Knowledgeable and helpful staff, a palpable passion for music and a good stock all used to be taken for granted in record stores. But with the number of retailers hugely diminished, it's good to be teaming up for this year's *Gramophone Classical Music Guide* with a store that has proved a haven for London's record enthusiasts for many years, Harold Moores. And the values that made it a must-visit destination continue to draw music lovers to Great Marlborough Street not just for the music but also for the enthusiasm and the warmth of the welcome.

THE
GRAMOPHONE
CLASSICAL
MUSIC
GUIDE
2011

CONTENTS

EDITOR James Jolly
SUB-EDITOR David Threasher
ART EDITOR Rupert Gale

CONTRIBUTORS
Andrew Achenbach, Nicholas Anderson, Nalen Anthoni, Mike Ashman, Mary Berry,
Alan Blyth, Joan Chissell, Philip Clark, Robert Cowan, Peter Dickinson, Jed Distler, Duncan Druce,
John Duarte, Adrian Edwards, Richard Fairman, David Fallows, David Fanning, Andrew Farach-Colton,
Iain Fenlon, Hilary Finch, Fabrice Fitch, Jonathan Freeman-Attwood, Edward Greenfield,
David Gutman, Martyn Harry, Stephen Johnson, Lindsay Kemp, Tess Knighton, Andrew Lamb,
Richard Lawrence, Robert Layton, Ivan March, Ivan Moody, Bryce Morrison, Jeremy Nicholas,
Christopher Nickol, Patrick O'Connor, Michael Oliver, Richard Osborne, Tim Parry, Stephen Plaistow,
Peter Quantrill, Nicholas Rast, Guy Rickards, Malcolm Riley, Marc Rochester, Julie-Anne Sadie,
Stanley Sadie, Lionel Salter, Alan Sanders, Michael Scott Rohan, Edward Seckerson, Robert Seeley,
Pwyll ap Siôn, Harriet Smith, Ken Smith, John Steane, Michael Stewart, Jonathan Swain,
David Threasher, David Vickers, John Warrack, Richard Whitehouse, Arnold Whittall,
Richard Wigmore, Barry Witherden, William Yeoman.

PRODUCTION EDITOR Antony Craig
PRODUCTION CONTROLLER Ailsa Donovan
PUBLISHER Kate Law
PUBLISHING MANAGER Luca Da Re

PUBLISHING DIRECTOR Bob McDowell
GROUP DESIGN DIRECTOR Paul Harpin
GROUP EDITORIAL DIRECTOR Mark Paton
MANAGING DIRECTOR David Prasher
CHIEF EXECUTIVE Kevin Costello

© **haymarket media group 2010**
ISBN 9 780860 249528

SALES AND DISTRIBUTION

North America
Music Sales Corporation
257 Park Avenue South, New York, NY 10010 USA
Telephone (212) 254 2100 **Fax** (212) 254 2013

UK and Rest of World
Music Sales Ltd
Newmarket Rd, Bury St Edmunds, Suffolk IP33 3YB
Great Britain
Telephone +44 (0)1284 702600 **Fax** +44 (0)1284 768301
e-mail trade.enquiries@musicsales.com

Printed in England by
William Clowes Limited, Beccles, Suffolk

Published by haymarket consumer media

haymarket

Teddington Studios, Broom Road, Teddington
Middlesex TW11 9BE, United Kingdom

INTRODUCTION

By Marin Alsop, Music Director, Baltimore Symphony Orchestra

Can you imagine living without music? I can't: many things, but not music.
For us music lovers, immersion in the extraordinary sounds created
by our fellow human beings is one of life's most treasurable experiences. And,
I suspect, for most people, recorded music comprises the greatest
proportion of their listening. I've always loved listening to music. Some of my
greatest musical experiences have come from recordings – and of course
many of my most lasting musical discoveries too. I remember the first time
I understood the emotional power of music when I heard a recording
of the Brahms B flat Sextet; I simply wept at the beauty
and depth of the work.

My parents, both professional musicians in New York, often played for
recording sessions, so my experience with the recording process
came early. Then as a violinist, I too would do session work. It was a wonderful
grounding and at the time little did I know (though I fervently hoped) that
I would one day being standing *in front* of the orchestra, rather than sitting in it!
In my conducting career I've always ensured that recording was part
of the orchestra's profile. We did a dozen or so recordings when I was with the
Bournemouth Symphony and as soon as I was appointed to the Baltimore
Symphony I made sure that recordings became part of the orchestra's
diet once again. And I'm thrilled that our discs of Corigliano, Bernstein
and Dvořák have been so well received!

Among the many other pleasures music offers is the act of
sharing it with others, guiding friends to new discoveries, or to old
favourites. And that's exactly what this book does – with authority,
enthusiasm and, above all, passion.

FOREWORD

By James Jolly, Editor-in-Chief, Gramophone

As I'm writing this foreword, Mozart's *Magic Flute* is playing in the background. I was given it this morning (so no chance of having it reviewed in time for this year's Guide!) and it finds René Jacobs adding another milestone to his series of Mozart opera recordings for Harmonia Mundi. That such a set should emerge from an independent company (beautifully packaged and lavishly supported by a superb booklet) would have been almost unthinkable even 15 years ago – that would have been the territory of a major company. Today, for a *major* company to issue such a recording would also be quite an event! Things have changed very dramatically: the major company would definitely have recorded it live, whereas this Harmonia Mundi set is a studio production.

And that's just one of the many changes we've become used to in this new era for the classical music recording industry. If the first three quarters of the industry's life was guided by the large multinational concerns, I think the next important period is going to be steered by smaller, more 'boutique' concerns. The mix of winners at the annual *Gramophone* Awards has certainly become more finely balanced between these two different – but equally valid – approaches to the same goal. And of course, between those two poles comes Naxos, a company that has redefined the recorded scene more radically than anyone in the past half a century: and there are many of its recordings represented in these pages.

A look back over the 110-plus year history of recorded music reveals a number of important milestones: the advent of electric recording, the birth of stereo, the arrival of the LP, digital recording technology, the CD, the DVD, the SACD and now the download. To get the maximum choice, you'd ideally consume your music in a combination of formats: probably CD and download. But if you stick to tradition (the CD) you won't miss very much, and similarly if you've embraced digital wholeheartedly there's not going to be much that will slip by you. Once upon a time, a recording's availability tended to be a fairly black-and-white affair: 'It's available' or 'It's not'! Nowadays, recordings slip in and out of the catalogue and are nearly always offered as a download if their physical equivalent has disappeared from circulation. In compiling this Guide I've tended to check availability both with individual dealers and with the companies' own websites. And of course, certain discs may be available in one country and not in another. It's always worth shopping around.

The Gramophone Classical Music Guide has been evolving and growing for more than two decades, drawing not only on the hundreds of new reviews published in *Gramophone* over the course of each year but also building on a tradition of informed, quality criticism that goes back to 1923 when the magazine was founded by the writer Compton Mackenzie. His philosophy back then was to search out the finest writers in their field and build a panel of reviewers who were experts in their own areas – and that's a philosophy that remains all these years later. So don't expect the same writer to offer opinions on Bach cantatas and on Donizetti operas or Messiaen organ music. We like to inhabit our areas of expertise and gain some genuine perspective.

In selecting the reviews for the Guide I've not aimed at a comprehensive coverage of every single recording of every single work. Instead I've been guided by *Gramophone*'s critics to the best version, and where possible offered alternatives at different price-points as well as a historic version and one on DVD. For some of the most popular works of the repertoire a box of at-a-glance comments is offered (and of course if you want to look back through the 87 years of *Gramophone*'s reviews you can find the entire archive at **gramophone.co.uk**).

Recordings are discussed as they are coupled on the disc so you will find, say, the piano concertos of Grieg and Schumann (one of the most popular pairings on disc) discussed under Grieg – so if you fail to find a particular work a quick look at the index to couplings will reveal if that work is to be found elsewhere in the book.

A couple of weeks before this Guide went to press, the death was announced of the great conductor Sir Charles Mackerras: the huge number of recordings of his recommended in this book must stand as a lasting tribute not just to a great musician but also to a real 'record man', someone who enriched the catalogue for over a half a century.

DOWNLOADING

Downloading has become the norm for a new generation of music lovers: there are numerous teenagers who haven't even played a CD. Classical music fans are starting to dip their toes into this new world – and enjoying the experience. **James Jolly** offers an introduction to the sites and the music available for download.

It's hard to believe but in October 2011 the iPod will be celebrating its 10th birthday. Rarely has an invention dug its way so completely into our lives quite so quickly: and not just as a way of delivering music, but also as a style icon. Of course an iPod is only one way to store your music – in fact, you don't even *need* to make it portable. Your downloaded music can sit quite happily on your hard-drive.

When downloading made music available instantly and very conveniently, it was assumed that classical music would lag behind more 'contemporary' genres. Not a bit of it. It came as quite a surprise to the powers-that-be at Apple that classical music performed disproportionately to investment, and that far from sticking to traditional methods of consuming their music, classical music fans started downloading as enthusiastically as fans of pop, rock and jazz. And with a catalogue that is as broad as it is deep, downloading was a perfect way to control the 'long tail'. Vast catalogues can sit in cyberspace, taking up no warehouse space but in a state of permanent availability. And a decade into the downloading age, many of the original concerns about the medium have evaporated. Sound quality is no longer an issue as many sites offer not only lossless files (in other words the same quality as CD) but some even offer what they style 'studio master' files – which are in sound that is superior to the CD (though these tend to be very large and also quite costly): and what's more, you need to make sure you can actually tell the difference. It's amazing how satisfied many people are with MP3 sound at surprisingly low bit-rates.

The CD, though, isn't going to disappear overnight; but it will become just one of a number of formats on offer. Already a vast array of recordings are available as downloads – one glance through this guide will reveal the extent of the catalogue: the ➦ symbol alongside a disc's details shows that the recording is also available as a download. But first, let's dispel a few concerns.

If downloading is now the norm in your regular music acquisition, then you might want to consider ways that will allow you to break away from your computer and 'attach' your digital music collection to your hi-fi. There are now numerous, wireless ways of transmitting your music from your PC to your hi-fi. There is an increasing number of systems, too, that allow you to insert your player (more often than not an iPod) and offer remarkably good sound quality. It's also pretty easy to link your iPod/MP3 player using its cradle and a good old-fashioned cable. I regularly plug my iPod into my kitchen mini-system and am more than satisfied with the results (and a phono-to-headphones cable is a mandatory holiday accessory now that many hotels and apartments have hi-fi as standard).

With the advent of a new generation of Network Music Players, freedom and quality go hand in hand. The audiophile listener can listen to downloaded (and no doubt lossless) music with no degradation of sound quality. And with companies such as Linn, Gimell and Chandos offering studio-quality downloads, there is no reason why your music should not sound as good as (and in some cases better than) the equivalent CD. A good introduction to Network Music Players can be found on the Gimell website (**gimell.com**) and on the various manufacturers' sites (**logitech.com** and **linn.co.uk** among the market leaders).

Most people's MP3 players contain a combination of music that they've ripped (ie transferred from CD to their computer's hard-drive) and music that has been downloaded (the proportion is invariably a single-figure percentage of downloaded music). It makes sense to load your computer (especially if you are planning to take your music with you) with your favourite recordings and then supplement them with downloads as necessary. If you've a laptop, why not store some music there, then you'll always have something for those unplanned-for delays when music is the only balm!

The one genre that would seem ideally suited to download-only music is new music, where sales are invariably low. It's an option being explored by a number of orchestras, allowing people to capture the quality and experience of the ensemble performing in its own concert hall. The St Louis Symphony, under its dynamic music director David Robertson, has already embarked on an imaginative series that offers live recordings of works central to each season's music-making. With the cost savings made by not having to press CDs and print booklets, this could greatly benefit new music ventures.

Where?

For the purposes of this explanatory section, let's assume you are buying your music to transport around on an MP3 player – most people do and it's a staggeringly easy way of guaranteeing that you can hear pretty well whatever you want, whenever you want it. (But as already noted above, you need go no further than downloading it onto your computer and leaving it there to listen to.) However you choose to listen to your music, you will need to store it. Many DSPs (Digital Service Providers – basically download stores) offer a player that works with their offerings. The most wide-spread and probably the easiest to use is the iTunes version. It's better than most at coping with the sort of information that a classical music consumer will need: it's certainly visually appealing – clean and intuitive in the typical Apple house-style but it also easily allows you to alter the various information columns to suit your musical tastes. For example, with pop and rock music you may prefer a hierarchy that gives artist, album and song the dominant position. With classical music, you may prefer a line-up that works something like: composer / work / movement or subsection / artist / genre (chamber, instrumental, song, etc).

Searching for music on the various sites is still a far-from-ideal manoeuvre. Most sites are geared up to the rock/pop consumer for whom an artist's name is probably all that is necessary to home in on their various albums and from there the selection is simple. Imagine typing in Herbert von Karajan – the choice is immense and the whole process is like shooting in the dark. One of the best search engines is found on the **classicsonline.com** site – it allows a number of fields to be entered and invariably locates what you're looking for immediately. If the big DSPs want to be taken seriously by the classical consumer they will have to address the 'searchability' of their sites (though this presumes that the data on each recording is in some kind of useable form to start with – mention the word 'metadata' to anyone working in this field and they tend to roll their eyes in a state of horror).

So, you want to dip a toe into the fresh waters of downloading. What do you do?

How?

Until recently there weren't many options for the download enthusiast to organise and play his or her music. Apple's Jukebox has the enormous advantage in being part of the iTunes eco-system where music can be seamlessly acquired, stored and synchronised to your iPod. Get it at **apple.com/itunes**. There are versions for Mac and PC, so everyone is catered for. Once installed, the set-up process is very easy: you simply follow the instructions on the screen.

Passionato.com, the latest download site and one of the few totally dedicated to delivering classical music, also offers a bespoke player. And very classy it is too – it not only works well within the download environment of Passionato's download store, but it will also ingest your existing downloads and even add to the metadata (electronic 'catalogue' details) if it has it. And once you've started to build a collection within the player, Passionato will offer recommendations for further listening. It's like having your own 'old school' record store salesman on your desktop!

Sound quality is an important issue for many classical music enthusiasts, so before you start you need to decide what bit-rate you are happiest with. Many classical stores – Passionato and theclassicalshop among them – start at 320 Kbps, more than acceptable for all but the 'golden eared'.

I suggest you try ripping a few of your favourite CDs simply to get a feel for the quality you are happy with. On a PC go to 'Edit', then 'Preferences', click on 'Importing' and you will be offered a number of file-format options. Once the disc is ready for ripping, go to the 'iTunes' prompt at the top left of your screen. Click on it, and then on Preferences. Then in the centre of the tab which opens, click on 'Importing'. You will then be given the option for Setting. The default will probably be 128kbps AAC. Try importing using this setting. Next, using 'Get Info' (the Control-click/right-click option as described above), add 192 to the composer's name (say, Mozart192) and, using the Import option, import at 192kbps. You can do this as many times as you want with all permutations of file type and bit-rate – just make sure you label your files so that you can compare later. And of course you can go as high as lossless, but the file size will be substantially larger.

Now, choosing the usual way you'll be listening to your music – headphones or speakers – play each of the different imported options and be critical! Once you've decided on the amount of compression you can cope with (I would be hesitant to go below 192kbps AAC – piano music tends to fray a little at the edges), you're ready to load some music onto your computer. Of course if you've a laptop then you're pretty close to starting a portable music collection.

Now you are set up to download. Further on in this section I suggest some of the different sites to visit to find your music, but before you go mad and start downloading an entire new music collection it's worth pausing to consider how you'll find all the music you've bought.

You will be amazed at how quickly you can amass a substantial collection of music on your PC (usually through a combination of ripping

CDs and downloading) so it's a good idea to create a 'house style' for cataloguing the music. The information that accompanies a music file – whether acquired automatically on the web using a service like Gracenote (which is supplied largely by fellow enthusiasts in a kind of collective responsibility) or as supplied by the DSP – can arrive in a variety of styles. Decide early on how you are likely to sort though your music when you are looking for something to listen to. (One example of the inconsistency of web-based metadata services is the difference you will encounter between discs if you are ripping an opera: each CD can attract a completely different style of information that can waste an enormous amount of time if you then edit it manually. You can even get the information in different languages between discs – not exactly conducive to easy listening.)

If you listen to classical as well as other genres (pop, rock, jazz, world and so on), the chances are that you will sort your classical music initially by composer and your non-classical music by artist or album. For the eclectic music consumer I would recommend that you remove composer details from all kinds of music other than classical: this makes searching far quicker; and besides, the chances are that you've never heard of half the people who compose pop tunes. Relying on the genre column is one option but I've yet to encounter anyone who does this.

Simplicity is the key-note: pare the details down to the minimum.

Ludwig van Beethoven
Symphony No 3 in C minor, Op 55, 'Eroica'
Allegro con brio
Berlin Philharmonic Orchestra /
Herbert von Karajan

may satisfy the completist (or the librarian), but that's an awful lot of information to contain in the small window of an iPod (which actually has a larger window than many MP3 players). Why not settle for:

Beethoven
Symphony No 3
I (or first movt)
BPO / Karajan

It says exactly what is playing and gets the message across with economy and clarity. The best advice is to experiment and decide how much information you need to find your music quickly and efficiently. (Do be careful that you don't oversimplify your system – there is a risk that you could end up being offered all the first movements, followed by all the second movements and so on – and that risk is increased when you start adding multiple versions of a

particular work to your collection. And if you're especially completist you'll almost certainly run into trouble when you add a different version of a particular work by a single performer – say, Brendel's *Hammerklavier* Sonata, but that's probably not going to happen too often!)

Another decision that needs to be taken is whether to keep your music in its original album form (do you want the Bruch Violin Concerto always to deliver the Mendelssohn as well?) or to store your music as individual pieces.

There are strong arguments to be made for both approaches: on a purely practical level you'd be amazed how quickly you seem to be re-programming your iPod if you have broken up albums into individual pieces (though you can easily make a special playlist that includes all your favourite violin concertos, so you can have a feast of Maxim Vengerov in great concertos if you want).

Where to find your music

There are various different 'business models' in operation for purchasing music. There is the simple, pay for what you buy (the most traditional and still most popular): the average price for a new 'full-price' album is about £8. This is model used by iTunes, Passionato, the classicalshop, classicsonline and numerous others. A second model is the subscription, where a monthly payment allows you either unlimited access to music (though with certain restrictions) or a fixed number of downloads (the eMusic model – see below). Here, for the classical music enthusiast, is a guide to some of the best sites for acquiring music.

iTunes

The mother of all DSPs is iTunes: it's one of the biggest source of downloads across the entire range of genres and in the classical arena it carries an impressive selection. The advanced search ability makes finding a particular piece/ recording much easier, and it's also easy to see what other recordings a particular artist has made. Special offers occur frequently and as a site it's beautifully and seamlessly engineered – and if you're an iPod user couldn't be simpler. Also quite a few albums come with a little extra recorded especially for iTunes.

Amazon

Once upon a time iTunes could easily claim to be the biggest digital music store but the mighty, and equally global, Amazon – who have already turned themselves into one of the best-stocked and most efficient online retailers for CDs and DVDs (not to mention just everything else that can be relatively easily transported!) – has entered the download market. And there's now considerable debate about whether Amazon's site is bigger than iTunes. Who cares, as they both offer a huge range. Admittedly it's not as visually appealing as iTunes but for range and price it's a site you can't ignore – and nor should you, as there are some great deals here too.

eMusic

Up there among the top three comes **eMusic** (it has both **.com** and **.co.uk** sites). It operates a payment system that allows you a certain number of download tracks for a fixed fee (at the time of writing, 24 tracks for £9.99; £13.99 for 35 and £17.99 for 50). If you consider that most symphonies have just four movements and concertos have three, that's potentially a lot of music for very little money. If you add in the free 25 tracks eMusic gives you as an incentive to join (and which you can keep even if you don't stay with them), then this might be a good first destination to see if you enjoy acquiring your music in this new way. All eMusic downloads are DRM-free, which means that once you've bought it you can do whatever you like with it. (Incidentally, eMusic's Download Manager allows you store your music and control the audio files on your PC and seamlessly imports them into your iTunes jukebox or preferred player.)

The site focuses predominantly on independent companies – it contains recordings from Naxos, LSO Live, BIS, Ondine, SDG, Guild, Danacord and numerous others, and also does rather more editorialising than other sites, containing artist profiles, reviews and so on. The eMusic site does contain many gems, though finding them is always slightly difficult – you tend to stumble over them when you least expect it (and little serendipity is still nice to encounter in this too-often-streamlined world!).

Opus Arte & Passionato

There are a number of classical music-focused websites, some new, some with a few years' experience. Passionato offers a good cross-section of labels, with a slight leaning towards the majors. File size is 320kbps and some are offered also as lossless. The focus is very much on labels, though the search facility allows you to decide how you are going to find your music and is easy to use (**passionato.com**). Only just launched at the time of writing, Opus Arte's site (**opusarte.com**) also aims at a broad spectrum of labels, and has a few that Passionato doesn't; uniquely it also offers the Opus Arte videos for download – quite an appealing idea (and you will find a vast number of the company's productions in the pages that follow).

theclassicalshop

One destination that has been steadily growing in size and confidence is **theclassicalshop**, a digital store with an increasingly broad catalogue. Chandos, the site's host, launched this download site early in 2006 and suddenly we were offered over 6000 MP3 files of the company's deleted recordings. The range is too immense to list but if you're attracted to Chandos's unequalled catalogue of rarer British orchestral music this could well be the place for you. There are gems such as Bryden Thomson's *Gramophone* Award-winning Bax Fourth, works by Finzi, Kenneth Leighton and Rubbra, and more standard fare such as the complete Rachmaninov piano concertos played by Earl Wild, with Jascha Horenstein conducting. The remainder of the catalogue followed and now all new releases are offered digitally alongside the CD.

Labels other than Chandos to be found at theclassicalshop include Avie, Amon Ra, Brana, Coro, CRD, Doyen, Guild, LSO Live, Naxos, Nimbus, NMC, Onyx, Priory, Pristine, Quartz, Signum, Somm and Wigmore Hall Live.

This is a site worth visiting if you're a collector of music in lossless formats – pricing is keen and the selection superb.

classicsonline.com

Naxos, despite being well represented on the larger sites like iTunes and eMusic, also has its own website, which contains music from the labels the company distributes around the world (**classicsonline.com**). It's worth checking out, though you might find that acquiring Naxos material via eMusic is a more cost-effective method. The search engine, however, is probably the best around – so finding your music is no problem here.

Another destination within Naxos's world is the Naxos Music Library (**naxosmusiclibrary. com**), a website with a mine of information that contains biographies, sleeve-notes, histories of music and the ability to listen to everything in the Naxos catalogue as well as a host of distributed labels. All this comes for a modest annual fee. And the summer of 2010 saw the arrival of the Naxos Video Library – a similar concept to the Music Library with an impressive selection of videos (concerts, opera, ballet, documentaries and feature films). Initially, like the NML, it's aimed at educational institutions, but I'm sure that consumer demand will be considerable (**naxosvideolibrary.com**).

eclassical.com

Based in Sweden, this download store has been around since 1999 and so has a fair amount of experience. There is some helpful 'editorial' material to support the downloads (biographies, introductory notes on the music and so on) and a good selection of music. Performances are a little variable but there are some treasures to be found, so it's a site that's worth exploring when you've time on your hands (eclassical.com). Not surprisingly, there's good representation of the (Swedish) BIS label, and also a large quantity of recordings from Hänssler Classic. The site also suggests suitable music for moods: under 'After a divorce' it recommends three movements of Dvořák's *New World* Symphony which I can only assume is a hint that emigration might be a good idea…

pristineclassical.com

Pristine Audio (pristineclassical.com) has a dual role as remastering experts who offer their very fine transfers on custom-made CD or as downloads. Focusing on out-of-copyright recordings (in other words, public domain music recorded before 1960), it has amassed a large catalogue full of the great names of 20th-century music-making. Especially fascinating are the recordings that have emerged from the US and added a little balance to our somewhat Europe-centric perspective.

Pristine has been exploring new transfer methods recently and has been achieving some very impressive results. It's now become the norm for this 'ambient stereo' to be applied to the company's transfers and they do sound terrific, whether in MP3, or my preference, FLAC.

Another powerful reason to visit this site is that it offers the recordings issued in the late 1920s and early 1930s on *Gramophone*'s own label, the National Gramophonic Society. Fascinating chamber music releases – including Sir John Barbirolli's first recording – have been cleaned up with remarkable success.

Own-label websites

Why rely on others when you can do it yourself? This is a philosophy that has always fostered innovation and imagination – and, in the world of classical music, has been the biggest force for advance. A number of labels have launched their own digital stores. Top of the list must be Linn Records, not only because it's a classy little label in its own right, but also because its technical instructions and usability are second to none. In fact, I'd suggest anyone interested in downloading should spend some time on the Linn site reading the FAQ section. The answers are level-headed and honest – and extremely helpful (linnrecords.com).

Linn offers what it styles 'studio master' dowloads which come as either FLAC or WMA files – they sound superior to the CD quality and if you've the equipment that makes

them worth worth investigating. There are some terrific recordings to be had – not least of which are the two sets of late Mozart symphonies from Sir Charles Mackerras and the big Baroque choral works from the Dunedin Consort.

And if superb sound quality and Renaissance choral works are your thing, then make a bee-line to Gimell's site: the glorious recorded legacy of Peter Phillips's Tallis Scholars recordings is also available in a selection of different quality files – and the sound of the human voice, beautifully recorded, does really show off the standard of your playback equipment (gimell.com).

The UK wing of the vast Universal Music company, Universal Classics and Jazz, has launched its own site (classicsandjazz.co.uk) which is a useful destination for the gems of the Decca, DG and Philips catalogues, as well as a growing amount of jazz material. And since its launch, DRM has been dropped and the music is compatible with just about every MP3 player on the market.

If you're a fan of Deutsche Grammophon – the Yellow Label, and for many the classical music brand *par excellence* – then check out its own webshop (dgwebshop.com). It's a rhapsody in yellow that offers the entire DG catalogue in the environment of the company's activities, both present and past. Music here is DRM-free and competitively priced. Early in 2010 the site added the catalogues of its two sister companies, Decca and Philips, so the range has grown considerably. The site also contains some lively editorial.

The latest own-label site to launch – and a model of its kind – is Hyperion's (hyperion-records.co.uk). Stylishly designed, it has been incorporated seamlessly into Hyperion's existing site. You can set the downloading mode to MP3 or FLAC (interestingly priced the same) and the process is beautifully tailored. There are a number of very nice features: ease of access to the booklets, the ability to re-couple complex programmes where, say, a Mass is interleaved with chant (at the click of the mouse you can string the Mass movements together and lose the chant) and, most sensible of all, the opportunity to load your wallet with a predetermined sum and then dip into it for your downloads. It's such an obvious and sensible idea that I'm amazed other companies haven't adopted it. Pricing has been very carefully thought out and there's an incentive for pre-loading your wallet.

The Canadian label Analekta (analekta.com) has also unveiled its own download store and, like Hyperion, got so many things right. The catalogue is not immense but there are terrific recordings to be had there and the downloading experience encourages exploration. And the more you buy the sooner you will accumulate enough points for a free download.

Toccata Classics, the record-company arm of Toccata Press, furthers the aim of exploring the byways of classical music. As a label it has turned up some real treats: encountering Donald Tovey as composer rather than as the author of a series of splendid analytical essays on music has been a real ear-opener. Well, Toccata Classics has grasped the nettle and launched a download service that works well. If exotica from the Baroque to the present day appeals, log on to **toccataclassics.com**.

Mention of new music brings us to NMC, a record company that has been doing a unique service for new British music for many years. Having built up an impressive catalogue – and gained a few *Gramophone* Awards on the way – logic demanded that NMC make it available for downloading. And it's a splendid place to go for challenging and invariably deeply rewarding musical experiences (**nmc.greedbag.com**). Rather charmingly, you search for the composers using their first name rather than their surname – but I guess that just adds a touch of familiarity. There are also some excellent samplers that are great ways to see whether a particular composer appeals to you.

Spotify

Much ink has been spilled in speculation about Spotify, an initiative that seemingly offers you something for nothing! The site's model is simple: sign up and listen for free and you will encounter the occasional advert; sign up and pay a subscription and you will have access to a staggering catalogue at a higher bit-rate, and you won't hear any adverts either. The range of labels is very impressive and though the bulk of its users are sure to listen to pop and rock music there's more than enough classical music there to keep all but the choosiest listener happy for hours.

To the future

These are exciting times for music lovers: there has never been so much music available, and now the ways to get at it have become even easier. If you live miles from a record store (even if that store even stocks classical music), then downloading is an option you should explore. It will inevitably become the obvious way for record companies to keep their back-catalogues available – a truly appealing prospect.

100 NEW RECORDINGS

Of the more than 400 recordings that have entered *The Gramophone Classical Music Guide* this year, we single out 100 that have particularly caught our imagination – many of which fared well in the 2010 *Gramophone* Awards

Adès Violin Concerto etc
Anthony Marwood *vn* **COE / Thomas Adès**
(EMI)
Reviewed on page 9

Arnell. Bate. Chisholm Orchestral works
RSNO / Martin Yates
(Dutton)
Reviewed on page 29

Arnold Homage to the Queen etc
BBC Philharmonic / Rumon Gamba
(Chandos)
Reviewed on page 32

Bach Solo Violin Partitas Nos 2 & 3 etc
Isabelle Faust *vn* (Harmonia Mundi)
Reviewed on page 56

Bach Solo Violin Sonatas and Partitas
Alina Ibragimova *vn*
(Hyperion)
Reviewed on page 55

Bach Goldberg Variations
Andreas Staier *hpd* (Harmonia Mundi)
Reviewed on page 64

Bach Cantatas, Vol 2
Monteverdi Ch; EBS /
Sir John Eliot Gardiner (SDG)
Reviewed on page 80

Bach Mass in B minor
Dunedin Consort / John Butt (Linn)
Reviewed on page 91

Bednall Requiem
Chamber Choir of St Mary's Calne /
Edward Whiting (Regent)
Reviewed on page 129

Beethoven Piano Concertos Nos 4 & 5
Till Fellner *pf*
Montreal SO / Kent Nagano
(ECM New Series)
Reviewed on page 136

Beethoven Complete Piano Sonatas
Friedrich Gulda *pf*
(Orfeo)
Reviewed on page 162

Beethoven. Schubert. Mozart. Wagner
Opera Arias
Jonas Kaufmann; Mahler CO / Claudio Abbado
(Decca)
Reviewed on page 1361

Bowen
Piano Sonatas
Danny Driver *pf* (Hyperion)
Reviewed on page 242

Brahms Symphony No 1
Budapest Festival Orchestra / Iván Fischer
(Channel Classics)
Reviewed on page 251

Brahms Symphony No 3. Choral Works
Monteverdi Choir; Orchestre Révolutionnaire et Romantique / Sir John Eliot Gardiner
(SDG)
Reviewed on page 254

Brahms. Grieg. Schumann
Cello Sonatas
Mstislav Rostropovich *vc*
Benjamin Britten, Sviatoslav Richter *pfs*
(BBC Legends)
Reviewed on page 262

Brahms. Ravel. Stravinsky. Scarlatti
'Transformation'
Yuja Wang *pf* (DG)
Reviewed on page 1349

Brahms. Rachmaninov. Ravel. Schubert
Works for Two Pianos
Martha Argerich, Nelson Freire *pfs*
(DG)
Reviewed on page 1330

Brahms Die schöne Magelone Romances
Dietrich Fischer-Dieskau *bar*
Sviatoslav Richter *pf*
(BBC Legends)
Reviewed on page 269

Briggs Messe pour Notre Dame
Choir of Trinity College, Cambridge /
Stephen Layton; David Briggs
(Hyperion)
Reviewed on page 274

Britten Quatre Chansons françaises.
Les illuminations **Finzi** Dies Natalis
Delius A Late Lark
Susan Gritton *sop*
BBC SO / Edward Gardner
(Chandos)
Reviewed on page 286

Byrd 'Infelix ego'
The Cardinall's Musick / Andrew Carwood
(Hyperion)
Reviewed on page 324

Mozart
Mitridate, re di Ponto
Adam Fischer (Dacapo)
Reviewed on page 816

Prokofiev Piano Concertos Nos 2 & 3
Freddy Kempf *pf*
Bergen PO / Andrew Litton
(BIS)
Reviewed on page 871

Prokofiev Romeo and Juliet
LSO / Valery Gergiev
(LSO Live)
Reviewed on page 874

Prokofiev String Quartets Nos 1 & 2
Pavel Haas Quartet (Supraphon)
Reviewed on page 875

Prokofiev Piano Sonatas
Anne-Marie McDermott (Bridge)
Reviewed on page 876

Rachmaninov. Tchaikovsky Piano Trios
Vadim Repin *vn* **Mischa Maisky** *vc*
Lang Lang *pf*
(DG)
Reviewed on page 912

Ravel Orchestral Works
Rotterdam PO / Yannick Nézet-Séguin
(EMI)
Reviewed on page 925

Reger Solo Viola Suites
Bach Solo Cello Suites Nos 1 & 2 (arr va)
Tabea Zimmermann *va*
(Myrios Classics)
Reviewed on page 936

Rossini Songs
Mireille Delunsch *sop*, et al
Malcolm Martineau *pf* (Opera Rara)
Reviewed on page 950

Rossini 'Colbran the Muse'
Joyce DiDonato *mez*
Santa Cecilia Chor & Orch / Edoardo Müller
(Virgin Classics)
Reviewed on page 953

Saariaho L'amour de loin
Kent Nagano (Harmonia Mundi)
Reviewed on page 974

Schubert Symphonies Nos 4 & 5
Netherlands CO / Gordan Nikolitch
(Pentatone)
Reviewed on page 1002

Schubert String Quintet. String Quartets
Valentin Erben *vc*
Belcea Quartet (EMI)
Reviewed on page 1008

Schubert Piano Sonatas
Imogen Cooper *pf* (Avie)
Reviewed on page 1013

Schubert Impromptus
David Fray *pf* (Virgin Classics)
Reviewed on page 1016

Schubert 'Heliopolis' – Lieder
Matthias Goerne *bar* **Ingo Metzmacher** *pf*
(Harmonia Mundi)
Reviewed on page 1018

Schubert Winterreise
Mark Padmore *ten* **Paul Lewis** *pf*
(Harmonia Mundi)
Reviewed on page 1029

Schumann Lieder
Bernarda Fink *mez* **Roger Vignoles** *pf*
(Harmonia Mundi)
Reviewed on page 1049

Schütz Weihnachtshistorie
Paul Hillier (Dacapo)
Reviewed on page 1051

Shchedrin Concertos for Orchestra
Bournemouth SO / Kyrill Karabits
(Naxos)
Reviewed on page 1060

Sheppard Media vita
Stile Antico (Harmonia Mundi)
Reviewed on page 1062

Sor Minuets etc
William Carter *gtr* (Linn)
Reviewed on page 1100

R Strauss Rosenkavalier Suite
CBSO / Andriss Nelsons (Orfeo)
Reviewed on page 1120

Stravinsky The Fairy's Kiss. Scènes de ballet
BBC Scottish SO / Ilan Volkov
(Hyperion)
Reviewed on page 1141

Stravinsky Complete Works for Violin and Piano
Anthony Marwood *vn* **Thomas Adès** *pf*
(Hyperion)
Reviewed on page 767

Sullivan Ivanhoe
David Lloyd-Jones (Chandos)
Reviewed on page 1147

Tchaikovsky Complete Works for Piano
and Orchestra
Stephen Hough *pf*
**Minnesota Orchestra /
Osmo Vänskä**
(Hyperion)
Reviewed on page 1168

Records of the Year

The annual *Gramophone* Awards celebrate the best in recorded music – listed below are the best of the best, the winners of the Records of the Year

1977 (Opera)
Janáček
Kát'a Kabanová
Vienna State Opera Chorus; Vienna Philharmonic Orchestra / Sir Charles Mackerras
Decca ② 421 852-2DH2   *Reviewed page 644*

1978 (Opera)
Puccini
La fanciulla del West
Soloists; Royal Opera House Chorus and Orchestra, Covent Garden / Zubin Mehta
DG ② 474 840-2GOR2   *Reviewed page 885*

1979 (Chamber)
Haydn
Piano Trios
Beaux Arts Trio
Philips ⑨ 432 061-2PM9   *Reviewed page 582*

1980 (Opera)
Janáček
From the House of the Dead
Soloists; Vienna State Opera Chorus; Vienna Philharmonic Orchestra / Sir Charles Mackerras
Decca ② 430 375-2DH2   *Reviewed page 642*

1981 (Opera)
Wagner
Parsifal
Soloists; Chorus of the Deutsche Oper, Berlin; Berlin Philharmonic Orchestra / Herbert von Karajan
DG ④ 413 347-2GH4   *Reviewed page 1281*

1982-83 (Concerto)
Tippett
Triple Concerto
György Pauk; Nobuko Imai; Ralph Kirshbaum; London Symphony Orchestra / Sir Colin Davis
Decca 470 196-2

1984 (Orchestral)
Mahler
Symphony No 9
Berlin Philharmonic Orchestra / Herbert von Karajan
DG ② 474 537-2 DGR   *Reviewed page 722*

1985 (Concerto)
Elgar
Violin Concerto
Nigel Kennedy vn
London Philharmonic Orchestra / Vernon Handley
EMI 345793-2   *Reviewed page 436*

1986 (Opera)
Rossini
Il viaggio a Reims
Soloists; Prague Philharmonic Chorus; Chamber Orchestra of Europe / Claudio Abbado
DG ② 415 498-2GH2

1987 (Early music)
Josquin Desprez
Masses – Pange lingua; La sol fa re mi
The Tallis Scholars / Peter Phillips
Gimell CDGIM009   *Reviewed page 647*

1988 (Orchestral)
Mahler
Symphony No 2, 'Resurrection'
Soloists; City of Birmingham Symphony Orchestra and Chorus / Sir Simon Rattle
EMI ② 747962-8   *Reviewed page 714*

1989 (Chamber)
Bartók
String Quartets Nos 1-6
Emerson Quartet
DG ② 423 657-2GH2   *Reviewed page 115*

1990 (Opera)
Prokofiev
The Love for Three Oranges
Soloists; Chorus and Orchestra of Lyon Opéra / Kent Nagano
Virgin Classics ② 358694-2

1991 (Choral)
Beethoven
Mass in D, 'Missa solemnis'
Soloists; Monteverdi Choir; English Baroque Soloists / Sir John Eliot Gardiner
Archiv Produktion 429 779-2AH   *Reviewed page 174*

1992 (Orchestral)
Beethoven
Symphonies Nos 1-9
Chamber Orchestra of Europe /
Nikolaus Harnoncourt
Teldec ⑤ 0927 49768-2   *Reviewed page 141*

1993 (Solo vocal)
Grieg
Songs
Anne Sofie von Otter *mez*
Bengt Forsberg *pf*
DG 476 1815 GGR   *Reviewed page 515*

1994 (Instrumental)
Debussy
Préludes
Krystian Zimerman *pf*
DG ② 435 773-2GH2   *Reviewed page ???*

1995 (Concerto)
Prokofiev Violin Concerto No 1
Shostakovich Violin Concerto No 1
Maxim Vengerov *vn*
London Symphony Orchestra /
Mstislav Rostropovich
Teldec 4509 89143-2   *Reviewed page 871*

1996 (Concerto)
Sauer. Scharwenka
Piano Concertos
Stephen Hough *pf* **City of Birmingham**
Symphony Orchestra / Lawrence Foster
Hyperion CDA66790   *Reviewed page 989*

1997 (Opera)
Puccini
La rondine
Soloists; London Voices;
London Symphony Orchestra / Antonio Pappano
EMI ② 556338-2   *Reviewed page 889*

1998 (Choral)
Martin
Mass for Double Choir. Passacaille.
Pizzetti Messa di Requiem. De Profundis
Westminster Cathedral Choir / James O'Donnell
Hyperion CDA67017   *Reviewed page 730*

1999 (Opera)
Dvořák
Rusalka
Soloists; Kühn Mixed Choir;
Czech Philharmonic Orchestra /
Sir Charles Mackerras
Decca ③ 460 568-2DHO3   *Reviewed page 428*

2000 (Orchestral)
Mahler
Symphony No 10 (ed Cooke)
Berlin Philharmonic Orchestra /
Sir Simon Rattle
EMI 556972-2   *Reviewed page 724*

2001 (Orchestral)
Vaughan Williams
A London Symphony (original 1913 version)
Butterworth
The Banks of Green Willow
London Symphony Orchestra / Richard Hickox
Chandos CHAN9902; 🅮 CHSA5501
                                          Reviewed page 1209

2002 (Concerto)
Saint-Saëns
Piano Concertos Nos 1-5. Wedding Cake.
Rapsodie d'Auvergne. Africa
Stephen Hough *pf* **City of Birmingham**
Symphony Orchestra / Sakari Oramo
Hyperion ② CDA67331/2   *Reviewed page 976*

2003 (Chamber)
Schumann
String Quartets Nos 1 and 3
Zehetmair Quartet
ECM 472 169-2   *Reviewed page 1036*

2004 (Opera)
Mozart
Le nozze di Figaro
Collegium Vocale; Concerto Köln /
René Jacobs
Harmonia Mundi HMC90 1818/20;
🅮 HMC80 1818/20   *Reviewed page 817*

2005 (Baroque vocal)
JS Bach
Cantatas Vol 1
Soloists; Monteverdi Choir; English Baroque
Soloists / Sir John Eliot Gardiner
SDG SDG101   *Reviewed page 80*

2006 (Orchestral)
Mahler
Symphony No 6
Berlin Philharmonic Orchestra / Claudio Abbado
DG 477 5684GSA2   *Reviewed page 719*

2007 (Orchestral)
Brahms
Piano Concertos Nos 1 & 2
Nelson Friere; Gewandhaus Orchestra /
Riccardo Chailly
Decca 475 7637DX2   *Reviewed page 245*

2008 (Instrumental)
Beethoven
Piano Sonatas Vol 4
Paul Lewis
Harmonia Mundi HMC90 1909/11
                                          Reviewed page 166

2009 (Orchestral)
Debussy. Fauré. Ravel
String Quartets
Quatuor Ebène
Virgin Classics 519045-2   *Reviewed page 375*

SUGGESTED BASIC LIBRARY

ORCHESTRAL

Bach Brandenburg Concertos
Bach Concerto for two violins
Bach Orchestral Suites
Barber Adagio for strings
Barber Violin Concerto
Bartók Concerto for Orchestra
Bartók The Miraculous Mandarin
Bartók Violin Concerto No 2
Beethoven Complete symphonies
Beethoven Piano Concertos Nos 4 and 5
Beethoven Violin Concerto
Berg Violin Concerto
Berlioz Symphonie fantastique
Brahms Complete symphonies
Brahms Piano Concerto No 1
Brahms Violin Concerto
Britten Young Person's Guide to the Orchestra
Bruch Violin Concerto No 1
Bruckner Symphonies Nos 4, 5, 8 and 9
Chopin Piano Concertos
Copland Appalachian Spring
Copland Fanfare for the Common Man
Corelli 12 Concerti grossi, Op 6
Delibes Coppélia
Debussy Jeux
Debussy La mer
Debussy Prélude à L'après-midi d'un faune
Dvořák Cello Concerto
Dvořák Symphony No 9, 'New World'
Elgar Cello Concerto
Elgar Enigma Variations
Elgar String music
Elgar Symphonies Nos 1 and 2
Elgar Violin Concerto
Falla Noches en los jardines de España
Gershwin Rhapsody in Blue
Górecki Symphony No 3
Grieg Peer Gynt Suite
Grieg Piano Concerto
Handel Fireworks Music
Handel Water Music
Haydn Cello Concerto in C
Haydn London Symphonies
Haydn Trumpet Concerto
Holst The Planets
Ives Three Places in New England
Mahler Symphonies Nos 5 and 9
Mendelssohn A Midsummer Night's Dream
Mendelssohn Hebrides Overture
Mendelssohn Symphony No 4 , 'Italian'
Mendelssohn Violin Concerto
Messiaen Turangalîla Symphony
Mozart Clarinet Concerto
Mozart Horn Concerto No 4
Mozart Piano Concertos Nos 20-27
Mozart Serenade for 13 Winds
Mozart Symphonies Nos 40 and 41
Mussorgsky Pictures at an Exhibition
Pärt Tabula rasa
Prokofiev Lieutenant Kijé
Prokofiev Peter and the Wolf
Prokofiev Piano Concerto No 3
Prokofiev Romeo and Juliet

Prokofiev Symphonies Nos 1 and 5
Rachmaninov Paganini Rhapsody
Rachmaninov Piano Concertos Nos 2 and 3
Rachmaninov Symphony No 2
Ravel Boléro
Ravel Daphnis et Chloé
Ravel Piano Concerto in G
Respighi Roman Trilogy
Rimsky-Korsakov Scheherazade
Rodrigo Concierto de Aranjuez
Rossini Overtures
Saint-Saëns Le carnaval des animaux
Saint-Saëns Piano Concerto No 2
Saint-Saëns Symphony No 3
Schoenberg Five Orchestral Pieces, Op 16
Schoenberg Variations for Orchestra, Op 31
Schubert Symphony No 8, 'Unfinished'
Schumann Piano Concerto
Shostakovich Cello Concerto No 1
Shostakovich Piano Concerto No 2
Shostakovich Symphonies Nos 5 and 10
Sibelius Finlandia
Sibelius Symphonies Nos 2 and 5
Sibelius Tapiola
Sibelius Violin Concerto
Smetana Má vlast
Strauss J II Waltzes
Strauss R Alpine Symphony
Strauss R Also sprach Zarathustra
Strauss R Till Eulenspiegel
Stravinsky Agon
Stravinsky The Rite of Spring
Stravinsky The Firebird
Tchaikovsky Romeo and Juliet
Tchaikovsky 1812 Overture
Tchaikovsky Ballets – The Nutcracker,
  Sleeping Beauty and Swan Lake
Tchaikovsky Piano Concerto No 1
Tchaikovsky Symphonies Nos 4-6
Tchaikovsky Violin Concerto
Vaughan Williams Symphony No 2, 'London'
Vaughan Williams Symphony No 5
Vaughan Williams Tallis Fantasia
Vaughan Williams The Lark Ascending
Vivaldi The Four Seasons
Walton Violin and Viola Concertos

CHAMBER

Bartók String Quartets
Beethoven Piano Trio in B flat, Op 97, 'Archduke'
Beethoven String Quartets [late]
Beethoven Violin Sonatas
Borodin String Quartet No 2
Brahms Clarinet Quintet
Debussy Sonata for Flute, Viola and Harp
Debussy String Quartet
Dvořák String Quartet No 12
Franck Violin Sonata
Haydn String Quartets, Opp 20 and 76
Mendelssohn Octet
Mozart Clarinet Quintet
Mozart String Quartet in C, K465, 'Dissonance'
Mozart String Quintet in G minor, K516
Ravel String Quartet

Reich Different Trains
Schubert Piano Quintet, 'Trout'
Schubert Piano Trios
Schubert Arpeggione Sonata in A minor, D821
Schubert String Quartet No 14
Schubert String Quintet
Shostakovich String Quartet No 8

INSTRUMENTAL

Bach Cello Suites
Bach Das wohltemperierte Klavier
Bach Goldberg Variations
Bach Solo Violin Sonatas and Partitas
Beethoven Complete piano sonatas
Beethoven Diabelli Variations
Biber Mystery Sonatas
Brahms Variations on a Theme of Paganini
Chopin Nocturnes
Chopin Piano Sonata No 2
Chopin Preludes
Debussy Children's Corner Suite
Debussy Préludes
Grieg Lyric Pieces
Haydn Piano Sonata E flat major, HobXVI/52
Liszt Piano Sonata
Mozart Piano Sonata No 11 in A, K331
Paganini 24 Caprices
Prokofiev Piano Sonata No 7
Ravel Gaspard de la nuit
Satie Piano works
Schubert Impromptus
Schubert Piano Sonata in B flat, D960
Schubert Wandererfantasie
Schumann Carnaval
Schumann Kinderszenen
Schumann Kreiserleriana

VOCAL

Allegri Miserere
Bach Cantatas – No 82 'Ich habe genug' and
    140 'Wachet auf'
Bach Magnificat
Bach Mass in B minor
Bach St Matthew Passion
Beethoven Missa solemnis
Berlioz Grande messe des morts
Berlioz L'enfance du Christ
Berlioz Les nuits d'été
Brahms Ein deutsches Requiem
Britten Serenade
Britten War Requiem
Bruckner Motets
Byrd Masses for 3, 4 and 5 voices
Canteloube Chants d'Auvergne
Duruflé Requiem
Elgar The Dream of Gerontius
Fauré Requiem
Handel Coronation Anthems
Handel Dixit Dominus
Handel Messiah
Haydn Nelson Mass
Haydn The Creation
Howells Hymnus Paradisi

Mahler Das Lied von der Erde
Mahler Kindertotenlieder
Mendelssohn Elijah
Monteverdi 1610 Vespers
Monteverdi Madrigals, Book 8
Mozart Mass in C minor
Mozart Requiem
Orff Carmina burana
Palestrina Missa Papae Marcelli
R Strauss Four Last Songs
Rachmaninov Vespers
Ravel Shéhérazade
Schubert Winterreise
Schumann Dichterliebe
Tallis Spem in alium
Vaughan Williams Serenade to Music
Verdi Requiem
Victoria Requiem
Vivaldi Gloria in D, RV589
Walton Belshazzar's Feast

OPERA, OPERETTA & STAGE WORKS

Bartók Duke Bluebeard's Castle
Beethoven Fidelio
Bellini Norma
Berg Wozzeck
Bernstein West Side Story
Bizet Carmen
Bizet Les pêcheurs de perles
Britten Peter Grimes
Britten Turn of the Screw
Debussy Pelléas et Mélisande
Gershwin Porgy and Bess
Gluck Orfeo ed Euridice
Handel Alcina
Handel Giulio Cesare
Handel Rinaldo
Janáček The Cunning Little Vixen
Lehár Die lustige Witwe
Leoncavallo Pagliacci
Mascagni Cavalleria rusticana
Monteverdi L'Orfeo
Mozart Die Zauberflöte
Mozart Don Giovanni
Mozart Le nozze di Figaro
Mussorgsky Boris Godunov
Puccini La bohème
Puccini Madama Butterfly
Puccini Tosca
Puccini Turandot
R Strauss Der Rosenkavalier
Rossini Il barbiere di Siviglia
Strauss J II Die Fledermaus
Sullivan The Pirates of Penzance
Tchaikovsky Eugene Onegin
Verdi Aida
Verdi Il trovatore
Verdi La traviata
Verdi Otello
Verdi Rigoletto
Wagner Der Ring des Nibelungen
Wagner Tristan und Isolde
Weber Der Freischütz

1000 YEARS OF MUSIC

The story of classical music is a long and complex one, but **Jeremy Nicholas** has risen to the challenge of telling it once again. Here he offers a guided tour of the key players and movements that have made classical music the rich art-form that today still entrances, moves and uplifts.

Fixing a date for 'the beginning of music' is as elusive as pin-pointing the millennium in which dinosaurs became extinct. 1000 AD merely provides a convenient starting point for the birth of modern Western music. It was around that date when the idea first occurred of combining several voices to sing a melody; it was the time, too, when the Church, for so long the most important influence and inspiration on the development of music, recognised a need to standardise the single-line unaccompanied chants that had been used for centuries in sacred ceremonies.

This early Christian music, derived from Greek songs and from the chanting used in synagogues, had evolved into what we now call plainsong, plainchant or Gregorian chant, the traditional music of the Western Church – a single melodic line, usually sung without accompaniment. (The Gregorian chant melodies sung today date from after the death of Pope Gregory in 604 AD.) Without any accepted written system to denote the pitch or length of a note, the scoring of music was inevitably a haphazard affair.

Guido d'Arezzo, a Benedictine monk whose life as a teacher and musical theorist usefully coincided with the Church's need for musical unification, is generally credited with the introduction of a stave of horizontal lines by which one could accurately record the pitch of notes. He also came up with what we now call the tonic sol-fa system, used by singers, in which notes are named by their position in the scale, as opposed to being named after letters of the alphabet (a practice derived from the ancient Greeks).

Still there was no method of notating the length of a note. Without this, it is difficult to see how any sense of rhythm could be measured. Some scholars say that this was defined by the natural accentuation and emphasis of speech patterns and that therefore no special device was needed – the singers (without a conductor, of course) provided their own 'flow' and expression.

With two of the three main elements of music – i.e. Melody and Rhythm – in the process of being codified, the idea of Harmony came into the world. Naturally, not all the singers in a choir would have the same vocal range, a problem for the comfortable unison singing of the psalms. So voices began to be divided according to natural range, chanting the Plainsong in parallel lines at two pitches, five notes apart (C-G for example) The gap between the two notes is called an interval, thus the singers sang the interval of a perfect fifth. From this apparently simple concept, but which took so long to implement, the idea grew that while one line sang the Plainsong (the 'tenor' or 'holding' part), others could weave another tune around it.

Rules were drawn up as to which part of the service could use which type of intervals. Gradually, the interval of a third (C-E), for long considered to be a dischord, was allowed. Within the moderately short time-scale of a century, we have Pérotin of Notre Dame – one of the early masters of Polyphony – writing music for three and four voices.

Parallel to the development of liturgical (Church) music ran the flowering of the secular music of the troubadours, the poet-musicians who sang of beautiful ladies, chivalry, spring and suchlike. These were the successors of the court minstrels, employed to sing the great sagas and legends, who themselves had their less-educated counterparts in the jongleurs, itinerant singers and instrumentalists. Nobly-born for the most part, the troubadours came from Provence and Aquitaine (the trouvères, their northern counterparts, and the minnesingers of Germany were almost contemporary). Only about 60 manuscripts of troubadour and trouvère poetry survive today and few of them contain musical notation which, again, have indications only of pitch but not of note length.

These 200 years witnessed the birth of harmony, of modern musical notation, the dance and song craze which pervaded Europe during the time of the Crusades and the complex structure of the troubadours' poetry – more than enough to ignite the imagination of Renaissance man.

From melody to harmony

The study and use of chords is what we call Harmony. Diaphony – 'two-voiced' music – dominated all musical composition till the 13th century; this two-part singing as applied to plainchant was also called organum. Voices would sing an octave apart (C-C), a perfect fifth (C-G), a perfect fourth (C-F) or a major third (C-E) apart.

Polyphony is also concerned with the sounding of more than one note, but through melody – the word means 'many-sounds', 'many-voiced'. The addition of a third, fourth or more independent musical lines sung or sounded together was the next obvious development, and it was the extraordinary Philippe de Vitry, a French bishop, musical theorist, composer, poet and diplomat, who showed the way forward in a famous book called The New Art – *Ars Nova* (as opposed to the *Ars Antiqua* of Guido d'Arezzo). Time-signatures indicated a rhythm for the music and improvements in notation symbolised note lengths – the ancestors of our minim, breve and semibreve. Guillaume de Machaut (another French priest, poet and composer) took de Vitry's ideas a stage further and wrote both secular songs and settings of the Mass (1364 – the earliest known complete setting by one composer) with three and four polyphonic voices.

Though France was the musical centre of Europe at this time, Italy was developing its own *ars nova* independently with music that reflected the warmth and sensuality of the country, in contrast to the more intellectual Gallic writing. England, less affected by *ars nova*, did not make a significant contribution to any musical development until the arrival of John Dunstable. Living in France as the court composer to the Duke of Burgundy (the younger brother of Henry V), Dunstable used rhythmic phrases, traditional plainchant and added other free parts, combining them into a flowing, mellifluous style. Nearly 60 pieces of his music still survive.

Dunstable in turn influenced the Burgundian composers Guillaume Dufay and Gilles Binchois, whose music can be said to be the stylistic bridge between *ars nova* and the fully developed polyphony of the 15th century. The technical aspects of musical composition and the almost mathematical fascination with note combination began slowly to open the door to the personality of a composer being reflected in his music.

Out of the church

By the middle of the 15th century, the royal palaces and the great houses of the noblemen had usurped the Church as the single most important influence on the course of music (in 1416, Henry V of England employed more than 30 voices in the Chapel Royal while the Papal Chapel had only nine). One by-product was the closer relationship between secular music and the music of the Church, a cross-pollination which benefited the development of both. The musicians who passed through the Burgundian court disseminated its style and learning to all points of the European compass.

The most noticeable advances during this period were the increased freedom composers gave to their vocal lines and the difference in the treatment of the texts they set. Previously, words had to fit the music; now the reverse was the case and this is no better illustrated than by the work of one of the next generation of composers to become renowned throughout Europe, Josquin Desprez. His music incorporates a greater variety of expression than any previously – there are even flashes of quirky humour – and includes attempts at symbolism where the musical ideas match those of the text. With various voices singing in polyphony, it is difficult to follow the words; where the subject called for the words to be heard clearly, Josquin wrote music that had the different voices singing different notes but the same words at the same time – chordal music, in other words. Not surprisingly, Josquin has been called 'the first composer whose music appeals to our modern sense of art'. After him, it is easy for our ears to follow the development of music into the language which is familiar to us today through the works of the great classical composers of two centuries later.

The 16th century witnessed four major musical phenomena: the polyphonic school reached its zenith, the tradition of instrumental music was founded, the first opera was produced and music began to be printed for the first time. For most people, the opportunity to see and read music had simply not been there; musicians could now, for the first time, stand around a score printed in a book and sing or play their part. Limited and expensive though it was, music was now available. No wonder it flourished so rapidly.

It's hard to conceive now of the central importance of the Christian Church at this time. The buildings which the men of the Renaissance erected with such splendour and confidence symbolised the age of 're-birth' and the music of the time rose to fill the naves of the great European cathedrals. Palestrina in Italy, Lassus in the Netherlands and Byrd in England carried on from where Josquin had left off to produce complex and richly expressive works which took the art of polyphonic writing for the voice to new heights and demonstrated man's ability to express his faith with a glory and fervour that no previous century had matched.

How was this rich cloth of musical gold woven? One distinguished writer on music, Percy Scholes, drew an illuminating analogy on musical 'fabric' when discussing the music of Palestrina. 'Woven' he felt, was an appropriate word for this kind of composition. 'The music consists of the intertwining of a fixed number of strands. And as [the composer] weaves he is producing a 'woof' as well as a 'warp'. Looked at as warp the composition is a horizontal combination of melodies; looked at as woof it is a perpendicular collection of chords. The composer necessarily has both aspects in his mind as he pens his piece, but the horizontal (or 'warp') aspect is probably uppermost with him. Such music as this we speak of as 'Contrapuntal' or as 'in Counterpoint'. The 'woof' (= perpendicular, ie 'Harmonic') element is there, but is less observable than the 'warp' (= horizontal, i.e. 'Contrapuntal'). A moment's thought will show that all Contrapuntal music must also be Harmonic, and a second moment's thought that not all Harmonic music need be Counterpoint.'

It had taken 1000 years from the earliest Plainsong for the tradition to develop into the elaborate, highly sophisticated art form, which produced such masterpieces as Palestrina's *Stabat mater*, Victoria's *Ave verum Corpus* and Byrd's *O Quam Gloriosum*.

Now, new preoccupations challenged composers. The reverent, lush choral works of the Church, mainly from Northern Europe, became fertilised by the lively, sunny dances and songs of the south. The secular counterparts of the church musicians led to the madrigal, a contrapuntal setting of a poem, usually about 12 lines in length, and whose subject was usually amorous or pastoral. The emphasis was on the quality of word-setting and the form proved remarkably popular if short-lived – especially in England (perhaps because of our great literary heritage) where the likes of Gibbons, Weelkes and Morley were the madrigal's finest exponents.

The madrigal and the birth of opera

The madrigals, like the liturgical motets and settings of the Mass, were all for unaccompanied voices – that was how the vast majority of music produced up to this time was conceived. It wasn't until the end of the 14th century that instrumental music began to emerge as an art-form in its own right. The recorder, lute, viol and spinet had played their part in dance music and in accompanying voices (occasionally replacing them) but now composers such as Byrd, Gibbons, Farnaby and Frescobaldi began to write music for specific instruments, though it must be said that the art form did not truly flourish until the Baroque era. Musicians would join together to play a series of varying dance tunes, forming a loosely-constructed suite; or a player might improvise his own tune round another's – a 'fancy' or 'fantasia'; or they might compose variations on a tune played over the same repeating bass line – 'variations on a ground' as it's called. Other innovations were by the Italians Andrea Gabrieli (c1510-86) – the first to combine voices with brass instruments – and his nephew Giovanni (1557-1612), whose antiphonal effects for choirs of brass instruments might have written for our modern stereo systems.

And it was from Italy that the next important step in musical history was taken. Indeed Italy was the country – actually a collection of small independent states at the time, ruled by a number of affluent and cultured families – which would dominate the musical world for a century and a half from 1600. Such was the power of Italian influence at this time that music adopted the language as its lingua franca. To this day, composers almost universally write their performance directions in Italian. One particular word, opera, described a new art form: that of combining drama and music. No one had thought of the concept till the end of the 16th century.

In the late 16th century, artists, writers and architects became interested in the ancient cultures of Greece and Rome. In Florence, a group of the artistic intelligentsia became interested in how the ancient Greek dramas were performed. Experimenting with declaiming the more poetic passages and using a few chords of instrumental music to accompany other passages in natural speech rhythm, the idea of music reflecting, supporting and commenting upon dramatic action was born: *dramma per musica* ('drama by means of music'), a play with a musical setting.

Into the ring then came one of the supreme musicians of history, Claudio Monteverdi. He did not write the first opera (that honour goes to Jacopo Peri and his *Dafne*, now lost, of 1594 or 1597) but with one work, *Orfeo* (1607) he drew up the future possibilities of the medium. Solo singers were given a dramatic character to portray and florid songs to sing, there were choruses, dances, orchestral interludes, scenery. Opera was a markedly different entertainment to anything that had gone before but, more importantly, it was a completely new way of using music.

The right instruments

Monteverdi's successors such as Pier Cavalli and Marc'Antonio Cesti developed a type of flowing, lyrical song inspired by the flow of spoken Italian – bel canto ('beautiful singing') which in turn encouraged the prominence of the singer. Dramatic truth soon went out of the window in favour of the elaborate vocal displays of the opera soloists – composers were only too happy to provide what their new public wanted – and no class of singers were more popular than the castrati. Feted wherever they appeared, the castrati, who had had their testicles removed as young boys to preserve their high voices, were highly paid and immensely popular, a not dissimilar phenomenon to The Three Tenors of today (with two small differences). The practice of castration to produce an entertainer, an extraordinarily barbaric concept, was only halted in the early 19th century. The last castrato, Alessandro Moreschi, actually survived until 1922 and made a dozen or so records in 1902.

St Paul had written that women should keep silent in church. They were therefore not available for the taxing high lines in church music. If the origins of the castrati could be laid firmly at the door of the Church, similar dogma can also be held responsible for the slow progress of instrumental composition. From the earliest times the Church had voiced its disapproval of the practice. St Jerome had declared that no Christian maiden should know what a lyre or flute looked like (let alone hear what they sounded like). The weakening of the Church's authority after the Reformation encouraged composers in the writing of instrumental music for groups, music moreover that took into account the relative strengths and colours of the different instruments, another new concept. The same change of emphasis led also to a flood of brilliant instrumental soloists. Among them was a brilliant Italian-born violinist named Jean-Baptiste Lully who went to France in 1646. Here he worked for King Louis XIV, the extravagant builder of Versailles who employed 120 musicians in various bands. An orchestra of 'Twenty-four Violins' provided music at the French court; with Lully's addition of flutes, oboes, bassoons, trumpets and timpani, the modern orchestra began to emerge.

Another important by-product of the Italian opera was the introduction of the sonata – the term originally simply meant a piece to be sounded (played), as opposed to sung (cantata). Although it quickly took on a variety of forms, the sonata began with the Italian violinists imitating the vocal display elements of opera – a single melody played against a harmonised background or, if you like, accompanied by chords. This was a huge difference from the choral works of a century before driven by their polyphonic interweavings. Now there was music which, even if there was no background accompaniment, the listener's ears could supply the harmony mentally – you could tell where the tune was going to resolve, you could sense its shape and destination more easily. With the musical emphasis on harmony – a key feature of the coming century and a half – rhythm began to take an increasingly important part. Chordal patterns naturally fall in sequences, in regular measures or bars. Listen to a chaconne by Purcell or Handel and you realise that the theme is not a tune but a sequence of chords. Measuring the beats in a bar (*one-two* or *one-two-three* or *one-two-three-four* – the emphasis always on the first beat) gives the music a sense of form and helps its onward progress. Phrases lead the ear to the next sequence like the dialogue between two people, exchanging thoughts in single words, in short sentences or in long paragraphs. Sing a simple hymn tune like *All people that on earth do dwell* and you are aware of what music had now acquired – a strong tonal centre.

Makers of musical instruments responded by adapting and improving instruments: the great Italian violin makers Stradivari, Amati and Guarneri, the Ruckers family of Antwerp with its harpsichords and the Harris family of England building organs.

A final contribution to this period was made by Italian opera. The use of the orchestra in opera naturally led to the expression of dramatic musical ideas – one reason why the Italian orchestra developed faster than elsewhere. Round about the start of the 18th century composers began to write overtures in three sections (fast-slow-fast), providing the model for the classical sonata form used in instrumental pieces, concertos and symphonies for the next 200 years and more.

Thus this 'homophonic' period, emphasising music with a single melody and harmonic accompaniment, melted seamlessly during the 17th century into the Baroque era of Vivaldi, Bach and Handel.

The concerto is born

The concerto developed from the dance suites popular in Italy at the beginning of the 17th century, known as the *sonata da camera*. Originally a composition that contrasted two groups of instrumentalists with each other, the form developed into the *concerto grosso* ('great concerto') of which the first leading exponent was Arcangelo Corelli. Here a group of solo string instrumentalists alternate with the main body of strings in a work, usually of three or four movements. Geminiani, Albinoni, Torelli, Handel and others contributed to the form. The solo concerto was but a short step from here where a soloist is contrasted with (later pitted against) the orchestra. No concertos of this period have achieved the popularity of Vivaldi's whose 500 essays in the genre (mainly for strings but sometimes for wind instruments) are the product of one of the most remarkable musical minds of the early 18th century. *The Four Seasons*, among the best known and most frequently-played pieces of classical music, illustrates the new concept.

Northern Europe provided the springboard for the rapid development of keyboard music: the North German school of organ music, founded by Frescobaldi and Sweelinck a century before, with its interest in contrapuntal writing, laid the way for the likes of Pachelbel and Buxtehude whose line reached its peak in the great works of Bach. Meanwhile Rameau and Couperin in France were producing short descriptive harpsichord pieces (as well as operas) in a style that is called 'rococo' – from the French *rocaille*, a term originally alluding to fancy shell and scroll work in art. It was predominantly diverting rather than elevating and rococo usefully defines the character of lighter music written in the Baroque period, especially when contrasted with the works of the two musical heavyweights of the time, Johann Sebastian Bach and George Frideric Handel.

Bach in his own time was considered old-fashioned, a provincial composer from central Germany. But his music contains some of the noblest and most sublime expressions of the human spirit and with him the art of contrapuntal writing reached its zenith. The 48 Preludes and Fugues for *The Well-Tempered Clavier* explore all the permutations of fugal writing in all the major and minor keys; his final work, *The Art of Fugue* (left incomplete at his death) takes a mathematical delight in the interweaving of contrapuntal variations on the same theme. Yet the technical brilliance of Bach's music is subsumed in the expressive power of his compositions, in particular his organ music, church cantatas and the great *St Matthew Passion* and Mass in B minor. His instrumental music is evidence that he was by no means always the stern God-fearing Lutheran – the exuberant six *Brandenburg Concertos* show that he was well acquainted with the sunny Italian way of doing things and many of his most beautiful and deepest thoughts are reserved for the concertos and orchestral suites. His influence on composers and musicians down the years has been immeasurable. For many he remains the foundation stone of their art.

Bach's great contemporary, Handel, also came from Germany but in contrast was a widely travelled, man-of-the-world who settled in England and became a shrewd entrepreneur and manipulator of musical affairs. In instrumental forms, such as the *concerto grosso*, Handel was equally at home writing in homophonic or polyphonic style and introduced a variety of wind/string combinations in his colourful scoring. He developed the typical 17th-century dance suite into such famous (and still immensely popular) occasional works as *The Water Music* and *Royal Fireworks Music*. Opera was a field into which Bach never ventured but Handel – between 1711 and 1729, – produced nearly 30 operas in the Italian style until the public tired of these when, ever the pragmatist, he turned to oratorio. An oratorio is an extended setting of a (usually) religious text in dramatic form but which does not require scenery or stage action. Handel's have an immense dramatic and emotional range and often employ daring harmonies, never mind the unending stream of glorious melodies and uplifting choruses

Bach was the last great composer to be employed by the church, fittingly, for the church had been the mainspring for the progress of polyphonic music and Bach was the *ne plus ultra* of the style. Henceforward, musical patronage came from the nobility and the nobility preferred music that was elegant, entertaining and definitely not smacking of anything 'churchy'. Following the 17th century's example of the French court and Italian principalities, every European duke worth his salt aspired to his own orchestra and music director. One such was the court of Mannheim where an orchestra under the direction of Johann Stamitz raised orchestral playing to a standard unheard of previously. A new era, breaking away from the contrapuntal writing of the later Baroque, was ushered in.

The Classical Era

The term 'Classical Music' has two meanings: used to describe any music which is supposedly 'heavy' (as opposed to pop or jazz as in 'I can't stand classical music') and also a certain period in the development of music, the Classical era. This can be summarised as music which is notable for its masterly economy of form and resources and for its lack of overt emotionalism. If Bach and Handel dominated the first half of the 17th century, Haydn and Mozart are their counterparts for the latter half and represent all the virtues of the Classical style.

This can be traced back to a generation or so before the birth of Haydn to the rococo style of Couperin and Rameau and, more powerfully, in the invigorating keyboard works of Domenico Scarlatti whose more than 500 short sonatas composed in his sixties demonstrate a brilliance that only Bach equalled. Scarlatti, though, writing on a smaller scale, had the specific intent of delighting and instructing his pupil, the Queen of Spain. His near-contemporary Georg Philipp Telemann brought the rococo style to Germany. Lighter and even more fecund than Bach, Telemann was held in far greater esteem in his lifetime than Johann Sebastian. Despite his stated credo ('He who writes for the many does better work than he who writes only for the few... I have always aimed at facility. Music ought not to be an effort, an occult science') the two greatly admired each other to such an extent that Bach named his son Carl Philipp Emanuel after Telemann and chose him as godfather.

CPE Bach's music represents a cross-roads between the Franco-Italian rococo and the emerging classical schools – indeed, in some of his keyboard music he seems to anticipate Beethoven. His piano sonatas, making use of the expressive powers of the newly invented pianoforte, lead us to redefine the term 'sonata' as used in the previous century. Now the sonata became a formalised structure with related keys and themes. These Bach developed into extended movements, as opposed to the short movements of the Baroque form. Listening to CPE, perhaps the most original and daring composer of the mid-18th century, one becomes aware of the serious and comical, the inspired and the routine, lying side by side with engaging unpredictability.

Parallel to this was the work of Johann Stamitz. His music is rarely heard today yet he and his son Carl (1746-1801) were pioneers in the development of the symphony. This form had grown out of the short quick-slow-quick one-movement overtures or sinfonias of Italian opera. Stamitz, in the employ of the Mannheim court, had one of the most distinguished orchestras in Europe under his direction. The symphonies he wrote were to be the pattern for those of Haydn and Mozart – in them we can see, as in CPE Bach's sonatas, use of related keys, two contrasted first movement subjects (themes) and the graceful working out and development of material. He was the first to introduce the clarinet into the orchestra (and was probably the first to write a concerto for the instrument), also allowing the brass and woodwind greater prominence. His orchestral crescendos, a novel effect at this time, were said to have excited audiences to rise from their seats.

Italy had dominated the musical world of the 17th and early 18th centuries with its operas and great violinists. From the middle of the 18th century, the centre of musical pre-eminence moved to Vienna, a position it would retain until the last of the Hapsburg emperors in the early years of the 20th century. The Hapsburgs loved music and imported the best foreign musicians to court; the imperial chapel became a second centre of musical excellence. Equally important was Vienna's location at the centre of Europe. With the Viennese court as its focus, all kinds of influences met and mingled from nearby Germany, Bohemia and Italy.

Sonata form and the symphony

There is less than half a century between the death of Handel (1759) and the first performance of Beethoven's *Fidelio* (1809). Bach and Handel were still composing when Haydn was a teenager. To compare the individual 'sound world' of any of these four composers is to hear amazingly rapid progress in musical thinking. Without doubt, the most important element of this was the development of the sonata and symphonic forms. During this period, a typical example generally followed the same basic pattern: four movements – 1) the longest, sometimes with a slow introduction, 2) slow movement, 3) minuet, 4) fast, short and light in character. Working within this formal structure, each movement in turn had its own internal structure and order of progress. Most of Haydn's and Mozart's sonatas,

symphonies and chamber music are written in accordance with this pattern and three-quarters of all Beethoven's music conforms to 'sonata form' in one way or another.

Haydn's contribution to musical history is immense, he was nicknamed 'the father of the symphony' (despite Stamitz's prior claim) and was progenitor of the string quartet. Like all his well-trained contemporaries, Haydn had a thorough knowledge of polyphony and counterpoint (and, indeed, was not averse to using it) but his music is predominantly homophonic. His 104 symphonies cover a wide range of expression and harmonic ingenuity. The same is true of the string quartets. With its perfect balance of string sound (two violins, viola and cello), the implicit economy in the scoring, the precision and elegance in the handling of the medium, the string quartet is the quintessential Classical art form.

Mozart composed 41 symphonies and in the later ones (try the famous opening of No 40 in G minor) enters a realm beyond Haydn's – searching, moving and far from impersonal. This is even more true of the great series of piano concertos, among music's most sublime creations, where the writing becomes deeply involved – the slow movement of the A major Concerto (K488) is grief-stricken, anticipating the writing of a future generation. It was Mozart, too, who raised opera to new heights. Gluck had single-handedly broken away from the ossified, singer-dominated Italian opera and shown in works such as *Orfeo ed Euridice* (1762) that music must correspond to the mood and style of the piece, colour and complement the stage action; arias should be part of the continuous action and not merely stuck in to display the singer's vocal talents. Mozart went further and in his four masterpieces *The Marriage of Figaro*, *Così fan tutte*, *Don Giovanni* and *The Magic Flute* revealed more realistic characters, truer emotions (and, of course, incomparably greater music) than anything that had gone before. Here, for the first time, opera reflected the foibles and aspirations of mankind, themes on which the Romantic composers were to dwell at length.

The Age of Revolution

'The Old Order Changeth': for the first half of the 19th century, Europe, taking its cue from the French Revolution and American War of Independence, was imbued with a spirit of general political unrest, culminating in the 1848 uprisings. Nationalism, the struggle for individual freedom and self-expression were reflected and indeed created by all the arts – the one fed off the other. The neat, well-ordered regime of the periwig and minuet gave way to the impetuous, passionate world of the tousle-headed revolutionary.

Ludwig van Beethoven coupled his genius for music with profoundly held political beliefs and an almost religious certainty about his purpose. With the possible exception of Wagner, no other composer has, single-handedly, changed the course of music so dramatically and continued to develop and experiment throughout his entire career. His early music, built on the Classical paths trod by Haydn and Mozart, demonstrates his individuality in taking established musical structures and re-shaping them to his own ends. Unusual keys and harmonic relationships are explored, while as early as the Third Symphony (*Eroica*), the music is vastly more inventive and cogent than anything Mozart achieved even in a late masterpiece like the *Jupiter*. Six more symphonies followed, all different in character, all attempting new goals of human expression, culminating in the great *Choral* Symphony (No 9) with its ecstatic final choral movement celebrating man's existence. No wonder so many composers felt daunted by attempting the symphonic form after Beethoven and that few ever attempted more than the magic Beethovenian number of nine.

His chamber music tells a similar story, building on the classical form of the string quartet, gradually making it his own (listen to the Middle Period *Razumovsky* quartets) until the final group of late quartets which contain music of profound spirituality and deeply felt personal statements – light years from the recent world of his illustrious predecessors. The cycle of 32 piano sonatas reflect a similar portrait of his life's journey; the final three of his five piano concertos and the sublime Violin Concerto are on a par with the symphonies and quartets. His single opera *Fidelio*, while not a success as a piece of theatre, seems to express all the themes that Beethoven held most dear – his belief in the brotherhood of man, his disgust at revolutionaries-turned-dictators, the redeeming strength of human love. All this was achieved, romantically enough, while he himself struggled with profound deafness. Beethoven's unquenchable spirit and his ability to use music to express himself places him in the forefront of man's creative achievements. 'Come the man, come the moment' – Beethoven's lifespan helpfully delineates the late classical period and the early Romantics. His music is the titanic span between the two.

Those who followed revered him as a god. Schubert, the next great Viennese master, 27 years younger but who survived him by a mere 18 months, was in awe of Beethoven. He did not progress the symphonic or sonata forms, there was no revolutionary zeal in his make-up. What he gave was the gift of melody. Schubert is arguably the greatest tunesmith the world has ever known and in his more than 600 songs established the German song (or Lied) tradition.

From his *Erlkönig* (1815) onwards, Schubert unerringly caught the heart of a poem's meaning and reflected it in his setting. For the first time, too, the piano assumed equal importance with the vocal part, painting a tone picture or catching the mood of the piece in its accompaniment.

And it was the new iron-strung pianos which came to be the favoured instrument of the first part of the Romantic era. A bewildering number of composer-pianists were born just after the turn of the century, the most prominent of whom were Liszt, Chopin, Schumann and Mendelssohn. Of these, Mendelssohn relied on the elegant, traditional structures of Classicism in which to wrap his refined poetic and melodic gifts. Many of his piano works (his *Songs Without Words*, for example) and orchestral pieces (*Hebrides* Overture and *Italian* Symphony, No 4) describe nature, places, emotions and so forth. Schumann, too, favoured such short musical essays with titles like *Traümerei* and *Des Abends* to evoke a mood or occasion – 'characteristic pieces' they were called, 'programme music' later on. The undisputed master of the romantic keyboard style was Frédéric Chopin. Almost his entire oeuvre is devoted to the piano in a string of highly individual and expressive works composed in the short period of 20 years. Fifty years after his early death in 1849, composers were still writing pieces heavily influenced by him. Chopin rarely used descriptive titles for his work (beyond such labels as Nocturne, Berceuse or Barcarolle). The technical and lyrical possibilities of the instrument were raised to new heights in such masterpieces as the Four Ballades, the final two (of three) piano sonatas and the many short dance-based compositions. Most of these derived from his homeland of Poland and, as a self-imposed exile living in Paris, Chopin was naturally drawn to expressing his love of his country. Nationalism of a much more fervent kind was to be a key factor in the music of composers writing later in the Romantic tradition (Chopin himself, incidentally, disliked being labelled 'a Romantic').

But to truly define 'the Romantic era' in music, we have to look at the three composers who dominated the musical world for the second and third quarters of the 19th century and who pushed music onward to the dawn of the next: Liszt, Berlioz and Wagner.

The Romantics

Rebellion and freedom of expression lie at the heart of the Romantic movement in music, literature, painting and architecture, a self-conscious breaking of the bonds and belief in the right of the artist. Liszt, Byronic in looks and temperament, the greatest pianist of the day, gave us the solo piano recital, the 'symphonic poem' – the extended orchestral equivalent of Schumann's 'characteristic pieces' – and a bewildering variety of music in all shapes and forms. The B minor Piano Sonata, in which all the elements of traditional sonata form are subsumed into an organic whole, is one of the cornerstones of the repertory; his final piano works anticipate the harmonies of Debussy, Bartók and beyond. While all of his music is by no means profound – there's a great deal of gloss and glitter – his adventurous scores and his patronage and encouragement of any young composer who came to him made him one of the most influential musical geniuses of the entire century.

Berlioz was not a pianist. Perhaps that is why he is the most important composer of the period in terms of orchestral writing. He based his music on 'the direct reaction of feeling' and could summon up with extraordinary vividness the supernatural, say, or the countryside or ardent lovers. Like Liszt, he never wrote a formal symphony: Liszt's *Faust Symphony* and Berlioz's *Symphonie fantastique* are 'programmatic' and rely on their literary inspiration for their structure. Berlioz wrote on an epic scale, employing huge forces to convey his vision: the *Grande Messe des Morts*, for example, requires a tenor solo, brass bands and a massive chorus as well as an expanded orchestra. Théophile Gautier, whose *Nuits d'été* Berlioz set to music, summed Berlioz up thus: '[He] represents the romantic musical idea, the breaking up of old moulds, the substitution of new forms for unvaried square rhythms, a complex and competent richness of orchestration, truth of local colour, unexpected effects in sound, tumultuous and Shakespearean depth of passion, amorous or melancholy dreaminess, longings and questionings of the soul, infinite and mysterious sentiments not to be rendered in words, and that something more than all which escapes language but may be divined in music.' Technical improvements in the manufacture of orchestral instruments – the brass and woodwind especially – helped composers like Berlioz achieve their ends, for the modern instruments provided a wider range and variety of sound. This additional colour in the composer's orchestral palette encouraged more extended (sometimes seemingly formless) works. The prop of the symphonic structure was needed less, though, writing this at the beginning of the 21st century, many still enjoy the challenges of composing in that form.

The third Titan of the Romantics was the most written- and talked-about composer of all time: Richard Wagner. As intelligent and industrious as he was ruthless and egocentric, Wagner's great achievement was *The Ring of the Nibelungen*, a cycle of four operas which took opera from the realm of entertainment to a quasi-religious experience. Influenced by Beethoven, Mozart (held to be the first truly German operatic composer) and Meyerbeer (whose sense of epic theatre, design and orchestration impressed him), Wagner's vision was to create a work that was a fusion of all the arts – literature, painting and music. He called his vision 'music-drama'.

Some of his ideas had been anticipated 40 years earlier by Carl Maria von Weber, one of the first to insist on total control of all aspects of the production of his work and who, as early as 1817, wrote of his desire to fuse all art forms into one great new form. Weber's opera *Der Freischütz*, the first German Romantic opera, was a milestone in the development of these ideas, using German mythology as its subject.

Wagner decided that the music must grow from the libretto (he supplied his own), that there must be no display arias for their own sake, inserted just to please the public; the music, like the opera's narrative flow, must never cease, for the music is equally important in the telling of the story and commenting on the action and characters; leitmotivs, short musical phrases associated with different characters and moods, would recur throughout the score to underpin and bind the whole work. The orchestral contribution was at least as important as the vocal element. But Wagner was more than just an operatic reformer. He opened up a new harmonic language, especially in the use of chromaticism (see page XXXI). This had not only a profound influence on succeeding generations of composers but led logically to the atonal music of the 20th century.

Not all composers fell under Wagner's spell. Brahms was the epitome of traditional musical thought. His four symphonies are far nearer the style of Beethoven than those of Mendelssohn or Schumann, and the first of these was not written until 1875, when Wagner had all but completed *The Ring*. Indeed Brahms is by far the most classical of the German Romantics. He wrote little programme music and no operas. It's a curious coincidence that he distinguished himself in the very musical forms that Wagner chose to ignore – the fields of chamber music, concertos, variation writing and symphonies.

Verdi v Wagner

It was only in old age that Giuseppe Verdi adopted some of Wagner's musical ideas. The Italian represents the culmination of the different school of opera. Wagner's operas are the descendants of Beethoven and Weber; Verdi's developed from the comic masterpieces of Rossini and the Romantic dramas by Bellini and Donizetti. With the famous trilogy of *Rigoletto* (1851), *Il trovatore* (1853) and *La traviata* (1853), Verdi combined his mastery of drama with a flow of unforgettable lyrical melodies, creating masterpieces of the genre of which the public has never tired. *Don Carlos* (1867), *Aida* (1871), *Otello* (1887) and *Falstaff* (1893) show a development and tirelessly searching mind that remain among the great miracles of music.

One thing that Wagner and Verdi had in common was their fierce patriotism. In his own lifetime, Verdi was held as a potent symbol of Italian independence, while Wagner espoused the dubious theories which made him such hero of the Third Reich. During the course of the century, Western music, now dominated by German tradition and forms, began to be more and more influenced by the rise of nationalism. Composers wanted to reflect the character and cultural identity of their native lands by using material and forms which derived from their own country. Russia was the foremost in the surge of nationalism that now fertilised the Late Romantic era. Glinka was the first important Russian composer to use Russian subjects and folk tunes in his opera A Life for the Tsar. Influenced by the Italian tradition, it nevertheless succeeded in conveying typical Russian song and harmony and had a profound effect on Borodin, Balakirev, Cui, Mussorgsky and Rimsky-Korsakov – the so-called 'Mighty Five' (or 'Mighty Handful' – though Cui is hardly 'mighty' compared with the genius of his peers).

Tchaikovsky, the most accomplished of all his Russian contemporaries, paid lip-service to the Nationalists, composing largely in the German tradition. Elsewhere in Europe, nationalist schools of music arose: in Bohemia there were Smetana, Dvořák and Janáček; in Scandinavia, Nielsen, Grieg and Sinding; in Finland, Sibelius, whose seven symphonies developed the medium in a highly arresting and individual way; in Spain, Albéniz, Granados and de Falla. Britain and the United States were slow in developing a nationalist school: Parry and Elgar wrote firmly in the German manner and it was not until the later arrival of Vaughan Williams and Holst that a 'British' (or at any rate 'English') sound began to emerge. America was a curious case. Its first native composer of any note, Gottschalk, used indigenous native rhythms for his (mainly) piano works as early as the 1850s – South American, New Orleans and Cuban elements are boldly to the fore. It took another half century before any music directly derived from American folk material began to assert itself in the form of jazz.

The dates for each period of music must be treated flexibly. The Romantic period embraces a wide divergence of personal styles and represents a long and rapid period in Western music's development. In common with every aspect of life, the art developed at an ever-increasing pace. Parallel to the growth of Nationalism, came the Italian *verismo* school of opera, the school of Realism or Naturalism

epitomised by the works of Puccini, Leoncavallo and Mascagni, whose subjects were drawn from contemporary life presented with heightened violence and emotions. During the closing years of the period, emerging under the influence of Wagner, came the neo-Romantics whose use of massive symphonic structures and elaborate orchestration is heard in the music of Bruckner, Mahler, Scriabin and the early works of Richard Strauss.

The Nationalists

Towards the end of the century there was a reaction against the excesses of the Romantics – the too-obvious heart-on-sleeve approach, the emotional over-indulgence, the extra-musical programmes and philosophies began to pal. Just as the Baroque period had melted into the Classical period, the Classical drifted into the early Romantic era, so the close of the 19th century saw a tendency toward bold experimentation in new styles and techniques. Coinciding with the French Impressionist movement in painting and poetry, came Impressionist music, epitomised by the daring (at the time), personal harmonic idiom of Claude Debussy. Here emphasis was put not on the subject of a piece of music but on an emotion or sensation aroused by the subject. His music is just as closely organised as anything in the classical German manner but, using the whole-tone scale and fresh harmonies, Debussy conjures up a sensuous, atmospheric spell in his piano music and orchestral works. The fastidious Maurice Ravel followed in his footsteps with exotic evocations of light and colour, later tinged with jazz references.

By the turn of the century, it was no longer possible to define a dominant general musical trend. Under its many fragmented divisions we can only label the successor of the Classical and Romantic periods somewhat lamely 'Modern Music'.

Igor Stravinsky studied with one of music's great orchestrators, Rimsky-Korsakov. He orchestrated some of Beethoven's piano sonatas as an exercise; he worked at counterpoint and learnt about classical forms – in other words, a sound, traditional conservatoire training. In less than a decade, we find Stravinsky writing music that is a world away from that of his mentor. *The Firebird* (1909), *Petrushka* (1911) and *The Rite of Spring* (1913), his three ballet masterpieces, became progressively more adventurous: in *Petrushka* we find bitonal passages (ie music written in two keys simultaneously), dissonant chords, a new rhythmic freedom and a percussive orchestral quality; in *The Rite of Spring*, a score which provoked a riot at its première, Stravinsky reduced all the elements of music to reinforce rhythm. Debussy and Schoenberg in certain of their works reduced music to the vertical effect of simultaneously sounding notes, so Stravinsky reduced melody and harmony to rhythm. As Alec Harman and Wilfred Mellers put it in their *Man and His Music*: 'Harmony without melody and rhythm, rhythm without melody and harmony, are static. Both the pandemonium of Stravinsky's *Rite of Spring* and Debussy's *Voiles* deprive music of the sense of motion from one point to another. Though they started from diametrically opposed points, both composers mark a radical departure from the traditions of European music since the Renaissance.'

Stravinsky went on to write in a number of other styles throughout his remarkable career, dominating the musical world for 50 years, in the same way that his almost exact contemporary Pablo Picasso dominated his field. Arguably, no other composer this century has exercised a greater influence than Stravinsky – Debussy and Ravel were less wide-ranging, Sibelius and Bartók less daring, Schoenberg and Webern less accessible.

Arnold Schoenberg is Stravinsky's only rival as the musical colossus of the age – to some he opened the door on a whole new world of musical thought that is as exciting as it is challenging; to others he is the bogey man of music, who sent it spiralling out of reach to the ordinary man in the street until, nearly one hundred years later, it has revealed itself as a cul de sac.

Since the Renaissance, all music had a tonal centre. No matter how far away from the tonic – the basic key – the music wandered, the listener was always conscious of the inevitability of a final return to that centre. Increasingly towards the end of the 19th century, music began to incorporate intervals outside the prevailing diatonic scale with the result that a work would feature an extraordinary amount of modulation. This is known as chromatic writing, since intervals from the chromatic scale (not the diatonic scale) are used to harmonise a piece. Listen, for instance, to Wagner's later works and to those of Mahler and Richard Strauss which followed closely on their heels. Hearing them, it becomes less clear as to which key the piece is written in, its tonal centre less obvious. What Schoenberg did was follow logically on from this and ask 'If I can introduce these chromatic notes into my music, can a particular key be said to exist at all? Why should any note be foreign to any given key? Harmony is simply the sounding together of notes, so why shouldn't the 12 semitones of the chromatic scale be accorded equal significance?'

The Second Viennese School

The theories and music of the so-called Second Viennese School – in succession to the First Viennese School of Haydn, Mozart et al – put the listener's expectations on a wrong footing. There are none of the familiar features of chords we recognise, tunes we can hum or rhythms we can tap our feet to. Only the traditional manner of indicating on the score individual notes, time-signatures and expression marks remain. Because the vast majority of the music we are exposed to when growing up is tonal, it is fairly easy to assimilate a Beethoven symphony on a first hearing. Because serial music is written in a completely foreign language with which most of us have no reference points, its effect is like listening to a Scandinavian epic poem spoken in Japanese. The music lover has to acquire a knowledge of the language – in other words, the musical technique involved in the composition – before it can be appreciated. There are comparatively few who have the time to study Scandinavian poetry in Japanese translation, as it were.

Not all composers were attracted to the new technique but dissonance, atonality and the abandonment of melody are strong features of many composers' work this century. Very little serial or atonal music has established itself in the regular concert repertoire; still less has found its way into the hearts and affections of the ordinary music-loving public. This, to jump forward in time, is especially true of music written since the Second World War. A list of works from the pens of world-famous contemporary composers will elicit a blank response form the majority of people. The avant-garde of today is taking far longer to become assimilated than the avant-garde of previous centuries. Opinions are deeply divided over the merits of a composer like Charles Ives, for example, whose polyrhythmic, polytonal works are far too complex for them ever to achieve popularity; Stockhausen, Birtwistle, Cage, Carter, Berio, Nono (the list is endless) will remain a closed book for most people. Yet each of these composers have a huge and fanatical following in certain quarters. Musical development will always, hopefully, have daring, fantastical innovators, examining new possibilities, expressing themselves in new and original ways. Whether they will ever find a broad, responsive and appreciative audience, only time will tell. Most new commissions have a première, a broadcast (if they're lucky) and are then consigned to oblivion – in whatever musical language they're written.

The other path taken by music this century is the one which retains its link with tonality and (increasingly, nowadays) with melody. Harsh and acid though some of Prokofiev's music may be, his style is a tangible descendant of the Romantics. Shostakovich too, sharing Prokofiev's love of the spiky, humorous and satirical, as well as the sombre and introspective, follows on from the same tradition. Rachmaninov to an even greater degree wrote in the late-

Romantic vein, producing some of the most popular symphonies and concertos written this century. In France, the most important composers after Ravel and Debussy were Honegger, Milhaud and Poulenc, three disparate composers un-usefully grouped together as Les Six (the other three made negligible contributions) and all influenced by the whimsical and eccentric Eric Satie. The most significant French composer since the Impressionists is Oliver Messiaen who introduced elements of Indian music and bird-song into the language of Western music. Pierre Boulez, whose complex works are often based on mathematical relationships, and Karlheinz Stockhausen, whose scores for his innovative electronic music are represented by charts and diagrams, are both pupils of Messiaen.

No longer does one school of musical thought prevail. There seems little to link the socio-political operas of Kurt Weill and their brittle, haunting melodies with his contemporary Paul Hindemith and his dense, contrapuntal neo-classical idiom. Far less does Aaron Copland, born only five years later in 1900, have any connection with either. The first conspicuously great American-born composer, Copland used in his music folk material, the sixths and sevenths intervals of the blues, echoes of cowboy songs, jazz and the memory of Jewish synagogues. His *Appalachian Spring* (1944) has been compared by one critic to Vaughan Williams's *Pastoral Symphony*.

The British legacy

And what has happened to British music this century? The Purcell centenary of 1895 stimulated interest in the great heritage of England's musical past; the English Folk Song Society was founded in 1898; the London Promenade Concerts were inaugurated in 1895 and suddenly, 'the land without music' found itself in the midst of a musical renaissance. No one deserves more credit for the revival of the nation's musical fortunes than Ralph Vaughan Williams and Gustav Holst. Vaughan Williams took as his creed the belief that 'The Art of Music above all other arts is the expression of the soul of the nation'. English Tudor music, medieval tonalities and folk song attracted him, composing in what might loosely be called a romantic neo-classical style, using counterpoint, classical forms (such as the symphony and the fugue) and modern harmony. Holst was inspired similarly but also drew inspiration from the east – his most famous piece, *The Planets*, from the ideas of Chaldean astrology. Of the succeeding generation, the most important have been Benjamin Britten, Michael Tippett and William Walton. Britten especially, with his many stage works, established English music on the

international stage, writing for a wide variety of mediums including an opera for television (*Owen Wingrave*). *Peter Grimes, Billy Budd, War Requiem, Serenade for Tenor, Horn and Strings, The Young Person's Guide to the Orchestra* – the list of works he composed since the Second World War now in the regular concert repertoire is remarkably high. Walton's outstanding contributions were made before the war with *Façade, Belshazzar's Feast*, the Viola Concerto and the First Symphony. Tippett has had less lasting success compared with his two contemporaries but *A Child of Our Time* (1941), the Concerto for Double String Orchestra (1939) and the *Fantasia Concertante on a Theme of Corelli* (1953) will undoubtedly stay the course.

Of the more recent generations of British composers, it is still too early to say with any certainty who and what will be remembered in the great scheme of things 50 years hence. Elizabeth Lutyens, Humphrey Searle and the so-called Manchester School of Peter Maxwell Davies, Harrison Birtwistle and Alexander Goehr have their champions and devoted admirers; they do not always mix comfortably with the likes of Richard Rodney Bennett, Malcolm Arnold and George Lloyd – to name those born prior to the War and who each enjoy a loyal following.

A contemporary postscript

Music written in our own time, *writes James Jolly*, remains a divisive art-form, with battle lines drawn up by its partisans. Here are some guides for exploring new music.

One of the strongest 'schools' – and one which drew people in from 'outside' the classical world – were the so-called Minimalists. Steve Reich (b1936), Philip Glass (b1936) and John Adams (b1947) are the three leading representatives, writing music that relies on repeated notes or phrases and which creates wave-like patterns as the phrases interact. All three have developed musical voices that won audience's hearts. Philip Glass has moved effortlessly between the opera-house, concert-hall and film studio, though latterly he has returned to purely abstract composition. John Adams has successfully managed to woo the critics as well as his public. Works such as his recent opera *Doctor Atomic* have an assured place in the repertoire, and his orchestral works are performed with regularity. One of Steve Reich's latest composition, his *Daniel Variations*, a work who impetus was the murder by Islamic extremists of the journalist Daniel Pearl, is a powerful and imaginative response to contemporary events. As *The New Yorker* put it, 'In the most recent pieces Reich has consolidated four decades of invention. Neon-lit textures have given way to dense, dusky landscapes, with tender lyrical passages at the heart of each piece. It's as if Reich were finally letting himself look back in time, perhaps even indulging a secret Romantic urge.'

Currently enjoying huge popularity on both sides of the Atlantic is the Argentinian-Jewish composer Osvaldo Golijov. His music represents 'fusion' at a very high level of sophistication and crosses boundaries with ease. His Lorca opera *Ainadamar*, recorded by DG (and included in this guide) is a magical creation, beautifully presented. His boundary-crossing music has touched a contemporary chord and the reverberations have filled concert-halls the world over.

Henryk Górecki (b1933), Arvo Pärt (b1935) and John Tavener (b1944) sprang to huge popularity during the 1980s with their individual and often gentle voices enhanced by a strong spiritual dimension. Górecki's Third Symphony was one of the musical phenomena of the day – a work of enormous popularity, made a virtual cult by its air-play on Classic FM. John Tavener looks to his deeply held Greek Orthodox beliefs for inspiration and has created a stream of haunting works. His cello concerto *The Protecting Veil* achieved enormous popularity and very quickly chalked up five recordings. Most recently he has written a *concertante* work for violinist Nicola Benedetti.

Oliver Knussen (b1952) grew up under the influence of Benjamin Britten, the then dominant voice in British music. His best known works are his two one-act operas *Higglety Pigglety Pop!* and *Where the Wild Things Are*; his *Ophelia Dances* and Symphonies Nos 2 and 3 reveal the work of a master craftsman. Born less than a decade later, George Benjamin (b1960) established his credentials while still a child. A pupil of Messiaen and Goehr, and friend of Boulez, his first work of significance was *Ringed by the Flat Horizon*. His fine ear for colour has created some wonderfully translucent scores, an approach no doubt enhanced by his skill as a conductor.

Benjamin's contemporary Mark-Anthony Turnage (b1960) enjoys popularity and patronage on both sides of the Atlantic – he is a composer in residence with both the London Philharmonic and the Chicago Symphony. His high-octane earlier works like *Greek*, *Blood on the Floor* and *Three Screaming Popes* (after Francis Bacon's disturbing triptych) have been succeeded by a more lyrical musical language. Many of his LPO commissions have been recorded and give a valuable insight into a the development of a major compositional voice.

Marc-André Dalvabie (b1961) is a French composer worth listening out for – his studies with Boulez and Murail clearly unleashed a fascination with texture and colour, and sometimes it's hard to reconcile Dalbavie's musical training with the actual sound of his music. It can be lush in the extreme but it is beautifully crafted.

Back in the UK, though he has taught in the US for the past few years, Julian Anderson (b1967) has been collecting a loyal following. His fascinating for and love of folk-music gives his works a dimension often lacking in new music – and he is not afraid of melody: his can strikingly beautiful music. His *Book of Hours* (2005) weaves electronics into an orchestral palette to rewarding effect and *Eden*, from 2005, explores the potential of non-tempered tuning.

The golden boy of music in the English-speaking world is the prodigiously gifted Thomas Adès (b1971) whose grasps of musical forms as diverse as an opera and a piano quintet has stunned his audiences. His orchestral *Asyla* (1999) was selected by Simon Rattle for his inaugural concert with the Berlin Philharmonic and the same performers have since given the premiere of *Tevot* (2007): the work was lauded by critics in London and New York. His operas *Powder Her Face* (1995) and *The Tempest* (2004) have both entered the operatic repertory – the Met has announced performances in its 2012-3 of *The Tempest*. His Violin Concerto was premiered at the BBC Proms and a subsequent London performance was recorded and released as a download by EMI.

The contemporary music scene is a rich and vibrant one – there is no shortage of talent and there is a loyal audience for new music. And it is also good to see so many high-profile musicians devoting their energies to performing new music. Vladimir Jurowski regularly conducts Turnage's music, Marin Alsop champions the music of Christopher Rouse, John Corigliano and Jennifer Higdon, Simon Rattle ensures that new music features prominently in Berlin. Conductors such as David Robertson, Esa-Pekka Salonen, Daniel Barenboim, Michael Tilson Thomas, Claudio Abbado and Riccardo Chailly all display a passion for the new. And with instrumentalists such as Anne-Sophie Mutter, Pierre-Laurent Aimard and Emanuel Pahud commissioning new works, the art form's profile stays visible at a very high level. Filter down through the world of music and the levels of passion and commitment increase even more... and the audiences come to listen.

HOW TO USE THE GUIDE

The presentation and design of this *Guide* is similar to that of its parent publication, *Gramophone*. Reviews of works generally appear in the following sequence: Orchestral, Chamber, Instrumental, Vocal/Choral and Opera.

The title for each review contains the following information: composer(s), work(s), artist(s), record company or label, price range, catalogue number and recording date. The circled numeral before the catalogue number indicates the number of discs (if there is more than one), while the timing and mode of recording are given in brackets afterwards. (The abbreviations AAD/ADD/DDD denote analogue or digital stages in the recording/editing or mixing/mastering or transcription processes in CD manufacture.) All other abbreviations used in this *Guide* are given below.

Where three or more composers are represented on a single disc, the review generally appears in the Collections section which starts on page 1323.

The indexes are divided into an artists' index and an index to couplings – an index of works reviewed under other composers. For example, you'll find Prokofiev's Third Piano Concerto with Martha Argerich reviewed under its Bartók Concerto No 3 coupling; to find the page number simply look in the couplings index under Prokofiev.

All recordings are flagged with one or more of the symbols explained below.

KEY TO SYMBOLS

Ⓕ Full price £11 and over
Ⓜ Medium price £8-£10·99
Ⓑ Budget price £6-£7·99
Ⓢ Super-budget price £5·99 and below

Ⓗ Denotes a Historic recording and generally applies to pre-1960 recordings. It can also be an indication that the recording quality may not be up to the highest standards

Ⓟ Denotes recordings where period instruments are used

⤷ Denotes recordings that are available as downloads

Simply the best
An unrivalled version, a cornerstone of the catalogue. A real gem!

OOO Classic
Gramophone Award-winners and recordings of legendary status

OO Outstanding
Outstanding performance and fine sound/transfer

O Strongly recommended
Not a top choice but none the less a fine recording

No disc
Recommended
Good performance with the odd reservation

(S/N/T/t)
(after the recording details)
Synopsis, notes, texts and translation if included in the CD package

ABBREVIATIONS

aas	all available separately	**mndl**	mandolin
alto	countertenor/male alto	**narr**	narrator
anon	anonymous	**oas**	only available separately
arr	arranged	**ob**	oboe
attrib	attributed	**Op**	opus
b	born	**orig**	original
bar	baritone	**org**	organ
bass-bar	bass-baritone	**perc**	percussion
bn	bassoon	**pf**	piano
c	circa (about)	**picc**	piccolo
cl	clarinet	**pub**	publisher/published
clav	clavichord	**rec**	recorder
compl	completed	**recons**	reconstructed
cont	continuo	**rev**	revised
contr	contralto	**sax**	saxophone
cor ang	cor anglais	**sngr**	singer
cpsr	composer	**sop**	soprano
cpte(d)	complete(d)	**spkr**	speaker
d	died	**stg**	string
db	double bass	**synth**	synthesizer
dig pf	digital piano	**tbn**	trombone
dir	director	**ten**	tenor
ed	edited (by)/edition	**timp**	timpani
exc	excerpt	**tpt**	trumpet
fl	flute	**trad**	traditional
fl	flourished	**trans**	transcribed
fp	fortepiano	**treb**	treble
gtr	guitar	**va**	viola
harm	harmonium	**va da gamba**	viola da gamba
hn	horn	**vars**	variations
hp	harp	**vc**	cello
hpd	harpsichord	**vib**	vibraphone
keybd	keyboard	**vn**	violin
lte	lute	**voc**	vocal/vocalist
mez	mezzo-soprano	**wds**	words

THE REVIEWS

THE
GRAMOPHONE
CLASSICAL
MUSIC
GUIDE

2011

Carl Friedrich Abel   German 1723-1787

Abel studied the bass viol, first with his father, and later came into contact with the Bach family in Leipzig. In 1743 he is known to have been a member of the court orchestra in Dresden under the directorship of Hasse. He moved to London during the 1758-59 season and remained there until his death. The bulk of his music is instrumental, and it is his works for viol that have secured his reputation today.

Mr Abel's Fine Airs
Susanne Heinrich *va da gamba*
Hyperion CDA67628 (78' · DDD)   Ⓟ**OO**▷

Carl Friedrich Abel is usually thought of as a genial symphonist much in the mould of his London concert-promoting business partner JC Bach, but this delightful release shows that anyone considering on that basis not to delve further into Abel's output is missing not only an important side of the man, but indeed his very core. Abel was one of the last masters of the viola da gamba, and in these unaccompanied pieces he reveals an intimate art which instantly makes sense of the affection and reverence in which he was held by his friends, they being the ones who got to hear him improvising at home in front of the fire and left touching accounts of his power to stir their emotions. 'He was the Sterne of music' is how one described him, which is saying something.

Susanne Heinrich has chosen 24 solo gamba pieces from the 30 contained in a manuscript in the New York Public Library which surely represent the kind of music Abel played in those domestic musical occasions. Unencumbered by showy virtuosity, they are never less than supremely elegant, yet at their best exhibit profound sentiment in the word's exquisite 18th-century sense. Four of the pieces are grouped together to make a sonata, but the others are free-standing and range from deeply felt *adagios* to lightly arpeggiated preludes, and from suave minuets to the occasional faintly rustic dance. Heinrich brings to them exactly the right blend of emotional involvement and earnest good taste, and finds pleasing resonance and smoothness in her instrument, such that even nearly 80 minutes of solo gamba never tires the ear. An unsuspected and atmospheric gem.

The Drexel Manuscript – Suite in D major; Suite in D minor; Suite in D major; Two Pieces in A major
Paolo Pandolfo *va da gamba*
Glossa GCD920410 (79' · DDD)   Ⓟ**OO**

Carl Friedrich Abel was a close friend of Johann Christian Bach, with whom he later appeared in London in the celebrated Bach-Abel Concerts (1774-82). Among his other friends was the painter Thomas Gainsborough, a passionate amateur violist, whose portrait of Abel hangs in London's National Portrait Gallery. Gainsbor-

ough was the owner of the Drexel Manuscript, containing 29 pieces for solo bass viol.

We are treated on this CD to all but one – a fragment. Paolo Pandolfo has arranged them, appropriately, into two suites in D major and one in D minor, concluding with two pieces in A major. Anyone familiar with the elder Bach's solo cello suites will immediately appreciate the influences as well as the originality and relative modernity of Abel's music. Pandolfo, considered by many to be the finest violist of our day, has already recorded several of the cello suites on the viol. But whereas the Suites present the modern player with awkward challenges (the Sixth in particular), Abel's music (like that of Marais) is supremely crafted for his instrument.

In Pandolfo's hands, Abel's music is highly communicative – packed with ideas, oft-repeated and always varied. His strong sense of overall form, both in freely expressed (preludes and slow movements) and more structured movements (dances and rondos), allows him to indulge in dynamic moments of silence, heightening the impression of monologue, and even dialogue. Technically wondrous, few could perform these delightful pieces with the skill, eloquence and sheer panache Pandolfo brings to them.

Adolphe Adam   French 1803-1856

Adam devoted his entire career to music for the theatre and was astonishingly prolific: he wrote one opera for every year of his life (he died just short of his 53rd birthday). This meant that he was turning out as many as three operas per season at the height of his powers. Among them is the once-popular Si j'étais roi but he's remembered today only for his perennially appealing ballet Giselle (1841). There are, in fact, two other pieces by Adam which have survived: his song Cantique de Noël is revived each Christmas (it was even featured in the film Home Alone) and his Variations on 'Ah, vous dirai-je maman?' (we know the tune as 'Twinkle, twinkle little star') from his 1849 opera Le Toréador remains a sensational (if silly) test of soprano coloratura agility. One of French music's great melodists, Adam enjoyed an incredibly successful career but he was not a great businessman. In the revolution of 1848 he lost all his savings and incurred so many debts that he spent the rest of his life in poverty.

Giselle

Giselle
**Royal Opera House Orchestra, Covent Garden /
Richard Bonynge**
Double Decca ② 452 185-2DF2 (126' · DDD)   Ⓜ**O**▷

Giselle has drawn harsh words from the more superior music critics, but the public has taken it to heart for its atmospheric writing and tender and haunting themes. The text used here is the complete original score; Bonynge's desire to re-record it lies in matters of performance and interpretation. Reviews of his previous version, made with the Monte Carlo Opera Orchestra in 1970, spoke of the limitations of the woodwind and brass, and suggested that a little more rehearsal time might have brought benefits. Here the musicians of the Royal Opera House bring both a confidence of attack and a refinement that aren't quite achieved by the Monte Carlo players. That same extra confidence of attack is displayed by Bonynge himself. Each of the discs of this issue is between one-and-a-half and two minutes longer than the older recording, but the dramatic moments are more vigorously attacked and the slower ones more lovingly caressed – always to considerable effect. Add recorded sound that's warmer and more spacious, and there's no hesitation in acknowledging the superiority of this version over the old. Without a doubt, this represents the first-choice version of Adam's complete score.

John Adams   American b1947

John Adams studied composition at Harvard where his teachers included Kirchner, Kim, Del Tredici and Sessions. Influenced by the music of Steve Reich he started exploring minimalism, and works from this period include Shaker Loops (1978), Harmonium for orchestra with choir (1981), the exuberant, parodistic Grand Pianola Music (1982), the opera Nixon in China (1987) and a Violin Concerto (1994). Deeply affected by the events of September 11, 2001, Adams wrote a work for chorus, children's chorus, orchestra and pre-recorded tape as a commission from the New York Philharmonic and Lincoln Center's Great Performers series, On the Transmigration of Souls: it was premiered in September 2002.

His opera Doctor Atomic (2005) is again based on true events; the story concerns the creation of the atomic bomb; the work was premiered in San Francisco. Adams has since created a symphony from the work.

Violin Concerto

Adams Violin Concerto
Corigliano The Red Violin – Chaconne
Enescu Romanian Rhapsody No 1 (arr Waxman)
Wagner/Waxman Tristan and Isolde Fantasia[a]
Chloë Hanslip vn [a]**Charles Owen** pf
Royal Philharmonic Orchestra / Leonard Slatkin
Naxos 8 559302 (64' · DDD)   ⑤☺➤

As an overall concept this album is a mess. Franz Waxman's arrangement of Enescu's *First Romanian Rhapsody* is positioned before the Adams Concerto and sounds like an encore before the main event. Waxman's *Tristan and Isolde Fantasia* pushes Wagner towards Cecil B DeMille histrionics, while John Corigliano's hacked-together Chaconne is episodic

and rhetorical and is severely lacking in the material department.

This is a pity because nothing should hide the fact that Chloë Hanslip is the sort of musician every teenager forced to practise their scales dreams of becoming. The richness and clarity of her tone is beyond learning, and she demonstrates such profound empathy for John Adams's 1993 Violin Concerto that Gidon Kremer (Nonesuch) can consider himself completely outplayed. This is the sort of performance that secures a reputation for life.

The first movement is a particular challenge, as an unwinding melodic line generates itself over a quarter-hour span. Kremer plays the notes mechanically but Hanslip deconstructs their meaning and pieces together a cogent narrative direction that's a bona fide interpretation. The sing-song ballad quality of the slow middle movement unlocks her lyrical imagination, while the tricky *moto perpetuo* of the violin part zigzags and breakdances across occasional Nancarrow-like rhythmic overlays in an exuberant finale. Assertive and enthused accompaniment from Slatkin and the RPO, too – everybody's doing Adams the greatest of service.

The Dharma at Big Sur

The Dharma at Big Sur[a].
My Father Knew Charles Ives[b]
[a]**Tracy Silverman** elec vn [b]**Bill Houghton** tpt
BBC Symphony Orchestra / John Adams
Nonesuch ② 7559 79857-2 (54' · DDD)   ⓕ

Both Charles Ives and John Adams grew up in New England and both have a healthy magpie attitude to their source material. Adams begins *My Father Knew Charles Ives* with the trademark solo trumpet writing he regularly deploys whenever he wants to evoke Ives: here it's like a camera slowly panning towards an Ivesian landscape far below. Brass-band music marches onwards and the famous 'false' last chord of Ives's Second Symphony flashes by. It's difficult to say what exactly Adams has created. It falls somewhere between direct quotation and constructivist allusion, like hearing deconstructed 'picture postcard' Ives. It's fun for sure, and the BBC Symphony Orchestra relish its follies.

Borrowing the experimental composer Lou Harrison's ideas about non-tempered tuning – as Adams does in his Jack Kerouac-inspired electric violin concerto *The Dharma at Big Sur* – gives another spin to a familiar Adams sound world. Tracy Silverman's folksy material in the concerto partly evolved from his own improvisations, and I fear a one-size-fits-all world-music patois is just around the corner. Nevertheless, the opening section is quite beautiful as non-tempered chords sensuously ebb and flow, and Adams integrates Silverman into his developing argument with a strategic sense of purpose. In the cathartic second section harmonic impetus races ahead, as gong-like sounds in the orchestra suggest inner stillness – a trademark Adams hook reborn.

Chamber Symphony

Chamber Symphony. Grand Pianola Music
London Sinfonietta / John Adams
Nonesuch 7559 79219-2 (53' · DDD)   ⒻO

A loud bash on an old tin can, and they're off – yelping, tapping, chattering, chasing to and fro, like a barn-yard full of loopy professors. And to think that the prime mover for John Adams's madcap Chamber Symphony (1992) was its 'eponymous predecessor', Schoenberg's Op 9. Even the instrumentation is similar, save that Adams has added synthesiser, jazz-style percussion, trumpet and trombone. It's a raw piece, with the merest suggestion of repose in the central 'Aria with Walking Bass' and a 'Roadrunner' finale that includes a manic violin cadenza followed by an ingenious passage where synthesiser, bass clarinet, bassoon and horn crank up for the panic-stricken home straight. It might not be exactly rich in tunes, but it's maddeningly moreish, a high-speed comedy where all the characters are temporarily on holiday from their more serious selves.

In complete contrast, the far gentler *Grand Pianola Music* (1971) provides a relatively 'easy' listen, with its smooth-driving motor rhythms, sensual female voices, warming waves of brass tone and occasional bouts of thumping excitement. Clichés there certainly are, especially the 'big tune' that crowns the third section, 'On the Dominant Divide', which is probably most effective when, towards the end of the work, it slims down to basic harmonic constituents. *Grand Pianola Music* is a sort of aural truck ride, with smooth tarmac, plenty of scenic incident, a glowing sunset on the far horizon and a closing cadence that rather unexpectedly recalls Sibelius. Both performances are fine and the recordings are superb.

El Dorado

Adams El Dorado **Busoni** Berceuse élégiaque, Op 42 (arr Adams)[a] **Liszt** La lugubre gondola, S200 No 1 (arr Adams)[a]
Hallé Orchestra / Kent Nagano; [a]**London Sinfonietta / John Adams**
Nonesuch 7559 79359-2 (47' · DDD)   ⒻO

El Dorado is a dramatic commentary on irreconcilable opposites: chromaticism versus pure modalities, malignancy versus rude health, and man's destructive impulses versus the unspoiled glory of unpopulated landscapes. Adams claims to have composed the second movement, 'Soledades' – the one 'without man' – in seven days. Indeed, the whole work appeared to him as a sort of apparition, 'alarmingly complete in its details, even before I wrote down a single sketch'.

The first movement, 'A Dream of Gold', opens to sinister held chords, pensive shufflings and rising clouds of string tone. The last section charges forth like some maniacal spectre, racing out of control then stopping dead. By contrast, 'Soledades' weaves a delicate web of sound, at least initially, with unmistakably Sibelian undertones. The ending, however, suggests a tranquil death. Overall, the recording of *El Dorado* reproduces a dynamic sound curve. The performance itself is deft and well paced, very much on a par with Adams's own performances of his Busoni and Liszt arrangements.

The *Berceuse élégiaque* is beautifully realised, while the richly coloured orchestration of Liszt's late *La lugubre gondola* is in total contrast to other, more austere, readings. Winds and solo strings are used to sensitive effect and the playing is uniformly excellent.

Gnarly Buttons

Gnarly Buttons. John's Book of Alleged Dances
Michael Collins cl **Kronos Quartet** (David Harrington, John Sherba vns Hank Dutt va Joan Jeanrenaud vc)
London Sinfonietta / John Adams
Nonesuch 7559 79465-2 (61' · DDD)   ⒻO

John's Book of Alleged Dances (the equivocation in the title refers to dance steps that have yet to be invented) is prime-cut Adams – fidgety, tuneful, teeming with invention and all but tactile in its aural variety; its use of the prepared piano is fascinating. We start by following a streetcar from town to coast and back again, then visit 'Toot Nipple' with 'chainsaw triads on the cello'. There's a raw-edged 'Hoe-Down' for leader David Harrington, a 'Pavane' for cellist Joan Jeanrenaud and a doleful Habanera. 'Hammer & Chisel' are contractor friends who construct to a knotty toccata; a slithery 'Alligator Escalator' employs reptilian harmonics and a chirpy 'Serenade' pays subtle homage to Beethoven and Schubert. These and more are kept on a high flame by the Kronos Quartet, whereas *Gnarly Buttons* calls on the combined talents of Michael Collins and the London Sinfonietta.

A more intense piece by far, its dry but colourful demeanour occasionally recalls Schoenberg's similarly spice-flavoured Serenade. The first movement is based on a Protestant shape-note hymn; the second is a 'Mad-Cow' hoe-down; and the third is a warming song of sure-fire hit potential. Collins does Adams proud, and so does the London Sinfonietta. The recordings are first-rate.

Harmonielehre

Harmonielehre. The Chairman Dances. Two Fanfares – Tromba lontana; Short Ride in a Fast Machine
City of Birmingham Symphony Orchestra / Sir Simon Rattle
EMI 555051-2 (62' · DDD)   ⓂO▷

3

Harmonielehre was inspired by a dream vision of a massive tanker that suddenly took flight, displaying a 'beautiful brownish-orange oxide on the bottom part of its hull'; the setting was just off San Francisco Bay Bridge. 'Those pounding E minor chords are like a grinding of gears,' says John Adams of its violent, gunshot opening. Scored for a huge orchestra and structured in three contrasted sections, *Harmonielehre* is probably the nearest thing on offer to a minimalist symphony, and for that reason alone it could well appeal beyond the élite coterie of minimalist-fanciers.

Rattle's recording has great heft and dynamic range, an informative balance and a vivid sense of aural perspective. The brass components of those opening chords have enormous weight and presence, and the ringing marimbas thereafter a bright complexion. Adams's frequent requests for subtle tempo transitions are deftly honoured by the conductor.

Naive and Sentimental Music

Naive and Sentimental Music
Los Angeles Philharmonic Orchestra / Esa-Pekka Salonen
Nonesuch 7559 79636-2 (44' · DDD)   Ⓕ**OO**

The title is adapted from *On Naïve and Sentimental Poetry*, a 1795 essay by Schiller, who regarded the naive artist as one for whom art is a natural form of expression, and who creates without concern for historical significance; the sentimental artist is all too aware that he and his art stand apart, and what he creates reflects this chasm. 'This particular piece,' Adams writes, 'perhaps more than any of my others, attempts to allow the naive in me to speak, to let it play freely.' A symphony in all but name, *Naïve and Sentimental Music* (1999) is cast in three movements. The first is an 'essay on melody,' built around an expansive theme that unfolds in long strands. Adams's harmonic sensitivity and structural control are breathtaking. And the entire movement unfolds as organically as the melody that's its *idée fixe*. Adams titled the finale 'Chain to the Rhythm'. Melody takes a back seat to what quickly becomes a dazzling and increasingly ominous *moto perpetuo*. *Naïve and Sentimental Music* is dedicated to Esa-Pekka Salonen and the LAPO, who premiered it in February 1999. Though the fiendishly difficult finale could perhaps be played more tautly, the overall interpretation is very persuasive indeed.

China Gates

China Gates. Phrygian Gates.
American Berserk. Hallelujah Junctiona
Ralph Van Raat, ªMaarten Van Veen pfs
Naxos 8 559285 (52' · DDD)   Ⓢ**OO**⊕

China Gates and *Phrygian Gates* from 1977-78 show Adams defining his own style as opposed to the classical minimalists such as Riley, Reich and Glass. *China Gates* is under six minutes and consistently delicate, while *Phrygian Gates* is a blockbuster of nearly 25. In *Phrygian Gates* the repetition is constant but there are also abrupt dislocations which function like film cuts – or the electronic gate which is meant by these titles. The technique is the same in the larger concert works as well as the operas that have made Adams famous. There seems to be no obvious reason why one texture ends and another begins, but that's the point of the discontinuity – and it goes back to Satie and Stravinsky.

American Berserk (2000) is the most recent piece and both words in the title are justified. From an early age Adams was surrounded by popular music and jazz on equal terms with classical composers. That background figures here with the crazier improvisational Ives and – very obviously – the swinging mechanical complexities of Conlon Nancarrow's studies for player piano. As in *Grand Pianola Music*, it's extravagantly entertaining.

In the exhilarating two-piano *Hallelujah Junction* (1996) Nancarrow again stands as godfather and you can hear the rhythmic hallelujahs as it belts on to its hilarious climax.

The Dutch pianists, cleanly recorded, deliver everything with consistent aplomb.

El Niño

El Niño
Dawn Upshaw sop **Lorraine Hunt Lieberson** mez **Willard White** bass **London Voices; Theatre of Voices; Deutsches Symphony Orchestra, Berlin / Kent Nagano**
Nonesuch ② 7559 79634-2 (111' · DDD · T/t)   Ⓕ**OO**

El Niño is an ecstatic celebration of Christ's birth, at once ethereal and fiercely driven, and as remote from homely 'Seasonal' images as Greenland is from Bethlehem. The pain and alienation of birth is as much a part of Adams's ground plan as the Holy Child whose universal significance has kept the legend alive.

Maybe it's coincidence that the score opens like a robust relation of Reich's *The Desert Music*, but given the Biblical setting, the idea of desert isn't exactly inappropriate. Bach is another probable reference-point. And yet any influences are absorbed among the pages of a score that, aside from its melodic appeal and considerable rhythmic (ie, quasi-minimalist) vitality, can toy delicately with guitar and harpsichord or breathe fire through trombones and low woodwinds. Adams's facility for musical word-painting at times levels with Benjamin Britten's. Voices and characters intertwine or juxtapose with a skill that only a seasoned opera composer could summon.

Countertenors echo ancient church modes, initially as Gabriel in dialogue with Mary, sweetly sung by Dawn Upshaw, then reporting on the Babe 'that leaped in her womb' and standing by as Joseph (a grainy-voiced Willard White) struggles with the concept of Mary's pregnancy. The choice of texts, many written by Hispanic women, was selected in collaboration with Peter Sellars. The overall aim seems less to tell a consistent story than to create narrative images within a spiritual context. The episodes, whether inwardly lyrical or outwardly aggressive, have an urgency, or relevance, that reaches beyond religious edification. It brings the Christmas story alive. But, be warned – this is no starlit Cosy Encounter. The performance can't be faulted, and the recording achieves a true aural perspective. Very strongly recommended.

El Niño
Dawn Upshaw sop **Lorraine Hunt Lieberson** mez **Willard White** bar **Maîtrise de Paris Children's Choir; London Voices; Theatre of Voices; Deutsches Symphonie-Orchester Berlin / Kent Nagano**
Stage director **Peter Sellars**
Video director **Peter Maniura**
ArtHaus Musik **DVD** 100 220 (147' · 16:9 · 2.0 · 0 · N)
Includes 'Making Of' documentary   Ⓕ●

'An opera by John Adams' says the packaging. Not quite. This is the composer's multi-cultural, postfeminist, quasi-minimalist take on Handel's *Messiah*, drawing on sources ranging from the pre-Christian prophets to 20th-century Hispanic women writers. While designed to allow fully staged productions, the concept and its musical realisation bring us closer to oratorio. Adams's musical language is predictably inclusive. There's a prominent role for three Brittenish countertenors, Broadway and popular idioms are more or less willingly embraced, and the use of repetition is sometimes reminiscent of Philip Glass in his heyday. *El Niño*'s sound world is delicate and lustrous, and, although Part 1 can seem a mite static with a surfeit of vocal recitative, there are fewer longueurs in Part 2. If not perhaps the unqualified masterpiece acclaimed by some critics, this is an effective and often truly affecting score: derivative, to be sure, yet obstinately fresh.

The performance as such is pretty much beyond criticism. The main characters are on top form, combining absolute vocal assurance with dramatic flair – and none more so than Lorraine Hunt Lieberson. The crisp DVD images certainly help explain the sensational impact of the European premiere, a multimedia extravaganza from Peter Sellars's top drawer in which dance and film interact quirkily with the exertions of chorus and soloists. . Strongly recommended.

The Death of Klinghoffer

The Death of Klinghoffer
Sanford Sylvan bar Leon Klinghoffer **Stephanie Friedman** mez Omar **James Maddalena** bar First Officer **Thomas Hammons** bar First Officer **Thomas**

Young sngr Molqui **Eugene Perry** bar Mamoud **Sheila Nadler** mez Marilyn Klinghoffer **London Opera Orchestra Chorus; Lyon Opera Orchestra / Kent Nagano**
Nonesuch ② 7559 79281-2 (135' · DDD · N/T)   Ⓕ

How many living composers do you suppose would happily watch their scores lead a short life, relevant but finite? Not many; but John Adams might be one. First *Nixon in China*, then *The Death of Klinghoffer*: rarely before has a composer snatched subjects from yesterday's news and made operas out of them. Admittedly, themes of lasting significance lurk beneath this work's immediate surface: conflict between cultures and ideologies, rival claims to ancestral lands, human rights in general. Specifically, however, it takes us back no further than October 1985, when Palestinian terrorists hijacked the Italian cruise liner *Achille Lauro* and murdered wheelchair-bound passenger Leon Klinghoffer. The opera guides us through those events, albeit in an oblique fashion. Whatever the long-term fate of the opera, Alice Goodman's libretto certainly deserves to be spared from oblivion. It's eloquent and beautiful, compassionate and humanitarian, rich in imagery and spacious in its sentence-structure. If *The Death of Klinghoffer* finally disappoints, it's because the marriage of words and music is so fragile. The opera's musical language is firmly rooted in tradition, but it's doubtful if anyone will come away from it with a memorable lyric moment lodged in the mind. The recording uses the cast of the original production, and contains no weak links. As you expect from Adams, the score has been superbly orchestrated, and it's done full justice by the Lyon Opera Orchestra.

The Death of Klinghoffer
Sanford Sylvan bar Klinghoffer **Christopher Maltman** bar Captain **Yvonne Howard** mez Marilyn Klinghoffer **Tom Randle** ten Molqi **Kamel Boutros** bar Mamoud **Leigh Melrose** bar Rambo **Emil Marwa** act Omar (sung by **Susan Bickley** mez) **London Symphony Chorus and Orchestra / John Adams** Video director **Penny Woolcock**
Decca **DVD** 074 189-9DH (166' · DDD; NTSC · 16:9 · PCM stereo & 5.1 · 0)
Includes a 'Making of...' documentary   Ⓕ

At the time of issue, *Klinghoffer* had yet to be performed in the US, and Penny Woolcock's live-action film, shot on location, won't do much to quieten the controversies that kept it off the stage. She fleshes out the opera's philosophies, inasmuch as the composer discussed production details with her, and was thereby at least complicit in the choice of images. *Klinghoffer* is more an oratorio than an opera, and she uses the choruses and non-dramatic stretches to fill out the characters with flashbacks to 1940s Palestine and even historical footage of Nazi Germany.

This is Adams's slowest stage piece, and Woolcock's close, hand-held camerawork tests severely the singers' acting, particularly when they aren't singing. The singers were actually recorded live during the on-location filming, after the orchestra was recorded. The payoff is immense: synchronisation is perfect, and what we hear goes believably with what we see. Even in these trying circumstances, the vocalism and acting are outstanding.

So, does the film show librettist Alice Goodman and stage director Peter Sellars's scenario to be anti-Semitic and sympathetic to terrorism, as some of its American critics claim? The film does round out the terrorists' characters, but there's a balanced portrayal, showing the good and the bad of both Jews and Palestinians. The terrorists show regret after the killing, but there is also a stoning where a Palestinian mob gets drunk on its own brutality. Some of the Jewish tourists are parodies early on, but Marilyn Klinghoffer comes to take on towering dignity and strength. Most of those who've criticised the politics are responding to what they want to see in the opera than what's actually there.

Woolcock has turned *Klinghoffer* into a fairly gripping visual drama; but her success shows up the musical deficiencies: encountered as an opera rather than a film, it may be of no more than topical interest.

Doctor Atomic

Doctor Atomic
Gerald Finley bar J Robert Oppenheimer **Jessica Rivera** sop Kitty Oppenheimer **Eric Owens** bass General Leslie Groves **Richard Paul Fink** bar Edward Teller **James Maddalena** bar Jack Hubbard **Thomas Glenn** ten Robert Wilson **Jay Hunter Morris** ten Captain James Nolan **Ellen Rabiner** mez Pasqualita **Netherlands Opera Chorus; Netherlands Philharmonic Orchestra / Lawrence Renes** Stage and video director **Peter Sellars** Opus Arte 📀 OA0998D (3h 50' · NTSC · 16:9 · PCM stereo and DTS 5.1 · 0). Includes bonus interview with Peter Sellars, mini documentary, cast gallery and illustrated synopsis　　　　　　　Ⓟ●○○○

Doctor Atomic is the most dramatic subject matter of any John Adams opera and musically the most inconsistent. Indeed, as subject matter goes, *Doctor Atomic* could hardly be more apocalyptic. The work's principal character is J Robert Oppenheimer, the scientist who developed the atomic bomb during the Second World War from its earliest prototype through to the test bomb that was detonated in 1945 at a secret site in New Mexico. The opera's first act takes place a month before the test; the second act is set on the day itself, with a finale that strategically plays with our perception of time as the bomb is about to be detonated.

Adams's first opera, *Nixon in China*, rattled along with a note-specific clarity that flickered like newsreel; he paints *Doctor Atomic* in broader brushstrokes, using post-Bernard Herrmann suspense tactics and angsty chromatic swells to portray charged emotions. But an underlying

weakness is the stubbornly unmemorable and melodically colourless vocal writing, leading to one-dimensional characterisations. Adams and librettist Peter Sellars's decision to incorporate poetry by John Donne and Muriel Rukeyser into the opera only highlights the functional flavour of Sellars's own words as the balance is flipped towards contrived artifice. No complaints about the performance though. Gerald Finley carries the problems of the world on his shoulders as Oppenheimer and the Netherlands Philharmonic and Lawrence Renes play like it's the best score since *Fidelio*.

I Was Looking at the Ceiling...

I Was Looking at the Ceiling and Then I Saw the Sky **Martina Mühlpointner** sngr Consuelo Kimako **Xavier Trotman** sngr Dewain Markus **Alexander Neisser** sngr Rick **Jeannette Friedrich** sngr Leila **Darius de Haas** sngr David **Lilith Gardell** sngr Tiffany **Jonas Holst** sngr Mike **Freiburg Young Opera Company; The Band of Holst-Sinfonietta / Klaus Simon** Naxos ② 8 669003/4 (116' · DDD · S/N)　　Ⓢ→

John Adams's stylistic range is vast, yet even in such a diverse output, *I Was Looking at the Ceiling and Then I Saw the Sky* (1995) stands apart. Conceived, in the composer's words, as 'a Broadway-style show', it draws its musical inspiration from popular song, moving from doo-wop to gospel, from pop ballad to the blues. The text, a poetic piece of social and political commentary by June Jordan, introduces us to seven young Angelenos whose intertwined lives are transformed by the 1994 Northridge earthquake. There's no recitative, no spoken dialogue; the story is told through song and ensemble. This posed a problem when Nonesuch issued a composer-conducted recording of excerpts in 1998, cutting seven of the 22 vocal numbers. Here, Naxos gives us the complete score.

It hard to state that the narrative flows a whole lot more smoothly when the show is heard in its entirety. There are still quite a few jarring gaps, although one certainly gets a better sense of the characters as well as a heightened sense of drama. Missing from the Nonesuch recording, for example, was the crucial post-earthquake scene involving Tiffany, Mike and Rick – the score's longest number.

As for the performance: the Freiburg-based Holst-Sinfonietta Band plays its intricate part with tightly coiled energy for conductor Klaus Simon; the mostly German cast copes reasonably well with the different American dialects (only Lilith Gardell's Tiffany fails to convince); and although the women's voices can turn shrill when pressed, all the singers sound fresh and youthful. Indeed, Martina Mühlpointner may not have the extraordinary tonal richness of Audra McDonald (Nonesuch) but her wide-eyed rendition of 'Consuelo's Dream' – one of the piece's prettiest and most effective numbers – is also deeply affecting. Not all the songs in *Ceiling/Sky* are as successful as this one but I'd guess that there's enough here to make this daring experiment in American musical theatre attractive to more than just Adams's fans.

Nixon in China

Nixon in China
Sanford Sylvan *bar* Chou en-Lai **James Maddalena** *bar* Richard Nixon **Thomas Hammons** *bar* Henry Kissinger **Mari Opatz** *mez* Nancy T'ang, First Secretary to Mao **Stephanie Friedman** *mez* Second Secretary to Mao **Marion Dry** *mez* Third Secretary to Mao **John Duykers** *ten* Mao Tse-Tung **Carolann Page** *sop* Pat Nixon **Trudy Ellen Craney** *sop* Chiang Ch'ing **St Luke's Chorus and Orchestra / Edo de Waart**
Nonesuch ② 7559-79177-2 (144' · DDD · T) Ⓕ

Whatever its weaknesses, there's no denying that *Nixon in China* is striking. Structured curiously, its three acts reduce from three scenes to two, and then to one, and they diminish proportionally in duration from more than an hour in Act 1 to the unbroken 30-minute span of Act 3. This last act, played out in the statesmen's bedrooms, is a weary sequence of dialogues and soliloquies, ending in a curious but calculated state of anticlimax. Preceding this, though, is a run of colourful scenes that symbolise the main events without imposing any artificial sense of dramatic shape. By the end of the work, the public faces have given way to private lives; even Nixon and Chairman Mao emerge as mere mortals rather than mythical demi-gods.

The music serves the libretto deftly in fast-moving dialogue but the reflective and rhapsodic portions of text seem to leave Adams baffled, the melodic lines wandering aimlessly, short on intrinsic musical interest and rarely moving the singers to expressive performances. In the handling of spectacle and scene-setting, by contrast, Adams is in his element. He freely avails himself of any idiom, any oblique references or musical quotation that serves as a means to an end. Some passages would be unthinkable without the operas of Philip Glass; elsewhere lie uncanny ghosts of 1930s Stravinsky. Magpie just about sums this score up. The singing is sympathetic, with James Maddalena as an aptly volatile Nixon and Trudy Ellen Craney coping admirably with the coloratura lines of Madam Mao.

Additional recommendation

Nixon in China
Soloists; Colorado Symphony Orchestra / Alsop
Naxos ② 8 669022/4 (154' · DDD) Ⓢ🅑➤
A live recording that may lack the precision of the de Waart (above), but for a dramatically cogent, well-acted budget-price alternative, Alsop's set has a lot going for it.

Further listening

The Wound-dresser
Coupled with Short Ride in a Fast Machine. Shaker Loops. Berceuse élégiaque
Gunn *bar* **Bournemouth Symphony Orchestra / Alsop**
Naxos 8 559031 (62' · DDD) Ⓢ🅑➤
A near-perfect Adams primer containing his tender and powerful meditation, to words by Walt Whitman, on the subject of those lost to Aids, touchingly performed by Nathan Gunn.

Richard Addinsell British 1904-1977

Adinsell studied both at the Royal College of Music in London and in Vienna. In 1933 he moved to the USA and focused on writing for the movies. His enormously popular Warsaw Concerto, in the style of Rachmaninov, was written for the 1941 film Dangerous Moonlight and started something a brief trend for mini-romantic piano concertos in films.

Warsaw Concerto

Warsaw Concerto (arr Douglas)[b].The Admirable Crichton[a] – Polka and Galop; Waltz Sequence ([a]reconstructed by P Lane) The Black Rose – Suite[a]. Blithe Spirit[a] – Prelude; Waltz. Goodbye Mr Chips – Suite[ac]. Love on the Dole – Suite[a]. Out of the Clouds – Flame Tango (arr Sharples). Scrooge – Suite (arr S Bernstein)[c]. Tom Brown's Schooldays – Overture[a]
[b]**Martin Roscoe** *pf* [c]**Manchester Cathedral Choir;** [c]**Chetham's Chamber Choir; BBC Philharmonic Orchestra / Rumon Gamba**
Chandos CHAN10046 (80' · DDD) Ⓕ🅞➤

None of the modern versions of the *Warsaw Concerto* seems to have the freshness, urgency and lack of self-indulgence of this very fine version. That's a pointer to the high level of playing and interpretation to be found throughout this ever fascinating and altogether quite delightful selection of Addinsell's film music. Though Rachmaninov comes so immediately and vividly to mind in the most celebrated of Addinsell's creations, that was strictly for the purposes of its film context. Elsewhere you're more likely to be reminded of Vaughan Williams, Ravel or Eric Coates. Pastiche was an inevitable part of a film composer's armoury, but the very real inventive gifts displayed in the *Warsaw Concerto* are also evident throughout this collection. About half the music has already been recorded in other Addinsell collections, but not with the chorus that's especially effective here in the 'School Song' from *Goodbye Mr Chips*. Of the new items the sumptuously lyrical finale to the music for *The Black Rose* is particularly fine (expertly reconstructed, like much else here, by Philip Lane), as are the dances from the

Addinsell Orchestral

1957 film *The Admirable Crichton*. It's by no means just nostalgia that makes Addinsell's film music well worth exploring, and this generously filled CD is undoubtedly the best single-CD selection available.

Additional recommendation

Addinsell Warsaw Concerto
Coupled with **Beaver** Portrait of Isla **Rózsa**
Spellbound Concerto. **Rota** The Legend of the Glass
Mountain **RR Bennett** Murder on the Orient Express
– excs **Bath** Cornish Rhapsody **Herrmann** Concerto
Macabre **Williams** The Dream of Olwen **Pennario**
Midnight on the Cliffs
Fowke *pf* RTÉ Concert Orchestra / O'Duinn
Naxos 8 554323 (74' · DDD)   ⑤🅑
Fowke plays all the pieces with affection and panache. If you've always wished that the *Warsaw Concerto* were longer, this is for you.

Film Music

Blithe Spirit – Prelude; Waltz. Encore – Miniature
Overture. Gaslight – Prelude. Parisienne – 1885.
Southern Rhapsody. Waltz of the Toreadors – March;
The General on Parade; Waltz (all arr Lane). Fire over
England – Suite (arr Zalva). Passionate Friends –
Lover's Moon. South Riding – Prelude. A Christmas
Caro – Suite (arr S Bernstein). WRNS March
Robert Gibbs *vn* **Peter Lawson** *pf* **Royal Ballet
Sinfonia** / **Kenneth Alwyn**
ASV White Line CDWHL2115 (68' · DDD)   Ⓜ⚫

Nobody should imagine that the *Warsaw Concerto* is all that's worth hearing from this fine composer. Addinsell had a natural feel for richly tuneful, romantic music in the best tradition of British light music. The diverse commissions he fulfilled served to turn these gifts to contrasted musical styles; these provide a rewardingly varied programme.

The most familiar music will probably be the swaggering march and haunting waltz from the *Waltz of the Toreadors*. Others will know the prelude and waltz from David Lean's film of *Blithe Spirit* or the suite from *A Christmas Carol*. Perennial favourites are the invigorating *WRNS March*, the delightfully mysterious prelude to the 1939 film of *Gaslight* and the waltz from the stage play *Parisienne*. The last has been given a splendid Glazunovian orchestration by compiler, producer, arranger and annotator Philip Lane, who again leaves us in his debt, as do conductor Kenneth Alwyn and the admirable Royal Ballet Sinfonia.

Additional recommendation

Film music
Goodbye Mr Chips – exc. Ring around the moon –
exc. Smokey Mountains Concerto. The Isle of
Apples. The Prince and the Showgirl – exc. Tune in
G. Tom Brown's Schooldays – exc. Festival. Journey

to Romance. Fire over England – exc. A Tale of Two
Cities – exc
Martin, Elms *pfs* **BBC Concert Orchestra** / **Alwyn**
Marco Polo 8 223732 (68' · DDD)   Ⓕ
A most attractive release. Much of the orchestral material for this recording was prepared by Philip Lane, who also provides the informative notes. Fine performances, too.

Thomas Adès   British b1971

One of the leading lights in contemporary classical music, pianist/conductor/composer Adès's meteoric rise to international musical prominence has been phenomenal. He gained early success as a pianist, winning second prize in the 1989 BBC Young Musician of the Year, then read music at King's College, Cambridge (1989-92). Among the works from his student years are his first opus, Five Eliot Landscapes (1990) and the Chamber Symphony (1990) – his first work to receive a professional performance. In 1993 he became Composer in Association to the Hallé Orchestra for whom he wrote The Origin of the Harp (1994) and These Premises Are Alarmed (1996). His most performed work, Living Toys (1993), brought him widespread critical acclaim, though it was the chamber opera Powder Her Face (1995) that earned him an international reputation.

In 1998 he became artistic director of the Birmingham Contemporary Music Group and the following year, for his first large-scale orchestral work, Asyla (1997), he received the Ernst von Siemens Prize and the Grawemeyer Award. Also in 1999 he became joint artistic director of the Aldeburgh Festival. His most recent opera, The Tempest, was a commission from the Royal Opera House, Covent Garden. Adès's compositions showed exceptional assurance of style and technique from the start, and his success had much to do with the unmistakable presence of a personal accent in music which blends vividness of detail with a clear sense of compelling overall design. His recent piano concerto, In Seven Days, is a collaboration with his partner, the Israeli video-artist, Tal Rosner. It was premiered in London in April 2008. Other recent works include the orchestral score, Tevot (2007) premiered by the Berlin Philharmonic under Sir Simon Rattle, a longstanding champion of Adès's music.

Adès also maintains a busy schedule as both a pianist and conductor.

Asyla

Asyla[bc]. ...but all shall be well[bd]. Chamber
Symphony[ad]. Concerto conciso[ae]. These Premises
Are Alarmed[bd]
[a]**Birmingham Contemporary Music Group**; [b]**City
of Birmingham Symphony Orchestra** / [c]**Sir Simon
Rattle**, [d]**Thomas Adès** [e]*pf*
EMI 556818-2 (61' · DDD)   Ⓕ⚫🅑

This CD includes the *Chamber Symphony*, the work that first aroused interest in Adès's work when he was 18, set alongside *Asyla*, a recent un-chamber symphony and his first work for full orchestra. The progression between them is remarkable: the *Chamber Symphony* has both real invention and real economy, and its use of jazz elements is neither patronising nor culinary. Maybe its last movement adds little of consequence to the preceding three, but *Asyla* genuinely grows from the grave, rather Brittenish horn line that sets it going through the strong drama of the central movements to the almost Sibelian climax of the finale. Adès's own voice is clearly audible throughout, elegant, coolly intelligent but urgent.

These Premises Sre Alarmed, a sinewy toccata of bright colour and urgent energy, was written for the opening of the Bridgewater Hall, Manchester. In the *Concerto conciso* Adès perhaps takes his pleasure in simple intervals and brief motifs a little too far. However, *...but all shall be well* is something else again. It develops abundant, earnest melody from a pair of simple phrases in an impressively sustained argument that reaches a powerful and satisfying climax. Fine performances, admirably recorded.

Chamber Symphony

Adès Chamber Symphony **Higdon** Percussion Concerto[a] **MacMillan** The Confession of Isobel Gowdie
[a]**Colin Currie** *perc*
London Philharmonic Orchestra / Marin Alsop
LPO LPO0035 (61' · DDD)   Ⓜ

Not the least notable aspects of this CD are the two works, both dating from 1990, that launched their composers' careers. In Thomas Adès's *Chamber Symphony*, an often oblique musical syntax binds fragmentary ideas and textures into a cumulative whole; its motifs moving purposefully through a 'slow movement' and 'scherzo' before finding repose in an exquisite coda. All the more pity, then, that this vivid but fallible reading does not quite match that by the composer.

Where Adès intrigues listeners, James MacMillan fairly bludgeons them into submission with *The Confession of Isobel Gowdie*, though this depiction of a 17th-century Scottish woman tortured then burnt at the stake for witchcraft could hardly afford to be self-effacing. And the initial accumulation of intensity, spilling over into an extended onslaught then recalling the opening in expressively heightened terms before the accusatory final *crescendo*, is nothing if not powerful. Marin Alsop has its measure, while the LPO give everything in an account that should convince those hearing the piece for the first time.

Jennifer Higdon's Percussion Concerto (2005) might also be found engaging on first hearing. The solo part, dispatched with aplomb by Colin Currie, is disappointingly limited in its invention and rhythmic profile, while the orchestral part – a mild distillation of Stravinskian and

Coplandesque gestures – is unlikely to set the pulse racing. The sound and booklet are on a par with earlier LPO releases, however, making this disc well worth investigating for the Mac-Millan alone.

Violin Concerto

Violin Concerto, 'Concentric Paths'[b]. Tevot[a]. Three Studies after Couperin[c]. Powder Her Face – Suite[d]
[b]**Anthony Marwood** *vn* [a]**Berlin Philharmonic Orchestra / Sir Simon Rattle**; [bc]**Chamber Orchestra of Europe / Thomas Adès**; [d]**National Youth Orchestra of Great Britain / Paul Daniel**
EMI 457813-2 (67' · DDD)   Ⓕ ⦿⦿⊕

EMI's commitment to Thomas Adès continues with this miscellany of recent works. Its Hebrew title referring to structures of security in time of flux, *Tevot* is an eventful 22 minutes. From a shimmering opening that erupts in energetic exchanges, it builds a momentum underpinned by the antagonism between tuned anvils and an oboe-led chorale. Reaching an expressive plateau, the piece recalls its start via a descent that gives the stratospheric violin writing a definite harmonic context, before the climactic final section attempts more overt tonal closure. The extent to which this ingenious take on post-minimalist facets enriches Adès's idiom is open to question but the BPO is responsive to its technical challenges, though more densely scored passages are not helped by the 'dead' ambience.

The Violin Concerto was previously a download-only release. Written for Anthony Marwood, the capricious outer movements enclose a central chaconne whose lyrically intense solo writing contrasts with the orchestra's volatile textures. Marwood is eloquence itself and Adès secures disciplined playing from a COE that is equally inside the understated yet characterful *Three Studies after Couperin*. Finally, the NYO gives its all in a suite from Adès's first opera *Powder Her Face*: an Overture that luridly hints at events to come, a Waltz where the Duchess's 'arrival' and the Waitress's yearning are tellingly fused, then a Finale relating the Duchess's downfall via a tango of grim humour. A fine calling-card for this rare masterpiece among recent English opera, it rounds off a highly thought-provoking disc.

Piano Quintet

Adès Piano Quintet[a]
Schubert Piano Quintet, 'Trout'[b]
Thomas Adès *pf* [b]**Corin Long** *db*
[a]**Arditti Quartet** (Irvine Arditti, Graeme Jennings *vns* Dov Scheindlin *va* Rohan de Saram *vc*); [b]**Members of the Belcea Quartet** (Corina Belcea *vn* Krzysztof Chorzelski *va* Alasdair Tait *vc*)
EMI 557664-2 (62' · DDD)   Ⓕ ⦿⦿⊕

Thomas Adès features both as composer and pianist on this release: two piano quintets which, though composed 182 years apart, are equally alive with formal and expressive provocations. That said, expression per se is not really an issue in Adès's Piano Quintet (2001). The single movement places its sonata-form emphasis so the near-literal repeat of an already evolving exposition takes on a strongly developmental feel, with the development then assuming the guise of a varied reprise, and the brief recapitulation becoming almost a transition that anticipates the coda.

It all amounts to an intriguing rethink of an age-old medium, though one whose musical material is so geared up to the unfolding of the formal process as to evince little intrinsic memorability beyond the pervasive opening motif. Adès and the Ardittis ensure a reading of unremitting clarity, with perhaps a didactic element such as seems more than appropriate to the work itself.

Outwardly, nothing could be less didactic than the near-effortless spontaneity of Schubert's *Trout* Quintet – though its often unpredictable formal transitions confirm the benign influence of Haydn and early Beethoven, while its taciturn tonal progressions anticipate the composer's instrumental works of the 1820s. These are qualities to which Adès and the Belcea Quartet are responsive: listen to the hushed intensity going into the codetta of the first movement's exposition, the tellingly unquiet repose which opens the *Andante*'s second half, or the lucidly drawn contrast between the last two variations of the fourth movement – making the return of *Die Forelle* itself the more arresting.

As an overall reading, it lacks the unforced naturalness of Clifford Curzon and members of the Vienna Octet, or the sense of discovery which Alfred Brendel et al manage to convey with an even greater communicative zeal. Recorded sound, with the instrumental interplay palpably defined if lacking the final degree of spatial depth, is well suited to the interpretative stance that these performances bracingly convey.

The Tempest

The Tempest
Simon Keenlyside bar Prospero **Kate Royal** sop Miranda **Toby Spence** ten Ferdinand **Ian Bostridge** ten Caliban **Cyndia Sieden** sop Ariel **Philip Langridge** ten King of Naples **Donald Kaasch** ten Antonio **Jonathan Summers** bar Sebastian **David Cordier** counterten Trinculo **Stephen Richardson** bass-bar Stefano **Graeme Danby** bass Gonzalo **Chorus and Orchestra of the Royal Opera House, Covent Garden / Thomas Adès**
EMI ② 695234-2 (118' · DDD · S/T/N)
Recorded live in 2007   ℗●●●▶

Thomas Adès's 'ism'-defying output gains in variety all the time, but whatever he comes up with in the future it is likely that *The Tempest* will remain one of his most significant achievements. Premiered at Covent Garden in 2004, and recorded there at the 2007

revival, Adès's second opera succeeds where most *Tempest* adaptations have failed: in adding something to Shakespeare's magical and inherently lyrical scenario. From the tornado-like prelude to Ariel's stratospheric yet ethereal 'Five fathoms deep' the music illuminates rather than merely illustrates the drama. It may not be a flawless masterpiece: Meredith Oakes's otherwise musical libretto relies on some clunky rhythms, and Adès could occasionally have tightened his writing, notably in Act 3, but it is one of the most viable and stageworthy of modern British operas. Most of this recording's cast created their roles, and the performances have a lived-in feel.

Yet even the newcomer, Kate Royal as Miranda, is fully inside her part and sings alluringly. For many, the most memorable writing in *The Tempest* comes attached to Ariel's vocal high-wire act. Few coloratura sopranos are able to dispatch it like Cyndia Sieden, whose sound lends special colour to the performance, and it is hardly her fault that her stratospheric flights leave the words almost unintelligible.

Simon Keenlyside, on the young side as Prospero, mixes brain and baritonal brawn in his characteristically charismatic way. Ian Bostridge sings unstintingly as a wonderfully weird Caliban and his Peter Pears-ish voice strengthens the impression of the character as an outsider. His younger tenor colleague, Toby Spence, is a fine Ferdinand. Philip Langridge's King of Naples and Jonathan Summers's Sebastian represent luxury casting in a recording made under the composer's own baton. The playing of the Covent Garden orchestra is another luxury, no, a necessity, given the brilliantly conceived and demanding orchestral aspect of this piece.

Alexander Agricola
Franco-Flemish 1446-1506

As with so musicians of his day, Agricola worked in the courts of Italy (Milan, Florence and Naples) and in France (he was attached to the court of Philip the Handsome for the last eight years of his life). He not only wrote music but was celebrated as a singer. His output was predominantly vocal and included eight Masses and nearly two dozen sacred vocal works. His musical language looks to the North, and to Ockeghem in particular, witnessed by his writing long lines of contrapuntal complexity.

Vocal Works

A la mignonne de fortune. Adieu m'amour.   ℗
Adieu m'amour II. Allez, regretz. Ay je rien fait.
Cecsus non iudicat de coloribus. De tous biens plaine. De tous biens plaine II. De tous biens plaine III. Et qui la dira. Fortuna desperata. Guarde vostre visage. Guarde vostre visage II. Guarde vostre visage III. J'ay beau huer. S'il vous plaist. Soit loing ou pres. Sonnes muses melodieusement

Ensemble Unicorn (Bernhard Landauer *counterten*
Johannes Chum *ten* Colin Mason *bass-bar* Marco
Ambrosini *fiddle* Nora Kallai *vihuela d'arco* Thomas
Wimmer *vihuela d'arco/lte* Riccardo Delfino *hp/snare
hp*) / **Michael Posch** *rec*
Naxos 8 553840 (65' · DDD)   ⑤ⓞⓞⒹ➔

Agricola was praised by his contemporaries for
the bizarre turn of his inspiration, and his music
likened to quicksilver. By the standards of the
period this is a highly unusual turn of phrase,
but remains spot-on. The Ferrara Ensemble
anthology, the first ever devoted to the composer, focused on the secular music, both
instrumental and vocal, precisely the area covered by Michael Posch and Ensemble Unicorn
in this most satisfying disc. Where there's duplication (surprisingly little, in fact) the performances compare with those of the Ferrara
Ensemble, although the style of singing is very
different. The voices are more up front and less
inflected, perhaps the better to match the high
instruments with which they're sometimes doubled. But the tensile quality of Agricola's lines
comes through none the less, as does the miraculous inventiveness and charm of his music.
Further, much of what's new to the catalogue
really is indispensible, for example Agricola's
most famous song, 'Allez, regretz'. Unicorn
keeps its improvisations and excursions to a
minimum, and the music is the better for it.
This disc would be indispensable at full price,
let alone super-budget. It really is a must-have.

'Chansons'
Agricola De tous biens plaine I. De tous biens plaine
II. Pater meus agricola est. En actendant. Fortuna
desparata. Je n'ay dueil. De tous biens plaine III.
Dung aultre amer I. De tous biens plaine IV. Comme
femme desconfortee I. Comme femme desconfortee
II. Comme femme desconfortee III. Se je fais bien.
Tout a part moy II. De tous biens plaine V. Vostre
hault bruit. Dung aultre amer II. Dung aultre amer III
Fitch Agricologies – Agricola I: Comme femme a
2/4; Agricola III/Obrecht canon I: De tous biens
plaine a 4 **Isaac** Si dormiero **Ninot le Petit** Si bibero
crathere pleno
Michael Chance *counterten* **Fretwork** (Richard
Boothby, Richard Campbell, Wendy Gillespie,
Susanna Pell, Asako Morikawa, Richard Tunnicliffe
viols)
Harmonia Mundi HMU90 7421 (75' · DDD · T/t)   ⓕ

Alexander Agricola, the quincentenary of whose
death fell in 2006, is not over-represented in the
catalogue so this disc, then, is very welcome.

Fretwork take hold of this frequently unpredictable music (all but one of the pieces are
performed in new editions by composer Fabrice
Fitch) with confidence. They produce performances of exuberance, proving that what a
contemporary of the composer called his
'bizarre and crazy manner', as Fitch notes, can
either be subverted or assumed to be, in fact,
less crazy than it might appear and give impressive musical results. The chansons also prove

that Agricola was a fine melodist: his contrapuntal strangeness elsewhere (perhaps best shown
here in the freely composed *Pater meus agricola
est*) is probably no greater than that of Ockeghem or Obrecht, both of whose counterpoint is
frequently thoroughly eccentric.

A unique feature of this anthology is that it
includes two parts from Fitch's cycle of *Agricologies*, a work in several movements for Fretwork
and the Kreutzer Quartet. The material for the
work comes from Agricola, or material used by
him, and Fitch makes a point of working, in the
first, with his melodic quirkiness and, in the very
brief second, with his counterpoint, a remarkable texture being produced by the performers
tapping on the strings rather than plucking or
bowing. An impressive disc on all counts, which
should do much to restore Agricola's obscure
profile to the light.

Kalevi Aho   Finnish b1949

*Aho studied at the Sibelius Academy in Helsinki
under Einojuhani Rautavaara and with Boris
Blacher in West Berlin. He has taught at Helsinki
University and the Sibelius Academy, but since 1993
has been a freelance composer. His extensive output
includes much orchestral music and several operas.*

Clarinet Concerto

Aho Clarinet Concerto **Nielsen** Clarinet Concerto
Martin Fröst *cl*
Lahti Symphony Orchestra / Osmo Vänskä
BIS ⓢ BIS-SACD1463 (54' · DDD)   ⓕⓞⓞⓞⒹ➔

Kalevi Aho's Concerto starts arrestingly but
without a trace of the attention-seeking that
afflicts certain other clarinet concertos of
recent times. There is something in Aho's five
continuous movements that recalls Nielsen's
directness and free-flowing succession of ideas,
and the cadenza that forms the second movement even brings momentary echoes of
Nielsen's uncompromising skirls and flourishes. But the Finn's sights are set more on the
starkly elemental than on the quirkily personal.
For Aho the *Vivace con brio* third movement is
the 'centre and culmination', and it is certainly
exuberant – dangerous, even – in its restless
virtuosity, rather like Strauss's *Till Eulenspiegel*
driven mad by inner demons. After this a sad
slow movement brings sober reflection, and an
Epilogue concludes the work on a note of mystery. There can have been few equally impressive head-on engagements with the concerto
medium in recent years.

There are eight or so modern accounts of the
Nielsen Clarinet Concerto in the catalogue.
Most have fine qualities. Yet for sureness of
idiomatic touch none dislodges Ib Erikson's
classic 1954 Danish accounts (now available on
Dutton). Closer to the mark than any modern
rivals is this new issue from Martin Fröst, the

clarinettist of the moment for all-round artistry allied to adventurous approach to repertoire. He seems to have Nielsen's irascible masterpiece in his bloodstream, as surely as he has its technical contortions under his fingers. Vänskä ensures that the Lahti players are never fazed by the exposed edges in the accompaniment, and only the very drawn-out final bars come across as slightly self-conscious. Detail for detail, phrase for phrase, this team takes the palm over the old Danish recording, even before considering BIS's immeasurably superior sound quality. Even so, Erikson and Wöldike remain a benchmark for insight into the character of the piece. In sum, a CD of rare distinction.

Orchestral Works

Symphony No 11ᵃ. Symphonic Dances
ᵃ**Kroumata Percussion Ensemble** (John Eriksson, Anders Holdar, Leif Karlsson, Anders Loguin, Ulrik Nilsson, Johan Silvmark *perc*) **Lahti Symphony Orchestra / Osmo Vänskä**
BIS BIS-CD1336 (61' · DDD)   Ⓕ▷

Aho's *Symphonic Dances* (2001) bear the subtitle 'Hommage à Uuno Klami' – and therein lies the clue to the work's genesis. Klami (1900-1961), one of the leading Finnish composers of the last century, had high hopes for his large-scale, *Kalevala*-inspired ballet *Pyörteitä*, but by the time of his death had managed to orchestrate only the second of its three acts. Aho orchestrated Act 1 in 1988. During 2000, no material having come to light for the final act, he embarked on completing Klami's *magnum opus*, bolstered by the prospect of a production at the Finnish National Ballet. In the event, that belated premiere never materialised, and it was left to Osmo Vänskä and the Lahti SO to champion Aho's 'Third Act' in the concert hall. A thoroughly approachable, 27-minute creation of exhilarating drive and colour, its four movements take their names from Klami's original synopsis. It's stunningly well served here by artists and production crew alike.

Symphony No 11 is almost as rewarding. It grew out of a commission for an orchestral work involving the Kroumata Percussion Ensemble, and is cast in three movements, the last of which distils a wondrous stillness and inner calm. It also serves as a perfect foil to the first two movements, both of which demonstrate Aho's comprehensive mastery of rhythm, timbre and drama. Again, the performance is a definitive one and BIS's engineering breathtaking in its realism.

Concert for Chamber Orchestra – The Book of Questionsᵃ; Viola Concertoᵇ; Symphony No 14, 'Rituals'ᶜ
ᵃ**Monica Groop** *mez* ᵇ**Anna Kreetta Gribajcevic** *va* ᶜ**Herman Rechberger** *darabuka/djembe* ᶜ**Jukka Koski** *gong/tam* **Chamber Orchestra of Lapland / John Storgårds**

BIS BIS-CD1686 (80' · DDD)   Ⓕ

Following the *Luosto* Symphony's premiere, Aho wanted to write on a smaller scale, for chamber orchestra. In the event, however, he produced a concert full of three interlinked works (2006-07) that, while performable separately, taken together 'form some sort of great "meta-symphony"'.

The concert opens with *The Book of Questions*, a half-hour-long song-cycle to lines from Neruda's final collection. Absent is the lushness of the *Chinese Songs*: the opening and closing sections are spoken and not until the fourth section does anything like their radiance of vocal writing emerge; by the 10th there is a hint of Aho's old teacher Rautavaara. Monica Groop sings as beautifully as she may, but the cycle's restraint is all-pervasive. Not so in the Viola Concerto which starts from the same chord with which the cycle concludes (in concert the soloists play tag while the music is still sounding); this is the more familiar Aho, dramatic, lyric, rhythmically vital.

The Fourteenth Symphony (*Rituals*) forms the concert's second half, exchanging singer and viola player for two percussionists, the first performing on the Arabian darabuka and African djembe (Aho confesses he is 'bored' with Western drums). Their special timbres infuse the three main sections called 'Incantation', separated by two interludes and a Procession in which the second percussionist takes centre stage with an array of gongs. At a few points the spirit of Hovhaness hovers dimly over proceedings but Aho's personal voice is too strong to succumb to pastiche. The performances here are strong and compelling, the soloists at the top of their game and BIS's recording (made in Rovaniemi Church) superb as always.

Jehan Alain   French 1911-1940

Jehan Alain falls into that line of major French composer-organists. At the Paris Conservatoire his professors included Marcel Dupré and Paul Dukas and in his twenties he was organist of St Nicolas de Maisons Lafitte in Paris. His musical language – he wrote almost exclusively for the organ – draws on Debussy's influence but tonally he pre-dated Olivier Messiaen and his exploration of Eastern musics. He was killed in action in 1940, but his legacy has been loyally championed by his sister, Marie-Claire Alain, one of the leading organists of our time.

Organ Works

Suite. Climat. Prélude et Fugue. Choral dorien. Choral phrygien. Aria. Variations sur 'Lucis créator'. Berceuse sur deux notes qui cornent. Deux préludes profanes. Monodie. Ballade en mode phrygien. Choral cistercian pour une élévation. Variations sur un thème de Clément Janequin. Le jardin suspendu. Litanies. Fantasmagorie. Trois danses. Quatre pièces.

Grave. Petite pièce. Intermezzo. Lamento. Premiere fantaisie. Deuxième fantaisie. Deux dances à Agni Yavishta. Cinque pièces faciles – Complainte à la mode ancienne; Fugue en mode de Fa; Verset-Choral; Berceuse. Postlude pour l'office de Complies. Page 21 du huitième cahier de notes de Jehan Alain
Kevin Bowyer org
Nimbus ② NI5551/2 (146' · DDD). Recorded on the Marcussen Organ, Chapel of St Augustine, Tonbridge School, Kent Ⓕ❍❍❍➔

This is the most comprehensive and impressive recording yet of Alain's organ music. Bowyer offers nine pieces not included on Eric Lebrun's two-disc survey from Naxos. These may not be among the composer's most substantial creations, but Alain enthusiasts wouldn't like to be without any of them, least of all the intensely moving page from one of Alain's notebooks setting out his musical reactions to the death, in a mountaineering accident, of his sister, Marie-Odile. Bowyer's performances are thought-provoking, stimulating and often inspired. His tempi aren't especially quick, though he does turn out the fastest performance ever recorded of the *Intermezzo*. Yet even here the choice of speed is symptomatic of his approach; nobody could deny that when played so rapidly the work takes on a new dimension. Nimbus achieves a near-perfect balance between clarity and atmosphere on the new Marcussen in Tonbridge School's rebuilt Chapel. When the disarming dialogue between a single reed and the flutes of the charming *Petite pièce* can be revealed in such detail nobody could realistically ask for a better setting for this magical music. Bowyer proves to be an unusually perceptive and persuasive advocate of Alain's music. It will probably be a long time before a serious contender to this outstanding release comes along.

Alain Trois danses. Le jardin suspendu.
Aria. Litanies, Op 79. Variations sur
'Lucis creator'. Deux dances à Agni
Yavishta **Duruflé** Danses pour orchestre,
Op 6 – Danse lente (arr Whitehead).
Prélude et fugue sur le nom d'Alain, Op 7
William Whitehead org
Chandos CHAN10315 (74' · DDD)
Played on the Oberthür organ of Saint-Etienne
Cathedral, Auxerre Ⓕ❍❍➔

With its futuristic console and its aurally shattering battery of chamade reeds, this astonishing 1986-built Oberthür organ is the perfect vehicle for this programme.

One is acutely aware of the terrible loss to French music when Jehan Alain was killed by a German sniper at the Battle of Saumur in 1940. His best known organ pieces are all here, including *Litanies*, *Le jardin suspendu* and the masterful *Trois danses*, completed just before his death. With his fondness for ostinatos, Eastern-influenced modes and irregular rhythms, Alain is

almost a proto-minimalist. The little-known *Aria* is a gem worthy of greater exposure. Although the recordings of the composer's sister, Marie-Claire Alain, have long remained the benchmark, Whitehead's more spacious approach reveals greater clarity. His sense of rhythmic bounce, coupled with a fastidious choice of colour, creates a strongly atmospheric performance. The recording, too, is outstanding.

Duruflé's music, while less experimental, is just as compelling. Whitehead's transcription of the *Danse lente* works well and should become a repertoire regular. The final track, the memorial *Prélude et fugue sur le nom d'Alain* bobs and weaves with a dramatic fervour. A winning disc.

Isaac Albéniz   Spanish 1860-1909

Albéniz's early life is one of the most extraordinary of any musician. In fact his whole life was something of an adventure. He was taught the elements of piano playing by his sister when he was just one year old and made his début at the age of four, improvising at a public concert. His father, a tax inspector with an eye to producing some extra revenue, exploited him as a child prodigy before his mother took him to Paris (aged seven) to study privately under the great Marmontel, teacher of Bizet and Debussy.

Albéniz returned to Spain but soon ran away from home, living rough and supporting himself by playing the piano as a vaudeville stunt – standing with the keyboard behind him, he would play with the backs of his fingers, palms upwards...dressed as a musketeer with a rapier at his side. Aged 12, after many more incidents, he stowed away in a ship bound for Buenos Aires. Thereafter he made his way via Cuba to the USA, giving concerts in New York and San Francisco before re-crossing the Atlantic and performing in Liverpool, London and Leipzig.

At 15, he decided to take himself more seriously but simply didn't have the self-discipline necessary to study systematically. At different times he came into contact with Liszt (in Budapest), d'Indy and Dukas (in Paris) and, more importantly, the Spanish composer and musicologist Felipe Pedrell (1841-1922). Pedrell's passionate belief in Spanish folk music and dance aroused Albéniz to become a serious composer and encouraged him to turn to Spanish idioms for inspiration. It took him some time to find that it was the piano that suited his talents best. He moved to Paris in 1893, writing unsuccessful zarzuelas, and then met a wealthy English banker, Francis Money-Coutts. Albéniz was paid an annual stipend of $5000 to set to music the appalling librettos that Money-Coutts wrote in his spare time under the pseudonym Mountjoy. This led to an (abandoned) Arthurian trilogy.

But it was his piano music that made him famous, with its essentially Spanish flavour, and after 1896 he moved between Paris, Barcelona and Nice to compose and teach. The last years of his life were marred by tragedy: his daughter died, his wife became sick with an incurable disease and his own health deteriorated, a victim of Bright's disease.

Iberia

Iberia. Navarra. España: Souvenirs.
La Vega. Yvonne en visite! – La révérence!;
Joyeuse rencontre et quelques...
Marc-André Hamelin pf
Hyperion ② CDA67476/7 (126' · DDD)

Here's the most immaculate, effortless and refined of all *Iberias*. Where others fight to stay afloat, Marc-André Hamelin rides the crest of every formidable wave with nonchalant ease and poetry. Did Albéniz, as Rubinstein once claimed, need a helping hand in *Iberia*, simplifying textures for greater clarity, brilliance and accessibility? Hamelin's musical grace mocks the very question. His 'Evocación', audaciously free and perfumed, makes you hang on every note, and although characteristically cool, elegant and supple, he's true to the heart of Albéniz's incomparable tapestry of southern Spain. Try 'Almeria' and you'll hear playing of jewelled perfection, a mesmerising dreamworld rudely interrupted by 'Lavapiés', where every one of the composer's torrents of notes is made crystal clear.

Again, when has 'Málaga' been played with greater fluency and imaginative delicacy? Perhaps such playing is a compensation for Rubinstein's legendary but never recorded performance. Certainly in its suppleness and transparency it has a Chopinesque rather than Lisztian bias, but Hamelin gives us all the notes and he's recorded in sound as natural and refined as his playing.

After *Iberia* there's *La Vega*, inspired by the plains surrounding Granada, by a 'land of flowers and sapphire skies'. This surely ranks among the greatest recordings of a Spanish piano work. Limpid, haunting and evocative, it resolves every complexity in rapt poetry. For added measure he gives us 'Yvonne en visite', a hilarious imitation of a pianist who stumbles from note to note, tenacious but incompetent. Finally, there is 'Navarra', complete with William Bolcom's coda, a lengthy and witty résumé and cadenza rather than de Sévérac's brief conclusion. Comparison with Larrocha's benchmark Albéniz is inevitable. But Hamelin's is radically different in both execution and character, and she, for all her magisterial command, is no match for him in musical grace and fluency.

Hamelin's Albéniz proudly but nonchalantly raises a new and astonishing standard.

Merlin

Merlin
David Wilson-Johnson bar Merlin **Eva Marton** sop Morgan le Fay **Stuart Skelton** ten King Arthur **Carol Vaness** sop Nivian **Ángel Ódena** bar Mordred **Victor Garcia Sierra** bass King Lot of Orkney **Ángel Rodriguez** ten Gawain **Juan Tomás Martinez** bar Sir Ector de Maris **Federico Gallar** bar Sir Pellinore **Eduardo Santamaria** ten Kay **Stephen Morscheck** bass Archbishop of Canterbury **Madrid Community Children's Choir Madrid Symphony Chorus and Orchestra / José De Eusebio** Stage director **John Dew** Video director **Toni Bargalló**
BBC/Opus Arte ② *DVD* OA0888D (184' · 16:9 · 2.0 & 5.1 · 0 · N). Recorded live at the Teatro Real, Madrid, on June 9, 2003. Includes interviews with José de Eusebio, Eva Marton and David Wilson-Johnson   Ⓕ**O**

Decca's release of its outstanding recording of Albéniz's *Merlin* marked a turning-point in our appreciation of this Spanish composer, best known for his colourful nationalistic piano music. José de Eusebio, conductor and force behind that project, followed it with a full staging of the opera in Madrid; this DVD is the result.

The staging certainly adds to one's involvement. When you can see the young Arthur drawing Excalibur from the stone, the Wagnerian echoes become clearer, even if Albéniz is much more diatonic. John Dew's direction sets out the story clearly, and the stylised sets and costumes are medieval enough to create the right atmosphere, but with a touch of science fiction.

Though the cast isn't as starry as that on disc (with Plácido Domingo as King Arthur), there's obvious benefit in having English speakers in three of the principal parts, David Wilson-Johnson commanding and noble as Merlin, with American tenor Stuart Skelton as Arthur, powerful rather than subtle, and Carol Vaness, also American, as Nivian. The big snag is the singer who might have been counted the star, Eva Marton as the evil Morgan le Fay. The unsteadiness of her voice, so extreme that one can hardly tell what pitch she's aiming at, may convey the wickedness of the character. She acts convincingly, but is painful on the ear. Ángel Odena characterises her son Mordred well but also has bouts of unsteadiness; Victor Garcia Sierra, as King Lot of Orkney, is another wobbler.

Happily, the chorus is first-rate, and Eusebio draws warmly committed playing from the Madrid Symphony Orchestra. With so rare an opera it's a pity that the booklet contains no synopsis, though there's compensation in having English subtitles available, even if that underlines the banality and incomprehensibility of the doggerel verses of Francis Burdett Money-Coutts's libretto. Outweighing any flaws, though, what shines out is the richness and variety of Albéniz's musical inspiration.

Tomaso Albinoni   Italian 1671-1751

Although Albinoni was a prolific and much admired composer (he produced 53 operas – all long since forgotten; JS Bach not only transcribed some of his works but borrowed some of his tunes) he is remembered now for just one work. The trouble is, he didn't write it. In 1958, a distinguished Albinoni scholar, Remo Giazotto, revealed that the Adagio was all that remained of a Trio Sonata in G minor. Of that fragment only the bass and some scribbled ideas for violin had survived. In 1945 he had put the two together and, feeling that the music had a mystic quality and was therefore probably intended as a church sonata, decided that there should be an organ accompaniment (rather than a harpsichord). There are many other works by Albinoni that have survived and none more attractive than the Oboe Concerto in D minor, Op 9 No 2 (the slow movement is utterly beguiling); try also the Trumpet Concerto in D major, Op 7 No 6 and the Double Oboe Concerto, Op 9 No 3.

Concerti a cinque, Opp 5, 7 & 9

Op 5 – No 1 in B flat **No 2** in F **No 3** in D **No 4** in G **No 5** in A minor **No 6** in A **No 7** in D minor **No 8** in F **No 9** in E minor **No 10** in A **No 11** in G minor **No 12** in C

Op 7 – No 1 in D **No 2** in C **No 3** in B flat **No 4** in G **No 5** in C **No 6** in D **No 7** in A **No 8** in D **No 9** in F **No 10** in B flat **No 11** in C **No 12** in C

Op 9 – No 1 in B flat **No 2** in D minor **No 3** in F **No 4** in A **No 5** in C **No 6** in G **No 7** in D **No 8** in G minor **No 9** in C **No 10** in F **No 11** in B flat **No 12** in D

Concerti a cinque, Op 5   Ⓟ
Collegium Musicum 90 / Simon Standage vn
Chandos Chaconne CHAN0663 (76' · DDD)   ⒻⓄⒺↂ

Albinoni might be described as a specialist in the medium of the Concerto *a cinque*, of which he composed 54, published at intervals during almost half his productive life. The first six appeared in his Op 2 (1700), together with six sonatas from which they inherited some structural features, and were followed in 1707 by the 12 of Op 5. They were 'halfway houses' on the road to the violin concerto *per se* as we know it – and as Vivaldi established it four years later. Virtuoso passages for a solo violin appear only *en passant* in flanking movements and 'symmetrically' in the *Adagios* of Nos 3, 6, 9 and 12. Each Concerto is in three-movement form and all the finales are fugal, as they are in the Op 2, though in their simplicity they sound rather like rondos.

There was little by way of innovation in Albinoni's concertos, which leant on past examples and stressed some of their most durable features, but the lyricism of the *Adagios* of Nos 2, 5, 8 and 11 (again symmetrically placed) was indeed new. Their strength is in his gift of

melodic invention, their clearly defined form and thematic material, their conciseness – a virtue that didn't survive in some of his later concertos – and their vitality and freshness. The recording and annotation are of the highest standard, and of the performances it might be said that if they're ever bettered in any respect, we and Albinoni will indeed be fortunate.

CHAN0579 – Op 7 Nos 3, 6, 9 & 12.   Ⓟ
Op 9 Nos 2, 5, 8 & 11
CHAN0602 – Op 7 Nos 1, 2, 4 & 5.
Op 9 Nos 1, 3, 4 & 6. Sinfonia in G minor
CHAN0610 – Op 7 Nos 7, 8, 10 & 11.
Op 9 Nos 7, 9, 10 & 12
Anthony Robson, Catherine Latham obs
Collegium Musicum 90 / Simon Standage vn
Chandos Chaconne CHAN0579/0602/0610
(oas: 72', 63' & 65' · DDD)   ⒻⓄↂ

Albinoni's Op 7 and Op 9 consist of four concertos *with* (rather than *for*, as the composer insisted) one oboe, four with two oboes and four for strings only. Overall, the last show a strong family resemblance, with vivacious outer movements and suave slow movements that tend to be more chromatic; but the Op 9 string concertos include a solo violin part, at times very elaborate. The first volume contains the works for solo oboe and strings. Albinoni treats the oboe like a voice and the slow movements have tunes that stay in the mind. The second volume contains the string and double-oboe concertos. All are three-movement *da chiesa* works, with cheerful outer movements and slow ones that often remind you that Albinoni wrote a good deal of vocal music. The two oboes 'sing' together for the most part, either in thirds or in unison. The concertos on Vol 3 for two oboes display rather more individuality – the joyous finale of Op 7 No 11 intriguingly sharpens the fourth of the scale, Op 9 No 9 allows the oboes more independence of each other, while in the outer movements of Op 9 No 12 the oboes put up a good pretence at being trumpets.

Anthony Robson and Catherine Latham contribute deftly to the spirit of enjoyment that emanates from the whole of this disc. Collegium Musicum 90 is one of the very best Baroque bands around and here the players are in their element. The recorded balance is just right, keeping soloists and strings in equal perspective.

Hugo Alfvén   Swedish 1872-1960

Alfvén's early study (at the Stockholm Conservatory) was also combined with tuition as a painter. He later worked as a choirmaster and professor at Uppsala University (1910-39). His musical language makes great use of colour and an almost 'visual' feel for programmatic expression. His output includes five symphonies, a considerable body of choral music and songs.

Swedish Rhapsodies

Swedish Rhapsodies – No 1, Op 19, 'Midsummer Vigil'; No 2, Op 24, 'Upsala-rapsodi'; No 3, 'Dalarapsodi'. A Legend of the Skerries, Op 20. Gustav Adolf II, Op 49 – Elegy
Iceland Symphony Orchestra / Petri Sakari
Chandos CHAN9313 (70' · DDD)   Ⓕ Ⓑ➤

Petri Sakari gives us the most natural, unaffected and satisfying *Midsummer Vigil* to be heard on disc. He's light in touch, responsive to each passing mood and every dynamic nuance, self-effacing and completely at the service of the composer. Moreover, in the *Upsala-rapsodi* and its later companion he's fresher and more persuasive than any of his rivals on record. Even the Wagnerian-Straussian echoes from the *Skerries* sound convincing. The only reservation concerns the *Elegy* from the incidental music to Ludwig Nordström's play about Gustav Adolf II, which might have benefited from greater reticence. Unusually for Sakari, he doesn't tell the tale simply or let the music speak for itself. The recorded sound is refreshingly free from analytical point-making; everything is there in the right perspective, although listeners whose first response is to find the recording recessed will find that a higher level of playback than usual will produce impressively natural results on high-grade equipment.

Charles-Valentin Alkan
French 1813-1888

Alkan is one of the most puzzling cases of 'composer neglect'. He wrote piano music at a level consistent with the greatest contemporary writers for the instrument – Chopin, Schumann, Liszt, Brahms – introduced new forms and produced music every bit as inventive as his peers. Yet he was all but forgotten until a few decades ago. Since then the advocacy of a few pianists has persuaded many people that Alkan, like Chopin and Liszt, was a genius.

He was a strange, bitter man, a misanthrope who had two homes in Paris (one of them in the Square d'Orléans, where he was a neighbour of Chopin and George Sand) so that he could avoid visitors. He was a formidable pianist (Liszt declared that Alkan had the greatest technique he had ever known) but seldom played in public. He had an illegitimate son with the wondrous name of Elie Miriam Delaborde who shared his home with two apes and 121 cockatoos. Having been passed over for a major position at the Conservatoire, ignored and (as he saw it) humiliated, he withdrew from public life, still yearning for official recognition. Today, it's the nature of his death that evokes a reaction at the mention of his name, rather than his music: he was crushed to death

by a falling bookcase. The legend of his having reached up for a copy of the Talmud which, miraculously, remained clutched in his hand, may be a romanticised version of the event.

It's easy to see why his music dropped out of sight. It was advanced for its day; he did little to promote it himself; it is ferociously difficult to play, putting it out of reach to all but a few top-flight virtuosos; he had few contemporary champions. By the time that anyone bothered to investigate this 'Berlioz of the piano', musical tastes had changed and Debussy, Bartók and Schoenberg had set new fashions. For anyone remotely interested in the piano, Alkan will provide an exciting, not to say jaw-dropping, experience.

Sonate de concert

Alkan Sonate de concert, Op 47 **Chopin** Cello Sonata, Op 65
Alban Gerhardt *vc* **Steven Osborne** *pf*
Hyperion CDA67624 (63' · DDD)   Ⓕ Ⓞ

Alkan's Sonata has been recorded several times before, yet it has remained obstinately in the wings of the cello repertoire. This new version must surely drag it centre-stage. It is a masterpiece: meaty, melodic and, as with most of Alkan's music, extremely demanding to play – Mendelssohn with balls. The *Allegretto* second movement with its sly, pungent harmonies and the mystical, almost impressionistic slow movement especially are further proof, if it were needed, of Alkan's genius.

Chopin's Cello Sonata, his final major work and the last published in his lifetime, has never lacked champions, despite the notorious problems of balance in the first movement. Here the musical line is focused and unambiguous, though the *da capo* repeat turns what is by far the longest movement (usually about 10 minutes) into one approaching 15, making it quite disproportionate to the scale of the other three. However, it offers the chance to hear twice the heart-catching little motif at 2'42" which has rarely been played so affectingly. Both performances from this outstanding partnership are out of the top drawer, fresh, spontaneous and beautifully recorded.

Concerto for Solo Piano

Concerto for Solo Piano, Op 39 Nos 8-10. Troisième recueil de chants – Book 3, Op 65
Marc-André Hamelin *pf*
Hyperion CDA67569 (68' · DDD)   Ⓕ ⓄⓄⓄ➤

This is Marc-André Hamelin's second recording of the Alkan Concerto for Solo Piano (the first for Music & Arts dates from 1992) and he now trumps his previous ace with a performance of the Concerto of such brilliance and lucidity that one can only listen in awe and amazement. Scaling even the most ferocious hurdles with yards to spare, he is blessedly free to explore the very heart of Alkan's bewildering interplay of austerity and monstrous elaboration. In the gigantic first movement you can hear avalanches of notes given with the rarest focus and trenchancy. And whether you turn to the finale's helter-skelter pages (with their curious Eastern underpinnings) or the baleful central *Adagio*, you can only marvel at such a unique mix of blazing if nonchalantly deployed virtuosity and poetic conviction.

For his substantial encore Hamelin gives us Alkan's *Troisième recueil de chants* where outward convention vies with that sinister and pervasive oddity so central to this composer's nature. No 3 is a near bitonal canon, No 4 a polonaise with memories of the Etudes from which the Concerto is drawn and a crazy, race-away coda, while the concluding Barcarolle contains ironic echoes of Liszt's *Au lac de Wallenstadt*.

All this is superbly recorded and presented, prompting some not unreasonable conjecture: if Liszt feared Alkan's mastery as a pianist he may well have feared Hamelin's.

Grand duo concertante, Op 21

Grand duo concertante in F sharp minor, Op 21. Sonate de concert in E, Op 47. Trio in G minor, Op 30
Trio Alkan (Kolja Lessing *vn* Bernhard Schwarz *vc* Rainer Klaas *pf*)
Naxos 8 555352 (75' · DDD) ⓈⒷ▸

As this disc so persuasively reveals, there are a number of Alkan's chamber works that are long overdue for serious consideration. His violin sonata, the *Grand duo concertante*, for instance, is so thoroughly original and masterly in invention that it should have acquired for itself a prominent place in the French violin sonata repertoire. The somewhat unconventional tonal layout of the bold and memorable first movement suggests, at times, the harmonic world of Berlioz, but perhaps more strikingly looks forward, both here and in the final movement, to the melodic, Gallic charm of the Fauré sonatas.

The *Sonate de concert* for cello and piano is perhaps Alkan's finest and most important contribution to chamber music. Although clearly rooted in the classical tradition, it shouts Alkan from every page. The second movement, in *siciliano* style, is a fine example of Alkan whimsy; in the slow movement, Alkan draws musical inspiration from his Jewish faith to create a serene and somewhat mystical oasis of calm before launching into the helter-skelter activity of the finale. The earlier Piano Trio of 1841 is perhaps even more classical in design and utterance, and is certainly more terse and economical in its use of material. However, it's no easy ride for the performers. The *Scherzo* is strangely prophetic of Tchaikovsky in places and is graced with a fiendishly difficult finale. The performances are quite superb. Klaas copes admirably with all the keyboard pyrotechnics thrown at him, and Lessing and Schwarz provide performances of dedication and great understanding. Recording is full-bodied and close.

48 Esquisses, Op 63

48 Esquisses
Steven Osborne *pf*
Hyperion CDA67377 (75' · DDD) ⒻⒷ▸

Here's a superlative record of music to confound the sceptics, including the soloist himself, who, in a witty, concentrated essay, expresses his surprise at discovering Alkan's *Esquisses* and their journey into intimacy rather than gargantuan bravura. Not that these 48 fragments, many of them of a teasing and enigmatic brevity, could be by any other composer. Gnomic, introspective, full of odd twists and turns of phrase and expression, they invariably catch you unawares.

In 'Confidence', a Field-like innocence is countered by enough surprises to declare the composer's identity. 'Les soupirs' is so much more than a foretaste of Debussian impressionism. 'Inflexibilité' holds the listener in a vicelike grip and the change from charm ('Petite marche villageoise') to grimness ('Morituri te salutant') is typical of Alkan's volatile yet rigorous command of the widest variety of ideas and pastiches. 'Le frisson', 'Pseudo-naïveté', 'Délire', 'Fais Dodo', 'L'homme aux sabots' – the titles predict an eccentricity that's none the less qualified by a formidable intellectual focus.

Osborne's performances are of a sensitivity, radiance and finesse rarely encountered from even the finest pianists. He floats the opening of 'La vision' in a magical haze or nimbus of sound, peppers the keyboard with an immaculate virtuosity in 'La staccatissimo', relishes the Norwegien tang of 'Début de quatuor' and brings a wicked *frisson* to 'Les diablotins', where Alkan's little devils are hustled from the field almost as if the composer had lost patience with his own grotesque creation.

Misha Donat's notes are as affectionate as they are perceptive, and Hyperion's sound is of demonstration quality. An invaluable disc.

Organ Works

11 Grands préludes et un transcription. Benedictus, Op 54. 12 Etudes pour les pieds seulement – Nos 1-6
Kevin Bowyer *org*
Toccata Classics TOCC0030 (76' · DDD)
Played on the organ of Blackburn Cathedral ⒻⒷ▸

This disc scores top marks in every department. Kevin Bowyer displays his customary polish, felicity and technical mastery, playing with an assurance made all the more astounding since this programme – none of it previously recorded – is hardly standard repertoire, certainly outside France.

By all accounts Alkan's organ technique equalled his command of the piano. In 1834 he gained the *premier prix d'orgue* at the Paris Conservatoire and he maintained close friendships with César Franck and Lefébure-Wély, dedicatees respectively of the *Grands préludes* and the *Douze études*. The first half-dozen of the *Etudes* – played on the pedals alone – are strikingly original and much more than mere technical exercises. Dupré considered them to be 'the complete and indispensable foundation of pedal technique'. The *Grands préludes* are equally engrossing and entertaining, especially the fiendish 10th, which Ronald Smith termed a 'Cossack Dance'. As the final notes of the transcription of Handel's 'Behold, and See' hover, teasingly, on a half close, succeeding volumes are eagerly awaited.

Blackburn Cathedral's magnificent Walker/Wood organ (superbly captured by sound engineer Lance Andrews) combined with Bowyer's effortless artistry and Malcolm MacDonald's masterful notes make this a must-have recommendation.

Pro organo. 12 Etudes pour les pieds seulement – Nos 7-12. 11 Pièces dans le style réligieux, et un transcription du Messie de Handel, Op 72
Kevin Bowyer *org*
Toccata TOCC0031 (74' · DDD)
Played on the organ of Blackburn Cathedral   Ⓕ

Pro organo, two minutes' worth of harmless and innocent tranquillity, opens this second volume of Kevin Bowyer's Alkan cycle, but it is a false dawn. You have to wait until the final track for anything so soothing to crop up again. Everything else is as challenging to the listener as it must be to the performer, but luckily in Bowyer we have a performer who not only guides us through the music with the assurance of one who sees nothing out of the ordinary in Alkan's musical language but who cuts through the immense technical difficulties like a hot knife through butter.

Bowyer's breathtaking footwork in the final six of the *Etudes pour les pieds seulement* doesn't diminish the slightly circus-like melodrama of these astonishing pieces which range from the tempestuous No 7 to the dark No 11 by way of the jaunty (but, as Malcolm MacDonald's excellent booklet-notes point out, fiendishly difficult) Ninth.

The remainder of the disc is given over to all 12 pieces in Alkan's Op 72, an opus with a typically unambiguously wordy title. Handel informs the first of these, majestically striding along, at once pompous and celebratory, both characteristics (as well as the vivid final echo effects) magnificently highlighted by the regal splendour of Blackburn Cathedral's matchless Walker/Wood, the cathedral's heady acoustic and a superlative recording from Toccata Classics. There then follows a series of increasingly complex and demanding pieces which, were it not for the amazing intensity of Bowyer's interpretative vision and his wonderful use of organ colour, would prove insurmountably daunting to most listeners. As it is we are treated to some of the most vividly focused and technically fluent organ playing imaginable.

It seems curious that Alkan rounded his Op 72 off with a simple transcription of the 'Pastoral Symphony' from *Messiah*. But it turns out to be a stroke of genius, restoring calm after so much, as MacDonald puts it, 'tortured and sardonic' writing.

Gregorio Allegri   Italian c1582-1652

Allegri was a singer and composer at the cathedrals of Fermo and Tivoli, and later maestro di cappella of Spirito in Sassia, Rome, and a singer in the papal choir. He composed many of his works for this choir and that of S Maria in Vallicella. His reputation rests on his Miserere, a psalm-setting traditionally sung every Holy Week by the papal choir: it is basically a simple five-part chant, transformed by interpolated ornamented passages for a four-part solo choir which reaches top C (rare at that time). These passages were a closely guarded secret for many years; Mozart wrote out the work from memory when he was 14. Allegri was at his best in the a cappella style, as in his five Masses; he also published three books of more up-to-date small-scale concertato church music. The work has become one of the all-time favourite classics – largely due to the recording made by King's College, Cambridge (listed below).

Miserere mei

Allegri Miserere mei (two versions) **Palestrina** Missa Papae Marcelli. Stabat mater. Tu es Petrus
Tallis Scholars / Peter Phillips
Gimell CDGIM041 (76' · DDD · T/t)   ⒻⓄⓄ▷

It's about 25 years since the Tallis Scholars' debut recording, which included the *Pope Marcellus* Mass and Allegri's *Miserere*; and in 1994 they issued a video (also available as a CD) of a concert in the Sistine Chapel commemorating the 400th anniversary of Palestrina's death. This third recording has far more in common with the latter interpretation than with the first, and in essentials little seems to have changed in 10 years, but the wholly ethereal approach a quarter-century ago is now changed into something more robust. That's attributable as much to the difference in the singers' timbres as to a change in Peter Phillips's view of these works.

This new recording's principal innovation is the inclusion of two different readings of the Allegri (or rather, the modern-day elaboration of it that bears his name – a distinction that Phillips's booklet-notes don't acknowledge): one sung quite 'straight', and the other with embellishments to the famous top line evolved over many years (and countless live performances) by soprano Deborah Roberts. This is the main reason for recommending the disc, even though the ornaments to the opening verses are a little slow to get off the ground. By the end, the excitement is undeniable.

Miserere mei (two versions). Missa Vidi turbam magnam. De ore prudentis. Repleti sunt omnes. Cantate domino
A Sei Voci / Bernard Fabre-Garrus
with **Dominique Ferran** org
Naïve E8524 (62' · DDD · T/t)   Ⓕ

Allegri's setting of the psalm *Miserere mei* is presented in two versions. The first is sung with ornamentation added by the French musicologist Jean Lionnet following 17th-century models, while the second presents the Burney-Alfieri version familiar from the classic 1963 Willcocks recording (below). A Sei Voci produce a rather varied sound, which is at times somewhat flat and white but at its best is imbued with an appropriate Italianate edge. For the most part the embellishments are negotiated with style and verve; just occasionally they're fuzzy or insecure. *Miserere mei* apart, hardly any of Allegri's music is heard either liturgically or in the concert hall. By training a pupil of Nanino, a distinguished follower of Palestrina, his best music is written confidently in the High Renaissance contrapuntal manner. The six-voice *Missa Vidi turbam magnam*, composed on one of his own motets, is a fine work, and shows that the *stile antico*, far from being a mere academic exercise, could still be vividly sonorous and dramatic, qualities which are brought out in this reading. The disc is nicely rounded out with a selection of short continuo motets in the popular new manner, well established in Northern Italy, which was becoming fashionable in Rome.

Allegri Miserere mei **Palestrina** Stabat mater a 8. Hodie beata virgo. Senex puerem portabat. Magnificat a 8. Litanie de Beata Virgine Maria I
Roy Goodman treb **King's College Choir, Cambridge / Sir David Willcocks**
Decca Legends 466 373-2DM (56' · ADD)
Recorded 1963-64   ⓂⓄⓄⓄ➔

It's doubtful if any recording made by the choir of King's College, Cambridge, in the fertile Willcocks era, will prove more enduring than this celebrated performance of Allegri's *Miserere*. Admittedly there are more authentic versions in the catalogue, authentic not only in that they use the original Latin words where Willcocks opts for an English translation, but also in the sense that they search for a style less obviously redolent of choral evensong and the Anglican tradition. At the farthest extreme from King's, other versions strip Allegri's score of its various 18th- and 19th-century accretions – a nice piece of musical archaeology which, ironically, reveals the utter plainness of the *Miserere* when denied its familiar jewels, and sounds like an impostor when dressed up in even more garish baubles.

For many the richly communicative singing of King's remains the ideal, however far removed it may be from the orginal intentions of Allegri. The *Miserere* is accompanied here by some classic Palestrina performances, which are still as fresh as when they were recorded in 1964. Some tape hiss intrudes, but otherwise the sound is excellent. A fabulous disc.

Eyvind Alnæs   Norwegian 1872-1932

Alnæs studied with Peter Lindeman and Iver Holter at the Christiana Music and Organ School; he later studied with Reinecke. An organist as well as conductor, he founded the Norsk Komonistforening. Among his output are numerous songs and choral works, as well as two symphonies.

Piano Concerto

Alnæs Piano Concerto, Op 27
Sinding Piano Concerto, Op 6
Piers Lane pf **Bergen Philharmonic Orchestra / Andrew Litton**
Hyperion CDA67555 (65' · DDD)   ⒻⓄ

For the 42nd issue in its 'Romantic Piano Concerto' series, Hyperion turns for inspiration to Norway and, in a first recording of Eyvind Alnæs's Concerto, they light up the sky like an aurora borealis. Here is music very much for those in love with the most succulent Romanticism, with lush, lavishly decorated melodies and a *fin de siècle* array of props. The opening *Allegro moderato* follows one sumptuous gesture with another and in the central *Lento* the pianist weaves starry figuration around the orchestra's full-blooded outcry. In the finale all fashionable gloom is cast aside for a rollicking waltz guaranteed to sweep its dancers off the floor. So for those wishing to venture beyond the Grieg or MacDowell concertos such music is heaven-sent, particularly when played by Piers Lane with such enviable poetry, fluency and aplomb.

Few pianists could have entered into the Romantic spirit more infectiously, though even he is hard-pressed to make a convincing case for Sinding's less heart-warming Concerto. Here, the music remains more effortful than inspired, huffing and puffing its way through one inflated gesture after another. Yet listening to Lane in the finale is to be reminded of playing as to the Romantic manner born. Andrew Litton and the Bergen Philharmonic are a perfect foil for their scintillating and indefatigable soloist, and Hyperion's sound balance is impeccable.

William Alwyn   British 1905-1985

Alwyn studied at the Royal Academy of Music, where he later worked for a substantial part of his life (1926-55). He later took up composition full-time and combined a prolific career as a composer for films (he wrote more than 60 scores) with a broad and strong output of concert music, written in an obviously English late-Romantic idiom but one by no means without modernist leanings. He was a great craftsman, something demonstrated over five symphonies, two string quartets, an opera (Miss Julie) and songs.

Piano Concertos

Piano Concertos[ab] – No 1; No 2. Sonata alla toccata[a]. Derby Day[b]
[a]Peter Donohoe *pf* [b]**Bournemouth Symphony Orchestra / James Judd**
Naxos 8 557590 (60' · DDD)

Alwyn (whose centenary year fell in 2005) is a composer of strong communicative gifts and the best of his music exhibits a disarming emotional candour, generous lyricism, powerful sense of argument and superior craftsmanship. If not as tautly constructed as, say, the Second, Third or Fifth Symphonies, the Second Piano Concerto undoubtedly makes pleasurable listening. It was commissioned for the 1960 Proms, where its big-boned theatricality and unabashed ardour would surely have gone down a treat had the dedicatee, the Dutch virtuoso Cor de Groot, not been struck down by sudden paralysis of his right arm. As a consequence, the work remained unheard until Howard Shelley's passionate 1993 Chandos recording with Hickox and the LSO (reviewed below). If anything, Peter Donohoe proves an even more dashing soloist and he is supported to the hilt by James Judd and an audibly fired-up Bournemouth SO. An airy, tastefully balanced production, too. Similarly, these accomplished newcomers set out a most persuasive case for the much earlier, single-movement First Concerto, a likeable offering with echoes of Ireland and Walton, written in 1930 for Alwyn's fellow RAM graduate and good friend, Clifford Curzon.

Canny programming allows us to hear the bustling 1960 overture *Derby Day* that Alwyn fashioned as a replacement for the ill-starred Second Concerto. Judd's spry performance is in every way the equal of both its fine predecessors, and the disc concludes with the exuberant *Sonata alla toccata*. This was composed in 1945-46 for Denis Matthews and Donohoe dispatches it with purposeful aplomb and dazzling technical prowess. Yet another Naxos winner.

Piano Concerto No 2. Symphony No 5, 'Hydriotaphia'. Sinfonietta for Strings
Howard Shelley *pf*
London Symphony Orchestra / Richard Hickox
Chandos CHAN9196 (74' · DDD)   ⓕⓄ🅑➛

Piano Concerto No 2 opens heroically and contains a good deal of rhetoric, yet the string writing has a romantic sweep and the *Andante* proves to be the highlight of the piece. Howard Shelley plays with bravura and

appealing sensitivity. The Fifth Symphony is a cogent argument distilled into one movement with four sub-sections. The energetically kaleidoscopic first section is sharply contrasted by a melancholy *Andante*. A violent *Scherzo* is followed by a curiously ambivalent finale which provides a moving and compelling, if equivocal, apotheosis. The richly expansive Sinfonietta, almost twice as long as the symphony, is very much in the English tradition of string writing. It's vigorous in the first movement and hauntingly atmospheric in the beautiful but disconsolate *Adagio*. The unpredictable finale begins impulsively before the mood changes completely and becomes altogether more subdued and muted in feeling. The obviously dedicated LSO is particularly responsive in the masterly Sinfonietta.

Symphonies

Symphonies – No 1; No 3
Royal Liverpool Philharmonic Orchestra / David Lloyd-Jones
Naxos 8 557648 (69' · DDD)   Ⓢ🅑➛

Completed in 1956 and premiered that year by Beecham, the third of William Alwyn's five symphonies won approval for its taut logic from no less an authority than Hans Keller, while John Ireland declared it the finest British symphony since Elgar's Second. The work's cogent drive registers to the full in Lloyd-Jones's thrusting conception, which clocks in at just over half an hour (the composer takes nearly 33 minutes, Hickox more than 34). At the same time, this score's lyrical ardour, giddy beauty and serene poetry are more potently conveyed on Alwyn's 1972 recording, where the combination of a less clinical acoustic (Watford Town Hall), Kenneth Wilkinson's superbly integrated balance and the LPO's richer body of string-tone makes for more involving listening.

When it comes to the the First Symphony of 1949, honours are more evenly divided. Dedicated to Barbirolli (who gave the first performance with the Hallé), this is a rather more effusive and looser-limbed statement than the Third; but its heart is always in the right place and there's plenty of red-blooded melodic appeal (the playful *Scherzo* is especially fetching). Again, Lloyd-Jones's clear-headed, muscular account shaves a couple of minutes off both his rivals' and the RLPO respond with unstinting spirit. To be honest, each of the three versions satisfies, though Hickox and the LSO sound particularly fired up (audibly revelling in the wide-screen splendour of Alwyn's sumptuous orchestration).

Overall, another eminently enjoyable disc in this useful series.

Symphonies – No 2; No 5, 'Hydriotaphia'. Harp Concerto, 'Lyra angelica'[a]
[a]**Suzanne Willison** *hp*

**Royal Liverpool Philharmonic Orchestra /
David Lloyd-Jones**
Naxos 8 557647 (70' · DDD).................................Ⓢ▶

All three works here show the composer at the
height of his powers. The Second Symphony
(1953) was Alwyn's own favourite of his five. Economically argued and cast in two parts, it's a stirring, heartfelt creation, full of striking invention
and resplendently scored. Impressive, too, is the
Fifth from 1973 (dedicated 'to the immortal
memory of Sir Thomas Browne', from whose
1658 elegiac discourse *Hydriotaphia* the work
derives its inspiration), a tightly organised single-
movement essay of considerable emotional
impact and touching sincerity. Lloyd-Jones provides a tauter, more convincingly paced view than
either of the earlier recordings but the RLPO,
enthusiastically though they respond, can't quite
match Richard Hickox's LSO (Chandos, only
available as a download) in terms of tonal sheen.

Sandwiched between the symphonies comes
Lyra angelica, the ravishing concerto for harp
and string orchestra that Alwyn penned in
1953-54. Inspired by lines from *Christ's Victorie
and Triumph* (1610) by the English metaphysical poet Giles Fletcher, it's a work of unbounded
lyrical beauty and leaves an indelibly rapt
impression here.

The immaculate soloist, Suzanne Willison, is
placed well forward in the sound picture without any undue masking of detail. In the symphonies, on the other hand, the orchestral balance is
neither as effortlessly natural nor helpfully
transparent as that struck by the Lyrita engineers three decades earlier – and the distant toot
of a car horn breaks the spell after the *diminuendo a niente* conclusion of No 2's first half.
Small niggles but not enough to withhold a
solid recommendation.

Additional recommendations

Symphonies Nos 2, 3 and 5
London Philharmonic Orchestra / Alwyn
Lyrita SRCD228 (77' · ADD)   Ⓕ▶
  A must if you've caught the Alwyn bug: three very
  different symphonies given superb performances.

Elizabethan Dances. Festival March. The Magic
Island. Concerto for Oboe, Harp and Strings[a]. The
Innumerable Dance – An English Overture.
Aphrodite in Aulis
[a]**Small** ob [a]**Hudson** hp
**Royal Liverpool Philharmonic Orchestra /
Lloyd-Jones**
Naxos 8 570144 (71' · DDD)   Ⓢ▶
  A delightful pendant to Naxos's Alwyn series with
  nimble performances by the RLPO.

Film Music

The Crimson Pirate – Overture. Green Girdle –
excerpts. Take my Life – Aria[a]. A Night to Remember
– Main Title. Suite from The Card. Suite from Desert

Victory – excerpts. Svengali – Aria: Libera me[ab.] Suite
from The Winslow Boy. In Search of the Castaways –
excerpts. Suite from State Secret – excerpts.
[a]**Susan Bullock** sop [b]**Canzonetta; BBC
Philharmonic Orchestra / Rumon Gamba**
Chandos CHAN9959 (77' · DDD)   Ⓕ▶

With vintage British films of the 1940s and '50s
you expected a major orchestral film score. William Alwyn, alongside Malcolm Arnold, supplied
some of the finest examples. His orchestral flair
and the ready lyrical flow of his themes brought
much that was memorable, and Philip Lane's
reconstructions from the original soundtracks
continually remind us of his melodic gifts, never
more effectively than in the opening pot-pourri
from *The Crimson Pirate*, which is teeming with
lively ideas and nautical colour. In *Take my Life*
Alwyn composed a pastiche aria for the operatic
heroine, and wrote yet another for *Svengali*, both
powerfully sung here by Susan Bullock.

The delectably light-hearted score for *The
Card* is a quite perfect, whimsical portrayal of
the engagingly resourceful hero (played by Alec
Guinness) of one of Arnold Bennett's most
endearing lighter novels. It opens, appropriately, with a (human) whistle, but includes both
a lively ball sequence and a nice touch of sentimental romantic nostalgia, exquisitely scored;
the 'Coachride to Bursley' is a delightful *moto
perpetuo scherzando*, and the finale is equally
charming and capricious. There's a fine 'Ship's
Waltz' and a rumbustious 'Rumba' for *In Search
of the Castaways*, while the wartime epic *Desert
Victory* opens *nobilmente*, and closes in similarly
patriotic mood with a grandiloquent march. As
shown by the main title for *A Night to Remember*
Alwyn wasn't a purveyor of flamboyant Holly-
woodian theme tunes, but his music always
added much to the background atmosphere,
and for the most part stands up very well on its
own, especially when it's as superbly played and
recorded as it is here.

Chamber music

String Quartets –
No 1; No 2, 'Spring Waters'; No 3. Novelette
Maggini Quartet (Lorraine McAslan, David Angel
vns Martin Outram va Michal Kaznowski vc)
Naxos 8 570560 (69' · DDD)   Ⓢ●▶

Between 1920 and 1936 Alwyn wrote no fewer
than 13 string quartets, but it was not until 1953
that the 48-year-old composer produced what
he regarded as his official No 1. A splendid
achievement it is, too, as consummately crafted,
organically integrated and emotionally involving as the mighty Second and Third Symphonies flanking it, and reaching genuine heights in
the *Adagio* slow movement (literally so, in fact,
as the first violin climbs into the stratosphere to
heart-stoppingly beautiful effect).

Completed in September 1975, the Second
Quartet is a much darker beast and derives its
subtitle *Spring Waters* from Turgenev's epony-

mous novel. The composer's description of the central *Allegro scherzando* as recalling 'the lost turbulence of youth and young love, but seen "as through a glass darkly"' strikes to the heart of this gritty, uncommonly terse essay, which ends in a mood of hard-won triumph. The two-movement Third Quartet of 1984 proved to be Alwyn's swansong and if anything boasts the most idiomatically assured writing of the three. It's also a deeply moving work, with a rapt lyrical flow, clear-sighted logic and exquisite refinement of which Ravel himself would have been proud.

The *Novelette* (a winsome miniature from 1938-39) rounds off yet another absorbing anthology from the Magginis, who play with the utmost perception and have been vividly recorded.

Concerto for Flute and Eight Wind Instruments[a]. Flute Sonata[b]. Trio for Flute, Cello and Piano[c]. Naiades[d]. Divertimento[e]. French Suite[f]
Philippa Davies fl **Nash Ensemble** ([a]Gareth Hulse, [a]Katie Clemmow obs [a]Richard Hosford, [a]Marie Lloyd cls [a]Gareth Newman, [a]Robin Kennard bns [a]Richard Watkins, [a]Tim Anderson hns [e]Malin Broman vn [e]Louise Williams va [c]Paul Watkins vc [de]Lucy Wakeford hp bclan Brown pf)
Dutton Digital Epoch CDLX7176 (77' · DDD)   Ⓜ

The Dutton anthology centres around Alwyn's ouptut for flute. Indeed, it was as a flautist that the 15-year-old Alwyn gained admission to the Royal Academy of Music in 1920, later joining the ranks of the LSO (with whom he frequently performed under Elgar's baton), so it comes as no surprise that he writes with such fluency and understanding for the instrument. Of the six works here particularly appealing is *Naiades*, a pellucid, often ravishing fantasy-sonata for flute and harp composed in 1971 for Christopher Hyde-Smith and Marisa Robles. William Bennett was the lucky dedicatee of the engaging 1980 Concerto, while the distinguished French virtuoso René Le Roy premiered the resourceful (and technically demanding) *Divertimento* that Alwyn wrote for the 1941 ISCM Festival in New York.

Ten years later, Alwyn fashioned his two-movement Trio for Le Roy, pianist Jacques Février and composer-cellist Roger Albin. It's a most fetching creation, as is the compact Sonata from 1948. The *French Suite* (1937) is a graceful reworking of 18th-century airs for flute, violin, viola and harp. Needless to say, Philippa Davies performs with phenomenal control, sensitivity and panache throughout, and her colleagues in the Nash Ensemble tender immaculate support. Strongly recommended.

Rhapsody[a]. Sonata Impromptu[b]. Ballade[c]. Two Songs[d]. Three Songs[e]. Sonatina[f]. Three Winter Poems[g]. Chaconne for Tom[h]
[de]**Jeremy Huw Williams** bar
[h]**John Turner** rec [bc]**Roger Chase** va
[cf]**Andrew Ball**, [adeh]**Iain Burnside** pfs

[g]**Bridge Quartet** ([abdf]Madeleine Mitchell, Catherine Schofield vns [a]Michael Schofield va [a]Lucy Wilding vc)
Naxos 8 570340 (72' · DDD)   Ⓢ ⤷

Having surveyed William Alwyn's orchestral output with such conspicuous success, Naxos now turns its attention to the chamber and vocal music. Just three of the eight items on this useful anthology have previously been recorded: the urgently expressive Rhapsody for piano quartet and strikingly resourceful *Sonata Impromptu* for violin and viola were completed in 1939, the latter written for (and premiered by) Frederick Grinke and Watson Forbes, while the ravishing *Three Winter Poems* for string quartet date from early in 1948 and bear a dedication to Alwyn's teacher at the RAM, Sir John McEwen (who died that same year aged 80). All are well worth getting to know and display the fastidious craft and generosity of feeling that are characteristic of their creator.

Of the music new to the catalogue, the 1939 *Ballade* for viola and piano combines full-throated ardour and wistfulness in a manner which suggests a more than passing acquaintance with Bax's powerful Viola Sonata. The 1933 Sonatina for violin and piano wears a sunnier demeanour, and we're also treated to five exquisite settings of poetry by Trevor Blakemore (1879-1953) and the composer himself (Alwyn was an accomplished flautist and painter to boot). The disc concludes with the pithy (and witty) *Chaconne for Tom* (1982), part of an 80th-birthday tribute devised by recorder player John Turner for the Lancastrian composer Thomas Pitfield (1903-99).

Performances throughout reflect great credit on all concerned in their scrupulous preparation and unquenchable conviction. Sound and balance, too, give no real cause for complaint. Alwyn's growing band of admirers needn't hold back.

Julian Anderson   British b1967

Early study with John Lambert, Alexander Goehr and Tristan Murail was supplemented by summer courses in composition by Oliver Knussen, Per Nørgard and György Ligeti. He won the Royal Philharmonic Society's Young Composer Prize in 1993 and has held composer-in-residence posts with Sinfonia 21 (1997-2000), the CBSO (2000-05) and the Cleveland Orchestra (2005-07). His music is characterised by an unashamed use of melody allied to a strongly rhythmic drive. He draws on folk traditions, particularly from Eastern Europe, and is also fascinated by the modality of Indian ragas. Major works include Diptych (1990), The Crazed Moon (1997), a moving memorial to a fellow composer, The Stations of the Sun (1998) and Alhambra Fantasy (2000). His Symphony of 2004 won him a British Composer Award. His work Alleluia was premiered at the re-opening of London's Royal Festival Hall in June 2007.

Alhambra Fantasy

Alhambra Fantasy[a]. Khorovod[a]. The Stations of the Sun[b]. The Crazed Moon[b]. Diptych[b]
[a]**London Sinfonietta;** [b]**BBC Symphony Orchestra /** [ab]**Oliver Knussen**
Ondine ODE1012-2 (77' · DDD)   Ⓕ**ⓄⓄⓄ**🔊

For more than a decade British composer Julian Anderson has been consolidating his reputation as a leading talent. This first CD shows that talent at full stretch. The music is always direct in its tone of voice and unfailingly approachable without turning its back on all contact with progressive modernism. It has the benefit here of superbly prepared and executed performances, recorded with fine responsiveness to instrumental colour and textural balance.

The earliest work, *Diptych*, is already formidably accomplished in its control of gradually intensifying formal design but it is in *Khorovod*, Anderson's first London Sinfonietta commission, that his feeling for balancing resonant harmonic densities and spontaneous melodic flow comes into its own. Anderson filters his admiration for such powerful contemporary presences as Per Nørgård and Tristan Murail through aspects of folk and popular music which are most immediately evident in the rhythmic and motivic profile of the piece. The result of such conjunctions could be mindlessly disparate but Anderson's knack for dramatising unexpected compatibilities makes for an enthralling structure of genuine substance, and this kind of process is replicated on the more ambitious scale of his 1998 Proms commission *The Stations of the Sun*, as well as in a second, no less rewarding Sinfonietta piece, *Alhambra Fantasy*.

The Stations of the Sun is complemented by *The Crazed Moon*, written slightly earlier, whose much darker, dance-free character indicates that Anderson is well able to inhabit quite different emotional spheres with equal success. With this release Ondine has made an impressive start to the Anderson discography; it is high time that Anderson was given his due.

Book of Hours

Eden[a]. Imagin'd Corners[b]. Four American Choruses[c]. Symphony[d]. Book of Hours[e]
[e]**Lamberto Coccioli;** [e]**Scott Wilson** *elecs*
[e]**Birmingham Contemporary Music Group /**
[e]**Oliver Knussen; City of Birmingham Symphony**
[c]**Chorus and** [abd]**Orchestra /** [a]**Martyn Brabbins,**
[c]**Simon Halsey,** [bd]**Sakari Oramo**
NMC NMCD121 (80' · DDD)   Ⓕ🔊

This, the magnificent follow-up to the Ondine Julian Anderson disc (see above), contains the five works he wrote for Birmingham forces during his years as CBSO composer-in-association (2000-05). The recordings were made at different times in different places but the strongest impression is of a group of compositions exploring closely related ideas and beliefs. The opening of the Symphony is emblematic, evolving from attenuated noises to the trills, arabesques and fanfares of a pastoral dawn-music. You might pick up hints of Tippett's *Ritual Dances*, Nicholas Maw's *Odyssey*, even of Ravel's *Daphnis et Chloé*.

But the music never falls back on simple imitation, and while it seems to share Tippett's modern construction of Utopia – of aspiration inseparable from uncertainty and doubt – the subtle intricacy of Anderson's approach to harmony, and to the interplay between tempered and non-tempered tunings, reinforces its strongly personal, authentically contemporary quality. Similar images are powerfully projected at the end of *Book of Hours* for instrumental ensemble and live electronics, when an artless, folk-like tune is challenged by much darker, denser materials, and again in the shorter orchestral works *Eden* and *Imagin'd Corners*. In all these scores the luminous yet abrasive resonance of the textures counters the risks of old-style pastoral complacency.

As John Fallas's well-informed notes point out, Anderson's is not an escapist vision of Utopia. Hope is always 'uncertain', and in the *Four American Choruses*, setting verses from Ira Sankey's evangelical hymns collection, the music seems to question as much as to endorse the simple religious sentiments of the texts.

Even if these works receive more polished performances in future years, the present recordings are all special in the imagination and excitement they convey.

Leroy Anderson   American 1908-75

He studied with Piston and Enescu (composition) at Harvard where, from 1930 to 1934, he pursued studies in German and Scandinavian languages. In the early 1930s he tutored at Radcliffe College (1930-32), directed the Harvard University Band (1931-35), and conducted and arranged music for dance bands. In 1936 he composed an arrangement of Harvard songs for the conductor of the Boston Pops, Arthur Fiedler. The growth of Pops concerts around the nation consolidated his popularity, and a 1953 study named him the American composer most frequently performed by native orchestras.

Orchestral Works

'Orchestral Music, Vol 3'
Harvard Sketches. Melody on Two Notes. Mother's Whistler. The Penny-Whistle Song. The Phantom Regiment. Plink, Plank, Plunk! Promenade. Sandpaper Ballet. Sarabande. Serenata. Old MacDonald had a Farm. Sleigh Ride. Suite of Carols. The Typewriter[b]. A Trumpeter's Lullaby[a]. The Syncopated Clock **Gershwin** (arr Anderson) Wintergreen for President **M Willson** (arr Anderson) Seventy-Six Trombones

Anderson Orchestral

[a]Catherine Moore tpt [b]Alasdair Malloy typewriter
BBC Concert Orchestra / Leonard Slatkin
Naxos American Classics 8 559357 (62' · DDD)
Ⓢ❶➔

This volume has its quota of favourites – *Plink, Plank, Plunk!*, *Sandpaper Ballet*, *Sleigh Ride*, *The Typewriter* and *The Syncopated Clock* among them, though there are also several pieces never before recorded. *Mother's Whistler* especially is so immediately engaging that one can only wonder why. Though the charm of other pieces such as *Melody on Two Notes* may be less immediate, it is ultimately hardly less real.

Of the rest, *Harvard Sketches* is a successor to the *Harvard Fantasy* that first attracted Arthur Fiedler to Anderson's gifts in 1936. Like Vol 2, this also has its share of Anderson adaptations, including one of his suites of carols – this time for brass – and three straight arrangements. Perhaps 'straight' is not an apt description, though, in so far as Anderson was ever one to add his own distinctive twist. In *Old MacDonald Had a Farm* he introduces some distinctly comical additional effects, while in *Seventy-Six Trombones* he cleverly highlights the debt Meredith Willson owed to the marches of Sousa.

Performances are technically and interpretatively outstanding, with utmost fidelity to the style and tempi of Anderson's own recordings. Richard S Ginell's notes add to our appreciation of a composer too readily taken for granted.

'Orchestral Music, Vol 4'
Irish Suite. Summer Skies. Scottish Suite.
Blue Tango[a]. Forgotten Dreams[a]. Belle of the Ball[ab].
Alma mater. A Christmas Festival
MacDowell To a Wild Rose (orch L Anderson)
[a]**Kim Criswell** sop [b]**William Dazeley** bar
BBC Concert Orchestra / Leonard Slatkin
Naxos American Classics 8 559381 (60' · DDD) Ⓢ➔

'Orchestral Music, Vol 5'
Goldilocks – selection[a]. Suite of Carols (version for woodwinds)
[a]**Kim Criswell** sop [a]**William Dazeley** bar
BBC Concert Orchestra / Leonard Slatkin
Naxos American Classics 8 559382 (52' · DDD) Ⓢ➔

On Volume 4 of this Naxos series, only the delightful *Summer Skies* falls into the familiar format of Anderson orchestral miniature. The rest constitutes arrangements, including Anderson's exquisitely wrought orchestration of MacDowell's *To a Wild Rose*. If the inclusion of vocal arrangements of *Blue Tango*, *Forgotten Dreams* and *Belle of the Ball* in a collection of orchestral works seems strange, few will object to the chance to hear Tin Pan Alley's attempts to capitalise on Anderson's successes.

The *Irish Suite* (the main item on this disc) – a clever compilation of Irish folk tunes – has already been recorded by Fiedler, Anderson himself (four movements only) and Fennell, and is done here with no less grace, charm and excitement. On the back of its success, Ander-

son conceived his *Scottish Suite*, but he completed only four of the planned six movements, recorded only two, and then withdrew the suite altogether. Though overall nowhere near as clever a piece as its predecessor, it's good to have the whole included here; 'Turn ye to me' is especially beautifully done.

Previous volumes in this series have included suites of carols; however, the arrangement of less devotional melodies within the Christmas overture heard here seems to me much the most attractive of such seasonal offerings.

Another of Anderson's Christmas selections (this time for woodwind) appears on Volume 5, a CD that's otherwise given over wholly to music from the only Anderson theatre score ever to reach Broadway. We have here a good proportion of *Goldilocks* (a misleading title, for the show is about a quarrelling actress and a millionaire who eventually acknowledge their love), though it's by no means as comprehensive as the original Broadway cast version. It's not made clear why – in a less than overfilled CD – the selection is so restricted. In fact, it's less a representation of the show per se than a concert suite – an ad hoc compilation of show extracts and Anderson's own concert arrangements. Thus it offers something different for those who know the show as much as for those who don't. Kim Criswell and William Dazeley do the vocal items justice, and as ever Leonard Slatkin and the BBC Concert Orchestra provide performances full of panache which are absolutely in the authentic Anderson orchestral style.

Those who have followed the series so far will find these successors no less superbly performed, recorded and annotated.

Volkmar Andreae   Swiss 1879-1962

Andreae was known equally as a conductor and composer. After study in Cologne and work as a répétiteur at the Munich Hofoper, he settled in Zürich where he became a major figure in musical life for the next half-century. He was also president of the Schweizerische Tonkünstlerverein (1920-25). Like most of his output, his operas date from the early part of his career: Ratcliff, after Heine's tragedy, was first staged in Duisburg (1914), and Abenteuer des Casanova, a group of four one-act works, in Dresden (1924). His musical language in squarely in the Romantic tradition, with use of the orchestra in the Straussian idiom.

Piano Trios – No 1, Op 1; No 2, Op 14
Locrian Ensemble (Rita Manning vn
Justin Pearson vc Kathy Rockhill pf)
Guild GMCD7307 (65' · DDD)   Ⓕ

Volkmar Andreae's First Piano Trio appeared in 1901, the Second Trio arriving in 1914. Like much music written by conductors, the works have undeservedly fallen by the wayside. Both trios open with an immediately endearing main theme and their invention thoughout is consistently memorable. The influence of Brahms is strong (especially in the richly scored slow movements) but in the central *scherzando* section of the *Adagio* of No 1 there is a lighter mood that reminds one a little of the easier-going Dvořák. The attractive lilting finale, too, has similar reminders. The *Adagio* of the Second Trio, whose first movement is obviously more mature, has a profound expressive depth and its gentle ending is wonderfully serene. The third movement moves swiftly at first but its lyricism predominates in a yearning middle section; then the opening theme dances back and combines with the lyrical material. The finale gallops into action and is essentially light-hearted, but again the richly lyrical melody is at its core. Both works deserve to be in the performing repertoire.

Accomplished and warm-hearted performances by the ideally balanced Locrian Trio, and the recording is first class. If you enjoy the chamber music of Brahms and Dvořák, do try this coupling; you won't be disappointed.

George Antheil   American 1900-1959

George Antheil studied in the US with Sternberg and Bloch before moving to Berlin in 1922 to experience modernist developments at first hand. He incorporated elements of jazz into his music, but also made considerable use of repetitive rhythmic writing and 'non-musical' tools like abstract noise. His most celebrated work is the Ballet mécanique of 1925 for an ensemble of pianos and percussion which includes electric bells and propellers. His opera Transatlantic (1930, Frankfurt) was a satire on American political life. In 1936 he settled in Los Angeles, where his compositions included symphonies, operas, vocal, chamber and piano music.

Symphonies

Symphonies – No 1, 'Zingareska';
No 6, 'after Delacroix'. Archipelago
**Frankfurt Radio Symphony Orchestra /
Hugh Wolff**
CPO CPO999 604-2 (63' · DDD)   Ⓕ❍

In 1923 Antheil gave a piano recital of his own music at the Théâtre des Champs-Elysées in Paris which created the kind of sensation not seen since *The Rite of Spring* 10 years earlier. Erik Satie was there and applauded vigorously, refusing to be deterred by Milhaud. You can see why. His Symphony No 1, *Zingareska* (*Gypsy Song*), comes from the same year as that spectacular piano recital and Antheil was uncertain about it. The gypsy element perhaps covers his own unsettled existence between the USA, Berlin and Paris, but it also symbolises his own kind of style-modulation long before he could have heard anything by Ives. We're now starting to enjoy Antheil's bare-faced kleptomania on its own terms. Indeed, there are some lovely things in this young man's music, often beautifully scored and hovering hazardously between *Petrushka* and *Parade*; you never quite know what's going to happen next. In spite of his bravado Antheil had soul – take the delicious opening of the *Doloroso* third movement with celesta background to the oboe or the melodies over ostinato patterns in the middle of the final ragtime – the one which starts at 1'26" gets so close to the first of Stravinsky's *Five Easy Pieces* for piano duet as to be actionable.

It's a pity that Symphony No 6 (partly based on Delacroix's picture *Liberty leading the people*) duplicates the National Symphony Orchestra of the Ukraine under Kuchar on Naxos, since both are strong performances of this substantial piece from 1948. Antheil pays another debt to Satie since the *Larghetto* is a slow *Gymnopédie*, an oasis of calm between patriotic war music. The riotous *Archipelago*, subtitled 'Rhumba', is in the tradition of Gottschalk but, via Gershwin's *Cuban Overture*, is pure 1930s and ends a most impressive and enjoyable case for orchestral Antheil from three different decades.

Symphony No 3 'American'. McKonkey's Ferry.
Capital of the World – Suite. Tom Sawyer.
Hot-Time Dance
**Frankfurt Radio Symphony Orchestra /
Hugh Wolff**
CPO CPO777 040-2 (61' · DDD)   Ⓕ

George Antheil is doing well on disc and he is lucky here to have a conductor of the calibre of Hugh Wolff taking up his cause and reviving a Frankfurt connection going back to the premiere of *Transatlantic*, the opera acclaimed there in 1930 but not seen in his native US for another 50 years.

Antheil was hesitant about his Third Symphony, written during the 1930s when he was returning from a decade spent mostly in Europe and exploring his own country. He broke off to write film scores and fulfil other commitments so it was picked up and put down, then revised in 1945. In its first recording, the Third is more successful than commentators have suggested, but as attractive tableaux rather than a symphonic entity. Antheil wanted to write American music and the breezy syncopations of the third movement show common ground with Copland, who in 1926 regarded Antheil as having 'the greatest gift of any young American now writing'.

If the Third Symphony is transitional, Antheil was very much in his stride during the 1940s. The short overture *Tom Sawyer* is an endearing evocation of Mark Twain's hero, and *Hot-Time Dance*, premiered at the Boston Pops in 1949, is characteristically swaggering and irrepressible – Antheil's orchestration can stand up with the most blatant Shostakovich; either would be a smash-hit encore. *Capital of the World*, a ballet based on Hemingway's short story, was premiered on television then staged at the Met in 1953. This is the suite, a suave and polished example of Antheil's late style. Wolff once again makes the most of everything.

Symphonies – No 4, '1942'; No 5, 'Joyous'.
Decatur at Algiers
Frankfurt Radio Symphony Orchestra /
Hugh Wolff
CPO CPO999 706-2 (63' · DDD)   Ⓕ

Symphony No 4, written in the worst years of the war, gets an ebullient performance which has the edge over its Ukrainian rival since the recorded sound is richer. The music employs juxtapositions, exactly like cinematic cuts, that have little to do with symphonic development and are less dominated by Stravinsky than some of Antheil's earlier works. The tunes are memorable. The novelty here is *Decatur at Algiers*, called a nocturne although it's based on Stephen Decatur conquering the Barbary pirates in the early 1800s. There's an attractive Arabic flavour about the spooky principal theme on the oboe. This release also brings the Fifth Symphony – first recorded by the Vienna Philharmonia under Herbert Haefner in 1952 – back into the catalogue. This is a war symphony too. Antheil lost his brother in the conflict and dedicated the symphony to 'the young dead of all countries who sacrificed everything'.

The first movement is continuously bustling in an idiom which crosses Stravinsky with jazz: it works. The *Adagio molto* is an elegiac *siciliano*, and the finale is a pot-pourri which raises constant echoes – that's how musical kleptomania operates. Almost at the start Antheil recalls the opening of Shostakovich's Fifth in homage to America's wartime ally. These are fine performances, well recorded too – another impressive case for later Antheil on his own terms.

Ballet mécanique

Ballet mécanique (rev 1953). Serenade for Strings No 1. Symphony for Five Instruments.
Concert for Chamber Orchestra
Philadelphia Virtuosi Chamber Orchestra /
Daniel Spalding
Naxos 8 559060 (61' · DDD)   ⓈⒷ►

Although *Ballet mécanique* is the inevitable selling-point here, the 1953 revision eschews many of the sonic and rhythmic excesses that give the work its infamy and, to be honest, its musical appeal. Spalding secures a zestful performance from the Philadelphia Virtuosi, less frenetic than the Ensemble Modern, with the interlocking ostinatos of pianos and percussion readily invoking *Les noces* in sound if not substance. The other works give a good overview of Antheil's changing idiom over the greater part of his career. From 1948, the First Serenade might seem a continuation of his inter-war neo-classicism, yet the chromatic unease that per-

meates the brusque outer movements, and the plaintive solos and chill *sul ponticelli* of the *Andante* intimate deeper emotions. The Symphony of 1923 offers a statement of stylistic intent to rival Stravinsky's Octet, though the astringent polytonal writing is more akin to Milhaud's Chamber Symphonies. Nine years on, and the *Concert* finds the eclipsed composer pursuing understated yet intriguing directions. The succession of mini-ensembles, linked by a varied ritornello for the whole group, may have its basis in Stravinsky's *Symphonies of Wind Instruments*, but Antheil's piece is formally open-ended and emotionally anything but cathartic. Characterful and well-prepared performances, cleanly recorded, and informative notes.

Anton Arensky   Russian 1861-1906

After study in St Petersburg with Rimsky-Korskov, Arensky, a pianist as well as a composer, became professor of harmony at the Moscow Conservatoire where his pupils included Rachmaninov, Scriabin and Glière. His musical influences were highly eclectic and his output included three operas, two symphonies and a number of concertos, as well as choral and chamber music.

Violin Concerto

Arensky Violin Concerto, Op 54
Taneyev Suite de concert, Op 28
Ilya Gringolts vn **BBC Scottish Symphony Orchestra / Ilan Volkov**
Hyperion CDA67642 (60' · DDD) Ⓕ

Arensky's Concerto is a continuous, four-in-one, 20-minute movement, Mendelssohnian in style, elegantly turned at every stage, and with a relatively undemanding solo part that would be perfect for students looking for something other than Bruch to limber up on. Taneyev's Suite is far more ambitious, not to say hybrid in form, encompassing a neo-Baroque Prelude and Gavotte, a Schumannesque 'folktale', a Theme with seven variations and coda, and a final Tarantella, all in a 40-minute structure that needs a soloist of outstanding technical command and expressive range.

Ilya Gringolts is fine advocate for both works, combining brilliance and idiomatic sensitivity, and enjoying fine support from Volkov and the BBC Scottish. In short, another superbly conceived and truthfully recorded addition to Hyperion's 'Romantic Violin Concerto' series.

Piano Concerto

Piano Concerto, Op 2ª. Fantasia on Russian Folksongs, Op 48ª. To the Memory of Suvorov.
Symphonic Scherzo

ªKonstantin Scherbakov *pf*
Russian Philharmonic Orchestra /
Dmitry Yablonsky
Naxos 8 570526 (49' · DDD)   Ⓢ➛

Arensky's Piano Concerto has never enjoyed a particularly good press, and given its near-plagiaristic closeness to Liszt and Chopin it is not hard to see why. The finale's slavish adherence to 5/4 metre was already noted as wearisome by Tchaikovsky. Even when blessed with the wholehearted advocacy of a fully tooled-up virtuoso such as Konstantin Scherbakov, the work has little of the sweep and none of the distinctive temperament of Rachmaninov's debut concerto a decade later; nor is it as mature or as assured as Arensky's own Violin Concerto, from the same year as the Rachmaninov. In essence, then, this comes from the pen of a gifted final-year student, heading in 1881 for Gold Medal graduation from Rimsky-Korsakov's class, and it sounds no better or worse than that. As so often with such run-of-the-mill pieces, there are passing details to be savoured, such as a prefiguring of one of the most characteristic turns in Sibelius's Violin Concerto near the opening of Arensky's slow movement.

Some of the same critical reservations apply to the undated (but probably early and certainly no more than routine) *Symphonic Scherzo*. And though the *Fantasia on Russian Folksongs* has more assurance than the Concerto, it is the ceremonial tone of the four-and-a-half-minute *To the Memory of Suvorov* (a general in the Russo-Turkish War of 1787-92) that proves the most memorable thing on the disc. Intrinsic musical quality apart, the excellent solo playing, serviceable orchestral support and decent recording and documentation combine to make this a recommendable gap-filler.

Piano works

Arabesques, Op 67. Etudes, Op 74. Forgotten
Rhythms, Op 28. Morceaux, Op 42. Preludes, Op 63
Anthony Goldstone *pf*
Divine Art DDA25085 (71' · DDD)   Ⓕ

Salon music in the best sense, such writing is raised by Anthony Goldstone to a still higher level. And, as he points out in his admirable accompanying essay, if Rimsky-Korsakov was dismissive ('he will soon be forgotten'), such disparagement was countered by enthusiasm from both Tchaikovsky and Taneyev.

Here, then, is a stream of encores to surprise and delight an audience. The first of the Op 63 Preludes is indelibly Russian and so is the peal of bells commencing No 2. No 6 looks ahead to Medtner's exquisite *Fairy Tale*, Op 9 No 3, also in G, while the *Forgotten Rhythms* are more exploratory, though with memories of Brahms in No 5. Chopin, too, is remembered in the fourth of the Op 74 Etudes (his Op 25 No 12 study), yet, more generally, Arensky runs the gamut of an essentially Russian Romantic pianism. Short in length but often sizeable in virtuoso demands, all this music is played by Goldstone with unflagging musical energy and brio.

Thomas Arne   British 1710-1778

Arne was the Eton-educated son of an upholsterer and coffin-maker. Like most of his contemporaries, his music has a resemblance to Handel's while retaining Arne's distinctive voice. Some of his best work was for the theatre – masques, operas and incidental music for plays. Despite numerous alternatives by others, it is his settings of Shakespeare songs which remain the only versions generally known ('Where the bee sucks' from The Tempest and 'When Daisies Pied' from Love's Labours Lost, for example).

But it is as the composer of 'Rule Britannia' that his name survives. This was first heard at Clivedon (the Prince of Wales's residence in Buckinghamshire) on August 1, 1740. It comes from the masque Alfred written to commemorate the succession of the House of Hanover and it concludes with the patriotic 'Ode in Honour of Great Britain'. 'Rule Britannia / Britannia rules the waves' (or 'rule the waves' as it was originally – and with an entirely different meaning) has been a national anthem ever since, an immovable part of the Last Night of the Proms. More than 250 years on it still manages to stir the cockles. Perhaps Wagner was right when he said that the first eight notes sum up the whole British character.

Eight Overtures

Eight Overtures in 8 Parts. Alfred – Overture.   ℗
Thomas and Sally – Overture
Collegium Musicum 90 / Simon Standage *vn*
Chandos Chaconne CHAN0722 (70' · DDD)   ⒻⓄ➛

Collegium Musicum 90 rarely get the adulation they deserve. This anthology of overtures by Arne, featuring a who's who of the English period-instrument scene, is a charming disc of beautifully played and brightly executed performances. Simon Standage nurtures affectionate interpretations and his violin-playing still perpetuates the impeccable stylishness and musical taste that made his pioneering recordings with Pinnock and Hogwood so enduring.

The Overture to the English comic opera *Thomas and Sally* (1760) gets things off to a splendid start; its Scotch gavotte features masterful, witty playing from bassoonist Sally Jackson. The bulk of the disc is devoted to 'Eight Overtures in 8 Parts' that Arne published in 1751. Peter Holman's informative booklet-notes say these overtures were probably extracted from introductions to vocal works, many of which are now lost. Among the finest moments are the vivacious opening *Presto* of Overture No 3 and the invigorated horn blasts and chuckling oboes in the middle movement of No 4. Trumpeters Crispian Steele-Perkins and David Black-adder provide grandeur in the bright Overture to Arne's setting of Milton's *Comus* (No 7). Although those devoted to pleading Arne's cause would love to hear a recording of such fine quality of *Comus*, or the oratorio *Judith*, this collection is comfortably among the strongest advocacies of Arne's merits on CD.

Artaxerxes

Artaxerxes   ℗
Christopher Robson counterten Artaxerxes
Ian Partridge ten Artabanes **Patricia Spence** mez
Arbaces **Richard Edgar-Wilson** ten Rimenes
Catherine Bott sop Mandane **Philippa Hyde** sop
Semira **The Parley of Instruments / Roy Goodman**
Hyperion CDA67051/2 (140' · DDD · T/N)   ℗**O**➔

This is a work of great historical importance and musically fascinating. Arne, the leading English composer of his time for the theatre, wanted to write serious as well as comic English operas, and decided that Italian *opera seria* should serve, on the literary side, as his model; he chose the most famous of all the Metastasio librettos, *Artaserse*, as the basis for his first (and last) attempt at the genre. It's generally supposed that the translation was his own work. He performed the opera at Covent Garden in 1762 with considerable success, and it remained a favourite for many years. He never followed up that success, and nor, regrettably, did anyone else. English vocal music of this period has quite a distinctive manner, being tuneful, rather short-breathed, often with a faintly 'folky' flavour. It doesn't naturally reflect the exalted emotional manner of an *opera seria* text. Nevertheless, the music is enormously enjoyable, full of good melodies, richly orchestrated, never (unlike Italian operas of the time) long-winded. Several of its numbers became popular favourites in Arne's time, and for long after.

Much of the best and most deeply felt music goes to Arbaces, very finely and expressively sung by Patricia Spence. She uses more vibrato than anyone else in the cast but her warmth of tone and expressive power are ample justification. Mandane, Arbaces's beloved, composed for Arne's mistress Charlotte Brent, is another rewarding part and is finely sung here by Catherine Bott, who can encompass both the charming English ditties and the more Italianate virtuoso pieces. Christopher Robson makes an excellent Artaxerxes, although this castrato part is bound to be testing for a countertenor and he's often covered by the orchestra. Arne's orchestral style here is very rich, with much prominent wind writing; sometimes the singers don't ride the full textures very comfortably. Roy Goodman's accompaniments aren't generally very subtle. The original score doesn't survive complete, a victim (like so many) of the frequent theatre fires of the time; Peter Holman has done an unobtrusive and stylish job of reconstructing some of the lost recitatives. This recording is recommended warmly to anyone curious about this byway of 18th-century opera, and to anyone drawn to Arne's very appealing melodic style.

Richard Arnell   British 1917-2009

English composer and conductor. He studied at the RCM – numbering John Ireland among his teachers – winning the Farrar composition prize in 1938. Visiting New York for the World Fair, he found himself stranded in the US when war broke out. He stayed until 1947 and returned with a much more significant reputation in the US than at home. He was music consultant to the North American service of the BBC during the war years. In 1948 he became a professor of composition at Trinity College of Music and taught there until 1987. Arnell's music has an immediately recognisable style. As a composer, he is known mainly for his instrumental music, including six symphonies, two violin concertos and six string quartets. He has also written for the stage (Beecham recorded his ballet Punch and the Child) and produced a considerable amount of film music. He is admired for his skills as an orchestrator.

Symphonies

Symphonies – No 1, Op 31; No 6, 'The Anvil',
Op 171. Sinfonia quasi variazioni, Op 13
Royal Scottish National Orchestra / Martin Yates
Dutton Epoch CDLX7217 (58' · DDD)   Ⓜ

Dutton's revelatory cycle of Richard Arnell's symphonies reaches a fitting culmination with this highly stimulating anthology. It's launched in arresting fashion by the *Sinfonia quasi variazioni* of 1941, an economical and inventive canvas of considerable dramatic and emotional scope premiered by Beecham in March of the following year.

By contrast, the First (1943) of Arnell's six numbered symphonies wears an altogether more restrained, urbane and finely chiselled demeanour. This, too, dates from Arnell's prolific New York sojourn, and both Beecham and Bernard Herrmann were early exponents of a work which Arnell initially designated as a 'Chamber Symphony' on the manuscript but which is surely rather more deserving of the epithet 'Classical Symphony'.

Over half a century separates it and the completion of the Sixth Symphony (1992-94). Lasting just under 14 minutes, this is an enigmatic, often uncompromisingly gritty statement, with something of the bare-faced agitation and autobiographical resonance of Malcolm Arnold's symphonic output. Its four parts run without a break and there are key roles for anvil (best heed the warning on the rear sleeve about replay levels!) and piano.

As on previous volumes, Martin Yates's clear-headed interpretations fairly crackle with conviction, and the Dutton microphones capture the RSNO's spirited and eloquent contribution to extremely vivid, if occasionally raw effect.

Symphonies – No 4, Op 52; No 5, Op 77
Royal Scottish National Orchestra / Martin Yates
Dutton Epoch CDLX7194 (64' · DDD)   Ⓜ

Written in London between 1955 and 1957 and revised seven years later, Richard Arnell's Fifth Symphony is an enormously sincere, patiently argued statement, full of rhetorical grandeur and unapologetically epic in countenance. Its centrepiece comprises a memorable conflation of slow movement and scherzo which is flanked in turn by two imposing *Andante*s, the second of which builds impressively to a jubilant peroration. One could easily imagine the piece going down a treat at the Proms, where it would make a refreshing alternative to, say, a Mahler or Shostakovich symphony.

The Fourth is more concise and no less involving. Begun in New York in the spring of 1948 and finished in London that July, it was premiered in a BBC studio broadcast under Charles Groves and soon taken up by dedicatee Leon Barzin, Barbirolli and Beecham. Its subsequent, almost wholesale neglect is hard to fathom, such is the communicative fervour of those arching lyrical lines in the eloquent central *Andante con moto* in particular. Nor is there an ounce of flab in the substantial first movement or enviably terse finale.

As in the Fifth, Yates and a fired-up RSNO give their all, and the sound is immensely full-blooded to boot, though the comparatively unflattering acoustic of Glasgow's Henry Wood Hall imparts a touch of steeliness when the decibels rise. No matter; if you enjoyed Naxos's recent Alwyn cycle, chances are you'll feel right at home here too.

Orchestral works

Arnell Prelude, 'Black Mountain', Op 46. Robert Flaherty: Impression, Op 87 **Bate** Symphony No 3 **Chisholm** Pictures from Dante (after Doré)
Royal Scottish National Orchestra / Martin Yates
Dutton Epoch CDLX7239 (74' · DDD)   Ⓜ

Richard Arnell's brief *Black Mountain* Prelude and 20-minute *Robert Flaherty: Impression* (with clear touches of Copland) both honour the American director of *Nanook of the North*, and they provide further worthwhile examples of the Arnell style familiar from those earlier CDs. Rewarding, too, is Erik Chisholm's richly scored *Pictures from Dante*, whose two movements ('Inferno' and 'Paradise') grip from the start with the evocation of Gustave Doré's illustration of Dante and his spirit-guide Virgil peering into the abyss.

Yet the major interest of this CD must surely lie elsewhere. Dutton's earlier issue of Stanley Bate's Viola Concerto aroused anticipation of the work recognised as this composer's master-

piece – his Third Symphony, composed in New York in 1940. Such anticipation will not be disappointed. Reflecting wartime tensions, it's an immediately striking and highly cohesive work, with brooding outer movements marked by big, brash music full of telling themes, building up to rousing climaxes, and brilliantly orchestrated. The more sparingly scored central *Andante* is no less arresting. Bate is clearly a composer who has something to say and who knows how to say it, and it's immensely sad that such music has languished unheard for so long.

Martin Yates and the RSNO seem understandably swept away with the gripping music, and excellent sound helps make this one of the most impressive Dutton discs of recent years.

Concerto capriccioso, Op 70ª. Harlequin in April, Op 63. Punch and the Child.
ªLorraine McAslan *vn* BBC Concert Orchestra / **Martin Yates**
Dutton Epoch CDLX7227 (77' · DDD)   Ⓜ

Punch and the Child is sprightly, satirical, episodic music, and if Beecham's interpretation perhaps has a more spontaneous swagger, it's still splendidly done here.

Harlequin in April was Arnell's most enduring ballet in the theatre; it's a version of the Everyman theme, representing man's journey from birth to death. It's a decidedly more substantial score than *Punch and the Child*, with longer movements and altogether deeper intent, possessing some of the sound quality of Holst's *The Planets* to add to the suggestion of Prokofiev that permeates much of Arnell's finely orchestrated music.

The concluding *Concerto capriccioso* is really Arnell's second violin concerto. Though apparently never performed in Britain until this recording, it's an endearingly inventive and moving work, with sweet lyricism masking technical challenges for the soloist which include a second movement that's played solo.

These Arnell recordings provide the perfect demonstration of how CD has opened up access to neglected music with much to enjoy – especially when performed and recorded as expertly as here.

Sir Malcolm Arnold   British 1921-2006

Arnold was born into a musical family but it was Louis Armstrong who inspired him to take up the trumpet at the age of 12. Arnold studied with Gordon Jacob at the Royal College of Music, London, and in 1941 joined the LPO as a trumpeter, leaving in 1948 to devote himself to composition. His versatility led him to write for almost every medium, most notably for the cinema where his scores include Inn of the Sixth Happiness, The Sound Barrier, Whistle Down the Wind, The Angry Silence, Tunes of Glory, The Heroes of Telemark and, most memorably, The

Bridge on the River Kwai. The latter, which won him an Academy Award, revitalised Kenneth Alford's 1914 march Colonel Bogey. Arnold had his personal problems – his unashamedly autobiographical Eighth Symphony depicts a suicide attempt – but the range of his work, its superb craftsmanship, coupled with his gift for melody and pungent rhythms, will ensure that more of his work survives than that of many of his contemporaries.

His most important works are orchestral (nine symphonies, 1951-82; numerous light and serious pieces). His language is diatonic, owing something to Walton and Sibelius, and the scoring is dramatically brilliant, Berlioz being his acknowledged model. A fluent, versatile composer, he has written scores for nearly 100 films. Perhaps because of his long involvement in films, Arnold never wrote a full-length opera. He claimed never to have found the ideal subject or librettist. By all accounts, though, despite his lack of formal education, he was exceptionally well-read, and it is possible that far from being insensitive to words he was if anything over-responsive.

Concertos

Arnold Clarinet Concerto No 2, Op 115 **Copland** Concerto for Clarinet and String Orchestra with Harp and Piano **Hindemith** Clarinet Concerto
Martin Fröst c/ **Malmö Symphony Orchestra /
Lan Shui**
BIS BIS-CD893 (57' · DDD)   Ⓕ ◐◑➔

All three of these concertos were written for Benny Goodman, but, not surprisingly, it's the Arnold work which most fully exploits his dedicatee's jazz background. The first movement is a typical Arnoldian *scherzando*, with an irrepressible *Tam O'Shanter/Beckus the Dandipratt* audacity. Fröst and Lan Shui clearly relish its verve and energy, and then bring a seductive richness to the main theme of the slow movement. Yet they don't miss the plangent emotional ambivalence later, for there are characteristic moments of Arnold-like darkness here too. The outrageous showstopper finale, with its rooty-tooty clarinet tune and orchestral whoops, also has a surprise up its sleeve in its sudden lyrical interlude; but one and all let their hair down for the boisterous reprise.

At the haunting opening of the Copland concerto, Martin Fröst's clarinet steals in magically on a half-tone. Lan Shui's sympathetic and flexible support contributes to a memorable performance of Copland's masterly first movement, with the coda gently fading into the cadenza. The Hindemith concerto which follows produces a characteristic sinewy lyricism in the first of its four movements, with some nicely touched-in brass and woodwind comments. Again Fröst cajoles the ear with his pliable line and the effect is unexpectedly mellow. With extremely fine recording and marvellous solo playing, this triptych will be hard to surpass.

Concerto for Piano Duet and Strings, Op 32ª.
Concerto for Two Pianos, Three Hands, and

Orchestra, Op 104ª. Beckus the Dandipratt, Op 5.
Fantasy on a Theme of John Field, Op 116
ªPhillip Dyson, ªKevin Sargent *pfs*
Ulster Orchestra / Esa Heikkilä
Naxos 8 570531 (67' · DDD)   Ⓢ ➔

The three major *concertante* works here reflect in a moving way the strange contradictions in Arnold's character, the mixture of lyrical warmth, popular inspiration and, in complete contrast, the darkness of Arnold's deeply depressive side, which at times had him consigned to psychiatric hospitals.

The longest work is the *Fantasy on a Theme of John Field*, the theme being one of the Nocturnes, a favourite work with Arnold's mother. Field, like Arnold, was alcoholic and depressive, and that made him a sympathetic figure to Arnold when the composer was living in Dublin. In effect, it is a set of variations which for the most part are dark but which end with a lyrical Rachmaninov-like passage.

The Concerto for Piano Duet and Strings dates from 1951, a time of frenetic activity which in a very short while produced a whole sequence of works including several film scores but which also resulted in distressing treatment for his depression. The work brings busy and brilliant passagework for the soloists in the first movement, a still and intense passacaglia slow movement and a relentlessly high-spirited finale.

The Concerto for Two Pianos was written for Cyril Smith and Phyllis Sellick after Smith lost the use of his left hand, and represents Arnold's lighter side, notably in the big tune of the central slow movement, first cousin to the great surging second subject theme in the Fifth Symphony. The work ends with a delightful rumba full of cross-rhythms.

The overture *Beckus the Dandipratt* is an exuberant comedy overture, with particularly brilliant writing for the brass – Arnold at the time was first trumpet in the LPO.

Phillip Dyson and Kevin Sargent are brilliant and alert piano soloists, with the young Finnish conductor Esa Heikkilä drawing dazzling playing from the Ulster Orchestra, vividly recorded.

Symphonies

Symphonies – No 1, Op 22; No 2, Op 40
London Symphony Orchestra / Richard Hickox
Chandos CHAN9335 (61' · DDD)   Ⓕ ◐➔

Here's an entirely appropriate coupling of the first two symphonies, superbly played by the LSO and given demonstration sound in what's surely an ideal acoustic for this music, with striking depth and amplitude and a wholly natural brilliance. The dynamic range is wide but the moments of spectacle – and there are quite a few – bring no discomfort. Richard Hickox shows himself to be thoroughly at home in both symphonies and the readings have a natural flow and urgency, with the two slow movements bringing haunting, atmospheric feeling.

The three-movement First Symphony opens with thrusting confidence on strings and horns, and at its climax, where the strings soar against angry brass ostinatos, the playing generates great intensity; then at the start of the slow movement the purity of the flute solo brings a calm serenity, which returns at the close. The plangent lyrical melancholia of the expansive march theme of the finale is filled out by some superb horn playing, which is enormously compelling. The first movement of Symphony No 2 brings a most winning clarinet solo (Arnold's fund of melodic ideas seems to be inexhaustible). There's an energetic, bustling *Scherzo* to follow, but again it's the slow movement that you remember, for its elegiac opening, its arresting climax and its lovely epilogue-like close. Above all, these are real performances without any of the inhibitions of 'studio' recording.

Symphonies – No 3, Op 63; No 4, Op 71
National Symphony Orchestra of Ireland /
Andrew Penny
Naxos 8 553739 (69' · DDD)   ⓈO🅑►

These recordings of two of Arnold's finest symphonies carry the composer's imprimatur (he attended the sessions). Penny is clearly right inside every bar, and the orchestra play with impressive ensemble and feeling, and above all great freshness and spontaneity.

The Naxos recording's concert-hall ambience has been beautifully caught. One of the finest players in Dublin is the principal oboe, whose solos often bring a specially plangent quality, particularly in the slow movement of No 3, where there's a real sense of desolation. The finale then lightens the mood with its kaleidoscope of wind and brass and a wispy string melody that soon becomes more fulsome. Penny's momentum and characterisation here are superb, as is the orchestral response. Similarly the winningly scored opening of the Fourth Symphony flashes with colour: that marvellous tune (2'44") is played with captivating delicacy by the violins. The exquisitely fragile *Scherzo* is etched with gossamer lightness and the slow movement is shaped by Penny with fine lyrical feeling and the most subtle use of light and shade. Its romanticism is heart-warming, yet is also balanced by Arnold's underlying unease. The boisterous fugal finale has some of the best playing of all.

Symphonies – No 5, Op 74; No 6, Op 95
London Symphony Orchestra / Richard Hickox
Chandos CHAN9385 (58' · DDD)   ⒻO🅑►

Arnold's Fifth is one of his most accessible and rewarding works. The inspiration for the work was the early deaths of several of Arnold's friends and colleagues: Dennis Brain, Frederick Thurston, David Paltenghi and Gerard Hoffnung. They are all remembered in the first movement and Hoffnung's spirit pops up in the third and fourth. The Chandos recording is richly resonant and reinforces the impression

that in Hickox's hands the *Andante* has an added degree of acceptance in its elegiac close, while the last two movements are colourfully expansive. The Sixth Symphony is nothing like as comfortable as the Fifth, with a bleak unease in the unrelenting energy of the first movement, which becomes even more discomfiting in the desolate start to the *Lento*. This leads to a forlorn suggestion of a funeral march, which then ironically quickens in pace but is suddenly cut down; the drum strokes become menacingly powerful and the despairing mood of the movement's opening returns. Hickox handles this quite superbly and grips the listener in the music's pessimism, which then lifts completely with the energetic syncopated trumpet theme of the rondo finale. Although later there are moments of ambiguity, and dissonant reminders of the earlier music, these are eclipsed by the thrilling life-asserting coda.

Symphonies – No 7, Op 113; No 8, Op 124;
No 9, Op 128. Oboe Concerto, Op 39[a]
[a]**Jennifer Galloway** *ob*
BBC Philharmonic Orchestra / Rumon Gamba
Chandos ② CHAN9967 (116' · DDD)   Ⓜ🅑►

In No 7 Gamba takes a more urgent approach than does Andrew Penny in his account for Naxos. With weightier orchestral sound, helped by a full, atmospheric Chandos recording, Gamba is even more compelling, though in that first movement the ragtime march halfway through loses some of its grotesquerie at a faster speed. At a more flowing speed in the slow movement Gamba is warmer than Penny, less chilly. One consistent advantage of Gamba's faster speeds is that the extra challenge to the orchestra brings out an element of daring, almost always an advantage in writing that's surreal in its sharp juxtapositions of ideas and mood, with Mahlerian references to popular music. That's specially true of the *Giubiloso* third movement of No 9. Penny and his Irish players by comparison seem almost too well-behaved, though the transparency of the sound lets you hear the heaviest textures clearly.

The final Mahlerian slow movement of the Ninth is also warmer, weightier and more measured with Gamba than with Penny, though both sustain the slow, spare writing superbly, with Gamba bringing an extra velvety warmth to the final movements of consolation. The Oboe Concerto makes a welcome supplement on that second disc, with Gamba and his excellent soloist, Jennifer Galloway, bringing out the wit and biting jauntiness of earlier Arnold.

Additional recommendations

Symphonies Nos 5 and 6
National Symphony Orchestra of Ireland / Penny
Naxos 8 552000 (57' · DDD)   Ⓢ🅑►
A good bargain alternative worth considering.

Overtures

Anniversary Overture. Beckus the Dandipratt. The
Fair Field. A Flourish for Orchestra. A Grand, Grand
Festival Overture. Peterloo. Robert Kett. The Smoke.
A Sussex Overture. Tam O'Shanter
BBC Philharmonic Orchestra / Rumon Gamba
Chandos CHAN10293 (76' · DDD)   ⓕⓞ🠖

Arnold's genius was particularly suited to
smallscale orchestral works, and every one of
these examples shows his orchestral personality
at its exuberant best. *Beckus the Dandipratt* came
first, in 1943, a portrait which has the wit of
Strauss's *Till* and the harum-scarum quality of
Walton's *Scapino*. *Tam O'Shanter*, a brilliantly
droll portrayal drawing on the Burns poem, has
a spectacular climax bringing an orchestral
realisation of bagpipes. The *Grand, Grand Festival Overture*, written for a 1956 Gerard Hoffnung festival, is remembered for including
parts for four vacuum cleaners and the floor
polisher. But this piece isn't just about high
spirits; it has a really good tune, too. There's
another memorable tune in the vivid *Peterloo*,
which is more of a Lisztian tone-poem.

The brief *Anniversary Overture* was for a
Hong Kong fireworks spectacular, while
The Smoke brings a sultry atmosphere in its
middle section.

The Fair Field celebrates the Croydon Concert Hall (with its superb acoustics), *A Sussex
Overture* is jauntily characteristic, while the
Orchestral Flourish, not surprisingly, brings
resplendent brass. The lively *Robert Kett* Overture is a recording premiere. The Chandos
recording is of the demonstration class.

Dances

English Dances – Set 1, Op 27; Set 2, Op 33.
Four Scottish Dances, Op 59. Four Cornish
Dances, Op 91. Four Irish Dances, Op 126.
Four Welsh Dances, Op 138
Queensland Symphony Orchestra / Andrew Penny
Naxos 8 553526 (55' · DDD)   ⓢⓞ🠖

This set includes the *Four Welsh Dances*,
not otherwise available on CD. These were the
last to be written, and their mood follows on naturally from the ambivalence of the *Irish Dances*.
Penny's tempos are very like Arnold's own in his
superb set made with the LPO for Lyrita. Where
there's a difference, Penny is slightly faster, but
the effect is marginal. The greater character of
the LPO under Arnold shows in the very first of
the *English Dances*, notably at the reprise, which is
more warmly positive.

The Queensland Hall is reverberant, and
detail is generally less well focused than on the
Lyrita disc; yet so vivid is Arnold's scoring that
not much is missed. The lovely *Mesto* third
English Dance is beautifully done in Queensland, and in the second set of *English Dances*,
the *Con brio* and *Giubiloso* have all the necessary
colour and flair. The Australian orchestra has
obviously warmed up for the Scottish set and

the inebriated Glaswegian is nicely observed.
For some the lyrical third *Scottish Dance* is one
of the most beautiful and memorable of all
Arnold's many fine tunes. Penny treats it gently; his coda is particularly delicate, but at its
appearance on the full strings the composer is
that little bit more romantic. However, Penny's closing dance, a Highland fling, is superb
in its drunken abandon.

In the opening *Cornish Dance* that follows,
Penny captures the mysterious evocation of
deserted copper mines well, and in the *Irish
Dances*, written some 20 years later, he captures the fragile mood of the central *Commodo*
and *Piacevole* tenderly. This is altogether an
excellent and inexpensive collection.

Ballet music

Homage to the Queen, Op 42 – Suite. Rinaldo and
Armida, Op 49. Sweeney Todd – Concert Suite,
Op 68a. Electra, Op 79
BBC Philharmonic Orchestra / Rumon Gamba
Chandos CHAN10550 (76' · DDD)   ⓕⓞ🠖

Commissioned to mark the 1953 Coronation and
choreographed by Frederick Ashton, *Homage to
the Queen* enjoyed a glitzy Covent Garden premiere on the evening of the big day itself (June 2).
Based around a scenario involving the Four Elements, it's an enormously fetching creation, from
which the composer subsequently extracted the
present crowd-pleasing 20-minute suite, and
whose brazenly festive and memorably swaggering outer portions frame four numbers: a bustling
'Dance of the Insects' leads to 'Water', succeeded
in turn by an explosive 'Fire Dance' and quite
ravishingly lovely 'Pas de deux'.

The following year brought the one-act
'dance-drama' *Rinaldo and Armida*, another considerable achievement, full of first-rate invention and manifesting a sure dramatic instinct.
The darkly comic *Sweeney Todd* was conceived in
1959 for the Royal Ballet's touring company,
and David Ellis's 1984 concert suite (compiled
under the composer's supervision) makes deliciously entertaining listening – fans of Arnold's
impeccably crafted and irresistibly tuneful output for the silver screen will feel right at home.
Rounding off a generous programme is *Electra*
(1963): the idiom is frequently astringent in the
manner of the Sixth and Seventh Symphonies
but there's no gainsaying the communicative
force behind the notes nor the imaginative
resource of Arnold's scoring.

The BBC Philharmonic respond with commendable polish and gusto for Rumon Gamba.

Film Music

Trapeze – Suite. No Love for Johnnie – Suite. David
Copperfield – Suite. Stolen Face – Ballade or Piano and
Orchestra[b]. The Belles of St Trinian's – Comedy Suite[c].
The Captain's Paradise – Postcard from the Med (all
arr Lane). You Know What Sailors Are – Scherzetto[a].

The Holly and The Ivy – Fantasy on Christmas Carols (both arr Palmer). The Roots of Heaven – Overture. Symphonic Study, 'Machines', Op 30
ªJohn Bradbury *cl* ᵇPhillip Dyson, ᶜPaul Janes *pfs*
BBC Philharmonic Orchestra / Rumon Gamba
Chandos CHAN9851 (79' · DDD)　　　ⒻⓄⓄ➔

Almost all the film music here comes from the 1950s, when memorable ideas were pouring out of Arnold, and his unique orchestral palette was already glowing luminously.

The suite arranged by Philip Lane from *Trapeze* is quite outstanding in the quality of its invention, including a swinging tune for the horns in the Prelude, an engaging blues for saxophone and guitar to follow, an ebullient circus march, and a deliciously lugubrious 'Elephant waltz' for tuba duet, while the closing sequence opens hauntingly and then introduces an accordion to remind us we're in Paris. The suite from *David Copperfield* has a fine lyrical opening sweep, then introduces a delightfully quirky, syncopated *moto perpetuo* representing 'The Micawbers'. This features a solo clarinet, and Christopher Palmer has arranged another witty clarinet *Scherzetto* from an equally winning theme used in *You Know What Sailors Are*.

The *concertante* Ballade for Piano and Orchestra adeptly arranged by Lane from *Stolen Face* is less memorable, but the overture from *The Roots of Heaven* (provided for the film's New York premiere) opens with a splendid Hollywood/Waltonesque flourish, then follows with more catchy syncopation and a lilting waltz tune. Perhaps the most tender, romantic writing comes in *No Love for Johnnie* (after another rousing march). The irrepressible score for *The Belles of St Trinian's* (the composer's favourite film) has something of the audacious sparkle of Ibert's *Divertissement*, and if *The Holly and the Ivy* brings a rather predictable collection of familiar carols, for the most part fully scored and not particularly individual, the jaunty samba from *The Captain's Paradise*, which memorably had Alec Guinness in the bigamous title-role, makes a splendid finale.

The performances have plenty of zest, and the flow of bittersweet lyrical writing is poignantly caught by Rumon Gamba and the excellent BBC Philharmonic in a recording of top Chandos quality. If you enjoy film music, it doesn't come any better than this.

String quartets

String Quartets – No 1, Op 23; No 2, Op 118. Phantasy for String Quartet, 'Vita abundans'
Maggini Quartet (Laurence Jackson, David Angel *vns* Martin Outram *va* Michal Kaznowski *vc*)
Naxos 8 557762 (57' · DDD)　　　Ⓢ➔

Here's a disc to demonstrate Arnold's gift of bringing out from whatever medium he is using sounds that are utterly original. Even in the very early *Phantasy*, he was using quartet writing with a confidence and originality which

rightly won him a prize in the Cobbett competition in 1941.

In both of the numbered quartets Arnold opens abrasively, almost as though he is seeking to demonstrate his modernity before relaxing into a more approachable, lyrical idiom. In No 1 (1949) the opening brings high entries for all four instruments, and if later there are one or two indications that he was influenced by the quartets of Bartók, particularly in the *Scherzo*, the echoes are only peripheral and in no way obscure the composer's originality. The *Andante* brings a poignant melody, leading into the energetic finale.

The Second Quartet (1975) is generally sparer, with the bold opening involving the instruments in pairs, leading to a sequence of bold and striking ideas, well contrasted. For all the profusion of material, there is nothing perfunctory about the result. Nor is there in the opening solo violin passage, leading to an *Allegro vivace* main section like a Celtic dance.

The *Andante* is spare and dark in its 'desolate polyphony', deeply meditative in the Maggini's superb performance, leading to a powerful climax and a hushed close. The finale opens with a violin melody over tremolos, a piece full of elusive shifts linked by the main theme, resolving in a warm, broad melody, and final emphatic chords. The Maggini performances achieve new standards and their bargain disc offers a valuable supplement in the *Phantasy*.

Piano works

Arnold Two Piano Pieces – Prelude; Romance. Piano Sonata. Variations on a Ukrainian Folksong **Lambert** Elegiac Blues. Elegy. Piano Sonata. Suite in Three Movements
Mark Bebbington *pf*
Somm New Horizons SOMMCD062 (77' · DDD)　Ⓕ

Mark Bebbington's 85th-birthday tribute to the late Sir Malcolm Arnold starts with his first substantial piano composition, the Piano Sonata in B minor from 1942. After a concise opening movement, a wistful *Andante con moto* leads without a break into the *Alla marcia* finale, whose element of ironic burlesque suggests an acquaintance with Prokofiev and Shostakovich. The Piano Pieces, completed the following year, already possess that bittersweet tang characteristic of the composer. However, the meatiest Arnold offering here is the absorbing 1944 *Variations on a Ukrainian Folksong*. Bebbington is a splendidly intrepidly communicative and an unruffled advocate. He also benefits from a superbly rounded, firmly focused sound-picture.

Bebbington proves equally at home in the music of Constant Lambert. His interpretation of the magnificent 1929 Sonata that bridges the gap between *The Rio Grande* (1927) and the Piano Concerto (1930-31) has all the stylish aplomb, improvisatory freedom and infectious swagger one could wish for. The finale hurtles menacingly towards its grim apotheosis, after which the skies darken further still for the inconsolable *Elegy* that Lambert wrote in 1938. The three-movement Suite from 1925 is full of daring, ear-tickling invention (sample the hallucinatory opening *Andante*) and a striking achievement for someone barely out of their teens. The sweetly touching *Elegiac Blues* of 1927 (written within days of the news of the early death of singer Florence Mills) rounds off another high-class collection from this intelligent and tasteful performer.

Samuel Arnold   British 1740-1802

A hugely prolific composer, Arnold was also an organist, conductor, editor and musical entrepreneur who mounted stage works in Marylebone Gardens which he owned. Arnold was composer and music director of the Little Theatre in London for 25 years writing numerous operas and stage works. In addition to that post he was also organist at the Chapel Royal and at Westminster Abbey, and was in charge of the Lenten oratorios at Drury Lane. He was also a great champion of Handel's music, overseeing a complete Handel edition.

Six Overtures

Six Overtures, Op 8. Macbeth. Polly – Overture
Toronto Camerata / Kevin Mallon
Naxos 8 557484 (76' · DDD)   ⑤⮕

Arnold's Op 8 Overtures are in fact three-movement symphonies, and in truth pretty light fare, their standardised *galant* clichés presenting the amiable countenance of a JC Bach or an early Mozart without capturing their more refined features or finding their kind of momentum.

Of more interest is the stage music. Like many a theatre man, he is not afraid to make the odd pragmatic borrowing, and in his incidental music to *Macbeth* he bypasses the play's supernatural element and emphasises its Scottishness by importing several authentic folk tunes, each given a pleasingly sensitive orchestral arrangement. His own original music includes a rattling military march and an ever-so-slightly Scottish-sounding Minuet for the Banquet scene. In the overture to *Polly*, sequel to *The Beggar's Opera*, Arnold again shows his theatrical nous by conjuring up the past in a medley of some of the earlier work's well known tunes. Under Kevin Mallon the modern instruments of Toronto Camerata play with style, accuracy and commitment.

Sergio Assad   Mexican b1952

Born in Mococa, São Paulo, Brazil, Sergio Assad began composing for the guitar almost as soon as he

began playing the instrument. He learned Brazilian folk melodies from his father. Aged 14 he was arranging and writing for the guitar duo he had formed with his brother, Odair. Still in his teens he and Odair began their studies under Monina Tavora, a former pupil of Andrés Segovia. Assad later went on to study conducting and composition at the Escola Nacional de Música in Rio de Janeiro, and worked with Brazilian composition teacher Esther Scliar. Assad has taught masterclasses in conservatories, universities and music schools throughout the world. He is currently on faculty at the San Francisco Conservatory of Music.

Interchange

Assad Interchange **Rodrigo** Concierto Andaluz
Los Angeles Guitar Quartet (William Kanengiser, John Dearman, Scott Tennant, Matthew Greif gtrs)
Delaware Symphony Orchestra / David Amado
Telarc TEL31754-02 (55' · DDD)   Ⓕ

At last, the Los Angeles Guitar Quartet's first concerto disc. And as if that's not enough to make the mental soundboards of classical guitar aficionados everywhere vibrate with excitement, it contains the world premiere recording of Sergio Assad's colourful, eclectic and enormously accomplished five-movement work for four guitars and orchestra, *Interchange*, written for the LAGQ.

Rodrigo's *Concierto Andaluz* was written for legendary guitar quartet Los Romeros nearly 45 years beforehand and subsequently recorded by them in 1967 and 1979. Both recordings exhibit a relaxed, natural musicality. The LAGQ's account is more tense and exciting; the festive last movement in particular overflows with an affection and *joie de vivre* that is quite special.

In the booklet Sergio Assad writes: '*Interchange* represents my intentions of using traditional musical styles of the world blended as a whole organic unit, while at the same time suggesting a casual meeting of different people on an LA freeway.' Each of the first four movements, which vary in style from Sephardic, flamenco and Asian through to Latin and North American jazz and blues, is dedicated to a different member of the LAGQ; the fifth movement, 'Crossings', combines material from the previous four movements. It's a superb work with some fine solo writing not only for the guitars but the woodwinds especially; both the LAGQ and the excellent Delaware SO under David Amado seize on the drama and exoticism inherent in the music, making it their own.

Georges Auric   French 1899-1983

Auric studied at the Paris Conservatoire and with d'Indy at the Schola Cantorum (1914-16), becoming acquainted with Satie, Milhaud and Honegger. He was a member of Les Six, wrote ballets for Diaghilev (Les fâcheux, 1923) and film scores for Cocteau and others (he scored a number of Ealing comedies). He was also a music critic. In 1962 he took up the post of director of the Opéra National de Paris and then chairman of SACEM, the French Performing Rights Society. Auric continued to write classical chamber music, especially for winds, even dabbling with serial techniques.

Film Music

Suites – Caesar and Cleopatra; Dead of Night;
Father Brown; The Innocents[a]; It always rains on
a Sunday; The Lavender Hill Mob; Moulin Rouge[b];
Passport to Pimlico; The Titfield Thunderbolt;
Hue and Cry – Overture
BBC Philharmonic Orchestra / Rumon Gamba with
[a]**Anthea Kempston,** [b]**Mary Carewe** sops
Chandos CHAN9774 (74' · DDD)　　　Ⓕ**Ο🅑➔**

All the scores here (expertly reconstructed by Philip Lane) are from British films, for which Auric wrote some 30; but he also wrote another 100 or so for French, German, Italian and American movies. It was in fact by a French film – René Clair's delightful satire *A nous la liberté* – that he first won our hearts in 1932; it wasn't until the end of the war that he was taken up by Denham and Ealing. Auric, not one for the 'hit tune' score beloved by commercial exploiters, nevertheless showed in his *Moulin Rouge* waltz that he too could command the popular style. On this disc he's heard running the gamut through the grandiose or the dramatic (*It always rains on a Sunday*, one of his finest pieces), the menacing (the unforgettably scary *Dead of Night*) and the atmospheric ('At the Sphinx' in *Caesar and Cleopatra*) to the swirling gaiety of *The Titfield Thunderbolt*, the perky *Passport to Pimlico* and the ebullient high spirits of *Hue and Cry*. From the gusto of the playing throughout, it seems clear that the BBC Philharmonic enjoyed making this disc: understandably so.

Further listening

The Ladykillers
Royal Ballet Sinfonia / Alwyn
Silva Screen FILMCD177 (61' · DDD)　　　　Ⓕ
A splendid collection of scores for Ealing comedies played with lashings of gusto and a great feeling for this now sadly lost idiom. A 1997 *Gramophone* Award winner.

Richard Ayres　　　English b1965

In 1986 Ayres followed Morton Feldman's classes at the Darmstadt and Dartington summer schools, an experience that decided him on a career in music. He studied composition, electronic music and trombone at Huddersfield Polytechnic. Since September 1989 he has lived and worked in the Netherlands. He followed the postgraduate composition course at the Royal Conservatoire in The Hague, studying with Louis Andriessen. He was appointed teacher of composition at the Royal Conservatoire in 2004. From 1990 Richard Ayres has worked as composer, receiving performances from numerous ensembles. In September 1994 he was awarded the International Gaudeamus prize for composition and in 2003 he was awarded the Vermeulen Prize, the highest award for a composition in the Netherlands.

NONcertos

'NONcertos and others'
No 31: NONcerto for Trumpet[a]. No 36: NONcerto for Horn[b]. No 37b for Orchestra[c]
[b]**Wim Timmermans** hn [a]**Marco Blaauw** tpt
[c]**Frankfurt Radio Symphony Orchestra;**
[a]**musikFabrik;** [b]**ASKO Ensemble /**
Roland Kluttig
NMC NMCD162 (64'· DDD)　　　Ⓕ**ΟΟΟ🅑➔**

Richard Ayres has amassed a notable catalogue, the inscrutability of whose numbering belies its range of approach and sheer diversity of expression, of which these works afford a good overview. Whether or not No 37*b* (2006) aspires to symphonic pretensions, its formal symmetry and cumulative momentum suggest a singular attempt to reinvent the genre – reinforced by the sense that the composer's often fanciful movement headings are but a means of detracting attention from musical processes 'serious' in spite of themselves. The other pieces are among the 'NONcertos' in which Ayres more directly (though no less quirkily) tackles the thorny issue of the concerto: No 36 (2002) sends the horn on an unlikely journey that culminates in the theme-and-variations evocation of Anna Filipiova and her disappearance, while No 31 (1998) draws the trumpet into an eventful dialogue taking in an affecting – and unaffected – 'Elegy for Alfred Schnittke' en route to an uproariously 'rhapsodic' finale.

This latter work is heard here in a formidable performance that is also available on a Donemus release which surveys the composer's earlier output. Few who possess this disc, however, will begrudge having it once more in a different and no less enlightening context. The other performances are hardly less inside the Ayres idiom and there is a detailed contextual article by Christopher Fox to complement the composer's own observations. Would that all musical postmodernism were as intriguing and provocative as this!

Grażyna Bacewicz　　　Polish 1909-1969

Grażyna Bacewicz, of Lithuanian descent, was given her first encouragement towards music by her father. She later studied at the Warsaw Conservatory and then in Paris under the guidance of Nadia Boulanger. Alongside composition she also studied the *violin, working for while with Carl Flesch. Her career embraced three strands: as a composer (and much of her output employed the violin), as a player (for many years she led the Polish Radio orchestra) and as a teacher (she was professor at the State Conservatory in Łódź). Her music has been steadily growing a large following and her representation on disc is now considerable.*

Violin Concertos

Violin Concertos – No 1; No 3; No 7. Overture
Joanna Kurkowicz vn **Polish National Radio Symphony Orchestra / Lukasz Borowicz**
Chandos CHAN10533 (64' · DDD)   ⑁⮞

Bacewicz is no mere 'missing link' between Szymanowski and Lutosławski but a distinctive creative presence in her own right. This group of concertos for violin – an instrument Bacewicz herself played professionally – reveals a strong personality allied to a special skill in designing unhackneyed yet workable form-schemes.

Concerto No 1 (1937) shows her resourceful and not unsceptical way with the kind of neo-classicism she encountered when studying in Paris, the orchestra challenging as well as supporting the soloist in ways which are often overtly dramatic. Eleven years and a cataclysmic world war later, Concerto No 3 has a deeper expressiveness, not without its folk-like tinges, and although the drama is still vivid there is a tendency, at least in the slow movement, to fall back on a rather featureless fervour just when strength of focus is most needed. Eighteen years on, and reacting to such new Polish initiatives as Penderecki's 'sonorism', Concerto No 7 (1965) is especially memorable for the way in which Bacewicz avoids the pitfall of featurelessness with a new blend of eloquence and austerity.

It's tantalising to sense here the kind of innovations which the composer might have worked with even more productively had she lived further into her sixties. As it is, the value and originality of what she did achieve is very well conveyed by Joanna Kurkowicz's polished yet passionate playing, backed to the hilt in slightly over-resonant but texturally lucid recordings, made in Warsaw, by Lukasz Borowicz and the Polish Radio orchestra.

Orchestral works

Concerto for String Orchestra. Music for Strings, Trumpets and Percussion. Sinfonietta. Symphony
New London Orchestra / Ronald Corp
Hyperion CDA67783 (67' · DDD)   ⑁⮞

The Sinfonietta (1935) reveals a lively, characterful style that not only evokes the Paris-based Martinů but suggests affinities with Bacewicz's fellow Boulanger-pupil Lennox Berkeley and even with the warmly expressive counterpoints of Tippett's Concerto for Double String Orchestra, written four years later. Grim war-

time experiences might account for the fact that the Symphony (1946) is weightier, more earnest and possibly too busy and dense at times, although Bacewicz's ability to introduce strong contrasts without disrupting deeper continuity remains impressive.

Two years further on, and the Concerto for String Orchestra manages a striking balance between energetic propulsion and a more elegiac, eloquent spirit, with concise forms incorporating striking interactions between solo and *tutti* lines. Another 10 years, and Bacewicz was in the thick of a cultural upheaval that saw music in Poland facing new challenges and new opportunities. Music for Strings, Trumpets and Percussion is far more than an anarchic gesture of dissent, digging deep into a heritage that seems rooted in *The Rite of Spring* and other more recent radical forays yet never lapsing into mere imitation. This is music of lament and even of protest, but it has a positive spirit concerned to communicate no less urgently and distinctively than the composer's more 'orthodox' earlier pieces.

Ronald Corp and his New London Orchestra are generally persuasive in what is often quite tricky instrumental writing: the recording is fine.

Carl Philipp Emanuel Bach
German 1714-1788

CPE was the second (surviving) son of Johann Sebastian. After lessons with his father he studied law before turning to music. The flute-playing Frederick the Great of Prussia hired him as a keyboard player when he was Crown Prince and, on becoming king in 1740, appointed him as chamber musician to his court in Potsdam. Carl Philipp Emanuel stayed there for the next 28 years, awaiting the royal call to make music and composing a vast amount of varied music in the anterooms between times. He also wrote a remarkable book, Essay on the True Art of Playing Keyboard Instruments, which is one of the most explicit and informative testimonies we have on how music was played in the 18th century. After Berlin and Potsdam, CPE moved to Hamburg to succeed his godfather Telemann as director of music of the five main churches. Here he remained for the rest of his life.

Apart from his influential book, CPE Bach's importance in musical history rests on his pioneering of the Sonata-Symphony. Instead of the musically disconnected separate movements (suites) fashionable hitherto, CPE thought about contrasting different moods and developing the thematic material in certain ways. In both his orchestral and keyboard writing you can hear these thematic contrasts heightening the drama in the music. A transitional composer – his earliest works appeared when his father was still alive – he led the way into the new Classical period and even (in some works) presaged the later Romantic school with works of clear personal emotional involvement. Carl Philipp Emanuel's music is eminently approachable, full of quirky, angular subjects which swoop in unexpectedly, with virile, bustling allegros and pensive, yearning slow movements of surprising candidness, whirling passages for the soloists' fingers in the concertos, and plenty of wit and exuberance.

Cello Concertos

Cello Concertos – A minor, H432; B flat, H436; A, H439
Timothy Hugh vc **Bournemouth Sinfonietta / Richard Studt**
Naxos 8 553298 (71' · DDD)   ⑤ᴮ⁺

Timothy Hugh's bow dances in the flanking movements and is matched by those of the Bournemouth Sinfonietta, alert to every nuance and disposed to throw their weight around only as much as is fitting. However, it's the slow movements that are the heart of these works. All are tinged with sadness, but none more than the *Largo* of the A major Concerto, where Hugh's abated vibrato, attenuated lines and resistance to the excessive squeezing of *appoggiaturas* express a sadness that's held within, not spilt in salt tears.

Keyboard Concertos

Harpsichord Concertos – G minor, H409;   ℗
A, H411; D, H421
Miklós Spányi hpd **Concerto Armonico / Péter Szüts**
BIS BIS-CD767 (68' · DDD)   ℉ᴮ⁺

Keyboard Concertos – D, H414;   ℗
E, H417; A, H422
Concerto Armonico / Miklós Spányi fp
BIS BIS-CD785 (74' · DDD)   ℉ᴮ⁺

Keyboard Concertos – E minor, H418;   ℗
B flat, H429; G minor, H442
Miklós Spányi fp **Concerto Armonico / Péter Szüts** vn
BIS BIS-CD786 (73' · DDD)   ℉ᴮ⁺

These concertos demonstrate the emerging inventiveness of CPE's musical personality within the trend towards public concerts in the mid-18th century. In fits and starts there are those sparsely etched landscapes which at their best can captivate us. If decorum is sometimes overworked, Bach's originality is even more remarkable given that the ritornello structure inherited from his father's generation, with its alternating solo and string sections, is less easy to sustain in a relatively uncontrapuntal style. Contrast is therefore a key element, and Bach needs a soloist who can discern how the relationship between the harpsichord and the orchestra can be manipulated to good effect. Miklós Spányi and Concerto Armonico, led by Péter Szüts, give wonderfully lucid, flexible and clearly articulated readings.

Symphonies

CPE Bach Sinfonias, H663-66 – No 1 in D; No 2 in E flat; No 3 in F; No 4 in G **WF Bach** Sinfonia in F **Salzburg Chamber Philharmonic Orchestra / Yoon K Lee**
Naxos 8 553289 (52' · DDD)   ⑤ᴮ⁺

The exhilarating CPE Bach symphonies presented here aren't the more frequently recorded, surprise-filled string symphonies of 1773 (H657-62), but the set of four for strings, flutes, oboes, bassoons and horns which Bach wrote a couple of years later. They are no less astonishing. Bewildering changes of direction, disorientating rhythmic games and unexpected solos all turn up in this nervous, excitable music, which for originality and life-force could surely only have been matched in its day by that of Haydn.

The Salzburg Chamber Philharmonic, under its founder Yoon K Lee, turns in crisp, spirited and (the odd moment of slack tuning apart) disciplined performances which do the music full justice. They aren't timid about making the most of Bach's strong contrasts, although they produce them more by the release of some thunderous *forte* passages than by the pursuit of too many unearthly *pianissimos*.

The overall effect is wholly convincing, and only in the symphony by Emanuel's older brother Wilhelm Friedemann – more old-fashioned and less successful as a piece – does the use of modern instruments begin to get in the way of the spirit of music. An undeniably good buy.

Symphonies Nos 1-4, Wq183. Cello Concerto, H439 Wq172ᵃ
ᵃ**Alison McGillivray** vc
The English Concert / Andrew Manze   ℗
Harmonia Mundi HMU90 7403 (64' · DDD)   ℉ᴮ⁺

These four symphonies from 1775 emerge from their performances by The English Concert sounding like the work of a forceful and original master, one perhaps out to shock with his sudden changes of direction, jagged melody lines and surprise silences, but whose expressive integrity never seems under threat. Andrew Manze, as is to be expected, revels in their extremes, not just at the local level but over wider spans too, as in the first minute of Wq183 No 4, when he rides the swell from opening nervy string unison to triumphant orchestral tutti with great aplomb.

These are performances full of life which, while not always matching the perfections of ensemble and intonation attained by some of this orchestra's top European counterparts, certainly leave a strong image of CPE Bach as a creative force. The sequence is broken up by a cello concerto, an earlier and less forward-looking work (as concertos often are), but a fine one nevertheless, with a hauntingly emotional slow movement. Soloist Alison McGillivray plays with the silver-toned elegance of some smooth-voiced tenor.

Chamber Works

Quartet for Keyboard, Flute, Viola and Continuo   **P** in D, H538. Viola da gamba Sonata in G minor, Wq88 – Larghetto. Trio Sonatas – Two Violins and Continuo in C minor, H579; Flute, Violin and Continuo in C, H571. Solo Flute Sonata in A minor, H562
Florilegium (Ashley Solomon *fl* Rachel Podger *vn/va* Lucy Russell *vn* Daniel Yeadon *vc/va da gamba* Neal Peres da Costa *hpd/fp*)
Channel Classics CCS11197 (59' · DDD) Ⓕ**O**➸

More than half a century separates the earliest and the latest of the works here. The C major Trio Sonata was one of Bach's earliest compositions, written at the age of 17 more or less under his father's supervision, and the D major Quartet was composed in the last year of his life, while he was Music Director in Hamburg. The remaining items date from his time at the court of Frederick the Great. The C minor Sonata is extraordinary, a programmatic work 'portraying a conversation between a Sanguineus and a Melancholicus' who disagree throughout the first two movements, but the former's outlook prevails in the finale. The talented Florilegium players bring out to the full the bewilderingly diverse character of this sonata.

If the Sonata for unaccompanied flute was written for Frederick, as seems likely, he must have been quite skilled, able to cope with some virtuoso passagework. Ashley Solomon's performance is most persuasive. How far Carl Philipp developed is shown by the late quartet, an attractive composition which, besides promoting the keyboard (fortepiano here) from a mere continuo to prominent solo status, is already in the style of the Viennese classics in form, and links the first two movements. The whole disc is strongly recommended.

Keyboard Sonatas

Keyboard Sonatas – H47 Wq65/17; H29 Wq48/6; H25 Wq48/2; H27 Wq48/4; H50 Wq52/1
Danny Driver *pf*
Hyperion CDA67786 (78' · DDD) Ⓕ

CPE Bach offers so much more than eccentricity and in this recital of five sonatas Danny Driver makes his superlative case for music that is as inventive as it is unsettling. Playing with imperturbable authority, he captures all of the mercurial fits and starts of the G minor Sonata (H47) – almost as if Bach were unable to decide on his direction. And here, in particular, you sense Haydn's delight rather than censure in such a startling and adventurous journey. The strange, gawky nature of the third movement even anticipates Schumann's wilder dreams. Again, the beguiling solace of the central *Adagio*

is enlivened with sufficient forward-looking dissonance to take it somehow out of time and place.

In the *Adagio* of the A major Sonata (H29) gaiety quickly collapses into a Feste-like melancholy, though even Shakespeare's clown hardly sings more disquietingly of life's difficulties. The finale from the same Sonata has a mischievous feline delicacy; and if the last three sonatas on this recital are more conventional, they are still subject to all of Bach's mood-swings. It would be impossible to over-estimate Driver's impeccable technique and musicianship, and also a winning warmth. This is surely one of the finest of all recent keyboard issues and Hyperion's sound and presentation are ideal.

Die Auferstehung und Himmelfahrt Jesu

Die Auferstehung und Himmelfahrt Jesu   **P**
Uta Schwabe *sop* **Christoph Genz** *ten* **Stephan Genz** *bar* **Ex Tempore; La Petite Bande / Sigiswald Kuijken**
Hyperion CDA67364 (73' · DDD· T/t) Ⓕ**O**

CPE Bach is much better known for his instrumental works, which are numerous, than his vocal, which are few: but his short oratorio *Die Auferstehung und Himmelfahrt Jesu* ('The Resurrection and Ascension of Jesus'), a late work which was written in the 1770s, has a strong claim to be reckoned among his most original and his finest. It certainly proclaims his originality in its opening bars, a sombre and mysterious passage for cellos and basses alone, and the ensuing chorus at least hints at the grandeur and sense of the momentous that distinguishes his father's great choral works.

The narrative is sung by a tenor in a series of recitatives, mostly starting *secco* but increasingly coloured by orchestral textures as they gather emotional force. Here they're impressively done by Christoph Genz, with subtle and refined shading of the tone and a quiet intensity of expression. The soprano aria, warmly and touchingly done by Uta Schwabe, with a mournful first part and a joyous second, is a particularly expressive piece, although arguably it's outshone by the duet that follows, with its attractive use of two flutes to accompany the soprano and its typical use of appoggiaturas and the dissonances they create to heighten the expression.

Sigiswald Kuijken's lively but sensitive and thoughtful direction, and his attention to details of the instrumental texture, ensure that the work gets the performance it merits.

Johann Christian Bach
German 1735-1782

Like his siblings, Johann Christian (JS Bach's youngest son) most probably studied initially with his father. On JS's death, JC lived with his brother CPE in Berlin, and studied with him too. He moved to Italy, embraced the Roman Catholic faith and was appointed organist at Milan Cathedral. He also wrote a number of stage works which were mounted in Turin and Naples. In 1762 he moved to London where he lived for the remainder of his life, earning himself the nickname the 'London' (or 'English') Bach. His music successfully blends a fine technique (a legacy of his German upbringing) with an Italian freedom and elegance.

He continued to write operas and became a successful teacher (to, among others, the children of the monarch), but perhaps his greatest contribution to musical life in England was as an impresario. With his friend CF Abel, he launched a concert series to expose Londoners to the best and latest music from mainland Europe. Among the outlets for his music were the Pleasure Gardens at Vauxhall. His last years were not happy: his music lost its popularity and he experienced financial difficulties.

Keyboard concertos

Six Concertos for Keyboard and Strings, Op 7   [P]
No 1 in C; No 2 in F; No 3 in D; No 4 in B flat;
No 5 in E flat; No 6 in G
Members of the **Hanover Band** (Graham Cracknell,
Anna McDonald *vns* Sebastian Comberti *vc*) /
Anthony Halstead *fp*
CPO CPO999 600-2 (73' · DDD)   (F)(O)

On Halstead's previous disc of JC Bach's keyboard concertos, he employed nine strings from the Hanover Band; but the present Op 7 concertos, like those of Op 1, call for only two violins and cello. He played the Op 1 work on the harpsichord, as specified on the title-page of the original edition: here he plays a fortepiano on the grounds that not only does the title-page of Op 7 designate 'Harpsichord or Piano Forte', but also that the fortepiano had made considerable headway in London in the seven years since the Op 1 appeared in 1763. The most interesting of these concertos are the last two of the set, each in three movements. No 5 is particularly fine, not merely because of its brilliant keyboard writing (notably in its finale) but because the sturdy initial *Allegro di molto* is more mature in style, with fresh material appearing in the development, and because of its deeply expressive, almost Mozartian, *Andante*. No 6 is distinguished by its central movement's long cantilena lines and for an extraordinary key-move near the end of the finale. Halstead's playing is a model of neatness and crisp rhythmicality: his decorations are in good taste, and in No 5 he adopts the composer's own cadenzas. His string colleagues are excellent. In short, a very pleasing disc.

Harpsichord Concertos – D minor; B flat; F minor   [P]
Hanover Band / Anthony Halstead *hpd*
CPO CPO999 393-2 (57' · DDD)   (F)

The works of JC Bach's Berlin years are almost indistinguishable from those of his brother, CPE, and anyone putting on this disc could be excused for thinking the first movement of the D minor Concerto – with its purposeful, energetic scales, its stark textures, its heavily used motifs, its rushing harpsichord writing, its sombre minor key and its total lack of lyricism – to be wholly CPE's work. In fact it's a very accomplished piece for a composer less than 20 years old and there are glimmerings of JC's own voice in the *Adagio affettuoso* that follows; it still sounds like North German music, untouched by Italian softness and sunshine, but the harpsichord cantilena certainly has a more personal expressive character and so does some of the string writing in the ritornellos and accompaniment. The slow movements throughout seem individual and appealing in a sense that CPE's aren't. The quick movements, especially in the B flat Concerto, contain gestures of the abrupt and musically violent kind that CPE so often used. The finale of the D minor has a curious element of fantasy and an imaginative use of *pizzicato* behind the first solo entry.

Halstead uses a small orchestra, strings only, 3.3.1.1.1, which is quite sufficient and very alert. The solo playing is extremely fluent and indeed brilliant; Halstead plays with ample energy and rhythmic precision and realises the elaborate melodic lines effectively.

Symphonies concertantes

Symphonies concertantes – F, T287 No 2;   [P]
B flat, T287 No 7; D
Anthony Robson *ob* **Jeremy Ward** *bn* **Graham
Cracknell, Anna McDonald** *vns* **Sebastian Comberti**
vc **Hanover Band / Anthony Halstead**
CPO CPO999 537-2 (52' · DDD)   (F)(O)

The *symphonie concertante*, predominantly lighthearted, allotted a more prominent role to the solo instruments than did the *concerto grosso*. The earliest of the present three works is that in F, and the JC Bach scholar Ernest Warburton speculates that the choice of a solo oboe and bassoon suggests that it may have been written in 1761 for Naples, where Bach's opera *Catone in Utica* called for outstanding players of just these instruments. It's a cheerfully engaging two-movement work that takes the bassoon up into the tenor register: its first movement is unorthodox in shape. The D major work, in three movements, likewise ends in a minuet, with a trio in the minor for a change. Overall, the writing places more emphasis on virtuosity for the two soloists, and both in the energetic first movement and the more formal second there's a lengthy cadenza. The most notable *symphonie concertante* here, however, is that in B flat, long considered lost and rediscovered only in 1996: this is its first recording. Probably composed for JC's London concerts in the late 1770s, it allows the orchestra greater say; the initial ritornellos in the first two movements are unusually long. In the *Larghetto* the solo cello drops out, leaving the violin long, sweetly pungent cantilenas – a strikingly fine movement. Halstead secures neat performances of finesse of all three works, which also benefit from skilful soloists and well-balanced recording. Delightful.

Symphonies

Six Symphonies, Op 6 – No 1 in G; No 2 in D;   **P**
No 3 in E flat; No 4 in B flat; No 5 in E flat;
No 6 in G minor
Hanover Band / Anthony Halstead
CPO CPO999 298-2 (56' · DDD)   Ⓕ

In the Op 6 Symphonies the frothy Italianate music of the composer's Italian and early London years was behind him; these pieces, dating from the late 1760s, while still Italian-influenced in their formal clarity and melodic style, are sturdier, more carefully composed, more symphonic. Both the E flat works have something of the solidity and warmth associated with that key, and each has a C minor *Andante*. The G major's first movement has the confident ring and thematic contrasts of his mature music, and the D major contains Mannheim *crescendos* and some delightful textures, with flutes and divided violas, in its charming, slightly playful middle movement.

The set ends with Bach's single minor-key symphony in G minor, very similar in spirit to Mozart's No 25; this piece, often recorded before, shows an unfamiliar side to his musical personality. Anthony Halstead and his players convey the music's strength and spirit convincingly. Admirers of the London Bach and his music needn't hesitate.

Symphonies – Op 9: No 1 in B flat; No 2 in E flat;   **P**
No 3 in B flat; B flat, Sieber No 1; E flat, Sieber No 2;
E flat (ed Warburton)
Hanover Band / Anthony Halstead
CPO CPO999 487-2 (60' · DDD)   ⒻⓄ

This disc offers the Op 9 Symphonies published in The Hague in 1773, two of them in two versions, along with a little-known symphony. Ernest Warburton explains in his notes that the usual texts for these works, with oboes and horns, are in his view arrangements of originals calling for clarinets – still rarities in most European orchestras at the time – and bassoon, in which form one of them was published in Paris. Here, then, Op 9 Nos 1 and 2 are done twice over to allow comparison; and certainly the versions differ markedly in flavour with clarinets and bassoon. The E-flat work, No 2, one of Bach's finest and most vigorously argued symphonies, comes out particularly well, with quite a different ring to its tuttis.

The E flat Symphony is an attractive work, with an eloquent violin line in the *Andante*, and a

charming final gavotte. Of the works played twice, the B flat is lightish, probably originally an opera overture; the E flat has more substance and notably a C minor slow movement with a melody of a haunting, graceful beauty. The third Op 9 Symphony is a brisk little piece which again started life as an overture. Halstead directs with his usual style and shapeliness.

Overtures

Overtures – Gioas, re di Giuda; Adriano in Siria;   **P**
Zanaida; Orione. La clemenza di Scipione – Overture;
No 5, March in G; No 22, March in E flat. Carattaco –
Overture; No 20, March in B flat; No 26, March in G.
Symphony in D, Schmitt Op 18 No 1
Hanover Band / Anthony Halstead
CPO CPO999 488-2 (58' · DDD)   ⒻⓄ

Small-scale but elegantly fashioned, melodious and pleasurable music: it's no wonder that the London public in the 1760s and 1770s took JC to their hearts. Here we have the overtures to six works of his that were performed at the King's Theatre in the Haymarket. The most striking feature about all these works, apart from their vigorous openings, is the freedom in the use of wind instruments: *Zanaida* has *soli* clarinets, and the trio of *Orione*'s minuet is for wind band only, as are passages in *Adriano*, the E flat March in *Clemenza* and the brilliant final *Presto* of *Carattaco*. The Hanover Band's playing is vital and fresh, rhythmically crisp and tonally clean-cut; the recording is first rate.

Johann Sebastian Bach
German 1685-1750

Seven generations of Bachs were professional musicians and their north German dynasty can be traced back to the early 16th century and beyond. None of them earned more than a local reputation and, surprising as it may seem, 'the supreme arbiter and law-giver of music', Johann Sebastian himself, achieved only limited fame during his lifetime. Music was in the blood, his musical gifts taken for granted by his family and himself. He never saw himself as exceptional, just a pious Lutheran artisan doing his best with a gift that was as much a part of him as his unquestioning religious belief.

Bach had little systematic training in his youth. It's said that at nine he almost ruined his eyesight from secretly copying out by moonlight an entire library of instrumental music to which he had been denied access. He was nine when both his parents died (his father was a respected violinist) and he was sent to live with his older brother Johann Christoph. None too happy at having an extra mouth to feed, Johann Christoph treated his new charge peremptorily and without much sympathy, though grudgingly gave him lessons on the harpsichord.

At 15, Johann Sebastian gained a position in the

choir at Lüneburg where he was able at last to indulge in every possible musical pursuit, soaking up scores, composing and studying the organ, clavichord and violin. Several times he tramped the 30 miles to Hamburg to hear the greatest organist of the day, Johann Adam Reinken, and he travelled the 60 miles to Celle for his first experience of French music. Though Bach led an unadventurous and parochial life, his thirst for every musical experience open to him, his curiosity and his willingness to absorb what other practitioners of the art were involved in, played an important part in the extraordinary diversity of the great music he was to write. His most famous journey was to Lübeck where the celebrated organist Dieterich Buxtehude gave recitals and a weekly instrumental concert.

At the time, Bach had obtained an appointment as organist at Arnstadt, aged just 19. He obtained leave of absence and, so legend has it, walked to Lübeck, a distance of 213 miles. The outcome, anyway, was a prolonged absence of four months which did not endear him any to the burghers of Arnstadt; neither did the strange music that young Bach returned with, for, perhaps recalling Buxtehude's playing, he began interpolating elaborate cadenzas and variations into the staid chorales.

Soon he was off. In June 1707 he went to Mühlhausen as organist and four months later, at the age of 22, married his cousin Maria Barbara. The following year saw the very first publication of a piece of his own music, the cantata Gott ist mein König; at the same time he left Mühlhausen to become court organist to Duke Wilhelm Ernst of Weimar. Here he stayed more or less contentedly, was made Konzertmeister (conductor) of the court orchestra in 1714 and composed some of his finest organ works including the Passacaglia and Fugue in C minor and many of the great preludes and fugues. Here, too, the future King Frederick I of Sweden heard him, recording that Bach's feet 'flew over the pedalboard as if they had wings'. In 1717 came further advancement when he accepted the position of music director to Prince Leopold of Anhalt in Cöthen. Duke Wilhelm, for some reason, at first refused to allow Bach to take up his new post and held him under arrest for a month. When at last Bach arrived in Cöthen, it was the start of one of his most fruitful periods as a composer, one which saw the appearance of the Brandenburg Concertos and the first book of the Well-Tempered Clavier. In 1720 he accompanied the Prince on a visit to Karlsbad and it was there that he learnt of his wife's death.

He lived as a widower for a year with his seven children before marrying his second wife, Anna Magdalena Wilcken, a daughter of the court trumpeter at Weissenfels, now immortalised in The Little Clavier Book of Anna Magdalena, the short pieces which Bach wrote for her study of the harpsichord. Is there a budding young pianist anywhere who hasn't played at least one of them? During their happy married life, she bore him a further 13 children though no fewer than six of Bach's 20 children did not survive into adulthood.

In 1722 the Cantor of Leipzig died and Bach applied for this prestigious post. The authorities first offered it to Telemann (who declined it) and then to Christoph Graupner (who was unable to take up the appointment). Third choice Bach succeeded to the title in April 1723. This was the job he retained for the rest of his life. His arduous duties as cantor involved playing the organ, teaching Latin and music in the Thomasschule, writing music for the services of two churches (Nicolaikirche and Thomaskirche) and directing the music and training the musicians of a further two. The living conditions were cold and damp, the salary parsimonious and Bach found himself fighting a running battle with the church authorities who were always trying to defraud him. Yet the music that flowed from his pen – and there was a great deal – is some of the greatest spiritual music ever written including the Mass in B minor, the St John and St Matthew Passions, the Christmas Oratorio as well as nearly 300 church cantatas. From this period, too, come the Goldberg Variations, the Italian Concerto, the Partitas and the second book of The Well-Tempered Clavier.

One of Bach's sons, Carl Philipp Emanuel, was Kapellmeister to King Frederick the Great and Bach visited him in Potsdam in 1747. The story goes that when Bach arrived, Frederick broke off the music-making and exclaimed, 'Old Bach is here!' and without permitting him to change his clothes, plonked Bach down at the keyboard. Later, Bach composed a six-part fugue on a theme of Frederick the Great – this was The Musical Offering, written in gratitude for his welcome.

By the end of his, life, Bach's eyesight was failing due to cataracts. In the spring of 1749 he was persuaded to have an operation performed on them by the same British optician, John Taylor, who had earlier treated Handel for the same affliction unsuccessfully. It left Bach almost completely blind. His sight then miraculously returned (possibly the cataract receded spontaneously), allowing him to feverishly copy and revise what was to be his final work, The Art of Fugue. Ten days later he died of a cerebral haemorrhage. He was 65 years old.

Bach was buried in the churchyard of St John in Leipzig. No identification marked the spot. Then, in 1895, his body was exhumed and photographs taken of his skeleton. On July 28, 1949, on the 199th anniversary of his death, Bach's coffin was transferred to the choir room of the Thomaskirche.

Bach is to music what Leonardo da Vinci is to art and Aristotle is to philosophy, one of the supreme creative geniuses of history. The amazing fact is that he was essentially a self-taught, provincial musician; he did not write music in a fever of inspiration like Beethoven, say, nor was he motivated by the same holy dedication to art as Wagner. For Bach, it was always 'For the glory of the most high God alone', as he wrote. 'I was obliged to work hard; whoever is equally industrious will succeed just as well.' He wasn't considered to be anything special in his day. His son Carl Philipp Emanuel referred to him as 'old peruke' – he was an old fogey, writing in a style that was already going out of fashion, the Baroque polyphonic school. He made little impression in the way of developing existing forms or inventing new ones. Little of his music was published or performed after his death and, though it was by no means completely ignored as is often stated (we know that Haydn, Mozart and Beethoven, for instance, all played his keyboard works), it was not until Mendelssohn's revival of the St Matthew Passion in Berlin in 1829 that the gradual reassessment of Bach's true worth was begun.

It wasn't as though he was a sophisticated intellectual either. Far from it. His letters and notes betray an uneducated hand and mind – his German is littered with grammatical mistakes, he knew little of the other arts and read mainly theological books. It is one of the most extraordinary paradoxes in musical history that a mind of such low culture could produce music of such unparalleled assurance, beauty and, yes, complexity. As the critic Ernest Newman observed, 'Truly, we have as yet barely the glimmer of an understanding of what the musical faculty is, and how it works.'

What makes Bach the great composer that he unarguably is? If we say that the Baroque era began (roughly) in 1600 with Monteverdi and ended in 1750, then Johann Sebastian represented the inevitable culmination of all Baroque styles: the contrapuntal German school, the melodic, singing Italian school and the elegant dance-based French school. As a young man he had absorbed the works of Palestrina and Frescobaldi, knew the more recent works of Vivaldi and Albinoni, of Froberger, Pachelbel and Buxtehude and, as we've seen, made strenuous efforts to acquaint himself with all the great German musicians of the day. It is not just his extraordinary capacity to think in counterpoint (its combined musicality, ingenuity and unforced complexity are of a different order to anything else being written) but his superior harmonic sense that set him apart. A Vivaldi concerto bowls along on fairly predictable lines; Bach was daring, taking the music into unexpected areas. It made people complain, so curious did it sound to contemporary ears.

The word 'Bach' itself means 'stream' in German. Hence Beethoven's famous saying: 'Nicht Bach aber Meer haben wir hier' ('Not a stream but a whole ocean'). Two further curiosities: Bach's very name is a musical theme. Our note B natural is the note H in German nomenclature; our note B flat is known as B in Germany. Thus the surname produces its own four-note motif. In The Art of Fugue, Bach produced an encyclopaedic work using every contrapuntal device imaginable based on a single theme. It was calculated to appeal to the visual senses as well as the aural and it's a moot point whether Bach ever intended the cycle to be performed. The work remained unfinished at his death. On the very last page, Bach had begun a fugue adding his name as one of the themes - B flat, A, C, B natural. It was the final thing he wrote.

Unlike Handel, who wrote for his patrons and his public, Bach was motivated only by a need to express himself. It is deeply personal music which yet speaks to mankind at large and the amount he wrote is simply staggering. When the task of gathering together and publishing all his music was undertaken, the project took 46 years to complete. Someone once calculated that if a present day copyist were to write out all of Bach's music (including all the parts, as Bach did) it would take 70 years. How he did it, with all his other duties of conducting, teaching, playing the organ and (an old but pertinent chestnut) fathering 20 children, he explained himself with characteristic modesty: 'I worked hard.'

Keyboard Concertos

No 1, D minor, **BWV1052**; No 2, E, **BWV1053**; No 3, D, **BWV1054**; No 4, A, **BWV1055**; No 5, F minor, **BWV1056**; No 6, F, **BWV1057**; No 7, G minor, **BWV1058**; No 8, D minor, **BWV1059**

Harpsichord Concertos – No 1, BWV1052; No 4, BWV1055; No 5, BWV1056; No 7, BWV1058
Bertrand Cuiller hpd
Stradivaria Ensemble / Daniel Cuiller
Mirare MIR085 (58' · DDD)   Ⓕ❶❶❶▷

This is an outstanding recital of Bach chamber-music playing in which four concertos bask in their own colours with a rare combination of infectious energy, quicksilver alertness among a single-string ensemble and not a hint of the affectedness which has blighted so many performances of these works in recent years.

Bertrand Cuiller plays his red-blooded harpsichord (a copy of an anonymous French instrument) with dazzling virtuosity, wit and lyricism, each of the players seeming unusually responsive to the soloist's inflections. Take the D minor, whose outer movements are mesmerisingly gilded by Cuiller and his colleagues, where the *Adagio* is shaped with compelling coherence and pungency.

The G minor Concerto is not often performed in this pragmatic transcription but here, and in the more intimate and familiar exchanges of the F minor (BWV1056, and only surviving in this form), rhythmic character and well-judged embellishment spring effusively from strong and directed bass-lines. There is an authority, too, in the ringing tenderness of the second movement of the G minor, whose bittersweet affekt is underpinned by an exquisite 'heavy laden' rhetorical accentuation. If the intonation is a touch 'gamey' here, and perhaps a little less acceptably in the equivalent point in the A major, nothing can detract from the thoughtfulness, personality and fun which radiate from this wonderful recital.

Harpsichord Concertos – No 1, BWV1052;   Ⓟ
No 3, BWV1054. Concerto for Flute, Violin,
Harpsichord and Strings in A minor, BWV1044. Das
wohltemperierte Klavier, BWV846-93 – Preludes and
Fugues: F, BWV880; B, BWV892
Le Concert Français / Pierre Hantaï hpd
Naïve E8837 (70' · DDD)   Ⓜ❶❶

The concertos come over well. Ensembles are tautly controlled, and the string playing effectively articulated, although on occasion the first violin is a little too favoured in the recorded balance. However, the string playing is so unanimous in sound and purpose that there's little to worry about in this department. Hantaï himself is impressive for his wonderfully rhythmic playing, the clarity with which he interprets both his own keyboard textures and those which support and punctuate it, and not least for his supple, muscular concept of the music. These are extraordinarily invigorating performances, which draw the listener deep into the harmonic and contrapuntal complexities and conceits of Bach's art. Take for instance the elusive *Adagio* of BWV1052, where careful punctuation and sensitive interaction between solo and *tutti* make for a rewarding coherence. In the A minor Triple Concerto, Hantaï is joined by his flautist brother, Marc, and François Fernandez, the violinist leader of the ensemble. The work is a Leipzig arrangement of movements from earlier pieces not in concerto form. The opening *Allegro* is a little too heavy, but the essentially three-part texture of the middle movement is realised with affection. A stimulating disc.

Keyboard Concertos, Vol 1 – No 1, BWV1052; No 7, BWV1058. Triple Concerto, BWV1044[a].
Brandenburg Concerto No 5, BWV1050[a]
Angela Hewitt pf [a]**Alison Mitchell** fl **Australian Chamber Orchestra / Richard Tognetti** [a]vn
Hyperion CDA67307 (77' · DDD)　　Ⓕ❶❶❶Ⓑ

Keyboard Concertos, Vol 2 – No 2, BWV1053; No 3, BWV1054; No 4, BWV1055; No 5, BWV1056; No 6, BWV1057[a]
Angela Hewitt pf
[a]**Alison Mitchell**, [a]**Emma Sholl** fls **Australian Chamber Orchestra / Richard Tognetti** vn
Hyperion CDA67308 (76' · DDD)　　Ⓕ❶❶❶Ⓑ
Also available as a two-CD set CDA67607/8

These are not entirely modern-instrument performances. Angela Hewitt includes, as she says, 'a harpsichord in its traditional role as continuo'. Combining old and new isn't unusual because in the early years of period performing practices, the likes of Thurston Dart, Raymond Leppard and George Malcolm married a harpsichord to modern strings and wind. What's unusual here is the melding of two different types of keyboard, one sharply transient, the other ductile; and just how their functions dovetail with one another may be heard in the slow movement of the *Brandenburg* Concerto No 5. Hewitt also adds a cello to the continuo while contributing *notes inégales*, *appogiature* and other embellishments to her own line. The result is a potent artistic synergy between the musicians.

Hewitt doesn't slavishly follow a formula, though. In the *Adagio* of No 1 and the *Adagio e piano sempre* of No 3 (where she is most intense because both remind her of Passion music), she omits the keyboard's bass notes for the exposition of the theme but only in No 1 does she play them for its return at the end. In these instances, in the *Andante* of No 7 and elsewhere, she also varies the prominence of her left hand to give the *ripieno* string bass a strong presence too, while delineating the right hand melody most feelingly.

Interpretative decisions are intelligently applied; and Hewitt is at her best in the slow movements, all of which are played with the fin-

est sensibility. If a more sinewy approach to a few of the outer movements might not have come amiss, her ability to gauge the critical notes of phrases so as to maintain an elastically accented rhythm offers ample compensation; and the consummate Australian Chamber Orchestra is with her every step of the way. The flute is placed backward in BWV1044 but otherwise recorded balance and sound ensure unimpeded concentration on the performances. Small changes in level between some works are easily adjusted. A superb pair of discs.

Keyboard Concertos – No1, BWV1052; No 2, BWV1053; No 4, BWV1055
Academy of St Martin in the Fields / Murray Perahia pf
Sony Classical SK89245 (53' · DDD)　　Ⓕ❶❶Ⓑ

Soloist-conducted piano concertos can sometimes mean compromise, even chaos…but not in this case. As soloist, Perahia is his usual stylish, discreet and pianistically refined self. He takes the D minor Concerto's opening at a fair lick, a hot foot sprinter embellishing the line with taste and affecting a little *ritardando*, just as the mood momentarily brightens, à la Edwin Fischer. Elsewhere, he's very much his own man, intensifying his tone for rising sequences or softening it to the most rarefied murmur. His command of colour is as striking here as it is on his CD of the *Goldberg* Variations, especially in the *Adagio*, which approaches cantorial heights of intensity.

As for the E major and A major Concertos, elegance is more of the essence than fire, but there too Perahia delivers. He has a way of accenting without jabbing the keys, tracing counterpoint while keeping the top line well to the fore. And how nice to hear the warming tone of a theorbo (bass lute) in the E major Concerto's central Siciliano, a beautiful performance, more ornamental than cantorial, in keeping with the more decorative nature of the music.

Rivals are plentiful, but credible contenders at this level of interpretation are rare. Sviatoslav Richter plays with incredible control while keeping every note alive, but some might find his manner too austere. And while Edwin Fischer is consistently spontaneous, he's rather less elegant than Perahia – and his version of the A major Concerto sounds as if it's 'Busonified'. András Schiff, like Perahia, commands a wide range of colours, though the binding force of Perahia's concentration – always a boon in his latest recordings – leaves the stronger impression. The carefully balanced Sony recordings keep the sound frame tight and lively.

Keyboard Concertos – No 3, BWV1054; No 5, BWV1056; No 6, BWV1057; No 7, BWV1058
Academy of St Martin in the Fields / Murray Perahia pf
Sony Classical SK89690 (54' · DDD)　　Ⓕ❶❶Ⓑ

As well as being immensely vital, Perahia's Bach is profoundly pianistic, not in any exhibitionistic sense, but in the way tempo, dynamics and nuance register without undue exaggeration. Perahia's *staccato* never loses quality, even when soft – try the opening movement of the Sixth Concerto. And yet he's just as capable of increasing the pressure as he sees fit: listen out for his brightening tone at 5'16" into the same movement, or the extraordinary dexterity of his finger work from around 1'45" into the finale, a fair match for any fiddler tackling the same passage in the parallel Fourth *Brandenburg* Concerto. The counterpoint-crazy Glenn Gould is the benchmark here, wonderfully absorbing as ever, but this warmer, more discreet and more overtly decorative version is preferable. The sound is beautifully clear (violin desks are antiphonally placed) with impressive richness in the bass. Nothing much more to say except, don't hesitate – life's too short.

Violin Concertos, Double Concertos

Violin Concertos – A minor, **BWV1041**; E, **BWV1042**. Double Concertos – Two Violins and Strings in D minor, **BWV1043**; Oboe, Violin and Strings in C minor, **BWV1060**

Violin Concertos – BWV1041-42.
Double Concertos – BWV1043[b]; BWV1060[a]
[a]**Albrecht Mayer** ob [b]**Daniel Stabrawa** vn **Berlin Philharmonic Orchestra / Nigel Kennedy** vn
EMI 557016-2 (59' · DDD)   Ⓕ Ⓞ ▷

Bach isn't a composer you generally associate with Nigel Kennedy, but this recording of the four most popular concertos is far more than a dutiful 250th anniversary offering. Kennedy is nothing if not characterful, taking a positive, often robust view of Bach. It isn't just his breathtakingly fast speeds in finales and in some first movements, too, that will have listeners pricking up their ears, but often a fierceness of manner which can initially take you aback. With brilliant playing not just from the soloist but from the Berlin Philharmonic, the results are certainly exciting. The power of Bach's writing is reinforced thanks also to the rather close recorded balance in the Jesus-Christus Kirche.

However fast Kennedy's speeds in *Allegros*, he counters any feeling of breathlessness not just in his clean articulation, but in his fine detailing. The Berlin players respond sympathetically, but aren't always quite so adept at springing rhythms at such fast speeds. By contrast, slow movements tend to be taken broadly, but there again Kennedy has thought through his expressive phrasing in detail, consciously pointing rhythms, shading dynamics and colouring tone. Any reservations over Kennedy's readings don't detract their positive strength.

In the Double Concerto Daniel Stabrawa makes a perfectly matched partner, and in the Concerto for oboe and violin there's no question of his seeking to overshadow the fine artistry of the warm-toned Berlin oboist Albrecht

Mayer. These are the visions of an exceptional artist, helped by warm, full sound.

Violin Concertos – BWV1041-42. Double Concerto, BWV1043[b]. Brandenburg Concerto No 5[ab].
Daniel Hope vn with [a]**Jaime Martin** fl
[b]**Marieke Blankestijn** vn **Kristian Bezuidenhout** hpd
Chamber Orchestra of Europe
Warner Classics 2564 62545-2 (64' · DDD)   Ⓕ Ⓑ ▸

First impressions suggest a high-energy, tightly accented approach, 'period'-schooled while retaining an element of modern-instrument intensity, mostly in the slow movements. Daniel Hope sees to it that the bass-line is firm and prominent, which tends to underline the sense of urgency. The Double Concerto's *Largo* focuses two well-matched players responding to, rather than mirroring, each other, invariably with one using more vibrato than the other. Outer movements are fast and buoyant (the A minor's gigue-allegro really whizzes along) and in the E major, Hope whirls into the first movement's second idea like a dervish possessed. Embellishment is legion, both along the solo line and in the discreetly balanced but lavishly stated continuo. The results approximate, more than usual with this music, dance models of the day, yet Hope always allows the slower music to breathe.

Plenty of air around the notes in the Fifth *Brandenburg* Concerto, too. Again the spirit of the dance is all-pervasive, but come the solo harpsichord cadenza, although Kristian Bezuidenhout plays brilliantly, the intrusive bending of tempo isn't entirely convincing. This sort of approach has become fairly popular: Rinaldo Alessandrini's set of *Brandenburg*s for Naïve is similarly individualistic. In most other respects this is a refreshing, often enlightening programme, very well recorded.

Violin Concertos – BWV1041-42[a]. Double Concertos – BWV1043[b]; BWV1060 (arr Fischer)[c]
[abc]**Ryo Terakado**, [b]**Natsumi Wakamatsu** vns
[c]**Marcel Ponseele** ob **Bach Collegium Japan / Masaaki Suzuki**
BIS BIS-CD961 (59' · DDD)   Ⓕ Ⓞ ▸   Ⓟ

These aren't just 'authentic' performances, they're also outstandingly musical ones. There's happy animation in the flanking movements – bows are lifted from or stopped on the strings to ensure the cleanest of textures – and a warmth of expression in the slow ones which comes from a deeper source than mere academic study.

The admirable soloist in the A minor and E major concertos, Ryo Terakado, and his partner in the Double Concerto, Natsumi Wakamatsu, both studied with Sigiswald Kuijken in The Hague and served with various Baroque ensembles in Europe before returning to Japan. It shows in the beautifully 'vocalised' shaping of their lines. Not once do they or their ripieno colleagues jar the ear with acidic sounds, and in the *Andante* of the A minor Concerto Terakado achieves a *pianissimo* that's near-miraculous in its quality. Marcel Ponseele, the only European on parade, has a comparably distinguished pedigree. In the reconstructed Concerto BWV1060 his fluency, rounded tone and clean articulation are second to none, and he makes the *Adagio* one of the serenely lovely high spots of the entire programme. As for the ripieno, you couldn't ask for better, and they're recorded in excellent balance with the soloists. Suzuki directs the whole with sure hands.

Additional recommendation

Violin Concertos – BWV1041-42.   🅟
Double Concertos – BWV1043; BWV1060
Podger *vn* **Academy of Ancient Music / Manze** *vn*
Harmonia Mundi HMU90 7155 (57' · DDD)   🄵
Manze projects a highly developed sense of fantasy in his interpretations and, for the most part, it proves immensely effective.

Brandenburg Concertos

No 1 in F, BWV1046; **No 2** in F, BWV1047;
No 3 in G, BWV1048; **No 4** in G, BWV1049;
No 5 in D, BWV1050; **No 6** in B flat, BWV1051

Brandenburg Concertos Nos 1-6.   🅟
Cantata No 174 – Sinfonia
Concerto Italiano / Rinaldo Alessandrini
Naïve ③ (2 CDs + 1 📀) OP30412 (100' · DDD)
                                                🄵🅓🅞🅞🅞🄳➔
Also includes DVD 'Rinaldo Alessandrini and Concerto Italiano record the Brandenburg Concertos', a film by Phillippe Béziat

How do you embark on a new addition to the vast pile of *Brandenburg Concerto* recordings? Do you go for a radical interpretation set to make people jump, laugh or recoil in surprise? Or do you perform them more or less as other good performers have but just try to do it better? Rinaldo Alessandrini and Concerto Italiano have gone for the latter approach and succeeded brilliantly. There is perhaps no Baroque group around today that can do the simple and obvious things to such exciting effect.

This is not to say that their *Brandenburg*s have no distinguishing features – just that, where they do, they spring from eminent good sense, as, for instance, in No 3 when the two central link chords come attached to a harpsichord flourish which has arisen directly from the first movement's final chord; or the abrupt ending of No 2; or any number of places where an inner part is brought out with the help of a generously drawn *legato* so that you are left wondering why you never noticed it before.

Indeed, clarity of texture is one of this recording's most glorious virtues, offering a view of the contrapuntal wonders of the music that has not always been available. This is particularly striking in the potentially murky, homogeneous textures of Nos 3 and 6; but the other, more colourfully scored concertos are just as lucidly done – a triumph of the balancer's art, obviously, but surely just as much a result of clear-headed thinking on the part of the performers. Equally enlivening is a tight attention to articulative detail and tasteful ornamentation which keeps the music buoyant and forward-moving at all times.

Technically, things are not always perfect: the horn players struggle sometimes to keep up in No 1 and the solo trumpet part in No 2 is a bit harum-scarum. But the performances are so joyous and fresh that, in their straightforward but deeply musical way, they are the most invigorating newcomers to the *Brandenburg* fold since Musica Antiqua Köln's provocative recording of the mid-1980s.

Bonuses come in the form of the Sinfonia to Cantata 174 (a version of the first movement of Concerto No 3 to which lusty oboes and horns have been added) and a curious 'patch take' of the shorter, swirling first version of the harpsichord cadenza to No 5. There is also a pleasingly unhyperbolic DVD of the sessions including interviews with Alessandrini.

Brandenburg Concertos Nos 1-6   🅟
**European Brandenburg Ensemble /
Trevor Pinnock**
Avie ② AV2119 (94' · DDD)   🄜🅞🅞🅞🄳➔

When Trevor Pinnock first recorded the *Brandenburgs* with The English Concert for Archiv in 1982, period performances of these works were relatively rare; today they abound, and it has become harder to make a mark in music that does not readily admit a wide range of interpretations. Not that Pinnock need worry about that at this point in his career. This new recording, made with an ensemble hand-picked for the job, is a 60th-birthday present to himself, and is just what such a project should be: talented musicians relishing each other's company in music of truly inspiring greatness.

Unsurprisingly, it reflects the increased playing standards of 25 years of period-instrument growth. Only Pinnock himself remains from that first line-up, and while the players then were a high-class team, the players of the European Brandenburg Ensemble include some of the finest of today's Baroque chamber players, and there is a relaxed expertise about their performances which seems to allow them to communicate directly and without technical or ideological hindrance. A hint of over-exuberant thickness in the texture of Concerto No 1 is perhaps a reflection of this, but elsewhere it is good to hear playing from the likes of violinist Kati Debretzeni, flautist Katy Bircher and the excellent David Blackadder on trumpet that is bold and confident without straying into coarseness. The clarity achieved in Nos 4, 5 and 6 also has a more natural air

BACH BRANDENBURG CONCERTOS – IN BRIEF

European Brandenburg Ensemble / Trevor Pinnock
Avie ② AV2119 (94' · DDD)　　　　Ⓜ❍❍❍➔
A triumphant return 25 years on with some classy playing from Pinnock's ensemble. This is chamber-music-making writ large.

Concerto Italiano / Rinaldo Alessandrini
Naïve ② OP30412 (100' · DDD)　　　　Ⓕ❍❍❍
Bach's concertos given a truly 21st-century make-over courtesy of these imaginative Italian musicians. Sensational!

Il Giardino Armonico
Warner Elatus ② 2564 61773-2 (95' · DDD)　Ⓜ➔
Another Italian set of the concertos – full of life and imagination. Continuo work is a constant joy and there are some notable solo contributions. A fun set.

Orchestra of the Age of Enlightenment
Virgin Classics ② 561552-2 (93' · DDD)　　Ⓑ❍
Often taken at quite a lick, these period performances never sound rushed but rather imbued with a spirit of dance.

Tafelmusik / Jeanne Lamon
Sony Classical ② S2K66289 (93' · DDD)　　Ⓜ❍
One of the finest period performances with a broad extrovert flair that occasionally flirts with danger but excites as a result.

Boston Baroque / Martin Pearlman
Telarc CD80368/54 (93' · DDD)　　　　Ⓕ❍
Not quite on the level of their Bach Suites, these are highly enjoyable performances with plenty to marvel at and superbly recorded.

ASMF / Sir Neville Marriner
Philips ② 468 549-2PM2 (98' · ADD)　　Ⓜ❍
Middle-of-the-road performances that show the Marriner/ASMF style at its best: *de luxe* soloists add to the allure of the set.

English CO / Benjamin Britten
Decca ② 443 847-2DF2 (128' · ADD)　　　Ⓑ
A historic set, made in 1968, and one great composer's take on another. Slightly dated in approach but still worth sampling.

Brandenburg Consort / Roy Goodman
Hyperion ② CDD22001 (96' · DDD)　　　　Ⓜ
There are sleeker period performances around but few that have as much character or charm.

The English Concert / Trevor Pinnock
DG Blue 471 720-2ABL (Nos 1-3), 474 220-2ABL (Nos 4-6) (99' · DDD)　　　　Ⓜ❍➔
Something of a modern classic, but only available on two single CDs, Pinnock's period performance interpretations are swift but never rushed, and magnificently played.

than the 'studio-y' balance of the Archiv set, no doubt helped by the decision to use a violone at pitch rather than the more usual octave below. The pensive violin improvisation which links the two movements of No 3 is surely a miscalculation, feeling like more of a hold-up than it need be; more lastingly refreshing to my ears were the subtle relaxations of tension in the first movement of No 6, these days so often given the hard-drive treatment.

This is not a *Brandenburg* set that seeks to score points, and all that is needed from us is to sit back and enjoy its relaxed, celebratory spirit.

Brandenburg Concertos Nos 1-6　　　　Ⓟ
English Baroque Soloists / Kati Debretzeni vn,
Sir John Eliot Gardiner
Soli Deo Gloria ② SDG707 (92' · DDD)　Ⓕ❍❍Ⓑ➔

Considering his vast experience as a Bach conductor, it comes as a surprise to find that Sir John Eliot Gardiner has not recorded the *Brandenburgs* before. But then, as he asks in his booklet-note, 'what is a conductor to do in this repertoire?' Well, quite. Since period instruments brought with them increasing acceptance that this is really chamber rather than orchestral music, recordings in which the director has not been among the instrumentalists have grown fewer. In fact, Gardiner only conducts Nos 1 and 2 here, these being the grandest; for Nos 3-5 he yields the stage to the English Baroque Soloists's excellent leader Kati Debretzeni, while No 6 apparently has no director at all. Gardiner's role in these, he says, was 'to facilitate and encourage', to 'give the players some feedback', and then to sit in the audience.

Nice work if you can get it, you might think, but actually these performances are recognisable enough as being in the Gardiner mould. There is the usual clarity of texture and detail; few accounts of Nos 3 and 6 have such chiselled edges and unobtrusively assertive inner parts. The dynamic contours are strong and meaningful. Tempi are brisk, and while they are not hard-driven in the way they might have been 20 years ago, the finale of No 2 charges to a startlingly abrupt finish. More recent Gardineresque trends can be observed in the tender care taken to characterise the various episodes in the finale of No 1, or in the wisdom and freedom with which he seeks out, but does not overplay, latent bass-line hemiolas in the third movements of Nos 1 and 3. Indeed, the controlled skill with which the joy of such movements is communicated by Gardiner's players – with Debretzeni, trumpeter Neil Brough, recorder-player and flautist Rachel Beckett and harpsichordist Malcolm Proud among the soloists – is one of the greatest pleasures of this set.

The recordings, made in concert, are lucid and democratically balanced but may strike some as a touch dry, while the act of splicing together live performances may be the reason for the odd little tempo shift or bumpy edit. Some may prefer a smoother-lined and more spaciously recorded account of these works but these are undeniably *Brandenburgs* of flair and understanding.

Brandenburg Concerto No 5, BWV1050[a].
Concerto for Flute, Violin, Harpsichord, BWV1044[a].
Italian Concerto, BWV971
[a]**Jaime Martin** *fl* [a]**Kenneth Sillito** *vn*
[a]**Jakob Lindberg** *theorbo*
[a]**Academy of St Martin in the Fields /
Murray Perahia** *pf*
Sony Classical SK87326 (55' · DDD)　　Ⓕ❶❶❶➟

Murray Perahia is first among equals in the concertos, and the whole production is infused with a sense of spontaneous musical interplay. The sense of engagement is infectious. The cadenza of the *Brandenburg* is reminiscent of Alfred Cortot in its bell-like voicing, elegance and, just before the orchestra's return, cumulative excitement.

There are, in a sense, two Perahias at work: the first a non-percussive front-man whose evenly deployed runs are a joy, unlike some who more approximate a hard stick being drawn past iron railings. And then there's the keyboard poet within the orchestra, who even when playing *mezzoforte* or *piano* manages to project a full tone. The presence of a theorbo helps flavour the two concerto slow movements, the Triple Concerto especially. Superb solo playing, too, flautist Jaime Martin producing a memorably plangent tone.

As on previous Perahia Bach concerto recordings, the overriding impression is of intelligence, sensitivity and drama tempered by humility. The *Italian Concerto* begs the by-now familiar question as to how one pair of hands can command so many simultaneous dynamic grades without sounding strained or self-conscious. The outer movements are colourful but never prettified, the principal melody of the central *Andante* like a memory of classic *bel canto*. An exceptional CD.

Brandenburg Concertos Nos 1-6
Orchestra Mozart / Claudio Abbado
Video director **Andreas Morell**
Medici Arts Ⓕ 🅳🆅🅳 205 6738 (100' · NTSC · 16:9 ·
PCM stereo, 5.1 and DTS 5.1 · 0)
Recorded live at the Teatro Municipale Romolo Valli,
Reggio Emilia, in 2007　　　　　Ⓕ❶❶

Here Claudio Abbado is gambolling among the *Brandenburg Concertos* in this straightforward TV-style concert film, recorded in the classic 19th-century opera house at Reggio Emilia during an Italian tour in spring 2007.

The orchestra is at first glance a curious gathering, mixing 'Baroque' players such as violinist Giuliano Carmignola and harpsichordist Otta-

vio Dantone with 'modern' names such as trumpeter Reinhold Friedrich and 'un-Baroque' recorder-player Michala Petri. Furthermore, a look round the instruments reveals mostly modern models, some hybrids (for instance Jacques Zoon's wooden, multi-keyed flute) and a sprinkling of Baroque bows. Mind you, most younger players these days are well versed in Baroque style whatever they play on, and the tenor of these performances is firmly consistent with current ideas of what Baroque music ought to sound like.

So what, then, does Abbado bring to pieces that these days are rarely considered to require a conductor? Well, in the performance itself, not a lot; his batonless beating is minimal, at times barely perceptible, and in Concerto No 6 he is not even on stage. But these are Bach interpretations very much. in his image, as detailed and humane as in any Mahler symphony, and infused with a musical sensitivity that is ever-present yet refuses to draw attention to itself. In music that is surely more for players than conductors, he allows fine soloists such as Carmignola, Zoon and the two yearningly exquisite viola soloists in No 6 to shine, yet has clearly worked hard to ensure that every note is in precisely the right place, every tempo convinces, and the texture is always deliciously transparent.

Miscellaneous Concertos

Flute Concerto, BWV1050a. Orchestral
Suite No 2, BWV1067. Flute Concerto (after
BWV209/1, BWV173a/2 & BWV207/3, ed Zimei)
Marcello Gatti *fl*
Aurora Ensemble (Rossella Croce *vn* Joanna
Huszcza *va* Judith-Maria Olofsson *vc* Riccardo
Coelati *vion* Michele Barchi *hpd*) /
Enrico Gatti *vn*
Glossa GCD921204 (56' · DDD)　　　　　Ⓕ

Three pieces: a new concerto, an old friend in a (not very) different guise, and a repertory staple. The 'new concerto' is a reconstruction by Francesco Zimei based on movements from three of Bach's secular cantatas. In his booklet-note, Zimei sets out the reasoning behind his choice: it reads convincingly and, more important, the result sounds convincing as well.

The 'old friend', billed as a Triple Concerto, is none other than the Fifth *Brandenburg Concerto* in an earlier version, BWV1050a. Most of us would be hard pressed to spot the difference – minor variations of figuration, mostly in the harpsichord part, and four bars less in the third movement – with two exceptions: there's no satisfying chord to herald the reprise in that movement, and the famous harpsichord cadenza consists of only 18 bars.

The 'repertory staple' is, of course, the Second Orchestral Suite. Marcello Gatti, Michele Barchi and the single strings of Ensemble Aurora are all superb, playing with grace and style. This disc is very warmly recommended.

BACH ORCHESTRAL SUITES –
IN BRIEF

**(Nos 1-3) English Baroque Soloists /
Sir John Eliot Gardiner**
Erato 8573 82931-2 (97' · DDD)　　　ⒻⒶⓄⒹ▸
Gardiner has a wonderful way with Bach
and he and his fine players float this music
with a real lightness and flair. Only Nos 1-3.

The English Concert / Trevor Pinnock
Archiv ② 477 6348GGP (76' · DDD)　　　Ⓜ️Ⓔ▸
A most enjoyable romp through Bach's suites
with some delicious solo work and always an
engaging rhythmic drive and flair.

Boston Baroque / Martin Pearlman
Telarc CD80619 (74' · ADD)　　　ⓂⓄ
A set of performances that pays great attention to detail and nuance. Pearlman is a Bach
conductor of imagination and flair.

Brandenburg Consort / Roy Goodman
Hyperion ② CDD22002 (113' · DDD)　　　Ⓜ
Sometimes Goodman's players are hard-
pressed by the speeds he chooses but they
cope manfully and deliver the suites with
great flair and sparkle.

**Freiburg Baroque Orchestra /
Gottfried von der Goltz**
EuroArts 🆅 205 0316 (95' · NTSC · 16:9 · 5.1 · 0)
　　　Ⓕ
Never mind the serious faces, this is a fine set
of the suites to rival the best audio-only ver-
sions. The film is dutiful but not thrilling!

Philharmonia Orchestra / Otto Klemperer
Testament ② SBT2131 (138' · ADD)　　　Ⓕ
From 1954, the very grand post-war Bach
style is displayed by Klemperer and the great
Philharmonia Orchestra. Some stunning solo
work but it's all very large scale.

Concert des Nations / Jordi Savall
Naïve Astrée ES9958 (61' · DDD)　　　Ⓜ
A breath of Mediterranean warmth adds an
appealing glow to the suites. A fine reminder
of one of Spain's leading period ensembles
and its charismatic music director.

ASMF / Neville Marriner
EMI Encore 586083-2 (72' · ADD)　　　Ⓑ
Marriner's 1984 set of the suites also fits onto
a single disc and conveys much of the spirit if
not the letter of the authentic movement.
A stylish undertaking.

AAM / Christopher Hogwood
Double Decca ② 458 069-2OF2 (118' · DDD)　　Ⓑ
A reading great refinement but also full of
vibrant detail. With swift tempi and a keen
alertness to rhythmic variety, this is a fine
period instrument version. Coupled now with
the Double Harpsichord Concerto.

Orchestral Suites

C, **BWV1066**; B minor, **BWV1067**; D, **BWV1068**; D,
BWV1069

Orchestral Suites, BWV1066-69　　　Ⓟ
Boston Baroque / Martin Pearlman
Telarc CD80619 (74 '·DDD)　　　ⒻⓄ

Scholars are now sure that Bach did not plan his
four orchestral suites as a set – unlike the six
Brandenburg Concertos. It seems likely, then, that
the stylistic diversity exhibited in the suites is
inadvertent, not, as in the case of the *Brandenburgs*, an overt display of compositional virtuosity. On recordings, however, the suites are usually presented as an entity, so the fact that each
has its own identifiable personality actually has
taken on interpretive significance.

On this Telarc disc, Martin Pearlman effectively delineates the unique character of each
work. The C major Suite is essentially lyrical, its
phrases unfolding in long, florid arcs; the B minor
suite is more fidgety, particularly in the Overture,
with its tense trills; and the two D major suites
combine grandeur and gaiety. Yet Pearlman
remains true to the specific nature of each dance
form, as well – listen to the four bourées in succession (the only dance that appears in every
suite), for example, and you will find a remarkable
consistency of tempo and spirit.

Special attention has also been paid to details
of instrumental balance, with admirably transparent results. Some might prefer a bit more
thrust and bite from the trumpets in the D major
works, where Pearlman prefers to blend the
brass into the orchestral fabric, but the sound is
still exhilaratingly brilliant.

The crystalline quality of Telarc's recording
reveals a few slight imperfections in the strings'
intonation; otherwise Boston Baroque's virtuosity
and élan leaves little to be desired. Indeed, the
Bostonians' interpretation is a strong contender
in a crowded field.

Orchestral Suites, BWV1066-69　　　Ⓟ
Ensemble Sonnerie / Monica Huggett
Avie AV2171 (74' · DDD)　　　ⒻⓄⓄⒹ▸

'Orchestral Suites for a young prince' is what
this release advertises, in reference to the fact
that Sonnerie perform Bach's familiar suites in
versions adapted to conform to how they might
have been if (as seems likely) they were originally written for Prince Leopold of Anhalt-
Cöthen, Bach's employer from 1717 to 1723,
instead of in the versions in which they survive
today, dating from his Leipzig years. It is partly
a matter of scale – the Cöthen court band, like
Sonnerie, was essentially a large chamber group
– but there is more to it than that: Suites Nos 3
and 4 are shorn of their trumpets and drums,
while No 2, the B minor 'flute suite', has been
reconstituted in an A minor version with an
oboe as its lead instrument.

Gonzalo X Ruiz, who made the reconstruction and plays the oboe in it, makes a convincing case in his booklet-note and, more clinchingly, in his performance, which demonstrates the fluency and dynamic control of a flute, as well as its ability to blend smoothly with the strings. In the low-lying opening, indeed, you might even be fooled momentarily into thinking a flute was playing, and only in the variation section of the Polonaise does it sound as if one might be more at ease. Suites Nos 3 and 4 gain enormously in clarity and lightness, as would be expected, but while No 4 retains its spark and character in the slighter scoring, No 3 does occasionally sounds like a piece in which something has gone missing.

Nothing lacks from Sonnerie's playing, however, which is generously shaped, beautifully judged for pace and balance, and attractively recorded. This may not, by its very nature, be a Bach Suites recording to oust all others, but it is certainly a classy one.

Orchestral Suites – No 1, BWV1066; No 4, BWV1069.
Sonata for Violin and Harpsichord No 4 , BWV1017.
Cantata No 21, 'Ich hatte viel Bekümmernis',
BWV21 – Sinfonia
Amandine Beyer vn
Le Concert Français / Pierre Hantaï hpd
Mirare MIR017 (69' · DDD)   Ⓕ

Converting a reputation as a distinguished solo harpsichordist into one as an orchestral director is not an obvious path these days. Performances of Bach's Suites are usually led from the continuo keyboard, though Pierre Hantaï would argue that greater control of detail can be best effected with a dedicated conductor at the helm. We know from Hantaï's thoughtful and challenging performances (his *Goldbergs* as prime examples) that each part of a journey needs appropriate attention with a view to its contribution to the whole. It is this, above all, which provides us with two suites where the dances cannot have felt more mutually integrated than here.

The curtain-raising Fourth Suite is a case in point after a blisteringly incisive, restless and punchy overture – one which both here and in the First Suite carries its Gallic ostentation to heights which Bach may have witnessed in the faux French courts of early-18th-century Germany. Instead of presenting diversely stylised vignettes, Hantaï brings a consistently infectious *réjouissance* to each movement until the final dance of that name. The scope is one of contained characterisation, carefully chiselled and fleet-of-foot articulation counterbalanced by delicately nuanced *legato*s and natural resonance.

The great C major First Suite is no less considered and polished. If generally rather clipped and fey, it comes as a welcome release after a hard, edgy, metronomic and small-scale performance of the C minor Sonata for violin and obbligato harpsichord, a work which deserves far greater expressive exploration than we hear

from Hantaï and violinist Amandine Beyer.

In sum, here are interesting alternative readings of two great orchestral suites, lovingly nurtured but strangely ephemeral in effect – as perhaps these recreational works should be.

Trio Sonatas

E flat, **BWV525**; C minor, **BWV526**; D minor, **BWV527**; E minor, **BWV528**; C, **BWV529**; G, **BWV530**

Trio Sonatas, BWV525-30.   Ⓟ
Purcell Quartet (Catherine Weiss, Catherine Mackintosh vns Robert Woolley hpd Richard Boothby va da gamba)
Chandos Chaconne CHAN0654 (73' · DDD)   ⒻⒷ▸

'Too good to be left only to organists' is how Richard Boothby cheekily describes Bach's six delightful 'organ trios', in which the organist's two hands play one of the upper lines each, while the bass is played on the pedals. Such is the integrity of this texture in Bach's writing that transferral of this music to a 'true' trio sonata line-up of two melody instruments and continuo is a relatively simple and satisfactory task, and there seems to have been no shortage in recent years of musicians who would agree with Boothby to the point of making their own arrangements for various small ensembles. On disc, these have often served as filler items. Recordings of all six are rarer.

Boothby's arrangements for the Purcell Quartet differ from the others currently available in involving no wind instruments. He shows considerable imagination, however, in convincingly varying the scoring between just two violins, viola da gamba and harpsichord, transferring the melodic line to his own viola da gamba whenever the tessitura demands in some movements, making it a full-blown partner in the dialogue in others, and also awarding the harpsichord a melodic role in BWV530.

Typically for the Purcell Quartet, the performances offer a sweet sound and a clarity of texture which is all to the good in such intricately and ingeniously contrapuntal music. Generally speaking, however, these performances are enjoyable for their lightness and tenderness (try the slow movement of BWV529). If you want something livelier, and do not necessarily require all six sonatas, you may just favour the Palladian Ensemble's characteristically alert recording of four of them on Linn (see below).

Additional recommendation

Trio Sonatas, BWV525, 527, 529, 530   Ⓟ
Coupled with: Four Duets, BWV802-05.
14 Verschiedene Canones, BWV1087
Palladian Ensemble
Linn CKD036 (75' · DDD)   Ⓕ
   Refreshingly committed performances which stray from old paths in stimulating ways and show off the corporate style of the Palladian Ensemble.

Flute Sonatas

B minor, **BWV1030**; E flat, **BWV1031**; A, **BWV1032**;
C, **BWV1033**; E minor, **BWV1034**; E, **BWV1035**

Flute Sonatas – B minor, BWV1030;   **P**
C, BWV1033; E minor, BWV1034; E, BWV1035.
Solo Flute Partita in A minor, BWV1013.
Ashley Solomon *fl* **Terence Charlston** *hpd*
Channel Classics CCS15798 (71' · DDD)   Ⓕ**OO**

This is an impressive and enjoyable CD that
easily bears repeated listening. There's a soothing quality to the Baroque flute, and its gentle,
slightly reedy tone is captured very well here.
It's closely recorded in a church acoustic to
give a brilliant tone with added depth. Today's
makers of the Baroque flute are producing
highly refined instruments, exemplified here
by the Rod Cameron copy of a Denner, which
has a strong, even tone and good balance of
register, allowing highly accomplished performers like Ashley Solomon complete technical freedom.

This recording isn't merely music therapy,
however, but a genuine musical experience. His
performance of the unaccompanied A minor
Partita, for example, is nothing short of commanding: the control in articulation and breathing allows the phrasing to be flexible and
unfussy. It's the directness of his interpretations
that's so telling; there's almost none of that
slightly coy *rubato* that some other flautists use
to disguise the need to breathe. Rather, Solomon ensures that the phrases are neither choppy
nor fragmented. He has an excellent sense of the
longer line and the harmonic pull beneath
Bach's wonderfully melodic writing. The faster
movements are perhaps the most successful, full
of buoyancy and energy without seeming rushed
or pushed. Try the second movement of the
E minor Sonata, for example, or that of the
C major. Slow movements are far from inexpressive, but again refreshingly direct: he never
wallows (a good example is the introductory
movement of the E major Sonata).

Solomon is well partnered by Terence Charlston on a rich-toned Ruckers-copy harpsichord.
Even if you already have a version of Bach's flute
works on CD this can be strongly recommended, and it makes an equally good first-time
buy too. Prepare to be uplifted.

Six Sonatas, BWV1030-35ª. Sonata, BWV1020.
Trio Sonata, BWV1039ᵇ
Emmanuel Pahud *fl* **Trevor Pinnock** *hpd*
with ᵃᵇ**Jonathan Manson** *vc* ᵇ**Silvia Careddu** *fl*
EMI ② 217443-2 (101' · DDD)   Ⓜ**O**🠪

Bach flute sonata recordings on modern instruments are not unknown but a 'complete' set of
all seven authentic and doubtful works, plus the
Sonata for two flutes and continuo (better
known as the G major Gamba Sonata), is bit of a
rarity. That said, we can be glad that the excel-

lent Emmanuel Pahud is the one to have taken
up the challenge, for this is a recording of great
skill and refinement which should give considerable pleasure. He has teamed up with distinguished Baroque-specialising partners to achieve
results that are technically assured and stylistically confident.

The most immediately attractive feature of
these performances is their touching and gentle
beauty; Pahud never forces the sound and maintains an evenly controlled tone at all times, with
no tightening on high notes or straining on low
ones. It is true that he is without the constant
subtle shadings possible on a Baroque wooden
flute, but for the most part Pahud's playing shows
a sensitive concern for detailed and enlivening
articulation without being slave to it, and a keen
sense of the music's greater rise and fall, revealed
in some drowsily relaxed slow movements.

The recording is not generous to the harpsichord, which, while crisply caressed as ever by
Pinnock, is too far back to contribute as meaningfully as it should in the sonatas where it has
an obbligato role equal to the flute's, and neither
is there any great sweetening of sound for compensation. But this is fine stuff nevertheless.

Lute Works

Suites – G minor, **BWV995**; E minor, **BWV996**;
C minor, **BWV997**; E, **BWV1006a**
Prelude, Fugue and Allegro in E flat, **BWV998**
Prelude in C minor, **BWV999**
Fugue in G minor, **BWV1000**

Lute Suites – BWV995-97, 1006a. Prelude, Fugue and
Allegro in E flat, BWV998. Prelude in C minor,
BWV999. Fugue in G minor, BWV1000
Stephan Schmidt *gtr*
Naïve ② V4861 (98' · DDD)   Ⓕ**OOO**

Whether or not the description of these as 'lute'
works is justified has long been a matter for
debate, and in their annotation Stephan Schmidt
and Claude Chauvel inevitably fail to resolve the
matter, though they lean more in the direction
of 'yes' than most. In a sense it matters little, for
the works have been performed and recorded on
a variety of other plucked-string instruments –
harpsichord and lute-harpsichord as well as
guitar – in exemplary fashion. The 'standard'
six-string guitar is a baritone instrument, but its
lowest register isn't extended enough to avoid
the need for compromises; accordingly guitars
with more strings (the extra ones at the bass end)
have been in use for over 30 years. Now
Schmidt, using 10 strings, sets a new benchmark
with this magnificent set. The extra four strings
give firmer bass and more resonant bass lines, as
did Söllscher's five, and free the player's left
hand from the restriction of having to hold
many of them down.

Schmidt's touch is happily light in the
galanteries and in the Loure of BWV1006a, but
there's gravity in the unhurried sarabandes –
such variations apply not only to pace but to

spirit, too. He knows when to embellish (which he does with elegance) and when not. His *rubato* 'bends' a little more than Söllscher's and he's less conservative in his approach to embellishment – but attitudes to such matters have since eased. If there's a better version of these works on any kind of guitar in terms of content and recording quality we have yet to hear it.

Suites – BWV995; BWV1006a. Sonata No 1, BWV1001
Paul O'Dette *lte*
Harmonia Mundi HMU90 7438 (68' · DDD)   Ⓕ Ⓑ➔

Bach never wrote directly for lute; his works for the instrument are transcriptions from his pre-existing music or were written for the lute-harpsichord (Lautenwerk), an instrument designed to imitate the lute. The A minor Suite, BWV995, *Pièces pour la Luth à Luth à Schouster*, is an arrangement of the Cello Suite BWV1011; the Partita in E major is an arrangement of the Partita BWV1006 for solo violin, transposed to F major. The Sonata in G minor is an arrangement by O'Dette of the Sonata in G minor for solo violin BWV1001, modelled after the arrangement of its fugue for lute by Johann Christian Weyrauch, a friend of Bach's.

A direct comparison with Hopkinson Smith's magisterial readings (Astrée) is revealing. He treats the dance in the abstract. His pulse is flexible, his expressive shading copious. O'Dette is determined to restore the dance proper. The rhythmic outlines are sharply defined by a judicious use of *staccato* bass notes and extensive employment of notes *inégales* and other French-style embellishments. That's not to say that O'Dette isn't alive to a more improvisatory quality, especially in the preludes and the Sonata in G minor. But in short, with his readings, the body dances; with Smith's, the soul. Neither approach is superior to the other – it's merely a matter of emphasis.

Viola da gamba Sonatas

Bach Three Viola da gamba Sonatas, BWV1027-29
CPE Bach Viola da gamba Sonata, H559 Wq137
Daniel Müller-Schott *vc* **Angela Hewitt** *pf*
Orfeo C693 071A (55' · DDD) Ⓕ

From the moment the cello starts its suave tread over the piano's gently rising bass and sustained right-hand trill at the beginning of the G major Sonata, you know this is going to be a disc to sit back and enjoy. Daniel Müller-Schott and Angela Hewitt may have substituted modern instruments for the viola da gamba and harpsichord Bach had in mind but nothing in this superb music's original character has been lost – this is as clear-textured and as vividly articulated a performance as you could hope to hear. Indeed, it has gained much by the sheer musical feeling and intelligence that these two players have put into it, aided by

extra warmth from Müller-Schott's cello (achieved without resorting to excessive vibrato) and from the delicate dynamic subtleties of Hewitt's piano playing.

There are some memorable moments here. Architecturally, too, they consistently get things just right. With a perfect balance between instruments, this is playing which gives nothing but a glow of pleasure, that not even what sounds like some weary tuning at the piano's top end can dispel.

All Bach gamba sonata discs need a filler, and the choice here is a sonata by CPE Bach, rather more romantically drawn by Müller-Schott and with a continuo accompaniment less well suited to the piano. But then this disc is worth your money for the JS alone.

Additional recommendation

Viola da gamba Sonatas, BWV1027-29
Coupled with: Trio Sonata in C, BWV529   Ⓟ
Savall *va da gamba* **Koopman** *hpd*
Alia Vox AV9812 (59' · DDD)   Ⓕ
A significant Bach gamba release. Savall and Koopman conjure performances whose sheer rightness and creative warmth make the music sound invigoratingly fresh.

Violin Sonatas

No 1 in B minor, BWV1014; **No 2** in A, BWV1015;
No 3 in E, BWV1016; **No 4** in C minor, BWV1017;
No 5 in F, BWV1018; **No 6** in G, BWV1019
Violin Sonatas Nos 1-6, BWV1014-19   Ⓟ
Sonata for Violin and Continuo in G, BWV1019a[a].
Cantabile, BWV1019a/2. Sonatas for Violin and
Continuo[a] – No 2 in G, BWV1021; No 4 in E minor,
BWV1023
Rachel Podger *vn* [a]**Jonathan Manson** *va da gamba*
Trevor Pinnock *hpd*
Channel Classics ② CCS14798 (139' · DDD)   ❋❋❋

A recording of Bach's violin sonatas that really hits the spot. Rachel Podger has already attracted much praise for her recordings of the solo violin music, but is heard here to even better advantage in the Six Sonatas for violin and obbligato harpsichord, BWV1014-19, for which she's joined by Trevor Pinnock.

The two make a fine match. Both are uncomplicated, instinctive musicians with a sure technical command and sound stylistic sense, and in works as robust and complete as these, that's most of the battle already won. But this is also music of great poetry, and, without straining unduly to make their points, Podger and Pinnock bring this out superbly; Pinnock's harpsichord is gently resonant and softly voiced, and Podger coaxes a lyrical flexibility out of her violin, its singing qualities enhanced thanks to a restrained but telling use of vibrato – one which also enables her to play more consistently and blessedly in tune than almost any other Baroque fiddler currently in business.

BACH CELLO SUITES – IN BRIEF

Mstislav Rostropovich
EMI ② 555363-2 (147′ · DDD)   Ⓕ❍🅑➔
Big-hearted, bold-gestured Bach from one of the greatest cellists of our time. Here is emotion writ large but done with such passion it's hard not to be won over.

Heinrich Schiff
EMI ② 586534-2 (124′ · DDD)   Ⓑ❍❍➔
One of the finest modern-instrument performances that takes academic advances into account, making for a delightfully buoyant set of the suites. Quite a bargain.

Pablo Casals
EMI mono ② 562611-2 (130′ · ADD)   Ⓜ❍➔
or Naxos mono ② 8 110915/6 (149′)   Ⓢ❍➔
A historic set from the 1930s which shows off the integrity and artistry of the man who rescued these works for posterity. Warts and all, these have to be heard.

Pierre Fournier
DG ② 449 711-2GOR2 (139′ · ADD)   Ⓜ❍❍❍➔
For many the classic performances: expressive, full-bodied yet never threatening to overwhelm the music. Fournier clearly adores this music and it shows.

Yo-Yo Ma
Sony Classical ② 82876 78751-2 (143′ · DDD) Ⓜ❍➔
The first of Ma's two cycles of the suites and at the price well worth considering for this fine cellist's innate musicality.

Pieter Wispelwey
Channel Classics ② CCS12298 (140′ · DDD) Ⓕ❍❍
Another cellist with two sets to his name offers a period approach that positively dances with a lightness of touch and songfulness. A real *tour de force*.

Truls Mørk
Virgin Classics ② 545650-2 (141′ · DDD)   Ⓕ🅑➔
A modern interpretation that brings many lessons from the period-instrument movement. It has a terrific 'rightness' about it and really dances.

Steven Isserlis
Hyperion ② CDA67541/2 (137′ · DDD)   Ⓕ❍❍❍➔
He bided his time before taking these works into the studio but the wait has been worth it because these are wonderfully lived-in and thought-about interpretations. Experience shines from every note. A modern classic?

Mischa Maisky
DG ③ 463 314-2GH3 (136′ · DDD)   Ⓕ🅑➔
Another cellist who felt the need to return to these infinitely rewarding pieces. He has so much more to say, albeit in a big, quasi-romantic style. Also has a fascinating CD-ROM extra.

It's difficult to single out details of this recording for comment; there just seems to be such a tremendous feeling of overall 'rightness' to it. Maybe the finale of Sonata No 2 seems rather frantic and the wonderful *Adagio ma non tanto* of No 3 a touch lumpy, but there really isn't much else to criticise. And there are true gems to be enjoyed in the opening movement of BWV1014, where the violin makes an almost imperceptible initial entry, or the warm embrace of BWV1017's *Adagio*, or practically any of the sparkling fast movements, played with invigorating rhythmic drive and clarity.

This recording's closest period rival, that of Andrew Manze and Richard Egarr, shows a typical wealth of new ideas and inspired moves but is less satisfying as a whole, and suffers from some intonationally hairy moments and a less precisely pointed sound. The only period recording to touch Podger and Pinnock for technical assurance is that of Fabio Biondi and Rinaldo Alessandrini, but in both sound and interpretation it's heavy-handed compared with the spontaneous musicianship and airy texture on display here, and rather meanly it gives the six obbligato sonatas only. Though all the recent recordings of these sonatas have had their merits, this – two discs for the price of one – is, quite simply, the best yet.

Solo Cello Suites

No 1 in G, BWV1007; **No 2** in D minor, BWV1008;
No 3 in C, BWV1009; **No 4** in E flat, BWV1010;
No 5 in C minor, BWV1011; **No 6** in D, BWV1012
Solo Cello Suites Nos 1-6
Pierre Fournier *vc*
DG The Originals ② 449 711-2GOR2 (139′ · ADD)
Recorded 1961-63   Ⓜ❍❍❍➔

Of all the great cellists, Pierre Fournier came closer to the heart of the music than almost any other. He seems to have possessed all the virtues of his fellow cellists without yielding to any of their self-indulgences. He could be brilliant in execution – his technique was second to none, as he proves throughout this set – profound in utterance, aristocratic in poise and wonderfully coherent in his understanding of Bach's articulation and phrases.

We need look no further than the *Prelude* of the First Suite in G major to find the supreme artistry which characterises each and every moment of these performances. There are very occasionally notes which fail to reach their centre but they're few and far between, and Fournier's intonation compares favourably with that of some of his virtuoso companions. Fournier's *rubato* is held tightly in rein and when he does apply it, it's in the interests of enlivening aspects of Bach's formal writing. He can sparkle too, as he does in many of the faster dance-orientated movements such as courantes, gavottes and bourrées; in the sarabandes, he invariably strikes a note of grandeur coupled with a concentration amounting at times almost to abstraction. Above all, his Bach playing is crowned with an eloquence, a lyricism and a grasp of the music's formal and stylistic content which will not easily be matched. Fine recorded sound and strongly commended on virtually all counts.

Solo Cello Suites Nos 1-6*.   Ⓗ
English Suite No 6 in D, BWV811 – Gavotte I; Gavotte II (arr Pollain). Musicalisches Gesangbuch – Komm, süsser Tod, BWV478 (arr Siloti). Violin Sonata, BWV1003 – Andante (arr Siloti). Orchestral Suite No 3 in D, BWV1068 – Air (arr Siloti). Toccata, Adagio and Fugue in C, BWV564 – Adagio
Pablo Casals vc with **Nikolai Mednikoff, Blas-Net, Otto Schulf** pfs
*EMI mono 562611-2 (132' · ADD)   Ⓜ🅞🅑

Naxos Historical mono ② 8 110915/6 (149' · ADD)
Recorded 1927-39   Ⓢ🅞🅑

When these recordings first appeared back in the 1930s and 40s, Bach for solo cello was a singular and esoteric concept. Casals had rediscovered the Suites for modern ears and his probing, albeit highly idiosyncratic, playing was a mandatory recommendation. Indeed, in those days it was the only recommendation. Nowadays, his achievement is still beyond question, but there will be some listeners who won't like what they hear.

After, say, the elegantly tapered playing of János Starker, Casals can initially sound wilful and ungainly. His bow seems to slice through chords like a meat cleaver. His intonation wanders, and his fingers press down on the strings so forcefully that a note 'pings' even before the bow is drawn. Casals reels and rhapsodises as if blind drunk on expressive freedom.

However, this impression is only transitory. What at first sounds gruff, even off-hand soon registers as boldly assertive. The intonation isn't so much 'faulty' as expressively employed, and as for those pre-echoing 'pings', they soon cease to matter – much as Glenn Gould's mumbling did years later. Time teaches you that the speaking tone, the poetic *tenutos*, the irresistible lilt in faster dance movements and the varied approach to vibrato were part of a grand musical plan, one that's now cherishable.

Casals makes a singular musical experience out of every movement. Try the Courante and Sarabande of the Fifth Suite – muscular resolve followed by profound self-communing.

Transfer-wise, things could hardly have gone better. True, there's some surface noise, but the sound has considerable realism and the broad contours of Casals's tone are untroubled by excessive filtering. A rival package from Pearl (identical couplings plus a transcription from a Bach-Vivaldi Concerto) reports a fatter cello sound with less well focused contours. EMI's set offers only the Suites in transfers that, while admirably clear, are rather less natural than Ward Marston's for Naxos.

Solo Cello Suites Nos 1-6
Traditional The Song of the Birds (arr Beamish)
Steven Isserlis vc
Hyperion ② CDA67541/2 (137' · DDD)   Ⓕ🅞🅞🅞🅑

Steven Isserlis clearly venerates Casals as an important figure in the suites' history, even paying touching homage to him by appending a performance of a Catalan folksong. Like Casals, Isserlis bided his time before committing them to disc, and he has looked for interpretative guidance to extra-musical ideas. Isserlis proposes a detailed concept. For him the Suites suggest a meditative cycle on the life of Christ, rather like Biber's Mystery Sonatas. He points out that this is 'a personal feeling, not a theory', but it has to be said that once you know that he is thinking of the Agony in the Garden during the darkly questioning Second Suite (the five stark chords towards the end of the Prélude representing the wounds of Christ), the Crucifixion in the wearily troubled Fifth or the Resurrection in the joyous Sixth, it adds immense power and interest to his performances.

But then, this is also the most wonderful celloplaying, surely among the most consistently beautiful to have been heard in this demanding music, as well as the most musically alert and vivid. Not everyone will like the brisk tempi (though the Allemandes, for instance, gain in architectural coherence), but few will fail to be charmed by Isserlis's sweetly singing tone, his perfectly voiced chords and superb control of articulation and dynamic – the way the final chord of the First Prélude dies away is spellbinding. There are so many other delights: the subtle comings and goings of the Third Prélude, the nobly poised Fifth Allemande, the swaggering climax that is the Sixth Gigue – to name but a few. Suffice to say that Isserlis's Bach is a major entrant into an already highly distinguished field, and a disc many will want to return to again and again.

Solo Cello Suites Nos 1-6   Ⓟ
Pieter Wispelwey vc
Channel Classics ② CCS12298 (140' · DDD)   Ⓕ🅞🅞

Pieter Wispelwey is equally at home on Baroque and modern instruments. These performances are carefully prepared, beautifully executed and most eloquently expressed. The instruments, too, sound well, Wispelwey having chosen an early 18th-century cello by Barak Norman for the first five Suites, and a five-stringed *violoncello piccolo* by an unidentified craftsman for the special requirements of the Sixth.

Wispelwey is an imaginative player with a highly developed sense of fantasy. These qualities are as welcome in his performances of Bach as they're to be treated with circumspection in his almost entirely fanciful written introduction to the music. Preludes come across especially well since it's in these wonderfully varied opening movements, with their rhetorical diversity, that the performer can give rein most freely to his or her most natural conversational inflexions. And he makes the most of that thrilling climax at the peak of a chromatic accent through a full scale and a half. Sarabandes are profound and reflective without being weighty, and allemandes graceful and substantial. The *galanteries*, by contrast, are lightly bowed and redolent of playful and demonstrative gestures. That, to an extent, is true also of the courantes, while the gigues are firmly projected, full-toned and splendidly robust.

Wispelwey's set of Bach's Cello Suites, then, is deserving of praise. If you're familiar with the gruff grandeur of Pablo Casals, or the aristocratic nobility of Fournier, then these performances will throw an entirely different light on the music, more conversational and with airier discourse. You may never want to be without the two earlier sets, but Wispelwey's version sits comfortably on the uppermost range of the period-instrument performance ladder.

Solo Violin Sonatas & Partitas

Sonatas – **No 1** in G minor, BWV1001; **No 2** in A minor, BWV1003; **No 3** in C, BWV1005.
Partitas – **No 1** in B minor, BWV1002; **No 2** in D minor, BWV1004; **No 3** in E, BWV1006

CCS12198: Sonata No 1. Partitas Nos 1 & 2   Ⓟ
CCS14498: Sonatas Nos 2 & 3. Partita No 3
Rachel Podger *vn*
Channel Classics ② CCSSEL2498 (142' · DDD)
Ⓕ**❍❍❍**

 Hitherto we have heard Rachel Podger only in early chamber works and as Andrew Manze's partner in Bach double concertos: here now, at last, is an opportunity to hear her on her own. And you couldn't be more on your own than in Bach's mercilessly revealing Solo Sonatas and Partitas, perhaps the ultimate test of technical mastery, expressiveness, structural phrasing and deep musical perception for a violinist. Playing a Baroque instrument, Podger challenges comparison with the much praised and individual reading by Monica Huggett: she has many of the same virtues – flawless intonation, warm tone, expressive nuances, clear understanding of the proper balance of internal strands – but her approach is sometimes markedly different. This is most obvious in the great D minor Chaconne, in which Huggett's rhythmical flexibility worried some people, but in which Podger, here as elsewhere, while fully characterising the varied repetitions of the ground, is intent on building up the cumulative effect. One pleasing general feature of her playing, indeed, is her firm but unassertive rhythmic sense; others are the absence of any suspicion that technical difficulties exist (instead a calm control, as in the G minor's Siciliano), her subtle phrasing (as in the B minor Corrente, with the fleetest of *doubles*), the cross-rhythms of her G minor *Presto* and, most strikingly, the poetic feeling with which she

imbues the initial *Adagio* of the G minor Sonata. She touches in chords lightly: though some might have been split downwards rather than upwards so as to preserve the continuity of a lower part (for example, in bar 5 of the B minor Allemande, bar 10 of the Chaconne and in the 18th and 19th bars of its major section). Her D minor Giga is stunning. Altogether a most impressive and rewarding disc.

As a matter of tactics disregarding the printed order of the works, the second disc opens in the most effective way with a joyous performance of the ever-invigorating E major *Preludio*. At once we can recognise Podger's splendid rhythmic and tonal vitality (not merely Bach's marked terraced dynamics but pulsatingly alive gradations within phrases), her extremely subtle accentuations and harmonic awareness (note her change of colour at the move from E to C sharp major in bar 33), are all within total technical assurances. The Gavotte en Rondeau is buoyantly dance-like, and in the most natural way she elaborates its final statement (throughout the Partita her ornamentation is stylish and convincing). She takes the Giga at a restrained pace that allows of all kinds of tiny rhythmic nuances. Only a rather cut-up performance of the Loure detracts.

In the sonatas she shows other sterling qualities. She preserves the shape in the A minor Grave's ornate tangle of notes; she judges to a nicety the balance of the melodic line against the plodding accompanimental quavers of the *Andante*; she imbues the C major's *Adagio* with a hauntingly poetic musing atmosphere, and her lucid part-playing of its Fuga could scarcely be bettered. In the Fuga of the A minor Sonata, however, she unexpectedly allows herself considerable rhythmic freedom in order to point the structure. The final track is a stunning performance of the C major's closing *Allegro assai* which would bring any audience to its feet.

Solo Violin Sonatas and Partitas, BWV1001-06
Gidon Kremer *vn*
ECM New Series ② 476 7291 (131' · DDD)   Ⓕ

Are a beautiful sound and a warm, singing tone as important to you as intelligent, stylish interpretation in Bach's Sonatas and Partitas? If so, you probably won't sympathise with Gidon Kremer's seeming determination to bypass his instrument in pursuit of musical truths, nor the hard-hitting, raw, squeezed-out quality of many notes above the stave and loud broken chords (although Kremer's intonation is, for the most part, absolutely dead-on).

The utterly unprettified G minor and C major Sonatas' *adagios*, for example, are brisker and grittier than what one usually hears. While many treat the B minor Partita's opening Allemande as an expansive aria, Kremer's headlong tempo, emphatic double-dotting and pronounced dynamic contrasts realise the music's French ouverture implications, making it easy to slip into the following Double movement unnoticed. Following a dazzling sprint through the *Presto* Double Kremer reduces the Sarabande and Double to a studied and rather precious whisper.

Kremer shapes the three sonatas' fugues in large, dramatic arcs, intensified by subtle tempo fluctuations. His unusually soft playing of the D minor Chaconne's most virtuoso passages convinces more than his dynamic exaggerations in bars 32-33. Similarly, the E major Partita's archly phrased Gavotte and Rondeau contrast with Kremer's imaginatively inflected, tough, driving dispatch of the Preludio.

With Kremer's earlier solo Bach set unavailable, his equally controversial yet more evolved (and better engineered) remakes offer ample food for thought, if not quite a first choice.

Solo Violin Sonatas and Partitas, BWV1001-06
Viktoria Mullova *vn*
Onyx ② ONYX4040 (132' · DDD)   Ⓕ

Viktoria Mullova plays a gut-strung Guadagnini (in modern set-up) at low pitch, using a Baroque-style bow, so it's with the period instrument Bach recordings that Mullova can be most usefully compared.

These are outstanding performances, however, whatever category they belong to. Mullova brings together several ideal qualities for a Bach player. Firstly, there's a secure sense of style, apparent equally in the rhythm and character of each of the Partitas' dances, and in the ornamented introductory movements of the first two Sonatas. Then there's her superior, virtuoso's technique, producing beautifully precise tuning and, in the fugal movements, finely controlled, varied and euphonious playing of the most densely polyphonic passages. To this we can add her deep musical understanding; by means of subtle emphasis and natural dynamic contrasts, she draws our attention to the beauty of Bach's harmonic progressions and to the balance and grandeur of his designs. Even on the few occasions where Mullova isn't entirely convincing the poise and sheer quality of the playing remains extremely persuasive.

There have been many fine recent recordings of these works, but this one is definitely not to be missed.

Solo Violin Sonatas and Partitas, BWV1001-06
Christian Tetzlaff *vn*
Hänssler Classic ② CD98 250 (130' · DDD)   Ⓕ❶❷❸

Christian Tetzlaff, always one of the most thoughtful, imaginative violinists, has obviously found Bach's solo works a stimulating and rewarding challenge. Technically, he's most impressive: using a modern bow, he can achieve, with each phrase, the kind of subtle give and take that's normally the preserve of the best Baroque violinists. His chord playing, too, shows wonderful control; in the more densely polyphonic

pieces – the Chaconne and the fugues in the three sonatas – it seems there's often little choice between aggressive accentuation and rhythmic distortion caused by spreading the chords. Tetzlaff, however, manages to avoid both pitfalls, with varied arpeggiation that never fails to take account of the music's rhythmic requirements.

The performances have a remarkable air of spontaneity, the result of a pervasive *rubato*, especially notable in the ornamented opening movements of the first two sonatas, and in the freer sections of the Chaconne. There's a sense of line and balance that ensures that each departure from metronomic regularity sounds entirely natural, unlocking the music's expressive potential. This is even felt when, in a few movements in the partitas, the dance character suggests a more regular, metrical pulse. Apart from this, it's notable how Tetzlaff realises the virtuosity of Bach's violin writing – the *moto perpetuo* finales of the sonatas sound truly thrilling, full of temperament and fire. Do investigate this outstanding set.

Solo Violin Sonatas and Partitas, BWV1001-06
Itzhak Perlman *vn*
EMI ② 476811-2 (143' · DDD)   Ⓜ❶❷❸

These works are brutally difficult to play, not least in securing accurate intonation and in minimising the disruptive effect of hacking out the three- and four-note chords but, given today's Olympian standards, technical shortcomings may be tolerated only in performances that are musically relevatory.

Technically Perlman is beyond reproach; chords are traversed deftly and in the *Adagio* of Sonata No 3 skilfully subjugated to the melodic line, and his differentiation between marked *pianos* and *fortes* is very clear. There's brilliance in the faster movements, delicacy in the *galanteries*, and except perhaps for the Allemande of Partita No 2, grave expressiveness in the slower ones; stylistic misfits are far fewer than those of, say, Sándor Végh or Nathan Milstein (1971), and all repeats are offered – usually with some changes of dynamics.

Bach with a fair degree of gloss maybe, but a version by one of today's greatest violinists that's justly popular.

Solo Violin Sonatas and Partitas, BWV1001-06
Alina Ibragimova *vn*
Hyperion ② CDA67691/2 (139' · DDD)   Ⓕ❶❷❸

Alina Ibragimova's Bach comes as something of a revelation. The finesse we've previously admired in her playing is here combined with thoughtful stylistic awareness (she's studied Baroque violin with Adrian Butterfield) and a distinctive, individual approach. She plays with very little vibrato, often none at all, so that variations in volume and colour all come from the bow, allowing her to present the musical shapes in a clear yet unemphatic way. She eschews the usual violinistic attempts, through big tone and heavy emphasis, to underline the grandeur of Bach's designs; the Chaconne ends quietly, and the peroration of the Fugue in the Third Sonata, whose exposition returns to round the movement off, is achieved through a slight broadening of the tempo.

Ibragimova's playing is uncommonly neat, with precise fingerwork and relaxed management of the bow; the virtuoso finale of the Third Sonata sparkles effortlessly while remaining for the most part at a *piano* dynamic. She plays unequal quavers in the Third Partita's Minuet as naturally as if she'd grown up in the 18th century. And finally, all her stylishness and technical refinement is at the service of an ingrained understanding of the music; she makes us feel where the points of harmonic tension and emphasis are, and she's able to do it without distorting the surface of the music.

Hearing this set, some listeners may miss a more vigorous, forceful character or long for a warmer tone and more sustained playing, but these airy, poised, deeply felt performances deserve to find wide appreciation.

Solo Violin Partitas – No 2, BWV1004; No 3, BWV1006. Solo Violin Sonata No 3, BWV1005
Isabelle Faust vn
Harmonia Mundi HMC90 2059 (69' · DDD) Ⓜ️ⓄⓄⒷ⟶

Gone are the days when the choice for performances of the Solo Sonatas and Partitas was a simple one between modern style and instrument on the one hand and historically informed Baroque violin playing on the other. Nowadays there's a whole range of approaches. Like Alina Ibragimova (see above), Faust – using a modern instrumental set-up and bow – employs little vibrato and employs the detailed marking of slurs in Bach's autograph as a guide to phrasing and accentuation. But whereas Ibragimova's performances are notable for their delicacy and intimate scale, Faust is bolder and more outgoing, introducing imaginative ornamentation into repeated sections. Quite often her playing allows a generous measure of rhythmic freedom – as in the Second Partita's Sarabande, for example; at other times she's concerned to maintain a strong momentum. The Chaconne is the most notable example of this: in her hands it sounds like the representation of a vast procession, moving forward inexorably.

The Third Partita's Prelude has a similar onward drive that's in no way mechanical – constantly varied bow strokes express perfectly the changes in harmonic speed and fluctuation of intensity. In short: Isabelle Faust has a magnificent grasp of this music. Hear her if you can!

English Suites, BWV806-11

Six English Suites, BWV806-11
Glenn Gould pf
Sony Classical Glenn Gould Edition ② SM2K52606 (112' · ADD). Recorded 1971-73　Ⓜ️Ⓞ

BWV806-8 also available on Glenn Gould Anniversary Edition SMK87765; BWV809-11 on SMK87766　Ⓞ

There has been no more original genius of the keyboard than Glenn Gould, but this has drawbacks as well as thrilling advantages. He can sacrifice depth of feeling for a relentless and quixotic sense of adventure. Yet love it or deride it, every bar of these lovingly remastered discs tingles with *joie de vivre* and an unequalled force and vitality. Try the opening of the First Suite. Is such freedom glorious or maddening, or is the way the odd note is nonchalantly flicked in the following sustained argument a naughty alternative to Bach's intention? The *pizzicato* bass in the second Double from the same Suite is perhaps another instance of an idiosyncrasy bordering on whimsy, an enlivenment or rejuvenation that at least remains open to question. But listen to him in virtually any of the sarabandes and you'll find a tranquillity and equilibrium that can silence such criticism. Even at his most piquant and outrageous his playing remains, mysteriously, all of a piece. The fiercely chromatic, labyrinthine argument concluding the Fifth Suite is thrown off with a unique brio, one of those moments when you realise how he can lift Bach out of all possible time-warps and make him one of music's truest modernists.

Six English Suites, BWV806-11
Murray Perahia pf
Sony Classical ② 88697 31050-2 (128' · DDD)
　Ⓜ️ⓄⓄⓄⒷ⟶

Murray Perahia's *English Suites* (his first Bach recordings) originally appeared as full-price individual releases, beginning with Nos 1, 3 and 6 in 1997, followed by Nos 2, 4 and 5 in 1998. Now programmed in numerical order, the performances have more than worn well. No matter how full-bodied and luminous his sonority, Perahia is a line player first and foremost, achieving clear, colourfully diversified textures mainly through finger power and hand balance. Perahia's Sarabandes are firmly etched and the Courantes propulsive. Ornaments are adventurous and he brings rhythmic drive to the quicker movements. The superb sound adds further value to an attractively priced reissue that collectors seeking the *English Suites* on the piano ought to seriously consider.

Bach English Suites – No 2, BWV807[a]; No 3, BWV808. Italian Concerto, BWV971. Toccata, BWV911[a]. Capriccio, BWV992[a] **Gulda** Prelude and Fugue
Friedrich Gulda pf
DG [a]mono 477 8020GH (72' · ADD)　ⒻⒷ⟶

Lovingly compiled from a mix of live and studio recordings by his son Paul, all these performances tell us that Gulda's legendary eccentricity was countered by an acutely economic and disciplined style and uncompromising musical integrity. For Gulda, Bach was 'a pillar of moral support' but for Paul Gulda, his father's life was full of foibles and oddities rather than airs and graces, and his lifelong attempt to reconcile the Apollonian and Dionysian elements in music were shown in his special reverence for Mozart and Beethoven. But here, his Bach is of a crystalline clarity combined with an innate musicality that erases all possible dryness or pedantry. The *Italian Concerto*'s opening *Allegro* is both sturdy and magnificently assured, the central *Andante* magically fine-spun while the final *Presto* is a marvel of exuberant virtuosity. Gulda's way with the *English Suites* just possibly tells us the source of Martha Argerich's dazzling Bach (Gulda was a guiding force and mentor to her) and throughout all these performances you are made gloriously aware of Bach as a contemporary, a composer for all time. The *Aria de postiglione* is springy and piquant while for his final offering, his own *Prelude and Fugue*, Gulda whisks us to New York's Birdland, the jazz club where, after playing Beethoven recitals at Carnegie Hall, he would jam away with his esteemed colleagues into the small hours.

Excellently recorded and lavishly illustrated, this special disc is part of 'an ocean of music' (Argerich) left by a very special pianist.

Toccata in C minor, BWV911. Partita No 2 in C minor, BWV826. English Suite No 2 in A minor, BWV807
Martha Argerich *pf*
DG The Originals 463 604-2GOR (50' · ADD)
Recorded 1979　　　　Ⓜ**Ⓞ**🔂

This recital, first issued in 1980, has an extraordinary authority and panache. Argerich's attack in the C minor Toccata could hardly be bolder or more incisive, a classic instance of virtuosity all the more clear and potent for being so firmly but never rigidly controlled. Here, as elsewhere, her discipline is no less remarkable than her unflagging brio and relish of Bach's glory. Again, in the Second Partita, her playing is quite without those excesses or mannerisms that too often pass for authenticity, and in the *Andante* immediately following the Sinfonie she's expressive yet clear and precise, her following *Allegro* a marvel of high-speed yet always musical bravura. True, some may question her way with the Courante from the Second English Suite, finding it hard-driven, even overbearing, yet her eloquence in the following sublime Sarabande creates its own hypnotic authority. The dynamic range of these towering, intensely musical performances has been excellently captured by DG.

French Suites, BWV812-17

Six French Suites, BWV812-17. Sonata in D minor, BWV964. Five Preludes, BWV924-28. Prelude in G minor, BWV930. Six Preludes, BWV933-38. Five Preludes, BWV939-43. Prelude in C minor, BWV999. Prelude and Fugue in A minor, BWV894

Angela Hewitt *pf*
Hyperion ② CDA67121/2 (151' · DDD)　　Ⓕ**Ⓞ**

Even the most out-and-out purists who blench at the thought of Bach on the piano will find it hard not to be won over by Angela Hewitt's artistry. Eschewing all hieratic pretentiousness on the one hand and self-regarding eccentricities on the other, she gives us Bach performances that aren't only admirable in style but marked by poise, and what used to be called a 'quiet hand': 'chaste' might not be too fanciful a term, so long as that does not suggest any lack of vitality. There's intelligence in her carefully thought-out phrasing and subtle variety of articulation: gradations of sound are always alive without their becoming precious. The bulk of this recording is devoted to the *French Suites*. Particularly enjoyable is the lightness of her treatment of the Airs of Nos 2 and 4, the vigour of No 5's Bourrée and the freshness of No 6's Allemande; the extra decorations she adds in repeats everywhere sound properly spontaneous and are in the best of taste; ornaments are always cleanly played and matched up in imitative voices.

Keyboard Partitas, BWV825-30

B flat, **BWV825**; C minor, **BWV826**; A minor, **BWV827**; D, **BWV828**; G, **BWV829**; E minor, **BWV830**

Six Keyboard Partitas, BWV825-30　　　　Ⓟ
Trevor Pinnock *hpd*
Hänssler Classic ② CD92 115 (149' · DDD)　Ⓜ**ⓄⓄⓄ**

The six Partitas are virtually a compendium of Bach's keyboard styles, with toccatas and French overtures, fugues and fantasies and all manner of dances. Trevor Pinnock rises to a new level of mastery in his new recording of them. We all know about the brilliance of his fingerwork and his beautifully sprung, ebullient rhythms; but here he goes further, showing a true grandeur of manner that embraces Bach at his most serious and pensive, his most learned, and – above all – his most vividly rhetorical. Pinnock takes his time over the music: these are measured readings of the partitas, thought through, viewed whole. The natural and spontaneous musicianship of old is still there, but now it's given extra depth and meaning through the carefully judged articulation, the tiny moments of hesitation, all within a fluent larger rhythm, that lend extra point and shape to a phrase, a group of phrases, an entire musical paragraph.

The warm, rather resonant recording beautifully captures the rich sound of his instrument – a David Way copy from 1983 of a Hemsch original – as well as the detail of his playing. There could hardly have been a happier return to the recording studio for Pinnock than this fine set.

Six Keyboard Partitas, BWV825-30
Angela Hewitt pf
Hyperion ② CDA67191/2 (143' · DDD)　ⒻOⒹ⁺

If Bach is to be played on the piano, this is the
kind of way to do it. Inherent in all Hewitt's
playing is a rhythmic vitality, always under
control, that sweeps you along with its
momentum, subtly varied articulation, dynamics that follow the natural rise or fall of phrases
without exaggerations, an appreciation of
Bach's harmonic tensions, an ability to differentiate between the strength of contrapuntal
lines, and an unfailing clarity of texture.

This is a sane and sensible interpretation,
deeply musicianly and devoid of eccentricity.
Her attitude, rather like Toscanini's, is to accept
the text *com' è scritto* and then to make legitimate
adjustments, so we get double-dotting and
assimilation of rhythms. Technically she's
immaculate, with the cleanest possible ornaments. In the great E minor Sarabande Hewitt is
justifiably emotional, without becoming soggy:
only in the first half of the A minor Allemande is
there a hint of coyness. No, the whole disc gives
unalloyed pleasure.

Keyboard Partitas – No 1, No 5, No 6
Murray Perahia pf
Sony Classical 88697 44361-2 (70' · DDD)　ⒻOOⒹ⁺

Keyboard Partitas – No 2, No 3, No 4
Murray Perahia pf
Sony Classical 88697 22695-2 (60' · DDD)　ⒻOOⒹ⁺

In Murray Perahia's hands, Bach's Partitas not
only work well on the modern concert grand but
also sound completely at home. The pianist's
vibrant and variegated sonority perpetually
sings, while his contrapuntal acumen leaves no
detail unconsidered nor unduly fussed over. His
tempi always seem right for what the music has
to express, as opposed to what Perahia wants to
express in the music.

A few examples should suffice to pinpoint what
makes these performances special. For instance,
the C minor No 2's Allemande and A minor
No 3's Corrente's two-part textures gorgeously
showcase Perahia's fluent, utterly natural conversational give and take between the hands.
The C minor Rondeaux's dance-like profile
acquires uncommon and welcome gravitas due
to Perahia's measured pulse and a non-legato
touch that avoids any hint of percussive residue.
The D major Partita No 4 easily takes its place
alongside versions by Kapell, Gould, Weissenberg, Hewitt, Tureck and Goode. Strong
melodic projection, inner "swing" and a sense of
air in between the notes characterise the Corrente, Aria and Menuet. In both the Allemande
and Sarabande he gives the decorative right-
hand lines their full lyrical due, while his left
hand provides a strong, decisive underpinning.
Even at a brisk tempo, the Gigue speaks clearly
and eloquently, with every accent, syncopation

and cross-rhythmic gesture perfectly placed.
Stylish, well considered and discreet embellishments flavour the repeats in all three works.

The high standards of stylish perception and
pianistic finesse Murray Perahia brought to
Bach's Partitas Nos 2, 3 and 4 happily inform
Nos 1, 5 and 6, where beauty and strength
merge as one. Perahia's *legato* and detached
articulations are always meaningful and tonally
varied without exaggeration or contrivance, and
each note of every ornament sings out with
unforced exactitude. Repeats vary in regard to
touch, voicings, accents, embellishments, but
with discretion and the utmost in expressive
economy. All of these virtues add up to one of
the most thoughtful, well proportioned and fastidiously detailed B flat Partita accounts in
recent memory, capped by an unusually loud yet
unaggresive Gigue. Picture Glenn Gould's
razor-sharp contrapuntal fingerwork fused with
Edwin Fischer's velvet touch to get the gist of
the E minor Partita's *Tempo di Gavotta* or the
completely natural specificity with which Perahia apreggiates the Sarabande's chords.

Some might wish for more animation and
point in the Allemande, yet Perahia's supreme
command of the music's conversational give-
and-take more than justifies his lyrical, leisurely
point of view. If you seek the Bach Partitas on
piano in state-of-the-art sound, Perahia easily
warrants top honours.

Keyboard Partitas – No 1, No 3; No 6
Richard Goode pf
Nonesuch 7559 79698-2 (65' · DDD)　ⒻOOO

 In this second volume of Richard
Goode's complete set of Bach Partitas
there's the sense of a distinguished lin-
eage, a tradition of Bach piano playing with a
Classical-Romantic bent that reaches back to
Harold Samuel via Borowsky, Horszowski,
Schnabel and Serkin. Like them (though not
specifically in the Partitas) Goode treats line as
paramount, stressing counterpoint only where
and when it serves an expressive end, as in the
First Partita's Allemande. Like Schnabel, Goode
can occasionally accelerate a phrase to focus its
place in the larger context. The use of *crescendo* is
subtle yet telling (the Corrente) and the way
phrases breathe, suggests hours spent focusing
on a precise *rubato*.

This is glorious music, and there's barely a
second when you aren't aware of that. Everything flows from the logic of the line, and
when perspectives do change (at around 46
seconds into the A minor Partita's opening
two-part Fantasia, for example, where the
lower voice takes the lead) the option seems
inevitable.

Everything essential to the spirit is here: dance
and reverie, clarity and form, digital brilliance.
Goode never forces his tone and although he has
a secure sense of rhythm – the faster dances
trip along rather than rush – there's no hint of
the obsessive drive indulged by the post-Gould

school. That, too, can be exciting, but Goode's inner explorations of Bach will probably yield longer-term satisfaction. This is an exceptionally fine set.

Disc 1: 'Bach Performance on the Piano' –
An Illustrated Lecture. Disc 2: Chromatic Fantasia and Fugue, BWV903. Italian Concerto, BWV971. Partita No 4, BWV828
Angela Hewitt pf
Video director **Uli Aumüller**
Hyperion ② 🗚 DVDA68001 (3h 30' · NTSC · 16:9 · PCM stereo, 2.0, 5.1 and DTS 5.1 · 0)   Ⓕ

Angela Hewitt has been giving illustrated lecture recitals on Bach performance for some time but not, on this showing, direct to camera. Though she becomes more fluent and confident over the 148 minutes, for most of the time she resembles the Queen delivering her Christmas message to the Commonwealth. Is she reading off an autocue? Her measured and articulated delivery with nary an 'um' or 'er' suggests that she is; if she isn't, then it sounds as though she is, and reading a script which, moreover, has been written to be published in a book rather than spoken aloud.

Its seven chapters are divided into 36 sections, each one fading to black-out and up again: usefully cued but tiresome to watch. The whole exercise would have been better on CD. What Hewitt has to say is full of wisdom and perspicacity, liberally illustrating the talk at her Fazioli piano (it is filmed in the Fazioli factory). But who is it aimed at? The conservatory student (useful), the teacher (instructive), the amateur Bach player (daunting) or the general public (illuminating but esoteric)?

Disc two is a live recital filmed in the Fazioli concert hall where Hewitt puts into practice what she has been preaching: her poise, clarity of voicing, spontaneity, wonderful finger *legato* and palpable joy in performing these works is a masterclass in itself.

Das wohltemperirte Clavier

48 Preludes and Fugues –
Book 1 BWV846-69; **Book 2** BWV870-93

Das wohltemperierte Clavier   Ⓗ
8 110651/2: Book 1
8 110653/4: Book 2
Edwin Fischer pf
Naxos Historical mono ② (107' & 126' · ADD)
Recorded 1933-36   Ⓢ❶❶❶

Edwin Fischer's recording of the '48' was the first by a pianist of the set, and probably remains the finest of all. Fischer might have agreed with András Schiff that Bach is the 'most romantic of all composers', for his superfine musicianship seems to live and breathe in another world. His sonority is as

ravishing as it's apt, never beautiful for its own sake, and graced with a pedal technique so subtle that it results in a light and shade, a subdued sparkle or pointed sense of repartee that eludes lesser artists. No matter what complexity Bach throws at him, Fischer resolves it with a disarming poise and limpidity. All this is a far cry from, say, Glenn Gould's egotism in the '48'. Fischer showed a deep humility before great art, making the singling out of one or another of his performances an impertinence.

In Book 2, you could hardly imagine a more seraphic utterance in No 3, later contrasted with the most skittish *allegro* reply. He possessed a touch with 'the strength and softness of a lion's velvet paw', and there are few recordings from which today's generation of pianists could learn so much; could absorb his way of transforming a supposedly learned tome into a fountain of limitless magic and resource. Here he is, then, at his most sublimely poised and unruffled, at bargain price in beautifully restored sound.

Das wohltemperirte Clavier, BWV846-93
Angela Hewitt pf
Hyperion ④ CDA67741/4 (4h 31' · DDD)
Recorded live   Ⓕ❶❶❶➔

Listening to Angela Hewitt's latest thoughts on Bach's *Well-Tempered Clavier* alongside her late-1990s Hyperion cycle (reviewed below), it appears that her interpretations haven't changed so much as evolved, intensified and, most important, internalised. This perception is enhanced by a closer sonic image, plus the leaner, more timbrally diverse qualities of Hewitt's Fazioli concert grand that contrast with her earlier recording's mellower, more uniform Steinway. Yet one readily credits Hewitt's pianistic prowess for more acutely differentiated *legato* and detached articulation this time around, together with a wider range of melodic inflection. This adds considerable textural dimension to fugues whose close counterpoint is extremely difficult to voice and clarify. Hewitt's uncommonly brisk and elegantly poised G sharp minor Book 2 Fugue has acquired conversational light and shade. Rubati hinted at earlier re-emerge in fuller, more purposeful bloom: compare both readings of the E flat major Book 1 Prelude and the E major Book 2 Fugue, for example. Perhaps one could pigeonhole Hewitt I as characterised by dance, while Hewitt II mainly celebrates song. While both versions hold equal validity and stature, Hewitt's remake ultimately digs deeper, with more personalised poetry. Perhaps she'll revisit the *Goldberg Variations* next?

Das wohltemperirte Clavier
CDA67301/2 – Book 1
CDA67303/4 – Book 2
Angela Hewitt pf
Hyperion ④ CDA67301/2 and CDA67303/4
(117' & 148' · DDD)   Ⓕ❶❶➔

Admirers of Canadian pianist Angela Hewitt's lightly articulated and elegantly phrased Bach playing won't be disappointed by this recording. These qualities characterise the playing of each and every one of these profoundly didactic yet sublimely poetic pieces. Her restrained use of the sustaining pedal, her consequently clearly spoken articulation, and the resultant lucidity of musical thought, bring to mind the recorded performances of Edwin Fischer. Hewitt certainly sounds more comfortable in a studio than Fischer ever did, and her technique is more consistently disciplined than his was under these circumstances. Her reflective view of the more inward-looking fugues, such as the lyrical one in E flat minor, is most attractive. Taut, but with a suppleness that's entirely devoid of stiffness, this is indeed cogent and gracefully beautiful playing of a high order. You may sense, from time to time, an overtly intense element of subjective thought in her understanding of the music, a quality which seems to be endorsed by occasional references in her lively, illuminating and detailed introduction, to Bach's 'sense of inner peace', and so on. However, to conclude on a thoroughly positive and enthusiastic note, these are performances of Book 1 that you'll want to hear many times over. The recording and instrument sound well, too.

Hewitt's Book 2 is a delight to both ear and mind. Everything is in the best taste and free of exhibitionism. There are subtle tonal nuances, natural rises and falls of dynamics, well-defined differentiation of contrapuntal lines and appreciation of the expressive implications of Bach's chromaticisms. Throughout her playing of these preludes and fugues – several longer, more mature and more demanding than those of Book 1 – there's a sense of unhurried poise, with flowing rhythm. The air of tranquillity is underlined by her frequent adoption of very quiet openings, many of which then take on a warmer tone towards the end – even the E major Fugue, which Landowska labelled 'combative', is handled quietly, yet she's able to sound contemplative (as in the E major Fugue) without lapsing into Tureckian reverentiality.

Just occasionally Bach's more intense movements tempt her into emotional *rubatos* which, though musically affecting, take Bach out of his century, and not everyone will care for the big *allargandos* she makes at the ends of some of the earlier movements. Otherwise these are musicianly and imaginative performances.

Das wohltemperirte Clavier – Book 1
Maurizio Pollini pf
DG ② 477 8078GH2 (110' · DDD)   Ⓕ**Ο**Ⓑ

Maurizio Pollini performed Bach's *Well-Tempered Clavier* Book 1 back in 1985 and his playing was straightforward, somewhat austere, well judged in terms of tempi, and ornamentally conservative. Apparently the pianist examined the music anew before finally committing his interpretations to disc nearly a quarter of a cen-

tury later. Although earlier impressions remain intact, there's greater fluidity and warmth now. Pollini will have none of the agogic stresses, dynamic hairpins and tiny *rubatos* sprinkled throughout Angela Hewitt's 2008 remakes (see above) and he avoids tempo modification as much as possible without managing to sound the least bit metronomic.

How does he do this? Close listening reveals minute changes in tone colour, subtle and strategic deployment of the piano's *una corda* pedal, plus long phrases and fugal textures that have beginnings, middles and ends but no dead spots. A good example of this is the A minor Fugue, where the often entangled polyphony emerges with uncommon differentiation and character. Also notice introspective Preludes such as the E flat minor and B flat minor, where the accompanying chords' moving parts fully present themselves without artificial highlighting. A few aggressively dispatched Preludes yield slightly blurry results (the G minor) and at least one tiny wrong note (in the C minor) that slipped past Pollini's perfectionist radar.

Some listeners may be turned off by the distant and slightly over-resonant engineering while others may more readily embrace its concert-hall realism, plus the fact that Pollini's habitual vocal grunts and groans recede more into the background.

Das wohltemperirte Clavier – Book 2
Masaaki Suzuki hpd
BIS ② BIS-CD1513/4 (160' · DDD)   Ⓕ**ΟΟΟ**Ⓑ

More than a decade has lapsed between instalments of Masaaki Suzuki's *Well-Tempered Clavier*. However, Book 2 was worth the wait. It lives up to Book 1's high artistic and sonic standards, and possibly surpasses them.

Suzuki's intelligent virtuosity operates on several levels. A vocal sensibility consistently determines how phrases begin, end and follow one another to their ultimate destinations. No matter what the basic tempo may be, breath pauses and agogic adjustments naturally mesh into the flow of Bach's lines, rather than work against them. Textural variety also manifests itself through Masaaki's subtle fingerwork. One also senses that Suzuki seriously pondered when and how to arpeggiate chords for maximum expressive and structural purpose, as the C sharp major, F minor and F sharp minor Preludes revealingly display. Yet the D major and B minor Fugues prove that Suzuki can deliver straightforward, even brash vitality when he choses.

As before, Suzuki plays an attractive and vibrantly recorded Willem Kroesbergen harpsichord modelled on a period Ruckers instrument, and Yo Tomita provides fascinating, informative booklet-notes. In all, Suzuki's heartfelt synthesis of scholarship and musicality will provide repeated listening pleasure in one of the finest harpsichord recordings of Book 2 available.

Das wohltemperirte Clavier – Book 2
Daniel Barenboim pf
Warner Classics ③ 2564 61940-2 (164' · DDD)   Ⓕ

There have been times when Barenboim's omnivorous musical appetite has threatened his musical stability and reflection but here, revisiting Bach – a childhood 'friend' – his individuality and poetic richness erase all stale notions of pedantry or aridity. There is no sense of received wisdom, only a vital act of recreation that captures Bach's masterpiece in all its first glory and magnitude; no simple-minded notions of period style or strict parameters but a moving sense of music of a timeless veracity.

The romantic influences of Furtwängler and Edwin Fischer can be sensed throughout. What a triumphant sense of homecoming he achieves in the Fugue from No 2, what musical rather than academic authenticity in the doubling or filling-out of the Sixth Prelude. His flight through the 15th Prelude is a marvel of lightness and vivacity and in the Fugue from No 17 every voice is given its due without a trace of that heavy underlining beloved by those intent on explaining their explanation.

Purists may quibble over this or that phrase or detail (and few performances of the 48 have been so richly coloured or inflected) but that is surely their loss. For Barenboim, Bach is the most 'romantic' of composers and his imaginative fullness and delicacy laugh to scorn a less bold or inclusive view. How Jacqueline du Pré, Barenboim's late wife, would have warmed to such performances; this is music-making after her own heart. Superb sound.

Das wohltemperirte Clavier – Book 1: Nos 1-12ª; Nos 13-24ᵇ; Book 2: Nos 1-12ᶜ; Nos 13-24ᵈ
ªaAndrei Gavrilov, ᵇJoanna MacGregor, ᶜNikolai Demidenko, ᵈAngela Hewitt
Video directors ªᵇKaren Whiteside, ᶜᵈPeter Mumford
EuroArts ② 𝗗𝗩𝗗 205 0309 (4h 20' · 16:9 · PCM stereo & 5.1 · 0)   Ⓕ

In February 2000 BBC Wales and EuroArts Music co-produced Bach's complete *Well-Tempered Clavier* for television, dividing the work between four very different pianists filmed in four visually distinct venues. Rather than impart a concert performance continuity between the pieces, the directors treat each Prelude and Fugue as a separate entity in terms of lighting, camera angles, placement of the piano, extramusical imagery (kept to a minimum), as well as the pianists' wardrobe and hairstyles.

Collectors familiar with Andrei Gavrilov's romantically tinged, pianistic Bach *French* Suites won't register much surprise as to how he treats Book 1's first 12 Preludes and Fugues. Contrapuntal rigour takes a back seat to melodic nuance and tone colour in his languid, slightly sedate way. It's interesting how his pianism contrasts with the stark visual impact of Walsall's Art Gallery. Conversely, the gothic, shadowy

detail Whiteside conveys in Barcelona's Güell Palace differs from Joanna McGregor's leaner propulsion throughout the rest of Book 1.

While she and Gavrilov use the printed score, Nikolai Demidenko and Angela Hewitt play Book 2 from memory. The plangent clarity of Demidenko's Fazioli concert grand stands out in Nos 1-12 (the other pianists perform on Steinways). Several tempo choices are wayward, such as an over-fast and flippant F minor Prelude. However, his linear clarity in the difficult-to-balance C sharp major Prelude and rhythmic swagger in the D major Prelude greatly impress.

Of the four pianists, Angela Hewitt commands the widest variety of articulations and inner dynamics, together with her finely honed ability to follow Bach's lines through to their final destination without sounding the least bit studied. Cogent examples include the long-lined refinement of the G sharp minor Prelude and Fugue, the G major Prelude's lilting, conversational trajectory, and the B major Prelude's delicate yet firmly centred fingerwork. In the B flat minor Prelude the camera zooms in on Hewitt from above, allowing one to observe how she achieves her superior *legato* through fingers and hand balance alone. Aside from optional titles, the menu offers no bells and whistles to supplement the programme, but the audio engineering boasts ample warmth and presence.

Bach Das wohltemperirte Clavier – BWV847; BWV851; BWV852; BWV854; BWV855; BWV856; BWV857; BWV860; BWV862; BWV864; BWV866
Bach/Busoni Nun komm' der Heiden Heiland, BWV659. Ich ruf' zu dir, Herr Jesu Christ, BWV639. Wachet auf, ruft uns die Stimme, BWV645
Brahms Schmücke dich O liebe Seele, Op 122 No 5
Edna Stern pf
Zig-Zag Territoires ZZT090104 (65' · DDD)   Ⓕ

If you prefer Bach on the piano served up in heaping Romantic portions, accompanied by dollops of creamy tone, tapered phrases and languishing tenutos, Edna Stern's ravishing pianism will turn your ears to jelly. Few modern pianists can pull off this approach, but Stern's sincerity, conviction and masterful control of the instrument prove utterly disarming. Her wide array of *legato* pedallings in the Busoni and Brahms choral prelude arrangements spill over into a selection of Preludes and Fugues from *The Well-Tempered Clavier*, Book 1, without ever obscuring the profile and direction of Bach's contrapuntal lines. Her unpressured fluidity in the F minor Fugue is a case in point. Likewise, the A major Fugue's cross-rhythmic phrases take on a curvaceous, playful character, while the B flat major Prelude's arpeggiated patterns unsystematically alternate between blurry and dry. Stern's *rubato* in the E minor Fugue dismantles the work's toccata-like drive, as if Pablo Casals's cello bow was guiding her fingers. And in contrast to more overtly virtuoso, incisive renditions of the G major Prelude and Fugue, Stern relaxes within her chosen fast tempi. Perhaps her ordering the programme according to key relationships explains how easily each work slips into the next. In short, a disc that will cause unrepentant pianophiles to jump for joy while historically informed performance mavens duck for cover.

and shapely rubato that never threatens to become anachronistic. Her readings of the C minor Fantasia and the *Chromatic* Fantasia and Fugue are as eloquent and stimulating as any yet recorded by a harpsichordist.

Inventions, BWV772-801

15 Two-Part Inventions, BWV772-86. 15 Three-Part Inventions, 'Sinfonias', BWV787-801. French Suite No 5, BWV816
Till Fellner pf
ECM New Series 476 6355 (68' · DDD)　Ⓕ❍●Ⓑ→

While Bach may have conceived his Inventions and Sinfonias as teaching pieces, Till Fellner's intelligent and characterful pianism consistently embraces the music behind the method book. Varied articulations and well conceived scaling of dynamics imbue the pianist's natural propensity for generating singing lines with shapely expression. Cogent examples of this include the E major Invention's subtle off-beat accentuations between the hands, the C major's unpressured dialogues, the D minor's incisive vitality, and the F major Sinfonia's easy bounce and gentle spring. The often protracted D minor Sinfonia retains its melodic poignancy at Fellner's headlong pace, although his tapered phrasing of the F minor Sinfonia's theme grows predictable with each repetition.

Purists may also take issue with the tonal haze and mist resulting from Fellner's liberal pedalling in the E major Sinfonia or, in the G major French Suite, the pianist's soft-grained Allemande and Loure. However, the Sarabande's simple eloquence plus the crisply pointed Bourrée and Gigue more than compensate. All told, the Inventions and Sinfonias in Fellner's hands rank alongside the catalogue's strongest piano versions and benefit from ECM's superior, state-of-the-art engineering.

15 Two-Part Inventions, BWV772-86. 15 Three-Part Inventions, BWV787-801. Chromatic Fantasia and Fugue in D minor, BWV903. Fantasia in C minor, BWV906
Angela Hewitt pf
Hyperion CDA66746 (63' · DDD)　Ⓕ❍Ⓑ→

Angela Hewitt's approach may be gleaned from her refreshingly lucid annotation, or simply by listening to what she does. 'A skilful player can [bring out the different voices] with different colours' and 'To be capable of producing a true *legato* without using the pedal will serve a pianist well in any repertoire.' She puts her fingers where her thoughts are. She never upsets the balance of the lines that it's in the nature of the harpsichord to yield, and her economy with the sustaining pedal helps preserve their clarity.

The two- and three-part Inventions are treated as music in their own right, not simply as invaluable exercises; each is given its distinctive character, with a wonderful variety of sensitive touch

Toccatas, BWV910-16

F sharp minor, **BWV910**; C minor, **BWV911**; D, **BWV912**; D minor, **BWV913**; E minor, **BWV914**; G minor, **BWV915**; G, **BWV916**

Toccatas, BWV910-16
Angela Hewitt pf
Hyperion CDA67310 (69' · DDD)　Ⓕ❍●❍Ⓑ→

As Angela Hewitt tells us in her exemplary accompanying essay, Bach's Toccatas were inspired by Buxtehude's '*stylus fantasticus* – a very unrestrained and free way of composing, using dramatic and extravagant rhetorical gestures'. For Wanda Landowska, they seemed initially 'incoherent and disparate' and it takes an exceptional artist to make such wonders both stand out and unite. Yet Angela Hewitt – always responsive to such a teasing mix of discipline and wildness – presents even the most audacious surprises with a superb and unfaltering sense of balance and perspective. Time and again she shows us that it's possible to be personal and characterful without resorting to self-serving and distorting idiosyncrasy. Everything is delightfully devoid of pedantry or over-emphasis; few pianists have worn their enviable expertise in Bach more lightly. In the F sharp minor Toccata everything is meticulously graded, and in the dazzling D major Toccata, which so fittingly closes her programme, not even Bach's most ebullient virtuosity can induce her to rush; everything emerges with a clarity that never excludes expressive beauty. Her performances could hardly be more stylish or impeccable, more vital or refined; and, as a crowning touch, Hyperion's sound is superb.

Goldberg Variations, BWV988

Goldberg Variations
Murray Perahia pf
Sony Classical SK89243 (73' · DDD)　Ⓕ❍●❍Ⓑ→

 Murray Perahia's *Goldberg* Variations aren't just colourful, or virtuoso, or thorough in terms of repeats, but profoundly moving as well. Here you sense that what's being played isn't so much 'Bach' as an inevitable musical sequence with a life of its own, music where the themes, harmonies and contrapuntal strands await a mind strong enough to connect them.

Rosalyn Tureck was the first recorded Goldbergian to take the structural route, and her EMI/Philips set remains among the most cogent of older alternatives. And while Glenn Gould achieves formidable levels of concentration, his gargantuan personality does occasionally intrude. Perahia brooks neither distraction nor unwanted mannerism. Yes, there are fine-tipped details and prominent emphases, but the way themes are traced and followed through suggests a performance where the shape of a phrase is dictated mostly by its place in the larger scheme of things. Perahia never strikes a brittle note, yet his control and projection of rhythm are impeccable. He can trace the most exquisite *cantabile*, even while attending to salient counterpoint, and although clear voicing is a consistent attribute of his performance, so is flexibility. Like Hewitt, he surpasses himself. It's just that in his case the act of surpassing takes him that little bit further. A wonderful CD.

Goldberg Variations
Angela Hewitt pf
Hyperion CDA67305 (72' · DDD)   Ⓕ**OO**▷

Name your leading interpretative preferences in the *Goldberg Variations*, and there's bound to be someone on disc who expresses them. Leaving aside numerous harpsichord versions, the current catalogue is notably rich in colourful piano alternatives. Two things strike you about Hewitt's *Goldbergs* from the start: first, that she can summon many dynamic grades simultaneously; and second, that her variations between repeats aren't restricted to matters of voicing. For example, in Variation 13, she accelerates her phrases as if caught on a spontaneous impulse, then relaxes for the response. When she plays the variation's first half again she significantly modifies her tone and *rubato*, then opts for a more formal approach to the second half. All this in just over four and a half minutes!

Her mastery of the keyboard is exemplary. She can launch an elegant *staccato* or allow one voice to weave an ivy-like thread, while others argue above it. Beyond a seamless account of the pivotal Variation 25, Hewitt rattles off manic trills in Var 23 and favours a grand, free-wheeling approach for Var 29. This disc is strongly recommended.

Goldberg Variations
Glenn Gould pf
Sony Classical SK93070 (51' · DDD).
Recorded 1981   Ⓕ**OOO**▷

Also available coupled with 1955 Variations on Sony
SM2K87703   Ⓕ▷

 This astonishing performance was recorded 26 years after Gould's legendary 1955 disc (see below). Gould was not in the habit of re-recording but a growing unease with that earlier performance made him turn once again to a timeless masterpiece and try, via a radically altered outlook, for a more definitive account.

By his own admission he had, during those intervening years, discovered 'slowness' or a meditative quality far removed from flashing fingers and pianistic glory. And it's this 'autumnal repose' that adds such a deeply imaginative dimension to Gould's unimpeded clarity and pin-point definition. The Aria is now mesmerically slow. The tremulous confidences of Variation 13 in the 1955 performance give way to something more forthright, more trenchantly and determinedly voiced, while Var 19's previously light and dancing measures are humorously slow and precise. Var 21 is painted in the boldest of oils, so to speak and, most importantly of all, Var 25 is far less romantically susceptible than before and has an almost confrontational assurance. The Aria's return, too, is overwhelming in its profound sense of solace and resolution. This is surely the finest of Gould's recordings.

Goldberg Variations[a]   Ⓗ
Das wohltemperirte Clavier, Book 2 – Nos 33 & 38
Glenn Gould pf
Sony Classical mono SMK52594 (46' · ADD) [a]Recorded
1955   Ⓜ**O**

Also available coupled with 1981 Variations on Sony
SM2K87703   Ⓕ

Gould's pianistic skills have been universally and freely acknowledged, but his musical vision has elicited a range of critical response that has few parallels in this century. The view that Bach was a mere mathematical genius and little more has long passed, but it has its echoes in Gould's approach; he was fascinated by the structure of the music and was supremely skilful in showing the Jacquard-loom patterns woven by its contrapuntal threads. Every structural detail is exposed with crystal clarity, but, switching metaphors, what's revealed is a marvellously designed and executed building, inhabited only by a caretaker. An overall time of 38 minutes doesn't seem unreasonable for the *Goldberg Variations* (here shorn of every repeat) but the statistic is misleading: many variations pass at breakneck speeds. As an exposition of the music's mechanism this is a remarkable performance but, despite occasional intrusions of sing-along and sparing use of the pedals (music first, pianism second), it says little of Bach's humanity.

Two Fugues from the '48' extend the playing time to the lower limit of respectability. Neither is hurried and No 33 proceeds with the solemnity that some others perceived to be its due. The sound quality of the recordings is impressive, but overall this is probably of archival rather than definitive interest.

Goldberg Variations
András Schiff pf
ECM New Series 472 185-2 (71' · DDD)   Ⓕ**O**

Whatever your likes or dislikes in the *Goldbergs*, Schiff will surely elicit a positive reaction, more so than with his 1982 Decca recording, which, though similarly felicitous, had little of the dar-

BACH GOLDBERG VARIATIONS –
IN BRIEF

Murray Perahia pf
Sony Classical SK89243 (73' · DDD)
ⒻⓄⓄⓄ🅑➔
Ⓖ A magnificent achievement combining
superb control of the piano with a probing intellect that's also deeply moving. This is
an outstanding modern performance.

Angela Hewitt pf
Hyperion CDA67305 (72' · DDD)　　ⒻⓄⓄ
The Bach player of our day brings to the
Goldbergs every quality that makes her
approach to this composer so appealing – a
commandingly wide dynamic range and a
palette full of colours. A very fine and
judiciously subtle achievement.

Glenn Gould pf
Sony Classical SMK52594 (78' · ADD)　　ⓂⓄⓄ
Sony Classical SK93070 (72' · ADD)　　ⓂⓄⓄ
Sony Classical offer both Gould's 1955
recording (listed first) and his 1981 remake
(second). The 1955 version has the freshness
of youth and Gould's historic approach to
Bach pianism. The 1981 version has a more
meditative quality that is equally fascinating.
(For an absorbing lesson in developing interpretation try hunting for the twin-pack that
combines both versions – SM2K87703)

Wanda Landowska hpd
EMI mono 567200-2 (73' · ADD)　　ⓂⓄ
A historic document of the woman who put the
harpsichord back on the map. Her Pleyel
instrument makes a fine sound and she plays
with great taste and spirit. It *does* sound its age.

Wilhelm Kempff pf
DG 439 978-2GGA (63' · ADD)　　ⒻⓄ
A great pianist heard in 1969 in a version
that sounds pretty romantic in approach but
which just drips with irresistible musicality
and intelligence.

Kenneth Gilbert hpd
Harmonia Mundi HMA195 1240 (77' · DDD) ⒻⓄⓄ
A deeply impressive performance from a
very serious musician and a very fine harpsichordist: this is not a reading laden with display
but it has an appealing honesty.

András Schiff pf
ECM New Series 472 185-2 (71' · DDD)　　ⒻⓄ
A piano version of these boundlessly fruitful
variations that has much to say and does so
with an appealing style and a greater sense of
danger than on his previous set for Decca.

Julian Rachlin vn **Nobuko Imai** va **Mischa Maisky** vc
DG 477 6378GH (80' · DDD)　　Ⓕ🅑➔
An intriguing piano trio version from three
fine chamber musicians. Worth trying…

ing, imagination and scale of this live remake.
After Perahia's probing intellect, Hewitt's sense
of fantasy and Tureck's sepulchral *gravitas*,
Schiff is the master colourist who, like Gould in
his later Sony recording, achieves impressive
continuity between variations. Contrasts, too,
and never more so than in the sequence of variations Nos 20-22, taking us from brilliantly realised syncopations, to a glowering canon in sevenths, then dipping suddenly for the intimate
stile antico of the four-part Variation 22. As for
overall style, repeats are often embellished,
sometimes radically varied. He has an occasional
tendency to spread chords (Var 15), obviously
loves to dance (the irresistibly lilting Var 18),
relishes an elegant turn of phrase (Var 13) and
has a keen ear for Bach's wit (the tripping exuberance of Var 23). This is a fascinating, beautiful, deeply pondered and profoundly pianistic
account. While not 'authentic' in the scholarly
sense, it's appreciative of Baroque manners and
ornamentation. It's also beautifully recorded on
a mellow, finely tuned Steinway.

Goldberg Variations, BWV988
Andreas Staier hpd
Harmonia Mundi ② (CD + 📀) HMC90 2058
(81' · DDD)　　ⒻⓄⓄ🅑➔

Andreas Staier is clearly in love. Having walked
out with Anthony Sidey's copy of a giant 1734
Hass harpsichord in two previous recital discs,
he here plights his troth by choosing it for his
first *Goldberg Variations*. The instrument has
plenty of seductions – lute stop, buff stop, even
a thunderous 16-foot register – and Staier is
ready to fall under their spell. And why not? It
makes perfect sense to offer a *Goldberg* rich
with the colours made available by the last
flowerings of harpsichord technology, especially as the trend in recent decades for a more
monochrome sound world makes it an exciting
novelty. So sit back and let yourself be wooed
by the sheer 'bigness' of Variations 4, 10
and 29, the other-worldly lute-stop reediness
in No 15 followed by the explosive introduction of the 16-foot in the overture-like No 16,
the partnership of buff and 'natural' registers
delightfully clarifying the crossing-over of
parts in No 20 (echoes of the Moog here), or
the eerie combination of left-hand lute stop
and right-hand 'natural' in the *Black Pearl*,
No 25.

The *Black Pearl*, by the way, also demonstrates to perfection Staier's ability to bring a
complex melodic line to life on the harpsichord with subtle articulation and rhythmic
displacement, a timely reminder that it takes
two to make a good match. Happily, Staier's
effortless virtuosity (hear the trills in Variation 28!) and sensible musicianship go
together to make this a strong *Goldberg* to set
beside admired alternatives. The instrument
is undoubtedly a major star here but that need
not stop us from recognising its player as a
master harpsichordist.

Keyboard Works

Duets, BWV802-05. French Overture in B minor,
BWV831. Italian Concerto, BWV971. Capriccios –
in B flat, BWV992; in E, BWV993
Angela Hewitt pf
Hyperion CDA67306 (69' · DDD)　　Ⓕ**OO**ⴑ

Here is an attractive recital of five varied pieces
or suites of pieces, familiar and not so familiar,
played with Hewitt's expected intelligence and
finish and not a little verve. In her very readable
introduction, Hewitt quotes a contemporary
review of the *Italian Concerto* describing Bach
not only as a great master but as someone 'who
has almost alone taken possession of the clavier',
and whose compositions are exceedingly difficult to play 'because the efficiency of his own
limbs sets his standards'.

They still are, and Hewitt conveys the
feeling that the challenges aren't just to be
met but should be sensed as integral to successful performance. By giving the quick numbers
plenty of pace she makes the music sound
difficult in the right way. No question of
hustling them along, but rather of touching
the core of the rhythmic energy and of making
all the lines, throughout the texture, directional
and lively. Hewitt's isn't a monumental
Bach, rooted to the spot, but one that makes
us curious as to what lies around the next
corner. The brilliant outer movements of
the *Italian Concerto*, the long fugal section
of the *French Overture*, the second and fourth
of the Duets (those extraordinary studies
in two-part writing) are all successes of her
musical dynamic and high-stepping style.
And the Echo movement of the *French
Overture* (track 28) has a positively theatrical
allure, like something out of Rameau –
wonderful!

What she can't disguise, however, is that some
of the movements in this great suite 'in the
French style' lie uneasily on the piano, especially
when the sonorities characteristic of a two-
manual harpsichord are transcribed as if for a
piano without sustaining pedal. If only she'd
allow herself a dab of it now and then; the music
needs to hang in the air a bit, and the 18th-
century harpsichord was, after all, an instrument
of mass as well as point, richer in colour and
weight of sound than Hewitt's pencil-lines and
sometimes rather brittle and over-articulated
manner suggest.

On the other hand, her characterisation of
the two early Capriccios in terms of the modern piano is a *tour de force* – sparky, fresh, as if
improvised. The greatness of the rest of the
music here may put them in the shade, a little,
but they're delightful. Bach aged 17, trying his
hand at programme music? Well, the Capriccio
'on the departure of his beloved brother'
remained his only example of it, but it's a
reminder too that there was nothing he
couldn't do. A stimulating disc, and beautiful
sound.

'Per cembalo solo...'　　Ⓟ
Chromatic Fantasia and Fugue in D minor, BWV903.
Fantasia and Fugue in A minor, BWV904. Fantasia in
C minor, BWV906. Sonata in A minor, BWV965.
Italian Concerto, BWV971. Concerto in D, BWV972
(after Vivaldi: Concerto, Op 3 No 9 RV230).
Concerto in G, BWV973 (after Vivaldi: Concerto,
Op 7 No 8 RV299).
Richard Egarr hpd
Harmonia Mundi HMU90 7329 (79' · DDD)　　Ⓕ**O**

Richard Egarr is the doyen of English
harpsichordists at present, displaying uninhibited virtuosity, rhetorical and dramatic sensibilities, and an ear for refinement of sound. This
discriminating recital combines the familiar
(including a marvellously dapper *Italian Concerto*) with more pragmatic and intimate Bachian
creations which are too often lost in the crevices
of the expert's discography. The two Vivaldi
concertos are idiomatic, thrilling and revealing
exposés of Bach's hands-on approach to mastering new styles. Perhaps more diverting still is the
Fantasia and Fugue in A minor, where Egarr
shrewdly considers the intense coexistence of
contrapuntal and textural relationships in the
fantasia, before a fugue of extraordinary clarity
of interpretative design. This is playing of real
stature.

The remarkable Sonata in A minor, after
Bach's aged spiritual mentor Reinken, might
have been arranged as early as 1703; it's a masterful demonstration of a young man in full
creative flow. Egarr has the edge on Staier's
penetrating but relatively dry execution; here
we have a quasi-Toccata and Fugue of dazzling
colour and affirmation before an Allemande
portrayed with somewhat looser stitching, a
highly affecting manipulation of rhythm. This
exquisite recital ends with the mature, unfinished Fantasia and Fugue in C minor, with
Egarr's own reworking of the fugue.

French Suite No 5 in G, BWV816. Partita No 1　Ⓟ
in B flat, BWV825. Three Minuets, BWV841-43.
Klavierbüchlein for WF Bach – Preludes: C,
BWV924; D, BWV925; D minor, BWV926; F,
BWV927; F, BWV928; G minor, BWV930. Preludes,
BWV939-43. Fugue in C, BWV953. Fughetta in C
minor, BWV961. Italian Concerto, BWV971.
Prelude in C minor, BWV999. Anna Magdalena
Notenbuch – Minuets: G, BWV*Anh*114;
G minor, BWV*Anh*115
Richard Egarr hpd
EMI Debut 569700-2 (78' · DDD)　　Ⓑ**OO**ⴑ

Richard Egarr's programme is an attractive
one in which three major solo harpsichord
works – the Partita (BWV825), the *French Suite*
(BWV816), and the *Italian Concerto* (BWV971)
– are interspersed with Preludes, Minuets
and two Fugues from the Kellner Collection,
the *Clavier-Büchlein* for Wilhelm Friedemann
Bach, 'the son I love, the one who fills me with
joy', and the *Notenbuch* for Bach's second wife,
Anna Magdalena. The character of Egarr's

instrument, a copy by Joel Katzman of a 1638 Ruckers, has been effectively recorded, capturing its warm timbre in an intimate, domestic-sounding ambience.

Egarr's B flat Partita is an unhurried affair, reflective in its Prelude and Allemande and rhythmically supple. Some readers may not at once respond to the extent to which he leans on notes, thereby breaking up that strict regularity of pulse that used to be the order of the day. His articulation and rhythmic flexibility are both illuminating and communicative. The music breathes, and with each breath comes a natural pause in the declamation allowing for rhetorical gesture and a feeling for scansion. Just occasionally in the Sarabande phrases are a little too clipped and skimped over, but such instances, both here and in the *French Suite*, are both few and far between. Each of the little Preludes and Minuets is lovingly shaped and played with a sense of affection for, and understanding of, the music's poetry. In short this is an outstanding disc, both for Egarr's technically accomplished playing and for his delicacy of feeling.

'The Secret Bach' Ⓟ
Partite diverse sopra 'O Gott, du frommer Gott', BWV767. Klavierbüchlein für WF Bach – Menuet in G, BWV841; Menuet in G, BWV843; Allemande in G minor, BWV836. Chromatic Fantasia and Fugue in D minor, BWV903a. Adagio in G, BWV968. Fugue in G minor, BWV1000. Violin Partita No 2 in D minor, BWV1004 (arr Mortensen)
Christopher Hogwood clav
Metronome METCD1056 (72' · DDD) Ⓕ

Christopher Hogwood's incisive mind regularly leads to strong and imaginative concepts: this, the first of a series of clavichord discs dedicated to Bach, Handel, Haydn, Mozart and Beethoven, is a perfect example. The clavichord has a history of domestic usage, the intimate nature of its utterances seeming both exquisite and slightly enigmatic. Its main mechanical feature of stretching strings gives the player the 'touch' to grade dynamics, alter pitch through vibrating and other idiomatic colouring. We know that Bach loved the instrument. Hogwood uses three clavichords of very particular tonal quality. In his thoughtful and devotional reading of *O Gott, du frommer Gott*, he plays a Schmahl copy from Finchcocks with a lovely cushioned and even tone. A Bodechtel clavichord provides contrast for the shorter vignettes, while a larger Hass is used for the *Chromatic* Fantasia and the Partita in A minor (a transcription of the violin Partita in D minor) – it's as extrovert and bold as you get with a clavichord. The chaconne, arranged by Lars Ulrik Mortensen, contains a few questionable harmonic and figurative quirks, but Hogwood glides through them fluidly and genially. It leads the mind and ears into revitalised pastures of how this music can be experienced afresh.

Bach Italian Concerto, BWV971. Partitas – No 1, BWV825: excerpts; No 5, BWV829; No 6, BWV830. French Suite No 5, BWV816 – Gigue. Jesu, Joy of Man's Desiring (arr M Hess) **Beethoven** Piano Sonata No 17, 'Tempest', Op 31 No 2. Bagatelle, Op 33 No 1
Walter Gieseking pf
Naxos Historical mono 8 111353 (79' · ADD)
Recorded 1931-40 ⓈⓄ▸

Although Gieseking's phenomenal aural sensitivity earned him a unique reputation in French piano music, his repertoire was all-embracing. All the more reason then to celebrate Naxos's release of Gieseking's Bach and Beethoven made when this unique artist was at the height of his career. Here you will search in vain for the sort of muddles or confusions that would sometimes plague his performances (evidence of his proud boast that he did little practice).

His Bach has a peerless lightness, grace and natural beauty, the reverse of Teutonic earnestness and heaviness. The *Andante* from the *Italian Concerto*, a tirelessly ornamented aria, is given with an enviable poise and lucidity while in the Gigue from the First Partita his playing is, again, the opposite of a more familiar cold-hearted virtuosity, making you regret that there are only excerpts from this exquisite masterpiece. In the Fifth Partita (given complete) Gieseking shows the most subtle virtuosity and is no less convincing in the Sixth Partita's more strenuous and concentrated demands.

Beethoven's *Tempest* Sonata is given without first- or last-movement repeats and is taken, in those outer movements, at such a pace that there are occasional dangers that the music's character is whisked out of existence (the finale is, after all, marked *allegretto*). For encores there are Beethoven's E flat Bagatelle from Op 33 and the Bach-Hess *Jesu, Joy of Man's Desiring* where Gieseking plays with admirable restraint while not quite equalling Dame Myra's own inimitable poise.

The Art of Fugue, BWV1080

The Art of Fugue
Pierre-Laurent Aimard pf
DG 477 7345GH (79' · DDD) ⒻⓄ▸

This is Bach-playing to listen to every day, fresh, spry and well modulated. If spirituality is to be found in *The Art of Fugue*, Aimard seems to say, it will not be through slow tempi, dynamic extremes or the quasi-religious trappings arrayed by the likes of Sokolov, Kocsis, Koroliov and Nikolaieva. The tripping, French swagger of Contrapuncti 2 and 6 and the smart Italian cut of No 9 fit neatly under the fingers. Freedom is found within the interplay of voices rather than any fancy phrasing: in fact the mirror fugues and canons are so unfussily done that you'd never guess without a score to hand how much a single musician can look and sound like Mr Messy while playing them.

This is not to imply dryness or inflexibility on Aimard's part. He follows Tovey in finding

No 3 to be 'one of Bach's most beautiful pieces of quiet chromatic slow music', after which the extraordinary cadences of No 4 are necessarily pedalled and clipped, even chirpy: the envoi of a true Kapellmeister. The great unfinished fugue is especially fascinating, gradually accumulating kinesis until the surge of B-A-C-H pulls us towards its unattained apotheosis with colossal force. Applied with more plain-spoken authority, such emphatic strength of wrist and will rather chews up the Tenth's preludial bars and the expansive, chorale-fantasia conclusion of the Fifth, though with equal force one senses that, in this case, they had to be so. Perhaps no pianist since Charles Rosen has so persuasively demonstrated that this contrapuntal encyclopedia is to be heard as well as read.

are expected to relate speed to time signatures without other guidance – Fretwork's judgements are difficult to fault. Turn to the Canon alla Duodecima, or alternatively Contrapunctus 9, where the required swift pulse does not preclude expressive articulation; and then to Contrapunctus 10, where four-in-a-bar is reflected in a slower pace that also allows more space for a keener, but not overt, subjective response. Indeed, throughout their idiomatically phrased, impressively cohesive and clean-textured exploration of the work, these thoughtful musicians don't italicise anything.

In sum, Fretwork opt for a quiet, controlled intensity that perhaps needs extended listening to be fully appreciated. The recording certainly won't stand in your way. It's expertly balanced, the acoustic giving both ambience and intimacy.

Bach The Art of Fugue – Contrapuncti 1-11; Ⓟ
Fuga **Mozart** Five Fugues, K405. Fugue in G minor, K401/K375e
Phantasm (Laurence Dreyfus, Wendy Gillespie, Jonathan Manson, Markku Luolajan-Mikkola viols)
3Imax PSC1135 (65' · DDD) Ⓗ Ⓞ

Seeing that we enjoy Bach and Mozart on a modern piano, should we demur at their music being played on an equally anachronistic consort of viols? Leaving aside the argument advanced in Laurence Dreyfus's note that much viol consort music was fugal in texture anyway, the fact is that the contrapuntal lines here emerge with great clarity and with a subtlety of timbre, articulation and dynamics beyond even the ablest keyboard player, thanks to Phantasm's accomplished and expressive performances.

The group offers the first 11 Contrapuncti, without the canons or mirror fugues, but plus the final uncompleted *chef d'oeuvre* that was to have crowned the project; Phantasm's playing offers new insights into Bach's prodigious mind. In his transcriptions for string quartet of fugues from the '48', Mozart – who, it's reported, constantly had Bach's volume lying open on his piano – made a few small adjustments to details of rhythm and part-writing; and the process also fired him to write several fugues of his own, including the one in G minor (for piano solo or duet) here. Phantasm, despite a slight tendency to hurry, brings a smile to the lips by its intonation, precision and, above all, musicality.

The Art of Fugue Ⓟ
Fretwork (Richard Boothby, Richard Campbell, Wendy Gillespie, Julia Hodgson, William Hunt, Susanna Pell viols)
Harmonia Mundi HMU90 7296 (76' · DDD) Ⓕ Ⓞ Ⓞ

Though *The Art of Fugue* is usually considered a composition for keyboard, the timbre of strings, especially viols played and reproduced this way, does give the music another dimension.

Though there are no tempo directions for the 20 pieces that comprise this work – performers

---

Organ Trio Sonatas, BWV525-30

No **1** in E flat, BWV525 No **2** in C minor, BWV526
No **3** in D minor, BWV527 No **4** in E minor, BWV528
No **5** in C, BWV529 No **6** in G, BWV530

Trio Sonatas Nos 1-6
Kay Johannsen org
Hänssler Classic CD92 099 (78' · DDD).
Recorded on the Metzler organ of the Stadtkirche, Stein am Rhein, Switzerland Ⓕ Ⓞ Ⓞ

Kay Johannsen's performance is distinguished by uniformly stylish, immaculately tailored readings of the Trio Sonatas. Johannsen has verve, spirit and musical persuasiveness, the organ is ideal both for these sparkling performances and the transparency of the musical textures (and Johannsen has chosen a glorious Swiss Metzler – this time the 1992 instrument in the Municipal Church of Stein am Rhein), and Hänssler Classic's recording has exceptional presence and clarity.

Schübler Chorales, BWV645-50

Preludes and Fugues – C, BWV545; E flat, BWV552, 'St Anne'. Trio Sonata in E minor, BWV528. Largo in A minor, BWV529. Fantasia in C minor, BWV562. Schübler Chorales, BWV645-50
Piet Kee org
Chandos Chaconne CHAN0590 (66' · DDD)
Recorded on the Schnitger organ of the Martinikerk, Groningen, Netherlands Ⓕ Ⓞ Ⓓ ➔

This is playing of heart-warming humanity and spiritual equilibrium, combining deep thought with complete spontaneity. Kee's control of the long, singing line goes hand in hand with a poetic command of Baroque instrumental articulation. Dip anywhere into the Schübler Chorales or to either of the Trio Sonata slow movements and you can hear the separate melodic lines not only given individual character, shape and direction but also combined with ease and gentle authority. Tempos in extrovert move-ments are unusually moderate, Bach's markings of *Vivace* and *Allegro* being taken by Kee as indi-cations of mood rather than velocity, and yet the musical discourse is involving and full of wit, helped by registrations that are both simple and wise. The disc is crowned by a magnificent per-formance of the Prelude and Fugue in E-flat, one that fully exploits the vivid contrasts of theme and texture and yet binds the work into a structural unity without a hint of haste or stiff-ness. Rightly, the recording presents this refined, robust organ as heard within its natural acoustic habitat and Kee has subtly absorbed the church's acoustic into his interpretations.

Clavier-Übung III, BWV669-89

Clavier-Übung III, BWV669-89. Duets, BWV802-05.
Fugue in E flat, BWV552 No 2
Kay Johannsen org
Hänssler Edition Bachakademie ② 92 101 (100' · DDD)
Recorded on the Erasmus-Bielfeldt organ,
St Wilhadi, Stade   Ⓕ**O**

These discs transport the listener back to 1736, the date of the Erasmus-Bielfeldt organ recorded here. Three years later Bach published the third part of his *Clavier-Übung*, an academically aus-tere title which disguises one of his most sym-bolic and liturgically important cycles. He had high hopes for the commercial success of the volume and its successor, the *Goldberg Varia-tions*. The *Clavier-Übung* features the so-called Organ Mass. A Hymn Mass, it uses Lutheran texts and melodies in one major and several minor arrangements.

The two discs open and close with the Prelude and Fugue in E flat, BWV552. From the Prelude's first notes it's clear that Johan-nsen's playing is of the highest calibre. There's emotional involvement without a superfluity of ornamentation and *rubato*. Here, too, is tenderness, flamboyance, attack and rhythmic drive. In Johannsen's hands the listener is sub-tly drawn to the core of the music, its complex-ity simplified through his beautifully balanced registrations. Highlights include the extended prelude on *Vater unser im Himmelreich*, BWV682, and those on *Aus tiefer Not*, BWV686/687.

The Four Duets are stylistically related and unified through an ascending key sequence which, as the notes mention, represent the Passion, Easter, Ascension and Pentecost. The superb booklet includes notes on the individ-ual registrations employed. First-rate record-ing quality.

Chorale Preludes, BWV1090-1120

Chorale Preludes – Neumeister Collection,
BWV1090-1120; Ach Gott und Herr, BWV714;
Der Tag, der ist freudenreich, BWV719; Vater unser
im Himmelreich, BWV737; Ach Herr, mich armen

Sünder, BWV742; Machs mit mir, Gott, nach deiner
Güt, BWV957
Christopher Herrick org
Hyperion CDA67215 (80' · DDD)   Ⓕ

These 38 chorale preludes come from a collection of 83 pieces compiled in the 18th century by Johann Gottfried Neumeister that eventually made its way to Yale University, where it was discovered by the Bach scholar Christoph Wolff. Bach's preludes are early works, and as Wolff so aptly wrote: 'Already there is innovation. There's a degree of original-ity and sophistication that is really quite remark-able.' Herrick gives clear, attractive perform-ances with rhythmic articulation and lively ornamentation. Some listeners may find his playing too calculated and self-conscious, but these are sprightly readings, free of excessive mannerism. The most enjoyable aspect of the CD is the way Herrick gives each chorale prel-ude its own distinct sound world, despite having only a nine-stop, one-manual Metzler organ. This instrument is one of the most beautiful organs imaginable, and Herrick achieves a pleasing variety of colour. Some may find the organ a little too closely miked.

Organ Works

Trio Sonata No 1 in E flat, BWV525. Fantasia and
Fugue in G minor, BWV542. Toccata and Fugue in
D minor, BWV565. Pastorale in F, BWV590. Organ
Concerto No 1 in G, BWV592. Erbarm' dich mein,
O Herre Gott, BWV721. Aus tiefer Not schrei ich
zu dir, BWV1099
Kevin Bowyer org
Nimbus NI5280 (67' · DDD)
Recorded on the Marcussen organ of St Hans Kirke,
Odense, Denmark   Ⓕ

This disc includes the best-known of all Bach's organ pieces – although some would dispute that it's an organ piece or even that Bach wrote it; Bowyer's account of the Toccata and Fugue in D minor is invigorating, exciting and very fast. It sets the scene for a CD of virtuoso performances and sound musicianship. The whole is a well-cho-sen, self-contained programme which also includes an indisputably 'great' organ work, a Trio Sonata, a transcription Bach made of an effervescent concerto by Ernst, a youthful chorale prelude as well as one from a collection only dis-covered in 1985 and one real oddity. Much thought has gone into the choice of organ and this instrument serves its purpose admirably; roaring magnificently in the *Fantasia* and emulating the tranquil sounds so characteristic of the *Pastorale*.

Kevin Bowyer's Nimbus recordings of the complete Bach organ works are now also available as an eight-disc set of MP3 files at budget price.

Short Preludes and Fugues, BWV553-60. Fantasia
con imitazione in B minor, BWV563. Fugue in

C minor, BWV575. Toccatas – G minor, BWV915;
G, BWV916. Fugues on themes of Albinoni –
A, BWV950; B minor, BWV951
Kevin Bowyer org
Nimbus NI5377 (74' · DDD)
Recorded on the Marcussen organ of St Hans Kirke,
Odense, Denmark   (F)

Critical opinion and academic argument may deter others, but Bowyer is content to let the music speak for itself, whether it's 'by JS Bach, JL Krebs or AN Other'. The music here speaks with absolute conviction. A gloriously dramatic rhetoric is brought to the two toccatas (BWV915 and 916). Harpsichordists may claim these as their own, but who could deny this lovely Odense organ the opportunity to glitter with such flamboyant music? The eight 'short' Preludes and Fugues have a muscular, clean-shaven feel to them underlined by plain and simple registrations. While other recordings of such indefinable pieces seem like scraps from the cutting-room floor, Bowyer sets them firmly in the mainstream of high Baroque organ music.

Prelude and Fugue in A minor, BWV551. Trio in C minor, BWV585. Canzona in D minor, BWV588. Wo soll ich fliehen hin, BWV694. Christum wir sollen loben schon, BWV696. Nun komm, der Heiden Heiland, BWV699. Gottes Sohn ist kommen, BWV703. In dich hab' ich gehoffet, BWV712. Fantasia: Jesu, meine Freude, BWV713. Ach Gott und Herr, BWV714. Gelobet seist du, Jesu Christ, BWV723. Lobt Gott, ihr Christen gmein, BWV732. Nun freut euch, lieben Christen g'mein, BWV734. Wie schön leucht' der Morgenstern, BWV739. Ach Gott, vom Himmel sieh' darein, BWV741. Auf meinen lieben Gott, BWV744. Herr Jesu Christ, mein's Lebens Licht, BWV750. O Vater, allmächtiger Gott, BWV758. Vater unser im Himmelreich, BWV762. Wie schön leuchtet der Morgenstern, BWV763. Prelude and Fugue in A minor, BWV894. Toccatas – D, BWV912; D minor, BWV913. Concerto in D minor, BWV974.
Kevin Bowyer org
Nimbus ③ NI5669/70 (3h 19' · DDD)
Recorded on the Marcussen organ of St Hans Kirke,
Odense, Denmark   (F)O

This is probably by far and away the best release so far in this comprehensive survey of Bach's organ works. What distinguishes it is, first of all, the recorded sound, which has lost that underlying feeling of artificiality in its mix between instrument and acoustic which has occasionally surfaced in previous Nimbus recordings from the Hanskirche in Odense. Most of all, however, the outstanding feature is Bowyer's own playing. Always able to come up with enjoyable and eminently listenable performances as a result of his phenomenal technique and intense musicianship, his playing here has real authority. There may be stylistic quibbles (Bowyer's ornamentation can be a little too sparing), but few would argue that the playing lacks real understanding of the music's essential spirit. You sense here a level of empa-thy with the world of Bach which has been missing from earlier releases. The chorale preludes are sweet sounding but really do sound like the musings of a great master on both the chorale melodies and their texts, while the handful of large-scale display works here seem to look beyond superficial virtuosity and into the mind of a composer for whom every note of music (good or mediocre) was of real intrinsic value. Those not so far tempted to explore this gargantuan series could do a lot worse than invest in this release.

Allein Gott in der Höh sei Ehr: BWV715; BWV717; BWV711; BWV260. Christ lag in Todesbanden: BWV4[a]; BWV695. Fugue on a Theme by Corelli in B minor, BWV579. Herr Jesu Christ, dich zu uns wend: BWV332[a]; BWV655. Jesus Christus unser Heiland: BWV363[a]; BWV688. Preludes and Fugues – C minor, BWV549; G, BWV550; E flat, BWV552. Prelude in A minor, BWV569. O Lamm Gottes, unschuldig: BWV401[a]; BWV618. Schmücke dich, o liebe Seele: BWV180[a]; BWV654. Trio Sonata No 1 in E flat, BWV525. Valet will ich dir geben· BWV415[a]; BWV736
[a]**Caroline Magalhaes** mez [a]**Philippe Froeliger** ten
Francis Jacob org
Zig-Zag Territoires ② ZZT001001 (90' · DDD)
Recorded on the Aubertin organ of the Parish Church, Saessolsheim, Alsace   (F)O

This might look like just another organ recital, but in reality it celebrates the remarkable phil-anthropy of a small Alsatian community who have collectively funded, over nine years, a beautiful organ in Saessolsheim in the north of Alsace. Here it's played by a local son, Francis Jacob, an accomplished young player whose programme is an imaginative cross-section of Bach's organ works. He's not afraid to play a fugue without a prelude if he feels it serves the greater architectural good of the programme. Indeed, his ideals of passing through carefully ordered genres, keys and colourific possibili-ties are engaging and perceptive.

The performances are striking for the ebullience and vitality of Jacob's fast playing, which is rhythmically assured and with a strong feel for instrumental timbre, not just organ sound – the key to discovering allusions and subtexts as the Bach player must. Lift and imme-diacy of articulation prevail over endless swathes of *legato*. How refreshing it is to hear such glowing colours in the opening chorale prelude, *Valet will ich dir geben*.

However invigorating Jacob's playing though, there's a tendency to resist the poetic instinct, as if he's mistaking it for indulgence. *Schmücke dich* sounds unyielding, calculated and even wearing. He produces an idiosyncratic equivalent in the middle movement of the Trio Sonata in C major (what possessed him to break this restful melody up into little squares?), and yet all is forgiven in a deeply touching *O Lamm Gottes*, a chorale marvellously disguised as a taut canonic web irradiating ethereal harmonic consequences –

this is where the expressive effect of dissonance is more at consonance with the underlying conceit than consonance could ever be! Jacob rattles off *Allein Gott* with supreme dexterity, and the dazzling upper partials are further evident in a compellingly neurotic reading of the A minor Prelude.

The programme of two short CDs ends with the E flat *St Anne* Fugue, not as grand or mature in conception as some, but carefully considered and, like most of this recording, it conveys a notably immediate, 'one-off' and animated musical presence.

Preludes and Fugues – E minor, BWV533; G minor, BWV535; D minor, BWV539; D minor, BWV549a; G, BWV550. Prelude in A minor, BWV551. Fantasia in A minor, BWV561. Fantasia con imitazione in B minor, BWV563. Toccata and Fugue in E, BWV566. Preludes – in G, BWV568; A minor, BWV569. Fantasia in C, BWV570. Fugues – C minor, BWV575; G, BWV576; G, BWV577, 'Jig Fugue'; G minor, BWV578. Trios – D minor, BWV583; C minor, BWV585; G, BWV586. Aria in F, BWV587. Canzona in D minor, BWV588. Allabreve in D, BWV589. Pastorale in F, BWV590. Four Duets, BWV802-05. Trio Sonata in G, BWV1027a. Musikalisches Opfer, BWV1079 – Ricercar a 3; Ricercar a 6
Christopher Herrick *org*
Hyperion ③ CDA67211/2 (156' · DDD)
Recorded on the organ of the Stadtkirche,
Rheinfelden, Switzerland   Ⓕ**OOᐅ**

Some might be tempted to describe what we have here as the 'scrapings from the barrel', for when you've taken out the chorale-based works, the trio sonatas, the concertos and the big preludes, fantasias, toccatas, passacaglias and fugues this is what's left. However, you could be tempted almost to prefer these crumbs from the table of great genius to those stupendous musical feasts which are everybody's idea of the real JS Bach. And when you have those crumbs seasoned with such loving care, such elegance and such finesse as Christopher Herrick gives to, say, the G minor fugue (BWV578) or the enchanting Trio Sonata (BWV1027a), you realise that here's music every bit as worthy of close attention as anything Bach wrote for the organ. In matters of registration, tempo, articulation and phrasing, Herrick displays immaculate taste.

This is playing of the very highest order. The modest two-manual Metzler, built in 1992, makes an enchanting sound, and the recording fully supports the superlative artistry of the playing.

Sacred Cantatas

No 1 Wie schön leuchtet der Morgenstern; No 2 Ach Gott, vom Himmel sieh darein; No 3 Ach Gott, wie manches Herzeleid; No 4 Christ lag in Todes Banden; No 5 Wo soll ich fliehen hin; No 6 Bleib bei uns; No 7 Christ unser Herr zum Jordan kam; No 8 Liebster Gott, wenn werd ich sterben?; No 9 Es ist das Heil uns kommen her; No 10 Meine Seel erhebt den Herren; No 11 Lobet Gott in seinen Reichen (Ascension Oratorio); No 12 Weinen, Klagen, Sorgen, Zagen; No 13 Meine Seufzer, meine Tränen; No 14 Wär Gott nicht mit uns diese Zeit; No 15 (spurious); No 16 Herr Gott, dich loben wir; No 17 Wer Dank opfert, der preiset mich; No 18 Gleichwie der Regen und Schnee; No 19 Es erhub sich ein Streit; No 20 O Ewigket, du Donnerwort

No 21 Ich hatte viel Bekümmernis; No 22 Jesus nahm zu sich die Zwölfe; No 23 Du wahrer Gott und Davids Sohn; No 24 Ein ungefärbt Gemüte; No 25 Es ist nich Gesundes an meinem Liebe; No 26 Ach wie flüchtig, ach wie nichtig; No 27 We weiss, wie nahe mir mein Ende; No 28 Gottlob! nun gebt das Jahr zu Ende; No 29 Wir danke dir, Gott; No 30 Freue dich, erlöste Schar; No 31 Der Himmel lacht! die Erde jubilieret; No 32 Liebster Jesu, mein Verlangen; No 33 Allein zu dir, Herr Jesu Christ; No 34 O ewiges Feuer, O Ursprung der Liebe; No 35 Geist und Seele wird verwirret; No 36 Schwingt freudig euch empor; No 37 Wer da gläubet und getauft wird; No 38 Aus tiefer Not schrei ich zu dir; No 39 Brich dem Hungrigen dein Brot; No 40 Dazu ist erschienen der Sohn Gottes

No 41 Jesu, nun sei gepreiset; No 42 Am Abend aber desselbigen Sabbats; No 43 Gott fähret auf mit Jauchzen; No 44 Sie werden euch in die Bann tun; No 45 Es ist dir gesagt, Mensch, was gut ist; No 46 Schauet doch und sehet; No 47 Wer sich selbst erhöhet; No 48 Ich elender Mensch, wer wird mich erlösen; No 49 Ich geh und suche mit Verlangen; No 50 Nun ist das Heil und die Kraft; No 51 Jauchzet Gott in allen Landen!; No 52 Falsche Welt, dir trau ich nicht; No 53 (spurious); No 54 Widerstehe doch der Sünde; No 55 Ich armer Mensch, ich Sündenknecht; No 56 Ich will den Kreuzstab gerne tragen; No 57 Selig ist der Mann; No 58 Ach Gott, wie manches Herzeleid; No 59 Wer mich liebet, der wird mein Wort halten; No 60 O Ewigkeit, du Donnerwort

No 61 Nun komm, der Heiden Heiland; No 62 Nun komm, der Heiden Heiland; No 63 Christen, ätzet diesen Tag; No 64 Sehet, welch eine Liebe; No 65 Sie werden aus Saba alle kommen; No 66 Erfreut euch, ihr Herzen; No 67 Halt im Gedächtnis Jesum Christ; No 68 Also hat Gott die Welt geliebet; No 69 Lobe den Herrn, meine Seele; No 70 Wachet! betet! betet! wachet!; No 71 Gott ist mein König; No 72 Alles nur nach Gottes Willen; No 73 Herr, wie du willt, so schicks mit mir; No 74 Wie mich liebet, der wird mein Wort halten; No 75 Die Elenden sollen essen; No 76 Die Himmel erzählen die Ehre Gottes; No 77 Du sollt Gott, deinen Herren, lieben; No 78 Jesu, der du meine Seele; No 79 Gott der Herr ist Sonn und Schild; No 80 Ein feste Burg ist unser Gott; No 81 Jesus schläft, was soll ich hoffen?; No 82 Ich habe genug; No 83 Erfreute Zeit im neuen Bunde; No 84 Ich bin vergnügt mit meinem Glücke; No 85 Ich bin ein guter Hirt; No 86 Wahrlich, wahrlich, ich sage euch; No 87 Bisher habt ihr nichts gebeten; No 88 Siehe, ich will viel Fischer aussenden; No 89 Was soll ich aus dir machen, Ephraim?; No 90 Es reisset euch ein schrecklich Ende; **No 91** Gelobet seist du, Jesu Christ; **No 92** Ich hab in Gottes Herz und Sinn; **No 93** Wer nur den lieben Gott lässt walten; **No 94** Was frag ich nach der Welt; **No 95** Christus, der ist mein Leben; **No 96** Herr Christ, der einge Gottessohn; **No 97** In allen meinene Taten; **No 98** Was Gott tut, das ist wohlgetan; **No 99** Was Gott tut, das ist wohlgetan; **No 100** Was Gott tut, das ist wohlgetan

No 101 Nimm von uns, Herr, du treuer Gott; **No 102** Herr, deine Augen sehen nach dem Glauben; **No 103** Ihr werdet weinen und heulen; **No 104** Du Hirte Israel, höre; **No 105** Herr, gehe nicht ins Gericht; **No 106** Gottes Zeit ist die allerbeste Zeit, 'Actus tragicus'; **No 107** Was willst du dich betrüben; **No 108** Es ist euch gut, dass ich hingehe; **No 109** Ich glaube, lieber Herr, hilf meinem Unglauben!; **No 110** Unser Mund sei voll Lachens; **No 111** Was mein Gott will, das g'scheh allzeit; **No 112** Der Herr ist mein getreuer Hirt; **No 113** Herr Jesu Christ, du höchstes Gut; **No 114** Ach, lieben Christen, seid getrost; **No 115** Mache dich, mein Geist, bereit; **No 116** Du Friedefürst, Herr Jesu Christ; **No 117** Sei Lob und Ehr dem höchsten Gut; **No 118** O Jesu Christ, mein Lebens Licht; **No 119** Preise Jerusalem, den Herrn; **No 120a** Herr Gott, Beherrscher aller Dinge; **No 120b** Gott, man lobet dich in der Stille

No 121 Christum wir sollen loben schon; **No 122** Das neugeborne Kindelein; **No 123** Liebster Immanuel, Herzog der Frommen; **No 124** Meinen Jesum lass ich nicht; **No 125** Mit Fried und Freud ich fahr dahin; **No 126** Erhalt uns, Herr, bei deinem Wort; **No 127** Herr Jesu Christ, wahr' Mensch und Gott; **No 128** Auf Christi Himmelfahrt allein; **No 129** Gelobet sei der Herr, mein Gott; **No 130** Herr Gott, dich loben alle wir; **No 131** Aus der Tiefen rufe ich, Herr, zu dir; **No 132** Bereitet die Wege, bereitet di Bahn!; **No 133** Ich freue mich in dir; **No 134** Ein Herz, das seinen Jesum lebend weiss; **No 135** Ach Herr, mich armen Sünder; **No 136** Erforsche mich, Gott, und erfahre mein Herz; **No 137** Lobe den Herren, den mächtigen König der Ehren; **No 138** Warum berübst du dich, mein Herz?; **No 139** Wohl dem, der sich auf seinen Gott; **No 140** Wachet auf, ruft uns die Stimme

Nos 141-42 (spurious); **No 143** Lobe den Herr, meine Seele; **No 144** Nimm, was dein ist, und gehe hin; **No 145** Ich lebe, mein Herze, zu deinem Ergötzen; **No 146** Wir müssen durch viel Trübsal; **No 147** Herz und Mund und Tat und Leben; **No 148** Bringet dem Herrn Ehre seines Namens; **No 149** Man singet mit Freuden vom Sieg; **No 150** Nach dir, Herr, verlanget mich; **No 151** Süsser Trost, mein Jesus kömmt; **No 152** Tritt auf die Glaubensbahn; **No 153** Schau, lieber Gott, wie meine Feind; **No 154** Mein liebster Jesus ist verloren; **No 155** Mein Gott, wie lang, ach lange; **No 156** Ich steh mit einem Fuss im Grabe; **No 157** Ich lasse dich nicht, du segnest mich denn; **No 158** Der Friede sei mit dir; **No 159** Sehet, wir gehn hinauf gen Jerusalem

No 160 (spurious); **No 161** Komm, du süsse Todesstunde; **No 162** Ach! ich sehe, jetzt, da ich zur Hochzeit gehe; **No 163** Nur jedem das Seine; **No 164** Ihr, die ihr euch von Christo nennet; **No 165**

O heilges Geist- und Wasserbad; **No 166** Wo gehest du hin?; **No 167** Ihr Menschen, rühmet Gottes Liebe; **No 168** Tue Rechnung! Donnerwort; **No 169** Gott soll allein mein Herze haben; **No 170** Vergnügte Ruh', beliebte Seelenlust; **No 171** Gott, wie dein Name, so ist auch dein Ruhm; **No 172** Erschallet, ihr Lieder; **No 173** Erhöhtes Fleisch und Blut; **No 174** Ich liebe den Höchsten von ganzem Gemüte; **No 175** Er rufet seinen Schafen mit Namen; **No 176** Es ist ein trotzig, und verzagt Ding; **No 177** Ich ruf zu dir, Herr Jesu Christ; **No 178** Wo Gott der Herr nicht bei uns hält; **No 179** Siehe zu, dass deine Gottesfurcht; **No 180** Schmücke dich, o liebe Seele

No 181 Leichtgesinnte Flattergeister; **No 182** Himmelskönig, sei willkommen; **No 183** Sie werden euch in den Bann tun; **No 184** Erwünschtes Freudenlicht; **No 185** Barmherziges Herze der ewigen Liebe; **No 186** Ärgre dich, o Seele, nicht; **No-187** Es wartet alles auf dich; **No 188** Ich habe meine Zuversicht; **No 189** (spurious); **No 190** Singet dem Herrn ein neues Lied!; **No 191** Gloria in excelsis Deo; **No 192** Nun danket alle Gott; **No 193** Ihr Tore zu Zion; **No 194** Höchsterwünschtes Freudenfest; **No 195** Dem Gerechten muss das Licht; **No 196** Der Herr denket an uns; **No 197** Gott ist unsre Zuversicht; **No 197a** Ehre sei Gott in der Höhe; **No 198** Lass Fürstin, lass noch einen Strahl, 'Trauer Ode'; **No 199** Mein Herze schwimmt in Blut; **No 200** Bekennen will ich seinen Namen

---

Volume 1 – Nos 16, 33, 37, 42, 56, 61, 72, 80, Ⓟ 82, 97, 113, 132, 133, 170. **Volume 2** – Nos 22, 23, 44, 54, 57, 85, 86, 92, 98, 111, 114, 135, 155, 159, 165, 167, 188. **Volume 3** – Nos 17, 35, 87, 90, 99, 106, 117, 123, 153, 161, 168, 172, 173, 182, 199. **Volume 4** – Nos 7, 13, 45, 69, 81, 102, 116, 122, 130, 138, 144, 149, 150, 169, 196. **Volume 5** – Nos 6, 26, 27, 46, 55, 94, 96, 107, 115, 139, 156, 163, 164, 178, 179. **Volume 6** – Nos 2, 3, 8, 60, 62, 78, 93, 103, 128, 145, 151, 154, 171, 185, 186, 192. **Volume 7** – Nos 9, 36, 47, 73, 91, 110, 121, 125, 129, 152, 157, 166, 184, 198. **Volume 8** – Nos 18, 30, 40, 49, 79, 84, 88, 89, 100, 108, 136, 140, 176, 187, 194. **Volume 9** – Nos 1, 5, 14, 20, 32, 38, 50, 51, 58, 63, 83, 104, 109, 162, 183, 195. **Volume 10** – Nos 21, 25, 28, 39, 43, 48, 52, 59, 65, 75, 119, 137, 143, 146, 175, 180, 197. **Volume 11** – Nos 4, 10, 12, 64, 70, 71, 74, 76, 95, 101, 105, 124, 127, 131, 134, 158, 177. **Volume 12** – Nos 19, 24, 29, 31, 34, 41, 66, 67, 68, 77, 112, 120, 126, 147, 148, 174, 181
Ruth Holton, Marjon Strijk sops **Sytse Buwalda** counterten **Marcel Beekman, Martinus Leusink, Nico van der Meel, Knut Schoch** tens **Bas Ramselaar** bass **Holland Boys Choir; Netherlands Bach Collegium / Pieter Jan Leusink**
Brilliant Boxes (12 five-disc sets) 99363/99364/ 99367/99368/99370/99371/99373/99374/99377-80 (61h 31' · DDD · T) Ⓢ⊙

Brilliant Classics, through licensing and creative plundering of old catalogues, has contrived its own Bach Edition. Rather more surprising is that within this patchwork of miscellaneous performances comes a brand new set of the complete cantatas. How on earth can such a project be viable as a realistic competitor to the meticulously prepared work of leading exponents, or even prudent financially? The answer lies in the spirit of the task, one clearly designed to provide a large audience with the opportunity to experience all these masterworks on period instruments, at an affordable price. A ridiculous price actually. The practice of speed-recording represents quite an art in itself, attempting to engender inspiration while also ensuring acceptable standards of performance and recording – all within an intensive low-budget schedule. Unsurprisingly then, Pieter Jan Leusink's standard-sized Holland Boys Choir and Netherlands Bach Collegium deliver a rather uneven collection of performances with highs and lows in close proximity.

Volumes 1-8: Some readings are simply too indistinct to warrant comparison with more considered and glamorous competition, doubtless in those cases where not enough time has been allowed for the performers to find their interpretative feet beyond merely 'getting it together'. Some, like that of the 'Trauer Ode', miss the point with overt force dispatching fragrant delicacy, while a healthy number constitute refreshing accounts disarmingly caught at the point of discovery. You take the rough with the smooth in this roller-coaster enterprise.

If there's one overriding Achilles heel, it's the unreliability of the solo singing. The tenor contributions, in particular, too often undermine Leusink's generally bright and well-judged conceptions. Volume 5 is a case in point, where Knut Schoch, in the solo tenor cantata, No 55, is simply not up to the task. Judging by the qualities the less ubiquitous Marcel Beekman demonstrates in a beautifully executed No 164, he would have been a better first choice throughout. The most seasoned of the tenors, Nico van der Meel, becomes more authoritative as the set progresses. Soprano Marjon Strijk often finds Bach's taxing melisma a squiggle too far, in marked contrast to the expert if somewhat recessed singing of Ruth Holton and the excellent bass contributions of Bas Ramselaar (they also combine well in their many duets, such as the rollicking No 49). Ramselaar is the best singer on the set and would, for the most part, grace any of the current series; he has the grainy intimacy of Klaus Mertens, and also a burly resonance when it suits him. His reading of *Ich will den Kreuzstab*, No 56, is a commendable achievement by any standards, and there are fine arias in the splendid Ascension works, Nos 37 and 128, as well as in 36, 100 and 108.

Further on the credit side, the boy-led choruses can irradiate a compellingly sure-footed and unmannered perspective of Bach, as in Nos 33 and 97 and in the refreshing and unselfconscious clarity of intent sweetly imparted in Nos 94, 6 and 117; the chorales are also luminously immediate and affecting.

Other cantatas are rather down-played, such as Nos 139 and 62, but are still worthy and enjoyable as honest performances in an unpretentious Kappellmeister mould. If there's a shortage of refinement and blend in No 133 or spit and polish

in the rhythmically exacting Nos 26 and 33, bright and energetic declamation is agreeably more the rule than the exception in Leusink's no-airs-and-graces approach. In the general firmament of new cantata recordings, these spontaneous performances stand comparison more in terms of individual movements (many, including several mentioned above, of real conviction and distinction) than complete pieces. Of the handful of cantatas where a special vision of the whole work is unanimously conveyed, with the performers firing on all cylinders, highlights are (in no particular order) Nos 57, 87, 33, 42, 192, 45, 88, 176, 125 and 129. If the choral movements are the best things in these sets, there are still some memorable arias (to counter an abundance of ropey ones) with which Volumes 1, 2, 4, 6, and 8 are particularly well endowed.

Volumes 9-12: Here, Leusink traverses the final peak with far more consistently enduring accounts than the comparative 'hit or miss' of the earlier readings, though unsurprisingly for an enterprise designed around tight rehearse-record schedules, there will always be scrappy moments.

More encouragingly, there's also a striking and rare quality here that shines through more strongly than in most of the earlier volumes, and gives Leusink and his Dutch colleagues genuine credentials. It's the unmannered and straightforward approach to delivering the essence of the work, the honesty and means to get directly to its heart through real 'performance', often at the point of discovery. In this respect it recalls the earlier recordings from Leonhardt/Harnoncourt, a set that should be increasingly revisited for that very reason. For all the 'al dente' movements here, there are as many refreshingly uninhibited and distinguished readings, notably Nos 119, 43, 74, 197, 127, 104 and 148. There's a keen ear for the fundamental 'conceit' of the music upon which spontaneous music-making happens 'as if live'; unassuming, common sensical and unegotistical, the earthy Kapellmeister approach reminds one of the unspectacular (and occasionally a touch unimaginative) but free-breathing performances by the likes of Karl Ristenpart, Wolfgang Gönnenwein, Fritz Lehmann, Felix Prohaska and Fritz Werner in the 1950s and '60s.

Ears attuned to the refined and homogeneous textures of the top Baroque orchestras will find the grainy and sometimes rather thin violins altogether too disturbing. Others may find this more acceptable and, at times, even liberating, especially when joined by the wonderfully colourful wind playing and robust brass playing; the oboe of Peter Frankenberg, in particular, is one of the set's greatest qualities, though not far behind is the trumpet consort, led by Susan Williams. Notable again is the outstanding bass singing of Bas Ramselaar, whose resonant warmth and musicianly response to text is the most significant vocal strength in the set. Also to be admired are the two main sopranos, Ruth Holton and Marjon Strijk. Both have a vocal timbre of the effervescent and light variety though they bring much radiance and projection to their music-making, and far more accuracy in matters of tuning than in the earlier boxes. Holton sings splendidly in the two demanding arias in No 75, with breeziness in No 52 and loving understanding in the stunning *cantabile* of No 120 (which Bach used in a later version of the G major Violin Sonata), and with great cultivation in BWV31. She sails through the treacherous No 51 with great élan. Strijk brings considerable fluency to her arias in both Nos 25 and 28.

The alto part is less appealingly taken. Sytse Buwalda should not have been lumbered with the responsibility for all the alto arias, several movements of which represent some of Bach's most treasured examples of reflective ardour (why not use mezzos, contraltos and even boy altos for these parts, rather than the often excellent but over-used countertenor?). Despite Buwalda's unsteadiness, he occasionally delivers something reasonable though, such as in Nos 148 and 83. Exactly the same complaint can be levelled at Knut Schoch, a courageous tenor but one without the capacity for variation of colour in his sound, as you hear and expects from both Paul Agnew for Koopman (Erato) or Gerd Türk for Suzuki (BIS). Too often, the upper tessitura just isn't there or else he can't control it. Luckily, Nico van der Meel is wheeled out for the big ones and he's splendid in both 'Ja, tausendmal tausend' in No 43, as well as No 74. In No 31, he's redolent of the deeply touching singing of Helmut Krebs for Werner. Also used is Marcel Beekman, who shines in No 48 and projects a palpable *joie de vivre* with Ramselaar in the fine duet, 'Wie will ich mich freuen' from No 146, as does Holton with Ramselaar in the duet of No 32.

The boy-led Holland Choir and 'period' band, Netherlands Bach Collegium, are again central to the success and distinctive essence of this series. The teamwork in the choir is admirably demonstrated in some of the most difficult pieces, such as the large 'da capo' chorus of No 34, the fervent No 197 and infectiously crackling No 70, resulting in white-hot expositions of thrilling proportions. Leusink's success elsewhere comes largely through his admirably well-judged feeling for tempos and a means of accentuation which drives the music forward inexorably. But there's a fine line here between luminous vitality and panic; the latter afflicts control in some choruses where Bach just can't be learnt in a rush: Nos 65, 48 and 137 are examples where phrases are snatched, or over-sung, to the detriment of both textural cohesion and intonation, as well as general quality of sound. In sum, these readings deserve to be recognised, primarily for their attractive and well measured strides, but also for a lack of dogma or self-importance. Hard-driven and intermittently rough in places (especially string intonation), they're nevertheless consistently honest, rarely disastrous, and occasionally illuminating statements. Bachians, old and new, should investigate the series with an eager

circumspection, taking the rough with the smooth but relishing the open-hearted spirit of the enterprise. The best performances will bring the listener close to the solar plexus of Bach's 'Kantatenwelt'.

'Cantatas, Volume 34' **P**
Cantatas Nos 1, 126 & 127
Carolyn Sampson sop **Robin Blaze** counterten
Gerd Türk ten **Peter Kooij** bass
Bach Collegium Japan / Masaaki Suzuki
BIS ⊕ BIS-SACD1551 (60' · DDD · T/t) **F**

On March 25, 1725, Bach celebrated the Feast of the Annunciation and Palm Sunday with a special cantata, *Wie schön leuchtet der Morgenstern* ('How beautifully shines the morning star'), a work of breathtaking atmosphere and delicate ardour. Masaaki Suzuki's poised grandeur brings considerable richness to this marvellous score, a sparkling duo of solo violins offset deftly against the full ivory texture of high horns and low oboes in the chorus, and joined by top-drawer solo singing. If Gardiner brings more immediate emotion and Koopman a little more élan, Suzuki captures the moment with sustained warmth and intensity.

Equally striking in this volume of pieces from the unfinished chorale-cantata cycle (the second 'Jahrgang') is the graphic immediacy of Bach Collegium Japan; there have been occasions recently when rhetorical projection has become rather too smoothed over, neutral and objectivised. Not so in Nos 126 and 127, the former leaving no stone unturned in its spiky outbursts (trumpet fanfares in wrathful and unusual minor keys) to reflect the 'murderous intent of Pope and Turks'!

The evocative Quinquagesima work *Herr Jesu Christ, wahr' Mensch und Gott* is a pre-Passiontide lament of sublime quality and, again, Suzuki hits the mark with heightened characterisation and, especially, meticulous care with 'Die Seele ruht'. There are not many extended arias here but this masterpiece for soprano, solo oboe and two punctuating recorders and *pizzicato* continuo (for 'Sterbeglocken' – knells of death) is exquisitely performed by Carolyn Sampson. All in all, a disc to be cherished.

'Cantatas, Volume 29' **P**
Cantatas Nos 2, 3, 38 & 135
Dorothee Mields sop **Pascal Bertin** counterten
Gerd Türk ten **Peter Kooij** bass **Bach Collegium Japan / Masaaki Suzuki**
BIS ⊕ BIS-SACD1461 (72' · DDD/DSD · T/t) **F**

The theme of these four works from Bach's second cycle of cantatas at Leipzig is almost universally concerned with the journey from despair towards longed-for reconciliation and the victory over sin. Masaaki Suzuki has chosen three works from the Trinity season of 1724, and the Epiphany cantata, *Ach Gott, wie manches Herzeleid* (No 3) from early 1725. Again, no Japanese soloists appear in this volume, yet the singers all produce worthy contributions in arias which mainly provide solace after the gloomy sentiments of the opening movement.

The chorus of No 2 is a case in point, a chorale fantasia whose austere and semi-inspired (it's all comparative) motet style can appear, in less capable hands, dour to the point of inertia. The work is soon lifted by the revelation of God's cross in 'Fire purifies silver', a strikingly contrasting *à la mode* aria sung with compelling involvement from Gerd Türk. The patience of Suzuki's glowing chorus with its doubling trombones builds with sustained gravitas here and in the highly suggestive contours of No 38, *Aus tiefer Not*, a work inspired by Luther's Phrygian hymn and where succour is harder to unearth.

One really can't but admire Suzuki's judgement when confronted with the contemplative. There are high-points in all the choruses: No 3 arches with eloquence, the hopeful but long-suffering oboe sequences countering the biting, dissonant language. Likewise, the pacing of *Ach Herr, mich armen Sünder* (No 135) results in a naturally incremental voyage of genuine discovery. Occasionally the arias pursue generic smoothness over greater articulation of sentiment. Such is the case in the fine duet 'Wenn Sorgen' (from No 3), where the strings never make the most of the wonderful 'leap' of joyful praise to Jesus. In sum, another serious addition to this most consistent of Bach series.

'Cantatas, Volume 5'   Ⓟ
Cantatas Nos 18, 143, 152, 155 & 161
Midori Suzuki, Ingrid Schmithüsen sops **Yoshikazu Mera** counterten **Makoto Sakurada** ten **Peter Kooij** bass **Bach Collegium Japan / Masaaki Suzuki**
BIS BIS-CD841 (78' · DDD · T/t)   ⒻOO

The fifth volume of Bach's sacred cantatas performed by the Bach Collegium Japan continues their Weimar survey with five pieces written between *c*1713 and 1716. It begins with No 18, performed in its Weimar version – Bach later revived it for Leipzig, adding two treble recorders to the purely string texture of the upper parts of the earlier composition. The scoring of No 152 is more diverse, featuring in its opening Sinfonia a viola d'amore, viola da gamba, oboe and recorder.

A conspicuous feature of No 155 is its melancholy duet for alto and tenor with bassoon obbligato. While the vocal writing sustains something of the character of a lament the wonderfully athletic, arpeggiated bassoon solo provides a magical third voice. The accompanying essay is confused here, emphasising the importance of a solo oboe which in fact has no place at all in this work. No 161 is a piece of sustained beauty, scored for a pair of treble recorders, obbligato organ, strings and continuo. Bach's authorship of No 143 has sometimes been questioned. Much of it is un-Bach-like, yet at times it's hard to envisage another composer's hand.

The performances are of unmatched excel-

lence. Suzuki's direction never falters and his solo vocalists go from strength to strength as the series progresses. Suzuki makes a richly rewarding contribution with beautifully poised singing, a crystal-clear voice and an upper range that only very occasionally sounds at all threatened. Mera and Sakurada sustain a delicately balanced partnership in the elegiac duet of No 155, the limpid bassoon-playing completing this trio of outstanding beauty. Kooij is a tower of strength, a sympathetic partner to Suzuki in the dance-like duet between Jesus and the Soul (No 152), and resonantly affirmative in his aria from the same cantata. But the highest praise should go to Mera and Sakurada for their affecting performance in No 161. All the elements of this superb cantata are understood and deeply felt by all concerned. The disc is admirably recorded and, apart from the aforementioned confusion, painstakingly and informatively documented.

'Cantatas, Volume 6'   Ⓟ
Cantatas Nos 21 & 31
Monika Frimmer sop **Gerd Türk** ten **Peter Kooij** bass **Bach Collegium Japan / Masaaki Suzuki**
BIS BIS-CD851 (68' · DDD · T/t)   Ⓕ

Both of these are Weimar compositions, dating from *c*1713 and 1715 respectively, and both were later sung at Leipzig. Where No 21 is concerned, the performance history is complex since Bach, who clearly and understandably set great store by this extended and profoundly expressive piece, made no fewer than four versions of it. Following what was probably its second Weimar performance, in 1714, Bach produced a new version which he used as a test-piece in Hamburg's Jacobikirche, when applying for an organist's post there in 1720. It's this version, for soprano and bass soloists only, in which the parts are transposed from C minor to D minor that forms the basis of the present recording. Suzuki offers listeners an opportunity, by way of an appendix, of hearing Bach's alternative thoughts on certain sections of the cantata. These are meticulously prepared and affectingly declaimed performances. Listen, for instance, to the beautifully articulated and delicately placed bassoon quavers in the poignant opening Sinfonia of No 21. This is most sensitively done and an auspicious beginning to the work. String playing isn't always quite as clean as it could be but the instrumental expertise is impressive. The solo line-up is strong, with Monika Frimmer sustaining several demanding soprano arias with eloquence and tonal warmth. Gerd Türk and Peter Kooij are secure and expressive, and the singing of the 18-voice choir of women's and men's voices is impressive, though tenors sound strained in the first chorus of No 21.

'Cantatas, Volume 8'   Ⓟ
Cantatas Nos 22, 23 & 75
Midori Suzuki sop **Yoshikazu Mera** counterten

Gerd Türk ten **Peter Kooij** bass **Bach Collegium Japan / Masaaki Suzuki** org
BIS BIS-CD901 (64' · DDD · T/t)   Ⓕ●●

This eighth volume of Bach Collegium Japan's Bach cantata series bridges the period between Bach's departure from Cöthen and his arrival at Leipzig, early in 1723. *Du wahrer Gott und Davids Sohn* (No 23) was mainly written at Cöthen, while *Jesus nahm zu sich die Zwölfe* (No 22) must have been composed almost immediately on Bach's reaching Leipzig. The remaining cantata, *Die Elenden sollen essen* is on an altogether grander scale, in two parts, each of seven movements. The performances maintain the high standards of singing, playing and scholarship set by the previous issues in this series. There are little insecurities here and there – the oboes, which play a prominent role in each of the three pieces, aren't always perfectly in agreement over tuning – but the careful thought given to the words, their significance and declamation, and the skill with which they're enlivened by the realisation of Bach's expressive musical vocabulary, remain immensely satisfying. The disciplined, perceptively phrased and beautifully sustained singing of the two choral numbers of No 23 illuminate the words at every turn, savouring the seemingly infinite expressive nuances of the music. As for No 75, we can only imagine the astonishment with which Leipzig ears must have attuned to its music. In this absolutely superb piece Bach entertains us with a breathtaking stylistic diversity. Polyphony, fugue, chorale fantasia, *da capo* aria, instrumental sinfonia, varied recitative, wonderful oboe writing and a rhythmic *richesse* all contribute to the special distinction both of this cantata and No 76.

Lose no time in becoming acquainted with this one. It reaches, you might say, those parts that other performances do not.

'Cantatas, Volume 28'   Ⓟ
Cantatas Nos 26, 62, 116 & 139
Yukari Nonoshita sop **Robin Blaze** counterten
Makoto Sakurada ten **Peter Kooij** bass
Bach Collegium Japan / Masaaki Suzuki
BIS BIS-SACD1451 (69' · DDD · T/t)   Ⓕ●Ⓓ➔

This volume takes its name from Bach's second and least-established setting based on the great Advent hymn *Nun komm, der Heiden Heiland* (No 62), composed in 1724 to inaugurate the new church year in Leipzig. If not quite boasting the magisterial imagery of his earlier effort from Weimar, the spirit of Luther's celebrated purloining of 'Veni redemptor gentium' lives on, especially in a brilliant opening concerto-style chorus whose unambiguous thematic character perfectly inhabits the hopes of the new season.

Masaaki Suzuki delivers a less visceral performance than some but derives a most effective contrast between the ecstatic fragrance of the first aria and the 'militant, tumultuous continuo theme of the second,' as Dürr puts it.

The latter, 'Streite, siege', is sung with considerable gusto by Peter Kooij but it is the contemplative elements to which Suzuki is most naturally drawn. The opening of *Wohl dem, der sich auf seinen Gott* (No 139) is a case in point, where the affectionate oboi d'amore provide a tender backdrop to a particularly reassuring treatment of Bach's most elegant of harmonic strategies. The return of Robin Blaze to the series brings a similarly involved and reflective musicianship to the anguished strains in 'Ach, unaussprechlich ist die Not' in No 116.

Elsewhere there is an urgent account of the graphic and succinct *Ach wie flüchtig* (No 26) in which Bach alights gleefully on the triviality and materialism of man's life; images of time and opportunity flash past us with striking immediacy here. This was a popular cantata in the pre-period era but few recordings maintain the focus of the conceit as effectively as Suzuki.

Less telling is the opening chorus of No 116 (*Du Friedefürst*) which, for all its tidy articulation and refined shaping, contains little of the rich repository of nuances, large and small, which Nikolaus Harnoncourt so effortlessly instils. For all the many beauties bestowed on us from Bach Collegium Japan over the past 27 volumes, that ageing series soberingly reminds us of a kind of musical assumption which oxygenated the best cantata performances then – qualities somehow less easily uncovered these days. The Super Audio option, used in the series for the first time, offers an even more luminous presence to the sound than the extant stereo picture.

'Cantatas, Vol 39'   Ⓟ
Cantatas Nos 28, 68, 85, 175 & 183
Carolyn Sampson sop **Robin Blaze** counterten **Gerd Türk** ten **Peter Kooij** bass **Bach Collegium, Japan / Masaaki Suzuki**
BIS BIS-SACD1641 (78' · DDD · T/t)   Ⓕ

None of these five cantatas extends beyond a quarter of an hour and yet the wealth of material is brilliantly compressed in a manner which followers of Bach's chorale cantata *Jahrgang*, his second cycle from Trinity 1724, would have come to expect. Before the following Easter, the composer had abandoned the cycle – at least partly, one imagines, as a result of some upset with the church authorities – and resumed with the conventional model where the music takes the gospel as catalyst for poetic inspiration.

Vol 39 from Masaaki Suzuki introduces us initially to the outstanding Whit Monday cantata, No 68, *Also hat Gott die Welt geliebt* ('God so loved the world') in a performance of uncharacteristically ruddy complexion by Collegium Bach Japan. The *siciliana* rhythm is elegantly turned here but lacks intensity. Likewise, the bubbling radiance of 'Mein gläubiges Herze' ('My heart ever faithful', as early English arrangers have known it) is short of the genial *joie de vivre* which Agnes Giebel famously brings to Fritz Werner's performance (Erato).

If the texts of Marianne von Ziegler for Nos 68, 175 and 183 (sadly, she collaborated with Bach on only nine works) afford a special luminosity of imagery which Bach clearly found profoundly arresting, Suzuki is equally committed to Neumeister's effervescent representation of God's gifts of the past year in the Christmas Cantata *Gottlob!*, No 28. After Carolyn Sampson's authoritative opening aria, the great motet movement on the chorale, 'Nun lob, mein Seel, den Herren', finds a happy balance between textural refinement and declamatory zeal.

These are, indeed, fine performances with notable contributions from all the soloists (and obbligato instruments – apart from some laboured violoncello piccolo playing in BWV183, albeit played on the shoulder, "da spalla"), though no single one falls into that special category where an association between work and performer is formed for instant recall.

'Cantatas, Volume 30'   **P**
Cantata No 51. Cantata No 210, O holder Tag, erwünschte Zeit – Aria: Spielet, ihr beseelten Lieder. Alles mit Gott und nichts ohn' ihn, BWV1127
Carolyn Sampson sop
Bach Collegium Japan / Masaaki Suzuki
BIS ⚛ BIS-SACD1471 (74' · DDD/DSD · T/t)   **F** ●

Of Bach's 12 sacred solo cantatas, *Jauchzet Gott* stands as a virtuoso concert piece without peer. No other work – with the possible exception of the secular cantata *O holder Tag* – pushes the soprano voice to such dazzling limits of coloratura. While Bach is thought to have used the work for a Trinity Sunday, perhaps in 1730, its provenance would appear to lie in the same celebratory context as *O holder Tag* (an aria of which is included as a 'bonus' track here), where courtly entertainment and panegyric often encouraged Bach to impress a potentially influential audience.

Carolyn Sampson joins a notable and plentiful list of fine sopranos who have tackled the work on record. She sails through it with controlled authority, encouraged by Masaaki Suzuki's spacious approach to tempi until, that is, the Choral and Alleluja where she and the admirable solo trumpeter (Toshio Shimada) pick off each fiendish run with a brilliant, almost nonchalant ease. Still, this is not a performance where Suzuki seeks to liberate the musicians towards true exultance: perfection is all but achieved, but rather as a geometric proof than the kind of genuine uplift we get from Stich-Randall, Giebel or Stader. Sampson's performance still remains highly accomplished and her natural poetic instincts are wonderfully realised in the recitative 'Wir beten' and the delectable but slight *Alles mit Gott*. Suzuki presents all 12 verses in a 48-minute marathon which no manner of variation and embellishment can sustain: maybe it's rather too much of a good thing.

'Cantatas, Volume 19'   **P**
Cantatas Nos 37, 86, 104 & 166
Yukari Nonoshita sop **Robin Blaze** counterten
Makoto Sakurada ten **Stephan MacLeod** bass
Bach Collegium Japan / Masaaki Suzuki
BIS BIS-CD1261 (64' · DDD · T/t)   **F**

The first work on this CD is a little-known gem, No 86, *Wahrlich, wahrlich, ich sage euch* ('Verily, I say unto you'). Succinct and imploring, the listener follows the doctrinal and attentive tone set so marvellously by a composer arrested by the intensity of Christ's promise: 'Whatsoever ye shall ask the Father in my name, he will give it you.' Suzuki, as ever, chooses exceptionally well-judged tempi throughout, leaves no stone unturned in his confident preparedness and also introduces a fine new bass to the series, Stephan MacLeod, as the 'vox Christi'.

Of the other three works here, none is particularly long but each contains a central movement of special significance. In No 37 it's the chorale duet of a stanza from 'How brightly shines the morning star', sung with disarming fluency by Yukari Nonoshita and Robin Blaze, and in No 166, the tidy tenor Makoto Sakurada gives a sensitive, if somewhat under-nourished, account of 'Ich will an den Himmel denken'. This cantata also boasts a ravishing and peerless 'Man nehme sich in Acht' from Blaze.

In the great bass aria 'Beglückte Herde', MacLeod gives a gentle and soft-grained performance (very much in the spirit of Suzuki's usual bass, Peter Kooij) as Christ's sheep are offered the rewards of faith. Some will wish for a more involving performance of this highly original work, as Richter provides (from 1973) – with a majestic Fischer-Dieskau – and the radiant spontaneity of Pieter Jan Leusink, which arguably boasts the best bass singing in recent years from Bas Ramselaar.

Suzuki's volume will, however, satisfy many tastes. These are consistently impressive performances, beautifully recorded and Suzuki communicates Bach with unalloyed joy.

'Cantatas, Volume 15'   **P**
Cantatas Nos 40, 60, 70 & 90
Yukari Nonoshita sop **Robin Blaze** counterten
Gerd Türk ten **Peter Kooij** bass **Bach Collegium Japan / Masaaki Suzuki**
BIS BIS-CD1111 (68' · DDD · T/t)   **F**

Masaaki Suzuki here brings us four more fine cantatas, of which *Wachet! betet! betet! wachet!* (No 70) stands apart as one of Bach's most graphically dramatic and cohesive choral achievements. The first movement is justly celebrated, its tautness, forbidding fanfares and diminished chords representing the coming of Christ and the Last Judgement. The apocalyptic backdrop fascinated early interpreters of Bach in the 1950s and '60s, notably Felix Prohaska with his menacing pacing and sepia-like textures offset against a Viennese elegance.

Suzuki's direction is more pressing and urgent in style; his less theatrical, more meticulous approach allows the filigree in the instrumental writing to emerge in a way too rarely heard. Koopman (Erato) has the edge in conveying a more harrowing perspective to the first movement, but the remainder of the cantata is beautifully crafted by Suzuki, demonstrating the artistic conviction and vocal bravura of Robin Blaze in 'Wenn kommt' (though his soaring tones are heard to even better effect in No 60). The pivotal aria in No 70 is the radiant 'Hebt euer Haupt empor', a succinct piece whose openheartedness requires something more than Gerd Türk and Suzuki can give.

The most compelling performances on this disc are in the busy counterpoint, such as the opening chorus of No 40, 'Dazu ist erschienen', the vibrant tenor aria 'Christenkinder', which shows off BCJ's exemplary wind section, and (to return to the horror of Judgement) the peerlessly executed bass aria of No 90, where Peter Kooij and the obbligato trumpet of Toshio Shimada find the perfect synergy. But it's in the stirring and decidedly prescient *Sturm und Drang* quality of No 60, *O Ewigkeit, du Donnerwort*, that Suzuki's infectious grasp of pulse, biting accentuation and luminous textures take fullest flight: he entertains no half-measures in the opening chorus. All round, yet another prestigious addition to the series.

'Cantatas, Volume 14'   P
Cantatas Nos 48, 89, 109 & 148
Midori Suzuki sop **Robin Blaze** counterten
Gerd Türk ten **Chiyuki Urano** bass **Bach Collegium Japan / Masaaki Suzuki**
BIS BIS-CD1081 (66' · DDD · T/t)   F

Masaaki Suzuki's considered approach to this oeuvre is what marks him out as a distinctive voice in current Bach performance. This volume reveals much of the best in the series so far: consistently good singing, a sustained familiarity with the music (not always to be taken for granted in the studio) beyond mere pristine executancy, and Suzuki's guiding hand which is especially attentive to the textual motivation in Bach's music.

A broader approach seems to win the day for much in this disc, as can be admired in the defining logic of the fine opening fugal chorus of *Bringet dem Herrn* (No 148), whose resplendent contrapuntal bravura takes thrilling flight in the chapel's ringing acoustic. Here, and rather less so in the relatively unpolished Leusink reading, the paragraphs connect in a way which ensures an inexorable momentum and sustained uplift – which was rarely achieved in performances of this work from the early days of Bach cantata recordings. The instrumental and obbligato playing throughout is of a high order (if not perhaps boasting the depth of string quality of Koopman), doubtless inspired by the alto and tenor of Robin Blaze and Gerd Türk respectively – who are the main soloists in all four

works. Both sing with delectation and authority. In No 109 Suzuki eschews over-characterisation and instead accentuates the instrumental profile as the means of gathering the disparate melodic ideas. There are many other highlights here. The plangent opening lament-chorus of No 48 is slower than Koopman's, but it's a remarkably controlled, even and luminous creation. If not always emotionally exhaustive, Bach Collegium Japan explore the naked emptiness in this work, leaving you feeling properly wrung out. A notable achievement.

'Cantatas, Volume 38'   P
Cantatas Nos 52, 55, 58 & 82
Carolyn Sampson sop **Gerd Türk** ten **Peter Kooij** bass **Bach Collegium Japan / Masaaki Suzuki**
BIS BIS-SACD1631 (66' · DSD · T/t)   F

As the honeymoon period of Bach's appointment began to wear off, two or three years after his arrival in Leipzig, the composer's cantatas became less central to his creative life. More works by other composers began to appear in the church calendar as energy was increasingly focused towards new large-scale projects, of which the *St Matthew Passion* was the most pressing at the time these four solo cantatas were composed.

Smaller resources may also suggest a shortage of adequate forces in Leipzig in the months between late 1726 and early 1727 but there is no let-up in quality. This latest Bach Collegium volume includes one of the most celebrated of all bass-baritone cantatas, *Ich habe genug*, in a reading of profoundly felt utterance by the experienced Peter Kooij. This is an even and fluent version, if in 'Schlummert ein' a touch too objective and laid-back. Yet the world-weariness of this great slumber aria is beautifully caught by Masaaki Suzuki in both the textural sensibility and rhythmic nuance of the ensemble. Unforced and natural, this is a reading reminding us of the simplicity of the work's unalloyed beauty.

Carolyn Sampson grows in stature as a Bachian in her exquisite musical judgement and technical assurance, not least in the outstanding tuning and allure of 'Ich halt es mit lieben Gott' (from *Falsche Welt*, No 52, which includes a rather sleepy performance of its Sinfonia, from the earliest version of *Brandenburg* No 1). *Ich armer Mensch* is the only extant solo tenor cantata, a piece for whom man's inherent sinfulness is prevalent in supplicatory chromaticism, but hampered here by a tired-sounding Gerd Türk and some uncharacteristically sour intonation from the flautist, Liliko Maeda.

Sampson and Kooij share the delights of No 58, *Ach Gott, wie manches*, a symmetrical and passionately conceived work framed by splendid duets in which the bass paraphrases the soprano chorale (the symbol of Soul and God) – transformed from a tortured chaconne in a cathartic concerto romp. This is a fine close to another largely successful addition to this distinguished series.

'Cantatas, Volume 43'   ℗
Cantatas Nos 57, 110 & 151
Hana Blažíková sop **Robin Blaze** counterten
Gerd Türk ten **Peter Kooij** bass
Bach Collegium Japan / Masaaki Suzuki
BIS ⊕ BIS-SACD1761 (62' · DDD)   Ⓕ

From the outset, the Bach Collegium Japan deliver these 1725 Christmas pieces with supreme vitality and exuberance. Initially, there's the reworking of the overture from the Fourth Orchestral Suite, now transformed into the virtuoso chorus of No 110 to depict mouths 'filled with laughter' at the news of Christmas Day's regal arrival.

Elsewhere these cantatas are defined by notable solo contributions. In *Unser mund* Gerd Türk delivers his open-hearted 'Ihr gedanken' with studied poise. Robin Blaze and Peter Kooij each appear comfortably embedded in George Christian Lehms's inward-looking texts, but one is no less struck by the gusto of debutante soprano, Hana Blažíková.

More daunting for Blažíková is how she responds to the heavy history of great singers in *Selig ist der Mann*, the great 'concerto in dialogo' for two solo voices. Boxing Day is of course the Feast of St Stephen where the Gospel prophesies the consolation of God's love but with the caveat of inevitable persecution. Bach took special care in setting the text here, not least where Vox Christi's divinity is relayed through a subtle blend of the doctrinal and other-worldliness.

If Kooij struggles to meet the authority of Barry McDaniel for Fritz Werner (though Kooij is magnificent in the rage aria here), Blažíková projects a penetrating radiance with admirable focus and impeccable tuning in 'Ich wunschte mir den Tod'. *Süsser Trost*, with its undisputed masterpiece of an opening aria, dominates this third cantata and Blažíková's sweet consolation takes us to a different place there. Overall this volume is a fine addition to Suzuki's distinguished series.

'Cantatas, Volume 21'   ℗
Cantatas Nos 65, 81, 83 & 190
Robin Blaze counterten **James Gilchrist** ten
Peter Kooij bass **Bach Collegium Japan /**
Masaaki Suzuki
BIS BIS-CD1311 (70' · DDD · T/t)   ⒻⓄ

Another meticulously prepared volume in this distinguished series comprises the late festivities of Christmas 1724 and two Epiphany works from a few weeks later. Taken from the first of Bach's annual cantata cycles, these four works reveal the astonishing variety and textual (and textural) coloration which the composer exercised in this period of free-wheeling creativity from his early months of employment in Leipzig.

While the instrumentation of horns, recorders, oboes da caccia and strings in No 65 captures the spiciness of eastern promise, Suzuki

imbues the whole with a relaxed and soft-grained pastoral regality. This is further exemplified in the easy delivery of the aria 'Nimm mich dir zu eigen' in which James Gilchrist performs with supreme awareness, beckoning the listener to inhabit his world: this is exceptionally characterised singing by any standards and Suzuki shouldn't look back.

No less successful is the way Bach Collegium Japan embraces the Christmas message in the incomplete Cantata No 190. Imaginative reconstruction can bring this work to life and Masaaki Suzuki has found a majestic solution to the opening chorus, which his namesake realises with abandon.

Cantata No 81 is a mesmerisingly compact piece in which St Matthew's account of Jesus calming the storm provides arresting imagery for three fine arias. The middle movement is the set-piece *par excellence*, truly operatic in its posturing bravura and burning focus of conceit. Gilchrist again brings tremendous commitment and open-heartedness with the kind of cultivated vocal élan of great Bach tenors in the Helmut Krebs and Anton Dermota mould. Both Robin Blaze and Peter Kooij perform their arias with customary distinction. Altogether, an extremely fine volume, finer than any rival.

'Cantatas, Volume 2'   ℗
Cantatas Nos 71, 106 & 131
Midori Suzuki, Aki Yanagisawa sops **Yoshikazu**
Mera counterten **Gerd Türk** ten **Peter Kooij** bass
Bach Collegium Japan / Masaaki Suzuki
BIS BIS-CD781 (63' · DDD · T/t)   Ⓕ

Here these artists are abreast of current thinking concerning Baroque style, yet sometimes you find yourself longing for a little more expression and a little less fashionable orthodoxy. The three cantatas included here are among Bach's earliest essays in the form. Nos 106 and 131 (*c*1707) belong to the Mühlhausen period, while No 71 was written in 1708. By and large, Suzuki has chosen effective tempos, though there are notable exceptions. One of these affects the beautiful Sonatina for recorders and viola da gamba that introduces the *Actus tragicus* (No 106), a funeral piece of startling intensity. Suzuki feels too slow here, adding a full 40 seconds on to performances by virtually all his rivals. Elsewhere, and above all in his choice of soloists, Suzuki fields an exceptional team. We can feel this especially in the effortlessly projected singing of Midori Suzuki (Nos 71 and 131) and Aki Yanagisawa (No 106), the uncluttered declamation of Gerd Türk, and the resonant contributions by Peter Kooij. The countertenor here lacks either conviction or consistent aural charm. The choir is well drilled and, as with the solo element, the voices respond urgently to the spirit of the text. Listen to the thrice supplicatory 'Israel' in the concluding chorus of No 131 for one such example.

'Cantatas, Volume 26'   P
Cantatas No 96, 122 & 180
Yukari Nonoshita sop **Timothy Kenworthy-Brown**
counterten **Makoto Sakurada** ten **Peter Kooij** bass
Bach Collegium Japan / Masaaki Suzuki hpd
BIS BIS-CD1401 (53' · DDD · T/t)   F

Although Bach never completed the second cycle of cantatas, he left us with an extraordinary range of solutions for how the chorale can inspire fantasy and invention. Some pieces are magnificent, others darned good and a few (dare one say) a touch severe. Such an example of 'magnificent' is the highly wrought *Schmücke dich* from October 1724, the *ne plus ultra* cantata for many, where the invitation to the feast provided Bach with radiant images of the hospitality of God's kingdom.

Masaaki Suzuki brings an especially balletic prospect to the opening chorus with strong, driving bass-lines and a dazzling sense of expectancy. One has never felt so sure of Bach's delight in an exceptional melody. This is counterbalanced by a soft-grained and lucid reading of the tenor aria 'Ermuntre dich' by Makoto Sakurada and then, fleetingly, an accompanied recitative introducing yet another countertenor to the series in the attractive and polished warmth of Timothy Kenworthy-Brown.

More heartening than anything is to hear soprano Yukari Nonoshita developing into a Bach singer of real stature. Both in *Schmücke dich* and the startlingly original inner movements of *Das neugeborne Kindelein* she conveys the gentle, compassionate honesty of Agnes Giebel.

Cantata No 96 is a less integrated piece but boasts some dazzling sopranino recorder playing in the opening chorus which Suzuki imbues with indulgent delight in Bach's glorious orchestration. Peter Kooij's 'Bald zur Rechten' deftly imparts the timid and halting steps of the Christian's human vulnerability. Another success chalked up in this riveting series.

'Cantatas, Volume 10'   P
Cantatas Nos 105ª, 179 & 186ᵇ
Miah Persson sop ᵃᵇ**Robin Blaze** counterten **Makoto
Sakurada** ten **Peter Kooij** bass **Bach Collegium
Japan / Masaaki Suzuki**
BIS BIS-CD951 (63' · DDD · T/t)   FO

Bach Collegium Japan's eloquent advance into the rich repository of cantatas composed during Bach's first year at Leipzig is distinguished in Vol 10 by Masaaki Suzuki's remarkable instinct for the emotional core of each of these three works. Experiencing *Herr, gehe nicht ins Gericht* (No 105) reveals a sense of open-hearted fervour and contemplation, never for a minute cloying or self-regarding at the expense of vibrant expression. This is a work embued with a rich discography, yet what Suzuki uniquely achieves, compelling in the opening chorus, is an intensity born of subtle contrast in vocal and instrumental articulation, underpinned by his uncanny ability to choose a tempo which provides for lyrical intimacy and

organic gesture, as the respective texts demand. Suzuki grasps the magnificent nobility of the composer's inspired musical commentary on the human soul in No 105. Miah Persson exhibits sustained control and delectable purity of tone in the continuo-less 'Wie zittern und wanken' and 'Liebster Gott' from No 179. With Peter Kooij's cathartic recitative singing (preparing the spirit of salvation) and the beautifully balanced tenor aria and final chorale, Herreweghe's elegant and fragrant 1990 account, a clear leader until now, has a companion on the top rung.

The bipartite Trinity cantata, *Ärgre dich, o Seele, nicht* (No 186), revised from a Weimar version of 1716, conveys equally Suzuki's assurance and vision. Perhaps the choruses which frame Part 1 are a touch short on gravitas (and tuning is intermittently awry in the first) but here, and in the formidable opening movement of No 179 rhythmic incision is the order of the day. This is another first-rate achievement (the soloists are slightly recessed but the recorded sound is excellent). Arguably the most complete and mature offering in the series so far.

'Cantatas, Volume 32'   P
Cantatas Nos 111, 123, 124, & 125
Yukari Nonoshita sop **Robin Blaze** counterten
Andreas Weller ten **Peter Kooij** bass
Bach Collegium Japan / Masaaki Suzuki hpd
BIS   BIS-SACD1501 (74' · DDD · T/t)   FB

Masaaki Suzuki takes us further into the second year of Bach's post in Leipzig with four fine cantatas which sit at the solar plexus of the second cycle in New Year 1725 – the unfinished series of works whose primary catalyst was the hymn of the week and not the usual gospel reading. The quality and maturity of Bach's vocal writing is revealed here in works which are still fighting for recognition. No 111 is the exception, with Bach's taut representation of God's might and also celebrated for the great duet, 'So geh ich mit behertzten Schritten' ('So I go with heartened steps') which Robin Blaze and Andreas Weller perform with exultant esprit.

Bach Collegium Japan are at their most persuasive in the superficially dour but incrementally magisterial opening choruses of both Nos 125 and 123, the latter a brilliant slow-burn contemplation of faith (and hope) with predominant falling motifs from the tender opening of the hymn. Suzuki paces this with as much warmth and understanding as he does in No 124, where a sweetly running oboe d'amore line threads its way through the galant minuet.

With *Mit Fried und Freud* we enter into another meditation on death, one in which Suzuki traverses Bach's extraordinary tonal excursions in the opening chorus, matched only by the succeeding aria where the blind disciple seeks Christ. Robin Blaze is quite exquisite here, as are the poignant oboe and flute obbligati which reflect the fragile human condition in a way strikingly akin to the mysteries and musical language of the *St Matthew Passion*. Suzuki and his musicians can be content that they have pulled out all the stops for one of Bach's most mesmerising creations.

'Cantatas, Vol 16' Ⓟ
Cantatas Nos 119ᵇ & 194ᵃ
ᵇYoshie Hida, ᵃYukari Nonoshita *sops*
ᵇKirsten Sollek-Avella *contr* ᵃMakoto Sakurada *ten*
ᵃJochen Kupfer *bar* ᵇPeter Kooij *bass*
Bach Collegium Japan / Masaaki Suzuki
BIS BIS-CD1131 (63' · DDD · T/t) Ⓕ

Masaaki Suzuki gives No 194 a fittingly airy charm, heard most infectiously in 'Hilf, Gott' where an underlying Gavotte (with resonances of the final movement of the *Wedding* Cantata, No 202) finds bright-eyed soprano, Yukari Nonoshita, in confident and beguiling voice. She's most accomplished throughout and delectably joins the gentle and receptive baritone Jochen Kupfer in 'O wie wohl' ist uns geschehn', a bucolic minuet-style duet. This is, all told, the most persuasive reading on disc, and supersedes both Rilling's stiff reading and even Harnoncourt's cultivated (if slightly hit-and-miss) performance, notable also for the presence of a young Thomas Hampson.

Harnoncourt, however, comes out better in one of the grandest French-overture cantatas Bach was to write, 'Preise Jerusalem' (No 119). Composed to honour the new Leipzig town council, Bach really pushed the boat out. Suzuki never quite boasts either the grand sonic cohesion of Philippe Herreweghe's urgent account or the thrilling characterisation of Harnoncourt. Strongly recommended nevertheless for Suzuki's superb reading of No 194.

'Cantatas, Volume 1: London' Ⓟ
Cantatas Nos 7, 20, 30, 39, 75 & 167
Gillian Keith, Joanne Lunn *sops*
Wilke te Brummelstroete *contr*
Paul Agnew *ten* Dietrich Henschel *bass*
Monteverdi Choir; English Baroque Soloists /
Sir John Eliot Gardiner
Soli Deo Gloria ② SDG101 (149' · DDD · T/t)
Recorded live at St Giles Cripplegate, London,
June 23-26, 2000 ⓂⒺⒺⒺ➔

'Cantatas, Volume 8: Bremen/Santiago de
Compostela' Ⓟ
Cantatas Nos 8, 27, 51, 95, 99, 100, 138 & 161
Katharine Fuge, Malin Hartelius *sops*
William Towers, Robin Tyson *countertens*
James Gilchrist, Mark Padmore *tens*
Thomas Guthrie, Peter Harvey *basses*
Monteverdi Choir; English Baroque Soloists /
Sir John Eliot Gardiner
Soli Deo Gloria ② SDG104 (145' · DDD · T/t)
Recorded live at the Unser Lieben Frauen, Bremen,
Germany, September 28, 2000, and Santo Domingo
de Bonaval, Santiago de Compostela, Spain,
October 7, 2000 ⓂⒺⒺⒺ➔

In 2000 John Eliot Gardiner commemorated the 250th anniversary of Bach's death with theBach Cantata Pilgrimage, a year-long European tour by the English Baroque Soloists and Monteverdi Choir that presented all of Bach's extant cantatas on the appropriate liturgical feast days. Here are the first two instalments of the complete cycle. Soli Deo Gloria's presentation is first class. The CDs are cased in a handsomely designed hardbound book, complete with texts, translations and Gardiner's extensive, informative notes based on a journal he kept during the pilgrimage.

The interpretations are consistently fine – often superb, in fact – with surprisingly few wrong steps or disappointments, especially given the unusually gruelling performance schedule that produced them. Among the many mind-blowing, beautiful moments is the deliciously syncopated contralto aria from No 30, sung with poise by Wilke te Brummelstroete and graced by playing of magical delicacy from the EBS. And there's the extraordinary opening chorus of No 8, with its seemingly endless melodic tendrils, chiming flute part and plucked strings, sounding like a celestial dance. Special mention must be made of the artistry of tenor Mark Padmore, who maintains his sweet, ringingly clear tone even in the demanding leaps and roulades of his aria in No 95.

It's in delicate or intimate music that Gardiner shines most luminously, and some may find that he unduly emphasises the contemplative. His thoughtful, refined approach is strikingly similar to Suzuki's cycle on BIS, though Gardiner's versions sound just a bit warmer. Although his interpretations offer the finest attributes of period practice – transparency and litheness – there's a long-breathed musicality here that can be lacking in other accounts.

'Cantatas, Volume 2: Paris/Zürich'
Bach Cantatas Nos 2, 10, 21, 76 & 135. Concerto
for Flute, Violin and Harpsichord, BWV1044ᶜ
Schütz Die Himmel erzählen die Ehre Gottes,
SWV386ᵃ
Lisa Larsson, Katharine Fuge *sops*
Daniel Taylor, Robin Tyson *altos*
James Gilchrist, Vernon Kirk *tens*
Stephen Varcoe, Jonathan Brown *basses*
Monteverdi Choir; English Baroque Soloists /
Sir John Eliot Gardiner
Soli Deo Gloria ② SDG165 (147' · DDD · T/t)
Recorded live at Basilique Saint-Denis, Paris, on July
2-3, 2000; Fraumünster, Zürich, on July 8-9, 2000
ⓂⒺ➔

The centrepiece here is the breathtaking *Ich hatte viel Bekümmernis* (No 21), arguably Bach's most significant vocal work to date (1713/14), where he consciously assembled a masterful blend of rhetorical elements (antiquated motet to *à la mode* oratorio) for a journey from profound despair to raw exultation. Gardiner's reading is graphic and visceral – patient in its gradual unfolding over 40 minutes – but notable less for choral focus and general consistency among his soloists than for specific landmarks of intensity. Katharine Fuge's poignant singing of the lament 'Seufzer, Tränen' ('Sighing, weeping') is compelling, as is Gardiner's sympathetic and unforced handling of a work in which overstressed appoggiaturas can easily become a wearing inflection. What, one wonders, would contemporary audiences have made of the almost sensual exchange (rather played up) between Jesus and the Soul that begins Part 2?

The concerts from the more resonant Saint-Denis, Paris, a week earlier, yield even better results overall, including a cultivated and purposeful No 2, a work whose austere chorale can inhibit the best. As so often in the Pilgrimage, James Gilchrist stands out but Lisa Larsson and Stephen Varcoe also contribute memorably in the highly articulated and image-laden arias which constitute No 10, a work based on the German *Magnificat* which merits some comparison with Bach's later, famous *Magnificat* setting.

Preceded by the grandeur of Schütz in heavenly mode, No 76 affords a no less striking reading in this most urgently impressive of extended cantatas. Bach was 'exhibiting' for only the second time after his appointment to Leipzig and he sets out his stall with studied deliberation. Despite a tendency to rush the fugal opening chorus, Gardiner presents a lucid and captivating vision of Bach's virtuoso imagination in the enrichment of 'The Word'. Gardiner refers to the piece as evergreen and the work has never sounded as fresh.

'Cantatas, Volume 3: Tewkesbury/Mühlhausen' Ⓟ
Cantatas Nos 24, 71, 88, No 93, 131, 177, 185
Joanne Lunn sop **Magdalena Kožená** mez **Nathalie Stutzmann** contr **William Towers** counterten **Paul Agnew, Kobie van Rensburg** tens **Peter Harvey, Nicolas Testé** basses **Monteverdi Choir; English Baroque Soloists / Sir John Eliot Gardiner**
Soli Deo Gloria ② SDG141 (138' · DDD · T/t)
Recorded live at Tewkesbury Abbey on July 16, 2000; Blausiuskirche, Mühlhausen, on July 23, 2000 ⒻⒹ➔

'Cantatas, Volume 27: Blythburgh/Kirkwall' Ⓟ
Cantatas – Nos 129, 165, 175, 176, 184 & No 194.
Brandenburg Concerto No 3, BWV1048
Ruth Holton, Lisa Larsson sops **Nathalie Stutzmann** contr **Daniel Taylor** counterten **Christoph Genz** ten **Peter Harvey, Stephan Loges** basses **Monteverdi Choir; English Baroque Soloists / Sir John Eliot Gardiner**
Soli Deo Gloria ② SDG138 (111' · DDD · T/t)
Recorded live at the Holy Trinity, Blythburgh, on June 13, 2000; St Magnus Cathedral, Kirkwall, on June 18, 2000 ⒻⒹ➔

The spread of locations – from Mühlhausen to Kirkwall – complements and intensifies the extraordinary range of cantatas in these rich and varied offerings from Sir John Eliot Gardiner.

Those who thought that, perhaps, the best fruits of the Pilgrimage had already been tasted, can think again with these two latest volumes.

One is reminded here – in works mainly for the extended summer months of the Trinity season – that the experience of touring so many masterpieces in such a short space of time obviated all dangers of homogeneity, comfort zones or complacency. Some exhaustion and rough-edgedness, yes, and just occasionally there's not quite enough time for the performers to get under the skin of a particular work, yet such instances are impressively infrequent.

Gardiner and his forces rise here to each challenge (as the Pilgrimage had now passed the halfway point) with, it seems, a creative regimen of Bachian proportions: just as Bach efficiently identified how to react with supreme concentration and speed according to the compositional demands of the week, so these 21st-century performers adapt robustly to the seasonal implications within this pattern of ever-changing locales.

The proof is in the imagination and wide compass of these performances – objectively assessed after nearly eight years – where the intense archaic idioms of *Aus der Tiefen* (No 131) and the municipal bravura of *Gott ist mein König* (No 71), performed in the Mühlhausen church for which they were written, are accentuated in quiet, contemplative dignity and surface finery, respectively. For Gardiner the emotional stakes are high and this possible memorial cantata for a horrific town fire is especially moving.

Bach's own engagement with a text or liturgical 'problem' depended largely on personal circumstances and this means that some cantatas make for challenging listening. Gardiner recognises this in his note for the austere *Ein ungefärbt Gemüte* (No 24), where the Gospel paraphrase of 'ye would that men should do to you, do ye even so to them' is reflected in a fiddly chorus of contrapuntal finger-wagging, a caveat of hypocrisy which then implores us to constancy.

Gardiner is a master of delivering these hard enigmatic pieces with renewed logic and understanding, aided in No 185 by the fine duet of Magdalena Kožená and Paul Agnew and, then, alto Nathalie Stutzmann in the delectable 'Sei bemüht in dieser Zeit' (where the successful sower reaps a splendid harvest). This is, in fact, far from enigmatic but one of those courtly Weimar arias whose inimitable generosity of spirit, not least in its ordered periodic phrasing, requires assiduous refinement in voicing, which is exactly what the beautiful oboe-and-strings blend provides.

If the cantatas discussed this far are included in the unusually rich Vol 3, Vol 27 from Blythburgh and Kirkwall is only marginally less uniformly good. Both volumes are characterised by choral and instrumental contributions of the most imploring and thrilling extremes (for instance, the glowing chorus to No 177, Bach's provocative take on Marianne von Ziegler's text in No 176 and the ecstatic trumpetings of *Gelobet*, No 129).

Many of the arias for Whit Tuesday and Trinity Sunday comprise reused material from secular cantatas at Cöthen and hence the bright-eyed and bushy-tailed gavottes, minuets and bourrées, which appear regularly. Nothing better captures Bach's endless capacity for exuding inner succour than the luminous, gentle melodic contours of 'Was des Höchsten' (from No 194), although it's only one example in another treasure chest of cantatas, whose jewels continue to glisten for the new pilgrim-collectors.

'Cantatas, Volume 4: Ansbach/Haddington'
Bach Cantatas Nos 9, 107, 170, 186 & 187
Kuhnau/Bach Der Gerechte kommt um[a]
Katharine Fuge, Joanne Lunn sops
Michael Chance, Richard Wyn Roberts countertens
James Gilchrist, Kobie van Rensburg tens **Stephan Loges, Stephen Varcoe** basses **Monteverdi Choir; English Baroque Soloists / Sir John Eliot Gardiner**
Soli Deo Gloria ② SDG156 (121' · DDD · T/t)
Recorded live at St Gumbertus, Ansbach, on July 30, 2000; St Mary's, Haddington, on August 5 & 6, 2000   ⓂⒷ→

As the longest season in the liturgical calendar, Trinity is represented by the largest corpus from within Bach's cantata oeuvre, covering a remarkable range of gospel- and epistle-inspired texts for Bach to set – from victory over death and restoration of faith over doubt, to God's power to relieve the hungry. High summer in 2000 saw the pilgrimage move back and forth between Scotland and Germany – between Ansbach and the late-medieval church in Haddington in the Scottish Lowlands.

The first programme, from the wonderfully named St Gumbertus in the Franconian town, is linked together by two of Bach's finest arias from Nos 9 and 170 respectively: the grim tenor aria 'Wir waren schon zu tief gesunken' is presented with typical rhetorical insight by James Gilchrist, while 'Wie jammern' from the celebrated solo-alto cantata *Vergnügte Ruh* presents the insidious wiles of the devil with breathtaking imagery. Michael Chance gives a compellingly theatrical performance whose 'liveness' brings added colour and risk, even if pitching is occasionally variable.

Sir John Eliot Gardiner brings great sensitivity to the remaining movements of No 9 (with its light and distinctly mature interweaving flute and oboe d'amore lines), especially the spacious geniality of the opening chorus and the ingenious duet 'Herr, du siehst'. This is a cantata written in the early 1730s which Bach interpolated to fill an empty gap in his second cycle of 1724-25 – as a form of good housekeeping.

The Haddington concert conveys an especially cohesive sense of gentleness, character and intimacy, largely unified by the nature and high quality of the opening movements. The languid exhortation 'not to fret' in *Ärgre dich* (No 186) is expressive in its soft-grained sympathetic gaze; it is given an appropriately introverted reading

by the full ensemble, as Katharine Fuge and Richard Wyn Roberts exclaim with suitable candour in their duet-gigue on the words 'O soul, be true'.

No less penetrating is Gardiner's account of No 107 but the pick of the crop – certainly in choral terms – is the sensational and woefully little-known *Es wartet*, No 187, whose opening canvas is strikingly extensive. Not all the solo contributions here are of equal merit in this second disc. One could quibble, too, over some over-exaggerated articulation, but overall the prime colours of these great pieces are undimmed, glowing with customary zeal.

'Cantatas, Volume 5: Rendsburg/Braunschweig'   Ⓟ
Cantatas Nos 45, 46, 101, 102, 136 & 178
Joanne Lunn sop **Daniel Taylor, Robin Tyson** countertens **Christoph Genz** ten **Gotthold Schwarz, Brindley Sherratt** basses **Monteverdi Choir; English Baroque Soloists / Sir John Eliot Gardiner**
Soli Deo Gloria ② SDG147 (119' · DDD)
Recorded live at the Christkirche, Rendsburg, on August 13, 2000; Braunschweig Cathedral on August 27, 2000   Ⓕ

Our Pilgrimage travels to Rendsburg and Braunschweig for a selection from Bach's 'golden years' of vocal writing, 1723-25. The immediacy of the sound in the former seems almost ideal for the intensity of *Wo Gott der Herr*, which thrusts us into an unyielding paranoia about God's indifference to our plight. Gardiner summons an impressive, generative agitation that illuminates the imagery of shipwreck in the bass aria, as well as the tenor aria with its declamatory 'Schweig, schweig' (Be silent) which, despite its final consolation, reeks of dissembling. Brindley Sherratt and Christophe Genz deliver exceptional realisations.

The short journey to the resonant Braunschweig involves a new solo team and performances which are altogether more transporting. If one reveres the 'Qui tollis' from the B minor Mass, doesn't the opening of *Schauet doch* in its original context of dissolute lamentation say even more? Certainly, Gardiner uses it brilliantly to take off with one of Bach's most jarring fugal exegeses. Equally breathtaking is the traumatic opening chorus, on Luther's hymn 'Vater unser', of No 101 with its almost flagellatory appoggiaturas to depict the breaking of Satan's hold.

In Nos 46 and 102 (with another sensational opening chorus), the arias and obbligato contributions are remarkable. Gardiner calls No 102's 'Dein Wetter' one of Bach's rare 'tsunami' arias: bass Gotthold Schwarz carries this image ideally, accompanied by the fine trumpet-playing of Gabriele Cassone.

If not flawless compared to the studio series, this Pilgrimage encourages a heart-warming depth of engagement with the music.

'Cantatas, Volume 9: Lund/Leipzig'   Ⓟ
Cantatas Nos 47, 96, 114, 116, 148 & 169. Der Geist

hilft unser Schwachheit auf, BWV226. Vor deinen
Thron ich hiermit, BWV668
Katharine Fuge sop **Frances Bourne, Nathalie
Stutzmann** mezs **Charles Humphries, Robin Tyson**
countertens **Christoph Genz, Mark Padmore** ten
Stephan Loges, Gotthold Schwarz basses
**Monteverdi Choir; English Baroque Soloists /
Sir John Eliot Gardiner**
Soli Deo Gloria ② SDG159 (138' · DDD · T/t)
Recorded live at Allhelgonakyrkan, Lund, on October
14, 2000; Thomaskirche, Leipzig, on October 22, 2000
Ⓜ❶❷➔

If 'rating' Bach cantatas is a perilous business,
Nos 148, 114 or 47 undeniably fall outside the
category where the incremental impact of the
whole work can be said to transport the listener
into another sphere altogether. Each, however,
contains some exceptional movements, including ebullient choruses and one or two memorable arias. The opening salvos of the thrusting
No 148 are less gripping than might have been
the case given more time (the *concertante* trumpet also seems a touch recessed), but Gardiner
manages to convey an exceptional logic in the
restless rhetorical figures of 'Ach, lieben Christen', a piece which plays fascinatingly on the
contradictions of divine encouragement and
admonishment.

This cantata also includes the aria 'Wo wird in
diesem Jammertale', a model of the extended
soul-searching tableau in which, here, the singer
and obbligato flute are co-subsumed within a
vale of sorrow. It is beguilingly delivered by
tenor Mark Padmore and flautist Rachel Beckett, the highlight of the Lund programme,
alongside a delightfully measured performance
of the motet *Der Geist hilft*.

The introduction of young solo singers brings
many fresh nuances to the 17th Trinity Sunday
works, though the experienced team for the 18th
Sunday from St Thomas's, Leipzig, provides
rather more consistent and embedded readings.
One of Bach's most incandescent and gracious
choruses, 'Herr Christ, der ein'ge Gottessohn'
(No 96) compels Gardiner to draw richly on the
irradiating tonal and textural contrasts of lyrical
choral writing under the stellar filigree of a sopranino recorder.

The resolute confidence of Gotthold Schwarz's
characterful singing in this work prepares us for
an electrifying account of the Sinfonia of No 169
(Howard Moody's obbligato organ playing a lesson in unfussy finesse), which itself heralds Bach's
least celebrated but, arguably, most refined and
mature alto cantata. Nathalie Stutzmann sails
through each portion with her inimitable diction
and plush allure. The centrepiece is, of course,
Bach's brilliant reworking of the Siciliano from
the Concerto, BWV1053, and Gardiner takes
this briskly enough for Stutzmann to shape the
extensive embellishments within an especially
elegant phraseology. Another stellar stage.

'Cantatas, Volume 13: Cologne/Lüneberg'   Ⓟ
Cantatas Nos 36, 61, 62, 70a, 132 & 147

Joanne Lunn, Brigitte Geller sops
Michael Chance, William Towers countertens
Jan Kobow ten **Dietrich Henschel** bar
**Monteverdi Choir; English Baroque Soloists /
Sir John Eliot Gardiner**
Soli Deo Gloria ② SDG162 (134' · DDD · T/t)
Recorded live at St Maria im Kapitol, Cologne, and
Michaeliskirche, Lüneburg, in December 2000
Ⓜ❶❷➔

If the church year begins in Advent, Gardiner's
Pilgrimage had to wait until the home-straight
of the millennial project before engaging with
the six cantatas for the first and fourth Sundays.
The concert in Cologne presents Nos 61, 62
and 36 in a repeat triptych of his 1992 accounts
(Archiv). Now the regal opening of Bach's first
setting of *Nun komm, der Heiden Heiland* has
become articulated with an even greater gestural
purpose, as indeed has the later, edgy and dramatic concerted setting.

The slower tempi here and in the other cantatas are largely governed by the resonant
acoustic of St Maria im Kapitol. The performances from this leg of the tour provide welcome alternative readings to the earlier version
(No 36 perhaps rather less), which remains one
of Gardiner's most durable Bach studio
recordings of cantatas; here the arias are altogether less lyrically inclined or characterised.
Jan Kobow's tame 'Bewundert' from No 62 is
not a patch on Anthony Rolfe Johnson's wonderful reading; only Dietrich Henschel's purposeful call to arms of 'Streite, siege' and the
ingenious and delectable chorale-duet from
No 36 seem to improve on Gardiner's previous
encounter.

These are, all the same, creditable performances of three marvellous works but the visit to
Lüneburg the next week brings rather more
musical sustenance. The fluency and dramatic
immediacy of *Wachet! betet!* (No 70) is telling
indeed. Most impressive is the panache and
finely judged pacing of the subsequent movements – in which Henschel is again supreme. No
132 receives an exceptional performance, the
line led by soprano Brigitte Geller and Henschel
with real class, and so too the ubiquitous *Herz
und Mund* (No 147). It is as powerful and effective a performance as you're likely to hear of a
perennial favourite.

'Cantatas, Volume 23: Arnstadt/Echternach'   Ⓟ
Cantatas – Nos 42, 67, 85, 104, 112, 150 & 158
Gillian Keith, Katharine Fuge sops
Daniel Taylor, William Towers countertens
Charles Daniels, Norbert Meyn tens
Stephen Varcoe bass **Monteverdi Choir;
English Baroque Orchestra /
Sir John Eliot Gardiner**
Soli Deo Gloria ② SDG131 (111' · DDD · T/t)
Recorded live at Johann-Sebastian-Bach-Kirche,
Arnstadt, on April 29 & 30, 2000; Basilique
St Willibrord, Echternach, on May 7, 2000   Ⓕ❶➔
The seven cantatas here, nominally represent-
ing the works for the two Sundays after Easter,

cover an unusual range from No 150 to the dazzling maturity of three pastoral cantatas from three different cycles in Leipzig. As Gardiner reminds us in his entertaining diary, the Neue Kirche in Arnstadt is now named after its teenage protégé organist and it seems appropriate that the early cantata *Nach dir, Herr, verlangen mich* should appear at the very place in which it probably received its premiere. One observes the ostentation of youth where Bach rolls out his command of past and current *musica lingua* as an advertisement of his ability.

The performances from Arnstadt are generally fresh and satisfying, and in No 150 there is a real sense of occasion. There are significant challenges in the burly orchestral concerto movement which opens *Am Abend* (No 42) and its long meandering aria 'Wo zwei und drei', bravely negotiated by Daniel Taylor but which, for me, cries out for the embracing security of a fine mezzo or contralto. The bold *Halt im Gedächtnis* (No 67) receives a committed reading but the extraordinarily dramatic scene with bass and chorus (where Christ brings peace and assurance to his ostracised disciples) fails to resonate with special moment.

The more durable performances come from Echternach in Luxembourg. *Du Hirte Israel* (No 104) is a gloriously poised work, unassuming on the surface and yet requiring the judgement to 'lift' each balletic movement without pushing the pace. Gardiner is only thwarted from hitting the spot by generally uneventful solo singing.

Ich bin ein guter Hirt (No 85), on the other hand, conveys the delicate and subtle pastoral conceits of 'Christ, the good shepherd' with endlessly alluring dialogues between on-form singers and instrumentalists, notably some disarmingly beautiful oboe playing, a performance of real distinction. The concise No 112 (following Psalm 23 to the letter) glows with the same ardour. It is indeed the second disc which establishes the longer-term credentials in this richly endowed and unique series.

'Cantatas, Volume 10: Potsdam/Wittenberg'　Ⓟ
Cantatas Nos 5, 48, 56, 79, 80, 90 & 192
Joanne Lunn *sop* **William Towers** *counterten*
James Gilchrist *ten* **Peter Harvey** *bass*
**Monteverdi Choir; English Baroque Soloists /
Sir John Eliot Gardiner**
Soli Deo Gloria ② SDG110 (122' · DDD · T/t)
Recorded live at the Erlöserkirche, Potsdam,
on October 29, 2000; the Schlosskirche, Wittenberg,
on October 31, 2000　ⒻⓄⒹ

There is unpredictable excitement in the random way the fruits of John Eliot Gardiner's Bach Pilgrimage are being released, as the next steps of that memorable year are retraced with autumn cantatas from Leipzig (19th Sunday after Trinity) and three Reformation pieces. Volume 10 represents another compelling reminder of what Gardiner can achieve in

Bach when he has the wind behind him – 'living' these works appears to have fired the imagination.

The largest work here is *Ein feste Burg* (No 80) whose gothic arches of sound find rasping advocacy in the Schlosskirche on the site where Luther preached. His famous hymn is most effectively fortified with a rousing bass sackbut in the first chorus. Here and in the outstanding sister-piece *Gott, der Herr* (No 79), the performances are distinguished by a palpable immediacy. The cathartic duet 'Wie selig' (No 80) from William Towers and James Gilchrist is a treasure.

The quality of music never lets up in Potsdam. *Wo soll ich fliehen hin* (No 5) is one of the finest of Bach's chorale cantatas, its hymn nurtured by an arresting concerto style which conveys the gnawing presence of sin and the yearning to escape its insidious influence. The contrast between its opening fantasia and the radiant tenor aria 'Ergiesse' is skilfully negotiated: James Gilchrist relishes the transformation of the chorus's 'flight' motif into one of tactile pleasure as the divine spring washes away all man's blemishes.

Mention must be made of Peter Harvey's cultivated and flexible bass. Joanne Lunn is perhaps not ideal but the chorus and orchestra are in stirring form and the recorded sound is captivating.

'Cantatas, Volume 17: Berlin'　Ⓟ
Cantatas Nos 16, 41, 58, 143, 153 & 171
Ruth Holton *sop* **Lucy Ballard, Sally Bruce-Payne**
contrs **Charles Humphries** *counterten*
James Gilchrist *ten* **Peter Harvey** *bass*
**Monteverdi Choir; English Baroque Soloists /
Sir John Eliot Gardiner**
Soli Deo Gloria ② SDG150 (96' · DDD · T/t)
Recorded live at the Gethsemanekirche, Berlin, on
January 1 & 2, 2000　Ⓜ ⓄⓄⒹ

Performed on the first days of the new millennium, this Pilgrimage volume has an especially candid coherence about it. These six New Year cantatas consistently speak of new prospect and a consolidated ambition to serve God's purpose.

If trumpets predominate in the festive exulting of the first four cantatas, the forces diminish markedly in Nos 153 and 58, partly because the theme of joy is startlingly checked by the fear of evil influence but, also, because Bach's hardworking troupe would have been sung-out after a busy Christmas. The resonant Gethsemanekirche in Berlin is beautifully handled throughout by both Gardiner and his engineers.

Most stirring perhaps is the bold canvas of *Jesu, nun sei gepreiset*, whose energetic climbs (with, in the opening chorus, one exceptional break to wave farewell on the words 'that we in prosperous peace have completed the old year') are negotiated with exceptional bravura. Then, later, there's a pastoral aria with oboe contours of shepherding solace that one recognises from the *Christmas Oratorio*.

If pickings are rich here, the 'guardian' arias are most illuminatingly realised by James Gilchrist, notably in 'Woferne' from the same cantata, whose piccolo cello circumnavigates the all-encompassing grace of the vocal line. Possibly even more beguiling is the conceit of untainted bliss in 'Geliebter Jesu' in No 16 with its stunning oboe da caccia accompaniment. Bach instils an innocence and trust here which Peter Harvey virtuosically sets up in the great solo nestling between the exhortations of the maverick aria-chorus, 'Lasst uns jauchzen'.

The opening cantata, No 143, may be a spurious work: there's something of the apprentice about it. This could not be further from the truth in the concise masterpieces No 153 and 58. In the former, there's something touching about Sally Bruce-Payne emerging from the Monteverdi Choir to sing her cathartic 'Soll ich meinen' after the mental breakdown of 'Stürmt nur' (a fine 'rage' aria). *Ach Gott, wie manches Herzeleid* is given a slightly brittle reading here. Gardiner reminds us again here that his hit-rate is exceptionally high.

'Cantatas, Volume 19: Greenwich/Romsey' [P]
Cantatas Nos 3, 13, 14, 26, 81, 155.
Jesu, meine Freude, BWV227
Joanne Lunn, Katharine Fuge *sops*
William Towers, Richard Wyn Roberts *countertens*
Julian Podger, Paul Agnew *tens* **Gerald Finley,**
Peter Harvey *basses* **Monteverdi Choir; English**
Baroque Soloists / Sir John Eliot Gardiner
Soli Deo Gloria ② SDG115 (128' · DDD · T/t)
Recorded live at the Old Royal Naval College,
Greenwich, London, on January 16-17, 2000; Romsey
Abbey, Hampshire, on January 30, 2000   ℗●◗▸

Gardiner's performance of *Ach Gott, wie manches Herzeleid* bends the ear towards the power of doleful dissonance, as the opening chorus wends its way through the 'narrow path of sorrow' with all the emblematic trappings of the operatic chaconne. Equally compelling is the taut, cathartic duet 'Wenn Sorgen', where Joanne Lunn and Richard Wyn Roberts chase each other in canonic bliss – in what Gardiner describes as Bach's 'Singin' in the Rain'.

Indeed, it is the naturalness of the solo singing that marks out this latest volume. Not always smoothed out or glamorous, the response is always fresh, engaged and alive to text. Roberts proclaims his consoling chorale in Meine Seufzer with a fervour encapsulated in the opening aria by the passionate angst of Julian Podger's exhortation and – if it seemed possible – yet greater despair from the slightly uneven but characterful Gerald Finley in 'Achzen und erbärmlich Weinen'.

William Towers brings a telling control and declamation to the fine opening aria of *Jesus schläft*. Gardiner rightly asserts that few places reveal the operatic Bach more triumphantly than the peerlessly graphic aria 'Die schäumenden Wellen' – especially in the slightly more forgiving space of Romsey Abbey, allowing Paul Agnew to let rip brilliantly. Bach is not just profoundly arrested by the raging sea but also by the implications of faith following Jesus's calming miracle in Peter Harvey's authoritative 'Vox Christi' scena. The bonus of the great motet *Jesu, meine Freude*, performed with customary vividness if not polish by the Monteverdi Choir, completes another memorable addition to the series.

'Cantatas, Volume 20: Naarden/Southwell'   [P]
Cantatas Nos 18, 84, 92, 126, 144 & 181
Angharad Gruffydd Jones, Gillian Keith, Miah
Persson *sop* **Wilke te Brummelstroete, Robin**
Tyson *countertens* **James Gilchrist, James Oxley**
tens **Jonathan Brown, Stephan Loges** *basses*
Monteverdi Choir; English Baroque Soloists /
Sir John Eliot Gardiner
Soli Deo Gloria ② SDG153 (95' · DDD · T/t)
Recorded live at the Grote Kerk, Naarden,
on February 20, 2000; Southwell Minster on
February 27, 2000   Ⓜ●◗▸

The weeks leading up to Lent carry a preparatory message which unifies these latest Pilgrimage cantatas: namely, one of expressing gratitude for spiritual blessings and – as specifically articulated in the wonderful minuet alto aria of the first work, BWV144 – the robust exhortation to 'be happy with your lot and get going'.

Gardiner's rapt performances launch themselves magnificently from the 'standing start' (as he aptly calls it) of the above-mentioned piece, whose opening chorus is stripped of all indulgence, in both setting and rendering, to the unequivocal aggression of 'Erhalt uns', via the emotional extremes in the chorale cantata, *Ich hab in Gottes Herz und Sinn*, whose muscular hymn by Paul Gerhardt is worked over by Bach in juxtapositions of extraordinary range.

Then, on a more reflective note, comes the solo soprano cantata *Ich bin vernügt*, receiving a measured, rhetorically questing reading from Miah Persson. If not instantly radiant, this is terrific Bach-singing and Persson extends her fine contribution with a wonderfully moving 'Meinem Hirten', the last aria in No 92: one of those irresistible vignettes of unswerving discipleship in pastoral mode.

Likewise, there are outstanding contributions from the compellingly focused James Oxley in the 'rage' aria 'Seht, seht!' ('See, see how all things snap, break, fall'), almost Schreier-like in its onomatopoeic designs, Stephan Loges's suitably avaricious and pettifogging representation of those who 'devour the seed' in No 181 and the invigorated Monteverdi Choir extending the conceit, in No 126, in perhaps the most angry piece Bach ever composed. Spoiling for a fight, 'fending off murderous Papists and Turks' – an odd sentiment to be conveying in these ecumenical times – Gardiner's forces are on splendid form in another exceptional volume.

'Cantatas, Volume 22: Eisenach'   [P]
Cantatas Nos 4, 6, 31, 66, 134 & 145

Angharad Gruffydd Jones, Gillian Keith sops
Daniel Taylor counterten James Gilchrist ten
Stephen Varcoe bass Monteverdi Choir; English
Baroque Soloists / Sir John Eliot Gardiner
Soli Deo Gloria ② SDG128 (121' · DDD · T/t)
Recorded live at the Georgenkirche, Eisenach, on
April 23-25, 2000   Ⓜ ❶ ❶ ➡

Easter 2000 had strong historical resonances for
Sir John Eliot Gardiner's cantata pilgrims, as
these outstanding works were performed in St
George's, Eisenach, where Bach was baptised,
and only a stone's throw from Wartburg Castle
where Luther completed his New Testament
translations.

One can only guess what inspired an unusually
visceral reading of *Christ lag in Todesbanden*
(arguably Bach's first great creation), with a
plethora of extremes from the Monteverdi
Choir. One might quibble with moments where
orchestral gestures are a little exaggerated but
this is a performance where the sinuous lines and
the momentum of liturgical ritual allow Luther's
great hymn to take us tantalisingly to the brink
of Christ's victory.

The Easter cantatas receive some ebullient readings. Erfreut euch boasts one of Bach's longest
choral movements and the composer (and Gardiner) demands vigilance from his virtuoso
ensemble, whose roulades of quicksilver scales
shed all the fear of the preceding weeks. Despite a
few uncertainties in the chromatic solos of the
middle section, this is a powerful account whose
spiritual core is found in the central recitative-duet
between the allegorical characters Hope and Fear.

The presence of James Gilchrist in any Bach
recording raises the stakes and his singing in the
little-known pearl *Ein Herz* is an infectious display of the new believer's ecstatic joy, expressed
disarmingly in his first aria and reinforced in the
duet with alto 'Wir danken and preisen'.

This volume continues to present the riches of
the Pilgrimage with admirable consistency;
rough edges aside, there is a unique sense of
exploration and devotion to the music which
comes from the palpable adrenalin of live performance in an oeuvre which has, historically,
been studio-bound. *Bleib' bei uns*, with its strong
St John Passion undertones, is an embodiment of
the best in the millennial journey and receives
one of the most concentrated and telling performances on disc.

'Cantatas, Volume 21: Cambridge/Norfolk' Ⓟ
Cantatas Nos 1, 22, 23, 54, 127, 159 & 182
Ruth Holton, Malin Hartelius sops
Claudia Schubert, Nathalie Stutzmann contrs
James Gilchrist, James Oxley tens
Peter Harvey bass Monteverdi Choir;
Trinity College Choir, Cambridge;
English Baroque Soloists /
Sir John Eliot Gardiner
Soli Deo Gloria ② SDG118 (135' · DDD · T/t)
Recorded live at King's College Chapel, Cambridge,
on March 5, 2000; Walpole St Peter, Norfolk, on
March 26, 2000   Ⓜ ❶ ➡

This eclectic selection covers works for Quinquagesima, the Annunciation, Palm Sunday and
Oculi (the third Sunday in Lent) in arguably the
least even of the seven releases so far. Yet there
are significant contributions smattered throughout, not least Nathalie Stutzmann's purple-
clad *Widerstehe* (No 54). This true contralto
imparts a captivating resilience in the face of
sin's devious tricks.

Inspired by the chamber-like ecclesiastical
works of Bach's Weimar period, the reduced
string ensemble lends a similar intimacy to No
182, though both works suffer from some scrappy
playing that clearly could not be rectified simply
by dropping in 'patches' from before or after.
Stutzmann, however, projects just the right sense
of involvement without forcing the issue.

Wie schön leuchtet der Morgenstern (No 1) is the
major work here – a masterpiece of understated
majesty and gentle celebration (for the Annunciation) where Bach appears to alight on the
morning star as a direct resonance of Epiphany;
such musical connections within the cantata
oeuvre, throughout the church calendar, provide listeners with endless sources of fascination.
Gardiner's performance is more an example of a
splendid occasion captured rather than a notable
addition to a distinguished discography.

Cantatas Nos 22 and 23 were Bach's first to
have been performed at Leipzig, audition pieces
for the post of Thomascantor before his eventual
appointment. Both were performed in the same
service on the morning of February 7, 1723.
Given the Lenten context, Bach hardly had a
chance to flex his muscles in opulent
displays of orchestration but he makes up for this
with two pieces of subtle stylistic range. *Jesus
nahm zu sich die Zwölfe* (No 22) is strikingly
prescient of Passion narrative as Christ prepares
for his death with melismas of distilled sadness
and acceptance of destiny. Peter Harvey's is an
affecting performance, as is the incrementally
impressive *Du wahrer Gott* (No 23), of which
Gardiner completely has the measure.

One special movement to bottle? 'Es ist vollbracht' from No 159 – arguably even better than
the setting of the words at the end of the *St John
Passion*. Heartfelt singing from Harvey is
adorned by playing from oboist Marcel Ponseele which is as exquisite as you'll ever hear.

'Jesu, deine Passion'   Ⓟ
Cantatas Nos 22, 23, 127 & 159
Dorothee Mields sop Matthew White counterten
Jan Kobow ten Peter Kooij bass Collegium Vocale,
Ghent / Philippe Herreweghe
Harmonia Mundi HMC90 1998 (64' · DDD· T/t)   Ⓕ

'Jesu, deine Passion' represents one of Collegium Vocale Gent's most outstanding Bach
projects for quite a while. Not least the power of
the Quinquagesima (the start of the fasting
before Easter) message – the preparation and
prescience for all things 'Passion' – gathers Herreweghe into a contemplative world in which he
feels most responsive.

The four works here are all masterpieces (sure, No 22 was probably composed in a hurry as a pre-Sermon accompaniment to No 23 as the dual audition pieces for Leipzig), rich in imagery and beguiling in the pure intricacy and invention of Bach's emotional world. Where does one begin? *Du wahrer Gott is*, at last, establishing itself as one of Bach's most profoundly crafted creations; Herreweghe asserts his luminous *a cappella* principles with an almost galant turn.

Elsewhere we hear Peter Kooy, mostly in good voice. *Es ist vollbracht* from No 159 is a restrained affair but effective nonetheless, especially with the exquisite oboe-playing of Marcel Ponseele. This aria would grace the *St Matthew Passion* with its Picander-esque sensibility (not least the setting of the words 'Welt, gute Nacht!', redolent of 'Mache dich').

This is, above all, a highly atmospheric programme, often overwhelming in content. *Herr Jesu Christ, wahr' Mensch und Gott* (No 127) is another corker: the opening chorus sublime in its incandescent contrapuntal mastery and then the main aria, 'Die Seele ruht', whose funeral bells (through recorders and *pizzicato*) are beautifully portrayed in Dorothee Mield's brittle but awestruck delivery.

Cantatas Nos 51 (arr W F Bach), 202 & 210　　　　　ℙ
Christine Schäfer *sop* **Musica Antiqua Köln / Reinhard Goebel** *vn*
DG 459 621-2GH (62' · DDD · T/t)　　　　　Ⓕ**Ⓞ**ⒹＧ

Of the two wedding cantatas, *Weichet nur, betrübte Schatten* (No 202) ranks among Bach's best-loved, but the other, *O holder Tag, erwünschte Zeit* (No 210), is much less heard. To these, Christine Schäfer adds another Bach favourite, *Jauchzet Gott in allen Landen!* (No 51) which, although not specifically for a wedding, confirms propriety in a nuptial context.

The partnership of Schäfer and Reinhard Goebel with his Musica Antiqua Köln is an interesting one, and rewarding more often than not. Schäfer is a spirited singer with a bright tone and an agile technique. Her clearly articulated phrases accord well with Goebel's well-defined instrumental contours and colourfully characterised rhythms – the fourth aria of No 210, in the rhythm of a polonaise, is admirably enlivened in these respects – and her well-controlled vibrato is a pleasure throughout.

If Emma Kirkby's performance of this piece and No 202 is more understated than the present one there's still an underlying expressive subtlety and a warmth of vocal timbre in her singing which may prove the more rewarding and enduring. The opening aria of No 202, a sublime piece of musical imagery, points up some of the essential differences between the two approaches: Schäfer declamatory, demonstrative and bright toned, with an edge to the voice, Kirkby, warm toned, alluring and exercising superb control throughout. On the other hand Schäfer's even technique, with its easier access to the highest notes of the range,

often has the edge over Kirkby in more virtuoso movements. And in No 210 Schäfer's vocal brilliance and unfailing security, together with Goebel's lively if on occasion provocative gestures, make one of the most alert and interesting performances of the piece. Schäfer also rises brilliantly to the occasion in No 51. A stimulating and often satisfying release.

Cantatas Nos 63[a], 91, 121 & 133. Magnificat, BWV243[a]
Dorothee Mields, [a]**Carolyn Sampson** *sops*　　ℙ
Ingeborg Danz *contr* **Mark Padmore** *ten* **Peter Kooij,** [a]**Sebastian Noack** *basses* **Collegium Vocale, Ghent / Philippe Herreweghe**
Harmonia Mundi ② HMC90 1781/2;
🔊 HMC80 1781/2 (117' · DDD · T/t)　　　　　Ⓕ

Bach composed Christmas music for more than 30 years of his professional life, but none in such a short a space of time as when he arrived at Leipzig in 1723. He used the relatively quiet Advent period to prepare for the onslaught of commitments around Christmas. This recording celebrates his vibrant representation of all the major themes of the season.

The *Magnificat* was his major contribution in his first year, as it was needed for Christmas Day. One his few works in Latin, this grandiloquent 16-movement canticle enabled the new Cantor to make his mark with a supreme exhibition of compositional mastery and acoustical opulence. Today's audiences usually hear the *Magnificat* in D, but it was originally composed in E flat, with four interpolated movements reflecting the special seasonal context. Philippe Herreweghe presents as tailored and tonally refined a reading as you are likely to find, as indeed he did in his more intimate but prosaic account of the D major version from 1990. This new performance also ranks with the best in terms of varied coloration and sonic choral brilliance.

Bach's Christmas cantatas from 1723 and 1724 comprise works of fascinating range. *Christen, ätzet diesen Tag* (No 63) is another extrovert celebration, with trumpets and drums, originally conceived in Weimar and smartened up for its new surroundings. Most interesting is 'Christen wir sollen', which presents the idea of thanksgiving as coming from within the dark recesses of Advent, preparation and expectation; Collegium Vocale are supreme in austerity, and the distilled *stilo antico*.

Herreweghe can be a touch anodyne, but this is a mild gripe for what is, overall, an outstanding collection of performances to celebrate a Bach Christmas – beyond the great Oratorio.

Cantatas Nos 82 & 199[a]　　　　　ℙ
Concerto for Oboe, Violin and Strings, BWV1060
[a]**Emma Kirkby** *sop* **Katharina Arfken** *ob* **Freiburg Baroque Orchestra / Gottfried von der Goltz** *vn*
Carus 83 302 (62' · DDD · T/t)　　　　　Ⓕ**ⓄⓄ**

One of the world's brightest Baroque ensembles performing with one of the world's most admired

Baroque sopranos is an enticing proposition. What's more, the solo cantatas on offer here are two of Bach's most moving: No 82, *Ich habe genug*, that serene contemplation of the afterlife; and No 199, *Mein Herze schwimmt im Blut*, a relatively early work with a text that moves from the wallowing self-pity of the sinner to joyful relief in God's mercy. Each contains music of great humanity and beauty, and each, too, contains an aria of aching breadth and nobility – the justly celebrated 'Schlummert ein' in the case of *Ich habe genug*, and in *Mein Herze* the humble but assured supplication of 'Tief gebückt'.

Both could have been written for Emma Kirkby, who's perhaps at her best in this kind of long-breathed, melodically sublime music, in which pure beauty of vocal sound counts for so much. The support of the Freiburg Baroque Orchestra is total, combining tightness of ensemble with such flexibility and sensitivity to the job of accompaniment that you really feel they're 'playing the words'. The Freiburgers also give one of the most satisfyingly thoroughbred accounts of the Violin and Oboe Concerto on disc. Add a recorded sound which perfectly combines bloom, clarity and internal balance, and you've a CD to treasure.

Cantatas Nos 82 & 199
Lorraine Hunt Lieberson *mez* **Peggy Pearson** *ob*
Orchestra of Emmanuel Music / Craig Smith
Nonesuch 7559 79692-2 (51' · DDD · T/t)   Ⓕ**OO**

Lorraine Hunt Lieberson's performances of these two cantatas are like deeply personal, supplicatory confessionals. The American mezzosoprano has a dark and well-focused sound, and brings words and music to life through a wealth of imaginative detail. The Orchestra of Emmanuel Music (a Boston-based church that incorporates the Bach cantata cycle into its regular liturgy) provides warm-hearted, rich-toned support from 11 strings plus bassoon, and Peggy Pearson shapes the obbligato oboe d'amore parts with exquisite sensitivity. A stunning and remarkably affecting achievement all around.

Cantatas Nos 80 & 147
Ingrid Kertesi *sops* **Judit Nemeth** *mez* **Jozsef Mukk**
ten **István Gáti** *bar* **Hungarian Radio Chorus; Failoni**
Chamber Orchestra, Budapest / Mátyás Antál
Naxos 8 550642 (54' · DDD)   Ⓢ�'t

Cantatas Nos 51 & 208
Ingrid Kertesi, Julia Pászthy *sops* **Judit Nemeth**
mez **Jozsef Mukk** *ten* **István Gáti** *bar* **Hungarian**
Radio Chorus; Failoni Chamber Orchestra, Budapest / Mátyás Antál
Naxos 8 550643 (50' · DDD)   Ⓢ➟

Naxos include here four of Bach's most celebrated and accessible cantatas. The performances are far removed in character from the complete Harnoncourt and Leonhardt edition on Teldec; women rather than boys sing all the soprano and alto solos, the Hungarian Radio Chorus is a mixed male and female ensemble and the Failoni Chamber Orchestra of Budapest plays modern rather than period instruments. However, for much of the time this is enjoyable spirited music-making which, in its choice of tempos, its understanding of recitative and its feeling for the lyricism of Bach's writing compares favourably with rival modern instrument versions. The disappointment lies partly in the choice of edition and solution to instrumentation. *Sheep may safely graze* (No 208) is without the treble recorders which Bach specifically asked for and which intensify the pastoral idyll. Here, furthermore the flutes are rather distantly balanced giving them a somewhat irrelevant role which is far from Bach's intention.

More serious is the decision to follow the inflated version of the first and fifth movements of *Ein feste Burg* (No 80) penned by Bach's eldest son, Wilhelm Friedemann shortly after his father's death. Here Friedemann added three trumpets and a kettledrum to the original texture of oboes and strings, and though some may prefer the more overt sense of occasion and the emphasis of the church militant, that this achieves, the scoring of the original is unquestionably effective and in keeping with the piece as a whole. Much else here is sensitively and unsentimentally performed. 'Jesu, joy of man's desiring' (from No 147) is perhaps a shade on the slow side.

Most affecting of all though, is the canonic alto/tenor duet from No 80 whose tender writing for oboe da caccia and violin has long been for some one of the purplest of all passages in the entire Bach cantata canon. The soprano Ingrid Kertesi negotiates the many difficulties of *Jauchzet Gott in allen Landen!* fluently and with a youthful zeal and few will be disappointed by her spirited artistry. These are two mainly very enjoyable discs which can be confidently recommended. Clear recorded sound.

Cantata No 198. Mass, BWV234.
Prelude and Fugue, BWV544.
Herzlich tut mich verlangen, BWV727
Katharine Fuge *sop* **Carlos Mena** *counterten*
Jan Kobow *ten* **Stephan MacLeod** *bass* **Francis**
Jacob *org* **Ricercar Consort / Philippe Pierlot**
Mirare MIR030 (78' · DDD · T/t)   Ⓕ

Rather gentler than the reconstruction culture of recent years, the Ricercar Consort ask the listener to contemplate the mourning for the Queen of Poland, Princess Christiane Eberhardine – in 1727, through a 'funerary monument' conceived around Bach's *Trauer* or Funeral Ode, the Mass in A major and contemporaneous organ pieces. We have no evidence that the Mass or the instrumental music appeared in the 'catalfalque in sound' (to quote Gilles Cantagrel), the memorial ceremony which occurred a month after the Queen's death and for which Bach was commissioned to write his exquisite Ode, but that is of little matter.

Whatever one's view on single-voiced Bach, the performances here are among the most persuasive in this medium. Philippe Pierlot understands the music from the thorough bass up – which one imagines should be common enough; yet so often a properly directed bass in Bach is traded for contrapuntal panache and facile rhythmic gesture. The Mass may lack a certain dramatic presence in the stunningly original exchanges in the *Gloria*, reconstituted from Cantata No 67 with its memorable Vox Christi 'scena' of Jesus's blessing bestowed on mankind. However, the vitality, interest and warmth of the opening, as in all the choruses on the disc, are determined above all by textural definition and characterful instrumental playing, the flutes beautifully appointed throughout.

The Ode is a remarkable example of a Bachian synergy between a carefully selected palette of light pastels (lutes, gambas, recorders, oboes d'amores and strings) and a melodic flavour and nostalgic intensity drawn from a Passion-inspired language, ideally crafted around the Enlightenment poetry of the young Leipzig humanist, Johann Christoph Gottshed. Its unique atmosphere is captured here, though as so often in single-voiced readings, the solo voices don't always have as much to say out of the collective realm. Francis Jacob's organ playing is both searchingly fluid and articulated. With the odd misgiving, this is a compelling and instinctive new Bach recording.

Additional recommendation

Cantatas Nos 39, 73, 93, 105, 107 & 131   **P**
Collegium Vocale, Ghent / Herreweghe
Virgin Veritas ② 562025-2 (120' · DDD)   Ⓜ🅑➔
This is a veritable treasure trove. The pick of the bunch is No 105, *Herr gehe nicht ins Gericht*, delivered with glowing intensity, led by the shimmering Barbara Schlick. Herreweghe and his beautifully blended ensemble give deeply considered performances.

Secular Cantatas, BWV201-16

No 201 Der Streit zwischen Phoebus und Pan;
No 202 Weichet nur, betrübte Schatten; **No 203** (doubtful); **No 204** Ich bin in mir vergnügt; **No 205** Der zufriedengestellte Äolus; **No 206** Schleicht, spielende Wellen; **No 207** Vereinigte Zwietracht der wechselnden; **No 208** Was mir behagt, ist nur die muntre Jagd; **No 209** Non sa che sia dolore; **No 210** O holder Tag, erwünschte Zeit; **No 211** Schweigt stille, plaudert nicht, 'Coffee'; **No 212** Mer hahn en neue Oberkeet, 'Peasant'; **No 213** Hercules auf dem Scheidewege; **No 214** Tönet, ihr Pauken!; **No 215** Preise dein Glücke, gesegnetes Sachsen; **No 216** Vergnügte Pleissenstadt

Cantatas Nos 207 & 214   **P**
Carolyn Sampson sop **Ingeborg Danz** contr
Mark Padmore ten **Peter Kooij** bass **Collegium Vocale, Ghent / Philippe Herreweghe**
Harmonia Mundi HMC90 1860 (56' · DDD · T/t)   Ⓕ

Whether parody or prototype, Bach's handful of secular cantatas present the face of a municipal composer who often sought to enhance his reputation by rising to special occasions. These two works are exceptional examples.

In *Vereinigte Zwietracht*, the subject is a popular professor named Kortte, whose inauguration in late 1726 encouraged his devoted students to commission a congratulatory work. For *Tönet, ihr Pauken!* from 1733 the purpose is more openly self-promotional as Bach sought, as he did in the dedication of his Mass of the same year, to ingratiate himself with the King of Poland and Elector of Saxony. This is, quite coincidentally, a brilliantly conceived homage cantata to the Elector's wife.

As usual, allegorical figures convey prized human qualities in various degrees of panegyric and yet the sensibilities in the music are far from obsequious. In recasting the third movement of the third *Brandenburg* Concerto for No 207, the tone is set for something compelling and moving. Philippe Herreweghe is equal to both with a performance of elegance and due restraint. Collegium Vocale – as their name suggests – relish the lines, the textural possibilities (note the mellow, dignified oboe sound) and the rhetorical detail. Mark Padmore's aria on 'Diligence' is a beautifully poetic and fluent reading and the later duet between Honour (Carolyn Sampson) and Happiness (Peter Kooij) trips with an effortless glee.

Tönet is the original source for movements which Bach was to recondition for the *Christmas Oratorio*. The opening movement is all but identical to the equivalent in the Oratorio but others present fascinating textual deviations which require, especially in the bass aria that was to become 'Grosser Herr', an adaptable ear for music so familiar.

Again, Herreweghe pitches the work just right, with consummate performances from the radiant Sampson (probably her best Bach work to date) and the soft-grained focus of contralto Ingeborg Danz. Her sincere and unsolicitous 'Gratitude', from No 207, with its winning obbligato flutes and mesmerising bass-line (it arches, hovers, rises and sinks), is exquisite. Kooij has rather less edge and character to his voice than in recent years but that's a small gripe in a release of considerable aplomb and exceptional vitality.

Cantatas Nos 211 & 212   **P**
Emma Kirkby sop **Rogers Covey-Crump** ten
David Thomas bass **Academy of Ancient Music / Christopher Hogwood**
L'Oiseau-Lyre 417 621-2OH (52' · DDD · T/t)   Ⓕ🅞➔

These two most delightful of Bach's secular cantatas here receive sparkling performances fully alive to the humour and invention of the music. The *Coffee* Cantata illustrates a family altercation over a current enthusiasm, the drinking of coffee. A narrator tells the story while the soprano and bass soloists confront each other in a series of delightful arias. Thomas brings out the crabby dyspeptic side of Schlendrian's character imaginatively and Kirkby makes a charming minx-like Lieschen. Covey-Crump's sweet light tenor acts as a good foil. The *Peasant* Cantata also takes the form of a dialogue, here between a somewhat dull and simple young man and his sweetheart Mieke, a girl who intends to better herself. Through the 24 short movements Bach conjures up a wonderfully rustic picture with some vivid dance numbers and rumbustious ritornellos. The soloists' nicely rounded characterisations emerge with great humour and Hogwood directs with vitality and sprightly rhythmic control. The recording is excellent.

Mass in B minor, BWV232

Mass in B minor   P
Carol Hall, Lynne Dawson, Nancy Argenta, Patrizia Kwella sops Mary Nichols mez Michael Chance alto Howard Milner, Wynford Evans tens Stephen Varcoe bar Richard Lloyd Morgan bass
English Baroque Soloists; Monteverdi Choir / Sir John Eliot Gardiner
Archiv ② 415 514-2AH2 (106' · DDD · T/t) Ⓕ**OOO**ᗡ→

Gardiner bases his forces on the famous memorandum which Bach handed to the Leipzig town council in 1730 outlining the vocal and instrumental requirements for performances of his church music. This results in a larger ripieno group. Gardiner also includes a harpsichord as well as an organ, the simultaneous playing of which, in Wolff's words, was 'a practice that can probably be assumed to be normative in the great majority of Bach's church music'. Gardiner uses women's voices for the soprano solo and ripieno lines and also a male alto soloist and male alto ripieno singers.

This is a fine achievement. Here the many strong points of his direction – a vital rhythmic understanding, a clear and positive sense of purpose, and a naturally affective response to Bach's music, combine in forming a concept of the work which not only explores its eneffable mysteries but also savours the magnificence of its architecture. The solo vocal line-up is a strong one and there are few weak moments; most of the soloists sing in the ripieno group as well, though Patrizia Kwella and Lynne Dawson appear to be exceptions to the rule. Nancy Argenta's 'Laudamus te', in which she is lightly partnered by Elizabeth Wilcock's sensitive violin playing is very fine and the singing of Mary Nichols who provides an expressive and well-balanced partnership with Patrizia Kwella in the 'Et in unum Dominum' deserves special mention. Michael Chance gives a beautifully controlled account of the 'Agnus Dei' and there are assured contributions elsewhere from Wynford Evans and Stephen Varcoe.

The crowning achievement of Gardiner's recording lies in the vitality, accuracy and

homogeneity of the ripieno singing it is in no sense intended to underplay the considerable virtues of the soloists and the orchestra; but this, after all, is first a vocal work and foremost a choral one. The ripieno singing at its very best – as it is for example, in the 'Et resurrexit' – is thrilling and gives a fervent imprint to the entire work. There is a spontaneity about this singing to which few listeners could remain indifferent. Gardiner's choruses are immediately striking and handled with such skill and rigorous discipline that repeated hearing in no sense diminishes their impact.

Mass in B minor   P
Carolyn Sampson, Rachel Nicholls sops
Robin Blaze counterten Gerd Türk ten Peter Kooij bass Bach Collegium Japan / Masaaki Suzuki
BIS ② .℗. BIS-SACD1701/2 (108' · DDD/DSD · T/t)
Ⓕᗡ→

This is, as you would expect from Masaaki Suzuki, a B minor performance of extraordinary devotional weight, as its resonant surround sound irradiates the score in a patiently constructed explication. The reflective objectivity may seem a little too tantalising as the strangely uncharacterised 'Christe eleison' duet is dogged by the kind of over-regulated articulations in the strings from which Bach Collegium Japan can still suffer.

Yet, after the somewhat lugubrious *Kyrie*, the *Gloria* fairly crackles and Suzuki's careful voicing between singers and instrumentalists generates extraordinary revelations (such as the consoling beauty of the 'Qui tollis' and, later, a remarkable reading of the *Sanctus*). The choral movements are admirably unhurried but purposeful. The solo movements are more variable: intonation takes time to settle early on, especially in the 'Laudamus te', and the 'Quoniam' is shorn of its eloquent grandeur in a prosaic romp, but 'Et in unum Dominum' reveals its expectant delights, as does Blaze's heart-stopping *Agnus Dei*.

Comparing this to Frieder Bernius's vital account with his Stuttgart forces (see below), the over-riding feeling with Suzuki is that generic beauty of sound, 'good judgement' and expert production (though the stereo picture is preferable to the undefined Super Audio) are collectively not quite enough. Preference remains with Bernius whose reverence for Bach's consummate compendium brings greater inner dialogue, colour and emotional risk and – apart from the expert soloists here – just a touch more quality. Still, this is a rounded and impressive reading whose 'Dona nobis pacem' encapsulates the best of Suzuki: committed, life-affirming and generous.

Mass in B minor   P
Mechthild Bach sop Daniel Taylor counterten
Marcus Ullmann ten Raimund Nolte bass
Stuttgart Chamber Choir; Stuttgart Baroque

Orchestra / Frieder Bernius
Carus ② 83 211 (101' · DDD · T/t)   Ⓕ**O**

Frieder Bernius gives us a B minor Mass which neither sits obediently in the groove of seasoned reverence nor resorts to well-worn and predictable period reflexes. It is a reading whose invigorating momentum is underpinned by a confident bass presence and an immediacy which resolutely ignores the heavy burden of posterity from which performances regularly suffer.

To say that the buoyant, syncopated *concertante*-like second *Kyrie* heralds an iconoclastic journey would be an exaggeration but Bernius knowingly approaches the Latin text as a means of liberating the abstract brilliance and lyricism inherent in Bach's great edifice. The 'Et in terra pax' is exquisitely judged with every one of those aspiring figures each yielding a little more ambition, as is the case in the urgent 'Gratias agimus' – though perhaps too driven for some. The same is true in both the 'Qui sedes' and *Agnus Dei* (despite the introduction being alarmingly faster than the initial vocal strains), sung by the refined Daniel Taylor, where both are approached with an easy and open-ended fluidity which avoids the obvious pit-falls of 'stop-start' between solo movements and the virtuoso ensemble 'concerti'.

Bernius repeatedly seeks a close alliance between his singers and instrumentalists with eloquent arched lines and yet without an obsession for homogeneity at the expense of individual character in the ensemble. The 'Crucifixus' is given an unselfconscious and gently accentuated reading, the chromatic ground and the flute and string 'pointings' instinctively realised. If the 'Confiteor' falls slightly short, the large choruses are open-breathed and thrilling. The Stuttgart Chamber Choir are full of vim and alertness and the trumpet playing is cataclysmically brilliant throughout. Of the solo singers, special mention must be made of the bass, Raimund Nolte, whose soft-grained 'Et in Spiritum Sanctum' stands out, though it is the effect of the combined ingredients which makes this the most striking and satisfying Mass in B minor to have appeared in years.

Mass in B minor
Susan Hamilton, Cecilia Osmond *sops* **Margot Oitzinger** *alt* **Thomas Hobbs** *ten* **Matthew Brook** *bass* **Dunedin Consort and Players / John Butt**
Linn ② ⊕ CKD354 (102' · DDD/DSD)   Ⓕ**OO**➔

In the booklet John Butt – Bach research specialist and author of the Cambridge Handbook on the Mass in B minor – explains his thoughts about historically informed performance practice (one voice per part, following the evidence outlined in the writings of Joshua Rifkin and Andrew Parrott), and discusses his choice to make the first recording of Rifkin's recent edition. Butt's interpretation owes firm allegiance to the 'OVPP' creed that will not please every-

one (even if detractors have not yet produced a single scrap of proof to refute it), but the Dunedin Consort and Players are never perfunctory or merely dogmatic. This performance demands to be heard.

Butt has considered every musical connection, context, texture and form. Not only do the individual movements feel spot-on in articulation and *Affekt* but the free-flowing pacing from one section to the next makes it easy for the listener to be pulled along. Each section of the Roman Ordinary is envisaged as continuous music, so there are no pregnant pauses between solo and choral movements. The first chords of the 'Kyrie' are sung boldly by the 10 singers (five 'principals' and another five 'ripienists'), and the solemn fugue is performed with gentle ardency; every gesture, detail, suspension and arching line is judged and executed with transparency, flexibility and rhetorical potency.

Thomas Hobbs and Matthew Brook sing the principal lower-voice contrapuntal passages with sensitive blend and superb intonation: they also declaim their solo movements with confidence and eloquence. The higher-voiced principals are marginally less successful: the combination of Susan Hamilton and Cecilia Osmond in the duet 'Christe eleison' occasionally threatens fragility but perhaps more authoritative and smoother-toned soprano soloists would have been less adaptable in the choruses. The galant character adopted by Butt's elegant harpsichord continuo, Patrick Beaugiraud's poignant oboe and tasteful strings during 'Qui sedes' proceeds without pause into 'Quoniam'; Anneke Scott's sparky horn playing and Matthew Brook's conversational authority conspire to take no prisoners, and the momentum carries through into a knock-out 'Cum Sancto Spiritu'.

Once upon a time the bravery of minimal forces tackling this repertoire was ridiculed by sniffy sceptics. Butt and the Dunedins might not change any entrenched minds; but the climax of 'Gratias agimus tibi' is as bold, resonant and glorious as anything one would expect (and not always get) from larger forces. The opening of the 'Gloria' bursts forth with radiant splendour but also has a dance-like lilt, and with Bach's intricate writing emerges as a compelling dialogue.

The Dunedin Consort's singing conveys the ebb, flow and shading of Bach's choruses with ease and naturalness. The sonorities of full homophonic chords concluding the grandest choruses are thrilling, whereas the densely polyphonic choral passages always possess clarity and logic thanks to the disciplined interplay of the singers.

Many excellent recordings of this monumental work cater for different tastes and priorities, and although an excellent one-voice-per-part version is nothing new, Butt's insightful direction and scholarship, integrated with the Dunedin's extremely accomplished instrumental playing and consort singing, amount to an enthralling and revelatory collective interpretation of the Mass in B minor.

BACH B MINOR MASS – IN BRIEF

Soloists; Monteverdi Ch; English Baroque Soloists / Sir John Eliot Gardiner
Archiv ② 415 514-2AH2 (106' · DDD)   Ⓕ❍❍❍❍▷
Ⓖ Stunning choral singing with fine solo work drawn from the choir. A performance that successfully captures the majesty of the work but also uncovers its intimacy.

Soloists; Tölz Boys' Choir; The Kings' Consort / Robert King
Hyperion ② CDD22051 (110' · DDD)   Ⓑ❍❍
A light-filled, fresh approach to the great Mass. The South German boys blend well with the English men's voices and the whole performance has an uplifting, celebratory feel.

Soloists; New Philharmonic Choir and Orchestra / Carlo Maria Giulini
BBC Legends ② BBCL4062-2 (138' · ADD)   Ⓕ
Recorded in St Paul's Cathedral in 1972, this is a performance on a large scale with broad tempi. The soloists and orchestra are superb, though the choir is rather indistinct.

Soloists; Viennensis Chorus; Concentus Musicus Wien / Nikolaus Harnoncourt
Teldec ② 4509-95517-2 (107' · ADD)   Ⓜ
Harnoncourt always has something fascinating and powerful to impart when he conducts Bach. His fine team of soloists does him proud in this recording from 1968.

Soloists; Bavarian Radio Chorus and Orchestra / Eugen Jochum
EMI ② 586537-2 (122' · DDD)   Ⓑ❍❍
If you're looking for modern instruments, superb soloists and a conductor totally in sympathy with this piece, Eugen Jochum's 1980 performance is well worth considering.

Soloists; Bach Collegium Japan / Masaaki Suzuki
BIS ② ♫ BIS-SACD1701/2 (108' · DDD)   Ⓕ▷
A moving, devotionally poised reading from this tried-and-trusted line-up.

Soloists; Stuttgart Chamber Choir; Stuttgart Baroque Orchestra / Frieder Bernius
Carus ② 83 211 (101' · DDD)   Ⓕ❍
A very striking and satisfying version of Bach's great Mass. Full of the spirit of discovery.

Soloists; Maîtrise de Notre-Dame, Paris; Ensemble Orchestral de Paris / John Nelson
Virgin Classics ✇ 370636-9 (153' · NTSC · 16:9 · 2.0 and 5.0 · 0)   Ⓕ
By no means perfect – there are some silly editing mishaps and awkward entries – but this performance is very much John Nelson's vision of the work. He has clearly thought long and hard about the B minor Mass and his passion and dedication shows. There is a real sense of occasion here.

Mass in B minor
Jenny Hill sop **Dame Janet Baker** contr **Peter Pears** ten **John Shirley-Quirk** bass **New Philharmonia Chorus and Orchestra / Carlo Maria Giulini**
BBC Legends ② BBCL4062-2 (138' · ADD) Recorded live at St Paul's Cathedral, London, in 1972   Ⓜ▷

In these days of period-instrument hegemony in the performance of Bach, this 'old-fashioned' B minor Mass may be considered an anachronism among younger collectors, but it has its own validity in terms of Giulini's absolute commitment to the work in hand and in the thoroughness of the execution. The downside of the large-scale approach can be heard in the somewhat lumbering account of 'Qui tollis', its upside in the grave, measured 'Gratias agimus' where the successive entries of the same idea are unerringly propelled. 'Et incarnatus est' and 'Crucifixus' in the *Credo* have a wonderful inwardness, the 'Sanctus' a power unavailable to a smaller choir.

When it comes to the soloists this performance wins hands down over authenticity. Janet Baker, on top form, is warm, vibrant, above all communicative with her words. Shirley-Quirk, in both his solos, is confident and bold in his vocal projection, secure and full in tone. There's no one to match them today. Jenny Hill sings purely and with fresh feeling. Only Peter Pears, already in his sixties, disappoints. The recording catches both the St Pauls' reverberation and the sense of a notable occasion.

Mass in B minor
Ruth Ziesak sop **Joyce DiDonato** mez **Daniel Taylor** counterten **Dietrich Henschel** bar **Maîtrise de Notre-Dame, Paris; Ensemble Orchestral de Paris / John Nelson**
Video director **Olivier Simonnet**
Virgin Classics ✇ 370636-9 (153' · NTSC · 16:9 · 2.0 and 5.0 · 0)   Ⓕ
Recorded live at the Cathedral of Notre-Dame, Paris, in March 2006

In a short interview before this concert in Notre-Dame Cathedral, John Nelson calls this performance 'a culmination of my experience with Bach' and it is one which is characterised by the conductor's highly considered and distilled understanding of the score. This is evident in his decisive direction, which is a model of clarity. The tempi are beautifully judged, the monumental choruses are chiselled lovingly and the image-laden and reflective movements – reaching a tortured sadness and composed dignity in a superbly judged 'Crucifixus' – all conspire towards a magisterial and logical conclusion in the 'Dona nobis pacem', where heart and head seem happily entwined.

What prevents this from being as memorable are both the capability of the forces, beyond a certain level, and the flawed filming – random and quick-fire shots from all manner of angles. The results are profoundly restless. There are far too many occasions where dubbing is ineptly handled, not least in the 'Laudamus te', where the admirable Joyce DiDonato is suddenly out of kilter with proceedings with an edit (26'39") using a patch where the tempo is far too fast. Comedy is the order of the day at the end of the 'Cum Sanctu Spiritu', where Nelson is filmed bringing off the ensemble at least two beats after the music has ended.

The Ensemble Orchestral de Paris perform in a fairly prosaic fashion by today's 'informed' standards and Nelson has a habit of accentuating appoggiaturas into submission; only the vibrant personality of the bassoons (notable in both bass 'arias') and the slick trumpeting ring out with complete confidence. The choir are committed and well drilled and Ruth Ziesak is the pick of the soloists, apart from an 'Et in unum' which is full of gratuitous accents – maybe in an attempt to encourage Daniel Taylor to take his head out of his copy. This DVD is not quite what it promises, though John Nelson's motivation and vision certainly bring a real sense of occasion.

Lutheran Masses, BWV233-36

F, **BWV233**; A, **BWV234**; G minor, **BWV235**; G, **BWV236**

Masses, BWV233 & 236. Trio Sonata in C,   **P**
BWV529 (arr Boothby)
Nancy Argenta sop **Michael Chance** counterten
Mark Padmore ten **Peter Harvey** bass
Purcell Quartet (Catherine Mackintosh, Catherine Weiss vns Richard Boothby vc Robert Woolley org)
Chandos Chaconne CHAN0653 (65' · DDD · T/t) Ⓕ**O**▸

The absurd prejudice that long deprived us of adequate recordings of Bach's four Lutheran Masses (or short Masses, as they're also known because, in accordance with Lutheran usage, they set only the *Kyrie* and *Gloria*) seems finally to have died a death. The Masses' crime has been to be made up almost entirely of paraphrases of cantata movements from the 1720s, yet Bach is Bach, whatever the circumstances, and this is wonderful music which, like the B minor Mass, offers sober old-style polyphonic choral movements of impressive cumulative power alongside choruses of almost physical excitement and clamour and some first-rate arias with instrumental obbligato.

As with volume 1, a one-to-a-part approach is taken, with the four vocal soloists also forming the choir and the Purcell Quartet being augmented by whatever extra instruments are needed. The result doesn't sound at all underpowered, and gains considerably over Herreweghe's typically well-turned but more traditional choral approach in vividness of texture and harmony, crispness of attack and a madrigalian litheness of expressive response.

The recording allows just the right amount of bloom without becoming washy. There are times when the two higher voices sound further

forward than the others, and Michael Chance occasionally disappears a bit towards the bottom of his range, but in general this release brings nothing but pleasure both in the music and in the stylish and lively performances.

Magnificat in D, BWV243

Bach Magnificat in D   **P**
Vivaldi Ostro picta, RV642. Gloria in D, RV589
Emma Kirkby, Tessa Bonner sops **Michael Chance** counterten **John Mark Ainsley** ten **Stephen Varcoe** bar **Collegium Musicum 90 Chorus and Orchestra /** **Richard Hickox**
Chandos CHAN0518 (64' · DDD · T/t) Ⓕ**O**▸

Hickox sets effective tempi in Bach's *Magnificat* and points up the many striking contrasts in colour and texture with which the piece abounds. From among the many successful features of the recording Stephen Varcoe's 'Quia fecit mihi magna' and the 'Et misericordia' sung by Michael Chance and John Mark Ainsley stand out. Vivaldi's *Gloria*, RV589 is the better known of two settings by the composer in D major. In this programme it's prefaced by an introductory motet *Ostro picta*, which may well in fact belong to the *Gloria* and is here sung with warmth and radiance by Emma Kirkby. Hickox's performance of this evergreen vocal masterpiece comes over with conviction. It's gracefully phrased, sensitively sung and affectingly paced with an admirable rapport between vocalists and instrumentalists. The sound is first rate.

Magnificat in D. Mass, BWV235. Fuga sopra il   **P**
Magnificat (Meine Seele erhebt den Herren),
BWV733. Prelude and Fugue, BWV541
Maria Keohane, Anna Zander sops **Carlos Mena** alto **Hans-Jörg Mammel** ten **Stephan MacLeod** bass **Francis Jacob** org **Ricercar Consort /** **Philippe Pierlot**
Mirare MIR102 (65' · DDD)
Includes bonus DVD, 'Magnificat' – a film by Pierre-Hubert Martin   Ⓕ**OOO**▸

Presented as a grand work with a single-voice chorus, this reading of the *Magnificat* is vitally conceived and multi-dimensional. So often the blend of a madrigal-sized choir detracts from a necessary corporate impact but such is the keen characterisation of the text and the willingness to 'come and go' in the texture that the Ricercar Consort convey, in the exultant framing movements and 'Omnes generationes', a rare combination of visceral rhythmic verve and vocal energy.

The solo movements are also bursting with personality, soprano Anna Zander delivering a robustly fluent 'Et exultavit' and her counterpart, Maria Keohane, a sensually captivating 'Quia respexit', whose oboe d'amore obbligato dovetails her lines with imploring beauty. If the alto, Carlos Mena, is the least vocally poised, then his

'Esurientes' is still exceptionally judged and his duetting with tenor Hans-Jörg Mammel in 'Et misericordia' sensitively projected. As throughout, all the singing is complemented by delectable instrumental accompaniments. 'Suscepit Israel' is the highlight, however: a bittersweet Carissimi-like trio of mesmerising fragility.

The G minor Mass represents a clever juxtaposition of conceits with the Magnificat, as Bach revisits choice cantata movements and parodies them so successfully that this lesser-known example from the four so-called 'Lutheran Masses' reminds us what they can communicate so specially with such a finely blended and integrated ensemble as the Ricercar Ensemble. Francis Jacob provides considered accounts of two significant solo organ works: supremely refined playing which articulates the ambitions of an exceptionally distinguished project.

St Matthew Passion, BWV244

St Matthew Passion   **P**
Anthony Rolfe Johnson ten Evangelist Andreas
Schmidt bar Christus Barbara Bonney, Ann
Monoyios sops Anne Sofie von Otter mez Michael
Chance counterten Howard Crook ten Olaf Bär bar
Cornelius Hauptmann bass London Oratory Junior
Choir; Monteverdi Choir; English Baroque Soloists
/ Sir John Eliot Gardiner
Archiv ③ 427 648-2AH3 (167' · DDD · T/t)
Ⓕ❍❍❍➼

What makes Gardiner's *St Matthew Passion* stand out in the face of stiff competition is, more than anything, his vivid sense of theatre. Bach's score is, after all, a sacred drama and Gardiner interprets this aspect of the work with lively and colourful conviction. That in itself isn't sufficient to ensure a fine performance, but here we have a first-rate group of solo voices, immediately responsive choral groups and refined obbligato and orchestral playing. Anthony Rolfe Johnson declaims the Evangelist's role with clarity, authority and the subtle inflexion of an accomplished story-teller. Ann Monoyios, Howard Crook and Olaf Bär also make strong contributions but it's Michael Chance's 'Erbarme dich', tenderly accompanied by the violin obbligato, which sets the seal of distinction on the performance. Singing and playing of this calibre deserve to win many friends and Gardiner's deeply felt account of Bach's great Passion does the music considerable justice. Clear recorded sound.

St Matthew Passion   **P**
Christoph Prégardien ten Evangelist Matthias
Goerne bar Christus Christine Schäfer, Dorothea
Röschmann sops Bernarda Fink, Elisabeth von
Magnus contrs Michael Schade, Markus Schäfer
tens Dietrich Henschel, Oliver Widmer basses
Vienna Boys' Choir; Arnold Schoenberg Choir;
Concentus Musicus Wien / Nikolaus Harnoncourt

Teldec ③ 2564 64347-2 (163' · DDD · T/t). Includes
enhanced CD with full autograph score   Ⓕ❍❍❍

Harnoncourt waited over 30 years to return to the 'Great Passion', which, but for his live Concertgebouw recording, he last recorded in 1970 when he had completed only a handful of cantatas in Teldec's defining series. Harnoncourt's revisitation presents a unique statement, one that can't fail to make an impression. Recorded in the sumptuous acoustic of the Jesuitenkirche in Vienna, there's a detectable flavour of southern European oratorio, ebulliently theatrical, immediate and free-breathing, and without the austerity of North German rhetoric. What's recognisably perceived as 'spiritual' in the carefully coiffured renderings of Suzuki (BIS) and Herreweghe (Harmonia Mundi) has no place here. Harnoncourt's religiosity isn't imposed but stands rather in a lifetime of musical distillation. This is instantly obvious in the opening chorus, where bridal imagery (in the music's secular, balletic lift) is juxtaposed with the physical imagery of what's at stake (in the broad, enduring bow strokes). While Suzuki's visceral chorale is more spine-tingling, the refinement here of 'Sehet, Wohin?' amid inexorable, paradoxically unquestioning direction, is masterful.

Pacing Part 1 is no easy task, and many a tank has been emptied before reaching what the great Bach scholar Friederich Smend called 'the central message of the work' (encompasssing Nos 46-49). Harnoncourt neither dallies unduly with the chorales nor charges through them; they skilfully counterbalance the remarkably incandescent narrative of Prégardien's Evangelist. The tenor shows a supreme attention to detail (even if his singing is sometimes effortful), and his dialogue with Matthias Goerne's vital Christus is especially compelling. Harnoncourt gives 'Blute nur' a touch of characteristic melodrama, but none can doubt how Dorothea Röschmann and the orchestra, between them, project its expressive core.

The strikingly cultivated crowd scenes of the well-drilled, medium-sized Arnold Schoenberg Choir make a strong contrast with the relatively brazen chorus in Harnoncourt's 1970 version. Unlike the specialists of the pioneering years, Harnoncourt hand-picks his soloists from the widest possible pool. Apart from the excellent Röschmann, Christine Schäfer impresses here far more than in her rather harried solo Bach disc (DG). More relaxed and controlled, she sings with acute coloration and stillness in 'Aus Liebe'. With Bernarda Fink's beguiling 'Erbarme dich' and Michael Schade's resplendent 'Geduld', only Oliver Widmer (who sings 'Gebt mir') gives less than unalloyed pleasure. The pick of the crop is Dietrich Henschel, who sings with great warmth and penetration with a 'Mache dich' to stand alongside (if not to rival) Fischer-Dieskau for Karl Richter. But with even these wonderful contributions, it still takes clarity of vision to graphically propel the drama yet also ponder it reverentially. Again, Harnoncourt leaves his mark with his unerring compassion at most of the critical points.

Finally, mention should be made of Concentus Musicus, grainy and luminous in ensemble, the obbligato wind a far cry from the softer-edged and rounded tonal world of almost all other 'period' groups. In short, this is the most culturally alert reading in years and a truly original and illuminating experience.

St Matthew Passion
Nicholas Mulroy ten Evangelist **Matthew Brook** bar Christus **Susan Hamilton, Cecilia Osmond** sops **Clare Wilkinson, Annie Gill** contr **Nicholas Mulroy, Malcolm Bennett** tens **Matthew Brook, Brian Bannatyne-Scott** basses **Dunedin Consort and Players / John Butt**
Linn ② 💿 CKD313 (161' · DDD)　　　Ⓕ🅾➤

Having swept the board with their Award-winning *Messiah*, John Butt and the Dunedin Consort and Players proceed headlong into the *summa* of dramatic religious masterpieces. One imagines, however, that this highly singular approach has been marinating in Butt's mind for years. This is a reading (the first to draw on the 1742 performing version with its re-allocation of continuo instruments) where scholarly and musical penetration is indivisible in the strength of the approach and the unswerving commitment of the 'players'.

And 'players' they are – except that Butt argues here for a new dramatic understanding of the *Matthew* (note the curious de-sanctification) where the work challenges the notion of 'parts' in an opera, towards various 'voices' which reflect the listener's absorption of the conflicting positions – both biographical and emotional – of the main protagonists and the most far-flung thresholds of human experience. This is achieved using the main singers, from the eight principal voices, in different contexts. Hence, as Butt explains in his illuminating note, the Evangelist may rally us to lament as an allegorical 'Daughter of Zion' in the opening chorus before darting in and out of the story in recitatives, chorus, aria and chorales, mixing up the past and present, first person and third person, in a web of intense and coherent narrative and reflection.

All of this presupposes a one-to-a-part troupe where all these subtle character combinations can be perceived. With such a spectacularly clear and balanced sound from Philip Hobbs, these ambitious perspectives are powerfully realised; refreshingly, too, Bach's 'novel in sound' is presented in a small inter-reliant ensemble without the need for tiresome dogmatic mantras on historical rectitude. Indeed, often so entwined are the textures that singers' vowels are shadowed by instruments in a close-knit rapport of exceptional immediacy.

For those steeped in both recent and old schools, this performance will resonate with both, though it is not always so easy to summarise how. The thread of intensity is achieved

largely by the focus and roundness of the Dunedin Consort's palette, the thrusting legatos (when called for) and the welcome presence of a strong, directed bass-line.

Such responses are relatively superficial because Butt's *St Matthew* is truly original in spheres resonating beyond established parameters. As his story-teller, Nicholas Mulroy brings his own striking naturalness of delivery, clarity of diction and honesty. At the start of Part 2, especially, there are moments of disarming reportage, such as the encounter with the High Priest where the Evangelist conveys a sickened response to Christ's humiliation and a gutting catch in his voice at the emptiness of Peter's denial. Yet it is Mulroy's identification with the outstanding Christus of Matthew Brook which raises the stakes in this performance. The timing between the two and the realism of the musical choreography is both remarkably patient and animated.

The only downside of a single-part *St Matthew* is that, while the singers – in Butt's words – 'become familiar to us as the piece progresses', this only works to advantage if they have the tonal and musical range to sustain such an extended and exposed vision. For all the stylistic nuancing and deft ensemble work of the sopranos, their arias rarely lift themselves beyond the generic. 'Ich will dir' sounds unsure and snatched and 'So ist mein Jesus gefangen' fails to demarcate the almost cosmic mystery ('moon and light have set in their anguish') alongside the admirable discipline of the crowd's graphic interjections.

No recorded *St Matthew Passion* comes without its blemishes but few parade such a compellingly fresh and raw realism, one so strongly identifiable by its wilful clarity of intent that it asks new questions about what this great work can say to us.

St Matthew Passion
Johannes Chum ten Evangelist **Hanno Müller-Brachmann** bass Christus **Christina Landshammer** sop **Marie-Claude Chappuis** alto **Maximilian Schmitt** ten **Thomas Quasthoff, Klaus Häger** basses **St Thomas Church Choir, Leipzig; Tölz Boys' Choir; Leipzig Gewandhaus Orchestra / Riccardo Chailly**
Decca ② 478 2194DX2 (160' · DDD) Ⓕ

Riccardo Chailly uses modern instruments including similarly pitched oboes d'amore and viola da gamba, to support all-male choirs with a separate boys' choir, and male and female soloists. It's clear that he has studied this many-faceted masterpiece deeply, but rejects the compromises that the composer had been forced to accept. And, in an interpretation conceived on a greater scale of involvement, Chailly tries to reach out to an ideal Bach might have had in mind. He doesn't lessen the significance of the Eucharist and empowers Johannes Chum and Hanno Müller-Brachmann to achieve heights of eloquence. All musicians in this performance are similarly empowered.

BACH ST MATTHEW PASSION – IN BRIEF

Soloists; Monteverdi Choir; English Baroque Soloists / Sir John Eliot Gardiner
Archiv ③ 427 648-2AH3 (167' · DDD) Ⓕ❶❶❶Ⓑ⇾
Ⓖ A stunning achievement, projected with powerful conviction. (Also available coupled with the B minor Mass and *St John Passion* – 469 769-2AB9: a real bargain.)

Soloists; Arnold Schoenberg Choir; Concentus Musicus Wien / Nikolaus Harnoncourt
Teldec ③ 2564 64347-2 (163' · DDD) Ⓕ❶❶❶Ⓑ⇾
Ⓖ With its ROM-capabilities offering the full autograph score, and Harnoncourt's long experience and sympathy for the work, this is one of the triumphs of recent times.

Soloists; Gabrieli Players / Paul McCreesh
Archiv ③ 474 200-2AH2 (161' · DDD) Ⓕ❶❶Ⓑ⇾
There's a brightness and lightness that comes from a one-to-a-part approach but you must decide whether it sacrifices some of the work's nobility.

Soloists; Choir and Orchestra of the Eighteenth Century / Frans Brüggen
Philips ② 473 263-2PH2 (160' · DDD) Ⓕ❶❶Ⓑ⇾
A wonderfully human and humane approach from Brüggen, who eloquently brings out the heart of the work, with its powerful emotional currents.

Soloists; Bach Collegium Japan / Masaaki Suzuki
BIS ③ BIS-CD1000/2 (164' · DDD) Ⓕ❶Ⓑ⇾
Suzuki touches the deep spiritual core of this universal drama and inspires his colleagues to scale truly dizzying heights. Beautifully recorded.

Soloists; Philharmonia Chorus and Orchestra / Otto Klemperer
EMI ③ 567538-2 (223' · ADD) Ⓜ❶
Bach on a large canvas from 1962 with fine soloists and the great Philharmonia Chorus. A strong, devotional reading with broad tempi – light years away from today's approach.

Soloists; Dunedin Consort and Players / John Butt
Linn ② ⊞ CKD313 (161' · DDD) Ⓕ❶Ⓑ⇾
A superb follow-up to their *Messiah*, and carrying the same conviction and passion. This is a *Matthew Passion* with a sense of being put on by a 'company'. It has drama but it also has tremendous intimacy.

Soloists; Hungarian Festival Choir and State Symphony Orchestra / Géza Oberfrank
Naxos ③ 8 550832/4 (163' · DDD) Ⓢ
Don't overlook this fine, modern-instrument set. There are no musical compromises and these fine Hungarian musicians sing and play with real conviction.

It falls to Chailly to point the unflinching emotional thrust of these pieces; and his interpretation of 'Können Tränen' is astonishingly far-sighted in thought and depth of feeling. Inspirationally, he establishes parity with the two violins by substituting a string bass line for the softer organ continuo (legitimate, as is Chailly's practice of switching to bassoons) which intensifies the expressive possibilities of this alto aria; and Marie-Claude Chappuis is alive to every nuance and inflection he uncovers at a daringly slow but flexible tempo. The death of Christ is anticipated; and as the end approaches Chailly tightens the tension. Jesus's cry in the darkness, 'My God, My God, why have you abandoned me?' reflects utter hopelessness, his demise on the Cross all the more sorrowful because the Evangelist's words are so unerringly timed and enunciated.

Decca's production team manages perspectives well, skilfully capturing the realism of Chailly 'live' as he resolutely claws his way into the anguish within this work of profound spirituality, betrayal and public execution. And he hurts.

St John Passion, BWV245

St John Passion Ⓟ
Gerd Türk *ten* Evangelist **Chiyuki Urano** *bass*
Christus **Ingrid Schmidthüsen, Yoshie Hida** *sops*
Yoshikazu Mera *counterten* **Makoto Sakurada** *ten*
Peter Kooij *bass* Bach Collegium Japan /
Masaaki Suzuki
BIS ② BIS-CD921/2 (110' · DDD · T/t) Ⓕ❶❶Ⓑ⇾

Bach seems to have performed his *St John Passion* on four Good Fridays during his tenure as Thomaskantor at Leipzig. However, he continued to make significant revisions right up to the last performance under his direction, on April 4, 1749. Of the four versions, the second, dating from 1725, contains the most distinctive revisions, the first version (1724) and the last bearing close affinity with one another. Masaaki Suzuki and his talented Bach Collegium Japan have chosen Bach's latest version. All has evidently been carefully prepared and deeply considered: what's refreshing about their approach is the importance afforded to the relationship between text and music, to the theological source of Bach's inspiration, and the emotional impact of the story and music on its audience. Some of their thoughts may strike readers as simplistic, even perhaps a shade sentimental, but on the strength of this fervent performance we can hardly question their sincerity.

The role of the Evangelist is sung with clarity and lightness of inflexion by Gerd Türk. His performance is eloquently measured, his phrasing well shaped and his articulation engagingly varied. All this makes him a riveting story-teller. The role of Jesus is taken by Chiyuki Urano, warm-toned and resonant. Ingrid Schmidthüsen and Yoshikazu Mera make strongly appealing contributions and Peter Kooij is satisfying and affecting.

Excellent, too, are the contributions of the Collegium's choir of women's and men's voices. Choral and instrumental articulation is incisive, propelling the rhythms with energy. The performance draws you in from the start. This is a major recording event, and an eminently satisfying one.

St John Passion (sung in English)
Sir Peter Pears ten Evangelist **Gwynne Howell** bass Christus **Heather Harper, Jenny Hill** sops **Alfreda Hodgson** contr **Robert Tear, Russell Burgess, John Tobin, Adrian Thompson** tens **John Shirley-Quirk** bar **Wandsworth School Boys' Choir; English Chamber Orchestra / Benjamin Britten**
Double Decca ② 443 859-2DF2 (130' · ADD)
Recorded 1971   ⓂⓄⓄ▷

Britten's recording of the *St John Passion* is very special indeed. Apparently he preferred to perform this Bach choral work because of its natural potential for drama. This account takes over the listener completely. The soloists are all splendid, though Heather Harper must be singled out, and the choral response is inspirational in its moments of fervour. Peter Pears is a superb Evangelist; Britten's direction is urgent and volatile; the Wandsworth School Boys' Choir sings out full-throatedly and the English Chamber Orchestra underpins the whole performance with gloriously rich string textures. The analogue recording offers a demonstration of ambient fullness, vividness of detail and natural balance. In fact, it's as if a live performance at The Maltings, Snape, has been transported to the area just beyond your speakers.

St John Passion   Ⓟ
James Gilchrist ten Evangelist **John Bernays** bass Christus **Eamonn Dougan** bass Pilatus **Joe Littlewood** sop **James Bowman** counterten **Matthew Beale** ten **Colin Baldy** bass **New College Choir, Oxford; Collegium Novum / Edward Higginbottom**
Naxos ② 8 557296/7 (110' · DDD · T/t)   Ⓢ▷

When you hear the ominous first chorus of Bach's *St John Passion* sung and played like this, liturgical ritual and visceral human drama make for an unusually intense experience. The bass line pulsates, the boys articulate the words with supreme clarity and the steady speed provides the movement with just the right length – a consideration too often neglected.

Recorded in New College, Oxford, the resident choristers, choral scholars and lay clerks appear to be entirely at ease with the special juxtaposition of quicksilver action and warm reflection which Bach demands in his choruses and chorales. Edward Higginbottom delivers a palpable sense of narrative, unfussy, as if habit lies at the root of its being. Just listen to the searing choral chromaticisms as Christ is brought before Caiaphas, the startlingly urgent declamations as the crowd bays for blood or the distraught tenderness of James Bowman in 'Es ist vollbracht'.

The Evangelist is the established tenor James Gilchrist, whose alert and straightforward singing makes his performance wholly believable. Of the current generation of choristers, Joe Littlewood reminds us that English choirboys can sing German music beautifully and convey the emotional essence of the text with maturity and purpose. His 'Ich folge' is a delight.

There's the odd strain in Matthew Beale's testing tenor arias but a pleasing timbre, as indeed there is in John Bernays' proud but unblustering Christus. If there's a general tendency, it's to allow the music to speak in its own time within a relaxed beat. The rest is instinct, experience and letting what will be, be. In such light comes this refreshing and captivating new interpretation.

St John Passion   Ⓟ
Markus Brutscher ten Evangelist **Ruth Holton** sop **Bogna Bartosz** contr **Thomas Laske** bar **Tom Sol** bass **Cologne Chamber Choir; Collegium Cartusianum / Peter Neumann**
Dabringhaus und Grimm ② MDG332 0983-2
(114' · DDD · T/t)   ⒻⓄ

Bach never entirely settled on a single view of the *St John* and there are at least four known versions, from Good Friday 1724 (Bach's first Easter in Leipzig) to a performance the year before he died. Peter Neumann expounds here on the virtues of the second, dating from a year after the first. The differences are neither extensive nor merely cosmetic; such is Bach's skilful pacing of the narrative that the original conception can shift markedly with an ever-so-slight nudge. The most immediate difference is the replacement of the austere, imagery-laden opening chorus, 'Herr, unser Herrscher', with the chorale fantasy 'O Mensch, bewein', later employed to conclude Part 1 of the *St Matthew*.

To the unsuspecting, this is the St John Passion that can have you thinking you're playing the beginning of the second disc of the St Matthew; this and two further movements demonstrate Bach's obsession – as with the cantatas of the period – with employing chorales as integral raw material. Yet perhaps more striking still is the interpolation of new arias, possibly derived from an earlier Passion setting conceived in Weimar. These arias, 'Himmel reisse' and 'Zerschmettert mich', are far more animated and graphic than anything in the earlier version. More remarkable still is 'Zerschmettert', performed with dazzling immediacy by Evangelist and tenor soloist Markus Brutscher. This is a superb piece of theatrical posturing of the sort that Handel and Telemann would have filched for their opera, had they only known. The one casualty in this version is 'Erwäge', a perennial favourite.

Given that the majority of the work remains common to all, this account should not be judged merely on its special properties. Neumann conveys strong musical ideas throughout: the choruses are wonderfully attentive to contrapuntal detail, and mesmerisingly varied in articulation. You can forget how beautifully crafted and selected the chorale tunes are in this work, and Neumann allows the music to breathe so that they represent a kind of caesura in the otherwise intense narrative.

Brutscher is a reliable, if somewhat monochrome Evangelist. His technical ease and superb intonation are noteworthy, but often he chooses to remain studiously uninvolved. Ruth Holton is made for the bright-eyed discipleship of 'Ich folge', but there's more to her Bach than youthful piping, as we can hear in her sensitive account of 'Zerfliesse, mein Herze'. However, the soloists individually aren't what marks out this recording; rather it's Neumann's corporate, controlled and intimate concept. He moves skilfully between incandescence and emotionally charged intensity. This is, then, a persuasive testament to Bach's most radically different version of the St John.

St John Passion   **P**
Caroline Stam sop **Peter de Groot** counterten
Charles Daniels, Gerd Türk tens **Stephan MacLeod,**
Bas Ramselaar basses **Netherlands Bach Society /**
Jos van Veldhoven
Channel Classics ② CCSSA22005 (112' · DDD/
DSD · T/t)   **F O**

This is the most beautifully packaged account of the *St John Passion* on the market. The performance is cushioned by informative essays and sharp reproductions of paintings and objects from the Museum Catharijneconvent, Utrecht. Such extras can illuminate an understanding of the music so long as the performance lives up to expectations. Thankfully it does.

Veldhoven brings his distinctive angle to the *St John* by presenting it as a notional 'first version'. Among some judicious tinkering, he ignores Bach's last-minute addition of flutes, made before the premiere in April 1724, and promotes an atmosphere of private devotion where the one-to-a-part ensemble allows for a distilled immediacy in the arias and flexible and varied choral contributions. This is a reading that shows that the argument for size in Bach's chorus – large or small – is better fought on musical grounds than musicological ones.

The Netherlands Bach Society, and Veldhoven especially, are more drawn to rhetorical effect than poetic instinct. The chorales are sometimes over-pointed and even precious, and string articulation rather unyielding, but little detracts from a profoundly luminous sense throughout, led by the supremely clear-sighted Evangelist of Gerd Türk. The other voices, soloists and ripienists alike, make a fine and colourful impression, especially in the crowd scenes, where Veldhoven presents them as a more questing, equivocal and three-dimensional group than the incessant hectoring of an uncompromising lynch mob.

This *St John* holds a special place in a notable catalogue of which, in their different ways, Gardiner, Fasolis, Higginbottom and

Suzuki are all leading lights. Veldhoven is thoughtful and effective, even if he never quite takes flight and allows the music to be expressed on the widest emotional canvas. The Super Audio sound is suitably rich and all-embracing.

St John Passion
Gerd Türk ten Evangelist **Stephen MacLeod** bass
Christus **Midori Suzuki** sop **Robin Blaze** counterten
Chiyuki Urano bass-bar **Bach Collegium Japan /**
Masaaki Suzuki Video director **Shokichi Amano**
TDK **DVD** DV-BAJPN (120' · 16:9 · 2.0 · 0)   **F**

With his outstanding series of choral recordings for BIS, Masaaki Suzuki has rightly established a high reputation for stylish interpretations of Bach. As he explains in a brief interview which comes as a supplement on this DVD, he had intensive training in period performance in Holland. Certainly, his vigour and sensitivity in Bach defies any idea that Japanese culture has been a barrier in authentically interpreting Bach. Suzuki recorded the *St John Passion* for BIS back in 1998. This DVD version marks a special performance recorded on the anniversary on 28 July 2000 of Bach's birth 250 years earlier. In essence the interpretation remains the same, with fresh, light textures and generally brisk speeds which yet allow for depth of feeling, and the sense of occasion is irresistible.

Gerd Türk gives an achingly beautiful performance, with his profound involvement all the more evident when seen as well as heard. Türk also sings the tenor arias, and the other soloists also have double roles, singing in the 16-strong choir before stepping forward when needed as soloists: Stephen MacLeod singing Christus as well as the bass arias, Chiyuki Urano singing Pilate and other incidental solos, Robin Blaze a superb alto soloist and the ravishing Midori Suzuki in the two soprano arias.

First-rate sound too. The leaflet offers minimal information and no text, though one can plumb into subtitles, either the original German or the English translation, but not both together.

St Luke Passion, BWV246 (attrib)

St Luke Passion (attrib)   **P**
Mona Spägele sop **Christiane Iven** contr
Rufus Müller, Harry van Berne tens **Stephan**
Schreckenberger, Marcus Sandmann basses **Alsfeld**
Vocal Ensemble; Bremen Baroque Orchestra /
Wolfgang Helbich
CPO ② CPO999 293-2 (106' · DDD · T/t)   **F O**

Though it isn't a genuine Bach work, those who love his music will want to investigate the *St Luke Passion*. In terms of scale, rhetorical intensity, structural and stylistic sophistication, musical invention and artistic ambition generally, it finds no common ground with his two extant Passions. But there's much that's intimate and touching about it. The meditative element comes less from contemplative arias than from a continuous and freshly fashioned narrative, although the arias, with their favoured wind obbligato parts, are often skilled and affecting. Wolfgang Helbich and his Bremen forces pitch the dramatic climate just about right throughout. Smoothly articulated, unmannered and technically accomplished, the chorales and *turba* scenes are especially well judged. The Evangelist, Rufus Müller, conveys the Gospel with soft-grained clarity and understated dignity and the other soloists do more than justice to the six arias.

Christmas Oratorio, BWV248

Christmas Oratorio **℗**
Monika Frimmer sop **Yoshikazu Mera** counterten
Gerd Türk ten **Peter Kooij** bass **Bach Collegium
Japan / Masaaki Suzuki**
BIS ② BIS-CD941/2 (145' · DDD · T/t)   Ⓕ**Ⓞ**▶

The six cantatas that make up Bach's *Christmas Oratorio* are part of a unified work celebrating not just Christmas itself but also the New Year and Epiphany. Masaaki Suzuki faces plentiful if not invariably stiff competition in this work. In fact, it outstrips most of its rivals, in respect both of vocal and instrumental considerations. A notable quality in Masaaki Suzuki's direction is his feeling for naturally expressive contours, allowing the music to breathe freely. Best of all, perhaps, is his refusal to pay even lip service to Bach's supposed predilection for fast tempos. Everything here seems to be exceptionally well judged, which isn't to say that the pace of individual movements is necessarily slower than those in competing versions but that it's more interrelated with a concept of each section as a whole, and more textually conscious than some.

The soloists are generally very good indeed. Yoshikazu Mera makes a distinctive contribution and Gerd Türk is a communicative singer whose light articulation suits his partly narrative role. Peter Kooij never puts a foot wrong, while Monika Frimmer makes a favourable impression in her duet with Kooij, 'Herr, dein Mitleid, dein Erbarmen'. A small, well-balanced choir of technical agility and an accomplished quorum of instrumentalists set the seal on an outstanding achievement. The finest all-round performance of the *Christmas Oratorio* on disc.

Christmas Oratorio
Sibylla Rubens sop **Ingeborg Danz** contr
James Taylor, Marcus Ullmann tens **Hanno Müller-Brachmann** bass **Gächinger Kantorei;
Stuttgart Bach Collegium / Helmuth Rilling**
Hänssler Classic ② CD92 076 (144' · DDD · T/t) Ⓜ**Ⓞ**▶

Energetic director Helmut Rilling is more fired up than ever here. The choruses crackle with thrilling fervour and a blistering attack and shine to notes which, alongside a forthright Gächinger Kantorei, carry the day persuasively on modern instruments. There will always be those for whom Rilling represents an inflexibility of phrasing and unyielding articulation in Bach, paradoxically more reminiscent of the least alluring elements of period performance than the 'ebb and flow' of mainstream consciousness. This recording doubtless reinforces the odd prejudice, though the habitually hard-edged orchestral textures of the Bach Collegium Stuttgart seem more mollifying and warm hearted in movements such as the pastoral Sinfonia at the beginning of Part 2 and the divinely inspired 'Schlafe, mein Liebster' later in the same cantata (it must be said now, flawed by a tiresomely repeated pull-up before the second phrase).

James Taylor is a natural Evangelist: articulate, discriminating, exacting if not emotionally candid. He also retains focus throughout the events of each tableau and gives clearly etched readings. Yet much of the credit must also go to the outstanding solo singing. Sibylla Rubens and Hanno Müller-Brachmann are stunning in the pivotal duet of Part 3, 'Herr, dein Mitleid', and Ingeborg Danz sings with exquisite and gentle poise in the scene-setting 'Bereite dich, Zion'. If her 'Schlafe' is a touch disappointing, then that reflects the weight of expectation which surrounds this central aria. If you prefer a mezzo to a countertenor, then only Anne Sofie von Otter for Gardiner or Christa Ludwig for Richter can better her largely satisfying contribution. Müller-Brachmann is a fine bass soloist in 'Grosser Herr' and as movingly intimate as Michael George for Philip Pickett in the recitative with chorale, 'Immanuel, O süsses Wort'. Rubens is on really terrific form throughout, and her 'Nur in Wink' in Part 6 is a model of outstanding Bach singing.

There's a spiritual containment which serves its purpose here – there's absolutely no sentimental guff – and yet it perhaps trespasses into the clinical too readily. Rilling, as ever, raises hopes and only intermittently fulfils them, but this is still a distinguished reading.

Motets, BWV225-30

Six Motets, BWV225-30. Motet, 'Ich lasse dich nicht',
BWV*Anh*159. Motet, 'O Jesu Christ, mein Lebens
Licht', BWV118 (alternate version)
Bach Collegium Japan / Masaaki Suzuki
BIS ⏺ BIS-SACD1841 (75' · DDD)   Ⓕ

With instruments or unaccompanied? Masaaki Suzuki comes heavily down on the side of the former. As there is an authentic orchestral accompaniment to *Der Geist hilft* – the first choir doubled by strings, the second by woodwind – he quite reasonably adopts the practice in *Singet dem Herrn* and *Fürchte dich nicht*. Where the choirs are united, in the fugal sections, the resulting sonorities are sumptuous. Elsewhere the accompaniment is scaled down to continuo and various combinations of strings, as in the fugue in *Jesu, meine Freude*. The exception is *O Jesu Christ*, BWV118, with its high parts for two 'litui'. Litui are explained in the booklet-note as 'probably meaning horns' but on this recording they sound more like cornetts. Whatever the instruments, they are quite beautifully played.

Mention of BWV118, which though described as a motet is more like a cantata movement, indicates that this disc ranges beyond the usual half-dozen; indeed, it also includes *Ich lasse dich nicht*, BWV*Anh*159, sometimes attributed to Bach's uncle, Johann Christoph. This consists of an antiphonal section for double choir and a single-choir treatment of a chorale tune: much like *Fürchte dich nicht*, in fact. More problematic is the authorship of *Lobet den Herrn*, with its independent continuo part.

Enough of these textual musings. The performances are splendid. After its solemn beginning, *Komm, Jesu, komm* is light, almost flirtatious in places; and the *staccato* of 'ich stärke dich' in *Fürchte dich nicht* is equally appealing. In *Jesu, meine Freude*, Suzuki finds a perfect balance between drama and lyricism, and *Singet dem Herrn* is full of rhythmic vitality. Recommended with all possible enthusiasm.

Wilhelm Friedemann Bach
German 1710-1784

Wilhelm Friedemann was Johann Sebastian's eldest son. He attended the Leipzig Thomasschule and therefore would have studied with his father. After university, he became organist at the Dresden Sophienkirche and later at the Liebfrauenkirche, Halle. He left under something of a cloud in 1764. He also lived in Brunswick and Berlin but rarely settled down and was clearly a difficult man, and his true potential never seems to have been realised.

Early in his career he focused on music for the keyboard (and he was by all accounts a very fine player); in Dresden his music tended to be orchestral; at Halle he wrote vocal music for the church before ending up writing chamber and keyboard works. His music tends to look Janus-like both back (his father's influence is evident) and forward, though without the dynamsim and imagination of his brother CPE.

Keyboard works

Harpsichord Sonatas – FK3; FK7. Fantasies – FK19; FK23; FKnv2. Polonaises – No 1; No 7; No 8; No 11. Fugues – No 1; No 2; No 3; No 6.
Maude Gratton *hpd/clav*
Mirare MIR088 (65' · DDD) Ⓕ

In Wilhelm Friedemann Bach's Fantasias, the music trips over itself in its rush towards the next harmonic goal, sometimes appearing to collapse several progressions within a single gesture. The

Polonaises, which ensured that his name survived into the 19th century before his father's was rediscovered, are more ordered but famously shot through with unexpected, startling effusions. The fugues, similarly, alternate between contrapuntal passages and more discursive episodes, and the sonatas (a form Wilhelm Friedemann seems to have pioneered) are filled with the excitement of new formal and expressive possibilities. The music flirts with incoherence and sometimes tips the precarious balance; but this recital is so well constructed that every piece hits the bullseye.

This is, in short, one of the best single selections of WF Bach's keyboard music. Maude Gratton's instinct for programming reveals great maturity and perception, and her playing is simply captivating, seeming to follow the composer in his flights of fancy and excesses of rigour with equal deftness. She's not afraid to share in his risk-taking either; it takes a sure touch to extract percussive effects from a clavichord without sacrificing pitch. The pathos of the slow movements is restrained but palpable: this is playing of real purpose and subtlety, and music that demands to be heard.

Cantatas

Cantatas – Lasset uns ablegen die Werke der Finsternis, F80. Es ist eine Stimme eines Predigers in der Wüste, F89   Ⓟ
Barbara Schlick *sop* **Claudia Schubert** *contr* **Wilfried Jochens** *ten* **Stephan Schreckenberger** *bass* **Rheinische Kantorei; Das Kleine Konzert / Hermann Max**
Capriccio 10 425 (54' · DDD · T/t)   Ⓕ�Ｏ

This disc makes a valuable contribution towards a fuller understanding of this highly gifted but complex member of the Bach clan. In the mid-1740s Wilhelm Friedemann was appointed Director of Music and organist at the Liebfrauenkirche at Halle. He remained in the post for almost 20 years, a period which witnessed the composition and performance of all the cantatas represented here. Among the many delights to be found in this music are those occasioned by Friedemann's disparate, even opposing terms of reference. In other words the stylistic vocabulary is both rich and varied, often harking back to a strong paternal influence – what better one has there ever been? JS Bach's idiom, for instance, is startlingly apparent in the opening chorus of the Advent cantata, F80 ('Let us cast off the works of darkness'). Both the arias of this fine cantata are of high quality, the first, for soprano with obbligato flute ably demonstrating how carefully Friedemann thought out his declamation.

For the most part the performances are excellent. The four soloists are first-rate, Barbara Schlick and Wilfried Jochens in particular; and the singing of the Rheinische Kantorei is effective, though just occasionally its component 16 voices sound under threat from Bach's sometimes exacting requirements.

Imaginative programming and sympathetic performances add to this musical revelation.

remarkable and a deeply moving achievement. Both performances are fine, that of the chamber settings beyond praise in its quiet intimacy.

Simon Bainbridge   English b1952

Bainbridge studied with John Lambert at the Royal College of Music in London and with Gunther Schuller at Tanglewood; American music, in particular Ives and Reich, has been a major influence. Among his most characteristic pieces are the Viola Concerto (1976), Concertante in moto perpetuo (1983) and Fantasia for two orchestras (1984). In 1997 Bainbridge won the Grawemeyer Award for Ad ora incerta (1993), an orchestral song-cycle for mezzo-soprano and bassoon on poems by Primo Levi. Other major scores include Scherzi (2000), heard at the Last Night of the Proms in 2005, the 30-minute Diptych for orchestra (2007) and Music Space Reflection, a work for 28 players inspired by and written to be performed inside buildings designed by architect Daniel Libeskind. Among recent works is Tenebrae, a setting of Paul Celan premiered by the Hilliard Ensemble and Arditti Quartet at Wigmore Hall, London.

Ad ora incerta

Ad ora incerta (Four orchestral songs from Primo Levi)[a]. Four Primo Levi Settings[b]
Susan Bickley *mez* [a]**Kim Walker** *bn* [b]**Nash Ensemble;** [a]**BBC Symphony Orchestra / Martyn Brabbins**
NMC NMCD059 (54' · DDD · T/t)   Ⓟ ⓄⒹ►

At the beginning of the fourth Primo Levi setting in *Ad ora incerta* (a depiction of the ghastly chemical factory attached to Auschwitz that Levi miraculously survived) there's a slow orchestral *crescendo*, like the panning of a camera to reveal the full horror of the scene. What follows isn't a shout of protest but sober lyricism, and when that *crescendo* returns it introduces an eloquently poignant melody. Simon Bainbridge is an uncommonly fine musical dramatist. He lets the words speak, and distils his music so as to clarify them. In *Ad ora incerta* the vocalist has a companion, a solo bassoon. Because that fourth poem repeatedly speaks of a dead companion, of course, but also in the way the bassoon shadows or reflects the voice, there's also a subtle and moving suggestion that after Auschwitz Levi lacked and longed for a companion, a fellow survivor who would understand his memories in ways that none of us can. It's scarcely believable that these beautiful but painful poems could be set to music; certainly not with the delicate and imaginative sympathy that Bainbridge shows here.

The four chamber settings are still sparer but no less gravely beautiful. In the seven brief lines of the first of them Levi distils the impossibility of communicating his experiences yet the imperative need to try. Bainbridge's setting conveys that, but adds the most restrained and loving pity. It's a

Edgar Bainton   English 1880-1956

Bainton studied under Stanford and Walford Davies at the Royal College of Music where fellow students and friends included George Dyson and Rutland Boughton. In 1901 he joined the Newcastle Conservatory (teaching piano and composition) and was appointed principal a few years later. Following internment in Germany during the First World War, Bainton resumed his activities in Newcastle, moving in 1933 to Australia as director of the New South Wales State Conservatorium, Sydney. His musical language is richly late-romantic with a strong sense of harmony but also a generous lyrical gift. He wrote four symphonies and a considerable body of work for chorus.

Orchestral works

Three Pieces for Orchestra. Pavane, Idyll and Bacchanal. The Golden River, Op 16. Concerto fantasia[a]
[a]**Margaret Fingerhut** *pf*
BBC Philharmonic Orchestra / Paul Daniel
Chandos CHAN10460 (69' · DDD)   Ⓟ ⓄⒹ►

All four works were composed prior to Bainton's permanent move to Australia in 1934, by far the most ambitious being the *Concerto fantasia* for piano and orchestra which won Bainton his second Carnegie Award. It is cast in four movements, launched by a solo cadenza destined to reappear at salient points throughout the work's half-hour course. Margaret Fingerhut's limpid pianism proves tailor-made for such a gorgeously lyrical, tenderly poetic and subtly integrated offering, which bids farewell in the sunset glow of a somewhat Baxian epilogue.

Bainton himself was the soloist for the 1921 world premiere of the *Concerto fantasia* in Bournemouth, where it shared a programme with the extremely fetching *Three Pieces for Orchestra* (1916-20). These grew out of incidental music for two Shakespeare productions in Ruhleben Camp near Berlin, where Bainton was held during the First World War, and are followed here by another most attractive triptych, the *Pavane, Idyll and Bacchanal* that Bainton wrote in 1924 for amateur groups but which requires a high level of technical expertise.

Unheard for the best part of a century, the four-movement suite *The Golden River* (1908, but revised four years later) derives its inspiration from a short story by John Ruskin and packs plenty of touching and colourful invention into its 16-minute span.

The BBC Philharmonic under the sympathetic baton of Paul Daniel seem to enjoy the experience. Excellent sound.

Sir Edward Bairstow English 1874-1946

English organist, composer and conductor. He studied with John Farmer at Balliol College, Oxford, and was articled to Frederick Bridge at Westminster Abbey, where he received organ tuition from the assistant organist Walter Alcock. On being appointed to Leeds parish church in 1907, he became organist to the Leeds Festival of that year and of 1910 and, later, conductor of the Leeds Philharmonic Society (from 1917 until his death). In 1913 he was appointed organist at York Minster and was made professor of music at Durham in 1927. An accomplished performer and accompanist, he was also in frequent demand as a lecturer and guest speaker. Bairstow's compositions are mainly for the church.

Choral works

Blessed City, heavenly Salem. Evening Services – in D; in G. If the Lord had not helped me. Jesu, the very thought of Thee. Let all mortal flesh keep silence. Lord, Thou hast been our refuge. Save us, O Lord. Five Poems of the Spirit[a]
St John's College Choir, Cambridge; Britten Sinfonia / David Hill with [a]**Roderick Williams** *bar* **Paul Provost** *org*
Hyperion CDA67497 (63' · DDD · T/t)   Ⓟ**O**▷

An excellent disc in regard both to the standard of performance and to the selection of Bairstow's music. And to that should be added straight away the quality of recorded sound, for in choral music of this type it is particularly important to allow for enough reverberance and sense of space without loss of clarity; also to balance choir and organ so as to keep a focus upon the singers and their words while enabling the organist to exploit the full range of the instrument in tone and volume. The recommendation for this new issue is confirmed most decisively by the inclusion of the *Five Poems of the Spirit*. Completed in 1944, it remained unpublished till after Bairstow's death. The orchestration was provided by Sir Ernest Bullock, and with its baritone solos and (largely) early-17th-century texts it stands, not unworthily, alongside Vaughan Williams's *Five Mystical Songs*. Particularly memorable is the fourth, Raleigh's 'Give me my scallop-shell of quiet', but all are attractive. Roderick Williams is the ideally suited soloist and the Britten Sinfonia do justice to a delightful score. In the accompanied anthems and services the organ parts are played with skilful registration by Paul Provost, and the choir sing throughout with their customary expressiveness and variety of colour: exquisitely (for instance) in the unaccompanied *Jesu, the very thought of Thee*.

Michael William Balfe Irish 1808-70

Balfe was the most successful composer of operas in English in the 19th century, a reputation grounded

on *his hugely popular work, The Bohemian Girl. He started his profesional career as a violinist in the Drury Lane orchestra before discovering his voice, a fine baritone (he made his stage debut in Weber's Der Freischütz). He studied composition with Paer in Rome where his first opera was premiered. His reputation was sealed with The Siege of Rochelle (1835). During his career he composed dozens of operas, all revealing an innate understanding of the voice. Characterisation was not a strong suit of his writing, the success of his works relying more on the 'hit' numbers he could invariably be relied upon to produce. In addition to singing and composing, Balfe developed quite a reputation as a conductor, taking charge of the Italian Opera at Her Majesty's Theatre in London fron 1846 until 1852.*

Falstaff

Falstaff
Marcel Vanaud *bar* Falstaff **Majella Cullagh** *sop* Mrs Ford **Sam McElroy** *bar* Ford **Barry Banks** *ten* Fenton **Tara Erraught** *sop* Annetta **Nyle Wolfe** *bar* Mr Page **Victoria Massey** *mez* Mrs Smith **Brendan Collins** *bar* Giorgio **Edel O'Brien** *mez* Mrs Quickly
National Chamber Choir of Ireland; RTÉ Concert Orchestra / Marco Zambelli
RTÉ Lyric FM ② CD119 (143' · DDD)   Ⓟ**OO**

This mighty impressive recording of a public performance in Dublin of Balfe's 1838 Italian opera *Falstaff* is no more likely to shift allegiance of fans of Verdi's or Vaughan Williams's operatic treatment of Shakespeare's *Merry Wives of Windsor* to Balfe than to Nicolai. However, it should have surer and wider appeal today than the melodramatic 'with one bound our heroine was free' operas such as *The Bohemian Girl* for which Balfe is most famed.

It's a score full of good tunes. From the joyous overture onwards, it's also a score full of skilfully worked numbers, several of which enjoyed favour on both sides of the English Channel for some years afterwards. The splendid trio for the ladies who receive a love letter from Falstaff (three in this version) has already been recorded; but others are no less impressive, including a duet for Ford and Falstaff and solos for Fenton and Mrs Ford. The latter two roles, written for Rubini and Grisi, contain fiendishly challenging writing that at times threatens to defeat Majella Cullagh. However, her final solo – along with that of the wholly admirable Barry Banks – justly receives the most enthusiastic applause of the evening. Altogether the recording is strongly sung and conducted, and it should be essential listening for any lover of Italian opera of its period.

The Maid of Artois

The Maid of Artois
Kay Jordan *sop* Isoline, Maid of Artois **Stephen Anthony Brown** *ten* Jules de Montangon **Jonathan Pugsley** *bass-bar* Marquis de Chateau-Vieux **John Molloy** *bass* Sans Regret **Rebecca Rudge** *sop*

Coralie **George Hulbert** bar Synnelet **Annette Reis-Dunne** sop Ninka **Adrian Lawson** bar Martin **Geoffrey Brocklehurst** bass Count Saulnier **John Elliott** ten Centinel **Victorian Opera Chorus and Orchestra / Philip Mackenzie**
Campion ② CAMEO2042/3 (148' · DDD · S/T/N) Ⓕ

All credit to Victorian Opera for undertaking the huge task of preparing performing material to record and document another Balfe opera as ably as they have here. In quality of composition, performance and recording alike, this is the most convincing exposition of Balfe's abilities to date – *The Bohemian Girl* not excluded.

Here in *The Maid of Artois*, with a libretto based on *Manon Lescaut*, there are winning melodies, flowing sub-Donizettian arias and ensembles, and imaginative orchestral scoring. Only infrequently does the piece lapse into mere British balladry. The work was composed for the celebrated Malibran, and it would be misleading to pretend that either Kay Jordan or Stephen Anthony Brown has complete control of the sometimes fiendishly high extremes of the heroine's and hero's music. Yet, within more comfortable range, both sing hugely impressively, and they get admirable support in key roles from Jonathan Pugsley and John Molloy, as well as from a strong chorus and orchestra under the inspired conducting of Philip Mackenzie.

On this showing Balfe deserves to be heard, and this set is commended warmly to lovers of early-19th-century opera.

Sir Granville Bantock British 1868-1946

After study at both Trinity College of Music and the Royal Academy of Music, Bantock pursued the dual career of conductor and teacher (he was professor at the University of Birmingham from 1908 to 1934). He was a major champion of music by his contemporaries, including Sibelius (who returned the favour by dedicating his Third Symphony to Bantock). He wrote a large amount of orchestral and large-scale choral works. Though his music was performed quite regularly during his lifetime, his reputation diminished until many of his works were recorded by Chandos and Hyperion (often under the baton of Vernon Handley). Key works of his are the oratorio Omar Khayyám (1906-09), the overture The Pierrot of the Minute (1908), the Hebridean Symphony (1915) and the Pagan Symphony (1928).

Pagan Symphony

Pagan Symphony. Fifine at the Fair.
Two Heroic Ballads
Royal Philharmonic Orchestra / Vernon Handley
Hyperion CDA66630 (80' · DDD · T/t) ⒻⓄ🄑

This collection confirms Bantock as a composer of real achievement whose music has been undeservedly neglected. He was a superb technician,

and his impressively large-scale structures have a real urgency. Or perhaps we should say, a real enjoyment. Despite the potentially tragic undertones of *Fifine at the Fair*, both works are almost untroubled, filled instead with the geniality of a craftsman joyfully exercising a craft of which he's master. The cleverness of the thematic transformations can make you smile with pleasure once you've worked out what he's doing – and then smile again at the realisation that the result of the transformation isn't an arid piece of technique for technique's sake, but another jolly good tune. And it's all very beautifully scored. He was a master of the orchestra. Can he be just a bit too clever, forever finding yet another ingenious and delightful thing to do with a scale-figure? Possibly, but he's never dull. Is real emotional depth lacking, despite hints of it whenever the wronged wife appears in *Fifine*? Maybe; possibly he was more given to enjoying than to pondering. The performances are stunning, the recordings most sumptuous. The two *Heroic Ballads*, for all that they're concerned with Cuchullan and his ilk, have not a shred of Irish Sea mist hanging around them: they're bold, colourful and stirring.

Pierrot of the Minute

Christ in the Wilderness – The Wilderness and the Solitary Place[a]. Overture to a Greek Tragedy. Pierrot of the Minute. Three Scenes from 'The Song of Songs'[ab]
[ab]**Elizabeth Connell** sop [b]**Kim Begley** ten
RPO / Vernon Handley
Hyperion CDA67395 (78' · DDD) ⒻⓇ🄑

Written quickly over the summer of 1908 and premiered at that year's Three Choirs Festival in Worcester, Bantock's comedy overture *Pierrot of the Minute* enjoyed much success before the First World War. It's a charming work, and Vernon Handley and the RPO deliver a performance of atmospheric delicacy and wit. Three years later Worcester also played host to the first performance of the *Overture to a Greek Tragedy*, an imposing curtain-raiser. Handley extracts every ounce of drama and lyricism from Bantock's ripely colourful inspiration; the majestically paced reading attains a moving nobility in the radiant, rather Straussian peroration.

From Bantock's two-and-a-half-hour setting of *The Song of Songs* (1912-26) come excerpts from three of the five scenes (or 'Days'). The Second Day and love duet from the Fifth Day are thematically related, and frame a purely orchestral sequence from the Third Day. In their respective roles of the Shulamite and her Shepherd lover, Elizabeth Connell and Kim Begley rise admirably to the wide-ranging vocal challenges. Connell also makes an affectionate showing in 'The Wilderness and the Solitary Place', a pretty, gently exotic six-minute aria from the 1907 oratorio *Christ in the Wilderness*. Excellent sound.

Sonatas

Cello Sonatas[a] – No 1 in B minor; No 2 in F sharp
minor. Solo Cello Sonata in G minor. Hamabdil[b].
Pibroch[b]. Elegiac Poem[a]
Andrew Fuller vc with [a]**Michael Dussek** pf [a]**Lucy
Wakeford** hp
Dutton Laboratories Epoch CDLX7107 (75' · DDD) Ⓜ

There are some rewarding discoveries here,
not least the two sonatas for cello and piano.
Both were penned during the first half of the
1940s, though the sketches for the B minor
Sonata date back to 1900. The latter is a finely
sculpted, generously lyrical creation, boasting
a particularly lovely slow movement. For the
scherzo Bantock pressed into service his earlier
Fantastic Poem of 1925, and the whole work
ends in a mood of autumnal nostalgia. The
impulse for the unaccompanied G minor
Sonata appears to have been Kodály's magnificent example in the genre: Bantock had heard
Beatrice Harrison give the British première in
1924. Cast in four compact movements, it's an
uncommonly well-knit essay and a demanding
workout for any aspiring virtuoso (as the giddy
moto perpetuo of the finale attests). We also get
two offerings for cello and harp: particularly
striking is *Pibroch*, a wonderfully affecting
'Highland lament'.

Andrew Fuller is an accomplished artist, mellow of tone and technically secure; he enjoys
sympathetic support from Michael Dussek.
Lucy Wakeford, too, contributes most beautifully. With eminently truthful sound and balance throughout, this enterprising collection
deserves a warm welcome.

Additional recommendation

Violin Sonatas Nos 1 & 2. Coronach (Pro patria mori).
Salve regina, 'Hail Queen of Heaven'
McAslan vn **Dussek** pf
Dutton Epoch CDLX7119 (64' · DDD) Ⓜ
   Works of bright-eyed vigour, deftness of touch and
   impeccable craftsmanship. Lorraine McAslan and
   Michael Dussek are consistently compelling and
   sure-footed.

Omar Khayyám

Omar Khayyám
Olivia Robinson sop **Catherine Wyn-Rogers**, **Siân
Menna** mezs **Toby Spence** ten **Roderick Williams**
bar **Edward Price** bass **BBC Symphony Chorus and
Orchestra / Vernon Handley**
Chandos ③ 💿 CHSA5051 (172' · DDD) ⒻⓄⓄⒹ⁺

London-born Granville Bantock used his early
championship of contemporaries – Strauss,
Debussy and especially Sibelius, who became a
close friend and correspondent – to enrich his
own Wagner-nourished sonorities and dramatic ambitions. Because he was British, he
fought shy of opera, channelling his gift for
theatre into song-cycles (he wrote 40),
symphonic tone-poems (he once planned a
24-work cycle), forward-looking multi-media
events (*Apollo and the Seaman* for film projection and orchestra) and oratorios (a 700-page
score of *Christus*).

Writing in the age of Mahler's Eighth and
Elgar's three major oratorios, Bantock found
101 quatrains of 12th-century Persian philosophical poetry – in the then widely read (and
very free) rendering of Pre-Raphaelite poet
Edward Fitzgerald – an irresistible challenge.
He set Fitzgerald's work by feeding his natural
gift for effective scoring and mood illustration
with his own first-hand impressions of the Middle East. It is to his credit that, throughout the
nearly three-hour performance span, genuine
symphonic interest rarely flags. His large
orchestra calls for two complete, antiphonally
placed, string sections, as well as the extra wind
and brass that his European heroes were deploy-
ing. The choral part becomes virtuoso in its
frequent use of unaccompanied, tricky-to-pitch
passages, while three named soloists, the
Beloved (mezzo), the Poet (tenor) and the Philosopher (baritone) are continually 'onstage' in
roles of operatic length.

This first recording reflects the detail and passion of Vernon Handley's championing of Bantock's kaleidoscopic output, and Stephen Jackson ensures that the choral input is similarly
lively and fresh. Toby Spence brings a bright
mix of Italianate slancio and English declamation to the Poet, combining well with Catherine
Wyn-Rogers's more controlled reading of the
Beloved in substantial (and *Parsifal*-like) duets in
Parts 1 and 3 (a highlight and a good starting-
point for samplers). Chandos's sound is suitably
lush, occasionally at the expense of the chorus's
diction. It's what recordings should be for, and
should encourage future festival performances.

Samuel Barber   American 1910-1981

*Born in West Chester, Pennsylvania, Barber showed
an early aptitude for music and studied at Philadelphia's Curtis Institute both as a singer (he had a fine
baritone voice) and as a composer. One of his earliest
works was his setting of Matthew Arnold's Dover
Beach which he himself performed (and recorded)
with string quartet. His musical language was unashamedly romantic and his biggest break came when
Toscanini performed the Adagio from his String
Quartet in a transcription for full strings – the
broadcast put Barber squarely on the musical map
and the work has gone on to be his greatest hit. Many
of his orchestral works from this period were performed by leading orchestras and conductors in the
US: his overture The School for Scandal (1933),
First Symphony (1936) and First Essay (1937). Of
his operas, Vanessa (1958) has enjoyed renewed popularity and even Antony and Cleopatra, written for
the opening of the new Met in New York, receives the*

occasional performance. His lyrical Violin Concerto is, alongside his Adagio, Barber's most performed and recorded work.

Violin Concerto

Barber Violin Concerto **Bloch** Baal Shem
Walton Violin Concerto
Joshua Bell vn **Baltimore Symphony Orchestra / David Zinman**
Decca 476 1723DGR (68' · DDD) Ⓕ**OOO**➔

Bell's coupling of the Barber Violin Concerto with Walton and Bloch brings together three highly romantic *concertante* works. Bell is placed less forward in the Barber than in the rich-sounding recordings of Gil Shaham and Itzhak Perlman, but if anything the results are even more intense. In the central slow movement the opening oboe solo leads to a magically hushed first entry for the violin, and the balance of the soloist also allows a quicksilver lightness for the rushing triplets in the *moto perpetuo* finale. Shaham may find more humour in that brief movement, but Bell's view is equally valid.

From an American perspective, Walton can well be seen as Barber's British counterpart. The playing of this American orchestra is warmly idiomatic, defying the idea that non-British orchestras find Walton difficult. Bell gives a commanding account – his expansive treatment of the central cadenza of the first movement, making it more deeply reflective – is most appealing. Not just there but in many gentle moments the rapt intensity of his playing is magnetic. Bell's is among the finest versions ever, with Bloch's own 1939 orchestration of *Baal Shem* offering a fine, unusual makeweight.

Barber Violin Concerto **E Meyer** Violin Concerto
Hilary Hahn vn **Saint Paul Chamber Orchestra / Hugh Wolff**
Sony Classical SK89029 (50' · DDD) Ⓕ**OO**➔

The 19-year-old Hilary Hahn once again shows her natural feeling for the American brand of late Romanticism, bringing out heartfelt emotion without overplaying it. There have been a number of outstanding versions of the Barber Concerto in recent years and Hahn's is among the finest ever. She stands between the urgently, fullbloodedly romantic Shaham and the more meditative Bell. It's partly a question of recording balances. The latter has the advantage of a recording which, setting him a little further back, allows *pianissimos* to be registered in a genuine hush. Hahn, like Shaham, is placed well forward, and it's hardly her fault that dynamic contrasts are reduced. The use of a chamber orchestra also affects the balance. The extra weight in the orchestral sound on the DG and Decca discs is here compensated by the incisiveness of the St Paul Chamber Orchestra under Hugh Wolff,

with textures a fraction clearer in detail. Even so, in the long introduction to the *Andante* a smaller body of strings, however refined, can't quite match in ear-catching beauty the bigger string sections of the LSO and Baltimore Symphony. What Hahn and Wolff nicely achieve between them, though, is a distinction between the first two movements, both of them predominantly lyrical. Deceptively, the first is marked *Allegro* (hardly sounding it), but here it's registered as a taut first movement leading to a powerful climax. Speeds in both the first two movements are a fraction broader than with either rival, but Hahn reserves her big coup for the *Presto* finale which is noticeably faster than either rival's, offering quicksilver brilliance and pinpoint articulation.

Meyer's Concerto makes an apt coupling. Unashamedly tonal and freely lyrical, it opens with a yearning folk-like melody that echoes Vaughan Williams, and there's also a folk-like, pentatonic cut to some of the writing in both of the two substantial movements. It's amazing what variety Meyer achieves (a string player himself), considering that conscious limitation of having a sustained drone underlying his argument. Hahn plays with passionate commitment, amply justifying her choice of so approachable a new piece for this important issue.

Barber Violin Concerto **Korngold** Violin Concerto, Op 35. Much Ado About Nothing, Op 11 – The maiden in the bridal chamber; Dogberry and Verges; Intermezzo; Hornpipe
Gil Shaham vn **London Symphony Orchestra / André Previn** pf
DG 439 886-2GH (71' · DDD) Ⓕ**O**➔

This performance of the Barber, warm and rich with the sound close and immediate, brings out the work's bolder side, allowing moments that aren't too distant from the world of Hollywood music (no disparagement there) and aptly the Korngold emerges as a central work in that genre. There have been subtler readings of Barber's lovely concerto, with the soloist not always helped by the close balance, but it's good to have a sharp distinction drawn between the purposeful lyricism of the first movement, marked *Allegro*, and the tender lyricism of the heavenly *Andante*. In the finale Shaham brings out the fun behind the movement's manic energy, with Previn pointing the Waltonian wit.

In the Korngold, Gil Shaham may not have quite the flair and panache of the dedicatee, Jascha Heifetz, in his incomparable reading (reviewed under Korngold), but he's warm and committed. What emerges again and again is how electric the playing of the LSO is under Previn, rich and full as well as committed. The recording helps, clear and immediate.

The suite from Korngold's incidental music to *Much ado about nothing*, dating from his early precocious period in Vienna, provides a delightful and apt filler, with Previn, as pianist, just as understanding and imaginative an accom-

BARBER VIOLIN CONCERTO – IN BRIEF

Joshua Bell; Baltimore SO / Zinman
Decca 476 1723DGR ⓂOOOOD→
An intense, beautifully conceived
performance, with the violin naturally
balanced. Zinman is a hugely sympathetic
partner. Coupled with Walton and Bloch.
A *Gramophone* Award-winner.

Hilary Hahn; St Paul CO / Wolff
Sony Classical 509970 89029-2 ⒻOO
A more transparent, smaller-scale perform-
ance that finds Hilary Hahn on fine form,
bringing out the lyricism of the work.
Coupled with Edgar Meyer's Concerto.

Gil Shaham; LSO / Previn
DG 439 886-2GH ⒻOD→
A rich, luxurious, Hollywood-style performance that makes the work sound bigger than
usual. Coupled, appropriately, with Korngold's wonderfully high-cholesterol Violin
Concerto and some violin and piano works.

James Buswell; RSNO / Alsop
Naxos 8 559044 ⓈD→
A strong, muscular performance, fresh and
spontaneous-sounding. The RSNO, nearing
the end of their Barber cycle with Marin
Alsop, have the measure of the idiom.

Isaac Stern; NYPO / Bernstein
Sony Classical SMK63088 Ⓑ
One of the first recordings of the work and
still one of the best. Isaac Stern's unique
sound and personality shine through the
somewhat dated sound.

Elmar Oliviera; St Louis SO / Slatkin
EMI 586561-2 ⓈO
A very fine budget-price version and a
welcome return to the catalogue, especially
as it comes in a superb two-disc Barber compilation that makes a perfect introduction.

Itzhak Perlman; Boston SO / Slatkin
EMI 562600-2 ⒷOOD→
Itzhak Perlman's elegant and honeyed performance returns at budget price as part of a
most appealing all-American programme
(Bernstein and Foss). Ozawa is a superb
accompanist.

Transcribed for flute and orchestra
Stinton; Philharmonia / Bedford
Regis RRC1100 Ⓢ
Really no more than a curiosity because the
Violin Concerto was so evidently conceived
for a string instrument that a transcriptions
seems unnecessary but Stinton makes a brave
stab at the work and the last movement, it
must be admitted, does work rather well
on the flute.

panist, and Shaham yearningly warm without
sentimentality, clean and precise in attack.

Additional recommendations

Violin Concerto
Coupled with: Souvenirs, Op 28. Serenade for Strings,
Op 1. Music for a Scene from Shelley, Op 7
Buswell vn **Royal Scottish National Orchestra /
Alsop**
Naxos 8 559044 (64' · DDD) ⓈD→
A fine performance, notable for its easy
spontaneity and unforced eloquence.

Symphonies Nos 1 and 2

Symphonies – No 1, Op 9; No 2, Op 19.
First Essay for Orchestra, Op 12. The School
for Scandal Overture, Op 5
Royal Scottish National Orchestra / Marin Alsop
Naxos 8 559024 (70' · DDD) ⓈOD→

That Marin Alsop is a musician of outstanding
gifts is amply reinforced by this all-Barber
anthology. In her red-blooded rendering of the
wartime Second Symphony, she shows just what
a powerfully inspired creation it is, extracting
every ounce of sinewy logic from its fraught
outer movements, while distilling wonder and
atmosphere in the haunting central *Andante, un
poco mosso*. No less convincing is her reading of
the magnificent First Symphony, always acutely
responsive to the music's daring expressive
scope and building climaxes of riveting cumulative intensity. In its unhurried authority, big
heart and epic thrust, it's the kind of interpretation you could have imagined from Bernstein in
his NYPO heyday. Elsewhere, she brings an
aptly bardic quality to the outer portions of the
First Essay, while few could fail to respond to the
twinkling affection and gentle wit she lavishes
on the irresistible *School for Scandal* Overture.
Were the orchestral contribution just a fraction
more polished, this would be a world-beater.
Zinman's stylish 1991 anthology with the Baltimore SO tends to throw into sharper relief the
relative shortcomings of Alsop's hard-working
Scots (their fiddles especially lack something in
silk-spun refinement and tone when playing
above the stave). The expert engineering can't
quite disguise the acoustical shortcomings of
Glasgow's Henry Wood Hall, but the result is
tonally truthful and conveys plenty of impact
when required.

Adagio for Strings, Op 11

Barber Adagio for Strings **Bernstein** Candide –
Overture **Copland** Appalachian Spring – Ballet
Schuman American Festival Overture
**Los Angeles Philharmonic Orchestra /
Leonard Bernstein**
DG Galleria 439 528-2GGA (54' · DDD)
Recorded live 1982 ⓂOD→

This is a beautiful collection of American music, lovingly and brilliantly performed. With Barber's lovely *Adagio* you might fear that Bernstein would 'do a Nimrod' and present it with exaggerated expressiveness. Although the tempo is very slow indeed, the extra hesitations aren't excessive and the Los Angeles strings play with angelic refinement and sweetness, as they do also in the many hushed sequences of the Copland ballet. There the live recording made in San Francisco in a dryish acoustic brings a degree of constriction at heavy *tuttis*, but the advantages of digital recording in this beautiful score are obvious, not least at the climax of the haunting variations on the Shaker hymn, *Simple Gifts*. To the three favourite works here is added William Schuman's brazenly extrovert overture with its virtuoso opening section, its quiet *fugato*, ominously introduced, and a brazen conclusion to match the opening. It's a splendid work, almost as joyously inspired as Bernstein's *Candide* Overture, with the composer here adopting a fairly relaxed speed, though with a wild coda.

Piano Sonata, Op 26

Piano Sonata, Op 26. Excursions, Op 20. Nocturne, Op 33, 'Homage to John Field'. Three Sketches. Ballade, Op 46. Interludes—No 1, Intermezzo. Souvenirs, Op 28
Daniel Pollack pf
Naxos 8 550992 (72' · DDD)   ⑤⊕

Daniel Pollack studied with (among others) Rosina Lhévinne and Wilhelm Kempf. His playing exudes confidence, especially in the more rhythmic and forthright passages. In his hands the Sonata is powerfully driven and crisply articulated, creating a palpable sense of raw energy and excitement. His full sonorities and sense of shape in the *Interlude* and the *Ballade* are also impressive, and while his tempo in the latter may seem a shade fast, it adds to the essential restlessness of the piece. In the more lyrical works, notably the *Nocturne*, however, Pollack's handling is too brusque, trampling roughshod over the contrast between passion and delicacy. The dance pieces of the *Excursions* and *Souvenirs* are generally more sensitive, and he effectively captures the diversity of distinctive flavours, from the slow blues (*Excursions*) to the Schottische (*Souvenirs*). Horowitz inevitably remains the benchmark in the Sonata, and his virtuoso fire is in a class of its own. Nevertheless, despite the poor recorded sound from Naxos's problematic Santa Rosa studio, this is an enjoyable disc and quite a bargain.

Knoxville: Summer of 1915, Op 24

Knoxville: Summer of 1915, Op 24[a].
Essays for Orchestra – No 2, Op 17; No 3, Op 47.
Toccata festiva, Op 36[b]

[a]**Karina Gauvin** sop [b]**Thomas Trotter** org
Royal Scottish National Orchestra / Marin Alsop
Naxos 8 559134 (57' · DDD · T)   ⑤OO⊕

Karina Gauvin and Marin Alsop take a nostalgic view of *Knoxville: Summer of 1915*. Theirs is an adult's bittersweet reminiscence rather than a child's innocent view. The outer sections sway slowly, the phrases longingly caressed as if soprano and orchestra were loath to let them go. Gauvin sings smoothly, generally emphasising song over text, though she's alive to James Agee's fragrant imagery, and varies the colour of her voice appropriately. With deeply expressive playing from the Royal Scottish National Orchestra, the result is ravishing; this is one of the finest versions of *Knoxville* to date.

Alsop's tautly argued Second Essay is equally satisfying. She resists the temptation to stretch the tempo at climactic moments, creating a strong sense of momentum; you're swept along by the music's powerful current.

Knoxville and the Essays pack a nice sonic punch. If only Thomas Trotter's brilliant execution of the solo organ part in the *Toccata Festiva* were recorded with greater presence than the acoustic of Paisley Abbey allows. The *Toccata* may not be top-drawer Barber, but it has its moments. Nevertheless, Alsop's ear-opening Barber series reaches a new high-point with this instalment. Strongly recommended.

Additional recommendation

Knoxville: Summer of 1915
Coupled with works by **Menotti**, **Harbison** and **Stravinsky**
Upshaw sop **Orchestra of St Luke's / Zinman**
Nonesuch 7559 79187-2 (44' · DDD)   ⑤⊕
Dawn Upshaw captures the childish innocence of Barber's gorgeous scena in a programme of comparable vocal treats.

Songs

Dover Beach, Op 3[a]. Hermit Songs, Op 29. Mélodies passagères, Op 2. Three Songs, Op 10. Four Songs, Op 13 – No 3, Sure on this shining night; No 4, Nocturne. In the dark pinewood. The Beggar's Song. There's nae lark
Gerald Finley bar **Julius Drake** pf
[a]**Aronowitz Ensemble** (Magnus Johnston, Nadia Wijzenbeek vns Jennifer Stumm va Guy Johnston vc)
Hyperion CDA67528 (62' · DDD · T)   ⑤OOO⊕

Performances of this calibre emphasise Barber's stature in the mainstream of 20th-century song composers. The tradition is Anglo-American and *There's nae lark*, written when Barber was 16 to a poem by Swinburne in imitation Scots, could even be by Quilter. But Barber soon gets into his stride and by the time he reached his Three Songs, Op 10, there's a rare kind of intensity as impressive as anything on this CD. The poems are from James Joyce's *Chamber Music*; Barber set a few more, such as *In the dark pinewood* included here; but what a tragedy he never set the whole cycle that could have been an American *Winterreise*. The *Hermit Songs*, fey and whimsically amusing, are probably the best-known set.

'Sure on the shining shore' is vintage Barber, and Finley and Drake are impeccable (as are the Aronowitz Quartet in *Dover Beach*). The French songs, to poems by Rilke, who did write in French, have less character, but the single songs are all gems. An outstanding release.

Agnus Dei, Op 11

Barber Twelfth Night, Op 42 No 1. To be Sung on the water, Op 42 No 2. Reincarnations, Op 16. Agnus Dei, Op 11. Heaven-Haven. Sure on this shining night. The Monk and his Cat. The Virgin Martyrs, Op 8 No 1. Let down the bars, O Death, Op 8 No 2. God's Grandeur **Schuman** Perceptions. Mail Order Madrigals
Anthony Saunders pf **Joyful Company of Singers / Peter Broadbent**
ASV CDDCA939 (66' · DDD · T)   ⒡⊙

Newcomers should make haste to track 6 for a pleasant surprise. Here they will encounter Samuel Barber's indestructible *Adagio* in its alternative and mellifluous 1967 vocal guise, set to the text of the *Agnus Dei*. Peter Broadbent's Joyful Company of Singers acquit themselves extremely well. Also to be particularly relished are the exquisite Op 42 pairing of *Twelfth Night* and *To be sung on the water*, the carefree lilt of *The monk and his cat* and, above all, the majestic, strikingly ambitious 1938 setting of Gerald Manley Hopkins's sonnet, *God's Grandeur* (perhaps the single most impressive achievement on the disc). Further delights are provided by Barber's countryman and contemporary, William Schuman. The concise, beautifully sculpted *Perceptions* (1982) are settings of choice aphorisms from the pen of Walt Whitman, while the *Mail Order Madrigals* (1972) wittily utilise the flowery prose drawn from advertisements contained within a Sears and Roebuck catalogue of 1897. A most attractive issue, in short, excellently produced and engineered.

Vanessa, Op 32

Vanessa
Christine Brewer sop Vanessa **Susan Graham** mez Erika **Catherine Wyn-Rogers** mez Baroness **William Burden** ten Anatol **Neal Davies** bass-bar The Old Doctor **BBC Singers; BBC Symphony Orchestra / Leonard Slatkin**
Chandos ② 🎵 CHSA5032 (123' · DDD/DSD · S/T/t/N)   ⒡⊙⊕

Gian Carlo Menotti took as his starting-point for the libretto of *Vanessa* the atmosphere of Isak Dinesen's *Seven Gothic Tales*. His story is original, but the ideas that fired him can be found in the stories. One of Dinesen's heroines lives a secluded life, and although beautiful, she's forlorn – 'she knew that she did not exist, for nobody ever looked at her'. Vanessa, too, has lived her adult life waiting for the return of her faithless admirer, Anatol. When he does come, it's an impostor.

For an opera that's so seldom performed, *Vanessa* has been accorded a generous three complete recordings. This new one, recorded in London's Barbican after a concert in 2003, has splendidly vivid sound. Leonard Slatkin draws full-blooded playing from the BBC Symphony Orchestra, accentuating Barber's use of yearning, Puccini-inspired melodies, laced with a few nods to Berg and Strauss. The weirdest music, that for the ball in Act 3, sounds like some kind of Western barn dance, even though the setting is northern Europe.

Excellent though Susan Graham is as Erika, Christine Brewer is so much in command, and in such splendid voice, there's no doubt it's Vanessa's story. One problem is that the three female voices sound a little similar: Catherine Wyn-Rogers is a youthful old Baroness.

Anatol, the greatest cad in opera since Pinkerton, is made almost sympathetic by William Burden. Neal Davies does what he can with the rather stock figure of the Doctor.

But listening at home one is conscious of an awful lot of generalised mood music. *Vanessa* was the last gasp of American *verismo*: its Met première in 1958 was in the same season as Bernstein's *West Side Story* on Broadway, and we all know what that led to.

Additional recommendations

Vanessa
Steber Vanessa **Elias** Erika **Resnik** Baroness **Gedda** Anatol **Tozzi** Old Doctor **New York Metropolitan Opera Chorus & Orchestra / Mitropoulos**
Sony Classical ② 88497 72400-1 (114' · ADD)   Ⓜ
The original-cast recording on RCA will always be irreplaceable. Brilliantly cast, it has the real feel of theatre. It is also Barber's first version, with four acts, and includes Vanessa's skating aria.

Richard Barrett   British b1959

Early studies in genetics were abandoned in favour of composition after an encounter with Michael Finnissy's work Alongside. He then studied with Brian Ferneyhough and Hans-Joachim Hespos at the Darmstadt Ferienkurse to which he returned later as a teacher. Barrett's music is characterised by an intensely fragmented, texture-focused approach. It is also notable for its extreme difficulty. He often employs electronics and leaves many decisions to the performers. Since 2003 he has been working on an eight-part cycle of compositions collectively entitled 'resistance & vision', of which the first (NO), fifth (Mesopotamia) and seventh (Nacht und Träume) have so far been completed and performed.

interference

interference[e]. transmission[b]. basalt[c]. air[d].
abglanzbeladen/auseinandergeschrieben[e].
knospend-gespaltener[f]
Elision ([b]Richard Barrett *elecs* [b]Daryl Buckley *elec gtr*
[a,f]Carl Rosman *cl* [c]Benjamin Marks *tbn* [a,e]Peter Neville
perc [d]Susan Pierotti *vn*)
NMC NMCD117 (64' · DDD)   (F)(B)→

The violent end of the world is perhaps dark
enough matter for Richard Barrett. His *interference* for contrabass clarinet, male voice and pedal
bass drum firmly punctuates the piece with
short, titanic stabs, played in true one-man-band
style with the foot. Simultaneously, contrabass
clarinettist Carl Rosman uses multiphonics,
throat-flutter and slap-tongue techniques while
vocalising a Latin text fragment from Lucretius'
apocalyptic poem *De rerum natura*. *interference* is
part of Barrett's larger *Dark Matter* work for
voices, ensemble and electronics but stands well
alone as a vehicle for extended technique on the
contrabass clarinet.

What sets Barrett apart is his unswerving
internal logic and consistency of style. While
others use extended technique to impress, the
works on this release use these in a natural and
unforced manner. The present disc carries this
through into a more intimate world of solo performances with members of new-music ensemble Elision. The impressive *transmission* closes
the disc with a *tour de force* for solo electric guitar
and live electronics, using a hybrid sound that
mixes acoustic and electric guitar output. Guitarist Daryl Buckley had a hand in devising the
guitar timbres that slide effortlessly from dense
electronic structures to fast, distorted passages
reminiscent of jazz-rock guitarist John
McLaughlin. The work ends with the sparse,
unamplified sound of the electric guitar. Buckley is to be congratulated on his near note-
perfect interpretation of a difficult, many-
layered score.

EARTH

Another Heavenly Day[a]. Negatives[a].
Codex I[b]. EARTH[c]. Ne songe plus à fuir[d]
[c]**Brett Kelly** *tbn* [c]**Peter Neville** *perc*
[d]**Friedrich Gauwerky** *vc* [a,b]**Elision**
NMC Ancora NMCD143 (79' · DDD)   (M)(B)→

Richard Barrett makes demands on the listener
only proportionately less than on the performer,
but his music is worth the attention of anyone
who believes that sound is a living entity in itself
rather than merely an expressive 'given'. The
bulk of this disc was first issued almost 15 years
ago and its reappearance is more than welcome,
confirming the consistency of Barrett's thinking
during the interim.

The shorter works demonstrate aspects of this
approach. *Ne songe plus à fuir* ('Dream no more
of fleeing') ruthlessly yet methodically dissects

the cello's sound world, while *EARTH* sets up an
abstract sequence of responses between trombone and percussion; one that *Another Heavenly
Day* takes to a more rarefied level with its fugitive yet arresting interplay of clarinet, electric
guitar and double bass. All three of these pieces
also form part of larger series – a typical Barrett
procedure conveyed *in toto* with the *Negatives*
cycle. Its five interrelated components variously
reflect and investigate each others' sound worlds
in a cumulative process that culminates with the
implosion of the final piece – in which percussion assumes the foreground to a point where
only piccolo and cello remain defiant.

Extended by the more recent *Codex I*, which
takes improvisational strategies to an extreme
without abandoning its conceptual focus, this
disc is a persuasive and representative way into
Barrett's music. The remastered sound, moreover, conveys more completely his concern to
make the recording integral to the performance
process rather than aiming for any unrealistic
'live' perspective.

Béla Bartók   Hungarian 1881-1945

*Bartók's early years – like his final ones – were spent
in economic hardship and poor health. His father, a
director of the local agricultural college, was a good
amateur pianist; his mother taught piano after her
husband's death (when Béla was seven), trekking
round from school to school with her young son and
daughter, eking out a living. Bartók suffered from
bronchitis and pneumonia and was treated (mistakenly) for curvature of the spine.*

*He was shy and highly introverted, a small, retir-
ing man who remained physically frail all his life. To
make up for it, he had a cast-iron will that brushed
aside rejection, incomprehension and failure. He
began composing aged nine and at 10 gave his first
concert as 'pianist-composer'. In 1894 the family
moved to Pressburg (Bratislava) where Bartók studied piano before enrolling at the Academy of Music in
Budapest.*

*In 1904, the year after graduating, he made a
discovery that changed his life. Up till then his musical heroes had been Richard Strauss, Liszt and his
slightly older fellow countryman Dohnányi. But
listening to Hungarian folk music galvanised his
creative thinking. With his friend Zoltán Kodály,
Bartók went on lengthy trips armed with an Edison
recording machine and a box of wax cylinders to collect systematically the folk tunes as performed by the
peasants of Hungary, Transylvania, Carpathia and
even as far afield as North Africa (1913) and Turkey
(1936). Their work, catalogued and documented,
was hailed as a major piece of ethnomusicology.*

*Thereafter, this music fed his soul and all his sub-
sequent music is imbued with the varied character of
his native folk music. The Budapest Academy offered
him a teaching post in 1907 (piano, not composition,
which Bartók always refused to teach) and he stayed
there until 1934. The more he composed, the more
his music became austere and experimental and,*

though it aroused strong opposition in his own country, outside Hungary his reputation grew steadily from a limited number of performances. Parallel to this was his burgeoning career as a pianist, predominantly in his own works.

Bartók saw that after the Anschluss in March 1938, it would be only a matter of time before Hungary fell to the Nazis. He was 58 years old, supporting his mother, wife and family – what was he to do? His mother's death in 1939 decided him. He would go to the United States. He was given a position at Columbia University and he composed and played a few concerts but the American public was indifferent. Though not totally impoverished at this time as legend has it, he certainly had very little money and his health went rapidly downhill when leukaemia was diagnosed.

Isolated, somewhat embittered at the lack of recognition and, worst of all, in increasing pain, Bartók's final completed score turned out to be his most popular, the Concerto for Orchestra. Before he died (of polycythemia), leaving a handful of works unfinished, he lamented: 'The trouble is that I have to go with so much still to say.'

Béla Bartók – the sound of his two names are the sounds of the two sides of his music, one soft and romantic, the other hard and angular. Without doubt, he's one of the century's most important and individual composers, though his influence on other composers is far more limited than is sometimes claimed. Some of his work is easily accessible (Concerto for Orchestra and the Third Piano Concerto, for instance); more often than not it makes tremendous demands on the listener. Musicians sing his praises for his intellectual rigour, for his totally uncompromising individuality and the personal sound world he dreamt up. They also like to rise to the particular technical demands Bartók makes on them. Connoisseurs of the genre are of the opinion that his six string quartets are the only original contribution to the medium since Beethoven.

Piano Concertos

No 1 Sz83; **No 2** Sz95; **No 3** Sz119

Piano Concertos Nos 1-3　　　　　　　Ⓗ
Géza Anda pf **Berlin Radio Symphony Orchestra / Ferenc Fricsay**
DG The Originals 447 399-2GOR (78' · ADD)
Recorded 1959-60　　　　　　　Ⓜ❶❶❶❶➔

Ⓖ　Much as you'd like to tout the new as the best, there are some older recordings where a very special chemistry spells 'definitive', and that pose an almost impossible challenge to subsequent rivals. Such is this 1959 recording of Bartók's Second Piano Concerto, a tough, playful, pianistically aristocratic performance where dialogue is consistently keen and spontaneity is captured on the wing (even throughout numerous sessions). The first movement is relentless but never tires the ear; the second displays two very different levels of tension, one slow and mysterious, the other

hectic but controlled; and although others might have thrown off the finale's octaves with even greater abandon, Anda's performance is the most successful in suggesting savage aggression barely held in check.

The Third Concerto is again beautifully moulded and carefully thought through. Moments such as the loving return from the second movement's chirpy central episode are quite unforgettable, while the finale is both nimble and full toned. The First Concerto was the last to be recorded and is perhaps the least successful of the three: here ensemble is occasionally loose, and characterisation less vivid than with some. Still, it's a fine performance and the current transfer has been lovingly effected.

Bartók Piano Concerto No 2[a] **Mozart** Piano Concertos – No 16, K451[b]; No 17, K453[c]
Géza Anda pf [a]**BBC Symphony Orchestra / Pierre Boulez**; [bc]**English Chamber Orchestra**
BBC Legends BBCL4247-2 (81' · ADD)
Recorded live at [b]BBC Studios, London, on November 27, 1968; Royal Festival Hall, London, on [a]December 5, 1973, and [c]April 9, 1975　　Ⓕ❶

Géza Anda's all-too-brief 30-year career (he died in 1976 at the age of 54) left us with a string of fine recordings including one of the first complete cycles of Mozart's concertos (for DG) and benchmark versions of all three of Bartók's. It is with these two vastly dissimilar composers featured here that Anda is indelibly linked.

From the first bar of K451, the least-played of all Mozart's mature keyboard concertos, you know you are in for something special. Anda, directing from the keyboard, launches the ECO into a true *allegro assai*, exuberantly matched by the piano's entry. This is Mozart-playing of a refined order, robust, sparkling and fully in tune with the entertainment character of the work. The sublime K453 is a live performance from over six years later, no less successful in its precision, stylishness and general high spirits, though the piano tone is slightly glassy compared to the more rounded studio sound of K451. In Pierre Boulez, Anda, who had been playing the Bartók concertos since the 1950s, had a sympathetic and experienced collaborator. This live 1973 performance of No 2 is played at a cracking pace, rich in detail and, in the treacherously difficult outer movements, simply thrilling. Yet few pianists (not even Pollini) have found on disc quite the same mesmerising, unsettling atmosphere as Anda does here in the central *Adagio*. This is a valuable and well-filled disc.

Bartók Piano Concerto No 3
Prokofiev Piano Concertos Nos 1 & 3
Martha Argerich pf
Montreal Symphony Orchestra / Charles Dutoit
EMI 556654-2 (70' · DDD)　　　　Ⓕ❶➔

As always with this most mercurial of virtuosos, Martha Argerich's playing is generated by the mood of the moment and many listeners may well be surprised at her relative geniality with Dutoit. Personal and vivacious throughout, she always allows the composer his own voice. This is particularly true in Bartók's Third Concerto where her rich experience in chamber music makes her often *primus inter pares*, a virtuoso who listens to her partners with the greatest care. In the *Adagio religioso* she achieves a poise that has sometimes eluded her in the past and her finale is specially characterful, her stealthy start to the concluding *Presto* allowing the final pages their full glory. Dutoit and the Montreal Symphony achieve a fine unity throughout, a sense of like-minded musicians at work.

All true musicians will recognise performances of a special magic and integrity. In the Prokofiev First Concerto, her opening is arguably more authentically *brioso* than ferocious, her overall view a refreshingly fanciful view of Prokofiev's youthful iconoclasm. The central *Andante assai* is inflected with an improvisatory freedom she probably wouldn't have risked earlier in her career and in the *Allegro scherzando* she trips the light fantastic, reserving a suitably tigerish attack for the final octave bravura display. Her performance of the Third Concerto is less fleet or nimble-fingered than in her early days but is more delectably alive to passing caprice. The recordings are clear and naturally balanced.

Additional recommendation

Piano Concertos Nos 1ª, 2ᵇ & 3ᶜ
ªZimerman, ᵇAndsnes, ᶜGrimaud *pfs* ªChicago SO; ᵇBPO; ᶜLSO / Boulez
DG download 447 5330GH (76' · DDD)   Ⓕ**OO➔**

Grimaud's Third is a winner; the Second with Andsnes has a fabulous finale, and Zimerman's First is brilliant in parts, if not quite a meeting of minds.

Viola Concerto, Sz120

Bartók Viola Concerto **Eötvös** Replica
Kurtág Movement for Viola and Orchestra
Kim Kashkashian *va* **Netherlands Radio Chamber Orchestra / Peter Eötvös**
ECM New Series 465 420-2 (50' · DDD)   Ⓕ**O➔**

Kashkashian's superbly engineered recording of the Bartók Viola Concerto bears witness to a total identification between performer and composer. Even the tiny pause bridging the opening and the secondary idea growing out of it, is perfectly judged. Kashkashian makes this music dance, not just in the finale but also in the way that she phrases and articulates the entire piece. Eötvös's conducting offers many parallel insights, not least towards the end of the first movement where a growing sense of agitation throws the succeeding *Adagio religioso* into a particularly favourable light. Eötvös employs Tibor Serly's completion, revising odd details and accommodating a few articu-

lations and phrasings that Kashkashian has herself instigated. If you need convincing that Bartók's Viola Concerto is a great work, then Kashkashian and Eötvös should, between them, do the trick.

Of the other pieces, Eötvös's *Replica* for viola and orchestra is astonishing music in which foggy harmonies hover between startled highs and raucous lows, then mutate into a strange, sickly pulsing. By contrast, György Kurtág's early *Movement for Viola and Orchestra* – two-thirds of a concerto Kurtág completed in 1953-4 – is relatively conventional, with plenty of virtuoso viola writing.

Bartók Viola Concerto **Hindemith** Trauermusik
Martinů Rhapsodie-concerto for Viola and Orchestra
Vladimír Bukač *va* **Czech Radio Symphony Orchestra / Vladimír Válek**
Calliope CAL9364 (47' · DDD)   Ⓕ

The combination of three fairly sombre viola pieces by major composers in exile hits the spot exactly: one extra work would have thrown the whole project out of kilter. Vladimír Bukač is violist of the Talich Quartet and it's interesting that rather than opt for the familiar Tibor Serly completion of Bartók's Viola Concerto, he appears to have used Peter Bartók's revision (one of several that have appeared since the 'original' was published in 1950). If you want to check Serly against Bartók *fils*, there's a giveaway in the first two bars where Serly answers the solo viola on *pizzicato* cellos and basses, and Peter Bartók opts for timpani. Thereafter differences between the two are both plentiful (many passages are completely rescored) and musically fascinating, the newer version claiming a far wider range of colours than its spartan predecessor.

Bukač offers a warm, emotionally committed performance of the Bartók, flexible, dusky-brown in tone and sensitively accompanied by Válek and the Czech Radio Symphony. The Hindemith *Trauermusik* for viola and string orchestra was famously written at breakneck speed while the viola player-composer was on a performing visit to London. George V had died the previous day, which meant that Hindemith's relatively upbeat *Schwanendreher* Concerto was deemed inappropriate for the occasion and the new piece, all seven minutes of it, was played in its place. Brief though it is, Hindemith's *Trauermusik* is one of his loveliest works, the poignant two-minute finale based on Bach's last chorale. Again, the performance radiates warmth but for me the highlight of this excellent disc is the *Rhapsodie-concerto* that Martinů wrote to a commission from the principal viola of George Szell's Cleveland Orchestra (Szell himself conducted the premiere in 1953). Martinů came up with a work cast in his most lyrical vein, music that while deeply nostalgic and mostly slow-moving does allow for a dash of dancing in the second of its two movements. Bukač's new recording is very persuasive and very well engineered. Again the orchestral playing is idiomatic and the conducting sympathetic and intelligent.

Violin Concertos Nos 1 & 2

Violin Concertos Nos 1 & 2
György Pauk vn
National Polish Radio Symphony Orchestra of Katowice / Antoni Wit
Naxos 8 554321 (62' . DDD)   Ⓢ🅑➔

The strongest aspect of these performances is soloist György Pauk's supremely idiomatic playing. He may not have the virtuosity of a Mullova or Midori, but there are only one or two moments when he sounds uncomfortable with the technical demands, and the Hungarian idioms of Concerto No 2 flow naturally from his bow, unexaggerated yet full of character. He's strikingly successful, too, at seeing each movement as a whole. It's so easy for the first movement of Concerto No 2, with its dramatic mood-swings, to sound disjointed, but here the march-tread of the opening remains somewhere in the background through most of the movement, giving it real coherence. The orchestral playing is accurate and spirited, but doesn't have the refinement that allows an orchestra like the Berlin Philharmonic to give such a strong sense of direction to the first movement of the First Concerto, and to accentuate the grotesque features of its second movement.

Pauk's interpretations, thoughtful and strongly felt, are essential listening for Bartók enthusiasts.

Additional recommendations

Violin Concertos Nos 1 and 2
Coupled with: Piano Concertos
Chung vn **Ashkenazy** pf **Chicago Symphony Orchestra, London Philharmonic Orchestra / Solti**
Decca Double ② 473 271-2DF2 (137' · DDD)   Ⓜ🅑➔
   Highly extrovert, likeable performances from Chung with Solti a like-minded collaborator. The piano concertos make a great package – Ashkenazy is on superb form.

Concerto for Two Pianos, Percussion and Orchestra, Sz115

Concerto for Two Pianos, Percussion and Orchestra[a].
Violin Concerto No 1, Sz36[b]. Viola Concerto, Sz120[c]
[b]**Gidon Kremer** vn [c]**Yuri Bashmet** va
[a]**Pierre-Laurent Aimard**, [a]**Tamara Stefanovich** pfs
[a]**Neil Percy**, [a]**Nigel Thomas** perc [bc]**Berlin Philharmonic Orchestra;** [a]**London Symphony Orchestra / Pierre Boulez**
DG 477 7440GH (70' · DDD)   Ⓕ🅞🅑➔

And so Pierre Boulez's DG survey of Bartók's major orchestral works draws to a close. This

final instalment opens with an Abbey Road taping of a masterpiece (the two-piano Sonata-turned-Concerto) then alternates two four-year-old Berlin Philharmonic recordings – the richly scored and erotically charged First Violin Concerto and the pared-down, largely ascetic Viola Concerto, an incomplete last testament rendered performable by the viola-player Tibor Serly. Yuri Bashmet treats the opening with considerable freedom and is consistently responsive to the score's more lyrical passages, though both he and Boulez bring a touch of menace to the closing moments of the slow movement.

Gidon Kremer sounds equally unfettered at the start of the Violin Concerto's gorgeous first movement but come the dizzy antics of the *Allegro giocoso* he engages more with play than with reverie. In fact from around 2'20" he sounds positively bored – very unlike him (he's a favourite player of mine).

Boulez has spoken about the 'Concerto' orchestration of the Sonata for Two Pianos and Percussion as adding 'a different dimension' to the Sonata, especially in the first movement, and he substantiates his claim with a performance that is typically transparent and attentive in matters of balancing, the brass fanfares at around 9'16" in the first movement so vividly reminiscent of parallel passages in the Second Piano Concerto. Pierre-Laurent Aimard and Tamara Stefanovich, although technically brilliant, keep a relatively low profile, which makes for added intimacy in the first movement's busy, often humorous badinage but rather mutes the rhythmic impact of the finale's opening. Greatly preferable is the stark, demonically driven spirit of the original – the Concerto pulls punches that the Sonata delivers in full – but Boulez's performance states a strong case for the plusher concerto alternative.

Concerto for Orchestra, Sz116

Concerto for Orchestra. Kossuth. Five Village Scenes.
Budapest Festival Orchestra / Iván Fischer
Philips 476 7255CC (67' · DDD)   Ⓜ🅞🅞🅞🅑➔

It is the flavour of this Concerto for Orchestra that wins the day. Just sample the subtle *portamento* that spices the string line at bars 52-53 (2'36") of the first movement, and the sombre colouring near the end of the movement, at 8'58". Fischer is a dab hand at shaping and inflecting the musical line, and his characterisation of the 'Giuoco delle coppie' – paced, incidentally, at the prescribed crotchet=94 – is second to none. He invests the 'Elegia' with the maximum respectable quota of passion and the 'Intermezzo interrotto' dances to a few added accents and the finale is a riot of sunshine and swirling skirts, except for the mysterious – and notoriously tricky – *più presto* coda, with its rushing *sul ponticello* string choirs, which Fischer articulates with great care. One senses that the players are being driven to the very limits of their abilities, which only serves to intensify the excitement.

Additional recommendation

Concerto for Orchestra
Coupled with: Music for Strings, Percussion and
Celesta. Hungarian Sketches
Chicago Symphony Orchestra / Reiner
RCA 09026 61504-2 (67' · ADD). Recorded 1955   Ⓜ**OO**

A classic recording by one of the master Bartók
conductors. With staggering playing by the
Chicago Symphony and recording that simply
doesn't sound its age, this is a magnificent
achievement. RCA's sound reportage of the
Concerto for Orchestra has uncanny realism,
and if the climaxes are occasionally reined in,
the fervour of Reiner's direction more than
compensates. His couplings are excellent too.

The Miraculous Mandarin, Sz73

The Miraculous Mandarin. Hungarian Peasant Songs,
Sz100. Hungarian Sketches, Sz97. Romanian
Folkdances, Sz68. Transylvanian Dances, Sz96.
Romanian Dance, Sz47
**Hungarian Radio Chorus; Budapest Festival
Orchestra / Iván Fischer**
Philips Gramophone Awards Collection 476 1799
(67' · DDD)   Ⓜ**OOO**▷

As *Mandarins* go, they don't come more miraculous than this – a vivid, no-holds-barred
performance. Everything tells: the flavour is
right, the pacing too, and the sound has a toughened, raw-edged quality that's an essential constituent of Bartók's tonal language. Although
lurid, even seedy, in narrative detail, this is ultimately a tale of compassion, and Fischer never
forgets that. Observable detail, all of it musically
significant, occurs virtually by the minute. Delicacy trails bullish aggression, forcefulness alternates with almost graphic suggestiveness: it's all
there in the score. Fischer never vulgarises, brutalises or overstates the case; most important, he
underlines the quickly flickering, folkish elements in Bartók's musical language that other
conductors barely acknowledge.
 The strongly individual character of the Budapest Festival Orchestra is delightful. The strings
have a biting edge, the woodwinds a gypsy-style
reediness, while brass and percussion are forceful and incisive but never raucous. This is Hun-
garian-grown Bartók that actually *sounds* Hungarian; if only other European orchestras would
reclaim parallel levels of individuality.

The Wooden Prince, Sz60

The Wooden Prince. Kossuth, Sz21
**Hungarian National Philharmonic Orchestra /
Zoltán Kocsis**
Hungaroton ⊛ HSACD32502 (72' · DDD/DSD)   Ⓕ

Kocsis's account of *Kossuth* is terrific – the best
we now have. The budding composer's youthful
essay has rarely sounded more engaging,

**BARTÓK'S CONCERTO FOR
ORCHESTRA – IN BRIEF**

Budapest Festival Orchestra / Iván Fischer
Philips 476 7255CC (67' · DDD)   Ⓜ**OOO**▷
Ⓖ A tremendous modern performance
 with lashings of character and some
really stunning orchestral work. Fischer
negotiates all the changes of tempo and
rhythm with his customary panache.

Chicago SO / Fritz Reiner
RCA 09026 61504-2 (76' · ADD)   Ⓜ**OO**
Recorded in 1955, this still sounds stunning
and Reiner's interpretation has the idiomatic
feel of someone who has really lived with the
score. This is Bartók with an iron grip, but
thrilling none the less. Coupled with the
Music for Strings, Percussion and Celesta.

Chicago SO / Sir Georg Solti
Decca ② 470 516-2DF2 (138' · DDD)   Ⓜ▷
This powerful recording from another great
Hungarian conductor comes as part of a most
appealing Bartók collection. Rather brightly
recorded though!

**Concertgebouw Orchestra /
Eduard van Beinum**
Dutton mono CDK1206 (69' · ADD)   Ⓜ
A wonderfully vital and exciting performance
from one of the Netherlands' greatest conductors – the ex-Decca sound is remarkable
for the early 1950s.

Boston SO / Serge Koussevitzky
Naxos mono 8 110105 (59' · DDD)   Ⓢ**O**
A radio relay of an early Boston performance
under the man who commissioned the work.
This has all the energy, excitement and sense
of discovery of a creator's recording (it even
has the original ending).

Chicago SO / Pierre Boulez
DG 437 826-2GH (60' · DDD)   Ⓕ▷
A master Bartók conductor with one of the
great Bartók orchestras in a reading that
shows off both the work's and the players'
virtuosity. This is a very exciting modern
account of this extraordinary creation.

Berlin PO / Herbert von Karajan
DG 457 890-2GGA (71' · ADD)   Ⓜ▷
This is one of a number of recordings
Karajan made of the work. His quest to seek
out the beautiful did somewhat take the
pungency out of much of the writing.

Philadelphia Orchestra / Christoph Eschenbach
Ondine ⊛ ODE1072-5 (69' · DDD)   Ⓕ**O**
With playing as beautiful as on the Karajan
version, Eschenbach offers more grit and
bite. Enterprisingly coupled with Klein and
Martinů, this is a very fine version in very well
engineered (live) sound.

for example in the tangy portrait at the start of the piece, the Wagnerian picture of 'The Battlefield', and the cynical minor-key distortion of the Austrian Hymn in the eighth section, the bizarre way Hungarian and Austrian motives collide. *Heldenleben* is an obvious forebear and Kocsis directs a performance that suggests a paprika-flavoured variant on Straussian exuberance.

The Wooden Prince ballet has enjoyed a rather more distinguished recorded history than Kossuth, with Fischer, Boulez and, from the analogue era, Dorati offering the best versions thus far. As with Bartók's piano music, Kocsis is a master of idiomatic *rubato*, of holding the crest of a phrase (the first dance) and of course he fully understands, even relishes, the rustic element (ie, the fourth dance with its spicy *col legno* strings). Like Fischer, he knows how to focus a narrative, for example the drooping brass glissandi when the prince is 'in greatest despair'. And there's the humour – the tipsy-sounding bassoon as the disorderly prince unsuccessfully attempts to dance with the princess. Swathes of post-impressionist tone-painting (the enchantment scene) alternate with passages of great delicacy and Hungaroton's fairly close-set recording captures it all vividly. If you already have Fischer's equally fine *Wooden Prince* stick with it, but if you haven't and the present coupling appeals then I would wholeheartedly recommend this new CD.

Additional recommendation

The Wooden Prince
Bournemouth SO / Alsop
Naxos 8 570534 (53' · DDD) ⓈⒹ►

Alsop and her orchestra do justice to Bartók's most overtly romantic large-scale score; it's a performance that will surely appeal beyond the ranks of Bartók devotees to balletomanes generally, not to mention lovers of *fin de siècle* musical excess.

String Quartets

No 1 Sz40; **No 2** Sz67; **No 3** Sz85; **No 4** Sz91; **No 5** Sz102; **No 6** Sz114

String Quartets Nos 1-6
Belcea Quartet (Corina Belcea, Lara Samuel vns Krzysztof Chorzelski va Alasdair Tait vc)
EMI ② 394400-2 (157' · DDD) ⒻⓄⓄⓄ►

Bartók's quartets are one of the great musical collision points between modernism and romanticism. How to handle the tension between their expressive gestures and constructivist designs is one of the abiding issues for performers and one reason why even the plethora of fine available recordings cannot remotely exhaust their riches. Getting the best of all worlds interpretatively is hardly a realistic aim. Even so, there are long stretches where

the Belceas come as close to the ideal as any ensemble on disc.

Try the first few minutes of Quartets Nos 2 and 3, and marvel at the gradation of *forte* and *fortissimo*, of *piano* and *pianissimo*, which helps to give entire movements far more convincing shape than less precisely observant ensembles achieve. Try the outer movements of No 5 and marvel at the gear-changes negotiated smoothly, instantly and unanimously, yet never as ends in themselves, always accompanied by a sense of expressive-dramatic purpose. Try virtually every movement in fact, and revel, as the Belceas do, in the interplay of the lines, even in passages where others seem thankful just to come through unscathed.

Clearly immense thought has been given to tone quality. In the first movement of No 1, for instance, the Belceas point the periodic arrivals on consonant harmonies by withdrawing vibrato, and instantly the as yet not fully mature Bartók's straggly structure gains sharpness of profile. They apply the same ploy in the much tauter environment of the first movement of No 5, and with similarly revelatory results. At the other extreme, their sustained tonal intensity makes the most barbaric onrushes exhilarating rather than exhausting, neither too streamlined nor too effortful. When the score is bare of instructions, as in the first slow movement of No 5, they take it at its word and uncover a hypnotic, staring blankness. And when the invitation to humour is extended, as in the finale of the same quartet, they seize it with full-blooded, yet never self-serving, relish.

Before surrendering to the power of these performances, one wondered if there was going to be enough ethnic tang and zest, enough wildness and strangeness, enough sultry longing. We've certainly heard more of those qualities in the first two quartets. Yet the central movement of No 2 is marked *molto capriccioso*, not *barbaro*, and that's exactly what comes across, while the coda is pushed daringly close to the edge, sounding like the distant fluttering of giant moths – not as precisely by the book as the Emersons but vastly more imaginative and emotionally telling – while the slow finale has a superbly intense accumulation at its heart.

Pushed for a general reservation, perhaps when a 'speaking' quality is needed in the quasi-recitatives, the first violin's colleagues don't quite match her for idiomatic insight. And do the Belceas get to the heart of the matter in the trauma-shaded No 6? Not quite – not by comparison with The Lindsays, anyway, who are generally more prepared to tolerate rough edges for the sake of emotional revelation.

In short, the Belceas are more than worthy rivals to the best on disc and EMI's recording quality is just right.

String Quartets Nos 1-6
Takács Quartet (Edward Dusinberre, Károly Schranz vns Roger Tapping va András Fejér vc)

Decca ② 455 297-2DH2 (152' · DDD) Ⓕ❶❶❶❶▷

These performances provide more impressive sampling points than can be enumerated in a single review. The First Quartet's oscillating tempo-shifts work wonderfully well, all with total naturalness. Characterisation is equally strong elsewhere, not least the first movement of the Debussian arpeggios of the Second Quartet, and the second movement where Fejér races back into the rustic opening subject. The nightmare climax in the last movement has rarely sounded more prophetic of the great *Divertimento*'s central movement. The middle quartets work very well, with prominent inner voices in the Third and plenty of swagger in the Fourth. The high spots of No 4 are Fejér's improvisational cello solo in the third movement and a finale where the violent opening is a hefty *legato* to compare with the sharper, more Stravinskian attack of, say, the Tokyo Quartet. Likewise, the sudden dance-like episode in the first movement of the Fifth Quartet, savage music played from the pit of the stomach, while the third movement's bleary-eyed viola melody over teeming violin triplets suggests peasants in caricature.

The Takács are responsive to Bartók's sardonic humour – the 'barrel-organ' episode at the end of the Fifth Quartet, and the corny 'Burletta' in the third movement of the Sixth. The Sixth itself has some of the saddest, wildest and wisest music written in the last 100 years: the opening viola solo recalls Mahler's Tenth and the close fades to a mysterious question. Throughout the cycle, Bartók's metronome markings are treated more as guidelines than literal commands. The playing imparts Bartók's all-embracing humanity. If the greatest string quartets after Beethoven are still unknown to you, this set may well prove the musical journey of a lifetime. The recording has ambient, full-bodied sound that's more reminiscent of the concert hall than the studio.

Bartók String Quartet No 5
Hindemith String Quartet No 4, Op 22
Zehetmair Quartet (Thomas Zehetmair, Kuba Jakowicz *vns* Ruth Killius *va* Ursula Smith *vc*)
ECM New Series 476 5779 (51' · DDD) Ⓕ❶❶

A few seconds into the first movement of this extraordinary version of the Fifth Quartet check whether the dynamics are being played as written – many aren't. The Zehetmairs career around the notes like bikers on a zig-zag course, tracing arches at speed with what sounds like the least effort. At the fervid build-up nearly three minutes in they lunge at the music *fortissimo* though for the starkly syncopated passage a few seconds later their *legato* handling of the viola/cello lines tends to soften the argument's impact. It'll take some getting used to, but persevere. There's savagery, too – for example where Bartók asks the leader to play *ff stridente* and Zehetmair all but saws through his fiddle.

BARTÓK STRING QUARTETS – IN BRIEF

Many of the classic sets of Bartók's string quartets are currently unavailable on CD in the local catalogue but are available for download or through international distribution.

Belcea Quartet
EMI ② 394400-2 (157' · DDD) Ⓕ❶❶❶❶▷
💎 A set of real distinction: the Belcea show flair and imagination aplenty. Their playing is first-rate and their feeling for Bartók's language total.

Emerson Quartet
DG ② download 423 657-2GH2 (149' · DDD) Ⓑ❶❶❶❶▷
💎 One of the three *Gramophone* Award-winning sets of these seminal 20th-century quartets. High-powered and totally accurate – this is one of the most virtuoso recordings.

Tokyo Quartet
DG ② download 477 6658GC (159' · ADD) Ⓜ❶❶▷
These are gentler but infinitely subtle performances with great attention to colour and texture.

Takács Quartet
Decca ② 455 297-2DH2 (152' · DDD) Ⓕ❶❶❶❶▷
💎 The most recent award-winning set and possibly the finest all-round set of the six quartets. The Takács Quartet play every note as if it were their last – the conviction positively crackles from the speakers.

Hagen Quartet
DG ② download 463 576-2GH2 (154' · DDD) Ⓕ❶❶❶❶▷
💎 Adventurous, imaginative performances from one of the younger quartets with a lovely consistency of approach throughout. There's real fire in their playing, as well as a truly songful lyricism.

Juilliard Quartet
Pearl mono ② GEMS0147 (156' · ADD) Ⓜ❶
This 1950s set originally from CBS is mightily impressive. As the first cycle to be recorded as such it was something of a milestone, and that quality of novelty and discovery shines through magnificently.

Keller Quartet
Warner Apex ② 2564 62686-2 (149' · DDD) Ⓑ❶❶▷
A fine bargain cycle well worth considering if you're on a tight budget. As Hungarians the Kellers have an innate feel for the idiom, and the digital recording is beautifully handled.

Don't expect either a comfortable or a familiar ride. The two symmetrically placed slow movements embrace vivid, often rough-hewn textures, from a quiet chalky treble to fierce full chords. Perhaps the most satisfying movements are the *Scherzo alla bulgarese* and the finale: both suggest an element of rustic dance, the finale's quieter music sounding eerily effective, especially at speed.

Hindemith's somewhat drier Fourth Quartet (1921) predates Bartók's Fifth by some 13 years. Like the Bartók it is cast in five rather than the usual four movements, the first opening to a slow, shadowy fugato which soon flares to near-rage. Both here and in the ferocious *Scherzo* the Zehetmair Quartet capture the music's radical spirit, much as they do for the equivocal, gently marching slow movement.

This is a fascinating CD. With the Zehetmairs you're rarely aware of bar-lines, more a constant flow of ideas, a compelling journey with a stated destination but with little need of pedantic sign-posting en route. You sense that the written notes have been fully absorbed and that the playing has become, in a sense, pure instinct.

String Quartets Nos 5 & 6
Arcanto Quartet (Antje Weithaas, Daniel Sepec *vns* Tabea Zimmermann *va* Jean-Guihen Queyras *vc*) Harmonia Mundi HMC90 1963 (60' · DDD)   Ⓕ**OO**

Quite exceptional, this…and on many levels. For one, the playing is superb, the biting attack of the Fifth Quartet's opening, its precision, energy and tempered rhythmic momentum, not to mention the accuracy of intonation throughout. Everything tells, nothing sounds rushed. Just as remarkable are the gentler episodes in the two interrupted slow movements, barely sighing in the first, scarily building to a maelstrom in the second. Humour is a priority in the *Scherzo*, which wafts in quietly then, towards the end, after a sudden snap, scurries back into the night. The finale often proves a stumbling block but not here, again strongly driven, the two madcap minuet episodes raising a smile, the first toying with atonalism (the timing here is crucially spot-on), the other a dazed minuet. No doubt about it, this is one of the most impressive, the most human accounts of Bartók No 5 to have appeared for a long time.

Though merely five years old as an ensemble, the Arcanto Quartet have clocked up considerable pooled experience. And they didn't enter into quartet playing lightly, having previously tried out other instrumental formations. What's for sure is that any internal disharmony would have surfaced in Bartók's fragile last quartet, another memorable performance. Again, everything is well articulated, tiny motifs that otherwise go for nothing are made clear, curving glissandi shaped as if carefully planed and the haunting motif that prefaces each movement and dominates the last is sustained with maximum expressive intensity. Echoes of folk music tail rarefied abstract

invention, and the alternation of slapstick comedy and implied tragedy is underlined, though never too heavily. It's another winner, purposeful yet refined.

Violin Sonatas, Rhapsodies, Contrasts

Violin Sonatas – No 1 Sz75; **No 2** Sz76
Rhapsodies – No 1 Sz86 **No 2** Sz89
Contrasts Sz111. **Solo Violin Sonata** Sz117

Violin Sonatas Nos 1 & 2. Solo Violin Sonata
Christian Tetzlaff *vn* **Leif Ove Andsnes** *pf*
Virgin Classics 545668-2 (79' · DDD)   Ⓕ**OOO**▷

Christian Tetzlaff's tone is grainy and lightly-brushed, his inward approach most evident in the Solo Sonata, a work he plays with sovereign command – and with greater freedom than on his more straightlaced 1991 Virgin Classics recording, which veered less towards the Sandór Végh axis than this new version does. Here Tetzlaff makes more of the fugue's shifting perspectives and relishes Bartók's bold chord constructions. Other players may at times employ a richer tone palette but few take a more thoughtful interpretative standpoint on what is after all the finest unaccompanied violin sonata since Bach.

The two duo sonatas are also beautifully done. Tezlaff again proves both focused and expressive, though among modern rivals you might prefer Faust's questing expressiveness, and György Pauk's Naxos coupling offers honest musical reportage. But what makes these performances more or less indispensable is the character and control of Leif Ove Andsnes's piano playing, its fastidious deployment of tone and immaculate timing. The clarion alarms in the outer movements of the First Sonata, where tonality is stretched to its limits, ring out without percussive overkill. The Second Sonata's folksy *Allegretto* is strong and tidy but with the unmistakable sense of earth under foot. Andsnes is the stronger personality, Tetzlaff the more confidential, yielding presence (wonderful in the First Sonata's *Adagio*); an ideal anima-animus performing relationship.

This is chamber music playing of the highest order, candid and straightforward enough for a basic library recommendation but also rich enough in subtleties to satisfy even the most discerning connoisseur.

Violin Sonatas Nos 1 & 2. Contrasts, Sz111
Kálmán Berkes *cl* **György Pauk** *vn* **Jenő Jandó** *pf*
Naxos 8 550749 (75' · DDD)   Ⓢ▷

Readers who habitually fight shy of Bartók's provocatively astringent piano writing might at first find these endlessly fascinating works rather unpalatable, the First Sonata especially. But careful scrutiny reveals manifold beauties which, once absorbed, tend to haunt the memory and prompt repeated listening. Jenö Jandó's piano playing is fairly forthright yet without the naked agression of, say, Sviatoslav Richter. And it provides an effective foil for György Pauk's warm tone and fluid solo line, especially in the First Sonata, where ungainly tone production could so easily compound the listener's discomfort. Here, however, the interpretation is at once thoughtful and well shaped, and fully appreciative of the mysterious 'night music' that sits at the heart of the *Adagio*.

The Second Sonata is both gentler and more improvisatory, its language and structure – although still pretty formidable – somewhat in the manner of a rhapsody. Pauk and Jandó again hit the target, and the full-bodied recording makes for a homogeneous sound picture. To have a spirited performance of the multi-faceted *Contrasts* (with Kálmán Berkes on clarinet) as a bonus certainly helps promote this well-annotated CD to the front line of competition. A confident mainstream recommendation, then, and superb value for money.

Rhapsodies Nos 1 & 2. Contrasts. Solo Violin Sonata. Six Romanian Folk Dances, Sz56 (arr Székely)
Michael Collins *cl* **Krysia Osostowicz** *vn* **Susan Tomes** *pf*
Helios CDH55149 (72' · DDD)　　　　　Ⓕ**O**

Unusually for a composer who wrote so much fine chamber music Bartók wasn't himself a string player. But he did enjoy close artistic understanding with a succession of prominent violin virtuosos, including the Hungarians Jelly d'Arányi, Joseph Szigeti and Zoltán Székely, and, towards the end of his life, Yehudi Menuhin. It was Menuhin who commissioned the Sonata for solo violin, but Bartók died before he could hear him play it – Menuhin was unhappy with the occasional passages in quarter-tones and the composer had reserved judgement on his proposal to omit them. It was Menuhin's edition which was later printed and which has been most often played and recorded; but Krysia Osostowicz returns to the original and, more importantly, plays the whole work with intelligence, imaginative flair and consummate skill.

The Sonata is the most substantial work on this disc, but the rest of the programme is no less thoughtfully prepared or idiomatically delivered. There's the additional attraction of an extremely well balanced and natural-sounding recording. As a complement to the string quartets, which are at the very heart of Bartók's output, this is a most recommendable disc.

Violin Duos

Bartók 44 Duos for Two Violins, Sz98
Kurtág Ligatura – Message to Frances-Marie, Op 31b
Ligeti Ballad and Dance
András Keller, János Pilz *vns*
ECM New Series 465 849-2 (58' · DDD)　　　Ⓕ**O**

Hearing top-grade quartet violinists tackle these flavoured educational duos is a delight, though not an original one. (The Emerson's co-leaders Eugene Drucker and Philip Setzer have already done likewise, albeit to quite different effect.) All, or virtually all, is revealed right from the opening 'Transylvanian Dance' where the newcomers' phrasing and rhythm are appropriately unbuttoned, their combined tone full but unforced. (Note: Keller and Pilz actually start at the end with Duo 'No 44'.) Bartók's original plan had been to place the easiest pieces first, then gradually pile on the challenges as the series progressed. However, for concert purposes he sanctioned the idea of not playing them in order.

Their chosen sequence is very well planned. The interpretative axis centres principally on harmony and rhythm, and characterisation is always vivid. In general the slower pieces leave the strongest impression: that's where these players harbour their most personal responses, but then the slowest pieces probably are the best. Though Sándor Végh's accounts with Alberto Lysy are rather more earthy, the advantage of this version is that it seems to have been conceived with continuous listening in mind: the ear never tires.

It would be easy to pigeonhole this set as veering in the general direction of the Végh's Bartók, just as the Keller's Bartók quartet cycle does, then make a parallel observation of Drucker and Setzer as representing the less stylised manner of their own Emerson Quartet. Which would be fairly accurate and explain a preference for this disc, where an extra shot of interpretative re-creativeness ultimately wins the day. The sound quality is spacious and pleasingly full bodied.

Piano Works

For Children, Sz42. The First Term at the Piano, Sz53. 15 Hungarian Peasant Songs, Sz71. Three Hungarian Folksongs from the Csík District, Sz35a. Hungarian Folktunes, Sz66. Eight Improvisations on Hungarian Peasant Songs, Sz74. Three Rondos on (Slovak) Folktunes, Sz84. Romanian Christmas Carols, Sz57. Six Romanian Folkdances, Sz56. Two Romanian Dances, Sz43. Suite, Sz62, with original Andante. Piano Sonata, Sz80. Sonatina, Sz55. 14 Bagatelles, Sz38. Four Dirges, Sz45. Petite Suite, Sz105. Violin Duos, Sz98 (arr Sándor) – No 1, Teasing Song; No 17, Marching Song; No 35, Ruthenian kolomejka; No 42, Arabian Song; No 44, Transylvanian Dance. 10 Easy Pieces, Sz39. Allegro barbaro, Sz49. Out of doors, Sz81. Seven Sketches, Sz44. Two Elegies, Sz41. Three Burlesques, Sz47. Nine Little Pieces, Sz82. Three Studies, Sz72
György Sándor *pf*
Sony Classical ④ SB4K87949 (4h 27' · DDD)　　Ⓑ**O**

There can't be many pianists on the current circuit whose fund of experience extends to working with a major 20th-century master; but of those still recording, György Sándor must surely take pride of place. Sándor prepared Bartók's first two piano concertos under the composer's guidance and gave the world premieres of the Third Concerto and the piano version of the *Dance Suite*. The present collection is Sándor's second survey of Bartók's piano music and contains all the major works apart from *Mikrokosmos*.

Many of these performances are exceptionally fine, even though the passage of time has witnessed something of a reduction in Sándor's pianistic powers, mostly where maximum stamina and high velocity fingerwork are required (as in the first *Burlesque*). However, you may be astonished at the heft, energy and puckish humour of Sándor's 1994 recording of the Piano Sonata, a more characterful rendition than its predecessor, with a particularly brilliant account of the folkish *Allegro molto* finale. The *Allegro barbaro* is similarly 'on the beam', while Sándor brings a cordial warmth to the various collections of ethnic pieces, the *Romanian Christmas Carols* especially.

His phrasing, rubato, expressive nuancing, attention to counterpoint and command of tone suggest the touch of a master, while his imagination relishes the exploratory nature of the *Improvisations, Bagatelles* and *Miraculous Mandarin*-style *Studies*. Sándor connects with all the music's abundant qualities: harmonic or rhythmic innovation, powerful emotion, humour, introspection, ethnic variety and the scope and complexity of Bartók's piano writing in general. Intuitive interpreters, especially those who knew and understand the composers they perform, are becoming a rare breed. In that respect alone, Sándor's Bartók deserves an honoured place in every serious CD collection of 20th-century piano music.

Bartók Kossuth, Sz21 – Funeral March. Mikrokosmos, Book 6, Sz107 – Dance in Bulgarian Rhythm Nos 1-6. Three Rondos on Slovak Folktunes, Sz84. Seven Sketches, Sz44 **D Scarlatti** Keyboard Sonatas – Kk3; Kk9; Kk17; Kk58; Kk82; Kk135; Kk159; Kk380; Kk430; Kk420; Kk491
Dejan Lazić pf
Channel Classics ⊕ CCSSA23407 (79' · DDD)   Ⓕ

An exciting idea this...and it works! After all, Bartók greatly admired Scarlatti: he even recorded a couple of his sonatas. Both composers were innovators and combined a strong feeling for rhythm with an audacious sense of harmony.

Dejan Lazic wastes no time in establishing his credentials as a Scarlatti player. He opens the programme with a somewhat militaristic-sounding C major piece, K420, and already it's all there – the light, resilient touch, the crisp (and often free) approach to rhythm, nimble passagework and an obvious appreciation of subsidiary material. The last of that particular Scarlatti trio, a filigree piece in F, segues beautifully with the first of Bartók's *Three Rondos on Slovak Folktunes* (in C), the principal common denominator here, as so often elsewhere, the dance element.

Lazic has a very individual Bartók style; he's no literalist, as illustrated by his emphatic handling of the syncopated main motif of the last Rondo. Again the segue from Bartók (third Rondo) to Scarlatti (the processional D major Sonata,

K491) is imaginative, though the switch from the gaily skipping D major Sonata (K159) to the first of Bartók's haunting *Seven Sketches* is more surprising. Lazic personalises the sequence in a most compelling way. He then gently breaks their spell with Scarlatti's D minor ('Pastoral') and interestingly sandwiches a dramatic piano version (Bartók's own) of the *Kossuth* Funeral March between lively sonatas in F major and A minor. Perhaps the most effective segue finds the flamenco strumming of Scarlatti's K135 (E major) acting as a prelude to the first of six *Dances in Bulgarian Rhythm* which conclude Bartók's Mikrokosmos. Here Lazic underlines the individual character of each dance, tenderising the fourth (a tribute to Gershwin) with expressive arpeggios, and focusing the fifth's dizzying rhythmic ambiguities.

You reach the journey's end eager to start all over again – or maybe work out another Scarlatti-Bartók sequence. The potential is limitless and let's hope that that this first volume of a series called 'Liaisons' doesn't preclude a second Scarlatti-Bartók sequence.

Additional recommendation

Solo piano works, etc   Ⓗ
Bartók pf
Pearl mono GEMMCD9166 (69' · ADD)   Ⓜ
This Bartók-plays-Bartók compilation offers full-bodied transfers of some fascinating commercial recordings, including the first *Romanian Dances*, *Allegro barbaro* and Liszt's 'Sursum corda'.

Duke Bluebeard's Castle

Duke Bluebeard's Castle
John Tomlinson bass Bluebeard **Anne Sofie von Otter** mez Judith **Sándor Elès** spkr **Berlin Philharmonic Orchestra / Bernard Haitink**
EMI 556162-2 (63' · DDD · N/T/t)   Ⓕ ⦿⦿Ⓓ→

Bernard Haitink's poetic axis is vividly anticipated in the rarely recorded spoken prologue where Sándor Elès bids us search beneath the story's surface. Elès's timing and his sensitivity to word-colouring and the rhythmic inflexions of his native language greet the Gothic imagery of Bartók's solemn opening bars. The main characters soon establish very definite personalities, Bluebeard/Tomlinson as commanding, inscrutable and just a little arrogant, von Otter/Judith as profoundly frightened but filled with curiosity. Haitink and the Berlin Philharmonic paint a rich aural backdrop that's neither too slow nor overly lugubrious and that shows due appreciation of Bartók's seamless scoring, especially in terms of the woodwind. The disembodied sighs that greet Judith's violent hammering on the first door mark a momentary retreat from the Philharmonie's ambient acoustic (or so it seems) and in so doing suggest – quite appropriately – a chilling 'world beyond'. Judith's shock as she recoils in horror is conveyed in clipped, halting tones by von Otter (note too how seductively she manipulates Bluebeard into opening the first door).

Beyond the expansive introduction come the doors themselves, and here too Haitink balances the 'outer' and 'inner' aspects of Bartók's score to perfection – whether in the torture chamber, the glowing textures of 'The Secret Garden' or the Brucknerian expanses of the fifth door, 'Bluebeard's Kingdom' (the opera's structural apex), launched here on a series of epic *crescendos*. Von Otter's stunned responses suggest lonely disorientation within a vast space, whereas the sullenness of the 'Lake of Tears' prompts an exquisite blending of instrumental timbres, most particularly between brass and woodwind. Haitink draws an aching curve to the string writing, but when Judith rushes panic-stricken towards the seventh door, fearful of Bluebeard's secret murders, he effects a gradual but cumulatively thrilling *accelerando*. The internment itself is devastating, while Bluebeard's helpless retreat marks a slow journey back to the questioning void. Recording live can have its pitfalls, but here the atmosphere is electric, the grasp of Bartók's sombre tone-painting – whether sung or played – absolute.

EMI's engineering favours a full sound stage rather than picking out specific instrumental details, but the overall effect remains comprehensively satisfying.

Duke Bluebeard's Castle
Gustáv Beláček bass Bluebeard
Andrea Meláth *mez* Judith
Bournemouth Symphony Orchestra / Marin Alsop
Naxos 8 660928 (58' · DDD) ⓢ🕪

Duke Bluebeard's Castle is in many ways the ideal opera for CD; stage action is less of the essence than a highly descriptive orchestral score, and the 'plot' provides as much mental as visual stimulation. There are plenty of good *Bluebeard*s on disc, and this new Naxos production is a welcome addition to the ranks. Imaginative moments are in generous supply. For example, Judith's blasé, low-key response to Bluebeard's pride as he throws open the Castle's fifth door, her implied rolling eyes at his 'spacious country', a passage thrillingly prepared by Marin Alsop and the orchestra. There's the feverish orchestral build-up approaching the sixth door, the lake of tears, and at the moment when Judith asks Bluebeard to tell her who he had loved before her – less 'asks' in this context than dares to enquire in the thrall of a terrible fear. Andrea Meláth sounds stunned, even terror-stricken, and Alsop draws a sickly-grey backdrop from her Bournemouth players. Best of all is the faltering path to the seventh door: 'I have guessed your secret,' cries Judith, and Alsop charts the tortuous course of this terrible moment to perfection. In context it proves the drama's high-point, more overwhelming in fact than the internment which isn't quite as effective as on some rivals.

Less impressive is Meláth's response to the 'mountains of gold' beyond the third door. The voices here are good but uneven, Meláth often impressive in the higher registers but lacking in colour (and tonal quality) at mid-range and with a tendency to excessive vibrato. Gustáv Beláček's Bluebeard is theatrically characterful but vocally grey, though his animated singing of the opening sequence is appealing. Alsop has the measure of the score. Certainly this *Bluebeard* is more than good enough to introduce a great and compelling work but if pressured to choose while ignoring of the price-tag Haitink's (see above) is still the one to go for.

Duke Bluebeard's Castle
Elena Zhidkova *mez* Judith **Sir Willard White**
bass-bar Bluebeard **London Symphony Orchestra /**
Valery Gergiev
LSO Live 🕪 LSO0685 (59' · DDD/DSD · S/T/t/N)
Recorded live 2009 ⒷⓄ🕪

Most recordings of *Duke Bluebeard's Castle* have their pivotal moments. With Valery Gergiev, the pivotal moment is the sombre burbling of the lake of tears where Judith is transfixed by the water's unearthly hush and Bluebeard explains, 'tears, my Judith, tears, tears…'. Gergiev sustains a pretty slow tempo while clarinet and low strings embrace both protagonists with long, expressive lines. The opera's later episodes, such as the accelerating blood-rush as Judith susses the shocking truth (Gergiev and his players are on tremendous form here), Bluebeard pondering his past wives and the overwhelming moment when Judith at last joins them, all suggest similar levels of thoughtfulness, sense of theatre and sensitivity to mood.

Interestingly, the Prologue is spoken in English (by Sir Willard himself) whereas the opera is sung in Hungarian. White does fairly well with the Hungarian though his vibrato tends to widen a little under pressure. Elena Zhidkova isn't the most seductive of Judiths – she sounds a mite too needy – and like White, the beat of her vibrato can be distracting, but she acts well and her singing generates considerable intensity. Gergiev keeps the Prologue on the move but one misses an element of shock as the first door reveals the torture chamber. The damp-squib effect is further underlined by Zhidkova's rather feeble 'Jaj' ('woe'). The castle's armoury, too, hardly inspires fear or terror, but Gergiev comes into his own when delving among Bluebeard's treasures, a brightly glistening blend of sonorities, and basking in his fragrant gardens. The fifth door is spoiled somewhat by Zhidkova entering fractionally off cue but the panoramic impact of the LSO's playing partially compensates.

If comparisons are less of the essence than hopping aboard an operatic masterpiece for the first time then rest assured, Gergiev, his orchestra and his singers offer good accounts of themselves and, by extension, of Bartók too.

Duke Bluebeard's Castle (sung in English)
John Tomlinson *bar* Bluebeard

Sally Burgess mez Judith
Opera North Orchestra / Richard Farnes
Chandos CHAN3133 (63' · DDD) Ⓕ Ⓑ→

This recording grew from performances by Opera North but the absence of a visual element hardly matters. Nor in this instance does the language issue either. *Bluebeard* is perfect food for the mind's theatre, the tale of a man alone (as John Tomlinson reminds us in the cryptic spoken prologue) and while under normal circumstances Hungarian would win over any translation, here vivid vocal acting and clarity of diction more than compensate. And there's Farnes's conducting, which even from as early as the introduction counters the pervading darkness with deftly pointed woodwind phrases and a light, expressive curve to the string lines.

Tomlinson's Bluebeard is godlike, cautioning and doleful, the voice hugely resonant. Sally Burgess sounds old enough to know better than to stray thoughtlessly from her father's home. When Judith first views the castle's interior she sounds suitably tremulous and awestruck, though when she blurts out the words 'tell me why the doors are bolted?' an air of petulance spells trouble: her command to 'open!' cues forceful thwacks on timps and bass drum. And so the drama unfolds, Burgess's Judith, shrewish and fatally curious, Tomlinson's Bluebeard, inwardly tortured but fired by Judith's dark beauty. The instruments of torture, the armaments, mountains of gold, tender flowers and spacious kingdom, all are graphically tone-painted, Farnes delivering with distinction every time – though when Burgess gasps at the kingdom newly revealed she keeps her high C fairly short. Tomlinson's most sensitive moment, as so often with him in this work, comes when he recalls his former wives, and Farnes's comes at the 'lake of tears', the perfect dovetailing of winds and strings, mournful but also extremely beautiful. The later climactic moments are delivered with enormous power, the sum effect very moving.

For a thoroughly sympathetic, theatrically effective English-language *Bluebeard's Castle*, this new release is about as good as it's likely to get.

Additional recommendation

Duke Bluebeard's Castle
Berry bass-bar Bluebeard **Ludwig** mez Judith
LSO / Kertész
Decca Legends download 466 377-2DM
(59' · ADD · T/t) Ⓜ Ⓞ Ⓑ→
Recorded in 1965, the husband-and-wife team of Walter Berry and Christa Ludwig convey more the sense of a woman discovering sinister aspects of the man she loves than an inquisitive shrew intent on plundering Bluebeard's every secret.

Sir Arnold Bax
British 1883-1953

Bax studied at the Royal College of Music, London (1900-05). After discovering the poetry of Yeats,

with which he was deeply impressed, he strongly identified with Irish Celtic culture. Drawing on many sources (Strauss, Debussy, Ravel, Elgar), he created a style of luxuriant chromatic harmony, rich ornament and broad melody, notably deployed in his tone-poems The Garden of Fand (1916), November Woods (1917) and Tintagel (1919). Other important works of this period include his First Quartet (1918) and Second Piano Sonata (1919). In the 1920s his music became clearer in outline and more contrapuntal, though without losing its wide range of harmonic resource: Sibelius became an influence. His main works were now symphonies, seven written 1922-39, though he remained a prolific composer in all non-theatrical genres. In 1942 he was made Master of the King's Music, after which he composed little.*

Symphonic Variations

Symphonic Variations. Concertante for Piano (Left Hand) and Orchestra
Ashley Wass pf
Bournemouth Symphony Orchestra / James Judd
Naxos 8 570774 (68' · DDD) Ⓢ Ⓞ Ⓞ Ⓑ→

Composed between 1916 and 1918, the *Symphonic Variations* for piano and orchestra bear a dedication to Bax's muse and lover, Harriet Cohen. It's an expansive and highly virtuoso work in two parts, whose six sections are apportioned titles ('The Temple' being the most eye-catching) that tantalisingly suggest some underlying programme. Borrowings from Bax's own First Violin Sonata and (more crucially) his 1916 setting of George 'AE' Russell's poem *Parting*, add a further layer of autobiographical intrigue. Best to sit back and let the piece weave its uniquely potent spell, for it contains page after page as raptly beautiful and ecstatically sensuous as even Bax ever conceived.

James Judd keeps a firm hand on the structural and motivic tiller and there's no disputing that Ashley Wass is the most stylish, characterful and charismatic of the three soloists to have recorded the work: the way he shapes the spellbinding opening paragraph of the final section ('Triumph', one of Bax's symphonic epilogues in all but name) is sheer magic and betokens a true poet of the keyboard.

The 1949 *Concertante*, written (again) for Harriet Cohen after she had lost the use of her right hand in a domestic accident, is smaller fry – but it can boast an absolute gem of a slow movement. Again, the performance is a very persuasive one. A hearty welcome for this conspicuously successful pairing.

Complete Symphonies

Symphonies Nos 1-7.
Rogue's Comedy Overture. Tintagel
BBC Philharmonic Orchestra / Vernon Handley
Chandos ⑤ CHAN10122 (5h 55' · DDD)
Includes an interview with Vernon Handley by Andrew McGregor Ⓜ Ⓞ Ⓞ Ⓞ Ⓑ→

This Bax symphony cycle comes under the baton of the composer's doughtiest champion, and superlatives are in order. Even seasoned Baxians will be startled by the propulsive vigour and sinewy strength of these performances.

In its uncompromising thrust and snarling tragedy, Handley's account of the First Symphony packs an almighty punch, but also quarries great detail from Bax's darkly opulent orchestration. In the closing pages the motto theme's sanguine tread is soon snuffed out, as the shredded nerve-ends of this music are exposed as never before.

The wild and brooding Second generates less heady sensuality than either the Thomson or Myer Fredman's pioneering Lyrita version, but there's ample compensation in the chaste beauty and enviable authority of Handley's conception. Scrupulous attention is paid to thematic unity and the many contrapuntal and harmonic felicities that bind together the progress of this extraordinary canvas. The BBC Philharmonic respond with such eager application that it's easy to forgive some slight loss of composure in the build-up to the cataclysmic pinnacle.

There can be no reservations about the Third, an interpretation that's by far the finest since Barbirolli's 1943-4 world première recording with the Hallé. Bax's iridescent textures shimmer and glow, bass lines stalk with reassuring logic and solidity, and these exemplary artists distil all the poetry and mystery in the ravishing slow movement and epilogue. Deeply moving is Handley's tender, unforced handling of the first movement's *Lento moderato* secondary material.

Handley's previous recording of the Fourth is comprehensively outflanked by this bracing remake. If you've ever regarded the Fourth as something of a loose-limbed interloper in the Bax canon, this will make you think again, such is the muscular rigour Handley locates in this lovable creation. At the same time, there's playful affection, rhythmic bite and pagan splendour of both outer movements.

Revelations abound, too, in the Fifth. Handley plots a superbly inevitable course through the first movement. At the start of the slow movement the glinting brilliance and sheen of the orchestral playing take the breath away, as does the richness of the lower strings in the first subject. The finale is stunning, its whirlwind *Allegro* a veritable bevy of cackling demons.

The bass ostinato that launches the Sixth picks up where the epilogue of the Fifth left off. A taut course is steered through this stormy first movement, though in some ways Norman Del Mar's recording got closer still to the essence of Bax's driven inspiration. The succeeding *Lento* has a gentle radiance that's very affecting. However, it's in the innovatory finale where Handley pulls ahead of the competition, cannily keeping some power in reserve, and locating a transcendental wonder in the epilogue.

Handley's Seventh is wonderfully wise and characterful music-making, the first movement in particular sounding for all the world as if it

was set down in a single take. There's bags of temperament about the performance, as well as an entrancing freedom, flexibility and purposefulness that proclaim an intimate knowledge of and total trust in the composer's intentions. The BBC Philharmonic respond with unflagging spirit and tremendous body of tone.

A majestic *Tintagel* and rollicking account of the 1936 *Rogue's Comedy Overture* complete the feast. Disc 5 houses an hour-long conversation about Bax the symphonist between the conductor and Andrew McGregor. Stephen Rinker's engineering does fabulous justice to Bax's imaginative and individual orchestration, particularly towards the lower end of the spectrum. The set is magnificent; its insights copious.

Symphonies – selected

Symphony No 2. November Woods
Royal Scottish National Orchestra /
David Lloyd-Jones
Naxos 8 554093 (57' · DDD)   ⓈⓄ🅑➤

From the grinding dissonances at the outset through to the inconsolable coda, Lloyd-Jones and his orchestra bring out the unremitting toughness of Bax's uncompromising, breathtakingly scored Second Symphony; even the gorgeous secondary material in the first movement offers an occasional shaft of pale, wintry sunlight. It helps, too, that Lloyd-Jones has clearly thought hard about the task in hand. How lucidly, for example, he expounds the arresting introduction, where the symphony's main building-blocks are laid out before us, and how well he brings out the distinctive tenor of Bax's highly imaginative writing for low wind and brass. The Scottish brass have a field-day.

Lloyd-Jones proves an equally clear-sighted navigator through the storm-buffeted landscape of *November Woods*, for many people, Bax's greatest tone-poem. Thoroughly refreshing in its enthusiasm and exhilarating sense of orchestral spectacle, this recording has a physical impact and emotional involvement that genuinely compel. A veritable blockbuster.

Symphonies Nos 2[a] & 5[b]
London Philharmonic Orchestra / [a]**Myer Fredman,**
[b]**Raymond Leppard**
Lyrita SRCD233 (78' · ADD)   Ⓕ🅞🅞🅑➤

Here's a majestic (and long overdue) return to currency for two cornerstones of the Lyrita catalogue. The LPO respond with all the edge-of-seat excitement of new discovery, particularly so in the turbulent Second Symphony, where an impassioned and inspired Myer Fredman secures playing of terrific fire, dedication and spontaneity. If Raymond Leppard's account of the Fifth operates at a slightly lower voltage, his cannily paced, sensitive and meticulously prepared reading none the less remains a most distinguished contribution to the Bax discography.

Both these vintage displays were marvellously engineered by Decca personnel working within the benign acoustic of Walthamstow Town Hall. A hugely rewarding reissue.

Symphony No 3. The Happy Forest
Royal Scottish National Orchestra /
David Lloyd-Jones
Naxos 8 553608 (54' · DDD)   ⑤●🅑➤

Dedicated to Sir Henry Wood, Bax's Symphony No 3 boasts arguably the richest store of memorable melodic invention to be found in any of the composer's cycle of seven, culminating in an inspired epilogue of wondrous, jaw-dropping beauty. David Lloyd-Jones's clear-headed, purposeful conducting of this intoxicating repertoire is the most judiciously paced and satisfyingly cogent Bax Third we've had since Barbirolli's pioneering 1943-4 Hallé account. Moreover, not only does Lloyd-Jones keep a firm hand on the tiller, he also draws some enthusiastic playing from the RSNO, which responds throughout with commendable polish and keen application.

Finely poised, affectingly full-throated solo work from principal horn and trumpet illuminates the progress of the ensuing Lento, whose ravishing landscape Lloyd-Jones surveys in less lingering fashion than either Barbirolli or Thomson. The first half of the finale, too, is a great success, Lloyd-Jones negotiating the fiendish twists and turns dictated by Bax's copious tempo markings with impressive aplomb. Only in the epilogue do you feel a need for a touch more rapt poetry. Tim Handley's excellently balanced recording is rich and refined, though the perspective is perhaps fractionally closer than ideal for The Happy Forest, which receives a performance of bounding vigour, gleeful mischief and muscular fibre; just that last, crucial drop of enchantment remains elusive. No matter, a disc not to be missed.

Symphony No 4. Nympholept.
Overture to a Picaresque Comedy
Royal Scottish National Orchestra /
David Lloyd-Jones
Naxos 8 555343 (65' · DDD)   ⑤●🅑➤

David Lloyd-Jones and the RSNO continue their stimulating championship of Bax with this extremely persuasive account of the Fourth Symphony. It's at once the most exuberantly inventive and most colourful of the cycle (the instrumentation includes six horns and organ). Lloyd-Jones steers a tauter, more athletic course through the eventful first movement than his *Gramophone* Award-winning rival (Bryden Thomson on Chandos), yet there's no want of playful affection, and the orchestral playing satisfyingly combines polish and eagerness. In the gorgeous central *Lento moderato* Lloyd-Jones perceptively evokes a bracing,

northerly chill wafting across Bax's dappled seascape. The unashamedly affirmative finale is a great success, its festive pomp and twinkling sense of fun conveyed with personable panache and swagger. If the symphony's jubilant closing pages reverberate in Thomson's version with just that crucial bit of extra weight and splendour in Belfast's Ulster Hall, Tim Handley's expert sound and balance do ample justice to Bax's distinctive scoring and his writing for low woodwind in particular. The *Overture to a Picaresque Comedy* makes an apt and boisterous curtain-raiser, Lloyd-Jones's rip-roaring rendering knocking Thomson's limp LPO version into a cocked hat. *Nympholept* could hardly form a greater contrast: a ravishing nature-poem in Bax's most enchanted Celtic vein. Again, this sensitive account is far preferable to Thomson's curiously laboured conception. Altogether a superb release.

Symphony No 5.
The Tale the Pine Trees Knew
Royal Scottish National Orchestra /
David Lloyd-Jones
Naxos 8 554509 (58' · DDD)   ⑤●🅑➤

The Fifth is perhaps the most characteristic of Bax's symphonies. For all the music's powerful range of emotion and its seemingly bewildering profusion of material and countless moments of bewitching beauty, its resourceful symphonic processes aren't easy to assimilate on first hearing. Lloyd-Jones's intelligent and purposeful direction pays handsome dividends, and a well-drilled RSNO responds with sensitivity and enthusiasm. Lloyd-Jones excels in the opening movement's tightly knit canvas, its epic ambition matched by a compelling sense of momentum, architectural grandeur and organic 'wholeness'. In the slow movement Lloyd-Jones paints a chillier, more troubled landscape than does Bryden Thomson (Chandos). The finale's main *Allegro* sets out with gleeful dash and a fine rhythmic snap to its heels. Lloyd-Jones judges that tricky, crisis-ridden transition into the epilogue well, and the apotheosis is a hard-won, grudging victory. The 1931 tone-poem *The Tale the Pine Trees Knew* makes an ideal bedfellow, foreshadowing as it does the bracingly 'northern' (to quote the composer) demeanour of the Fifth. Lloyd-Jones's comparatively extrovert treatment of the work's exultant final climax works perfectly convincingly within the context of his overall conception. Another eminently truthful, judiciously balanced sound picture from producer/engineer Tim Handley.

Symphony No 6[a]. Irish Landscape[b]. Overture to Adventure[c]. Rogue's Comedy Overture[c]. Overture: Work in Progress[c]
[a]**New Philharmonia Orchestra / Norman Del Mar**;
[bc]**Royal Philharmonic Orchestra / Vernon Handley**
Lyrita SRCD296 (76' · [ab]ADD/DDD)   Ⓕ●●🅑➤

Here's yet another valuable reissue from Lyrita's vaults. Norman Del Mar's pioneering 1966 account of Bax's Sixth Symphony has held up extremely well. Occupying an interpretative middle ground between the thrilling thrust and narrative coherence of Vernon Handley's much-praised recording (part of his *Gramophone* Award-winning cycle – see page 115) and the colourfully expressive languor of Bryden Thomson's, Del Mar may be the most satisfying of the lot. Like Handley, Del Mar makes sense of the symphony's unusual structure (the finale is a fierce scherzo positioned between a dark introduction and elegiac epilogue) while allowing one to savour more of the details. The result remains the most emotionally potent on disc. Note, for instance, how warmly the New Philharmonia strings sing their opening cantilena at the beginning of the slow movement. And although he is not as graceful as Handley, Del Mar brings far more character and incident to the finale's scherzo section.

The CD is rounded out with shorter works performed by Handley and the RPO, including a succinctly passionate, though somewhat rough-edged, reading of the atmospheric *Irish Landscape* (1913). The conductor's recording of the *Rogue's Comedy Overture* (1936), on the above-mentioned Chandos set, is slightly more frisky than this one – but only slightly. And while neither the *Overture to Adventure* (1936) nor the *Overture: Work in Progress* (1943) is top-drawer Bax, both are attractively vivacious and dispatched with élan.

Symphony No 6. Into the Twilight. Summer Music
Royal Scottish National Orchestra /
David Lloyd-Jones
Naxos 8 557144 (58' · DDD) Ⓢ**O**➔

David Lloyd-Jones's Bax series goes from strength to strength with this clear-headed interpretation of the exhilarating Sixth Symphony (arguably the last work to show the composer at creative white heat).

Lloyd-Jones rides the tempest of the opening movement with particular success, while still allowing himself plenty of expressive leeway for the ravishing secondary material. In the central *Lento* he paints a bleakly beautiful, snow-flecked landscape. As for the ambitious finale (a *tour de force* of structural innovation and thematic integration), the conductor steers a superbly confident course, and the RSNO respond with unflagging spirit and no mean skill.

Both Lloyd-Jones's fill-ups are sensitively done, although *Into the Twilight* doesn't equal the fragrant beauty and haunting allure of Thomson's intoxicating Ulster version. Unfortunately, the sound, while enormously vivid and wide ranging, is neither quite as natural in timbre nor judiciously blended as on previous instalments (bigger *tutti*s tend towards an aggressive blur). None the less, a firm recommendation.

Additional recommendations

Symphony No 3
Coupled with: Violin Concerto Ⓗ
Kersey *vn* **Hallé Orchestra / Barbirolli;**
BBC Symphony Orchestra / Boult
Dutton Epoch CDLX7111 (73' · ADD)
Recorded 1943-44 Ⓜ**O**

Barbirolli's recording of Bax's Third was the first of any Bax symphony and is a spellbinding achievement. No account on disc since can match it for authority and depth of feeling. The transfer boasts remarkable body and miraculously quiet surfaces.

Tone-Poems

In memoriam. Concertante for Piano (Left-Hand) and Orchestra[a]. The Bard of the Dimbovitza[b]
[b]**Jean Rigby** *mez* [a]**Margaret Fingerhut** *pf*
BBC Philharmonic Orchestra / Vernon Handley
Chandos CHAN9715 (77' · DDD) Ⓕ**OO**➔

The glorious tune that dominates the 1916 tone-poem *In memoriam* will be familiar to many Bax enthusiasts from its use in his 1948 film score for David Lean's *Oliver Twist*, and to hear it in its original surroundings is both a moving and thrilling experience. It had long been assumed that the 32-year-old composer never got round to scoring this deeply felt elegy so it's pleasing to find that Vernon Handley and the BBC Philharmonic do full justice to its opulent yet iridescent sound world, with its strong echoes of *The Garden of Fand* and *Nympholept*.

The *Concertante* for left-hand piano and orchestra, written for Harriet Cohen after a domestic accident had disabled her right hand, isn't top-drawer Bax, but remains a most appealing creation, with a central *Moderato tranquillo* in the composer's sweetest lyrical vein. Margaret Fingerhut is a deft, sympathetic soloist.

The five orchestral songs that make up *The Bard of the Dimbovitza*, setting poems allegedly based on Romanian folk-songs, contain not a hint of local colour but are purest Bax, the harmonic idiom and overall mood strikingly similar to his *Enchanted Summer*. Jean Rigby vividly characterises the dialogue in the last two songs ('My girdle I hung on a tree-top tall' and 'Spinning Song'), while bringing plenty of drama to the almost operatic scena that's 'The Well of Tears'. Some typically lustrous Chandos engineering adorns this valuable triptych of recorded premières, and the issue as a whole deserves the heartiest of welcomes.

The Garden of Fand. In the Faery Hills. November Woods. Sinfonietta
BBC Philharmonic Orchestra / Vernon Handley
Chandos CHAN10362 (76' · DDD) Ⓕ**B**➔

In the Faery Hills and *The Garden of Fand* are among Bax's loveliest and most loveable creations, and though the windswept *November*

Woods is far less tuneful, its emotional undercurrents run unfathomably deep. Bryden Thomson's shimmering, sensuous interpretations of these scores, recorded for Chandos some 20 years ago, laid bare the music's Impressionist roots; Vernon Handley (in an encore to his *Gramophone* Award-winning set of Bax's symphonies – see page 115) takes a tougher, more vigorous view. The only place he's notably slower than Thomson is in *November Woods*, yet how much darker and more ominous are the leaden skies that Handley paints. Indeed, even in such sensitive hands as Boult's, some of the stormier passages sound rather like film music, while Handley's deliberate focus on motivic clarity brings out a Wagnerian grandeur and gravity that strengthen the work's narrative backbone.

In *The Garden of Fand* and *In the Faery Hills* Handley adopts brisk tempi, occasionally pushing the music into a kind of giddy ecstasy that makes Thomson's fragrant, graceful readings sound downright languorous. If only the BBC Philharmonic were as flatteringly recorded as Thomson's Ulster Orchestra or, for that matter, the RSNO in David Lloyd-Jones's superb Naxos cycle. Lloyd-Jones's dynamic direction is similar in spirit to Handley's, in fact, and almost as arrestingly characterised – but not quite. This restless, syncopated score may not be top-drawer Bax but the Manchester musicians play it with the fervour of true believers.

Three Northern Ballads. Nympholept. Red Autumn. The Happy Forest. Into the Twilight
BBC Philharmonic Orchestra / Vernon Handley
Chandos CHAN10446 (77' · DDD)　　Ⓕ❶❷❸❹

Vernon Handley's revelatory Bax odyssey for Chandos comes up trumps once again with this generous feast spanning a quarter of a century from the enchanted Donegal glens of the youthful *Into the Twilight* (1908) to the rugged, wintry seascape of the Second *Northern Ballad*, completed in 1934. The latter is flanked by its roistering and plaintive predecessor and the darkly opulent *Prelude for a Solemn Occasion* (also known as *Northern Ballad* No 3). Whether Bax ever envisaged them as a self-contained entity is pure conjecture but, when presented with such swaggering commitment, they do comprise a deeply stirring and evocative sequence.

Elsewhere, *Into the Twilight* receives ideally radiant, heartfelt treatment – and you'll wait a lifetime to hear the ecstatic *Nympholept* better done. *The Happy Forest* raises the bar in its lightness of touch, iridescent glow and twinkling fun. The gale-tossed *Red Autumn* (more familiar in its two-piano garb) is clad in a remarkably idiomatic new orchestration by Graham Parlett.

So, gloriously assured music-making from first measure to last, and it's a relief to be able to report that Chandos's spectacularly ample and informative sound has all the natural bloom and crucial mid-range warmth that the companion disc (above) lacked. An unmissable treat.

Bax Tintagel **Rachmaninov** Symphony No 3, Op 44
London Philharmonic Orchestra / Osmo Vänskä
LPO LPO0036 (53' · DDD)
Recorded live at the Royal Festival Hall, London, on December 8, 2007　　Ⓜ❶Ⓑ▸

Vänskä's *Tintagel* has real fire in its belly allied to a surging momentum, and he uncovers many a fleck of exquisite detail within Bax's endlessly resourceful and wondrously evocative scoring. The ecstatic B major sunburst that heralds the second subject's unforgettable return has all the thrusting ardour one could wish for. The justly enthusiastic applause bursts in somewhat too precipitately for comfort.

The Rachmaninov (complete with exposition repeat in the first movement) is just as involving, not quite as volatile or heart-on-sleeve as some but intensely refreshing all the same in its zestful swagger, scrupulous preparation, limpid beauty and concern for the bigger scheme (how shrewd of Vänskä to keep in reserve such a scintillating burst of energy for the headlong closing pages). The engineering does ample justice to some splendidly selfless and thoroughly invigorating music-making, though in the Bax you might need to crank up the volume a notch higher than usual. A strongly recommendable issue.

Additional recommendations

November Woods
Coupled with: Northern Ballad No 1. Mediterranean. The Garden of Fand. Tintagel
LPO / Boult
Lyrita SRCD231 (62' · ADD)　　ⒻⒷ▸
Boult's performance of this tone-poem is masterly and he generates a great deal of tension, atmosphere and drama.

The Truth about the Russian Dancers. From Dusk till Dawn
LPO / Thomson
Chandos CHAN10457 (67' · DDD)　　Ⓜ❶Ⓑ▸
Not top-drawer Bax, admittedly, but the LPO under Bryden Thomson relish both scores' undeniable period charm and they have been sumptuously served by Chandos. A really enjoyable disc.

Tintagel
Coupled with: **Vaughan Williams** Symphony No 5
Philharmonia Orchestra; London Symphony Orchestra / Barbirolli
EMI British Composers 565110-2 (54' · ADD)　　Ⓑ
Bax's rugged, windswept seascape finds Barbirolli in his element, and his reading is on the whole more passionately involving than either Boult's or Thomson's.

String Quartets

String Quartets Nos 1 & 2
Maggini Quartet (Laurence Jackson, David Angel *vns* Martin Outram *va* Michal Kaznowski *vc*)
Naxos 8 555282 (54' · DDD)　　ⓈⒷ▸

Had Dvořák written an *Irish* Quartet to sit along-side his delectable *American*, it might well have sounded like the start of Bax's First String Quartet. Completed in 1918, this is one of Bax's most endearing and approachable scores. The clean-cut opening *Allegretto semplice* positively beams with happiness, and it's succeeded by a wistfully intimate slow movement. The finale begins and finishes in a mood of pagan revelry, though there's time for a ravishing episode in Bax's sweetest lyrical vein, its indelible tune a close cousin to the folksong *The Fair Hills of Ireland*. The Second Quartet of 1924-5 proves an altogether tougher nut to crack. Conceived at the same time as the Second Symphony, it's a knotty, densely plotted creation, as harmonically daring as Bax ever ventured and demanding formidable concentration from performers and listeners alike.

The Maggini Quartet do Bax absolutely proud, their performances striking an ideal balance between urgent expression and purposeful clarity. Both rival readings on Chandos have considerable strengths, but the Maggini's scrupulously dedicated advocacy will captivate both seasoned Baxians and newcomers alike. An outstanding coupling in every way.

String Quartet No 3. Adagio ma non troppo, 'Cathaleen-ni-Hoolihan'. Lyrical Interlude for String Quintet[a]
Maggini Quartet (Laurence Jackson, David Angel *vn* Martin Outram *va* Michal Kaznowski *vc*) with
[a]**Garfield Jackson** *va*
Naxos 8 555953 (57' · DDD)   Ⓢ**O**Ⓞ**➔**

Bax composed the last of his three mature string quartets between May and September 1936, inscribing it to the Griller Quartet who gave the first performance on the BBC National Programme the following May. An appealing, cogently structured 37-minute work, it's cast (unusually for Bax) in four movements, the joyous first of which 'was probably influenced by the coming of spring in beautiful Kenmare' (to quote the composer's own descriptive notes in *The Radio Times*). An Irish flavour also permeates the bardic *Poco lento*, while the third movement's 'dreamy, remotely romantic' trio melody is eventually cleverly welded to the 'rather sinister and malicious' *scherzo* material. The vigorous finale builds up a fine head of steam and incorporates a wistful backward glance just before the close that's entirely characteristic of its creator.

The Maggini Quartet forge a well-paced and concentrated interpretation, playing with assurance, infectious rhythmic snap and heartwarming dedication. They are joined by violist Garfield Jackson for the haunting *Lyrical Interlude* from 1922 (a reworking of the slow movement from Bax's ambitious String Quintet of 1908), and there's another rarity in the shape of the lovely *Adagio ma non troppo* centrepiece from the 1903 String Quartet in E major that Bax orchestrated two years later as his first tone-poem, *Cathaleen-ni-Hoolihan*.

Throughout, the sound is faithful in timbre and the balance most musically judged.

Violin Sonatas

Violin Sonatas – in G minor; No 1 in E.
Ballad. Legend
Robert Gibbs *vn* **Mary Mei-Loc Wu** *pf*
ASV CDDCA1127 (61' · DDD)   Ⓕ

The First Sonata is a passionate, deeply personal outpouring, essayed here with rapt understanding and tender intimacy. The rival Chandos performance may exhibit rather more in the way of commanding projection and urgent expression, but these newcomers' keen poetic instincts are never in doubt. Both the *Legend* and *Ballad* date from the First World War years (of the broodingly elegiac *Legend* – much liked by Vaughan Williams, apparently – Bax later recalled to violinist May Harrison that it 'came straight out of the horror of that time'), whereas the single-movement Sonata in G minor is an amiable, confidently argued student effort from November 1901. Again, Gibbs and Wu lend consistently idiomatic and warm-hearted advocacy to this material. A very appealing collection, in short, and a mandatory purchase for confirmed Baxians.

Violin Sonata No 2. Ballad. Legend.
Allegro appassionato. Sonata in F.
Laurence Jackson *vn* **Ashley Wass** *pf*
Naxos 8 570094 (74' · DDD)   Ⓢ**➔**

Cast in four linked movements and held together by a motto theme which also appears in the 1917 tone-poem *November Woods*, Bax's storm-tossed Second Violin Sonata was conceived during the summer of 1915 at a time of great personal upheaval for the 31-year-old composer and comprehensively overhauled six years later. Be it in the seductive sway of the second movement (a ghostly waltz enigmatically entitled 'The Grey Dancer in the Twilight') or hair-raising final climax prior to the ecstatically serene epilogue, these dashingly poised newcomers give of their considerable best, with CBSO leader Laurence Jackson formidably secure in the solo part's more scarily vertiginous exploits. No one coming to this music for the first time will be left unstirred by its piercing beauty, urgency of expression and vaulting ambition.

In any case, what lifts this collection into the indispensable category are the spellbinding performances of the darkly smouldering *Legend* and *Ballad* from 1915 and 1916 respectively, as well as the *Allegro appassionato* in G minor (a likeable student effort from 1901) and unpublished F major Sonata of 1928 (which Bax subsequently recast as his captivating Nonet). The Potton Hall sound in these last four items (emanating from sessions a year after those for the Second Sonata) is particularly handsome and true, and the disc as a whole represents yet another 'must have' within this extensive series.

Viola Sonata

Legend. Viola Sonata. Concert Piece. Trio[a]
[a]**Laurence Jackson** vn **Martin Outram** va
Julian Rolton pf
Naxos 8 557784 (61' · DDD)   ⓈⒹ▸

Here is a stunningly coordinated reading of urgent drive, bold contrasts and edge-of-seat drama reminiscent of dedicatee Lionel Tertis's even fleeter 1929 recording with the composer and manages to knock more than four minutes off that of their transatlantic rivals. It's sensationally exciting in its way, but there's no escaping the fact that others convey the greater bardic poetry and affectionate warmth. Although a tad dry, Naxos's sound is accommodating.

Reservations evaporate in the flamboyant *Concert Piece* (1904) and wintry *Legend* from 1929, both convincingly done, and proceedings conclude with the 1906 Trio in one movement for piano, violin and viola. In his autobiography *Farewell, My Youth*, Bax witheringly refers to it as 'a derivative and formless farrago', but the 'Irish' skip some five minutes in is characteristic. This dashing performance has real fire in its belly.

Don't let the minor niggles concerning the sonata deter you. Expertly annnotated by Lewis Foreman, here's a release that all Baxians should check out.

Clarinet Sonatas

Clarinet Sonatas[ad] – in E (1901); in D (1934).
Folk-Tale[cd]. Piano Trio[abd]. Romance[ad]. Trio[abd]
[a]**Robert Plane** cl **Gould Piano Trio**
([b]Lucy Gould vn [c]Alice Neary vc [d]Benjamin Frith pf)
Naxos 8 557698 (77' · DDD)   ⓈⒹ▸

Bax's engaging Clarinet Sonata of 1934 has been lucky on disc, with distinguished versions from Janet Hilton, Emma Johnson and Michael Collins happily still adorning the catalogue. Robert Plane's irreproachably alert and stylish account with Benjamin Frith leaves a similarly delightful impression. Plane's timbre could hardly be more alluring and he strikes up a tangible rapport with Frith. The pleasures continue with the 1945-46 Piano Trio, Bax's final chamber offering, which finds him at his most economical and relaxed. It gets a first-rate performance from the Gould Trio, who bring plenty of bite and sparkle to the rhythmically buoyant finale. In the wistful and brooding *Folk-Tale* (first performed in 1918) Alice Neary and Frith do full justice to what is an unexpectedly powerful eight-minute essay.

But what makes this generously timed Naxos CD essential listening are three world-premiere recordings. Both the one-movement Sonata in E and Romance for clarinet and piano date from 1901 and may well have been conceived as parts of a larger work. The 1906 'Trio in one movement for piano, violin and viola' was the first extended score Bax deemed worthy for publica-

tion, a decision he later regretted (he described it as a 'derivative and formless farrago'); it is performed here with the viola part taken by the clarinet, an option sanctioned by the composer.

Neither of the clarinet pieces is likely to set the world alight, whereas the fluent and predominantly extrovert 17-minute Trio contains tantalising glimpses of greater achievements to come. Enthusiasts can rest assured that these admirably agile and idiomatic performers give Bax's youthful inspiration every chance to shine; indeed, it's impossible to imagine a more convincing account of the Trio.

Chamber Works

Nonet. Oboe Quintet. Elegiac Trio. Clarinet Sonata. Harp Quintet
Nash Ensemble (Philippa Davies fl Gareth Hulse ob Michael Collins cl Marcia Crayford, Iris Juda, Elizabeth Wexler vns Roger Chase va Christopher van Kampen vc Duncan McTier db Skaila Kanga hp Ian Brown pf)
Hyperion CDA66807 (73' · DDD)   Ⓕ⊙⊙

A truly first-rate modern recording of Bax's Nonet. What a bewitching creation it is, overflowing with invention and breathtakingly imaginative in its instrumental resource (the sounds created are often almost orchestral). Bax worked on the Nonet at the same time (1929-30) as he was composing his Third Symphony and there are striking similarities between the two. The Nash Ensemble gives a masterly, infinitely subtle reading.

The remainder of the disc brings comparable pleasure. The delightful Oboe Quintet (written for Leon Goossens in 1922) receives immensely characterful treatment, especially the jaunty, Irish-jig finale (such richly communicative playing). The same is true of the lovely Harp Quintet, essayed here with rapt intensity and delicious poise. In the hands of these stylish artists, the *Elegiac Trio* possesses a delicacy and poignancy that are really quite captivating. That just leaves the engaging Clarinet Sonata, a work that has fared well in the recording studio over the last few years. Suffice to report, Michael Collins and Ian Brown are compelling advocates, and theirs is a performance to set beside (if not supersede) all rivals. Beautiful sound throughout.

Elegiac Trio[a]. Fantasy Sonata[b]. Quintet for Harp and Strings[c]. Sonata for Flute and Harp[d]
Mobius ([ad]Lorna McGhee fl [c]Kanako Ito, [c]Philippe Honoré vns [abc]Ashan Pillai va [c]Martin Storey vc Alison Nicholls hp)
Naxos 8 554507 (65' · DDD)   Ⓢ⊙⊙▸

Mobius is a gifted young London-based ensemble of seven prize-winning instrumentalists from four different countries, and their scrupulously shaded, fervent playing betokens a very real empathy with this gorgeous repertoire. In both the *Elegiac Trio* and Harp Quintet these artists favour a more boldly etched, less delicately evanescent approach than that of the Nash Ensemble (which is perhaps marginally more successful in distilling the poignant heartache of two works indissolubly associated with the tragic events of the 1916 Easter Rising). Especially valuable is the impassioned rendering of the marvellous *Fantasy Sonata* for harp and viola of 1927. Certainly, harpist Alison Nicholls (a beguiling presence throughout) copes heroically with the daunting technical demands of Bax's writing (tailored for the virtuosity of the great Russian harpist, Maria Korchinska); moreover, she's splendidly partnered by violist Ashan Pillai. Likewise, the engagingly relaxed Sonata for Flute and Harp emerges with delightful freshness, its plangent central 'Cavatina' as haunting as ever. Sound and balance are just fine. Terrific value and strongly recommended.

Additional recommendation

Octet. String Quintet. Concerto. Threnody and Scherzo. In memoriam
Fingerhut pf **ASMF Chbr Ens**
Chandos CHAN9602 (72' · DDD)　　　Ⓟ🅞🅑➤
This is a beautiful and enterprising collection. In the single-movement String Quintet Bax draws some luscious, almost orchestral sonorities from his chosen forces. The sound is warm and transparent.

Piano Sonatas

Piano Sonatas – No 1 in F sharp minor; No 2 in G. Burlesque. In a Vodka Shop. Nereid. Dream in exile
Ashley Wass pf
Naxos 8 557439 (77' · DDD)　　　Ⓢ🅞🅞🅞➤

Not only does this gifted young pianist possess a rock-solid technique and striking keyboard finesse, his penetrating accounts of both these large-scale, single-movement sonatas make you sit up and listen. So it is that in the bracing First Sonata (written in 1910 during Bax's sojourn in Russia and Ukraine) Ashley Wass finds the balance between epic and introspective. More than that, he brings out the music's brazen Slavic fervour with its echoes of Scriabin and Rachmaninov (the coda's pealing bells toll with magnificent cumulative impact). He paces its turbulent successor of 1919 with cogency and concentration. Even more than the magisterial John McCabe, Wass takes us on a genuine voyage of discovery: the control, sense of colour and dynamic range are remarkable, and his tone never hardens under pressure.
Of the four couplings, *Dream in Exile* stands out. The sound throughout is vividly truthful.

Songs

Far in a Western Brookland[b]. The Market Girl[b]. A Milking Sian[a]. The Song in the Twilight[a]. To Eire[b].

The White Peace[b]. A Celtic Song Cycle[a]. The Fairies[b]. Youth[b]. Parting[b]. A Lullaby[a]. Roundel[b]. When I was one and twenty[b]. The Enchanted Fiddle[b]. When we are lost[b]
[a]**Jean Rigby** mez [b]**Ian Partridge** ten
Michael Dussek pf
Dutton Laboratories Epoch CDLX7136 (78' · DDD)　Ⓜ

With the exception of *The White Peace* (a favourite of John McCormack), Bax's songs have been largely and undeservedly neglected. Ian Partridge sings with his customary sensitivity and intelligence, responding with particular eloquence to the grateful melodic lines of *To Eire* (1910) and the yearningly ecstatic *Parting*. The latter appeared in the aftermath of the 1916 Easter Uprising, and its haunting strains are heard again in the epilogue of the Symphonic Variations completed two years later. Likewise, the opening phrase of the 1914 Chaucer-setting *Roundel* will already be familiar to listeners to the tone-poem *Nympholept*. Jean Rigby works wonders with the youthful *Celtic Song Cycle*, and imparts almost operatic scope to the quietly intense *Song in the Twilight*. She's impressive, too, in *A Lullaby*, a 1910 setting of one of Bax's own poems, conceived in the middle of an unrequited love-affair with a Ukrainian girl, Natalia Skarginska. Michael Dussek's accompaniments are a model of scrupulous musicality.

Antonio Bazzini　　　Italian 1818-1897

Italian violinist, composer and teacher. He was a pupil of a Brescian violinist, Faustino Camisani (Camesani); encouraged by Paganini, he began his concert career at an early age and became one of the most highly regarded artists of his time. Written in the classic forms of the German school, Bazzini's chamber works earned him a central place in the Italian instrumental renaissance of the 19th century.

Works for violin and piano

La ronde des lutins, Op 25. Trois morceaux lyriques, Op 41. Calabrese, Op 34 No 6. Le carillon d'Arras, Op 36. Deux morceaux de salon, Op 12. Deux grande études, Op 49. Trois morceaux en forme de sonate, Op 44
Chloë Hanslip vn **Caspar Frantz** pf
Naxos 8 570800 (71' · DDD)　　　Ⓢ🅞➤

Among 19th-century violinist/composers, Antonio Bazzini was probably the most successful in escaping from exclusive specialisation in the virtuoso repertoire. His compositions include operas, sacred music, orchestral works and chamber music, so it's rather sad that he should be remembered today by a single piece, the scintillating *Ronde des lutins* ('Dance of the Goblins'). Chloë Hanslip demonstrates most persuasively that, even among his violin showpieces, it isn't a one-off. The items in her recital may make for fairly undemanding listening, the idiom may not be strikingly original, but Bazzini has the knack of integrating post-Paganini virtuoso features into a romantic style that's sophisticated, subtle and tasteful. The *cantabile* items are very appealing – the central Romance in the *Trois morceaux en forme de sonate* could rival the ubiquitous Massenet *Méditation* were it to become better known – and the Op 49 Etudes are particularly interesting, the first a *moto perpetuo* with very original accented dissonances, the second a delightful scherzo with elegant double-stopping and lively cross accents, and an unexpectedly lyrical central section.

Hanslip certainly has the confidence and technique for this repertoire: more importantly, she's able to engage with each piece, bringing out its particular expressive character. For the Romance in Op 44, for instance, she produces a soft, sensuous tone, quite different from her sound in the plaintive, ornate Nocturne from Op 41. Caspar Frantz accompanies very stylishly throughout, and Hanslip's musical personality, graceful and with spontaneous verve, brings everything to life. It's lovely violin-playing!

Amy Beach   American 1867-1944

Born in New Hampshire in the US, Amy Marcy Cheney Beach showed prodigious musical talent at an early age. She later studied with her mother She gave her first public recital aged seven, and in 1885 she made her debut with the Boston Symphony. After her marriage to Dr Henry Beach, she reduced her public appearances to one concert per year and devoted herself to composition. After his death in 1910 she resumed a performing career. Beach composed works in many genres, including a Mass, a symphony, a Piano Concerto, chamber works, piano solo and vocal works in a Romantic idiom.

Piano Concerto

Piano Concerto in C sharp minor, Op 45[a]. Symphony in E minor, Op 32, 'Gaelic'
[a]**Alan Feinberg** pf **Nashville Symphony Orchestra / Kenneth Schermerhorn**
Naxos 8 559139 (79' · DDD)   ⓢ🄳➤

Composed in 1898-99, Amy Beach's ambitious, singularly impressive Piano Concerto is at long last coming in from the cold. An expansively rhetorical *Allegro moderato* launches the work before a playful *perpetuum mobile* scherzo and moody *Largo* (described by its creator as a 'dark, tragic lament'); the finale goes with a delightful swing. In fact, it's a rewarding achievement all round, full of brilliantly idiomatic solo writing (Beach was a virtuoso pianist herself and performed the work many times) and lent further autobiographical intrigue by its assimilation of thematic material from three early songs.

Alan Feinberg brings more charisma to bear than Joanne Polk on her rival account for Arabesque, without any loss of delicacy or poetry, and his collaboration with Kenneth Schermerhorn and the Nashville Symphony undoubtedly generates greater thrust and spontaneity. The recording, too, is more pleasingly spacious, if a little lacking in body.

Following the success of her 1889 Mass in E flat, Beach knew that she needed to produce a large-scale symphony to cement her reputation; it was the Boston premiere of Dvořák's *New World* that finally spurred her into action. Responding to the Czech master's exhortation that American composers should turn to spirituals, plantation songs and minstrel-show music for inspiration, Beach selected four Irish melodies of 'simple, rugged and unpretentious beauty', moulding any additional themes 'in the same idiom and spirit'.

That the *Gaelic* Symphony (1894-96) won golden opinions from the outset comes as no surprise, given its big heart, irresistible charm and confident progress. Schermerhorn and his eager Nashville band give a convincingly paced, tidy performance with real fire in its belly and plenty of character. A thoroughly enjoyable issue.

Sally Beamish   British b1956

English composer and viola player, active in Scotland. Though drawn to composition, she studied the violin and the viola at the RNCM and worked for around 10 years as a viola player with several London ensembles. In 1986 she received her first professional commission, for Dances and Nocturnes; in 1989 she moved to Scotland where, aided by an Arts Council bursary, she began to concentrate on composition. She founded the Chamber Group of Scotland with James MacMillan and her husband Robert Irvine. Her distinctive music draws on many different sources. Motherhood has been an important inspiration. The concerto form has become her trademark medium and she has composed works for soloists including cellists Robert Cohen and Steven Isserlis, viola player Tabea Zimmermann, trumpeter Håkan Hardenberger, flautist Sharon Bezaly and percussionists Colin Currie and Evelyn Glennie. She has also worked on several projects with saxophonist Branford Marsalis, who has performed two of her concertos.

Viola Concerto No 2, 'The Seafarer'[a]. Whitescape. Sangsters
[a]**Tabea Zimmermann** va
Swedish Chamber Orchestra / Ola Rudner
BIS BIS-CD1241 (59' · DDD)   Ⓕ

From 1998 to 2002 Sally Beamish enjoyed a four-year dual residency with the Swedish and Scottish chamber orchestras. The compositional results included this trio of orchestral works, which are among her best: there's the kind of creative confidence and certainty, couched in unmistakable personal tones, which, in assured performances, well recorded, makes for a first-rate CD.

The common factor lies in the way all three works respond to the chilly essences of very northern landscapes. The earliest, *Whitescape* (2000), is particularly bold in suggesting the monstrous in nature (it has links with Beamish's Mary Shelley opera), and is also impressively direct in expression, regularly cutting back on tendencies to elaborate its material and setting its strong, stark climax in a forbidding but never merely austere context.

More impressively still, the Second Viola Concerto (2001) takes a fresh look at the genre's standard three-movement form. Beamish makes reference to an Anglo-Saxon poem which sets the travails of seafarers, aware of storms and the cries of birds, alongside visions of heavenly life after death. Against this background she charts a progression from brooding, rhapsodic material, within which quirky contrasts, percussion prominent, make highly effective incursions, towards a kind of repose – not exactly serene in spirit, but founded in rich, lucid harmony. This fine work has the added benefit of Tabea Zimmermann's marvellously characterful performance.

Sangsters (2002) is also rooted in a poem – a modern one in Scots – which shows how birds, seals and humans adapt to nature and celebrate their different worlds. The second of the three movements is marginally less characterful and cogent than the rest, but for the most part Beamish sustains the high level of invention and imagination which the disc as a whole embodies. No praise is too great for the excellence of the Swedish Chamber Orchestra and their conductor Ola Rudner: never has musical northern-ness seemed more inviting!

David Bednall
British *b*1979

Bednall studied at Sherborne and at Queen's College, Oxford, where he was organ scholar. He later studied with Naji Hakim and David Briggs, and in 2000 was appointed organ scholar at Gloucester Cathedral. He was a prize-winner in Improvisation and Performance at the examination for Fellow of the Royal College of Organists in 2002, and has given recitals at L'Eglise de La Trinité, Paris, Westminster, St Paul's and many other cathedrals. He balances a busy career as composer and organist, combining extensive freelance commitments with the position of sub-organist at Bristol Cathedral, PhD Studies in Composition with John Pickard at the University of Bristol and directorship of the University Singers.

Requiem

Requiemᵃ. O come let us sing. Salvator mundi.
Let all the world
ᵃ**Philip Dukes** *va* ᵃ**David Bednall** *org* **Chamber Choir**

of St Mary's, Calne / Edward Whiting
Regent REGCD327 (64' · DDD) Ⓕ**OOO**

With each new exposure to the music of David Bednall, one is ever more impressed with both the quality of his writing and its originality. Here, with the evocative passage for viola and organ which opens his Requiem, we have something quite special. It helps, of course, that accompanying the richly expressive playing of Philip Dukes we have the composer himself at the organ, and with the entry of the impeccably poised Chamber Choir from St Mary's School, Calne in Wiltshire, we are clearly hearing performers who are deeply committed to a work which they themselves premiered in November 2008. But the music stretches far beyond the commitment of these superb performers and makes a significant new contribution to the already fertile genre of Latin Requiems composed by English composers. Echoes of the Duruflé may resound a little too strongly for comfort in the 'Domine Jesu Christe' but otherwise the work shows considerable distinction.

Edward Whiting has achieved a remarkable sound from his choir of 43 girls aged 14-18, their unison singing moulded to perfection and the lovely nuances of tone colour and phrase-shaping delicately and subtly managed. Once or twice the sound may take on a slightly bland quality but this is invariably dissipated by Bednall's resourceful organ support. It's hard to imagine many other organists achieving the same compelling quasi-orchestral effects as he does on the Marlborough College Chapel organ used in this recording.

As a new addition to the Requiem repertoire as well as a performance in its own right, this disc is a resounding success and the addition of three unaccompanied motets only adds to the very high regard earned by both composer and choir. By any standards this is an impressive achievement.

Ludwig van Beethoven
German 1770-1827

'There are and there will be thousands of princes,' wrote Beethoven to Prince Lichnowsky. 'There is only one Beethoven.' People approach Beethoven with a feeling of awe and reverence. Whether you like his music or not, it is an appropriate response for his achievements make him one of the supreme creative geniuses of history, up there with Leonardo, Michelangelo and Shakespeare (in fact someone once said that 'where Shakespeare ends, Beethoven begins'). In one short burst he dragged music from the Classicism of the 18th century into the Romantic era, one which dominated musical thinking for a hundred years. What he did was genuinely courageous – his single-minded vision, idealism, determination and personal bravery are indeed awe-inspiring.

Beethoven was convinced that the 'van' in his name indicated noble birth and he allowed the rumour to circulate that he was the love-child of

Friedrich Wilhelm II (or even – and more improbably – Frederick the Great). In fact his family was of Dutch descent. His grandfather had been a choir director in Louvain.

Beethoven had a thoroughly miserable childhood thanks to his alcoholic brute of a father (a singer in the Electoral Chapel in Bonn). Fired by ambitions to turn his gifted son into a second Mozart, Johann van Beethoven would keep him slaving at the piano all night, raining blows on him when he made a mistake. Young Ludwig was an unprepossessing-looking child, he had no friends, he was clumsy and untidy in appearance and the only warmth he knew came from his mother. Johann and his fellow drinker Tobias Pfeiffer were his first teachers; various others contributed to his early musical study of the violin, organ, piano and horn. His first work to be published was Nine Variations for piano on a March of Dressler which he composed when he was 12. His first important lessons came from the court organist Christian Neefe who recognised and nurtured Beethoven's talent. At 14, the Elector Maximilian made him deputy court organist.

While on a visit to Bonn, Beethoven's mother died. His father's alcoholism cost him his job, obliging Beethoven to earn enough money to keep the family (he had two younger brothers). This he did by playing the viola in a theatre orchestra and giving piano lessons to the wealthy widow of a court councillor. Among the influential admirers he met at this time was Count Ferdinand Waldstein, later immortalised by the dedication of one of Beethoven' sonatas.

In 1792 he studied briefly and unprofitably with Haydn in Vienna (which became his home for the rest of his life) before lessons in counterpoint from Albrechtsberger and vocal composition with Salieri. Haydn, it must be said, though as intolerant of Beethoven's crude manners as he was of his disregard for the normal rules of harmony, was moved to remark that Beethoven made the impression of 'a man who has several heads, several hearts and several souls'.

In 1795 Beethoven made his debut in Vienna and his reputation as a virtuoso pianist and composer spread rapidly. Though it remained a secret between his doctor and himself for many years, we know that Beethoven was aware of impending deafness as early as his 26th year – otosclerosis was certainly part of the cause (an abnormal growth of honeycomb bone in the inner ear) accompanied by tinnitus, but a contributory factor was syphilis, the symptoms of which show up in the life mask made in 1812 and in the photograph taken of his skull in 1863 when the body was exhumed.

In a document dated 1802 and not discovered till after his death, Beethoven wrote poignantly of his condition, aware that the most important sense to him, that of hearing, was going to be taken away. This is the so-called Heiligenstadt Testament, written in the village of Heiligenstadt near Vienna.

His predicament spurred him to a furious spell of creativity and, in the circumstances, it is quite remarkable that he was able to compose such music – of every shape and form, embracing tragedy and joy – without apparent reference to his physical state ('coolness under the fire of creative fantasy' was how Schubert summed up Beethoven's genius). During this period he presented his Third Piano Concerto

and the Kreutzer Sonata, his oratorio Christus am Oelberge, the Waldstein, Appassionata and Moonlight Sonatas as well as his Symphony No 3 (the Eroica).

And still the music came pouring out: the first version of Fidelio was given in 1805, followed by the Razumovsky string quartets, Symphonies Nos 4, 5 and 6, the Violin Concerto, the Triple Concerto and a number of piano sonatas. Beethoven was offered the well-paid position of Kapellmeister of Kassel by King Jerome Bonaparte of Westphalia but, despite his financial difficulties (his income from various patrons was uncertain), he decided to stay in Vienna.

The inexorable progress of Beethoven's deafness made him increasingly irritable, over-sensitive, scornful and petulant, more inclined to retreat into himself and shun society. He exaggerated his poverty (he kept his shares and bonds locked up in a secret drawer) and assiduously studied the winning numbers in the Austrian national lottery in the hope of making a fortune. Beethoven was also irredeemably untidy – his handwriting was all but indecipherable – and many manuscripts bear the circle made by using them as a cover for his soup or chamber pot. But his belief in himself and what he was doing was intense and woe betide anyone who didn't acknowledge that. Many close friends were banished for ever for trifling incidents; others believed in him and supported him unsparingly: Prince Lobkowitz, Countess Erdödy, for instance, and (especially) the Archduke Rudolph – all tolerated his foibles and stuck loyally by him. Beethoven knew that he was breaking new ground. 'With whom need I be afraid of measuring my strength?' he once boasted proudly. To prove it, one masterpiece followed another – the Fifth Piano Concerto (the Emperor), Symphonies Nos 7 and 8, the Les adieux Piano Sonata.

The years 1812 to 1817 saw a marked decline in the amount of music and in its adventurousness. And this led to the third and final phase of his development as a composer beginning in 1818 – and with a vengeance! It saw the appearance of the mammoth Hammerklavier Piano Sonata and it heralded the beginning of arguably his greatest and most productive period, the one which brought the Ninth 'Choral' Symphony, the Missa solemnis and the late string quartets. During this decade, deprived of a wife and family, Beethoven sought to find a surrogate son in the form of his nephew Karl, whose father died in 1815. He regarded Karl's mother as unfit to bring up the boy and engaged in a series of sordid and bitter court quarrels in an attempt to become his guardian. He finally won the case in 1820 and for the next six years stifled him with avuncular affection in a pathetic attempt to gain his love and reform Karl's dissolute ways. Karl, in return, piled up enormous debts, regarded his uncle with some contempt and finally attempted to commit suicide. At length, he joined the army and went on to enjoy a normal life.

Beethoven was totally deaf after 1818. Just as those who have never fought in a war can never properly conceive its true terrors, so we can never imagine what deafness can have been like for one of the greatest composers of history. His touching faith in every new 'hearing remedy' that came on the market bears witness to his undying hope for a cure.

His only means of conversation with his fellow men was through conversation books – everything that anybody wanted to say to Beethoven was written down first (he would answer orally). The most heart-rending demonstration of his affliction is the famous occasion of the premiere of the Ninth Symphony in May 1824, which the composer insisted on conducting himself, though stone deaf. It's said that as the Symphony ended, Beethoven was several bars adrift from the orchestra and continued to conduct even as a storm of enthusiastic applause broke out. The contralto soloist, Caroline Ungher, at length came over to him, and gently turned him round to face the audience. Only then did the audience realise that Beethoven had not heard anything that had been going on and, wrote Sir George Grove, '[it] acted like an electric shock on all present. A volcanic explosion of sympathy and admiration followed which was repeated again and again and again and seemed as if it would never end'. There must have been a few tears shed that night.

In 1826 Beethoven caught a cold while visiting his brother; the cold developed into pneumonia; jaundice and dropsy set in after that. His death on the afternoon of March 26 came in the middle of a violent thunderstorm, a coincidence which has appealed to the more romantically inclined biographers. In fact, there was an electrical storm over Vienna that day but the other legend, that of the dying Beethoven raising his fists to Heaven in a last defiant gesture, must be a fanciful invention considering his feeble physical state. His last words were reported to have been: 'I shall hear in heaven.' For his funeral, schools closed, people stayed away from work and all Vienna mourned. Franz Schubert was one of the torch-bearers.

'The first of Beethoven's compositions are music,' wrote the critic Eduard Hanslick. 'In his last compositions Beethoven makes music.' There is a direct parallel between the political climate of the time and Beethoven's music. Just as the French Revolution overthrew established authority and spread a wave of rebellion throughout Europe, so Beethoven with equal defiance and decisiveness overthrew accepted musical form, traditional harmony and structure and the neat, well-ordered ways of the so-recent worlds of Haydn and Mozart. Beethoven's credo was the entirely new one expressed in the writings of the philosophers of the Enlightenment such as Rousseau and Voltaire: the creative ego has the right to express itself in its own way without fear or hindrance. As a devout republican, Beethoven (and indeed his music) shouts from the rooftops, 'I, too, am King!'

Piano Concertos

No 1 in C, Op 15; No 2 in B flat, Op 19; No 3 in C minor, Op 37; No 4 in G, Op 58; No 5 in E flat, Op 73, 'Emperor'

Complete Piano Concertos

Piano Concertos Nos 1-5
Pierre-Laurent Aimard pf **Chamber Orchestra of Europe / Nikolaus Harnoncourt**
Teldec ③ 0927 47334-2 (184' · DDD) Ⓜ❶❷❸▣▸

Ⓖ The freshness of this set is remarkable. You do not have to listen far to be swept up by its spirit of renewal and discovery, and in Pierre-Laurent Aimard as soloist Harnoncourt has made an inspired choice. Theirs aren't eccentric readings of these old warhorses – far from it. But they could be called idiosyncratic – from Harnoncourt would you have expected anything else?

These are modern performances which have acquired richness and some of their focus from curiosity about playing styles and sound production of the past. Harnoncourt favours leaner string textures than the norm and gets his players in the excellent COE to command a wide range of expressive weight and accent; this they do with an immediacy of effect that's striking. Yet there's a satisfying body to the string sound, too.

The playing seems to have recourse to eloquence without having to strive for it, and that's characteristic of Aimard's contribution as well. Strong contrasts are explored and big moments encompassed as part of an unforced continuity in which nothing is hurried. The big moments do indeed stand out: one of them is the famous exchange of dramatic gestures between piano and orchestra in the development of the E flat Concerto's (No 5's) first movement; another the equally dramatic but very different exchange when the piano re-enters at the start of the development in the first movement of the G major Concerto (No 4). At these junctures, conductor and pianist allow the gestures to disrupt the rhythmic continuity. Over the top? No, but risky maybe, and if you've strong views about what Beethoven's rubrics permit, or have swallowed a metronome, you may react strongly. For make no mistake, Aimard is as intrepid an explorer here as Harnoncourt – by conviction, not simply by adoption.

Technically he's superbly equipped. This is evident everywhere, but especially in the finales, brimful of spontaneous touches and delight in their eventfulness and in the pleasure of playing them. The finale of the *Emperor* tingles with a continuously vital, constantly modulated dynamic life that it rarely receives; so many players make it merely rousing. And among the first movements, that of the G major Concerto is a quite exceptional achievement for the way Harnoncourt and his soloist find space for the fullest characterisation of the lyricism and diversity of the solo part – Aimard begins almost as if improvising the opening statement, outside time – while integrating these qualities with the larger scheme. It's the most complex movement in the concertos and he manages to make it sound both directional and free as a bird.

The first movement of the E flat Concerto is nearly as good, lacking only the all-seeing vision and authority Brendel brings to it, and perhaps a touch of Brendel's ability to inhabit and define its remoter regions. In general, Aimard imposes himself as a personality less than Brendel. In spite of being different exercises, their distinction touches at several points and is comparable in degree. What Aimard doesn't match is the

BEETHOVEN THE FIVE PIANO CONCERTOS – IN BRIEF

Daniel Barenboim; New Philharmonia / Otto Klemperer
EMI ③ 763360-2   ⑧❍⤷
Youth and experience combine for a set of the concertos that constantly reveals new facets of the works. Klemperer draws playing of fierce commitment from the orchestra. The coupling is the *Choral Fantasy*.

Pierre-Laurent Aimard; COE / Nikolaus Harnoncourt
Teldec ③ 0927 47334-2   ⑧❍❍❍⤷
An inspirational set with a truly impressive freshness and spontaneity (partly due to the set's having been recorded live). This is very much a Beethoven set for the new century.

Maurizio Pollini; BPO / Claudio Abbado
DG ③ 439 770-2GH3   ⑥❍⤷
Pollini's second cycle (the first with the VPO remains available) is a fine achievement with Abbado a sympathetic partner. Pollini may shy away from Beethoven's jokes but he thrives on the majesty and grandeur.

Murray Perahia: Concertgebouw Orchestra / Bernard Haitink
Sony Classical ③ S3K44575   ⑥❍❍⤷
Limpid, spontaneous and wonderfully poetic, Perahia is a magnificent interpreter. With glorious sound, this is one of the most 'complete' of all concerto cycles.

Alfred Brendel; VPO / Simon Rattle
Philips ③ 462 781-2PH3   ⑤❍⤷
Two musicians completely in tune with each and an orchestra that really understands this music makes for a richly rewarding encounter. The slow movements are magnificent. A set of probing intellectual rigour married to years of Beethoven experience.

Wilhelm Kempff; BPO / Paul van Kempen Ⓗ
DG ⑤ 474 024-2GOM5   ⑤❍❍❍⤷
A classic set (Kempff's first) withstands the passing of years remarkably well. Kempff's lucid yet poetic way with Beethoven is enormously satisfying. There's a real sense of delight here. (It forms part of a set focusing on Kempff's complete concerto recordings for DG.)

Radu Lupu; Israel PO / Zubin Mehta
Decca ④ 475 4065DC4 (4h 50' · ADD)   Ⓜ❍⤷
A new recording from Lupu seems unlikely so all the more reason to cherish these supreme interpretations form the 1970s. Lupu's lyricism is illustrated on every page and he brings myriad detail to these very fine performances. They form part of four-disc Beethoven set that also includes sonatas and a superb Quintet for Piano and Winds.

variety of sound and the amplitude of Brendel's expressiveness in the first two concertos' slow movements. Balances are good, with the piano placed in a concert-hall perspective.

This set balances imagination and rigour, providing much delight and refreshment, and playing that will blow you away.

Piano Concertos Nos 1-5
Evgeny Kissin pf
London Symphony Orchestra / Sir Colin Davis
EMI ③ 206311-2 (180' · DDD)   ⑧❍❍⤷

It has been clear for some time that Evgeny Kissin is a Beethoven player of rare pedigree and distinction, the finest Russian-born Beethovenian since Emil Gilels. Twelve years ago he recorded the Second and Fifth concertos in performances of flair and élan with the Philharmonia under James Levine (Sony Classical – reviewed below). His own playing was vital and fluent, the technique awesome, not least his ability to refine tone and taper dynamics in those high-lying passages where Beethoven's expressive powers are at their most rarefied.

The new recordings were made in the autumn of 2007 at Abbey Road and it must be said that the piano sound is a thing of quite exceptional beauty, well forward though not unpleasingly so. Doubts linger about the handling of the difficult-to-judge orchestral *ritornelli* that launch the three earliest concertos. The playing has a slightly sullen feel to it, set back on its heels rhythmically, that Kissin's arrival decisively transforms. Was there at the outset a gap in expectation between the orchestra and its soloist? If so, it quickly dissolves as the real music-making gets under way.

Nowadays Sir Colin is more in love with the music's lyric aspect, audibly so at times. The unfurling of the strings' rapt eight-bar rejoinder to the piano's opening statement in the Fourth Concerto can rarely have been more memorably realised. After such an opening, Kissin has every right to spend the next 20 minutes contemplating the heavens in his own uniquely affecting way, ably abetted by his attentive accompanists.

Despite Davis's slowish tempo, Kissin announces himself in the Second Concerto with playing of great brilliance and vernal loveliness. The entire performance is a success, not least the finale where Kissin throws down the gauntlet to the orchestra with a driving molto allegro that sets up to perfection a typically Beethovenian jest in which high seriousness is made to crook its knee to the life-affirming power of play.

Kissin also sets a cracking pace in the Rondo of the rather grander First Concerto, though is this a true *allegro scherzando*? Beethoven loved to shock but after a slowish albeit beautifully articulated opening movement (where Kissin aptly and intriguingly uses Beethoven's shorter second cadenza) and a sublime account of the *Largo*, this rabid assault on the finale rather unbalances the whole.

There is no such lack of balance in the Third Concerto on which many a pianist-conductor combination has come to grief. Once past that rather dourly played *ritornello*, Kissin and Davis realise the concerto as well as some and better than many.

We know from their earlier recordings how fine both soloist and conductor are in the *Emperor* Concerto and this new version does not disappoint. Kissin's realisation of the big opening cadenza is broadly phrased in the Russian manner, subtler and less extreme than Pletnev in his recent DG recording.

As in the Fourth Concerto, the agogic freedom Kissin allows himself in moments of visionary meditation is underwritten both by the orchestra and his own capacity to return swiftly and pointedly to the *tempo primo*.

A sterner producer might have persuaded Davis to provide a grunt-free start to the string recitative that begins the slow movement of the Fourth Concerto. The exchanges, stilted at first, shed self-consciousness as the dialogue evolves and quietens. And the finale is a delight, the scherzando and visionary elements held in perfect balance. (An unlooked-for bonus is the fact that the set is being offered at budget price!)

Piano Concertos Nos 1-5
Richard Goode pf
Budapest Festival Orchestra / Iván Fischer
Nonesuch ③ 7559 79928-3 (168' · DDD)   Ⓕ

This is not a set that immediately fires the imagination, nor is it in all respects a perfectly 'finished' production. That said, it contains fine accounts of the elusive Third Concerto and the imperturbably splendid Fifth.

The two early concertos receive disappointing performances. Though Fischer and his Budapest players provide brisk, no-nonsense support, soloist Richard Goode appears to be in the grip of a self-denying ordinance, happy to provide an accurate tally of the notes but not much inclined to report upon them. Narrowness of dynamic and expressive range is complemented by a similar narrowness of dramatic vision.

In the Third Concerto the clouds lift. Here is freshness and attack, real poetry in the first movement development, a recapitulation that matters and a superbly calibrated account of Beethoven's built-in cadenza. In the finale of the Third, there is nothing daemonic. Rather, there is a sense of an uncomplicated dance to the music of time. Richard Goode's way with the opening of the Fourth Concerto also has a somewhat balletic feel to it. His reading has a gracious, clean-cut quality which deserves a more aurally sensitive, less matter-of-fact accompaniment than it receives here from the Budapest players. In the slow movement, the orchestral summonses are given a strangely militaristic character.

After which, everything comes right in the Fifth Concerto. This is a straightforward performance of the old school, with clean symphonic lines and classy articulation from the soloist; one of those readings of the *Emperor* that manages to combine lightness of spirit with a proper sense of heroic endeavour.

The piano sound, dull-toned in the two early concertos, is brighter and more robust in the later works without being absolutely in the first flight of excellence.

Piano Concertos Nos 1-5
Murray Perahia pf
Concertgebouw Orchestra / Bernard Haitink
Sony Classical ③ S3K44575
(178' · DDD)   ⓂⓄⒶ

Perahia's account of the C minor Concerto (No 3) is a joy from start to finish, wonderfully conceived, executed conducted and recorded. The single issue, coupled with this account of the G major Concerto (No 4), began life by winning the 1986 *Gramophone* Concerto Award. In these two concertos, and in the two earlier ones, Perahia and Haitink are difficult to fault. The First Concerto is especially well done with a quick first movement and the apt and delightful inclusion in the finale of a cadenza that Beethoven sketched in 1800. If Perahia is anywhere slightly below par it's in the *Emperor* Concerto. The reading gives us an emergent view of the work, undiscursive but perhaps at times lacking in a certain largeness of vision and purpose. For that we must return to Kempff or Arrau, which only confirms the pitfalls of buying cycles rather than separate performances. However, the Perahia cycle is one of the most consistently accomplished of those currently available; the recordings are a joy to listen to.

Piano Concertos Nos 1-5.
Choral Fantasia in C minor, Op 80
Daniel Barenboim pf **John Alldis Choir;**
New Philharmonia Orchestra / Otto Klemperer
EMI ④ 763360-2 (3h 31' · ADD). Recorded 1967 ⓂⓄⒶ

Klemperer had done concert cycles, perhaps most memorably in London in the 1950s with Claudio Arrau but his decision to record the piano concertos at the age of 82 came as a result of his admiration for the most precociously talented of all young Beethoven pianists at the time, Daniel Barenboim. Barenboim was 25 and about to embark on what was to be an exceptionally fine cycle of the Beethoven piano sonatas. He was steeped in Beethoven and perhaps peculiarly well suited to the concertos which, we should not forget, are essentially a young man's music. It was a fascinating pairing, Klemperer and Barenboim contrasted in age and to some extent in temperament but at the same time symbiotically at one musically. Had this not been the case, Barenboim would have been swamped, lost in the wash of Klemperer's accompaniments which deliver the orchestral argument and the orchestral detail with an articulacy and authority unique in the history of these works on record.

The performance of the B flat Concerto, the first historically if not numerically, is a typical joy, full of fire and grace and unstoppably vital. Given Klemperer's propensity for taking slow tempos in Beethoven, you might imagine him being taken for a ride by the young Barenboim in the B flat and C major finales. But not a bit of it. It's Klemperer, as much as his youthful soloist, who seems to be the driving force here. Rarely on record has the slow movement of the C major Concerto been played with so natural a sense of concentrated calm, the whole thing profoundly collected on the spiritual plane. One of the joys of the Barenboim/Klemperer cycle is its occasional unpredictability: rock-solid readings that none the less incorporate a sense of 'today we try it this way'.

Ensemble is mostly first rate during the cycle. The tricky coda of the first movement of the C minor Concerto is both rapt and dramatic. But in the coda of the first movement of the G major there's little doubt that Klemperer drags the pulse. And elsewhere there are some occasionally awkward adjustments to be made between soloist and orchestra. At the time of its initial appearance, the *Emperor* performance was generally adjudged a success. Again it's broadly conceived. At first the finale seems a little staid; but later the 6/8 rhythms are made to dance and the performance has a burning energy by the end. So does the account of the *Choral Fantasia*. Given Klemperer's magisterial style and authority, this set could have emerged as five symphonies with piano obbligato. In fact, it's a set of rare authority and spontaneity, and given the slightly unconventional idea of the soloist as *primus inter pares*, it's probably unique.

Piano Concertos Nos 1-5
Alfred Brendel *pf* **Vienna Philharmonic Orchestra / Sir Simon Rattle**
Philips ③ 462 781-2PH3 (178' · DDD)   Ⓕ**Ⓞ▷**

Happily, Alfred Brendel's fourth recorded cycle of the Beethoven piano concertos shares with the previous three qualities of energy, sensibility, intellectual rigour and high pianistic finish which made the earlier recordings so interesting. Brendel has always played all five slow movements supremely well, drawing the orchestra around him like a celebrant at the communion table and here we have even finer performances than previously.

In the two early concertos the Vienna Philharmonic's playing has a sweetness and allure, in the grander, later works a black-browed power, that's specially its own. Brendel's playing in the early concertos recalls his fine recordings of the early sonatas and the early and late *Bagatelles*, but it's as a private person impatient with the conventions and frock-coated formalities of the concertos as 'public' works. With No 3 we move into a different world. This is a marvellous performance from all three partners, purposeful and robust, the tonic C minor the cue for a reading full of darkness and menace, basses to the fore, drums at the

ready. The finale is particularly ominous (relieved only by a lustrous clarinet solo) after an account of the slow movement, full toned yet deeply quiet, the like of which is rarely heard. The C minor Concerto's heroic antitype, the *Emperor* in E flat, fares less well. Not the slow movement or finale, but the first movement which is slower than previously, to no very good effect. Perhaps interpreters nowadays are less happy than their predecessors were with Beethoven's heroic persona. Back in the private world of the Fourth Concerto, soloist, orchestra and conductor are at their inspired best. Brendel's glittering, wonderfully propelled account of the solo part is superbly backed by playing of real fire and sensitivity. The recordings are first rate.

Piano Concertos Nos 1ª & 2ᵇ   Ⓗ
Solomon *pf* **Philharmonia Orchestra / ª Herbert Menges,** ᵇ**André Cluytens**
Testament ᵇmono SBT1219 (63' · ADD)   Ⓕ**Ⓞ**

Piano Concertos Nos 3ª & 4ᵇ   Ⓗ
Solomon *pf* **Philharmonia Orchestra / ªMenges,** ᵇ**Cluytens**
Testament ᵇmono SBT1220 (70' · ADD)   Ⓕ**Ⓞ**

Beethoven Piano Concerto No 5 **Mozart** Piano   Ⓗ
Sonatas – No 11 in A, K331; No 17 in D, K576
Solomon *pf* **Philharmonia Orchestra / Menges**
Testament mono SBT1221 (74' · ADD)   Ⓕ**Ⓞ**
All recorded 1952-56

Here on three CDs are Solomon's legendary 1952-56 recordings of the Beethoven piano concertos and two Mozart piano sonatas, a felicitous coupling. Time and again Beethoven's exuberant, unpredictable nature is qualified by playing of a supreme poise and equanimity that omits so little of his essential character. It's also one of Solomon's cardinal qualities that he makes it impertinent to single out this or that detail, offering instead a seamless argument as supple and natural as it's understated.

Solomon makes the slow movements the expressive centres of each concerto, and here his ability to sustain an *Adagio* or *Largo* is without equal. This is notably true of the first two concertos, where such writing becomes music to soothe the savage breast rather than awake more immediate emotions. In the outer movements his superfine technique and musicianship make light of every difficulty, and at 6'55" in the Second Concerto, after an impatient if very Beethovenian entry, he re-creates a magical sense of stillness and repose.

In the Third Concerto the *Largo* is impeccably controlled and so, too, is the central *Andante con moto* from the Fourth Concerto. Solomon's momentary lack of control in the first movement at 9'37" is, perhaps, an indication of problems caused by Cluytens' less than vital or stimulating partnership. And yet the finale could hardly be more *vivace*, with all the clarity and grace for which Solomon was celebrated.

In the *Emperor* Concerto Solomon somehow bridges the gap between the Fourth and Fifth Concertos. His immaculate ease and buoyancy in the double-note descent just before the first movement's conclusion, his limpid and serene traversal of the central *Adagio* are pure Solomon, and his finale is among the least opaque on record. Surprises include the shorter cadenza in the First Concerto, Clara Schumann's cadenza in the Third (enterprising if less distinguished than Beethoven's own magnificent offering) and a few teasing elaborations in the two cadenzas from the Fourth.

The recordings come up well (though the sound in the Fifth needs some opening out; it lacks ring and brilliance), and the Mozart sonatas are a delectable bonus. Listening to Solomon's peerless pianism and musicianship, the critic discards pen and paper and listens in awe, wonder and affection.

Piano Concertos – selected

Piano Concertos Nos 1 & 2
Murray Perahia *pf* **Concertgebouw Orchestra / Bernard Haitink**
Sony Classical SK42177 (70' · DDD)   Ⓕ**OⒹ**

It's a pleasure here to salute such all-round excellence: a very remarkable soloist, superb orchestral playing and direction, and a recording which gets everything right, offering the kind of sound picture and natural perspective of solo piano with orchestra as we might experience them from a good seat in the Concertgebouw itself, where these performances were recorded.

Precision, clarity of expression, variety of character, beauty of sound: these are the qualities Haitink and Perahia sustain, and through which their readings gain an illuminating force. And it's perhaps in the slow movements that the illumination brings the most distinguished results. Their raptness and distinctive colouring are established from the first notes, and the inward quality of the expression takes breath as if there was nothing to the business of delineating these great set-pieces, so special among the achievements of Beethoven's first maturity, except to sing them through. Perahia has the gift of reducing his voice to the quietest level and still remaining eloquent. The poise of the playing is classical, his authority unblemished by any hint of exaggeration or false emphasis.

Piano Concertos Nos 1 & 2
Yefim Bronfman *pf*
Tonhalle Orchestra, Zürich / David Zinman
Arte Nova 82876 82587-2 (67' · DDD)   Ⓢ**OOOⒹ**

This Zürich performance of the First Concerto is beautifully articulated. True, there are moments of grandeur but the overall impression is of a poised, at times chamber-like traversal, with sculpted pianism and crisply pointed orchestral support. The sensation of shared listening,

between Bronfman and the players and between the players themselves, is at its most acute in the First Concerto's *Largo*, which although kept on a fairly tight rein is extremely supple (the woodwinds in particular excel). In the finale, Bronfman and the Tonhalle provide a clear, shapely aural picture.

Bronfman's B flat Concerto (No 2) has the expected composure, the many running passages in the first movement polished if relatively understated. Again the slow movement is full of unaffected poetry and the finale (with the odd added embellishment) is appropriately buoyant – has Bronfman ever played better?

Piano Concertos – Nos 2 & 3
François-Frédéric Guy *pf* **Radio France Philharmonic Orchestra / Philippe Jordan**
Naïve V5179 (60' · DDD)   Ⓕ**OⒹ**

What a joy François-Frederic Guy's performances are. Brilliant and direct in the finest French tradition, they are also alive with passing felicities, whether illuminating an early pioneering spirit or a change into what EM Forster once called 'Beethoven's C minor of life'. In the Second Concerto Guy's exuberance and poetry go hand in hand. The first movement's startlingly original cadenza is played with unfaltering assurance and the hushed magic with which Guy handles the main theme of the central *Adagio* sounds a special note. A dazzling finale, too, finds ample time for individual nuance and pointed characterisation, making his sense of contrast in the Third Concerto all the more remarkable. Here both he and Jordan take a qualified view of Beethoven's *con brio*, conveying an atmosphere of foreboding, of minor-key unease resolved in an inward-looking *Largo* where everything is experienced afresh. The finale is unusually restrained but, again, there is nothing of the studio and everything of a life experience. Guy's reading ranks high in a crowded catalogue.

Piano Concertos – No 2; WoO4. Rondo, WoO6
Ronald Brautigam *pf*
Norrköping Symphony Orchestra / Andrew Parrott
BIS 🔊 BIS-SACD1792 (58' · DDD/DSD)   Ⓕ**OOⒹ**

Beethoven's early E flat Piano Concerto, WoO4, ought to be better known. Written around 1784 when he was 14, it survives in a manuscript copy of the piano part that Beethoven later annotated and amended. The orchestral tuttis were also written into the manuscript, along with indications that the scoring was for two flutes, two horns and strings. The first modern performance was given by Edwin Fischer in Potsdam in 1943 in a realisation by Willy Hess.

The piano-writing suggests the alliance of virtuoso execution with an already distinctive musical voice. In later life, Beethoven rarely chose so charming a rondo subject as he does here, but the discourse in the two earlier movements is decidedly Beethovenian: doubly so in this superbly articulated performance by Dutch pianist Ronald Brautigam. A follower and pupil of the late Rudolf Serkin – the influence is evident – Brautigam is also the editor of this new reconstruction.

His account of the B flat, Second Concerto, interestingly coupled with a none too remarkable earlier finale Beethoven wrote for the concerto, is first-rate. It is intriguing that Brautigam deploys a modern Steinway, matching this, with fine Dutch pragmatism, to the period manner of the Norrköping players under Andrew Parrott. The strings lack weight in their rebuttal of the piano's skittishness in bar 23 of the B flat Concerto's finale; for Beethoven's joke to work they need to put on a braver show than this before they capitulate. A terrific disc, nonetheless.

Piano Concertos Nos 3 & 4
Murray Perahia pf
Concertgebouw Orchestra / Bernard Haitink
Sony Classical SK39814 (70' · DDD)   ⓂOOOⒹ

These performances have rightly been described as exceptional. They were directly compared to Alfred Brendel's accounts with James Levine (on Philips) but in the event, there's little to choose between these two distinguished soloists. The first movements are brilliantly and sensitively etched (Perahia uses Beethoven's bigger first cadenza in the first movement of the G major Concerto). Tempos are steady but with a fine degree of forward projection. Once past the daunting opening solo, Perahia plays the C minor's slow movement with great sureness and subtlety of touch; and with Haitink as his partner the exchanges in the G major's slow movement are memorably brought off. Note the superior quality of the Sony recordings and the wonderfully judicious accompaniments prepared for Perahia by the Concertgebouw Orchestra under Haitink, who's exemplary.

Beethoven Piano Concerto No 3[a]
Grieg Piano Concerto[b]
Emil Gilels pf [a]**Philharmonia Orchestra**; [b]**Finnish Radio Symphony Orchestra / Paavo Berglund**
Video Artists International 📀 VAIDVD4472 (86' · 4:3 · PCM mono · 0). Recorded live in [b]1983, [a]1984   Ⓕ

This is the seventh volume from VAI of live performances of the great Russian pianist. If you insist on crisp colours and high definition you must look elsewhere: the second-generation picture quality boasts a characteristic hue of various shades of predominantly murky browns, greens and greys. No matter – the sound is fine.

As to the performances, it may be significant that whereas there are around 10 different commercially available accounts of Gilels in Beethoven's Third Piano Concerto, there is only one of the Grieg. The Beethoven is impressive

without being outstanding (unlike, for example, Gilels's incomparable Beethoven Fourth with Leopold Ludwig) with sharply contrasted episodes, eloquently clear phrasing, unhurried tempi – the second movement lasts nearly 11 minutes – and not a few smudges in the finale. The genial Paavo Berglund offers rock-steady support.

In the Grieg, the two outer movements seem altogether too portentous and heavy-handed. Gilels makes the work sound like Tchaikovsky and in passages such as the concluding *poco più allegro* of the first movement is decidedly flat-footed. There are, also, rather too many *tutti* downbeats where conductor and soloist fail to coincide. In mitigation there is an exquisitely played *Adagio*. This is repeated as an encore after the enthusiastic reception by the Helsinki audience.

So – Gilels in familiar and unfamiliar territory: never less than stimulating and of vital interest. As is customary from this label, there are no notes on the music or performers.

Piano Concertos Nos 4 & 5, 'Emperor'
Till Fellner pf **Montreal Symphony Orchestra / Kent Nagano**
ECM New Series 476 3315 (73' · DDD)   ⒻOOOⒹ

Till Fellner, always among the more quietly celebrated pianists, together with Kent Nagano and the Montreal SO gives us two of the most supremely satisfying performances of both these concertos on record. This is a dream partnership with soloist and conductor working hand-in-glove, and even when you conjure with so many glorious names in such core repertoire (from Schnabel to Lupu) you will rarely hear playing of such an enviable, unimpeded musical grace and fluency.

Fellner surely belongs among that elite who Charles Rosen so memorably defined as those who, while they appear to do nothing, achieve everything. His playing is subtly rather than ostentatiously coloured and inflected, and if others might be thought more vivid or personal, Fellner's and Nagano's ease and naturalness always allow Beethoven his own voice. Fellner's still small voice of calm in the Fourth Concerto's central *Andante con moto* is one among many glories. Balance and sound are pleasingly natural and this memorable issue is crowned with a short but intriguing essay by Paul Griffiths.

Piano Concerto No 4. Piano Concerto, Op 61a
Ronald Brautigam pf **Norrköping Symphony Orchestra / Andrew Parrott**
BIS 🎵 BIS-SACD1693 (68' · DDD)   ⒻOⒹ

'I truly believe that what the composer wanted was chamber music rather than a battle between orchestra and soloist.' So claims Ronald Brautigam in a brief but informative booklet interview, which helps explain why the 'Orpheus placating the Furies' slow movement of the Fourth Concerto sounds more like a brisk telling-off. Still, it fits the mood of the performance which, aside from the expected lightness of touch (a Steinway D played with admirable bounce and precision), introduces some additional filigree that Barry Cooper has deciphered from manuscript annotations that show what actual notes Beethoven may have played at the work's 1808 premiere.

The first signs of change arrive around six minutes into the first movement when a descending scale is embellished with trills followed by some very decorative tinkling before a brief visit to the minor and a return to an exuberant statement of the lovely second theme. And that's just for openers: there are plenty more textual surprises – in the development section, for example, and in the finale. The key issue seems to be if this Cooper 'revision' was the version that you had always known and someone came up with the now-familiar published score as an alternative, would you then prefer the published score? Almost certainly the answer would be 'yes'. Most listeners would probably agree, but hearing this animated and intelligently voiced performance (no vibrato among the strings by the way) at least poses the question, as well as presenting an interestingly ornate variant on a much-loved musical text.

The CD also offers us a very crisp reading of the piano version of the Violin Concerto, which works well apart from the re-entry into the main body of the first movement after Beethoven's admittedly ingenious cadenza, a moment that only really works its magic on the violin. That aside, the sound is beautifully balanced, with Brautigam's lidless piano set well within the orchestra.

Piano Concertos Nos 4 & 5, 'Emperor'
Emil Gilels pf **Philharmonia Orchestra /**   [H]
Leopold Ludwig
Testament SBT1095 (73' · ADD). Recorded 1957 Ⓕ**OO**

This is one of the most – perhaps *the* most – perfect accounts of the Fourth Concerto recorded. Poetry and virtuosity are held in perfect poise, with Ludwig and the Philharmonia providing a near-ideal accompaniment. The recording is also very fine, though be sure to gauge the levels correctly by first sampling one of the *tutti*s. If the volume is set too high at the start, you'll miss the stealing magic of Gilels's and the orchestra's initial entries and you'll be further discomfited by tape hiss.

The recording of the *Emperor* Concerto is also pretty good, not quite on a par with that of the Fourth. Ludwig and the orchestra tend to follow Gilels rather than always integrate with him and there are times, too, especially in the slow movement, when Gilels's playing borders on the self-indulgent. This isn't, however, sufficient reason for overlooking this fine and important reissue.

Piano Concerto No 5, 'Emperor'
Murray Perahia pf
Concertgebouw Orchestra / Bernard Haitink

Sony Classical SK42330 (42' · DDD)   Ⓜ**OOO**➔

Ⓖ This is a superb performance though not as generous as in its previous coupling where it came with Perahia's Award-winning Fourth. This is an excellent *Emperor*, on a level with the best. Comparisons with other pianists, at this level, can be rather futile. It's a splendidly engineered recording, with a natural concert-hall type of balance, and there's good presence to the sound and depth to the perspective. The presentation of the orchestral detail allows you to delight in it, and perhaps to discover new subtleties, without a moment of unease as to whether anything has been forced into the wrong kind of relief. Perahia's performance has the freshness and natural authority we have come to expect of him in Beethoven. His reading might be described as uncomplicated if that didn't risk implying that it's in some way lightweight, or that he plays like a child of nature. The weight is certainly there, in sound (when he wants it) as in expression.

Perahia himself has spoken of the happy experience of making this Beethoven cycle with Haitink (the other concertos including the complete set are reviewed above). It has indeed been a successful collaboration, and a joyous quality about the music-making communicates itself quite strongly from the beginning.

Piano Concerto No 5, 'Emperor'[a]. Choral Fantasia[ab]. Meeresstille und glückliche Fahrt[b]
[a]**Yefim Bronfman** pf [b]**Swiss Chamber Choir; Tonhalle Orchestra, Zürich / David Zinman**
Arte Nova 82876 82585-2 (64' · DDD)   Ⓑ**OO**➔

Rather than opt for superficial barnstorming, Yefim Bronfman and David Zinman offer us a discreet, subtly voiced and above all durable *Emperor*, that rewards listening with increasing musical dividends. Bronfman plays with a light, precise though never brittle touch, always phrasing elegantly and dipping his tone whenever important instrumental lines need to be heard. There are numerous details that reveal how minutely all the participants are listening to each other. The slow movement unfolds in a mood of unruffled calm, Bronfman's first entry gentle, delicate, with an appropriate, even touching simplicity. The finale is brisk and energetic and the way Bronfman keeps accompanying rhythmic figurations light and well buoyed is most appealing.

The fill-ups are worthwhile, the *Choral Fantasy*'s long solo opening more thoughtful than usual and with a bright, easy-going contribution from the chorus. Nothing is ever forced or overstated and the contrast in the seven-minute *Calm Sea and Prosperous Voyage* between worrying stillness and the first signs of a redeeming breeze, ingeniously painted by slowly swirling triplets, is superbly handled.

It is hard to imagine anyone being less than satisfied with Bronfman and Zinman, the Tonhalle Orchestra scoring top marks for teamwork,

137

BEETHOVEN PIANO CONCERTO NO 5, 'EMPEROR' – IN BRIEF

Murray Perahia; Concertgebouw Orchestra / Bernard Haitink
Sony Classical SMK89711 (73' · DDD) Ⓜ●○○
Ⓖ A superb performance of real authority but above all of true poetry. Beautifully accompanied by the great Dutch orchestra. Coupled with an equally fine No 4.

Wilhelm Kempff; Berlin PO / Ferdinand Leitner
DG 447 402-2GOR (70' · ADD) Ⓜ●○
A magnificent, aristocratic interpretation from Kempff's second (stereo) cycle (with No 4). Still sounding very good for its 1962 vintage.

Evgeny Kissin; Philharmonia / James Levine
Sony Classical SK62926 (69' · DDD) Ⓕ●○
The young Russian pianist reveals himself to be an artist of great articulacy, brilliance and sensitivity. Coupled with a lively No 1.

Emil Gilels; Philharmonia / Leopold Ludwig Ⓗ
Testament SBT1095 (73' · DDD) Ⓕ
A fine *Emperor* coupled with a superb Fourth. Gilels was a commanding Beethoven interpreter. There is some hiss from the 1957 tape; otherwise fine at reasonable levels.

Maurizio Pollini; Vienna PO / Karl Böhm
DG download 439 483-2GCL (71' · ADD) Ⓑ☐➔
A cooler Beethoven than Pollini later gave with Abbado but certainly spontaneous and fresh-sounding (coupled with No 4).

Leon Fleisher; Cleveland Orchestra / George Szell
Sony Classical SBK46549 (74' · DDD) Ⓑ●
High-octane Beethoven from Fleisher and Szell: commanding, virtuoso and iron-willed. Not for the faint-hearted! Coupled with a fine Triple Concerto.

Solomon; Philharmonia / Herbert Menges Ⓗ
Testament mono SBT1221 (74' · ADD) Ⓕ●
A stunning *Emperor* for its classical poise, ease and limpid fingerwork. A reminder of one of the UK's greatest pianists. Coupled with two Mozart piano sonatas.

Robert Levin fp **Orchestre Révolutionnaire et Romantique / Sir John Eliot Gardiner**
Archiv download 447 771-2AH (71' · DDD) Ⓕ☐➔
A most successful period-instrument *Emperor*: the combination of Levin's fantasy and Gardiner's drama pays dividends. The coupled *Choral Fantasy* with Gardiner's superb Monteverdi Choir is magnificent.

Edwin Fischer; Philharmonia / Wilhelm Furtwängler Ⓗ
EMI mono 574800-2 (78' · ADD) Ⓕ●○
A great *Emperor* for its sense of grandeur and majesty. A superb collaboration from 1951.

their woodwinds sounding fully on a par with Europe's best. Superbly balanced sound helps clinch an unmissable bargain.

Piano Concerto No 5, 'Emperor'.
Triple Concerto, Op 56[a]
Leon Fleisher, [a]**Eugene Istomin** pfs [a]**Isaac Stern** vn **Leonard Rose** vc **Cleveland Orchestra / George Szell;** [a]**Philadelphia Orchestra / Eugene Ormandy**
Sony Classical SBK46549 (74' · ADD)
Recorded 1961, [a]1964 Ⓑ●

Leon Fleisher's recording of the *Emperor* is very powerful indeed. He was relatively young at the time and obviously George Szell had a considerable influence on the reading, but the solo playing is remarkably fresh and its pianistic authority is striking. That great octave passage in the first movement, just before the recapitulation, is enormously commanding, and Fleisher's lyrical playing, in the slow movement especially, has striking poise. Szell keeps the voltage high throughout, but for all its excitement this is by no means a hard-driven, unfeeling interpretation. The recording is bright, bold and forward in the CBS 1960s manner, and the Severance Hall acoustic prevents any ugliness.

A splendid *Emperor*, then, but what makes this disc even more enticing is the inclusion of an equally distinguished version of the Triple Concerto, recorded in Philadelphia Town Hall (a much more successful venue than many used over the years for this great orchestra). The very gentle opening by the orchestra is full of anticipatory tension, and at the beginning of the slow movement Ormandy's preparation for Rose's glorious cello solo demonstrates what a superb accompanist he is. Indeed, this is no mere accompaniment, but a complete partnership. Although Stern's personality dominates marginally, the three soloists play together like a chamber-music team, without in any way submerging their individuality. The sound is very good for its time.

Additional recommendation

Piano Concertos Nos 2 & 3
Argerich pf **Mahler CO / Abbado**
DG download 477 5026GH (64' · DDD) Ⓕ●○○➔
Martha Argerich's long-awaited recording of Beethoven's Third Concerto appears with the Second, music she's relished over the years. But whether novel or familiar, both performances are of a quality rarely encountered.

Violin Concerto in D, Op 61

Violin Concerto. Romances
Christian Tetzlaff vn
Tonhalle Orchestra, Zürich / David Zinman
Arte Nova 82876 76994-2 (56' · DDD) Ⓕ●○○

This superb Beethoven disc from Christian Tetzlaff is a real winner. The main stumbling-block on so many rival recordings of this work is a sort of romantic reverence, a trend challenged by Zehetmair, Kremer and others – and now Tetzlaff. For all its many moments of profound repose, Beethoven's Violin Concerto is a forthright, heroic piece, with boldly militaristic first-movement tutti and a rollicking finale which Tetzlaff invests with numerous added colours.

Following on the heals of Zehetmair, Kremer and Schneiderhan, Tetzlaff performs the violin version of the cadenza that Beethoven wrote for his piano transcription of the work, a playful excursion and a snug fit for his overall interpretation. Tempi are brisk without hurrying, the slow movement has an unruffled serenity and a lively added cadenza in the finale helps accentuate the pervading sense of play. Excellent booklet-notes explain the work's genesis and the basic drift of Tetzlaff's approach and the two Romances that complete the programme are performed with the same chaste lyricism.

Violin Concerto
Itzhak Perlman *vn* **Philharmonia Orchestra / Carlo Maria Giulini**
EMI Great Recordings of the Century 566900-2
(44' · DDD) Ⓜ❶❶❶▷

This is a very distinguished performance, as much from Giulini as from Perlman. Early on Giulini makes clear the importance of recognising the difference between *forte* and *fortissimo* in Beethoven – for example the *ff* of bars 73 and 74 and the which surrounds them; and the marvellous way he gets the Philharmonia to play *sfp* is a pleasure in itself. The liquid smoothness of the winds is another joy.

The slow movement has the utmost calm beauty from both soloist and orchestra, while Perlman plays the finale at an admirably swift speed, yet with all the flexibility it needs, so that it really dances lightly. The clarity of the orchestral texture is outstanding too. The bassoon, for example, sings its solos in the finale easily and without the least forcing. A real Great Recording of the Century!

Violin Concerto. Romances
Gidon Kremer *vn* **Chamber Orchestra of Europe / Nikolaus Harnoncourt**
Warner Elatus 0927 49773-2 (57' · DDD)
Recorded live 1992 Ⓜ❶▷

Gidon Kremer offers one of his most commanding performances, both polished and full of flair, magnetically spontaneous from first to last. Rarely do you hear such consistently pure tone in this work and the orchestral writing too is superbly realised. It has become customary to treat the long first movement as expansively as possible but Kremer takes a more urgent view, and after his thoughtful and dedicated, slightly understated reading of the slow movement, he and Harnoncourt round the performance off magically with a finale that skips along the more

infectiously thanks to light, clean articulation and textures. Traditional performances seem heavyweight by comparison. The controversial point for some will be the cadenza in the first movement where he uses a transcription of the big cadenza which Beethoven wrote for his piano arrangement of the work. However, this is altogether one of the most refreshing versions of the concerto ever committed to record, backed up by crisp, unsentimental readings of the two *Romances*.

Beethoven Violin Concerto[a] Ⓗ
Mendelssohn Violin Concerto in E minor, Op 64[b]
Yehudi Menuhin *vn* [a]**Philharmonia Orchestra**, [b]**Berlin Philharmonic Orchestra / Wilhelm Furtwängler**
EMI Great Recordings of the Century mono 566975-2
(71' · ADD). Recorded 1952-53 Ⓜ

Furtwängler and Menuhin recorded the Beethoven Concerto on two occasions, and this second version has an extraordinary quality of spirituality and profundity. Furtwängler's conducting of the opening *tutti* has a magnificently arresting, weighty quality, and Menuhin's response, profound and rich in re-creative imagination shows the two great artists in perfect accord. Their account of this movement is on the largest scale, yet they convey Beethoven's vision in a humane, approachable fashion. The slow movement has a highly concentrated yet serene character, with Menuhin's rapt, singing tone achieving rare eloquence, and the finale is superbly balanced, with an affecting sense of a shared, joyful experience. The recording sounds quite similar to the original LP issue, but the quality is quite acceptable.

The Mendelssohn was recorded a year earlier, and here remastering has brought a slight roughening in an orchestral sound which was never very ingratiating, though the defect isn't serious. Menuhin and Furtwängler float the first movement in an unhurriedly serene, elegantly shaped fashion. In the slow movement they achieve a touchingly tender, almost innocent quality and the finale, taken at a moderate tempo, has lightness and an appealingly eager character.

Beethoven Violin Concerto[a] Ⓗ
Brahms Violin Concerto in D, Op 77[b]
Jascha Heifetz *vn* [a]**NBC Symphony Orchestra / Arturo Toscanini**; [b]**Boston Symphony Orchestra / Serge Koussevitzky**
Naxos Historical mono 8 110936 (77' · AAD)
Recorded [a]1939, [b]1940 Ⓢ❶❶❶

 'An old diamond in the rough' is how Robert C Marsh (*Toscanini and the Art of Orchestra Performance*; London: 1956) recalled the original Victor 78s of this 1940 Heifetz Studio 8-H recording of the Beethoven. Of the LP reissue he wrote: 'On the whole, the recording is so dead and artificial that at times the thin line of violin sound reminds one of something from the golden age of Thomas Edison's tinfoil cylinder rather than 1940.' Early CD transfers suggested that all wasn't lost but even they barely anticipated the extraordinary fineness of the sound we now have on this transfer by archivist and restorer Mark Obert-Thorn.

The performance itself is one of the most remarkable the gramophone has ever given us. The visionary, high *tessitura* violin writing is realised by Heifetz with a technical surety which is indistinguishable, in the final analysis, from his sense of the work as one of Beethoven's most sublime explorations of that world (in Schiller's phrase) 'above the stars where He must dwell'. Those who would query the 'depth' of Heifetz's reading miss this point entirely. To adapt Oscar Wilde, it is they who are in the gutter, Heifetz who is looking at the stars.

As for Toscanini's contribution, it, too, is masterly. Now that we can actually hear the performance, the orchestral *tutti*s seem beautifully balanced both within themselves and *vis-à-vis* the soloist. As for the actual accompaniment, it's discreet and self-effacing, fiery yet refined, and always wondrously subtle.

In the case of the Brahms, it's more reasonable to argue that there are other ways of playing the concerto. Heifetz's isn't a Romantic reading. It's lean, athletic, classical, aristocratic, finely drawn, an approach which wears exceptionally well on record. The Brahms enjoys another impeccable transfer. Musically and technically, this is a real thoroughbred of a release, unignorable at any price.

Beethoven Violin Concerto[a]   **H**
Tchaikovsky Violin Concerto in D, Op 35[b]
Bronisław Huberman *vn* [a]**Vienna Philharmonic Orchestra / George Szell;** [b]**Staatskapelle Berlin / William Steinberg**
Naxos Historical mono 8 110903 (67' · AAD)
Recorded [a]1934, [b]1928   Ⓢ**OO**☐►

Virtuoso violinist Bronislaw Huberman was an idealist, an ardent Pan-European and co-founder (with William Steinberg) of the Israel Philharmonic. He was, in a sense, the prototype for such present-day fiddling mavericks as Kremer, Zehetmair, Tetzlaff and Kennedy. Huberman's open letter to the conductor Wilhelm Furtwängler, in which he pledged support of the persecuted, and refused to perform in Nazi Germany, has become famous, and his astringent though frequently dazzling playing translates that steely resolve into musical terms.

This Naxos coupling is very nearly the answer to a prayer. Huberman's interpretation is more in line with, say, Zehetmair and Brüggen than the stately readings of Kreisler, Szigeti, Menuhin or David Oistrakh. His lively speeds and darting inflections spin silver beams where others opt for (for some misplaced) 'Olympian' heights. The luminosity of the reading, its radiance and refusal to dawdle, run counter to the languid sweetness favoured by various of his peers and successors.

The 1929 Tchaikovsky recording is peerless. Huberman's first entry reveals all: elastic phrasing, sweeping *portamento*s and generous *rubato* stamp a giant personality. Thereafter, quicksilver bowing and a steely *spiccato* level with the best of the period. Brahms loved Huberman's playing (he promised the budding youngster a *Fantasy* but never lived to compose it), and no wonder, given the veiled beauty of his tone (*Canzonetta*) and the uninhibited swagger of his bravura style (finale).

You simply have to hear Huberman's recording, and Naxos's give-away price makes it a mandatory purchase. However, the transfer of the Beethoven, although perfectly adequate, is rather spoiled by excessive digital noise reduction. On one occasion in the first movement, the violinist momentarily disappears; in the second movement two chords inadvertently become one. But these technical reservations will likely prove trifling for anyone who has never heard Huberman before. There are no greater violin recordings in existence.

Additional recommendation

Violin Concerto. Romances   Ⓟ
Zehetmair *vn* **Orchestra of the 18th Century / Brüggen**
Philips download 462 123-2PH (54' · DDD) Ⓕ**OO**☐►
This is a great performance, one that simply has to be heard. The use of period instruments adds extra fibre to the aural mix, and Brüggen's conducting has a pressing urgency about it that, again, intensifies the drama. Limited availability on CD.

Triple Concerto in C, Op 56

Beethoven Triple Concerto[a]
Brahms Double Concerto in A minor, Op 102[b]
David Oistrakh *vn* **Mstislav Rostropovich** *vc*
Sviatoslav Richter *pf* [a]**Berlin Philharmonic Orchestra / Herbert von Karajan;**
[b]**Cleveland Orchestra / George Szell**
EMI Great Recordings of the Century mono 566902-2 (70' · ADD). Recorded 1969   Ⓜ**OO**☐►

These are illustrious performances and make a splendid coupling. EMI planned for a long time to assemble this starry line-up of soloists, conductor and orchestra for Beethoven's Triple Concerto, and the artists don't disappoint, bringing sweetness as well as strength to a work which in lesser hands can sound clumsy and long winded. The recording, made in a Berlin church in 1969, is warm, spacious and well balanced, placing the soloists in a gentle spotlight. The account of Brahms's Double Concerto is perhaps the most powerful recorded performance since the days of Heifetz and Feuermann or Thibaud and Casals. The recording has come up extremely well in this remastering: although the sound isn't as smooth as can be achieved nowadays, this is soon forgotten, and you're caught up in the magnificent music-making.

Triple Concerto. Choral Fantasia in C minor, Op 80.
Rondo in B flat, WoO6
Pierre-Laurent Aimard *pf* **Thomas Zehetmair** *vn*
Clemens Hagen *vc* **Arnold Schoenberg Choir;**
Chamber Orchestra of Europe / Nikolaus
Harnoncourt
Warner Classics 2564 60602-2 (66' · DDD)
Recorded live

Listening to the opening tutti on this joyful new
Triple Concerto, you can just picture Nikolaus
Harnoncourt cueing his strings, perched slightly
forwards, impatiently waiting for that first, pregnant *forte*. This is a big, affable, blustery Triple,
the soloists completing the sound canvas rather
than dominating it, a genuine collaborative effort.
So beside the Beethovenian strut to this performance there's poetry too. Yet thoughtfulness never
spells timidity; Hagen and Thomas Zehetmair
throw caution to the winds near the end of the
first movement. The Concerto's *Largo* is simplicity itself, rather like a song without words, but it's
the finale that is likely to raise the most smiles, a
rumbustious affair, uninhibited without coursing
out of control. Harnoncourt and his team go for
the burn, always brilliant but, more importantly,
full of character and humour.

The fill-ups (like the Concerto, recorded at
concerts in Graz) are hardly less engaging. The
little B flat Rondo is bubbly from the start,
Aimard and the orchestra maintaining a feeling
of chamber collaboration. And then the *Choral
Fantasia*, so often clunky on disc but here aided
by Aimard's sense of style – his arpeggios in the
long opening solo have so much colour – and by
Harnoncourt's relaxed approach to the music
that follows, each variation imaginatively tended
within a larger framework. The singing is excellent, the sound both warm and realistic. As 'feel-
good' Beethoven programmes go, this is about
as enjoyable as it gets, though a high level of
musical insight further enhances one's pleasure.

Symphonies

No 1 in C, Op 21; **No 2** in D, Op 36; **No 3** in E flat, Op
55, 'Eroica'; **No 4** in B flat, Op 60; **No 5** in C minor,
Op 67; **No 6** in F, Op 68, 'Pastoral; **No 7** in A, Op 92;
No 8 in F, Op 93; **No 9** in D minor, Op 125, 'Choral'

Complete Symphonies

Symphonies Nos 1-9
Charlotte Margiono *sop* **Birgit Remmert** *mez*
Rudolf Schasching *ten* **Robert Holl** *bass* **Arnold**
Schoenberg Choir; Chamber Orchestra of Europe /
Nikolaus Harnoncourt
Warner Elatus ⑤ 0927 49768-2 (5h 58' · DDD)
Recorded live 1990-91

 Brimful of intrepid character and interpretative incident, this is surely one of
the most stimulating Beethoven symphony cycles of recent times. As Harnoncourt
himself states in the booklet: 'It has always been

my conviction that music is not there to soothe
people's nerves…but rather to open their eyes, to
give them a good shaking, even to frighten them.'
So it transpires that there's a re-creative daring
about Harnoncourt's conducting – in essence an
embracement of recent scholarly developments
and his own pungent sense of characterisation –
which is consistently illuminating, thus leaving
the listener with the uncanny sensation that he or
she is encountering this great music for the first
time. In all this Harnoncourt is backed to the hilt
by some superbly responsive, miraculously
assured playing from the COE: their personable,
unforced assimilation of his specific demands,
allied to his intimate knowledge of the inner
workings of these scores, make for wonderfully
fresh, punchy results. In this respect Nos 6-8 in
particular prove immensely rewarding, but the
Eroica and the Fourth, too, are little short of
superb. This is a cycle which excitingly reaffirms
the life-enhancing mastery of Beethoven's vision
for many years to come.

Symphonies Nos 1-9
Gundula Janowitz *sop* **Hilde Rössel-Majdan** *contr*
Waldemar Kmentt *ten* **Walter Berry** *bass*
Vienna Singverein; Berlin Philharmonic Orchestra /
Herbert von Karajan
DG Collectors Edition ⑤ 463 088-2GB5 (5h 32' · ADD
· T/t). Recorded 1961-62 Ⓜ ⚫

This was the first set of the Nine to be planned,
recorded and sold as an integral cycle. It was also
a set that had been extremely carefully positioned from the interpretative point of view.
Where Karajan's 1950s Philharmonia cycle had
elements in it that owed a certain amount to the
old German school of Beethoven interpretation,
the new-found virtuosity of the Berliners
allowed him to approach more nearly the fierce
beauty and lean-toned fiery m anner of Toscanini's Beethoven style as Karajan had first encountered it in its halcyon age in the mid-1930s.
Nothing demonstrates this better than the 1962
recording of the Fourth Symphony, fiery and
radiant as Karajan's reading had not previously
been, and never would be again. The old shibbo-
leth among writers and musicians that the even-
numbered symphonies were somehow less dramatic than the odd-numbered ones meant
nothing to Karajan. His accounts of the Second,
Fourth, Sixth and Eighth Symphonies were
every bit as intense as their allegedly sturdier
neighbours. Only in the Seventh Symphony's
third movement Trio and the Menuetto of the
Eighth Symphony – where he continued to follow Wagner's idea of this as an essentially stately
dance, a kind of surrogate slow movement – did
he deviate significantly from the Toscanini
model. And it worked. True, the first movement
of the *Pastoral* Symphony was a touch airless,
lacking some of the easy wonderment of Karajan's old Philharmonia recording. But, then,
Toscanini himself had never managed to replicate the unique charm of his pre-war English
recording with the BBC SO.

The original review of the cycle entered a number of caveats, some of which still pertain, though it's the lack of certain repeats and the non-antiphonal dispensation of the violins that may worry some most nowadays. What so enthused us back then was the urgency of the music-making, its vitality and, ultimately, a fierce sense of joy that had its natural point of culmination in a thrillingly played and eloquently sung account of the finale of the Ninth. The playing of the new rejuvenated BPO dazzled throughout, as did Günther Hermanns recordings: clean and clear, and daringly 'lit' with a bright shimmer of reverberation. The recordings have always transferred effortlessly to CD and the present reissue is no exception.

Symphonies Nos 1-9
Karita Mattila sop **Violeta Urmana** mez **Thomas Moser** ten **Thomas Quasthoff** bass-bar **Eric Ericson Chamber Choir; Swedish Radio Choir; Berlin Philharmonic Orchestra / Claudio Abbado**
DG ⑤ 477 5864GM5 (5h 46' · DDD)   ⑧❶❷❸➤
Nos 1-8 from TDK and EuroArts DVD originals

The finest of fine lines can divide routine and revelation. Seven years on from the release of a studio set of the nine, Abbado reveals doubts of his own. The Ninth excepted, the original DG set has been consigned to history, its place taken on CD by live performances given by Abbado and the Berliners in Renzo Piano's acclaimed new Santa Cecilia hall in Rome in February 2001. Originally recorded for DVD, this Rome cycle now emerges as Abbado's 'legacy' choice.

Hindsight tells us that the original set was premature, recorded before the project had established a purpose beyond that of providing the obligatory Beethoven cycle Abbado owed the orchestra; recorded, too, before players or engineers were conversant with the soundscapes needed to create Abbado's vision of a vital yet at the same time properly autochthonous Beethoven manner.

Where the Berlin set lacked emotional intensity and sonic immediacy, the Rome cycle provides both. As early as the slow movement of the First Symphony, it is evident that the warmer, more intimate Rome sound is helping concentrate our minds; the performance too is more strongly characterised, the finale markedly so.

The First, Third, Fifth and Seventh symphonies are the principal beneficiaries here. An examination of the relative timings tells us little beyond the fact that the Rome performances may occasionally be a touch broader. In practice, this has little to do with tempo, everything to do with shape and commitment – with concentration of tone and intensity of phrasing.

Abbado's claim that the Rome performances 'marked a significant advance in terms of style, spirit, and technique' is best illustrated in the Seventh Symphony. In Berlin, the finale seemed driven and over-quick; in Rome, everything is absorbed and of a piece. The more closely focused sound also helps. The individual string

sections, the violins in particular, are far more clearly defined, an important factor when Abbado's retention of non-antiphonal layouts might be thought (wrongly as it turns out) to take the edge off the drama.

With the even-numbered symphonies it is more a case of swings and roundabouts. The Rome *Pastoral* is less vernal, the Eighth fiercer and more monumental, albeit not entirely settled rhythmically in the outer movements. The Fourth is again outstanding, though fuller-bodied and more overtly songful. The Berlin Ninth remains. It is a pretty good performance with an outstandingly well realised finale. What happened to the Rome Ninth is not explained. Ever since student days in Vienna with Toscanini fanatic Hans Swarowsky, Abbado has been in semi-permanent revolt against the Italian school of Beethoven interpretation. In these vibrant Rome performances he achieves an intensity of effect his hero Furtwängler just might have approved.

Symphonies Nos 1-9   ℗
Luba Orgonášová sop **Anne Sofie von Otter** mez **Anthony Rolfe Johnson** ten **Gilles Cachemaille** bar **Monteverdi Choir; Orchestre Révolutionnaire et Romantique / Sir John Eliot Gardiner**
Archiv ⑤ 439 900-2AH5 (5h 28' · DDD)
                                        ⑤❶❷❸➤

This set is remarkable and many will rate it as Mr Knightley rates Emma Woodhouse 'faultless in spite of her faults'. In his booklet essay, Peter Czorny tells us that the recordings are offered in the hope of transporting the listener back 'to that moment when this music burst forth into a world of heroes, wars and revolution, creating its own world of the sublime and ineffable'. This theme is developed by Gardiner in a robust 20-minute talk on the project that comes free on a sixth CD. Gardiner's opinion that Beethoven wanted his musicians to live dangerously has some peculiar consequences.

Symphony No 1: The opening is superbly judged. Gardiner doesn't overplay the *Adagio molto*, and the *Allegro con brio*, often played with a fatal languor by members of the old German School, is pretty quick. After his absurdly brisk reading of the second movement, Gardiner goes on to conduct dazzlingly successful accounts of the *Scherzo* and finale. Symphony No 2: This is very fine throughout. By following the written tempo markings and his own musical instincts Gardiner produces a perfomance of the first movement that opens out the drama most compellingly. Symphony No 3: More *révolutionnaire* than *romantique*. A very fast first movement gets within spitting distance of an impossible metronome mark. That and keen texturing make for tremendous dramatic urgency. Unfortunately, there's also too little accommodation *en route* of the rich cargo of ideas that Beethoven has shipped into this movement. In their haste to get to the recapitulation itself, Gardiner and his players are decidedly unpoised. He's superb in the last two movements; but these are considerably less than half the story where the *Eroica* is concerned. Symphony No 4: An unusually quick introductory and brisk *Allegro vivace*. Gardiner treats the pivotal drum entry before the recapitulation atmospherically. Glorious slow movement, impossibly quick finale.

Symphony No 5: Here is the stuff of which revolutions are made. Gardiner plays the piece pretty straight, and at white heat. The orchestra is superb, helped by the Francophone bias of its sound base. That said, the *Scherzo* (with repeat) is surely too fast. It starts briskly and not especially quietly. The pace drops back for the Trio, which is just as well since the strings are hard-pressed to articulate clearly. The finale is also very fast, again ahead of what's generally regarded as a good metronome. There's a grandeur to the Scherzo-cum-finale that could be seen to reflect a vision that transcends the politics of revolution. Still, for its *éclat terrible*, this is unbeatable. The slow movement is also superbly shaped and directed.

Symphony No 6: Despite some lovely playing in the slow movement and an air of brisk efficiency, this is a rather joyless *Pastoral*. Nor is it a spiritually uplifting one. The *Scherzo* – 'A merry gathering of country folk' – is a very high-speed affair. At such a pace the various amusing false entries rather lose their point; to play in this village band you would need to be a virtuoso, and teetotal to boot.

Symphony No 7: A glorious performance. The introduction sets the scene with an ideal blend of weight and anticipation. The *Vivace* has a splendid dance feel and a power that's wholly unforced. *Scherzo* and finale are also superbly paced. The *Allegretto* is eloquent with a sense of barely sublimated grieving. The recording is magnificent. Symphony No 8: In general, the symphony thrives on the Gardiner approach, though in the finale the emphasis is again on high-speed locomotion.

Symphony No 9: The first movement has never been dispatched as rapidly as here. In fact, Gardiner doesn't get the bit between the teeth until bar 51, so the celebrated introduction has room to breathe. But he isn't entirely inflexible, and he and his players show remarkable skill in making busy detail tell. Yet a lot does go by the board. The slow movement is also played very quickly. However, the finale is superb. Tempos are unerringly chosen, the choral singing is beyond criticism, and there's a rare expressive quality to the singing of the solo quartet. High quality playing from the orchestra and often exceptional Archiv sound. At best, the physical and intellectual vitality of this music-making brings us close to the *Ding an sich*. It's a best that occurs only intermittently. That it occurs at all is perhaps a sufficient miracle.

Symphonies Nos 1-9
Ruth Ziesak *sop* **Birgit Remmert** *contr* **Steve Davislim** *ten* **Detlef Roth** *bar* **Swiss Chamber Choir; Zürich Tonhalle Orchestra / David Zinman**

BEETHOVEN SYMPHONIES – IN BRIEF

CO of Europe / Nikolaus Harnoncourt
Teldec ⑤ 3984 28144-2 (10h 40' · DDD)
®0000➔

A groundbreaking set which harnessed fresh ideas, totally committed playing and a *Gramophone* Record of the Year now economically coupled with more Beethoven works. It should be seriously considered.

Zürich Tonhalle / David Zinman
Arte Nova ⑤ 74321 65410-2 (5h 36' · DDD)
⑤00

Another set that blends modern instruments and a historically aware approach. There's a freshness and sparkle here that's very hard to resist. Only the Ninth slightly disappoints.

BPO / Claudio Abbado
DG ⑤ 477 5864GM5 (5h 46' · DDD) ®00
Caught live in Rome and originally issued as the soundtrack to the DVD, Abbado's second Berlin cycle is magnificent, a superb memento of his years with the BPO.

London Classical Players / Sir Roger NorringtonⓅ
Virgin Classics ⑤ 561943-2 (5h 53' · DDD) ®00
A fine period-instrument cycle – Nos 2 and 8 won a *Gramophone* Award – with a fine sense of excitement and an intoxicating feeling for the adventure of such a project.

Orchestre Révolutionaire et Romantique / Ⓟ
Sir John Eliot Gardiner
Archiv ⑤ 439 900-2AH5 (5h 28' · DDD) Ⓕ00
A superb, carefully considered and very theatrical cycle: this is Beethoven straight off the stage. The playing on period instruments is very fine and the recording nicely handled.

Berlin PO / Herbert von Karajan
DG ⑤ 463 088-2 (5h 32' · ADD) ®00
Dating from 1961-62, Karajan's second cycle was the first cycle recorded and released as such. It's still fresh and imaginative, boasting a real sense of discovery and excitement.

Vienna PO / Sir Simon Rattle
EMI ⑤ 557445-2 (5h 42' · DDD) Ⓜ
Recorded live, this is a controversial set. Much admired in some quarters, it's lacking in the joy that's so central to this music. Rattle's 'period' approach sits uneasily with the lush, romantic style of the VPO. Sample first…

Scottish CO, Philharmonia /
Sir Charles Mackerras
Hyperion ⑤ CDS44301/5 (5h 36' · DDD) ®000
Ripeness is all! Mackerras, caught live at the 2006 Edinburgh Festival, offers a magnificent cycle (the only regret is a change of orchestra for the Ninth). This is historically informed Beethoven, but so full of humanity and life.

Arte Nova Classics ⑤ 74321 65410-2 (5h 36' · DDD)
Ⓢ**OO**

Also available separately
74321 63645-2 – Nos 1 & 2 (54')
74321 59214-2 – Nos 3 & 4 (75')
74321 49695-2 – Nos 5 & 6 (74')
74321 56341-2 – Nos 7 & 8 (61')
74321 65411-2 – No 9 (73')

Viewed overall, the performances of Nos 1, 4, 6 and 8 are the best in this set, though there's a certain levelling of dynamics in the Eighth. In the Seventh and the Fifth, the finales might have benefited from a wider curve of dynamics and a little more in the way of tonal weight. On the other hand, Zinman's fleet-footed *Eroica* grows on you, and the Fourth is among the most vivacious accounts available. As to the Ninth, the *Scherzo*'s super-fast Trio makes particular sense at the very end of the movement where Trio and outer section engage in a brief comic tussle. The fast first movement is suitably dangerous and while the finale will no doubt court controversy (primarily for some unusual tempo relations), the *Adagio* sounds matter-of-fact, even a little impatient. Indeed, it's the one movement in this cycle that seems to misfire.

Zinman has used Bärenreiter's new edition of Beethoven's texts, although the extra appoggiaturas and ornaments, invariably sewn along the woodwind lines – were inserted by the conductor, based on sound musicological principles. All repeats are observed, and so are the majority of Beethoven's metronome markings. What matters most is the overall character of Zinman's Beethoven which is swift, lean, exhilarating and transparent. The Tonhalle copes bravely, often with exceptional skill, and the recordings easily compare with their best full-price rivals.

And the best bargain alternatives? Günter Wand's sense of structure (RCA) draws a sympathetic response, while Leinsdorf's solid, strong-arm Beethoven also has much to commend it (RCA). Karajan's 1962 cycle is surely the best of four (see above) and although Mackerras (Classics for Pleasure), like Zinman, sheds revealing beams of light here and there, this Zurich set has the greater impact. Those who favour the darker, weightier, more obviously 'heroic' Beethoven known (wrongly, perhaps) as 'old school' will probably not respond quite so readily, but they should still give Zinman a try. On balance, his cycle remains the best bargain digital option. Besides, Arte Nova's asking price is so ludicrously cheap that it's worth buying on impulse, if only for the sake of a refreshing change. Just try to have someone else's *Choral* in reserve.

Additional recommendations

Symphonies Nos 1-9

Wiens *sop* **Hartwig** *contr* **Lewis** *ten* **Hermann** *bar*
Hamburg State Opera Chorus; North German Radio Chorus; North German RSO / Wand

RCA Red Seal ⑤ 74321 20277-2
Ⓜ
(5h 56' · DDD · aas)

Consistently inspired: Wand's tempi are superbly judged, the orchestral balance ideal, and in the Ninth the soloists make a first-rate team.

Symphonies Nos 1-9[a]. Overtures – Coriolan, Op 62; Egmont, Op 84; Die Geschöpfe des Prometheus, Op 43
[a]**Schütz Choir of London; London Classical Players / Sir Roger Norrington**
Virgin Classics ② 561943-2 (5h 53' · DDD)
Recorded 1986-88
Ⓢ**OO**⊕

This was a trailblazing set that collected a *Gramophone* Award for Symphonies Nos 2 and 8. Norrington made much of Beethoven's metronome marks but also brought great drama and excitement to these well-known scores.

Symphonies Nos 1-9. Overtures – Coriolan; Egmont; Die Geschöpfe des Prometheus; Die Ruinen von Athen (and March); Die Weihe des Hauses
Anima Eterna / Jos van Immerseel
Zig-Zag Territoires ⑥ ZZT080402/6 (5h 08 · DDD)
Recorded 2008
Ⓜ**OO**⊕

A fine period-instrument set without a whiff of the routine to it: thrilling and reassuring by turns with many more hits than misses. The small size of the band (23 players and 33 in the Ninth) makes for some very punchy phrasing. Well worth trying.

Symphonies – selected

Symphonies Nos 1 & 4. Egmont Overture, Op 84[a]
Berlin Philharmonic Orchestra / Herbert von Karajan
DG Galleria 419 048-2GGA (64' · ADD) Recorded
[a]1969, 1975-76
Ⓜ**O**⊕

The opening of the First, perfectly timed and chorded, announces playing of rare pedigree, though the *Allegro* itself, taken at a gently ruminative pace, is a surprise. The autumnal side of Karajan's make-up is one we don't often see. It's a beautifully shaped reading, with glorious wind playing and a nobly sustained through-rhythm. The mellow *Andante*, like the Minuet and Trio, emerges as a miracle of instrumental ensemble, a reminder of how, summer by summer, Karajan encouraged his players to make chamber music together on vacation. After so gentle a start, the finale seems strangely quick. Orchestrally, it's the finest quick Beethoven playing imaginable and for all the aerial excitement the final *fortissimo* peaks are compelling placed.

Karajan's instinctively dynamic approach to Beethoven is modified in the Fourth by a contrasted but equally strong feel for the German symphonic tradition. The performance strikes deepest at the points of stasis midway through each of the first three movements. Indeed, the sonority of the performance is remarkable throughout, with great use made of bass and cello colourings (something which the BPO had perfected by this time) and a huge dynamic range – implicit in the score from massive *tutti* chords down to the most perfectly regulated quiet drum rolls. It's in such playing, as subtle as it is creatively alive, that the flame of Beethoven's genius can be seen to burn brightly on. The *Egmont* Overture, played superbly and surprisingly swiftly, makes a welcome filler.

Symphonies – Nos 2 & 7
Minnesota Orchestra / Osmo Vänskä
BIS ⊕ BIS-SACD1816 (76' · DDD/DSD)   Ⓕ**O**➛

This coupling of the Second and Seventh symphonies points up what Rob Cowan has called Vänskä's ability to 'focus the music's rhythmic profile with unwavering control'. Not that the performances are control-orientated. Even where the metronomes are good and speed is of the essence, as in the finale of the Second Symphony, quickness does not preclude ease.

In the Seventh Symphony, Vänskä keeps the harmonic drama in as sharp a focus as the rhythmic. The pulse may be quicker, the sound tauter, but the epic first movement breathes here much as Klemperer would have allowed it to breathe. With Vänskä, old insights are not necessarily invalid insights. In the *Allegretto* and third-movement Trio there is a reversion, not to old-fashioned Teutonic slowness, but to thoughtful tempi that are on the measured side of quick.

What is truly outstanding here is the transparency of the texturing and the meticulous integration of phrase shape and accent within the rhythmic continuum. Everything is audible but since Vänskä is not a didactic conductor nothing is italicised or underlined. That said, the violins' extraordinarily precise articulation of the Second Symphony's notorious seventh bar, with its arch of double-dotted trilled quavers and interior grace notes, may shock collectors used to the old pre-Bärenreiter fudges.

The BIS recording has exceptional clarity, with finely judged reverberation times, and a dynamic range that catches every gradation of the orchestra's scrupulously judged sound profile right down to *pianissimi* of quite astonishing beauty and restraint.

Symphonies No 2 & 6, 'Pastoral'
London Symphony Orchestra / Bernard Haitink
LSO Live LSO0082 (76' · DDD); ⊕ LSO0582.
Recorded live 2005   Ⓢ ➛

Very appealing, this – the punchy, neatly packed sound; the way the timps thwack away at the right-hand side of the stage, the antiphonally placed fiddles busying to and fro, Haitink's unmannered, high-energy but essentially non-aggressive approach to both symphonies. The first thing that strikes you about the *Pastoral* is its sensitive shaping. The second is the lively pacing, but never breathless or unduly hurried. The 'Scene by the brook' ebbs and flows at roughly the prescribed speed and yet the LSO's playing, ever warm-hearted, never adopts 'period' affectations: it's as if the laudable old guard has had a

wash, a brush-up and a slight change of heart regarding tempo and articulation. The 'Peasants' Merrymaking' enjoys something of Toscanini's bacchanalian drive, the storm a measure of his dynamism.

The Second Symphony is formal but fun. The opening *Adagio molto* is pretty powerful, the principal *allegro* light on its feet but rock-steady and with an imposing and firmly held bass-line. Again, Haitink keeps the slow movement on the move without sacrificing gravitas.

Both readings are profoundly satisfying, the work of musicians who know the scores backwards, love playing them and know what not to do. To say that they provide a new benchmark would be crass; but Haitink and the LSO seem set to provide one of the top Beethoven symphony cycles of the digital era.

Symphonies Nos 2 & 6, 'Pastoral'
**Royal Flemish Philharmonic Orchestra /
Philippe Herreweghe**
Pentatone ⊕ PTC5186 314 (73' · DDD/DSD)   Ⓕ**B**➛

For Philippe Herreweghe, Beethoven's metronome markings are sacrosanct even when the composer appears to contradict himself in the first movement of the Sixth Symphony. The written instruction is *Allegro ma non troppo* yet the speed indication is a swift minim=66. By easing or tightening phrases and being flexible within a spirited pulse, Herreweghe makes the written instruction fit the speed indication. The music could have sounded harried but it doesn't. This is how he conducts both works; and Beethoven's express wishes are vindicated.

It all begins most arrestingly as the Second Symphony crackles into vibrant life, brass cutting through the fabric, woodwind to the fore. Vibrato-less strings may be a touch etiolated at the upper end but their otherwise un-coagulated tone is revealed in an astutely balanced and transparent SACD recording. Incisive drive in the outer movements nicely complements a lyrically felt slow movement, as does a similarly felt 'Scene by the Brook' in the *Pastoral*. Herreweghe doesn't linger here, even for the birdcalls towards the end; yet there is a feeling of gently undulant repose before the 'Peasants' Merrymaking' which is ebulliently bucolic as Beethoven envisaged. The storm is stormy rather than cyclonic; and Herreweghe coaxes wind-playing of opaline radiance to launch a 'Shepherds' Hymn' that swings in relaxed, songful 6/8 time. Beethoven always knew what he wanted in terms of pacing. Herreweghe and his expert band not only obey his tempi, they do so most artistically as well. Excellent indeed.

Symphonies – Nos 3, 'Eroica', & 4
Basle Chamber Orchestra / Giovanni Antonini
Sony Classical ② ⊕ 88697 19252-2 (79' · DDD/DSD)   Ⓜ**O**➛

It is rare nowadays, even in the daredevil world of period performance, to come across a performance of Beethoven's *Eroica* Symphony that makes this revolutionary piece seem new-minted. Here though is just such a performance. Giovanni Antonini has been mentioned in the same breath as Toscanini, which may seem odd given Antonini's origins as a recorder- and Baroque flute-player and founder member of Il Giardino Armonico. Yet one can see how the comparison arose. The mix of drive and acumen is indeed extraordinary.

Not that the Maestro could, or would, have approved of Antonini's megalomaniac account of the Fourth Symphony where tempi, always a notch faster than Toscanini's own, are driven to extremes and where there is barely a *cantabile* in sight, even in the slow movement. This is the Fourth Symphony on a war-footing, brutal and unreflecting, with some odd sonorities to boot. The *pianissimo* timpani rolls, to whose care Beethoven entrusts the first movement's most magical transitions, rattle like rain on a corrugated iron roof.

Period performers like to live dangerously. Even so, it is difficult to reconcile the conductor who so brutalises the Fourth Symphony with the sure-footed interpreter of the *Eroica*. Here is a musician who understands the *Eroica* from within, dramatically, logistically and imaginatively. A musician, moreover, who can project that understanding into an orchestral performance that glows white in the furnace. The *Marcia funebre* is particularly fine with a characteristically forward-moving pulse, finely chiselled phrasing and strikingly 'French' sonorities.

Symphony No 3, 'Eroica'.
Overtures – Leonore Nos 1 & 2
Philharmonia Orchestra / Otto Klemperer　🄷
EMI Great Recordings of the Century mono 567740-2
(76' · ADD). Recorded 1954-55　Ⓜ❶❶❶➔

In 1955 the Philharmonia Orchestra was at the peak of its powers. And what cogency there is sustaining and feeding the drama. Where other orchestras and conductors whip themselves into a terrible lather at the start of the finale, Klemperer and the Philharmonia sail majestically on. This is a great performance, steady yet purposeful, with textures that seem hewn out of granite. There's no exposition repeat, and the trumpets blaze out illicitly in the first movement coda, but this is still one of the great *Eroicas* on record. As Karajan announced to Klemperer after flying in to a concert performance around this time: 'I have come only to thank you, and say that I hope I shall live to conduct the Funeral March as well as you have done'. In the *Leonore* Overtures, recorded in 1954, the playing is a bit more rough-edged.

'Eroica'
A film by Simon Cellan Jones
Ian Hart Beethoven **Tim Piggott-Smith** Count Dietrichstein **Jack Davenport** Prince Lobkowitz
Fenella Woolgar Princess Lobkowitz **Claire Skinner**

Josephine **Lucy Akhurst** Therese **Frank Finlay** Haydn **Leo Bill** Ferdinand Ries
Music performed by the **Orchestre Révolutionnaire et Romantique / Sir John Eliot Gardiner**
Opus Arte 📀 OA0908D (129' · 16:9 · PCM stereo and DTS 5.1 · 0). Includes a complete performance of Symphony No 3, 'Eroica'　Ⓕ

'June 1804' says the legend at the film's opening. Denis Matthews (in his Master Musicians volume) thought it was six months later that the *Eroica* was given a first run-through in the palace of Prince Lobkowitz, but had that been so we should have been denied Beethoven and his pupil Ferdinand Ries tramping river banks, and Beethoven and the object of his unrequited love lazing idly in the palace courtyard, so June it is. Let's not complain: historical verisimilitude is always going to be at a premium in such reconstructions, and the makers of this BBC film do not take us for fools. They use what we know of the people and places concerned to invent a plausible narrative of politics, love and anger that, most importantly, centres on the music.

In fact the domestic scale of the setting is a powerful reminder of the work's vast reach and capacity to shock. Potential purchasers will have to judge for themselves whether they are likely to be bothered by the soundtrack being palpably separate from the visuals, or the orchestra being visibly smaller than the sum of its excellent parts. The recording is instrumental in bringing film and symphony to life: winds to the fore, bassoons and growly double-basses balefully ever-present.

In the *Eroica* itself, Gardiner's first movement (without its repeat) has a bare and remorseless intensity; his own previous DG recording is nearer Beethoven's metronome mark and some distance further from the expressive force of this new recording. The *Scherzo* is a little plainly phrased but Gardiner springs his surprise with the finale. A tempo that seems at first tepid grows around the music, allowing the fugue its due weight, the flute solo its pathos and horns their full measure of glory.

The film's producers think the performance worth hearing on a separate set of tracks, without noises off: there are only so many times that you will want to hear Beethoven tell Ries to 'piss off' after his pupil has interrupted halfway through the first movement. In a further act of charity, Opus Arte spares us the otherwise ubiquitous musical excerpt over the title menus. The enterprise is probably a one-off but it's tempting to imagine what this team could do with the Fifth, or even the Ninth.

Symphonies Nos 4 & 5
Minnesota Orchestra / Osmo Vänskä
BIS 🅂 BIS-SACD1416 (67' · DDD/DSD)　Ⓕ❶❶❶➔

It was during Osmo Vänskä's time with the BBC Scottish SO that his Beethoven began winning golden opinions. His reading of the Fourth is fiery but not relentless. Metronome marks are important but not mandatory. Transparent textures and a rigorous way with dynamics also feature. Of particular interest is the skill with which he continuously keeps in view the bass line, and thus the music's harmonic contour, never easy, given the 'open' nature of Beethoven's scoring.

The Minnesota Orchestra are extraordinarily proficient: fleet-footed and articulate, though tonally they have less in reserve than the Berlin or Vienna orchestras. This can be a limitation in the Fifth, where the sound occasionally edges towards coarseness but it makes little or no difference in the Fourth, even in the *Adagio*. What Vänskä sacrifices in lyric poetry he makes up for in justness of rhythm and chasteness of texture. Skilful as BIS's engineers are in dealing with the quietest passages, finding an optimum playback level for the vibrant but *pianissimo*-strewn Fourth takes time and patience.

The performance of the dynamically less problematic Fifth also also bristles with character. Typically, *Scherzo* and finale are bound to one another structurally but not tamed emotionally.

Symphonies Nos 4 & /
Manchester Camerata / Douglas Boyd
Avie AV2169 (74' · DDD)   Ⓕ ⦿⦿⦿➔

Thirty years ago, 'chamber orchestra' Beethoven was considered to be a mildly interesting eccentricity; nowadays it is practically *de rigueur*. The Chamber Orchestra of Europe blazed the trail. Douglas Boyd was its principal oboe for many years, though more recently his widely recognised drive and musical acumen have been put at the service of the long-established and nowadays upwardly mobile Manchester Camerata. This, surely, is one of their finest records.

The Camerata do not use period instruments (under Boyd they do not even use period layouts), nor is Boyd an interpretative absolutist. Harnoncourt and Abbado, his old bosses at the COE, have probably helped determine his approach, yet there is no sense that these are hand-me-down readings. The switch of roles has clearly refocused his interest in the music and rekindled it: an experience the orchestra evidently shares.

There is aggression in the performances, but it is an artistically contained aggression. The playing, with its gutsy, tensile strings and characterful lead woodwinds, has a powerfully communicative quality. Both readings are rhythmically strong, though the delayed string entry at the start of the hushed return to the dominant in the second subject group of the first movement of the Seventh (bars 141-42) is still a surprise. As this happens three times, twice in the exposition and again in the recapitulation, it is clearly no accident.

The recordings are superb. For once we have an in-house, orchestra-live product that actually works on record, with a sharply focused bespoke production (no applause) that vividly conveys the no-holds-barred immediacy of the music-making.

Symphonies – Nos 5 & 6, 'Pastoral'
Basle Chamber Orchestra / Giovanni Antonini
Sony Classical 88697 64816-2 (70' · DDD)   Ⓕ

The Fifth and Sixth make almost as stimulating a pair as the Fourth and Fifth, developing as they do several of the same ideas in different ways, and Antonini is at least as good at what brings the two symphonies together as what sets them apart, such as instrumental theatre. We're made aware with unusual force not just of the withholding of trombones until the Fifth's finale and the breaking of the *Pastoral*'s storm, but also the entry and sporadic reappearance of the trumpets in the 'Peasants' Dance'. Antonini is very clear about when, in both symphonies, Beethoven's impossible runs of semiquavers in the bass are to play an active, melodic role and when they should recede to a wash of brown watercolour. The first clarinet of the Basle Chamber Orchestra has the time of his life in the Sixth.

Especially impressive is Antonini's sense of rhythm. These performances really swing. Beethoven's play with pedal-points and motivic layers in the two slow movements is joyfully enacted, showing how counterpoint can take a back seat in classical discourse to patterning and variation, but the point when the game becomes serious is also acutely felt.

There is something of a pantheistic celebration about both these performances that offers and commands not just respect but a rather thrilling demand for your attention.

Symphonies Nos 5 & 7
Vienna Philharmonic Orchestra / Carlos Kleiber
DG The Originals 447 400-2GOR (72' · ADD)
Recorded 1974   Ⓜ ⦿⦿⦿➔

The recording of the Fifth, always very fine, comes up superbly in this transfer. What, though, of the Seventh, an equally distinguished performance though always perceptibly greyer-sounding on LP, and on CD? The result is a performance of genius that now speaks to us freely and openly for the first time. In some ways this is a more important document than the famous Fifth.

Great recordings of the Seventh, greatly played and conducted, but with first and second violins divided left and right, are as rare as gold dust. Freshly refurbished, this Kleiber Seventh would go right to the top of any short list of recommendable Sevenths. It's wonderful to have these two legendary performances so expertly restored.

Symphonies Nos 5[a] & 7[b]   Ⓗ
New York Philharmonic Symphony Orchestra / Arturo Toscanini
Naxos Historical mono 8 110840 (77' · ADD)
Recorded in New York [b]1936, [a]live 1933   Ⓢ ⦿⦿⦿➔

Toscanini is a near-impossible act to follow. But then in a sense he was fortunate. He didn't have

BEETHOVEN SYMPHONY NO 5 – IN BRIEF

Vienna Philharmonic Orchestra / Carlos Kleiber
DG The Originals 447 400-2GOR   Ⓜ❍❶❶❷➔
Ⓖ This is one of those legendary recordings that everyone knows about but which quite takes the breath every time it's played. Kleiber paces the work magnificently and draws from the great VPO playing of an unparalleled intensity and beauty. Also available as a single download from iTunes.

Minnesota Orchestra / Osmo Vänskä
BIS ⓢⓐⓒⓓ BIS-SACD1416   Ⓕ❍❶❶❷➔
This disc, coupled with the Fourth Symphony, launched a new cycle and what a start! Vänskä's keen ear for orchestral texture and rhythmic bite makes for a thrilling ride: the sound may occasionally coarsen but that's an effect he's probably after.

New York Philharmonic Symphony Orchestra / Arturo Toscanini   Ⓗ
Naxos Historical mono 8 110840   Ⓢ❍❶❶❷➔
If you can cope with the 1936 sound, here's a Fifth that positively blazes. Other Toscanini performances are better drilled but few achieved this incendiary quality when the music catches light. Thrilling.

London Classical Players / Sir Roger Norrington
Virgin Veritas 562489-2   Ⓜ❍Ⓑ➔
One of the first 'period' Fifths and still a performance to take note of – Norrington manages very successfully to convey that coiled-spring intensity right from the start. When the finale finally explodes, the punch of the LCP is really impressive

Zürich Tonhalle / David Zinman
Arte Nova 74321 49695-2   Ⓜ❍
Zinman's Beethoven – fleet of foot and with a zestful spring in its step – has gathered a substantial following. In the Fifth, his period-informed approach makes for a reading of agility but with an appealing dramatic bite.

Concertgebouw Orchestra / Wolfgang Sawallisch
EMI ② 573326-2   Ⓑ❍
Coupled with Nos 4, 6 and 7, Sawallisch offers a traditional big-band approach, but a sane and very rewarding one. Don't expect any surprises from the interpretation – but then they are supplied in plenty by this extraordinary score.

Royal Liverpool Philharmonic Orchestra / Sir Charles Mackerras
Classics for Pleasure 572849-2   Ⓢ❍❍
A richly rewarding pairing with No 7 that finds Sir Charles inspiring his players to performances of agility and intensity, though with a nice period feel.

Ⓖ a fat record catalogue full of Rostrum Greats to live up to and he wasn't under pressure to say something new, or at least something different. On the contrary, Toscanini's avowed mission was to clean up where others had indulged in interpretative excess. And he could as well have been cleaning up for the future.

There are numerous Toscanini Fifths in public or private circulation, at least four of them dating from the 1930s. This one is lithe, dynamic and consistently commanding. Comparing it with Toscanini's 1952 NBC recording finds numberless instances where a natural easing of pace helps underline essential transitions, such as the quiet alternation of winds and strings that holds the tension at the centre of the first movement. The glow of the string playing towards the close of the second movement has no parallel with the 1952 version and while the NBC *Scherzo* is better drilled, this finale really blazes. Mark Obert-Thorn has done a first-rate job with the sound, focusing the orchestra's whispered *pianissimo*s while keeping surface noise to a minimum.

The commercially released 1936 New York Seventh has already been hailed as a classic. As with the Fifth, Toscanini's ability to gauge pauses to the nth degree – in this case the rests that separate the finale's opening *fortissimo* rallying calls – is truly inimitable. The nobility and the visceral thrill of Toscanini's pre-war version remains unchallenged. The transfer is excellent.

Symphonies Nos 5 & 6   Ⓟ
London Classical Players / Sir Roger Norrington
Virgin Veritas 562489-2 (74' · DDD)   Ⓜ❍Ⓑ➔

Norrington conducts an enjoyable, memorable account of the Fifth. He throws off the introduction to the first movement with crisp brilliance, and the *Allegro* conveys enormous underlying energy. His *Andante* is beautifully phrased and flows most delicately; in the bustling double bass theme at the centre of the *Scherzo* the bowing is light, the effect refined and offering easy virtuosity. Norrington's finale is strongly accented, his horns broadly sonorous, partly as a result of the resonant EMI sound.

The *Pastoral* is also a revelation. Norrington adopts a swift tempo in the joyous first movement but there's no hint of that relentless, driven quality we've sometimes had on record. He's fully up to tempo in the vibrant *tuttis*; elsewhere he's most careful to allow the music to dance and breathe, the transitions always most sensitively moulded. It's also a joy to hear this symphony on period instruments. This *Pastoral* is a real voyage of aural discovery. Sometimes the wind tuning isn't 100 per cent true, at others it's simply a matter of Norrington teasing us with the timing of a trill's release or pointing up dissonances that usually get smoothed over. The sound is wonderfully clear and trenchant.

Beethoven Symphony No 6, 'Pastoral'[a]
Schubert Symphony No 5 in B flat, D485[b]
Vienna Philharmonic Orchestra / Karl Böhm
DG The Originals 447 433-2GOR (74' · ADD)
Recorded [a]1971, [b]1979   Ⓜ❍❍❍❱

Karl Böhm's Beethoven is a compound of earth and fire. His VPO recording of Beethoven's Sixth of 1971 dominated the LP catalogue for over a decade, and has done pretty well on CD on its various appearances. His reading is generally glorious and it remains one of the finest accounts of the work ever recorded. It still sounds well and the performance (with the first-movement exposition repeat included) has an unfolding naturalness and a balance between form and lyrical impulse that's totally satisfying. The brook flows untroubled and the finale is quite lovely, with a wonderfully expansive climax.

The Schubert dates from the end of Böhm's recording career. It's a superb version of this lovely symphony, another work that suited Böhm especially well. The reading is weighty but graceful, with a most beautifully phrased *Andante* (worthy of a Furtwängler), a bold Minuet and a thrilling finale. The recording is splendid. If you admire Böhm this is a worthy way to remember his special gifts.

Symphony No 7. Triple Concerto
Gordan Nikolitch vn **Tim Hugh** vc **Lars Vogt** pf
London Symphony Orchestra / Bernard Haitink
LSO Live ⓈⓂ LSO0578 (75' · DDD)   Ⓜ❱
Recorded live 2005

Nothing like having your expectations challenged, especially in Beethoven where interpretative templates tend to settle for good. Past experience of Bernard Haitink in the symphonies left an impression of worthiness and generalised musicality; but the first instalment of the conductor's projected live Beethoven symphony cycle with the London Symphony Orchestra witnesses a significantly increased adrenalin count. As well as being vital and intelligently thought through, Haitink's new Seventh honours all repeats and has the inestimable advantage of spatially divided violin desks, particularly telling in the clear but relatively dry Barbican Hall acoustic. The first movement's bracing rhythms gambol rather than storm and there's genuine tenderness in the *Allegretto*. The *Scherzo*'s dancing gait and the unforced momentum of the finale is very attractive.

What's strong about Haitink's excellent Triple Concerto is its sense of architecture, the way Haitink builds the opening *tutti* so that the climactic passage where winds alternate with strings (2'04") establishes a real sense of arrival. Interesting Haitink's soloists seem more integrated within the rest of the band than some versions, less in terms of sound than overall playing-style: inspired moments include Tim Hugh's rapt opening phrases in the second movement. James Mallinson's integrated sound-picture for LSO Live is very pleasing.

Symphony No 9, 'Choral'
Helena Juntunen sop **Katarina Karnéus** mez
Daniel Norman ten **Neal Davies** bass
Minnesota Chorale and Orchestra / Osmo Vänskä
BIS Ⓢ BIS-SACD1616 (66' · DDD · T/t)   ⒻⓄ❱

Vänskä offers a radical re-think of Beethoven's *Choral* Symphony, a youthful, brave statement, free of iconic influences. Considered in purely musical terms, his version would better fit the idea of revolution through renewal.

The opening of Vänskä's *Choral*, though deathly quiet, is chiselled and precise, the first *tutti* like a fireball from the heavens, much aided by a hugely dynamic recording. Within a mere minute or two, one quality has made its mark with maximum force, namely rhythm, tight as a drum – that, and an astonishing power of projection. But what is really striking is the muscularity of the playing, its clipped, propulsive phrasing, quite unlike any other modern-instrument version of the Ninth. Suddenly this quirky first movement sounds like tough-grained middle-period Beethoven, the fugal writing at its centre granitic and purposeful, the music's many calculated repetitions unnervingly obsessive. The contrast with the Bacchanalian *Scherzo* is more marked than usual, Vänskä again focusing the music's rhythmic profile with unwavering control. The *Adagio*'s quiet opening is breathtaking and although the variations that follow are seamlessly interwoven, the effect is anything but rigid.

Vänskä's finale returns us to the shock and awe of his first moment, with a decisive, tight-lipped opening (the fast tempo held absolutely firm), warmly phrased counterpoint surrounding the 'Ode to Joy' build-up and then, with the unleashing of the voices, an excellent group of soloists and a well drilled chorus who sing as if they really know (and mean) what they're singing. The tenor's March episode is fairly swift, leading to a razor-sharp fugue. And when the chorus enters, well... In a word, Vänskä's finale is full of zeal.

Symphony No 9, 'Choral'
Christiane Oelze sop **Petra Lang** contr
Klaus Florian Vogt ten **Matthias Goerne** bar
**Deutsche Kammerchor; Deutsche
Kammerphilharmonie Bremen / Paavo Järvi**
RCA Red Seal Ⓢ 88697 57606-2 (64' · DDD/DSD)
   ⒻⓄ❱

With any good Ninth the prospect of an imminent onslaught should posit itself right from the opening bars, and Järvi's certainly does that. The curve from deathly quiet to fearfully loud is swift and decisive, and the die is cast for a dramatic and stylishly shaped performance. There's power to spare. The *Scherzo* opens like a clipped call to arms: there'll be no slacking here, obviously, and the very fast Trio includes some vividly shaped wind *crescendos*.

The *Adagio* subscribes to current thinking as to what the Ninth's slow movement should sound like (or rather, how Beethoven himself might have imagined it to sound), serene and pure in tone with never a hint of the broad pacing and vibrant projection favoured by previous generations. Järvi opts for maximum shock value as he cues the finale to crash in on the tail of the *Adagio* virtually *attacca*, which works well except that there's a marked contrast between the hot-headed brass and timpani combination and the rather camp-sounding, vibrato-free response from the basses. The remainder of Järvi's finale is superb, and excellently sung (especially by Matthias Goerne and the Deutsche Kammerchor), with beautifully traced counterpoint from the bassoons as the 'Ode to Joy' theme builds, a sparky march leading to a chipper fugue and a noble *Andante maestoso* where the wind accompaniment approximates the sound of an organ. Like Furtwängler many years before him, Järvi whips the closing section into a *prestissimo* frenzy, having allowed himself some small degree of flexibility earlier on in the symphony.

This is without doubt a worthy climax to a very fine cycle. One or two digressions from the textual norm suggest that, as in previous volumes, the musical text used is the Bärenreiter 'New Urtext Edition'.

Symphony No 9, 'Choral' 🄷
Aase Nordmo-Løvberg *sop* **Christa Ludwig** *mez* **Waldemar Kmentt** *ten* **Hans Hotter** *bass-bar* **Philharmonia Chorus and Orchestra / Otto Klemperer**
Testament SBT1177 (71' · ADD)
Recorded live 1957 🄕 **OO**

This is a revelatory live recording by EMI's engineers of Klemperer's performance of the Ninth Symphony at the Royal Festival Hall, immediately before his 1957 EMI recording. Where the studio recording gives us a frontal, ground-level view of the players spread out across the spaces of the Kingsway Hall, this live Festival Hall recording offers us that special Klemperer balance which gave particular prominence to the winds and the timpani. Strings, and in the finale the chorus, are nicely focused; but from where we sit, somewhere above the first oboe, it's winds and timpani that are the centre of interest. No one would have dared balance a studio recording this way, yet this is far closer to what a Klemperer performance really sounded like.

There are a couple of oddities in the finale. In the preliminary orchestral statement of the 'joy' theme, the bassoon descant drowns out the violas and cellos; then, later on, we get a less than clear view of the tenor. (A blessed relief, perhaps, given Kmentt's thin, dried-out sound here.) Interpretatively, the two performances are identical, though the live performance is just that bit more intense. The first movement does not benefit greatly but the Scherzo is transformed; what rather lumbers in the studio is here a thrilling dance of the Titans. The finale is wonderfully performed, thrillingly articulated by the newly founded Philharmonia Chorus and the Philharmonia players. Detail after detail

shines out, etched into the imagination by the playing and the persistently enquiring recording.

Symphony No 9, 'Choral' 🄷
Maria Stader *sop* **Grace Hoffman** *mez* **Waldemar Kmentt** *ten* **Hans Hotter** *bass-bar* **North German Radio Chorus; Cologne Radio Chorus and Symphony Orchestra / Otto Klemperer**
Medici Masters MM031-2 (73' · ADD). Recorded live at the Funkhaus, Cologne, in January 1958 Ⓜ

Does this Ninth differ radically in its shape, thrust and strength from either EMI's studio recording, made six weeks previously, or Testament's recension of the concert immediately prior to the sessions, with its additional and inspiring sense of occasion? No, however enthusiastically Colin Anderson's booklet-note argues for a quickening here (the *Adagio*) and greater breadth there (the *Scherzo*), though the constancy in itself is both a recommendation of something trusted and treasured, and no cause to pass by, secure in the assumption that you've heard it all before.

The two North German choruses may show less collective discipline than their exhaustively drilled London counterparts but the Cologne orchestra's sound, occasionally gritty and diffuse, now familiar to international listeners through recordings by Erich Kleiber and Günter Wand, rises to quite terrifying heights at the climax of the first movement, mercifully undistorted and with plenty of timbral colour preserved in the remastering. Try the cello recitative of the finale which is done just as Beethoven instructs, in the character of a recitative but *in tempo*.

In case anyone persists in the tired dichotomy of Klemperer the firebrand (Kroll and Budapest Opera days) and patrician (Philharmonia years), it's worth pointing out that at 14 minutes, this *Adagio* is barely a minute longer than Mackerras and the Philharmonia (Hyperion), and no less sensitive in its regard for the interplay of the two given tempi. His security and flexibility in moving from one to another, and the disciplined liberation of the movement's central horn solo (as well as much of the finale), puts most conductors, ancient and modern, to shame.

Symphony No 9, 'Choral' 🄷
Elisabeth Schwarzkopf *sop* **Elsa Cavelti** *mez* **Ernst Haefliger** *ten* **Otto Edelmann** *bass* **Lucerne Festival Chorus; Philharmonia Orchestra / Wilhelm Furtwängler**
Tahra mono FURT1054/7(78' · ADD)
Recorded live 1954 🄕 **OOO**

 The 40th anniversary of Furtwängler's death on November 30, 1954, brought forth a rich crop of reissues and remasterings, most notably on the French label Tahra, which secured the rights to publish limited editions of some of Furtwängler's most important (and, it must be said, most frequently pirated) live recordings. Some of Furtwängler's finest performances of Beethoven's music were given in the last months of his life, an odd paradox given his failing health, and by November the apparent extinction of his will to live. Yet this Lucerne Ninth is a seismic utterance, the final heroic regrouping of musical and psychic powers that in certain works of the repertory have this gangling figure towering over all his rivals. This is arguably the greatest of all Furtwängler's recordings of the symphony. Walter Legge wanted to acquire the performance as EMI's official replacement for the momentous 1951 Bayreuth account, but it wasn't to be. Since then, there have been various 'unofficial' editions. The Tahra differs in being 'official', well transferred, and further enhanced by a few introductory remarks made by Furtwängler himself.

Here, the most significant section is that in which Furtwängler sees the problem of interpreting the Ninth as one that effectively postdates the performing culture into which it was born. Furtwängler understood the Ninth as well as any conductor in the 20th century. You can argue this way or that over the pacing of the slow movement (though we defy anyone to say that his performance is anything other than deeply eloquent) or the leisurely speed of the second movement Trio. In the all-important first movement, though, there's no doubt that Beethoven's written tempo markings and frequent subsequent modifications clearly presuppose the kind of uniquely singing, flexible, harmonically searching (but by no means too slow) reading Furtwängler invariably gave us.

Additional recommendation

Symphony No 9
Wiens *sop* Hartwig *mez* Lewis *ten* Hermann *bass*
Hamburg State Opera Chorus; North German Radio Symphony Orchestra and Chorus / Wand
RCA Red Seal 74321 68005-2 (66' · DDD)   Ⓢ
A real bargain. Wand's 1986 recording enshrines a wonderfully wise and humane Ninth, unerringly paced and always intensely refreshing in its lean purposefulness, if at times lacking that last ounce of lump-in-the-throat universality.

Septet, Op 20

Septet in E flat, Op 20. Piano Quintet in E flat, Op 16. Sextet in E flat, Op 81*b*
Ottó Rácz *ob* József Balogh *cl* József Vajda *bn* Jenö Keveházi, János Keveházi, Sándor Berki *hns* Ildikó Hegyi, Péter Popa *vns* Győző Máthé *va* Peter Szabó *vc* István Toth *db*
Naxos 8 553090 (74' · DDD)   Ⓢ🠖

These talented Hungarian players offer a fluent, responsive account of the Septet that highlights the music's intimate chamber character – delight in the music's elegance and perfect balance of

instrumental forces. In the present instance, vivid recording creates a clear, natural ambience for this alert, sensitively blended ensemble. In the Sextet, horn players, Jenö and János Keveházi play with subtlety and panache as required, their tone spontaneous and free. This excellent, value-for-money Naxos disc also offers an elegant, well-turned performance of Beethoven's E flat Quintet.

Piano Quintet, Op 16

Beethoven Piano Quintet in E flat, Op 16   Ⓗ
Mozart Piano Quintet in E flat, K452.
Sinfonia concertante in E flat, K297*b*ᵃ
Walter Gieseking *pf* **Philharmonia Wind Quartet**
(Sidney Sutcliffe *ob* Bernard Walton *cl* Dennis Brain *hn* Cecil James *bn*) ᵃ**Philharmonia Orchestra / Herbert von Karajan**
Testament mono SBT1091 (80' · ADD)
Recorded 1955   Ⓟ🟊🟊

There have never been any doubts about these performances. The horn playing in the *Sinfonia concertante* is unsurpassable and in the quintets Gieseking's lightness and his clarity and sense of style is simply beyond praise. The tempos are on the slow side in the first movement of the Mozart and the finale of the Beethoven but somehow with Gieseking, slow tempos have a way of seeming to be just about right. Richard Osborne's excellent notes quote a letter from Sidney Sutcliffe of touching modesty. Speaking of their run-through of the Mozart, he says, 'On reaching the *Allegro moderato*, the great man played two bars at an absolutely perfect tempo and then stopped and asked in the most gentle and hesitant manner, "Will that be all right for you?" So it was a most happy occasion although I found it a grave responsibility matching the artistry of my colleagues when Bernard [Walton], Cecil [James] and Dennis [Brain] were producing sounds of breath-taking beauty.' Breathtaking is the right word for all concerned here on one of the great chamber music records of the LP era. Considerable pains have been taken with the transfers, which now sound fresh and full bodied. Thoroughly recommended.

String Quartets

Op 18: No 1 in F; No 2 in G; No 3 in D;
No 4 in C minor; No 5 in A; No 6 in B flat
Middle Quartets: Op 59 'Rasumovsky': No 1 in F; No 2 in E minor; No 3 in C Op 74 in E flat, 'Harp'; Op 95 in F minor, 'Serioso'
'Late' Quartets: Op 127 in E flat; Op 130 in B flat; Op 131 in C sharp; Op 132 in A minor; Op 135 in F
Grosse Fuge in B flat, Op 133

Complete String Quartets

Complete String Quartets. Grosse Fuge
Quartetto Italiano (Paolo Borciani, Elisa Pegreffi *vns*

BEETHOVEN STRING QUARTETS OP 18 – IN BRIEF

Tokyo Quartet
Harmonia Mundi ② HMU90 7436/7　Ⓜ❍❍❍
A superb achievement that manages wonderfully to combine the wisdom of years with the ability to convey the startling originality of these six quartets. The actual sound these four players make is stunning.

Takács Quartet
Decca ② 470 848-2DH2　Ⓜ❍❍
The Takács bring tremendous intensity to these six quartets: this is playing of enormous contrasts, with barely audible *pianissimos* turing to sledgehammer *fortissimos* with amazing control. Listening to this you sense the music in a way that few other groups permit.

Alban Berg Quartet
EMI ② 562778-2　Ⓑ❍
Elegant, aristocratic playing from one of the great European ensembles. You rarely find playing of this cultivation that digs so deeply into the music. A real bargain drawn from the ABQ's first (studio) cycle.

The Lindsays
ASV ③ CDDCA1111/3　Ⓑ❍❍
The UK's greatest string quartet returned to the Beethoven for a second recorded cycle and offered readings that are even more satisfying than their first cycle. Speeds have quickened, the textures have lightened but nothing of the intensity is sacrificed. They add the String Quintet which takes the set on to a third disc.

Leipzig Quartet
MDG 307 0853-2, 0855-2 & 0856-2　Ⓕ❍❍
Deeply rewarding musicianship and a complete lack of showmanship make these performances well worth hearing. There's a lovely sheen to their sound and they are constantly alive to Beethoven's imaginative world.

Talich Quartet
Calliope CAL9633, CAL9634　Ⓜ
If you are drawn to the Talich's very individual approach this set might be worth considering, though it's not at the level we have come to expect in the later, greater works. They still sound wonderfully inspired by this music. The sound could benefit from a little more space around it.

Mirò Quartet
Vanguard Classics ② ATMCD1655　Ⓕ
A set of lively, dancing playing from one of the shooting stars on the US chamber music scene. These Op 18 quartets have a fizzing, modern feel to them that makes them very appealing.

Piero Farulli *va* Franco Rossi *vc*)
Philips ⑩ 454 062-2PB10 (544' · ADD)
Recorded 1967-75　Ⓑ❍❍
The String Quartets, Op 59 Nos 2 & 3 are also available on Pentatone ⨷ PTC5186 176 (70' · ADD)
　Ⓕ❍❍

It goes without saying that no one ensemble can unlock all the secrets contained in these quartets. The Quartetto Italiano's claims are strongest in the Op 18 Quartets. They offer eminently civilised, thoughtful and aristocratic readings. Their approach is reticent but they also convey a strong sense of making music in domestic surroundings. Quite frankly, you couldn't do very much better than this set. In the middle-period quartets the Italians are hardly less distinguished, even though there are times when the Végh offer deeper insights, as in the slow movement of Op 59 No 1. Taken in isolation, however, the Quartetto Italiano remain eminently satisfying both musically and as recorded sound. As far as sound quality is concerned, it's rich and warm. In Opp 74 and 95, they more than hold their own against all comers. These are finely proportioned readings, poised and articulate.

The gain in clarity because of the remastering entails a very slight loss of warmth in the middle register, but as recordings the late quartets, made between 1967 and 1969, can hold their own against their modern rivals. Not all of these received universal acclaim at the time of their first release. The opening fugue of Op 131 is too slow at four-in-the-bar and far more *espressivo* than it should be, but, overall, these performances still strike a finely judged balance between beauty and truth, and are ultimately more satisfying and searching than most of their rivals.

Complete String Quartets
Alexander Quartet (Zakarias Grafilo, Frederick Lifsitz *vns* Paul Yarbrough *va* Sandy Wilson *vc*)
Foghorn ⑨ CD2005 (8h 42' · DDD)　Ⓑ❍

There's a great deal to enjoy here: try the first couple of minutes of the First Quartet where you'll note the keen attack, an intelligent approach to dynamics and the teasing manipulation of musical rests, extending them by a millisecond or so, a ploy that the San Francisco-based Alexander Quartet use on various occasions throughout the cycle. All four instruments are by Francis Kuttner and carry labels dated 1987, the violins and cello being based on Stradivari models, the viola made to a personal specification. They sound wonderful, tonally firm yet warm and 'woody; with impressive potential for powerful projection. The overall approach is taut, animated and, wherever all four players are busily conversing, distinguished by a welcome refusal to promote any one particular voice.

The Op 18 set goes swimmingly, each piece granted its very different character, the amiable 'rocking-chair' opening of No 5, for example, lively but relaxed and with a real fizz to the opening *Allegro con brio* of No 6. Particularly fine is the veiled urgency of the C minor (No 4), where in the first movement the Alexanders' insistence on transparency pays off (too often inner lines coagulate) and the Haydnesque *Andante scherzoso* marks a playful and unexpected contrast. That element of the unexpected is a crucial feature of all 16 works, especially in the middle five, the three *Razumovskys* bearing the heaviest expressive load, in this case headed by No 2 which the Alexanders argue as persuasively and as forcefully as any recorded ensemble in the last 10 years.

Also impressive is the Alexander's candidly expressive way with the 'late' quartets, Op 130 ending with its revised finale rather than with its rightful *Grosse Fuge*, which in this case works because the 'parent' performance doesn't actually feel as if it's heading towards a full-blown catharsis. There have been more ethereal accounts of Op 131 but Op 127 is memorably sonorous and as heard here Op 135's high-point is its dramatic finale. And there's the heavenly, long-breathed *Molto adagio* of Op 132, skilfully sustained by the Alexanders, serving as both sick room and prayer before a delirious and – in this context – energetic thanksgiving for recovery (at bar 31). It's the sort of musical experience that changes lives.

The recordings have great presence and body but with such a hugely experienced engineer/producer as Judith Sherman at the desk one would hardly expect less. So it's a definite thumbs up. This set makes a partial claim on all fronts and were you to choose it above its rivals you'd not be short-changed, certainly not given the excellent sound.

Complete String Quartets
Végh Quartet (Sándor Végh, Sándor Zöldy vns
Georges Janzer va Paul Szábo vc)
Astrée Naïve ⑩ V4871 (8h 46′ · ADD)
Recorded 1974   Ⓑ**OO**

The Végh's classic accounts of the String Quartets are in a completely different league from any of their rivals: there's no cultivation of surface polish but there's no lack of elegance and finesse. Above all, there's no attempt to glamorise their sound. In Op 18 No 1 they find the *tempo giusto* right at the beginning and they find more depth in the slow movement than anyone else on record. Végh himself floats the melodic line in this movement in a most imaginative way and is wonderfully supported. In the civilised exchanges that open Op18 No 2 the Végh brings alight touch to bear, and has an elegance and wit that's almost unmatched and great refinement of tone. There were complaints of the bottom-heavy recording when it appeared on LP, and it's less transparent and lifelike than more modern recordings.

The *Rasumovsky* set is admirable for its alertness of articulation, rhythmic grasp and flexibility and its subtle range of tone-colour. The effortlessness with which the dialogue proceeds silences criticism. The Végh brings special insights to this

inexhaustible music. The style and the quality of perception seem so remarkable and so well sustained here that any deficiencies can be overlooked. There are lapses in tone and intonation, most of them on the part of the leader, yet what a musician he is, and what a remarkable guide to the visionary content of these quartets. Where the music demands most in such matters he's never wanting. These are neither the most 'perfect' nor the most sumptuously recorded accounts available, yet they are the deepest and most searching. When listening to them you're conscious only of Beethoven's own voice. The transfers give a slightly firmer focus and sharper detail, though that slight bottom-heaviness still remains.

String Quartets Op 18

CDDCA1111: String Quartets, Op 18 Nos 1-3
CDDCA1112: String Quartets, Op 18 Nos 4 & 5.
String Quartet in F, H34
CDDCA1113: String Quartet, Op 18 No 6.
String Quintet in C, Op 29ᵃ
The Lindsays (Peter Cropper, Ronald Birks vns
Roger Bigley va Bernard Gregor Smith vc) with
ᵃ**Louise Williams** va
ASV CDDCA1111-3 (oas: 78′, 66′, 58′ · DDD)   Ⓕ**O**

It's wonderful how The Lindsays, after a career of more than 30 years, could still sound so fresh and spontaneous. From the start of Op 18 No 1 we feel that every phrase is shaped individually, the music felt as it's being played. The dynamics are beautifully differentiated; *pianissimo* always has an altered sound compared with *piano*. Presenting the sense of the music and its emotions is always a priority, which leads to some daring interpretative decisions. The fast and fantastical finale of the Op 29 Quintet, with its scary *tremolos* and wild-sounding *rubato* in the first violin arpeggios is one example of a no-holds-barred approach that gets into the character of the music in a way that a more measured style couldn't. It's a splendid idea to include this neglected quintet as well as Beethoven's brilliant arrangement of the Op 14 No 1 Piano Sonata; the Quintet's rich, often complex, textures are relished, helping us to hear this work as a halfway house between the C major Quintets of Mozart and Schubert.

Despite the air of spontaneity, The Lindsays' interpretations of Op 18 remain very similar to those they offered us 20 years ago. The new recordings are certainly crisper and more immediate than their analogue predecessors, yet the sound has a warmth that enhances the often very atmospheric playing to be found, for instance, in the mysterious *pianissimo* passages at the ends of the slow movements of Nos 3 and 6. The main difference in the playing is that the new performances are generally faster, brighter and rhythmically lighter, with clearer articulation. The earlier version of No 2's highly ornamented *Adagio* has a beautiful sustained sound; in this recording Peter Cropper plays the melody with more fantasy, giving a powerful, rhetorical expression to each phrase. The slight increase in speed of most of the *allegros* brings them more into line with Beethoven's often challenging metronome marks: as a result there's more sparkle and excitement, and the light touch means there's rarely any sense of strain. The two Minuets, in Nos 4 and 5, benefit from being played faster; the passionate C minor character in No 4 is brought out most persuasively. For the *Adagio* of No 6 The Lindsays, in common with most other groups, adopt a more flowing speed than Beethoven's very slow suggestion, and their new recording is noticeably faster than the old. Yet, this is one of the most finely played movements in the set, with soft, sensuous tone, delicate ornamentation, and mysterious, tenuous unisons.

For the *Adagio* of No 1, on the other hand, Beethoven provides what seems a very fast tempo). The Lindsays play it a good deal slower – their earlier version has a particularly impressive, concentrated atmosphere. The 1933 Busch Quartet recording, however, shows how it's possible for the movement to sound even more impressive at a speed close to Beethoven's mark; the fiercely dramatic interruptions lose the somewhat ponderous effect they have when taken more slowly.

With these much-recorded quartets – in their way just as challenging to the performers as the later works – but there is no group that brings out better the startling range of the youthful Beethoven's imagination.

String Quartets, Op 18
Tokyo Quartet (Martin Beaver, Kikuei Ikeda *vns* Kazuhide Isolmura *va* Clive Greensmith *vc*)
Harmonia Mundi ② HMU90 7436/7 (146′ · DDD)
Ⓕ**OOO**

Enjoyable as other digital recordings of Beethoven's first quartets by (for example) the Takács and Lindsay Quartets are, this new Tokyo set just about pips all rivals to the post. The reason is primarily one of balance, not only within the group itself but also in terms of overall musical judgement – whether relating to tempo, dynamics or emphases, or simply the way the players combine a sense of classical style with an appreciation of Beethoven's startling originality. Even as early as No 1's pensive opening, you notice how skilfully rests are being gauged, contrasts in colour and inflection, too: the way the clipped first motif leads into its sweetly imploring extension a couple of bars later. The *Scherzo*'s skipping gait, incisive but lightly dispatched, is another source of pleasure, and so is the seemingly effortless swirl of the closing *Allegro*. The old quartet cliché about 'leaning together' is here a principal attribute. At times it could be just one person playing.

The qualifying *ma non tanto* of the C minor's opening *Allegro* is pointedly observed: dramatic impact is sustained while composure is maintained. The crispness of the *Andante scherzoso* and the cannily calculated crescendi at the start of the finale is oustanding. Few ensembles have

characterised the A major's cantering first idea as happily as the Tokyos do here, while the ethereal and texturally variegated middle movements anticipate the very different world of Beethoven's 'late' quartets. Beautifully blended recordings, too: if you're after a top-ranking digital set of Op 18, you couldn't do better.

String Quartets, Op 18
Takács Quartet (Edward Dusinberre, Károly Schranz *vns* Roger Tapping *va* András Fejér *vc*)
Decca ② 470 848-2DH2 (148′ · DDD)
Ⓕ**OO**▶

Robert Simpson disagreed with writers who believed that Beethoven's backward glances to Haydn and Mozart in his Op 18 set were so obvious as to distract attention from his own individuality. The Takács disagree, too. They concede the tradition, but those glances are far from obvious. From the beginning this is Beethoven through and through. The opening bars of Op 18 No 1 are soft yet terse. The answering calls are conciliatory, but the suspense is palpable. And, in a trenchant *Allegro con brio*, every *sforzando* is used to raise the tension, especially in the development. There are no concessions to surface beauty, and the message isn't subdued.

The Takács are particular about dynamics. The *fortissimo* chord near the finish of the slow movement is startling, and the build-up from *pianissimo* is as impressive as the drop back to the end. The *Adagio*, though directed to be both impassioned and tender, tends to be fervent, while fine inflections to the line ensure that the fairly swift tempo doesn't appear hurried. Conversely, the *Adagio ma non troppo* of No 6 is compassionately slow but continuously mobile: these musicians don't overlay textures with fatty tissue. Despite wide separation, ensemble is always close-knit. Just how close may be appreciated in the *scherzos*, which are tight and cohesive. That of No 4 has, in addition, precise give and take between the contrapuntal lines. The Takács play them in a way that leads the ear on without ignoring the expressive demands of the unusual marking *Andante scherzoso quasi Allegretto*.

String Quartets, Op 18 Nos 3 & 6
Leipzig Quartet (Andreas Seidel, Tilman Büning *vn* Ivo Bauer *vc* Matthias Moosdorf *vc*)
Dabringhaus und Grimm MDG307 0856-2
(51′ · DDD)
Ⓕ**O**

These are performances of exceptional finesse and integrity. Such qualities are immediately apparent at the opening of No 6 where, amid the splendidly vigorous, bustling atmosphere, they manage to give the answering phrases in violin and cello a gentler articulation. The second movement of this Quartet, though marked *Adagio ma non troppo*, has a surprisingly slow metronome mark, which the Leipzigers observe, their fine sense of line allowing the music to flow easily even at this spacious tempo, and they impart an especially chilling aspect to the sinister minor-key middle section.

The D major Quartet starts sweetly and gently, gradually and effortlessly picking up more liveliness as the movement progresses. The *Andante* flows easily, with notably rich, dark-hued tone in the passages in low register, and the third movement winningly combines a lively tempo with a slightly wistful manner.

In short, these must be among the most persuasively played, finely recorded Op 18 performances available. There are places where you might prefer other versions – The Lindsays' spontaneity in the finale of No 6, or the joyful virtuosity of the Emerson in the last movement of No 3 – but, overall, the Leipzig Quartet is as satisfying as any.

String Quartets Op 59, 'Razumovsky'

String Quartets, Op 59 Nos 1-3. String Quartet Op 74
Takács Quartet (Edward Dusinberre, Károly Schranz
vns Roger Tapping *va* András Fejér *vc*)
Decca ② 470 847-2DH2 (144' ·DDD) Ⓕ❶❶❶↦

The Takács do a fine job here: controlled, well paced and impeccably balanced. They manage to balance the music's vertical and horizontal aspects beautifully, long-breathed contrapuntal lines gliding serenely above a sharp, occasionally dramatic accompaniment – masterful playing indeed and typical of this first lap of the Takács' projected Beethoven cycle.

The Takács hold both line and rhythm in Op 59 No 1 with imposing control. Their manner of badinage in the mischievously hocketing second movement is more intense than the rival account by The Lindsays, and their tempi consistently swifter. In Op 59 No 3 the Takács approximate the Busch in a broad, soulful *Andante con moto*. And in the fugal finale they're almost on a par with the Emersons, whose demonic DG account is one of the most viscerally exciting quartet recordings around. The finale of Op 59 No 2 is a tautly braced canter whereas in the *Scherzo* of the *Harp*, Op 74, taken at a hair-raising lick, the Takács make obsessive music of the dominating four-note idea – and there's absolutely no let up in tension for the cello-led trio. Indeed, the Takács' *Harp* is one of the finest ever recorded, with fiery reportage of the first movement's central development and a delightfully playful account of the finale, the 'tipsy' first variation especially.

The jewel, then, is Op 59 No 2, though you'd be hard pressed to find a rival digital set of Opp 59 and 74 that's better overall. Andrew Keener's recording (St George's, Bristol) reports a realistic 'edge' within a sympathetic acoustic. You won't find a finer quartet recording anywhere.

String Quartets, Op 59 – Nos 2 & 3
Brodsky Quartet (Andrew Haveron, Ian Belton *vns*
Paul Cassidy *va* Jacqueline Thomas *vc*)

Brodsky Records BRD3502 (71' · DDD) Ⓕ

This isn't just another *Rasumovsky* recording: the Brodskys manage to sound thoroughly individual without ever seeming eccentric or one-sided. They pay close attention to detail – balance, articulation and accentuation are all carefully controlled – but as part of a performance full of conviction. One might argue that the interpretation is in places excessively literal: in the second quartet's first movement, for instance, where Beethoven writes *staccato* dots only at the start of a passage, it seems likely he intended the same articulation to persist. But the Brodsky performance, becoming smoother after the first bar, is convincing enough to prompt one to question such an assumption.

For the majority of movements the Brodskys stay close to Beethoven's metronome indications: the extraordinarily swift *Presto* finale of No 2 is revelatory and, in No 3, the flowing *Andante con moto quasi allegretto*, and the following Minuet, spacious and truly *grazioso*, would surely have pleased the composer. No 2's *Molto adagio* moves serenely onwards at Beethoven's suggested 60 beats per minute: it's a lovely performance, but there's no doubt that groups adopting a slower speed – the Takács or the Busch, for example – achieve greater intensity. The Brodskys don't always observe the metronome marks, however. For No 3's finale the tempo is slower than in many versions; but what's lost in brilliance is gained in dramatic power. And in No 2's opening *Allegro*, moderate and unhurried, we may miss something of the music's impulsive, disturbed character but can focus on a wealth of expressive detail. So it's well worth hearing this, however many *Razumovsky*s you have on your shelves.

Late String Quartets

String Quartets, Opp 95, 127, 130, 131, 132 & 135.
Grosse Fuge.
Takács Quartet (Edward Dusinberre, Károly Schranz
vns Roger Tapping *va* András Fejér *vc*)
Decca ③ 470 849-2DH3 (3h 40' · DDD) Ⓕ❶❶❶↦

 Interpreters of the late quartets have to convey what at times sounds like a stream of musical consciousness while respecting the many written markings. The Takács do better than most. For openers, they had access to the new Henle Edition and have made use of some textual changes – nothing too drastic but encouraging evidence of a good musical conscience. In Op 130 they take the long first-movement exposition repeat, using the *Grosse Fuge* as the rightful finale (Beethoven's original intention) which, in the context of their fiery reading of the fugue, works well. Contemporary incredulity at the sheer scale and complexity of the fugue caused Beethoven to offer a simpler alternative finale, in which they again play the repeat, which helps balance the 'alternative' structure.

BEETHOVEN LATE STRING QUARTETS – IN BRIEF

Quartetto Italiano
Philips ③ 464 684-2PM3 (216' · ADD)   Ⓜ❶❶🅑⟶
'Civilised', 'aristocratic', 'thoughtful' are some of the words often used to describe this great Italian ensemble's approach. Their late quartets were recorded in the late 1960s and still sound very fine. A notable achievement.

Talich Quartet
Calliope CAL9637/8/9 (213' · DDD)   Ⓕ❶
A powerfully intimate set which conveys the impression of four outstanding chamber musicians playing for each other – music-making eavesdropped upon, rather than projected to an imagined audience. A fine set.

Busch Quartet
Pearl mono ③ GEMS0053 (220' · ADD)   Ⓜ❶
A wonderfully human and humane experience: this is quartet-playing of towering achievement that satisfies at every level. The sound, from the 1930s, is evidently somewhat antique but the passion and understanding shines down the years.

Lindsay Quartet
ASV ③ CDDCS403 (220' · DDD)   Ⓜ❶
A *Gramophone* Award-winner back in the 1980s and deservedly so, for this is very impressive quartet playing. The Lindsays have lived long with this music and, though their newer cycle may plumb deeper, this first set is still a notable achievement.

Hollywood Quartet   Ⓗ
Testament ③ SBT3082 (193' · ADD)   Ⓕ❶
A very fine set from the late 1950s featuring the superb Los Angeles-based quartet. Their technical address is considerable and, unlike some American quartets from later generations, they don't overproject this music – it remains appropriately and rightly 'chamber music'.

Takács Quartet
Decca ③ 470 849-2DH3 (200' · DDD)   Ⓕ❶❶❶🅑⟶
Ⓖ A staggering achievement to crown a magnificent cycle: the Takács evidently appreciate this music both as musical argument and as sound, and it shows in every bar of these beautifully recorded performances.

Alban Berg Quartet
EMI ③ 768230-2 (193' · ADD)   Ⓕ❶🅑⟶
A quartet that has always divided opinion: can their playing be *too* beautiful? This set from their second (live) cycle has an extraordinary sense of concentration. There may not be the anger and anguish of the Takács's performances but they have clearly thought long and hard about this amazing music.

The Takács evidently appreciate this music both as musical argument and as sound. Try their glassy *sul ponticello* at the end of Op 131's *Scherzo*, or the many instances where plucked and bowed passages are fastidiously balanced. Attenuated inflections are honoured virtually to the letter, textures carefully differentiated, musical pauses intuitively well-timed and inner voices nearly always transparent.

This set completes one of the best available Beethoven quartet cycles, possibly the finest in an already rich digital market, more probing than the pristine Emersons or Alban Bergs (live), more refined than the gutsy and persuasive Lindsays, and less consciously stylised than the Juilliards (and always with the historic Busch Quartet as an essential reference).

String Quartets, Opp 95 & 132
Talich Quartet (Petr Messiereur, Jan Kvapil *vns* Jan Talich *va* Evzen Rattai *vc*)
Calliope Approche CAL5639 (68' · ADD)
Recorded 1977-79   Ⓜ❶

After the expansive canvas of the Op 59 quartets and the *Eroica*, Beethoven's F minor Quartet, Op 95, displays musical thinking of the utmost compression. The first movement is a highly concentrated sonata design, which encompasses in its four minutes almost as much drama as a full-scale opera. With it comes one of the greatest masterpieces of his last years, the A minor, Op 132. The isolation wrought first by his deafness and secondly, by the change in fashion of which he complained in the early 1820s, forced Beethoven in on himself. Op-132 with its other-worldly *Heiliger Dankgesang*, written on his recovery from an illness, is music neither of the 1820s nor of Vienna, it belongs to that art which transcends time and place. Though other performances may be technically more perfect, these are interpretations that come closer to the spirit of this great music than any other on CD.

The Talich Quartet's readings bring a total dedication to this music: their performances are innocent of artifice and completely selfless. There's no attempt to impress with their own virtuosity or to draw attention to themselves. The recordings are eminently faithful and natural, not overbright but the effect is thoroughly pleasing.

String Quartets, Opp 95 & 127
The Lindsays (Peter Cropper, Ronald Birks *vns* Robin Ireland *va* Bernard Gregor-Smith *vc*)
ASV CDDCA1116 (59' · DDD)   Ⓕ❶❶❶

The prospect of actually listening to Beethoven never loses its appeal. It's also clear that The Lindsays approach Beethoven's quartets with undiminished enthusiasm. This is immediately apparent in the physical energy with which they attack the opening of Op 95. Along with enthusiasm comes a deep understanding, expressed most strikingly in the way their fine internal balance is adapted to allow important subsidiary lines to make their effect. Nothing as crude as making a decision to 'bring out' an inner part; just the feeling that each player knows how much pressure is needed to fulfil a line's potential. Such expressive detail allied to a lovely *dolce* sound makes a contrapuntal movement like Op 95's *Allegretto* especially memorable.

The Lindsays aren't the smoothest, slickest ensemble to have recorded this music. In the *Scherzo* of Op 95 the Quartetto Italiano's tone is more blemish-free, and the fast coda to this quartet's finale sees the Emerson Quartet create a more brilliant, sparkling impression. But such things only become noticeable with comparative listening; if you stick with The Lindsays what will impress you is the splendid rhythm and drive of the Op 95 *Scherzo*, the magnificent, rich sound, without any sense of aggressiveness or strain, at the start of Op 127, the way the expression is sustained throughout the great *adagio* variations of Op 127, and the delicate, magical atmosphere established at the beginning of this quartet's final section. A hugely compelling set.

String Quartets, Op 59 No 2, Op 130
Talich Quartet (Petr Messiereur, Jan Kvapil vns Jan Talich va Evzen Rattai vc)
Calliope CAL5637 (73' · ADD). Recorded 1977-80 Ⓕ

The advantage of this Talich recording is that it couples a masterpiece from Beethoven's middle period, the great E minor Quartet, Op 59 No 2, with one of the greatest of his last years. The B flat, Op 130, was the third of the late quartets to be composed and at its first performance in 1826 its last movement, the *Grosse Fuge*, baffled his contemporaries. Later that same year, he substituted the present finale. The Talich Quartet has a no less impressive technical command than other ensembles but theirs are essentially private performances, which are a privilege to overhear, rather than the overprojected 'public' accounts that so often appear on record nowadays.

String Quartets, Opp 132 & 135
Cleveland Quartet (William Preucil, Peter Salaff vns James Dunham va Paul Katz vc)
Telarc CD80427 (69' · DDD) Ⓕ

The Cleveland Quartet are upholders of tradition, rather than seekers after new truths. One of this ensemble's most notable characteristics is its rich, warm tone, well captured here. The first movement of the A minor Quartet, Op 132, has a level of emotional commitment that's quite compelling – all the details of this complex music fall into place and contribute to the overall effect.

If the rest isn't quite so outstanding it's still very good, with a lovely swinging rhythm to the second movement, and delightfully sprightly accounts of the *Andante* episodes in the slow movement – absolutely 'feeling new strength', as Beethoven's caption puts it. Their Op 135 is also very impressive. The *Lento* is deeply felt, their

rich sound coming into its own. And the finale must be one of the best versions on record – spirited, touching, playful, as the music's mood demands.

Beethoven String Quartet Op 135
(arr Prooijen) **Walton** Sonata for Strings
Amsterdam Sinfonietta
Channel Classics CCSSA23005 (55' · DDD/DSD) Ⓕ

As the booklet asks, why Beethoven and Walton? The answer is, the Walton has become a favourite work with this superb Dutch ensemble and it was felt appropriate to couple it with another arrangement of a string quartet, the last Beethoven wrote. Walton made the imaginative arrangement of his A minor Quartet at the prompting of Neville Marriner, who wanted a work for the Academy of St Martin in the Fields. The arrangement of the Beethoven by Marijn van Prooijen similarly adapts the original without inflating it.

As the booklet-note says, the Amsterdam Sinfonietta aim to preserve the intimate character of the works. In this they contrast their approach to that of Bernstein and the VPO (DG), in which he uses a full body of strings. With the Amsterdam players showing the give-and-take, ebb-and-flow of small chamber groups, they achieve rare refinement and natural warmth.

The bite and precision of the Amsterdam account is most impressive, with the rhythmic lift of the *Scherzo* and of the finale after the ominous opening bringing a joyful lightness. Yet it is the sublime *Lento* slow movement which achieves the greatest heights in playing of hushed dedication. This new version of the Walton is more intimate than the LPO full-strings Chandos rival. It is true that Walton freely sets the full ensemble in contrast with passages for solo strings, as at the very start, but the Amsterdam performance brings out that terracing of sound more clearly, helped by the refined recording. As in the Beethoven, the heart of the performance comes in the lovely *Lento* movement.

The Sonata emerges as a fair match for other great British string pieces – Elgar's *Introduction and Allegro* and Vaughan Williams's *Tallis* Fantasia, for example. It's a work which neatly spans the gap between the early Walton, passionate and electrifying, and his later refined and carefully considered style.

Piano Trios

Op 1: No 1 in E flat; **No 2** in G; **No 3** in C minor
Op 11 in B flat
Op 38 in E flat
Op 70: No 1 in D, 'Ghost'; **No 2** in E flat
Op 97 in B flat, 'Archduke'

Complete Piano Trios
Piano Trios, Opp 1, 11, 38, 70, 97; WoO38 & 39.
Variations, Opp 44 & 121a. Trio in D (after Symphony

No 2). Triosatz
Beaux Arts Trio (Isidore Cohen *vn* Bernard
Greenhouse *vc* Menahem Pressler *pf*)
Philips ⑤ 468 411-2 (356' · DDD/ADD)
Recorded 1980   Ⓜ●

Growing older doesn't always mean growing
wiser, though in the case of the Beaux Arts
Trio and Beethoven the passage of some 20-
odd years signalled a rare and fruitful broadening of musical vision. In the period between
their two recordings of the Beethoven Piano
Trios there had been just one personnel
change – Daniel Guilet was replaced by ex-
Juilliard Quartet second violin Isidore Cohen.
The principal route of the Beaux Arts' interpretative development was forged by the pianist, Menahem Pressler, whose increased tonal
subtlety and willingness to widen expressive
dynamics lent the trio a whole new palette of
colours. Just listen to the opening of Op 1
No 2's ineffably deep *Largo con espressione*.

Heard superficially, there's not that much in it
between the Pressler of the 1960s and of 1980,
but labour the comparison and you'll soon hear
the benefits of a more variegated touch and a
freer approach to phrasing. There are many
other plus-points. The *Archduke*, for example, is
at once softer-grained and more wistful than its
energetic predecessor and you couldn't hope for
a happier rendition of the Septet transcription
(the E flat Trio, Op 38).

Philips' sound quality is just as good as the
original: clear, full-bodied and well balanced.
Given the price, the superior sound quality,
the comprehensive coverage of repertoire and
the profundity of the Beaux Art's later interpretative standpoint, this new reissue justifies a
front-ranking recommendation. So much is said
with so much feeling – and so little fuss – that
you're drawn back again and again.

Piano Trios – selected

Piano Trios, Op 1 Nos 1 & 2; WoO38
Florestan Trio (Susan Tomes *pf*
Anthony Marwood *vn* Richard Lester *vc*)
Hyperion CDA67393 (72' · DDD)   Ⓕ●Ⓑ⟶

Piano Trios. Op 1 No 3; Op 11. Variations in E flat, Op
44
Florestan Trio
Hyperion CDA67466 (61' · DDD)   Ⓕ●●Ⓑ⟶

Piano Trios, Op 70 Nos 1 & 2. Allegretto, WoO39
Florestan Trio
Hyperion CDA67327 (60' · DDD)   Ⓕ●Ⓑ⟶

These three discs comprise the Florestan Trio's
Beethoven series. Their thoughtfulness throughout has been impressive; their overall style
avoids heaviness, keeping the textures light and
airy, and giving every phrase individual life and
character. Occasionally the liveliness can seem
relentless, but their bubbling vitality is a natural
response to Beethoven's inventiveness. And

their care for detail makes the early and not fully
characteristic Variations in E flat (Op 44) into an
absorbing, thoroughly entertaining piece. The
recorded sound and balance are equally fine.

String Trios

Op 3 in E flat.
Op 9: No 1 in G; **No 2** in D; **No 3** in C minor

String Trio, Op 3; Serenade in D, Op 8
Leopold String Trio (Marianne Thorsen *vn*
Sarah-Jane Bradley *va* Kate Gould *vc*)
Hyperion CDA67253 (73' · DDD)   Ⓕ●Ⓑ⟶

String Trios, Op 9
Leopold String Trio
Hyperion CDA67254 (77' · DDD)   Ⓕ●Ⓑ⟶
Both discs available through Hyperion's Archive Service

The Leopold String Trio demonstrate the kind
of virtues that come from long study together:
polished ensemble, excellent intonation and
notably consistent and well-conceived interpretations. Just occasionally the viola is swamped by
the outer voices, but overall it's a particularly
well-balanced and recorded set. They show that
a restrained style can bring out the inward aspect
to the music. On the fourth track of Op 8, where
Beethoven alternates a sombre *Adagio* with a
facetiously jolly *Scherzo*, the stark yet gentle
Leopold playing of the slow music expresses
more pathos and melancholy than the intensity
of other versions. And the Leopold's care and
respect for the text also tips the balance in its
favour – in Op 3's second Minuet, for example,
Marianne Thorsen's beautiful and exact interpretation is winning. In Op 9 No 1's *Scherzo*,
another splendidly poised and spirited reading,
there's a special bonus – a second Trio, omitted
from most editions. It's an attractive bit of music
and gives the movement a new dimension.

String Quintets

String Quintets, Opp 4 & 29
Nash Ensemble (Marianne Thorsen,
Malin Broman *vns* Lawrence Power,
Philip Dukes *vas* Paul Watkins *vc*)
Hyperion CDA67693 (63' · DDD)   Ⓕ●

The Nash Ensemble here give flawless, superbly
disciplined performances of Beethoven's two
string quintets. Op 4 is the composer's transcription of the wind octet that he wrote in
emulation of Mozart's great examples of *Harmoniemusik*, the wind octets in E flat and C minor.
Op 29, on the other hand, is Beethoven's first
completely original exploitation of the genre.

It is fascinating to find how Beethoven developed his arguments by rewriting wind music for
strings, as Richard Wigmore explains in his
excellent note. Key modulations are more
adventurous and textures lightened, making this
by far the finer work. The Nash players, care-

fully balanced and helped by the transparent recording, bring out the inner lines with admirable clarity. The slow movement, marked simply andante, is free-flowing with a warmly lyrical violin solo, while the mis-titled *Menuetto più allegretto* is the most dashing scherzo, full of wit, and the finale is a dance-like rondo. The performance of Op 29 in C brings similar qualities, with clean separation and well chosen speeds on the fast side. What especially comes out is the originality of the finale, with its bizarre opening, chromatic passages and striking dynamic contrasts. Warmly welcomed for its first-rate sound and immaculate performances.

Cello Sonatas

No 1 Op 5 No 1 in F; **No 2** Op 5 No 2 in G minor; **No 3** Op 69 in A; **No 4** Op 102 No 1 in C; **No 5** Op 102 No 2 in D

Cello Sonatas, Op 102 Nos 1 & 2. Duo in E flat, WoO32. Variations on 'See the conqu'ring hero comes'
Maria Kliegol vc **Tabea Zimmermann** va **Nina Tichman** pf
Naxos 8 555787 (59' · DDD)   Ⓢ**O**➪

Complete Works for Cello and Piano
Miklós Perényi vc **András Schiff** pf
ECM New Series ② 472 401-2 (151' · DDD) Ⓕ**OO**➪

Maria Kliegel and Nina Tichman conclude their three-volume Beethoven exploration with fine-toned, vigorous performances of the last two sonatas. Most sets of the cello- and-piano music fit onto two CDs; Naxos's more liberal allowance permits the inclusion of extra items, in this case the Duo, with 'Two Obbligato Eyeglasses', for viola and cello; not, perhaps, one of the young Beethoven's finest achievements, but most imaginatively written for the two instruments. Tabea Zimmermann's spirited playing prompts regret that Beethoven never wrote a *concertante* work for viola.

In the sonatas and variations Tichman and Kliegel make a well-matched pair. They favour firm, rounded tone and strong, expressive projection, and are equally convincing in the passionate A minor *Allegro* that forms the second part of the Fourth Sonata's first movement, and in the preceding *Andante*, where warm sound and soaring lines perfectly express the music's romantic spirit. What's missing, perhaps, is a range of tone colour that can suggest mystery or solemnity. And in the variations, Kliegel is inclined to phrase in a smooth, somewhat bland way, where a more articulated, 18th-century style would be more in order. The passages in dialogue between the instruments, however, are most beautifully realised.

Turning to András Schiff and Miklós Perényi, the first impression is of a much lighter sound. The piano, indeed, might seem quite brittle, if it weren't for Schiff's beautiful *cantabile* touch and his exceptional ability to balance chords – Beet-

hoven's gruffest harmonies form part of a texture that's richly coloured and always clear. It's the kind of thing we normally only experience with the best period-instrument players.

In contrast to the finely matched pairing of Tichman and Kliegel, Perényi and Schiff appear as distinct, contrasting characters – Perényi suave and elegant, and though demonstrating a wide expressive range, always staying within the boundaries of what is polished and unexaggerated, Schiff much more volatile and extreme. In the high-spirited finales of the first two sonatas you can easily imagine the tempestuous young composer performing before the King of Prussia.

But this contrast of styles doesn't result in unbalanced performances. There are, maybe, one or two places (in the Third Sonata's first movement, for example) where where you might welcome more intensity from Perényi, but overall his playing has all the vigour and commitment one could wish for. And where it's necessary to achieve perfect unity, the two come together in the most inspiring way. The most remarkable instance of this is Op 102's fugal finale, a movement that's often been perceived as impressive rather than attractive, but these two artists match articulation, note-lengths, volume and tone colour in such a way as to make the music seem beautiful as well as uplifting. An outstanding set.

Complete Works for Cello and Piano
Adrian Brendel vc **Alfred Brendel** pf
Philips ② 475 379-2PX2 (148' · DDD) Ⓕ**OOO**➪

Ⓖ The Brendels, father and son, give us Beethoven's complete works for piano and cello. You'll have to search long and hard to hear performances of a comparable warmth and humanity or joy in music-making. Sumptuously recorded and lavishly presented (including engaging family photographs), the sonatas are offered in a sequence that gives the listener an increased sense of Beethoven's awe-inspiring scope and range.

CD 1 juxtaposes early, middle and late sonatas with a joyous encore in the Variations on Mozart's 'Ein Mädchen oder Weibchen'. CD 2 gives us the Variations on 'See the conqu'ring hero comes' from Handel's *Judas Maccabaeus*, continues with the remaining two sonatas and ends with the other *Magic Flute* Variations, on 'Bei Männern'.

Pianist and cellist are united by a rare unity of purpose and stylistic consistency, whether in strength and exuberance, an enriching sense of complexity or in other-worldly calm (often abruptly terminated). What eloquence they achieve in the opening *Adagio* of the Second Sonata, what musical energy in the following *Allegro molto tanto presto*, instances where Beethoven's volatility is always tempered by the Brendels' seasoned musicianship.

In Op 102 No 2 Beethoven's far-reaching and still bewildering utterance, there is a quiet strength and lucidity; time and again a direction such as *Allegro vivace* is exactly that and not stretched, as in more urgently, even neurotically, propelled performances. Their glowing expressiveness at 10'57" in Sonata No 3 is 'interior' yet never at the expense of impetus, and Adrian Brendel's *ad libitum* lead into the concluding *Allegro* is memorable – improvisatory and relaxed. Both players display rhythmic resilience in the final Rondo from Sonata No 1, and what open-hearted delight and *joie de vivre* there is in the sets of variations.

The Brendels offer an invaluable additions to the recordings of these masterpieces.

Complete Works for Cello and Piano
Antonio Meneses vc **Menahem Pressler** pf
Avie ② AV2103 (154' · DDD)   Ⓕ**OO**B⇥

Between them, Menahem Pressler and Antonio Meneses offer us a rare listening privilege, with playing that is at once intimate, conversational, reposeful, intelligent and, above all, simple in its musical intentions, which are, or seem to be, to present the music without excessive interpretative intervention. Not that these are in any way bland performances: Pressler may now be a venerable 84 but his wisdom isn't at a high premium, either mentally or physically: both his mind and to a large extent his fingers are still remarkably agile. Maybe the call to arms in the first movement of the Third Sonata, Op 69, sounds less forceful than on some rival versions, but it certainly doesn't drag and the crucial virtue is concentration: throughout this set both players hold the line without letting it flag and although moments of rapt intensity are far too plentiful to catalogue in detail.

The outer movements of both Op 102 sonatas achieve clarity without clatter (some pianists force an excessively hard tone here) but if you fancy a prime sampling of Meneses/Pressler magic, then sample the *Conqu'ring Hero Variations*, starting with the chorale-like piano variation then picking up the tempo before relaxing again for some slow-breathing dialogue. There's nothing sensational about it, no showing off or theatrical arching of eyebrows, just the joy of hearing two seasoned players getting it absolutely right. A rare privilege, and a credible, gently stated alternative to more forthright sets.

Cello Sonatas – No 1, Op 5 No 1;
No 2, Op 5 No 2; No 3, Op 69
Daniel Müller-Schott vc **Angela Hewitt** pf
Hyperion CDA67633 (78' · DDD)   Ⓕ**O**B⇥

Daniel Müller-Schott and Angela Hewitt give Beethoven's first three cello sonatas a nimble and colourful outing. Their musical 'dress' sense is immaculate, with never so much as a quaver out of place, no hint of ungainliness or aggression and a cultivated sound world which, whether presented singly or in duet, is consistently smooth. Their duo engagement is compelling and their repertoire of gestures – vivid

dynamics, tiny instances of expressive *rubato*, suspended breathing and so on – is exceedingly broad. Sometimes the reverie might be considered a little overplayed. At the opening of the A major Third Sonata's brief *Adagio* third movement Hewitt's dreamily sculpted phrasing verges on sounding Chopinesque, though poetic in effect and poignantly responded to by Müller-Schott.

These performances are full of interesting ideas: there's rarely a bar without a subtle bend somewhere along the line and yet the various *allegros* are sparky in the best sense of the term, rhythmically crisp and alert, especially the rondo finale of the G minor Sonata, which is deliciously pointed by Hewitt. Those in search of a more overtly masculine approach to Beethoven would probably be better off elsewhere but Müller-Schott and Hewitt provide a bright, decorative antidote to their more austere rivals. The recorded sound is beautifully balanced.

Additional recommendation

Cello Sonata No 3, Op 69
Coupled with: Sonata in E flat, Op 64; 12 Variations on 'Ein Mädchen oder Weibchen', Op 66
Kliegel vc **Tichman** pf
Naxos 8 555786 (77' · DDD)   ⓈB⇥
A sound recommendation, both for the rare Op 64 (an arrangement of the Op 3 String Trio) and as an excellent bargain version of the more familiar items. Kliegel and Tichman give highly sympathetic performances; in the A major Sonata their playing has a breadth and confidence that easily encompasses the music's great emotional range.

Variations for Cello

12 Variations on Handel's 'See the conqu'ring   Ⓟ
hero comes', WoO45. 12 Variations on Mozart's 'Ein Mädchen oder Weibchen', Op 66. Seven Variations on Mozart's 'Bei Männern, welche Liebe fühlen', WoO46. Horn Sonata, Op 17 (arr vc)
Pieter Wispelwey vc **Lois Shapiro** fp
Channel Classics CCS6494 (45' · DDD)   Ⓕ**O**

There are only 45 minutes of it, but this recital teems with fresh insights in the irresistible serendipity of its playing. Lois Shapiro partners Wispelwey's 1701 cello on a 1780 Viennese fortepiano whose wiry energies she unleashes in an attention-grabbing opening theme for Handel's *See the conqu'ring hero comes*. Her bright-eyed first variation glints as phrases dart from dynamic shadow to light and back again. Then the cello's lean, slightly astringent voice makes itself felt in no uncertain terms before the keyboard gets its own back in mercurial scale passages. The players' delight in teasing, sparring and debating with each other comes into its own in the variations on *Ein Mädchen oder Weibchen*. The theme itself struts forward cheekily, only to peck its way through the first variation, before the cello makes the most of the wry harmonic subtext of the second. In the seventh, one half of a shared phrase caresses and preens the other; the 10th casts the shadow of Papageno's noose. Each player's imagination and technique is tested to the full in an absorbing account of the more abstracted *Bei Männern* variations. The world of *Singspiel* isn't far away, either, in this performance of the Sonata, Op 17: Wispelwey and Shapiro summon up the nascent world of Marzelline and Jacquino in their quick, ardent responses to the music and to each other.

Violin Sonatas

Op 12: No 1 in D; **No 2** in A; **No 3** in E flat
Op 23 in A minor **Op 24** in F, 'Spring'
Op 30: No 1 in A; **No 2** in C minor; **No 3** in G
Op 47 in A, 'Kreutzer' **Op 96** in G

Complete Violin Sonatas
Itzhak Perlman *vn* **Vladimir Ashkenazy** *pf*
Decca Ovation ④ 421 453-2DM4 (3h 59' · ADD)
Recorded 1973 75   ⓂⓄ◐🅑

Although Beethoven designated these works as 'for piano and violin', following Mozart's example, it's unlikely that he thought of the piano as leading the proceedings, or the violin either, for that matter: both instruments are equal partners, and in that sense this is true chamber music. Perlman and Ashkenazy are artists of the first rank and there's much pleasure to be derived from their set. Such an imaginative musician as Ashkenazy brings great subtlety to these works composed by a supreme pianist-composer. And the better the pianist is in this music, the better does the violinist play. Discernment is matched by spontaneity and the whole series is remarkably fine, while their celebrated performance of the *Kreutzer* Sonata has quite superb eloquence and vitality. The recording boasts unusually truthful violin sound capturing all the colour of Perlman's playing.

Complete Violin Sonatas   Ⓗ
Wolfgang Schneiderhan *vn* **Wilhelm Kempff** *pf*
DG The Originals ③ 463 605-2GOR3 (3h 56' · ADD)
Recorded 1952   ⓂⓄ🅑

In the 1950s these recordings would have probably given a very up-to-date impression; the playing is extremely clean – there's never a hint of sentimental violin slides or over-use of the sustaining pedal. But nearly half a century later, perhaps we're more conscious of the old-world virtues – Schneiderhan's beautiful *legato* bowing and gentle vibrato, Kempff's full, unforced tone, and a flexible approach from both artists, with finely graded *ritardandos* and subtle variations of tempo.
Though not regular sonata partners, Kempff and Schneiderhan have an admirable collective sense of rhythm. They favour moderate, poised speeds, and so tend to miss something of the

impulsive quality of early Beethoven. And, in the same way, their dedication to pure, well-balanced, unforced tone means that the grotesque element in such a movement as the finale of Op 30 No 2 is underplayed. It's a delight to hear them find so many ways of interpreting Beethoven's frequent *sforzando* markings, from sharp accents to the expressive melodic emphasis they give to the theme of the *Kreutzer* Sonata's variations. But quite often Kempff downgrades or ignores these accents, smoothing away any angular corners, and this tendency towards blandness occasionally leads to disappointingly inexpressive playing, at the start of the *Spring* Sonata, for instance, where Schneiderhan's beautifully lyrical opening doesn't elicit a comparable response from the piano.

If there are a few let-downs, however, there are far more moments where the characteristically moderate, unexaggerated approach bears rich dividends. Schneiderhan's beautiful singing tone is a constant delight; witness the intensely vocal style of Op 24's finale and the luminous sound of his high register in the last of the *Kreutzer* variations. Similarly, Kempff's continual care for clear textures and his finely balanced chordal playing seem to offer glimpses into the essence of Beethoven's thought. The mono sound is beautifully clear and well balanced.

Violin Sonatas – No 1, Op 12 No 1; No 4,
Op 23; No 7, Op 30 No 2; No 8, Op 30 No 3
Alina Ibragimova *vn* **Cédric Tiberghien** *pf*
Wigmore Hall Live WHLIVE0036 (82' · DDD)
Recorded live 2009   ⓂⓄ◐🅑

These performances are brimful of life; there's a sense of joy and freedom, with fast passagework that's exceptionally clear and even, and expressiveness that ranges from extreme delicacy to passionate intensity. The liveliness has another aspect, too: Alina Ibragimova and Cédric Tiberghien have clearly thought about each phrase, every expression mark, with such detailed individuality as to banish routine interpretation. As a result, the character of each sonata emerges with vivid clarity – the outer movements of the First Sonata show the extraordinary impulsiveness of the young Beethoven's creativity, while in Op 23's finale subtle modifications of tempo accentuate the sense of constant surprise as the music changes direction. Ibragimova's way with the accompanying passages deserves special praise: cutting vibrato to a minimum, she blends perfectly with the piano's left hand, and in Op 30 No 3's middle movement her change of tone on taking up the melodic line is most beautiful. In Op 30 No 2, the most substantial of these sonatas, we can feel the strong emotional involvement of both players, not through ultra-intense tone or heavy emphasis but by means of rhythmic drive (in the first movement) and through long-term phrasing – in the *Adagio* we feel each extended phrase as a single shape. As live performances these are remarkably free from blemishes but whether or not they've been cleaned up with retakes, the sense of occasion, of living the music as it unfolds, is very strong.

Piano Sonatas

No 1 in F minor, Op 2 No 1 **No 2** in A, Op 2 No 2 **No 3** in C, Op 2 No 3 **No 4** in E flat, Op 7 **No 5** in C, Op 10 No 1 **No 6** in F, Op 10 No 2 **No 7** in D, Op 10 No 3 **No 8** in C minor, Op 13, 'Pathétique' **No 9** in E, Op 14 No 1 **No 10** in G, Op 14 No 2 **No 11** in B flat, Op 22 **No 12** in A flat, Op 26 **No 13** in E flat, Op 27 No 1, 'Quasi una fantasia' **No 14** in C sharp minor, Op 27 No 2, 'Moonlight' **No 15** in D, Op 28, 'Pastoral' **No 16** in G, Op 31 No 1 **No 17** in D minor, Op 31 No 2 'Tempest' **No 18** in E flat, Op 31 No 3 **No 19** in G minor, Op 49 No 1 **No 20** in G, Op 49 No 2 **No 21** in C minor, Op 53, 'Waldstein' **No 22** in F, Op 4 **No 23** in F minor, Op 57 'Appassionata' **No 24** in F sharp, Op 78 **No 25** in G, Op 79 **No 26** in E flat, Op 81a, 'Les adieux' **No 27** in E minor, Op 90 **No 28** in A, Op 101 **No 29** in B flat, Op 106, 'Hammerklavier' **No 30** in E, Op 109 **No 31** in A flat, Op 110 **No 32** in C minor, Op 111

Piano Sonatas Nos 1-32
Richard Goode pf
Nonesuch ⑩ 7559 79328-2 (10h 8' · DDD)   Ⓜ**OO**

You may have a doubt as to whether all the playing represents everything Goode is capable of: sometimes he disappoints, slightly, by appearing to hold back from the listener the boldness and fullness of communication the greatest players achieve. You might say that, for all their insight and illumination, some of the performances lack the final leap and a degree of transcendence. But his playing is so very likeable: the finish, technical and musical, is immaculate, but on top of that he's exciting. His sound always makes you listen. His feeling for it and for fine gradations of sound from one end of his wide dynamic range to the other are those of a virtuoso, and inform everything he does. When he's more obviously on virtuoso territory, he responds to the demands for brilliance and thrilling projection as to the manner born. He's constantly inside the music, and what a lively, cultivated, lucid and stimulating guide he is. There's nothing diffident or half-hearted about the way he makes this cycle of Beethoven resound wonderfully, the earlier sonatas appearing no less masterly or characteristic of their composer than the later. His interpretation of the A major Sonata, Op 101, is one of the finest ever put on record.

Piano Sonatas Nos 1-32
Friedrich Gulda pf
Brilliant Classics ⑨ 92773 (9h 58' · ADD)   Ⓢ**O**

Friedrich Gulda's stereo Beethoven sonata cycle from the late 1960s differs from his 1950s mono/stereo Decca Beethoven cycle in that the rhythms are tighter, tempi are generally faster, the sonority is more astringent, and the composer's fingerprint accents are harder-hitting. Tonal warmth, geniality and spacious introspection play little part in Gulda's expressive game plan, and that may not sit well with collectors who gravitate towards Arrau's full-bodied rhetoric or Kempff's intimately scaled, multi-hued conceptions. Perhaps the Op 10 triumvirate best typifies Gulda's chosen Beethoven style: the C minor Sonata's finale truly takes the composer's controversial *Prestissimo* at face value. The three Op 31 works and the Op 26 'Funeral March' Sonata receive unusual and refreshingly stark, headlong readings. Yet Gulda is anything but predictable. If the *Appassionata*'s unyielding drive and gaunt patina are positively Brechtian, he pulls the *Waldstein* apart to a fault.

Among the late sonatas, tension and severity serve Gulda's Opp 109 and 110 less well than in his remarkably concentrated *Hammerklavier*. And who'd have expected such an affectionately nuanced Op 54, Op 28 or *Pathétique* slow movement? All told, the pianist's occasional idiosyncracies and misfired moments are but a tiny price to pay for a stimulating, absorbing Beethoven cycle whose virtues proudly stand the test of time. The recording is closely miked, slightly dry yet decidedly impactful.

Piano Sonatas Nos 1-32. Diabelli Variations, Op 120. Ⓗ
Eroica Variations, Op 35. Six Bagatelles, Op 126
Friedrich Gulda pf
Orfeo mono C808 109L (10h 50' · ADD)
Recorded 1953, 1954 & 1957   Ⓜ**OOO**

Orfeo's nine-CD set of the complete Beethoven piano sonatas (plus the *Eroica* and *Diabelli* Variations, and the *Bagatelles* Op 126, all from 1957) is no mere duplication of what we already have. Indeed, this 1953-54 Austrian Radio sonata cycle falls almost exactly midway between the constituent parts of the Gulda cycle that Decca issued on LP (and subsequently reissued as an 11-CD set in its Original Masters series).

Oddly enough the first point of contrast to hit home, specifically in the early sonatas, is the enormous superiority of Orfeo's recordings, which are clearer, better focused and generally far more listenable than their Decca counterparts. As to the performances, take the slow movement of Op 7 which has greater breadth than on the 1957 Decca (stereo) recording (Gulda's Amadeo version – now on Brilliant Classics, see above – was swifter even than the Decca), and where the poise and pacing are pretty close to perfect. The first movement of the Decca *Moonlight*, infamous in its day, swims in a sea of sustain pedal, an effect that Gulda hadn't yet hit upon in the early 1950s, much to one's relief. The *Tempest*, *Waldstein* and *Appassionata* sonatas are startlingly red-blooded (the *Waldstein*'s first movement in particular is charged with an unusually high level of nervous energy) and the later sonatas capture that almost inexpressible combination of physical confrontation and spiritual engagement that only the greatest Beethovenians can muster. Gulda was always at his best in the last three sonatas but his Decca *Hammerklavier*, for all its trimness and brilliance, rarely matches this one for impact.

Gulda could charm, too, and you'd have to go a long way to find a more lyrical reading of the G major Sonata, Op 14 No 2. It is hardly credible that all this interpretative accomplishment was achieved by a pianist who, at the time, was still only in his early twenties, and who would subsequently divide his musical activities between the Viennese classics and varieties of jazz.

There are certain records that seem to capture the very moment when a fledgling virtuoso first confronts a great corpus of musical work, and this marvellous set represents such a confrontation. Highly recommended.

Piano Sonatas Nos 1-32   H
Artur Schnabel *pf*
EMI Références mono ⑩ 763765-2 (10h 5' · ADD)
Recorded 1932-38   Ⓜ○○

Schnabel was almost ideologically committed to extreme tempos; something you might say Beethoven's music thrives on, always provided the interpreter can bring it off. By and large he did. There are some famous gabbles in this sonata cycle, notably at the start of the *Hammerklavier*, with him going for broke. In fact, Schnabel also held that 'It is a mistake to imagine that all notes should be played with equal intensity or even be clearly audible. In order to clarify the music it is often necessary to make certain notes obscure.' If it's true, as some contemporary witnesses aver, that Schnabel was a flawless wizard in the period pre-1930, there's still plenty of wizardry left in these post-1930 Beethoven recordings. They are virtuoso readings that demonstrate a blazing intensity of interpretative vision as well as breathtaking manner of execution. Even when a dazzlingly articulate reading like that of the *Waldstein* is home and dry, the abiding impression in its aftermath is one of Schnabel's (and Beethoven's) astonishing physical and imaginative daring. And if this suggests recklessness, well, in many other instances the facts are quite other, for Schnabel has a great sense of decorum. He can, in many of the smaller sonatas and some of the late ones, be impeccably mannered, stylish and urbane. Equally he can be devilish or coarse. At the other extreme, he's indubitably the master of the genuinely slow movement.

For the recorded sound, there's nothing that can be done about the occasional patch of wow or discoloration but, in general, the old recordings come up very freshly.

Piano Sonatas Nos 1-32   H
Wilhelm Kempff *pf*
DG Dokumente mono ⑧ 447 966-2GDO8 (8h 31' · ADD). Includes bonus disc, 'Wilhelm Kempff – An All-Round Musician'. Recorded 1951-56   Ⓜ○○○

Ⓖ Wilhelm Kempff was the most inspirational of Beethoven pianists. Those who have cherished his earlier stereo cycle for its magical spontaneity will find Kempff's qualities even more intensely conveyed in this mono set, recorded between 1951 and 1956. Amazingly the sound has more body and warmth than the stereo, with Kempff's unmatched transparency and clarity of articulation even more vividly caught, both in sparkling *Allegros* and in deeply dedicated slow movements. If in places he's even more personal, some might say wilful, regularly surprising you with a new revelation, the magnetism is even more intense, as in the great *Adagio* of the *Hammerklavier* or the final variations of Op-111, at once more rapt and more impulsive, flowing more freely. The bonus disc, entitled 'An All-Round Musician', celebrates Kempff's achievement in words and music, on the organ in Bach, on the piano in Brahms and Chopin as well as in a Bachian improvisation, all sounding exceptionally transparent and lyrical. Fascinatingly, his pre-war recordings of the Beethoven sonatas on 78s are represented too. Here we have his 1936 recording of the *Pathétique*, with the central *Adagio* markedly broader and more heavily pointed than in the mono LP version of 20 years later.

Piano Sonatas Nos 1-32
Daniel Barenboim *pf*
Video directors **Andy Sommer** and **Alan Miller**
EMI ⑥ DVD 368993-9
(10h 20' · NTSC · 16:9 · PCM stereo and 5.1 · 0)
Recorded live at the Deutsche Staatsoper, Berlin, in June and July 2005   Ⓕ○○

For those seeking a home-video Beethoven cycle featuring an established, internationally acclaimed artist, Barenboim's is the only game in town for now. The musical results synthesise the best qualities of Barenboim's two earlier (audio only) cycles (the EMI from the 1960s and the DG from the early 1980s). More than 20 years on, the 62-year-old pianist revisits many of the rhetorical nuances he favoured in his youth, but now applies them within a context of greater expressive economy and structural cohesion. This particularly holds true in difficult-to-sustain slow movements such as those in Op 2 No 3, Op 7, the *Tempest* and the *Hammerklavier*, along with movements in variation form (Op 26's first movement, the *Appassionata*'s *Andante con moto* and Op 111's majestically unfolding Arietta).

Notwithstanding tiny inaccuracies, imbalances and occasional pounding in louder moments that are inevitable in a live, minimally edited concert, Barenboim's technique remains never less than solid and world-class. His body language isn't particularly eye-catching, except that he often raises his hands high at the end of big, declamatory phrases, and makes conducting gestures with the left hand while the right hand plays alone.

BEETHOVEN'S COMPLETE PIANO SONATAS – IN BRIEF

Paul Lewis
Harmonia Mundi ⑩ HMC90 1902, 1903/5, 1906/8, 1909/11 Ⓕ❍❍Ⓑ→
Spread over four volumes, Paul Lewis offers a sonata cycle of great intellectual strength but also of real poetry and imagination. This is Beethoven-playing that doesn't smile that often but it has an integrity that jumps out of every bar. Here's a young artist not afraid to throw down the gauntlet to his elders.

Artur Schnabel Ⓗ
EMI Références mono ⑩ 763765-2 Ⓜ❍❍Ⓑ→
Also availably singly from Naxos
This was the first Beethoven piano sonata cycle ever recorded: Schnabel went into the studio for HMV during the 1930s and recorded a cycle that for many remains the greatest. Technically fallible he may be from time to time, but he offers the real Beethoven: a man of contrasts, of contradictions even, but someone with poetry in his every fibre.

Wilhelm Kempff Ⓗ
DG Dokumente mono ⑧ 447 966-2GDO8 Ⓜ❍❍❍
Though Kempff recorded a stereo cycle a decade later, this mono set from the 1950s has an intensity married to his characteristic intensity that makes it the preferred cycle. There is a transparency to his sound that remains undimmed all these years later.

Friedrich Gulda
Brilliant Classics ⑨ 92773 Ⓢ❍
Gulda's second sonata cycle is a real bargain: performances of flair and imagination. Accents are forceful and there's a really bracing sense of rediscovery about these interpretations. A fascinating document from a fascinating musician.

Stephen Kovacevich
EMI ⑨ 562700-2 Ⓑ❍❍Ⓑ→
Recorded between 1992 and 2003, Kovacevich's cycle is a magnificent achievement (and it is particularly well priced). Kovacevich never lets you relax into the music and he constantly draws attention to the challenges Beethoven makes to his interpreters and to his listeners. A triumphant success crowned by some outstanding individual interpretations (such as the *Hammerklavier*).

Alfred Brendel
Philips ⑩ download 446 909-2PH10 Ⓕ❍❍Ⓑ→
An intellectually rigorous yet deeply poetic response to these extraordinary works. Brendel has devoted a lifetime to these sonatas and brings that experience to bear in way that will guarantee hours of rewards. (Not currently listed on CD, but available to download.)

However, the set's most provocative revelations appear on the final two discs in the form of masterclasses in Chicago in 2005. Six young pianists (including familiar names such as Lang Lang, Jonathan Biss and Alessio Bax) each play a movement from a sonata. Barenboim acknowledges the performances' positive attributes, then gets down to work. He guides the pianists through details of articulation, tempo relationships, dynamics, pedalling and harmonic motion, helping their interpretations attain greater clarity and specificity. Judging from the post-session questions, it's clear that the audience has been listening nearly as well as the teacher. We then return to Barenboim in Berlin and replay that recently dissected sonata movement with the benefit of newly enlightened ears and sharpened insights. Does the pianist practise what he preaches? Well, maybe 90 per cent of the time, yes.

SBT1188 – Piano Sonatas – Nos 1, 3 & 32 Ⓗ
SBT1189 – Piano Sonatas – Nos 7, 8, 13 & 14
SBT1190 – Piano Sonatas – Nos 17, 18, 21 & 22
SBT1191 – Piano Sonatas – Nos 26, 27 & 29
SBT1192 – Piano Sonatas – Nos 23, 28, 30 & 31
Solomon *pf*
Testament mono/stereo SBT1188/92 (oas: 73', 78', 80', 78' & 79' · ADD). Recorded 1951-56 Ⓕ

By the autumn of 1956, when a stroke ended Solomon's career at the absurdly early age of 54, he'd recorded 18 of the Beethoven piano sonatas, 12 of which had been released. Had his career continued, the cycle would almost certainly have been revised and completed. The immediate rivals would have been the two cycles Wilhelm Kempff recorded for Deutsche Grammophon (mono 1951-6, stereo 1964-5) and the pre-war Schnabel recordings which EMI reissued in its series Great Recordings of the Century in 1963-4. In the event, Solomon's cycle remained incomplete, as did later Emil Gilels's not dissimilar DG cycle.

Some will fret over this but sanguine folk will reflect that all the 'important' sonatas are here in performances that can generally be reckoned 'representative'. Testament's Paul Baily has done a first-rate job on the transfers and the layouts: five CDs, each packed to the gunnels, each logically planned. The only sonata that's significantly out of sequence is Op 111 (No 32), yet curiously, that's the one performance from among the late, great sonatas which isn't entirely up to scratch. Here you might think back to Schnabel. Alongside Schnabel's reading, Solomon's sounds scampered (in the first movement), lacking in depth (in the second), and oddly unspontaneous, as though haunted by the knowledge of the older reading. The rather hollow-sounding 1951 recording doesn't help.

Op 111 is coupled here (SBT1188) with two of the Op 2 sonatas (Nos 1 and 3), the playing by turns fiery and lucid, gracious and gay. If anything's missing, it's the sense of tragic pathos Schnabel finds in the slow movement of the

C major Sonata and his radical recklessness of spirit in the two finales.

The second disc contains celebrated readings of the *Moonlight* (No 14) and the *Pathétique* (No 8). Solomon's reading of the opening movement of the *Moonlight* is famously long-breathed, his reading of the opening movement of the *Pathétique*, and the *Moonlight*'s finale, wonderfully tense and austere.

The remaining three discs are, quite simply, indispensable, Solomon at the peak of his powers as a Beethoven player. In sonata after sonata, we hear virtuosity of the finest and most discriminating kind put at the service of some of the loftiest yet most physically beautiful and physically exciting music known to man. Solomon was famous for the Cistercian clarity of his quick playing (the *Waldstein* – No-21, and *Appassionata* – No 23, sonatas *passim*) and for the concentrated calm of his playing of the great slow movements (this 1952 recording of the *Hammerklavier* – No 29, as fine an example as any). Underpinning both these phenomena is a quality of dynamic control that both gratifies the eye (Beethoven's text lifted off the page with rare precision) and bewitches the ear. It's this latter point which gives Solomon his special ability to define for us that element of unalloyed wonder in Beethoven's writing, those moments when we're brought to what TS Eliot called 'the still point of the turning world'.

There are minor disappointments on each of these three final discs. The 1951 recording of Op 54 (SBT1190) is dowdily recorded and would almost certainly have been remade had circumstances allowed. Both the 1956 Op 90 (SBT1191) and the 1954 Op 101 (SBT1192) are good without being a match for what we have elsewhere on the discs. In the case of Op 90, this is Solomon's legendary elucidation of the *Hammerklavier* Sonata and his well-nigh definitive account of *Les adieux*, a performance, humane and vivid, that's fine almost beyond belief.

'Complete Piano Sonatas, Vol 1'
Piano Sonatas – No 5, Op 10 No 1; No 6, Op 10 No 2; No 7, Op 10 No 3; No 8, 'Pathétique', Op 13
Martin Roscoe pf
Deux-Elles DXL1161 (76' · DDD)   Ⓕ**O**▶

Martin Roscoe, on the first volume of his sonata cycle (it will be the first complete recording of Barry Cooper's new ABRSM edition), brings a rugged approach to the *Pathétique*. Preceding this are the three Op 10 Sonatas. Beethoven has not quite shaken off Haydn and Mozart and yet, in the wonderful slow movements of Nos 1 and 3, has moved light years away. Coloured perhaps by a personal fondness for Op 10, Roscoe's way with them is nigh-on perfect, lightly pedalled, full of a youthful vitality and impudence as though the ink was still wet on the paper. Try and hear his handling of the C minor Sonata's *Adagio*, a heartbreaking cry of regret that only a refined pianist with the wisdom of experience could

bring off quite as well as this. Recorded with drawing-room intimacy at Potton Hall, further volumes are eagerly awaited.

Piano Sonatas – Nos 3, 8, 'Pathétique', & 15, 'Pastoral'
Angela Hewitt pf
Hyperion Ⓢ SACDA67605 (74' · DDD)   Ⓕ**B**▶

The *Pastoral* Sonata leads off Angela Hewitt's second Beethoven sonata cycle instalment, and she taps into the music's overall geniality while also paying heed to its darker corners. In the first movement, her accompaniments are full and resonant, yet convey a murmuring, disembodied aura, while she gauges the development section's silences and transitions to particularly dramatic effect. She also plays the central movements well, although the *Andante*'s *staccato* left-hand lines are more characterfully bassoon-like in Stephen Kovacevich's hands, and some might prefer Richard Goode's more impetuous, angular fingerwork in the *Scherzo*. Yet Hewitt's conversational give-and-take between the droning left-hand ostinato and the main theme at the Rondo finale's outset is quite wonderful.

Having enjoyed Hewitt's edgy, fervent *Appassionata*, her *Pathétique* seems underplayed and studio-bound by comparison. Her fastidious, occasionally rounded-off execution softens the outer movements' ardour and momentum.

Hewitt's way with the C major Sonata, Op 2 No 3, boasts considerable profile and personality. Her tempo fluctuations in the first movement (the lyrical G major theme, for example) illuminate rather than detract from the structure, while the *Andante* appears more internally animated than one would guess from its nearly eight-minute timing. The contrapuntal acumen that distinguishes Hewitt's Baroque interpretations brilliantly comes to the fore in the *Scherzo*. In contrast to the pouncing scintillation Kovacevich and Richter bring to the *Allegro assai*, Hewitt evokes Rubinstein's urbane poise and patrician control, and treats the display passages in the manner of rapid melodies. Small wonder that Hewitt considers this one of Beethoven's most fulfilling sonatas to perform. In addition to Hyperion's superb sound, Hewitt, as usual, provides her own penetrating, vividly articulate annotations.

Piano Sonatas Nos 4, 7 & 23, 'Appassionata'
Angela Hewitt pf
Hyperion Ⓢ SACDA67518 (77' · DDD)   Ⓕ**B**▶

Angela Hewitt's first instalment in a projected Beethoven sonata cycle for Hyperion offers intelligent, stylish and often illuminating interpretations. The contrapuntal acumen she regularly brings to Bach suits Beethoven's linear trajectory, as borne out by Hewitt's astute (yet never fussy) care over inner voices and bass-lines. She takes Beethoven's characteristic dynamic contrasts on faith but not to extreme, discontinuous ends, while her ear for uncovering melodic outlines of rapid arpeggios ensures that these figurations don't sound 'notey'. In addition, Hewitt's strong left hand lends uncommon clarity and direction to passages such as the double notes in No 4's first movement, or the motoric sequences in No 7's Rondo.

Occasional telltale signs of pre-planning include Hewitt's tendency to hesitate a split second before Beethoven's trademark *subito pianos*, thereby softening one's sense of surprise. Her protracted treatment of No 4's *Largo* might have benefited from Claudio Arrau's gravitas and sustaining power. Fusing poetry and passion, Hewitt lets her long hair down and her fingers run wild in the *Appassionata*'s first movement. She continues with a brisk and well unified account of the central variations, and suffuses her powerful, headlong finale with cutting accents and perceptive modifications of the basic pulse. The Fazioli piano's lean bass and bright treble characterise the kind of timbral differentiation one often associates with instruments of Beethoven's time. Hyperion's SACD surround sound better absorbs the engineering's resonant ambience than conventional two-channel playback's relatively flatter sound-stage.

Piano Sonatas – Nos 5, 6, 7 & 8, 'Pathétique'
András Schiff pf
ECM New Series 476 3100 (77' · DDD)   Ⓕ

András Schiff's sharp attention to detail spills over from the first volume in his projected Beethoven cycle into this recital, although he sometimes crosses the thin line separating astute perception and finicky mannerism. The exaggerated quality of his clipped chords and staccato passages proves mincing and ultimately monotonous in No 6's outer movements, although some of the intricate left-hand runs attain uncommon clarity.

Surprisingly, Schiff holds back in No 5's finale, maintaining a comfortable *allegro*, whereas Beethoven marks *prestissimo*, in contrast to the thrust and momentum Glenn Gould, Stephen Kovacevich and, more recently, Gerhard Oppitz generate. Although Schiff makes the most of No 7's finale's questioning silences, others bring more gravity and desolation to the sonata's great slow movement (Arrau and Schnabel, for example).

Yet Schiff's subtle tempo modifications in the first movement add expressive dimension to the hurling octaves, while numerous left-hand counterlines zoom to the forefront. He similarly modifies the *Pathétique*'s first movement's basic tempo so that the bass tremolos have enough room to resonate and breathe, and follows the Rudolf Serkin tradition of repeating the introduction. Intense right- and left-hand interplay vibrantly unhinges the slow movement from its comfort zone, while Schiff's adherence to Beethoven's careful dynamic differentiations restores the Rondo's long lost thematic spice.

Heed these reservations: but respect Schiff's forethought, integrity and utter lack of routine.

Piano Sonatas – Nos 9, 10, 12 & 15, 'Pastoral'
Murray Perahia pf
Sony Classical 88697 32646-2 (71' · DDD)   ⒻOOⒷ

Perahia is a quiet Beethovenian, referring not to his dynamics but his utterly unhistrionic approach. Though you might want higher voltages running through some works, the sonatas here respond well to such a temperament. The opening of the variation set in Op 26, for instance, is simplicity itself, and Perahia's swiftly flowing second movement is beautifully judged. If anything is missing from these readings, it's a certain irreverent humour. Perahia's playing is so well honed that sometimes that last aspect seems to have been tamed, though he brings an effective sense of unease to the finale of the work.

His *Pastoral*, on the other hand, is a joyous balance of warmth of sound (how he makes the piano sing) in the outer movements, both simultaneously anchored by, and tensing against, a pedal note of D, and the shadowy *Andante*. A thought-provoking essay by Jeremy Siepmann and a well balanced recording match the quality of the playing.

'Piano Sonatas, Volume 1'
Piano Sonatas – Nos 16, 17, 'Tempest', & 18
Paul Lewis pf
Harmonia Mundi HMC90 1902 (74' · DDD)   ⒻOOⒷ

'Piano Sonatas, Volume 2'
Piano Sonatas – Nos 8, 'Pathétique', 9, 10, 11, 21, 'Waldstein', 24, 25, 27, 28 & 29, 'Hammerklavier'
Paul Lewis pf
Harmonia Mundi ③ HMC90 1903/5 (3h 27' · DDD)
ⒻOOⒷ

'Piano Sonatas, Volume 3'
Piano Sonatas – Nos 1-4, 12, 13, 'quasi una fantasia', 14, 'Moonlight', 22 & 23, 'Appassionata'
Paul Lewis pf
Harmonia Mundi ③ HMC90 1906/8 (3h 9' · DDD)
ⒻOOOⒷ

'Piano Sonatas, Volume 4'
Nos 5, 6, 7, 15, 'Pastoral', 19, 20, 26, 'Les adieux', 30, 31 & 32
Paul Lewis pf
Harmonia Mundi ③ HMC90 1909/11 (3h 4' · DDD)
ⒻOOOⒷ

Paul Lewis's Beethoven sonata cycle shows him playing down all possible roughness and angularity in favour of a richly humane and predominantly lyrical beauty. Again, here is nothing of that glossy, impersonal sheen beloved of too many young pianists, but a subtly nuanced perception beneath an immaculate surface.

His technique, honed on many ultra-demanding areas of the repertoire allows him an imaginative and poetic latitude only given to a musical elite. Telescoped phrasing, rapid scrambles for security, waywardness and pedantry he gladly leaves to others, firmly but gently guiding you to the very heart of the composer. His *Appassionata* is characterised by muted gunfire, as if the sonata's warlike elements were heard from a distance. Yet the lucidity with which he views such violence easily makes others' more rampant virtuosity become sound and fury, signifying little. His way, too, with the teasing toccata-like finales of Nos 12 and 22 is typical of his lyrical restraint, a far cry, indeed, from a more overt brilliance. How superbly he captures Beethoven's over-the-shoulder glance at Haydn, his great predecessor, yet gives you all of his forward-looking Romanticism in the early F minor Sonata (No 1). Again, how many pianists could achieve such unfaltering poise and sensitivity in No 4's *Largo, con gran espressione*?

Sometimes his warmth and flexibility suggest Beethoven seen, as it were, through Schubert's eyes (the finale to Op 31 No 1), and he often suggests a darker, more serious side to the composer's laughter and high jinks. But he plays Beethoven's humorous afterthought at the close of the Op 31 No 1's *Allegro vivace* as to the manner born and his *presto* coda to the finale becomes a joyous chase.

His way with the so-called *Tempest* Sonata is a reminder, too, of his outwardly relaxed mastery, quite without a sign of a skewed or telescoped phrase and with page after page given with a quiet but superbly focused intensity. His *Adagio* is gravely processional, his finale acutely yet subtly and unobtrusively characterised.

Even the composer's relatively carefree or lightweight gestures are invested with a drama and significance that illuminate them in a novel but wholly natural light. Here is one of those rare pianists who can charge even a single note or momentary pause with drama and significance and convince you, for example, that his lyrical, often darkly introspective way with Beethoven's pulsing *con brio* brilliance in the *Waldstein* Sonata is a viable, indeed, memorable alternative to convention.

So, too, is his way with the *Hammerklavier*, that most daunting of masterpieces, where he tells us that even when the composer is at his most elemental he remains deeply human and vulnerable. Not for him Schnabel's headlong attempt to obey Beethoven's wild first-movement metronome mark; nor does he view the vast spans of the *Adagio* as 'like the icy heart of some remote mountain lake' (JWN Sullivan) but rather a place of ineffable sadness. And here as elsewhere he is able to relish every detail of the composer's ever-expanding argument while maintaining a flawless sense of line and continuity.

These performances are a transparent act of musical love and devotion. Nothing is exaggerated yet virtually everything is included. Of all the modern versions of the sonatas, Lewis's is surely the most eloquent and persuasive. And, as in previous issues, Harmonia Mundi's sound is of demonstration quality.

Beethoven Piano Sonatas Nos 8, 23 & 31 Ⓗ
Handel Keyboard Suite in D minor, HWV428 – Prelude; Air and Variations; Presto. Chaconne and Variations in G, HWV435
Edwin Fischer pf
APR Signature mono APR5502 (72' · AAD)
Recorded 1931-38 ⓂⓄⓄ

On this invaluable disc are some of Fischer's finest and most legendary performances. His very first published recording (1931) of the Handel Chaconne, for example, was made at a time when his matchless *leggiero* and radiant tone were unimpeded by obvious blemishes or erratic pianism. Both this performance and that of the pieces from the Suite No 3 are endowed with an improvisatory magic, a strength and grace and supreme assurance. Fischer commences the *Pathétique* with a scrupulous adherence to Beethoven's *fp* marking, a sudden shift of sound that's fascinatingly modernist or prophetic. The *Allegro di molto e con brio* is exactly that, dancing with an irrepressible lightness and urgency; in the slow octave descent just before the final outburst there's a rapt 'all-passion-spent' quality, something that Fischer was able to achieve with supreme naturalness, without even a hint of artifice or calculated effect.

All past vicissitudes are finally resolved in Sonata, Op 110 (No 31) in a blaze of heroic glory, and time and time again he makes you pause to consider key points and details that have somehow eluded others. There's a richness and humanity here that was uniquely Fischer's.

Piano Sonatas Nos 8, 'Pathétique, 14, 'Moonlight', 15, 'Pastoral', 17, 'Tempest', 21, 'Waldstein', 23, 'Appassionata', & 26, 'Les adieux'
Alfred Brendel pf
Philips Duo ② 438 730-2PM2 (152' · ADD)
Recorded 1970-77 ⓂⓄ➡

The Philips reissue, with seven of Beethoven's most popular sonatas admirably played by Alfred Brendel, is in every way an outstanding bargain, and is well worth obtaining, even if duplication is involved. All the performances are authoritative and offer consistently distinguished playing, while the recording is very realistic indeed. The *Tempest* resonates in the memory and the central movements of the *Pastoral* are most beautifully shaped. The *Pathétique*, *Moonlight* and *Appassionata* all bring deeply satisfying readings that are compellingly conceived and freshly executed. This set can be recommended without any reservations.

Piano Sonatas – No 14, 'Moonlight', 21, 'Waldstein', 26, 'Les adieux', & No 31
Nelson Freire pf
Decca 475 8155DH (69' · DDD) ⒻⓄ➡

What's not to admire about Nelson Freire's brilliantly virtuoso, heartfelt and utterly alive Beethoven interpretations? They're pianistically oriented in terms of tone colour and symmetry, yet never feel the least bit four-square, and convey vivid communicative immediacy, even when Freire tends to hurry in hot anticipation of a dramatic build that lies just a few steps ahead. Freire takes the *Waldstein* first movement's *Allegro con brio* directive to scintillating heart, as the sweeping scales jump out of your loudspeakers like white lightning and the development section's relentless left-hand arpeggios gain urgency through unusual accentuations. He also generates plenty of tonal magic from the *Rondo*'s unconventional long pedal markings and galvanic momentum in the prestissimo coda. Some may prefer a more austere, contained *Adagio molto*, yet one could make a case for Freire's unfolding animation as being true to this music's intended introductory function.

In *Les adieux*, Freire fuses Solomon's incredibly poised fingerwork and Schnabel's passionate sweep into his own individualised *tour de force*. Other Op 110 performances may offer more breadth and spirituality, yet Freire's carefully gauged tempo relationships in the hard-to-pace Fugue pay no less expressive dividends. Also notice that Freire, like Claudio Arrau, takes trouble to make the first movement's rapid left-hand figurations clear and distinct. The *Moonlight*'s *Adagio sostenuto* is beautifully sung out, while the *Allegretto*'s varied articulations sound as how they read on the page. So do those of the finale. You won't find Kovacevich's shock and awe, but rather a masterclass in steady cumulation that should reveal more with each listening.

Beethoven Piano Sonatas – Nos 15, 'Pastoral', & 23, 'Appassionata' **Schubert** Piano Sonata No 21, D960
Andreas Haefliger pf
Avie ② AV2148 (91' · DDD)   Ⓑ➔

Haefliger's innate affinity for Beethoven's largely lyrical *Pastoral* Sonata manifests itself via the pianist's relaxed tempi and ample tone. Taste and proportion govern his penchant for rhetorical broadenings and tenuti. Although Haefliger tempers Beethoven's characteristic *subito* dynamics more than he ought to, he pays special heed to matters of articulation. You'll notice how he distinguishes the slurs and staccati in the *Scherzo*'s main theme, whereas many pianists treat these notes equally. The *Appassionata*'s outer movements achieve a happy fusion of drama, cumulative sweep and textural clarity. Haefliger's keen attention to the *Andante con moto*'s left-hand lines rivets the attention to the point that one barely notices how he bumps up the variations' tempi in bite-size increments.

With exposition repeat in tow, Haefliger sculpts the Schubert B flat's lengthy first movement in long arcs propelled more by songful than symphonic impulses (the way he pulls back from certain high notes, for instance). And here's the surprise: for some reason, Haefliger races through the first ending nearly twice as fast as it's written. Strange. Similar breadth and vocally informed phrasing inform the *Andante*

sostenuto. The *Scherzo*'s Trio expands and contracts as Haefliger magnifies the bass-note syncopations, while the finale convinces entirely. You get a strong sense of concert-hall realism if you play these discs at a loud volume.

'Complete Works for Solo Piano, Vol 6'
Piano Sonatas Nos 21-25
Ronald Brautigam fp
BIS ⬚ BIS-SACD1573 (73' · DDD/DSD)   Ⓕ●➔

Volume 6 in Ronald Brautigam's Beethoven cycle offers stunning performances that are technically breathtaking, stylistically astute, emotionally intense and musically alive in every moment. What is more, they make the most compelling case on disc for period instruments in this repertoire. Go to the *Waldstein*'s Rondo, for example, to hear uncommon textural differentiation from register to register, where Beethoven's controversial long pedal markings make sense, the left-hand figurations emerge with rare shape and purpose, and the octave glissandi in the coda are light as feathers.

In both the *Waldstein*'s and *Appassionata*'s first movements, Brautigam's fast tempi generate drama and tension, not so much through sheer speed as by way of characterful thematic contrasts, pointed accents and subtle yet expressively powerful modifications of the basic pulse. The slightly militant edge with which Brautigam phrases the graceful main theme in the Op 54 Sonata's first movement makes the subsequent octaves in triplets sound less jarring in context. At first one fears that his brisk pace for the second movement leaves Beethoven's humbler *Allegretto* directive at the starting-gate, but the clarity of the toccata-like part writing and off-beat accents make Brautigam's conception work. By contrast, the little Op 79 Sonata's outer movements are comparatively sedate and graceful.

Wonderful sound quality too, in both SACD and conventional two-channel formats. Don't pass up this amazing release!

Piano Sonatas Nos 27-32   🅷
Solomon pf
EMI Références mono/stereo ② 764708-2 (141' · ADD)
Recorded 1951-56   Ⓜ●○○

Solomon's 1952 recording of the *Hammerklavier* Sonata is one of the greatest of the century. At the heart of his performance there's as calm and searching an account of the slow movement as you're ever likely to hear. And the outer movements are also wonderfully well done. Music that's so easy to muddle and arrest is here fierily played; Solomon at his lucid, quick-witted best.

The CD transfer is astonishing. It's as though previously we have merely been eavesdropping on the performance; now, decades later, we're finally in the presence of the thing itself. It's all profoundly moving. What's more, EMI has retained the juxtaposition of the 1969 LP reissue: Solomon's glorious account of the A major Sonata, No 28 as the *Hammerklavier*'s proud harbinger. We must be grateful that Solomon had completed his recording of these six late sonatas before his career was abruptly ended by a stroke in the latter part of 1956.

The Sonatas Nos 27 and 31, were recorded in August 1956. In retrospect the warning signs were already there; yet listening to these edited tapes you'd hardly know anything was amiss. There's the odd fumble in the *Scherzo* of No 31; but, if anything, the playing has even greater resolve, both in No 31 and in a songful (but never sentimental) account of No 27. The recordings of Nos 30 and 32 date from 1951. Sonata No 30, is very fine; No 32 is, by Solomon's standards, a shade wooden in places, both as a performance and as a recording.

Still, this is a wonderful set, and very much a collectors' item.

Piano Sonatas Nos 28-32
Maurizio Pollini pf
DG The Originals ② 449 740-2GOR2 (126' · ADD)
Recorded 1975-77   Ⓜ❶❶❶

This reissued DG Originals set makes an exceptionally neat package. Consistent praise has been heaped on these recordings since they won the Instrumental Record Award in 1977. One of Pollini's greatest strengths is his ability to stand up to the accumulated momentum of Beethoven's structure, but he can also build on it so as to leave the impression of one huge exhalation of creative breath. In the first movement of the Hammerklavier the astonishing technical assurance has you on the edge of your seat with excitement. His controlled vehemence is without rival in the outer movements, and though he doesn't get right to the bottom of No 29's poetry, his far-sighted phrasing and paragraphing is again remarkable.

In the last three sonatas there are others who stop to peer deeper into some of the psychic chasms, but Pollini's mastery of integration and continuous growth, and his ability to hold potentially conflicting musical demands in balance, are again sources of wonderment. In terms of the qualities just mentioned, who is Pollini's equal? Other than small touches of pre-echo in No 32, there's nothing here to distract from the exalted quality of both the music and the playing.

Piano Sonatas – Nos 29, 'Hammerklavier'ᵃ & 31ᵇ
Rudolf Serkin pf
BBC Legends ᵃmono BBCL4241-2 (66' · ADD)
Recorded live at the Royal Festival Hall, London, on ᵃMay 13, 1968 and ᵇJune 16, 1971   Ⓕ❶

Rudolf Serkin was one of music's greatest overreachers, at his finest lifting his capacity audiences into the most exalted regions of the mind and imagination. And here, in two incomparable performances taken from two London recitals, his candour and intensity are of a searing force and conviction. Others may plough a smoother

furrow but smooth furrows have little to do with the *Hammerklavier* Sonata's epic and intimidating utterance. Caressing *pianissimi* or magical, multicoloured nuance were hardly Serkin's way, even when he chose less obviously daunting repertoire, and as he himself put it, 'the piano has always been less interesting to me than the music'. In this sense he was Horowitz's polar opposite and here in late Beethoven nothing stands between you and the composer.

In the first movement of the *Hammerklavier* there is no question of emulating Schnabel's ill-advised attempt at Beethoven's supposed metronome markings so that the music's force and eloquence have rarely been more powerfully paced and unfolded. Again, whether storming the heavens or making time stand still (and you will hear both in the *Adagio sostenuto*'s closing pages) Serkin makes you aware that beneath the mask of the benignly smiling 'Rudy' lay a ferocious missionary zeal. Once more, in Op 110 everything is achieved by essentially gritty musical rather than pianistic means so that what can initially seem literal and forbidding takes on a sublime perspective. Serkin was, quite simply, a unique voice and presence and, as these excellently transferred recordings tell us, true musical stature is only achieved by unfaltering commitment and an awareness that you can never do enough for music.

Diabelli Variations, Op 120

Beethoven Diabelli Variations
Bach Partita No 4, BWV828
Stephen Kovacevich pf
Onyx ONYX4035 (78' · DDD)   Ⓕ❶❶❶❶▸

Kovacevich writes in his introduction to this new set that it was the *Diabelli* Variations – via the Serkin recording – that first made him love Beethoven. It's a reading that still holds its head high today, and just a decade later, in 1968, Kovacevich set down his own recording, rightly acclaimed and something of a calling-card for the young pianist. But what of this new performance, made 40 years later? What is immediately striking is the sense of a cumulative whole, the tension and indeed speed with which he approaches the work. The work's juxtapositions of the sublime and the ridiculous are presented with a vividness that sounds more live than studio-bound.

Kovacevich emphasises the sense of continuous development with a certain fleetness of finger: his opening theme sets quite a pace, and dances more lightly than many rival versions. It's certainly faster than his own earlier recording. But more important is the sense that Kovacevich has now encompassed the extremes of the work more fully. His understanding of Beethoven's juxtapositions of beauty and crudity, reflection and action, and the sheer dynamic range, are fully exposed in this new version, which captures the piano sound beautifully.

Kovacevich has, in the intervening decades between his first and second *Diabelli*s, recorded a complete sonata cycle and again that familiarity with Beethoven's language in the final years shows and, again and again, Kovacevich reveals how that humour can tip over into something far more menacing. Perhaps in his younger days Beethoven would have ended the set with the fugue, but instead we get a final addition: a switch to C major and an utter change in mood, with a graceful, quasi-Mozartian idea, whirled ever higher. It's as enigmatic and undefinable as anything Beethoven wrote and a transcendent ending to this remarkable performance.

Kovacevich might be less associated with Bach, but let's not forget that his teacher was that consummate Bachian, Myra Hess. He treads a middle path between the tonally slimline, rhythmically motivated readings of Angela Hewitt and the more obviously romantic ones of Cédric Tiberghien. And it's an enlightening partner to the *Diabelli* Variations, not only in its basis in dance rhythms but also in its scope and its extrovert demeanour, whose tone is set with the grand Ouverture. Altogether, a disc to treasure.

Diabelli Variations
Piotr Anderszewski *pf*
Virgin Classics 545468-2 (63' · DDD)   Ⓕ**OO**Ⓑ

This is the most intelligent, searching and delightful account of the *Diabelli* Variations to have reached us since Brendel's. It gives opportunities everywhere to admire a superfine control of every aspect of piano playing, but that isn't the great thing about it, splendid though the finish is. The performance is entirely composer-led, driven by the music, not by ideas *about* the music, and in that sense you hardly notice the means to the end at all. It's an account of the *Diabelli* based on a much closer reading of the text than you usually get, and you've only to hear the theme and the first variation to perceive an exceptional balance of rigour and imagination: rigour in the way Anderszewski has thought about every inflection marked by Beethoven; imagination, evident here and throughout, in the quality with which he has realised them in terms of expression and vividness of character. His rhythm is tremendous.

More remarkable still is his feeling for dynamics, so copiously prescribed in this work and yet treated with approximation by so many players. He's not one to play the daredevil, and you could say his tempos in the quick numbers are sometimes surprisingly moderate; but he isn't a sober-sides. He has fingers which are always saying something, a varied and attractive sound, usually built from the bass up, and that rare ability to get from one thing to another with pinpoint accuracy, expressively speaking, as if forging sonority and character with a laser. A fine recording, and the sound is at an apt distance. An outstanding issue.

Diabelli Variations   Ⓗ
Piano Sonata No 32, Op 111. Polonaise, Op 89
Julius Katchen *pf*

Decca Heritage Masters 478 1727DC (77' · ADD)   Ⓢ
Recorded 1953, 1954, 1968

This reissue is a reminder of a prodigiously gifted pianist who died tragically at the age of 42. His recording of Beethoven's *Diabelli* Variations was first issued in 1953, while Op 111 was to follow a year later when it was coupled with the *Appassionata* Sonata. Katchen once claimed that his studies in philosophy helped him to come closer to the heart of Op 120, a towering masterpiece, and together with Bach's *Goldbergs* the greatest set of keyboard variations ever composed. And returning after many years to this performance tells you how Katchen made light of every difficulty while at the same time discarding a more profound or speculative viewpoint. The confidence, ease and facility remain daunting and the playing is never less than sensitive and musicianly. Yet at the same time it is difficult to sense the sustained eloquence and intensity of, say, Schnabel or, more recently, Richter, Kovacevich and Anderszewski.

Relatively speaking Katchen's is a lightweight conception with everything kept smartly on the move. You won't easily hear a more coruscating technique than in, for example, Variations 10 and 26, but it is only in the second movement of Op 111 that Katchen achieves much of the heaven-sent wonder and repose that eludes him elsewhere. As an encore he includes the C major Polonaise, recorded in 1968, a virtuoso oddity and squib tossed off with astonishing energy and aplomb. Decca's transfers are excellent.

Piano Variations

32 Variations on an Original Theme in C minor, WoO80.
Six Variations on an Original Theme in F, Op 34.
Fifteen Variations and a Fugue on an Original Theme in E flat, 'Eroica', Op 35. Six Variations on an Original Theme, 'Die Ruinen von Athen', Op 76. Six Variations on an Original Theme in G, WoO77. Seven Variations in C on 'God save the King', WoO78. Five Variations in D on 'Rule Britannia', WoO79.
Cédric Tiberghien *pf*
Harmonia Mundi HMC90 1775 (76' · DDD)   Ⓕ**OO**

Cédric Tiberghien commences the *Eroica* Variations with a meticulous weight and balance of textures and although exceptionally delicate and precise, rarely misses the force and energy underlining one of Beethoven's lithest, most vigorous arguments. He sinks gratefully into reflection in Variation 8 and his musicianship in the richly ornamented *Largo* of Variation 15 is at once individual but unsullied by personal idiosyncrasy. Again, in the *32 Variations* in C minor – that compendium of classical virtuosity – Tiberghien is meticulous but never severe, precisely yet generously registering the mood and character of each brief Variation in a manner that may well have caused Beethoven to alter his unfavourable opinion of his work ('Beethoven, what a fool you have been!'). His *stretto* in Variations 21-2 makes the dark place of Variation 23 sound unusually mysterious while Variations 10-11 show an unfaltering assurance and style.

Tiberghien is no less outstanding in less demanding fare, relishing the explosive whimsy of the *Rule Britannia* and *God save the King* Variations, with their mock solemnity and affectionate digs at British assumptions of superiority. Here, clearly, is a pianist to watch. Harmonia Mundi's sound is excellent, making this an altogether exceptional disc.

Bagatelles

Bagatelles – Op 33; Op 119; C minor, WoO52; C, WoO56. Rondos – Op 51: No 1 in C; No 2 in G; C, WoO48; A, WoO49. Six Minuets, WoO10. Polonaise in C, Op 89. Andante favori in F, WoO57. Variations – Six in F on an Original Theme, Op 34; Nine in C minor on a March by Dressler, WoO63; Six in F on a Swiss Song, WoO64; 24 in D on Righini's 'Venni amore', WoO65; 12 in C on Haibel's 'Menuet à la Viganò', WoO68; Six in G on Paisiello's 'Nel cor più non mi sento', WoO70
Mikhail Pletnev *pf*
DG ② 457 493 2GH2 (152' · DDD)

From the very first notes of the *Dressler* Variations – Beethoven's first-known composition, dating from 1782 – it's clear that Pletnev is a master of piano texture, and that he's going to use his mastery not only to ravish the ear but to delight the mind. His nuances in the simple Swiss theme and its artless variations are quite delicious. At the opposite extreme, the grand set of 24 Variations on Righini's 'Venni amore', WoO65, come across as a dry run for later cycles such as the *Eroica* or even the *Diabelli* Variations, both in overall design and in certain idiosyncratic details. Technical *tours de force* abound; Pletnev negotiates them all not only with phenomenal pianistic aplomb but, where appropriate, dry wit. It's a fascinating glimpse into the laboratory of the 20-year-old Beethoven's mind.

In the two early Rondos Pletnev is freer than some might wish with the notated dynamics, phrasing and articulation, and his touch suggests at times that he's thinking more of Scarlatti than of Beethoven. Nevertheless the most startling moments of whimsy in these pieces aren't his but the composer's. By contrast, in the Vienna-period Rondos of Op 51 he seems to be thinking forward to the age of Lisztian rhetoric. But the fact that he's never satisfied with the default response to the surface of the music is much to be welcomed, and almost always his initiatives are stylish and effective. Similarly the bagatelles radiate openness to all sorts of possibilities. In some instances Brendel finds more of a rough-and-tumble edginess; but Pletnev's range of touch and tonal nuance outstrips them both and brings rewards of its own, as in the proto-Schubertian touches of Op 119.

Instrument and recording quality are near to ideal. An outstanding issue.

Cantatas

Cantata on the Death of the Emperor Joseph II, WoO87. Cantata on the Accession of the Emperor Leopold II, WoO88. Opferlied, Op 121*b*. Meeresstille und glückliche Fahrt, Op 112
Janice Watson, Judith Howarth *sops* **Jean Rigby** *mez* **John Mark Ainsley** *ten* **José van Dam** *bass-bar* **Corydon Singers and Orchestra / Matthew Best**
Hyperion CDA66880 (80' · DDD· T/t)

Beethoven was only 19 when he was commissioned to write this 40-minute cantata on the emperor's death. It was never performed, the musicians claiming it was too difficult, and remained buried for almost a century. Arguably Beethoven's first major masterpiece, it was one of his few early unpublished works of which he approved. When he came to write *Fidelio*, he used the soaring theme from the first of the soprano arias here, 'Da stiegen die Menschen an's Licht', for Leonore's sublime moment in the finale, 'O Gott! Welch' ein Augenblick'. The tragic C minor power of the choruses framing the work is equally memorable. Dramatic tension is kept taut through all seven sections, with recitatives indicating the young composer's thirst to write opera. Matthew Best conducts a superb performance, fresh, incisive and deeply moving, with excellent soloists as well as a fine chorus. In this first cantata the solo quartet simply contribute to the opening and closing choruses.

The second cantata, only a little more than half the length of the first, was written soon after, when Leopold II had succeeded as emperor. This second work is less ambitious, expressing less deep emotions, yet it anticipates later masterpieces. Much more specific is the way that the finale of the cantata, 'Heil! Stürzet nieder, Millionen', clearly looks forward to the finale of the Ninth Symphony, a point reinforced by the key of D major. The two shorter pieces, both dating from Beethoven's difficult interim period between middle and late, with Jean Rigby as soloist in the *Opferlied*, make a generous fill-up, performed with equal dedication. With plenty of air round the chorus, the recording has ample weight yet is transparent enough to clarify even the heaviest textures. A revelatory issue.

Songs

Sechs Gellert Lieder, Op 48. Lieder – Op 52: No 3, Das Liedchen von der Ruhe; No 4, Mailied; Op 75: No 2, Neue Liebe, neues Leben; No 3, Aus Goethes Faust; Op 83: No 1, Wonne der Wehmut; No 2, Sehnsucht. Adelaide, Op 46. An die Hoffnung, Op 94. An die ferne Geliebte, Op 98. Klage, WoO113. Der Liebende, WoO139. An die Geliebte, WoO140
Stephan Genz *bar* **Roger Vignoles** *pf*
Hyperion CDA67055 (69' · DDD · T/t)

 The young baritone Stephan Genz is in the first bloom of his youthful prime. Beethoven's setting of Goethe's 'Mailied', with its lightly breathed, springing words, could have been written with Genz in mind. Roger Vignoles, Genz's regular accompanist, contributes an irresistible bounding energy and even a sense of mischief to one of Beethoven's most spontaneous yet subtle settings, 'Neue Liebe, neues Leben'; and an elusive sense of yearning is created as the voice tugs against the piano line in 'Sehnsucht'. The six *Gellert Lieder* form the centrepiece of this recital: Beethoven's song cycle, *An die ferne Geliebte*, its grand finale. The intensity of Genz's cry 'Is there a God?' in *An die Hoffnung*, at the start of the disc, gives some indication of the *gravitas* he brings to his firmly enunciated 'spiritual songs' of Gellert. Genz and Vignoles have here reinstated a number of the original verses omitted by Beethoven in the first printed edition, creating a greater sense of balance and proportion within the set. The concluding song cycle is quite simply one of the best performances currently available. Fresh and bright of tone, awe-filled and beautifully paced and scaled, Genz's singing is modulated exquisitely from song to song by Vignoles's sentient piano accompaniment.

Beethoven An die ferne Geliebte
Schubert Schwanengesang
Matthias Goerne bar **Alfred Brendel** pf
Decca 475 6011DH (72' · DDD · T/t)
Recorded live 2003   Ⓕ**ⓄⓄ**☞

Matthias Goerne and Alfred Brendel form one of the great Lieder partnerships of the day. The sympathy between them goes beyond skilful ensemble, and beyond shared enjoyment of the wealth of illustration in Schubert, into a deep understanding of the poetry as he composed it. There is no surprise that these two thoughtful artists should produce powerful performances of the most inward-looking Heine songs – the suffering power of 'Der Atlas', the misery from which the harmony allows no escape in 'Die Stadt', the terror of 'Der Doppelgänger'. In its beauty, their shared phrasing springs from an understanding of the meaning of each poem, so that the lighter ones are scarcely less affecting. 'Das Fischermädchen' has a slightly knowing lilt, catching Heine's typical irony in the girl's false wooing. In 'Der Abschied' Goerne's young man sings happily as he sets off while Brendel's merry trot tells us that the horse has caught his mood. Their mutual understanding completely solves such a difficult song as 'Kriegers Ahnung'. And the Beethoven cycle moves in a steady progress not into the usual triumphant assertion but into a warmth of belief that song may truly join the parted lovers. Music-making of genius.

Als die Geliebte sich trennen wollte, WoO132. An die Geliebte, WoO140. Vier Arietten und ein Duett, Op 82. Das Geheimnis, WoO145. In questa tomba oscura, WoO133. Der Kuss, Op 128. Sechs Lieder von Gellert, Op 48. Acht Lieder, Op 52. Sechs

Lieder, Op 75. Der Mann von Wort, Op 99. Sehnsucht, WoO134. Sehnsucht, WoO146. Seufzer eines Ungeliebten und Gegenliebe, WoO188
Ann Murray mez **Roderick Williams** bar
Iain Burnside pf
Signum Classics ② SIGCD139 (87' · DDD)   Ⓜ☞

Beethoven was a reluctant song composer, avowedly frustrated by the limitations of the human voice – and, one suspects, the genre's limited scope for motivic-symphonic development. Yet he still left over 80 songs, ranging from agreeable trifles and Italianate scenas to the gravely majestic Gellert Lieder and the song-cycle *An die ferne Geliebte*. Mirroring Beethoven's life, the distant, unattainable beloved is a recurrent obsession here, whether in three settings of 'An die Geliebte' or four of Mignon's yearning 'Nur wer die Sehnsucht kennt', the last surely in Schubert's mind when he composed his famous setting of 1826. Elsewhere we have ingenuous quasi folksongs, the sombre 'In questa tomba oscura', and a clutch of comic songs, by turns lusty, viciously satirical (Mephistopheles's 'Song of the Flea' from *Faust*) or coyly erotic ('Der Kuss').

Two thirds of the numbers on this pair of CDs go to Roderick Williams, whose clean, mellifluous timbre, firm legato and expressive diction are well nigh ideal. The Gellert Lieder can be a bit of a bore when performed as lofty hymns: Williams sings them as personal dramas of the soul. At the other end of the spectrum he sings a slyly lubricious 'Der Kuss', colouring and timing to perfection, characterises the 'Song of the Flea' with gusto, and even brings off the potentially tedious 'Urians Reise um die Welt', a 14-verse travelogue related by a blinkered bore.

Ann Murray is, as ever, a thoughtful interpreter; and when she sings softly – as in her touching performances of the 'Nur wer die Sehnsucht kennt' settings or 'An den fernen Geliebten' – she gives pleasure. At *mezzo forte* and above her tone tends to grow squally – marring, say, her deeply felt 'Kennst du das Land' and 'Liebes-klage'. This proviso aside, these discs offer many unsuspected delights, enhanced throughout by Iain Burnside's vividly imagined and, where appropriate, witty keyboard commentaries and epilogues.

Irish, Welsh and Scottish Songs

Irish Songs, WoO152 – No 1, The Return to Ulster[b]; No 5, On the Massacre of Glencoe[b]; No 6, What shall I do to shew how much I love her[b]; No 8, Come draw we round a cheerful ring[b]; No 9, The Soldier's Dream[c]; No 19, Wife, Children and Friends[abc]; WoO153 – No 4, Since greybeards inform us that youth will decay[b]; No 9, The kiss, dear maid, thy lip has left[c]; WoO154 – No 3, The Farewell Song[b]; No 4, The Pulse of an Irishman[c]. Welsh Songs, WoO155 – No 2, The Monks of Bangor's March[bc]; No 9, To the Aeolian Harp[a]; No 14, The Dream[ab]; No 19, The Vale of Clwyd[a]; No 22, Constancy[bc]; No 25, The Parting Kiss[b]. Scottish

Songs, Op 108 – No 5, The sweetest lad was Jamie[a]; No 8, The lovely lass of Inverness[a]; No 11, Oh! thou art the lad of my heart, Willy[a]; No 13, Come fill, fill, my good fellow[abc]; No 20, Faithfu' Johnie[a]; No 24, Again, my Lyre[b]; WoO156 – Womankind[abc]. God save the King!, WoO157[abc]

[a]**Sophie Daneman** sop [b]**Paul Agnew** ten
[c]**Peter Harvey** bar **Alessandro Moccia** vn
Alix Verzier vc **Jérôme Hantaï** fp
Astrée Naïve E8850 (71' · DDD· N/T/t)   Ⓕ

Here's an excellent selection of Beethoven's 140 folksong arrangements, performed with all due care and accomplishment, spirit and affection. They're a joy: the songs in themselves, for a start, but more especially Beethoven's work on them. Or put it another way: 'work' is exactly what it does not sound like. It sounds as though he met these tunes (sent him, mostly, by George Thomson of Edinburgh), took to them like magic, found something in each that warmed his heart or set him dancing, and eventually, sorry when the verses had run out, made him add a ritornello or coda like a pat on the back to send each on its way.

Each number is a delight, but among the favourites are *Faithfu' Johnie*, with its deep cello underlining the heart's affections, *The Pulse of an Irishman*, both rumbustious and delicate in its fun, and, unexpectedly, *God save the King*, in which, in spite of its two peremptory calls to attention, Beethoven seems to be doing anything but. A special feature is the use of period instruments, effective in the more dramatic arrangements such as *The Return to Ulster* and the jovial party-pieces, *Come, fill, fill, my good fellows* and *Since greybeards inform us*. All three singers contribute ably, and the occasional collaborations in duet and trio are welcome.

Mass in C, Op 86

Mass in C. Ah! perfido, Op 65.   Ⓟ
Meeresstille und glückliche Fahrt, Op 112
Charlotte Margiono sop **Catherine Robbin** mez
William Kendall ten **Alastair Miles** bar **Monteverdi Choir; Orchestre Révolutionnaire et Romantique / Sir John Eliot Gardiner**
Archiv 435 391-2AH (62' · DDD · T/t)
                              ⒻⓄⓄ▷

Gardiner's genius is in evidence here. The *Kyrie eleison* is a plea for mercy but its opening bars speak of comfort: there's almost the simple good faith of a quiet, very Germanic carol about them. Gardiner sets a mood of deliberate seriousness, with lowered period, pitch and a tempo rather slower than that suggested by Beethoven's direction: *Andante con moto, assai vivace, quasi allegretto ma non troppo*. He also appears to have encouraged the soloists, especially the soprano, to shape and shade the phrases, so intensifying the feeling of seriousness and deliberation. Happily, this policy prevails for only a short time, and to some extent the music itself goes out to meet it. As the second *Kyrie* (fol-

lowing the *Christe*) moves towards its climax, the *fortissimo* brings suspensions where the alto part grinds against the soprano, and then come sudden *fortissimos* with intense modulations and momentary discords, all of which are particularly vivid in this performance. What follows has the same exhilarating quality as that which was so applauded in Gardiner's *Missa solemnis* and, just as he did there, Gardiner is constantly illuminating detail while maintaining an apparently easy natural rightness throughout.

Again, an outstanding contribution is made by the Monteverdi Choir. Splendidly athletic, for instance, are the leaps of a seventh in the fugal 'Hosanna'. The tone-painting of *Meeresstille* finds them marvellously alert and vivid in articulation. *Ah! perfido* brings a similar sense of renewal: there isn't even a momentary suspicion of concert routine, but rather as though it's part of an exceptionally intense performance of *Fidelio*. Charlotte Margiono sings the angry passages with the concentration of a Schwarzkopf, and brings to those that are gentler-toned a special beauty of her own. Other soloists in the Mass sing well if without distinction. Distinction is certainly a word to use of the disc as a whole.

Mass in C[a]. Meeresstille und glückliche Fahrt, Op 112. Elegischer Gesang, Op 118
[a]**Rebecca Evans** sop [a]**Pamela Helen Stephen** mez
[a]**Mark Padmore** ten [a]**Stephen Varcoe** bar **Collegium Musicum 90 / Richard Hickox**
Chandos Chaconne CHAN0703 (56' · DDD · T/t)   ⒻⒹ▷

Beethoven's Mass in C, like Haydn's late masterpieces and the Masses of Hummel, was written on commission from Prince Esterházy for the nameday of the Princess. Puzzlingly, Beethoven's 1807 contribution was counted a failure: the prince described the music as 'totally ridiculous'. Beethoven starts his setting more conventionally than Haydn did in his late masses. Where Haydn brilliantly gave his *Kyries* a symphonic flavour, Beethoven is devotional in a simpler, more innocent style. That's surely apt in a prayer for mercy, even if you note the Beethovenian modulations and dissonances, individual touches well brought out in Richard Hickox's performance.

Hickox, with an excellent quartet of soloists, gives full-blooded performances that bring out the exuberance of the inspiration. Where Gardiner brings out the work's drama with phenomenally crisp singing and playing, there's an infectious joy to Hickox's reading, in which, with a choir of 24 singers, a closer focus and a marginally more intimate acoustic, the words can be heard more clearly.

Throughout the liturgy one Beethoven took nothing on trust, thinking afresh rather than relying on convention, as when the *Credo*'s first eight bars are quiet before the full outburst of affirmation from the choir, and the setting of 'Et resurrexit' begins with a baritone solo, not with a choral or orchestral outburst. The setting of 'passus' just before it has extraordinary intensity, just it does in the later *Missa*. Hickox brings out such points with clarity, with period forces making the music sound not just more vital but more modern.

The Mass is coupled with the lovely Goethe setting *Meeresstille und glückliche Fahrt*, and the *Elegischer Gesang*, written in a simple, homophonic style to commemorate the passing of a noble friend's wife.

Mass in D, 'Missa solemnis', Op 123

Missa solemnis **P**
Charlotte Margiono *sop* **Catherine Robbin** *mez* **William Kendall** *ten* **Alastair Miles** *bass* **Monteverdi Choir; English Baroque Soloists / Sir John Eliot Gardiner**
Archiv 429 779-2AH (72' · DDD · T/t)

The *Missa solemnis* is one of the supreme masterpieces of the 19th century, but attempts to record a genuinely great performance have over many years run into difficulties. Usually the greatness itself is flawed, perhaps in the quality of the solo singers or in passages where the conductor's approach is too idiosyncratic or momentarily not up to the challenge of Beethoven's inspiration. The strain on the choir, especially its sopranos, is notorious; similarly the technical problems of balance by producer and engineers. This performance mixes discipline and spontaneous creativity; the rhythms are magically alive and the intricate texture of sound is made wonderfully clear. The great fugues of the *Gloria* and *Credo* achieve their proper Dionysiac sense of exalted liberation. Gardiner uses a choir of 36 and an orchestra of 60 playing on period instruments, aiming at a 'leaner and fitter' sound. The exceptional clarity of his smaller body of singers and players, their meticulous responsiveness to direction and concentrated attention to detail is impressive; yet you're aware of it *as* a performance. Sometimes, as in the first sounding of drums and trumpets signifying war, Gardiner's additional intensity brings a real gain.

Missa solemnis **P**
Eva Mei *sop* **Marjana Lipovšek** *contr* **Anthony Rolfe Johnson** *ten* **Robert Holl** *bass* **Arnold Schoenberg Choir; Chamber Orchestra of Europe / Nikolaus Harnoncourt**
Teldec ② 9031 74884-2 (81' · DDD · T/t)
Recorded live 1992 **B○○**

There are many marvellous performances in the catalogue of Beethoven's great Mass. Gardiner catches the greatness, rises to it with his uncanny freshness of perception, and secures a performance virtually without fault. Levine (DG, and currently out of the catalogue), with conventional forces, presents a large-scale performance, not universally liked, but which impresses you almost unequivocally on every hearing. Harnoncourt is very different from either of the others, but brings at least equally the stamp of

devotion and high attainment. Choir and orchestra achieve wonderful precision and clarity of articulation; they're sensitive to the needs of shading, to the ever-shifting balance of the parts, and to the purpose of cross-rhythms which at first may look like anarchy.

The soloists, who all meet their immense individual challenges, work intelligently as a quartet. It might be good simply to stop there and say, 'Enjoy it'. But once comparisons start, such simplicity begins to melt. Gardiner's performance is recorded more brightly and sharply. Returning to Harnoncourt after listening to that for a few minutes you feel a relative remoteness of contact with the sound. Moving then to Levine, there's again a more immediate presence in the sound. Yet in this three-way comparison Harnoncourt emerges as a kind of halfway-house between Gardiner and Levine, and not quite as colourful as either. You might opt for Gardiner because his performance is confined to a single disc. Yet, listening again to the *Credo*, there's something almost military in the way his people march along, and, as Harnoncourt stresses, the whole Mass is above all 'an appeal for peace'. This is a performance of great integrity: that is, it's a complete, consistent whole, and all its parts are sound.

Additional recommendation

Missa solemnis **H**
Coupled with: Symphony No 7
Cherubini Anacréon – Overture. **Mozart** Symphony No 35 in D, 'Haffner', K385
Milanov *sop* **Thorborg** *mez* **Pataky** *ten* **Moscona** *bass* **BBC Choral Society; BBC Symphony Orchestra / Toscanini**
BBC Legends mono ② BBCL4016-2 (145' · ADD)
Recorded live 1939 **M○○**
This is an absolute triumph and utterly gripping. The transfer eschews excessive de-hissing for a quiet sea of surface noise that soon ceases to matter.

Fidelio

Fidelio
Inga Nielsen *sop* Leonore **Gösta Winbergh** *ten* Florestan **Alan Titus** *bar* Don Pizarro **Kurt Moll** *bass* Rocco **Edith Lienbacher** *sop* Marzelline **Herwig Pecoraro** *ten* Jaquino **Wolfgang Glashof** *bass* Don Fernando **Péter Pálinkás** *ten* First Prisoner **József Moldvay** *bass* Second Prisoner **Hungarian Radio Chorus; Nicolaus Esterházy Sinfonia / Michael Halász**
Naxos ② 8 660070/1 (114' · DDD· D) **S○○**

Naxos has an uncanny knack for choosing the right artists for its operatic ventures. On this occasion, four of the singers are among the better known in the field, each judiciously cast. Halász projects every facet of the score, inspiring his forces to live every moment of the plot in words and music. This isn't an interpretation in the romantic, quasi-philosophical mode of Furwängler or Klemperer, rather one that alerts the mind and ear to the human agony of it all.

Nielsen's Leonore is no projection of subservient femininity but a tormented wife seeking to save her husband, her plight expressed in every key phrase. She doesn't provide the heroic sounds of a Nilsson (Maazel) or all the warmth of Rysanek (Fricsay), but her slimmer, more compact tone exactly fits this performance. Winberg is a Florestan equal to his Leonore in vocal and interpretative assets. Not even Heppner (Davis) or Seiffert (Harnoncourt), among modern interpreters, sings the role better. His voice poised between the lyrical and the heroic, his tone warm, his technique firm, Florestan's scene can seldom have been so satisfyingly sung and enacted. As Marzelline, Edith Lienbacher is something of a discovery, catching the eagerness, also the sense of nerves a-jangle predicated by the part.

The dialogue, rather drastically foreshortened, is well spoken by all and intelligently directed. The orchestral and choral singing need fear no comparisons, and the recording has plenty of presence, no tricks. This is a performance that fulfils almost all the demands made on its principals and at the price should be eagerly sought after: its most notable predecessors are matched, if not surpassed.

Fidelio
Sena Jurinac sop Leonore **Jon Vickers** ten Florestan **Hans Hotter** bass-bar Don Pizarro **Gottlob Frick** bass Rocco **Elsie Morison** sop Marzelline **John Dobson** ten Jaquino **Forbes Robinson** bass Don Fernando **Chorus and and Orchestra of the Royal Opera House, Covent Garden / Otto Klemperer**
Testament mono ② SBT2 1328 (143' · ADD · T/t)
Ⓕ**OOO**

Here is the first night of Otto Klemperer's legendary 1961 *Fidelio*, from the Royal Opera House, to challenge his noted studio set from a year later. This confirms the Achilles' heel of Walter Legge, EMI's leading mogul at the time, in his unwillingness to record live occasions, probably because he liked to have every aspect of a recording under his control. In this case there is more to it than that. Klemperer wanted, in the studio, to retain his Covent Garden cast; Legge preferred to make changes with two exceptions (Jon Vickers and Gottlob Frick). On the evidence of this magnificent issue, Klemperer was right. Not only are the singers, by and large, better equipped for their roles, but given the electricity of the occasion the conductor's interpretation is more vital (often faster tempi) and even more eloquent. For his own staging, Klemperer decided to include far more dialogue than is usually heard so that we have as much a play with music as an opera. The singers speak and act with such feeling and immediacy, most particularly Jurinac, Hotter and Frick, as to justify the added text. Add to that the dedication on all

---

BEETHOVEN'S MISSA SOLEMNIS – IN BRIEF

Margiono; Robbin; Kendall; Miles; Monteverdi Choir; English Baroque Soloists / Sir John Eliot Gardiner   Ⓟ
Archiv 429 779-2AH (72' · DDD)
Ⓕ**OOO**▷

Ⓖ *Gramophone*'s 1991 Record of the Year. Magnificent choral singing, four superb soloists and the fervent, committed playing of the EBS under Gardiner's incandescent direction. Lean and lithe and terrifically powerful.

Mei; Lipovšek; Rolfe Johnson; Holl; Arnold Schoenberg Choir; CO of Europe / Nikolaus Harnoncourt
Teldec ② 9031 74884-2 (81' · DDD)   Ⓑ**OO**
Period manners and modern instruments combined to great effect: it may lack the dynamism of the Gardiner or the monumental quality of the Levine but there's binding integrity that makes this a very powerful experience. The soloists are well matched and the COE play their hearts out.

Studer; Norman; Domingo; Moll; Leipzig Radio Chorus; Swedish Radio Choir; Vienna PO / James Levine
DG ② 435 770-2GH2 (83' · DDD)   Ⓕ**O**▷
A truly festive performance in memory of Karajan recorded at the Salzburg Festival. This is grand, majestic Beethoven that's mighty impressive and deeply moving.

Orgonášová; Larsson; Trost; Selig; Swiss Chamber Choir; Zürich Tonhalle Orchestra / David Zinman
Arte Nova 74321 87074-2 (66' · DDD)   Ⓢ**O**
A *Missa solemnis* for the 21st century – the lessons of the period-instrument movement have been well and truly absorbed into this thrillingly vital and low-calorie performance.

Mannion; Remmert; Taylor; Hauptmann; La   Ⓟ Chapelle Royale; Collegium Vocale; Orchestre des Champs-Elysées / Philippe Herreweghe
Harmonia Mundi ② HMC90 1557 (140' · DDD)   Ⓕ
Another successful period-instrument version, recorded live, that captures the questing spirituality at the heart of this great Mass. Four light-voiced, young soloists add to the performance's considerable appeal.

Milanov; Thorborg; von Pataky; Moscona;   Ⓗ BBC Choral Society; BBC SO / Arturo Toscanini
BBC Legends ② BBCL4016-2 (145')   Ⓕ
Milanov; Castagna; Björling; Kipnis; Westminster Choir; NBC SO / Arturo Toscanini
Istituto Discografico Italiano IDIS6365 (79') Ⓜ**OO**
Beethoven at white heat in 1939 and 1940, both with more humanity than the classic RCA set. This was a work that Toscanini adored – and it shows in every bar.

sides to Klemperer, and you can imagine why this was such a special occasion.

Compared to Christa Ludwig on Klemperer's studio version, Sena Jurinac creates a more believable and vulnerable Leonore. Her heartfelt sympathy with the role is evident in every line she speaks and sings, most notably in key phrases in her duet with Rocco near the end of Act 1 and the melodrama in Act 2. Once past some first night nerves evident in 'Abscheulicher!' she proves an ideal Leonore. Vickers, even in these early days of his career, is inclined to sentimentalise his Florestan with scoops and lachrymose effects, but all is forgiven when he provides the heroic thrust and inner feeling which the part demands and which is so notably absent from the Florestan on the recent Rattle version. Frick's Rocco is, if possible, even more admirable than on the studio set, expressing the jailor's terrible dilemma in the kind of incisive, warm tones few other basses on disc match.

It is incomprehensible that Legge preferred as Pizarro the too-comfortable sounding Walter Berry to Hans Hotter. Hotter, usually known for his noble roles, is here the epitome of evil, a threatening force of nature, his voice and diction full of menace so that he can be forgiven one or two wobbles in his aria. The young lovers are personably sung and enacted by Elsie Morison and John Dobson, and another Royal Opera stalwart, Forbes Robinson, is a dignified Don Fernando. There was a fuss at the time about Klemperer's inclusion of *Leonore* III, but he fully justifies it by his electrifying interpretation. He insisted on placing the wind in the middle of the orchestra spectrum, and the balance is improved throughout as a result. His reading overall has the stature and sense of the work's philosophical basis which will be familiar to those who know his discs of the symphonies.

Harnoncourt is almost bound to be controversial somewhere. If many speeds are to their advantage just on the measured side of the customary, as in the Dungeon quartet, allowing us for once to hear every strand of the argument, that for 'O namenlose Freude' is uncommonly moderate. At this pace, Leonore and Florestan seem to be conducting a gentle exchange of deeply felt emotions on an interior level rather than allowing their pent-up emotions to burst forth in an explosion of joy, as is more usual.

The dialogue is delivered in an understated fashion. Two vocal interpretations stand out for excellent singing and pungent characterisation. Once Leiferkus's Pizarro takes centre-stage the action lifts on to a new, more tense plane. This vicious little dictator with his incisive diction, spoken and sung, and his biting, vital voice is a commanding presence. But Evil is up against an equally arresting advocate of Good in Margiono's gloriously sung and read Leonore. Hers isn't the quasi-dramatic soprano usually associated with the part, but she never sounds strained in the context of a more lyrical, smaller-scale performance. Seiffert fills Florestan with more refulgent tone than any other tenor on recent recordings – the high tessitura of his aria's close causes him no distress at all – but it must be admitted that there's little of the *Schmerz* in the tone found, quite differently, in the recording of Vickers (Klemperer). In that sense, though, he fits into Harnoncourt's well-ordered scheme of things. The only piece of miscasting is Don Fernando: a role that needs a solid bass with strong low notes has been given to a high baritone who sounds anything but authoritative. Harnoncourt has opted for a professional chamber choir to second the superb Chamber Orchestra of Europe. By the side of the superb Teldec recording, the Klemperer and Maazel sound less than immediate.

Fidelio
Charlotte Margiono sop Leonore **Peter Seiffert** ten Florestan **Sergei Leiferkus** bar Pizarro **László Polgár** bass Rocco **Barbara Bonney** sop Marzelline **Deon van der Walt** ten Jaquino **Boje Skovhus** bar Don Fernando **Reinaldo Macias** ten First Prisoner **Robert Florianschütz** bass Second Prisoner **Arnold Schoenberg Choir; Chamber Orchestra of Europe / Nikolaus Harnoncourt**
Teldec ② 4509 94560-2 (119' · DDD· T/t)   ⑫**OO**
Highlights available on Warner Apex 0927 401374-2   ⑤

Everything Harnoncourt touches leaves a sense of a country rediscovered: we listen to the piece in hand with new ears. So it is again here. Beethoven's sole but intractable opera has seldom emerged from the recording studio, or indeed the theatre, with such clarity of texture, such promptness of rhythm, such unity of purpose on all sides. This is a reading that gives full play to winds and horns, making you aware, whether it's in the Overture, Pizarro's aria, Leonore's big scena or the Prelude to Act-2, just how important they are to the structure and character of each movement. Where tempos are concerned,

---

Fidelio
Anja Kampe sop Leonore **Lisa Milne** sop Marzelline **Brindley Sherratt** bass Rocco **Peter Coleman-Wright** bar Don Pizarro **Andrew Kennedy** ten Jaquino **Torsten Kerl** ten Florestan **Henry Waddington** bass Don Fernando **Nathan Vale** ten First Prisoner **Anthony Cleverton** bass Second Prisoner **Glyndebourne Chorus; London Philharmonic Orchestra / Sir Mark Elder**
Glyndebourne Festival Opera ② GFOCD004/6 (121' · DDD · T/t). Recorded live in August 2006   ⑫**O**

Fidelio, so difficult to bring off in the theatre, is an ideal opera for listening to at home. In this recording we have the best of both worlds: all the intensity of stage performances without the irritations of Deborah Warner's production.

As one expects from Glyndebourne performances, the teamwork of the singers is impeccable. But the highest praise must be reserved for Sir Mark Elder. Whereas his predecessor, when the production was first staged in 2001, raced through the score as though he had a train to catch, Elder paces it almost to perfection. He instils confidence from the start with a weighty account of the Overture. The opening scene, before Fidelio appears, has the right lightness of touch. The mood darkens when Don Pizarro enters (after much stage clatter). His vengeance aria works up to a terrific climax, albeit with understated horns at 'in seiner letzten Stunde' (compare Klemperer's Philharmonia!). Elder's steady speeds, his close attention to *crescendos* and *sforzandos*, reflect the drama in the most wonderful way. There are just two places where it seems that his instinct deserted him: the lingering at the beginning of 'Euch werde Lohn' (and at the reprise), and the speedy, almost perfunctory response to the first trumpet-call. Against that, one could cite numerous examples of his sensitivity, such as the dying fall of the Act 1 finale.

That finale, of course, includes the Prisoners' Chorus: the Glyndebourne Chorus sing it beautifully and it's Beethoven's fault, not theirs, if they sound improbably robust. The Act 2 finale, where the prisoners are joined by 'the people', is another matter: a jubilant outburst, gloriously sung.

The cast is excellent, especially Torsten Kerl, deeply moving in his aria. Minor drawbacks include an editing slip that adds a half-bar to the Act 2 quartet and a not wholly accurate translation of the libretto. The competition is formidable, but Elder can hold his head high in their company.

Fidelio
Hildegard Behrens *mez* Leonore **James King** *ten*
Florestan **Donald McIntyre** *bass-bar* Don Pizarro
Kurt Moll *bass* Rocco **Lucia Popp** *sop* Marzelline
Norbert Orth *ten* Jaquino **Nikolaus Hillebrand** *bass*
Don Fernando **Friedrich Lenz** *ten* First Prisoner **Hans Wilbrink** *bar* Second Prisoner **Bavarian State Orchestra and Opera Chorus / Karl Böhm**
Orfeo d'Or ② C560 012I (141' · ADD)
Recorded live 1978   Ⓜ️**OO**

At 84 this was to be Böhm's last *Fidelio*, and he knew it. Yet absolutely no allowances have to be made for his age in this life-enhancing, dramatically alert reading, quite on a par with his earlier versions of the work on disc. Indeed this now joins those other legendary live performances by great conductors of the past – Böhm himself in 1944 in Vienna, Bruno Walter at the Met in the same year, Toscanini at a concert in New York in 1945 and Furtwängler at Salzburg in 1950. But, of course, this one is vastly superior in sound. Everyone seems determined to give of their best. None more than Hildegard Behrens, the very epitome of the dedicated, highly strung wife on a rescue mission and singing her heart out at all the important moments, not least in her 'Abscheulicher!'. She far surpasses her performance for Solti on Decca a year later. By her side throughout is the sterling, warm, authoritative Rocco of Kurt Moll in a reading that surpasses his own high standards on other versions. James King, though his voice had dried out a

BEETHOVEN'S FIDELIO – IN BRIEF

Inga Nielsen *Leonore* **Gösta Windbergh** *Florestan*
Alan Titus *Don Pizarro* **Hungarian Radio Chorus, Nicolaus Esterházy Sinfonia / Michael Halász**
Naxos ② 8 660070/1 (114' · ADD)   Ⓢ**OO**
At bargain price, a good place to start: a vivid performance with stellar leading singers and good, dramatic conducting.

Christa Ludwig *Leonore* **Jon Vickers** *Florestan*
Walter Berry *Don Pizarro* **Philharmonia Chorus and Orchestra / Otto Klemperer**
EMI download 567364-2 (143' · ADD)   Ⓜ️**OO**▷
Often considered a definitive recording, Klemperer's is a massive, granitic reading harking back to symphonic Beethoven, with a cast of heroic stature. Ludwig is a dark-toned, dramatic soprano Leonore, but Vickers is unforgettable in Florestan's suffering. Great value now it's at mid-price (if you can still find it on CD), but don't overlook the live Klemperer set on Testament noted below…

Charlotte Margiono *Leonore* **Peter Seiffert** *Florestan* **Sergei Leiferkus** *Don Pizarro* **Arnold Schoenberg Choir, CO of Europe / Nikolaus Harnoncourt**
Teldec ② 4509 94560-2 (119' · ADD)   Ⓕ
An attempt at an intimate interpretation, with a lighter-voiced cast in which Seiffert's vigorous Florestan stands out. Harnoncourt's eccentric tempi and the deliberately understated drama won't suit everyone.

Hildegard Behrens *Leonore* **James King** *Florestan* **Donald McIntyre** *Don Pizarro* **Bavarian State Opera Chorus and Orchestra / Karl Böhm**
Orfeo ② C560 012I (141' · ADD)   Ⓜ️**O**
A 1978 theatre performance, well recorded but with some resultant noise and stagey dialogue delivery, this is an intense, dramatic reading with a brilliant Leonore in Hildegard Behrens.

Sena Jurinac *Leonore* **Jon Vickers** *Florestan* **Hans Hotter** *Don Pizarro* **Royal Opera House Chorus and Orchestra / Otto Klemperer**
Testament ② SBT2 1328 (143' · ADD)   Ⓕ**OOO**
A performance of tremendous authority and stature taken live from the stage of Covent Garden. A superb cast headed by Jurinac's deeply moving Leonore.

Anja Kampe *Leonore* **Torsten Kerl** *Florestan* **Peter Coleman-Wright** *Don Pizarro* **Glyndebourne Chorus; London Philharmonic Orchestra / Sir Mark Elder**
Glyndebourne Festival Opera ② GFOCD004/6 (121' · DDD)   Ⓕ**O**
A very fine memento of a thrillingly dramatic Glyndebourne performance. Paced to perfection, it unfolds with colossal theatricality and poetry, and it is strongly cast, too.

little by 1978, sings a Florestan imbued with anguish.

As Pizarro, McIntyre, in powerful voice, is evil personified. For all the vocal glories, Böhm remains the evening's hero. Above all, he makes the opera living drama. Were this *Fidelio* his only work that survived for us to judge him by, it would be enough to clinch his reputation as a great conductor. There's more dialogue than we usually hear either in the theatre or on disc. There's also a deal of stage action. None of that should deter you from hearing such a truthful enactment of this masterpiece, few if any better on CD.

Fidelio
Gabriela Beňačková sop Leonore **Josef Protschka** ten Florestan **Monte Pederson** bar Don Pizarro **Robert Lloyd** bass Rocco **Marie McLaughlin** sop Marzelline **Neill Archer** ten Jaquino **Hans Tschammer** bass-bar Don Fernando **Lynton Atkinson** ten First Prisoner **Mark Beesley** bar Second Prisoner **Royal Opera House Chorus and Orchestra, Covent Garden / Christoph von Dohnányi**
Stage director **Adolf Dresen**
Video director **Derek Bailey**
ArtHaus Musik ☼ 100 074 (129' · Regions 2 & 5) Ⓕ ●

'Triumph! Triumph! Triumph!' as nasty Pizarro exultantly cries. He's in for a disappointment, of course. Not so the listener and viewer of this performance, which is caught in fine sound and skilfully filmed. Pizarro will, for instance, have no place in the great festival of light that is the finale. Here the rejoicing is so powerful that we switch off the DVD player and go to bed with the surge and sequence of inspired creation fully in possession, convinced that in the whole of opera there's nothing to match it. That's the sign of a great *Fidelio*, and it means that, throughout, the proportions, structure and balance of the work have been rendered with clarity and conviction. That in turn means that the opening scene – the Marzelline-Jaquino duet and the solos which might seem to be from some other opera – has been integrated, so that the work is a journey from light into the blackest tunnel and out again into an infinitely greater light.

A prime contribution to the success of this process is made by the portrayal of Rocco, the gaoler. Instead of the bumbling, coarse-grained character of convention, Robert Lloyd presents a full human being, a man with a rueful-realistic twinkle, and above all a loving father. This of itself guards against the alien introduction of comic opera, and helps to fashion the role so that even here our concern is with real humanity. Leonore is the radiant Beňačková, and she presents a problem. The camera reveals unsparingly a disguise which just possibly might pass in the theatre. It says much for her singing, and for something in the spirit of her performance, that the willing suspension of disbelief can prevail as well as it does. In all other respects the visual element satisfies well; and musically, under Dohnányi's direction, this is a memorable and moving *Fidelio*.

Fidelio
Camilla Nylund sop Leonore **Jonas Kaufmann** ten Florestan **Alfred Muff** bass Don Pizarro **László Polgár** bass Rocco **Elizabeth Magnuson** sop Marzelline **Christoph Strehl** ten Jaquino **Günther Groissböck** bass Don Fernando **Bogusław Bidzinski** ten First Prisoner **Gabriel Bermúdez** bass Second Prisoner **Zürich Opera House Chorus and Orchestra / Nikolaus Harnoncourt**
Stage director **Jürgen Flimm**
Video director **Felix Breisach**
TDK ☼ DV-OPFID (134' · 16:9 · PCM stereo, 5.1 & DTS 5.1 · 0). Recorded live at the Opernhaus, Zürich, on February 15, 2004　　　　　　Ⓕ●●

Harnoncourt's predominantly light but dramatic reading harks back to the 18th century rather than forward to the 19th, with romantic feeling at a premium. The orchestra foretells the rest in its crisply accented rhythms, clean sound and sense of the impending drama: they play splendidly. However, the thrust of Beethoven's universal message sometimes goes missing by comparison with the Dohnányi on DVD.

The simple, somewhat geometric sets, sensitively lit, house a direction that's sometimes fussy in detail. Jürgen Flimm offers a fairly minimalist production concentrating on the characters of the principals. Marzelline (the bright-voiced Elizabeth Magnuson) and Jaquino are preparing guns and ammunition for the troops. She is bossy, he slightly sadistic. By contrast, Rocco – a wonderfully moving, warm and eloquent performance from László Polgár – is kindly, cowed by his surroundings, and alert to every nuance of feeling in those around him. His body language and his eyes tell us everything about the jailer's torment.

Leonore, in the arresting figure of Camilla Nylund, is slim and appealing, truly believable as a young man. Her singing, in the modern way, is lighter than one would have expected of yore. Every note is well placed, united into a real *legato* projected on a compact, firm tone. Jonas Kaufmann's Florestan, also a more youthful portrayal than usual, sings with accuracy and feeling, though he may find more in the words and notes in years to come. He and Nylund make 'O namenlose Freude', taken at an extraordinarily slow tempo, more an inward expression of release than the usual excited one. Alfred Muff's Pizarro, more conventional, is always a hateful presence, as he should be.

The sound could be a bit more immediate; the video direction is for the most part perceptive.

Additional recommendation

Fidelio
Janowitz Leonore **Kollo** Florestan **Sotin** Don Pizarro **Jungwirth** Rocco **Popp** Marzelline **Vienna State Opera Chorus and Orchestra / Bernstein**
Stage and video director **Otto Schenk**
DG ☼ 073 4159GH Ⓕ
　Bernstein conducts with all his heart – and with the occasional eccentricities as regards tempo that

went with the package. By 1978 he was God in Vienna and the VPO play superbly for a conductor they had come to love. Otto Schenk's staging remains a marvel of sensible action, pertinent handling of the singers and clarity of action. Gundula Janowitz has a lovely voice but her acting is unconvincing. René Kollo sings with strength and conviction as Florestan and acts effectively. Dialogue is cut to the minimum. Sound and video direction (by Schenk himself) are both excellent.

Vincenzo Bellini
Italian 1801-1835

Of the Famous Three of Italian opera (Rossini, Donizetti, Bellini), it was Bellini who did the most to develop the medium to which he devoted his career. Rossini and Donizetti could toss off three or four operas a year; Bellini struggled with each one, shaping, structuring, experimenting.

What did he bring that was new? One clue can be had from a remark he made to a friend after listening to Pergolesi's Stabat mater. 'If I could write one melody as beautiful as this, I would not mind dying young like Pergolesi,' a hauntingly prescient wish. All of Bellini's operas are gloriously melodic, with arias full of long-breathed, arching phrases, the epitome of the Italian bel canto style. Opera composers had written beautiful melodies before, of course, but had never matched the intensity that Bellini achieved. He did this by seriously considering the dramatic content of the libretto and writing music which reflected the emotion of the characters and their situation in the story. This was a big move away from the purely decorative vocal displays of the past and was one of the key elements in the development of Italian opera.

Bellini made the most of writing for particular singers and several of them, reckoned to be among the greatest of the century, frequently appeared together in his operas – Pasta, Grisi, Tamburini, Lablache and, most electrifying of all, Rubini. He was the Pavarotti of his day, not much of an actor but with a huge vocal range.

Although Bellini came from a family of musicians (both his father and grandfather were organists and maestri di cappella), a musical career was strongly opposed. But when the Duke and Duchess of San Martino offered to fund his studies at the Real Conservatorio di Musica in Naples, the family relented. Bellini proved a diligent student and wrote his first opera while in his final year. This, Adelson e Salvini (first performed by fellow students in 1825) was such a success that he was commissioned to write another for the following Carnival season in Naples. Not every composer has such fairy-tale boosts to their youthful aspirations. For the next decade, Bellini produced an average of one opera per year for the major Italian houses. Il Pirata (premiered at la Scala in 1827) set the seal on his fame and established the Bellini style but it was La Sonnambula (1830) and Norma (1831) that are the two masterpieces which have never lost their place in the international repertoire.

In 1833 Bellini paid a visit to London and then settled in Paris where he befriended Rossini (living in early retirement) and Chopin. The two younger men had much in common – slim, aristocratic-looking, delicate and highly appealing to members of the opposite sex. But listen to their music and there are more interesting comparisons: Bellini's music is concerned with the voice and the vocal line (the orchestral accompaniment simply provides harmonic and rhythmic support); a Chopin nocturne has exactly the same qualities and, for example, the slow movement of the early Piano Concerto in E minor is just like a Bellini aria for the keyboard. Each composer influenced the other. More important was the influence of Bellini's music on the young Verdi (listen to some of his earliest efforts such as Oberto and Nabucco).

What might Bellini have achieved if he had lived longer? One feels that he was just getting into his stride, for each successive work is an advance on the previous one, but his career lasted just 10 years. He was a few weeks short of his 34th birthday when he died in a house outside Paris from an acute inflammation of the large intestine and an abscess of the liver, a particularly unromantic way to go for this archetypal Romantic.

I Capuleti e i Montecchi

I Capuleti e i Montecchi
Anna Netrebko sop Giulietta **Elīna Garanča** mez Romeo **Joseph Calleja** ten Tebaldo **Robert Gleadow** bass Lorenzo **Tiziano Bracci** bass-bar Capellio **Vienna Singakademie; Vienna Symphony Orchestra / Fabio Luisi**
DG ② 477 8031GH2 (128' · DDD · S/T/t/N) Ⓕ**OO**▷

Bellini's version of the Romeo and Juliet story has notched up quite an impressive discography considering that is not performed that often. This new set boasts three of the most admired singers of the moment, all of them in fine form. The performance is dominated by Elīna Garanča's Romeo; she easily suggests both the swaggering duellist and the lovelorn youth. There are times when her rich, velvety tones sound almost like a soprano, and in the duets with Anna Netrebko's Juliet, the two voices seem naturally to complement each other. The slow section of their Act 1 'Ah, crudel, d'onor ragioni' develops into an almost Norma-like blend of scales and trills. Netrebko sings the beautiful lament 'Oh! Quante volte' with considerable feeling, although the voice is beginning to sound a bit mature now for the innocent daughter of the Capulets. This is all to her advantage in the more tragic Act 2 'Morte io non temo' as she contemplates taking the poison.

I Capuleti e i Montecchi was one of the last important operas to employ a mezzo as the masculine lead. The tenor who sings Tebaldo needs to be of equal strength to balance the drama, and Joseph Calleja rises to the challenge of his two-part Act 1 aria, 'È serbata a questo acciaro' with virile strength. The duet in Act 2, when Tebaldo and Romeo are about to fight but then learn of Juliet's death, finds Garanča and Calleja striking sparks off each other; despite the beauty of the final tomb-scene duet, this confrontation is the highlight of the proceedings.

Robert Gleadow makes a strong impression as Friar Laurence, and Tiziano Bracci is impressive as Capellio. Fabio Luisi leads the Vienna forces in a performance which, though obviously sympathetic to the voices, manages to accentuate the drama. It's certainly a star vehicle but also a satisfying account of Bellini's near-masterpiece, and one which now leads the field.

I Capuleti e i Montecchi

Patrizia Ciofi sop Giulietta **Clara Polito** mez Romeo **Danilo Formaggia** ten Tebaldo **Federico Sacchi** bass Capellio **Nicola Amodio** bass Lorenzo **Orchestra Internazionale d'Italia / Luciano Acocella**
Stage director **Denis Krief**
Video director **Marco Scalfi**
Dynamic 📀 DV33504 (136' · NTSC · 16:9 · 2.0, DTS 5.1 and ODS · 0). Recorded live at the Martina Franca Festival, Italy, in August 2005   Ⓕ🔵🔵

This *Capuleti e i Montecchi* is one of the best versions of this opera on disc. The edition used is the one Bellini made for La Scala a few months after the Venice premiere in 1830. The main difference is that Friar Lawrence here is a tenor (the excellent Nicola Amodio), and Juliet's solo in Act 2 is a continuous aria, rather than being punctuated by interjections from her father. Patrizia Ciofi gives this a really passionate performance: she is an ideal Juliet, youthful in appearance, in no way overextended by Bellini's long vocal lines. Clara Polito makes a tremendous Romeo, adding some effective flourishes in the cabaletta to her Act 1 aria and joining Danilo Formaggia as Tybalt in an exciting account of their fight duet in Act 2. Federico Sacchi is a thunderous Capulet, and the chorus makes an always positive contribution.

Luciano Acocella and the Orchestra Internazionale d'Italia make the opera sound quite the equal of Bellini's later, more famous works, but as Wagner wrote of it, 'there is true passion and emotion there'. Denis Krief's production is straightforward and always concentrated on the drama. It is played in modern dress, the Montagues and Capulets obviously on opposite sides in some unforgiving sectarian civil war, the men brandishing machine guns and revolvers. It works extremely well on its own terms, and the setting of the Ducal Palace in Martina Franca makes a perfect backdrop: recommended.

Norma

Norma
Maria Callas sop Norma **Christa Ludwig** mez Adalgisa **Franco Corelli** ten Pollione **Nicola Zaccaria** bass Oroveso **Piero De Palma** ten Flavio **Edda Vincenzi** sop Clotilde **Chorus and Orchestra of La Scala, Milan / Tullio Serafin**
EMI ③ 566428-2 (161' · ADD· T/t)
Recorded 1960   Ⓜ🔵🔵🔵➾

Norma   Ⓗ
Maria Callas sop Norma **Ebe Stignani** mez Adalgisa **Mario Filippeschi** ten Pollione **Nicola Rossi-Lemeni** bass Oroveso **Paolo Caroli** ten Flavio **Rina Cavallari** sop Clotilde **Chorus and Orchestra of La Scala, Milan / Tullio Serafin**
EMI Callas Edition mono ② 556271-2 (160' · ADD· T/t). Recorded 1954.   Ⓕ🔵🔵➾

Norma may be considered the most potent of Bellini's operas, in its subject – the secret love of a Druid priestess for a Roman general – and its musical content. It has some of the most eloquent music written for the soprano voice. The title-role has always been coveted by dramatic sopranos, but there have been few in the history of the opera who have completely fulfilled its considerable vocal and histrionic demands: in recent times the leading exponent has been Maria Callas.

Is the 1960 recording better or worse than the 1954 recording? The answer can't be put in a word. But those who heard Callas sing Norma at Covent Garden in 1953-4, and then again, slim, in 1957, will know the difference. The facts are that in 1954 the voice above the stave was fuller, more solid and more certain, but that in 1960 the middle timbres were more beautiful and more expressive; and, further, that an interpretation which was always magnificent had deepened in finesse, flexibility and dramatic poignancy.

The emphasis you give to these facts must be a matter of personal opinion. Certainly Callas's voice lets her down again and again, often when she essays some of her most beautiful effects. The F wobbles when it should crown a heart-rending 'Oh rimembranza'; the G wobbles in an exquisitely conceived 'Son io' – and yet how much more moving it is than the simpler, if steadier *messa di voce* of the earlier set. There are people who have a kind of tone-deafness to the timbres of Callas's later voice, who don't respond to one of the most affecting and eloquent of all sounds. They'll stick to the earlier set. But ardent Callas collectors will probably find that it's the later one to which they will be listening again and again, not unaware of its faults, but still more keenly responsive to its beauties. 'Casta Diva', by the way, is sung in F, as in 1954 – not in the original G, as in the Covent Garden performances of June 1953. The big duet with Adalgisa is again down a tone, 'Deh! con te' in B flat, 'Mira, o Norma' in E flat, and the change is once again effected in the recitative phrase 'nel romano campo'. Callas doesn't decorate the music. Adalgisa, a soprano role, is as usual taken by a mezzo. Ludwig blends beautifully with Callas in the low-key 'Mira, o Norma' (though her downward scales are as ill-defined as her colleague's). She's no veteran Adalgisa, but youthful and impetuous except when she lets the rhythm get heavy, and Serafin does nothing to correct her.

On the earlier set, Stignani is a worthy partner, while Filippeschi is rough but quite effective. On both sets, Serafin restores the beautiful quiet coda to the 'Guerra' chorus, and on both sets,

Callas disappointingly doesn't float over the close of that slow rising *arpeggio*. In the later set, the conducting is spacious, unhurried, elevated and eloquent. Only in his handling of the mounting tension and the two great climaxes and releases of the finale, might you prefer the earlier version. The La Scala playing is superlative, and the recording is excellent.

Norma
Edita Gruberová *sop* Norma **Elīna Garanča** *sop* Adalgisa **Aquiles Machado** *ten* Pollione **Alastair Miles** *bass* Oroveso **Judith Howarth** *mez* Clotilde **Ray M Wade** *ten* Flavio **Rastatt Vocal Ensemble; Rhineland Palatinate Philharmonic Orchestra / Friedrich Haider**
Nightingale Classics ② NC040245 (145' · DDD · S/T/t/N). Recorded live 2004   Ⓕ🔵

'Nothing is played for as willed theatrical pathos or as melodrama, but simply as the predicament of a woman whose emotional being is totally real and whose singing voice is its unique and irreplaceable expression.' That was the verdict on Maria Callas's Norma from a *Gramophone* survey in 2002. Something very similar can now be said of Edita Gruberová's Norma, and to it will have to be added notice of the extraordinary radiance of her voice.

That requires a further note of wonder, for Gruberová was in her 58th year at the time of these performances. Her voice, as recorded recently, had begun to show its age – which this singing does not do. The purity and Tetrazzini-like radiance of tone seem scarcely diminished; the years have brought an underlying maturity to the voice and have enabled her to acquire the rare art of infusing her high, bright soprano with warmth and depth of feeling; and the occasionally intrusive unfocused tones which we have known in the past are hardly in evidence at all. 'Casta diva' is sung in the high, original key of G, the decorations in verse two being ingenious, neat and natural. The pain of those crucial 'debate' recitatives ('Vanne, e li cela entrambi', 'Dormono entrambi!', 'Ei tornerà') is marvellously actual and the climax of the great role is reached with vocal and emotional reserves still to draw on.

The Adalgisa, Elīna Garanča, is also an exceptional singer: pure and rich in tone, extensive in range, accomplished in technique and intelligently expressive. Aquiles Machado makes a sturdy, resonant Pollione: no brute but not very interesting either. Alastair Miles brings an authoritative manner to support his true *basso cantante* singing. And Judith Howarth is luxury casting as Clotilde. The Rastatt Vocal Ensemble give the Druids more life (young and responsive to rhythm) than usual.

The Rhineland Palatinate State Philharmonic play with relish and Haider conducts with firmness and an effective feeling for tempo (sometimes refreshingly brisk). Recording is clear and well balanced, and the only textual grumble is that the lovely 'Sun-god' chorus ('A mirare il

trionfo dei figli') is omitted, as regrettably and by this time inexcusably it still generally is.

Norma
Montserrat Caballé *sop* Norma **Josephine Veasey** *sop* Adalgisa **Jon Vickers** *ten* Pollione **Agostino Ferrin** *bass* Oroveso **Gino Sinimberghi** *ten* Flavio **Marisa Zotti** *mez* Clotilde **Teatro Regio di Torino Chorus and Orchestra / Giuseppe Patanè** *Stage director* **Sandro Sequi** *Video director* **Pierre Jourdan**
Hardy Classic Video 📀 HCD4003 (161' · 4:3 · 1.0 · 0) Recorded live 1974   Ⓕ🔵🔵🔵

G Here in Orange, France, on a windswept, night in 1974, they had greatness itself. Pierre Jourdan's film of the event is a priceless document, first of all, in the history of the opera. Stage-settings of *Norma* are usually hopeless: an offence to the eye, a chafing confutation of the spirit by gross matter. The ancient Roman amphitheatre is at any rate worthy and appropriate, and the Mistral, which threatened to close down the whole show and turn away an audience estimated at 10,000, adds a fine reminder of the power of Nature as it sets the druidical robes billowing and attacks the microphones.

The vastness of the stage provides a further challenge to the man in charge, and although conductor Giuseppe Patanè's star is somewhat eclipsed in the general view of things, he deserves congratulation for two contrary achievements – holding the ensemble together and giving the soloists freedom. But it's their night, and particularly Caballé's. She called it the greatest single performance of her career. In certain passages it's hard to think of any voice we've known that could sound more lovely; but, more than that, the great role is sung and acted with such well-founded assurance that for once it fulfils its own legend, the embodiment of musical-dramatic sublimity in 19th-century opera. Of the others in the cast it must for now suffice to say that they're worthy partners.

Norma
Edita Gruberová *sop* Norma **Sonia Ganassi** *sop* Adalgisa **Zoran Todorovich** *ten* Pollione **Roberto Scandiuzzi** *bass* Oroveso **Markus Herzog** *ten* Flavio **Cynthia Jansen** *mez* Clotilde **Bavarian State Opera Chorus and Orchestra / Friedrich Haider**
Stage director **Jürgen Rose**
Video director **Brian Large**
DG ② 📀 073 4219GH2
(155' · NTSC · 16:9 · PCM stereo & DTS 5.0 · 0) Includes a 'Making of' documentary and Gruberová discography.   Ⓕ🔵

Edita Gruberová waited until 2006 to sing Norma on stage for the first time. In this production from Munich she is revealed as the greatest Norma of today. Her singing and acting bring out the complete portrait of the guilt-ridden priestess, trapped between her sense of duty to her religion and country, and the sickening prospect of losing her lover and her children. Gruberová brings a lifetime's experience of singing *bel canto* opera and caresses Bellini's vocal lines with many subtle touches. Almost entirely absent is that mannerism of sliding between notes which has marred some of her singing in the past. Every phrase is moulded with the feeling and reticence of a great artist.

Jürgen Rose, in total control of the production – stage direction, lighting, costumes and sets – succeeds where many have failed in the past. The action seems to be taking place in the aftermath of some terrible conflict. The middle-eastern costumes suggest the Iraq war, but the whole concept is more ambitious than merely to rely on familiar signs. Norma's tribe seems to have returned to its ancient religion as a refuge from the surrounding chaos. The semi-abstract sets are beautiful, the costumes simple. The priestesses' hands are stained with symbolic woad. The men carry machine guns and wear black woollen masks. Norma's dwelling is an underground bunker.

Sonia Ganassi makes a sympathetic Adalgisa, and she and Gruberová sing both the great duets with exquisite tenderness. There is a touching moment when Adalgisa first confesses her love and Norma removes the girl's veil, as if to free her from her vows. Zoran Todorovich is a charismatic and virile Pollione. In the first act his singing seems rather over-loud at moments, but he is a fine actor and rises to the challenge of the final scene, where Gruberová begins 'In mia man' while he is bound to the altar with ropes.

Roberto Scandiuzzi makes the most of the somewhat ungrateful part of Oroveso. He too is very moving in the closing ensemble, as he forgives Norma and agrees to care for her children. Friedrich Haider conducts the Munich forces with fine urgency and an impeccable understanding of the grand sweep of this notoriously tricky work. The whole undertaking is a triumph for all concerned, above all Gruberová and Jürgen Rose.

I Puritani
Eduardo Valdes ten Bruno **Franco Vassallo** bar
Riccardo **Anna Netrebko** sop Elvira **John Relyea**
bass Giorgio **Eric Cutler** ten Arturo **Valerian
Ruminski** bass Gualtiero **Maria Zifchak** mez
Enrichetta **Metropolitan Opera Ballet, Chorus and
Orchestra, New York / Patrick Summers**
Stage director **Sandro Sequi**
Video director **Gary Halvorson**
DG ② 💿 073 4421GH2 (149' · NTSC · HD ·
16:9 · PCM stereo and DTS 5.1 · 0)
Includes 'Backstage at the Met with Anna Netrebko,
Renée Fleming and Beverly Sills' Ⓕ**OO**

Although *I Puritani* was performed during the Metropolitan Opera's first season in 1883, it had not been seen there for decades until this production by Sandro Sequi was unveiled in 1976. It was one of the greatest triumphs for the partnership of Joan Sutherland and Luciano Pavarotti, and it is to the credit of all concerned in this recent revival that one soon forgets names from the past and enjoys what is a spirited attempt to evoke mid-19th-century style.

Although it is very much an opera for four singers – the original 'Puritani quartet' of Grisi, Rubini, Tamburini and Lablache entered into legend – this is essentially Anna Netrebko's evening. In her tightly waisted costumes, her pale face framed by a dark wig, she succeeds in dominating the action both by her singing and by her physical presence, using sudden, jerky movements to suggest Elvira's unhinged state. At the climax of the mad scene in Act 2, she flings herself on the floor and, with her head hanging over the orchestra pit, launches the second verse of 'Vien, diletto'. She negotiates both 'Son vergin vezzosa' and 'Oh vieni al tempio' with brilliance in Act 1, and has more than enough stamina left in Act 3 to match Eric Cutler as Arturo in the vertiginous 'Vieni fra queste braccia'. If there is something missing from her singing it is the ability to invest Carlo Pepoli's verses with an edge of pathos beyond what is already there in Bellini's languid melodies.

Cutler makes a good cavalier hero, especially in the desperate plea of 'Credeasi, misera!'. As usual, the baritone and bass, Franco Vassallo and John Relyea, bring down the house with 'Suoni la tromba' at the end of Act 2. After more than 30 years, the sets and costumes by Ming Cho Lee and Peter J Hall look very handsome. Whether you consider the production quaint or merely traditional, it is something of a relief not to have to battle with an elaborate political concept. Patrick Summers conducts the Met forces always with consideration for the singers. The photography is excellent, and there are some intriguing glimpses of the singers backstage, including an interval feature in which Renée Fleming is the interviewer, chatting to Netrebko in her dressing-room.

La Sonnambula

La Sonnambula Ⓗ
Maria Callas sop Amina **Cesare Valletti** ten Elvino
Giuseppe Modesti bass Rodolfo **Eugenia Ratti** sop
Lisa **Gabriella Carturan** mez Teresa **Pierluigi
Latinucci** bass Alessio **Giuseppe Nessi** ten Notary
**La Scala, Milan Chorus and Orchestra /
Leonard Bernstein**
EMI mono ② 567906-2 (141' · ADD · N/T/t)
Recorded live in 1955 Ⓜ**OO**

This important historical document comes from live performances at La Scala in 1955 when the diva was at the height of her powers. Callas gives a more vital performance here than on the set recorded in the studio. The only drawback is the intrusive distortion at climactic moments.

It was Callas's particular genius to find exactly the appropriate mode of expression for every role she tackled. Here Callas gives us Amina, the shy, vulnerable sleepwalker. Bernstein and Callas join forces (having performed *Médée* together the previous year) for an utterly charming account of *Sonnambula*. The conductor's feeling for rhythm and colour and Callas's subtle responses to her fragile role are everywhere felt. And it isn't only Callas and Bernstein who make this set so unmissable. Cesare Valletti – a still underrated artist – is as sensitive and involved an Elvino as any on disc and he duets to perfection with Callas, Bernstein giving them the space to phrase as only they can phrase. And Giuseppe Modesti is a warm Rodolfo. Not to be missed.

La Sonnambula
Cecilia Bartoli *mez* Amina **Juan Diego Flórez** *ten* Elvino **Ildebrando D'Arcangelo** *bass* Rodolfo **Gemma Bertagnolli** *sop* Lisa **Liliana Nikiteanu** *mez* Teresa **Peter Kálmán** *bass* Alessio **Zürich Opera House Chorus; La Scintilla Orchestra, Zürich / Alessandro De Marchi**
L'Oiseau-Lyre ② 478 1087DHO2 (134' · DDD) Ⓟ**Ⓞ**▶

In this first recording of the new critical edition of Bellini's pastoral romance Juan Diego Flórez and Cecilia Bartoli are well matched. Bellini composed the role of Amina for Giuditta Pasta, who was also the first Norma and Beatrice di Tenda. As the 19th century progressed the roles were generally assigned to different kinds of voices – Norma becoming the province of heavier, dramatic sopranos, Amina a favourite with lighter coloratura sopranos, Jenny Lind, Patti and Tetrazzini among them. Pasta, though, was basically what we would think of as a mezzo-soprano nowadays, and the new edition has realigned the part in a slightly lower tessitura. Although the booklet says that this is the longest version of the score yet recorded, in its text it does not differ significantly from existing recordings. So the difference in the new edition is more in the general texture, and played as it is here on period instruments by the Orchestra La Scintilla conducted by Alessandro De Marchi, the sound is warmer, more in keeping with the mood of *opera semi-seria*.

The problem with *La sonnambula* is the lack of action during the first hour. The characters introduce themselves in arias and duets but nothing happens, the only hint of drama being provided by the arrival of the Count, the new master of the castle. The bass aria 'Vi ravviso' became a great favourite with Victorian soloists, and it is given an elegant performance here by Ildebrando D'Arcangelo. The other significant subsidiary role is that of Lisa, the flirty innkeeper, and Gemma Bertagnolli sings both her arias with spirit. *Sonnambula*, though, stands or falls on the *bel canto* expertise of its two main protagonists, and on this occasion they are both on great form. Bartoli's decorations in the second verse of 'Sovra il sen la mano', the cabaletta of her entrance aria, are delivered in that typical, slightly hushed 'confidential' manner of hers. De Marchi lets her have a *rallentando* towards the end, with a cou-

ple of dips down into the contralto range that make about as extreme a contrast as possible with the brilliant effects above the stave that Callas, Sutherland and more recently Dessay achieve in their various recordings. The highlight of the first scene, and indeed of the whole recording, is the duet 'Son geloso del zefiro' which gives Flórez and Bartoli an opportunity to demonstrate both exquisite piano passagework and some welcome passionate utterance.

It is the ensemble in the second scene of Act 1, 'D'un pensiero', that provides the moment of high drama. Flórez is in his element as the apparently betrayed lover, and Bartoli's distress is convincing, even though she cannot quite equal – who could? – Callas's sense of outrage as she realises her predicament. In Act 2 Florez sings the vehement aria 'Ah! perchè non posso odiarti' with all his accustomed vigour.

What, though of the most famous passage in the whole opera, the sleepwalking aria, 'Ah, non credea'? Bartoli maintains a beautiful line throughout the aria, without any intrusive 'expressive' elements that can sometimes distort this, perhaps the ultimate Bellinian cantilena. 'Ah, non giunge' is joyful, with many pretty decorations but the quieter atmosphere here is in keeping with the whole conception of this, very much a new view of *La Sonnambula*. It is highly enjoyable, and one to sit alongside the 1962 Sutherland-Bonynge set, and of Callas's recordings, although it is in poor sound, the 1955 live La Scala version conducted by Bernstein.

La Sonnambula
Natalie Dessay *sop* Amina **Juan Diego Flórez** *ten* Elvino **Michele Pertusi** *bass* Count Rodolfo **Jennifer Black** *sop* Lisa **Jane Bunnell** *mez* Teresa **Jeremy Galyon** *bass* Alessio **Bernard Fitch** *ten* Notary **Metropolitan Opera Ballet, Chorus and Orchestra, New York / Evelino Pidò**
Stage director **Mary Zimmerman**
Decca 📀 074 3357DH (145' · NTSC · 16:9 · LPCM Stereo and DTS 5.1 · 0). Recorded live 2009 Ⓕ

The Company is only rehearsing Bellini's opera, which they intend to perform in a largely traditional style of production. This is a pre-dress rehearsal, at any rate to start with. So how about that for an idea? It may sound like a straight thumbs-down. But it works. The saving grace is that gradually the rehearsal is forgotten, re-emerging only in the finale where the chorus enter in costume and the principals are fitted up with theirs in the bars before Amina's cabaletta. One may say 'Well, in that case why not give the performance "straight" from the start?' But in the theatre, one has sometimes felt more than a touch of initial impatience with what can appear to be an irredeemably vacuous entertainment, both dramatically and musically, and this device has the effect (even if unintentionally) of channelling such impulses of rejection towards the production rather than the opera. Then, almost without knowing it, one is drawn into the work itself, rejoicing in the power of song and even (with the ensemble 'D'un pensiero') experiencing emotions that run deeper than one may have supposed.

Natalie Dessay wins hearts more by her acting and attractive personality than by her singing which is, of course, entirely up to the demands upon it in terms of range and fluency of technique but less than golden in tone or reliably even in voice-production. Juan Diego Flórez has an abundance of all that is required and enjoys a well-deserved ovation after his solo in Act 2. Michele Pertusi is a personable Count but there is no poetry in his aria. The others do well, as does the unimaginatively directed chorus. Evelino Pidò conducts with judicious flexibility.

La Sonnambula
Dame Joan Sutherland sop Amina **Nicola Monti** ten
Elvino **Fernando Corena** bass Count Rodolfo
Margreta Elkins mez Teresa **Sylvia Stahlman** sop
Lisa **Giovanni Foiani** bass Alessio **Angelo Mercuriali**
ten Notary **Chorus and Orchestra of the Maggio**
Musicale Fiorentino / Richard Bonynge
Decca ② 448 966-2DMO2 (136' · ADD · T/t)
Recorded 1962   Ⓜ❶❶▷

La sonnambula was Bonynge's and Sutherland's first Bellini recording. Sutherland's Amina in the early 1960s was sung with extraordinary freedom and exuberance. It's difficult to describe her in the role: it's felt. She doesn't touch a thrilling nerve of passion as Callas can; but in the final scene – a wonderfully sustained and imaginative piece of dramatic, as well as delicate and brilliant singing – she's very moving. Far more so, in fact, than Callas, who overloaded 'Ah! non credea' and made 'Ah non giunge' too artful. It's no good comparing Sutherland with Callas at this late stage, though it's inevitable here, especially as the Elvino, Nicola Monti, sings the role on both sets. Callas does superb things in the coloratura of 'Sovra il sen', Sutherland is full of dramatic fire in the scene in the inn – the tone, the note-shaping is simply exquisite. And Bonynge excels in conducting the choruses. (Currently not listed on CD, but available to download.)

La straniera

La straniera
Patrizia Ciofi sop Alaide **Mark Stone** bar Baron of
Valdeburgo **Dario Schmunck** ten Arturo **Enkelejda**
Shkosa mez Isoletta **Graeme Broadbent** bass Prior
of the Knights Hospitallers **Roland Wood** bass-bar
Lord of Montolino **Aled Hall** ten Osburgo **Geoffrey**
Mitchell Choir; London Philharmonic Orchestra /
David Parry
Opera Rara ② ORC38 (141' · DDD)   Ⓟ❶

La straniera was Bellini's fourth opera, first performed at La Scala in February 1829. The libretto concerns the woes of the exiled Queen of France, Agnese, who is obliged to live incognito in Brittany as Alaide – 'The Stranger'. She spends the whole opera refusing to tell anyone, including her beloved Arturo, who she really is. When he at last finds out – at his wedding to another woman – he stabs himself to death at the Queen's feet. It is a blood-and-thunder piece of gothic melodrama, with the inevitable courtroom scene in which the heroine is wrongly accused.

Renata Scotto, Montserrat Caballé and Elena Souliotis have sung the work but this set is the first studio recording of the work, and Opera Rara has done it proud. David Parry leads the LPO in a gripping account of a tricky piece. Patrizia Ciofi is meltingly pathetic and then imperious when necessary. Dario Schmunck makes a virile and ardent Arturo, and in the crucial role of Valdeburgo (also in disguise, he is Agnese's brother), Mark Stone is suitably warrior-like. In the rather ungrateful role of the 'other woman', Enkelejda Shkosa gets quite a jolly little rondo towards the end of Act 2. Among the other highlights are a catchy hunters' chorus and the trio in which the two men fight for the stranger's affection. The scene in Act 1, when they both end up in the lake apparently drowning, is a rousing finale. The contributions of the Geoffrey Mitchell Choir are splendid. A must for lovers of the *bel canto* repertory.

George Benjamin   British b1960

Benjamin studied at the Paris Conservatoire with Messiaen and at Cambridge with Alexander Goehr; Ligeti and Boulez have been other influences. The first work to bring him major attention was the orchestral piece Ringed by the Flat Horizon (1980), conducted by fellow student Mark Elder – it was performed at the Proms that August, making him the youngest living composer ever to have had music performed at the Proms. His first opera Into the Little Hill (to a libretto by Martin Crimp) was premiered in Paris in 2006; it received its London premiere at the Royal Opera House in February 2009.

Benjamin taught composition at the Royal College of Music, London, for 16 years, where he became the first Prince Consort Professor of Composition before he was named Henry Purcell Professor of Composition at King's College, London, in 2001. As a conductor he regularly appears with some of the world's leading ensembles and orchestras. His most recent work, Duet for piano and orchestra, was commissioned by Roche for the 2008 Lucerne Festival, where he was Composer-in-Residence, and was premiered there by Pierre-Laurent Aimard and the Cleveland Orchestra under Franz Welser-Möst.

Antara

Ringed by the Flat Horizon[a]. A Mind of Winter[b].
At First Light[c]. Panorama[d]. Antara[e]
[b]**Penelope Walmsley-Clark** sop
[e]**Sebastian Bell**, [e]**Richard Blake** fls
[c]**Gareth Hulse** ob [b]**Paul Archibald** tpt
[a]**Ross Pople** vc [e]**Pierre-Laurent Aimard**,
[e]**Ichiro Nodaira** pfs [a]**BBC Symphony Orchestra /**

Mark Elder, [bce]London Sinfonietta /
George Benjamin [d]electronics
Nimbus NI5643 (71' · DDD · T)   ℗**OO**⊕

Between March 1979, when *Ringed by the Flat
Horizon* was begun, and March 1987, when
Antara was completed, foundations of remarkable potential were well and truly laid, and it's
fascinating to be able to trace that process
through four such different George Benjamin
works. There are, of course, five items on the
disc, but the 2'24" of *Panorama* – a beguiling,
all-too-brief indication of Benjamin's work
using pre-recorded tape – form a study for
Antara rather than a wholly independent conception. The overall impression is certainly one
of progress, in that the accomplished but in
some ways rather stiff procedures to be heard in
Ringed by the Flat Horizon led directly to the
magnificently fluent setting of Wallace Stevens
in *A Mind of Winter*, in which lucid instrumental
textures provide the ideal foil for a brilliantly
resourceful vocal line. In *At first light*, the stylistic spectrum opens up further, with clear hints of
Varèse and even Xenakis. This disc is an essential document of the music of our time.

Sudden Time

Sudden Time[a]. Upon Silence[b]. Upon Silence[c]. Octet[d].
Three Inventions[d]
[bc]**Susan Bickley** *mez* [a]**London Philharmonic
Orchestra,** [bd]**London Sinfonietta,** [c]**Fretwork /
George Benjamin**
Nimbus NI5505 (65' · DDD · T)   ℗**OO**

Sudden Time is here reissued in the context of a
range of other works which underline its distinctive textural refinement and expressive conviction. *Upon Silence* (1993) is a setting for mezzo-
soprano and five viols of a poem by Yeats in
which textures of exceptional subtlety reflect a
response to the text which is captivating in its
blend of spontaneity and stylisation. The alternative version, with the viols replaced by a septet
of violas, cellos and double basses is no less
imaginative, while obviously lacking the unique
quality – old instruments used in an entirely
viable modern way – of the original.
Three Inventions (1994) has ear-opening
instrumental effects on every page, but these
never detract from the essential processes of
argument and cogent form-building in music
perhaps more urgently expressive (especially in
the third piece) than anything else of Benjamin's. With the astonishingly precocious
Octet, written in 1979, when the composer was
18, and with highly effective recordings of
definitive performances, this disc is an outstanding success.

Into the Little Hill

Into the Little Hill[a]. Dance Figures[b]. Sometime Voices[c]
[a]**Anu Komsi** *sop* [a]**Hilary Summers** *contr*

[c]**Dietrich Henschel** *bar* [b]**BBC Symphony
Orchestra / Oliver Knussen;** [c]**Deutsches
Symphony Orchestra, Berlin / Kent Nagano;**
[a]**Ensemble Modern / Franck Ollu**
Nimbus NI5828 (63' · DDD). Recorded live   ℗

George Benjamin's 36-minute 'lyric tale' *Into the
Little Hill* taps into the rich vein of English
music theatre stemming from Benjamin Britten's church parables, Alexander Goehr's *Triptych* and Harrison Birtwistle's smaller-scale dramas, such as *The Io Passion*. Martin Crimp's
concise text, made even more concise by Benjamin's omissions (shown in the admirably
detailed booklet) shapes a version of the Pied
Piper story to highlight contemporary anxieties
about fragile political and social structures.
But fragile is exactly what Benjamin's music is
not. The drama's rituals are far from reassuring,
and the music's eerie colours (cornets, basset-
horns, cimbalom) are the stuff of rat-infested
nightmare. As always with Benjamin at his best,
sonic refinement and formal lucidity lay the
foundations for a uniquely involving musical
experience, and having the story enacted and
narrated by just two singers fits the sinister
expressionism of the musical style to perfection.
Instead of expansive melodic lyricism the tale
demands a vocal idiom that shifts disconcertingly between fearful reticence and shrill ferocity. The recorded sound is not in itself especially
vivid, but with Anu Komsi, Hilary Summers and
the 15-strong Ensemble Modern all responding
to Franck Ollu's direction with razor-sharp alacrity, this unsettling piece exerts a vice-like grip.
The scene for *Into the Little Hill* is set by Benjamin's daringly economical portrait of Shakespeare's Caliban (*Sometime Voices*) and the
haunting sequence of orchestral miniatures
comprising *Dance Figures*. Both these performances are also from live concerts, and both get
to the heart of Benjamin's finely balanced and
powerfully sculpted sound images. This is an
outstanding release.

Richard Rodney Bennett
British *b*1936

*One of the very few contemporary composers who can
straddle the worlds of serious and light music. Even
fewer are as prolific; however, no further names spring
to mind of those who, in addition to these accomplishments, can also play brilliant jazz piano, do a neat
cabaret turn and be equally highly regarded in each of
these different areas. Richard Rodney Bennett is, in
fact, the complete musician. Few listening to his popular film scores for Murder on the Orient Express,
Nicholas and Alexander, Far From the Madding
Crowd, Equus and Yanks (to name but a handful)
would connect him with his operas The Mines of Sulphur, the advanced choral work Spells and the astonishing variety of instruments for which he has written
concertos. He studied with Lennox Berkeley and
Howard Ferguson in London before taking private*

lessons from Boulez in Paris. His Second Symphony was commissioned by Leonard Bernstein and the New York Philharmonic, making his reputation in the United States, where he now lives. Under-valued and under-rated in his own country.

Concertante Piano Music

'Complete Works for Piano and Orchestra'
Piano Concerto. Dream Dancing. Reflections on a Theme of William Walton. Party Piece
Martin Jones pf **RTÉ National Symphony Orchestra of Ireland / David Angus**
Metronome METCD1071 (66' · DDD)   Ⓕ

You could hardly wish for a more sympathetic and scintillating soloist than Martin Jones, his playing offset by a no less idiomatic response from the RTÉ orchestra under David Angus. Metronome's sound and balance, too, are exemplary.

The Piano Concerto (1968) was inspired (and first performed) by Stephen Kovacevich and mirrors not only that great pianist's expertise but also Bennett's own virtuoso prowess. Jones meets every challenge. Bennett's skill is contained within a scrupulous impersonality, breaking out in *Party Piece* into Gershwin-inspired high jinks. Bennett's *Reflections on a Theme of William Walton* are wide-ranging and varied, and there is much to admire in *Dream Dancing* with its hallucinogenic *Adagio tranquillo* and Debussy-inspired *Molto vivo* (which quotes directly from *Masques*).

Film music

Murder on the Orient Express – Suite. Far from the Madding Crowd – Suite. Lady Caroline Lamb – Elegy[a]. Tender is the Night – Nicole's Theme. Enchanted April – Suite[b]. Four Weddings and a Funeral – Love Theme
[a]**Philip Dukes** va [b]**Cynthia Miller** ondes martenot
BBC Philharmonic Orchestra / Rumon Gamba
Chandos Movies CHAN9867 (70' · DDD)   Ⓕ ⦿ ▶

Richard Rodney Bennett possesses a natural flair for composing for both big screen or small. The concept of presenting the music in suites makes the best possible case for it.

It's a measure of his standing in the film world that all these scores were issued on disc concurrently with the film. The earliest, *Far from the Madding Crowd* (1967), belongs to another era sonically speaking, but on this sumptuously recorded disc you can imagine yourself back in that state-of-the-art Odeon, Marble Arch, as the curtains parted to reveal Hardy's Dorset landscape on its giant curved screen. Like that film, *Lady Caroline Lamb* was presented on its initial run as a road-show attraction, with an Overture, Entr'acte and Exit Music on the soundtrack, played respectively before the showing, during the intermission and after the film.

The Suite reveals Bennett's fondness for a lyrical line at its most impassioned, with Philip

Duke's eloquent viola-playing going to the heart of the story of this aristocratic lady's doomed affair with Byron. *Enchanted April* moves us to the sunshine of Italy, where the colours of the percussion and ondes martenot lend a sweet fragrance to the scene.

From television comes *Tender is the Night – Nicole's Theme*, a popular foxtrot, 20s style, representing Scott Fitzgerald's ill-fated character Nicole Diver, inspired by his wife Zelda. Period dance music plays a part, too, in *Murder on the Orient Express*. Conductor Rumon Gamba knows just how to levitate Bennett's celebrated train waltz theme, and the response of his orchestra throughout this disc suggests that they can turn their hand to the idiom of this music at the flick of a wrist.

Partita. Reflections on a Sixteenth Century Tune. Songs before Sleep[a]. Reflections on a Scottish Folk Song[b]
[a]**Jonathan Lemalu** bar [b]**Paul Watkins** vc
Philharmonia Orchestra / Richard Hickox
Chandos CHAN10389 (76' · DDD)   Ⓕ ▶

It's hard to imagine a more beguiling start to this series or a more appealing introduction to Richard Rodney Bennett than this CD. It begins with a Partita that has a spring in its step and the breeze of the countryside blowing through it. Bennett's way with fashioning long strands of melody is a special feature of his lyrical writing. It's a gift he may owe, in part, to the songwriters he admires, like Kern and Arlen.

A chanson by Josquin provides the theme for the *Reflections on a Sixteenth Century Tune*, which enshrines a homage to Peter Warlock. The scoring is breathtaking, with soloists highlighted against the muted string ensemble. Jonathan Lemalu characterises *Before Sleep* well with colour, dynamics and some exquisite quiet singing in the upper voice.

Reflections on a Scottish Folk Song ('Ca' the yowes') was written in memory of the Queen Mother. It's the most substantial piece here, with a formidable cello part played with great feeling by Paul Watkins. It's hard to imagine anyone not being enraptured by this CD.

Choral Works

Sea Change[a]. Verses. Out of your Sleep. Puer nobis. A Good-Night. Susanni. A Farewell to Arms[b]. Missa brevis. There is no rose. That younge child. Sweet was the song. Lullay mine liking. What sweeter music
Cambridge Singers / John Rutter with [a]**Charles Fullbrook** bells [b]**Sue Dorey** vc
Collegium ⬚ CSACD901 (75' · DDD · T/t)
Ⓕ ⦿ ⦿ ▶

Hard to believe, but this is the first CD devoted solely to Sir Richard Rodney Bennett's extensive choral output. That it's a richly rewarding body of work is nowhere better exemplified than in the curtain-raiser, *Sea Change* (1984) a marvellously effective, 17-minute cycle to texts by Shakespeare, Andrew Marvell and Edmund Spenser. The Spenser setting thrillingly evokes the terrible monsters encountered by Sir Guyon during a stormy sea voyage by employing a technique akin to *Sprechgesang*, while the concluding 'Full fathom five' is a worthy successor to Vaughan Williams's setting in his *Three Shakespeare Songs*.

Whereas *Sea Change* minimally and subtly deploys tubular bells, *A Farewell to Arms* (2001) memorably incorporates an extensive role for solo cello and sets the same poems by Ralph Knevet and George Peele that Finzi first brought together for his 1945 diptych. It's a tenderly moving creation, as is the part-song 'A Good-Night' (1999) from the sequence *A Garland for Linda*. If Britten's shadow looms large over the *Missa brevis* (1990) for Canterbury Cathedral Choir, it's a no less appealing creation for all that.

Bouquets all round to John Rutter and his Cambridge Singers; theirs is *a cappella* singing of a very high order. Exemplary presentation and admirable sound, tastefully balanced within the comparatively intimate acoustic of the LSO's home, St Luke's in the City of London. A delightful anthology.

Additional recommendation

The Mines of Sulphur
Soloists; Glimmerglass Opera Orchestra / Stewart Robertson
Chandos ② ⊛ CHSA5036 (107' · DDD)   Ⓕ Ⓓ▸

The Mines of Sulphur was a commission from Sadler's Wells, premiered in 1965. It was a considerable success. *The Mines* is a gripping thriller set in an isolated, decaying country house. The oscillation between lyrical arioso and violence is compelling; there are countless examples of evocative scoring; and the word-setting is realistic and well enunciated. Everyone is well cast and directed in this astonishingly assured first full-length opera.

Alban Berg
Austrian 1885-1935

Berg is the most expressive and accessible of the group of composers who wrote using the discipline of 12-tone (serial) composition. Along with Schoenberg and Webern, he was the best-known of the so-called Second Viennese School. Very little of his music is known to the general public though his most important works were composed 60 and more years ago. Conductors and concert programme planners have doggedly included them in concerts, productions of his operatic masterpiece Wozzeck come and go but for the broad spectrum of music lovers Berg's music remains 'difficult'. However, there are some enriching pieces to get to grips with and in most of them, behind the atonality, are glimpses of the more conventional worlds of Mahler and Richard Strauss.

Berg came from a musical family and had written a group of songs by the age of 15 without any formal training. He worked first as a clerk in the government

and then, in 1904, met Arnold Schoenberg, which proved to be the turning-point of his life. Over the next six years, the relationship between them developed from master and pupil into one of friendship and colleagues. Berg's drift from conventional harmony to the new school of thought was gradual but his music attracted fierce hostility. The first performance of his Altenberg Lieder in 1913 provoked a riot and the premiere of Wozzeck – for which the conductor Erich Kleiber needed no less than 137 rehearsals – produced a storm of violent criticism. 'I had the sensation of having been not in a public theatre but in an insane asylum. On the stage, in the orchestra, in the stalls – plain madmen,' thundered the Deutsche Zeitung. Undeterred, Berg followed Wozzeck with the Chamber Concerto (dedicated to Schoenberg on his 50th birthday) and a second opera Lulu (left incomplete). With the Nazis' rise to power Berg's music was labelled 'degenerate', and as performances of his work diminished, so did his income. Work on Lulu was interrupted by the composition of his Violin Concerto in the spring of 1935. In September he was bitten by an insect which caused an abscess on his back. Though this was treated, three months later the abscess burst internally and he died, despite two operations, from blood poisoning at the age of 51.

Violin Concerto

Berg Violin Concerto **Stravinsky** Violin Concerto in D **Ravel** Tzigane[a]
Itzhak Perlman vn **Boston Symphony Orchestra / Seiji Ozawa;** [a]**New York Philharmonic Orchestra / Zubin Mehta**
DG The Originals download *447 445-2GOR* (57' · ADD/[a]DDD). Recorded 1978   Ⓜ Ⓞ Ⓞ Ⓓ▸

Perlman's account of the Berg Violin Concerto with the Boston orchestra under Ozawa has long occupied a respected place in the catalogue. The original reviewer in *Gramophone* in March 1980 was completely convinced by Perlman's 'commanding purposefulness'. As to the recording, he wrote that 'though Perlman's violin – beautifully caught – is closer than some will like, there's no question of crude spotlighting'.

Twenty years later and in a different competitive climate, his favourable verdict still holds good. Perlman is also a little too close in the *Tzigane*, the recording of which sets him very firmly front-stage again. But this is playing of stature and still among the best available versions. There are more desirable recordings now available of the Stravinsky.

Violin Concerto. Lyric Suite (original version)   Ⓗ
Louis Krasner vn **Galimir Quartet** (Felix Galimir, Adrienne Galimir *vns* Renee Galimir *va* Marguerite Galimir *vc*) **BBC Symphony Orchestra / Anton Webern**
Testament mono SBT1004 (57' · ADD) Recorded 1936   Ⓕ Ⓞ Ⓞ Ⓞ

This is an extraordinary issue of more than mere documentary interest. Krasner commissioned the Violin Concerto and had just given the first performance at the 1936 ISCM Festival in Barcelona (with Hermann Scherchen conducting) only three months after Berg's death. Webern was to have conducted,but withdrew at the last moment much to the consternation of the BBC who had booked him for the following month with some misgivings. Fortunately adequate rehearsal time had been allotted, and the players of the BBC Symphony Orchestra proved more expert in coping with the score than their Barcelona colleagues. Webern had appeared on a number of occasions with the orchestra, but no recording of him survives in the BBC Archives. Berg's death had shocked the musical world, though not as much as the death of the 18-year-old Manon Gropius had shaken the composer, who wrote the concerto as a memorial to her.

What's most striking about this performance is its glowing intensity. There's no sense of the bar-line or of the music ever being 'moved on'; time seems to stand still, yet there's also a natural sense of musical pace. The surface noise on this recording, made before an invited audience in the Concert Hall of Broadcasting House, London, can't disguise the care with which the textures are balanced and the finesse of the wind players. This was only the work's second performance, yet the players sound as if they'd lived with the music all their lives. It has all the anguish and poignancy the music demands, and Krasner is an eloquent exponent. The opening bars suffer from some minor audience coughs and the surface noise and moments of distortion call for a tolerance that's well worth extending.

The Galimir Quartet specialised in contemporary music and its playing has commendable ensemble and dedication. Unfortunately its pioneering account of the *Lyric Suite*, recorded shortly before the performance of the Violin Concerto, was hampered by a very dry acoustic that must have deterred many listeners. It was the only version for many years, and in spite of its musical excellence can't have made many new friends for the work. But this shouldn't deter collectors from acquiring this remarkable issue.

Berg Violin Concerto[a] **Janáček** Sinfonietta[b]
Tippett Concerto for Double String Orchestra[c]
[a]**Edith Peinemann** vn
BBC Symphony Orchestra / Rudolf Kempe
BBC Legends BBCL4215-2 (78' · ADD)
Recorded live at the [ac]Royal Festival Hall, London, in 1976, [b]Fairfield Hall, Croydon, in 1975   Ⓕ

Did his mastery of mainstream European orchestral music leave Rudolf Kempe at a loss when confronted with Tippett's Utopian synthesis of Tudor polyphony and English folksong in the Concerto for Double String Orchestra? Not a bit of it. There may be a bustling, Hindemithian weight to the first movement's busy textures, an unexpected but not inapposite touch of Straussian opulence in the slow movement, and a lack of truly sprung rhythm in the finale. But this reading never sells Tippett short, and

even in a rather airless recording, the symphonic ambitions that underpin the music's pastoral and pictorial elements are very well realised.

The sound quality in the Berg Concerto is similarly constrained, yet the strengths of the performance cannot be denied. By some standards Edith Peinemann may appear self-effacing, but her technique is secure, her commitment to the piece absolute: in music which has ample flamboyance built in she is never timid or tentative. Kempe ensures that the first movement flows effortlessly around its evocations of the dance, and even if you prefer the later stages of the second movement to move on a bit more than they do here, Kempe's flair for balancing the music's intricate moods and even more intricate strands of texture is admirable. With a lively and eloquent account of Janáček's *Sinfonietta* thrown in, clear as a bell despite the limitations of the recording, this is a refreshing disc: a reminder of the all-round virtues of the BBC SO in its post-Boulez phase, and of Kempe's special ability to bring not just care but a degree of charisma to performances of 20th-century classics.

Additional recommendation

Berg Violin Concerto
Coupled with: **Rihm** Gesungene Zeit
Mutter vn **Chicago SO / Levine**
DG download 437 093-2GH (52' · DDD)   ⒻⓄＢ•
Mutter fusing ice and fire to powerful results in music she is perfectly suited to. Levine is a superb partner. Terrific sound too – try and track down the CD, but the download is always available.

Chamber Concerto

Berg Chamber Concerto[a]
Mozart Serenade, 'Gran partita', K361
[a]**Christian Tetzlaff** vn [a]**Mitsuko Uchida** pf
Ensemble Intercontemporain / Pierre Boulez
Decca 478 0316DH (80' · DDD)   ⒻⓄⓄⓄＢ•

Lucky number 13: Boulez has come up with a characteristically inventive pairing of Mozart's great wind serenade with Berg's *Chamber Concerto*. OK, he's cheated slightly, in that Mozart's original stipulation was for a double bass rather than a contrabassoon (though it's a common enough substitution), and the wind instruments used by Berg and Mozart are not identical. But conceptually it's a winner; and musically too, with Old Vienna coming face to face with its more turbulent post-First World War self.

The sheer scale of the work, too, suggests that this was an august occasion. Within the seven movements of the *Gran Partita*, Mozart deftly moves between the worlds of the military band, traditional Harmoniemusik and, of course, opera, both *seria* and *buffa*. The (sadly uncredited) members of Ensemble Intercontemporain clearly relish the opportunity to venture into earlier territory, and the playing, as you'd expect, is supremely accomplished and in perfect accord. But much more than that, there's a sense of fun, of genial affection for the music. Whether in the fluid lines of the tender *Adagio* or the yearning *Andante*, or in the bustling, concise finale, where everything – in the true spirit of *opera buffa* – seems to come right, Boulez makes plain his relish for the work. This serenade, he reminds us, is so much more than merely an attractive backdrop for the goings-on of Viennese life.

Berg's *Chamber Concerto* was written for the 50th birthday of his friend and mentor Arnold Schoenberg. It's a work that has endlessly fascinated theorists, not just for Berg's very particular way of using Schoenberg's serial methods, but also for his obsessive interest in numerology, which is touched on with great lucidity by Boulez in the booklet. But although it's useful for the performers to be able to dissect the piece in such a manner, for the listener it is hardly any more essential than an in-depth knowledge of fugal techniques is for the enjoyment of late Beethoven quartets. Boulez has been here before, of course, memorably recording the concerto with Barenboim and Zukerman, and he knows his way round the piece's stickier points and its occasionally intransigently dense wind textures. But what makes Mitsuko Uchida and Christian Tetzlaff outstanding is their feeling for the piece's inherent theatricality.

The writing for wind instruments is hardly less original, whether in sustained, organ-like chords or the extreme sonorities at the end of the movement, where textures are sunk as low as can be against a heaven-bound violin. Finally the soloists come face to face for the *Rondo ritmico*, which begins with a swirling cadenza. The freedom of the two players here is extraordinary, undoubtedly helped by the fact that they toured the work before taking it into the studio.

The real achievement here is that most people will buy the disc for either the Mozart or the Berg, not both. But in listening to it, they'll discover something new and utterly remarkable. Lucky 13 indeed.

Piano Sonata, Op 1

Berg Piano Sonata, Op 1 **Schoenberg** Drei Klavierstücke, Op 11. Sechs Klavierstücke, Op 19. Fünf Klavierstücke, Op 23. Piano Suite, Op 25. Klavierstücke, Op 33a & Op 33b **Webern** Variations, Op 27
Peter Hill pf
Naxos 8 553870 (79' · DDD)   Ⓢ**OO**▷

When interviewed by *Gramophone* back in September 1989, Peter Hill said he felt he had things to say about the Schoenberg piano works which had not been said on record. Here is the complete vindication of that statement. These are scrupulously prepared performances, with all the polyphonic strands clarified and all the myriad articulation marks respected. In order to accommodate that detail and let it speak musically, Hill takes tempos on the relaxed side of

Schoenberg's frequently rather manic metronome indications. The first two of the Op 11 pieces gain a gravity that might have surprised the composer, and the fourth piece of Op 23 loses some of the suggested *schwungvoll* character. Yet there's no lack of brilliance and velocity in such pieces as the Gigue from Op 25, and time and again Hill's thoughtfulness and search for expressiveness and beauty of sound justify his spacious approach.

Hill probes with equal subtlety, sympathy and high intelligence in the Webern Variations, while in the Berg Sonata, Hill's unforced lyricism, inwardness and flexibility of phrasing are again immensely appealing. Apart from its amazing value for money, Naxos's first-rate recording quality, Peter Hill's own lucid booklet-essay, and what sounds like an ideally regulated instrument, all contribute to the outstanding success of this issue.

Seven Early Songs

Seven Early Songs. Three Orchestral Pieces, Op 6. Der Wein
Anne Sofie von Otter *mez* **Vienna Philharmonic Orchestra / Claudio Abbado**
DG 445 846-2GH (49' · DDD · T/t)   Ⓕ**O**▷

Anne Sofie von Otter included the *Seven Early Songs* on a recital disc (no longer available on CD). Singing with orchestra, von Otter naturally works on a larger scale. The words are more firmly bound into the vocal line; there isn't the detailed give-and-take that's possible with a pianist. But the outline of her interpretation remains that of a true Lieder singer, always lighting upon unexpected subtleties of colour and emphasis to inflect the poetry. In all this Abbado is an equal partner. Von Otter needs careful accompaniment in the concert hall if she's to dominate an orchestra and Abbado, in co-operation with DG's technical team, has produced a balance that never drowns her, but still sounds fairly natural. In *Der Wein*, Berg's late concert aria, von Otter and Abbado catch the lilt of the jazz rhythms. In the *Seven Early Songs* are they a touch too cool? Perhaps, but in the final song, 'Sommertage', they throw caution to the winds and end the cycle on a passionate high.

Abbado has recorded the *Three Orchestral Pieces* before and his 1970s recording has long been one of the standard versions of this work. The opportunity to see how his thoughts have developed since then brings more surprises than might have been expected.

In short, his outlook is progressing from the Italianate to the Germanic. No doubt the influence of the Vienna Philharmonic Orchestra has much to do with this and their marvellously eloquent playing is one of the prime attractions of the disc.

In their company Abbado finds more depth and complexity in the music than before, although that does mean that the March loses the Bartókian attack and driving rhythms that made his first version so exciting.

Lulu

Lulu (orchestration of Act 3 completed by Friedrich Cerha)
Teresa Stratas sop Lulu **Franz Mazura** bar Dr Schön, Jack **Kenneth Riegel** ten Alwa **Yvonne Minton** mez Countess Geschwitz **Robert Tear** ten The Painter, A Negro **Toni Blankenheim** bar Schigolch, Professor of Medicine, The Police Officer **Gerd Nienstedt** bass An Animal-tamer, Rodrigo **Helmut Pampuch** ten The Prince, The Manservant, The Marquis **Jules Bastin** bass The Theatre Manager, The Banker **Hanna Schwarz** mez A Dresser in the Theatre, High School Boy, A Groom **Jane Manning** sop A 15-year-old Girl **Ursula Boese** mez Her Mother **Anna Ringart** mez A Lady Artist **Claude Meloni** bar A Journalist **Pierre-Yves Le-Maigat** bass A Manservant **Paris Opéra Orchestra / Pierre Boulez**
DG ③ download 476 2524GGR3 (172' · ADD · S/T/t/N)
Recorded 1979   Ⓜ ❶❶❶❶➡

This is a masterpiece that fulfils all the requirements for a commercial smash hit – it's sexy, violent, cunning, sophisticated, hopelessly complicated and emotionally draining. The meaningful but gloriously over-the-top story-line, after two tragedies by Frank Wedekind, deserves acknowledgement, but what matters is that Berg's music is magnificent, Romantic enough to engage the passions of listeners normally repelled by 12-tone music, and cerebral enough to keep eggheads fully employed.

It's opulent yet subtle (saxophone and piano lend the score a hint of jazz-tinted decadence), with countless telling thematic inter-relations and much vivid tonal character-painting. Berg left it incomplete (he orchestrated only 390 of the Third Act's 1326 bars), but Friedrich Cerha's painstaking reconstruction is a major achievement, especially considering the complicated web of Berg's musical tapestry. This recording first opened our ears to the 'real' Lulu in 1979.

The performance is highly distinguished. Teresa Stratas is an insinuating yet vulnerable Lulu, Yvonne Minton a sensuous Gräfin Geschwitz and Robert Tear an ardent artist. Dr Schön is tellingly portrayed by Franz Mazura, Kenneth Riegel is highly creditable as Schön's son and that Boulez himself is both watchful of detail and responsive to the drama, hardly needs saying. It's not an easy listen, but it'll keep you on your toes for a stimulating, even exasperating evening.

Lulu (sung in English)
Lisa Saffer sop Lulu **Robert Hayward** bar Dr Schön, Jack the Ripper **John Graham-Hall** ten Alwa **Susan Parry** mez Countess Geschwitz **Gwynne Howell** bass Schigolch **Graeme Danby** bass Professor of Medicine, Theatre Manager, Banker **Robert Poulton** bar Animal Tamer, Athlete **Alan Oke** ten Manservant,

Prince, Marquis **Roger Begley** spkr Police Commissioner **Claire Mitcher** sop Girl **Jane Powell** mez Her Mother **Moira Harris** sop Lady Artist **Toby Stafford-Allen** bar Journalist **Anna Burford** mez Dresser, School Boy **English National Opera Orchestra / Paul Daniel**
Chandos ③ CHAN3130 (166' · DDD · S/T/N)   Ⓜ❶➡

The 2002 production of Berg's Lulu by Richard Jones is generally agreed to be one of the best things to come from troubled English National Opera in recent years. Chandos has done everyone a favour by transferring its 2005 revival lock, stock and smoking revolver from the opera house to the studio.

This is important for several reasons. Lulu can seem forbidding to the uninitiated. Its amoral characters, its sordid plot, its enigmatic anti-heroine, its complex (and masterful) formal design: all these aspects repel some as much as they attract others. Yet cabaret burlesque is as integral to the opera's make-up as high operatic tragedy. Paul Daniel and the Chandos engineers don't let us forget it. Piano, saxophone and vibraphone get the prominence they deserve. The farcical comings and goings in Parisian salon and London garret alike spring to life without the inevitable noises-off and dropouts of an in-house recording.

Richard Stokes has rendered Wedekind's demotic text aptly and brilliantly enough for anyone who will not wrinkle their noses at (say) the Acrobat's refrain of 'Bugger, bugger, bugger it!' And the ENO orchestra swing where the Paris Opéra for Boulez are stiff. It should come as no surprise that Böhm and the Viennese know their way around a quickstep and a tango; likewise Daniel and his players really get under the skin of Berg's 'English Waltz' in Act 3.

So consistent an overall vision is perhaps bound to reduce the starring role of Lulu herself. In Jones's production, Lisa Saffer projected her onstage as a fantasy-u-like for her many admirers. Without the sublime confidence of an Anja Silja, the vulnerability of a Constance Haumann or the hauteur of a Teresa Stratas, she brings unruffled poise and a shapely, silken tone that would not be out of place in Wolf. Nor is it here; as Dr Schön observes, after Lulu has shot him and poured herself a glass of champagne, 'You never change'. Robert Hayward's Schön is gruff, like his Wotan: a bully reduced to bluster. It is Countess Geschwitz who must convey whatever redemptive transformation Berg (not Wedekind) has to offer, and Susan Parry is equal to the task, moving from mannish suavity to an intensely moving Liebestod. John Graham-Hall is no more of a cipher than most Alwas – a Wunderlich or a Bostridge may be too much to hope for.

The many smaller parts are well taken and distinctly enunciated but the most definitive portrayal here is Gwynne Howell's Schigolch, weary and pervy and always with the emphasis on the gesang, not the sprech.

Original-language recordings will hardly go out of fashion, nor ones with more Mahlerian breadth and depth of feeling; for both, Christine

Schäfer needs to be seen in Graham Vick's production on DVD (see below). But for *Lulu* in the raw, a *Rosenkavalier* with no underwear, this is one to go for.

Lulu

Christine Schäfer *sop* Lulu **Wolfgang Schöne** *bar* Dr Schön, Jack the Ripper **David Kuebler** *ten* Alwa **Kathryn Harries** *mez* Countess Geschwitz **Stephan Drakulich** *ten* Painter, Negro **Norman Bailey** *bass* Schigolch **Jonathan Veira** *bass* Professor of Medicine, Banker, Theatre Manager **Donald Maxwell** *bass* Animal-tamer, Athlete **Neil Jenkins** *ten* Prince, Manservant, Marquis **Patricia Bardon** *contr* Dresser, High-School Boy, Groom **London Philharmonic Orchestra / Sir Andrew Davis**
Stage director **Graham Vick**
Video director **Humphrey Burton**
Warner Music Vision/NVC Arts **DVD** 0630 15533-2 (183' · NTSC · 4:3 · PCM stereo · 2-6)   Ⓕ**OO**

Warner has reissued Glyndebourne's 1996 staging of all three acts of *Lulu*, a much-lauded affair that won the *Gramophone* Award for Best Video in 1997. Graham Vick's direction is admirable not only for what it achieves but also for what it avoids. With its redbrick interior, upward-curving staircase and minimal furnishings, the stage-set has a spartan air, enlivened by a central hole in the floor through which characters disappear and emerge according to the needs of the drama. Costumes have a generalised present-day feel, and the recourse to mobile phones was a prescient touch. Crucially, this staging doesn't encumber the opera with a specious extra-musical concept or smother it with designer cleverness. The filmed interlude in Act 2 is both a pragmatic realisation of Berg's concept and faithful to the spirit of his intentions: a triumph of dramatic common sense.

Schäfer's Lulu is the best sung and most beautifully voiced yet recorded: diffident, even distanced at the outset, yet assuredly in control as she closes down Dr Schön's emotional space at the end of Act 1 and evincing real expressive pain at her degradation in Acts 2 and 3. Wolfgang Schöne has the right hollow authority for Dr Schön, and brings an appropriately Mr Hyde-like demeanour to his Jack the Ripper *alter ego*, while David Kuebler's fantasising Alwa is the most complete rendition since Kenneth Riegel's for Boulez. Aloof in her initial emotional exchanges, Kathryn Harries goes on to to find quiet strength and nobility in Countess Geschwitz. Stephan Drakulich's seedy-looking Painter is unusually accurate, Donald Maxwell's Athlete over-acted to the point of caricature, while Norman Bailey's Schigolch has a wiliness that makes the part more substantial than usual.

Davis conducts with a sure awareness of short-term incident and long-term tension. His sense of dramatic pace makes the best case yet for the first scene of Act 3, its mosaic-like succession of exchanges throwing the the second scene's

seamless intensity into greater relief. Friedrich Cerha's realisation of this act has come in for its share of criticism, but makes for a musical and dramatic whole such as Berg is unlikely to have altered appreciably had he lived to complete the work.

As directed for video, Humphrey Burton goes to town on facial asides and long-range stares. The picture reproduces with the expected sharpness of focus, though the sound throws the orchestra a little too far forward – giving voices a slightly distanced, though never unfocused quality. Subtitles are clear and to the point, and the 33 chapter selections well-placed for ease of access. On DVD this performance is now a clear first choice.

Wozzeck

Wozzeck

Franz Grundheber *bar* Wozzeck **Hildegard Behrens** *sop* Marie **Heinz Zednik** *ten* Captain **Aage Haugland** *bass* Doctor **Philip Langridge** *ten* Andres **Walter Raffeiner** *ten* Drum-Major **Anna Gonda** *mez* Margret **Alfred Šramek** *bass* First Apprentice **Alexander Maly** *bar* Second Apprentice **Peter Jelosits** *ten* Idiot **Vienna Boys' Choir; Vienna State Opera Chorus; Vienna Philharmonic Orchestra / Claudio Abbado**
DG ② download *423 587-2GH2* (89' · DDD · T/t)
Recorded live 1987   Ⓕ**O**B▸

A live recording, in every sense of the word. The cast is uniformly excellent, with Grundheber good both at the wretched pathos of Wozzeck's predicament and his helpless bitterness, and Behrens as an outstandingly intelligent and involving Marie, even the occasional touch of strain in her voice heightening her characterisation. The Vienna Philharmonic responds superbly to Abbado's ferociously close-to-the-edge direction.

It's a live recording with a bit of a difference, mark you: the perspectives are those of a theatre, not a recording studio. The orchestra is laid out as it would be in an opera-house pit and the movement of singers on stage means that voices are occasionally overwhelmed. The result is effective: the crowded inn-scenes, the arrival and departure of the military band, the sense of characters actually reacting to each other, not to a microphone, makes for a grippingly theatrical experience. This version has a raw urgency, a sense of bitter protest and angry pity that are quite compelling and uncomfortably eloquent. (Currently not listed on CD; well worth tracking down internationally or downloading.)

Wozzeck (sung in English)
Andrew Shore *bar* Wozzeck **Dame Josephine Barstow** *sop* Marie **Alan Woodrow** *ten* Drum Major **Peter Bronder** *ten* Andres **Stuart Kale** *ten* Captain **Clive Bayley** *bass* Doctor **Jean Rigby** *contr* Margret **Leslie John Flanagan, Iain Paterson** *basses* Apprentices **John Graham-Hall** *ten* Idiot **Susan**

Singh Choristers; Geoffrey Mitchell Choir;
Philharmonia Orchestra / Paul Daniel
Chandos/Peter Moores Foundation Opera in English
② CHAN3094 (92' · DDD · N/T)　　　　ⓂⒹ→

This is a fine *Wozzeck*; the perfect complement to the outstanding Abbado version which has been the top recommendation for so long. Abbado's was recorded live in Vienna, and any studio recording of an opera risks sounding score-bound when compared with a real, live performance in the theatre. But with *Wozzeck* a studio ambience can bring real advantages, especially if it underlines the kind of claustrophobic intimacy and obsessiveness which theatrical histrionics inevitably broaden and – in some instances – coarsen. Ranting and raving are kept to a minimum in Paul Daniel's interpretation, and the result is intensely moving without in any way underplaying the music's visceral dramatic power.

One result of Daniel's concentrated yet warmly expressive moulding of the score is a strong sense of its late-Romantic background in Strauss and also in Mahler. The Philharmonia play superbly throughout, and the recording successfully balances a spacious orchestral canvas of the widest dynamic range while placing the voices effectively. Nor are there any weak links in the cast, with three tenors, John Graham-Hall, Stuart Kale and Alan Woodrow, making particularly telling contributions. Josephine Barstow has one or two squally moments in delineating Marie's bewilderment and fear, but her voice remains in remarkably good shape, and the character's conflicting impulses are brilliantly conveyed. Shore is one of the best operatic baritones of our time, and he dominates the drama with an utterly convincing blend of the menacing and the pathetic. Moreover, his way with the text is exemplary.

This performance proves that an English *Wozzeck* can easily match the impact of the best German performances. Its virtues are such that it makes as powerful a case for this extraordinary work as any other version.

Wozzeck
Toni Blankenheim *bar* Wozzeck **Sena Jurinac** *sop*
Marie **Richard Cassilly** *ten* Drum Major **Peter Haage**
ten Andres **Gerhard Unger** *ten* Captain **Hans Sotin**
bass Doctor **Kurt Marschner** *ten* Idiot **Kurt Moll**
bass First Apprentice **Franz Grundheber** *bar* Second
Apprentice **Elisabeth Steiner** *contr* Margret
**Hamburg State Opera Chorus; Hamburg State
Philharmonic Orchestra / Bruno Maderna**
Video director **Rolf Liebermann**
ArtHaus Musik 🆅 101 277
(106' · NTSC · 4:3 · PCM mono · 0)　　　　Ⓕ

Wozzeck is perfect for the small screen, as the composer and intendant Rolf Liebermann intuited when he made his seventh and, he thought, best TV opera film by decamping the Hamburg State Opera to a castle in southern Germany.

The many short scenes, abrupt shifts of perspective and concentrated dialogue are no more or less macabre, pitiful and comic than a month in the life of Weatherfield's Coronation Street. Willi Reich points out in his monograph on the composer that *Wie arme Leut* ('We Poor People') 'summarises the whole social milieu of the work'. Just so, the orchestra squeezes into your sitting room like a busy night at the Rovers Return.

Liebermann could not have picked a better conductor for the job. Bruno Maderna's studies with Hermann Scherchen, his uneasy blood-brotherhood with Boulez and the Darmstadt bunch and his own creative analysis of Renaissance music in performance and composition make him ideally equipped to eschew the broad strokes of an opera-house production, even one as finely tuned as Abbado's, for a more expansive, analytical approach that zeros in on the structural fundamentals of Berg's score just as the camera registers every flicker of naivety (Andres), lust (Marie) and uncomprehending despair (Wozzeck) in relentless close-up.

Toni Blankenheim presents a noble, wretched Everyman, one who only at the last buckles under torment into insanity. Sena Jurinac plays Marie in the tradition of lighter voices such as Danco and Seefried, more agile and believably seductive-pathetic than the Wagnerian assumptions by (say) Polaski or Behrens. The remainder of the cast has strength in depth, and they all heed Berg's injunction to treat their lines as though singing *Il trovatore* instead of his *Sprechstimme* instructions in the score: even Gerhard Unger's hysterically admonishing Captain is sung rather than shrieked.

The considerable problems of the TV opera enterprise are overcome, triumphantly so: synchronisation is almost perfect, and the total commitment of all the singers is such as to suspend disbelief when their voices are coming from a generous studio acoustic while we see them outdoors – often with breath visible in the chill. It is an oppressively claustrophobic, deeply sobering experience, and so it should be.

Wozzeck
Franz Grundheber *bar* Wozzeck **Hildegard Behrens**
sop Marie **Walter Raffeiner** *ten* Drum Major **Philip
Langridge** *ten* Andres **Heinz Zednik** *ten* Captain
Aage Haugland *bass* Doctor **Anna Gonda** *contr*
Margret **Alfred Sramek** *bass* First Apprentice
Alexander Maly *bar* Second Apprentice **Peter
Jelosits** *ten* Madman **Vienna State Opera Chorus
and Orchestra / Claudio Abbado**
Stage director **Adolf Dresen**
Video director **Brian Large**
ArtHaus Musik 🆅 100 256 (97' · 4:3 · 2.0 · 2 & 5)　Ⓕ

Coarse conducting and highly approximate singing have been so readily excused in 'difficult' idioms such as *Wozzeck*'s that they became almost expected, obscuring the music's beauty and emotional intensity. Not so, in this welcome DVD appearance of an appropriately Viennese production. Abbado recognises the late Romantic lyricism that unifies the score, but emphasises translucent textures rather than Teutonic density, while still unleashing Berg's nascent Expressionist snarls with vividly theatrical force. The singers, too, treat the vocal line with greater respect than was once the norm, especially Grundheber's memorable Wozzeck. Behrens sings Marie's anguished, tender lines with intense beauty and keen characterisation, suggesting a sluttishness almost sanctified by her capacity for love. Zednik's steely-toned, neurotic Captain becomes unusually sinister, a sort of hellish Laurel to the late Aage Haugland's Hardy. Adolf Dresen, sometimes a dull producer, here creates a quite effective world whose derelict interiors and expansively desolate marshlands reflect its alienation of human feeling. Sliding sets keep the short scenes moving crisply, but lowering the curtain during interludes leaves Brian Large's excellent visual direction with only conductor and orchestra, to the detriment of tension. Striking and involving none the less.

Additional recommendation

Wozzeck
Falkman Wozzeck **Dalayman** Marie **Qvale** Captain
Swedish Opera Chorus & Orchestra / Segerstam
Naxos ② 8 660076/7 (100' · DDD)   ⑤🅑
   A few minor quibbles apart – both the Captain and the Doctor are portrayed as being more 'normal' than usual, and the orchestral balance is a little skewed in places – this is close to being a giant among *Wozzeck* recordings.

Luciano Berio   Italian 1925-2003

Berio's first studies were with his father and grandfather, both organists and composers, and later with Giorgio Federico Ghedini at the Milan Conservatory. In 1951 at Tanglewood he met Luigi Dallapiccola, who steered him towards and beyond 12-note composition in such works as his cycle of settings of James Joyce, Chamber Music for voice and trio (1953). Other major musical figures in his early life were Maderna, Pousseur and Stockhausen, whom he encountered in Basle in 1954, and Berio became a key member of the Darmstadt circle.

While working for Italian radio in Milan (1955-61) he focused on electonic music, producing Sequenza I for flute (1958, the first of a cycle), Circles (1960) and Epifanie (1961). For most of the next decade he worked in the USA, teaching and composing, his main works being the Dante-esque Laborintus II for voices and orchestra (1965), the Sinfonia for similar resources (1969, which employs quotations from Mahler) and Opera (1970). Two more operas, La vera storia (1982) and Un re in ascolto

(1984) followed to libretti by Italo Calvino. His marriage in 1950 to soprano Cathy Berberian produced some of his most enduring works, including Folk Songs, which they recorded together and which today is one of his most performed works.

Sinfonia

Sinfonia. Eindrücke
Regis Pasquier vn **New Swingle Singers; French National Orchestra / Pierre Boulez**
Erato 2564 69707-5 (45' · DDD)   ⑤🅞

This was the first complete recording of Berio's *Sinfonia*. Previously this absorbing and bewilderingly complex work was available only in the four-movement version that Berio himself prepared in 1969 for the first performance with the Swingle Singers and the New York Philharmonic Orchestra. Within a few months, he'd completed a fifth and final movement which, though ostensibly an appendix, arguably stands as the apotheosis of the entire work; for it's genuinely a 'sounding together' (sinfonia) of the preceding movements, a rich sequence of reminiscences, just as the celebrated third movement leads us through memories of the standard orchestral repertoire in a kind of stream of subconsciousness. To hear the work in its completed form is a revelation, and for this reason alone Boulez's performance must be said to supersede Berio's own. To complete the disc he chose one of Berio's less-familiar orchestral works, *Eindrücke* ('Impressions', 1973-4). This is a complete contrast: a vast monody, projected by the string orchestra against the stuttering interjections and lingering trills of the wind and percussion, a stark and uncompromising conception. Again, the reading is a powerful one. This is a most important issue, far too good to miss.

Chamber Works

Notturno. Quartetto. Sincronie. Glosse
Arditti Quartet (Irvine Arditti, Graeme Jennings vns
Dov Scheindlin va Rohan de Saram vc)
Naïve Montaigne MO782155 (62' · DDD)   Ⓕ

Berio's music for string quartet, if hardly central to his composing life, contains much that's characteristic and impressive. The two pairs of compositions are separated by a 30-year gap, yet it's fascinating to hear how clearly *Sincronie* (1963-4) anticipates the manner of *Notturno* (1993) in the wide range of its materials, from simple to complex, and the skill with which a large-scale single-movement structure is balanced and sustained. *Sincronie* and *Notturno* give us Berio at his best. Just as *Sincronie* uses its initial perception about the homogeneity of the four string instruments as the starting point for an enthrallingly spontaneous journey which never loses its sense of direction, so *Notturno* ventures well beyond the connotations of tranquil repose into the kind of dark, concentrated volatility which Berio has made his own. *Notturno* was recorded some years ago by the Alban Berg Quartet (EMI), the Arditti's all-Berio programme is more persuasive. These new performances are no less persuasive, bringing the music to fascinating life, with the help of a recording that's well-nigh ideal.

Stanze

Stanze[a] **Schubert/Berio** Rendering
[a]**Dietrich Henschel** bar [a]**French Army Chorus;**
Orchestre de Paris / Christoph Eschenbach
Ondine ODE1059-2 (64' · DDD · T/t)
[a]Recorded live 2004   Ⓕ🅑➔

Stanze, a sequence of five songs for baritone, male chorus and orchestra, was Berio's last completed work, premiered after his death in 2003. Though the title is Italian – and means 'rooms', not 'verses', indicating the distinct character of each individual movement – only the texts for movements two and three are in that language. The third movement sets an English version of a whimsical poem by Alfred Brendel and the outer movements are both to German texts – the first Paul Celan's *Tenebrae*, the last translated from the Hebrew of Dan Pagis.

The movements are indeed diverse and it could be that, after hearing them, Berio would have had second thoughts, if not about the order then about some details of the balance between voice and orchestra. Even the admirable Dietrich Henschel has difficulty adhering to the dynamics as marked in the score – perhaps he should have been more forwardly balanced. But this is a live recording of the premiere. Given the work's importance, it's a pity that it couldn't have been taken into the studio and worked on more intensively. Yet this Ondine release captures the emotional power of a special occasion, all five movements coloured by the brooding atmosphere established at the outset in Celan's great threnody.

Christoph Eschenbach has recorded *Rendering* before and although his new reading of Berio's idiosyncratic filling-out of the sketches for Schubert's Tenth Symphony is excellent in its way, it seems a pity that a different and more substantial orchestral work, not otherwise available, couldn't have been included instead.

Folk Songs

Berio Recital I for Cathy[a]. 11 Folk Songs[b] **Weill** (arr Berio; sung in English) Die Dreigroschenoper – Ballade von der sexuellen Hörigkeit. Marie Galante – Le grand Lustucru. Happy End – Surabaya-Johnny
Cathy Berberian mez [a]**London Sinfonietta;**
[b]**Juilliard Ensemble / Luciano Berio**
RCA Victor Gold Seal 09026 62540-2 (65' · ADD · T)
Recorded 1972   Ⓜ🅞🅞

These are classic recordings that no contemporary music enthusiast or Berberian/Berio admirer will want to be without. This disc could be regarded as a fitting tribute to Cathy Berberian and her inimitable vocal genius. As an artist she was unique. As a champion of contemporary music (particularly that of Berio, her ex-husband) she was second to none – not only for her interpretative prowess but also the inspirational quality of her highly individual style. These pieces were all composed, or arranged for her, by Berio. *Recital I for Cathy* makes use of Berberian's dramatic training in a composition in which the vocalist, frustrated by the non-appearance of her pianist, struggles through the programme while sharing a Beckett-like stream-of-consciousness monologue with her audience. her performance here is a monumental *tour de force*. Another example of the extraordinary qualities of Berberian's voice can be found in the celebrated *Folk Songs* of 1964. The three Weill songs reveal Berberian as a natural interpreter of his music (perhaps the best since Lotte Lenya). A wonderful tribute to a phenomenal talent.

Additional recommendations:

Berio Folk Songs[a]
Coupled with: **Golijov** Ayre[b]
Upshaw sop [a]**O'Connor** fl [a]**Palmer** cl [a]**Gottlieb,**
[a]**Poland** perc [a]**Ljova** va [a]**Friedlander** vc [a]**Kibbey** hp
[b]**Andalucian Dogs**
DG download 477 5414GH (62' · DDD · T/t) Ⓕ🅞🅞➔

Dawn Upshaw taps into the core of each song with an intensity and abandon that is likely to astonish many listeners. She is less playful than Berberian but she is in some ways more expressive, and her deeply felt interpretation offers its own joys and revelations. (Not universally listed on CD.)

Sequenzas – I-VIII, IXa, IXb & X-XIII, 'Chanson'
Castellani sop **Cherrier** fl **Hadady** ob **Damiens** cl
Gallois bn **Wirth** alto sax **Cassone** tpt **Sluchin** tbn
Conquer vn **Desjardins** va **Cambreling** hp **Fisk** gtr
Boffard pf **Anzellotti** accordion
DG ③ download 457 038-2GH3 (158' · DDD)
Ⓕ🅞🅞🅞➔

Berio's sequence of solo compositions complements his larger-scale vocal and orchestral works in various productive ways. These discs are a definitive document and a wonderful reminder of why Berio's music matters. (Not available on CD in all countries but always downloadable.)

Lennox Berkeley   British 1903-1989

After University at Oxford, Berkeley studied with Nadia Boulanger in Paris (1927-32), and there came into contact with Stravinsky and Poulenc, who was to remain a lifelong friend. In London, later, he worked for the BBC (1942-45) and taught at the RAM (1946-68). His output is large, including a full-length opera, three one-acters (including the comedy A Dinner Engagement), four symphonies, sacred music (Missa brevis with organ, 1960), songs, chamber and piano music. His early music has a distinct French accent but he was also influenced by neo-classical experiments of the 1930s. Late in his life, like Stravinsky, he incorporated serial techniques as his music took on a darker coloration. His music, and that of his son, Michael, is been well represented in the Chandos catalogue.

String Quartets

String Quartets Nos 1-3
Maggini Quartet (Lorraine McAslan, David Angel vns Martin Outram va Michal Kaznowski vc)
Naxos 8 570415 (63' · DDD)   ⑤🅑▸

The Maggini turn their attention to Sir Lennox Berkeley, giving us all three of these landmarks in 20th-century British chamber music with the first recordings of Nos 1 and 3.

The First, the longest of the three, is a revelation. Virtually unknown, it has usually been regarded as just an early work from 1935. Nothing could be more wrong since it's teeming with ideas and ingenious string quartet textures. There are plenty of Berkeley fingerprints, such as the regular pulse of the second movement supporting diatonic melodies in counterpoint; the high spirits of the *Scherzo*; and the final theme and variations, which anticipates examples later in the Two-Piano Concerto and the Violin and Piano Sonatina.

The Second (1942) has an eloquent slow movement in what the composer called free form is a fine example of Berkeley's completely individual melodic and harmonic style. By the time of No 3 (1970) Berkeley was in his slightly tougher, final phase. But it is recognisably the same composer and his spiritual roots emerge in the connections between a simple setting of *Hail, Holy Queen* and the slow movement.

These performances are simply magnificent. Clean and immediate sound, perhaps slightly shrill. But the main thing is that at last these outstanding chamber works are available. A legacy comparable to Britten's? See what you think – at a bargain price.

Additional recommendation

String Quartet No 2
Coupled with: **M Berkeley** Abstract Mirror^a.
Magnetic Field
Chilingirian Quartet with ^a**Thomas Carroll** vc
Chandos CHAN10364 (55' · DDD)   Ⓕ

A fine performance coupled with two pieces by Berkeley's son, Michael. *Magnetic Field* of 1995 explores, à la Purcell, a single middle-register F and in the quintet *Abstract Mirror* there's a special richness about the two cellos.

Choral music

Missa brevis, Op 57^{ae}. A Festival Anthem, Op 21 No 2^{cde}. Three Latin Motets, Op 83 No 1. Magnificat

and Nunc dimittis, Op 99^{be}. Crux fidelis, Op 43 No 1^d. Three Pieces, Op 72 – No 1, Toccata^e. Look Up Sweet Babe, Op 43 No 2^{ce}. The Lord is my Shepherd, Op 91 No 1^{be}
^a**Julian Gregory,** ^b**Benjamin Durrant,** ^c**James Geidt** trebs ^d**Allan Clayton** ten ^e**Johnny Vaughan** org **St John's College Choir, Cambridge / Christopher Robinson**
Naxos 8 557277 (75' · DDD)   ⑤🅑▸

Lennox Berkeley's church music has now entered the cathedral lists – both Anglican and Roman – to an extent unthinkable even 10 years ago. He was a pious Catholic, and much of his music is rooted in his deep spiritual convictions His personal kind of melody and harmony sounds like nobody else. This is particularly evident in the most familiar of his religious works here – the 1960 *Missa Brevis* for Westminster Cathedral, which Britten much admired, and *The Lord is my shepherd* for Chichester. Just as typical are *Look up sweet babe* and the ecstatic George Herbert setting which forms the central section of the expansive *Festival Anthem*. Once heard, these tunes are difficult to forget.

The Mass for five voices and Three Latin Motets, written for this choir in 1972, are more austere but, like the eloquent sacred works of his friend Poulenc, they clearly come from the same imagination as the composer's other works. And quite late in life Berkeley boldly brings the discoveries of his more advanced later music into the *Magnificat* and *Nunc Dimittis*.

This is an impressive collection which merits repeated hearings. The choir sounds well and boasts fine soloists.

Operas

A Dinner Engagement
Roderick Williams bar Earl of Dunmow **Yvonne Kenny** sop Countess of Dunmow **Claire Rutter** sop Susan **Jean Rigby** mez Mrs Kneebone **Anne Collins** mez HRH The Grand Duchess of Monteblanco **Robin Leggate** ten HRH Prince Philippe **Blake Fischer** ten Errand Boy **City of London Sinfonia / Richard Hickox**
Chandos CHAN10219 (60' · DDD · N/T)   Ⓕ⚫

A Dinner Engagement (Aldeburgh, 1954) was written for Britten's English Opera Group, suited their resources and philosophy admirably and was much admired by Britten himself. This jewel of a one-act comic opera has somehow escaped the record catalogue for half a century.

The period is that of British kitchen-sink theatre in the 1950s; however, this kitchen is an aristocratic one. Lord and Lady Dunmow, living in desperately reduced circumstances, have invited the Grand Duchess of Monteblanco to dinner. The Dunmows ardently hope that the Duchess's batchelor son, Prince Philippe, might be interested in their daughter Susan. Paul Dehn's libretto abounds in amusing incidents *en route* to a happy ending. The layout of the opera is an impeccable blend of aria and recitative; the scoring is colourful and effective; and the piece is full of memorable tunes.

Anne Collins as the Duchess is magnificent; Claire Rutter as Susan is enchanting; Robin Leggate makes a mellifluously charming Prince. This is an all-star cast, and the Mozartian ensembles are scintillating. Once again enormous credit to Richard Hickox, whose total understanding of Berkeley's music gives him unrivalled authority in this long-delayed début. Well recorded, too.

Ruth
Jean Rigby mez Ruth **Mark Tucker** ten Boaz
Yvonne Kenny sop Naomi **Clare Rutter** sop
Orpah **Roderick Williams** bar Head Reaper **Joyful Company of Singers; City of London Sinfonia / Richard Hickox**
Chandos CHAN10301 (79' · DDD · S/T/N) ℗Đ

Much has changed for Lennox Berkeley on disc in the past few years thanks to the superb advocacy of Richard Hickox. When *A Dinner Engagement* was released (see above) we wondered how this scintillating jewel of a comic opera could have escaped the catalogue for 50 years. Now *Ruth* – just as fine – shows the religious side of Berkeley, stemming from his *Four Teresa of Avila Poems* written nine years earlier.

Ruth is based on the biblical story and was adapted by Eric Crozier. At the opening of the first of the three scenes, Naomi is returning dejected to her homeland with her two daughters-in-law after all have lost their husbands. Ruth stays to support Naomi; after some resistance to Ruth as a foreigner, the workers on the estate of Boaz, a distant kinsman, are persuaded to allow her to work with them. The climax comes in the last scene, in which Ruth, urged by Naomi, cautiously offers herself to Boaz in marriage. He accepts her, announces his decision to the people, and all ends with rejoicing.

Every detail of this touching story is depicted with typical Berkeley finesse; the set-piece arias are precisely focused and memorable, and the scoring is masterly. Hickox's pacing is consistently right. Jean Rigby as Ruth is charming but firm in resolve when needed and Yvonne Kenny is a dignified and vocally imposing Naomi. Much of the drama is carried by these two women but all the roles are well cast and effective. There are plenty of lively choruses for the reapers, projected with panache.

Hector Berlioz   French 1803-1869

The arch-Romantic composer, Berlioz's life was all that you'd expect – turbulent, passionate, ecstatic and melancholic by turn, eccentric, excessive, egotistic. His influence on modern orchestral sound was profound; he propagated the ideal of programme music (music that describes works of art or literature). It was a remarkable life and the best account of it is his own, arguably the finest autobiography of any composer.

Berlioz's father was a country doctor practising near Grenoble who was musical enough to give his son his first lessons on the flute, though dead set against music as a career. (Later Berlioz took up the guitar but, unusually for a composer, never became proficient on any instrument.)

At his father's behest, he entered the school of medicine in Paris in 1821 in order to become a doctor, taking private music lessons the while from Jean François Lesueur. In 1824 he abandoned his medical studies in order to devote himself entirely to music and, aged 22, enrolled at the Paris Conservatoire where Lesueur taught him composition and Anton Reicha counterpoint and fugue.

In September 1827 Berlioz became infatuated with an Irish actress named Harriet Smithson after he'd seen her as Ophelia in a production of Hamlet given in Paris. Berlioz knew no English (Miss Smithson knew no French) and his attempts to contact her met with no success; he bombarded her with love letters which at first startled her and then terrified her; he put on a concert of his works to impress her; he rented rooms near her – all to no avail. Instead, he transferred his affections to a young pianist, Camille Moke, who became a kind of surrogate Harriet. During the next three years, Berlioz worked on a symphony, a musical autobiography, a gigantic love letter to the real object of his affections which turned out to be his most enduring masterpiece, his Symphonie fantastique. It received its first performance at the Paris Conservatoire in December 1830, a date Berlioz timed to the return to Paris of his grande passion. The work was given to great acclaim, though Miss Smithson was not present at the occasion. 'Alas,' wrote Berlioz, 'I learnt afterwards that, absorbed in her own brilliant career, she never even heard of my name, my struggles, my concert, or my success!' What that astute critic Robert Schumann wrote of Berlioz the musician was equally true of Berlioz the man: 'Berlioz does not try to be pleasing and elegant; what he hates, he grasps fiercely by the hair; what he loves, he almost crushes in his fervour.'

The ultimate accolade for a student of music was to win the Prix de Rome, awarded since 1803 by the French Academy of Fine Arts. The recipient was entitled to study gratis in Rome for four years, living at the Villa Medici. Berlioz's first effort was rejected in 1827; his second effort in 1828 won second prize; he tried again in 1829 but no awards were given that year. Finally, at the fourth attempt, he won the prize with his La mort de Sardanapale, though it was so poorly performed that Berlioz angrily threw the score at the musicians.

He duly set off for Italy in 1830. It proved to be a disaster. Not one to take kindly to prescribed musical rules, Berlioz also disliked the food and the music. When rumours reached him that Camille had taken a lover, he was incandescent with rage and left Rome for Paris, disguising himself as a lady's maid, intent on killing both Camille and her amour. In Genoa, however, he lost his disguise and the wait for a replacement gave him time to cool down. He returned meekly to Rome.

Returning to Paris in 1832, he discovered Harriet was also in the city again and arranged a second performance of the *Symphonie fantastique* for her. This time, the bewildered actress came, heard and was conquered. After a feverish courtship Berlioz and Harriet Smithson were married in October 1833. 'We trust,' wrote the ungallant Court Journal, 'this marriage will ensure the happiness of an amiable young woman, as well as secure us against her reappearance on the English boards.' Predictably, the union was not a success and, after a volatile few years spent in poverty, they decided to live apart. Berlioz took up with a second-rate singer called Marie Recio but he never quite forgot Harriet and, towards the end of her life when she had become an invalid, Berlioz was solicitous and tender in her predicament. She died in March 1853. A year later, Berlioz married Marie, a scarcely more successful partnership and in which he again outlived his wife.

The same concert that brought Harriet and Berlioz together brought an important benefactor to the impoverished composer. Niccolò Paganini, then at the height of his considerable fame, commissioned a work for his newly acquired viola. The result was *Harold en Italie*, inspired by Byron's poem 'Childe Harold' but whereas Paganini had hoped for a virtuoso vehicle for this unusual combination, Berlioz wrote a symphony with a viola obbligato – it would not produce the effect Paganini needed and he never played it. Throughout the following two decades, Berlioz composed industriously, controversial (for, after all, he was the avant-garde of his day) and increasingly successful. Commissions came from the government, he became a music critic (from 1833 to 1863 he wrote for the influential *Journal des Débats*) and began his career as a conductor. In 1838, so legend has it, Paganini turned up again in Berlioz's life: after a performance of the rejected viola concerto on December 16, the great violinist appeared on stage and knelt in homage to him, overwhelmed by hearing for the first time the work he had commissioned. The next day, he sent a message to Berlioz: 'Beethoven is dead and Berlioz alone can revive him.' With it came a cheque for 20,000 francs.

The money enabled Berlioz to write the ambitious work he had dreamed of – the dramatic symphony *Romeo and Juliet* in which he wanted to relive his first feelings of love on seeing Harriet Smithson. The work was given its premiere the following November and in the audience was a young, unknown composer called Richard Wagner. It took him by storm and 'impetuously fanned the flame of my personal feeling for music and poetry'.

With another government commission for a large-scale work (Grande symphonie funèbre et triomphale), Berlioz entered into a period of unsurpassed grandeur and grandiloquence in terms of orchestral writing. The large forces he employed to play his works (and those of others) had never been assembled before. Such excesses prompted a barrage of ridicule from sceptical critics and caricaturists. It's said that he conducted the Grande symphonie funèbre et triomphale with a drawn sword while marching through the streets of Paris; in 1844 he conducted a concert including Beethoven's Fifth Symphony with 36 double basses, Weber's overture to Der Freischütz with 24 horns and Moses' Prayer (from Rossini's opera) with 25 harps – 1022 performers in all. This was exceeded in 1855 by an orchestra, military band and chorus of 1200 for his celebratory L'Impériale.

Tours of England and Russia ensued, a festival of his music at Weimar (produced by the ever-generous Liszt) was given in 1852, opera and stage compositions flowed from him – it looks like the portrait of a successful, admired composer. Yet Berlioz had no cult following, unlike Wagner and Liszt; he wrote no solo works with which his name could appear regularly on concert programmes; he had enormous difficulty in seeing his operas and stage works mounted regularly. The final years of Berlioz's life were miserable: he believed he was a failure as a composer and conductor in his own country; he knew his most productive days were over – a fact that deeply depressed him; his health began to give out and his marriage was unhappy. The death of his only child (a son from his marriage to Harriet Smithson) of yellow fever in Havana came as a final blow.

At his funeral, his body was carried by Gounod, Ambroise Thomas and other famous French musicians to its final resting place in Montmartre. The music was his own funeral march from the Grande symphonie funèbre et triomphale.

Symphonie fantastique, Op 14

Symphonie fantastique.
Béatrice et Bénédict – Overture
London Symphony Orchestra / Sir Colin Davis
LSO Live LSO0007 (65' · DDD)　　　Ⓢ**OO**ⴅ

This LSO performance of the *Symphonie fantastique* is in many ways the subtlest of Davis's four accounts to date, conveying more mystery, with *pianissimos* of extreme delicacy beautifully caught. There's an overall gain, too, from having a live recording of a work with such an individual structure, with its hesitations and pauses. In overall timings it's marginally longer than earlier versions, maybe also reflecting the conditions of a live performance, even though some of this must have been put together from rehearsal tapes as there's no applause at the end.

The *Béatrice et Bénédict* Overture is taken from the complete recording of the opera on the same label, and makes both a welcome bonus and a tempting sampler. Though the disc comes at super-budget price, it offers splendid notes by David Cairns, author of the definitive, prize-winning biography of the composer.

Berlioz Symphonie fantastique **Mozart** Symphony No 35, 'Haffner', K385 **Sibelius** Finlandia
Philharmonia Orchestra / Charles Dutoit
Decca Concerts　　　　　　Ⓜⴅ only
Recorded live 2006

Historically informed performances really are 'informing' the most conventional of Romantic symphony concerts. Even 10 years ago would the *Andante* of Mozart's *Haffner*, given here with conventional, albeit reduced forces, have moved on at this light, swift tread, woodwinds at the back

BERLIOZ'S SYMPHONIE FANTASTIQUE – IN BRIEF

Lamoureux Orchestra / Igor Markevitch
DG 447 406-2GOR (71' · ADD)　　　Ⓜ☙
Of the many recordings with French orchestras, Igor Markevitch's extraordinarily characterful 1961 version is perhaps the most tangily idiomatic. A bonus is the remarkably undated sound.

French National Radio Orchestra / Sir Thomas Beecham　　　Ⓗ
EMI 567971-2 (75' · ADD)　　　Ⓜ
Sir Thomas at his inimitable best: an elegant and exciting interpretation, full of panache. Beecham's thrilling 1958 *Le corsaire* with the RPO provides a cherishable bonus.

Mahler CO / Marc Minkowski
DG download *474 209-2GH* (81' · DDD)　　　Ⓕ☙
A daring and characterful *Symphonie fantastique* that blends period sensibility with the bite of modern instruments. His approach makes the drama of the work more daring than usual, even though he inclines towards slower speeds en route. Well worth hearing…

ORR / Sir John Eliot Gardiner
Philips download *434 402-2PH* (53' · DDD)　　　ⒻⒸ☙
Gardiner brings out the daring originality of Berlioz's visionary inspiration and draws hugely spirited yet refined playing from his period-instrument band. Exemplary sound and balance, too.

Hallé Orchestra / Sir John Barbirolli　　　Ⓗ
Dutton CDEA5504 (69' · ADD)　　　Ⓑ
Dating from 1947, a splendidly combustible reading from this magnetic partnership. Barbirolli had a particular affection for this score, and it shows.

London Symphony Orchestra / Sir Colin Davis
LSO Live LSO0007 (65' · DDD)　　　ⓈⒸ☙
The *Symphonie fantastique* has long been a Davis speciality. Captured live at the Barbican in September 2000, this is Sir Colin's fourth recording of it and arguably his most masterly yet.

Philharmonia Orchestra / Charles Dutoit
Decca Concerts Download only　　　☙
Less suave than his Montreal performance, Dutoit finds more bite and excitement in this download-only Decca Concert. Doesn't oust the Davis performances but it is elegant and Gallic none the less.

RAI SO, Turin / Sergiu Celibidache
Opus Arte ᴅᴠᴅ OA0977D (58' · NTSC · 0)　　　Ⓕ
A fascinating glimpse of a master-magician at work. Filmed in black and white, this is a gem of observation as Celibidache creates an elegant performance of Berlioz's symphony.

of the orchestra rightly given parity with the string band. In the opening *Allegro*, too, the winds rightly have their say as the main motivators of rhythmic interest. This reading makes a subtle contrast to the 19th-century weight at either end of the programme. *Finlandia* also goes well – alert, not as gloomy and raspy as some, a tone-poem rather than nationalistic stomping.

The Berlioz, too, has picked up some period sonorities. Dutoit finds more drama in the tricky opening movement (and its exposition repeat) than he did in his perfect but prim Montreal recording (Decca), and plays the Ball scene as a story rather than a mere dance movement. His cor anglais and oboe soloists have taken on some French tang and really act out in sound the parts of Romeo and Juliet (or Hector and Harriet) in the country. The Scaffold begins with promising roughness in the brass but, on the whole, these last two movements feel too beautiful, too purely symphonic: no nasty slithering basses nor eardrum-damaging winds in this Witches' Sabbath.

Closely recorded but with real presence, this is a concert to be appreciated as an effective programme in itself, rather than to be matched off against comparative recordings.

Symphonie fantastique
RAI Symphony Orchestra, Turin / Sergiu Celibidache
Opus Arte ᴅᴠᴅ OA0977D
(58' · NTSC · 4:3 black & white · PCM mono · 0)　　　Ⓕ

1969 is long enough ago in the history of sound and vision to feel primitive compared to today's technology, but Opus Arte has buffed up this black-and-white Italian TV original to some purpose. As has Maestro Celibidache Turin's RAI orchestra, whose every section shows off the care of his characteristically detailed rehearsal. It translates into a reading whose tempi and dynamics have been tailored with the care of a wonderful listener to the band and the hall at hand.

This *Fantastique* is not an especially dramatic or grandstanding performance – only the final pages of the 'Witches' Round' put the players under stress. But it is one where everyone has time and space to play with comfort and expression, to live fully in the rits of Celibidache's graceful, rather miniaturist waltz, to enjoy the pulsing, guitar-like accompaniments as the *idée fixe* gets under way for the first time in 'Passions', or to dig in with force (but never crudity) to a serious, steady 'March to the Scaffold'.

As an interpretation though per se this performance remains, intentionally perhaps, on the page, with the notes and the music viewed through an essentially 20th-century brain, as played smoothly by a 'modern' orchestra. Celibidache is totally uninterested in the dirtiness of some of Berlioz's bass and brass writing, or the Weber-like shrieks of the high wind, or the orchestral opera going on within the symphony.

A stylish, detailed note by Misha Donat and sensitive work by RAI's camera director – following the score's high-points without indulging in visual ping-pong – add to the value of a release that promises to be the first of a series.

Additional recommendations

Symphonie fantastique   **P**
ORR / Gardiner
Philips download *434 402-2PH* (53' · DDD)   ⓕ**O**↪

Endless fascination and enjoyment here! A period instrument performance to set beside other well-loved interpretations with a modern orchestra. Worth trying to track down a CD, or downloading.

Symphonie fantastique.
Coupled with: Herminie[a].
[a]**Legay** *sop* **Les Musiciens du Louvre; Mahler CO / Minkowski**
DG download *474 209-2GH* (81' . DDD)   ⓕ↪

Recorded live, this characterful version breaks new ground in bringing together the talented performers of the Mahler CO, using modern instruments, and wind players from Minkowski's period orchestra, Les Musiciens du Louvre. Some listeners will find themselves jumping up to change volume levels, such is the dynamic range of DG's all-embracing recording. (Restricted availability on CD.)

Harold en Italie, Op 16

Harold en Italie. Les Troyens – Ballet Music
Tabea Zimmermann *va* **London Symphony Orchestra / Sir Colin Davis**
LSO Live LSO0040 (52' · DDD)   Ⓢ**O**↪

Yet again Sir Colin Davis demonstrates his mastery as a Berlioz interpreter. It's fascinating to compare this latest version of *Harold en Italie* with his 1975 Philips version with Nobuko Imai as soloist, and the 1962 HMV one, no longer available, with Yehudi Menuhin.

Most noticeable is the extra tautness of Davis's interpretation, with speeds consistently faster, sometimes markedly so. The textures are sparer, sharper and lighter, bringing an extra incisiveness all round. The soloist, the magnificent Tabea Zimmermann, is balanced as part of the orchestra instead of being spotlit. The beauty of her tone, with its nut-brown colours on the C-string, is never masked, but at the other end of the spectrum the balance allows *pianissimo*s of a delicacy never achieved by the excellent Nobuko Imai, even though she may well have been playing just as quietly, or by the relaxed and rich-toned Menuhin, who prefers lyrical expansion to urgency.

The fierceness of the *Allegro*s, with their quirky bursts of high dynamic contrasts, is enhanced on the new disc. The first movement, 'Harold in the Mountains', is markedly faster and tauter this time (some 2'30" shorter than with Menuhin), and the more flowing speed for the second movement, 'Pilgrims' March', establishes the feeling of a procession, with the surprisingly gentle dynamic markings meticulously observed. Though the third movement 'Sere-

nade' the skipping rhythms are infectious, with dotted rhythms sparklingly pointed by the oboists at the start, and the 'Brigands' Orgy' of the finale clearly gains in dramatic flair from the extra incisiveness.

The Ballet Music, taken from Davis's prize-winning LSO Live version of *Les troyens* makes an atmospheric bonus.

Harold en Italie. Le corsaire – Overture.   **H**
King Lear – Overture[a]. Trojan March
Frederick Riddle *va* **Royal Philharmonic Orchestra;**
[a]**BBC Symphony Orchestra / Sir Thomas Beecham**
BBC Legends/IMG Artists mono BBCL4065-2
(72' · ADD). Recorded live 1951, 1954,1956   Ⓜ**OO**

These radio recordings of Beecham in full flight could not be more welcome. The mono sound is limited but beefy and immediate, with fine transfers by Paul Baily, even though the opening *Corsaire* Overture is taken from an acetate disc, not a tape. What above all hits you hard from first to last is that Beecham in such live performances of Berlioz conveyed a manic intensity, a red-blooded thrust that brings out to the full the characterful wildness in this ever-original composer, making almost any rival seem cool.

So, the *Corsaire* Overture has a fierceness and thrust entirely apt to the Byronic subject, culminating in a swaggering climax that verges on the frenetic. It will have you laughing with joy. You find a similar approach in Beecham's studio performances of this overture, but this is even more uninhibited in its excitement. *King Lear* – with the BBC Symphony Orchestra, not the RPO – surges with warmth in the lyrical first half, before similarly building excitement in the *Allegro*.

Harold in Italy, recorded in 1956 in the dry acoustic of the Usher Hall, Edinburgh, with the dynamic range compressed so as to magnify *pianissimos*, as at the very start, is specially valuable for having as soloist Beecham's chosen leader of his viola section, Frederick Riddle, who made the first recording of the Walton Viola Concerto in 1937 with the composer conducting, arguably still the finest ever interpretation, and here his expressive warmth and responsiveness to Beecham's volatile inspiration make up for the sort of intonation problems that the viola at that period always seemed to invite, even with players of this calibre. The pauseful tenderness of the *Adagio* section just after the start of the finale, is similarly magnetic, thanks to both conductor and soloist, bringing out the parallel in the review of themes with the finale of Beethoven's Ninth. The *Trojan March* makes a swaggering encore, a performance the more electrifying for being recorded at the opening concert of the Colston Hall in Bristol in 1951.

Overtures

Overtures – Les francs-juges, Op 3. Waverley, Op 1.
King Lear, Op 4. Le carnaval romain, Op 9. Béatrice

et Bénédict. Le corsaire, Op 21. Benvenuto Cellini
Staatskapelle Dresden / Sir Colin Davis
RCA Victor Red Seal 09026 68790-2 (74' · DDD)ⓕ**OO**

Berlioz's seven overtures fit comfortably into an hour and a quarter, in performances that reflect Sir Colin's long absorption with music that remains difficult, original, surprising. The most extrovert, the Ball Scene in *Le carnaval romain*, is exhilaratingly played, but done so without the strenuous attempts after excitement at all costs, through speed and volume, which are all too familiar. The music is more interesting than that, its tensions more dramatic. What are perhaps the two hardest overtures to play successfully, *Waverley* and *King Lear*, benefit from some understatement, especially in the quieter sections when, particularly in *Lear*, a sense of trouble animates the music. As elsewhere, Berlioz's melodies made out of awkward rhythms and uneven metres call for a skilled hand: nowhere is this more evident than at the opening of *Benvenuto Cellini*, whose oddity doesn't immediately strike the listener but whose 'rightness' is proved by its wonderful verve. Davis handles this superbly, as in different vein he does the soft music answering the opening of *Le carnaval romain*, in which he's given some beautiful playing (especially from the cor anglais) by the Dresden orchestra. It responds to his understanding of the different levels of tension and expression, as well as different dynamic levels, at which Berlioz can make his effects, such as at the start of *Les francs-juges*. Sometimes a slight emphasis in the accompaniment, even the touch of warmth on a single note, can illuminate much in the melody. It's all beautifully done.

Additional recommendation

Overtures – Le carnaval romain; Le corsaire; Les   **H**
francs-juges; King Lear; Waverley. Les Troyens – Act 3
Prelude; March
RPO / Beecham
Sony Classical SMK89807 (69' · ADD)
Recorded 1950s   Ⓜ
  Astonishing performances. All are played with a
  wonderful shaping of phrases and with a fiery
  attack and zest that are utterly satisfying.

Roméo et Juliette, Op 17

Roméo et Juliette
Daniela Barcellona mez **Kenneth Tarver** ten **Orlin
Anastassov** bass **London Symphony Chorus and
Orchestra / Sir Colin Davis**
LSO Live LSO0003 (99' · DDD)   Ⓢ**OO**▷

This recording of Berlioz's masterpiece builds in important ways on what Sir Colin has revealed to us in his two previous versions, both for Philips, and preserves what by any reckoning was an electrifying event at the Barbican. The recording was edited from two separate concerts, so ironing out irritating flaws of the moment, while offering the extra dramatic thrust of a live performance.

That's most strikingly illustrated in the concluding chorus, a passage that has often been felt to let the rest of the work down, but which here provides an incandescent climax, silencing any doubts. That said, the differences between this live recording and Davis's two studio ones are less a question of interpretation than of recording balance and quality. Davis's view of the work has remained fundamentally unchanged, though his speeds at the Barbican are marginally broader until the concluding sections from Juliet's funeral onwards, which now flow more easily. The live recording may not match in opulence either the 1993 one with the Vienna Philharmonic or the 1968 one with the LSO, for the Barbican acoustic is drier. Yet the refinement of the sound this time, with orchestra and chorus set at a slight distance, brings *pianissimos* of breathtaking delicacy, focused in fine detail. Not only the Love scene but the choral recitatives gain greatly from that, as does the lovely passage before the Love scene where the Capulets return home after the party. The three young soloists are first-rate, characterising strongly. A fine modern recording at such a reasonable price.

Grande Messe des morts, Op 5

Grande Messe des morts, Op 5[a]. Te Deum, Op 22[b]
[a]**Ronald Dowd**, [b]**Franco Tagliavini** tens [b]**Nicolas
Kynaston** org **Wandsworth School Boys' Choir;
London Symphony Chorus and Orchestra /
Sir Colin Davis**
Philips 50 Great Recordings ② 464 689-2PM2
(144' · ADD · T/t). Recorded 1969   Ⓜ**OO**

The similarities between these two great choral works – the monumental style and blend of austerity and brilliance – make them an ideal coupling. Both are tremendous sonic showpieces, and although Sir Colin Davis's Berlioz cycle dates back over 30 years, the performances remain among the front runners.

The key is Davis's ability to concentrate on the inner meaning of the music, rather than its outward effects. In the *Grande Messe des morts*, conductors as various as Maazel, Levine and Ozawa have failed to see any more than generalised beauty and grandeur, but Davis is always alive to the specific emotion of the moment, whether it's the pleading of the 'Quaerens me' or the angular pain of the 'Lacrymosa'. His chorus is stretched, especially in the underweight tenor section (Berlioz prescribes 60 tenors, adding helpfully that the numbers may be doubled or tripled if space permits) and Ronald Dowd isn't entirely comfortable in the solo part of the 'Sanctus'. But in all other respects this is a high-quality performance of vision and imagination.

The splendid *Te Deum* is given a performance of comparable virtues, and Philips' natural sound stands up well to recent competition.

Grande Messe des morts, Op 5
Keith Ikaia-Purdy ten **Saxon State Opera Choir;**

Dresden Symphony Chorus; Dresden
Singakademie; Staatskapelle Dresden /
Sir Colin Davis
Profil ② PH07014 (90' · DDD)
Recorded live 1994   Ⓕ●

The *Grande Messe des morts* was recorded one year
short of the 50th anniversary of the day that
dawned to reveal to Dresdeners the devastation of
their city. For many years, Dresden was not an
easy city for Englishmen to visit; but attitudes
change, and it was certainly a moving gesture for
Davis to conduct this performance. The Kreuz-
kirche has been beautifully reconstructed, and it
has beautiful acoustics that welcome Berlioz's
wide-ranging demands.

The quieter moments fare best here: the
strange chords in the *Hostias*, with a firm trombone seeming to project overtones in the flutes;
the soft cor anglais and bassoon lines over cellos
and basses in the *Quid sum miser*; the unaccompanied choral *Quarens me*, which the Dresden
choirs sing most sensitively; the high sounds of
the *Sanctus*, with Keith Ikaia-Purdy an elegant if
slightly operatic tenor. The acoustic seems positively to welcome these, and it can well accommodate, though not without some loss of verbal
clarity, the great clamour of the *Dies irae* and the
snapping rhythms of the *Lacrymosa*, which have
a cut that Davis achieves more sharply than any
other conductor. This is his only recording of
the work since his classic 1969 version, and his
grasp of the music remains supreme.

Grande Messe des morts   Ⓗ
Richard Lewis *ten* **Royal Philharmonic Chorus and
Orchestra / Sir Thomas Beecham**
BBC Music Legends mono BBCL4011-2
(78' · ADD · T/t). Recorded live 1959.   Ⓜ●

Almost 60 years to the day since his first Berlioz
performance, Beecham conducted the *Grande
Messe des morts* in the Albert Hall. Though the
Dies irae thunders out tremendously, and the
'Lachrymosa' has a wonderful snap on the off-
beat chords, it's the quieter movements that
characterise what's, after all, a Requiem Mass.
Beecham's response to them is with a lifetime's
devotion to one of the composers who had been
closest to his heart. The 'Quid sum miser' has an
enchanting clarity; the long, hushed end of the
'Offertoire', as Berlioz lingers over the gently
alternating notes that suffuse the invention, is
finely judged; the *Sanctus* is eloquently sung by
Lewis and the splendid chorus; the return of the
opening 'Te decet hymnus', near the close of the
whole work, is sublime. Such things aren't
achieved without the attention to detail with
which Beecham used to complain people did not
credit him. How wrong. His orchestral parts were
always covered with powerful blue pencil marks
and the signature 'TB', so that it was impossible
to mistake intentions which players would then
shape for him in rehearsal. Here, the detail is
exquisite. Occasionally he takes his own view, not
Berlioz's, about phrasing; and the orchestra con-

tains not a whiff of an ophicleide. No matter.
This is a recording of a great occasion – full in
recording, scarcely bothered by audience noise –
but also of a marvellous performance.

Te Deum, Op 22

Te Deum
Roberto Alagna *ten* **Marie-Claire Alain** *org*
**European Union and Maîtrise d'Antony Childrens
Choirs; Orchestre de Paris Chorus; Orchestre de
Paris / John Nelson**
Virgin Classics 545449-2 (58' · DDD)   Ⓕ●Ⓑ

Berlioz's *Te Deum* has been relatively neglected
on disc in comparison with his other major works.
This latest version has John Nelson as an incisive,
understanding conductor of Berlioz, revelling in
the weight of choral sound, balancing his forces
beautifully. He's helped here by fuller, more
detailed digital sound than on previous versions.

The organ sound may be less transparent
than it might be, but the authentic French
timbre of the Cavaillé-Coll organ of the
Madeleine in Paris blends beautifully in the
ensemble, and Marie-Claire Alain, as you
might expect, is the most idiomatic soloist,
making her non-French rivals seem rather
square by comparison. It makes for luxury
casting, too, to have Roberto Alagna as an
imaginative, idiomatic tenor soloist in the
prayer, 'Te ergo quaesumus', warmly
persuasive and full of temperament.

An additional plus-point for the new issue,
even in relation to Sir Colin Davis's now classic
version for Philips (see below), isn't only the
fuller, more open recorded sound but the interesting bonus provided. The two extra instrumental movements included here were written
by Berlioz expressly for performances celebrating victory, both with military overtones. On
CD either can easily be left out, yet Berlioz, even
at his most populist, never fails to grab the listener's attention.

Additional recommendation

Coupled with: Grande Messe des morts
Dowd, Tagliavini *tens* **Kynaston** *org* **Wandsworth
School Boys' Choir; LSO & Chor / C Davis**
Philips 50 Great Recordings ② 464 689-2PM2
(144' · ADD) Recorded 1969   Ⓜ●●Ⓑ
A classic recording and an ideal coupling: these performances remain among the front-runners, though
the chorus sounds rather stretched at times. Philips'
natural sound quality stands up well (reviewed opposite under *Grande Messe*).

La damnation de Faust, Op 24

La damnation de Faust
Enkelejda Shkosa *mez* **Giuseppe Sabbatini**
ten **David Wilson-Johnson** *bar* **Michele Pertusi** *bass*
London Symphony Orchestra and Chorus /

Sir Colin Davis
LSO Live ② LSO0008 (132' · DDD · T/t)

Ⓢ🄾🄾🄳

This *Damnation de Faust* matches and even out-shines previous sets at whatever price, not least in the gripping drama of the performance, the more intense for being recorded live. Even more than in his classic 1973 recording for Philips, Davis involves you in the painful quandry obsessing Faust, never letting tension slip for a moment.

There may be different views over Giuseppe Sabbatini's portrayal of the central character. He's more overtly emotional than any of his immediate rivals. In the heat of the moment he tends to resort to an Italianate style, with the hint of a half-sob or the occasional phrase which is only half vocalised. Purists may resist, yet with his firm, golden, finely shaded tone and his radiant treatment of the highest-lying passages the impact is intensely characterful and involving.

As for Davis, the differences between his reading here and in 1973 are ones of detail and refinement, for there's an extra lightness and resilience in the playing of the current LSO, as in Mephistopheles' Flea song, which is more wittily pointed than before. The little snarling flourishes which herald Mephistopheles' arrival have you sitting up immediately, while the excitement generated in a number such as the Trio at the end of Part 3 leaves you breathless.

Michele Pertusi as Mephistopheles matches Sabbatini in the red-blooded fervour of his singing, weighty yet agile, and Enkelejda Shkosa is a warm, vibrant Marguerite, with a flicker in the voice giving a hint of the heroine's vulnerability. Not just the LSO but the London Symphony Chorus, too, are in searing form, and the recording brings out the detail of Berlioz's orchestration with ideal transparency, though the transfer is at rather a low level, needing fair amplifications for full impact. Davis is given wonderfully refined sound, with any problems from the Barbican acoustic completely eliminated. An astonishing bargain.

La damnation de Faust
Susan Graham *sop* **Thomas Moser** *ten* **José van Dam** *bass-bar* **Frédéric Caton** *bass;* **Chorus and Orchestra of Opéra de Lyon / Kent Nagano**
Erato ② 0630 10692-2 (122' · DDD · T/t)   Ⓜ🄾

New versions of *Faust* appear regularly, but one as good this is rare. At its centre is a perception of Berlioz's extraordinary vision, in all its colour and variety and humour and pessimism, and the ability to realise this in a broad downward sweep while setting every detail sharply in place. It's a work about the steady failure of consolations in a romantic world rejecting God, until all Faust's sensations are numbed and Mephistopheles has him trapped in the hell of no feeling. Every stage of the progress is mercilessly depicted here. The chorus is brilliant in all its roles, offering in turn the lively charms of peasant life, raptures of faith in the Easter Hymn, beery roistering in Auer-

bach's Cellar that grows as foul as a drunken party, cheerful student Latin bawls; later they sing with delicacy as Mephistopheles's spirits of temptation and finally become a vicious pack of demons. Nagano takes the Hungarian March at a pace that grows hectic as the dream of military glory turns hollow. It's all brilliantly realised.

There's the same care for orchestral detail. Nagano seems to be conducting from the New Berlioz Edition score, and he uses his imagination with it. He has an unerring sense of tempo, balancing weight of tone against speed, and he can light upon the telling contrapuntal line, or point a detail of instrumental colour or even a single note (like the snarl in the Ride to the Abyss), elements that give Berlioz's marvellous orchestration its expressive quality.

José van Dam is outstanding as Mephistopheles, curling his voice round phrases with hideous elegance, relishing the mock-jollity of the Serenade and the Song of the Flea, taunting Faust with lulling sweetness on the banks of the Elbe, yet also disclosing the sadness of the fallen spirit. Thomas Moser sings gravely and reflectively as he's first discovered on the plains of Hungary, and rises nobly to the challenge of the Invocation to Nature, but is almost at his finest in the many recitative passages as he twists and turns in Mephistopheles's grasp.

Susan Graham doesn't match these two superb performances but sings her two arias simply and well. This version sets Nagano among the outstanding Berlioz conductors of the day.

La damnation de Faust
Vesselina Kasarova *mez* **Paul Groves** *ten* **Willard White** *bass* **Andreas Macco** *bass* **San Sebastian People's Choral Society; Tölz Boys' Choir; Staatskapelle Berlin / Sylvain Cambreling**
Stage directors **Alex Olle, Carlos Pedrissa**
Video director **Alexandre Tarta**
ArtHaus Musik 🄳🆅🄳 100 003 (146' · DDD)   Ⓕ🄾🄾🄾

 This production was the sensation of the 1999 Salzburg Festival, and this riveting DVD captures most of the excitement that must have been felt at the time in the evocative Felsenreitschule. The staging is a joint venture. The spectacular scenic realisation of Berlioz's 'Légende dramatique' originated with the Spanish theatre troupe La Fura dels Baus; the staging itself is the work of Olle and Pedrissa. The sets and costumes were conceived by the Spanish sculptor Jaume Piensa.

The results were described in the press as 'extreme theatre' – and one can see why when viewing the virtuoso treatment of the vast stage area. It's dominated by a transparent cylinder which serves all sorts of purposes, depicting in particular the soul-searching struggles of Faust and Méphistophélès; while the complex choral movements and an elaborate lighting plot are all carried out without a hint of a hitch.

The producer certainly managed to inspire all the participants to heights of interpretative skill. Cambreling and the Berlin Staatskapelle perform with discipline and fire, wanting only that extra dedicated vision evinced by Colin Davis and the LSO on CD. Kasarova and Willard White, stage beings to their fingertips, sing and act with total conviction. Kasarova is the vulnerable, insecure, beautiful Marguerite to the life, every gesture and facial expression supporting her intense reading of the glorious music Berlioz wrote for her. Her vision of the great Romance is idiosyncratic to say the least, but a triumph of erotic communication on its own account, a cross between Callas and Ewing at their most individual. White is commanding throughout – at once demonic, cynical, relaxed and satirical, his huge voice absolutely in command of the role. Groves isn't quite on his colleagues' level of accomplishment, but acts and sings with the awe and sense of identity-seeking which this production requires of its Faust. The sound, as on most DVDs, is exemplary. Highly recommended.

L'enfance du Christ, Op 25

L'enfance du Christ
Jean Rigby mez **John Aler, Peter Evans** tens **Gerald Finley, Robert Poulton** bars **Alastair Miles, Gwynne Howell** basses **St Paul's Cathedral Choir; Corydon Singers and Orchestra / Matthew Best**
Hyperion Dyad ② CDD22067 (101' · DDD · T/t) Ⓑⵔ

Best treats *L'enfance du Christ* as overtly operatic, not so much by cast movements or varied microphone placings as by his pacing of the action and by encouraging his artists to throw themselves wholeheartedly into the emotions of the story. He gets off to a tremendous start with a superb reading by a black-voiced Alastair Miles as a Herod haunted by his dream and startled into belligerent wakefulness by the arrival of Polydorus. Later, there's desperate urgency in the appeals for shelter by Joseph (an otherwise gently lyrical Gerald Finley), harshly rebuffed by the chorus. And, throughout, there are spatial perspectives – the soldiers' patrol advancing (from practically inaudible pizzicatos) to centre-stage and going off again; and a beautifully hushed and atmospheric faraway 'Amen' at the end. Balance in general is excellent.

The clear enunciation (in very good French) of nearly everyone is a plus point. The chorus's response to the mood and meaning of words is always alert and sensitive, matched by the nuanced orchestral playing. The scurrying of the Ishmaelite family to help, played really *pianissimo*, is vividly graphic; and their home entertainment on two flutes and a harp, which can mark a drop in the interest, here has great charm. But overall it's Best's pacing which makes this recording distinctive. This recording stands comparison well with its much-praised predecessors.

Messe solennelle

Messe solennelle (also includes revised version   Ⓟ
of Resurrexit)

Donna Brown sop **Jean-Luc Viala** ten **Gilles Cachemaille** bar **Monteverdi Choir; Orchestre Révolutionnaire et Romantique / Sir John Eliot Gardiner**
Philips 464 688-2PM (61' · DDD · T/t)
Recorded live 1993   Ⓜⵔⵔⵔ▸

The reappearance of Berlioz's lost Mass of 1824 is the most exciting musical discovery of modern times. To an incredulous meeting of the New Berlioz Edition in 1992 the General Editor, Hugh Macdonald, announced that a Belgian choirmaster, Frans Moors, had made contact with news of an improbable find in an Antwerp organ loft. Gardiner with his Monteverdi Choir and Orchestre Révolutionnaire et Romantique gave performances in Bremen, Vienna, Madrid, Rome and Westminster Cathedral. This is a live recording of that last, thrilling occasion.

Why did Berlioz abandon the work? Only the *Resurrexit* was retained, though it was rewritten: both versions are included here. Some of it, but not much, is dull: the *Offertory* and *Sanctus* sit rather stolidly with the rest. He was unfair on what he denounced in an angry scribble on the MS as an 'execrable' fugue. Some is disconcertingly awkward, and Gardiner tells in the notes to this record of his and the singers' and players' confusion – until they all came together and suddenly the music made sense. The best of the work is superb: among this one may count the *Incarnatus*, the *O Salutaris* and the lovely *Agnus Dei*. The latter was too good to lose, and survives in another form in the *Te Deum*. So do other ideas: it was at first disconcerting to hear the chorus singing 'Laudamus te. Benedicimus te' to the Carnival music from *Benvenuto Cellini*, more so than to hear the slow movement of the *Symphonie fantastique* in the beautiful *Gratias*.

Once these and other associations are overcome, the work coheres remarkably well. Yet perhaps it did not do so well enough for Berlioz, and perhaps he was dissatisfied with the conjunction of some rather academic music with ideas that were too original, indeed too beautiful, to make a satisfying whole. Who knows whether he might have been made to think twice about abandoning the work had he heard a performance such as this? In any case, this is a recording of a great musical event, not to be missed.

Cantatas

Herminie[a]. La mort de Cléopâtre[b]. La mort d'Orphée[c]. La mort de Sardanapale[c]
[a]**Michèle Lagrange** sop [b]**Béatrice Uria-Monzon** mez [c]**Daniel Galvez Vallejo** ten **Choeur Régional Nord, Pas de Calais; Lille National Orchestra / Jean-Claude Casadesus**
Naxos 8 555810 (61' · DDD)   Ⓢ▸

To have on a single disc Berlioz's four attempts at the Prix de Rome, or at least as much of them as survives, was one of the most enjoyable fruits of the bicentenary year. Together they present a vivid portrait of the composer in his twenties, a

Janus figure looking at once back to Gluck and forward to the more highly coloured, Romantic products of the mid-19th century. These four works are all the more extraordinary for being based on a format devised by someone else – something Berlioz preferred to avoid after *Benvenuto Cellini*; even here he couldn't resist adding at times to the texts provided.

He tried to destroy *La mort de Sardanapale*, his prize-winning cantata of 1830, and only its end has survived by accident. Like its predecessors, it deals with an extreme situation. To that extent they all chimed in with Berlioz's natural propensities for shaking and stirring audiences, even to the point of aural discomfort. It's fascinating to find so many features of the mature Berlioz already in place: the ubiquitous diminished sevenths, the hitching up of tonalities by semitones, the love of descending scales (as in the wonderful line for Cléopâtre's 'Il n'en est plus pour moi que l'éternelle nuit', which could be Dido in *Les troyens* some 30 years later). The poetic Berlioz is also in evidence, notably in the beautiful Nature-music that opens *La mort d'Orphée*, his earliest attempt from 1827.

The contribution of the solo singers on this disc belongs more to the 19th century than to the 18th, which is possibly what Berlioz would have wanted. That's to say, all three voices are dramatic in size and style. There's some spreading at the top of all three above *mezzo forte*, but in giving their all they're merely taking a cue from Berlioz's orchestra, which, under Casadesus's firm direction, miraculously already sounds like the Berlioz we know. In softer passages all three are excellent.

Les nuits d'été, Op 7

Berlioz Les nuits d'été[a] **Ravel** Shéhérazade[a]
Debussy Trois chansons de Bilitis[b] **Poulenc**
Banalities[b] – Chansons d'Orkenise; Hôtel[c].
La courte paille[b] – Le carafon; La reine de coeur[c].
Chansons villageoises[b] – Les gars qui vont à la fête.
Deux poèmes de Louis Aragon[b]
Régine Crespin sop [b]**John Wustman** pf
[a]**Suisse Romande Orchestra / Ernest Ansermet**
Decca The Originals 475 7712DOR (68' · ADD · T/t)
Recorded [a]1963, [bc]1967 (M)**OOOO**→

Crespin's *Nuits d'été* has always been the interpretation by which others have been assessed and, listening to it again, there's no reason to challenge the verdict. In terms of idiomatic and natural French, languorous tone and understanding of the poetry's and the music's meaning, it stands above all other versions without any question. Even Dame Janet Baker's appreciable reading sounds a trifle affected in its vocal grammar besides Crespin's, particularly as regards the determinedly bright, jolly tone employed by the British artist in the first and last songs, whose joyous moods Crespin encompasses without resort to contrivance. Crespin's tempos are also ideally chosen.

The only drawback to her version is the sometimes slack accompanying of Ansermet, not that Barbirolli is ideal in that respect. Crespin's *Shéhérazade* is even more in a class of its own than her account of the Berlioz too. As soon as she launches seductively into 'Asie' we know that singer and music are perfectly matched, and the last two songs are even better.

As if this weren't enough, we have Crespin's *Chansons de Bilitis* from a later recital, a performance that wonderfully suggests the distant lassitude of poem and music, and a group of Poulenc songs from the same 1969 record of which the sad, elegiac 'C' (*Deux poèmes*) is the plum. Anyone who thinks that some of Crespin's successors fully understand how to interpret *mélodies* must hear this record.

Les nuits d'été. Herminie
Mireille Delunsch sop **Brigitte Balleys** mez
**Orchestre des Champs-Elysées, Paris /
Philippe Herreweghe**
Harmonia Mundi HMC90 1522 (54' · DDD · T/t)
(F)**OO**

It isn't fanciful to hear decided pre-echoes in *Herminie* of Cassandra's fateful, searing music (quite apart from the dry-run for the *Symphonie fantastique*'s main motif). This extraordinary work of 1828, almost as arresting as its near-contemporary *Cléopâtre*, receives a grand rendering from Mireille Delunsch, who sings it in a compact, direct manner. Her tone is narrow and focused, her French diction clear. Herreweghe and his orchestra adopt a lean sound, surely close to that of Berlioz's time. Delunsch enters into the inner agony of the distraught, frustrated Herminie with a will. Her interpretation is absorbing from start to finish.

The recording imparts a slight glare to her tone as it does to that of Balleys in the much more familiar *Nuits d'été*, but that's hardly enough to detract from an idiomatic, unfussy reading. Her voice doesn't luxuriate in the more sensual moments of the cycle as does Régine Crespin's in her famous version (currently unavailable on CD, listed 'In Brief') but it has a clarity of profile and a definition of phrase and, where strength of feeling is called for, Balleys provides it, as in 'Au cimetière' and 'Absence'. This makes a sensible pairing with the cantata. What may also influence your choice is, again, Herreweghe's lean, well-pointed support which often emphasises, rightly, the striking originality of Berlioz's scoring.

Berlioz Les nuits d'été, Op 7[a]
Chausson Poème de l'amour et de la mer, Op 19[b]
Schoenberg Gurrelieder – Song of the Wood Dove[c]
Dame Janet Baker mez [a]**London Philharmonic
Orchestra / Carlo Maria Giulini;** [bc]**London
Symphony Orchestra /** [b]**Evgeny Svetlanov,**
[c]**Norman del Mar**
BBC Legends BBCL4077-2 (75' · ADD · N)

Recorded live [a]1975, [b]1975, [c]1963   Ⓕ❍

These three absorbing interpretations are a welcome addition to the growing discography of Dame Janet in live performances, where the *frisson* of a 'real' occasion adds an extra immediacy to her readings. Dame Janet recorded *Nuits d'étés* some 10 years earlier with Barbirolli, when speeds were on the slow side. Here they're even more deliberate, possibly the longest 'Le spectre de la rose' on disc. The extra time allows the singer to bring an even deeper sense of mystery and longing to the four middle songs. Has 'Absence' ever sounded so sad and eloquent? Her ability to control a wide range of dynamic effects is astonishing. Giulini and the LPO couldn't be more supportive.

All the recordings are a tribute to the BBC's recording expertise, giving more presence to the voice than is often the case today. Apart from one disfiguring cough in the Berlioz, the presence of an audience is hardly intrusive.

Additional recommendation

Les nuits d'été   Ⓗ
Coupled with: Symphonie fantastique. Roméo et Juliette – Queen Mab Scherzo. Overtures – Benvenuto Cellini; Béatrice et Bénédict. Le carnaval romain. Le corsaire. Les Troyens – Chasse royale et orage
De los Angeles *sop* **Boston SO / Munch**
RCA Red Seal Artistes et Répertoires
② 74321 84587-2 (129' · ADD)   Ⓜ❍❍

De los Angeles's *Nuits d'été* still remains a benchmark by which all others are judged; she has all the vocal range and variety of expression needed for these songs. It's a shame, though, that no stereo tapes exist for these 1955 sessions. The performances of the overtures are electric.

Songs

Mélodies, Op 19 – No 2, Les champs; No 6, Le Chasseur danois. Mélodies, Op 13 – No 1, Le matin; No 2, Petit oiseau, chant de paysan; No 4, Le Jeune pâtre breton[c]; No 5, Le Chant des Bretons. Mélodies, 'Irlande', Op 2 – Le coucher du soleil; Chant guerrier[b]; La belle voyageuse; Chanson à boire[b]; Chant sacré[a]; L'origine de la harpe; Adieu Bessy; Elégie en prose. Roméo et Juliette, Op 17 – Premiers transports[d]
Jérôme Corréas *bass-bar* **Arthur Schoonderwoerd** *pf* with [a]**Claire Brua,** [a]**Marie-Bénénedicte Souquet** *sops* [b]**Alain Gabriel,** [a]**Jean-Francois Novelli,** [a]**Jean-Francois Lombard** *tens* [a]**Vincent Deliau** *bar* [c]**Claude Maury** *hn* [d]**Christophe Coin** *vc*
Alpha ALPHA024 (58' · DDD · T/t)   Ⓕ

It's surprising that Berlioz's songs aren't better known. Anyone who thinks *Les nuits d'été* constitutes a summary of his vocal production need only listen to this disc to be disabused. Jérôme Corréas has so far tended to specialise in Baroque music and his dark, warm bass-baritone is surpris-

BERLIOZ LES NUITS D'ÉTÉ – IN BRIEF

Régine Crespin; SRO / Ernest Ansermet
Decca 475 7712DOR (69' · ADD)   Ⓜ❍❍❍☐➤
The classic recording in which every nuance has been scrupulously articulated. Gorgeous.

Janet Baker; New Philharmonia / Sir John Barbirolli
EMI 562788-2 (78' · ADD)   Ⓜ❍❍❍
The version that for many vies with the Crespin. Baker in 1967 is on top form and her rapport with Barbirolli conjures some moments of breathtaking allure.

Janet Baker; LPO / Carlo Maria Giulini
BBC Legends BBCL4077-2 (75' · ADD)   Ⓕ❍❍❍
A live recording from 1975 shines a light on different areas than her earlier version – speeds here tend to be quite slow.

Anne Sofie von Otter; Berlin PO / James Levine
DG 445 823-2GH (63' · DDD)   Ⓟ☐➤
An early von Otter foray into the French repertoire – it's good but nowhere as full of the insight she customarily brings to the French repertoire these days.

Susan Graham; ROH Orchestra / John Nelson
Sony Classical SK62730 (61' · DDD)   Ⓕ❍❍
A wonderfully imaginative, carefully moulded performance: perhaps the most complete interpretation since the celebrated Régine Crespin version. A modern classic.

Diana Montague; Catherine Robbin; Howard Crook; Gilles Cachemaille; Lyon Opera Orchestra / Sir John Eliot Gardiner
Apex 0927 49583-2 (63' · ADD)   Ⓑ❍☐➤
The most successful of the multi-voice recordings and a set that showed early on (1989) Gardiner's wonderful way with Berlioz. A real bargain, too.

David Daniels; Ensemble Orchestral de Paris / John Nelson
Virgin Classics 545646-2 (69' · DDD)   Ⓕ☐➤
A reasonably successful countertenor version but the mezzos generally find more to say in these magical songs.

Isabel Vernet; Laurent Martin *pf*
Ligia LIDI0201032 (57' · ADD)   Ⓑ
One of the handful of recordings with piano uncovers many subtleties and insights.

Brigitte Balleys; Champs-Elysées Orchestra / Philippe Herreweghe
Harmonia Mundi HMC90 1522 (54' · ADD)   Ⓕ❍❍
Fine singing from Brigitte Balleys but Philippe Herreweghe's control of his French orchestra is a thing of wonder.

ingly flexible in its articulation, with an especially tender *mezza voce*. Berlioz's roots aren't generally thought to extend further back than Gluck, but Corréas's well-focused tone and shapely phrasing is ideal for this music. Certainly Berlioz's vocal lines, asymmetrical and often plain weird, have little to do with Viennese Classicism. Corréas embraces the asymmetry, but is ingenious in finding some logic in the composer's most outlandish effusions, and you can hear every word. Arthur Schoonderwoerd draws wonderful sounds from an 1836 Pleyel and in a song like *Elégie en prose* you can sense Duparc in the making. The other supporting artists are all excellent – a particularl joy is Christophe Coin's cello playing in the marvellous 'Premiers transports'. The spacious church acoustic, with up to a three-second echo, isn't ideal, but then traffic-free venues in Paris are hard to find.

Béatrice et Bénédict

Béatrice et Bénédict
Susan Graham *sop* Béatrice **Jean-Luc Viala** *ten* Bénédict **Sylvia McNair** *sop* Héro **Catherine Robbin** *mez* Ursule **Gilles Cachemaille** *bar* Claudio **Gabriel Bacquier** *bar* Somarone **Vincent Le Texier** *bass* Don Pedro **Philippe Magnant** *spkr* Léonato **Lyon Opera Chorus and Orchestra / John Nelson**
Erato MusiFrance ② 2292 45773-2 (111' · DDD · T/t)
Ⓕ🔴

We have to note that the title isn't a French version of *Much Ado about Nothing*. Berlioz takes the two principal characters of Shakespeare's play and constructs an opera around them. The comedy centres on the trick that is played on the pair by their friends, producing love out of apparent antipathy. Much of the charm lies in the more incidental matters of choruses, dances, the magical 'Nocturne' duet for Béatrice and Héro, and the curious addition of the character Somarone, a music-master who rehearses the choir in one of his own compositions. There's also a good deal of spoken dialogue. Perhaps surprisingly, the extra dialogue is a point in its favour, for it's done very effectively by good French actors and it makes for a cohesive, Shakespearian entertainment. John Nelson secures a well-pointed performance of the score, and with excellent playing by the Lyon Orchestra. Susan Graham and Jean-Luc Viala are attractively vivid and nimble in style, and Sylvia McNair makes a lovely impression in Héro's big solo. The veteran Gabriel Bacquier plays the music-master with genuine panache and without overmuch clownage. There's good work by the supporting cast and the chorus and the recording is finely produced.

Benvenuto Cellini

Benvenuto Cellini
Gregory Kunde *ten* Benvenuto Cellini **Laurent Naouri** *bass* Balducci **Jean-François Lapointe** *bass*

Fieramosca **Patrizia Ciofi** *sop* Teresa **Joyce DiDonato** *mez* Ascanio **Radio France Chorus; French National Orchestra / John Nelson**
Virgin Classics ③ 545706-2 (3h 8' · DDD · S/T/t/N)
Recorded live 2003   Ⓕ🔴🅱▸

Thanks to to Hugh Macdonald's brilliant work for the *New Berlioz Edition* the 1838 Paris Opéra version of *Benvenuto Cellini* is once again performable; this adds almost half an hour's music to the Colin Davis recording of 1972 (Philips, nla). It's a splendid achievement. Macdonald's notes are an exemplary guide to the music's youthful genius, and David Cairns's original translation for the Davis recording is augmented by Lisa Hobbs, alongside the French.

Each of the singers responds with a quick understanding to the unexpected, eloquent contours of the recitatives, none more so than Gregory Kunde, who can phrase elegantly Cellini's wistful aria longing for a shepherd's simple life, but also prove an ardent suitor for Teresa, and challenge his adversaries with an heroic, defiant *brio*. Patrizia Ciofi can sound a little timid for him, and for Teresa's light vivacity, though she sings fluently and gracefully. Jean-François Lapointe characterises the devious Fieramosca wittily, and joins the two other two cleverly in the brilliant *tour de force* of their trio. There's a high-spirited performance of Ascanio from Joyce Di Donato that includes witty imitations of the men, and Laurent Naouri vigorously struts his hour on the stage as Teresa's father Balducci.

Berlioz's reckless demands on the orchestra are brilliantly answered. The recording engineers have done extraordinarily well in conveying so much detail even when matters are hurtling full tilt in the Roman Carnival scene and in the final casting of the Perseus. John Nelson steers it all with a sure hand and total conviction.

Les Troyens

Les Troyens
Ben Heppner *ten* Aeneas **Michelle DeYoung** *mez* Dido **Petra Lang** *mez* Cassandra **Sara Mingardo** *mez* Anna **Peter Mattei** *bar* Choroebus **Stephen Milling** *bass* Narbal **Kenneth Tarver** *ten* Iopas **Toby Spence** *ten* Hylas **Orlin Annastassov** *bass* Ghost of Hector **Tigran Martirossian** *bass* Panthous **Isabelle Cals** *mez* Ascanio **Alan Ewing** *bass* Priam **Guang Yang** *mez* Hecuba **Andrew Greenan** *bass* First Sentry **Roderick Earle** *bass* Second Sentry **Bülent Bezdüz** *ten* Helenus **Leigh Melrose** *bass* A Trojan Soldier, Mercury **Mark Stone** *bar* A Greek Chieftain **London Symphony Chorus and Orchestra / Sir Colin Davis**
LSO Live ④ LSO0010 (4h' · DDD)   Ⓢ🔴🔴🔴🅱▸

 Colin Davis's 1969 recording remains a landmark event, the first time this grand opera of Meyerbeerian length, spectacular *éclat* and Wagnerian artistic ambition had found its way complete onto LP. It effectively changed views about Berlioz the opera composer and orchestral genius and has for many remained the yardstick by which all later performances have been judged. Although studio recorded, it was based on the Covent Garden casting of the day – Jon Vickers's heroic Aeneas and Josephine Veasey's voluptuous Dido – with a couple of Frenchmen to boost the ranks of lesser Trojans and Carthaginians.

The tantalising glimpses of Régine Crespin's Cassandra and Dido belong to a now lost tradition which none of the singing on the new LSO disc quite emulates – with the possible exception of the delightful young French mezzo Isabelle Cals as Ascagnio. Part for part, however, the LSO have assembled a cast which challenges without comprehensively surpassing that of the earlier Davis recording. Some of the *comprimario* singers are without doubt their predecessors' superiors: the handsome-voiced Peter Mattei is a nobler-toned, more youthful and romantic-sounding Choroebus in his fraught interview with his 'vierge adorée', Cassandra; Sara Mingardo's sumptuous contralto is luxury casting for Dido's sister beside the admirable but plain Heather Begg. And as the Carthaginian court poet, Iopas, Kenneth Tarver's tone catches the microphone just that bit more sweetly than Ian Partridge's.

Any account of *Les Troyens*, however, stands or falls by the casting of the three central characters – Cassandra, Aeneas and Dido – and this the LSO has done with exceptional results. Michelle DeYoung was originally assigned Cassandre, but was 'promoted' to Didon when Olga Borodina fell ill. Her replacement as Cassandra, the German dramatic mezzo Petra Lang, was a revelation at the Barbican, a passionate prophetess, thrilling in her imprecations against the Greeks and heroic in her suicide as Troy is consumed in flames at the close of Act 2.

Her French has a slightly 'thick' Germanic flavour but she makes every word tell and she has the grand rhetorical manner Berlioz learned from Gluck and Cherubini to the manner born.

It's hard to imagine today – vocally at least –a more musical, more romantic, more impetuous Aeneas than Ben Heppner who brings real stylish distinction and heroic bravura to bear. Michelle DeYoung's Dido isn't quite so successful. Her big, bright-toned voice is less warm than Veasey's and she has a tendency to 'yowl' on climactic notes. She doesn't really convey Dido's regal bearing either: her imperiousness is that of a bossy housekeeper rather than a great founding Queen. That said, she rises to a magnificent 'Adieu, fier cité' and works herself into a Medea-like rage when she threatens to serve a dismembered Ascanio as her perjured lover's dinner.

What really makes this issue indispensable is Davis's conducting of an LSO on incandescent form. The 'world's greatest Berlioz conductor' seems to become ever more convinced of the greatness of this astonishing score and revels, with greater conviction than ever, in its magical

orchestral effects and its grand theatrical rhetoric. For Davis and his orchestra – and the splendid immediacy of the live recording – this account of *Les Troyens* is first choice at any price. This set is a must-buy.

Additional recommendations

Ferrer Didon, Cassandre **Giraudeau** Enée   Ⓗ
Cambon Chorèbe, Narba **BBC Theatre Chorus; Royal Philharmonic Orchestra / Beecham**
Malibran-Music mono ④ CDRG162 (3h 46' · ADD)
Broadcast 1947   Ⓕ**OOO**

One of the most important documents ever to appear from previously unavailable archives. Beecham is at least Davis's peer here. An arresting, inspiriting performance, which has the benefit of a superb French cast.

Les Troyens
Susan Graham *mez* Dido **Gregory Kunde** *ten* Aeneas **Anna Caterina Antonacci** *sop* Cassandra **Ludovic Tezier** *bar* Choroebus **Renata Pokupic** *conti* Anna **Laurent Naouri** *bass* Narbal **Nicolas Testé** *bass* Pantheus **Stéphanie d'Oustrac** *mez* Ascanius **Mark Padmore** *ten* Iopas **Topi Lehtipuu** *ten* Hylas, Helenus **Monteverdi Choir; Théâtre du Châtelet Chorus, Paris; Orchestre Révolutionnaire et Romantique / Sir John Eliot Gardiner**
Stage director **Yannis Kokkos**
Video director **Peter Maniura**
BBC/Opus Arte ② ▶️**DVD** OA0900D (5h 12' · NTSC · S/s/N · 16:9 · PCM Stereo, DTS 5.1 · 0). Recorded live. Includes documentary, cast gallery   Ⓕ**OOO**

Les Troyens hasn't fared well on DVD, but this superb authentic-instrument performance of October 2003 from the Théâtre du Châtelet, Paris, equals Sir Colin Davis's pioneering original. Orchestrally it's everything we've come to expect from Gardiner's Berlioz, his tempi swift and dynamic, sharing the composer's delight in complex rhythmic interplay, yet always propelling the drama. Passages like Andromache's entrance and Hector's ghost nevertheless have their proper gravitas and sombre hues against the brighter shades of Carthage. Colour is the great gift of the period instruments, revealing a wide range of sonorities, and creating a sense of freshness and discovery. The effect is sometimes rawer, sometimes more classical, but almost always more complex and dramatic than the homogenised modern sound.

Gardiner's singers, too, could hardly be more committed. Anna Caterina Antonacci is a fiery Cassandra, superbly classical-looking, so wrung and tormented that some moments of strain scarcely matter. Gregory Kunde tackles Aeneas with ringing tone, looks and acts pretty well, and brings a welcome *bel canto* touch to the gorgeous duet. Susan Graham, though, needs no caveats: a radiant Dido, queenly yet youthful, lyrical and lighter-toned than Janet Baker, but in her final despair no less tragically moving. Other roles are generally excellent. The mostly youthful chorus sounds marvellous, and is a constant force in Yannis Kokkos's moderately modern production.

The stage is plain and bare, capped by a reflector in which most of the décor appears: an Italian Renaissance cityscape for Troy, and the Horse only as a menacing head. Carthage is a classical vision of white walls and blue sea with stylised ships. The Trojans wear the inescapable greatcoats the brutal Greeks, inevitably, American combat gear, and the Carthaginians vaguely North African whites and pastels. This is a mostly straightforward, lively staging which lets characters and drama speak for themselves, and so works well on screen. The magnificent high-definition recording does it ample sonic and visual justice.

For anyone who loves *Les Troyens*, this is a revelatory and essential performance.

Les Troyens (sung in English)
Blanche Thebom mez Dido **Jon Vickers** ten Aeneas
Amy Shuard sop Cassandra **Jess Walters** bar
Corebus **Lauris Elms** mez Anna **David Kelly** bass
Narbal **Michael Langdon** bass Panthus **Joan Carlyle**
sop Ascanius **Richard Verreau** ten Iopas **Forbes**
Robinson bass Priam **Noreen Berry** contr Hecuba
Dermot Troy ten Hylas **Edgar Evans** ten Helenus
Joseph Rouleau bass Ghost of Hector **Robert**
Allman bar Greek Captain **Alan Beale** bar Mercury
Chorus and Orchestra of the Royal Opera House,
Covent Garden / Rafael Kubelík
Testament mono ④ SBT4 1443 (3h 45' · ADD)
Recorded live 1957. Also includes Jon Vickers in
conversation with Jon Tolansky, recorded 1998   Ⓕ

This 1957 production of Berlioz's epic five-act opera was the first modern attempt to stage the whole work in one evening at a major house. Sir David Webster, the pioneering manager of Covent Garden, and the then musical director, Rafael Kubelík, had set their hearts on bringing the work to the stage in as complete a form as possible. Sir John Gielgud was the director, and it must be in some measure due to his influence that the diction of all concerned is so clear, declaiming Edward Dent's translation.

It is difficult not to approach this historic broadcast without some feeling of awe. There was no tradition of performing the work in modern France (indeed, it had never been performed there complete). The material available, long before any definitive edition had been made, was in poor condition, and in some instances inaccurate. Everyone involved was approaching his or her role for the first time. Yet from the moment Amy Shuard as Cassandra utters 'The Greeks have quit the plane', one is gripped by the recording, the performance and, as always, above all the work itself.

Shuard was on the threshold of her international career then. She made hardly any commercial recordings but in recent years several off-the-air issues have emerged, of which this is one of the most vivid. Blanche Thebom, as Dido, does not immediately make such an

impact, yet by the time the love duet, 'O sweet night', is reached one is captivated by her warm personality. Jon Vickers's Aeneas is well known: he recorded the role complete and in French some 12 years later for Sir Colin Davis and Philips; here, singing in English, and more youthful-sounding, he makes a superbly positive hero. His great aria in the final act, 'There is no turning back', is one of the many highlights of the set. There are so many other names that might be singled out; but suffice to say that the whole is a fine souvenir of the Covent Garden ensemble in that time. (The sound is adequate for a 52-year-old tape, splendidly remastered by Paul Baily.)

Lord Berners   British 1883-1950

English composer, writer and painter Lord Berners was essentially self-taught and was proof that a jack of all trades can be a master of a good deal of them! He was a friend of Stravinsky, Casella, Walton and Lambert, and his music has something of their surface lustre. His early works (mainly songs and piano pieces) are mostly small-scale and quite French in feel. His larger scores are mainly for the stage and include a number of ballets, including The Triumph of Neptune (1926), Luna Park (1930) and A Wedding Bouquet (1936). He also wrote the film score for Nicholas Nickleby (1947). The epitaph on his gravestone reads: 'Here lies Lord Berners / One of life's learners / Thanks be to the Lord / He never was bored.'

Songs / Solo piano works

Polka. Le poisson d'or. Dispute entre le papillon et le crapaud. Trois petites marches funèbres. Fragments psychologiques. March. The Expulsion from Paradise. Valse. Lieder Album[a]. Trois chansons[a]. Three English Songs[a]. Dialogue between Tom Filuter and his Man by Ned the Dog Stealer[a]. Three Songs[a]. Red Roses and Red Noses[a]. Come on Algernon[a]
[a]**Ian Partridge** ten **Len Vorster** pf
Marco Polo 8 225159 (52' · DDD · T/t)   ⒻⒹ➔

The minuscule, dejected, lovelorn *Le poisson d'or*, based on Lord Berners' own poem, has a distant Debussian inheritance, while the *Trois petites marches* and *Fragments psychologiques* are Satie-esque, and not just for their bizarre titles. Yet they, too, have a distinct avant-garde precocity, and 'Un soupir' (the third of the *Fragments*) brings a pensive dolour all its own. Berners' sense of fun erupts in the simulated German *Lieder Album* (the seriousness underpinned with a twinkle), and the French *Trois chansons* are naturally idiomatic, with 'La fiancée du timbalier' engagingly light-hearted. The English songs are most winning. *Tom Filuter's* dialogue changes mood chimerically, and the *Three Songs* of 1921 are like a re-discovery of the English folksong idiom, while the sentimental *Red Roses and Red Noses* has an endearingly flowing lyrical line. It's followed by the irrepressible *Come on Algernon*. It makes a delightful pay-off to end the recital.

Ian Partridge obviously relishes all the stylistic changes like a vocal chameleon, while Len Vorster backs him up splendidly and is completely at home in the solo piano music.

Le carrosse du Saint-Sacrement

Le carrosse du Saint-Sacrement[a].
Fanfare[b]. Caprice péruvien[c]
[a]**Ian Caddy** bass Viceroy [a]**Alexander Oliver** ten Martinez [a]**John Winfield** ten Balthasar [a]**Cynthia Buchan** mez La Périchole [a]**Thomas Lawlor** bar Thomas d'Esquivel [a]**Anthony Smith** bass Bishop of Lima [a]**BBC Scottish Symphony Orchestra / Nicholas Cleobury;** [b]**Royal Ballet Sinfonia / Gavin Sutherland;** [c]**RTE Sinfonietta / David Lloyd-Jones**
Marco Polo 8 225155 (79' · DDD · T/t)

Berners' one-act was neglected after its 1924 Paris premiere under Ansermet until the BBC Radio 3 revival in 1983, which is issued here for the first time. The libretto is adapted from a short story by Mérimée, also used in Offenbach's *La Périchole*. The attractive score has Such Berners fingerprints as the rhythms of his cynical 'Funeral March for a Rich Aunt' and Spanish effects, daringly close to Chabrier, to suit the Peruvian setting. The leading lady, La Périchole, is a young actress carrying on with the jealous, gout-ridden Viceroy. Their extended duet in Scene 4 develops as a fascinating alliance of scoundrels. At the end of it, she prises the Viceroy's brand-new coach out of him so she can parade in it to the cathedral and eclipse her rivals in Lima. After a spectacular ride, including a collision, she upstages everyone by giving the carriage to the church to take the sacrament to the dying. Chris de Souza's excellent radio production used a translation by Adam Pollock of the French libretto. The diction of all the characters is clear: everyone is well cast, especially Cynthia Buchan and Ian Caddy. The *Caprice péruvien* is a later compilation based on music from the opera. Both orchestras are adequate, decently recorded, but above all *Le carrosse* is an enchanting discovery in British comic opera.

Leonard Bernstein   American 1918-1990

'One-man bridge' would be an appropriate description for Bernstein. Like no other musician of his age, he was able to straddle the extremes of the musical world – an intellectual, a composer who wrote complex symphonies and 12-tone music but who was equally happy playing piano and writing Broadway musicals, able to take his adoring public with him down most of the roads he chose to travel. His appetite for music and his zest for life, his passion to share his enthusiasms, his versatility and boundless energy leave one breathless. As conductor,

composer, educator and pianist, 'Lenny' dominated American musical life for four decades.

He was actually born Louis, the son of Russian-Jewish immigrants, but changed his name by deed poll aged 16 to avoid confusion with other Louis Bernsteins in the family. He had private piano lessons as a child before going to Harvard University where began a succession of distinguished mentors who oversaw the development of a prodigious talent – Walter Piston and Edward Burlingame Hill for counterpoint, fugue and orchestration, followed, at the Curtis Institute, by Fritz Reiner for conducting and Isabella Vengerova for piano. Scholarships enabled him to attend courses at Tanglewood, Massachusetts, in 1940 and 1941 where he studied under the great conductor, publisher and patron Serge Koussevitzky.

Bernstein became Koussevitzky's protégé, his assistant at Tanglewood, before being made assistant to the legendary Artur Rodzinski at the New York Philharmonic. Fairy-tale stuff – and better was to come. In November 1943 he was called upon at very short notice to take over a difficult concert for the indisposed Bruno Walter. Rodzinski was out of town and the young Bernstein scored a huge personal triumph. Overnight he was famous and the occasion gave a kick-start to one of the most brilliant conducting careers in American history, crowned by being made conductor of the New York Philharmonic in 1958 and, on resigning in 1969 to give more time to composition, 'conductor laureate'. His animal energy on the podium was compulsive. In concerts and books, on radio and television, Bernstein was the supreme communicator and the Young People's Concerts he presented from 1958 to 1973 must have introduced millions to the music he so obviously loved.

Bernstein seemed to need little time before discovering his own distinctive voice of strongly lyrical, jazz-slanted music full of his Jewish heritage. The 1940s and '50s saw the appearance of a bewildering variety of musical works in all shapes and forms including his Symphonies Nos 1 and 2, Clarinet Sonata, Prelude, Fugue and Riffs, his film score for On the Waterfront (1954) as well as a Broadway career. This came as a result of his 1944 ballet Fancy Free which was subsequently adapted into the musical comedy On the Town; that in turn led to another (Wonderful Town) and then, most spectacularly, to West Side Story. Less commercially successful but with interesting and delightful scores were the comedy operetta Candide and the one-act opera Trouble in Tahiti (Bernstein supplying his own text – his other writing talents included poetry and he published a number of sonnets and other poems). In the '60s came a series of religious works – his Symphony No 3 (Kaddish), the Chichester Psalms (commissioned by the Dean of Chichester and first performed in 1965) and a Mass (written for the opening of the John F Kennedy Center for the Performing Arts in Washington, DC, in 1971).

He married Chilean actress Felicia Montealagre in 1951 (she died in 1978) but Bernstein's sexual drive was devoted mainly to members of his own sex. One young man was due to go to America to study with Bernstein. 'Be careful,' his father warned. 'Leonard Bernstein is gay.' The young man looked up in wonder. 'Is there nothing that man can't do?' he said in admiration.

Symphonies

Symphony No 1, 'Jeremiah'[a]. Concerto for Orchestra,
'Jubilee Games'[b]
[a]**Helen Medlyn** mez [b]**Nathan Gunn** bar **New
Zealand Symphony Orchestra / James Judd**
Naxos 8 559100 (55' · DDD) Ⓢ▷

In life, Leonard Bernstein ran into criticism for
programming his own concert music. Now he's
gone, it seems we can't get enough of it – and in
a variety of performance styles. Latterday champions such as Michael Tilson Thomas and
Marin Alsop still go for the idiomatic jugular.
Less extrovert interpreters – David Zinman and
Kent Nagano spring to mind – downplay the
bravado to discover a fresher transparency. On
this disc James Judd, British-born but for many
years Florida-based, seems closer to the second
camp while remaining remarkably faithful to the
composer's own overall timings in both pieces.

Keeping a stiff upper lip isn't an option in the
Concerto for Orchestra, one of Bernstein's
most exploratory and frankly uneven scores.
Some of its music is very beautiful, though it
isn't easy to see what it has to do with the rest.
Judd sometimes trumps the composer's own
wilder performance with his paler, more neutral tone.

Competition is fiercer in the coupling. The
scherzo of the *Jeremiah*, rowdy, raw and rhetorical
in the composer's New York recording, is brought
that much closer to the symphonic mainstream
here, the New Zealand winds relatively polite and
in tune. The portentous, hieratic tendencies of the
last movement may even be less apparent when
the singer is an Australasian crossover artist rather
than the customary *grande dame*. The sonorities
are lighter and the voltage a little lower than you
might be used to. A genuine bargain even so, with
recorded sound way ahead of the super-budget
norm. There are full if not always felicitously
expressed notes. Newcomers needn't hesitate.

Bernstein Symphony No 2, 'The Age of Anxiety'
Bolcom Piano Concerto
Marc-André Hamelin pf **Ulster Orchestra /
Dmitry Sitkovetsky**
Hyperion CDA67170 (59' · DDD) Ⓕ▷

After Hamelin's fantastic virtuosity in the outrageously difficult Godowsky *Studies on Chopin's
Etudes* (for which he won the *Gramophone*
Instrumental Award 2000) these two works for
piano and orchestra are – for him – mere bagatelles. But this is an impressive release since it
contains the most convincing account of Bernstein's Symphony No 2 (1949) in recent years.

The whole piece is Bernstein's obsessive
response to Auden's poem *The Age of Anxiety*,
published the year before, about four characters struggling to sort themselves out in New
York City. Even though Auden apparently
disliked it, you can increasingly hear Bernstein's Symphony as saturated with the poem,

its ideas and atmosphere. Often programmatic, it represents a particularly original
approach to piano and orchestra and is personal in countless ways – the gentleness of the
soft opening and its mystical descending scale,
the precisely engineered variations, memorable tunes, a splendid jazzy *Scherzo* and so on.
Hamelin and the Ulster Orchestra in fine form
under Sitkovetsky deliver a well-paced and
cogent performance right up to the deliberately inflated, optimistic ending.

Bolcom is one of the most idiosyncratic American composers of the next generation. His 1976
Piano Concerto draws widely on various types of
popular music, which he's always performed
superbly. The Concerto was written in memory of
his teacher, Darius Milhaud, who'd have loved it.
The opening movement is captivatingly serene
until the blue notes get out of hand; the slow
movement is more stable and serious; but the
finale comes over as a riotous celebration of
Americana. Unfortunately Bolcom intended it to
be ironic, as a kind of anti-bicentennial tribute.
But tunes like these have a habit of occupying
centre-stage on their own terms. Hamelin is again
utterly scrupulous and idiomatic, and delivers all
the musical styles with supreme confidence –
nobody could have mixed them up like Bolcom.

Symphony No 3, 'Kaddish'[a]. Chichester Psalms[b]
[a]**Yvonne Kenny** sop [b]**Michael Small**
treb [a]**Willard White** spkr **Liverpool Metropolitan
Cathedral Choir; Liverpool Philharmonic Youth
Choir; Royal Liverpool Philharmonic Choir and
Orchestra / Gerard Schwarz**
Naxos American Classics/Milken Archive 8 559456
(56' · DDD) Ⓢ▷

The word 'chutzpah' might have been invented
for Leonard Bernstein's *Kaddish* Symphony.
Not content with challenging the great deity in
the sky, Bernstein also takes on the credo of
1960s 12-tone orthodoxies in his third symphony – a far greater sin in the eyes of some.
'Every son defies his father, fights him…only to
return to him closer and more secure than
before,' Bernstein wrote as he explained how
Jewish theology informed his score. And as his
speaker rages against God, down in the orchestra there's a furious debate about what Bernstein
perceived as the crisis in modern music.

The raw material of Bernstein's score is a
dialectical clash between paternal tonality and
'errant' 12-tone music, although it's hard to
imagine a more hummable tone-row. This cen-
trifugal tension powers the symphony on, and
Gerard Schwarz conveys the unfolding drama
with strategic clarity. Ironically in the circumstances, Bernstein's own pull-no-punches 1977
DG recording with the Israel PO must hang
heavy over any conductor approaching the
piece. One giant tick in Schwarz's plus-column
is Willard White, a less mannered speaker than
Bernstein's Michael Wager. The orchestra and
voices, too, sound as if they're taking pleasure in
Bernstein's highly inventive scoring, running

the spectrum of his jazzy big-band swagger and post-Darmstadt atonal webs with ease.

In comparison to Kaddish's angst, *Chichester Psalms* is a cathartic work that, to paraphrase, requires little more than reading the lines without tripping over the lopsided time signatures. Schwarz energises the Technicolor opening movement, although choral vulnerabilities detract from the work's conclusion. None the less, a disc Bernstein fans will relish.

Fancy Free

Candide – Overture. West Side Story – Symphonic Dances. On the Waterfront – Symphonic Suite. Fancy Free
New York Philharmonic Orchestra /
Leonard Bernstein
Sony Classical Bernstein Century 82796 92728-2
(69' · ADD). Recorded 1960-63   Ⓜ**OO**

These performances have long been considered definitive. All but *Fancy Free* were taped in New York's Manhattan Center in the early 1960s, a problematic venue in which the original sound engineers sought to reconcile the close-miking of individual sections and sometimes individual players with a substantial reverberation period. The results have a synthetic, larger-than-life quality which suits most of the music here. The exception is the Overture to *Candide*, a more driven sort of reading, the brashness of Broadway insufficiently tempered by the rapid figurations of Rossini, the academicism of Brahms, the *joie de vivre* of Offenbach: subtler details tend to disappear into a fog of resonance. In the Symphonic Dances from *West Side Story*, the players eschew the customary shouts in the 'Mambo' but it's doubtful whether there will ever be a more idiomatic reading of what was then essentially 'new music'. The score, by no means a straightforward 'greatest hits' selection, had only recently been unveiled, with Lukas Foss conducting, at a gala concert intended to raise funds for the NYPO pension fund. Here certainly was the 'aura of show business' which so irked Harold Schonberg, the influential music critic of the *New York Times*: Bernstein's own recording from March 6th has the quality of an unanswerable rejoinder. *On the Waterfront* is if anything even more intense, its lyrical core dispatched with an overwhelming ardour. Last up is what's almost the best of all possible *Fancy Free*s. It was originally sung in inimitable style by Billie Holiday.

Chichester Psalms

Bernstein Chichester Psalms **Barber** Agnus Dei, Op 11 **Copland** In the Beginning. Four Motets – Help us, O Lord; Have mercy on us, O my Lord; Sing ye praises to our King
Dominic Martelli treb **Catherine Denley** mez **Rachel Masters** hp **Gary Kettel** perc **Thomas Trotter** org
Corydon Singers / Matthew Best
Hyperion CDA66219 (54' · DDD · T)   Ⓕ

Half of this programme is devoted to unaccompanied choral music by Copland: *In the Beginning*, a striking 15-minute 'Creation' for mixed four-part chorus and solo mezzo (which is eloquently executed by Catherine Denley) written in 1947, and three of four short motets he composed in 1921, while studying with Nadia Boulanger in Paris. The performance of the *Chichester Psalms* recorded here uses Bernstein's own reduced (but very effective) instrumentation of organ, harp and percussion, but follows the composer's New York precedent in employing a mixed chorus – although the illusion of a cathedral choir is persuasively conveyed. It's very impressive.

The singing of the Corydon Singers under Matthew Best is very fine, and the vivid recording, which gives the voices a pleasant bloom while avoiding the resonance of King's College Chapel, reproduces the instrumental accompaniment, notably the percussion, with electrifying impact. Best's soloist is Dominic Martelli, and very sweetly he sings too. The disc is completed by Barber's setting of the *Agnus Dei* from 1967 and is an arrangement of the famous *Adagio for Strings*.

This imaginative and enterprising programme is extremely well sung and vividly recorded.

Chichester Psalms[a]. On the Waterfront – Symphonic Suite. On the Town – Three Dance Episodes
[a]**Thomas Kelly** treb [a]**Elizabeth Franklin-Kitchen** sop [a]**Victoria Nayler** contr [a]**Jeremy Budd** ten [a]**Paul Charrier** bass **Bournemouth Symphony** [a]**Chorus and Orchestra / Marin Alsop**
Naxos 8 559177 (49' · DDD)   Ⓢ**OO**▶

Some years ago Andrew Litton presided over a memorable all-Bernstein concert for Virgin Classics that showed that the Bournemouth orchestra could swing with the best of them; now it's the turn of new principal conductor Marin Alsop to put them through their paces. Very sassily they strut, too, in the exuberant outer numbers of *On the Town*. It's a similar tale in the symphonic suite from *On the Waterfront*. Alsop displays a special sympathy for this score's intimate undertow, investing softer music with a tingling atmosphere and lyrical poetry that consistently ignite the imagination, and moulding the love theme with a warmth and vulnerability that all but match the composer's NYPO version. Not that there's any lack of red-blooded drama or brazen spectacle, even though Mike Clements's otherwise excitingly dynamic sound-frame exposes some slight thinness of violin tone. The account of the *Chichester Psalms* is polished, communicative and beautifully sprung, attaining eloquent heights in the soothing setting of Psalm 23 for boy treble and mixed choir, as well as the strings' impassioned plea that launches the last movement.

A conspicuous success. The playing-time is comparatively stingy, but, given the superior quality of the music-making and the low Naxos price-tag, not many should complain.

Mass

Mass
Jubilant Sykes bar **Peabody Children's Chorus;
Morgan State University Choir and Marching
Band; Baltimore Symphony Orchestra /
Marin Alsop**
Naxos American Classics ② 8 559622/3
(104' · DDD · T)   ⓢ❍❍❍❍➔

Bernstein's relationship with God is dangerous,
probing, transformational. There are those, of
course, who proffer that Bernstein thought he
was God, that's why he could stand in defiance
against Him. But *Mass* reveals a man thirsting for
faith but petrified of blind acceptance. Bernstein's
religion was muscular and intellectualised, and
the experience of *Mass* expands, rather than contracts, the further you travel towards the essence
of its cosmology.

Alsop's Jubilant Sykes is the best of all possible
Celebrants. There can be few roles in contemporary music theatre that demand so many sides
of a performer. He must disentangle music of
gnarly complexity; he needs an operatic sensibility but must also swing like a hipster jazzer and
declaim with authentic rockist swank. Sykes's
voice shakes with James Brown's ecstasy, snarls
with Janis Joplin-like indigence and projects
through the labyrinth of Bernstein's tricky
melodic contours like any trained voice would.
He was born to play this part.

Although she doesn't drive things quite as far
as Bernstein, Alsop is pacy, creating a dramatic
slipstream that is powered relentlessly onwards
by the awkward discontinuities and jagged narrative. Even if the atheist cannot quite love the
God-fearing D major affirmation of the final
scene, it doesn't matter. The journey, the process of discovery, counts for more.

Candide

Candide (1988 final version)
Jerry Hadley ten Candide **June Anderson** sop
Cunegonde **Adolph Green** ten Dr Pangloss, Martin
Christa Ludwig mez Old Lady **Nicolai Gedda** ten
Governor, Vanderdendur, Ragotski **Della Jones** mez
Paquette **Kurt Ollmann** bar Maximilian, Captain,
Jesuit Father **Neil Jenkins** ten Merchant, Inquisitor,
Prince Charles Edward **Richard Suart** bass Junkman,
Inquisitor, King Hermann Augustus **John Treleaven**
ten Alchemist, Inquisitor, Sultan Achmet, Crook
Lindsay Benson bar Doctor, Inquisitor, King
Stanislaus **Clive Bayley** bar Bear-Keeper, Inquisitor,
Tsar Ivan **London Symphony Chorus and Orchestra
/ Leonard Bernstein**
DG ② 474 472-GTA2 (112' · DDD · N/T)   ⑧❍❍❍➔

Ⓖ Here's musical comedy, grand opera,
operetta, satire, melodrama, all rolled
into one. We can thank John Mauceri
for much of the restoration work: his 1988 Scottish Opera production was the spur for this
recording and prompted exhaustive reappraisal.

Numbers like 'We Are Women', 'Martin's
Laughing Song' and 'Nothing More Than This'
have rarely been heard, if at all. The last mentioned, Candide's 'aria of disillusionment', is
one of the enduring glories of the score, reinstated where Bernstein always wanted it (but
where no producer would have it), near the very
end of the show. Bernstein called it his 'Puccini
aria', and that it is – bittersweet, long-breathed,
supported, enriched and ennobled by its inspiring string counterpoint. And this is but one of
many forgotten gems.

It was an inspiration on someone's part
(probably Bernstein's) to persuade the great
and versatile Christa Ludwig and Nicolai
Gedda (in his sixties and still hurling out top
Bs) to fill the principal character roles. To say
they do so ripely is to do them scant justice.
Bernstein's old sparring partner Adolph Green
braves the tongue-twisting and many-hatted
Dr Pangloss with his own highly individual
form of *Sprechstimme*, Jerry Hadley sings the
title role most beautifully, *con amore*, and June
Anderson has all the notes, and more, for the
faithless, air-headed Cunegonde. It's just a pity
that someone didn't tell her that discretion is
the better part of comedy. 'Glitter and Be Gay'
is much funnier for being played straighter,
odd as it may sound. Otherwise, the supporting roles are all well taken and the London
Symphony Chorus has a field-day in each of its
collective guises.

Having waited so long to commit every last
note (or thereabouts) of his cherished score to
disc, there are moments here where Bernstein
seems almost reluctant to move on. His tempos are measured, to say the least, the score
fleshier now in every respect: even that raciest
of Overtures has now acquired a more deliberate gait, a more opulent tone. But Bernstein
would be Bernstein, and there are moments
where you're more than grateful for his indulgence: the grandiose chorales, the panoramic
orchestra-scapes (sumptuously recorded), and
of course, that thrilling finale – the best of all
possible Bernstein anthems at the slowest of all
possible speeds – and why not (prepare to hold
your breath at the choral *a cappella*). You're
unlikely to be disappointed by this disc.

West Side Story

West Side Story
Dame Kiri Te Kanawa sop Maria (Nina Bernstein)
José Carreras ten Tony (Alexander Bernstein)
Tatiana Troyanos mez Anita **Kurt Ollmann** bar Riff
Marilyn Horne mez Offstage voice **chorus and
orchestra / Leonard Bernstein**
DG 457 199-2GH (77' · DDD · N/T)   ⑤❍❍➔

If the job of a 'crossover' record is to shatter
preconceptions on both sides of any musical
fence, then this is the greatest ever. Not all the
aficionados of Broadway musicals are going to
warm to de facto operatic treatment of *West Side
Story*: not all opera-lovers or devotees of Bern-

stein as star conductor are going to rate *West Side Story* as an equivalent to opera. But any listener who keeps any sort of open mind, forgetting the constriction of barriers, must recognise this historic disc as superb entertainment and great music-making on every level, with an emotional impact closely akin to that of a Puccini opera. That of course is the doing of Leonard Bernstein as conductor as well as composer. It's astonishing that before this recording he had never conducted his most famous work.

Te Kanawa may not be a soprano you'd cast as Maria on stage, yet the beauty of the voice, its combination of richness, delicacy and purity, brings out the musical strengths of Bernstein's inspiration. Similarly, with Carreras as Tony, it's self-evident to point out how such a voice brings out the pure beauty of the big melodies like 'Maria' or 'Tonight', but even a sharp number like his first solo, 'Something's coming', with floated *pianissimos* and subtly graded *crescendos* allied to sharp rhythms, makes it more clearly a question-mark song, full of expectation, more than just a point number. Marilyn Horne is in glorious voice, while Tatiana Troyanos will surprise you as Anita with the way she could switch her naturally beautiful operatic voice into a New York throaty snarl. Troyanos, it appears, was brought up in exactly the area of the West Side, where the story is supposed to be set, which makes her natural affinity with the idiom less surprising. Kurt Ollmann, American too, as Riff equally finds a very confident balance between the traditions of opera and those of the musical. Diction may not always be so clear as with less rich-toned singers, but Carreras manages a very passable American accent and Dame Kiri a creditable Spanish-American one. The speed with which the piece moves is astounding, not just as superb entertainment but as a Shakespearean tragedy modernised and intensified.

West Side Story – The Making of the Recording
Kiri Te Kanawa *sop* Tatiana Troyanos *mez* José Carreras *ten* Kurt Ollman *bar* orchestra and chorus / Leonard Bernstein
Film director **Christopher Swann**
DG 📀 073 017-9GH (89' · NTSC · 4:3 · 2.0 · 0)
Filmed during the recording sessions in 1984 Ⓕ⊙

This is the famous – or notorious – documentary about the 'operatic' recording of Bernstein's best-loved work (reviewed on page 187), a considerable popular and critical success that overrode the rather silly crossover controversy it aroused. Seeing it again in this excellent DVD transfer emphasises both the strengths and weaknesses of Bernstein's approach. Unquestionably the music is fine enough to stand the weight of the operatic treatment, and it's a pleasure to watch him rejuvenated by rediscovering his own score. However, the visual element shows that, despite his denials, even the youngest and freshest trained voices do add an extra layer of artificiality. Kurt Ollmann and the other Jets sound altogether too mannered, for all the

heavy accents, and the chattering teenyboppers more like housewives. Te Kanawa, with her popular background, is at least at home in the idiom, and her songs benefit from the richer colour and *legato*; but Troyanos, for all her authentically comic West-Sidese, sounds inescapably middle-aged and blowsy for a girlish role. And Carreras is ludicrously condemned to play the all-American boy. This miscasting causes him painful struggles with diction and tempo, especially in the fiendishly difficult 'Something's Coming!' number, and Bernstein's refusal to allow for this clearly provokes the ugly scenes in which the composer petulantly humiliates him – not his finest moment. But Carreras and the others obviously love the music so much that, while they can't obscure these handicaps, they largely transcend them. A fascinating record of a great composer/conductor.

Wonderful Town

Wonderful Town
Kim Criswell *sop* Ruth **Audra McDonald** *sop* Eileen **Thomas Hampson** *bar* Baker **Brent Barrett** *sngr* Wreck **Rodney Gilfry** *bar* Guide, First Editor, Frank **Carl Daymond** *bar* Second Editor, Chick Clark **Timothy Robinson** *ten* Lonigan **Michael Dore** *bass* First Man, Cadet, Third Cop, Villager **Lynton Atkinson** *ten* Second Man, Second Cop **Simone Sauphanor** *sngr* First Girl **Melanie Marshall** *mez* Second Girl **Kimberly Cobb** *sngr* Violet **Robert Fardell** *sngr* First Cop **London Voices; Birmingham Contemporary Music Group / Sir Simon Rattle**
EMI 518175-2 (67' · DDD · N/t) Ⓜ⊙⊙☞

The Birmingham Contemporary Music Group, with key brass and sax personnel bumped in from the West End, play the Overture with great attitude, trumpets with the throttle full out and a bevy of saxes licking everyone into shape. Check out the Original Cast album (on Sony) and you'll find it's faster, tighter – not much, but enough to sound like NYC in the fast lane; crude and sassy with plenty of grime in the mix. Accept the fact that Rattle's is a pristine *Wonderful Town*, temporarily divorced from its smart book (Joseph Fields and Jerome Chodorov), out of context, and, to some extent, out of its element, and you'll have a good time. No one in the Original Broadway Cast can come within spitting distance of the vocal talent assembled here. Kim Criswell's Ruth has to live with Rosalind Russell's keys – in the bass-baritone range. Where Russell had about three notes in her voice – all dubious – Criswell has them all but doesn't have too much occasion to use them. So she works the lyric of 'One Hundred Easy Ways' a little harder than Russell – a piranha to Russell's shark. Audra McDonald as Sister Eileen uses every part of her versatile voice, wrapping it round a lyric like the two are inseparable, and sings 'A Little Bit in Love' with such contentment that it's as if she's giving herself a big, well-deserved hug. It's a gorgeous voice and the microphone loves her. It loves Hampson, too, and though he will never quite erradicate the 'formality' from his delivery he's rarely sounded quite so unassuming as here imagining his 'Quiet Girl'.

Of the big set-pieces, 'Conversation Piece' sounds as if it could have been lifted from a performance of the show. When the village kids get in on the action that's quite a stretch for Simon Halsey's London Voices. Now and again you catch their English choral tradition, but not long enough for it to get in the way. 'Conga!' sounds sufficiently inebriated and they sound right at home on 'Christopher Street'. You get slightly more *Wonderful Town* for your money with Rattle (a couple of reprises for a start). Don Walker's feisty orchestrations get more of an airing with the addition of 'Conquering New York', a dance number which demonstrates how ready Lenny was to raid his bottom drawer by reusing *Prelude, Fugue and Riffs*.

Documentary

Leonard Bernstein: 'Reflections'
A film by **Peter Rosen**
Medici Arts 📀 307 8728
(70' · NTSC · 4:3 · 5.1 and DTS 5.1 · 0)
Includes bonus performance of Milhaud's Le boeuf sur le toit, recorded in Paris, 1976   Ⓕ**OO**

Peter Rosen's compelling 50-minute film portrait was made in 1977 and seen worldwide – except in the USA, where it was not released, for some reason, until September 2008, nearly two decades after Bernstein's death in 1990. Pivotal to the documentary is this iconic genius of American music rehearsing and conducting a 1977 retrospective of his music in Tel Aviv, amazingly the first such celebration ever mounted. As Rosen notes: 'At the time the film would have been more of a current story about the Leonard Bernstein Festival in Israel…now it's a historic record to be treasured as a look back in time, and a reminder of Bernstein's universal contribution.'

Interspersed with the all-too-brief extracts from *Serenade*, Symphonic Dances from *West Side Story*, *Kaddish* (Symphony No 3) and *Mass*, we see Bernstein reflecting on his life and music, shot in Carnegie Hall (scene of his legendary 1943 debut) and his studio overlooking New York's Central Park. What a charismatic talker he is – straight to camera, unprompted, measured, fluent, thought-provoking, self-deprecating and fascinating about the creative process. Chain-smoking heroically (in fact the only time he hasn't got a ciggy in his hand is when there's a baton in it), Bernstein tells us the story behind the last-minute deputation for Bruno Walter in the broadcast concert that was to make him an overnight star, and his sceptical father's moving reaction.

Epithets such as 'conservative' and 'retrogressive' were routinely flung at him by the more progressive critics who could neither understand why he wrote Broadway musicals nor why he eschewed serial techniques (which, of course, he did not, parts of *Kaddish* illustrating the

point). Bernstein, as he tells us resignedly, was merely reflecting the polycultural society in which he thrived. He concludes with a passionate defence of tonality – the root deep in the earth of all musical creation – to which composers are now returning after their trip up the cul-de-sac of dodecaphony. As a communicator both through his music and his verbal eloquence, Bernstein had few peers in the latter part of the last century, and his body of work will surely outlast those of others who do not share his life-affirming credo.

Franz Adolf Berwald
Swedish 1796-1868

Composer and violinist Franz Berwald is one of the most important musicans Sweden has produced. A true polymath, Berwald followed a number of non-musical professions during his life: he ran an orthopaedic institute, a glassworks and a sawmill. He played in the Stockholm court orchestra (following in his father's footsteps) between 1812 and 1828, during which time he was also composing his remarkably original music. As well as body of finely crafted chamber works, he left four full-length symphonies, the most remarkable of which is the Symphonie singulière of 1845, a work of great individuality. Although he did teach (he was professor of composition at the Swedish Royal Academy), his music had to wait until the 20th century before its startling inventiveness and energy were recognised.

Symphonies

Symphonies – No 1 in G minor, 'Sinfonie sérieuse'; No 2 in D, 'Sinfonie capricieuse'; No 3 in C, 'Sinfonie singulière'; No 4 in E flat. Konzertstück for Bassoon and Orchestra
Christian Davidsson *bn* **Malmö Symphony Orchestra / Sixten Ehrling**
BIS ② BIS-CD795/6 (131' · DDD)   Ⓕ**O🅑**

As might be expected, given Sixten Ehrling's excellent account of the *Singulière* and the E flat Symphonies with the LSO for Decca way back in the late 1960s and his no less impressive 1970 Swedish Radio version of the *Sérieuse*, the performances are *echt*-Berwald. Ehrling gives us plenty of space without ever lingering too lovingly. Even apart from the *tempo giusto*, you feel rather more comfortable with Ehrling's handling of phrasing and balance. He's very attentive to dynamic markings and sometimes, as at the beginning of the *Sinfonie singulière*, pianissimo becomes *pianopiano-pianissimo*!

The recording reproduces these dynamic extremes flawlessly. The Malmö Concert Hall, where this set was made, has a good acoustic. The recordings are generally excellent, though there seems to be more back-to-front perspective and air around the players in the *Singulière* and E flat Symphonies than in the *Sérieuse*. In short, Ehrling and his fine players bring us closer to the spirit of this music than do any of the current rivals.

Additional recommendations

Symphonies Nos 1-4. Symphony in A. Overture – Estrella de Soria; The Queen of Golconda
Swedish RSO / Goodman
Hyperion Dyad ② CDD22043   Ⓑ➔
Neat performances of Berwald's main symphonic output played with style and affection by a Swedish orchestra and a highly musical conductor.

Piano Trios Nos 2 & 4. Grand Septet. Duo. Piano Quintet. Quintet for Piano and Winds.
Gaudier Ensemble
Hyperion Dyad ② CDD22053   ⒷⓄ➔
A delightfully performed introduction to Berwald the chamber-music composer – and the rewards are quite as enchanting as with his orchestral music. The Gaudier Ensemble judges things to perfection. Beautifully recorded, too.

Heinrich Biber   Bohemian 1644-1704

Born in Bohemia, Biber worked in Kroměříž and Graz before settling in Salzburg in 1670, where he remained for the rest of his life. He became Kapellmeister to Maximillian Gandolph von Kuenberg, the Archbishop of Salzburg, and soon consolidated his position by publishing his own music and achieving acclaim both as a violinist of great virtuosity and as a composer. He was raised to the nobility by the Emperor in 1790, becoming Biber von Bibern. Maximillian's successor Johann Ernst, Count Thun, appointed him lord high steward.

His violin music exercised considerable influence on the composers to Austria's south, such as Ucellini and Farina in Italy, and on the German school led by Schmelzer: his formidable armoury of virtuoso techniques were way beyond anything employed by his contemporaries (he played in the sixth and seventh positions and used myriad double-stops). Notable among these violin works are his Mystery or Rosary Sonatas, 15 sonatas for violin and continuo which illustrate the 15 Mysteries of the Rosary; the work concludes with a long passacaglia for solo violin.

For his archbishop, Biber wrote a number of large-scale Masses and choral works, the most ambitous being the 53-part Missa Salisburgensis (1628); most of these works exploit the spacious interior of Salzburg Cathedral and the opportunity for elaborate layout of his forces.

Balletti

Arias a 4 in A. Ballettae a 4 violettae. Balletti a 6 in C. Balletti lamentabili a 4 in E minor. Harmonia Romana. Trombet undt musicalischer Taffeldienst
Ars Antiqua Austria / Gunar Letzbor *vn*
Symphonia SY95143 (75' · DDD)   Ⓕ

The Baroque palace of Kremsier was the summer residence of Prince-Bishop Karl Liechtenstein-Kastelkorn of Olmütz, an ardent music lover. During his rule, 1664-95, the palace library acquired what's a precious collection of manuscripts. This programme features some of the ensemble music by Biber from that source, though the authenticity of the *Harmonia Romana* anthology, some of whose dances are on the disc, hasn't been established. In any case, the sequence put together by violinist and director Gunar Letzbor is entertaining and very well executed. Most is for strings, but there are contributions from variously sized recorders, too, as well as some splendidly gruff, earthy and inebriate interjections from bass, Michael Oman, as the Nightwatchman.

Letzbor has built his programme around an idea of a Carnival feast at the bishop's court: the bishop enters to a fanfare; dance music greets the guests; a nightwatchman passes by; table music during dinner; dancing; the nightwatchman passes by again, this time drunk; peasant dancing; midnight, the end of Carnival and the beginning of Lent. The revelry is concluded by the 12 strokes of midnight sounded on what sounds like a school bell. The notion comes off well, for the scheme allows for a degree of musical contrast, both of sound and mood. Biber's dances are enchanting for the fullness of their character and for their rhythmic bite, and Ars Antiqua bring them to life with vigour, imagination and style. The group offers us well over an hour of first-class entertainment in which only the Bishop's festive board and the contents of his cellar aren't shared with us. The disc is superbly recorded.

Mensa sonora

Mensa sonora seu musica instrumentalis. Sonata in A for Violin and Continuo
Purcell Quartet (Catherine Mackintosh, Catherine Weiss *vns* Richard Boothby *vion* Robert Woolley *hpd*) with Jane Rogers *va*
Chandos Chaconne CHAN0748 (59' · DDD)   Ⓕ➔

Mensa sonora, published in Salzburg in 1680, is scored for four-part strings and basso continuo. It consists of six suites of mainly very short dance movements and could be seen as the least substantial of Biber's instrumental collections. But the consistently high level of craftsmanship and imagination transforms what might have been purely functional music. We're continually delighted by Biber's contrapuntal dexterity, by the beautiful sonorities and by the way he introduces a deeper level of expression into the longer movements. There are moments, too, of startling originality – the pointillist treatment of the arpeggio motif at the start of Suite No 3, and the astonishing ending to the last suite, where the musical discourse is broken into smaller and smaller fragments.

The Purcell Quartet bring out these and many more facets of the music with playing that's always lively and sweetly tuned. The many decisions on tempo and character are well taken – even the more surprising ones, such as the very moderate, smooth first Gigue in Suite No 5, sound entirely convincing in context.

The Violin Sonata comes at the disc's mid-point; its broader canvas, with improvisatory passagework over static bass notes, a toccata-like episode in dotted rhythms and a substantial set of variations, makes an excellent contrast with *Mensa sonora*'s miniature movements. Catherine Mackintosh has this demanding music at her fingertips. Her manner avoids the extravagance of some Baroque violinists but she can be relied on to project the expressive, rhetorical character that's always present in Biber's figuration. Strongly recommended.

Mystery Sonatas

Mystery Sonatas ℗
John Holloway vn **Davitt Moroney** org/hpd
Tragicomedia (Stephen Stubbs lte/chitarrone Erin Headley va da gamba/ lirone Andrew Lawrence-King hp/regal)
Virgin Classics Veritas ② 562062-2 (131' · DDD)
Ⓜ❶❶❶❶↦

Biber's 15 *Mystery Sonatas* with their additional *Passacaglia* for unaccompanied violin were written in about 1678 and dedicated to his employer, the Archbishop of Salzburg. Each Sonata is inspired by a section of the Rosary devotion of the Catholic Church which offered a system of meditation on 15 Mysteries from the lives of Jesus and the Virgin Mary. The music isn't, strictly speaking, programmatic, though often vividly illustrative of events which took place in the life of Christ.

All but two of the 16 pieces require *scordatura* or retuning of the violin strings; in this way Biber not only facilitated some of the fingerings but also achieved sounds otherwise unavailable to him. The Sonatas are disposed into three groups of five: Joyful, Sorrowful and Glorious Mysteries whose contrasting states are affectingly evoked in music ranging from a spirit reflecting South German Baroque exuberance to one of profound contemplation. John Holloway plays with imaginative sensibility. He's supported by a first-rate continuo group whose instruments include Baroque lute, chitarrone, viola da gamba, a 15-string lirone, double harp and regal.

Additional recommendations

Les Veilleurs de Nuit / Piérot vn
Alpha ② ALPHA038 (120' · DDD)   Ⓕ
A wonderful combination of virtuosity and poise characterise this set, and Alice Piérot and her colleagues respond with great imagination.

Beznosiuk vn **Tunnicliffe** va da gamba
Roblou hpd with **T West** spkr
Avie ② AV0038 (157' · DDD)   Ⓕ❶↦

Timothy West reads from the Jesuit Rosary psalter before each sonata. Again, great imagination is employed to bring these powerful works to life for a new generation.

Manze vn **Egarr** org/hpd with **McGillivray** vc
Harmonia Mundi ② HMU90 7321/2 (141' · DDD)
Ⓕ❶❶

Andrew Manze offers a rapt and intimate version of these pieces and his virtuosity and flair in this repertoire are never in question.

Violin Sonatas

Eight Sonatas for Violin and Continuo ℗
(1681). Sonata violino solo representativa in A.
Sonata, 'La Pastorella'. Passacaglia for Solo Lute.
Mystery Sonatas – Passacaglia in G-minor
Romanesca (Andrew Manze vn Nigel North lte/ theorbo John Toll hpd/org)
Harmonia Mundi ② HMX290 7344/45 (127' · DDD)
Ⓜ❶❶❶❶↦

While the more famous *Mystery Sonatas* have quickly found friends, the 1681 set is still largely unknown. Yet what's immediately noticeable from this premiere recording of the sonatas is that Biber isn't only a legendary virtuoso, probably never bettered in the 17th or 18th centuries, but one of the most inventive composers of his age: bold and exciting, certainly, but also elusive, mercurial and mysterious. Most of the works are preludes, arias and variations of an unregulated nature: improvisatory preludes over naked pedals and lucid arias juxtaposing with eccentric rhetorical conceits are mixed up in an unpredictable phantasm of contrast, and yet at its best it all adds up to a unified structure of considerable potency. Andrew Manze is the player *par excellence* for music that requires a considered response to complement the adventurous spirit of the virtuoso. This is masterful playing in which he doesn't overcharacterise Biber's volatile temperament. The preludes are sweet and restrained, yet there's also a held-back, almost smouldering quality, skilfully pitched against the free-wheeling energy of the fast music.

Eight Sonatas for Violin and Continuo – Nos 3, 4, 6 & 7.
Sonata No 81 in A. Sonata No 84 in E
John Holloway vn **Aloysia Assenbaum** org
Lars Ulrik Mortensen hpd
ECM New Series 472 084-2 (77' · DDD)   Ⓕ❶❶❶↦

 John Holloway has contributed as much as anyone to modern-day recognition of Biber's status as one of the greatest of all violinist-composers. In his notes he draws attention to the difference in character between the sonatas in normal tuning and those that asl for *scordatura* or altered tunings, citing the latter (Nos 4 and 6 from the published set) as 'more intimate, more personal'. But actually this is the side which comes across most strongly in these performances anyway, at the expense of the extrovert maybe, but with no shortage of effective musical moments nevertheless; the point halfway through the Sixth Sonata when the violin re-emerges retuned and with a veiled new sound is managed with ghostly beauty.

With the violin resonating pleasingly through the many double- and triple-stoppings, and Holloway's bowing demonstrating a delicious lightness and freedom, these fundamentally inward, tonally aware performances also seem to have more of the smell of the 17th century about them than their current rivals (including Manze's, reviewed above),which push the violin's sound out a bit more. A respectfully resonant recording is a help here, as is the gentle but effectively unfussy continuo support of harpsichord and organ.

Anyone who already has the Manze need have no qualms about adding this one to their collection.

'Der Türken Anmarsch'
Biber Eight Sonatas for Violin and Continuo – Nos 1, 2, 5 & 8 **Muffat** Violin Sonata in D **Biber/A Schmelzer** Violin Sonata in A minor, 'Victory of the Christians over the Turks'
John Holloway vn **Aloysia Assenbaum** org
Lars Ulrik Mortensen hpd
ECM New Series 472 432-2 (63' · DDD)   ⒻⒹ→

John Holloway plays four sonatas from the set of eight Biber published in 1681 and also dedicated to the archbishop. First, however, comes a curiosity: an adaptation by Andreas Anton Schmelzer (son of the better-known Johann Heinrich) of Biber's 'Crucifixion' sonata, transposed up a tone and retitled as a representation of the siege of Vienna in 1683. It's difficult, though, to detect any difference other than some small changes to the Praeludium and an extra movement at the end.

The 1681 sonatas show Biber's propensity for rhapsodic flights over a pedal point and for variations on a ground bass. In the imitative writing of No 8, the double-stopping is so skilfully done that it's hard to believe that Holloway hasn't cloned himself. In this sonata especially, there's some nicely pointed continuo playing. The Muffat is a *sonata da chiesa*, with a return to the first movement at the end. Here and throughout the disc Holloway plays with a most appealing warmth and a faultless technique.

Masses

Missa Bruxellensis   Ⓟ
La Capella Reial de Catalunya;
Le Concert des Nations / Jordi Savall
Alia Vox AV9808 (52' · DDD · T)   ⒻOO

Modern technology and expert engineering allow us to bask in Biber's magnificent-sounding and spaciously conceived masses, complete with all the glistening attention to detail, the visceral *tutti* impact and the delicate textural contrasts which constitute some of Baroque music's most opulent expressions of earthly potency. Salzburg Cathedral provided exceptional acoustical possibilities. Biber, in his mass, could satisfy the potentate by adorning the unique status of Salzburg as the court with everything. The problem, however, with the *Missa Bruxellensis* – so called since it was discovered in Brussels – is that it appears to serve its purpose more as a professional job than as a vehicle for extended inspiration. Even so, a world premiere recording of a monumental work by a major composer isn't to be sniffed at, especially when directed by Jordi Savall. He lets Biber's score roll out unassumingly; even if at the expense of fine tuning and exacting ensemble, the final sections of the *Credo* are immensely stylish, and the 'Miserere' from the *Gloria* has the dignity of a spontaneous event rather than a contrived vignette.

The recorded sound has a mixed success, taken from sessions held in the original location; there's a natural sense of the cathedral acoustic, though not, happily, at the expense of immediacy in the solo sections. Less satisfactory are the strident upper frequencies, in particular the solo sopranos. Gripes aside, this will delight collectors who relish fortress-like recordings.

Biber Missa Christi resurgentisa. Sonatae tam aris quam aulis servientes – Fanfare No 1; Fanfare No 4. 12 Sonatas, 'Fidicinium sacro-profanum' – I; III; V; VII; XI. Sonata a 6 **JH Schmelzer** 13 Sonatas, 'Sacro-profanus concentus musicus' – XII
ªChoir of The English Consort;
The English Concert / Andrew Manze
Harmonia Mundi HMU90 7397 (78' · DDD · T/t)   Ⓕ

Missa Christi resurgentis. Mystery Sonatas – The Resurrectiona
New York Collegium / Andrew Parrott with
ªIngrid Matthews vn ªEric Milnes org
Kleos Classics KL5135 (74' · DDD/DSD · T/t)   Ⓕ

The *Missa Christi resurgentis* seems to have lain in obscurity for centuries, known about but otherwise ignored, until brought to life by James Clements and published by A-R Editions in the US. The New York Collegium gave the first modern performance in 2003 and The English Concert followed a year later with the European premiere. The recordings differ in the way the music is presented: both are very welcome.

After perhaps descending to the crypt to sneer at the tomb of Prince-Archbishop Hieronymus Colloredo, Mozart's employer, the visitor to the Baroque cathedral of Salzburg cannot fail to be impressed by the interior with its four galleries. Biber, who had joined the service of the Archbishop Maximilian Gandolph in 1670, made full use of the cathedral's spatial opportunities: two four-part choirs are complemented by string and brass groups used, like Venetian *cori spezzati*, both antiphonally and in combination.

The Mass was probably written for Easter 1674. It begins with a sonata, the strings answering the brass. Andrew Manze takes it straight; while Andrew Parrott, by slurring the second and third notes, adds an appealing rakishness to the phrase. 'Christe eleison' sees the first of several appearances by three basses, a difficult ensemble to balance. The Americans, with a light first bass, make it sound quite airy. The English Concert, at a slower speed and a lower pitch, tend to growl away in their boots. The 'Et exspecto' section of the *Credo* finds Manze's sopranos singing high with a real sense of awe. In general, the singing of the Choir of The English Concert is the more accomplished: some of the solo work in Parrott's choir sounds tentative and the boy alto causes moments of unease for the listener. The orchestral playing is first-rate on both recordings.

Which to choose must depend on the supplementary pieces. Manze includes five sonatas for strings. The tonal palette is limited, as is usual for the time, to the home key with occasional excursions to the relative major or minor. The first movement of the Sonata a 6 for trumpet and strings reappears on the American disc. Here, however, the context is that of an actual service. It starts with an alternatim setting of the introit *Resurrexi* by Johann Stadlmayr and includes, as well as the chanting of the epistle and gospel, organ pieces by Kerll and Poglietti. There are also two string sonatas from the *Sonatae tam aris* collection, one of which includes a fugue theme that anticipates the *Allegro* of Handel's *Concerto grosso*, Op 3 No 2.

Gilles Binchois
French c1400-1460

Along with Dufay and Dunstable, Binchois was among the most important composers of the early 15th century. His early life was spent in Mons and Lille, and he is also supposed to have entered the service of William Pole, Earl of Suffolk. In the 1420s he joined the Burgundian court chapel where he was appointed a secretary to the court in about 1437. He held posts in Bruges, Mons, Cassel and Soignies, where he finally retired, enjoying a pension from the Burgundian court.

His music was hugely influential on his contemporaries and on the those composers who followed. His gift for melody was well-known and his music has a transparency that makes it very impressive, and even at his most intricate he is wonderfully clear. As well as writing for the church, Binchois left a substantial body of secular music, including love songs and songs of chivalry.

Sacred works

Binchois Nove cantum melodie. Domitor Hectoris. Kyrie. Sanctus. Agnus Dei **Dufay** Mass for St Anthony Abbot
Binchois Consort (Mark Chambers, William Towers *countertens* Edwin Simpson, Nick Todd, Matthew

Vine, Christopher Watson *tens*) / **Andrew Kirkman**
Hyperion CDA67474 (71' · DDD)   Ⓕ℗➤

The Binchois Consort finally turn their attentions to the composer whose name they bear. The contrast between Dufay and Binchois is every bit as striking in sacred music as in the secular. Binchois's Mass movements trip along very un-solemnly, a worthy foil to the stately Dufay; but the high-point is his single surviving isorhythmic motet, here seamlessly reconstructed by Philip Weller.

It is fascinating to hear a familiar voice like Binchois's speaking in a language one's not used to from him. If the tempo chosen for the piece stretches the singers more than usually (albeit exhilaratingly), in the rest of the Dufay programme they are masterful. The verse of the Offertory has one of those spine-tingling moments (a high countertenor f' conjured out of nowhere) that hits the bull's eye every time you hear it.

Judith Bingham
British b1952

Early study with Alan Bush, Eric Fenby and John Hall led to two years of tutorials with Hans Keller whom Bingham counts as a major influence. In 1977 she won the BBC Young Composer of the Year Award which led to BBC commissions and a series of works for brass band. Recent composition prizes include the Barlow Prize for a cappella music in 2004, two British Composer Awards in 2004 (choral and liturgical), one in 2006 (choral), and the instrumental award in 2008. Bingham was a member of the BBC Singers for many years, and between 2004 and 2009 she was their Composer in Association, during which time she wrote a number of choral works.

Choral works

'Remoter Worlds'
Gleams of a Remoter World. The Shepheardes Calender. Water Lilies. Irish Tenebrae[a]. Unpredictable but Providential. Beneath these Alien Stars[b]. Ghost Towns of the American West
BBC Singers / David Hill with [a]**Olivia Robinson** *sop* [a]**Krysia Osostowicz** *vn* [ab]**Iain Farrington** *org* [a]**Richard Benjafield**, [a]**Chris Brannick** *perc*
Signum Classics SIGCD144 (71' · DDD)   Ⓕ

Judith Bingham's discography is slowly catching up with her increasingly impressive body of work. Unsurprisingly, the releases to date have concentrated on her choral music and it is heartening to see the BBC Singers – with whom she sang as a permanent member for 12 years and has been Associate Composer for the past four – perform a whole disc's worth of repertoire mostly unavailable otherwise.

The Shepheardes Calender, a triptych written in 2006 for the St Louis Chamber Choir receives a polished and refined account, with great bite and drive. There is an expressive resonance to the central setting of Psalm 23 (in a variant textual version) and the opening 'Winter' is icy as befits the words. *Unpredictable but Providential* (1992, rev 2007) is a delightful skit on Elizabethan word-setting and *Beneath these Alien Stars* (2001), like the larger *Ghost Towns of the American West* (2005), sets poems by the Mormon poet Vesta Pearce Crawford.

The major item is *Irish Tenebrae* (1990, rev 1992 and 2007), a remarkable cantata in seven sections for solo and choral voices, violin, organ and percussion. Inspired by the composer's part-Irish origins, the Troubles and a love of Irish folksong, the work is a tremendous achievement, Britten-like in its range and variety – and expressive acuity – yet distinctly Binghamian in its sound (though quite unlike its couplings). The performances by all concerned are superb, from the opening *Gleams of a Remoter World* (1997) and *Water Lilies* (1999) to the larger pieces. Strongly recommended.

The Secret Garden[a]. Salt in the Blood. First Light. The Darkness is no Darkness. The Snow Descends[b]
Thomas Trotter org **BBC Symphony Chorus;**
[b]**Fine Arts Brass / Stephen Jackson**
Naxos 8 570346 (68' · DDD)   Ⓢ▷
[a]Recorded live

All five works on this disc reveal a distinctive voice writing in a recognisably modern idiom which combines clarity of thought and complexity of vision. Bingham's music draws audiences in, without alienating them or compromising her expressive integrity. *Salt in the Blood* (1995) is a prime example, a large musical – at times theatrical – tapestry of British sea-song, weaving in existing shanties and invented hornpipes to retell the tale of two sailors' rivalry as to who was the better dancer. Bingham thinks convincingly in long spans, as her 2004 Prom commission *The Secret Garden* confirms (given here in a live performance). *First Light* (2001) and the brief *The Darkness is no Darkness* (1993) engage with the English choral tradition to an unusual degree, the latter – a reinterpretation of a Wesley hymn – in particular.

The performances all round are first rate and the recorded sound is excellent, which is no less than Bingham deserves. The BBC Symphony Chorus sing with gusto and Fine Arts Brass relish some fine brass writing, not least in *The Snow Descends* (1997), an atmospheric paraphrase for brass of one of Bingham's choral works. Recommended.

Sir Harrison Birtwistle   British b1934

Birtwistle studied clarinet and composition at the Royal Manchester College of Music (1952-55), where he was part of a highly talented group of students alongside Peter Maxwell Davies, Alexander

Goehr, John Ogdon and Elgar Howarth. He sold his clarinets to devote himself full-time to composition and having won a scholarship to Princeton he wrote his first opera, Punch and Judy, a work which sealed his reputation. He devoted himself to music theatre in the 1970s and early '80s, a period which culminated in The Mask of Orpheus in 1986. And this highly fruitful time also saw the creation of some of his most important scores: Secret Theatre, Silbury Air and Carmen Arcadiae Mechanicae Perputuum. His most recent opera, Minotaur, was premiered at the Royal Opera House, Covent Garden, in 2008 to great acclaim. His music is frequently performed by some of the world's leading conductors: Boulez, Barenboim, Dohnányi, Rattle, Pappano and Welser-Möst among them. He was awarded a KBE in 1988 and a CH in 2001.

Orchestral works

Secret Theatre. Silbury Air. Carmen Arcadiae Mechanicae Perpetuum
London Sinfonietta / Elgar Howarth
NMC Ancora NMCD148 (58' · DDD)   Ⓜ

When these recordings first appeared Birtwistle enthusiasts were still absorbing the impact of three 1986 premieres, *Earth Dances*, *The Mask of Orpheus* and *Yan Tan Tethera* – works which helped to catapult a highly regarded composer into something as close to superstardom as contemporary classical music can provide. *Secret Theatre*, the longest of the three works, was itself a mere three years old in 1987: more than two decades on, its elaboration and refinement of basic formal and textural elements present in *Silbury Air* and *Carmen Arcadiae Mechanicae Perpetuum* (both from 1977) is ever more striking. Written between *The Mask of Orpheus* and the no less epic enterprise of *Earth Dances*, *Secret Theatre* really does mark a great leap forward, and this performance captures the special, pioneering dedication and enthusiasm which Elgar Howarth and the London Sinfonietta were able to summon up in those days. The recording, even with sensitive remastering, can't give a full picture of the spatial processes at work, involving the tension and interaction between separated individuals and groups, but it is still a highly charged, eloquent account of one of the composer's most powerful and most personal scores.

The more starkly differentiated mechanisms of the other pieces now seem like relatively unelaborated blueprints for the riches to follow, and despite the very different connotations of their titles – the Wiltshire landscape in *Silbury Air*, a Paul Klee canvas in *Carmen Arcadiae* – there are evident similarities, as well as moments which now sound unexpectedly derivative (for example, of Ligeti at the opening of *Silbury Air*). But that simply reinforces Birtwistle's importance as part of the European modernist mainstream, something to which his substantial and distinctive contribution remains a thing to wonder at.

Additional recommendation

Theseus Game[a]. Earth Dances[b]
[a]**Ensemble Modern / Brabbins, Valade;** [b]**Boulez**
DG download *477 070-2GH* (67' · DDD)
Recorded live   (F)🔘➤

Theseus Game (2002-03) offers clear visual contrasts: an ensemble of 30 players has two conductors, and there's a central space at the front of the platform for the succession of soloists who emerge from the ensemble. *Earth Dances* (1985-86) demands total surrender; as the music unwinds to its end, spasms of the seismic dance stand in the way of any comforting sense of fulfilment or resolution.

Five Distances

Five Distances[a]. The Silk House Tattoo[b]. 17 Tate Riffs[c]
[b]**John Wallace,** [b]**Adam Wright** *tpts* [b]**Sam Walton**
perc [a]**Gallimaufry Ensemble** (Louisa Dennehy *fl* Holly Fawcett *ob* Peter Sparks *cl* Siona Crosdale *bn* Nicholas Wolmark *hn*) [c]**Royal Academy of Music Chamber Ensemble**
Royal Academy of Music RAM019 (29' · DDD)   (M)

To coincide with the composer's 70th birthday, the Royal Academy of Music released a sequence of Birtwistle recordings made by staff and students in 2001. *Five Distances* for wind quintet (1992) has been recorded before, and this version risks substituting a generalised resonance for a strong sense of actual separation between the players. Yet it's very well played and persuasively shaped. Distance and resonance are even more basic to *The Silk House Tattoo* (1993) with its circling, echoing trumpets kept in line by a peremptory drummer, and to *17 Tate Riffs* (2000), Birtwistle's characteristically ritualised response to a commission for the opening ceremony of Tate Modern, with 15 players spread around the cavernous Turbine Hall. No recording can match the far-flung aural vistas of the original location but this one is well worth having as a reminder of how – even on the smallest timescale – Birtwistle can hint at the wider formal perspectives and grander mythic themes which form his usual terrain.

Piano Works

The Axe Manual[a]. Harrison's Clocks. Hector's Dawn. Berceuse de Jeanne. Précis. Sad Song. Oockooing Bird. Ostinato with Melody. Betty Freeman: Her Tango. Saraband: The King's Farewell
Nicolas Hodges *pf* [a]**Claire Edwardes** *perc*
Metronome METCD1074 (71' · DDD)   (F)

Though most of the items in this indispensable collection of Birtwistle's keyboard music last five minutes or less, two are on a scale commensurate with the orchestral *Triumph of Time* or *Secret Theatre*.

In *Harrison's Clocks* (1997-98) simultaneously unfolding strata demonstrate that 'interde-

pendent independence' of which Birtwistle often speaks. On one level, the music is potently mechanical, welded together from clearly defined rhythmic patterns which recur and collide like meshing cogs. Yet lying behind these mechanics is that background of complex associations with myth and ritual that's never far away in any Birtwistle composition, even the shortest and simplest.

The first recording of *The Axe Manual* (2000) reveals it as an exuberant and, in its central stages, delicate essay in 'extending' piano sound by means of metal and wood percussion. It turns fascination with tone-colour and texture into an absorbing musical drama, a battle with and against time that has an intensely human urgency and passion. It's a tribute to the quality of the WDR Cologne recording, excellent throughout, that the balance between the two performers seems so effortlessly right.

Nicolas Hodges is an accomplished guide to these varied perspectives, never over-nuancing the understated poetry of the miniatures, but meeting with total authority all the technical and interpretative challenges of the larger works.

Harrison's Clocks
Joanna MacGregor *pf*
SoundCircus SC004 (26' · DDD)   (M)

Even if Harrison Birtwistle was not knowingly named after John Harrison, the 18th-century clockmaker discussed in Dava Sobel's recent best-seller *Longitude*, his recurrent concern with musical mechanisms, whose 'ticking' regularity is the perfect foil for other, much less predictable elements, makes him the ideal composer to celebrate the pioneer of navigational chronometers. The recurring patterns which dominate the first of these five pieces (composed in 1998) are deceptive in that they create a relatively mild-mannered, even static effect, with contrast confined to brief episodes marking the movement's main formal divisions. But if this leads you to expect a sequence of neo-classical toccatas, the explosive fragmentation of the second piece will soon disabuse you, and in the hair-raisingly intense third movement the implacable power of the composer's invention takes the breath away.

Joanna MacGregor meets the demands with interest, bringing the music vividly to life, and the recording is excellent. Indispensable.

Vocal works

The Field of Sorrow[ac]. Verses for Ensembles[c]. Nenia: The Death of Orpheus[ab]
[a]**Jane Manning** *sop* [b]**The Matrix / Alan Hacker;** [c]**London Sinfonietta / David Atherton**
Lyrita SRCD306 (56' · ADD). Recorded 1975   (F)

This trio of compositions charts Harrison Birtwistle's transition from the brutal mechanics and plaintive lyricism of his first opera *Punch and Judy* (1967) to the more subtle expressive qualities and more expansive forms of his second, *The Mask of Orpheus*, begun in 1973. The recordings, especially of *Verses* (1969), show their age, but the performances remain uniquely arresting, unsurpassed in their eager response to the challenges and rewards these scores offered to David Atherton, Alan Hacker and their colleagues.

Listening to *Verses* today, its well-nigh half hour of improvisatory drumming interspersed with woodwind and brass riffs recalling Varèse and Tippett, you can see why Birtwistle felt the need to open himself up to the kind of mythic subject matter that the *Orpheus* pieces explore. *Verses* has its quieter moments but they tend to sound drained of expression, and the strategy of moving the players around the platform makes little impact in a parched analogue recording. The great leap forward in *Nenia: The Death of Orpheus* (1972) is obvious and profound. Birtwistle might not have been immediately confident enough in his vocal writing to dispense with a battery of effects close to the kind of thing Berio had devised for Cathy Berberian, but Jane Manning's brilliant account, especially in the soft yet intense speech of the final section, helps to underline that new-found mastery of slow but certain pacing – drifting with a purpose – that would be a Birtwistle feature from then on.

The Field of Sorrow (1972) further concentrates form and expression with consistent, complementary textural layering and richly focused lyricism. That Birtwistle has remained faithful to such principles ever since is evidence not of a lack of fresh ideas but of his awareness that he had found a winning, infinitely adaptable formula. This disc is valuable above all in reminding today's listeners of where and when that formula was first deployed.

Operas

Punch and Judy
Stephen Roberts *bar* Punch **Jan DeGaetani** *mez* Judy, Fortune-teller **Phyllis Bryn-Julson** *sop* Pretty Polly, Witch **David Wilson-Johnson** *bar* Choregos, Jack Ketch **Philip Langridge** *ten* Lawyer **John Tomlinson** *bass* Doctor
London Sinfonietta / David Atherton
NMC Ancora ② NMCD138 (103' · ADD) **Ⓜ❍❍❍↦**

It's almost 40 years since the 1968 premiere of *Punch and Judy*, celebrated in legend as a rude gesture in the face of Aldeburgh primness, and with hindsight as one of the finest achievements by Britten's most gifted British successor in the field of opera composition.

Good though it would be to have a new performance, the chances of something recent outclassing this 1979 version are remote. David Atherton has total empathy with the tricky blend of short numbers and culminative intensity, and draws brilliantly polished and characterful playing from the London Sinfonietta. The

dream cast is headed by Stephen Roberts's stunning portrayal of Mr Punch as a demented Oxbridge choral scholar, and by David Wilson-Johnson's suave, sinister Master of Ceremonies, while Philip Langridge and John Tomlinson make telling contributions. This, it need hardly be said, is not 'slice of life' opera, but the characters are animated and individualised, as they should be, through music which fits Stephen Pruslin's hilariously concise word-games like a glove. And if all this weren't enough, the fabulous Phyllis Bryn-Julson comes into her own in the final stages, a succession of vivid, poignant musical moments which Birtwistle has never bettered. And given NMC's no-deletion policy, this classic set is here to stay. No collection should be without it.

The Mask of Orpheus
Jon Garrison *ten* Orpheus: Man **Peter Bronder** *ten* Orpheus: Myth, Hades **Jean Rigby** *mez* Euridice: Woman **Anne-Marie Owens** *mez* Euridice: Myth, Persephone **Alan Opie** *bar* Aristaeus: Man **Omar Ebrahim** *bar* Aristaeus: Myth, Charon **Marie Angel** *sop* Aristeus: Oracle of the Dead, Hecate **Arwel Huw Morgan** *bar* Caller **Stephen Allen** *ten* Priest, First Judge **Nicholas Folwell** *bar* Priest, Second Judge **Stephen Richardson** *bass* Priest, Third Judge **Juliet Booth** *sop* Woman, First Fury **Philippa Dames-Longworth** *sop* Woman, Second Fury **Elizabeth McCormack** *mez* Woman, Third Fury **Ian Dearden** *sound diffusion* **BBC Singers; BBC Symphony Orchestra / Sir Andrew Davis, Martyn Brabbins**
NMC NMCD050 ③ (162' · DDD · N/T) **Ⓜ❍❍❍↦**

Birtwistle's opera is about the Orpheus myth, but the familiar story has been fragmented. Each of the principal characters is represented by two singers and a (silent) dancer, and much of what happens isn't directly described in the libretto. Without following the libretto you won't be able to follow everything being sung; at times very little (the text is sometimes broken up; some passages, including much of Act 3, are sung in an invented language). Rituals are often at their most powerful when they appeal to the imagination rather than to reason, and here the sense of ritual is awesomely powerful. It's an extraordinarily patterned opera, with many varied repetitions, all meticulously labelled ('First Structure of Decision', 'Second Time Shift' and so on) in the score. The ritual repetitions, the elaborate patternings and allegorical structures make their own effect. In the boldest of these, the 17 'arches' over which Orpheus passes in his quest for Euridice in Act 2, Birtwistle aids comprehension by quite extensive use of speech. But the music says far more than the sometimes enigmatic words, and the ceremonial retelling of the whole story in Act 3 would perhaps have less impact if the words of the song verses were comprehensible. Birtwistle communicates his refracted but gripping myth with, above all, orchestral colour: an orchestra of wind, percussion and plucked instruments (plus tape, sampler and a small chorus) used with vivid mastery. The sheer sound of this opera is quite haunting and moving. *The Mask of Orpheus* is a masterpiece, and this performance is fully worthy of it. There are no weak links at all in the extremely fine cast. Although it's unfair to single out any singer for special mention, Jon Garrison's portrayal of Orpheus the Man is outstanding. The recording, direct and pungent but by no means lacking in atmosphere, leaves nothing to be desired.

The Minotaur

John Tomlinson bass The Minotaur **Johan Reuter** bar Theseus **Christine Rice** mez Ariadne **Andrew Watts** counterten Snake Priestess **Philip Langridge** ten Hiereus **Chorus and Orchestra of the Royal Opera House, Covent Garden / Antonio Pappano**
Stage director **Stephen Langridge**
Video director **Jonathan Haswell**
Opus Arte 📀 OA1000D (175' · NTSC · 16:9 · PCM stereo and DTS 5.1 · 0)
Extra features include the documentary 'Myth Is Universal'   Ⓕ**OO**

Birtwistle's latest large-scale music drama, written for Covent Garden, is a quite different experience on DVD: what might have been planned by composer and stage director to be witnessed from a distance is shown in unsparing close-up. But this seething, monumental reinvention of one of the most disquieting Greek myths – with a pithy libretto by David Harsent – is neither betrayed nor diminished by this excellent film.

Only in its final stages does the opera's focus shift decisively to the doomed Minotaur from the scheming Ariadne, and the drama's most essential point is that this Ariadne – as different from Strauss's as Birtwistle's Orpheus is different from Gluck's – is in her own way as much of a monster as the half-man/half-bull. These demanding roles are projected with maximum musical eloquence by Christine Rice and Sir John Tomlinson, no doubt because – as Rice makes clear in the absorbing 30-minute documentary that accompanies the performance – what is demanding is also intensely rewarding to singers prepared to commit themselves to a steep learning curve. Equal commitment is evident in Johan Reuter's Theseus, the conventions of heroic posturing given new depth and relevance in text, music and vocal acting alike.

The filming reinforces the strengths of Stephen Langridge's tightly controlled, potently expressive production in an economical yet atmospheric setting, with the whole ensemble totally engaged in the drama's dark enterprise. We see little of Antonio Pappano and his orchestra, but the excellent sound never lets us escape the inexorable magnetism of the instrumental continuum. As Stephen Langridge says in the documentary, this is 'a very dark piece', and a first hearing might not reveal its subtlety of pacing, the care it takes to avoid being merely

unremitting. Repeated hearings underline that, in the end, this tragedy is the more convincing for the way its turn towards pathos does not involve any false consolation.

Georges Bizet   French 1838-1875

Think of Bizet and you think of Carmen. Most people would have to think hard to name another work. Perhaps it comes as a surprise to learn that he began his career as a child prodigy on the piano, entering the Paris Conservatoire when he was only nine. (He was the son of professional musicians, his father a singing teacher, his mother a fine pianist herself.) He wrote about 150 pieces for the piano, though of them only a set of piano duets is still played today; by the age of 17 he had written his first symphony, quite the equal of anything Mozart or Mendelssohn wrote at the same age. He won the coveted Prix de Rome in 1857 and went off to Italy to study, joined two years later by his lifelong friend Ernest Guiraud, the 1859 prize winner. It was altogether a promising start and his natural talent soon attracted attention. Then it all went off course.

The problem was Bizet's incredible facility which made it difficult for him to decide on any one project; those he did land on generally turned out to be failures. Throughout the 1860s, Bizet wrote a string of unsuccessful operas. He had an unerring eye for a weak libretto and a penchant for setting them to uneven music – works like The Pearl Fishers and The Fair Maid of Perth. Ideas that initially filled him with enthusiasm were abandoned and he found it difficult to focus his creative energies, happy to settle for an undemanding way of life. This included a relationship with the fantastic adventuress Céleste Mogador, his neighbour in Le Vésinet, the little village just outside Paris where Bizet lived in the cottage his father had built, overlooking the banks of the Seine. By the time he was 30, he had little to show for all his early promise.

He was a plump young man with a short temper and an addiction to chocolate, cakes and petit fours. He was always to be seen elegantly dressed and invariably nibbling a bon-bon. In 1869 he married the daughter of Jacques Halévy, his old professor at the Conservatory and the composer of an immensely popular opera of the day called La Juive. (Geneviève Bizet was later to become the model for Proust's Princesse de Guermantes.) More aborted schemes followed and then, slowly, it all began to take shape. He wrote an opera called Djamileh in 1872. Now, although it was another disastrous failure (due in part to the total miscasting of the title-role) many discerned an originality and lyrical gift that hitherto had not been recognised (the opera later became a great favourite of Mahler's). In 1871, too, Bizet had come up with some delightful pieces for piano duet entitled Jeux d'enfants. At the same time he received a commission from the Opéra-Comique and was able to write to a friend of 'the absolute certainty of having found my path'. The libretto was by two experienced men of the theatre who had provided the libretti for some of Offenbach's successes: Henri Meilhac and Ludovic

Halévy (*a cousin of Bizet's wife*). *The opera was to be Carmen. Meanwhile, Bizet had produced the incidental music for Daudet's play L'Arlésienne. In the theatre, the music was a failure but, having rescored some of the music and formed it into a suite, Bizet found he had a success on his hands at last.*

The struggle to mount Carmen and the reaction of the first night audience to its subject matter must, however, have disheartened Bizet further. 'A definite and hopeless flop,' Bizet pronounced after its unenthusiastic reception. In fact, he had been paid a handsome 25,000 francs for the score by his publisher and had been made a Chevalier of the Légion d'honneur on the eve of the premiere but, nevertheless, he was right in his initial assessment. Fate decreed that he should not live to see his masterpiece acclaimed. On the evening of the 31st performance of Carmen, Bizet died of a heart attack brought on by a throat affliction (probably cancer) from which he had suffered intermittently since his days in Rome. He was 36. Carmen rapidly grew in popularity. Had Bizet lived another few months he would have experienced its total triumph; another three years and he would have seen it produced in almost every major opera house in Europe.

Orchestral works

Symphony in Cᵃ. L'Arlésienneᵇ – Suites Nos 1 & 2 **H**
ᵃ**French National Radio Symphony Orchestra;**
ᵇ**Royal Philharmonic Orchestra / Sir Thomas Beecham**
EMI 567231-2 (65' · ADD). Recorded 1956-59 Ⓕ**OOD**

In Beecham's hands the Symphony in C is made to sound wonderfully songful and although the French orchestral playing is less than ideally polished, the *joie de vivre* of Beecham's performance is irresistible. What makes this disc doubly desirable are the marvellous RPO wind solos (and, of course, the haunting strings in the *Adagietto*) in *L'Arlésienne*. The performances of these two suites stand head and shoulders above present CD competition, their loving finesse mixes evocative magic (the 'Intermezzo' of No 2) with wonderful rhythmic vivacity (the closing 'Farandole'). The refurbishing of the recordings is remarkably successful, especially *L'Arlésienne*.

Carmen – Prélude; Entractes 1, 2 and 3. L'Arlésienne – Suites Nos 1 and 2; Incidental Music
Lyon Opera Chorus; Les Musiciens du Louvre-Grenoble / Marc Minkowski
Naïve V5130 (59' · DDD) Ⓕ**OOOD**

Couplings of the *Carmen* and *L'Arlésienne* suites have long been a favourite, and Minkowski's new disc has the best of all worlds in demonstrating a Beechamesque flair (the opening cymbal crash of the *Carmen* Suite is immediately arresting) and in including three suites from *L'Arlésienne*, their content well thought out and lovingly prepared. They consist of the familiar First Suite (as Bizet designed it), the Second, arranged after the composer's death by

Ernest Guiraud, including the borrowed Menuet from *La jolie fille de Perth*, and a third suite of excerpts from the original score. The collection is a delight, not least because of the beautifully elegant orchestral playing. Minkowski's choice of tempi and crisp pointing of the woodwind are admirable – in the first Entr'acte from *Carmen*, for instance, and the Minuet which follows. The Farandole too, is given a splendid lift by Minkowski's virtual double-dotting, while the flute solos in both *Carmen* and *L'Arlésienne* all have a delicious delicacy. There is much pleasure too, from the sensitive phrasing and the light and shade of the playing. *L'Arlésienne*'s famous *Adagietto* is very affecting at the slower pacing, and it touchingly returns before the final reprise of the exuberant Farandole, heard first with men's voices and then full choir in imitation.

The choral singing is splendid and the playing of Les Musiciens du Louvre-Grenoble alternates sparkle with delicacy of colour and feeling, while the recording and sumptuous packaging are first-class. This is now a clear first choice on virtually all counts for those wanting a disc combining music from *Carmen* and *L'Arlésienne*.

Carmen

Carmen
Angela Gheorghiu sop Carmen **Roberto Alagna** ten Don José **Inva Mula** sop Micaëla **Thomas Hampson** bar Escamillo **Elizabeth Vidal** sop Frasquita **Isabelle Cals** sop Mercédès **Nicolas Rivenq** ten Dancaïre **Yann Beuron** ten Remendado **Ludovic Tézier** bar Moralès **Nicolas Cavallier** bass Zuniga **Toulouse Children's Choir; Les Eléments; Toulouse Capitole Orchestra / Michel Plasson**
EMI ② 557434-2 (157' · DDD · N/T/t) Ⓕ**OD**

Michel Plasson draws some very fine playing indeed from the Toulouse orchestra, and his choice of speeds seems just right, never resorting to extreme effects. The one moment when things get a bit sluggish is in the Card scene, but he is, perhaps rightly, more concerned with letting Gheorghiu have as much breathing space as she needs; the chest tone she uses for the cries of 'La mort!' is amazingly forceful. Her portrayal has little of the easy sensuality of such celebrated interpreters as Grace Bumbry or Teresa Berganza. But Gheorghiu and Roberto Alagna have obviously worked very hard to achieve some fine moments, a beautifully soft ending to 'Là-bas, dans la montagne', and an almost visible change of mood towards the end of the Séguedille, as Carmen begins to work her charms. Gheorghiu can't help sounding rather imperious at times, and there's no exchange of remarks at the moment when she throws the flower.

Alagna has done nothing better recently: he's really inside the character, and portrays the man's descent into degradation. There's little sense of him pushing the tone – as in his Manrico – although his voice is much lighter than many other famous Don Josés. This is all in his

BIZET'S CARMEN – IN BRIEF

Leontyne Price Carmen **Franco Corelli** Don José
Mirella Freni Micaëla **Robert Merrill** Escamillo
VPO / **Herbert von Karajan**
RCA ③ 74321 39495-2 (160' · ADD)　Ⓜ〇〇
One of Price's greatest studio achievements,
one of Corelli's richest, and Freni at her most
charming. Conducted a little effortlessly.

Angela Gheorghiu Carmen **Roberto Alagna**
Don José **Inva Mula** Micaëla **Thomas Hampson**
Escamillo **Toulouse Capitole Orchestra /**
Michel Plasson
EMI ③ 557434-2 (157' · DDD)　Ⓕ〇Ⓓ➔
The husband-and-wife team of Gheorghiu
and Alagna really strike sparks off each other,
and the tenor has rarely done anything better
on disc.

Jessye Norman Carmen **Neil Shicoff** Don José
Mirella Freni Micaëla **Simon Estes** Escamillo
French National Orchestra / **Seiji Ozawa**
Decca ③ 470 417-2DOC3 (161' · DDD)　Ⓑ➔
A surprise success – Jessye Norman might
not appear to be a natural Carmen but she
sings with real insight and intelligence.
Shicoff's José, too, is magnificent.

Victoria de los Angeles Carmen **Nicolai Gedda**
Don José **Janine Micheau** Micaëla **Ernst Blanc**
Escamillo French National Radio Orchestra /
Sir Thomas Beecham
EMI ③ 567357-2 (162' · DDD)　Ⓕ〇〇〇Ⓓ➔
A classic recording, superbly cast and con-
ducted with a lightness of touch by Beecham
that has rarely been equalled.

Teresa Berganza Carmen **Plácido Domingo**
Don José **Ileana Cotrubas** Micaëla **Sherill Milnes**
Escamillo LSO / **Claudio Abbado**
DG ② 477 5342GOR2 (157' · DDD)　Ⓜ〇
Even the sluggishly delivered dialogue
can't detract from the theatricality of this
much-loved recording. Berganza is an aristocratic Carmen, and Cotrubas one of the
loveliest Micaëlas.

Maria Callas Carmen **Nicolai Gedda** Don José
Andrea Guiot Micaëla **Robert Massard**
Escamillo **Orchestre de Paris / Georges Prêtre**
EMI ② 556281-2 (146' · ADD)　ⓂⒹ➔
Callas is Callas and demands to be heard: this
isn't conventional but, wow, it works. Gedda
sounds more comfortable chez Beecham…

Julia Migenes Carmen **Plácido Domingo** Don
José **Faith Esham** Micaëla **Ruggero Raimondi**
Escamillo French National Orchestra / **Lorin**
Maazel
Erato ② 2292 45207-2 (151' · DDD)　Ⓜ〇
The soundtrack to a successful film version
finds Migenes a fiery, earthy Carmen and
Domingo once again proves his worth as a
singing actor of real class.

favour, though, for moments such as the beautifully realised ending to 'Parle-moi de ma mère'.

Other roles are well taken: Thomas Hampson
presents Escamillo as a very jovial sort of fellow,
Inva Mula as Micaëla is better in the Act 1 duet
than she is in her aria. The sound is uncomplicated, though Carmen's castanets (some very
classy playing) seem to be coming from quite a
distance away from her.

With dozens of *Carmen*s available on disc, it's
impossible to recommend only one. This will be
a pleasure for the many admirers of Plasson,
Gheorghiu and Alagna. Once you get to the
final duet in this 21st-century *Carmen*, you
should find yourself completely gripped – by
Alagna, who, while sounding distraught, still
manages to produce some lovely tone, and by
Gheorghiu, who, though she may never sing the
role on stage, is a remarkably dramatic lady-in-
distress for the microphone.

Carmen　　　　　　　　　　　　　　　Ⓗ
Victoria de los Angeles sop Carmen **Nicolai**
Gedda ten Don José **Janine Micheau** sop Micaëla
Ernst Blanc bar Escamillo **Denise Monteil** sop
Frasquita **Marcelle Croisier** mez Mercédès
Monique Linval sop Mercédès **Jean-Christoph**
Benoit bar Dancaïre **Michel Hamel** ten
Remendado **Bernard Plantey** bass Moralès **Xavier**
Depraz bass Zuniga **Les Petits Chanteurs de**
Versailles; French National Radio Choir and
Symphony Orchestra / Sir Thomas Beecham
EMI Great Recordings of the Century ③ 567357-2
(162' · ADD) Recorded 1958-59　Ⓜ〇〇〇Ⓓ➔

This classic Beecham set stands the
test of time, sparkling, swaggering
and seducing in a way that's uniquely
Beecham's. It now comes in the EMI Great
Recordings of the Century series, with brightened, freshened and clarified sound. As Richard Osborne points out in his brilliant, informative note, there were serious problems at the
sessions – a second series was organised 15
months after the first (hence the two Mercédès) – but you would never realise there had
been difficulties, either from the performance
or the firmly focused, spacious recording in
which the atmospheric offstage effects are vividly caught.

What's so individual is the way that Beecham
points rhythms to captivate the ear, as well as his
persuasive moulding of phrases. Witness the
sensuous way he coaxes the string phrase leading
into the second half of the Don José/Micaëla
duet in Act 2, 'Parle-moi de ma mère!' (disc 1,
track 9, 3'47"). In those qualities Beecham is
matched by Victoria de los Angeles in the title-
role.

Osborne reveals that Beecham's original
choice of heroine was the Swedish mezzo Kerstin Meyer. After all, de los Angeles – Mimì in
Beecham's *Bohème* recording – is hardly an
obvious candidate for such a fire-eating role.
But there's far more to Carmen than is conveyed in that conventional approach, and de

los Angeles instantly establishes her as a seductive, provocative character with wickedly sparkling eyes. In her opening solo, the Habanera, her delicious downward *portamento* on 'Je t'aime' is irresistible. The Carmen quality which de los Angeles doesn't have in her regular armoury, though, is a snarl. Instead she consistently uses her golden tone to tantalise and provoke, as in the magically sultry moment leading into 'Là-bas dans la montagne' in her Act 2 duet with José just after the Flower song (disc 2, track 13). At that point Beecham, too, subtly pressing the music forward, is a fellow magician. Then at the very end, in Act 4, de los Angeles does finally muster a snarl in the culminating phrase 'laisse-moi passer' ('Well stab me then, or let me pass').

In a way, Nicolai Gedda's portrait of Don José is just as remarkable. He was at his peak, and sings not just with refinement and imagination but with deep passion, leading you on in the widest expressive range in the Flower song. Janine Micheau makes a bright, clear Micaëla, very French in tone, and Ernst Blanc, if not the most characterful Escamillo, makes the bullfighter a forthright, heroic character, singing with firm, clear tone.

The rest of the cast, all French, make an excellent team, as is clear in ensembles: the sparkling account of the Act 2 Quintet or the opening of the Card scene, or the swaggering march ensemble as the smugglers depart in Act 3. A magic set now made all the more enticing in this mid-price reissue.

Carmen
Teresa Berganza *sop* Carmen **Plácido Domingo** *ten* Don José **Ileana Cotrubas** *sop* Micaëla **Sherrill Milnes** *bar* Escamillo **Yvonne Kenny** *sop* Frasquita **Alicia Nafé** *mez* Mercédès **Robert Lloyd** *bass* Zuniga **Stuart Harling** *bar* Moralès **Gordon Sandison** *bar* Dancaïre **Geoffrey Pogson** *ten* Remendado **Ambrosian Singers; London Symphony Orchestra / Claudio Abbado**
DG ② 477 5342GOR2 (157' · ADD · N/T/t) Ⓜ◉◐▶

This notable recording followed immediately on from the famous Faggioni production at the 1977 Edinburgh Festival, a staging finely observed enough still to remain with those who were there. In it Berganza declared her aim of rescuing the role from bad traditions and from its insults to Spanish womanhood. Her reading was restrained, haughty, but no less attractive and haunting for that. She developed the character, as she does on the recording, from carefree gypsy to tragic woman and, in doing so, is scrupulous in her obedience to Bizet's notes, rhythms and dynamics. Nothing is exaggerated yet nothing is left out in this sensuous but never overtly sensual portrayal, bewitchingly sung. Maybe you don't feel the full engagement of her emotions in her entanglement with José, but better a slight reticence than overacting. Migenes, on the Maazel set, is more immediately seductive, and occasionally more varied in

tonal colouring, but Berganza is the more subtle artist. She works in keen rapport with Abbado, who brings clarity of texture, Mediterranean fire and intense concentration to the score.

You may find more elegance, more Gallic wit in, say, Beecham's famous EMI set, but only Maazel of other conductors comes near Abbado's emphasis on close-knit ensemble and histrionic strength – and both their sets come as the result of experience of 'real' performances. Domingo benefits here, as on the Maazel in the same way, being more involved in affairs. Like his Carmen, he sometimes lacks variety of colour in his singing, but its sheer musicality and, in the last two acts, power, count for much. Sherrill Milnes is at once virile and fatuous as Escamillo should be. Cotrubas makes a vulnerable, touching Micaëla. The dialogue is heavily foreshortened compared to rival sets. Abbado chooses some of the questionable Oeser alternatives, but – apart from the one in the finale – they aren't disturbing. The recording is first-rate.

Carmen
Christa Ludwig *mez* Carmen **James King** *ten* Don José **Eberhard Waechter** *bar* Escamillo **Jeanette Pilou** *sop* Micaëla **Lucia Popp** *sop* Frasquita **Margarita Lilova** *bar* Mercédès **Oskar Czerwenka** *bar* Zuniga **Reid Bunger** *bar* Moralès **Murray Dickie** *ten* Remendado **Erich Kunz** *ten* Dancaïre **Vienna State Opera Chorus; Vienna State Opera Orchestra / Lorin Maazel**
Orfeo ② C733 082I (145' · ADD · T/t)
Recorded live at the Staatsoper, Vienna, on February 19, 1966 Ⓜ

In this 1966 live recording conductor Lorin Maazel adopts some rather extreme tempi, for instance rather stately in the introduction to the Toreador's song, but elsewhere seeming a bit rushed. As the evening progresses, however, the performance gains considerably in dramatic fervour.

Christa Ludwig was fond of the title-role; she made a complete recording of it in German for EMI, conducted by Horst Stein, but as she explained in her autobiography: 'I'm personally the exact opposite of Carmen…I made her shameless, fearless, amoral and high-spirited.' Hers is a gypsy in the Viennese tradition of Maria Jeritza; in Acts 1 and 2 it's very much a star turn, but once things turn nasty in Act 3, Ludwig rises to the challenge and makes a tragic, proud figure. Her French is pretty good, although she has a bit of trouble with 'tu' and 'tout'.

James King recorded very little outside the German repertory for which he was best known. He overdoes the emotion a bit at the end of Act 1, but this is a valuable souvenir of this great trouper in one of his favourite parts. Jeanette Pilou was a lovely soprano, not well enough represented on disc, although she also made a studio recording as Micaëla under Jean Martinon. Lucia Popp is luxury casting as Frasquita, her unmistakable voice riding over the quintet, with Erich Kunz, no less, as Le Dancaïre. Eberhard Waechter must have cut a glamorous fig-ure as Escamillo, and he too is impressive in his command of the original language. As Gottfried Kraus explains in the booklet, until this produc-tion by Otto Schenk the opera had often been given in polyglot performances, principals sing-ing in French or Italian, chorus and compri-marios in German!

The mono sound is adequate, the stage noises atmospheric rather than distracting, and at the centre a pair of great singers, Ludwig and King, inhabiting their roles, aided by the dynamic leadership provided by Maazel: a heady dose of nostalgia.

Carmen
Julia Migenes *mez* Carmen **Plácido Domingo** *ten*
Don José **Faith Esham** *sop* Micaëla **Ruggero**
Raimondi *bass* Escamillo **Lilian Watson** *sop*
Frasquita **Susan Daniel** *mez* Mercédès
Jean-Philippe Lafont *bar* Dancaïre **Gérard Garino**
ten Remendado **François Le Roux** *bar* Moralès
John Paul Bogart *bass* Zuniga **French Radio**
Chorus; French Radio Children's Chorus;
French National Orchestra / Lorin Maazel
Erato ② 2292 45207-2 (151' · DDD · T/t)   Ⓕ**OO**

Too many recordings of *Carmen* have blown up the work to proportions beyond its author's intentions but here Maazel adopts a brisk, light-weight approach that seems to come close to what Bizet wanted. Similarly Julia Migenes approaches the title part in an immediate, vivid way, exuding the gypsy's allure and suggesting Carmen's fierce temper and smouldering eroti-cism; she develops the character intelligently into the fatalistic person of the card scene and finale. Her singing isn't conventionally smooth but it's compelling throughout. Plácido Domingo has made Don José very much his own, and here he sings with unstinting involve-ment and finesse. Ruggero Raimondi is a macho Toreador though Faith Esham is a somewhat pallid Micaëla.

Carmen
Maria Ewing *mez* Carmen **Jacques Trussell** *ten* Don
José **Miriam Gauci** *sop* Micaëla **Rosemary Ashe** *sop*
Frasquita **Ludmilla Andrew** *sop* Mercédès **Alain**
Fondary *bar* Escamillo **Emile Belcourt** *ten*
Remendado **David Hamilton** *bar* Dancaïre **Rodney**
McCann *bass-bar* Zuniga **Christopher Blades** *bass*
Moralès **Ambrosian Opera Chorus; National**
Philharmonic Orchestra / Jacques Delacôte
Stage director **Steven Pimlott**
Video director **Gavin Taylor**
Stax Entertainment 📀 MAWA131 (165' · 4:3 ·
5.1 · 0). Recorded live 1989   Ⓕ**OO**

This DVD derives from a television relay from Earl's Court in June 1989, an unexpectedly suc-cessful staging in the barn-like venue. The tri-umph of the event was almost entirely due to Steven Pimlott's highly imaginative use of the huge space, presenting the work in the round on

a large dais with a kind of moving platform sur-rounding it.

Maria Ewing's Carmen, as on her other two video interpretations of the role (Glynde-bourne and Covent Garden), is an earthily mesmeric, wholly sensual and elemental gypsy, conceived perfectly for her own character yet marching with Bizet's concept. She's in won-derful voice, with many subtle emphases of word and tone to bring her solos to life. Trus-sell is a good foil, at once fiery, vulnerable, tetchy, and he sings with a combination of plangency and power. Fondary delivers his native French and the character of Escamillo with unerringly economic strength as to the manner born. Gauci is a limpid, lyrical, prop-erly ingenuous Micaëla.

Delacôte is a near-ideal conductor of this score, an elegant, sensitive, vibrant reading that hits all the right spots. The work is played superbly by the National Philharmonic, who are heard to far better effect here than in the origi-nal venue. The sound-enhancement occasion-ally produces odd effects, but they hardly detract from enjoyment of the riveting performance. Subtitles are provided, but in the last two acts they're out of sync with the action.

Les pêcheurs de perles

Les pêcheurs de perles
Barbara Hendricks *sop* Leïla **John Aler** *ten* Nadir
Gino Quilico *bar* Zurga **Jean-Philippe Courtis** *bass*
Nourabad **Toulouse Capitole Chorus and Orchestra**
/ Michel Plasson
EMI ② 749837-2 (127' · DDD · T/t)   Ⓕ**O**▶

Let a tenor and a baritone signify that they're willing to oblige with a duet, and the cry will go up for *The Pearl Fishers*. It's highly unlikely that many of the company present will know what the duet is about – it recalls the past, proclaims eternal friendship and nearly ends up in a quar-rel – but the melody and the sound of two fine voices blending in its harmonies will be quite sufficient. In fact there's much more to the opera than the duet; and the EMI recording goes further than previous versions in giving a complete account of a score remarkable for its unity as well as for the attractiveness of individ-ual numbers.

It's a lyrical opera, and the voices need to be young and graceful. Barbara Hendricks and John Aler fulfil those requirements, she with a light, silvery timbre, he with a high tenor admi-rably suited to the tessitura of his solos. The third main character, the baritone whose role is central to the drama, assumes his rightful place here: Gino Quilico brings true distinction to the part, and his aria in Act 3 is one of the highlights. Though Plasson's direction at first is rather square, the performance grows in respon-siveness. It's a pity the accompanying notes aren't stronger in textual detail, for the full score given here stimulates interest in its history. One of the changes made in the original score of

1863 concerns the celebrated duet itself, the first version of which is given in an appendix. It ends in a style you'd swear owed much to the 'friendship' duet in Verdi's *Don Carlos* – except that Bizet came first.

Sir Arthur Bliss   British 1891-1975

After attending Rugby School and Cambridge, Bliss embarked on studies with Stanford at the Royal College of Music, but the First World War intervened. After the war he made a name for himself with a series of ironic, slightly French-influenced works such as Rout (1920), which sets nonsense words. A major turning-point was his Colour Symphony of 1922, a work that explores the significance of heraldic colours; it signalled a move towards a more traditionally British orchestral language. The Introduction and Allegro (1926) and Music for Strings (1935) are also in this vein. His feel for the screen and stage is demonstrated in the ballets Checkmate (1937), Miracle in the Gorbals (1944) and Adam Zero (1946), and the film score for Things to Come (1935). Among his orchestral works are concertos for piano (1938), violin (1955) and cello (1970). But his later works tended to overshadowed by the output of his younger colleagues like Britten, Dutilleux and Lutosławski. In 1953 he was appointed Master of the Queen's Music.

Cello Concerto

Cello Concerto. Music for Strings.
Two Studies
Tim Hugh vc **English Northern Philharmonia /
David Lloyd-Jones**
Naxos 8 553383 (64' · DDD)   Ⓢ**O**▷

This is a first-rate performance of Bliss's Cello Concerto from Tim Hugh, stylishly and sympathetically partnered by David Lloyd-Jones and the English Northern Philharmonia. The work is a delightful creation, ideally proportioned, impeccably crafted and full of the most beguiling invention. Hugh plays with commanding assurance, great beauty of tone and rapt commitment, and the accompaniment is sprightly and sensitive to match. What makes this release indispensable to all Bliss admirers is the inclusion of the *Two Studies*. These date from 1921 and were believed lost until they turned up in the composer's papers after his death in 1975. The first is a memorably chaste, coolly serene affair, scored with delicious poise, whereas the second is an energetic, good-humoured and occasionally face-pulling romp.

That just leaves the tremendous *Music for Strings*, which is where, alas, reservations must be raised. This superb score displays and demands a formidable technical facility, and Bliss's exhilaratingly well-judged writing would surely test any string section. It would be idle to pretend that the hard-working strings of the

English Northern Philharmonia are ideally secure exponents. The work is well served by Lloyd-Jones's clear-headed, expressive interpretation, but in the finale's crucial introductory bars his approach is oddly perfunctory. The Cello Concerto and the *Two Studies* alone though, will probably be enticement enough for many listeners. The recorded sound is excitingly realistic.

Piano Concerto

Piano Concerto in B flat. Concerto for Two Pianos and Orchestra[a]. Sonata for Piano
Peter Donohoe, [a]**Martin Roscoe** pfs **Royal Scottish National Orchestra / David Lloyd-Jones**
Naxos 8 557146 (73' · DDD)   Ⓢ▷

In recent times Bliss's swaggering Piano Concerto (written in 1938-39 for Solomon) has found a champion in Peter Donohoe, and it's good that he's been able to set down his powerful interpretation as part of Naxos's British Piano Concertos series. As those thunderous octaves at the outset demonstrate, Bliss's bravura writing holds no terrors for Donohoe and he generates a satisfying rapport with David Lloyd-Jones and the RSNO. Theirs is a beautifully prepared and attentive reading which grips from start to finish. The bittersweet central *Adagietto* casts an especially potent spell, while both outer movements harness blistering virtuosity to supple affection. All told, a worthy modern counterpart to the thrilling historic displays from Solomon and Mewton-Wood.

No less compelling is the buoyant account of the Concerto for Two Pianos: an infectiously enjoyable, single-movement work that began life in 1921 as a Concerto for Piano, Tenor and Strings (that same year, Bliss embarked on his *Colour Symphony*, of which there are fleeting echoes here). The present revision dates from 1950; 18 years later, Bliss overhauled the piece one last time for the three-hand partnership of Phyllis Sellick and Cyril Smith. As in the Piano Concerto, the recording is a touch bright and clangorous, but the ear soon adjusts.

No such technical qualms surround Donohoe's intelligent and accomplished performance of the Sonata composed in 1952 for Noel Mewton-Wood. With his commanding presence and rich tonal palette, Donohoe again exhibits a remarkable empathy with Bliss's red-blooded inspiration. This rewarding Naxos disc deserves every success.

Additional recommendation

Piano Concerto in B flat[a]. Adam Zero[b]
Solomon pf [a]**NYPSO / Boult;** [b]**Royal Opera House Orchestra, Covent Garden / Lambert**   Ⓗ
APR mono APR5627 (61' · DDD). Recorded [a]1939 (live), [b]1946   Ⓜ
    Solomon, for whose sovereign technique the Concerto was designed, plays like a man possessed.

His partnership with Boult operates at the highest level of excitement, eloquence and dedication.

A Colour Symphony

A Colour Symphony. Adam Zero
English Northern Philharmonia / David Lloyd-Jones
Naxos 8 553460 (74' · DDD)   ⑤◯◯↦

David Lloyd-Jones's exciting and idiomatic account of *A Colour Symphony* proves more than a match for all current competition, including the composer's own 1955 recording so spectacularly transferred by Dutton Laboratories. Speeds are judged to perfection – nicely flowing for the first and third movements, not too hectic for the flashing *Scherzo* – and countless details in Bliss's stunning orchestral canvas are deftly attended to. Phrasing is sensitive and affectionate, solo work is consistently excellent (the slow movement's delicate woodwind arabesques are exquisitely voiced), and *tuttis* open out superbly in a technically fine recording from Naxos (magnificently keen-voiced horns throughout).

Whereas *A Colour Symphony* was inspired by the heraldic associations of four different colours (one for each movement), the theme of *Adam Zero* is the inexorable life-cycle of humankind. In its entirety, this 1946 ballet score does admittedly have its occasional *longueurs*, but for the most part Bliss's invention is of high quality. Certainly, the vivid exuberance and theatrical swagger of numbers like 'Dance of Spring' and 'Dance of Summer' have strong appeal. Equally, the limpid beauty of both the 'Love Dance' and the hieratic 'Bridal Ceremony' which immediately ensues isn't easily banished, while the darkly insistent 'Dance with Death' distils a gentle poignancy which is most haunting.

Orchestral works

Meditations on a Theme by John Blow.
Metamorphic Variations
Bournemouth Symphony Orchestra / David Lloyd Jones
Naxos 8 572316 (73' · DDD)   ⑤◯◯↦

Did Sir Arthur Bliss write a finer work than the *Meditations on a Theme of John Blow* (1955)? A beautifully balanced set of expanded variations on a theme from the Sinfonia to Blow's setting of Psalm 23, Bliss's score is a glowing exhibition of his compositional prowess. Its sequence of Introduction, five Meditations, Interlude and Finale bear superscriptions from the psalm – excepting the *scherzando* third meditation, 'Lambs' – which colour the characters of each section. But, as Giles Easterbrook notes in the booklet, there is a parallel expressive strand running throughout the work, of memorial to the fallen of the Great War in which Bliss had served and his brother was killed. And somehow

it achieves greater weight than *Morning Heroes*.

The inspiration behind *Metamorphic Variations* (1972) was George Dannatt's triptych *Tantris*, based on the Tristan legend. Composed nine years after Bliss's retirement from large-scale composition, this kaleidoscopic score turned into his largest abstract orchestral piece. Its 14 variations each bear a descriptive title – eg 'Ballet', 'Assertion', 'Speculation' – collectively comprising a *tour de force* of the octogenarian composer's art.

Meditations has been recorded before but the newcomer is beautifully played, well paced and boasts the finest sound to date. Recommended.

Checkmate

Checkmate. Mêlée fantasque
Royal Scottish National Orchestra / David Lloyd-Jones
Naxos 8 557641 (65' · DDD)   ⑤↦

Bliss composed *Checkmate* at the behest of dancer and choreographer Ninette de Valois to mark the Vic-Wells Ballet's inaugural visit to Paris in June 1937. A keen chess player, Bliss devised the scenario himself, the original idea having germinated some 14 years before in a dinner conversation with the Russian ballerina Tamara Karsavina. Lasting some 53 minutes, it's a mightily impressive achievement, scored with sumptuous skill and crammed full of first-rate, colourful invention, much of which will already be familiar from the six-movement concert suite.

Now comes a compelling account of the complete ballet from David Lloyd-Jones and the RSNO, who respond with commendable polish and ebullient swagger. Lloyd-Jones's characteristically lucid conception possesses just that crucial bit more dramatic tension, expressive scope and thrust – and how pliantly he moulds those ravishing melodic tendrils in 'Entry of the Black Queen' (where there's some particularly disarming wind playing). Some occasionally raucous brass sonorities aside, the engineering is enormously vivid, the slightly unflattering acoustic appropriately akin to that of the theatre-pit.

The *Mêlée fantasque* (written in 1921 in memory of the painter Claude Lovat Fraser) makes a delightful curtain-raiser, with Lloyd-Jones extracting just that bit more vitality from this by turns exuberant and touching dance-poem than the composer (always an accomplished interpreter of his own music). A real bargain.

Additional recommendation

Bliss Checkmate – Suite. **Lambert** Horoscope – Suite. **Walton** Façade – Suites Nos 1 & 2
English Northern Sinfonia / David Lloyd-Jones
Hyperion Helios CDH55099 (74' · DDD)   ⑧◯↦
A delicious trio of British ballet scores performed with zest and an ideal feel for pacing. The recording, too, is near perfect.

Chamber Works

Piano Quartet in A minor, T6a. Viola Sonata.
Oboe Quintet, T44
Maggini Quartet (Laurence Jackson, David Angel
vns Martin Outram va Michal Kaznowski vc) with
Peter Donohoe pf **Nicholas Daniel** ob
Naxos 8 555931 (62' · DDD)   ⓈⒹ→

The Maggini Quartet and Peter Donohoe give a
commanding performance of the Piano Quartet, locating an underlying toughness of argument and urgency of expression in both outer
movements to make one regret all the more
forcefully the budding composer's decision to
withdraw the piece following his demobilisation
in 1919.

The Viola Sonata was written in 1933 for
Lionel Tertis. If Bliss's inspiration lacks the
distinctive melodic profile and organic mastery
of, say, Walton's Viola Concerto of four years
previously, the work as a whole is still worth getting to know. The Maggini's viola player, Martin Outram, makes commendably light of the
solo part's at times hair raising demands and
Donohoe offers exemplary support.

But the jewel in this anthology is the Oboe
Quintet that Bliss composed in 1927 for Leon
Goossens. Elegance and resourcefulness are the
watchwords in the first two movements, whose
bittersweet lyricism forms an effective contrast
with the exuberant festivities of the finale.
Nicholas Daniel and the Maggini give a spry,
ideally proportioned reading. Production-values throughout are of a high order. Very
warmly recommended.

Bliss Viola Sonata, T52 **Bridge** Allegro appassionato,
H82. Serenade, H23. Norse Legend, H60. Pensiero,
H53a. Souvenir, H48. Berceuse, H8. Gondoliera, H80
Delius Violin Sonata No 3, RTVIII/10 (arr Tertis)
Enikő Magyar va **Tadashi Imai** pf
Naxos 8 572407 (67' · DDD) Ⓢ

Fashioned for the great Lionel Tertis, Bliss's
imposing Viola Sonata of 1933 has been enjoying a renaissance on disc: this fine new recording
by Hungarian viola player Enikő Magyar is the
fifth in almost as many years. Confidently partnered by Tadashi Imai, Magyar gives a most
compelling interpretation which, in its rewarding marriage of youthful vigour and songful
grace.

Tertis's own arrangement of Delius's Third
Violin Sonata was published in 1932, the virtuoso having sought and received the wheelchair-bound composer's approval on a visit to Grez-sur-Loing the previous year. It's an effective and
accomplished piece of work, and these sensitive
artists are fully attuned to the music's intensely
lyrical flow and inimitably Delian sunset glow
(the valedictory finale being especially moving).
The sequence of seven pieces by Frank Bridge
(an admirable viola player in his own right) date
from between 1901 and 1908. The winsome

Berceuse, *Serenade* and *Norse Legend* were later
orchestrated; just two (*Pensiero* and *Allegro
appassionato*) were originally conceived for viola
and piano. Once again, Magyar and Imai are
utterly convincing protagonists of all this attractive material.

Throw in sound that is undistractingly truthful, Lewis Foreman's helpfully detailed notes
and Naxos's enticing price-tag, and it certainly
adds up to a healthy recommendation.

A Knot of Riddles

Two American Poems[ag]. Seven American Poems[cg].
Angels of the Mind[ag]. The Ballads of the Four
Seasons[ag]. A Knot of Riddles[chi]. Two Love Songs[cg].
Two Nursery Rhymes[aef]. Three Romantic Songs[bg].
Three Songs[bg]. Four Songs[adf]. At the Window[bg].
Auvergnat[bg]. A Child's Prayer[ag]. Elegiac Sonnet[bhi].
The Fallow Deer at the Lonely House[bg]. The
Hammers[bg]. Rich or Poor[ag]. Simples[bg]. Three Jolly
Gentlemen[ag]. 'Tis time, I think, by Wenlock Town[bg].
The Tramps[cg]. When I was one-and-twenty[cg].
The Tempest[bcg] – The Storm; Overture and Act 1,
Scene 1
[a]**Geraldine McGreevy** sop [b]**Toby Spence** ten [c]**Henry
Herford** bar [d]**Leo Phillips** vn [e]**Michael Collins** cl
[f]**John Lenehan** pf [g]**Kathron Sturrock** pf [h]**Nash
Ensemble** / [i]**Martyn Brabbins**
Hyperion ② CDA67188/9 (123' · DDD · T)   ⒻⓄ

Nearly all Bliss's songs are here (only a few
orchestral ones are omitted) but they're of uneven
quality and are presented in almost random
order, with no sense given of Bliss's development
as a song-writer. It was a mistake to include the
Two Love Songs, which are in fact the vocal movements of Bliss's beautiful *Serenade* for baritone
and orchestra. Kathron Sturrock, throughout a
wonderfully musical and responsive accompanist,
does her best to make Bliss's piano reductions
seem pianistic; but despite her they just sound
clumpy.

The finest songs here are mostly on the second
disc. Kathleen Raine's poems drew the best from
the composer – simple eloquence, bold, shining
gestures and memorable images including a fine
nocturne: they're masterly, and would alone
make investigating this pair of discs worthwhile.
Geraldine McGreevy sings them simply, purely
and very movingly, as she does the progression
from lyric charm to bare strength of *The Ballads
of the Four Seasons*. Also on CD2 is *The Tempest*;
this vivid storm scene is all that survives of some
1921 incidental music to Shakespeare's play, set
with striking originality for two voices, trumpet,
trombone and five percussion players. Things of
such quality are rarer on CD1, though the *Three
Songs* to poems by WH Davies are all strong,
Bliss's setting of "When I was one-and-twenty"
has a blithe insouciance, and several of the other
sets contain pleasing discoveries, like the elegantly witty 'A Bookworm' from *A Knot of Riddles* or the charming 'Christmas Carol' that
opens *Four Songs*. McGreevy is the best of the
singers, but both Herford and Spence are com-

Bliss Vocal

mitted advocates. The best of these songs (about half) are of a quality to make their present neglect seem inexplicable.

Ernest Bloch   Swiss/American 1880-1959

Bloch studied in Switzerland, Belgium and Germany before moving to the USA in 1916 (taking US citizenship in 1924). He taught in Cleveland (1920-25), San Francisco (1925-30) and Berkeley (1940-52). His early works, including the opera Macbeth (1910) draw on a rich late-romantic language with echoes of Strauss and Debussy. This was followed by an interest in neo-classical composition (Piano Quintet No 1 of 1923 and Concerto grosso No 1 of 1925 being prime examples). He also studied Jewish music and produced a number of works that adhere to Jewish principles and to Jewish themes (including the ever-popular Schelomo); this interest culminated in his epic Sacred Service (Avodath hakodesh).

Symphony in C sharp minor

Symphony in C sharp minor. Schelomo
Torleif Thedéen vc **Malmö Symphony Orchestra / Lev Markiz**
BIS BIS-CD576 (78' · DDD)   Ⓕ

Bloch's early symphony is an endearing and at times impressive showcase for a young composer (he was 23) endowed by nature and nurture with all the gifts save individuality (though there are hints in the later movements that that too is on the way). He can write impressively strong, expansive melodies, develop them with real ingenuity and build them into monumental climaxes. Climax-building, indeed, is what young Bloch seems most interested in at this stage, that and a love for all the rich contrasts of colour and texture that a big orchestra can provide. He's so adept at pulling out still more stops when you thought there could hardly be any left that you're scarcely ever made impatient by the occasional feeling that this or that movement could have ended two or three minutes earlier.

It's a pleasure, too, to listen for fulfilled echoes of that youthful exuberance in the mature 'biblical rhapsody' Schelomo. Just as Lev Markiz adroitly avoids any impression of overpadded grossness in the symphony, so he and his fine soloist find more than richly embroidered oriental voluptuousness in this portrait of King Solomon; there's gravity and even poignancy to the music as well, and Thedéen's subtle variety of tone colour provides shadow and delicacy as well as richness. The recording is excellent.

Violin Sonatas

Violin Sonatas – No 1; No 2, 'Poème mystique'. Suite hébraïque. Abodah. Melody
Miriam Kramer vn **Simon Over** pf

Naxos 8 554460 (75' · DDD)   ⓈⓄ➔

Miriam Kramer's programme might usefully serve as a sort of 'Bloch starter-pack', with the delightful *Suite hébraïque* as its tuneful opener. 'Rapsodie', the Suite's first movement, harbours a noble melody reminiscent of top-drawer Max Bruch and Kramer's performance of it could hardly be more heartfelt. Both violin sonatas are given extremely good performances, that of the Second particularly fine especially in the ecstatic, double-stopped statements of the central theme. The combination of Kramer's musicianship and Naxos's price will be irresistible to most repertory explorers.

Bloch Baal Shem. Suite hébraïque. Solo Violin Suites – No 1; No 2 **Ben-Haim** Berceuse sfaradite. Solo Violin Sonata. Improvisation and Dance
Hagai Shaham vn **Arnon Erez** pf
Hyperion CDA67571 (74' · DDD)   Ⓕ

Bloch's two unaccompanied suites date from 1958, the year before his death; they combine a chromatic idiom with a strong sense of tonality. Occasionally the music seems to lack individuality – the third movement of the First Suite is almost like pastiche Bach and its final cadence is academically predictable – but more often one's attention is caught and held by the expressive melodic writing and, in both suites, by a compelling sense of continuity. Shaham revels in Bloch's demanding yet imaginatively idiomatic violin writing. In the solo suites, as well as the more extravagantly emotional pieces with piano on Jewish themes, he enters wholeheartedly into the feeling of the music yet retains a measure of balance and restraint – the vibrato isn't exaggerated and a feeling of rhapsodic freedom is achieved without sacrificing natural flow.

Bloch's popularity has waned somewhat in recent decades, and the Israeli composer Paul Ben-Haim (1897-1984) is even more poorly represented in the CD catalogue. His Solo Sonata, written for Yehudi Menuhin, is, however, a masterly work, not at all original in form and idiom, perhaps, but full of memorable ideas. Shaham's playing of the central *Lento e sotto voce* is stunningly beautiful. And the *Improvisation and Dance*, a folk-style showpiece after the manner of the Bartók rhapsodies, inspires both Shaham and Erez to brilliant feats of virtuosity.

Piano Quintets

Piano Quintets[a] – No 1; No 2. Landscapes. Night. Two Pieces
[a]**Piers Lane** pf **Goldner Quartet** (Dene Olding, Dimity Hall vns Irina Morozova va Julian Smiles vc)
Hyperion CDA67638 (70' · DDD)   ⒻⓄⓄⓄ

A fabulous CD this, easily the best recording of Bloch's chamber music in years. The First Quintet, a product of the early 1920s, seems to combine the acerbic drive of middle-period

Bartók with the kind of veiled sensuality one associates more with Chausson or Fauré. Bloch's use of quarter-tones, aimed at intensifying the work's already heightened emotional atmosphere, requires careful handling, and the Goldner Quartet make them sound both musically striking and entirely natural. If you need a sampling-point, try the finale's opening, where the sense of urgency will hold you riveted.

The real revelation here is the Second Piano Trio (1957). The language recalls the First Quintet's stronger elements, with tone-rows this time rather than quarter-tones, though again their employment is musical rather than 'political'. Amazing to think that this was Bloch's last chamber work (he was already suffering from cancer when he wrote it), the combination of raw energy and mysticism suggesting the mind of a much younger man, much as Janáček's late chamber music does. The Quintet's quiet coda is rapturously beautiful and the blending of voices between Piers Lane and the Goldners simply could not be bettered. The short quartet bonuses suggest that a Goldner Bloch quartet cycle would be a good idea. But that's one for the future; as for this current release, the music is truly wonderful, the playing entirely sympathetic and the sound perfectly balanced.

Additional recommednation

Schelomo. Sacred Service. Concerto grosso No 1. Violin Concerto. Solo Violin Suites Nos 1 & 3.
Rostropovich; Orch Nat de France / Bernstein; Utah SO / Abravanel; Grier; ASMF / Marriner; Menuhin; Philh / Kletzki
EMI Gemini ② 456319-2 (119' ADD)　　ⒷＯＯ⯈
A near-ideal Bloch taster with first-rate performances of all the works, including a terrific account of the *Concerto grosso* from Marriner's ASMF and a heart-felt *Schelomo* from Rostropovich.

John Blow
British 1649-1708

Though born in Nottinghamshire, Blow trained in London as a Chapel Royal chorister and was then organist of Westminster Abbey (1668-79). In 1674 he both became a Gentleman of the Chapel Royal and Master of the Children. Henry Purcell served an apprenticeship under him. While still active at the Chapel Royal, he was Master of the Choristers at St Paul's Cathedral from 1687 to 1703, and in 1695 he returned to Westminster Abbey as organist, succeeding Purcell.

Though nowadays somewhat overshadowed by Purcell, Blow is a major figure in English music at the same time as his great pupil. He was a prolific composer over a large range of styles and genres. The majority of his work is for the church, with anthems the most well-represented. Venus and Adonis (1685), a small-scale opera written for the court, was his only dramatic work, but betrays a strong sense of the daramatic. His Ode on the Death of Mr Henry Purcell

(1696), a duet with instrumental accompaniment, is a masterpiece of poignant expression.

Ode on the Death of Purcell

Blow Sonata in A. Ground in G minor.　　Ⓟ
Fugue in G minor. Suite in G. Ground in C minor. An Ode on the Death of Mr Henry Purcell[ab]
Purcell Birthday Ode, Z331 – Sweetness of Nature[ab]. Here let my life[a]. Oedipus – Music for a while[a]. St Cecilia's Day Ode, Z328 – In vain the am'rous flute
[ab]**Gérard Lesne**, [b]**Steve Dugardin** countertens **La Canzona** (Pierre Hamon, Sébastien Marq recs Elisabeth Joyé clav Philippe Pierlot va da gamba Vincent Dumestre theorbo)
Virgin Veritas 545342-2 (64' · DDD · T/t)　　ⒻＯＯ⯈

The teacher who has even one pupil who becomes even more distinguished than himself is fortunate; in Purcell, Blow had one such. And when that pupil's death precedes his own he has cause for genuine grief, as Blow did. One of Purcell's songs, here alternated with instrumental pieces by Blow, contains the line 'Nor let my homely death embroider'd be with scutcheon or with elegy', but it's one with which Blow and others could not concur. In a programmatic *tour de force* Blow's profoundly beautiful vocal tribute to Purcell comes at the end. Few countertenors are as finely matched in artistry and vocal quality as Lesne and Dugardin, who, in both the solo songs and duets, wring every drop of emotion from the texts with sincerity, technically effortless *messa di voce* and admirably clear diction. In Blow's *Ode on the Death of Mr Henry Purcell*, the risk that the recorders may cover the singers is avoided. The instrumental support faithfully shadows every vocal nuance throughout. Much of Blow's instrumental music was unpublished in his time and has remained unrecorded – some first-time pieces here. Where violins were originally specified, as in the A major Trio Sonata, in this recording they're replaced by recorders, and the harpsichord Suite in G minor is a modern compilation from various sources. Altogether this album is pure, unalloyed delight.

Luigi Boccherini
Italian 1743-1805

Who knows Boccherini's name today for any reason other than his celebrated Minuet, used in films and television possibly more than any other piece as a shorthand way of conveying 18th-century elegance and refinement? Many will remember it being used to marvellous effect in the 1955 Ealing comedy The Ladykillers. The minuet (in A major) comes from the String Quintet in E, Op 13 No 3 published about 1775. He also wrote a further 124 string quintets, 102 string quartets and an enormous pile of other chamber music. Boccherini was highly regarded in his day, so much so that he was said to be 'the wife of Haydn' (musically speaking, of course!). Much of what he wrote is very fine and ought to be better known (his elegant piano quintets, for example, his eight surviving guitar quintets – No 4 in D has an infectiously lively Fandango finale – and the once-popular Cello Sonata in A). He was a cello virtuoso. Of his concertos for the instrument, there's a fine one in G (G480 from 1770) but that most often heard is one in a souped-up arrangement by the 19th-century cellist Friedrich Grützmacher (Concerto in B flat, G482), a Romantic conflation of two different works.

Cello Concertos

Cello Concertos – No 4 in C, G477; No 6 in D, G479; No 7 in G, G480; No 8 in C, G481
Tim Hugh vc **Scottish Chamber Orchestra / Anthony Halstead**
Naxos 8 553571 (74' · DDD)

This disc is a winner, the first of a series of all 12 Boccherini cello concertos, beautifully performed on modern instruments but with concern for period practice and superbly recorded. Each concerto has its individual delights, but the formula in all four works is similar, with strong, foursquare first movements, slow movements that sound rather Handelian, and galloping finales in triple time.

Many collectors will be concerned about the Boccherini Cello Concerto beloved of generations in Grützmacher's corrupt edition. Many years ago Jacqueline du Pré was questioned about choosing it for her recording: she promptly justified herself, saying, 'But the slow movement is so lovely'. She was quite right, as her classic recording makes clear, but that movement was transferred from another work, in fact No 7 in G, one of the four works here. Tim Hugh's dedicated account of this lovely G minor movement is a high-spot of this issue, with rapt, hushed playing not just from the soloist but also from the excellent Scottish Chamber Orchestra under Anthony Halstead. Hugh offers substantial cadenzas not just in the first movements of each work, but in slow movements and finales too, though none is as extended as the almost-two-minute meditation in the G minor slow movement. Halstead, as a period specialist and a horn virtuoso as well as a conductor, matches his soloist in the dedication of these performances, clarifying textures and encouraging Hugh to choose speeds on the fast side, with easily flowing slow movements and outer movements which test the soloist's virtuosity to the very limit, without sounding breathless. Not just for those who know only the old Grützmacher concerto, all this will be a delightful discovery.

'Simply Baroque'
Boccherini Cello Concertos – No 5 in D, G478; No 7 in G, G480 **Bach** Cantatas: No 22, Jesus nahm zu sich die Zwölfe: Choral – Ertöt' uns durch dein' Güte; No 136, Erforsche mich, Gott, und erfahre mein Herz: Choral – Dein Blut, der edle Saft; No 147,

Herz und Mund und Tat und Leben: Choral – Jesu bleibet meine Freude; No 163, Nur jedem das Seine: Aria – Lass mein Herz die Münze sein; No 167, Ihr Menschen, rühmet Gottes Liebe: Choral – Sei Lob und Preis mit Ehren. St Matthew Passion, BWV244 – Erbarme dich. Orgel-Büchlein – Ich ruf' zu dir, BWV639. Schübler Chorales – Kommst du nun, Jesu, von Himmel herunter, BWV650. Orchestral Suite No 3 in D, BWV1068 – Air (all arr Koopman)
Yo-Yo Ma vc **Amsterdam Baroque Orchestra / Ton Koopman** hpd/org
Sony Classical SK60680 (69' · DDD)

This appealing compilation is extremely imaginative: nine movements from Bach sensitively arranged for cello and chamber orchestra, plus an attractive pair of Boccherini cello concertos. Yo-Yo Ma's Stradivarius was altered for the occasion by luthier Charles Beare, and Ma uses a Baroque bow. As superior 'light' listening goes, it's difficult to think of a happier 70 minutes' worth. It also provides an ideal 'soft-option' introduction to the sound of period instruments. The *St Matthew Passion*'s 'Erbarme dich' becomes a cleverly worked duet for violin and cello, always flowing and discreet, aided by responsive strings and a tactile lute continuo. Ton Koopman's harpsichord brushes *Jesu, Joy of Man's Desiring* into action with a flourish, answered by a mellifluous mix of solo cello, strings and winds. Bassoon and cello join forces for a swaggering 'Lass mein Herz die Münze sein', before the brief chorale 'Dein Blut, der edle Saft'. Last comes the inevitable 'Air' from the Third Orchestral Suite, tellingly arranged (as a duet for cellos) and superbly played. In fact, Koopman's 'second' cello – his lead cellist Jaap ter Linden – is every bit as eloquent as the star act.

Listening to the two Boccherini works on this marvellous CD reminds you again of Ma's uncanny technical facility, at once elegant and unselfconsciously virtuoso. Ton Koopman provides the cadenzas and the performances are pure delight.

String Quintets

String Quintets, Op 25 – No 1 in D minor, G295; No 4 in C, G298; No 6 in A minor, G300. String Quintet, Op 11 No 5 – Minuet
Europa Galante (Fabio Biondi, Enrico Casazza vns Ernesto Braucher va Maurizio Naddeo, Antonio Fantinuoli vcs)
Virgin Veritas 545421-2 (60' · DDD)

The frustration of those who seek to identify Boccherini's works by their opus numbers may end in their being taken into care by sympathetic men in white coats. The first three of the six string sextets listed in his own catalogue as Op 25 were first published as Op 36, No 4 as Op 47 No 9, and No 6 as Op 47 No 5. The six of his Op 11, from the Fifth of which the 'amputated' and very famous Minuet is taken, appeared as Op 13 and his own Op 13 became Op 20.

Thank goodness for Gérard, here also the annotator, by whom be guided when in any doubt! Given that Boccherini wrote 100 string quintets it isn't surprising that none of the three from Op 25 on this disc has any other listed recording. These three quintets serve as a persuasive introduction to his music, full of melodic invention, harmony that knows when and for how long to remain static or flowing, or ready to spring surprises, great variety of form, and a kaleidoscope of sounds that could have been imagined only by an accomplished and venturesome virtuoso – which Boccherini was of the cello.

If the music itself is persuasive it becomes irresistible in these performances on period instruments (or copies thereof) at slightly lower pitch than today's standard, wielded by players of the highest calibre and sensitivity. The Font family quartet with whom Boccherini played at the Madrid court of Don Luis must have revelled in these quintets; in these recordings we come as close to sharing that experience as it's possible to get. An absolute must.

String Quintets – in E, G275; in F minor, G348; in G minor, G351
Richard Lester vc **Vanbrugh Quartet** (Gregory Ellis, Keith Pascoe vns Simon Aspell va Christopher Marwood vc)
Hyperion CDA67287 (62' · DDD) Ⓕ**O**

With more than 100 Boccherini cello quintets to choose from, the problem for anyone wanting to make recordings is which to choose. The E major G275 (formerly Op 13 No 5) makes an obvious first choice, when the third movement is the music universally associated with the very name of Boccherini, his Minuet. It's particularly refreshing in the Vanbrugh performance to hear it set in context against the work's other three movements, with their approach, light and crisp, paying obvious tribute to period practice in the choice of tempo – far faster than one usually associates with 'Boccherini's Minuet'.

The format of a string quintet with two cellos instead of two violas was very much Boccherini's special genre. Himself a cellist, it allowed him to free at least one of the cellos from following the bass line, so as to soar lyrically. To have this fascinating music vividly recorded in such fine performances, both polished and refreshing, with Richard Lester a perfect partner for the prize-winning Vanbrugh Quartet, makes an ideal sampler disc.

String Quartets

String Quartets, Op 32 – No 3 in D, G203; No 4 in C, G204; No 5 in G minor, G205; No 6 in A, G206
Quartetto Borciani (Fulvio Luciani, Elena Ponzoni vns Roberto Tarenzi va Claudia Ravetto vc)
Naxos 8 555043 (79' · DDD) Ⓢ**→**

Boccherini was a little less indulgent in his string quartets than in his string quintets, which are more numerous: here he couldn't allow so many fanciful flights for the cello into the upper reaches of the treble clef, nor could he create textures of quite such luxuriance. But the range of invention in these four works, composed in his compositional prime in 1780, is extraordinarily wide. The gem of this group is the A major work, with its graceful 6/8 opening, its pathetic, chromatic *Andantino lentarello*, its haunting little minuet with its echoing open E strings, and its brilliant and ebullient finale. This was recorded many, many years ago by the Carmirelli Quartet (for Decca), whose Boccherini style was a model. The present group, the Quartetto Borciani, probably play it more perfectly in a sense, but the magic isn't quite so well captured. Named after the leader of the much admired Quartetto Italiano, this group play in a manner close to their model, with passion, intensity and accuracy, and their soft playing is wonderfully smooth and controlled, with a fine, veiled sound. In the quick movements they're a little sharper, more incisive in articulation than sometimes seems ideal for this music (they use modern instruments), but certainly the result is enormously spirited. This is very fine quartet playing and immensely endearing music; you can hardly ask for more.

Stabat mater

Boccherini Stabat mater, G532 (1800 vers)[a]
Astorga Stabat mater[b]
Susan Gritton, [a]**Sarah Fox** sops **Susan Bickley** mez
Paul Agnew ten [b]**Peter Harvey** bass [b]**The King's Consort Choir; The King's Consort / Robert King**
Hyperion 🔊 SACDA67108 (73' · DDD · T/t) Ⓕ**O→**

These settings of the same text by two Italian composers (more exactly, Sicilian in the case of Astorga), who spent much of their lives in Spain, vary from each other both by the different groupings of the lines into movements and by the stylistic changes that had taken place in music in the course of the at least half century that separates them. Astorga's earlier setting has a good deal more contrapuntal writing, especially in three of its four choruses, as well as some diversity of style: more ornate in the double duet 'Quis est homo' and, in particular, the extremely florid, almost operatic, final 'Amen', but gently pathetic in the instrumental introduction and the soprano solo 'Sancta mater'. Intensity of feeling is heard in the duet stanza voicing the desire to weep with the distraught Mary, and the chorus sings expressively throughout, though 'Virgo virginum praeclara' sounds altogether too cheerful, and in the initial chorus the tenor line obtrudes rather edgily. Boccherini's is by far the more remarkable and beautiful setting. Originally written in 1781 for solo soprano, it was expanded in 1800 for three solo voices: fears that this could lead to a more 'symphonic' sound are dispelled by

Robert King's use of only seven instrumental-ists. King has a fine team of vocalists who on the whole blend well, an important considera-tion since only four of the 11 sections of the work are single-voice settings. The anguished melancholy of the opening and the grave seren-ity of the ending enclose a finely planned diver-sity of treatments, from the intense 'Quae moerebat' or the lyrical 'Fac ut portem' (both admirably sung by Sarah Fox) to the vigorous 'Tui nati' or the vehemently passionate 'Fac me plagis vulnerari' (for all three singers). The performance is accomplished and polished but the recording venue tends to amplify singers' higher notes out of proportion.

William Bolcom
American b1938

Bolcom studied with Milhaud at Mills College, with Leland Smith at Stanford and with Olivier Messiaen at the Paris Conservatoire. He began teaching at the University of Michigan in 1973, a post he held until 2008. As a pianist he regularly performs with his wife, soprano Joan Morris, and they have developed an appealing and infectiously enjoyable cabaret-style presentation that crosses boundaries and genres. His works are eclectic and often highly ambitous in scale: they include an epic setting of Blake's Songs of Innocence and Experience for soloists, choirs and orchestra (1956-81). He has written three operas, eight symphonies and numerous songs. His 12 New Études for Piano won him a Pulitzer Prize in 1988.

Violin Sonatas

Complete Violin Sonatas
Solomia Soroka *vn* **Arthur Greene** *pf*
Naxos 8 559150 (77' · DDD)   Ⓢ☞

These four violin and piano sonatas cover a period of almost 40 years. Bolcom gave up violin lessons with relief at the age of about 10 when his instrument was stolen from his father's car, but he has retained a strong affection for the fiddle and the sonatas represent his more serious side rather than the rumbustious ragtimer.

The First Sonata comes from 1956, Bolcom's freshman year at the University of Washington, Seattle, but was revised later. The Second Sonata arose 20 years later, after he met jazz violinist Joe Venuti, and it was completed in memoriam. In the first movement the violin sings in a gentle bluesy manner over regular pat-terns in the piano; 'Brutal', which follows, is as tough as anything in Ives. There are conven-tional triads in both the last two movements and the whole piece affectionately recalls some of Venuti's own licks.

The other two sonatas come from the mid-1990s. The Third is subtitled *Stamba* ('Weird') and, admittedly, you never quite know what is

going to happen next. A mini-*scherzo* is a scrap of tarantella, then the finale fuses tangos and Arab music. The last one is another virtuoso piece, at times hyperactive, where everything is confi-dently delivered by this brilliant duo.

Songs of Innocence and Experience

Songs of Innocence. Songs of Experience
Christine Brewer, Measha Brueggergosman, Ilana Davidson, Linda Hohenfeld, Carmen Pelton *sops* **Joan Morris** *mez* **Marietta Simpson** *contr* **Thomas Young** *ten* **Nmon Ford** *bar* **Nathan Lee Graham** *sngr* **Peter 'Madcat' Ruth** *harc/sngr* **Michigan State University Children's Choir; Orpheus Singers; Choir, Chamber Choir, Musical Society Choral Union, Contemporary Directions Ensemble and Symphony Orchestra of Michigan University / Leonard Slatkin**
Naxos American Classics ② 8 559216/8
(138' · DDD · T)   Ⓢ☞

This is a *magnum opus* that occupied Bolcom for 25 years, starting as early as 1956. He's drawn on a wide range of musical styles to parallel Blake's method of moving from sophisticated to almost folk idioms. In some features – diatonic writing, English text and children's voices – Britten's *Spring Symphony* is in the background, but Bol-com is defined by the styles he juxtaposes with carefully calculated transitions in between. Some of the most memorable moments involve popular idioms, evoking his ragtime perform-ances or the songs he recorded so vividly with his wife Joan Morris. The word-setting is straightforward, reflecting the strophic poems, and refreshingly free from elaboration. The *Songs of Innocence* are charming and pastoral but in the *Songs of Experience* there's real anger at the human predicament.

This recording is based on a live performance with massive forces comprising 10 soloists, three choirs totalling almost 350 singers and a full symphony orchestra plus a harmonica and vari-ous extra electronic players and percussion. Nathan Lee Graham is an actor-singer who can project his catchy tunes and spoken poems; Joan Morris exercises all her magic in a range of styles, but Thomas Young seems too consist-ently declamatory. Christine Brewer is magiste-rial in numbers that reflect the modernistic side of Bolcom, and Carmen Pelton has a rare purity of sound.

This unique Blake spectacular makes a cumu-lative impact that represents Bolcom's wide sty-listic embrace at its most ambitious.

Songs

I will breathe a mountain. Casino Paradise – Night make my day; My father the gangster. Greatshot – You cannot have me now (or The Military Orgy). The Digital Wonder Watch. The Last Days of Mankind. Mary. Songs to Dance. Tillinghast Duo. Three Songs

from The Wind in the Willows. Dynamite Tonite –
When we built the church
Carole Farley sop **William Bolcom** pf
Naxos American Classics 8 559249 (64' · DDD · T)
Ⓢ**O**➔

Bolcom has always exemplified his eclectic
American heritage in a distinctly personal way.
As a pianist he's known for superb LPs of ragtime, Gershwin, Milhaud and songs with his
wife Joan Morris. This collection of his songs
with piano with Carole Farley, another performer of remarkable versatility, covers a range
of styles from various periods; there are cycles
and single songs.

Most of the accompaniments are hyperactively
virtuoso, drawing on the full compass of the
piano – a refreshing change from so much of the
literature, but you're left wondering who else
could play them like this. There are moments of
repose, some in the witty mini-cycle *Songs to
Dance* from 1989. *I will breathe a mountain* (1990)
sets 10 American women poets, each song
reflecting their personalities in a different style.
'The Fish' is an amusing poem by Elizabeth
Bishop, a helter-skelter ride as dizzy as some of
Sondheim's patter-songs. 'Messing about in
boats', one of three poems based on *The Wind in
the Willows*, makes an easy-going habanera.

This is a fascinating collection from one of
the most individual American composers,
who shouldn't be forgotten in the minimalist
onslaught. Full texts of songs are an asset, it's
vividly recorded and is delivered with effervescent enthusiasm by both performers.

Alexander Borodin   Russian 1833-1887

*Few people get two bites at the cherry but Borodin is a
rare example. No other great composer has achieved
that sobriquet while achieving equal eminence in
another, entirely different field of work. For a full-
time professional scientist to compose works of such
originality and beauty as the Polovtsian Dances
(from Prince Igor) and the String Quartet No 2 is a
minor miracle. Borodin's first published work was
not a song or a sonata but a paper, 'On the Action of
Ethyl Iodide on Hydrobenzamide and Amarine'. His
first tour of Europe was not as a concert pianist but
for scientific study.*

*His origins were as exceptional: he was the illegiti-
mate son of a Georgian prince, Ghedeanov, and the
wife of an army doctor. As was the custom of the time,
he was registered as the lawful child of one of Ghedeanov's serfs, one Porfiry Borodin. He learnt to
speak several foreign languages and was taught to
play the flute, but it was his love and natural bent for
science and, in particular, chemistry that dominated
his professional life. He graduated with honours from
the Academy of Medicine in St Petersburg in 1856
and by the mid-1860s was a professor in the Academy
of Physicians. No wonder that so much of Borodin's
music was abandoned or left incomplete at his death
– his public duties as an eminent scientist and*

*research chemist left him no time for systematic com-
position. This for Borodin was, in any case, a slow
process. Compared with Rimsky-Korsakov, his
craftsmanship was modest, but his feeling for orchestral colour and rhythm, his extraordinary melodic
gifts and innate evocative powers were the equal of
the other four Russian composers who came to be
known as 'the Mighty Handful' – Balakirev, Cui,
Mussorgsky and Rimsky-Korsakov. His meeting in
1862 with the charismatic Balakirev produced the
same effect as on the others, a passionate desire to
write music that reflected Russia and the Russian
people. In much of his music you can hear that
enchanting, unique mix of the sensuous Orient and
the melancholic Russian, the exotic Oriental strain
dominating, a characteristic that greatly appealed to
the young Debussy.*

*Borodin's wife, Ekaterina (or Catherine) Proto-
popova, whom he married in 1863, was an excellent
pianist and, as an admirer of Schumann and Wagner, exerted no little influence on her husband's
music. Liszt, too, helped his growing reputation and
championed a number of his works (Borodin was in
Germany in 1877 for scientific purposes but found
the time to drop in on the Wizard of Weimar and the
two men quickly became firm friends). Throughout
the 1870s Borodin worked fitfully on various compositions but during the last decade of his life produced
very little – the two string quartets, In the Steppes of
Central Asia and a suite for piano. After his death
(from a burst artery in the heart) Rimsky-Korsakov
and Glazunov, ever the generous colleagues, prepared or completed much of Borodin's music for performance. In 1953 Robert Wright and George For-
rest produced their musical Kismet whose themes are
almost entirely taken from Borodin's work.*

Symphonies

Symphony No 2 (two performances)   Ⓗ
[a]**NBC Symphony Orchestra / Erich Kleiber;**
[b]**Stuttgart Radio Symphony Orchestra / Carlos
Kleiber**
Hänssler Classic CD93 116 (52' · ADD)
Recorded live [a]1947, [b]1972   Ⓕ

Keen collectors may have acquired these off-air
recordings in previous, more or less illicit incarnations but, in placing them back to back,
Hänssler's authorised release allows us to make
instructive comparison between Kleiber father
and son. It's obvious here that Carlos has lifted
key interpretative features from his father's
marked-up score, and, in all probability, the
recording too. Even so, his is the more remarkable of the two performances. He takes the
music seriously, imparting a unique level of
intensity to the argument, without moulding
melodic lines with what we think of as idiomatic
'Russian' warmth.

In the first movement, both Kleibers eschew
the grandiose rhetoric; Carlos has the edge in
the development, hurtling forward with astonishing power. Surprisingly, perhaps, he makes
more of the second movement, too, even relaxing a little for the Trio's local colour where

235

Erich stiffens up. Neither *Andante* can boast a truly Russian-sounding horn but Carlos comes closer. He's also a notch faster than Erich; even if the Stuttgart players aren't always quite on top of his demands, they struggle manfully with his no doubt fanatical insistence on crisp and resilient rhythms at high speed. When everything comes together, as in the finale's dash for the finishing line, the results are sensational.

The SWR studio relay has come up reasonably well, whereas the 1947 NBC broadcast (with audience) is inevitably rather dry and limited. Enthusiasts shouldn't hesitate.

Additional recommendations

Symphony No 2[a]
Coupled with: Symphony No 3 (unfinished)[b].
Prince Igor – Overture; Polovtsian Dances[c]
[a]LSO / Martinon [b]SRO / Ansermet [c]LSO / Solti
Decca Eloquence 467 482-2DH (66' · ADD)
Recorded 1961-66) ⒷⵔⓇ

Martinon draws a thrilling performance from the LSO, an orchestra on top form. Solti's contributions are equalling thrilling – what playing!

String Quartets

String Quartets – No 1 in A; No 2 in D.
String Sextet in D minor[a]
The Lindsays (Peter Cropper, Ronald Birks vns Robin Ireland va Bernard Gregor-Smith vc) [a]**Louise Williams** va [a]**Raphael Wallfisch** vc
ASV CDDCA1143 (73' · DDD) ⒻⓄ

Borodin's two string quartets have been coupled several times, and for a long time the most idiomatic versions were those made by the Borodin Quartet, who set the standard and persuaded many that they should be heard more often. The Lindsays don't ape these interpretations: for instance, they take the *Scherzo* of No 1 much more steadily than the fleeting performance of the Borodins, more as a dance than a *scherzo*, and they tackle the rather problematic finale of No 2 after their own fashion, by means of well-judged structural emphases, making a strong and just conclusion to the work. It isn't an easy movement, and like some other parts of the quartet, such as the spectral central section of the *Scherzo*, they manage the textures beautifully.

There's a less easy flow to the opening of No 2, and sensitively as The Lindsays play the much-traduced *Andante*, it's difficult not to feel the well-loved melody coming more instinctively, less lavishly, from the Borodins. Nevertheless, these are characteristically sensitive, thoughtful interpretations from a quartet whose fine work has brought us so much.

Unusually, they find room for the two surviving movements of Borodin's String Sextet, a lively *Allegro* in which, as is often remarked, Borodin seems to be taking Mendelssohn on at his own game, and a pleasant *Andante*. It's an agreeable addition to an attractive coupling.

Prince Igor

Prince Igor
Mikhail Kit bar Igor **Galina Gorchakova** sop Yaroslavna **Gegam Grigorian** ten Vladimir **Vladimir Ognovenko** bass Prince Galitzky **Bulat Minjelkiev** bass Khan Kontchak **Olga Borodina** mez Kontchakovna **Nikolai Gassiev** ten Ovlour **Georgy Selezniev** bass Skula **Konstantin Pluzhnikov** ten Eroshka **Evgenia Perlasova** mez Nurse **Tatyana Novikova** sop Polovtsian Maiden **Kirov Opera Chorus and Orchestra / Valery Gergiev**
Philips ③ download *442 537-2PH3*
(3h 29' · DDD · N/T/t) ⒻⵔⓇ

Prince Igor, even after 18 years of work, remained unfinished at Borodin's death in 1887, and it was finally completed by Rimsky-Korsakov and Glazunov. Borodin's main problem with *Prince Igor* was the daunting task of turning what was principally an undramatic subject into a convincing stage work. In many ways he never really succeeded in this and the end result comes over more as a series of epic scenes rather than a musical drama.

Despite this, however, the impression is given of a rounded whole, and it contains some of Borodin's most poignant and moving music, rich in oriental imagery and full of vitality. Curious things happen long before the official surprises of this vitally fresh *Prince Igor*, not least in the Overture, where Gergiev takes the horn's beautiful melody at a very slow pace. Gergiev is anxious to prepare us for the weighty events which follow and his particular point with the theme is to relate it to its place in the opera as the heart of Igor's great aria. There, in league with the bass-baritonal timbre of Gergiev's prince, Mikhail Kit, it solemnly underlines the fact that this is an aria of potency frustrated, sung by a hero who spends most of the opera in captivity; and that's further emphasised by a second aria which no listener will ever have heard before. It's the most significant of the passages discovered among Borodin's papers, rejected by Rimsky-Korsakov in his otherwise sensitive tribute to Borodin's memory but specially orchestrated for this recording by Yuri Faliek.

The other problem with the *Prince Igor* we already know is the way that Act 3 rather weakly follows its much more imposing Polovtsian predecessor. Gergiev obviates both that, and the problem of too much time initially spent in Igor's home town of Putivl, by referring to a structural outline of Borodin's dating from 1883 which proposes alternating the Russian and Polovtsian acts. In the theatre, we might still want the famous Polovtsian *divertissement* as a centrepiece; but on the recording the new order works splendidly, not least because Gergiev is at his fluent best in the scenes of Galitzky's dissipation and Yaroslavna's despair, now making up the opera's second act. While Borodina executes Kontchakovna's seductive chromaticisms with astonishing breath control and focus of tone, Bulat Minjelkiev's Kontchak is a little too free and easy, at least next to Ognovenko's perfectly gauged Galitzky, a rogue who needs the extra rebellion music of the more recent version to show more threatening colours. There's just the right degree of relaxation, too, about his drunken supporters Skula and Eroshka. It takes two Russian character-singers to make sense of this pair – 'with our wine and our cunning we will never die in Russia', they tell us truthfully – and their comical capitulation on Igor's return wins respect for Borodin's daring happy-end transition here.

It's beautifully paced by Pluzhnikov, Selezniev and their conductor, and crowned by a choral cry of joy which brings a marvellous rush of tearful adrenalin. That leaves us with Gorchakova, so touching in Yaroslavna's first aria but not always projecting the text very vividly and clearly not at her best in the big scena of the last act. Still, in terms of long-term vision, orchestral detail and strength of ensemble, Gergiev is ahead of the competition.

Dmitry Bortnyansky
Ukrainian 1751-1825

Bortnyansky studied in Italy from 1769; his first operas were given there, 1776-78. Returning to Russia in 1779, he became Kapellmeister at the St Petersburg court and in 1796 director. His many Russian sacred pieces (later edited by Tchaikovsky) are notable for their Italianate lyricism and skilful counterpoint. He also wrote operas, cantatas and instrumental pieces, notably a Sinfonia concertante (1790).

Sacred Concertos

Sacred Concertos – No 17, How amiable are thy tabernacles, O Lord of hosts!; No 18, It is a good thing to give thanks unto the Lord; No 19, The Lord said unto my Lord: sit thou at my right hand; No 20, In thee, O Lord, do I put my trust; No 21, He that dwelleth in the secret place of the most high; No 22, The Lord is my light and my salvation; No 23, Blessed is the people that know the joyful sound
Russian State Symphonic Cappella / Valéry Polyansky
Chandos CHAN9840 (66' · DDD · T/t)   Ⓕ●

Bortnyansky has been mostly ignored in the West until quite recently. Tchaikovsky's disparaging comments on editing his sacred concertos also show he was not universally appreciated in his native Russia, but he has never lost his place in the repertoire of the Russian Orthodox Church and, as this series shows, these works are finely crafted pieces with an endless variety of invention.

This is Volume 3, and it contains some real gems. Concerto No 19 is a *locus classicus* of Bortnyansky's considerable lyrical power, though he also employs his neo-Baroque fugal writing to impressive effect, but No 20 is even more convincing, each movement containing a substructure characterised by different musical moods. Tchaikovsky complained that the con-

certos used 'stagey or even operatic' techniques, and that's quite true, but it's done with consummate elegance, as you may hear in No 22. The Russian State Symphonic Cappella understand this music, in all its manifestations, completely responding to its subtlest nuances.

Rutland Boughton
British 1878-1960

Boughton studied briefly at the RCM but was mostly self-taught. While teaching in Birmingham (1905-11) he developed his ideas on the basis of Wagner and William Morris socialism, and put them into practice at his Glastonbury festivals (1914-27), where several of his operas were first produced, including The Immortal Hour (1914); this had immense success when staged in London in 1922. After the collapse of the Glastonbury venture he retired to farm, write and compose, and in 1945 completed his Arthurian cycle of five operas, in which Wagnerianism gives way to a simpler folksong manner.

The Immortal Hour

The Immortal Hour
Roderick Kennedy bass Dalua **Anne Dawson** sop Etain **David Wilson-Johnson** bar Eochaidh **Maldwyn Davies** ten Midir **Geoffrey Mitchell Choir; English Chamber Orchestra / Alan G Melville**
Hyperion ② CDD22040 (125' · DDD · N/T)   Ⓜ

The Immortal Hour is part of theatrical folklore: in London in the early 1920s it ran, unprecedentedly, for 216 consecutive performances and, shortly afterwards, for a further 160 at the first of several revivals. Within a decade it had been played a thousand times. Many in those audiences returned repeatedly, fascinated by the otherworldly mystery of the plot (it concerns the love of a mortal king, Eochaidh, for the faery princess Etain and the destruction of their happiness by her nostalgic longing for the Land of the Ever Young) and by the gentle, lyrical simplicity of its music. In the bleak aftermath of 1918, with civil war in Ireland, political instability at home and the names of Hitler, Mussolini and Stalin emerging from obscurity into the headlines, what blessed escapism this blend of Celtic myth and folk-tinged pentatonic sweetness must have been. Boughton's score still has the power to evoke that world, immediately and effortlessly.

It's quiet, sweet music, muted in colour and softly plaintive, and whenever the plot demands more than this the opera sags. Midir, the visitant from the Land of the Ever Young who lures Etain away from the mortal world, really needs music of dangerously heady, Dionysiac incandescence, but Boughton's vocabulary can run to nothing more transported than the prettily lilting Faery Song and some pages of folksy lyricism with a few showy high notes. No less seriously the music has little dramatic grip. Despite all this, *The Immortal*

Hour does have a quality, difficult to define, that's genuinely alluring. It's there in the touching purity of Étain's music (and how movingly Anne Dawson sings the role). It's there in the moments of true darkness that the music achieves: Dalua, the tormented Lord of Shadow conjures up something of the sombre shudder of the supernatural world.

The performance could hardly speak more eloquently for the opera. Alan G Melville allows the music to emerge from and retreat into shadowy silences; all the principal singers are accomplished and the superb chorus has been placed so as to evoke a sense of space.

Lili Boulanger   French 1893-1918

Lili Boulanger, the younger sister of the teacher Nadia, studied at the Paris Conservatoire and won the Prix de Rome aged 19 for her Faust et Hélène. Her composing life was short but productive: most important are her psalm settings, most notably Psalm 130, Du fond de l'abîme. Her music greatly influenced Honegger.

Psalms

Psalms – 24[b]; 129[d]; 130, 'Du fond de l'abîme'[abd]. Pour les funérailles d'un soldat[cd]. D'un soir triste. D'un matin du printemps. Vieille prière bouddhique[bd]
[a]**Sonia de Beaufort** *mez* [b]**Martial Defontaine** *ten* [c]**Vincent le Texier** *bar* [d]**Namur Symphonic Chorus; Luxembourg Philharmonic Orchestra / Mark Stringer**
Timpani 1C1046 (67' · DDD · T/t)   Ⓕ❍

The name of the remarkable teacher and conductor Nadia Boulanger is famous throughout the musical world, but her sister Lili (six years younger), phenomenally gifted – she was the first woman to win the Premier Prix de Rome (while Nadia had attained only a Second Prix) – showed promise of at least equal distinction. Always of delicate health, her death at the age of 24 was a tragedy for music. Apart from works written in her early teens, which she later destroyed, her composing career lasted a mere seven years; but the quality of these compositions is arresting.

Except for parts of *D'un matin du printemps* (originally for violin and piano, and orchestrated only two months before her death), a grave, even sombre air permeates her works, which are heavily tinged with modal thinking. Her idiom is strong, with a bold harmonic sense and an individual feeling for scoring (her stirring Psalm 24, for example, has the unusual combination of brass, timpani, harp and organ with the male voices): the beatific ending of Psalm 129 is heart-easing after the earlier harshness of 'Hard as they have harried me, they have not overcome me' (words significantly applicable to her own determined spirit). Her choral works are comparable to the best of Roussel or Honegger, but her Psalm 130 (dedicated to her father's mem-

ory), with its exotic scale and chromaticisms, has more affinity with Bloch and is, without much doubt, a masterpiece. A disc not to be missed.

Faust et Hélène

D'un matin du printemps. D'un soir triste. Faust et Hélène[a]. Psalm 24[b]. Psalm 130, 'Du fond de l'abîme'[c]
[a]**Lynne Dawson** *sop* [c]**Ann Murray** *mez* [a]**Bonaventura Bottone,** [bc]**Neil MacKenzie** *tens* [a]**Jason Howard** *bar* [bc]**City of Birmingham Symphony Orchestra Chorus; BBC Philharmonic Orchestra / Yan Pascal Tortelier**
Chandos CHAN9745 (74' · DDD · T/t)   Ⓕ❍❍❍▷

This disc largely duplicates Mark Stringer's programme on the Timpani label mentioned above (inevitably, since in her mere 24 years of life Lili's output was limited). The performances here are first-class, and splendidly recorded too. The eloquent sombreness of *D'un soir triste* tugs at the heart, *D'un matin du printemps* is deliciously airy and optimistic, Psalm 24 is given tremendous attack by orchestra and chorus and the powerful Psalm 130 is presented as the masterly, heartfelt work it is. The major work here, though, is the 30-minute cantata *Faust et Hélène* in its first recording. No wonder that it won the 1913 Premier Prix de Rome: the jury must have been thunderstruck by the maturity of this entry from a 19-year-old. It blends lyricism of striking beauty, rapturous fervour, emotional anguish and tense drama with, for a young composer, an astonishing sureness of touch in overall structure, freshness of invention, technical brilliance and imaginative scoring. It seems to have inspired the present performers, among whom it's almost invidious to praise Bonaventura Bottone.

Pierre Boulez   French b1925

Boulez studied with Messiaen at the Paris Conservatoire and then with Andrée Vaurabourg (Honegger's wife) and René Leibowitz. He developed an interest in 12-tone composition. Major early scores include Le visage nuptial and le soleil des eaux, and his Second Piano Sonata of 1948. Soon Boulez was developing the concept of the 12-tone technique to embrace all of music's armoury (dynamics, mode of attack, organisation of pitch). In the 1950s he came into contact with Stockhausen, with whom he became a leader of the European avant-garde, teaching at Darmstadt from 1955 to 1967). A key work from this period is Le marteau sans maître (1954), for contralto with alto flute, viola, guitar and percussion.

In the mid-1950s Boulez took up conducting and instituted a concert series, the Domaine Musical, to provide an outlet for new music. By the mid-1960s he was widely known as a conductor, becoming chief conductor of the BBC SO (1971-74) and the New York PO (1971-78). His performing career necessarily limited the time he could devote to composition and his output reduced. Pli selon pli for soprano and orchestra

(1962) is an important work from the early 1960s though Boulez has returned to it to revise repeatedly. Other works, notably Eclat/Multiples for tuned percussion ensemble and orchestra, also remain in progress.

Since the mid-1970s Boulez has been director of the Institut de Recherche et Coordination Acoustique/Musique (IRCAM), a studio in Paris where his main work has been Répons for orchestra and digital equipment. As a conductor he continues to work with the world's greatest ensembles, and records prolifically.

Rituel in memoriam Bruno Maderna

Rituel in memoriam Bruno Maderna[a]. Eclat/Multiples[b]
[a]**BBC Symphony Orchestra,** [b]**Ensemble Intercontemporain / Pierre Boulez**
Sony Classical SMK45839 (52' · ADD/DDD)
Recorded 1976-82   Ⓜ

Whatever's involved in the 20-bit technology used by Sony Classical to enhance the original CBS recordings of these works, the result is a very immediate and clear sound-picture. The sound does justice to a disc that can be recommended without reservation: magisterial performances by fine musicians of two masterworks by a leading contemporary composer. Boulez's casting off of post-Debussian refinements in *Eclat/Multiples* is enormously invigorating, and there's little of the stately, Messiaen-like processional writing that dominates *Rituel*. Here, two very different facets of Boulez's musical personality come into mutually illuminating confrontation, and this recording is frustrating only to the extent that the work itself remains unfinished. Maybe what's most radical about Boulez is that Western music's traditional concern with preparing and achieving a definitive ending has ceased to be necessary. In which case, of course, the way in which *Rituel* draws to a close could represent a concession to convention he now regrets.

In its CD transfer *Rituel* seems more than ever in thrall to the chiming, clattering percussion spread through the orchestra, which shepherds the various instrumental groups like so many anxious guardians. The source of *Rituel* lies in Boulez's tribute to Stravinsky, and the music – a massive public act of mourning, not a private expression of grief – is in some respects more appropriate as a memorial for the great Russian than for the genial Maderna. Solemn, hieratic, carved from blocks of harmonic marble by a master musical sculptor, *Rituel* is a fitting homage for a composer who learned to keep his emotions under strict control.

Piano Sonatas

Piano Sonatas Nos 1-3
Idil Biret pf
Naxos 8 553353 (64' · DDD)   Ⓢ**Ⓞ➤**

It sometimes seems as if Boulez has spent a lifetime paying the penalty for having found com-

position so easy as a young man. The first two piano sonatas, works of his early twenties, are formidably assured in technique and tremendously rich in ideas. Those sections of the Third Sonata released for performance sound cold and tentative by comparison. Or is it that the Third Sonata's much more extreme rejection of tradition is itself a triumph, an authentic modernity that stands out the more prominently for its individualism? Such thoughts are inspired by Idil Biret's absorbing disc. In the first movement of the First Sonata the broader picture proves to be well fleshed out, the argument kept on the move, the young composer's impatience and arrogance palpable in Biret's steely touch and the rather dry but never harsh recorded sound.

The Second Sonata is no less confidently played. Its power suggests why such experiments as No 3 represents could never be a last word for Boulez. This disc isn't the first to bring us the three sonatas together, but Biret's musical persuasiveness, and the up-to-date sound, earn it a strong recommendation.

Pli selon pli

Pli selon pli
Christine Schäfer sop
Ensemble Intercontemporain / Pierre Boulez
DG download 471 344-2GH (70' · DDD · N/T/t)
                                                        Ⓕ**Ⓞ➤**

This is the third recording of *Pli selon pli*, with the Ensemble Intercontemporain expanded to 57 players, fitting the composer's definitive conception of the work as enhanced chamber music. Moreover, this is in effect a first recording, since it incorporates the revisions which Boulez made to the first and fourth movements during the 1980s. The recording was, as he wryly notes, the result of assiduous preparation, with no insecurity or 'panic'. It's a remarkably polished, gravely expressive account, as if he now sees his 'portrait of Mallarmé' more as a ritual homage to the radical 19th-century poet than as a multivalent, urgent, even angry sketch of the kind of intransigent creativity that few of Boulez's contemporaries were committed to at the time of the work's genesis (1957-60). But, even without panic, there can be no such thing as a sanitised, lushly comforting *Pli selon Pli*. The music remains Boulez's most extended engagement with the modernist aesthetic.

The recording is technically immaculate, with the intricate tapestry woven around guitar, mandolin and harps and the labyrinthine interactions between families of flutes, horns and lower strings especially well managed. Christine Schäfer sings serenely and securely, with an admirable poetic presence. Although you can imagine other performances recapturing more of the score's original fire and fury, this is an imposing representation of a work which sums up the composer's vision of art and life in the years before he found his way to a viable electro-acoustic technique and a more stable view of musical structure.

Pli selon pli[a]. Les soleil des eaux[b]. Le visage nuptial[c].
Figures, Doubles, Prismes
[abc]**Phyllis Bryn-Julson** sop [c]**Elisabeth Laurence** mez
[bc]**BBC Singers; BBC Symphony Orchestra /**
Pierre Boulez
Warner Classics Apex ② 2564 62083-2
(129' · DDD · T/t)   ⑧●❍❍❍❶

 This is a super-budget-price reissue of four of Boulez's most imposing earlier works. True, the 1981 *Pli selon pli* doesn't give you his most recent thoughts on his endlessly evolving Mallarmé portrait – for that you need the DG account reviewed above. But this BBC version, a *Gramophone* Award-winner in 1983, remains a very satisfying document of its time. A special strength of the set as a whole is the vividness with which it demonstrates what has been lost in Boulez's complete abandonment of writing for the voice since the 1980s.

The large-scale cantata *Le visage nuptial*, originally composed in 1946, but performed here in the revised version from 1988-89, has an expressive incandescence and a sustained dramatic power that not only reconcile you to René Char's convoluted verse but provoke the thought that Boulez might, after all, be contemporary music's greatest opera composer manqué. The BBC Singers have have probably never done anything finer on disc.

More subversive dynamism can be heard in the expansive, eruptive monumentality of the orchestral *Figures, Doubles, Prismes*, strikingly enigmatic in its commitment to strongly sustained oppositions, and bringing back the composer's own 1985 reading. Add to all this the fascinating feline glitter of *Le soleil des eaux* and you have a 'portrait de Boulez' of exceptional quality.

Additional recommendation

Le marteau sans maître[a]. Dérive 1 & 2
[a]**Summers** contr **EIC / Pierre Boulez**
DG download 477 5327GH (69' · DDD · T/t) ⑤●❍❍❶
This is notable for a new recording of *Le marteau sans maître*: a score now half a century old and sounding more urgently volatile than ever in this superbly crafted performance. With the finest present-day sound quality, this DG release is outstanding in every way: try and find a CD version!

York Bowen   British 1884-1961

Bowen studied at the Royal College of Music, London, played the violin and horn, and became known as a fine pianist and a productive composer who wrote in a Romantic style and in many forms. Sorabji considered that he wrote for the piano 'with the mastery of Rachmaninov and Medtner', and Saint-Saëns, hearing him aged 19, thought him 'the most remarkable of the young British composers'. As a pianist he recorded the first ever disc of Beethoven's Fourth Piano Concerto, and performed with many leading players including Kreisler, Szigeti and Zimbalist. He taught at the Royal Academy, being elected a Fellow aged 23 and named Professor at 25. As well as numerous chamber works and works for solo piano, he also wrote three piano concertos. His music is at last enjoying a deserved revival thanks to the efforts of Hyperion, Dutton and Chandos.

Concertos

Piano Concertos[a] – No 2, 'Concertstück', Op 17;
No 3, 'Fantasia', Op 23. Symphonic Fantasia, Op 16
[a]**Michael Dussek** pf
BBC Concert Orchestra / Vernon Handley
Dutton Epoch CDLX7187 (75' · DDD) Ⓜ

The Second and Third Piano Concertos, together with the ambitious *Symphonic Fantasia*, make a fine follow-up to the coupling of the First Piano Concerto and Violin Concerto. Such largesse deserves the highest praise and it is easy to see a wry if grateful smile crossing Bowen's face if he were alive as he remembered his dismissal by modernists who viewed him as little better than a seashell washed ashore in a ruthlessly unaccommodating age.

Today, Bowen's unapologetic romanticism has found several champions taken by his warmth and sincerity and an open-hearted nostalgia for less brittle, over-sophisticated times. How hard it is to resist the appeal of the Second Concerto's *Lento espressivo*. How easy to imagine an elegantly attired audience greeting the finale's virtuoso close with gloved plaudits, sighing with delight over present if fast-receding conservative values. The rippling charm of the Third Concerto's central *Andante grazioso* and the finale's sunlit capers are sure to please.

So, too, is the *Symphonic Fantasia*, an ideal ballet score where the third movement's nodal and expressive centre is countered by the fifth movement's proud ceremonial stance. All this is superbly performed by Vernon Handley while Michael Dussek plays with brilliant facility and the warmest musical commitment. Dutton's sound is excellent.

Piano Concertos – No 3, 'Fantasia', Op 23; No 4,
Op 88
Danny Driver pf
BBC Scottish Symphony Orchestra /
Martyn Brabbins
Hyperion CDA67659 (61' · DDD) ⑤●❍❶

Sorabji, in the final essay of *Mi Contra Fa*, declared York Bowen to be 'at the present time [1947], the one English composer whose work can justly be said to be that of a great Master of the [piano]'. Hearing these two works, it's hard to deny that Sorabji had a point.

It takes a particular kind of pianistic sensibility to take up Bowen's virtuoso challenges and 'sell' them. Danny Driver certainly lives up to his surname. He, Brabbins and the punchy Scottish orchestra play Bowen as if he were standard repertoire with the added zest of a live performance. The 1908 four-movements-in-one Third Concerto (aka *Fantasia*), with its surging climaxes and soaring themes, offers 17 minutes of instant gratification, though it's a pity Hyperion did not provide separate tracks for the work's distinct sections.

The much longer (42'53") Fourth Concerto (1937) is generally darker in character, no less attractive but even more rewarding. The writing veers between magical impressionism and passionate bravura outbursts couched in Straussian orchestral textures. Thrilling stuff. Driver, again, is firmly in the spotlight. This is his first recording for Hyperion. His recording of the complete York Bowen piano sonatas is reviewed below.

Bowen Viola Concerto **C Forsyth** Viola Concerto
Lawrence Power va BBC Scottish Symphony
Orchestra / Martyn Brabbins
Hyperion CDA67546 (63' · DDD)   ⓕ❍❍❍❍▸

During the decade leading up to the First World War, York Bowen, one of the brightest and most prolific young talents in British music, produced no fewer than three piano concertos, two symphonies, a concert overture, *Symphonic Fantasia*, *Concertstücke* for piano and orchestra and a tone-poem, *The Lament of Tasso*. His exquisitely polished and sure-footed Viola Concerto in C minor was written for Lionel Tertis (viola professor at the Royal Academy of Music), who first performed it in March 1908. Lasting nearly 36 minutes, each of its three movements serves up a heady flow of intoxicating melody, all clothed in the deftest orchestral garb (there's a definite Russian tang to proceedings – Bowen clearly knew and loved his Tchaikovsky, Borodin and Rimsky-Korsakov). This new performance is beyond criticism. Not only does Lawrence Power effortlessly surmount every technical challenge, he forms a scintillating partnership with Martyn Brabbins and an uncommonly well-prepared BBC Scottish SO.

A pupil of Stanford, Greenwich-born Cecil Forsyth (1870-1941) played the viola in Henry Wood's Queen's Hall Orchestra (as, indeed, did Bowen) before emigrating to the USA in 1914. His G minor Concerto (in all likelihood the first for viola by a British composer) was premiered in 1903 by the French virtuoso (and its dedicatee) Emile Férir. Beside its its present companion it strikes a rather more conventional note, but remains an appealingly lyrical and sturdily crafted achievement. The performance is everything one could desire, and the recording is wonderfully ripe and glowing.

Violin Concertoᵃ. Piano Concerto No 1ᵇ
ᵃ**Lorraine McAslan** vn ᵇ**Michael Dussek** pf
BBC Concert Orchestra / Vernon Handley
Dutton Epoch CDLX7169 (64' · DDD)   Ⓜ

York Bowen's Viola Concerto was quite a discovery last year so getting to know his Violin Concerto was an intriguing prospect. Finished in 1913 but not performed until 1920, it was briefly taken up by May Harrison but failed to establish itself. This exemplary first commercial recording reveals another substantial, exquisitely scored and unjustly forgotten Bowen gem which lovers of the Tchaikovsky, Elgar and Delius concertos should waste no time in seeking out.

The slow movement proves especially fetching, evincing a most engaging poetry and warm-hearted lyricism, while the finale serves up many opportunities for virtuoso display and ends with the clinching return of the horns' rousing call to arms. Lorraine McAslan gives a technically brilliant, sweet-toned account. Vernon Handley, too, well and truly in his element, secures memorably responsive, glowingly affectionate playing from the BBC Concert Orchestra.

The First Piano Concerto was written a decade earlier and first performed by the 19-year-old composer at London's Queen's Hall in December 1903. If less distinctive than its bedfellow, it's a thoroughly attractive piece, whose cheeky central *Scherzo* (which nods towards Saint-Saëns) precedes an extended, at times unashamedly Tchaikovskian, finale (with an exceedingly catchy main theme). This performance is outstanding, with Michael Dussek admirably stylish and Handley offering the most malleable support. The Watford Town Hall production marries amplitude and warmth to realistic balance.

String Quartets

String Quartets – No 2 in D minor, Op 41;
No 3 in G, Op 46b. Phantasy Quintet, Op 93ᵃ
ᵃ**Timothy Lines** bcl **Archaeus Quartet** (Ann Hooley, Bridget Davey vns Elizabeth Turnbull va Martin Thomas vc)
British Music Society BMS426CD (70' · DDD)   ⓕ

Published in 1922 after scooping a Carnegie Trust Award, York Bowen's Second String Quartet proves a most endearing discovery. Brimful of sweet-toothed yet never cloying melodic charm and written with consummate virtuosity for the medium, it's a fluent, poised and readily assimilable creation which merits immediate investigation by anyone with a penchant for, say, Bax or Korngold. Its unpublished successor was probably conceived about the same time and again boasts a wealth of big-hearted, felicitous invention. Both works follow the same classical ground-plan, comprising two soundly constructed, sonata-form outer movements which frame a tenderly reflective slow movement in straightforward ternary form, and both certainly merit their resuscitation here. A similar technical mastery, harmonic pungency and generously lyrical cast inform Bowen's later *Phantasy Quintet* for the unusual combination of bass clarinet and string quartet, a single-movement essay of considerable imagination and frequently haunting beauty.

The Archaeus Quartet are sterling advocates of all this rewarding material. Timothy Lines, too, contributes most sensitively in the Quintet, and the sound is vivid to match. A stimulating and enjoyable release.

Viola Sonatas

Viola Sonatas – No 1 in C minor; No 2 in F.
Phantasy, Op 54
James Boyd va **Bengt Forsberg** pf
Dutton Epoch CDLX7126 (72' · DDD)   Ⓜ

A valuable survey of three early Bowen offerings fashioned for that great British viola player, Lionel Tertis (1876-1975). Not surprisingly, given Tertis's phenomenal technique and tone-production, each piece here makes exceptional demands. Happily, James Boyd is fully equal to the task. What's more, he forges a marvellously eloquent alliance with Bengt Forsberg, their playing brimful of affectionate understanding while retaining a sense of freshness in discovery.

Both sonatas date from 1905 and were premiered at London's Aeolian Hall by Tertis, with the 21-year-old composer at the piano, in May 1905 and February 1906 respectively. Described by its dedicatee as 'a vivacious and light-hearted work', the First Sonata comprises an expansive and confident *Allegro moderato*, a songful slow movement in ternary form (whose principal melody hints at Lowell Mason's 1856 hymntune for *Nearer, my God, to Thee*) and an unusually meaty finale, where sheer high spirits win out in the end. Its F major successor follows pretty much the same pattern, though the slow movement now quarries a darker vein of expression, while the concluding *Allegro giocoso* yields plenty of opportunity for cheeky display. Boasting admirable sound and balance, this is a gem of a disc.

Viola Sonatas – No 1; No 2. Romances – in D flat major; in A major. Fantasia, Op 41 No 1ª. Phantasy, Op 54. Allegro de concert. Melody for the G string. Melody for the C string. Rhapsody **Beethoven/ Bowen** Piano Sonata, 'Moonlight', Op 27 No 2 – I
Lawrence Power va **Simon Crawford-Phillips** pf with ªPhilip Dukes, ªJames Boyd, ªScott Dickinson vas
Hyperion ② CDA67651/2 (123' · DDD)   ⒻⓄ

Inspired by the incomparable Lionel Tertis, his friend and colleague at the Royal Academy of Music, Bowen wrote music for the viola of such richness and fantasy that its long neglect is one of music's saddest mysteries. True, Bowen's delight in resurrecting the glamour of the past and archaisms too long uncherished, sat uneasily with the engulfing modernism of his age. Bowen, like Medtner, had little wish to move with the times, and yet if his music is endearingly old-fashioned it is also full of surprises and of a harmonic language and idiom peculiarly his own. Only a puritan could fail to respond to Bowen's warmth and exquisite craftsmanship in, for example the *Fantasia*, two *Romances* and the

two *Melodies* where his sense of elegy takes on a double meaning: the aftermath of the war and the loss of what he saw as the departure of civilised creativity.

Both discs are beautifully planned, opening with sizeable sonatas and continuing with shorter works before ending with more large-scale offerings, and the performances could hardly be more glowing. Bowen's writing for both instruments is more than demanding yet nothing detracts from Lawrence Power's and Simon Crawford-Phillips's enviable fluency and achievement. Once again Hyperion has hit the jackpot in a much-needed revival and the sound and balance are exemplary.

Piano works

Complete Piano Sonatas
Danny Driver pf
Hyperion CDA67751/2 (119' · DDD)   Ⓕ②ⓄⓄⓄⒹ▸

No better example of Hyperion's founding principles could be imagined than this disc of three premiere recordings contributing to the first survey of the complete sonatas by an unjustly neglected composer. There really is no longer any excuse for pianists to ignore the music of York Bowen or for concert promoters to reject it as obscure music by a minor composer.

Francis Pott provides a superb and perceptive overview of the six works in his accompanying booklet, noting the development of (and various influences on) Bowen. One catches glimpses in the early Sonatas Nos 1 and 2 (*c*1901) and No 3 (1912) of Chopin, Mendelssohn and most notably MacDowell (the slow movement of the B minor Sonata is reminiscent of "AD MDCXX", one of the *Sea Pieces*). Sonata No 4 appears to be lost. The *Short Sonata*, Op 35 No 1 (1922) has hints of Delius. In Nos 5 (1923) and 6 (1961) one at last finds some justification in Bowen being labelled the 'English Rachmaninov'.

Danny Driver is the ideal advocate for this glorious music, playing with razor-sharp articulation and a rich, organ-like sonority while characterising Bowen's ruminative slow movements with tender introspection and an improvisatory air, a particular pleasure of these two discs. Driver is an artist who is able to transcend the sterile surrounds of the studio and give 'real' performances.

Piano Sonata No 5, Op 72. Fantasia, Op 132. Nocturne, Op 78. Four Bagatelles, Op 147. Siciliano e Toccatina, Op 128. Two Intermezzi, Op 141. Two Preludes. Ripples, Op 100 No 1. Evening Calm
Joop Celis pf
Chandos CHAN10410 (74' · DDD)   Ⓕ

The major offering here is York Bowen's Fifth Sonata, music on a heroic scale, heavily indebted to Rachmaninov's Second Sonata, music that had clearly got under Bowen's skin. Yet the cross-fertilisation of Russian and English idioms is richly personal and such superbly crafted writing is a constant reminder of a composer in love with the piano. Again, as old-timers will recall, Bowen was a master pianist in his own and other people's music. The central *Andante* broods with a wholly Russian sense of romantic darkness and despondency, and the finale's dazzling rhetoric includes a ghostly recall of the first movement's fanfares before ending in a blaze of virtuoso glory. Not everything speaks with this level of inspiration yet all this music is composed with an innate understanding of a sheerly pianistic magic.

Bowen's *Fantasia* is hugely ambitious and *Evening Calm* also outstays its welcome. But the First Intermezzo's Schumannesque charm is beguiling and so is the delightfully off-centre *Siciliano e Toccatina*. However, not a single piece on this excellently recorded disc could be in more sensitive or magisterial hands. Joop Celis confirms his stature at every point.

Further listening

Bowen Flute Sonata
Coupled with: **Arnold** Flute Sonata
L Berkeley Sonatina **Hamilton** Spring Days
D Matthews Duet Variations **Maw** Sonatina
Khaner fl **Abramovic** pf
Avie AV0016 (65' · DDD)   Ⓕ

The Bowen Sonata is a real discovery; a strong and characterful piece full of Gallic lyricism, underpinned with ample, and always interesting, keyboard writing. A fascinating programme.

William Boyce   British 1711-1779

Boyce was a St Paul's Cathedral chorister and an organ pupil of Maurice Greene after his voice broke. From 1734 he held organist's posts in London and from 1736 was a composer to the Chapel Royal, writing anthems and services. He was named Master of the King's Music in 1755. Boyce was among the most highly thought-of English composers of his day, though his music had become somewhat old-fashioned by the time of his death. Deafness blighted his performing career, and when he could no longer play the organ he devoted himself to the compilation Cathedral Music, started by his teacher, Maurice Greene – many of the pieces are still used in the Anglican service today. His reputation waned during the 19th century and modern interest in his music was created by Constant Lambert who edited and often performed Boyce's works, notably the Symphonys.

Eight Symphonys, Op 2

Eight Symphonys, Op 2   Ⓟ
The English Concert / Trevor Pinnock hpd
Archiv 419 631-2AH (60' · DDD)   ⒻⓄ▸

William Boyce's eight Symphonys (his own spelling) aren't symphonies in the modern sense, but a collection, issued for concert use, of overtures he had composed over nearly 20 years for theatre pieces and court odes. They represent English 18th-century music at its unpretentious best, notably in their formal unorthodoxy. The performances are a delight – cleanly articulated, decisive in rhythm, just in tempo. The French overture-like movements that open Nos 6 and 7 are crisp and brilliant; the more Italianate first movements, like those of Nos 2 and 4, have a splendid swing. And the tone of gentle melancholy behind the fine, expansive D minor first movement of No 8 is particularly well caught. Three of the symphonies have middle movements marked *Vivace*, which often leads conductors into unsuitably quick tempi; but Pinnock obviously knows that, in 18th-century England, *Vivace* meant a speed not much above *Andante*, and for once these movements make proper sense: they're lively, to be sure, but not fast. This disc comfortably surpasses any rivals in both style and accomplishment. The sound of the modest-sized band is brightly and truly reproduced.

Eight Symphonys
Aradia Ensemble / Kevin Mallon
Naxos 8 557278 (62' · DDD)   ⓈⒷ▸

While Trevor Pinnock (see above) or Christopher Hogwood might justifiably retain benchmark status, Kevin Mallon and his Canadian period-instrument Aradia Ensemble offer a nicely judged and pleasantly played alternative, vibrantly conveying the difficult blend of dance-like wit and muscular energy in Boyce's music.

Apart from the list of participants being wildly incorrect (a choir where none exists, horns overlooked, no organ and uncredited harpsichord), the only mild reservation is that the over-reverberant recorded sound conceals occasional problems with intonation and washes everything in a mushy soup that does not always assist transparency and clarity. However, the acoustic lends an attractive bloom to the horns in Symphony No 4, and the effect of the resonant trumpets and timpani in Symphony No 5 is invigorating. If you are curious about Boyce's orchestral music, then this is an ideal place to start.

Johannes Brahms   German 1833-1897

Eduard Marxsen, who taught the young Brahms, heard of Mendelssohn's death in 1847 and said: 'A master of the art is gone; a greater one arises in Brahms', a remarkably accurate prediction to make about a 14-year-old student. (The two remained friends for the rest of Marxsen's life and Brahms dedicated his great Piano Concerto in B flat to him.) Brahms's father was an impecunious double-bass player, eventually good enough for the Hamburg Philharmonic. At the age of six Brahms was discovered to have perfect pitch and a natural talent for the piano. He made his first public appearance playing chamber music at the age of 10. A passing American impresario heard him and offered the wunderkind an American tour, but his teacher Otto Cossel forbade it before turning him over to Marxsen.

To supplement his income, the teenager played in taverns and, some say, bordellos. It remains a moot point whether this period left its psychological scars. His parents were an ill-matched couple and he frequently witnessed their violent arguments as a child; some have suggested he may have been impotent. Whatever the reason, Brahms never married and seems to have resorted to prostitutes when the need arose. In the 1880s, so the story goes, Brahms entered a somewhat dubious establishment and was accosted by a well-known prostitute with the greeting 'Professor, play us some dance music,' whereupon the great composer sat down at the piano and entertained the assembled company. Brahms sublimated his love and desire for women in his music. 'At least,' he said, recognising his awkwardness with women, 'it has saved me from opera and marriage.'

He began to compose, too, but when he met up with the Hungarian violinist Eduard Reményi, Brahms leapt at the chance of becoming his accompanist and off they went on tour. It proved to be a fortuitous move. In Hanover, he was introduced to Reményi's old student friend, violinist Joseph Joachim, only 22 years old but already Konzertmeister to the King. Brahms and Joachim formed a firm friendship and Joachim, who was part of the Liszt circle, took Brahms with him to Weimar to meet the great man. Of more significance was Joachim's introduction to Robert and Clara Schumann, then living in Düsseldorf. There's a brief note in Schumann's diary recording the event. It reads simply: 'Brahms to see me (a genius).' In his last article for the Neue Zeitschrift für Musik, Schumann wrote of Brahms as a young eagle and predicted great things from him. In fact, so enamoured did the Schumanns become of the young man that they invited him to move into their house. Schumann introduced Brahms to his publishers Breitkopf und Härtel who published his early works. When Schumann tried to commit suicide, Brahms was there at Clara's side to help and comfort; he was there with her when Schumann died in 1856.

There's no doubt that Brahms was in love with Clara but doubtful whether the relationship ever developed into anything more than a platonic friendship. They decided to go their separate ways after Robert's death but Brahms's correspondence with her reveals a deep spiritual and artistic affinity – it was probably the most profound human relationship Brahms ever experienced. Only a few years later, he was castigated by his friends for compromising a young singer named Agathe von Siebold. She inspired many songs and attracted him immensely but after he became engaged to her he wrote: 'I love you. I must see you again. But I cannot wear fetters...' Agathe naturally broke off the engagement.

Meanwhile, he had written his magnificent First Piano Concerto. It was hissed at its premiere in 1859 and the year later he had a further disappointment

when he was turned down for the conductorship of the Hamburg Philharmonic. Then an invitation to conduct in Vienna, his mother's death in 1865 and father's remarriage, loosened his ties with Hamburg. Eventually, in 1872, he decided to make the Austrian capital his base. His German Requiem and Alto Rhapsody from the late 1860s made him famous but it was the next two decades which saw the flowering of his genius. He was offered the conductorship of the famed Gesellschaft der Musikfreunde in 1872 but was so consumed with the need to compose that he resigned in 1875. Within three years he had completed his Symphonies Nos 1 and 2, the Violin Concerto and the Academic Festival and Tragic overtures. From the rigours of conducting and playing his music all over Europe, Brahms escaped every summer to the country, either to stay in Baden-Baden where Clara Schumann had a house or to Ischl where Johann Strauss II had a villa (the two men were good friends).

In 1878 he was taken to Italy by a surgeon friend, the first of many visits to a country he came to love. Masterpiece followed masterpiece in the 1880s: the B flat Piano Concerto, the Third and Fourth Symphonies and the Double Concerto for violin and cello. In the 1890s he abandoned larger forms and concentrated on chamber music and more intimate, personal piano works, all tinged with nostalgia and a warm, steady glow of autumnal romanticism. Perhaps they reflected a growing realisation of life's transience: it seemed as though all those who mattered to him were dying and when Clara Schumann too died in 1896, it affected him deeply. His appearance deteriorated, his energy disappeared and he was persuaded to see a doctor. Only months after Clara's death, he too had gone, like his father, from cancer of the liver.

Brahms had much in common with Beethoven. Short in stature, unable or unwilling to have lasting relationships with women, bad tempered and lovers of the countryside, they even walked about Vienna in the same way with head forward and hands clasped behind the back. Like Beethoven, Brahms had an unhappy childhood and was a prickly, uncompromising man. He nevertheless had a wonderfully generous side to him when the mood took him – his help and encouragement to young composers such as Dvořák and Greig who needed a leg up. He was a sociable man who attracted many friends but he could be quite remarkably tactless on occasion, blunt to the point of gruffness, grumpy and cruelly sarcastic in later life, characteristics that didn't make his relations with other people any easier. After one party in Vienna, it's said Brahms left saying, 'If there's anybody here I haven't insulted, I apologise.'

Younger members of the New German School, the Liszt- and Wagnerites, sneered at his rock-like loyalty to classical thought and design. Some, like Hugo Wolf, a Wagner follower, bitterly attacked Brahms. Tchaikovsky had no time for him at all. 'I have played over the music of that scoundrel Brahms,' he confided in his diary. 'What a giftless bastard!' One element is lacking in his music and that is wit. 'When Brahms is in extra good spirits,' quipped his friend the violinist Hellmesberger, 'he sings "The grave is my joy".' It's all serious stuff, there's no superficial prettiness and few hints at empty virtuosity in his keyboard writing – it's all logically worked out by a meticulous, perfectionist craftsman. Some find him a *turgid Teutonic. Certainly a lot of his music, especially his early work, can sound thick-textured and plodding. But Brahms's many masterpieces have a confidence and ebullience, an irresistible lyricism and melodic charm that have no sign of losing their appeal and rich rewards more than a century after his death.*

Piano Concertos

No 1 in D minor, Op 15; **No 2** in B flat, Op 83

Piano Concertos Nos 1 & 2
Nelson Freire pf **Gewandhaus Orchestra, Leipzig / Riccardo Chailly**
Decca ② 475 7637DX2 (95' · DDD). Recorded live
Ⓜ❶❶❶❶➔

This is the Brahms piano concerto set we've been waiting for. Nelson Freire and Riccardo Chailly offer interpretations that triumphantly fuse immediacy and insight, power and lyricism, and incandescent virtuosity that leaves few details unturned, yet always with the big picture in clear sight. The D minor's headlong opening *tutti* updates Szell/Cleveland's patented fire and brimstone with a warmth of tone that manages to convey both line and mass as few others do. Timpani and brass proudly step up to the fore in both concertos, while frequently buried lines emerge from the gnarly textures with uncommon clarity and specificity. In Chailly's hands, a genuine chamber music aesthetic consistently governs the lustrous warmth of Brahms's underrated orchestrations, to say nothing of the heights to which the conductor has led his revitalised Leipzig Gewandhaus ensemble.

Balanced within the orchestra as an equal partner, Freire is completely on top of and inside both works' solo parts, from No 1's fervent yet cogently shaped octave outbursts and the B flat's graceful, light-footed finale to both slow movements' unforced simplicity, organic flow and freedom from sentimentality. No doubt that the presence of an audience fuels the palpable give and take between soloist and conductor. Just as the Szell/Cleveland cycles with Serkin and Fleisher, and Gilels/Jochum (reviewed below) were benchmarks in their day, these gorgeously engineered, stunningly executed and temperamentally generous performances will stand as points of reference for generations to come.

Piano Concertos Nos 1 & 2.
Seven Piano Pieces, Op 116
Emil Gilels pf **Berlin Philharmonic Orchestra / Eugen Jochum**
DG The Originals ② 447 446-2GOR2 (125' · ADD)
Recorded 1972-75
Ⓜ❶❶❶➔

The booklet-notes make reference to the original *Gramophone* review, in which Gilels and Jochum were praised for 'a rapt songfulness that in no way detracts from Brahms's heroism, and so comes

BRAHMS PIANO CONCERTOS – IN BRIEF

Nelson Freire
Gewandhaus Orchestra, Leipzig / Riccardo Chailly
Decca ② 475 7637DX2 (95' · DDD)   Ⓜ❶❶❶❶➔
A magnificent achievement that finds a pianist of enormous integrity supported by a conductor with excellent Brahms credentials at the helm of a newly reinvigorated orchestra. This set – a Brahms concerto set for the new millennium – took *Gramophone*'s Record of the Year Award in 2007.

Emil Gilels
Berlin PO / Eugen Jochum
DG ② 447 446-2GOR2 (125' · ADD)   Ⓜ❶❶❶➔
This is a modern classic: awe-inspiring piano playing and accompaniments of weight, power and great sympathy. Unmissable.

Rudolf Serkin
Cleveland Orchestra / George Szell
Sony Classical ② 82796 93447-2, 07464 48166-2 (64' & 67' · ADD)   Ⓑ
A fine memento of a great partnerhsip and one of the glories of the US orchestral scene, the Cleveland Orchestra. These are wonderfully intense performances but the sound takes a bit of getting used to. Available in various couplings: here Mendelssohn and solo Brahms.

Stephen Hough
BBC SO / Sir Andrew Davis
Virgin Classics ② 561412-2 (100' · DDD)   Ⓑ➔
Hough's set of these two mighty concertos is remarkably successful, with delicacy matched by considerable power, but there's a luminosity here that's very attractive.

Daniel Barenboim
Philharmonia, Vienna PO / Sir John Barbirolli
EMI ② 572649-2 (146' · ADD)   Ⓜ
An often overlooked pair of performances but a superb one none the less. The First Concerto is magnificent, with the partnership of pianist and conductor at its most inspired. There's a wonderful freshness about both finales, and the 1960s sound is excellent.

Emanuel Ax
Chicago SO / James Levine, Boston SO / Bernard Haitink
Sony Classical ② 88697 03510-2 (134' · DDD)   Ⓑ
A recoupling that finds Ax purveying poetry and passion in equal measure. The First, with Levine in charge, is magnificent, and though Haitink can be a little generalised there is much to win the heart in the performance of No 2.

BRAHMS VIOLIN CONCERTO – IN BRIEF

Joshua Bell; Cleveland Orchestra / Christoph von Dohnányi
Decca 475 6703-5DF2   Ⓕ❍◗
Sweet-toned and subtle, Bell is an appealing soloist with a winning spontaneity that reveals great depths of feeling. Dohnányi displays his Brahmsian credentials to fine effect. (Coupled with the Schumann, Tchaikovsky and Wieniawski No 2.)

Jascha Heifetz; Chicago SO / Fritz Reiner   Ⓗ
RCA mono 88888 03034-2   Ⓕ❍◗
This is a high-octane, high-velocity performance in which Heifetz's legendary virtuosity is matched by some staggering playing by the Chicago orchestra under Reiner. This is no autumnal vision of the work but an athletic, graceful display. (Coupled with the Tchaikovsky.)

Gil Shaham; Berlin Philharmonic Orchestra / Claudio Abbado
DG 469 529-2GH   Ⓕ❑◗
Coupled with the Double Concerto, this is one of the most impressive of modern versions, intense and full of imagination. Recorded live, it shows Shaham at his spontaneous best.

David Oistrakh; London Philharmonic Orchestra / Norman Del Mar
BBC Legends BBCL4102-2   Ⓕ❑◗
This is great violin playing: Oistrakh is on superb form, playing with his customary warmth. Well accompanied by Norman Del Mar, this builds up to a finale of thrilling power. Inevitably, the 1960 recording shows its years.

Julia Fischer; Netherlands Philharmonic Orchestra / Yakov Kreizberg
Pentatone ⊛ PTC5186 066   Ⓕ❍
A hugely impressive reading of this huge concerto from one of the brightest of the new generation of violin stars. Kreizberg is a model accompanist and together with his characterful young soloist gives a performance that demands to be heard.

Ginette Neveu; Philharmonia Orchestra / Issay Dobrowen   Ⓗ
Dutton mono CDBP9710   Ⓜ
Dutton improves on EMI's own transfer of this magnificent performance, giving it a winning warmth and body. Neveu was a commanding violinist and there's never a moment's doubt that she has the measure (and beyond) of this great work. Her technique is astounding and the accuracy of her playing an object lesson in great musicianship.

closer to that unique and complex combination of attitudes that for me is Brahms more than any other performances of these concertos I have ever heard, on records or otherwise'. It might be added that Jochum and the Berlin Philharmonic make plain sailing where others struggle with choppy cross-currents (admittedly sometimes to Brahms's advantage) and that the recordings don't sound their age. Other interpreters have perhaps probed a little deeper here and there; neither concerto rests content with a single interpretation, the Second especially. As for the Seven Piano Pieces, Gilels viewed the opus as a single piece, a musical novella in several chapters.

Brahms Piano Concerto No 1, Op 15 **Brahms/ Schoenberg** Piano Quartet No 1, Op 25
Daniel Barenboim pf **Berlin Philharmonic Orchestra / Sir Simon Rattle**
EuroArts 𝐃𝐕𝐃 202 0108 (102' · NTSC · 16:9 · PCM Stereo 5.1 · 0)   Ⓕ

These extraordinary performances were recorded live at the Herodes Atticus Odeon in Athens in 2004 and offer the first musical encounter between Daniel Barenboim and Simon Rattle. One-time rivals for the post of principal conductor of the Berlin Philharmonic, they here unite, happy to pay tribute to each other in a performance of Brahms's First Piano Concerto of an epic grandeur and raw emotional intensity. Barenboim, pianist, conductor and political activist, has clearly reached the pinnacle of a dazzling career that has ranged from prodigy to the fullest maturity. Caught on this form, few musicians can approach him in stature. Rattle launches the opening *tutti* with an explosive force, and after an oddly stiff and self-conscious entry he quickly declares his true status, playing with a dark eloquence and with a breadth and range of inflection that allows him to savour every detail. Rarely can the first movement's coda have emerged with such frenzied emotion, and here in particular both Barenboim and Rattle combine to sound like King Lear raging against the universe. The second movement, Brahms's response to Schumann's attempted suicide, is weighted with an almost unbearable significance and intensity, and in the finale Wolf's strange dictum, 'Brahms cannot exult', is turned topsy-turvy.

The performance ends in a storm of applause and presentation of an outsize bouquet to Barenboim who graciously plucks out a single rose for his partner in glory. A playful tug-of-war follows as both artists seek to acknowledge each other's achievement. Schoenberg's 1937 orchestral arrangement of Brahms's G minor Piano Quartet follows, a glowing tribute from one composer to another, recreated in all its richness by Rattle and the orchestra. Their way with the gypsy finale, aptly described as showing Brahms's taste for 'vigorous horseplay', brings this momentous occasion to a close. There are more flowers and a standing ovation from an audience both elated and exhausted.

Violin Concerto in D, Op 77

Brahms Violin Concerto[a]
Schumann Violin Concerto[a] **Tchaikovsky** Violin
Concerto[b] **Wieniawski** Violin Concerto No 2[b]
Joshua Bell vn
Cleveland Orchestra / [a]**Christoph von Dohnányi,**
[b]**Vladimir Ashkenazy**
Decca ② 475 6703-5DF2 (134' · DDD)   Ⓜ❶➾

Bell's first entry in the Brahms instantly reveals
the soloist's love of bravura display, his gift for
turning a phrase individually in a way that catches
the ear, always sounding spontaneous, never self-
conscious. Regularly one registers moments of
new magic, not least when, in the most delicate
half-tones, *pianissimos* seem to convey an inner
communion, after which the impact of bravura
fortissimos is all the more dramatic. He rounds off
the movement with his own big cadenza and a
magically hushed link into the coda, rapt and
intense. The slow movement, sweet and songful,
gains too from Bell's love of playing really softly,
not least in stratospheric registers. In the finale the
vein of fantasy is less apparent. Next to others this
can seem a little plain. Dohnányi and the Cleveland Orchestra provide weighty and sympathetic
support and the generous Schumann, Tchaikovsky and Wieniawski couplings in commanding
performances adds to the attractions of the set.
    In the Schumann Dohnányi and the Cleveland
Orchestra add to the weight and dramatic
impact of a performance that defies the old idea
of this as an impossibly flawed piece, with Bell
bringing out charm as well as power. With
full and atmospheric Cleveland sound, well-
balanced, the Tchaikovsky makes an excellent
choice, particularly if you fancy the Wieniawski
Second Concerto for coupling. Bell may not
quite match Perlman in either of his recordings
for his individual poetry, but within its less
searching compass Bell's is a masterly performance, full of flair.

Brahms Violin Concerto
Tchaikovsky Violin Concerto in D, Op 35
Jascha Heifetz vn **Chicago Symphony Orchestra /**
Fritz Reiner   Ⓗ
RCA Victor Living Stereo 88888 03034-2 (64' · ADD)
Recorded 1955, 1957   Ⓜ❶➾
This combination appears unbeatable. You
may think that Reiner starts the opening *tutti* at
an extraordinarily quick speed – until you
remember that he's going to accompany no less
a virtuoso than Heifetz, so he's merely taking it
to match his soloist's performance. You'll like
this if you think that this concerto is too often
played in the kind of 'autumnal' manner often
attributed to Brahms's compositions but which
really shouldn't apply to many of them. With
Heifetz it's played with respect but without any
kind of reverent hushed awe. The slow movement is lovely and the finale is a winner, the
playing of an exuberant young man, yet Heifetz
was over 50 when he made this record. Reiner

conducts the fast movement with a fiery rhythmic impetus that incandescently matches the
exhilarating yet unforced bravura of his great
soloist. It's confident throughout – and just
listen to his real *staccato*, a rare thing from
violinists.
    The RCA recording comes up extraordinarily
well – although the soloist is balanced forwardly,
he's naturally focused and the Chicago acoustic
ensures a convincing concert-hall balance. If anything, the remastering of the Tchaikovsky is even
more remarkable, considering that originally
Heifetz was apparently placed right up against the
microphone. You soon adapt to the closeness
when the fiddle-playing is so peerless; and Heifetz
colours Tchaikovsky's melodies ravishingly.

Violin Concerto, Op 77. Double Concerto, Op 102[a]
Julia Fischer vn [a]**Daniel Müller-Schott** vc
Netherlands Philharmonic Orchestra /
Yakov Kreizberg
Pentatone ⬥ PTC5186 066 (73' · DDD/DSD)   Ⓕ❶

Julia Fischer offers this ideal Brahms coupling in
strong and sympathetic readings, joined in the
Double Concerto by her brilliant young compatriot, cellist Daniel Müller-Schott. In the Violin
Concerto, Fischer takes an expansive view of the
first movement, freely varying the tempo as she
did in her outstanding version of the Tchaikovsky Concerto. The 23-minute timing even
underestimates her spaciousness, as she uses an
unidentified cadenza rather shorter than the
usual Joachim one (the booklet incorrectly says
it's the Joachim).
    Others offer tauter and brisker accounts of the
first movement but Fischer amply justifies her
spacious and flexible speeds in the feeling of
spontaneity. Her performance never feels self-
conscious or too studied and her range of tone
and dynamic is extreme, bringing *pianissimi* of
breathtaking delicacy. Fischer's slow movement,
too, is expansive while in the finale she lets the
tempo relax just enough to allow a persuasive
spring in the rhythms, bringing out the Hungarian dance flavour.
    The Double Concerto is not nearly as expan-
sive: no doubt the influence of Müller-Schott
was important here as the cello takes the lead in
introducing each theme, with the cellist matching his partner in warmth and brilliance. Fischer
and Müller-Schott are relaxed and easily lyrical
in the slow movement, brilliant and thrusting in
the finale. An outstanding disc which stands
high on the list of this perfect coupling.

Double Concerto, Op 102

Double Concerto, Op 102[a]. Clarinet Quintet, Op 115[b]
Renaud Capuçon vn **Gautier Capuçon** vc
[b]**Paul Meyer** cl
[b]**Aki Saulière** vn [b]**Béatrice Muthelet** va
[a]**Gustav Mahler Jugendorchester /**
Myung-Whun Chung
Virgin Classics 395147-2 (72' · DDD)   Ⓕ❶➾

The stellar young Capuçon brothers seem incapable of setting a foot wrong on disc and they put their considerable chamber-music experience to great use in Brahms's final orchestral work, with cellist Gautier Capuçon proving an eloquent lead in the vehement first movement.

The other striking aspect about this performance is the sheer range of colour, not only from the soloists but also from the Gustav Mahler Youth Orchestra, who play their hearts out for Myung-Whun Chung in this most symphonic of concertos. If Oistrakh and Fournier are still irresistible in the slow movement, offering a perfect balance of melodic lines that are lovingly cherished but never saccharine, the Capuçons are still very impressive, and their finale is full of vitality, making much of the folk-tinged inflections and achieving a seemingly telepathic unanimity in their shared passages.

For a change from the usual concerto companion we get Brahms's Clarinet Quintet, written in 1891, four years after the Double Concerto. In this coupling it's easy to hear the Quintet's famous autumnal quality prefigured in the outer sections of the concerto's *Andante*. Paul Meyer is an ideal protagonist, producing a wide array of mellow shadings in the opening movement, yet never underplaying the more agitated passages within the piece, notably the *Presto* of the third movement. The quartet is minutely responsive to Meyer's every move and even seasoned Brahms aficionados will find new detail to relish in both the performances here.

Brahms Double Concerto
Schumann Cello Concerto in A minor, Op 129
Ilya Kaler vn **Maria Kliegel** vc **National Symphony Orchestra of Ireland / Andrew Constantine**
Naxos 8 550938 (59' · DDD)　　Ⓢ🅑➔

The Brahms and Schumann concertos make an excellent and apt coupling, here given warmly spontaneous-sounding performances, very well recorded. The violinist, Ilya Kaler, is as clean in attack and intonation as Maria Kliegel. Kliegel in her opening cadenza allows herself full freedom, but any feeling that this is to be an easygoing, small-scale reading is dispelled in the main *Allegro*, which is clean and fresh, sharp in attack, helped by full-bodied sound. Kaler and Kliegel make the second subject tenderly expressive without using exaggerated *rubato*. Similarly there's no self-indulgence in the soaring main melody of the central *Andante*, but no lack of warmth or tenderness either. The finale is then unhurried but has dance-rhythms so beautifully sprung and such delicate pointing of phrases that any lack of animal excitement is amply replaced by wit and a sense of fun.

In the Schumann Kliegel takes a spacious, lyrical view of the first movement, using a soft-grained tone at the start with wide vibrato. She then builds up the power of the performance, and with Constantine providing sympathetic accompaniment, the spontaneous expression is most compelling. So, too, is the simple, dedicated playing in the central *Langsam*, and, as in the Brahms, Kliegel brings witty pointing to the finale, not least in the second subject. The balance of the soloists is good.

Double Concerto[a]. Symphony No 2 in D, Op 73
[a]**Gordan Nikolitch** vn [a]**Tim Hugh** vc
London Symphony Orchestra / Bernard Haitink
LSO Live LSO0043 (75' · DDD)　　Ⓢ🅞🅞➔

Labels such as LSO Live bring altered priorities and fresh perspectives. When did a studio-based company last contemplate recording Brahms's Double Concerto with soloists drawn from within the orchestra? Brahms wrote the work with Joachim and his colleague in the Joachim Quartet, Robert Hausmann, in mind. It has a chamber-music dimension to it, yet it's also a work of real symphonic power. Haitink's accompaniment is superb, allowing the soloists the space for the lyric outpourings at the heart of the work. The sweet-toned Gordan Nikolitch and the burlier-sounding, though endlessly responsive Tim Hugh are perfectly matched, and grow ever closer and more eloquent as the romantic, at times almost operatic, colloquy of the two opening movements unfolds. After which, slippered ease and remembered passion is the order of the day in a sweetly judged reading of the finale. The recording, rich and immediate, brings out the tactile quality of Brahms's writing.

Haitink's 1990 Boston recording of the symphony has a certain Mediterranean glow to it. In this imposing and beautifully shaded new LSO performance, we return north again with a reading that's weightier and even more cleanly articulated than his 1973 Amsterdam version.

Symphonies

No 1 in C minor **No 2** in D **No 3** in F **No 4** in E minor

---

Symphonies Nos 1-4. Variations on a Theme by Haydn, Op 56a. Tragic Overture
Staatskapelle Dresden / Kurt Sanderling
RCA ③ 09478 69220-2 (197' · ADD)
Recorded 1971-72　　Ⓑ🅞🅞

Kurt Sanderling has recorded the Brahms symphonies twice (his first set, with the Berlin Symphony Orchestra, is available on Capriccio), but what started out as solid, patient and well built broadened significantly, and in doing so stressed the epic element that was always implicit in the first recordings: the first movement of the later First Symphony is slower than its predecessor by over two minutes. Sanderling's great strength is in the way he handles Brahms's choppy, obdurate string writing, whether in the First Symphony's strutting first movement *Allegro* or the opening *Allegro non troppo* of the Fourth. Tempi are consistently held firm, the lyrical passages allowed their due only within a solid structural frame (the Third Symphony's middle movement, for example) and first-movement repeats omitted. As ever, it's the Third Symphony that underlines specific interpretative differences between conductors – the first movement especially, a vigorous *Allegro con brio* that, for some reason or other, defeats even the greatest maestros. Sanderling takes a majestic, even marmoreal option that seems misguided: the gestures are grand, certainly, but the music remains rooted to earth. And if ever a piece said 'come fly with me', it's the first movement of Brahms's Third Symphony.

In short, Sanderling is sturdy, intelligently phrased, warmly played, fairly well recorded (the strings are a little grainy) and supplemented by equally well-considered accounts of the *Haydn* Variations and *Tragic Overture*.

Symphonies Nos 1-4
Berlin Philharmonic Orchestra / Sir Simon Rattle
EM ③ 267254-2 (151' · DDD)
Recorded live at the Philharmonie, Berlin   ⒷⒽ➔

Consistently satisfying cycles of the four Brahms symphonies are rare on record. Not the least of the problems is the dichotomy that exists between the First and Third symphonies – both deeply personal works – and their musical antitypes, the organically conceived and wondrously self-sufficient Second and Fourth symphonies. It requires a particular kind of mind and technique to cope with these immensities.

Forging a comparable discourse with the Berlin Philharmonic is no easy task, as Simon Rattle is no doubt shrewdly aware. Furtwängler had his own methods, drawing without fear or favour on the orchestra's richly layered sound and visceral manner. A First and Third man, he highlighted the darker elements of the Second and treated the Fourth as unmitigated tragedy. Karajan, a Second and Fourth man who spent 50 years grappling with the First like a climber confronting some unattainable Alpine peak, first clarified the Berlin sound, then rebuilt it to epic proportions, as we can hear in his 1987 DG recording of the First or the tumultuous performance of that same symphony he conducted in London in October 1988 (Testament).

After Rattle's radically styled Vienna Philharmonic Beethoven cycle, you might imagine that his Brahms would be closer to Harnoncourt's than Karajan's. This is not the case. Taking on the mantle of conductor as custodian, he has gone back to the pre-1989 way of doing things. Where Harnoncourt rather underplays the First Symphony, giving it a decorous Schumannesque feel, Rattle's reading is one in which the inwardness and charm of the exquisitely realised inner movements offset the breadth and lyric power of the surrounding drama. Less riven than Furtwängler's reading or the later Karajan's, it is a powerfully directed performance, measured and humane.

The EMI recording is an 'in concert' affair, more closely focused, with a less natural-sounding ambience than the recording Teldec gave Harnoncourt in this same hall. Impressive in the First Symphony, it seems cloudier and more claustrophobic in the Second. Clearly the reading has something to do with this, with its bottom-heavy string sound and evened-out dynamics. There's a lack of narrative variation here; too little play of light and shade as we journey through the symphony's changing landscapes.

We return to memorability in the Third where we hear again the kind of exquisitely quiet string- and horn-playing – the inner movements rich in beauty and quiet foreboding – which we missed in the Second. Here Rattle's finely moulded direction sustains the discourse. Tension occasionally slackens in meditative passages but this is preferable to the unnuanced approach we have in the Second Symphony.

Sadly the performance of the Fourth is again bottom-heavy, with slowish tempi that rob the music of its edge and tragic severity. Still, two successes out of four is not bad. In the great Brahms handicap that's about par for the course.

Symphonies Nos 1-4. Variations on a Theme by Haydn. Tragic Overture. Academic Festival Overture, Op 80. Hungarian Dances – No 1 in G minor; No 3 in F; No 10 in F. Serenades – No 1 in D, Op 11; No 2 in A, Op 16
Concertgebouw Orchestra / Bernard Haitink
Philips Bernard Haitink Symphony Edition ④
442 068-2PB4 (4h 51' · ADD). Recorded 1970-80   Ⓑ⒪

Concertgebouw standards at the time of Haitink's survey (1970-80) left little to be desired. Perhaps the clarinets don't always overcome reservations about their tone and intonation with the sensitivity of their phrasing; but the horns invariably do, and more often than not Brahms's favourite instrument is a source of joy in these recordings, blazing gloriously at appropriate moments (especially in the Fourth Symphony), or opening up and sustaining huge vistas in the 'dawn' of the First's finale. As to the strings, Haitink's insistence on firmly defined (though never over-emphatic) rhythms from the bass-lines up is altogether exceptional; there are countless examples, but most memorable of all is the cellos' and basses' ostinato that sees the Second Symphony's finale in the home straight. What an articulate, integrated Brahms sound this is, too; a case of conductor and engineers easily achieving their aims working in a familiar acoustic. The only movement you may initially find overly sober is the first of the Third Symphony, taken very broadly, though it's determined and imposing, and the launching of the coda is stupendously powerful. There's no better way of getting to know Brahms's orchestral works on a budget.

Symphonies Nos 1-4. Variations on a Theme by Haydn. Academic Festival Overture. Tragic Overture

BRAHMS SYMPHONIES – IN BRIEF

Hallé Orchestra / James Loughran
CfP ③ 575753-2 (279' · ADD)   ⑧●
A longtime favourite: honest, muscular, with a fine sweep and sense of architecture. The Second Symphony is magnificent.

Berlin PO / Nikolaus Harnoncourt
Teldec ③ 0630 13136-2 (214' · DDD)   Ⓕ●●▷
A fresh approach to four classics played with total conviction by a band with a tradition.

Berlin PO / Herbert von Karajan
DG ② 453 097-2GTA2 (156' · ADD)   Ⓜ●▷
From the late 1970s, the BPO's Brahms sound glows under Karajan's total command. (Don't confuse this with his later, more expensive, very similar digital recordings.)

Philharmonia / Otto Klemperer
EMI ② 562742-2 (156' · ADD)   Ⓜ●▷
A set that shows Klemperer at his finest: there is a power and strength that inspires real admiration. The Philharmonia plays with burning passion.

Staatskapelle Dresden / Kurt Sanderling
RCA ② 09478 69220-2 (197' · ADD)   ⑧●●
Perfectly proportioned, sturdy readings from a master conductor and great ensemble.

Concertgebouw Orchestra / Bernard Haitink
Philips ④ 442 068-2PB4 (291' · ADD)   ⑧●
Exquisitely phrased, elegant Brahms from one of the world's great orchestras.

Berlin PO, Vienna PO / Wilhelm Furtwängler Ⓗ
EMI mono ④ 565513-2 (219' · ADD)   Ⓜ●
Perhaps *the* historic choice (1948-52) and a fine example of Furtwängler's incandescent art: the Fourth positively drips with tragedy.

Philharmonia Orchestra / Arturo Toscanini Ⓗ
Testament ② SBT3167 (200' · ADD)   Ⓕ●●
From 1952, the Italian maestro's singing way with Brahms is gloriously conveyed.

Berlin PO / Claudio Abbado
DG ④ 435 683-2GH4 (246' · DDD)   Ⓕ●▷
One of the finest of modern Brahms cycles with stylish, sleek orchestral work.

North German RSO / Günter Wand
RCA ③ 74321 89103-2 (158' · DDD)   Ⓕ●
Wonderfully wise, beautifully prepared performances that speak of a lifetime's love of this music and thorough familiarity with it.

Scottish CO / Sir Charles Mackerras
Telarc ③ CD80450 (199' · DDD)   Ⓕ
An interesting historic approach that uses an orchestra of the same size as the one Brahms had at Meiningen – fresh and light on its feet.

**Berlin Philharmonic Orchestra /
Nikolaus Harnoncourt**
Teldec ③ 0630-13136-2 (214' · DDD)   Ⓕ●●

Any fears that Nikolaus Harnoncourt's Brahms will be quirky, provocative or abrasive can be dispelled. There are interpretative novelties (freshly considered articulation and clarified counterpoint) and the Berlin strings project a smooth, curvaceous profile. Harnoncourt makes a beeline for the brass, and the horns in particular. The live recordings have remarkable presence and are mostly cough-free.

The First Symphony's opening *Un poco sostenuto* seems a trifle soft-grained but the pounding basses from bar 25 are beautifully caught and the first-movement *Allegro* is both powerful and broadly paced. The *Andante sostenuto* slow movement is both limpid and conversational, with trance-like dialogue between oboe and clarinet and sparing use of vibrato among the strings. Harnoncourt makes real chamber music of the third movement, though he drives the Trio section to a fierce climax, and the finale's first accelerating *pizzicatos* are truly *stringendo poco a poco* – the excitement certainly mounts, but only gradually. The Second Symphony's first movement is relatively restrained. Harnoncourt's strategy is to deliver a sombre exposition and a toughened development. Again, the slow movement is fluid and intimate, with some tender string playing. The third movement's rustling Trio is disarmingly delicate and the finale, tightly held, keenly inflected and heavily accented: the coda threatens to break free and the effect is thrilling.

First impressions of the Third Symphony suggest a marginal drop in intensity, yet the first movement's peroration is so powerful that there's a retrospective suspicion that all the foregoing was mere preparation. The middle movements work well but the rough-hewn, flexibly phrased finale really makes the performance.

Like the Third, the Fourth opens with less import than some of its older rivals, yet the development intensifies perceptibly, the recapitulation's hushed *piano dolce* opening bars are held on the edge of a breath and the coda is recklessly headstrong. The slow movement has some heartfelt moments, the top-gear *Scherzo* is quite exhilarating and the finale, forged with the noble inevitability of a Baroque passacaglia. Ultimately, Harnoncourt delivers a fine and tragic Fourth.

Harnoncourt's Brahms is the perfect antidote to predictability and interpretative complacency.

Symphonies Nos 1-4. Tragic Overture.   Ⓗ
Variations on a Theme by Haydn
Philharmonia Orchestra / Arturo Toscanini
Testament mono ④ SBT3167 (3h 20' · ADD)
Recorded live 1952   Ⓕ●●

The concerts recorded here preserve the two legendary occasions in the autumn of 1952 when in a Brahms cycle at the Royal Festival Hall Toscanini conducted the Philharmonia Orchestra, then only six years old but already the front runner among London orchestras. The recording itself, now legendary, has generated pirated versions, but never before has the original made by EMI, under the supervision of Walter Legge, been officially released. Testament's remastering is a revelation. This new set brings the clearest of demonstrations that the RCA recordings of Toscanini and the NBC Symphony Orchestra made during the last years of his life (including his Brahms cycle of the very same 12-month period) give only an imperfect picture of a conductor who at the time, and for a generation or so previously, was almost universally counted the greatest in the world. That reputation has been eroded over the years, but this issue may help to put the record straight.

Take for example the quite different NBC version of No 3 that he recorded in New York barely a month after this performance: as Alan Sanders says in his note, a 'rhythmically staid recording which entirely lacked the lyricism and eloquence of the Philharmonia performance'. His description points to the marked contrasts, not only in No 3 but in all four symphonies. Whereas the New York performances, resonant and superbly drilled, have a hardness and rigidity, with the dynamic contrasts ironed out, thus eliminating *pianissimos* (partly a question of recording balance), the Philharmonia's consistently bring a moulding of phrase and subtlety of rubato which bears out the regular Toscanini instructions to 'Sing!'. And in contrast with most Toscanini recordings, the hushed playing is magical. The New York players, by comparison, seem to have forgotten how to respond to the finer subtleties of this notorious taskmaster among conductors. The extra flexibility of the Philharmonia performances over the NBC has an interesting effect on tempo too. Whereas in No 1 the NBC speeds of 1951 are faster, not just than those of the Philharmonia but of the 1941 NBC performance, in the other three symphonies the Philharmonia timings tend to be a degree quicker, notably in No 3, where for example the *Andante* flows far better.

Additional recommendation

Symphonies Nos 1-4
Coupled with: Violin Concerto[a]. Alto Rhapsody[b].
Hungarian Dances
[a]**Hasson** vn [b]**Greevy** mez [a]**LPO; Hallé Orchestra / Loughran**
Classics for Pleasure ④ 575753-2
(4h 39' · ADD). Recorded mid-1970s   Ⓑ

Loughran's cycle had a very loyal following on LP. It still sounds pretty good some 25 years on. He knows how to build a Brahms symphony not only towards its climax but from its bass-line; his choice of tempo rarely falters. And No 2 is a sheer delight. Add a glorious *Alto Rhapsody* and a cultivated Violin Concerto and you've a real bargain.

Brahms Symphony No 1. Begräbnisgesang, Op 13[a].
Schicksalslied, Op 54[a]
Mendelssohn Mitten wir in Leben sind, Op 23[a]
[a]**Monteverdi Choir; Orchestre Révolutionnaire et Romantique / Sir John Eliot Gardiner**
Soli Deo Gloria SDG702 (75' · DDD)   Ⓕ**OO**B

Part of a project whose purpose is to contextualise Brahms's four symphonies and *German Requiem*, this is a record that needs to be heard chronologically and complete, not cherry-picked for individual items.

Sir John Eliot Gardiner's project promises to bring into play the work of Schütz, Palestrina, and Bach, along with choral pieces by admired contemporaries. Here Felix Mendelssohn is the representative 'other', his superb *Mitten wir*, composed three years before Brahms's birth. It is flanked by Brahms's *Begräbnisgesang* (1858), a threnody for chorus, winds and timpani that openly anticipates the second movement of the *German Requiem*, and the sublime yet troubled Hölderlin-inspired *Schicksalslied* ('Song of Destiny', 1868-71) which can be seen as a pendant to the Requiem.

Brahms's setting of Hölderlin's poem was controversial. Where Hölderlin supplants his opening vision of celestial quiet with images of the hell of earthly existence, Brahms ends by revisiting that celestial vision in a ruefully beautiful orchestral coda in C major. *Schicksalslied* tells us a good deal about the First Symphony. In Gardiner's powerful juxtaposition, the descent from that rueful C major coda to the C minor of the symphony's tumultuous opening is a true *coup de théâtre*, the terrible enactment of another Fall.

These are intensely dramatic performances, powerful and unmanicured. The gathering drama of the three choral pieces is channelled and unleashed in a towering account of the First Symphony's opening movement. When Klemperer conducted the symphony in Los Angeles in 1941 a player recalled: "He drove, as in a huge chariot, to the highest planes of expression." There is something of that spirit here in Gardiner's gaunt, no-holds-barred account of the work.

The use of period instruments and their deployment in the brooding acoustic of Paris's Salle Wagram are clearly factors in the performance's wider impact. It has to be said that the playing in the symphony's middle movements is rather rough and ready. In the third movement, which under Gardiner is neither *allegretto* nor *grazioso*, Sir Charles Mackerras's historically informed Scottish Chamber Orchestra version (Telarc) is much to be preferred. Not that comparisons matter. This is a mighty Brahms First which, like the programme it inhabits, is a thing sufficient unto itself.

Symphony No 1. Variations on a Theme by Haydn, Op 56a. Hungarian Dance No 14 (arr Fischer)
Budapest Festival Orchestra / Iván Fischer
Channel Classics ⟨S⟩ CCSSA28309
(67' · DDD/DSD)   Ⓕ**OO**B

The decision to begin this disc with Iván Fischer's own arrangement for strings of Brahms's soulful Hungarian Dance in D minor puts down a marker. This is Brahms seen from the perspective of the borderlands to the east of Vienna, Brahms Hungarian-style.

Fischer and his decidedly classy Budapest orchestra treat the Variations as an affectionate tribute to Haydn, an east-of-Vienna man if ever there was one. Finely sprung and nicely styled, the performance even has its own *zigeunerisch* dimension – in the finale where Brahms's witty and heroic use of the triangle is neatly pointed. A superlative recording helps.

And what of the symphony, which Fischer describes with Polonius-like elaboration as Brahms's first 'German Hungarian Gypsy Swiss Austrian symphony'? This too is a vibrant affair, stylish and alert, played with clarity and sheen (and the merest hint of string *portamento*).

Fischer brings out the dance element in the first-movement *Allegro*, the music's youthful purpose. After a slow movement exquisitely voiced by the orchestra, the third movement has a pace and grace that again seems decidedly Hungarian. Fisher is comprehensively floored by the weirdly fluctuating *pizzicato* transition near the start of the finale but poise and momentum are soon restored. The symphony's peroration is more than usually fiery.

This is a more extrovert reading than many you will hear, less burdened. Conscious of this, and perhaps wanting to have the best of both worlds, Fischer plays the lyric sections of the first movement rather broadly and begins drawing down the coda a whole 20 bars before the brief 15-bar *meno allegro* Brahms asks for. Furtwängler did something similar but subtly and disarmingly. Since Fischer's command of a subtly fluctuating pulse is not in the Furtwängler league, the effect seems manufactured. Better conduct your own Brahms well than someone else's badly. Happily, for most of the performance Fischer does just that.

Brahms Symphony No 1 **Wagner** Siegfried Idyll. 🄷
Siegfried – Siegfried's horn-call
Dennis Brain *hn*
Philharmonia Orchestra / Guido Cantelli
Testament mono SBT1012 (62' · ADD)
Recorded 1947-53
Ⓕ⚫

Cantelli conducts an interpretation which is free of any idiosyncrasy. Yet there's an extraordinary electricity in his conducting, a sense of concentration and conviction which lifts the performance into one of the greatest ever set down on record. The fiery young Italian makes the vintage Philharmonia play in an inspired fashion, and the 1953 mono recording is very acceptable.

A slightly edgy string sound betrays the 1951 origin of the *Siegfried Idyll* recording, but the performance has a tenderness, warmth and eloquence which has never been surpassed. Dennis Brain's exuberant horn-call completes a very desirable Testament disc.

Brahms Symphony No 1[a]
Mozart Symphony No 36, 'Linz', K425[b]
Philharmonia Orchestra / Carlo Maria Giulini
BBC Legends [a]mono BBCL4175-2 (76' · ADD)
Recorded live [a]1962; [b] 1982
Ⓕ

Giulini appears to have taken Mozart's festive and eloquent *Linz* Symphony into his repertory when he was in his mid-50s, though as we know from his unsurpassed recording of *Don Giovanni*, his interpretations which arrived, as it were, out of the blue, always came fully formed. This live 1982 Proms performance (Giulini made no commercial recording of the *Linz*) is a joy to hear: vital, companionable, generous-spirited.

The celebrated recording which Bruno Walter made, with attendant rehearsal sequences, with the Columbia SO in 1955 for CBS was very similar. Indeed, that may well have been Giulini's model (he had greatly admired Walter's conducting when he played under him in Rome's Augusteo Orchestra in the 1930s). 'Authenticists' will no doubt sniff at the full-bodied sonorities here (did Mozart dream of anything less?) and the non-antiphonal disposition of the violins, though they would be ill-advised to do so. Rarely has the symphony's important second violin part been as carefully, or as eloquently, attended to as here.

And, of course, Giulini knows the symphony's anatomical make-up as well as anyone. At the technical level, this is a wonderfully articulated performance, with clean yet pliant rhythms (the work's trademark trills tautly but expressively attended to), and well terraced wind and string sonorities. The only thing to be regretted is an exposition repeat in the finale.

The Brahms could not be more different. Recorded at the 1962 Edinburgh Festival in dry, immediate, somewhat acidulous mono sound, it bears about as much relation to the Mozart as a Fragonard landscape does to a grainy black-and-white photograph of Berlin after the blitz. This is a quite literally terrific performance. The physiognomy is recognisably that of Giulini's three studio recordings: powerful, imposing, superbly sculpted. What those recordings don't have is the sense of a performance taking shape in the shadow of an apocalypse. So great is the tension, Giulini even moves the finale's big tune on at a half-decent pace, something he was generally loath to do.

Symphonies Nos 1 and 2
West German Radio Symphony Orchestra, Cologne / Semyon Bychkov
Video director **Hans Hadulla**
ArtHaus Musik 📀 101 243 (98' · NTSC · 16:9 · PCM stereo, 5.1 and DTS 5.1 · 0). Also includes 'The Horizon Moves With You' – a portrait of Semyon Bychkov
Ⓕ

It's a long time since we've had such satisfying accounts of either work, free of any idiosyncrasies, adeptly paced and in a clear, warm acoustic. The oboe(s), clarinet(s) and horns make outstanding contributions. Visually, Hans Hadulla (director) and Lothar Mattner (editor) are classy and imaginative without being intrusive (except, arguably, at the end of the First Symphony); they make the most of the medium and eschew any gimmickry. Particularly fine are the long steadicam shots that introduce and end each performance.

The documentary on Bychkov also comes highly recommended – international locations, crisply and atmospherically shot, eloquent contributions from the conductor, and a particularly touching sequence as he celebrates the 95th birthday of his teacher, Ilya Musin.

Symphony No 2. Hungarian Dances Nos 1, 3, 10, 17, 18, 19, 20 & 21
London Philharmonic Orchestra / Marin Alsop
Naxos 8 557429 (65' · DDD)   Ⓢ🅑➔

This is a late-summer idyll of a performance, easily paced, nicely judged and warmly played. For first-time buyers it will provide unalloyed pleasure; for older hands it will satisfy without necessarily enlightening or surprising.

It is one of those Brahms performances whose centre of gravity is in the violas, cellos and horns. This is apt to the symphony's lyrical, ruminative character, though there are times when the music is robbed of its light and shade. In the finale, for example, one rather misses the chill-before-dawn mood of the lead-in to the recapitulation; and one needs a keener differentiation of horn and trumpet tone to catch the final page's incomparable D major blaze. Alsop's account of the third movement is strong in contrast, the oboe-led *Allegretto grazioso* strangely muted, the quicker 2/4 section done more or less to perfection. That said, you might think the slow movement under-characterised: insufficiently distinct in tone and temper from the first.

The symphony was recorded in Blackheath Concert Hall, the *Hungarian Dances* in Watford's Colosseum: a bigger, brawnier acoustic that doesn't suit the music quite so well. In dance No 18 in D, one of Dvořák's orchestrations, there is a noisy, cluttered feel to the performance. By contrast, the alfresco No 3 in F, winningly and economically orchestrated by Brahms himself, is played with real charm and style.

Brahms Symphony No 2[a]   🄷
Beethoven Symphony No 2 in D, Op 36[b]
Royal Philharmonic Orchestra /
Sir Thomas Beecham
BBC Legends mono BBCL4099-2 (70' · ADD)
Recorded live in [b]1956, [a]1956   Ⓕ🅞

Beecham was no Brahmsian but he loved the Second Symphony and was one of its most persuasive interpreters. In 1936 he made a much-admired recording with the newly founded LPO. Reviewing Beecham's stereo remake in *Gramophone* in June 1960, William Mann recalled: 'I grew up with his 78 set and remember it with keen pleasure. It was light and sunny and full of charm, though perfectly strong; some peo-

ple probably thought it a reading that lacked nobility.' The remake, recorded in 1958-59, wasn't as well liked as the 78rpm original. This live 1956 Edinburgh Festival performance is superior in almost every respect to that laboriously assembled studio version, and left the festival audience flabbergasted, walking on air.

In the studio the rip-roaring conclusion seemed contrived, but here it electrifies sense. If there's a whiff of the circus about the Edinburgh performance – Beecham audibly urging his players on like a shiny-hatted ringmaster, the final chord sounding defiantly on even as it drowns in a sea of applause – it's largely to do with the fact that the performance is live. The actual reading is exemplary: a thrilling denouement thrillingly realised. And in the earlier movements Beecham's reading is everything William Mann remembered it as – sunny and full of charm but also, by 1956, wise and wondering, too. The mono sound is first-rate.

The Beethoven is less interesting, though this Maida Vale broadcast is every bit as vital as the generally well-respected EMI studio recording which Beecham and the RPO made that same winter. Buy it for the Brahms.

Symphony No 3. Tragic Overture. Schicksalslied
Ernst-Senff Choir; Berlin Philharmonic Orchestra /
Claudio Abbado
DG 429 765-2GH (68' · DDD)   Ⓟ🅞➔

This disc is gloriously programmed for straight-through listening. It gets off to a cracking start with an urgently impassioned *Tragic Overture* in which the credentials of the Berlin Philharmonic to make a richly idiomatic, Brahmsian sound-are substantially reaffirmed. A wide-eyed, breathtaking account of the *Schicksalslied* ('Song of Destiny') follows to provide sound contrast before the wonders of the Third Symphony are freshly explored. This is a reading of the Symphony to be savoured; it's underpinned throughout by a rhythmic vitality which binds the four movements together with a forward thrust, making the end inevitable right from the opening bars. Even in the moments of repose and, especially, the warmly felt *Andante*, Abbado never lets the music forget its ultimate goal. Despite this, there are many moments of wonderful solo and orchestral playing along the way in which there's time to delight, and Abbado seems to bring out that affable, Bohemian-woods, Dvořák-like element in Brahms's music to a peculiar degree in this performance. The Symphony is recorded with a particular richness and some may find the heady waltz of the third movement done too lushly, emphasised by Abbado's lingering tempo. Nevertheless, this is splendid stuff, and not to be missed.

Symphony No 3. Variations on a Theme by Haydn
London Philharmonic Orchestra / Marin Alsop
Naxos 8 557430 (56' · DDD)   Ⓢ🅞🅞➔

Brand new budget-price recordings which can rub shoulders with the best are rarer than one imagines but this fine new Brahms disc probably comes into that category. Finding a recommendable Brahms Third is more difficult than one might suppose. Since Felix Weingartner made his very fine LPO recording in 1938, the number of great, or even successful, Thirds can probably be listed on the fingers of two hands.

Marin Alsop's reading is certainly fine: dark of hue, lyrical and long drawn, though never, even for a moment, comatose. Rhythm is good, articulation keen, phrasing exquisite, the reading's crepuscular colours glowingly realised by the LPO. The reading has a quality of melancholy, a wistfulness crossed with a sense of incipient tragedy, which is almost Elgarian (Elgar's fascination with the piece is well attested).

Readings such as Furtwängler's and Sanderling's, which are more inclined to tower and course, may not have allowed themselves to be overtopped by the *Haydn* Variations, yet there is something rather wonderful about the transition we have here from dark to light. It is a long time since we had a performance of the Variations as well grounded and as keenly profiled as this. Winds are splendidly to the fore: skirling flutes, songful oboes, grumbling descants on the horns 'in deep B'. It is, above all, a reading of great character: the horn-led sixth variation a burgherly jaunt, the seventh variation a handsome galliard, the finale a *Meistersinger*-like revel.

Symphony No 3. Einförmig ist der Liebe Gram, Op 113 No 13[a]. Es tönt ein voller Harfenklang, Op 17 No 1[a]. Gesang der Parzen, Op 89[a]. Ich schwing mein Horn ins Jammertal, Op 41 No 1[a]. Nachtwache I, Op 104 No 1[a]. Nänie, Op 82[a]
[a]**Monteverdi Choir; Orchestre Révolutionnaire et Romantique / Sir John Eliot Gardiner**
Soli Deo Gloria SDG704 (70' · DDD · T/t)
Recorded live in 2007 & 2008   Ⓕ ❶ ❷

The six choral items on this disc take us to the very heart of the enigma that is Brahms. It was not for nothing that Malcolm MacDonald began his superb and now shamefully out-of-print Master Musicians Brahms with a two-page preface on the Op 113 canon for female voices, *Einförmig ist der Liebe Gram*. Ingeniously laid out as a four-part canon in the sopranos accompanied by a two-part canon in the altos, it uses as its theme the emotionally drained melody of the hurdy-gurdy man's song at the end of Schubert's *Winterreise*.

Gardiner takes the canon fairly swiftly – a high-wire act of *a cappella* singing that intensifies the mood while focusing the craft. Taking up more than half the disc, the choral items are its obvious glory, though as on previous discs Gardiner sets his face against anything that could be construed as false consolation. In his element in *Song of the Fates*, he gives the sublime *Nänie* an unusually taut, sharp-edged feel.

Song of the Fates prefaces the Third Symphony, *Nänie* acts as its epilogue. It is superb planning.

The symphony, however, receives a performance that will divide opinion – so extreme yet so finely realised is Gardiner's interpretative take on the work. The outer movements are taken more rapidly than on any of the 70 or more versions on record. A brisk tempo and forward winds can work wonders in this work, as Klemperer proved to glorious effect. With an expert period ensemble at his command, Gardiner takes this approach to an extreme. Memorably as the inner movements are shaped, the finale is overdriven. But then *Nänie* breaks in with its redeeming touch.

Symphony No 4
Vienna Philharmonic Orchestra / Carlos Kleiber
DG The Originals 457 706-2GOR (40' · DDD) Ⓜ ❶ ❷ ❸

Kleiber's charismatic 1981 Vienna recording, a classic of sorts and still sounding exceptionally well, continues to stand its ground. From the beginning, he keeps the speed fairly steady. In the first movement's coda, he scores over many of his rivals with prominent horns and a particularly exciting conclusion. He opens the second movement in a rather perfunctory manner, but the Vienna cellos make a beautiful sound in the *piano dolce* second subject. In the *Scherzo*, Kleiber pulls back for the two accented notes that dominate the first theme, an interesting gesture that lends the music an appropriately swaggering gait. This, arguably, is his finest movement – also from 4'48", where he keeps the timpani's triplets crystal-clear, then pushes his horns very much to the fore. Overall, Kleiber in the Fourth is the knight with shining breast-plate, bold, handsome, outgoing, relatively straightforward and (this will court controversy) perhaps just a little superficial.

Symphony No 4. Hungarian Dances Nos 2, 4, 5, 6, 7, 8 & 9 (orch Breiner)
London Philharmonic Orchestra / Marin Alsop
Naxos 8 570233 (65' · DDD)   Ⓢ ❶ ❷

The LPO, London's finest Brahms ensemble, has been in vintage form during this cycle under Marin Alsop's measured and thoughtful direction. Not since the classically incisive Loughran/Hallé recordings of the mid-1970s has there been a more obviously collectable budget-price Brahms set.

Alsop's reading of the Fourth Symphony is not dissimilar to Sir Adrian Boult's 1972 LPO recording. Like Boult, Alsop is happy to establish a tempo and emotional trajectory for each movement and leave it at that – a plausible view given the astonishing degree of thematic integration that underpins the work.

As elsewhere in the cycle, tempi tend to be measured. The *Andante moderato* is downright slow, though Alsop manages to maintain line and interest. The *Scherzo*, happily, is a true *Allegro giocoso*, which is important. By acting out the role of a conventional finale, the *Scherzo* leaves the actual finale free to enact its own tragic destiny.

The recording sounds well if played at a decent level. In the *Scherzo*, the triangle (deliciously placed and recorded in the *Hungarian Dances*) is more an impression than a presence. There is also an editing glitch midway through the movement, not the first in this series. The seven *Hungarian Dances*, unorchestrated by Brahms, are heard in newly commissioned orchestrations by Peter Breiner. The thudding fairground timpani in No 6 doesn't appeal. Elsewhere, piquancy is the watchword, with stylish playing from the LPO, gamesomely led.

Symphony No 4. Hungarian Dances – selection
(orch Brahms; Dvořák)
Pittsburgh Symphony Orchestra / Marek Janowski
Pentatone ☻ PTC5186 309 (57' · DDD/DSD) Ⓕ❍⮞

It's been true for many years now that American orchestras have been sounding more middle-European, but the Pittsburgh Symphony could easily be mistaken for a top German orchestra, like Leipzig or Dresden, in this music. Listen to the slow movement of the Fourth Symphony where Marek Janowski really has his players leaning into the harmonic radiance of the writing. All those wondrous transfigurations evolve so naturally and so dreamily that the brawny exuberance of the *Scherzo* – tough and resilient in Janowski's hands – really does come as an unexpected blast.

Approaches differ greatly with regard to the highly innovative first movement, the whole of which constitutes a development of sorts. So, how soon do the darkening clouds descend? For some they cannot descend soon enough. But here it's as if Janowski is delaying the inevitable right through to the high anxiety of the final pages. He tightens the screw relatively late in the movement. The slow movement then restores some sense of prior well-being and inner calm, as does the still centre of the finale with its tranquil flute and trombone-led chorale variation. The refulgence of the playing is a constant source of pleasure.

The *Hungarian Dances* come in Brahms's and Dvořák's orchestrations, their kinship self-evident. They are earthy and sinewy with plenty of surge factor in the lower strings and the requisite cheekiness in the phrasing exemplified by those traditionally tantalising hesitations and stomping downbeats.

Serenade No 1, Op 11

Brahms Serenade No 1 **Schumann** Cello Concerto[a]
[a]**Natalia Gutman** vc
Mahler Chamber Orchestra / Claudio Abbado
DG download 476 5786GH (73' · DDD) Ⓕ❍⮞
Recorded live

The most enjoyable feature of this superbly engineered CD is the high level of musical interrelation that it more or less consistently conveys, between Natalia Gutman and the orchestra in the Schumann, and between Abbado and his young players in both works. Gutman's playing, like Abbado's conducting, is communicative and conversational, earnestly so at times, her tone mostly warm in texture, her bowing seamless and in the quieter sections quite ravishing, although she's also capable of muscular attack. For a sustained sense of musical line, try the opening minute or so of the slow movement – note how easily the music breathes, even at a relatively slow tempo. The effect is of poignancy beyond words. The finale is playful and fairly genial, and the clarity of Gutman's articulation means that the solo line never sounds merely 'busy'. The orchestra is there with her every bar of the way, ever responsive, attentive and affectionate.

Schumann's Cello Concerto is a late work whereas Brahms's First Serenade is relatively early. Abbado's performance is chamber-like, modestly individual and for the most part beautifully played by the Mahler CO. Just listen to the easeful charm of the opening and the adoring way Abbado draws the first movement's second subject, gradually slowing the tempo before picking it up again for a return to the otherwise pervasive ebullience. No single movement anticipates the later, equivocal Brahms more tellingly than the whimsical *Scherzo*, thoughtfully played here, while the tripping finale is both assertive and delicate – though, again, the second set is poetically underlined. This is prime-quality Abbado: points are made but never overstated, and there's always the sense that quality musicians are working together with a common musical aim. Who could possibly ask for more?

String Sextets

No 1 in B flat, Op 18; **No 2** in G, Op 36

String Sextets Nos 1 & 2
Raphael Ensemble (James Clark, Elizabeth Wexler *vns* Sally Beamish, Roger Tapping *vas* Andrea Hess, Rhydian Shaxson *vcs*)
Hyperion CDA66276 (74' · DDD) Ⓕ❍⮞

Completed after the First Piano Concerto but still comparatively early works, the Sextets are typified by lush textures, ardent emotion and wonderfully memorable melodic lines. The first is the warmer, more heart-on-the-sleeve piece, balancing with complete naturalness a splendidly lyrical first movement, an urgent, dark set of intricate variations, a lively rustic dance of a *Scherzo*, and a placidly flowing finale. The second inhabits at first a more mysterious world of half-shadows, occasionally rent by glorious moments of sunlight. The finale, however, casts off doubt and ends with affirmation. Both works are very susceptible to differing modes of interpretation, and the Raphael Ensemble has established distinctive views of each, allowing the richness of the texture its head without obscuring the lines, and selecting characteristically distinct tone qualities to typify the two works. The recording is clear and analytic without robbing the sound of its warmth and depth. An impressive recording debut for this ensemble.

String Sextets Nos 1 & 2
Nash Ensemble (Marianne Thorsen, Malin Broman vns Lawrence Power, Philip Dukes vas Paul Watkins, Tim Hugh vcs)
Onyx ONYX4019 (77' · DDD)   Ⓕ**O**▷

There is real precision and polish of ensemble here that marks the Nash performances out. The players appear to be listening keenly and responding to one another. The Nash omit exposition repeats in the first movement of each sextet, unlike the older versions. As a sampler try the delectable third movement *Scherzo* of No 1, which with the Nash Ensemble is beautifully and wittily sprung, one of the gems of Brahms's chamber music.

Clarinet Quintet in B minor, Op 115

Clarinet Quintet. Clarinet Trio in A minor, Op 114
Thea King *cl* **Karina Georgian** *vc* **Clifford Benson** *pf*
Gabrieli Quartet (Kenneth Sillito, Brendan O'Reilly vns Ian Jewel va Keith Harvey vc)
Hyperion CDA66107 (65' · DDD)   Ⓕ**O**

These players' tempo in the Clarinet Quintet is more leisurely than most of their rivals. In the faster flanking movements of the Trio, a stronger forward drive mightn't have come amiss. On the other hand, they allow themselves time to savour every bar to the full. Striking in both these performances is their underlying warmth of heart. You'll respond easily to their quality of good-natured, unforced civility. The ensemble is excellent, with the clarinet very much one of the team, never assuming the role of soloist in a quasi-chamber concerto.

Thea King's phrasing is unfailingly perceptive and stylish, and her undemonstrative, wise artistry in both works is most appealing. In the Trio, the sumptuous-sounding cello is impressive, which at times makes you feel that Brahms could just as well have called the work a cello trio. This is a disc which will bear frequent repetition. Playing such as this, committed and serious, yet at the same time relaxed and spontaneous, isn't easy to contrive in the recording studio, and Hyperion has done well to capture these interpretations on the wing. The sound is very good indeed, mellow and natural.

Clarinet Quintet.
String Quartet No 2 in A minor, Op 51 No 2
Karl Leister *cl* **Leipzig Quartet**
(Andreas Seidel, Tilman Büning vns Ivo Bauer va Matthias Moosdorf vc)
Dabringhaus und Grimm MDG307 0719-2 (71' · DDD)   Ⓕ

One of the most attractive qualities of this version of a well-loved quintet is the skill with

which the artists, abetted by the record producer, have integrated the clarinet into the string textures. Having listened more creatively than any other composer to Mozart's example, Brahms allows the clarinet to become part of the tone colour in the string ensemble; and he has also followed the implications, as not all his interpreters seem to understand. Here, the little falling third theme, one of his lifelong obsessions, moves in and out of the musical texture with wonderful subtlety, so that the return of the opening figure at the very end needs no special emphasis but is a natural conclusion.

Leister is an artist of long skill and experience, and also of great musical intelligence; the qualities tell. They also mean that there's no need to confer upon the performance anything approaching the sentimentality which can afflict it, in the name of 'nostalgia' as the old composer looks affectionately back on his life's work. This is quite a robust performance, clearly appreciated by the enthusiastic young string quartet, who give a suitably matching account of the Op 51 work. There are, of course, any number of performances of the quintet, but this is unique.

Clarinet Quintet. Trio for Horn, Violin and Piano   Ⓗ
in E flat, Op 40
Reginald Kell *cl* **Aubrey Brain** *hn* **Rudolf Serkin** *pf*
Busch Quartet (Adolf Busch, Gosta Andreasson vns Karl Doktor va Hermann Busch vc)
Pearl mono GEMMCD0007 (63' · ADD) or Testament SBT1001 (63' · ADD)   Ⓜ/Ⓕ**OO**

There's no need, at this remove of time, for further praise to be lavished on these performances. This account of the Horn Trio remains at, or very near, the top of any list of recorded rivals. HMV's recording of this somewhat idiosyncratic combination of instruments survives well and has been cleanly, honestly transferred. However, the performance of the Clarinet Quintet will give you even deeper pleasure. Where nowadays do we hear playing of such emotional range, such probing intensity? Here the Busch Quartet and Reginald Kell out-sing and out-search most rivals in the work's autumnal aspect but also make everything seem alive and doubly intense with their fierce and intense response to the music's wild mood-swings. It helps to have a clarinettist who can coo like a dove and exult like a gipsy; but, in the end, the performance's genius rests in the players' profound and unflinching identification with Brahms's shifting moods.

Clarinet/Viola Sonatas, Op 120 Nos 1 & 2

Clarinet Sonatas Nos 1 & 2. Clarinet Trio, Op 114ª
Martin Fröst *cl* ª**Torleif Thedéen** *vc*
Roland Pöntinen *pf*
BIS ⎗ BIS-SACD1353 (67' · DDD/DSD)   Ⓕ▷

The Trio tends to be the neglected one among the great clarinet works from Brahms's mellow last period, usually coupled with the Clarinet Quintet as though a poor relation. That is grossly unfair to a work which, while maybe not on such a grand scale as the Quintet, has over its four compact movements both profundity and charm. BIS, however, has put it with the sonatas, works on a scale closer to the Trio, and an excellent and successful coupling it is.

Young Swedish clarinettist Martin Fröst has established himself as a leading soloist, appearing with many of the most important European orchestras and inspiring works from composers including Penderecki. He tends to favour speeds on the fast side in the Trio, which means that the second movement *Andante* may lack the meditative depth one finds elsewhere but which has an easy flow. The dramatic bite and thrust of the outer movements is enhanced by relatively urgent speeds, with the coda of the first fading away on a ghostly scalic passage.

Cellist Torleif Thedéen matches Fröst in imaginative playing but pianist Roland Pöntinen, placed backward in the recording balance, is less individual. None the less this is a generously filled CDs and the couplings are apt.

Clarinet Sonatas (trans flute and piano)
Schumann Drei Romanzen, Op 94
C Schumann Drei Romanzen, Op 22 (all arr Khaner)
Jeffrey Khaner *fl* **Charles Abramovic** *pf*
Avie AV2075 (62' · DDD)　　　　　　Ⓕ▷

With the poignant flute solo in the middle of the passacaglia finale of the Fourth Symphony among the most tenderly reflective passages in all Brahms, it is sad that he did not write any work specifically for the flute. That, no doubt among other considerations, was what led Jeffrey Khaner, the distinguished principal flute of the Philadelphia Orchestra, to make his transcriptions of the two Brahms clarinet sonatas.

As one would expect, his alterations to the solo parts are discreet, involving occasional octave transpositions upwards and, more rarely, downwards. In many of the changes it seems that Khaner has been concerned not so much whether the flute can actually play Brahms's written notes but what is more effective on the lighter instrument.

Naturally the replacement of the clarinet by the flute brings a marked change of character. While these late chamber works in their clarinet versions – or in the viola alternatives which the composer himself suggested – have an autumnal quality, the freshness of flute tone brings more of a spring-like feeling. Khaner also demonstrates that though flute tone in its lightness is fresher and brighter than clarinet tone, it is also generally gentler, with such passages as the running quavers in the finale of the First Sonata made more delicate. Yet sensitive as Khaner's arrangements are, it is hard to imagine many people actually preferring these flute versions to the originals: they simply make a splendid showpiece for an outstanding flautist.

Much the same can be said of the Romances by Robert and Clara Schumann, though there is a stronger case for flute transcriptions of Robert's pieces: he suggested the violin or clarinet as an alternative to the oboe which he originally had in mind. The charming Clara pieces were written specifically for violin but again Khaner's transcriptions could not be more sensitive, nor the playing more inspired. In all these works he is greatly helped by the brilliant, warmly understanding accompaniment of Charles Abramovic.

Viola Sonatas Nos 1 & 2. Trio, Op 114[a]
Lawrence Power *va* [a]**Tim Hugh** *vc*
Simon Crawford-Phillips *pf*
Hyperion CDA67584 (65' · DDD)　　　　Ⓕ▷

Viola players have reason to be grateful to Brahms for giving them the chance to perform the two Op 120 sonatas, originally for clarinet. It's less well known that he similarly provided a viola part as alternative to clarinet for the Op 114 Trio. For the sonatas he reworked the part, adding a few chords and double stops, as well as transposing some of it downwards (to exploit the instrument's generally lower tessitura) but in the Trio he contented himself with a simple transcription. In Lawrence Power's hands the extensive use of the viola's upper register poses no problem; he commands a wide tonal spectrum throughout his range, and there's no sense of strain. The Trio does lose something without clarinet, sounding more monochrome as the viola and cello blend together. This blending can, of course, be an advantage – the two string instruments in octaves, in the *Adagio*, make a wonderful sound. And this is a very fine performance, of exceptional expressive range, from extreme delicacy to thrilling power.

The sonatas as played here will surely demonstrate (even to clarinettists) that the viola version is in no way second best. Particularly enjoyable in the Second Sonata is the second movement's dark passion, relieved by glowing intensity in the middle section, where Simon Crawford-Phillips manages exactly to convey Brahms's *forte ma dolce e ben cantando*. The final variations are just as impressive, each one so well characterised yet perfectly paced so that the coda seems an inevitable climax to the whole work.

Trios – Op 40[a]; Op 114[b]. Viola Sonatas Nos 1[c] & 2[d]. Violin Sonata No 1, Op 78 (arr Klengel/Rysanov)[e]
Maxim Rysanov *va* [a]**Boris Brovtsyn** *vn*
[b]**Kristine Blaumane** *vc* [ace]**Katya Apekisheva**,
[bd]**Jacob Katsnelson** *pfs*
Onyx Classics ② ONYX4033
(125' · DDD)　　　　　　　　　　Ⓜ○Ⓑ▷

Brahms was the first to admit that he hadn't entirely solved the new problems of balance in the works that replace the clarinet with a viola (the clarinet sonatas and the Op 114 Trio). With recording, of course, some help can be given. The viola is well forward in the performances by Rysanov, and this suits the music's extrovert, eloquent manner. In the First Sonata, in which Rysanov is accompanied by the excellent Katya Apekisheva, the music is more freely phrased, with a humorous sense of the latent waltz in the *Allegretto* and plenty of vigour in the finale. In the Op 114 Trio, the outside movements benefit from the vivid sense of melodic direction provided by Rysanov and Katsnelson.

The G major Violin Sonata was also written for Joachim, and arranged for viola not by Brahms but by his publisher Simrock's editor Paul Klengel. Transposing it from G down a fourth to D to accommodate the viola loses the music something of its elegance, but this is a persuasive performance. Persuasiveness is also needed in Op 40, which began life as the Horn Trio. Not all the cheerful vigour that Rysanov and Apekisheva provide can make the finale seem anything but a piece of hunting exuberance, but they do splendidly with the *Scherzo* and the *Adagio mesto*.

Piano Quintet in F minor, Op 34

Brahms Piano Quintet
Schumann Piano Quintet, Op 44
Leif Ove Andsnes *pf* **Artemis Quartet**
Virgin Classics 395143-2 (69' · DDD) Ⓕ**OO**🅑➔

Leif Ove Andsnes has an uncanny knack of revealing the inner truth of the music he plays without recourse to excessive gimmickry. He also has exquisite taste when it comes to choosing his chamber music collaborators, as this pairing of the two cornerstones of the piano quintet repertoire demonstrates.

Schumann's Quintet has become the most famous of his chamber works, with its boundless energy and melodic generosity. Andsnes and the Artemis let the notes speak for themselves, never lingering too lovingly on mere details. It's an approach that serves the work well, and an ideal instrumental balance helps illuminate the work's compelling textures throughout.

It's a similar story in the Brahms. Andsnes and the Artemis are alive to all the possibilities in the pregnant opening phrases of each movement and maintain the intensity of the impetuous passion implicit in this youthful music. The Brahms hasn't fared as well on disc as the Schumann and this recording of it can certainly take its place among the finest. As for the Schumann, it's undoubtedly up there with the best.

Piano Quintet^a. String Quartet No 2, Op 51 No 2
^a**Stephen Hough** *pf*
Takács Quartet (Edward Dusinberre, Károly Schranz *vns* Geraldine Walther *va* András Fejér *vc*)
Hyperion CDA67551 (73' · DDD) Ⓟ🅑➔

In the Brahms Second Quartet the Takács find a most appealing lightness of touch. They reveal anew the extraordinarily imaginative way in which the work begins, and breathe air into the intricate textures which precede the vacillating second theme. There's an absolute unanimity to their playing, but a fetching liveliness too. Compared to such groups as the Alban Berg, who revel in the lushness of Brahms's writing, the Takács are more febrile and transparent. Their third movement creeps in, skittering, but there's no lack of sweetness of tone when required. And the fugal section has a spring in its step. Brahms isn't all seriousness, they remind us.

The other major selling-point of this disc is the Piano Quintet, for which the Takács are joined by Stephen Hough. There's nothing cosy about this latest reading, which has fire and passion aplenty, and the recording places Hough pleasingly within the overall texture rather than unduly spotlighting him. There's a feeling of coming together of ideas, with these artists – masters of colour all of them – sparking off one another in a very unstudio-ish way. And throughout, Hough's virtuosity makes light of Brahms's unforgiving textures.

Brahms Piano Quintet **Schubert** Piano Quintet in A, D667, 'Trout'
Sir Clifford Curzon *pf* **Amadeus Quartet** (Norbert Brainin, Siegmund Nissel *vns* Peter Schidlof *va* Martin Lovett *vc*) with **James Edward Merrett** *db*
BBC Legends ② BBCL4009-2 (82' · ADD)
Recorded live 1974, 1971 Ⓜ**OO**

The 1971 recording of the Schubert sounds marginally better than the 1974 Brahms, but the visceral excitement generated by the Brahms Quintet has to be heard to be believed. It would be fairly easy to imagine a tidier performance, but not one that's more spontaneous or inspired. Sir Clifford Curzon's grand vision registers within a few bars of the opening movement and heats to near boiling-point by the start of the recapitulation. The emotional temperature rises even higher for the second movement.

The distinction of the performance resides in the co-operation of all five players, which reaches unprecedented heights in the finale. No wonder the audience explodes: it's doubtful that anyone present has heard a finer performance since. The *Trout*'s repeated exposition is even more exciting than its first statement, and there's some gentle tempo acceleration during the development. True, the strings make a fractionally late entrance at the beginning of the *Andante*, but the vitality of the *Scherzo* would be hard to beat, while the Theme and Variations features notable playing from Lovett. There's an amusing spot of premature congratulation when applause momentarily breaks in at the end of the *Allegro giusto*'s exposition, but it soon withers to silence for a joyous finale. Here the recording rather favours the strings, but better that than have the piano drown everyone else out. Wonderful stuff, all of it.

Piano Quintet
Andreas Staier pf **Leipzig Quartet** (Andreas
Seidel, Tilmann Büning vns Ivo Bauer va Matthias
Moosdorf vc)
Dabringhaus und Grimm MDG307 1218-2
(39' · DDD)　　　　　　　　　　Ⓜ️ⓄⓄ

Here's something quite unusual! Andreas
Staier is playing a Steinway model-D dating
from 1901; not exactly contemporary with the
Quintet (1865), but producing a noticeably
lighter sound than its modern counterpart, and
taking us closer to what would have been
familiar to Brahms.

On this excellent recording we're aware that
the dominating resonance of the present-day
concert grand is missing; the balance shifts in
favour of the strings, making the work seem
more colourful, less sombre. The first movement and the *Scherzo* are especially successful,
with full, resonant *tuttis* contrasting dramatically with the more tenuous, atmospheric music.
The Leipzig Quartet maintain a notably pure
sound, without excessive vibrato, adding to the
feeling of transparency.

Other performers, such as Peter Serkin and
the Guarneri Quartet, have delved more
searchingly into the Quintet's emotional content, bringing out the moments of deep
pathos or soaring lyricism. But Staier and the
Leipzigers will expand your view of this great
work.

Piano Quartets

No 1 in G minor, Op 25; **No 2** in A, Op 26;
No 3 in C minor, Op 60
Piano Quartets Nos 1-3[a]. Three Pieces, Op 117
Marc-André Hamelin pf
[a]**Leopold String Trio** (Marianne Thorsen vn
Lawrence Power va Kate Gould vc)
Hyperion ② CDA67471/2 (142' · DDD)　ⒻⓄⓄ➌

Brahms's finest chamber works are the quintets
and sextets, whereas in the smaller line-ups textures can sometimes get clogged, as if the composer had metaphorically donned one overcoat
too many. His three piano quartets sometimes
exhibit this tendency but in performances as fine
as these it is triumphantly surmounted with a
combination of brisk speeds and an extraordinary collective *joie de vivre*.

The First Quartet opens simply, with Hamelin
shaping the line beautifully but unaffectedly, the
Leopold players gradually entering, their playing filled with ardour. The finale is irresistibly
ebullient, with a jaw-dropping ending. The
other impressive aspect is the sense of absolute
precision, which lightens the textures and keeps
edges crisp. Sample, for instance, the *Scherzo* of
No 3 which can, in some hands, sound positively
elephantine. Not here though, Hamelin dealing
with Brahms's dense chords as easily as if they
were single lines.

The epic Second Quartet, more a symphony
than a quartet, is a considerable challenge to

players and audience. Hamelin and the Leopold
get to the heart of the matter in the soulful *Poco
adagio* and while they in no way lack heft when
it's needed, there's always a dancing quality to
their playing which does much to illuminate
textures. This music certainly benefits from
their defiantly un-Germanic approach. Hamelin
signs off with the Op 117 *Intermezzi*, elegantly
played.

Piano Quartet No 1. Four Ballades, Op 10
Emil Gilels pf members of the **Amadeus Quartet**
(Norbert Brainin vn Peter Schidlof va Martin Lovett
vc)
DG The Originals 447 407-2GOR (65' · ADD)
Recorded 1970, 1975　　　　　　Ⓜ️Ⓞ➌

This is an outstanding performance of Brahms's
G minor Piano Quartet, unforgettable for its
spontaneity and uninhibited Romantic warmth
and verve. The booklet reminds us that this 1970
recording made history since 'a contract between
an artist from the Soviet Union and a Western
label was a sensational event in cultural diplomacy'. Reproduced with respect for the sound
quality of its time, the playing has a glowing
strength and intensity throughout. Only in the
first movement's opulent textures does the keyboard occasionally dominate. From Emil Gilels
we're also given a maturely unhurried, essentially
'inward' recording of Brahms's youthful *Ballades*.

Piano Quartet No 3[a]. Double Concerto[b]
Isaac Stern vn [a]**Jaime Laredo** va Yo-Yo Ma vc
[a]**Emanuel Ax** pf [b]**Chicago Symphony Orchestra /
Claudio Abbado**
Sony Classical 509970 90405-2 (68' · DDD)　ⒻⓄⓄⓄ

The piano quartets have all the power
and lyricism that we associate with
Brahms's music; but alongside a wealth
of melodic and harmonic invention there are
some shadows: all we know of Brahms's life suggests that he was never a happy man. Even if this
is reflected in the music, and especially the
C minor Quartet, all is kept in proportion and
there's no overt soul-bearing. The present performance with its exuberant sweep is particularly telling, and although no detail is missed the
players offer an overall strength. Sadly the
Third Piano Quartet is the only one of the set
now available from these formidable musicians.
In place of the first two quartets we now have a
fine performance of the Double Concerto, Stern
and Ma displaying the subtlety of chamber
musicians, Abbado a faithful collaborator.

String Quintets

String Quintets – No 1, Op 88; No 2, Op 111
Nash Ensemble (Marianne Thorsen, Malin
Broman vns Lawrence Power va Paul Watkins vc)
with **Philip Dukes** va
Onyx Classics ONYX4043 (56' · DDD)　　ⒻⓄⓄ➌

Brahms, by adding a second viola to the string quartet line-up, revelled in the richness such bulking-out in the mid-range afforded him. The two string quintets (1882 and 1890) are essentially sunny creations, conceived during happy times in Bad Ischl. The First Quintet strikes a characteristic Brahmsian balance between economy and expansiveness, telescoping slow movement and *scherzo* into the single span of the central variations, and framing this with the autumnal, Schubertian unfolding of the opening *Allegro non troppo* and the Beethovenian contrapuntal discursiveness of the final *Allegro energico.* Brahms conceived the Second Quintet as his final work and in one of the most striking openings in all chamber music, upper-string sirens blaze off in hot pursuit of a drive-by cello solo. The slow movement and waltzish Intermezzo are in Brahms's elegiac mode, while the finale demonstrates his love of Hungarian gypsy music.

The Nash Ensemble are nothing less than the London regiment of chamber music's crack troops, and they present this joyful, compelling music in its best light. Recorded with appealing immediacy.

String Quartets

No 1 in C minor, Op 51 No 1; **No 2** in A minor, Op 51; **No 3** in B flat, Op 67

String Quartets Nos 1 & 3
Takács Quartet (Edward Dusinberre, Károly Schranz vns Geraldine Walther va András Fejér vc)
Hyperion CDA67552 (65' · DDD) Ⓕ**OO**

Viola to the fore in the third movement, *Agitato,* of No 3; and Geraldine Walther, firm-toned and assertive, rises to the occasion as the only un-muted instrumentalist here. Agitation isn't consistently maintained though because the Takács Quartet tend to ease the tension in places. Yet there is no slack in the other movements. This close-knit group unanimously stretch or tighten the rhythm, achieving evenly matched dynamics such as the *sotto voce* sequences in the opening *Vivace,* the hushed *dolce e grazioso* in the recapitulation of the *Andante* and the stilled peace of the G flat sixth variation in the finale. Walther is well in the picture in this movement so whereas elsewhere she appears occasionally to lose focus.

Not so in No 1. Her place on the right of the ensemble is firmly assured here. The work is 'commonly held to be representative of Brahms's austerity and asceticism' (Edwin Evans), and these epithets are apposite for the Takács, spare of style and tone. The players' control over the first movement doesn't preclude a range of *rubato* that serves to sharpen the musical argument. Nor does it preclude a linear drive that knits the six themes of the last movement into a coherent whole, while they do not let up on the melancholy of the middle movements, the third particularly dark. The recording is tonally credible but is widely separated.

String Quartets Nos 1 & 2
Cleveland Quartet (William Preucil, Peter Salaff vns James Dunham va Paul Katz vc)
Telarc CD80346 (68' · DDD) Ⓕ

Though the Cleveland Quartet has changed both its leader and viola player in recent years, all the old tonal opulence is still very much there. So is all the old fire, and equally, the determination to wring the last drop of expression from even the most intimate confession. In short, you'd be unlikely to meet a more overtly romantic composer than the Brahms you meet here. In the C minor Quartet's *Romanze* some might in fact prefer the very mellow but more emotionally reticent Borodin Quartet, or the Alban Berg with their ethereally withdrawn *pianissimo.* In the bolder flanking movements it's as compulsive as the highly strung, impressionable Alban Berg while often finding a broader, suaver, melodic sweep. Opulent sound.

Clarinet Trio in A minor, Op 114

Brahms Clarinet Trio **Holbrooke** Clarinet Quintet Ⓗ No 1 in G, Op 27 No 1 **Weber** Clarinet Concertino in E flat, J109
Reginald Kell cl **Anthony Pini** vc **Louis Kentner** pf
Willoughby Quartet (Louis Willoughby, Kenneth Skeaping vns Aubrey Appleton va Vivian Joseph vc)
orchestra / **Walter Goehr**
Testament mono SBT1002 (54' · ADD)
Recorded 1941 Ⓕ

In the rapturous love-duet between clarinet and cello in the *Adagio* of the Clarinet Trio, Reginald Kell's tonal warmth and beauty seem more than ever appropriate. Elsewhere in this work, though, despite his liquid sound and finesse of dynamics he's all but outshone by the eloquent lyricism and passion of that superb player Anthony Pini. Together with Kentner's understanding collaboration, never over-assertive but always supportive, an admirably cohesive team is formed, alive to Brahms's interplay of interest and changes of mood. Kell is the star of the Quintet by Josef Holbrooke which has fallen into total neglect; frankly the present diffuse work (concocted out of previous compositions) will not prompt much reevaluation of his status. Nevertheless, it offers great opportunities for *cantabile* clarinet playing in the central *Canzonet* and for fluent virtuosity in the finale: Kell excels in both. Not unexpectedly the Weber *Concertino,* every clarinettist's party-piece, finds him displaying, besides an easy technical brilliance, beauty of tone, a charming sense of phrase and sensitive dynamic nuances. Goehr's orchestral accompaniment is clean and alert.

Piano Trios

No 1 in B, Op 8; **No 2** in C, Op 87; **No 3** in C minor, Op 101

Piano Trios Nos 1-3. Horn Trio in E flat, Op 40
Clarinet Trio in A minor, Op 114
Richard Hosford cl **Stephen Stirling** hn **Florestan
Trio** (Anthony Marwood vn Richard Lester vc Susan
Tomes pf)
Hyperion ② CDA67251/2 (137' · DDD)　　Ⓕ**O**▷

Aided by an especially clear, vivid, yet spacious
recording, the Florestan Trio and their two colleagues allow us to hear far more of this music
than usual – the elaborate decoration of Op 114's
Adagio, or the sinister detail of the more delicate
passages in Op 8's *Scherzo*. Much of the credit for
this goes to Susan Tomes; her playing is an
object-lesson in sensitivity and in matching the
other voices. Balance and blend are a special feature of these performances. Anthony Marwood
and Richard Lester match their sounds perfectly
for the lovely duet passages in the slow movements of Opp 8 and 101. Less expected, and less
usual, is the matching of violin and horn, cello
and clarinet. But perhaps the single outstanding
feature of all the performances is the way the
music is shaped. It's not only that the phrases are
projected clearly and expressively – the approach
moves outwards to encompass the music's larger
paragraphs and, indeed, whole movements.
These are very desirable recordings, then.

Additional recommendation

Piano Trios Nos 1 & 2
Augustin Dumay vn **Jian Wang** vc
Maria João Pires pf
DG download 447 055-2GH (67' · DDD)　　Ⓕ**O**▷
The duo of Augustin Dumay and Maria João Pires
have found themselves a true soul mate in the Chinese cellist Jian Wang, as this, their first disc of
piano trios, engagingly shows. Poetic and powerful,
this is glorious chamber music-making.

Cello Sonatas

No 1 in E minor, Op 38; No 2 in F, Op 99

Cello Sonatas Nos 1 & 2
Mstislav Rostropovich vc **Rudolf Serkin** pf
DG 410 510-2GH (58' · DDD)　　Ⓕ**O**▷

Our younger generation of cello soloists seems
to favour a tone production which balances a
refined upper range with a middle and lower
register that's strong and well focused, rather
than expansively rich and resonant. Readers will
not need to be told that Rostropovich's solo
image is definitely not of this ilk: his musical
personality is in every sense larger than life and
in this magnificent coupling of the cello sonatas,
in partnership with Rudolf Serkin, the very forward balance of the recording exaggerates this
impression in the most vivid way. By comparison the piano image – to the right of and behind
the cello – is more reticent in timbre and seldom
matches Rostropovich's rich flood of sound,

which isn't, of course, to suggest that Serkin fails
to project the music, merely that the microphone placing makes Rostropovich very much
the dominating artist. This passionately warm-
hearted and ripely Brahmsian music-making
almost overwhelms the listener in its sheer
impact. But with playing of this calibre, with
both artists wonderfully attuned to each other's
responses, every nuance tells and Brahms's bold
melodic lines soar out from the speakers to capture the imagination, and provide an enthralling
musical experience in each and every work.

Cello Sonatas Nos 1 & 2 **Dvořák** Silent Woods.
Rondo **Suk** Ballade, Op 3 No 1. Serenade, Op 3 No 2
Steven Isserlis vc **Stephen Hough** pf
Hyperion CDA67529 (74' · DDD)　　Ⓕ**OO**

In 1984 Steven Isserlis made excellent recordings
for Hyperion of the Brahms sonatas with Peter
Evans; this time he's added some substantial extra
items – the two Suk pieces, wonderfully played,
are particularly welcome. The new recording is
fuller in sound and more realistic; Stephen
Hough's commanding playing of Brahms's 'big'
piano parts could, one feels, overpower the cello
but, thanks to his sensitivity, this never happens.

In the sonatas, the timings are in nearly every
case slightly shorter, due not to any very different tempi but because the music now flows
more easily, with less sense of effort. Some listeners may miss the intensity of Evans's
involvement with the music but the new versions have a wonderful sense of line, and
Hough's more detached approach comes with
vivid characterisation – seen in the sinister
colours of No 2's *Allegro passionato*, for example,
or the limpid, elegant playing of No 1's *Allegretto quasi menuetto*.

Only in one place, the finale of No 2, is there
the feeling that Hough's fluency creates a problem: repeating the opening theme, he pushes on
in a way that detracts from the sunny, contented
atmosphere at the start. These are deeply considered, immensely satisfying accounts. Isserlis
and Hough make a formidable team.

Cello Sonatas Nos 1 & 2. Anklänge, Op 7 No 3.
Die Mainacht, Op 43 No 2
Anthony Leroy vc **Sandra Moubarak** pf
Zig-Zag Territoires ZZT070202 (63' · DDD)　　Ⓕ**O**

Brahms's cello sonatas tackle head on the real
problem of balancing the cello's potentially gruff
lowest register and singing high tones with the
piano, but he does not make matters easy for
himself. Some of the piano textures are very thick
and there are places in this recording where the
problems are barely solved: the start of the
F major Second Sonata and the finale of the
E minor No 1 are cases in point. He is at least
considerate enough to refine the piano textures
when he risks asking the cello to play the flowing
theme of this finale with the tricky slurred
pizzicato, and this comes off excellently here.

The performances are exceptional. Anthony Leroy and Sandra Moubarak have a real understanding of Brahms's unusually long phrases. In the great sweeping melody of the opening of the E minor Sonata they begin pensively and are not afraid to use considerable freedom of tempo change at the peak of the exposition before returning to this inwardness. The *Adagio*, another very long and varied melody, is beautifully phrased, as is the middle section of the third movement, its marking dolce espressivo constrasting with the general *Allegro passionato*. The E minor Sonata's Minuet has a delightful lilt, and they go with a will at the difficult final fugue. There are also charming performances of the two songs included as fill-ups.

Brahms Cello Sonata No 1ª **Grieg** Cello Sonata, Op 36ª **Shostakovich** Cello Sonata, Op 40ᵇ
Mstislav Rostropovich vc
ᵇ**Benjamin Britten**, ª**Sviatoslav Richter** pfs
BBC Legends BBCL4263-2 (81' · ADD)
Recorded live at the Parish Church, Aldeburgh, in June 1964   Ⓕ**OO**

Joyful anticipation at 80 minutes of previously unreleased live performances from Aldeburgh, given by two Russian giants and their composer-pianist mutual friend, is temporarily dampened by the recorded sound, which is distractingly hissy and acoustically less than grateful, especially for the piano. But the discomfort passes, thanks to passionate communication, matched by formidable intellectual control and sparking off against it. Richter offers no apologies for the chunkiness of Brahms's piano writing, but the amplitude and range of Rostropovich's tone show that no such apologies are needed. Neither player is embarrassed by the obviousness of Grieg's melodrama; instead they do everything they can to maximise it, and both they and the music emerge triumphant.

With Britten as accompanist, the first movement of the Shostakovich is if anything even more driven than in Rostropovich's account with the composer, but any hint of loss of character is soon forgotten as the large-scale vision and sheer presence of the playing work their magic. Admittedly a few spills accompany the thrills – the tricky conclusion to the *Scherzo* for one, and the piano's last note for another – but that is merely a concomitant of music-making that has its sights set far beyond perfection. All three performances are documents to treasure, and Tully Potter's sympathetic accompanying essay is another bonus.

Violin Sonatas

No 1 in G, Op 78; **No 2** in A, Op 100;
No 3 in D minor, Op 108

Violin Sonatas Nos 1-3
Itzhak Perlman vn **Vladimir Ashkenazy** pf

EMI Great Recordings of the Century 566893-2 (70' · DDD)   Ⓜ**OO**Ⓑ➔

If anyone doubts that these three sonatas represent Brahms at his most blissfully lyrical, then this is an essential set to hear. The trouble-free happiness of these mellow inspirations, all written after the main body of Brahms's orchestral music had been completed, comes over richly and seductively in these fine performances. In their sureness and flawless confidence, they carry you along cocooned in rich sound. Perlman consistently produces rich, full-bodied tone, an excellent illustration being the way that he evokes a happy, trouble-free mood in the melody which opens the second movement *Adagio* of No 3. The obverse of this is that with such consistent richness and warmth, the three sonatas come to sound more alike than they usually do, or maybe should, a point which comes out the more from playing them in sequence. It's true that Perlman does quite often play softly, but for some tastes he's placed too close to the microphone, and the actual dynamic level stays rather high, however gently he's playing. This isn't to say that with sharp imagination and superbly clean articulation from the pianist, these performances lack range of expression – in particular, there's the rhythmic pointing, which gives a Hungarian or a Slavonic tang to such passages as the first contrasting episode in the 'raindrop' finale of No 1 or the contrasting *vivace* passages in the second movement of No 2, where the last *pizzicato* reprise is made totally delectable. These performances are both distinctive and authoritative. The recording is bright, with a good sense of atmosphere to give bite to the piano tone without diminishing the warmth of Perlman's violin.

Violin Sonatas Nos 1-3. Sonata 'FAE' – Scherzo
Renaud Capuçon vn **Nicholas Angelich** pf
Virgin Classics 545731-2 (79' · DDD)   Ⓕ Ⓑ➔

Capuçon and Angelich make a wonderfully well-matched team, with a command of genuine *rubato* (pressing forward in order to make room for subsequent holding back) that gives a truly authentic impression. Each detail of the music is expressively convincing: it seems that it's a priority for Angelich and Capuçon to feel the music. This can lead them sometimes to go against Brahms's expressed intentions. The theme at 3'18" in the first movement of Op 78 is marked to be in tempo (after a *ritardando*) but here the speed suddenly becomes faster, and the dynamic much louder than the written *pianissimo*. Similarly, in the *Presto agitato* finale of Op 108 the quieter passages are taken more slowly.

These are occasional lapses: overall the performances are beautifully considered, tending towards an expansive, romantic view of Brahms, but with a care for balance and proportion. The *FAE* Scherzo, for example, has all the necessary youthful exuberance, but it's coupled with a fine feeling for balance between the parts and for rhythmic character. And, throughout, there's a magnificent sense of line: Capuçon plays the great G-string melodies in Op 108's *Adagio* and Op 100's finale with rich, opulent sound but his vibrato is never too prominent – the most important thing is the shape of the melody.

enchanting vivacity and lightness. The rapid chording of Variation 3 holds no terrors for them and, throughout, their virtuosity is as fearless as it is musical. This is a fine and well recorded addition to the sisters' discography.

Violin Sonatas Nos 1-3. Sonata 'FAE' – Scherzo
Nikolaj Znaider *vn* **Yefim Bronfman** *pf*
RCA Red Seal 88697 06106-2 (71' · DDD) Ⓕ**O**Ⓓ⁺

Brahms's Op 78 Violin Sonata, the first of his three, comes closer to a work of some wistfulness, the opening phrase taking on, with Nikolaj Znaider and Yefim Bronfman, a gentle melancholy that suits the music well. The hesitancy of this dotted phrase marks the whole of the sonata's invention, and is picked up with touching effect, as Clara Schumann was moved to find, when Brahms quotes an earlier song in the finale. This is all sensitively done.

So is the Second Sonata, with delightful touches: when the *Andante* gives way to a faster section, it is here played as gaily as a Brahms waltz, one that turns faintly spectral on its return with the *pizzicato* violin. Perhaps the finale, *Presto agitato*, deserves more extrovert agitation, but these are most thoughtful and sympathetic performances. There is also room on the disc for the lively *scherzo* which, as a young man, Brahms wrote for a composite sonata, with movements by Schumann and Albert Dietrich.

Sonata for Two Pianos, Op 34b

Sonata for Two Pianos. Waltzes, Op 39 – Nos 1, 2, 11, 14, 15 and 16. Hungarian Dances – Nos 5 & 17
Saint-Saëns Variations on a Theme of Beethoven
Güher Pekinel, Süher Pekinel *pfs*
Warner Classics 2564 61959-2 (67' · DDD) Ⓕ Ⓓ⁺

A quick glance at Warner Classics's note reminds us that the twin sisters Güher and Süher Pekinel studied with Serkin, Arrau, Yvonne Loriod and Horszowski, a formidable pedigree reflected in performances of rare brilliance and pinpoint definition. Their crystalline clarity and verve erase the very real threats of strenuousness, opacity and coagulated textures in the Brahms Sonata, music exposed to severe criticism from Clara Schumann before its final reincarnation as the Piano Quintet.

The Pekinels achieve exactly the right note of foreboding at the start of the first movement development. They also give us a true oasis of calm in the *Andante* before racing through the *Scherzo* at a tempo sufficiently precipitate to tempt fate. But their command and control win the day at every point and never more so than in the finale's concluding *Presto non troppo*, whirled to an exhilarating close with total assurance.

After such a weighty offering the Waltzes and *Hungarian Dances* provide charming and scintillating relief, and, moving from Germany to France, the Pekinels' performance of Saint-Saëns's *Variations on a Theme of Beethoven* is of an

Piano Works

Piano Sonatas – No 1 in C, Op 1; No 2 in F sharp minor, Op 2; No 3 in F minor, Op 5. Variations on a Theme by Paganini, Op 35. Variations and Fugue on a Theme by Handel, Op 24. Four Ballades, Op 10ᵇ. Variations on a Theme by Schumann, Op 9. Variations on an Original Theme, Op 21 No 1. Variations on a Hungarian Song, Op 21 No 2. Waltzes, Op 39. Two Rhapsodies, Op 79. Scherzo in E flat minor, Op 4. Piano Pieces – Op 76; Op 116; Op 117; Op 118; Op 119. Hungarian Dancesᵃ Ⓗ
Julius Katchen, ᵃ**Jean-Pierre Marty** *pfs*
Decca London Ⓖ 455 247-2LC6 (388' · ADD)
Recorded 1962-66 Ⓑ**OO**

The American pianist Julius Katchen made his name in the early 1950s and died in 1969, but although he's generally thought of as a distinguished figure from the last generation, it's salutary to realise that he would probably be performing today if his career had not ended when he was only 42. Even so, his legacy of recordings reminds us of his gifts and the breadth of his repertory, and the present Brahms cycle has distinction. It begins with an account of the *Paganini* Variations that gives ample proof of his assured technique: the playing tells us at once that the challenging variations in sixths (Nos 1 and 2 in Book 1) held no terrors for him, and the athleticism here is matched by a fluency in the *leggiero* writing of the variation that follows. In this work, though, you're generally made more aware of a keyboard virtuoso than a poet; there are other performances which balance these two qualities more finely. Tempi tend to rapidity, too, and the piano sound tends to have a hardish brilliance. However, he does bring a gentler quality to the three other sets of variations here, not least in his freer use of rubato and tonal nuance, as witness (say) the serene Variations Nos 11-12 in the big *Handel* set, where the recording from three years earlier is easier on the ear. Here, as elsewhere, there's a little tape hiss, but not enough to distract.

Poetry is to be found in good measure in Katchen's playing of the Four Ballades, Op 10. These pieces belie the composer's youth in their deep introspection, though the pianist takes a brisk view of the *Andante con moto* tempo in No 4. The 16 Waltzes of Op 39 are attractive too in their crispness and charm, and the early *Scherzo* in E flat minor has the right dour vigour. The three sonatas are also impressive in their strong, energetic interpretative grasp, though you could wish that the first-movement repeat of No 1 had been observed. Also, slow movements could have a still more inward quality to convey that brooding self-communion which is so characteristic of this composer (though that of Sonata

No 3 in F minor is pretty near it). But the great F minor Sonata is spacious and thoughtful as well as leonine, and this is a noble performance, well recorded in 1966.

The shorter pieces are finely done also. Katchen is in his element in the Two Rhapsodies of Op 79, balancing the stormy and lyrical qualities to perfection. The Fantasias, Op 116, aren't so well recorded (the sound is a bit muffled). However, the playing is masterly, with tragedy, twilight mystery and storm and stress fully playing their part and giving a golden glow to such pieces as the lovely E major Intermezzo which is No 6 of the set and the A major Intermezzo, Op 118 No 2. Possibly more sensuous gypsy charm could be found in, say, the B minor Capriccio of Op 76, but it's very attractive playing and the playful C major Intermezzo in Op 119 is delightful, as is the tender lullaby that begins Op 117.

Only the first 10 of the 21 Hungarian Dances exist in the composer's own (very difficult) version for piano solo, and in the others, written for piano duet, Katchen is joined by Jean-Pierre Marty; there's plenty of fire here and much to enjoy. Altogether, this Brahms set is a fine memorial to Katchen and a worthy issue.

Piano Sonata No 2. Three Pieces, Op 117.
Eight Pieces, Op 76
Libor Novacek pf
Landor LAN285 (76' · DDD)　　　　　　　ⒻⓄ

Libor Novacek shows himself deeply sensitive to the interior light burning beneath the surface of Brahms's often dark-hued later masterpieces. What unfaltering poise and tonal translucence he achieves throughout Opp 76 and 117. Less ebullient than, say, Rubinstein or Perahia in the second Capriccio from Op 76, his playing is so finely 'worked' and controlled that even here he captures a reflection and nostalgia at the heart of such music. His poetic refinement in No 6 is exquisite and if Novacek dims the radiance of No 8, keeping his exultance on a tight rein, he remains musicianly to his fingertips. Here once more he locates an underlying poetry denied to less subtle or less engaging pianists.

A master of inwardness, he also sets the storm clouds scudding menacingly across No 6 and shows that he's as swashbuckling as the best of them in the early F sharp minor Sonata, resolving every thorny and perverse difficulty with ease and lucidity. The Landor sound (Potton Hall in Suffolk) is of demonstration quality.

Piano Sonata No 3. Hungarian Dances – No 1 in G minor; No 2 in D minor; No 3 in F; No 6 in D flat; No 7 in A. Eight Pieces, Op 76 – No 2, Capriccio in B minor; No 7, Intermezzo in A minor
Evgeny Kissin pf
RCA Red Seal 82876 52737-2 (56' · DDD)　　ⒻⒹ→

Kissin opens the F minor Sonata with an imperious thrust, and in the octave outburst at 4'46"

again proves himself a fearless virtuoso; few pianists of any generation would even consider such a whirlwind tempo. For some, his *rubato*, heated and intense, will seem overbearing, yet he finds the still centre at the heart of the *Andante*. He thunders to the heavens the final climax (*molto appassionato*) and launches the *Scherzo* as though with a rush of blood to the head. He may be a less subtle poet of the keyboard in this sonata than, say, Radu Lupu, but his searing projection carries its own rewards, and every bar of Brahms's early and rhetorical masterpiece is marked by his overwhelming technique and magisterial temperament.

In Op 76 No 2 you'd hardly mistake the pressure he exerts for Rubinstein's or Perahia's patrician grace, but it says much for his conviction that in No 7 he can so audaciously replace the composer's *semplice* direction with his own more elaborate notion of style. But it's in five of the *Hungarian Dances* that his extrovert nature finds its truest outlet: in No 6 his performance is of an astounding verve and resilience. Here's virtuosity in the grandest of grand manners, and RCA's sound, for once, is as red-blooded as the playing.

Piano Sonata No 3. 16 Waltzes, Op 39
Antti Siirala pf
Ondine ODE1044-2 (62' · DDD)　　　　ⒻⓄⓄⒹ→

Antti Siirala has been a serial entrant of piano competitions. He wins most of them, including the Beethoven, London, Dublin and Leeds (2003) events, but Siirala is a great deal more than a jury-pleaser. This is a strikingly good disc, notable both for the full-bodied, golden tone of the piano (superbly recorded) and his ability to hold together both long movements and large structures with playing of refined musicality. After the first two pages of the F minor Sonata other mighty performances spring to mind – Katchen, Solomon, of course, Grainger and Bauer from an even earlier era. After the leonine first movement comes the long nocturnal narrative of the second. To hear Siirala at his most expressive, try the final section (*andante molto*) from 9'02", sensitive to every nuance, deeply felt and aching with regret. He characterises the rumbustious *Scherzo* and its chorale-like Trio equally well, and builds to the impassioned climax of the finale with abandon.

Siirala brings colour and imagination to the Op 39 Waltzes. He makes subtle use of all the repeats, and the sighing falls of No 12 are beautifully done, though it's debatable whether almost all the left hand of the famous A flat waltz (No 15) should be played *staccato* (only the first four bars and six towards the end are so marked). It's a detail, to be sure, an aspect of the music to which Siirala, otherwise, pays admirable attention.

Two Rhapsodies, Op 79. Three Intermezzos, Op 117.
Six Piano Pieces, Op 118. Four Piano Pieces, Op 119
Radu Lupu pf
Decca 417 599-2DH (71' · ADD). Recorded 1970s　Ⓕ

Here are 71 minutes of the finest Brahms piano music, played by one of the outstanding Brahms exponents of our day. What's most treasurable about it is the quiet rapture of some of the most quintessentially Brahmsian moments; for example, the way Lupu sleepwalks into the last section of Op 117 No 3 and the revelation in Op 118 No 2 that the inversion of the theme is even more beautiful than its original statement. The Op 79 *Rhapsodies* are perhaps a fraction less memorable. Decca's recording sounds a little bottom-heavy, in the manner of certain Ashkenazy records of this vintage, and in the heavier textures of the Rhapsodies Lupu compounds the problem by reinforcing the bass with octaves and even fifths. Still, this remains as fine a selection of Brahms's piano works as you're likely to find on one disc.

Brahms Piano Sonata No 3   Ⓗ
Liszt La leggierezza, S144 No 2a. Années de pèlerinage, première année, S160, 'Suisse' – Au bord d'une source[a]. Hungarian Rhapsody No 15 in A minor, S244[b] **Schumann** Carnaval, Op 9
Solomon pf
Testament mono SBT1084 (79' · ADD)
Recorded 1952; [a]1930, [b]1932   Ⓕ❂❂

Solomon's 1952 recordings of Schumann's *Carnaval* and the Brahms Sonata in F minor are essential for the desert island, so this well-produced compilation, generously filled out with Liszt, recommends itself. If you've heard tell of Solomon's reputation but don't know his work, or perhaps know only his Beethoven, snap it up. The sound has come up astonishingly well, also in the Liszt pieces which were made in 1930 and 1932. Solomon's performance of 'Au bord d'une source' is a match for Liszt's poetic inspiration, as few recordings of it are. Technical address and refinement on this level constitute a small miracle.

Piano Pieces – Op 116; Op 117; Op 118; Op 119
Markus Groh pf
Avie ⌖ AV2136 (79' · DDD)   Ⓕ❍▷

Markus Groh's supreme control of the instrument and sensitivity regarding timbre and texture enable him convincingly to stretch the Op 117 No 1 Intermezzo's middle section to its arguable breaking-point. The same goes for his full-throated, polyphonically aware conceptions of the A major and G minor Capriccios from Op 116. The Intermezzi, Op 118 No 6 and Op 119 No 1, elicit brooding, weighty interpretations that still manage to convey shape and sustaining power. Notable too are Groh's slightly agitated take on Op 117 No 3's *con moto* directive, with more varied *legato* articulation than one commonly hears. The pianist's ample tone and deft delineation of the Op 116 No 7 Capriccio's gnarly textures are all the more impressive once you realise how discreetly he employs the sustain pedal. To be certain, some selections meet with less success: for example,

the little C major Intermezzo, Op 119 No 3 (made famous by Myra Hess), is voiced to perfection yet never takes wing; nor does the cycle's closing Rhapsody break out from Groh's four-square shell.

Still, for a single-disc release that includes all four 'late' Brahms piano works, Groh more than holds his own alongside more seasoned performances. The dryish room ambience characterising Avie's engineering via conventional two-channel and headphone playback appreciably opens up when experienced in surround-sound.

---

16 Waltzes, Op 39. 10 Hungarian Dances
Idil Biret pf
Naxos 8 550355 (52' · DDD)   Ⓢ▷

Both the Waltzes and the *Hungarian Dances* are extremely demanding in their two-hand form, and in the latter collection you could often believe that the 20 fingers of two duettists must be involved, so many notes are being played in all registers (for an example, try No 8 in A minor). However, the technical problems hold no terrors for this pianist and her performances are convincing and attractive. What more need be said about this playing of music in which Brahms portrayed, in turn, sophisticated Vienna and untamed Hungary? Well, not a great deal. The quicker Waltzes have plenty of vivacity, and the slower ones are lyrical in an aptly Viennese manner. Tempi, textures, phrasing, *rubato* and pedalling are well managed and the playing has a very convincing blend of subtlety and simplicity. She treats these 16 pieces as a sequence, as Brahms's key structure allows, and leaves relatively little gap between them. The *Hungarian Dances* have a darkly surging Magyar energy and sound that are very pleasing: indeed, Biret seems totally at home in this music. The recording is a bit larger than life, but perfectly acceptable.

Brahms Choral Preludes, Op 122 (arr Mandyczewski)
Febel Seven Choral Arrangements after JS Bach
Reger Choral Fantasia on 'Rejoice My Soul', Op 30
Yaara Tal, Andreas Groethuysen pfs
Sony Classical 88697 12146-2 (65' · DDD)   Ⓕ

Brahms's 11 Chorale Preludes for organ have been arranged for solo piano by a number of composers including Busoni and Paul Juon, but here we have the world premiere of versions for four-hands-one-piano by Brahms's friend Eusebius Mandyczewski (1857-1929). Brahms knew he was dying when he wrote them and most of the chosen chorales are concerned with death, so the music is not exactly calculated to put a spring in your step, but these faithful translations are welcome discoveries. In fact, I'm not sure I don't prefer them to the originals, at least when played by this superb duo. Listen to the best known of the set, the haunting harmonisation of *Es ist ein Ros' entsprungen*, to which Tal and Groethuysen bring an affecting simplicity, reminding us of the art that conceals art.

BRAHMS'S EIN DEUTSCHES REQUIEM – IN BRIEF

Schwarzkopf; Fischer-Dieskau; Philharmonia Chorus and Orchestra / Otto Klemperer
EMI 566903-2 (69' · DDD)   Ⓜ❹❹❹▷
A genuine Great Recording of the Century: two superb soloists, a great choir and orchestra, and a conductor whose rugged feeling for the music pays colossal dividends.

Margiono; Gilfry; Monteverdi Choir; Orchestre Révolutionnaire et Romantique / Sir John Eliot Gardiner
Philips 478 2119DOR (66' · DDD)   Ⓑ❹❹▷
Gardiner's magnificent choir cover themselves in glory here: this is a performance charactersied by great clarity and transparency that makes this a wonderfully light-filled spiritual experience. Beautiful playing from the period strings.

Röschmann; Quasthoff; Berlin Radio Chorus; Berlin Philharmonic Orchestra / Sir Simon Rattle
EMI 365393-2 (67' · DDD)   Ⓕ❹❹▷
Rattle has long cherished this work and the BPO has a long tradition of performing it. It is a beautiful, burnished interpretation with choral singing to match the wondrous playing of the Berlin orchestra. Only Quasthoff's rather flappy singing detracts a little.

Grümmer; Fischer-Dieskau; St Hedwig's Cathedral Choir; Berlin PO / Rudolf Kempe Ⓗ
EMI mono 764705-2 (76' · SDD)   Ⓜ
The earliest of Fischer-Dieskau's numerous recordings of the work finds him, in 1955, in glorious voice – as is Elisabeth Grümmer. Kempe's interpretation is deeply moving.

Janowitz; Waechter; Vienna Singverein; Berlin Philharmonic Orchestra / Herbert von Karajan
DG 463 661-2GOR (77' · ADD)   Ⓜ
DG 📀 073 4398GH (79' · NTSC · 0)
Two glorious soloists – Waechter mellow toned and wonderfully humane, Janowitz almost instrumental in her purity – add to Karajan's soft-grained performance. A long-time favourite that still sounds good. Karajan's video version is also worth considering: same line-up except for José van Dam as the (excellent) baritone soloist.

Bonney; Terfel; Swedish Radio Choir; Eric Ericson Chamber Choir; Berlin PO / Claudio Abbado
TDK 📀 DV-MUSIK (140')   Ⓕ❹
Though the CD version of this performance is currently available, the DVD makes a fine alternative. Made in Vienna's striking Musikverein, it has been sensitively filmed by Bob Coles and presents a deeply impressive reading in a beautifully understated way. Excellent performances.

The Reger Fantasy in the composer's arrangement (1899) of his organ original (1898) was unearthed by the duo and premiered by them in 2004. Seven of the chorale's nine verses, notated throughout the score by Reger, inspire a sequence of seven variations culminating in a complex three-part canon.

Reinhard Febel (b1952), on the other hand, takes six different Bach chorale preludes (*Wo soll ich fliehen hin?* is treated twice) and leaves the originals intact for one pianist while the other supplements additional layers using contemporary devices. I found these quite mesmerising, especially the barely audible overtones in the first version of *Wo soll ich fliehen hin?* and the disconcerting dissonant chords that float above *Allein Gott in der Höh sei Her.*

Ein deutsches Requiem, Op 45

Ein deutsches Requiem
Elisabeth Schwarzkopf *sop* **Dietrich Fischer-Dieskau** *bar* **Philharmonia Chorus and Orchestra / Otto Klemperer**
EMI Great Recordings of the Century 566903-2
(69' · ADD · T/t). Recorded 1961   Ⓜ❹❹❹▷

Brahms's *German Requiem*, a work of great concentration and spiritual intensity, is rather surprisingly the creation of a man barely 30 years old. Klemperer's reading of this mighty work has long been famous: rugged, at times surprisingly fleet and with a juggernaut power. The superb Philharmonia is joined by its excellent chorus and two magnificent soloists – Schwarzkopf offering comfort in an endless stream of pure tone and the superb solo contribution from Fischer-Dieskau, still unequalled, taking us closer to the work's emotional, theological and musical sources than any other. Digital remastering hasn't entirely eliminated tape noise, but the engineers appear to have encountered few problems with the original tapes. A uniquely revealing account of the work.

Ein deutsches Requiem
Dorothea Röschmann *sop* **Thomas Quasthoff** *bar* **Berlin Radio Chorus; Berlin Philharmonic Orchestra / Sir Simon Rattle**
EMI 365393-2 (67' · DDD · T/t)   Ⓕ❹❹▷

This is a lovely performance, sensitive to the work's consolatory mood, free-moving and sweetly sung. Rattle's reading does not obscure Brahms's debt to Schütz, Bach and the other great pre-classical German Protestant composers, but it stresses more the work's roots in the new German school: to the influence, above all, of Brahms's cherished and much mourned mentor, Robert Schumann.

This is not a period performance in the sense of attempting to conjure forth period sounds. The opening colloquy for violas and divided cellos is pure Berlin (Nikisch would have recognised the sound, as would the young Karajan).

The singing is awed and reverential, with ravishing *pianissimi* from the superb Berlin Radio Chorus. What we have here is not authenticity of sound but authenticity of feeling and effect. Has there ever been a swifter performance of the fourth movement, 'Wie lieblich sind deine Wohnungen', or a more calming one? A flowing tempo which creates a sense of deep repose suggests that most sought-after of all qualities in an interpreter, the art that disguises art.

Throughout, Rattle strikes a shrewd balance between the work's affective nature and its narrative power. Tempi are brisk in the two movements with baritone solo which carry much of the work's doctrine. The great choral codas to the second, third and sixth movements are also superbly judged. In the great choral peroration to the penultimate movement, space is provided for the words to tell, as Brahms clearly intends.

Thomas Quasthoff, who seems a little out of sorts, is no match for Fischer-Dieskau on Klemperer's unignorably splendid recording (reviewed above); and Dorothea Röschmann's reedy tone and tight vibrato in 'Ihr habt nun Traurigkeit' may not appeal either. Still, the movement is so persuasively shaped that, heard in context, it, too, 'speaks' to us through the sonic squall. Internal balances between choir, soloists, and orchestra are generally well judged: apt to a performance which treats this great memorial prose poem with a mixture of acumen and affection that is entirely special.

Ein deutsches Requiem   Ⓟ
Charlotte Margiono *sop* **Rodney Gilfry** *bar*
Monteverdi Choir; Orchestre Révolutionnaire et Romantique / Sir John Eliot Gardiner
Philips 478 2119DOR (66' · DDD· T/t)   Ⓑ❶❶❶➔

Gardiner's performance is notable for its intensity and fervour, and for the superb singing of his choir: splendidly firm and secure attacks and phrasing, always with fine tonal quality, meticulous attention to dynamic nuances, and alertness to verbal meaning and nuance. The solo baritone is a real find: an admirably focused voice with cleanly projected words and sensitive tonal gradations: if the soprano, pure-voiced and consoling, seems slightly less distinguished, it may be that she's set a trifle too far from the microphone. Pains have been taken to bring out contrapuntal strands with clarity, in both the chorus and the orchestra; and here the employment of period instruments and of selective string vibrato makes a significant contribution. In the past Gardiner has been accused of minimising the spiritual quality of religious works; but not in this outstanding performance.

Ein deutsches Requiem (London Version)
Sandrine Piau *sop* **Stéphane Degout** *bar* **Boris Berezovsky, Brigitte Engerer** *pfs* **Accentus Chamber Choir / Laurence Equilbey**
Naïve V4956 (65' · DDD · T/t)   Ⓕ

It was in Wimpole Street in 1871, at the home of a leading surgeon and his musical wife, that the London first performance of Brahms's *Deutsches Requiem* was given, two years before it was introduced to the British public at large and with orchestral scoring. The arrangement for piano duet was the composer's own, made at the urgent request of his publisher. The occasion was essentially a domestic one, with a small invited audience, piano duettists and singers who, having sung of all flesh being grass, would doubtless have found cold meats laid out for them in the dining room and a glass of wine to refresh the spirits.

This recording successfully presents the Requiem as chamber music. An earlier performance on Opus 111 suggested a final piano rehearsal, the orchestra being expected next week. Here the piano part is played on two instruments, achieving a far more satisfying musical finish. The playing is sensitive, with a singing tone most of the time, and a keen ear for the differentiation between parts or melodic strands. Sandrine Piau is clear-toned and well in control after a very slightly tremulous start; Stéphane Degout, a fine baritone, isn't particularly expressive here but admirable in quality and phrasing. The choir sing with fresh, well-matched tones and care for detail. Choice of tempo seems unerringly right: that is but one of many reasons we have to be grateful to Laurence Equilbey, the conductor.

Ein deutsches Requiem
Gundula Janowitz *sop* **José van Dam** *bass-bar*
Vienna Singverein; Berlin Philharmonic Orchestra / Herbert von Karajan
Video director **Herbert von Karajan**
DG 𝔻𝕍𝔻 073 4398GH
(79' · NTSC · 4:3 · PCM stereo and DTS 5.1 · 0)
Recorded live in Salzburg in March 1978   Ⓕ❶

You can see the Vienna Singverein in this Easter Festival performance spaced across the back of the Felsenreitschule, but the sound mix – supervised by Karajan – mingles them with the orchestra to an intriguing and unprecendented extent. The result is quite different from the closely communicative *German Requiem* recently recorded by Simon Rattle (reviewed above).

Sometimes one feels it has been done to spare the chorus, or spare us from them. There are too many occasions on which the orchestra comes in after an *a cappella* section and finds the chorus has dropped by a fraction to take the performance entirely seriously. But there is also much to admire and even love here: the relatively swift outer movements, the genuinely awe-ful *Marschmässig* at the start of 'Denn alles Fleisch', and the genteel, beneficent relaxation of its interlude, like peasants by Poussin – and you could feel the character of text, sound and interpretation even with the sound off, just as Karajan's hands build, mould and then smother a conflagration on the same movement's final chord.

The tempo for the third movement is slow for the vocal lines – José van Dam is nobly stentorian – but perfect for the minatory dialogue between timpani and horns and its subsequent, syncopated fragmentation. Janowitz achieves the communion in her movement that had been shaped with these performers many times, but, as ever in Karajan's interpretation of the Requiem, the sixth movement never recovers from its pedantic opening trudge, and is not improved by a cussedly obtrusive electric organ. Stepping over this Achilles heel, however, this is a loving document of a work, time and place.

Choral Works

Two Motets, Op 74. Fest- und Gedenksprüche,
Op 109. Three Motets, Op 110. Missa Canonica.
Two Motets, Op 29
RIAS Chamber Choir, Berlin / Marcus Creed
Harmonia Mundi HMC90 1591 (61' · DDD · T/t) Ⓕ

These are wonderful pieces, which, hearing, you would suppose to be all heart, looking at, you think must be all brain, and in fact are compounded of both, the one feeding upon and stimulating the other. In no other area of his work is Brahms quite so conscious of his heritage. Writing in the midday of Romanticism, he finds the great formal, contrapuntal tradition not a weight upon him but a refreshment. He draws upon Schütz as upon Bach, and from the Italian polyphonists and masters of the double choir as well as from his own German background. The innocent ear would never suspect the mathematical intricacies, the musical logic, and yet it tells, even without conscious recognition: the workmanship is clear, and the emotion which would in any case go out to greet such strong, vivid word-setting is immeasurably enhanced. A striking example is provided by the three movements, all that survive, from the *Missa Canonica*. The *Sanctus* is set in deeply reverential mood and, like the flowing triple-time *Benedictus*, betrays nothing of its origin as an academic exercise. The *Agnus Dei* is overtly polyphonic, yet that too gives way to a gently lyrical mode, in the 'Dona nobis pacem'. They were published in 1984 and this is their first recording. The motets, of course, have been recorded many times and very well too, yet, on balance, no more satisfyingly than they are here. The RIAS Chamber Choir produces a fine quality of homogeneous tone and, under Marcus Creed, shows itself fully responsive to both words and music. This disc carries a strong recommendation, especially for its inclusion of the surviving *Missa Canonica* fragments.

Gesänge – Op 17; Op 42; Op 104. Sieben Lieder,
Op 62. Deutsche Volkslieder, WoO33 – In stiller Nacht
Stefan Jezierski, Manfred Klier hns ᵃ**Marie-Pierre
Langlamet** hp **RIAS Chamber Choir, Berlin /
Marcus Creed**
Harmonia Mundi HMC90 1592 (62' · DDD · T/t) Ⓕ

The RIAS Chamber Choir's blend of voices is impeccable and the tone-quality perfectly lovely. They're sensitive to word and phrase,

responding as one to their conductor's shading and shaping. The performances give pleasure and complete satisfaction. The sheer beauty of sound preserves the gentle, romantic qualities of the music faithfully; and there's never any question of dullness, for text and music are both lovingly tendered. The pieces themselves always have more to them than you think at first, and the sureness of Brahms's feeling for choral sound impresses immediately. All are unaccompanied save Op 17, where the harp and horns bring a delightful enrichment. This is quiet, late-night listening, of the kind that helps to ease the day into retrospective contentment.

Liebeslieder, Op 52

Liebeslieder. Neue Liebeslieder, Op 65.
Three Quartets, Op 64
Edith Mathis sop **Brigitte Fassbaender** mez
Peter Schreier ten **Dietrich Fischer-Dieskau** bar
Karl Engel, Wolfgang Sawallisch pfs
DG 423 133-2GH (55' · DDD · T/t) ⒻⓄ🅑

These delightful works will be eagerly snapped up by lovers of these seemingly simple but, in fact, quite complex settings for one, two or four voices. The performances are thoroughly idiomatic, both as regards the singers and pianists, with full value given to the words and their meaning. It isn't merely a question of fine singing, which with this quartet can be more or less taken for granted: the subtlety and charm of the interpretations makes what can all too often be a dreary sequence of three-four numbers into a poetic response to the nature of the waltz. There's an intelligent give-and-take between the soloists, so that voices move in and out of the limelight, as the skilful recording allows, and an extra dimension of the music is disclosed here that's too often obscured. The immediate sound is here a great advantage. This is a very worthwhile and welcome reissue of a most attractive individual record.

Songs

Vier ernste Gesänge, Op 121. Neun Lieder, Op 69.
Sechs Lieder, Op 86. Zwei Lieder, Op 91ᵃ
Marie-Nicole Lemieux contr ᵃ**Nicolò Eugelmi** va
Michael McMahon pf
Analekta AN29906 (68' · DDD · T/t) ⒻⓄ🅑

The absorbing six songs that make up Op 86 are all easily encompassed by Marie-Nicole Lemieux, not least because her technique is so secure that she can pay attention to the meaning of each song. 'Feldeinsamkeit', so inwardly sung, and 'Todessehnen' receive particularly thoughtful readings, all supported finely by Michael McMahon's perceptive playing.

The nine songs of Op 69 are expressly designed for a woman and have their moments, but they're among the less inspired in Brahms's large output of Lieder. Not so, of course, the two songs with viola – the admirable Nicolò

Eugelmi here. To these gently lulling, timeless pieces, Lemieux brings the sovereign virtues of firm line and apt phrasing.

The CD reaches its zenith in Brahms's last and greatest Lieder, his *Vier ernste Gesänge*. Lemieux rises to their challenge. The interpretations are properly earnest, but intimate, never overblown. Her partner is again exemplary in his discreet yet positive playing.

A natural acoustic adds to the pleasure to be gained from this sensibly planned recital, which is highly recommended.

Brahms[a] 15 Romanzen aus 'Die schöne Magelone', Op 33 **Schubert**[b] An die Freunde, D654. Auf der Donau, D553. Heliopolis II, D754. Fischerweise, D881. Prometheus, D674. Der Wanderer an den Mond, D870. Der Wanderer, D649
Dietrich Fischer-Dieskau bar
[a]**Sviatoslav Richter**, [b]**Benjamin Britten** pf
BBC Legends BBCL4255-2 (76' · ADD) (F)
Recorded live at [a]Aldeburgh Parish Church on June 20, 1965; [b]The Maltings, Snape, on June 8, 1972   (F)

The year 1965 was the one which brought Fischer-Dieskau to Aldeburgh. More surprisingly, it brought Brahms also (Brahms being the composer of whom Britten said that he liked a little every now and again to remind himself how bad he was). The 15 Romances comprising what we know as *Die schöne Magelone* were at that time a rarity, so that the prospect of a performance by Fischer-Dieskau with Sviatoslav Richter was a major event. Britten turned the pages.

It comes now to a subtler form of life than it had probably ever enjoyed before, and indeed this is a more totally satisfying version than even Fischer-Dieskau's studio recordings with Richter and Barenboim. The hearty, roistering mode of the opening moves almost immediately through a kaleidoscope of changes, with the tenderest expression irradiating the third song ('Sind es Schmerzen'), the simplest, most transparent texture in the Schumannesque fourth ('Liebe kam aus fernen Landen') and a magical sense of gentle movement downstream in the one famous song, 'Ruhe, Süssliebchen'. In all of those great handfuls of notes which Brahms confers upon the pianist with such largesse, Richter never smudges or lets slip a single one, and the two great artists work together as though this were the performance of a single mind.

And so it is, though in a very different style, with the Schubert group dating from a concert in 1972. The eager tread and silvery tone of 'Der Wanderer an den Mond' will remain a precious memory, as will the other 'Wanderer' song, the relatively unfamiliar D649. All here is in the finest spirit of music-making, the superb professionalism not quenching the love, freshness and intimacy of (in the literal sense) the amateur.

Mainacht. An die Nachtigall, Op 46 No 4. Sonntag, Op 47 No 3. Der Gang zum Liebchen, Op 48 No 1. Fünf Lieder, Op 49 – No 1, Am Sonntag Morgen; No 4, Wiegenlied. Dein blaues Auge, Op 59 No 8. Geheimnis, Op 71 No 3. Fünf Lieder, Op 72 – No 1, Alte Liebe; No 4, Verzagen. Vergebliches Ständchen, Op 84 No 4. Mädchenlied, Op 85 No 3. Sechs Lieder, Op 86 – No 1, Therese; No 2, Feldeinsamkeit. Sapphische Ode, Op 94 No 4. Sieben Lieder, Op 95 – No 1, Das Mädchen; No 2, Bei dir sind meine Gedanken; No 4, Der Jäger; No 6, Mädchenlied. Der Tod, das ist die kühle Nacht, Op 96 No 1. Nachtigall, Op 97 No 1. Fünf Lieder, Op 105 – No 1, Wie Melodien zieht es mir; No 4, Auf dem Kirchhofe. Ständchen, Op 106 No 1. Fünf Lieder, Op 107 – No 3, Das Mädchen spricht; No 5, Mädchenlied
Bernarda Fink mez **Roger Vignoles** pf
Harmonia Mundi HMC90 1926 (63' · DDD · T/t)   (F)

'Bei dir sind meine Gedanken', one of Brahms's happiest songs, makes an inviting aperitif. Buoyed by the evanescent shimmer of Roger Vignoles's accompaniment, Bernarda Fink is all confiding eagerness, phrasing deftly and gracefully and showing a natural feeling for Brahmsian *rubato*. One would expect Fink's warm, luminous mezzo, flecked by darker, deeper tints, to be near ideal for, say, the nostalgia of 'Alte Liebe' or the many songs of elegiac loss and heartbreak, all touchingly done here. But having thought of her as an essentially 'serious' singer, dignified, eloquent, the vivacity and 'face' she brings to 'Bei dir sind meine Gedanken' and other lighter songs is sheer delight. 'Ständchen', here more sunlit than moonlit, is charmingly characterised, with an affectionate caress on the dreaming girl's 'Vergiss nicht mein'. Fink is playfully coquettish without archness in the delicious 'Spanisches Lied', and sings 'Vergebliches Ständchen' with an outgoing boldness and witty touches of timing – and the tender lingering on the penultimate 'Mein Knab' suggests that the boy's luck may soon be about to change.

Other singers have brought a more intense yearning to 'Die Mainacht' and found greater mystery amid the slumberous balm of 'Feldeinsamkeit'. But Fink's flowing performances, sensitively shaped and inflected, are never less than satisfying. It is good to be reminded, too, that, for all its melancholy, 'Die Mainacht' is also a song of spring, suffused by warm major-key harmonies, with a hint of excited anticipation at the line 'Wann, o lächelndes Bild'. On the face of it, Fink's lyric mezzo would seem to be on the light side for 'Von ewiger Liebe'. But with Vignoles imaginatively 'orchestrating' the keyboard part, she gives a finely graded, deeply moving performance, vividly contrasting the contained passion of the boy's words with the girl's gentle candour. The glowing climactic avowal of eternal love is truly overwhelming, setting the seal on a Brahms recital of rare distinction.

Liebestreu, Op 3 No 1. Spanisches Lied, Op 6 No 1. Anklänge, Op 7 No 3. Der Schmied, Op 19 No 4. Vier Lieder, Op 43 – No 1, Von ewiger Liebe; No 2, Die

Von ewiger Liebe, Op 43 No 1[b]. An die Nachtigall, Op 46 No 4[c]. Herbstgefühl, Op 48 No 7[c]. Neun Lieder, Op 63 – No 5, Junge Lieder I, 'Meine Liebe

ist grün'ᶜ; No 8, Heimweh II , 'O wüsst ich doch den Weg zur'ᵃ. Abendregen, Op 70 No 4ᶜ. Geheimnis, Op 71 No 3ᵃ. Fünf Lieder, Op 72 – No 2, Sommerfädenᶜ; No 3, O kühler Waldᵃ; No 4, Verzagenᶜ. Vergebliches Ständchen, Op 84 No 4ᶜ. Sechs Lieder, Op 86ᶜ – No 2, Feldeinsamkeit; No 3, Nachtwandler. Vier Lieder, Op 96 – Der Tod, das ist die kühle Nachtᶜ; Wir wandeltenᵃ; Meerfahrtᵃ. Komm bald, Op 97 No 5ᶜ. Auf dem Kirchhofe, Op 105 No 4ᵃ. Fünf Lieder, Op 106ᵃ – No 1, Ständchen; No 5, Ein Wanderer. Fünf Lieder, Op 107ᵃ – No 3, Das Mädchen spricht; No 5, Mädchenlied. Mondnachtᵃ. Regenliedᵃ
Dame Janet Baker mez
ᵃᵇ**Ernest Lush**, ᶜ**Paul Hamburger** pfs
BBC Legends ᵃᶜmono BBCL4200-2 (70' · ADD).
Recorded in ᵇ1960; ᵃ1961; ᶜ1968   Ⓕ

Listening to these Brahms songs culled from BBC broadcasts one realises just why Dame Janet's reputation continues to remain so high and why so many of her successors don't quite match her standards. To every song here, familiar or unfamiliar, she brings her special ability of making it her own and reaching to its heart. It's an almost uncanny gift, and not one easy to explain, but it makes every song in this programme momentous. Wondrous is the sustained half-voice with which she invests 'Nachtwandler' with its intimate, sad feeling.

Then there's the outpouring of joy that is 'Meine Liebe ist grün' to which she brings the most lustrous tone and an outgoing manner, and finally the gentle sense of fun, never overdone, which she brings to the very familiar 'Vergebliches Ständchen'.

If Brahms had written no other songs than 'Feldeinsamkeit', 'Der Tod, das ist die kühle Nacht' and 'Von ewiger Liebe', he would surely be hailed as a great Lieder composer. Baker obviously understands their astonishing high quality. The first is sung, as it should be, with a kind of inner wonder, each amazing line given its full due. In the second, a Liebestod *avant la lettre*, she sings with the proper impassioned feeling, while the last, a happier statement of eternal love, is sung with the rugged conviction that always showed the singer at her very best.

Lush and Hamburger, especially the latter, are fully cognisant of what to do with Brahms's intricate writing for the piano. The sound is admirable, catching early Baker in full flow.

Neun Gesänge, Op 69. Vier Gesänge, Op 70.
Fünf Gesänge, Op 71. Fünf Gesänge, Op 72
Juliane Banse sop **Andreas Schmidt** bar
Helmut Deutsch pf
CPO CPO999 446-2 (56' · DDD · T/t)   Ⓜ

Of all the leading composers of Lieder, Brahms suffers more than any other through neglect, with so little of his output in the field ever appearing on recital programmes. There's some reason for this, given that his contribution to the genre is uneven, as you can judge listening to the uninspired settings of minor poets comprising

Op 69. But just when you think the composer might have been on auto-pilot in his songs of the mid-1870s, along come the four pieces of Op 70 to make you revise your opinion. The impressionistic 'Lerchengesang', the reflective 'Serenade' and the better-known 'Abendregen' all show the composer in his most imaginative mode, alive to words and their inner meaning. The inspiration is more intermittent in Opp 71 and 72, but the better of the songs here – the Hölty 'Minnelied' and Bretano 'O kühler Wald' – rank with the finest in Brahms's output.

Both Banse and Schmidt are at their appreciable best as regards voice and interpretation, Banse always inside her readings, Schmidt producing tone that's consistently warm and appealing. She alternates convincingly between passion and lighter emotions. He's particularly well suited by the whole of Op 72, giving a nicely ebullient account of 'Unüberwindlich', a Goethe setting that ends the programme. Deutsch is fully up to the exigent demands of the piano parts, often almost like solos in themselves.

Havergal Brian   British 1876-1972

Despite his lack of any formal musical education, Havergal Brian dedicated his life to music, creating numerous vast symphonies and large-scale choral works. He received encouragement from Elgar and Henry Wood who conducted the English Suite and For Valour. His primary source of income was as a journalist and critic – he was assistant editor of Musical Opinion from 1927 until 1940 – and he championed many then-unfashionable composers such as Bruckner, Mahler and Schoenberg. His musical language is late-Romantic and lush, and invariably expressed on a colossal scale. He tended increasingly to explore his ideas through motivic development and contrapuntal means rather than relying on traditional techniques such as sonata form.

Orchestral Works

Violin Concertoᵃ. Symphony No 18. The Jolly Miller.
ᵃ**Marat Bisengaliev** vn
BBC Scottish Symphony Orchestra / Lionel Friend
Naxos 8 557775 (55' · DDD)   ⓈⓄⓄ▷

The late Robert Simpson once referred to Havergal Brian as the 'Original Awkward Cuss raised to the level of genius'. A highly misunderstood composer, one either loves (sadly the minority) or hates his music. Michael Oliver clearly liked it, as his review of the original release shows, where he waxed lyrical over the kind of compositional processes, games even, that Brian played in his Violin Concerto (1934-35). He described the performance of Kazakh virtuoso Marat Bisengaliev as 'jaw-droppingly' good; hearing it again it really does sound like one of the finest British violin concertos, worthy of comparison with Elgar's, Walton's,

Britten's, Stevens's and McCabe's. Tony Kime's excellent recording catches all the subtle detail of the solo writing – especially when so wonderfully well played – along with the *tuttis'* massive splendour.

The best is saved until last, however, with the Symphony No 18 (1961), long a personal favourite. Written in gratitude for Bryan Fairfax, conductor of the *Gothic*'s premiere that year, it is one of Brian's most beguiling march-fantasies, scored for a fairly standard orchestra. All the typical late Brian fingerprints are present, the bold, craggy harmonies, expressive dislocations and haunting melody. Lionel Friend directs a crisp and crystal clear account of this quarter-hour gem. Very strongly recommended.

Symphony No 1, 'Gothic'
Honor Sheppard *sop* **Shirley Minty** *contr* **Ronald Dowd** *ten* **Roger Stalman** *bass* **Hampstead Choral Society; Emanuel School Choir; Orpington Junior Singers; BBC Chorus, Choral Society and Symphony Orchestra / Sir Adrian Boult**
Testament ② SBT2 1454 (115' · ADD)
Recorded live at the Royal Albert Hall, London, in 1966   Ⓕ**OO**

There is a super photograph on the back of Testament's booklet showing Boult rehearsing the *Gothic* in the Royal Albert Hall using a megaphone, as if the most natural thing in the world, to communicate with the farthest-flung members of the vast forces under his baton.

The performance Boult elicited from the hundreds of players and singers remains a superb achievement, even if only two of the four additional brass ensembles required were used on the night. Boult takes a measured view (just listen to the memorable stamping orchestral gesture at the outset), keeping the end – some 104 minutes away – in focus. Boult achieves great grandeur in the magnificent *Lento espressivo e solenne* second movement and great fantasy in the *Vivace* third.

Brian Symphonies[a] – No 6, 'Sinfonia tragica'; No 16
Cooke Symphony No 3[b]
London Philharmonic Orchestra / [a]**Myer Fredman;** [b]**Nicholas Braithwaite**
Lyrita SRCD295 (60' · ADD)   Ⓕ◗▸

Havergal Brian's Sixth and Sixteenth Symphonies were recorded in April 1973. The Sixth (1948), incorporating material from an abandoned opera on Synge's *Deirdre of the Sorrows*, is highly illustrative with atmospheric orchestration, a gorgeous, full-blooded romantic melody in the slow central section and a dramatic finale. Completely convincing symphonically, it plays continuously in an effective three-in-one design.

A marvellous example of Brian's late polyphony, the Sixteenth (1960) is the finest of a group of five single-movement symphonies that sig-

nalled the start of his final compositional phase (1959-68), in which he completed no fewer than 20 symphonies. It too has its dramatic and evocative aspects, possibly derived from his reading of Herodotus while composing the work. But it is as absolute music that the work succeeds brilliantly. These performances, directed by Myer Fredman, still sound excellent.

It is a shame that No 24 was not available to complete an all-Brian disc, but the inclusion of Arnold Cooke's Third (1967) will not disappoint. Certainly, there are stylistic differences; not for nothing was Cooke described (or derided?) as the 'English Hindemith', but the influence of his German teacher never hampered his expressive mission. The Third's outer movements are brisk and vigorous but its heart is the central *Lento*, which opens like a missing interlude from *Mathis der Maler*. Another first-class performance, too. Full marks to Lyrita for its remastering, especially in dealing with Brian's singular orchestral soundscapes. Strongly recommended.

Frank Bridge   British 1879-1941

Bridge studied with Stanford at the Royal College of Music. He played the viola in a number of string quartets, most notably the English String Quartet, and conducted, sometimes deputising for Henry Wood, before devoting himself to composition, receiving the patronage of Elizabeth Sprague Coolidge. He privately tutored a number of pupils, most famously Benjamin Britten, who later championed his teacher's music.

Bridge's early works, including the orchestral suite The Sea (1911) and the symphonic poem Summer (1914), are late-Romantic in language, close in style to the works of Bax and Delius. After the First World War his interests turned towards the developments taking place in mainland Europe and some of his chamber works – the Third (1926) and Fourth (1937) Quartets, for example – are highly chromatic, reflecting his admiration for Alban Berg.

Orchestral Works

Lament, H117. Oration (Concerto elegiaco), H180[a].
Rebus, H191. Allegro moderato, H192. A Prayer[b]
[a]**Alban Gerhardt** *vc* **BBC National** [b]**Chorus and Orchestra of Wales / Richard Hickox**
Chandos CHAN10188 (77' · DDD)   Ⓕ◗▸

Here's probably the most appealing and varied instalment in Richard Hickox's Frank Bridge series for Chandos. The disc's highlight is a superb performance of the 1930 'Concerto elegiaco' *Oration*, in which Hickox teams up with the gifted German cellist Alban Gerhardt. High drama and emotional candour are the keynotes to a riveting display. But there's no want of intimacy or compassion in the more contemplative passages, and the result is a trenchant interpretation that does justice to one of the towering masterpieces of British music.

The 1940 *Rebus* overture is as invigorating and impeccably crafted a concert-opener as any British composer has yet produced. The touching *Lament* (1915) is sensitively done, but Hickox and company seem less comfortable in Anthony Pople's completion of the patiently argued opening *Allegro moderato* from a projected symphony for strings upon which Bridge was working at the time of his death in 1941. Fortunately, there's a glowing account of *A Prayer*, Bridge's only composition for chorus and orchestra, a moving and often hauntingly beautiful setting from 1916-18 of words from *The Imitation of Christ* by Thomas à Kempis. Minor strictures notwithstanding, this is an essential purchase for *Oration* alone – and the music itself deserves the widest dissemination.

Adoration, H57[b]. Berceuse, H8. Berceuse, H9[a]. Blow out, you bugles, H132[b]. Chant d'espérance, H18 No 2. Love went a-riding, H114[b]. Mantle of Blue, H131[a]. The Pageant of London, H98. A Royal Night of Variety, H184. Serenade, H23. Three Tagore Songs, H164[a] – Day after Day; Speak to me, my love!. Thy hand in mine, H124[b]. Where she lies asleep, H113[b]
[a]**Sarah Connolly** *mez* [b]**Philip Langridge** *ten* **BBC National Orchestra of Wales / Richard Hickox**
Chandos CHAN10310 (62' · DDD · T/t)   Ⓕ➲

No fewer than 10 first recordings adorn this, the last instalment in Hickox's valuable Bridge series. Philip Langridge is in ardent voice for the first five tracks, the fourth of which, 'Love went a-riding', remains the composer's best-known song. It sounds exhilaratingly new-minted in its sumptuous orchestral garb and is framed here by two companion settings of words by Mary Coleridge, 'Where she lies asleep' and 'Thy hand in mine'. Particularly striking is the big-scale treatment afforded to Rupert Brooke's 'Blow out, you bugles', written in 1918 for the tenor Gervase Elwes and whose incorporation of the Last Post movingly anticipates Bridge's own towering *Oration* for cello and orchestra of a dozen years later.

Sarah Connolly is wonderfully eloquent in the haunting and often inspired 1922-24 Tagore diptych for mezzo and orchestra and also excels in the very early 'Berceuse' (a remarkably assured setting of Dorothy Wordsworth from 1901) and affecting 'Mantle of blue' (1918, and orchestrated 16 years later, to words by the Irish poet Padraic Colum). The programme concludes with five purely instrumental items, the most extended of which is the 1911 suite for wind band, *The Pageant of London*. Expertly fashioned, it makes for a diverting enough quarter of an hour (the 'Pavane' in the middle movement was destined to reappear 15 years later in Warlock's *Capriol Suite*). The tuneful *Serenade* exudes plenty of sepia-tinted charm, as does the wistful little 'Berceuse'.

Throw in some spick and span orchestral playing and Chandos's commendably natural engineering, not to mention Paul Hindmarsh's scholarly notes, and you have a job well done.

Allegro moderato, H192. Dance Poem, H111. Dance Rhapsody, H84. Two Poems, H118. Rebus, H191
London Philharmonic Orchestra / Nicholas Braithwaite
Lyrita SRCD243 (72' · DDD)   ⒻⓄ➲

How, one wonders, can such a rapturously tuneful work as Bridge's *Dance Rhapsody* (1908) be so shamefully neglected: it deserves to be as popular as, say, Ravel's *La valse*! The intense songfulness of the strings' inner voices and the general fervour of the London Philharmonic's playing is thrilling throughout. In the more elusive (yet still alluring) *Dance Poem* (1913), Braithwaite unflinchingly explores the music's darker corners, finding a tragic vein that Hickox misses, though the newer account moves with admirable grace.

Braithwaite is magically sensitive, too, in the vaguely Delian world of the *Two Poems* (1916); 'The Open Air' sustains a fragile atmosphere of mystery and 'The Story of my Heart' is simultaneously passionate and mercurial. The extreme contrasts of character contained in the *Rebus* overture (1940) are crisply delineated – and note how the LPO revel in the passages of glittering, Straussian opulence. As for the *Allegro moderato* (a loose-limbed movement that Bridge left unfinished at his death in 1941), Hickox's taut, focused reading provides a semblance of symphonic cohesion, while Braithwaite elicits the stronger emotional charge. It's hard to imagine being without either recording.

Additional recommendation

The Sea, H100. Summer, H116. Two Poems, H118. Enter Spring, H174
New Zealand Symphony Orchestra / James Judd
Naxos 8 557167 (63' · DDD)   Ⓢ➲
   A hearty, sensibly paced account of *Enter Spring*, a gorgeous *Summer*. Despite any minor reservations, an enjoyable concert and very decent value.

String Quintet, H7 / String Sextet, H107

String Quintet in E minor, H7[a]. String Sextet in E flat, H107[b]. Lament[c]
[b]**Raphael Ensemble** ([a]James Clark, [a]David Adams *vns* [ac]Louise Williams, [ac]Asdis Valdimarsdottír *vas* [a]Andrea Hess, Tim Gill *vcs*)
Hyperion CDA67426 (66' · DDD)   Ⓕ➲

Bridge was a star student at the RCM, and his E minor String Quintet from 1901, one of four chamber offerings he wrote at that time, reveals a burgeoning talent. Cast in four movements and lasting just over half an hour, it's an accomplished achievement. A scrupulous craft and pleasing sense of proportion attest to lessons well learnt under Stanford's tutelage, yet there's already a strongly emergent personality in pages such as the third-movement Trio section. The finale, too, shows enviable skills, the poignant backward glance to the work's opening just before the close being particularly effective. It's preceded by a powerfully wrought *Lament* for two violas first performed by Lionel Tertis and the composer at London's Aeolian (now Wigmore) Hall in March 1912. Both works are worthy of resuscitation and both are superbly served here.

So too is the Sextet (1906-12) in an even more persuasive performance than that by the Academy of St Martin in the Fields Chamber Ensemble on Chandos. The Raphael Ensemble produce a leaner, more subtly shaded sonority, allied to an extra re-creative spark and expressive urgency (witness the edgy anxiety they locate in the *Scherzo* at the heart of the work). And the opening *Allegro moderato* is surveyed with due appreciation of its lyrical grace and elegant architecture; likewise, the finale combines pliancy and thrust. A delightful anthology, highly recommended.

String Quartets

String Quartets – No 1 in E minor, 'Bologna', H70; No 3, H175
Maggini Quartet (Laurence Jackson, David Angel, *vns* Martin Outram *va* Michal Kaznowski *vc*)
Naxos 8 557133 (60' · DDD)　　　　　Ⓢ🄱➔

Even by the high standards of previous Maggini/Naxos offerings, this is an exceptionally fine disc. If you don't know Frank Bridge's First Quartet of 1906, its ardour and melodic fecundity compel investigation. The Maggini Quartet give a performance to match, of sweep, assurance and affection. At the same time, their rapt concentration and daring range of expression (especially in the slow movement) banish for good any vestige of salon-room cosiness; the return of the opening material at the quartet's close has never seemed more wistfully inevitable.

That the Magginis are no less attuned to the far more challenging sound world of the 1926 Third Quartet is at once evident from the articulate authority and thrust they impart to the introductory bars (which sow the seeds for so much that follows). Both this work and the searching Piano Sonata, completed the previous year, represent the first wholly convincing examples of Bridge's liberating brand of English expressionism. The Magginis are scrupulously alive to the anguished introspection which runs through the work: the ghostly visions that stalk the central *Andante con moto* and finale's twilit coda linger long in the memory here. A superb coupling, impeccably captured by the Walton/Thomason production team and well annotated by Andrew Burn.

String Quartets – No 2; No 4. Phantasy[a]
Maggini Quartet ([a]Laurence Jackson, David Angel *vns* [a]Martin Outram *va* [a]Michal Kaznowski *vc*)
with [a]**Martin Roscoe** *pf*
Naxos 8 557283 (60' · DDD)　　　Ⓢ🄾🄾🄾➔

 Bridge's glorious Second Quartet, written in 1915 and winner of that year's Cobbett Prize, is arguably his first true

chamber masterwork, superbly realised on every level (the finale is a *tour de force* of motivic integration) and full of the most engagingly fresh invention and invigorating part-writing. The last of his four quartets (completed in 1937) represents more of a challenge, but strong emotions stir beneath its uncompromising surface. Once again, the finale proves a fitting summation, and Bridge's technical command of the medium is absolute. Leaner and more 'classically' compact than its towering predecessor from 1926, this searching score will afford the patient listener plentiful long-term rewards.

The Brindisi Quartet's coupling has served us handsomely over the past dozen years but must now yield to this Naxos release. These are exemplary, scrupulously prepared readings from the Magginis, who play with unquenchable fire, keen intelligence and immaculate polish throughout. Joined by the admirable Martin Roscoe, they also offer a considerable bonus in the shape of the lovely *Phantasy* Piano Quartet of 1909-10.

With vividly realistic, beautifully balanced sound from the experienced Walton/Thomason production-team and succinct annotation by Andrew Burn, this is an unmissable disc.

Piano Trio No 2

Piano Trio No 2, H178. Phantasie Trio, H79.
Miniatures – Set 1, H87; Set 2, H88; Set 3, H89.
Jack Liebeck *vn* **Alexander Chaushian** *vc*
Ashley Wass *pf*
Naxos 8 570792 (73' · DDD)　　　　Ⓢ🄾🄱➔

How encouraging to see Ashley Wass branching into Bridge's chamber output – and with such gifted colleagues, too. This Naxos version of the adorable, Cobbett Prize-winning *Phantasie Trio* is an adroit and boldly characterised affair. The three sets of *Miniatures* probably date from the following year and comprise nine exquisitely crafted and tuneful morsels originally intended for domestic use. They're best dipped into rather than played at one stretch, but all are dispatched with sizzling panache and evident relish by these elegant performers.

Of course, the masterpiece here is the epic Second Piano Trio of 1929, one of Bridge's most cogent, questing and durable utterances, whose radical language so bamboozled the largely conservative British critics of the period. Wass and company lend it exhilarating advocacy in a realisation of enviable security, unswerving concentration and burning conviction. Tip-top production values and exemplary notes set the seal on an irresistible bargain.

Additional recommednation

Phantasie Trio, H79. Piano Trio No 2, H178.
Miniatures – H88: Romance; Intermezzo;
H89: Valse russe; Hornpipe
Bernard Roberts Trio

Black Box BBM1028 (57' · DDD)   Ⓕ

These are utterly sympathetic, beautifully prepared performances from this fine family group. The centrepiece is the Second Piano Trio, a work of searing intensity and astounding individuality.

Piano Quintet

Piano Quintet, H49a[a]. Three Idylls, H67. String Quartet No 4, H188
[a]**Piers Lane** pf **Goldner Quartet**
(Dene Olding, Dimity Hall vns Irini Morozova va Julian Smiles vc)
Hyperion CDA67726 (65' · DDD)   Ⓕ

Frank Bridge's comprehensive 1912 revision of his D minor Piano Quintet from seven years before remains the sole comparative dud in his early chamber output – and not even this splendidly articulate rendering from Piers Lane and the Goldners can persuade otherwise. The original work's four movements are condensed to three, its centrepiece a gratefully lyrical amalgam of slow movement and *scherzo* enclosed within one of Bridge's arch-like 'phantasy' structures. Alas, the opening movement (after a promising start) soon drifts into a worryingly humdrum, sequential lassitude, and the finale fails to provide sufficient ballast to counterbalance what has preceded it.

The *Three Idylls* of 1906 are an infinitely more enticing proposition – exquisitely crafted, keenly proportioned and supremely touching miniatures for string quartet, the second of which later provided the 23-year-old Britten with the theme for his Op 10 Variations for string orchestra. The Fourth Quartet is utterly different again. Completed in 1937 after a near-fatal bout of bronchitis, this is arguably Bridge's most rivetingly cogent and harmonically bracing statement, evincing a deftness, compassion and unerring intellectual scope that beg comparison with the greatest 20th-century examples in the medium.

These unfailingly sympathetic, flexible and exhilaratingly assured performances have been most truthfully captured. So, despite reservations surrounding the Quintet, this is clearly a release to investigate.

Cello Sonata in D minor, H125

Bridge Cello Sonata. Meditation. Spring Song. Serenade. Berceuse. Scherzo. Elégie. Mélodie. Cradle Song **Britten** Cello Sonata in C, Op 65
Øystein Birkeland vc **Vebjørn Anvik** pf
Simax PSC1160 (70' · DDD)   Ⓕ

The Norwegian duo of Øystein Birkeland and Vebjørn Anvik lend gloriously unaffected and formidably lucid advocacy to Bridge's masterwork, his Cello Sonata, the strength and nobility of their playing always ideally counterbalanced by tender restraint and songful intimacy. These

superbly stylish performers prove no less responsive to the poetic charms of Bridge the miniaturist.

The winsome *Serenade* of 1903 is a fresh-faced delight here, while the 1902 *Scherzo* fairly twinkles with humour. How memorably, too, they sustain the long-breathed ardour of both the *Elégie* (1904) and *Mélodie* (written in 1911 and dedicated to the cellist Felix Salmond).

Sandwiched between the Bridge Sonata and a sequence of miniatures comes a really fine account of the Cello Sonata that Britten penned for Rostropovich in 1960-61. Here, too, Birkeland and Anvik form an intelligent, scrupulously observant partnership, their playing as thoughtful as it's intense, though not even they can match the extraordinary fluidity that Rostropovich and Britten bring to the work's opening bars on their inspirational premiere recording for Decca.

Among digital contenders, however, this beautifully engineered and sensitively balanced recording is as good as any and more imposing than most. Calum MacDonald contributes the exemplary booklet essay. All told, a very positive recommendation.

David Briggs   British b1962

Briggs studied the organ with Jean Langlais before winning a host of competitions. He is Organist Emeritus of Gloucester Cathedral, where he directed the music for eight years (having been organist at Hereford and Truro Cathedrals). While at Gloucester, he oversaw the complete rebuilding of the Cathedral organ by Nicholson, and directed the Three Choirs Festivals. His organ transcriptions of orchestral symphonies – including Schubert's Eighth, Tchaikovsky's Fourth, Bruckner's Seventh and Mahler's Fifth and Sixth – are becoming increasingly popular and have been praised for helping make organ music accessible to broader audiences. He is also a prolific composer and his works range from full scale oratorios to works for solo instruments.

Messe pour Notre-Dame

Messe pour Notre-Dame. I will lift up mine eyes. The Trinity College Service. Te Deum laudamus. Toccata on Te Deum laudamus. O Lord, support us
Choir of Trinity College, Cambridge / Stephen Layton with **David Briggs** org
Hyperion CDA67808 (73' · DDD)   Ⓕ

  David Briggs is an unashamed admirer of the school of 20th-century French organist improvisers/composers, and the influence of Dupré, Duruflé, Langlais and Messiaen is clearly evident in his music. Notable features are a sensuous harmonic language, intricate organ textures and richly layered vocal writing. The harmony may originate in keyboard improvising but Briggs's skill as a choral composer enables the choir to inhabit this adventurous musical landscape. The result is a happy marriage between the modern French school of organ improvising and the British choral tradition nurtured by our cathedral and collegiate choirs.

The strongest musical influence comes from Pierre Cochereau, legendary organist of Paris's Notre-Dame Cathedral, and some of his improvisations (preserved through recordings) are woven into the musical tapestry of the *Messe pour Notre-Dame*. Briggs's Mass setting is one of the most colourful ever written, while his prayerful approach to the *Magnificat* and *Nunc dimittis* matches the emotional intensity of Howells's settings.

The Choir of Trinity College, Cambridge, sing superbly under the expert direction of Stephen Layton; wonderful quiet, melting *legato* phrases and passionate *forte* sections. The composer himself, playing the Gloucester Cathedral organ, provides impeccable accompaniments and stunning improvisations. This recording is one of the finest CDs of sacred choral and organ music you'll ever hear; listeners who are churchgoers and non-believers alike will find this disc a profoundly moving experience.

Benjamin Britten   British 1913-1976

England's most significant composer in the second half of the 20th century was born on St Cecilia's Day. The patron saint of music blessed Britten with precocious gifts for he began playing the piano at two and was reading symphony and opera scores in bed at the age of seven. By his 10th birthday he had completed an oratorio and a string quartet; by 16 he had produced a symphony, six quartets, 10 piano sonatas and other smaller works – some of the material from these juvenile works were later incorporated into one of his first mature works, Simple Symphony (1934).

Britten was the son of a dental surgeon and a mother who was a fair amateur pianist. He had a good education, adding the viola to his sporting and musical accomplishments at school before studying with the major influence on his musical development, Frank Bridge. Later, at the Royal College of Music, John Ireland was his composition teacher; Arthur Benjamin (of 'Jamaica Rumba' fame) taught him piano. Britten's unique voice was quick in arriving and soon after completing his studies he was commissioned to write the music for a number of innovative documentary films, most notably Night Mail for the GPO film unit. In this he collaborated with the second figure who was to influence his thinking, the poet WH Auden.

Not only did Auden provide the text for Britten's first song-cycle (On this Island) and reveal to him the beauties of poetry and awareness of the possibilities of setting words and music, but he enforced Britten's pacifist convictions. When Auden departed for America in 1939, Britten and his friend, tenor Peter Pears, followed him a few months later feeling, in his own words, 'muddled, fed-up and looking for work, longing to be used'. Before this, the first performances

of Variations on a Theme of Frank Bridge had taken place at the Salzburg Festival (1937) and in London. Aaron Copland reviewed it: 'The piece is what we would call a knock-out.' Not yet 30, Britten was firmly on his way.

While in America he produced his first big orchestral work (Sinfonia da Requiem, 1940) and his first dramatic work, the operetta Paul Bunyan, which was – as Britten put it – 'politely spat at'. In 1942, with the war going badly for Britain and feeling homesick, he decided to return home. He appeared before the Tribunal of Conscientious Objectors and was exempted from military duty, prepared to do what he could for the war effort without sacrificing his pacifist ideals. He was allowed to continue composing as long as he took part in concerts promoted by CEMA (Council for the Encouragement of Music and the Arts). Britten, apart from being a fine and exacting conductor of his own works, was always an excellent pianist (he was the soloist in the premiere of his Piano Concerto in 1939). His Mozart playing was exquisite but as an accompanist in recital or as a chamber musician he was up there among the best.

Before the end of the war he had produced two of his most enduring works, the Ceremony of Carols and the Serenade for Tenor, Horn and Strings, but it was his opera Peter Grimes that made him internationally famous. This was the result of a commission from the Koussevitzky Foundation in America. The resumption of artistic activity after the conflict and the re-opening of the Sadler's Wells theatre made this a keenly anticipated event and produced one of the most memorable first nights in British music. Peter Grimes was hailed as milestone in modern opera.

With only two opera companies established in Britain, Britten founded the English Opera Group. Then in 1948 he, with Eric Crozier and Peter Pears, founded the Aldeburgh Festival, then, as now, an indispensable national flagship of musical excellence. He and Pears had made their base in the Suffolk village and it was remain their home for the rest of their lives together. A string of operas followed Peter Grimes, some with the expected full orchestra, some scored for a mere 12 instruments, facilitating performances and showing the composer to be a master of inventiveness with limited forces. The Rape of Lucretia (1946), Albert Herring, Billy Budd, The Turn of the Screw, A Midsummer Night's Dream and Death in Venice (1973) have all, to a lesser or greater degree, established themselves in the repertoires of opera houses the world over.

Britten was particularly adept at writing music for children, accessible without being condescending, and works like Let's Make an Opera, Noye's Fludde and The Young Person's Guide to the Orchestra have had a stimulating, not to say inspirational, effect on generations of young people. In 1961 he received a commission to celebrate the consecration of the newly built Coventry Cathedral to replace the building bombed in the war. The result was his powerful and profound War Requiem, using the words of the Latin Mass and the poems of the First World War poet Wilfred Owen.

In 1967 the tiny Jubilee Hall in Aldeburgh was replaced by the conversion of part of The Maltings at Snape into a larger concert and opera hall. Two years later it was destroyed by fire. The phoenix which rose from the ashes has proved to be among the outstanding concert halls of Europe and it was here that the first performance of Britten's last major composition, Death in Venice, was given in 1973. As with so much of his work, his partner Peter Pears was the inspiration behind it, as much a confessional piece as an autobiographical one. Whether or not you are a fan of Pears's voice, no one can deny the enormous influence exerted by Pears on Britten during the course of their nearly four decades together. Few other composers' partners, straight or gay, can claim to have dominated a composer's creative life to the same extent.

During work on Death in Venice, it became clear to Britten that the heart condition from which he had suffered was likely to be fatal and in the last few years of his life he was reduced to doing very little. He had been made a Companion of Honour as early as 1952 and awarded the most coveted British award, the Order of Merit, in 1965; less than six months before his death he was elevated to the peerage, the first composer ever to be made a Lord. Britten wrote in a stunning variety of styles without ever losing the unmistakable 'Britten sound'. More memorable than the melodies he wrote are the haunting moods and atmospheres he conjures up. The brooding, bleak flatness of the East Anglian landscape forever hovers round him. His friendship with some of the greatest artists of the day (including, most notably, horn-player Dennis Brain, cellist Mstislav Rostropovich and pianist Sviatoslav Richter) encouraged music which delights in virtuosity. The sea, too, played a major part in his creative process. 'My parents' house directly faced the sea,' he wrote, 'and my childhood was coloured by the fierce storms that sometimes drove ships into our coast and ate away whole stretches of the neighbouring cliffs.' Britten came of age in 1934, the year in which Elgar, Holst and Delius died. He rapidly dragged British music into another era – his own.

Piano Concerto in D, Op 13

Piano Concerto. Violin Concerto, Op 15
Mark Lubotsky vn **Sviatoslav Richter** pf
English Chamber Orchestra / Benjamin Britten
Decca British Music Collection 473 715-2 (67' · ADD)
Recorded 1970 Ⓜ️Ⓑ️➔

Just after Britten's performances were released on LP in 1971, the composer admitted with some pride that Sviatoslav Richter had learnt his Piano Concerto 'entirely off his own bat', and had revealed a Russianness that was in the score. Britten was attracted to Shostakovich during the late 1930s, when it was written, and the bravado, brittleness and flashy virtuosity of the writing, in the march-like finale most of all, at first caused many to be wary of it, even to think it somehow outside the composer's style. Now we know his music better, it's easier to accept, particularly in this sparkling yet sensitive performance.

The Violin Concerto dates from the following year, 1939, and it, too, has its self-conscious virtuosity, but it's its rich nostalgic lyricism which strikes to the heart and the quiet elegiac ending is

unforgettable. Compared to Richter in the other work, Mark Lubotsky isn't always the master of its hair-raising difficulties, notably in the *Scherzo*, which has passages of double artificial harmonics that even Heifetz wanted simplified before he would play it (Britten refused), but this is still a lovely account. Fine recordings.

Piano Concerto, Op 13 (incl both versions of the third movement). Young Apollo, Op 16. Diversions, Op 21
Steven Osborne pf **BBC Scottish Symphony Orchestra / Ilan Volkov**
Hyperion CDA67625 (71' · DDD) Ⓕ🄾

Commissioned as a 24-year-old to compose and perform a piano concerto for the 1938 Proms, Britten played safe. None of the edginess he might have filched from Bartók or Stravinsky, no Bergian angst: instead, the models are Prokofiev, Shostakovich and Ravel, and in these terms he doesn't miss a trick, at least before the finale's rather perfunctory final gallop. Most of the piece takes a genuinely fresh look at pianistic conventions, and Steven Osborne yields nothing to the great Sviatoslav Richter in the punchiness and fine-tuned filigree of his playing. No skating over the surface here, with Ilan Volkov and the BBC Scottish SO adept at teasing out the music's symphonic subtext, as well as its piquant orchestral effects.

Britten replaced the original slow movement in 1945, possibly because it spent too much time in waltz-like regions already visited in the second movement. This disc adds it anyway, alongside two other scores for piano and orchestra. *Young Apollo* (1939) was not heard for half a century after its premiere, perhaps discarded by Britten because its fanfare-like material was more effectively deployed in *Les illuminations* (also 1939). It's a quirky piece, difficult to programme, a euphorically unguarded response to Keats's vision of male beauty in *Hyperion*.

Diversions is on a much grander scale, its style making even clearer those debts to Mahler which Britten had allowed to surface now and again in the concerto. The multifarious challenges to the single-handed soloist create moments of strong emotional depth and, as throughout the disc, Osborne and his colleagues make the best possible case for pieces which have tended to be placed on the outer fringes of the Britten canon. The recordings, made in Glasgow's Henry Wood Hall, have ample depth of sonority and vividness of colour.

Violin Concerto in D minor, Op 15

Britten Violin Concerto **Walton** Viola Concerto
Maxim Vengerov vn/va **London Symphony Orchestra / Mstislav Rostropovich**
EMI 557510-2 (64' · DDD) Ⓕ️Ⓑ️➔

When artists of the stature of Vengerov and Rostropovich tackle English music it's often a revelation, and here's some of the most ravishing string playing ever heard in either of these masterpieces. But these readings don't always follow convention, let alone metronome markings, and there's at least one choice of tempo that may have traditionalists spluttering in protest. As you might expect with Rostropovich as conductor, the Britten is the less controversial of the two readings. The soloist's first entry over crisply sprung ostinato repetitions on bassoon and harp is marked *dolcissimo*, and the sweetness of Vengerov's playing in the high-lying cantilena is nothing short of heavenly. Here and throughout the work his free expressiveness, his use of *rubato*, far from sounding forced, reflects a seemingly spontaneous understanding, the creative insight of a major artist, rapt and intense. Rostropovich and the LSO match him in their warm expressiveness. The full-blooded recording not only covers the widest dynamic range throughout, but brings out many inner details in the orchestral writing normally obscured.

That's also true of the Russians' reading of the Walton Viola Concerto, with Vengerov evidently just as much at ease on the viola as the violin. Yet the timings alone will bear witness to the individuality of the reading. Vengerov is even more expansive than Kennedy or Bashmet, and the wonder is that, with Rostropovich in total sympathy, he sustains the slow tempo with rapt intensity, pure and tender with no hint of soupiness of the kind that mars the Kennedy version. Unconventional as it is, this is a reading that demands to be heard, even if Waltonians won't want it as their only choice.

Additional recommendations

Violin Concerto
Coupled with **Beethoven** Violin Concerto
J Jansen *vn* **Deutsche Kammerphilharmonie, LSO / P Järvi**
Decca 478 1530 (71' · DDD) Ⓕ**OO**▷
A stunningly recorded and brilliantly played performance by Jansen, who clearly understands this amazing score. A fine, punchy Beethoven comes as an unusual coupling.

Violin Concerto[a]
Coupled with Cello Symphony[b]
[a]**Hirsch** *vn* [b]**Tim Hugh** *vc* **BBC Scottish SO / Yuasa**
Naxos 8 553882 (68' · DDD) Ⓢ▷

Not only does Rebecca Hirsch make light of the solo part's fiendish technical difficulties, her playing evinces a beguiling lyrical beauty that's breathtaking. In the *Cello Symphony*, Tim Hugh displays a profound musicality, great subtlety of tone and affecting lyrical ardour. Sound and balance are generally very good indeed.

Cello Symphony, Op 68

Cello Symphony[a]. Sinfonia da Requiem, Op 20[b].
Cantata misericordium, Op 69[c]

Mstislav Rostropovich *vc* **Sir Peter Pears** *ten* **Dietrich Fischer-Dieskau** *bar* [a]**English Chamber Orchestra,** [b]**New Philharmonia Orchestra,** [c]**London Symphony Chorus and Orchestra / Benjamin Britten**
Decca London 425 100-2LM (75' · ADD · T/t)
Recorded 1964 Ⓜ**O**▷

The Cello Symphony, written in 1963 as part of a series for the great Russian cellist Mstislav Rostropovich, was the first major sonata-form work written since the *Sinfonia*. The idea of a struggle between soloist and orchestra, implicit in the traditional concerto, has no part here; it's a conversation between the two. Rostropovich plays with a depth of feeling that has never quite been equalled in other recordings and the playing of the English Chamber Orchestra has great bite. The recording, too, is extraordinarily fine for its years.

From the opening drumbeat the *Sinfonia* employs a sonata form with dramatic power, although the tone is never fierce or savage; it has an implacable tread and momentum. The central movement, 'Dies irae', however, has a real sense of fury, satirical in its biting comment – the flutter-tongued wind writing rattling its defiance. The closing 'Requiem aeternam' is a movement of restrained beauty. The New Philharmonia play superbly. The *Cantata misericordium* was written in 1962 as a commission from the Red Cross. It takes the story of the Good Samaritan and is scored for tenor and baritone soloists, chorus, string quartet and orchestra. It's a universal plea for charity and receives a powerful reading. A must for any Britten enthusiast.

Additional recommendations

Cello Symphony[a]
Coupled with **Elgar** Cello Concerto
Mørk *vc* **City of Birmingham Symphony Orchestra / Rattle**
Virgin Classics 545356-2 Ⓜ**OO**
Truls Mørk plays this powerful work as if his life depended on it: it's his second recording of the work and long familiarity has clearly paid off. In Rattle and the CBSO he has truly supportive partners. (And the Elgar as coupling is a refreshingly unsentimental performance that never, alas, quite takes wing as it might, fine though it is.)

'Frank Bridge' Variations, Op 10

Variations on a Theme of Frank Bridge, Op 10. The Young Person's Guide to the Orchestra, Op 34. Four Sea Interludes, Op 33a. Passacaglia, Op 33b
BBC Symphony Orchestra / Sir Andrew Davis
Warner Apex 8573 89082-2 (68' · DDD) Ⓢ▷

The real reason for investing in this bargain reissue is Davis's exceptionally insightful account of the *Variations*. After a deceptively low-key 'Introduction and Theme', this quickly develops into a reading of striking application and abundant character, plumbing genuine depths in the 'Funeral March' and 'Chant', and conveying an overwhelming sense of pathos towards the close. Of course, no home should be without the composer's uniquely authoritative 1966 account with the ECO on Decca but, as 'big-band' contenders go, there's no more perceptive rendering than Davis's.

The couplings include a thoroughly professional, no-frills *Young Person's Guide*, finely played and with a delectable rhythmic snap in the variation for percussion in particular. What's missing is harder to define: that sense of playfulness, fun even, you hear in, say, Hickox's excellent account for Chandos, which remains the pick of the digital crop, though Britten's own classic LSO recording is also an absolute must. Davis's *Four Sea Interludes* are agreeable enough in their comparatively breezy, uncomplicated manner, and it's always a pleasure to hear the imposing *Passacaglia* given with such intensity. Overall, well worth its modest outlay.

The Young Person's Guide ..., Op 34

The Young Person's Guide to the Orchestra. Simple Symphony, Op 4[a]. A Spring Symphony, Op 44 – Spring, the sweet spring. Noyes Fludde[b] – Noye, Noye, take thou thy company ... Sir! heare are lions. Serenade for Tenor, Horn and Strings, Op 31 – Nocturne. Folk Songs – The Plough Boy; Early One Morning. Billy Budd – Interlude and Sea Shanties. A Ceremony of Carols, Op 28 – Adam lay i-bounden. A Hymn to the Virgin. War Requiem – Lacrimosa. Peter Grimes – Interlude (Dawn)
Sir Peter Pears ten **Barry Tuckwell** hn **various soloists; choirs, choruses and orchestras, London Symphony Orchestra,** [ab]**English Chamber Orchestra / Benjamin Britten** pf [b]**Norman Del Mar**
Decca 436 990-2DWO (74' · ADD). Recorded 1963-68
Ⓜ●🅑➔

This reissue includes the composer's own 1963 recording of *The Young Person's Guide to the Orchestra* with the LSO and his complete 1968 ECO version of the *Simple Symphony*. The latter is delightfully fresh and is unforgettable for the joyful bounce of the 'Playful Pizzicato', helped by the resonant acoustic of The Maltings, Snape. In *The Young Person's Guide*, without the now somewhat rather dated text, he adopts quick, demanding tempi, with more spacious ones for the more introspective sections. This is beautiful playing, possessing wit and brilliance, with all kinds of memorable touches. Even if this transfer is a little dry in sonority, this disc is invaluable for these two performances alone. As a bonus we're offered 10 short excerpts from other major Britten works.

Film music

'Britten on Film'
Britten When you're feeling like expressing your

affection[ad]. Night Mail[dg]. Way to the Sea[dg]. The Tocher (Rossini Suite)[fg]. The King's Stamp[g]. Negroes[abcg]. Telegrams[fg]. Peace of Britain[g]. Men Behind the Meters[g]. Coal Face[bcdeg]
[a]**Mary Carewe** sop [b]**Daniel Auchincloss** ten [c]**Adam Green** bar [d]**Simon Russell Beale** narr [d]**Malcolm Wilson** pf [e]**City of Birmingham Symphony Orchestra Chorus;** [f]**Choir of King Edward's School, Birmingham;** [g]**Birmingham Contemporary Music Group / Martyn Brabbins**
NMC NMCD112 (79' · DDD)   Ⓕ🅑➔

In the mid-1930s, in his early twenties, Britten wrote film scores, giving him an unrivalled opportunity to hear his own music immediately after it had been composed. He learnt to apply his imagination to visual effects and drama – this was the genesis of the great opera composer. His colleagues included WH Auden, intimidatingly erudite and sometimes bullying, who was a formative influence on Britten at this impressionable period.

This generous 79-minute collection consists of the film music without the film, so if you have once seen some of the better known ones such as *Night Mail* or *Coal Face* your visual memory fills the gap. An excellent feature is the provision of Auden's texts as well as thorough documentary material from Philip Reed.

There are familiar elements in *The Tocher (Rossini Suite)*, which overlaps with Britten's *Soirées musicales* based on Rossini, and it's odd to find Britten arranging Balfe's 'I dreamt that I dwelt in marble halls' in a film about the gas industry. Surprisingly often the musical ideas are strong enough on their own but some extracts such as *The King's Stamp* (commemorating the George V Silver Jubilee issue of 1935) consist of bits and pieces that weren't meant to cohere and don't. Simon Russell Beale is the narrator and his rather low-pitched voice is sometimes drowned by the instruments: he also drops his voice at the end of sentences. The track-listing has gone awry at the start of *The Negroes*, which begins with a passage very close to Kurt Weill. But most of this material is well worth having at least for its pre-echoes and is admirably performed.

Miscellaneous works

'Unknown Britten'
In memoriam Dennis Brain[ae]. Les illuminations[be]. Movements for a Clarinet Concerto (ed C Matthews)[ce]. Rondo concertante[de]. Untitled Fragment for Strings[e]. Variations[d]
[b]**Sandrine Piau** sop [c]**Michael Collins** cl [a]**Michael Thompson**, [a]**Richard Watkins**, [a]**Peter Francomb**, [a]**Chris Griffiths** hns [d]**Rolf Hind** pf [e]**Northern Sinfonia / Thomas Zehetmair**
NMC NMCD140 (78' · DDD)   Ⓕ●●🅑➔

The eight (!) previously unrecorded works presented on this disc span the length of Britten's career. Two come from 1930, when he was 16 and newly enrolled at the Royal College of Music: a three-minute sliver of a piece for string orchestra and two unfinished yet far more substantive movements of a *Rondo concertante* for piano and strings (the latter's loose ends have been handsomely sewn up by Colin Matthews). Both fragments are finely textured, harmonically adventurous and assured, and full of striking ideas.

Les illuminations (1939-40) is quite well known, of course. But here, in addition to the song-cycle, we have three songs (in Matthews's orchestration) discarded from the published version. 'Phrase' is extremely brief and has a prefatory, recitative-like character. In the exquisitely evocative 'Aube', however, Britten magically illustrates one of Rimbaud's ecstatic visions; why he thought this song to be disposable is incomprehensible. An intense, almost Mahlerian sense of yearning makes 'A une raison' engrossing, too.

Britten began writing a Clarinet Concerto for Benny Goodman in 1941, during his final months in the US. The first movement was complete (in short score) when he returned to the UK in 1942 but the project was abandoned. Matthews has orchestrated this rhythmically playful piece as well as the 1941 *Mazurka elegiaca* (originally for two pianos), and filled out the sketches for another unfinished work from this same period to create three 'Movements for a Clarinet Concerto'. It's an attractive and sturdy score that brings to light some marvellous music. Indeed, the wave-like passages in the first movement foreshadow *Peter Grimes*.

Matthews has also masterfully realised *In memoriam Dennis Brain* (1958), an anguished, angry and affecting work for four horns and strings. Since Brain, who was killed in a car crash, played a crucial role in the creation of the Serenade (1943), Britten freely quotes the 'Lyke-Wake Dirge', the darkest song from that song-cycle. And, finally – for solo piano – an unfinished set of theme and variations intended for the 1966 Leeds Competition. Improvisatory, ruminative (note the use of repeated notes) and exploratory in its use of extended tonality, it is a small but significant cobblestone in the path towards Britten's late style.

All the performances are superb. Sandrine Piau's stylish and imaginative interpretation of *Les illuminations* is one of the best soprano versions on disc, in fact. Michael Collins's easy virtuosity in the Clarinet Concerto is a joy. And throughout, Thomas Zehetmair elicits razor-sharp, sensitively shaped playing from the Northern Sinfonia. In short, this is one of the most important Britten recordings in many a year.

String Quartets

No 1 in D, Op 25; **No 2** in C, Op 36; **No 3** Op 94

String Quartets Nos 1-3. Three Divertimentos
Belcea Quartet (Corina Belcea, Lara Samuel vns
Krzysztof Chorzelski va Alasdair Tait vc)

EMI ② 557968-2 (115' · DDD)   Ⓕ**OOO**▸

Ⓖ The Belcea Quartet have become prominent players on the chamber-music scene. In the concert hall, their rather balletic style of performance can be alienating, but in these Britten recordings you can appreciate their high level of technical accomplishment without the risk of visual distraction.

Collectors familiar with any of the earlier sets of the quartets may not warm immediately to the Belcea's exceptionally dramatic way with the music's contrasting materials. But almost nothing is forced or eccentric here. The hell-for-leather tempo adopted for the First's finale is genuinely exciting, not a scramble, and although there are a few obtrusive, fussy details in the outer movements of No 2 the overall impression is powerfully convincing. No 3 is even better, at least in the earlier movements, bringing a sense of barely suppressed anger to some of Britten's most personal and allusive music. In the last movement the phrasing is occasionally over-pointed: yet, despite tempi that make this account significantly faster than the excellent Magginis and considerably faster than the stately Brodskys, the effect reinforces the true consistency of tone and character which underpins this notably diverse score. This is one of the best-engineered quartet discs you might hope to hear.

String Quartets – No 2; No 3. Three Divertimentos
Elias Quartet (Sara Bitlloch, Donald Grant vns Martin
Saving va Marie Bitlloch vc)
Sonimage SON10903 (70' · DDD)   Ⓕ**OOO**

Selection to BBC Radio 3's New Generation Artists has clearly made the Elias Quartet a group to watch. The quality of quartet playing here is high by any standard. As part of their preparation the Elias players studied with Norbert Brainin of the Amadeus Quartet, who gave the premiere of Britten's Third Quartet. A comparison with the Amadeus's famed authority in these works (Decca) does the newcomers no harm: they are as expert in the fast movements and, where sensitivity is called for, the Elias players give themselves more elbow room to delve deep into the music.

These are highly sensitive, touching performances. Occasionally in the Second Quartet the Elias flirt with emotional indulgence but there is a wonderful pensiveness here and a real appreciation of the beauty of sound and colour, aided by a fine recording. In the Third Quartet the gently pulsing rhythms of the opening already evoke the lapping waves of Venice and the very hushed *sul ponticello* effects at the start of the finale are as subtle as a fine mist, through which the quotations from *Death in Venice* sing with heartfelt yearning. If the Amadeus Quartet focus on Britten the master of rhythm, these lyrical Elias performances remind us he was primarily a composer of vocal music. The playing in the *Three Divertimentos* is just as imaginative. Those who are looking to have all three Britten quartets may choose the admirable two-CD set by the Belcea Quartet (see above). Nobody who buys this new disc is likely to regret it.

String Quartet No 2; String Quartets – in D (1931); in F (1928)
Sorrel Quartet (Gina McCormack, Catherine Yates vns Vicci Wardman va Helen Thatcher vc)
Chandos CHAN9664 (74' · DDD)   ⒻO

The Sorrel Quartet can claim a significant 'first' in its account of the recently resurrected F major Quartet from 1928. At 15 Britten was nothing if not precocious, and although the ideas in this substantial piece offer few hints of his mature style, he was already using the medium to excellent effect. Three years later, in the D major Quartet which has been a repertory item since Britten revised it in 1974, there are signs of a more individual voice; this is an attractive performance, well shaped and effectively characterised. Nevertheless, it's on the interpretation of the Quartet No 2 that the disc must be judged. The Sorrel's naturalness and feeling for line are much in evidence. Tempi for the first movement are broader than most rivals, but they serve an approach which makes a virtue of reticence, and still manages to be quite gripping. It has just about the best sound currently available (with The Maltings, Snape, providing an ideal acoustic), and the otherwise unrecorded F major Quartet adds strength to the recommendation of this noteworthy disc.

Phantasy Quartet

Britten Phantasy Quartet, Op 2[acde] **Dohnányi** Serenade, Op 10[cde] **Mozart** Oboe Quartet, K370[acde]. Die Zauberflöte[ac] – Der Vogelfänger bin ich ja; Ach, ich fühl's; Der Hölle Rache. Adagio, K580[abcde]
François Leleux [a]ob/[b]cor ang [c]**Lisa Batiashvili** vn [d]**Lawrence Power** va [e]**Sebastian Klinger** vc
Sony Classical 88697 28585-2 (64' · DDD)   Ⓕ

Distinguished soloists do not always make distinguished chamber musicians. Here they do; and unsuspected depths in the music are plumbed. A measure of daring seems implicit in their control of fine *pianissimi* and tonal halflights at the beginning of Britten's *Phantasy Quartet*. The initial notes marked to be played on the fingerboard of a muted cello emanate from an inky nothingness, to be gradually joined by the viola and violin playing in a similar fashion. And there is no rude awakening from oboist François Leleux; his softly reedy tone steals in to reinforce the delicate texture.

This is no flash in the pan. Technique, both individual and corporate, is consummate, a vehicle for a penetrating intelligence that reaches beyond the limitations of musical notation. Leleux avoids a narrow dynamic range and blunt attack, instead producing within the scope of his instrument a ductile expressiveness of the sort that is usually heard from strings. The inter-

pretation of Mozart's Oboe Quartet is sure to meet the expectations of many a dream, as will the C minor Adagio where an eloquent case is made for a piece not often heard. Ditto Dohnányi's Trio, Lisa Batiashvili as unobtrusively cogent a leader here as she is the duo partner in the arias from *Die Zauberflöte*. Bewitching performances!

Solo Cello Suites

No 1, Op 72; **No 2**, Op 80; **No 3**, Op 87
Solo Cello Suites Nos 1 & 2. Cello Sonata, Op 65
Mstislav Rostropovich vc **Benjamin Britten** pf
Decca London 421 859-2LM (68' · ADD)
Recorded 1961-69   ⓂOOO

 This is a classic recording of the Cello Sonata, with Rostropovich and Britten playing with an authority impossible to surpass, and is here coupled with the unaccompanied First and Second Cello Suites. The suggestive, often biting humour masks darker feelings. However, Britten manages, just, to keep his devil under control. Rostropovich's and Britten's characterisation in the opening *Dialogo* is stunning and their subdued humour in the *Scherzo-pizzicato* also works well. In the *Elegia* and the final *Moto perpetuo*, again, no one quite approaches the passion and energy of Rostropovich. This work, like the two Suites, was written for him and he still remains the real heavyweight in all three pieces. Their transfer to CD is remarkably successful; it's difficult to believe that these recordings were made in the 1960s.

Solo Cello Suites Nos 1-3
Jean-Guihen Queyras vc
Harmonia Mundi Les Nouveaux Interprètes
HMN91 1670 (65' · DDD)   ⒷO

Britten's three Cello Suites have all the strength of musical character to sustain a permanent place in the repertory. Inspired by the personality and technique of Mstislav Rostropovich, they're remarkable for the way in which they acknowledge yet at the same time distance themselves from the great precedent of Bach's Cello Suites. The best performers (like Rostropovich himself, though he has never recorded No 3) are equally at ease with the music's Bach-like contrapuntal ingenuity and its lyric intensity, where Britten's own most personal voice is heard. Queyras has such a fine sense of phrase that his slower speeds do not sound unconvincing, and his technically superb playing has an impressive consistency of style. The quality of the recording is another plus, with the close focus needed to ensure that all the details tell. The only disappointment came in the final track, with the Russian Prayer for the Dead that ends Suite No 3. Here, of all places, Queyras is simply too fast. Nevertheless, this lapse isn't so great as to deprive the disc of a place in this guide.

War Requiem, Op 66

War Requiem[a]. Sinfonia da Requiem, Op 20. Ballad of Heroes, Op 14[b]
Heather Harper sop [a]**Philip Langridge,** [b]**Martyn Hill** tens **John Shirley-Quirk** bar [a]**St Paul's Cathedral Choir; London Symphony Chorus and Orchestra / Richard Hickox**
Chandos ② CHAN8983/4 (125' · DDD · T/t)
Ⓕ**OOO**▷

Ⓖ Britten's *War Requiem* is the composer's most public statement of his pacifism. The work is cast in six movements and calls for massive forces: full chorus, soprano soloist and full orchestra evoke mourning, supplication and guilty apprehension; boys' voices with chamber organ, the passive calm of a liturgy which points beyond death; tenor and baritone soloists with chamber orchestra, the passionate outcry of the doomed victims of war. The most recent challenger to the composer's classic Decca version offers up-to-date recording, excellently managed to suggest the various perspectives of the vast work, and possibly the most convincing execution of the choral writing to date under the direction of a conductor, Richard Hickox, who's a past master at obtaining the best from a choir in terms of dynamic contrast and vocal emphasis. Add to that his empathy with all that the work has to say and you've a cogent reason for acquiring this version even before you come to the excellent work of the soloists. In her recording swansong, Harper at last commits to disc a part she created. It's right that her special accents and impeccable shaping of the soprano's contribution have been preserved for posterity.

Shirley-Quirk, always closely associated with the piece, sings the three baritone solos and duets with rugged strength and dedicated intensity. He's matched by Langridge's compelling and insightful reading, with his notes and words more dramatic than Pears's approach. The inclusion of two additional pieces, neither of them short, helps to give this version an added advantage even if the *Ballad of Heroes* is one of Britten's slighter works.

War Requiem
Stefania Woytowicz sop **Peter Pears** ten **Hans Wilbrink** bar **Wandsworth School Boys' Choir; Melos Ensemble; New Philharmonia Orchestra and Chorus / Carlo Maria Giulini**
BBC Legends BBCL4046-2 (79' · ADD · T)
Recorded live 1969
Ⓜ**OO**

This performance is a revelation. As the authoritative note makes clear, Britten and Giulini had a mutual respect for and an admiration of each other's work. Here they combine to give a performance that's a true Legend, as this BBC series has it. Giulini's reading is as dramatic and viscerally exciting as any rival version. The music leaps from the page newminted in his histrionically taut hands, the

BRITTEN'S WAR REQUIEM – IN BRIEF

Vishnevskaya; Pears; Fischer-Dieskau; Bach Choir; Highgate School Choir; Melos Ens; LSO & Chorus / Benjamin Britten
Decca ② 475 7511DOR2 (132' · ADD) Ⓕ**OOO**▷
Ⓖ A true recording classic, sounding more resplendent than ever in its latest 24-bit remastering. It also now contains a fascinating 50-minute rehearsal sequence.

Brewer; Griffey; LPO & Choir / Kurt Masur
LPO ② LPO0010 (83' · DDD) Ⓕ
With moments of searing insight and power this is a fine if not outstanding reading. Masur's soloists were better on his Teldec recording, though Finley, as always, brings superior musicianship and intelligence to the baritone solos.

Curtin; Di Virgilio; Krause; Chorus Pro Musica; Columbus Boychoir; Boston SO / Leinsdorf
VAI 📀 VAIDVD4429 (89' · PAL · 4:3 black and white · 1.0 · 0). Ⓜ**O**
The *War Requiem*'s US premiere is a genuine moment in history and captured for posterity on this excellent film. Leinsdorf is superb and holds the entire work together, and also draws from his fine soloists performances of genuine distinction.

Harper; Langridge; Shirley-Quirk; St Paul's Cathedral Choir; London Symphony Chorus & Orchestra / Richard Hickox
Chandos ② CHAN8983/4 (125' · DDD) Ⓕ**OOO**▷
Now available at mid-price, Richard Hickox's admirably incisive and dedicated realisation rightly triumphed in both the Choral and Engineering categories at the 1992 *Gramophone* Awards. Generously coupled with the *Sinfonia da Requiem* and *Ballad of Heroes*.

Woytowicz; Pears; Wilbrink; Wandsworth School Boys' Choir; Melos Ensemble / Britten; New Philharmonia Chorus & Orchestra / Carlo Maria Giulini
BBC Legends BBCL4046-2 (79' · ADD) Ⓜ**OO**
An unmissable live recording from April 1969. Giulini's thrustingly intense and superbly sung account fits snugly onto a single disc. Britten himself directs the chamber forces in the Wilfred Owen settings. A remarkable document.

Dasch; Taylor; Gerhaher; Aurelius Sängerknaben Calw; Stuttgart Festival Ensemble / Robin Engelen, Helmuth Rilling
Hänssler Classic ② 📀 CD98 507 (83' · DDD) Ⓕ**OOO**▷
A wonderful new recording with three superb soloists, excellent choral work and a fine control of the different orchestral perspectives. The SACD recording makes it well worth considering.

rhythmic tension at times quite astonishing. For instance, the sixth movement, 'Libera me', is simply earth-shattering in its effect, every bar, every word, every instrument sung and played to the hilt – and so it is throughout, with the peculiar, and in this case peculiarly right, acoustics of the Albert Hall adding its own measure of *verité* to the inspired occasion.

The performance of the New Philharmonia forces, under the man who was at the time their favourite conductor after Klemperer, is at once technically assured and wholly dedicated. Only perhaps the classic Decca recording comes near equalling it in this respect, and that doesn't quite have the electrifying atmosphere found on this astonishing occasion. Nor have the Wandsworth Boys' Choir, placed up in the Hall's gallery, been surpassed.

The soloists also seem to realise the special quality of the occasion. Pears surpasses even his own creator's reading on the Decca set, singing with the sustained concentration and vocal acuity that were so much his hallmarks in Britten's music. The soprano Stefania Woytowicz, who at the time made something of a speciality of this work, has very much the vocal timbre of Vishnevskaya, for whom the part was written, and perhaps a shade more sensitivity. She's certainly the best soprano on any version, and Wilbrink comes near being the best baritone. He may not be quite as varied or subtle as Decca's Fischer-Dieskau, nor as confident as Chandos's Shirley-Quirk, but he has a more beautiful voice than either, with a plangency in his tone that's so right for this music.

Most of all it's the sum of the parts that so impresses here, as does the truthfulness of the sound, preferable to that on the Chandos set.

War Requiem
Galina Vishnevskaya *sop* **Peter Pears** *ten*
Dietrich Fischer-Dieskau *bar* **Simon Preston** *org*
Bach Choir; Highgate School Choir; Melos Ensemble; London Symphony Orchestra /
Benjamin Britten
Decca ② 475 7511DOR2 (132' · DDD · T/t)
Recorded 1963. Includes previously unreleased
rehearsal sequence Ⓟ❶❷❸❹➔

Decca has used the most recent digital and Cedar technology to improve the original sound, under the overall supervision of veteran technician James Lock. This is one of the great performances of recording history. As an imaginative bonus, Decca gives us the first issue of a long rehearsal tape made by the producer John Culshaw without Britten's approval. When Culshaw presented it to the composer on his 50th birthday, Britten was 'appalled', considering it 'an unauthorised invasion of a territory exclusively his own and his performers'', as Donald Mitchell relates in the booklet. Now Mitchell believes that we should be allowed 'to assess the tape as a contribution to our knowledge of him [Britten] as a performer and interpreter of his own

music and to our understanding of the *War Requiem* itself'.

Throughout this fascinating document you hear evidence of Britten's vision of his own music, his astonishing ear for timbre and intimate details, above all his wonderful encouragement of all his forces, culminating in his heart-warming words of thanks at the end of the sessions, not to mention his tension-breaking humour and a couple of sharp comments from Vishnevskaya, who's unsurpassed as soprano soloist. The merit of this groundbreaking performance is that it so arrestingly conveys Britten's intentions. We're lucky to have not only Britten's irreplaceable reading refurbished, but also his commentary suggested by the rehearsal sequences.

War Requiem
Annette Dasch *sop* **James Taylor** *ten* **Christian Gerhaher** *bar* **Aurelius Sängerknaben Calw;**
Stuttgart Festival Ensemble / Robin Engelen,
Helmuth Rilling
Hänssler Classic ② CD98 507 (83' · DDD)
Recorded live Ⓕ❶❷❸❹➔

A wonderful performance and a most moving experience. Critically, one must keep the experience (subjective) as distant from the relatively objective facts of the performance as possible: on this occasion that wasn't very easy, or even desirable. Certainly all the elements in this complex organisation are well served. The soloists are admirable, Annette Dasch pure in tone, powerfully concentrated in style, James Taylor a tenor whose voice can respond to what is gentle and compassionate in his music as to the unsparing harshness, and Christian Gerhaher authoritative, humane and (like the others) entirely firm in his singing. The choir is fine in blend, precision and enunciation; the boys' choir, too, ideal in its embodiment of unsanctimonious sanctity. For the chamber ensemble and full orchestra, only admiration, as for the recording's producer and engineer who have dealt so well with the difficult task of keeping these elements distinct and unifying them at the same time. Above all, we must honour their conductor, whose mature guidance is everywhere in evidence.

It's the sense of unity that has distinguished this experience of the *War Requiem* most especially. Rarely has it moved with such logic. That seems a strange word to use in the description of what was so deeply emotional, yet it's right. For the first time the work moved with the single-minded force of a geometrical theorem. Darkness and light, war and peace, noise and quiet are the unifying opposites throughout. The selection and sequence of Owen's poems are so well-fitting that the line – can you call it 'of argument'? – is unbroken and all goes forward to the almost painful easement of 'Let us sleep now'. Do try it for yourself.

War Requiem
Phyllis Curtin sop **Nicholas Di Virgilio** ten
Tom Krause bar **Chorus Pro Musica;**
Columbus Boychoir; Boston Symphony Orchestra /
Erich Leinsdorf
VAI 📀 VAIDVD4429 (89' · PAL · 4:3 black and white ·
1.0 · 0). Recorded live at the Tanglewood Festival,
USA, on July 27, 1963   Ⓕ**O**

'It makes criticism impertinent,' thought Peter Shaffer of the *War Requiem*, and for all Stravinsky's grousing that any such criticism would be 'as if one had failed to stand up for *God Save the Queen*' the piece still carries as much sense of occasion as it evidently did at this, its American premiere in 1963, a year after its fraught first performance. What a contrast. The alfresco acoustic of the Tanglewood Music Shed may have been no more favourable in its way than that of Coventry Cathedral, though, you might think miraculously, there is no trace of indistinctness or inadequacy about the stereo sound preserved by WGBH Boston to accompany its telecast.

Nor is there about the performance, which was evidently prepared with all the care that such an occasion merited. The hero of the hour is preeminently Leinsdorf, who picked the work as the centrepiece of his first season as Tanglewood's music director. Whatever else the *War Requiem* stands for, its performance here serves as a conducting masterclass. Leinsdorf stands ramrod-straight, no baton, and his timing and pacing are equally impeccable, honed by his years in the pit at the Met. When he raises his left hand, infrequently, it is either to conduct the chamber ensemble to his left or to indicate 'too loud'. When both arms are aloft and the eyes blaze at the climax of the *Sanctus*, on the upbeat to the 'Hosanna', the response is electrifying, as though all heaven's angels had joined the already excellent Chorus Pro Musica.

It would be easy but misleading to equate the unyielding body language with the interpretation: a strict, dry-eyed tempo for the 'Lacrymosa' makes all the more sense when it eventually contrasts so poignantly with the tenor's desperate cry of 'Was it for this the clay grew tall', as though the ancient liturgy was cracking under the strain of expressive necessity.

The booklet-note accurately summarises Nicholas Di Virgilio's contribution as having 'a robust and honest American style', though he rises to the challenge in the brief but crucial *Agnus Dei* and is less troubled by the *passaggio* between D and F than many Britten tenors past and present. As Di Virgilio does elsewhere, the Finnish baritone Tom Krause perhaps responds more to Britten's setting than to Owen's poetry in 'Be slowly lifted up', though the trumpet obbligato is something of a highlight, and the singer ratchets up the tension for the apocalyptic recapitulation of the *Dies irae*. Phyllis Curtin's soprano matches Leinsdorf for unobtrusive clarity – and she never scoops, despite every Verdian invitation to do so. A one-off event invites excuses for slips of all kinds, but

there are none, and the breathless hush from the 11,000-strong audience suggests that the stoic power latent in Britten's testament affected them as it might anyone watching almost 50 years hence.

AMDG

AMDG. Choral Dances from 'Gloriana'. Chorale after an Old French Carol. Five Flower Songs, Op 47. A Hymn to the Virgin. Sacred and Profane, Op 91
Polyphony / Stephen Layton
Hyperion CDA67140 (62' · DDD)   Ⓕ**OOO**▷

The programme is delightful and the choir excellent. *AMDG* presents as formidable a challenge to its singers as any of Britten's compositions for unaccompanied choir. In fact that's sometimes suggested as the reason why, having written it for an expert group in 1939 and realising that its chances of frequent performance were slim, Britten never prepared the work for publication. It's a pity he couldn't have heard Stephen Layton's Polyphony! Even more than the Finzi Singers, their predecessors on record, they've worked it into the system so that they have the sense of it clearly in their mind and can make the word-setting fresh and spontaneous. 'God's Grandeur' (*allegro con fuoco*) has the fire: the Finzis seem almost cautious by comparison. In 'The Soldier' Polyphony catch the swing of the triplets and dotted notes with more panache and make more of the words. They also bring out the tender lyricism in 'Prayer II' and grasp more decisively the *con moto*, *Vivace* and *Avanti!* markings in 'O Deus, ego amo te'.

In the *Five Flower Songs* Polyphony have a young tone and their numbers allow them to convey a sense of round-the-table intimacy. In the Choral Dances from *Gloriana*, Polyphony improve on the Finzi Singers' performance with crisper rhythms and a clearer acoustic. *Sacred and Profane*, like *AMDG* a work for virtuosos, is given with wonderful confidence and imagination. A wonderful disc.

Additional recommendation

AMDG
Coupled with: Hymns – to St Peter, Op 56a; of St Columba; to the Virgin; to St Cecilia, Op 27. Rejoice in the Lamb, Op 30. Choral Dances from Gloriana
Finzi Singers / Spicer with **Lumsden** org
Chandos CHAN9511 (67' · DDD · T)   Ⓕ
Very enjoyable performances from this expert choir, successfully directed by Paul Spicer.

The World of the Spirit

An American Overture. King Arthur – Suite (arr Hindmarsh). The World of the Spirit (arr Hindmarsh)
Susan Chilcott sop **Pamela Helen Stephen** mez
Martyn Hill ten **Stephen Varcoe** bar **Hannah**

Gordon, Cormac Rigby *spkrs* **Britten Singers;**
BBC Philharmonic Orchestra / Richard Hickox
Chandos CHAN9487 (79' · DDD · T)　　　　Ⓕ Ⓑ➔

Hickox's performance of the Coplandesque *An American Overture* has exemplary polish, commitment and dash. The remaining items owe their revival to the efforts of Paul Hindmarsh. Britten wrote his incidental music for a BBC radio dramatisation of the King Arthur legend in 1937. It was the first of his 28 radio commissions and contains much high-quality invention. Hindmarsh has fashioned the 23-year-old composer's inventive inspiration into a terrific four-movement orchestral suite lasting some 25 minutes, which Hickox and the BBC PO devour with audible relish.

The 'radio cantata' *The World of the Spirit* dates from May 1938. Commissioned by the BBC as a successor to *The Company of Heaven* (1937), it intersperses sung and spoken texts chosen by R Ellis Roberts. Again, Britten's fertile compositional powers are much in evidence. The work contains a whole string of memorable numbers, from the lilting barcarolle-like treatment of Emily Brontë's 'With wide-embracing love', via the joyful strut and swagger of Part 2's concluding 'The Spirit of the Lord' with its unmistakable echoes of Walton's *Belshazzar's Feast*, to a strikingly imaginative setting of Gerard Manley Hopkins's 'God's Grandeur'. Framing the 42-minute edifice are two radiant settings of the Whitsuntide plainsong, *Veni Creator Spiritus* – an idea possibly inspired by a recent encounter with Mahler's Eighth Symphony at the Queen's Hall under Sir Henry Wood.

The recording is superbly wide in its range and offers a realistic quality.

A Ceremony of Carols, Op 28

A Ceremony of Carols. Missa brevis in D, Op 63.
A Hymn to the Virgin. A Hymn of St Columba,
'Regis regum rectissimi'. Jubilate Deo in E flat.
Deus in adjutorum meum
Sioned Williams *hp* **Westminster Cathedral Choir /**
David Hill with **James O'Donnell** *org*
Hyperion CDA66220 (49' · DDD · T)　　　　Ⓕ Ⓞ Ⓑ➔

A Ceremony of Carols sets nine medieval and 16th-century poems between the 'Hodie' of the plainsong Vespers. The sole accompanying instrument is a harp, but given the right acoustic, sensitive attention to the words and fine rhythmic control the piece has a remarkable richness and depth. The Westminster Cathedral Choir performs this work beautifully; diction is immaculate and the acoustic halo surrounding the voices gives a festive glow to the performance. A fascinating *Jubilate* and *A Hymn to the Virgin*, while lacking the invention and subtlety of *A Ceremony*, intrigue with some particularly felicitous use of harmony and rhythm. *Deus in adjutorum meum* employs the choir without accompaniment and has an initial purity that

gradually builds up in texture as the psalm (No 70) gathers momentum.

The *Missa brevis* was written for this very choir and George Malcolm's nurturing of a tonal brightness in the choir allowed Britten to use the voices in a more flexible and instrumental manner than usual. The effect is glorious. St Columba founded the monastery on the Scottish island of Iona and Britten's hymn sets his simple and forthright prayer with deceptive simplicity and directness. The choir sings beautifully and the recording is first rate.

Hymn to St Cecilia, Op 27

Rejoice in the Lamb, Op 30. Te Deum in C. Jubilate
Deo in C. Antiphon, Op 56b. A Hymn to the Virgin.
Festival Te Deum, Op 32. Missa brevis in D, Op 63.
Hymn to St Peter, Op 56a. A Hymn of St Columba.
Prelude and Fugue on a Theme of Vittoria.
Hymn to St Cecilia
St John's College Choir, Cambridge /
Christopher Robinson with **Ian Farrington** *org*
Naxos 8 554791 (74' · DDD)　　　　Ⓢ Ⓑ➔

As with other recent records from St John's, there's a freshness, almost a feeling of adventure and a sense that all this choral discipline is an easy yoke. These are excellent performances, the opening item setting a standard which is to be maintained throughout. Buoyant rhythms, precise accentuations and well-pointed contrasts are features of the singing; and the playing of Ian Farrington in accompaniments that are often difficult and always demanding of maximum alertness is outstanding. Outstanding, too, is the contribution of the trebles. In tone they preserve the traditional John's sound, without exaggerating its so-called continental element. But what impresses most is the sense of imaginative involvement. It's there, for instance, in the *Kyrie* of the *Missa brevis*, and most of all in the 'I cannot grow' section of *A Hymn to St Cecilia*. To this they bring a distinctive excitement, a wide-eyed, breathlessly playful feeling of childlike wonder. The programme itself is highly attractive. The 'hymns' are fully developed compositions, and the canticles are notably independent of tradition (for instance, a quietly meditative note of praise is struck at the start of both *Te Deums*). The *Missa brevis* makes inventive use of its forces; and *Rejoice in the Lamb*, a masterly expression of the liberal spirit, never ceases to amaze with its evocation of the cat Jeoffry, valiant mouse and staff-struck poet. Recorded sound isn't as vivid as the performances, but this remains a very likeable disc.

Serenade, Op 31

Serenade for Tenor, Horn and Strings, Op 31ᵃ　Ⓗ
Folksongsᵇ – The Bonny Earl o' Moray; Avenging and
Bright; The Last Rose of Summer; Sally in our Alley
Walton Façadeᶜ
ᵃᵇᶜ**Sir Peter Pears** *ten/spkr* ᶜ**Dame Edith Sitwell** *spkr*
ᵃ**Dennis Brain** *hn* ᵇ**Benjamin Britten** *pf* ᵃ**Boyd Neel**

String Orchestra / Benjamin Britten; ᶜEnglish
Opera Group Ensemble / Anthony Collins
Decca 468 801-2DM (74' · ADD/DDD)
Recorded 1953-54   Ⓜ●●

This disc includes one of the great highlights of
the whole Britten discography, that first magical
recording of the *Serenade*, with Pears in fresh,
youthful voice and Dennis Brain's marvellous
horn obbligatos, creating *frisson*-making echoes
in Tennyson, dark melancholy in Blake, and rippling away exuberantly in Johnson's 'Hymn to
Diana'. What playing! The transfer is faithful;
but why on earth couldn't Decca have removed
the surface rustle, and above all, the clicks? The
coupled Walton *Façade*, however, was a consummate technical and artistic miracle of Decca's mono era. Edith Sitwell and Pears deliver
the engagingly preposterous words with bravura
insouciance, Collins conducting the English
Opera Group Ensemble with matching wit and
flair, and even today the 1953 recording sounds
almost like stereo.

Serenade, Les illuminations, Op 18. Nocturno, Op 60.
Ian Bostridge ten **Radek Baborák** hn **Berlin
Philharmonic Orchestra / Sir Simon Rattle**
EMI 558049-2 (75' · DDD · T/t)   Ⓕ●●☞

This recording offers a profoundly considered
and technically immaculate traversal of Britten's
three great and varied cycles for tenor and
orchestra, conceived with Pears's voice in mind.
Authoritative as the recordings by composer and
tenor may be, there is plenty of room for new
insights into such complex and inspired scores.
Bostridge's particular gift for lighting texts
from within, and projecting so immediately
their images, comes into its own arrestingly in
the *Nocturne*. With his vocal agility and vital
word-painting at their most assured – allied to
surely the most virtuoso account of the obbligato parts yet heard, and Rattle supremely alert
– this reading sets a standard hard to equal. Add
a perfectly balanced recording and you have an
ideal result.
Not that the accounts of the earlier cycles are
far behind in going to the heart of the matter.
Bostridge catches all the fantasy and irony of *Les
illuminations* and projects the text with a biting
delivery that stops just the right side of caricature. Rattle and his orchestra are once again
aware of Britten's subtleties of rhythm and
instrumentation.
The *Serenade*, most easily accessible of the
three works, demonstrates the advantages of
recording after live performances. Everything
seems fresh-minted and immediate, nowhere
more so than in Radek Baborák's bold yet sensitive horn playing. Some of the verbal over-
emphases that are now part of Bostridge's vocal
persona might not have been approved by the
composer but for the most part they second the
plangent beauty of his voice, which is evident
throughout these very personal and satisfying
interpretations. Bostridge writes illuminating

notes in the booklet, too, adding to the disc's
value.

Songs

Harmonia Sacra – Lord! I have sinned; Hymn to God
the Father; A Hymn on Divine Musick. This way to the
Tomb – Evening; Morning; Night. Night covers up
the rigid land. Fish in the unruffled lakes. To lie flat on
the back with the knees flexed. A poison tree. When
you're feeling like expressing your affection. Not
even summer yet. The red cockatoo. Wild with
passion. If thou wilt ease thine heart. Cradle song for
Eleanor. Birthday song for Erwin. Um Mitternacht.
The Holy Sonnets of John Donne, Op 35
Ian Bostridge ten **Graham Johnson** pf
Hyperion CDA66823 (65' · DDD · T)   Ⓕ�D☞

Bostridge is in the royal line of Britten's tenor
interpreters. Indeed his imaginative response to
words and music may come closer than any to
Pears himself. He's heard here in a veritable
cornucopia of mostly unfamiliar and unknown
songs (the Donne cycle apart), mainly from the
earliest period of Britten's song-writing career
when his inspiration was perhaps at its most free
and spontaneous. The three settings from Ronald Duncan's *This way to the Tomb* nicely match
that poet's florid, vocabulary-rich style as Britten was to do again two years later in *Lucretia*,
with 'Night', based on a B minor ground bass, a
particularly arresting piece. The Auden settings,
roughly contemporaneous with *On this Island*, all
reflect Britten's empathy with the poet at that
time. The third, 'To lie flat on the back', evinces
Britten's gift for writing in racy mode, as does
'When you're feeling like expressing your affection', very much in the style of *Cabaret Songs*.
Much deeper emotions are stirred by the two
superb Beddoes settings ('Wild with passion'
and 'If thou wilt ease thine heart'), written when
the composer and Pears were on a ship returning home in 1942. 'The red cockatoo' itself is an
early setting of Waley to whom Britten returned
in *Songs from the Chinese*.
All these revelatory songs are performed with
full understanding and innate beauty by Bostridge and Johnson, who obviously have a close
artistic rapport. The *Donne* Sonnets are as
demanding on singer and pianist as anything
Britten wrote, hence their previously small representation in the catalogue. Both artists pierce
to the core of these electrifying songs, written
after, and affected by, Britten's visit to Belsen
with Menuhin in 1945. The recording catches
the immediacy of these riveting performances. A
richly satisfying issue.

'Britten Abroad'
Six Hölderlin Fragments, Op 61ᵃ. Seven Sonnets of
Michelangelo, Op 22ᵃ. The Poet's Echo, Op 76ᵃ.
Um Mitternachtᵇ. Eight French Folksongsᵇ
ᵇ**Susan Gritton** sop ᵃ**Mark Padmore** ten
Iain Burnside pf
Signum Classics SIGCD122 (74' · DDD)   Ⓕ●

285

Britten is 'abroad' here in the sense that he is occupied with foreign texts. He is also away in time. The breadth of cultural reference is large, involving four languages, none of them his own. The recital, then, challenges its listeners as well as its performers.

And how these two singers have grown, both in voice and artistry. The languages assist in the sense we have of them as being transformed. Mark Padmore in Italian, Susan Gritton in Russian show themselves in new guises. Each is inescapably performing in the shadow of a great original; but even as (in our minds) we hear Pears and Vishnevskaya, recognising that their voices are written into these songs, we can acknowledge these younger artists as worthy successors, and (to be honest) part of us is glad to be hearing them instead. Padmore has now quite a full-bodied ring to his voice at a *forte* (hear him in the strong affirmations of the last sonnet), and Gritton commands an aristocratic concentration of tone, unshakably firm and precise in its placing.

Iain Burnside more than copes with the formidable technical difficulties, and in many songs (for instance, the last of the Pushkin poems with its ticking clock, or the spinning-wheel in 'Fileuse' mingling past and present in the old woman's thoughts) we bless the imaginative touch. Recorded sound is fine, as are John Evans's introductory notes.

'Before Life & After'
Britten The Holy Sonnets of John Donne, Op 35.
Folksong Arrangements – There's none to soothe;
The Miller of Dee; Sail on, sail on; At the mid hour of
night; I wonder as I wander. Winter Words, Op 52
Purcell/Britten An Evening Hymn on a Ground, 'Now
that the sun hath veil'd his light', Z193. Job's Curse,
'Let the night perish', Z191. A Morning Hymn, 'Thou
wakeful shepherd', Z198
Mark Padmore ten **Roger Vignoles** pf
Harmonia Mundi HMU90 7443 (72' · DDD) Ⓕ**ⒺⒾ**

The two song-cycles that Mark Padmore pairs on this disc are highly contrasted. *The Holy Sonnets of John Donne* were composed in 1945, soon after Britten's visit to German concentration camps, and the stark immediacy of that experience can be heard in the composer's own recordings. Padmore and Roger Vignoles, his warm-toned accompanist, take a more reflective line. Tempi are slower, the emotions feel more consoling, and at the core of the cycle is some heartfelt singing in the sixth and most beautiful setting, 'Since she whom I loved'.

The vivid picture-painting of *Winter Words* helps make it probably Britten's most popular song-cycle with piano. Several of the Thomas Hardy poems evoke a time of innocence now lost, a familiar Britten theme, and the evocative performance by Padmore and Vignoles captures that sense of longing particularly well. The portrait of the lone boy traveller on the Great Western could be more vivid (Vignoles's train jogs along somewhat sluggishly), but otherwise Pad-

more dramatises the narrative songs with subtlety and imagination.

Padmore also includes three of Britten's Purcell realisations and a handful of the lesser-known folksongs, all impeccably sung. Harmonia Mundi's presentation is excellent.

Britten Quatre Chansons françaises. Les
illuminations, Op 18 **Delius** A Late Lark **Finzi** Dies
natalis, Op 8
Susan Gritton sop
BBC Symphony Orchestra / Edward Gardner
Chandos CHAN10590 (68' · DDD) Ⓕ**ⒺⒾ**

The pleasures here are many. Finzi's *Dies natalis* opens the programme and right from the outset one can hardly fail to be struck by the exquisite (but never self-aware) sheen of the BBC SO's response. Edward Gardner directs with the utmost sensitivity, shaping Finzi's arching melodic lines with gratifying elasticity and always displaying a genuinely sophisticated feel for texture. Susan Gritton, too, sings with heartfelt empathy, radiance and intelligence, and her alliance with Gardner certainly distils the necessary tingle-factor. Just occasionally her lustrous tone hardens a fraction when she ascends the heights in "The Rapture". A small niggle and scarcely enough to take the shine off an account which grows with every hearing.

Gardner's view of *Les illuminations* likewise excites in its imaginative spark, scrupulous observation and lucid thrust. Gritton's assumption is pleasingly fresh and agile even though it may not match, say, the incomparable Heather Harper in her comprehensive understanding of Britten's masterly score; nor is her French diction all it might be. Otherwise, there's little with which to take issue, and she reserves her very best form for Britten's astonishingly precocious *Quatre Chansons françaises*. Delius's *A Late Lark* makes a gorgeous postscript.

Chandos's outstandingly realistic, truthfully balanced sound emanates from the BBC SO's Maida Vale home, and there are personable and informative notes by Andrew Burn. All in all, a very positive recommendation.

Albert Herring, Op 39

Albert Herring
Christopher Gillett ten Albert Herring **Josephine
Barstow** sop Lady Billows **Felicity Palmer** contr
Florence Pike **Peter Savidge** bar Mr Gedge **Robert
Lloyd** bass Superintendent Budd **Stuart Kale** ten Mr
Upfold **Susan Gritton** sop Miss Wordsworth **Della
Jones** mez Mrs Herring **Gerald Finley** bar Sid **Ann
Taylor** mez Nancy **Yvette Bonner** sop Emmie
Témimé Bowling sop Cis **Matthew Long** treb Harry
Northern Sinfonia / Steuart Bedford
Naxos ② 8 660107/8 (142' · DDD)
Libretto available with UK copies only Ⓢ**ⒺⒾ**

Vivid as Hickox's traversal of the score for Chandos may be, Bedford's is just that much more alert, crisper. With his long experience of Britten in the theatre, dating back to *Death in Venice* under the composer's aegis, his timing carries unique authority and, in better sound than the old Decca set can now offer, he even has the edge over the composer's obviously definitive reading. Bedford's players are at least as accomplished as Hickox's, and are caught in a more immediate, less reverberant acoustic.

As for the singers, in almost every case Bedford's are the equal of, or superior to, Hickox's and several surpass Britten's. For instance, Albert was never one of Peter Pears's happiest assumptions; Christopher Gillett makes a more credible mother's boy and does well when he decides to break loose. Where the crucial role of Lady Billows is concerned, Josephine Barstow's commanding performance may not quite be on a par with Sylvia Fisher for Britten, but the difference is small. Susan Gritton gives us a dotty and cleanly sung Miss Wordsworth (Margaret Ritchie, the role's creator, must have sounded like this), Robert Lloyd is a simpleton of a Budd (as well sung as any), and Felicity Palmer makes a wonderfully fussy Florence Pike.

It only remains to laud once again the score's many delights as regards technical mastery and subtle characterisation, and to suggest you hurry off to enjoy a real bargain.

Albert Herring H

Peter Pears *ten* Albert Herring **Sylvia Fisher** *sop* Lady Billows **Johanna Peters** *contr* Florence Pike **John Noble** *bar* Mr George **Owen Brannigan** *bass* Mr Budd **Edgar Evans** *ten* Mr Upford **April Cantelo** *sop* Mrs Wordsworth **Sheila Rex** *mez* Mrs Herring **Joseph Ward** *ten* Sid **Catherine Wilson** *mez* Nancy **English Chamber Orchestra / Benjamin Britten** Decca London ② 421 849-2LH2 (138' · ADD · N/T) Recorded 1964 ⒻⓄⒹ

Also available in the Complete Britten Operas Volume 1, also containing Owen Wingrave, Billy Budd and Peter Grimes (475 6020DC8 – eight discs)

Having shown us the grim and nasty side of Aldeburgh life at the beginning of the 19th century in *Peter Grimes*, Britten had fun with its parochial aspects at the end of the century in his comic opera *Albert Herring*, a tale of a mother-dominated shop assistant elected May King because of his virtue, and who is slipped a laced drink at his crowning and goes off for a night on the tiles, after which he asserts himself. For some tastes, it's proved too parochial; some who otherwise admire the composer are repelled by its self-regarding whimsicality. The possible cure for these people is to listen to Britten's own recording, here marvellously transferred to CD and showing again what a genius the producer John Culshaw was. Britten finds all the humour in the piece, but he gives it a cutting edge and is totally successful in conveying the proximity of comedy to tragedy in the remarkable ensemble where Albert is thought to have been killed. With the English Chamber Orchestra on peak

form, all kinds of Bergian echoes in the score are revealed and some, too, of Verdi's *Falstaff* (Act 3). There's also Peter Pears's brilliant performance as Albert, a genuine piece of perceptive singing-acting. The cast is well nigh ideal. If only Britten had written more comic operas.

Albert Herring H

Peter Pears *ten* Albert Herring **Nancy Evans** *mez* Nancy **Joan Cross** *sop* Lady Billows **Gladys Parr** *contr* Florence Pike **Margaret Ritchie** *sop* Miss Wordsworth **Otakar Kraus** *bar* Mr Gedge **Roy Ashton** *ten* Mr Upfold **Norman Lumsden** *bass* Superintendent Budd **Denis Dowling** *bar* Sid **Catherine Lawson** *mez* Mrs Herring **English Opera Group / Benjamin Britten** Nimbus ③ NI5824/6 (133' · ADD · N/T) Recorded live at the Theatre Royal, Copenhagen, on September 15, 1949 Ⓑ

This recording of *Albert Herring* is of considerable historical interest. By the time Benjamin Britten conducted the Decca studio version in 1964, both he and Peter Pears were finding it difficult to recapture the guileless comic spirit so evident here. Plenty of tenors have been able to suggest Albert's blithe gormlessness more naturally than Pears, but in September 1949 (two years after the opera's first performance at Glyndebourne) there was a lightness and flexibility to his voice which could modulate effortlessly into the more dramatic vein the role also calls for.

Nimbus provides a complete version of Eric Crozier's spick-and-span libretto, which comes as close as any Britten set to being self-sufficient as a performable stage play. Some verbal details get lost in a recording that initially seems to be favouring the pit at the expense of the stage, but ears soon adjust to the balance, and the ensemble's experience with, and relish for, this tricky score (all but two were members of the Glyndebourne cast) shines out. The line-up includes particularly characterful contributions from Margaret Ritchie and Otakar Kraus, but there are no weak links, and none of the singers sinks into caricature – something which can easily happen in less tightly knit performances. Britten conducts with immense vitality and needle-sharp attention to shifting moods, evoking frequent but never distracting laughter from an attentive audience. He rewards them with a brief speech at the end, quoting Albert's crucial line: 'Thank you very much!'

A 1949 recording of an opera set in 1900 is a period piece twice over, and the cut-glass vowels of Joan Cross and Nancy Evans suggest degrees of gentility that help to highlight the satirical social nuances of the story, and its knife-edge avoidance of mere cosiness. The booklet gives full details of how the original tapes were made, and the CD transfers and edits have been well done. Tape changes lead to two brief gaps in the opera. The second, near the start of Act 2 scene 2, is the more regrettable, but even this can't honestly be said to damage the special value of this splendid performance.

Billy Budd, Op 50

Billy Budd.
The Holy Sonnets of John Donne, Op 35[a].
Songs and Proverbs of William Blake, Op 74[a]
Peter Glossop bar Billy Budd [a]**Peter Pears** ten
Captain Vere **Michael Langdon** bass John Claggart
John Shirley-Quirk bar Mr Redburn **Bryan Drake**
bar Mr Flint **David Kelly** bass Mr Ratcliffe **Gregory
Dempsey** ten Red Whiskers **David Bowman** bar
Donald **Owen Brannigan** bass Dansker **Robert Tear**
ten Novice **Robert Bowman** ten Squeak **Delme
Bryn-Jones** bar Bosun **Eric Garrett** bar First Mate
Nigel Rogers ten Maintop **Benjamin Luxon** bar
Novice's Friend **Geoffrey Coleby** bar Arthur Jones
[a]**Dietrich Fischer-Dieskau** bar; Ambrosian Opera
Chorus; London Symphony Orchestra /
Benjamin Britten [a]pf
Decca London ③ 417 428-2LH3 (3h 25' · ADD · N/T)
Recorded 1961   Ⓟ❶❶⮕

Billy Budd is remarkable in having been composed for male voices, yet not once is there any
lack of colour or variety. Britten marvellously
supports the tenor, baritone and bass voices with
extraordinary flair in the use of brass and woodwind. This was the last operatic recording John
Culshaw produced for Decca and he again
showed himself unsurpassed at creating a theatrical atmosphere in the studio. Although there
have been several striking and brilliant stage
productions of this opera in recent years, not to
mention Nagano's recording, it must also be
said that both technically and interpretatively
this Britten/Culshaw collaboration represents
the touchstone for any that follows it, particularly in the matter of Britten's conducting.
Where Britten is superb is in the dramatic tautness with which he unfolds the score and his
unobtrusive highlighting of such poignant detail
as the use of the saxophone after the flogging.
But most of all, he focuses with total clarity on
the intimate human drama against the background of life aboard the ship.

And what a cast he had, headed by Peter Pears
as Vere, conveying a natural authoritarianism
which makes his unwilling but dutiful role as
'the messenger of death' more understandable,
if no more agreeable. Peter Glossop's Billy Budd
is a virile performance, with nothing of the
'goody-goody' about him. Nor is there any particular homo-eroticism about his relationship
with Michael Langdon's black-voiced Claggart:
it's a straight conflict between good and evil, and
all the more horrifying for its stark simplicity.
Add to these principals John Shirley-Quirk,
Bryan Drake and David Kelly as the officers,
Owen Brannigan as Dansker and Robert Tear
and Benjamin Luxon in the small roles of the
novice and his friend, and the adjective 'classic'
can be applied to this recording with a clear
conscience. Also on the discs are two of Britten's
most sombre song-cycles, the *Donne* Sonnets
and the *Blake Songs and Proverbs*, the former with
Pears, the latter with Fischer-Dieskau, and both
incomparably accompanied by Britten. They

make ideal complements to *Billy Budd*. This is
without doubt a vintage set.

Billy Budd
Simon Keenlyside bar Billy Budd **Philip Langridge**
ten Captain Vere **John Tomlinson** bass John
Claggart **Alan Opie** bar Mr Redburn **Matthew Best**
bass-bar Mr Flint **Alan Ewing** bass Lt Ratcliffe **Francis
Egerton** ten Red Whiskers **Quentin Hayes** bar
Donald **Clive Bayley** bass Dansker **Mark Padmore**
ten Novice **Richard Coxon** ten Squeak **Timothy
DuFore** bar Bosun **Christopher Keyte** bar Bosun
Richard Whitehouse bar Second Mate, Gunner's
Mate **Daniel Norman** ten Maintop **Roderick
Williams** bar Novice's Friend, Arthur Jones **Alex
Johnson** treb Cabin Boy **Tiffin Boys' Choir; London
Symphony Chorus and Orchestra / Richard Hickox**
Chandos ③ CHAN9826 (165' · DDD · N/T)   Ⓟ❶❶⮕

Britten's score is so often praised that we tend to
neglect the distinction of Forster and Crozier's
libretto, sung in this set with unerring conviction
by its three principals. Keenlyside and Langridge
deserve special mention for their arresting sensitivity throughout the final scenes, when they
make the utterances of Billy and Vere so poetic
and moving: refined tone allied to eloquent
phrasing – the epitome of English singing at its
very best. Keenlyside has a voice of just the right
weight and an appreciation of how Billy must be
at once sympathetic and manly. From first to last
you realise the lad's personal magnetism in vocal
terms alone, explaining the crew's admiration for
his qualities. Langridge is the complete Vere,
suggesting the man's easy command of men, his
poetic soul, his agony of mind at the awful decision placed in his hands to sacrifice Billy. At the
opposite end of the human spectrum, Claggart's
dark, twisted being and his depravity of thought
are ideally realised by Tomlinson, give or take
one or two moments of unsteadiness when his
voice comes under pressure. In supporting roles
there's also much to admire. Mark Padmore conveys all the Novice's terror in a very immediate,
tortured manner. Clive Bayley's Dansker is full of
canny wisdom. Alan Opie is a resolute Mr Redburn. Matthew Best is an appropriately powerful
Mr Flint, though his large, gritty bass-baritone
records uneasily.

Hickox conducts with all his old zest for marshalling large forces, searching out every cranny
of the score, and the London Symphony forces
respond with real virtuosity. Speeds now and
again sound a shade too deliberate, and there's not
always quite that sense of an ongoing continuum
you feel in both of Britten's readings, which are by
and large tauter. But the Chandos, using the
revised two-act version, comes into most direct
competition with Britten's later Decca set. The
latter still sounds well, though inevitably it hasn't
the aural range of the Chandos recording. Yet
nobody will ever quite catch the creative tension
the composer brings to his own work. For all that,
the Chandos set benefits from this trio of imaginative singers, and most newcomers will be satisfied
with its appreciable achievement.

Billy Budd (original four-act version)
Thomas Hampson bar Billy Budd **Anthony Rolfe Johnson** ten Captain Vere **Eric Halfvarson** bass-bar John Claggart **Russell Smythe** bar Mr Redburn **Gidon Saks** bass Mr Flint **Simon Wilding** bass Mr Ratcliffe **Martyn Hill** ten Red Whiskers **Christopher Maltman** bar Donald **Richard Van Allan** bass Dansker **Andrew Burden** ten Novice **Christopher Gillett** ten Squeak **Matthew Hargreaves** bass Bosun **Ashley Holland** bass First Mate **Simon Thorpe** bar Second Mate, Arthur Jones **Robert Johnston** ten Maintop **William Dazeley** bar Novice's Friend **Manchester Boys' Choir; Northern Voices; Hallé Choir and Orchestra / Kent Nagano**
Erato ② 3984-21631-2 (148' · DDD · N/T)   Ⓜ▸

This recording is an exciting achievement; it restores to circulation the original four-act version of the score. The crucial difference between this and Britten's two-act revision is a scene at the close of what's here Act 1, in which 'Starry' Vere addresses his crew and is hailed by them as the sailors' champion, thus establishing the relationship between captain and foretopman. It's an important scene, though musically not particularly distinguished. You can quite see why Britten wanted a tauter two-act drama. Nagano gives us a wonderfully full-bodied and detailed account of the score. There are electrifying moments, not least the battle scene, where the listener feels very much in the middle of things, and the end of Act 3 where those tremendous and ominous series of chords represent Vere telling Budd of the sentence of death. Britten, in his studio recording, prefers a leaner sound and a slightly tauter approach all-round – in his hands you feel the tension of the personal relationships even more sharply than with Nagano.

Hampson is very good, singing with all his customary beauty of voice and intelligence of style, though he imparts a touch of self-consciousness that goes against the grain of the writing. Halfvarson, as Budd's antagonist, the evil Claggart, gives us a mighty presence, singing with power and bite, though not always a steady tone. Rolfe Johnson sings his heart out as he presents Vere's tormented soul. For the rest, Gidon Saks makes a dominant Mr Flint, the sailing-master, Richard Van Allan, is here, predictably, a characterful Dansker, and Andrew Burden stands out as a properly scared Novice, far preferable to Tear's placid reading on Decca. The sum here is greater than the parts, and this set can be heartily recommended.

The recording possesses an amazingly wide spectrum of sound: indeed, sometimes the orchestra is simply too loud.

Curlew River, Op 71

Curlew River
Peter Pears ten Madwoman **John Shirley-Quirk** bar Ferryman **Harold Blackburn** bass Abbot **Bryan Drake** bar Traveller **Bruce Webb** treb Voice of the Spirit **English Opera Group / Benjamin Britten** and **Viola Tunnard**

Decca London 421 858-2LM (69' · ADD · T)
Recorded 1965   ⓂOO▸

Curlew River captured completely the composer's fascination with the Japanese Noh play on which it was based. The recording, produced by John Culshaw, was made in Orford Church, and the atmosphere of this unforgettable occasion is preserved. The procession of monks at the beginning and end comes towards us and recedes, just as if we were sitting in a pew. Pears's performance as the Madwoman is one of his finest and most touching, while Shirley-Quirk and Drake are equally authoritative. The voice of the Madwoman's dead son is devoid of the sentimentality that might have been a peril if any treble other than Bruce Webb had sung it, and the inventive and beguiling orchestral score is marvellously played. With the composer and Viola Tunnard directing the performance, this is in a class of its own.

Death in Venice, Op 88

Death in Venice
Peter Pears ten Gustav von Aschenbach **John Shirley-Quirk** bar Traveller, Elderly Fop, Old Gondolier, Hotel Manager, Hotel Barber, Leader of the Players, Voice of Dionysus **James Bowman** countertenor Voice of Apollo **Kenneth Bowen** ten Hotel Porter **Peter Leeming** bass Travel Clerk **Neville Williams** bass-bar **Penelope MacKay** sop Strolling Players **Iris Saunders** sop Strawberry-seller **English Opera Group Chorus; English Chamber Orchestra / Steuart Bedford**
Decca London ② 425 669-2LH2 (145' · ADD · N/T)
Recorded 1973   ⒻOO▸

Also available in the Complete Britten Operas Volume 2, also containing A Midsummer Night's Dream, The Rape of Lucretia, The Turn of the Screw and Gloriana (475 60296CD10 – 10 discs)

In his insert-notes, Christopher Palmer has pertinent things to say about the sexual climate of Britten's last opera, *Death in Venice*; but these seem to become of less consequence as you listen to the music. Its potency and inventiveness create this opera's disturbing and intense atmosphere, each episode heightened dramatically by instrumental colouring. Under Bedford's direction each scene is fully integrated into a fluent and convincing whole. This recording was made while Britten was very ill; it omits Aschenbach's first recitative ('I have always kept a close watch over my development as a writer …'), given as an optional cut in the vocal score, which was published after the recording was made, by which time Britten had changed his mind about this cut and wished it had been included in the recording. Pears's Aschenbach, a very English conception, is a masterly performance, matched by John Shirley-Quirk's assumption of the six characters who are Aschenbach's messengers of death and the Voice of Dionysus.

Death in Venice

Philip Langridge *ten* Gustav von Aschenbach **Alan Opie** *bar* Traveller, Elderly Fop, Old Gondolier, Hotel Manager, Hotel Barber, Leader of the Players, Voice of Dionysus **Michael Chance** *counterten* Voice of Apollo **BBC Singers; City of London Sinfonia / Richard Hickox**
Chandos ② CHAN10280 (152' · DDD · S/T/t/N)
Ⓕ**OO**➔

This recording in Richard Hickox's Britten series is beautifully played and recorded, and in its all-important central role reunites Hickox with Philip Langridge, so compelling in their earlier set of *Peter Grimes*. Britten tailored the role of Aschenbach so perfectly for Peter Pears's inimitable tenor that it's unlikely any other singer will find it an easy fit. A few years earlier Langridge might have been more adept than he is here at handling some of the high-lying lyrical lines, but the compromises in this department are worth making for a singer who's so penetrating in dramatic insight. Hardly a page of the score passes without his vivid delivery opening up some new dimension of the role. As the drama deepens he progressively strips the soul of Aschenbach bare.

His two main colleagues perform to an equally high level. Alan Opie is still in his vocal prime and all seven of his multifarious Dionysiac characters are sharply delineated. The excellent Michael Chance is more ethereal as the Voice of Apollo than James Bowman, and for that reason is preferable by a whisker.

As always, Hickox takes his time over the score, but there's less sense of self-indulgence than in some of his earlier Britten recordings. He draws playing of high quality and generosity of feeling from the City of London Sinfonia. Add an exemplary choral contribution from the BBC Singers and a typically atmospheric Chandos recording, and there's no reason to resist.

Gloriana, Op 53

Gloriana
Sarah Walker *sop* Queen Elizabeth I **Anthony Rolfe Johnson** *ten* Earl of Essex **Jean Rigby** *mez* Countess of Essex **Neil Howlett** *bar* Lord Mountjoy **Alan Opie** *bar* Sir Robert Cecil **Elizabeth Vaughan** *sop* Lady Rich **Richard Van Allan** *bass* Sir Walter Raleigh **Malcolm Donnelly** *bar* Henry Cuffe
ENO Chorus and Orchestra / Mark Elder
Stage director **Colin Graham**
Video director **Derek Bailey**
ArtHaus Musik Ⓕ *DVD* 102 097
(147' · NTSC · 4:3 · PCM stereo · 0)   Ⓕ
Recorded live at the Coliseum, London, in 1984

It was this staging that conclusively restored the work to the repertory when directed with such utter conviction in Alix Stone's and Colin Graham's evocative sets, and Stone's proud costumes. Many fine singers graced the title-part over the years. Sarah Walker is

among the foremost of them. Barstow is, of course, unforgettable, but Walker's portrayal stands up to the comparison and, though a mezzo, she has no trouble with high-line passages.

At the time ENO still boasted fine ensembles. Every other member of the cast surpasses its Opera North counterpart: Rolfe Johnson's manly, hot-headed and finely sung Essex, Richard Van Allan's menacing Raleigh, Jean Rigby's moving Frances Essex, Alan Opie's sly Cecil. Over all presides Mark Elder, projecting a grandly conceived yet subtle account of the whole score, played with acumen by the ENO orchestra. This is an experience of a great company in full flight and should not be missed; it gives the score in its entirety, allowing us to hear what a dramatically varied and superbly crafted piece of work Britten's opera has proved to be.

Noye's Fludde / The Golden Vanity

Noye's Fludde
Owen Brannigan *bass* Noye **Sheila Rex** *mez* Mrs Noye **David Pinto** *treb* Sem **Darian Angadi** *treb* Ham **Stephen Alexander** *treb* Jaffett **Trevor Anthony** *spkr* The Voice of God **Caroline Clack** *sop* Mrs Sem **Maria-Thérèse Pinto** *sop* Mrs Ham **Eileen O'Donnovan** *sop* Mrs Jaffett **Chorus; English Opera Group Orchestra; An East Suffolk Children's Orchestra / Norman Del Mar**

The Golden Vanity
Mark Emney *treb* Captain **John Wojciechowski** *treb* Bosun **Barnaby Jago** *treb* Cabin-boy **Adrian Thompson** *treb* Captain **Terry Lovell** *treb* Bosun **Benjamin Britten** *pf* **Wandsworth School Boys' Choir / Russell Burgess**
Decca London 436 397-2LM (66' · ADD · T)
Recorded 1961, 1966.   Ⓕ

Britten wrote these two works for children, but don't imagine that they're cosy and childish. Many of his friends thought that there remained much of the child in him, and this clearly comes out in the boisterous high spirits of some of this music. By and large, *Noye's Fludde* and *The Golden Vanity* are happy works. *Noye's Fludde* makes invigorating listening. This 1961 performance is immensely vivid, and the enthusiasm of the young singers and instrumentalists is infectious. All the children of East Suffolk seem to be involved in the enterprise: consorts of recorders, bands of bugles, peals of handbell-ringers, plenty of violins, a few lower strings, seven percussion players, child soloists, and a choir as big as you like, enough to give full representation to the 49 different species of animal mentioned in the text. Then three grown-ups, and the English Chamber Orchestra. The skill and imaginative power with which Britten has used these forces defy adequate description. There are inevitably rough edges in the singing and playing, but the spirit is there in abundance.

The same is true of *The Golden Vanity*, and although there's more conscious vocal skill in the singing of the Wandsworth School Boys' Choir, it never gets in the way of the presentation, which bubbles with life.

Owen Wingrave, Op 85

Owen Wingrave
Peter Colman-Wright bar Owen Wingrave **Alan Opie** bar Spencer Coyle **James Gilchrist** ten Lechmere **Elizabeth Connell** sop Miss Wingrave **Janice Watson** sop Mrs Coyle **Sarah Fox** sop Mrs Julian **Pamela Helen Stephen** mez Kate **Robin Leggate** ten Sir Philip Wingrave; Narrator **Tiffin School Boys' Choir; City of London Sinfonia / Richard Hickox**
Chandos ② CHAN10473 (107' · DDD · S/T/N) Ⓕ🅑➔

After experimenting with smaller-scale forms of musical theatre throughout the 1960s, Britten returned to 'grand' opera in *Owen Wingrave*, based on Henry James's pacifist debate about following the flag or one's conscience. Premiered as a TV commission, *Wingrave* enjoyed unmerited Cinderella status among Britten's stage works until the recent TV film conducted by Kent Nagano (with Gerald Finley in the title-role – see below) and an innovative stage production by Tim Hopkins at Covent Garden's Linbury Studio in 2007.

Over the years Richard Hickox used his studio skills to telling effect in the vocal works of Britten. In this recording following concert performances, Peter Coleman-Wright is most adept at conveying Owen's pain and troubled conscience the while never giving way to an over-emotionalism untrue to anyone brought up in a soldier's family. Alan Opie, in what is in many ways the beau rôle of the military tutor Spencer Coyle, achieves both a superb neutrality and an evident empathy with Owen's decision to quit the military life. Robin Leggate avoids caricature (or simple Peter Pears homage) in the small but essential role of the family termagant, General Sir Philip Wingrave. The women are no less characterful, with an especially sympathetic reading of Coyle's wife from Janice Watson.

Throughout *Wingrave*, Britten's cunning reworking of rhythmic structures and harmonic devices pioneered as early as *Peter Grimes* reaches a new level of plasticity and sophistication. The shimmer of orchestral sound – sometimes impressionistic, sometimes Gamelan-influenced, sometimes wholly percussive – is a still insufficiently appreciated wonder of 1970s operatic writing. The core duets of Coyle/Wingrave, Wingrave/Lechmere and Wingrave/Kate (in which she sets the reluctant soldier the challenge of spending a night alone in the haunted room) are anchored on a sophisticated version of the tonal atonal structures on which Britten had once based *The Turn of the Screw*. It lends the drama an amazing tensile strength, closely parallel to the Berg operas which Britten wanted to get to know better in the 1930s but was discouraged by his teachers from approaching too closely.

The new set, in Chandos's customary natural, comfortable sound, becomes the first recording in any medium to do the work full musical and dramatic justice. It should also satisfy the curiosity of those who wonder why its devotees hail *Wingrave* as Britten's greatest completed opera.

Owen Wingrave
Gerald Finley bar Owen Wingrave **Peter Savidge** bar Spencer Coyle **Hilton Marlton** ten Lechmere **Josephine Barstow** sop Miss Wingrave **Anne Dawson** sop Mrs Coyle **Elizabeth Gale** sop Mrs Julian **Charlotte Hellekant** mez Kate **Martyn Hill** ten Sir Philip Wingrave **Andrew Burden** nar **Deutsches Symphony Orchestra, Berlin / Kent Nagano** Video director Margaret Williams
ArtHaus Musik 📀 100 372 (150' · 16:9 · PCM stereo · 2 & 5). Includes 'Benjamin Britten: The Hidden Heart' – a film directed by Teresa Griffiths Ⓕ🅞🅞

Britten's penultimate opera was planned to be equally effective on television or in the opera house, but it was its first stage production at Covent Garden that made the bigger impact. Now this film version, imaginatively directed by Margaret Williams and tautly conducted by Kent Nagano, helps swing the balance the other way.

There's almost nothing stagey about the opera here. The camera roams freely indoors and out, using cleverly executed angles to follow members of the fearsome Wingrave family at their ancestral home, and throwing in flashbacks and voice-overs wherever they might be apposite – much as one might expect of an adaptation of a literary classic. In fact, the period has been updated to the 1950s, which necessitates some minor changes to Myfanwy Piper's libretto (no need to escort the ladies to their bedchambers by candlelight any more), but this handsome version in all other respects stays close to Britten's intentions.

Gerald Finley is a tower of strength as Owen Wingrave, completely believable as the sturdy but sensitive scion of an upper-crust family. The other singers are well cast, and play expertly to the camera.

The 'special feature' on the disc, Teresa Griffiths's three-part biographical film, *Benjamin Britten: The Hidden Heart*, lasts as long as the opera. It focuses on three major works – *Peter Grimes*, the *War Requiem* and *Death in Venice* – and, while its message is somewhat diffuse and the editorial style jumps irritatingly from image to image as if afraid to let the camera come to rest, it does include a wealth of fleeting extracts showing Britten and Pears in performance. Those alone are enough to make it a desirable collector's item.

Peter Grimes, Op 33

Peter Grimes   Ⓗ
Peter Pears ten Peter Grimes **Claire Watson** sop Ellen Orford **James Pease** bass Captain

BRITTEN'S PETER GRIMES – IN BRIEF

Peter Pears *Peter Grimes* **Claire Watson** *Ellen Orford* **James Pease** *Balstrode* **ROH Chorus & Orchestra / Benjamin Britten**
Decca Legends ② 467 682-2DL2 (142' · ADD)
Ⓕ❍❍❍❶➔

Ⓖ A uniquely authoritative set. Britten's Covent Garden forces respond magnificently, and Pears is simply unforgettable in the title-role specially written for him. John Culshaw's newly remastered 1958 production barely begins to show its years.

Jon Vickers *Peter Grimes* **Heather Harper** *Ellen Orford* **Jonathan Summers** *Balstrode*
ROH Chorus & Orchestra / Sir Colin Davis
Philips ② 462 847-2PM2 (146' · ADD) Ⓜ❶➔
Davis conducts an intensely refreshing performance, dominated by Jon Vickers's searingly passionate Grimes. Heather Harper, too, is quite superb as Ellen Orford.

Anthony Rolfe Johnson *Peter Grimes* **Felicity Lott** *Ellen Orford* **Thomas Allen** *Balstrode*
ROH Chorus & Orchestra / Bernard Haitink
EMI ② 754832-2 (145' · DDD) Ⓕ
Haitink's 1993 set boasts a strong cast, most notably Felicity Lott's outstandingly sympathetic and secure Ellen Orford. Anthony Rolfe Johnson's Grimes is not always as involving as one might wish, and the whole venture lacks the whiff of greasepaint that marks out the composer's own classic version.

Philip Langridge *Peter Grimes* **Janice Watson** *Ellen Orford* **Alan Opie** *Balstrode* **Opera London, London Sym Chorus, City of London Sinfonia / Richard Hickox**
Chandos ② CHAN9447/8 (147' · DDD) Ⓕ❍❍
Philip Langridge's Grimes is one of the glories of our age, and Alan Opie's Balstrode is another triumphant assumption. Hickox is in his element.

Glenn Winslade *Peter Grimes* **Janice Watson** *Ellen Orford* **Anthony Michaels-Moore** *Balstrode*
London Symphony Chorus and Orchestra / Sir Colin Davis
LSO Live ② LSO0054 (143' · DDD) Ⓢ❶➔
A stunning achievement for conductor, chorus and orchestra, and while the performances of the soloists may not match those of Davis's earlier recording, the strikingly powerful LSO forces demand to be heard.

Christopher Ventris *Peter Grimes* **Emily Magee** *Ellen Orford* **Alfred Muff** *Balstrode* **Zurich Opera Chorus and Orchestra / Franz Welser-Möst**
EMI ② 🄳🅅🄳 500971-9 (150' · NTSC · 16:9 · PCM stereo, 5.1 and DTS 5.1 · 0)
Quite simply phenomenal – a vision that steps outside the tradition and triumphs!

Balstrode **Jean Watson** *contr* Auntie **Raymond Nilsson** *ten* Bob Boles **Owen Brannigan** *bass* Swallow **Lauris Elms** *mez* Mrs Sedley **Sir Geraint Evans** *bar* Ned Keene **John Lanigan** *ten* Rector **David Kelly** *bass* Hobson **Marion Studholme** *sop* First Niece **Iris Kells** *sop* Second Niece **Chorus and Orchestra of the Royal Opera House, Covent Garden / Benjamin Britten**
Decca ② 467 682-2DL2 (142' · ADD · N/T)
Recorded 1958 Ⓕ❍❍❍❶➔

Also available in the Complete Britten Operas
Volume 1, also containing Albert Herring, Owen Wingrave, Billy Budd (475 6020DC8 – eight discs)

Ⓖ The Decca set, which in 1958 introduced this opera to many listeners, has never been superseded in its refinement or insight. Britten's conducting, lithe and lucid, reveals his work as a complex, ambiguous drama. Peter Pears, in the title-role written for him, brings unsurpassed detail of nuance to Grimes's words while never losing sight of the essential plainness of the man's speech. The rest of the cast form a vivid portrait gallery of characters. The recording is as live and clear as if it had been made yesterday, and takes the listener right on to the stage. The bustle of activity and sound effects realise nicely Britten's own masterly painting of dramatic foreground and background.

Peter Grimes
Philip Langridge *ten* Grimes **Janice Watson** *sop* Ellen Orford **Alan Opie** *bar* Captain Balstrode **Amaral Gunson** *mez* Auntie **John Graham-Hall** *ten* Bob Boles **John Connell** *bass* Swallow **Anne Collins** *contr* Mrs Sedley **Roderick Williams** *bar* Ned Keene **John Fryatt** *ten* Rector **Matthew Best** *bass* Hobson **Yvonne Barclay** *sop* First Niece **Pamela Helen Stephen** *mez* Second Niece **London Symphony Chorus; City of London Sinfonia / Richard Hickox**
Chandos ② CHAN9447/8 (147' · DDD · N/T)Ⓕ❍❍❶➔

Any reading that so potently confirms the genius of this piece must have a distinguished place in the discography. In the first place there's Langridge's tense, sinewy, sensitive Grimes. Predictably he rises to the challenge of the Mad Scene; this is a man hugely to be pitied, yet there's a touch of resignation, of finding some sort of peace at last, after all the agony of the soul. His portrayal is tense and immediate, and a match for that of Pears in personal identification – listen to the eager touch at 'We strained in the wind'. The next composite heroes are the members of the chorus. Electrifying as their rivals are, the LSO singers, trained by Stephen Westrop, seem just that much more arresting, not least in the hue-and-cry of Act 3, quite terrifying in its immediacy as recorded by Chandos. Hickox's interpretation has little to fear from the distinguished competition. Many details are placed with special care, particularly in the Interludes and the parodistic dances in

Act 3, and whole episodes, such as the Grimes-Balstrode dispute in Act 1, have seldom sounded so dramatic. Once or twice one would have liked a firmer forward movement, as in the fifth Interlude, but the sense of total music-theatre is present throughout.

Of the other soloists, the one comparative disappointment is Janice Watson's Ellen Orford. She sings the part with tone as lovely as any of her rivals on disc and with carefully wrought phrasing, but doesn't have the experience to stand out from the village regulars. Britten's set remains *hors concours* but Hickox is the finest of the modern recordings: as sound it's quite spectacular, vast in range, with well-managed perspectives and just enough hints of stage action to be convincing.

Peter Grimes
Christopher Ventris *ten* Peter Grimes **Emily Magee**
sop Ellen Orford **Alfred Muff** *bar* Balstrode **Liliana**
Nikiteanu *contr* Auntie **Sandra Trattnigg** *sop* Niece I
Liuba Chuchrova *sop* Niece II **Rudolf Schasching**
ten Bob Boles **Richard Angas** *bass* Swallow **Cornelia**
Kallisch *mez* Mrs Sedley **Martin Zysset** *ten* Rev
Horace Adams **Cheyne Davidson** *bar* Ned Keene
Valeriy Murga *bass* Hobson
Zurich Opera House Chorus and Orchestra /
Franz Welser-Möst
Stage director **David Pountney**
Video director **Felix Breisach**
EMI ② *DVD* 500971-9 (150' · NTSC · 16:9 · PCM
stereo, 5.1 and DTS 5.1 · 0)
Recorded live in December 2005   Ⓕ**OO**

Peter's line 'Where the walls themselves gossip of inquest' – his cry of pain to Ellen after the coroner's open verdict on the loss of his first apprentice – cues the scenery and concept. The Borough, some of its citizens mounted on chairs and pillars permanently suspended above an unchanging set, is never absent from this stylised, Brechtian (and Weillian) production. Pountney's stage has no room for naturalistic clutter – no real boats, no fishing nets, no beach.

The English director's characters step out of years of 'English' ambiguity into a light of glaring every-man (and woman)-for-himself selfishness. Balstrode listens to Grimes (Christopher Ventris, riveting) but only once (the capstan ensemble) does anything to help him; in the pub he gropes the women as much as Boles. Auntie, a red-headed Widow Begbick played with Oscar-winning charisma by Liliana Nikiteanu, and her Nieces are, quite openly, a Madame and her whores. Hobson, another terrifyingly intense portrayal, is a lazy, uncooperative psychopath, roused only by drink and the prospect of violence. Ellen is allowed more intimacy with Peter than one often sees but, as soon as she realises his obsessive work methods will never change, her 'Peter – we've failed' is final, provoking Grimes to inevitable self-destruction. In a penultimate Mad scene of haunting, almost religious (or sacrilegious) beauty, she and Balstrode sit with a dead boy each draped across

their laps, either side of the constantly see-sawing Peter on a stylised boat platform with a cross-like mast. Unforgettable.

Welser-Möst's reading of the score is hardly less innovative, reminding one with its forward, motoric winds of some great, lost Shostakovich score and, in the dance music so present in the pub scenes, of contemporaries Weill and Gershwin.

No *Grimes* on film is without some distinctive merit but this new EMI issue is carried by its cast, phenomenal chorus contribution, director and conductor to an important new interpretative level.

Additional recommendation

Peter Grimes
Vickers Peter Grimes **Harper** Ellen Orford **Royal**
Opera House Chorus and Orchestra / C Davis
Philips 462 847-2PM2 (146' · ADD)   Ⓜ🅑➤
   A mid-price alternative which enshrines the wonderfully drawn Grimes of Jon Vickers and the touching, immensely human Ellen of Heather Harper. Colin Davis's conducting, too, displays his love of the score.

The Turn of the Screw, Op 54

The Turn of the Screw   🅗
Sir Peter Pears *ten* Prologue, Peter Quint **Jennifer**
Vyvyan *sop* Governess **David Hemmings** *treb* Miles
Olive Dyer *sop* Flora **Joan Cross** *sop* Mrs Grose
Arda Mandikian *sop* Miss Jessel **English Opera**
Group Orchestra / Benjamin Britten
Decca London mono ② 425 672-2LH2
(105' · ADD · N/T). Recorded 1955   Ⓕ**OO**

Also available in the Complete Britten Operas
Volume 2, also containing A Midsummer Night's
Dream, The Rape of Lucretia, Death in Venice, Gloriana
(475 60296DC10 – 10 discs)

As Sir Colin Davis has shown on Philips, there's room for an alternative interpretation of this remarkable work, but this superb first recording will remain as documentary-historical evidence of the highest importance and value. Will there ever be a better performance, let alone recording, of *The Turn of the Screw* than this by the original cast, recorded less than four months after the 1954 Venice premiere?

This score is Britten at his greatest, expressing good and evil with equal ambivalence, evoking the tense and sinister atmosphere of Bly by inspired use of the chamber orchestra and imparting vivid and truthful life to every character in the story. As one listens, transfixed, all that matters is Britten's genius as a composer. Jennifer Vyvyan's portrayal of the Governess is a classic characterisation, her vocal subtleties illuminating every facet of the role, and she has the perfect foil in Joan Cross's motherly and uncomplicated Mrs Grose. The glittering malevolence of Pears's Quint, luring David Hemmings's incomparable Miles to destruction; the tragic tones of Arda Mandikian's Miss Jessel; Olive Dyer's spiteful Flora – how fortunate we are that these performances are preserved. As with all the Decca/Britten reissues, the transfer is a triumph.

The Turn of the Screw
Ian Bostridge ten Prologue, Peter Quint **Joan Rodgers** sop Governess **Vivien Tierney** sop Miss Jessel **Julian Leang** treb Miles **Caroline Wise** sop Flora **Jane Henschel** sop Mrs Grose **Gustav Mahler Chamber Orchestra** / **Daniel Harding**
Virgin Classics ② 545521-2 (106' · DDD · N/T/t)
Ⓕ**OOO**

This absorbing version of Britten's arresting masterpiece, derived from Henry James's ever-mysterious short story, is based on the stage performances given by London's Royal Opera in Deborah Warner's controversial staging. It offers a considerable challenge to both the premiere recording, conducted by the composer, and the more recent version conducted by Steuart Bedford. The new recording catches all the sinister fascination of Britten's most tautly composed opera score, so aptly matched to James's tale and to Myfanwy Piper's evocative libretto.

Daniel Harding extracts the greatest tension from both the finely wrought writing for the chamber ensemble and from the well-balanced and, by and large, exemplary cast. He's helped by the clearest and most detailed recording the work has yet received.

When discussing the merits of the casts one is comparing three teams of undoubted excellence. Nevertheless there are distinctions to be made. As on stage, Joan Rodgers nicely balances the need to suggest the ingenuous and the excitable side of the Governess's nature, which she conveys in a performance that combines clarity of diction with the vocal verities. Bostridge's ethereal, other-worldly, eerily magnetic Quint provides an interesting contrast with Philip Langridge's more forceful and present assumption for Bedford. Both are preferable to Pears's more mannered singing on the pioneering set, but that, needless to say, has its own authority. On the other hand neither Vivian Tierney nor Nadine Secunde (Bedford) quite match the searing sadness of Arda Mandikian's dark-hued Miss Jessel for Britten. In the case of Mrs Grose, Jane Henschel, imposingly as she sings, sounds a trifle too stock-operatic in her responses to words and notes beside the particular gentility of Joan Cross (Britten) or the marvellously detailed and intensely uttered interpretation of Phyllis Cannan (Bedford).

This is an utterly absorbing version. Given its masterly engineering and sense of atmosphere it is, by a hair's breadth, preferable to the Bedford among stereo recordings. The composer's set remains both a historic document and the tautest reading, but most will prefer and be satisfied with the conviction and the sound of this newcomer.

The Turn of the Screw
Helen Field sop Governess **Menai Davies** mez Mrs Grose **Richard Greager** ten Peter Quint, Prologue **Phyllis Cannan** sop Miss Jessel **Machiko Obata** sop Flora **Samuel Linay** treb Miles **Stuttgart Radio Symphony Orchestra** / **Steuart Bedford**
Stage director **Michael Hampe**
Video director **Claus Viller**
ArtHaus Musik 🎬 100 198 (114' · 4:3 · 2.0 · 2-8)
Recorded live 1990
Ⓕ**O**

Michael Hampe clearly places the audience in the expected quandary as to whether the ghosts are 'real' or a product of the Governess's vivid imagination. The concept is underlined by Helen Field, who makes the role very much her own by her intelligent acting and fine singing of it. The young Samuel Linay could hardly be bettered as Miles, suggesting the boy's innocence and his devilment while singing purely and accurately. Menai Davies brings out all Mrs Grose's generous character and her slight befuddlement at events beyond her ken. Phyllis Cannan is at once a menacing and unearthly Miss Jessel. Richard Greager sings splendidly as Quint but rather misses out on the character's menace. The Flora, as so often with this part, looks too mature. The instrumental playing is superb. The sound balance and video direction faultless. Along with the fine rival version (below), this opera is very lucky on DVD.

The Turn of the Screw
Mark Padmore ten Peter Quint **Lisa Milne** sop Governess **Catrin Wyn-Davies** sop Miss Jessel **Diana Montague** sop Mrs Grose **Nicholas Kirby Johnson** treb Miles **Caroline Wise** sop Flora **City of London Sinfonia** / **Richard Hickox**
Video director **Katie Mitchell**
Opus Arte 📀 OA0907D (117' · 16:9 · PCM stereo · 0)
Extra features include Synopsis and Cast Gallery
Ⓕ**OOO**

This film was much lauded when shown on BBC2. Katie Mitchell's arresting production opens up the story, taking it into the countryside and producing spooky and louring images to create the mysterious and dangerous aura of Bly, which does no harm to the intentions of Henry James and Benjamin Britten. Mitchell allows the characters' interior monologues to be heard while the singers' mouths remain closed – especially apt for the role of the Governess.

For about two-thirds of the work the director keeps within the boundaries stipulated by Britten and librettist Myfanwy Piper, making us fully aware of the ambiguities of the participants and their relationships. But in the third part she rather allows her ideas to get out of hand, the nightmarish images becoming too surreal, especially for the ghosts and the children, although she recovers in time to make the final struggle between the Governess and Quint for Miles's soul an arresting close. We're left, as we should be, uncertain at the state of the Governess's mind and the exact powers of the ghosts.

Richard Hickox commands every aspect of the tricky score, lovingly executed by members of his City of London Sinfonia, even if the balance with the singers sometimes goes awry. The cast is splendid. Nicholas Kirby Johnson as Miles achieves just the right balance between innocence and knowingness. His singing is fluent and pointed, as is that of Caroline Wise, a teenage Flora with a lively presence, expressive eyes and a malleable voice. Lisa Milne, unflatteringly garbed, is rather too confident of voice and mien as the Governess. Although she sings with her customary clarity of line and word, she doesn't suggest the nervous vulnerability of Jennifer Vyvyan, who created the role. Diana Montague is a gratifyingly sympathetic Mrs Grose, using body language to convey just the right feeling of apprehension and concern over the fate of her charges. Mark Padmore is among the best of Quints, vocally and histrionically. Catryn Wyn-Davies is a properly wild and scary Miss Jessel. All in all, this is the version to have.

Leo Brouwer
Cuban b1939

Born in Cuba, Brouwer was encouraged by his music-loving physician father to learn the guitar. He studied with Isaaca Nicola and then at the Hartt College of Music, and later at Juilliard with Persichetti and Stefan Wolpe. The work of Iannis Xenakis was a huge influence and his music successfully fuses a Cuban accent with more modernist leanings. He has held a number of major musical posts in Cuba and is invloved with the Concurso y Festival Internacional du Guitarra de la Habana.

Guitar Concerto

Guitar Concerto No 5, 'Helsinki' **Albéniz/Brouwer** Iberia Suite **Lennon-McCartney/Brouwer** From Yesterday to Penny Lane
Timo Korhonen gtr **Tampere Philharmonic Orchestra / Tuomas Ollila**
Ondine ODE979-2 (66' · DDD)   Ⓕ**O**

The Concerto No 5, *Helsinki*, was commissioned for the Helsinki Festival but contains no musical reference to that city. As Brouwer explains: 'I compose in Space or in Lightness and Heaviness,' referring to the titles of the first two movements, but whether he ever does so in 'Luminosity', the title of the third, we aren't told. It's a substantial work that's none the worse for its lack of memorable tunes – except to those who regard them as essential. Brouwer's fingerprints abound, especially in the first movement's gestures, made familiar in other (solo) pieces. He has an intimate knowledge of the guitar, and uses the orchestra skilfully and imaginatively. Renaissance composers didn't hesitate to use popular and folk tunes, so why shouldn't today's

do likewise? Brouwer describes The Beatles' tunes as 'folksongs of today' and the seven in this recording are set in a variety of pastiche forms, à la Wagner, Hindemith, Stravinsky et al, a pleasing counterbalance to the serious business of the Concerto. Timo Korhonen is a superb guitarist who takes everything in his clean-fingered stride. The Tampere orchestra shares his zest, and the recording is first-class.

John Browne
English fl c1490

Browne may have been the John (or William) Browne, clerk of Windsor, who died in 1479, or the lawyer and rector of West Tilbury who died in 1498. The Eton Choirbook originally contained 11 antiphons and four Magnificats by him, of which only nine antiphons (two incomplete) and a fragment of a Magnificat remain.

Motets

Music from the Eton Choirbook
O Maria Salvatoris mater. Salve regina. Stabat iuxta Christi crucem. Stabat mater dolorosa. O regina mundi clara
The Tallis Scholars / Peter Phillips
Gimell CDGIM036 (71' · DDD · T/t)   Ⓕ**OOO**▷

By any other name, John Browne would surely be recognised as one of the very greatest English composers. The fact that fewer than 10 works survive intact in the Eton Choirbook (practically the only source transmitting his music anyway) only adds to his mysterious aura; the music sends normally dispassionate specialists reaching for superlatives. He stands head and shoulders above the other Eton composers, and it's high time he was accorded an anthology of his own. The discography of early polyphonic music has made such great strides that 'landmark' recordings are fewer and further between; yet this can hardly be described as anything else.

An index of Browne's stature is the variety of scorings he deploys. His eight-voice *O Maria Salvatoris mater* was considered extraordinary enough to be given pride of place in the Eton Choirbook, and each of the three six-voice pieces included here is scored differently. No other Eton composer wrote so much six-voice music excluding trebles. Two of his pieces in this mould (*Stabat iuxta Christi crucem* and *O regina mundi*) are here recorded convincingly for the first time. Phillips's line-up of men's voices (especially on the top lines) is as superb as Browne's must have been, for an exceptional keenness of focus is needed to prevent the thick texture from becoming stodgy; as it is, the sound of six parts jostling in a compass of under two octaves is thrilling.

But the pieces with trebles have long been reckoned Browne's masterpieces; as such, they

BRUCH'S VIOLIN CONCERTO NO 1 – IN BRIEF

Nathan Milstein; NYPSO / Sir John Barbirolli Ⓗ
Biddulph LAB096 (77' · ADD)   Ⓜ️Ⓞ
Milstein captured on peak form in this memorable 1942 alliance with Barbirolli. A generous sequence of assorted bon-bons make up the remainder.

Jascha Heifetz; New SO of London /   Ⓗ
Sir Malcolm Sargent
RCA 09026 61745-2 (65' · ADD)   Ⓜ️Ⓞ
A delectable souvenir of Jascha Heifetz's incomparable gifts. Similarly superlative accounts of Bruch's *Scottish Fantasy* and Vieuxtemps's Fifth Concerto make for ideal bedfellows.

Josef Suk; Czech Philharmonic Orchestra /
Karel Ančerl
Supraphon SU3663-2 (79' · ADD)   Ⓜ️Ⓞ
An irresistibly songful, warm-hearted performance. Suk's sweet, silky tone gives much pleasure, and he generates a profoundly satisfying rapport with Ančerl.

Nigel Kennedy; English Chamber Orchestra /
Jeffrey Tate
EMI 518173-2 (69' · DDD)   Ⓜ️Ⓞ⯈
A powerful reading that's also full of poetry from a youthful Kennedy. It's not been out of the catalogue in 20 years and it's not surprising: this is Kennedy at his most poetic.

Kyung Wha Chung; London Philharmonic
Orchestra / Klaus Tennstedt
EMI 503410-2 (70' · DDD)   ⒻⓄⓄ
A freer, more impulsive account than Chung's own earlier Decca recording with Kempe. Tennstedt and the LPO tender powerful support.

Itzhak Perlman; Concertgebouw Orchestra /
Bernard Haitink
EMI 356523-2 (77' · DDD)   Ⓜ️⯈
Sweetness and poetry characterise this likeable performance by one of the fiddle's greats. Haitink is a sympathetic accompanist.

Maxim Vengerov; Leipzig Gewandhaus
Orchestra / Kurt Masur
Teldec 4509 90875-2 (51' · DDD)   Ⓜ️Ⓞ
The 19-year-old Vengerov's first concerto disc is a winner all the way. Wonderfully vital, raptly expressive playing that never fails to lift the spirits.

SCO / Jaime Laredo
Regis RRC1152 (54' · DDD)   ⓈⓄ
A lovely, sweet-toned version if you're on a budget. Directed from the violin by Laredo, the Scottish CO are wonderfully fleet of foot but also capable of power (as at the start of the first movement).

have been recorded several times before. Phillips sees Browne as a mystical figure, and his choice of tempi in the *Stabat mater* and *O Maria* reflects this. His singers articulate it so convincingly as to suspend disbelief absolutely. The Tallis Scholars are to be heard at their best in this repertory; this recording confirms that. If you don't know Browne's music, you simply must hear this.

Max Bruch   German 1838-1920

To most people the name Bruch means just one work, his Violin Concerto No 1 in G minor. There's a little more to him than that. He wrote symphonies (his first at the age of 14), operas and oratorios (he was particularly adept at writing for large vocal forces and was regarded as a choral composer of genius during his time). By his mid-twenties he was famous, considered to be the equal of Brahms and a worthy successor to Mendelssohn.

Bruch had a peripatetic career teaching music in Cologne, conducting and composing all over Germany, moving from Berlin to Leipzig to Dresden and on to Munich. In 1867 he was made director of the court orchestra in Sonderhausen (his predecessors had been Spohr and Weber) before returning to Berlin three years later. In 1880 he was invited to become the conductor of the Liverpool Philharmonic Orchestra and stayed in England for three years. (He married his German wife the week before he arrived.) Then he was off to America, returning in 1891 to become professor of composition at the Hochschule für Musik in Berlin. He was said to be self-centred and dictatorial ('in personal appearance,' remarked a contemporary, 'Bruch is by no means as majestic as one would suppose from his works'), not the sort of personality to adapt to the new world of Debussy and Stravinsky. His son's death in the First World War left him depressed; his choral music – as with other composers – fell out of fashion. No wonder this child of the 19th century died embittered, bewildered that his once exalted reputation had shrunk to nothing.

Clarinet and Viola Concerto, Op 88

Clarinet and Viola Concerto in E minor.
Romance, Op 85. Eight Pieces, Op 83
Paul Meyer *cl* **Gérard Caussé** *va* **François-René**
Duchâble *pf* **Orchestra of the Opéra National**
de Lyon / Kent Nagano
Apex 8573 89229-2 (65' · DDD)   Ⓢ

The Double Concerto and the Eight Pieces both stem from Bruch's later years as a composer, by which time he was ill and tiring, also embittered and resentful of the successes being enjoyed by Strauss and Debussy (the latter 'an unqualified scribbler'). His Concerto isn't only a backward-looking and inward-looking work: it's the music of a weary composer with little more to say but the habit of a lifetime in saying it. The technique doesn't fail, though the last movement is thinly stretched; the manner is still lyrical, and makes graceful use both of the solo instruments and of the accompaniments. This is unusually disposed so that the chamber orchestra of the first movement gradually swells in numbers until it's virtually a full symphony orchestra for the finale. Some problems ensue for the viola, which is in any case cast in a secondary role to the clarinet.

Parity is restored with the Eight Pieces, though Bruch wrote them for the talents of his son Max Felix, a gifted clarinettist whose performance of these pieces earned him favourable comparison with the great Richard Mühlfeld from the conductor Fritz Steinbach. They are pleasant pieces, sometimes drawing on the tonal companionship which Mozart discovered the instruments to have in his *Kegelstatt* Trio, sometimes contrasting them with opposing kinds of music.

Violin Concerto No 1, Op 26

Bruch Violin Concerto No 1ª
Beethoven Violin Concerto in D, Op 61ᵇ
Kyung Wha Chung vn ªRoyal Concertgebouw Orchestra; ᵇLondon Philharmonic Orchestra / Klaus Tennstedt
EMI 503410-2 (70' · DDD). ᵇRecorded live 1989 Ⓜ ⦿⦿

Kyung Wha Chung has recorded both of these concertos before, but these performances not only have the benefit of more modern sound but are more spontaneous in their expressive warmth. The Bruch was recorded in the studio and reflects Chung's growing ease in a recording environment. Notoriously, she dislikes the constraints of recording, when she's so essentially spontaneous in her expressiveness. Here her *rubato* is freer, so that in the first movement the opening theme is more impulsive, and her freedom in the second subject conveys the sort of magic you find in her live performances. The slow movement brings extreme contrasts of dynamic and expression from orchestra as well as soloist, and the finale is again impulsive in its bravura.

The Beethoven is a live recording. Chung sustains spacious speeds very persuasively indeed. She's freely flexible in her approach to Beethoven, as Tennstedt is too, but magnetically keeping an overall command. The element of vulnerability in Chung's reading adds to the emotional weight, above all in the slow movement, which in its wistful tenderness is among the most beautiful on disc. As for the outer movements, they're full of flair, with a live event bringing few if any flaws of ensemble. Altogether, an exceptionally attractive release.

Serenade, Op 75

Serenade, Op 75. Scottish Fantasy, Op 46.
Maxim Fedotov vn

Russian Philharmonic Orchestra / Dmitry Yablonsky
Naxos 8 557395 (73' · DDD) Ⓢ⊳

Though the *Scottish Fantasy*, with its wealth of traditional melodies, ripely presented, is firmly based in the repertory, most of Bruch's other *concertante* works for violin are largely unknown. Here's one of the most ambitious, the Serenade, dating from 1900, 20 years after the Fantasy. Its breadth and weight belies the lightweight title. It's a warm and fluent work in Bruch's high-Romantic style, built on clearly defined themes that lack only the last degree of memorability of the Fantasy. The third of the four movements, a dreamy, lyrical *Notturno*, comes nearest to matching the Fantasy's natural glow, but the other movements have striking moments, too. Bruch had the idea of putting this substantial work among his numbered concertos but changed his mind.

Maxim Fedotov gives a warm, thrusting performance of both the Serenade and the Fantasy. He may be a little short on mystery and tenderness but his bravura playing, helped by full-blooded accompaniment from Dmitry Yablonsky, makes the results consistently compelling.

Anton Bruckner   Austrian 1824-1896

'*I never had a more serious pupil than you,*' remarked Bruckner's renowned teacher of counterpoint, Simon Sechter. Certainly, no one could ever accuse Bruckner of being frivolous and quite how this unsophisticated, obsequious boor came to write nine symphonies of such originality and epic splendour is one of music's contradictions. You don't turn to Bruckner the man or the musician for the light touch. His worship of Wagner verged on the neurotic for, really, there is something worrying about his debasement before the composer of Tristan. The dedication of his Third Symphony to Wagner reads: 'To the eminent Excellency Richard Wagner the Unattainable, World-Famous, and Exalted Master of Poetry and Music, in Deepest Reverence Dedicated by Anton Bruckner'; before the two men eventually met, Bruckner would sit and stare at his idol in silent admiration, and after hearing Parsifal for the first time, fell on his knees in front of Wagner crying, 'Master – I worship you'. His soliciting of honours, his craving for recognition and lack of self-confidence, allied with an unprepossessing appearance and a predilection for unattainable young girls, paints a disagreeable picture. The reverse of the coin is that of the humble peasant ill at ease in society, devoutly religious (most of his works were inscribed 'Omnia ad majorem Dei gloriam') and a personality of almost childlike simplicity and ingenuousness. God, Wagner and Music were his three deities.

He was the son of a village schoolmaster whose duties included playing the organ in church and teaching music. When his father died in 1837,

Bruckner enrolled as a chorister in the secluded monastery of St Florian where he studied organ, piano, violin and theory. The story of his life until he was 40 was one of continual study, with an income derived from various meagre teaching and organ posts. Few major composers have waited so long before finding their voice. He was 31 when he began studying with Sechter in Vienna and remained with him on and off until 1861. His lack of confidence in his abilities as a composer led him onwards to more extended studies (this time of Italian and German polyphony – especially Bach) until, like Saul on the road to Damascus, the blinding light of Wagner hit him when he attended the first performance of Tristan und Isolde in Munich in 1865. All these rules and theories he had been assiduously absorbing had to be abandoned – for that was what Wagner had done.

The year 1868 saw the arrival of his first important works, though one of them, the Mass in F minor, had been prefaced by depression and a nervous breakdown which included a spell of numeromania – an obsession with counting. But if Wagner had opened the door, it also put obstacles in the way of recognition. There was indecently fierce opposition to Wagner and all his works in Vienna (orchestrated by the influential critic Eduard Hanslick, whom Wagner caricatured as Beckmesser in his opera Die Meistersinger von Nürnberg). Anyone who was so clearly under the influence of Wagner was also the subject of attack and his Third Symphony was greeted with catcalls from the anti-Wagner pro-Brahms faction of the audience at the premiere. Few people remained in the hall to applaud. The Fourth Symphony, given in Vienna under the great conductor Hans Richter, was better received and later Richter recalled the pathetic gesture of thanks that the tearfully thankful composer made after the first performance. 'Take it!' Bruckner said, squeezing a gulden into Richter's hand. 'Drink a pitcher of beer to my health.' Richter wore the coin on his watch chain for the rest of his life 'as a memento of the day on which I wept'.

In 1884 the tide turned. After conducting the premiere of Bruckner's Seventh Symphony, the charismatic Artur Nikisch wrote, 'Since Beethoven there had been nothing that could even approach it'. During the last 35 years of his life, Bruckner combined composition with teaching and held a number of prestigious appointments in Vienna, at the Conservatoire, the University and St Anna College.

Throughout his life Bruckner searched for a woman with whom to share his life. He was 43 when he fell in love with a 17-year-old, whose parents put a stop to the relationship. He fell for another 17-year-old in his mid-fifties. Though the parents in this instance gave the relationship their blessing, the young girl tired of Bruckner and his passionate letters went unanswered. Later still he became infatuated with the 14-year-old daughter of his first love – that came to nothing and at 70 he proposed to a young chambermaid. Her refusal to convert to Catholicism ended that. Piety and pubescent girls are not an attractive combination. Bruckner died a virgin and was buried under the organ at St Florian.

Symphonies

No 00 in F minor, 'Study Symphony'; **No 0** in D minor, 'Die Nullte'; **No 1** in C minor; **No 2** in C minor; **No 3** in D minor; **No 4** in E flat, 'Romantic'; **No 5** in B flat; **No 6** in A; **No 7** in E; **No 8** in C minor; **No 9** in D minor

Symphonies – Nos 1 (Linz version), 2, 3 (1889 version, ed Nowak), 4-7, 8 (ed Haas) & 9
**Berlin Philharmonic Orchestra /
Herbert von Karajan**
DG ⑨ Karajan Symphony Edition 477 7580GB9
(8h 40' · ADD/DDD). Recorded 1975-81   Ⓜ❍❍❍❍▸

Karajan's understanding of the slow but powerful currents that flow beneath the surfaces of symphonies like the Fifth or Nos 7-9 has never been bettered, but at the same time he shows how much more there is to be reckoned with: strong emotions, a deep poetic sensitivity (a Bruckner symphony can evoke landscapes as vividly as Mahler or Vaughan Williams) and a gift for singing melody that at times rivals even Schubert. It hardly needs saying that there's no such thing as a perfect record cycle, and Karajan's collection of the numbered Bruckner symphonies (unfortunately he never recorded 'No 0') has its weaknesses. The early First and Second Symphonies can be a little heavy-footed and, as with so many Bruckner sets, there's a suspicion that more time might have been spent getting to know the fine but elusive Sixth. However, none of these performances is without its major insights, and in the best of them – particularly Nos 3, 5, 7, 8 and 9 – those who haven't stopped their ears to Karajan will find that whatever else he may have been, there was a side to him that could only be described as 'visionary'. As for the recordings: climaxes can sound a touch overblown in some of the earlier symphonies, but overall the image is well focused and atmospheric. A valuable set, and a landmark in the history of Bruckner recording.

Additional recommendation

Symphonies Nos 1-9
**Berlin Philharmonic Orchestra; Berlin Radio SO /
Jochum**
DG ⑨ 469 810-2GB9 (9h 12' · ADD)
Recorded 1958-68   Ⓑ▸
If you're used to Karajan's Bruckner, Jochum's approach can appear rather stop-start. But he was a great Brucknerian, and his highly charged, romantically intense, seemingly spontaneous approach will appeal to many. This is a great set with few real weaknesses, except for the Eighth.

Symphonies Nos 1 (ed Carragan) & 3 – Bewegt, quasi Andante (1876 version)
Royal Scottish National Orchestra / Georg Tintner
Naxos 8 554430 (76' · DDD)   Ⓢ❍▸

Some of the outstanding performances in the late Georg Tintner's Naxos Bruckner series have been of the early symphonies. 'Your young men shall see visions,' says the Prophet Joel. It has been Tintner's skill to conjure vision by marrying sharpness of detail and youthful diction with a daring breadth of utterance. He did this in his recording of the Symphony No 3 and he does it again here in a fine account of the First recorded in Glasgow's Henry Wood Hall with the RSNO at the top of its considerable form.

Timings of individual movements confirm a broad reading, as broad as Václav Neumann's on his old Leipzig set. But where Neumann's performance ended up sounding soulful and ponderous, Tintner's is as fresh as could be. Bruckner called this a 'cheeky little minx' of a symphony. Tintner shows it to be that, and more. (Bruckner's own generally unavailing pursuit of cheeky post-pubescent minxes clearly fed a rich and lively fantasy life which the symphony vividly charts. Or so Freudians might have us believe.)

The announcement that this is the 'world premiere recording' of the 'unrevised Linz version' shouldn't cause seasoned collectors to throw out cherished extant recordings of the 1866 'Linz' (as opposed to 1890-91 'Vienna') version. The emendations Bruckner made in 1877 to the 1866 text are fairly minor. That said, future interpreters may want to follow Tintner in using this plainer Haas/Carragan edition rather than the 1955 Nowak edition which, in typically meddling style, incorporates the 1877 changes into the original text. The plainness of the orchestration at the very end of the symphony is absolutely right for a peroration that's both prompt and ingenious.

The fill-up is rather more intriguing textually. It's the largely forgotten 1876 revision of the original 1873 version of the *Adagio* of the Third Symphony. The changes include a quicker tempo, a gentle elaboration of the violin figurations near the start, and a disastrous attempt to underpin the lead to the final climax with a new *Tannhäuser*-like violin accompaniment. Since this is funny in the wrong way, it could be said nicely to complement the main work on the disc which is funny (and fun) in all the right ways.

Symphony No 2 (ed Carragan)
National Symphony Orchestra of Ireland /
Georg Tintner
Naxos 8 554006 (71' · DDD)

This exceptional recording by veteran Austrian conductor Georg Tintner is in a league of its own. It's a beautifully shaped performance, characterfully played and vividly recorded. What's more, it is in effect a gramophone 'first', for though the original, 1872 version of Bruckner's Second Symphony has been recorded elsewhere, this is the first to reach a wider market. Not that the differences between editions are hugely significant. What the earlier 1872 version principally offers is the reversal of the order of the two inner movements (the *Scherzo* now

comes before the *Andante*), a full clutch of repeats in the *Scherzo* and Trio, a rather longer development section in the finale, various small changes to the orchestration and the absence of some of the more meretricious tempo markings. What's appealing about the 'full monty' is the feeling it gives of the symphony's Schubertian pedigree: heavenly length joining hands with a deep sense of melancholy and melodic *Angst*. Which brings us to Tintner's reading of the symphony, which is shrewd and affectionate, tellingly phrased and beautifully paced, the moves away from and back to the basic pulse nicely handled. This is Bruckner conducting of the old school. There's also something reassuringly old-fashioned about the playing of the National Symphony Orchestra of Ireland. The entire orchestra has the character of a well-to-do country cousin who's blessedly innocent of the more tiresome aspects of metropolitan life. This is an exceptional recording.

Symphony No 2 (1877 Novak edition)
Vienna Symphony Orchestra / Carlo Maria Giulini
Testament SBT1210 (59' · ADD). Recorded 1974   Ⓕ

Perhaps the greatest of all recordings of the work, spacious, involved, profoundly human. So persuasive is Giulini's interpretation, it makes it almost impossible to take seriously the attempt at a more detached, monumental approach found in Daniel Barenboim's relatively recent Teldec performance. Giulini's ability to convey fervour without sentimentality is little short of miraculous, and it's clear from the way the early stages of the first movement effortlessly project an ideal balance between the lyrical and the dramatic that this reading will be exceptional. The recording might not have the dynamic range of current digital issues, and resonance can sound rather artificial in louder passages. There's also an obtrusive extension of the trumpet triplets seven bars before the end of the first movement. But such things count for less than nothing in the face of a performance which culminates in a finale of such glowing spontaneity you could almost believe that the orchestra are playing it for the first time, and that neither they (nor any other orchestra) will ever play it better.

A fuller and more authentic text of the symphony is available at super-bargain price in Georg Tintner's fine account of the 1872 edition (on Naxos; reviewed above). Serious collectors will need both. Yet the last thing you're likely to feel after hearing Giulini is that there's something inauthentic about this Bruckner. Matters musicological fade to vanishing point, given such communicative genius.

Symphony No 3 (1877/78 version)
Wagner Lohengrin – Act 1, Prelude; Act 3, Prelude
South West German Radio Symphony Orchestra /
Michael Gielen
Hänssler Faszination Musik **CD**93 031 (67' · DDD)
      Ⓕ ●●●

The Bruckner is the thing here. This is a truly inspired performance, keenly argued, swift and clean-limbed, yet one that's also sensitive to the characteristic Brucknerian musings in lyric subjects and at points of transitions. Haitink may create more space in the finale's polka-cum-chorale in his 1988 Vienna recording but his account of the finale runs into gearing problems of its own later on.

The Gielen was made over three days in May 1999 in the Festspielhaus in Baden-Baden. It was evidently made with care; yet it sounds live. It even 'settles' as a real performance might, the orchestra shifting focus a few minutes into the first movement as the players begin to illuminate the drama from within rather than merely sounding it from without. Like Haitink, Gielen includes the scampering coda to the third movement which Bruckner added to this 1877 revision in January 1878. It's a curious afterthought which can sound trite. Not so here. Gielen's performance of the *Scherzo* and Trio is so lithe and fiery you half expect the music to race on beyond its accredited end.

Brucknerians who lust after the weight and unfailing security of the Berlin or Vienna string ensembles may have a few reservations about this Gielen version. The Gielen is *hors concours* principally because of the intuitive brilliance of a reading which profiles so vividly the ardent, aspiring mood of a provincial musician, intoxicated by his craft, giving his all in the service of the god Wagner to whom the work was dedicated.

Symphony No 3 (1873 version)
**Stuttgart Radio Symphony Orchestra /
Sir Roger Norrington**
Hänssler Classic CD93 217 (61' · DDD)   Ⓕ**O**🔂

Since he first recorded the symphony in 1995, Sir Roger has modified his tempo in the first movement. His brisk though no longer over-quick tempo works superbly with and through the spare, pellucid, finely honed texturing he draws from the Stuttgart orchestra, an ensemble which under his guidance has brought the art of playing modern instruments in old ways to a new pitch of excellence. There are wind and string sonorities here such as you would expect to hear in music of the Baroque period, something that suits early Bruckner especially well.

The vibrato-free Stuttgart strings play with a purity and simplicity that merits the epithet Cistercian. There are spellbinding moments of quiet at the start and finish of the first movement development and throughout the slow movement (a requiem, in part, for Bruckner's lately deceased mother). The all-in-one *Scherzo* and Trio is also betwitchingly done, fiery but with grace and charm to spare.

One thing Sir Roger has not modified is his quick-fire treatment of the finale's second theme: the counterpointing of polka and chorale inspired by Bruckner's experience of hearing dance music issuing from a house while nearby a revered colleague lay in his coffin. Karl Böhm in

his wonderfully idiomatic VPO recording of the 1889 version takes this at a leisurely 52 bars per minute, the usual pace for a *Polka française* (as opposed to *Schnell-Polka*) in Viennese ballrooms at the time. That reservation aside, this is a touching and exhilarating new account of the Third.

Symphony No 3 (1889 version, ed Nowak)
Mozarteum Orchestra, Salzburg / Ivor Bolton
Oehms OC722 (58' · DDD)   Ⓕ

Though you might wonder at the idea of the Salzburg Mozarteum Orchestra playing Bruckner, they have been doing so for many years. Joseph Schröcksnadel's history of the orchestra reproduces a poster from July 1928 advertising a performance of the Fifth Symphony conducted by Bernhard Paumgartner in the Cathedral Square. In 2004 Ivor Bolton took over as music director, and judging by this excellent 2007 Bruckner Third, it would seem that he has made a difference.

The deftness and buoyancy with which the opening string ostinatos are realised indicate qualities of grace and manoeuvrability that more than make up for the fact that the orchestra will never command the weight or fire-power of, say, Böhm's Vienna Philharmonic, an ensemble that also brings to the third- and fourth-movement dance subjects a properly Austrian tread.

There have been outstanding versions of this 1889 version from Wand, Karajan, Böhm and others besides. However, with few of these surviving as single-CD releases, this admirable new Oehms CD might be said to have the market at its mercy.

Symphonies – No 3 (1889); No 4, 'Romantic'
(1880, ed Nowak)
**Royal Concertgebouw Orchestra, Amsterdam /
Mariss Jansons**
RCO Live ② 🎵 RCO09002 (125' · DDD/DSD)
Recorded live 2007, 2008   Ⓕ**O**🔂

In these powerfully articulated accounts of Bruckner's Third and Fourth symphonies, Mariss Jansons exhibits the quality that Karajan attributed to the great Czech conductor Václav Talich: "He had a great genius for…drawing the orchestra together and controlling it as a single expressive instrument."

This is particularly evident in the finale of the Fourth Symphony. Though Bruckner spent years trying to get this movement right, it can still sound inadequate in a less than first-rate performance. That is not the case here. Jansons's grasp of the relative importance of individual ideas within the competing hierarchies of thematic material is as impressive as his marrying of a properly measured opening pulse with a strong yet unforced forward motion.

Though the Third Symphony is less difficult to bring off, there have been few better-directed accounts on record than this. If there is a limitation, it lies with the Dutch orchestra's northern manner. Finely as Jansons shapes the polka-cum-chorale in the symphony's finale, others have managed it better. Nor do the horn or bassoon sections have the kind of sound characteristics that have helped establish the superiority of Vienna and Munich Philharmonic accounts of the Fourth Symphony under Böhm, Abbado, Celibidache and Kempe.

The horns are further disadvantaged by a somewhat distant recorded balance, unlike that of the cellos which can be too immediate. Concertgebouw Live generally gives us a closer, darker sound than that of Concertgebouw recordings made in an empty hall under studio conditions. A striking pair of discs none the less.

Symphony No 4
Berlin Philharmonic Orchestra / Günter Wand
RCA Victor Red Seal 09026 68839-2 (69' · DDD)
Recorded live 1997   Ⓕ❍❍❍❍▷

The pacing of each movement is majestic. Not too fast in the first movement; a slow, contemplative tread in the second; animated, but capable of opening out into something more leisurely in the *Scherzo*; varied, but with the sense of an underlying slow pulse in the finale. Wand allows himself some fairly generous *rubato* from time to time, halting slightly on the high unaccompanied cello phrase in the first movement second subject. From the start there's something about his performance that puts it in a different league from rivals. There's the depth and richness of the string sound in the opening tremolo. A few seconds later the Berlin Philharmonic's principal horn intones the opening phrases so magically and majestically that it's hard to believe you aren't listening to a real voice – a superhuman larynx, not just a contraption of brass and valves. The sound is, to some extent, the orchestra's own, but there's a feeling that the players are giving extra for Wand, something with more inner life; and the unaffected eloquence and shapeliness of the phrasing is all Wand. It carries you along even when the *rubato* ought to jar, as it does sometimes in other versions.

This is a concert performance, and feels like one. Things that work in concert aren't always ideal solutions on a repeatable commercial recording. Take Wand's big *ritardando* at the fleeting reference to Brünnhilde's Magic Sleep motif in the finale – the effect might pall after a couple of playings. But then he does ease very effectively into the weird *pianissimo* cello and bass figures that follow, triplet quavers gradually becoming triplet crotchets. The sound quality is excellent.

Symphony No 4
Vienna Philharmonic Orchestra / Karl Böhm
Decca Legends 466 374-2DM (68' · ADD)
Recorded 1973   Ⓜ❍❍❍❍▷

Böhm's VPO account of the Fourth Symphony has the unmistakable stamp of greatness. It was

made in the Sofiensaal in Vienna with its helpful acoustic; for though you can detect a whisper of tape-hiss if you put your ear against the loudspeaker, in almost every other way the sound is realistic and warm. There's a roundness in the brass tone with plenty of bite and fullness but no unwanted rasp – especially important in this symphony. Böhm's Fourth is at the head of the field irrespective of price. The warmth as well as the mystery of Bruckner are far more compellingly conveyed in Böhm's spacious view than with any other conductor.

Bruckner Symphony No 4[a] **Vaughan Williams**
Fantasia on a Theme by Thomas Tallis[b]
London Symphony Orchestra / István Kertész
BBC Legends BBCL4264-2 (78' · ADD)
Recorded live at the Royal Festival Hall, London in
[a]1964, [b]1966   Ⓕ❍❍

There can have been few finer live performances of the Fourth on record than this. Valuable in itself, it is also a document of rare interest where the LSO is concerned.

The performance of the Bruckner took place in London in March 1964, three months before the death of the LSO's revered chief conductor, Pierre Monteux. The well nigh symbiotic relationship between orchestra and conductor that is evident on every page of this Bruckner Fourth is a pointer to why the LSO later chose the 35-year-old Kertész as its new principal conductor.

So what we have here is Monteux's clear-sighted yet mellow-sounding LSO led by a superbly gifted young musician at his relaxed and decisive best. 'Wonderful sense of rhythm, great sense of line and phrasing, but incredibly immature as a person' was one player's retrospective on Kertész. Here happily it is the musical qualities that count.

Kertész's role model for the Fourth Symphony was Bruno Walter who, like Klemperer, played this most vital yet at the same time lyrical of Bruckner symphonies with a judicious mixture of pace and relaxation. The playing is superb, as is the recording.

The microphones are set further back for the Vaughan Williams, giving bloom and perspective to a performance of some grandeur and eloquence. Happily, there is time to exit before the applause which BBC Legends insists on preserving but which in the privacy of one's own room ruins the sense of completion and quiet at the music's end.

Symphony No 4
**Royal Concertgebouw Orchestra /
Nikolaus Harnoncourt**
Warner Elatus 2564 60129-2 (65' · DDD)   Ⓜ▷

If you're expecting something controversial here you'll probably be disappointed. Harnoncourt's Bruckner Fourth is nothing like as provocative as his Beethoven. It's relatively fast, but not startlingly so. If Harnoncourt's first movement is

BRUCKNER SYMPHONY NO 4 – IN BRIEF

Vienna PO / Karl Böhm
Decca 446 374-2DM (68' · ADD)　Ⓜ❍❍❍▷
A classic performance from 1973, in which both orchestra and conductor rise to the challenge with one of the freshest, most endearing interpretations ever recorded. (Also coupled with a fine No 3 on an excellent Double Decca, 448 098-2DM2.)

Berlin PO / Günter Wand
RCA 09026 68839-2 (69' · DDD)　Ⓕ❍❍❍
Recorded live at the Philharmonie, Berlin, in 1997, and taking a *Gramophone* Award on its release, this is a fine souvenir of the Wand way with Bruckner: thoughful, structurally as safe as houses and beautifully phrased, every note lavished with attention. Truly inspired.

Berlin PO / Herbert von Karajan
EMI 768872 (70' · ADD)　Ⓜ❍▷
Berlin PO / Herbert von Karajan
DG 439 522-2GGA (64' · ADD)　Ⓜ▷
The EMI was Karajan's first recording of the work (1970) and demonstrates his credentials as a Brucknerian. Beautifully recorded, it still sounds splendid. The DG version dates from five years later. Both show an innate grasp of the work's architecture.

Royal Concertgebouw Orchestra / Nikolaus Harnoncourt
Warner Elatus 2564 60129-2 (65' · DDD)　Ⓜ▷
A fresh and refreshing view of Bruckner's Fourth, more exciting than is usual with a delightful rustic gait and very light on its toes. Well worth considering for a slightly unconventional approach to Bruckner.

Royal Scottish National Orchestra / Georg Tintner
Naxos 8 554128 (73' · DDD)　Ⓢ▷
A CD that matches value with musical insight: Tintner was an experienced Brucknerian and gives a reading full of poetry and delightful incident. Good playing from the RSNO. A real bargain.

Philharmonia Orchestra / Lovro von Matačić Ⓗ
Testament mono SBT1050 (76' · ADD)　Ⓕ
Coupled with a stereo recording of the rarely encountered Overture in G minor, von Matačić's 1954 Bruckner Fourth is a fine one, though for many the Schalk edition used, with its substantial cuts, may count against it.

Staatskapelle Dresden / Herbert Blomstedt
Dal Segno DSPRC045 (76' · ADD)　Ⓜ❍❍
Originally issued on the Denon label, this is a very fine, beautifully judged and, above all, musical performance. The sound is still mighty fine.

more gripping, more like a symphonic drama than usual, that has more to do with the crisp, clear rhythmic articulation than with the number of crotchets per minute. The solo woodwind and horn playing that follows is lovely, expansive enough; what else would you expect from the Concertgebouw in Bruckner? This is an unusually compelling Bruckner Fourth – exciting throughout the first movement and *Scherzo*, and in passages like the problematical Brucknerian Ride of the Valkyries that erupts after the finale's bucolic second theme. In many more traditional Bruckner performances the bass often seems to move in sustained, undifferentiated pedal points. In Harnoncourt's version you're often aware of a deep pulsation – like the throbbing repeated notes that open the finale – continuing, however discreetly, while the tunes unfold above. To hear the finale's second theme in this version is to be reminded that Bruckner was an excellent dancer, light on his feet until he was nearly 70. Of course, you shouldn't confuse the man with the musical personality, but why should Bruckner always sound heavy, sedentary, as though slowly digesting a gigantic meal? Harnoncourt provides us with the light-footedness, while allowing the music to unfold at its own speed, to take time. There's no question that Harnoncourt must be considered a serious contender in Bruckner.

Symphonies – No 4, 'Romantic'; No 7
Munich Philharmonic / Christian Thielemann
Video Director **Agnes Méth**
C Major 📀 701908 (156' · NTSC · 16:9 · PCM Stereo and DTS 5.1 · 0)　Ⓕ❍❍

One of the world's finest Bruckner ensembles, the Munich Philharmonic has already recorded classic accounts of the Fourth Symphony under Kempe and Celibidache. Christian Thielemann's performance is comparably fine, not least for the orchestral playing which has the kind of concentration of tone and attack one used to associate with the Berlin Philharmonic in this repertory. Thielemann's podium manner is that of a general calmly surveying the landscape spread out before him. Like Fritz Reiner, he tends to keep baton and body movements to a minimum with an unblinking gaze controlling proceedings in a 180° field of vision.

Harald Reiter's booklet essay speaks of 'the apparent paradox between total commitment to the task in hand and at the same time a highly effective, conscious and intellectual organisational power'. Dynamic control is masterly, paragraphs are clearly marked, silences fully exploited, climaxes expertly tiered. The slow movement is taken at a slower tempo than Bruckner requests. On CD it might hang fire; seen as well as heard, it works perfectly well. There is a thrilling account of the *Scherzo* and a properly broad-based approach to the finale. Agnes Méth's video direction is excellent. As reportage it is superb, as a piece of visually conceived musical analysis the camerawork outscores even the finest programme essay.

The performance of the Seventh Symphony, also filmed in the Festspielhaus Baden-Baden, begins with what are in effect two slow movements, culminating in the sombre funeral rites, memorably realised, of the second movement coda. Though the lights go up in the last movements this is not quite as easy a recommendation as that of the Fourth which is set to be a DVD Bruckner classic.

Symphony No 5
Philharmonia Orchestra / Benjamin Zander
Telarc ② 2CD80706 (149' · DDD)   ⓂOOOⒺ→
Includes bonus disc of Benjamin Zander discussing
Bruckner Symphony No 5

Yet another Bruckner Fifth? Not exactly. The performance, which has its own distinction, comes with an 80-minute bonus disc of unusual quality and interest. Not since the halcyon days of Antony Hopkins 'Talking About Music' has there been a commentary as lucid, as approachable and yet as musically satisfying as this.

Devised by Zander and his co-producer David St George, it is a multifaceted essay. Mapping the symphony has pride of place and is superbly done. It also thrives on a rich array of music examples tucked with consummate skill in, around and beneath the narrative.

Another distinctive touch is his breathing new life into the old cathedral analogy. The CD comes with a foldaway leaflet. On one side is a cathedral floor-plan, on the other the structure of the Fifth Symphony laid over that same plan. Nor does Zander stop there. His profound and often moving remarks on time, space, spiritual struggle and spiritual renewal grow naturally out of this.

His trump card is his father Walter Zander, who died in 1993 at the age of 95. In the summer of 1918, while fighting on the Russian front, Walter was sent a score of Bruckner's Fifth Symphony by his mother. His letters home with their comments on what the music meant to him have only recently reappeared. These, too, have been woven into the narrative, and very remarkable they are.

Despite his father's urging, Zander did not study the symphony until he was past 60. Antony Hopkins once said that some of his best scripts are written on works he knew little about before writing. Zander seems to have been similarly blessed, creating a remarkable narrative and complementing it with a performance of great lucidity and drive. If the finely geared playing seems a touch lightweight in places, turning up the level of the beautifully judged Watford Coliseum recording helps bulk out the vertical dimension.

Symphony No 5 (ed Haas/Nowak)
**Vienna Philharmonic Orchestra /
Nikolaus Harnoncourt**
RCA Red Seal 〰 82876 60749-2 (73' · DDD/DSD)
Recorded live 2004. Includes a disc of rehearsal
excerpts   ⒻOO

Nikolaus Harnoncourt's Fifth is more a realisation than an interpretation, musically vivid but spiritually serene. Serene but not slow. By the clock, this is one of the quickest Fifths on record, though only the *Adagio* is taken more swiftly than usual. It was here that Bruckner began the symphony in the pit of despair in 1875 with a keening oboe melody he marked 'Sehr langsam' but scored *alla breve*. Harnoncourt treats it *allegretto* after the manner of a threnody by Bach or Mozart, whose Requiem is quoted during the course of the movement. Furtwängler, surprisingly, took a similar view of the movement.

The 'liveness' of the live performance owes much to Harnoncourt – his persona fuelling the music-making not the concept, which is as it should be – though the superlative playing of the Vienna Philharmonic is also a factor. The light-fingered realisation of the exquisite string traceries is a constant source of wonder; *tuttis* are glowing and unforced. The hall of the Musik-verein helps, too; with an audience present it offers a uniquely natural-sounding Bruckner acoustic. This is a performance of rare vision and strength.

Symphony No 6
**Stuttgart Radio Symphony Orchestra /
Sir Roger Norrington**
Hänssler Classic ② CD93 219 (52' · DDD)
Recorded live   ⒻOⒺ→

Bruckner's Sixth has always been the most elusive of the composer's mature symphonies. Treat it 'as a kind of music we have never heard before', wrote an admiring Donald Tovey in 1935. But few have. Only that grand old iconoclast Otto Klemperer, and now Sir Roger, have had the courage to recognise the piece as an epic off-the-wall revel.

Not that Norrington downplays the symphony's moments of introspection. No symphony, not even Beethoven's revel in A, can be a total knees-up. Norrington is aware where the outer movement song-subjects and their attendant harmonic adventures are going to land us. Even more than Klemperer (see below), he takes the main themes of these movements at quite a lick (the finale especially so, at some cost to orchestral equanimity in the lyric countersubject) though as with Klemperer the pulse of the lyric subjects remains proportionate. Where Norrington is fearless is in Bruckner's on-the-spot shifts of tempo or key. But, then, he has always rather relished the shock of the obvious.

It is difficult to outsmart Klemperer in the *Adagio* since he too divides his fiddles and deploys minimal vibrato. He is also a touch quicker than Norrington and has a more keenly recorded first oboe. That said, Norrington generates real tension in the harmonically indeterminate climax before the recapitulation. And Norrington's is the more gamesome third movement, the downbeats in the *Scherzo*'s plodding string ostinato cheekily accented. With its rustic vigour and devil-may-care insouciance, this is a performance that really does tell it as it is.

Symphony No 6
Deutsches Symphony Orchestra, Berlin / Kent Nagano
Harmonia Mundi HMC90 1901 (57' · DDD)　　ⒻⒹ➤

'Bruckner's Sixth Symphony is not easy to play,' says Habakuk Traber in his fine booklet essay. Nor is it easy to conduct; witness the fact that no one these past 40 years has seriously challenged Klemperer's sublimely direct account of the work (see below). In fact, Kent Nagano's reading is not unlike Klemperer's: purposeful and big-boned. Even in the finale, where Nagano takes too brisk an opening tempo and thereafter does too much stopping and starting for comfort, the performance coheres inasmuch as he appears to have an overview of the work, and the will to enforce it.

In a symphony where, as Traber suggests, the home key of A major is easier to perceive on the printed page than to hear in performance, conductors often end up not seeing the wood for the trees. Nagano, happily, appears to have moved to higher ground. Like Klemperer, he establishes moments of real gravitational pull, ensuring that the first movement's critical passages – the exposition, the glorious transition to the recapitulation, and the celebrated coda which sent Sir Donald Tovey into such raptures – are commandingly done. The slow movement, the work's epicentre, is played with great solemnity, serious and fine, and the *Scherzo* is more or less perfectly judged.

The recording, made in the Berlin Philharmonie, is clear and robust with woodwind and brass well in the picture.

Additional recommendation

Symphony No 6
Coupled with: **Gluck/Wagner** Iphigénie en Aulide – Overture **Humperdinck** Hänsel und Gretel – Overture
New Philh, Philh / Klemperer
EMI download 562621-2 (80' · ADD)　　ⓂⓄⓄⓄ➤
Klemperer's performance is masterly from first note to last. It is a performance by turns lofty, tender and serene, but it is, above all, a structurally cogent performance and within the compass of its steady-treading tempi an intensely exciting one. (Not currently listed, but worth tracking down.)

Symphony No 7 (ed Haas)
Vienna Philharmonic Orchestra / Herbert von Karajan
DG Karajan Gold 439 037-2GHS (66' · DDD)　　ⒻⓄ

The Vienna Philharmonic features on what was Karajan's last recording, an idiomatic account of Bruckner's Seventh Symphony, lighter and more classical in feel than either of his two Berlin recordings yet loftier, too. As

for the original-image bit-processing you need go no further than the first fluttered violin *tremolando* and the cellos' rapt entry in the third bar to realise how ravishingly 'present' the performance is in this reprocessing. Or go to the end of the symphony and hear how the great E major peroration is even more transparent than before, the octave drop of bass trombone and bass tuba 13 bars from home the kind of delightfully euphoric detail that in 1989 only the more assiduous score-reader would have been conscious of hearing. This remastered Seventh is definitely pure gold.

Symphony No 7 (ed Haas)
Stuttgart Radio Symphony Orchestra / Sir Roger Norrington
Hänssler Classic CD93 243 (55' · DDD)　　Ⓕ

Symphony No 7 (ed Nowak)
Frankfurt Radio Symphony Orchestra / Paavo Järvi
RCA Red Seal Ⓢ 88697 38997-2
(67' · DDD/DSD)　　ⒻⓄⓄ➤

Sir Roger Norrington's Bruckner Seventh might not be quite the work that one knows and loves, but under his informed scrutiny it bounds at speed, donning the expected vibrato-free string lines. The idea of having a first movement that is significantly faster than anyone else's is based on the theory that because the outer movements share thematic cells they should also share tempi, *allegro moderato* being in essence very similar to *bewegt, doch nicht zu schnell*, 'fast but lively'. The initial impression is 'chaste and with haste', the opening less warmly cosseted than usual, but by the time we reach the second set proper we really are in the fast lane. Suddenly music that in days of yore was filled with ardour and a certain strain of Romantic idealism becomes a garrulous outgrowth of classical symphonic argument, admittedly something that was always implied but never so clearly focused. The noble rising string chords near the start of the *Adagio* sound strangely disembodied; and although Norrington exhibits a sure sense of line and keeps textures illuminated from within, there's no real warmth, repose or exultation (though the *Adagio*'s climax, played here without percussion, is powerful enough). The *Adagio*'s tempo is only marginally faster than the norm whereas the last two movements respond well to regular pacing and less eccentric characterisation, although at the very end of the symphony the brass's reference back to the work's opening phrase is rather mannered. Come the closing chord, and the audience remains silent – stunned, before some rather tentative applause implies 'what the...?' Clearly this was not what they were expecting. Paavo Järvi's Seventh inhabits – no, creates – quite another world, and not just because of his very different view of the music. Here we have two German radio orchestras sounding as if they hail from different continents, one couched in cold, pure air, the other, Järvi's, enjoying a comfortably mild climate. As to the differences in interpretation, while Järvi's first movement runs to a conservative 21'54", Norrington's is a breakneck 15'08", a fairly dramatic contrast in comparison with the two *Adagios* where the variation in tempo amounts to less than three minutes (which in itself is quite significant). Not that tempo is, strictly speaking, as much of the essence as you would imagine, certainly not in this context.

Järvi offers an extremely beautiful performance, responsively played and, most crucially, sensitive to key transitions. There are many subtleties, while the finale's angrily strutting second set will have your woofers quaking. Incidentally, in Järvi's *Adagio* those hymn-like string chords are mightily sonorous and the no-holds-barred climax – with percussion this time – is extremely effective though the *ritardando* "in" is perhaps a mite excessive.

By now it will be fairly obvious that Järvi's Seventh is the more convincing, but Norrington's sense of daring, his energy and conviction, and the way he inspires his players to focus exactly the performance he wants has a huge appal. In a sense what we have here are two quite different symphonies, and the great virtue of Norrington's is that no one knows it – yet.

Symphony No 7 (ed Haas)
Royal Scottish National Orchestra / Georg Tintner
Naxos 8 554269 (66' · DDD)   ⑤🅓➔

In the absence of recommendable budget or super-budget recordings of Bruckner's Seventh Symphony, this will do nicely. It's a finely schooled performance, chaste and discreet, with a notable reading of the *Adagio* which lies at the heart of the work. Tintner sees this very much as a piece, the first (G major) climax finely achieved, the later, greater climax splendidly 'placed'. The coda, Bruckner's lament for the dead Wagner, is played relatively swiftly, touchingly and without bombast. In general, his reading of the score is loyal without being in any sense dull or hidebound. In an ideal world, the playing of the first violins would be more consistently secure *in alt*. In particular, you have the feeling that both the players and the engineers (the engineering is generally excellent) would have benefited from a chance to refine and tidy parts of the performance of the first movement. A notable bargain, none the less.

Symphony No 8 (ed Haas)
London Philharmonic Orchestra / Klaus Tennstedt
LPO LPO0032 (74' · ADD)   Ⓜ**OO**

Tennstedt's performance of Bruckner's mighty Eighth Symphony is high on adrenalin from the very first minute and remains so for the next 73. There were times during the performance when, had the laws of physics permitted it, the speakers would have glowed white. Not all Brucknerians will approve of so unremittingly intense a performance – the *Scherzo*, for example, treated as a rip-roaring festive joust – though it is impossible

---

BRUCKNER'S SYMPHONY NO 8 – IN BRIEF

Vienna PO / Herbert von Karajan
DG download only (83' · DDD)   Ⓕ**OOO**➔
Bruckner's longest *Adagio* has perhaps never radiated such warmth as in Karajan's last and most integrated recording of the Eighth, with the Vienna Philharmonic more flexible than their Berlin rivals for the conductor.

Hallé Orchestra / Sir John Barbirolli
BBC Legends BBCL4067-2 (74' · ADD)   Ⓕ**OO**
An electric live performance – the last Barbirolli gave in London – in which the tragic first movement casts a baleful shadow over the rest. Not for the faint-hearted, nor for those who like their Bruckner opulent.

Vienna PO / Carlo Maria Giulini
DG ② 445 529-2GMA2 (88' · DDD)   Ⓜ**OO**
Giulini takes such loving, paternal care over inner parts that his spacious tempi rarely register as such. Opulence never obscures the sure-footed journey from C minor to major.

Berlin PO / Günter Wand
RCA ② 74321 82866-2 (87' · DDD)   Ⓕ**OOO**
The last of Günter Wand's recordings of the work, but one that shows an ever-deepening desire to present all of its many sides, from the unrelieved tension of the first movement, through the Olympian dance of the *Scherzo* to the finale's unifying triumph.

North German RSO / Günter Wand
RCA 09026 68047-2 (88' · DDD)   Ⓕ**OO**
Wand's second recording of the work with 'his' orchestra, and many would say his finest of all. Lübeck Cathedral's acoustic bestows its own benediction – the audience is understandably awed into silence.

Vienna PO / Pierre Boulez
DG 459 678-2GH (76' · DDD)
TDK 📀 DV-VOPBR (95 mins)   Ⓕ**O**
Boulez's famed clarity of ear results not in the antiseptic traversal some might expect but lends a startling clarity and sense of purpose to Bruckner's symphonic argument. A superbly 'terraced' orchestral balance in the best Bruckner tradition.

Vienna PO / Wilhelm Furtwängler   Ⓗ
Music & Arts CD764 (77' · ADD)   Ⓜ**OO**
Furtwängler judged this work the finest of all symphonies. Hear this terror-filled, mid-war performance and you understand why.

Munich PO / Sergiu Celibidache
EMI ② 556696-2 (107' · DDD)   Ⓕ
Bruckner never sounds the same again once heard through Celibidache's patient, prismatic analysis. You'll love it or you'll hate it.

to fault Tennstedt on the cogency and long-term reach of the reading. When it comes to seeing the symphony whole, hewn as it were from a single block of marble, he is up there with the best: Barbirolli, Furtwängler, Karajan, Klemperer. The players, the brass in particular, are also high on adrenalin. Given the dry, bright, somewhat unaccommodating Festival Hall acoustic, this doesn't always make for easy listening. The audience greets the performance with its own ecstatic yawp. But, then, they heard the real thing, not this all too brazen aural précis.

Symphony No 8 in C minor (ed Haas)
Hallé Orchestra / Sir John Barbirolli
BBC Legends BBCL4067-2 (74' · ADD)
Recorded live 1970   Ⓕ**OO**

At the time of this concert in May 1970 there were just three recordings of Bruckner's Eighth Symphony in the catalogue; now there are more than 50, and counting. This performance is that rare thing, an intensely dramatic Bruckner Eighth. It isn't often that you hear an account of the turbulent first movement as thrilling as this. The jagged downward slashes of the trumpets are terrible to experience, yet the space that opens up after the vast and glorious E flat cadence 40 bars later is the very reverse, a way to heaven even from the gates of hell. The odd stumble in the brass, the occasional cough are immaterial. This isn't a performance for those who measure out their life in coffee spoons. The *Scherzo* is ferociously quick with a Trio of compensating loftiness. The loftiness returns in the *Adagio* which Barbirolli again projects urgently and with a full heart. Plaintive winds, trenchant brass and speaking strings, full-bodied and emotionally intent, build the heaven on earth that Bruckner envisions. To hear why this is great music-making, listen to the coda and the gloriously articulated long string recitative that underpins it. The finale, too, is fairly gripping, though there's a brief tired patch midway.

The Festival Hall's fierce acoustic suits the performance well and the engineering is spectacular for its day. Barbirolli was mortally ill when this concert took place. He died just 10 weeks later. 'This might be the old man's last, so let's make it a good one,' the players were saying at the time. By all accounts, Karajan's last live Bruckner Eighth was a lofty, out-of-life experience. Barbirolli's is the very opposite, a case of 'Do not go gentle into that good night / Rage, rage against the dying of the light.' It's a one-off, eloquent beyond measure: the boldest, bravest Bruckner Eighth on record.

Symphony No 8 in C minor (ed Haas)
Berlin Philharmonic Orchestra / Günter Wand
RCA Red Seal ② 74321 82866-2 (87' · DDD)
Recorded live 2001   Ⓕ**OOO**

Few readings have been more assiduously toured or generally acclaimed than Wand's

Bruckner Eighth yet Wand himself struggled to better on record the exact and far-seeing account of the symphony he made with the Cologne RSO in 1979. In January 2001 he harnessed the Berlin Bruckner sound to his own particular ends, a potentially Sisyphean task for a man then nearing his 90th birthday.

And the rewards are here. This Eighth is exceptionally fine. When in the *Scherzo* you sense that the mountains themselves are beginning to dance, you know you're onto a good thing; on this occasion, Olympus itself seems to have caught the terpsichorean bug. Not that anything is exaggerated or overblown. Wand knows where each peak is and how best to approach it. His reading is broader than it was 20 years ago, yet nowhere is there any sense of unwanted stasis. Wand draws from the orchestra, the brass and strings in particular, sound of great power and transparency which the engineers have translated in a recording of uncommon reach and splendour. This is a grand and worthy memento for the tens of thousands who heard Wand conduct the symphony in the concert hall.

Symphony No 8 (ed Nowak)
Berlin Philharmonic Orchestra / Carlo Maria Giulini
Testament ② SBT2 1436 (85' · DDD)
Recorded live in 1984   Ⓕ**OO**

As with much of the music he conducted, Carlo Maria Giulini took his time to come to Bruckner. He first amazed the musical world in 1974 with a superb account of the then rarely played Second Symphony. In the years that followed, it was the mighty Eighth Symphony that most preoccupied Giulini. Again he struck gold, conjuring forth performances worthy to be set beside Furtwängler's or Karajan's. In May 1984 he made his own memorable recording with the Vienna Philharmonic, now available to download from DG.

No matter. This Berlin Philharmonic performance, recorded in concert in February 1984, four months before the DG recording, is very much on a par with its studio rival, such is the power and long-term command of Giulini's conducting, the quality and refinement of the playing and the extraordinary staying-power of the Berlin orchestra throughout this 85-minute quest. If anything, the great *Adagio* is even more impressive, benefiting from the added tautness live music-making can bring. The Philharmonie-derived radio sound is a touch closer and more confined than that of the bespoke studio version made in Vienna's Musikverein but it is a marginal matter, no real bar to enjoyment.

Symphony No 9
Berlin Philharmonic Orchestra / Daniel Barenboim
Elatus 0927 46746-2 (63' · DDD). Recorded live   Ⓜ**O**

This is an outstanding version of Bruckner's Ninth Symphony. Like Karajan's reading on DG, it's essentially a 'central' account of the score that attempts neither extreme breadth of utterance nor sharp-edged drama. Rather it's a reading that combines long lines, flowing but astutely nuanced, and sonorities that are full-bodied yet always finely balanced. The outer movements have great rhetorical and emotional power; the *Scherzo* is thunderous and glinting by turns. The *Adagio* begins very slowly but, for once, Barenboim gets away with it, the movement growing organically rather than remaining still-born near the start. This is a live performance and, as you would expect, it's superbly executed, the playing every bit as fine as it is on the Karajan recording. But even that doesn't compete with the natural splendours of this issue. This is superb Bruckner sound, spacious and clear, with strings, woodwind and brass at once unerringly 'placed' and finely matched. Given good engineering and the kind of astute playing we have from Barenboim and the Berliners, the Philharmonie is far from being the acoustic lemon it's sometimes said to be. This is a front-runner for this symphony.

Symphony No 9
Hallé Orchestra / Cristian Mandeal
Hallé CDHLL7524 (62' · DDD)　　　Ⓕ**OO**

This is as fine a Bruckner Ninth as any we have had on record from an English orchestra. It was made in July 2007 during the 61-year-old Romanian Cristian Mandeal's three-year spell as the Hallé's principal guest conductor.

Mid-career Mandeal worked with two noted Brucknerians, Karajan and Celibidache. Happily his Ninth is less bewilderingly long-drawn than Celibidache's. His tempi at the beginning of the two outer movements are unusually broad yet he has the art of growing the music, of easing the pulse on after the initial exordium to the point where a broad, flexible yet forward-moving pulse has been established. There is thus nothing broken-backed about his handling of the first movement's great double exposition as there is with some conductors.

The Hallé's realisation of the reading is finely moulded, powerful where necessary, and distinguished above all by the sustained intensity of the playing in the music's quietest passages. This is not 'Hallé live' but a properly made studio recording. And it shows. The treacherous wind passages in the great concluding *Adagio* are all expertly managed, as is the awesome but awkward *Scherzo*, which Mandeal plays with a pace and élan comparable to that of Sigmund von Hausegger on his pioneering 1938 recording of Bruckner's original score.

The recording is very fine. There is great clarity of detail yet enough atmosphere to convey the work's numinous element.

Symphony No 9
Vienna Philharmonic Orchestra /
Nikolaus Harnoncourt

RCA Red Seal ② 82876 54332-2 (131' · DDD)
Includes a workshop concert with commentary by
Harnoncourt　　　　　　　　　　　　　　Ⓕ

Harnoncourt's flirtations with Bruckner haven't always impressed. He didn't seem to 'know' the symphonies as the old master Brucknerians did. But this live Salzburg Ninth is glorious. There's no sense here of fallible rhythms or a conductor not being able to see the wood for the trees. Like all great interpreters of the Ninth, Harnoncourt treats the opening movement as a vast tripartite structure – exposition, countervailing statement and coda – which can be taken in a single glance. Nor is there any falling off in the *Scherzo* or the great concluding *Adagio*, both of which are beautifully paced and expertly realised in terms of each new harmonic salient. In beauty of sound and accuracy and articulacy of ensemble, the Vienna Philharmonic matches, even occasionally surpasses, its own high standards in this work. All of which must have helped the Teldex engineers, who make the acoustically problematic Grosses Festspielhaus sound like one of the great Bruckner halls.

Additional recommendations

Symphony No 9
Saarbrücken Radio Symphony Orchestra /
Skrowaczewski
Arte Nova Classics 74321 80781-2 (61' · DDD)　Ⓢ
　A very closely controlled performance. Skrowaczewski has taken enormous care over the preparation of the performance and the results tell in orchestral playing of a quality and articulacy that few ensembles could rival.

Symphony No 9
Stuttgart Radio Symphony Orchestra /
Carlo Maria Giulini
Video director **Agnes Meth**
ArtHaus Musik **DVD** 101 065
(123' · 4:3 · PCM stereo · 0)　　　　　　　Ⓕ

'My intention always has been to arrive at human contact without enforcing authority … The great mystery of music-making requires real friendship among those who work together.' So said Carlo Maria Giulini, than living in seclusion in Milan. From the first few moments of the rehearsal, you know that he practises what he preaches, a gracious, spiritual presence whose stature doesn't preclude him from apologising at one point to the solo horn for suggesting a misleading dynamic: 'Sorry, that is my mistake – it sounds too much like Debussy.' If you're unfamiliar with Bruckner's Ninth (the one he left incomplete at his death), then this absorbing hour-long sequence will prove a stimulating, unmissable introduction; for aspiring conductors and Brucknerphiles, this and the live concert performance are an essential purchase for repeated viewing.

Masses

No 1 in D minor; **No 2** in E minor; **No 3** in F minor

Masses Nos 1ª, 2 & 3ᵇª
Edith Mathis, ᵇ**Maria Stader** sops ª**Marga Schiml,**
ᵇ**Claudia Hellmann** mezzos ª**Wiesław Ochman,**
ᵇ**Ernst Haefliger** tens ª**Karl Ridderbusch,**
ᵇ**Kim Borg** basses **Bavarian Radio Chorus and
Symphony Orchestra / Eugen Jochum**
DG ② The Originals 447 409-2GOR2 (148' · ADD · T/t)
Recorded ª1963, ᵇ1971, ᶜ1972. ⓂⓄⒷ→

Like Bruckner, Eugen Jochum came from a
devout Catholic family and began his musical life
as a church organist. He would have known the
Mass texts more or less inside out, which explains
why his readings focus not on the sung parts –
which, for the most part, present the text in a
relatively four-square fashion – but on the
orchestral writing which, given the gloriously
full-bodied playing of the Bavarian orchestra, so
lusciously illuminates familiar words. He
approaches the Masses with many of the same
ideas he so eloquently propounds in his recordings of the symphonies and the music unfolds
with a measured, almost relaxed pace which creates a sense of vast spaciousness. This can have its
drawbacks: you can be so entranced by the beautifully moulded orchestral introduction to the
Benedictus from the D minor Mass that the entry
of a rather full-throated Marga Schiml comes as a
rude interruption. DG's transfers are extraordinarily good – they really seem to have produced a
sound which combines the warmth of the original
LP with the clarity of detail we expect from CD.

Mass No 2ª. Ave Maria. Christus factus est. Locus iste.
Os justi. Pange lingua, 'Tantum ergo'. Vexilla regis.
Virga Jesse floruit
Polyphony; ª**Britten Sinfonia / Stephen Layton**
Hyperion CDA67629 (70' · DDD · T/t) ⒻⓄⒷ→

Hyperion long ago paid signal service to Bruckner's mature settings of the Mass with recordings
by Matthew Best's Corydon Singers of all three
(see review of the F minor below). Interestingly,
their 1985 recording of the E minor Mass has also
been re-reissued on the budget Helios label, providing pretty powerful opposition to any new
release, let alone one at full price. But while the
Corydons were the choir *par excellence* on Hyperion in the 1980s and '90s, the torch has been passed
to Polyphony, whose sound is, if anything, even
more smoothly rounded, more fully blended and
more sumptuous. In Stephen Layton, too, they
have a director who is every bit as openly communicative, and while Best reveals the soul of Bruckner's sacred utterings more intensely, Layton (who
also uses the 1882 version), produces such gorgeous sound from his singers that the overall listening experience is infinitely satisfying.
There's no doubt that the latest Hyperion
recording, made in Ely Cathedral, has more

presence and atmosphere than that made over
20 years earlier in St Alban's Church, Holborn.
That certainly helps produce an ideal balance
between wind ensemble and singers, the delicate
woodwind flutterings of the *Benedictus* providing
a delicious undercurrent to the broad, spacious
choral lines. The rare moments of climax are
nicely restrained and never impinge on the overall calmness of Bruckner's setting.
Splendid as the performance of the Mass is, the
seven unaccompanied motets which surround it
on this disc are absolute gems. An ethereal
account of *Ave Maria* has a breadth and grandeur which belies its short time-span; as the
vocal lines crowd in on each other, the effect is
nothing short of electrifying. And popular as it
is, if there is to be a 'definitive' interpretation on
disc of *Locus iste*, this has to be it. Put simply,
we're unlikely to hear choral singing as fine as
this for a good few years to come.

Mass No 3. Psalm 150 in C
Juliet Booth sop **Jean Rigby** mez **John Mark
Ainsley** ten **Gwynne Howell** bass **Corydon Singers
and Orchestra / Matthew Best**
Helios download CDA66599 (68' · DDD · T/t) ⒻⒷ→

The F minor Mass can certainly be regarded as
being among the finest music Bruckner ever created. The intensity of religious feeling is heightened rather than diminished by the sumptuous
orchestral support, and the soaring melodies
and opulent harmonies are somehow purified
and enriched by the devotional character of
these familiar texts. Matthew Best's performance, by understating the music's abundant richness, gives tremendous point to the inner conviction of Bruckner's faith. His orchestra,
sounding as if it has been playing this music all
its days, plays with commendable discretion,
balancing admirably with a relatively small choral body. As with everything the Corydon Singers and Best turn their hands to, it's an impeccable performance, infused with real artistry and
sensitive musicianship. Enhanced by the glorious solo voices from a high-powered team this is
a CD of rare depth and conviction.

Te Deum

Te Deumª. Symphony No 1
ª**Jessye Norman** sop ª**Yvonne Minton** mez
ª**David Rendall** ten ª**Samuel Ramey** bass
Chicago Symphony ª**Chorus and Orchestra
/ Daniel Barenboim**
DG download 435 068-2GGA (69' ·DDD) Ⓜ Ⓑ→

The download-only reissue of this 1980 Chicago
recording of the boisterous First Symphony (in
its original Linz version of 1866) under Barenboim is a very attractive choice, particularly if you
don't mind adding to your collection a superb –
eloquently sung, expertly played, exceptionally
well recorded – account of Bruckner's mighty *Te
Deum*. In it, the Chicago Symphony Chorus

boasts basses to challenge the magnificent Samuel Ramey himself. The tenor could be better matched, though hardly more ardent. As for Jessye Norman's all-too-brief contribution, it so ravishes the ear as to leave one frustrated that Bruckner did not entrust more of the work to the siren-voiced daughters of Eve.

In the symphony, Barenboim is witty, affectionate and vital and the Chicago playing is sumptuous without in any way being bland or suffocating. Here and there one might long for the countrified tread of Jochum, a German Bruckner conductor of the old school, but one can understand DG's desire to give the best of this Barenboim Bruckner cycle another airing.

Antoine Brumel · French c1460-c1515

Little is known of Brumel's early life, though he was certainly born in France. He sang at Notre Dame, Chartres, from 1483 until 1486; afterwards he held posts in Geneva and Laon. In 1498 he took charge of the choirboys at Notre Dame, Paris, and in 1501 he was a singer at the Chambéry court of the Duke of Savoy. From 1506 to 1510 he was choirmaster to Alfonso I d'Este in Ferrara, a post in which he succeeded Jacob Obrecht. He stayed in Italy where, at 'a ripe old age', he died. The bulk of his music is sacred, notably Masses (15 survive complete) and motets.

Missa Et ecce terrae motus

Missa Et ecce terrae motus
Ensemble Clément Janequin; Toulouse Saqueboutiers / Dominique Visse
Harmonia Mundi HMC90 1738 (58' · DDD · T/t) Ⓕ

Until somebody finds Ockeghem's 36-voice motet (which almost certainly did exist), Brumel's so-called 'Earthquake Mass' must count as the earliest seriously large composition – not just in its 12 voices, used together almost throughout, but also in its sheer length.

Another reason it's so long is that Dominique Visse likes to linger over particular passages and bring out some of the inside details. This is most welcome, because the previous two recordings of the cycle (Paul Van Nevel in 1990 and Peter Phillips in 1992) tended to keep a steady tempo and charge past much of the lovely inner writing Visse makes more audible. Especially in the 'Benedictus' and the *Agnus Dei*, he reveals new glories in this enormously complicated score. His flexibility of tempo also makes it possible for the singers to give more value to the texts, which is again a welcome change.

His recording is fundamentally different in other ways, too. Whereas Phillips had 24 voices and no instruments, and Van Nevel had four instruments, Visse has 12 voices and 12 instruments. Whether Brumel is likely to have had such forces around 1500 seems unlikely, but it

brings certain advantages: it makes it possible to pitch the whole thing fairly low without losing clarity on the crucial bottom lines and to have men singing the top line.

The result has a slightly nasal quality that isn't at all in line with what we expect here; those who dislike this may be a lot happier with the direct brilliance of the Tallis Scholars under Peter Phillips. But it's a beautifully balanced ensemble with a coherent and unusual sound; and it brings out unexpectedly different qualities in the music. If you love this work, one of the most fascinating and original of the years around 1500, you'll want this recording alongside the others.

Gavin Bryars · British b1943

Bryars studied philosophy at Sheffield University and music privately; in the 1960s he played in jazz groups as a double-bass player, and he has lectured at Leicester Polytechnic (now De Montfort University) where he founded the music department. Early influences included Morton Feldman, Earle Brown and the minimalist composers. One of his earliest works, The Sinking of the Titanic (1969), allows the performers to choose a number of sound sources and create the music from them. And his best-known work, Jesus' Blood Never Failed Me Yet (1971) is structured over a loop of a homeless man improvising a hymn. His has written a Cello Concerto, three operas, three string quartets as well as ballet scores, including one, Biped (2001) for Merce Cunningham.

String Quartets

String Quartets – No 1, 'Between the National and the Bristol'; No 2; No 3. Die letzten Tage
Lyric Quartet (Jonathan Carney, Edmund Coxon vns Nick Barr va David Daniels vc)
Black Box BBM1079 (63' · DDD) Ⓕ

A quiet strain of melancholy passes through all three of Gavin Bryars's string quartets, though the Third and latest – which was commissioned by, and is dedicated to, the Lyric Quartet – has a bardic feel to it that's quite unlike the others. Part of the reason lies in the use of pure intervals which in turn reflects a passing preoccupation with the world of early music.

Bryars's original plan for the First Quartet had been to create a sort of compositional séance where memories of such past masters as Ysaÿe, Hindemith and Schoenberg would be conjured musically. In the event it's the Second Quartet that's more suggestive of musical side-references: to John Adams of *Shaker Loops* and the Schoenberg of *Verklärte Nacht*, though these are probably just coincidental similarities.

All that needs to be said about the music Bryars says himself in the booklet-note, much as he did for the Balanescu Quartet's Argo CD of the first two quartets. There the coupling is *Die letzten*

Tage for two violins but this disc will hold the greater appeal for those. building their quartet repertoire on CD. Comparing the two versions finds the colour-conscious Balanescu employing a subtler range of nuance while the Lyric press for greater emphases and rather more in the way of inner voice detail. Either disc will probably find you returning to this haunting, though by no means immobile, music again and again.

Choral works

Bryars Lauda 22. Lauda 23. Lauda 24. Glorious Hill.
Cadman Requiem. **Ešenvalds** Legende de la femme emmurée **Vasks** Zilis zina **Anonymous** Fammi cantar l'amor. Dammi conforto Dio
**Latvian Radio Choir / Ieva Ezeriete,
Kaspars Putnins, Sigvards Klava**
GB Records BCGBCD09 (78' · DDD)   Ⓕ Ⓑ→

Gavin Bryars's music and the special qualities of the Latvian Radio Choir fit one another like hand and glove. And the glorious acoustic of Riga Cathedral lends its aura to his *Cadman Requiem* and two 13th-century chants (the latter chosen because they relate to, and effectively offset, the three Bryars *Laude*).

All this music has a restrained purity that never admits suspicions of opportunism, in the way some work in this spiritual minimalist field does. There is more floridity to Eriks Ešenvalds's *Legend of the Walled-up Woman*, but this too feels like part of the natural voice of the music and its subject matter. Only in Pēteris Vasks's *Zilis zina* does the impression surface of special effects for special effects' sake. And even that can be taken as an effective vehicle for this remarkable choir to display the full range of its talents.

Bryars's 12-minute *Glorious Hill*, which lends its title to this generously filled disc, sets a marvellous Italian Renaissance text that imagines God addressing Adam as He confers free will on mankind. Even more powerful in its inspiration and consistent in its focus is the *Cadman Requiem*, composed in memory of a friend killed in the 1988 Lockerbie disaster. In this new version with organ rather than strings or viols, the music is utterly gripping, and affinities with the Fauré Requiem stand out in ways not previously registered. Overall then, an eminently collectable disc, beautifully sung and recorded from first note to last.

Geoffrey Burgon   British b1941

Burgon started his music studies with the intention of becoming a jazz trumpeter, but once at the Guildhall School of Music an interest in composition took over. He wrote a number of successful ballet scores for the Ballet Rambert and London Contemporary Dance Theatre. In 1976 his Requiem was heard at the Three Choirs Festival and shortly afterwards the BBC adaptation of John la Carré's Tinker, Tailor,

Soldier…Spy put him on the map through its use of the Nunc dimittis as its theme music. In 1981 he wrote the score for Brideshead Revisited: Burgon resisted the subsequent offers from Hollywood to concentrate on concert music. He has produced a substantial opus embracing all genres from sacred works to film and TV scores.

Concertos

Viola Concerto, 'Ghosts of the Dance'[a].
Cello Concerto[b]. Merciless Beauty[c]
[a]**Philip Dukes** *va* [b]**Josephine Knight** *vc*
[c]**Sarah Connolly** *mez* **City of London Sinfonia /
Rumon Gamba**
Chandos CHAN10592 (63' · DDD)   Ⓕ Ⓑ→

Despite its surface simplicity, Burgon's music remains difficult to pin down. Having come to composition relatively late, a distinguished career in film and TV soundtracks has produced a musical style that continues to evade easy classification. There's something strangely familiar yet distant about Burgon.

Rather apt, then, that this recording's centrepiece should be a viola concerto subtitled *Ghosts of the Dance*. Written in 2008, the work's ambiguous subject matter is reflected in quixotic changes of mood and tempo, most noticeable in the opening movement. Burgon's sparse orchestration adds to a heightened sense of disembodiment. The dark, hypnotic second movement (a *quasi tango*) is especially effective, vividly characterised by soloist Philip Dukes.

The other concerto on this disc, for cello, is less striking, partly because Burgon eschews his concentrated style for a more expansive narrative approach. As a result, the musical thread woven by the solo cello threatens at times to become entangled in its own circular patterns and frequent pauses suggest creative dead ends rather than new openings.

Listeners will no doubt detect the influence of film composition in Burgon's concert music and in the song-cycle *Merciless Beauty* its impact is as subtle as it is profound. Sung here by mezzo-soprano Sarah Connolly, Burgon's tightly focused style generates some truly arresting moments, especially in the two 'Anna' songs. A film sensibility may lie at the core of Burgon's musical personality but there is much here in terms of expressive weight and musical content to ensure that his music stands firm without the need for visual support.

William Busch   British 1901-1945

Busch studied the piano in Berlin with Leonid Kreutzer – and to some extent with Backhaus and Egon Petri – and harmony and composition with Hugo Leichtentritt. From 1924 onwards he completed his training in London. He first became known as a pianist, making his debut in London in 1927, and later in Berlin and New York. During the 1930s he was well known in England and was a regular broadcaster. However, composition was his chief interest, and from about 1935 he devoted more and more time to it. For several years before his early death he was a sick man, often unable to work. It was in pursuit of better health that he settled at Woolacombe, Devon, where his last compositions, mainly elegiac in tone, were written.

Concertos

Cello Concerto[a]. Piano Concerto[b]
[a]**Raphael Wallfisch** vc [b]**Piers Lane** pf
Royal Philharmonic Orchestra / Vernon Handley
Lyrita SRCD320 (52' · DDD)　　　　　　　Ⓟ Ⓑ➔

Here's another rewarding discovery courtesy of Lyrita, this time two substantial concertos by a composer born in London in 1901 to naturalised German parents. William Busch initially studied piano in Berlin with Wilhelm Backhaus and Egon Petri in the early 1920s, as well as composition under John Ireland, Alan Bush (his close friend and near-contemporary) and Bernard van Dieren.

Nerves scuppered a promising career on the concert platform, so from the mid-1930s onwards Busch decided to devote himself full-time to composition. He died tragically young, aged just 43, the victim of a brain haemorrhage, shortly after the birth of his daughter, Julia.

The Cello Concerto bears a dedication to Florence Hooton (who first performed it at a 1941 Prom) and proves a beautifully wrought, enviably terse yet warm-hearted score, its modal lyricism and appealingly ruminative manner strikingly prescient of Finzi's gorgeous Cello Concerto (lovers of the latter should most certainly lend an ear). Premiered in January 1939 with the composer as soloist partnered by Sir Adrian Boult and the BBC SO, the Piano Concerto wears a knottier, more harmonically adventurous demeanour which shows a shrewd awareness of continental trends audaciously out of kilter with attitudes prevailing within the British musical establishment of the period, its meaty opening *Allegro* and finale (a resourceful theme and 32 variations) framing a bittersweet central *Allegretto tranquillo*.

As one might expect from the calibre of the artists involved, the performances are all one could wish for. Eminently truthful sound and balance, too, for this enterprising coupling, which is definitely worth seeking out.

Alan Bush　　　　　　　British 1900-1995

Bush studied at the Royal Academy of Music and privately with John Ireland, going on to study musicology and philosophy at Berlin University. He also studied the piano under Moiseiwitsch and Schnabel. In 1925 he began teaching at the RAM and in 1936,

already a committed communist, founded the Workers' Music Association, later becoming its president. He taught at the RAM until 1978. After the war he simplified his style and began a series of operas expressing his political beliefs, though he had to endure an embargo on performance of his music: Wat Tyler (1953), Men of Blackmoor (1960), The Sugar Reapers (1966) and Joe Hill (1970) were all produced in East Germany. His output includes four symphonies and a Piano Concerto which includes a male chorus in the last movement, declaiming a Communist text.

Chamber Works

Three Concert Studies, Op 31[abd]. Two Easy Pieces[ad]. Two Melodies, Op 47[ac]. Sonatina, Op 88[ac]. Concert Piece, Op 17[ad]. Summer Valley, Op 125[ad]
[a]**Catherine Summerhayes** pf **Adam Summerhayes** [b]vn/[c]va [d]**Joseph Spooner** vc
Meridian CDE84458 (67' · DDD)　　　　　　Ⓕ

The challengingly rhapsodic *Concert Piece* for cello and piano was written prophetically as war clouds were gathering in Europe. The music's angst expresses real despair, the harmony bleakly astringent. Yet there's a touching central cantilena of the utmost sadness before the malevolent closing section with its march rhythms builds to an urgent and uncompromising climax. One then turns to the balm of the Sonatina for viola with its pastoral atmosphere (the opening and close might almost be by Vaughan Williams) or the lovely, very English evocation of a *Summer Valley* (ravishingly played here). These three artists have obviously lived with this music and play very sympathetically indeed and with fine ensemble.

There's all the expressive power needed in Op 17, while the central 'Nocturne' of the Op 31 *Concert-Studies* for piano trio is haunting in its gentle atmospheric feeling, and the closing 'Alla Bulgaria' great fun. The two charming *Easy Pieces* for cello, and the pair for viola (both with piano) show Bush's disarming melodic gift.

In short, this CD combines excitement and real stimulation, lyrical strength and musical pleasure, in varying measure. Let John Amis, who wrote the booklet-notes, have the final word. He tells us that 'Bush was a delightful man' who 'wrote music for head and heart, and many times managed to combine the two elements…these [works] are all masterly and endearing.'

Ferruccio Busoni　　　Italian/German 1866-1924

With an Italian clarinettist for a father and an Italian-German concert-pianist (Anna Weiss) for a mother, it was not surprising that their extravagantly named offspring should become a musician. Busoni was playing the piano in public from the age of eight, made his debut in Vienna at 10 and con-

ducted his own choral work in Graz, to where the family had moved, at the age of 12. For the rest of his life, he managed to combine the role of international virtuoso (and Busoni was one of the great pianists of history) with that of composer, developing his own complex theories of music and art. A man of formidable intellect, he sought to combine in his art the warmth of Italy and the formality of Germany; he postulated the idea that the octave could be divided into 36 intervals among other avant-garde theories; he advocated the possibilities of electronic music and microtonal music – not that any of this made any appearances in his own works. He was strictly a classicist at heart and couldn't bring himself to write music as daring as his theoretical ideas. Little of Busoni's music has survived beyond the many masterly transcriptions he made of Bach's instrumental works which have remained standard repertoire for pianists all over the world.

He held various teaching posts throughout his career (Helsingfors – where one of his students was Sibelius – Moscow, New England, Bologna) but was based mainly in Berlin with his wife and two sons. Among the pianists and other musicians who passed through his hands were Egon Petri, Dimitri Mitropoulos, Percy Grainger, Kurt Weill and the extreme avant-gardist Edgar Varèse but, in the end, when he died of kidney disease aged 57, it was clear that his strongest influence was on the next generation of pianists – not as a trail-blazing composer.

Piano Concerto

Piano Concerto
Marc-André Hamelin pf Men's Voices of the
**City of Birmingham Symphony Chorus and
Orchestra / Mark Elder**
Hyperion CDA67143 (72' · DDD)   Ⓕ**OO**

Busoni's Piano Concerto has never become a repertoire piece. It fits awkwardly into a concert programme, due to its length and its choral finale, and the extreme difficulty of its solo writing can't quite disguise the fact that it's really more of a symphony with an elaborate piano part than a real concerto. This new recording might just change all that, for like no other performance (not even Garrick Ohlsson's stunning account on Telarc) it proves what a richly enjoyable piece it is. Without in the least understating the grandeur of the central movement (or its Faustian pointers to Busoni's later style), it finds humour not only of the gallows kind in the first *Scherzo* (even a touch of irony to its nostalgic centre), while the brilliant tarantella second *Scherzo* is often very funny indeed: Busoni celebrates his Italian ancestry, but at times bursts into helpless laughter at it as well. Hamelin obviously loves the work's opportunities for grand romantic pianism and barnstorming, and he has a fine ear for its stark boldness. Elder is splendidly eloquent, from the nobly Brahmsian introduction to the full-throatedly sung finale. Both are at their best in the central *Pezzo serioso*, which is grand and grave, but alert to the presence of Chopin as well as Liszt. The recording is

warm and spacious, the piano at times just a touch (but forgivably) close. This is a remarkable performance.

Violin Concerto

Violin Concerto[a]. Violin Sonata No 2[b]
Frank Peter Zimmermann vn
[b]**Enrico Pace** pf [a]**RAI National Symphony Orchestra
/ John Storgårds**
Sony Classical SK94497 (54' · DDD)   Ⓕ

Frank Peter Zimmermann performs an inestimable service by coupling two of the most approachable works by a master too often sidelined as excessively prolix. Prior to hearing this assured and musically persuasive account of the Violin Concerto, only Joseph Szigeti and Adolf Busch have really made it work.

It's an early piece, premiered in Berlin in 1897, a three-movement structure that plays without a break. Busoni himself called the Concerto 'good…if unpretentious', quietly original, too, though near the start you'll hear a short passage that replicates almost to the note the transition from first to second subjects in the first movement of Brahms's Violin Concerto. Busoni's Concerto is at its darkest in the *Quasi andante* where solo and orchestral voices are beautifully integrated. The bustling finale is filled with typically Busonian playfulness, felicitously scored music that's stylishly played by Zimmermann – his tonal polish and technical mastery reminiscent at times of both Milstein and David Oistrakh.

The half-hour Violin Sonata, a seminal piece from 1900, opens more like the Busoni we know and love (or not, as the case may be) and owes an obvious debt to both Beethoven and Schubert. The first movement is mostly sombre and austere, the *Scherzo* a manic tarantella, then after a brief slow movement there's a set of variations based on a chorale-like theme, a world on its own that incorporates elements of dance, fugue and virtuoso display. The transition to the closing *Allegro* unmistakably echoes Schubert's great C major Fantasy. Again Zimmermann comes up trumps with a modern benchmark, matched in spirit and expertise by his pianist Enrico Pace. A marvellous disc, not to be missed on any count.

Orchestral Works

Turandot – Concert Suite, Op 41. Sarabande und Cortège: Zwei Studien zu Doktor Faust, Op 51. Berceuse élégiaque, Op 42
**Hong Kong Philharmonic Orchestra /
Samuel Wong**
Naxos 8 555373 (71' · DDD)   ⓈⒹ▸

Of the six works recorded here, two are essential for anyone interested in Busoni: the *Berceuse élégiaque* and the *Sarabande und Cortège*. Samuel Wong, music director of the Hong Kong Philharmonic, is on this reading an interesting artist.

He takes the *Berceuse élégiaque*, for example, at a very slow tempo and indeed its pace suggests mournful sighing rather than the rocking of a cradle. The extraordinary end of the piece, string chords with the dark glow of gong strokes, is quite magical, partly because it's so sombrely slow. In the *Cortège*, also a touch slow, he misses something of Busoni's mercurial quality but imparts a lovely nobility to its string counter-subject.

Every one of the *Turandot* suite's movements is entertaining, two are Busoni at his most imaginative (the strikingly malign fourth and the sinister seventh) and they're all brilliantly and characterfully played. Wong's intriguing musicality and Naxos's bargain price make this a worthwhile issue.

Piano Works

Sieben Elegien. Perpetuum mobile. Prélude et Etude en arpèges. Sieben Kurze Stücke zur Pflege des polyphonen Spiel
Roland Pöntinen *pf*
CPO CPO999 853 2 (73' · DDD)   Ⓟ

Few composers have more resolutely avoided popularity than Busoni. Like Rachmaninov and Liszt he took a jaundiced view of his career as a virtuoso pianist, seeing it as a vainglorious alternative to the serious business of composition. Is this why his work so often exudes an atmosphere of dark intellectuality and desolation? Such music, in Alfred Brendel's words, only 'begins to glow when the right eye falls on it', and in Roland Pöntinen it surely has an ideal interpreter. His playing is subtly and brilliantly judged and, whether in the far-reaching Elegies, the more didactic *Kurze Stücke* or in the *Perpetuum mobile*, where Busoni temporarily rises from the slough of despond, his sympathy and virtuosity are unfailing. The recordings are excellent; those looking for an uneasy rather than comfortable experience need look no further.

Busoni Fantasia contrappuntistica, K255/6.
Liszt/Busoni Fantasia and Fugue, 'Ad nos, ad salutarem undam' **Mozart/Busoni** Piano Concerto No 9, K271 – Andantino
Hamish Milne *pf*
Hyperion CDA67677 (71' · DDD)   Ⓟ Ⓞ

This daunting and inspired coupling is played by Hamish Milne with an uplifting musical authority. Indeed, aided by Hyperion's superb sound (rich and resonant throughout the entire register), you are made to realise that the *Ad nos* Fantasy – a massive tribute to Busoni as transcriber – is not only among his finest achievements but (as Milne suggests in his accompanying notes) transcends Liszt's original organ work and seemingly takes on a life of its own. The central *Adagio* in particular has all of Liszt's obsessive and ecstatic wheeling round an idea

yet is unmistakably stamped with Busoni's own intimidating power. And it is here in particular that Milne offers playing of the rarest refinement and sensitivity before launching the final fugue in a blaze of virtuosity.

Busoni's *Fantasia contrappuntistica* takes such music to a further extreme. Among the composer's most formidable works, its colossal range and scope tell you that Busoni's music can seem like a mighty mountain range glimpsed behind clouds. Again, Milne's performance is of an unfaltering beauty and lucidity. As an extra he sandwiches Busoni's transcription of the *Andantino* from Mozart's *Jeunehomme* Concerto between these two peaks, a rarity where Mozart's sublimity is coloured by Busoni's altogether more forbidding personality. Milne may playfully claim in his notes that he would 'like to play like Bill Evans and Ahmad Jamal and sing like Flagstad', but we should surely be mightily grateful for his own unmistakable personality.

Die Brautwahl

Die Brautwahl
Siegfried Vogel *bass* Voswinkel **Carola Höhn** *sop* Albertine **Graham Clark** *ten* Thusman **Vinson Cole** *ten* Lehsen **Pär Lindskog** *ten* Baron Bensch **Roman Trekel** *bar* Leonhard **Günter von Kannen** *bar* Manasse **Chorus of the Deutsche Staatsoper, Berlin; Staatskapelle Berlin / Daniel Barenboim**
Teldec ② 3984 25250-2 (116' · DDD · N/T/t)   Ⓟ Ⓞ ➔

Busoni's first mature opera occupied him for seven years (1905-11). He may not have been as natural a man of the theatre as Richard Strauss, but *Die Brautwahl* has plenty of fine music in it – at times foreshadowing the splendours of *Doktor Faust*. This 1992 Berlin production used a version made by Antony Beaumont, whose completion of *Doktor Faust* was a great success. As Beaumont explains in the booklet, we get only about two-thirds of the whole, and all aspects of the opera's subject-matter may not be ideally balanced. This 'fantastic comedy' is based on a story by ETA Hoffmann, with the climactic scene in which a bride is chosen (hence the title) leaning heavily on *The Merchant of Venice*. The action is set in Berlin, but there are echoes of Wagner's Nuremberg in the text and characterisation. Musically, Busoni keeps his distance from Wagner, and the music is attractive, ranging widely in character.

This performance is a strong one, with a certain, untroublesome amount of stage noise. No doubt reflecting the staging, the recording occasionally recesses the singers, but the energy and command of Barenboim's conducting are never in doubt. The energy does not mean that anything is rushed, and the romantic episodes are warmly moulded, the scenes of fantasy properly attentive to matters of colour and texture. Roman Trekel, a warm yet dramatically resonant baritone, makes a strong impression as Leonhard. He's the perfect foil to Graham Clark, who tackles the role of Thusman with relish, and with considerable technical skill in music which demands lyrical sensitivity as well as comic agility.

Doktor Faust

Doktor Faust
Dietrich Henschel *bar* Doktor Faust **Markus Hollop**
bass Wagner, Master of Ceremonies **Kim Begley** *ten*
Mephistopheles **Torsten Kerl** *ten* Duke of Parma **Eva
Jenis** *sop* Duchess of Parma **Detlef Roth** *bar* Soldier
William Dazeley *bar* Natural Philosopher **Eberhard
Lorenz** *ten* Lieutenant **Frédéric Caton** *bass*
Theologian **Jérôme Varnier** *bass* Jurist **Dietrich
Fischer-Dieskau** *spkr* Poet **Geneva Grand Theatre
Chorus; Chorus and Orchestra of the Opéra
National de Lyon / Kent Nagano**
Erato ③ 3984 25501-2 (196' · DDD · N/T/t) Ⓜ️Ⓞ➔

Finally we have a recording that not only provides the full, uncut text, as completed by Busoni's pupil Philipp Jarnach soon after the composer's death, but also offers as supplements Antony Beaumont's very different realisations of parts of the opera's later stages. So complete is this version, indeed, that it includes the spoken prologues and epilogues, with Dietrich Fischer-Dieskau providing a poignant link to DG's heavily cut 1969 recording.

Given that Beaumont worked from sketches and other information of which Jarnach was unaware (or chose to ignore), there can be no question as to which of the two is the more genuinely Busonian, and the extended closing scene in Beaumont's version has a persuasive gravity and sense of fulfilment quite different from Jarnach's more terse yet slightly melodramatic completion. Nevertheless, it will take a sensibility more refined than most not to be swept away by the sheer visceral power of Jarnach's rendering of the death of Faust.

Dietrich Henschel displays considerable style and stamina during his two extended monologues in the opera's final stages, and although his singing isn't entirely free of straining for effect, or of bluster, the character's tortured humanity is vividly conveyed. Kim Begley makes a considerable success of the other principal role, although, in an ideal world, Mephistopheles would manage more variety. But Begley tackles the many demanding aspects of the part with panache and, in the scintillating ballad, wit and menace are in perfect balance. Other parts are adequately taken, though articulation of the German text varies in clarity and accuracy.

This variability is one reason why the performance takes some time to take wing: another, more fundamental reason concerns the rather dry nature of the recording itself. At times, principal voices are backwardly placed, and, even when they aren't, one suspects that the brilliance of the orchestral sound is being damped down in order to ensure their audibility. Nevertheless, Nagano's shaping of this extremely demanding score is neither inflexible nor inexpressive. *Doktor Faust* can at last be heard in a recording

that, in the end, reaches and reveals its essence, and whose documentary value is inestimable.

Doktor Faust
Thomas Hampson *bar* Doktor Faust **Günther
Groissböck** *bass* Wagner; Master of Ceremonies
Gregory Kunde *ten* Mephistopheles **Reinaldo
Macias** *ten* Duke of Parma; Soldier **Sandra Trattnigg**
sop Duchess of Parma **Martin Zysset** *ten* Lieutenant
Andreas Winkler *ten* 1st Student from Cracow **Thilo
Dahlmann** *bass-bar* 2nd Student from Cracow
Matthew Leigh *bar* 3rd Student from Cracow
Giuseppe Scorsin *bass* Gravis **Tomasz Slawinski**
bass Levis **Gabriel Bermúdez** *bar* Asmodus **Randall
Ball** *ten* Belzebuth **Miroslav Christoff** *ten* Megäros
**Zürich Opera House Chorus and Orchestra /
Philippe Jordan**
Stage director **Klaus Michael Grüber**
Video director **Felix Breisach**
ArtHaus Musik ② 📀 101 283 (172' · NTSC · 16:9 ·
PCM stereo, 5.1 and DTS 5.1 · 0)
Recorded live in 2006   Ⓕ

Presented here is Philipp Jarnach's version (completed for the premiere, unaware of the composer's notes for its unfinished sections, realised only by Antony Beaumont 60 years later) which Philippe Jordan prefers on musical grounds, 'whether it really fits with the rest of the work or not'. He approves of Jarnach's use of Wagnerian leitmotif and darker conclusion, finding it 'simply overwhelming' and Beaumont's more positive finale 'drier'. Jarnach's version is – unavoidably – a misrepresentation of Busoni's vision and stylistically jars the moment it starts. Beaumont's may be a musicologist's rather than composer's edition but it gives us more of Busoni's intentions.

That aside, this production has many strengths. Hampson, after seeming ill-at-ease in the first Prelude, audibly grows into the role. Trattnigg is beguiling as the Duchess and Macias shines as the Soldier (Gretchen's grief-stricken brother) and pompous Duke. The show is stolen, however, by Gregory Kunde's Mephistopheles, a portrayal vocally superb throughout and brilliantly acted. The Zürich Opera House Chorus are excellent. Some of Jordan's tempi are a tad measured but the orchestra's playing is assured.

There are minor annoyances: for instance in Prelude 1, why do the Students not bring Faust the book, key and paper they sing about? A major omission is the Students' serenade to Wagner (Faust's former familius) at the start of the final scene. Wagner's replacement of Faust as Rector is included in the sung text and meaningless without its representation onstage. Musically, the cut section provides vital contrast between the defiance of the second scene's close and the denouement. Felix Breisach's video direction is commendably unfussy, catching both the scale of the production's biggest moments as well as Kunde's mischievous expressions. The Devil is truly in the detail.

Martin Butler English b1960

Butler studied piano and composition at the RNCM and the University of Manchester (1978-82), following which he undertook postgraduate studies with Babbitt and JK Randall at Princeton University (1983-87). He became a lecturer at the University of Sussex in 1988 and was later appointed reader in music. Also in 1988 he was awarded the Mendelssohn Scholarship which enabled him to work at Tempo Reale, Berio's electro-acoustic studio in Florence, on Graffiti. Butler has forged a distinctive musical identity rooted, on the one hand, in the European tradition of Stravinsky and Berio, and, on the other, in American folk and popular music, and minimalism.

Chamber works

American Rounds. Funérailles[a]. Nathaniel's Mobile[a]. Sequenza notturna[b]. Siward's River Song[c]. Suzanne's River Song[d]. Walden Snow[e] **D Scarlatti** Sonatas (arr Butler) – Kk119; Kk215
Schubert Ensemble of London
([bd]Simon Blendis *vn* [be]Douglas Paterson *va* [bc]Jane Salmon *vc* Peter Buckoke *db* [abcde]William Howard *pf*)
NMC NMCD120 (72' · DDD) Ⓕ☐▶

Martin Butler's contribution to the chamber domain has been a significant one. All of these pieces were written over the past decade with the Schubert Ensemble in mind: the earliest being *American Rounds* – which combines American folk idioms with a rhythmic impetus whose Stravinskian incisiveness is anything but mindlessly post-minimalist. Equally engaging are the 'River Songs' derived from the chamber opera *A Better Place*, its restrained yet evocative mood distilled in the threnody for Siward and the effulgent lyricism of that for Suzanne. On a lighter note, the two Scarlatti transcriptions – respectively vigorous and poetic – evince a keen ingenuity. The most striking works, however, are the two piano pieces: *Nathaniel's Mobile* – which intercuts linear and harmonised melody so the music evolves, without intensifying, towards its conclusion; and *Funérailles*, which adds a more disruptive element that opens out the music's dynamic and emotional range on the way to its quiet yet restive close. *Sequenza notturna* passes through several expressive vignettes, given focus by the unassuming viola melody that underpins them, while *Walden Snow* is a 'postcard' from New England of touching limpidity.

The performances are as sensitive and assured as one would expect from the Schubert Ensemble, continuing their laudable contribution to British new music, and the sound is a model of chamber balance. Informative notes from John Fallas, and a disc that should extend the audience for a composer whose idiom – distinctive but accessible and never remotely facile – is nowhere better represented than here.

George Butterworth British 1885-1916

After school at Eton and university at Trinity College, Oxford, Butterworth pursued his passion for music first by collecting folksongs (inspired by the work of Cecil Sharp and Vaughan Williams). Butterworth also studied folk dancing, particularly Morris dancing. He was instrumental in encouraging VW to write his London Symphony and, having had to reconstruct the score with Edward Dent, the full score having been lost, VW dedicated the piece to him. He combined the careers of teaching (Radley), music criticism and composing until he was called up at the outbreak of the First World War. He served as a lieutenant in the Durham Light Infantry and was killed in action, aged 31. He was recommended for the Military Cross. Of his relatively small output, Butterworth is best known for his settings of AE Housman (particularly for A Shropshire Lad) and for his orchestral work The Banks of Green Willow.

Songs

'The Complete Butterworth Songbook'
A Shropshire Lad. Eleven Folksongs from Sussex. Love Blows as the Wind Blows. Bredon Hill and Other Songs from 'A Shropshire Lad'. Haste on, my joys!. I will make you brooches. I fear thy kisses. Requiescat
Mark Stone *bar* **Stephen Barlow** *pf*
Stone Records 506019 2780024 (71' · DDD) Ⓕ❌❌

The label is Mark Stone's, his the informative notes, and he is of course also the very good singer: we are much indebted to him. Most of us know Butterworth in association with AE Housman – the *Shropshire Lad Rhapsody* and the six songs, with possibly a few additional songs such as 'Bredon Hill'. As for Butterworth's life, as Mark Stone says, what is still best known about that is his death at the age of 31 on the Western Front in 1916. Its poignancy is driven home by this collection of his songs, which helps greatly to clarify an individuality both sympathetic and distinctive.

It will also do no harm at all to Mark Stone's already considerable reputation as a singer. As many amateur baritones will have discovered, the *Shropshire Lad* songs do not always sit as comfortably on the voice as may be supposed. The third song, 'Look not in my eyes', is an example, and it suits Mark Stone admirably. Stephen Barlow is his excellent pianist and together they give a particularly fine performance of 'On the idle hill of summer', the masterpiece among the Housman settings. Enjoyable too are the folksong arrangements, and an unexpected bonus is a short piece of film (playable on a PC) in which Butterworth is seen dancing.

Dieterich Buxtehude German c1637-1707

Better known for his influence on JS Bach than for any of the influential music itself, Buxtehude was one of the greatest organists of his day. In 1668 he suc-

*ceeded one Franz Tunder as organist of the Marien-
kirche in Lübeck, among the prime musical posts in
Germany. One of the conditions attached to the post
was that the newcomer should marry the incumbent's
daughter – which Buxtehude duly did. Some 35 years
later the German composer Johann Mattheson
applied to be his successor and took his friend Handel
with him. 'We listened with much attention as good
artists,' he wrote, 'but as a matrimonial alliance was
proposed for which neither of us had the slightest
inclination, we departed having had much enjoyment'. All five of Buxtehude's daughters were singularly lacking in appeal apparently.*

*Lübeck became a Mecca for German musicians.
Bach, aged 20, is supposed to have walked the 200
miles from Arnstadt just to hear Buxtehude play,
overstayed his leave of absence and almost lost his job.
Whether or not the story is true, the effect of Buxtehude's vocal and keyboard works on Bach, one of the
most important composers in musical history, was
crucial.*

Organ works

Complete Organ Works
Bernard Foccroulle org
with **Bernarda Fink** mez **Dirk Snellings** bass
Ricercar ⑤ RIC250 (6h 50' · DDD)   Ⓕ**O**

What better way to mark the 300th anniversary
of Buxtehude's death in 1707 than with this
wonderful box-set? Its 77 tracks reaffirm what a
central figure Buxtehude was to subsequent
generations of Northern European organists
working in the German Lutheran tradition.

These recordings (made between 2003 and
2006) are played on two historic Schnitger
instruments in the Ludgerikirche, Norden,
and the Martinkerk, Groningen, two recent
organs in Hoogstraten (near Antwerp) and the
German Church, Stockholm, and the reconstructed Lorentz-Frietzsch organ in Helsingor's
St Maria Church, parts of which Buxtehude
himself played.

The 19 organ praeludia form the core of
Buxtehude's organ oeuvre and are considered
his most important contributions to the 17th-
century literature. Their quasi-improvisatory
flair and brilliance always sounds spontaneous, at times quite extrovert. Foccroulle wisely
contrasts them with the much plainer devotional chorale settings. He teases endlessly
fresh solo timbres from these striking instruments. The variety of tuning temperaments
keeps the ear alert and the playing is constantly inspiring.

The careful juxtaposition of pieces means that
each disc makes a highly satisfying programme in
its own right. By way of an epilogue the set concludes with the poignant *Klag-Lied* for organ and
vocal duet. Other complete Buxtehude organ sets
have clearly been superseded by this release.

'Opera omnia VIII – Organ Works, Vol 3'
Auf meinen lieben Gott, BuxWV179. Canzonetta,

BuxWV225. Ciacona, BuxWV159. Durch Adams Fall
ist ganz verderbt, BuxWV183. Erhalt uns, Herr, bei
deinem Wort, BuxWV185. Es spricht der Unweisen
Mund wohl, BuxWV187. Fugue, BuxWV176. Herr Jesu
Christ, ich weiss gar wohl, BuxWV193. Komm, heiliger
Geist, Herre Gott, BuxWV200. Nun lob mein Seel'
den Herren – BuxWV213; BuxWV214; BuxWV215.
Prelude and Fugue, BuxWV145 – Prelude.
Praeludiums – BuxWV149; BuxWV140; BuxWV137;
BuxWV148
Ton Koopman org
Challenge Classics CC72247 (66' · DDD). Played on
the Schnitger organ of St Jacobi Kirche, Hamburg   Ⓕ

Koopman's programme displays examples of
the five distinct genres of improvisatory
styles central to the organist's craft in Lutheran
Germany: multi-sectional *Pedaliter* preludes,
freer large-scale preludes in the *stylus phantasti-
cus*, ostinato-based pieces and two types of
chorale movements. And where better to present a selection of Buxtehude's broad compositional spectrum than the oft-recorded 1693
Schnitger organ in Hamburg's St Jacobi
Church?

Koopman's approach remains refreshingly
free, radical even, the no-nonsense opening
Prelude in G minor setting the tone for that
which follows. Ornamentation is tastefully
florid and melodic lines are allowed to sing out
naturally. Tempo changes seem effortless and
Koopman achieves a near-perfect balance of
dextral clarity and pace. The warm Hamburg
acoustic helps.

Among the many highlights, mention must be
made of the Chaconne in C minor. Koopman
obviously relishes the piece's innovations (a
direct inspiration for JS Bach). In addition, the
setting of the chorale *Nun lob mein Seel'* combined with verses 2 and 3 of BuxWV213 makes a
logical set of four variations. The Schnitger's
wealth of registers never tires the ear. Its soothing, limpid flutes and sparkling and spitting
upperwork are superbly captured by sound engineer Adriaan Verstijnen. He presents a deep
sound stage, with plenty of ambience and sense
of height, an effect enhanced by the floor-
wobbling 32-foot registers.

'Opera omnia X – Organ Works, Vol 5'
Bruhns Nun komm der Heiden Heiland. Prelude and
Fugue in E minor No 1, 'The Great' – Praeludium
Prelude and Fugue in E minor No 2 – Praeludium
Prelude and Fugue in G – Praeludium **Buxtehude**
Herr Christ, der einig Gottes Sohn, BuxWV191. Herr
Christ, der einig Gottes Sohn, BuxWV192. Ich dank
dir, lieber Herre, BuxWV194. Magnificat primi toni,
'Dorian', BuxWV204. Magnificat noni toni,
BuxWV205. Mensch, willt du leben seliglich,
BuxWV206. Nun bitten wir den heilgen Geist,
BuxWV208. Nun bitten wir den heilgen Geist,
BuxWV209. Prelude and Fugue, BuxWV142 –
Praeludium. Prelude and Fugue, BuxWV151 –
Praeludium. Prelude and Fugue, Phrygian, BuxWV152
– Prelude. Prelude and Fugue, BuxWV143 –
Praeludium. Prelude and Fugue, BuxWV158 –

Praeambulum. Te Deum laudamus, BuxWV218.
Toccata and Fugue, BuxWV155 – Toccata. Von Gott
will ich nicht lassen, BuxWV221. Wär Gott nicht mit
uns diese Zeit, BuxWV222. Praeludium, BuxWV153.
Praeludium, BuxWV136. Praeludium, BuxWV150
Ton Koopman org
Challenge Classics ② CC72249 (113' · DDD)
Played on the Bielfeldt organ of St Wilhadi, Stade Ⓕ

This two-CD release concludes Ton Koopman's
complete survey of Buxtehude's organ and harpsichord works. He plays on a three-manual
organ which was built between 1731 and 1735
by Erasmus Bielfeldt. Its silvery choruses are
perfectly matched to Koopman's fresh – almost
flighty – approach to Buxtehude's *stylus phantas-
ticus*. The recording's sound stage has a clear
sense of depth and breadth. Majestic, rotund
climaxes are handled as adeptly as the smaller-
scale manuals-only passages. Tonal combinations are constantly refreshed. The hurdy-gurdy
effect in the chorale prelude *Von Gott will ich
nicht lassen* is especially engaging. Pedal solos
(whether at 16-, eight- or four-feet pitches) cut
through with ease.

As in the previous instalments these discs
include a contrasting mixture of extended multi-
sectional preludes and three types of chorale-
based works: compact polyphonic settings,
elaborate and highly expressive fantasias, and
pieces based on Latin liturgical melodies. Right-
hand solo voicings are particularly plangent in
the second category.

The second CD is made up with the complete
surviving organ works of Nicolaus Bruhns
(1665-97), a gifted pupil of Buxtehude. Bruhns
displays a young man's exuberance and desire to
display his technical prowess, and is no slavish
copier of his teacher. His idiom is highly distinctive and his keyboard writing beautifully balanced.

Each disc makes a satisfying recital on its own.
Key juxtapositions and tempo changes between
tracks make perfect sense and the playing,
recording and documentation are first rate.
Koopman has done Buxtehude proud.

Harpsichord works

'Opera omnia VI – Harpsichord Works, Vol 2'
Aria, BuxWV246. Aria and Three Variations,
BuxWV249. Canzona, BuxWV166. Canzonetta,
BuxWV168. Courante, BuxWVAnh6. Rofilis,
BuxWV248. Toccata and Fugue, BuxWV165. Suites –
BuxWV227; BuxWV229; BuxWV236; BuxWV237;
BuxWV239; BuxWV240; BuxWV241; BuxWV244;
BuxWVdeest
Ton Koopman hpd
Challenge Classics ② CC72245 (97' · DDD)   Ⓕ

Performing on two copies of Stefanini and
Ruckers harpsichords, Ton Koopman completes the exquisite solo *oeuvre* by Buxtehude
with captivating élan. For a musician with somewhat precipitous tendencies, Koopman here
delivers a considered programme of mainly

standard four-movement suites, interpolated
with other contemporaneous genres, from variations to the flamboyance of the *stylus phantasti-
cus* of toccatas and the like.

Koopman's most significant achievement is
the poetry he brings to Buxtehude's cultivated
and understated world of pre-Telemann domestic music. This is where the Suites appear as the
apogee of a tradition which Froberger honed
and which Bach extended in his early works.
Indeed, keen ears will notice the prescient
melodic seeds of the *English Suites* and, more
specifically, the Canzona in C whose turns perhaps inspired the ambitious young Turk in the
Capriccio in E (BWV993).

That aside, witness the sheer richness of Buxtehude's luminous textures, as well as the finely
drawn and grateful melodic contours. The
opening Aria in C (with 10 variations) reveals
the warmth of both Buxtehude's hypnotically
life-affirming variations and Koopman's concentrated placement and esprit.

Within such compositional calibre and refinement, Koopman also explores a steeliness in the
investigative lines of the fine C major Suite
which concludes the first disc; as throughout,
the tempo relationships between movements are
thoughtfully rendered, with the 'gamey' mean-
tone tuning and elegant characterisation all
conspiring towards a notable 'world premiere'
set of harpsichord recordings. In sum, an outstanding release in this enterprising series.

Membra Jesu nostri, BuxWV75

Membra Jesu nostri   Ⓟ
**The Sixteen; Symphony of Harmony and Invention
/ Harry Christophers**
Linn CKD141 (61' · DDD · T/t)   ⒻⒹ➔

Composed in 1680, this group of seven tiny
cantatas – each meditating on a part of Christ's
body (feet, knees, hands, side, breast, heart and
face) – represents an extreme in formal compression. Each cantata has just six movements:
an instrumental introduction, a choral setting of
the relevant Biblical citation, three short solo
arias, and a repeat of the chorus. Few of those
movements last more than 90 seconds and some
are a lot shorter. But the real catch is that the
solo arias are all on texts consisting of 80-syllable
trochaic lines: Buxtehude sets the vast majority
of them to four-bar phrases, which can lead to
musical predictability. The first task of musicians is to counteract the numbing regularity of
those phrases. They approach this by adopting a
generally very smooth rhythmic style, benefiting much from the marvellous continuo group
of Paul Nicholson (organ), Jane Coe (cello) and
Elizabeth Kenny (theorbo): all three superbly
resourceful in their range of colours and attacks,
without ever interrupting the music's flow.
Above this the violins of David Woodstock and
Walter Reiter glow or sparkle as the music
requires. In line with today's best practice, the
choruses are taken just by the five excellent solo

singers, led by Carolyn Sampson in luscious form. A wonderfully moving account of Buxtehude's remarkable cycle of cantatas.

Sacred Cantatas

Sacred Cantatas   🅿
Fuga, BuxWV174. Ich habe Lust abzuscheiden, BuxWV47[abc]. Ich halte es dafür, BuxWV48[bc]. Jesu meine Freude, BuxWV60[abc]. Mein herz ist bereit, BuxWV73[cd]. Herr, wenn ich nur dich hab, BuxWV38[b]. Salve, Jesu, Patris gnate unigenite, BuxWV94[ab]. Jesu dulcis memoria, BuxWV56[ab]. Cantate Domino, BuxWV12[abc]
[a]**Emma Kirkby**, [b]**Suzie LeBlanc** *sops* [c]**Peter Harvey** *bass* [d]**Clare Salaman** *vn* **Purcell Quartet** (Catherine Mackintosh *vn/va* Catherine Weiss *vn* Richard Boothby *bar vio* Robert Woolley *org*)
Chandos Chaconne CHAN0691 (76' · DDD · T/t) Ⓕ🅑➔

Setting various German and Latin texts for solo voices, violins and continuo, these sacred cantatas are typical products of the late 17th century in their pragmatic approach to form.

Here are patchworks such as *Jesu dulcis memoria* and *Salve, Jesu, Patris gnate unigenite*; chorale or song variations such as *Jesu, meine Freude*; and others, like *Ich halte es dafür* and *Ich habe Lust abzuscheiden*, which combine the two. *Cantate Domino* is liltingly Italianate, *Mein Herz ist bereit* is an agile showpiece for solo bass, while *Herr, wenn ich nur dich hab* is a set of variations over a ground bass. The Purcell Quartet's essential string sound has always been sweet, airy and lucid, and it's interesting to hear how that has been transferred here from the instrumental sphere to the vocal. To this end the choice of singers is important, and on this occasion they could hardly have picked more shrewdly: Emma Kirkby and Suzie LeBlanc make an excellent pairing, distinguishable from each other in both voice and approach, yet at the same time superbly matched in duet; and Peter Harvey has the friendliest of bass voices, his alert account of *Mein Herz ist bereit*, set against the thrillingly radiant background of three violins, being one of the disc's highlights.

An expert recording in an amenable acoustic completes a release of many refined pleasures.

Fried- und Freudenreiche Hinfart, BuxWV76. Gen Himmel zu dem Vater mein, BuxWV32. Singet dem Herrn ein neues Lied, BuxWV98. Was mich auf dieser Welt betrübt, BuxWV105. Herr, wenn ich nur dich hab, BuxWV38. Sicut Moses exaltavit serpentem, BuxWV97. O dulcis Jesu, BuxWV83. O fröhliche Stunden, BuxWV84. Schaffe in mir, Gott, BuxWV95
Emma Kirkby *sop* **John Holloway, Manfred Kraemer** *vns* **Jaap ter Linden** *va da gamba* **Lars Ulrik Mortensen** *org/hpd*
Naxos 8 557251 (72' · DDD)   Ⓢ

Those enamoured of opulent voices may wonder why Emma Kirkby is the undisputed first lady of early music, but this anthology of Buxtehude's music for solo voice and instruments captures much of what makes her so special: she has acute awareness of dance forms in her delivery of rhythms (even in slower music), a crystal-clear tone, superb agility in quick passages and a marvellous sense of rhetorical communication. The mournfully sublime *Klaglied* (BuxWV76 No 2) is movingly performed. Also superb is the lovely 12-minute *O dulcis Jesu*.

Ritornellos are beautifully articulated by violinists John Holloway and Manfred Kraemer, and Lars Ulrik Mortensen's organ continuo is delightful. The programme is 100 per cent authentic Buxtehude, spellbindingly performed, with an excellent essay by the leading authority Kerala Snyder (although sung texts are not included). Emma Kirkby and her accomplices do more to illustrate why he is the supreme genius of the generation before JS Bach.

'Opera omnia XI – Vocal Works, Vol 4'
Gott fähret auf mit Jauchzen, BuxWV33. Jesu dulcis memoria, BuxWV56. Erfreue dich, Erde!, BuxWV26. Lobe den Herrn, meine Seele, BuxWV 71. O Gott, wir danken deiner Güt, BuxWV86. Canite Jesu nostro, BuxWV11. Erhalt uns, Herr, bei deinem Wort, BuxWV27. Att du, Jesu, vil mig höra, BuxWV8. Man singet mit Freuden vom Sieg, BuxWVAnh2. Frohlocket mit Händen, BuxWV29. Wo soll ich fliehen hin?, BuxWV112. Ist es recht, dass man dem Kaiser Zinse?, BuxWV54. Also hat Gott die Welt geliebet, BuxWV5. In te, Domine, speravi, BuxWV53. Herr, nun lässt du deinen Diener, BuxWV37. Jesu, meine Freud und Lust, BuxWV59. Das neugeborne Kindelein, BuxWV13
Amsterdam Baroque Choir and Orchestra / Ton Koopman
Challenge Classics ② CC72250 (131' · DDD)   Ⓕ

The 11th volume of Ton Koopman's complete series of Buxtehude's works (the fourth to include vocal music) was recorded in batches across a two-year period. It is uncertain which of Buxtehude's extant compositions were intended for his famous Abendmusik concerts at the Marienkirche in Lübeck although Christoph Wolff speculates in his booklet commentary that some of the arias, sacred concertos and cantatas in this anthology might have resembled the kind of repertoire the composer performed on such occasions.

The cornetts, trumpets, trombones and timpani in the introductory sonata of *Gott fähret auf mit Jauchzen* emphasise Buxtehude's Italianate leanings; the colourful splendour produces an exciting sound, although Koopman ensures that the trio of soloists (Bettina Pahn, Miriam Meyer and Klaus Mertens) are never swamped by the impact of the full instrumental passages. Buxtehude's more intimate music is perhaps the most beguiling: Siri Thornhill and Meyer combine to lovely effect in the strophic duet *Jesu dulcis memoria*, and the long concerto *Lobe den Herrn, meine Seele* is ardently sung by Jörg Dürmüller (even if his voice seems more effortful than usual). The vocal quintet that performs *O Gott, wir danken deiner Güt* is impeccably balanced and expressive, and the trio *Canite Jesu nostro* is a radiant and springy encouragement to praise God with 'zithers, cymbals and organs'. A finely paced performance of the substantial chorale cantata *Wo soll ich fliehen hin?* contains particularly beautiful string ritornellos but the highpoint of the anthology is Johannette Zomer's stylish performance of the virtuoso concerto *Also hat Gott die Welt geliebet*.

The Amsterdam Baroque Choir sings with conviction and flair; its unbridled sopranos overpower the choral sections of the grander cantatas and the inner parts are less distinct than some other conductors might insist upon. Koopman's organ continuo playing may be fussily ornamental for some tastes but he provides an interesting short note in which he contemplates the value of works that are of doubtful authenticity: a couple are included in this anthology, most notably the anonymous but splendidly thrilling *Man singet mit Freuden vom Sieg*. Koopman's advocacy for Buxtehude continues to produce fruits that will nourish any music lover appreciative of German sacred repertoire before Bach.

Quemadmodum desiderat cervus, BuxWV92. Singet dem Herrn ein neues Lied, BuxWV98. Lobe den Herren, meine Seele, BuxWV71. Herr, wenn ich nur dich hab, BuxWV38. O fröhliche Stunden, BuxWV84. Herr, nun lässt du deinen Diener, BuxWV37. Fugue, BuxWV175. Toccata and Fugue, BuxWV164
Hans Jörg Mammel ten **La Fenice / Jean Tubéry**
Alpha ALPHA113 (56' · DDD · T/t)   Ⓕ

This collection of Buxtehude's church concertos (and a few other miscellaneous bits) has been hand-picked and thoughtfully researched by the outstanding German tenor Hans Jörg Mammel. Any admirers of the warm musicianship of Jean Tubéry and his ensemble La Fenice will not hesitate to investigate this. The richly exotic continuo group (including harp and theorbo) and cornetts put Buxtehude's instrumentation into glorious Technicolor (*Quemadmodum desiderat cervus*, for example). When a more restrained approach to scoring is taken the results are equally sublime. For example, the effect of the solo voice, violin, viola da gamba and keyboard continuo unfurls gloriously without unnecessary additives in *Singet dem Herrn*.

It is not rare to hear Buxtehude's intimately scaled church music sung by sopranos, countertenors and even basses, but it seems that tenors have infrequently got in on the act. Mammel is an assured singer of intelligent quality, and, although he often sounds rooted in his baritonal chest voice, his occasional excursions upwards prove to be particularly well rounded and sweetly judged, and his agile singing is well illustrated by the tricky coloratura in *Herr, nun lässt du deinen Diener*. It seems as if he has genuinely absorbed the meaning of texts and is narrating a story rather than merely singing lovely pious

music. Also, full marks to Alpha for yet another lovingly prepared recording with its customary emphasis on fine artwork.

William Byrd   English 1543-1623

If Tallis was the first important English composer, Byrd was the first English composer of genius, unquestionably the greatest of the Elizabethan era. He, more than anyone – even Purcell – can claim to be the father of British music.

Byrd may have studied under Tallis as a young man. What is certain is that at the age of only 20 he was appointed organist of Lincoln Cathedral and in 1572 he moved to London to become joint organist of the Chapel Royal with Tallis. The two of them obtained the exclusive licence to publish music in England, in effect an early attempt to establish copyright. After Tallis's death, the licence passed wholly into Byrd's hands: he was an astute businessman and well able to look after himself during protracted litigation over ownership of the property in Essex to which he moved in 1593 with his second wife.

Like Tallis, Byrd was an ardent Catholic as well as being a royal musician and wrote for both the Roman and English Churches (which says something for the state of religious tolerance under Elizabeth I, though it must be said that much of his Latin music was written for private worship). Byrd's range was far wider than Tallis's, however, and his liturgical music, motets, madrigals, chamber and keyboard works show him to be among the most complete musicians of the age.

What exactly did he add to the musical language? Just as JS Bach was to do, Byrd combined the passionate with the intellectual. He was adventurous in his harmony and experiments with structure, the music had great rhythmic variety and complex syncopation to an unprecedented degree and he was more free in his melodic ideas than his contemporaries. Listening to Byrd's music you can hear many apparently 'wrong notes' (discords) where the independent intertwining melodic parts clash harmonically in passing before being resolved. Such collisions seem totally logical – and nothing out of the ordinary to our modern ears – but Byrd was at the cutting edge of new music. 'What I have written are not misprints,' he once said. Obviously he felt a need to make this clear!

Consort works

Byrd Fantasia a 5, BE17/8. Browning a 5, BE17/10. Ⓟ Fantasias a 6, BE17/13-14. In nomines a 5, BE17/19-22 **Mico** Fancies a 4 Nos 4a, 5-7, 9, 10, 14, 18 & 19. Pavans a 4 Nos 2-4
Phantasm (Laurence Dreyfus, Wendy Gillespie, Jonathan Manson, Markku Luolajan-Mikkola *viols*) with **Martha McGaughey, Alison McGillivray** *viols*
Simax PSC1143 (60' · DDD)   Ⓕ

The odd juxtaposition of Byrd's very finest chamber music with pieces by Richard Mico may seem rather like pairing late Beethoven with Vanhal but it works extremely well. Though Mico has been little regarded, much of his music shows absolute mastery (his Pavan No 4 is in some ways one of the most perfect and beautiful examples of the simple eight-bar pavane). The Mico selection includes two pieces that are by no means certainly his (*Fancies* Nos 18 and 19); but they're still fine work. Phantasm play this music with immaculate control and balance, finding many telling details that might elude less careful musicians. Some listeners may be a touch less happy with the Byrd, feeling that the honeyed sounds cover certain details, that the speed of *Browning* loses the work's harmonic and contrapuntal magic, that the myriad changes in the grand six-voice *fantasias* could benefit from greater lightness of touch. But that would be like saying that only the English can perform Elgar idiomatically. What Phantasm bring to this music is a clear and unusual view of the music. Moreover, they present what's absolutely the best of Byrd's consort work, omitting the troublesome first *In nomine* and the less perfect first six-part *Fantasia*. The four *Fantasias* and the four *In nomines* on this disc are the core of Byrd's claim to stand among the world's greatest composers of chamber music. The performances convincingly support that claim.

Complete Keyboard Works

23 Pavans and Galliards (with two additional [P] Pavans and five Galliards). 14 sets of Variations. 11 Fantasias. 11 Grounds. Nine Preludes. Miscellanea and variant versions
Davitt Moroney chbr org/clav/hpd/muselar virg/org
Hyperion ⑦ CDA66551/7 (8h 17' · DDD) Ⓜ**OOO**☞)
Selected highlights available on Ⓕ CDA66558

The three volumes of keyboard music added in 1950 as an afterthought to Edmund Fellowes's edition of Byrd have only slowly made their full impact as containing one of the most remarkable and innovative repertories in the history of music. A much-needed new edition by Alan Brown (1969-71) was followed by Oliver Neighbour's important critical study (1978), which perhaps for the first time made it clear that Byrd wasn't just another of the 'Elizabethan Virginalists' but stood head and shoulders above all his contemporaries – in range, contrapuntal technique, melodic invention and above all formal control and imagination. Davitt Moroney has completed the picture by presenting the entire body of music on seven CDs. The results here are a triumph for all concerned. Moroney has the music in his hands, head and soul. There are so many fine details in his playing that it's hard to know where to begin in its praise: the wonderful clarity of the part-writing; the superb energy of the playing; the glittering virtuosity; the ability to vary the colours and move from the ineffably light and whimsical to the seriously confrontational; the constant delicate flexibility of his metre; or his compelling grasp of Byrd's often difficult formal designs.

Moroney approached this Everest of a project over many years, in constant consultation with Brown and particularly Neighbour (who, appropriately enough, plays the 'third hand' for the duet *Fantasia* on disc 4). The engineers have coped well with the different recording venues and occasions. Six different instruments are used to vary the colour and to fit the different styles of the music. The most novel is the muselar virginal, a marvellously earthy instrument with a refreshingly noisy action. The others are plainly chosen with loving care. A harpsichord by Hubert Bédard (after Ruckers) tends to be used for the lighter pieces, while he chooses one by Reinhard von Nagel (after Couchet) for some of the more serious works. Neatly enough, the set ends with a prelude already heard on Ahrend's Toulouse organ, now played on four different instruments in turn (omitting only the chamber organ). Alongside all this, Moroney has provided the most detailed set of notes: 200 pages of wide-ranging erudition (in English and French) including a key to the 'BK' numbers of the Brown edition which are used throughout his running prose. So when you've got through the 497 minutes needed to listen to the discs, you still have several hours of reading to do.

Masses

Masses – for Three Voices; for Four Voices; for Five Voices (ed Skinner). Fantasias[a] – in G, 'A Voluntary for My Ladye Nevell'; in D minor; C, 'A Fancie for My Ladye Nevell'
[a]**Patrick Russill** org **The Cardinall's Musick / Andrew Carwood**
ASV Gaudeamus CDGAU206 (79' · DDD · T/t)
Ⓕ**OOO**

This is incomparable music by one of the greatest English composers and it was high time for someone to take a fresh look at these works in the light of more recent research and of changing attitudes to performance practice.

Byrd had composed his three settings of the Ordinary of the Mass in troubled times for the small recusant Catholic community that still remained in England in spite of persecution. The settings would have been sung, in all probability, during festive, albeit furtive, celebrations of the old time-honoured Roman liturgy, in private chapels in the depths of the country, at places such as Ingatestone, the seat of Byrd's principal patron, Sir John Petre. Andrew Carwood has recorded them in the Fitzalan Chapel of Arundel Castle, a small but lofty building with a clear resonance that enables the inner voices of the part-writing to come through straight and clean. It hasn't the aura of King's College Chapel, but is probably easier to manage than, say, Winchester Cathedral or Merton College Chapel.

Carwood uses two voices to a part in all three Masses. In comparison with rival recordings he's alone in selecting high voices for the three-part Mass, transposed up a minor third, which introduces a note of surprising lightness and grace. He, too, is alone in taking the initiative of using an all-male choir for the four-part Mass – alto, tenor, baritone, bass. This close, low texture, together with the transposition down an augmented fourth, adds a fitting sense of gravity to the performance. In particular, it heightens the poignancy of such passages as the 'dona nobis pacem' in the *Agnus Dei*, with its series of suspensions in the drooping phrases leading to the final cadence.

That dimension of understanding is precisely what this recording by The Cardinall's Musick so keenly demonstrates. Theirs is a simplicity of style that belies simplistic criticism. Vibrato is used sparingly: 40 years on, some listeners might consider its constant use by a King's Choir of the late 1950s almost too overpowering. Carwood chooses his tempi with care, avoiding the modern tendency to speed everything up inordinately.

The interesting historical note on the whole background is a good pointer to what the listener may experience as the music unfolds.

Masses – for Three Voices; for Four Voices; for Five Voices. Motet – Ave verum corpus a 4
The Tallis Scholars / Peter Phillips
Gimell CDGIM345 (67' · DDD · T/t) Ⓕ🅞🅞🅓➔

Byrd was a fervently committed Roman Catholic and he helped enormously to enrich the music of the English Church. His Mass settings were made for the many recusant Catholic worshippers who held services in private. They were published between 1593 and 1595 and are creations of great feeling. The contrapuntal writing has a much closer texture and fibre than the Masses of Palestrina and there's an austerity and rigour that's allowed to blossom and expand with the text. The beautifully restrained and mellow recording, made in Merton College Chapel, Oxford, fully captures the measure of the music and restores the awe and mystery of music that familiarity can dim.

'Playing Elizabeth's Tune'
Ave verum corpus. Great Service – Magnificat. Masses – for Three Voices; for Four Voices; for Five Voices. Ne irascaris Domine. O Lord make thy servant. Prevent us, O lord. Tristitia et anxietas. Vigilate. Tribue, Domine. Diffusa est gratia. Nunc dimittis servum tuum
The Tallis Scholars / Peter Phillips
Video directors **Philip George, Rhodri Huw**
Gimell 📀 GIMDP901 (184' · 16:9 · PCM stereo & 5.0 · 0). Includes a documentary about the life and music of Byrd, presented by Charles Hazlewood Ⓕ

In 2002 the Tallis Scholars recorded an audio-visual Byrd-fest in three parts: a concert-format sequence of some of his sacred music in the atmospheric setting of Tewkesbury Abbey; a documentary of his life and his relationship

to his powerful patroness, Queen Elizabeth I; and, as an 'audio bonus', another outing for the Scholars' outstanding version of the three Byrd Masses, recorded in Merton College Chapel.

Charles Hazlewood fronts the documentary; casually attired and casually unshaven, he has a degree of ease, if not exactly charm, in front of the camera. He traces adeptly and fluently the different phases of Byrd's career, with stunning visuals of Lincoln Cathedral, the Chapel Royal and Ingatestone Hall as impressive backdrops. The whole is lent authority through the erudite but accessible contributions of experts on Reformation England (Christopher Haigh) and Byrd's music (David Skinner). Hazlewood sums up by talking about the hidden depths of passion in Byrd's music, and its range, though given that the documentary is slanted towards his development as a composer of church music, we get only background snippets of his keyboard and consort music. Nevertheless, the tale is well told, not least with added visual elements such as shots of 16th-century documentation, the original printed editions of Byrd's music and his own beautifully penned autograph.

As to the performances, it's interesting to hear Peter Phillips emphasise the passionate nature of Byrd's sacred music, when this aspect is fairly understated in the Tallis Scholars' performances. This isn't to say that they don't have a high degree of intensity at times: on the whole they capture the ebb and flow of the music well, but there's a sense of distance. Phillips talks of getting right inside, of 'ticking along with the music', and that's what he does above all. This may not be the only way to perform Byrd's music but it's still very impressive in the ethereal clarity of the overall sound, and in the total commitment and rare understanding resulting from these musicians' years of experience.

The Great Service

The Great Service. My Ladye Nevells Booke – Fancie in C; Voluntary a 3. Christ rising again. O Lord, make thy servant Elizabeth. Prevent us, O lord. Sing joyfully unto God our strength. Out of the deep. How long shall mine enemies?
Westminster Abbey Choir / James O'Donnell with **Robert Quinney** org
Hyperion CDA67533 (76' · DDD · T/t) Ⓕ➔

This particular work needs no introduction; indeed, some fine recordings already exist of this set, which has become a particular favourite of modern choirs. The atmosphere one associates with this combination of 'artist and repertoire' is present in abundance: warmth and intimacy combined with a certain reserve. At times the latter quality is perhaps too marked, or could have been leavened with a hint of extroversion: the opening track, perhaps, *O Lord, make thy servant Elizabeth*. On the other hand the final selection, *Sing joyfully* (which, like the opening track, is sung *a cappella*) does indeed sound joyful.

In *The Great Service* itself, the character of the interpretations is entirely appropriate, and the choir may be heard at its best there. Its warmth of tone is due to the admixture throughout *The Great Service* of a chamber organ, sensitively handled by Robert Quinney. In the anthem *Christ rising again* the two treble soloists (accompanied by the organ) alternate with the full choir, a strategy that seems unconvincing because the music doesn't always lend itself to so strongly sectional an approach. Otherwise it's very polished and confident performance. Quinney gives equally fluent renditions of the Voluntary and 'Fancie for My Ladye Nevell', completing a disc that fulfils its brief with distinction.

Cantiones sacrae

Cantiones sacrae (1575) – Tribue, Domine. Siderum rector. Domine secundum. Fantasias – C; D. Attollite portas. Miserere mihi. Aspice Domine. Peccantem me quotidie. Salvator mundi II. O lux, beata Trinitas
New College Choir, Oxford / Edward Higginbottom with **Timothy Morris** *org*
CRD CRD3492 (64' · DDD · T/t)   Ⓜ▷

There's so much wonderful six-part writing in this attractive selection from the 1575 *Cantiones sacrae* that such a medium appears in a new light, particularly when performed by the choir and in the acoustic of New College Chapel – where, as Edward Higginbottom reminds us, they 'have been rehearsing for 500 years'. The beauty and balance of the musical architecture is constantly conveyed to the listener, particularly in the six-part writing. It doesn't matter whether these compositions were intended for liturgical or domestic use, or as a noble offering to the Queen: from a purely musical point of view they're superb. To give a single example, the little Vespers hymn *O lux, beata Trinitas* displays consummate craftsmanship through the ingenious use of the number three – three high, then three low voices, three diverse voices, a canon three-in-one, three strophes, triple time, and so on, building up to a tremendous final 'Amen'. The point made by this recording is that it all sounds natural, uncontrived, magnificent. The three organ pieces are a welcome addition: with their brilliant fingerwork and gentle registrations they present a charming and lively contrast to the vocal settings.

Cantiones sacrae (1589) – Vigilate; In resurrectione tua; Aspice Domine de sede; Ne irascaris Domine. Propers for the Feast of the Purification – Ave regina caelorum; Adorna thalamum; O quam gloriosum; Tribulationes civitatum; Domine secundum multitudinem; Laetentur caeli
The Cardinall's Musick / Andrew Carwood
ASV Gaudeamus CDGAU309 (71' · DDD · T/t)   Ⓕ

ASV's Byrd Edition presents Propers for Candlemas (also known as the 'Feast of the Purifica-

tion'), and further motets from the 1589 *Cantiones sacrae*, many of them composed to strengthen the spirits of the Queen's loyal Catholic subjects in those troubled and highly dangerous times. Which goes to explain the high proportion of sorrowful or penitential texts, the frequent cries for deliverance (*Aspice Domine, Ne irascaris, Tribulationes*), and the mastery with which Byrd sets them. This historical background, vital to an understanding of the music, doesn't exclude the possibility of a joyful outcome: Byrd can also contemplate the ultimate joys of heaven (*O quam gloriosum, Laetentur caeli*).

The choir enters deeply into an understanding of what lies behind these pieces. And Byrd is never averse to raising his singers' spirits by introducing a jaunty rhythm – the crowing cock in *Vigilate*, for example – or a bright, rising theme to inspire hope. The choir responds with sustained restraint, perfect balance and crisp rhythms.

The settings of the Propers for Candlemas offer a short recital of their own, this time in the full context of the liturgy for this ancient feast, and following the whole course of events as the story unfolds. A thoroughly satisfying disc.

Gradualia

Gradualia, Vol 1: Saturday Lady Masses in Advent. Domine quis habitabit. Omni tempore benedic Deum. Christe redemptor omnium. Sermone blando a 3. Miserere. Ne perdas cum implis. Lamentations of Jeremiah. Christe, qui lux es a 5. Christe qui lux es a 4. Sanctus. Audivi vocem de caelo. Vide Dominum quoniam tribulor. Peccavi super numerum (all ed Skinner)
The Cardinall's Musick; Frideswide Consort
(Caroline Kershaw, Jane Downer, Christine Garratt, Jean McCreery *recs*) / **Andrew Carwood**
ASV Gaudeamus CDGAU170 (70' · DDD · T/t)   Ⓕ

This is a great start to The Cardinall's Musick's project to record Byrd's complete output. On the disc, some of the shorter motets are entrusted to The Cardinall's' habitual instrumental accomplices, the Frideswide Consort. A full list of sources is given for each piece, along with appropriate editorial commentary. Since Byrd set certain texts a number of times, such precision seems only sensible. Much of this music is new to the CD catalogue, and even in this selection of largely unpublished motets, there are impressive finds (the nine-voice *Domine quis habitabit*, for instance). This repertory is the mother's-milk of English choristers, and of the younger generation of English vocal ensembles The Cardinall's Musick remains perhaps the closest to that tradition outside of actual choral establishments. So they respond to Byrd with a suavity and confidence born of longstanding acquaintance. The expansive penitential pieces, such as the early *Lamentations*, are far removed from the small-scale forms of the *Gradualia*. The Cardinall's Musick respond effectively to these different functions and moods, and the recording complements them admirably.

Gradualia, Vol 2: Nativity of our Lord Jesus Christ –
Puer natus est; Viderunt…omnes fines terrae;
Dies sanctificatus; Tui sunt coeli; Viderunt
omnes fines terrae; Hodie Christus natus est;
O admirabile commercium; O magnum mysterium.
Ave regina caelorum. O salutaris hostia. Confitemini
Domino. In exitu Israel (with Sheppard and Mundy).
Laudate pueri Dominum. Decantabat populus.
Deus in adjutorium. Ad Dominum cum tribularer
(all ed Skinner)
The Cardinall's Musick / Andrew Carwood
ASV Gaudeamus CDGAU178 (73' · DDD · T/t)   ⒻⓄ

This second volume of The Cardinall's Musick's Byrd edition is, if anything, more impressive than the first. It may be a matter of programming, for the works recorded here seem to be of a higher overall calibre: even an obviously experimental piece such as *O salutaris hostia* could have been included on merit alone – yet this appears to be its first recording. Complete surveys sometimes turn up items of lesser interest, yet they also allow one to hear pieces that might have difficulty in finding a home elsewhere: witness the responsory *In exitu Israel*, an intriguing collaborative effort by Byrd and his contemporaries, Mundy and Sheppard. Finally, one can judge for oneself the authenticity of works that modern scholarship has deemed doubtful (such as the opening *Ave regina caelorum*). Most of the pieces here involve male altos on the top line. The centrepiece is a collection of Propers from the *Gradualia* of 1607, this time for the Nativity. As on their first set, Skinner's and Carwood's decision to structure each volume around a set of Propers proves an astute piece of programming, integrating shorter items as it does (such as the various *Alleluia* settings) within a framework that allows them their own space. The singers are on very fine form indeed. It takes confidence to carry off *O salutaris hostia*, whose fierce false relations could so easily have sounded merely wilful. Only in the final, extended settings does the pace flag: the disc's last moments are rather ponderous. That aside, this is a disc to delight Byrd lovers everywhere.

'Assumpta est Maria'
Gradualia – Propers for the Nativity of the Virgin;
Propers for the Annunciation of the Virgin; Propers
for the Assumption of the Virgin. Quem terra, pontus,
aethera. Salve regina. O gloriosa Domina. Memento,
salutis auctor. Salve sola Dei genetrix. Ave maris
stella
The Cardinall's Musick / Andrew Carwood
Hyperion CDA67675 (70' · DDD · T/t)   ⒻⓄⓄⓄ▷

In a monumental series devoted to Byrd's choral music in Latin, this is the third volume comprising motets and hymns to the Virgin. All are from

the collection called *Gradualia* published in 1605. Most are settings for five voices, the programme being varied by the inclusion of some for three, which, as Andrew Carwood remarks in his introductory notes, are 'intimate examples of chamber music', reminding us of their likely purpose, serving a small domestic community of Roman Catholics living in what were for them still insecure times. Carwood also points out that the manner of these compositions suggests that Byrd had found contentment, and is in contrast to the mood of those earlier pieces which lament the persecution, identifying (for instance) with the plight of Rachel weeping for her children. The motets in the present volume are further enlivened by the inclusion of Alleluias, proper only for Easter but finding in this way a deserved place in the complete edition.

Most striking in their sustained vigour are the two motets for the Annunciation to the Virgin, *Vultum tuum* and *Diffusa est gratia*. The happy spirit and concentrated invention of the first are capped by a particularly joyous Alleluia, and the second takes unexpected flight in triple time as it tells how the virgins will be led to the King's temple. Others (*Gaudeamus omnes* a prime example) rejoice in syncopation. Often the Amens come as a final enfolding grace. Some of the three-part hymns are masterly in their technical assurance, setting the voices free to wander and with the lightest touch recalling them to the fold for a cadence. Try *Memento, salutis auctor*: exquisitely wrought.

To the singers and their director is due an additional hymn of praise, though there is an impression here of faces turned downwards and not at all expressive of the cheerful text: very hard to sound happy with voices ironed out as is generally deemed necessary to lose all trace of their natural vibrancy. Later the impression is somewhat dispelled. For that and all else, much gratitude.

Gradualia, Vol 1/ii: Miscellaneous and Office Text –
Laetania. Gradualia, Vol 2: Feast of Saints Peter and
Paul – Introit: Nunc scio vere; Gradual: Constitues
eos…Domine; Alleluia: Solve iubente Deo; Antiphon:
Hodie Simon Petrus; Antiphon: Tu es pastor ovium;
Antiphon: Quodcunque ligaveris. Liber secundus
sacrarum cantionum – Descendit de caelis; Miserere
mei, Deus; Circumdederunt me dolores mortis;
Recordare, Domine; Exsurge, quare obdormis,
Domine?; Levemus corda; Haec dicit Dominus
The Cardinall's Musick / Andrew Carwood
Hyperion CDA67653 (68' · DDD · T/t)   ⒻⓄ▷

Andrew Carwood's programme-note begins with a comment on the motet *Haec dicit Dominus* with which the programme ends. The lament of Rachel weeping for her children is thematic, if indeed we are to see these *Cantiones sacrae* of 1591 as a cry on behalf of the old, true believers besieged in a Protestant stronghold. As Rachel wept then, so (it is suggested) does the Church now. And yet there is hope ('et est spes') and this is the message reiterated throughout these heartfelt works of a master craftsman.

This is the 11th volume in The Cardinall's Musick's edition of Byrd's Latin settings. Apart from the *Cantiones*, the other major source is the *Gradualia* of 1607, probably written for the Catholics of Ingatestone Hall in Essex. The Litany from Book 2 (1605) is the principal variant in the mode of composition, which is dense in imitative polyphony, usually in six parts, concentrated in the intensity of their utterance. Particularly fine examples are the *Miserere mei, Deus* and the vigorous *Exsurge, quare obdormis, Domine?* with its strong, well defined climax.

The performances are admirably directed, responsive to words, clear in their exposition of counterpoint, carefully blended in the homophonic passages. The Cardinall's Musick is an expert body of singers who know exactly what they are doing. Even so, balance and tone are not everywhere ideal: the bass-line, for instance, though utterly reliable, has been so stripped of natural vibrancy that the tone is dulled. A small point, no doubt, in relation to the riches their work is opening up.

'Byrd Edition, Vol 13'
Cunctis diebus. Domine, non sum dignus. Domine salva nos. Gradualia, Vol 1/i: Feast of All Saints – Introit: Gaudeamus omnes; Gradual: Timete Dominum; Alleluia: Venite ad me; Offertory: Iustorum animae; Communion: Beati mundo corde. Gradualia, Vol 1/ii: Miscellaneous and Office Texts – Visita quaesumus, Domine; Deo gratias haec dies. Gradualia, Vol 2 – Venite exultemus Domino. Laudate Dominum. Liber secundus sacrarum cantionum – Afflicti pro peccatis nostris; Cantate Domino; Infelix ego
The Cardinall's Musick / Andrew Carwood
Hyperion CDA67779 (61' · DDD)   Ⓕ❶❷❸❹➔

The membership of The Cardinall's Musick has remained virtually unchanged in the many years their Byrd Edition has taken to complete. As with the last few volumes, this final instalment combines excerpts from the 1591 *Cantiones sacrae* and the Propers from Feast of All Saints from the later, monumental *Gradualia* of 1605/07. It's a mixture also of the celebratory, as though the singers were congratulating themselves on a job well done – as well they might – and the penitential, concluding with the full ensemble in a finely judged and quite extrovert *Infelix ego*, surely one of Byrd's most memorable motets.

Yet the same might be said of so much of this music, the craftsmanship of which is impeccable, and the expression seemingly so heartfelt (try the marvellously restrained *Iustorum animae*, for example). Most of it's taken with trebles on the top lines (as the spirited opener, *Venite exultemus Domino*) but when the line-up consists only of men (as in *Domine, non sum dignus* and *Domine salva nos*), the blend of voices is perhaps still more convincing. There is and has been much to praise, and at a time when early music ensembles are finding it increasingly difficult to get concerts or make records,

the commitment of singers and label alike is a cause for gratitude, perhaps even optimism.

Music for Holy Week and Easter

Plorans plorabit. Passio Domini nostri Jesu Christe secundum Johannem[a]. Adoramus te[bc]. Vespers for Holy Saturday[a]. Mass Propers for Easter Day. Haec dies. Angelus Domini. Mane vobiscum. Post dies octo. Christus resurgens
The Cardinall's Musick / Andrew Carwood [a]ten
with [b]**Robin Tyson** counterten [c]**Patrick Russill** org
ASV Gaudeamus CDGAU214 (76' · DDD · T/t)
                                                   Ⓕ❶❷

The sixth volume of the Byrd Edition is a landmark recording, covering most of Byrd's Holy Week and Easter music, from the St John's Passion choruses for Good Friday to the Octave day of Easter, and including miniature Vespers at the end of the Easter Vigil, and the whole of the Proper of the Mass for Easter Day.

The opening motet, *Plorans plorabit*, recalling the Lamentations chanted earlier in the week, is a stern reminder of the recusant atmosphere in which Byrd lived out his religious beliefs. The straightforward Passion choruses are rightly set into their proper context, an edition of St John's Passion prepared by Byrd's Roman contemporary, Guidetti. Admirably sung, Carwood maintains throughout a remarkable balance between drama and restraint. A gentle consort song, *Adoramus te*, fills the space in the listener's imagination between the burial of Christ and his rising from the dead. The miniature Vespers follow, sung, almost with bated breath, to Byrd's simple three-part settings of the two antiphons, with a correction of Bretts's suggested psalm-tone for the single – and shortest – psalm.

The Mass *Resurrexi* is exhilarating, with surging themes, rhythmic interplay and bursts of joy. Byrd, unable to resist word-painting suggestive of an earthquake at the Offertory, introduces here a note of merriment into a particularly serious liturgy, and doesn't entirely avoid it elsewhere. Thankfully it was under- rather than overplayed.

The solemn final four-part processional *Christus resurgens* is a triumphant restatement of the Easter message: total joy.

Consort Songs

All in a garden green. La volta No 1 in G, 'Lady   Ⓟ
Morley'. O mistress mine I must. Wolsey's Wild.
O Lord, how vain are all our delights. Psalmes, Sonets and Songs – Who likes to love; My mind to me a kingdom is; Farewell, false love. Triumph with pleasant melody. Truth at the First. Ad Dominum cum tribularer. Cantiones sacrae – Attollite portas; da mihi auxilium; Domine secundum actum meum; Miserere mihi, Domine
Sophie Yates virg
I Fagiolini / Robert Hollingworth; Fretwork
Chandos Chaconne CHAN0578 (73' · DDD · T/t) Ⓕ❶

This disc adopts an imaginative approach to programming Byrd's music by presenting works in different genres grouped together to demonstrate a single stage in his development. It includes Latin motets, keyboard dances and variations on popular songs of the day, and sacred and secular songs (and a dialogue) with viols. There's so much here that wins our admiration: the dazzling contrapuntal elaboration of *Attollite portas*, the close-knit texture of *Da mihi auxilium* and the massive *Ad Dominum cum tribularer*; the exuberant variations on *O mistress mine* (neatly played by Sophie Yates) and Byrd's melodic gift in the strophic *O Lord, how vain*. The singers' adoption of period pronunciation – for example, 'rejoice' emerges as 'rejwace' – affects the tuning and the musical sound, it's claimed here, but without rather clearer enunciation the point remains not proven. Probably more upsetting to many will be the Anglicised pronunciation of Latin.

The viol consort gives stylish support and is well balanced, the Fagiolini sopranos occasionally 'catch the mike' on high notes (eg in the passionate pleas of *Miserere mihi, Domine*), and the recorded level of the virginals might have been a little higher without falsifying its tone. But these are minor criticisms of a most rewarding disc.

Rejoice unto the Lord. Ah, silly soul. Come to me, grief, for ever. Constant Penelope. Lullaby my sweet little baby. O dear life. O God that guides the cheerful sun. O that most rare breast. Ye sacred muses. An aged dame. Psalmes, Songs and Sonnets – How vain the toils that mortal men do take; Who likes to love; All as a sea
Robin Blaze *counterten* **Concordia** (Emilia Benjamin, Reiko Ichise, Joanna Levine, Mark Levy, Alison McGillivray *viols* Elizabeth Kenny *lte*)
Hyperion CDA67397 (67' · DDD · T/t) Ⓕ Ⓓ➤

The subject-matter of these songs is wide ranging, from a triumphant celebration of an Elizabethan anniversary, *Rejoice unto the Lord*, to the two laments on the death of Sir Philip Sidney, the quietly poignant funeral song *Come to me, grief, for ever*, and the deeply felt sonnet *O that most rare breast*, the text attributed to Sir Edward Dyer, one of Sidney's circle of poets. A third lament, *Ye sacred muses*, was Byrd's personal, most moving tribute to his great master: 'Tallis is dead, and music dies'.

The performance brings out two seemingly contradictory points. One is the importance Byrd gives to the soloist's line. He admires the fine natural voice, so rare, he says, 'as there is not one among a thousand, that hath it...' He'd have appreciated the voice and art of Robin Blaze, whose sympathetic interpretation of Byrd's melodic style, the rests, the patterning of the phrases and the syncopation, is remarkable. The second point is the way in which viols and lute become an integral part of 'a carol for New Yeares Day' – *O God that guides the cheerful sun*. Their imitation of the movements of the voice in the

little tableau of the old lady tumbling over on top of the hill, spilling her lapful of skulls, is equally delightful (*An aged dame*). And the sprightly rhythms in *All as a sea* brought home the analogy between human life and life on the ocean wave.

Fantasias – a 6 Nos 2 & 3. Pavan and Galliard a 6, BE17/15. Gradualia, Vol 1/ii: Miscellaneous and Office Text – In manus tuas, Domine. Constant Penelope[a]. Content is rich[a]. My mistress had a little dog[a]. The Noble famous Queen[a]. O Lord how vain are all our delights[a]. O you that hear this voice[a]. Psalmes, Sonets and Songs[a] – My mind to me a kingdom is; O that most rare breast. Truth at the First[a]. Out of the Orient crystal skies[a]. O Lord, bow down thine... He that all earthy pleasure scorns[a]
[a]**Emma Kirkby** *sop* **Fretwork** (Richard Boothby, Richard Campbell, Wendy Gillespie, Julia Hodgson, William Hunt, Susanna Pell *viols*)
Harmonia Mundi HMU90 7383 (75' · DDD · T/t) Ⓕ

Byrd's consort songs reveal a homelier, more personal aspect than his sterner sacred music. Many have texts reflecting the earlier part of his life, the reign of Edward VI, a time of moralising piety: *He that all earthly pleasure scorns* would be an obvious example, or *Content is rich*. But that particular song becomes fast and witty in this performance, almost tongue-in-cheek: it's as if the singer has joined the viols and uses a vocal technique to match their bowing.

Emma Kirkby's versatile performance brings these delightful items to life, and Fretwork fill out the texture with sensitive imitative polyphony. Sometimes the soprano's almost-too-perfect clarity of articulation tends to obscure the subtlety of the musical phrasing: Byrd makes a point of measuring the English text with extreme care, and the gentle cross-rhythms he creates are essential, adding to the life and flow of the composition.

The well-chosen programme is interspersed with five instrumental pieces, three Fantasias for viols, and a delightful pairing and sharing Pavan and Galliard. Fretwork excel here with their vibrant rhythms and gorgeous interplay of parts.

John Cage

Cage was one of the most influential composers of the 20th century thanks to his experiments with chance music and his employment of standard instruments in non-standard uses. He studied with Henry Cowell and Arnold Schoenberg, but another major influence as the music of the East. The I Ching became a constant composing guide throughout his life. His most celebrated work is the non-music, 4'3", a piece that employs silence for that given duration – and that can be performed by any player or ensemble. Throughout his life he wrote music for dance companies, notably for Merce Cunningham, alongside his concert works,

As well as being a composer Cage produced prints and scupltural works, and he maintained a busy schedule as a lecturer and teacher. Cage's influence stretched far beyond the 'classical' arena with rock musicians being inspired by his electronic works and his musical philosophies.

The Seasons

The Seasons. Suite for Toy Piano[a]. Concerto for Prepared Piano and Orchestra[b]. Seventy-Four (Versions A & B)[c]
Margaret Leng Tan [a]toy pf/[b]prepared pf **American Composers Orchestra / Dennis Russell Davies**
ECM New Series 465 140-2 (76' · DDD)　　Ⓟ**O**Ⓑ

This is an enchanting CD, every item a sheer delight. Margaret Leng Tan worked with Cage in the last decade of his life, and her earlier recordings show a special sympathy for Cage's keyboard music. The second of her New Albion CDs included the piano solo version of *The Seasons*, and Cage was honest enough to admit to her that he had help from Virgil Thomson and Lou Harrison in making the orchestral version recorded here. The result is Cage at his most poetic, evoking each of the four seasons in lovely changing colours.

There are two realisations of one of the last of what are called Cage's 'Number Pieces', *Seventy-Four*, written for the American Composers Orchestra a few months before his death in 1992. This seamless garment of sustained sound in two overlapping parts is an immensely moving document from a unique human being at the end of his life. Anyone who responds to the spiritual minimalism of Pärt, Górecki or Tavener will understand, especially in these dedicated performances.

The Concerto for Prepared Piano (1951) takes its rightful place as the major classic for the transformed instrument with orchestra – a status emphasised by this fastidious performance with its delicate sonic tapestry, including discreet radio, all reflecting Cage's absorption with oriental philosophy. Tan has recorded the Suite for Toy Piano (1948) before. This time the sound is closer, you can hear her in-breath just before some movements, and we could have done with more precise rhythms. Lou Harrison's orchestration is perfectly in the spirit and makes a fascinating complement – Cage writing memorable tunes!

This disc shows that much of Cage has now entered the mainstream and that his music is unique.

Number Pieces

Three[2]. Seven. Ten[a]. Fourteen
The Barton Workshop / James Fulkerson [a]tbn
Megadisc MCD7801 (79' · DDD)　　Ⓕ

Cage's late 'Number Pieces' transform the act of subversion into a thing of majorly profound beauty. Musicians are given material framed by 'time brackets' that indicate how long each sound lasts. The different instrumental parts aren't meant to coordinate, and the random overlapping of colliding time brackets creates a texture where harmony without function and over-exposed instrumental timbre fuse with clandestine intent.

The Barton Workshop's survey of four 'Number Pieces' is dominated by a monumental 30-minute performance of *Ten* (1991). The wind players dig deep into the fervent beauty of a carefully conceived microtonal patois. The piano is deployed to add pointed perspective, with inside-of-the-instrument stabs cutting across the fluidly sustained grid of the wind and strings. The structure is punctuated by wild card percussion strokes, the whole unfolding construct growing holistically from the DNA of the material and the process the composer has set up.

Three[2] (1991) for three percussionists teases by hovering on a precipice of inaudibility, a device that overturns expectations of percussion music. The piece stutters between momentum and interruption, and the coolly abstract process is embedded with unexpectedly potent drama. Two earlier ensemble works – *Fourteen* (1990) and *Seven* (1988) – are perhaps slightly arid in their realisation but this is a beautiful and worthy disc none the less.

Piano works

Music for Piano – 1; 2; 3; 4-19; 20; 21-36; 37-52; 53-68; 69-84; 85. Music for…Two Pianos I/II; Three Pianos; Four Pianos; Five Pianos. Electronic Music for Two Pianos
Steffen Schleiermacher pf
Dabringhaus und Grimm ② MDG613 0784-2 (153' · DDD)　　Ⓕ

This set is devoted to the *Music for Piano* series almost entirely written in the 1950s, which is neglected and mostly unavailable. You can see why performers have found these pieces less attractive. After Cage's crisis year of 1952, which saw him produce the so-called silent piece *4'33"*, he was obsessed with removing his own tastes and desires from his compositions. Before he became fully committed to the *I Ching*'s random numbers he marked out imperfections in the manuscript paper he was using as a way of getting the notes. He said he looked at his paper and suddenly realised that all the music was there. This procedure also settled the density of notes on the page. In the whole series the performer is left to decide dynamics and pace in a continuity dominated by single notes. If this sounds austere, we're reckoning without Schleiermacher's ingenuity. Cage specifies various types of sound production, apart from the use of the keys: primarily plucking the strings from inside or muting them. As in Schleiermacher's prepared piano recordings, the quality of sound has been carefully considered. A muted low note or a single plucked string can be marvellously evocative in conjunction with conventionally produced pitches. The ambience of the prepared piano isn't far away. Further, Schleiermacher avails himself of Cage's provision for several of these pieces to be played together, which he does at intervals in the series. Since we've heard the same pieces solo, the superimposed versions bring back familiar material in a fascinating way. Fastidiously researched and performed, Schleiermacher says he's taken the pieces seriously. In so doing he's begun a new chapter of virtually unknown Cage.

In a Landscape. A Metamorphosis. The Seasons. Ophelia. Two Pieces (c1935). Two Pieces (1946). Quest
Herbert Henck pf
ECM New Series 476 1515 (69' · DDD)　　　Ⓕ Ⓑ▸

The shock here is that this is simply piano music – no preparations, nothing played from the inside, every detail notated. *In a Landscape*, with a dozen recordings already, tops Cage's greatest hits. It was written for dance, can be played on harp or piano, and again exercises its uncanny, mesmeric powers in this performance by Herbert Henck, who takes it much more slowly than the marked tempo. But Henck's performances throughout are fastidious in representing every detail of the scores. The longest work, *The Seasons* (1947), was a ballet for Lincoln Kirstein which, like the *Sonatas and Interludes*, shows Cage's interest in Indian philosophy before he moved on to Zen. At this period, perceptibly under the influence of Satie, Cage would assemble a collection of attractive sounds and then rotate them automatically, a procedure that became his trademark. The *Two Pieces* (1946) use some of the same autonomous sonorities as *The Seasons* in a different context.

Some of these early pieces are not linked to dance but stem from Cage's study with Schoenberg and his development of his own kind of row technique. Late in life Cage liked his early keyboard pieces but found *A Metamorphosis* the least interesting. These are fascinating documents, well recorded, which bring this part of Cage's enormous output quite naturally into the mainstream of 20th-century piano music.

Sonatas and Interludes
Yuji Takahashi prpf
Fylkingen Records FYCD1010 (58' · ADD)
Recorded 1965　　　Ⓕ

Written between February 1946 and March 1948, the *Sonatas and Interludes* were, at the time of this recording, still quite new, although already established as core contemporary repertoire. Even when they were premiered they were accepted as among the least controversial of Cage's works: the somewhat conservative journal *Musical America* welcomed them as 'quite enchanting'. Cage had devised the prepared piano in 1940. Wanting a percussion ensemble for a dance piece but having room only for a piano, he began to transform the instrument into a substitute gamelan. In the *Sonatas and Interludes* he explored the timbral possibilities further, here and there extending them by the use of contact mikes.

These pieces, often structured in accordance with complicated mathematical schemes, leave little to chance. The preparation of the piano is a long and meticulous process, and Cage provided precise directions. Nevertheless, performers need to make choices, and the results can be very different.

The benchmark recording by Aleck Karis (on Bridge) is certainly an impressive, powerful, virtuoso performance. Yet, compared with Takahashi's fresh-sounding reading, with its endlessly subtle gradations and reflective approach, evoking the image of a musical archaeologist's brush carefully revealing ancient, magical inscriptions, Karis sounds too burly, sometimes seeming to fall prey to the contemporary tendency to confuse aggression with conviction. Takahashi is a marvellous guide through the mystery and strange beauty of these appealing pieces.

Litany for the Whale

Litany for the Whale. Aria No 2. Five. The Wonderful Widow of Eighteen Springs. Solo No 22. Experiences No 2. Thirty-six Mesostics re and not re Marcel Duchamp. Aria (arr Hillier). The Year Begins to be Ripe
Theatre of Voices (Paul Elliott, Andrea Fullington, Allison Zelles, Terry Riley *vocs* Alan Bennett *voc/closed pf* Shabda Owens *voc/electronics*) /
Paul Hillier voc
Harmonia Mundi HMU90 7279 (72' · DDD · T/t)　Ⓜ

This is a landmark for Cage, Paul Hillier's group and everyone else. Hillier says he's been interested in Cage for years and here his own considerable advocacy has turned Cage into a troubadour of our global village. The Theatre of Voices' collection jumps right in at the deep end with *Litany for the Whale* (1980), a 25-minute monody with two uncannily similar voices (Alan Bennett and Paul Elliott) using only five notes in antiphonal phrases. Shut your eyes and this ritual could almost be Gregorian chant. The scope narrows to three notes in *The Wonderful Widow*, where the closed piano part is slightly subdued, and the same three recur in *Thirty-six Mesostics*, spoken by American minimalist Terry Riley and sung by Hillier.

Cage's *Aria* (1958), for Cathy Berberian, has been associated with one voice but this realisation for seven voices and electronic sounds is thoroughly idiomatic. *Experiences No 2*, another monody to a poem by EE Cummings, is beautifully sung, but the precisely notated pauses aren't always accurate. *Aria No 2* is a fastidious mix of extended vocal techniques by Alan Bennett with weather sounds. Cage convinces us of the musical beauty of rainfall, water and thunder. *Five* is a vocal version of one of Cage's late number pieces. This type of sustained writing is ideal for voices and there are meditative qualities in all these performances. The close-microphone breathing in *Solo No 22* is, like everything else here, artistic and well engineered.

---

49 Waltzes for the Five Boroughs

49 Waltzes for the Five Boroughs
Video director **Don Gillespie**
Mode **DVD** MODE204 (127' · NTSC · 4:3 · 2.0 · 0)   (F)

In 1977 Cage devised this do-it-yourself environmental piece based on 147 New York street locations selected by using chance operations. The conception was realised complete only in 1994/95 when Don Gillespie and colleagues decided to visit all these places and video whatever they saw and heard. So the 49 Waltzes (three sections each = 147 places) are simply film with no other soundtrack apart from what is heard at the time. It's a celebration of ordinary life in urban and residential streets. Refreshingly there's no background music, no asinine commentator, and the visual aspect dominates so that it's more film than music. Cage enjoyed the sound of what happens – so here it is for just over two hours.

In each shot the camera swings out and back from a fixed position; and apart from endless ordinary streets there's a subway station, the Bronx Zoological Gardens, Cunningham Park in Queens, and JFK. The random processes often focus on Staten Island and the whole series ends picturesquely with the sound of gulls and waves at Weir Creek Park in the Bronx. Birds are the soloists elsewhere too. As people go about their business there's surprisingly little conventional music, apart from operetta on tap in a record store and the occasional car radio. The team has realised exactly what Cage intended in the most conscientious way; excellent documentation in three languages.

Antonio Caldara   Italian c1670-1736

Caldara was a chorister at St Mark's, Venice, and became a multi-talented musician who excelled on the viol, cello and keyboard. He served as maestro di cappella da chiesa e dal teatro to the Duke of Mantua at the turn of the 18th century, and maestro di cappella to Prince Ruspoli in Rome between 1709 and 1716. Thereafter he was vice-Kapellmeister at the court in Vienna, a post he held until his death. He earned a reputation for his dramatic works, which included cantatas and oratorios. His output (over 3000 pieces) was one of the largest of his generation. His operas and oratorios make him an important figure in the dramatic tradition of the 18th century.

Maddalena ai piedi di Cristo

Maddalena ai piedi di Cristo
Maria-Cristina Kiehr, Rosa Dominguez *sops*

Bernarda Fink *contr* **Andreas Scholl** *counterten*
Gerd Türk *ten* **Ulrich Messthaler** *bass* **Schola Cantorum Basiliensis** / **René Jacobs**
Harmonia Mundi ② HMC90 5221/2 (126' · DDD · T/t)
(F)OOO

Caldara was the most prolific and famous oratorio composer of his day and this one, written around 1700, is wonderfully rich in fresh and attractive invention. Practically devoid of external action, it's dramatically tense and concentrates on the struggle between the forces of good and evil, the sinner Magdalen being urged towards penitence by her sister Martha; the roles of Christ and a Pharisee are considerably smaller. The work opens arrestingly, with an agitated sinfonia followed by the hypnotic aria 'Dormi, o cara'; then come another 27 brief *da capo* arias with their associated recitatives – ensembles scarcely exist. But there's no lack of variety: some arias, flanked by an orchestral ritornello, are accompanied only by a continuo instrument; others are furnished with different usages of the five-part strings.

René Jacobs furthers the dramatic impact by his pacing; and his casting is flawless. He has the highly effective idea of differentiating the parts of Earthly and Celestial Love by allocating the former to a mezzo and the latter to a countertenor. Both are excellent, but so are all the participants. It seems invidious to single out highlights but outstanding are the aria 'Diletti' for Magdalen (Kiehr) and the succeeding ornate 'Vattene' for Martha (Dominguez) and, even more, two florid arias from Scholl rejoicing in the eventual triumph of good, and two, passionately delivered by Fink, of fury by evil at its overthrow. You're urged to acquire this disc.

Cantatas

12 Suonate da camera, Op 2 – in B flat; in A; in F; in G minor. 12 Cantate da camera a voce sola, Op 3ª – Il silentio; L'anniversario amoroso; La fama. Vicino a un rivoletto[a]
Four Nations Ensemble ([a]Jennifer Lane *mez* Ryan Brown, Claire Jolivet *vns* Loretta O'Sullivan *vc*) / **Andrew Appel** *hpd*
ASV Gaudeamus CDGAU347 (68' · DDD · T/t)   (F)

This very agreeable disc samples the two chamber genres favoured by Caldara, prolific writer of operas and oratorios in Venice, Rome and Vienna. The sonatas are in the Corelli mould of *sonate da camera*, but half a generation on – more regular in their patterns, rather perkier in their manner, their counterpoint always beautifully dovetailed. The voice behind them isn't especially original but the music is always pleasingly and elegantly formed. Four of the 12 sonatas of Op 2 are recorded here, including the last of the set, which in the Corelli tradition is an extended ground-bass movement, carried off with a lot of ingenuity. There's wit, too, in some of these pieces: try for example the sparkling little Corrente from No 8. The Four Nations Ensemble play them with real feeling for the idiom as well as impeccable technique, and the recorded sound is bright and true.

It's principally as a vocal composer that Caldara is known, and Jennifer Lane, possessor of a full and warmly musical voice, makes the most of his graceful and shapely lines while always giving due weight and sense to the words. There's plenty of appealing, if again not specially distinctive, music in the three cantatas here, but the gem is *Vicino a un rivoletto*, where the first aria has an *obbligato* for violin and the second one for cello, which, exquisitely played by Loretta O'Sullivan, unmistakably represents the heart swooning with pain, and coupled with Lane's singing does so to very moving effect.

Joseph Canteloube   French 1879-1957

In one respect, Canteloube could be called the French Vaughan Williams: their careers were contemporaneous and dominated by the folksongs of their respective countries. Both went to extraordinary lengths to go out into the countryside and collect material with all the alacrity of butterfly collectors. (There all similarity between the two stops; Vaughan Williams was a far superior creative force.)

Canteloube had piano lessons from Amélie Doetzer, a former pupil of Chopin, but more importantly studied composition with the austere Vincent d'Indy. Did d'Indy's Symphony on a French Mountain Song of 1887, based on Cévennes folksong, inspire Canteloube? At any rate, from 1900 until the end of his life he travelled all over France in search of folk material, using the elements in the music he found to revivify contemporary French music.

Between 1923 and 1955 he published four sets of songs he'd discovered in the Auvergne, that dramatic and mountainous area dominated by its chain of puys – extinct volcanic peaks. First he set them for piano and voice, later orchestrating them in opulent fashion – and this is the form in which they're most often heard. It's charming, idiosyncratic and indispensable music, albeit by a minor figure.

Chants d'Auvergne

Canteloube Chants d'Auvergne – La pastoura als camps; Baïlèro; Lï'o de rotso; Ound' onorèn gorda; Obal, din lou Limouzi; Pastourelle; L'Antouèno; La pastrouletta è lo chibaliè; La delïssádo; N'aï pas iéu de mio; Lo calhé; Lo fiolaï'ré; Passo pel prat; Lou boussu; Brezairola; Maluros qu'o uno fenno. Jou l'pount d'o Mirabel; Oï, ayaï; Pour l'enfant; Chut, chut; Pastorale; Lou coucut; Postouro sé tu m'aymo; Quand z-èyro petituono; Té, l'co tèl; Uno jionto postouro; Hél beyla-z-y-dau fél; Obal, din lo combuèlo; Là-haut, sur le rocher; Lou diziou bé **Villa-Lobos** Bachianas brasileiras No 5

Dame Kiri Te Kanawa *sop* **English Chamber Orchestra / Jeffrey Tate**
Double Decca ② 444 995-2DF2 (111' · DDD · T/t) Ⓜ🄱➔

Te Kanawa's richly sensuous approach to these delightful songs is very seductive, especially when the accompaniments by Jeffrey Tate and the ECO are so warmly supportive and the sound so opulent. Her account of the most famous number, 'Baïlèro', must be the most relaxed on record, yet she sustains its repetitions with a sensuous, gentle beauty of line, supported by lovely wind playing from the orchestra which seems to float in the air. There's a resonance given to the sound, which means that certain of the brighter, more obviously folksy numbers lose a little of their rustic sharpness. However, the overall effect is very appealing, particularly when her voice (recorded in the early 1980s) is so young and fresh.

As an encore we are offered the Villa-Lobos *Bachianas brasileiras* No 5, an 'Aria' for soprano and cellos. The result is ravishing, almost decadent at its softly intoned reprise. An enticing disc.

Chants d'Auvergne – Baïlèro; Lï'o dè rotso; Ound' onorèn gorda; Obal, din lou Limouzi; L'Antouèno; La delïssádo; N'aï' pas iéu de mio; Lo calhé; Lo fiolaï'ré; Passo pel prat; Brezairola; Oï, ayaï; Pour l'enfant; Chut, chut; Lou coucut; Tè, l'co, tè!; Uno jionto postouro; La pastoura als camps; Pastourelle; La pastrouletta è lo chibaliè; Lou boussu; Malurous qu'o uno fenno; Jou l'pount d'o Mirabel; Pastorale
Frederica von Stade *mez* **Royal Philharmonic Orchestra / Antonio de Almeida**
Sony Classical Essential Classics SBK63063 (73' · DDD)   ⒷB

This Sony selection with Frederica von Stade is an old friend. Two sets of recordings have been combined and all the best-known songs are here in conventional performances.

Von Stade varies her tone according to the sense of each song, but the overall mood is less sharp, more comfortable if you like, than with some. The RPO sounds rich and, at generally broad speeds, Antonio de Almeida provides big-orchestra accompaniments. You'll probably find that the consoling romanticism of the *Songs of the Auvergne* on this tried-and-trusted disc is more what you had in mind.

Chants d'Auvergne – La pastoura als camps; Baïlèro; Lï'o dè rotso; Ound' onorèn gorda; O bal, din lou Limousi; Pastourelle; L'Antouèno; La delïssádo; N'aï pas iéu de mïo; Lo calhé; Passo pel prat; Lou boussu; Brezairola; Malurous qu'o uno Fenno; Jou l'pount d'o Mirabel; Oï, ayaï; Lou coucut; Quand z-èyro petituono; Uno jionto postouro; Là-haut, sur le rocher; Lou diziou bé
Véronique Gens *sop* **Lille National Orchestra / Jean-Claude Casadesus**
Naxos 8 557491 (62' · DDD · T/t)   ⓈⓄ➔

Each decade finds its favourite soloist for the *Chants d'Auvergne*: in the 1960s it was Natania Devrath, the '70s had Victoria de los Angeles, the '80s Kiri Te Kanawa, the '90s Dawn Upshaw. They weren't French, whereas Véronique Gens is quite at home in the dialect, as she comes from the Auvergne. Her singing is smooth and delicate, with plenty of body in the tone for some of the earthier moments.

In all, five volumes of Auvergne songs were published between 1923 and 1955. Each singer naturally includes 'Baïlèro', the most famous, and Gens doesn't disappoint in this. The 20 other songs range from the sad 'Uno jionto postouro', the lament of the girl whose lover has deserted her, to 'Malurous qu'o ono Fenno', the jaunty exposé of unhappy couples.

Jean-Claude Casadesus and the Lille orchestra bring out all the little details in the score, such as the lovely woodwind solos that link the three Bourrées. Perhaps this will become the interpretation for the 2000s.

Chants d'Auvergne – La pastrouletta è lo chibaliè; Lo fiolairé; Pour l'enfant; Chut, chut; Pastorale; Postouro sé tu m'aymo; Tè, l'co, tè!; Hé! beyla-z-y-dau fé!; Obal, din lo combuèlo. Triptyque. Chants de France – Auprès de ma blonde; Où irai-je me plaindre?; Au prè de la rose; Délicieuses cimes; Réveillez-vous!; D'où venez-vous fillette?

Véronique Gens *sop*
Lille National Orchestra / Serge Baudo
Naxos 8 570338 (57' · DDD)

For her second CD devoted to Joseph Canteloube's vocal music, Véronique Gens has looked beyond the celebrated, much-recorded *Chants d'Auvergne* and back to *Tryptique*, composed in 1913. Canteloube dedicated this to Maggie Teyte but the First World War interrupted its progress, and it was not until 1923 that Jane Campredon gave the premiere, with the Colonne orchestra conducted by Gabriel Pierné.

A setting of three poems by Roger Frêne, its lush, not to say extravagant orchestration anticipates Canteloube's later folksong settings. The influence of both Ravel and Debussy is obvious, maybe also Stravinsky (it was, after all, the year of *The Rite of Spring*). The first section, 'Offrande à l'été' is an ardent love song, with some pretty giddy scoring for harps. The central 'Lunaire' has a more mysterious, yearning feel, with a lovely little dissonance at the word 'cendre', as the poet imagines the leaves turning to ash. The finale, 'Hymne dans l'aurore' is an ecstatic prayer to Pan, celebrating every wonder of nature. The final cry, 'Mon âme s'ouvre ainsi qu'une aube étincellante! O Pan!' is marked in the score *crescendo en grandissant*, and Gens, Serge Baudo and the Lille orchestra rise to the moment with splendid force. It is really surprising that this work has not become better known; any soprano wanting to look beyond the obvious repertory should welcome it.

The rest of the disc is taken up with those remaining Auvergne songs not included on the

earlier issue, conducted by Jean-Claude Casadesus. Once again, Gens proves that an authentic knowledge of the dialect is a great advantage. The much later group from *Chants de France* makes a pleasant end to the recital, but it is *Tryptique* that has to be heard.

Elliott Carter   American b1908

Carter studied at Harvard, at the Ecole Normale de Musique in Paris and also with Nadia Boulanger. Back in the USA he worked as musical director of Ballet Caravan and as a teacher. Despite an early fascination for – and love of – the music of mavericks such as Varèse and Ives, Carter's first compositions looked more to the language of Stravinsky. But soon he abandoned tonality with pieces like his Piano Sonata of 1946. In the 1950s his output became more complex, and the forces for which he wrote reduced. He returned to writing for voices in the mid-1970s and also, encouraged by a number of high-profile performers including Daniel Barenboim and Pierre Boulez, started to write for large instrumental ensembles. Despite his advanced years (he was 100 in 2008), Carter is extraordinarily productive: in his nineties he produced over 40 new works. His most recent work was a flute concerto premiered in February 2010 under the baton of James Levine in Boston.

Piano Concerto

Piano Concerto. Concerto for Orchestra.
Three Occasions
Ursula Oppens *pf*
**South West German Radio Symphony Orchestra /
Michael Gielen**
Arte Nova 74321 27773-2 (62' · DDD)   Ⓢ

Oppens and Gielen have collaborated in a recording of the Piano Concerto before, and their long familiarity with the work brings an air of confidence to an account which is admirable in its feeling for the essential character as well as the formal logic of a score whose shoals of notes will defeat all but the most dedicated of interpreters. Gielen's ability to bring a convincing sense of shape and a persuasive expressive profile to complex music is no less apparent in an admirable reading of the Concerto for Orchestra. Again and again, the solo lines marked in the score are brought out, although the recording isn't able to give ideal clarity to the highly detailed string writing (a compositional problem, perhaps). But Gielen's is as compelling a presentation of this turbulent yet strangely affirmative music as one could hope to hear.

In *Three Occasions* Gielen is weighty, perhaps to excess in the often delicate third piece. Nevertheless, the interpretation is full of character, and the orchestra confirms its excellence in this demanding repertory. Recommended, despite the inadequate insert-notes.

Violin Concerto

'The Music of Elliott Carter, Vol 6'
Violin Concerto[a]. Four Lauds[b]. Holiday Overture[c]
[ab]**Rolf Schulte** vn [ac]**Odense Symphony Orchestra /**
[a]**Justin Brown,** [c]**Donald Palma**
Bridge BRIDGE9177 (58' · DDD)   (F)

'The Music of Elliott Carter, Vol 7'
Dialogues[a]. Boston Concerto[b]. Cello Concerto[c].
ASKO Concerto[d]
[a]**Nicolas Hodges** pf [c]**Fred Sherry** vc
[d]**ASKO Ensemble;** [a]**London Sinfonietta**
[bc]**BBC Symphony Orchestra / Oliver Knussen**
Bridge BRIDGE9184 (62' · DDD)   (F)

There are composers who get a second wind late in their career – and then there's Elliott Carter. Late bloomers such as Verdi (to whom he's often compared) usually make a dramatic coda to their careers, but Carter's burst of productivity in his nineties actually revealed a noticeable change in musical direction. Their respective rate of maturity notwithstanding, a more fitting comparison would be Ginastera, another composer who began in an accessible folkloric style, turned almost excessively complex in middle age, and reconciled the two in his late maturity.

Having these two volumes of Bridge's Elliott Carter series arrive almost concurrently helps put the composer's career in perspective. Despite the pleasing tonality and unapologetic American-ness of Carter's 1945 *Holiday Overture* (the connection with Ives's *Holidays Symphony* worn handily in its title), the dense counterpoint and rhythmic complexity are none the less already in place. The aggressively modernist Carter we usually think of came of age shortly afterwards and is still going strong in the Violin Concerto (1990), where musical lines remain unrestrained by tonality or conventional rhythmic pulse.

Those lines may not be as individualistic as in the composer's chamber works but they none the less need firm guidance from the podium. Justin Brown shows a sure sense of each line and its destination, making instrumental outbursts more purposeful and less impulsive than they might otherwise seem. It provides, in fact, a nearly unified orchestral front against Rolf Schulte's fairly lyrical solo playing, with textural contrasts duly marking emotional contrasts.

Four Lauds for solo violin, part of a series of short virtuoso works, traces Carter's more recent transition from the assertive *Riconoscenza per Goffredo Petrassi* (1984) to the more freely 'romantic' (the composer's own description) *Rhapsodic Musings* (2000). Though hardly as prevalent as his chamber works, the inner musical lines remain surprisingly vital, setting up a palpable internal counterpoint that Schulte deftly navigates.

At first glance, *Dialogues* (2003) would seem to be in the old Carter model, where different musical lines unfold with such clearly delineated personalities that they're often compared to characters in a play. Carter describes the piece as a conversation between piano and orchestra but the lively discourse continues with little of his former abrasiveness. This is civilised cocktail chatter rather than a raucous town meeting, with musical points respecting each other's space rather than yelling each other down. The Cello Concerto (2001), by contrast, is more a solo oration with some periodic cheers from the crowd. A full decade away from the Violin Concerto, the piece falls back much more squarely on traditional string phrasing and playing technique, but under soloist Fred Sherry the rhetoric is less of a crutch than a platform to make the main points clear and fresh.

Without the benefit of soloists, the remaining *concerto grosso* works here, the *ASKO Concerto* (2000) and the *Boston Concerto* (2002), indeed confirm a change in Carter's musical approach. It might be too much of a stretch to blame this new-found clarity on the composer writing his first opera in 1999 (at the age of 90!) but clearly Carter has started letting his musical ideas sing as well as shout.

Additional recommendation

Symphonia: sum fluxae pretium speia. Clarinet Concerto[b]
[b]**Collins** cl [a]**BBC SO,** [b]**London Sinf / Knussen**
DG download 459 660-2GH (64' · DDD)   (F)OOOB→

In Knussen's supremely authoritative interpretation, the sound quality has been meticulously managed in order to help the listener trace the gradually emerging and steadily unfolding arcs of eloquent melody. It takes time to appreciate how *Symphonia*'s extraordinary variety of pace contributes to the music's melodic and harmonic coherence. The performance of the more approachable Clarinet Concerto will leave you breathless with admiration, not only for Carter's inventiveness but also for the brilliance with which the score is realised by these dedicated artists.

String Quartets – No 2; No 3; No 4
Pacifica Quartet (Simin Ganatra, Sibbi Bernhardsson vns Masumi Per Rostad va Brandon Vamos vc)
Naxos 8 559363 (74' · DDD)   (S)O B→

This disc finds the composer exploring the genre's potential for conversation and confrontation. The Second Quartet (1959) sees its members as a divisive, even dysfunctional foursome – compressing the four movements while interspersing them with cadenzas in which the introspection, impulsiveness and exhibitionism of viola, cello and first violin are offset by the uniformity of the second violin. The Pacifica enter into the discourse with relish, while at times evincing Mozartian poise. The Third Quartet (1971) sets up an opposition between duos of first violin and cello, against second violin and viola in a continuous and vivid juxtaposition of movement types always meaningful in context. Adopting a degree of expressive license, the Pacifica rightly give the sheer velocity of the material its head right through to the seismic energy of the closing pages.

The Fourth Quartet (1986) can seem a retrenchment in its more equable dialogue over four outwardly traditional movements but this does not account for a deft superimposing of elements across movements in a powerfully cumulative argument, any final 'coming together' being undermined by the coda's fragmentation. Not a work likely to yield its secrets easily, yet the Pacifica add appreciably to its understanding. Both sound and booklet-notes are of a high standard, thus making this disc an indispensable acquisition.

Resurrection Symphony or a take on 'death and transfiguration', Casella's Second manages to prefigure the worst kind of movie-music bathos, though even Cecil B de Mille might have baulked at having his more sentimental images so relentlessly underlined.

Fast-forward 16 years and Mahler has yielded to Stravinsky as the model of choice. *Scarlattiana* (1926) is a contribution to post-*Pulcinella* neo-classicism and in places it equals the vitality and charm with which Stravinsky reshaped his early 18th-century materials. Its besetting sin is the same as that of the Symphony No 2: laying on with a trowel what is better sketched in fine point. But Martin Roscoe is a witty, trenchant piano soloist and the Chandos sound brings out all the piquancy of Casella's artfully un-18th-century orchestration.

Alfredo Casella   Italian 1883-1947

Casella was born into a family with a strong musical heritage: his gradfather was a friend of Paganini's and a professional cellist, as were his father and two brothers. He studied at the Paris Conservatoire where Fauré taught him compositon and fellow students were Enescu and Ravel. He was much influenced by the music of Debussy, though his own music inclined more to the language of Mahler and Strauss. He taught in Rome while establishing a career as a fine pianist (he was a member of a piano trio, the Trio Italiano). He played a major role in the resuscitation of the music of Vivaldi and during the 1930s wrote a number of neo-classical works in the style of Stravinsky's Pulcinella. He was conductor of the Boston Pops during the 1920s. Unusually for an Italian he did not seem particularly interested in writing operas (he only wrote two), instead concentrating on large-scale orchestral music and a substantial number of chamber works.

Orchestral works

Symphony No 2, Op 12. Scarlattiana, Op 44a
aMartin Roscoe pf BBC Philharmonic Orchestra / Gianandrea Noseda
Chandos CHAN10605 (77' · DDD)   ⒻⒷ

Bartók, Berg, Stravinsky, Szymanowski, Webern – these composers, all born in the early 1880s, are just some of Alfredo Casella's close contemporaries. Does his relative neglect tell us more about their (unfair?) dominance than about the quality of his music? This courageous Chandos disc offers the curious a way to find out.

Casella spent his formative musical years in Paris but it was Mahler rather than Debussy who was the inspiration for the Symphony No 2 (1908-10). This 50-minute would-be epic is given a splendidly forthright performance by Gianandrea Noseda and the BBC Philharmonic but not for a moment is one persuaded that its hyped-up bombast and soft-centred pseudo-eloquence were a match for the authentically raw and searing qualities of Mahler himself. As a

Francesco Cavalli   Italian 1602-1676

Cavalli (who took his name from his patron) joined the choir of St Mark's in Venice, singing first as a treble and then as a tenor. In his thirties he became second organist at St Mark's. His operas were soon taken up in a number of Italian centres, and 1660-62 saw his Ercole amante staged in Paris. He composed six more operas but his musical life continued at St Mark's and in 1668 he was appointed its maestro di cappella. Despite his appointment at a major cathedral, Cavalli's surviving sacred output is relatively modest, his reputation resting more on his operas and stagings in the past five decades of works such as Didone, Ormindo, Calisto and Egisto have revealed him to be of the major figures of dramatic music post-Monteverdi.

Ercole amante

Ercole amante
Luca Pisaroni bass-bar Ercole **Veronica Cangemi** sop Iole **Anna Bonitatibus** mez Giunone **Jeremy Ovenden** ten Hyllo **Anna Maria Panzarella** sop Deianira **Marlin Miller** ten Licco **Umberto Chiummo** bass-bar Nettuno, Tevere, Spirit of Eutyro **Wilke te Brummelstroete** mez Bellezza, Venere **Johannette Zomer** sop Cinzia, Parsitea, Spirit of Clerica **Mark Tucker** ten Mercurio, Spirit of Laomedonte **Tim Mead** counterten Paggio, Spirit of Bussiride
Chorus of Netherlands Opera; Concerto Köln / Ivor Bolton
Stage director **David Alden**
Opus Arte 🅳🆅🅳 0A1020D; 🔵 OABD7050D
(4h 21' · 1080i · PCM and 5.0 · 0)   Ⓕⓞ

Director David Alden's stagings of early operas, often conducted by Ivor Bolton, have revelled in the diversity, humanity and comedy of these multi-discipline works. *Ercole amante* ('Hercules as Lover') was Cavalli's offering for the Paris wedding of Louis XIV. *Ercole* spins the tale of the self-satisfied, over-ambitious semi-divine hero over-reaching himself, and coming to grief on Earth but bliss in the heavens. His quest is to abandon wife Deianira in favour of Iole, his son Hyllo's beloved. In this, Ercole is egged on or misguided by goddesses Venere and Giunone, and comic servants Licco and Paggio. He is brought down by a conspiracy of the wronged starring the return from the underworld of Iole's father Eutyro and ghostly colleagues. All this is abundantly clear in Alden's production – but there's not a syllable about it in Opus Arte's pretty but generalised booklet.

The production, like the piece, is moving, funny and literally action-packed. Alden knows well when to fill or empty his stage. All the effects that Paris's famous 1660s Salle des Machines provided – Giunone flying in, Nettuno rising from the sea on a huge boat – are here. There is also a stream of little comic decorations like Hyllo's trainers, Ercole's huge 12-pack of Heineken and the representation of Sonno ('sleep') by a character dancer. Jonathan Lunn's choreography is, rightly, not restricted to the 'dance sections' and moves seamlessly from Lully to Lady Gaga.

The look of the show – designer Paul Steinberg, lighting by Adam Silverman – is 'modern' in the sense that 17th-century Italian Baroque is realised through eyes informed by 20th-century American painting and comic strips. Coloured printed wallpapers and rich red, blue and yellow costumes dominate. The prologue scenes at court, the descent to the scary black-and-white underworld with Eutyro coming out of his coffin, and the gold and blue of Ercole's heavenly apotheosis, are as lavish as a Sun King could want – and seem well served by the depth and definition of the Blu-ray pictures. For the soloists' costumes Constance Hoffman uses a similarly heightened, modern-refracted period look, with Ercole as hero sporting a long blond wig (good for flicking), overall plastic body prosthetics, boxing shorts and platform heels.

Cavalli seems to have been especially stirred by the plight of Hyllo, the antics of the comics and the long section in which Eutyro and other dead are recruited against Ercole. Bolton leads his large authentic-instrument forces with gusto. They include an exceptional battery of continuo instruments to make dark noises in the storm interludes. It's invidious to pick from such a real ensemble cast but Umberto Chiummo (as always) gives great comic and sinister detail to his three roles, Jeremy Ovenden sings beautifully as the put-upon son and Anna Bonitatibus is a flighty, controlling Juno. Hugely recommended.

Statira, Principessa di Persia

Statira, Principessa di Persia
Roberta Invernizzi sop Statira **Dionisia di Vico** mez Cloridaspe **Maria Ercolano** sop Ermosilla, Usimano **Giuseppe de Vittorio** ten Elissena **Giuseppe Naviglio** bass Plutone, Nicarico, Dario **Maria Grazia Schiavo** sop Floralba **Daniela del Monaco** contr Brimonte **Rosario Totaro** ten Vaffrino **Roberta Andalò** sop Maga, Eurillo **Stefano di Fraia** ten Marcurio,

Brisante **Valentina Varriale** sop Messo **Cappella de' Turchini / Antonio Florio**
Opus 111 ② OP30382 (139' · DDD · N/T/t)   Ⓕ

The plot of *Statira*, first produced in Venice in 1656, is a convoluted mixture of supernatural hatred and royal love triangles. It's given here in a revised form that includes comic scenes probably inserted for a performance at Naples 10 years later as part of the festivities celebrating the coronation of King Philip IV of Spain. The Cappella de' Turchini present a refined performance. The prominent continuo section juggle the busy demands of the music with seeming ease. *Ritornelli* are consistently infectious and irresistibly dance-like. The playing is generally first class, exemplified by the mournful yet tasteful string playing in Ermosilla's aria 'Menfi, mia Patria, Regno'.

There are few moments of intense drama in an opera that seems to have been devised primarily as entertainment rather than a profound experience. The final chorus declares that 'After all sufferings, all joy comes at last', but the preceding drama doesn't present a credible exploration of suffering. It's only when the plot grows more desperate in Act 3 that *Statira* becomes notably riveting, but there are delectable moments to enjoy. During the prologue the band plays beautifully, while a malcontent sorceress plots revenge on the Arabian King Cloridaspe with caustic glee. Meanwhile, the king has fallen in love with Statira, and their love is subsequently challenged and threatened before all ends happily. Roberta Invernizzi in the title-role is more muscular than most 'early music' sopranos but lacks nothing in finesse and clarity in the rapturous night scene that opens the opera. The outstanding aria of the recording is Invernizzi's exuberantly heroic 'La tromba orgogliosa', although her lament 'Lassa che fò' is an equally potent moment.

The opera's plenteous comic scenes are hammed up, but the plain-speaking servant characters have dated worse than the conventional *opera seria* lovers that monopolise the best arias. Mountains of recitative are delivered with sparkle, and Antonio Florio judges each scene effectively. The quality of the recording is indisputable, and Opus 111 deserves immense credit for continuing to reveal fascinating lesser-known repertoire. This recording is an indispensable indication of operatic style in the under-represented period between Monteverdi and Handel, and those interested in buying it shouldn't hesitate.

Emmanuel Chabrier French 1841-1894

An affluent background (his father was a successful barrister in the Auvergne) allowed Chabrier to lead the life of a well-off cultured dilettante. His many friends included not only leading musicians including

Fauré and d'Indy but the writers Verlaine and Zola as well as artists such as Renoir and Manet (in fact, not only did Manet die in his arms but he also owned, among his Renoirs and Sisleys, Manet's *Un bar aux Folies-Bergère*). After only a dozen or so years composing, Chabrier died aged just 53.

His music was influenced by two childhood Spanish piano teachers and, especially, by Wagner, whose scores he laboriously copied and studied. His first success was with an operetta called *L'étoile*, written when he was still a civil servant; others like *Gwendoline* (1886) and *Le roi malgré lui* (1887) prospered less well, though their overtures are worth hearing, as are his heady and exuberant piano pieces. His *Joyeuse marche* (1888) is a worthy companion to *España*.

Piano works

Habañera. Impromptu. 10 Pièces pittoresques. Cinq Pièces posthumes - Aubade; Ballabile; Caprice; Feuillet d'album; Ronde Champêtre
Angela Hewitt pf
Hyperion CDA67515 (76 '·DDD)   ⓕⓞⓞⒹ

Chabrier's name lives on primarily through *España* and *Marche joyeuse*. His tiny output for piano is far too rarely encountered in the concert hall or on recordings, yet he is a delightful, self-contained original. From his total of a mere 26 titles, Angela Hewitt plays 18 on this little gem of a disc. It sounds as though the piano was recorded in some deserted *fin de siècle* spa hotel – and so it proves, for Hewitt's richly coloured Fazioli was captured in 'Das Kulturzentrum Grand Hotel, Dobbiaco, Italy'. In fact, whenever there is an exposed soft passage in the upper treble in this programme, the same atmospheric effect engages the ear momentarily; in the more robust items, it is hardly noticeable. As to Hewitt's performances, they are as affectionate, warm, lyrical and charming as one could wish, underlining but not exaggerating Chabrier's deliciously predictable unpredictability.

Additional recommendation

Suite pastorale. Habanera. España. Larghetto. Prélude pastoral. Joyeuse marche. Gwendoline – Overture. Le roi malgré lui – Fête polonaise
VPO / Gardiner
DG download 447 751-2GH (66' · DDD)   ⓕⓞⒹ
Gardiner draws some superbly responsive playing from the VPO and a first-class recording, while warm, leaves all detail clear, and sweeps the board with a set of outstanding, exuberant performances.

Marc-Antoine Charpentier
French 1643-1704

After study in Rome, most likely with Carissimi, Charpentier returned to France and entered the serv-

ice of the Duchess of Guise and worked with Molière on his stage works. After his 17-year service to the Guise household, he was music teacher to Philippe, Duke of Chartres (later Duke of Orleans and Regent of France). From 1698 until his death he held the post of maître de musique of the Saint-Chapelle. One of his most famous compositions during his tenure was the Mass Assumpta est Maria. Another of his best-known works is his setting of the Te Deum, and specifically its prelude, employed as the signature tune of the European Braodcsting Union. Thanks to pioneering work by William Christie and Les Arts Florissants, Charpentier's genius as a composer for the stage has been duly recognised.

Mass, H1

Mass, H1. Te Deum, H147. Precatio pro filio regis, Ⓟ H166. Panis quem ego dabo, H275. Canticum Zachariae, H345, 'Benedictus Dominus Deus'
Le Concert Spirituel / Hervé Niquet
Naxos 8 553175 (57' · DDD · T/t)   ⓈⒹ

This early Mass is a beautiful piece, intimately scored for voices with two melody instruments and continuo. The Mass is harmonically richly inventive with passages of vivid word-painting. Taken as a whole the work is generously endowed with subtle inflexions, a pervasive element of contemplation, and effectively varied rhythmic juxtapositions which enliven the text and hold our attention.

The *Te Deum*, for four soloists, four-part choir and *colla parte* instruments, isn't that one for which Charpentier is renowned but a smaller, later piece belonging to the last years of his life. Modest in scale it may be but musically it's impressive and emotionally satisfying. The choir and instrumentalists of Le Concert Spirituel are on their usual lively form. Some of the solo vocal contributions are more focused than others but the choir maintains a high standard of vocal blend and secure intonation. The recorded sound is very good indeed and Niquet directs with stylistic assurance.

Te Deum, H146

Te Deum, H146. Dixit Dominus, H202. Domine salvum fac regem, H291. In honorem S Ludovici Regis Galliae canticum, H365. Marches pour les trompettes, H547
Le Concert Spirituel / Hervé Niquet
Glossa GCD921603 (55' · DDD)   ⓕⓞ

Hervé Niquet and his ensemble are old hands at the French *grand motet* for choir and instruments by now, and Charpentier in particular has been well served by them. Here they move into familiar ground in the form of the best-known of his *Te Deum* settings, prefaced by two scurrying, delightful little marches and coupled with three motets not currently available elsewhere. These last should be good enough reason to acquire the disc, but even for those who have a *Te Deum* or two in their collection already, Niquet's reading of it is another. With a choir of 12 and a one-to-a-part band, this is as limpid and lithe a performance of the piece as you're likely to hear. Niquet chooses some fleet tempi, but also injects the music with a catchy rhythmic lilt and an attention to declamatory detail that constantly keeps the music alive. And when a smoother arch is required, as in the choral soprano setting of 'te ergo quaesumus', he can touch the heart too. Good recorded sound and balance make this a disc to have.

Vesper Psalms / Magnificat, H72

Charpentier Beatus vir, H221. Laudate pueri, H149. Laetatus sum, H216. Nisi Dominus, H150. Lauda Jerusalem, H210. Ave maris stella, H60. Magnificat, H72. Salve regina, H24 **Nivers** Antiphonarium Monasticum, Antiennes I-VI
Le Concert Spirituel / Hervé Niquet
Naxos 8 553174 (61' · DDD · T/t)   ⑤➔

This release offers a liturgical reconstruction of the Vespers office. The five Vesper psalms and *Magnificat* belong to different periods in Charpentier's life and the six antiphons are by his organist-composer contemporary, Nivers. The reconstruction works well and Le Concert Spirituel, under Hervé Niquet, demonstrates its rapport with Charpentier's music. The vocal sound is fresh and the wide range of musical *Affekt* shows off a greater diversity of tonal colour. Tenors and basses incline towards a roughness of timbre here and there yet, overall, the bright and full-blooded choral sound is pleasing and vital. Some may find the recording balance of the psalms and canticle a fraction too close, creating the atmosphere of a drawing-room Vespers rather than one in more spacious, ecclesiastical surroundings. The antiphons fare much better in this respect, having a deeper aural perspective. This is a richly rewarding programme of music which never disappoints.

Leçons de Ténèbres du Vendredi Saint

Leçons de Ténèbres de la Semaine Sainte de 1692 – H135; H136; H137. Méditations pour le Carême – H380; H381; H386; H387; H388
Thibaut Lenaerts, Cyril Auvity countertens **Pierre Evreux, Ian Honeyman** tens **Alain Buet, Ronan Nédélec** bars **Le Concert Spirituel / Hervé Niquet**
Glossa GCD921604 (59' · DDD · T/t)   Ⓕ

Messe de Monsieur de Mauroy, H6
Marie-Louise Duthoit, Claire Gouton sops **Serge Goubiod** counterten **Pierre Evreux** ten **Christophe Sam** bass **Le Concert Spirituel / Hervé Niquet**
Glossa GCD921602 (66' · DDD · T/t)   Ⓕ

It almost goes without saying that a Hervé Niquet recording of Charpentier is going to be a thing of beauty. Whether it's in the long build-up to the

top of the grand arch that's the opening *Kyrie* of the *Messe de Monsieur de Mauroy*, or the ardent twists and dissonances with which the first of the *Leçons de Ténèbres* announces itself, it only takes a few moments for Niquet's expert team of singers and instrumentalists to draw us into the achingly expressive world of 17th-century France.

Composed around 1691, this is the longest of his 11 Masses, and its many sections seem to move effortlessly from one to another, creating a constantly shifting range of subtle responses to text – some sweet, some stirring, some lilting and some weighty – while successfully maintaining the work's continuity.

Charpentier composed 31 incomplete sets of *Leçons de Ténèbres*, those intense settings of the Lamentations of Jeremiah that were so popular in Holy Week in France during the mid-Baroque period, and which produced some of its most ravishing musical moments. Scored for six male voices, strings, flutes and continuo, this set moves between straightforward declamation and music of increasing harmonic and dramatic urgency to present a striking evocation of the desolation of the ruined Jerusalem.

These performances are exquisitely judged, showing an unerring feel for the music's expressive ebb and flow. Two releases of thorough desirability.

Dialogus inter angelum et pastores, H406

Dialogus inter angelum et pastores, H406[a]. Mors ⓟ Saülis et Jonathae, 'Cum essent congregata ad praelium', H403[b]. Sacrificium Abrahae, H402[c]
[bc]**Jaël Azzaretti**, [bc]**Marie-Louise Duthoit** sops
[bc]**Benjamin Clee** counterten **Jean-François Novelli**, [bc]**Nicholas Bauchau** tens **Ronan Nédélec**, [bc]**Raimonds Spogis** basses **Il Seminario Musicale / Gérard Lesne** counterten
Naïve Astrée E8821 (68' · DDD)   Ⓕ❍

French countertenor Gérard Lesne and Il Seminario Musicale manage to bring Charpentier's three miniature oratorios vividly to life. The works employ narrators – sometimes a solo voice, sometimes the chorus – in a highly dramatic series of instrumental and vocal movements, carefully tinged with suspensions and chromatic inflections. Both *Mors Saülis et Jonathae* and *Sacrificium Abrahae* rely on tightly constructed dialogues cast in recitative. Lesne intensifies the characterisation by associating particular combinations of continuo instruments and organ stops with each of the interlocutors. Melodic, melismatic movements are reserved for moments of powerful emotion, as when David weeps for his brother Saul.

Although Il Seminario Musicale take pride in performing without a conductor, they wouldn't produce the precision of ensemble so evident in this recording but for the vigilance of the continuo players. The absence of a principal interpreter is audible and here, as in less complex chamber music, the effect is highly desirable. Lesne delivers a string of inspiring performances in a raft of roles – as do Jean-François Novelli as David and Abraham and the bass Raimonds Spogis as Samuel.

Christmas Music

Canticum in nativitatem Domini, 'Usquequo avertis', H416. Dialogus inter angelos et pastores Judeae in nativitatem Domini, H420. Noël: un flambeau, Janette, Isabelle!, H460c
Aradia Ensemble / Kevin Mallon
Naxos 8 557036 (62' · DDD) ⑤⮞

Perhaps few composers have produced as much beautiful Christmas music as Charpentier. Both oratorios recorded here are generously laid out for soloists, chorus and a sweet-toned, atmospherically nocturnal ensemble of recorders and strings, a grand motet-style line-up which Charpentier uses to create a work with clear dramatic pretensions. Thus, in addition to the ravishing choral writing of the kind at which Charpentier excelled, each oratorio has a gentle instrumental number to represent night (an archetype taken straight from the dreamy *sommeils* of French Baroque opera), followed by a tootly little dance-chorus to represent the 'awakening of the shepherds', and later on a perky march to send them off to Bethlehem. In this way Charpentier's faultless music brings together his own contemporary world and that of the New Testament in an utterly beguiling mixture of richness and simplicity.

The Toronto-based Aradia Ensemble are superbly attuned to the music's atmosphere. Perhaps an extra ounce of vocal refinement could have been drawn from the choir, but more important is that these performances show an unfailing appreciation of style, taste and sheer beauty of sound. The result is a Christmas treat for us all.

Opera arias

'Ombre de mon amant'
Charpentier Medée – Ouverture; Princesse c'est sur vous; Quel prix de mon amour; Croiras-tu mon malheur...Dieux témoins de la foy que l'ingrat m'a donnée; Prelude, scene 4; C'en est fait, on m'y force; Avant que d'éclater...Malgré sa noire trahison; Prelude, scene 5; Noires filles du Styx; Venez mêler à mes poison; Prelude, scene 7; Je voy le Don fatal; Premier air pour les Démons; Dieu du Cocyte et des Royaumes sombres; Entrée des Démons. Prélude instrumental et chansonette, 'Auprès du feu l'on fait l'amour', H446. Chanson à danser, 'Celle qui fait mon tourment', H450. Suite a 4, H545 – Prelude; Gigue angloise; Gigue francoise **M Lambert** Airs de cour – Ma bergère est tendre et fidèle; Ombre de mon amant; Vos mépris chaque jour **Rameau** Les fêtes d'Hébé – Air gracieux pour Zéphyre et les Grâces; Ariette de l'Amour, 'Vole, Zéphyre'; Tambourins I & II; Première Entrée La Poésie; Air tendre; Pour le Génie de Mars; La Victoire; Chaconne. Hippolyte et Aricie – Prelude, Act 3; Cruelle mère des amours; Quelle plainte en ces lieux m'appelle?

Anne Sofie von Otter *mez*
Les Arts Florissants / William Christie
Archiv Produktion 477 8610AH (65' · DDD) Ⓕ◐⮞

The title of this disc is taken from an air by Michel Lambert, who is perhaps better known as the father-in-law of Lully than as a composer. There is no Lully here: but Anne Sofie von Otter, who claims French Baroque music as 'a new love affair', sang a very fine Médée in *Thésée* recently in Paris. And it's Medea, but Charpentier's rather than Lully's, who dominates this excellent recital. In Act 3, Medea takes her revenge on the faithless Jason by poisoning the robe demanded by her rival. Von Otter sounds utterly wretched in Medea's lament for her lost love, then she intensifies her tone as she summons up demons and monsters. It's a pity that the last chorus is cut.

The third composer to be featured is Rameau, with two airs from *Hippolyte et Aricie* enclosing a sequence of dances and an ariette from *Les fêtes d'Hébé*. Phaedra is another vengeful character with a sympathetic side and von Otter conveys Phaedra's various emotions with consummate skill. Buy the disc, then move on to William Christie's complete versions of *Médée* and *Hippolyte et Aricie* on Erato. One mustn't forget Lambert: three tender chansons, exquisitely sung and played.

Actéon, H481

Actéon Ⓟ
Dominique Visse *counterten* Actéon **Agnès Mellon** *sop* Diane **Guillemette Laurens** *mez* Junon **Jill Feldman** *sop* Arthébuze **Françoise Paut** *sop* Hyale
Les Arts Florissants Vocal Ensemble
La Comtesse d'Escarbagnas/Le mariage Forcé, H494 – Ouverture
Michel Laplénie *ten* **Philippe Cantor** *ten*
Les Arts Florissants Ensemble / William Christie
Harmonia Mundi Musique d'abord HMA195 1095 (47' · ADD). Recorded 1981 Ⓑ◯◯◯

 Charpentier's little vignette opera is an astonishingly rich score containing most, if not all, the ingredients of a *tragédie-lyrique*. There's a profusion of fine choruses and dances but an overture which departs somewhat from the standard Lullian pattern. *Actéon* is made up of six well-contrasted short scenes. The first of them is musically the most colourful with appealing evocations of *La chasse* and a riotous dance as the hunters go in search of their quarry. The second scene is much gentler with a tender air for Diana, pastoral reflections from her followers and a recurring chorus of nymphs which recalls passages in Blow's *Venus and Adonis*. Jill Feldman as Arthebuze, one of Diana's attendants, is admirably languid in her air disdaining love's ardour. Scene 3 discloses a pensive Actéon who, while reflecting on matters of the heart, stumbles upon Diana and her retinue in a state of *déshabillé*. Actéon's defence is touching and is delicately portrayed by Dominique Visse. The fourth tableau begins with Actéon's discovery that he has been turned into a stag: 'A horrible fur enwraps me', he cries and, at this point Visse cleverly alters the character of his voice: 'Ma parole n'est plus qu'une confuse voix'. A poignant *symphonie* follows. In the fifth tableau Actéon is torn to pieces by his own hounds and, in the sixth and final scene, Junon, imperious as ever, explains to the hunters what they have just done. A chorus of grief mingled with anger sung by Actéon's followers brings this little *opera de chasse* to an end.

Christie directs the work from beginning to end with conviction and assurance. The action is well paced and there's an intensity of expression, a fervour, which gives a touching emphasis to the drama.

Médée, H491

Médée   Ⓟ
Lorraine Hunt *sop* Médée **Bernard Deletré** *bass*
Créon **Monique Zanetti** *sop* Créuse **Mark Padmore**
ten Jason **Jean-Marc Salzmann** *bar* Oronte **Noémi
Rime** *sop* Nérine **Les Arts Florissants /
William Christie**
Erato ③ 4509 96558-2 (195' · DDD · T/t)   ⒻⓄⓄ

Lorraine Hunt's Medea is something of a *tour de force*. She invests every word with meaning and produces the widest range of colour to express all the emotional nuances in Medea's complex character – jealousy, indignation, tenderness, sorrow, fury, malignity and outright barbarism: she's outstanding in Act 3, one of the most superb acts in all Baroque opera, in which she has no fewer than four great monologues, the first with affecting chromatic harmonies, the second accompanied by feverish rushing strings, the third the sombre 'Noires filles du Styx' with its eerie modulations, the fourth with dark orchestral colours. Charpentier's orchestration and texture, indeed, are wonderfully effective: string writing varies between extreme delicacy (beautifully played here) and savage agitation; the cool sound of the recorders is refreshing and the many dances featuring recorders and oboes are enchanting. As Jason, Mark Padmore, a real *haute-contre*, sings with admirable ease and intelligence and the tragic Creusa, poisoned by the vengeful Medea, is the light-voiced Monique Zanetti, the very embodiment of youthful innocence and charm: her death scene, still protesting her love for Jason, is most moving. A notable detail in all the principals, incidentally, is their absorption of *agréments*, with Hunt showing special mastery in this regard. All told, a considerable achievement, and a triumph for Christie.

Ernest Chausson   French 1855-1899

As a man of private means (his father was a building contractor who made a fortune from rebuilding the centre of Paris), Chausson never had to struggle to

make a living. He'd already got a law degree and was married with a family by the time he decided to enrol at the Paris Conservatoire. Though he withdrew after a few months, he was able to study privately with César Franck for three years and it's Franck and Wagner who were the main influences on his music. A major creative talent had finally established itself by the end of his short life; its development and fruition were not to be.

His Poème, Op 25, is a richly lyrical masterpiece for violin and orchestra, composed in 1896 and dedicated to the great Eugène Ysaÿe who gave its first performance in London exactly a week after the premature death of Chausson in a bicycling accident. (While on a summer holiday near Limay, he lost control going down a steep hill and was smashed to death against a stone wall.)

Symphony in B flat, Op 20

Symphony in B flat. Viviane, Op 5. Soir de fête, Op 32. La têmpete – Air de danse; Danse rustique
BBC Philharmonic Orchestra / Yan Pascal Tortelier
Chandos CHAN9650 (67' · DDD)   ⒻⓄ➛

There are at least two misconceptions to put right about Franck's arguably most gifted pupil. The first, which this disc dispels admirably, is that the majority of Chausson's music, in the manner of his *Poème*, is endlessly melancholic or elegiac. The second, which the disc doesn't dispel quite so well, is that in his orchestral writing never managed to free itself from Wagner's embrace. Never *entirely* perhaps, but by the time the 43-year-old composer came to write his last orchestral piece, the nocturnal *Soir de fête* included here, his escape from Wagner was well under way, and who knows where it might have led, had it not been for his tragically early death the following year? The outer sections of *Soir de fête* have something about them of 'the vibrating, dancing rhythms of the atmosphere' of Debussy's later *Fêtes*. The programme as a whole, the overall richness of the orchestral process – whether Wagnerian, Franckian, Straussian or Chaussonian – is well served by the full-bodied sound of Tortelier's BBC Philharmonic.

The Symphony, like Franck's, is cyclical, but not otherwise as indebted to the older composer as is often suggested. There are none of Franck's organ-loft sonorities anywhere in this wonderfully variegated, open-air orchestration. This is the finest modern recording of the Symphony now available. Each movement is superbly built, and Chandos's recording is truly impressive, although in the excerpts from Chausson's incidental music for *The Tempest*, the sound is perhaps a little bulky.

Chausson Symphony in B flat **Franck** Symphony
Liège Philharmonic Orchestra / Louis Langrée
Accord 476 8069 (72' · DDD)   ⒻⓄⓄ

It is apt that this excellent new version of the Franck Symphony, the most important orchestral work by the greatest of Belgian composers, should come from a Belgian orchestra. It is good, too, that it is coupled with a symphony by a composer closely associated with him, Chausson's Op 20. It may come as a surprise to find what a refined body the Liège orchestra is under Louis Langrée: their Franck could hardly be more idiomatic, with subtle nuances of phrasing and variations of tempo reflecting the players' affection for the music.

The performance of the Chausson is equally persuasive and the result is totally idiomatic. Langrée again opts for a flowing speed in the central slow movement, this time marked *Très lent* – very slow – but never sounds at all rushed. The clarity and immediacy of the sound add to the impact.

Piano Trio in G minor, Op 3

Chausson Piano Trio **Ravel** Piano Trio
Pascal Rogé pf **Mie Kobayashi** vn
Yoko Hasegawa vc
Onyx ONYX4008 (58' · DDD)   Ⓕ⊖→

Pascal Rogé heads up this thoughtful disc of French trios. He has described his gods as Bach, Beethoven and Schumann, with Poulenc, Debussy and Satie as his friends. And so, too, are Ravel and Chausson, to judge by his finely sensitive performances.

Ravel's swaying, insinuating opening theme could hardly be played more lucidly or affectionately and its final return is full of hushed magic, a far cry from smarter, more metropolitan and impersonal readings. The *Pantoum* is vivacious rather than aggressive and the entire performance, even in moments of heightened drama and intensity, is unforced, its sparkle gentle rather than metallic or self-consciously virtuoso.

Chausson's early Trio is remote from such ultra-Gallic refinement and sophistication, its opening *Pas trop lent* romantically troubled in a style clearly deriving from César Franck's recently completed Piano Quintet. The second-movement *Vite*, on the other hand, falls like manna from heaven after so much chromatic turbulence. Both here and in the finale Chausson breaks out into a reassuring lightness which has its origins in Saint-Saëns. Such alternating solace and despair are beautifully realised by Rogé and his colleagues. The warm and fluid Onyx sound reflects performances of a quiet but unmistakable authority.

Additional recommendation

Piano Trio
Coupled with Poème, Op 25 (arr cpsr).
Andante et Allegro. Pièce, Op 39
Neidich cl **Graffin** vn **Hoffman** vc **Devoyon** pf
Chilingirian Qt
Hyperion CDA67028 (62' · DDD)   Ⓕ⊖→

Opulent sound and wonderfully committed playing makes this a real winner and an ideal disc if you want an all-Chausson programme.

Poème de l'amour et de la mer, Op 19

Poème de l'amour et de la mer
Debussy Cinq poèmes de Charles Baudelaire
(arr Adams) – Le balcon; Harmonie du soir; Le jet d'eau; Recueillement **Ravel** Shéhérazade
Susan Graham sop **BBC Symphony Orchestra /
Yan Pascal Tortelier**
Warner Classics 2564 61938-2 (63' · DDD · T/t)
                              Ⓕ❶❶❶⊖→

Ⓖ⃝ Only a brave, or foolhardy, composer sets about reorchestrating Debussy. Yet that's what John Adams has done, in 'Le jet d'eau', the third of Debussy's *Cinq poèmes de Charles Baudelaire*, the first four of which Adams has chosen to score for a modern orchestra. He's done an effective job, and if it makes the songs sound more boisterous, less mysterious than in the usual version for voice and piano, he's probably doing his soloist a big favour. By common consent, these are the most difficult of all Debussy's early songs. Susan Graham seems totally in command: her *diminuendo* on the words 'Et le charme des soirs' is tender, and is echoed a few bars later by Adams providing a nostalgic woodwind for the reference to those firelit evenings, 'par l'audeur du charbon'.

There's a lovely photograph, taken in 1893, the year of *Poème de l'amour et de la mer*. It shows Debussy, at Chausson's house, playing the piano. Both composers are in white shirts, surrounded by a peaceful group of family and friends, all in summer clothes, the windows open. This is the sort of mood this disc evokes. Yan Pascal Tortelier and Susan Graham give Chausson's work a well nigh perfect performance, capturing the sense of quiet regret at the memory of springtime love that has faded, and of a story that is never quite told.

As for Ravel's *Shéhérazade*, like nearly all mezzo-sopranos, Graham is stretched to the limits of her resources by the big climactic phrases in 'Asie'. She sings a hushed, beautiful 'La flûte enchantée' and a rather too sad 'L'indifférent', but it's all done with a fine line, with the BBC Symphony Orchestra playing Ravel's music with a good deal of passion.

Chausson Poème de l'amour et de la mer
Vierne Les Djinns, Op 35. Eros, Op 37.
Ballade du désespéré, Op 61. Psyché, Op 33
Steve Davislim ten
Queensland Orchestra / Guillaume Tourniaire
Melba ⊕⃝ MR301123 (77' · DDD)   Ⓕ

Here is a side of Louis Vierne few of us will have encountered before: angry, bitter, vengeful and simply bursting with passion and high emotion. As the excellent notes that come with this attractively packaged disc point out, Vierne had every reason to feel angry, bitter and vengeful. But while we may be inclined to say 'poor old Vierne' when we read of his blindness, messy divorce, turbulent affairs of the heart and so on, we should privately rejoice that personal adversity gave rise to such inspired music. These are four brilliantly crafted songs with almost Wagnerian orchestral accompaniments which are dazzlingly reflected in performances of breathtaking intensity.

The immediate inclination with the Vierne songs is to compare them – highly favourably – with those of his German contemporaries, Mahler and Strauss. But there is a noble tradition of French song with orchestral accompaniment, and the impressive French conductor, Guillaume Tourniaire, chooses Chausson's *Poème de l'amour et de la mer* as a companion piece. Certainly Australian tenor Steve Davislim is every bit as impressive here as in the Vierne – and this is highly distinguished singing by any reckoning – while the Queensland Orchestra, on absolutely cracking form, clearly relish the opulence of Chausson's orchestral textures, not least towards the end of the first movement where we get a bracing dose of *La mer*. But the net result of these fervently inspired performances and the generous and fulsome recorded sound is to emphasise the astonishing emotional potency of Vierne's songs above Chausson's more colour-oriented writing.

On every count, this is a magnificent release. It is also a truly revelatory one.

Luigi Cherubini   Italian 1760-1842

Cherubini was a major figure in French music in the five decades spanning the turn of the 19th century, admired by Beethoven, Schumann, Brahms and Berlioz. He studied in Italy (Bologna and Milan) and was soon producing operas in London and Paris where he settled in 1786. His second French opera, Lodoïska (Paris, 1791), established his substantial reputation and this was followed in 1797 by Médée and in 1800 by Les deux journées. He was also a prolific composer for the church and his sacred output incudes seven Masses and two Requiems. His reputation has started to grow once again – Maria Callas championed Médée and Riccardo Muti is a fine performer of his Masses. His skill as an orchestrator of flair and imagination is demonstrated by his opera overtures and his small body of symphonic works.

Mass No 1 in C minor

Mass No 1 in C minor. Marche funèbre
**Corydon Singers; Corydon Orchestra /
Matthew Best**
Hyperion CDA66805 (54' · DDD · T/t)   (F)(B)→

It would be an oversimplification to suggest that Matthew Best emphasises the Beethoven rather than the Berlioz aspect of the main work here; but he does seem less interested in the fascinating use of colour as an element in the actual invention than in the rugged moral strength and the force of the statements. The

recording reflects this emphasis, and is firm and clear without being especially subtle over orchestral detail. The choir delivers the 'Dies irae' powerfully, and much dramatic vigour is recalled in the fugue traditionally reserved for 'Quam olim Abrahae'. Berlioz, however, was satirical about Cherubini's fugues, and saved his admiration for the wonderful long *decrescendo* that ends the *Agnus Dei*. This is beautifully controlled here.

Best includes the tremendous *Marche funèbre*, inspiration here again for Berlioz. Best handles this superbly, opening with a merciless percussion crash and sustaining the pace and mood unrelentingly. It sounds more original than ever, a funeral march that, rather than mourn or honour, rages against the dying of the light.

Requiem in C minor

Requiem[a]. Marche funèbre
[a]**Gruppo Vocale Cantemus; Italian Swiss Radio**
[a]**Chorus and Orchestra / Diego Fasolis**
Naxos 8 554749 (56' · DDD · T/t)   (S)(B)→

Cherubini's C minor Requiem was admired by both Berlioz and Beethoven, with good reason, since both owed a great deal to a work that isn't far short of a masterpiece. For Beethoven, the music's rugged strength and the force of the statements held much; Berlioz, often mocking and unfair to Cherubini, responded warmly to the use of instrumental colour as part of the actual invention. To oversimplify, if Christoph Spering and his Cologne artists (Opus 111) give a more colourful, 'Berliozian' performance, Matthew Best and the Corydon Singers (Hyperion) respond to the 'Beethovenian' aspect of the music. Of course, there's much more to it than that. Both are excellent performances.

So is the present one. Certainly it has more of an emotional charge in the 'Dies irae' than Spering's which, once the trump has sounded, gathers the voices with nervous intensity rather than the urgent drama that both Best and Fasolis discover. Best and Fasolis also produce great vigour for the 'Quam olim Abrahae' fugue. No one can make very much of the *Sanctus*, a surprisingly weak movement; all respond sensitively to the strange 'Pie Jesu', Best and Fasolis with rather sharper definition of phrasing.

All three open with the tremendous *Marche funèbre*, another piece that inspired Berlioz when he came to write his *Hamlet* funeral march. Excellent as the new performance is, those who acquired Best, in particular, can rest content.

Fryderyk Chopin   Polish 1810-1849

Few composers command such universal love as Chopin; even fewer have such a high proportion of their entire output remaining in the active repertoire. He's the only great composer whose every work involves the piano - no symphonies, operas or choral works and only a handful of compositions that involve other instruments. He wrote just under 200 works; 169 of these are for solo piano.

The greatest of all Polish composers had a French father, Nicholas, who had gone to Poland as a young man and become a tutor to the family of Countess Skarbek at Żelazowa Wola. His mother was the Countess's lady in waiting, herself from Polish nobility. This dual nationality is reflected in Chopin's music – the epic struggle of the Poles and the refined elegance of the French. Shortly after Frédéric's birth, the family moved to Warsaw where his father had a teaching post.

Chopin had his first piano lessons from Adalbert Zwyny in 1816, a local all-round musician, and made his public debut at nine. He then became a piano student of Joseph Elsner, director of the Warsaw Conservatory. It's largely thanks to Elsner and Zwyny that Chopin developed into the original creative force he became: they let him develop in his own way.

A friend of Chopin's father invited him to Berlin and in 1829 he gave two concerts in Vienna, including his Variations on Mozart's 'Là ci darem la mano' after which Schumann made his famous judgement: 'Hats off, gentlemen! A genius.'

The fading attractions of Warsaw, further diminished by his unrequited love of a young singer, persuaded him to leave Poland. Before he left, his old teacher Elsner presented him with a silver urn of Polish earth with the admonishment 'May you never forget your native land wherever you go, nor cease to love it with a warm and faithful heart'. The urn was buried with Chopin when he died.

Despite a Polish revolt against Russian rule soon afterwards, Chopin headed for Vienna (probably he would have been too physically frail to serve in the army in any case). After some time in Stuttgart, intending to travel to London, he stopped off in Paris in 1831. It remained his home for the rest of his life.

His Paris debut in January 1832 was not a success. The Parisians did not take to his playing or music immediately and Chopin thought for a time of leaving for America. His destiny was changed by Prince Radziwiłł who introduced him to the salon of Baron Jacques de Rothschild. Here Chopin triumphed and from then on his career as a composer (and highly paid teacher) was a story of unbroken success.

Chopin was a sensitive, fastidious man who never enjoyed exactly robust health. The rich, privileged world of the aristocratic and wealthy salons not only appealed to his snobbish instincts (he liked to mingle with money and beautiful women) but provided the perfect ambience for his music and his particular style of playing. Audiences admired his cantabile (singing) touch. Where Liszt was the thunderous, virtuoso showman, Chopin was the refined, undemonstrative poet, noted for his rubato, the effect whereby notes are not played in strict tempo but subtly lengthened and shortened 'like a trees' leaves in the breeze', as Liszt described it.

His first great love in Paris was the flirtatious daughter of Count Wodzińska. The family put a stop to the affair. His next was perhaps the most unlikely woman of his circle: Aurore Dupin (Mme Dudevant), the radical, free-thinking novelist who called

herself George Sand. By no means good-looking (photographs bear witness), she smoked cigars and wore men's clothing. 'What a repellent woman she is,' was Chopin's reaction when he first set eyes on her. 'Is she really a woman? I'm ready to doubt it.' Nevertheless she exercised a fascination for Chopin and a relationship developed which lasted for 10 years, a mother figure who became the love of his life. One of her personal letters implies that the physical side of their life was embraced less than enthusiastically by the composer.

In 1838 George Sand travelled to Majorca with her son and daughter and Chopin joined her there. Instead of the paradise they hoped for, it turned into a disaster with inhospitable and antagonistic locals, damp, wet weather and the breakdown of Chopin's health. He began having haemorrhages and hallucinations and it was only a prompt departure for the mainland that saved his life (he had another haemorrhage in Barcelona).

For the next few years, Chopin was at the height of his creative powers, respected and internationally famous. His health deteriorated and he became more consumptive year by year.

The increasingly tense relationship with George Sand came to an end in 1848. Sand seemed comparatively unaffected; 'Chopin,' said Liszt, 'felt and often repeated that in breaking this long affection, this powerful bond, he had broken his life.' A Scottish pupil of Chopin, Jane Stirling, persuaded him to make a trip to England and Scotland with her but this and a few fundraising concerts undermined his health further and when he returned to Paris he became a virtual recluse, too weak to compose or teach.

He gave strict instructions that all his unpublished manuscripts be destroyed. Chopin had a good idea of his worth and was determined that only his best work should survive. He died on October 17, 1849, from consumption and was buried in Père Lachaise cemetery next to his friend Bellini.

More than any other, Chopin is responsible for the development of modern piano technique and style. His influence on succeeding generations of writers of piano music was profound and inescapable. He dreamt up a whole range of new colours, harmonies and means of expression in which he exploited every facet of the new developments in piano construction. The larger keyboard (seven octaves) and improved mechanism opened up new possibilities of musical expression. He possessed an altogether richer and deeper poetic insight than the myriad pianist-composers who flourished during his lifetime.

Piano Concertos

No 1 in E minor, Op 11; **No 2** in F minor, Op 21

Piano Concertos Nos 1 & 2
Martha Argerich pf
Montreal Symphony Orchestra / Charles Dutoit
EMI 556798-2 (69' · DDD)   Ⓟ❍❍❍❍➔

Martha Argerich's first commercially released recordings of the Chopin concertos were for

DG; No 1 in 1968, No 2 in 1978. Here she revisits both concertos and offers an act of re-creative daring, of an alternating reverie and passion that flashes fire with a thousand different lights. Indeed, her earlier performances are infinitely less witty, personal and eruptive, less inclined to explore, albeit with the most spontaneous caprice and insouciance, so many new facets, angles and possibilities. Now, everything is accomplished without a care for studios and microphones and with a degree of involvement that suggests an increase rather than a diminution of her love for these works. The recordings are impressively natural and if Dutoit occasionally seems awed if not cowed into anonymity by his soloist (the opening *tuttis* to the slow movements of both concertos are less memorable than they should be) he sets off Argerich's charisma to an exceptional degree. Argerich's light burns brighter than ever. Rarely in their entire history have the Chopin concertos received performances of a more teasing allure, brilliance and idiosyncrasy.

Piano Concertos Nos 1 & 2
Murray Perahia pf
Israel Philharmonic Orchestra / Zubin Mehta
Sony Classical SMK87323 (76' · DDD)
Recorded live 1989   Ⓜ️🔘▶️

Perahia has never made any secret of his liking for the 'inspirational heat-of-the-moment' of a live performance as opposed to a studio recording, where 'sometimes things get tame'. As enthusiastic audience applause (discreetly rationed on the disc) makes plain, these two concertos were recorded live at Tel Aviv's Mann Auditorium. Whether they were subsequently 'doctored' we don't know, but the finished product brings us a Perahia miraculously combining exceptional finesse with an equally exceptional urgency. In all but the finale of No 1 (where Pollini on EMI beats him by a minute) his timings throughout both works are considerably faster than most of his rivals on disc. Was this prompted by 'inspirational heat-of-the-moment'? Or was it a deliberate attempt to come closer than others do to the surprisingly briskish metronome markings printed in the Eulenburg scores? The two slow movements are distinguished by exquisitely limpid *cantabile* and superfine delicacy of decorative detail while again conveying urgent undercurrents. But in a guessing-game perhaps it would be the two finales that would most betray the identity of the soloist. Not only are they faster, but they are also of a more scintillating, *scherzando*-like lightness. The recording is first rate.

Piano Concertos – Nos 1ᵃ & 2ᵇ
Arthur Rubinstein pf ᵃ**Los Angeles Philharmonic Orchestra / Alfred Wallenstein**; ᵇ**NBC Symphony Orchestra / William Steinberg**
Naxos Historical mono 8 111296 (67' · ADD)
Recorded ᵃ1953, ᵇ1946   Ⓢ🔘🔘▶️

Mercifully uncut, unlike Rubinstein's previous discs of both concertos with Barbirolli, these are astonishing performances, occasionally, particularly in the Second Concerto, content simply to astonish. Here there is an almost arrogant dismissal of all difficulties and a prima donna stance sometimes hard to square with some of Chopin's more delicate and ornate confidences. In the scintillating coda Rubinstein takes his bravura to a spine-tingling edge, but in, for example, the *Larghetto*'s central storms there is a brusque, streamlined indifference to the music's finer qualities.

In the First Concerto, while recognisably the same pianist, Rubinstein is altogether more subtle, following his characteristic exuberance and extroversion with playing of a rapt magic and delicacy. The music may be sent smartly on its way by both conductor and soloist, but the patrician ease, nonchalant glitter and authority of Rubinstein's playing are uniquely his to command. These are both extraordinary performances by an extraordinary pianist, though of the two, the First Concerto is the more affecting. Mark Obert-Thorn's restoration of the 1953 sound is a model of remastery though even he cannot make the 1946 Second Concerto sound less than cramped.

Piano Concertos Nos 1ᵃ & 2ᵇ   Ⓗ
Noel Mewton-Wood pf ᵃ**Netherlands Philharmonic Orchestra**, ᵇ**Zürich Symphony Orchestra / Walter Goehr**
Dante Historical Piano Collection HPC105 (69' · ADD)
Recorded c1951, 1948   Ⓕ

Inconsolable after the death of his partner Bill Fredricks, Noel Mewton-Wood (1922-53) committed suicide and robbed the world of a musical genius. Born in Melbourne, he included, in his London-based career, work with Schnabel, a debut (in Beethoven's Third Concerto) with Sir Thomas Beecham, the frequent replacement of Benjamin Britten as Peter Pears's musical collaborator and, mercifully for the present generation, the making of several recordings taken from his eclectic and enterprising repertoire.

Amazingly, in his incomparably sensitive and robust hands, the Chopin concertos seem as though heard for the first time, their passions and intimacies virtually recreated on the spot. Who of today's pianists would or could risk such candour or phrase and articulate Chopin's early intricacy with such alternating strength and delicacy? The notes (in French only) suggest parallels with Solomon, Anatole Kitain and Murray Perahia, yet as with all truly great artists, Mewton-Wood's playing defies comparison, however exalted. No more vital or individual performances exist on record. The orchestra is hardly a model of precision or refinement but the recordings have come up remarkably well.

Piano Concerto No 1. Ballade in G minor, Op 23 . Nocturnes – Nos 4 & 5, Op 15 Nos 1 & 2; Nos 7 & 8,

Op 27. Polonaise No 6, Op 53, 'Heroic'
Maurizio Pollini pf **Philharmonia Orchestra /**
Paul Kletzki
EMI 567548-2 (73' · ADD). Recorded 1960-68 Ⓜ❍❍↻

This disc is a classic. The concerto was recorded shortly after the 18-year-old pianist's victory at the Warsaw competition in 1959. Nowadays we might expect a wider dynamic range to allow greater power in the first movement's *tuttis*, but in all other respects the recording completely belies its age, with a near perfect balance between soloist and orchestra. This is very much Pollini's disc, just as the First Concerto is very much the soloist's show, but effacing as the accompaniment is, Pollini's keyboard miracles of poetry and refinement could not have been achieved without one of the most characterful and responsive accounts of that accompaniment ever committed to tape. The expressive range of the Philharmonia on top form under Kletzki is exceptional, as is the accord between soloist and conductor in phrasing and shading. The solo items are a further reminder of Pollini's effortless bravura and aristocratic poise.

Piano Concerto No 1, Op 11ᵃ. Four Balladesᵇ.
Barcarolle, Op 60ᶜ. Nocturnes – No 5, Op 15
No 2ᵈ; No 13, Op 48 No 1ᵉ; No 17, Op 62 No 1ᶠ.
Preludes, Op 28ᵍ. Waltz No 14, Op posthʰ
Gulda Epitaph for a Loveⁱ
Friedrich Gulda pf
ᵃ**London Philharmonic Orchestra / Sir Adrian Boult**
DG ᵃᵇᶜᵈᵉᵍmono ② 477 8724GH2 (150' · ADD)
Recorded ᵃ1954; live in ᵇᵍʰ1955, ᵈ1956, ᶜᵉ1960, ᶠⁱ1986
Ⓜ❍❐↻

Here in all his glory is Friedrich Gulda the ultimate maverick pianist, yet beneath his determined assault on what he saw as the stuffy conventions of the music world (the Viennese world in particular) lay a pianist of genius aptly described by Martha Argerich, his one-time protégée, as 'the most extraordinary and brilliant man I ever met'.

Certainly all the live performances on these discs create a towering tribute to Chopin. Forever the nonconformist, Gulda may sometimes be wilful and irascible but he is never less than mesmeric and fascinating. Time and again he casts a novel and intense light on even the most familiar phrase, making you hang on every note. Try Prelude No 14 for a virtuoso savagery beyond the world of other more 'civilised' pianists, or No 13 where Gulda's rapture makes the music stretch seemingly to infinity. Again there may be moments in the Ballades and Barcarolle where the playing verges on hysteria but the sheer mastery and strength are like an elemental force of nature. Even when he takes a rough hand to some of Chopin's more intimate confessions, his way with his selection of Nocturnes creates a sense of drama and occasion light years away from more recent recordings.

The First Concerto is given in Balakirev's touched-up version and if in the studio Gulda's

playing is more disciplined, less free-thinking, it is also of a special imaginative delicacy and engagement. The programme ends with Gulda's own *Epitaph for a Love*, a strange mixed-up jazz effusion that includes some very odd vocals in Viennese dialect and a phantom reference to Chopin's C minor Prelude. The pianist's son, Paul Gulda, writes a moving and informative essay clarifying much of his father's complexity and telling us, perhaps not surprisingly, that Alfred Cortot was among his chief musical idols.

Piano Concerto No 2ᵃ.   Ⓗ
Ballade No 1, Op 23. Mazurka No 35,
Op 56 No 3. Etudes, Op 10 – Nos 6, 8 & 9.
Scherzo No 4, Op 54. Andante spianato
and Grande polonaise, Op 22
Arthur Rubinstein pf ᵃ**Philharmonia Orchestra /**
Carlo Maria Giulini
BBC Legends mono BBCL4105-2 (78' · ADD)
Recorded live 1959; ᵃ1961   Ⓕ❍

Rubinstein remains the most elegant and life-affirming of all great Chopin pianists, his patrician ease and stylistic distinction the envy and despair of lesser mortals. Above all he understood a central paradox, that Chopin was in love with the human voice, yet sensing the limitation of words and a single vocal line confided his deepest, most fiery and intimate thoughts to the piano, an instrument of a supposed percussive limitation. No pianist has played Chopin with a more translucent and uncluttered tone, with a greater sense of singing 'line', of vocal breathing and inspiration. His *rubato* was personal and inimitable, a subtle bending of the phrase, an ebb and flow. Above all there was his sovereign naturalness. Audiences felt transported, indeed transfigured by his playing.

These wondrous performances transport you to another world. True, there are tiny slips of finger and concentration, yet they do nothing to qualify a sense of supreme mastery. In the Concerto, where, despite a once traditional and disfiguring cut in the opening *tutti*, he's memorably partnered by Giulini, Rubinstein achieves a flawless balance between Chopin's ever-elusive mix of poise and intensity. In his recital his reading of the great C minor Mazurka surely numbers among the greatest of all Chopin performances in its play of light and shade, of brio and introspection.

But all these performances are memorable, haunting one over the years and now, thankfully, available in beautifully remastered sound.

Piano Concertos Nos 1 & 2 (chamber versions)
Fumiko Shiraga pf **Jan-Inge Haukås** db **Yggdrasil**
Quartet (Fredrik Paulsson, Per Oman vns Robert
Westlund va Per Nyström vc)
BIS BIS-CD847 (72' · DDD)   Ⓕ❍

This is one of the most exciting Chopin recordings in recent years because it confronts and deepens the uneasiness that Chopin lovers have with his concertos. They are more comfortable as chamber works, the chamber works he never succeeded in writing when he confronted that form head on. If you find Chopin's ideas inflated when cast in orchestral form, this recording will remove the last traces of doubt. Pianist Fumiko Shiraga has reduced the scope of the music, and wisely so. The heroism and grandeur is of the sort one finds in Schumann's piano-chamber context; the dynamic and expressive extremes that Shiraga achieves are no less compelling than a pianist unleashed against a large orchestra. Shiraga doubles in some *tutti* passages – a surprise at first, but again a wise decision. She adds gravity and fullness to the Yggdrasil Quartet's excellent accompaniment while remaining hidden, diligently underscoring but never overbearing.

Cello Works

Cello Sonata in G minor, Op 65. Polonaise brillante in C, Op 3 (ed Feuermann). Grande duo concertante in E on themes from Meyerbeer's 'Robert le Diable'. Nocturne in C sharp minor, Op posth (arr Piatigorsky) Etude in E minor, Op 25 No 7 (arr Glazunov). Waltz in A minor, Op 34 No 2 (arr Ginzburg). Etude in D minor, Op 10 No 6 (arr Glazunov)
Maria Kliegel vc **Bernd Glemser** pf
Naxos 8 553159 (64' · DDD)   ⓈⒷ▸

Here are Chopin's complete works for cello and piano complemented by an intriguing garland of encores. Performed with youthful relish, impressively balanced and recorded, this is a notable offering. Clearly, Kliegel and Glemser have few reservations concerning the sonata's surprisingly Germanic overtones. Recognisably Chopin in virtually every bar, there remains an oddly Schumannesque bias, particularly in the finale's tortuous argument – an irony when you consider that Chopin had so little time for his adoring colleague. Yet this awkward and courageous reaching out towards a terser form of expression is resolved by both artists with great vitality and, throughout, they create an infectious sense of a live rather than studio performance. Kliegel and Glemser are no less uninhibited in Chopin's earlier show-pieces, written at a time when the composer had a passing passion for grand opera and for what he dismissed as 'glittering trifles'. Their additions (transcriptions by Glazunov, Piatigorsky and Ginzburg) remind us how singers, violinists and cellists beg, borrow or steal Chopin from pianists at their peril. As Chopin put it, 'the piano is my solid ground; on that I stand the straightest', and his muse has proved oddly and magically resistant to change or transcription. Still, even though the selection often suggests an alien opacity, the performances are most warmly committed.

Piano Sonatas

No 1 in C minor, Op 4; **No 2** in B flat minor, Op 35; **No 3** in B minor, Op 58

Piano Sonatas Nos 2ª & 3ᵇ. Scherzo No 3, Op 39ᶜ
Martha Argerich pf
DG 419 055-2GGA (56' · ADD)
Recorded ª1975, ᵇ1967, ᶜ1961   ⓂⓄⓄⒷ▸

Here, simply and assuredly, is one of the most magisterial talents in the entire history of piano playing. She's hardly a comfortable companion, confirming your preconceptions. Indeed, she sets your heart and mind reeling so that you positively cry out for respite from her dazzling and super-sensitive enquiry. But she's surely a great musician first and a great pianist second. From her, Chopin is hardly the most balanced or classically biased of the Romantics. She can tear all complacency aside. How she keeps you on the *qui vive* in the Second and Third Sonatas. Is the Funeral March too brisk, an expression of sadness for the death of a distant relative rather than grief for a nation? Is the delicate rhythmic play at the heart of the Third Sonata's *Scherzo* virtually spun out of existence? Such qualms or queries tend to be whirled into extinction by more significant felicities. Who but Argerich, with her subtle half-pedalling, could conjure so baleful and macabre a picture of 'winds whistling over graveyards' in the Second Sonata's finale, or achieve such heart-stopping exultance in the final pages of the Third Sonata (this performance is early Argerich with a vengeance, alive with a nervous brio). And if her free spirit leaves us tantalised, thirsting for Chopin's First, Second and Fourth as well as his Third Scherzos, for example, she has also left us overwhelmingly enriched, for ever in her debt.

Piano Sonata No 2. Ballade No 2, Op 38.
Mazurkas Nos 22-25, Op 33. Waltzes Nos 2-4,
Op 34. Impromptu No 2, Op 36
Maurizio Pollini pf
DG 477 7626GH (57' · DDD)   Ⓕ Ⓞ Ⓑ▸

The programme embraces Chopin's Opp 33-38 with the exception of the two Nocturnes, Op 37, though they're not played in chronological order. Pollini begins with a magnificent account of the Ballade No 2, the maelstrom that erupts after the pastoral first page sounding like a howl of despair. The four Mazurkas, Op 33, and three Waltzes, Op 34, not only form a contrast to the Ballade but are themselves contrasted with each other. The F sharp major Impromptu, almost a mini-ballade, is heard in another refined account, Pollini relishing the *leggiero jeu perlé* scale passagework at the close. In the Second Sonata, Pollini unites what Schumann called 'four of [Chopin's] wildest children' into a family, a feat managed by few pianists, the first movement (with a *da capo* repeat) leading quite naturally into the *Scherzo* and so on.

It'd be difficult for Pollini to produce an ugly sound (and he doesn't here), but while the piano is captured from a slight distance (say the front row of the stalls), the pianist's frequent nasal intakes of breath are recorded in close-up.

Piano Sonata No 2. Four Scherzos
Simon Trpčeski pf
EMI 375586-2 (65' · DDD)   Ⓕ**OO**Ⓑ⟶

From Simon Trpčeski, Chopin's music boils with a Heathcliff-like defiance. Here is no drawing-room dandy but a composer who truly rages against the dying of the light. Yet just as awe replaces critical scrutiny when faced with Trpčeski's formidable mastery, you remember how such towering virtuosity is complemented by an equally remarkable refinement. If few pianists have stormed the Second Sonata's first movement more heroically, even fewer have played the Funeral March's central Elysian Trio with such poise and concentration.

The four Scherzos, too, offer a similar combination of superlatives, one where a thrusting youthful impetuosity is balanced by lyrical introspection (try Chopin's central *molto più lento* reworking of the Polish carol 'Sleep little Jesus'). Such unfaltering style and assurance are enough to make lesser pianists weep with envy and, more generally, there is an almost palpable sense of Chopin's irony, when he called three of his most savage utterances 'scherzo' (literally meaning a joke). Trpčeski's dizzying voltage and aplomb, superbly recorded, represent the finest modern alternative.

Piano Sonatas Nos 2 & 3. Fantasie, Op 49
Arthur Rubinstein pf
RCA Victor Red Seal 09026 63046-2 (61' · ADD)
Recorded 1960s   Ⓜ

In the Chopin sonatas it's difficult to think of which performance to choose as the greatest. Aside from the Funeral March itself, Rubinstein's account of the Second Sonata is a bit too imperious; the Third is much more thrilling, with considerable technical risks being taken both in the first movement and the finale. His own feeling for quiet nuances in the *Largo* of this work is quite superb, and here too Pollini on DG achieves an innocence that's disarming. Pollini's disc is the most perfect, both in terms of the pianist's technical accomplishment and the lucid piano sound, with nothing that offends the ear. The middle treble range in Rubinstein's piano sound has a hollow resonance. Rubinstein tackles the F minor Fantasie in rather a heavy-handed manner, with more power than searching drama. If you want your Chopin sonatas balanced and formally cohesive, then Rubinstein is for you.

Piano Sonatas – No 2 & 3.
Barcarolle, Op 60. Berceuse, Op 57.
Nocturnes – No 7, Op 27 No 1; No 8, Op 27 No 2.
Marc-André Hamelin pf
Hyperion CDA67706 (77' · DDD)   Ⓕ**OO**

This is a disc that takes you by stealth. Not simply because it opens almost unassumingly, with a finely wrought Berceuse, but because it was only after several listenings that one realises just how good it is. This is Hamelin's second recording of the Second Sonata and it shows how much his pianism has developed during the intervening time.

Hamelin's playing is refreshingly free from the 'inverted comma' school of profundity, and he lets the music speak through him most eloquently; he doesn't get carried away with the subtext of the Second's Funeral March, keeping it flowing (with desynchronisation of the hands subtly done) and all the more effective as a result. In the slow movement of the Third he finds time to dream without ever becoming portentous, and is every bit the equal of Nelson Freire, whose Chopin sonatas have rightly won considerable praise. Predictably, Hamelin is wonderful in such things as the *Scherzo* of the Third and the visceral finale of the Second, though perhaps slower than you might expect in the neurotic *Scherzo* of No 2. In the finale of the Third he doesn't begin the build-up too soon, as can be a temptation, and even has a skip in his step.

The addition of two Nocturnes and the sublime Barcarolle simply confirm that though Hamelin has made many fabulous discs, particularly in repertoire of superhuman virtuosity, this is one of his very finest achievements to date.

Piano Sonatas Nos 2 & 3. Etudes – Op 10; Op 25.
Impromptus – No 1, Op 29; No 2, Op 36; No 3, Op 51. Fantaisie-impromptu, Op 66
Janina Fialkowska pf
ATMA Classique ② ACD2 2554 (137' · DDD) Ⓜ**OOO**

Lesser mortals may well weep with envy at such unfaltering authority and one hesitates even to imagine the hours of work behind such magnificence. What a glittering and assured curtain-raiser to the Op 10 Etudes; and if she can command with the best of them she can just as easily take you into her confidence. No 3 is, for once, truly *Lento* though with a marked sense of character in the central *Poco più animato*, while in No 6 Fialkowska is hauntingly responsive to Chopin's nameless malaise. How perfectly she judges the echoing mountain-calls in No 9, while even the most seasoned pianist might despair over her fleetness in the Op 25 Etude 'in thirds'.

Elsewhere she is grand and imperious in the Second Sonata, storming the first movement's climax in towering and heroic fashion, and her demonic pace and drive make a true Mephisto-*scherzo* of the second movement. Her finale, while hardly *sotto voce*, opts for a more ferocious but intriguingly voiced alternative and she has all of the four Impromptus' lighter charm and caprice at her fingertips. Her B minor Sonata is as thoughtful as it is masterly and if one occasionally misses the seductive tonal allure and magical *cantabile* of a Cortot or Perahia (most notably in the *Largo*), there's admiration aplenty for such clarity, strength of purpose and musical integrity. Fialkowska offers an unfailing balance of sense and sensibility. Well recorded, she has done her one time mentor, Arthur Rubinstein, proud.

Piano Sonata No 2. Four Scherzos.
Nocturnes – No 16, Op 55 No 2; No 17, Op 62
No 1; No 18, Op 62 No 2; No 19, Op 72 No 1
Louis Lortie pf
Chandos CHAN10588 (80' · DDD)   ⓕⓄ🠊

The booklet's 'note from the performer' for this first volume of a planned series of Chopin discs by Lortie raised a silent cheer. Other pianists should take note. Taking his lead from the days when pianists would improvise between selections to get the audience in the right mood, Lortie uses a Nocturne in a closely related key to preface each Scherzo. 'I believe, moreover, that nobody really wants to sit down and listen to pieces of a single genre in a row…This practice…makes more sense by allowing the listener to enjoy the contents in one stretch.'

It's a credo that serves Chopin's genius far better than the default approach (it complements each Nocturne just as much as it does the Scherzos), the more so when the performances are as richly coloured and deftly articulated as these. Along the way there are some lovely individual touches like the way Lortie varies the dynamics in the exposition repeat of the First Scherzo, and the way he tiptoes querulously into the minor-key episode of the Third Scherzo. The soundscape of the recording is bit man-alone-in-empty-studio, and a *da capo* (rather than *doppio movimento*) repeat in the Sonata's first movement always sounds clumsy. But these are minor cavils. This is Chopin playing of a superior order.

Piano Sonata No 3. Mazurkas Nos 36-38, Op 59.
Nocturne No 4, Op 15 No 1. Polonaise No 6, Op 53,
'Heroic'. Scherzo No 3, Op 39
Martha Argerich pf
EMI 556805-2 (52' · ADD). Recorded 1965   ⓕ🠊

Argerich's pianism is remarkable for combining seemingly effortless technical resource with temperamental volatility. Yet the vehemence of her playing is seldom to the disadvantage of the extraordinary subtlety of her art. Moreover, despite the limits she places on her repertory, such is the spontaneity of her approach that each of her interpretations, no matter how familiar in broad outline, is characterised by a profusion of contrasting details beneath the surface. In the B minor Sonata she omits the first-movement repeats. Such a formal contraction can contribute to the momentum with which the movement unfolds. Ironically, however, she seems to rein in the propulsive power for which she's renowned, appearing instead to be seeking at every turn to exploit a deeply felt exprssive lyricism to offset the febrile intensity of the most energetic figurational devices. This has the virtue of allowing us a less hectic view of subsidiary elements within the music, which elsewhere can too often be overwhelmed by the sheer turbulence of the action.

CHOPIN'S PIANO SONATA NO 2 – IN BRIEF

Martha Argerich
DG 419 055-2GGA (56' · ADD)   ⓜⓄⓄ🠊
Coupled with the Third Sonata and the Scherzo No 3, this disc shows off Argerich's mastery of this music. You never quite know what will happen next, which only adds to the excitement! Red-blooded Chopin, for sure.

Vladimir Ashkenazy
Decca download 448 123-2DM (76' · ADD)   ⓜ🠊
Ashkenazy's Chopin is wonderfully poetic, and this disc contains all three sonatas. His way with the slow movements – try the Funeral March – is very appealing.

Murray Perahia
Sony Classical MK76242 (50' · DDD)   ⓜⓄ🠊
Beautifully played, intellectually probing Chopin with an great emphasis on detail and incidental delights. Coupled with the Third Piano Sonata – another joy.

Arthur Rubinstein
RCA 09026 63046-2 (61' · ADD)   ⓜⓄⓄ
Rubinstein is the Chopin pianist *par excellence* for many people, and listening to him in the Second and Third Sonatas it's easy to agree. Poetry flows from his fingers with ease, and his way with the most subtle nuance is quite breathtaking.

Maurizio Pollini
DG 415 346-2GH (52' · DDD)   ⓕⓄ🠊
This is Chopin playing of great power and feeling: there's no hint of the chilliness of which Pollini is occasionally accused.

Ivo Pogorelich
DD download 463 678-2GOR (73' · ADD)   ⓑⓄ🠊
Perhaps Pogorelich's most controversial recording, but in 1981, as his recorded debut, it established him as a player of quite extraordinary technique and temperament. It's coupled, unusually, with Ravel's *Gaspard de la nuit* and Prokofiev's Piano Sonata No 6.

Simon Trpčeski pf
EMI 375586-2 (65' · DDD)   ⓜⓄⓄ🠊
Power and poetry fuse magnificently for the young Macedonian pianist. He wears his considerable virtuosity lightly and gives the sonata a really heroic face: this is not salon Chopin but living drama.

Emil Gilels   Ⓗ
Testament SBT1089 (64' · ADD)   ⓕ
The great Russian pianist, far too little represented on record in Chopin, proves to be a magnificent interpreter, full of majestic gesture and noble utterance. This is resonant playing (coupled, oddly, with Mozart and Shostakovich).

Some of the most satisfying playing on the disc comes in her account of the Op 59 Mazurkas. There's a vulnerability as well as an affecting wistfulness about the playing which captures the elusiveness of the idiom, with its harmonic ambiguities, with rare acuity. At the other end of the scale, the excitement she generates in the A flat Polonaise is of an order that goes far beyond mere effect. If these accounts do not necessarily outstrip her other recordings, they nevertheless offer an intriguing insight into a 'work in progress' from a pianistic giant whose artistry continues to fascinate and perplex.

Piano Sonata No 3ᶜ Ballade No 1, Op 23ᵃ. Etude,
Op 10 No 4ᵇ. Mazurkasᵇ – No 15, Op 24 No 2; No 23,
Op 33 No 2; No 26, Op 41 No 1; No 27, Op 41 No 2;
Nos 36-38, Op 59. Nocturnesᵇ – No 4, Op 15 No 1;
No 16, Op 55 No 2.
Martha Argerich *pf*
DG 477 7557GH (64' · DDD)
Recorded in ᵃ1959; ᵇ1967; ᶜlive at the Hochschule für
Musik, Berlin, on March 15, 1967   Ⓕ**ⓄⒷ▸**

Argerich first came to international prominence in 1965 when she won the Chopin Competition. The first track on this CD dates from six years earlier, a blistering performance of the G minor Ballade recently unearthed in the archives of Deutschlandradio Kultur (formerly RIAS) in Berlin. The work is new to Argerich's discography but, though it will not worry her legions of admirers, neither the recorded sound nor the duff piano are things of aural beauty.

There is a marked improvement in these respects in the following selections of Mazurkas and Nocturnes recorded in a different RIAS studio eight years later with, inevitably, a greater depth and maturity to the playing. Before these, there is a quite dazzling performance of the Op 10 C sharp minor Etude, not the fastest on disc (though fairly brisk) but one of the fastest that also makes musical sense. This and the Mazurkas Op 24 No 2, Op 33 No 2 and Op 41 Nos 1 and 4 are also works Argerich has not otherwise recorded. From the playing here, it's no wonder she won the Chopin Competition. Likewise the three Mazurkas Op 59, discovered in the vaults of West German Radio (WDR) in Cologne, she captures their intimacy and lightning changes of mood to perfection.

Then the B minor Sonata, a live performance at the Berlin Hochschule für Musik. Though she over-reaches herself in the first part of the *Scherzo*, this is even better than her familiar studio recording of two months earlier. In the finale (for once truly *agitato*) she sweeps all before her with breathless exhilaration.

Piano Sonata No 3. Mazurkas – No 13, Op 17 No 4;
No 17, Op 24 No 4; No 20, Op 30 No 3; No 23,
Op 33 No 2; No 32, Op 50 No 3; No 34, Op 56 No 2;
No 38, Op 59 No 3; No 39, Op 63 No 1; No 40,
Op 63 No 2; No 41, Op 63 No 3; No 49, Op 68 No 4

Evgeny Kissin *pf*
RCA Victor Red Seal 09026 62542-2 (65' · DDD)
Recorded live 1993   Ⓕ**Ⓞ**

Kissin is among the master-pianists of our time. What magnificence and assertion he finds in the B minor Sonata's opening, what menace in the following uprush of chromatic scales, his deliberate pedal haze capturing one of Chopin's most truly modernist moments. He may relish left-hand counter-melody in the return of the second subject and elsewhere, yet such detail is offered within the context of the whole. A momentary failure of concentration in the *Scherzo* comes as reassuring evidence of human fallibility but elsewhere one can only marvel at a manner so trenchant, musicianly and resolutely unsentimental. The equestrian finale is among the most lucid on record and concludes in a controlled triumph that has the audience cheering to the heavens.

The 12 Mazurkas are no less remarkable for their strength and discretion. Everything unfolds with complete naturalness and authority. The beautifully idiomatic *rubato* is so stylishly applied that you're only aware of the finest fluctuations of pulse and emotion. Few pianists have gone to the heart of the matter with such assurance (always excepting Arthur Rubinstein). The recording captures Kissin's clear, unnarcissistic sonority admirably and audience noise is minimal.

Four Ballades

No 1 in G minor, Op 23; **No 2** in F, Op 38;
No 3 in A flat, Op 47; **No 4** in F minor, Op 52

Four Ballades.
Mazurkas – No 7, Op 7 No 3; No 13, Op 17 No 4;
No 23, Op 33 No 2. Waltzes – No 1, Op 18; No 5,
Op 42; No 7, Op 64 No 2. Etudes, Op 10 – No 3;
No 4. Nocturne No 4, Op 15 No 1
Murray Perahia *pf*
Sony Classical SK64399 (61' · DDD)   Ⓕ**ⓄⓄⓄⒷ▸**

 This is surely the greatest, certainly the richest, of Perahia's many exemplary recordings. Once again his performances are graced with rare and classic attributes and now, to supreme clarity, tonal elegance and musical perspective, he adds an even stronger poetic profile, a surer sense of the inflammatory rhetoric underpinning Chopin's surface equilibrium. In other words the vividness and immediacy are as remarkable as the finesse. And here, arguably, is the oblique but telling influence of Horowitz whom Perahia befriended during the last months of the old wizard's life. Listen to the First Ballade's second subject and you'll hear *rubato* like the most subtle pulsing or musical breathing. Try the opening of the Third and you'll note an ideal poise and lucidity, something rarely achieved in these outwardly insouciant pages. From Perahia the waltzes are marvels of liquid brilliance and urbanity. Even Lipatti hardly achieved such an enchanting lilt or buoyancy, such a beguiling sense of light and shade. In the mazurkas, too, Perahia's tiptoe delicacy and tonal iridescence (particularly in Op 7 No 3 in F minor) make the music dance and spin as if caught in some magical hallucinatory haze. Finally, two contrasting Etudes, and whether in ardent lyricism (Op 10 No 3) or shot-from-guns virtuosity (Op 10 No 4) Perahia's playing is sheer perfection. The recording beautifully captures his instantly recognisable, glistening sound world.

Four Ballades. Four Scherzos
Stephen Hough pf
Hyperion CDA67456 (72' · DDD)   ⒻOO

This is astonishing piano playing; Chopin interpretation that, at its best, fully measures up to the greatness of these pieces. Stephen Hough's accounts offer plenty of refreshment to spirit and senses.

The distribution is interesting, chronological but alternating one of each, which may not make a recital to consume at one go but helps to point up these pieces' diversity and individual character, as well as Chopin's mastery of large forms. Hough is unfailingly thoughtful; there isn't a note that hasn't been cared for. Just a few of them (Third Ballade, for example) are picked out of the texture and strung together for our delectation in a way that might strike you as otiose if you're in a sober-sides kind of mood. The surfaces of his presentations are very 'worked', more indicative of application, maybe, than of organic growth. But this isn't superficial playing – the performances catch fire.

He inclines to the accepted view that Chopin's large forms have a 'plot' that culminates in a tumult or a whirlwind of activity. The tempest in the coda of the Fourth Ballade might have been a mite less furious, to let the ear have more time to register what's going on. The closing pages of No 1, on the other hand, have an exemplary finish and allure. Most distinguished of the Ballades is No 2, where Hough perceives the invasion of one kind of music by another in all its subtlety and lays out a spellbinding seven-minute drama.

He has interesting points to make in the Scherzos, too. Where many a player is content to let recurring sections and paragraphs register simply as the music we heard before, with him they sound different in some degree, affected by what's come in between. Hough is always doing something, though sometimes you might wish he were doing less. This is an issue out of the ordinary; welcome, too, for being handsomely recorded and produced.

Ballades Nos 3 & 4. Mazurkas – No 36, Op 59 No 1; No 37, Op 59 No 2; No 38, Op 59 No 3; No 39, Op 63

No 1; No 40, Op 63 No 2; No 41, Op 63 No 3; No 49, Op 68 No 4. Polonaises – No 5, Op 44; No 6, 'Heroic', Op 53
Piotr Anderszewski pf
Virgin Classics 545619-2 (60' · DDD)   ⒻOOⒹ

Following his celebrated earlier discs of Beethoven, Mozart and Bach, 34-year-old Piotr Anderszewski gives us an exceptionally powerful and seductive Chopin recital. He prefers a subtly chosen programme to complete sets of the Mazurkas, Ballades or Polonaises, and his often phenomenally acute and sensitive awareness of Chopin's constantly shifting perspective has you reliving every bar of such incomparable music.

In the three Op 59 Mazurkas (a notably rich part of Chopin's deeply confessional diary) he achieves a rare sense of brooding introspection, close to neurosis, with bittersweet mood-swings that shift from resignation to flashes of anger. Then there's the F minor Mazurka, Op 63 No 2, taken for once at a true *lento*, a dark place indeed for Anderszewski, with only relative light in the central idea to lessen the mood of heart-stopping despondency. Again, in both the Ballades his sharply original ideas combine with a total responsibility to the score; seldom can the letter and spirit of the composer be united so flawlessly.

Eyebrows may be raised in the A flat Polonaise but this is no obvious celebration of triumph over adversity, rather a re-creation of music which lives again in all its initial audacity. Here, in this great young pianist's incomparable hands, and in Virgin's excellent sound, is living proof that Chopin's music is forever new, forever revelatory.

Four Ballades. Nocturnes – No 2, Op 9 No 2 (two recordings); No 4, Op 15 No 1; No 5, Op 15 No 2; No 7, Op 27 No 1; No 15, Op 55 No 1; No 16, Op 55 No 2   Ⓗ
Alfred Cortot pf
Naxos Historical mono 8 111245 (62' · ADD)
From HMV originals, recorded 1929-51   ⓈⒹ

This fifth and final release of Cortot's 78rpm Chopin recordings is surely the jewel in the crown. Here, the 1929 rather than the more familiar 1933 set of the Ballades blazes with a passion, brilliance and poetic audacity that set the pulses racing and the mind reeling. Here is a great artist who seized the opportunity to achieve ever greater heights of eloquence and rhetorical verve. Superbly restored by Mark Obert-Thorn, every performance is charged with a heady and consuming poetry that confirms Daniel Barenboim's claim that 'Cortot discovered the opium in Chopin'. Take the First Ballade's opening, where Cortot is every inch the bardic poet, free, rhapsodic and inimitable; or hear him in the *Presto con fuoco* storms of the Second Ballade, where he plays as if pursued by the furies of hell.

Again, even when inaccuracies fly in all directions in the heat of the chase, no other pianist has approached the Third Ballade's central C sharp minor turbulence with such daring or recreative force. Cortot was never one to hold back in the interests of decorum and in the Fourth Ballade he stretches the parameters of Chopin's poetry to the very edge, his playing close to being consumed in its own ecstasy.

His selection of Nocturnes (sadly his projected Chopin survey was never completed) pulse with the same alluring quality, suggesting the reverse of Rubinstein's more patrician elegance. True, for today's more antiseptic and 'tasteful' practitioners such artistic conviction and originality will seem extravagant or even camp. Yet there is surely no living pianist who could or would attempt to emulate such heart-stopping poetry. Maria Callas herself would have been among the first to pay tribute to Cortot's *cantabile*, an unequalled 'singing' at the piano.

Etudes

Etudes, Opp 10 & 25
Murray Perahia pf
Sony Classical SK61885 (56' · DDD)   Ⓟ**ⓄⓄⓄ**Ⓑ⟶

Perahia brings order and lucidity to the heart of Chopin's most audacious fire-storms and in, for example, Etudes Nos 1 and 4 from Op 10, you're made aware of an incomparable mix of poetry and precision. Perahia's may be a wholly modern voice yet he truly speaks in the spirit of his revered masters of the past, of Cortot and Fischer in particular, and this, allied with his immaculate, infinitely polished and shaded pianism, gives his performances the rarest distinction and quality.

How superb and unfaltering is his mastery in No 1, that magnificent curtain-raiser to Op 10, how magical his improvisatory touch in its closing page. His textural translucency and musical breathing, his *rubato* in No 3, like that of Rubinstein, is that of a great and natural singer of the keyboard. Chopin would surely have cried out once again, 'ah, mon patrie!' if he had heard this performance.

No 8 is delightfully rumbustious, and just when you note a touch of evasion in his rapid spin through the morbid near-Wagnerian chromaticism of No 6 you find yourself relishing his cool tempo, a musical ease and flexibility that give new meaning to Chopin's prescribed *con molto espressione*. On the other hand No 7 from Op 25 unfolds with the truest, most memorable sense of its *lento* elegy. And where else have you heard a more impassioned or articulate *Revolutionary* Etude? Perahia's is the finest of all modern discs of the Etudes, and Sony's sound captures all his artistry.

Etudes, Opp 10 & 25
Maurizio Pollini pf
DG 413 794-2GH (56' · ADD). Recorded 1972 Ⓟ**Ⓞ**⟶

The 24 Etudes of Chopin's Opp 10 and 25, although dating from his twenties, remain among the most perfect specimens of the genre ever known, with all technical challenges – and they are formidable – dissolved into the purest poetry. With his own transcendental technique (and there are few living pianists who can rival it), Pollini makes you unaware that problems even exist – as for instance in Op 10 No 10 in A flat, where the listener is swept along in an effortless stream of melody. The first and last of the same set in C major and C minor have an imperious strength and drive; likewise the last three impassioned outpourings of Op 25. Lifelong dislike of a heart worn on the sleeve makes him less than intimately confiding in more personal contexts such as No 3 in E major and No 6 in E flat minor from Op 10, or the nostalgic middle section of No 5 in E minor and the searing No 7 in C sharp minor from Op 25. Like the playing, so the recording itself could profitably be a little warmer at times, but it's a princely disc all the same.

Fantasie in F minor, Op 49

Fantasie, Op 49. Waltzes – No 2, Op 34 No 1;
No 3, Op 34 No 2; No 5, Op 42. Polonaise
No 5, Op 44. Nocturnes – No 1, Op 27
No 1; No 2, Op 27 No 2; No 10,
Op 32 No 2. Scherzo No 2, Op 31
Evgeny Kissin pf
RCA Victor Red Seal 09026 60445-2 (67' · DDD)
Recorded live 1993   Ⓕ

Evgeny Kissin's playing at 21 (when these performances were recorded) quite easily outmatches that of the young Ashkenazy and Pollini – and most particularly in terms of the maturity of his musicianship. The programme launches off with a reading of the great F minor Fantasie, which, though a bit measured, is integrated to perfection. The power and determination of the performance certainly make one sit up and listen, but at the same time it would be difficult not to be moved by the heartfelt lyricism of the melodic passages. Although Kissin may be a little unsmiling in the three Waltzes, at least he has admirable sophistication in being able to add interest to the interpretations. His control in the tricky A flat, Op 42, is quite amazing. The Nocturne in C sharp minor is a jewel. This reading is among the most darkly imaginative and pianistically refined on disc. The disc ends with a powerfully glittering performance of the Second Scherzo.

Mazurkas

Nos 1-64: Op 6 Nos 1-4 **(1-4)**; Op 7 Nos 1-5 **(5-9)**;
Op 17 Nos 1-4 **(10-13)**; Op 24 Nos 1-4 **(14-17)**;
Op 30 Nos 1-4 **(18-21)**; Op 33 Nos 1-4 **(22-25)**;
Op 41 Nos 1-4 **(26-29)**; Op 50 Nos 1-3 **(30-32)**;
Op 56 Nos 1-3 **(33-35)**; Op 59 Nos 1-3 **(36-38)**;
Op 63 Nos 1-3 **(39-41)**; Op 67 Nos 1-4 **(42-45)**;
Op 68 Nos 1-4 **(46-49)**; Op posth **(50-64)**

Mazurkas Nos 1-51
Arthur Rubinstein pf
RCA Victor Red Seal ② 09026 63050-2 (140' · ADD)
Recorded 1960s Ⓑ**OO**

Recording in the studio, rather than at a live concert, quite naturally leads to a safe and uniform approach, which doesn't really serve the inspired inventiveness of the music. In some ways these recordings suffer from this. If you compare Rubinstein's readings here with those he recorded on 78rpm discs in 1938-39, you immediately notice that an element of fantasy and caprice has given way to a more sober view of the music. The Mazurkas are so intricate in their variety of moods that the successful pianist has to be able to treat each one as an entity, contrasting the emotional content within the context of that particular piece. Rubinstein, with his serious approach, lends the music more weight than is usual and he wholly avoids trivialising it with over-snappy rhythms. With him many of the lesser-known Mazurkas come to life, such as the E flat minor, Op 6 No 4, with its insistent little motif that pervades the whole piece. His phrasing is free and flexible and he has utter appreciation of the delicacy of Chopin's ideas. He doesn't, however, take an improvisatory approach. Rubinstein judges to perfection which details to bring out so as to give each piece a special character. He convinces one that he has made this music his own. When you hear Rubinstein tackle the C sharp minor Mazurka, Op 53 No 3, you at once know that he fully comprehends the depth of this, perhaps the greatest of them all. He ranges from the pathos of the opening to a persuasive tonal grandeur in the more assertive parts, and yet is able to relate the two. The recording has a number of blemishes: the piano is too closely recorded, the loud passages are hollow-toned, especially in the bass, and there is little sparkle to the sound.

Mazurkas Nos 1-52, 55, 56, 59-62
Vladimir Ashkenazy pf
Double Decca 448 086-2DF2 (143' · DDD/ADD)
Recorded 1976-85 Ⓑ**OO**▷

Vladimir Ashkenazy made his integral set of the Mazurkas over a decade. He has always played the Mazurkas outstandingly. He does so again here, giving complete satisfaction. The set includes all those published posthumously and the revised version of Op 68 No 4; so his is the most comprehensive survey in the current catalogue. Ashkenazy memorably catches their volatile character, and their essential sadness. Consider, for example, the delicacy and untrammelled spontaneity with which he approaches these works. He shows the most exquisite sensibility, each item strongly though never insistently characterised. His accounts of the Mazurkas of Opp 6 and 7, for instance, offer a genuine alternative to Rubinstein. Nine pieces in all, they were Chopin's first published sets and their piquancy, the richness of their ideas, is here made very apparent. One is given

a sense of something completely new having entered music. Although there are fine things in all the groups, Op 24 is the first Mazurka set of uniformly high quality and No 4 is Chopin's first great work in the genre.

On hearing them together like this one appreciates the cumulative effect which the composer intended, and Ashkenazy makes a hypersensitive response to their quickly changing moods. The recorded sound has the warmth, fullness and immediacy typical of this series, with a nice bloom to the piano tone.

Mazurkas Nos 1-51[a]; No 23, Op 33 No 2[b]; Ⓗ
No 35, Op 56 No 3[e]; No 41, Op 63 No 3[f].
Waltzes – No 2, Op 34 No 1[c]; No 7, Op 64 No 2[d]
Arthur Rubinstein pf
Naxos Historical mono ② 8 110656/7 (137' · ADD)
Recorded [cd]1928-30, [bef]1930-32, [a]1939 Ⓢ**O**▷

Nocturnes, Nos 1-19[a]. Four Scherzos[b] Ⓗ
Arthur Rubinstein pf
Naxos Historical mono ② 8 110659/60 (132' · ADD)
Recorded [b]1932, [a]1936-37 Ⓢ▷

It's controversial to say so, but such playing makes a mockery of present-day standards. All these performances prove that Rubinstein played the piano as naturally as a bird flies or a fish swims. He was simply in his element, and never more so than in Chopin. Who else has given us the Nocturnes with such ravishing inwardness, pianistic sheen and a *bel canto* to rival the finest singer? Decorative *fioriture* are spun off like so much silk, and whether or not you consider Op 15 No 2 'inseparable from champagne and truffles' and Op 27 No 1 a portrait of 'a corpse washed ashore on a Venetian lagoon', or hear the nightingales of Nohant in Op 62 No 1 and the chant of the monks of Valdemosa in Op 15 No 3 and Op 37 No 1, you can hardly remain unaffected by Rubinstein's unique artistry. His feline ease in the double-note flow of Op 37 No 2, or the way he lightens the darkness of the great C minor Nocturne without losing an ounce of its tragedy, all form part of the genius that made him the most celebrated of all Chopin pianists.

Rubinstein's Mazurkas are equally the stuff of legends. Chopin's most subtle and confessional diary, they transcend their humble origins and become in Rubinstein's hands an ever-audacious series of miniatures extending from the neurasthenic to the radiant, from Chopin's nagging child (Op 17 No 3) to the unfurling of proud ceremonial colours (Opp 63 No 1). What heartache he conveys in Op 63 No 3; and when he takes Op 67 No 3 been more intimately confided, its banal association with *Les sylphides* more blissfully resolved? Chopin's final composition, Op 68 No 4, becomes a valediction encouraging rather than forbidding weeping, Rubinstein's *rubato* the caressing magic that created a furore at his unforgettable recitals.

Finally the Scherzos, played with an outrageous but enthralling disregard for safety. Only a pedant will underline the odd mis-hit or pock-mark in the context of such sky-rocketing bravura and poetic impulse. As an added bonus there are additional recordings of three Mazurkas and two Waltzes, the A flat Op 34 No 1 alive with dizzying virtuoso trickery. The sleeve-note writer may comically mistake the Mazurkas for the Polonaises in referring to Schumann's oft-misquoted description, 'guns [sic] buried in flowers', but that's a mere spot on Naxos's blazing sun. No more life-affirming Chopin exists.

Mazurkas – Nos 2, 7, 10, 13, 15, 17, 20, 22, 23, 27, 29, 32, 34, 35, 37, 39, 40, 41, 45, 47 & 49
Vassily Primakov pf
Bridge BRIDGE9289 (62' · DDD)   Ⓕ

In his subtly planned selection of 21 Mazurkas Vassily Primakov shows a special sense of a Slavic melancholy and gaiety at the heart of what is surely Chopin's most deeply confessional diary. Hyper-sensitive to mood-swings, his poetic insight is backed by deft and immaculate pianism. Try the opening of Op 17 No 1 in B flat minor, or hear him in the teasingly enigmatic start and close of Op 24 No 2 in C, and you are clearly in the presence of a most fascinating and individual young artist. Op 33 No 1 in G sharp minor is confided in a daringly slow tempo, adding to its introspection, while Op 56 No 2 in C is gloriously rumbustious. Op 41 No 4 in A flat is gracefully and piquantly inflected, but Primakov surely reserves his ultimate triumph for the end. His Op 17 No 4 in A minor is worth the price of the disc alone, memorably refined in sound, colour and nuance. And while nothing can eclipse Arthur Rubinstein's 1939 set of the Mazurkas (Naxos, reviewed above), Primakov's less patrician manner creates its own ambience and style. Bridge's sound is admirable.

Nocturnes

No 1 in B flat minor, Op 9; **No 2** in E flat, Op 9; **No 3** in B, Op 9; **No 4** in F, Op 15; **No 5** in F sharp, Op 15; **No 6** in G minor, Op 15; **No 7** in C sharp minor, Op 27; **No 8** in D flat, Op 27; **No 9** in B flat, Op 32; **No 10** in A flat, Op 32; **No 11** in G minor, Op 37; **No 12** in G, Op 37; **No 13** in C minor, Op 48; **No 14** in F sharp minor, Op 48; **No 15** in F minor, Op 55; **No 16** in E flat, Op 55; **No 17** in B flat, Op 62; **No 18** in E, Op 62; **No 19** in E minor, Op 72; **No 20** in C sharp minor, Op posth; **No 21** in C minor, Op posth

---

Nocturnes Nos 1-19
Maria João Pires pf
DG ② 447 096-2GH2 (109' · DDD)   ⒻⓄⓄⓄ▸

Passion rather than insouciance is Pires's keynote. Here is an intensity and drama that scorn all complacent salon or drawing-room expecta-

tions. How she relishes Chopin's central storms, creating a vivid and spectacular yet unhistrionic contrast with all surrounding serenity or 'embalmed darkness'. The *con fuoco* of Op 15 No 1 erupts in a fine fury and in the first *Nocturne*, Op 9 No 1, Pires's sharp observance of Chopin's *appassionato* marking comes like a prophecy of the coda's sudden blaze. Chopin, she informs us in no uncertain terms, was no sentimentalist. More intimately, in Op 15 No 3 (where the music's wavering sense of irresolution led to the sobriquet 'the Hamlet Nocturne') Pires makes you hang on to every note in the coda's curious, echoing chimes, and in the *dolcissimo* conclusion to No 8 (Op 27 No 2) there's an unforgettable sense of 'all passion spent', of gradually ebbing emotion. Pires with her burning clarity has reinforced our sense of Chopin's stature and created a new range of possibilities (showing us that there's life after Rubinstein). Naturally, Rubinstein's legendary cycles possess a graciousness, an ease and elegance reflecting, perhaps, a long-vanished *belle époque*. Yet moving ahead, one has no hesitation in declaring Maria João Pires among the most eloquent master-musicians of our time.

Nocturnes Nos 1-20
Nelson Freire pf
Decca ② 478 2182DX2 (102' · DDD)   ⒻⓄⒷ▸

For Freire the Nocturnes are tirelessly experimental, an opalescent world of shifting moods and colours. Too serious to be overtly glamorous or heart-stopping, his warm-hearted performances eschew a concert-hall brio in favour of intimacy, almost as if played in the privacy of one's own room. Not that he is immune to those sudden flashes of anger never far from Chopin's always volatile nature. He is dramatically alive to the startling end to the Field-like B major Nocturne, Op 32 No 1, with its muffled timpani strokes and a sudden, chilling menace. The posthumous E minor Nocturne, too, which, as the sleeve-notes usefully tell us, is a late rather than early work, emerges pained and drawn, reminding you of Delacroix's celebrated portrait of Chopin. But overall Freire is at his finest in readings which are pensive and conciliatory. He is truly *lento* in the G minor Nocturne with its obsessive questioning and *religioso* conclusion, and time and again he makes you see these works as truly night pieces, music of an 'embalmed darkness' (to quote Keats). True, there are moments when a once legendary and impeccable technique stiffens (in the double-note flow of the G major Nocturne), yet this is less than marginal in music-making so personal and reflective.

Nocturnes Nos 1-21
Bernard d'Ascoli pf
Athene Minerva ② 23 201 (105' · DDD)   ⒻⓄ

Even in a heavily competitive market place this ranks among the most remarkable of

Chopin Nocturne recordings. Courting controversy at one level yet burningly sincere at another, Bernard d'Ascoli goes his own heart-warming way unburdened by tradition. From him, the Nocturnes are not a world of sweet dreams but possess a troubled and assertive life. True, simplicity is hardly his byword (in Nos 1, 6 and 11, his intense *rubato* often tugs against the music's natural line) yet such bold and declamatory playing is never less than enlivening, positively forbidding the listener to sink into complacency or repose. An impetuous thrust given to the D flat Nocturne's long-breathed Italianate lines, and the sudden plunge into darkness at the end of Op 32 No 1, are two among many examples of performances of a living, breathing presence, the reverse of studio-bound.

The two extra posthumous Nocturnes are added for good measure and the ever-popular Op 9 No 2 comes complete with flashing variants authorised by the composer. The recordings are vivid and immediate and the oustanding notes (a provocative side-swipe at Fauré notwithstanding) are by the pianist himself.

Polonaises

No 1 in C sharp minor, Op 26; **No 2** in E flat minor, Op 26; **No 3** in A, Op 40, 'Military'; **No 4** in C minor, Op 40; **No 5** in F sharp minor, Op 44; **No 6** in A flat, Op 53, 'Heroic'; **No 7** in A flat, Op 61, 'Polonaise-fantaisie'; **No 8** in D minor, Op 71; **No 9** in B flat, Op 71; **No 10** in F minor, Op 71; **No 11** in B flat minor; **No 12** in G flat; **No 13** in G minor; **No 14** in B flat; **No 15** in A flat; **No 16** in G sharp minor

Polonaises Nos 1-7. Andante spianato and
Grande polonaise, Op 22
Arthur Rubinstein pf
Naxos Historical mono 8 110661 (64' · ADD)
Recorded 1934-35 ⓈⓄⓄⓄ▶

Here, in all their glory, are Rubinstein's 1934-35 recordings of Chopin's six mature Polonaises framed by examples of his early and late genius (Opp 22 and 61 respectively). Together with his early discs of the Mazurkas, Scherzos and Nocturnes, these performances remain classics of an unassailable calibre, their richness and character increased rather than diminished by the passage of time.

For Schumann, the Polonaises were 'cannons buried in flowers' and whether epic or confiding, stark or florid, their national and personal fervour is realised to perfection by Rubinstein. Listen to the *Andante spianato* from Op 22 and you'll hear a matchless *cantabile*, a tribute to a *bel canto* so often at the heart of Chopin's elusive and heroic genius. Try the central *meno mosso* from the First Polonaise and witness an imaginative freedom that can make all possible rivals sound stiff and ungainly by comparison. The colours of the A major Polonaise are unfurled with a rare sense of its ceremonial nature, and the darker, indeed tragic, character of its sombre C minor companion is no less

surely caught. The two 'big' Polonaises, Opp 44 and 53, are offered with a fearless bravura (you can almost hear the audience's uproar after Rubinstein's thunderous conclusion to the latter), rhythmic impetus and idiomatic command beyond criticism.

The simple truth is that Rubinstein played the piano as a fish swims in water, free to phrase and inflect with a magic peculiarly his own, to make, in Liszt's words, 'emotion speak, weep and sing and sigh'. The sound may seem dated but Naxos's transfers are excellent, and to think that all this is offered at a bargain price...

Polonaises Nos 1-7
Maurizio Pollini pf
DG The Originals 457 711-2GOR (62' · ADD)
Recorded 1975 ⓂⓄⓄ▶

This is Pollini in all his early glory, in expertly transferred performances. Shorn of all virtuoso compromise or indulgence, the majestic force of his command is indissolubly integrated with the seriousness of his heroic impulse. Rarely will you be compelled into such awareness of the underlying malaise beneath the outward and nationalist defiance of the *Polonaises*. The tension and menace at the start of No 2 are almost palpable, its storming and disconsolate continuation made a true mirror of Poland's clouded history. The C minor *Polonaise*'s denouement, too, emerges with a chilling sense of finality, and Pollini's way with the pounding audacity commencing at 3'00" in the epic F sharp minor *Polonaise* is like some ruthless prophecy of every percussive, anti-lyrical gesture to come. At 7'59" Chopin's flame-throwing interjections are volcanic, and if there's ample poetic delicacy and compensation (notably in the *Polonaise-fantaisie*, always among Chopin's most profoundly speculative masterpieces), it's the more elemental side of his genius, his 'cannons' rather than 'flowers' that are made to sear and haunt the memory. Other pianists may be more outwardly beguiling, but Pollini's magnificently unsettling Chopin can be as imperious and unarguable as any on record. That his performances are also deeply moving is a tribute to his unique status.

Polonaises Nos 1-16. Allegro de concert, Op 46.
Etudes – F minor, Op posth; A flat, Op posth; D flat,
Op posth. Tarantelle, Op 43. Fugue in A minor. Album-
leaf in E. Polish Songs, Op 74 – Spring. Galop marquis.
Berceuse, Op 57. Barcarolle, Op 60. Two Bourrées
Vladimir Ashkenazy pf
Double Decca ② 452 167-2DF2 (145' · DDD/ADD)
Recorded 1974-84 Ⓑ▶

Ashkenazy's Chopin hardly needs any further advocacy. His distinguished and virtually complete survey rests alongside the Rubinstein recordings in general esteem. The 16 Polonaises were not recorded in sets but individually, or in small groups, which is one reason why they sound so fresh, with Ashkenazy striking a sensitive artistic balance between poetic feeling and the commanding bravura that one takes for granted in the more extrovert pieces, with their Polish patriotic style. The recordings vary between analogue and digital, and the recording venues are as different as the Kingsway Hall, St John's, Smith Square, and All Saints, Petersham; but the realism of the piano sound is remarkably consistent. A series of shorter pieces is included on the second disc and the playing is always distinguished. Among the major items, the gentle Berceuse is quite melting, while the *Allegro de concert* and Barcarolle are hardly less memorable.

Preludes, Op 28

No 1 in C; **No 2** in A minor; **No 3** in G; **No 4** in E minor; **No 5** in D; **No 6** in B minor; **No 7** in A; **No 8** in F sharp minor; **No 9** in E; **No 10** in C sharp minor; **No 11** in B; **No 12** in G sharp minor; **No 13** in F sharp; **No 14** in E flat minor; **No 15** in D flat; **No 16** in B flat minor; **No 17** in A flat; **No 18** in F minor; **No 19** in E flat; **No 20** in C minor; **No 21** in B flat; **No 22** in G minor; **No 23** in F; **No 24** in D minor; **No 25** in C sharp minor; Op 45; **No 26** in A flat, Op *posth*

Preludes Nos 1-26[a]. Barcarolle, Op 60[b]. Polonaise No 6, Op 53, 'Heroic'[c]. Scherzo No 2, Op 31[d]
Martha Argerich pf
DG Galleria 415 836-2GGA (62' · ADD)
Recorded [a]1977, [b]1961, [c]1967, [d]1975   Ⓜ️Ⓞ🅱️➕

Professor Zurawlew, the founder of the Chopin Competition in Warsaw, was once asked which one of the prize-winners he would pick as having been his favourite. The answer came back immediately: Martha Argerich. This disc could explain why. There are very few recordings of the 24 Preludes that have such a perfect combination of temperamental virtuosity and compelling artistic insight. Argerich has the technical equipment to do whatever she wishes with the music. Whether it's in the haunting, dark melancholy of No 2 in A minor or the lightning turmoil of No 16 in B flat minor, she's profoundly impressive. It's these sharp changes of mood that make her performance scintillatingly unpredictable. In the Barcarolle there's no relaxed ease on which the melodies of the right hand are constructed, as is conventional, but more the piece emerges as a stormy odyssey through life, with moments of visionary awareness. Argerich is on firmer ground in the Polonaise, where her power and technical security reign triumphant. The CD ends with a rippling and yet slightly aggressive reading of the Second Scherzo. This is very much the playing of a pianist who lives in the 'fast lane' of life. The sound quality is a bit reverberant, an effect heightened by the fact that Argerich has a tendency to overpedal.

Preludes Nos 1-24
Grigory Sokolov pf
Opus 111 OP30-336 (47' · DDD). Recorded live 1990 Ⓕ

Grigory Sokolov is an uncompromising, exclusively serious rather than commercial artist and has consequently paid a price. Even today, he remains an awe-inspiring figure to connoisseurs rather than a wider public. His recordings, too, are sadly few, though this reissue reaffirms him as among the most formidable and characterful pianists of our time. So deeply is every bar, indeed, every note, weighed and considered that each Prelude emerges in a new and arresting light. True, he can bear down so intensely that Chopin isn't always allowed his truest or most natural voice. But glories far outweigh queries. Prelude No 2 is authentically *lento* and lugubrious, its morbidity realised quite without a cool and over-familiar evasion. Again, just as you wonder whether No 13, an idyllic Nocturne, needs such strenuous pleading, you find yourself at No 16, played with a thunderous and lavishly pedalled aplomb, and to a reading of No 17 inflected with rare affection. What daring in No 18, what imaginative delicacy in No 19 (that flight into a cloudless azure), what aerial magic in No 23 with its audacious close, and when have you heard a more dramatic dip from *fortissimo* to *pianissimo* in the elegaic and processional C minor Prelude (No 20)?

The sound captures Sokolov's immense dynamic range exceptionally well, and even if you're a lover of understatement or of Cortot's careless and unforgettable rapture you'll surely admit that this is among the most powerfully individual of all Chopin recordings.

Chopin Preludes Nos 1-24[a] **Mendelssohn** Ⓗ
(arr Rachmaninov) A Midsummer Night's Dream[b] – Scherzo **Prokofiev** Suggestion diabolique, Op 4 No 4[c] **Rachmaninov** Lilacs[d]. Moment musical in E minor, Op 16 No 4[e] . Preludes – G, Op 32 No 5[f]; B minor, Op 32 No 10[g] **Schumann** Kinderszenen, Op 15[h] **Stravinsky** Etude, Op 7 No 4[i] **Vallier** Toccatina[j] **Weber** Piano Sonata No 1 in C – Rondo, 'Perpetuum mobile'[k]
Benno Moiseiwitsch pf
Testament SBT1196 (78' · ADD). Recorded [h]1930, [i]1938, [b]1939, [g]1940, [a,d]1948, [c,j,k]1950, [e,f]1956   Ⓕ🅾️🅾️

Benno Moiseiwitsch's love affair with the piano spawned numerous fine recordings, though few match this superlative 1948 set of Chopin's Preludes. The First Prelude is candid and forthright, whereas No 4's *Largo* projects an outspoken top line (and note how sensitively Moiseiwitsch negotiates the accompaniment's constantly shifting harmonies). Desynchronised chords mark the opening of Prelude No 6, while the same Prelude's quiet close segues almost imperceptibly into the gnomic A major (a parallel sense of transition marries Nos 10 and 11). Bryce Morrison, in his booklet-notes for Testament, singles out No 16 for its dexterity, but the more oratorical Nos 18 and 22 are particularly notable too for their especially keen sense of narrative.

But the greatness of these performances lies beyond detail. Much of the magic resides in Moiseiwitsch's ability to balance close-up and landscape, cultivating the individual phrase while keeping an eye on whole paragraphs. His touch, pedalling and attention to contrapuntal side-play are remarkable. These are profoundly individual readings that positively teem with incident. But which CD to choose? Testament's transfer achieves a marginally clearer sound frame, APR (APR5575) a touch more warmth but a tad more surface noise. One minor criticism of Testament's disc: there's a very slight drop in pitch between the end of the 14th Prelude and the beginning of the 15th – not a full semitone, but noticeable enough to trouble those with perfect or relative pitch. APR's transfer is spot-on.

Choosing between the two programmes is more problematic. APR's all-Chopin sequence includes fluent accounts of the four Ballades, the Fourth a first ever release. Odd smudges hardly matter in the face of such compelling musicianship. In the B flat Polonaise it's fascinating to compare Moiseiwitsch with fellow Leschetizky pupil Ignaz Friedman, the one restrained and elegant, the other (Friedman) pointed and rhythmically fierce. Likewise in the A flat Ballade, where Friedman invests the 'Galloping Horse' second set (Winston Churchill's description) with extra impetus, Moiseiwitsch's musical manners are far milder.

Testament's makeweights highlight Moiseiwitsch's virtuosity, most memorably in Rachmaninov's reworking of the *Scherzo* from the *Midsummer Night's Dream*, which is heard to even better advantage than on the arranger's own recording. So much happens, so quickly and at so many dynamic levels, you can hardly credit the results to a single pair of hands. A Rachmaninov sequence includes a stereo G major Prelude (Op 32 No 5) and a justly famous 1940 account of the sombre B minor Prelude, Op 32 No 10. His primary-coloured 1930 recording of *Kinderszenen* is a joy. In contrast, lightning reflexes benefit textually bolstered Weber and the dry wit of Prokofiev, Stravinsky and John Vallier.

Those fancying an 'Essential Moiseiwitsch' collection should plump for Testament, though Chopin's magnificent Ballades are a significant enough draw to push the scales in APR's direction. It really is a matter of repertory preferences. Both discs are extremely well annotated.

Four Scherzos

No 1 in B minor, Op 20; **No 2** in B flat minor, Op 31; **No 3** in C sharp minor, Op 39; **No 4** in E, Op 54

Four Scherzos
Ivo Pogorelich pf
DG 439 947-2GH (42' · DDD)　　　Ⓕ**O**Ⓑ⊕

Love him or hate him, Pogorelich guarantees a response. Chopin for the faint-hearted this isn't; original, provocative, challenging, daring, it emphatically is. Nevertheless, if Pogorelich's most unconventional ideas approach wilful eccentricity, the rewards far outweigh any reservations. True, if they weren't reinforced by such transcendent pianism Pogorelich's interpreta-

tions wouldn't carry nearly the same authority or conviction; but it's precisely the marrying of his imaginative scope with his extraordinary technical resource that opens up such startling expressive possibilities.

The First and Second Scherzos show the juxtaposition of extremes at its most intense, stretching the limits of the musically viable. Predictably, the outer sections of the B minor Scherzo are incredibly fast, possessed of an almost demonic drive, while the central Polish carol ('Sleep little Jesus') is unusually slow and luxuriously sustained. But such extremes, of character as much as tempo, place enormous tension on the musical structure, and this is most evident in the B flat minor Scherzo. Make no mistake, Pogorelich's playing is astounding, from the imperious opening to the lingering and ravishing middle section, where his sublime lyrical simplicity is of the deepest inward poetry.

To sum up, a recording like this isn't easy. Some may find Pogorelich's probing individualism too overwhelming. There are more ideas crammed into under 42 minutes than on many discs almost twice the length, although most collectors will still feel short-changed by the playing time. This may not be Chopin for every day, but the force of Pogorelich's musical personality subtly and irrevocably shapes one's view of the music. A truly extraordinary disc.

Waltzes

No 1 in E flat, Op 18; **No 2** in A flat, Op 34 No 1; **No 3** in A minor, Op 34 No 2; **No 4** in F, Op 34 No 3; **No 5** in A flat, Op 42; **No 6** in D flat, Op 64 No 1; **No 7** in C sharp minor, Op 64 No 2; **No 8** in A flat, Op 64 No 3; **No 9** in A flat, Op 69 No 1; **No 10** in E minor, Op 69 No 2; **No 11** in G flat, Op 70 No 1; **No 12** in F minor, Op 70 No 2; **No 13** in D flat, Op 70 No 3; **No 14** in E minor, Op *posth*; **No 15** in E, Op *posth*; **No 16** in A flat, Op *posth*; **No 17** in E flat, Op *posth*; **No 18** in E flat, Op *posth*; **No 19** in A minor, Op *posth*

Waltzes Nos 1-14
Arthur Rubinstein pf
RCA Red Seal 09026 63047-2 (50' · ADD)
Recorded 1960s　　　　　　Ⓑ**O**

There has in recent years been a tendency to take Rubinstein's imposing series of Chopin recordings from the mid-1960s for granted, but to hear them digitally refurbished soon puts a stop to that. His tone doesn't have much luxuriance, being quite chiselled; yet a finely tuned sensibility is evident throughout. This is at once demonstrated by his direct interpretation of Op 18, its elegance explicit. His reading of Op 34 No 1 is *brillante*, as per Chopin's title. In Op 34 No 2 Rubinstein judges everything faultlessly, distilling the sorrowful yet cannily varied grace of this piece. The two finest here are Opp 42 and 64 No 2, and with the former Rubinstein excels in the unification of its diverse elements, its rises and falls of intensity, its hurryings forward and holdings back. This is also true of his reading of Op 64 No 2, the yearning of whose brief *più lento* section is memorable indeed. The sole fault of this issue is that conventional programming leads to the mature Waltzes, which were published by Chopin himself, coming first, the lesser, posthumously printed items last. Not all of these are early but they have less substance than Opp 18-64, and should come first.

Complete Waltzes
Ingrid Fliter pf
EMI 698351-2 (68' · DDD)　　　Ⓕ❍❍❍➻

Presenting them in their published order, followed by the 11 posthumous waltzes with and without opus numbers, Ingrid Fliter sets a new benchmark for the complete Waltzes. From beginning to end, this is among the finest Chopin recordings of recent years.

Why? Each waltz emerges as if a great actress were reading a short story, each with its own colour and character. Fliter's 'timing' (meaning her phrasing and *rubato*) is judged to perfection; her tempi are near ideal; she never loses sight of Chopin the poet or reinvents him as a red-blooded virtuoso. In addition, the superbly voiced piano is realistically recorded, neither too distant in that impersonal back-of-an-empty-hall way nor so close that the instrument is not allowed to sing.

Dip into any section of any Waltz at random and you will hear a version to supersede, or at least rival, your current personal favourite. Fliter stays faithful to the spirit of the composer without denying her own keyboard personality.

Complete Waltzes
Alice Sara Ott pf
DG 477 8095GH (57' · DDD)　　　Ⓕ❍❍➻

Only just out of her teens, Alice Sara Ott – half-German and half-Japanese – gives us a performance of the Waltzes as touching, piquant and scintillating as on any modern recording. She leaves you to marvel at her instinct for Chopin's poetic ambiguity, his alternating melancholy and exuberance, his ultra-Slavonic hope and despair, her playing backed by the sheen of an immaculate technique and pianism. You will go a long way to hear the A minor Waltz confided with a greater sense of its intimacy or the following F major Waltz given with such contrasting brio and expressive freedom. Her D flat Waltz, Op 64, is sufficiently stylish and elegant to make nonsense of its sobriquet, 'Minute' Waltz, and she catches the B minor Waltz's gentle but querulous mood to perfection. Playing from autograph manuscripts, she relishes the more florid harmony and ornamentation of, for example, Nos 8, 9 and 10, and includes all the posthumous Waltzes, ending with the *Allegretto* in A minor and making it a haunting and touching valediction. (DG's sound is ideal and their presentation could hardly be more lavish.)

Waltzes Nos 1-14. Mazurka No 32, Op 50 No 3. ⒽBarcarolle, Op 60. Nocturne in D flat, Op 27 No 2
Dinu Lipatti pf
EMI Great Recordings of the Century mono
566904-2 (65' · ADD)
Recorded 1947-50　　　Ⓜ❍❍❍➻

 As a former pupil of Cortot, it wasn't perhaps surprising that Lipatti always kept a special place in his heart for Chopin. And thanks primarily to the 14 Waltzes, played in a non-chronological sequence of his own choosing, it's doubtful if the disc will ever find itself long absent from the catalogue. Like the solitary Mazurka, they were recorded in Geneva during his remarkable renewal of strength in the summer of 1950. The Nocturne and Barcarolle date back to visits to EMI's Abbey Road studio in 1947 and 1948 respectively. Just once or twice in the Waltzes you might feel tempted to question his sharp tempo changes for mood contrast within one and the same piece – as for instance in No 9 in A flat, Op 69 No 1. However, for the most part his mercurial lightness, fleetness and charm are pure delight. His Nocturne in D flat has long been hailed as one of the finest versions currently available. And even though we know he himself (one of the greatest perfectionists) was not completely happy about the Barcarolle, for the rest of us this glowing performance has a strength of direction and shapeliness all its own. In fuller contexts there's just a trace of plumminess in the recorded sound.

Miscellanous piano recitals

'Journal intime'
Mazurkas – No 6, Op 7 No 2; No 11, Op 17 No 2; No 13, Op 17 No 4; No 41, Op 63 No 3; No 47, Op 68 No 2. Ballades – No 1, Op 23; No 2, Op 38. Fantasie, Op. 49. Nocturnes – No 2, Op 9 No 2; No 20, Op *posth*. Prelude, Op 28 No. 4. Trois Ecossaises, Op 72 No 3. Contredanse, KKAnhIa/4. Impromptu No 4, 'Fantaisie-Impromptu', Op 66
Alexandre Tharaud pf
Virgin Classics 457845-2 (64' · DDD)　　　Ⓕ❍❍➻

Here, in memorably refined and stylish performances, Tharaud is wonderfully enterprising, mixing the familiar and unfamiliar, the large-scale (despite his disc's title, 'Journal intime') and the miniature. Everything is arrestingly personal yet never exaggerated or inflated, and his way with five Mazurkas, in particular, is very much at the heart of their confessional nature.

One misses the Berceuse, surely the most magical of all Chopin's intimate creations, but relishes the variety achieved by including such grand works as the Fantasie and the First and Second Ballades. Here, as so often with Tharaud, there is an aristocratic balance of sense and sensibility, though his brilliant fury in the Second Ballade's *Presto* storm is breathtaking, the left-hand octaves hurtling towards their apex like guided missiles.

Finally, in the evergreen E flat Nocturne, Op 9 No 2, Tharaud may be less enchanting than, say,

Cherkassky but it is also a salutary reminder that Chopin was the most classically biased of the great keyboard composers. Finely recorded, this is an original and exemplary addition to Chopin's bicentenary year.

'Late Masterpieces'
Barcarolle, Op 60. Berceuse, Op 57. Mazurkas –
Op 63 No 2; Op 63 No 3; Op 67 No 4; Op 68 No 4.
Nocturnes, Op 62 Nos 1 & 2. Piano Sonata No 3.
Polonaise-fantaisie, Op 61
Stephen Hough pf
Hyperion CDA67764 (73' · DDD) Ⓕ**OO**➔

A new Hough disc is one of life's pleasures. You know the programme will have been carefully considered and nurtured, every aspect of the performance and recording attended to in the finest detail, matched by Hyperion's exacting standards of presentation. Hough's Chopin can be a little emotionally chilly in a studio-perfect environment but here, for the most part, he transcends the lonely confines of St George's (Bristol) to offer a masterclass in pianistic command and stylistic poise with the most heartfelt playing of any of his recent recordings. There are few who can elucidate the question-and-answer phrasing of Chopin's music with Hough's transparency and unaffected simplicity. Just listen to the opening Barcarolle, the selection of four Mazurkas, two Nocturnes and the closing Berceuse. At the centre of the recital is a masterly performance of the enigmatic *Polonaise-fantaisie*. In Hough's hands, this discursive, experimental piece of great depth and beauty becomes an operatic aria. It seems to cry out for lyrics and a soprano.

After the first movement of the B minor Sonata (without the exposition repeat), Hough takes the *Scherzo* at a conservative *molto vivace*, while the finale, after one of those long-spun *cantilena* movements that Hough does so well, is an acutely executed studio recording. The disc's striking cover has the Bowler-hatted Hough gazing at a Rothko abstract. The connection between Bowler, Rothko and Chopin is the subject of a thought-provoking essay by the pianist.

Muzio Clementi   Italian/British 1752-1832

Italian-born Clementi started his studies in Rome before being all but adopted by Sir Peter Beckford who brought him to live on his estate in Dorset. There he honed his craft both as a composer and as a considerable keyboard virtuoso. In 1774 he moved to London where he established his reputation as a conductor and impresario in addition to his compisitional and keyboard skills.

Between 1780 and 1785 he toured extensively in Europe and in 1781 he took part in a widely publicised keyboard 'duel' with Mozart – a contest that was declared a tie. He took up teaching and in 1798 he established a music publishing firm in whose cata-

logue were works by Beethoven. He also founded a piano-making company.

Much of his output features the piano but he also wrote a handful of symphonies in a late-Classical style. His style did take into account the new demand for Romantic sensibility in music but he was essentially a Classical artist, though his keyboard dexterity was considerable. He wrote a couple of treatises on keyboard playing: Introduction to the Art of Playing on the Piano Forte (1801) and the comprehensive keyboard collection Gradus ad Parnassum (1817-26).

Keyboard Sonatas

Keyboard Sonatas – F minor, Op 13 No 6; F, Ⓟ
Op 33 No 2; G minor, Op 34 No 2. Musical
Characteristics, Op 19 – Preludio I alla Haydn;
Preludio I alla Mozart. Capriccio in B flat, Op 17.
Fantasie with Variations, 'Au clair de lune', Op 48
Andreas Staier fp
Teldec Das Alte Werk 2564 69613-6 (68' · DDD)
Ⓜ**OOO**

One's inclined to think of Clementi as a rather dry composer, however brilliant, but there's nothing remotely dry about this CD, which is full of expressive and often powerful music. Partly it's the instrument: on the fortepiano Clementi's music has a sharpness of impact that it lacks on a modern grand, and also a gently poetic, often almost mysterious ring that carries overtones of early Romanticism, especially in some of the slower music. But the chief responsibility belongs with Andreas Staier, who's clearly fired by the music and discovers so many layers of expression in it.

Essentially he plays three sonatas with a framework of single pieces surrounding them. Two of those pieces come from Clementi's *Musical Characteristics*, a group of short preludes published in 1787 and imitating Haydn and Mozart as well as Sterkel, Kozeluch and Vaňhal. Interestingly, these lively pieces indicate the features of the two composers that Clementi regarded as distinctive. Then there's a *Capriccio*, a charming piece demanding (and receiving) crisp and athletic fingerwork. The final item is a brilliant and imaginative fantasy on *Au clair de lune*, which Clementi varies in some highly inventive ways. This is a late work, from about 1820, and its style is comparable with mature Beethoven.

Of the three sonatas, the last (Op 33 No 2, 1794) is an elegantly written piece, in effect in two movements. Staier is masterly in his command of Clementi's dialectic and of the slightly quirky character of some of his themes, as in the first movement's finale. Op 34 No 2 is a big G minor work: its *Adagio* draws beautifully shapely and pointed playing from Staier, and the finale, another elaborate and extended movement, is impassioned music, powerfully done. The first of the sonatas, the earlier F minor work (1785), seems in some ways the most 'Romantic' in tone, with its *Allegro agitato* carrying hints of menace and darkness (enhanced by Staier's sensitive pedalling and misty textures), its eloquent *Largo*, where the melodic line is enunciated with real pathos, and its stormy final *Presto*. In all, Staier's reconciliation of the poetic and imaginative content of this music, with his command of its structure and its arguments, makes this one of the most impressive fortepiano discs in memory.

Piano Sonatas – WoO3; Op 13 Nos 4-6; Op 20; Op 23; Op 24
Howard Shelley *pf*
Hyperion ② CDA67729 (122' · DDD)   Ⓕ**Ⓞ**➔

The third volume of Howard Shelley's invaluable survey of Clementi's piano sonatas confirms every expectation. Once more you are left to marvel at his unfailing brilliance and musicianship, qualities that can lift and enliven even the most predictable and mechanical gestures. There may be possible thefts from Mozart (who disliked Clementi) and prophecies of Beethoven but, more generally, it would be difficult to imagine all these works, whether slight or distinguished, given with greater skill, zest and affection. Every finger-twisting challenge is met with effortless ease, energy and grace, and Hyperion's sound is, as usual, of demonstration quality.

Eric Coates   British 1886-1957

Coates studied at the Royal Academy of Music both as a composer and as a viola player (with Lionel Tertis). He worked as an orchestral viola player (under both Beecham and Wood) for seven years before taking up composition full-time, writing light orchestral music and some 100 songs. One of his earliest champions was Edward Elgar. His best-known works are his London Suite, The Dam Busters March and By the Sleepy Lagoon (still used as the theme music for BBC Radio 4's Desert Island Discs).

Light Orchestral Works

Sweet Seventeen. Summer Afternoon. Impressions of a Princess[a]. Salute the Soldier. Two Light Syncopated Pieces. For Your Delight. The Unknown Singer[a]. I Sing to You. Coquette. Over to You. Idyll. Under the Stars. By the Tamarisk. Mirage. Last Love. The Green Land[a]
[a]**Peter Hughes** *sax*
BBC Concert Orchestra / John Wilson
ASV White Line CDWHL2107 (79' · DDD)   Ⓜ

The title of these pieces won't ring much of a bell with any but the most avid Coates fans. Indeed, four pieces are here recorded for the first time. But what delights there are! It goes without saying that Coates's craftsmanship is in evidence from start to finish. Yet so often, one wonders just *why* a particular piece never quite made it in the way his most popular works did. Isn't *Summer Afternoon* every bit as delightful as

By the Sleepy Lagoon? And wouldn't *Salute the Soldier* have served just as well as other marches as a radio signature tune? Most simply, aren't *Under the Stars, For Your Delight* and others just simply such utter charmers? The BBC Concert Orchestra plays beautifully, and the conductor seems thoroughly imbued with the Coates style. The recorded sound is crisp and clean, too. You are urged to sample the pleasures of this splendid collection.

The Enchanted Garden. Footlights.
London Bridge. Two Symphonic Rhapsodies.
The Three Men. Dancing Nights.
Idyll. Four Centuries Suite – 20th Century Rhythm
**London Philharmonic Orchestra /
Barry Wordsworth**
Lyrita SRCD213 (76' · DDD)   Ⓕ➔

'Boult Conducts Coates'
Coates The Dam Busters – March[a]. From Meadow to Mayfair[b]. The Merrymakers[b]. Summer Days[b]. The Three Bears[b]. The Three Elizabeths – Youth of Britain: The Princess Elizabeth[b] **Delius** Marche-caprice, RTVI/6[b] **Grainger** Children's March: Over the Hills and Far Away, RMTB4[a] **Holst** Suite No 1, H105 – March[a] **Rossini/Britten** Soirées musicales, Op 9 – March[a] **Vaughan Williams** The Wasps – March-past of the Kitchen Utensils[b] **Walton** Hamlet – Finale (Funeral March)[a]
[a]**London Philharmonic Orchestra;**
[b]**New Philharmonia Orchestra / Sir Adrian Boult**
Lyrita SRCD246 (63' · ADD)   Ⓕ**ⓄⓄⓄ**➔

Fans of Eric Coates and Sir Adrian Boult are in for a field-day as Lyrita at long last restores to currency the 87-year-old maestro's much-loved 1976 concert with the New Philharmonia alongside a previously unreleased collection delivered with polish and enthusiasm by the LPO under Barry Wordsworth. There can be no real grumbles about the production values (though a touch more ventilation and bloom would have been nice), and Wordsworth directs proceedings with chipper ebullience.

Especially valuable here is the 1938 ballet *The Enchanted Garden*, Coates's biggest orchestral canvas, opulently scored and full of the most warm-hearted invention. Other plums include the roistering '20th Century Rhythm' from the 1941 *Four Centuries* suite, glittering concert waltz *Footlights* (1939) and exuberant 1934 march *London Bridge* (the follow-up to the previous year's indelible *Knightsbridge*).

However, there's no disputing the step-up in class when one turns to Boult's famous selection, which radiates a tingling spontaneity and beaming affection that are very special. For evidence of a master at work, just listen to the way Boult caresses the glorious second subject in *The Merrymakers*; and what vernal freshness and unruffled elegance he brings to the witty *Three Bears* fantasy and entrancing *Summer Days* suite (a great favourite of Elgar's, and whose fragrant centrepiece possesses a truly heady beauty). The rest of the CD is filled out with seven treats from

Lyrita's 1978 'Sir Adrian Boult Conducts Marches' anthology. Grainger's irresistible *Over the Hills and Far Away* in particular fairly bounds along with irrepressible vigour – as, for that matter, does Coates's *The Dam Busters* – and Delius's *Marche-caprice* has a captivating twinkle in its eye. The sound remains crisp and nicely detailed. A joyous tonic indeed – they don't make 'em like this any more!

Samuel Coleridge-Taylor
British 1875-1912

Born to a Sierra Leonian father and an English mother, Coleridge-Taylor studied violin, singing and composition (with Stanford) at the RCM. Best known for his cantata Hiawatha's Wedding Feast (1898) – performed annually at the Royal Albert Hall to packed audiences – he wrote incidental music for the theatre as well as concert works. He taught composition and was a fine conductor. He was also active in his work to give black performers more opportunities for work within the music world.

Violin Concerto in G minor, Op 80

Coleridge-Taylor Violin Concerto
Dvořák Violin Concerto in A minor, B108
Philippe Graffin vn **Johannesburg Philharmonic Orchestra / Michael Hankinson**
Avie AV0044 (63' · DDD)   Ⓕ🅑➤

The resurgence of interest in the music of Samuel Coleridge-Taylor reaches another milestone with this long-overdue first recording of his Violin Concerto. Coleridge-Taylor completed it in 1911 for the American virtuoso Maud Powell but never lived to hear a note. Abetted by polished and passionate playing from the recently formed Johannesburg PO under its British-born chief Michael Hankinson, Philippe Graffin triumphantly demonstrates what an effective, endearing work it is, acutely responsive as he is to its bittersweet lyricism while equally relishing the many opportunities for solo display in both outer movements.

The choice of Dvořák's Concerto as a coupling would no doubt have pleased Coleridge-Taylor; the Czech master was his favourite composer. Again, there's no missing the whole-hearted commitment of all involved. Admittedly, there are times when you're aware that the orchestra isn't in the luxury class, but Graffin plays with such vibrant character and imagination, and the whole venture radiates such a life-affirming spontaneity and joy in music-making that any drawbacks dwindle into insignificance.

Additional recommendation

Violin Concerto
Coupled with **Somervell** Violin Concerto

Marwood vn **BBC Scottish SO / Brabbins**
Hyperion CDA67420 (65' · DDD)   Ⓕ
The coupling with Arthur Somervell's English pastoral Concerto of 1930 is interesting. Marwood's unflashy, sweet-toned playing lends the right note of enchantment and authenticity to these forgotten scores.

Chamber Works

Clarinet Quintet, Op 10[a].
Piano Quintet, Op 1[b]. Ballade, Op 73[c]
Nash Ensemble ([a]Richard Hosford *cl* [ab]Marianne Thorsen, [b]Malin Broman, [a]Benjamin Nabarro vns [ab]Lawrence Power va [ab]Paul Watkins vc [bc]Ian Brown pf)
Hyperion CDA67590 (69' · DDD)   Ⓕ🅑➤

Coleridge-Taylor is enjoying a decent innings at present. The performance of the 1895 Clarinet Quintet is superb: it comes as no surprise to learn that these consummate artists had given a memorable live rendering at the Wigmore Hall just a few weeks previously. The work emerges as a quite astonishingly mature achievement for a 19-year-old, its pleasing sense of architecture and ambition reinforced by the inclusion of the first-movement exposition repeat. What's more, the slow movement is now revealed as so much more than just a songful interlude, its 'deepest sensibility' (to quote Lionel Harrison's admirable annotation) and wistful tenderness that recalls the ravishing Air from Parry's *An English Suite*.

The even earlier Piano Quintet (1893) may be marginally less assured but likewise manifests a tumbling lyricism and joyful spontaneity worthy of Dvořák, and well merits the entrancingly poised championship it receives here. The 13-minute Ballade in C minor for violin and piano was written in 1907 for the Anglo-Russian virtuoso Michael Zacherewitsch (1879-1953), who had made his debut at the age of 12 playing the Tchaikovsky Concerto under the composer's baton.

Backed up by a blemish-free production from the Keener/Eadon team and attractively presented, this is a most welcome and engaging release.

Arnold Cooke
British 1906-2005

Cooke studied with Dent at Cambridge (1925-28, BA, MusB; MusD 1948) and with Hindemith at the Berlin Hochschule für Musik (1929-32). He spent a year as music director of the Festival Theatre, Cambridge (following Walter Leigh, an earlier Hindemith pupil), and then taught composition at the Manchester College of Music from 1933 to 1938. After war service in the Navy he was appointed professor of harmony, counterpoint and composition at Trinity College of Music, where he remained from 1947 until his retirement in 1978. A pianist and cellist himself, Cooke wrote chamber music and vocal music for soloists, for children and for choirs. His woodwind writing is especially grateful and, like Hindemith, he has written successfully for the organ.

Symphony No 1

Symphony No 1. Concerto for Strings.
Jabez and the Devil – Suite
London Philharmonic Orchestra /
Nicholas Braithwaite
Lyrita SRCD203 (70' · DDD) ⓕ ⒟➤

The first of Arnold Cooke's five symphonies was completed in 1947 and premiered under Sir Adrian Boult in a BBC broadcast two years later. At first glance both the home tonality and formal plan might imply a nod or two towards Walton's First Symphony from the previous decade. However, it doesn't take very long to discover that the most fruitful influence is that of Hindemith (Cooke's teacher at the Berlin Hochschule für Musik from 1929 to 1932); anyone who responds to the German master's *Mathis der Maler*, Symphony in E flat or *Symphonia serena* should most certainly lend an ear. Closer to home, annotator Calum MacDonald also perceives a timeless, deep-rooted quality in Cooke's fad-free music that suggests a kinship with Rubbra (witness the long-breathed polyphony of the heartfelt slow movement). In sum, a work of impeccable resourcefulness, cogent argument and affecting sincerity that invites and repays repeated listening.

The symphony is flanked by the 1948 Concerto in D for string orchestra (a bracingly assured, big-hearted essay in three movements, which features some grateful writing for the section principals) and a splendidly colourful and diverting 18-minute suite from the 1959 ballet *Jabez and the Devil* (eventually staged at Covent Garden in September 1961). Kenneth Wilkinson's 1974 Kingsway Hall sound in the latter boasts fabulous bite and presence still, but the two other works (taped in 1988-89) have likewise been ripely captured by the microphones, and Nicholas Braithwaite helms the LPO with scrupulous care and infectious commitment throughout. Definitely one for the 'want' list!

Aaron Copland   American 1900-1990

Born in a humble street in Brooklyn, the son of Lithuanian immigrants, Copland is generally regarded as the first indisputably great American composer. The piano came easily to him and, after he'd graduated from the local high school, he had lessons in harmony and counterpoint from the eminent (though conservative) teacher and composer Rubin Goldmark. His first published piece, The Cat and the Mouse, appeared in 1920.

He was able to scrape together enough to go to Paris to study with the doyenne of European teachers, Nadia Boulanger. Here, during his four years at the New School for Americans at Fontainebleau

(1921-25), Copland was introduced to an enormous range of musical influences, all of which he was encouraged to absorb – jazz, the neo-classicism of Stravinsky and the whimsicality of Les Six made a particularly strong impression on him and colour the first period of his mature compositions. With a thorough grounding in composition and orchestration under his belt, he returned to America where he became involved in a wide range of musical activities, working as a pianist in a hotel, as a lecturer and organiser of various musical societies, as well as composing.

Conductor, publisher and patron of music Serge Koussevitzky became an influential champion of his music throughout his tenure as conductor of the Boston Symphony Orchestra, an incalculable boost to Copland's growing reputation. Between 1930 and 1936 he entered a phase of experimental and dissonant writing (Variations and the Piano Sonata, for instance, are difficult works) before discovering the power of American folk idioms. Here his music is as essentially American as Mussorgky's or Stravinsky's is Russian – El Salón México, the ballets Billy the Kid, Rodeo and Appalachian Spring are as American as apple pie. His Lincoln Portrait, using texts from Lincoln's speeches and letters, has been performed (for better or worse, but generally worse) by world leaders. His patriotic Fanfare for the Common Man (1942) has been used for the opening of every type of formal ceremony. Some of Copland's film music (The Red Pony, for example, Our Town and Of Mice and Men) is among the most distinguished ever written (he won an Oscar in 1950 for the score of The Heiress). In a nutshell, Copland managed the difficult feat of becoming a popular classical composer while retaining the respect of critics and the 'serious musical establishment'. In his later works, Copland reverted to serial techniques, writing in a far less approachable, more austere manner.

Whatever one thinks of his virtually unknown middle- and late-period music, Copland has to be admired for his steadfast independence and unwillingness to court popularity for its own sake.

Early Symphonies

Symphony No 1. Short Symphony. Dance Symphony
Bournemouth Symphony Orchestra / Marin Alsop
Naxos American Classics 8 559359 (59' · DDD) Ⓢ ⓞ➤

There are two attractions here: the only current recording of the *Short Symphony* and a fine recording of Symphony No 1 – at last. It started life as the Symphony for Organ and Orchestra, written for Copland's teacher Nadia Boulanger whose performances launched his career in 1925. Six years later the reworking of the score without organ was first performed but it has never made much headway. Alsop and the Bournemouth players make a fine case for this neglected score with many characteristics of mature Copland.

There are also two versions of Copland's *Short Symphony*. It was first played in Mexico City under Carlos Chávez in 1934 but the rhythmic difficulties were considered so great that the American premiere had to wait 10 years. Meanwhile, despairing of orchestral performances, Copland made the version for sextet. There are no difficulties now for the Bournemouth SO but one might have hoped for more sparkle and a better recording.

There are odd circumstances about the *Dance Symphony* too. It was taken from the ballet *Grohg* – never performed – that Copland wrote during his student years in Paris. In the absence of a full recording of *Grohg*, the *Dance Symphony* completes an essential CD.

Symphony No 3

Symphony No 3. Billy the Kid – Suite
New Zealand Symphony Orchestra / James Judd
Naxos American Classics 8 559106 (64' · DDD) ⑤●🕪

The first of Copland's three popular ballets is coupled here with what's arguably the greatest American symphony. Judd's first movement has more dynamic range than Eiji Oue's performance (below) and the long lines feel better paced. The second movement is the rumbustious *Scherzo* in Copland's most extrovert manner. Judd's interpretation works, and makes Oue seem a trifle pedestrian, closer to Copland's own performances than the dazzle that Bernstein brought to this kind of texture. The New Zealand strings aren't as precise in the taxing high opening as Oue's Minnesota players but, when it eventually comes, the fanfare and the subtle textures surrounding it are completely convincing.

The verdict on this efficient and sympathetic performance will be affected by its being the best buy around now. The suite from *Billy the Kid* gets thoroughly idiomatic treatment too and the coupling will encourage lovers of the most folksy Copland to recognise and enjoy the same composer in the big symphony.

Symphony No 3. Appalachian Spring.
Fanfare for the Common Man
Minnesota Orchestra / Eiji Oue
Reference Recordings RR93CD (72' · DDD) ⑤●

As an opening salute, the *Fanfare for the Common Man* makes a good centenary tribute and prepares listeners for its appearance in the finale of the Third Symphony. It also shows off the prowess of the Minnesota brass. The version of *Appalachian Spring* here is the suite, not the full ballet, and it's well paced under Oue although occasionally lacking attack in the strings where Copland said he wanted 'bitten out *marcato*'.

Significant earlier versions of the Third Symphony have included Copland's rather understated treatment with the New Philharmonia and Bernstein's much better projected interpretation on DG. Yet Oue's approach is compelling, falling midway between Copland's objectivity and Bernstein's dramatisation. The soft, long lines of the first movement move inexorably towards the first

COPLAND'S APPALACHIAN SPRING – IN BRIEF

San Francisco SO / Michael Tilson Thomas
RCA 09026 63511-2 (77' · DDD) ⑤❍❍❍
◈ The complete 35-minute score in its guise for full orchestra, surveyed with acute perception by Tilson Thomas and his peerlessly refined band. Sensational, spectacularly natural sound.

Los Angeles PO / Leonard Bernstein
DG 439 528-2GGA (54' · DDD) Ⓜ❍🕪
The popular 1945 suite in the performance of a lifetime. Lenny at his most charismatic and raptly understanding. Marvellous orchestral playing.

Boston SO / Serge Koussevitzky
Biddulph WHL050 (80' · ADD) Ⓜ
Koussevitzky's 1945 account was the suite's world premiere recording, a blazingly committed display with a coda as touchingly serene as you could hope to hear.

London SO / Aaron Copland
Sony SMK89874 (77' · ADD) Ⓜ
The suite receives an eminently sprightly, forthright performance under Copland's lead, though it's perhaps neither quite as distinctive nor as radiant as his own 1959 RCA Boston predecessor.

Atlanta SO / Robert Spano
Telarc CD80596 (69' · DDD) ⑤❍
A beautifully sprung account of the suite from this burgeoning partnership. Barber's tremendous First Symphony and approachable new works by Jennifer Higdon and Christopher Theofanidis complete a varied programme.

Detroit SO / Antal Dorati
Decca 430 705-2DM (74' · DDD) Ⓜ🕪
Glowingly caught by the Decca microphones, Dorati's uncomplicated Detroit account of the 1945 suite will give pleasure. Part of a supremely enjoyable all-Copland concert.

Seattle SO / Gerard Schwarz
Delos DE3154 (62' · DDD) Ⓕ
Another lucid, gently perceptive reading of the 1945 suite. Enterprisingly coupled with the Piano Concerto and *Symphonic Ode*, and handsomely engineered by Delos.

Atlanta SO / Louis Lane
Telarc CD80074 (68' · DDD) Ⓜ
Louis Lane offers the ballet suite in a performance that has a real feel of the theatre about it: you could almost imagine that these musicians had played in the pit for a while. Telarc's sound is all you could wish for. Part of an appealing Copland programme.

climax, and Copland's translucent scoring tells in its purely personal way. The *Scherzo* is a controlled riot, again showing off the brass – the orchestra's best feature – and the finale is convincing. The recorded sound is spectacular too.

Additional recommendation

Coupled with Quiet City
New York PO / Bernstein
DG download 419 170-2GH   ⓂⓄ▷

Still a wonderful performance, with Bernstein's unique insight into and sympathy for Copland's music reaping huge rewards.

Ballets

Appalachian Spring. Billy the Kid – Orchestral Suite. Rodeo – Four Dance Episodes
San Francisco Symphony Orchestra / Michael Tilson Thomas
RCA Red Seal 09026 63703-2 (77' · DDD)   ⓂⓄⓄⓄ▷

 For *Appalachian Spring* Tilson Thomas boldly opts for the rarely heard full orchestral version of the complete ballet score. This includes an extra 10 or so minutes of fretful, dark-hued music omitted from the familiar suite, after which that glorious final statement of *Simple Gifts* seems to emerge with even greater éclat and emotional release than usual. Elsewhere, these newcomers distil all the tender poetry and dewy freshness you could wish for, while bringing a marvellously supple spring and athletic purpose to any faster music.

Under Tilson Thomas, the suite from *Billy the Kid* opens with a real sense of 'once upon a time' wonder, the illimitable expanses of the prairie stretching out before our very eyes. The ensuing street scene soon generates an infectious rhythmic snap, and there's a wonderfully affecting contribution from the SFSO's principal trumpet during the card game at night. Best of all is 'Billy's death', as poignantly intoned as you've ever heard it. Absolutely no grumbles, either, about the four *Rodeo* dance episodes. Tilson Thomas sees to it that 'Buckaroo Holiday' packs all the requisite punch and high-kicking swagger, while the two middle numbers ravish the ear in their disarming beauty. Moreover, the concluding 'Hoe-Down' goes with terrific, toe-tapping gusto, though the orchestra's delirious whoops of delight may perhaps strike some listeners as too much of a good thing. Boasting opulent, exhilaratingly expansive recorded sound, this is a corker of a release.

El Salón México[a]. Danzón cubano[b]. An Outdoor Overture[b]. Quiet City[b]. Our Town[b]. Las agachadas[a]. Fanfare for the Common Man[b]. Lincoln Portrait[b]. Appalachian Spring – Suite[b]. Rodeo – Four Dance Episodes[b]. Billy the Kid – Orchestral Suite[b]. Music for Movies[c]. Letter from Home[b]. John Henry[b]. Symphony No 3[c]. Clarinet Concerto[d]
Benny Goodman *cl* **Henry Fonda** *narr*

[a]**New England Conservatory Chorus;** [b]**London Symphony Orchestra;** [c]**New Philharmonia Orchestra;** [d]**Columbia Symphony Orchestra / Aaron Copland**
Sony Classical ③ SM3K46559 (226' · ADD)
Recorded 1963-76   Ⓜ
Single 'Copland conducts Copland' disc available on Sony Classical Ⓜ SMK89874 includes Appalachian Spring, Fanfare for the Common Man, Rodeo – Four Dance Episodes, Old American Songs (with William Warfield) & Billy the Kid – Celebration

This offers a welcome gathering of a lot of Copland's own performances. Only *Las agachadas* ('The shake-down song') for unaccompanied chorus is new to the British catalogue; this is a rather lame performance and nobody would buy the three-CD set for that. The oldest recording is the Clarinet Concerto with Benny Goodman – the second of the two he made under Copland. *Lincoln Portrait* with Henry Fonda is disappointing, but apart from earlier recordings in Spanish and Portuguese, this, made in 1968, is the only one under Copland. He was surprisingly modest about interpretation and wrote (in *Copland on Music*; New York: 1960): 'Composers rarely can be depended upon to know the correct tempi at which their music should proceed.' All the same it's a pleasure to have Copland as both composer and interpreter in some of his most delightful shorter works such as *Letter from Home*, *John Henry*, *Quiet City* and *An Outdoor Overture*. All told, this is an economical way to build up a collection of his performances which provide such an insight into his personality.

The Red Pony – Suite. Rodeo – Four Dance Episodes. Letter from Home. Music for Radio, 'Prairie Journal'
Buffalo Philharmonic Orchestra / JoAnn Falletta
Naxos American Classics 8 559240 (60' · DDD)   Ⓢ▷

This attractive anthology represents Copland the Populist, to quote the title of Tilson Thomas's stunning RCA disc of all three ballets with the San Francisco Symphony. There are two suites, one from film and one from ballet, plus a couple of less familiar short pieces written for radio.

The least recorded of these is *Prairie Journal*, which had an odd genesis. It was commissioned by CBS Radio in 1936, premiered simply as *Music for Radio*, and their massive audience was invited to send in suggestions for a better title. A thousand people responded and Copland chose *Saga of the Prairie* – even at this stage listeners thought his music evoked the western scene. Copland changed the title much later. In both this piece and *Letter from Home* – as he admitted, a slightly sentimental picture of our boys at the front receiving mail in 1944 – he was taking the mass medium of radio seriously.

He did the same with films, as *The Red Pony* shows. The suite was performed in 1948 before the Steinbeck film was released. It's full of diatonic tunes you think you've known all your life, pure triads and Copland's characteristic snappy scoring. These are lively performances in the Copland tradition, although *Letter from Home* seems fast and at times the orchestra lacks finesse.

Piano Quartet

Movement[a]. Two Pieces[a]. Vitebsk[b]. Piano Quartet[c]. Sextet[d]
[d]**Michael Collins** *cl* [bcd]**Martin Roscoe** *pf* [ad]**Vanbrugh Quartet** ([bc]Gregory Ellis, Keith Pascoe *vns* [c]Simon Aspell *va* [bc]Christopher Marwood *vc*)
ASV CDDCA1081 (65' · DDD)　　　　　　　　　(F)

This fine collection of Copland's small output of chamber music offers the first British recording of *Movement*, a characteristically introspective piece from his student years in Paris which shares a theme with the Symphony for Organ and Orchestra. The Two Pieces (1928) are also rarities well worth having, the rapid second one embodying to perfection the ideals of Nadia Boulanger's teaching.

Then there are the three major chamber works, starting with *Vitebsk*, the 1929 trio based on a Jewish folk theme. This is a commanding performance, which makes the most of the off key quarter-tones and is thoroughly adroit in the central *Allegro*. The Sextet is a genuine chamber piece, although it was an arrangement of the *Short Symphony* which was found too difficult for most orchestras in 1933 and had to wait until 1944 for its American premiere. With Collins and Roscoe the Vanbrugh give an accomplished performance of the Sextet's sparklingly affirmative rhythms.

The Piano Quartet (1950) is in the same slow-quick-slow layout as *Vitebsk*. Like the final slow movement of the Piano Sonata, its outer movements have a sublime immobility. Written while Copland was working on his great cycle, *Twelve Poems of Emily Dickinson*, the first two movements of this impressive quartet enter new territory, Copland tentatively exploring serial techniques. A few exposed string phrases lack finesse, and some soft details in the piano are almost lost at the end of the first movement and more seriously at the end of the last movement when the dissonant note in the last chord is inaudible. But this is a valuable collection, well worth acquiring to have all these works together, played – and recorded – like this.

Twelve Poems of Emily Dickinson

Four Piano Blues. Twelve Poems of Emily Dickinson. Night. Pastorale. Poet's Song. Old American Songs – Set 1; Set 2
Susan Chilcott *sop* **Iain Burnside** *pf*
Black Box BBM1074 (69' · DDD · T)　　　(F)(O)

In this excellent selection Susan Chilcott and Iain Burnside grasp the subtlety of Copland's idiom. The two sets of *Old American Songs* are rightly sung in an American accent in a range of styles from the soulful-nostalgic of 'Long time ago' to the knockabout comedy of 'I bought me a cat'. But 'Simple Gifts', so well known from *Appalachian Spring*, is taken well below the marked tempo.

Copland's settings of Emily Dickinson are given with the commanding authority that this great cycle deserves. The competition on CD consists of Roberta Alexander with Roger Vignoles, where there are minor flaws, and Barbara Bonney with André Previn, which isn't an all-Copland disc. Neither of Copland's own recordings is still available. Even in this company Chilcott is impressive, with an enviable control of the wide leaps from top to bottom. Her breath control is so good that she can easily sustain the last note of 'I could not stop for death' for its full length, symbolising eternity. In each song every mood is right, although the recorded balance varies.

The early songs are interesting. Copland set his friend Aaron Schaffer's poem 'Night' when he was only 18 and Debussy's impressionism still avant-garde. But *Pastorale* three years later, just before he went to study with Nadia Boulanger in Paris, shows real personality.

Arcangelo Corelli　　Italian 1653-1713

Coming from a wealthy family near Bologna, Corelli showed an early talent for the violin, and after spending the first part of his career in Rome, Paris (where Lully thwarted his hopes) and Germany, he returned to Rome for the rest of his life. His patron was the wealthy music loving Cardinal Ottoboni (nephew of Pope Alexander VIII) and Corelli provided the music for his household. The fame of the Monday concerts held there spread all over Europe and Corelli's reputation as the leading violinist of his day together with the widespread publication of his music placed him among the most influential musicians of the period. You can see this not only in the music of Purcell, Vivaldi, Handel and Bach but also in what he introduced to the art of violin playing – such things as asking the performer to play more than one note with a single bow stroke (before this it was always one note for each stroke) and playing two or three strings at the same time (double- and triple-stopping). His pupils Geminiani and Locatelli in turn passed on what they had learnt.

Corelli was buried in the Pantheon in Rome near Raphael, leaving an estate of about £6000 (an exceptional amount in those days) and a collection of over a hundred paintings, including works by Bruegel and Poussin.

He insisted that the string players in his orchestra should all bow in the same way, a practice which led to unprecedented accuracy in performance and, said a contemporary, 'an amazing effect, even to the eye, as well as the ear'. In this Corelli was the main founder of modern orchestral playing and the composer who fashioned two new musical forms: the Baroque trio and solo sonata, and the concerto grosso (a four- or five-movement work), the forerunner of the modern concerto: a solo passage interplays and contrasts with the whole orchestra (or tutti).

His music itself is passionless, balanced, almost mechanical, but the slow movements show the lyrical powers of the violin as never before with great dignity and serenity, and the fast outer movements are crisp, concise and jolly – in other words, the classical form of Baroque music.

Concerti grossi

12 Concerti grossi, Op 6 – No 1 in D; No 2 in F; No 3 in C minor; No 4 in D; No 5 in B flat; No 6 in F; No 7 in D; No 8 in G minor; No 9 in F; No 10 in C; No-11 in B flat; No 12 in F
The English Concert / Trevor Pinnock
Archiv ② 459 451-2ATA2 (130' · DDD)   Ⓑ**OOO**➔

In his working life of about 40 years Corelli must have produced a great deal of orchestral music, yet the 12 Concerti grossi, Op 6, form the bulk of what's survived. Their original versions are mostly lost; what we know today are those published in Amsterdam by Estienne Roger. These had been assembled from movements Corelli had written over a period of years, and which he'd carefully polished and revised. The first eight are of the *da chiesa* type, the last four the *da camera* type, which essentially means that the latter have dance movements, the former don't. The number of movements in each varies from four to seven. All feature the interplay of a group of soloists, the concertino (two violins and a cello) and the orchestra, the ripieno, whose size, as Corelli wrote, could be flexible. These are masterpieces of their genre, much admired in their day, and very influential. The scores leave scope for embellishment, and the players of The English Concert take full advantage of them.

Trio Sonatas

Trio Sonatas, Opp 1ª,2ᵇ,3ᶜ & 4ᵈ
Purcell Quartet (Catherine Mackintosh, ᵃᵇᶜElizabeth Wallfisch, ᵈCatherine Weiss *vns* Richard Boothby *vc*) with **Jakob Lindberg** *theorbo* **Robert Woolley** ᵇᵈ*hpd/*ᵃᶜ*org*
Chaconne Classics ④ CHAN0692/4 (4h 36' · DDD)
                                        Ⓜ**O**➔

Corelli's chamber music was reprinted 84 times during his lifetime and 31 more during the rest of the 18th century, a record most composers would envy even today. The Sonatas of Opp 1 and 3 are *da chiesa*, those of Opp 2 and 4 are *da camera* (with dance-titled movements). They are small gems: most have four movements, and their durations range from five and a half to seven and a half minutes, within which they pack a wealth of invention, pure beauty and variety of pace and mood. Surviving evidence suggests that they were played at a much lower pitch than today's standard, the lower string tension adding warmth and opulence to the sound. Catherine Mackintosh takes full advantage of the works' opportunities for pliant phrasing and added embellishments; Elizabeth Wallfisch 'converses' with her in her own characteristic way, while Catherine Weiss follows her example more closely. The Purcell Quartet's oneness of

thought and timing is a joy to hear and the recording is superb in all respects.

Violin Sonatas, Op 5

Violin Sonatas, Op 5
Andrew Manze *vn* **Richard Egarr** *hpd*
Harmonia Mundi ② HMU90 7298/9 (131' · DDD)
                                    Ⓜ**OO**➔

Accounts of Corelli's violin playing tell us that his eyes would glow 'red as fire' and his face contort, but evidence of this volatile character has not not always been easy to detect in the written notes of the violin sonatas. If anyone is going to find him, however, it's Andrew Manze, who has repeatedly demonstrated that the heart of Baroque music lies beyond what's on the printed page. At a time when improvisational flair and spontaneity have never been a more exciting part of Baroque music-making, Manze and his accompanist Richard Egarr are the masters of it, and here they have produced a Corelli recording which is nothing short of revelatory.

Not that it's unthinkingly wild or bizarre. Manze may have adorned the music with his customarily liberal decoration of extra double-stops, flowery arabesques and emphatic gestures – and Egarr may have performed his usual extraordinary feats at the keyboard, devising an array of inventive keyboard textures which ranges from luxurious feather-bed arpeggios and swirls to daring, stabbing left-hand double octaves (no other continuo player manages to sound so much as if his fingers were a direct extension of his imagination) – but this is still Corelli with a measure of north Italian dignity.

The resulting balance between restraint and urgency is compelling, because the performers, you feel, aren't out to shock but to search for something new and real. This really is Corelli as you haven't heard him before. The performances reach a high technical standard, as does the recording, though strangely long gaps are left between some of the movements. This vital, ear-opening disc is in a category of its own, classic music in a classic recording.

John Corigliano   American b1938

After studying at Columbia University, Corigliano worked as a music programmer for the New York Times radio station WQXR, and as music director for WBAI. He also produced recordings for Columbia Masterworks and worked with Leonard Bernstein on the Young People's Concerts series for CBS. He has taught at the Manhattan School, the Juilliard School and Lehman College, CUNY, where he was named distinguished professor in 1984. During the period 1987-90 he served as the first composer-in-residence of the Chicago SO. Corigliano's first period, which he described as a 'tense, histrionic outgrowth of the "clean" American sound of Barber, Copland, Harris and Schuman', extends from the Violin Sonata (1963) through the choral symphony A Dylan Thomas Trilogy (1960-76). The Oboe Concerto (1975) and, more definitively, the Clarinet Concerto (1977), introduced by Bernstein and the New York PO, inaugurated a change in style, abandoning an earlier restriction to conventional notation and embracing an 'architectural' method of composition. Many of Corigliano's mature orchestral works have experimented with the physical placement of players: offstage instrumentalists figure prominently in both Troubadours and Symphony No 1; The Ghosts of Versailles features an orchestra onstage as well as in the pit, and both the Flute Concerto and the Clarinet Concerto conclude with dialogue between players onstage and in the auditorium. This concern reached an apotheosis of sorts with Circus Maximus (Symphony No 3, 2005).

Symphony No 3

Symphony No 3, 'Circus Maximus'. Gazebo Dances
University of Texas Wind Ensemble / Jerry Junkin
Naxos 8 559601 (53' · DDD)   ⓈⒹ→

Just as Corigliano's First Symphony embodied his anger about Aids, this spectacular based on the vast Roman arena the Circus Maximus finds 'parallels between the high decadence of Rome and our present time'. Corigliano rightly slates our entertainment-dominated culture and compares today's ubiquitous obsession with violence to the ancient Romans enjoying the sight of lions devouring human beings for amusement. This is heady stuff and nowhere more so than in the extravagant resources of Circus Maximus itself.

There's a stage band of 37 players plus four to five percussionists; a 'surround band' with 22 players including 11 trumpets and three percussionists; and a marching band that moves down the centre of the auditorium in track 6 and, like everything else, is stunningly caught by the sound engineers. As if that wasn't enough, the work ends with a sustained high note followed by a blast from a 12-bore shotgun! Some sections are as laceratingly violent as Varèse, and there are sirens and whistles too. But there's some repose in 'Night Music I' with its uncanny tapestry of animal sounds, even if 'Night Music II' evolves into a nightmare through dotted rhythms. The following 'Prayer' is sustained triadic relief.

The American wind band has a noble tradition and Corigliano has added a substantial work to the repertoire. The Gazebo Dances, originally for piano duet, are affable early pieces with a waltz that falls out of step and a hectic tarantella.

The Red Violin Concerto

The Red Violin Concerto[a]. Violin Sonata[b]
Joshua Bell vn [b]**Jeremy Denk** pf [a]**Baltimore
Symphony Orchestra / Marin Alsop**
Sony Classical 82876 88060-2 (62' · DDD)   ⒻⓄⒹ→

With his 70th birthday in 2009 and decorated with many awards, John Corigliano is one of the most prominent American composers of his generation. Thirty years ago his Clarinet Concerto made a strong initial impact and the Red Violin is his fifth concerto, with a new one for percussion to follow.

Corigliano's score for François Girard's film The Red Violin (1997) was the starting-point for the latest concerto. Even before the film was finished the composer extracted a Chaconne for violin and orchestra, which eventually became the first movement of the concerto. He felt that a single movement would get lost compared with a full-scale concerto.

And this is exactly what he has delivered – a romantic, dramatic, lyrical four-movement work with luxuriant orchestral textures that benefited from starting life as a film. In his essay in the booklet Corigliano says this context encouraged him to write with fewer inhibitions; things flowed easily, but he has cunningly adapted the work to the concert hall. Even further, the Red Violin Concerto is a resourceful vehicle for the eloquence and panache of Joshua Bell, who gave the premiere in 2003. The opening movement now seems long but the ghostly Scherzo is concise and throughout there is a special rapt atmosphere in pianissimo passages.

Bell and Jeremy Denk give a polished performance of the 1963 Violin Sonata that fuses neoclassical and American styles. Ideal performances well recorded.

Additional recommendation

Violin Sonata[a].
Coupled with The Red Violin Caprices. **V Thomson**
Five Ladies[a]. Three Portraits[a]. Eight Portraits
Quint vn [a]**Wolfram** pf
Naxos 8 559364 (65' · DDD)   ⓈⓄⒹ→

Quint and Wolfram make the sonata sound just as impressive as Bell and Denk (above). In the Virgil Thomson works, Quint's panache is stunning and this CD offers some of the most attractive music for solo violin in the entire repertoire.

William Cornysh   English 1468-1523

Cornysh was Master of the Children at the Chapel Royal, a post he held until his death. He was also responsible for the musical and dramatic entertainments at Henry VIII's court, and during important diplomatic events such as at the Field of the Cloth of Gold and visits to and from the courts of France and the Holy Roman Empire. Several of his sacred vocal works are in the Eton Choirbook.

Magnificat

Salve regina. Ave Maria, mater Dei. Gaude virgo mater Christi. Magnificat. Ah, Robin. Adieu, adieu,

my heartes lust. Adieu courage. Woefully arrayed.
Stabat mater
The Tallis Scholars / Peter Phillips
Gimell CDGIM014 (65' · DDD · T)   ⓕ

Cornysh's music is a riot of abundant, often seemingly wild melody, constantly in search of wanton, abstract, daredevil ideas. Take, for example, the extraordinary conclusion to the five-part *Magnificat*, where pairs of voices are challenged with music of gradually increasing complexity, peaking in an exchange of quite hair-raising virtuosity between the sopranos – and all this just for the words 'and ever shall be, world without end'! As far as the sacred works are concerned, the Tallis Scholars respond magnificently to Cornysh's audacious imagination. Theirs is a majestic and glorious sound, to be relished in full in the *Stabat mater*, a huge piece that survives incomplete and for which the late Frank Harrison composed treble parts that may even trump Cornysh himself in their sheer bravura. Marginally less striking in The Tallis Scholars' performances are the short partsongs and the carol *Woefully arrayed*, robbed as they are here of some of their latent expressiveness and strength by being sung (admittedly very beautifully) in an inappropriately resonant building, and in rounded modern English vowels. But judged as a whole this disc must be reckoned an outstanding success.

Louis Couperin   French c1626-1661

Louis was the first Couperin to achieve acclaim in the world of music in France, and his descendants maintained that position for more than two and a half centuries. He was organist of St Gervais in Paris and wrote music is for keyboard: some 70 fugues, plainchant settings and other pieces for organ, and about 135 for harpsichord, consisting of preludes and dances.

Suites

L Couperin Suites – in F; in A; in D; in A; in F; in C. Pavane in F sharp minor **Froberger** Le tombeau de Monsieur Blancheroche
Skip Sempé hpd
Alpha ALPHA066 (79' · DDD)   ⓕ**OO**

Louis Couperin, less famous than his nephew, François 'Le Grand', was nevertheless one of the greatest harpsichord composers of the 17th century, a creator of suites of beautifully honed miniatures cast predominantly in the standard French dance-forms of the day (Allemande, Courante, Sarabande and so on) exuding all the noble expressiveness and lyrical melancholy of their age.

He finds an ideal interpreter in Skip Sempé, a player who relishes the sheer sound of the harpsichord and knows how to exploit its glorious resonance. Sempé achieves this by means of

probably the most exquisite touch you'll ever hear on the instrument, leaving him in control of the tone at every turn. Chords are spread lovingly, ornaments tumble easily into one another, all without a hint of unwelcome percussiveness or jangliness – every note seems to have been deftly caressed into being.

He also shows us just how much he enjoys the bass sonority of his harpsichord (a compliant French copy by Bruce Kennedy) by throwing in a low-lying transcription of a Marais gamba piece; another guest composer is Froberger, who answers Couperin's Prelude in explicit imitation of his style, with his sombrely magnificent *Tombeau de Monsieur Blancheroche*. A minute lack of improvisatory flow in the unmeasured Preludes is scarcely worth mentioning when so much else in Sempé's playing gives unalloyed pleasure. This is demonstration-class musicianship at the harpsichord.

François Couperin   French 1668-1733

The most prominent representative (thus 'Le Grand') of a famous family of musicians whose dynasty began in the 1620s and expired when the last male Couperin died two centuries later – French rivals to the German Bachs. François spent most of his musical life in the service of the French court as a harpsichordist and organist, composing sacred music and chamber works for the royal pleasure of King Louis XIV.

The field in which he achieved his most lasting success was the extraordinary harpsichord works he composed towards the end of his life. Between 1713 and 1730 he published four volumes of his Pièces de clavecin. These amount to 230 pieces in 27 ordres (Couperin's name for suites), each ordre a series of dances. They all have whimsical, witty or descriptive titles like 'The Little Windmills', 'The Knitters', etc, and many that defy translation because of their reference to topical subjects (Les tic-toc-choc, for instance, which described the work of Mme Guillotine). The Romantics were keen on this kind of thing and, later, Debussy and Satie in their piano pieces. They are musical postcards of the court, sketches of Couperin's life and personality.

His book L'art de toucher le clavecin (1716) had an enormous influence on succeeding generations of keyboard players. Alfred Einstein wrote perceptively that 'in Couperin we see the beginnings of the French musical predilection for the exquisite, for studied brilliance, emotional discretion and roguish charm extending to sly wit'. It was not for nothing that Ravel wrote his Le tombeau de Couperin in tribute 200 years later.

Pièces de clavecin

Quatre Livres de pièces de clavecin
Michael Borgstede hpd
Brilliant Classics ⑪ 93082 (11h 17' · DDD)   Ⓢ

Couperin's creative world can be a difficult one to enter as a listener; not everyone finds its refined expression and intimacy of thought involving, bound up as it is in the Watteauesque subtleties of early-18th-century French court society, and shot through with enigmatic character pieces named after people and preoccupations long gone and forgotten. Yet once one has put such ephemeral matters out of one's mind – and this set forces one to, since there is little room for explanations in the skinny booklet – then this great music stands revealed as able to speak for itself with all the eloquence of a Chopin ballade or a Debussy prélude.

Michael Borgstede's spruce performances of the four published books of *Pièces de clavecin* plus the eight Préludes from *L'art de toucher le clavecin* keep drawing one back for further doses, to revel not only in the sheer poetry, imagination and individuality of Couperin's musical personality, but also its classical balance and poise. The compact *ordres* (or suites) of the later books in particular offer meticulously planned sets of varied yet complementary character pieces in perfect 'drop-in'-sized sequences.

Borgstede's two instruments, one Flemish and one German, are not always voiced with perfect precision and their tuning sounds a little tired on occasion. A box of goodies to snap up.

L'art de toucher le clavecin – Prélude No 6 in **P**
B minor. Troisième livre de pièces de clavecin –
Treizième ordre; Quatorzième ordre; Quinzième
ordre
Robert Kohnen *hpd* **Barthold Kuijken** *fl*
Accent ACC9399D (64' · DDD)   Ⓕ

Kohnen's playing is rhythmically incisive, fastidious in detail – Couperin was hot on that – and full of character. If, on first acquaintance, his realisation of Couperin's vignette 'Les lis naissans' (*Ordre* No 13) seems a shade spiky then his lyrical approach to the flowing 6/8 melody of the rondeau 'Les rozeaux', which follows, reassures us that Kohnen does have the poetry of the music at heart, and intends that it should be so. Less appealing are Kohnen's somewhat intrusive vocal introductions to 'Les folies françoises'. This information is provided in the booklet so it hardly needs to be reiterated. In a concert recital such snatches of actuality can be effective; on a disc, after repeated listening, they become an unwelcome interruption. Occasional departures from the norm in the following two *ordres* are of an altogether more agreeable nature. In 'Le rossignol-en-amour' (*Ordre* No 14) Kohnen takes Couperin up on his suggestion to use a transverse flute, played here with a beautifully rounded tone by Barthold Kuijken. Likewise, in the jaunty rondeau 'La Julliet', the trio texture is realised by flute and harpsichord rather than the more usual two-harpsichord texture. This piece is beautifully done, as is the subtly bell-like 'Carillon de Cithère' which follows it. In short, a stylish and entertaining release which is as likely as any to draw the cautious listener into Couperin's refined, allusory and metaphor-laden idiom.

F Couperin Livres de clavecin, Books I-IV – selection
Duphly La Pothouïn
Alexandre Tharaud *pf*
Harmonia Mundi HMC90 1956 (65' · DDD)   Ⓕ➔

Alexandre Tharaud's disc of Rameau keyboard works was a refreshing demonstration that French harpsichord music can be convincingly transferred to the piano, twiddles and all, if its essential character is respected and understood. Now he attempts the seemingly tougher task of doing the same for the more delicate Couperin, and again emerges with honour. Reactions to a disc like this can only be personal, but Tharaud's unapologetically pianistic approach not only yields highly attractive results but also gets closer to Couperin's true spirit.

Mind you, he only chooses works that he considers suitable to the piano, selecting from right across Couperin's output rather than playing whole suites. Arguably, he gets it wrong only twice, in 'La visionnaire' and the great B minor Passacaille, fulsome formal pieces both, whose grandeur the piano somehow manages to dull. Yet for the most part the music sounds beautifully at home. Poetic wonders such as 'La muse plantine', 'Les ombres errantes' and the iconic 'Les baricades mistérieuses' are played with tender sensitivity of mind and touch, while 'Le carillon de Cithére' is a glistening vision of a Watteauesque paradise. Elsewhere, 'Le tic-toc-choc' and 'Les tours de passe-passe' are enlivened by off-beat accents, 'Bruit de guerre' thrills with its added drum part, and 'Muséte de taverni', multi-tracked into a work *à 5 mains*, rattles away like some delicious missing movement from *L'arlésienne*. Tharaud closes with a piece by Duphly, relishing its dark melancholy and, not for the first time on this disc, evoking another great keyboard poet, Robert Schumann. This is a release which successfully recognises and celebrates Couperin's genius, and you cannot ask for much more than that.

Armand-Louis Couperin
French c1727-1789

Armand-Louis was a member of the great Couperin dynasty – a son of one of Louis's cousins (see page 364). Aged 21 he inherited his father's post as organist at St Gervais, Paris. He married Elisabeth-Antionette Blanchet, daughter of the great harpsichord maker. Such was his reputation as an improviser that he was mentioned by Burney. He left a substantial oeuvre at the time of his death which resulted from a traffic accident as he rushed from Vespers at St Gervais.

Harpsichord works

Pièces de clavecin – La victoire; Allemande;
Courante: La De Croissy; Les Caqueteuses; La
Grégoire; L'Intrépide; Première menuet; Deuxième

menuet; L'Arlequine ou la Adam; La Blanchet; La de Boisgelou; La Foucquet; La Semillante, ou La Joly; La Turpin; Première gavotte; Deuxième gavotte; Première menuet; Deuxième menuet; La du Breüil; La Chéron; L'Affligée; L'Enjoué; Les tendres sentimens; Rondeau gracieux

Sophie Yates hpd

Chandos Chaconne CHAN0718 (80' · DDD) Ⓕ Ⓑ⊕

According to accounts Armand-Louis Couperin was a likeable man whose life was led free from strife and uncorrupted by ambition, and it is not fanciful to say that such are the qualities which inform his harpsichord music. Mostly rather rangy character pieces, though with a sprinkling of dances, they show the bold textural richness of the later French harpsichordist-composers, if without the galloping imagination of figures such as Rameau, Balbastre or Royer. Instead, they prefer to inhabit a contented rococo world, into which they bring considerable professional polish.

If that makes the pieces sound predominantly 'pleasant', well, so they are…as agreeable a body of solo harpsichord music as any. But they are not vapid and neither are they easy, and we can be grateful that this selection has fallen to a player as technically assured and as musically sympathetic as Sophie Yates. Whether skipping through the wide-spread arpeggios and scales of 'La Semillante', firing out the repeated notes of 'Les Caqueteuses' or tumbling down the helter-skelters of 'L'Enjoué', she exudes invigorating virtuosity. Yet she shows delicacy, too, in the little gavottes and minuets, and sensitivity in the melancholy 'L'Affligée' (a piece somewhat reminiscent of Rameau's *L'Enharmonique*). Her harpsichord, a copy of a 1749 Goujon, sounds superb, being resonant without boominess and clear-voiced without excessive punchiness of attack. One of Sophie Yates's best yet.

Henry Cowell   American 1897-1965

Henry Cowell was a hugely influential American composer who helped the cause of new music enormously. As a composer he was experimenting with clusters of notes in his piano music before he'd even started his official studies (which he pursued in New York and California). He was a publisher (his New Music Edition published scores by mavericks such as Ives and Ruggles) and a writer (his 1930 book New Muscial Resources was much studied). He later taught at the Peabody Conservatory (1951-56) and Columbia University (1949-65).

His early music experimented with new sounds, including the piano clusters (Advertisement from 1914, for example) and strumming on the piano's strings. In the 1930s his music became more tonal and drew a lot on folk music but later he returned to his more exploratory earlier experimental style.

His musical output is vast and includes 21 symphonies (and many concertos), nearly 200 chamber works, over 200 piano pieces, operas, and incidental and film music.

Miscellaneous Works

Deep Color[a]. Fabrica. Fairy Answer[a]. Tiger[a]. Violin Suite[b]. Quartet for Flute, Oboe, Cello and Harpsichord[c]. Polyphonica[d]. Three Anti-Modernist Songs[e]. Irish Suite[f]
[e]**Ellen Lang** mez [c]**Jayn Rosenfeld** fl [c]**Marsha Heller** ob [b]**Mia Wu** vn [c]**Maria Kitsopoulos** vc **Cheryl Seltzer** [bef]pf/[c]hpd [df]**Continuum** /[de]**Joel Sachs** [a]pf
Naxos American Classics 8 559192 (66' · DDD) Ⓢ Ⓑ⊕

Set of Five[a]. The Banshee[b]. Vestiges[b]. Euphoria[b]. What's This?[b] Elegie[b]. Six Casual Developments[c]. Homage to Iran[d]. Piece for Piano with Strings[e]. Two Songs[f] – Sunset; Rest
[f]**Raymond Murcell** bar [c]**David Krakauer** cl [a]**Gordon Gottlieb** perc [d]**Mark Steinberg**, [a]**Marilyn Dubow** vns [bdef]**Cheryl Seltzer** pf [be]**Continuum** / **Joel Sachs** [a]pf/[d]perc
Naxos American Classics 8 559193 (60' · DDD) Ⓢ Ⓑ⊕

Henry Cowell was an avant-garde pioneer with his tone-clusters; became a multi-culturalist, some of whose music falls midway between East and West; and was an inspiration to younger American composers such as John Cage and Lou Harrison. His use of the insides of the piano has borne fruit in the work of George Crumb. Cowell said he wanted to 'live in the whole world of music' and wrote almost 1000 works to prove it. Many of these are unknown but his position in the record catalogue has been improving steadily since his centenary in 1997.

Cowell recorded three of the group of four piano pieces on the first CD in 1962; his aggressive *Tiger* is better phrased and slower than Joel Sachs's and thus more comprehensible but *Deep Color* is barely known. Both the Suite for violin and piano (1925) and the much later Quartet for flute, oboe, cello and harpsichord are neo-Baroque. The Bach-with-clusters approach at first seems surreal but the *Andante calmato* is magical. *Polyphonica* is a bracing study in the kind of dissonant textures fashionable in the late 1920s but the *Irish Suite* is quite different. It's an expanded version for piano and small orchestra of three earlier pieces played directly on the piano strings. The first is *Banshee* (the original version is on the second CD) named after the ghost which wails at the time of a death. The ravishing new sounds in all three pieces – amazing for 1929 – are uniquely Cowell's.

In 1956 he spent some time in the Middle East; one result was the *Homage to Iran* for violin, piano and drums. As elsewhere, he ingeniously adapts ethnic materials in a manner that falls midway between the two cultures. The *Six Casual Developments* (1933) for clarinet and piano are vivid epigrammatic miniatures. The *Set of Five* (1952) is for violin, piano and varied percussion, used to provide an ethnic flavour. The final *Vigoroso* is spacious and declamatory with a surprise in the middle – a duet for celesta and prepared piano.

These two CDs provide a judiciously chosen sample of Cowell's work on a small scale; the performances are fine; enthusiasts for Cowell will certainly want both.

George Crumb
American b1929

Crumb has gathered a cult following, largely due to his string quartet Black Angels of 1970. He has never distanced himself from the music of the Classical and Romantic eras, and has developed a musical language that creates an atmospheric chiaroscuro. He often employs musical quotations. Surprisingly, he has written very little for orchestra, preferring instead more intimate forces, as well as small vocal ensembles. After initially being influenced by Webern, Crumb became interested in exploring unusual timbres. He often asks for instruments to be played in unusual ways and several of his pieces are written for electrically amplified instruments. Crumb has earned his living primarily from teaching. His first teaching job was at a college in Virginia, before he became professor of piano and composition at the University of Colorado in 1958. In 1965 he began a long association with the University of Pennsylvania, becoming Annenberg Professor of the Humanities in 1983. Some of his most prominent students include Margaret Brouwer, Uri Caine, Christopher Rouse, Osvaldo Golijov and Jennifer Higdon.

Songs, Drones and Refrains of Death

Songs, Drones and Refrains of Death[a]. Quest
Ensemble New Art ([a]Nicholas Isherwood *bass-bar*
Hugo Read *sax* Alexander Swete *gtr* Peter
Degenhardt *kybds* Silke Aichorn *hp* Carmen Erb,
Hans-Peter Achberger *perc* Franzisco Obieta *db*) /
Fuat Kent
Naxos American Classics 8 559290 (55' · DDD) ⑤ⓑ→

This disc will bring Crumb to a wider audience with two substantial works, one early and one late. *Songs, Drones and Refrains of Death* was completed in 1968 and has all the hallmarks of Crumb's magical sound world. It's one of several pieces stemming from the poetry of Federico García Lorca. Nicholas Isherwood, after many live performances, is totally in command of this spooky territory and delivers his lines with great clarity (full texts of the four poems are available online). 'The Song of the Rider' is a spine-chilling counterpart to Schubert's *Erlkönig* – both scenarios end in death, a consistent presence throughout both in the poems and in the movements called 'Death-Drones'.

Written in 1994, *Quest* shows Crumb still finding unusual sonorities for his six players with prominent guitar. So we hear the Appalachian hammer dulcimer, the African talking drum, the Mexican rainstick, and sometimes the guitar and harp are interwoven. Crumb admits that he had some trouble in finding a final form for *Quest*: there is no programme but he pondered a couple of gloomy phrases from Dante and Lorca.

Alexander Swete plays electric guitar in *Songs, Drones* and acoustic guitar in *Quest*, which becomes a showpiece for him (it was written for David Starobin). It's now good to have both these works together, well recorded, with notes by the composer.

Bernhard Crusell
Finnish 1775-1839

Crusell studied the clarinet from an early age before joining a military band in Sveaborg; he later travelled to Stockholm to became a court musician. He studied the clarinet in Berlin in 1798 and in 1803 went to Paris to study composition with Gossec. He later held posts as music director in the Swedish court chapel and royal regiment. His compositions including numerous works for clarinet (including three concertos). He also made Swedish translations of operas by Mozart, Rossini and others.

Clarinet Concertos

Clarinet Concertos – No 1 in E flat, Op 1; No 2 in
F minor, Op 5; No 3 in B flat, Op 11
Kari Kriikku *cl* **Finnish Radio Symphony Orchestra**
/ Sakari Oramo
Ondine ODE965-2 (64' · DDD) ⑤ⓑ→

With full, bright, immediate sound, Finnish clarinettist Kari Kriikku gives dazzling performances of these three delightful clarinet concertos. In many ways he's even more daring than his rivals, regularly choosing speeds that stretch virtuosity to the limit, particularly in the finales. Those of Nos 1 and 2 may be marked merely *allegretto*, but Kriikku, by choosing exceptionally fast speeds, brings out an extra *scherzando* quality, often sharp and spiky, in which Crusell's characteristic dotted rhythms are delightfully crisp. The almost impossibly rapid tonguing never seems to get in the way of detailed characterisation.

Emma Johnson in her recordings is altogether more relaxed, regularly adopting speeds rather broader, extremely so in the *Alla polacca* which ends No 3. Consistently, her pointing of rhythm brings out the fun in the writing, and in her comparably broad approach to slow movements she finds extra poetry. Partly as a result of the immediacy of the recording, Kriikku's *pianissimos* aren't as extreme, yet in flair and panache Kriikku is second to none, superbly supported by the crisp, purposeful playing of the Finnish National Radio orchestra under Sakari Oramo.

An excellent disc, guaranteed to win friends for these sparkling works.

Marc-André Dalbavie
French b1961

Dalbavie had his first piano lesson aged six and within two years he had already won his first national competition. He attended the Conservatoire National Supérieure de Musique in Paris and followed this with study with John Cage and at the Academia Chigiana in Siena. Between 1983 and '89 he studied composition with Tristan Murail; he has also worked with Boulez and at IRCAM. His works include a Piano Concerto written for Leif Ove Andsnes and a number of orchestral works, many drawing their inspiration from music of the Middle Ages.

Concertos

Violin Concerto[a]. Color. Ciaccona
[a]**Eiichi Chijiiwa** vn **Orchestre de Paris /**
Christoph Eschenbach
Naïve MO782162 (64' · DDD)
Recorded live 2001-03   (F)

Marc-André Dalbavie is one of the more visible French composers of his generation and as such he is able to draw upon musicians of real distinction. Indeed, he could hardly hope for better live performances than those on this recording. The latter point is eloquently made by Eiichi Chijiiwa, who handles the many bravura passages of the Violin Concerto's solo part seemingly effortlessly. So it is disconcerting to turn to the music and find so little of substance.

Dalbavie can certainly write for show: in his hands the orchestra has a glitzy patina, at times reminiscent in its allure of film music, and the soloist in the Concerto has much to do. The composer/conductor knows the repertoire of modernist orchestral and ensemble scores very well, and in not a few instances one can even identify specific works that he references; the problem is that this isn't done it seems in any playful spirit of postmodernism. Perhaps his signature (an element that occurs in all three scores) is the unfolding of slow, steady scalar passages, or of chords whose tessituras gradually ascend or descend, expand or contract. These simple gestures may betoken the accessibility to which he aspires (according to the booklet-notes) but the end result is a kind of modernism-lite, likely to frustrate as many listeners as it flatters.

Dalbavie Flute Concerto[a] **Jarrell** Flute Concerto,
'...un temps de silence...'[b] **Pintscher** Transir[c]
Emmanuel Pahud fl **Radio France Philharmonic**
Orchestra / [a]**Peter Eötvös,** [b]**Pascal Rophé,**
[c]**Matthias Pintscher**
EMI 501226-2 (55' · DDD)   (F)(O)(+)

Like other high-profile wind players, Emmanuel Pahud has sought to compensate for the dearth of pre-1900 concertos by commissioning contemporaries. These three works provide a well balanced programme, and high standards of playing and recording combine to make this a release to be reckoned with.

Marc-André Dalbavie has no hang-ups about evoking both the languor and the energy of Ravel's *Daphnis et Chloé* – and the music is all the better for the kind of tongue-in-cheek approach which leads Pahud himself to make comparisons with Ibert. It works because there are no half-measures: both the opulence and the tenderness seem genuine and well judged in terms of Dalbavie's own personal angle on contemporary idioms. After this, Michael Jarrell's *...un temps de silence...* and Matthias Pintscher's *Transir* are a good deal more intense. Jarrell risks over-indulging the defining features of his idiom – fast and febrile at one extreme, quietly whispering at

the other. But there's enough drama to keep the piece in focus, and Pahud's way with its intricate flurries and withdrawn musings is mesmerisingly fastidious.

Transir is the most radical of the three works in its addiction to fragmentation, brief expressionistic outbursts articulating what might be heard as an extended modernist mad scene. Even if the work's dedication to the memory of a composer called Dominic Transir is not a joke, 'transir' also happens to be the French verb for 'to paralyse, to chill to the bone'. This is indeed profoundly chilly music, constantly on the verge of freezing solid, never thawing into expansiveness. After it, Dalbavie's unaffected warmth seems even more seductive than it otherwise might.

Luigi Dallapiccola   Italian 1904-1975

Dallapiccola studied at the conservatoire in Florence in the 1920s, becoming a professor there in 1931, a post he retained until 1967. He numbered Luciano Berio among his pupils. His early interest in Wagner's music was supplanted by a fascination with the works of Debussy and later works by Busoni, Berg and Webern. His Il prigioniero, one of his operas, sealed his reputation after the Second World War and also revealed his strong political views, especially his passionate opposition to fascism. As he aged his music took on a more sensuous feel, in sharp opposition to the raw intensity of his early works.

Orchestral works

Dialoghi[a]. Variazioni. Due Pezzi. Three Questions with
Two Answers
[a]**Jean-Guihen Queyras** vc **RAI National Symphony**
Orchestra / Pascal Rophé
Stradivarius STR33698 (61' · DDD)   (F)

This new collection of Dallapiccola's later orchestral works is more than welcome. As Mario Ruffi's informative booklet-note points out, their emergence was largely due to the composer's success in the United States, as opposed to the hostility aroused in his native Italy – notably the Milan premiere of *Due Pezzi* (1947), an orchestral expansion of violin-and-piano originals whose inspiration in frescos by Piero della Francesca is here made the more explicit.

In the *Pezzi*, Pascal Rophé makes great sense of its subtle timbral continuity and downplays the overtly rhetorical in the 'Fanfara e Fuga'. Rophé shapes the *Variazioni* (1954) into a cohesive and cumulative whole, emphasising the emotional impact that arises out of technical rigour. The new disc includes the first modern recording of *Dialoghi* (1960) – the most hermetic of all Dallapiccola's works in its inwardness and glacial, though never inexpressive, harmonies, played with keen eloquence by Jean-Guihen Queyras. A satellite to the in-progress *Ulisse, Three Questions with Two Answers* (1963) fairly encapsulates the opera's metaphysical concerns in its motivic richness and sense of grand vistas – whether of nature or humanity – aspiring towards the infinite.

Rophé obtains responsive playing from Turin's RAI orchestra, with sound that brings out detail and atmosphere in equal measure. Strongly recommended.

Orchestral Works, Vol 2
Partita[a]. Quattro Liriche di Antonio Machado[a].
Dialoghi[b]. Three Questions with Two Answers
[a]**Gillian Keith** *sop* [b]**Paul Watkins** *vc*
BBC Philharmonic / Gianandrea Noseda
Chandos CHAN10561 (67' · DDD)   Ⓕ**OO**▷

The wait for Volume 2 in Chandos's Dallapiccola series has been well worthwhile. It includes two of the composer's most refined and characterful instrumental scores, written within two years of each other, and both are performed here with the kind of balance between striking details and a sense of evolving overall shape which it's all too easy to take for granted in music that is a good deal more intricate than it may sound at first hearing.

Dialoghi (1960) is a fine example of Dallapiccola's ability to rethink traditional genres like the concerto in refreshing and stimulating ways. Economical and intense, it is never merely austere in that 'post-Webern' fashion so familiar around 1960, and Paul Watkins brings ideal eloquence and spontaneity to the solo part. *Three Questions with Two Answers* (1963) is closely linked to the opera *Ulisse* but lacks that troubled work's occasional looseness and lack of focus. There's a spirit of stoic intensity, brooding but never merely despairing, conveyed by luminous orchestral textures, all beautifully caught in excellent recorded sound.

The early *Partita* (1930-32) is on a much lower creative level, with moments of Respighian, even Puccinian flamboyance failing to offset a prevailing blandness which Dallapiccola soon learnt to avoid. Gillian Keith does her best in the final vocal movement but comes into her own in the orchestral version of the brief but exhilarating Machado settings, originally written with piano accompaniment. Recommended especially for those who don't believe that 12-note music can be joyful, it is one of Dallapiccola's most perfect works.

Peter Maxwell Davies   British *b*1934

Everyone knows his name, some of us may recognise the titles of some of his pieces, a few may have heard of the famous composer who lives on the Orkney island of Hoy. How many of us could identify a note of his many compositions is a moot point. Yet Sir Peter, though he writes as obtusely as any contemporary composer, has also written some of the most accessible of new works. Few though, beyond school choirs and

the odd festival chorus, have really taken his music to their hearts. And, in common with his peers, his critical reputation is in no way matched by his success with the public. Nevertheless, here is a knight of the realm, hailed like his student colleague Sir Harrison Birtwistle, as the leading light of his generation, a great British composer.

After the Manchester (now Royal) College of Music where he was part of the 'Manchester Group' of Birtwistle, Elgar Howarth and John Ogdon intent on promoting the avant-gardists of Europe, Davies went off to Rome on a scholarship and served as director of music at Cirencester Grammar School for three years, a period which stimulated his lifelong interest in writing for young people. In 1968, after a period with Roger Sessions at Princeton University, a round-the-world lecture tour and a spell as composer-in-residence at Adelaide University, he returned to London. Here, with Birtwistle, he founded the Pierrot Players (later The Fires of London), a chamber group at whom Davies directed much of his output, including the haunting music-theatre piece Eight Songs for a Mad King. Medieval and Renaissance music had always played an important part in his make-up, as now did the sights and sounds of the sea and the bleak Scottish landscape (An Orkney Wedding with Sunrise and Runes from a Holy Island are two works with which to conduct initial explorations of Davies's complex world).

In 1971 Davies moved to Orkney and the St Magnus Festival which he founded there has seen the premiere of many of his works since then. He campaigns fervently for the causes closest to his heart: Britain's musical life and its orchestras, as well as taking up the anti-nuclear banner and being a committed environmentalist. Given that, it was somewhat surprising that he accepted the title of Master of the Queen's Music im 2004, a role at which he has proved himself not only well suited but in which he has acquited himself with great style.

String Quartets

Naxos Quartets Nos 1 & 2
Maggini Quartet (Laurence Jackson, David Angel *vns* Martin Outram *va* Michal Kaznowski *vc*)
Naxos 8 557396 (75 ' · DDD)   Ⓢ**OO**▷

This first instalment of Sir Peter Maxwell Davies's ambitious series of 10 Naxos Quartets indicates that it's shaping up to be quite a journey. The septuagenarian composer rises superbly to the technical challenges of the medium. The first two movements of the First Quartet evince a formal strength, expressive scope and thematic ingenuity that launch the cycle in sure-footed fashion; both attain a dramatic and emotional resolution in some arresting unison writing. The compact concluding *Scherzo* could hardly provide a bolder contrast; its ghostly, will-o'-the-wisp dialogue will re-emerge in the Third Quartet.

There are four movements in the Second Quartet, the second and third of which comprise a self-contained diptych (and the former's recitative first half harks back to No 1's *Largo* centrepiece). The outer movements are more expansive. An expectant *Lento* introduction leads to a bracing *Allegro*, its progress stimulating and satisfyingly proportioned. The *Lento flessibile* finale is finer still: a memorably serene and utterly inevitable essay.

The Magginis are most accurate and cogent guides, realistically recorded within the sympathetic acoustic of Potton Hall in Suffolk. A most rewarding coupling.

Additional recommendations

Naxos Quartets Nos 3 & 4
Maggini Quartet
Naxos 8 557397 (56' · DDD)   Ⓢ☐►

The impression of great things given by the first two quartets in the Naxos cycle is amply confirmed by this no less rewarding second volume. The Magginis once again play with superlative poise and intelligence. Both sound and balance are first-rate.

Naxos Quartets Nos 9 & 10
Maggini Quartet
Naxos 8 557400 (64' · DDD)   Ⓢ◐►

The Magginis perform with the no-holds-barred commitment and jaw-dropping technical acumen we have come to expect from them throughout this massive project. Splendidly rich sound and a most truthful balance, too. (The complete Naxos Quartets are also available in a five-CD set, 8 505225.)

Choral music

Missa parvula[ab]. Mass[abc]. Dum complerentur[a]. Veni Sancte Spiritus[a]. Veni Creator Spiritus[b]. Reliqui domum meum[b]
[a]**Westminster Cathedral Choir / Martin Baker** with
[b]**Robert Quinney**, [c]**Robert Houssart** orgs
Hyperion CDA67454 (67' · DDD· T/t)   Ⓕ

Under David Hill and subsequently James O'Donnell the choir of Westminster Cathedral established a tradition of excellent recordings for Hyperion. That tradition is as strong as ever under Martin Baker, who became Master of the Music in 2000. Like his immediate predecessors, Baker is exploring repertoire which isn't just challenging and unusual, but of real value.

The *Missa parvula* for unison boys' voices vividly recalls Britten's *Missa brevis* both in its terse musical language and understated emotion. The opening of the Mass occupies the same sound world as the *Missa parvula* and it's only with the thrilling and lavishly scored *Gloria* that it's apparent we are now into a work of much greater depth and impact. This is a hugely impressive performance, as much for the astonishing effect of the two organs as for the often magical choral effects. Baker entices some of the most wonderful singing from his choir here while Roberts Quinney and Houssart revel in their virtuoso interplay. Hyperion's recording

captures the full effect of Maxwell Davies's astonishing writing.

A revelatory disc for those keen to know what sort of 'establishment' music we might expect from the new Master of the Queen's Music.

Music Theatre

Mr Emmet Takes a Walk
Adrian Clarke bar Mr Emmet **Jonathan Best** bass Mr Todd, Security, Waiter, Heating Engineer, Piano Teacher, Gabor **Rebecca Caine** sop Ka, Woman in Café, Reception, Maid, Housekeeper, Crone, Varoomschka
Psappha / Etienne Siebens
Psappha PSACD1002 (75' · DDD · T/N)   Ⓕ

Sir Peter Maxwell Davies regards *Mr Emmet Takes a Walk* (2000) as his music-theatre swansong, and in the 20-minute discussion with Paul Driver that follows this performance he muses on the various ways in which it can be linked to his earlier operas and dramatic works, from *Taverner* to *The Doctor of Myddfai*. As a chamber opera, or 'dramatic sonata', in which the citation and distortion of earlier musics are prominent, there are even stronger links with *Eight Songs for a Mad King* and *The Martyrdom of St Magnus*. Mr Emmet is a martyr too, driven to suicide by the self-doubt and disorientation that can so easily afflict middle management in the modern age.

With a pithy libretto by David Pountney, a cast of three and a versatile ensemble of just 10 players, the piece delivers a scary yet ultimately poignant portrait of psychological crack-up. It might not have the universal resonance of a *Wozzeck* or a *Grimes*, but Maxwell Davies is a past master of the economical, vividly expressive gesture. The best music in *Emmet* is instrumental – culminating in the archetypally dreamy yet intense cello solo that accompanies Emmet to his doom. The vocal writing is less characterful but the excellent and versatile cast make sure that it functions potently in the inexorable unfolding of the drama. Psappha and their conductor Etienne Siebens are brilliant in support, and the booklet presents the full text in an admirably clear format. Recorded with maximum attention to clarity and atmosphere, this is an exemplary release.

Taverner
Martyn Hill ten John Taverner **David Wilson-Johnson** bar Jester **Stephen Richardson** bass Henry VIII **Fiona Kimm** mez Virgin Mary **Michael Chance** counterten Priest, God **Quentin Hayes** bar White Abbot **Peter Sidhom** bar Richard Taverner **Stuart Kale** ten Cardinal, Archbishop **Fretwork; New London Children's Choir; London Sinfonietta Voices; His Majestys Sagbutts & Cornetts; BBC Symphony Orchestra / Oliver Knussen**
NMC ② NMCD157 (117' · DDD)   Ⓕ❶❷❸►

On the one hand, sublimely euphonious sacred music; on the other hand, the primitive barbarity of torture and burnings at the stake. This was the reality of England around the time of the Reformation, as imagined and recreated by Davies in his first and most important opera, in which the living idioms of contemporary music strive to achieve a more potent relation to that conflicted reality than did the music of its anti-heroic composer-protagonist, John Taverner.

That this is only possible through collisions between opposed elements which generate huge intensity and a burning sense of compassionate outrage is manifest throughout this remarkable score. It reaches its apotheosis as expressionistic lament confronts foursquare hymnody, and Taverner's own music, allowed the last word, fades into emptiness. All this is an immense challenge to the performers, and although the 1972 Covent Garden staging, revived in 1983, made heroic efforts to do justice to the opera's inordinate demands, it was only with this BBC recording, broadcast in April 1997, that it was possible to experience the full power of the musical drama.

Of the stalwart team of solo singers, Martyn Hill, Quentin Hayes and Stuart Kale are particularly successful in their lyrical shaping of lines which can so easily become tortuously shapeless. In those places where the score provides detailed dynamic markings, it is sometimes impossible to attain the ideals which these represent. More importantly, however, conductor Oliver Knussen keeps the goals in view and the climaxes in proportion, with the strings of the BBC SO tirelessly eloquent in the searing final stages. For the most part, too, the recording balances the diverse, often superimposed sound sources, ancient and modern, with great success. At the climactic point when the townspeople proclaim that 'this is the work of John Taverner, musician, servant of the King', a more forwardly balanced choral presence might have been desirable, but this is scarcely a major defect.

It has taken a long time for *Taverner* to appear but the wait has been worthwhile. There could scarcely be a more important issue to mark the year of the composer's 75th birthday.

Brett Dean   Australian b1961

Dean studied at the Queensland Conservatorium and from 1985 to 1999 was a viola player in the Berlin Philharmonic Orchestra. In 2000 he decided to pursue a career as a freelance artist and returned to Australia. He became established as a composer in his own right through worldwide performances of the ballet One of a Kind *(Nederlands Dans Theater, choreographer Jiří Kylián) and by the clarinet concerto* Ariel's Music, *which won an award from the UNESCO International Rostrum of Composers. Dean was artistic director of the Australian National Academy of Music in Melbourne until June 2010. Leading interpreters of his music include Simon Rattle, Markus Stenz, Simone Young, Frank Peter Zimmermann and Daniel Harding.*

Orchestral music

Water Music[a]. Pastoral Symphony[b]. The Siduri Dances[c]. Carlo[d]
[c]**Sharon Bezaly** *fl* [a]**Raschèr Saxophone Quartet** (Kenneth Coon, Christine Rall, Elliot Riley, Bruce Weinberger *saxs*); **Swedish Chamber Orchestra /** [c]**Brett Dean,** [abd]**HK Gruber**
BIS BIS-CD1576 (75' · DDD) Ⓕ

The four works here span the decade of Brett Dean's transition from viola player to composer, underlining both his technical resourcefulness and his environmental concerns. *Water Music* elides the timbral disparity of saxophone quartet and chamber orchestra with evident finesse – outlining a course in which water as 'sound' and 'image' is ultimately defined by its 'absence'. This passing from idealised present to starkly imagined future is realised even more directly in *Pastoral Symphony*, in which a pervasive use of samples is the active context for a tightly argued discourse on pollution and deforestation – one that is no less musical for its being so graphically represented.

Siduri Dances is the expansion of an earlier work for solo flute, with Sharon Bezaly encompassing its pivoting between restraint and abandon with her customary poise. Musically, though, *Carlo* is a more engrossing listen: a portrait in sound of the late-Renaissance aristocrat-composer Carlo Gesualdo, whose life and music Dean rightly considers inseparable. Concrete allusions to Gesualdo's music (via tape) and direct vocal interjections (via sampler) are presented in a continuous process that reveals more through closing in on itself – hence the suffocating climactic chord. This is rendered with powerful immediacy, as is everything else on a disc that, alongside informative booklet-notes, can be well recommended to Dean admirers and newcomers alike.

Claude Debussy   French 1862-1918

The refined taste and exquisitely coloured music of Debussy belonged to a man born above his parent's china shop on the outskirts of Paris. Neither his mother or father seems to have shown much interest in his development and it was his aunt Clémentine who was the one to notice his musical gifts. She kept a dress shop and when she and her wealthy amour removed to Cannes in 1871, Debussy visited her there and had his first piano lessons. Back in Paris, he had further lessons from a pupil of Chopin. Just three years later he was good enough to play Chopin's F minor Concerto, having entered the Paris Conservatoire aged 10. About the same time, he started to compose.

His teachers found him charming, while one fellow student described him as 'uncommunicative, surly and not attractive to his friends'. His piano teachers were the finest and he was thought to be headed for a career as a virtuoso. Early on, his few intimates noticed his impeccable taste and quiet obstinacy. Later he would surround himself with fine books and pictures, dressing in beautifully cut clothes (usually sporting a broad-brimmed hat) and eating the best caviar, for he was something of a gourmet.

In 1880 Debussy was recommended as household pianist to Mme Nadezhda von Meck, Tchaikovsky's patron. He was to teach her children and play four-hands with them. He was not quite 18 at the time and travelled to Switzerland, Italy and Russia with the family, staying in Moscow and the family estate in the summers of 1881 and 1882. During 1881-84 he prepared himself for the Prix de Rome and won the much-coveted prize at the second attempt with a can-tata (L'enfant prodigue). At the Villa Medici in Rome he had the chance to meet Liszt. The great master introduced him to the music of Lassus and Palestrina (whose austere spirituality rubbed off on Debussy); Liszt's subtle pedalling when he played the piano also gave him ideas.

Back in Paris in 1886, living with his parents, he fell under the influence of Wagner's music though he was to reject it fairly swiftly, with the exception of Parsifal, a work in which he delighted for the rest of his life. Other influences were at work which resulted in music that was to be the very antithesis of Wagnerism. First there was the eccentric Erik Satie. He encouraged Debussy to write music that was not hidebound by academic tradition – 'Break the rules, defy convention' could have been his credo – and to find inspiration in the paintings of Claude Monet, Cézanne, Renoir, Pis-sarro and others. Three influential exhibitions from 1874 to 1877 had led to the term 'impressionism' being used to describe their work. Edgar Allan Poe, too, fascinated him, as he did all the symbolist poets (for a while Debussy worked on an orchestral work based on The Fall of the House of Usher). Yet another influence on his development was the Grande Exposition Uni-verselle of 1889 where he first heard a Javanese gamelan orchestra and fell in love with its exotic tex-tures and counterpoint to which, he said, 'in compari-son that of Palestrina is a child's game'.

In the late 1880s he met up with Gabrielle Dupont – 'green-eyed Gaby'. They lived in a shabby apartment in Montmartre while Debussy struggled to make ends meet. He wrote a String Suartet (1893) and the Prélude à L'après midi d'une faune the following year, the two works with which we may say that Impression-ism in music was born. Gradually he began to make a name for himself. After 10 years, Gaby's reward for her support and care while her lover established him-self was to be thrown over in 1899 when Debussy upped and married Rosalie Texier. Gaby Dupont shot herself, survived and disappeared into oblivion. Only five years later, Debussy grew tired of Rosalie ('the sound of her voice makes my blood run cold,' he once said) and took up with Emma Bardac, the wife of a wealthy banker.

Debussy divorced in 1904 and married Emma in October 1905. Older than Debussy, she already had grown children; their only child together was born before Emma was divorced. This was Debussy's adored Chouchou, to whom he dedicated his Children's Cor-ner suite. She died in 1919 aged 14.

By the turn of the century, Debussy's music had begun to reach a wider public. His opera Pelléas et Mélisande was produced in 1902. Though controver-

sial and opposed by Maeterlinck on whose play the opera was based, it won him many admirers and made his name internationally famous. He received the Légion d'Honneur and was made an advisor on the board of the Conservatoire. Financially secure from his second marriage and with increasing success as a com-poser, Debussy had at last 'arrived'.

He travelled all over Europe and (in 1913) even as far afield as Moscow and St Petersburg but from 1909 his health started to deteriorate. He suffered from fre-quent haemorrhages and in 1915 underwent an operation for bowel cancer. He had a second operation; radium and morphine were administered but it was no use. From the beginning of 1918 he could not leave his room and died there at the end of March.

Orchestral Works

Images. Berceuse héroïque[a]. Danse sacrée et danse profane[b]. Jeux. Nocturnes. Marche écossaise sur un thème populaire. Prélude à L'après-midi d'un faune. La mer. Première rapsodie[bc]
[b]**Vera Badings** hp [c]**George Pieterson** cl
Concertgebouw Orchestra / [a]**Eduard van Beinum, Bernard Haitink**
Philips Duo ② 438 742-2PM (141' · ADD)
Recorded [b]1957, 1976-79   Ⓜ ❶❶❶❶▷

Ⓖ Philips has repackaged Haitink's late-1970s recordings on two CDs for the price of one. Space has also been found for Debussy's last orchestral work, the short *Berceuse héroïque* conducted by Eduard van Bei-num (in excellent 1957 stereo). In every respect this package is a bargain. In *La mer*, like the 1964 Karajan on DG Galleria, there's a concern for refinement and fluidity of gesture, for a subtle illumination of texture; and both display a col-ourist's knowledge and use of an individually apt variety of orchestral tone and timbre. It's the wind playing that you remember in Haitink's *Images*: the melancholy and disconsolate oboe d'amore in 'Gigues'; and from 'Ibéria', the gor-geous oboe solo in 'Les parfums de la nuit', and the carousing clarinets and raucous trumpets in the succeeding holiday festivities. And here, as elsewhere in the set, the Concertgebouw acous-tic plays a vital role. Haitink's *Jeux* is slower and freer than average, and possessed of a near-miraculous precision, definition and delicacy. The jewel in this set, for many, will be the *Noc-turnes*, principally for the purity of the strings in 'Nuages', the dazzling richness and majesty of the central procession in 'Fêtes', and the cool beauty and composure of 'Sirènes'. Haitink opts for an ethereal distance; there may be passages where you're unsure if they're singing or not, but the effect is magical.

Debussy La mer. Prélude à L'après-midi d'un faune
Ravel Daphnis et Chloé – Suite No 2. Boléro
Berlin Philharmonic Orchestra /
Herbert von Karajan
DG Galleria 427 250-2GGA (64' · ADD)
Recorded 1964-65   Ⓜ ❶❶❶❶▷

Beautifully recorded, controlled and aristocratic, these performances show a scrupulous regard for the composers' wishes. The sound of the Berlin strings is sumptuous, with detail well placed and in a generally natural perspective. It's a joy to relish the beauty of the playing in such clear, well-defined sound. It has that indefinable quality that one can more readily recognise than describe, a magic that makes one forget the performer and transports one into the composer's world. You can either be seduced by some of the most sheerly beautiful orchestral sound recorded, or appreciate it for its wide-ranging imagery and its properly mobile pacing; whichever, it's one of the great recorded *La mers* and one of the classics of the gramophone. Karajan's interpretation of *Prélude à L'après-midi d'un faune* remains one of the most beautiful readings committed to record – the first flute, Karl-heinz Zöller, plays like a wizard. *Boléro* is slow and steady (but Karajan risks floating the early solos). This is also a ravishing account of the Second Suite from *Daphnis et Chloé*.

La mer. La boîte à joujoux (arr Caplet).
Prélude à L'après-midi d'un faune. Three Préludes (arr C Matthews)
Berlin Philharmonic Orchestra / Sir Simon Rattle
EMI 558045-2 (79' · DDD). Recorded live 2004
ⓕ❶❶❶🅑▸

Karajan and the Berlin Philharmonic's perfumed, pictorial 1964 recordings of Debussy's *Prélude à L'après-midi d'un faune* and *La mer* (see above) have come to be revered – and rightly so, as they possess a remarkable frisson. Rattle's interpretations, recorded live, are markedly less urgent; with nary a noise from the audience, one might even mistake them for studio recordings. Yet these new accounts, too, have the ability to engross and sometimes even astonish. Note, for example, the sinuous swoop of the flutes and clarinets at the beginning of 'Jeux de vagues' in *La mer*, or the shimmering rustle of strings at 1'00" in the *Prélude* – both almost tactile sensations.

Of course, one counts on Rattle to elucidate detail, and here the clarification of the music's intricately layered textures is revelatory. Karajan appears more intent on blending colours, creating a kind of sonic kaleidoscope that, coupled with a strong narrative thrust, can make Debussy sound a little like Rimsky-Korsakov. Subtlety may be part of the issue. Karajan, for example, heightens dynamic contrast whereas Rattle grades the dynamics as per Debussy's instructions (he's one of the few conductors who seems to have noticed that there's but one *fortissimo* in the *Prélude*).

The makeweights are especially valuable. There aren't that many recordings of *La boîte à joujoux* in the catalogue and this zestful, gracefully droll performance is among the best. As in the *Prélude* and *La mer*, the conductor's supple tempo manipulations convey a real feeling of spontaneity. Colin Matthews's scoring of three

DEBUSSY LA MER – IN BRIEF

Concertgebouw Orchestra / Bernard Haitink
Philips 438 742-2PM   Ⓜ❶❶❶🅑▸

A glorious performance that finds Haitink in masterly control of his magnificent Dutch orchestra: beautifully recorded in the Concertgebouw's near-perfect acoustic, this is a miracle of refinement. A *Gramophone* Award winner.

Berlin PO / Herbert von Karajan
DG 427 250-2GGA   Ⓜ❶❶❶🅑▸

A classic recording from 1964 proving that a German orchestra and Austrian conductor can get under the skin of this elusive score. Karajan's feeling for the ebb and flow is supreme.

Berlin PO / Simon Rattle
EMI 558045-2   ⓕ❶❶❶🅑▸

A modern classic perhaps? Rattle offers a cooler Debussy than Karajan but his generation of Berliners cede nothing to their great predecessors in beauty of tone and virtuosity. A glorious programme.

Lucerne Festival Orchestra / Claudio Abbado
DG 477 5082GH2   ⓕ🅑▸

Abbado's much-lauded ability to paint with an orchestra is here beautifully confirmed with a reading of iridescent colourings. The Lucerne orchestra plays superbly, and the recording is handled with great skill.

Philharmonia / Guido Cantelli   Ⓗ
Testament SBT1011   ⓕ

A historic account that shows what a amazing conducting talent was lost to the world with Cantelli's early death. The Philharmonia, at a vintage period in their history, play magnificently.

London PO / Serge Baudo
Classics for Pleasure 586167-2   Ⓢ

A really marvellous Debussy collection at budget price. Baudo sculpts this music with a masterly hand and the LPO play superbly. A Debussy 'primer' well worth considering.

Hallé / Sir Mark Elder
Hallé CDHLL7513   Ⓜ❶❶🅑▸

Yet another snapshot of the reinvigorated Hallé playing with lashings of personality. Elder's is a rhapsodic seascape achieving a Barbirolli-like poetry.

NBC SO / Arturo Toscanini   Ⓗ
Naxos mono 8 110811/2   Ⓢ🅑▸

A valuable glimpse of Toscanini in French repertoire – there's an electricity as well as an awareness of light that makes these fascinating performances. The couplings are of Debussy rarities.

piano *Préludes* evokes Debussy's sound world with preternatural accuracy.

The turbulence of 'Ce qu'a vu le vent d'Ouest' and sparkle of 'Feux d'artifice' are most impressive, though 'Feuilles mortes', with its hauntingly desolate atmosphere, is perhaps finer still. In short, a dazzling disc.

La mer. Préludes (arr C Matthews) – Le vent
dans la plaine; Les sons et les parfums; Ce qu'a vu le
vent d'Ouest; La fille aux cheveux de lin; La danse de
Puck; Minstrels; Brouillards; Feuilles mortes;
La puerta del Vino; Général Lavine; Canope;
Les tierces alternées
Hallé Orchestra / Mark Elder
Hallé CDHLL7513 (67' · DDD)   Ⓜ️ⓄⒶⒷ

Mark Elder has achieved an astonishing transformation at the Hallé, and there is no better example of his achievement than in this immensely compelling account of *La mer*, which in refinement of detail, warmth of atmosphere and the sheer brilliance of the playing is comparable with any in the catalogue.

The *pianissimo* opening has an evocative sense of mystery. Elder's control of phrase and shaping of line has the most subtle *rubato* and infinitely varied dynamic, always seeming spontanous. The tension is high but there are moments of languor – the sunshine on the water glowing on the horns is magical, and the closing of the first section moves from sensuous feeling to grandeur.

'Jeux de vagues' glitters, bringing solo instrumental playing of great delicacy and an exotic colouring, with an underlying rhapsodical feeling that reminds me of Barbirolli, the lustre of the strings exquisite at the becalmed close. The spectacular 'Dialogue du vent et de la mer' opens darkly, even ominously, and has haunting evocation at its gentle central section, yet Elder generates exhilaration and ardour at the climax with the racing waves of the orchestra's virtuosity. The recording is extraordinarily vivid.

What makes this disc unmissable is the equally fine playing (and lustrous recording) in Colin Matthews's imaginative orchestration of 12 of Debussy's piano *Préludes*. Forget the piano originals, these are far more than 'orchestrations': the music is completely and creatively rethought in orchestral terms. Altogether a remarkable achievement.

Debussy Jeux. Préludes (arr C Matthews) –
Danseuses de Delphes; Voiles; Les collines
d'Anacapri; Des pas sur la neige; La sérénade
interrompué; La cathédrale engloutie; Les fées sont
d'exquises; Bruyères; Les terrasses des audiences;
Ondine; Homage à S Pickwick Esq, PPMPC; Feux
d'artifice **C** Matthews Postlude: Monsieur Croche
Hallé Orchestra / Mark Elder
Hallé CDHLL7518 (74' · DDD)   Ⓟ️ⓄⒷ

The diaphanous atmospheric detail from the strings and subtle wind colouring in *Jeux*,

Debussy's *poème dansé*, require great delicacy of feeling and sensuous caressing from the violins in the moments of restrained ecstasy, which are exquisitely realised here. The transparent acoustic of the Bridgewater Hall and the balancing skill of producer Andrew Keener add to the allure of this miraculous score, with the violent climax superbly graduated and the closing pages returning spontaneously to the opening mood.

The programme is completed by 12 more of Colin Matthews's highly imaginative orchestrations of Debussy's piano *Préludes*, and these have even more distinction than the first group, which came in harness with Mark Elder's compelling Hallé account of *La mer* (see above). The shimmering textures Matthews creates from the 'Danseuses de Delphes', 'Des pas sur la neige' and 'Les fées sont d'exquises' are even more translucently exotic, balanced by the luxuriance of 'Bruyères'. If not quite matching Stokowski's famous over-the-top transcription, 'La cathédrale engloutie' produces a splendidly expansive, watery spectacle, tolling bell included, which is sonorously moving. However, 'S Pickwick Esq', with its side drum and mock-solemn national anthem snippet on the brass, feels rather too heavily pompous, not witty enough, and 'Feux d'artifice', too, is a bit of a damp squib – it sounds much more effective in its barer piano original. Moreover, Colin Matthews's own *Monsieur Croche* makes an exuberantly brilliant postlude, even if its helter-skelter progress obviously includes very few crochets. Altogether this is a fascinating and rewarding disc and is well worth aquiring to make a pair, alongside its illustrious companion.

Pelléas et Mélisande – Symphonie (arr Constant).
Suite bergamasque – Clair de lune (orch Caplet).
Nocturnes[a]. Berceuse héroïque. Etudes (orch Jarrell)
– No 9, Pour les notes répétées; No 10, Pour les
sonorités opposées; No 12, Pour les accords
[a]**MDR Radio Choir, Leipzig; Orchestre National de
Lyon / Jun Märkl**
Naxos 8 570993 (74' · DDD)   Ⓢ️ⓄⒷ

The two major items here are the set of three *Nocturnes*, central to Debussy's output, and the substantial symphonic suite from *Pelléas et Mélisande* that Marius Constant put together using almost entirely the opera's evocative orchestral interludes. Märkl's performance is warm and idiomatic, and the only reservation is that almost inevitably there is rather a lack of contrast in music that moves slowly. It is none the less a valuable item, adding to the outstanding performance of the three *Nocturnes* which is the high-point of the whole collection. The first, 'Nuages', is supremely evocative with refined strings and a cor anglais solo that stands out in the terracing of textures. 'Fêtes' is richly seductive in its bright colours. The passage where one hears a procession from afar on muted trumpets is wonderfully achieved, with crisply precise triplets leading up to a powerful climax before fading away again.

The longest of the three *Nocturnes*, 'Sirènes', brings a vital contribution from the Leipzig choir attached to the other orchestra with which Märkl is associated, the Leipzig Radio Symphony. Their chording and ensemble is flawless. The Caplet orchestration of the piano piece 'Clair de lune' is beautifully wrought and here given a sumptuous performance.

The *Berceuse héroïque* is similarly evocative, with its distant fanfares and its climactic reference to the Belgian National Anthem. The three *Etudes*, orchestrated by Michael Jarrell as recently as 1991, represent a different approach; a degree sharper, appropriate enough for some of Debussy's most advanced music, and pointing forward to a new generation of composers. A richly satisfying collection, immaculately recorded, with its full measure of rarities.

Nocturnes – Nuages; Fêtes
Prélude à L'après-midi d'un faune. Le martyre de Saint-Sébastien – symphonic fragments. La mer
Philharmonia Orchestra / Guido Cantelli
Testament mono SBT1011 (67' · ADD)
Recorded 1954-55   ⒻO

The death of Guido Cantelli in an air crash at the age of 36 in 1956 was a terrible loss. In a career lasting just 13 years he made his way right to the top, although at the end of his life he was still developing and maturing, and would surely have been one of the most important artists of our time. Fortunately he made a number of superlative recordings and this disc, which contains all his Debussy, shows why concert audiences in the 1950s were bowled over by him.

It's a pity that he never conducted all three *Nocturnes*, for 'Nuages' flows beautifully and expressively and he chooses just the right tempo for 'Fêtes'. He doesn't press this piece too hard as most conductors do, and its colour and piquant personality thus flower freshly and easily. *L'après-midi* is also given plenty of room to breathe: the playing cool, elegant, beautifully poised, yet very eloquent. In *La mer* Cantelli avoids the ham-fisted, overdramatic approach of so many conductors, and instead we have a performance with clear, gleaming textures. The first movement ebbs and flows in a movingly poetic fashion: every detail makes its effect and everything is perfectly in scale. The middle movement is taken quite briskly, but phrasing is hypersensitive and appropriately fluid. In the last movement there's plenty of drama and excitement, although climaxes are kept within bounds in a way which paradoxically makes for a greater effect than if they were given Brucknerian proportions, as they often are.

During Cantelli's lifetime *Le martyre de Saint-Sébastien* was strangely regarded as a tired, feeble work, yet he conducted the 'Symphonic fragments' quite frequently. His approach is very much of the concert hall in that he gives the four pieces a life of their own rather than relating them to the unfolding drama. However, he still

captures the music's peculiarly fervent, religious-cum-exotic flavour very effectively. The Philharmonia plays with extraordinary subtlety, and the recordings sound very well indeed.

String Quartet in G minor, Op 10

Debussy String Quartet **Ravel** String Quartet
Dutilleux Ainsi la nuit
Belcea Quartet (Corina Belcea, Laura Samuel *vns* Krzysztof Chorzelski *va* Alasdair Tait *vc*)
EMI Debut 574020-2 (71' · DDD)   ⒷOOOⒹ

Ⓖ This CD is the work of a highly talented, exceptionally well-integrated ensemble. Their excellent balance is highlighted by crystal-clear recording. This is quartet-playing of great musicality, with a wonderful sense of interaction. They find a near ideal transparency in the Ravel, its subtleties beautifully articulated.

The denser, less light-filled style of the Debussy, too, is perfectly weighted – this is a work they've clearly played on numerous occasions, and their performance has a feeling of a work truly inhabited by its players. And the Dutilleux is exquisitely observed, its fragmentary structure creatively embraced by these young musicians. And if all that weren't enough, this disc comes at budget price.

Debussy String Quartet **Fauré** String Quartet, Op 121 **Ravel** String Quartet
Quatuor Ebène (Pierre Colombet, Gabriel Le Magadure *vns* Mathieu Herzog *va* Raphaël Merlin *vc*)
Virgin Classics 519045-2 (80' · DDD)   ⒻOOOⒹ

Ⓖ Among the many breathtaking moments on the Ebène Quartet's CD, there is one in particular that keeps calling one back. It occurs at around 1'14" into the Ravel's slow movement, the second set, which enters like a bittersweet memory before a literal recollection of the Quartet's opening motif. Other subtle details of interpretation include the chord at 2'03" that underpins a transformation of the first subject before the same chord leads directly into the second subject – and when it does, utterly changing in character, turning warmer, more openly inviting. The ebb and flow of the passage at 5'29" where the second subject rides above an arpeggiated accompaniment, music that looks both forwards to Debussy's own *La mer* and backwards to Rimsky's *Sheherazade* (or so it seems). There's a fluidity to the Ebène's playing of both works that suits the music's character, a mood of wistfulness too that the Ravel especially benefits from. This improvisatory approach is hardly surprising from an ensemble that is also celebrated for its jazz performances.

It was a brilliant idea to include Fauré's late Quartet which, in a sense, provides the linchpin for all three works, the Ravel having been composed in Fauré's class to mark the 10th annivsary

DEBUSSY'S STRING QUARTET – IN BRIEF

Belcea Quartet
EMI Debut 574020-2   ⑧**OOO**🏵️▸

The fast-rising Belcea Quartet serve this enchanting score with exquisite sensitivity and understanding. Like the Juilliard on Sony, they also offer quartets by Ravel and Dutilleux.

Juilliard Quartet
Sony Classical 82796 92622-2   Ⓕ
A wealth of wisdom and interpretative insight informs the Juilliard Quartet's third recording of Debussy's masterpiece. As well as the popular coupling of Ravel's Quartet, we also get Dutilleux's sole contribution to the genre (*Ainsi la nuit*).

Melos Quartet
DG download 463 082-2GGA   Ⓜ**OO**▸
Another distinguished account, fastidiously prepared and beautifully balanced by the DG engineers. Likewise, the Ravel Quartet coupling falls ravishingly on the ear.

Hagen Quartet
DG download 437 836-2GH   Ⓕ▸
In terms of terms of virtuosity and sumptuous tonal refinement the youthful Hagen Quartet are second to none, though their artistry is perhaps not entirely without a certain self-conscious mastery.

Ebène Quartet
Virgin Classics 519045-2   Ⓕ**OOO**🏵️▸

A recording that will give enormous pleasure for its subtlety and style – a real winner. (It generously adds the Ravel and the Fauré.)

Alban Berg Quartet
EMI 567550-2   ⑧
Gorgeously played and recorded, there's a tonal glow that is very seductive but these do sounded rather over-rehearsed interpretations that lack a little in freshness.

Formosa Quartet
EMI 366557-2   ⑧
A stylish debut on disc for this young quartet: they may not as yet plumb the depths but they have style and technique aplenty. Unusually coupled with Wolf and Mozart (his Quartet No 14, K387).

Dante Quartet
Hyperion CDA67759   **OO**▸
As well as the seemingly mandatory Ravel Quartet, the young Dantes add Ravel's Violin Sonata No 2 (leader Krysia Osostowicz and Simon Crawford-Philips) to complete a beautifully played and recorded French trio.

of Debussy's Quartet, and which is dedicated to Fauré. An extraordinary work by any standards, ethereal and other-worldly with themes that seem constantly to be drawn skywards, Fauré's Quartet responds well to the Ebène's sensitised approach.

Anyone requiring this particular trio of works won't be disappointed, which makes the various pairings of the Ravel and Debussy quartets on their own seem somewhat less enticing.

Piano Trio

Debussy Piano Trio in G **Fauré** Piano Trio in D minor, Op 120 **Ravel** Piano Trio in A minor
Florestan Trio (Anthony Marwood *vn*
Richard Lester *vc* Susan Tomes *pf*)
Hyperion CDA67114 (66' · DDD)   Ⓕ**O**🏵️▸

The Florestan Trio has the ability to adapt its style to different kinds of music without any loss of conviction. After Brahms and Schumann comes this French disc showing it equally adept at entering the 1880 salon world of Debussy's youthful Trio, Ravel's brilliant exotic idiom, and the intimate, intense thoughts of Fauré's old age. In the quicker movements Susan Tomes's playing is remarkably light and precise. The finale of the Fauré, for example, has a *scherzando* quality that throws into relief the seriousness of the strings' initial gesture. The string players are always ready to modify their sound to produce special expressive effects – the eerily quiet unison passage in Fauré's *Andante* (track 2, 2'54") and the vibrato-less duet in the Ravel *Passacaille* (track 10, 5'15") – sounding wonderfully remote and antique. The clarity of the Hyperion recording allows the fantastical detail in the Ravel *Pantoum* to emerge. In the Debussy, the Florestan favour elegance rather than trying to search out expressive depths. Their freshness, imagination and purposeful directness makes this a top choice.

Sonata for Flute, Viola and Harp

Sonata for Flute, Viola and Harp[a]. Prélude à L'après-midi d'un faune (arr Samazeuilh)[b]. Syrinx[b]. La flûte de Pan[c]. Chansons de Bilitis[d]
[cd]**Irène Jacob** *spkr* **Philippe Bernold**, [d]**Mathieu Dufour** *fls* [a]**Gérard Caussé** *va* [ad]**Isabelle Moretti**, [d]**Germaine Lorenzini** *hps* **Ariane Jacob** [b]*pf/*[d]*celesta*
Harmonia Mundi HMC90 1647 (50' · DDD · T)   Ⓕ

The high-point of this disc is a beautifully sensitive performance of Debussy's elusive late sonata, a 'terribly sad' work according to the composer himself, but also containing in its latter two movements an uneasy kind of high spirits born of desperation. The opening and close of the first movement provide two of those haunting moments at which French composers seem to excel. Philippe Bernold is a player of delicate, refined tone whose descents to the edge of sound are hypnotic in their effect; and with his two partners the performance rivals those recordings hitherto cherished as yard-sticks – the classic Melos of 1962 and the Nash of 1991. Bernold captures the spirit of rapture in *Syrinx*, which is heard both in its usual form as an unaccompanied solo and as it was originally intended, as incidental music to a play, *Psyché*. Unfortunately Irène Jacob, who reads the text admirably, is too distantly placed in relation to the flute. The same criticism applies to the erotic *Chansons de Bilitis* poems. It was Debussy's own idea to make a transcription for flute and piano of the *Prélude à L'après-midi d'un faune*; but imaginatively as Samazeuilh wrote this and Ariane Jacob plays the piano part, the sensuous magic of this score suffers from this reduction of colour.

Cello Sonata

Debussy Sonata for Cello and Piano. Valse 'La plus que lente'. Scherzo. Intermezzo **Poulenc** Sonata for Cello and Piano. Suite française. Bagatelle. Sérénade
Jean-Guihen Queyras vc **Alexandre Tharaud** pf
Harmonia Mundi HMC90 2012 (63' · DDD)   Ⓕ🅑➔

Vividly captured in a warm acoustic, Queyras and Tharaud's is an intimate approach which exactly suits the two short sonatas of Debussy and Poulenc, the former with its abrupt changes of direction and unpredictable mood-swings, the latter brimful of Poulencian wit and, not surprisingly as it was sketched in 1940 (completed in 1948), replete with some self-plagiarising from *Babar*.

These are fine accounts, the programme made even more attractive by the inclusion of the seven short movements of Poulenc's *Suite française* (1935) based on 16th-century dances by Claude Gervaise. It's a charmer. Apart from this, there are five other short works by the two composers making a truly delightful whole.

Complete Piano Works

Préludes, Books 1 & 2. Pour le piano.   🄷
Estampes . Images, Sets 1 & 2. Children's Corner. 12 Etudes. D'un cahier d'esquisses. Rêverie. Valse romantique. Masques. L'isle joyeuse. La plus que lente. Le petit nègre. Berceuse héroïque. Hommage à Haydn. Danse bohémienne. Mazurka. Deux Arabesques. Nocturne. Tarantelle styrienne. Ballade. Suite bergamasque. Fantaisie[a]
Walter Gieseking pf [a]**Hessian Radio Orchestra, Frankfurt / Kurt Schröder**
EMI mono ④ 565855-2 (4h 36' · ADD)
Recorded 1951-55   Ⓜ🅞🅞🅞

The complete Préludes are also available on EMI Great Recordings of the Century 567233-2   Ⓜ🅞🅞➔

 Gieseking's insight and iridescence in Debussy are so compelling and hypnotic that they prompt either a book or a blank page – an unsatisfactory state where criticism is concerned! First and foremost, there's Gieseking's sonority, of such delicacy and variety that it can complement Debussy's witty and ironic

desire to write music 'for an instrument without hammers', for a pantheistic art sufficiently suggestive to evoke and transcend the play of the elements themselves ('the wind, the sky, the sea…'). Lack of meticulousness seems a small price to pay for such an elemental uproar in 'Ce qu'a vu le vent d'ouest', and Puck's elfin pulse and chatter (*pp aérian*) are caught with an uncanny deftness and precision. The final Debussian magic may not lie in a literal observance of the score, in the unfailing dotting and crossing of every objective and picturesque instruction, yet it's the start or foundation of a great performance.

More domestically, no one has ever captured the sense in *Children's Corner* of a lost and enchanted land, of childhood re-experienced through adult tears and laughter, as Gieseking does here. 'Pour les tierces', from the *Etudes*, may get off to a shaky start but, again, in Debussy's final masterpiece, Gieseking's artistry tugs at and haunts the imagination. Try 'Pour les sonorités opposées', the expressive centre of the *Etudes*, and you may well wonder when you've heard playing more subtly gauged or articulated, or the sort of interaction with a composer's spirit that can make modern alternatives seem so parsimonious by comparison. So here's that peerless palette of colour and texture, of a light and shade used with a nonchalant but precise expertise to illuminate every facet of Debussy's imagination.

An added bonus, a 1951 performance of the *Fantaisie* for piano and orchestra, completes an incomparable set of discs. The transfers are a real triumph.

Etudes

Etudes – Books 1 & 2
Mitsuko Uchida pf
Philips 475 7559POR (47' · DDD)   Ⓜ🅞➔

The harmonic language and continuity of the *Etudes* is elusive even by Debussy's standards, and it takes an artist of rare gifts to play them 'from within', at the same time as negotiating their finger-knotting intricacies. Mitsuko Uchida is such an artist. On first hearing perhaps rather hyperactive, her playing wins you over by its bravura and sheer relish, eventually disarming criticism altogether. This isn't just the finest recorded version of the *Etudes*; it's also one of the finest examples of recorded piano playing in modern times, matched by sound quality of outstanding clarity.

Etudes. Images
Pierre-Laurent Aimard pf
Teldec 8573 83940-2 (72' · DDD)   Ⓕ🅞🅞➔

With Pierre-Laurent Aimard the sheer freshness and novelty of this music come across strongly. So does the ardour; whereas some players are content with mood and atmosphere, his communication of feeling is acute. There are passages of extraordinary violence in this music, especially in the Etudes; he makes them still sound modern. Others would favour letting sonorities hang longer in the air. You couldn't ask for more colour or greater sensibility, but he isn't a charmer. He has edge and likes sonority to work directly on the business in hand. He always goes for the movement and the thrust of what's written; those used to a more spacious and laid-back view of the *Images*, in particular, may occasionally be disconcerted.

This is a Debussy record of high class, hugely stimulating. Aimard's version of the *Etudes* is up there with the very best. Technically, he's a wizard, without a chink in his armour; but he's the best kind of technician, playing like a composer, and letting the music drive him.

'Complete Works for Solo Piano, Vol 4'
Images. 12 Etudes. Etude retrouvée (ed Howat)
Jean-Efflam Bavouzet pf
Chandos CHAN10497 (76' · DDD)   Ⓕ❍❍❍❍Ɖ▸

Jean-Efflam Bavouzet's flexible virtuosity and innate grasp of Debussy's style and sound world yields ravishing, freshly minted interpretations of the *Images* and *Etudes* that proudly rank with (and sometimes surpass) the catalogue's reference versions. The *Images* gain welcome nourishment from Bavouzet's portfolio of ravishing colour shadings and articulations, while easily absorbing such pianistic liberties as playing one hand before the other, à la Michelangeli. His headlong, impulsive 'Hommage à Rameau' contrasts with similarly nuanced yet more austere readings. In 'Poissons d'or', he sneaks a few piranhas into the fishbowl as he modifies Debussy's *aussi léger que possible* directive with volatile dynamic hairpins and witty accents. 'Et la lune descend sur le temple qui fût' also rivets your attention via his seductive *legato* and three-dimensional textures.

Bavouzet's *Etudes* remake may well be the best yet. As you follow the intelligently contoured left-hand counterlines of 'Pour les tierces' you almost don't notice the fluency and easy evenness of Bavouzet's right-hand double notes. On the other hand, in 'Pour les huit doigts' and 'Pour les degrés chromatiques' he favours melodic inflection and linear motion over Aimard's and Uchida's smoother, scintillating surfaces.

The difficult leaps of 'Pour les accords' have rarely sounded less like technical feats and more like music, and 'Pour les arpèges composés' rivals Horowitz's 1965 reading for harmonic pointing and sexiness. Bavouzet precedes this Etude with a full-bodied, emotionally generous performance of its recently rediscovered earlier version, *Etude retrouvée*. This attractively engineered release will reveal more and more details to savour with each rehearing – guaranteed!

Images

Images. Le petit nègre. Children's Corner. La plus que lente. Valse romantique. Tarantelle styrienne.

Mazurka. Suite bergamasque. Hommage à Haydn. Elégie. Berceuse héroïque. Page d'album. Etudes. Etude retrouvée
Jean-Yves Thibaudet pf
Decca ② 460 247-2DH2 (151' · DDD)   Ⓕ Ɖ▸

Jean-Yves Thibaudet's Debussy cycle is a cornucopia of delights. The 12 *Etudes* could hardly be presented more personally or vivaciously. Nos 6 and 7 are marvels of bright-eyed irony and humour, while Nos 8 and 9 contrast a haunting alternation of lassitude and hyperactivity with razor-sharp cascades of repeated notes. His timing in the central *lento, molto rubato* of No 12 is memorably acute; throughout, you're aware of a pianist with a penchant for spare pedalling and a refined brilliance, far remote from, say, Gieseking's celebrated, opalescent magic. He takes a brisk hand to the *Children's Corner* suite (*allegro* rather than *allegretto* in 'Serenade for the Doll', hardly *modérément animé* in 'The Snow is Dancing') but even here his spruce technique and vitality are never less than enlivening. In the *Suite bergamasque* he dances the 'Menuet' with an unusual sense of its underlying grace and gravity, and his 'Clair de lune' is exceptionally silvery and transparent. Both books of *Images* are given with a rare sense of epiphany or illumination, of flashing fins and sunlight in 'Poissons d'or' and of a timeless sense of archaism in 'Hommage à Rameau'. Decca's presentation and sound are, respectively, lavish and natural. If you want to hear Debussy new-minted, with air-spun and scintillating textures, Thibaudet is your man.

Préludes

Préludes – Books 1 & 2
Krystian Zimerman pf
DG ② 435 773-2GH2 (84' · DDD)   Ⓜ❍❍❍❍Ɖ▸

Two discs, retailing at a high mid-price and playing for a total of 84 minutes? The playing and the recording had better be in the luxury class. Fortunately they are. Zimerman is the very model of a modern virtuoso. His overriding aim is vivid projection of character. His quasi-orchestral range of dynamic and attack, based on close attention to textual detail (there are countless felicities in his observation of phrase-markings) and maximum clarity of articulation, is the means to that end. As a result, he draws out the many connections in this music with the romantic tradition, especially in pianistic *tours de force* such as 'Les collines d'Anacapri', 'Ce qu'a vu le vent d'ouest' and 'Feux d'artifice', which are treated to a dazzling Lisztian *élan*.

At the other extreme Zimerman displays an exquisite refinement of touch that makes the quieter pieces both evocative and touching. Such sensitively conceived and wonderfully executed Debussy playing stands, at the very least, on a level with a classic recording such as Gieseking's. The instrument selected is itself

DEBUSSY'S PRÉLUDES – IN BRIEF

Walter Gieseking ⊞
EMI 567233-2 (71' · AAD) ⓂOOO

🔷 Gieseking's classic recording of the *Préludes* dates from 1953-54 and remains unsurpassed in extracting the elusive poetry of the more delicate pieces. This is one of the greatest of all piano recordings, and one of the greatest of Debussy's music.

Krystian Zimerman
DG ② 435 773-2GH2 (84' · DDD) ⓂOOOB

🔷 Larger in scale if perhaps less obviously idiomatic, Zimerman's compelling revivification tips over onto a second disc. This is high-octane playing for our own times, with the widest dynamic range and very tangible digital sound. It took a *Gramophone* Award on its release.

Noriko Ogawa
BIS BIS-CD1205 (76' · DDD) ⒻOO
The second instalment of Ogawa's Debussy survey includes a fine account of the First Book of *Préludes* in unbeatably natural sound.

Martino Tirimo
Regis RRC1111 (78' · DDD) ⓈO
Complete on one super-bargain CD, Tirimo's set offers excellent value, his sensitive playing enhanced by fine digital sound.

Jean-Yves Thibaudet
Decca ② 452 022-2DH2 (157' · DDD) Ⓕ
Always a crisp and articulate pianist, Thibaudet's *Préludes* display greater freedom and imagination than is sometimes the case with him. The eruptive, lightly pedalled *Feux d'artifice* is a particular highlight. This is Volume 1 of his first-rate survey of the complete Debussy piano music.

Jos van Immerseel
Channel Classics CCS4892 (54' · DDD) Ⓕ
This is something of a curiosity and certainly isn't a prime recommendation: van Immerseel uses an 1897 Erard piano for the First Book of *Préludes*, as well as the *Images oubliées*. It's certainly worth hearing for its special note of authenticity. When not played loudly the piano makes a delightful sound, but Immerseel isn't the most imaginative of players.

Jacques Rouvier
Dal Segno DSPRC043 (78' · DDD) ⓂOO
Rouvier is one of the most stylish and elegant interpreters of this repertoire: wonderfully alive the variety of nuance and colour in these extraordinary pieces. Under his fingers, each prelude becomes a sparkling miniature.

something of a star and DG's recording combines opulence with razor-sharp clarity.

Préludes – Books 1 & 2 ⊞
Walter Gieseking pf
EMI Great Recordings of the Century 567233-2 (71' · ADD) (in USA: 567262-2) Recorded 1953-4
ⓂOOOB

🔷 Gieseking's set of both Books of the *Préludes* is one of the great classics of the gramophone. The individual insights are endless, so is the extraordinary feeling for the music's evocation and atmosphere. The 1953-54 recordings just missed the stereo era, but the Abbey Road mono sound is first-class. Don't miss it.

Préludes – Books 1 & 2
Steven Osborne pf
Hyperion CDA67530 (78' · DDD) ⒻOO

Steven Osborne tells us that in preparing this recording he was struck 'by the enormous scope of these preludes. What other collection of pieces manages to create so many utterly distinct and compelling worlds?' But he has prepared well, and every prelude glows, always rich in atmosphere.

The opening 'Danseuses de Delphes' has a commandingly grave serenity and 'Voiles' floats effortlessly. Yet 'Les collines d'Anacapri' dances with sparkling rhythmic vitality and 'La danse de Puck' is deliciously capricious. Osborne's delicacy of feeling (and texture) is at its most magical in the soft footfalls 'sur la neige', although 'Feuilles mortes' has similar moments of evocative quietness. The unpredictability of 'Le vent dans la plaine' is matched by the simulated violence of 'Ce qu'a vu le vent d'Ouest', and the thrilling climax of 'La cathédrale engloutie' has rich depth and sonority. By contrast, 'La fille aux cheveux de lin' has a ravishing simplicity, without sentimentalising. 'S Pickwick' brings a momentary smile but his eccentricity is banished by the calm of 'Canope' and the joyful virtuosity of 'Les tièrces alternées'.

Osborne's virtuosity is never for its own sake and always reflects the music's spirit. The obvious comparison is with Zimerman's stunningly vivid recording; but his extraordinarily brilliant playing is at times almost over-projected and Osborne's natural spontaneity and powerful conveying of inner feeling is every bit as telling – less intense but deeply satisfying. The Hyperion recording is very realistic.

Préludes – Book 1. D'un cahier d'esquisses.
Children's Corner. Suite bergamasque – Clair de lune
Nelson Freire pf
Decca 478 1111DH (63' · DDD) ⒻOB

Nelson Freire, the legendary Brazilian pianist and longtime musical partner of Martha Argerich, turns to Debussy. In the accompanying notes he confesses to a special empathy for Debussy and you will be hard pressed to find a recital of comparable warmth, affection and finesse. Here, there is no need for spurious gestures and inflections; everything is given with a supreme naturalness and a perfectly accommodated virtuosity that declare Freire a master pianist throughout. When have you heard 'Voiles' given with a greater sense of its mystery or witnessed playing throughout Book 1 of the *Préludes* more delicate, rapt and precise? There is lightly worn fantasy and expertise in 'La sérénade interrompue' and the direction *Profondément calme (dans une brume doucement sonore)* is distilled into something close to perfection. Always Freire 'evokes rather than spells out'; and has one ever heard a more subtle or engaging way with 'Dr Gradus ad Parnassum' (from the *Children's Corner Suite*)? *Clair de lune*, added, as it were, as an encore, is dreamy and magically remote, making you long for further Debussy from this artist. Decca's sound is warm and brilliant.

Préludes – Book 1. D'un cahier d'esquisses. Morceau de concours. La plus que lente. Hommage à Joseph Haydn. Le petit nègre. Children's Corner
Noriko Ogawa *pf*
BIS BIS-CD1205 (76' · DDD)   Ⓕ**OO**

Every bar of these performances confirms Ogawa as a most elegant, scrupulously sensitive interpreter of 'music like a dream from which one draws away the veil' (Debussy). She achieves a magical transparency throughout Book 1 of the *Préludes* with her refined pedalling and cool command of texture and colour. In 'Voiles' she makes you readily recall Cortot's heady description of 'the flight of the white wing on the crooning sea toward the horizon bright with the setting sun' while maintaining her own individuality. Her hushed start before the start of the whirling tarantella in 'Les collines d'Anacapri' is one of many haunting touches; and her playing of 'Des pas sur la neige', the Arctic centre of Book 1 of the *Préludes*, suggests some ultimate desolation. In *Children's Corner* she never turns 'Doctor Gradus', marked *modérément animé*, into a glittering *presto* and finds time to convey its mix of guile and sophistication. You could hardly find a more skilful or sympathetic artist from the younger generation. BIS's demonstration sound quality crowns this superb issue.

Préludes – Book 2. Berceuse héroïque. La boîte à joujoux. Elégie. Pièce pour l'oeuvre du 'Vêtement du blessé'.
Noriko Ogawa *pf*
BIS BIS-CD1355 (80' · DDD)   Ⓕ**OO**

Volume 3 of Noriko Ogawa's highly praised Debussy cycle includes a superlative performance of *La boîte à joujoux* that's worth the price of the disc alone. Here, the wildest selection of characters, folk tunes and operas – whether gentle or uncouth, charmers or roustabouts – twirl and tap-dance their way through an intricate variety of steps clearly inspired by Stravinsky's *Petrushka*. Ogawa responds to every fleeting whimsicality with such clarity and refinement that you are lost in wonder and almost forget that the piano version finally outstays its welcome.

On more authentic pianistic ground, Ogawa wears her sense of Debussian mystery lightly, taking a sometimes disappointingly open-ended view of some of the composer's most poignant and interior thoughts. Scrupulously modern in her approach, she scorns all sentimental evasion but, while she's never less than musicianly, one would have liked a greater awareness of elegy in the *Berceuse héroïque*, and, in the *Préludes*, more of the whirring evanescence and less of the superficially abstract, étude-like character in 'Les tierces alternées'.

'Brouillards' and 'Canope' are other coolly perceived evocations and Ogawa is surely happier when not confined by so many *pianissimo* demands. 'Feux d'artifice' and 'La puerto del vino' are outstanding examples of her virtuosity at its most superfine and characterful.

These, then, are masterly performances even when they hardly sound like music composed 'for an instrument without hammers'. The sound, like the playing, is close, bright and intense.

Additional recommendation

Préludes – Books 1 & 2
Tirimo *pf*
Regis RRC1111 (78' · DDD)   Ⓢ**O**
It would be hard to find a more quietly stylish or subtle account than that offered by Tirimo. His undemonstrative mastery makes him among the finest Debussy interpreters on disc.

Miscellaneous Piano Works

Ballade. Berceuse héroïque. Danse bohémienne. Elégie. Six Epigraphes antiques. Trois Estampes. Hommage à Haydn. Trois Images oubliées. Mazurka. Morceau de concours. Nocturne. Page d'album. Le petit nègre. La plus que lente. Pour le piano. Rêverie. Tarantelle styrienne. Valse romantique. Roi Lear, L107 – Le sommeil de Lear. Les soirs illuminés par l'ardeur du charbon
Alain Planès *pf*
Harmonia Mundi ② HMC90 1947/8 (114' · DDD)   Ⓕ

Alain Planès at long last concludes his Harmonia Mundi Debussy cycle with a two-disc set that upholds his excellent standards. There's much to savour. Sample the pianist's warm, intelligently modulated sonority and calm sense of line in the first two *Images oubliées* and the Sarabande from *Pour le piano*. Then clear your palate vis-à-vis Planès's vivacious, dry-point articulation in 'Jardins sous la pluie' that evokes cascading raindrops of all shapes and sizes. Perhaps it's slightly un-kosher to raid piano duet masterworks for soloistic purposes, yet Planès's sophisticated textural layering in a two-handed transcription of the *Six Epigraphes antiques* nearly made me forget the original. The pianist also lavishes care and consideration over the short pieces. *Le plus que lent* emerges less like a vignette than an epic, whose unexpected mood-swings and tempo fluctuations convinced me only after several auditions. But Planès's lush, serious and cannily voiced *Rêverie* conveys a depth of feeling beyond the salonish norm many pianists prefer. The *Mazurka* and *Le petit nègre* gain sharpened rhythmic spring through Plainès's measured, firmly held basic tempi. Aside from a few jangled moments like the climaxes of *Pour le piano*'s Prélude and *Tarentelle styrienne*, Harmonia Mundi's engineering does full justice to the pianist's attractive-sounding Steinway.

Deux Arabesques. Children's Corner. Six Images.
Suite bergamasque – Clair de lune
Simon Trpčeski pf
EMI 500272-2 (62' · DDD)   Ⓕ🅑➔

Simon Trpčeski turns to Debussy's withdrawn poetry and fantasy with an ease and delicacy that suggest, once more, a wholly exceptional artist. He is, perhaps above all, harmonically aware, with every change of colour and sonority subtly underpinned, making you doubly aware of Debussy's chiaroscuro, his infinite play of light and shade. The First Arabesque could hardly be more charming or insinuating, the Second thrown off with all the requisite perkiness and vivacity.

In *Children's Corner* Trpčeski's 'Dr Gradus' is truly *modérément* and a far cry from a once fashionable virtuoso rush as well as much received French wisdom. His 'Golliwogg' is superbly cantankerous and up-front, though with plenty of sly winks and nudges when required, and in extreme contrast, in 'Et la lune descend sur le temple qui fut' (*Images*, Bk 2) you will hear an ideally balanced chording and a tonal translucency inseparable from great Debussy-playing. The end, too (*pianissimo* and *lointain*) is memorably evocative. True, there is a momentary loss of focus at the end of 'Poissons d'or' where the final shift of emphasis is blurred, but such tiny lapses are like spots on the sun. Trpčeski's way with 'Clair de lune' makes you long to hear him in the complete *Suite bergamasque*.

'Complete Works for Piano, Volume 2'
Ballade. D'un cahier d'esquisses. Estampes. Trois
Images oubliées. L'isle joyeuse. Masques. Pour le
piano. Tarentelle styrienne. Valse romantique
Jean-Efflam Bavouzet pf
Chandos CHAN10443 (66' · DDD)   ⒻⓄⓄ➔

While Bavouzet is no slouch in the tone-colour department, his interpretations do not primarily concern themselves with sound-painting. Instead he focuses upon clarity of textures, rhythmic precision, well differentiated articulation, plus scrupulous balances between the hands and

within chords. Timbral variety and tonal allure arise from these elements working together. As you listen to Bavouzet's effortless rhythmic lilt and buoyant sense of line in the *Tarantelle styrienne*, *Masques* and 'Jardins sous la pluie', or his firm bass underpinnings and impeccably calibrated arabesques throughout *L'isle joyeuse*, you don't perceive the 'hammerless' piano of Debussy's dreams. Instead, the piano's innards morph into a finely honed chamber orchestra. Similarly in 'Pagodes', Bavouzet's sharply profiled melodies shed welcome animated light on a piece that's often interpreted too flaccidly. Some might favour a warmer, more curvaceous way with the *Valse romantique* but Bavouzet's shapelier urgency proves more convincing in *Pour le piano*'s central Sarabande, as well as its earlier incarnation in the cycle of 'forgotten' *Images*. The recorded sound is never less than pleasing.

'Complete Works for Piano, Volume 3'
Deux Arabesques. Berceuse héroïque. Children's
Corner. Danse bohémienne. Elégie. Hommage à
Haydn. Mazurka. Morceau de concours. Nocturne.
Page d'album. Le petit nègre. La plus que lente.
Rêverie. Suite bergamasque
Jean-Efflam Bavouzet pf
Chandos CHAN10467 (72' · DDD)   ⒻⓄⓄⓄ➔

'Complete Works for Piano, Volume 3'
Berceuse héroïque. D'un cahier d'esquisses.
Hommage à Haydn. Six Images. L'isle joyeuse. Page
d'album. Pour le piano. Rêverie. Tarentelle styrienne
Pascal Rogé pf
Onyx ONYX4028 (78' · DDD)   ⒻⓄⓄ➔

Volume 3 of Jean-Efflam Bavouzet's superb Debussy cycle links mostly early miniatures with the *Suite bergamasque* and *Children's Corner*. Once more he turns conventional notions of 'impressionism' topsy-turvy, cleansing Debussy of years of dust and accretion and recreating him in every bar in a sparkling and pristine light. Fiercely energised yet superfine, his performances are not for those with comfortable drawing-room notions of Debussy, and rarely in my experience has a pianist so faultlessly or precisely achieved his aims.

All sentimentality is erased from the *Nocturne*'s enchanting evanescence and just when he momentarily has you wishing that his formidable directness would melt into something more heart-easing, he makes you gasp at his flawless balance of sense and sensibility. He makes something audaciously epic out of *Hommage à Haydn* and the startling hesitancy in the opening of 'The Snow is Dancing' is convincing rather than idiosyncratic. His recital ends on a desolating note with the *Berceuse héroïque*'s phantom battle-cries and bugle-calls memorably evoked. The superbly recorded disc includes his own remarkable essay. This could well be the finest and most challenging of all Debussy piano cycles.

A greater study in contrast in 'composer and interpreter' would be hard to imagine than between Bavouzet and Pascal Rogé. Where

Bavouzet breaks out into blazing Mediterranean sunlight, Rogé (radically enriching his earlier Decca Debussy discs) is happy to withdraw into shadow-land. Time and again his playing suggests emotion recollected in tranquillity rather than turmoil; and in, say, 'Hommage à Rameau' or the Sarabande from *Pour le piano* he discovers the mysterious, still centre of Debussy's art. 'Poissons d'or' is a marvellous distillation of indolence and flashing disruption, and 'Mouvement' is a perky and vivacious rejoinder to all former introspection. And so too is the *Toccata*, played with unerring ease and grace, and with many ear-catching details.

To summarise, the ever-elusive truth lies somewhere between Rogé the dreamer, Bavouzet the sinewy but always musical athlete, Thibaudet, the teasing wit and sophisticate and, of course, the legendary Gieseking. You pays your money and you takes your choice...

'Complete Works for Piano, Volume 5'
Khamma. Le boîte à joujoux. Jeux – Poème dansé
Jean-Efflam Bavouzet pf
Chandos CHAN10545 (65' · DDD)　　Ⓕ ❶❶❶❶➡

Debussy was in the habit of preparing a short score before orchestrating a work, and what's striking is that these three stage pieces sound as pianistic as Stravinsky's – indeed in *Le boîte à joujoux* there are a fair few echoes of *Petrushka*. It's also full of more overt borrowings, too, both from Debussy's own music and that of others, notably Mendelssohn's Wedding March and the Soldiers' Chorus from Gounod's *Faust*, gently taken down a peg or two. The figures and the far-fetched action come alive in Bavouzet's hands, from the tender, far-off opening phrases right up to the final tableau with its hints of Schumann's *Carnaval* and its strangely ambiguous ending.

This series has been as much an exploration of the mind of Debussy as a traversal of the works themselves. Bavouzet combines a probing intellect with a sensuality of touch that is enthralling. That's never more telling than in *Khamma* and *Jeux*, the latter Bavouzet's second transcription of the work, having already made one for two pianos.

Khamma suffered from two things: the fact that the dancer Maud Allan – who commissioned it – was simultaneously indecisive and a control freak, and its proximity to the It-girl among sacrificial virgins, that of Stravinsky's *Rite*. Though the settings, musically and geographically, are quite different, it prompted one of Debussy's most adventurous scores; more's the pity he never completed the orchestration. But Bavouzet shows that it can stand alone as a piano work every bit as compellingly as *Petrushka* or Ravel's *La valse*.

As for that remarkable work, it's extraordinary first of all that such a complex score could be articulated by just one pair of hands – at times it does sound as if Bavouzet must have sprouted an extra pair. The fact that he knows every semi-

quaver intimately allows him a profound knowledge of its detail but also the way it works: you become aware of the sinews that give this music its shape and its power, aspects that tend to be enveloped by Debussy's orchestration.

Altogether, a remarkable achievement, and the disc is every bit as essential – perhaps more so for the rarity of the repertoire – as previous instalments.

Pelléas et Mélisande

Pelléas et Mélisande
Hans Wilbrink bar Pelléas **Denise Duval** sop Mélisande **Michel Roux** bar Golaud **Anne Reynolds** mez Geneviève **Guus Hoekman** bass Arkel **Rosine Brédy** sop Yniold **John Shirley-Quirk** bass-bar A Doctor **Glyndebourne Festival Chorus; Royal Philharmonic Orchestra / Vittorio Gui**
Glyndebourne Festival Opera ③ GFOCD003-63 (164' · ADD). Recorded live 1963　　Ⓜ❶

If Gui's reading is 'Italianate', this is because it gives considerable though never excessive weight to the drama's emotional intensity. The idea that Debussy's opera is reticent from start to finish is a myth, and in this close-up recording the turbulent anguish of the orchestral interludes is especially vivid. When the focus is on the voices, the orchestra suffers to a degree in the restricted balance. That bright hard edge which is the accursed associate of digital remastering is evident here too, though never to a disabling extent: better a hard edge than a pervasive lack of clarity.

In 1963 Glyndebourne fielded a cast of French, Dutch and English singers whose handling of the French text stands up well in comparison with the best recent recordings. There is the minor incongruity of a very feminine Yniold, and also a Pelléas (Hans Wilbrink) whose occasionally strained moments suggest dramatic engagement rather than musical weakness. Gui's Denise Duval is a persuasive, convincingly youthful Mélisande – although Act 1 scene 2 does rather underline the fact that Anna Reynolds, singing the mother of Golaud and Pelléas, was actually 10 years younger than Duval. The Golaud, Michel Roux, had recorded the role in 1955 and again in 1962 but he was not the first singer to find the Glyndebourne experience uniquely energising, and there is no lack of force in his telling portrayal of this most maddeningly obtuse of operatic characters. Guus Hoekman is an eloquent Arkel, and John Shirley-Quirk has all the necessary gravitas as the Doctor in Act 5. The packaging comes with full text (four languages) and production photographs but no biographies of the performers.

Pelléas et Mélisande
Wolfgang Holzmair bar Pelléas **Anne Sofie von Otter** sop Mélisande **Laurent Naouri** bar Golaud **Alain Vernhes** bass Arkel **Hanna Schaer** mez Geneviève **Florence Couderc** sop Yniold **Jérôme Varnier** bar A Doctor, A Shepherd **Radio France Chorus;**

French National Orchestra / Bernard Haitink
Naïve ③ V4923 (160' · DDD · T/t)　　　Ⓜ○

Bernard Haitink has always had a soft spot for French music, where his control of texture and pace often brings out beauties and strengths that other conductors do not find. *Pelléas et Mélisande*, for which long-term flow is a crucial requirement, is ideally suited to his talents. He has the ability, like a good games player, to create his own time and space. He gives us a deeply serious and powerful interpretation of the opera.

Throughout, the beauty, energy and brilliance of the orchestral playing ride over an undertow of melancholy and impending disaster, echoing that 'strange air' Mélisande has of someone who, in Arkel's words, 'is always waiting for some great sorrow in the sunshine in a lovely garden'. Haitink is well served by his singers. Holzmair is a fresh-voiced, ardent but elegant Pelléas, and innocent enough to make his entrapment plausible. Even the slight signs of tiring on his high notes in Act 4 can be heard as portraying vulnerability. Von Otter plays Mélisande in the traditional way as timid and fatally seductive. But she brings more vibrato to her top notes than some other interpreters and this gives her timidity a slightly used, passive-aggressive colouring, as though she has employed her don't-touch-me gambit several times in the past, and has found it works.

Laurent Naouri is a supremely intelligent Golaud, slow to jealousy and anger, but terrifying when the dam finally bursts. By contrast, in the final act he's the image of a spiritually lost soul and his choked cries of 'Mélisande!' are truly heart-rending. Alain Vernhes's Arkel has that 'goodness' in his tone that the composer wanted, though his pitching, hitherto perfect, wanders somewhat in Act 5.

Pelléas et Mélisande
Neill Archer *bar* Pelléas **Alison Hagley** *sop*
Mélisande **Donald Maxwell** *bar* Golaud **Kenneth Cox** *bass* Arkel **Penelope Walker** *contr* Geneviève **Samuel Burkey** *treb* Yniold **Peter Massocchi** *bar*
A Doctor, A Shepherd **Welsh National Opera Chorus and Orchestra / Pierre Boulez**
Stage and Video director **Peter Stein**
DG ② 📀 073 030-9GH2 (158' · NTSC · 4:3 · 2.0, 5.1 & DTS 5.1 · 0). Includes picture gallery, 'Pelléas at Welsh National Opera'. Notes included
Recorded live 1992　　　Ⓕ○○○

This is, in every respect, a model of what a DVD ought to be, a perfect realisation in picture and sound of Debussy's sole and inspired opera. Peter Stein staged the work for Welsh National Opera in 1992 and won universal praise, as did Pierre Boulez for his conducting.

Within austere, wholly appropriate sets, beautifully lit by Jean Kalman, Stein catches the very essence of this singular and elusive piece. Each of the 15 scenes is given its own distinctive décor in which the action is played out on several levels – high for the tower scenes, low for the eerie, subterranean grottoes, for instance. A master-

DEBUSSY'S PELLÉAS ET MÉLISANDE – IN BRIEF

Jacques Jansen *Pelléas* **Iréne Joachim** *Mélisande* **Henri Etcheverry** *Golaud* **Yvonne Gouverné Choir / Roger Desormière**
EMI ③ 761038-2 (3h 16' · AAD)　　Ⓜ○○
A truly historic 1941 recording that transcends limited sound with superbly idiomatic performances by a native French cast, a great advantage in this opera, with Jacques Jansen's still youthful Pelléas and Iréne Joachim's glass-clear Mélisande.

Wolfgang Holzmair *Pelléas* **Anne Sofie von Otter** *Mélisande* **Laurent Naouri** *Golaud* **Radio France Chorus, French National Orchestra / Bernard Haitink**
Naïve ③ V4923 (160' · DDD)　　　Ⓜ○
Though the international cast is quite impressive, Haitink's conducting, luminous but highly dramatic, is the star of this concert recording.

François Le Roux *Pelléas* **Colette Alliot-Lugaz** *Mélisande* **José van Dam** *Golaud* **Chorus and Orchestra of the Lyon Opera / John Eliot Gardiner** *Dir* **Pierre Strosser**
ArtHaus Musik ② 📀 100 100 (147')　　　Ⓕ
With luminous, diaphanous conducting from Gardiner and exquisite lighting, this is a wonderfully atmospheric performance. The cast is excellent, making this a strong contender not only for video but also for the music-making.

Richard Sitwell *Pelléas* **Frederica von Stade** *Mélisande* **José van Dam** *Golaud* **Deutsche Oper Berlin Chorus, Berlin PO / Herbert von Karajan**
EMI ③ 567057-2 (162' · ADD)　　　Ⓜ
Pelléas meets *Tristan* in this extraordinary and – for many – misguided set, with a decent cast and superb orchestral playing subjected to an over-romantic, glutinous interpretation.

Neill Archer *Pelléas* **Alison Hagley** *Mélisande* **Donald Maxwell** *Golaud* **Welsh National Opera Chorus and Orchestra / Pierre Boulez** *Dir* **Peter Stein**
DG ② 📀 073 030-9GH2 (158')　　　Ⓕ
A grittier, more psychologically acute approach than the Strosser for Gardiner. Stein and Boulez are scrupulously faithful to Debussy's instructions and the eye is perfect led along by the ebb and flow of the music.

François Le Roux *Pelléas* **Maria Ewing** *Mélisande* **José van Dam** *Golaud* **Vienna State Opera Chorus, Vienna PO / Claudio Abbado**
DG ③ 435 344-2GH2 (148' · DDD)　　　Ⓕ
A large-scale but beautifully translucent performance, very well recorded, with probably the best modern cast on disc, appropriately Francophone except for Maria Ewing's unconventional and strikingly seductive Mélisande.

stroke is the subtle evolution from one scene to another in view of the audience, offering a visual counterpoint to the interludes.

Stein sees that Debussy's instructions are scrupulously observed. In fact, as a whole, this is an object-lesson in modern staging. Stein and his collaborators reflect the ebb and flow of crude realism and fragile dream-life that permeate the score, which Boulez has identified as lying at its heart. Director and conductor worked closely with each other over a six-week rehearsal period, something unlikely to occur today, so Boulez's interpretation is in complete accord with the staging, his musical direction at once direct and luminous, timbres finely balanced one with the other.

The cast also benefited from the long gestation. Alison Hagley catches ideally the paradox that is Mélisande, candour married to duplicity, and sings the enigmatic character with an acute ear for French syllables. Neill Archer, though not quite as responsive to the French language, is a poetic, youthfully ardent Pelléas. Donald Maxwell's Golaud rightly stands at the centre of the production, conveying guilt, jealousy and self-torment in tellingly intense tones. Kenneth Cox is a grave, world-weary Arkel, Penelope Walker a properly dignified, compassionate Geneviève. The treble singing Yniold is remarkably assured. This is a riveting experience.

Pelléas et Mélisande
Le Roux Pelléas **Alliot-Lugaz** Mélisande **Van Dam** Golaud **Chorus and Orchestra of the Lyon Opera / Gardiner**
Stage director **Pierre Strosser**
Video director **Jean-François Jung**
ArtHaus Musik ② 🆅 100 100 (147' · Regions 2 & 5)
Recorded 1987   Ⓕ**OO**

On DVD, with superb lighting and camerawork, the results are even more convincing than in the theatre. Gardiner conducts a translucent, firmly shaped account. His interpretation brings the piece even more clearly into a post-Wagnerian world of sound, and the Lyon Orchestra play up to the hilt. The entirely French cast is one of the best to record the work, challenging the hegemony of the audio-only versions.

Additional recommendation

Stilwell Pelléas **von Stade** Mélisande
Berlin Philharmonic Orchestra / Karajan
EMI 567057-2 (162' · ADD)   Ⓜ**B→**

A controversial recording: too 'hot-house' for some but full of breathtaking playing and a heartbreakingly touching pair of lovers. This was clearly a labour of love for the great Austrian conductor.

Léo Delibes   French 1836-1891

After early lessons with his mother, Delibes entered the Paris Conservatoire at the age of 12 but this

precocious start led only to jobs as organist and accompanist (Adolphe Adam, the composer of Giselle, recommended him to a post at the Théâtre Lyrique in 1853) and as chorusmaster (he assisted Gounod, Berlioz and Bizet). He had a hit with his very first work for the stage, a light-hearted one-act operetta called Deux sous de charbon. That set the seal on his career, for Delibes became a complete man of the theatre. His ballet La source (later revived as Naila) presented by the Paris Opéra in 1866, was his first break, followed four years later by a second ballet commission, Coppélia. With another ballet, Sylvia, 10 years later, Delibes achieved lasting fame as one of the great melodists of music. His deft and imaginative orchestration won him many admirers including Tchaikovsky (you can hear the influence that Delibes had on his own ballet music) and, later, Stravinsky. Delibes was not as successful with his operas. That is not until, almost out of the blue, came his exotic masterpiece Lakmé in 1883.

None of Delibes's music has pretensions to depth or high aesthetic ideals like some of his contemporaries. He wrote expertly crafted, delicately drawn scores of tuneful, characterful music.

Sylvia

Delibes Sylvia **Saint-Saëns** Henry VIII – Ballet-divertissement
Razumovsky Sinfonia / Andrew Mogrelia
Naxos ② 8 553338/9 (114' · DDD)   Ⓢ**B→**

Of Delibes's two full-length ballets, *Coppélia* is the more obviously popular, the one with the bigger tunes and the greater number of recordings. However, *Sylvia* is also a superbly crafted score, full of haunting melodies. Andrew Mogrelia's Naxos series is one to be collected and treasured: there's loving care applied to selection of tempi, shaping of phrases, orchestral balance and refinement of instrumental detail. Here you thrill to *Sylvia*'s Act 1 Fanfare, marvel at the control of tempo and refinement of instrumental detail in the 'Valse lente' and 'Entrée du sorcier', and revel in the sheer ebullience of Sylvia's return in Act 2. The inclusion of the ballet music from Saint-Saëns's *Henry VIII* was an admirably enterprising move, even though it doesn't amount to anything major apart from the 'Danse de la gitane', being essentially a collection of mock 'Olde Britishe' dances. All the same, a quite remarkable bargain.

Lakmé

Lakmé
Natalie Dessay *sop* Lakmé **Gregory Kunde** *ten* Gérald **José van Dam** *bass-bar* Nilakantha **Delphine Haidan** *mez* Mallika **Franck Leguérinel** *bar* Frédéric **Patricia Petibon** *sop* Ellen **Xenia Konsek** *sop* Rose **Bernadette Antoine** *sop* Mistress Bentson **Charles Burles** *ten* Hadji **Toulouse Capitole Chorus and Orchestra / Michel Plasson**
EMI ② 556569-2 (144' · DDD · T/t)   Ⓕ**O**

Opera audiences in 19th-century Paris may never have visited India, but they loved to dream about it. After the successes enjoyed by *Les pêcheurs de perles* and *Le roi de Lahore*, Delibes knew what he was doing when he chose to set an adaptation of Pierre Loti's exotic Indian novel *Rarahu*, and duly scored a hit with his opera *Lakmé* at the Opéra-Comique in 1883. The opera is nothing without a star in the title-role. Natalie Dessay is certainly that and yet she never fails to remember that Delibes's heroine must be fragile and sensitive. Her Bell Song, brilliantly sung, is also intent on telling a story. Her singing of the death scene, with its delicate *fil de voce* perfectly poised each time the high A comes round, is heartfelt and leaves no doubt that this is a Lakmé who deserves to go to heaven. EMI found a worthy tenor to partner her. Gregory Kunde, as Gérald, is at ease at the top of his voice. At the first entrance of the colonial Brits, Frédéric describes Gérald as a poet and Kunde lives up to the promise by phrasing his opening solo, 'Fantaisie aux divins mensonges', with poetic sensibility. In the duets he and Dessay are tender young love personified. The supporting cast is also a decent one.

Michel Plasson gives the music room to breathe and is able to conjure a dreamy atmosphere in the scenes of romance. His Toulouse orchestra is adequate, if not exceptional, and the recording is of a good standard. What reason is there to resist?

Frederick Delius
British 1862-1934

The sound world of Delius is immediately recognisable – warm, luminous orchestral colours, hazy, impressionistic tone pictures tinged with a romantic glow. Hard to hum a Delius tune (yet they're there) or to see where the music's going (he was at his best fantasising, dreaming, drifting), yet the ravishing, luminous beauty of his music is equally hard to resist. No one (unless you include popular music arrangers) followed in his footsteps. He belonged to no tradition; he led nowhere.

His father, Julius Delius, was a successful Prussian industrialist who had settled in Bradford, the owner of a wool company. Frederick was destined to follow in his footsteps and in 1882 was sent over to run the orange groves his father had purchased in Solano, Florida. Here, he had a Damascus-like conversion: hearing the close harmony of the African-American singers wafting across the St John River he realised that music must be his life. (His Appalachia Suite, variations on an old slave song, reflect his time there.) He'd brought his violin with him – Delius was good enough to make a favourable impression with the Mendelssohn Concerto – and on a trip to Jacksonville in search of a piano, met up with an American organist called Thomas F Ward who gave him lessons in music theory. In six months, so Delius said, he learnt more from Ward than in the three years of formal training he undertook subsequently at the Leipzig Conservatory (father Delius relented in

the face of his son's determination and the oranges were left to ripen under someone else's care). '[Ward] showed wonderful insight in helping me to find out just how much in the way of traditional technique would be useful for me.'

However uncongenial he found Leipzig, one benefit was meeting Grieg there and the two became close friends. Indeed, Scandinavia exercised a lifelong hold over Delius's imagination and music (he'd first travelled there as a young man) and when, after graduating in 1888, he moved to Paris, he mixed with painters and poets (more than musicians) who were predominantly Scandinavian.

Delius married the painter Jelka Rosen in 1897 and moved to the village of Grez-sur-Loing near Paris which was to remain his home for the rest of his life. He became increasingly reclusive. Visitors were rarely welcomed and when they were invited chez Delius, they would often be met with profound silence or dismissed abruptly when the host could stand their company no longer.

From the age of 40, his unique voice began to assert itself; the pleasant but derivative works of the previous two decades gave way to the distinctive Delius sound – A Mass of Life, Sea Drift, Brigg Fair and In a Summer Garden. Germany took to his music readily and England too, after a reluctant start, mainly due to Thomas Beecham, a lifelong ardent champion of Delius's music.

The Deliuses spent the war years in England and Norway but by the early 1920s his creative powers faltered. Paralysis and blindness set in, the result of contracting syphilis in Paris in the 1890s. That might have been that had it not been for the intervention of the young Yorkshire musician Eric Fenby who offered his services as amanuensis to the ailing Delius. Beecham organised a festival of six concerts in 1929 devoted entirely to Delius's music which the composer attended (he mounted a second in 1949). 'He was carried in his invalid chair, propped up by cushions, down the gangway to a waiting ambulance,' wrote his sister. 'All that the pressmen could see was a figure with silvered hair, wearing a grey felt hat, a heavy overcoat, with his sightless eyes shielded by tortoise-shell glasses and a pale, wrinkled, ascetic face.' This was the first and only time Delius heard his music cheered to the echo by his compatriots. It was his last public appearance.

The final four years of his life were spent in excruciating pain alleviated by constant doses of morphine. When he died, he was buried at Grez but a year later friends arranged for the transferral of his body to England where he was buried in the quiet country churchyard of Limpsfield in Surrey.

Orchestral Works

Appalachia[d]. Brigg Fair[a].　　　　　　　　　**H**
Koanga[b] – La Calinda (arr Fenby).
Hassan[c] – Closing scene. Irmelin Prelude[b].
[c]**Jan van der Gucht** ten [c]**Royal Opera House Chorus, Covent Garden;** [d]**BBC Chorus;** [a]**Symphony Orchestra;** [bcd]**London Philharmonic Orchestra / Sir Thomas Beecham**
Naxos Historical mono 8 110906 (66' · AAD)
Recorded [a]1928-29, 1938　　　　　　　　Ⓢ**O**▶

385

There always was a unique alchemy between the art of Sir Thomas Beecham and the music of Frederick Delius, to be heard in every bar of this remarkable January 1938 recording of *Appalachia*. It's a performance of beaming dedication, wistful heartache and rapt wonder, leaving the listener in no doubt about Sir Thomas's boundless love for a work that served as his introduction to the composer. (He later recalled how the 1907 London premiere under Fritz Cassirer left him 'startled and electrified'.) By July 1938 Beecham and the LPO had committed to disc the three remaining items that eventually made up the Delius Society's lavishly presented third and final volume of the composer's music issued by Columbia Records; suffice it to say, *La Calinda* skips along entrancingly here, while no true Delian could fail to respond to Beecham's ineffably poignant way with both the closing scene from *Hassan* and the lovely *Irmelin Prelude*.

Naxos's curtain-raiser, *Brigg Fair*, was recorded towards the end of the previous decade. Some seven months separated the two days required to produce a reading of unforgettable tenderness and bewitching poetry (the results of an even earlier session in July 1928 having been rejected altogether), although some will still hold a slight preference for the second of Sir Thomas's three versions (a gloriously intuitive display with the newly formed RPO from November 1946).

David Lennick's transfers have been admirably managed, *Appalachia* now sounding rather more open and full bodied than on a rival Dutton compilation. Throw in a lively and informative booklet-essay from Lyndon Jenkins, not to mention the absurdly low price-tag, and it should be abundantly clear that this is a self-recommending issue.

Fantastic Dance. Dance Rhapsodies Nos 1[a] & 2.
A Song of the High Hills. Three Preludes.
Zum Carnival
Maryetta Midgley *sop* **Vernon Midgley** *ten*
Eric Parkin *pf* **Ambrosian Singers**
Royal Philharmonic Orchestra / Eric Fenby,
[a]**Norman Del Mar**
Unicorn-Kanchana Souvenir UKCD2071 (65' · DDD) Ⓜ

Irmelin Prelude. A Song of Summer. A Late Lark.
Piano Concerto in C minor[a]. Violin Concerto[b]
Anthony Rolfe Johnson *ten* **Ralph Holmes** *vn*
Philip Fowke *pf* **Royal Philharmonic Orchestra /**
Eric Fenby, [a]**Norman Del Mar,** [b]**Vernon Handley**
Unicorn-Kanchana Souvenir UKCD2072 (71' · DDD) Ⓜ

Koanga – La Calinda (arr Fenby). Idyll: Once I passed through a populous city. Songs of Sunset. A Village Romeo and Juliet – The Walk to the Paradise Garden[a]
Felicity Lott *sop* **Sarah Walker** *mez* **Thomas Allen**
bar **Ambrosian Singers; Royal Philharmonic**
Orchestra / Eric Fenby, [a]**Norman Del Mar**
Unicorn-Kanchana Souvenir UKCD2073 (73' · DDD)
All recorded 1981-90 ⓂⒺ

The unique insight that the late Eric Fenby would bring as an interpreter of Delius was the reason for many of these Unicorn recordings, but we owe the idea and its realisation to their producer, Christopher Palmer. As well as providing Delians with some of the most illuminating text on the music, Palmer, in the studio, and especially in a work like *A Song of the High Hills*, was able to put his understanding (and Fenby's, of course) into practice. You don't need the score of *A Song of the High Hills* to tell you that the passage from 9'54" represents 'The wide far distance, the great solitude'. What you're listening to – totally spellbound – couldn't be anything else (or by anyone else).

Ralph Holmes's recording of the Violin Concerto is a warm, leisurely reading. The Piano Concerto, as recorded here, is a grand showstopper in the best Romantic piano concerto tradition, yet Fowke and Del Mar alert you to all the Delian reverie in the making (the dynamic range of Fowke's piano is colossal). But the outlay for Vol 2 is justified by Anthony Rolfe Johnson alone, in the all too brief six-minute *A Late Lark* ('one of Delius's works that is surely entirely without flaw', as Trevor Harvey put it in his original review).

In Vol 3, Fenby's control in *Songs of Sunset* doesn't always match his insight (choral work is often sloppy and too distantly recorded); the recent Hickox or the 1957 Beecham is to be preferred. But without Fenby in the recording studio (or at Grez!), we would never have had *Idyll*: Whitman texts combined with a late reworking of music from an earlyish opera, *Margot la Rouge*, to provide a reflective then rapturous love duet that looks back to Delius's Paris as well as to his *Paris* – this makes Volume 3 indispensable, especially as sung and played here.

And a very considerable bonus to be found in Vol 3 is Del Mar's previously unissued *Walk to the Paradise Garden*. This isn't the Beecham version for reduced orchestra, though it incorporates many of Beecham's dynamics and tempo indications. Most assuredly, it's a *Walk* on the grandest (11'00" to Beecham's 8'38"), most passionate scale (there's not a bar-line in earshot, either), and turns out to be yet another of these three discs' memorials to inspired Delians who died in our, but before their, time.

On Hearing the First Cuckoo in Spring. Brigg Fair.
In a Summer Garden. Paris: The Song of a Great City.
Summer Night on the River. A Village Romeo and
Juliet – The Walk to the Paradise Garden
BBC Symphony Orchestra / Sir Andrew Davis
Warner Apex 8573 89084-2 (77' · DDD) ⓈⒷ

This *Brigg Fair* is unique. What a lovely surprise to hear real London sparrows sharing the air space of St Augustine's Church with Delius's translated Lincolnshire larks (flute and clarinet) in the opening minutes of the work, albeit much more distantly. Very effective too are those almost still pools of string sound (early morning mists?), given the extended boundaries of this acoustic, and the familiar warmth and depth of tone Davis draws from the orchestra's strings. In the final magnificently broad climax (pealing bells, for once, very clear), you can't fail to be impressed by the depth, coherence and articulacy of the sound – hallmarks, indeed, of the entire disc.

Davis's strings come into their own in *The Walk to the Paradise Garden*. For *In a Summer Garden*, Davis mutes his strings more often than Delius asks; but the reading's delicacy of texture and hazy, suffusing warmth are difficult to resist.

American Rhapsody. Fantastic Dance. Marche caprice. Three Small Tone Poems. Two Pieces for Small Orchestra. A Song Before Sunrise. A Village Romeo and Juliet – The Walk to the Paradise Garden
Royal Scottish National Orchestra / David Lloyd-Jones
Naxos 8 557143 (64' · DDD)   ⑤→

A chronologically wide-ranging programme starts with Bizet-meets-Elgar in *Marche caprice* (composed in Paris in 1889) and finishes with the flourishes of the 1931 *Fantastic Dance* that Delius inscribed to his amanuensis Eric Fenby. There are two further rarities: the fragrant *Spring Morning* of 1890, which breathes a distinctly Norwegian air, and the colourful *American Rhapsody* of 1896, an embryonic (and purely orchestral) dry run for the towering *Appalachia* of six years later.

Lloyd-Jones's flowing yet deeply felt way with *The Walk to the Paradise Garden* leaves a less artfully self-conscious impression than Mark Elder's silky Hallé version. The only reservation applies to the Two Pieces for small orchestra, *On Hearing the First Cuckoo in Spring* and *Summer Night on the River*, both of which are too robust to work their full magic. (Thomas Beecham and Norman Del Mar remain unsurpassed in this 1911-12 diptych; the same goes for *A Song Before Sunrise*.) Otherwise, the RSNO respond attentively throughout.

Hiawatha (ed Threlfall). Caprice and Elegy (arr Tertis)[b]. Double Concerto (arr Tertis)[ab]. Légende[a]. Suite[a]
[a]**Philippe Graffin** *vn* [b]**Sarah-Jane Bradley** *va*
BBC Concert Orchestra / David Lloyd-Jones
Dutton Epoch CDLX7226 (72' · DDD) Ⓜ

Composed in 1888 at the tail-end of Delius's Leipzig sojourn, the tone-poem *Hiawatha* remained incomplete and unheard until the Delius Trust invited Robert Threlfall to produce a performing version. It's a charming discovery, its wholly disarming lyricism and fragrant poetry bringing irresistible echoes of the captivating *Florida Suite* completed the previous year. It's also fascinating to encounter an idea (the oboe's winsome second subject, conceivably

representing Minnehaha) that Delius would later flesh out to even more potently expressive effect in his 1899 nocturne *Paris*. The BBC Concert Orchestra respond with commitment under David Lloyd-Jones's alert lead.

Four *concertante* offerings make up the remainder. Both the Suite for violin and orchestra (dating from the same year as *Hiawatha*) and *Légende* (1895) will already be familiar to longstanding enthusiasts from Ralph Holmes's pioneering recordings from 1984 with Vernon Handley and the RPO. These newcomers are less inclined to linger, but Graffin all but matches Holmes's eloquence, even roughening up his tone a little in the second-movement *Intermezzo*. Lionel Tertis's reworkings for viola suit the shadowy *Caprice and Elegy* (written in 1930 for Beatrice Harrison) more than the masterly Double Concerto (conceived, again, for Beatrice and her sister May), where, although Lloyd-Jones paces proceedings admirably, there's rather less sense of soloistic interplay and fruitful dialogue.

Suffice to say, everything has been cleanly recorded by the Dutton production team, and Robert Threlfall supplies an exemplary booklet essay. A job very well done, then, and mandatory listening for devoted Delians.

Additional recommendations

Brigg Fair. Dance Rhapsody No 2.   Ⓗ
On Hearing the First Cuckoo in Spring. Summer Night on the River. A Song Before Summer. Intermezzo (arr Fenby). Irmelin Prelude. Sleighride. Summer Evening (ed & arr Beecham). Florida Suite (rev & ed Beecham) – Daybreak; Dance
RPO / Beecham
EMI download 567552-2 (77' · ADD)   Ⓜ→

Brigg Fair. A Song Before Sunrise. Songs from   Ⓗ
the Norwegian. Hassan – excerpts. Dance Rhapsodies Nos 1 & 2. On Hearing the First Cuckoo in Spring. Summer Night on the River. Danish Songs. Irmelin Prelude.
Suddaby *sop* **Thomas** *contr* **RPO / Beecham**
Dutton CDLX7028 (77' · ADD)   Ⓜ

Two superb reissues containing superlative performances from Beecham and the RPO, both beautifully remastered and at mid-price. At least one of these discs of these should be on every classical enthusiast's shelf (the EMI is not currently listed on CD but the download is).

Violin Sonatas

Violin Sonatas Nos 1-3. Cello Sonata
Ralph Holmes *vn* **Julian Lloyd Webber** *vc*
Eric Fenby *pf*
Unicorn-Kanchana Souvenir UKCD2074
(65' · ADD/DDD). Recorded 1972-81   Ⓜ

This is selfless, utterly dedicated music-making, always spontaneous-sounding yet never losing the organic thread of Delius's remarkable, free-flowing inspiration. There's a slight fragility to

Holmes's distinctive, silvery tone that's extremely moving, and Fenby, though no virtuoso practitioner, accompanies with intuitive sympathy. The recording of the piano (the instrument used is the three-quarter Ibach grand left to Fenby by Delius himself) remains a touch boxy and wanting in bloom, though the balance is otherwise natural and the overall effect nicely intimate. In the Cello Sonata Lloyd Webber and Fenby adopt a mellow, notably ruminative approach.

A Mass of Life

A Mass of Life[a]. Requiem[ba]
[a]Joan Rodgers, [b]Rebecca Evans sops [a]Jean Rigby mez [a]Nigel Robson ten Peter Coleman-Wright bar Waynflete Singers; Bournemouth Symphony Chorus and Orchestra / Richard Hickox
Chandos ② CHAN9515 (129' · DDD · T/t) Ⓕ℗➔

This is only the third commercial recording of *A Mass of Life*. The previous two recordings were the 1952 Beecham (no longer available) and the 1971 Groves on EMI. You might imagine modern recording would best place this vast canvas between your loudspeakers. And yes, Hickox's dynamic peaks are marginally higher, his perspectives marginally wider and deeper. Actually, some of this has as much to do with Hickox's own pacing and shading as the engineering. In general, this 'idealised' light- and air-filled sound brings a sharper, bright presence for the chorus, and such things as the piccolo trilling atop the final 'Hymn to Joy'. What it doesn't bring is the sense of performers in a specific acoustic space. But the chorus shines in the prominent role which the Chandos balance gives them, with ringing attack for all entries where it's needed, and singing as confident as it's sensitive, even if one has to make the odd allowance for not quite perfect pitching on high (Delius's demands are extreme) and moments where they're too loud. The soloists are fine; Hickox's baritone has a good line in stirring, virile address, though little of Benjamin Luxon's nobility, inwardness and true *legato*. What makes the Hickox *Mass* preferable to the Groves (but only just) is the conductor's inspired handling of each part's central dance panels. Hickox makes you believe in them, with a judicious drive, lift to the rhythms, and really incisive, eager singing and playing. As a coupling, Hickox has only the second commercial recording of the Requiem: more Nietzsche, but this time dogma not poetry, all the more unpalatable/ embarrassing (regardless of your faith) for being in English, but containing much unique Delius.

Sea Drift

Sea Drift. Songs of Sunset. Songs of Farewell
Sally Burgess mez Bryn Terfel bass-bar Waynflete Singers; Southern Voices; Bournemouth Symphony Chorus and Orchestra / Richard Hickox
Chandos CHAN9214 (77' · DDD · T) Ⓕ❶❶❶❶➔

 Sea Drift is a sublime conjunction of Whitman's poetry and Delius's music describing love, loss and unhappy resignation, with the sea (as Christopher Palmer put it) as 'symbol and agent of parting'. Written in 1903-04 (the same years as Debussy's *La mer*), it's surely Delius's masterpiece; right from the swaying opening bars its spell is enduring and hypnotic. Hickox in his second recording of the work now gives us the finest recorded post-Beecham *Sea Drift*. The shaping of the opening falling woodwind figures at a slow tempo more than usually (and very beautifully) portends the sad turn of events; and the climax is broad and superbly co-ordinated. Terfel's bar-by-bar characterisation (and glorious voice) conveys the full expressive range of the role from impassioned appeal to gentle call without artifice; and the choral singing is superb. The whole is recorded with warmth, spaciousness, depth and clarity.

Songs

The Song of the High Hills, RTII/6[b] Eventyr, 'Once upon a time', RTVI/23. Sleigh ride (Winter night), RTVI/7. Five Songs from the Norwegian, RTV/5[a] (arr Holten)
[a]Henriette Bonde-Hansen, [b]Helle Høyer Hansen sops [b]John Kjøller ten [b]Aarhus Chamber Choir; [b]Aarhus University Choir; Aarhus Symphony Orchestra / Bo Holten
Danacord DACOCD592 (66' · DDD · T/t) Ⓕ❶❶❶

Bo Holten and the excellent Aarhus Symphony Orchestra include here a collection of Delius works inspired by Norway, a country to which he was specially attracted. His first major visit was in 1887 during a summer vacation while studying at the Leipzig Conservatory, when he spent more than six weeks joyfully exploring fjords, moors and mountains.

Later that year his Leipzig contemporary, Christian Sinding, introduced him to Grieg, for whom as a Christmas present Delius wrote *Sleigh Ride*, a piano piece buried for many years that finally surfaced in the composer's orchestration in 1946, long after his death. It's a jolly little piece, not at all Delian in style, that by rights should have been a popular hit from the start; here it's given a delightful, lightly sprung performance.

The *Five Songs from the Norwegian* were written the following year in 1888 in gratitude for Grieg's intervention with Delius's father over giving him an allowance so as to devote himself to composition. Dedicated to Grieg's wife, they're charming pieces, setting poems by Bjornsen and others that Grieg himself had set, and are here made the more seductive in Bo Holten's sensitive orchestrations, with Henriette Bonde-Hansen the fresh, pure-toned soprano. The most ambitious Delius work inspired by Norway is *The Song of the High Hills*, the most substantial item on the disc. Though Beecham recorded it in the days of 78, it has been curiously neglected on disc; over its 25-minute span it offers some of the most hauntingly atmospheric music that Delius ever wrote, notably in the passages for wordless choir. Holten conducts a beautiful, refined performance which keeps the music moving, never letting it meander, building to powerful climaxes, thrillingly recorded. With a wide dynamic range the sound is evocatively atmospheric, not least in the offstage choral passages.

Fennimore and Gerda – Intermezzo. Lebenstanz, RTVI/15. An Arabesque, RTII/7[bc]. Sakuntala[b]. The Page Sat in the Lofty Tower[a]. In Bliss we Walked with Laughter[a]. Two Brown Eyes[a]. I Hear in the Night[a]. Two Danish Songs, RTV/21 – The Violet[b]; Autumn[a]. Seven Danish Songs, RTIII/4[a]. Summer Landscape, RTV/24[b]
[a]**Henriette Bonde-Hansen** sop [b]**Johan Reuter** bar
[c]**Danish National Opera Chorus;** [c]**Aarhus Chamber Choir; Aarhus Symphony Orchestra / Bo Holten**
Danacord DACOCD536 (70' · DDD · T/t)   (F)

This collection of Delius's Danish inspirations, beautifully performed and recorded, makes a delightful disc, including as it does rarities that are otherwise unavailable. Even if 'masterworks' is a bit of an exaggeration, the pieces here all show Delius at his most characteristic, drawing on his deep sympathy for Scandinavia and its culture. Significantly, the performances under Bo Holten tend to be faster and often more passionate than those on rival recordings, such as in Unicorn's admirable Delius Collection.

An Arabesque dates from 1911 but all the other vocal items were written much earlier. In many ways the conventional picture we have of Delius, as the blind and paralysed composer of his later years, is misleading, failing to reflect what we know of the younger man, active and virile, a point that Bo Holten has clearly registered. It's good to have the *Seven Danish Songs* of 1897 as a group in Delius's own sensuous orchestrations. The self-quotations in the ballad-like 'Irmelin Rose' are the more telling in orchestral form, and the most beautiful song of all, 'Summer Nights', is magically transformed in its atmospheric evocation of a sunset.

Delius also orchestrated two separate Danish songs, 'The Violet' and *Summer Landscape* as well as *Sakuntala*, prompting Holten to orchestrate the five other Danish songs, which here form another orchestral cycle. These, too, are more beautiful than with piano, even though Holten is less distinctive than Delius himself in his use of orchestral colour, notably in woodwind writing. All these songs are sung in the original language, where the Unicorn series opted for the English translations which Delius either made himself or approved. The two singers here may not be as characterful as such British soloists as Felicity Lott, Sarah Walker or Thomas Allen (in *An Arabesque*), but they both have fresh young voices, clear and precise, with Henriette Bonde-Hansen shading her bright

soprano down to the gentlest *pianissimos*. The choral singing, too, is excellent in *An Arabesque*.

The *Fennimore and Gerda* Intermezzo is relatively well known, but *Lebenstanz* ('Life's Dance'), inspired by a play of Helge Rode, is a rarity, otherwise available only on Unicorn conducted by Norman Del Mar. Here, too, Holten opts for marginally faster speeds in a piece depicting (in the composer's words) 'the turbulence, the joy, energy, great striving of youth'. The dance sections – one of them surprisingly Straussian – are punctuated by typically reflective passages, and the depiction of death at the end is peaceful and not at all tragic.

The Aarhus Symphony Orchestra respond warmly to Holten's idiomatic direction, and the refined playing is quite closely balanced in a helpful acoustic.

Five Partsongs (1887). Her ute skal gildet staa. Irmelin Rose (arr Lubin). On Craig Dhu. Wanderer's Song. Midsummer Song. The splendour falls on castle walls. Two Songs for Children. To be sung of a summer night on the water. A Village Romeo and Juliet – The Dream of Sali and Vrenchen (arr Fenby). Appalachia – Oh, Honey, I am going down the river (arr Suchoff). Irmelin – Away, far away to the woods. Hassan – Chorus behind the scenes; Chorus of Beggars and Dancing Girls
Joanna Nolan sop **Stephen Douse** ten **Andrew Ball** pf **Mark Brafield** org **Elysian Singers of London / Matthew Greenall**
Somm SOMMCD210 (50' · DDD · T/t)   (F)

Delius had a special relationship with the collective human voice, and the songs here are presented chronologically, which allows us to follow pleasurably the development of his style. The extracts from *A Village Romeo and Juliet* and *Appalachia* prolong what would otherwise be a rather brief encounter and their accompaniments also provide contrast of timbre, but they do need to be heard in context to 'take off'. The 'essential' Delius comes with *On Craig Dhu* – experience of nature not so much tinged by melancholy as perceived through it, a haunting evocation in grey; and the setting of Tennyson's 'The splendour falls on castle walls', as characteristically Delius as Britten's setting of it in his *Serenade* is Britten.

Though the singing itself deserves a generally warm welcome, not all Delius's chromatic wanderings are as confidently charted as they might be. The sopranos seem the strongest contingent, and the ones most often in the expressive spotlight. Nor are the soloists ideal, the tenor sounding unhappy in the higher regions of 'To be sung of a summer night on the water'. And on occasions, as in the first of those two songs, one might have wished for more varied pacing and dynamic shading from the conductor. But the world of Delius performance is one where devotees are used to taking the roundabouts with the swings, and this is the only all-Delius collection of its kind on the market.

Film

'Song of Summer'

Max Adrian Frederick Delius **Maureen Pryor** Jelka
Delius **Christopher Gable** Eric Fenby **David Collings**
Percy Grainger **Geraldine Sherman** Girl next door
Elizabeth Ercy Maid **Roger Worrod** Bruder
Film director **Ken Russell**
BFI *DVD* BFIVD518 (72' · 4:3 · 1.0 · 0). Made for the
BBC in 1968. Includes director's commentary and on-
screen biography. Ⓕ**OO**

Ken Russell's extraordinarily compelling and
intensely moving *Song of Summer* remains, quite
simply, a joy from start to finish, arguably the
controversial director's finest achievement to
date and a landmark in the history of British
television. Based on Eric Fenby's 1936 memoir
Delius as I knew him (Faber & Faber: 1981), *Song
of Summer* tells of Delius's syphilis-wracked final
years and the remarkable relationship that
develops between the blind, crippled composer
and his gifted, tirelessly devoted amanuensis.
The screenplay (by Russell and Fenby) fairly
teems with intelligent observation, darkly mischievous humour and compassionate warmth.
Indeed, the film's chief fascination lies in its
subtle exploration of the profoundly contradictory nature of Delius's life and art ('I can't reconcile such hardness with such lovely music,'
says Fenby, just after Delius's wife, Jelka, has
filled him in on her unfaithful husband's wanton
sexual exploits from years past).

Memorable characterisations abound. As the
by turns irascible yet vulnerable composer, Max
Adrian gives a performance of towering eloquence. Christopher Gable, too, is totally
believable in the role of Fenby, while Maureen
Pryor makes a touching Jelka. There's also a
boisterous cameo from David Collings as Percy
Grainger. Dick Best's luminous black-and-
white photography comes up with pristine
freshness, and Russell himself provides a typically candid and personable commentary. All
told, a real treat.

'Discovering Delius – A Portrait of Frederick Delius (1862-1934)'

Includes contributions from **Sir Charles Mackerras,
Julian Lloyd Webber, Tasmin Little, Thomas
Hampson** and the **Brindisi Quartet**
Directed and narrated by **Derek Bailey**
Digital Classics *DVD* DCD1009DC
(60' · 4:3 · PCM stereo · 0) Ⓕ

Derek Bailey's 1993 film for the Delius Trust
offers a gentle introduction to Delius's life and
music. The life chronology, however, is mud-
dling. Nine minutes in and we are already covering Delius's final years via a clip of Max Adrian
and Christopher Gable in Ken Russell's unforgettable 1962 film, before being whisked back to
Norwegian fjords and Paris student days. Of one
thing we are left in no doubt: England and English music were not for Delius, and, as we are

told in the opening sequence, he did not see
himself as an English composer. The Bradford-
born son of a wealthy first-generation German
wool merchant, he left for Florida as soon as he
was able in order to manage an orange plantation. After America came Scandinavia, Leipzig
(where he befriended Grieg), Paris and Italy
before Grez-sur-Loing, France, where he lived
for the last 40 years of his life.

The film is valuable for the contributions of
two musicians sadly no longer with us: Eric
Fenby (*d*1997), Delius's amanuensis from 1928,
and the critic Felix Aprahamian (*d*2005) who, at
the time of filming, was one of only four people
left alive to have visited Delius at Grez-sur-
Loing. Robert Threlfall, longtime custodian of
the Delius Trust reveals, somewhat horrify-
ingly, that Beecham, Delius's foremost champion, entered his own performance directions in
ineradicable blue crayon directly onto Delius's
manuscript scores.

Here, too, are the young(er) Thomas Hampson, Tasmin Little and Julian Lloyd Webber.
The latter plays part of the Cello Sonata using
the very same instrument on which Delius first
heard the work; Little, beautifully expressive as
she is in part of the Violin Concerto, is particularly moving as she speaks of what she believes to
be Delius's great lost loves – a negro girl and the
son she bore him – and the effect this had on his
music thereafter with its constant 'yearning for
the unattainable'.

Henry Desmarest   French 1661-1741

*Desmarest sang as a boy in Louis XIV's chapel where
he came into contact with Lully and become one of his
most outstanding pupils. His first opera was given at
Versailles in 1682. He was maître de chapelle at a
Jesuit college. His connection with the court at
Versailles ended suddenly in 1699 when a relationship with one of his pupils forced him into exile. After
five years in Spain, Desmarest returned to France
and to the Duchy of Lorraine where he remained, in
the role of surintendant de la musique, until a royal
pardon was granted in 1720. He wrote about
20 stage works as well as grands motets, cantatas,
airs and sonatas.*

Grands Motets Lorrains

Grands Motets Lorrains – Usquequo, Domine; Ⓟ
Lauda Jerusalem; Domine, ne in furore
Sophie Daneman, Rebecca Ockenden *sops* **Paul
Agnew** *ten* **Laurent Slaars** *bar* **Arnaud Marzorati**
bass **Les Arts Florissants / William Christie**
Erato 8573 80223-2 (68' · DDD · T/t) Ⓕ**OO**

If Henry Desmarest hasn't yet joined other
French Baroque composers among the ranks of
the Great Rediscovered, here's a disc which ought
to help him on his way. These three *grands motets*
were composed between 1708 and 1715, the early

years of his time as musical director to the court of the Duke of Lorraine. Scored for soloists, choir and orchestra, each is a multi-sectional psalm-setting lasting about 20 minutes. What's immediately striking isn't only how strong-boned and well-written the music is, but also how contrasted; here are moments of supreme tenderness, powerful intensity, robust grandeur and uplifting rhythmic vigour. And if a tendency towards melancholy is unsurprising given that two of these psalm-texts are penitential, who's to say that we aren't also witnessing a reflection of the unhappy circumstances of this composer's life?

Such music couldn't have fallen into better hands than Christie's. His talent is to see the work as a totality, with the result that the music never fails to punch its full expressive weight. With Sophie Daneman and Paul Agnew excellent among the soloists, and choral singing which remains unfailingly vivid and alert throughout, these are vibrant performances that don't put a foot wrong. The recording is clear and nicely balanced, though an unusual profusion of extraneous noises is an irritant. Even so, this is a must-buy for French Baroque fans.

Peter Dickinson
English b1934

Dickinson is an English composer, musicologist and pianist. He studied organ at Queens' College, Cambridge. In 1958 he became a student at the Juilliard School in New York City, where he studied with Bernard Wagenaar and encountered the works of experimental composers such as Cowell, Cage, and Edgard Varèse. Returning to England in 1962, he established courses in improvisation and experimental music at the College of St Mark and St John, Chelsea. After a lectureship at Birmingham, he became the first professor of music at Keele University in 1974, where he created an important centre for the study of American music. He served as chair of music at Goldsmiths' College, University of London, from 1991 to 1997, and in 1996 became a Fellow and head of music at the Institute of United States Studies in London.

As a prolific writer, he has often shown his varied interests in American music. He wrote a series of articles on improvisation in 1964, and more recently has discussed postmodernism, coining the term 'style modulation' to describe the weaving together of serious and popular or past and present music. The term can be applied to his own music, which adds a mix of ragtime, jazz, serial music and even electronic playback to more traditional types of instrumental musical forms.

Organ Music

Complete Solo Organ Works
Jennifer Bate org
Naxos 8 572169 (78' · DDD)
Played on the organs of St John's, Duncan Terrace, St James's, Muswell Hill, and St Dominic's Priory, London
Ⓢ Ⓞ ▶

The student pieces that begin this fascinating disc demonstrate the expected ability to identify with the musical worlds of Vaughan Williams and Herbert Howells, though one piece at least – the *Postlude on Adeste fideles* – shows signs of a more abrasive idiom, as if Ives were waiting in the wings. The *Meditation on Murder in the Cathedral* is another, quite different kind of early acknowledgement that the dissonance and a sense of disquiet so common in contemporary concert music by 1958 could be no less relevant to the organ loft.

When Dickinson exchanged Cambridge for New York in the late 1950s, that potential for responding to changes taking place in the wider musical world began to be realised with interest. The organ works from the 1960s which followed his return to the UK reveal the edgy, angular perspectives stemming from Dickinson's familiarity with composers as different as Copland and Cage. However, neither *Three Statements* nor *Paraphrase 1* are pale imitations of such composers – nor, for that matter, of other Dickinson enthusiasts such as Satie and Berners. Only with the exuberant, ebullient absorption of blues and rag music found in *Blue Rose Variations* (1985) do specific stylistic associations emerge, and this piece remains an invigorating blast of fresh air, a kind of secular equivalent to Messiaen's ecstatic spiritual dances.

The Dickinson journey is traced here in supremely well articulated and strongly characterised performances by Jennifer Bate. The three organs involved are recorded with maximum fidelity and no sense of distortion, even in the loudest passages. The disc is a fine birthday tribute to a composer who has escaped the confines of the predictable without ever ceasing to communicate.

Vocal works

Lullaby from 'The Unicorns'[a]. Mass of the Apocalypse[b]. Larkin's Jazz[c]. Five Forgeries[d]. Five Early Pieces[e]. Air[f]. Metamorphosis[f]
[b]**Jo Maggs** sop [b]**Meriel Dickinson** mez [b]**Donald Reeves** spkr [c]**Henry Herford** bar/spkr [a][f]**Duke Dobing** fl [b]**James Holland**, [b]**David Johnson** perc [b]**John Alley**, [a][d][e]**Peter Dickinson**, [d][e]**John Flinders** pfs [b]**St James's Singers**; [c]**Nash Ensemble** / [b]**Ivor Bolton**; [c]**Lionel Friend**
Naxos 8 572287 (79' · DDD)
Ⓢ ▶

Peter Dickinson and Philip Larkin make a surprisingly plausible pairing. The essential Englishness of their voices – Dickinson's infused with Britten and Lennox Berkeley, Larkin as England's miserablist-in-chief – was coloured by an engagement with American culture, radically so in Dickinson's case. In his booklet-note Dickinson recalls meeting Larkin to discuss a collaboration but his 1989 composition for voice and ensemble, *Larkin's Jazz*, was inspired by jazz performances he heard at Larkin's memorial service. With King Oliver's 'Riverside Blues' and Bechet's 'Blue Horizon' as models, Dickinson created a musical gumbo by returning Larkin's jazz-inspired poems to source, interwoven around instrumental commentaries.

The Nash Ensemble – augmented with saxophonist John Harle and trumpeter Paul Archibald – make an unexpectedly decent fist at evoking New Orleans salty-dog funk, responding to Dickinson's slyly astute caricatures. Plummy Henry Herford sounds incongruously schoolmasterly as he intones about Bechet. But perhaps that's the point: stiff Englishness admiring of, but alien from, the music? That was Larkin's jazz.

Mass of the Apocalypse (1984) makes an apt coupling. Using the Apocalypse story from the Book of Revelation as an allegory for contemporary concerns, Dickinson contrasts formal compositional procedures – like the harmonic cycle underpinning the 'Kyrie' – with stylistic lurches towards the blues and, in the 'Kyrie', overlaid strata of (presumably) uncoordinated choral speaking – a neat way of expressing early '80s angst about the state we were in. There are also hints of Tippett's granite lyricism in the flute and piano *Lullaby*, the most intriguing of the accompanying miniatures.

words for rain and wind. This exhilarating essay for solo cello is executed with charismatic brilliance by Rohan de Saram. That there's far more to his music than mere sound-effects is confirmed by the Second String Quartet, a fizzing firework display as exuberant as it's poetic and a supremely imaginative rethinking of the traditional quartet. In *Traumwerk*, 12 miniatures for two violins, Dillon seizes the opportunity to devise a sequence of sharply drawn character pieces whose variety of mood ranges from sly comedy to unbridled ferocity. As always with this composer, nothing about the medium – like the contrast between playing vibrato and non-vibrato – is taken for granted. The persuasive technical and interpretative virtuosity of all the performers on this CD should not be taken for granted either, and the various recordings are all superb.

the soadie waste[ac]. Del cuarto elemento[d]. Dillug-Kefitsah[a]. Traumwerk Book III[ad]. black/nebulae[ab].
[a]**Noriko Kawai**, [b]**Hiroaki Takenouchi** pfs
[c]**Arditti Quartet** ([d]Irvine Arditti, Ashot Sarkissjan vns
Ralf Ehlers va Lucas Fels vc)
NMC NMCD131 (76′ · DDD)   (F)

The 27-year period covered by this group of compositions, taking James Dillon from his mid-twenties to his early fifties, could hardly fail to outline substantial changes. *Dillug-Kefitsah* (1976) might well be fully representative in its relish for weird titles and joyful technical radicalism, shifting between gentleness and turbulence in thoroughly disconcerting ways. But it gives little sign of the delight in forceful pattern-making and affectionate allusion to a Glaswegian location that makes *the soadie waste* (2003) such a bracing and engaging experience. The more confidently international Dillon's range of reference, the more resourceful his acknowledgement of his native Scots roots becomes.

The two big works here, *black/nebulae* (1994) and *Traumwerk Book III* (completed 2002) belong to a time when Dillon was deep in larger-scale projects. Yet neither sounds remotely like music of reduced ambition or limited scope. The space/time drama underpinning *black/nebulae* promotes a surface that seethes and erupts in 20 effortlessly sustained minutes of duo-pianistic bravura, in which meticulous coordination is as crucial as assertive independence. The 12 miniatures of the *Traumwerk* collection are even more fastidious in their intricacy, yet the result is often playful, even nonchalant, as Irvine Arditti and Noriko Kawai make light (apparently) of the formidable challenges presented. Arditti is also characteristically arresting in the 10-minute solo piece Dillon wrote for him in 1988 and named after the fourth element, water. The music, a miniature drama, is not merely liquid-like in its fluidity but is constantly reaching and retreating from boiling-point.

These performances benefit greatly from the crystal-clear Potton Hall acoustics. With luck,

James Dillon   British b1950

He studied music and linguistics at London University but was self-taught as a composer. His music, influenced by Ferneyhough and Finnissy, is characterised by wild complexity and extreme instrumental demands. His early works are for solo instruments or small ensembles – Once Upon a Time for eight instruments (1980), East 11th St NY 10003 for six percussionists (1982) – but in Überschreiten for 16 instruments (1986) and his first orchestral score Helle Nacht (1987) he began to extend his techniques to larger forces.

Chamber Works

String Quartet No 2[a]. Parjanya-vata[b].
Traumwerk[c]. Vernal Showers[d]
[a]**Arditti Quartet** ([cd]Irvine Arditti vn David Alberman vn Garth Knox va [b]Rohan de Saram vc) [c]**Graeme Jennings** vn [d]**Nieuw Ensemble / Ed Spanjaard**
Auvidis Montaigne MO782046 (67′ · DDD)   (F)

For a composer with James Dillon's avant-garde credentials, the title *Vernal Showers* might lead you to expect a send-up of English pastoralism. In fact, there's nothing the least frivolous or forbidding about this response to Coleridge's *The Nightingale*. The music invokes the glittering cascades of sudden downpours while the sun still shines, and even the nocturnal song of the nightingale, without compromising Dillon's very personal blend of inventiveness and carefully weighted structuring.

Parjanya-vata is an appropriate partner for *Vernal Showers*, its title involving two Sanskrit some of Dillon's more substantial works from recent years will turn up on disc before too long.

The Book of Elements

The Book of Elements
Noriko Kawai pf
NMC ② NMCD091 (83′ · DDD)

There's a marvellously flamboyant spontaneity and exuberance *The Book of Elements*, demonstrating his view of the elements – air, water and so on – as standing for 'different forms of energy'. Energy is life, life is both time and transience, and the composer's over-riding concern is with images of impermanence and flux. These determine musical processes that speak of the inherent fragility of life and the essential sadness of attempts to construct something relatively stable and permanent in sound.

The work, composed between 1996 and 2003, is in five volumes with a clear formal trajectory, comprising 11, 7, 5, 3 and 1 pieces respectively. The listener is kept enthralled, not only by allusions to familiar generic prototypes (toccata or *moto perpetuo* at one extreme, nocturne or threnody at the other), but also by a musical language that plays with perceptions about centricity: repeated notes or chords reconfigure traditional, even tonal identities as much as they contradict them. All this is accomplished with a mastery of piano style in which the entire history of keyboard virtuosity from Frescobaldi to Ligeti is thrown into the melting pot.

The Book of Elements began with a commission from Roger Woodward, and Rolf Hind, Nicolas Hodges and Ian Pace have all been associated with individual volumes. But Noriko Kawai has become most closely involved with this music, and she offers an unfailingly persuasive realisation, helped by a recording of exemplary immediacy and atmosphere. While she has ample reserves of strength for the many episodes of turbulence, the delicacy with which she plays the soft yet immensely intricate polyphony of the third piece of Volume 3 is even more remarkable.

Dillon manages to use all the instrument's traditional technical devices for prolonging sound with barely a hint of cliché. The final dispersal of energy at the end of the fifth volume, coming as it does after a positive *Hammerklavier* of trills and tremolos, is one of the great moments of early 21st-century music, simply because it speaks as much of affirmation as of dissolution. It sets the seal on a memorable release.

Philomela
Anu Komsi sop Philomela **Susan Narucki** sop Procne
Lionel Peintre ten Tereus **Remix Ensemble / Jurjen Hempel**
Aeon ② AECD0986 (91′ · DDD)

In the great tradition of radical composers, James Dillon manages to be provocative and persuasive in more or less equal measure. He calls *Philomela* (completed in 2004) 'music/théâtre' rather than 'opera', mixing English and French to underline its hybrid nature: and the instruments push the voices to the margins while at the same time positively enhancing the expressionistic tension that comes from the drama's mythic-tragic theme. All the same, it's difficult not to feel that the work belongs with Britten's *The Rape of Lucretia* and Birtwistle's *The Mask of Orpheus*, ritualising an inordinate act of violence or moment of loss, and wringing maximum intensity from an essentially austere dramatic enactment.

The composer admits to a range of associations – Baroque opera, Noh theatre – and never ceases to worry away at music's ability to do something more than merely aestheticise matters of life and death. But what use are CDs when so much depends on mime, movement, and various other visual effects? Surely only a DVD could adequately convey the elemental force of this jet-black representation of the story of Philomela, her tongue torn out by her maddened brother-in-law, and who then conspires with her sister to kill her young nephew in revenge. As an ending, the gods metamorphose the characters into birds – Philomela herself into that arch-emblem of spontaneous musical magic, the nightingale.

The visual dimension is vital. Yet Dillon's music, with its rich weave of aggressive eloquence and obsessively evolving sound-patterns, is fully equal to the task of making the turbulent ritual seem real to the ears alone. If the text on its own seems to court ridicule at times with its Dadaist eroticism, the music is no less incautious in refusing to shrink from the horror-movie implications of its theme. To turn these potential banalities into strengths is a remarkable achievement, and Dillon can be heard at his most potently expressive in the extraordinary duet for cello and double bass that builds into the closing instrumental chorale. The impact would be far less direct without the bold close-miking and amplification captured in this recording, challenging the collective virtuosity of singers and players – a challenge they meet with considerable success. Philomela demands to be heard: but the sooner it can also be seen more widely than has so far been the case, the better.

Ernö Dohnányi Hungarian 1877-1960

Dohnányi (who preferred the German 'Ernst von' as a Christian name) began his career as a virtuoso pianist. He made many recordings – including two versions of the Variations – but abandoned full-time concerts and touring to concentrate on composing and teaching in Berlin and Budapest (his pupils included Sir Georg Solti). The Second World War brought personal tragedy: of his two sons, Hans was executed for his role in the abortive attempt on Hitler's life and

*the other was killed in combat. After the war he set-
tled in America and came to be regarded rather as the
Grand Old Man of Hungarian Music. His grandson
is the distinguished conductor Christoph von
Dohnányi.*

Variations on a Nursery Theme, Op 25

Variations on a Nursery Theme[a] Der Schleier der
Pierrette – Pierrot's Love-lament; Waltz-rondo; Merry
Funeral March; Wedding waltz. Suite for Orchestra,
Op 19.
[a]**Howard Shelley** *pf*
BBC Philharmonic Orchestra / Matthias Bamert
Chandos CHAN9733 (70' · DDD)　　　Ⓕ🅑➔

Dohnányi's penchant for quality musical entertainment bore popular fruit with his perennially fresh *Variations on a Nursery Theme.*
Howard Shelley's performance is a model of
wit and style, blending in with the orchestra
whenever the moment seems right and employing an ideal brand of *rubato*. Bamert's conducting is properly portentous in the Introduction
and charming elsewhere, whether in the music-
box delights of the fifth variation, the animated
bustle of the sixth or the seventh's novel scoring (plenty for the bassoons and bass drum).
Kocsis and Fischer's is still marginally the best
version overall, but Shelley and Bamert are no
less musical.

Lovely, too, is the F sharp minor Suite, especially the opening *Andante con variazioni* which
seems to straddle the worlds of Dvořák and
Elgar (try the serene string choirs from 9'35").
The stamping *Scherzo* brings to mind the
Scherzo from Bruckner's Ninth Symphony, and
the tuneful Rondo finale has a striking resemblance to a key passage in the *Rondo-burleske* in
Mahler's Ninth.

Also included is the very first recording of *The
Veil of Pierrette*, four scenes from a mimed
entertainment dating from 1908-09. The best
movement is the exuberant 'Wedding Waltz'
(track 21), rumbustious music, carefree and
beautifully scored. Chandos has come up with a
dazzlingly realistic recording. A peach of a
disc.

Ruralia hungarica

Suite, Op 19. Ruralia hungarica. American Rhapsody
Danubia Symphony Orchestra / Domonkos Héja
Warner Classics 2564 62409-2 (71' · DDD)　　Ⓕ🅑➔

Good to have Dohnányi delivered in bright,
local packaging. The substantial Suite, Op 19,
revisits Brahmsian vistas, the string writing
especially, and at around the seven-minute
mark into the sizeable theme-and-variations
first movement there's a vivid premonition of
Bartók and Bluebeard's cache of jewels (put
together some 10 years later). Clean, incisive,
light in texture – Héja's still-young orchestra is
all of these and projects a subtly individual

personality, at once grainy and slimline, if not
yet quite the equal of Iván Fischer's more
colourful Budapest Festival band. The Danubia's playing of the Suite's *Scherzo* (echoes of
the Russian late-Romantics) and momentarily
Mahlerian finale is quite brilliant, whereas the
strings do very nicely in the exotic *Romanza*
slow movement.

The somewhat later suite *Ruralia hungarica* is
less 'earth under the fingernails' (which is what
Bartók and Kodály were offering) than peasant
life spied from the business lounge. The suite's
lyrical centrepiece is the dusky, rhapsodic *Adagio
non troppo*, widely known out of context as a
'Gypsy Andante'. If you don't immediately
recognise it, be patient: the big theme sweeps in
at around the two-minute mark. The more
memorable of the fast movements, pungently
played here, is the pentatonic *Presto* with its
coincidental echoes of American-Indian music,
while the finale is charmingly childlike in its
simplicity.

How different the relatively late and infinitely
more complex *American Rhapsody*, a melange of
traditional tunes woven into a contrapuntal
tapestry that would have made even Reger green
with envy. Good to hear once or twice, especially when played with conviction and just a
touch of wistfulness – which is how it's played
here. Good sound.

Violin Sonata

Dohnányi Violin Sonata, Op 21. Ruralia hungarica,
Op 32c. Suite for Orchestra, Op 19 – Romanza
(arr Heifetz) **Janáček** Violin Sonata. Dumka.
Romance. Allegro. On an Overgrown Path – A blown-
away leaf (arr J Štědroň)
Hagai Shaham *vn* **Arnon Erez** *pf*
Hyperion CDA67699 (71' · DDD)　　　Ⓕ🅑➔

Janáček and Dohnányi present an interesting
contrast, both growing up within the Germanic
Romantic milieu while conscious of a separate
national identity. Janáček, however, departed in
an increasingly radical way from the tradition,
whereas Dohnányi's outlook remained conservative, adapting rather than discarding his heritage. His 1912 Sonata often suggests Brahms
but with a more modern sense of unease and
restlessness. Shaham and Erez give an excellent
performance, Shaham's seductive tone and elegant phrasing being well matched by Erez's
sensitive touch. The *Ruralia hungarica* pieces
show the composer's more nationalistic side but
are still fairly traditional in their approach to
folk material. Shaham is in his element here –
the brilliant final piece carefree and dashing in
style, the preceding, improvisatory *Andante
rubato alla zingaresca* graceful and stylish. Some
listeners, however, may prefer a more intense,
dramatic way with this piece.

The Janáček items range over 40 years, from
the quite formal *Romance* to the mature Sonata.
Of particular interest is the Allegro – the discarded original finale of the Sonata, which uses

material subsequently incorporated into the Sonata's third movement. Again, these are all appealing, finely judged performances, but I do feel in the Sonata that this immensely polished, civilised playing fails to express some of the raw emotion. However, this is still a very fine recital.

Piano Quintets

Piano Quintets[a] – No 1 in C minor, Op 1; No 2 in E flat minor, Op 26. Suite in the Old Style, Op 24
[a]**Vanbrugh Quartet** (Gregory Ellis, Elizabeth Charleson vns Simon Aspell va Christopher Marwood vc)
Martin Roscoe pf
ASV CDDCA915 (70' · DDD)   Ⓕ

Dohnányi's First Piano Quintet, Op 1, written when the composer was only 18, is a work of abounding confidence and energy that's played here with suitable verve and exuberance. Roscoe and the Vanbrugh Quartet luxuriate in lush, romantic textures in the first movement, and delight in the melodic exchanges of the warmly expressive *Adagio*. Moreover, their expression of Hungarian flavour, evident in the *Scherzo*'s jaunty cross-rhythms and the engagingly dance-like finale, has considerable charm.

The Second Quintet, written some 19 years later, shows a striking advance in technique. Sensitive evocation of atmosphere in the first movement by Roscoe and the Vanbrugh Quartet highlights both Dohnányi's more searching harmonic language and his remarkably fresh and imaginative approach to form.

The performers deftly blend the *Intermezzo*'s faintly Viennese character with the flamboyant toccata material, and the final movement's fusion of slow movement and finale is ingeniously turned from sombre minor to radiant major. Both the quintets display Dohnányi's considerable pianistic skills; the *Suite in the Old Style* being a highly effective display of the composer's parody of Baroque keyboard techniques. Roscoe's evident sympathy for his music contributes to this arrestingly persuasive account, which fully exploits the work's rich variety of style and technique.

Gaetano Donizetti   Italian 1797-1848

Imagine composing over 20 operas – some of them highly successful at the time - before finding your own individual way of doing things. That's what happened to the incredibly prolific Donizetti.

His father, a weaver and later a pawnbroker, would not countenance a musical career for his son at first but eventually reluctantly allowed him to go to the Bergamo School of Music. Here Donizetti devoured the scores of his idol Rossini (who was only five years older), determined to be another opera composer in the same mould. So his first opera, Enrico di Borgogna (1818) and the next 22 were written by the hand of Donizetti but with the voice of Rossini. He couldn't have known that Rossini would stop *writing operas in 1829 but the strange fact is that as soon as Rossini did 'retire' (at 37) Donizetti grabbed the mantle, as it were, and started writing in his own distinctive style.*

His finest operas were produced after 1830 – Anna Bolena, L'elisir d'amore, Maria Stuarda, Lucia di Lammermoor, Don Pasquale – some sentimental and tragic, some witty and subtle, 70 in all. As in the Rossini-influenced days, he could turn out as many as three or four a year and was said to have sketched and written the last act of La favorita in a few hours. Not all have stood the test of time – one wonders what such quixotic titles as Alfredo il grande, Alina, regina di Golconda and Elisabetta al castello di Kenilworth contain. At any rate, Donizetti dashed all over Europe in the 1830s and '40s producing, supervising and composing his operas, acclaimed in Vienna and Paris just as much as he was in his native Italy.

With the appearance of Don Pasquale in 1843, Donizetti reached the height of his creative powers, for then Fate intervened. He had never got over the death in 1837 of his adored wife and began suffering bouts of fever and headaches, accompanied by intense depression and hallucinations. He continued to work through 1844 but in 1845 had a paralytic stroke and lapsed into insanity in the final stages of syphilis.

Anna Bolena

Anna Bolena
Maria Callas sop Anna Bolena **Nicola Rossi-**   Ⓗ
Lemeni bass Enrico VIII **Giulietta Simionato** mez
Giovanna Seymour **Gianni Raimondi** ten Riccardo
Percy **Plinio Clabassi** bass Rochefort **Gabriella**
Carturan mez Smeton **Luigi Rumbo** ten Hervey
Chorus and Orchestra of La Scala, Milan /
Gianandrea Gavazzeni
EMI mono ② 566471-2 (140' · ADD · T/t)
Recorded live 1957   Ⓜ▷

One of Callas's unique qualities was to inspire an audience with the sense of a great occasion, and to key up a sympathetic conductor into the production of something to match her own intensity and the public's expectations. Here she gives one of her finest performances. The first impression is a vocal one, in the sense of the sheer beauty of sound. Then, in the first solo, 'Come innocente giovane', addressing Jane Seymour, she's so clean in the cut of the voice and the style of its usage, delicate in her *fioriture*, often exquisite in her shading, that anyone, ignorant of the Callas legend, would know immediately that this is an artist of patrician status. There are marvellous incidental moments, and magnificent *crescendos*, into, for instance, 'per pietà delmio spavento' and 'segnata è la mia sorte', culminating in the Tower scene.

Unfortunately, the singers at her side hardly measure up. Simionato has a splendid voice that nevertheless bumps as it goes into the low register and isn't reliably steady in many passages, while the manner is too imperious and unresponsive. The tenor role has been reduced by Gavazzeni's cuts, but Gianni Raimondi makes limited impression in what remains; and, as the King, Rossi-Lemeni produces that big but somewhat woolly tone that became increasingly characteristic. Even so, the great ensembles still prove worthy of the event, and the recording, which is clear without harshness or other distortion, conveys the special quality of this memorable evening with remarkable vividness and fidelity.

For those who insist on a modern recording, there's an imaginatively conducted 1994 performance on Nightingale Classics by Elio Boncompagni, with Edita Gruberová in the title-role. But this Callas/Gavazzeni set is in a different class altogether.

Dom Sébastien, roi de Portugal

Dom Sébastien, roi de Portugal
Vesselina Kasarova mez Zayda **Giuseppe Filianoti** ten Dom Sébastien **Alastair Miles** bass Dom Juam de Sylva **Simon Keenlyside** bar Abayaldos **Carmelo Carrado Caruso** bar Camoëns **Robert Gleadow** bass Dom Henrique **John Upperton** ten Dom Antonio **Andrew Slater** bass Ben-Sélim
Chorus and Orchestra of the Royal Opera House, Covent Garden / Mark Elder
Opera Rara ③ ORC33 (176' · DDD · S/T/t/N) Ⓕ**OO**

As is usual in this series, Jeremy Commons writes a well informed and judicious introductory essay, and he seems convinced. It was, he says, Donizetti's most ambitious opera. But the nature of that ambition is indicated by the remark of Donizetti which he has just quoted: 'If you could see what a frightening spectacle it presents: Portuguese, Arabs, Procession of Inquisitors, Royal Procession with funeral bier, the subterranean chambers of the Inquisition.' In other words, grand entertainment for the Paris Opéra: big, expensive, sensational. Preferable, surely, is the ambition which produced *Lucia di Lammermoor* and *Don Pasquale*.

The performance raises fewer questions, though enough is said about textual revisions for the Vienna premiere to make one wonder whether the Paris original is indeed always the best version. More immediately, some doubts arise about the casting. It seems strange that the major role of Camoëns (who on his return to Lisbon has one of the two best-known arias) should be given to a baritone whose voice-production is so unsteady when at hand is Simon Keenlyside, whose own role, well as he sings it, hardly makes best use of a singer of his quality. Something similar is true of Alastair Miles, whose sympathetic *basso cantante* is not a natural choice for the vindictive Grand Inquisitor. The two principals, however, are truly excellent: Kasarova so rich in voice and vivid in expression, Filianoti a tenor with brilliantly focused tone impressively supporting his place at the centre of the opera. Orchestra and chorus are at all times responsive, and Mark Elder conducts with energy and imagination. If you need convincing, here are three passages in which opera and

recording might be sampled at their best: Zayda's duets with Sébastien (Act 2) and with Abayaldos (Act 3), and the grand ensemble of Act 4.

Don Pasquale

Don Pasquale
Renato Bruson bar Don Pasquale **Eva Mei** sop Norina **Frank Lopardo** ten Ernesto **Thomas Allen** bar Malatesta **Alfredo Giacomotti** bass Notary **Bavarian Radio Chorus; Munich Radio Orchestra / Roberto Abbado**
RCA Victor Red Seal ② 09026 61924-2
(120' · DDD · T/t) Ⓕ

Roberto Abbado balances equally the witty and more serious sides of this score, finding a gratifying lightness in the 'A quel vecchio' section of the Act 1 finale and creating a delightful sense of expectancy as Pasquale preens himself while awaiting his intended bride. Abbado plays the score complete and respects Donizetti's intentions. This set has many strengths and few weaknesses. Pasquale is usually assigned to a veteran singer and with Bruson you hear a voice hardly touched by time and a technique still in perfect repair. Apart from weak low notes, he sings and acts the part with real face, and his vital diction is a pleasure to hear. He works well with Thomas Allen's nimble, wily Malatesta, an inspired piece of casting. Like Bruson, Allen sings every note truly and relishes his words.

Eva Mei's Norina is an ebullient creature with a smile in her tone. The edge to her voice seems just right for Norina though others may find it tends towards the acerbic under pressure. Her skills in coloratura are as exemplary as you would expect from a reigning Queen of the Night. Lopardo is that rare thing, a tenor who can sing in an exquisite half-voice, yet has the metal in his tone to suggest something heroic in 'È se fia', the cabaletta to 'Cercherò lontana terra', which in turn is sung in a plangent, loving way, just right. The recording here is exemplary.

L'elisir d'amore

L'elisir d'amore
Mariella Devia sop Adina **Roberto Alagna** ten Nemorino **Pietro Spagnoli** bar Belcore **Bruno Praticò** bar Dulcamara **Francesca Provvisionato** mez Giannetta **Tallis Chamber Choir; English Chamber Orchestra / Marcello Viotti**
Erato ② 4509 98483-2 (129' · DDD) Ⓜ**B→**

This set is a delight, making one fall in love all over again with this delightful comedy of pastoral life. Roberto Alagna, disciple of Pavarotti, sings Nemorino with all his mentor's charm and a rather lighter tone appropriate to the role. He also evinces just the right sense of vulnerability and false bravado that lies at the heart of Nemorino's predicament. He's partnered by Mariella Devia who has every characteristic needed for the role of Adina. With a fine sense of buoyant rhythm, she sings fleetly and uses the coloratura to enhance her reading. She can spin a long, elegiac line where it's needed, and her pure yet full tone blends well with that of her colleagues. She also suggests all Adina's high spirits and flirtatious nature. The other principals, though not as amusing in their interpretations as some predecessors, enter into the ensemble feeling of the performance. All are helped by the lively but controlled conducting of Viotti and by the ideal recording.

L'elisir d'amore
Mirella Freni sop Adina **Luigi Alva** ten Nemorino
Emily Maire sop Giannetta **Enzo Sordello** bar
Belcore **Sesto Bruscantini** bass Dulcamara
Glyndebourne Festival Chorus; Royal Philharmonic Orchestra / Carlo Felice Cillario
Glyndebourne Festival Opera mono ②
GFOCD005-62 (125' · ADD)
Recorded live in June 1962   Ⓕ

Glyndebourne's first go at *Elisir* at the start of the 1960s is an essentially un-serious affair, taking its cues from the pretty story-book naturalism of Franco Zeffirelli's staging, Bruscantini's always near-the-top Dulcamara and maestro Cillario's laid-back conducting. But real enjoyment is to be had from their combined experience. Cillario and his players (the RPO just after Beecham) are never over-heavy or thumpy, and Bruscantini is nearly always good to hear. Only the Act 2 barcarolle duet is a Venetian lagoon and a half too much, and the orchestra's stage banda sound like they've rivalled the audience in long-interval imbibing. But the real star is Freni – a gorgeous-voiced mix of tease, wit and seriousness, whose success in a role she kept in her repertoire until the 1980s was important in escalating her international career. And, mostly, Alva, whose more-upper-class-than-usual Nemorino is good at finding playboy self-illusion in the voice.

The basic sound feels its 47-year vintage, although careful transfer work has given important human and instrumental voices more space and presence than they might have had.

L'elisir d'amore (sung in English)
Mary Plazas sop Adina **Barry Banks** ten Nemorino
Ashley Holland bass Belcore **Andrew Shore** bar
Dulcamara **Helen Williams** sop Giannetta
Geoffrey Mitchell Choir; Philharmonia Orchestra / David Parry
Chandos Opera in English Series ② CHAN3027
(133' · DDD · T)   ⒻⒹ→

'Prima la musica' no doubt, but in this instance the words should perhaps take their share of the credit first. The late Arthur Jacobs, who was an expert on Arthur Sullivan, provides a translation that might almost be the work of WS Gilbert. A resourceful vocabulary and a keen ear for verbal rhythms are its main technical assets, and a natural sense of humour rather than the untiring facetiousness of a self-conscious clever-dick is the source of its wit. Dulcamara is a Gilbertian figure

to start with, so the translator isn't forcing an entrance for his hobby-horse, and any inventions are all in the spirit of the thing. The Gilbertian element emerges again when Andrew Shore, in the Barcarolle, sings his part of 'elderly Senator' in the tones of Sir Henry Lytton. Generally his portrayal is well sung and gracefully turned, as is Ashley Holland's Sergeant Belcore. The lovers have light, well-matched voices, Mary Plazas avoiding the pert, hard character-note and vocal tone that can make Adina so unsympathetic, and Barry Banks giving particular pleasure with the freedom and clarity of his upper notes.

The playing of the Philharmonia under David Parry calls for special remark: from the Overture onwards there are passages in the score that find a flavour, their own by rights but usually lost because not sought-out. The recording is one of the series' best.

L'elisir d'amore
Angela Gheorghiu sop Adina **Roberto Alagna** ten
Nemorino **Roberto Scaltriti** bar Belcore **Simone Alaimo** bass Dulcamara **Elena Dan** sop Giannetta
Lyon National Opera Chorus and Orchestra / Evelino Pidò Stage director **Frank Dunlop**
Video director **Brian Large**
Decca 🅳🆅🅳 074 103-9DH (177' · 16:9 · 2.0 & 5.1 · 0)
Includes documentary 'Love Potion', a behind-the-scenes look at the making of the production   Ⓕ

Frank Dunlop's witty, unvarnished view of Donizetti's country comedy, updated to the 1930s, is delightful to see, wondrous to hear. Gheorghiu and Alagna make an ideal partnership as capricious girl and shy bumpkin. They both act and sing their roles to near perfection in a staging that exposes the heart and heartlessness as much as the fun of this work.

Singing with every care for tone and nuance, Gheorghiu presents Adina as by turns haughty, flighty, concerned, annoyed when the other girls paw him, and finally tender when love at last triumphs, and she finds the vocal equivalent for each mood. Not so versatile vocally, but always tidy and responsive to the text, Alagna makes an attractively naive, emotionally vulnerable Nemorino. Scaltriti's Belcore is made deliberately unsympathetic by Dunlop and at times he seems to be overblowing his basically attractive voice. There need be no reservations about Alaimo's witty yet genial Dulcamara: all the *buffo* elements of the part are there but never exaggerated. Evelino Pidò conducts a trim account of the score, his often fast speeds justified by the way his singers enjoy them in terms of athletic delivery. Brian Large's video direction is predictably exemplary. The sound and widescreen picture make us feel present at an obviously enjoyable night at the opera.

La fille du régiment

La fille du régiment
Joan Sutherland sop Marie **Luciano Pavarotti** ten
Tonio **Spiro Malas** bass Sulpice **Monica Sinclair** contr

Marquise **Edith Coates** *contr* Duchess **Jules Bruyère**
bass Hortensius **Eric Garrett** *bar* Corporal **Alan
Jones** *ten* Peasant **Chorus and Orchestra of the
Royal Opera House, Covent Garden / Richard
Bonynge**
Decca ② 414 520-2DH2 (107' · ADD · T/t)
Recorded 1968   Ⓕ**OOɕ**

Even Joan Sutherland has rarely, if ever, made
an opera recording so totally enjoyable and
involving as this. With the same cast (including chorus and orchestra) as at Covent Garden, it was recorded immediately after a series
of live performances in the Royal Opera
House, and both the comedy and the pathos
come over with an intensity born of communication with live audiences. That impression is
the more vivid on this superb CD transfer. As
with some of Decca's early CD transfers, you
could do with more bands to separate items
and it strikes one as odd not to indicate separately the most spectacular of Luciano Pavarotti's contributions, his brief but important
solo in the finale to Act 1, which was the specific piece which prompted the much-advertised
boast 'King of the High Cs'. For those who
want to find it, it comes at 2'58" in track 13 of
the first disc. Dazzling as the young Pavarotti's
singing is, it's Sutherland's performance
which, above all, gives glamour to the set, for
here in the tomboy Marie she found a character through whom she could at once display
her vocal brilliance, her ability to convey
pathos and equally her sense of fun. The reunion of Marie with the men of her regiment and
later with Tonio makes one of the most heart-
warming operatic scenes on record.

The recording is one of Decca's most brilliant,
not perhaps quite so clear on inner detail as
some, but more atmospheric. Though there are
one or two deliberately comic touches that
approach the limit of vulgarity, the production is
generally admirable. The sound at once takes
one to the theatre, without any feeling of a cold,
empty studio.

Lucia di Lammermoor

Lucia di Lammermoor
Maria Callas *sop* Lucia **Ferruccio Tagliavini** *ten* Ⓗ
Edgardo **Piero Cappuccilli** *bar* Enrico **Bernard
Ladysz** *bass* Raimondo **Leonard del Ferro** *ten* Arturo
Margreta Elkins *mez* Alisa **Renzo Casellato** *ten*
Normanno **Philharmonia Chorus and Orchestra /
Tullio Serafin**
EMI Callas Edition ② 556284-2 (142 minutes · ADD ·
T/t). Recorded 1959
                        Ⓕ**OOOɕ**

Ⓖ   Callas was certainly more fallible here
    than in her first Lucia for Serafin in
    1953 but the subtleties of interpreta-
tion are much greater; she's the very epitome of
Scott's gentle yet ardently intense heroine, and
the special way she inflects words and notes lifts
every passage in which she's concerned out of

the ordinary gamut of soprano singing. In that
sense she's unique, and this is certainly one of
the first offerings to give to an innocent ear or a
doubter to help convince them of Callas's greatness. The earlier part of the Mad scene provides
the most convincing evidence of all. Then the
pathos of 'Alfin son tua', even more that of 'Del
ciel clemente' are here incredibly eloquent, and
the coloratura is finer than it was in 1953, if not
always so secure at the top. Tagliavini, after a
rocky start, offers a secure, pleasing, involving
Edgardo. Cappuccilli, then in his early prime, is
a forceful but not insensitive Enrico, Bernard
Ladysz a sound Raimondo. Serafin is a far more
thoughtful, expressive Donizettian than his
rivals on other sets, confirming this as the most
persuasive recorded account of the opera.

Additional recommendations

Lucia di Lamermoor   Ⓗ
Callas *Lucia* **di Stefano** *Edgardo* **Berlin RIAS
Symphony Orchestra / Karajan**
EMI mono ② 566438-2 (119' · ADD). Recorded live Ⓜ
   A great event: two great musicians striking sparks
   off each other. Karajan directs a white-hot per-
   formance and Callas sings with huge passion.

Sutherland *Lucia* **Pavarotti** *Edgardo* **ROHO /
Bonynge**
Decca ② 478 1513DH3 (140' · ADD). Recorded 1971
                        Ⓕ**OOɕ**
   Sutherland's second commercial recording finds
   her on great form in one of her signature roles.
   Pavarotti is a stylish Edgardo and Bonynge is the
   most sympathetic of conductors.

Lucrezia Borgia

Lucrezia Borgia
Edita Gruberová *sop* Lucrezia Borgia **Pavol Breslik**
ten Gennaro **Franco Vassallo** *bar* Don Alfonso **Alice
Coote** *contr* Orsini **Steven Humes** *bass* Gubetta
**Bavarian State Opera Chorus; Bavarian State
Orchestra / Bertrand de Billy**
Stage director **Christof Loy**
Medici Arts ② 𝐃𝐕𝐃 207 2458 (3h 7' · NTSC · 16:9 ·
PCM stereo, 5.1 · DTS 5.1 · 0). Recorded live at the
Nationaltheater, Munich, in July 2009
Includes bonus documentary, 'The Art of Bel canto:
Edita Gruberová' – a portrait by Claus Wischmann
and Stefan Pannen   Ⓕ

Christof Loy's serious contemporary production has simple modern clothes (mostly suits)
and little scenery apart from a back wall with the
inscription LUCREZIA BORGIA – important
for Gennaro's crime of removing the B – and
wooden-backed chairs. Entries, exits and who is
onstage are treated in deconstructionist fashion.
This is exciting in Act 2 where the constant
presence of the Duca (Alfonso) and his oily
henchman Rustighello at Princess Negroni's
party is not realistic but hugely underlines the
threat to Gennaro, Maffio Orsini and their

friends visiting Ferrara. When these young men are murdered by Borgia poison, they sit and turn facing upstage.

The Slovak soprano legend Edita Gruberová is now 63. Concentrating increasingly on *bel canto* roles, she's more singer than singing actress. In collaboration with Loy she produces a dramatic performance of concentration, at its most convincing in Act 2 where her age meshes well with the character of distraught mother. There are, of course, the odd slips of intonation but huge experience guides her through the role with style. The handsome Slovak tenor Pavol Breslik is a star Gennaro of passion and agility, and Alice Coote is a convincingly butch Maffio. The orchestra play richly for de Billy who sounds at home in this repertoire. Sound and Brian Large's filming do the project justice. The documentary has clips of early Gruberová on black-and-white Czech TV and whiles away a pleasant not-quite hour.

Maria Stuarda

Maria Stuarda
Laura Polverelli *sop* Elisabetta **Maria Pia Piscitelli** *sop* Maria Stuarda **Giovanna Lanza** *mez* Anna Kennedy **Roberto De Biasio** *ten* Roberto, conte di Leicester **Simone Alberghini** *bar* Talbot **Mario Cassi** *bass* Cecil **Coro Lirico Marchigiano 'V Bellini'; FORM (Orchestra Filarmonica Marchigiana) / Riccardo Frizza**
Naxos ② 8 660261/2 (117' · DDD)   ⓢ🔊

This release is the soundtrack of a Pier Luigi Pizzi production at the Sferisterio Opera Festival in August 2007, an outdoor event at a sizeable theatre in Macerata, Italy, a film of which has been released on Naxos DVD.

Ironically, here is very much the kind of ensemble performance at which, in the early Callas/Sutherland era, the movers and shakers of the London-orientated record industry would have sniffed loudly. Praise be, it has a cast full of real Italians. Maria Pia Piscitelli's red-blooded portrayal of Mary is suitably gracious and put-upon, and manages pride and inflexibility too. Act 2's 'Guarda: sui prati appare, o nube! che lieve per l'aria ti aggiri' and 'Nella pace del mesto riposo' are delivered with power, beauty and high notes to burn. Later in Act 3 Mary's confession to the disguised Talbot is well coloured and her progress to the scaffold emotional without recourse to self-pity. Roberto de Biasio is a charismatic yet evidently selfish Leicester. He has bright and secure Italianate tone with quick vibrato – like a voice from an earlier age – and an intelligent range of expression and tonal colour.

Laura Polverelli, enjoying the vocal acrobatics on offer, fields a more nuanced characterisation of Elisabetta than the vindictive, bitchy, jealous harpy the character can become in performance. Riccardo Frizza leads the proceedings with a stylish hand, encompassing the intriguing extra dimension of the third act, where Donizetti and librettist Giuseppe Bardari go some way towards presenting Mary's death as Catholic martyrdom. The recording is more than serviceably vivid for live performance conditions. Of course, no serious *bel canto* lover will turn their back on what Caballé, Gruberová and Sutherland have to offer on rival sets. But as an overall performance finely conducted and as an economical way of acquiring a compelling opera, the Naxos release is most useful.

Maria Stuarda (sung in English)
Janet Baker *mez* Maria Stuarda **Rosalind Plowright** *sop* Elisabetta **David Rendall** *ten* Leicester **John Tomlinson** *bass* Talbot **Alan Opie** *bar* Cecil **Angela Bostock** *sop* Anna **English National Opera Chorus and Orchestra / Sir Charles Mackerras**
Chandos Opera in English Series ② CHAN3017 (136' · ADD · N/t). Recorded live 1982   Ⓜ🔊

This revival celebrates the association of Janet Baker and Charles Mackerras within the context of the ENO company and one of its most memorable productions. For those who saw this, the set will call the stage back to mind with wonderful vividness; but the appeal goes well beyond that, preserving a performance stamped with the strong individuality that confers the status of a gramophone classic. This brought a personal triumph for Janet Baker and it impresses afresh by the distinctiveness of her vocal characterisation. It isn't every singer who reflects, or re-creates, the distinctive identities through vocal colour and 'registration'. Everyone who was there will remember the 'Royal bastard!' in confrontation with Elizabeth, but equally powerful, and more regal, is her command – 'Be silent! Leave me!' – to the Lord Chancellor of England who brings to Fotheringay news of her condemnation to death. By contrast, the quieter moments can be immensely moving, as, for instance, in the line in which she acknowledges an unexpected generosity in her great opponent. In that role, Rosalind Plowright gives what surely must have been one of the supreme performances of her career. The writing for Elizabeth makes immense demands of the singer, and in these fearsome opening solos the technical challenges are triumphantly met.

John Tomlinson's massive bass commands attention (which it doesn't then always reward with evenness of production). The male soloists have not the most grateful of roles, but Alan Opie's Cecil shows its quality in the duet with Elizabeth, and David Rendall endows the ineffectual Leicester with plenty of Italianate ardour. The chorus has limited opportunities, and has certainly been heard to better advantage on other occasions.

A word of warning must be added concerning texts which involve cuts and adaptations. The transpositions are defended as standard practice when an exceptional mezzo-soprano (such as Malibran) took a soprano role, in the present instance merely conforming to the lower orchestral pitch of Donizetti's time. However, it's unlikely that at this date the set would be bought or rejected with this kind of consideration foremost.

What remains are the strong positives, most notably the vitality of Mackerras's conducting and the glory of Baker's singing. Also, for those to whom this is a priority, the opera is given in clear English.

Parisina

Parisina
Carmen Giannattasio sop Parisina **José Bros** ten Ugo **Dario Solari** bar Azzo **Nicola Ulivieri** bass-bar Ernesto **Ann Taylor** mez Imelda **Geoffrey Mitchell Choir; London Philharmonic Orchestra / David Parry**
Opera Rara ③ ORC40 (162' · DDD · S/T/t/N) Ⓟ**OO**

Parisina's music was written in a hurry. The starry librettist Felice Romani, multi-commissioned into a schedule of Lorenzo da Ponte-type pressure, delivered late for the March 1833 Carnival season in Florence. He took the action from Byron's popular contemporary sex-and-jealousy poem. Parisina, the wife of Azzo, a 15th-century Duke of Ferrara, has fallen in love with Ugo, who will turn out to be a child of Azzo's previous marriage. Azzo's reaction to his wife's desired but never realised infidelity is to have Ugo murdered, and to present Parisina with the corpse in a manner that anticipates Puccini's *Tosca* and *Tabarro*.

The opera looks beyond decorative *bel canto* towards the urgent, direct style that would become Verdi's hallmark – an almost *verismo* approach in which, instead of leaving violence offstage to be described in torrents of beautiful (or mad) singing, the audience was confronted directly with the hero's murdered corpse.

While Acts 1 and 2 are substantial, Act 3 is manically (and brilliantly) short – an obvious forerunner of Verdi's desire to end an evening quickly – in its focus on Azzo's revenge. Opera Rara's recording is led by Carmen Giannattasio, a sometime student of Leyla Gencer. Her Act 3 defiance of Azzo, the ingenious *Romanza* in Act 2, and her fatalistic 'Forse un destin che intendere' are agile in decoration, expressive and well acted – a cunning piece of casting. The Spanish tenor José Bros displays enough metal in the voice to catch Ugo's Percy-like desperation in returning obsessively to Parisina's hostile court.

Uruguayan baritone Dario Solari is beautiful and supple in Azzo's Act 1 hymn to his wife, although he is a very cultivated bad guy in the *Otello*-like scene in Act 2 where he observes Parisina sleeping and overhears her muttering Ugo's name. Nicola Ulivieri's young, grainy yet flexible bass gives point to Ernesto's announcement of Ugo's true parentage. Parisina's lady in waiting, Imelda, is alertly taken by Ann Taylor's warm mezzo.

The horns at Parisina's entrance and the spooky bird-calls in Act 3, or the river 'traffic' in Act 2 which Verdi may well have recalled for Act 3 of *Aida*, show off Donizetti's imaginative use of scoring to second dramatic points. David Parry's well paced conducting is especially aware of these touches. Ardent Donizettians will have other *Parisinas* but the quality of the present recording, musically and technically, demands that cognoscenti should invest again, and should tempt those for whom the opera's name has remained merely an entry on a complete works list.

Poliuto

Poliuto   Ⓗ
Franco Corelli ten Poliuto **Maria Callas** sop Paolina **Ettore Bastianini** bar Severo **Nicola Zaccaria** bass Callistene **Piero de Palma** ten Nearco **Rinaldo Pelizzoni** ten Felice **Virgilio Carbonari, Giuseppe Morresi** basses Christians **Chorus and Orchestra of La Scala, Milan / Antonino Votto**
EMI mono ② 565448-2 (111' · ADD · T/t)
Recorded live 1960   Ⓜ

This is the first appearance of this recording in the official canon, by incorporation into EMI's Callas Edition; and the quality is certainly an improvement on the previous 'unofficial' incarnation. The sound is clear and faithful to the timbre of the voices, which are slightly favoured in the balance at the expense of the orchestra. With it comes unforgettable testimony to what was clearly a great night at La Scala. Its place in the Callas history owes less to the importance of this new role in her repertory than to the triumph of her return to the house she had left in high dudgeon in 1958. The part of Paolina in this Roman tragedy is restricted in opportunities and leaves the centre of the stage to the tenor. In other ways it suits her remarkably well, the second act in particular involving the heroine in grievous emotional stress with music that here runs deep enough to give it validity.

There's a big part for the chorus, which sings with fine Italian sonority. Nicola Zaccaria, La Scala's leading *basso cantabile*, has not quite the sumptuous quality of his predecessors, Pasero and Pinza, but is still in their tradition. Ettore Bastianini is rapturously received and, though wanting in polish and variety of expression, uses his firm and resonant voice to exciting effect. The tenor *comprimario* Piero de Palma cuts a by no means inadequate vocal figure by the side of Corelli, who's mostly stupendous: it isn't just the ring and range of voice that impress, but a genuinely responsive art, his aria 'Lasciando la terra' in Act 3 providing a fine example. It's for his part in the opera, quite as much as for Callas's, that the recording will be valued.

Rosmonda d'Inghilterra

Rosmonda d'Inghilterra
Renée Fleming sop Rosmonda **Bruce Ford** ten Enrico II **Nelly Miricioiu** sop Leonora di Guienna

Alastair Miles bass Gualtiero Clifford **Diana Montague** mez Arturo **Geoffrey Mitchell Choir; Philharmonia Orchestra / David Parry**
Opera Rara ② ORC13 (150' · DDD · T/t)　　Ⓕ

The performance of this, Donizetti's 41st opera, could hardly be improved. And there's scarcely more than a single item in which Donizetti seems not to be writing with genuine creativity. Parry conducts with what feels like a natural rightness and the playing of the Philharmonia is of unvaryingly high quality – the Overture is one of Donizetti's best, and the orchestral score shares interest on equable terms with the voice-parts. These include two virtuoso roles for sopranos, who in the final scene confront each other in duet. As Rosmonda, Renée Fleming shows once again that not only has she one of the most lovely voices of our time but that she's also a highly accomplished technician and a sympathetic stylist. Nelly Miricioiu is the older woman, the Queen whose music encompasses a wide range of emotions with an adaptable vocal character to match. She fits the second act more happily than the first, where for much of the time the tone appears to have lost its familiar incisive thrust. Bruce Ford is an excellent, incisive Enrico, and Alastair Miles makes an authoritative father and councillor as Clifford. The *travesto* role of Arturo is taken by the ever welcome Diana Montague, and it's good to find that a solo has been dutifully included for 'him' in Act 2, even if it's a less than inspired piece of music. The only complaint concerns balance, which sometimes accords prominence and recession in a somewhat arbitrary way. The opera and performance, however, are strong enough to take that on board.

Jonathan Dove　　British b1959

Jonathan Dove is best known as a composer of operas and choral music. His output includes a dozen operas, including the successful airport-comedy Flight, which premiered at Glyndebourne; it has since been broadcast on television and performed to acclaim in the Netherlands and Belgium, and has recently received its US premiere at the St Louis Opera. He has arranged a number of operas for English Touring Opera and the City of Birmingham Touring Opera (now Birmingham Opera Company), including in 1990 an 18-player two-evening adaptation of Wagner's Der Ring des Nibelungen.

Operas

Siren Song
Brad Cooper ten Davey Palmer **Mattijs van de Woerd** bar Jonathan Reed **Amaryllis Dieltiens** sop Diana Reed **Mark Omvlee** ten Regulator **Marijn Zwitserlood** bass-bar Captain **John Edward Serrano** spkr Wireless Operator
Siren Ensemble / Henk Guittart
Chandos CHAN10472 (78' · DDD · S/T/N)

Recorded live at the Grachtenfestival, Amsterdam, in August 2007　　ⒻⒷ▶

Not since Benjamin Britten has a British composer succeeded in writing operas which communicate with such clarity and coherence to their audience as those by Jonathan Dove. The secret to his success lies partly in his experiences of writing 'community' operas, resulting in refreshingly open and accessible works. But there's also plenty of grit and grime beneath the polished veneer of his streamlined style, especially when the plot is as equally compelling and disturbing as it is in *Siren Song*.

The opera recounts the true story of a Royal Navy sailor (Davey) who becomes the victim of an elaborate hoax. Duped by means of letter exchanges into believing that the beautiful and alluring Diana lies waiting for him on terra firma upon completing Navy service, the hapless sailor parts with thousands of pounds in anticipation of marital bliss, all of which lines the pockets of Jonathan, the perpetrator of this ruse.

Dove's dramatic skill lies in his ability to create a seamless continuity by weaving cell-like musical figures from one scene to the next. His subtle manipulation of an undulating pattern first heard in the opening seascape scene is adapted to accompany a whole host of other states and situations. Given the seafaring setting, it's hardly surprising that echoes of Debussy's *La mer*, Britten's *Peter Grimes* and Adams's *The Death of Klinghoffer* rise to the surface. Dove also shares with the latter composer an ability to generate large-scale structures from the simplest of musical means. But it is testimony to the Englishman's eclecticism that he skilfully appropriates such references into a language undeniably his own.

This live recording possesses its fair share of onstage clanks and offstage coughs, but at least they all lend an air of vraisemblance to proceedings, and the opera's rapid descent into the depths of deceit and desperation is effectively portrayed, despite the absence of visuals.

The Adventures of Pinocchio
Victoria Simmonds mez Pinocchio **Jonathan Summers** bar Geppetto **Mary Plazas** sop Blue Fairy **Rebecca Bottone** sop Cricket, Parrot **Graeme Broadbent** bass Puppeteer, Ape-Judge, Ringmaster, Big Green Fisherman **Allan Clayton** ten Lampwick **Mark Wilde** ten Cat **James Laing** counterten Fox, Coachman **Carole Wilson** mez Pigeon, Snail
Chorus and Orchestra of Opera North / David Parry
Stage director **Martin Duncan**
Opus Arte ② 📀 OA1005D (3h 33' · NTSC · 16:9 · PCM stereo and DTS 5.1 · 0)　　Ⓕ
Recorded live at Sadler's Wells Theatre, London, in 2008. Includes Interviews, Synopsis and Cast gallery

The story of Pinocchio, as told by Carlo Collodi, is best known through the Disney cartoon version, an equivocal movie generally less sympathetic than other Disney features, but giving a graphic if partial view of the story. Jonathan Dove with his librettist, Alasdair Middleton, in this operatic version in two substantial acts gives a much fuller idea of the story, starting with the moment when Gepetto the woodman finds a talking log in the forest.

Gepetto is about to chop it up when it speaks to him demanding that he preserve it, later demanding that he should bring out the secret it contains, nothing less than the puppet, Pinocchio, who kicks him as his legs appear. Dove tells the story in brief scenes, 12 in Act 1, nine in Act 2, which carry the story on swiftly and effectively, going on to one sequence involving a circus – cue for pastiche circus music – and one when Pinocchio and Gepetto are trapped inside a whale, from which they escape thanks to Pinocchio's cunning in realising that this asthmatic animal is asleep with its mouth open. Generally the scenes follow the development of Pinocchio from rebellious puppet to kind and considerate boy.

Dove's writing characteristically is colourful and vigorous, with inventive instrumentation, as when Pinocchio refuses to pull a cart when asked by a stranger, denying that he is a donkey – at which Dove has the orchestra briefly making a hee-haw sound. Dove's sharp, jazzy syncopations add to the attractions of the writing, which is generally easily lyrical. This, believe it or not, is Dove's 21st opera, though few are as long or ambitious as this one, which was written for Opera North and given its premiere in 2007.

The performance, filmed live, is excellent, with a cast which includes a number of the singers discovered by the Peter Moores Foundation, and conducted very ably by David Parry, the Foundation's regular conductor. A very welcome issue of a most attractive new opera.

John Dowland   English c1563-1626

During his life Dowland was known as much for his virtuoso lute-playing and his singing as he was for his music. Like many of his musical contemporaries he was much-travelled: he served the English ambassador in Paris (1580-84) and travelled in Europe, visiting the courts of Brunswick, Kassel, Nuremberg and cities in Italy. From 1598 Dowland worked at the court of Christian IV of Denmark, though he continued to publish in London. King Christian paid Dowland astronomical sums; his salary was 500 daler a year, making him one of the highest-paid servants of the Danish court. Though Dowland was highly regarded by King Christian, he was not the ideal servant, often overstaying his leave when he went to England on publishing business or for other reasons. This led to his dismissal in 1606 and he returned to England. In early 1612 he secured a post as one of James I's lutenists. There are few compositions dating from the moment of his royal appointment until his death in London in 1626: while the date of his burial is recorded, the exact date of his death is not known. Two major influences on Dowland's music were the popular consort songs and the

dance music of the day. Most of Dowland's music is for his own instrument, the lute. It includes several books of solo lute works, lute songs (for one voice and lute), part-songs with lute accompaniment, and several pieces for viol consort with lute.

Lute Works

A Fancy, P73. Pavana Dowlandi Angli. Doulands ▣ rounde battell galyarde, P39. The Erle of Darbies galliard, P44. Mistris Norrishis delight, P77. A Jig, P78. Galliard, P76. Une jeune fillette, P93. Gagliarda, P103. Squires galliard. A Fancy, P72. Sir Henry Umptons funerall. Captayne Pipers galliard, P88. A Fantasie, P1 **Bacheler** (arr ?) The Earl of Essex galliard, P89 **Moritz, Landgrave of Hessen** (arr Dowland?) Pavin **Joachim Van Den Hove** Pavana Lachrimae **Holborne** Hasellwoods galliard **R Dowland** Sir Thomas Monson, his Pavin and Galliard. Almande
Paul O'Dette *lte*
Harmonia Mundi HMU90 7164 (73' · DDD)   Ⓕ

Given the odd transmission of John Dowland's lute music, any 'complete' recording of it is inevitably going to include a fair number of works that can have had little to do with him. Paul O'Dette has boldly put most of these together in his fifth and last volume, adding for good measure the three surviving works of the master's son, Robert Dowland. O'Dette is engagingly candid in expressing his views about the various works and their various degrees of authenticity. The only works he seems to think authentic are the *Sir Thomas Monson* pavan and galliard that survive only under the name of Robert Dowland. The collection is none the less fascinating for all that. They are nearly all thoroughly worthwhile pieces, some of them very good indeed; and he ends with what he considers a late adaptation of one of Dowland's most famous fantasies. O'Dette continues to show that in terms of sheer freedom of technique he's hard to challenge among today's lutenists: the often complicated counterpoint is always crystal clear and he invariably conveys the strongest possible feeling for the formal design of the works. Anyone who's fascinated by the work of the prince of lutenists will want to have this disc.

Preludium, P98. Fantasias – P6; P71. Pavans – ▣ Lachrimae, P15; The Lady Russell's Pavan, P17; Pavana Johan Douland, P94; La mia Barbara, P95. Galliards – Frog Galliard, P23; Galliard (upon a galliard by Dan Bachelar), P28; The Lord Viscount Lisle, his Galliard, P38; The Earl of Essex, his Galliard, P42a; Galliard to Lachrimae, P46; A Galliard, P82; Galliard on 'Awake sweet love', P92. An Almand, P96. My Lord Willoughby's Welcome Home, P66a. Loth to departe, P69. The Shoemakers Wife, a Toy, P58. Coranto, P100. Come away, P60
Paul O'Dette *lte*
Harmonia Mundi HMU90 7163 (64' · DDD)   Ⓕ

Cadential trills played on one string are a recurrent problem for performers; the less well equipped use a *rallentando* or slur them, while guitarists tend to play them across two strings. No one is more adept at delivering them cleanly and in tempo than O'Dette. It's in the suppleness of his phrasing, clarity of his contrapuntal lines and attention to the functional purpose of every note that he's pre-eminent – and has the edge over Lindberg. This disc has all the virtues of its predecessors, and though it's doubtful that the Earl of Essex would have been happy to dance his galliard at O'Dette's pace, you can share the sentiment of its last track – you'll be loath to leave it.

'A Dream'
Almains – Sir John Smith his Almain, P47; My Lady Hunsdons Allmande (Puffe), P54. Settings of Ballads and Other Popular Tunes – Fortune my foe, P62. Fantasies and Other Contrapuntal Pieces – Fantasie, P1; Farwell, P3; A Fancy, P73. Galliards – Melancholy Galliard, P25; Galliard (upon a galliard by Dan Bachelar), P28; The Battle Galliard (The King of Denmarke his Galliard), P40; K Darcyes Galliard, P41; The Earl of Essex his Galliard, P42; The Right Honourable Lady Rich her Galliard, P43; The Right Honourable the Lady Cliftons Spirit, P45. Frogg Galliard, P90. Jigs, Corantos, Toys, etc – Mrs Whites Nothing, P56. Pavans – Semper Dowland Semper Dolens, P9; Lachrimae, P15; A Dream, P75; La mia Barbara, P95 **Moritz** Pavan
Hopkinson Smith *lte*
Naïve E8896 (69' · DDD)　　　　　　　　　Ⓕ

Hopkinson Smith's latest collection, 'A Dream', invites the listener '…to penetrate the world of the inner senses that is the domain of the lute'. An elegantly constructed programme (built around groups of Hilliard-like portraits and melancholy flights of fancy) tropes sonnet-like at the wonderful *Farwell*, a magical, troubling fantasy that treats its chromatically rising theme contrapuntally while somehow tying all the preceding emotional strands in the programme together. This propels the listener lachrymoneously (*sic* – Smith's word) into an even darker dwelling-place than was expected. In fact, this is the genius of the disc, and what makes it a genuinely moving experience.

Smith's playing, too, is elegant rather than overtly virtuoso, although he has technique to burn, as anyone who's familiar with his numerous recordings will tell you. He prefers a more suggestive, diffuse approach to Dowland's music (compared with, say, Paul O'Dette). As a result, the numerous diminutions serve to intensify the character of each piece in a profound and subtle way.

Lute Songs

The First Booke of Songes or Ayres – If my　　　Ⓟ
complaints could passions moue; Can she excuse my wrongs with vertues cloake; Deare if you change ile neuer chuse againe; Go Cristall teares; Sleepe wayward thoughts; All ye whom loue or fortune hath betraide; Come againe: sweet loue doth now enuite; Awake sweet loue thou art returnd. The Second

Booke of Songs or Ayres – I saw my Lady weepe; Flow my teares fall from your springs; Sorrow sorrow stay, lend true repentant teares; Tymes eldest sonne, old age the heire of ease; Then sit thee down, and say thy 'Nunc Dimitis'; When others sings 'Venite exultemus'; If fluds of tears could clense my follies past; Fine knacks for Ladies, cheap, choise, braue and new; Come ye heavie states of night; Shall I sue, shall I seeke for grace
Paul Agnew *ten* **Christopher Wilson** *lte*　　　Ⓕ
Metronome METCD1010 (59' · DDD · T)

Paul Agnew is light of step in the quicker songs, and he languishes longer than most over the variously sorrowful ones. Many of his choices now enjoy 'pop' status, but his inclusion of the beautiful trilogy of which 'Tymes eldest sonne' is the first part is particularly welcome. He receives the most sensitive of support from Wilson, clearly articulated, warm in tone, and perfectly complementary in completing the contrapuntal textures – neither intrusively nor coyly balanced with the voice. Dowland's lute songs have generated many fine recordings, as they richly deserve, and here's one more, beautifully presented, with a booklet containing all the texts.

Lachrimae, or Seaven Teares

Lachrimae, or Seaven Teares.　　　　　　　　　Ⓟ
First Booke of Songs[a] – Come heavy sleepe; Go teares. Second Booke of Songs[a] – Sorrow stay; I saw my Lady weepe; Flow my teares
Paul O'Dette *lte* **The King's Noyse** ([a]Ellen Hargis *sop* Robert Mealy, Scott Metcalfe, Margriet Tindemans *vas* Emily Walhout *bvn*) **David Douglass** *vn*
Harmonia Mundi HMU90 7275 (75' · DDD · T/t) ⒻⓄⓄ

The Seaven Teares are the heart of *Lachrimae*; the purpose of the other 14 items is unknown – were they intended to be played together with the Pavans, and if so, in what order?

This present recording is superb in every way. Ellen Hargis sings in sensitive response to her texts and her diction is almost clear enough to make the printed ones in the inlay booklet redundant. The violins of The King's Noyse have a rounder and less edgy sound than those of the Parley of Instruments, and their dynamic ebb and flow is as eloquent as that of Ellen Hargis's voice. The recording itself and the annotation are superb.

With so many options available you pays your money and you takes your choice. Our choice rests firmly with this recording.

Rihards Dubra　　　　　　　Latvian *b*1964

Born in Riga, Dubra lives in Jurmala where he started piano studies at the Music School aged seven. He continued his studies of music theory at the Emils Darzins Special Music School in Riga, and studied composition with Adolfs Skulte at the Latvian Music

Academy and finally at the Latvian Music Academy where he graduated with an MA in composition. He also worked as a teacher of music theory and composition at the Music College in Jurmala. Much of his music is sacred.

Vocal Works

'Hail, Queen of Heaven'
Oculus non vidit. Ave Maria I. Ave Maria III. Miserere mei. Hail, Queen of Heaven. Duo Seraphim. Felix namque es. Stetit Angelus. Gloria Patri. Missa de Spiritu Sancto. Ubi caritas
Royal Holloway Choir / Rupert Gough with **Alexander Norman** org
Hyperion CDA67799 (66' · DDD · T/t)　　　🄯🅑➜

In this so-called postmodern age (and in the case of Latvian composer Rihards Dubra, a post-Soviet age of religious freedom), the rediscovery of a numinous aesthetic inspired by the Middle Ages and the Renaissance has fuelled the creation of a new wave of tonally based church music, one that has ignited a popularity among choirs not only for its pragmatism but also for its exploration of new techniques and reinterpretations of older precepts (one thinks here especially of Tavener, Pärt and Gabriel Jackson). Simplicity is often central to Dubra's structural conceptions of pieces such as *Oculus non vidit*, the luminously tonal *Ave Maria III* and the more baldly minimalist-conceived *Gloria Patri*. Much of Dubra's harmonic world is transparently diatonic, as are many of his progressions, but his most profound effects are often derived from carefully placed moments of chromaticism, ethereal aleatoric passages, mantra-like repetitions, sonorous parallelisms, unusual chordal doublings, striking 'sound moments' of rapturous texture (such as the word 'Christ' in *Hail, Queen of Heaven*, by far the most substantial piece in this programme) and closely knit processes of suspension and resolution (take the *Kyrie* of the *Missa de Spiritu Sancto*). Dubra's natural home is a mood of controlled meditation and lyrical clarity as in *Felix namque es* and the more overtly experimental rhythmical and textural techniques of *Stetit Angelus* but, at times, a more lively exuberance is evident in *Duo Seraphim*. This style is well handled by the Choir of Royal Holloway, whose clean-edged sound, under Gough's sympathetic direction, warms to the generous acoustic of St Alban's, Holborn.

Guillaume Dufay　　　French c1400-1474

As the central figure in the Burgundian School, he was the most famous and influential composer in Europe in the mid-15th century. He trained as a chorister at Cambrai Cathedral, and later appears to have entered the service of the Malatesta family in Pesaro. After a brief return to Cambrai, he was back in Italy – in Bologna and Rome. During this period *Dufay also began his long association with the Este family in Ferrara, some of the most important musical patrons of the Renaissance, with whom he probably had become acquainted during the days of his association with the Malatesta family; Rimini and Ferrara are not only geographically close, but the two families were related by marriage, and Dufay composed at least one ballade for Niccolò III, Marquis of Ferrara. He spent his later years back at Cambrai, where he was visited – such was his fame – by such musicians as Binchois, Tinctoris and Ockeghem.*

Dufay wrote in most of the common forms of the day, including Masses, motets, Magnificats and hymns. None of his surviving music is specifically instrumental, although instruments were certainly used for some of his secular music, especially for the lower parts; all of his sacred music is vocal.

Sacred Music

'Sacred Music from Bologna, Q15'
O sancte Sebastiane. Supremum est mortalibus bonum. Vasilissa, ergo gaude. O gemma, lux et speculum. Kyrie, 'Fons bonitatis'. O beate Sebastiane. Gloria, Q15 No 107. Credo, Q15 No 108. Sanctus and Benedictus, Q15 No 104. Inclita stella maris. Agnus Dei, Q15 No 105. Gloria, 'Spiritus et alme'
The Clerks' Group (William Missin *counterten* Lucy Ballard *alt* Chris Watson, Matthew Vine *tens* Jonathan Arnold *bass*) / **Edward Wickham** *bass*
Signum SIGCD023 (60' · DDD · T/t)　　　🄯🄾🅑➜

This recording focuses on sacred works by Dufay from a 15th-century manuscript preserved at Bologna and known as Q15. This is a complex source, compiled over a number of years in northern Italy, and containing a wide range of polyphonic repertory, including diverse works by the great Dufay.

This CD isn't in any sense a reconstruction but a carefully selected anthology of not necessarily very familiar pieces by Dufay. Indeed, this is a really superb recording: vocal lines are well shaped and the sonorities achieved through accuracy of ensemble and pacing result in performances that are decidedly sensual, even dance-like, at times.

Just try the four-voice *Gloria* or the isorhythmic motet *Supremum est mortalibus bonum*, in praise of peace. This extraordinary work, composed to commemorate the signing of a peace treaty between the Pope and Holy Roman Emperor-elect in 1433, combines just about every musical technique and idiom available to a composer in the first half of the 15th century, complete with, in this interpretation by The Clerks' Group, improvised vocal flourishes on the block chords declaiming the names of the signatories.

Vocal agility – notably in the faster-moving upper parts of *Inclita stella maris* – and a text-centred intensity of projection are hallmarks of this excellent group: only in the three-voice setting of *O beate Sebastiane*, a plea for delivery from the plague, does the approach seem too cool. Elsewhere, even in familiar texts such as the

Sanctus, there's a real sense of engagement. If you've yet to discover the delights of Dufay, this is an excellent place to start; Dufay fans can't fail to be delighted.

Missa Se la face ay pale. Venite benedicti. Gloriosus Deus. Iudicabunt sancti. Mirabilis Deus. Gaudete iusti. O très piteulx. Se la face ay pale. Magnanime gentis
Binchois Consort (Mark Chambers, William Towers *altos* George Pooley, Christopher Watson, Edwin Simpson, Matthew Vine *tens* Giles Underwood, William Gaunt *basses*) / **Andrew Kirkman**
Hyperion CDA67715 (72' · DDD)　　　Ⓕ●Ⓞ→

Se la face ay pale remains Dufay's most approachable Mass – very much a tune with accompaniment, one that is assembled as though elegance of line was Dufay's main criterion of musical excellence. And Andrew Kirkman chooses to treat it as such: at least, he essentially persuades the singers on the contratenor line to keep well down so that borrowed melody in the tenor can come through while allowing the top line to stand out as it must. What the Binchois Consort do here sounds both transparent and natural. The balance is superb; and all lines are presented in a free and supple manner that projects the music very well. This is easy, effortless musicianship.

Meanwhile Kirkman intersperses the five Ordinary movements with movements for the Proper for St Maurice. Much of the music is in three or two voices only, so sounding different from the *Missa Se la face ay pale* and contrasting with it neatly. Only the glowing Offertory is in four voices. Metrical complexities in the *Alleluia* and in the *Offertory* add neat spice to the music. Special credit here should be given to the soloists who sing the long and exposed duos: these have lines and phrases that seem to go on for ever, so they are astonishingly hard to sing, and these musicians do them marvellously.

To fill out the disc they perform three more Dufay pieces that can be associated with the court of Savoy: the song *Se la face ay pale* is heard in the rarer four-voice version that may not have anything to do with Dufay but is delightful and eminently worth hearing, especially in a spirited performance like this; the famous *Lament for Constantinople*, a touch less transparent than one might wish; and the motet *Magnanime gentis*, sounding as though it was done in a hurry at the end of an exhausting session.

'The Fall of Constantinople'
Anonymous Hierarchical Entrance Rite for a Byzantine Divine Liturgy. Kyrie **Dufay** Vasilissa ergo gaude. Apostolo glorioso. Ecclesiae militantis. Lamentatio Sanctae Matris Ecclesiae Constantinopolitanae **Manuel Chrysaphes the Lampadarios** Lament for the Fall of Constantinople **Manuel Gazes the Lampadarios** Hymn for Great Compline **Plousiadenos** Canon in honour of Thomas Aquinas: Ode 1. Communion Verse for Mid-Pentecost. Canon for the Council of Florence: Ode 5

Cappella Romana / Alexander Lingas
Cappella Romana CR402CD (74' · DDD)　　　Ⓕ

English-speaking audiences commonly associate Greek Orthodox plainchant with the music of John Tavener, whose work draws substantially from its ethos. This recording confronts plainchant with the compositions of another Western composer, albeit one from the 15th century, when the two Christian churches were nearly reunited after a thousand-year split. It's even likely that Dufay's singers and their Eastern counterparts had a chance to hear each other in Florence. But these attempts at reconciliation came to nothing, and in 1453 came the event after which this disc is named, and to which Dufay devoted a commemorative lament, which concludes this recital very movingly.

The performance of Western polyphony with voices trained in, or inflected by, Eastern chant is not unfamiliar – Ensemble Organum have been doing it for years. To do so, it's not necessary to invoke a context within which the two might have commingled; as Alexander Lingas observes in his informative note, it's likely that the Greeks found Dufay's polyphony 'incomprehensible'. But it must have been a fascinating confrontation, and it's that sense of occasion that's conveyed here. The range of performance options for the plainchant itself is surprisingly diverse, and an intriguing new light is shed on Dufay's motets: the five-voice *Apostolo glorioso* is particularly striking, although *Ecclesiae militantis* is a touch less sure. The singers are miked more distantly than is usual nowadays for polyphony, but this only adds to the sense of pleasurable unfamiliarity.

Jacques Duphly　　French 1715-1789

Duphly was a French harpsichordist and organist, and the composer of bright, vivacious and attractive keyboard music. An early aptitude as a keyboard player suggested to him that he would do better as a specialist of the harpsichord in Paris than as an organist in Rouen. So in 1742 he settled in Paris, making his name as a harpsichordist, teacher and composer. He was praised for his light touch and a great ability to bring out the character of the pieces. He was considered by Pascal Taskin, the harpsichord maker, to be one of the best teachers in Paris.

He started publishing books of original harpsichord music in 1744. His popularity continued to increase into the 1760s, and he published more: in all, he published four volumes of harpsichord music (1744, 1748, 1756 and 1768). Book 4 of his harpsichord music contains the enchanting (and still regularly played today) rondeau, 'La Pothoüin'.

Harpsichord works

Allemandes – in C; in D. Courante. Courante La Boucon. Chaconne. La de Belombre. La Félix. La

Forqueray. Les Grâces. Médée. La Millettina.
Rondeau. Rondeau: La Pothoüin. La Vanlo
Elisabeth Joyé hpd
Alpha ALPHA150 (75' · DDD)   Ⓕ🅱➡

There are three stars on this beautiful harpsichord disc: Elisabeth Joyé, whose playing is a
model of graceful musicianship; Jacques Duphly,
a composer from the post-Rameau, final decades
of the French harpsichord era; and a superbly
voiced anonymous 18th-century French harpsichord from the chateau d'Assas, near Montpellier.

Joyé has chosen 14 pieces from the four books
Duphly published between 1744 and 1768, and
though athletic numbers such as the demonic
Médée, the whirling *La de Belombre* and the
Scarlatti-esque *La Vanlo* duly appear, her decision to balance them with gentler creations such
as *Les Grâces*, *La Pothoüin*, rondeaux and two
finely turned Allemande-Courante pairings
gives her the chance to show off both the wondrous sound of her historic instrument – mellow, richly characterful of tone, each note with a
firm but kindly attack – and the easy gait of her
own playing. Joyé's way with the music is calm,
not prone to exciting extremes and beautifully
attuned to this particular music and instrument;
the way she allows the splendid Chaconne to
gather effect with assured and unhurried step is
truly compelling. This release – as ever, stunningly presented by Alpha – should be a harpsichord lover's treat.

Paul Dukas   French 1865-1935

*Dukas puts in a strong challenge for the 'most boring
life of a composer' award. He devoted all his life to
studying, teaching and composing music in Paris, a
mild-mannered, self-centred man. He was certainly
self-critical: he completed very little music after 1910
and just before his death destroyed most of what he had
written. As well as his hugely popular L'apprenti sorcier (1897), his finest works are his mammoth Piano
Sonata (1900), the opera Ariane et Barbe-Bleue
(1907) and an exotic ballet La péri (1912). As a critic
he was known for his breadth of sympathy and as a
scholar he was a scrupulous editor of Beethoven,
Couperin, Rameau and Scarlatti.*

The Sorcerer's Apprentice

Dukas The Sorcerer's Apprentice
Saint-Saëns Symphony No 3, 'Organ'
Simon Preston org
Berlin Philharmonic Orchestra / James Levine
DG 419 617-2GH (47' · DDD)   Ⓕ🅱➡

Levine's account of Dukas's masterpiece is still
the best in the catalogue. He chooses a fast basic
tempo but justifies his speed by the lightness of
his touch; and the clean articulation and rhythmic
bounce of the Berlin Phil's playing help consider-

ably. The climax is thrilling, but Levine reserves
something for the moment when the sorcerer
returns to quell the flood. In all, it provides a
marvellous finish to an exhilarating listening
experience. Levine's performance of Saint-
Saëns's Third Symphony is also among the best
available. The balance between the orchestra and
organ, here played powerfully by Simon Preston,
is well judged and the overall acoustic very convincing. Levine directs a grippingly individual
reading, full of drama and with a consistently
imaginative response to the score's detail. The
organ entry in the finale is quite magnificent, the
excitement of Preston's thundering out the main
theme physical in its impact. The music expands
and blossoms magnificently, helped by the spectacular dynamic range of the recording.

Piano Sonata

Dukas Piano Sonata **Decaux** Clairs de lune
Marc-André Hamelin pf
Hyperion CDA67513 (65' · DDD)   Ⓕ🅱➡

Dukas's E flat minor Sonata (1900) is a rare
(the only?) French example of the form from
this period. Lasting more than 45 minutes,
each of its four movements is underpinned by
almost unremitting motion. The chromaticism of the first owes an obvious debt to
Franck; the second has prescient touches of
Scriabin and Debussy; the outer sections of the
third are an Alkanesque toccata with a haunting *mystérieuse* central section, while the
equally virtuoso finale shows that while Dukas
remains firmly his own man, he also knew his
Schumann and Liszt.

Hamelin, one needs hardly say, makes light of
any difficulty, clarifying complex textures and
subtly highlighting different voices with myriad keyboard colours. It is this facility that
sometimes leads to a certain coolness and lack
of (audible) engagement. Not here: this performance has an expressive power and intense
emotional involvement that make it one of his
most successful recordings – and that is saying
something.

For those who have never previously encountered Dukas's companion on this CD, Abel
Decaux (1869-1943) – and you'd not be alone
– was a French organist (pupil of Widor and
Guilmant) who studied composition with
Massenet. What the composer of *Manon* and
Werther would have made of the four pieces
that comprise *Clairs de lune* (note the plural),
one can only guess. Written between 1900 and
1907, they were not published till a year after
Massenet's death in 1912. Listen blindfold and
you might think, as Roger Nichols points out
in his informative notes, that you were listening to Schoenberg or Debussy – except that
Decaux's pieces pre-date both of them. Not
for everyday listening, but fascinating nevertheless and a further example of this great pianist's extraordinary musical *savoir faire* and his
invaluable, unflagging curiosity.

Ariane et Barbe-Bleu

Ariane et Barbe-Bleu
Lori Phillips sop Ariane **Patricia Bardon** mez Nurse
Peter Rose bass Barbe-Bleu **Laura Vlasak Nolen**
mez Sélysette **Ana James** sop Ygraine **Daphne**
Touchais sop Mélisande **Sarah-Jane Davies** sop
Bellangère **Graeme Danby** bass Old Peasant **BBC**
Singers and Symphony Orchestra / Leon Botstein
Telarc ② CD80680 (115' · DDD · S/T/t/N)   ⒻO▷

If you think the libretto of *Pelléas et Mélisande* is
impenetrable, try making sense of this: Maurice
Maeterlinck's 'prequel' in which Mélisande is one
of Bluebeard's imprisoned wives. They are rescued
by his latest victim, Ariane, but refuse to leave their
tormentor; they prefer his dark castle to the threat
posed by the world outside, to which, at the final
curtain, Ariane and her faithful nurse return.

Georgette Leblanc, Maeterlinck's longtime
companion, had been disappointed not to get the
role of Mélisande in Debussy's opera in 1902, and
there is some feeling that Maeterlinck was offering her a consolation prize – she sang the title-
role at the Opéra-Comique premiere in 1907.
Ariane is seldom offstage – conversely, Bluebeard
hardly appears, and has only a few lines to sing.
There is very little action as such, although the
crowd of angry peasants break in occasionally
with threats against their monstrous lord.

The effect is more like a symphonic poem.
There are wonderful moments: when Ariane
unlocks the doors of the rooms containing gems;
when she breaks open the window and lets light
into the dungeon; and in the long final scene as
she slowly leaves Bluebeard and his harem to
their fate. The subject matter – sexual abuse, the
victim's need for their torturer, and the power of
suggestion – ought to make the opera attractive
for an imaginative theatre director. Leon Botstein makes the strongest possible case for the
opera in this new recording, the BBC SO playing Dukas's elaborate score with great élan.

Lori Phillips sings Ariane with great feeling; her
voice is rather too similar to that of Patricia Bardon
as the Nurse, who also makes a strong impression.
Of the other wives, not all of whom sing, Laura
Vlasak Nolen has the most substantial part as Sélysette, who declares 'Oh! Tu es pâle, Mélisande…ta
robe est en lambeaux', as if she were anticipating
Pelléas's words in Debussy's opera.

It would be easy to ridicule some of the more
obvious psychological symbolism with which
Maeterlinck has weighed down his story and it
was destined to be Dukas's only completed
opera. But if you have never encountered *Ariane*
et Barbe-Bleu it is an instructive and rewarding
experience.

Henry Du Mont   French 1610-1684

After early posts as organist at Maastricht Cathedral
and study in Liège, Henry De Thier moved to Paris
as organist at St Paul and later compositeur de
musique de la Chapelle Royale and maître de la
musique de la Reine. From this time he used the
name Du Mont (or Dumont) in place of De Thier.
From 1652 he was harpsichordist at the court of the
Duke of Anjou (Philippe I, Duke of Orléans, a
brother of Louis XIV), and in 1660 he obtained that
post to the young queen Marie-Thérése. In 1663 he
became 'maître' of the Chapelle Royale in Versailles,
in 1672 he became sous-maître de la musique du Roy
(with Pierre Robert) and in 1673 he became Master
of the Queen's Music. He is best-known for his sacred
music and above all for his motets.

Grands motets

'Grands motets pour la chapelle de
Louis XIV au Louvre'
Allemandes. Allemande grave. Dialogus de anima.
Super flumina Babylonis. Benedic anima mea. Ecce
iste venit. Pavane
Pierre Robert Ensemble / Frédéric Desenclos org
Alpha ALPHA069 (73' · DDD · T/t)   ⒻOO

Henry Du Mont has long been credited as one
of the creators, alongside Lully, of the *grand*
motet, the opulent style of church composition
for soloists, choir and orchestra associated with
Louis XIV's chapel at Versailles. The Pierre
Robert Ensemble take a different view. Noting
that Du Mont's 20 *Motets pour la Chapelle du Roy*,
printed two years after his death in 1684, contain the kind of clumsy viola parts reconcilable
with the work of a publisher's hack, they propose that such 'posthumous tawdry' can be dispensed with to reveal the originals as more intimate works for five solo singers, two violins and
continuo, probably written for pre-Versailles
times at the Louvre palace. It's in this form that
they present three of the motets here, emphasising their argument by adding the semi-dramatic
Dialogus de anima, scored for the same line-up.

When performed and recorded as beautifully
and sensitively as they are here, Du Mont's plangent harmonies and dissonances reach into the
listener's heart with sensuous clarity. These are
near-perfect performances by an ensemble ideal
for such ravishing music, and who, in Marcel
Beekman, have an *haute-contre* of striking quality.
Frédéric Desenclos's tidy organ solos break up the
programme nicely, but the motets are the stars.

John Dunstaple   English c1390-1453

Dunstaple is generally acknowledged as the first
great English composer, one with an influence that
stretched into mainland Europe: Dufay certainly
knew his music. Not much is known of his life, but he
is known to have served Queen Joan of Navarre,
second wife of Henry IV, and was part of the house-
hold of Henry, Duke of Gloucester, in 1438. In the
late 1430s he held lands in northern France. It has
been suggested too that he was also an astronomer.

His epitaph (at St Stephen's, Walbrook) describes him as 'prince of music'.

Sacred Works

Descendi in ortum meum. Ave maris stella. Gloria in canon. Speciosa facta es. Sub tuam protectionem. Veni, Sancte spiritus / Veni creator spiritus. Albanus roseo rutilat / Quoque ferundus eras / Albanus domini laudus. Specialis virgo. Preco preheminencie / Precursor premittitur / textless / Inter natos mulierum. O crux gloriosa. Salve regina mater mire. Missa Rex seculorum
Orlando Consort
Metronome METCD1009 (74' · DDD · T/t) Ⓕ ⊙⊙⊙

This disc contains three of Dunstaple's well-known motets – *Preco preheminencie*, *Veni veni* and *Albanus* – but the rest are rarely performed. For some of the delicious antiphons, it's hard to see why: *Salve regina mater mire* is particularly striking – one of those pieces that sounds far more impressive than it looks on the page. There are also some total novelties. The canonic *Gloria* was discovered in Russia: it's a massively inventive work that adds a substantial new dimension to our knowledge of Dunstaple. And *Descendi in ortum meum*, though discovered and published a quarter of a century ago, surely stands as the latest known work of its composer: a magnificent piece that builds an entirely new kind of edifice with the materials of his characteristic style. Most impressive of all, though, is the Mass, *Rex seculorum*, which ends the disc. This may or may not be by Dunstaple – which is probably why it has never been recorded. Whoever the composer, though, it's a key work in the history of the polyphonic Mass cycle, brimming with invention. The Orlando Consort has a wonderfully forward style that beautifully matches the music and helps the listener to understand why Dunstaple achieved such an enormous reputation on the continental mainland. If they're occasionally a touch rough, these are classic performances that will be hard to challenge.

Henri Duparc   French 1848-1933

After study with César Franck, Duparc embarked on a short career as a composer. A serious psychological condition forced him to abandon creative work at the age of 36, leaving a small but beautiful legacy, much of which is influenced by the music of Wagner. His wonderfully subtle response to poetry has given us 13 exquisite songs, a number of which have orchestral accompaniments.

Mélodies

L'invitation au voyage. Sérénade florentine. Extase. Chanson triste. Le manoir de Rosemonde. Lamento. Au pays où se fait la guerre. La fuite. La vague et la cloche. Sérénade. Testament. Phidylé. Romance de Mignon. Elégie. Le galop. Soupir. La vie antérieure
Danielle Borst sop **François Le Roux** bar
Jeff Cohen pf
REM REM311049 (63' · DDD · T/t)   Ⓕ

If you consider Duparc's songs the most rewarding in the French language you'll rejoice at this issue. Without hesitation, we would say Le Roux's are the most successful performances of these masterpieces in miniature since the war. In his foreword to this issue the veteran composer Henri Sauguet comments: 'The interpretations of François Le Roux and Danielle Borst are remarkable, not just for their vocal qualities and their emotional commitment but also for their exemplary use of words, which illustrates perfectly the profound unity of poetry and music.' That almost says all that needs to be said, at any rate about Le Roux who has the lion's share of the burden. His voice can sometimes take on a rough edge but his understanding of the Duparc idiom is second to none, rivalling that of Panzéra and Bernac in the distant past, precisely because he realises what French can convey when sung with scrupulous care over diction.

Added to that he and his admirable pianist, Jeff Cohen, seem almost always to find exactly the right tempo for each *mélodie*. Le Roux is partnered in *La fuite* by Borst, another dedicated Duparcian who catches some of its trance-like beauty. The recorded sound is ideal. A 'must' for anyone interested in great performances of *mélodies*.

Marcel Dupré   French 1886-1971

One of France's major organist-composers, Dupré studied with Guilmant, Vierne and Widor at the Paris Conservatoire, returning as professor of organ, a post he held from 1926 to 1954 (among his pupils were Jehan Alain and Marie-Claire Alain, Pierre Cochereau, Jeanne Demessieux, Jean Guillou, Jean Langlais and Olivier Messiaen). Succeeding Widor, he also served as organist of St Sulpice from 1934 until his death in 1971. His own music is characterised by great virtuosity and a harmonic language that explored modality.

Organ Works

'Complete Organ Works, Volume 9'
Entrée, méditation, sortie, Op 62. Les nymphéas, Op 54. Suite bretonne, Op 21. Poème héroïque, Op 33 (arr cpsr)
Jeremy Filsell org
Guild GMCD7188 (63' · DDD). Recorded on the organ of St Boniface Episcopal Church, Sarasota, Florida Ⓕ ⊙

It's sometimes the case that the reputation of great composers rests on a handful of works. With Dupré it's the two symphonies, the Op 7 Preludes and Fugues and the *Noël* Variations for which he's best known, but these compositions form a tiny proportion of his entire output. One of the many benefits of Guild's series is the discovery of hidden treasures, and much of the music on Volume 9 deserves to be heard more frequently.

The revelation here is *Les nymphéas*. This is a beautiful work, even as original as Debussy's *Images*, *Nocturnes* or the quieter moments of *Jeux*. It would make a marvellous orchestral suite; indeed, much of Dupré's organ writing has a quasi-orchestral character, and reflects his love and knowledge of the vast tonal palette of 20th-century instruments. You can also tell that, like Messiaen, he was an experienced writer of piano and chamber music.

We're indebted to Filsell for his special arrangement of *Les nymphéas* for this CD, and for his excellent performances throughout this volume. The choice of the organ at St Boniface, Florida, was a good one as it provides sensuous colours for the softer movements, plus glockenspiel effects for the *Suite bretonne*. The playing is backed up by fine recorded sound and comprehensive programme notes. There's no doubt that this series is setting the standard for Dupré interpreters of the future and will be a landmark in the history of organ recordings.

'Complete Organ Works, Volume 10'
Le chemin de la croix, Op 29
Jeremy Filsell *org*
Guild GMCD7193 (56' · DDD)   Ⓕ**OO**

'Complete Organ Works, Volume 11'
Vêpres du commun des fêtes de la Sainte-Vierge, Op 18. Choral et Fugue, Op 57. Regina coeli, Op 64
Vocal Quartet; Jeremy Filsell *org*
Guild GMCD7198 (55' · DDD)   Ⓕ**OO**

'Complete Organ Works, Volume 12'
79 Chorales, Op 28
Jeremy Filsell *org*
Guild GMCD7203 (72' · DDD)   Ⓕ**OO**

All recorded on the organ of St Boniface Episcopal Church, Sarasota, Florida

---

Thinking about 20th-century French music after Debussy and Ravel, the names of Messiaen and the members of Les Six would probably spring to mind. However, at the same time organists such as Vierne, Tournemire, Alain, Langlais and Dupré himself were writing music every bit as original and as intense as the aforementioned composers. One of the many benefits of Guild's series (which concludes with these three volumes) is the opportunity to discover just how fine a composer Dupré was. Perhaps more than any of his contemporaries he managed to embrace both the sacred and the secular with utter conviction. *Le chemin de la croix* is one of his major works, and is a landmark piece of musical drama. One can hear links with the *Symphonie-Passion* of six years earlier, and David Gammie in his comprehensive accompanying notes points out the influence of these works on Duruflé's Requiem and Messiaen's *Les corps glo-*

rieux. Filsell gives a suitably dramatic performance with some telling *rallentandos* at climactic moments.

All three compositions on Volume 11 were inspired by Gregorian chant, and each movement is preceded on this CD by the singing of the verse on which it's based. The vocal quartet includes the CD's producer Adrian Peacock and Filsell himself – an inspired and appropriate piece of programming. Listening to Filsell's flowing, atmospheric playing it's easy to imagine oneself sitting in a vast, incense-laden Parisian church, with glorious improvised music coming from the west-end *grand orgue*.

Dupré is remembered for writing music of extreme technical complexity, but Volume 12 shows that he was well capable of composing pieces for organs and organists of modest resources. The 79 Chorales take hymn tunes which were all used by Bach as the basis for chorale-preludes. Many of Dupré's chorales are effective Bachian pastiches, but a handful have the unmistakable 20th-century French idiom. Again, Filsell's performances are beyond reproach, and he shows that Dupré was able to match JSB for solemnity and piety.

As is so often the case Naxos provides healthy competition, and Volume 11 of its Dupré series has a very fine performance of *Le chemin de la croix* from Mary Preston. She brings a greater clarity to the music, helped by the drier acoustic of the Meyerson Symphony Center at Dallas. However, Filsell in the more resonant acoustic of St Boniface Church, Sarasota, Florida, brings more warmth, passion and drama to his interpretations, and this, coupled with Gammie's excellent insert-notes, sways the balance in favour of the Guild series.

In all 12 volumes Filsell's playing has been consistently superb, and what has been most impressive is that his virtuosity has always been the servant of the music. The St Boniface organ may not have the éclat of a Cavaillé-Coll, but its clarity and attack enhance Dupré's complex textures, and the recordings are suitably warm and atmospheric. We must salute Filsell for what must surely rank as one of the greatest achievements in organ recordings.

Additional recommendation

Le chemin de la croix, Op 29
van Oosten *org*
Dabringhaus und Grimm MDG316 0953-2   Ⓕ
Playing one of the finest extant Cavaillé-Colls captured in a recording of exemplary clarity, depth and presence, van Oosten gives a performance which exposes the very heart of Dupré's creation.

Choral Works

Dupré La France au Calvaire, Op 49[a] **Alain**
O Salutaris **Langlais** Festival Alleluia **Messiaen**
O sacrum convivium!
[a]**Helen Neeves** *sop* [a]**Catherine Denley** *mez*

[a]Matthew Beale *ten* [a]Colin Campbell *bar* **Jeremy Filsell** *org* **Vasari Singers / Jeremy Backhouse**
Guild GMCD7239 (78' · DDD · T/t)   Ⓕ**OO**

La France au Calvaire is an astonishing work, setting, to quote the booklet-note, 'a curious libretto' by René Herval who, like Dupré, was a native of Rouen. Appalled by the devastation wrought on his native city during the Second World War, Dupré vents all his anger and passion into this 65-minute oratorio, its movements dedicated to six French saints and framed by a Prologue and Final. Principally known for his organ music, it might seem strange to question Dupré's use of the organ here as the sole means of instrumental accompaniment. But despite Jeremy Filsell's stunning virtuosity and brilliant handling of the not always perfectly in tune Douai Abbey organ, the score seems to cry out for an orchestra.

No such reservations about the performance: in a word, stunning. The bleak ugliness of Christ nailed to the cross is compellingly portrayed by Matthew Beale, Catherine Denley makes an arresting France appealing for forgiveness for her misguided people, Colin Campbell fulfils the dual roles of St Denis and the voice of Christ with suitable gravitas and authority, and Helen Neeves is a beautifully innocent St Clotilde (magically set against a decidedly Messiaenic organ backdrop).

As for Jeremy Backhouse and his superb Vasari Singers, they excel even by their own high standards. The three motets which share the disc seem in comparison a trifle disappointing. But that disappointment is only because the motets precede a work of extraordinary emotional impact and a performance of exceptional power.

Additional recommendation

Quatre motets, Op 9[a]. De profundis, Op 18. Ave verum, Op 34 No 1. La france au Calvaire, Op 49 – Final. Deux motets, Op 53
Vasari Singers / Backhouse with **Filsell,** [a]**Curror** *orgs*
Guild GMCD7220   Ⓕ
    Here is truly impressive choral music. True, the organ does figure prominently, occasionally assuming a decidedly virtuoso role, but it's clearly always the servant of the choir, and for the most part it's the choral lines rather than the organ accompaniments which require the greatest virtuosity. And every ounce of the Vasari Singers' artistry is called into play.

Maurice Duruflé   French 1902-1986

After singing as a chorister at the Rouen Cathedral Choir School, Duruflé studied piano and organ before moving to Paris, where he took private organ lessons with Charles Tournemire (whom he assisted at Basilique Ste-Clotilde). In 1920 Duruflé entered

the Conservatoire de Paris, eventually graduating with first prizes in organ, harmony, piano accompaniment and composition. In 1927 Louis Vierne nominated him as his assistant at Notre-Dame. Duruflé became titular organist of St-Étienne-du-Mont in Paris in 1929, a position he held for the rest of his life. In 1939 he gave the premiere of Francis Poulenc's Concerto for Organ, Strings and Timpani; he had advised Poulenc on the registrations of the organ part. In 1943 he became professor of harmony at the Conservatoire de Paris, where he worked until 1970. In 1947 Duruflé wrote what is probably the most famous of his few pieces: the Requiem.

Organ Works

'Veni Creator: The Complete Organ Music'
Scherzo, Op 2. Prélude, Adagio et Choral varié sur le thème de 'Veni Creator', Op 4. Suite, Op 5. Prélude et Fugue sur le nom d'Alain, Op 7. Fugue sur le thème du Carillon des Heures de la Cathédrale de Soissons, Op 12. Prélude sur l'Introït de l'Epiphanie, Op 13. Meditation, Op posth
Hans Fagius *org*
BIS BIS-CD1304 (71' · DDD). Played on the 1928 Frobenius organ at Århus Cathedral, Denmark   Ⓕ

Listeners to his *Requiem* will recognise Duruflé's conservative and intensely personal musical language as heard in his organ music. The influence of Debussy, Dukas, Ravel, Tournemire and Vierne is evident, and like these composers Duruflé provides detailed performance indications. Hans Fagius, a former student of Duruflé's, scrupulously observes all the scores' markings, and this is one reason why he's now the top recommendation for this repertoire.

His performances have a flexible, seamless flow, and the playing has a slight understated quality which gives more clarity and impact than Eric Lebrun's flamboyant accounts. Fagius's interpretations are close in spirit to the recordings by the composer and his wife Marie-Madeleine Duruflé-Chevalier, and it's a shame that their authoritative performances are marred by poor sound quality. By contrast, BIS's recording of the 89-stop four-manual organ in Århus Cathedral is superbly realistic. The choice of this instrument was inspired; it has all the appropriate colours and it's set in a warm, generous acoustic.

Another bonus is the inclusion of the sensuous and recently discovered *Meditation*. Although the recordings by Lebrun and the Duruflés are very good, they must now stand aside and let this BIS disc take the place of honour, for this is a truly distinguished release of one of the finest bodies of organ music you'll ever hear.

Requiem

Requiem. Prélude et Fugue sur le nom d'Alain, Op 7. Quatre Motets sur des thèmes grégoriens, Op 10 **Fauré** Requiem, Op 48. Cantique de Jean Racine, Op 11. Messe basse **Poulenc** Mass in G. Salve regina. Exultate Deo. Litanies à la Vierge Noire

Jonathon Bond, Andrew Brunt, Robert King trebs
Benjamin Luxon bar Christopher Keyte bass
St John's College Choir, Cambridge; Academy of
St Martin in the Fields / George Guest with
Stephen Cleobury org
Double Decca ② 436 486-2DF2 (149' · ADD)
Recorded 1969-76   Ⓜ️▶️

Here's almost two and a half hours of bliss. These
are recordings to set aside for the time when, as
the prayer says, 'the busy world is hushed'. Asked
to characterise Fauré's and Duruflé's Requiems
as compared with others, we might suggest words
such as 'delicate', 'meditative', 'undramatic'; but
that last would be a mistake. These performances
certainly do not go out of their way to 'be' dramatic or anything else other than faithful to the
music, but one is struck by the power exercised by
those rare moments that rise to a *forte* and above.
The choir is surely at its best, the trebles with
their fine clear-cut, distinctive tone, the tenors (so
important in the Fauré) graceful and refined
without being precious, the altos exceptionally
good, and only the basses just occasionally and
briefly plummy or obtrusive in some way.

The Poulenc works further test a choir's virtuosity, yet in the extremely difficult Mass the choir
seem secure, and in the *Salve regina* they catch the
necessary tenderness. The treble soloists sing
beautifully, Christopher Keyte dramatises almost
too convincingly in Duruflé's 'tremens factus',
and Benjamin Luxon, his production less even,
builds finely in Fauré's *Libera me*. These recordings have a vividness, certainly in the choral
sound, that modern recordings generally lack.

Duruflé Requiem[a]. **Fauré** Requiem, Op 48[b]. Pavane[c]
[b]**Robert Chilcott** treb [a]**Janet Baker** mez [b]**John Carol
Case,** [a]**Stephen Roberts** bars [ab]**Choir of King's
College Cambridge;** [bc]**New Philharmonia
Orchestra /** [bc]**Sir David Willcocks,**
[a]**Sir Philip Ledger** with [a]**John Butt** org
EMI Great Recordings of the Century 379994-2
(65' · ADD). Recorded [bc]1968 & [a]1982   Ⓜ️Ⓞ▶️

The first decision to be made is between the
orchestral and the organ-accompanied versions
of this most serene and other-worldly of Requiems. Duruflé expresses profundities with the
most restrained and subtle of musical means,
and in a performance as scrupulously responsive
as this, those subtleties need no orchestra to
intensify them.

It is a very rare experience indeed to be able to
describe a recording as near as can be to absolute
perfection from start to finish, but this Fauré
Requiem truly provides this experience. For the
happy result the highest praise must go first and
foremost to David Willcocks's inspiring and
most sensitive direction of the exquisite work.

Additional recommendation

Requiem
Coupled with **Fauré** Requiem

Murray; Allen; Corydon Singers; ECO / Best
Hyperion CDA67070 (75' · DDD)   ⒻⓄ
Beautifully judged performance of these two
favourite (and similar) French Requiems. The
glory of both performances is the choral work.

Henri Dutilleux   French b1916

*Dutilleux studied with the Gallons, Büsser and
Emmanuel at the Paris Conservatoire. He worked as
head of music production for French Radio from
1945 to 1963, and served as professor of composition
at the Ecole Normale de Musique, Paris, from 1961
to 1970. He was appointed to the staff of the Paris
Conservatoire in 1970. Though his early work
clearly stems from the same tradition as Debussy,
Ravel, Roussel and Honegger, he soon established his
own voice and has followed a lone track with music of
great beauty and delicacy, mostly for instrumental,
rather than vocal, forces.*

Concertos

Cello Concerto, 'Tout un monde lointain'. Métaboles.
Mystère de l'instant
Boris Pergamenschikov vc **BBC Philharmonic
Orchestra / Yan Pascal Tortelier**
Chandos CHAN9565 (60' · DDD)   Ⓕ▶️

This is the third issue in Chandos's Dutilleux
series with the BBC Phil and Yan Pascal Tortelier.
The virtues of those earlier issues remain evident
here, with meticulously prepared, well-played
performances, and recordings carefully adapted to
the colouristic subtlety and textural delicacy of the
music. *Métaboles* is particularly tricky to bring off,
but this version is admirable in the way it builds
through some dangerously episodic writing to
underline the power of the principal climaxes,
though a more sharply delineated sound picture
could have reinforced these contrasts even more
appropriately. Boris Pergamenschikov is an eloquent soloist in the Cello Concerto. Tortelier's
account of *Mystère de l'instant* – using a full orchestral complement of strings – is excellently done.
As with *Métaboles*, the structure is shaped with
great flexibility and feeling for its ebb and flow,
and this emerges as a highly dramatic score,
despite the inherent reticence of Dutilleux's style.

Violin Concerto, 'L'arbre des songes'. Timbres,
espace, mouvement. Deux Sonnets de Jean Cassou
(orch cpsr) **Alain** (orch Dutilleux) Prière pour nous
autres charnels
Olivier Charlier vn **Martyn Hill** ten **Neal Davies** bar
BBC Philharmonic Orchestra / Yan Pascal Tortelier
Chandos CHAN9504 (58' · DDD · T/t)   ⒻⓄ

Timbres, espace, mouvement (1978, revised 1991)
can be counted as Dutilleux's best orchestral
composition, at once rooted in tradition yet
persistently sceptical about conventional 'sym-

phonic' values. It's a tricky score to bring off, and Tortelier is successful in negotiating its twists and turns of form. In the Violin Concerto (1985) Tortelier again favours a symphonic approach, and very effective it is too, with a soloist who's authoritative without being overly self-assertive. The disc also includes Dutilleux's orchestral arrangement of his Cassou settings, and also his orchestration, made in 1944, of Jehan Alain's touching prayer. Well-characterised contributions from Martyn Hill and Neal Davies complete this valuable release.

Symphony No 1

Symphony No 1. Cello Concerto, 'Tout un monde lointain'[a]. Timbres, espace, mouvement
[a]**Jean-Guihen Queyras** vc **Bordeaux-Aquitaine National Orchestra / Hans Graf**
Arte Nova 74321 92813-2 (80' · DDD)   Ⓢ

The traditional French virtues of lightness, elegance, wit and so on are all very well, but they don't take us far with Dutilleux's music on their own. It's wonderfully inspiriting to hear, albeit under an Austrian conductor, an orchestra from the long underfunded French provinces finding this music's power, passion and eloquence.

Hans Graf enjoys Dutilleux's confidence, and from this recording it's easy to see why. The detail is all here, but so is the control of long paragraphs – few recordings of the slow movement of the First Symphony are as moving as this. The sound may not have quite the brilliance of the Chandos set, but do we always have to have brilliance?

Similarly, Jean-Guihen Queyras may not produce Rostropovich's matchless tone high up on the A string; but he has his own things to say and says them with authority. In *Timbres, espace, mouvement*, Graf impresses on us the sheer curiousness of many of the textures, just as Van Gogh's 1889 picture *La nuit étoilée*, which inspired the work, stands far apart from so much contemporary painting.

The First Symphony is especially welcome. Amid all the congratulations after its first public performance in 1952, Pierre Boulez pointedly turned his back on the composer. The usual explanation is that Dutilleux, eschewing the 12-note system, was clearly one of those who were, in Boulez's words, 'inadequate to the times'. Or was the younger man all too aware of this music's quality? Happily, these fences have been mended since. But the work is undoubtedly a masterpiece and the final resolution on to D flat major one of the great moments of 20th-century music.

Pascal Dusapin   French b1955

Pascal Dusapin studied arts and aesthetics at the Sorbonne before attending seminars by Iannis Xenakis. He was composer-in-residence at the Lyon National Orchestra, 1993-94. His compositions cover most genres, including four operas. His music is characterised by high levels of intensity achieved through very economic means.

Perelà

Perelà
John Graham-Hall ten Perelà **Isabelle Philippe** sop La Reine **Chantal Perraud** sop La Fille d'Alloro **Martine Mahé** contr Une Pauvre Vieille **Nora Gubisch** mez La Marquise Olivia di Bellonda **Daniel Gundlach** counterten L'Archevêque **Gilles Yanetti** spkr Le Perroquet **Isabelle Pierre** spkr La Jeune Fille à la Flûte **Montpellier Opera Chorus; Montpellier National Orchestra / Alain Altinoglu**
Naïve Montaigne ② MO782168 (122' · DDD · S/T/t/N)
Recorded live 2003   Ⓜ

Pascal Dusapin is among the most significant composers at work today and it is good to see Naïve releasing this live account of his fourth stage work. *Perelà* is derived from Aldo Palazzeschi's 1911 futurist novel *Perelà uomo di fumo*. It concerns the eponymous hero's metamorphosis into existence, his arrival in a corrupt and decadent city – where he is first fêted as its saviour, then, after the accidental suicide of an admirer, condemned for his subversive influence – and his trial and incarceration, from where he returns to the ether.

It's a story which resonates in the past or present, from which Dusapin has fashioned not a narrow polemic or a moralistic opera, but one rich in incident of a necessarily symbolic yet never abstruse nature – an opera, moreover, whose complex textural and rhythmic interplay are derived from relatively simple harmonic means, ensuring musical cohesion over the course of 10 'chapters' which are widely contrasted in content and impact.

The opening chapter presents Perelà – created from the mothers Pena, Rete and Lama, the first two letters of each forming his name, and themselves reiterated as a kind of mantric trinity – on his way to the city, where he is accorded 'celebrity status', only to be knocked off a pedestal he never sought to occupy. Later chapters include a garish ball, with its onstage orchestra and massed choir, a strange meeting with the Queen where the main conversation is provided by her parrot's repetition of 'Dieu', and the magical scene in which the solitary Perelà encounters a girl with a flute – the disembodied sonorities an understated pointer to his final evanescence.

The recording is an assured one. John Graham-Hall is superb in the title-role, its high tessitura accommodated with little strain. Nora Gubisch is commanding as the Marchesa whose hypochondria is not unempathetic, as witness her impassioned defence of Perelà in the trial scene. Isabelle Philippe's neutral tone is ideal for the Queen, as is Daniel Gundlach's hectoring falsetto for the Archbishop; the remaining roles are all characterfully delivered.

Alain Altinoglu directs with evident concern for the bigger picture, in sound which, for all its stage intrusions, has a realistic placement of voices and orchestra.

Antonin Dvořák   Bohemian 1841-1904

The greatest of all Czech composers whose best works are among the finest of the second half of the 19th century, recognised internationally and a hero among his countrymen, died impoverished. The violinist Fritz Kreisler went to visit him at his home in 1903 and said the scene recalled something out of La bohème. Dvořák had sold all his music for a pittance and all the money from his tours and stay in America had gone. 'I had been playing some of Dvořák's Slavonic Dances,' wrote Kreisler, 'and visited the old man to pay my respects. I asked him whether he had nothing further for me to play. "Look through that pile," said the sick composer, indicating a pile of unorganised papers. "Maybe you can find something." I did. It was the Humoresque.' (Now one of Dvořák's best-known pieces, the Humoresque was transcribed for violin and piano by Kreisler, achieving enormous popularity.)

If his father had had his way, Dvořák would have followed in his footsteps and become a butcher. Instead his extraordinary musical gifts led him elsewhere, though recognition was a long time coming. He learnt the violin as a child, became a chorister in his native village and played in local orchestras. Financed by an uncle, when Dvořák was 12 he was sent away to study music and learn German. The headmaster of the school, Antonín Liehmann, was an excellent musician who taught Dvořák not only the piano, viola and organ but also gave him a good grounding in music theory.

Throughout the 1860s he was an orchestral violinist and viola player, performing in cafés and theatres, and composing prolifically. He played in a concert of Wagner excerpts conducted by the composer himself and came under his spell, later playing in the Prague National Theatre Orchestra under the father of Czech music, Smetana. Life was a struggle both financially and creatively. Dvořák lived for music and nothing else but trains. Like Hindemith half a century later, Dvořák was one of music's great trainspotters, knew all the timetables from the Franz-Josef Station in Prague off by heart and often said that he would have liked to have invented the steam locomotive, 'one of the highest achievements of the human spirit,' he said.

In 1873 he abandoned the orchestra for the organ loft (St Adalbert's in Prague), a less demanding job which gave him more time to compose. The same year he married his former pupil, Anna Cermaková. Suddenly, a string of marvellous pieces appeared (including the Serenade for strings), news of his music spread and before five years had elapsed he found himself recognised throughout Europe as a major creative force. What Dvořák had done was to recognise that what he had been writing up till 1873 was derivative, a copy of Wagner, Brahms and other German post-Romantics. As soon as he turned to Czech nationalism and began using the musical character and folk rhythms of his native land, a personal, fresh, distinctive voice emerged. His Symphony No 3 won him a national prize as well as the respect of Brahms (who was on the jury) and the relationship between the two men devel-

oped into one of lifelong friendship. Brahms was instrumental in finding a publisher for the younger man's work and Dvořák went on to win the Austrian State prize four years in succession.

Dvořák's frequent visits to England during the 1880s spread his fame further – his choral works were eagerly lapped up – and he was awarded many prestigious honours culminating in 1891 when he was made a professor of composition at the Prague Conservatory, awarded an honorary doctorate by Cambridge University as well as being offered the directorship of the National Conservatory of New York at an annual salary of $15,000. Dvořák moved to the States in 1893, after a string of farewell European tours. A combination of homesickness and the discovery of American indigenous folk music combined to inspire a string of masterpieces, including the 'New World' Symphony, the Cello Concerto and the 'American' String Quartet.

On returning to Prague, he resumed his professorship, was made director of the Conservatory in 1901 and appointed a life member of the Austrian House of Lords, the first musician to be so honoured. During this final period, Dvořák turned to writing symphonic poems based on old Czech legends and, especially, operas including the only one which remains in today's repertoire, Rusalka. Though his last months were clouded by the fiasco of his new opera Armida (he died of an apoplectic stroke six weeks after its premiere), his death was marked by a national day of mourning.

Cello Concerto in B minor, B191

Cello Concerto[a]. Symphonic Variations
[a]**Pieter Wispelwey** vc
Budapest Festival Orchestra / Iván Fischer
Channel Classics .🎵. CCSSA25807 (63' · DDD)
Recorded live at the Budapest National Concert Hall, Palace of Arts, in 2006
Ⓕ**ⓄⓄⓄ**Ⓑ➤

Here we have an outstanding version of Dvořák's Cello Concerto, one to rival any version in the catalogue and imaginatively coupled with the much earlier *Symphonic Variations*. Pieter Wispelwey crowns his previous releases in this electrifying live recording, brilliantly accompanied by the Budapest Festival Orchestra under Iván Fischer.

It includes applause at the end of each performance, suggesting there is far less editing here than in many other live recordings. That ties in with the high-voltage performances, well recorded in atmospheric and finely detailed sound, with the soloist well balanced in the concerto. Wispelwey's playing is marked by crisp attack and exceptionally clean articulation, and though he allows an easing for the transition into the great second-subject melody, as well as in the mysterious G sharp minor reference to it in the central development section, he keeps romantic freedom well in check.

Wispelwey's first-movement climax is triumphant, with the orchestra weighty in *tuttis*, while the slow movement finds the soloist flexible, with magical shading of *pianissimos* leading to the hushed close. The finale is crisp and clean, with

DVOŘÁK CELLO CONCERTO – IN BRIEF

Mstislav Rostropovich; Berlin PO / Herbert von Karajan
DG 447 413-2GOR   Ⓜ❍❍❍❐

Ⓖ A longtime favourite, with sympathetic accompaniment from Karajan and his Berlin orchestra and pliant, flexible playing from Rostropovich at his most charismatic.

Mstislav Rostropovich; USSR SO / Evgeni Svetlanov
BBC Legends BBCL4110-2   Ⓕ❍
Recorded at London's Royal Albert Hall the very day in 1968 when Soviet tanks rolled in Prague, this is a performance of extremes: orchestra and conductor sound like they want to dispatch it as quickly as possible, while the soloist uses the piece to project his pain and guilt. It is hugely powerful, though the mono sound is somewhat constricted.

Pieter Wispelwey; Budapest Fest Orch / Iván Fischer
Channel Classics 🔊 CCSSA25807   Ⓕ❍❍❍
Straight to the top of the pile: a magnificent achievement from everyone concerned.

Yo-Yo Ma; New York PO / Kurt Masur
Sony Classical SK93027   Ⓕ
A very fine modern version of this popular work: Yo-Yo Ma betters his already fine first version, offering playing of both powerful discipline and apparent free-flying spontaneity. This is not Ma in sophisticated mode but rather offering a direct simplicity that pays huge dividends in this ebulliently melodious music.

Pablo Casals; Czech PO / George Szell
Dutton mono CDEA5002   Ⓜ
Casals's 1937 recording with the Czech Philharmonic is a classic with wonderfully idiomatic playing by the orchestra, gloriously directed by George Szell. This is a performance of incandescent beauty, the cellist's bow seemingly striking sparks off the string as he launches into the work's richly Romantic melodies.

Gautier Capuçon; Frankfurt RSO / Paavo Järvi
Virgin Classics 519035-2   Ⓕ❍❐
A strong and characterful version of the Dvořák coupled with the Victor Herbert work that inspired its composition. Sensitively accompanied.

Pierre Fournier; Philharmonia / Rafael Kubelík
Testament SBT1016   Ⓕ
The first of Fournier's three recordings dates from 1948 and displays his customary ease and grace as a soloist. Kubelík conducts idiomatically, drawing excellent playing from the young Philharmonia.

some wonderfully ripe-sounding horns suggesting Viennese influence. The hushed epilogue is refined, leading to a powerful final cadence.

In the *Symphonic Variations* Fischer holds the structure cleanly together, crisply defining each of the 27 brief variations and the fugal finale. One marvels anew at Dvořák's inventive elaborations on a simple theme, on a par with the *Slavonic Dances*. An outstanding disc.

Dvořák Cello Concerto
Tchaikovsky Variations on a Rococo Theme, Op 33
Mstislav Rostropovich vc **Berlin Philharmonic Orchestra / Herbert von Karajan**
DG The Originals 447 413-2GOR (60' · ADD)
Recorded 1968   Ⓜ❍❍❍❐

Ⓖ There have been a number of outstanding recordings of the Dvořák Concerto since this DG record was made, but none to match it for the warmth of lyrical feeling, the sheer strength of personality of the cello playing and the distinction of the partnership between Karajan and Rostropovich. Any moments of romantic licence from the latter, who's obviously deeply in love with the music, are set against Karajan's overall grip on the proceedings. The orchestral playing is superb. You've only to listen to the beautiful introduction of the secondary theme of the first movement by the principal horn to realise that the BPO is going to match its illustrious soloist in eloquence, while Rostropovich's many moments of poetic introspection never for a moment interfere with the sense of a spontaneous forward flow. The recording is as near perfect as any made by DG in that vintage analogue era. It gives the cello a highly realistic presence, and if the passionate *fortissimo* violins lose just a fraction in fullness, and there seems to be, comparably, just a slight loss of resonance in the bass, the sound picture has an impressively clear and vivid focus.

In the coupled Tchaikovsky *Rococo* Variations, Rostropovich uses the published score rather than the original version. However, he plays with such masterly Russian fervour and elegance that any criticism is disarmed. The music itself continually demonstrates Tchaikovsky's astonishing lyrical fecundity, as one tune leads to another, all growing organically from the charming 'rococo' theme. The recording is marvellously refined. The description 'legendary' isn't a whit too strong for a disc of this calibre.

Dvořák Cello Concerto
Herbert Cello Concerto No 2, Op 30
Gautier Capuçon vc
Frankfurt Radio Symphony Orchestra / Paavo Järvi
Virgin Classics 519035-2 (61' · DDD)   Ⓕ❍❐

Though the name of Victor Herbert is nowadays associated above all with Broadway musicals like *Naughty Marietta*, Herbert was in fact a multi-talented musician, one of the world's leading cello virtuosos of the time and the composer of two cello concertos which greatly influenced Dvořák in the United States to write his supreme masterpiece. That makes this coupling of Dvořák's Cello Concerto with the second and finer of Herbert's an apt one, and Gautier Capuçon gives distinctive, characterful and intense performances of both works, well supported by Paavo Järvi and the Frankfurt orchestra, especially strong in its brass section.

In the Dvořák the fruity-toned Frankfurt horn gives a beautiful account of the great second-subject melody even though it is dangerously slow. In the exposition with soloist, Capuçon takes that section a fraction faster and the result is magical. As in the Herbert the slow movement is deeply elegiac, while the incisive finale leads to a dedicated account of the beautiful epilogue. Altogether a version of this much-recorded work which stands comparison with any in the catalogue, made the more attractive by the coupling.

Dvořák Cello Concerto[a]
Schumann Cello Concerto in A minor, Op 129[b]
Tchaikovsky Pezzo capriccioso in B minor, Op 62[c]
Mstislav Rostropovich vc [a]**USSR State Symphony Orchestra / Evgeni Svetlanov;** [b]**London Symphony Orchestra;** [c]**English Chamber Orchestra /** [bc]**Benjamin Britten**
BBC Legends/IMG Artists [ab]mono BBCL4110-2
(71' · ADD). Recorded live [ac]1968, [b]1961   Ⓕ**Ⓞ**

Truly legendary performances are rare, but this heroic account of the Dvořák Concerto deserves its place on collectors' shelves alongside such classics as Mravinsky's Shostakovich Eighth or Horenstein's Mahler *Symphony of a Thousand*. This concert offers us a piece of history in sound that raises questions about music and politics, music and personality, music and identity.

In the Cold War era, no Western tour by Russian artists was entirely without political resonance, and this London Prom took place on the very day that Soviet tanks rolled into Prague. With demonstrators outside the Royal Albert Hall, there was also dissent within. The performers might not have been directly to blame, yet had they not been dispatched knowingly, as cultural ambassadors? Svetlanov, at least, was something of an apparatchik. Moreover, the programme featured the Dvořák Concerto – an intensely nostalgic and nationalistic score, a natural focus for strong emotions.

On this privately sourced, somewhat compressed-sounding mono tape, you can hear the unease as Svetlanov and his raw-toned band tear into the work as if determined to get it over with as quickly as possible. It's the cellist, already in tears, whose transparently honest playing wins the audience over, as his sense of guilt and fury is transmuted into a potent requiem for the Czech Spring. The restated second subject is forcefully projected, suitably gutsy and passionate at the start, but it's the development that strikes deepest. Never has the first theme's metamorphosis from resolute, relatively short-breathed march to elegy struck home so movingly. The finale is

almost too rushed until the tender, unmistakably tragic coda arrives, presenting an extreme and all the more moving contrast.

The Schumann, though scarcely epoch-making in the same way, was recorded on the occasion of the cellist's first visit to the Aldeburgh Festival. It receives a glorious interpretation. The sound, considerably more refined and open, is still mono only with the orchestra rather backwardly placed. Strongly recommended.

Piano and Violin Concertos

Dvořák Piano Concerto
Schumann Piano Concerto in A minor, Op 54
Paolo Giacometti pf **Arnhem Philharmonic Orchestra / Michel Tilkin**
Channel Classics CCS17898 (71' · DDD)   Ⓕ

To say that Paolo Giacometti measures up well to the classic versions is to say a great deal. His playing has all the energy, sparkle, poetry and technical finish you could wish. He approaches the Dvořák with an admirable mixture of respect and enjoyment. And his Schumann is as urgent as the composer's markings suggest it should be, yet without sacrificing natural characterisation for the sake of making that point. Nor do the Dutch orchestra and conductor sound in any way out of their depth; on the contrary, they're clearly as engaged as their soloist in warm, lively music-making. The Channel Classics recording is also rich and well balanced. If the Schumann/Dvořák coupling is just what you're looking for, there's no need to hesitate.

Piano Concerto[a]. The Golden Spinning-Wheel, B197
[a]**Pierre-Laurent Aimard** pf **Royal Concertgebouw Orchestra, Amsterdam / Nikolaus Harnoncourt**
Teldec 8573 87630-2 (68' · DDD)   Ⓕ**Ⓞ**▶

Straight to the top of the list for this one! Even on its best showings Dvořák's Piano Concerto has never quite managed to cast off its Cinderella rags. With this recording, the ball beckons, and there's no time limit. Granted, Brahms is still securely in the background and the concerto is hardly as pianistic as the best of its concerto-peers but the beauty of this performance is its utter naturalness, Pierre-Laurent Aimard easing around the solo part as if he's been playing it all his life, and Nikolaus Harnoncourt's sympathy for the work obvious from the start. Together they make the most of the score's drama, giving the lie to Dvořák's supposedly ineffective piano writing. Albrecht Gaud's excellent booklet-note credits the long-prevalent revision by Vilém Kurz as giving the part 'not only a more effective form' but also the virtue of extra clarity. Yet it appears that the original is used here and redeemed. Richter's clarity and Firkušný's knowing accent remain attractive, but Aimard's combination of intelligence and informality win the day. A magnificent CD.

Violin Concerto[a]. Piano Concerto[b]
[a]James Ehnes vn **[b]Rustem Hayroudinoff** pf
BBC Philharmonic Orchestra / Gianandrea Noseda
Chandos CHAN10309 (71' · DDD) Ⓕ▶

The Russian pianist Rustem Hayroudinoff gives a commanding performance of the Dvořák Piano Concerto, always a tricky work to play thanks to unpianistic piano writing. Hayroudinoff basically follows the composer's original piano text but modifies it in places where he feels the original is ineffective in favour of Vilém Kurz's 'performing version'. Yet where he feels that Kurz's changes 'seem to push the piano part too far in the direction of a typical Romantic concerto', he has 'found his own solutions for staying true to Dvořák's intentions'. Controversial or not, the result is a performance in which Hayroudinoff brings out the joyful, carefree quality of Dvořák's inspiration, demonstrating what a wonderful fund of good melodies it contains. The clarity of his articulation in the trickiest passagework is phenomenal, and his phrasing in the central *Andante sostenuto* is limpidly beautiful. Helped by full, rich sound which yet allows fine detail, Noseda and the BBC Philharmonic match the subtlety and point of the soloist's playing, establishing this as an outstanding modern version.

Having Dvořák's Violin and Piano Concertos on a single disc makes an apt and generous coupling. Canadian violinist James Ehnes gives a strong, incisive performance with speeds on the fast side in the first two movements and with the *furiant* finale bitingly fresh. His rapid vibrato gives a distinctive timbre to his playing, making the slow movement less warmly romantic than it is in some rival versions, yet Ehnes offers real magnetism in his performance.

The recording, generally well-balanced, is yet less full and warm than in the Piano Concerto: strangely so, as both recordings were made by the same conductor and orchestra in the same venue.

Additional recommendations

Violin Concerto
Coupled with Violin Sonata, B106[b]. Sonatina, B183[b]
Liebeck vn [b]**Apekisheva** pf [a]**RSNO / Walker**
Sony Classical 88697 49963-2 ⒻＯ▶
From the Concerto's opening bars you are aware of being in the presence of an extremely confident player, someone sure of his ability to present a persuasive view of the music. It's such a strong, idiomatic performance, and the chamber works are equally fine.

Violin Concerto
Coupled with **Dvořák** Romance, B39 **Szymanowski** Violin Concerto No 1
Steinbacher vn **Berlin RSO / Janowski**
Pentatone ⓟ PTC5186 353 Ⓕ▶
Pentatone's recording brings out the flair and the exceptional expressive contrasts in Steinbacher's playing. From this recording one would imagine

that hers is not a big tone but it is an opulent one, cushioned by ample if well controlled vibrato. That opulence makes her playing of the heartfelt melody in the slow movement of the concerto winningly rich.

Violin Concerto
Coupled with **Suk** Fantasy
Suk vn **Czech Philharmonic Orchestra / Ančerl**
Supraphon SU1928-2 (69' · ADD) Ⓜ
A distinguished performance from this all-Czech line-up.

Symphonies

No 1 in C minor, B9, 'The Bells of Zlonice'; No 2 in B flat, B12; No 3 in E flat, B34; No 4 in D minor, B41; No 5 in F, B54; No 6 in D, B112; No 7 in D minor, B141; No 8 in G, B163; No 9 in E minor, B178, 'From the New World'

Complete Symphonies

Symphonies Nos 1-9. Scherzo capriccioso, B131. Overtures – In Nature's Realm, B168; Carnival, B169; My Home, B125a
London Symphony Orchestra / István Kertész
Decca ⓑ 430 046-2LC6 (7h 11' · ADD)
Recorded 1963-66 ⒷＯＯ▶

István Kertész recorded the Dvořák symphonies in the mid-1960s and his integral cycle quickly achieved classic status; his exhilarating and vital account of the Eighth Symphony rapidly became a special landmark in the catalogue. The original LPs are now collectors' items. These magnificent interpretations became available again in 1992, in glitteringly refined digitally remastered sound, and it's a tribute to the memory of this tragically short-lived conductor that this cycle continues to set the standard by which others are judged. He was the first conductor to attract serious collectors to the early Dvořák symphonies, and his jubilant advocacy of the unfamiliar First Symphony has never been superseded. This work offers surprising insights into the development of Dvořák's mature style, as does the Second Symphony. Kertész shows that Symphonies Nos 3 and 4 have much more earthy resilience than many commentators might have us believe, insisting that Dvořák's preoccupation with the music of Wagner and Liszt had reached its zenith during this period. The challenging rhetoric of the Fourth has never found a more glorious resolution than here, with Kertész drawing playing of quite gripping intensity from the LSO. The Fifth Symphony and, to a still greater extent, the Sixth reveal Dvořák's clear affinity with the music of Brahms. Kertész's superb reading of the Sixth, however, shows just how individual and naturally expressive this underrated work actually is, while the playing in the great climax of the opening movement and the vigorous final peroration remains tremendously exciting. In the great final trilogy, he triumphs nobly with the craggy resilience of the Seventh Symphony, and he brings a dynamic thrust and momentum to the Eighth. His *New World* is by turns indomitable and searchingly lyrical.

The six-disc set also offers assertive and brilliant readings of the Overtures *Carnival, In Nature's Realm* and the rarely heard *My Home*, together with a lucid and heroic account of the *Scherzo capriccioso*. These definitive performances have been skilfully reprocessed, the sound is astonishingly good, even by modern standards, and the playing of the London Symphony Orchestra is often daringly brilliant.

Symphonies – selected

Symphonies Nos 5, 7, 8 & 9
Oslo Philharmonic Orchestra / Mariss Jansons
Brilliant Classics 92779 (131' · DDD)　Ⓢ🅾🅾

With such lovable music, affectionate treatment pays even greater dividends, and Jansons's Fifth is pure joy. The pastoral opening with its theme for two clarinets over shimmering strings is wonderfully subtle and relaxed, and the EMI engineers have produced sound in the difficult acoustic of the Oslo Konserthus that gives just the bloom needed, combined with warmth and clarity. Jansons's Dvořák now fully matches the achievement of his Oslo Tchaikovsky series for Chandos. As in his Tchaikovsky, Jansons has a way of drawing out expressive phrasing to make it sound totally natural, without self-consciousness.

The slow movement is warmly lyrical, but also refined, and the playing of the Oslo orchestra polished, with cleaner textures enhanced by the recording. The *Scherzo* is done with a playful lilt, and with the horn whoops more exuberant than in any of the rival versions. Jansons crowns his reading with an account of the finale which at the start dramatically hammers home the surprise of Dvořák's use of the minor mode and his deliberate avoidance of establishing the home key of F major. The arrival of that key at last is then all the more warmly satisfying, leading almost at once to the lusciousness of D flat major and the soaring second subject, where the Oslo violins play with a passion to make others seem uncommitted.

In every way except one this is a model performance. Maybe influenced by Dvořák's disowning of the exposition repeat marks in No 6, Jansons – as in his *New World* – fails to observe that first movement repeat here too. His accounts of the last three symphonies make this a super-budget collection to treasure.

Symphony No 6. The Wild Dove
Czech Philharmonic Orchestra / Jiří Bělohlávek
Chandos CHAN9170 (63' · DDD)　Ⓕ🅳➔

Bělohlávek has referred to his Czech orchestra's 'singing art of playing' and its 'mellow sound', and indeed it's Bohemia's woods, fields and wild-

life, rather than energetic village green festivities, that linger in the memory here. Perhaps you shouldn't expect a Czech Philharmonic performance to 'go' or leap about excitedly in the manner of Kertész's with the LSO; in these days of high adrenalin, high contrast and high definition, there's a lot to be said for a less assertive and vigorous approach, always artlessly sung, and for this orchestra's Old World timbres, lending a Brahmsian fireside glow, for example, to the Symphony's first movement second subject on cellos and horns (beautifully eased in by Bělohlávek). These horns, always more rounded in tone than their rasping counterparts in London (Kertész), bear an obvious family resemblance to the woodwind, not only in timbre, but also in the use of vibrato (again, that 'singing art of playing'). And the 'silver moon' flute is one of this disc's principal joys. Bělohlávek also projects the drama of *The Wild Dove* with relish. Chandos guarantees a sepia-toned warmth throughout.

Symphony No 6. The Golden Spinning-Wheel, B197
Czech Philharmonic Orchestra / Sir Charles Mackerras
Supraphon SU3771-2 (71' · DDD)　Ⓕ🅳➔

Sir Charles Mackerras's vibrant interpretation easily holds its own in the most venerable company. Not only are the Czech Philharmonic, recorded live in October 2002, at their articulate and spirited best, but Mackerras directs the outer movements with a pliancy and keen sense of long-term proportion reminiscent of his mentor Talich, as well as Rowicki's magnificent (and sadly deleted) 1965 LSO account. He also extracts every ounce of songful poetry from the sublime slow movement, while the *Furiant* cross-rhythms of the *Scherzo* skip to the manner born. The performance as a whole has a spine-tingling thrust, meriting a place alongside any of its distinguished rivals.

The Golden Spinning-Wheel is a studio recording from June 2001. A splendidly opulent and atmospheric reading, observant and affectionate, if without quite the narrative flair and expressive scope of Harnoncourt's riveting Concertgebouw account.

Symphony No 7. Nocturne in B, B47. The Water Goblin
Czech Philharmonic Orchestra / Jiří Bělohlávek
Chandos CHAN9391 (69' · DDD)　Ⓕ🅳➔

Bělohlávek is a lucid, sure-footed guide through Dvořák's mightiest symphonic utterance, and his sympathetic direction combines both warmhearted naturalness and total fidelity to the score (dynamics are scrupulously attended to throughout). If it sounds just a little under-energised next to other vividly dramatic accounts, the sheer unforced eloquence and lyrical fervour of the playing always give enormous pleasure. Certainly, the first movement's secondary material glows with affectionate warmth, while the sublime *Poco adagio* emerges seamlessly, its songful rapture and nostalgic vein captured as to the manner born by this great orchestra (listen out for some gorgeous work from the principal flute, clarinet and horn).

The *Scherzo* trips along with an infectious, rhythmic spring, as well as an engaging poise and clarity; moreover, the dark-hued, unsettling Trio (a casualty in so many rival performances) is handled with equal perception. The finale, too, is immensely pleasing, marrying symphonic thrust with weighty rhetoric rather in the manner of Colin Davis's distinguished Amsterdam account. The closing bars are very broad and imposing indeed. A performance of considerable dignity and no mean stature, benefiting from vibrant Chandos engineering. The symphony is followed by a long-breathed, slumbering account of the *Nocturne* (gloriously played by the Czech PO strings) and the disc concludes with a fine *Water goblin*. Again, the orchestral response is as disciplined and poised as you could hope to hear.

Symphonies Nos 7 & 8
Philharmonia Orchestra / Sir Charles Mackerras
Signum Classics SIGCD183 (74' · DDD)
Recorded live in 2008   ⓅⓄ⮑

Sir Charles Mackerras himself provides potent rivalry in the form of a Classics for Pleasure double-pack where all three late Dvořák symphonies come coupled with the *Symphonic Variations*. These 2008 live Philharmonia versions of Symphonies Nos 7 and 8 are in general mellower than their 1991-92 predecessors, subtler too in terms of shading and the more expressive tone of various inner voices. The CfP recordings are more sharply focused and have rather more of an 'edge' than this Signum production, while energy levels are marginally higher. What is appealing about the new disc is the naturalness of both readings, always unaffected yet with plenty of discernible character. The Seventh suggests both autumnal thickets and summer skies, though the overall temperature never quite matches Kubelík's Berlin recording. Tempi are flexibly negotiated and there's plenty of light and shade among the textures. The Eighth is extrovert and brightly lit, with one or two telling climactic *ritardandos* in the first movement and a breathtaking dip to *pianissimo* just before the horns sound their alarm in the second. The finale isn't quite as rumbustious as its LPO predecessor but the *Allegretto grazioso* third movement yields sweetness to spare, much aided by some well employed *portamentos*.

Symphonies Nos 7 & 8
Baltimore Symphony Orchestra / Marin Alsop
Naxos 8 572112 (74' · DDD)
Recorded live in 2009   ⓂⓄⓄ⮑

The amount of felicitous detail here is more than enough to justify purchase, even if you already own one or more versions of either

work. In the darkly dramatic finale Alsop allows herself just enough expressive leeway to sweeten the pill without spoiling the line – in the cello-dominated second subject, for example, where the pulse eases ever so slightly. Only the first movement seems rather too strait-laced, with next to no deviation in tempo throughout. This is restless, autumnal music that surely demands a more rhapsodic approach, whereas in the Eighth Alsop turns on her heels and opts for subtle expressiveness, delivering one of the most tender accounts of the finale's wind-down coda since Bruno Walter. Again the first movement is very 'straight' but this time, with less weathered music, the approach works better: no tiresome *ritardandos* impede the flow and there's an impressive contrast between chamber-style intimacy in the quieter passages and impressive, full-blown climaxes. The third movement's Trio is just a little pallid (rather that though than excessive schmaltz) but heard overall the performance works extremely well, and both recordings are thoughtfully balanced.

As to recent rivals in the same coupling, Mackerras and the Philharmonia, also recorded live (see above), offer bags of spontaneity and at times even more warmth, though Alsop's Baltimore orchestra parades a refined tonal profile that pays its own special dividends. Still, Alsop should please both the eager newcomer on the lookout for a recommendation and the seasoned collector who knows and loves the music but fancies listening between the staves. There'll be no disappointment on either score.

Symphonies Nos 8 & 9, 'From the New World'
Berlin Philharmonic Orchestra / Rafael Kubelík
DG The Originals 447 412-2GOR (73' · ADD)
Recorded 1972   ⓂⓄⓄ⮑

These accounts are quite magnificent, and their claims on the allegiance of collectors remain strong. Their freshness and vigour remind one of what it was like to hear these symphonies for the first time. The atmosphere is authentic in feeling and the sense of nature seems uncommonly acute. Kubelík has captured the enthusiasm of his players and generates a sense of excitement and poetry. The playing of the Berlin Philharmonic is marvellously eloquent and, as is often the case, a joy in itself. The woodwinds phrase with great poetic feeling and imagination, and all the departments of this great orchestra respond with sensitivity and virtuosity.

The recording has great dynamic range and encompasses the most featherweight string *pianissimos* to the fullest orchestral *tutti* without discomfort. The listener is placed well back in the hall so that the woodwind, though they blend beautifully, may seem a little too recessed for some tastes, though it should be said that there's no lack of vividness, power or impact. The balance and the timbre of each instrument is natural and truthful; nothing is made larger than life and Kubelík has a natural warmth and flexibility. This will remain high on any list of recommendations for it has a vernal freshness that's wholly reviving.

Symphonies Nos 8 & 9, 'From the New World'
Budapest Festival Orchestra / Iván Fischer
Philips 464 640-2PH (78' · DDD)   Ⓕ❶❶➡

Ten years earlier Fischer recorded the Eighth Symphony with the same orchestra at the same venue. In terms of timings, the two readings are remarkably similar, and yet the later performance is warmer, more malleable and significantly more spontaneous. Both employ expressive string slides (a Fischer characteristic in Slavic music), most noticeably at the end of the *Scherzo*, where a snappy *portamento* on fiddles is echoed by the brass. Philips' recording has an extended dynamic range and a fuller, closer string sound.

While the Eighth, then, is given a bouncy, lyrical performance, 'localised' with the odd gypsy inflection, the *New World*, on the other hand, is intense and energetic. Indeed, it's some tribute to Fischer's musical perception that he views the two works in entirely different terms. Small dynamic details invariably tell with a new-found freshness. Just try sampling the difference between *forte* and *sforzando* among the basses in the first movement and the softness of the second subject, for once a genuine *ppp*. These and similar markings register even if you're not following the music with a score. Accents, too, are keenly observed, articulation is carefully judged and the string choirs have real bite. Indeed, there isn't a more enjoyable digital *New World* on the current market. Fischer's CD is a consistent joy, and is thoroughly recommended.

Symphony No 9, 'From the New World'
Symphonic Variations, B70
Baltimore Symphony Orchestra / Marin Alsop
Naxos 8 570714 (65' · DDD)   Ⓢ❶➡

Dvořák's *New World* has already been recorded by almost everyone who matters! But Marin Alsop makes it very much her own, with her fine Baltimore orchestra responding with an account full of warmth moments of high drama, and, above all, finely paced with a flowing, spontaneous feeling. One notes the delightful flute playing, the bold, strong trombones in *tuttis*, and the luminous grace of the strings, immediately apparent at the affectionate opening of both first and second movements. The delicate close of the *Largo*, after the songful repeat of the beautifully simple and very lovely cor anglais melody, is memorable. The movement's central episodes are equally poetic, particularly the gentle clarinet theme over the murmuring bass *pizzicatos*.

The *Scherzo* bursts in, and the finale has all the impetus one could want. Yet overall, Alsop's is not a histrionic reading but one full of affectionate touches, the appealing little nudge at the end of the second subject of the first movement for instance, while the closing retrospective section of the finale is particularly satisfying.

What makes this disc doubly recommendable is the superb account of the *Symphonic Variations*, inspired but surprisingly neglected. It is a work which after the mysterious opening *Lento e molto tranquillo*, which is perfectly captured here, needs to move on flexibly but with plenty of impetus, capturing the continual changes of mood and colour. The extraordinary variety of invention and scoring captivates the ear, sometimes perky, sometimes gentle (like the enchanting little repeated-note flute solo, followed immediately by gruff trombones), until it reaches its genial fugal apotheosis and the performance sweeps to its folksy, grandiloquent close. The recording is outstanding in every way, well balanced and vivid in detail.

Symphony No 9, 'From the New World'.
The Water Goblin, B195
**Royal Concertgebouw Orchestra /
Nikolaus Harnoncourt**
Teldec 3984 25254-2 (64' · DDD)   Ⓕ❶➡

Harnoncourt has some distinguished Concergebouw forebears, not least structure-conscious Sir Colin Davis and combustible Antal Dorati (both Philips). This, though, beats them all. Auspicious happenings register within the first few pages: carefully drawn woodwind lines; basses that calm meticulously from fierce *fortissimo* to tense *pianissimo*; provocative bassoons and an effortless passage into the lovely flute melody at 2'58". At the start of the development section *piano* violins really are played *leggiero* (lightly), a significant detail that most rivals gloss over. Middle and lower voices are granted their full flavour and the violin desks are divided. Harnoncourt's *Largo* is something of a minor miracle. Undulating clarinets register against shimmering string *tremolandos* and, beyond the beautifully judged approach to the *Meno* passage (bar 78), you suddenly hear quiet second-violin *pizzicato* chords (7'00") that you almost never notice in concert. The finale itself never sags, and for the home straight Harnoncourt treads a course somewhere between the printed *Allegro con fuoco* and the expressive broadening that Dvořák later sanctioned. Most admirable about Harnoncourt's Dvořák is its close proximity to nature: barely a minute passes that isn't somewhere touched by verdure or sunshine.

For the couplings, Harnoncourt gives us *The Water Goblin*, the most folk-like of Dvořák's Erben tone-poems where, as in the Symphony, middle voices rise to the fore and the stamping outer sections are played with great rhythmic bite. If you think that you know the *New World* back-to-front then Harnoncourt will have you thinking again.

Additional recommendations

Symphony No 6
Coupled with **Janáček** Sinfonietta
Bavarian Radio Symphony Orchestra / Kubelík

Orfeo C552 011B (70' · ADD). Recorded live 1981 Ⓕ
A cherishable document captured in wholly
acceptable sound and a must-buy for all devotees
of this conductor. Live performance lends the
Sixth an easy, free-wheeling spontaneity and a
songful poetry that his studio version lacks. The
slow movement is an especial delight.

Symphony No 7
London Symphony Orchestra / C Davis
LSO Live LSO0014 (40' · DDD) Ⓢ▶
Davis masterminds a performance of authority.
His approach is more flexible and generously
expressive than his outstanding 1975 account
but there's no want of symphonic thrust. That
set still reigns supreme but at the price this is
one to snap up.

Symphonies Nos 7, 8 & 9
Coupled with Romance in F minorª. Symphonic
Variations
ª**Gonley** vn ª**English Chamber Orchestra, London
Philharmonic Orchestra / Mackerras**
Classics for Pleasure ② 575761-2 (150' · DDD) Ⓑ
These are winning performances – rhythms
delightfully sprung, detail closely observed and
completely without point-scoring. The Seventh
and Eighth are the gems here, but the rest in no
way disappoints.

Symphony No 8
Coupled with The Noon Witch
Concertgebouw / Harnoncourt
Teldec 3984 24487-2 (51' · DDD) Ⓕ▶
A typical Harnoncourt interpretation with a
freshness of approach and attention to colour
and detail that spell 'winner'.

Symphony No 9
Coupled with Slavonic Dances, B83 – Nos 6, 8;
B147 – No 2
New York Philharmonic Orchestra / Masur
Apex 8573 89085-2 (60' · DDD)
No 9 recorded live 1991 Ⓢ●
The slow movement is particularly outstanding,
with straight, simple phrasing conveying a deeply
emotional intensity. Though recorded live, Masur
achieves a precision of ensemble to rival that of a
studio performance.

Symphony No 9
Coupled with Othello. In Nature's Realm.
Czech Philharmonic Orchestra / Ančerl
Supraphon SU3662-2 (70' · ADD) Ⓜ
A truly great, remarkably unforced interpretation,
consistently illuminating and displaying an iron
grip unmatched on disc.

Symphony No 9
Coupled with **Beethoven** Leonore Overture No 3.
Prokofiev The Love for Three Oranges – Suite
BBC Symphony Orchestra / Kempe
BBC Legends BBCL4056-2 (71' · ADD)
Recorded live 1975 Ⓜ
A visionary reading, deeply meditative in the slow
movement. The BBC SO, on exceptional form,
have *pianissimos* of breathtaking delicacy. The

extreme dynamic contrasts are beautifully caught
and the sound is vivid and fresh.

American Suite, B190

Dvořák American Suite
Suk Scherzo fantastique, Op 25. Serenade, Op 6
Prague Philharmonia / Jakub Hrůša
Supraphon SU3882-2 (66' · DDD) Ⓕ

Still in his mid-twenties, Jakub Hrůša is a conductor to look out for. A pupil of Jiří Bělohlávek,
he has built up a formidable career in Europe
and America. Here he draws superb playing
from the orchestra which Bělohlávek founded.
Dvořák's *American Suite* can easily seem square
and uninspired but Hrůša directs a magical performance. The descending opening phrase
immediately brings echoes of a spiritual. It is
fresh and rustic-sounding, growing more magnetic as it is repeated in melodic ostinato. The
Trio brings a brisk idea like a *Slavonic Dance*, and
the lively second-movement *Allegro* offers a lyrical Trio. The *Moderato* third movement echoes a
polonaise or polacca in its light and jaunty dotted
rhythms. The fourth movement is a warmly lyrical Nocturne opening with a lovely oboe theme,
while the vigorous finale brings folk-like accented
repeated chords again with oboe prominent,
slowing down before a final brisk pay-off.
The two items by Josef Suk are given similarly
fresh and inspired performances. Suk was still in
his teens and a pupil of Dvořák when in 1892 he
completed his Serenade for Strings, and it
remains one of his most delightful works. There
are many echoes of Dvořák, not least in the long
third-movement *Adagio*; but already Suk was
beginning to reveal a distinctive voice, and the
writing for strings throughout is astonishingly
assured for a teenager.
The *Scherzo fantastique* is darker and more distinctive, inventive in its contrasted sections, with
a swinging episode in triple-time lightening the
mood with a waltz-like episode. Again Hrůša's
performance could not be more winning, and the
Supraphon recording is full and vivid.

Czech Suite, B93

Czech Suite. Festival March, B88. The Hero's Song,
B199. Hussite Overture, B132
**Polish National Radio Symphony Orchestra /
Antoni Wit**
Naxos 8 553005 (65' · DDD) Ⓢ▶

The Hero's Song, a colourful, rather sprawling
tone-poem, was Dvořák's last orchestral work
and isn't an easy piece to bring off. Wit finds
genuine nobility in it, while his gentle, mellow
way with the lovely *Czech Suite* also gives much
pleasure. The opening 'Praeludium' is just a
touch sleepy, but there's no want of lyrical
affection or rhythmic bounce elsewhere and
the whole performance radiates an idiomatic,
old-world charm that really is most appealing.

As for the *Hussite* Overture, Wit's clear-headed reading impressively combines dignity and excitement. Given such finely disciplined orchestral playing, the results are again both eloquent and characterful. This just leaves the rousing *Festival March* of 1879, splendidly done here, with the excellent Katowice brass sounding resplendent in their introductory call to arms. Recordings throughout possess a most agreeable bloom and transparency.

Dvořák Czech Suite **Suk** Pohadka, Op 16
Czech Philharmonic Orchestra / Zdeněk Mácal
Octavia ⊗ OVCL00296 (53' · DDD/DSD)   Ⓕ

Though the performers and the works are all Czech, the technicians behind this issue are all Japanese, with the exception of two assistant engineers. The result is technically superb, bringing out the vivid qualities of Super Audio. Dvořák's *Czech Suite* reveals the composer at his most relaxed and winning, fresh and open, light and transparent, with a charming Polka as the second of the five movements, a *Sousedská* ('Fairy-tale') as the third and ending with a lively Furiant.

Suk's suite *Pohadka* makes an ideal coupling. The music was originally written as incidental music to a play, but Suk realised that in that form it would be heard by relatively few people and so devised this suite, which is much more accessible. The result is a delight, also with a Polka as the second movement, and with a bold finale full of cymbal clashes. You could hardly find performers more understanding than Mácal and the Czech Philharmonic.

Slavonic Dances, B83 & B147

Slavonic Dances
**Chamber Orchestra of Europe /
Nikolaus Harnoncourt**
Teldec 8573 81038-2 (73' · DDD)   Ⓕ**OO**☞

Each dance on this exciting disc is granted its rightful, rustic character. The *furiants* really move (Harnoncourt's readings of Op 46 Nos 1 and 8 are among the fastest on disc) and the Dumka of No 2 oscillates between tender reflection and feverish high spirits.

Harnoncourt's high energy levels never preclude delicacy, transparency or even the occasional suggestion of sentiment. Tempo relations have been thought through to the last semiquaver though in general they're more dramatic than rival Iván Fischer's (Philips). That Harnoncourt loves this music is beyond doubt, and that he understands it beyond question. He delves among Dvořák's inner voices, pulling them to the fore like a magician freeing a rabbit, while others seem happier to let the music speak for itself. The Chamber Orchestra of Europe play superbly, all swelling curves and attenuated lines, with their pooled individuality shedding fresh light on virtually every piece. If you don't know the music,

Harnoncourt will make you love it. And if you do know it, he'll make you love it even more.

Slavonic Dances
Cleveland Orchestra / George Szell
Sony Classical 69699 89845-2 (74' · ADD)
Recorded 1963-65   Ⓑ

This reissue is something of a revelation. Both discs have been lovingly remastered and the quality is an amazing improvement over the old LPs. The remastering engineers seem to have discovered a whole bottom octave in the sound, which before had appeared to lack richness and weight to support the brilliant upper range. The *Slavonic Dances* are offered as Szell recorded them, with no repeats cut, so the phenomenal orchestral virtuosity is revealed in all its glory. There's much evidence of the conductor's many captivatingly affectionate touches of *rubato* and, throughout, this large orchestra follows Szell's every whim, with playing full of lyrical fervour and subtlety of nuance, wonderful precision and a lilting rhythmic pulse. The recordings were made within the acoustics of Cleveland's Severance Hall, usually a pair of dances at a time. The result is infectiously spontaneous and this disc can't be recommended too highly; even if the close balance prevents any real *pianissimos* to register, the dynamic range of the music-making is still conveyed.

Additional recommendations

Slavonic Dances
Czech Philharmonic Orchestra / Sejna
Supraphon SU1916-2 (72' · ADD)   Ⓜ
Sejna secures some wonderfully lithe and vivacious playing from his superb Czech band – an exhilarating treat.

Tone-poems

The Water Goblin, B195. The Noon Witch, B196. The Golden Spinning-Wheel, B197. The Wild Dove, B198
Czech Philharmonic Orchestra / Sir Charles Mackerras
Supraphon SU4012-2 (80' · DDD)   Ⓕ**OO**☞

Premonitions of Janáček abound in these wonderful pieces and Sir Charles Mackerras seems to acknowledge the fact in performance, most particularly in *The Wild Dove*, which could easily have hailed from a first draft for *Taras Bulba*. Sir Charles also marks the Mendelssohnian drift of the big string theme in *The Golden Spinning-Wheel*, a performance full of warmth and vitality, very realistically recorded and surely the highlight of the disc. His performing style in this music often calls to mind his one-time teacher Václav Talich, the way dance rhythms are underlined but never overstated (the opening of *The Water Goblin*), the solidity of the playing and what seems like an intuitive understanding of the music's extraordinarily strong atmosphere, for example the palpable premonitions of late Mahler in *The Water Goblin*.

The one problem, such as it is, is in a significant and charismatic rival, namely Nikolaus Harnoncourt. Where Mackerras captures atmosphere, Harnoncourt relishes the music's mix of rustic dance forms and colouristic innovation. Mackerras offers the straighter option, which, good as it is, doesn't conjure quite the same degree of eerie magic, although his version does have the advantage of fitting onto just one CD.

Piano Quintet in A, B155

Piano Quintet in A. String Quintet in G, B49
Gaudier Ensemble (Marieke Blankestijn, Lesley Hatfield *vns* Iris Juda *va* Christoph Marks *vc* Stephen William *db* Susan Tomes *pf*)
Hyperion CDA66796 (66' · DDD)   Ⓕ

Pianist Susan Tomes, who encourages a performance of greater contrasts than the Melos Ensemble on Harmonia Mundi. For example, in the second movement *Dumka* there's more light and shade, and the *Scherzo* sparkles even more, leading to a jaunty, exuberant finale. The G major String Quintet, the earliest of the two which Dvořák wrote, the one with extra double bass, is similarly lighter than the Chilingirian Quartet on Chandos. The Chilingirian is just as strongly characterised as the Gaudier, with a firmer, fuller tone. Marieke Blankestijn's violin is thinner than Levon Chilingirian's, but it can be just as beautiful, as in the lovely high-floating second subject of the slow movement. A fine disc.

Piano Quintet in Aª. Bagatelles, B79[b]
Frank Braley [a]pf/[b]harm [a]**Ensemble Explorations**
([b]Christine Busch, [b]Hyunjong Kang *vns*
Anna Lewis-Deeva *va* [b]Roel Dieltiens *vc*)
Harmonia Mundi HMC90 1880 (54' · DDD)   Ⓕ

Recorded in warm, full sound, pianist Frank Braley leads an often fiery and impulsive account of Dvořák's masterly Piano Quintet (1887), using a vintage Steinway of 1874. The clarity of his articulation adds sparkle to his freely romantic reading, matched by the players of Ensemble Explorations.

In the slow movement, marked *Dumka*, Braley leads a reading poised in the slower sections, making an effective contrast with the faster sections, which are not as sharply different as in most dumka movements. The contrasts of tone and dynamic are most persuasive. In the third-movement Furiant, all three readings are fast and light, while the finale inspires Braley and his partners to spring the rhythms infectiously, with thrust and swagger.

The coupling brings a welcome rarity, written in 1878, the year of the first set of *Slavonic Dances*, for two violins, cello and harmonium, an instrument popular at the time, particularly in America. The sequence is delightful in its

exploiting of fresh ideas, and Braley readily adapts to the demands of the harmonium. It is not a generous coupling but a very attractive one, completing a first-rate disc, well recorded.

Piano Quartets

Piano Quartets – No 1 in D, B53; No 2 in E flat, B162
Domus (Krysia Ososstowicz *vn* Timothy Boulton *va* Richard Lester *vc* Susan Tomes *pf*)
Hyperion CDA66287 (70' · DDD)   Ⓕ

These are two very enjoyable works. Hans Keller's description of the opening pages of the E flat Quartet as 'childish' is staggering – this from the leading campaigner against 'posthumous critical torture'! 'Childlike' would be much more suitable, and this appealing characteristic is well brought out by the members of Domus: Susan Tomes's descent from incisive *fortissimo* clarity to *pianissimo* mystery in the opening bars is a delight, and fully prophetic of the kind of musicianship we're to hear. Two other unforgettable moments from this performance: the lovely return of the first movement second subject, with its heart-easing B major/E flat major modulation – very sensitive use of *rubato* here – and cellist Richard Lester's richly expressive solos at the beginning of the *Lento*.

The D major Quartet is a delightful, if not fully mature piece – it does tend to rely rather heavily on sequence and repetition. Domus makes sure we don't miss any of its virtues, but it doesn't force anything: the timing in the magical opening shift from D major to B major is finely judged, and Dvořák's wonderfully effortless melodies are affectionately shaped and shaded; admirable too the way Susan Tomes finds so much beauty in what often looks like conventionally decorative piano writing. In general the sound is very pleasing, intimate enough to draw one right into the performances without being intimidating, even in the somewhat histrionic second theme of the E flat Quartet's *Lento*. A richly rewarding disc.

String Quartets

No 1 in A, B8; **No 2** in B flat, B17; **No 3** in D, B18;
No 4 in E minor, B19; **No 5** in F minor, B37; **No 6** in A minor, B40; **No 7** in A minor, B45; **No 8** in E, B57;
No 9 in D minor, B75; **No 10** in E flat, B92; **No 11** in C, B121; **No 12** in F, B179, 'American'; **No 13** in G, B192; **No 14** in A flat, B193

String Quartets Nos 1-14; F, B120 (Fragment).
Cypresses, B152. Quartettsatz. Two Waltzes, B105
Prague Quartet (Břetislav Novotny, Karel Přibyl *vns* Lubomír Malý *va* Jan Sírc *vc*)
DG ⑨ 463 165-2GB9 (9h 49' · ADD)
Recorded 1975-77   Ⓑ**OO**

Like Schubert, Dvořák turned to the string quartet early in his career. The three complete quartets included in Vol 1 (Nos 1-3) show considerable facility in writing for strings (after all,

Dvořák was a violinist), but it took him some time to arrive at a fully idiomatic quartet style. He also had to learn to rein in his natural expansiveness: the Third Quartet spins out its modest material to an astonishing 70 minutes – the first movement alone is longer than the whole *American* Quartet! The outer movements of the No 4 in E minor (Vol 2) show him concentrating admirably, though the later shortened version of the central *Andante religioso* is a considerable improvement.

So the interest of Vol 1 (three discs) is largely musicological. Despite this, with playing so fresh and authoritative even the impossibly long-winded Third Quartet has rewards to offer. Each performance has a strong sense of purpose, but that doesn't mean an inability to enjoy all those charming Dvořákian byways. Technically the playing is admirable.

The enjoyment increases through Vol 2. The violin cavatina in the *Andante* of the Fifth Quartet has just the right gentle lilt. Listening to the Prague in the first movement of No 7 you realise how what looks on the page like very simple music can come glowingly to life in the right hands – and the way they handle the slightly tricky *poco più mosso* at the second subject is very impressive.

The finest work in Vol 2 (discs 4-6) is undoubtedly the D minor Quartet, No 9. Volume 3 contains three gems: the E flat Quartet (No 10), the *American* and No 13 in G major – the outstanding work of the collection. The Prague are very sensitive to dynamic contrast (Dvořák's markings are often surprisingly detailed). There's plenty of fine music on these nine well-filled discs, all of it well performed, and the recordings are generally creditable.

String Quartets Nos 12 & 13
Vlach Quartet, Prague (Jana Vlachová, Ondřej Kukal vns Petr Verner va Mikael Ericsson vc)
Naxos 8 553371 (69' · DDD)   Ⓢ➔

On the face of it, the Vlach Quartet's credentials would seem to be impeccable – the group's leader, Jana Vlachová, is the daughter of the great Josef Vlach – and, indeed, the players make a most pleasing impression on this vividly recorded Naxos coupling. They certainly produce a beguilingly rich, beautifully blended sound and bring to this music a big-hearted, songful fervour as well as textural mastery. What's more, Dvořák's characteristic, chugging cross-rhythms are handled with particular felicity. Interpretatively, their approach contrasts strongly with other readings in that the Vlach team adopt a coaxing, lyrically expressive stance (with the gorgeous slow movement of the *American* a highlight). In the case of the masterly G major Quartet, these gifted newcomers show fresh insights (they're especially perceptive in those wistful reminiscences at the heart of the finale).

'Old World – New World'
Cypresses, B152. String Quartets – Nos 10, 11, 13 & 14.

String Quintet, 'American', B180[a]
Emerson Quartet (Eugene Drucker, Philip Setzer vns Lawrence Dutton va David Finckel vc) with
[a]**Paul Neubauer** va
DG Ⓜ ③ 477 8765GH3 (3h 26' · DDD)

These fine recordings build on qualities that over the years have become indelibly associated with the Emerson's profile: clean-edged attack, a suave, subtly varied body of tone, fine-tuned personalities within the group and an overall clarity of vision. It would have been nice to have heard a new version of the *American* (they recorded it a quarter of a century ago), though the differences between the old and the new may well have amounted to little more than the odd greying whisker. All else seems much as it was, with the two 'late' masterpieces, Quartets Nos 13 and 14, earning the highest accolades performance-wise. Both are played with an involving level of dramatic animation and great tenderness.

This set is dedicated to the recently retired Guarneri Quartet, whose founding cellist David Soyer died in 2010: a timely opportunity to take down a recent CD reissue of the Guarneri's *American* Quintet with viola player Walter Trampler (RCA). There the temperature is marginally higher and the dancing element more obviously underlined, though the Emersons struck gold with Paul Neubauer, whose burnished tone fits the quartet like a very warm glove. After the two late quartets, other highlights are the jewel-like *Cypresses*, exceptional as played by the Emersons. In fact the only criticism of Nos 10 and 11 and the Quintet is a tendency towards excessively fine manners in music that quite often needs to connect with the earth, even occasionally get its hands dirty. But the virtues by far outweigh any shortcomings: this is really beautiful quartet playing, with inner parts that are both transparent and well integrated, and that gives the essential impression of four superb musicians sharing matters of vital import, albeit from the standpoint of camaraderie and understanding. The sound quality is intimate but within a gently ambient setting.

Additional recommendation

String Quartets Nos 12, 'American', & 13
Lindsay Quartet
ASV CDDCA797 (66' · DDD)   Ⓕ
Dedicated, typically probing accounts from the Lindsays; the great G major Quartet comes off especially well here.

Piano Trios

Piano Trios – No 3 in F minor, B130; No 4 in E minor, B166, 'Dumky'
Florestan Trio (Anthony Marwood vn Richard Lester vc Susan Tomes pf)
Hyperion CDA66895 (68' · DDD)   Ⓕ

A favourite and appropriate pairing – Dvořák's most passionate chamber work in harness with one of his most genial. The F minor Piano Trio (1883) was contemporaneous with the death of Dvořák's mother; it anticipates something of the storm and stress that characterises the great D minor Seventh Symphony (1884-85) and the Florestan Trio serves it well. All three players allow themselves plenty of expressive leeway and yet the musical line is neither distorted nor stretched too far. The second movement *Allegretto* is truly *grazioso* and the qualifying *meno mosso* perfectly judged. The finale is buoyant rather than especially rustic, whereas the more overtly colourful *Dumky* Trio inspires a sense of play and a vivid suggestion of local colour. Throughout the performance, the manifest 'song and dance' elements of the score (heartfelt melodies alternating with folk-style faster music) are keenly projected. The recordings are first rate, as are the insert-notes. If you're after a subtle, musically perceptive coupling of these two works, then you could hardly do better.

Piano Trios – No 3 in F minor, B130; No 4 in E minor, B166, 'Dumky'
Smetana Trio (Jitka Cechová *pf* Jana Vonášková-Nováková *vn* Jan Páleníček *vc*)
Supraphon SU3872-2 (67' · DDD)　　　Ⓕ

Not surprisingly, the performance by the Smetana Trio is thoroughly idiomatic, with the many *dumka* speed-changes sounding totally natural and spontaneous. What instantly strikes the ear is the delicacy, the piano relatively light to bring out the filigree textures of much of the writing.

They also play with a hushed concentration, keeping the different sections tautly woven together. In the fifth of the six movements, there is a delightful pay-off at the end, and the finale is taken at a thrillingly fast tempo, though light textures bring complete clarity.

In No 3 there is an apt if subtle shift in the recording balance, with the piano weightier, reflecting the Brahmsian quality of much of the writing. Though in the conventional four movements instead of the six of No 4, it is a work on a bigger scale. Not surprisingly, the Czech flavours are brought out strikingly. The Supraphon sound is excellent.

Works for Violin/Viola/Cello and Piano

Dvořák Romantic Pieces, B150. Rondo, B171. Sonatina, B183 **R Strauss** Romanze, AV75. Cello Sonata, Op 6. Morgen, Op 27 No 4
Mischa Maisky *vc* **Pavel Gililov** *pf*
DG 477 7465GH (75' · DDD)　　　ⒻⒹ▸

Richard Strauss's youthful Cello Sonata is often described as influenced by Mendelssohn. There are also touches of Brahms – and of Strauss himself. With hindsight, which is at least insight, the music shows not a few signs of the mature composer's harmonic colouring, and there is certainly plenty of his energy, sometimes doing duty for real invention. To this, Mischa Maisky and Pavel Gililov wholeheartedly respond, going at the powerful first movement with a panache that makes the most of the best in the music and sails airily through the odd clumsiness. Not even Maisky can do much for the rather flat *Andante* but he is well at ease with the separately composed *Romanze*, and with his own arrangement of the song 'Morgen', which does more than simply reiterate the vocal line.

Dvořák's Sonatina was originally a violin-and-piano piece for two of his children, and though Maisky takes it with a light touch, and despite clear and sympathetic piano accompaniment from Gililov, it does not really go as well on the cello. The last of the *Four Romantic Pieces*, which began life as a Trio and which Dvořák said he had hugely enjoyed writing, fares better in this arrangement; and the Rondo, in which it sounds as if Dvořák enjoyed himself more and more as it goes on, is charmingly played. An excellent recording deals admirably with the notorious balance problems of cello and piano.

'Songs My Great-Grandfather Taught Me'
Ten Biblical Songs, B185ᵃ. Seven Gypsy Melodies, 'Zigeunerlieder', B104. In Folk Tone, B146 – Good night, my darling; Nothing can change for me. Eight Love Songs, B160. The Maid Imprisoned, B62 No 11. Leave me alone, B157 No 1. Lullaby, B194
Josef Suk *vn/ᵃva* **Vladimir Ashkenazy** *pf*
Toccata Classics TOCC0100 (50' · DDD)　Ⓕ❶❶❶Ⓓ▸

Josef Suk celebrated his 80th birthday in August 2009; the following month he was in the studio with Vladimir Ashkenazy to record these transcriptions of 30 of his great-grandfather's songs. Readers familiar with Suk's immense and magnificent discography will be delighted to discover he's playing as well as ever. True, these songs aren't as taxing as the great concertos he's recorded in the past, but we can hear the same vibrant tone, pure intonation and confident musicianship that have thrilled us for many years.

In a recent interview, Suk, speaking about these transcriptions, said: 'As a violin or viola is without words I would have to find other ways to add variation.' In the *Gypsy Melodies* and the *Love Songs*, he achieves this partly by changing register for each verse, and as a performer he constantly varies repeated phrases with slight changes of articulation, accent and tone colour – an object lesson in the art of expressive performance. In most of these songs, moreover, Dvořák's melodic quality is strong enough to stand without text. And, in Ashkenazy's hands, the piano parts emerge as wonderfully colourful and evocative.

For the *Biblical Songs* (psalm-settings in Czech composed in 1894 in America) Suk turns to the viola – not just any viola, but the composer's own instrument. Listening to its dark, burnished tone, one wonders whether this was the instrument that played at the premiere of *The Bartered*

Bride and in the first, private performance of Smetana's quartet *From My Life*, with its celebrated opening viola solo.

Requiem, B165

Requiem. Mass in D, B153
Pilar Lorengar sop **Neil Ritchie** treb **Erzesébet Komlóssy** contr **Andrew Giles** counterten **Robert Ilosfalvy, Alan Byers** tens **Tom Krause** bar **Robert Morton** bass **Nicholas Cleobury** org **Ambrosian Singers; Christ Church Cathedral Choir, Oxford / Simon Preston; London Symphony Orchestra / István Kertész**
Double Decca ② 448 089-2DF2 (138' · ADD · T/t)
Recorded 1968 Ⓜ

Kertész's Requiem dates from 1968 and on all counts but one, it surpasses Karel Ančerl's classic 1959 set, reissued on DG in 1995 and coupled with Fischer-Dieskau's 1960 set of Dvořák's *Biblical Songs* with Jörg Demus. The exception is the rather too soft-grained singing of Pilar Lorengar as compared with the clear, more vibrant soprano of Maria Stader. But Lorengar's singing is particularly sensitive and appealing in the quieter passages. The lovely quality of Robert Ilosfalvy's voice tells beautifully in 'Liber scriptus proferetur' and in the opening section of the quartet, 'Recordare, Jesu pie'. Dvořák distributes short passages among the soloists impartially. They combine beautifully in the quartet, and the chorus with them in 'Pie Jesu Domine'. The hero of the occasion is Kertész. He gets choral singing and orchestral playing of the finest quality. It's abundantly evident that he cherishes a great love for this work. The Mass in D (sung in the original version with organ) sits well with the Requiem; Simon Preston produces a fine, well-balanced performance, with the Christ Church choristers on excellent form.

Requiem
Lisa Milne sop **Karen Cargill** mez **Peter Auty** ten **Peter Rose** bass **London Philharmonic Choir and Orchestra / Neeme Järvi**
LPO ② LPO0042 (85' · DDD) Ⓑ⯈

The classic recording of Dvořák's Requiem, Ančerl's, has found a place intermittently in the catalogue and held one permanently in the affections of those who admire this uneven but moving work. Ančerl's understanding of all that went into the music remains unrivalled. Others, notably Kertész and Sawallisch, have given smoother performances and been given richer recordings; and this new version from Neeme Järvi certainly does more detailed justice to Dvořák's eloquent orchestration.

Not the least of the problems for conductor, soloists and indeed recording engineers is his love of writing for the four soloists as a quartet, for instance in the 'Recordare' and the 'Pie Jesu'. This is not a work for soloistic egotism, beautifully though they sing; this is essentially an ensemble work, and one of Järvi's strengths lies

in allowing the choir to sing with an almost improvisatory fluency, though it is of course the product of a deep understanding and watchful control of Dvořák's melodic lines. These can be unexpected; the music here sounds natural and always expressive. Järvi makes his points without labouring them.

Even if there is something grittier and more heartfelt in the old Ančerl version, this new one is no less true to a remarkable setting of the ancient words.

Requiem[a]. Symphony No 8[b]
[a]**Krassimira Stoyanova** sop [a]**Mihoko Fujimura** mez [a]**Klaus Florian Vogt** ten [a]**Thomas Quasthoff** bass [a]**Vienna Singverein; Royal Concertgebouw Orchestra / Mariss Jansons**
RCO Live ② RCO10001 (60' · DDD)
Recorded live at the Concertgebouw, Amsterdam, in [a]2009 and [b]2008 Ⓕ⯈

Dvořák's wonderful Requiem differs from the major Masses of Haydn, Mozart, Beethoven, Verdi and Brahms in that its musical poetry turns inward and there's a sense of awe that at times approximates the larger choral works of Bruckner.

The 'Dies irae' is grimly insistent and the *Parsifal*-like use of brass and tam-tam at the start of the 'Tuba mirum' is supremely effective, though the lyrical 'Recordare' is very characteristic. The work's second part, which starts with the Offertorium, offers the greater comfort and generally lighter shades, the thundering central climax of the closing 'Agnus Dei' quite overwhelming on this magnificent recording. The singing is consistently fine, both solo and in ensemble, and the sheer range of colour achieved by the Vienna Singverein, whether in rapt *pianissimo* or when singing their hearts out in the 'Agnus Dei', at times defies belief.

The most recent rival to Jansons – with Neeme Järvi conducting the LPO's forces in full cry, and recorded at almost exactly the same time – was much praised (see above), and with good reason. It's a fair bit swifter than this Jansons version, though that exultant last climax makes less of an impact, principally because an important counter-idea at its crown is partially obscured. Also, there's some less-than-tight string ensemble early on in the 'Dies irae'. The fill-up on the present double-pack (Järvi's set doesn't have one) is a 'very Mariss Jansons' performance of the Eighth Symphony that toys with dynamics in pursuit of maximum expressive effect. It's a real performance and a worthy makeweight for a magnificent reading of the Requiem, which is a real feather in Jansons's cap, CD-wise. Both recordings are superb.

Mass in D, B153

Dvořák Mass in D **Eben** Prague Te Deum 1989
Janáček Our Father
Dagmar Mašková sop **Marta Beňačková** mez

Dvořák Vocal

Walter Coppola *ten* Peter Mikuláš *bass* Lydie Härtelová *hp* Josef Ksica *org* Prague Chamber Choir / Josef Pancík
ECM New Series 449 508-2 (59' · DDD · T/t) Ⓕ☐➤

This imaginative coupling brings together three fine pieces of Czech church music in skilled and sympathetic interpretations. Dvořák's Mass has received a number of good recorded performances; this one, in the original 1887 version with organ, has a very well-matched quartet of soloists who blend smoothly with each other and with the chamber choir. It's a work of particular intimacy and charm, and these qualities mark this performance.

Janáček's setting of the Lord's Prayer dates from 1906, and is in turn a meditative piece, not without vivid illustrative touches appropriate to a work originally designed to accompany a sequence of devotional pictures; and Petr Eben's *Prague Te Deum* coincided, in 1969, with a moment of apparent release from political oppression. It has something of Janáček's suddenness in the invention, and a graceful melodic manner. Each of these works is in its way inward, personal and reflective, but they all share a Czech character.

Stabat mater

Stabat mater. Psalm 149
Lívia Ághová *sop* Marga Schiml *contr* Aldo Baldin *ten* Luděk Vele *bass* Prague Children's Choir; Prague Philharmonic Choir; Czech Philharmonic Orchestra / Jiří Bělohlávek
Chandos ② CHAN8985/6 (96' · DDD) Ⓕ●

The 10 sections of the *Stabat mater* are well laid out for the different vocal and instrumental forces and so avoid the monotony which might seem inherent in this contemplative and deeply sombre text. This performance was recorded in Prague Castle, and in it we feel the full dignity and drama of the work, an oratorio in all but name. The four solo singers convey genuine fervour and one feels that their sound, which is quite unlike that of British singers, must be akin to what the composer originally imagined. If they're a touch operatic, that doesn't sound misplaced and they perform well together, as in the second verse quartet 'Quis est homo'. The choral singing is no less impressive, and indeed the whole performance under Bělohlávek gets the balance right between reverent simplicity and intensity of feeling. Psalm 149 is a setting of 'Sing unto the Lord a new song' for chorus and orchestra and its celebratory mood provides a fine complement to the other work.

Cypresses

Cypresses, B11ᵃ. Cypresses, B152ᵇ
ᵃTimothy Robinson *ten* ᵃGraham Johnson *pf*
ᵇDelmé Quartet (Galina Solodchin, John Trusler *vns* John Underwood *va* Jonathan Williams *vc*)
Somm SOMMCD236 (80' · DDD · T/t) Ⓕ

The charming sequence of 12 pieces for string quartet that Dvořák called *Cypresses* has been recorded fairly often, but the set of 18 folk-like songs on which they're based has been neglected. So this disc setting the two cycles side by side makes an illuminating coupling. His first essays in song-writing were inspired by his unrequited love for the elder of two sisters (he later married the younger one), and were not published in his lifetime. The cycle had to wait until 1983 for a first complete public performance. In their reflection of youthful love they provide a touching portrait of the young composer. Predictably, the quartet versions are subtler. The vocal line is generally transferred to violin or viola, with masterly transcription of the piano accompaniments, disguising their origin. A number were radically expanded.

The recording sets Timothy Robinson at a slight distance, and there's an occasional roughness to the top of his range. Still, he responds with warmth, and in idiomatic Czech, aided by responsive accompaniment from Graham Johnson. In the instrumental versions the Delmés phrase expressively within relatively broad speeds.

Songs

Seven Gypsy Melodies, B104. In Folk Tone, B146. Eight Love Songs, B160. Ten Biblical Songs, B185
Dagmar Pecková *mez* Irwin Gage *pf*
Supraphon SU3437-2 (69' · DDD · T/t) Ⓕ

These four cycles make an excellent and generous coupling, with Dagmar Pecková, brilliantly supported by Irwin Gage, a most persuasive advocate. Hers is an ideal voice, unmistakably Slavonic in timbre, yet firm and pure as well as rich. She retains a freshness specially apt for songs inviting a girlish manner, including Dvořák's most famous song, the fourth of the seven *Gypsy Melodies*, 'Songs my mother taught me', sounding fresh and new.

The four cycles represent the full span of Dvořák's career. The eight *Love Songs*, B160 may officially date from 1888, but Dvořák in fact reworked a selection from 18 songs he'd written passionately at high speed over 20 years earlier – charming pieces which already reveal his unquenchable lyrical gift. Next chronologically are the *Gypsy Songs* of 1900, bold and colourful, here nicely contrasted by Pecková and Gage with four simpler, less exotic songs, *In Folk Tone*, of six years later. Last and longest is the cycle of ten *Biblical Songs*, written in the United States in 1894, when he was feeling homesick. They are more often sung by male singers, gaining from weight and gravity, but here with the mezzo, Pecková, they prove just as moving and intense. The sound is clear and well balanced.

Seven Gypsy Melodies, B104. In Folk Tone, B146.

Eight Love Songs, B160. Four Songs, B124 – Oh what a perfect golden dream; Downcast am I, so often. Four Songs, B157 – Over her Embroidery; Springtide; At the Brook. Four Songs, B23 – Obstacles; Meditation; Lime Trees. Songs from the Dvur Králové Manuscript, B30
Bernarda Fink mez **Roger Vignoles** pf
Harmonia Mundi HMC90 1824 (69' · DDD)   Ⓕ

An all-Dvořák song recital may still seem a luxury. The *Gypsy Songs*, and not just their famous fourth ('Songs my mother taught me'), have found a secure place in the repertoire, but not much else is heard at all regularly either in recital or on disc. They may lack the variety of mood to constitute a fully satisfying programme on their own, but they never fail to give pleasure. One cause of the continued unfamiliarity of the B160 set is that Czech is an alien language to most recitalists. Not, however, to Argentinian mezzo Bernarda Fink, who comes from a Slovenian family, lived in Prague for a while and has made a special study of Czech music. Her diction is very clear. Her tone is rich and deep, and the manner has warmth and dignity, though these seem to be its limits. If you come to the *Gypsy Songs* with Anne Sofie von Otter's recording in mind, you'll miss, in Fink's singing, a lot of colour, imagination and temperament. But there may be some relief, too. Von Otter's recording with Bengt Forsberg is exciting but assertive. Fink and Vignoles may prove more companionable. But this new issue is most welcome: tasteful and often lovely performances and a generously comprehensive selection.

The Jacobin

The Jacobin
Václav Zítek bar Bohuš **Vilém Přibyl** ten Jiří **Daniela Sounová** sop Terinka **Karel Průša** bass Count Vilém **René Tuček** bar Adolf **Marcela Machotková** sop Julie **Karel Berman** bass Filip **Beno Blachut** ten Benda **Ivana Mixová** mez Lotinka **Kantilena Children's Chorus; Kühn Chorus; Brno State Philharmonic Orchestra / Jiří Pinkas**
Supraphon ② 11 2190-2 (155' · ADD · T/t)
Recorded 1977   Ⓕ

This was the first recording of Dvořák's charming village comedy – for the Jacobin of the title isn't a political activist but a young man, Bohuš, returning from exile in Paris to his stuffy old father, Count Vilém. The sub-plots include all manner of misunderstandings, and set in the middle of them is the touching figure of Benda, the fussy, rather pedantic but wholly moving music-master. Dvořák is known to have had in mind his own boyhood teacher, Antonín Liehmann, whose daughter gives her name, Terinka, to Benda's daughter. Beno Blachut celebrated his 64th birthday during the making of this set. His was a long career, as well as one of great distinction; he's still well able to get round the lines of this part, and gives an affecting picture of the old musician, never more so than in the

rehearsing of the welcome ode. This is an idea that's cropped up in opera before, but it's charmingly handled here.

Václav Zítek sings Bohuš pleasantly and Marcela Machotková trips away lightly as Julie. Vilém Přibyl sounds less than his most energetic, though his voice is in good fettle; and there's some lack of drive from Jiří Pinkas, who might have done more to bring out the often witty touches in Dvořák's scoring. Never mind: this revived version of a delightful piece can be safely recommended.

Kate and the Devil

Kate and the Devil
Anna Barová contr Kate **Richard Novák** bass Devil Marbuel **Miloš Ježil** ten Shepherd Jirka **Daniela Suryová** contr Kate's Mother **Jaroslav Horáček** bass Lucifer **Jan Hladík** bass Devil the Gate-keeper **Aleš Stáva** bass Devil the Guard **Brigita Sulcová** sop Princess **Natália Romanová** sop Chambermaid **Pavel Kamas** bass Marshall **Oldřich Polášek** ten Musician **Brno Janáček Opera Chorus and Orchestra / Jiří Pinkas**
Supraphon ② 11 1800-2 (119' · AAD · T/t)
Recorded 1979   Ⓕ

Though this was never one of the best Supraphon recordings, it's perfectly serviceable. The plot is complicated, and broadly speaking concerns the bossy Kate who, finding herself a wallflower at the village hop, angrily declares that she would dance with the Devil himself. Up there duly pops a junior devil, Marbuel, who carries her off to hell, where her ceaseless chatter wearies Lucifer himself. The diabolical company is only too happy to allow the shepherd Jirka to remove her again. Jirka, attractively sung by Miloš Ježil, also manages to help the wicked but later repentant Princess to escape the Devil's clutches, and all ends well. The work has a proper coherence, and much good humour besides. Anna Barová's Kate is strong and full of character, but manages not to exclude the charm that should underlie her rantings at Marbuel, who's handsomely sung by Richard Novák. Brigita Sulcová similarly makes much of the unsympathetic Princess. Jaroslav Horáček enjoys himself hugely as Lucifer and Jiří Pinkas accompanies them well.

The King and the Charcoal Burner

The King and the Charcoal Burner
Dalibor Jenis bar King Matyáš **Peter Mikuláš** bar Matěj **Michelle Breedt** contr Anna **Lívia Ághová** sop Liduška **Michal Lehotsky** ten Jeník **Markus Schäfer** ten Jindřich **Prague Chamber Choir; Cologne Radio Chorus and Symphony Orchestra / Gerd Albrecht**
Orfeo ② C678 062H (114' · DDD · S/T/t/N) Ⓕ
Recorded live 2005

Dvořák's delightful *The King and the Charcoal Burner* was the second opera that he wrote and the first to be staged. In its first form it was abandoned during rehearsal as being too complex and Wagnerian, which led the composer to rewrite the piece completely, simplifying its textures and material. There followed two more versions which together form the basis of this version, recorded at concert performances in Cologne with an excellent cast of young Czech singers under Albrecht, an ever-sympathetic advocate.

The piece vies with Smetana's *The Bartered Bride* in the freshness of its Czech flavours. This marked the emergence of Dvořák's mature style, benefiting in this instance from his experience as a player in the opera orchestra in Prague. Very attractive it is, if without the sharp memorability of the Smetana's most striking numbers. Well balanced sound with voices exceptionally clear, each of them well defined with clear diction.

Lívia Ághová in the soprano role of Liduška, the charcoal burner's daughter, sings with beautiful, pure tone. She is first heard at her spinning-wheel, before the arrival of her lover, Jeník, sung with comparable purity by tenor Michal Lehotsky. The King, strongly sung by baritone Dalibor Jenis, lost in the forest in Act 1, is given shelter by the charcoal burner, Matěj – Peter Mikuláš in splendid voice. Though the King is attracted to the lovely Liduška, he recognises her genuine love for Jeník, and, after a test he devises for her, gives his blessing to their union amid general rejoicing. The chorus is a key element in the work, reflecting Dvořák's original inspiration prompted by hearing *Meistersinger*, with the Prague Chamber Choir and the Radio Choir singing with crisp, fresh ensemble.

Rusalka

Rusalka
Renée Fleming sop Rusalka **Ben Heppner** ten Prince **Franz Hawlata** bass Watergnome **Dolora Zajick** mez Ježibaba **Eva Urbanová** sop Foreign Princess **Iván Kusnjer** bar Hunter, Gamekeeper **Zdena Kloubová** sop Turnspit **Lívia Ághová** sop First Woodsprite **Dana Burešová** mez Second Woodsprite **Hana Minutillo** contr Third Woodsprite **Kühn Mixed Choir; Czech Philharmonic Orchestra / Sir Charles Mackerras**
Decca ③ 460 568-2DHO3 (163' · DDD · T/t)
Ⓕ **OOO**B↦

Renée Fleming's tender and heart-warming account of Rusalka's Invocation to the Moon reflects the fact that the role of the lovelorn water nymph, taken by her in a highly successful production at the Met in New York, has become one of her favourites. Ben Heppner also has a special relationship with the opera, for the role of the Prince was the first he studied in depth as a student. He has sung it repeatedly since then, often opposite Renée Fleming, and both he and Mackerras have long harboured the ambition to make a complete recording.

The joy of this magnificent set, which won *Gramophone*'s Record of the Year 1999, is that in almost every way it fulfils every expectation and more, offering a recording with glowing sound that more than ever before reveals the richness and subtlety of Dvořák's score. As interpreted by Fleming and Mackerras, Rusalka's big aria at the start of Act 3, when having been rejected by the Prince, she seeks consolation in returning to the water, is as poignantly beautiful as the more celebrated Invocation to the Moon in Act 1, when she laments over loving a human. In addition, the climactic moments bring glorious top notes, firm and true up to B flat and B. Heppner, like Fleming, conveys his special affection for this music, unstrained up to top C, combining heroic power with lyric beauty.

Dolora Zajick as the Witch, Ježibaba, is characterful and fruity. Franz Hawlata as the Watergnome, Rusalka's father, is firm and dark, bringing a Wagnerian weight to the role. The engineers also thrillingly capture the off-stage effects so important in this opera, with the Watergnome balefully calling from the lake. Even the smaller roles have been cast from strength, all of them fresh, true and idiomatic. Strikingly, there isn't a hint of a Slavonic wobble from any of the singers. In the orchestra, too, the Czech horns are consistently rich and firm. And if anyone is worried about having four non-Czech principals, they're as idiomatic as any rivals.

The final glory of the set lies in the warmly understanding conducting of Charles Mackerras. In every way this matches and even outshines his supreme achievement in the Decca series of Janáček operas. In those you had the Vienna Philharmonic, but here the Czech Philharmonic is both a degree more idiomatic and just as opulent in tone, with superb solo work. The balance between voices and orchestra is well managed, with voices never drowned.

Rusalka
Cheryl Barker sop Rusalka **Rosario La Spina** ten Prince **Bruce Martin** bar Watergnome **Elizabeth Whitehouse** sop Foreign Princess **Anne-Marie Owens** mez Ježibaba **Sarah Crane, Taryn Fiebig** sops Wood Sprites **Dominica Matthews** mez Wood Sprites **Barry Ryan** bar Hunter, Gamekeeper **Sian Pendry** sop Kitchen Boy **Australian Opera Chorus and Orchestra / Richard Hickox**
Chandos ③ CHAN10449 (153' · DDD · S/T/t/N)
Recorded live at the Opera House, Sydney in March 2007
Ⓕ **OO**B↦

Richard Hickox has made a bold choice in Dvořák's last and greatest opera, *Rusalka*, given the near-definitive version conducted by Sir Charles Mackerras (see above). Yet even in face of such competition there is a strong case for his new version from Chandos.

Cheryl Barker may not have so creamily beautiful a voice as Renée Fleming but she sounds more aptly girlish and fresh. Her big Act 1 solo, the Invocation to the Moon, flows far more easily than in Fleming's very beautiful but very expansive version, an obvious advantage. Tenor Rosario La Spina as the Prince is younger-sounding, more virile and more expressive than the Heldentenor Ben Heppner on Decca. As for Hickox, he conducts this magical score with a bite that brings out the elements so closely related to the *Slavonic Dances*, and the recording, made live in the Sydney Opera House (a difficult venue), is clean and fresh.

The Australian cast, singing in Czech, sounds totally in tune with the Dvořák idiom, with each singer matching up to his or her Decca counterpart. Bruce Martin as the Water Goblin may not have so rich or well focused a voice as Franz Hawlata on Decca, but his is a strong and characterful performance, and as the witch Ježibaba, Anne-Marie Owens is satisfyingly rich and fruity, where her Decca counterpart is relatively thin-toned. There is also a gain in that this has been recorded live from a stage production, notably in the thrilling conclusion of the Second Act. Surprisingly, Renée Fleming in Act 2 is less assured than in the other acts, while Cheryl Barker is consistent throughout, and her performance culminates in a deeply moving account of Rusalka's final solo, with a thrilling build-up.

A final choice must remain marginal, but anyone who wants a new-minted version of one of the most magical of all operas – with the harp signalling the other-worldly magic of Rusalka as Water Nymph, more atmospherically recorded than on Decca – this new Chandos version makes an excellent choice.

Rusalka
Milada Subrtová *sop* Rusalka **Eduard Haken** *bass* Watergnome **Marie Ovčačíková** *contr* Ježibaba **Ivo Zídek** *ten* Prince **Alena Míková** *mez* Foreign Princess **Jadwiga Wysoczanská, Eva Hlobilová** *sops* **Věra Krilová** *contr* Woodsprites **Ivana Mixová** *sop* Kitchen Boy **Václav Bednář** *bar* Hunter, Gamekeeper **Prague National Theatre Chorus and Orchestra / Zdeněk Chalabala**
Supraphon ② SU0013-2 (149' · ADD · T/t)
Recorded 1961   Ⓕ ●

This excellent set boasts Eduard Haken, one of the great interpreters of the Watergnome, in robust voice, infusing the character with a rueful gentleness as well as a firmness of utterance. Ivo Zídek as the Prince was in his mid-thirties and in his prime at the time of this recording, singing ardently and tenderly and with a grace of phrasing that matches him well to Milada Subrtová's Rusalka. Hers is a beautiful performance, sensitive to the character's charm as well as to her fragility and pathos. The Slavonic tradition of the old watersprite legend places her in the line of the suffering heroine and it's a measure of Dvořák's success that her delicate appeal holds throughout quite a long opera, and her sinuous but never oversensual lines and the piercing harmony associated with her give her a unique appeal. Subrtová sings the part

with unfaltering sensitivity. Zdeněk Chalabala, who died only a couple of months after completing this recording, handles the score with great tenderness and an affection that shines through every bar. This is a beautiful performance. The recording comes up remarkably well, too.

Rusalka (sung in English)
Eilene Hannan *sop* Rusalka **Rodney Macann** *bass* Watergnome **Ann Howard** *mez* Witch **John Treleaven** *ten* Prince **Phyllis Cannan** *sop* Foreign Princess **Cathryn Pope, Eileen Hulse** *sops* **Linda McLeod** *mez* Woodsprites **Fiona Kimm** *sop* Kitchen Boy **Edward Byles** *ten* Gamekeeper **Christopher Booth-Jones** *bar* Hunter **English National Opera Orchestra / Mark Elder**
Stage director **David Pountney**
Video director **Derek Bailey**
ArtHaus Musik 🖸 102 019
(159' · NTSC · 4:3 · PCM stereo · 0).
Recorded live 1986   Ⓕ ●●

The power-house regime of music director Mark Elder and stage director David Pountney at ENO created many imaginative productions, of which this *Rusalka* was among the finest. They set the fairy-tale opera in an Edwardian nursery full of toys, with the Watergnome as Rusalka's grandfather in a wheelchair and the watersprite first seen on a swing with her feet bound together, very much an Alice in Wonderland figure. The Witch is a wicked aunt, sinister in black as she pronounces her curses: when Rusalka chooses human form, she snarls: 'You'll be dumb for evermore!'

The concept works well, with suggestions that it is all just a dream. Motivations, characterisation and storyline are clarified and the fantasy is intensified. In the title-role Eilene Hannan, with her clear, bright soprano, sings powerfully, and John Treleaven as the Prince shows no sign of strain, even if he does not cut a very romantic figure. Rodney Macann as the Watergnome tends to steal the show, his dark, incisive bass very characterful. Ann Howard is wonderfully menacing as the Witch, while the fluttering *vibrato* of Phyllis Cannan as the Foreign Princess adds to the exotic image (in Act 2, when most of the characters are dressed in white, she stands out in a crimson gown). The three Woodsprites are lively, and incidental characters are well taken.

Mark Elder draws warm incisive playing from the orchestra, adding to the dramatic impact and underpinning the moving final scene, when the Prince kisses Rusalka, knowing it will mean his death.

Film

'Deo Gratias – A Documentary on the life of Antonín Dvořák'
Written and directed by Martin Suchánek

Includes movements from Symphony No 9,
Piano Concerto, Cello Concerto, Slavonic
Dances, String Serenade, 'American' Quartet,
Biblical Songs, Te Deum
Artists include **Gustav Rivinius** vc **Martin Kasik** pf
**Škampa Qt; Czech PO / Kout, Košler, Neumann;
Prague Philharmonic / Bělohlávek; Prague SO /
Delogu**
Video directors **Jan Bonaventura, Adam Rezek**
Supraphon 📀 SU7007-9 (142' · NTSC · 16:9 · PCM
stereo & 2.0 · 0) Ⓕ

'Deo Gratias' ('Thanks be to God'), Dvořák's
final comment on his life, is an admirably direct
and informative documentary, with plenty of
illustrations of people and places, complemented by historic film.

The opening, shots of the 1969 moon landing,
are a surprise, though we learn that, aptly, the
New World Symphony was playing on Neil
Armstrong's headphones as he stepped onto the
lunar surface. Other points are less surprising
but more revealing: reports from Dvořák's first
music school were unflattering, for example, and
his New York salary as director of the Conservatoire was 30 times higher than what he was getting at home. The film contrasts the rapturous
reception he received in England, and later in
the United States, with the relative indifference
and even hostility that greeted him in Germany,
and covers the composition of key works, giving
us an engaging portrait.

It's a pity that the musical items are single
movements rather than complete works, but the
selection is fair. The *New World* finale and the
first movement of the Cello Concerto, with
soloist Gustav Rivinius, are vintage recordings,
but the brilliantly played Piano Concerto finale
is recent.

Sir George Dyson
British 1883-1964

*Dyson studied at the Royal College of Music. In 1914
he joined the Royal Fusiliers after being invalided
home with shell shock in 1916 and recovering, he
joined the Royal Air Force and became involved in
their military bands. In 1921 he took up posts as
music master at Wellington College and as professor
of composition at the Royal College of Music. He then
worked for 30 years as a school music teacher (at
Rugby, Wellington and Winchester), before being
appointed director of the Royal College of Music in
1937. His works include choral and orchestral pieces
(notably The Canterbury Pilgrims).*

Symphony

Symphony. Concerto da chiesa. At the Tabard Inn
**Bournemouth Symphony Orchestra /
David Lloyd-Jones**
Naxos 8 557720 (73' · DDD) Ⓢ➔

Acclaimed at its first performance in 1937,
Dyson's ambitious Symphony subsequently fell

into neglect as it followed on from a striking
sequence of symphonies written by British
composers in the 1930s such as Vaughan
Williams, Walton, Bax and Moeran. In the first
two movements, Dyson's determination to
strike a contemporary pose in an era symphonically dedicated to Sibelius seems to inhibit his
natural melodic gift, with often fragmentary
thematic material rarely developing into a
tune.

Yet in the third-movement variations – taking
the place of a *scherzo* – and most of all in the colourful finale, any inhibitions evaporate in warm,
free and colourful writing, echoing that in Dyson's Chaucerian choral work *The Canterbury
Pilgrims*. Helped by a clear, well-balanced recording, David Lloyd-Jones conducts a brilliant performance that clarifies textures noticeably.

Each of the three movements of the *Concerto da
chiesa* for strings of 1949 is based on a medieval
hymn melody, with *Veni Emmanuel* inspiring a
darkly dedicated slow first movement. It is
among Dyson's finest inspirations, a lament no
doubt reflecting his mood after the Second
World War. That melody returns transformed
at the end of the joyful finale, which is based on
the vigorous psalm tune *Laetatus sum*. The central *Allegretto* uses the carol-like *Corde natus* for
lightly scored and fanciful variations. As in
Elgar's Introduction and Allegro and Vaughan
Williams's *Tallis* Fantasia, solo strings are beautifully and atmospherically set against the full
string band, enhanced here by fine separation in
the Naxos recording.

Originally designed to introduce *The Canterbury
Pilgrims*, the overture *At the Tabard Inn* makes an
attractive addition to a well-filled disc. All three
works are superbly played and vividly recorded.

The Canterbury Pilgrims

The Canterbury Pilgrims. In Honour of the City.
At the Tabard Inn
Yvonne Kenny sop **Robert Tear** ten **Stephen
Roberts** bar **London Symphony Chorus and
Orchestra / Richard Hickox**
Chandos ② CHAN9531 (118' · DDD ·T) Ⓕ❶❶❶➔

 This superb offering of a full-length
cantata based on the Prologue to Chaucer's *Canterbury Tales* bears out its reputation as Dyson's masterpiece. It's a fresh, tuneful
work, aptly exuberant in its celebration of Chaucer. Following the scheme of Chaucer's Prologue,
the 12 movements, plus Envoi, present a sequence
of portraits, deftly varying the forces used, with the
three soloists well contrasted in their characterisations and with the chorus acting as both narrator
and commentator, providing an emotional focus
for the whole work in two heightened sequences,
the sixth and twelfth movements, moving and
noble portraits of the two characters who aroused
Dyson's deepest sympathy, the Clerk of Oxenford
and the Poor Parson of a Town. If the idiom is
undemanding, with occasional echoes of Vaughan
Williams's *A Sea Symphony* and with passages

reminiscent of Rachmaninov's *The Bells*, the cantata sustains its length well.

Outstanding among the soloists is Robert Tear who not only characterises brilliantly but sings with admirable fullness and warmth. The beautiful, fading close, when Tear as the Knight begins the first tale, moving slowly offstage, is most atmospherically done. Yvonne Kenny and Stephen Roberts sing well too, but are less distinctive both in timbre and expression. The London Symphony Chorus sings with incandescent tone, superbly recorded, and the orchestra brings out the clarity and colourfulness of Dyson's instrumentation.

Additional recommendation

Quo vadis
Barker sop **Rigby** mez **Langridge** ten **Williams** bar
BBC Nat Chor & Orch of Wales / Hickox
Chandos ② CHAN10061   Ⓕ**OO**Ⓑ
Dyson's idiom may not be as distinctive as that of those other 'agnostics at prayer', but with its lyrical warmth and fine control of texture, the result will delight all devotees of the English choral tradition.

Petr Eben   Czech 1929-2007

Born in northeastern Bohemia, Eben studied piano, and later cello and organ. The years of German occupation and the Second World War were especially difficult for him. Although Eben was raised as a Catholic, his father was a Jew and in 1943 Eben was expelled from school and interned by the Nazis in Buchenwald for the duration of the war.

After the war he was admitted to the Prague Academy for Music where he studied piano. Beginning in 1955 Eben taught for many years in the music history department at Charles University in Prague.

In 1990 he became professor of composition at the Academy of Performing Arts in Prague and president of the Prague Spring Festival. He was well-known for his improvisations on the piano and organ, but composition remained his main area of interest, and he wrote across a wide range of genres.

Piano Trio

Eben Piano Trio **Martinů** Piano Trio No 1, 'Cinq pièces brèves', H193 **Smetana** Piano Trio, Op 15 B104
Florestan Trio (Anthony Marwood vn
Richard Lester vc Susan Tomes pf)
Hyperion CDA67730 (57' · DDD)   Ⓕ**O**Ⓑ

An imaginatively planned programme which showcases, as the album's excellent annotator Robert Philip suggests, the 'Czech family', Smetana being the father, Martinů and Eben two of his most gifted sons. Martinů's pleasantly

diverting First Trio, subtitled *Cinq pièces brèves*, is very much of its time (1930), the third movement busily contrapuntal *à la* Hindemith, the fourth and fifth at times gently syncopated and with distant echoes of jazz. Eben's relatively recent Trio (1986) is musically rather more gripping, its style aphoristic, restless and inward, the work of a man with a keen ear and a probing spirit. Especially appealing is the way Eben fills musical rests with the retreating echoes of resonating piano chords (specifically in the first movement), and the impression of a chorale interrupted by conspiratorial chatter that dominates the third movement. This is the sort of score that the Florestans seem to relish, music full of subtle shades, many of them tucked carefully within subsidiary voices.

As to the Smetana, one always remembers it as being on the same large scale as the Tchaikovsky and Rachmaninov trios, but of course it isn't. The reason for the illusion is the amount of thematic and colouristic contrast that Smetana packs into each movement and the impact that those contrasts have. It's an immensely imposing piece, written in the wake of great personal loss, and the Florestans do it justice. All in all, this is an excellent programme, beautifully recorded.

John Eccles   English 1668-1735

Eccles's greatest talent is revealed in his many songs. Remarkable for their beautifully contoured melodies and impeccable prosody, they quickly capture the mood and subtleties of the poetry and are eminently singable. Eccles brought the Restoration tradition to its close. After Purcell's death in 1695 he was undoubtedly the greatest of the Restoration theatre composers. Continuing in Purcell's footsteps, The Judgment of Paris was the last of the masques.

The Judgement of Paris

The Judgement of Paris[a]. Three Mad Songs[b]
Roderick Williams bar Mercury **Benjamin Hulett** ten
Paris [b]**Susan Bickley** mez Juno [b]**Claire Booth** sop
Pallas [b]**Lucy Crowe** sop Venus [a]**Chorus of Early
Opera Company; Early Opera Company /
Christian Curnyn**
Chandos Chaconne CHAN0759 (62' · DDD) Ⓕ**OO**Ⓑ

Eccles's one-act 'semi-opera' (1701) calls for five solo singers, a choir and relatively modest instrumental resources – four-part strings, four trumpets, two recorders, kettledrums and continuo. Absent are castrati and countertenors. The music is tuneful, the boundaries between recitatives and airs often blurred. To address the lack of anguish or whiff of treachery in the masque, three 'mad' arias by the composer, each sung by a different soprano, are included at the end. The Early Opera Company band delivers delicately balanced homophonic accompaniments to the airs, varied by ground basses that remind us of Henry Purcell, and occasional solos, duos and quartets. As charming as it is, it doesn't bear comparison with *opera seria* of the day and, in particular, Handel's *Rinaldo*, presented to London audiences a decade later.

Christian Curnyn offers an unaffected, faithful reading of the printed score. If anything, it is understated, the instrumental forces reduced (the premiere employed 85 musicians in addition to the 'verse singers') and the recording acoustic intimate. Lucy Crowe's Venus may win the prize, but all of the soloists contribute beautifully judged portrayals.

Edward Elgar   British 1857-1934

Elgar's father was at the centre of Worcester's musical life, on friendly terms with the local gentry and clergy connected with the Anglican Cathedral. By the age of 12 his son was deputising for him at the organ and had taught himself (under father's guidance) the violin so that he could join in the music-making of local ensembles. He also won a reputation for his improvising abilities on the piano. Having left school at 15 and spent an unsuccessful year in a lawyer's office, he determined on some sort of career in music. This took the form of giving piano and violin lessons locally and, in 1879, being made bandmaster at the County Lunatic Asylum.

During his five years' involvement there, he wrote and arranged dozens of works for the motley ensemble to play at dances, entertainments and so forth – a formative experience, for he could experiment with every kind of instrumental combination at will. Simultaneously he played in an orchestra in Birmingham and conducted another amateur group in Worcester. By the time of his marriage in 1889, Elgar was thoroughly versed in the ways of composing – he would become an orchestrator of unsurpassed brilliance – and his new wife, Caroline Alice Roberts introduced him into moneyed society. It also gave his creative impetus and his musical ambitions the boost they needed. All of Elgar's important music was written during the 30 years of his marriage to Alice. They had one child, their daughter Carice, who was born in 1890 and died as recently as 1970.

The next 13 years saw the transformation of Elgar from a provincial small-time musician to a great composer of international standing, culminating in a knighthood in 1904. Orchestral and choral works were his main preoccupations. The demand for new choral works was insatiable and Elgar's lifelong connection with choirs and his immersion in the Catholic faith stood him in good stead – the success of his religious and secular cantatas The Black Knight, The Light of Life, King Olaf and Caractacus paving the way for his 1900 masterpiece The Dream of Gerontius. By then, Elgar's name was widely known as a composer of individuality and depth, especially after the appearance in 1899 of another masterpiece, perhaps his most loved work, the orchestral portaits of his friends featured in the Enigma Variations.

Now living in London, his religious faith receding, Elgar turned his attention to what he considered to be the pinnacle of the composer's art – the writing of a symphony. He achieved his ambition in no small measure, producing two masterworks, the first in 1908, the second in 1911. A third large-scale work, the inspired Violin Concerto, was premiered in 1910 by Fritz Kreisler.

Elgar was awarded the highest British honour for artists, the Order of Merit, in 1911; the next year saw the completion of his final large-scale choral work The Music Makers in which, in a weirdly prophetic vision, Elgar used thematic ideas from his past work, uniting them in one single conception. How could he have known what was to occur, for after his symphonic study Falstaff (1913) he wrote nothing more of importance until 1919; there's a final magnificent autumnal flourish with his Cello Concerto, String Quartet and Piano Quintet and then...nothing. After his wife's death in 1920, Elgar lost the urge to create (he tried hard, though unsuccessfully, to complete a Third Symphony). He was made Master of the King's Music in 1924 and given a baronetcy in 1931, but for the last 14 years of his life, returned to his roots in Worcester, he was all but silent as a composer.

Cello Concerto in E minor, Op 85

Cello Concerto. Sea Pictures
Jacqueline du Pré vc **Janet Baker** mez **London Symphony Orchestra / Sir John Barbirolli**
EMI 556219-2 (54' · ADD). Recorded 1965 ℗ ❶❶❶❷▷

Though both Jacqueline du Pré and Janet Baker were already well established and widely appreciated in 1965, this disc marked a turning point for both of them in their recording careers. With Barbirolli so warm-hearted and understanding an accompanist to each, these are both in every sense classic performances that can never be replaced.

Jacqueline du Pré's Elgar has been all the more appreciated, since her tragic illness took her away as a performer. In principle her *espressivo* may be too freely romantic, but the slow movement and epilogue remain supreme in their intensity, conveying in whispered *pianissimos* of daring delicacy an inner communion, while the bravura of the brilliant passages remains astonishing from an artist still only 20.

Until this recording, *Sea Pictures* had tended to be underprized even among Elgarians; but the passion, intensity and sheer beauty of this performance with each of the five songs sharply distinct rebutted any idea that – in reflection of verse of varying quality – it had anything of substandard Elgar in it. It's a work you'll probably never be able to listen to again without hearing in your mind Janet Baker's deeply individual phrasing on this disc. What strikes you most is the central relevance to Baker's whole career of the last stanza in 'Sabbath morning at sea', a radiant climax. 'He shall assist me to look higher' says the Barrett Browning poem, and the thrust of meaning as she sings it invariably conveys a *frisson* such as you rarely get on record.

Elgar Cello Concerto[a]
Bach Cello Suites[b] – No 1, BWV1007; No 2, BWV1008
Jacqueline du Pré vc [a]BBC Symphony Orchestra /
Sir John Barbirolli
Testament [b]mono SBT1388 (72' · ADD)
[a]Recorded live 1967   Ⓕ🔴🔴

Jacqueline du Pré was 20 when she recorded
Elgar's Cello Concerto with Barbirolli and the
LSO in August 1965 – an interpretation universally acclaimed for its profound expressiveness
(see above). A second recording, taped live in 1970
with Daniel Barenboim and the Philadelphia
Orchestra, has proved more controversial; du
Pré's radiant intensity remains undimmed but
instead of the nobility found in the EMI account
one hears desperation, or something close to it.

This new Testament disc makes public another
live document, recorded in Prague with Barbirolli and the BBC Symphony Orchestra. The
general shape of this performance resembles the
EMI recording, not surprisingly given that the
studio session had taken place a little more than
a year before. But while du Pré was always an
electric player, the voltage clearly increased
before an audience. One hears the difference
immediately as she digs into the opening solo
with startling urgency. Tempi, in general, are
noticeably faster; and although Barbirolli and
the orchestra occasionally fall behind, the phrasing is longer-breathed and the sections flow
more smoothly one into the other.

Du Pré (onstage and a year on from the EMI
version) finds a greater variety of mood in the
score. The *dolcissimo* Elgar asks for at fig 8 (starting at 3'58" in the first movement) evokes an
audible smile in the cellist's sound, for example.
Or try her magical way with the swooping
phrase at 3'10" in the *Adagio*: the high note is
floated beautifully in the studio but in concert
her tone and timing take one's breath away. Best
of all, perhaps, is the finale's *Poco più lento*
(beginning at 6'42"), where du Pré's playing has
an emotive force and eloquence akin to the
greatest Shakespearian oratory – Barbirolli and
the orchestra provide splendid support here.

Youthful (and previously released) interpretations of Bach's first two Cello Suites round out
the disc, but the Elgar here is valuable enough to
merit the highest possible recommendation.

Elgar Cello Concerto[a] **Bloch** Schelomo[a] **Kabalevsky**
Cello Concerto No 2 in G, Op 77[b] **Tchaikovsky**
Variations on a Rococo Theme, Op 33[c]. Nocturne,
Op 19 No 4[c]. Pezzo capriccioso, Op 62[c]. Andante
cantabile, Op 11[c] **R Strauss** Don Quixote[d]
Steven Isserlis vc [a]London Symphony Orchestra /
Richard Hickox; [b]London Philharmonic Orchestra /
Andrew Litton; [c]Chamber Orchestra of Europe /
Sir John Eliot Gardiner; [d]Minnesota Orchestra /
Edo de Waart
Virgin Classics 561490-2 (51' · DDD)   Ⓜ🔵➤

Cellists are apt to 'come of age' in recordings of
the Elgar. Isserlis was no exception. This is a
wonderful account of the Concerto – brave,

ELGAR'S CELLO CONCERTO – IN BRIEF

Daniel Müller-Schott vc
Oslo Philharmonic Orchestra / André Previn
Orfeo C621 061A (60' · DDD)   Ⓕ
A German-Norwegian-American version
that proves splendidly that Elgar's very Brit-
ish voice can travel the world.

Pablo Casals; BBC SO / Sir Adrian Boult
Biddulph LAB144 (79' · ADD)   Ⓜ
Backed by Boult at his authoritative best,
Casals brings an irresistible physicality and
capricious temperament to Elgar's nostalgic
inspiration. An account to hear.

**Jacqueline du Pré; BBC Symphony Orchestra /
Sir John Barbirolli**
Testament SBT1388 (72' · ADD)   Ⓕ🔴🔴
Made just over a year after the classic EMI
recording, here's another invaluable memento
of du Pré's musical genius. The extra adrenalin pumping at a public performance is obvious in every bar. A fantastic document…

**Jacqueline du Pré; London SO /
Sir John Barbirolli**
EMI 556219-2 (54' · ADD)   Ⓕ🔴🔴🔴➤
Ⓖ For countless collectors the world over,
du Pré's immortal 1965 recording with
Barbirolli and the LSO tugs at the heart-
strings like no other version before or since.

Steven Isserlis; London SO / Richard Hickox
Virgin Classics ③ 561490 2 (156' · DDD) Ⓜ🔵➤
Unusually self-effacing, Isserlis eschews
any vestige of overheated, heart-on-sleeve
exaggeration. Intimacy and wistfulness are
the keynotes.

Natalie Clein; RLPO / Vernon Handley
EMI 501409-2 (52' · DDD)   Ⓕ➤
A fine modern version from one of the UK's
most accomplished young cellists. It combines imagination and poetry with a wonderfully explansive view of the work.

Truls Mørk; CBSO / Sir Simon Rattle
Virgin Classics 545356-2 (65' · DDD)   Ⓢ➤
Mørk and Rattle form an intelligent, dignified and irreproachably stylish partnership.
Top-notch production values. Comes with
an equally compelling Britten Cello Symphony.

**Pieter Wispelwey; Netherlands RPO /
Jac van Steen**
Channel Classics CCS12998 (54' · DDD)   Ⓕ
Wispelwey is acutely alive to the strong strain
of classicism that runs through Elgar's
autumnal masterpiece. An unforced, deeply
satisfying reading, with splendidly bright-
eyed orchestral playing.

imaginative, individual – indeed, quite the most personal in its perception of the piece since the treasurable du Pré on EMI. And that, you'll appreciate, is saying something, though not, we hasten to add, that the two readings are in any outward sense similar. Far from it. With Isserlis, the emotional tug is considerably less overt, the emphasis more on shadow and subtext than open heartache. Yet the inner light is no less intense, the phrasing no less rhapsodic in manner than du Pré. On the contrary. This is free-range Elgar all right, and like du Pré it comes totally without affectation. Both Isserlis and du Pré take an appropriately generous line on the first movement's sorrowful song, with Isserlis the more reposeful, the more inclined to open out and savour key cadences. The *Scherzo* itself is quite simply better played than on any previous recording; the articulation and definition of the semiquaver 'fours' would, we're sure, have astonished even the composer himself. From a technical point of view Isserlis is easily the equal, and more, of any player currently before us. And if you still feel that du Pré really did have the last word where the epilogue is concerned, then listen to Isserlis sinking with heavy heart into those pages preceding the return of the opening declamation. He achieves a mesmerising fragility in the bars marked *lento* – one last backward glance, as it were – and the inwardness of the final *diminuendo* is something to be heard and remembered. Hickox and the LSO prove model collaborators. Don't on any account miss these performances.

Elgar Cello Concerto
Dvořák Cello Concerto in B minor, B191
Maria Kliegel vc
Royal Philharmonic Orchestra / Michael Halász
Naxos 8 550503 (73' · DDD) ⑤↠

The technical accomplishment of Kliegel's playing is balanced by a richness of musical insight that won't disappoint. The boldness of the opening soliloquy recalls du Pré at her finest, and yet Kliegel shares a yet deeper cup of grief in the world-weariness of the main first subject, carried with noble conviction. She takes a more improvisatory view in the lilting second group than du Pré.

The *Scherzo* is brilliantly done, and at a very fast tempo, but the conductor Michael Halász overlooks Elgar's precisely noted *a tempo* indication in response to the soloist's cantabile *largamente* statements at the end of each main section. The effect isn't only tedious, but is quite the reverse of the composer's intention, clearly stated in the score. The *Adagio* is thoughtfully played, avoiding unwelcome posturing or empty affectation, though Kliegel is, if anything, a little too cool and dispassionate here.

The finale is superbly paced, with the rumbustious militarism of the orchestration never allowed to dominate. The recording was made at Henry Wood Hall, and is full bodied and emphatic in major *tuttis*, yet one might have

wished the overall balance to favour the soloist more than it does.

Elgar Cello Concerto **Walton** Cello Concerto
Daniel Müller-Schott vc
Oslo Philharmonic Orchestra / André Previn
Orfeo C621 061A (60' · DDD) Ⓕ

The Elgar and Walton cello concertos make a perfect coupling and this is the second time André Previn has conducted the pairing on disc. The first, some 20 years ago, had Yo-Yo Ma, still near the beginning of his career, and the LSO. Here he's with the young German cellist Daniel Müller-Schott and his own Oslo Philharmonic in an equally idiomatic reading.

Significantly, Müller-Schott writes his own booklet-notes, demonstrating his warm affection for and understanding of both works. It is the passion of his playing that strikes home immediately – he uses a wider vibrato than Ma, and rather freer, less inhibited phrasing. That passion comes over not only in the slower music of the Elgar but also in the seemingly hesitating introduction to the second-movement *Scherzo*; and where Ma's reading of the slow movement is marked by refinement and nobility, Müller-Schott's is weightier. Similarly, in the central *Scherzo* of the Walton, where Ma is very fast and volatile, Müller-Schott is heavier-handed, though without losing the piece's sparkle.

The solo cello is balanced very far forward so that at the start of the Walton its sound obscures the subtle detail in the orchestration. That said, there is everything to enjoy in performances that are uninhibited, bringing out the warmth of both pieces. Many will forgive the odd balance when the performances are so convincing, even if Müller-Schott is not quite so imaginative or individual in his phrasing as Ma.

Cello Concerto[a]. Falstaff, Op 68[b]. Ⓗ
Nursery Suite[c]
[a]**Beatrice Harrison** vc
[bc]**London Symphony Orchestra;**
[a]**New Symphony Orchestra / Sir Edward Elgar**
Dutton mono CDBP9776 (76' · ADD)
From HMV originals ⑤●

It was Mike Dutton, when he was at EMI, who supervised the transfer of all of Elgar's electrical recordings. That set has been available only intermittently, which makes Dutton's revised transfers of these three works specially valuable, particularly the 1928 recording of the Cello Concerto with Beatrice Harrison. It now has a satisfying weight and body, though Harrison's wiry tone is not to everyone's taste and the intonation is occasionally suspect.

The *Falstaff*, made at the opening of EMI's Abbey Road Studios in 1931, has always been impressive in transfers, and the recording of the *Nursery Suite* made in the same year with the dedicatees, the Duke and Duchess of York and Princesses Elizabeth and Margaret present, comes out brightly and clearly. The Royals were particularly delighted with 'The Wagon Passes', with the whistling of the carter charmingly portrayed. The septuagenarian Elgar put love into his performance, as he did also in *Falstaff* with its swaggering Prince Hal theme and tragic epilogue which so echoes the epilogue of Strauss's *Don Quixote*.

Elgar (arr Tertis/Carpenter) Cello Concerto, Op 85
Schnittke Viola Concerto
David Aaron Carpenter va
Philharmonia Orchestra / Christoph Eschenbach
Ondine ODE1153-2 (65' · DDD) Ⓕ

In a recent interview, Carpenter spoke of his desire 'to put [the viola] out as a major solo instrument to rival the violin and cello', an aim which chimes with that of Lionel Tertis when he fashioned his transcription of Elgar's Cello Concerto in 1929. Tertis's clever makeover has now, in turn, been overhauled by Carpenter, yet the finished article still runs the risk of pointing up the music's exquisite, truly classical economy, deftness and poise at the expense of its aching intimacy, nostalgic glow and irresistible physicality. Nor will everyone warm to the enforced changes of register within Elgar's seamlessly conceived solo part. Carpenter gives a commandingly articulate display, and the Philharmonia are on immaculately scrubbed form under Christoph Eschenbach's thoughtful lead.

Carpenter's choice of the powerful Schnittke Concerto calls to mind Pieter Wispelwey's adventurous pairing of the Elgar and Lutosławski cello concertos (Channel Classics). Written for Yuri Bashmet in 1985, it is an excitingly intrepid and deeply sincere creation, as provocative in its wild extremes of mood as it is intriguing in its fruitful juxtaposition of old and new. However, such is the work's emotional clout and cumulative impact, you'll surely keep coming back for more. It helps, too, that Carpenter plays with superlative assurance and magnetic conviction, and he is backed to the hilt by Eschenbach and an audibly fired-up Philharmonia. Ondine's dryish sound and somewhat analytical balance suit Schnittke better than Elgar. All told, an impressive and bold debut.

Violin Concerto in B minor

Violin Concerto
Vaughan Williams The Lark Ascending
Nigel Kennedy vn **City of Birmingham Symphony Orchestra / Sir Simon Rattle**
EMI 556413-2 (72' · ADD) Ⓕ�O

Astonishingly, in the case of the first two movements at least, this release, recorded during the week following a live concert at Birmingham's Symphony Hall in July 1997, fully recreates the heady excitement of that memorable event. From every conceivable point of view – authority, panache, intelligence, intuitive poetry, tonal beauty and emotional maturity – Kennedy surpasses his 1985 *Gramophone* Award-winning

EMI Eminence recording (now on Classics for Pleasure). The first movement is a magnificent achievement all round, with tension levels extraordinarily high for a studio project. Rattle launches the proceedings in exemplary fashion, his direction passionate, ideally flexible and texturally lucid (the antiphonally divided violins help). The CBSO, too, is on top form. But it's Kennedy who rivets the attention from his commanding initial entry onwards. There's no hiding in this of all scores and Kennedy penetrates to the very essence of 'the soul enshrined within' in his melting presentation of the 'Windflower' theme – Elgar's *dolce semplice* realised to tear-spilling perfection. The slow movement is almost as fine. Only the finale oddly dissatisfies. Not in terms of technical address or co-ordination (both of which are stunning); rather, for all the supreme accomplishment on show, the results aren't terribly moving. Despite any lingering doubts about this last movement we're still left with an enormously stimulating and well-engineered display.

The fill-up is a provocative account of *The Lark Ascending*, which Kennedy (whose tone is ravishing) and Rattle spin out to 17 and a half minutes.

Violin Concerto
Gil Shaham vn **Chicago Symphony Orchestra / David Zinman**
Canary Classics CC06 (48' · DDD)
Recorded live at Orchestra Hall, Symphony Center, Chicago, in February 2007 ⒻO

It is good to welcome an all-American performance of this most British of concertos that is so thrillingly passionate. David Zinman has said that of all concertos this is his favourite, something confirmed in the playing he draws from the Chicago Symphony, its richness as well as its characteristic polish. The detail revealed in the long *tuttis* also demonstrates the care with which Zinman has prepared this performance. The recording on the Canary Classics label (Gil Shaham's own) is taken from live performances, and that adds to the impact, with the opulent sound matching the playing.

The playing of the orchestra finds a perfect counterpart in the performance of Gil Shaham, always one of the most sensitive and responsive of the high-powered violin virtuosos. Amazingly, he has performed this work some 20 times in the last 10 years. His range of tone and of dynamic is extreme, some might feel too much so, when some of his *pianissimos*, as in the second subject of the first movement, are so gentle that they can barely be heard against the orchestra. Though in that key passage he slows from the basic speed – something adopted by virtually every soloist in this work – there is nothing self-indulgent or sentimental in it, rather less so than in Kennedy's fine version with Vernon Handley conducting. Equally, Shaham's pronounced vibrato is always perfectly controlled.

The slow movement brings refinement and purity, while the main *Allegro* in the finale is fast and light, leading to a deeply dedicated account of the long accompanied cadenza. This now stands as one of the very finest versions of this concerto, and even though the disc, unlike most, offers no coupling, it is well worth the price. Under Solti as music director, the Chicago Orchestra produced one or two fine Elgar recordings, but the playing here is even warmer under Zinman.

Violin Concerto[a]. Serenade, Op 20.
[a]**James Ehnes** vn
Philharmonia Orchestra / Sir Andrew Davis
Onyx ONYX4025 (61' · DDD) Ⓕ**O**▷

Not since Nigel Kennedy's 1997 EMI remake with Sir Simon Rattle and the CBSO (see above) has the Elgar received a recording as thrillingly combustible, imaginative and involving as this. James Ehnes brings to this great concerto a rapt identification, tingling temperament and glowing ardour. Not only is Ehnes's technical address impeccable and intonation miraculously true, his contribution is remarkable for its intrepid emotional scope, athletic agility and (perhaps above all) jaw-dropping delicacy (nowhere more heart-tuggingly potent than in the finale's accompanied cadenza).

Ehnes is also fortunate in enjoying the support of Sir Andrew Davis, a proven Elgarian whose wonderfully perceptive conducting has authoritative sweep, elasticity and fiery passion to spare as well as a very special understanding of those moments of aching intimacy in which this of all scores abounds: what a ravishing backcloth he provides for the ineffable appearance of the 'Windflower' theme in the same movement; and how affecting are the strings' songful sighs in the ensuing *Andante*. One or two unruly timpani thwacks aside, the Philharmonia's response exhibits polish, grace and dedication.

Some might take issue with the sound which is a little shrouded and lacking something in alluring bloom (the actual balance is otherwise very much as you would hear from a seat in the stalls). No matter, this remains a performance of conspicuous pedigree and insight, guaranteed to make you fall in love all over again with this sublime music and which can only boost Ehnes's standing as one of the most gifted and charismatic fiddlers around. Davis's utterly unforced and ravishingly moving account of the entrancing Serenade makes a cherishable pendant.

Violin Concerto[a]. Cello Concerto[b] Ⓗ
[a]**Yehudi Menuhin** vn [b]**Beatrice Harrison** vc
[a]**London Symphony Orchestra,** [b]**New Symphony Orchestra / Sir Edward Elgar**
EMI Great Recordings of the Century mono
566979-2 (75' · AAD). Recorded 1932, 1928 Ⓜ**OOO**

Elgar's conducting for Menuhin in the Violin Concerto's opening orchestral *tutti* is magnifi-

cent, as is his solicitous, attentive accompaniment throughout the work. Menuhin's youthful, wonderfully intuitive musicianship in fact needed little 'instruction', and the success of the recording may be judged from the fact that there have been few periods in the years since it was first issued when it hasn't been available in some shape or form. Beatrice Harrison first studied the Cello Concerto for an abridged, pre-electric recording with Elgar conducting. So impressed was the composer then that he insisted that she should be the soloist whenever he conducted the work again. Their authoritative performance is deeply felt and highly expressive, but it has a quality of nobility and stoicism which comes as a refreshing change from some overindulgent modern performances.

Since the original matrices were destroyed, EMI's engineers had to return to the 1957 tape for this transfer; although the 1957 engineers did not quite capture all the body of the originals there's an impressive clarity in the transfer, now brightened a little more for CD. The 1970s transfer of the Harrison/Elgar Cello Concerto was impressively managed, and this reissue has given still more presence to the sound without any sense of falsification.

Elgar Violin Concerto[b] Delius Violin Concerto[a] Ⓗ
Albert Sammons vn [a]**Liverpool Philharmonic Orchestra / Malcolm Sargent;** [b]**New Queen's Hall Orchestra / Henry Wood**
Naxos Historical mono 8 110951 (67' · ADD)
Recorded [b]1929, [a]1944 Ⓢ**OOO**

Albert Sammons's 1929 account of Elgar's Violin Concerto with Sir Henry Wood and the New Queen's Hall Orchestra remains the finest version ever made, outstripping even the legendary Menuhin/Elgar collaboration from three years later in terms of authoritative grip, intuitive poetry and emotional candour. Previous transfers to CD have varied from satisfactory to merely tolerable and unacceptably botched. So it's a pleasure to encounter Mark Obert-Thorn's judicious restoration for Naxos.

Delius heard Sammons perform the Elgar in May 1915, and was so bowled over that he set about writing a concerto for the formidable virtuoso. Sammons premiered the work with Boult in January 1919 but had to wait a full quarter of a century before committing it to disc. Here is another irreplaceable document: Sammons was an assiduous champion of this glorious music, and although the solo playing hasn't quite the effortless technical mastery of its companion here, his wise and unforced interpretation penetrates to the very core of Delius's lovely vision. An admirable introduction to a truly great fiddler, irresistible at the price.

Additional recommendation

Violin Concerto
Kennedy vn **LPO / Handley**

Classics for Pleasure 575139-2 (54' · DDD) ⓑ❍❍❍
Kennedy's superb first recording of the Elgar Violin Concerto won the *Gramophone* Record of the Year in 1985 and is now at bargain price.

Symphonies

No 1 in A flat, Op 55; **No 2** in E flat, Op 63; **No 3** in C minor, Op 88 (realised A Payne)

Symphonies Nos 1 & 2. Cello Concerto.
Violin Concerto. 'Enigma' Variations.
Cockaigne, 'In London Town'. In the South,
'Alassio'. Froissart. Falstaff. Sea Pictures.
Chanson de matin. Chanson de nuit.
Elegy. Serenade. Introduction and Allegro.
Coronation March. Imperial March.
The Sanguine Fan. Contrasts
Featuring performances by **Janet Baker** *mez* **Alfredo**
Campoli, Rodney Friend, John Willison *vns* **John**
Chambers *va* **Paul Tortelier, Alexander Cameron**
vcs **David Bell** *org* **London Philharmonic Orchestra**
/ Sir Adrian Boult, Sir Edward Elgar, Vernon
Handley, Sir Charles Mackerras, Sir Landon
Ronald, Sir Georg Solti
LPO ⑤ LPO0016/20 (6h 25' · ADD/DDD)   Ⓜ

What a brilliant idea of the LPO to gather together Elgar recordings from many different sources, some rare and unexpected. They range from the composer's recordings with the newly founded LPO to Sir Charles Mackerras and Vernon Handley in the 1980s. Most Elgarians will know the great majority, but it is many years since the Campoli recording of the Violin Concerto, fresh and urgent, was freely available.

Most cherishable of all is a *Sea Pictures* with Janet Baker and Vernon Handley, a live recording from 1984 that was rescued from the Capital Radio archives; it's a wonderful alternative to the much-loved LSO/Barbirolli version. Baker's voice is still gloriously rich, and the live occasion inspires a performance of great urgency and intensity. The nobility in 'Sabbath Morning at Sea' is heart-stopping, from full-throated richness down to a hushed *pianissimo* on 'brooded soft on waters deep', and the attack in 'The Swimmer' is thrilling. Handley beautifully conjures up the surge of the sea in the brilliant orchestration.

Sir Adrian Boult is the principal contributor to the set in recordings from a number of labels. The excellent transfer gives wonderful body to the mono recording of the Violin Concerto while *Falstaff*, Boult's 1956 Nixa recording, has a restricted frequency range but still reveals plenty of detail, the close rhythm. It is good, too, to have Paul Tortelier's warm and steadily paced reading of the Cello Concerto, and Handley's noble CfP version of the Second Symphony is valuable for the use of organ to reinforce the bass at a key point in the finale. Mackerras's *Imperial March*, made for Reader's Digest, is a rarity, and his other contribution, a 1985 *Enigma* Variations (EMI Eminence), brings an unusually slow 'Nimrod'.

It is good to have Elgar's own beautiful account of the Serenade for Strings, spacious in the slow movement, and his *Froissart*. From the 1930s, too, an excellent *Coronation March* by Sir Landon Ronald sounds wonderfully rich for the period. Solti's Decca recordings have tingling clarity and brilliance, warmth and panache.

A wonderfully rich collection that all Elgarians should try to hear. Praise must go to the transfer engineers.

Symphonies Nos 1 & 2. Froissart, Op 19
Philharmonia Orchestra / Sir Andrew Davis
Signum ② SIGCD179 (112' · DDD)
Recorded live in 2007   Ⓜ❍🄳➤

Symphony No 1. Sea Pictures[a]
[a]**Janet Baker** *mez*
London Philharmonic Orchestra / Vernon Handley
LPO LPO0046 (64' · ADD)
Recorded live in 1984   Ⓜ❍🄳➤

The comparison with Davis's earlier recordings with the BBC SO, made in the studio and now reissued at super-budget price on Warner Apex, is that, as so often with Davis, a live occasion brings out an extra intensity. For example, the pause before the final rush of the coda in the first movement of the Second Symphony is significantly longer, making a greater impact.

Generally, in both symphonies Davis allows himself greater freedom in his use of *rubato*, phrasing warmly, so that the lovely third theme of the slow movement in the First Symphony is even more tender, and though the playing in both symphonies is marginally less polished in the live performance, the Elgarian thrust is greater and the sound fuller and more immediate. Also, the final coda of the finale in the First Symphony is even more thrilling, though all these differences are only marginal. The *Froissart* Overture, dating from early in Elgar's career, is also richly done.

In the First Symphony Vernon Handley's live version on the LPO's own label – now reissued, coupled with Dame Janet Baker's superb account of *Sea Pictures* (reviewed in detail above) – comes in surprisingly warm sound. Handley, an equally fine, idiomatic Elgarian, gives a reading just as rich and moving, with timings surprisingly similar to those of Davis. The *Scherzo* is particularly clean and well sprung. Those who just want the First Symphony may even prefer it to the Davis performances because of the coupling. In effect collectors can hardly go wrong with either of these recordings, both offering marvellous evidence of Elgar's mastery.

Symphonies Nos 1 & 2
London Philharmonic Orchestra / Sir Adrian Boult
Lyrita ② SRCD221 (100' · ADD)   Ⓕ❍❍

In 1968, when Sir Adrian Boult recorded the two Elgar Symphonies for Lyrita, he wrote an

ELGAR'S SYMPHONIES – IN BRIEF

London PO / Sir Georg Solti
Decca ② 443 856-2DF2 (135' · ADD)   Ⓜ

Solti drives hard in any faster music but both slow movements have a tingling concentration and rapt hush that are deeply affecting. The LPO respond brilliantly throughout; lustrous Decca sound, too.

**London Philharmonic Orchestra /
Sir Adrian Boult**
EMI ② 382151-2 (137' · ADD)   Ⓜ

A glorious memento of a great Elgarian. Not only does the set include the two symphonies but also *In the South*, the Introduction and Allegro and *Grania and Diarmid*.

SYMPHONY NO 1

Hallé Orchestra / Sir John Barbirolli
BBC Legends BBCL4106-2 (67' · DDD)   Ⓢ**OO**▷

The other great Elgarian knight: Barbirolli shares with Boult a profound feeling for this music and draws from the Hallé Orchestra playing of tremendous warmth and sweep. Just one of his six recordings, and a thing of joy none the less.

London SO / Sir Colin Davis
LSO Live LSO0017 (55' · DDD)   Ⓢ▷

Sir Colin's unhurried conception is crowned by a superbly exciting reading of the finale that sweeps all before it. The Barbican acoustic is not ideally opulent, but don't let that minor caveat put you off.

SYMPHONY NO 2

Hallé Orchestra / Sir John Barbirolli
EMI 764724-2 (66' · ADD)   Ⓜ**O**

A richly expansive performance, delivered by the Hallé *con amore*, with the slow movement in particular rising to an indescribable peak of emotion. One to snap up.

BBC SO / Sir Andrew Davis
Apex 0927 49586-2 (78' · DDD)   Ⓢ**OO**

Few rivals come close to equalling the all-round perception displayed by Sir Andrew Davis in his 1991 account of Elgar's multi-faceted masterpiece. With its meaty coupling of *In the South*, this is an exceptional bargain.

SYMPHONY NO 3

Bournemouth SO / Paul Daniel
Naxos 8 554719 (55' · DDD)   Ⓢ**OO**▷

One in the fast-growing discography for this newly created work, Daniel nails his Elgarian credentials to the mast with a reading that makes you believe wholeheartedly in every bar of this powerful work. The Bournemouth orchestra plays with burning conviction and the Naxos price makes it irresistible.

open letter to *Gramophone*, couched diplomatically but reflecting his fury that at the sessions his recording manager had forced him on technical grounds to have all the violins on the left instead of his usual habit of dividing them between the two sections. That said, and 40 years on, the comparisons with Boult's other recordings of the Elgar symphonies demonstrate very clearly how fine they are, arguably the finest versions he ever recorded.

Compared with the EMI versions recorded less than five years later, they are tauter, the ensemble noticeably crisper. The recording is brighter and clearer in this transfer. The difference is particularly marked in No 2 which, as Elgar said, was a work which Boult was the first conductor to make a success after the disappointing reception given at its premiere. The comparison is closer with the mono recording of No 2, which Boult recorded with the BBC SO in 1945, a superb performance but which is still marginally outshone by the Lyrita version.

Symphony No 1. Introduction and Allegro, Op 47
Hallé Orchestra / Sir John Barbirolli
BBC Legends BBCL4106-2 (67' · ADD)
Recorded live 1970   Ⓕ**O**

On July 24, 1970, Sir John Barbirolli conducted (and recorded) this inspired Hallé performance of Elgar's First Symphony in St Nicholas's Chapel as his major contribution to the King's Lynn Festival. Four days later he suffered a fatal heart attack. There could be no finer memorial, for the acoustic of the chapel provides a wonderfully warm glow and the richest amplitude for the Hallé brass and strings, without blunting the *fortissimos*. The depth of feeling and power in the performance has the genuine thrill of live music-making. For instance, there's an extraordinary central climax in the first movement, with the brass outbursts given a terrifying intensity; the apotheosis of the finale has similar emotional strength. Barbirolli invests the symphony's slow sad motto theme with a poignant nostalgia each time it appears; but most memorable of all is the richness of the opening of the *Adagio*, sustained throughout with Barbirolli's characteristic warmth of feeling, while the impassioned Hallé string playing is as rich in tone as it's heartfelt.

Fascinatingly, the interpretation looks back to his first 1956 Pye recording with his own orchestra (available on Dutton). Both performances play for a little over 52 minutes, and the timings of each movement and the flexible inner relationships of tempo are very close. But this final version matches and even surpasses that first venture in its surging forward momentum, and the sound is far richer, obviously more modern. Everyone has their favourite version among the six, but no Elgarian will be disappointed with this account.

Symphony No 1
London Symphony Orchestra / Sir Colin Davis

LSO Live LSO0017 (55' · DDD) Ⓢ🔵🔵➤

This thrillingly combustible account easily holds its own in the most exalted company. Davis's is a patient, noble conception, yet lacking absolutely nothing in thrusting drama, fresh-faced character and tender poetry. Certainly, Sir Colin steers a marvellously confident course through the epic first movement, the music-making always comprehensive in its emotional scope and hitting genuine heights in the development. The *Scherzo* is another great success, the glinting, defiant swagger of the outer portions counterbalanced by the delectable grace and point these eloquent players lavish on the Trio. Just one small interpretative quibble: Davis's inorganic slackening of tempo during the sublime transition into the slow movement (listen to Barbirolli's unforgettable 1956 Hallé account to hear how it should be done). As for the great *Adagio* itself, Davis's intensely devotional approach works beautifully. The finale positively surges with purposeful bite, fire and sinew, while the glorious closing pages really do raise the roof. The expertly balanced sound doesn't have quite the bloom that EMI and Decca achieved for Boult and Solti on their classic analogue versions, but it amply conveys the tingling electricity and physical impact of a special event. At this price, this is one to snap up.

Symphony No 1.
Organ Sonata No 1, Op 28 (orch Jacob)
BBC National Orchestra of Wales / Richard Hickox
Chandos 💿 CHSA5049 (78' · DDD) Ⓟ🔵🔵🔵➤

The SACD recording for this impressive Elgar First is spectacular: you really appreciate the sharpness of articulation of the Cardiff players. Hickox's interpretation is comparably impressive, particularly so in the first movement where he has a cunning way of presenting the great Elgarian melodies simply. In the tricky transition from two in a bar to three Hickox broadens the tempo where others follow the composer's example in keeping the minim beat steady; none the less he makes that moment a magnificent climax.

Hickox's control of such climaxes is masterly. In the *Scherzo* the articulation of the violins and the sharpness of attack is thrilling. In the great melodies of the slow movement Hickox tenderly brings out a songlike quality, making others seem a little studied. The delicate *pianissimo* as the third theme enters is breathtaking. The two great 'gulp' moments in the finale come at the climax of the passage where the theme of the slow introduction comes in augmentation; there Hickox comes near to matching Elgar himself in impact. Finally, he secures a superbly satisfying *crescendo* from the brass on the final chord.

The generous coupling adds to the attractions of the disc, an orchestration of a work which should be far better known. The qualities which make Hickox's reading of the Symphony so impressive come out here too.

Symphony No 1[a]. In the South, 'Alassio', Op 50[b] 🄷
London Philharmonic Orchestra / Sir Adrian Boult
Testament mono SBT1229 (69' · DDD)
Recorded [a]1949, [b]1955 Ⓕ🔵🔵🔵

The first wonder of this very welcome transfer is the astonishing quality of the sound, mono only but full-bodied and finely detailed to give a keener sense of presence than the rather disappointing CD transfer of the 1976 stereo version, with a surprisingly wide dynamic range for a 1949 recording. When Boult recorded that final stereo version, he was already 87, and though as ever the reading is a noble one, beautifully paced, it has nothing like the same thrust and tension as this recording of nearly three decades earlier. In particular the heavenly *Adagio* has an extra meditative intensity in the way that Boult presents each of the great lyrical themes. The finale in particular has a bite and thrust far beyond that of the later account.

Boult's recording of *In the South*, made in 1955, brings out his thrustful side even more strikingly, with urgent speeds giving way in the lovely 'Canto popolare' section to a honeyed beauty before an urgent yet finely controlled account of the coda. Sadly, the 1955 sound is shallower than that of six years earlier for the symphony, though there's ample weight for the brass theme of the second section.

Symphony No 2. In the South, 'Alassio', Op 50
BBC Symphony Orchestra / Sir Andrew Davis
Warner Apex 0927 49586-2 (78' · DDD) Ⓢ🔵🔵

In his finest achievement on record, Andrew Davis penetrates to the dark inner core of this great symphony. In the opening *Allegro vivace e nobilmente*, for example, how well he and his acutely responsive players gauge the varying moods of Elgar's glorious inspiration: be it in the exhilarating surge of that leaping introductory paragraph or the spectral, twilight world at the heart of this wonderful movement, no one is found wanting.

Davis's unerring structural sense never once deserts him, and the BBC Symphony Orchestra plays its heart out. Above all, it's in the many more reflective moments that Davis proves himself an outstandingly perceptive Elgarian, uncovering a vein of intimate anguish that touches to the very marrow; in this respect, his account of the slow movement is quite heart-rendingly poignant – undoubtedly the finest since Boult's incomparable 1944 performance with this very same orchestra – while the radiant sunset of the symphony's coda glows with luminous beauty.

Prefaced by an equally idiomatic, stirring *In the South*, this is an Elgar Second to set beside the very greatest. In every way a treasurable release.

Symphony No 2
BBC Philharmonic Orchestra / Sir Edward Downes
Naxos 8 550635 (56' · DDD) Ⓢ🔵➤

Here's further proof that Edward Downes was an Elgarian to be reckoned with. This account of the Second Symphony is up there with the very best. In the first movement, Downes steers a clear-sighted course: here's the same unexaggerated, splendidly authoritative conception heard from this conductor in the concert hall. Unlike some rivals on record, Downes resists the temptation to give too much too soon, and this feeling of power in reserve lends an extra cumulative intensity to the proceedings; indeed, the coda here is absolutely thrilling. The ensuing *Larghetto* sees Downes striking a near-perfect balance between introspection and heart-warming passion. Both the Rondo and finale are ideally paced – the former not too hectic, the latter flowing to perfection, culminating in an epilogue of rare delicacy.

Throughout, the BBC Philharmonic plays outstandingly for its former chief: the orchestra's golden-toned cello section must be singled out for special praise. Just a touch more clarity in *tuttis*, and the recording would have been ideal. A deeply sympathetic reading, possessing qualities to match any rival.

Symphony No 3
Bournemouth Symphony Orchestra / Paul Daniel
Naxos 8 554719 (55' · DDD)   ⑤◐◐🄳

How thrillingly urgent Elgar's unforgettably gaunt introductory bars sound here – a magnificent launch-pad for an interpretation of unswerving dedication, plentiful character and intelligence. Audibly galvanised by Paul Daniel's direction, the Bournemouth orchestra responds with infectious eagerness, polish and, most important, all the freshness of new discovery. In these newcomers' hands there's a rhythmic snap and athletic drive about the mighty opening movement that exhilarate. Where Davis perhaps scores over Daniel is in the spiritual, 'inner' dimension he brings to those ineffably beautiful bars at the start of the development section. Come the succeeding *Allegretto*, and Daniel's approach is more urgent, less evocative. The anguished slow movement welds a penetrating textural and harmonic clarity to a noble strength that's very moving. Best of all is the finale, which now emerges in a rather less piecemeal fashion than it does under Davis. Particularly good is the dark swagger that Daniel locates in both the *nobilmente* paragraphs, while the closing bars are magical, the final soft tam-tam stroke disappearing into the ether like some vast unanswered question. The sound is excellent in every respect. Another jewel in the Naxos crown, not to be missed.

Additional recommendation

Symphony No 3
BBC Symphony Orchestra / A Davis
NMC NMCD053 (56' · DDD)   Ⓕ
An eloquent, profoundly involving performance with demonstration-worthy sound.

Variations on an Original Theme, 'Enigma', Op 36

Enigma Variations. Cockaigne Overture, Op 40. Introduction and Allegro, Op 47. Serenade for Strings
BBC Symphony Orchestra / Sir Andrew Davis
Warner Apex 0927 41371-2 (74' · DDD)   ⑤🄳

These are four of the best Elgar performances on disc available. First, the recording is superb, with near-perfect balance and a really natural sound. Second, the playing of the BBC Symphony Orchestra is first-rate. Andrew Davis's conducting of all four works is inspired, as if he had forgotten all preconceived notions and other interpretations, gone back to the scores and given us what he found there. In *Cockaigne*, for example, the subtle use of *ritardando*, sanctioned in the score, gives the music that elasticity which Elgar considered to be an ideal requisite for interpreting his works. The poetry and wit of this masterpiece emerge with renewed freshness. As for the *Enigma* Variations, instead of wondering why another recording was thought necessary, you'll find yourself rejoicing that such a fine performance has been preserved to be set alongside other treasured versions. Each of the 'friends pictured within' is strongly characterised by Davis, but without exaggeration or interpretative quirks. Tempi are just right and the orchestral playing captures the authentic Elgarian sound in a manner Boult would have recognised. Similarly, in the Introduction and Allegro, how beautifully the string quartet is recorded, how magical are the gentle and so eloquent *pizzicatos* which punctuate the flow of the great melody. The fugue is played with real zest and enjoyment. This is music on a large scale and is played and conducted in that way, whereas the early Serenade is intimate and dewy-eyed and that's how it sounds here.

Enigma Variations. In the South, 'Alassio', Op 50. Serenade, Op 20
Philharmonia Orchestra / Sir Andrew Davis
Signum Classics SIGCD168 (67' · DDD)
Recorded live in 2007   Ⓕ◐🄳

Captured on the wing at Croydon's Fairfield Hall during Davis's sesquicentennial Elgar series from the spring of 2007, this *Enigma* Variations is also, on balance, his most compelling and characterful yet, evincing an eager application, easy flow and unforced wisdom that stem from long familiarity with the score. There are highlights aplenty: both 'Troyte' and 'GRS' bound along with a trim swagger, while Davis's 'Nimrod' comes close to the ideal in its humane, selfless glow. Best of all, perhaps, is 'EDU', an infectiously unbuttoned and finely paced culmination, with the organ adding a splendidly grandiloquent opulence to the coda. However, the stand-out offering here has to be *In the South*, which enshrines as personable, generously pliable and lucidly integrated a conception as one can ever recall. Davis invests Elgar's arching melodic lines with heartwarming lyrical fervour. What's more, the (uncredited) principal viola extracts every ounce of wistfulness from the sultry 'Canto popolare' at the work's evocative heart. Both *In the South* and the Serenade were recorded in London's Queen Elizabeth Hall – not an ideally spacious acoustic, you'd have thought, but in fact there's little to quibble with sonically.

Enigma Variations[e] Three Bavarian Dances, Op 27 – Lullaby[d]. **Barbirolli** An Elizabethan Suite[a] **Bax** The Garden of Fand[b] **Butterworth** A Shropshire Lad[c] **Ireland** The Forgotten Rite[f]. Mai-Dun[g]. These Things Shall Be[h] **Purcell** Suite for Strings[i] **Vaughan Williams** Fantasia on 'Greensleeves'[j]. Fantasia on a Theme by Thomas Tallis[k]
[h]**Parry Jones** ten **Hallé** [h]**Choir and Orchestra / Sir John Barbirolli**
Dutton mono ② CDSJB1022 (140' · ADD)
Recorded at Houldsworth Hall, Manchester [k]1946, [e]1947, [ih]1948; [d]Kingsway Hall, London 1947; [fg]Abbey Road Studio, London 1949; Free Trade Hall, Manchester [a]1954, [bci]1956   Ⓑ❍

The long-buried treasure here is Barbirolli's very first recording of Elgar's *Enigma* Variations, never previously issued. It was recorded in Manchester in May 1947, only months before Barbirolli made his first published recording at EMI's St John's Wood studio. This newly unearthed version narrowly becomes the favourite rather than the later one. Both versions are perfectly satisfying in terms of sound, but interpretatively this unpublished version brings added advantages. The opening statement of the theme is lighter, more flowing and less emphatic, while even more important, 'Nimrod' is more warmly emotional, more spontaneous in expression, and the 'EDU' finale, taken at a marginally slower tempo, has no hint of the breathlessness which slightly mars the October performance at the end, again more warmly spontaneous sounding. Significantly Barbirolli's later stereo version of *Enigma* also adopts the slightly broader, less hectic speed.

The two Vaughan Williams items have never appeared before on CD, and both are very welcome. They may be less weighty than Barbirolli's stereo remakes, but the *Tallis* Fantasia, featuring a vintage quartet of Hallé principals, separates the quartet more clearly from the main body than the version with the Sinfonia of London, and again is more warmly expressive. The extra lightness of *Greensleeves*, too, sounds more spontaneous. Disc 1 contains the shorter works of Bax, Butterworth and Ireland. The performances all have a passionate thrust typical of Barbirolli, with the tenor, Parry Jones, and the Hallé Chorus matching the orchestra in their commitment.

'Enigma' Variations[a]. Pomp and Circumstance Marches, Op 39[b]
[a]**London Symphony Orchestra,** [b]**London Philharmonic Orchestra / Sir Adrian Boult**

ELGAR ENIGMA VARIATIONS – IN BRIEF

Royal Albert Hall Orchestra / Sir Edward Elgar
EMI 566979-2 (67' · ADD)   Ⓜ
Elgar's own 1926 recording positively oozes spontaneity and fantasy. Harnessed to the 14-year-old Menuhin's legendary 1932 version (with the composer) of the Violin Concerto.

Hallé Orchestra / Sir John Barbirolli
Dutton ② CDSJB1022 (140' · ADD)   Ⓑ❍
The first of Sir John's four recordings. Never previously issued, it features irrepressible playing and conducting of rare perception. Other Hallé/Barbirolli highlights on this Dutton double-pack include Bax's *Garden of Fand* and Ireland's *Mai-Dun* and *The Forgotten Rite*.

Hallé Orchestra / Sir John Barbirolli
EMI/IMG Artists ② 575100-2 (150' · ADD)   Ⓜ
Barbirolli's first stereo *Enigma*, originally engineered by a Mercury production team for Pye, is a gloriously uninhibited conception. A heartwarming, indeed life-enhancing experience.

London SO / Pierre Monteux
Decca 452 303-2DCS (78' · ADD)   Ⓜ
Another vernally fresh interpretation from a great conductor. Monteux brings plenty of revealing insights to bear, the LSO are on top form and Decca's 1958 Kingsway Hall sound is astonishingly undated.

London SO / Sir Adrian Boult
EMI 567748-2 (55' · ADD)   Ⓜ❍❍↪
Sir Adrian's noble 1970 *Enigma* (the last of his four versions) dates from towards the start of his Indian summer in the recording studio, and remains a central recommendation.

Royal PO / Norman Del Mar
DG 429 713-2GGA (58' · ADD)   Ⓜ
The voluble expressive freedom of this interpretation owes much to the composer's own. Similarly, Del Mar invests the *Pomp and Circumstance* Marches with terrific élan.

Czech PO / Leopold Stokowski
Cala CACD0524 (76' · ADD)   Ⓜ
Stokowski's only Elgar recording enshrines an interpetation of abundant charisma and glowing affection. The sheer energy of it all is astounding, especially when you remember that the Old Magician had just turned 90!

Baltimore SO / David Zinman
Telarc CD80192 (62' · DDD)   Ⓜ
Now reissued at mid-price, Zinman's eagle-eyed, exceptionally poised account is a real tonic, and receives top-drawer Telarc sound to boot.

EMI 764015-2 (55' · ADD). Recorded 1970, 1976 Ⓜ️ⒶⒶ

Boult's 1970 recording of the *Enigma* Variations offers similar riches to those of Barbirolli with the additional bonus of a slightly superior recorded sound. Boult's account has authority, freshness and a beautiful sense of spontaneity: each variation emerges from the preceding one with a natural feeling of flow and progression. There's warmth and affection, coupled with an air of nobility and poise, and the listener is always acutely aware that this is a performance by a great conductor who's lived a lifetime with the music. You need only sample the passionate stirrings of Variation 1 (the composer's wife), the athletic and boisterous 'Troyte' variation, or the autumnal, elegiac glow of the famous 'Nimrod' variation to realise that this is a very special document indeed. The LSO, on top form, plays with superlative skill and poetry and the excellent recording has been exceptionally well transferred to CD. The *Pomp and Circumstance* Marches, recorded six years later with the London Philharmonic Orchestra, are invigoratingly fresh and direct – indeed the performances are so full of energy and good humour that it's hard to believe that Boult was in his late eighties at the time of recording! A classic.

Enigma Variations
BBC Symphony Orchestra / Sir Andrew Davis
Video director **Diana Hill**
Opus Arte 📀 OA0917D
(85' · 16:9 · PCM stereo & DTS 5.1 · 0)
Includes documentary, 'A Hidden Portrait'   Ⓕ

Sir Andrew Davis's warmly committed performance of the *Enigma* Variations, atmospherically recorded in Worcester Cathedral, introduces a highly enjoyable documentary about the work and the 'friends pictured within'. Davis suggests that each variation, as well as reflecting the character of a particular friend, reveals much about Elgar himself, 'like an actor playing many roles'. Each section is illustrated with archive material and period reconstructions, happily with no dialogue, only Davis's narration. He describes and analyses nine of the 14 variations with orchestral clips and illustrations played on the piano.

So the first variation, 'CAE', depicting Elgar's wife Alice, concentrating on the central major-key section of the theme, includes a brief, passionate climax, 'showing his depth of feeling'. 'RBT', subject of the third variation, was the treasurer of the local golf club, who got Elgar accepted as a member even though his social class was against him. We're shown what used to be the clubhouse, now set in waste land. 'Nimrod' depicts the publisher August Jaeger and Elgar walking together, and Davis points to echoes of the slow movement from Beethoven's *Pathétique* Sonata. The intermezzo, 'Dorabella', brings a good portrait of the young Dora Penny, but after a reference to her cycling, ends absurdly on shots of a modern couple roller-blading – an

example of fussy and intrusive visual illustration. Fairly enough, Davis favours the idea that the 13th variation, 'Romanza', represents not Lady Mary Lygon, as has generally been thought, but his first love, Helen Weaver, who emigrated to New Zealand. Irritating are the accompanying shots of a soulful modern teenager on Lambeth Bridge looking at a launch bearing his girlfriend away.

The performance itself has no unwanted intrusions – just a sepia photo of the subject as each variation begins – and is a fine one.

Falstaff, Op 68

Falstaff. Froissart, Op 19. Romance, Op 62[a]. Grania and Diarmid – Incidental Music and Funeral March
[a]**Graham Sheen** *bn* **BBC Symphony Orchestra / Sir Andrew Davis**
Warner Apex 2564 62200-2 (66' · DDD)   ⓈⒶⒶ

As digital *Falstaffs* go, Sir Andrew Davis's 1995 account with the BBC SO remains arguably the front-runner. If both Elgar himself and Barbirolli impart the greater vulnerability and compassion to the illimitably moving closing pages, the irresistible symphonic current coursing through Davis's meticulously observant conception provides ample compensation. The orchestral playing is splendid, the recording glowingly realistic (the experienced Keener/Faulkner production team working in one of their favourite haunts, St Augustine's in Kilburn).

The couplings are memorable, too. In *Froissart* Davis achieves an acutely perceptive balance between thrusting chivalry and wistful introspection (how tenderly he moulds Elgar's lyrical secondary material). The *Romance* for bassoon and orchestra comes off beautifully, as does the Funeral March from *Grania and Diarmid* (surely one of Elgar's noblest utterances). At its ludicrously low price, not to be missed.

Pomp and Circumstance Marches

Pomp and Circumstance, Op 39 – No 1 in D; No 2 in A minor; No 3 in C minor; No 4 in G; No 5 in C.

Pomp and Circumstance Marches Nos 1-5[b]
Overtures – Froissart; Cockaigne[a]
[a]**Philharmonia Orchestra,** [b]**New Philharmonic Orchestra / Sir John Barbirolli**
EMI British Composers 566323-2 (62' · ADD)   Ⓜ️Ⓑ➔

A splendid programme that finds Sir John celebrating London courtesy of Edward Elgar. The two overtures are beautifully done with ample shade to counterbalance the swagger. And it's a real treat to hear all five of the *Pomp and Circumstance* Marches, especially when played as sensitively as here. The rarely encountered Second and Fifth marches are superbly conducted; the Philharmonia are on top form.

Piano Quintet in A minor, Op 84

Piano Quintet[a]. Violin Sonata[b]
The Nash Ensemble ([b]Marcia Crayford, [a]Elizabeth
Layton vns [a]Roger Chase va [a]Christopher van Kampen
vc Ian Brown pf)
Hyperion Helios CDH55301 (65' · DDD) Ⓑ**O**

Nash Ensemble members Marcia Crayford and
Ian Brown give a most perceptive rendering of
the Elgar Violin Sonata, one of the finest on
disc. Crayford's admirably disciplined, exquisitely shaded contribution is a constant source of
pleasure; Brown is an exemplary partner, acutely
responsive and passionate, yet never forcing the
tone. In the Quintet the playing of the Nash
Ensemble evinces consummate refinement and
total dedication; their heartwarmingly eloquent
reading communicates strongly.

Violin Sonata in E minor, Op 82

Elgar Violin Sonata
Finzi Elegy in F, Op 22 **Walton** Violin Sonata
Daniel Hope vn **Simon Mulligan** pf
Nimbus NI5666 (62' · DDD) Ⓕ**OO**

 The coupling of the violin sonatas by
Elgar and Walton is a most satisfying
one, not unique on disc, and one which
provides fascinating parallels. The Finzi *Elegy* is
a very apt makeweight, the only surviving movement from a projected Violin Sonata written in
a hectic period for the composer at the beginning of the Second World War.

The Elgar elicits a performance of high contrasts both in dynamic range – Hope uses daringly extreme *pianissimos* – and in flexibility of
tempo. So in the first movement, the opening at
an urgent speed gives way to a very broad reading of the second subject, hushed and musingly
introspective. Yet such freedom of expression
goes with deep concentration, so that the structure is still firmly held together. In the finale,
Hope conveys an improvisational quality, again
using the widest dynamic range, finely matched
by Mulligan.

With Hope's sweet, finely focused violin tone
beautifully caught in the Nimbus recording –
full and warm but less reverberant than some –
and well balanced against the piano, this set
makes an outstanding recommendation.

Organ Sonatas

Organ Sonatas – No 1, Op 28; No 2, Op 87a
(trans I Atkins). Cantique, Op 3 No 1. Vesper
Voluntaries, Op 14. Chanson de matin (arr
AH Brewer). 'Enigma' Variations, Op 36 –
Nimrod (arr WH Harris). Pomp and Circumstance
March No 4, Op 39 (arr GR Sinclair)
Thomas Trotter org
Regent REGCD256 (75' · DDD). Played on the Father
Willis organ of Salisbury Cathedral Ⓕ

It is extraordinary that no major label has got
Thomas Trotter, the greatest British organist of
his generation, cuffed hands and feet for life. It
has been left to the small Wolverhampton-based
Regent label to do the honours – and it does him
proud. There are few organs better suited to
Elgar than Salisbury Cathedral's Willis. It
speaks with a mellifluous, unforced authority in
a clear acoustic that avoids the generalised rum-
blings of many English cathedrals. The G major
Sonata unfolds with impressive breadth and
command of structure, a dramatic contrast to
the intimate *Cantique*, a short work derived from
an early (1879) piece for wind quintet, and the
attractive eight *Vesper Voluntaries* of 1889.

Three of the final four works are transcriptions
by a Three Choirs triumvirate of Elgar's organist friends: the Organ Sonata No 2 arranged
from the *Severn Suite* by Ivor Atkins (Worcester), *Chanson de matin* (Herbert Brewer of
Gloucester) and *Pomp and Circumstance* March
No 4 by the work's dedicatee, George Sinclair of
Hereford – GRS and his bulldog Dan from the
Enigma Variations. From the latter, 'Nimrod' is
heard in the transcription by WH Harris
(St George's, Windsor) and it is only here that
one might have wished Trotter had opted for a
more measured pace and emotional response.
But throughout this superbly engineered recording his mastery of tonal gradation, innate stylistic sense and imaginative colouring make for a
recording as rewarding as it is timely.

The Black Knight, Op 25

The Black Knight. Scenes from the Bavarian
Highlands, Op 27
**London Symphony Chorus and Orchestra /
Richard Hickox**
Chandos CHAN9436 (61' · DDD · T) Ⓕ Ⓑ→

Elgar completed *The Black Knight* in 1893 and it
provided him with his first big success. The text
tells of a sinister, unnamed 'Prince of mighty
sway', whose appearance at the King's court
during the feast of Pentecost has disastrous consequences. Elgar's score boasts much attractive
invention, some of it strikingly eloquent and
prescient of greater offerings to come. The choral writing is always effective, the orchestration
already vivid and assured. Richard Hickox and
his forces are dab hands at this kind of fare and
their performance has great bloom and spaciousness. Similarly, in the tuneful, vernally
fresh *Scenes from the Bavarian Highlands*, Hickox
and his colleagues respond with commendable
spirit and pleasing polish. Typical of Chandos,
the recording is bright and clear, tonally beyond
reproach and with just the right balance between
choir and orchestra.

The Light of Life, Op 29

The Light of Life
Judith Howarth sop **Linda Finnie** mez **Arthur**

Davies *ten* John Shirley-Quirk *bar* London
Symphony Chorus and Orchestra / Richard Hickox
Chandos CHAN9208 (63' · DDD · T)   Ⓕ

In the glorious orchestral 'Meditation' Hickox's
conducting demonstrates a noble flexibility,
sensitivity to dynamic nuance and feeling for
climax. Equally the engineering, sumptuous yet
detailed, comes close to the ideal. The LSO and
Chorus contribute to proceedings in exemplary,
disciplined fashion. As the Blind Man, Arthur
Davies could hardly be more ardent, but his
slightly tremulous timbre won't be to all tastes.
John Shirley-Quirk, so eloquent and firm-toned
a Jesus for Groves (on EMI) back in 1980 now
shows signs of unsteadiness in the same part. On
the other hand, Linda Finnie and Judith
Howarth make a creditable showing. Hickox's
reading excels in precisely the areas where the
Groves was deficient, and vice versa. If you
already have the Groves reissue, hang on to it,
for it's by no means outclassed by the Hickox.
However, for anyone coming to this underrated
score for the first time, Hickox's must now be
the preferred version.

The Crown of India, Op 66

The Crown of India (orch Payne, ed Davis)ᵃ. Imperial
March, Op 32. The Coronation March, Op 65. The
Empire March
ᵃClare Shearer *mez* ᵃGerald Finley *bar* ᵃBarbara
Marten, ᵃDeborah McAndrew, ᵃJoanne Mitchell
spkrs ᵃSheffield Philharmonic Chorus;
BBC Philharmonic Orchestra / Sir Andrew Davis
Chandos ② CHAN10570 (152' · DDD · T/t)   Ⓜ

Sir Andrew Davis's first recording for Chandos
brings this extravagantly enjoyable resuscitation
of *The Crown of India*, an 'Imperial Masque in
Two Tableaux' written swiftly in response to a
lucrative fee from impresario Oswald Stoll (1866-
1942). Henry Hamilton's verse will doubtless
provoke titters, but Elgar's music (mostly compiled from discarded material in his sketchbooks)
is a different matter, displaying fertility of imagination, boldness of orchestral colour and an
arresting range of mood. As the notes say: 'It may
not be India, but it is Elgar, who did this sort of
thing better than anyone else.'

The demolition of the publisher's archives in
the early 1970s eradicated all existing orchestral
material but Anthony Payne has managed to
piece together the original score, drawing upon
the piano arrangement by Hugh Blair in addition to the five surviving movements that Elgar
selected for the already familiar suite premiered
at the 1912 Three Choirs Festival in Hereford.
The complete entertainment is housed on
Disc 1 but the majority of listeners may well
prefer Andrew Davis's own, altogether more
compact edition on the second disc, which omits
the spoken element (the two CDs sensibly retail
for the price of one).

The performance possesses all the sterling
virtues that we have come to expect from one of

this composer's most distinguished exponents.
Sir Andrew directs with contagious relish, no
little charisma (witness the glinting spectacle of
the 'March of the Mogul Emperors') and
instinctive ebb and flow, the BBC PO and Sheffield Philharmonic Choir acquitting themselves
in kind with admirable skill and commitment.
Both vocal soloists are excellent (Gerald Finley
projects marvellously in 'The Rule of England'),
and the three speakers do what they can with
Hamilton's clunky couplets. The fill-ups are
perceptively handled, too, not least the markedly subdued and darkly sumptuous *Coronation
March* of 1911, while both the *Imperial March*
(1896-97) and lesser-known *Empire March*
(1924) have confidence and burnished splendour to spare.

With its gloriously ample sound and attractive
artwork, this set should find favour with every
Elgar devotee.

The Dream of Gerontius, Op 38

The Dream of Gerontius
Alice Coote *mez* Paul Groves *ten* Bryn Terfel *bass-
bar* Hallé Youth Choir; Hallé Choir and Orchestra /
Sir Mark Elder
Hallé ② CDHLD7520 (94' · DDD · T/t)   Ⓜ ❶❶❶❷►

For all sorts of reasons Barbirolli's famous Hallé
account has lived in everyone's hearts for
decades. It still will, because there is something
about the immediacy and wholeheartedness of
its vision that speaks as directly as ever. Mark
Elder's approach is more elusive. He draws us
patiently, unerringly, into the profound mystery
of the piece, judiciously weighing its theatricality against its inwardness. It is reverent in the
best sense, with breathless *pianissimi* and a
potency of atmosphere that takes hold from the
moment we enter the dying man's room. Just
listen to the Hallé strings in the Prelude, or the
introduction to Part 2. The stylistic finesse of
the playing, the very particular articulation, the
inbred *portamento* – all these qualities are testament to the fantastic work Elder has done with
the orchestra.

It is, by a mile, the best-sounding *Gerontius* we
have had, handsome in its depth and breadth
with great spatial perspectives and a wonderful
sense of how the score is layered. Onto this
impressive sound stage comes Paul Groves's
Gerontius with a near-perfect blend of poetic
restraint and high emotionalism – though some
may feel that the 'operatic' hot-spots, 'Take me
away!' being, of course, the hottest of them – are
wanting in that last degree of heft. Elder and his
sound team might have given us something
more startling with that chord of 'utmost force'
in the moment Gerontius finally glimpses his
creator.

No lack of force or presence in Bryn Terfel's
proclamation to 'Go forth!' – the portals of
heaven open to that, as indeed they do with the
arrival of the heavenly host for the great 'Praise

to the Holiest' chorus. The Hallé Choir bravely gather momentum in that, thanks to Elder's insistence on clear rhythmic articulation, and he achieves a simply stonking *crescendo* on the final chord, leaving the organ to plumb infinite depths.

Of course, Janet Baker's timbre still haunts every measure of the Angel's music, but the wonderful Alice Coote conveys great confidentiality in her highly personalised reading. 'Softly and gently' is gloriously enveloping – and maybe that's the word which ultimately best describes this fine and most satisfying recording.

The Dream of Gerontius^a. Cello Concerto^b   **H**
Gladys Ripley contr **Heddle Nash** ten **Dennis Noble** bar **Norman Walker** bass **Paul Tortelier** vc **Huddersfield Choral Society;** ^b**BBC Symphony Orchestra;** ^a**Liverpool Philharmonic Orchestra / Sir Malcolm Sargent**
Testament mono ② SBT2025 (120' · ADD · T)
Recorded 1945-53   **F O 🡢**
Also available as a download or custom-made CD from www.pristineaudio.com

This pioneering set of *Gerontius* has come up newly minted in these superbly engineered transfers taken from 78rpm masters. That only enhances the incandescence and fervour of the reading itself, in virtually all respects the most convincing the work has received. Sargent's conducting, influenced by Elgar's, is direct, vital and urgently crafted with an inborn feeling for the work's ebb and flow, and an overall picture that comprehends the piece's spiritual meaning while realising its dramatic leanness and force. Heddle Nash's Gerontius is unrivalled in its conviction and inwardness. He'd been singing the part since 1930, and by 1945 the work was in his being; he sang it from memory and had mastered every facet. 'Take me away' is like a searing cry of pain from the depth of the singer's soul. Gladys Ripley is a natural and communicative Angel, her flexible and appealing tone always a pleasure. The Liverpool Philharmonic lives up to its reputation at the time as the country's leading orchestra (in particular the sonorous string section), and the members of the Huddersfield Choral Society sing as if their lives depended on it.

Tortelier's Cello Concerto presents the 'classical' approach as compared with the 'romantic' one of du Pré, and is the best of Tortelier's readings of the work on disc, with his tone and phrasing at their firmest and most telling. A considered and unaffected reading among the best ever committed to disc.

Elgar The Dream of Gerontius Parry Ode at a Solemn Music, 'Blest Pair of Sirens'. I was glad
Felicity Palmer sop **Arthur Davies** ten **Gwynne Howell** bass **London Symphony Orchestra and Chorus / Richard Hickox**
Chandos ② CHAN8641/2 (114' · DDD · T)   **M**

Hickox gives us a peculiarly immediate and urgent interpretation – not dissimilar from Rattle's on EMI – that has us thinking more than ever that *Gerontius* is an opera in everything but name, or at least a dramatic cantata, not an oratorio. His speeds tend to be quick, but only once, in 'Sanctus fortis', does the tempo feel hurried. Being a choral trainer of many years' standing, he naturally enough persuades his choirs to sing with an impressive unanimity of purpose and with perhaps a wider range of dynamics than any other conductor. Perhaps an element of dignity and grandeur such as you find in Boult's and Barbirolli's EMI readings, both appreciably more measured, is missing, but little else. The sound of the chorus and excellent orchestra surpasses that on the Rattle version, Watford Town Hall proving as ever a good venue for the recording of large forces.

Arthur Davies has a stronger, more secure voice than any other tenor who has recorded Gerontius and, unlike several of them, he's in his prime as a singer. 'Mary, pray for me' and 'Novissima hora est' are sung with the appropriate sweet sadness, the duet with the Angel tenderly, and he enters with terrified power at 'Take me away'. He doesn't have the individuality of utterance or special affinity with the text, as for instance at 'How still it is!', that you get with Heddle Nash (for Sargent) and Sir Peter Pears (for Britten), or even quite the agony of the soul projected by Mitchinson (for Rattle), but it's an appreciable performance, firmly projected. Felicity Palmer's Angel is less successful. The intentions are right, the understanding is there, but the means to carry them forward are faulty: her singing, once she puts pressure on the tone, is uncomfortable to hear. Gwynne Howell is just about the best Priest and Angel of the Agony in any version. His warm, firm bass-baritone easily encompasses the different tessituras of the two 'parts'. This is a fine modern version.

The Kingdom, Op 51

The Kingdom[a]. Coronation Ode, Op 44[b]
[a]**Margaret Price**, [b]**Felicity Lott** *sops* [a]**Yvonne Minton**
mez [b]**Alfreda Hodgson** *contr* [a]**Alexander Young**,
[b]**Richard Morton** *tens* [a]**John Shirley-Quirk**,
[b]**Stephen Roberts** *bars* [a]**London Philharmonic Choir
and Orchestra / Sir Adrian Boult;**
[b]**Cambridge University Musical Society Chorus;**
[b]**Choir of King's College Cambridge;** [b]**New
Philharmonia Orchestra / Philip Ledger**
EMI British Composers ② 764209-2 (130' · ADD) Ⓜ️Ⓞ

Boult was a passionate admirer of *The Kingdom* and, as ever, the unaffected devotion and authority of his advocacy is hard to resist. The two formidable contenders in the work are Leonard Slatkin and Richard Hickox. All three performers have much going for them. In short, Boult enjoys the strongest team of soloists, Hickox obtains the most disciplined and full-bodied choral work, and Slatkin secures the finest orchestral playing – indeed, the LPO are on inspired form, responding with an exemplary sensitivity, commitment and

concentration which also marked out Slatkin's magnificent account of the Symphony No 2 set down with this same group some 17 months later. Slatkin also benefits from perhaps the best engineering, with Boult's Kingsway Hall production now sounding just a little pale and hard-edged in comparison. Where the EMI release really comes up trumps, though, is in the shape of its generous fill-up, Philip Ledger's superb, swaggering reading of the *Coronation Ode*. Ultimately, then, the Boult, must take the palm, especially at mid-price, though no devoted Elgarian should miss hearing Slatkin's gloriously lucid conception either.

Sea Pictures, Op 37

Sea Pictures. The Music Makers
Sarah Connolly *mez* **Bournemouth Symphony
Chorus and Orchestra / Simon Wright**
Naxos 8 557710 (62' · DDD · T/t)   Ⓜ️⮞

The Music Makers is one of Elgar's most poignant and troubled utterances which movingly incorporates material from some of his greatest compositions, and it can hold its head high. Simon Wright steers a commendably clear-sighted course and coaxes an idiomatic response from his Bournemouth forces. Sarah Connolly proves scarcely less raptly responsive than Baker (for Boult), singing with glorious radiance, security and richness of tone; her delivery of the final line ('And a singer who sings no more') is deeply affecting.

Connolly also steps up to the mark in the *Sea Pictures* (which follows after too short a gap). Hers is a gripping, intelligent display, combining keen poetic and dramatic instinct with clarity of diction, all technical challenges effortlessly surmounted. A performance to hear alongside the classic Baker recording – reviewed on page 432.

Miscellaneous choral works

There is sweet music, Op 53 No 1. Deep in my soul.
O Wild West Wind. Owls (An Epitaph). As torrents in
summer. The Prince of Sleep. The Shower. The
Fountain. My love dwelt in a northern land, Op 18
No 3. Death on the Hills, Op 72. Love's Tempest, Op 73
No 1. Serenade. Evening Scene. Go, song of mine,
Op 57. Scenes from the Bavarian Highlands, Op 27
**Cambridge University Chamber Choir /
Christopher Robinson** with **Iain Farrington** *pf*
Naxos 8 570541 (75' · DDD · T)   Ⓢ️Ⓞ⮞

Plaudits to Christopher Robinson and the Cambridge University Chamber Choir for their keenly prepared and fervent exploration of this still under-appreciated repertoire. And what an absorbing creative portrait of the composer they give us, stretching from 1889 and 'My love dwelt in a northern land' to 1925 and the delectably assured setting of Walter de la Mare's 'The Prince of Sleep'. Other bewitching gems along the journey include 'As torrents in summer'(from the epilogue of the 1896 cantata *King Olaf*), 'Evening Scene' (1905) and 'Go, song of mine'

(1909). In the five items (Opp 71-73) from 1914 Elgar's treatment of the *a cappella* medium acquires an extra confidence (the writing at once dark, rich and penetrating), though perhaps the most sheerly gripping and diverse inspiration on this well filled anthology is to be found within the four Op 53 songs of 1907: sample the ear-tickling bitonality of 'There is sweet music' or ghostly gloom of 'Owls' (Elgar at his most daring and inscrutable).

One might hope for a fractionally tighter focus to what is an otherwise tonally true sound-picture (the words are not always ideally clear – Naxos does, thankfully, supply full texts). Otherwise, these commendably disciplined and infectiously spirited performances are sure to give pleasure. A tempting price, too!

Excerpts from Caractacus[a]; The Dream of Gerontius[c/d]; The Saga of King Olaf[e]; Sea Pictures[f]; The Spirit of England[h]. Carillon, Op 75[b]. Shepherd's Song, Op 16 No 1[g]. With Proud Thanksgiving[i]. 🎧

[h]**Elsie Suddaby**, [a]**Isobel Baillie** *sops* [c]**Astra Desmond**, [d]**Muriel Brunskill**, [f]**Mary Jarred** *contrs* [cde]**Heddle Nash**, [g]**Walter Widdop**, [a]**Edward Reach** *tens* [a]**Arthur Cranmer**, [a]**Edward Brown** *bars* [d]**Horace Stevens**, [c]**Keith Falkner** *basses* [g]**Helen Perkin** *pf* [a]**Hereford Choral Society**; [i]**Preston Cecilian Choir**; [dh]**BBC Choral Society**; [bi]**BBC Northern Orchestra / Crawford McNair**; [e]**BBC Opera Orchestra / Stanford Robinson**; [fh]**BBC Orchestra / Clarence Raybould**; [d]**BBC Symphony Orchestra / **[dh]**Adrian Boult**; [a]**City of Birmingham Orchestra / Percy Hull**; [c]**Hallé Choir and Orchestra / Malcolm Sargent**
Elgar Editions mono ③ EECD003/5 (3h 38' · ADD) BBC broadcast performances, recorded 1935-50   Ⓜ

This is one of the most exciting archival releases in recent years. The source is a collection of privately made recordings of BBC broadcasts between 1935 and 1950. Kenneth Leech was a remarkable man, an engineer employed originally on the railways, designing a searchlight for the Navy in wartime, composing and conducting works for orchestra, and living to be over 100. Putting his technical skills to the task of recording from the radio, he used aluminium discs running at 64rpm and applying 3-in-1 oil to reduce surface noise. The collection, which is now in the British Library, is particularly rich in Elgar, and it was on *Gramophone* critic Alan Blyth's urging that this compilation was issued to mark the 150th anniversary of Elgar's birth.

Everything here has its interest and value, but at the centre are two performances of *The Dream of Gerontius*: from 1935 under Sargent and 1936 under Boult. Both have Heddle Nash as Gerontius. Of the first, just over 70 minutes is preserved, with slightly over half an hour of the second, in separate excerpts but allowing all three soloists to be heard. Andrew Neill, in his introductory notes, does well to warn listeners about the fragmentary nature of the recordings, though much comes through with startling brightness; in particular, Nash's singing is heard

throughout with perfect clarity. And it is glorious! Sargent conducts admirably but (and this is the other dazzling glory of what we hear) Boult brings such a charge to his performance we see how his orchestra at just this time became one fit for Toscanini.

There are several performers who in these broadcasts come to life as they never did in the studio; or rather, we come much nearer to the experience of hearing them in reality. Elsie Suddaby emerges as a valiant soprano, strong in spirit and sure in the thrust of her voice. Mary Jarred takes to the *Sea Pictures* like a Valkyrie. Astra Desmond has something of her heroine Clara Butt about her. Keith Falkner brings an unexpected operatic thrill to his 'Proficiscere'. And there is a new Widdop, from 1935, when they had stopped recording him; and what a mistake that was! These are precious retrievals: blessings on Kenneth Leech and all concerned.

Film

'Elgar – A film by Ken Russell'

Peter Brett Mr Elgar **Rowena Gregory** Mrs Elgar **George McGrath** Sir Edward Elgar **Ken Russell** Himself
British Film Institute 📀 BFIVD524 (71' · 4:3 black & white · 1.0 · 2). Includes commentary by Ken Russell and Michael Kennedy, historical footage and photo gallery   Ⓕ 000

Originally screened in November 1962 as the 100th programme within the BBC's groundbreaking *Monitor* series, Ken Russell's *Elgar* has lost none of its power to entrance, stimulate and provoke. If you never caught the film on television, prepare to be bowled over by the perfect marriage of music and pictures, especially during the scenes shot on and around Elgar's beloved Malvern Hills (against which the purposeful stride of the Introduction and Allegro for strings acts as a marvellously apt backdrop). Any minor factual anomalies along the way pale into insignificance when set against film-making of such poetry, wit and imagination. Pioneering, too, in as much as it was made at a time when Elgar's reputation was at a comparatively low ebb. Indelible images come thick and fast: Elgar's burgeoning love for Alice is exquisitely conveyed by the delicate interplay of four hands on the keyboard performing the piano-duet arrangement of *Salut d'amour*; the jaw-dropping transformation of Worcestershire Beacon into the cross-topped hill at Calvary (to the strains of 'Sanctus fortis' from *Gerontius*); or the composer on his bicycle rushing through the dappled woodland and heather. The result is an undisputed classic of British television.

Extras include rare home-film footage of the Three Choirs Festivals of 1929, 1930 and 1932 (during which we also see Elgar relaxing at home), as well as a November 1931 Pathétone movie-reel of the 74-year-old composer conducting the LSO in *Land of Hope and Glory*. Not to be missed.

George Enescu   Romanian 1881-1955

*Composer, teacher and violinist, George Enescu stud-
ied in Vienna and at the Paris Conservatoire (1895-
99), and Paris would be where he focused his musical
life, though he returned often to Romania to teach
and conduct. His music is slowly being rediscovered,
and it is greatly admired for the way it incorporates
Romanian folk music with a modernist language
that owes much to Reger and early Schoenberg. His
output includes the opera Oedipe (1936), five symphonies and much chamber music.*

Romanian Rhapsodies

Poème roumain[a]. Romanian Rhapsodies – Nos 1 & 2.
Suites for Orchestra – Nos 1, 2 & 3, 'Villageoise'.
Symphonie concertante for Cello and Orchestra[b].
[b]**Franco Maggio-Ormezowski** *vc*
[b]**Jean-Paul Barrellon** *ob* [a]Male voices
of the **Chorus of the Colonne Orchestra and the
Audite Nova Vocal Ensemble; Monte Carlo
Philharmonic Orchestra / Lawrence Foster**
Apex ② 2564 62032-2 (158' · DDD)   ⑤↪

Enescu's three suites stand in relation to the
symphonies rather as Tchaikovsky's suites relate
to his symphonic works. The First opens with a
striking prelude for strings in unison which in
turn gives way to a gorgeous *Menuet lent*. The
more formal Second Suite (which falls between
the First and Second Symphonies) is based on
Baroque models, while the relatively 'late' Third
Suite, named *Villageoise* (it dates from 1938),
overflows with invention, whether imitations of
birdsong and children at play, or exquisite tone-
painting of nature by day and night. Foster also
offers us the early, 23-minute *Symphonie concertante* for cello and orchestra, his soloist Franco
Maggio-Ormezowski unfolding its generous
stream of melody with a warm, fluid tone.

Lawrence Foster's performances of these fascinating if occasionally over-effusive works provided a fitting tribute for the 50th anniversary of
Enescu's death (1955). Do give this music a try.
It combines the freshness of Dvořák with the
earth-and-spirit daring of Bartók; and while not
quite on a level with either, it comes pretty
damned close.

String Quartets, Op 22

String Quartets, Op 22 – No 1 in E flat; No 2 in G
Ad Libitum Quartet (Adrian Berescu, Serban
Mereuta *vns* Bogdan Bisoc *va* Filip Papa *vc*)
Naxos 8 554721 (74' · DDD)   ⑤●↪

Enescu's 1920 First Quartet crams so much into
45-odd minutes that even two or three hearings
barely scratch its surface. It's a veritable forest of
invention, fairly Brahmsian in texture, organic
in its thinking and frequently dramatic. The
second movement incorporates sundry embellishments and effects (including the use of *sul

ponticello), and the finale features variations on a
march-like theme. It will make wonderful if
challenging listening for anyone who values
quality ideas above economical structuring.

Although the two quartets share the single
opus number, they're years apart chronologically, aeons if you consider their contrasting
styles. The Second Quartet was Enescu's penultimate work, and breathes the heady aroma of
Romanian folk music, especially in the slow
movement and finale, which recall the world of
the far better-known Third Violin Sonata.
Shorter than the First Quartet by almost half,
the Second feels tighter and more agile.

The Ad Libitum Quartet do a fabulous job.
They attend to Enescu's endless technical
demands with a devotion that translates to
apparent effortlessness. Naxos's superior production secures a top recommendation and
unbeatable value too.

Violin Sonatas

'Complete Works for Violin and Piano, Vol 1'
Violin Sonatas – 'Torso' Sonata; No 2, Op 6.
Impressions d'enfance, Op 28
Remus Azoitei *vn* **Eduard Stan** *pf*
Hänssler Classic CD98 239 (61' · DDD)   ⑤

'Complete Works for Violin and Piano, Vol 2'
Violin Sonatas – No 1, Op 2; No 3, 'dans le caractère
populaire roumain', Op 25. Ballade, Op 4a. Hora
Unirei. Impromptu concertant. Andante malinconico.
Tarantelle
Remus Azoitei *vn* **Eduard Stan** *pf*
Hänssler Classic CD98 240 (70' · DDD)   ⑤

Like Béla Bartók, Romanian composer-violinist-
pianist George Enescu wrote violin music from
a fairly early age, even earlier in fact: both the
Ballade and *Tarantella* that feature on the second
disc of this admirable survey are the products of
a prodigiously gifted 14-year-old. Both are
world premiere recordings, forming part of a
sequence of unusual short pieces that includes a
racy *Hora Unirei* from 1917 (like an offbeat
waltz), a playful *Impromptu concertant* (1903) and
a brief but harmonically pungent *Andante
malinconico* that Enescu wrote for a sight-reading
competition just four years before he died. All
five miniatures showcase the refined but
vibrant performing style of Remus Azoitei, a
distinctive player whose sound world echoes
Enescu's own.

Azoitei's pianist Eduard Stan is memorably
supple in terms of both rhythm and touch, vital
attributes in the last and greatest of the violin
works, the Third Sonata, with its tricky transitions, complex but spirited dance sequences and
fiery climaxes, especially in the finale. Azoitei
and Stan combine temperament, mastery of
idiom and executive elegance in a very special
way. They shape the music beautifully, so that
what in some hands sounds like mere extended
improvisation (a desirable attribute admittedly)
also parades discernable form.

The five larger works all come off exceptionally well. Regarding the folky and atmospheric *Impressions d'enfance*, Azoitei gives the feeling of controlled rhapsodising, and so does his pianist. The earliest larger-scale work here is the First Sonata, another teenage essay, confident and fitfully memorable though predictably derivative, with Schumann coming most often to mind. Carl Flesch described the Second Sonata (1899) as 'one of the most important works of all sonata literature, whose neglect is totally unjustifiable'. If the repertoire appeals, no need to look any further.

Additional recommendation

Violin Sonata No 3
Coupled with Impressions d'enfance
Ravel Sonata for Violin and Piano in G. Tzigane
Kavakos *vn* **Nagy** *pf*
ECM New Series 476 053-2   (F)**OOD▸**

A compelling programme. These aren't 'showy' performances. Though Kavakos is audibly appreciative of the folk flavouring in Enescu's Third Sonata, he treats the abstract element as paramount, suggesting keen parallels with the violin sonatas of Bartók.

Einar Englund   Finnish 1916-1999

Englund studied with Palmgren and Carlsson at the Helsinki Academy (1933-41), with Copland at Tanglewood, and in Russia, where he was impressed by Prokofiev and Shostakovich. His works include five symphonies (1946-77), concertos and piano pieces.

Symphonies

Symphonies – No 2, 'Blackbird'; No 4, 'Dedicated to the Memory of a Great Artist'. Piano Concerto No 1[a]
[a]**Niklas Sivelöv** *pf* **Turku Philharmonic Orchestra / Jorma Panula**
Naxos 8 553758 (76' · DDD)   (S)**OD▸**

Einar Englund was the finest Finnish symphonist between Sibelius and Kokkonen, and the *Blackbird* Symphony is one of his best. You can hear why he so named it from the woodwind writing, particularly the solos for flute, although he grew wary of emphasising the title in later life. One of the most attractive features of all his music is its orchestration. Panula's account is superbly played, with excellent sound. The Fourth (1976), written in memory of Shostakovich, is less epic, though no less inventive. A chamber symphony for strings and percussion, its most effective movement is the sparkling but macabre *Scherzo*, 'Tempus fugit', haunted by the chiming of bells and the manic ticking of some outlandish clock. Here, as well as in the darkly poetic third span, 'Nostalgia', and concluding 'Epilogue', Panula finds great poetry. Naxos's

centrepiece, though, is the first of Englund's two piano concertos. Englund's own recording disappeared from the catalogue long ago, but Niklas Sivelöv proves a fine advocate.

Symphonies – No 4, 'Dedicated to the Memory of a Great Artist'; No 5, 'To the Memory of JK Paasikivi'. The Great Wall of China
Tampere Philharmonic Orchestra / Eri Klas
Ondine ODE961-2 (65' · DDD)   (F)

The Fifth Symphony (1977) was recorded on LP by Jukka-Pekka Saraste; Englund once said this was too fast, so he would probably have approved of Klas's better-judged version. Although titled *Sinfonia Fennica* ('Finnish' Symphony), the composer claimed it contained more of his wartime experiences than his famous *War* Symphony (No 1, 1946). In a bold, riveting single span, its full orchestration pairs very effectively with the strings and percussion of No 4. The suite from the incidental music to Max Frisch's *The Great Wall of China* (1949) is great fun. 'The Green Table Tango' and 'Rumba' reveal what an adept light/jazz composer he also was (under the pseudonym, Marcus Eje). The Tampere band are really put through their paces here and come through very well. If Panula's Naxos disc is still perhaps the best introduction to Englund's music, this disc should certainly be the next stop.

Manuel de Falla   Spanish 1876-1946

Felipe Pedrell, the éminence grise of Spanish nationalism in music, persuaded Falla (as he had Albéniz and Granados beforehand) to use his country's character and folklore with which to express himself in composition. But, rather like Grieg whose music he greatly admired, Falla preferred not to make direct use of folk melody but to capture the essence and the spirit of his native land as reflected in his own personality.

He began by writing zarzuelas (then as now, popular, light musical entertainments in Spain) and won a prize for his opera La vida breve (1905). After its success he decided to go to Paris for a few weeks. Here he met and befriended Debussy, Ravel and Dukas, became swept up in French musical life and ended by staying seven years. Influenced and greatly encouraged by them (listen to Debussy's Ibéria from Images and his piano prelude Soiré dans Grenade!), Falla found his own voice and made his way back to Spain in 1914. This blend of Impressionism and his own ambitions for Spanish music resulted in his three best-known works: Nights in the Gardens of Spain and the two ballet scores El Amor brujo and El sombrero de tres picos.

In 1922, Falla settled in Granada, leaving only infrequently to conduct or attend performances of his work. A lifelong bachelor, he was a recluse by nature, hated publicity and went out of his way to avoid attention. Stravinsky once described Falla as 'the most unpityingly religious person I have ever known

– and the least sensible to manifestations of humour'. Though from a wealthy family, he had no desire for money, possessions or honours, and all he wanted was to worship God, write music and lead a simple life. (This austerity comes across in his music – it's far more aloof and spare than the spontaneity, warmth and ebullience of Albéniz and Granados.) Towards the end of his life he became a hypochondriac: believing that a full moon was bad for his health, when such an occurrence was due in March or September, he refused to see anyone.

At first he sided with Franco during the Civil War but the anti-religious sentiment after the overthrow of the monarchy forced him into self-imposed exile, knowing that his frail health would never allow him to set foot in Spain again. So it was, but after his death at his home near Cordoba in Argentina, his body was brought back to be buried in the crypt of Cádiz Cathedral.

Nights in the Gardens of Spain

Falla El Amor brujo – ballet (complete)[a].
Noches en los jardines de España[b]. La vida breve –
Interlude and Dance
[a]**Sarah Walker** mez [b]**Margaret Fingerhut** pf
London Symphony Orchestra / Geoffrey Simon
Chandos CHAN10232X (57' · DDD)   Ⓜ Ⓞ ⤷

The coupling of the complete *El Amor brujo* and *Nights in the Gardens of Spain* is sensible as the works are broadly contemporary (although the latter had a longer gestation period). This recording has to compete with much-praised earlier issues, but Geoffrey Simon and the Chandos sound engineers have something new and fresh to offer. The brighter lighting of the Chandos disc, while bringing great vividness to the ballet, is particularly striking in the *concertante* work. At the end of the *Nights* Simon's broadening brings a powerful feeling of apotheosis. Margaret Fingerhut's playing responds splendidly to the changes of mood and has plenty of personality.

In *El Amor brujo* the singing of Sarah Walker with its vibrant, earthy vitality brings an added dimension of Flamenco drama at the outset, and she is especially fine in the passionate closing 'Bells of the Morning'. But in the set pieces like the 'Ritual Fire Dance', Simon's vigour and brilliance are very telling. The 'Interlude and Dance' from *La vida breve* makes a suitable encore.

Gabriel Fauré French 1845-1924

What a quiet, undramatic life he had. The son of a village schoolmaster promoted to assistant inspector of primary schools, Gabriel was the sixth (and unwelcome) child to be born to the family. He was fostered out until he was four and never seems to have enjoyed much warmth or family love. It's said that a blind woman heard the eight-year-old boy playing the

harmonium one day and urged his father to take him to Paris to study. Fauré was introduced to the newly opened Ecole Niedermeyer (the 'Ecole de musique religieuse et classique'). Niedermeyer was so impressed that he offered him a place at the school free of charge. When he died in 1861, Fauré's teacher became Saint-Saëns. The two developed a close friendship which was to last until Saint-Saëns's death.

Fauré's career thereafter is notable for its lack of thrust. He spent four years in Rennes as the church organist, returning to Paris in 1870 on the eve of the Franco-Prussian war (he joined the light infantry for a short spell). He found a succession of increasingly important organ posts, eventually landing the top job at the Madeleine in 1896; parallel to this he took conducting and composition classes at the Ecole Niedermeyer, becoming a professor of composition at the Paris Conservatoire. Meanwhile, he had married in 1883 the daughter of a successful sculptor.

As a link to the Impressionists and as a teacher of the future generation of French composers, Fauré was of the utmost importance. One only has to read the names of those who came under his undemonstrative tutelage: Ravel, Enescu, Roger-Ducasse, Florent Schmitt and arguably the greatest teacher of the 20th century, Nadia Boulanger. Unlike his contemporaries Chabrier, d'Indy and Lekeu, Fauré did not succumb to the fashionable habit of Wagner worship and throughout his songs and chamber work there is an unmistakable 'Frenchness' about the language. In larger forms he was unsuccessful (operas and symphonies were not his forte) but his songs and idiomatic piano and chamber music attracted a growing band of admirers from the mid-1870s.

Fauré was made director of the Conservatoire in 1905, a post he retained for 15 years until increasing deafness made it impossible for him to continue to carry out his duties. All through his tenure he was determined, rather pathetically, to keep his handicap a secret; close friends helped him in this and, though his final works (the Second Piano Quintet and the Trio in D minor) were written when he was stone deaf, when his predicament was revealed four years after his death, many people who knew him were shocked at the revelation.

'I have been reserved all my life,' he wrote in a letter to his wife, 'and have only been able to let myself go in certain situations.' To his son, Philippe, he confided 'For me…music exists to elevate us as far as possible above everyday existence'.

Ballade, Op 19

Fauré Ballade **Franck** Symphonic Variations, Op 46
d'Indy Symphonie sur un chant montagnard français
in G, Op 25
François-Joël Thiollier pf **National Symphony
Orchestra of Ireland / Antonio de Almeida**
Naxos 8 550754 (55' · DDD)   Ⓢ ⤷

François-Joël Thiollier's playing is individual, often impulsive but always idiomatic, helped by the sensitive, guiding hand of a conductor well acquainted with the music. A more high-profile production would probably have retaken those passages where piano and orchestra co-ordination is occasionally fractionally awry, such as in the last variation of the Franck, but it might also have seemed less spontaneous. Thiollier's *rubato* is always distinctive and attractive; the style, particularly and crucially in the Fauré, properly fluid. Both the piano and the orchestra's woodwind are discreetly prominent but internal balances are generally excellent.

Fauré Ballade[a] **Leigh** Concertino for Piano and Strings[b] **Mozart** Piano Concertos – No 15 in B flat, K450[c]; No 24 in C minor, K491[d]
Kathleen Long *pf* [ac]**National Symphony Orchestra;** [b]**Boyd Neel String Orchestra / Boyd Neel;** [d]**Concertgebouw Orch / Eduard van Beinum**
Dutton CDBP9714 (75' · ADD)
Recorded 1940s ⓢ🅾🅾

A richly experienced chamber musician, Kathleen Long (1896-1968) was partnered and praised by Casals, played Ravel's 'Ondine' to the composer and gave over 60 National Gallery concerts during the Second World War. Though her playing may initially seem too restrained, you find yourself wondering why you've never enjoyed music so much or been made so aware, however unobtrusively, of its innermost spirit. It's in Fauré's *Ballade* that she makes her finest impression. Indeed, it's difficult to imagine this magical work played more serenely or inwardly. Even French critics wary of foreign interpreters marvelled over this recording. Her affection is evident in every caressing bar and makes for a perfect conclusion to a delectable disc. Long was a born aristocrat of the keyboard and you'll look in vain for any overt or disfiguring drama in her lucid and stylish performance of Mozart's C minor Concerto. The recordings have come up well and the inclusion in the booklet of a 1950 *Gramophone* interview is an illuminating bonus.

Orchestral Works

Masques et bergamasques, Op 112. Ballade, Op 19[a]. Pavane, Op 50. Fantaisie, Op 79[b]. Pénélope – Overture. Elégie, Op 24[c]. Dolly Suite (orch Rabaud).
[b]**Richard Davis** *fl* [c]**Peter Dixon** *vc* [a]**Kathryn Stott** *pf*
BBC Philharmonic Orchestra / Yan Pascal Tortelier
Chandos CHAN9416 (72' · DDD) Ⓕ🅳➤

Masques et bergamasques, which takes its title from Verlaine's sad, mysterious poem *Clair de lune*, is a late stage work that the composer himself described as melancholy and nostalgic, but it's hardly Romantic, being instead pointedly neo-classical in character and shape. The playing here under Yan Pascal Tortelier is very satisfying, as are the elegant flute solos of the exquisitely delicate *Pavane*, performed here without the optional chorus, and in *Dolly*. The rarely heard Overture to the opera *Pénélope* is also effectively presented here.

The biggest *concertante* work here, the *Ballade* of 1881, is Fauré's orchestration of his piano

piece of the same name; it's gentle music that persuades and cajoles in a very Gallic way. Though not an overtly virtuoso utterance, it makes its own exacting technical demands on the soloist, among them being complete control of touch and pedalling. The highly regarded Fauréan Kathryn Stott meets these with consistent success.

There's little rhetoric and no bombast in Fauré's art, but how civilised he was, and what sympathetic interpreters serve him here! The recording is warm yet also delicate.

Piano Quintets

Piano Quintets – No 1, Op 89; No 2, Op 115
Cristina Ortiz *pf*
Fine Arts Quartet (Ralph Evans, Efim Boico *vns* Yuri Gandelsman *va* Wolfgang Laufer *vc*)
Naxos 8 570938 (63' · DDD) ⓢ🅾🅾🅾🅳➤

Ⓖ Fauré's last years were dogged by increasing deafness, an unhappy marriage, a wholesale neglect of even his finest works and a continuing grief over his father's death. True, the ceaseless flow of invention has puzzled many listeners ('verse innocent of punctuation') but for others the First Quintet's opening theme, heard beneath a spray of piano arpeggios, or the strange, archaic dance commencing the same work's finale are features that can haunt the imagination for ever. The whirling figuration, too, of the Second Quintet's *Allegro vivo* is again somehow part and parcel of an autumnal, other-worldly utterance that can be both heart-easing and disturbing.

Ideally balanced and recorded, Cristina Ortiz and the Fine Arts Quartet offer performances that are warmly affectionate, fluent and musicianly to the core. Surpassing even Domus's fine Hyperion disc (see below), these are outstanding readings and Ortiz in particular is memorably sensitive to Fauré's subtle and intricate piano-writing.

Additional recommendation

Piano Quintets Nos 1 & 2
Domus; Marwood *vn*
Hyperion CDA66766 Ⓕ🅾🅾🅾🅳➤
Domus play with an ardour and élan that would surely have delighted the composer ('people play me as if the blinds were down'). The recordings are superb.

Piano Quartets

Piano Quartets – No 1 in C minor, Op 15; No 2 in G minor, Op 45
Domus (Krysia Osostowicz *vn* Robin Ireland *va* Timothy Hugh *vc* Susan Tomes *pf*)
Hyperion CDA66166 (62' · DDD) Ⓕ🅾🅾🅾🅳➤

The First Piano Quartet reveals Fauré's debt to an earlier generation of composers, particularly

Mendelssohn. Yet already it has the refined sensuality, the elegance and the craftsmanship which were always to be hallmarks of his style and it's a thoroughly assured, highly enjoyable work which could come from no other composer's pen.

The Second Quartet is a more complex, darker work, but much less ready to yield its secrets. The comparatively agitated, quicksilver *Scherzo* impresses at once, however, and the complete work possesses considerable poetry and stature. Occasionally one might wish that Domus had a slightly more aristocratic, commanding approach to these scores, but the overall achievement is impressive, for their playing is both idiomatic and technically impeccable. The recording is faithful and well balanced.

Cello Works

Romance in A, Op 69[b]. Elégie, Op 24[b]. Cello Sonatas[b] – No 1 in D minor, Op 109; No 2 in G minor, Op 117. Allegretto moderato[a]. Sérénade, Op 98[b]. Sicilienne, Op 78[b]. Papillon, Op 77[b]. Andante[c]
Steven Isserlis, [a]**David Waterman** vcs
[b]**Pascal Devoyon** pf [c]**Francis Grier** org
RCA Victor Red Seal 09026 68049-2 (62' · DDD)   Ⓕ

This, surely, is the most 'complete' of Fauré's complete works for cello yet to appear. Isserlis has unearthed the original version of the *Romance*, Op 69 (entitled *Andante*), with a sustained, chordal accompaniment for organ in place of the piano's broken chordal semiquavers, and a gracious flourish from the cello by way of adieu. Mystically accompanied by Francis Grier at the organ of Eton College Chapel, the cello's song, restored to the church, seems to acquire more depth.

In the more familiar version of this work, as throughout the disc, Pascal Devoyon is a partner in a thousand, keenly aware of Isserlis's respect for the 'discretion, reticence and restraint' once hailed as the hallmarks of Fauré's style. In fact only in the noble *Elégie* do we discover the full breadth and richness of this cello's (a 1745 Guadagnini) tonal range.

A world war, plus the private trauma of incipient deafness, helps to explain the yawning gulf between the miniatures and the two sonatas of 1918 and 1922. Skipping through the score of the First you notice that only once does Fauré use a dynamic marking above *forte*, relying on the word *espressivo* to elicit just that little extra intensity at moments of climax. This is appreciated by both artists, most movingly in the central *Andante*. In the first movement, however, it's Devoyon's piquant accentuation that brings home the music's menace. The urgency and *Elégie*-evoking heart-throb of the G minor work again benefit from the immediacy of keyboard characterisation, and the variety of keyboard colour, underpinning this poetically introspective cellist's fine-spun line.

Cello Sonatas Nos 1 & 2. Berceuse, Op 16. Elégie, Ⓟ Op 24. Romance, Op 69. Trois Romances sans paroles, Op 17. Après un rêve, Op 7 No 1 (arr Casals). Vocalise-étude. Morceau de lecture. Serenade, Op 98. Papillon, Op 77. Sicilienne, Op 78
Xavier Gagnepain vc **Jean-Michel Dayez** pf
Zig-Zag Territoires ZZT070602 (73' · DDD)   ⒻOⒹ

Fauré's cello sonatas are not nearly so well known as his violin sonatas, but these two late works are well coupled with other cello works and some arrangements from songs (the ever-popular 'Après un rêve' among them). The big exception is the *Elégie*, the first work Fauré specially wrote for the cello, here played with the reprise of the opening theme magically hushed. The Op 16 *Berceuse* is not to be confused with the *Berceuse* from the *Dolly Suite*, and comes here in a version designed either for violin or cello. As an exception, *Papillon* is a light and brilliant virtuoso showpiece.

The centrepiece of the recital comes in the two sonatas, both late works, very compact in their structure, the first dating from 1917, the year when Debussy too devoted himself to chamber music, and the second from 1921, when the style is even more purified. Each is in three movements, lively outer ones framing hushed and intense slow ones. The *Andante* of No 2 brings a simple, dedicated melody accompanied by plain chords on the piano.

The unusual aspect of this issue is the use of period instruments, a 1902 Erard piano accompanying an 1878 cello made in France, not notably different in timbre from a traditional cello and a modern Steinway, but adding point to a fine issue, well recorded, and issued in celebration of the label's 10th anniversary.

Additional recommendation

Cello Sonatas Nos 1 & 2. Elégie, Op 24. Papillon, Op 77. Sérénade, Op 98. Après un rêve, Op 7 No 1
Kliegel vc **Tichman** pf
Naxos 8 557889   ⒮Ⓓ
> In both sonatas and in the shorter pieces Kliegel plays with an impressively wide dynamic range down to a mere whisper of *pianissimo*, perfectly articulated. She is on top form throughout.

Piano Works

Five Impromptus. Impromptu, Op 86. Thème et Variations in C sharp minor, Op 73. Trois Romances sans paroles, Op 17. Quatre valses-caprices. 13 Barcarolles. Ballade in F sharp, Op 19. 13 Nocturnes. Souvenirs de Bayreuth[a]. Pièces brèves, Op 84. Dolly, Op 56[a]. Nine Préludes, Op 103. Mazurka in B flat, Op 32
Kathryn Stott, [a]**Martin Roscoe** pfs
Hyperion ④ CDA66911/4 (4h 57' · DDD)   ⓂOOⒹ

Fauré's piano works are among the most subtly daunting in all keyboard literature. Encompassing Fauré's entire creative life, they range through an early, finely wrought eroticism via sporting with an aerial virtuosity as teasing and light as the elements themselves (the *Valses-caprices*) to the final desolation of his last years. There, in his most powerful works (Barcarolles Nos 7-11, Nocturnes Nos 11-13), he faithfully mirrors a pain that 'scintillates in full consciousness', a romantic agony prompted by increasing deafness and a lack of recognition that often seemed close to oblivion. Few compositions have reflected a darker night of the soul, and Fauré's anguish, expressed in both numbing resignation and unbridled anger, could surely only be exorcised by the articulation of such profound and disturbing emotional complexity. The task for the pianist, then, is immense, but in Kathryn Stott Fauré has a subtle and fearless champion. How thrilled Fauré would have been by the sheer immediacy of Stott's responses. Time and again she throws convention to the winds, and although it would be surprising if all her performances were consistent successes, disappointments are rare. Sometimes her *rubato* and luxuriant pedalling soften the outlines of Fauré's starkest, most austere utterances. But such quibbles remain quibbles. The Fourth Nocturne is gloriously supple, and the 13 Barcarolles show Stott acutely responsive to passion and finesse alike. The *Pièces brèves*, too, are played with rare affection. Stott proves herself a stylish and intriguing pianist.

---

13 Barcarolles   H
Germaine Thyssens-Valentin *pf*
Testament mono SBT1215 (72' · ADD)

13 Nocturnes
Germaine Thyssens-Valentin *pf*
Testament mono SBT1262 (80' · ADD)

Quatre Valses caprices.
Six Impromptus. Pièces brèves, Op 84
Germaine Thyssens-Valentin *pf*
Testament mono SBT1263 (73' · ADD)
All recorded 1956-59   Ⓕ**❍❍❍**

Germaine Thyssens-Valentin (1902-87) was a great and inspired pianist; occasionally one hears Fauré-playing that approaches or even occasionally equals hers, but none that surpasses it. This review could be filled with a catalogue of her qualities, but her intimacy of expression demands first place. Fauré's music has a confiding quality to it, as though it were a message intended for an audience of one, and Thyssens-Valentin is in perfect accord with this. Those messages, however, especially in the later Nocturnes and Barcarolles, are often of great profundity, and she has both the heart and the technique to convey them.

Her sound, first of all, is wonderfully beautiful, a combination of the subtlest colour and great delicacy of touch ensuring that contrapuntal voices are in perfect balance. She's a mistress of the most refined *rubato*, extreme finesse of articulation and smooth, singing line. Although she excels in quiet delicacy, her strength when required is formidable but even in the strongest *fortissimo* she never makes an ugly sound.

She is, blessedly, aware that Fauré had a sense of humour, and not only in the frank exuberance of the *Valses caprices*. Nor is she one of those artists that it takes a while to get used to. On each of these discs the first track is immediately characteristic of her. The first Nocturne has immaculate voice-leading and the lightest-fingered *leggierissimo* playing imaginable; the first Barcarolle is wonderfully tender, its second idea poised and liquid; the first *Valse caprice* has rich fantasy, dazzling brilliance and adorable wit.

The exploration of Fauré's emotional and technical range through the Barcarolles and especially the Nocturnes has never seemed so absorbing, the companion on that voyage never so prodigal with insight. Truly a great pianist.

Requiem, Op 48

Requiem (original version – ed Rutter). Motets –
Ave verum corpus; Tantum ergo; Ave Maria; Maria, mater gratiae. Cantique de Jean Racine, Op 11 (orch Rutter). Messe basse
Caroline Ashton, Ruth Holton *sops* **Stephen Varcoe** *bar* **Simon Standage** *vn* **John Scott** *org*
Cambridge Singers; City of London Sinfonia / John Rutter
Collegium COLCD109 (63' · ADD/DDD · T/t)
Recorded 1984   Ⓟ**❍❍❍**▷

Fauré began his Requiem in 1885, under the impact of the death of his father, but the work didn't take on the form in which we now know it until 15 years later. The familiar 1900 score, therefore, can't really be regarded as 'definitive'; it's a compromise, rather, between Fauré's original conception and what his publisher no doubt saw as the practicalities of concert performance. It's Fauré uncompromised that John Rutter has sought to restore in his edition of the seven-movement 1892 version, and his performance of it, using a chamber orchestra, a small choir and, in the 'Pie Jesu', a soprano who could easily be mistaken for a treble (Fauré's own early performances used a boy soloist) is a most convincing argument for accepting this score as more 'authentic' than the customary 1900 version.

The differences are audibly obvious, and most are no less obviously improvements. The almost omnipresent organ now sounds more like a continuo instrument than (as can easily happen with the 1900 score) an unwelcome thickening of an already dark orchestra. Above all, one is more aware than in any other recording that the sound in Fauré's head when he conceived the work wasn't that of a conventional orchestra but the rich, dark graininess of divided violas and cellos, the radiant luminosity of the work provided not by violins or woodwind but by the voices. It's thus more unified than the later revision as well

FAURÉ REQUIEM – IN BRIEF

Yan Pascal Tortelier
Chandos CHAN10113 (70' · DDD)　　　Ⓕ**O**Ⓑ
A warm and spacious mainstream perform-ance that comes as part of an all-Fauré collec-tion taking in the rarely heard *La naissance de Vénus*.

John Rutter
Collegium COLCD109 (63' · ADD)　　Ⓕ**OOO**Ⓑ
💎 Rutter's recording of his own edition of the original 1893 score retains its fasci-nation. The sound is more closely balanced than is usually the case with the larger-scale traditional readings.

Sir David Willcocks
EMI 764715-2 (42' · ADD)　　　　　Ⓜ**OO**
A much-loved LP version, documenting the excellence of the King's College Choir at its mid-1960s peak, and still sounding well.

Philippe Herreweghe
Harmonia Mundi HMC90 1771 (76' · DDD) Ⓕ**O**Ⓑ
Herreweghe, the first to tape Jean-Michel Nectoux's reconstruction of the composer's lightly scored original (Harmonia Mundi HMC90 1292), here gives new life to the 1901 version, again favouring surprisingly broad tempi. The coupling is unique: a period-instrument performance of the Franck Symphony.

George Guest
Decca ② 436 486-2DF2 (149' · ADD)　　　Ⓜ
Fresh, vivid and relatively small-scale, the Choir of St John's College, Cambridge, as taped in 1975, shines in a twofer of French choral classics.

Laurence Equilbey
Naïve V5137 (41' · ADD)　　　　　　Ⓕ**OOO**
A quite ravishing version of the Requiem from Accentus offering choral singing of exquisite purity and control.

Sir Neville Marriner
Philips 446 084-2PH (54' · DDD)　　　　　Ⓕ
With Sylvia McNair and Thomas Allen the outstanding soloists, Sir Neville Marriner's 1993 version uses the fuller orchestration and never lets the music drag. His unusual make-weight is a select group of French orchestral miniatures, exquisitely played.

Nadia Boulanger
BBC Legends BBCL4026-2 (75' · ADD)　　　Ⓕ
A blast from the past, Nadia Boulanger's performance has dignity and gravitas, while the rest of the programme, featuring music by Nadia's short-lived sister Lili, has even greater authority. She draws from her BBC forces a performance on a grand scale but also alive to the work's detail.

as being more intimate. Rutter's chorus is a fine one, immaculate of diction and pure of line; Stephen Varcoe's light and unforced baritone could well be just what Fauré had in mind and Caroline Ashton's absolute purity in her brief solo is most moving. The recording is excellent.

Requiem. Cantique de Jean Racine, Op 11
Sandrine Piau *sop* **Stéphane Degout** *bar* **Accentus Chamber Choir; French National Orchestra / Laurence Equilbey**
Naïve V5137 (41' · DDD)　　　　　　Ⓕ**OOO**

Can there may be a more profoundly beautiful recording of Fauré's Requiem out there? We defy any sensitive soul not to be transported into a state of near rapture by the unspeakably delicious *Sanctus*, the solo violin of Luc Héry floating ethereally above the choral and orches-tral textures like a skylark in full song.

What is it that makes this such a sublimely beautiful recording of a work which, let's face it, is more than generously represented in the cata-logues? (For the record, this is the original scor-ing of the work – organ with chamber orchestra minus violins – which was finally published in 1969.) It's not just the lovely sound produced by the three dozen voices of Accentus, unquestion-ably one of the really top-notch choirs around at the moment, or the angelic voices of the Maî-trise de Paris which point us heavenwards in the closing *In paradisum*. Nor can the credit for such unremitting loveliness be laid wholly at the feet of the members of the Orchestre National de France, handling this famous score with rare sensitivity and delicacy, or the wonderful pair of soloists. Stéphane Degout brings immeasurable poise to the *Hostias*, while Sandrine Piau's *Pie Jesu* has a wholly unaffected aura of purity and innocence – and has the string response to each line ever before been captured on disc with such utter gentleness?

These are all exceptional elements, but the two things which transform these are the recording's location and Laurence Equilbey's inspired direction. The famous Parisian church of St Clotilde imbues the whole thing with an atmosphere of warmth and great tranquillity, the organ pedals perfectly proportioned (and superbly captured by the Naïve engineers), while Equilbey shapes and caresses every single phrase, every line, every note with the kind of loving care few conductors ever lavish on such a well known and technically undemanding score. The result is a genuinely revelatory reading.

Fauré Requiem (1901 version)[a]　　　　Ⓟ
Franck Symphony in D minor
[a]**Collegium Vocale;** [a]**La Chapelle Royale; Champs-Elysées Orchestra, Paris / Philippe Herreweghe**
Harmonia Mundi HMC90 1771 (76' · DDD · T/t) Ⓕ**O**Ⓑ

Philippe Herreweghe's earlier recording of the Fauré *Requiem* (also Harmonia Mundi) used Jean-Michel Nectoux's edition of the original

1891 'chamber' score. This is the familiar 1901 version, with its full if curious orchestration, but in other respects this is a more 'authentic' reading than the earlier one. Period instruments are used, gut strings giving the sound a gentle luminescence, and instead of an organ Fauré's permitted alternative, a large harmonium, adds a reedy quality to the wind scoring. A shade more controversially, the work is sung in 'Gallican' Latin – 'Pié Zhesü' instead of 'Pie Yesou', 'Lüx perpétüa', and so on. Together with the other period details it makes the work sound distinctly Gallic: an admirable antidote to the Anglicised or even Anglicanised Fauré presented by the archetypally English cathedral and college choirs that have so often recorded it. Both soloists are excellent, Herreweghe's tempi are a little more alert than before and the recording is splendidly ample.

Alongside gut strings the big advantage of a period orchestra in Franck is the beautifully smooth sound of the horns. The overall sound is more transparent than usual, and Franck's reputation for dense over-scoring seems more than ever unjustified. It's a fine and idiomatic performance and hugely enjoyable. A fascinating coupling, strongly recommended.

Requiem[a]. Pavane. Cantique de Jean Racine, Op 11. La naissance de Vénus, Op 29[b]
[a]**Libby Crabtree**, [b]**Mary Plazas** sops [b]**Pamela Helen Stephen** mez[b]**Timothy Robinson** ten [ab]**James Rutherford** bass-bar
City of Birmingham Symphony Chorus;
BBC Philharmonic Orchestra / Yan Pascal Tortelier
Chandos CHAN10113 (70' · DDD · T/t) ⓕ ⓞⓓ

It was the French music publisher Hamelle who suggested that Fauré expand his 'petit Requiem' (1893 version – as restored by John Rutter) into a 'version symphonique' (1900). However, if you like Fauré's evergreen sung by a large chorus supported by symphonic-strength strings and brass then this new recording will suit nicely.

The disc's sound is consistently warm, reverberant and engaging. The chorus are in committed form: unanimous, well blended and balanced. Aside from one ugly glitch from the sopranos in the Requiem's *Sanctus* ('hosanna-RIN-excelsis'), they should be congratulated on their clear diction. Unlike Philippe Herreweghe's 'authentic' recording, no attempt has been made to sing the Latin text with a French accent. Yan Pascal Tortelier's tempi are perfectly sensible, though the opening *Kyrie* is well below the metronome marking. Both soloists control their fervour admirably, and the organist Jonathan Scott conjures up a wide variety of (presumably) electronic organ tone, including a delicious harmonium-type combination in the 'Pie Jesu'.

The enjoyable makeweights *Pavane* and *Cantique de Jean Racine* both breathe the calm air of the Requiem. But the disc's revelation is a wonderful performance of the rarely heard *La naissance de Vénus*, a 23-minute 'mythological scene' completed in 1895. It's a little gem.

Songs

'The Complete Songs – Volume 1, Au bord de l'eau'
Les matelots. Seule!. La chanson du pêcheur. Barcarolle, Op 7 No 3. Au bord de l'eau. Tarentelle, Op 10 No 2. Les berceaux. Larmes. Au cimetière. Cinq Mélodies de Venise. Pleurs d'or. La fleur qui va l'eau. Accompagnement. Mirages. C'est la paix!. L'horizon chimérique
Felicity Lott, Geraldine McGreevy, Jennifer Smith sops **Stella Doufexis** mez **John Mark Ainsley** ten **Stephen Varcoe, Christopher Maltman** bars **Graham Johnson** pf
Hyperion CDA67333 (69' · DDD · T/t) ⓕ ⓞⓞⓓ

Few singers would give over a whole evening to Fauré's songs on the concert platform, and choosing a way of presenting them on disc obviously poses problems. Previous sets had all the songs in chronological order; others chose poets or moods: Graham Johnson and company have begun with songs about water. This means a lot of dreaming and melancholy, whether in Gautier's 'Chanson du pêcheur' ('Ma belle amie est morte', also set by Berlioz), or Richepin's 'Au cimitière'. The latter is given a most beautiful rendition by John Mark Ainsley, who otherwise only sings on two tracks, with Jennifer Smith in the sentimental 'Pleurs d'or', and the homage to Venice and its lovers in Marc Monnier's 'Barcarolle'.

Three cycles are the main items here. Felicity Lott sings the *Cinq Mélodies de Venise*, which includes some of Fauré's best-known songs, 'Mandoline', 'En sourdine' and 'Green'. She brings to bear on them a lifetime's devotion to French song. Her other contribution is 'Au bord de l'eau', to a poem by Sully-Prudhomme. This is made to sound very sad; taken faster it can be quite merry; it's a celebration of love, as well as a meditation on the passing of time.

Stephen Varcoe sings *Mirages*, Fauré's penultimate cycle (1919). As Graham Johnson writes in his fascinating notes, these poems by Brimont permitted Fauré 'uneventful passion'. Christopher Maltman is the other featured singer, in five separate songs and *L'horizon chimérique*. All the performances are elegant and well-balanced, but one misses the extra slight note of acid that native French singers bring to Fauré's songs.

Hyperion's sound is impeccable and in both his playing and accompanying essay Graham Johnson penetrates to the heart of one of music's most subtle and enigmatic geniuses.

'The Complete Songs – Volume 2, Un paysage choisi'
Mai, Op 1 No 2[f]. Dans les ruines d'une abbaye, Op 2 No 1[g]. Sérénade toscane, Op 3 No 2[e]. Lydia, Op 4 No 2[f]. Three Songs, Op 5[g] – No 1, Chant d'automne; No 3, L'Absent. Tristesse, Op 6 No 2[b]. Après un rêve, Op 7 No 1[e]. Puisqu'ici-bas, Op 10 No 1[bd]. Three Songs, Op 18 – No 2, Le voyageur[h]; No 3, Automne[b]. La fée aux chansons, Op 27 No 2[b]. Noël, Op 43 No 1[e]. Clair de lune, Op 46 No 2[a]. Spleen, Op 51 No 3[g]. Prison, Op 83 No 1[h]. Dans la forêt de

septembre, Op 85 No 1ª. Chanson, Op 94ª. Les jardins clos, Op 106ᶜ. Il est né, le divin Enfantᵇ. En prièreᵇ
ᵃFelicity Lott, ᵇGeraldine McGreevy, ᶜJennifer Smith *sops* ᵈStella Doufexis *mez* ᵉJohn Mark Ainsley, ᶠJean-Paul Fouchécourt *tens* ᵍStephen Varcoe, ʰChristopher Maltman *bars* Graham Johnson *pf*
Hyperion CDA67334 (68' · DDD · T/t)   Ⓕ🅑➔

Volume 2 of Hyperion's superb Fauré song series takes its theme from 'Clair de lune' and an idealised landscape peopled with dreaming birds and sobbing fountains. It follows the composer from youth to old age, from the young charmer to the mature master to the inscrutable sage, imaginatively side-stepping all possible monotony. Fauré's dream world is a mirror of an occasionally innocent nature that received too many cruel knocks, reflected in music of light and darkness, courage and despair. All the singers involved in this ideally presented and recorded offering perform with a special ardour and commitment; Graham Johnson is, as always, a matchless partner and commentator.

Quatre Mélodies, Op 51. Cinq Mélodies, Op 58. Deux Mélodies, Op 76. Deux Mélodies, Op 83. Trois Mélodies, Op 85. Deux Mélodies, Op 87. Chanson, Op 94. Le Don silencieux, Op 92. Shylock, Op 57 – Chanson; Madrigal
Yann Beuron *ten* **Billy Eidi** *pf*
Timpani 1C1162 (53' · DDD)   Ⓕ

Here is music of a harmonic and rhythmic iridescence quickly shadowed by darker imaginings. The scope, too, is remarkable from a composer too frequently characterised as limited. 'Larmes' has a near-operatic declamation while 'La rose' is magically radiant. In the inimitable 'Mandoline' from the *Cinq Mélodies de Venise* a mischievous tripping charm 'softens to paint the shimmering of silk jackets, blue shadows and the halo of a pink-grey moon', a reminder that figures from the *commedia dell'arte* were central to Fauré's fantasy. Such music requires special qualities from both singer and pianist, and while Yann Beuron and Billy Eidi hardly eclipse memories of Gérard Souzay and Dalton Baldwin (Testament) or Hyperion's glorious four-disc set, their ardour and commitment are unmistakable. At once sensitive and strong, they are true to a clearly beloved composer whether in the voluptuously beautiful 'En sourdine' or in the heartbreaking reflection of 'Prison'. All lovers of a still misunderstood composer will want to add this well-recorded album to their collection.

Robert Fayrfax   British 1464-1521

After singing in the choir of the Chapel Royal, Fayrfax graduated MusB (1501) and MusD (1504) at Cambridge and was incorporated DMus at Oxford

(1511). At the beginning of Henry VIII's reign in 1509 he granted Fayrfax the annuity of a farm in Hampshire (with a lifetime award of 12 pennies a day). From 1516, for four consecutive years, he presented the king with collections of his compositions and received financial rewards. In 1520 he led the Chapel Royal in the state visit to France of the Field of the Cloth of Gold. He died in 1521, possibly at St Albans where he was buried. More compositions by him survive than by any composer of his day, and his output includes six cyclic Masses, two Magnificats as well as secular pieces.

Missa Regali ex Progenie

(ed Skinner). Antiphona Regali ex Progenie. Missa Regali ex Progenie. Lauda Vivi Alpha et O. Magnificat Regali. Alas, for lak of her presens. That was my woe
The Cardinall's Musick / Andrew Carwood
ASV Gaudeamus CDGAU185 (78' · DDD · T/t)   Ⓕ

Fayrfax's *Missa Regali ex Progenie* and *Magnificat Regali* are both early works, written before 1504, perhaps to impress his royal patron, and both, particularly the Mass, show signs that the composer had yet to settle into his stride. The longer, wordy movements of the Mass (the *Gloria* and *Credo*) seem elusive, as though he were note-spinning rather than weaving the contrapuntal texture, even if the hallmarks of greatness are all there. The Cardinall's Musick, with its by now almost instinctive understanding of his music, gives as convincing a performance as anyone.

The votive antiphon *Lauda Vivi Alpha et O*, with its coda in praise of Henry VIII, probably dates from the time of or shortly after his coronation in 1509. This extended homage to the Virgin is rich in textural resonances, and a double meaning of 'O rosa gratie redolentissima' ('Most sweetly scented rose') was surely intended. Here the long-drawn-out vocal lines, shifts in scoring and intellectual transitions of harmony of Fayrfax's mature style are much in evidence, and the work's richness is given its full due here. There's a striking contrast between this full-blown rose of a piece and the closed but equally perfectly formed rose-bud that is the duo 'That was my woe': it was a long way from ceremonial homage to semi-private entertainment in Tudor London. It's sung perfectly by Robin Blaze and Steven Harrold.

Magnificat, 'O bone Ihesu'

Magnificat, 'O bone Ihesu'. Missa O bone Ihesu. Salve regina. Most clere of colour. I love, loved and loved wolde I be. Benedicite!. What dreamed I?
(all ed Skinner)
The Cardinall's Musick / Andrew Carwood
ASV Gaudeamus CDGAU184 (76' · DDD · T/t)   Ⓕ🅞

The Cardinall's Musick put the focus here on Fayrfax's Mass *O bone Ihesu*. Tragically, only a single voice survives of the antiphon that was probably its model, so in that respect their recording can't be complete, unless David Skinner is prepared to indulge in the massive and quixotic task of reconstruction for this and other fragmentary survivals. But we do have a glorious *Magnificat* built on the same materials, one of the most widely distributed of all early Tudor works. By far the most commanding performance here is of that *Magnificat*: wonderfully controlled and perfectly tuned. The group is slightly rougher in the Mass and the *Salve regina*, a work that stands rather apart from the style we otherwise know from Fayrfax, and which may be one of his earliest surviving works. Intriguingly, this is the piece that seems to show the strongest debts to composers from the Continent (especially Brumel), giving important insights into the evolution of his music. Similarly, the three songs presented here, in performances that are skilled but slightly wooden, show a remarkable affinity with other mainland music, particularly that of Alexander Agricola. These little three-voice works, with their beautifully evocative texts, can without any doubt be counted among the glories of early Tudor music.

friend and mentor, Harold Samuel, and premiered by Myra Hess in April 1940, it's a cloud-hung, passionate and tightly organised canvas in three linked movements. Dame Myra went on to make an imperious recording (Biddulph), and there have been other notable accounts since. Fortunately, Raphael Terroni more than holds his own in such prestigious company, displaying both impressive technical security and gratefully rounded tone (all captured handsomely in Michael Ponder's production). He brings comparable eloquence and insight to the pithy and resourceful Five Bagatelles (the introspective *Molto moderato* No 4 will give you a good idea of Terroni's poetic reach), and he lends instinctive support to contralto Phillida Bannister in the 1951 song-cycle *Discovery* (of which the great Kathleen Ferrier was so fond).

The programme concludes with the captivating 1935-36 Partita in its two-piano guise, Terroni teaming up with Vadim Peaceman to give an immensely spirited rendering. A supremely enjoyable anthology overall, and not to be missed at Naxos price.

Howard Ferguson British 1908-1999

Ferguson was discovered as a 13-year-old pianist and invited to take lessons in London at the Royal College of Music, where he studied composition with RO Morris and conducting with Sir Malcolm Sargent. His compositional breakthrough came in 1933 with the Octet, widely regarded as his masterwork. Influenced by Brahms, he championed the music of friends Vaughan Williams and Finzi. A meticulous approach to craftsmanship produced a small output praised for its compositional perfection. In 1959, after making a final artistic statement in two oratorios (one of which was The Dream of the Rood), Ferguson abandoned composition to pursue musicological interests (including editions of early keyboard music and also the complete Schubert piano sonatas). During the Second World War, Ferguson helped Myra Hess run the popular, morale-boosting series of concerts at the National Gallery. From 1948 to 1963 he taught at the Royal Academy of Music, his students there including Richard Rodney Bennett and Cornelius Cardew.

Miscellaneous Works

Piano Sonata, Op 8. Five Bagatelles, Op 9. Discovery, Op 13ª. Partita, Op 5b^b
Raphael Terroni, ^b**Vadim Peaceman** pfs
ª**Phillida Bannister** contr
Naxos 8 572289 (60' · DDD) Ⓢ➔

Although Howard Ferguson may have decided to hang up his composing boots early (his final work, the large-scale cantata *The Dream of the Rood*, was completed in 1959), the 19 published works he did leave us are all of lasting quality. Take the epic, magnificently defiant Piano Sonata, for instance: written during 1938-40 in direct response to the sudden death of his close

Brian Ferneyhough British b1943

Ferneyhough studied at the Birmingham School of Music and then with Lennox Berkeley at the Royal Academy in London; he later worked with Ton Leeuw and Klaus Huber. He has followed a career as an academic at universities as varied as the University of California at San Diego, the Hague and Stanford. He has been associated with the New Complexity school, and while rejecting serialism has pursued a method of composition that embraces a formalist focus. His music is extremely complex and makes colossal demands on its performers. His work spans all genres and he was the recipient of the Ernst von Siemens Music Prize in 2007.

Funérailles

Funérailles I & IIª. Bone Alphabet^b.
Unsichtbare Farben^c
^b**Christian Dierstein** perc
ªMembers of the **Arditti Quartet** (^cIrvine Arditti vn Ralf Ehlers va Rohan da Saram vc); ª**Recherche Ensemble** (Melise Mellinger vn Barbara Maurer va Lucas Fels vc Uli Fussengger db Virginie Tarrête hp) / **Lucas Vis**
Stradivarius STR33739 (50' · DDD) Ⓕ

One of the particular attractions of this disc is its delineation of contrasts and continuities between Brian Ferneyhough's earlier and later compositions. The two *Funérailles*, which he worked on between 1969 and 1980, show the composer emerging from a turbulent expressionism which has affinities with the style of his principal teacher, Klaus Huber, into the kind of hyperfractured yet remarkably coherent manner of his full maturity. Ferneyhough doesn't approve of the two pieces being heard without other music in between, but even if his wishes are disregarded the second piece emerges as an extraordinarily radical analysis of its predecessor, bringing out the kind of aggressive eloquence that confirms Ferneyhough's position as one of the most resourceful expressionists of our time.

Bone Alphabet (1991) is a study of how register, colour and rhythm manifest themselves structurally in the absence of precise pitch patterns. The booklet-notes, tied as they are to certain timed events in the performance, are useful here, even if they risk suggesting that the music contains more obvious and extreme contrasts than this recording conveys.

With *Unsichtbare Farben* (1999) we are in the instrumental sound world that Ferneyhough has made his own, the paradoxical title – invisible colours – hinting at a music that aspires to transcend sound itself. It's not exactly that 'unheard melodies are sweeter' but that a music that constantly reaches towards silence can, under the right conditions, have a particularly poignant intensity. These performances are in safe, experienced hands, and the recordings are well conceived to convey the music's special refinements.

John Field

The 'inventor of the nocturne' came from a family of musicians. At the age of 12 he was taken by his ambitious father to London where he studied with Clementi. Not only that but he was also employed as a kind of salesroom demonstrator for Clementi's pianos. His mentor took him on a trip to Paris, Vienna and St Petersburg, where Field decided to settle. Perhaps he might have become an important composer but a succession of extra-marital affairs and too much drink meant that compositions appeared irregularly, though he was popular as a teacher (Glinka was among his pupils). From 1824 to 1831 he lived in Moscow, by which time he was already suffering from cancer. He returned to England in 1832 for concerts and an operation. Reunited with his mother, it is said that she hardly recognised him, he had aged so much. At the end of his resources, he toured round Europe before returning finally to Moscow in 1835 an alcoholic and incurably ill.

Field wrote almost exclusively for the piano and today he's remembered just for his Nocturnes, where the right hand plays a song-like melody accompanied by a flowing left hand. It was Chopin who developed the form. Compared with those miniature masterpieces, Field's are merely charming trifles but pleasant none the less.

Piano Concertos

Piano Concertos – No 1 in E flat, H27;
No 3 in E flat, H32
Benjamin Frith *pf* **Northern Sinfonia /
David Haslam**

Naxos 8 553770 (52' · DDD) ⓈⒶⓂ→

Benjamin Frith presents a very formidable challenge to rival versions, at super-budget price. Both works are played with effortless fluency, plus all the immediacy and freshness of new discovery. In No 1 Frith is acutely responsive to the delicate charm of the Scottish-inspired (*'Twas within a mile of Edinboro' Town*) slow movement. He makes one aware of Field's teasing delight in the unexpected in the smiling outer movements, to which he brings a wide range of tone, and piquant accentuation in the last. There's warm, sympathetic support from the Northern Sinfonia under David Haslam. The performers revel in the composer's surprises of modulation, rhythm and orchestral colouring, while from the soloist there isn't a trace of the perfunctory in passagework. The recording (in a resonant venue) might be thought over-forward and full, but it remains a true bargain.

Piano Concertos – No 2 in A flat, H31; Ⓟ
No 3 in E flat, H32
Andreas Staier *fp* **Concerto Köln / David Stern**
Warner Elatus 0927 49610-2 (62' · DDD) ⓂⒶⓄ→

For those who love the sound and capabilities of the modern piano, the fortepiano's thinner tone, distinctive timbre and more intimate dynamic scope (or, put another way, the lack of power) take some adjusting to. But once one is attuned to its tonal and colouristic possibilities, the daring nature of the piano writing emerges with striking force. Take the soloist's first entry in the Second Concerto, where the virtuoso power and originality delivers its full intended *frisson* and physicality when heard on an instrument being pushed to its limit. Andreas Staier is a brilliant pianist who allies dazzling technical élan to his acute musical insight and imagination. In the outer movements, his fingerwork is as precise and crystalline as his musical intelligence, with passagework assuming a quasi-melodic purpose, elevated to the level of what Gerald Abraham called 'significant line'.

The slow movement of the A flat Concerto, a brief contrasting *molto espressivo* song without words, is played with unaffected simplicity and clarity of line, while in the E flat Concerto, Staier follows Field's own practice of interpolating one of his nocturnes as a slow movement by playing the well-known work in C minor. Staier is a most poetic and inspiring advocate, yet the success of these performances is as much due to the extraordinary clarity and impact of Concerto Köln's orchestral playing. There's such an infectious generosity of spirit, such vivid character and crispness, with beautifully poised wind playing and a real bite from the brass and timpani. Try the opening of the finale of the Second Concerto, where, after the lilting melody is presented by the soloist, the full orchestra respond with invigorating gusto and rusticity, never losing their tonal blend or refinement. The recorded sound, too, is wonderfully clear and detailed.

Piano Concertos – No 5 in C, 'L'incendie par l'orage';
No 6 in C
Benjamin Frith pf **Northern Sinfonia /**
David Haslam
Naxos 8 554221 (57' · DDD)   ⓢ🄾🄳►

Benjamin Frith proves an ideal soloist in these attractive, decorative pieces. Like his close contemporary, Hummel, Field is much more adept at embroidering the themes which bubble from him than at developing them in a conventional way. The passagework which can seem just trivial needs both the virtuosity and the artistry of a pianist of charm such as Frith if it's to come fully alive and compel attention, as it does here. Frith's articulation is sparklingly clear throughout with rapid scales and decorations pearly and wonderfully even, helped by the relatively intimate acoustic of the theatre in Gosforth where the recordings were made.

The title of the Fifth Concerto, *L'incendie par l'orage* ('Fire from the Storm'), is inspired by the passage of storm music towards the end of the central development section in the first movement. Surprisingly Field, the inventor of the nocturne and inspirer of Chopin, here avoids a full slow movement, contenting himself instead with a slow introduction to the jaunty finale. At least he makes amends in the Sixth Concerto, where the central *Larghetto* slow movement is a nocturne in everything but name, with a soaring cantilena for the piano which might well have inspired Bellini. The finale is a sparkling polka-like movement, with breathtakingly elaborate passagework, which Frith rightly treats as fun music, a fine pay-off. Haslam and the Northern Sinfonia are well recorded, too, in the relatively small-scale acoustic.

Morton Feldman   American 1926-1987

One of American music's great originals, Morton Feldman received early musical instruction from Wallingford Riegger; he later worked with Stefan Wolpe but the truly significant encounter came in 1949 when he met John Cage. Heavily influenced by the art scene in post-war New York, Feldman started experimenting with allowing his performers to determine the durations within a given tempo while at the same time adhering to strictly noted pitches. One of Feldman's most celebrated – and approachable – works is Rothko Chapel, named after the place created by the painter for silent contemplation.

String Quartet

String Quartet
Group For Contemporary Music (Benjamin
Hudson, Carol Zeavin vns Lois Martin va

Joshua Gordan vc)
Naxos American Classics 8 559190 (79' · DDD)   ⓢ🄱►

Morton Feldman has made it to Naxos American Classics! But not with some of his more accessible pieces such as *Rothko Chapel* or *The Viola in my Life* but with the challenging late String Quartet (1979) – a single span lasting nearly 80 minutes. When the original incarnation of this fine performance appeared, it was easy to imagine Feldman at his piano fastidiously conceiving his sounds through some kind of psychic transmission that somehow penetrated the fog of his uniquely personal conceptual confusions.

The String Quartet is long but never boring. Within the gamut of slow and mostly soft sounds there's intriguing variety, and the players often ride a high wire of demanding harmonics. The occasional loud clusters – only nine of these – are like volcanic eruptions. By the time we reach the end Feldman has taught us to listen microscopically, and the stop-start of the final section seems almost agonisingly moving.

The Viola in my Life

The Viola in my Life I–IV
Marek Konstantynowicz va **Cikada Ensemble;**
Norwegian Radio Orchestra / Christian Eggen
ECM New Series 476 5777 (40' · DDD)   Ⓕ

Anyone wanting an introduction to Morton Feldman's ravishing sound world could do worse than sample this ECM album before gingerly proceeding to tougher fare.

The Viola in my Life, Feldman's nostalgic cycle portraying the intimate web of associations he had with the instrument, is far from hardcore. The four parts of the cycle add up to a 40-minute listen and Feldman doesn't reach for such alienated extremes. The Cikada Ensemble and the Norwegian Radio Orchestra are expert, but it's a shame viola player Marek Konstantynowicz tends towards the expressive hard-sell, overplaying gestures that Karen Phillips on Feldman's own recording (recently reissued on New World Records) keeps at an objective distance.

Paying full price for a 40-minute CD might make some smart. If so, the irony of a too-short Feldman CD won't be lost on others.

Gerald Finzi   British 1901-1956

Finzi studied privately with Farrar and Bairstow. Influenced by Elgar and Vaughan Williams as well as his teachers, he developed an intimate style and concentrated on songs, particularly settings of Hardy. Other works include a Clarinet Concerto (1949), a Cello Concerto (1955) and Dies natalis for high voice and strings (1939). He lived most of his life in the country composing and growing apples.

Cello Concerto, Op 40

Finzi Cello Concerto[a]
Leighton Cello Concerto, Op 31[b]
Raphael Wallfisch vc [a]**Royal Liverpool Philharmonic Orchestra / Vernon Handley;** [b]**Royal Scottish National Orchestra / Bryden Thomson**
Chandos CHAN9949 (72' · DDD)   Ⓕ🅑➔

The Cello Concerto is arguably Finzi's finest work, written at the very end of his life under the stress of knowing he was terminally ill. At just under 40 minutes it's planned on a massive scale. The first movement brings the darkest music, an extended *tutti* establishing a brooding tone of voice. The slow movement is in more characteristically tender pastoral vein, with a poignant tinge of melancholy, music originally conceived many years before its actual completion in 1951. Leighton's Cello Concerto is almost equally ambitious. Helped by full, warm Chandos sound, the Finzi receives a big, bold performance. With a good balance for the soloist, the panache of Wallfisch's playing comes over more forcefully, and the tenderness of the slow movement is reinforced at a more spacious speed.

Clarinet Concerto in C minor, Op 31

Clarinet Concerto. Five Bagatelles, Op 23 (orch Ashmore). Love's Labour's Lost – Soliloquies Nos 1-3. A Severn Rhapsody in D minor, Op 3. Romance in E flat, Op 11. Introit in F, Op 6
Robert Plane cl **Lesley Hatfield** vn
Northern Sinfonia / Howard Griffiths
Naxos 8 553566 (71' · DDD)   Ⓢ🅞➔

This is a highly commanding performance of Finzi's gorgeous Clarinet Concerto from Northern Sinfonia principal Robert Plane. With his bright, singing tone and effortless technical mastery, there's no shortage of intuitive poetry from Plane in the sublime central *Adagio*. Howard Griffiths's conducting is exemplary. We also get an atmospheric account of Lawrence Ashmore's idiomatic orchestration of the Five Bagatelles (with the poignant Romance a highlight), as well as exquisitely drawn renderings of both the Romance for strings and Three Soliloquies from Finzi's incidental music for a 1946 BBC production of *Love's Labour's Lost*. The fragrant, very early *Severn Rhapsody* (1923) makes a welcome return to the catalogue under Griffiths's deeply felt advocacy, and Lesley Hatfield makes a touching soloist in the radiant *Introit* (the slow movement of a withdrawn Violin Concerto). The sound and balance are extremely truthful, though the acoustic may be a little over-resonant for some tastes.

Clarinet Concerto. Love's Labour's Lost – Suite, Op 28. Prelude in F minor, Op 25. Romance in E flat, Op 11. Eclogue for piano and orchestra, Op 10
Alan Hacker cl **Martin Jones** pf

English String Orchestra / William Boughton
Nimbus NI5665 (65' · DDD)   Ⓕ

Several other Finzi issues available include the Clarinet Concerto. Alan Hacker, however, encompasses all his colleagues' virtues, providing special insights and revelling in the brilliant writing. He also adds something extra – an almost mystical realisation of the music's poetic vision which is deeply moving. This is in spite of the fact that the string playing sometimes lacks polish and precision. Finzi wrote incidental music for a BBC production of *Love's Labour's Lost* and expanded it for a later open-air production. It's tuneful, graceful music, but one can't feel that the stage was Finzi's world. The disc is completed by two interesting early pieces for strings, the Prelude and Romance, both wholly characteristic of the composer and very well played.

Additional recommendation

Clarinet Concerto
Coupled with: Cello Concerto
Denman cl **RPO / Handley**
Lyrita SRCD236 (70' · DDD)   Ⓕ🅑➔
 A gloriously mellow reading coupled with Yo-Yo Ma's first commercial recording of the Cello Concerto. Handley is on top form.

Violin Concerto

Violin Concerto[b]. Romance in E flat, Op 11[b]. Prelude in F minor, Op 25[b]. In Years Defaced[a] – To a Poet a Thousand Years Hence (orch C Matthews); When I set out for Lyonnesse (orch cpsr); In Years Defaced (orch Roberts); Tall Nettles (orch Alexander); At a Lunar Eclipse (orch Weir); Proud Songsters (orch Payne)
[a]**John Mark Ainsley** ten [b]**Tasmin Little** vn
City of London Sinfonia / Richard Hickox
Chandos CHAN9888 (55' · DDD · T)   Ⓕ🅞🅞➔

Finzi began work on his Concerto for small orchestra and solo violin in 1925, dedicating it to Sybil Eaton, a talented young violinist and the object of the 24-year-old composer's unrequited love. He harboured considerable doubts about the opening movement, however, and when Eaton eventually gave the premiere in 1927 under Sargent, the Queen's Hall audience heard only the second and third movements. When Vaughan Williams programmed the concerto the following year, Finzi penned another first movement. Neither he nor the critics found much to please them, though, and the work wasn't heard again in its entirety until the present artists revived it in 1999. The highlight is the central, characteristically rapt *Molto sereno* that Finzi later recast as his Op 6 Introit. Of the two vigorous flanking movements, the finale leaves the stronger impression, but the concerto thoroughly deserves its new lease of life, and Little and Hickox's sparkling and stylish advocacy will win it many new friends.

There's another first recording in the guise of the song-cycle *In Years Defaced*. Only one number, the 1928-32 setting of Hardy's 'When I set out for Lyonnesse', was actually orchestrated by Finzi, and, in an effort to place it in a more programme-friendly context, the Finzi Trust commissioned five contemporary composers to choose a song that might benefit from the extra colour an orchestral palette can provide. The resulting sequence is a joy from start to finish. Ainsley is a potent, irreproachably sensitive presence throughout this imaginative and rewarding creation. Again, Hickox and the City of London Sinfonia accompany to the manner born. Lovely, airy sound further enhances the appeal of this disc.

Dies natalis

Dies natalis, Op 8. Intimations of Immortality, Op 29
John Mark Ainsley ten **Corydon Singers and Orchestra / Matthew Best**
Hyperion CDA66876 (67' · DDD · T)   Ⓕ**OO**➔

What's central, and essential, is the capacity of Finzi's music to grow in the listener's mind over long years, deepening in appeal, strengthening in the conviction of its purpose. Moreover, these performances are marvellously good at clarifying the strengths. Rather more than their predecessors, they clarify structure and texture. The soloist is more distinctly focused in the recording balance, and this makes an important difference when the poet's words are such a vital element. Ainsley sings with grace and clarity. The small choir conveys a restrained presence in the *Intimations*; but for much of the time this kind of halo over the sound is appropriate, and in certain important passages the fewer numbers help to compensate with clearer definition. Highly recommended.

Finzi Dies natalis, Op 8[a]. Romance, Op 11
Walton Sonata for Strings
[a]**Toby Spence** ten
Scottish Ensemble / Jonathan Morton
Wigmore Hall Live WHLIVE0021 (64' · DDD)
Recorded live on October 13, 2007   Ⓕ➔

Tenor Toby Spence is the featured artist in this recital but the biggest work, taking up the second half of the programme, is Walton's Sonata for Strings, a fine work that has not been recorded nearly as often as it deserves. This is the piece, commissioned by Neville Marriner and the Academy of St Martin, that Walton brilliantly adapted from his String Quartet of 1947, making a work for strings in the great tradition of Elgar's Introduction and Allegro and Vaughan Williams's *Tallis* Fantasia.

Misleadingly, the Sonata opens with a passage for the string quartet alone, before developing into a full string piece when the opening theme is repeated. What comes out very clearly is not just how memorable Walton's thematic material is, but how clear the sonata-form structure is. In some ways this is the last of what one might regard as the pre-war Walton works, written when his partner, Alice, Lady Wimborne, was dying painfully of cancer.

The development section brings a strongly argued fugato, with the second-movement *Scherzo*, marked *presto*, bringing a dazzling arrangement of the quartet original. The slow movement is one of Walton's most beautiful, here given a deeply expressive performance by the Scottish Ensemble. Exceptionally for Walton, the reprise of the main material is extended, with the violas leading. The *Allegro molto* finale is vigorous with its cross rhythms and a more lyrical countersubject.

Toby Spence sings sensitively in Finzi's *Dies natalis*, setting words by the mystic poet Thomas Traherne, starting with a prose poem entitled 'Rhapsody'. That leads to three more poems, with a vigorous, exhilarating movement, 'Wonder', separating the two more reflective movements. It is among Finzi's finest works. The Romance for strings makes an attractive introduction to the programme. A first-rate issue.

Intimations of Immortality, Op 29

Finzi Intimations of Immortality[a]
Hadley The Trees so High[b]
[a]**Ian Partridge** ten [b]**Thomas Allen** bar [a]**Guildford Philharmonic** [b]**Choir and Orchestra; [b]New Philharmonia Orchestra / Vernon Handley**
Lyrita SRCD238 (77' · ADD · T)   Ⓕ➔

The works pair uncommonly well, especially in the way Finzi's opening follows Hadley's conclusion so naturally that the one might almost be a commentary on the other. And 'both of them speak of something that has gone': *The Trees* tells of wasted youth, the *Immortality* Ode of lost vision. There's a contrast in that Finzi's chosen text does not impose its form as Hadley's folksong does. The young man's life falls, very conveniently for the 'symphonic ballad', into four phases, or movements: youth, marriage, fatherhood, death. Wordsworth, on the other hand, alternately cheers himself up and relapses into sad acknowledgement of an unwelcome fact; he also speculates or, some would say, philosophises. In form, it doesn't help the musician and it leads Finzi, in its 'cheering up' vein, to be musically untrue to himself: he keeps thinking he's Walton, and can't get *Belshazzar's Feast* (of all surely alien works) out of his mind. It's a deeply moving composition nevertheless.

The recordings date from 1978 (Hadley) and 1975 (Finzi) and continue to impress as fine performances. They provide timely reminders that in Vernon Handley we had one of the best conductors of British music in this period. The orchestral playing gives pleasure throughout, while the Guildford choir is heard to better advantage in the Finzi. Both soloists are ideally suited, and if we make special mention of Ian Partridge it is because his is the major undertaking.

Josef Bohuslav Foerster

Czech 1859-1951

Foerster was born into an old Bohemian cantor family and continued the tradition by studying in Prague as a teacher and at the organ school. He later held appointments as organist and choirmaster. At the same time he was an active and influential teacher at the organ school and his harmony manual, Nauka o harmonii, was an important aid to study for a number of generations. He later developed an interest in Renaissance music, somethin that spilled over into his own music.

Concertos

Violin Concertos – No 1, Op 88[a]; No 2, Op 104
Ivan Zenatý vn
BBC Symphony Orchestra / Jiří Bělohlávek
Supraphon SU3691-2 (65' · DDD)
Recorded [a]live   Ⓕ🅓➔

Little of Foerster's large output is widely known, yet, as this finely played, splendidly recorded disc demonstrates, he's an enthralling composer. His chromatic, highly expressive harmonic style and sophisticated orchestral writing place him firmly in the company of late Romantics such as Strauss, Elgar and his friend Mahler, but his music, with its clearly defined phrases and lyrical tone, retains a distinctively Czech character. Sometimes the resemblance to his nationalist forebears is clear – the opening of the First Concerto recalls Smetana in passionate mood, and the *Andante* middle movement of No 2 evokes a Dvořák-like pastoral atmosphere. Foerster differs, however, in the way he indulges his lyrical gift; in place of the positive rhythmic drive characteristic of both Dvořák and Smetana his tendency is to allow energy to subside into dreamy reverie – often extremely beautiful, but, especially in the long first movement of the First Concerto, weakening the overall impact.

However, Foerster shows real originality. The First Concerto's third movement, a graceful, sensuous waltz with playful, decorative writing for the soloist, is unlike any other violin concerto finale I can think of. Op 104 is a more introspective work, with an unusual but satisfying form. After three or four minutes of what promises to be a mercurial finale, we're suddenly recalled to the sombre surroundings of the first movement, to hear a complete recapitulation, which Foerster had earlier omitted.

Ivan Zenatý plays with lovely tone and wide expressive range, contributing his own idiomatic cadenza to Op 88. The BBC SO under Bělohlávek matches his warmth and conviction.

Foerster Cello Concerto, Op 143 **Martinů** Cello Concerto No 1, H196 **Novák** Capriccio for Cello and Small Orchestra
Jiří Bárta vc **Prague Philharmonia / Jakub Hrůša**
Supraphon SU3989-2 (67' · DDD)   Ⓕ🅓➔

'Swinging' cello concertos aren't exactly thick on the ground, which makes Jan Novák's *Capriccio* (1958-59) a particular delight, with its saucy clarinets and saxophones and its lightly percussive ostinatos. It starts like Twenties show music, goes gently tiptoe for a 12-tone second movement then jives away happily for the closing *Allegro*, with 'Lennie' and 'Igor' never out of earshot for too long. Midway between the high jinks of Novák's *Capriccio* and the more formal expressive qualities of Foerster's Concerto comes the thrice-revised First Cello Concerto of Bohuslav Martinů. His characteristically off-beat rhythmic computations make their presence felt right from the dramatic opening bars but it is the work's haunting melodic profile that most lingers in the memory.

Josef Bohuslav Foerster's Concerto of 1931 is the earliest of the works programmed, as well as the most intense and the most obviously rooted in tradition (think of, for example, Dvořák and Suk). The work's heart is again its slow movement, where meaningful dialogue with other solo strings is so effective, the music often rather reminiscent of Chausson. Amazingly, this is the work's world premiere recording.

Jiří Bárta plays with a warm, unselfconscious expressiveness that connects with all three works, and the Prague Philharmonia is with him every step of the way. The sound is excellent, the solo cello profile especially good.

John Foulds

English 1880-1939

Largely self-taught, Foulds was the son of a Hallé Orchestra bassoonist, and he composed copiously from childhood. During the 1890s he acquired performing experience as a cellist in theatre and promenade orchestras in England and Wales; he also travelled on the Continent. In 1900 he joined the ranks of the Hallé's cello section under Richter, who encouraged Foulds as a conductor, taking him to Essen, where he met Delius, Humperdinck and Mahler. He also studied conducting with Lamoureux, Mahler and Nikisch.

A World Requiem (1919-21), composed in memory of the war dead of all nations, was adopted by the British Legion for the Armistice Night commemorations and performed each year for four years. He left London for Paris in 1927, and eventually travelled to India in 1935 where, among other things, he collected folk music, composed pieces for traditional Indian instrument ensembles and worked for a radio station.

Orchestral works

Three Mantras, Op 61b[a]. Mirage, Op 20. Lyra Celtica, Op 50[c]. Apotheosis (Elegy), Op 18[c]
[b]**Susan Bickley** mez [c]**Daniel Hope** vn
City of Birmingham [a]**Youth Chorus and Symphony Orchestra / Sakari Oramo**
Warner Classics 2564 61525-2 (78' · DDD)   Ⓕ❶❶❶➔

Sakari Oramo programmed plenty of 20th-century British music during his Birmingham tenure, a policy which bore spectacular fruit with this enterprising disc devoted to Manchester-born John Foulds. A self-taught figure, Foulds won some measure of fame in his lifetime with his light music and *World Requiem* (1919-21); later in his career, he developed an interest in theosophy and all things Eastern, and had spells in Paris and India (where he died of cholera).

The extraordinary *Three Mantras* (1919-30) originally served as the preludes to the three acts of Foulds's abandoned Sanskrit opera, *Avatara*. In the opening 'Mantra of Activity' Oramo daringly sets an even more propulsive tempo than does Barry Wordsworth on his pioneering Lyrita recording, yet with no loss of composure. A wordless female chorus inten-sifes the atmosphere of mystic awe that perme-ates the succeeding 'Mantra of Bliss'. The concluding 'Mantra of Will' strictly employs the seven-note modal scale of a South Indian raga. A daring, extended pause ushers in a flam-boyantly savage pay-off (here rather more transparent and tidier in execution than under Wordsworth).

Next comes *Lyra Celtica*, a concerto for word-less voice and orchestra written between 1917 and the mid-1920s for his wife, the soprano Maud McCarthy. In the event Foulds completed only two of the three movements (the finale remains a 150-bar fragment). It's an alluring discovery, which deploys both microtones and quarter-tones (a Foulds trademark). Mezzo Susan Bickley rises valiantly to the challenge.

By comparison, *Apotheosis* (1909) and *Mirage* (1910) strike a rather more conventional note, though Daniel Hope's contribution in the former locates the lyrical beauty in this heartfelt elegy in memory of Joachim. Richard Strauss looms large in *Mirage*, an opulent 23-minute tone-poem with much arresting incident, which Oramo and the CBSO do proud.

The sound is hugely vivid and Calum Mac-Donald's annotation a model of its kind. Don't miss this gem of a release.

April – England, Op 48 No 1. Dynamic Triptych, Op 88. Keltic Suite – Keltic Lament. Music-Pictures: Group III, Op 33. The Song of Ram Dass.
Peter Donohoe pf
City of Birmingham Orchestra / Sakari Oramo
Warner Classics 2564 62999-2 (61' · DDD)   Ⓕ◐➔

Extraordinary how Foulds's *Dynamic Triptych* opens, like an unstoppable current swirling around its seven-note mode, a tightly-woven study that goes to show how, given the right composer, confined harmony can work mira-cles. The slow second movement is cold but gripping, with strings that slide every now and then on a queasy bed of quarter-tones, the use of piano and timps fitfully anticipating Bartók's Second Concerto. The finale anticipates Martinů in the way that rhythmic patterns meet

or converge, occasionally even Prokofiev with some brilliant running passagework from Peter Donohoe, who gives a superb performance.

April – England is an earlier piece that was later revised, spontaneous and wide-eyed à la Copland to start with then quietening for a noble, slower section in the manner of a passacaglia. The *Music-Pictures* Group III is earlier still (1912), the first of them prophesying the Sibelius of *Tapiola* with a huge climax, the mostly playful 'Colum-bine' featuring yet more destabilising quarter-tones. The 'Old Greek Legend' has something of an Elgarian tread about it and the lively 'Toc-sin' finale ends just like the 'March to the Scaf-fold' from the *Symphonie fantastique*. In fact Ber-lioz is probably Foulds's nearest forebear; both men relished new sounds while holding fast to key aspects of tradition, and Foulds, like Berlioz, was a pretty stunning orchestrator.

As for the gorgeous 'Keltic Lament', how Stokowski would have basked in this amazing music! But, not having Mickey's magic wand to hand, Oramo and his Birmingham players will do very nicely. This is a really first-rate programme, a worthy follow-up to Oramo's first Foulds CD (see above) and a revealing window onto an unusual and innovative area of English music.

A World Requiem

A World Requiem
Jeanne-Michèle Charbonnet sop **Catherine Wyn-Rogers** mez **Stuart Skelton** ten **Gerald Finley** bar
Trinity Boys' Choir; Crouch End Festival Chorus; Philharmonia Chorus; BBC Symphony Chorus and Orchestra / Leon Botstein
Chandos ② ⅏ CHSA5058 (84' · DDD · T/t)
Recorded live at the Royal Albert Hall, London, on November 11, 2007   Ⓕ◐➔

Foulds conducted *A World Requiem*'s 1923 pre-miere at the Festival of Remembrance, using 1250 performers. This present performance, the first in more than 70 years, was given on Remembrance Day 2007, and, aside from a rather unwieldy soprano, is a triumph, with spe-cial praise due to baritone Gerald Finley and conductor Leon Botstein.

A World Requiem is the kind of piece that could only have grown from wholehearted sincerity, in this case a very personal and inspired response to the devastating losses and suffering in the First World War. Cast in 20 interlinking sections, much of the work's musical style emerges off the backs of Requiems by Verdi and Berlioz but what we actually hear is more reminiscent of Busoni, the sombre tread of the opening Requiem, the ethereal, half-lit solos and duets, and the searing climaxes, not to mention the spooky use of quarter-tones. The fifth move-ment 'Audite' includes a stirring summons to 'you men of all the continents', an impressive roll call of nations (individually named) and a plea for universal peace.

The contrast between the sombre-hued close of the first part and the day-bright opening of the second – a celebration of deliverance – could hardly be more telling. From here on, the mood and language become more esoteric and the scoring is often extremely delicate. Sections based on texts from Revelation and the Gospel of St John lead to an affirmation of Christ's spirit and the work ends in ecstatic joy.

Foulds's work is as ambitiously all-embracing as Mahler's Third or Eighth symphonies, and in its way almost as moving as Britten's *War Requiem* – though these are spontaneous reactions forged in the light of a first encounter. Posterity's work starts here but her ultimate verdict could well be pretty favourable. Calum MacDonald's booklet-notes serve as an invaluable listening aid.

Christopher Fox   British b1955

Born in York, Fox studied at the universities of Liverpool, Southampton and York, where his teachers included Hugh Wood and Jonathan Harvey. From 1984 to 1994 he was a member of the composition staff at the Darmstadt New Music Summer School. He is currently professor of music at Brunel University, a post he took up in 2006. His music is widely performed, broadcast and recorded. He is also a prolific writer on music. In addition to concert works, Fox has collaborated with artists on gallery works, and with the poet Ian Duhig on a 'musical box'.

Catalogue irraisoné

Catalogue irraisoné
Exaudi (Juliet Fraser, Julia Doyle *sops* Tom Williams *counterten* Jimmy Holliday *bass*) / James Weeks *spkr* with Christopher Fox *spkr*
Metier MSVCD92103 (53' · DDD)   Ⓕ

Here's some compositional reverse engineering. Christopher Fox describes his *Catalogue irraisoné* (1999-2001) as a 'parallel version of the same ideas in a different form' of his evening-long *Everything You Need To Know*. Defining *Everything* itself isn't easy. Commissioned by the Ives Ensemble with a stipulation that they didn't want conventionally formatted concert music, Fox devised a living and breathing sound installation using live instrumentalists and singers. *Catalogue irraisoné* distils that material for vocal ensemble Exaudi as 'a guide…like a catalogue for an exhibition of visual art' to his larger work. Everything you need to know about *Everything You Need To Know*.

Fox's choice of texts ranges from Dante and Virgil to an essay about artist Rachel Whiteread and an address by the president of Romania to the 1999 World Music Days; a puzzling compendium and, on a point of order, Metier could have helped our comprehension by reproducing the texts. But were they omitted by design? Fox is experimenting, he says, with the distinction between song, speech and declamation, deliber-

ately querying boundaries of comprehensibility, and Exaudi serve these technique-stretching demands keenly. Group director James Weeks snarls, shouts and whispers text as he stamps on the floor in rhythm; bass voice Jimmy Holliday is locked into an obsessive-compulsive melodic loop that collects new modules additively; soprano Juliet Fraser duets with 'natural' singing put against her voice filtered through a megaphone; Fox himself slips between speech and stylised *Sprechstimme*. The surface might be disarmingly simple, sometimes serene even, but there's a deeper wisdom at play that keeps these aphoristic statements rewinding in the imagination.

César Franck   Belgian/French 1822-1890

Name a famous Belgian! Well, here's one, even though he spent most of his life in Paris and became a naturalised Frenchman in 1873. Has there ever existed a milder, more humble man who was also a great composer than César Franck? His ambitions were simple: to serve music and God with equal reverence.

Franck began as a piano prodigy (he was 12 when his father sent him and his brother Joseph, a violinist, off on tour). After the Liège Conservatoire, he entered the Paris Conservatoire where his abilities to improvise and transpose on the organ and piano were legendary. Part of his first-year examination was to sight-read a concerto by Hummel. Some mischievous streak in him led him to transpose the entire thing at sight from A minor down to F sharp minor, an incredible feat.

Everything looked set for a successful and profitable career as a soloist – Franck's tyrannical father wanted nothing else from his talented son – but Franck was not interested and settled down to a routine that would alter little for the rest of his life: rising at half past five to compose for two hours, teaching pupils all over Paris and playing the organ at various churches. (He became organist at St Clotilde in 1858, a post he held for the rest of his life.)

People remembered him rushing from one appointment to another through the streets of Paris, his overcoat several sizes too large for him, his trousers too short, the absent-minded, sweet-natured music professor to a T, untouched by the lack of worldly recognition. 'He possessed the soul of a child,' wrote Debussy. 'The discovery of a beautiful harmony was sufficient to make him as happy as the day was long.' He was adored by his pupils at the Conservatoire where he was made organ professor in 1872. They included Lekeu (who died aged 24), Duparc, d'Indy, Chausson and Pierné.

Franck's marriage in 1848 to the daughter of a well-known actress – his family were horrified and broke off relations with him – was not a success. He discovered he had exchanged his overbearing father for an overbearing wife – she disliked his music and his lack of ambition even more. The love of his pupils was some recompense, in particular the Franco-Irish Augusta Holmès with whom it's said he had an affair (the Piano Quintet is a love letter to her and is full of erotic intensity).

His one taste of public success came in April 1890 with the premiere of his Quartet. Shortly after, he was on his way to a pupil when he was knocked down by a bus. Though he was able to carry on working – he even made it to the pupil's house for the lesson! – his physical condition deteriorated and he died of pleurisy.

Symphony in D minor

Symphony in D minor. Symphonic Variations[a].
Les Eolides
[a]**Louis Lortie** pf **BBC Philharmonic Orchestra /**
Yan Pascal Tortelier
Chandos CHAN9875 (62' · DDD)   Ⓕ**O**▶

With so many versions of the Symphony and the Symphonic Variations available, it's surprising that these two favourite orchestral works aren't coupled more often. Here Tortelier adds an attractive bonus in the evocative tone-poem *Les Eolides*. His reading of the Symphony is no less than five minutes shorter than both the Karajan and Chailly versions. The reading isn't in any way perfunctory, rushed or trivial, but one made fresher, eliminating any suspicion of the glutinous or sentimental, helped by a cleanly defined yet atmospheric recording. The slow introduction, promptly repeated, is all the more effective for being taken at a flowing speed, with no feeling of haste, and the main *Allegro* is fresh and alert, less smooth than with either Karajan or Chailly. Tortelier is far closer to Monteux in his feeling for the idiom than either Karajan or Chailly, both taking a weighty view. In tempo Tortelier is very similar to Karajan and Monteux in the central *Allegretto*, with fine gradations of dynamic and a slightly raw-sounding cor anglais adding to the freshness. It's in the finale that Tortelier is most distinctive, his fast, urgent speed for the *Allegro non troppo* challenging the players of the BBC Philharmonic to produce exciting rather than genial results.

Louis Lortie is the excellent soloist in the Symphonic Variations, spontaneously poetic in the slow sections, sparkling and light in the *scherzando* finale. Tortelier is again at his most warmly understanding in *Les Eolides*, a work that can seem wayward, but which here is made light and fanciful in its luminously scored evocation of the breezes of heaven.

Additional recommendation

Symphony in D minor   Ⓟ
Coupled with: **Fauré** Requiem
Champs Elysées Orchestra, Paris /
Philippe Herreweghe
Harmonia Mundi HMC90 1771 (76' · DDD · T/t) Ⓕ**O**▶
A striking period-instrument version that beautifully gauges the work's scale and ambition. Unusually coupled with Fauré's Requiem in an equally fine reading.

Symphonic Variations

Franck Symphonic Variations **Saint-Saëns** Piano Concerto – No 2, Op 22; No 5, 'Egyptian', Op 103
Jean-Yves Thibaudet pf
Suisse Romande Orchestra / Charles Dutoit
Decca 475 8764DH (66' · DDD)   Ⓕ▶

This scintillating disc finds Jean-Yves Thibaudet on notably effervescent form, revelling in Saint-Saëns's pianistic brio and intricacy. He makes a special case for the enchanting but still neglected *Egyptian* Concerto, commenced in Luxor, completed in Cairo and, according to the composer, reflecting 'the joy of a sea voyage'. He brings a recognisably French clarity and verve to the music's foaming figuration and captures all of its audacity (an imitation of croaking Nile frogs in the central *Andante* and pumping boat engines in the riotous finale). Hear his pinpoint brilliance in the opening *Allegro animato* where the pianist weaves a sparkling thread round the orchestral outline, his fast-paced avoidance of sententiousness in the long-winded *Andante* and his rush of adrenalin in the split-octave upsurge at the end of the concluding *Molto allegro*, and you are made conscious of a pianist whose virtuosity takes wing in exactly the way prescribed by the composer.

Much the same could be said of Thibaudet's performance of the Second Concerto, music which as one writer put it journeys from Bach to Offenbach. His *ad libitum* opening cadenza is complemented by flashing fingers elsewhere, and since there is inwardness as well as an irresistible élan and impetus in the Franck Variations, you could say that Thibaudet and France (or in Franck's case, Belgium) go together like a horse and carriage. Dutoit and the Suisse Romande are all of a piece with their high-flying soloist and Decca's balance and sound are exemplary.

String Quartet

Franck String Quartet **Fauré** String Quartet, Op 121
Dante Quartet (Krysia Osostowicz, Giles Francis vns Judith Busbridge va Bernard Gregor-Smith vc)
Hyperion CDA67664 (67' · DDD)   Ⓕ**O**▶

Two swansongs, and in each case it's the composer's only string quartet. But how different these works are – the Franck overflowing with invention, drama and passion, while Fauré's sparer textures and unchanging motion leave an impression of reflective melancholy. Roger Nichols's excellent notes point out, though, how the music of both composers has the quality of *intériorité*, of intimacy and self-examination.

This is a notably well-recorded disc; we're placed, it seems, right in the middle of the music-making, and from the opening bars of the Franck we feel the intensity of the Dante's commitment. You may consider that their intense approach, with powerful vibrato and bow pressure applied even to the voices filling out the harmony, tends to become rather wearing. The Dante performance is still a fine one, by turns vigorous and tender, and with impressive variety of expression.

In the Fauré there's a nice ebb and flow of feeling as the music progresses – in a leisurely way in the *Andante*, more purposeful in the outer movements. Others may have come closer to the heart of this elusive music, but you may prefer the Dante's more earthy approach. It's certainly playing of great accomplishment.

Piano Quintet in F minor

Franck Piano Quintet[a]
Mozart Clarinet Quintet in A, K581[b]
R Strauss Capriccio – Prelude[c]
Amadeus Quartet (Norbert Brainin, Siegmund Nissel vns Peter Schidlof va Martin Lovett vc) [b]**Gervase de Peyer** cl [a]**Clifford Curzon** pf [c]**Cecil Aronowitz** va [c]**William Pleeth** vc
BBC Legends [a]mono BBCL4061-2 (77' · ADD)
Recorded live [a]1960, [b]1966, [c]1971 Ⓜ❍❍❍

Rarely can a case for live rather than studio performances have been made more persuasively than by the present disc, a study in contrasts if ever there was one. The Amadeus Quartet was celebrated for its homogeneity (accusations from critics of a plush or *de luxe* style were rare), yet this superb ensemble could easily accommodate other radically different players, and here Curzon's legendary nervous intensity is accentuated by the Amadeus, who join him in a performance of the Franck Quintet so supercharged it virtually tears itself apart. Taken from a 1960 Aldeburgh Festival concert, it eclipses all others (even Curzon's revelatory Decca disc). Curzon and his colleagues hurl themselves at music which clearly they see as hardly needing a cooling agent. How free and rhapsodic is Curzon's reply to the Amadeus's opening *dramatico*, and what a savage explosion of pent-up energy from all the players at 7'02"! Intonation may suffer in the finale's equestrian nightmare, but the concluding pages are overwhelming, and Curzon's darting *crescendo*s at 3'56" and 58" are like snarls of defiance.

At the opposite end of the spectrum is Mozart's Clarinet Quintet, that assuaging and elusive glory of the repertoire, played with all Gervase de Peyer's serenity and elegance. Yet again, the performance is essentially live, and has the sort of vitality and imaginative subtlety less easy to achieve or even countenance in the studio. And the same could be said of Cecil Aronowitz and William Pleeth, who join the Amadeus for Strauss's Prelude to *Capriccio*, aptly described in the notes as 'a sumptuous effusion of very late Romanticism'. The recordings (1960-71) are vivid and immediate, and odd noises off only add to the sense of occasion. Finally, a word of warning: this performance of the Franck isn't for late-night listening: you'll sleep more peacefully after the Mozart.

String Quartet. Piano Quintet
Cristina Ortiz pf **Fine Arts Quartet** (Ralph Evans, Efim Boico vns Yuri Gandelsman va Wolfgang Laufer vc)
Naxos 8 572009 (79' · DDD) Ⓢ🅑➔

Since Cristina Ortiz first recorded the Piano Quintet in the 1970s, she has broadened and clarified her reading of music so turbulent and rawly emotional that it offended Liszt's notion of chamber music, Saint-Saëns's sense of musical decorum and, perhaps more understandably, Franck's wife who knew that such an outpouring was hardly inspired by her own comfortable and domestic nature. At all events Franck hurled his Pater Seraphicus image aside in one of music's most blazing and unsettling utterances. Ortiz and her colleagues realise all of Franck's pent-up feeling in a performance of a special musical refinement and commitment.

The Fine Arts Quartet, too, are entirely at home in the very different scope of the String Quartet, relishing both the music's contrapuntal intricacy and its full-blown Romanticism. They are notably successful in the second movement's hallucinatory, stop-go flight; almost as if Mendelssohn's fairy-tale *scherzos* had become darkened with unease. Naxos's sound is less than ideal in the Quartet but is beautifully and realistically balanced in the Quintet.

Cello Sonata in A

Franck Cello Sonata
Lekeu Cello Sonata in G **Ysaÿe** Solo Cello Sonata, Op 28. Rêve d'enfant, Op 14
Raphael Wallfisch vc **John York** pf
Cello Classics CC1009 (78' · DDD) Ⓕ❍❍

Raphael Wallfisch's and John York's playing in the Franck has an air of spontaneity and enjoyment which exudes a very natural ebb and flow, while the ample ambience allows them to make the most of the 'big' moments, such as the central climax in the finale.

The disc also scores through its imaginative programming, placing the two Franco-Belgian sonatas alongside music by the great violinist who inspired them. Ysaÿe's unaccompanied Cello Sonata is an impressive, sombre work; as in the more familiar violin sonatas, echoes of the Baroque are placed within an impressionistic context. Wallfisch's account is magnificent – full-blooded, yet very clear and precise.

The Lekeu, with its opulent, passionate piano part and predominantly lyrical string writing, transcribes just as effectively for the cello as does the Franck. And its grand emotions inspire a very wholehearted response. Thoroughly recommended.

Violin Sonata in A

Debussy Violin Sonata. Sonata for Flute, Viola and
Harp **Franck** Violin Sonata **Ravel** Introduction and
Allegro
Kyung-Wha Chung vn **Osian Ellis** hp **Radu Lupu** pf
Melos Ensemble
Decca 421 154-2DM (67' · ADD)
Recorded 1962-77   Ⓜ❍❍❍▷

 Here we have masterpieces from the
French tradition in excellent performances that have won the status of recording classics. Kyung-Wha Chung and Radu Lupu
are a fine duo who capture and convey the delicacy and poetry of the Franck Sonata as well as its
rapturous grandeur, and never can the strict
canonic treatment of the great tune in the finale
have sounded more spontaneous and joyful. They
are no less successful in the different world of the
elusive Sonata which was Debussy's last work,
with its smiles through tears and, in the finale, its
echoes of a Neapolitan tarantella. The 1977
recording is beautifully balanced, with a natural
sound given to both the violin and piano.

The Melos Ensemble recorded the Ravel
Introduction and Allegro 15 years before, but
here too the recording is a fine one for which no
allowances have to be made even by ears accustomed to good digital sound; as for the work
itself, this has an ethereal beauty that's nothing
short of magical, and Osian Ellis and his colleagues give it the most skilful and loving performance. A wonderful disc and a must-buy.

Franck Violin Sonata
Shostakovich Violin Sonata, Op 134
Sergey Khachatryan vn **Lusine Khachatryan** pf
Naïve V5122 (60' · DDD)   Ⓕ

The Khachatryans, brother and sister, make a
formidable team. The recording is exceptional,
too: finely balanced and with a wide dynamic
range. The sound is so beautiful that one wondered, at moments during the Shostakovich,
whether a harsher, more direct sonority might
paint this dark work's bleak sound-picture more
accurately, though it must be admitted that this
duo is able to give the maximum intensity and
force (as they clearly do in the ferocious second
movement) while maintaining top tonal quality.
At all events, this Shostakovich performance is
extremely impressive, the technical difficulties
seemingly of no account, and the vast design of the
final passacaglia compellingly sustained with playing that ranges from precise and delicate, through
mysterious and poetic, to the highest degree of
force and energy (in the two solo variations).

There's outstanding playing, too, in the Franck,
especially in the first movement, where the tonal
range of Sergey Khachatryan's lyrical phrases
gives them a powerful emotional pull. However,
the performance as a whole doesn't quite fulfil
this initial promise. The second movement lacks
the passionate drive that some bring to it: it's a

mistake, too, to allow the dynamic level to drop at
the appearance of the soaring second theme –
Franck only marks a *diminuendo* some bars later.
In the following *Recitativo-Fantasia*, the composer
again provides many clues; by virtually ignoring
his *poco accels* and *molto lentos* the Khachatryans
miss a crucial improvisatory element. It remains
an enjoyable performance, however – very
accomplished sonata-playing.

Piano Works

Prélude, choral et fugue. Prélude, aria et final. Grand
caprice. Les plaintes d'une poupée. Danse lente.
Chorale No 3 in A minor (arr Hough)
Stephen Hough pf
Hyperion CDA66918 (68' · DDD)   Ⓕ❍

Hough has a dream-ticket combination of virtues – astonishing agility, a faultless ear for texture, fine-tuned stylistic sensibility and an
exceptional understanding of harmonic and
structural tensions. He acknowledges all
Franck's nuances, notated and implied, without
ever disturbing the broader flow; he gives full
rein to the heroic Lisztian cascades, without
ever tipping over into melodrama. The only hint
of a nit to be picked would be that the *fortissimo*
arpeggiations in the 'Choral' don't ring as resonantly as they might. One can't imagine the
calm at the end of the 'Aria' being better
judged.

In their very different ways the almost comical
bravura of the *Grand caprice* and the salon charm
of the *Danse lente* and *Les plaintes d'une poupée* are
extremely difficult to bring off with success. Yet
anyone who has followed Hough's recording
career will know that this sort of thing is meat
and drink to him. As for his own transcription of
the A minor *Chorale*, the unavoidable adjective is
'awesome'.

Organ Works

Pièce héroïque in B minor. Cantabile in B. Fantaisie
in A. Grande pièce symphonique in F sharp minor,
Op 17. Pastorale in E, Op 19. Fantaisie in C, Op 16.
Prélude, fugue et variation in B minor, Op 18. Trois
Chorales – No 1 in E; No 2 in B minor; No 3 in A minor.
Prière in C sharp minor, Op 20. Final in B flat, Op 21
Marie-Claire Alain org
Erato ② 2564 61428-2 (152' · DDD). Recorded on the
Cavaillé-Coll organ, Saint-Etienne, Caen, France Ⓢ❍

Alain is a completely involved communicator.
More than anyone else she delves into the very
soul of these works. Thus we have an intensely
prayerful *Prière*, a majestically statuesque *Grande
pièce symphonique* while the *Chorales* are delivered
with an unexpected degree of fervour; perhaps
the Third is a shade overfervent since some of the
semiquaver figurations lack absolute clarity –
something which after one or two hearings serves
to heighten the excitement but which might, after
repeated listening, become irritating. This is a

highly authoritative release not just in terms of playing but also in Alain's accompanying notes. The Caen organ is a particularly fine specimen of a Cavaillé-Coll, dating from 1884 – 25 years after the St Clotilde organ for which Franck wrote much of this music. The recording captures it, and the church's atmosphere, effectively.

Girolamo Frescobaldi
Italian 1583-1643

Frescobaldi studied in Ferrara, and it was there that he came into contact with Gesualdo. After a period as organist of Santa Maria in Rome's Trastevere district, Frescobaldi travelled to Brussels before returning in 1608 to take up the post of organist of St Peter's, Rome. After a brief period working for the Gonazaga family in Mantua, Frescobaldi returned to Rome and stayed there until 1628 when he joined the Medici court as organist. He returned once again to Rome, by this time a composer and performer with an international reputation: among his pupils was the Austrian Froberger. The bulk of his output is for the keyboard though he did write for voices; but his vocal works are often considered of lesser interest because they lack the sophistication and imagination of his works for harpsichord or organ.

Canzonas

Il Primo libro delle canzoni – La Bernadina; La Donatina; L'Altera; La Tucchina o La Superba; L'Ambitiosa; La Plettenberger; La Lievoratta; La Samminiata; La Diodata; La Nobile; Canzona Prima a due bassi; Canzona Quinta a due canti; Canzona Seconda a due canti e basso; Canzona Quinta a 4; Canzona Quarta a due canti e basso; Tre Canzona a canto e basso; Canzona Prima a 4; Canzona Seconda a 4; Canzona trigesima quinta
Les Basses Réunies / Bruno Cocset vion
Alpha ALPHA053 (65' · DDD)　　　　　Ⓕ

As this ensemble's name implies, viols are the start here, and part of the disc's attraction lies in the novelty of hearing these pieces, which are played often enough, in an instrumentation that largely dispenses with the more usual winds. The only touch of non-string colour is provided by the cornetto.

The role of the continuo is immeasurably enhanced, becoming not so much a backdrop to the solo lines as their foundation. And the continuo section is rich indeed: harp, claviorganum, theorbo and harpsichord. When everything comes together the result is as colourful and ear-tickling as anything to be heard on other recordings of this repertoire.

The performances rise to the music's challenges with elegance and barely any technical strain. This is a disc that grows on you with repeated listening, and demonstrates that Frescobaldi's canzonas are no less inventive than his keyboard music.

Keyboard Works

Il Primo libro di Ricercari et Canzoni francese　　Ⓟ
Il Primo libro delle Fantasie
Sergio Vartolo hpd/org
Naxos ② 8 553547/8 (132' · DDD)　　　　Ⓢ Ⓞ ⮀

The *Fantasie* (1608) and *Ricercari* (1615) are the earliest of Frescobaldi's keyboard publications, and as neither has been issued complete before, to get both together, and at super-budget price, is treasure-trove indeed. Frescobaldi fanatics need read no further.

Vartolo's tendency to spin out the music at twice the length of most other interpreters can be rather off-putting, and doesn't always help the listener to grasp the overall design of formally complex pieces like the Toccatas. But these Fantasias and Ricercars are imitative, fugal pieces, more abstract in conception than the exuberant toccatas; recognising this, Vartolo avoids extreme tempi, and instead gives measured performances that gain in clarity what they have lost in eccentricity. These are (and this isn't intended to damn with faint praise) sensible performances, that give both composer and audience their due. Vartolo loosens up a bit in the playful *Canzoni francese* that conclude the book of Ricercars, but in this he follows the composer's lead, and demonstrates his own sensitivity to style.

Vartolo mostly performs on a modern copy of an Italian harpsichord, and on the organ of the Chiesa del Spirito Santo, Pistoia (built a few years after Frescobaldi's death). Suffice it to say that this recording would be a must-have at full price; as it is, you won't find better value anywhere.

Kenneth Fuchs
American b1956

Fuchs received his Bachelor of Music in composition from the University of Miami and his Master of Music and Doctor of Musical Arts degrees from the Juilliard School in New York City. His teachers included Milton Babbitt, David Diamond, Vincent Persichetti, David Del Tredici, Alfred Reed and Stanley Wolfe. He has worked in the music education system at various colleges: University of Oklahoma, the Manhattan School of Music, North Carolina School of the Arts and Juilliard School. He is currently Professor of Composition at the University of Connecticut. He has written for orchestra, band, chorus, jazz ensemble and chamber ensembles.

Orchestral works

Canticle to the Sun[a]. United Artists. Quiet in the Land[b]. Fire, Ice and Summer Bronze[b]. Autumn Rhythm[b]
[a]**Timothy Jones** hn
London Symphony Orchestra / JoAnn Falletta
[b]**members of the orchestra**
Naxos American Classics 8 559335 (64' · DDD)　　Ⓢ ⮀
Kenneth Fuchs is an energetic American com-

poser now in his mid-fifties who is based at the University of Connecticut. He has a wide range of compositions and is also involved in music education and administration. At Juilliard he was a contemporary of JoAnn Falletta, who very much wanted to make an orchestral CD of his music. The opportunity came in 2003 when she recorded a group of works with the LSO, which came out on Naxos in 2005. Fuchs was so stunned by the legendary expertise of the LSO in playing at sight for a recording that he wrote *United Artists* as a short tribute. It opens this second Naxos CD; a series of chamber works follows, and the disc closes with *Canticle to the Sun*, a horn concerto in which the British connection continues with the soloist Timothy Jones from the LSO.

United Artists is a kind of fanfare to this orchestra, who obviously enjoyed it – the idiom stems from Copland and early Carter. *Quiet in the Land* for mixed string and wind quintet is contemplative in mood, generally music of low density suitable for illustration. This aspect comes to the fore in *Autumn Rhythm*, inspired by the paintings of Jackson Pollock: it would make an apt soundtrack for a series of his pictures.

Canticle to the Sun is based on the familiar hymntune 'All Creatures of our God and King'. This is an imaginative idea where the soloist emerges from a tinkling backdrop and retains clear contact with the melody throughout, although it is never stated in full. The concerto adds up to a pastoral idyll with occasional spots for the timpani and lyrical cadenzas – all neatly played.

Andrea Gabrieli   Italian 1533-1585

Not a lot is known about Andrea Gabrieli's early career: most likely Venetian by birth, he may have been a pupil of Adrian Willaert at St Mark's, and in 1557-58 he was organist of S Geremia, Cannaregio. In 1562 he was travelling in Germany, where he encountered Lassus, and the two men inspried each other with their very different but complementary musical backgrounds. In 1566 he became organist of St Mark's, Venice, where he remained all his life.

His output was vast and wide-ranging, embracing secular as well as sacred music. His greatest legacy is the music he wrote for St Mark's which displays his intimate knowldge of the building, its acoustics and the spatial qualities that allow music to be experienced to best effect. He was the uncle of Giovanni Gabrieli (see below).

Madrigals

A Gabrieli 21 Madrigals – Caro dolce ben mio, perchè fuggire; Sento, sent'un rumor ch'al ciel si estolle; Mentr'io vi miro, vorrei pur sapere. Del gran Tuonante. Sassi, palae. Felici d'Adria. I'vo piangendo. Asia felice. O beltà rara. Laura soave. O-passi sparsi. Amami, vita mia. Lasso, Amor mi transporta. Hor ch'a noi torna. Voi non volete, donna. Io mi sento morire. Mirami, vita mia. Chi'nde darà la bose. Ancor che col

partire. Fuor fuori a sì bel canto. Dunque il commun poter **G Gabrieli** Canzoni – Canzon la spiritata
I Fagiolini; The English Cornett and Sackbut Ensemble / Robert Hollingworth
Chandos Chaconne CHAN0697 (77' · DDD · T/t) ⒻⒹ➔

Andrea Gabrieli has always been something of a textbook composer, whose reputation falls under the shadow of his more famous nephew, Giovanni, the composer *par excellence* of the grand Venetian polychoral manner. Though Andrea's music may not plumb the depths of Giovanni's best pieces, his compositional range displays a versatility that the writing of his more considered relation surely lacks. Whereas Giovanni concentrated on liturgical composition, Andrea explored the gamut of contemporary styles and forms, from madrigals and lighter secular writing to dialect texts, church music, instrumental works, experimental theatre-pieces and music for Venetian festivities.

This imaginatively constructed disc, punctuated by instrumental items, presents as a main course a selection of Andrea's settings of Italian texts. These reveal an unexpected emotional complexity, robust and lively works being contrasted with more reflective ones. The former are characterised by an energetic rhythmic drive and bright sonorities in the upper registers, the latter by a mellifluous and sensitive approach.

There are also a few oddities, notably 'Asia felice', composed for an outdoor celebration of the Battle of Lepanto in 1571 – suitably enlivened here with unscripted interventions of organ, sackbuts and cornets – and the boisterous rendition of the dialect text 'Chi'nde darà la bose al solfizar', which evocatively breathes the air of the streets and squares of Renaissance Venice. Anyone smitten with the musical traditions of this most fascinating of all cities shouldn't hesitate to buy this record.

Giovanni Gabrieli   Italian c1553/6-1612

Giovanni Gabrieli studied with his uncle Andrea (see above) and, like him, also worked briefly in Germany, also working with Lassus, before becoming organist at St Mark's in Venice; he was also attached to the Scuola Grande di San Rocco. He held both posts for the remainder of his life. Giovanni edited much of his uncle's music for publication, something which ensures its survival. His superior musicianship helped make St Mark's a centre of musical excellenace whose reputation spread far and wide through north Europe (one of his most prominent pupils was Heinrich Schütz). He focused on sacred and isntrumental music and his musical language is even more devloped than that of his uncle.

Sacrae symphoniae

The 16 Sonatas and Canzonas from Sacrae symphoniae. Toccata quinti toni. Three Toccatas. Ⓟ

Intonatione del noni toni
**His Majestys Sagbutts and Cornetts /
Timothy Roberts** org
Hyperion CDA66908 (75' · DDD)   ⓕ🄱▸

Giovanni Gabrieli's *Sacrae symphoniae* publication of 1597 is a mixed set of vocal and instrumental pieces and, in its grand design, preserves a
glorious heyday of textural opulence, intimate
and playful dialogue between galleries and unashamedly ostentatious virtuosity. His Majestys
Sagbutts and Cornetts have augmented their
chamber consort to form, as cornettist David
Staff proudly proclaims, 'the largest group of
cornett and sagbutt players to have been assembled from one city since the 17th century'. These
wonderful 16 canzonas and sonatas make up the
complete instrumental music of the 1597 collection. In essence it's the extensive juxtaposition
between sombre blocks and glittering small-scale
exchanges which gives the music its seminal quality of moving both inevitably and eventfully
towards a self-assured resolution, befitting its
aristocratic gait. Having a 'moderator' (in this
case the fine keyboardist, Timothy Roberts), as
opposed to an artistic director, is pragmatic and
democratic but there's the odd moment where a
strong artistic presence at the helm would have,
ironically perhaps, empowered the musicians
towards a more flexible and varied approach to
articulation and colour. That said, there are some
glorious and majestic sounds: you can fly to the
buzzing *Canzon duodecimi toni a 10*, bathe in the
fragrant harmonic mosaic of the three-choir *Canzon quarti toni a 15* and relish elsewhere the peculiarly delicate and sweet sounds of this ensemble.
Overall, a notable and distinctive achievement.

Chandos CHAN10026 (58' · DDD)   ⓕ🄱▸

Symphonies – No 3 in A minor, Op 15; No 6 in G
minor, Op 32. Andante (discarded first movement
from Symphony No 3). Echoes from Ossian, Op 1
Danish National RSO / Christopher Hogwood
Chandos CHAN9795 (77' · DDD)   ⓕ🄱▸

If not the most adventurous of composers, and in
his later years over-conservative, Gade in his
youth certainly had his moments. His inventiveness is evident in all four symphonies presented
here, albeit in very different ways. The Sixth
(1856-57) is perhaps the most perfect, Classical in
design although with a minatory feel suggestive at
times of middle-period Haydn. If it stays within
its own clearly defined harmonic and stylistic
limits, the First, Third and Fifth do not. No 1
(1842), based on an old ballad and incorporating
his own earlier setting of it, is bright and full of
life: no wonder Mendelssohn and the Leipzig
audience were enchanted.
   The Third (1846-47) is a different proposition, more Romantic in tone, its first movement
too much so, causing the composer to replace it
with a less radical opening span (the *Presto*
tempo marking of which must still have raised a
few eyebrows). The original *Andante – Allegro
energico* is included here in its first recording,
proving a fine if turbulent sonata *allegro*.
   The Fifth (1852) has a Mendelssohnian poise
and grace plus one startling – if ultimately still-
born – innovation: the piano as an orchestral
instrument. The Fifth is definitely not a concerto,
but a true symphony with an extended keyboard
part, sometimes as soloist, sometimes as colouristic device. The performances are all very nicely
drawn, the First and Fifth particularly so.

Niels Gade   Danish 1817-1890

*Gade trained as a violinist and played in the Royal
Orchestra, Copenhagen. Mendelssohn was an early
admirer of his music having premiered Gade's First
Symphony, and at Mendelssohn's invitation he went
to Leipzig as an assistant conductor of the Gewandhaus Orchestra (where Gade conducted the premiere
of Mendelssohn's E minor Violin Concerto). On
Mendelssohn's death Gade was appointed chief conductor of the Gewandhaus Orchestra but he was
forced to return to Coenhagen when the the war
between Prussia and Denmark broke out. Back in
Copenhagen he established a permanent orchestra
and choir which gave the premieres of five of his
symphonies and his large choral works. He held the
post of co-director of the Copenhagen Academy of
Music where his pupils included Grieg and Nielsen.*

Symphonies

Symphonies – No 1 in C minor, 'On Zealand's Fair
Plains', Op 5; No 5 in D minor, Op 25[a]
[a]**Ronald Brautigam** *pf* **Danish National Symphony
Orchestra / Christopher Hogwood**

Hans Gál   Austrian 1890-1987

*Gál studied with Eusebius Mandyczewski and Guido
Adler – formative influences that informed his later
dual life as a composer and an academic. His precocious
talent quickly assured a named for him and his works
were widely performed. His second opera Die heilige
Ente was performed in 20 opera houses. With the rise
of the Nazis he lost his job at the Mainz Conservatoire
where he was director and his music was no longer
performed. At the suggestion of Donald Tovey he
emigrated to the UK and from 1945 until his retirement he was a lecturer in music at Edinburgh University. He was also a co-founder of the Edinburgh Festival. His music, which numbers 110 published works, is
tonal in nature but never bland or reactionary. He
edited many of Brahms's major works and wrote books
on Brahms, Schubert, Wagner and Verdi.*

String Quartets

String Quartets – No 1, Op 16; No 4, Op 99.
Improvisations, Variations and Finale on a
Theme of Mozart

Edinburgh Quartet (Charles Mutter, Philip Burrin vns
Michael Beeston va Mark Bailey vc)
Meridian CDE84530 (72' · DDD)   (F)

String Quartets – No 2, Op 35; No 3, Op 95.
Five Intermezzi, Op 10
Edinburgh Quartet
Meridian CDE84531 (72' · DDD)   (F)

Hans Gál's sophisticated but accessible musical language pushes the boundaries of formal design just about as far as they will go without fracturing, his slow movements poignant and tightly woven, his *scherzos* and finales invariably touched by understated humour.

Although stylistically distinctive, the First Quartet seems to take a good many of its cues from Brahms, Mendelssohn and, in the finale, Reger, a high-point being a slow movement that opens to ethereal harmonics and generates considerable intensity. Gál had a gift for eloquent melodic invention and the opening of the Second Quartet wafts in among weeping cadences, lightening just a little for a wistful second idea. An underplayed strain of melancholy permeates the *Canzone*, placed third in a novel five-movement structure, and where gently arpeggiated cello chords suggest parallels with Dvořák.

The Third Quartet ferries us forwards by 40 more years. The playful *Scherzo* and finale frame another of Gál's memorably meditative slow movements, this one opening to an unaccompanied violin solo before the other strings gather round in what sounds like a consolatory embrace.

Gál published the last in 1972 when he was in his early eighties (though he still had some 15 years left to him), the introductory *Adagio* perhaps the most magical episode in the whole cycle, music that twice recurs later in a movement that subsequently gives way to another of Gál's wry *scherzos*. Like its predecessors it betrays the hand of someone steeped in the classical quartet tradition while at the same time having something uniquely his own to say. A set of five pleasantly diverting *Intermezzi* predates the cycle, and the *Improvisation, Variations and Finale on a Theme of Mozart* take us on a light-hearted excursion via the kind of writing Gál put to more 'serious' use for the masterly quartets. They provide the sort of music that seems to grow richer with each hearing, especially in such sympathetic performances. Very strongly recommended.

Piano Music

Complete Piano Works
Leon McCawley pf
Avie ③ AV2064 (3h 9' · DDD)   (F)(O)(O)(>)

To say that Hans Gál was unique is not to suggest that his work is quirky or inaccessible. Hardly a single track on this admirable and musically worthwhile collection lacks interest, colour or instant appeal. And yet Gál was no mindless lightweight: a strain of deeper mean-

ing invariably lingers somewhere beneath his compact and attractive surfaces.

The first thing to say about this set is that Leon McCawley's playing could hardly be bettered: virtually every bar betrays a level of perception that would surely have warmed the composer's heart. Take the very first track on the first CD, the opening movement of Gál's Op 28 Piano Sonata of 1927, the numerous decorative harmonic digressions even within the first 30 seconds, the way McCawley ever so slightly stresses them but without disrupting the flow. Then try the *Quasi menuetto* second movement, a playful charmer stylistically placed somewhere between Prokofiev and Finzi. The early Suite, Op 22, is a genial sequence slightly reminiscent of Korngold (the Minuet) whereas the two post-war Sonatinas display more of a neo-classical leaning. All this, plus the three early Sketches, three Pieces and three Preludes (the middle piece achingly beautiful), fill just the first disc.

But the best is yet to come: two CDs of Preludes and Fugues, the 24 preludes written mostly in hospital in 1960, one a day while recovering from illness; the fugues, serene and clear headed, the work of an unusually lucid 90-year-old. Both sets progress from their initial key (B for the Preludes, C for the Fugues) and ascend chromatically, with the last piece cast a semitone lower than the first. The Preludes are more akin to, say, Prokofiev's *Visions fugitives* than to Shostakovich's Preludes. The fugues, on the other hand, are rather more ascetic, pared to essentials but often intensely expressive.

So, a surprise journey that should encourage many a return visit, especially in performances as consistently sympathetic as these. Excellent sound.

Baldassare Galuppi   Italian 1706-85

Nicknamed 'Il Buranello' after his birthplace in the Venetian lagoon, Baldassare Galuppi is remembered today for inspiring a sonnet by Robert Browning rather than for his music. He was none the less a prolific composer, leaving a large number of operas, particularly opera buffa. He worked as maestro di capella at St Mark's in Venice as well as in London and St Petersburg (for Catherine the Great).

Opera arias

'Forgotten Arias of a Venetian Master'
L'Olimpiade – Superbo di me stesso. Scipione in Cartagine – Di madre ai cari amplessi. Il sagrifizio di Jephte – Ah, di Lete dall'onda profonda. Il trionfo della continenza – Cedo alla sorte. Antigono – È pena troppo barbara; Benché giusto a vendicarmi. Voi che languite. Concerti a quattro – G minor; B flat.
Catherine King mez **Il Canto di Orfeo /
Gianluca Capuano** hpd
Avie AV2116 (72' · DDD · T/t)   (F)(>)

Avie here marks Galuppi's 300th anniversary – largely forgotten amid the Mozart and Shostakovich junketings – with a clutch of *opera seria* arias from the 1730s and '40s, before he teamed up with the playwright Carlo Goldoni to become the most successful *opera buffa* composer of the day.

Metastasio, doyen of *opera seria* librettists, once complained that Galuppi's music failed to express fully the emotions of the poetry. He may have thought again if he had heard the gravely eloquent E minor aria from *Antigono*, where soft trumpets add their mournful gloss to the strings. If Galuppi's fiery bravura arias, à la Vivaldi, are less distinctive, his pathetic or soulful *arie d'affetto* reveal his feeling for graceful, shapely melody and delicate orchestral textures: say, in a touching aria from *Scipione in Cartagine* (again, subtly coloured by trumpets), or a number ('Voi che languite') from an unknown opera.

Though caught in an uncomfortably swimmy church acoustic, Catherine King sings these attractive arias with firm, clear tone (her predominantly 'straight' sound selectively warmed with vibrato), elegant phrasing and agile, precise coloratura. She is splendidly vehement in the virtuoso castrato aria 'Benché giusto a vendicarmi' from *Antigono*, tenderly musing in 'Voi che languite', and smoothly negotiates the wide leaps between registers in the *Scipione* aria.

Il Canto di Orfeo accompany with verve and imagination, and on their own give vivid performances of two of Galuppi's *Concerti a quattro* for solo strings: the sober, Corellian G minor, and the more galant concerto in B flat, whose racy finale the players deck out with all sorts of jokey effects, right up to their zany, Stravinskified ending. Outrageous, but fun.

John Gardner   English b1917

Gardner was organ scholar at Exeter College, Oxford (1935-39), where his teachers included Armstrong, Walker and Morris. After war service he was a répétiteur at the Covent Garden Opera Company (1946-52); tutor (1952-76) and director of music (1965-69) at Morley College; visiting director of music at St Paul's Girls' School (1962-75); and professor of harmony and counterpoint at the RAM (1956-86). His compositional career effectively recommenced with the premiere of the Symphony No 1 at the 1951 Cheltenham Festival under Barbirolli. Its success led to several major commissions including Cantiones sacrae (1951-52) for the Three Choirs Festival, and the opera The Moon and Sixpence (1954-57) for Sadler's Wells Opera. Gardner's music is characterised by skilful craftsmanship and an eclecticism often arising from the nature of a particular work.

Orchestral Works

Piano Concerto No 1, Op 34[a]. Symphony No 1, Op 2. Midsummer Ale, Op 73

[a]**Peter Donohoe** *pf* **Royal Scottish National Orchestra / David Lloyd-Jones**
Naxos 8 570406 (72' · DDD)   ⓈⒹ▸

This coupling of two of John Gardner's major works, plus a sparkling comedy overture, could not be more welcome. He celebrated his 90th birthday in 2007, and has always been astonishingly prolific; maybe one reason for his neglect when there is so much to choose from.

The First Symphony (1946-47), the most extended work on the new disc, is in four movements spanning more than 40 minutes. The idiom is more abrasive than in Gardner's later works, with a grinding slow introduction leading to an *Allegro* with echoes of Walton in its jazzy syncopations, though with sharper harmonies. A chattering *Scherzo* in triple time leads to a *Lento* slow movement with whole-tone passages and orchestration echoing Debussy and Ravel. The finale is strongly rhythmic. As always in Gardner's music the orchestration is brilliantly clear, and after an interlude of stillness, the work ends with a ripe and optimistic D major chord.

The First Piano Concerto (1957) offers a contrasted idiom in its percussive echoes of the Bartók concertos, suiting Peter Donohoe's strong style admirably in a performance brilliantly backed by the RSNO. The clangorous opening movement leads to a still slow movement with echoes of Bartók but also of John Ireland. The finale brings more echoes of Walton and Arnold in music that is invariably attractive and distinctive.

The disc is dazzlingly rounded off with the rumbustious comedy overture *Midsummer Ale*, which should bring renewed attention to the composer's most attractive music.

John Gay   British 1685-1732

Gay was a poet and playwright best known for The Beggar's Opera, to music by Johann Christoph Pepusch. A close friend of poet Alexander Pope, Gay developed a literary style that was to anatomise city life with great accuracy.

The Beggar's Opera

The Beggar's Opera (arr Britten)
Tom Randle *ten* Captain Macheath **Leah-Marian Jones** *mez* Polly Peachum **Sarah Fox** *sop* Lucy Lockit **Jeremy White** *bass* Mr Peachum **Susan Bickley** *mez* Mrs Peachum **Donald Maxwell** *bar* Lockit **Robert Anthony Gardiner** *ten/spkr* Filch **Frances McCafferty** *contr* Mrs Diana Trapes **City of London Sinfonia / Christian Curnyn**
Chandos ② CHAN10548 (118' · DDD · S/T/N)   ⒻⒹ▸

This is the latest release in the Britten opera cycle inaugurated by Richard Hickox. Although the conductor's death cast a shadow over the Royal Opera's production of *The Beggar's Opera* at the Linbury Theatre, the performances went ahead with Christian Curnyn as his replacement and this studio recording, made at Blackheath Concert Halls, features the same cast. The staging was criticised for failing to capture the satirical cut-and-thrust of John Gay's original, but in the recording the purely musical strengths shine through.

Anybody who enjoys Britten's folksong arrangements or Purcell realisations will recognise the same ingenuity at work here. The arrangements are busy with counterpoint – Britten himself worried that he was 'canonising the music' too much – and the sharp-edged timbres of the chamber scoring sometimes transport the listener off to the familiar world of *Albert Herring*. All this is well captured by the highly skilled playing that Curnyn gets from the City of London Sinfonia and Chandos's excellent recording gives every instrument a life of its own.

The main competitor to the new Chandos, however, is Argo's earlier studio recording conducted by Steuart Bedford. The Chandos is longer, mainly because a fuller (and slightly different) version of the dialogue is used, but otherwise honours are even. Tom Randle gives an attractive portrayal of Macheath as a lovable young rogue, though Philip Langridge on Argo makes more of the solo scene Britten gives Macheath near the end.

The two women – Leah-Marian Jones's Polly Peachum and Sarah Fox's Lucy Lockit – sing with less beauty than their counterparts but more character, mock Cockney accents and all. Jeremy White as Peachum and, especially, Donald Maxwell as Lockit relish Gay's brand of low humour. With the stage experience in mind, it is no surprise that supporting roles, such as Susan Bickley's low-life Mrs Peachum and Frances McCafferty's thickly Scottish Diana Trapes, come across the footlights strongly – plenty of rude vigour to make this a recommendable addition to the series.

Giuseppe Gazzaniga   Italian 1743-1818

Study in Venice and Naples (with Niccolò Piccinini), led ultimately to the post of maestro di capella at Crema Cathedral. He was a prolific composer of opera buffa though posterity has relegated him well below Paisiello and Cimarosa.

Don Giovanni

Don Giovanni
Roberto Iuliano ten Don Giovanni **Linda Campanella** sop Donna Elvira **Cristina Mantese** sop Donna Anna **Valentina Molinari** sop Maturina
Maurizio Leoni bass Pasquariello **Giorgio Trucco** ten Duca Ottavio **Alberto Rota** bass Commendatore
Dario Giorgelè ten Biagio **Claudia Grimaz** sop Donna Ximena **Luca Tamani** ten Lanterna
Teatro Donizetti Chorus, Bergamo; Fondazione Orchestra Stabile di Bergamo 'Gaetano Donizetti' / Pierangelo Pelucchi

Bongiovanni 📀 AB20002
(130' · NTSC · 4:3 · PCM stereo and 5.1 · 0)
Recorded live 2005   Ⓕ

The booklet flags the 'impressive similarity' between Giuseppe Gazzaniga's *Don Giovanni*, premiered in February 1787, and Mozart's masterpiece first heard in Prague later the same year. True, there are occasional superficial musical resemblances but what strikes you time and again is the fathomless gulf between Gazzaniga's casually structured one-act romp, designed as a play-within-a-play for the Venice Carnival, and Mozart's tragi-comic masterpiece.

The atmosphere of Carnival frivolity is epitomised by the bitchy duet for Donna Elvira and the peasant girl Maturina (Mozart's Zerlina), and the all-singing, all-dancing frolic after the Don's distinctly un-terrifying descent to hell. There are several pleasantly spirited *buffo* numbers, including a duet for Pasquariello (the Leporello character) and Elvira, at the point where in Mozart Leporello sings his Catalogue aria, and the jolly Spanish-flavoured music that introduces the peasant couple. Elvira's second aria, with cello obbligato, has a touching dignity. *Au fond*, though, Gazzaniga's characterisation is stereotyped, his instrumental textures thin (just what the Venetians expected in 1787), his harmonies limited and predictable. But for the story, no one would think of reviving this *Don Giovanni* today.

Still, anyone curious about the subsoil from which the Mozart-Da Ponte opera grew should find this Bergamo performance more than acceptable. Alessio Pizzech's production, drawing on the imagery of the commedia dell'arte and the Venice Carnival, is visually inventive, with the 'realistic' action – usually watched by one or more of Don Giovanni's victims – counterpointed by dreamlike pantomime and surreal montages, sometimes arresting, sometimes flitting by too rapidly as filmed for the small screen. Though there are no specially distinguished voices among the cast, all have lively stage personalities and (being Italian helps) really relish their words. Tenor Roberto Iuliano, a distinctly louche, fleshy Don, sings his recitatives with devil-may-care bravado and brings a measure of seductive grace to his one aria. As his sidekick, Maurizio Leoni reveals a robust baritone and deft comic timing, while the Elvira – by far the biggest female role – compensates for some shrillnesss above the stave with the ardour of her phrasing. Orchestral playing is adequate, no more. There are subtitles for the opera, though, frustratingly for non-Italian speakers, not for Alessio Pizzech's half-hour spoken prologue, centring, Ariadne-like, on rehearsal squabbles and clashes.

Francesco Geminiani   Italian 1687-1762

A pupil, in Rome, of Corelli and Alessandro Scarlatti, Geminiani became leader of the opera orchestra in Naples. He moved to London in 1714 and earned a huge reputation as a violin virtuoso and became one of the most influential teachers (of the violin and composition). He published a series of instrumental works, starting with the highly acclaimed Violin Sonatas, Op 1 (1716). In the 1730s he visted Ireland, the Netherlands and Paris. He settled in Dublin in 1759. His music betrays his Corellian training, but his musical langauge is more adventurous and he also wrote for more varied solo instruments.

Concerti grossi

Geminiani Concerti grossi (after Corelli, Op 5)[a]. [P]
Cello Sonata in D minor, Op 5 No 2[b] **Corelli/
Geminiani** Sonata for Violin and Cello in A,
Op 5 No 9a[c]
[bc]**David Watkin** vc [b]**Alison McGillivray** vc [b]**Richard
Egarr** hpd [a]**Academy of Ancient Music /
Andrew Manze** [c]vn
Harmonia Mundi ② HMU90 7261/2 (144′ · DDD)
(F)OO

Eighteenth-century English music lovers, it seems, were obsessed with the music of Corelli, in particular his concerti grossi; Manze's notes quote a lovely account of how, when the Op 6 concertos were first published in 1714, one London orchestra of gentlemen amateurs, led by a Mr Needler, couldn't stop themselves from playing through all 12 at one sitting. They were Corelli's only published concertos, however, so it isn't hard to see what a welcome sight the works presented on this disc must have been when they first appeared in the mid-1720s; immensely skilful arrangements by Corelli's London-based pupil Francesco Geminiani of the master's 12 violin sonatas, Op 5, they were to all intents a new set of Corelli concertos.

What held for Londoners back then should hold equally well for Baroque enthusiasts today; these ingeniously crafted concerti grossi are a delight, their musical effectiveness in no way compromised by their origins. Listeners familiar with Corelli's Op 5 will doubtless have fun spotting what Geminiani has done with them (which goes well beyond straightforward orchestration); those who do not know the originals can just enjoy the music for what it is, which is to say bright, tuneful and invigorating.

Where Manze's particular success lies is in conjuring the atmosphere of the past and in the sheer joyousness and freshness which these performances convey. It's as if Mr Needler and his friends were before us, revelling in an unexpected Corellian bonus. Listen to the Academy of Ancient Music lustily laying into the thick chords in the final movement of Concerto No 4, dragging back the tempo and then charging off again, and you can almost see the complicit grins on their faces.

Manze is free with his embellishments, throwing in double-stops, blue notes and all manner of flourishes with an abandon that won't be to everyone's taste, but which contribute hugely to the enthusiastic tenor of the music-making as a whole. The orchestra is in fine form, offering a full sound whose occasional slight rawness is no bad thing in performances of such strength, directness and honesty.

Roberto Gerhard
Spanish/British 1896-1970

Roberto Gerhard – born to a German-Swiss father and mother from the Alsace – studied in Barcelona with Enrique Granados and Felipe Pedrell, and in Vienna and Berlin with Arnold Schoenberg (1923-28). Back in Barcelona he became a major figure in bringing modernism to Spain, organising performances of the music of Schoenberg and Webern, above all at the 1936 ISCM Festival. His Republican sympathies meant that he had to leave Spain in 1939 and he finally settled in Cambridge where he concentrated on writing for the BBC and for theatre (Covent Garden mounted his ballet Don Quioxote, the RSC staged King Lear with his incidental music and the BBC broadcast the opera The Duenna).

His output, which successfully fused atonalism with a 'Spanish' flavour, includes four symphonies, a Concerto for Orchestra, concertos for violin, piano and harpsichord, the cantata The Plague (after Albert Camus), the ballets Pandora and Soirées de Barcelone, and pieces for a wide variety of chamber ensembles.

Symphonies

Symphony No 2. Concerto for Orchestra
BBC Symphony Orchestra / Matthias Bamert
Chandos CHAN9694 (55′ · DDD)   (F)(D)▶

Although the avowed purpose of Gerhard's *Concerto for Orchestra* (1965) was to highlight the orchestra as an entity rather than its constituent sections or instruments, and while it may not have the immediate universal appeal of, say, Kodály's or Bartók's works with the same title, it has never been surpassed for its imaginative handling of instrumental sonorities or for its virtuoso demands on the players. It has to be said right away that this is a stunning performance: not merely does the BBC SO rise spectacularly to the work's demands, but Bamert shows himself exceptionally skilful at securing internal balances. It's worth quoting Gerhard's own words: 'My favourite listener is one who does not read explanatory programme notes … I stand by the *sound* of my music, and it is the sound that must make the sense…a work of music takes shape only in the mind of the listener.'

Gerhard's Second Symphony has been represented on disc only by the revised version (*Metamorphosis*) which had had to be completed by Alan Boustead (available on Auvidis Montaigne); although Gerhard may have felt the original too cerebral, it was at least all his, and tough going as it undoubtedly is, it's very welcome to all interested in the mental processes of this quite exceptional musician. The opening of the work's second section, with its clicking percussion, is hauntingly mysterious, and the final nightmare palindrome *Scherzo* (of which only a fraction exists in the Boustead version) is one of his most astonishing creations. With first-class recording throughout, this must be regarded as an essential disc for all admirers of Gerhard.

Edward German   British 1862-1936

After study at the RAM with Ebenezer Prout, German joined the teaching staff of the Academy and during that period composed a number of works for the RAM orchestra. Visits to Germany, and particularly Bayreuth, in the late 1880s aroused an interest in opera. In 1888 he became music director of the Globe Theatre, composing incidental music for a number of Shakespeare productions. His two symphonies were admired by George Bernard Shaw. His most popular work, Merrie England (1902), is aligned more to the Savoy operas of Gilbert and Sullivan than to Grand German opera. He is widely credited as founding the light music school, inherited by composers such as Eric Coates and Haydn Wood.

Orchestral works

Symphony No 1. Romeo and Juliet – Prelude.
The Tempter – Overture. Hamlet. The Willow Song
BBC Concert Orchestra / John Wilson
Dutton Digital Epoch CDLX7156 (77' · DDD)   Ⓕ

This collection of Edward German's orchestral music – none of it duplicated from earlier sets – is perhaps generally less striking but all is warmly romantic and beautifully crafted music of real grace and refinement.

Two items derive from German's theatre commissions of the 1890s – the Overture to *The Tempter* and the *Romeo and Juliet* Prelude, which contains an especially beautiful love theme for strings. The longest single movement is the *Hamlet* symphonic poem, written for the 1897 Birmingham Festival and further demonstrating German's command of orchestral resources, if inviting questionable comparisons with Tchaikovsky's tone-poem of a few years earlier. *The Willow Song* was German's last work of any significance – a heartfelt outpouring for the Royal Academy of Music's centenary in 1922 but one that, at less than eight minutes, suggests a composer by then somewhat worked out. There are echoes of Tchaikovsky, too, as well as Dvořák and Parry in perhaps the major attraction here – the First Symphony, performed at the Crystal Palace in 1890 and never published for orchestra. Again it is full of arresting ideas and eminently tuneful, if never quite becoming an arresting entity.

John Wilson demonstrates an impressive feel for constructing larger forms. The result is a beautifully played and recorded CD that further fills out our knowledge of Britain's symphonic output before Elgar.

Tom Jones

Tom Jones
Marianne Hellgren Staykov *sop* Sophia **Richard Morrison** *bar* Tom Jones **Heather Shipp** *mez* Honour **Donald Maxwell** *bar* Squire Western **Simon Butteriss** *bar* Gregory **Richard Suart** *bar* Benjamin Partridge **Gaynor Keeble** *mez* Lady Bellaston **Giles Davies** *bar* An Officer **Paul Carey Jones** *bar* Mr Allworthy, Dobbin **Ashley Bremner** *bar* Blifil **Catrine Kirkman** *sop* Hostess **Rachel Harland** *sop* Betty **Elizabeth Menezes** *sop* Peggy **Iestyn Morris** *ten* Grizzle **National Festival Chorus and Orchestra / David Russell Hulme**
Naxos ② 8 660270/71 (110' · DDD)   Ⓢ Ⓞ ➔

Though *Merrie England* may come more immediately to mind among Edward German's stage output, his setting of a much compressed version of Fielding's *Tom Jones* is generally considered his theatrical masterpiece, fusing the genteel old English style for which German is renowned with something strikingly more robust. Against the English country setting, German produced a score with sturdily written ensembles as well as outstanding individual numbers. That the work deserves a complete recording is no more in doubt than that it has here received a worthy one.

David Russell Hulme, the conductor, has long made a special study of German's music, and his grasp of its scope and nuances is readily apparent. His pacing of the score is much more convincing than that of a 1972 BBC broadcast of a virtually complete version with dialogue. So too is his casting of the work, with such leading musical theatre comedians as Richard Suart and Simon Butteriss in support of the more lyrical leading singers. In those leading roles Richard Morrison and Marianne Hellgren Staykov do the work proud. The one major pity is that, at the end of the waltz song, Staykov attempts an optional high note that she doesn't quite reach. Since this is the showpiece of the score, it's an especial pity. However, to dwell on this one blemish would be to obscure the exceptionally fine achievement this recording otherwise is. Though we have no dialogue, the recording is not only musically complete but goes further still by including an appendix of three numbers written for the show but dropped along the way.

This release admirably makes the point that there was a great deal more to pre-First World War British musical theatre than just G&S.

George Gershwin   American 1898-1937

Is there anyone, from the most sophisticated to the musically illiterate, who doesn't get a kick out of Gershwin? No composer has done more to weld the two opposing cultures of serious and popular music together (a road that is still in the process of being mapped out, let alone built). The tragedy is that he didn't live long enough to develop all his ideas.

His father, Morris Gershovitz, bought a piano in 1910 initially for Ira, his elder son, but it was Jacob (later George) who took to it like a duck to water. Within four years he was good enough to get a job playing popular songs in music shops. He had some lessons with the top New York teachers (piano with Ernest Hutcheson and Charles Hambitzer, harmony with Edward Kilenyi and Rubin Goldmark) but no one can teach a composer the gifts with which Gershwin was blessed. Before he was 20 he had written a Broadway hit, La La Lucille. In the score was the hit song 'Swanee'. It sold more than a million copies in sheet music and over 2,250,000 records, setting him up for life. An early string quartet went by unnoticed as did a serious one-act opera while he turned out hit after hit musical containing songs like 'Fascinating Rhythm', 'Lady be Good' and 'The Man I Love', with lyrics usually by his brother Ira.

Gershwin was a man possessed of phenomenal energy and ambition and it was inevitable that he should want to prove himself in more demanding music. The bandleader Paul Whiteman provided the catalyst by asking for a concert piece. The result was Rhapsody in Blue. The first performance on February 12, 1924 (attended by the likes of Rachmaninov, Stravinsky and Toscanini) was a triumph – if controversial – and it made Gershwin internationally famous overnight.

The only question-mark was over his ability to orchestrate. Ferde Grofé, Paul Whiteman's arranger, had done the job on the Rhapsody. The following year Gershwin produced his Piano Concerto in F, orchestrated by himself. Successful as he was, while continuing to write Broadway shows Gershwin still felt under-educated musically and asked to study with Ravel and Nadia Boulanger. Ravel turned him down. 'Why do you want to be a second-rate Ravel,' he asked, 'when you're already a first-rate Gershwin?'

Other concert works followed (Second Rhapsody and Cuban Overture) but it was his inspired An American in Paris that scored his next success in the field. During the last years of his life he spoke of plans for a symphony, a string quartet, a ballet and a cantata based on the Gettysburg address. None of these was achieved. What he did complete was an ambitious folk opera based on the novel Porgy by Dubose and Dorothy Heyward. It was not immediately popular – some eminent black composers, including Duke Ellington, did not like it, the serious music critics sniffed at it and Gershwin's usual audience was bamboozled by its very seriousness. Its acceptance as one of the great operas of American music came only after Gershwin's premature death at the age of 38 from an inoperable brain tumour.

Bernstein conducted and played the music of Gershwin with the same naturalness he brought to his own music. Here, An American in Paris swings by with an instinctive sense of its origins in popular and film music; no stilted rhythms or four-squareness delay the work's progress, and where ripe schmaltz is wanted, ripe schmaltz is what we get, devoid of all embarrassment. Rhapsody in Blue is playful and teasing, constantly daring us to try to categorise its style, and then confounding our conclusions. Although the solo passages from individual players are beautifully taken, the orchestra captures the authentic flavour of Gershwin's and Bernstein's idiom, and Bernstein pushes them to transcend the printed scores. His own playing in the Rhapsody is tantalisingly unpredictable. The recording is clear and bright, perhaps a touch hard-edged, and a little of the richness of the original LP issue might have been preferred by some, especially as the editing is now made more obvious.

Complete Music for Piano and Orchestra:
Rhapsody in Blue. Second Rhapsody.
Variations on 'I Got Rhythm'. Piano Concerto in F
Anne-Marie McDermott pf
Dallas Symphony Orchestra / Justin Brown
Bridge BRIDGE9252 (73' · DDD)   ℗ ●●

It's rare enough to have all four Gershwin works for piano and orchestra on a single disc but rarer still for each one to come near or top of the class. First, and unusually enough, McDermott and her (British) conductor do Gershwin the courtesy of playing all the scores uncut and observing his dynamics and performance instructions to the letter. Typical of their meticulous attention to detail is the first bar of the coda (allegro con brio) in the Concerto's first movement, almost always played forte but marked (and rendered here) piano by the orchestra, mp by the soloist, allowing a crescendo over the following eight bars. A small point, maybe, but it is what the composer asked for and is all the more effective.

Such preparation would mean little, though, if the performances did not fly off the page with verve and confidence, rhythmic precision and real style. The slow movement of the Concerto in particular is wonderfully characterised, all smokey blues with decadent solos from the muted first trumpet. The Dallas strings lend a Hollywood swoon to the big tunes in the famous Rhapsody and the Concerto while the remaining two pieces are more coherent and convincing than in the hands of some far more famous names. Strongly recommended.

Rhapsody in Blue

Gershwin Rhapsody in Blue. An American in Paris   Ⓗ
Grofé Grande Canyon Suite
New York Philharmonic Orchestra /
Leonard Bernstein pf
Sony Classical SMK63086 (64' · ADD)
Recorded 1958-59   Ⓜ ● ▶

Additional recommendation

Rhapsody in Blue   Ⓗ
Coupled with: An American in Paris. Piano Concerto in F. Variations on 'I Got Rhythm'
Wild pf **Boston Pops Orchestra / Fiedler**
RCA Red Seal 74321 68019-2 (70' · ADD)
Recorded 1959-61   Ⓢ

Wild's pianism is often scintillating, and he generates an infectiously sparky rapport with Fiedler and the Bostonians, whose exuberant, gently affectionate *American in Paris* is a treat. RCA's sound is astonishingly undated.

Piano Concerto

Gershwin Piano Concerto in F
Ravel Piano Concerto in G
Hélène Grimaud pf
Baltimore Symphony Orchestra / David Zinman
Erato 0630 19571-2 (55' · DDD)   (F)**O**B+

Also available in a four-CD Apex set featuring
Grimaud in major piano concertos   (S)

This is a logical and satisfying coupling, and it is surprising that it hasn't been recorded more often. Both the Gershwin and Ravel concertos are heavily influenced by jazz. Gershwin's, written in 1925, is a strange mix of creative spontaneity and formal constraint. The fusion of popular and traditional elements clearly influenced Ravel, whose G major Concerto (completed in 1931) contains a seemingly incongruous, yet superbly constructed, juxtaposition of American blues and jazz, Iberian exoticism and neo-classicism.

Hélène Grimaud offers a straightforwardly romantic view of these works, especially of the Gershwin. She seems happiest with broad melodic lines, such as in Gershwin's first movement, which she shapes with a wholly natural and unforced beauty. Other pianists may go for a more rhythmically buoyant and propulsive approach, further playing up the jazz impulse, but Grimaud's sincerity succeeds on its own terms. There are times – most notably the slow movement of the Ravel – where her playing seems just a little too strait-laced or emotionally restricted. In this movement, her left-hand-before-right mannerism may irritate some listeners. But she can never be accused of 'milking' the music, and Ravel, who believed that a concerto should be 'light-hearted and brilliant, and not aim at profundity or at dramatic effects', would surely have approved.

Additional recommendation

Piano Concerto
Coupled with Rhapsody in Blue. Variations on 'I Got Rhythm'
Thibaudet pf **Baltimore SO / Alsop**
Decca 478 2189DH (57' · DDD)   (F)B+
    The rarity here is Grofé's arrangement for the Paul Whiteman Orchestra of Gershwin's Concerto, and this is currently the best version. Stylish and rhythmically buoyant, Thibaudet and Alsop adopt an unflashy approach to the Variations.

Piano Works

Of Thee I Sing – Prelude[a]; Jilted. Second Rhapsody[a].
The Shocking Miss Pilgrim – For you, for me, for

GERSHWIN RHAPSODY IN BLUE – IN BRIEF

Columbia SO / Bernstein pf   H
Sony Classical SMK63086 (64' · ADD)   M**O**B+
The free-wheeling zip and chutzpah of this famous 1958 recording are irresistible. Coupled with Lenny's abundantly charismatic renderings of Gershwin's *An American in Paris* and Grofé's *Grand Canyon* Suite.

McDermott; Dallas SO / Brown
Bridge BRIDGE9252 (73' · DDD)   M**OO**
A strongly recommendable anthology devoted to all of Gershwin's piano *concertante* works played with a terrific feel for the idiom.

London SO / Previn pf
EMI 566891-2 (65' · ADD)   M**O**
Previn's endearingly laid-back 1971 account sounds more glowing than ever in EMI's latest remastering. These artists' *An American in Paris* and Piano Concerto complete a fondly regarded Gershwin triptych.

Grimaud; Baltimore SO / Zinman
Erato 0630 19571-2 (55' · DDD)   (F)**O**B+
A beautifully shaped performance with an almost classical feel but Zinman and his Baltimore orchestra bring a nice touch of pizzazz. Cool, but rather elegant!

Gershwin pf roll **Columbia Jazz Band / Tilson Thomas**
Sony Classical 07464 39699-2 (71' · ADD)   (F)
Tilson Thomas's earliest recording cleverly fuses the composer's 1925 piano roll with Grofé's original jazz-band instrumentation. Coupled with *An American in Paris* and six of Gershwin's Broadway overtures.

San Franciscso SO / Tilson Thomas pf
Sony Classical 82876 60862-2 (77' · DDD) M**OO**B+
Tilson Thomas's second version (and his first directing from the piano) has heaps of temperament, and again employs the original 1924 scoring. Brightly recorded, this could well be a first choice for many.

Los Angeles PO / Bernstein
DG 477 6352GGP (56' · DDD)   (F)**O**B+
Charismatic, outrageous but with buckets of personality, Bernstein brings his inimitable flair to Gershwin's *Rhapsody* as part of an all-American programme. (This performance is available in various couplings depending on your territory.)

Donohoe; London Sinfonietta / Rattle
EMI 508996-2 (56' · DDD)   B)B+
The punchy jazz-band version given a terrific performance by Peter Donohoe (also available in a four-CD 'American Music' set from Rattle – 215014-2).

evermore. Cuban Overture[a]. Pardon My English –
Isn't it a pity?. Variations on 'I Got Rhythm'[a]. Catfish
Row[a]. Shall we dance? – Let's call the whole thing
off[a]; They can't take that away from me[a]. Goldwyn
Follies – Our love is here to stay
Jack Gibbons pf
ASV White Line CDWHL2082 (77' · DDD)
Items marked [a] arr Gibbons. Ⓜ

This disc is mostly comprised of Gibbons's own
arrangements, based on Gershwin's film music,
two-piano pieces, and in the case of the 'Catfish
Row' *Porgy and Bess* suite, his orchestrations. The
longest work is the *Second Rhapsody*, composed for
a scene in the Gershwins' first Hollywood movie,
Delicious. The film starred Janet Gaynor and
Charles Farrell, and in this sequence the heroine
wanders frightened through Manhattan – it might
be rechristened *A Scotswoman in New York*. George
Gershwin referred to the main tune as his
'Brahmsian theme' but today no one would
mistake it for anything but Gershwin.

The solo version of the *Cuban Overture* is Gibbons's own adaptation of Gershwin's four-hand
arrangement; like the 'Catfish Row' suite it
makes formidable demands on the pianist and
Gibbons gives them both virtuoso performances. The recital ends with three of the standards Gershwin wrote in Hollywood during the
last months of his life. 'They can't take that away
from me' must be a strong contender for the
greatest songs of the 20th century, and no one
hearing 'Our love is here to stay' can doubt that
a premonition of death lingered somewhere in
the composer's heart in the autumn of 1936.

Porgy and Bess

Porgy and Bess
Willard White bass Porgy **Cynthia Haymon** sop Bess
Harolyn Blackwell sop Clara **Cynthia Clarey** sop
Serena **Damon Evans** ten Sportin' Life **Marietta
Simpson** mez Maria **Gregg Baker** bar Crown
**Glyndebourne Chorus; London Philharmonic
Orchestra / Sir Simon Rattle**
EMI ③ 234430-2 (3h 9' · DDD · T/t) Ⓜ❶❶❶▷

The company, orchestra and conductor from the outstanding 1986 Glyndebourne production recreate a very real
sense of Gershwin's 'Catfish Row' community
on this complete recording. Such is its atmosphere and theatricality, we might easily be back
on the Glyndebourne stage. From the very first
bar it's clear just how instinctively attuned Rattle and this orchestra are to every aspect of a
multifaceted score. The cast, too, are so *right*, so
much a part of their roles, and so well integrated
into the whole, that one almost takes the excellence of their contributions for granted. Here is
one beautiful voice after another, beginning in
style with Harolyn Blackwell's radiant 'Summertime', which at Rattle's gorgeously lazy
tempo, is just about as beguiling as one could
wish. Willard White conveys both the simple
honesty and inner strength of Porgy without

milking the sentiment and Haymon's passionately sung Bess will go wherever a little flattery
and encouragement take her. As Sportin' Life,
Damon Evans not only relishes the burlesque
elements of the role but he really *sings* what's
written a lot more than is customary. But the
entire cast delivers throughout with all the
unstinting fervour of a Sunday revivalist meeting. Sample the final moments of the piece – 'Oh
Lawd, I'm on my way' – if that doesn't stir you,
nothing will.

Additional recommendation

Porgy and Bess Ⓗ
Warfield Porgy **L Price** Bess **Calloway** ten Sportin'
Life **McCurry** bar Crown **RIAS Light Orchestra,
Berlin / Smallens**
Guild mono ② GHCD2313/4 (139' · ADD) Ⓕ
Recorded live in 1952
A fascinating live recording of a US State Dept-
funded performance in Berlin, part of a tour that
gave the British, French, Italian, German, Czech
and Russian premieres of Gershwin's opera. William Warfield's Porgy is a noble achievement and
Price's voice is at its youthful best. The sound is
clear, well defined; the recording favours the
voices, but Alexander Smallens, who conducted the
first performance in 1935, somehow persuades
some really hot playing from the RIAS Light
Orchestra. No one who admires Gershwin's work
should ignore this unique document.

Carlo Gesualdo   Italian c1561-1613

*Probably still best known as the noble who murdered
his wife, Donna Maria d'Avalos, and her lover when
he caught them in flagrante delicto in 1590. And his
anguished, often fiercely dissonant music, merely
adds to the story – for many, his music a key to his
tortured soul. He was essentially an amateur musician but he was greatly influenced by the expressive
music of Luzzasco Luzzaschi. He left six books of
madrigals and three sacred collections in which his
setting of words is powerfully achieved. His reputation, which lay dormant until the 19th century, has
grown steadily and he is now considered one of the
major composers of the turn of the 17th century.*

Madrigals

Madrigals Books 1-3
**Gesualdo Consort, Amsterdam /
Harry van der Kamp**
CPO ② CPO777 138-2 (143' · DDD · T/t) Ⓕ

This must rank among the most important
recent additions to the madrigal discography,
and a landmark in that of Gesualdo. The composer's reputation rests largely on his last three
books of madrigals, which have been admirably
served; but the first three had so far been less

lucky. Their musical language is less strikingly 'original' than in the later books, and for that reason the interpretative challenge they represent is quite different.

This anthology succeeds brilliantly in dispelling the notion that Gesualdo was 'still finding his voice' in his earlier work. One's almost tempted to turn the traditional view on its head and regard the later music as a self-indulgently hyperbolised departure from the style of, say, the Third Book. Not quite believable, perhaps needless to say, but Harry van der Kamp and his singers have achieved something rather special here.

The Gesualdo Consort is a multinational ensemble, and though it includes no Italians, for sonic seduction they certainly rival their Italian counterparts while never losing sight of the music's rhetorical sense. The pleasure here consists in following Gesualdo's gradual widening of his technical and expressive resources: by the Third Book, the pieces are longer, the argument correspondingly more ambitious, the chromaticism more assertive. His 'Ancidetemi pur' (a re-reading of a set text in one of Arcadelt's most famous madrigals), for example, is very fine indeed. The singing is superb, with few slips to speak of, and none that detracts from the singers' expressive purpose. The continuo is unobtrusive but tastefully and sensitively deployed, and is given its head with a few keyboard intabulations that provide a welcome contrast.

Ahi, disperata vita. Sospirava il mio cor. O malnati messaggi. Non t'amo, o voce ingrata. Luci serene e chiare. Sparge la morte al mio Signor nel viso. Arde il mio cor. Occhi del mio cor vita. Mercè grido piangendo. Asciugate i begli ochi. Se la mia morte brami. Io parto. Ardita Zanzaretta. Ardo per te, mio bene. Instrumental items – Canzon francese. Io tacerò. Corrente, amanti
Les Arts Florissants / William Christie
Harmonia Mundi HMC90 1268 (55' · DDD · T/t)   Ⓕ

To many, Gesualdo is known above all for the *crime passionnel* that left his wife and her lover impaled on the same sword, but the notion that his highly charged music is the product of a tortured and unstable mind is, no doubt, over-romanticised. For this foray into the schizophrenic world of Gesualdo's five-voice madrigals, Les Arts Florissants have selected their programme from the last three books, pieces in which the highly mannered and exaggerated aspects of the composer's style reach their most extreme expression. Nevertheless, we should not think of all these works being undifferentiated in style, and one of the fascinations of this disc, which has been very carefully planned, is the insight it offers into the gradual emergence and sharpening of the features which characterise Gesualdo's late madrigalian manner.

Some of those elements can already be heard in *Sospirava il mio cor* from the Third Book, and by the last tracks they're present, with all their compositional distortions in full dress. William

Christie and Les Arts Florissants are no strangers to the aesthetic of the Italian madrigal in its last decades. This recording, like so many of their productions, is full of surprises on both the large and small scales. The first, of a general kind, is the decision to add continuo accompaniments *avant la lettre*. This is justifiable on historical grounds, though less certain is the precise way it has been done with some passages within a piece still left *a cappella*. Less justifiable, if only on artistic grounds, is the performance of two madrigals on instruments alone (*Io tacerò* and *Corrente, amanti*); it makes little sense to attempt such highly charged word-driven music in this way. What may also surprise is the rather understated, almost classically pure character of the interpretations, though it is a relief that the calculatedly neurotic and deliberately out-of-tune manner so often turned out for Gesualdo has here been eschewed. These are technically very fine and dramatically convincing and coherent readings which are certainly preferable to any other recordings of Gesualdo's madrigals currently available.

Tenebrae Responsories

Tenebrae Responsories for Maundy Thursday
King's Singers (David Hurley, Robin Tyson *countertens* Paul Phoenix *ten* Philip Lawson, Gabriel Crouch *bar* Stephen Connolly *bass*)
Signum SIGCD048 (66' · DDD)   ⒻＰ

It's perhaps in his music for Holy Week that Gesualdo's claim as a composer of real substance lies. By transferring his madrigal idiom to the sacred sphere so consummately, he shows he can work effectively within formal constraints that the secular works rarely impose. The formal severity of these Responses places in sharp relief his striking melodic turns and startling contrapuntal progressions. It's no wonder that vocal ensembles have been so attracted to them.

This recording joins a select and distinguished group, starting with the Hilliard Ensemble's complete set for ECM, and continuing with the Taverner Consort's set for Good Friday. The King's Singers have a brighter tone than the Hilliards, which makes for a more extrovert reading. In qualitative terms there's little to choose: perhaps in matters of intonation the Hilliards and the Taverners retain a slight edge. But this newcomer naturally takes its place alongside them in the front row, which speaks volumes for its quality.

Orlando Gibbons   British 1583-1625

Gibbons was born in Oxford and and was a chorister and student at King's College, Cambridge (where his brother was master if the choristers). He joined the Chapel Royal and, by 1615, was one of its organists (senior organist, 1625), a post he kept until his death.

In 1619 he became a keyboard player at court and in 1623 organist at Westminster Abbey. He was a hugely important musician and celebrated during his day, so his death, aged 41, caused great shock. He was hastily buried in Canterbury where a monument was later erected in his memory. A very versatile musician, Gibbons was perhaps the greatest composer of his age, renowned for his keyboard music, his music for viols and a number of madrigals (including the famous The Silver Swanne). His church anthems are works of great beauty and power (as, for example, See, the word is incarnate and This is the record of John).

Viol Works

Fantasias – a 3: Nos 1-4; a 6: Nos 1-6. Pavan and Galliard a 6. Three In nomines a 5 – No 1; No 2. Pavan and Galliard in A minor, 'Lord Salisbury', MBXX/18-19. Hosanna to the Son of David. O Lord, in thy wrath rebuke me not. Go from my window. Peascod time. The Silver Swanne **P**
Phantasm (Wendy Gillespie, Jonathan Manson, Markku Luolajan-Mikkola *viols*) / **Laurence Dreyfus** *viol* with **Asako Morikawa, Susanna Pell** *viols*
Avie AV0032 (72' · DDD)   Ⓕ❍❍❍❍▷

Phantasm is a superb ensemble. They now turn their attention to the viol music of Orlando Gibbons, with a focus on the central works that are definitely for viols and definitely by Gibbons: the six great fantasies for six viols, the four marvellous fantasies for three viols and a selection of what is otherwise best of his viol music in five and six parts. They play with vast assurance and verve, always attractive, always with fresh and varied textures, always beautifully balanced. This is often playing of a breathtaking virtuosity that communicates the music with irresistible vitality. Some listeners may feel that they hit poor Gibbons a little hard, occasionally losing track of the poetry that's his own special contribution; others could feel that some tempi are chosen simply for bravado, especially in the dazzling performance of *Go from my window* that ends the disc. But this is classy playing and a major contribution to the catalogue.

As a slightly eccentric *bonne bouche* they steer away from the music with a violone, preferring to offer arrangements of keyboard pieces and vocal anthems. This is presumably to stress the unquestionable truth that music in those days wasn't often genre-specific; but in the event it emphasises that the greatest of Gibbons' viol pieces are perfectly suited to that particular ensemble.

Keyboard Works

'The Woods So Wild'   **P**
Fantasias – in D minor, MBXX/5; in G, MBXX/6; in D minor, MBXX/7 (for double organ); in D minor, MBXX/8; in G minor, MBXX/9; in A minor, MBXX/10; in A minor, MBXX/11; in A minor, MBXX/12; in C, MBXX/13; in C, MBXX/14; Ground, MBXX/26. Italian Ground, MBXX/27. Pavan and Galliard in A minor, 'Lord Salisbury', MBXX/18-19. The Fairest Nymph,

MBXX/43. Preludes – in A minor, MBXX/1; G, MBXX/2; in D minor, MBXX/3; in A minor, MBXX/4; The Woods So Wild, MBXX/29. Galliard, MBXX/23. Pavans – MBXX/16; MBXX/17. Coranto, MBXX/39
John Toll *org/hpd*
Linn CKD125 (73' · DDD)   Ⓕ▷

John Toll succumbed to cancer in his early fifties, thus depriving the world of a supreme continuo player, in many ways unchallenged in his generation. This disc's quality deepens the sense of loss. The choice of Gibbons is itself intriguing for a man whose main career was in Baroque music. But it's clear from every note that this was a composer very close to Toll's heart, that he acknowledged the quiet poet who has perhaps the most distinctive voice of all composers from the age of Shakespeare.

Toll has focused on the most substantial works. All the Fantasias are here, as well as most of the Pavans; but most of the smaller dances are omitted. So we have a Gibbons of considerable seriousness, which Toll underlines by controlled playing that has not the slightest trace of self-indulgence. What we hear in Toll is the composer who was not just the 'best finger of that age' but also one of the finest contrapuntists and a man of marvellous musical imagination. The music is divided between two instruments. The late 17th-century organ at Adlington Hall sounds absolutely glorious, beautifully caught by the engineers, and played with sympathetic mastery; it's used not just for Fantasias but also for some of the music that one would more instinctively have thought intended for a harpsichord – with fascinating results. A modern Flemish-style harpsichord by Michael Johnson serves for the rest, but again not just for the dances. This is top-quality playing.

Sacred Vocal Works

O clap your hands. Great Lord of Lords. Hosanna to the Son of David. Prelude in G[a]. Out of the deep. See, see, the Word is incarnate. Preludes – No 3 in D minor, MBXX/3[a]. Lift up your heads. Almighty and everlasting God. First (Short) Service – No 6, Magnificat; No 7, Nunc dimittis. Second Service – No 3, Magnificat; No 4, Nunc dimittis. Fantazia of four parts[a]. O God, the king of glory. O Lord, in Thy wrath rebuke me not
Oxford Camerata / Jeremy Summerly with [a]**Laurence Cummings** *org*
Naxos 8 553130 (65' · DDD · T)   Ⓢ▷

The Oxford Camerata provides a representative selection of choral works by Gibbons, together with three of his organ pieces. The programme is introduced by a bright and busy performance of the eight-part *O clap your hands*, followed by the noble verse anthem *Great Lord of Lords* – and it's pleasing to hear in this piece, and in the other verse-anthems, the rich timbre of the counter-tenor Robin Blaze, a welcome acquisition for the Camerata, which has a great deal of vocal talent in its make-up. They tackle the gently moving *See, see, the Word is incarnate* with great confidence, together with the First and Second Services and the quiet collects with all the knowledge and aplomb of cathedral lay clerks or choral scholars from Oxford and Cambridge. Laurence Cummings plays two short preludes, the one in G major – a real test of agility – from *Parthenia* and that in D minor from Benjamin Cosyn's *Virginal Book*. The *Fantazia of four parts* is a most extraordinary work, quite hard to steady and control. A welcome addition to the programme.

Secular Vocal Works

Pavan and Galliard a 6. Fantasia a 2 No 1. Go from my window. Fantasias a 6 – Nos 3 & 5. Fantasia a 4 No 1 'for the great double bass'. Galliard a 3. In Nomine a 4. Pavan and Galliard in A minor, 'Lord Salisbury'. Prelude in G. Masks – Lincoln's Inn mask; The Fairest Nymph. Alman in G. Behold, thou hast made my days. Glorious and powerful God. The First Set of Madrigals and Mottets – Daintie fine bird; Faire is the rose; I weigh not fortune's frown; I see ambition never pleased; I feign not friendship where I hate; The Silver Swanne
Tessa Bonner sop **Timothy Roberts** keybds **Red Byrd; Rose Consort of Viols**
Naxos 8 550603 (68' · DDD · T)   ⓢ▷

Beautifully performed and finely recorded, this selection of Gibbons's music is especially attractive for its variety. At its richest it presents writing for voice and viols combined, five parts to each, or for viols alone, sometimes in six parts. In lightest, most transparent texture there's a charming piece for two viols. Three keyboard instruments are used for solos: virginals, harpsichord and organ. A soprano also sings solos to viol accompaniment. Moods and styles vary correspondingly. The *Masks* and *Alman* for virginals have a high-spirited, almost popular manner; the Fifth *Fantasia* includes some unusual chromaticism and harmonic developments that for a while almost anticipate Purcell.

Tessa Bonner sings with unvibrant purity; but most striking here is the pronunciation. It's one of the distinguishing marks of this curiously named group, Red Byrd, that they sing such music with vowel sounds modified to fit theories about the English in which it would originally have been sung. Thus the 'daintie fine bird' tells 'oi sing and doy', and the 'u' acquires a sort of umlaut in *I weigh not fortune's frown*, 'weigh' and 'frown' also having a measure of rusticity. Perhaps it's a good idea, but it does increase the desirability of printed texts in the booklet.

The instrumental music is finely played, and Timothy Roberts's keyboard solos are particularly skilful, in *legato* and fluency.

Eugène Gigout   French 1844-1925

Gigout studied with Saint-Saëns at the Ecole Niedermeyer. In 1863 he became organist of St Augustin, *Paris, a post he retained for 62 years. In 1911 he began teaching at the Conservatoire and his pupils included Boëllmann, Gagnon, Marchal, Messager and Roussel. Most of his substantial output is for organ.*

Organ Works

'The Complete Organ Works, Volume 1'
Rhapsodie sur des airs catalans. Suite de six pièces. Trois Pièces
Gerard Brooks org
Priory PRCD761 (77' · DDD). Played on the organ of Perpignan Cathedral, France   Ⓕ

For lovers of organ sound this disc is an absolute treasure. Perpignan's sumptuous Cavaillé-Coll isn't an organ of memorable solo stops but of deliciously blended, exquisitely balanced choruses. Full organ is warm and robust while its plentiful soft-stops have a subtlety and charm which, even in the face of the omnipresent action clatter, this recording captures with almost magical delicacy. The fourth of the *Suite de six pièces*, an *Andantino* in E minor, is lent distinction by the utter charm of the contrasting soft flute and string choruses, while the first of the *Trois pièces* dances across the manuals revealing tantalising glimpses of colour richly enhanced by the atmospheric acoustic of Perpignan's cathedral. All this is superbly captured in Priory's rich, mellow recording.

In his deft handling of the instrument and his keen sense of colour, Brooks proves that there's much more to organ playing than big virtuoso gestures. Which may be as well since there's little scope for such things here. Not only do all 10 pieces on this disc completely avoid the virtuoso and emotional excesses of Liszt, Widor and Vierne, but none stretches much over 10 minutes in duration. With the exception of the captivating *Rhapsodie sur des airs catalans*, all are relatively youthful works revealing a composer with a keen sense of structure and a penchant for contrapuntal argument. A most attractive release.

'The Complete Organ Works, Volume 2'
Suite de six pièces (pub 1881). Deux Pièces. Interludium. Méditation
Gerard Brooks org
Priory PRCD762 (72' · DDD). Played on the Cavaillé-Coll organ of St Ouen, Rouen   Ⓕ

'The Complete Organ Works, Volume 3'
Dix Pièces. Pièce Jubilaire. Poèmes Mystiques
Gerard Brooks org
Priory PRCD763 (75' · DDD). Played on the Cavaillé-Coll organ of St Etienne, Caen   Ⓕ

Before Gerard Brooks embarked on his complete cycle, only two of Gigout's solo organ pieces figured consistently on the *Gramophone* database. One of those, the 'Grand choeur dialogué' (the sixth of the 1881 *Suite de six pièces*), appears on the second disc of the series in a performance that makes it a highly treasurable release. Brooks imbues it with great majesty and splendour, letting it unfold with all the opulence of a regal procession. Such spacious playing allows us ample opportunity to savour the glorious sonic spectacle of the wonderful St Ouen organ in Rouen, an instrument frequently recorded, though never before with such stunning sound.

The third disc includes the most familiar of Gigout's organ works; the *Dix Pièces* published in Paris in 1892. There can be few organists who don't possess this tome, if only for the scintillating B minor Toccata, and it's been recorded frequently. Brooks's may not be the most impressive of these but he's impeccably faithful to the score and, playing on what's described as 'one of the finest surviving examples of Cavaillé-Coll's work', we have here an unquestionably authoritative version, not just of the Toccata but of all 10 pieces. Even those that pass most organists by are revealed as musical gems ideally suited to a resourceful organ. Organ recordings of this calibre are few and far between.

Alberto Ginastera

Argentinian 1916-1983

Ginastera studied at the National Conservatory in Buenos Aires and later joined the teaching staff there. His ballet Panambí established his reputation and he soon followed it with Estancia. Between 1945 and 1947 he visited the USA and attended Copland's courses at Tanglewood; thereafter his life was divided between Argentina and abroad. In 1971 he settled in Geneva. His music gradually lost its nationalistic style (recognisably from the same school as Bartók, Falla and Stravinsky) and he started to explore atonality.

Orchestral Works

Panambí, Op 1. Estancia, Op 8[a]
[a]**Luis Gaeta** *bass/narr*
London Symphony Orchestra / Gisèle Ben-Dor
Naxos 8 557582 (73' · DDD)   ⓈⒹ→

It was a characteristically bold step by the 21-year-old Ginastera to make his Op 1 an ambitiously scored orchestral ballet rather than a modest suite or chamber piece. Of course, he had written such works – mostly withdrawn and destroyed – but the one-act choreographic legend *Panambí* (1935-37) was several strides forward and as impressive a compositional debut as any.

Drawn from an Amerindian tribal legend, the plot concerns the love of Guirahu for the chief's daughter, Panambí, and the machinations of the local sorcerer, who also desires her. A battle between good and evil plays out across a single night, opening with wonderful, impressionistic moonlight and ending with a radiant hymn to the dawn. In between, the expertly scored music

is largely restrained, though with some electrifying episodes along the way.

Panambí betrays Ginastera's formative influences clearly, *The Rite of Spring* and Ravel in particular. The vividly achieved, primitivist atmosphere (not unlike the music of Revueltas) necessary for the story is absent from his follow-up ballet, *Estancia* (1941). Some of the latter's music is so well known, thanks to the popular Suite, that it may surprise that this recording of the whole was a premiere. Absent, too, is the self-consciousness of *Panambí* as a public statement; in *Estancia* one can hear Ginastera relax as he whips up a greater storm.

Gisèle Ben-Dor and the LSO are splendid throughout. Luis Gaeta makes a splendid soloist in *Estancia*. Recommended.

Overture to the Creole 'Faust', Op 9. Pampeana No 3, Op 24. Estancia, Op 8a. Glosses on Themes of Pablo Casals, Op 48
Berlin Symphony Orchestra / Gabriel Castagna
Chandos CHAN10152 (66' · DDD)   Ⓕ

Overture to the Creole 'Faust', Op 9. Pampeana No 3, Op 24. Estancia, Op 8a. Ollantay, Op 17
Odense Symphony Orchestra / Jan Wagner
Bridge BRIDGE9130 (57' · DDD)   Ⓕ

Either of these two well-produced discs would make a near-ideal introduction to this versatile composer's output, featuring three of his finest orchestral inspirations. If the suite from his ballet *Estancia* (1942) remains his best-known work, and its malambo finale one of the most famous pieces in Latin American music, the *Overture to the Creole 'Faust'* (1943) can't be far behind. Both are outgoing, 'popular' items, whereas the 'symphonic pastoral' *Pampeana No 3* (1954) is more obviously serious.

All three works receive committed performances on both discs. Castagna and the Berliners find a touch more magic in the *Pampeana*'s slower outer movements aided by Chandos's sumptuous sound, but the Danish players, led by their Venezuelan-born conductor, often have the edge in the swifter sections. In *Estancia*, the resonance of Chandos's recording works against the music: Bridge's drier, cleaner sound in the Carl Nielsen Hall in Odense is more successful. And while some of Jan Wagner's tempi seem a shade deliberate compared to Castagna's, he mostly justifies them by the pacing of each work *in toto*.

If there's little overall to choose between the newcomers, the fourth item on each may decide the matter. On Chandos comes a scintillating account of the second, full-orchestral version of the more harmonically advanced *Glosses on Themes of Pablo Casals*, originally written for strings to celebrate the Catalan cellist's centenary in 1976 and rescored a year later. In contrast, Bridge restores to the CD catalogue Ginastera's *Ollantay* (1947), a darkly colourful and dramatic folk-triptych that could be thought of as an Argentinian *Taras Bulba*.

If you want only one version of these pieces the Bridge is recommended.

Umberto Giordano   Italian 1867-1948

Giordano studied at the Naples Conservatory and, after displaying talent in a composition competition, was commissioned to write an opera. Mala vita was given in Rome in 1892: it was not a success. He moved to Milan, where his Andrea Chénier was given, at La Scala, in 1896; it was well received and established his reputation. His other regularly performed opera is Fedora (1898, Milan).

Andrea Chénier

Andrea Chénier
Plácido Domingo ten Andrea Chénier **Renata Scotto** sop Maddalena **Sherrill Milnes** bar Carlo Gérard **Michael Sénéchal** ten Incredible **Maria Ewing** mez Bersi **Gwendolyn Killebrew** mez Madelon **Jean Kraft** mez Countess **Allan Monk** bar Roucher **Terence Sharpe** bar Fléville **Stuart Harling** bass Fouquier Tinville **Isser Bushkin** bass Schmidt **Malcolm King** bass Dumas **Piero De Palma** ten Abate **Nigel Beavan** bass-bar Maestro di casa **Enzo Dara** bar Mathieu **John Alldis Choir; National Philharmonic Orchestra / James Levine**
RCA ② 88697 57615-2 (114' · ADD · T/t)   Ⓑ

Choosing between this recording and the Decca Chailly (currently available only as a download), it might seem sensible to start with the tenor in the title-role, and here a strong inclination would be to plump for RCA and Domingo: he's in splendid voice, with a touch of nobility to his manner that makes for a convincing portrayal of a poet. Pavarotti (Chailly) begins with a rather leather-lunged Improvviso, but he later finds poetry in the role as well, especially when responding to his soprano, Caballé, who's rather stretched by the more exhausting reaches of her role and sounds audibly grateful for the occasional opportunities he gives her to float rather than belt a high-lying phrase. However, Pavarotti is an *Italian* tenor, and his Italianate sense of line adds one per cent or so of elegance to some phrases that even Domingo can't match. Caballé does many things beautifully, and her fine-spun *pianissimo* and subtle shadings only occasionally sound mannered, but the role is undeniably half a size too big for her. So it is for Scotto, you might say, and a hint of strain is audible once or twice, in her timbre rather than her phrasing. It's her phrasing that tips the balance back to RCA: Scotto is as subtle a vocalist as Caballé, but she gives meaning and eloquence to every phrase without ever breaking the long line, which one can't always say of the Spanish soprano. Matters are about even as far as the baritones are concerned: Milnes acts admirably,

but refrains from over-acting, and the voice is rich and characterful. In the supporting cast, RCA's striking Bersi, vividly characterised Incredible, and their Roucher, too, aren't outmatched (only their Madelon, both fruity and acid – a grapefruit of a voice – is disappointing).

A lot of people will enjoy the huge energy and bustle of Levine's direction. It's vividly characterful, but a shade exhausting and overassertive. The flow of the music seems more natural in Chailly's hands, and orchestral detail is clearer. The Decca recording, too, is warmer.

Additional recommendation

Pavarotti Chénier **Nucci** Gerald **Caballé** Maddalena **Kuhlmann** Bersi **Varnay** Countess **NPO / Chailly**
Decca download 410 117-2DH2 (107' · DDD)
Swings and roudabouts when compared with the RCA set; Chailly tends to over-conduct and Pavarotti takes some time to warm up. Both Nucci and Caballé are on good form, Caballé displaying her customary great artistry on nearly every page.

Andrea Chénier
Franco Corelli ten Andrea Chénier **Celestina Casapietra** sop Maddalena **Piero Cappuccilli** bar Carlo Gérard **Ermanno Lorenzi** ten Incredibile **Gabriella Carturan** mez Countess **Giovanna di Rocco** mez Bersi **Luigi Roni** bass Roucher **Leonardo Monreale** bass Fléville **Mario Chiappi** bass Fouquier Tinville **Renzo Gonzales** bass Schmidt **Florindo Andreolli** ten Abate **Cristina Anghelakova** mez Madelon **Giorgio Giorgetti** bar Mathieu **Milan RAI Chorus and Orchestra / Bruno Bartoletti**
Stage director **Vaclav Kaslik**
Hardy Classic Video 📀 HCD4008
(110' · NTSC · 4:3 · 1.0 · 0)
Recorded at RAI TV Studios, Milan 1973   Ⓕ

This is something of a find – a production produced in Milan's television studios in 1973 that does more than justice to Giordano's *verismo* work about personal conflicts at the time of the French Revolution. It's directed, with considerable imagination, by the Czech Vaclav Kaslik, at the top of his profession in the '70s. In realistic period sets he unerringly creates the milieu of a degenerate aristocracy in Act 1 and of the raw mob-rule of the Revolution in the succeeding acts. The only drawback is the poor lip-sync.

Conductor Bruno Bartoletti makes certain we're unaware of the score's weaker moments and releases all the romantic passion in Giordano's highly charged writing for his principals. Chénier was one of Corelli's most notable roles so it's good that his splendid portrayal has been preserved for posterity. He doesn't disappoint with his excitingly trumpet-like tones and finely moulded phrasing of the composer's grateful writing for his tenor hero, and – although already 52 – he still looks the part of the glamorous, challenging poet.

Cappuccilli was famous for his Gérard and here – at the height of his powers – he projects all the man's conflicting feelings with enormous conviction on a stream of burnished tone. Celestina Casapietra, a generally underrated soprano from Genoa, is just what Maddalena should be, and sings with a nice combination of tenderness and intense feeling. She and Corelli do full justice to their duets. The RAI orchestra plays well, but unfortunately it's too backwardly placed as regards the singers.

Madame Sans-Gêne

Madame Sans-Gêne
Mirella Freni sop Caterina **Giorgio Merighi** ten Lefebvre **Mauro Buda** bar Napoleone **Andrea Zese** bar Fouche **Valter Borin** ten Neipperg **Antonio Feltracco** ten Vinaigre, Despreaux **Marzia Giaccaia** sop Toniotta, Carolina **Muriel Tomeo** sop Giulia **Federica Bragaglia** sop Principessa Elisa, La Rossa **Valerio Marletta** bar De Brigole **Riccardo Ristori** bar Gelsomino, Roustan **Alfio Grasso** bar Leroy **Muriel Tomao** sop Madame Bulow **Modena Teatro Comunale Chorus; Emilia Romagna 'Toscanini' Symphony Orchestra / Stefano Ranzani**
Dynamic ② CDS247 (123' · DDD · T/t)   Ⓕ

The plot of *Madame Sans-Gêne* is a rather charming variant on the theme of the Emperor's clothes; it's also about a star-struck girl who learns sense and returns to home and boyfriend. The premiere at La Scala in 1929 failed to impress, though Toscanini conducted and Toti Dal Monte sang the leading role. The score is elegantly lyrical and lively, modern in relation to *Chénier* as (say) *Gianni Schicchi* is in relation to *Manon Lescaut*.

Madame Sans-Gêne is a comedy whose story takes a serious turn in Act 3, which for a while seems about to topple over into tragedy. Napoleon, previously a figure in the background, appears in person and in a bad mood, but is charmed and shamed into a talk about old times with the genial heroine and all ends well. At first Madame Sans-Gêne, so-called, seems to be one of those tireless life-and-soul-of-the-party people who can be so wearing, but she develops into less of a turn and more of a character, while her chirpy vocal line eventually settles for a more rewarding warmth and lyricism. It's understandable that the role should be attractive to a star soprano who late in her career looks for something out of the way in which much is accomplished by personality. Mirella Freni's voice is still full bodied and to a large extent pure in quality but by this time had long forfeited the firm evenness of its prime. She gives a genuine performance – and (not far off her 64th birthday) a remarkable one. The best singing, however, is that of the tenor, Giorgio Merighi. Mauro Buda as Napoleon shows an almost tenorial baritone which it would be good to hear in a part with more opportunities. Ranzani conducts with spirit. As a recording this is a great deal more satisfactory than the currently available alternative, taken from an Italian radio transmission in 1957.

Mauro Giuliani   Italian 1781-1829

Born in Bisceglie, Giuliani studied the cello in Barletta but soon took up the guitar, which he mastered with great skill. He moved to Vienna and began to write works in the Classical style for the guitar; soon he was celebrated as the greatest living guitarist, teaching, performing and composing. He was also a cellist, playing in the premiere of Beethoven's Symphony No 7 (1813). He was acquainted with Rossini, Moscheles and Hummel, often giving chamber music concerts with some very illustrious partners. He returned to Italy in 1819 and restablished his career as composer and publisher. His works include three guitar concertos, sonatas, studies and variations for solo guitar, quartets and many duos for guitar, and songs.

Guitar Concerto No 1

Giuliani Guitar Concerto No 1 in A, Op 30
Schubert Sonata for Arpeggione and Piano in A minor, D821 (arr Williams)
John Williams gtr **Australian Chamber Orchestra**
Sony Classical SK63385 (52' · DDD)   ⒻⒹ+

The guitar has played a part in several adaptations of the Schubert A minor Sonata, substituting for either the arpeggione or the piano, but never before with a string orchestra in the supporting role, reversing the bowed/percussive relationship. Good arranging doesn't consist of literal adherence to the original score but, as here, in making small changes to take advantage of the new instrumentation. Rarely has such a transmutation been accomplished with greater conviction. Put any doubts or prejudices you may have on the back burner and enjoy familiar beauty in new clothing.

The Giuliani is familiar in every respect – except that of interpretation. What we have in this recording is the recognition of the relationship between instrumental and vocal music in Giuliani's work; it's apparent in his (and others') frequent adaptation of operatic music for the guitar, but has more or less escaped the attention of guitarists on record. The vocal quality of the writing is fully realised here, producing what might even be regarded as the first stylistically faithful recording of the First Concerto. The performances from both John Williams and the Australian Chamber Orchestra are exemplary and praise should also extend to the engineers who recorded them with such clarity and ideal balance. If you already have these works, don't let it deter you from adding this revelatory recording to your collection.

Philip Glass   American b1937

Born in Baltimore, Glass studied at the Juilliard School and with Boulanger in Paris (1964-66), and worked with the Indian musicians Ravi Shankar and Alla Rakha. His music, often described as minimalist, relies on repetition, often slightly out of sync so that wave patterns are formed: Glass prefers to describe it as 'music with repetitive structures'. Seminal early works include String Out *(1967-68) and* Music in Twelve Parts *(1971-74). His opera* Einstein on the Beach *was given at the Met in 1976 and secured his reputation. This was followed by further full-scale operas,* Satyagraha *(1980),* Akhnaten *(1984),* The Making of the Representative for Planet 8 *(1988) and* The Voyage *(1992). He has written a number of highly admired film-scores (*Kundun, The Hours *and* Notes on a Scandal *all won Academy Awards) as well as symphonies, concertos and string quartets. He is one of the few 'serious' composers today who has truly crossed over to attract an entire new audience.*

Cello Concerto

'The Concerto Project, Volume 1'
Cello Concerto[a]. Concerto Fantasy for Two
Timpanists and Orchestra[b]
[a]**Julian Lloyd Webber** *vc* [b]**Evelyn Glennie,**
[b]**Jonathan Haas** *perc* **Royal Liverpool Philharmonic
Orchestra / Gerard Schwarz**
Orange Mountain Music OMM0013 (45' · DDD) Ⓕ Ⓑ➤

The Cello Concerto was conceived when Julian Lloyd Webber asked Glass to compose a work for the cellist's 50th birthday. Lloyd Webber says the piece, premiered in October 2001, contains technical hurdles he had not seen before, particularly in the opening cadenza, but for the listener it's not a difficult work. That cadenza, underpinned by muffled, percussive figures from the orchestra, is dramatic, with an undercurrent of ambiguous emotion, but it's also lithe and attractive, evocative of the classics of cello literature, not least Bach and Elgar. There are passages where the debate between orchestra and soloist seems to contrast those often-copied, easily parodied Glass mannerisms with his more melodically and harmonically expansive work of recent years. The result is one of the most engaging, impressive and beautiful things Glass has done. The slow movement, lyrical and graceful, sets us up perfectly for the shock of the opening of the finale, which bursts in with one of those 'accelerating train' episodes he does so effectively.

The gestation of the timpani concerto was more problematic. Despite their tuneful capabilities, timpani are associated primarily with melodrama and bombast and aren't an ideal choice for a concerto solo instrument. There are 14 of them here, presumably due to the need to negotiate fairly rapid movement through different keys. It all works remarkably well in the event. The fast first movement has exciting, ritualistic solo parts, perhaps influenced by south-east Asian and Japanese traditions. The slow movement manages to make the drums sound lyrical, embedded in settings of regal brass and pastoral woodwind. The cadenza preceding the third movement, highly athletic as it is, proves to be a warm-up for Evelyn Glennie and Jonathan Haas before the technical *tour de force* of the finale.

Piano Concerto No 2

Piano Concerto No 2, 'After Lewis and Clark'[a].
Harpsichord Concerto[b]
[a]**Paul Barnes** *pf* [b]**Jillon Stoppels Dupree** *hpd*
[a]**R Carlos Nakai** *fl* **Northwest Chamber
Orchestra / Ralf Gothóni**
Orange Mountain Music OMM0030 (59' · DDD) Ⓕ Ⓑ➤

This is certainly one of the most enjoyable recent releases of Glass's music. There is something fresh about both works, though the Glass fingerprints naturally also abound. The Piano Concerto No 2 takes its cue from the exploits of Lewis and Clark, who made the first overland expedition in the US in 1804-06, and the first movement is suitably epic in its feeling (something at which Glass is very good), with much expansive, dark-hued writing. The second has a hauntingly beautiful contribution from a Native American flute, something so riveting (especially in the hands of R Carlos Nakai) that one wishes Glass would write an entire work for the instrument. Only in the third movement does there seem to be too much archetypal Glassian triumphalism; but even here, when the 'slipped' variation technique of the second section begins, one's attention is held very firmly by the strangeness of the result. Paul Barnes is a shining soloist.

The harpsichord offers different challenges, but Glass seems to relish those, too; this concerto, with its more transparent orchestration, occasionally exotically Eastern flourishes, baroquisms and frequently unexpected harmonic moves, works an almost alchemical magic with the composer's familiar simple arpeggiated material. The third movement blasts off like a rocket. Soloist Jillon Stoppels Dupree notes that she rarely steps outside the world of the Baroque but that she was 'entranced' by the concerto when she came to work on it. Entrancing is a pretty good description of her performance, too. Both concertos are splendidly accompanied by the Northwest Chamber Orchestra under Ralf Gothóni, and recorded sound is full without being over-resonant.

Symphonies

Symphony No 2. Orphée – Interlude. Concerto for
Saxophone Quartet and Orchestra
Raschèr Saxophone Quartet (Carina Raschèr *sop*
sax Harry Kinross White *alto sax* Bruce Weinberger
ten sax Kenneth Coon *bass sax*) **Vienna Radio
Symphony Orchestra, Stuttgart Chamber
Orchestra / Dennis Russell Davies**
Nonesuch 7559 79496-2 (69' · DDD) Ⓕ Ⓑ➤

Glass isn't a symphonist in the conventional sense, but neither was Messiaen. Glass himself has indicated that his large-scale orchestral works are conceived with their probable role in the conventions of concert programming in mind. This sounds outrageously manipulative when stated explicitly, but in fact it's nothing more than a description of the context of the symphonic form since its inception. He's also said that he devoted his earlier career to subtracting elements from his music and is now deciding what to put back in. In the case of this symphony, the specified element is polytonality, the presence of which in much 20th-century music is perhaps taken for granted. However, when it's added into this stripped-down and austere idiom, the results are certainly striking. The opening movement recalls the prelude to *Akhnaten*, the third and final movement reprises the chattering arpeggios of the composer's earlier works, closing with an exciting – and, indeed, viscera-loosening – *crescendo*. After recovering during the snippet from *Orphée*, we come to the marvellous Concerto. Conceived for performance either as a quartet or in this quartet-plus-orchestra version, this is a gloriously animated work, almost Coplandesque in many respects, yet remaining true to Glass's own vision. Despite being presented as the secondary work on this disc, its presence makes the whole recommendable.

Symphony No 3ᵃ. The CIVIL WarS – Interludes Nos 1 & 2ᵃ. The Voyage – Mechanical Balletᵇ. The Lightᵇ
ᵃStuttgart Radio Symphony Orchestra, ᵇVienna Radio Symphony Orchestra / Dennis Russell Davies
Nonesuch 7559 79581-2 (61' · DDD)   Ⓕ🄱➤

Comparing Glass's Third Symphony with his Second finds the forces reduced from full orchestra to strings, the overall timing reduced by virtually half and the number of movements increased from three to four. Glass No 2 is long breathed, atmospheric and occasionally suggestive of Brucknerian vistas, whereas Glass No 3 is texturally lean and harmonically more adventurous than much of his previous work. It also seems to have taken in influences from some fairly unexpected sources.

The first movement is sombre and march-like while the second, which is built on compound metres, kicks out in all directions, switching to a gutsy *staccato* at 2'59". The pulse is constant, but the tone has altered, sometimes sidling nearer to Sibelius, sometimes a stone's throw from Shostakovich. At the start of the brief finale, there's even a hint of Kurt Weill, but one thing is for sure: if you play the symphony blind, you might never guess that it's by Glass. The stylistic shift from mellow, arpeggiated dreamscape (a familiar Glassian aura that holds sway for most of *The Light*) to a sort of ecstatic acerbity, follows through to the rest of the work. But there's another presence – less of a surprise, perhaps – later in the long third movement when the Arvo Pärt of *Cantus* seems to join the fray.

The idea of external influence extends to the interludes from *The CIVIL WarS*, where, as annotator David Wright tells us, Tchaikovsky's *Nutcracker* gets a look in, particularly in the Second Interlude with its *pas-de-deux*-like downward

scales. 'Mechanical Ballet' (from *The Voyage*) and the expansive *The Light* are rather more what you'd expect from Glass: haunting narratives, always on the move yet tinged with melancholy. Even if you don't care for Glass's more familiar 'arpeggiated' style, do try the Third Symphony. It's different, and the performance is excellent.

Symphony No 7, 'Toltec'
Bruckner Orchestra Linz / Dennis Russell Davies
Orange Mountain Music OMM0061 (45' · DDD)   Ⓕ🄱➤

Film director Errol Morris once said that Glass does 'existential dread' better than anyone. It's true that the dark side of Glass's music has been put to good use in countless films and opera scores. Such moods have also been transferred into the symphonic medium. No 7, *Toltec*, is no exception. Composed in 2005, it forms a neat pair with No 5, *Requiem, Bardo, Nirmanakaya*, in that both symphonies draw upon texts to address meaning, existence and mortality.

The Toltec tradition, which was based in present-day Mexico and reached its peak during the end of the first millennium AD, provides a number of arresting images for each of the symphony's three movements: 'The Corn' (Ecology), 'The Sacred Root' or 'Hikuri' (Spiritual Enlightenment) and 'The Blue Deer' (Knowledge and Understanding). These subjects enable Glass to use the essential apparatus of his musical language once more: repetition and variation, rhythmic motion and momentum, patterns based on scales or broken chords, and terraced structures of tension and release. But Glass does not simply go through the motions here: the work plumbs great depths in the first movement and scales vast heights in the last. In between, the second movement's impressively harnessed massed choral textures evoke similar moments in Glass's powerful opera *Akhnaten*, which also looks towards the beliefs and practices of ancient civilisations. Benefiting from a generously rounded but clearly defined recording under Dennis Russell Davies, the *Toltec* is seriously worth considering, whether you are into 'existential dread' or not.

In the Upper Room

In the Upper Room
Philip Glass Ensemble / Michael Riesman
Orange Mountain Music OMM0056 (45' · DDD)   Ⓕ

Slightly over half the dances which Glass wrote for choreographer Twyla Tharp's *In the Upper Room* in 1986 were issued by CBS a year later under the title *Dance Pieces*, but this disc presents the complete cycle for the first time.

Comparing the two recordings makes for an interesting exercise in minimalist performance practice. When *Dance Pieces* was released, the trend was towards layering electronically manipulated and treated sounds over acoustic instruments to impart a more polished sheen to

Glass's music. The result was clinical and, one suspects, driven at the time by corporate pressures to make the music as commercial as possible. Twenty years later, and Glass has decided to revisit the original masters in order to try to recapture the live sound which accompanied the original ballet production.

There is certainly more warmth and depth here, with the ebullient, processional Dance IX benefiting in particular from a more three-dimensional sonic facelift. At the same time the reinstated dances do little to supplement any perceived deficit in the abridged version, or the need to restore some kind of cyclic unity to the work. The disc's highlight, Dance VIII, with its haunting, fragile piano figure is already present in the original version, as are most of the weightier, more extended movements. The 'missing' dances are on the whole short and somewhat transitional in nature. All this adds further weight to the fact that there were sound reasons for leaving them out in the first place, although Glass aficionados will no doubt be glad to receive the complete set.

String Quartets

Complete String Quartets (Nos 1-5)
Smith Quartet (Ian Humphries,
Darragh Morgan vns Nic Pendlebury va
Deidre Cooper vc)
Signum Classics ② SIGCD117 (89' · DDD)　　Ⓜ️▶️

If success was measured according to output and sales units alone, Glass would be head and shoulders above his contemporaries. His compositions for conventional combinations, including the five string quartets included on this disc, have already appeared on recordings by the Kronos and Duke quartets, but the Smith Quartet have been the first to release the complete cycle.

Quartets Nos 2 to 5, written between 1983 and 1991, form a neat and consistent set, from the enigmatic, introspective Second, via the expressive Third and quirkily bitonal Fourth, to the neo-romantic, almost Tchaikovskian opening gesture of the Fifth. The Smith Quartet's thoughtful and measured performance allows subtle metric, linear and textural features to rise unassumingly to the surface, enhanced on this recording by a clear, balanced stereo image, and played with characteristic precision and projection by the ensemble.

The First Quartet is something of an anomaly, however. Written soon after Glass's studies with Nadia Boulanger in Paris during the mid-1960s, it has been viewed either as a transitional work of marginal interest or a potent symbol of Glass's emerging minimalist style. What connects this work with later Glass – at least more than the Cageian silence – is the work's obsessive preoccupation with cyclical repetition, although the accompanying atonally charged atmosphere seems light years away from the lush harmonies of the Fifth Quartet.

Naqoyqatsi

Naqoyqatsi – Original Film Soundtrack
Yo-Yo Ma vc Members of the **Philip Glass Ensemble**
(Lisa Bielawa sop Jon Gibson, Richard Peck saxs
Andrew Sterman fl/picc/cl Michael Riesman kbd)
orchestra / Michael Riesman
Sony Classical SK87709 (77' · DDD)　　Ⓜ️Ⓞ️▶️

This is another colourful, barnstorming film score from Glass, and one that contains enough material of substance that it can stand quite successfully on its own. There are the expected Glass fingerprints – the powerful, pulsing, dark-hued 'heartbeat' opening, the rippling arpeggios of 'Religion', the clangorous vocal and orchestral writing in 'Intensive Time' and 'Point Blank', both of which recall parts of his opera Akhnaten – but there are also moments when he creates something quite new. In 'Massman' he explores the higher regions of the solo cello in some hauntingly lyrical music; and lyricism, of a non-Western kind, also characterises two remarkable sections for solo cello and percussion, 'New World' and 'Old World'. A more purely romantic sensibility is at work in 'Media Weather', as in other sections in passing, but it seems all of a piece with this interesting mixture of the familiar pulsing, glowing Glass and the less familiar, introspective lyrical composer. The performance is superb, and beautifully recorded.

Documentary

'A Portrait of Philip in 12 Parts'
Film director **Scott Hicks**
Drakes Avenue ② 📀 DAP7768
(115' · 16:9 · 2.0 and 5.1 · 0)
Extra features include Director's Commentary,
Extended Interviews, Trailer and Deleted Scenes　Ⓕ

Scott Hicks's documentary dates from Glass's 70th year (2007) and, unlike previous films (which have tended to concentrate on Glass's public persona), provides a fascinating and often revealing glimpse into the composer's personal and private life. It ostensibly portrays Glass as the gregarious, affectionate family man. There are interviews with close family and friends, and we get to see the composer relaxing in the kitchen, chopping garlic and making vegetarian pizza, entertaining friends while on retreat in one of his many rural dwellings, or going out on walks with his wife and kids. Fascinating insights are also provided by those who have worked professionally with Glass, not least by film directors such as Errol Morris, Godfrey Reggio and Woody Allen. And the downtown New York scene that fostered and developed Glass's talents in the early 1970s is vividly contextualised.

But the camera lens also reveals a different and altogether more uncomfortable reality. When Glass is not jet-setting across the globe either performing, recording and promoting his music, or receiving spiritual counselling sessions from

Buddhists and Shamanists, his workaholic habits result in long periods of self-imposed isolation from his family. What is gradually uncovered as the film shifts through its 12 parts is the composer's overwhelming sense of self-focus and obsessive desire to succeed, and the increasing strain this places on a close-knit network of people who appear to do little else other than attend to his every need and wish.

For Glass himself, one suspects that Hicks's film would make for rather uncomfortable viewing at times; but in a strange way, this is also what makes it so compelling. Glass's music is reflected in the very nature of his life – repetitively structured, mechanically controlled, totally determined. Yet one cannot help but admire the man's resolute purposefulness and drive. In making a film about Glass, Hicks has successfully shown what makes all great composers tick.

Alexander Glazunov

Russian/USSR 1865-1936

Glazunov studied with Rimsky-Korsakov and had his First Symphony performed when he was 16. In 1899 he was appointed to the St Petersburg Conservatory, which he directed from 1905 until leaving the Soviet Union in 1928. His importance in Russian music is considerable, not just because of his academic authority but because in his music he brought together many of the disparate elements of his contemporaries: from Rimsky he learnt a virtuoso treatment of orchestration, from Balakirev came a nationalist language, from Tchaikovsky he absorbed the melodic gift, and from Taneyev he took the skill of a contrapuntalist. While not being a particularly forward-looking composer, he was a powerful stabilising influence at a time of social and artistic turmoil. He wrote eight symphonies, five concertos (of which the Violin Concerto is the most well known), seven string quartets and a number of ballets (of which Raymonda is his masterpiece).

Violin Concerto in A minor, Op 82

Violin Concerto. Meditation, Op 32[a]
The Seasons, Op 67
[a]**Aaron Rosand** vn **Malaysian Philharmonic Orchestra / Kees Bakels**
Vox Classics VXP7907 (61' · DDD)   ⓕ❍

Aaron Rosand began recording for Vox in the late 1950s. Now in his seventies, his timbre and technique are as sure as ever. Moreover Rosand's very stylish playing of the delightful Glazunov Concerto brings a sense of having lived with this music over the decades, yet returning to it as to an old friend, with no possible hint of staleness. The beguiling opening theme floats off the bow with the most engaging warmth and an easy, natural *rubato*, which the conductor follows admirably. The richly shaped melody of the *Andante*, too,

goes straight to the heart of the music: again Rosand's timbre is warm, his phrasing ravishingly lyrical. The finale dances away jauntily, its spirited rhythmic charisma echoed by the orchestra.

In short, this performance is very good indeed, worthy of comparison with the finest on disc (including Vengerov, Shaham, Mutter) and, in its security of the solo line, even approaches Heifetz. The gentle, rhapsodic *Meditation* makes a splendid encore while the recording is admirable, with a completely natural balance.

Glazunov Violin Concerto[a]
Prokofiev Violin Concertos Nos 1 & 2[b]
Maxim Vengerov vn [a]**Berlin Philharmonic Orchestra / Claudio Abbado;** [b]**London Symphony Orchestra / Mstislav Rostropovich**
Warner Elatus 0927 49567-2 (DDD)   Ⓜ❍ᗕ

Vengerov turns Glazunov's war-horse concerto from a display piece into a work of far wider-ranging emotions. It's a remarkable account, with Vengerov making you appreciate afresh what a wonderful and varied sequence of melodies Glazunov offers. It's characteristic of Vengerov how he shades and contrasts his tone colours. He reserves his big, romantic tone for the third theme, where most rivals let loose sooner with less subtle results. His *rubato* is free but always spontaneous sounding, and the lolloping fourth section brings some delicious *portamento*. Predictably the dashing final section is spectacular in its brilliance, with orchestral textures fresh and clean.

Vengerov and Rostropovich take an unashamedly epic, wide-open-steppes view of Prokofiev's First Concerto rather than the pseudo-Ravelian one posited by Chung/Previn and Mintz/Abbado, but it works at least as well. His tone is gloriously rich, every note hit dead centre. No 2 is slightly less successful. The balance is partly to blame – the soloist rather too closely scrutinised – but there's also a lack of intimacy in the interpretation itself. Nevertheless, this is an extremely fine disc and comes thoroughly recommended.

Symphonies

Symphony No 6, Op 58. The Sea, Op 28.
Salomé, Op 90 – Introduction; Dance
Royal Scottish National Orchestra / José Serebrier
Warner Classics 2564 69627-0 (67' · DDD)   Ⓕ❍❍ᗕ

From the formidable list of rival versions of the Sixth, arguably Glazunov's most powerfully dramatic symphony, dating from 1896, this one from José Serebrier and the Royal Scottish National Orchestra is among the very finest, warm and approachable with Serebrier drawing beautifully moulded playing from the Scottish orchestra, with *rubato* perfectly judged and with the orchestra fine and resonant in vividly recorded, rich, unexaggerated sound.

Glazunov's lyrical second subjects were always striking, and the one in the first movement here is no exception. The structure is clearly defined with fine thrust from the performers, and with that theme coming thrillingly back *fortissimo* at the climax of the movement. The theme and seven variations which make up the second movement go with an easy flow, with the brassy climax of the seventh variation well controlled in its dynamic contrasts. The third movement is a charming *allegretto* with neo-classical overtones, while the finale is the most powerful movement of all with its Borodin echoes at the start and a most ingenious combination of sonata and double-variation form, all of which Serebrier brings out most persuasively.

The fill-ups, though much less powerful, are well worth hearing, two works that vie with the masterpieces of Debussy and Strauss. *La mer* of 1889 (antedating Debussy) is a richly evocative seascape with the harp prominent, hardly equalling Debussy's masterpiece but very attractive, while the Introduction and Dance from *Salomé*, more conventional than the rest, were from incidental music that Glazunov wrote for a production of the Oscar Wilde play in 1908. There is a powerful gesture at the start of the Introduction with Salomé's Dance predictably getting faster and faster and with the horn-writing adding to the exotic orientalism. Altogether a splendid issue.

Symphony No 8 in E flat, Op 83. Cantata in Memory of Pushkin's 100th Birthday, Op 65ᵃ. Lyric Poem in D flat, Op 12
ᵃ**Ludmila Kuznetsova** *mez* ᵃ**Vsevolod Grivnov** *ten*
Russian State Symphony ᵃ**Cappella and Orchestra / Valéry Polyansky**
Chandos CHAN9961 (67' · DDD · T/t)　　　Ⓕ⮕

Glazunov's Symphony No 8 opens confidently and lyrically, conductor Valéry Polyansky maintaining an easy-going momentum, later pressing forward, yet always holding the argument together. There's some lovely woodwind playing in the *Mesto* slow movement and the strings create a genuinely passionate climax. The *Scherzo* is given a purposeful thrust, and the finale doesn't outstay its welcome, with the chorale theme splendidly sonorous at the opening, the drive and tension of the playing well maintained to the end.

Also well captured here is the lovely *Poème lyrique*, admired by Tchaikovsky for its rich flow of Russian melancholy. But what makes this Chandos disc so very attractive is the *Cantata in Memory of Pushkin's 100th Birthday*, which is full of warmly lyrical ideas. Glazunov's flow of invention more than compensates for the doggerel poetry he was forced to set by the Grand Duke Constantine Romanov. The work is framed and interlaced by splendid, powerfully sung and very Russian choruses of gratitude. There's a lovely 'Berceuse' for the mezzo, here radiantly sung by Ludmila Kuznetsova, who redeems its sentimentality; a later aria of praise for the tenor is relished by Vsevolod Grivnov; finally comes a hymn in which the two soloists join, exultantly taken up by

the chorus, with a burst of joy at the close. This one of those happy works, full of melody, that makes you feel glad to be alive. A truly memorable performance then, and the Chandos recording is well up to house standards.

Additional recommendation

Suite caractéristique. Le chant du destin.
Deux Préludes
Moscow SO / Golovschin
Naxos 8 553857 (75' · DDD)　　　⑤Ⓞ⮕
An appealing collection of lesser orchetsral works including the eight-movement *Suite caractéristique*, an orchestral transcription of piano pieces. It's all played impressively and well recorded.

Reinhold Glière
Ukraine/USSR 1875-1956

Glière studied at the Moscow Conservatory under Taneyev, Ippolitov-Ivanov and Arensky: he later became professor of composition there (1920-41). His works, in the Russian nationalistic tradition of Borodin and Glazunov, include three symphonies, concertos and ballets (notably The Red Flower), as well as operas on central Asian themes.

Symphonies

Symphony No 3, 'Il'ya Mouromets', Op 42
London Symphony Orchestra / Leon Botstein
Telarc CD80609 (72' · DDD)　　　Ⓕ Ⓞ⮕

Recognisably breathing the same air as Stravinsky's *Firebird*, Scriabin's *Poem of Ecstasy* and Suk's *Asrael* Symphony, Glière's *Il'ya Mouromets* makes up in lusciousness and sweep what it slightly lacks in individuality, offering a superb vehicle for the modern orchestra and, indeed, for state-of-the-art hi-fi systems. The LSO and Leon Botstein have the edge in almost every respect over rival performances. Comparable to Downes in his tempi, albeit with a rather fleeter-footed finale, Botstein is less insistent in his accentuation and more emotionally generous with his phrasing, so the overall effect is less strenuous, more sensuously appealing, with the climaxes standing in higher relief. The LSO, on terrific form, command a slighter wider range of nuance, and Telarc's recording is a degree or two more spacious, without ever feeling overblown. Altogether, a very collectable disc.

Mikhail Glinka
Russian 1804-1857

Coming from a monied family, Glinka was financially secure all his life. He had a job with the Ministry of Communications in St Petersburg for a few years and was made Master of the Imperial Chapel.

Otherwise he relied on his mother's generosity and was able to indulge his passion for music without the need to worry about where the next rouble was coming from. His health, though, was never strong and this gave him the excuse to travel to warmer climes for recuperation.

Along the way he picked up his musical education. He was a natural pianist and had a few lessons with John Field in St Petersburg; he took singing lessons in Italy where he bumped into Bellini, Donizetti and Mendelssohn; a famous German theorist called Dehn taught him composition in Berlin; he befriended Russian literary giants Pushkin and Gogol. In 1834, on the death of his father, he returned home to take care of his family's affairs.

This haphazard, unfocused development culminated in the writing of an opera which changed the course of Russian music and which in turn had a significant effect on all music. Glinka's aim was to write a thoroughly Russian work, patriotic and nationalistic. 'As if by magic,' he wrote, 'the plan of the whole opera and the idea of the antithesis of Russian and Polish music, as well a many of the themes and even details of the working-out – all this flashed into my head in one stroke.' A Life for the Tsar was the first opera written by a Russian to quote Russian folksongs, to take a Russian subject and to be concerned with the peasants instead of the nobility.

Glinka followed this with another opera, Ruslan and Lyudmila, but its music was too advanced for the Russians of the day and it was not a success. He was to compose nothing of equal importance again. Depressed by the reaction to Ruslan, he took himself off on a tour of France and Spain, collecting folk tunes and trying to learn Spanish. 'My feet were all right,' he said, 'but I couldn't manage the castanets.' After further adventures in Warsaw, St Petersburg and Paris, he eventually fetched up in Berlin where he had come to study Bach and choral music. There he caught a cold and died.

Orchestral Works

Capriccio brillante on the 'Jota aragonesa'. Souvenir d'une nuit d'été à Madrid. Symphony on Two Russian Themes. Overture in D. Kamarinskaya. Valse-fantaisie. Ruslan and Lyudmila – Overture; Dance; Chernomor's March
BBC Philharmonic Orchestra / Vassily Sinaisky
Chandos CHAN9861 (71' · DDD)   Ⓕ

This is a more comprehensive survey than that available on ASV with the Armenian Philharmonic under Loris Tjeknavorian. Both conductors include the two 'Spanish Overtures', the *Valse-fantaisie* and *Kamarinskaya* in closely matched performances. Sinaisky is rather faster and brighter in the first 'Spanish Overture', *Capriccio brillante on the Jota aragonesa*, and in the second, *Souvenir d'une nuit d'été*, he reflects more subtly the French grace that also lies within the music. Both conductors give good, vivid performances of the *Valse-fantaisie* and *Kamarinskaya*, with recordings that do justice to Glinka's brilliant orchestration. Thereafter the repertoire parts company. While Tjeknavorian gives

the rest of his record up to a suite of six pieces from *A Life for the Tsar*, Sinaisky prefers *Ruslan and Lyudmila*, with a lively performance of the Overture and then the Act 3 dances and the dwarf Chernomor's grotesque little march. This gives him room for the early Overture in D, which doesn't often feature on records, and for the *Symphony on Two Russian Themes*. The work survives in only a single movement, but fascinatingly anticipates *Kamarinskaya*. For a highly enjoyable introduction to Glinka's orchestral music, indeed to his whole original way of thinking, this Chandos disc is the one to go for.

Christoph Gluck   Bohemian 1714-1787

His father was a forester and, like Handel's, actively discouraged his son from playing any musical instruments when it was obvious that he had such a talent. Gluck left home at 18 and for the next 25 years flitted all over Europe in pursuit of his musical career: first to Prague where he supported himself by playing at dances and singing in churches, then to Vienna, afterwards (in 1737) to Milan. Here he studied with Sammartini, one of the first symphonic composers, and Gluck absorbed all there was to know about Italian opera. Four years later he had his first success with Artaserse and decided to move on to London. He met Handel there who liked him but couldn't stand his music. Gluck kept a portrait of Handel in his bedroom for the rest of his life.

He left London to travel the length and breadth of Europe for the next 15 years as a composer and conductor, tossing off operas in the Italian style and becoming more and more dissatisfied with what he was doing. Eventually, he married the daughter of a wealthy Viennese banker which made him financially independent. Then in 1760, famous and successful as he was, collaborating with two others, he wrote a ballet, Don Juan, based on Molière's play, which broke with convention – it was more human, more truthful and aspired to far greater dramatic effect than anything currently on offer. In 1762 one of his collaborators, the extraordinary playwright, critic and lottery organiser Ranieri de' Calzabigi, who was entirely in tune with Gluck's ideas, came up with the libretto of Orfeo ed Euridice. It did for opera what Don Juan had done for ballet. Audiences had heard nothing like it before.

Neither had musicians. Gluck was a perfectionist with an acute ear and simply would not tolerate sloppy playing. His abrupt manner and dictatorial demands made him the Toscanini of his day, insisting that players repeat passages 20 or 30 times until he was satisfied with the result.

In 1773 he visited Paris with his wife and adopted daughter, a fine singer. Here he composed Iphigénie en Aulide and also produced it, after long rehearsals in which he had to correct acting and vocal styles that had not altered since the days of Lully. It precipitated a furore among French musicians and commentators, rival composers and music lovers. Even Queen Marie Antoinette played a small part in the battle by coming to the defence of Gluck (before her marriage, he'd taught the Austrian princess singing and harpsichord). In the end, the powerful Italian clique headed by the composer Niccolò Piccinni was defeated and Gluck returned to Vienna triumphant, though greatly saddened by the premature death of his daughter.

Perhaps his own health persuaded him to remain in Vienna after 1779 for he had suffered several 'apoplectic seizures' – probably minor thromboses. Hailed throughout Europe as its leading musical master, Gluck survived for a further eight years until a final stroke killed him.

Opera Arias

Italian Arias　　　　　　　　　　　　P

Antigono – Berenice, che fai?. La clemenza di Tito – Tremo fra' dubbi miei; Ah, taci, barbaro…Come potesti, oh Dio!; Se mai senti spirarti sul volto. La corona – Quel chiaro rio. Ezio – Misera, dove son!…Ah! non son io che parlo. Il Parnaso confuso – Di questa cetra in seno. La Semiramide riconosciuta – Ciascun siegua il suo stile…Maggior follia

Cecilia Bartoli mez

Akademie für Alte Musik Berlin / Bernhard Forck

Decca 467 248-2DH (68' · DDD · T/t)　　F OOOD

This is something very much out of the ordinary. These eight arias, taken variously from Gluck's early operas (those preceding his 'reforms' that began with Orfeo in 1762) or his non-reform later ones, are almost wholly unfamiliar, but they have great power and character; and they're sung with an extraordinary emotional force and technical skill, not to say a sheer beauty of tone, that can't be matched by any other singer today. Cecilia Bartoli's range is formidable. In the first aria, from La clemenza di Tito, she sings with trumpet-like tone and brilliance of attack, throwing off wide-spanning arpeggios with evident abandon and dispatching coloratura with fluency and precision, each note articulated and perfectly tuned. The second, an elegantly pathetic little piece from the later Il Parnaso confuso, is a tour de force of delicate, tender pianissimo singing. The third, from Ezio, begins with an orchestral recitative of thrilling dramatic urgency and goes on to an aria of great passion. Bartoli is described as a mezzo-soprano here, and her voice does indeed chiefly lie in that range; but most of these are soprano arias, and she happily goes well above the stave – there's one slightly squally high C sharp in the first aria but she's usually pretty comfortable in her top register. The accompaniments are splendidly sensitive and alert. A quite outstanding disc that no one who loves fine singing can miss.

Gluck Paride ed Elena – O del mio dolce ardor.　P Orfeo ed Euridice – Che puro ciel!; Che farò senza Euridice. Alceste – Non vi turbate **Haydn** Il mondo della luna – Una donna come me. Orlando Paladino – Ad un sguardo, a un cenno solo. La fedeltà premiata – Deh soccorri un'infelice **Mozart** Le nozze di Figaro – Voi che sapete. Don Giovanni – Batti, batti; Vedrai,

carino; In quali eccessi…Mi tradì quell'alma ingrata. Lucio Silla – Dunque sperar…Il tenero momento. La finta giardiniera – Dolce d'amor compagna. La clemenza di Tito – Ecco il punto, oh Vitellia…Non più di fiori

Anne Sofie von Otter mez

The English Concert / Trevor Pinnock hpd

Archiv 449 206-2AH (71' · DDD · T/t)　　F OD

For the sake of both vocal and family well-being, Anne Sofie von Otter has always followed the wise course of self-rationing in opera. This disc, an entirely personal selection of arias from the Viennese Classical period, means all the more to her including, as it does, arias sung by dramatic and passionate women 'most of whom', she admits in the accompanying notes, 'I have never performed on stage and, alas, probably never will'. They include La clemenza di Tito's Vitellia, whom she has irresistibly observed in her own role as Sesto: here she at last voices her guilt at implicating Sesto in her crime of passion, and expresses that unique fusion of sadness and desperation of 'Non più di fiori' in the eloquent company of Colin Lawson's basset horn, followed by Gluck's Alceste, again keenly observed by von Otter in a comprimario role. Gluck's Orfeo is familiar to her at first hand, and here The English Concert's introduction to the recitative preceding 'Che farò' creates exquisitely the 'nuova serena luce' of the Elysian fields against which her grief is the darker, the more plangent. The Mozart arias evoke memorable stage and concert performances by von Otter: a Cherubino whose phrasing combines with that of the wind soloists to create the warm breath of burgeoning sensuality in 'Voi che sapete'; a Cecilio (Lucio Silla) whose coloratura captures the thrilled anticipation of that 'tenero momento'; and a moustachioed Ramiro (La finta giardiniera) who pays ecstatic cantabile tribute to the power of love.

Alceste

Alceste　　　　　　　　　　　　　　　P

Teresa Ringholz sop Alcestis **Justin Lavender** ten Admetus **Jonas Degerfelt** ten Evander **Miriam Treichl** sop Ismene **Lars Martinsson** bar Herald Voice of Apollo **Adam Giertz** treb Eumelo **Emilie Clausen** treb Aspasia **Johan Lilja** bass High Priest Hercules, God of the Underworld **Mattias Nilsson** bar Bandit **Drottningholm Court Theatre Chorus and Orchestra / Arnold Östman**

Naxos ③ 8 660066/8 (147' · DDD · T/t)　　S D

Almost all critics of Gluck's two versions of Alceste – the Italian original, first given in Vienna in 1767, and the French revision or recomposition given in Paris in 1776 – regard the latter as superior: musically richer, more flexible, dramatically more persuasive, deeper in its treatment of the emotions and the humanity of the two central characters. But this performance of the Italian version treats the 1767 text on its own terms. Like the original Orfeo, the original

Alceste is an opera pared down, in accordance with Gluck's and his librettist Calzabigi's reform principles, to deal with just a single issue: it's concerned exclusively with Alceste's sacrifice of her life to save that of her husband, Admeto, King of Thessaly, and the emotions that each of them and those around them feel. The performance is deftly paced and transparent in its textures. There's no portentousness about Öst-man's direction, and the Drottningholm orchestra ensures that the detail of accompanying textures is clearly heard, playing gently and lightly in the dances.

Teresa Ringholz has a voice of modest dimensions, which she uses in a natural way, with little vibrato, firm, surely tuned, clear and well focused. She catches Alceste's increasingly passionate determination, at the close of Act 1, as her resolution to die to save her husband hardens, with its magnificent climax in 'Ombre, larve'. Her controlled manner – there's no outburst of grief when she bids her children farewell at the end of the act, for example – catches well the stylised nature of Gluck's expression. Justin Lavender, as Admeto, is slightly less successful. He has a generous tenor – fuller and weightier than that of the other tenor, Jonas Degerfelt, who sings gracefully and also with vitality – and he brings to the music a good deal of passion that occasionally threatens to go beyond the scale of the performance as a whole. The smaller roles are very adequately done. This recording conveys effectively the intensity and the integrity of Gluck's vision.

Alceste
Janet Baker *mez* Alceste **Robert Tear** *ten* Admète
John Shirley-Quirk *bar* High Priest, Infernal God
Maldwyn Davies *ten* Evandre **Philip Gelling** *bar*
Herald, Apollo **Jonathan Summers** *bar* Hercules
Matthew Best *bass* Oracle
**Chorus and Orchestra of the Royal Opera House,
Covent Garden / Charles Mackerras**
Royal Opera House Records ② ROHS010 (146' · ADD
· N/T/t). Recorded live on December 12, 1981 Ⓜ❍❍

It is wonderful to have Janet Baker's deeply moving portrayal (her farewell to Covent Garden) made available after all these years – if only it were on DVD! The sombre overture sets the scene: the orchestra under Charles Mackerras is admirable, trombones well to the fore, the unnecessary harpsichord a minor irritatant. In the opening number some wobbly sopranos obtrude from time to time, but in general the choral contribution is excellent, albeit in rather occluded sound. However, the grand sweep of Gluck's design, the chorus's 'Ô Dieux! Qu'allons nous devenir?' and 'Ô malheureuse Admète!' framing Alcestis' solos, is weakened by the omission of a whole section. Other regrettable cuts include the powerful restatement of the chorus at the end of Act 2 and chunks of the final Chaconne.

Even more unsettling is the frequency with which, by Mackerras's sleight of hand, Alcestis'

music abruptly shifts down a tone or a semitone. The booklet article praises Dame Janet for her singing of 'the repeated ascents from sustained A flat to A natural', but that is not what we hear. This is a pity, because it vitiates Gluck's tonal scheme, and it's when she is straining at the top of her range that Baker is at her most thrilling. The air in question is certainly gripping; but 'Divinités du Styx', sung at pitch, is stupendous.

In the scene where Admetus learns that Alcestis is sacrificing herself for him, the dramatic force that Baker and Tear bring to the accompanied recitative is exemplary. Make no mistake: gripes notwithstanding, this recording should be in every opera lover's collection.

Armide

Armide   Ⓟ
Mireille Delunsch *sop* Armide **Charles Workman**
ten Renaud **Laurent Naouri** *bar* Hidraot **Ewa Podles**
mez Hate **Françoise Masset** *sop* Phénice, Mélisse
Nicole Heaston *sop* Sidonie, Shepherdess, Lucinde
Yann Beuron *ten* Artémidore, Danish Knight **Brett
Polegato** *bar* Ubalde **Vincent le Texier** *bar* Aronte
Magdalena Kožená *mez* Pleasure **Valérie Gabail**
sop Naiad **Choeur des Musiciens du Louvre; Les
Musiciens du Louvre / Marc Minkowski**
Archiv ② 459 616-2AH2 (139' · DDD · T/t) Ⓕ❍▶

'Perhaps the best of all my works', said Gluck of his *Armide*. But this, the fifth of his seven 'reform operas', has never captured the public interest as have *Orfeo*, *Alceste*, the two *Iphigénies* and even *Paride ed Elena*. Its plot is thinnish, concerned only with the love of the pagan sorceress Armide, princess of Damascus, for the Christian knight and hero Renaud, and his enchantment, disenchantment and finally his abandonment of her. But *Armide* has two features that set it apart. One is the extraordinary soft, sensuous tone of the music; Gluck said that it was meant 'to produce a voluptuous sensation', and that if he were to suffer damnation it would be for the passionate love duet in Act 5. Certainly his orchestral writing here has a warmth, a colour and a richness going far beyond anything in his other reform operas (apart from parts of *Paride ed Elena*). Second, there are several great solo dramatic scenes, two of them for Armide.

The success of *Armide*, then, depends critically on the Armide herself. Here it goes to Mireille Delunsch, who brings to it a good deal of intensity but doesn't have command of a wide range of tone, and doesn't seem to make much use of her words. There's some graceful singing in the softer music and the scene where she can't bring herself to kill Renaud is finely done, though ultimately perhaps her singing lacks real emotional tension. Renaud is sung by Charles Workman, in a strong tenor, sounding almost baritonal at times, but then singing the sleep song, 'Plus j'observe ces lieux', with soft, sweet tone and much delicacy. The lovers' duet in Act 5 is sung gently and with much charm.

Among the other singers, Ewa Podles makes a strong impression as Hate with her large and steady voice. And Laurent Naouri shows a pleasant, firm baritone as Hidraot.

Minkowski makes much of the score's colour and flow. He uses a substantial orchestra, which plays lightly and flexibly and with rhythmic spring. He has a tendency towards quickish tempos here and there but is always attentive to the characterisation of individual numbers.

Iphigénie en Aulide

Iphigénie en Aulide
Lynne Dawson sop Iphigénie **José van Dam** bass
Agamemnon **Anne Sofie von Otter** mez
Clytemnestre **John Aler** ten Achille **Bernard Deletré**
bass Patrocle **Gilles Cachemaille** bass Calchas **René**
Schirrer bass Arcas **Guillemette Laurens** mez Diane
Ann Monoyios sop First Greek Woman, Slave
Isabelle Eschenbrenner sop Second Greek Woman
Monteverdi Choir; Lyon Opéra Orchestra /
Sir John Eliot Gardiner
Erato ② 2292 45003-2 (132' · DDD · T/t)   ⒻⓄⓄ

Gluck's first reform opera for Paris has tended to be overshadowed by his other *Iphigénie*, the *Tauride* one. But it does contain some superb things, of which perhaps the finest are the great monologues for Agamemnon. On this recording, José van Dam starts a little coolly; but this only adds force to his big moment at the end of the second act where he tussles with himself over the sacrifice of his daughter and – contemplating her death and the screams of the vengeful Eumenides – decides to flout the gods and face the consequences. The cast in general is strong. Lynne Dawson brings depth of expressive feeling to all she does and her Iphigenia, marked by a slightly grainy sound and much intensity, is very moving. John Aler's Achilles too is very fine and sings both with ardour and vitality. There's great force too in the singing of Anne Sofie von Otter as Clytemnestra. Gardiner's Monteverdi Choir sings with polish, perhaps seeming a little genteel for a crowd of angry Greek soldiers baying for Iphigenia's blood. But he gives a duly urgent account of the score, pressing it forward eagerly and keeping the tension at a high level even in the dance music. A period-instrument orchestra might have added a certain edge and vitality but this performance wants nothing in authority. Securely recommended.

Iphigénie en Tauride

Iphigénie en Tauride   Ⓟ
Christine Goerke sop Iphigénie **Vinson Cole** ten
Pylade **Rodney Gilfry** bar Oreste **Sharon Baker** sop
First Priestess, Greek Woman **Jayne West** sop
Second Priestess, Diana **Stephen Salters** bar
Thoas **Mark Andrew Cleveland** sngr Scythian
Mark Risinger sngr Minister of the Sanctuary
Boston Baroque / Martin Pearlman
Telarc ② CD80546 (134' · DDD · T/t)   ⒻⓄⓄ

'With Gluck, there's a long sweep to the drama,' says Martin Pearlman towards the end of his introductory talk about *Iphigénie*, included here at the end of the second CD. It's obvious from his performance that this is how he sees the work; and it's his capacity to sustain that 'long sweep' that makes this version so compelling.

Pearlman, using period instruments, draws vivid and dramatic playing from his admirable group. He's particularly successful in the various dances in the course of the opera, which, beautifully alive and springy in rhythm, never permit the drama to flag, but emerge as an integral part of it, not as decorative interludes. With these clear textures, Gluck's orchestral colouring comes across sharply as, too, does the lofty, hieratic quality of the work. There's tenderness as well, and it's thanks partly to Pearlman's sensitive timing that the opera's climactic moment – the sacrifice scene, where brother and sister at last recognise each other – is so intense and poignant.

Although it lies quite high, the role of Iphigenia is often assigned to a mezzo, as if to heighten the intensity. Christine Goerke is a true soprano, which allows softer tones and more femininity than one generally hears, but there's metal in her voice, too (she doesn't altogether forgo vibrato), and the weight of the tragedy is by no means underplayed: listen to 'O malheureuse Iphigénie' – enhanced by the fine line of the oboe obbligato – or to her impassioned singing of the noble aria at the beginning of Act 4. Rodney Gilfry provides a strong, manly Orestes and is successful in conveying the tortures he's suffering. Vinson Cole gives a sympathetic reading of Pylades – lyrical, shapely and expressively phrased. There's excellent choral singing.

The principal rival recordings both have rather starrier casts. Muti's is a big, modern opera-house performance, powerful and exciting, Gardiner's more stylish, more concentrated dramatically. But this set is just about first choice.

Orfeo ed Euridice

Orfeo ed Euridice   Ⓟ
Bernarda Fink contr Orfeo **Veronica Cangemi** sop
Euridice **Maria Cristina Kiehr** sop Amore **Berlin**
RIAS Chamber Choir; Freiburg Baroque Orchestra
/ René Jacobs
Harmonia Mundi ② HMC90 1742/3 (91' · DDD · T/t) Ⓕ

Orfeo comes in many guises. There's Gluck's original Italian version, composed for Vienna in 1762, his adjusted version for Parma in 1769, his French revision of 1774 for Paris, and then the numerous, posthumous compromise texts that seek the best of both worlds by incorporating sections of the French version within the framework of the Italian. This version is 'pure' Italian, and although this means forgoing such famous and affecting music as the Dance of the Blessed Spirits, 'Cet asile' and the enhanced ending to

'Che farò', as well as the big D minor Dance of the Furies, it does offer a much more concentrated experience.

The tone of the performance is set by the highly energetic Overture, with its forceful accents and its sharply defined textures and dynamics. Jacobs takes pains throughout to give a clear yet also rich quality to Gluck's highly original orchestral textures and to shape his phrases with style and awareness of the omnipresence of dance. However, it's the singer of Orpheus, even more than the conductor, who gives character to a performance of this work. Often nowadays it's sung by a countertenor in preference to the contralto long favoured in the role, which was composed for a castrato anyway. So which voice better suits the semi-divine Orpheus? Ultimately it depends on the artistry of the singer. Bernarda Fink sings the role here very beautifully and quite unaffectedly. Her great strength lies in her smooth, natural and very even tone and her command of line.

This is probably the best version of the Italian original with a woman as Orpheus, and can be recommended without hesitation to anyone who prefers to avoid the male alto voice. If you prefer to stick with the male voice the choice lies between Michael Chance's beautifully sung version under Frieder Bernius (Sony) and Derek Lee Ragin's ardent impersonation in Gardiner's account; both are revealing, in quite different ways, of this very special work.

Orphée et Eurydice
Juan Diego Flórez ten Orphée **Ainhoa Garmendia** sop Eurydice **Alessandra Marianelli** sop L'Amour **Chorus and Orchestra of Teatro Real, Madrid / Jesús López-Cobos**
Decca ② 478 2197DH2 (105' · DDD)
Recorded live at the Teatro Real, Madrid, in 2008   Ⓕ

There is no question where the spotlight falls in this recording. The glorious Italianate tenor of Juan Diego Flórez is the centre of attention throughout and was clearly the *raison d'être* of the three concert performances which this recording is taken.

Gluck fashioned the 1774 Paris version of *Orphée et Eurydice* to be sung by an *haute-contre*, a specially high breed of tenor, of which Rousseau complained: 'It is not natural in a man's voice…[and] always has some harshness and is rarely in tune.' Needless to say, the high quality of Flórez's singing never falters for a second. There is no harshness to be heard and his intonation is never suspect. From the opening scene he sings the most aristocratic of *legato* lines, which are a constant source of pleasure, and as an ace Rossini tenor has the agility needed for the showpiece aria 'L'espoir renaît'.

Is he a moving Orphée? Yes and no. The clean-cut Italianate style, combined with the glowing ardour of his tenor, imbues Flórez's Orphée with a distinctive classical fire but the effect remains generalised. He rarely responds in detail to the shifting moods of the drama, at least until 'J'ai perdu mon Eurydice', where the involvement suddenly feels complete. His main tenor rivals on disc include Léopold Simoneau and Nicolai Gedda, and it was unwise of the booklet-notes to reproach them for transposing down parts of the role. Flórez himself takes 'Laissez-vous toucher' in Act 2 and the duet 'Viens, suis un époux' in Act 3 down a semitone. Like them, he is singing with a conventional orchestra at modern pitch and even with transpositions is almost certainly reaching higher – he hits a high C sharp briefly – than Gluck would have expected.

The rest of the cast do not let him down. Ainhoa Garmendia makes a warmly sympathetic Eurydice, Alessandra Marianelli a gleaming L'Amour, and the live recording – as these were concert performances, there are no stage bumps and bangs – is perfectly acceptable. Jesús López-Cobos has rehearsed his Madrid orchestra and chorus with care. Incidentally, the ending of the score is rearranged here, with Gluck's concluding Chaconne cut and the ensemble 'L'Amour triomphe' moved to the end. The message is clear: Flórez, as the star of the evening, was needed to provide the final flourish, and that remains just as true of this recording.

Orphée et Eurydice
Magdalena Kožená ten Orphée **Madeline Bender** sop Eurydice **Patricia Petibon** sop L'Amour **Monteverdi Choir; Orchestre Révolutionnaire et Romantique / Sir John Eliot Gardiner**
Stage director **Robert Wilson**
Video director **Brian Large**
EMI *DVD* 216577-9 (100' · NTSC · 16:9 · PCM Stereo and DTS 5.0 · 0)   Ⓕ

Alceste
Anne Sofie von Otter mez Alceste **Paul Groves** ten Admète **Dietrich Henschel** bar High Priest, Hercules **Yann Beuron** ten Evandre **Ludovic Tézier** bar Herald, Apollo **Frédéric Caton** bass Oracle, Infernal God **Hjördis Thébault** mez Coryphée **Monteverdi Choir; English Baroque Soloists / Sir John Eliot Gardiner**
Stage director **Robert Wilson**
Video director **Brian Large**
EMI *DVD* 216570-9 (134' · NTSC · 16:9 · PCM stereo and DTS 5.0 · 0)   Ⓕ

Orphée et Eurydice is performed in the arrangement that Berlioz made in 1859 for the French mezzo-soprano Pauline Viardot. He based it on the later, Paris, version of the opera, but restored the part of Orpheus to the alto tessitura of the original. His influence can also be detected in this recording of *Alceste*, an opera which likewise exists in two versions: incensed at the way the brass interjections in 'Ombre, larve' were obscured by the extra notes required for 'Divinités du Styx', Berlioz proposed a simple change to 'Ombres, larves'; and his suggestion is adopted here by John Eliot Gardiner. You won't find it in the documentation accompanying the DVDs, because there isn't any. No synopsis, no background articles, no timings; not even a list of 'chapters', except on-screen. And some detailed help is necessary, because the purchaser, in the case of *Orphée et Eurydice*, is getting neither pure Gluck nor pure Gluck/Berlioz.

Robert Wilson's production of *Orphée et Eurydice* is spare, bordering on minimalist. A blue background; cypresses in Act 1; a rock in the bleak Elysian Fields. There are some striking stage pictures, such as Orpheus silhouetted during the Dance of the Furies (another Gardiner restoration, not in fact danced), and the couple positioned on different levels in Act 3. The acting is more movement and gesture than facial expression: effective as far as it goes, but the Blessed Spirits look pretty miserable. One miscalculation is the failure to show Orpheus disobeying the gods' commands by turning to look at Eurydice, thereby bringing about her second death. Magdalena Kožená, then virtually unknown, sings Orpheus superbly, including the bravura air in Act 1 (orchestrated, incidentally, by Saint-Saëns). The latter is remarkable for the cadenza, a joint effort by Berlioz, Saint-Saëns and Viardot herself. Madeline Bender and Patricia Petibon have much less to do, they do it well, but Petibon is not helped by the variable sound quality.

The two operas are connected by a suspended cube which, seen at the end of *Orphée et Eurydice*, reappears in the overture to *Alceste* and many times thereafter. The chorus is heard but not seen: a cop-out, surely, but the dancers replacing the singers on stage provide an unforgettable image when they appear, arms upraised, between the columns of the temple. Silhouette again, and gesture, too. Anne Sofie von Otter, severe, hair scraped back, is the picture of regal dignity at her first appearance. Later, unable to look at the husband for whom she is sacrificing her life, her pain is palpable; at the end, after Apollo has descended with the reprieve, the camera focuses on the gentle smile that she permits herself.

The sharp-eyed will have noticed that two orchestras are employed: same players, different pitch. Even at the lower pitch, some of *Alceste*'s music is transposed down. If von Otter is almost unbearably moving in the duets with Admetus, perhaps her finest moment is her scene, alone and terrified, at the entrance to Hades. Paul Groves as Admetus is almost as eloquent, and Dietrich Henschel, swinging an imaginary club, makes a hearty, no-nonsense Hercules. Both discs are well worth investigating.

Additional recommendations

Orfeo ed Euridice (abridged recording)　🅗
Ferrier Orfeo **Ayars** Euridice **Vlachopoulos** Amor
**Glyndebourne Festival Chorus; Southern
Philharmonic Orchestra / Stiedry**　🆂🅾
Dutton mono CDBP9730 (63' · ADD). Recorded 1947
Though the sound may initially prove a little distracting, Dutton have done their best to clean it up, and Ferrier's singing more than makes up for it.

Its beauty goes straight to the heart: a noble and intensely human Orfeo which deserves its place on every collector's shelves.

Orfeo ed Euridice
Baker Orfeo **Speiser** Euridice **Gale** Amor **LPO /
Leppard**
Erato ② 2292 45864-2　🅜🅞
A wonderful memento of Baker's Orfeo, a glorious characterisation with its ardent, heartfelt emotional response. Strong, sinuous accompaniment from Leppard.

Vladímir Godár　Slovak b1956

A musician of extraordinarily broad musical sympathies, Godár is one of Slovakia's most respected. A scholar as well as a composer, he works in film as well as in 'classical' repertoire. He is a great admirer of the music of Béla Bartók and has a comparable fascination with folk music – something that has emerged through his musical collaborations with singer Iva Bittová.

Choral works

'Mater'
Stálá matka (Stabat mater). Magnificat.
Maykomashmalon. Uspávanky (Lullabies).
Ecce puer. Regina coeli
Iva Bittová voc **Bratislava Conservatory Choir;
Solamente Naturali / Marek Štryncl**
ECM New Series 476 5689 (57' · DDD · T/t)　🅟🅑➔

To say that Vladímir Godár is a typical ECM discovery is certainly not to diminish either him or ECM. This Slovak composer uses a vocabulary in the works recorded here that will inevitably recall Górecki, and also at times Pärt and Tavener, though the music's emotional intensity, the particular way in which repetition is used and the use of certain sonorities and chords, relate much more to the Polish composer than the other two, very noticeably in the *Stabat mater*; aficionados of these composers will certainly enjoy what is recorded here. But though the music may recall them, it does not sound like any of them for any length of time: Godár has his own way of saying what he wants to say, which is, for him, intimately connected with what he calls 'musical archaeology', specifically Slovak culture, musical, literary and religious.

Thus there are works that draw upon Slovak translations of the *Magnificat* and *Stabat mater*, traditional lullabies, a Latin *Regina coeli* and, rather oddly, a single poem by James Joyce. The *Magnificat* is based very simply on the immediately recognisable first tone, for solo voice and dark string underpinning, but is interrupted by massive choral interjections of the word 'Magnificat' at its climax – a simple but effective device. There are conscious references to the Baroque at various points but folk monody – the archetypal lullaby of the mother – is what really holds all this material together.

Godár's transparent but strong style is greatly helped in this by the powerfully raw voice of the amazing Iva Bittová, but also by the precision of Solamente Naturali and the Bratislava choir.

Benjamin Godard   French 1849-1895

At the age of 10 he was enrolled at the Paris Conservatoire and although he was considered a child prodigy as a violinist, he did not win any prizes at the Conservatoire, and his submissions in 1863 and 1864 for the Prix de Rome were unsuccessful. A prodigious worker, he soon began to establish a reputation as a composer in Germany and Spain as well as in France. Godard composed works in most genres with the exception of church music, but ultimately he made his reputation as a composer of salon pieces for piano and of songs, albums of which were translated into English. His early promise did not really develop in his later works, although his early death from consumption meant that he had no chance to mature fully as a composer.

Concertante Violin Works

Concerto romantique, Op 35ª. Violin Concerto No 2, Op 131ª. Scènes poétiques, Op 46
ªChloë Hanslip vn Slovak State Philharmonic Orchestra, Košice / Kirk Trevor
Naxos 8 570554 (66' · DDD)   ⑤➔

Benjamin Godard was a prolific, fluent composer in many genres, but little of his output is familiar today. A string player (he'd been a pupil of Henri Vieuxtemps), he writes for the violin with great panache, and Chloë Hanslip is in her element, making the most of the showy passagework, enjoying finding the right tone of voice for the different styles of melody – elegiac, sensuous or graceful – and attacking with passion the dramatic recitatives that join the movements of the *Concerto romantique*. The orchestral writing in both concertos is full of colour, if occasionally rather brash, and is performed here with considerable dash and spirit. There are some delightful solo contributions from oboe, clarinet and viola, in dialogue with the violin, during the little *Canzonetta* that separates the slow movement and finale of the *Concerto romantique*. Neither concerto comes near to rivalling Bruch or Tchaikovsky, but Godard is a skilful composer; it's music that's formally satisfying, consistently entertaining and sometimes memorable and touching. Hanslip, who's to be congratulated for taking on such unfamiliar repertoire, seizes on these high-spots – the second theme in Op 131's first movement, the moment in Op 35's sombre *Adagio* when the first turn to the major is made – and finds just the right colour to emphasise

Godard's happy thought. The *Scènes poétiques* are really salon music transposed to the concert hall. Kirk Trevor and the orchestra relish the imaginative instrumental colouring, though the performance sounds a little like music learnt in the studio, rather than familiar from many concert outings.

Leopold Godowsky
Polish/American 1870-1938

An American pianist and composer of Polish birth, Godowsky toured widely from the age of nine, making his American debut in Boston in 1884. Tours of the USA and Canada followed and until 1900 he taught in Philadelphia and Chicago. Until the Second World War he continued to appear in Europe; his reputation as a Chopin interpreter was not enhanced by a series of elaborate Studies on the Etudes. His concert career ended in 1930.

Studies

53 Studies on Chopin's Etudes
Marc-André Hamelin pf
Hyperion ② CDA67411/2 (158' · DDD)   Ⓕ〇〇〇➔

Godowsky's 53 studies on Chopin's 27 studies are the *ne plus ultra* of Romantic intricacy. Godowsky's wily disclaimer that, far from wanting to 'improve' on Chopin's matchless originals, he merely wished to extend the parameters of technique, hardly convinces purists, who dismiss his *magnum opus* as an outrageous gilding of the lily, an unforgivable powdering and rouging of Chopin's genius. For others, Godowsky's ingenuity, his ear-tickling wit and elegance, create edifices, indeed 'miracles of rare device'. But if heated debate still rages around the music, the quality of Hamelin's recording is entirely uncontroversial. Rarely can such a gargantuan task have been accomplished with such strength, grace and agility, with an ease bordering on nonchalance. His virtuosity is pre-eminent because it's so musical, and it's impossible to think of another living pianist who could have carried off this enterprise with comparable success. In lesser hands these *Etudes* can seem overweight; with Hamelin, even the densest, seemingly impenetrable textures are kept as light as air and everything is mobile, fluent and adroit. And so, to evoke Schumann, it's 'hats off, gentlemen' to this handsomely presented and finely recorded set. A truly phenomenal achievement.

Godowsky 53 Studies on Chopin Etudes –
Op 10 Nos 1, 2 (2nd version), 4, 5 (2 versions), 6, 11 & 12; Op 25 Nos 1 (3rd version), 2 (2nd version) & 9. Triakontameron – No 11, Alt Wien. Waltz, Op 64 No 1
Chopin Etudes – Op 10 Nos 1, 2, 4, 5, 6 & 12; Op 25 Nos 1 & 5
Boris Berezovsky pf

Warner Classics 2564 62258-2 (55' · DDD)
Recorded live 2005　　　　　Ⓕ**OOO**⯈

Here, uniquely, you can hear Chopin and Chopin-Godowsky side by side, marvelling or shuddering at the way Chopin's original is turned topsy-turvy and transformed into 'something rich and strange'. Recorded live, Boris Berezovsky's performances of eight of Chopin's Studies and 11 of Godowsky's arrangements beggar description.

No more formidable young pianist exists and his stunning recital balances prodigies of virtuosity with an unfaltering musical integrity. His Op 10 No 1 study is *maestoso* indeed, and never more so than when Godowsky's massive carillon of sound is embellished with a counterpoint as imperious as the last trump. Chopin's originals are always musically rather than sensationally characterised, the reverse of, say, Cziffra's dazzling if infamous distortions, yet Berezovsky's way with Op 10 No 5 is of a rollicking bravura that few could equal.

In the left-hand-only studies his tone conjures up Neuhaus's description of Gilels, 'rich in noble metal, a 24 carat gold that we find in the voices of the great singers' and, throughout, you are also reminded of Shakespeare's words: 'O, it is excellent / To have a giant's strength, but it is tyrannous / To use it like a giant.' Here, caught 'on the wing', there is none of that diffidence that occasionally affects Berezovsky when at his least concentrated but rather playing in the grandest of grand Russian traditions.

For encores there are *Alt Wien*, as warm and affectionate as Cherkassky though without a trace of whimsy, and Godowsky's teasing elaboration of the *Minute* Waltz. Heard on this form Berezovsky is the pianist of your dreams; and it only remains to add that he plays the third rather than the second version of Op 25 No 1 and that Warner's sound is superb. Prolonged applause celebrates Berezovsky's phenomenal achievement.

J Strauss II/Godowsky Symphonic Metamorphis on Künsterleben. Symphonic Metamorphosis on Wein, Weib und Gesang. Symphonic Metamorphosis on Die Fledermaus **Godowsky** Walzermasken – Pastell; Französisch; Wienerisch; Portrait: Joh Str. Triakontameron – Rendezvous; Alt Wien; Terpsichorean Vindobona; The Salon; Memories. **O Strauss/Godowsky** The Last Waltz
Marc-André Hamelin pf
Hyperion CDA67626 (69' · DDD)　　　Ⓕ**OO**

Here's another release that testifies to Hamelin's cultured musicianship, extraordinary keyboard proficiency and unflappable tonal control. His key assets include the most together, impeccably voiced chords in the business, plus octaves, trills and rapid leaps that remain effortlessly even and focused, regardless of tempo.

All of this comes into delightful play over the course of the three big Strauss *Symphonic Metamorphoses*. Countless inner voices and contrapuntal rejoinders abound in these works, and Hamelin makes them audible and clear without resorting to the pianistic equivalent of red-ink underlining or pop-up windows. Furthermore, Hamelin is a seasoned and subtle orchestrator at the piano; notice how he achieves such eloquent shading of simultaneous *legato* and detached phrases with no more help from the sustain pedal than is necessary.

One could argue that Godowsky's pinpoint tempo modifications throughout *Wein, Weib und Gesang* might benefit from stronger characterisation, in the manner of Shura Cherkassky's admittedly more capricious Decca recording, although Hamelin eschews the older pianist's cuts; in fact, Hamelin plays all three *Metamorphoses* complete, as written. As it happens, the less demanding shorter selections from *Walzermasken*, *Triakontameron* and *The Last Waltz* inspire some of Hamelin's most poetic, lyrically inspired playing on disc.

All told, a stellar achievement, graced by Hyperion's close-up yet ample engineering, plus Godowsky biographer Jeremy Nicholas's thoroughly informative and penetrating annotations.

Heiner Goebbels　　　　　German b1952

Goebbels's compositions reflect his interests in theatre, noise, jazz, rock and critical views of the concert hall. His works have been much influenced by film, montage being a favourite technique; in Surrogate Cities, for example, a recording of Jewish chant is superimposed on the symphony orchestra. The ballet Red Run, which includes sections of improvised material and choreography for the musicians, was the first of several compositions on which Goebbels collaborated with the Ensemble Modern. He has also directed his own theatre and radio plays, frequently setting texts by Heiner Müller. He won the Prix Italia for the third time in 1996 for his radio play Roman Dogs.

Landschaft mit entfernten Verwandten

Landschaft mit entfernten Verwandten
Georg Nigl bar **David Bennet** voc **German Chamber Choir; Ensemble Modern / Franck Ollu**
ECM New Series 476 5383 (80' · DDD)　　Ⓕ**OO**

Heiner Goebbels has gone a considerable way to redefining what is possible in the theatrical sphere. First seen at Geneva in 2002, this work (its title translates as 'Landscape with Distant Relatives') is the first that he has called an 'opera', though his use of the term characteristically fights shy of overt historical associations. A diverse range of sources is utilised, the main ones being Gertrude Stein's 1945 *Wars I Have Seen* and poems by Henri Michaux – largely from the late 1940s – which provide a specific temporal and cultural framework.

Within this framework, Goebbels arranges his texts so they become 'objects' to be encountered over a two-part journey – and with an emphasis on parallels between concepts of war from the Renaissance and modern eras. Predictably, the composer casts his stylistic net wide – but apart from a couple of misfires, inclusion of such as Moroccan dance and Bollywood film musics with spirituals and 'down-home' Americana is as thought-provoking as it is engaging.

The performance is as involving as one would expect, but while it is no hardship that the texts are included only in their original language, the visual dimension is absent. This is a pity, as stills reproduced in the booklet make one hanker after a DVD presentation. As a soundtrack, however, this disc makes for an engrossing experience.

Osvaldo Golijov
Argentinian/Israeli b1960

Golijov grew up in an Eastern European Jewish household in La Plata, Argentina. After studying piano at the local conservatory and composition with Gerardo Gandini he moved to Israel in 1983, where he studied with Mark Kopytman at the Jerusalem Rubin Academy. Upon moving to the United States in 1986, Golijov earned his PhD at the University of Pennsylvania, where he studied with George Crumb, and was a fellow at Tanglewood, studying with Oliver Knussen. Golijov was one of the composers commissioned by the Internationale Bachakademie Stuttgart to write pieces for the Passion 2000 project in commemoration of JS Bach. Golijov's contribution was La Pasión según San Marcos (The Passion according to St Mark).

He has also composed for the Kronos Quartet and the St Lawrence Quartet, classical and Klezmer clarinetist David Krakauer and soprano Dawn Upshaw, who performed premieres of his opera Ainadamar. He composed for Francis Ford Coppola's movies Youth Without Youth and Tetro.

Oceana

Oceana[a]. Tenebrae[b]. Three Songs[c]
[c]**Luciana Souza** voc [c]**Dawn Upshaw** sop [a]**Elizabeth Remy Johnson** hp [a]**Jamie Haddad** perc [a]**Jay Anderson** db [a]**Scott Tennant**, [a]**John Dearman** gtrs [b]**Kronos Quartet**; [a]**Gwinnet Young Singers**; [ac]**Atlanta Symphony** [a]**Chorus and Orchestra / Robert Spano**
DG 477 6426GH (61' · DDD)   Ⓕ🄳➔

With its boldly flavoured mix of styles, Golijov's *Oceana* (1996) looks forward to the *St Mark Passion* (2000) – the work that put him on the musical map. The solo part was written for renowned Brazilian jazz singer Luciana Souza whose solos range from impassioned invocation to angular yet elegant breeziness. The choral part is of equal prominence, however, and some of it sounds surprisingly reminiscent of Philip Glass. The final section, 'Chorale of the Reef', makes the most powerful effect, with mesmeric, over-

lapping phrases, chant-like rhythms and darkly radiant harmonies. The Atlanta Chorus sing it with rapt conviction.

Oceana ebbs away to haunting silence, providing a natural segue to *Tenebrae* (2002), a lament for string quartet that somehow smiles through its tears. Generous arcs of slow-moving melody – often with trembling accompaniment – evoke the great Renaissance masters. Golijov introduces earthier elements – exotic scales, anxious heartbeats, flickering firelight – and the work comes full circle, concluding with a consoling meditation on a hopeful cadential gesture. Kronos, the dedicatees, give a heartfelt performance.

The Three Songs are drawn from diverse sources. 'Night of the Flying Horses' is adapted from Golijov's music for Sally Potter's film *The Man Who Cried*. The drop-dead gorgeous lullaby Dawn Upshaw intones at the beginning echoes Bizet's 'Je crois entendre encore' (an aria featured in the film), while the rhapsodic instrumental conclusion is inspired by Balkan gypsy band music. 'Lua descolorida' is yet another demonstration of Golijov's gift for melody – and for establishing an other-worldly atmosphere through the simplest means. Upshaw rightly describes it as the saddest C major song she knows. 'How slow the wind' (Emily Dickinson) taps into a vein of Mahlerian sorrow while ravishing the ear. Upshaw's love for this music is palpable in every bar, and Spano and the Atlanta Symphony provide firm yet supple emotional support. Absolutely not to be missed.

Ainadamar

Ainadamar
Dawn Upshaw sop Margarita Xirgu **Jessica Rivera** mez Nuria **Jesús Montoya** voc Ruiz Alonso (Arresting officer) **Eduardo Chama** voc José Tripaldi (Guard) **Sean Mayer** voc Maestro **Robb Asklof** voc Torero **Kelley O'Connor** voc Federico García Lorca **Atlanta Symphony Chorus and Orchestra / Robert Spano**
DG 477 6165GH (80' · DDD · N/T/t)   Ⓕ🄾➔

Osvaldo Golijov has based this dramatic work around the life and death (at the hands of a Franco-ist Civil War firing squad) of the Spanish poet Federico García Lorca. *Ainadamar* (the 'fountain of tears', the Moorish name for the site near Grenada where Lorca died in 1936) is neither history nor fiction, rather a symbolic account of reactions to key moments in the poet's life.

The text, translated back into Spanish by the composer, suits Golijov's eclectic and anarchic mix of musics. At the start you hear low pedal notes similar to those that launch *Das Rheingold* or *Also sprach Zarathustra*. Within minutes we are closer to 'prog-rock' tracks of the 1970s like Led Zeppelin's *Kashmir* – a meeting of classical strings and heavy-metal beat – or the soundscapes, featuring combinations of riffs and sound effects (here horses' hooves or, chillingly in context, echoing gunshots), of Roger Waters. From a vocal point of view the score is deeply stained by alternations of the Jewish chants of Golijov's mother religion, the *cante jondo* of the flamenco of Lorca's homeland, or the Argentinian tangos worked up to symphonic proportions by Piazzolla and his contemporaries. American minimalism (of the John Adams variety) has left its mark too in the obsessive use of repetitive cells or phrases.

The effect is compelling: these words and scenes cry out for music, and Golijov delivers in full measure. While the whole is anchored to a subject of emotional power – Lorca, freakishly like Pushkin, almost seemed to anticipate and prepare his own fate – the lack of a conventional narrative is a great plus. Like the controversial *Mass* of Leonard Bernstein, *Ainadamar* is part lament and part celebration, an action of the mind rather than of dramatic events. The comfortable-sounding recording originates in performances by the characteristically adventurous Roberto Spano and the Atlanta SO; not all the cast are as famous as Golijov's champion Dawn Upshaw but they partner her well in few-holds-barred commitment.

Nicolas Gombert   Flemish c1495-c1560

Probably a native of Flanders and possibly a pupil of Josquin (he composed a déploration on Josquin's death, 1545), Gombert was a singer (from 1526) and maître des enfants (from 1529) in Emperor Charles V's court chapel, with which he travelled in Europe and for which he also served unofficially as composer. He was canon of Notre Dame, Tournai, by 1534. By 1540 he had been dismissed from the imperial chapel but was probably pardoned (and granted a benefice) around 1552. Highly regarded by his contemporaries as a great innovator, he favoured dense textures and often used dark, rich timbres. He used pervading imitation more consistently than anyone of his own or an earlier generation, creating textures in which the voices tend to be equally important. All but two of his 10 extant Masses elaborate existing motets or chansons. His motets (over 160 survive) are his most representative works, each phrase of text having its own expressive motif worked through the texture. Other sacred works include eight fine Magnificats and multi-voice works. His chansons (over 70) are like the Netherlands motet only more animated and often conceived on a broad scale. His music continued to be printed until long after his death.

Motets

Ave Maria. Virgo sancta Catherina. Inviolata, integra, et casta es, Maria. Tribulatio et angustia. Hortus conclusus es. Aspice Domine quia facta est. Ne reminiscaris, Domine. Pater noster. Ave sanctissima Maria a 5. Ergone vitae
Brabant Ensemble / Stephen Rice
Hyperion CDA67614 (66' · DDD · T/t)   Ⓕ**OO**▷

This is the first disc to focus on the core of Gombert, his motets. What we know of his troubled life and extant music suggests that he

was not a '*Laetentur coeli*' sort of composer, and so the opening *Tribulatio et angustia* is well chosen, being both one of the finest of them and setting the mood for the rest. Barely a minute has passed before the first of many dark spots of extreme and focused dissonance, yet such harmonic knots never tie up the line. Indeed it's one of very few discs of this repertoire you can happily play in its entirety.

This is in part a tribute to Gombert, who went to the well so often and never returned empty-handed; but also to the Brabant Ensemble and Stephen Rice, who researched Gombert's motets for a doctorate. Rice believes in a largely steady *tactus*, which certainly suits the reflective nature of these works, but by encouraging an unusually individual and carefully balanced vocal response, he avoids the pitfalls of relentless consistency (the Tallis Scholars) and arrided elision (one-per-part groups like Henry's Eight and the Hilliard Ensemble). There is a welcome and (in this music) novel belief in the power of voices as voices rather than instrumental simulacra: try the sopranos halfway through *Hortus conclusus est* for erotic Mariolatry at its most disconcertingly sensual. Arise, make haste, as they sing, and hear this music.

Eugene Goossens   English 1893-1962

Born in London, Goossens started his musical education at the age of 10, spending a year at the Bruges Conservatory. After his return to England he gained a Liverpool Scholarship to the RCM (1907), where his professors included Stanford for composition. His contemporaries Benjamin, Bliss and Howells became his lifelong friends. He played the viola in Beecham's Queen's Hall Orchestra, attracting the conductor's attention and becoming his assistant. He played in the British concert premiere of Stravinsky's The Rite of Spring. He made his conducting debut at an RCM public concert with his first composition, Variations on a Chinese Theme. Goossens's success as a conductor may have overshadowed his prowess as a composer. Among his works as a composer are two symphonies (1940, 1945), two string quartets, two violin sonatas and a 'concertino' for octet among other chamber music. He wrote two operas; Don Juan de Manara was broadcast by the BBC in 1959.

Orchestral Works

Symphony No 1, Op 58. Phantasy Concerto, Op 60ᵃ
ᵃ**Howard Shelley** pf **Melbourne Symphony Orchestra / Richard Hickox**
Chandos ⊛ CHSA5068 (65' · DDD/DSD)   Ⓕ**O**▷

As swansongs go, this striking coupling of two of Sir Eugene Goossens's meatiest large-scale offerings under the baton of the late Richard Hickox really is something to cherish. The epic First Symphony of 1938-40 has not lacked passionate advocacy on disc but Hickox is more realistically recorded than any and draws argu-ably the most finely groomed orchestral play-ing. No one coming to this ambitious canvas for the first time could fail to be struck by Hickox's excitingly committed and typically red-blooded handling of what is a most impos-ing and rewarding creation.

The *Phantasy Concerto* dates from 1942 and this would appear to be its first commercial record-ing. Inspired in part by 'the fantastic and sinister character' of Edgar Allan Poe's *The Devil in the Belfry* and written for the Spanish pianist José Iturbi, it's an attractively spicy, densely plotted score in four linked movements lasting just over 25 minutes, in which the piano largely eschews ostentatious display in favour of a more *concer-tante* role ('conversational' was how Goossens described it). Howard Shelley is the fearless soloist and he receives alert support from Hickox and the Melbourne SO. Eminently truthful sound, too, with an astutely judged bal-ance throughout.

Henryk Górecki   Polish b1933

Górecki studied at the Katowice Conservatory (1955-60) and with Messiaen in Paris. His works of the 1950s and early 1960s were influenced by mod-ernist trends and spoke in a similar language to that of Nono, Penderecki and Stockhausen, but gradually his style became sparer and more minimal, and often drew on a sacred theme or text. His Third Symphony of 1976 was rediscovered in the early 1990s and put Górecki squarely on the musical map. Of the astounding success of the Nonesuch recording, Górecki commented: 'Perhaps people find something they need in this piece of music…somehow I hit the right note, something they were missing. Something somewhere had been lost to them. I feel that I instinc-tively knew what they needed.'

Symphonies

Symphony No 2, 'Copernican', Op 31ª.
Beatus vir, Op 38
ªZofia Kilanowicz sop Andrezej Dobber bar
Silesian Philharmonic Choir; Polish Radio Choir;
Polish National Radio Symphony Orchestra /
Antoni Wit
Naxos 8 555375 (67' · DDD)   ⓈⒹ▸

Górecki composed his Second Symphony in 1972 in response to a commission to mark the 500th anniversary of the birth of the Polish astronomer Nicolas Copernicus. It possesses a certain Janus-like quality in that it forms a bridge between his earlier 'modernist' works and his later 'reductionist' style, into which the ubiquitous Third Symphony falls. The Second Symphony comprises two movements, the first glancing back to the dissonance of earlier works, the second looking forward to more tonal pas-tures in which the seeds of the Third Symphony

are in abundant evidence. Górecki's *Copernican* Symphony is an unsung masterpiece, and a greater and more impressively constructed work than the Third.

Beatus vir was composed in 1977 in response to a commission to mark the 900th anniversary of the martyrdom of the Bishop of Cracow, Stanisław of Szczepanów. The opening pages are particularly striking and there are some mar-vellously scored moments in the remaining 24 minutes or so, though it doesn't attain the stat-ure of the Second Symphony. That said, this disc is thoroughly recommended to anyone wanting to expand their appreciation of Górecki beyond the Third. The *Copernican* Symphony more than justifies the price of the disc alone and the performances and recorded sound through-out are exceptionally fine.

Symphony No 3, 'Symphony of Sorrowful Songs',
Op 36
Dawn Upshaw sop **London Sinfonietta /
David Zinman**
Nonesuch 7559 79282-2 (54' · DDD)   Ⓕ〇〇〇Ⓓ▸

Górecki's Third Symphony has become leg-end. Composed in 1976, it's always had its champions and admirers within the contempo-rary music world, but in 1993 it found a new audience of undreamt-of proportions. A few weeks after its release, this Elektra Nonesuch release not only entered the top 10 in the clas-sical charts, but was also riding high in the UK pop album charts. It became the biggest selling disc of music by a contemporary classical com-poser.

The Symphony, subtitled *Symphony of Sorrow-ful Songs*, was composed during a period when Górecki's musical style was undergoing a radical change from avant-garde serialism to a more accessible style firmly anchored to tonal tradi-tions. The Symphony's three elegiac move-ments (or 'songs') form a triptych of laments for all the innocent victims of the Second World War and are a reflection upon man's inhumanity to man in general. The songs are beautifully and ethereally sung by Dawn Upshaw, and David Zinman and the London Sinfonietta provide an intense and committed performance of the shimmering orchestral writing. The recording quality is excellent.

Additional recommendation

Symphony No 3
Coupled with Three Pieces in Old Style
Kilanowicz sop **Katowice RSO / Wit**
Naxos 8 550822   Ⓢ〇〇Ⓓ▸
    This recording is virtually as good as the better-known Zinman version. The performance is exceptionally fine, although the acoustic is more resonant, the orchestral choirs less closely balanced and Antoni Wit isn't as meticulous as Zinman in his observance of minor details. Interpretatively, Wit leaves the more austere impression.

Kleines Requiem für eine Polka

Kleines Requiem für eine Polka, Op 66[a]. Harpsichord Concerto, Op 40[b]. Good Night, 'In memoriam Michael Vyner', Op 63
Dawn Upshaw sop **Sebastian Bell** fl
John Constable pf **Elisabeth Chojnacka** hpd
David Hockings perc **London Sinfonietta /**
[a]**David Zinman,** [b]**Markus Stenz**
Nonesuch 7559 79362-2 (59' · DDD)　　Ⓕ●Ⓞ↦

Like a small café huddled within the shadow of some ancient church, Górecki's *Kleines Requiem für eine Polka* (1993) evokes feelings of paradox. The opening movement suggests distracted tranquillity. This is followed by a grating *Allegro* which approximates the sort of vicious 'knees-up' that Shostakovich penned whenever he bared his teeth at empty celebration. Later, we're back within the tranquil interior of Górecki's imagination – and it's there that we stay.

The *Kleines Requiem für eine Polka* displays a profundity expressed via the simplest means. It's a pity, then, that the Harpsichord Concerto breaks the mood so quickly: one's initial impression is of a further violent 'episode' from the first work, although the stylistic contrast breaks the illusion soon enough. This is probably the most famous 20th-century harpsichord concerto after Falla's. Bach served as its creative prime mover, while Elisabeth Chojnacka is its dedicatee and most celebrated interpreter. Here she revels in the piece's playful aggression. It's an unrelenting display and in total contrast to *Good Night*, Górecki's deeply felt memorial to one of his staunchest supporters, Michael Vyner. The language is sombre, but never merely mournful. Mostly quiet and contemplative, *Good Night* is scored for alto flute, piano and tam-tam with Dawn Upshaw intoning Hamlet's 'flights of angels' in the closing movement. The work ends in a spirit of veiled ritual with a sequence of quiet gong strokes. The performance and recording are consistently fine.

Additional recommendation

Miserere, Op 44[a]. Amen, Op 35[a]. Euntes ibant et flebant, Op 32[a]. My Vistula, Grey Vistula, Op 46[b]. Broad waters, Op 39[b]
[a]**Chicago Sym Chor;** [a]**Chicago Lyric Opera Chor / Nelson;** [b]**Lira Chamb Chor / Ding**
Nonesuch 7559 79348-2 (67' · DDD · T/t)　Ⓕ●Ⓞ↦
　Lovers of the Third Symphony will fall under the *Miserere*'s spell straight away, but it should gain respect from those less easily swayed by the opulent orchestral textures of that work.

Louis Moreau Gottschalk
American 1829-1869

'*I was dreadfully sorry to hear of poor Gottschalk's death,*' wrote the American pianist Amy Fay. '*If anything more is in the papers about him you must send it to me, for the infatuation that I and 99,999 other American girls once felt for him still lingers in my breast.*' Gottschalk was the first American-born composer to achieve international success as a composer and virtuoso pianist. From an exotic background (Jewish London-born father, mother of French nobility), he was born a Creole and gained his musical education in Paris where he was sent when he was only 12. Here he became the darling of the salons; Berlioz and even Chopin praised his unique gifts.

Having returned to the States in 1853, he was lionised throughout his incessant and interminable perambulations all over the American continent (during the Civil War it's said he travelled 95,000 miles, giving 1100 concerts in the process). He spent much of his time in South America where he eventually ended his days. He was 40 years old.

During his lifetime his piano music was phenomenally popular. He thrilled his audiences with scintillating versions of national tunes and operatic themes, introduced for the first time the sensual dance rhythms of Latin America and, 50 years before Scott Joplin, was writing ragtime – all allied to disciplined European pianism. The last quarter of a century has seen a great revival of interest in his music. He may not be a Great Composer but he is certainly Great Fun.

Piano Works

Sospiro, RO214 Op 24. Marguerite, RO158 Op 92. Bataille, RO25 Op 64. Réponds-moi RO225 Op 50 (arr Wachtmann). Solitude, RO239 Op 65. Ballade No 8, RO16 Op 90. Tremolo, RO265 Op 58. Orfa, RO186 Op 71. El cocoyé, RO57 Op 80. Polka de salon, RO207 Op 1. Rayons d'azur, RO220 Op 77. La chasse du jeune Henri, RO54 Op 10
Philip Martin pf
Hyperion CDA67248 (68' · DDD)　　　　　　Ⓕ

There's very little of Gottschalk's piano music on CD that hasn't been recorded by Philip Martin, the ideal exponent, but here's another whole collection of surprises – again a real enchantment from start to finish. It's interesting to hear Gottschalk's Op 1, the *Polka de salon*, published in Paris, which he wrote in his mid-teens. No particular character yet but genuine charm. More typical of the pianist-composer as pop star is *El cocoyé*, which gives a local carnival tune a flashy setting and brought the house down for Gottschalk's first recital in Havana in 1854. *Solitude* is a pretty nocturne inspired by Lamartine, Chopinesque but simpler. The middle section is a fine example of Martin's totally natural, relaxed melodic playing which perfectly fits the serenity of Gottschalk's lyricism. Martin knows how to pace Gottschalk's Caribbean syncopations, too, and is up to all the pyrotechnics.

O ma charmante, épargnez-moi, RO182. Grande fantaisie triomphale sur l'hymne national brésilien, RO108. Melody in D flat. Bamboula, RO20. The Dying Poet, RO75. Grande étude de concert, RO116,

'Hercule'. The Last Hope, RO133. Murmures éoliens, RO176. Symphony No 1, RO5, 'La nuit des tropiques' – Andante (arr Napoleão). La chute des feuilles, RO55. Tournament Galop, RO264
Philip Martin pf
Hyperion CDA66915 (73' · DDD)   ℗⊙▷

It isn't only the playing here which gives such satisfaction, but the whole package is stylishly produced – Rousseau on the booklet cover and fine notes from Jeremy Nicholas. The piano sound from the fastidious Hyperion team is flawless. Martin, operating in a context where some pianists can hardly play softly at all, has a ravishing *pianissimo*. This makes *O ma charmante* and the perennial – but highly original – *The Last Hope* simply enchanting. Gottschalk is a real melodist. Martin understands the intimacies of the salon but he also lacks nothing in his transcendental virtuosity. The more flamboyant numbers such as *Tournament Galop* prove this. About 10 years after Gottschalk's death, his pianist colleague, Artur Napoleão, made a piano arrangement of the first movement of Symphony No 1 (*Night in the Tropics*) which Martin includes here. It's slightly drab compared with the orchestral version and soon feels repetitive. But don't let that put you off this outstanding continuation of Martin's Gottschalk series.

Charles-François Gounod
French 1818-1893

Gounod is an intriguing fellow, an endearing mix of the profane and sacred – rather like his music. His father was a clever but unsuccessful painter who died when Gounod was four but his mother, also a good artist, taught music and ran her late husband's lithography business successfully. Gounod picked up both arts quickly but it was after a performance of Rossini's Otello when he was 13 that decided him irrevocably on music as a profession. 'I felt as if I were in some temple,' he recalled later, 'as if a heavenly vision might shortly rise upon my sight...Oh that night! What rapture! What Elysium!'

His mother insisted on his having a thorough academic education before studying music. Gounod duly complied then, aged 18, entered the Paris Conservatoire. After three attempts he won the coveted Prix de Rome in 1839 and hurried off to immerse himself in Italy and its music. Unlike Berlioz, it proved a formative experience and he became captivated by the music of Palestrina, making a serious study of 16th-century ecclesiastical music. His absorption led him to start writing church music of his own.

When he left Rome to return to Paris, he did so by way of Vienna and Leipzig where he spent several days with Mendelssohn and heard the choral music of Bach for the first time. His first position on returning to Paris was as organist for Les Missions Etrangères (the Chapel for Foreign Missions). The early composers he had come to love were introduced into the services amid objections – they were not the same as the fashionable sentimental music played in most Catholic churches at that time. Gounod's profound religious nature led him to begin theological studies in preparation for entering the priesthood. The pull of music was too strong (and so, it proved, was that of the flesh) for him to progress beyond the novitiate stage. Nevertheless he affected the wearing of a clerical garb and signed himself 'Abbé Gounod' – rather like Liszt (who was challenged by similar temptations). Gounod was even known in some quarters as 'the philandering monk'. He was clearly one of those outgoing people whom most people cannot resist, a man of impish humour and enormous charm. The actor Edmund Got recorded in his diary that Gounod was 'as talented musically as he is exuberant and shamelessly pushy as a man'.

A chance meeting with the influential prima donna Pauline Viardot led her to ask Gounod to write an opera for her. Gounod had no difficulty in falling in love with one of her daughters (the eventual engagement, however, did not lead to marriage). Now, the only way for any composer to make money from music in Paris was from writing opera and, though he had had no experience of writing for the stage, Gounod set to his task with a will. The result was Sapho (1850) – not a huge success but enough of one to encourage him to write more.

In 1852 he was appointed conductor of the Orphéon (a union of choral societies), a position his new father-in-law had arranged, for Gounod married Agnes Zimmerman, the daughter of Pierre Zimmerman, the famous teacher of piano at the Paris Conservatoire. Four years later he began work on the opera that was to make him world famous, Faust.

After its premiere in 1859, Gounod was the most famous musician in France. He tried for the rest of his life to repeat its extraordinary effect – his own favourite La reine de Saba, Mireille and Roméo et Juliette were not failures but came nowhere near the popularity of Faust. To be strictly accurate, the first production was not an overwhelming triumph and Gounod had to wait another 10 years for its revival before it really took off to become the most popular French opera of the entire 19th century. In less than 50 years it had notched up over 2000 separate performances worldwide. No publisher would touch it at first; however, a newcomer in the publishing field, Choudens, took it up. It made the company's fortune.

At the outbreak of the Franco-Prussian war, Gounod and his wife, along with Viardot and other artists, fled to London. Here he remained from 1870 until 1875 – rather longer than the duration of the war. In London he stayed in Tavistock House, once the home of Dickens, with the eccentric and unstable Mrs Georgina Weldon whom Gounod seduced. After his wife returned indignantly to Paris, he seems to have remained there quite happily in a pleasant ménage à trois, Georgina managing Gounod's affairs. Gounod met with great success in England, founding the Gounod Choir.

He returned to Paris and for the last decade of his life turned to religious mysticism and the writing of liturgical music, but truth to tell, after 1870 produced little of significance. 'He might well have echoed Tennyson's despairing cry,' wrote Martin Cooper, 'that he was the greatest master of English living and had nothing to say.'

Symphonies

Symphonies No 1 & 2
**Orchestra of St John's, Smith Square /
John Lubbock**
ASV CDDCA981 (65' · DDD)   Ⓕ

Gounod's symphonies aren't brow-furrowing and don't represent any advance in symphonic thought beyond Schumann and Mendelssohn, but they reveal Gounod in the Gallic tradition of elegantly crafted works with a light touch. The melodious, classically built and witty First Symphony, with its delicate second-movement fugue and vivacious finale, isn't to be peremptorily brushed aside. The longer Second Symphony makes an attempt to sound more serious, especially in the first movement and the dramatic *Scherzo* – the cantilena of the *Larghetto* is beautifully shaped here – but high spirits return in the finale. John Lubbock and his St John's orchestra are adept at the crisply neat treatment that this music demands. His wind section is outstanding, but in the finale of No 1 the violins too show real virtuosity. A warm but clean recorded sound adds to our pleasure.

Mélodies

Où voulez-vous aller?[a]. Le soir[a]. Venise[a]. Ave Maria[b]. Sérénade[b]. Chanson de printemps[a]. Au rossignol[b]. Ce que je suis sans toi[a]. Envoi de fleurs[a]. La pâquerette[b]. Boléro[b]. Mignon[a]. Rêverie[a]. Ma belle amie est morte[b]. Loin du pays[a]. Clos ta paupière[a]. Prière[b]. L'absent[a]. Le temps des roses[a]. Biondina[c]. The Worker[c]. A lay of the early spring[c]. My true love hath my heart[b]. Oh happy home! Oh blessed flower![c]. The fountain mingles with the river[a]. Maid of Athens[c]. Beware! The Arrow and the Song[a]. Ilala: stances à la mémoire de Livingston[c]. If thou art sleeping, maiden[c]
[a]**Dame Felicity Lott** sop [b]**Ann Murray** mez
[c]**Anthony Rolfe Johnson** ten **Graham Johnson** pf
Hyperion ② CDA66801/2 (136' · DDD · T/t) ⒻⒹ→

This well-filled two-CD set is surely the most wide-ranging single issue of Gounod's *mélodies*. The first of the discs confirms the commonly held view of Gounod. Almost without exception the songs are pleasing and sentimental, a sweetly scented posy of hymns to flowers, of rêveries and serenades. The selection includes two settings of poems that Berlioz had used in *Les nuits d'été*, plumbing the depths of the poetry, where Gounod is content to skim across the surface. In chronological order, the songs show how little Gounod's music deepened, but also how evergreen was his inspiration in melody and harmony.

To turn to the second disc is to have all your prejudices overturned. This comprises non-French settings, for which Gounod dons first Italian garb for the song-cycle *Biondina*, and then English for a group of 10 songs written during his stay in London in the 1870s. The Italian cycle is a delight. It would be impossible to guess the composer, as Gounod exchanges his customary flowing themes and rippling arpeggios for an ardent, Tosti-like vocal line over dry *staccato* chords. Anthony Rolfe Johnson catches its mix of sunny lyricism and Gallic sensitivity to perfection.

All three singers are on their best form, Rolfe Johnson bringing an air of intimate seductiveness to Byron's *Maid of Athens*.

Gounod L'Arithmétique. Au printemps. D'un coeur qui t'aime. O ma belle rebelle. Mignon. Par une belle nuit. Sérénade. La siesta. Fleur des bois. Les vacances. Le banc de pierre. Donne-moi cette fleur Lalo Puisqu'ici bas. Aubade. Dansons! **Saint-Saëns** Clair de lune. Dans les coins bleus. El desdichado. Pastorale. Rêverie. Le rossignol. Le soir descend sur la colline. Viens!
Les Demoiselles de... (Sophie Marin-Degor sop Claire Brua mez Serge Cyferstein pf)
Alpha ALPHA033 (70' · DDD · T/t) ⒻOO

Every now and then a disc comes along that paralyses the critical faculties: you know you should be trying to be objective, but somehow cold analysis seems almost obscene. So it is here. Though just one word of warning: for some tastes, Sophie Marin-Degor's soprano may seem a little shrill at *forte* in the higher reaches. But then French sopranos have been taxed with this since forever, and we probably have to accept that it goes with the territory.

In all other respects that territory, as explored here, is the land where the oranges bloom; or, if you prefer, 'l'île heureuse'. Both Marin-Degor and Claire Brua come to this repertory from the world of Baroque music, and they bring with them a cleanness of articulation and phrasing that's wholly delightful, sensitively and tactfully supported by Serge Cyferstein. Apart from the sheer sonorous pleasure of the disc, the balance all three artists maintain between expressive moment and formal shaping is almost perfection itself: key words come over with just a little emphasis, but not so much that we're aware of some vocal coach in the background saying 'Bring out the verb here!' Similarly, rhythms are accurately observed, and delicate *rubato* generally reserved for cadences.

This disc is stylish, responsive, impeccable in ensemble and tuning, sensuous, witty, moving... (that's enough epithets): utterly unmissable.

Faust

Faust
Richard Leech ten Faust **Cheryl Studer** sop Marguerite **José van Dam** bar Méphistophélès **Thomas Hampson** bass Valentin **Martine Mahé** mez Siébel **Nadine Denize** sop Marthe **Marc Barrard** bar Wagner **French Army Chorus; Toulouse Capitole Choir and Orchestra / Michel Plasson**
EMI ② 556224-2 (3h 24' · DDD · T/t) ⒻOD→

Richard Leech as the hero sings his part with the fresh, eager tone, the easy *legato*, the sense of French style that it has so badly been wanting all these years, certainly since Nicolai Gedda essayed the role on the now rather aged Cluytens/EMI sets from 1953 and 1958. Gedda's voice may be more lyrical in the role, but Leech encompasses it with less effort, and creates a real character. It's extremely distinguished singing. Beside him he has an equally impressive loved one in Studer and antagonist van Dam. Studer finds herself another amenable *métier* in Gounod; her Marguerite isn't only sung with innate musicality, firm tone and expressive phrasing but also with a deep understanding of this style of French music in terms of nuance and the lighter touch. The Jewel song is a treasure, and to add to one's satisfaction Studer's French seems faultless.

Van Dam is a resolute, implacable Devil with a firm, even tone to second the insinuating characterisation. His voice may have dried out a little, but he remains a paragon of a stylist in all he attempts. The three French-speaking singers excel in subsidiary roles. Thomas Hampson is in places overextended as Valentin, a role that needs experience and perfect French.

Plasson almost but not quite kills the score with kindness. He so loves the piece that his tempi, especially in the more reflective moments, such as the start of the Garden scene, become much slower than the score predicates and demands. Against that must be set his respect for the minutiae of Gounod's often inspired writing for orchestra and a general warmth that lights the score from within. It was an inspired stroke to invite the French Army Chorus to sing the Soldiers' Chorus, delivered with such verve as to make it seem unhackneyed.

Faust (sung in English)
Paul Charles Clarke *ten* Faust **Mary Plazas** *sop* Marguerite **Alastair Miles** *bass* Méphistophélès **Gary Magee** *bar* Valentin **Diana Montague** *mez* Siébel **Sarah Walker** *mez* Marthe **Matthew Hargreaves** *bass* Wagner **Geoffrey Mitchell Choir; Philharmonia Orchestra / David Parry**
Chandos Opera in English Series ② CHAN3014 (3h 28' · DDD · N/T) Ⓕ Ⓑ→

After listening to this *Faust*, one can feel something very like awe. The structure is massive, the workmanship infinitely thorough, the boldness of stroke (dramatic and musical) almost breathtaking. No doubt the performance contributes to the awe. That's because in many ways it's a very good one, and partly because it underlines seriousness and grandeur. But it appears that David Parry has joined the swelling ranks of the slowcoaches. The Church scene and Faust's solo in the garden, for instance, are probably the slowest on record. Happily, there's nothing boring about it. This recording and its production keep the stage in view, and it's particularly good to have the chorus in such clear focus.

The principals, too, form a strongly gifted team. Paul Charles Clarke, the Faust, is an interesting tenor, thrustful both in tone and manner yet capable of gentleness and delicacy. He never lets us forget that this is *his* story; when he sings everything counts. By comparison, Alastair Miles's Méphistophélès seems a mild-mannered type with reserves of authority and a magnificent voice. The absence of overt devilry may pass as a virtue, but the absence of character is surely taking the disguise too far. Gounod's Mephisto is a joker, a man of the world and an exhibitionist; this one, rarely in the spotlight, loses it entirely when Marthe enters the garden in the person of Sarah Walker.

The Valentin, Gary Magee, has a fine, vibrant baritone and rises well to his high notes and big moments. Diana Montague is an excellent Siébel (and how she rises to hers). The Marguerite, Mary Plazas, is totally likeable, ingenuous but not winsomely so, touchingly sincere in her love and her loss, clean in the scale-work of her Jewel song, a little underpowered in the grand melody of the Church scene, but having a powerful high C in reserve. The English version by Christopher Cowell reads well.

Additional recommendations

Faust Ⓗ
Nash Faust **Licette** Marguerite **Easton** Méphistophélès **BBC Choir; orchestra / Beecham; Raybould**
Dutton mono ② 2CDAX2001 (138' · ADD) Ⓜ
Recorded in 1929-30, Beecham's English version enshrines two wonderful performances by Heddle Nash and Miriam Licette. They are object lessons in style and diction. Beecham conducts with the lightest of touches.

Faust
Hadley Faust **Gasdia** Marguerite **Ramey** Méphistophélès **Welsh National Opera Chorus and Orchestra / Rizzi**
Teldec ② 4509 90872-2 (3h 31' · DDD) Ⓕ
A wonderfully idiomatic and touching recording headed by Cecilia Gasdia and Jerry Hadley on top form. Rizzi can occasionally sound a little lax but this is still a set to consider.

Roméo et Juliette

Roméo et Juliette
Roberto Alagna *ten* Roméo **Angela Gheorghiu** *sop* Juliette **José van Dam** *bass-bar* Frère Laurent **Simon Keenlyside** *bar* Mercutio **Marie-Ange Todorovitch** *sop* Stéphano **Alain Fondary** *bar* Capulet **Claire Larcher** *mez* Gertrude **Daniel Galvez Vallejo** *ten* Tybalt **Didier Henry** *bar* Paris **Till Fechner** *bar* Grégorio **Guy Flechter** *ten* Benvolio **Alain Vernhes** *bar* Duc **Christophe Fel** *bass* Frère Jean **Toulouse Capitole Chorus and Orchestra / Michel Plasson**
EMI ③ 556123-2 (180' · DDD · T/t) Ⓕ Ⓞ

Michel Plasson is no stranger to this opera. He's recorded it once before for EMI in 1983, but compared with his earlier self Plasson is more assuredly his own man here, taking a broader view of the turbulent, dramatic opening. Then comes the chorus's introductory narration; the earlier Plasson recording puts great emphasis on story-telling, and isn't nearly as imaginative as the quieter, more intimate style he favours here, the chorus having more light and shade, better rhythmic pointing, more 'face'.

As Juliette Gheorghiu immediately makes her listeners echo the chorus's 'Ah! qu'elle est belle!', for the sound matches the imagined sight. Its beauty is more mature than Catherine Malfitano's (Plasson's earlier Juliette), but as the part develops towards tragedy so her warmer, richer tone is better able to embody the depth of feeling, and she brings a fine conviction to the despairing scene with Friar Laurence and to the scene of the potion.

Alagna's Romeo has youth on his side, and though he doesn't always sound too happy with the B flats of 'Ah, lève-toi, soleil', there are many, many things to enjoy. The opera also abounds in rewarding secondary roles – José Van Dam as the Friar is gravely firm and as fine as ever, while Simon Keenlyside is also excellent.

Roméo et Juliette
Roberto Alagna ten Roméo **Angela Gheorghiu** sop Juliette **Frantisek Zahradnicek** bass Frère Laurent **Vratislav Kríz** bar Mercutio **Ales Hendrych** bass Capulet **Zdenek Harvánek** bar Paris **Kühn Mixed Choir; Czech Philharmonic Chamber Orchestra / Anton Guadagno**
Film director **Barbara Willis Sweete**
ArtHaus Musik 📀 100 706 (90' · 16:9 · 2.0, 5.1 & DTS 5.1 · 0). Filmed on location in Zvikov Castle, Czech Republic, 2002 Ⓕ

Gounod's opera has been described as a love duet with interruptions; here the interruptions are much reduced. Other characters do indeed appear and sing a phrase or two from time to time, but Mercutio has no Queen Mab, Capulet no 'jeunes gens', the Friar none of those solos one calls less easily to mind, and Stephano the page is eliminated altogether.

Events are similarly compressed. Important news items such as Romeo's banishment and Juliet's impending marriage are relegated. Adjustments are made to such of the interruptions as remain (for instance, Romeo doesn't take part in the mourning, 'O jour de deuil', for Mercutio, but is seen walking away with Juliet who has watched the unfortunate events from her balcony and quite understands).

Indeed, there's a great deal of walking in this production. Juliet walks home after her first love duet and Romeo sings an abbreviated aria while walking towards the second. He walks up a staircase to the balcony, in fact a nice long gallery good for a gentle stroll. 'Ah, ne fuis pas encore' is also sung on the move and when we meet Romeo again, at dawn, he's still walking. The motif persists right up to the ambulatory death scene.

On the other hand, the countryside, the river, the castle and the weather are all so beautiful that it would be a sin to stay indoors, and as long as one takes this film for what it is (which isn't Gounod's five-act opera) there's much pleasure to be gained. Gheorghiu sings feelingly and with tone to match the natural beauties of earth and sky around her. Alagna, but for his habit of 'lifting' to notes, gives a stylish, sensitive performance and is in good voice. The love duets can rarely have been better sung, and that's what it's really all about.

Percy Grainger
American/Australian 1882-1961

Everyone knows Country Gardens (based on an English Morris dance) and probably Molly on the Shore, Shepherd's Hey, Mock Morris and Handel in the Strand. Their popularity has tended to overshadow the rest of Grainger's prolific and varied output and though he would never be put on a pedestal to join the pantheon of immortals, he is unorthodox, original and deserves better than to be dismissed by the more snooty arbiters of musical taste. There is a tendency to overlook real craftsmanship when it is put to (sometimes) frivolous use.

The amusing and bizarre aspects of his life are well-documented in John Bird's biography – his habit of jogging from one concert venue to the next with a heavy rucksack on his back; his abnormally close relation with his formidable mother Rose and her subsequent suicide; his predilection for physical self-flagellation; his 'blue-eyed' Nordic views; his substitution of Anglo-Saxon music terms for Italian and German ones (chamber music = room music, crescendo = louden, viola = middle-fiddle and other self-conscious eccentricities).

Grainger (born George Percy, he changed to his mother's maiden name of Aldridge later) first made his name as a concert pianist. His teacher in Melbourne, Louis Pabst, was actually a student of the great Anton Rubinstein and Grainger made a strong impression on all those who heard him. Among them were Grieg and Delius with both of whom he developed a strong friendship. After living in Britain for a time he settled in America where he took citizenship and, in 1926, married his 'Nordic Princess' Ella Viola Ström in the Hollywood Bowl before a paying audience of 20,000.

As a composer he was virtually self-taught and his best music relies on conventional harmonies, with an emphasis on vigorous rhythms and traditional tunes. He was tirelessly curious in trying out new combinations – he wrote for the solovox, theremin, marimba, harmonium, banjo and other underused instruments as well as experimenting with electronic instruments as early as 1937.

Orchestral Works

Green Bushes, BFMS12. Lord Maxwell's Goodnight, BFMS14 (both ed Barry Peter Ould). Hill Song No 2.

The Merry King, BFMS39[a]. Eastern Intermezzo.
Colonial Song, S1. Spoon river, AFMS2. The Power of
Rome and the Christian Heart. The Immovable Do.
County Derry Air, BFMS29. Ye Banks and Braes
O' Bonnie Doon, BFMS31. English Dance No 1
[a]**Paul Janes** pf **BBC Philharmonic Orchestra /
Richard Hickox**
Chandos Grainger Edition CHAN9839 (70' · DDD)
Ⓟ❶❶▶

Here's a recipe guaranteed to delight Grainger
acolytes and inquisitive newcomers alike: a liberal
sprinkling of old friends, three of the composer's
most ambitious creations and no fewer than four
world premiere recordings. Falling into the last
two categories comes the giddily inventive *English
Dance* No 1. Bearing the inscription 'For Cyril
Scott with long love', this is the work of which
Gabriel Fauré exclaimed: 'It's as if the total popu-
lation were a-dancing.' Hickox and company have
already set down this remarkable piece in its final
scoring from 1924-29; the present orchestration
dates from 1906-09 and wears an even more exuberantly colourful demeanour than its successor.
   Originally conceived in 1907 for 24 winds (in
which guise it can be heard on Chandos), the
bracing, somewhat Delian *Hill Song* No 2 is
played in its final incarnation from 1948 for
symphony orchestra. That same year, Grainger
accepted a commission for an even more ambitious wind-band creation, *The Power of Rome
and the Christian Heart*, based on ideas from as
far back as 1918 and given here with the
optional string parts. It's an imposing, oddly
moreish affair, whose second half borrows
material from the 1943 orchestral essay *Dreamery* (Chandos) as well as the first movement
('The Power of Love') of the marvellous *Danish
Folksong Suite*. From a clutch of indelible
favourites, to be singled out are the well-
upholstered 1919 orchestration of the
supremely touching *Colonial Song*, *Green Bushes*
and that memorably tangy 1920 harmonisation
of the *Irish Tune from County Derry*.
   Hickox secures a set of performances that are
simply past praise in their combination of stylish
swagger and heartwarming commitment to the
cause. Wonderful Chandos sound, too, irrepressibly vivid. Terrific stuff!

Additional recommendation

Youthful Suite. Molly on the Shore, BFMS1. Irish Tune
from County Derry, BFMS15. Shepherd's Hey,
BFMS16. Country Gardens. Early one Morning, BFMS
unnum. Handel in the Strand, RMTB2. Mock Morris,
RMTB1. Dreamery (ed Ould). The Warriors
(ed Servadei)
BBC PO / Hickox
Chandos Grainger Edition CHAN9584 (75' · DDD)
Ⓟ❶▶

Recorded in ripe, beautifully clean-cut sound,
this collection is a great success for all involved.
For *The Warriors*, Hickox uses a new critical edition and Grainger's orchestral palette has never
sounded more gloriously extravagant.

Music for Wind Band

The Power of Rome and the Christian Heart.
Children's March: Over the Hills and Far Away,
RMTB4. Bell Piece[a]. Blithe Bells. The Immovable Do.
Hill Songs – No 1; No 2. County Derry Air, BFMS29.
Marching Song of Democracy
[a]**James Gilchrist** ten **Royal Northern College of
Music Wind Orchestra / Timothy Reynish, Clark
Rundell**
Chandos Grainger Edition CHAN9630 (65' · DDD)
Ⓟ❶▶

Rundell's compelling realisation of the extraordinary *Hill Song* No 1 – regarded by Grainger
as one of his finest achievements and performed here in its original guise for two piccolos, six oboes, six cors anglais, six bassoons
and double bassoon – was actually made by
BBC Manchester back in 1992; the remaining
items date from 1997 and benefit from the
splendid sound and balance achieved by
Chandos.
   Another of Grainger's most striking wind-band
compositions opens the disc, namely the 12-
minute *The Power of Rome and the Christian Heart*.
Both the *Children's March* and *Bell Piece* feature
some unexpected vocal contributions. In the latter – a charming 'ramble' on John Dowland's
Now, O now I needs must part – Grainger incorporates a bell part specially written for his wife, Ella.
The delightfully piquant arrangements of *Blithe
Bells* and *The Immovable Do* date from March 1931
and November/December 1939 respectively.
These fine players equally revel in the 'scrunchy'
harmonies of the eventful version of *Irish Tune
from County Derry* (made in 1920 for military
band and pipe-organ). That just leaves the boisterous *Marching Song of Democracy*, which Rundell again directs as to the manner born.

Piano Works

'Piano Music for four hands, Volume 3'
Rondo. Crew of the Long Dragon. Fantasy on
George Gershwin's 'Porgy and Bess'. Ye Banks and
Braes, BFMS32. Tiger-Tiger, KS4/JBC9. Walking
Tune, RMTB3. **C Scott** Three Symphonic Dances.
Delius A Dance Rhapsody No 1, RTVI/18.
Grieg Knut Lurasens Halling II. **Addinsell** Festival.
Le Jeune La Bel'aronde. **Gershwin** Girl Crazy –
Embraceable you (all trans Grainger)
Penelope Thwaites, John Lavender pfs
Pearl SHECD9631 (78' · DDD)   Ⓕ

Volume 3 of Grainger's music for four hands
(Volume 2 is no longer available) contains
short original compositions and a number of
his transcriptions. These latter are fascinating
in their admirable combination of scrupulous
fidelity and creative rethinking for an entirely
different medium. You wouldn't necessarily
think that a transcription, even for two pianos,
of Delius's First *Dance Rhapsody* could possibly
work with any real degree of success. However,

the reality is that it works so well that some may even prefer Grainger's version to the original. In the *Porgy and Bess* Fantasy he treats the tunes with loving respect, but as a pianist he can't help seeing different ways of presenting them: the very big gestures in 'My man's gone now'; a searching little prelude to 'It ain't necessarily so' implying all sorts of interesting things that Grainger could have done with that slithery little tune if he weren't obliged to play it straight – which he then does, and with sparkling enjoyment.

Grainger Jutish Medley, DFMS8. Colonial Song, S1. Molly on the Shore, BFMS1. Harvest Hymn. Spoon River, AFMS1. Country Gardens, BFMS22. Walking Tune, RMTB3. Mock Morris, RMTB1. Ramble on Themes from Richard Strauss's 'Der Rosenkavalier'. Shepherd's Hey, BFMS4. Irish Tune from County Derry, BFMS6. Handel in the Strand, RMTB2. The Hunter in his Career, OEPM4. Scotch Strathspey and Reel, BFMS37. In a Nutshell Suite – No 4, The Gum-suckers March. The Merry King, BFMS38. In Dahomey **Stanford** (arr Grainger) Four Irish Dances, Op 89 – No 1, A March-Jig; No 4, A Reel
Marc-André Hamelin pf
Hyperion CDA66884 (73' · DDD)   Ⓕ

This is perhaps one of the most riveting and satis-fying anthologies of Grainger's music. Hamelin's superb control and artistry just about sweep the board if you're looking for a disc that not only brings you all the old favourites but also explores some of the less familiar music, such as Grainger's arrangements of two of Stanford's *Irish Dances*, the 'cakewalk smasher' *In Dahomey* or some of the rather less familiar folk-music settings such as *The Merry King* – the latter a delightful discovery. The deceptive ease with which Hamelin presents these pieces is quite breathtaking. The *Irish Tune from County Derry*, for instance, contains some exacting problems which call on the pianist to play *ppp* in the outer fingers and *mf* with the mid-dle in order to bring out the melody which Grainger places almost entirely within the middle register of the piano, and yet Hamelin makes it sound incredibly natural.

Piano Transcriptions

Grainger Beautiful Fresh Flower. Lullaby. Paraphrase on the Waltz of the Flowers from Tchaikovsky's Flower Waltz. Free Settings of Favourite Melodies – Brahms: Wiegenlied, Op 49 No 4; Handel: Hornpipe from the Water Music; Fauré: Nell, Op 18 No 1; Fauré: Après un rêve, Op 7 No 1; R Strauss: Rosenkavalier Ramble; Dowland: Now, O now, I needs must part. Gershwin Transcriptions – The Man I Love; Love Walked In **Scott** Handelian Rhapsody **Stanford** Irish Dances, Op 89 **Byrd** The Carman's Whistle **Delius** Air and Dance, RTVI/21
Piers Lane pf
Hyperion CDA67279 (75' · DDD)   Ⓕ**OO**

These short pieces range from simplicity to

elaboration, from innocence to experience; most of them are homages to many of Grainger's friends and honour his trenchant belief in the sort of folk-melody that crosses all barriers. Wherever you turn you'll hear music 'like a breath of spring air' (to quote Barry Peter Ould's excellent note) and, more para-doxically, transcriptions that show Grainger's originality.

Cyril Scott's *Handelian Rhapsody*, receiving its first recording, may suggest Scott and Grainger more than Handel but it's an intrigu-ing oddity and one which rises to an impressive grandeur. Stanford's Leprechaun is gentle and confiding rather than mischievous and the 'Ramble on Love' from *Der Rosenkavalier* is a sophisticated 'dish-up' of introspection and open-hearted virtuosity. All this music makes a wide variety of subtle and fierce demands, but Piers Lane, weaving his expertise with the lightest of touches, meets them with warmth and brio. Heartache, heart-ease or a tantalising mix of both all come within his style and every-thing is played with unfaltering command. Grainger's 'woggles' (his idiosyncratic term for *tremolandi*) can rarely have sounded more con-vincing and the Tchaikovsky Waltz is taken by storm in a magnificent display of red-blooded virtuosity.

The recording and presentation are immacu-late. This is a dazzling, affectionate tribute to the composer and pianist who once said: 'To know a world of beauty and not to be able to spread the knowledge of it is agonising.'

Songs

David of the White Rock[a]. Died for Love, BFMS10[a]. The Sprig of Thyme, BFMS24[a]. Willow, Willow, OEPM1[a]. Near Woodstock Town[a]. Early one morning[a]. In Bristol Town (arr Gibbs)[d]. Songs of the North[a] – No 2, This is no my plaid; No 3, Turn ye to me; No 4, Skye Boat Song; No 5, Weaving Song. The Bridegroom Grat[a]. The Land O' the Leal[a] (both arr Ould). Proud Vesseli[a] (ed Thwaites). Under a bridge[ac]. Hubby and Wifey, DFMS5[ac]. The Lonely Desert-Man sees the Tents of the Happy Tribes, RMTB9[abc]. Colonial Song[ab]. The Only Son, KS21[ab]. The Love Song of Har Dyal, KS11[ac]. A Song of Autumn[a]. Five Settings of Ella Grainger[a]. O Glorious, Golden Era[a]. Little Ole with his Umbrella[a]. Variations on Handel's 'The Harmonious Blacksmith'[a] (ed Ould). Harvest Hymn[ae]. After-word[a]
Della Jones mez [a]**Penelope Thwaites** pf with [b]**Mark Padmore** ten [c]**Stephen Varcoe** bar [d]**George Black** gtr [e]**John Lavender** pf
Chandos Grainger Edition CHAN9730 (74' · DDD · T)
                                                      Ⓕ**O**▶

Again Grainger amazes, amuses, arouses, intrigues. These 'Songs for mezzo' originate in Britain (with an excellent sequence of Scottish songs), Jutland and Australia. Some are folk-songs collected in the early years of the century; two have words by Kipling, five by Ella, Grainger's wife, and some have no words at all.

The latter are fortifying antidotes to those text-merchants who think that song is essentially 'about' the communication of words, whereas everybody knows that you sing (la-la, dee-dee, as in these of Grainger) because a tune has taken your fancy and singing it makes you feel better.

It's really Della Jones's record, or hers and that of the admirable Penelope Thwaites. But the menfolk appear occasionally and always to effect. Mark Padmore is a resourceful tenor with hints here that he has in reserve a vibrant, rather Italianate body of tone. Jones herself is a natural for Grainger: she has the spirit to match, and, like him, a certain ambiguity in her forthrightness, so that at times we're not quite sure what's serious and what's a bit of fun. The *Colonial Song* ('Sentimental No 1') is unashamedly nostalgic, but with an element of send-up too: in the piano solos especially a joyful passage of inspired improvisation that's both a joke and 'for real'. Also for real is the prime quality of this disc, with 15 tracks 'premiere recordings' and 14 'premiere recordings in this version'.

Enrique Granados   Spanish 1867-1916

Falla, Albéniz and Granados: the triumvirate responsible for the establishment of a modern Spanish school of music. In fact Granados's father was Cuban (an officer serving in the Spanish army) while his mother was a Mantañesan from Santander in the north (the elaborate ornamentation of the music of Montañesa is a notable characteristic of Granados's music). He was all set to make a career as a pianist, studying in Barcelona and, thanks to a wealthy patron, at the Paris Conservatoire. Returning to Spain he established himself as one of the leading Spanish musicians of the day – there are even some primitive recordings of his piano playing.

Some early piano pieces, Danzas españolas, proved immediately popular – one especially, but his masterpieces are without doubt the two books of piano pieces Goyescas. These were turned into a short opera and a production at the Paris Opéra was arranged. The outbreak of the First World War prevented this and the project was delayed until 1916, transferred to the Metropolitan Opera in New York. Granados and his wife crossed the Atlantic to attend the premiere. A newly composed Intermezzo greatly helped its modest success, a result of which was an invitation by President Wilson for Granados to play at the White House, thus delaying the return to Europe. When Granados and his wife did so, their ship the Sussex was torpedoed by a German submarine on the journey from Liverpool to Dieppe. Though the ship was brought back safely to port, Granados drowned attempting to save his wife.

Danzas españolas

Granados 12 Danzas españolas, Op 37.
7 Valses poéticos. Allegro di concierto.
El pelele. Danza lenta. Goyescas

Montsalvatge Divagación. Sonatine for Yvette
Alicia de Larrocha pf
RCA Victor Red Seal ② 74321 84610-2 (147' · DDD)
Ⓑ⊙

Alicia de Larrocha, that incomparable interpreter of the Spanish repertoire, here revisits many of her favourite musical haunts. And if some of her former edge and fire, her tonal and stylistic luxuriance are now replaced by more 'contained' and reflective qualities, her warmth and affection remain undimmed. Her *rubato*, while less lavishly deployed than before, is potent and alluring, and each and every dance is played with rare naturalness and authority. But if a touch of sobriety occasionally blunts the fullest impact of these fascinating, most aristocratic idealisations of local Spanish life and colour, the actual playing is never less than masterly. The *Valses poéticos* are offered as an engaging encore. The recordings have much less range and reverberance than her previous ones on Decca; however, all lovers of this repertoire will want to add this to their collection.

Goyescas

Granados Goyescas **Albéniz** Iberia. Navarra
Alicia de Larrocha pf
Double Decca ② 448 191-2DF2 (141' · ADD)
Recorded 1972-76
Ⓜ⊙⊙↦

Alicia de Larrocha has been playing these works, the greatest in the repertoire of Spanish piano music, all her life. Complete technical assurance in these extremely demanding works has now become taken for granted, and Larrocha isn't unique in mastering their terrors; but though there have been other distinguished interpreters, her readings have consistently remained a touchstone. She employs plenty of subtle *rubato* but possesses the ability to make it sound as natural as breathing. In the true sense of that much misused word, this is classical playing, free from any superimposed striving for effect but responding fully to the music's sense of colour; and even in the densest of textures she's able to control conflicting tonal levels. *Goyescas*, which can tempt the unwary into exaggerated 'expressiveness', brings forth a wealth of poetic nuance, without losing shape. The recorded quality throughout always was good and here emerges as fresh as ever. Anyone who doesn't already possess these recordings should not hesitate to acquire them now – all the more since the two discs together cost the same as one full-price one.

Alexandr Grechaninov
Russian/American 1864-1956

Grechaninov studied at the Moscow Conservatory (1881-90) and with Rimsky-Korsakov at the St Petersburg Conservatory (1890-93), and worked as a piano teacher and folksong arranger; in 1910 he received a pension for his liturgical music. But that ceased with the Revolution, and in 1925 he settled in Paris, moving to the USA in 1929. His large output (nearly 200 opus numbers) includes operas, five symphonies, Masses, songs and piano music.

All-Night Vigil

All-Night Vigil, Op 59. Nunc dimittis, Op 34 No 1. **P**
The Seven Days of the Passion, Op 58 – No 3, In Thy Kingdom[a]; No 6, Now the Powers of Heaven
[a]**James Bowman** counterten **Holst Singers / Stephen Layton**
Hyperion CDA67080 (63' · DDD · T/t)   Ⓕ**OO**

The *All-Night Vigil* is an outstanding achievement. Like Rachmaninov's famous setting, it's a selection of texts from the services of Vespers and Matins celebrated as a Vigil, though in current parish practice this lasts rather less than an entire night. Grechaninov sets fewer texts: the duration of the work is just over 47 minutes. Here we find the sustained chordal writing and slow-moving melodies oscillating around a few notes familiar from Rachmaninov, but Grechaninov has his own distinctive harmonic vocabulary, and his writing is less text-driven. Chant is an inspiration, but is also used in a different way from Rachmaninov: none is quoted in its entirety, the composer preferring instead to use fragments of various chants which are combined and juxtaposed with considerable freedom. He's a master of texture: listen to the astonishing darkness of sound produced by the scoring for lower voices in *Ot yunosti moyeya*, for example. Overall there's a feeling of luminosity in the writing, however, as well as an undeniable grandeur.

To round off the disc we're given three other liturgical works, including a dramatic setting of the Beatitudes (sung at the Divine Liturgy) with James Bowman as soloist. The Holst Singers under Stephen Layton are superb: they have a complete mastery of the style and the fine, rich choral timbre which the music demands. Very highly recommended.

Edvard Grieg   Norwegian 1843-1907

Grieg's great-grandfather was a Scot who emigrated to Bergen after the Battle of Culloden, changed his name from Greig and became British Consul there, a post subsequently held by his son and grandson. The music came from Edvard's mother, a talented amateur pianist, but it was largely due to the persuasion of Norwegian violinist Ole Bull, who heard the young Grieg play the piano, that a musical career came about. The parents were reluctant and Grieg, who'd had thoughts of becoming a priest, hated the Leipzig Conservatory where he was sent.

However, he had the opportunity of hearing Clara Schumann play her late husband's Concerto and

Wagner conduct Tannhäuser; the young Arthur Sullivan was a fellow student. Here, too, he developed pleurisy which left his left lung seriously impaired, bequeathing him precarious health and diminished energy for the rest of his life.

He returned not to Oslo but to Copenhagen in 1863; there the revered Niels Gade, founding father of the new Scandinavian school of composition and Denmark's leading composer, befriended Grieg, inspiring him to form the Euterpe Society dedicated to promoting Scandinavian music. This he did with the aid of another gifted young composer, Rikard Nordraak. 'From Nordraak,' wrote Grieg, 'I learnt for the first time to know the nature of Norwegian folk tunes and my own nature'. Alas, Nordraak died in 1866 at the age of 24 (though not before he'd written what is today's Norwegian national anthem).

In 1867 he married his cousin, the talented singer Nina Hagerup, who would become the chief interpreter of his songs, but a period of despair ensued: he had found the key to his own musical voice yet his missionary zeal in promoting Norwegian composers and its music met with opposition; then his first and only child, a 13-month old girl, died in 1869. It was a letter from Franz Liszt not only praising his music but inviting him to Rome that did more to encourage him than anything. After the meeting with Liszt in 1869, he returned to Norway and opened a Norwegian Academy of Music.

In 1869 he gave the first performance of his Piano Concerto, the work by which most people know him. This, with the first set of Lyric Pieces (for piano) and two violin sonatas that had already been published, established him as one of the foremost composers of the time. Ibsen approached him to write the incidental music for the stage version of his Peer Gynt (a job which occupied Grieg for two years). In a short time, Grieg had become so famous that the government granted him an annuity to relieve him of financial burdens so that he could concentrate on composing. Ironically, apart from the Holberg Suite, all his most successful works were written by the time he was 33.

He visited England frequently and was showered with honours and decorations wherever he went, a much-loved figure. But Grieg was a shy, retiring, modest man, a Republican not much impressed by medals and orders bestowed by Royalty (though he confessed they were useful for putting on the top layer of his trunks when travelling: 'The Customs officials are always so kind to me at the sight of them'). As he grew older, Grieg grew physically weaker and more reclusive, preferring the company of his wife and the tranquillity of his home at Troldhaugen overlooking the Hardanger fjord near Bergen.

He died of a heart attack and, following a state funeral, his ashes were sealed in the side of a cliff round the fjord at Troldhaugen.

Piano Concerto in A minor, Op 16

Grieg Piano Concerto **Schumann** Piano Concerto
Leif Ove Andsnes pf
Berlin Philharmonic Orchestra / Mariss Jansons
EMI 503419-2 (59' · DDD)   Ⓕ**OOO**▷

GRIEG PIANO CONCERTO –
IN BRIEF

Leif Ove Andsnes; Berlin PO / Mariss Jansons
EMI 557562-2 (59' · DDD)   Ⓕ❍❍❍❍❯
A commanding, intrepidly imaginative
account from one of the supreme pianists of
our times, its pleasures enhanced by Jansons's
immaculate, powerfully responsive backing
with the Berliners.

Dinu Lipatti; Philharmonia Orchestra /   Ⓗ
Alceo Galliera
EMI 767163-2 (71' · ADD)   Ⓜ
Very special playing from Dinu Lipatti; the
poetry and rapt beauty of this famous 1947
performance linger long in the memory.
Currently only available in a five-disc Lipatti
retrospective – pure gold all of it!

Murray Perahia; Bavarian RSO / Sir Colin Davis
Sony Classical 82796 92736-2 (60' · DDD) Ⓕ❍❍❯
A performance to delight all admirers of this
aristocrat of the keyboard. Sir Colin Davis
and the Bavarian RSO also distinguish themselves, as do the Sony engineers.

Benno Moiseiwitsch; Philharmonia Orchestra /   Ⓗ
Otto Ackermann
Testament SBT1187 (70' · ADD)   Ⓕ❍
Moiseiwitsch's vintage 1953 recording was
one of the mainstays of HMV's early LP cata-
logue.

Leif Ove Andsnes; Bergen PO /
Dmitri Kitaenko
Virgin The Classics 561996-2 (78' · DDD)   Ⓜ
Andsnes's earlier recording continues to
holds its own at mid-price. A softer-spoken
affair than his EMI remake, with poetry and
delicacy in perfect equilibrium.

Stephen Kovacevich; BBC SO / Sir Colin Davis
Philips 464 702-2PM (61' · ADD)   Ⓜ❍❍❯
Kovacevich's indelibly fresh performance has
enchanted for over three decades now.
Felicities abound, not least the agile bravura
of the first-movement cadenza and captivating skip of the finale.

Arturo Benedetti Michelangeli; New Phil-
harmonia Orch / Rafael Frühbeck de Burgos
BBC Legends BBCL4043-2 (69' · ADD)   Ⓜ❍❍❍
Ⓖ Simply breathtaking artistry from the
great Italian pianist. This June 1965
performance generates a joyous, edge-of-seat
ardour that grips from the first bar to the
last.

Solomon; Philharmonia / Herbert Menges   Ⓗ
Testament SBT1231 (75' · ADD)   Ⓕ❍❍
Recorded late in his career, this performance
still captures Solomon's power and incandescence. This is a wonderful memento of a
great pianist.

Ⓖ It was the Grieg Concerto that first
made the name of Leif Ove Andsnes
on disc in 1990. The interpretation
remains broadly the same, except that speeds are
now rather brisker. However many times he's
performed the Grieg, Andsnes retains a freshness
and expressiveness that always sounds spontaneous. That inspirational quality is more markedly
perceptible with the new version's faster tempi,
but the expressive flights remain just as broad. In
that contrast, he's firmly supported by Jansons
and the Berlin Philharmonic, with playing not
just refined but dramatic too in fiercely exciting
tuttis. Schumann's cello melodies are gloriously
warm, with textures in both works admirably
clear, and Andsnes fully responds to Schumann's
espressivo and *ritardando* requests.
   Though both Stephen Kovacevich and Murray Perahia are equally spontaneous, they tend
not to be quite so free in their expressive flights;
EMI's finely balanced digital sound and the
playing of the Berlin Philharmonic are also in
this version's favour. Andsnes also offers slightly
faster basic speeds than his rivals; particularly
enjoyable is the free-flowing tempo for the central *Andantino grazioso* of the Schumann, which
you'd never mistake for a simple *Andante*.

Grieg Piano Concerto **Saint-Saëns** Piano Concerto
No 2 **Schumann** Piano Concerto
Orchestra of Opera North / Howard Shelley pf
Chandos CHAN10509 (79' · DDD)   Ⓕ❍❍❯

What a good idea to add to that favourite among
LP couplings Saint-Saëns's most Bachian concerto, No 2. And the pleasure doesn't stop there.
Howard Shelley is one of those musicians who
quietly goes about his pianistic (and now conduc-
torly) business without grabbing the limelight
except for the odd award, but who is consistently
impressive, unfailingly musical and only goes into
the studio when he has something to say about a
work. That is certainly the case here.
   It's a particular delight to hear a reading of the
Schumann as fleet and joyous as this one. These
are intimate performances, an effect no doubt
enhanced by the fact that Shelley directs from
the piano. Intimate but also sharply characterised. And when virtuosity is required, Shelley
provides it in spades. Take the finale of the
Schumann: textures are wonderfully transparent, the dotted rhythms are perky and precise,
and there are plenty of striking colours from the
orchestra (which throughout the disc proves
itself a fine ensemble, with some particularly
outstanding wind-players).
   Shelley is just as persuasive in the Grieg, coaxing from the orchestra a real sense of narrative,
some lovely oboe-playing and allowing the big
tunes due space but never over-indulging them.
The concerto's irresistible yearning quality is
well caught too, particularly in the central
movement, where he is almost a match for
Lipatti. Again, tempi are generally fleet, and
Shelley pays attention both to the *marcato* marking of the finale and its folk tinges without over-

statement. These are certainly performances to put alongside the classics.

Technically, the Saint-Saëns is an ideal vehicle for Shelley's fingery kind of pianism and he is exceptional in the *Allegro scherzando*, the movement that out-Mendelssohns Mendelssohn. Again, the orchestra is utterly focused. The recorded quality here, as elsewhere, is exemplary.

Grieg Piano Concerto[b] **Debussy** Préludes – Book 1[a]
Arturo Benedetti Michelangeli pf
[b]**New Philharmonia Orchestra /**
Rafael Frühbeck de Burgos
BBC Legends [b]mono/[a]stereo BBCL4043-2
(69' · DDD/ADD). Recorded live [b]1965, [a]1982
Ⓜ❍❍❍

Somehow you feel it must be possible to deliver the hackneyed opening flourishes of the Grieg Concerto with real abandon and impetuosity, to get the orchestra to respond to them with genuine ardour, then for the soloist to combine flow, virtuoso dash, fantasy and noble eloquence and to crown the structural high-points in a way that lifts you out of your seat. Yet until you hear a performance like this one you may never quite believe it can be done. A sense of joyous rhapsody buoys up Michelangeli's playing from first note to last, yet everything is founded on a bedrock of high intelligence, taste and natural authority. Witness too the fabulous tone-colours he draws from the instrument. His slow movement is by turns balmy and ecstatic, and the finale has terrific drive. And the virtuosity…! If your hair isn't standing on end in the finale's coda you need an urgent medical check-up. Forget the boxy recording and the hissy background. This is a performance that entirely merits the hysterical cheers that greet it.

Seventeen years on, Michelangeli's Debussy also provokes rapturous applause, but in this instance it was probably partly a tribute to his by this time legendary status – he was 63 and rapidly becoming as famous for his cancellations as for his performances. There are marvels of pianism here, but an air of calculation hangs over much of the playing. Those who have Michelangeli's 1978 DG studio version will find little to prefer here, apart from the slightly warmer acoustic.

Grieg Piano Concerto **Schumann** Piano Concerto
Murray Perahia pf **Bavarian Radio Symphony Orchestra / Sir Colin Davis**
Sony Classical 82796 92736-2 (60' · DDD)
Recorded live 1987, 1988   Ⓕ❍❍❍▷

Despite the hazards, Murray Perahia delights in the inspirational heat-of-the-moment of a live recording. Though there are no claps, coughs or shuffles betraying the presence of an audience, we're told both concertos were recorded live at Munich's Philharmonie Gasteig. Of the two works, the Grieg is better served by the imme-

diacy and warmth of Perahia's response, whether through rhythmic bite in livelier dance tempo or total surrender to lyrical nostalgia elsewhere. Never is there the slightest sacrifice of artistic sensitivity or keyboard finesse.

His Schumann is no less ardent. In the spirited finale, as throughout the Grieg, any collector would be as happy with this performance as that of Kovacevich for Philips. But in the first two movements, it's Kovacevich who finds a simpler, more confiding note – as well as more artfully weaving the piano into the comparatively light texture as if it were part of the orchestra instead of a spotlit outsider. Davis goes all the way in both works to uphold Perahia in his open-hearted point-making, and the Bavarian Radio Symphony Orchestra gives him all he asks. The sound is more clear-cut than the old Philips.

Additional recommendation

Grieg Piano Concerto[a] **Schumann** Piano Concerto[a]. Romance in F sharp. Vogel als Prophet **Palmgren** West-Finnish Dance. Refrain de berceau
Moiseiwitsch pf [a]**Philharmonia / Ackermann**
Testament mono SBT1187 (70' · ADD)
Recorded 1941, [a]1953   Ⓕ❍

The Grieg Concerto sounds newly minted, with markings such as *tranquillo e cantabile* observed with special affection. The catalogue may be filled with more openly confrontational performances but Moiseiwitsch, who took music more by stealth than storm, elegantly eclipses the readings of so many more assertive keyboard tigers. For encores there are classic performances of Palmgren and Schumann.

Peer Gynt Suites

Grieg Peer Gynt – Suites Nos 1 & 2, Opp 46 & 55. Holberg Suite, Op 40 **Sibelius** Legends, Op 22 – No 2, The Swan of Tuonela. Kuolema – Valse triste, Op 44. Finlandia, Op 26
Berlin Philharmonic Orchestra / Herbert von Karajan
DG Karajan Gold 439 010-2GHS (78' · DDD) Ⓜ❍❍▷

Very impressive indeed. Somehow one feels that one could stretch out and touch the players, so vivid is the sound here. In the *Peer Gynt* movements, there's much greater range and separation. *Peer Gynt* is most beautifully done. At times you might think the wind could have been a shade more distant, particularly in the 'By the seashore' movement but there's no want of atmosphere here – quite the contrary! Not to put too fine a point on it, this is a marvellous recording. In the *Holberg Suite*, the sound has marvellous clarity and definition as well as exemplary range. For some tastes it may be a little too sophisticated but one's admiration for it remains undimmed. The playing throughout is beautifully cultured and there's wonderful lightness and delicacy.

The present issue is Karajan's third account of 'The Swan of Tuonela' and it's regrettable that he never committed to disc the four *Legends* in their entirety. It's as powerful and atmospheric an account as ever recorded, and the remaining two pieces, 'Valse triste' and *Finlandia*, reinforce the feeling that this partnership has never been equalled. The stirring account of *Finlandia* is incredibly wide-ranging – the orchestral playing is really in a class of its own.

Additional recommendation

Peer Gynt – Suites Nos 1 & 2. In Autumn. Symphonic Dances
CBSO / Oramo
Erato 8573 82917-2 (74' · DDD)   Ⓕ**Ⓞ**➤

  As soon as the strings respond to the flute near the beginning of *Peer Gynt*'s 'Morning' – longingly leaning on an expressive *ritardando* – you sense this is a quality production. Oramo's Grieg is keen-eared and with a sense of play that does credit both to Ibsen's dramatic prompt and the folk-music roots of the concert works.

String Quartets

Grieg String Quartets – No 1 in G minor, Op 27; No 2 in F, CW146 **Schumann** String Quartet No 1 in A minor, Op 41 No 1
Petersen Quartet (Conrad Muck, Gernot Süssmuth *vns* Friedemann Weigle *va* Hans-Jakob Eschenburg *vc*)
Capriccio 10 476 (75' · DDD)   Ⓕ

Grieg String Quartet No 1 in G minor, Op 27
Mendelssohn String Quartet No 2 in A minor, Op 13
Shanghai Quartet (WeiGang Li, HongGang Li *vns* Zheng Wang *va* James Wilson *vc*)
Delos DE3153 (64' · DDD)   Ⓕ**Ⓞ**

Since Grieg owed much to Schumann, coupling their quartets seems a good idea. These G minor and A minor Quartets were written when the composers were in their thirties, although Grieg was a few years older. Yet it's his work that sounds more youthfully passionate, while the Schumann is a rather self-conscious homage to his friend Mendelssohn and classical models. The Petersens invest the Grieg G minor Quartet with gravitas and are skilful in linking the disparate sections of its structure. Their recording has a natural balance and an impressively wide dynamic rang; it also copes well with Grieg's forceful, semi-orchestral string writing. The whole performance has vigour and tenderness in good proportion, and a truly Scandinavian feeling. The unfinished F major Quartet is another sensitive performance and the work sounds no more incomplete than Schubert's *Unfinished* Symphony.

The Schumann is no less enjoyable; the artists are fully inside its idiom and make a consistently beautiful and meaningful sound. The Shanghai Quartet's brightly lit account of the Mendelssohn suggests a rich store of interpretative

potential. Theirs is a sizzling, multi-coloured performance. The Grieg coupling is, if anything, even finer, with an *Allegro molto* first movement that truly is *ed agitato*, a warming *Romanze* and a superbly characterised *Intermezzo*. It's richly recorded.

Violin Sonatas

No 1 in F, Op 8; **No 2** in G, Op 13;
No 3 in C minor, Op 45

Violin Sonatas Nos 1-3
Henning Kraggerud *vn* **Helge Kjekshus** *pf*
Naxos 8 553904 (67' · DDD)   Ⓢ➤

This disc gives us consistently enjoyable performances. The two young Norwegians play with idiomatic style, and give the impression of expressing every aspect of the music. Their eagerness at the start of Op 8's first *Allegro* sets the tone; the *doloroso* opening of Op 13, the delicacy and serenity of the E major section of that sonata's middle movement, and the exciting 'Hall of the Mountain King' atmosphere they generate in the finale of Op 45 – these are just a few of the places where the pair convince us they've found exactly the right sound and manner of expression. Kraggerud's account of the 'big tune' in the last movement of Op 45, respecting all Grieg's marks of expression and phrasing, has real nobility. Highly recommendable.

Piano Works

Volume 1: Piano Sonata in E minor, Op 7. Funeral March for Rikard Nordraak, CW117. Melodies of Norway – The sirens' enticement. Stimmungen, Op 73. Transcriptions of Original Songs I, Op 41 – No 3, I love thee. Four Humoresques, Op 6. Four Piano Pieces, Op 1
Einar Steen-Nøkleberg *pf*
Naxos 8 550881 (72' · DDD)   Ⓢ➤

Volume 2: Two Improvisations on Norwegian Folksongs, Op 29. Melodies of Norway – A Ballad to Saint Olaf. 25 Norwegian Folksongs and Dances, Op 17. Transcriptions of Original Songs II, Op 52 – No 2, The first meeting. 19 Norwegian Folksongs, Op 66
Einar Steen-Nøkleberg *pf*
Naxos 8 550882 (70' · DDD)   Ⓢ➤

Volume 3: Four Album Leaves, Op 28. Six Poetic Tone-pictures, Op 3. Melodies of Norway – Iceland. Three Pictures from Life in the Country, Op 19. Three Pieces from 'Sigurd Jorsalfar', Op 56 – Prelude. Ballade in G minor, Op 24, 'in the form of variations on a Norwegian melody'
Einar Steen-Nøkleberg *pf*
Naxos 8 550883 (64' · DDD)   Ⓢ➤

Volume 4: Holberg Suite, Op 40. Melodies of Norway – I went to bed so late. Six Norwegian Mountain Melodies, CW134. Peer Gynt Suite No 1, Op 46 –

Morning. 17 Norwegian Peasant Dances, Op 72
Einar Steen-Nøkleberg pf
Naxos 8 550884 (71' · DDD) ⓈⒹ▸

These are the first four volumes of a complete Grieg cycle which stretches to no fewer than 14 discs. Since they are all at super-budget price they make a very competitive alternative to other complete or near-complete surveys. Einar Steen-Nøkleberg came to prominence during the 1970s and won numerous Norwegian and other prizes. He was professor of the piano at the Hanover Musikhochschule for a number of years and is the author of a monograph on Grieg's piano music and its interpretation.

Volume 1: The first disc juxtaposes early pieces, the Sonata, Op 7, the Op 6 *Humoresques* and the *Funeral March for Rikard Nordraak*, all written in the mid-1890s with his very last piano work, *Stimmungen* (or 'Moods'), Op 73. He plays these bold and original pieces with great flair and understanding. Whatever its limitations there's much greater range in Grieg's piano music than is commonly realised and Steen-Nøkleberg is attuned to the whole spectrum it covers, ranging from the Bartókian 'Mountaineer's Song' from Op 73 to the charm and innocence of the *Allegretto con grazia*, the third of the *Humoresques*, Op 6.

Volume 2: The *19 Norwegian Folksongs* (1896) are remarkable pieces as Grieg himself knew. He wrote to the Dutch composer, Julius Röntgen, of having 'put some hair-raising chromatic chords on paper. The excuse is that they originated not on the piano but in my mind.' Readers will recognise No 14 as the source of the theme for Delius's *On Hearing the First Cuckoo in Spring*. Steen-Nøkleberg plays them with great tonal finesse and consummate artistry.

Volume 3: The most substantial work on this disc is the *Ballade* which Grieg wrote on his parents' death. This recording can hold its own with the best in this healthy area of the catalogue – even if there are moments when Steen-Nøkleberg seems too discursive. Yet what an imaginative colour he produces in the *Adagio* variation when the music suddenly melts *pianissimo*.

Volume 4: The *Norwegian Peasant Dances* are amazing pieces for their period, and though their audacity and dissonance were later overtaken by Bartók, they still retain their capacity to surprise. The playing conveys the extraordinary character and originality of these pieces as do few others. The smaller pieces contained on this disc – as well as on its companions – are full of rewards.

Lyric Pieces, Book 1, Op 12 – No 1, Arietta; No 2, Waltz; No 5, Folksong; No 6, Norwegian; Book 2, Op 38 – No 6, Elegy; No 7, Waltz; No 8, Canon; Book 4 Op 47 – No 2, Album Leaf; No 3, Melody; No 4, Norwegian Dance; Book 5, Op 54 – No 3, March of the Trolls; No 4, Nocturne; Book 6, Op 57 – No 2, Gade; No 3, Illusion; No 6, Homesickness; Book 7, Op 62 – No 1, Sylph; No 4, Brooklet; No 5, Phantom; No 6, Homeward; Book 8, Op 65 – No 6,

Wedding Day at Troldhaugen; Book 9, Op 68 – No 3, At your Feet; No 4, Evening in the Mountains; No 5, Cradle Song; Book 10, Op 71 – No 6, Gone; No 7, Remembrances
Leif Ove Andsnes pf
EMI 557296-2 (68' · DDD). Played on Grieg's piano at the Grieg Troldhaugen Museum, Bergen ⒻⓄOOOD▸

 Once again on home ground, Andsnes reminds you of his capacity to go directly to the heart of the matter. Taking you on a journey of increasing subtlety and introspection, he makes you aware that so much of this music is for those long winter nights. At the same time the music is so richly varied: The insistent dactylic rhythm of 'Melody' creates a strange unsettling poetic ambience, while the central oasis of calm in 'Wedding Day at Troldhaugen' would surely melt a heart of stone.

All Andsnes's performances have that deceptive simplicity which is his touchstone. His playing is always sensitive, never sentimental and with a bracing and essential 'touch of the codfish' (Grieg) when required. And while one would never want to be without Gilels's rapt DG performances (see below), praise could hardly be too high for a pianist who so enviably captures the poignant nature of a composer who Tchaikovsky once claimed had 'a glance like a charming and candid child'. Grieg's piano, with its distinctive timbre, provides an added touch of nostalgia.

Lyric Pieces – Arietta, Op 12 No 1. Berceuse, Op 38 No 1. Butterfly, Op 43 No 1. Solitary Traveller, Op 43 No 2. Album Leaf, Op 47 No 3. Melody, Op 47 No 3. Norwegian Dance, 'Halling', Op 47 No 4. Nocturne, Op 54 No 4. Scherzo, Op 54 No 5. Homesickness, Op 57 No 6. Brooklet, Op 62 No 4. Homeward, Op 62 No 6. In ballad vein, Op 65 No 5. Grandmother's Minuet, Op 68 No 2. At your feet, Op 68 No 3. Cradle Song, Op 68 No 5. Once upon a time, Op 71 No 1. Puck, Op 71 No 3. Gone, Op 71 No 6. Remembrances, Op 71 No 7
Emil Gilels pf
DG The Originals 449 721-2GOR (56' · ADD) Recorded 1974 ⓂOOOD▸

 Here, surely, is a classic recording, one of calibre and status for all time. Rarely can a great artist have declared his love with such touching candour. By his own admission Gilels discovered in Grieg's *Lyric Pieces* a 'whole world of intimate feeling' and at the sessions where these were recorded fought tirelessly to capture their intricate mix of innocence and experience. The results are of an unblemished purity, grace and contained eloquence. He brings the same insight and concentration to these apparent trifles as he did to towering masterpieces of the classic repertoire. The programme proceeds chronologically and one can appreciate the gradual but marked development in Grieg's harmonic and expressive language – from the folksong-inspired early works to the more progressive and adventurous later ones. Gilels's fingerwork is exquisite and the sense of total involvement with the music almost religious in feeling. Never can Debussy's sniping estimate of Grieg, 'a pink bonbon filled with snow' (or DG's dreary accompanying notes) have seemed wider of the mark. The recordings remain as impeccable as the playing. This is a disc for everyone's desert island.

Lyric Pieces – selection. Holberg Suite, Op 40. Poetic Tone Pictures, Op 3
Katya Apekisheva pf
Quartz QTZ2061 (79' · DDD)   Ⓕ**OOO**▷

Cards on the table: Katya Apekisheva is a young pianist who has already achieved artistic greatness. Not even Emil Gilels, in his legendary DG Grieg recital, played more magically or, astonishingly, with greater finesse. How thrilled Irina Zaritskaya, Apekisheva's teacher, would have been if she had lived to hear the fruit of her work with this profoundly gifted artist. A sonority of beguiling warmth and refinement and a rare poetic empathy quickly make you listen mesmerised as Apekisheva captures the very essence of Grieg's genius.

Here, in her mixed programme, she tells you with an often painfully beautiful and unforced eloquence of how Grieg's romantic temperament was easily clouded by depression and unease, of the way, for example in 'Homesickness' and 'Vanished Days', a heartbreaking state of mind is only temporarily modified by memories of happier times. The sense of the *Lyric Pieces* as Grieg's confessional diary is everywhere in Apekisheva's recital. In the Aria from the *Holberg Suite* she is deeply sensitive to the way Grieg's love and respect for the 18th century is coloured by a near-Franckian chromaticism and dark introspection. These works and everything else on this beautifully recorded album suggest an artistic fervour and commitment given to very few in any generation.

Peer Gynt

Peer Gynt – The Bridal March Passes By; Prelude; Ⓗ
In the Hall of the Mountain King; Solveig's Song;
Prelude; Arab Dance; Anitra's Dance; Prelude;
Solveig's Cradle Song. Symphonic Dance, Op 64 –
Allegretto grazioso. In Autumn, Op 11. Old
Norwegian Romance with Variations, Op 51
Ilse Hollweg sop **Beecham Choral Society; Royal Philharmonic Orchestra / Sir Thomas Beecham**
EMI Great Recordings of the Century 566914-2
(77' · ADD). Recorded 1957   Ⓜ**OO**▷

Grieg's incidental music was an integral part of Ibsen's *Peer Gynt* and from this score Grieg later extracted the two familiar suites. This recording of excerpts from *Peer Gynt* goes back to 1957 but still sounds well and is most stylishly played. Included is the best known ('Anitra's Dance' is a delicate gem here) together with 'Solveig's Song' and 'Solveig's Cradle Song'. Beecham

uses Ilse Hollweg to advantage, her voice suggesting the innocence of the virtuous peasant heroine. There's also an effective use of the choral voices which are almost inevitably omitted in ordinary performances of the two well-known suites: the male chorus of trolls in the 'Hall of the Mountain King' are thrilling, and the women in the 'Arab Dance' are charming. The other two pieces are well worth having too; *Symphonic Dances* is a later, freshly pastoral work, while the overture *In Autumn* is an orchestral second version of an early piece for piano duet. This reissue is further enhanced by the first release in stereo of the *Old Norwegian Romance*.

Peer Gynt
Christiane Kohl sop Solveig **Boguslaw Bidzinski** ten
Peer Gynt **Agnieszka Adamczak, Huiling Zhu** sops
Angelica Voje mez **Chorus, Orchestra and Ballet of the Opera House, Zürich / Eivind Gullberg Jensen**
Choreographer **Heinz Spoerli**
Set designer **Florian Etti**
Video director **Andy Sommer**
Bel Air Classiques 🄳🅅🄳 BAC050 (110' · NTSC · 16:9 · PCM stereo, 5.1 & DTS 5.1 · 0). Includes additonal music by Brett Dean and Mark-Anthony Turnage   Ⓕ

Zürich Ballet chief Heinz Spoerli has created a passionately felt ballet from much of Grieg's score, some of Ibsen's dialogue (in German) and the borrowing of existing contemporary music. His choice and placing in the sequence of six pieces by Australian composer and ex-Berlin Philharmonic viola player Brett Dean and two by Mark-Anthony Turnage follow the darker, neurotic corners of Ibsen's play more closely than Grieg did – a kind of filling-in of the traditional incidental music.

The Turnage and Dean works also bring forth a freer, more modern form of dance and, in this choreography, strike more dramatic sparks than the lively but relatively conventional set-pieces sculpted by Spoerli to Grieg's main numbers. Turnage's jazzy *Scherzoid* follows, and intentionally disrupts, the comfortably familiar 'Morning Mood' in the Act 4 desert; it's used by Spoerli as an ambivalent meeting between newly rich (but always outsider) Peer and his potential Arabian friends or partners. Similar highlights are Dean's *Beggars and Angels* and *Shadow Music I*. Both provide staging opportunities for the many human and supernatural warnings Ibsen gives of Peer's demise on his return to Norway.

Spoerli's decision to double-cast Peer with dancer and actor is effective, as is his fast-rising conductor Eivind Gullberg Jensen's decisions to remain with a house rather than guest cast for the singing roles, and that all voices, even speaking ones, should come from offstage. Jensen is able to secure from the Zürich Opera orchestra a deft pit-band lightness – and Norwegian-ness – of touch in the Grieg numbers which can elude symphony orchestras in concerts of this material. His Dean and Turnage feel hardly less fluent. Good, representative filming and sound complete a project which, after a comfortable first half, strikes some suitably unsettling resonances in its full treatment of Ibsen's final two acts.

Songs

Haugtussa, Op 67. Two brown eyes, Op 5 No 1. I love but thee, Op 5 No 3. A Swan, Op 25 No 2. With a waterlily, Op 25 No 4. Hope, Op 26 No 1. Spring, Op 33 No 2. Beside the stream, Op 33 No 5. From Monte Pincio, Op 39 No 1. Six Songs, Op 48. Spring showers, Op 49 No 6. While I wait, Op 60 No 3. Farmyard Song, Op 61 No 3
Anne Sofie von Otter mez **Bengt Forsberg** pf
DG 477 6326GGP (68' · DDD · T/t) Ⓜ❍❍❍🅑➔

Ⓖ Von Otter is at the peak of her powers here, glorying in this repertoire. In the *Haugtussa* cycle she projects her imagination of the visionary herd-girl with absolute conviction. She's no less successful in the German settings that follow. The sad depths of 'One day, my thought' from Six Songs, Op 48, the hopelessness of Goethe's 'The time of roses' (Op 48 No 5), a setting of great beauty, are encompassed with unfettered ease, but so are the lighter pleasures of 'Lauf der Welt'. Even the familiar 'A Dream' (Op 48 No 6) emerges as new in her daringly big-boned reading. Her readings are immeasurably enhanced throughout by the imaginative playing of Bengt Forsberg. They breathe fresh life into 'A Swan' and in the almost as familiar 'With a waterlily', another superb Ibsen setting, the questing spirit expressed in the music is marvellously captured by the performers. This should be regarded as a 'must' for any collector.

Six Ibsen Songs, Op 25. Six Songs, Op 48. Melodies of the Heart, Op 5. Haugtussa, Op 67. The Princess, EG133
Katarina Karnéus mez **Julius Drake** pf
Hyperion CDA67670 (68' · DDD) Ⓕ❍❍🅑➔

Anne Sofie von Otter's Grieg recital for DG (see above) did much to encourage singers outside Scandinavia to bring back to the concert platform – and the public again to listen to – songs which their great-grandparents knew well but their parents had almost forgotten. Now another front-ranking Swedish mezzo-soprano has recorded core components of the Grieg song repertoire. Like her compatriot, Katarina Karnéus includes the Op 67 *Haugtussa* cycle, the Ibsen settings, the six German lyrics of Op 48 and the early Hans Christian Andersen *Melodies of the Heart*, adding, suitably, the less well known 'The Princess' to words by Bjørnstjerne Bjørnson.

Compare Karnéus, von Otter and Kirsten Flagstad (one of at least three recordings) in *Haugtussa*. Karnéus and Julius Drake are all over the imagery, scenery and sexuality of Garborg's verse novel in thrilling and well worked detail. Flagstad

may appear at first hearing to be limiting herself to heroic declamation and her pianist (regular collaborator Edwin McArthur) just mapping out the written notes, but her sheer joy in singing her own language, and the subtlety of her pointing of the text (a half-smile, a raised eyebrow) and cunning use of her large voice make their own points. Von Otter has something of both sides – a weightier tone and more reserve than Karnéus but a much wider colour range than Flagstad chooses to deploy – and Bengt Forsberg is a magician in these accompaniments.

Elsewhere the Karnéus performances are good and lively in the Scandinavian lyrics (a passionate 'Jeg elsker dig', a good range of moods in the Ibsen settings), more formal in the German settings. All Saints' Church in Finchley, north London, sounds especially resonant here, not everywhere an advantage in such text-oriented settings. Lots to enjoy and celebrate then, but don't ignore the competition.

Charles Griffes American 1884-1920

Griffes studied in his home-town of Elmire, New York state, and then travelled to Berlin to study with Humperdinck, where he remained from 1903 to 1907. On returning to the US he taught at the Hackley School for boys in Tarrytown, New York, a post which he held until his early death 13 years later. His early works draw their inspiration from the German Romantic tradition but his language moved closer to the French tradition. Debussy's music stands behind some of his piano music from the second decade of the century (The Pleasure-Dome of Kubla Khan, 1912; Roman Sketches, 1915-16) and songs. And French music with, perhaps, hint of Scriabin can be discerned in his orchestration.

Orchestral Works

Bacchanale. Clouds. Poem for Flute and Orchestra. The Pleasure-Dome of Kubla Khan. The White Peacock. Three Poems of Fiona McLeod. Three Tone-Pictures
Barbara Quintiliani sop **Carol Wincenc** fl
Buffalo Philharmonic Orchestra / JoAnn Falletta
Naxos 8 559164 (56' · DDD) Ⓢ❍➔

Griffes represents the high-point of American post-Romanticism. From his European training he inherited both the German and French traditions of Strauss and Debussy, fused them into something rich and strange, and in his later years became involved with Scriabin and oriental music. Much of his music has been regularly available on record, but this all-Griffes CD now makes the best showing for his hyper-sensitive responses to both literature and landscape.

Many of the works here are piano pieces fastidiously scored, with significant additions. *The White Peacock*, just possibly a cousin of Stravinsky's *Firebird*, is the first of the *Roman Sketches* for piano, all prefaced with stanzas by Fiona McLeod (a nom de plume for William Sharp): the impressionistic *Clouds* is the last of these. The orchestral opulence of the *Three Poems of Fiona McLeod*, steeped in baleful Celtic twilights, makes the piano version seem anaemic; they're compellingly sung here by Barbara Quintiliani.

In the *Three Tone-Pictures* every picturesque detail of harmonically qualified melody is subtly imagined. The same applies to the *Poem* for flute and orchestra, where the continuity has the instinctive flow of Delius, beautifully realised by Carol Wincenc. *The Pleasure-Dome of Kubla Khan*, the most extended work in this anthology, is an ecstatic response to Coleridge's opium-saturated masterpiece.

Conductor JoAnn Faletta is completely sympathetic throughout, and there are neatly delivered solos from many of the Buffalo players. This is a revelatory Griffes release, decently recorded with a wide dynamic range: strongly recommended.

Sofia Gubaidulina   Russian b1931

Gubaidulina studied at the Moscow Conservatory and during the 1960s and '70s wrote primarily chamber music, which often uses serial techniques, as in Night in Memphis of 1968. She then explored the potential of orchestral and vocal genres; her experiments in the role of rests culminated in the solo for conductor in the symphony Stimmen Verstummen (1986). Gubaidulina became better known abroad during the early 1980s through Gidon Kremer's championing of her violin concerto Offertorium. In 2000 Gubaidulina, along with Tan Dun, Osvaldo Golijov and Wolfgang Rihm, was commissioned by the Internationale Bachakademie Stuttgart project to write a piece for the Passion 2000 project in commemoration of JS Bach. Her contribution was the Johannes-Passion. In 2002 she followed this by the Johannes-Ostern ('Easter According to John'), commissioned by Hannover Rundfunk. The two works together form a 'diptych' on the death and resurrection of Christ, and constitute her largest work to date. Her work The Light at the End preceded Beethoven's Symphony No 9 in the 2005 BBC Proms. In 2007 her second violin concerto In tempus praesens was performed at the Lucerne Festival by Anne-Sophie Mutter.

Orchestral Works

Seven Last Words[a]. Flute Concerto, 'The Deceitful Face of Hope and of Despair'[b]
[b]**Sharon Bezaly** fl [a]**Torleif Thedéen** vc [a]**Mie Miki** accor **Gothenburg Symphony Orchestra /**
Mario Venzago
BIS ⏤ BIS-SACD1449 (61' · DDD/DSD)   ⓕⓄ➔

'Every interval,' Gubaidulina explains, 'creates a summation tone and a difference tone: an interval in the lowest register creates a difference tone which we recognise not as a tone but a pul-

sation.' At higher registers we 'hear the pulsation of the difference tone simultaneously with the original interval'. Gubaidulina sees this transition from pulse to tone and back (and, eventually, the loss of even the pulse) as a metaphor for hope and despair. *The Deceitful Face* Concerto exploits and explores this acoustical phenomenon and the emotional process of struggling against despair. As the piece unfolds, quiet passages inhabited by the flute soloist and other individual instruments are brutally invaded by outbursts from larger groupings. The flute part, impressively realised by Sharon Bezaly, finally gives way to the terrifying pulsing of the bass drum from which the piece first welled up.

Seven Last Words (1982) is a kind of companion piece to *In croce* (1979), in which cello and bajan (Russian accordion) moved towards an explosive meeting from their extreme registers. Again, the crossing of lines is among the structural devices used to symbolise crucifixion. As is her custom, Gubaidulina asks her soloists to venture beyond the standard techniques of their instruments but, as ever, she does so in the service of expressiveness, not novelty. Her thorough command of instrumental colour (and, indeed, temperature) is put to brilliant use in evoking the contradictory emotions associated with Good Friday, from the pain and despair of the participants to the implicit hope of believers.

Gubaidulina Violin Concerto, 'In tempus praesens'[b]
Bach Violin Concertos[a] – BWV1041; BWV1042
Anne-Sophie Mutter vn [a]**Trondheim Soloists;**
[b]**London Symphony Orchestra / Valery Gergiev**
DG 477 7450GH (62' · DDD)   ⓕⓄ➔

Anne-Sophie Mutter lost no time in recording the violin concerto written for her by Sofia Gubaidulina in 2006-07. In a single movement running for about 32 minutes, it shows the composer's concern to make a direct and immediate impact, avoiding complicated materials but using expansive forms. It's possible to sense the kind of allusions to Mahlerian archetypes that are no less prominent in Shostakovich or Schnittke. Yet Gubaidulina has her own very personal musical identity, and the concerto's strategies for playing off heights against depths, lament against affirmation, are powerfully realised. The risks of rambling, improvisatory musing are triumphantly avoided, and the work's final stages appear to bring starkly opposed images of extinction and rebirth into a strongly ambivalent conclusion that both affirms and questions resolution.

This darkly inviting music is splendidly performed. You'd expect the Mutter/Gergiev combination to be combustible, and there is certainly no reticence or half-measures in the way the music's expressive core, its play with visions of hell and heaven, is exposed. Gestures towards traditional consonant harmony stand out strangely, and dance-like patterns are clearly not going to survive for very long in a context where brooding and turbulence are the principal qualities. The resplendent recording celebrates the score's rich colouring while never allowing the solo line, played with all this performer's natural theatricality and poise, to lose its prominence. Maybe, at one particularly stark climax, the hammered rhythmic repetitions in the orchestra seem over-emphatic. But urgency rather than reticence drives Gubaidulina's thought, and this performance never lets you forget it.

It would have been good to hear these performers in Gubaidulina's other major work for violin and orchestra, *Offertorium*. Instead, the pair of Bach concertos speak of a distant musical world in which stability and spontaneity achieved an extraordinary conjunction. The performances are neat, tidy, dispatched with elegance and vigour. Yet they reinforce the gulf that musically separates then from now, and all-Gubaidulina discs are not as common as they should be.

De profundis[a]. Seven Words[b]. Ten Preludes[c]
[ab]**Elsbeth Moser** *bajan* [c]**Boris Pergamenschikov** *vc*
[b]**Munich Chamber Orchestra / Christoph Poppen**
ECM New Series 461 897-2 (72' · DDD)　　　Ⓕ🄱➔

Recordings of Sofia Gubaidulina's music differ markedly as to presentation. Elsbeth Moser and Boris Pergamenschikov interpret *Seven Last Words*, meditations rather than commentaries on the biblical texts, with chamber-like inwardness. Their fervent confrontation in movement IV has a transparency of texture, incisive strings kept to the rear, which offsets the gestural immediacy of the experience. The final movement isn't so much valedictory as implosive, draining away in a haze of sound and emotion. The premiere recording by Friedrich Lips and Vladimir Tonkha, briefly available on Melodiya, has an impact like no other, but this new recording has a distinct and searching identity of its own. It's enhanced by the companion pieces. The Ten Preludes have become staples of the modern repertoire, harnessing technique to a range of moods which work perfectly as a sequence. *De profundis* is a classic of its medium, and while Gerd Draugsvoll on BIS draws visceral emotion from this quirky mix of dissonance and incantation, Moser's lucid unfolding probes deeper. Sound, here and in the *Preludes*, is a model of solo balance.

Chamber Works

In croce[a]. 10 Preludes. Quaternion[b]
Alexander Ivashkin, [b]**Natalia Pavlutskaya**, [b]**Rachel Johnston**, [b]**Miranda Wilson** *vcs* [a]**Malcolm Hicks** *org*
Chandos CHAN9958 (56' · DDD)　　　　　Ⓕ🄱➔

A quaternion may be a mathematical operation, but there's nothing calculated or contrived about *Quaternion* for four cellos (1996), which here receives its first recording. At its best – as it certainly is here – Gubaidulina's music manages to combine a fiercely improvisatory freedom

with a satisfying sense of balance and coherence. On one level *Quaternion* concerns the contrast between the mundane and the transcendent. Yet although the music contains strikingly immediate evocations of both the earthy and the uncanny, it never suggests the withdrawn serenity of a spirituality that regards the real world as 'lost'. Ivashkin and his colleagues achieve marvels of co-ordination, as well as an astonishingly wide range of colour, qualities enhanced by a truthful and well-balanced recording.

Two earlier works complete the programme. The Ten Preludes for solo cello (1974) encapsulate energy and expressiveness to highly charged poetic effect. *In croce* for cello and organ (1979) transforms what could have been a simplistic exercise in the crossing over of two very different sound sources into a grippingly unpredictable drama of convergence and divergence. Both pieces have been recorded before, and you might welcome the chance to acquire the bargain-price version of *In croce* in its alternative arrangement for cello and accordion (Naxos). But Alexander Ivashkin is a fine player, unsurpassed in Gubaidulina's music.

Francisco Guerrero　　Spanish 1528-99

Guerrero was a pupil of Morales. Aged 17 he was appointed maestro de capilla of Jaén Cathedral and then vice-maestro and maestro of Seville Cathedral, a post he held from 1574 to 1599. He also visited Rome, Venice and the Holy Land – the return from which was somewhat fraught (including two attacks by pirates which left him penniless), but provided him with the material for a hugely popular book. He was the most important 16th-century Spanish composer of sacred music after Victoria, publishing 18 Masses and about 150 motets. Such was their power and approachability they remained in use in Spanish and Spanish-American cathedrals for more than two centuries after his death.

Missa de la Batalla Escoutez

Missa de la Batalla Escoutez[ab]. Pange lingua[a].　　Ⓟ
In exitu Israel[ab]. Duo Seraphim[a]. Regina coeli[b]
Magnificat[a]. Conditor alme siderum[a]
[a]**Westminster Cathedral Choir**; [b]**His Majestys Sagbutts and Cornetts / James O'Donnell**
Hyperion Helios CDH55340 (72' · DDD · T/t) Ⓑ🄾🄾➔

Despite his suggestive name, Guerrero's parody of Janequin's *La bataille de Marignan* isn't the work of a fighting man: fanfares and alarums are definitely off the agenda while he develops, in an often rather sober manner, the smooth counterpoint of his model. Only in the 'Osanna' does Guerrero let rip, a moment seized on with gusto by the choir and His Majestys Sagbutts and Cornetts. Guerrero spent his career at Seville Cathedral, where the chapter was one of the first in Spain to agree to the establishment of a permanent, salaried wind band to participate in processions and at other points in divine worship. It appears to have been one of Guerrero's duties to sort out what and when, and even how (scoring and ornamentation were part of his brief) the minstrels played.

The instruments (shawms, cornetts, sackbuts, dulcian and organ) subtly double the voices, adding depth to the sound, and strengthening major cadence points. Particularly striking is the earthy tone of the *bajón* (dulcian) reinforcing the bass-line in proto-continuo fashion. In fact, it's in the other items on this CD that the combination of voices and instruments really comes into its own. The setting of the psalm *In exitu Israel* experiments with Guerrero's forces (including cornetts and recorders), resulting in an opulence of sound more readily associated with Venetian music of the period. But this isn't just an exercise in applied musicology. These are well-paced, intelligent performances that get inside the skin of Guerrero's marvellous music. Don't be surprised to find yourself humming the Spanish chant for the hymn *Conditor alme siderum* after this compelling rendition. The musicianship is superb, the technical element entirely satisfactory and satisfying.

Additional recommendation

Guerrero Missa de la Batalla Escoutez. Lauda mater ecclesia. Tota pulchra es, Maria. Hymn: Vexilla Regis. Song of Songs: Ego flos campi. Pange lingua **Janequin** La guerre (La bataille de Marignan)
The Sixteen / Christophers
Coro COR16067 (69' · DDD · T/t) Ⓕ🅞🕪

To the Westminster Cathedral Choir's historically documented approach to performance The Sixteen now provide an *a cappella* alternative. The winds in the earlier recording helped James O'Donnell to evoke the martial atmosphere of the original Janequin song. The Sixteen take an altogether more placid approach throughout. It's a fine piece, and to have two contrasted interpretations of similar quality can only deepen one's appreciation of it.

Ivor Gurney   British 1890-1937

Early musical promise led to a scholarship, at 14, to the Royal College of Music where Gurney studied with Stanford. Stanford told Gurney's friend Herbert Howells that he was potentially 'the biggest of them all' but that he was 'unteachable'. The First World War interrrupted and Gurney was gassed in the trenches. After the war he returned to the RCM, where he studied with Vaughan Williams, but soon he was showing symptoms of bipolar disorder. By 1922 he had been declared insane and spent the rest of his life as a patient in various institutions. As well as being a composer of note, he was also a poet and his war poetry has guaranteed his reputation. He died of tuberculosis aged 47.

Songs

All night under the moon. The Apple Orchard. The boat is chafing. By a Bierside. Cathleen ni Houlihan. An Epitaph. Epitaph in Old Mode. The Fiddler of Dooney. Ha'nacker Mill. I will go with my father a-ploughing. Last hours. Nine of the Clock. On the Downs. The Scribe. The Ship. The Singer. Snow. Thou didst delight my eyes. When death to either shall come. Cradle Song. Lights Out. The Bonnie Earl of Murray. The Cherry Trees. Five Elizabethan Songs. The Latmian Shepherd. Fain would I change that note
Susan Bickley mez **Iain Burnside** pf
Naxos 8 572151 (72' · DDD)   Ⓢ🕪

Stanford considered Gurney the pupil of his who most clearly displayed the signs of 'genius'. Certainly, this collection of 30 songs, the latest in the Naxos English Song series, demonstrates that genius, above all in his feeling for English words, which is also demonstrated in his own poetry.

The writer of the excellent notes on this disc suggests very perceptively that Gurney's feeling for triplet hemiolas in his settings may owe something to his training as a chorister in Gloucester Cathedral, or even to his love of Brahms. Sadly, too few of these songs are well known. One of the more familiar is 'I will go with my father a-ploughing', folk-like and exuberant.

Otherwise the settings of John Masefield are especially memorable, notably 'By a Bierside' with a wonderful final climax, superbly conveyed here by Susan Bickley. Another poet close to Gurney was Edward Thomas, best-known for the glorious poem 'Adlestrop' and here represented by some of the most touching of the songs. It is interesting too that Gurney sets 'The Bonnie Earl of Murray' with a real Scottish tang, a song, incidentally, that Brahms set earlier.

Wherever you turn, these songs offer illumination and refreshment, splendidly captured not only by Susan Bickley but by her ever-sensitive accompanist, Iain Burnside.

Barry Guy   British b1947

A double-bass player as well as a composer, Guy's musical interests cross many genres. He is founder and artistic director of the London Jazz Composers Orchestra for whom he has written a number of works. Indeed nearly all his music derives from a personal relationship with the musicians he composes for – which also enables the improvisatory nature of music to connect at a remarkable keen level.

Folio

Folio
Muriel Cantoreggi, Maya Homburger vns
Barry Guy db **Munich Chamber Orchestra / Christoph Poppen**

ECM New Series 476 3053 (58' · DDD)   ⓟⒹ→

Barry Guy's *Folio* is a multi-movement cycle for string orchestra, inspired by a stage work by Nikolai Evreinov, *The Theatre of the Soul*, written in 1912. It is, in part, a reflection on the parallels between the historical situation of that time and place, and our own. Perhaps this dialogue of time and place explains the use of a Baroque and a modern violin among the work's soloists. The cycle brings together free-standing movements of varying length for string orchestra (which can be performed independently of the cycle), connected by a number of 'improvised commentaries' by a combination of the soloists and Barry Guy himself on the double bass. The bringing together of both improvised and through-composed music is another of the cycle's themes, and in several movements the two may occur simultaneously, with the soloist being given a choice of materials from which to draw upon.

The longest work is the 20-minute 'Postlude – Ortiz I – Postlude'. It alternates between quasi-spectral harmonic fields and chaotic episodes, all of which exploit the string orchestra's potential for timbral cohesion and sheer power. Guy's experience as a string player comes into its own here, and his own improvisations have real flair and a slightly understated virtuosity: one would have liked to hear more of them. The shorter movements are less contrasted within themselves, more concerned with a single idea. The intended overall structure is not easy to grasp at first hearing but the performance matches the composer's liking for striking, bold gestures and highly imaged detail. The work's 'quirkiness quotient' is consonant with a certain ECM house-style, with which its devotees will be instantly at home.

Pavel Haas   Czech 1899-1944

Haas studied composition at the Brno Conservatory in Janáček's masterclass (1920-22). He worked first in his father's business, then from 1935 as a private teacher of music theory, and finally taught music at the Jewish secondary in Brno. Haas took the style of Janáček as his starting-point, and came closer to Janáček's compositional method than any of his other pupils. However, he developed this in his own way and soon achieved a mature individuality. During the German Occupation he suffered persecution on account of his Jewish origins, performances of his compositions were banned, and neither he nor his wife were allowed to work. He was imprisoned in Terezín concentration camp (1941-44), where he continued to compose. Haas died in a gas chamber at Auschwitz.

String quartets

Haas String Quartets – No 1, Op 3; No 3, Op 15
Janáček String Quartet No 1, 'The Kreutzer Sonata'

Pavel Haas Quartet (Veronika Jarúšková, Marie Fuxová *vns* Pavel Nikl *va* Peter Jarúšek *vc*)
Supraphon SU3922-2 (55' · DDD)   ⓕ○○

This disc's *Gramophone* Award-winning predecessor coupled the second string quartets of Haas and Janáček (see below), superbly played and including optional percussion in Haas's finale. Haas's Second (subtitled *From the Monkey Mountains*) is an amazing piece, but the Third is surely his masterpiece. It is both more concise and more tautly argued than the Second, less a journey into fantastical realms than an urgent, astringent drama, rhythmically driven and intensely heartfelt. And no wonder, given that the Quartet was composed in 1938 when Haas and his family were already marked for tragedy as part of a racially mixed community where an active Nazi faction was ready to pounce. Haas was destined for Auschwitz (where he was killed in 1944) and although it would be fanciful to read prophecy into the pages of this marvellous and varied work, the candour and emotional unrest that it expresses have inevitable associations. The longest movement is the last, a theme with variations which closes with a brief but pungent fugue and at times seems prophetic of Prokofiev's folk-derived Second Quartet of 1941.

The First Quartet (1921) plays for a continuous, action-packed 14 minutes and so impressed Haas's mentor Janáček that he had it performed. Although less striking than the Third, the First inhabits a similar climate, where temperature and colour shift with a degree of rapidity that suggests Janáček's influence, though Haas's musical language has a softer edge. In the hands of the Pavel Haas Quartet Janáček's own powerfully emotive First Quartet positively glows; one cannot but help ponder what Haas himself might have achieved had he too lived to compose at the ripe old age of 69! The Haas Quartet negotiate Janáček's fervid narrative without over-playing the drama, and they obviously relish its novel and occasionally abrasive sound world. This is a superb release that deserves not merely to bask in the reflected glory of its predecessor, but to share in it. The sound is first-rate.

P Haas String Quartet No 2, 'From the Monkey Mountains', Op 7[a]
Janáček String Quartet No 2, 'Intimate Letters'.
[a]**Colin Currie** *perc* **Pavel Haas Quartet** (Veronika Jarúšková, Kateřina Gemrotová *vns* Pavel Nikl *va* Peter Jarúšek *vc*)
Supraphon SU3877-2 (58' · DDD)   ⓕ○○○

Ⓖ The catalogue is not short of recommendable versions of Janáček's *Intimate Letters* Quartet. But there are any number of ways of bringing its hyper-passionate declarations off the page, and this young Czech quartet have plenty of ideas of their own about that. Once or twice that leads them into an over-calculated delivery. But try the third movement at 2'58" where, having fined the texture down to a whisper, Janáček gives the first violin an electrifying outburst: it's hard to imagine if that contrast has been made more emotionally real on record.

But then there is the 1925 Second Quartet by the composer whose name the players have adopted. This is the kind of piece that may make you wonder why you haven't heard it before. After a first movement that tellingly redeploys a number of patent Janáčekisms, Haas slips into the grotesque humour of Stravinsky's *Three Pieces for String Quartet* and once again fashions a structure that transcends reliance on its model. In the finale whackiness goes a step further, with a rollicking jazz-folk fusion, brilliantly caught here together with the original drum-kit accompaniment that Haas suppressed following adverse criticism at the premiere. The PHQ's streamlined but full-blooded playing is more than welcome. Superb recording quality too.

Reynaldo Hahn

Venezuelan/French 1875-1947

Hahn studied with Massenet at the Paris Conservatoire. While in his teens he gained a reputation as a composer of songs, which he sang to his own accompaniment in fashionable salons, gaining admittance to Proust's circle. But after 1900 he concentrated on the theatre, as conductor (at the Opéra from 1945) and as a composer of ballets, operas and operettas (Ciboulette, 1923; Mozart, 1925).

Violin Concerto

Violin Concerto[ch]. Piano Concerto[dh].
Suite Hongroise[cdh]. Violin Sonata in C[ce]. Romance in A[ce]. Nocturne[ce]. Piano Quintet[eg]. Les feuilles blessées[bf]. Amour sans ailes[af]. Cinq petites chansons[af]. Neuf mélodies retrouvées[bf]. Méduse[af] – Chanson au bord de la fontaine; Danse, petite sirène. La dame aux camélias[af] – Mon rêve était d'avoir; C'est à Paris!; Au fil de l'eau
[a]**Catherine Dune** *sop* [b]**Didier Henry** *bar* [c]**Denis Clavier** *vn* [d]**Angeline Pondepeyre**, [e]**Dimitris Saroglou**, [f]**Stéphane Petitjean** *pfs* [g]**Quatuor Clavier** (Denis Clavier, Marie-France Razafimbadà *vns* Florian Wallez *va* Claire Breteau *vc*); [h]**Lorraine Philharmonic Orchestra / Fernand Quattrocchi**
Maguelone ③ MAG111 111 (3h 23' · DDD · T/t) Ⓜ

Both the Violin Concerto and the Piano Concerto belong to a period in Hahn's life when he knew that strange mixture of happiness and regret that comes to us all in our fifties. The great figures he had known in his youth were nearly all dead, the First World War had claimed many of his contemporaries, and the glamour that had once surrounded his name had faded. Yet in the Paris of the 1920s he had his biggest stage successes (*Ciboulette* and *Mozart*) and entered on the longest and happiest relationship of his life with the tenor Guy Ferrant; all this seems to be expressed in the slow move-

ment of the Violin Concerto. Here we have Hahn spinning a slow, languorous tune that hovers between dance and delirium. It's marked throughout *Tranquillo*, *Très calme*, *Amoroso* and *Sans rigueur*. Denis Clavier plays it with just the right air of restraint: as Jean Gallois writes in the notes, it's 'a song from the soul without pathos'.

The better-known Piano Concerto from 1930 is a slighter work. Perhaps its curious structure – the second movement lasts less than three minutes – makes it seem a little jokey. Those who already have a recording should not be deterred from hearing this excellent performance: Angeline Pondepeyre takes the opening somewhat slower than Magda Tagliaferro in the historic recording conducted by the composer, but she brings out the jazzy element more.

The second CD starts with the Violin Sonata, composed in 1926. Denis Clavier and Dimitris Saroglou give a first-rate performance, the opening movement a beautiful questioning theme which gives way to a second, more romantic melody. The *Romance* and *Nocturne* are both real salon pieces, and the *Romance* in particular has a haunting tune. As for the Piano Quintet, this has some of Hahn's most passionate music in the slow movement. It's impossible not to believe that this piece – composed in 1920-21 – isn't a commentary on the tragic events of 1914-18.

The Quintet may be Hahn's personal reaction to the war, but while actually in the trenches, he composed music which was as far removed from the horrors as possible. His *Five Little Songs* were dedicated to Jan Bathori; it's very difficult for modern singers to hit off the mood of deliberate naivety in these songs, but it's good to have at least this performance. Most of the other songs on the third CD in this set have not been recorded before: it's not difficult to see why; the heavy sentiment is so hard to take.

This set can't be recommended too highly. Three CDs might seem too much to the uninitiated, but if you only know his songs or operettas, these is a lot to surprise here.

Chamber Works

Premières valses[a]. Venezia (arr Pidoux)[b]. Piano Quartet[c]. Soliloque et forlane[d]. Cello Concerto (unfinished, ed Pollain)[e]
[be]**Roland Pidoux**, [b]**Pierre Cordier**, [b]**Renaud Guieu**, [b]**Antoine Lederlin**, [b]**Matthieu Lejeune**, [b]**Christophe Morin** *vcs* [c]**Quatuor Gabriel** ([ade]Yoko Kaneko *pf* Guillaume Plays *vn* [d]Vincent Aucante *va* Jérôme Pinget *vc*)
Maguelone MAG111 117 (72' · DDD) Ⓕ

According to Jean Gallois's notes for this invaluable disc, the Quartet in G for violin, viola, cello and piano, was completed just a month before Hahn died in January 1947. If that's so, it can be listened to as a farewell, something that inevitably invokes Hahn's friendship with Marcel Proust. And even if one were told that he'd composed the quartet when he was young and happy, it would still evoke a mood of regret and yearning. It's the beautiful *Andante*, the third movement, that's the heart of the piece. A song without words that seems to speak of the pain of long parting, of thoughts unspoken, it ends on a reflective note of acceptance. Even the dance-like final movement, which contains a perhaps unconscious quote from some of the music for Hahn's musical comedy *Mozart*, also has a bittersweet quality. The Quatuor Gabriel play it eloquently, without undue sentimentality.

The suite *Premières valses* for piano was composed in 1898, when Hahn was at the height of his youthful celebrity in Parisian society. The fifth waltz is subtitled 'A l'ombre rêveuse de Chopin', and the whole sequence seems to be a tribute to the style of the 1840s. Yoko Kaneko plays it with more emphasis on the Polish mood than Catherine Joly in her 1988 recording on Accord. This performance reveals more of the rhythmic inventiveness in these miniatures.

The romantic *Soliloque et forlane* was composed in 1937 as a test piece for the Conservatoire. Vincent Aucante and Kaneko bring out the playful Spanish quality in the *allegro scherzando* finale. Finally, Roland Pidoux's arrangement of Hahn's song cycle *Venezia* for cello sextet must be such an expensive proposition that you're unlikely to encounter it in the concert hall. The tunes are adorable.

Songs

A Chloris. Le rossignol des lilas. L'enamourée. Trois jours de vendange. Etudes latines – Lydé; Tyndaris; Phyllis. Les fontaines. Automne. Infidélité. Dans la nuit. D'une prison. Quand la nuit n'est pas étoilée. Fumée. Le printemps. Je me souviens. Quand je fus pris au pavillon. Paysage. Fêtes galantes. Nocturne. Mai. L'heure exquise. Offrande. Si mes vers avaient des ailes
Susan Graham sop **Roger Vignoles** pf
Sony Classical SK60168 (62' · DDD · T/t) Ⓕ🅾🅾➔

Susan Graham brings to these songs a voice of lovely quality, excellent French and – in keeping with Hahn's own insistence – gives overriding importance to clarity of enunciation, the verbal meaning governing the vocal colour. It's certainly better to savour these songs a few at a time, but the programme has been well put together to show Hahn's range, from the Bachian pastiche of 'A Chloris' or the antique simplicity of 'Lydé' to the adventurous harmonic progressions of 'Fumée', 'Le printemps' or 'Je me souviens', from the despairing pathos of 'D'une prison' to the light-heartedness of 'Quand je fus pris au pavillon', from the quiet rapture of 'Nocturne' to the passion of 'Dans la nuit' (a splendid miniature). His outstanding gift for lyricism is evident throughout; 'Le rossignol des lilas', for example, is enchanting. Susan Graham perfectly captures these songs' elegant intimacy with a wealth of nuance, from the gentle tone of 'L'enamourée' to the fullness of 'L'automne'; and the way she

floats the words 'l'heure exquise' is haunting. Roger Vignoles provides most sensitive partnership throughout: he has more scope in songs like 'Les fontaines' or 'Dans la nuit', but equally noteworthy is his subtle treatment of the repeated pattern of 'Infidélité'.

Douze rondels. Etudes latines. Si mes vers avaient des ailes. Paysage. Rêverie. Offrande. Mai. Infidélité. Seule. Les cygnes. Nocturne. Trois jours de vendange. D'une prison. Séraphine. L'heure exquise. Fêtes galantes. Quand la nuit n'est pas étoilée. Le plus beau présent. Sur l'eau. Le rossignol des lilas. A Chloris. Ma jeunesse. Puisque j'ai mis ma lèvre. La nymphe de la source. Au rossignol. Je me souviens. Mozart – Air de la lettre. O mon bel inconnu – C'est très vilain d'être infidèle. Ciboulette – C'est sa banlieue; Nous avons fait un beau voyage. Une revue – La dernière valse
Dame Felicity Lott sop **Susan Bickley** mez **Ian Bostridge** ten **Stephen Varcoe** bar **Graham Johnson, Chris Gould** pfs **London Schubert Chorale / Stephen Layton**
Hyperion ② CDA67141/2 (134' · DDD · T/t) Ⓕ🅾🅾➔

The two cycles, *Douze rondels* and *Etudes latines*, are linked by a common fascination with the past. The *Douze rondels* were composed to poems in a medieval metre, which allowed Hahn to try his hand at pastiche madrigals and courtly ballads. The *Etudes latines* cast their gaze back still further in time to Classical antiquity. For Hahn, that era seemed to represent the ultimate in purity and sensuality rolled into one. This collection of 10 songs is a real discovery and rivals late Fauré, both in its refinement and mesmerising simplicity of utterance. Apart from a few moments when one would like a more substantial tone, Stephen Varcoe's light baritone suits Hahn very well and he's a refreshingly unaffected interpreter, who sings with grace and feeling. Susan Bickley is better at the larger canvas of a piece like 'Quand la nuit n'est pas étoilée' than the more intimate songs but the most celebrated pair of all Hahn's *mélodies* goes to Dame Felicity Lott, whose sympathy for the French style could have no happier outlet. Both 'Si mes vers avaient des ailes' and 'L'heure exquise' are included here, the latter if not an hour, then at least two and a half minutes that are truly exquisite. They are both beautifully sung and are undisturbed by the discomfort around the top of the stave that sometimes mars Lott's singing elsewhere. At the end, she offers four operetta solos as an encore. Graham Johnson's accompaniments are as sensitive as ever. The piano could have been placed a little closer, but the voices have been well captured.

George Frideric Handel
German/British 1685-1759

Handel's father was a barber-surgeon and valet to the Prince of Saxe-Magdeburg. He was in his mid-sixties when his son was born and he hated music.

Somehow young Handel managed to learn the organ and spinet. From these unpromising beginnings flourished the greatest keyboard instrumentalist of the day – and it happened quickly. In 1693 the Duke of Saxe-Weissenfels heard the boy play the organ at one of the Sunday services, filled his pockets with gold coins and insisted that he was allowed to study music. Handel was put in the care of Zachau, the organist of the Lutheran church in Halle, who quickly realised he had a genius on his hands. After three years, Zachau confessed there was nothing more he could teach the boy. Handel was just 11. He doesn't appear to have had any further instruction from anybody.

After studying law for a while in Halle, he was organist at the Cathedral of Moritzburg – only 18 years old and already people were talking of 'the famous Handel' – and then moved to Hamburg, the seat of German opera. Fed up with the petty jealousies and cabals there, he moved to Italy in 1706 where he turned to writing opera in Florence and Venice and oratorio in Rome. All were triumphs and soon 'Il Sassone' ('The Saxon') was one of the most talked about musicians in Italy. Here he absorbed and studied all the current music being written and came into contact with such figures as Corelli, Alessandro Scarlatti and his son Domenico with whom he had a celebrated keyboard 'duel' to determine whom was the finer player. Result? Scarlatti was adjudged to be the better harpsichordist but Handel the finer organist. (Scarlatti admitted that till he heard Handel play the organ he had no conception of its powers.) The two retained a lifelong mutual admiration.

From Italy, Handel moved to Hanover in 1710 as court musician to the Elector of Hanover – a prescient decision as it turned out. After a year he was given leave to go to England where he wrote an opera (Rinaldo, 1711) which had an astonishing success. Back to Hanover – but London was too tempting and he returned to England and further triumphs. Time passed (two years in fact) and Handel was still absent from the Hanoverian court. When Queen Anne died in 1714, who should succeed her on the throne? None other than Handel's German employer, the Elector of Hanover.

If George I was displeased at his musician's cavalier attitude it didn't last long, for soon Handel had a royal pension of £400 a year – with an additional £200 from the Princess of Wales – and he was able to embark on a series of operas underwritten by the nobility and cast with the finest European singers. The Royal Academy of Music in London (not the famous music college which came later) was set up to present Italian opera and the entrepreneurial Handel was made its artistic director. He was, unassailably, the most powerful musician in the land.

Perhaps it was his very success or the fact that he was a foreigner or the fact that he was dictatorial in his demands, but he was frequently attacked and ridiculed. Despite royal patronage and his popularity with the public, despite his capacity for making friends and supporting the underprivileged, Handel found he had many enemies. One particular rival appeared in the form of Giovanni Bononcini and for a time there was intense competition as to who was the better composer. Handel saw him off in the end, of course, but not before the poet John Byrom had written:

> Some say, compared to Bononcini
> That Mynheer Handel's but a ninny.
> Others aver that he to Handel
> Is scarcely fit to hold a candle.
> Strange all this difference should be
> 'Twixt tweedledum and tweedledee.

And that's how the phrase was coined.

By the late 1720s, not long after Handel became a British citizen, public taste for Italian opera waned (the British had discovered John Gay's The Beggar's Opera to be more accessible and with tunes they already knew). Handel, now quite wealthy from shrewd investment, sank £10,000 of his own money into another Italian opera company and lost the lot.

Faced with bankruptcy and the debtors' prison, his health broke down (rheumatism set in and he suffered a paralytic stroke), he appears to have had some sort of breakdown and then...changed course. He wrote himself back into financial success and public favour by resurrecting a genre that was relatively unknown in England – the oratorio. These were dramatised Bible stories set to music, music of the same verve as the operas but with massive choruses and grand orchestral writing. Nothing like them had been heard before. In the interludes he would appear at the organ to play a concerto, improvising the brilliant solo part.

By 1741 Handel knew he had taken the right direction – public demand was overwhelming. Then in 1742, inspired by the invitation to Dublin by the Duke of Devonshire and the Lord Lieutenant to present one of his works for charity, came Messiah, written in a feverish 25 days, one of man's grandest musical achievements. A succession of oratorios followed – among them Semele, Judas Maccabaeus, Joshua and Solomon – showing Handel to be at the height of his creative powers. The 'great Handel' ruled the musical world again, only to be knocked sideways by another cruel blow. He became blind, a condition not helped by being once operated on by the same quack surgeon who attempted to save Bach's eyesight.

Indomitably, he continued to play the organ and conduct, one of the wonders of London, for people flocked to hear him. Handel knew his own worth and asked to be buried in Westminster Abbey – which he duly was, with a statue of him at his working table and the score of Messiah open at: 'I know that my Redeemer liveth'.

Organ Concertos, Opp 4 & 7

Op 4 – No 1 in G minor; No 2 in B flat;   **P**
No 3 in G minor; No 4 in F; No 5 in F
Op 7 – No 1 in B flat; No 2 in A;
No 3 in B flat; No 4 in D minor;
No 5 in G minor; No 6 in B flat.
Harp Concerto in B flat, Op 4 No 6
Paul Nicholson org **Frances Kelly** hp
The Brandenburg Consort / Roy Goodman hpd
Hyperion ② CDD22052 (154' · DDD)   Ⓜ▷

This recording was made at St Lawrence Whitchurch on an organ Handel must certainly have played. It sounds well under Paul Nicholson's hands. There's plenty of brightly glittering passagework and rich diapason sound in such movements as the passacaglia-like first of Op 7 No 1; while the softer side of the instrument is particularly appealing in Op 4 No 5, where Nicholson, doubtless conscious that this is a transcription of a recorder sonata, draws from it some very sweet sounds. It has a mechanical action, and here and there the incidental noise may be disconcerting. Still, it's authentic, so possibly we should be grateful to have it reproduced. There's some very lively and at times virtuoso playing from Nicholson in the quick movements, with sturdy rhythms, and some of the dance movements go with a good swing too.

Nicholson gives good, precise accounts of the various solo fugues and the transcriptions and improvisatory movements used here when Handel offered merely an *ad lib*. He's a thoughtful player; his added ornamentation is always musical, intelligent and stylish. However, in several movements over-deliberate orchestral phrasing or accentuation can be damaging; this happens quite often and sometimes affects Nicholson's playing. Op 4 No 6 is played on the harp, with some very delicate timing from Frances Kelly. The bright, clear recording captures happily the acoustic of this moderate-sized church.

Organ Concertos, Op 7[a]. Concerto in F major, HWV295. Chaconne, HWV442[b]. Chaconne, HWV485[b]. Fugue, HWV264[b]
[a]**Academy of Ancient Music /**
Richard Egarr [a]org/[b]hpd
Harmonia Mundi ② ⌕. HMC80 7447 (128' · DDD) Ⓕ

Richard Egarr and the AAM have prepared their own performing edition of Handel's Op 7 Organ Concertos, which has involved spontaneously creating *ad libitum* passages, or choosing other bits of Handel for the slow movements. The rich-sounding forces comprise 18 players, including oboes and bassoons; both their playing and Egarr's solo contributions are of an impeccably high order.

Taking his cue from Charles Burney's eyewitness accounts of Handel's own performances, Egarr takes a bold, improvisatory approach to the concertos. The *allegro* movements are enlivened by rapid keyboard flourishes, liberal ornamentation (especially during repeats of whole sections) and delightful variants to the basic printed rhythms in the manner of French Baroque composers. Particularly startling is the opening bitonal chord cluster of the A major Concerto, Op 7 No 2; Egarr acknowledges his debt to the 17th/18th-century writer Roger North for this daring harmonic gesture. On a lighter note, listeners will enjoy all the cuckoo calls plus other birdsong motifs that crop up during the *Cuckoo and the Nightingale* Concerto in F.

Throughout the two CDs, tempi are beautifully judged, with a degree of flexibility and an avoidance of excessive speeds in the fast movements. In the three works for solo harpsichord, Egarr's calm, measured pacing allows Handel's music to flow clearly and effortlessly. The opportunity to hear the splendid Chaconne in G, HWV442, is highly rewarding; and, as Egarr points out, it uses the same bass-line and harmonic progression as the first eight bars of Bach's *Goldberg Variations*.

Egarr's insert-notes and a lovely collection of paintings featuring 18th-century London make for a booklet whose excellence matches that of the distinguished music-making. The recording is highly detailed – possibly a bit too close-up for some listeners. Full marks to Egarr for his choice of the 1998 Handel House Museum organ for the concertos; this modern British instrument is a copy of the type of chamber organ known to Handel. This is a superb set from all concerned.

Additional recommendation

Six Organ Concertos, Op 4   Ⓟ
Halls *org* **Sonnerie / Huggett** *vn*
Avie AV2055 (73' · DDD)   ⒻⒹ►

Matthew Halls, using a fascinating Dutch chamber organ which is perfect for the intimately balanced ensemble, plays with admirable delicacy and affection. These chamber performances are smaller than those Handel would have directed but one never feels that Sonnerie are weak or underpowered.

Concerti grossi

Op 3, HWV312-17; **Op 6**, HWV319-30

Concerti grossi, Opp 3 and 6   Ⓟ
Handel & Haydn Society / Christopher Hogwood
Avie ③ (three CDs for the price of two) AV2065 (3h 36' · DDD)   ⒻⒹ►

The London music publisher John Walsh threw Handel's Op 3 together in 1734 by organising various single orchestral movements into concertos without the composer's creative involvement or permission; the result was a hotchpotch. But Op 6 features 12 new concertos that Handel had deliberately composed as a coherent set during September and October 1739. While Op 6 is undeniably Handel's monumental masterpiece for the orchestra, there are a lot of excellent recordings that do much to promote the variety and charm of Op 3.

For this recording Christopher Hogwood uses a performance edition that takes into account manuscript sources that pre-date Walsh's compilation. It is good to have the Handel & Haydn Society's disciplined and lean performances available again thanks to this newly compiled and remastered reissue. The opening of Op 3 No 2 has deliciously sprung rhythms and fine solo concertino playing; the sublime cello duet in the following *Largo* is sinewy yet tender, its melancholic mood enhanced by the restrained oboe solo. Handel later added oboes and bassoons to some of the Op 6 concertos when they were performed in the theatre but Hogwood prefers Handel's original scoring for string orchestra throughout.

The Handel & Haydn Society's alert enthusiasm is tangible throughout these polished and stylish readings, originally recorded by Decca's much lamented early-music division L'Oiseau-Lyre. Hogwood directs with natural sensitivity and his tastefully emphasised suspensions and relaxed shaping of cadences are consistently perfect. The finest Op 6 on disc? Maybe not, but there is ample here to satisfy the fussiest Handelians.

Concerti grossi, Op 3. Sonata a cinque, HWV288   🅟
Academy of Ancient Music / Richard Egarr
Harmonia Mundi HMU90 7415;
📀 HMU80 7415 (68' · DDD/DSD)   ⒻⓄ➔

Handel's Op 3 *Concerti grossi* was his first published set of concertos, although scholars have regarded the level of his personal involvement in John Walsh's 1734 edition with suspicion. Richard Egarr suggests that Handel might have had more of a hand in the compilation of Op 3 than hitherto identified. Fresh speculation is a healthy opportunity to reconsider matters but the truly significant aspect of this recording is the new attention brought to Handel's charming music. It is hard to think of a lovelier moment in all of Handel's orchestral works than the spellbinding cellos interweaving under a plaintive solo oboe in the *Largo* of No 2. Likewise, the immense personality of the solo organ runs during the finale of No 6 is a potently precocious display of Handel's genius at the keyboard. All such moments come across with vitality and passion.

The AAM has never committed Op 3 to disc before: under Egarr they sound as good as ever, perhaps even reinvigorated and a few degrees sparkier. These are for the most part lively performances full of fizzy finesse. There are several fine recordings that find a little more warmth, sentimentality and intimacy in the music, although the energetic brilliance so prominent in the AAM's crisply athletic playing has its own rewards. The musicians are unanimously immersed in the intricacies of the music, but special mention must be made of violinist Pavlo Beznosiuk's dazzling contribution to the dynamic finale of the 'Sonata a cinque' (a sort of violin concerto that Handel presumably composed for Corelli in Rome in about 1707).

Additional recommendation

Concerti grossi, Opp 3 & 6   🅟
Vienna Concentus Musicus / Harnoncourt
Teldec ④ 4509 95500-2 (3h 57' · ADD/DDD)
Recorded 1982-85   ⒷⓄ
The fact is that there's ferocious creativity in every

bar. Every opening slow movement is the prelude to a drama, every fugue a precisely related episode. The Vienna Concentus Musicus plays for the most part with a virtuosity and precision that's well highlighted by the slightly dry but transparent acoustic in which they're recorded.

Concerti grossi, Op 6   🅟
Il Giardino Armonico / Giovanni Antonini
L'Oiseau-Lyre ③ 478 0319DX3 (168' · DDD)   ⒷⓄ➔

One can overlook a few of Il Giardino Armonico's eccentricities to listen to some generally intoxicating performances of Handel's most masterful instrumental compositions. Much of the credit for the intricate passagework and dynamic excitement must be given to fiddler Enrico Onofri, whose playing sparkles with articulate energy. The plunging interplay between *concertino* and *ripieno* groups is exhilarating. The Polonaise in No 3 is astonishingly robust, with its droning bass thrashed out; it certainly brings out the daring brilliance of Handel's musical imagination, though it seems rather short on the pastoral charm that the composer surely intended. The opening *Largo* and *Allegro* of No 5 possess panache and the opening of No 10 is tautly dramatic, but one misses the airy wit that such music may also convey.

Il Giardino Armonico's playing is never clumsy but incisive muscular approaches in contrapuntal movements seem overly severe. It is possible to find a more measured elegance and shapely sentimentality in Handel's music, but there is plenty of highly spiced food for thought served by Il Giardino Armonico.

Concerti grossi, Op 6   🅟
Academy of Ancient Music / Andrew Manze vn
Harmonia Mundi ② HMU90 7228/9 (157' · DDD)   ⒻⓄ

With one stride, Harmonia Mundi has stolen a march on Chandos Chaconne's rival set of Handel's Op 6 with Simon Standage's Collegium Musicum 90; by juggling with the order, the 12 concertos have been accommodated on only two CDs. The AAM is on sparkling form, clearly enjoying itself under Andrew Manze's leadership. Performances are invigoratingly alert, splendidly neat (all those semiquaver figurations absolutely precise) and strongly rhythmical but not inflexible, with much dynamic gradation which ensures that phrases are always tonally alive and sound completely natural (even if more subtly nuanced than Handel's players ever dreamt of). Manze's basically light-footed approach is particularly appealing, and he sees to it that inner-part imitations are given their due weight.

Speeds are nearly all fast, occasionally questionably so (though exhilarating), as in the first *Allegro* of No 1, the big *Allegro* of No 6 and the *Allegro* in No 9. But Manze successfully brings out the character of all the movements, and the listener can't fail to love the vigorous kick of his No 7 hornpipe. He's mostly sparing in embellishing solo lines except in Nos 6 and 11. Altogether this is an issue of joyous vitality.

Concerti grossi, Op 6
Australian Brandenburg Orchestra / Paul Dyer hpd
ABC Classics ② ABC476 3436 (156' · DDD)   Ⓕ

Australia may seem a long way from Handel's London but there is no lack of engagement with his greatest set of orchestral compositions here; these are performances of style and understanding into which Paul Dyer and his fine period orchestra have plunged with freshness, buoyancy and joyful enthusiasm.

If there is nothing greatly radical in these interpretations, then, it hardly matters when the music is delivered with such straightforward energy, commitment and skill. Concertos Nos 2, 5, 7, 9 and 10 are especially successful, with the string players laying into their bowing with relish (the siciliana-like *Larghetto* of No 9 is richly drawn) and the concertino soloists delivering the occasional exuberant but shapely cadenza (a violin even breaks into tasteful double-stopping in No 1). No 8 has strongly punched *tutti* chords in the *Grave* movement and a final *Allegro* full of eager detail, and there is a delicious air of Frenchness to the first *Allegro* of No 10.

Concertos Nos 1, 4 and 6 lack a little of the sonic immediacy (and thus vibrancy) of the others, for instance, while Nos 9 and 11 suffer from an over-present harpsichord not evident elsewhere in the set. These are small prices to pay, however, for such immensely enjoyable and inspiriting performances.

Additional recommendation

Concerti grossi, Op 6 Nos 1-5, 6-9, 10-12; C, HWV318, 'Alexander's Feast'   Ⓟ
Collegium Musicum 90 / Simon Standage vn
Chandos Chaconne CHAN0600, CHAN0616,
CHAN0622 (62', 58' & 56' · DDD)   Ⓕ Ⓞ Ⓑ→

The performances are brimful of vitality, and the clean articulation and light, predominantly detached style give the music buoyancy and help to bring out Handel's often mischievous twinkle in the eye. Speeds are generally brisk, with boldly vigorous playing, but Standage's team can also spin a tranquil broad line. Dynamics throughout are subtly graded.

Water Music, HWV348-50

Water Music   Ⓟ
Simon Standage, Elizabeth Wilcock vns
The English Concert / Trevor Pinnock hpd
Archiv 477 756-2GOR (54' · DDD)   Ⓜ Ⓞ Ⓞ Ⓑ→

It's unlikely that George I ever witnessed performances that live up to this one. They are

sparkling; tempi are well judged and there's a truly majestic sweep to the opening F major French overture; that gets things off to a fine start but what follows is no less compelling with some notably fine woodwind playing, so often the disappointing element in performances on period instruments.

In the D major music it's the brass department that steals the show and here, horns and trumpets acquit themselves with distinction. Archiv has achieved a particularly satisfying sound in which all strands of the orchestral texture can be heard with clarity. In this suite the ceremonial atmosphere comes over particularly well, with resonant brass playing complemented by crisply articulated oboes.

The G major pieces are quite different from those in the previous groups, being lighter in texture and more closely dance-orientated. They are among the most engaging in the *Water Music* and especially, perhaps, the two little 'country dances', the boisterous character of which Pinnock captures nicely.

Water Music. Music for the Royal Fireworks   Ⓟ
L'Arte dell'Arco / Federico Guglielmo vn
CPO CPO777 312-2 (66' · DDD)   Ⓕ Ⓞ Ⓞ Ⓞ

The tradition of dividing the *Water Music* into three separate suites dates back to the 1950s. The suspicion that Handel envisaged it as one long sequence of movements has informed a couple of fine recordings but this disc by L'Arte dell'Arco is the first such recording to be made since the earliest surviving manuscript copy of the music (dating from 1718) was rediscovered in 2004.

The strings play with polish and alertness. Federico Guglielmo leads proceedings expertly from the violin; his few solo flourishes are direct yet courtly. The famous Hornpipe is splendidly done, with a radiant balance between the pairs of trumpets and horns (who relish some tasteful ornaments in the *da capo*), and lovely solo fiddle-playing during the middle section.

Generally these performances are pleasantly contoured, though the continuo team occasionally become intrusive in faster music. However, it is good to hear musicians confident enough to play the *Lentement* more slowly than has become common. The Bourrée is thrillingly quick. The Country Dance sparkles with conviviality, although the recorder is a little uneven.

The Ouverture from the *Music for the Royal Fireworks* is given a vibrant and engaging performance. Guglielmo and his forces achieve the rare feat of ensuring that 'La Réjouissance' is coherently shaped. CPO's translator of the booklet has done a poor job of what seems to have been an interesting note by Guglielmo ('cembalo' is consistently mistranslated as 'cymbals'!) but the disc is warmly recommended.

Water Music. Music for the Royal Fireworks
Aradia Ensemble / Kevin Mallon
Naxos 8 557764 (71' · DDD)   Ⓢ Ⓑ→

HANDEL FIREWORKS AND WATER MUSIC – IN BRIEF

Le Concert Spirituel / Hervé Niquet
Glossa GCD921606 (62' · DDD)   (F)

This comes closest of all 'authentic' recordings to gathering the forces Handel originally wrote for in both *Water* and *Fireworks*, with massed winds – horns using the natural intonation of their instruments to piquant effect – and some splendid drumming sessions! The sound is rather recessed to cope with the wide dynamic range, but the overall effect is stunning.

Le Concert des Nations / Jordi Savall
Astrée Naive ES9920 (74' · DDD)   (F)O

Using smaller though still substantial forces, Savall's performances are more refined than Niquet's but still very characterful, with a delightful sense of rhythmic swing, caught in less recessed sound.

London Classical Players / Roger Norrington
Virgin 545265-2 (69' · DDD)   (F)

Neatly articulated, 'cleaner' playing than either Niquet or Savall, though perhaps lacking something of the character they find. None the less the grandeur of the brass in the *Fireworks* is stirring.

Aradia Ensemble / Kevin Mallon
Naxos 8 557764 (71' · DDD)   (F)B+

Nicely conceived performances, full of detail and with an attractive sense of theatre. You may regret the added percussion but there's no denying the sense of occasion that Mallon creates with his Canadian ensemble.

L'Arte dell'Arco / Federico Guglielmo
CPO CPO777 312-2 (66' · DDD)   (M)OOOO

A terrific new disc for Handel Year that dismantles the traditional suites and presents the music in one long and, here, thrilling sequence. This is alert sprightly playing with plenty of excitement and genuine sense of occasion.

Berlin Philharmonic / Riccardo Muti
(Water Music only)
EMI 5864092 (60' · DDD)   (B)

A highly unlikely line-up and a throw-back to an earlier time! This is none the less a spirited performance of the *Water Music* at an appealingly low price.

LSO / Charles Mackerras (Fireworks only)
Testament SBT1253 (76' · ADD)   (F)O

A historic first attempt to gather the forces Handel originally scored the *Fireworks* for, but using modern instruments. Some of the speeds are a touch ponderous by today's standards, but the sound is excellent and the overall effect breathtaking.

The *Water Music* has traditionally been divided into three suites, as it is here, but a recently rediscovered early manuscript copy confirms that Handel originally created one long sequence of movements. A more regretful aspect of this recording is a superfluous percussionist rattling away on a tambourine in several movements (for example, the hornpipe in Suite No 1). Kevin Mallon claims that this 'was often the practice in the 18th century' but there is not a single piece of evidence that Handel would have agreed.

Mallon's performance is otherwise exemplary. Handel's melodies are nicely shaped, with colourful accompaniments that range between assertive energy and understated pathos. Resonant horns and elegant trumpets synthesise stylish wit and regal pomp in the famous 'Alla hornpipe' (Suite No 2). Brightness and subtlety co-exist with a charismatic swagger.

Mallon's sense of an attractive flowing pulse in the music carries through to the *Music for the Royal Fireworks*. The Ouverture has crisp, articulate phrasing, in which important details are stressed and then shade away to allow the next musical detail to come to the fore. The zesty Aradia Ensemble never succumb to monotonous tub-thumping. There is no shortage of excellent recordings that pair these beloved works together, but Mallon's interpretation is an attractive contender at budget price.

Water Music. Music for the Royal Fireworks, HWV351
Le Concert Spirituel / Hervé Niquet
Glossa GCD921606 (62' · DDD)   (F)

Hervé Niquet celebrated the 15th anniversary of his group Le Concert Spirituel by assembling a hundred musicians at the Arsenal de Metz to produce what is claimed as 'the first historical recording' of the *Fireworks Music* and *Water Music*. We've had many versions on period instruments but until now only one recording of the *Fireworks Music* has attempted to assemble period instruments in the numbers that Handel is known to have had originally. That's the 1989 version for Hyperion by Robert King with the King's Consort, but he was content with 62 wind, brass and percussion players; Niquet, as in the *Water Music*, adds massed strings too. Sir Charles Mackerras's flamboyant recording of the *Fireworks Music* using vast wind forces has reappeared on Testament with great success, but that dates from the days of Handel on modern instruments.

Niquet goes further than most of his rivals, not only in assembling these numbers, but in applying early performance techniques. When he reports that the nine horn players 'performed their parts without "correcting" the natural intonation of their instruments', with mean-tone temperament imposed on the whole orchestra, it makes one apprehensive that the results would be painful to the modern ear. Happily this isn't so. The rawness of brass tone is so well controlled that it tickles the ear delightfully.

The massed woodwind players (24 oboes, 15 flutes and recorders, and 14 bassoons) add to the weight and tang of the sound, and though only two percussionists are listed, they're balanced to give maximum impact, with a spectacular timpani cadenza in the Overture to the *Fireworks Music*. The bass drum and timpani in the Gigue which ends the G major *Water Music* Suite have similar panache.

The string sections are comparably large, but inevitably on gut strings their playing is less prominent, counterbalanced by such elaborations as the sparkling little cadenza for solo violin that links the Prelude and Hornpipe of the D major *Water Music* Suite.

As you'd expect, fast speeds predominate, sometimes so fast that they sound breathless: one marvels at the articulation of the wind and brass players in coping. Helped by atmospheric recording, one has a vivid impression of a grand ceremonial celebration. Niquet's is a fine achievement.

'Water Music – Recreating a Royal Spectacular'
The English Concert / Andrew Manze
Video director **Fergus O'Brien**
BBC/Opus Arte 📀 OA0930D
(78' · NTSC · 16:9 · PCM stereo and DTS 5.1 · 0) Ⓕ

This documentary's hypothesis for where, how and why Handel performed his famous orchestral suites on the Thames makes for enjoyable viewing. Social historian Philippa Glanville presents two documents that describe the original event in 1717 (although both have been familiar to Handelians since they were reprinted in 1955). Political historian Jeremy Black takes us around Greenwich and Venice looking for clues to a possible political agenda for the barge party, comparing it to the spectacular ceremonies of La Serenissima that might have captured the imaginations of impressionable young Englishmen on the Grand Tour. A barge is given a make-over so that it resembles what Handel's musicians might have floated on. The soundtrack of the orchestra's trip down the Thames is obviously a studio recording with superimposed sound effects of river noises, although an acoustician tests some of The English Concert's players on the river to prove scientifically that Handel knew what he was doing when orchestrating the music.

The only missing ingredient in this reconstruction project is the involvement of a music historian. There is no discussion of the *Water Music*'s context within Handel's fascinating career. Andrew Manze's presence gives musical muscle; but it is a welcome corrective that the booklet features an essay by Donald Burrows which manages to cover all the missing elements while gently amending a few of the documentary's less convincing conjectures.

Music for the Royal Fireworks, HWV351

Music for the Royal Fireworks[d] Ⓗ
Berenice, HWV38 – Overture (arr Whittaker)[a].
Concerti a due cori in F, HWV333 (arr Mackerras)[b].

Concertos[c] – in D, HWV335a; F, HWV331. Water Music, HWV38-50 (arr Harty)[e] – Allegro; Bourrée; Hornpipe; Allegro decisio
[d]**Wind Ensemble;** [ce]**London Symphony Orchestra; Pro Arte Orchestra**[b] **/ Charles Mackerras**
Testament SBT1253 (76' · ADD)
Recorded [ae]1956, [bd]1959, [c]1977 Ⓕ Ⓞ

Over the night of April 13-14, 1959, in St Gabriel's Church, Cricklewood, a recording session took place, historic in every way, when the young Charles Mackerras conducted a band of 62 wind players plus nine percussionists in Handel's *Music for the Royal Fireworks*. With no fewer than 26 oboists topping the ensemble, it was only possible to assemble such a band after all concerts and operas had finished for the day.

They began at 11pm and finished at 2.30 in the morning, yet so far from sounding tired or jaded, the players responded to the unique occasion with a fizzing account of Handel's six movements. The success of this extraordinary project fully justified Mackerras's determination to restore the astonishing array of instruments that Handel himself had assembled for the original performance in Green Park in April 1749.

It's thrilling to hear that 1959 recording, at last transferred to CD, with sound that's still of demonstration quality, full and spacious, with a wide stereo spread. It's true that Mackerras takes the introduction to the Overture and the Siciliana at speeds far slower than he would choose today, but this was a recording which marked a breakthrough in what later developed as the period performance movement.

As a coupling for the *Fireworks Music*, Mackerras devised a composite *Concerto a due cori* which draws on two works written with that title around 1747. It makes a splendid piece, in which the massed horns bray gloriously.

Whatever the degree of authenticity, this is an electrifying collection, superbly transferred.

Music for the Royal Fireworks.
Concerti per due cori, HWV332-334
Ensemble Zefiro / Alfredo Bernardini
Deutsche Harmonia Mundi 88697 36791-2
(69' · DDD) Ⓕ Ⓞ Ⓞ▶

The Italian ensemble Zefiro, directed by oboist Alfredo Bernardini, specialise in 18th-century music that gives prominence towards wind instruments. This lends itself to Handel's *Music for the Royal Fireworks*, written for the public celebrations of the Peace of Aix-la-Chapelle in London's Green Park (1749). Zefiro play the grand Ouverture with the perfect synthesis of splendour and dance-like charisma (too many versions possess too little of the latter). 'La réjouissance' trips along lightly without a hint of clumsiness, but still has ample juicy magnificence. There are several other good recordings available, but this zesty and fluid performance is a welcome change from stodgy readings in which everything is hammered home mercilessly. Zefiro bring a marvellous sense of light and shade to this music. Maybe Bernardini's sparkling and communicative approach would have been too subtle for the great British outdoors in 1749, but it is curious that this beautifully engineered recording was made outside in the cloisters of a former Jesuit college in Sicily.

Zefiro also perform all three of the *Concerti per due cori* (1747-48) that Handel arranged for orchestra and two 'choirs' of woodwind and brass. These were intended as entr'actes in oratorio concerts, and it is fun to play 'name that tune'. These shapely performances are phrased and paced to perfection, and exploit an enjoyable range of instrumental colours (whether oboe trios or bucolic horns, almost everything here feels right). This is one of the most enjoyable discs of Handel's orchestral music in a long time.

Orchestral and Ballet Music

Orchestral and Ballet Music from Alcina,   **P**
Ariodante, Arminio. Berenice, Rinaldo, Rodelinda and Serse
Collegium Musicum 90 / Simon Standage *vn*
Chandos Chaconne CHAN0650 (67' · DDD)   Ⓕ**O**Ⓑ➤

Handel's music is never more winsome than when it's written for special occasions, not least operas. Several of the items in this programme are arias, but they aren't sung. Like today's musicals, though not for calculated commercial reasons, some became what we would now term pops, and Handel reworked them as instrumental pieces, so no liberty has been taken here in presenting them in that form. The charm of this music hasn't escaped the notice of others in recording studios, but it has never been more persuasively captured than it is by Collegium Musicum 90. Other recordings exist of the complete operas and some of the individual instrumental items, but *Arminio* is represented by only one aria; there's nothing run-of-the-mill about the fugal subject of the Overture, or its treatment, and the Minuet is winsome and light of step. Collegium Musicum 90 fields a team of 32 players but their sound is marvellously light and transparent even when in full flood, and their use of period instruments (or copies thereof) leads also to a natural, revelatory balance. Flawless recording and excellent notes by Standage complete an outstanding issue.

Solo Sonatas, Op 1

12 Solo Sonatas, Op 1
Academy of Ancient Music (Rachel Brown *fl/rec*
Frank de Bruine *ob* Pavlo Beznosiuk *vn*) /
Richard Egarr *hpd*
Harmonia Mundi ② HMU90 7465/6 (148' · DDD)   Ⓕ

John Walsh senior's compilation of Handel's sonatas for solo instrument and basso continuo (first printed *c*1730 and retrospectively known as Opus 1) is a horrible mess from a scholarly per-spective. Walsh cobbled together the collection, often printing sonatas for the wrong instrument, in the wrong key, or with some wrong movements; some sonatas are clearly not even composed by Handel. In his booklet essay, Richard Egarr does an entertaining job of conveying the confusing history and contents of 'Op 1'.

Happily, there can be few qualms about the assured music-making. *Rubato* in slow movements sometimes disturbs the rhythmic pulse of Handel's writing, but otherwise the playing of the three principals of the Academy of Ancient Music sparkles, charms and soothes. Rachel Brown's recorder-playing is sweetly elegiac in leisurely music, and subtle yet playful in quicker movements (the conclusion of HWV369); likewise, Brown's flute-playing is gently conversational, and the unison opening of the *Allegro* in HWV363*b* is typical of the impressive understanding between Egarr and his soloists. Pavlo Beznosiuk's contributions are by turns tender and refined. The violinist receives the four sonatas that were clearly not by Handel but plays them gracefully enough for issues of attribution to be temporarily forgotten. Frank de Bruine's fluent oboe playing is a particular delight. Egarr has dispensed with cello doubling the bass-line of the keyboard accompaniments; his harpsichord realisations give sensitive support to the soloist in the limelight. The occasional flamboyant keyboard passages have plenty of crispness and character but are light enough to avoid dogmatically forcing the soloists to fight for attention.

Trio Sonatas

Trio Sonatas, Op 2, HWV386-391
Sonnerie (Wilbert Hazelzet *fl* Monica Huggett, Emilia Benjamin *vns* Joseph Crouch *vc* Matthew Halls *hpd*)
Avie AV0033 (66' · DDD)   Ⓕ Ⓑ➤

With their boldness of invention, their expressive range and their extraordinary variety of three-part textures, Handel's six Op 2 sonatas represent a peak of the trio sonata as a genre. Yet for some time there's been no complete recording of the set in the catalogue.

These are polished and sophisticated performances fill the gap admirably. There's much exquisitely turned detail, subtle timing, graceful shaping, and a happy sense of the musical logic. The two violinists play as if they were identical twins. Some listeners may feel these finely modulated performances lack the energy and freshness that ideally belong to the music, but there's a great deal to compensate for that, and you won't often hear this music more attentively, more lovingly played.

Trio Sonatas – Op 2; Op 5
Academy of Ancient Music / Richard Egarr *hpd*
Harmonia Mundi ② HMU90 7467/8 (142' · DDD)   Ⓕ

The Academy of Ancient Music's project to record all of Handel's works with opus numbers reaches its completion with this double-bill of 13 trio sonatas. Most are played by two violins (Pavlo Beznosiuk and Rodolfo Richter) and basso continuo (Joseph Crouch and Richard Egarr). The Op 2 set features two sonatas that specify slightly different scoring: flute in HWV386 and recorder in HWV389 (both played by Rachel Brown).

The interplay between the AAM is Baroque chamber-playing of the very highest order: sincerely conversational, emotive and finely nuanced. Egarr and Crouch are an outstanding continuo team, providing attentive yet uncluttered support to the two upper instruments. Brown and Beznosiuk play together with touching eloquence in the *Largo* of HWV386 and excel in the jaunty jig that concludes HWV389. Beznosiuk and Richter interweave to gorgeous effect in the *Largo* of HWV387. On a few occasions the slower music could perhaps have been trusted to play itself with a more literal rhythmical pulse, and sometimes things seem precious if compared to the best alternative recordings, but of course this may also be an unavoidable consequence of listening to an entire collection of works that were never designed by the composer to be sampled together in one long sitting.

Violin Sonatas

Violin Sonatas. Andante in A minor, HWV412.   **P**
Allegro in C minor, HWV408
Andrew Manze *vn* **Richard Egarr** *hpd*
Harmonia Mundi HMU90 7259
(77' · DDD)   **F D**

Uncertainty over the authenticity of the violin sonatas, coupled with the fact that Handel and his publisher were notoriously imprecise about which instruments his various solo sonatas were even intended for, has no doubt prevented many violinists from embracing them as they might in these scholarly times. But there's certainly a good CD's worth of material to be had, even if only five sonatas are thought to be definitely by Handel. Andrew Manze and Richard Egarr offer these, plus three questionable works originally published in one or other of two versions of Handel's Op 1 set of mixed solo sonatas and two authentic one-movement fragments. There isn't an unenjoyable note.

The recording was made immediately after this pair's *Gramophone* Award-winning set of sonatas by Pandolfi (Harmonia Mundi), and it shows them in the same world-beating form. These are performances brimming with vitality and imagination, transforming these sonatas from the polite, even rather staid music you might expect, into grand dramas full of incident, excitement and many little moments that make you sit up and listen. Manze's violin sings with wonderful, glowing tone (he's not afraid to use vibrato to achieve it), to which he adds a joyous assortment of flowery ornaments and emphatic double-stoppings. Egarr's contribution is no less crucial; surely the most inspired continuo improviser around at present, he draws an astounding and mercurial array of colours and textures from his harpsichord. Whatever he does, though, it's never routine. This is a great chamber-music recording, made by a duo who complement each other to perfection.

Flute Sonatas

Flute Sonatas – in E minor, HWV359b; in G,   **P**
HWV363b; in B minor, HWV367b; in A minor,
HWV374; in E minor, HWV375; in B minor, HWV376;
in D, HWV378; in E minor, HWV379
Barthold Kuijken *fl* **Wieland Kuijken** *va da gamba*
Robert Kohnen *hpd*
Accent ACC9180 (73' · DDD)   **F O**

In this recording of solo flute sonatas Barthold Kuijken plays pieces unquestionably by Handel as well as others over which doubt concerning his authorship has been cast in varying degrees. Certainly not all the pieces here were conceived for transverse flute – there are earlier versions of HWV363b and 367b, for example, for oboe and treble recorder, respectively; but we can well imagine that in Handel's day most, if not all, of these delightful sonatas were regarded among instrumentalists as more-or-less common property. Barthold Kuijken, with his eldest brother Wieland and Robert Kohnen, gives graceful and stylish performances. Kuijken is skilful in matters of ornamentation and is often adventurous, though invariably within the bounds of good taste. Dance movements are brisk and sprightly though he's careful to preserve their poise, and phrases are crisply articulated. This is of especial benefit to movements such as the lively *Vivace* of the B minor Sonata (HWV367b) which can proceed rather aimlessly when too *legato* an approach is favoured; and the virtuosity of these players pays off in the *Presto (Furioso)* movement that follows. In short, this is a delightful disc which should please both Handelians and most lovers of Baroque chamber music.

Recorder Sonatas

Sonatas for Recorder and Continuo – G minor,   **P**
HWV360; A minor, HWV362; in C, HWV365; in F,
HWV369; in B flat, HWV377. Sonata for Flute and
Continuo in B minor, HWV367b
Marion Verbruggen *rec/fl* **Jaap ter Linden** *vc*
Ton Koopman *hpd/org*
Harmonia Mundi HMU90 7151 (58' · DDD)   **F O**

These are lively, intelligent performances. The recorder playing is outstandingly fine, sweet in tone, pointed in articulation, perfectly tuned, technically very fluent, and informed by a good understanding of the art of ornamentation. Marion Verbruggen's real command of Handel's language is out of the ordinary. Some of Ton Koopman's accompaniments are a little busy (half are on the organ, half on the harpsichord), but it's all part of the sense of lively music-making that runs through this attractive disc.

Recorder Sonatas – in G minor, HWV360;
in A minor, HWV362; in C, HWV365; in D minor,
HMW367a; in F, HWV369; in B flat, HWV377.
Keyboard Suite in E, HWV430
Pamela Thorby rec **Richard Egarr** hpd/org
Linn CD/SACD ⬚ CKD223 (74' · DDD) Ⓕ◗➕

Pamela Thorby, a regular member of the Palladian Ensemble, demonstrates versatility and virtuosity beyond question and is imaginatively accompanied by Richard Egarr, who also contributes a sparkling account of the Harpsichord Suite in E major. The recording was made from facsimiles of the autograph manuscripts, and the performances are commensurately vivid and immediate. One feels constantly gripped by the music, as if every single note matters.

There's no compulsive need for a cello on the basso continuo part, and on this occasion Thorby and Egarr manage perfectly well without one. Egarr uses a chamber organ on some of the sonatas, and although it's not historically likely in Handel's chamber sonatas, its musical effect is pleasing, and increases textural variety while removing the threat of monotony across 74 minutes of intense brilliance.

___

Keyboard Works

Handel Keyboard Suites – in F, HWV427; in D minor,
HWV428; in E, HWV430. Chaconne in G, HWV435
D Scarlatti Keyboard Sonatas – in B minor, Kk27;
in D, Kk29; in E, Kk206; in A, Kk212; in C sharp minor,
Kk247; in D, Kk491; in A, Kk537
Murray Perahia pf
Sony Classical SK62785 (69' · DDD) Ⓕ◗◗◗◗➕

Ⓖ In his projection of line, mass and colour Perahia makes intelligent acknowledgement of the fact that none of this is piano music, but when it comes to communicating the forceful effects and the brilliance and readiness of finger for which these two great player-composers were renowned, inhibitions are thrown to the wind. Good! Nothing a pianist does in the *Harmonious Blacksmith* Variations in Handel's E major Suite, or the Air and Variations of the D minor Suite could surpass in vivacity and cumulative excitement what the expert harpsichordist commands, and you could say the same of Scarlatti's D major Sonata, Kk29; but Perahia is extraordinarily successful in translating these with the daredevil 'edge' they must have. Faster and yet faster! In the Handel (more than in the Scarlatti) his velocity may strike you as overdone; but one can see the sense of it. It's quite big playing throughout, yet not inflated. Admirable is the way the piano is addressed, with the keys touched rather than struck, and a sense conveyed that the music is coming to us through the tips of the fingers rather than the hammers of the instrument. While producing streams of beautifully moulded and inflected sound Perahia is a wizard at making you forget the percussive nature of the apparatus. There are movements in the Handel

where the musical qualities are dependent on instrumental sound, or contrasts of sound, which the piano just can't convincingly imitate. And in some of the Scarlatti one might have reservations about Perahia's tendency to idealise, to soften outlines and to make the bite less incisive.

If you can't bear to hear it on anything other than the harpsichord, this record won't be for you. But Perahia is an artist, not just a pianist, and has an experience to offer that's vivid and musically considered at the highest level – not at all second best. The virtuosity is special indeed, and there isn't a note that hasn't been savoured.

___

Keyboard Suites – in F sharp minor, HWV431; Ⓟ
in G minor, HWV432; in F minor, HWV433; in B flat,
HWV440; in G, HWV441; in G, HWV442 – Preludio
Sophie Yates hpd
Chandos CHAN0688 (71' · DDD) Ⓕ◗➕

Sophie Yates brings formidable technique and strong dramatic feeling to these suites. The works of the first collection (1720, HWV426-33) are the more demanding, each of them opening with a prelude (or overture) – complex, pensive, often sombre – with a large-scale, fully worked fugue. Yates plays these in an appropriately rhetorical manner, rhythmically taut yet with enough flexibility and attentiveness to the music's caesuras to shape and characterise it, at the same time giving it some sense of the improvisatory. Then she takes the fugues at a lively pace, just a touch too fast for the music to sound comfortable: this is brilliant, edge-of-your seat playing.

Her playing, with its thoughtful details of timing, clearly conveys the structure of the music. She finds the same grandeur of manner in the Passacaille that ends the G minor Suite. For the rest, it's mainly dance music: some lively courantes and exuberant gigues, sober and deliberate allemandes, spacious and noble sarabandes – the crisp and precise fingerwork in that of the B flat Suite in the Second Set (1733), with its intensely detailed line, is a delight.

These are the most appealing versions of Handel's suites: fresh, alive, with a real command of style and technique but also just a hint of risk about the playing. Handel's harpsichord music has sometimes been called dull, but there isn't a moment here when you'd believe that.

___

Handel Chaconne, HWV435. Keyboard Suites –
in F, HWV427; in F minor, HWV433
Haydn Keyboard Sonata No 62, HobXVI:52. Sonata
un piccolo divertimento: Variations, HobXVII/6.
Angela Hewitt pf
Hyperion CDA67736 (67' · DDD) Ⓕ◗➕

Isn't it odd to lump Handel with Haydn? Not for Haydn who, like Beethoven, thought Handel the greatest composer of all. Not for Angela Hewitt either, but for different reasons. She senses an emotional affinity between the composers, just as she senses religious connotations in the music of Bach.

In her booklet-note she also 'unashamedly' admits to sharing with him a relish for an old edition of Handel's Chaconne that differs from one based on other sources. And she observes the repeat only in the theme, not in the variations. 'Authenticists' might be dismayed and might even quail at her introspective *rubato* in the Suites, two of eight that Handel himself published in 1720 when George I granted him a Privilege of Copyright.

But that's Hewitt, individual, and equally probing in the deeper waters of Haydn's Variations where, towards the end, the music reflects a composer whose own faith seems to be sorely tested by personal tragedy. Hewitt is with him in his sobriety, lightness, fury and eventual exhaustion. Regrettably she omits the whimsical five bars – included in the autograph but not in Artaria's first published version – that bridge the last variation to the return of the theme. Yet all has to be forgiven as Hewitt unfolds the drama of the last sonata through proud gesture and pathos. Rhetoric may be understated but her point of view grows with repetition. The recording never stands in your way.

'The Secret Handel'
Handel Water Music, HWV348-50 – Air in F; Bourée and Hornpipe in F. Chaconne, HWV435. Concerto, HWV487 – Allegro; Andante. Six Fugues or Voluntaries, HWV605-10 – Fugue, HWV610. Eight Keyboard Suites, Set I – Suite No 3, HWV428; Suite No 5, HWV430. Air, HWV464. Air, HWV467. Suite, HWV446a. Minuet, HWV545. Minuet, HWV547. Minuet, HWV546. Air, HWV469. Allemande, HWV479. Courante, HWV489. Prelude on 'Jesu meine Freude', HWV480 **Krieger** Aria and 24 Variations **Zachow** Suite – Sarabande; Gigue
Christopher Hogwood, ᵃ**Derek Adlam** *clavs*
Metronome ② METCD1060 (99' · DDD)   Ⓕ

Alas, 'The Secret Handel' does not unveil any salacious facts about the composer's sexual orientation or hitherto unsuspected illegitimate offspring. However, Christopher Hogwood's illuminating booklet essay hints that the inclusion of a few short pieces by the Hallé organist Zachow and an aria and 24 variations by Krieger illustrate the kind of music that the young Handel might have copied in his long-lost manuscript keyboard book. Also, Hogwood's use of clavichord reflects the famous story that the boy Handel, forbidden to learn music by his disapproving father, smuggled a clavichord into his attic in order to practise secretly during the night.

On the first disc, which includes a version of Handel's third keyboard suite ornamented by Gottlieb Muffat, Hogwood plays an instrument built by the Hamburg keyboard builder Johann Albrecht Hass in 1761. Its plangent yet warm textures produce a fascinating sound, utterly different from the familiar hard brilliance of harpsichords. A fastidiously stylish performance of Aria and Variations in G (*The Harmonious Blacksmith*) is a fine advocacy for the clavichord's virtues. On disc 2, Hogwood plays two other key-

boards, including a magical-sounding Gräbner instrument (Dresden, 1761) that is similar to a small Italian clavichord now in Maidstone Museum that reputedly belonged to Handel. A few movements from the *Water Music* show how Handel's music might have been conceived before the compositional skeleton was garbed in orchestral flesh. Hogwood's thoughtfully prepared programme and articulate playing is a laudable fusion of scholarly detail and artistic insight.

Dixit Dominus, HWV232

Dixit Dominus. Laudate pueri Dominum, HWV237 Saeviat tellus, HWV240. Salve regina, HWV241
Annick Massis *sop* **Magdalena Koẑená** *mez*
Chœur des Musiciens du Louvre;
Les Musiciens du Louvre / Marc Minkowski
Archiv 459 627-2AH (78' · DDD · T/t)
            Ⓕ ⦿⦿▷

These pieces, written in Handel's early twenties, embody a kind of excitement and freedom, and a richness of ideas, that come from his contact with a different tradition and a sudden realisation that the musical world was larger and less constricted than he had imagined, tucked away in provincial middle and north Germany. You can hear him stretching his musical wings in this music. And it certainly doesn't fail to take off in these very lively performances. The quickish tempi habitually favoured by Marc Minkowski are by no means out of place here. The *Saeviat tellus*, although little recorded, is pretty familiar music, as Handel recycled most of it, notably the brilliant opening number in *Apollo e Dafne* and the lovely 'O nox dulcis' in *Agrippina*. This is a solo motet, as too is the *Salve regina*, notable for the expressive vocal leaps and chromatic writing in the 'Ad te clamamus' and the solo organ and string writing in the 'Eia ergo' that follows. *Laudate pueri*, which uses a choir, is another fresh and energetic piece: the choir of the Musiciens du Louvre do their pieces in rousing fashion, and there's some happy oboe playing, as well as fine singing from Koẑená, earlier on, in particular in the hugely spirited 'Excelsus super omnes'. The biggest item is the *Dixit Dominus*, where the choir sings very crisply. The illustrative settings of 'ruinas' tumbling down through the registers, and the 'conquassabit' that follows, are truly exciting; and the long closing chorus is done with due weight at quite a measured pace. These splendid performances truly capture the spirit of these marvellous pieces.

Handel Dixit Dominus
Caldara Crucifixus. Missa Dolorosa
Balthasar-Neumann Choir and Ensemble /
Thomas Hengelbrock
Deutsche Harmonia Mundi CD/SACD
82876 58792-2 (63' · DDD · T/t)   Ⓕ ⦿⦿▷

Handel's *Dixit Dominus*, the magnificent psalm-setting composed in Rome in 1707, seems to have an eternal power to startle and delight in equal measure. This performance captures the flamboyant tension and precocious genius that must have struck the 22-year-old's Roman patrons like a thunderbolt. The superb Balthasar-Neumann Choir possess laudable clarity and precision, although the in-house male soloists are less impressive than their rivals for John Eliot Gardiner and Andrew Parrott.

The soprano duet 'De torrente' is ideally hushed and plaintive, but apocalyptic moments such as 'Juravit Dominus' make Thomas Hengelbrock's version comparable with the most striking in the catalogue. The *staccato* chords on 'conquassabit' are delivered with impeccably controlled aggression. The orchestra is magnificent, with the contrast between first and second violins presented in thrilling SACD sound. Two theorbo players drive the music along with firm determination and make the opening of the 'Gloria' snap with an energetic bite.

Some of Hengelbrock's most important work has been the championing of Italian Baroque sacred music (especially Lotti). This time it's the turn of Antonio Caldara, a Venetian active in Rome at about the same time as Handel and was subsequently the most popular and prolific composer at the Viennese court of Emperor Charles VI. The *Kyrie* of the *Missa dolorosa*, composed in 1735, instantly establishes that Caldara was infinitely more than a mediocre talent blessed by good fortune, although the feeling persists that the Mass was made to fit circumstances rather than to endure for posterity. Its splendid moments range from the graceful bassoon solo in 'Domine Fili' to an abrasively dramatic 'Et resurrexit'. Caldara's reputation is further restored by the gorgeous 16-part *Crucifixus* which rounds off this exceptional disc. Highly recommended.

Coronation Anthems

Zadok the Priest, HWV258. **Let thy hand be strengthened**, HWV259. **The King shall rejoice**, HWV260. **My heart is inditing**, HWV261.

Coronation Anthems, HWV258-61. Ode for the Birthday of Queen Anne, 'Eternal Source of Light Divine', HWV74
Susan Gritton sop **Robin Blaze** counterten **Michael George** bass **King's College Choir, Cambridge; Academy of Ancient Music / Stephen Cleobury**
EMI 557140-2 (61' · DDD)　　　　Ⓕ**Ⓞ**➾

Recordings of the *Coronation Anthems* are usually winners – the old Willcocks one from King's, and the Preston from Westminster Abbey certainly were in their day – and this one certainly hits the mark. It's a traditional enough reading, without eccentricities, with plenty of energy and duly grand in scale: listen to the noble opening of *Zadok the Priest*, the introduction beautifully sustained and shaped, and then overwhelmingly grand at the choral entry, whose weight and power may surprise you, bearing in mind the quite modest size of the King's

choir. They know just how to manage this kind of music in the chapel acoustic, which is naturally appropriate to the music.

The other three are no less enjoyable. The clear young voices, free of the fuzziness and soft edges of most choirs, help in such movements as the first of *Let thy hand be strengthened*, or the lightly sprung first of *My heart is inditing* and its vigorous finale too. The *Ode for the Birthday of Queen Anne*, one of Handel's earliest settings of English words, is more of a rarity. This is a lively performance, with clear and light solo singing, notably from Robin Blaze. There are also admirable contributions from Susan Gritton and Michael George. Excellent choral singing, and the Academy of Ancient Music are on their toes throughout.

Coronation Anthems, HWV258-61. Messiah – Worthy is the Lamb; Amen. Jephtha – Overture. Organ Concerto, Op 4 No 4. Solomon – Arrival of the Queen of Sheba
The Sixteen / Harry Christophers
Coro COR16066 (70' · DDD · T)　　Ⓕ**ⓄⓄⓄ**➾

Ⓖ　There are plenty of very good recordings of these anthems but this new one leaps straight towards the top of the heap (those preferring to hear boy trebles might already admire the excellent version by King's College, Cambridge, under Cleobury, above).

We have come selfishly to expect reliability, stylishness and honest fine musicianship from Harry Christophers, his singers and instrumentalists. Yet these fresh, spontaneous and vivacious performances are revelatory. Not only is the choral singing wonderfully clear, perfectly enunciated, beautifully phrased and impeccably tuned, but also the orchestral playing – an aspect too often relegated to auto-pilot in this repertoire – is brilliantly alert, bold and lyrical. *Zadok the Priest* never fails to make a strong impression even in average performances (and The Sixteen's expertly judged reading is anything but average), but the special quality of this disc is that the other three lesser-known anthems also receive performances that allow them to shine just as brightly as the most famous (and shortest) anthem. *My heart is inditing* is radiantly performed ('The King shall have pleasure in her beauty' is gorgeously shaped), *The King shall rejoice* is splendidly poised and paced, and the first part of *Let thy hand be strengthened* conveys the perfect juxtaposition of forthrightness and elegance. Christophers's sure direction locks onto the musical interest and richness of each section in the longer anthems (some other good versions rely on good openings and grand conclusions, but the bits in between sometimes get a bit lost). Coupled with a sparkling account of the Organ Concerto Op 4 No 4 (superbly played by Alastair Ross, and with a magnificent choral 'Alleluia' finale created for the 1735 revival of *Athalia*), a couple of orchestral interludes and the last chorus of *Messiah*, the judicious programme avoids the overkill factor one sometimes encounters when all four anthems are heard consecutively.

Donald Burrows's booklet-note is ideally detailed and accessible, and overall this disc ranks as The Sixteen's most exciting achievement in its impressive Handel discography.

Chandos Anthems

O praise the Lord with one consent, HWV254. Let God arise, HWV256a. My song shall be alway, HWV252
Dame Emma Kirkby sop **Iestyn Davies** counterten **James Gilchrist** ten **Neal Davies** bass **Choir of Trinity College, Cambridge; Academy of Ancient Music / Stephen Layton**
Hyperion CDA67737 (66' · DDD · T)   Ⓕ〇

Here are three of the 11 so-called *Chandos Anthems* composed for James Brydges, the Earl of Carnarvon (from 1719 the First Duke of Chandos). Handel's music was tailor-made for fewer performers than those featured here. Nevertheless, the 40 members of the Choir of Trinity College, Cambridge, sing with flexibility and lightness. The opening chorus of *O praise the Lord with one consent* is crisply articulate and lightly shaped, and consonants are attacked with voracity. Most of the choral contributions have sweetness and delicacy. Stephen Layton lets the performers off the leash a little in the final pealing 'Alleluia' sections of each anthem, and in some dynamic passages of *Let God arise*, based on *Dixit Dominus*. The Academy of Ancient Music's playing is often understated, and the introductory sonatas of *Let God arise* and *My song shall be alway* feature convivial oboe solos played by Katharina Spreckelsen. The four illustrious soloists excel in numerous short movements. Iestyn Davies navigates some difficult low passages in 'Praise him, all ye that in his house' (HWV254) without traces of strain. Neal Davies is authoritative, James Gilchrist is on fine dramatic form in 'Like as the smoke vanisheth' (HWV256*a*), and Emma Kirkby shows her stylistic intelligence and masterful communication of text in the radiant opening of HWV252. It is enjoyable to hear some of Handel's lesser-known and more intimate English church music performed with such elegant restraint and skill.

Ode for St Cecilia's Day

Ode for St Cecilia's Day, HWV76.
Cecilia, volgi un sguardo, HWV89   Ⓟ
Carolyn Sampson sop **James Gilchrist** ten
Choir of The King's Consort;
The King's Consort / Robert King
Hyperion CDA67463 (78' · DDD · T/t)   Ⓕ〇〇〇

 This completes the series of recordings exploring the smaller works Handel inserted into his glorious setting of Dryden's *Alexander's Feast*. Robert King has previously recorded *The Choice of Hercules*, which

was created for the 1751 revival. The tenor cantata *Look down, harmonious Saint* was intended as the interlude for the original run in 1736, but was rejected in favour of *Cecilia, volgi un sguardo*. It's a splendid idea to pair this seldom-heard Italian cantata with Dryden's sublime *Ode for St Cecilia's Day* that Handel created to fulfil the same function three years later.

This is a mouth-watering performance of Handel's colourfully gorgeous ode. 'The trumpets' loud clangour' features Crispian Steele-Perkins on fine form, flautist Rachel Brown enchants in 'The soft complaining flute', and Jonathan Cohen's cello solo in 'What passion cannot Music raise and quell!' is sweetly inspired. The King's Consort and Choir perform with perfect juxtaposition of flamboyance and taste. James Gilchrist sings with authority: he's a Handel tenor of the highest order.

This recording is in a class of its own when it comes to the seemingly effortless, beautiful singing of Carolyn Sampson, now the best British early music soprano by quite some distance. She's sensitively partnered by organist Matthew Halls in the sublime 'But oh! what art can teach', which has a breathtaking poignancy. Notwithstanding many agreeable past achievements, King has seldom produced a disc of such outstanding conviction.

L'Allegro, il Penseroso..., HWV55

L'Allegro, il Penseroso, ed il Moderato   Ⓟ
Patrizia Kwella, Marie McLaughlin, Jennifer Smith sops **Michael Ginn** treb **Maldwyn Davies, Martyn Hill** tens **Stephen Varcoe** bar **Monteverdi Choir; English Baroque Soloists / Sir John Eliot Gardiner**
Erato ② 2292 45377-2 (116' · ADD · T/t)
Recorded 1980   Ⓜ〇〇〇

The score of *L'Allegro, il Penseroso ed il Moderato* is presented here virtually complete. The soprano aria 'But O, sad virgin' is omitted, which if you look at the marvellous opening for two cellos, seems savage indeed, but the music does rather lose its way in the long decorative passages for both voice and instruments, and its absence need not be regretted. The band is small and so is the superbly alert chorus. Playing and singing constantly delight by their delicacy. The three soprano soloists sound poised and clean-cut. Jennifer Smith's high notes are an especial joy. Handel wanted a boy treble for two arias and presumably knew that their words were never very clear; this one produces some pretty sounds. The succession of charming miniatures is interrupted in the middle of Part 2 by more substantial items and a blaze of brilliant coloratura from several soloists. Martyn Hill's 'These delights' is triumphantly good, and the choral singing is excitingly precise. The final chorus in Part 2, a fugue with four subjects, is sublime, but he did not bother himself unduly with the final chorus in Part 3. But in general this is very likeable music, its charm, conciseness and emphasis on word-painting unlike anything else in Handel. The sound quality is very good.

Additional recommendation

L'Allegro, il Penseroso ed il Moderato   Ⓟ
Anderson, Gritton, McFadden *sops* **Agnew** *ten*
Davies *bass* **The King's Consort & Choir / King**
Hyperion ② CDA67283/4 (138' · DDD · T/t)   Ⓕ

This is the first truly complete recording of Handel's delectable pastoral ode. Robert King gives full value to the tranquil reflectiveness that lies at the core of the work, favouring broad tempi and gravely expressive phrasing. Occasionally his approach seems a shade too reverential. But for the most part he directs this glorious music with affection and relish, abetted by vivid orchestral playing and a typically responsive contribution from the chorus.

Acis and Galatea, HWV49b

Acis and Galatea (original Cannons 1718 version)   Ⓟ
Susan Hamilton *sop* Galatea **Nicholas Mulroy** *ten*
Acis **Matthew Brook** *bass* Polyphemus **Thomas Hobbs** *ten* Damon **Nicholas Hurndall Smith** *ten* Coridon
Dunedin Consort & Players / John Butt
Linn ② 💿 CKD319 (95' · DDD)   ⒻⓄⓄ➔

Handel's *Acis and Galatea* has been recorded often, but the original version written for small-scale performance by only five singers (soprano, three tenors and bass) and a small band at Cannons in 1718 has almost never been properly revived. This beggars belief because the Cannons version text makes more dramatic sense and the musical scale of it is charming. It is certainly among Handel's most perfect creations. Thankfully, John Butt has researched the performing conditions and text of the Cannons *Acis*. The philological aspects of the Dunedin Consort & Players' new recording are impeccable, and, better still, the performance is utterly magical.

The Sinfonia brims with unforced personality, after which the pastoral chorus 'O the pleasure of the plains' is relaxed, with the oboes given enough space to weave their imitative lines clearly. The five singers and the band are beautifully in proportion with each other, and Linn's sound recording is stunningly good. Susan Hamilton's light, articulate soprano is preferable to an operatic voice in the role of Galatea. Nicholas Mulroy's Acis is resonant and suave, combining muscularity with elegance. The madrigal-like beauty of 'Wretched lovers' is breathtaking: the blend and understanding between the five singers is deeply satisfying, and the menacing music to convey the arrival of Polyphemus is astutely integrated. Matthew Brook's Polyphemus is extrovert, powerful and amusing, but also arouses pity and tenderness from the listener in 'I rage, I melt, I burn'. The dialogue between the hapless would-be seducer and the disgusted Galatea is superbly enacted by Brook and Hamilton. The roles of Damon and Coridon are admirably sung by Nicholas Hurndall Smith and Thomas Hobbs.

Butt's direction from the harpsichord is a role model of taste and style, and he insightfully conveys the elusive changing tone of the story from pastoral romp into personal tragedy. Previous versions of merit still possess enduring appeal, but it seems to me that the Dunedins have transformed the way in which we can understand and enjoy Handel's lovely early English masterpiece.

Acis and Galatea (arr Mendelssohn)
Julia Kleiter *sop* Galatea **Christoph Prégardien** *ten*
Acis **Wolf Matthias Friedrich** *bass* Polyphemus
Michael Slattery *ten* Damon
North German Radio Choir; Göttingen Festival Orchestra / Nicholas McGegan
Carus CARUS83 420 (73' · DDD)   Ⓕ

The virtues of *Acis and Galatea* were clear enough more than a century later for the 19-year-old Mendelssohn to arrange the work for the Berlin Sing-Akademie in 1828-29 (with a German version of the libretto prepared by his sister Fanny). One might uncharitably (but accurately) criticise that the teenage Mendelssohn's feverish excitement at discovering Handel led to him throwing everything he could (almost including the kitchen sink, so it seems) at the music. Unlike Mozart's more discreet and softer reorchestration of *Acis* (1788), there is an intense amount of intervention in Mendelssohn's orchestral score, which is tailored for a full-scale symphony orchestra and large chorus.

Nicholas McGegan and his Göttingen Festival Orchestra gave the modern premiere of Mendelssohn's score at the 2008 Göttingen Handel Festival, and the ensuing recording is crisply detailed. The most amusing effects are huge bursts of brass and timpani explosions associated with Polyphemus, who is sung with gusto by Wolf Matthias Friedrich. Acis is sung with a hint of strain by Christoph Prégardien, and Julia Kleiter's Galatea is efficient.

The NDR Choir are jovial or doleful as the music requires. McGegan directs with liveliness, and it's hard to imagine this arrangement receiving a better advocate. It's bombastic and clumsy in comparison to Handel's delightful original, but the young Mendelssohn's perspective is entertaining.

Alexander's Feast, HWV75

Alexander's Feast[a]. Organ Concerto, Op 4 No 1 HWV289[b]. Harp Concerto, Op 4 No 6 HWV294[c]
[a]**Nancy Argenta** *sop* **Alan Partridge** *ten* [a]**Michael George** *bass* [b]**Paul Nicholson** *org* [c]**Andrew Lawrence-King** *hp* **The Sixteen; Symphony of Harmony and Invention / Harry Christophers**
Coro ② COR16028 (116' · DDD · T)   Ⓜ➔

Alexander's Feast, an ode to St Cecilia by the long-dead John Dryden, was set by Handel in 1736 and revised many times. Subtitled 'The Power of Musick', it describes a banquet held by Alexander the Great after his victory over the Persians. The singing and playing of Timotheus inspire Alexander to drunkenness, pity, love and revenge, one after the other. What has this to do with the patron saint of music, you might well ask? The answer comes in a commentary towards the end, when Dryden contrasts Timotheus's pagan skills with the invention of the organ and the celestial connections of 'Divine Cecilia', who 'enlarg'd the former narrow bounds'.

The music is superb, and it's given a superb performance here. The Sixteen (actually 18, with two extra sopranos and an all-male alto line) are a little lightweight in the grander choruses but they sing with precision and unforced tone. Over a swiftly moving ground bass, 'The many rend the skies' goes with a swing; their finest moment, though, is their hushed contemplation of the Persian king lying dead on the field of battle. The lion's share of the solos goes to Nancy Argenta, whose fresh tones, admirably suited to 'War, he sung, is toil and trouble', are cunningly and effectively veiled for 'He chose a mournful muse', an accompanied recitative in the manner of 'Thy rebuke hath broken his heart'. Ian Partridge is superb in his subtle handling of the words, as he is with his wonderful breath control in 'Happy pair'. Michael George is perfect in 'Revenge, Timotheus cries': hissing snakes, flashing sparkles and all.

The orchestration is a constant delight. In some of the solo numbers Handel uses only violins and continuo; elsewhere he introduces a solo cello, a trumpet obbligato, recorders and horns. Best of all is the creepy middle section of 'Revenge, Timotheus cries', where he conjures up the 'ghastly band' of the Grecian dead with Neapolitan sixth cadences played by the violas and bassoons in octaves. All these opportunities are seized with relish by the Symphony of Harmony and Invention. In an unsuitable church acoustic, Harry Christophers sets unfailingly suitable tempi. And to add to our delight he includes the concertos detailed above that are integral to the piece.

Alexander Balus, HWV65

Alexander Balus   P
Lynne Dawson, Claron McFadden sops **Catherine Denley** mez **Charles Daniels** ten **Michael George** bass **New College Choir, Oxford; The King's Consort and Choir / Robert King**
Hyperion ② CDA67241/2 (156' · DDD · N/T)   F

Alexander Balus has never been one of Handel's more popular oratorios. That's mainly because its plot is by modern standards lacking in drama and motivation, and accordingly doesn't call forth the vein of his music that nowadays has the strongest appeal. It's essentially a sentimental drama, in which the interest centres on the characters' emotional reactions to their situations, amatory, political and religious, and these are rather static in the first two acts but much more powerful in the more eventful third with the deaths of both Alexander and Ptolomee.

Here we have a very capable, idiomatic, sensibly cast performance under Robert King. The choruses are especially accomplished. The New College Choir, supported by men from The King's Consort Choir, is confident, bright-toned and vigorous, clean in line and well balanced. Lynne Dawson sings beautifully in her firm and resonant soprano and her usual poised and unaffected style. Her singing of the lamenting music in the final act is particularly moving. Cleopatra has a couple of duets, one with some attractive interplay with the secondary character Aspasia, sung with much assurance by Claron McFadden. As Alexander, Catherine Denley sings with much confidence and directness in music that isn't all of special individuality. Jonathan is sung fluently and warmly, but very plainly, by Charles Daniels. Lastly there's Michael George, who's ideally suited to the villainous Ptolomee, with his forceful (but always musical) manner and the touch of blackness in his tone. The orchestral playing is accomplished, and often rather carefully shaped. The recitative moves at a steady but natural pace; ornamentation is generally modest. All Handelians will want to acquire this set, and others should not be put off by the indifferent press *Alexander Balus* has received from time to time.

Athalia, HWV52

Athalia   P
Joan Sutherland sop Athalia **Emma Kirkby** sop Josabeth **Aled Jones** treb Joas **James Bowman** counterten Joad **Anthony Rolfe Johnson** ten Mathan **David Thomas** bass Abner **New College Choir, Oxford; Academy of Ancient Music / Christopher Hogwood**
Decca Gramophone Awards Collection ② 475 201-2 (122' · DDD · N/T)   M**OOO**⟫

Athalia, composed for Oxford in 1733 to a libretto that draws on Racine's play, tells of the usurping, apostate Jewish queen Athalia, and her overthrow when the prophet Joad and his wife Josabeth bring the true heir, the boy Joas, to the throne. The action is feebly handled by the librettist, Samuel Humphreys; but several of the characters are quite strong and Handel grasps the opportunities offered him for striking music.

Athalia fares best of all, musically, as one would expect; and it was a brilliant stroke of imagination to ask Joan Sutherland to take the role here. She's a great Handelian, but not a figure you expect to see in early-music circles. In the event, the slight disparity of approach between her and the other members of the cast serves ideally to symbolise the separation of Athalia from her fellow Israelites. She uses more vibrato than the rest of the cast, but the singing is magnificent in its grandeur and its clear, bell-like, perfectly focused tone. Among the rest, Emma Kirkby is on her very best form, singing coolly, with poised musicianship, and with quite astonishing technical command at times. James Bowman, as Joad, has his moments, and always sounds well. David Thomas is dependable in the often very vigorous music for Abner; and as Athalia's priest, Mathan, Anthony Rolfe Johnson sings in shapely fashion. The boy Joas is sung, as it should be, by a boy, in this case Aled Jones, who gives a very controlled, exact performance, perhaps rather careful but of intense tonal beauty. At its best, the choral singing is first-rate, spirited, forthright and accurate, but it can have an air of the routine. There's much good, crisp orchestral playing, though some of the AAM's less positive characteristics are evident: an occasional moment of unsure ensemble, and a lack of broad shaping. These are however perfectionist quibbles: these discs, excellently recorded, give an admirable and often striking realisation of a choice work.

Esther, HWV50b

Esther (1732 version)   **P**
Rosemary Joshua, Rebecca Outram, Cecilia Osmond sops **Susan Bickley** mez **James Bowman** counterten **Angus Smith, Andrew Kennedy, Christopher Watson** tens **Christopher Purves** bar
**London Handel Choir and Orchestra /
Laurence Cummings**
Somm ② SOMMCD238/9 (137' · DDD)
Recorded live in March 2002   Ⓕ

This is a particularly welcome and important world premiere recording. Handel composed *Esther* in about 1718-20 for James Brydges, the Earl of Carnarvon (and later Duke of Chandos), using a libretto that was anonymously adapted from Thomas Brereton's English translation of a play by Racine. This slender work, containing only six scenes, lays a strong claim to being the first English oratorio, but Handel seems not to have considered performing it for a public audience until 1732, when the entrepreneurial composer thoroughly revised the score to fit his company of Italian opera singers (including Senesino, Strada and Montagnana, who all sang in English), and enlisted the aid of the writer Samuel Humphreys to expand the drama with additional scenes. This is the historic version of *Esther* that launched Handel's oratorio career in London, but it has remained inexplicably neglected in modern times.

Laurence Cummings is one of our finest and most natural Handelian conductors. The Israelite Woman's sensuous opening number 'Breathe soft, ye gales' (featuring recorders, oboes, bassoons, harp, theorbo, five-part strings and organ) is neatly judged by the impressive London Handel Orchestra. The superb choir is enthusiastic and masterful, and the two inserted Coronation Anthems *My heart is inditing* and *Zadok the Priest* (the latter given a parody text) are both performed magnificently. James Bowman sounds a little fragile in the most extensive coloratura passages written for Senesino in

'Endless fame', and the part of Mordecai seems uncomfortably low for Susan Bickley (which is not helped by the dragging speed of 'Dread not, righteous Queen, the danger'), but in general the soloists form a consistently solid team. Christopher Purves is marvellous as the scheming and bullying evil minister Haman, and is equally good at singing the pitiful and lyrical 'Turn not, O Queen, thy face away' when the villain fears his deserved doom.

The all-round excellence of this live concert performance from Handel's parish church, St George's, Hanover Square, makes it an essential treat for Handelians.

Israel in Egypt, HWV54

Israel in Egypt   **P**
Nancy Argenta, Emily Van Evera sops **Timothy Wilson** counterten **Anthony Rolfe Johnson** ten **David Thomas, Jeremy White** basses **Taverner Choir and Players / Andrew Parrott**
Virgin Classics Veritas ② 562155-2 (135' · DDD · T)
Ⓑ➔

Israel in Egypt, of all Handel's works, is the choral one *par excellence* – so much so, in fact, that it was something of a failure in Handel's own time because solo singing was much preferred to choral by the audiences. Andrew Parrott gives a complete performance of the work, in its original form: that's to say, prefaced by the noble funeral anthem for Queen Caroline, as adapted by Handel to serve as a song of mourning by the captive Israelites. This first part is predominantly slow, grave music, powerfully elegiac; the Taverner Choir shows itself to be firm and clean of line, well focused and strongly sustained. The chorus has its chance to be more energetic in the second part, with the famous and vivid Plague choruses – in which the orchestra too plays its part in the pictorial effects, with the fiddles illustrating in turn frogs, flies and hailstones. And last, in the third part, there's a generous supply of the stirring C major music in which Handel has the Israelites give their thanks to God, in some degree symbolising the English giving thanks for the Hanoverian monarchy and the Protestant succession. Be that as it may, the effect is splendid. The solo work is first-rate, too, with Nancy Argenta radiant in Miriam's music in the final scene and distinguished contributions from David Thomas and Anthony Rolfe Johnson.

Jephtha, HWV70

Jephtha   **P**
Lynne Dawson, Ruth Holton sops **Anne Sofie von Otter** mez **Michael Chance** counterten **Nigel Robson** ten **Stephen Varcoe** bar **Alastair Ross** hpd **Paul Nicholson** org **Monteverdi Choir; English Baroque Soloists / Sir John Eliot Gardiner**
Philips ③ 422 351-2PH3 (158' · DDD · T)   Ⓕ❶❷❸➔

Ⓖ *Jephtha* has the same basic story as several eastern Mediterranean myths familiar to the opera-goer (in *Idomeneo* and *Iphigénie en Aulide*, for example), of the father compelled to sacrifice his child. In the event Jephtha's daughter Iphis isn't sacrificed: when, Abraham-like, her father has shown himself willing to perform God's will, and she has shown herself ready to accept it, an angel happily intervenes and commutes her sentence to perpetual virginity. But not before the tragic situation has provoked some of the noblest music Handel wrote. From the moment that Jephtha sees that it's his daughter who has to fall victim to his improvident oath, the music, hitherto on a good but not outstanding level, acquires a new depth, above all in the sequence at the end of Act 2. This recording does the work full justice. It could scarcely have been better cast. Nigel Robson seems ideal as Jephtha. He has due weight as well as vigour, style as well as expressive force. Lynne Dawson's Iphis is also a real success. Sometimes this role is done in a girlishly 'innocent' vein; she does more than that, establishing the character in the appealing love duet in Part 1. Her firm, well focused, unaffected singing is just right for this role.

The other outstanding contribution comes from Michael Chance as Hamor, her unfortunate betrothed. Stephen Varcoe sings Zebul's music with due resonance and spirit, and Anne Sofie von Otter makes a distinguished contribution in Storgè's music: 'Scenes of horror' has a splendid attack and depth of tone, and 'Let other creatures die!' is spat out with rare power. Ruth Holton makes a pleasantly warm and mellifluous angel. The Monteverdi Choir is in fine voice, responsive to all that Gardiner asks of them. Here and there one might cavil at some of the dynamic shaping in the choruses, for example in 'Doubtful fear' in Act 3; and the Overture can be a trifle fussy in detail. But the broad vision of the work, the rhythmic energy that runs through it and the sheer excellence of the choral and orchestral contributions speak for themselves. Cuts are very few, and amply justified by authentic precedent. This recording is firmly recommended as the standard version of this great work.

Joseph and his Brethren, HWV59

Joseph and his Brethren   Ⓟ
Yvonne Kenny *sop* **Catherine Denley** *mez* **Connor Burrowes** *treb* **James Bowman** *counterten* **John Mark Ainsley** *ten* **Michael George** *bass*
New College Choir, Oxford; The King's Consort Choir; The King's Consort / **Robert King**
Hyperion ③ CDA67171/3 (164' · DDD · T/t)   Ⓕ

There's never been a complete, professional recording of *Joseph and his Brethren*, a neglect out of proportion to the merits of its music. It's full of good and characteristic things, and there are several scenes, including the extended denouement in the last act, that are very moving. The work begins splendidly, with an unusual overture her-

alding a deeply felt opening scene for Joseph, languishing in an Egyptian prison. The setting of his prophecy is effective, with seven bars of darting arpeggios for the years of plenty and seven of sparse harmonic writing, *adagio*, for the famine years. The rest of Act 1 celebrates Joseph's foresight, preferment and marriage to Asenath, Pharaoh's daughter. The highlights of Act 2 include a prison scene for Simeon, an agonised G minor accompanied recitative and aria, a beautiful, nostalgic idyll for Joseph, and scenes for Joseph with his brothers which incorporate a splendid outburst from Simeon, an aria from Benjamin and a moving chorus from the brothers, a sustained prayer and a richly worked fugue.

The soloists dispatch all this music with spirit and accuracy. James Bowman is in excellent voice in the title-role, full, rich and duly agile in the rapid music. *Joseph* is well suited to Robert King's way of conducting Handel. This isn't a specially dramatic performance, but carefully moulded and intelligently paced. The choir produces a sound that's bright and firm and the singing is resolute. King is particularly good at shaping the dynamics in a natural and unanimous way.

Messiah, HWV56

Messiah   Ⓟ
Arleen Auger *sop* **Anne Sofie von Otter** *mez* **Michael Chance** *counterten* **Howard Crook** *ten* **John Tomlinson** *bass* **The Choir of the English Concert; The English Concert / Trevor Pinnock**
Archiv ② 477 5904GOR2 (150' · DDD · T)
ⓂⓄⓄ▷

How authentic is authentic? Trevor Pinnock and The English Concert, while using period instruments, are guaranteed to appeal very widely to traditional lovers of Handel's masterpiece, who might as a rule opt for a performance with modern instruments. Pinnock gets the best of both worlds. A distinctive point is that, even more than his rivals, he brings out the impact of timpani and trumpets, above all in the 'Hallelujah' and 'Amen' choruses. There he stirs the blood in a way that even Sargent would have envied. Another point is that a genuine, dark, firm, bass soloist has been chosen, John Tomlinson, who's ripely resonant here. Traditionalists who lament the lack of dark bass tone and the predominance of baritonal shades in Handel today will doubtless raise a cheer, and if it comes to authenticity, Handel must surely have been thinking of just such a voice, rather than anything thinner or more discreet. Not only Tomlinson but Arleen Auger too will delight listeners of all Handelian persuasions. She has one of the sweetest, most ravishing soprano sounds on any of the current versions, and the warmth of expressiveness, whether strictly authentic or not, brings many of the most memorable moments in the whole performance. Try the close of 'I know that my Redeemer liveth', where the dramatic contrasts of dynamic are extreme and masterfully controlled, without a hint of sentimentality. The male alto, Michael Chance, also outshines his direct rivals in artistry and beauty of tone, but he's given only a proportion of the alto numbers. The majority are given to Anne Sofie von Otter. Hers is another beautiful voice, finely controlled. The recording is one of the finest available, with plenty of bloom and with inner clarity never making textures sound thin or over-analytical.

Messiah
Carolyn Sampson sop **Catherine Wyn-Rogers** contr
Mark Padmore ten **Christopher Purves** bass
The Sixteen; Orchestra of The Sixteen /
Harry Christophers
Coro ② COR16062 (145' · DDD)
Includes bonus excerpts disc of previous Handel
recordings by The Sixteen   Ⓜ**ⓄⓄ**➾

Over the past few decades Harry Christophers and The Sixteen have performed *Messiah* about 150 times. This new Coro recording presents them to better advantage than their uneven 1987 version for Hyperion: the choir remains excellent 21 years later but the orchestra and soloists are a vast improvement. Only one member of the choir and two orchestral players repeat their roles in the 2008 performance, and the violin section has swelled from seven to 12, which helps to produce a stronger theatrical sound. Christophers's interpretation nowadays is just over four minutes longer than it was in 1987, so there are no radical changes in his overall pacing, but taking a few things a notch slower suggests an increased confidence and maturity.

The contribution from the oboes is more telling and to the fore than one usually hears, although the prominence of the organ as a continuo instrument is seldom convincing (nor is the use of theorbo accompaniment in recitatives). The Sixteen's choral singing has clarity, balance, shapely moulding of contrapuntal lines and plenty of unforced power. When necessary, resonant homophonic grandeur is achieved without pomposity. The contrast between the playful and solemn parts of 'All we like sheep' is wondrously realised, and the soft sections of 'Since by man came death' are breathtaking.

Three of the soloists earned their spurs as members of The Sixteen. Mark Padmore, a choir member in 1987 and here making his third (and best) *Messiah* recording as a soloist, could be a little lighter in 'Comfort ye', but his evangelical communication of words is highly effective in 'Thy rebuke hath broken his heart'. Carolyn Sampson and the orchestra's violins relish an equal dialogue in 'Rejoice greatly', and her coloratura sparkles with clarity and assurance. Christopher Purves sings 'For behold, darkness shall cover the earth' more softly than one usually hears, and 'The trumpet shall sound' is lyrical and suave (with splendid obbligato from Robert Farley). Christophers conducts with finesse and integrity. This fine team performance is a safe

recommendation for anyone wanting to acquire an all-purpose 'period' *Messiah*.

Messiah
Julia Doyle sop **Iestyn Davies** counterten **Allan**
Clayton ten **Andrew Foster-Williams** bass
Polyphony; Britten Sinfonia / Stephen Layton
Hyperion ② CDA67800 (134' · DDD · T)   Ⓜ**Ⓞ**➾

Polyphony have given annual Christmas performances of *Messiah* at St John's, Smith Square, for 15 years and this Hyperion set is based on the 2008 run of performances featuring the Britten Sinfonia. Perhaps some might find the use of modern instruments (rather than period ones) a major talking-point. But it isn't as if hearing generally stylish 'traditional' performances of *Messiah* is rare.

There is a lot to like about this engaging performance. Allan Clayton's 'Comfort ye' conspicuously lacks its 'y', but in all other respects the four soloists are ideal. Julia Doyle is a charismatic Angel/narrator in the pastoral scene, and her embellished recapitulation of the line 'I know that my Redeemer liveth' is spine-tingling. Andrew Foster-Williams's singing is marvellous ('Why do the nations' is thrillingly dispatched, and he holds the listener in the palm of his hand as he confides 'Behold I tell you a mystery'). The well-rounded tone and technical precision of Iestyn Davies's singing is easy to enjoy, but it is equally significant that his ornamentation in 'But who may abide' is masterful for its stylish vocabulary and expressive wisdom (Layton's dramatic explosion of the strings for 'the refiner's fire' is startling).

There are a few stylistic solecisms that do not improve on Handel's practices. There is too much churchy organ in recitatives, and the use of solo violin in several arias is not preferable to unison fiddles, although the use of a solitary string bass note as the cue for 'Since by man came death' is effective. Proceedings are occasionally a shade over-conducted, too sculpted and self-conscious, but Layton's affection for the oratorio is frequently discernible, not least in the technical and communicative qualities of Polyphony's exceptional singing of the choruses. This *Messiah* is calculated to keep certain questions open, and one doesn't have to agree with all of the proposed answers in order to find it enjoyable. It certainly has strong musical appeal and a probing nature.

Messiah   Ⓟ
Henry Jenkinson, Otta Jones, Robert Brooks trebs
Iestyn Davies counterten **Toby Spence** ten
Eamonn Dougan bass **Academy of Ancient**
Music; New College Choir, Oxford /
Edward Higginbottom
Naxos ② 8 570131/2 (142' · DDD)   Ⓢ➾

Taking his cue from Handel's 1751 performances, Edward Higginbottom assigns all the soprano solos to some talented boy trebles from the Choir of New College, Oxford. Otta Jones's contribution to 'He shall feed his flock' and Henry Jenkinson's 'I know that my redeemer liveth' are lovely testaments to Higginbottom's crusading 30 years with his choir. At best, Higginbottom's choir produces some marvellous moments ('All we like sheep', and one of the finest 'Amen' fugues on disc). Higginbottom's direction does not boil with dramatic intensity but instead simmers along with patience, elegant judgement and articulate tastefulness.

Some familiar music bears ripe fruit when taken a shade slower than has become common in recent times ('Glory to God' is splendid rather than hurried, and all the better for it). Ex-scholar Toby Spence is on fine form in 'Rejoice greatly', and Iestyn Davies's poetic singing is another enjoyable feature, although one might hanker for a more dramatic treatment of 'shame and spitting' ('He was despised'). 'The trumpet shall sound' resounds with David Blackadder's magnificent playing, and the Academy of Ancient Music play Handel's orchestral parts immaculately. This Naxos release will appeal to those who want an affordable *Messiah* that is beautifully played, brightly sung, sweetly satisfying and unashamedly English in its sentimental roots.

Messiah (Dublin version, 1742)   ▣
Susan Hamilton *sop* **Clare Wilkinson, Annie Gill,**
Heather Cairncross *mez* **Nicholas Mulroy** *ten*
Matthew Brook *bar* **Edward Caswell** *bass*
Dunedin Consort / John Butt
Linn ⚌ CKD285 (138' · DDD · T)   Ⓕ❶❷❸❹➔

For an infinitely rewarding fresh look at Handel's most familiar music, look no further than the Dunedin Consort's performance of Handel's first version, premiered at Dublin in 1742. Bizarrely under-represented in concert and on disc, the Dublin score contains some fascinating music that Handel never reused, such as the substantial chorus 'Break forth into joy'. The exuberant direction by harpsichordist John Butt is meticulously stylish and utterly devoid of crassly pretentious egotism. The playing is unerringly spontaneous and dramatically integrated with singers who illustrate profound appreciation of text. Clare Wilkinson's 'He was despised' is most moving, Susan Hamilton effortlessly skips through a delicious 'Rejoice greatly', and bass Matthew Brook sings as if his life depends on it.

Butt bravely resolves to use the same forces Handel had at his disposal in Dublin, which means that the entire oratorio is sung by a dozen singers (with all soloists required to participate in the choruses, as Handel would have expected). Where this approach might risk worthy dull solos churned out by stalwart choir members, the Dunedin Consort's exemplary singers produce virtuoso choruses that are theatrically charged, splendidly poised and exquisitely blended. Old warhorses 'For unto us a child is born' and 'Surely he hath borne our griefs' are delightfully inspiring. Butt and the Dunedin

HANDEL'S MESSIAH – IN BRIEF

English Concert and Choir / Trevor Pinnock ▣
Archiv ② 423 630-2AH2 (150' · DDD)   Ⓕ❶❷➔
Grace and liveliness are the characteristics of Pinnock's fine performance that uses instruments Handel would have recognised, though, arguably, a smaller choir than he would have ideally wanted. Arleen Auger is outstanding in the aria 'I know that my redeemer liveth'.

Gabrieli Consort & Players / Paul McCreesh ▣
Archiv ② 453 464-2AH2 (130' · DDD)   Ⓕ❶❷➔
McCreesh favours drama above gracefulness, often to striking effect, though his chorus often sound slick rather than engaged with their text. However, he has a number of fine soloists, with Susan Gritton memorably touching in her two big arias.

London Sym Chorus & Orch / Sir Colin Davis
Philips ② 438 356-2PM2 (144' · ADD)   Ⓜ
This 1966 *Messiah*, once thought to be a fresh reinterpretation of a very British institution, ironically became the 'traditional' *Messiah* many of us knew before the rise of such conductors as Pinnock and Norrington. Colin Davis's intelligent direction, using modern orchestral forces, has moments of high drama, and he has a sterling line-up of soloists.

Collegium Musicum 90 / Richard Hickox ▣
Chandos ② CHAN0522/3 (141' · DDD)   Ⓕ
Although using authentic instruments, this is another fine performance in the post-Colin Davis tradition, with an excellent line-up of soloists (including the young Bryn Terfel) and excellent choral singing.

Academy of Ancient Music; New College Choir, Oxford / Edward Higginbottom ▣
Naxos ② 8 570131/2 (142' · DDD)   Ⓢ➔
A performance to show of the magnificent treble voices of the New College Choir. A well-thought-out, nicely scaled reading – and competitively price too.

Dunedin Consort / John Butt ▣
Linn ⚌ CKD285 (138' · DDD)   Ⓕ❶❷❸❹➔
A wonderfully fresh and uplifting attempt to take us back to the work's first performance. Butt draws on a small 'company' of a dozen singers and wonderfully balances intimacy and drama. The sound is first rate, too. A worthy *Gramophone* Award winner in 2007.

Huddersfield Choral Society; Liverpool PO / Malcolm Sargent Ⓗ
Dutton mono ② 2CDEA5010 (146' · ADD)   Ⓑ❶
For a generation of British listeners Sir Malcolm Sargent owned *Messiah*; here his 1946 recording has been lovingly cleaned up for the digital age.

Consort marry astute scholarship to sincere artistic expression and the result is comfortably the freshest, most natural, revelatory and transparently joyful *Messiah* to have appeared for a very long time. (It's also available as a download at numerous different bit-rates.)

Additional recommendation

Messiah   **H**
Baillie sop **Ripley** contr **Johnston** ten **Walker** bass
Huddersfield Choral Society; RLPO / Sargent
Dutton Essential Archive mono ② 2CDEA5010
(146' · ADD). Recorded 1946   **B O**

> From the 1940s until the early 1960s one of the greatest of regular British musical events was Malcolm Sargent's *Messiah*. He believed deeply in this music and he carried the listener with him. The sound itself is truly astounding. At bargain price it's an ideal investment for anyone who relishes an old-fashioned, large-scale approach to Handel's *Messiah*.

The Occasional Oratorio, HWV62

The Occasional Oratorio
Susan Gritton, Lisa Milne sops **James Bowman** **P**
counterten **John Mark Ainsley** ten **Michael George** bass **New College Choir, Oxford; The King's Consort / Robert King**
Hyperion ② CDA66961/2 (144' · DDD · T)   **F**

The occasion that called forth this work was the Jacobite rising of 1745 and its impending defeat. The Duke of Cumberland's victory at Culloden was yet to come. Handel, anticipating it, hit off the mood of the moment with a rousing piece full of appeals to patriotic feeling, partly through the traditional identification between the English Protestant culture of Hanoverian times with that of the biblical Hebrews. Much of the music comes from existing works, notably *Israel in Egypt*. The 'plot' pursues the familiar route of Anxiety-Prayer-Victory-Jubilation, but the work lacks the unity of theme and purpose of the great dramatic oratorios; if, however, you value Handel primarily because the music is so splendid you'll find a lot to relish here. King rises to the challenge of this sturdier side of Handel's muse and produces playing and singing full of punch and energy, and with that command of the broad Handelian paragraph without which the music lacks its proper stature.

The grand eight-part choruses, with the choir properly spaced, antiphonally, over the stereo span, make their due effect. King has a distinguished solo team. John Mark Ainsley's singing is particularly touching in the highly original 'Jehovah is my shield', where the rocking figures in the orchestra eventually turn out to symbolise sleep. Also very enjoyable is Susan Gritton's soprano, a sharply focused voice with a fine ring and due agility in the lively music and handled with taste and a keen feeling for

the shape of phrases in the contemplative airs. A fine set.

Parnasso in Festa

Parnasso in Festa
Diana Moore mez Apollo, Euterpe **Carolyn Sampson** sop Clio **Lucy Crowe** sop Orfeo **Rebecca Outram** sop Calliope **Ruth Clegg** mez Clori **Peter Harvey** bass Marte **Choir of the King's Consort; The King's Consort / Matthew Halls**
Hyperion ② CDA67701/2 (132' · DDD · T/t)   **F**

Parnasso in Festa was composed to mark the wedding in 1734 of Handel's favourite pupil, Princess Anne, to Prince William of Orange. A preview in the *Daily Journal* announced that the music was a mixture of 'single Songs, Duetto's, &c. intermix'd with Chorus's, some what in the Style of Oratorio's'. This was spot-on, as most of the numbers were recycled from *Athalia*, performed in Oxford the previous year but not yet heard in London. The setting is Mount Parnassus, where gods, Muses and assorted hangers-on are gathered to celebrate the marriage of Peleus and Thetis, the future parents of Achilles.

Much of the music is perfectly well suited to its new context. The Muse Clio's 'Verginelle dotte', for instance, is a perfect analogue to Josabeth's deathless 'Blooming virgins' in *Athalia*. And even when the sentiments are different – Clio's aria commending the happy pair to the care of the Graces is far removed from Athalia's 'My vengeance awakes me' – the result is not incongruous.

The cast is led by the superb Apollo of Diana Moore, a name new to me, who combines the range of a mezzo with the tone quality of a contralto. Her semiquaver runs in 'Torni pure', one of the few original numbers, are thrilling. With admirable support from Carolyn Sampson and the rest of the cast, and crisp choral and orchestral contributions under Matthew Halls, this recording should ensure that *Parnasso in Festa* will at last come into its own.

La Resurrezione, HWV47

La Resurrezione di Nostro Signor Gesù Cristo
Camilla Tilling, Kate Royal sops **Sonia Prina** mez **Toby Spence** ten **Luca Pisaroni** bass-bar
Le Concert d'Astrée / Emmanuelle Haïm hpd/org
Virgin Classics ② 694507-0 (112' · DDD)
Recorded live in April 2009   **F O O O B**

Handel's early Resurrection oratorio, written in 1708 during the young composer's Roman sojourn, is characterised by a freshness and vitality that he seldom matched in more mature works. That spirit shines through in Emmanuelle Haïm's excellent new recording with her Concert d'Astrée, played with all the expressive flair one has come to expect of her. In what might be described as the French manner in Handel, Haïm can be exaggerated in her tempi, lavishing care on the beautiful slower numbers; but that seems to me to be absolutely right, and preferable to some of the stiff-upper-lip English interpretations in a surprisingly full discography of this work.

After all, *La Resurrezione* is an opera in all but name, a sacred drama hiding behind the oratorio label because of the Papal ban on opera in Rome during that period. In common with many operas of the time – and fewer oratorios – there are no large choral forces required in this portrayal of the battle between protagonists of darkness and light. The path towards the ultimate victory of Christ's acolytes is portrayed in music of great brilliance and Handel must have made a profound impression on his Roman colleagues at the premiere – where the orchestra was led by none other than Corelli.

The international cast includes two Italians, whose verbal relish is especially good to hear. Luca Pisaroni makes a suitably villainous Lucifer and his virile bass-baritone is well up to the wide tessitura of the part; this is a devil who gets some of the most difficult tunes. Sonia Prina's contralto is heard to lovely effect in Mary Cleophas's pastoral music. The work's striking opening aria belongs to the Angel, taken here with plenty of presence by Swedish soprano Camilla Tilling. Two British singers complete the line-up and both give of their very best. Toby Spence is elegant in St John the Evangelist's music, and Kate Royal finds sumptuous beauty and emotional depth in the part of Mary Magdalene.

Saul, HWV53

Saul
Nancy Argenta, Susan Gritton, Susan Hemington Jones sops **Andreas Scholl** counterten **Paul Agnew, Mark Padmore, Tom Phillips, Angus Smith** tens **Julian Clarkson, Neal Davies, Jonathan Lemalu** basses **Gabrieli Consort and Players / Paul McCreesh**
Archiv ③ 474 510-2AH3 (166' · DDD · T/t)　　Ⓕ🅞🅑➔

The special strengths of Paul McCreesh's performance lie in the drama and the urgency he brings to the work, the keen sense of character he imparts to the music, the vigorous pacing that carries the action forward with the inevitability of a Greek tragedy. But *Saul* is a tragic work, and there's sometimes a want of the necessary gravitas. Nevertheless, this is a gripping and very inspiriting performance. The precision and flexibility of the Gabrieli Consort is a constant delight; the voices are fresh and bright, the words well articulated. The Gabrieli Players, too, produce a fine and distinctive period orchestral timbre. Andreas Scholl makes an ideal David, with sweetness and unusual depth of tone, exceptional precision of rhythm and perfectly clear words: if you try 'O Lord, whose mercies' you will buy this set. Enjoyable, too, is Nancy Argenta's natural, delicately phrased singing of Micah's music, and Susan Gritton's telling portrayal of Saul's elder

daughter, Merab. Saul himself, sometimes fiery, nearly always agonised, is effectively drawn by Neal Davies; and Mark Padmore's warm and gently graceful tenor is ideal for Jonathan's music.

There's no shortage of good recordings of this work. Gardiner's weighty version holds the field, but this version presents a serious challenge; the lightness and clarity, the livelier drama and the solo singing of Scholl in particular tell in favour of McCreesh.

Additional recommendation

Saul
Bell, Joshua sops **Zazzo** counterten **Bjarnason, Ovenden, Slattery** tens **Saks, Waddington** basses **RIAS Chamber Choir, Berlin; Concerto Köln / Jacobs**
Harmonia Mundi 🎧 HMC90 1877/8 (150' · DDD · T/t/N)　　　　　　　　Ⓕ

Jacobs's understanding of the dramatic workings of Baroque opera and oratorio is second to none and, as usual, his performance is outstandingly successful in linking Handel's sequences of numbers into a coherent whole. If it is dramatic involvement you want from *Saul*, then Jacobs's is the one to have, though it certainly should not turn you against McCreesh's classy product. If money is no object (and note that Jacobs gets his performance onto two discs to everyone else's three), you could do worse than treat yourself to more than one.

Semele, HWV58

Semele
Rosemary Joshua, Gail Pearson sops **Hilary Summers** contr **Stephen Wallace** counterten **Richard Croft** ten **Brindley Sharratt** bass **Chorus and Orchestra of the Early Opera Company / Christian Curnyn**
Chandos ③ CHAN0745 (170' · DDD)　　Ⓕ🅞🅞🅞➔

Of a handful of previous recordings of *Semele*, none was entirely satisfying. Which makes this new version – complete save for an aria for Cupid that Handel later pilfered for *Hercules* – all the more welcome. Christian Curnyn understands the unique *tinta* of this gorgeous score, and directs his spruce period band with a nice blend of nonchalant elegance and dramatic energy. Tempi are shrewdly judged, rhythms light and supple, and recitatives tumble inevitably into arias. The tragic denouement in Act 3 has due weight and intensity, whether in the tenderly inflected accompanied recitatives for Jupiter and Semele, or the awed chorus of Thebans after the heroine's incineration.

As at the English National Opera, Rosemary Joshua, radiant of tone, dazzling in coloratura, makes Semele far more than an over-sexed airhead. She is trills ethereally in 'The morning lark', distils a drowsy, erotic languor in 'O sleep, why dost thou leave me?', and ornaments her 'mirror' aria, 'Myself I shall adore', with dizzy glee. She is imploring and fiery by turns in her exchanges with Jupiter, and brings real pathos to the haunting siciliano 'Thus let my thanks be paid' and her sublime death scene. As Jupiter, Richard Croft fields a honeyed, sensuous tone (heard to advantage in a seductive 'Where're you walk') and formidable agility, though he could learn a thing or two about diction from Anthony Rolfe-Johnson (on Gardiner's Erato set).

Like Handel himself, Curnyn assigns the virago Juno and Semele's gentle sister Ino to the same singer. Hilary Summers, a true, deep contralto, characterises both roles well. Brindley Sherratt, with his oaky bass, offers vivid, witty cameos as Cadmus and Somnus, while Stephen Wallace sings Athamas's arias with smooth tone and a nimble florid technique, though a suspicion remains that the role lies a bit low for him. With excellent recorded sound and balance, and an informative essay from David Vickers, this becomes a clear first choice for an ever-enticing work.

Solomon, HWV67

Solomon   **P**
Andreas Scholl counterten **Inger Dam-Jensen, Susan Gritton, Alison Hagley** sops **Susan Bickley** mez **Paul Agnew** ten **Peter Harvey** bass **Gabrieli Consort and Players / Paul McCreesh**
Archiv ③ 459 688-2AH3 (161' · DDD · T)   Ⓕ**OO**➔

Solomon is universally recognised as one of Handel's finest masterpieces, not only with magnificent choruses, but more importantly containing rapturous love music, nature imagery, affecting emotion and the vividly portrayed dramatic scene of Solomon's famous judgement over the disputed infant. This is in fact the only dramatic part of the oratorio; and each of the female characters appears in only one of the work's three parts. Paul McCreesh, responsive to the work's stature, employs an orchestra of about 60 (including a serpent as the bass of the wind group) and presents the oratorio in the original 1749 version, full and uncut.

It's been argued that even in so splendid a work Handel was fallible enough to include some dead wood. McCreesh, however, stoutly defends the original structural balance. In one respect, though, he does depart from Handel's intentions. By the time *Solomon* was written, he was using no castratos in his oratorios, and the title-role was deliberately designed for a mezzo-soprano; but here the chance to secure the pre-eminent countertenor Andreas Scholl was irresistible. The colour of Handel's predominantly female vocal casting (only Zadok and the smaller-part Levite being exceptions) is thus slightly modified. This historical infidelity is one of the few possible reservations about the set, which is a notable achievement. McCreesh is fortunate in his cast, too. Predictably, Scholl becomes the central focus by his beauty of voice,

calm authority, charm and intelligent musicianship. Inger Dam-Jensen, as Solomon's queen, sounds suitably ecstatic in the florid 'Blessed the day' and amorous in 'With thee th'unsheltered moor', and her duet with Solomon flows with easy grace. To Susan Gritton falls the sublime 'Will the sun forget to streak', with its wonderful unison oboe-and-flute obbligato. As the high priest Zadok, Paul Agnew shines in the ornate 'See the tall palm'. A more positive and audible keyboard continuo would have been welcome, but this is a minor shortcoming, and the effect of the performance as a whole is deeply impressive, with such things as 'Will the sun', the grave interlude to 'With pious heart' and the elegiac chorus 'Draw the tear from hopeless love' haunting the listener's mind.

Solomon   **P**
Carolyn Sampson, Susan Gritton sops **Sarah Connolly** mez **Mark Padmore** ten **David Wilson-Johnson** bass **RIAS Chamber Choir, Berlin; Akademie für Alte Musik Berlin / Daniel Reuss**
Harmonia Mundi ② HMC90 1949/50
(155' · DDD · T/t)   Ⓕ

In his pioneering *Handel's Dramatic Oratorios and Masques* (OUP: 1959), Winton Dean advocated the excision of several arias (mainly for the priestly figures of Zadok and the Levite) and the replacement of the closing chorus by the monumental 'Praise the Lord' – a policy followed by John Eliot Gardiner (Philips), though not by the completist Paul McCreesh (Archiv – see above). In his new recording, Daniel Reuss ditches the final chorus, though he omits just two arias, neither lamented. He also makes puzzling internal cuts in the duet for Solomon and the first harlot, and, more damagingly, the gorgeous opening number of the masque.

That said, the Harmonia Mundi recording is almost unreservedly enjoyable. Abetted by his crack period orchestra and 40-strong chorus, Reuss is responsive alike to the oratorio's ceremonial splendour and its fragrant pastoral *tinta*. The versions by Gardiner and McCreesh, balanced rather more in favour of the voices, generate an extra weight and sonorous magnificence in the great double choruses. But the vitality and refinement of the Berlin choir is always compelling. With terrific controlled raucousness from antiphonal wind and brass, the opening chorus of Act 2 is as elementally thrilling as it should be. At the other extreme, the Nightingale chorus, taken slowly and secretively, is at least the equal of McCreesh's in drowsy amorous enchantment.

Where the earlier recordings each have at least one unsatisfactory soloist, Reuss's solo line-up could hardly be bettered. Handel cast the role of Solomon with a mezzo-soprano. Reuss does likewise with Sarah Connolly, who sings with glowing, even tone, ardour (in the love scene), and rapt inwardness in Solomon's two 'nature' arias. Susan Gritton makes a gently sensuous queen (her musing 'With thee th'unshelter'd moor I'd tread' a highlight) and probes the full poignancy and anguish of the first harlot's music. While yielding to Della Jones (Gardiner) and Susan Bickley (McCreesh) in sheer venom, Carolyn Sampson characterises with gusto as the second harlot, and beautifully softens her bright, vernal tone in 'Will the sun forget to streak?' The priests are in the expert hands of Mark Padmore (exemplary in his bouts of coloratura) and the gravely sonorous David Wilson-Johnson.

If you want this magnificent work complete, McCreesh's is the version to go for, while for consistently glorious Handel singing the new Harmonia Mundi recording, impressively directed by Reuss, takes the palm.

Theodora, HWV68

Theodora   P
Susan Gritton sop **Susan Bickley** mez **Robin Blaze** counterten **Paul Agnew, Angus Smith** tens **Neal Davies** bass **Gabrieli Consort and Players / Paul McCreesh**
Archiv ③ 469 061 2AH3 (3h 1' · DDD · T/t)
Ⓕ❍❍❍❍⊕

Theodora, Handel's penultimate oratorio, was a failure in his own time. Until relatively recently it remained a rarity, but lately it has come to be recognised as a masterpiece, although quite different in mood and treatment from most of his more familiar oratorios. This recording encourages attentive listening to its subtleties, because it's done with such affection, care and refinement. There's nothing sensational about it, no singer who overwhelms you with brilliance or virtuosity. But all the solo music is finely sung. Theodora herself is taken by Susan Gritton, who's won golden opinions recently, and will win more here for a great deal of lovely, clear and musicianly singing, with a quiet seriousness and unaffected intensity that are ideally suited to the role. Her presence at the centre of the tragic drama elevates it as a whole.

Irene, her fellow Christian, is sung with scarcely less distinction by Susan Bickley, coolly expressive in most of her music, more passionate in 'Defend her Heaven' in Act 2, a shapely performance with subtleties of timing. Didymus, originally a castrato role (very rare in oratorios), is sung by Robin Blaze, whose focused, even-toned countertenor – not a hint of the traditional hoot – serves well: this is fluent singing, with no great depth of tone, but very steady and controlled, with the detail precisely placed. As Septimius, Paul Agnew is in good voice, firm and full in tone, phrasing the music elegantly (although the Act 3 air is unconvincing, too bouncy and cheerful for the situation). Lastly, there's Neal Davies as the Roman ruler, Valens, whose excellent singing makes as persuasive a case as can be imagined for torturing Christians – his is a pleasantly grainy voice, with considerable warmth and

fullness of tone, well suited to a figure representing authority, and he despatches the divisions with assurance.

Ornamentation is appropriate and tasteful, and McCreesh takes the recitative at a natural and relaxed pace. His main contribution, however, is in the well-sprung rhythms he draws from his Gabrieli singers and players, in the way he allows the lines to breathe, and in the sense of purpose and direction he imparts to the bass line. Add to this a keen sense of the right pace for each number, and you've the recipe for an outstanding reading of this noble work.

Theodora
Dawn Upshaw, Lorraine Hunt sops **David Daniels** counterten **Richard Croft** ten **Frode Olsen** bass **Orchestra of the Age of Enlightenment / William Christie** Stage and video director **Peter Sellars**
Warner Music Vision/NVC Arts 🆅🆅 0630 15481-2 (3h 27' · NTSC · 4:3 · 2.0 · 2-6). Recorded live at Glyndebourne Opera House, 1996   Ⓕ❍❍❍

What a paradox it is that one of the great opera productions of our time should be of a work not intended for the stage. If you're repelled by the thought of Roman soldiers in US army uniforms and a Roman governor glad-handing like a US president, then think again. The score is of a matchless beauty, the production riveting, the individual performances flawless. Unmissable.

Cantatas

Aci, Galatea e Polifemo, HWV72   P
Sandrine Piau sop **Sara Mingardo** contr **Laurent Naouri** bar **Le Concert d'Astrée / Emmanuelle Haïm** hpd
Virgin Classics ② 545557-2 (99' · DDD · T/t) Ⓕ❍❍⊕

The cantata or serenata *a 3* (for three), *Aci, Galatea e Polifemo*, dates from Handel's visit to Naples in 1708, and it has almost nothing in common, except for its subject matter, with his exquisite English pastoral, *Acis and Galatea* for the Duke of Chandos's house at Cannons of 1718. As with so many of his Italian compositions, Handel used this enchanting creation of his youth as a sort of melody bank, lifting whole arias for insertion into his subsequent operas, so even if there are Handelians new to this work some of the music won't be entirely unfamiliar.

Aci, cast originally, one presumes, with a high soprano castrato, has two sublime arias, 'Qui l'augel da pianta in pianta' and his dying lament, 'Verso già l'alma col sangue' ('My soul pours out with my blood'). Both belong to Handel's most ravishing early inspirations, the first a simile aria in which the soprano voice 'competes' with birdsong supplied by oboe and violin solos, the second a wonderfully evocative representation of the dying hero's throbbing heart and intense anguish. This is top-flight stuff, and Aci's music is superbly sung by Sandrine Piau with her brilliant, steely yet still sweet soprano, used with quasi-instrumental technical accomplishment. Even though Galatea's music, written for a contralto, is less interesting, the Arcadian nymph is cast with the best singer here, the wonderful Sara Mingardo, one of the truly sublime Handelians of our time, who brings a dark sensuality to her love music and a heartbreaking outpouring of grief in the recative following Aci's death. Haïm's spirited and imaginative direction, her singers and a pristine modern recording weigh the balance in favour of this set.

'Delirio'   P
Aci, Galatea e Polifemo – Qui l'augel da pianta in pianta. Il delirio amoroso, 'Da quel giorno fatale', HWV99. Mi, palpita il cor, HWV132
Natalie Dessay sop **Le Concert d'Astrée /
Emmanuelle Haïm** hpd
Virgin Classics 332624-2 (62' · DDD · T/t)   (F)(B)➔

Handel created his cantata *Il delirio amoroso* while in Rome in early 1707. Its text was written by Cardinal Benedetto Pamphili. The unusual inclusion of some dance movements suggests that it might have been presented in a simple sort of staging. Emmanuelle Haïm directs a performance that is relaxed and breezy, although Le Concert d'Astrée – featuring two harpsichords and two lutes – is bigger than some orchestras used on recent Baroque opera recordings. There are lovely contributions from oboist Patrick Beaugiraud, and the violinist Stéphanie-Marie Degand provides finely executed solos during the first aria, 'Un pensiero voli in ciel'. Natalie Dessay's coloratura is honey-toned and sweet.

While amiable and technically impressive, proceedings are curiously superficial. There is emotional depth in this cantata that the resolutely frothy approach fails to reach. Dessay does not convey the ramblings of 'delirious love', unlike Ann Murray's poetic interpretation with Harry Christophers (Coro).

The lush beauty of Dessay's impressive tuning, clear timbre and fine technique is beyond doubt in the aria 'Qui l'augel da pianta' from the Naples serenata *Aci, Galatea e Polifemo*. Haïm chooses a bizarrely slow tempo whereby Handel's 6/8 becomes a very lethargic 3/4. Not much of Handel's vocal part is left intact during repeats, when Dessay and Haïm carry out some brutally over-elaborate recomposition. Dessay plucks out stratospheric notes at every opportunity, but there is more that could and should have been said in accordance to the parameters of Handel's notation. Nice though this disc is, it brings little depth or substance to Handel's music.

'Italian Cantatas, Vol 1: Le cantate per il Cardinal Pamphili'   P
Il delirio amoroso, 'Da quel giorno fatale', HWV99. Pensieri notturni di Filli, 'Nel dolce dell'oblio', HWV134. Tra le fiamme il consiglio, HWV170. Figlio

d'alte speranze, HWV113
Roberta Invernizzi sop
La Risonanza / Fabio Bonizzoni hpd
Glossa GCD921521 (66' · DDD · T/t)   (F)●

'Italian Cantatas, Vol 2: Le cantate per il   P
Marchese Ruspoli'
Armida abbandonata, HWV105[a]. Notte placida e cheta, HWV142[a]. Tu fedel? tu costante?, HWV171[a]. Alla caccia Diana cacciatrice, HWV79[ab]. Un'alma innamorata, HWV173[a]
[a]**Emanuela Galli,** [b]**Roberta Invernizzi** sops
La Risonanza / Fabio Bonizzoni hpd
Glossa GCD921522 (74' · DDD · T/t)   (F)●●●

'Italian Cantatas, Vol 3: Le cantate per   P
il Cardinal Ottoboni'
Ah! crudel nel pianto mio, HWV78. No se emenderá jamás, HWV140. Qual ti riveggio, oh Dio, HWV150. Spande ancor a mio dispetto, HWV165
Raffaella Milanesi sop **Salvo Vitale** bass
La Risonanza / Fabio Bonizzoni hpd
Glossa ② GCD921523 (67' · DDD)   (F)●●

'Italian Cantatas, Vol 4'   P
Aminta e Fillide, 'Arresta il passo', HWV83. Clori, mia bella Clori, HWV92
Nuria Rial, Maria Grazia Schiavo sops
La Risonanza / Fabio Bonizzoni hpd
Glossa GCD921524 (67' · DDD)   (F)●●

'Italian Cantatas, Vol 5'   P
Clori, Tirsi e Fileno, 'Cor fedele', HWV96
Roberta Invernizzi, Yetzabel Arias Fernández sops
Romina Basso mez **La Risonanza /
Fabio Bonizzoni** hpd
Glossa GCD921525 (75' · DDD)   (F)●●

'Le Cantate per il Marchese Ruspoli, Vol 6'   P
Alpestre monte, HWV81. Duello amoroso, 'Amarilli vezzosa', HWV82. Olinto, pastore arcade, 'Oh! Come chiare e belle', HWV143
Roberta Invernizzi, Yetzabel Arias Fernández sops
Romina Basso mez **La Risonanza / Fabio Bonizzoni** hpd
Glossa GCD921526 (69' · DDD)   (F)●●

La Risonanza's theatrically coloured playing has raised the performance standard for Handel's Italian cantatas. Bonizzoni's refreshing direction is entirely devoid of the coolly dispatched detachment or mannered feyness often found in this repertoire. This lovingly prepared series promises to be of the utmost importance to Handel lovers.

Recitatives are performed with perfect poetic clarity and dramatic timing. Bonizzoni's Italian ensemble astutely diagnoses and communicates the affect of each movement in some of the youthful Handel's most freely imaginative music. The balance between instruments is consistently fine, warm and lyrical. In particular, Bonizzoni has the admirable knack of conveying the strong rhetorical elements in Handel's vivacious music, and the entire performance is beautifully executed with subtlety and charm. This is an essential series from La Risonanza, whose project is shaping up to become the most rewarding Handelian discographic undertaking of recent years.

Notte placida e cheta, HWV142. Un' alma innamorata, HWV173. Figlio d'alte speranze, HWV113. Agrippina condotta a morire, HWV110. Concerto a quattro
Emma Kirkby sop **London Baroque**
BIS BIS-SACD1695 (67' · DDD/DSD)

The largest single legacy of Handel's years in Italy (in his early twenties) were around 100 chamber cantatas, from which Emma Kirkby and London Baroque have picked out four excellent examples from the 30 or so featuring one or two violins alongside the solo voice and continuo. In this they face strong competition from La Risonanza's series with Italian singers on Glossa, but the clash does no damage to either group as both have distinct virtues. For some, of course, the presence of Emma Kirkby will be enough to seal the deal, and indeed she is on superb form. Early on there are a few signs of a lack of her usual instrumental precision; but by the time she is showing off her artless virtuosity in the final aria of *Figlio d'alte speranze* and striding easily through 'Orrida, oscura', the first aria of the compellingly dramatic *Agrippina condotta a morire*, all worries have long been banished. Her interpretative intelligence and attention to words are a given but she can also catch a subtle mood, as in 'Quel povero core' from *Un' alma innamorata*, whose sense of resigned torment is enhanced by a sensitive contribution from the solo violin. Emanuela Galli captures this kind of intimate emotion even more affectingly in La Risonanza's performances, mind, but with a touch less vocal security.

The recorded sound, as often in London Baroque's recordings for BIS, is strangely resonant and steely. The 'Concerto a quattro' included here is claimed as a Handel work in its German 18th-century source but sounds like nothing of the kind.

Apollo e Dafne, 'La terra e liberata', HWV122. Crudel tiranno amor, HWV97
Nancy Argenta sop **Michael George** bass
Collegium Musicum 90 / Simon Standage
Chandos Chaconne CHAN0583 (58' · DDD · T/t)

Handel's *Apollo e Dafne* is a difficult work to put in context. Completed in Hanover in 1710 but possibly begun in Italy, its purpose isn't clear, while, as secular cantatas go, it's long (40 minutes) and ambitiously scored for two soloists and an orchestra of strings, oboes, flute, bassoon and continuo. But this isn't just a chunk of operatic experimentation: it sets its own, faster pace than the leisurely unfolding of a full-length Baroque stage work, yet its simple Ovidian episode, in which Apollo's pursuit of the nymph Dafne results in her transformation into a tree, is drawn with all the subtlety and skill of the

instinctive dramatic genius that Handel was.

This recording features the expert Handelian voices of Nancy Argenta and Michael George, and both convey their roles convincingly. Argenta's hard, clear tone seems just the thing for the nymph, who isn't required to be especially alluring but who does have to sound quick to anger and (literally) untouchable; and George strikes the right note as Apollo, bragging loudly at the opening of his superior skill in archery to Cupid before succumbing more gently, and in the end extremely touchingly, to Cupid's arts. The orchestra is bright and efficient, and the pacing of the work seems just right. This is superb Handel then, and, as if that were not enough, there's a bonus in the form of a shorter cantata for soprano and strings, *Crudel tiranno amor*. It's a beautiful piece indeed, and Argenta performs it perfectly.

German Arias, HWV202-10

Handel German Arias[a]
Telemann Musique de table – 'Paris' Quartets: G, E minor
[a]**Dorothea Röschmann** sop
Akademie für Alte Musik Berlin
Harmonia Mundi HMC90 1689 (79' · DDD · T/t)

Handel's nine German Arias aren't as well known nor as often recorded as they deserve, perhaps because, being devotional music, they're generally rather solemnly, even earnestly performed. Dorothea Röschmann sings them delightfully. There's no lack of seriousness, or intensity, where it's called for. The instrumental support is highly polished, but arguably too varied in colour: what's the justification for switching bass instruments for an aria's middle section? The obbligato part is shared between violin, flute and oboe: the oboe seems to be a mistake in the high part of 'Meine Seele', with a rather squealy effect – although Röschmann's exuberance at 'Alles jauchzet, alles lacht' ('all rejoice, all laugh') is happy. The Telemann 'Paris' Quartets set off the arias well. Some of the playing in the E minor work is a little sober, but the lively G major is done in lively and elegant fashion, with spruce rhythms. But Röschmann's Handel is the real joy: listen to 'Die ihr aus dunklen Grüften' and you won't be able to resist it.

Oratorio & Opera Arias

Belshazzar – Destructive War; Oh sacred oracles of truth. Jephtha – Dull delay, in piercing anguish; Up the dreadful steep ascending. Messiah – He was despised. Saul – O Lord, whose mercies; Brave Jonathan. Semele – Despair no more shall wound me; Your tuneful voice. Theodora – The raptur'd soul; Deeds of kindness; Kind Heav'n; Sweet rose and lily
David Daniels counterten **Paris Orchestral Ensemble / John Nelson**
Virgin Classics 545497-2 (67' · DDD · N/T)

The world's leading 'operatic' countertenor has sung on precious few of the abundant complete Handel recordings of the last decade so this selection of oratorio arias fills some of the gaps in the Daniels discography.

The American was to have sung Didymus in Paul McCreesh's Archiv recording of *Theodora* – the role of his Glyndebourne debut in Peter Sellars's controversial 1995 staging – but he was unable to fit the preceding concerts into his burgeoning international schedule and was replaced by Robin Blaze. Not surprisingly, he includes four of Didymus's arias in his oratorio album, and rejoices in the wonderful music Handel composed for the young Italian castrato, Gaetano Guadagni. The sensuous colours of Daniels' falsetto are ideal in this music, which he sings with beguiling erotic ambiguity.

The same goes for David's ravishing 'O Lord, whose mercies numberless' – a prayer whose yearning melismata suggest passions more earthly than godly – from *Saul*. There's little cause for complaint, except perhaps about the use of the modern-instrument Ensemble Orchestral de Paris rather than a period band, but at least John Nelson's conducting – particularly in the fast-moving numbers – is livelier than on his complete *L'Allegro*. In excellent sound, this glorious disc comes highly recommended.

Ariodante – E vivo ancora…Scherza infida in   **P**
grembo al drudo. Giulio Cesare – Cara speme,
questo core; Va tacito e nascosto; L'angue offeso mai
riposa; Al lampo dell'armi; Dall' ondoso periglio…
Aure, deh, per pietà. Rinaldo – Cara sposa; Venti,
turbini, prestate. Rodelinda – Pompe vane di
morte!…Dove sei?; Vivi tiranno!. Serse – Fronde
tenere…Ombra mai fù. Tamerlano – A dispetto
David Daniels counterten **Orchestra of the Age of
Enlightenment / Sir Roger Norrington**
Virgin Classics Veritas 545326-2 (69' · DDD · T/t)
Ⓕ**ⓄⓄ**B➔

The ever-increasing popularity of Handel and his contemporaries, and their employment of alto castratos, has encouraged the development of countertenors capable of similar vocal feats to the original interpreters of the heroic roles in these works. Among these David Daniels can certainly be counted as a leading contender. He displays and deploys his talent here in a wide range of arias reflective and dramatic. His amazing technique runs through Tamerlano's virtuoso 'A dispetto' and Bertarido's 'Vivi tiranno!' without a blemish in the sound and with every division in its place yet part of a confidently delivered whole: by and large Daniels's runs and embellishments are smoothly accomplished. In more reflective pieces such as Giulio Cesare's 'Aure, deh, per pietà' (he also tackles Sesto's 'Cara speme' from *Giulio Cesare*, a particularly liquid, subtle piece of singing), Bertarido's 'Dove sei?' and Ariodante's sad lament, 'Scherza infida', written for the great Senesino, he uses his impeccable Italian to express wide-ranging emotions. Throughout, Roger Norrington and the Orchestra of the Age of

Enlightenment give excellent support. The recording is blameless so there's every reason for readers to sample this fine exposition of the countertenor's art.

Hercules – Where shall I fly? Joshua – O had I   **P**
Jubal's lyre. Theodora – With darkness deep as is my
woe. Agrippina – Pensieri, voi mi tormentate. Alcina
– Ah! mio cor! Schernito sei! Amadigi di Gaula –
Desterò dall'empia Dite. Ariodante – Dopo notte,
atra e funesta; Scherza infida in grembo al drudo.
Giulio Cesare – Cara speme, questo core. Orlando –
Ah! stigie larve!…Già latra Cerbero…Vaghe pupille,
no, non piangete, no. Rinaldo – Lascia ch'io pianga
mia cruda sorte
Magdalena Kožená mez
Venice Baroque Orchestra / Andrea Marcon
Archiv 477 6547AH (76' · DDD)   Ⓕ B➔

With most items familiar from previous Handel aria anthologies, on paper this looks full of tired clichés. Thankfully, the stirring and passionate execution of Handel's music is anything but dull routine. Kožená and her Venetian accomplices might not be giving us anything deeply perceptive but everybody involved sounds as if they are engaged with the music. In particular, the Venice Baroque Orchestra sound admirably absorbed in the dramatic world of each aria.

Kožená has a good stab at this, too, but does not quite capture the personality and situation of each character. Alcina's heartbroken first encounter of a man being beyond her seductive power in 'Ah! mio cor!' is ravishing but its slowly creeping pathos is not a natural opener for a disc like this, and Kožená – albeit passionate – does not capture the depth of Alcina's complex psychological condition. An extrovert 'Cara speme' does not quite fit Sesto's emotional self-inquiry.

Kožená is much better at conveying the scheming Agrippina's anxious plea to the gods and 'Scherza infida' is finely judged, its best passages not too far off the benchmark set by Janet Baker, Sarah Connolly and Lorraine Hunt Lieberson (alas, it is let down by the staccato B section). The most convincing synthesis of musical outpouring and dramatic mood is Melissa's 'Desterò dall'empia dite' (from *Amadigi*).

In Dejanira's mad scene from *Hercules*, Kožená's affected vowels and hammed-up insanity rob it of the poignancy that understatement achieves much better; Dejanira is a distraught heroine, not a lunatic shrieking that the Martians have landed. A similar approach makes for an over-egged mad scene from *Orlando*. But despite the frequent limitation of one-dimensional characterisation, these appealing performances have strength and colour.

'Great Oratorio Duets'   **P**
Jephtha – These labours past. Joshua – Oh peerless
maid; Our limpid streams. Belshazzar – Great victor,
at your feet I bow. Susanna – When thou art nigh; To
my chaste Susanna's praise. Theodora – To see, thou
glorious son of worth; Streams of pleasure ever

flowing. Solomon – Welcome as the dawn of day;
Ev'ry joy that wisdom knows. Eternal Source of Light
Divine – Kind health descends. Saul – O fairest of ten
thousand fair; At persecution I can laugh. Deborah –
Where do thy armours raise me!; Smiling freedom,
lovely guest. Alexander Balus – Hail wedded love.
Esther – Let imitate her notes above.
Esther – Who calls my parting soul
Carolyn Sampson sop **Robin Blaze** counterten
**Orchestra of the Age of Enlightenment /
Nicholas Kraemer**
BIS 🔊 BIS-SACD1436 (71' · DDD/DSD · T)　　ⒻⒹ→

'Great Oratorio Duets'? It seems a strange concept at first – not many of these pieces have
made an individual name for themselves just yet.
But then the point of this disc is evidently to
bring together in mouthwatering partnership
two of the most dulcet-voiced young Baroque
singers Britain has to offer, and it does not take
long to discover that that is a very good idea
indeed. Carolyn Sampson's voice is bright and
clear yet warmed by judiciously selected and
moderated vibrato, while Robin Blaze has a
more distinctively tangy sound, but they fit each
other well and in their faultless display of Handelian style, lyricism and warmth they are in
total mental and spiritual accord.

The music, meanwhile, does indeed have
greatness. The vocal style of Handel's English
oratorios does not recreate the virtuoso flashiness of the Italian operas but speaks in a more
direct, lyrical manner, expressing with unimpeachable honesty all the sympathy and human
understanding for which their composer is so
revered. The majority here are love duets, but
with what variety, from carefree (examples from
Jephtha and *Susanna*) to chaste (*Deborah*) to
ambiguously melancholy (*Joshua* and *Saul*). The
forgiveness duet from *Esther* is indescribably
tender (especially in this performance), the duet
from *Saul* in which a love-drunk David is reluctant to leave when warned by his fiancée of
approaching danger is effortlessly theatrical, and
the two duets for the doomed lovers from *Theodora* are works of pure and noble genius. If the
performances in these last do not quite reach the
heartbreaking intensity of which Peter Sellars's
Glyndebourne production proved them capable,
it is hard to see how that could ever be achieved
in a recital; Sampson and Blaze surely manage as
well as anyone ever could. With intelligent,
kind-hearted accompaniments from Nicholas
Kraemer and the OAE, this is a truly beautiful
Handel recording, a disc to give pleasure for
years to come.

Acis and Galatea – I rage, I melt, I burn!…O ruddier
than the cherry. Alcina – Verdi prati, selve amene.
Alexander's Feast – Revenge, revenge, Timotheus
cries…Behold a ghastly band. Berenice – Si, tra i
ceppi e le ritorte. Giulio Cesare – Va tacito e
nascosto. Judas Maccabaeus – I feel the Deity
within…Arm, arm, ye brave!. Messiah – Thus saith
the Lord…But who may abide?; Why do the nations?;
Behold I tell you a mystery…The trumpet shall

sound. Orlando – O voi del mio poter…Sorge
infausta una procella. Samson – Honour and arms
scorn such a foe. Semele – Where'er you walk. Serse
– Fronde tenere…Ombra mai fù. Te Deum in D,
'Dettingen' – Vouchsafe, O Lord
Bryn Terfel bass-bar **Scottish Chamber Orchestra /
Sir Charles Mackerras**
DG 453 480-2GH (73' · DDD · T/t)　　ⒻⒹ→

'I feel', sings Terfel with assurance in his voice
matching the solemnly, expectantly, ceremonious opening bars; and then, the second time,
'I feel', but now with the awed conviction of one
who has experienced 'the Deity within'. The
adjustment, the change of expression, is small,
and no doubt when described sounds obvious
enough; but it's typical of the imaginative intelligence Terfel brings. And what of his singing, his
voice production, his care for *legato*? As to the latter, conflict always lurks as expressive emphasis,
shading and verbal naturalism assert their rights
in the face of pure beauty and the evenness of the
singing line. Terfel is one in whom the rival
claims work their way to a compromise, though if
one side has to win it will generally be the expressive element. A good example of the compromise
is the second track, the 'Vouchsafe, O Lord',
quietly and simply sung, preserving the movement's unity and yet with a power of feeling that,
at 'let thy mercy lighten upon us', is as overtly
emotional as an operatic aria.

The adapted arias, 'Where'er you walk', 'Verdi
prati' and 'Ombra mai fù', justify their inclusion
readily enough, and it's good to hear Terfel in
the solos from *Messiah*. The singing here incorporates a good deal of embellishment, some of it
of Mackerras's devising. He's excellent, sharing
with Terfel an appreciation of the zest in Handel. The recording is vivid and clean.

Alessandro – Brilla nell' alma un non inteso ancor. Ⓟ
Amadigi di Gaula – Ah spietato. Arianna in Creta –
Son qual stanco. Deidamia – M'hai resa infelice.
Faramondo – Combattuta da due venti. Giulio
Cesare – Che sento? oh Dio!; Se pietà di me
non senti. Orlando – Verdi piante, erbette liete.
Partenope – L'amor ed il destin. Rodelinda –
Ombre, piante. Scipione – Scoglio d'immota
fronte. Tamerlano – Cor di padre
Sandrine Piau sop **Les Talens Lyriques /
Christophe Rousset**
Naïve E8894 (67' · DDD · T/t)　　ⒻⓄⓄⓄ

Ⓖ　Sandrine Piau and Christophe Rousset
have been consistently stylish and
perceptive Handelians together. Their
musical flair and dramatic intelligence is marvellously captured here, and they have chosen arias
that explore the full range of Handel's genius.

The experience starts with the spectacular
'Scoglio d'immota fronte', and the subsequent
sequence weaves through wonderful contrasts.
It's hard to capture the full dramatic sense and
vivid personality of Handel's opera characters in a
studio recital, yet they hit the bullseye every time,
bringing out Cleopatra's despair, Rodelinda's

eloquent grief for her apparently deceased husband, the heartbroken sorceress Melissa in *Amadigi di Gaula*, Deidamia's distress at losing Achilles to the Trojan war, and Partenope's gorgeous charisma.

Although some *da capo* sections stray a little too far from Handel's notation for the comfort of scholars, they all enhance the drama of the text, and each cadenza, showing panache and taste, is a breath of fresh air. The playing of Les Talens Lyriques is a model of clarity, vitality and theatrical wit. It was an inspired decision to close the recital with the sublime understatement of 'Son qual stanco', featuring a heartbreaking cello solo by Atsushi Sakaï. Rousset and Piau achieve the perfect synthesis of elegance, extravagance and emotion. This may be the finest recital of Handel arias ever recorded.

'As steals the morn…'   P

L'Allegro, il Penseroso ed il Moderato – As steals the morn[a]. Esther – Tune your harps to cheerful strains. Jephtha – His mighty arm, with sudden blow; Waft her, angels, through the skies. Samson – Total eclipse; Did love constrain thee; Your charms to ruin led the way; Thus when the sun from's wat'ry bed; Let but that spirit. Il trionfo del Tempo e del Disinganno – Urne voi. Alceste – Enjoy the sweet Elysian grove. Rodelinda – Fatto inferno; Pastorello d'un povero armento. Semele – Where'er you walk. Tamerlano – Forte e lieto; Oh per me lieto, avventuroso giorno![ab]; Figlia mia
Mark Padmore ten
with [a]**Lucy Crowe** sop [b]**Robin Blaze** counterten
The English Concert / Andrew Manze
Harmonia Mundi HMU90 7422 (77' · DDD)   F○○B»

Underpinned by Andrew Manze's unobtrusive and warm-hearted English Concert, Mark Padmore uses his extraordinary diction and whispering chamber-like intimacy to remind us that the most exalted tenor arias from Handel's operas and oratorios can achieve true potency out of context.

Favourites like 'Where're you walk' and 'Waft her, angels' appear to grow out of this varied programme without the sense of being lifted for a compilation; Padmore is a master of taste, restraint and unassuming gesture. 'Pastorello d'un povero' is a touching vignette and the soft singing elsewhere contributes to a concentrated and affecting juxtaposition of human vice and virtue in the *Tamerlano* scenes. As throughout, Padmore saves the greatest emotional impact for the *da capos* where coloration reaches new heights.

Indeed, it is the joy in conveying the emotional core of each situation which marks out this disc. Graphic dramatic effects abound (not least the Sultan's gradual giving up the ghost in 'Figlia mia' with a croaking realism) but this is a disc which celebrates Handel's capacity for incisive human observation, achieved more through reflective means than showpiece coloratura. It's a persuasive and thoughtful approach.

Padmore's lowest register can seem a touch insubstantial but this is a small gripe in a disc boasting – as its parting shot – the duet 'As steals the morn', a performance with the fine Lucy Crowe at her most alluring.

'Heroes and Heroines'   P

Alcina – Act 3, Sinfonia; Sta nell'Ircana; Mi lusingha il dolce affetto; Entrée des songes agréables; Verdi prati. Ariodante – Act 2, Sinfonia; Scherza infida; Dopo notte. Hercules – Act 2, Sinfonia; Cease, ruler of the day; Where shall I fly. Solomon – Arrival of the Queen of Sheba; Will the sun forget to streak
Sarah Connolly mez **The Symphony of Harmony and Invention / Harry Christophers**
Coro COR16025 (65' · DDD)   F B»

Sarah Connolly is an exemplary Handel singer. Her recital is dominated by two roles she's performed at ENO, with arias from *Alcina* and *Ariodante*. 'Scherza infida' is an addictive mixture of vocal elegance and poignant desolation, and 'Mi lusingha' is sung with a beautiful simplicity that lacks for nothing in drama or passion. In contrast, the extravagant coloratura in 'Dopo notte' and the robust 'Sta nell'Ircana' capture the virtuoso thrills of heroic joy. In Dejanira's 'Where shall I fly?', she reminds us that taste and subtlety have an important place even in Handel's tormented and emotionally unstable creation. She avoids contrived intensity and allows the quality of the vocal writing to speak for itself.

Harry Christophers's direction is judicious, supportive yet never intrusive. It's pleasant to hear performances that are musically sensible, dramatically sensitive, and brave enough to apply understatement.

Ariodante – Dopo notte, atra e funesta.   P

Rodelinda – Fatto inferno è il mio petto; Pastorello d'un povero armento. Serse – Fronde tenere e belle; Ombra mai fù; Più che penso alle fiamme del core; Crude furie degl'orrido abissi. Tamerlano – Oh per me lieto, avventuroso giorno![a]; Figlia mia; Ciel e terra armi di sdegno; Tu spietato, il vedrai. La Resurrezione di Nostro Signor Gesù Cristo – Così la tortorella; Caro figlio
Rolando Villazón ten with
[a]**Rebecca Bottone** mez [a]**Jean Gadoullet** counterten
Gabrieli Players / Paul McCreesh
DG 477 8056GH (59' · DDD). Also available in a deluxe limited edition with DVD, 477 8057GH2
                                              F○B»

Until making this recording Rolando Villazón had sung 'barely a note of Handel in public'. There will be some who will question whether his superstar status justifies yet another Handel aria disc, but much of this is invigoratingly performed, and has a smacking impact that some half-hearted anthologies desperately lack. It may be more difficult for some to overlook the inclusion of castrato arias with the vocal part knocked down an octave, which spoils the way the music is balanced, and is unnecessary to what is otherwise a decent programme, no matter how pleasantly the booklet-note attempts to justify it. But it's fair to acknowledge that Villazón's choice to record 'Ombra mai fù' follows in the footsteps of Caruso and Tito Schipa.

It is splendid to hear a singer of abundant personality leaping into the suicide scene from *Tamerlano* with such dramatic authority. Listening to Villazón's lively rendition of Bajazet's 'Ciel e terra armi di sdegno', one's eager to see him sing the role on stage. He certainly sings extrovert arias very well, albeit in a slightly idiosyncratic way. Moreover, the enthusiasm seems infectious: McCreesh's Gabrieli Players have rarely sounded better and more dramatically attuned in this repertoire. Grimoaldo's anguished soliloquy from *Rodelinda*, which resolves into a gorgeous pastoral aria, is excellently accompanied by the orchestra, although Villazón's soft lyrical singing occasionally feels a bit closed in, as if a champion racehorse is being kept in a paddock that is too small; in this regard 'Caro figlio' from *La Resurrezione* is much better sung. This disc is zany in some ways, but offers fine rewards.

Alessandro – Overture; Sinfonia; Che vidi?;   **P**
No, più soffrir; Placa l'alma; Solitudine amate…Aure, fonti; Pur troppo veggio…Che tirannia d'Amor; Svanisci, oh reo timore…Dica il falso. Admeto – Il ritratto d'Admeto; La sorte mia vacilla; Quest'è dunque la fede…Vedrò fra poco. Riccardo Primo – Morte vieni…A me nel mio rossere…Quando non vede. Siroe – A costei, che dirò?; L'aura non sempre; Si diversi sembianti…Non vi piacque, ingiusti dei. Tolomeo – E dove, e dove mai…Fonti amiche; Ti pentirai, crudel
Catherine Bott, Emma Kirkby sops
Brandenburg Consort / Roy Goodman
Hyperion CDA66950 (76' · DDD · T/t)   Ⓕ**OO**

It was a happy idea to assemble a selection of Handel's arias written for the two sopranos whose famous rivalry coloured the last years of the first Royal Academy. Francesca Cuzzoni – impersonated here by Catherine Bott – was Handel's principal soprano from 1723, creating among other roles Cleopatra and Rodelinda. Faustina Bordoni – her roles here go to Emma Kirkby – arrived in 1726 and the two sang together in several operas including five new ones by Handel, all represented on this recording. Both were superlative singers and each had a characteristic style.

In his music composed for them, Handel clearly differentiated between their capacities, as this disc illustrates. The 'rival queens' first sang together in *Alessandro*, which is the opera most fully represented here. There are two of Cuzzoni's arias, one brilliant piece with rapid divisions, which Bott throws off in splendidly free fashion, and a pathetic one, a typical F minor *siciliano*, taken very slowly here, allowing plenty of time for some expressive elaboration in the *da capo*. Of Faustina's music we have the exquisite *scena* that opens Act 2, including the aria, 'Aure,

fonti', and the lively one with which the act closes. The aria typifies, in the way it demands and rewards precisely detailed singing, Handel's writing for her, and Kirkby's refinement of detail is remarkable. There's beautifully managed interplay between the singers in the *Alessandro* duet; they seem to feed one another with opportunities.

The programme is imaginatively put together and Goodman is a prompt and stylish accompanist. A thoroughly enjoyable disc.

'Duets'   **P**
Agrippina – No, no ch'io non apprezzo. Ariodante – Bramo haver mille vite. Giulio Cesare – Caro! Bella!. Ottone – Notte cara. Radamisto – Se teco vive il cor. Rodelinda – Io t'abbraccio. Sosarme – Per le porte del tormento. Tamerlano – Vivo in te. Belshazzar – Great victor, at your feet I bow. Theodora – To thee, thou glorious son of worth; Streams of pleasure ever flowing…Thither let our hearts aspire. Solomon – Welcome as the dawn of day
Rosemary Joshua sop **Sarah Connolly** mez
The English Concert / Harry Bicket hpd/org
Chandos Chaconne CHAN0767 (63' · DDD)   Ⓕ**OO**▶

Most collections concentrate on either opera or oratorio but Rosemary Joshua and Sarah Connolly mix things up: 10 of their 14 items are from operas in Italian but the other four are from English oratorios, although it was not a good idea to place the two great sublime duets from *Theodora* in the wrong order; the dramatic characterisation and context of these duets seems to have been subservient to superficial musical beauties. The programming of famous operatic duets alongside less obvious choices from *Ottone*, *Radamisto* and *Agrippina* assists a nice variety of styles, dramatic moods and works.

Connolly and Joshua are as outstanding a pair of Handel singers as one is likely to hear. Both deploy a slightly wider vibrato than seems ideal for the emotional suspensions of the vocal parts and the straight string tone of The English Concert in 'Io t'abbraccio', and the sorrowful and hopeless parting of Rodelinda and Bertarido fails to convey its full dramatic punch. Elsewhere the blend and connection between the two voices is immaculate, such as a tender performance of 'Great victor, at your feet I bow'; the lighter love duets, such as 'Bramo haver mille vite', are delightfully judged. 'Per le porte del tormento' is irresistibly gorgeous – and this is probably the loveliest interpretation of this duet on disc. 'Caro! Bella!' is conspicuously more affectionate than one usually hears.

The English Concert and Harry Bicket provide understated and efficient accompaniment but seldom reach deep into the dramatic personality of Handel's musical rhetoric. Jonathan Keates provides an expert yet friendly commentary on the music in his booklet-note, and fans of both composer and these two singers will be enchanted by the highly accomplished music-making.

'Amor e gelosia'   🅿

Admeto – Alma mia, dolce ristoro. Atalanta –
Amarilli?; Amarilli? Oh Dei! che vuoi?. Faramondo –
Del destin non mi lagno; Caro, tu m'accendi. Flavio –
Ricordati, mio ben. Muzio Scevola – Vivo senz'alma,
o bella. Orlando – Finché prendi. Poro – Caro amico
amplesso!; Perfidi! Ite di Poro a ricercar nel campo;
Se mai più sarò geloso; Se mai turbo il tuo riposo;
Act 3, Sinfonia; Lode agli Dei!; Se mai turbo il tuo
riposo. Rinaldo – Scherzano sul tuo volto. Rodelinda
– Non ti bastò, consorte; Io t'abbraccio. Serse – Gran
pena e gelosia!. Sosarme – Per le porte del
tormento. Teseo – Addio, mio caro bene. Silla – Mio
diletto, che pensi?; Sol per te, bell'idol mio
Patrizia Ciofi sop **Joyce Di Donato** mez
Il Complesso Barocco / Alan Curtis hpd
Virgin Classics 545628-2 (74' · DDD · T/t) Ⓕ🅞🅞🅞▶

Ⓖ The duets in Handel's operas are the
special treats, coming at climactic points
– most often two lovers' supposedly final
parting or their ultimate reunion. Try 'Io
t'abbraccio', from *Rodelinda* or the wonderful 'Per
la porte del tormento' from *Sosarme*. We have
several pieces from *Poro*, first the intense little
love duet in Act 2, and later the two arias in which
Poro and Cleofide swear eternal fidelity – which
they fling back at each other when, in a duet we
also hear, both believe themselves betrayed.
Then there's the delightful little minor-key duet
from *Faramondo*, the quarrel duet from *Atalanta*,
the charmingly playful piece from *Muzio Scevola*,
and the extraordinary one for the pleading Angelica and the furious, maddened Orlando. Handel's
understanding of the shades and accents of love
are something to marvel at.

All are most beautifully sung by Patrizia Ciofi
and Joyce DiDonato, who has just the right firmness and focus for a castrato role (as the mezzo
voices almost always are here); both phrase beautifully, articulate and express the words clearly
and tellingly, and ornament the *da capo* sections in
a natural and tasteful fashion. The accompaniments, done by a chamber group under Alan
Curtis with much refined timing of detail, add to
the pleasures of this truly delectable CD.

'Furore'   🅿

Arias from Admeto, Amadigi di Gaula, Ariodante,
Giulio Cesare, Hercules, Imeneo, Semele, Serse and
Teseo
Joyce DiDonato mez
Les Talens Lyriques / Christophe Rousset
Virgin Classics 519038-2 (75' · DDD)   Ⓕ🅞🅞▶

One of the most enjoyable 'gems from' Handel
discs in recent years was 'Amor e gelosia', a
recital of duets sung by Patrizia Ciofi and Joyce
DiDonato (see above). DiDonato now presents
a selection of arias, entitled 'Furore', that is just
as fine; indeed, it's superior in that the accompaniment is provided by a chamber orchestra
rather than the spare tones of the one-to-a-part
Il Complesso Barocco.

The pieces are by no means all 'furious'. But
most are passionate, and passion is something

that DiDonato does well. A good example is the
accompanied recitative 'Orride larve' from
Admeto, where the king rages at his fate. The
following aria is quite different, a calm acceptance of death that DiDonato sings with affecting simplicity.

Would that the same could be said of her
cadenzas and embellishments. As with many
other singers, the decorations hover on the borders of good taste; and starting the *da capo* of
'Sorge all'alma' a third higher was not a good
idea.

The selection is refreshingly unhackneyed,
'Scherza infida' from *Ariodante* and 'Where shall
I fly?' from *Hercules* being among the few predictable arias; and although there is an excerpt
from *Serse*, it isn't 'Ombra mai fù'. Full marks
for including some *secco* recitatives.

Admeto, re di Tessaglia, HWV22

Admeto   🅿
René Jacobs counterten Admeto **Rachel Yakar**
sop Alceste **Ulrik Cold** bass Ercole, Apollo **Rita
Dams** mez Orindo **James Bowman** counterten
Trasimede **Jill Gomez** sop Antigona **Max van
Egmond** bar Meraspe, A Voice **Il Complesso
Barocco / Alan Curtis**
Virgin Classics Veritas ② 561369-2
(3h 37' · ADD · N/T/t). Recorded 1979   Ⓕ

Admeto is full of fine things, particularly in its
music for the two women – Alceste, the nobly
self-sacrificing wife of King Admetus, and
Antigona, the princess he'd once wooed but
then rejected, who now returns after the
supposed death of Alceste. The plot, then, is
akin to Gluck's *Alceste*, but with an extra sub-
plot that allows for touches of wit and irony and
insights into human character.

When it was first released, the recording was
something of a pioneer in the use of period
instruments and performing conventions.
Things have moved on, of course: it seems a bit
dated now, heavier in manner than most Handel
opera recordings of recent years. And some of
the cast aren't wholly at home in a Baroque style
where little vibrato is wanted. One thinks in
particular of Rachel Yakar, but although her
articulation and attack aren't always ideally
clean she does bring a good deal of spirit to some
of the arias. Jill Gomez's lighter, bell-like voice
is more convincingly Handelian: she sings
Antigona's music charmingly and with due agility, and expressively too in the beautiful Act 2
siciliana. James Bowman is in his best voice as
Trasimede, Admetus's brother who loves
Antigona. René Jacobs, however, lacks the
heroic tones and the incisiveness that the role
demands. Ulrik Cold makes a strong Ercole,
with appropriately sturdy, masculine tone, and
Meraspe is neatly and very stylishly sung by Max
van Egmond.

Alan Curtis's direction is attentive to matters
of style, but he sometimes lets the bass-line plod.
Even so, Handelians needn't hesitate.

Agrippina, HWV6

Agrippina
Véronique Gens sop Agrippina **Philippe Jaroussky**
counterten Nero **Ingrid Perruche** sop Poppea **Nigel
Smith** bar Claudius **Thierry Grégoire** counterten
Otho **Bernard Deletré** bass Pallas **Fabrice Di Falco**
counterten Narcissus **Alain Buet** bass Lesbo
**La Grande Ecurie et La Chambre du Roy /
Jean-Claude Malgoire**
Stage director **Frédéric Fisbach**
Video director **Tiziano Mancini**
Dynamic *DVD* DV33431 (172' · NTSC · 4:3 · PCM
stereo, 5.1 & DTS 5.1 · 0). Recorded live at the
Théâtre Municipal, Tourcoing, March 2003   Ⓕ

Fisbach's production gives an amusing account, respectful yet inventive, of librettist Vincenzo Grimani's look at the shenanigans of ancient Rome. *Agrippina* shares three characters with *L'incoronazione di Poppea*, but at an earlier stage of the story, Poppea here being pursued by Otho, Nero and the emperor Claudius. Agrippina, Claudius's wife, spends the opera scheming to discredit Otho and to get Nero, her son by a previous marriage, designated as the next emperor.

The mood is light and ironic, but with a darker side as well. Against a minimalist set, above which French surtitles are, disconcertingly, sometimes visible, the costumes are exaggeratedly 18th-century. Poppea's yards of chiffon conceal two suitors simultaneously in a scene that anticipates *L'heure espagnole*. Nero, with rouged cheeks, sports an aubergine wig; the wigs of the other characters include various degrees of red, with a striking raspberry shade for Poppea. Otho wears no wig, perhaps to distinguish his genuine emotions from the buffoonery of Nero, Pallas and Narcissus.

In the accompanied recitative 'Otton, Otton' and the aria 'Voi che udite il mio lamento', with its aching suspensions in the strings, Thierry Grégoire gives moving expression to Otho's melancholy. As Claudius, Nigel Smith looks comically put out as Poppea fails to notice his preening, but strikes the right lyrical note with 'Vieni o cara'. To decorate the opening of 'Cade il mondo' and leave the *da capo* penny plain is surely to get things the wrong way round.

In the castrato role of Nero, Philippe Jaroussky shows an astonishing agility at soprano pitch. The penultimate aria, 'Come nube', is a *tour de force*. Ingrid Perruche has a nice lightness of touch for Poppea, as do Bernard Deletré as Pallas and Fabrice Di Falco as a mincing Narcissus. To Véronique Gens fall two of this delightful opera's best numbers: the heartfelt 'Pensieri' and the jaunty 'Ogni vento'. If she doesn't quite plumb the depths of the first, her performance overall is sharp and amusing.

Alcina, HWV34

Alcina
Joyce DiDonato sop Alcina **Karina Gauvin** sop

Morgana **Maite Beaumont** mez Ruggiero **Sonia
Prina** contr Bradamante **Kobie Van Rensburg** ten
Oronte **Vito Priante** bass Melisso **Laura Cherici** sop
Oberto **Il Complesso Barocco / Alan Curtis**
Archiv ③ 477 7374AH3 (3h 23' · DDD)   Ⓕ❶❶❶▷

Alan Curtis clearly welcomed the chance to add this masterpiece to the gradually expanding list of Handel operas he has recorded with Il Complesso Barocco. This *Alcina* is polished and passionate, the standard of *da capo* ornamentation unsurpassed. The acoustical environment of this recording is near-perfect. Every detail can be clearly heard, in part because of the minimal instrumental resources Curtis employs and his keen sense of the architecture and pacing of Handel's music.

Handel knew his singers' individual strengths and played to them. Curtis, too, knows how to coax the best from his singers. Joyce DiDonato, Maite Beaumont and Karina Gauvin have worked with him before and contribute vividly informed portrayals of the principal characters that stand comparison with the best performances on previous recordings. Technically, DiDonato is superb: her Alcina is a complex, feminine creature, vain and vindictive – listen to her spine-tingling performance of 'Ombre pallide' and the recitative that precedes it in Act 2. Beaumont is at ease in Carestini's role as Ruggiero – heroic when required (as in 'Bramo di trionfar', the discarded aria, originally in Act 1 scene 7, that Curtis reinstated) – and more than equal to the demands of the much-loved 'Verdi prati' (Act 2). Gauvin, her silk-clad Morgana fully as manipulative as Alcina, and Prina, the ever faithful Bradamante, each bring tremendous spirit and sensuousness to their roles. If Van Rensburg's Oronte wavers momentarily in Act 3, Priante's steadfast Melisso and Cherici's courageous Oberto show the way. This could well be the *Alcina* we've been waiting for.

Additional recommendation

Fleming Alcina **Dessay** Morgana **Kuhlmann**
Bradamante **Graham** Ruggiero **Les Arts Florissants
/ Christie** (coupled with Orlando, see page 558)
Erato ⑥ 2564-69653-2 (6h 59' · DDD · N/T/t)   Ⓕ❶

Fleming sings with great intensity. Her performance of this marvellous role is of a very high order. There are others to match. Susan Graham brings a firm, full mezzo, clear and agile. Kathleen Kuhlmann sings Bradamante with great vigour and resource and Natalie Dessay brings her full and warm soprano to Morgana's music. The orchestra is less aggressively 'period' in tone than some.

Ariodante, HWV33

Ariodante   Ⓟ
Anne Sofie von Otter mez Ariodante **Lynne
Dawson** sop Ginevra **Veronica Cangemi** sop Dalinda
Ewa Podles mez Polinesso **Richard Croft** ten

Lurcanio **Denis Sedov** bass King of Scotland **Luc Coadou** ten Odoardo **Choeur des Musiciens du Louvre; Les Musiciens du Louvre / Marc Minkowski**
Archiv ③ 457 271-2AH3 (178' · DDD · T/t)   Ⓕ Ⓞ ➔

Lynne Dawson is the star of this show. In Act 2, where Ginevra finds herself inexplicably rejected and condemned by everyone, Dawson brings real depth of tone and feeling to her E minor lament, 'Il mio crudel martoro'; in the final act she shines in the desolate miniature 'Io ti bacio' and brings much fire to the outburst 'Sì, morro'. But she never transgresses the canons of Baroque style. Von Otter, too, has much marvellous music – the aria 'Scherza infida' is one of Handel's greatest expressions of grief – and she sings it beautifully, but she isn't really at one with his idiom and seems to lack a natural feeling for the amplitude of Handel's lines.

Yet there's much to enjoy here too: the beauty of the actual sound, the immaculate control, the many telling and musicianly touches of phrasing. But the noble, climactic triumphant aria 'Dopo notte' doesn't have quite the effect it should. For that, however, Minkowski is partly to blame. Carried away, it almost seems, by the passion of the music, he's often inclined to go at it baldheaded, too fast and with a ferocity of accent that seems foreign to the style and dangerously close to ugly. Veronica Cangemi makes a charming Dalinda, light, spirited and duly agile, with some gently pathetic expression in the delightful *siciliana* song early in Act 2. Ewa Podles brings her large, resonant voice to Polinesso's music; and the King of Scotland's fatherly music is done with due fullness and warmth by Denis Sedov, who covers the two-octave range with comfort and resonance.

Despite the driven quality of Minkowski's performance, especially in the high dramatic music of the latter part of the opera, the sheer passion of this set does give it claims to be considered first choice. The admirable McGegan performance is possibly a safer buy, and in some respects it's a more stylish performance, but the singing here, Lynne Dawson's above all, is on balance superior.

Ariodante
Ann Murray mez Ariodante **Joan Rodgers** sop Ginevra **Lesley Garrett** sop Dalinda **Christopher Robson** counterten Polinesso **Paul Nilon** ten Lurcanio **Gwynne Howell** bass King of Scotland **Mark Le Brocq** ten Odoardo **English National Opera Chorus and Orchestra / Ivor Bolton**
Stage director **David Alden**
Video director **Kriss Rusmanis**
Arthaus Musik ⊚ᵈᵛᵈ 100 064
(178' · 16:9 · PCM stereo · 2, 3, 5)   Ⓕ Ⓞ

David Alden's staging of *Ariodante* was generally praised when it was first staged by WNO, a joint venture with ENO. This DVD is a recording of the much-admired revival at the ENO in 1996. Its appearance confirms the extraordinary per-

spicacity of Alden's production, which explains, from an almost Freudian viewpoint, the loves, hates, fears and fantasies of the principal characters so unerringly and deeply delineated in Handel's masterly score, in which aria after aria exposes new layers of emotional thrust and instability. Ann Murray gives a committed performance as the unhinged Ariodante and displays a physical and vocal virtuosity only occasionally vitiated by a harsh tone. The great arias 'Scherza infida' and 'Dopo notte' are just the climactic moments they should be. Joan Rodgers as Ginevra is hardly less impressive in her portrayal of the myriad feelings suggested by Handel and Alden.

Christopher Robson, as the villain Polinesso, is the very incarnation of evil lasciviousness, for which his edgy countertenor isn't inappropriate. Lesley Garrett gives Dalinda just the right touch of vulnerability as she submits to Polinesso's wiles while being sexually captivated by him. Gwynne Howell is the upright King to the life. Ivor Bolton conducts a vital, well-played account of the score with modern strings sounding very much like their period counterparts. Almost three hours of gripping music-drama pass in a trice, helped by the unbroken sequence of DVD. The sound is commendable, the picture superb.

Arminio, HWV36   Ⓟ

Arminio
Vivica Genaux sop Arminio **Geraldine McGreevy** sop Tusnelda **Dominique Labelle** sop Sigismondo **Manuela Custer** mez Ramise **Luigi Petroni** ten Varo **Syste Buwalda** counterten Tullio **Riccardo Ristori** bass Segeste **Il Complesso Barocco / Alan Curtis**
Virgin Veritas ② 545461-2 (147' · DDD · T/t)   Ⓕ

On the evidence of this very fine recording, *Arminio* can stand among the best of Handel's operas, full of beauty and imagination. The first number, a minor-key duet largely in dialogue for Arminio and his wife Tusnelda, is done with an intensity and vitality that immediately involves you in the action. In Act 2 a series of more expansive arias unfolds: a pair for Arminio, one noble and the other furious, a striking one, austerely scored for Tusnelda, a more playful piece for Arminio's sister Ramise, and a spacious one – also almost an oboe concerto movement – for Sigismondo. This sequence is crowned by a sombre aria for Arminio, with hints of a music that foreshadows 'He was despised', and a soft-textured, sensuous *siciliana* aria for Tusnelda. This is musically one of Handel's finest acts.

The performance is excellently directed by Alan Curtis, who paces the opera well, keeping the recitative moving and characterising the arias clearly. Dominique Labelle is of star quality, delicate, precise, rhythmic, powerful where she needs to be. The lower castrato part, the title-role, is sung by Vivica Genaux, whose focused, slightly grainy voice serves ideally – there's singing of real brilliance here. Geraldine

McGreevy gives a lot of pleasure too with her commanding singing in the *prima donna* role. *Arminio* isn't of the stamp of, say, *Giulio Cesare* or *Alcina*, but it has a lot of splendid music in it and is hugely enjoyable. Recommended.

Arianna in Creta, HWV32

Arianna in Creta   ℗
Mata Katsuli *sop* Arianna **Mary-Ellen Nesi** *mez*
Teseo **Irini Karaianni** *mez* Carilda **Marita Paparizou**
mez Tauride **Theodora Baka** *mez* Alceste **Petros**
Magoulas *bass* Minos **Orchestra of Patras /**
George Petrou
Dabringhaus und Grimm ② MDG603 1375-2
(131' · DDD · T/t/N)   Ⓕ

This is the first commercial recording of *Arianna in Creta* but, just as importantly, it is also the last of Handel's surviving operas to be issued on CD. Handel, according to his usual practice for the London stage, chose to set an old Italian libretto: *Arianna e Teseo* set by Leonardo Leo for Rome in 1729, although a few of Handel's aria texts were instead taken from a pasticcio that his new London rival Porpora had organised at Naples in 1721.

Handel's opera portrays Theseus' love affair with the Cretan King Minos' daughter Ariadne, the hero's victory over the Minotaur, and his escape from the labyrinth. It ends happily, with the sentiment that love overcomes cruelty. None of the later dejection when Ariadne is forsaken on Naxos is portrayed.

Curiously, Porpora and the 'Opera of the Nobility' organised *Arianna in Nasso* at Lincoln's Inn Fields on December 29, 1733, just under a month before Handel's treatment of the Theseus and Ariadne story could make it to the King's Theatre stage. However, Handel's opera was a much greater success, notching up 16 performances and earning a prompt revival at the beginning of the following season. Produced between *Orlando* and *Ariodante*, *Arianna in Creta* does not quite match the pinnacles that surround it in the chronology of Handel's works but this new recording illustrates that it is high time Arianna's reputation was restored.

The cocky villain Tauride, who spends the opera spouting off at Teseo, opens proceedings with 'Mirami' (a marvellous portrayal of swaggering arrogance, not quite captured by the Orchestra of Patras's elegant phrasing but sung resolutely by Marita Paparizou) and the spectacular 'Qual leon' (featuring two magnificent horns, although it is rushed a fraction here). The secondary lovers Carilda and Alceste get a few impressive scenes too, especially Alceste's sublime 'Son qual stanco pellegrino' with a mellifluous cello solo (the soprano castrato Carlo Scalzi might have stolen the show with this in 1734). Soprano Mata Katsuli delivers Arianna's taxing arias with sensitivity.

However, the towering figure of the opera is Mary-Ellen Nesi's heroic Teseo. This was the first role Handel composed for the star castrato Carestini and every aria is a gem: 'Nel pugnar' is an extensive florid showpiece; sentimental reconciliation is tenderly expressed in 'Sdegnata sei con me'; and Handel rises to the challenge of the Minotaur scene with a stirring accompanied recitative and a dashing heroic aria ('Qùi ti sfido').

George Petrou has a firm grasp on Handelian style and presents a persuasive case for the opera's merits. The predominantly Greek cast and period-instrument orchestra will not be familiar to many but, despite some approximate orchestral intonation, they reveal that *Arianna in Creta* is well worth investigation.

Ezio, HWV29

Ezio   ℗
Sonia Prina *sop* Valentiniano **Ann Hallenberg** *mez*
Ezio **Anicio Zorzi Giustiniani** *ten* Massimo **Karina**
Gauvin *sop* Fulvia **Marianne Andersen** *mez* Onoria
Vito Priante *bass* Varo **Il Complesso Barocco /**
Alan Curtis
Archiv ③ 477 8073AH3 (3h 6' · DDD· T/t)   ⒻⓄⓄ➤

Ezio is like a Roman thriller. Those wanting superficial thrills and glamorous wit from their Baroque operas might not know what to make of it, and the original audience in 1732 certainly didn't (it was one of Handel's worst commercial flops). However, it frequently shows the composer at his most masterful.

Alan Curtis sagely allows Handel's music to speak for itself unhindered by artificial gimmicks: ritornellos are subtle, continuo accompaniment of recitatives is exemplary for its pacing and judgement, and singers declaim their texts with utmost clarity. The sole disadvantage is that more passionate music is underplayed and lightweight, which means that sometimes it lacks dramatic punch and expressiveness. For instance, the dance-like courtliness in the overture is elegantly moulded but could do with some fiery intensity, and the final chorus is curiously underdone. So much of the performance is musically meticulous, but it would have flourished with a few more degrees of dramatic heat.

'Ecco alle mie catene', an emotional prison-scene aria at the end of Act 2, is sensitively sung by Ann Hallenberg but Il Complesso Barocco sound underpowered; a better synergy between instruments and voice is achieved in 'Se la mia vita'. Fulvia's dazzling *aria di bravura* 'La mia costanza' is impressive for Karina Gauvin's articulate stylishness and a fantastic cadenza. Sonia Prina's singing is admirable. Anicio Zorzi Giustiniani's fast runs are a bit dry in the superbly played 'Và! dal furor portata'. The unusual instrumentation for flutes and violette in Onoria's 'Quanto mai felice' is excellently played. Vito Priante sings Varo's splendid trumpet aria 'Già risonar d'intorno' with robust precision (Curtis adds a timpani part). Overall, this is an excellent and much-needed first complete recording, and confirms that *Ezio* is a fascinating serious drama.

Faramondo, HWV39

Faramondo   **P**
Max Emanuel Cencic *counterten* Faramondo **Sophie Karthäuser** *sop* Clotilde **Marina de Liso** *mez* Rosimonda **In-Sung Sim** *bass* Gustavo **Philippe Jaroussky** *counterten* Adolfo **Xavier Sabata** *counterten* Gernando **Fulvio Bettini** *bar* Teobaldo **Terry Wey** *counterten* Childerico
Swiss Radio Chorus; I Barocchisti / Diego Fasolis
Virgin Classics ③ 216611-2 (166' · DDD)   ⒻⓄ➀

Faramondo (1738) was written after the remnants of the Opera of the Nobility and Handel's opera company merged together for one peculiar and unsuccessful season at the King's Theatre. Virgin Classics has made much of the fact that this is the first Handel opera recording in which all the male characters are sung at the correct pitch by male singers, but several of the illustrious countertenors involved occasionally drop a few notes down an octave in order to conserve their larynxes.

I Barocchisti's playing of the fine *concerto grosso*-style Overture is zesty. Handel's scoring of the chorus 'Pera, pera' doesn't include the drums and trumpets employed here, and a few more euros could have been saved by not using unhistorical organ and guitar in the continuo group. Sophie Karthäuser's light navigation of Clotilde's arias provides some nice moments ('Combattuta da due venti' is eloquent rather than tempestuous, but none the worse for a bit of measured clarity and detail in its oscillating orchestral figures). Philippe Jaroussky and Max Emanuel Cencic each give attractive performances of virtuoso arias. Adolfo's slow aria 'Se a' piedi tuoi morrò' is delightful for its polished orchestral playing and Jaroussky's pleasant singing. Cencic's high-lying tessitura and brilliant coloratura are almost flawless. Xavier Sabata demonstrates his muskier voice in the enraged 'Voglio che mora, sì', but hams up his *da capo* too much. Marina de Liso gives a stunning performance of Rosimonda's turbulent 'Sì, l'intendesti, sì' (in which Diego Fasolis brings out exciting details in the accompaniment), and the bass villain Gustavo is resonantly sung by In-Sung Sim. Fasolis's direction is exemplary for its warmly authoritative expressiveness and fluent mastery over detail. *Faramondo* is revealed as a much better score than previously thought.

Fernando, re di Castiglia, HWV30

Fernando, re di Castiglia   **P**
Lawrence Zazzo *counterten* Fernando **Veronica Cangemi** *sop* Elvida **Marianna Pizzolato** *sop* Isabella **Max Emanuel Cencic** *counterten* Sancio **Filippo Adami** *ten* Dioniso **Antonio Abete** *bass-bar* Altomaro **Neal Banerjee** *ten* Alfonso
Il Complesso Barocco / Alan Curtis

Virgin Classics ② 365483-2 (149' · DDD)   Ⓕ

Fernando is the abandoned first draft of Handel's opera *Sosarme* (1732). We do not know why Handel changed almost all the character names, the location of the action and the title during the composition process, but in either guise the opera is full of top-drawer music. Alan Curtis has decided to reconstruct *Fernando* for philological reasons, although maybe the desire to bring us another 'premiere' had something to do with it.

Curtis's pacing and shaping of Handel's music is consistently subtle, astutely rhetorical and firmly connected to the libretto text. Although it might be possible to explore firmer muscularity and create a more vivid sense of surprise in the quicker music, there is something to be said for Curtis's shrewd reservation of such effects for when it is truly vital for the drama. For instance, Marianna Pizzolato's powerful arias 'Vado al campo' and 'Cuor di madre e cuor di moglie' are potently delivered moments of severe agitated passion that are all the more effective for the sweeter elegance that pervades much of this lovely score. The sublime duet 'Per le porte' is sung with poetic intimacy by Lawrence Zazzo and Veronica Cangemi. Zazzo sings his elegantly heroic aria 'Alle sfere della gloria' with supple clarity. Max Emanuel Cencic is impressive as the reticent Sancio, unwilling to be used as a pawn in his ruthless grandfather Altomaro's Machiavellian plans to tear the royal family apart. Antonio Abete gives an ideal account of the villain's arias.

The only weak link is Filippo Adami's vocally deficient Dionisio: natural Italian declamation in his extrovert recitatives is not enough to carry him through under-achieving blustery accounts of magnificent arias that deserve better. Il Complesso Barocco are excellent: *ritornelli* are intelligently weighted and phrased and instrumental contributions are patiently integrated with the singing. There are a few cuts to recitatives, but overall *Fernando* is one of Curtis's most consistent and pleasing Handel opera recordings.

Giulio Cesare, HWV17

Giulio Cesare   **P**
Jennifer Larmore *mez* Giulio Cesare **Barbara Schlick** *sop* Cleopatra **Bernarda Fink** *mez* Cornelia **Marianne Rørholm** *mez* Sesto **Derek Lee Ragin** *counterten* Tolomeo **Furio Zanasi** *bass* Achilla **Olivier Lallouette** *bar* Curio **Dominique Visse** *counterten* Nireno **Concerto Köln / René Jacobs**
Harmonia Mundi ③ HMC90 1385/7 (4h 3' · DDD · T/t)   ⒻⓄⓄⓄ➀

 Handel's greatest heroic opera sports no fewer than eight principal characters and one of the largest orchestras he ever used. Undoubtedly this, and the singing of Francesca Cuzzoni (Cleopatra) and Senesino (Caesar), helped to launch *Giulio*

Cesare into the enduring popularity that it enjoys to this day. But it's primarily the quality of the music, with barely a weak number in four hours of entertainment, that's made it such a favourite with audiences. Here the period instruments are an immediate advantage in giving extra 'bite' to the many moments of high drama without threatening to drown the singers in *forte* passages.

This performance is a particularly fine one with an excellent cast; Caesar, originally sung by a castrato, is here taken by the young mezzo, Jennifer Larmore. She brings weight and integrity to the role, seemingly untroubled by the demands of the final triumphant aria, 'Qual torrente'. Occasionally her vibrato becomes intrusive, but that's a minor quibble in a performance of this stature. Handel could just as well have called his opera 'Cleopatra' as she's the pivotal element in the drama, a role taken here by Barbara Schlick and sung with acuity and imagination. If Cleopatra represents strength in a woman, then Cornelia is surely the tragic figure, at the mercy of events. Her first aria, 'Priva son', here taken very slowly, shows Bernarda Fink to be more than equal to the role, admirable in her steady tone and dignity of character. Derek Lee Ragin's treacherous Ptolemy is also memorable, venom and fire injected into his agile voice.

A first-rate cast is supported by René Jacobs and Concerto Köln on fine form, though the continuo line is sometimes less than ideally clear. The recording is excellent.

Giulio Cesare   P
Kristina Hammarström *mez* Giulio Cesare **Emanuela Galli** *sop* Cleopatra **Mary-Ellen Nesi** *mez* Sesto **Irini Karaianni** *mez* Cornelia **Romina Basso** *mez* Tolomeo **Tassis Christoyannis** *bar* Achilla **Petros Magoulas** *bass* Curio **Nikos Spanatis** *counterten* Nireno
Orchestra of Patras / George Petrou
Dabringhaus und Grimm ③ MDG609 1604-2
(3h 52' · DDD)   Ⓜ OOO

This new recording of Handel's complete 1724 text, studio-made but based on a stage production in Thessaloniki, comfortably holds its own with the two fine versions from René Jacobs (see above) and Marc Minkowski. George Petrou directs his alert period band with style and sensibility. His tempo choices are occasionally extreme – languorously protracted in Cornelia's lament 'Priva son d'ogni conforto', frenetically driven in Caesar's 'Qual torrente'. Several times, especially in the first act, one wanted the extended *secco* recitatives to move more fluently. But despite minor quibbles, the performance, animated by a colourful continuo battalion (two harpsichords, plus strumming theorbo), equals Minkowski, and surpasses Jacobs, in theatrical verve.

Giulio Cesare is in essence a celebration of the power of sex, embodied in the infinitely alluring figure of Cleopatra. Barbara Schlick, for Jacobs, was bright and nimble, but distinctly virginal,

while Magdalena Kožená, for Minkowski, combined sensuality with a certain regal detachment. Emanuela Galli certainly generates a stronger sexual charge than either. She sings her playful numbers in the first act with knowing, coquettish grace, then finds warmer, more voluptuous colourings for the ravishing 'Parnassus' tableau, 'V'adoro pupille'. After Cleopatra has herself succumbed to the passion she aroused in Caesar, Galli brings a tragic intensity and individuality of nuance to 'Se pietà' and 'Piangerò'. Occasionally, though, her taste in ornamentation seems questionable – more Verdi's Violetta than Handel's Cleopatra.

Dubiously extravagant *da capo* embellishments also mar one or two other arias. Still, with the partial exception of Irini Karaianni's dignified but rather matt-toned Cornelia (far less affecting than Jacobs's Bernarda Fink), the singers, all round, compare well with their counterparts on the rival recordings. Swedish mezzo Kristina Hammarström has both the swashbuckling vigour for Caesar's heroic arias and the intense inwardness for his great soliloquy at Pompey's tomb. Though inclined to go berserk in *da capos*, Romina Basso's androgynous contralto makes a superb Tolomeo: sleazy, insinuating, neurotically unstable, yet without the hint of camp petulance that countertenors in the role seem unable to avoid. She uses her words more vividly than any of the other singers bar Mary-Ellen Nesi, whose Sextus – fiery, headstrong and thrillingly sung – is surely the finest on disc. Sextus's magnificent 'vengeance' aria 'L'angue offeso' is a highlight of the whole performance. The incisive-toned Tassis Christoyannis makes a high-testosterone, impulsive Achilla.

Here's a *Giulio Cesare* to return to at least as often as the rival versions, for much superb Handel singing, for the lively and inventive continuo playing, and for a dramatic flair and immediacy that, at its best, eclipses all comers.

Giulio Cesare (sung in English)
Dame Janet Baker *mez* Giulio Cesare **Valerie Masterson** *sop* Cleopatra **Sarah Walker** *mez* Cornelia **Della Jones** *mez* Sextus **James Bowman** *counterten* Ptolemy **John Tomlinson** *bass* Achillas **Christopher Booth-Jones** *bar* Curio **David James** *counterten* Nirenus **English National Opera Chorus and Orchestra / Sir Charles Mackerras**
Chandos Opera in English Series ③ CHAN3019
(4h 4' · DDD · N)   Ⓜ O⯈

This opera was a personal triumph for Dame Janet. As Caesar, she arms the voice with an impregnable firmness, outgoing and adventurous. Valerie Masterson shares the honours with Dame Janet, a Cleopatra whose bright voice gains humanity through ordeal. The tinkle of surface-wear clears delightfully in her later arias, sung with a pure tone and high accomplishment. As a total production, *Julius Caesar* was an outstanding achievement in ENO's history. Strongly cast, it had a noble Cornelia in Sarah Walker, a high-spirited Sextus in Della Jones,

HANDEL GIULIO CESARE – IN BRIEF

Jennifer Larmore *Giulio Cesare* **Barbara Schlick**
Cleopatra **Concerto Köln / René Jacobs**
Harmonia Mundi HMC90 1385/7   Ⓜ️❍❍❍

🅖 A superb performance that took a
Gramophone Award back in 1991. Jennifer Larmore is a powerful and technically
magnificent Caesar, Barbara Schlick an
imaginative and sweet-voiced Cleopatra, and
Derek Lee Ragin a suitably poisonous
Ptolemy. Jacobs demonstrates his mastery
of 18th-century theatre with the superb
Concerto Köln.

Dame Janet Baker *Giulio Cesare*
Valerie Masterson *Cleopatra*
ENO / Sir Charles Mackerras
Chandos CHAN3019   Ⓜ️❍

An outstanding performance from 1984 that
enshrines Janet Baker's extraordinarily complete portrayal of Caesar. Valerie Masterson
is a superb Cleopatra, bright-toned and
coquettish. James Bowman sings well as
Ptolemy, though he could perhaps be
nastier! Mackerras's command of the score is
magnificent.

Dame Janet Baker *Giulio Cesare*
Valerie Masterson *Cleopatra*
ENO / Sir Charles Mackerras
ArtHaus Musik 📀 100 308   Ⓜ️❍

John Copley's English National Opera production is here taken into the studio and
reveals the magnificent cast on top form,
all revolving around Baker's emotionally
powerful Caesar. Mackerras drives the score
forward with his customary élan ensuring a
performance of real dramatic intensity.

Marijana Mijanovic *Giulio Cesare* **Magdalena
Kožená** *Cleopatra* **Les Musiciens du Louvre /
Marc Minkowski**
Archiv 474 210-2AH3   Ⓕ❍➡️

A strong challenger to the Jacobs set, with
Majanovic a strong Caesar and Kožená a fine
Cleopatra (though perhaps lacking the *n*th
degree of voluptuousness). Anne Sofie von
Otter is a superb Sextus and Charlotte Hellekant a noble Cornelia. Minkowski's direction
is generally pretty swift, though he can linger
at particularly lovely moments.

Andreas Scholl *Giulio Cesare* **Inger Dam-Jensen**
Cleopatra **Concerto Copenhagen /
Lars Ulrik Larsen**
Harmonia Mundi 📀 HMD990 9008/9   Ⓕ❍

The same production as on the EuroArts version (see right) conducted by Hickox, but
here with Andreas Scholl lifting it to even
greater heights. He has developed as an actor
and his singing, it almost goes without saying, is superlative. But the rest of the cast is
very fine too, and Larsen directs with an
exquisite feeling for Handelian style.

and in James Bowman a Ptolemy whose only
fault was that his voice lacked meanness of timbre appropriate to the odious character. John
Tomlinson's massive bass also commands attention. Mackerras's conducting is impeccable and
the opera is given in clear, creditable English.
(See next review for the video equivalent.)

Giulio Cesare (sung in English)
Janet Baker *mez* Giulio Cesare **Valerie Masterson**
sop Cleopatra **Sarah Walker** *mez* Cornelia **Della
Jones** *mez* Sextus **James Bowman** *counterten*
Ptolemy **John Tomlinson** *bass* Achillas **Brian Casey**
sngr Pothinus **John Kitchiner** *bar* Curio **Tom Emlyn
Williams** *counterten* Nirenus **English National
Opera Chorus and Orchestra / Sir Charles
Mackerras**
Stage director **John Copley**
Video director **John Michael Phillips**
ArtHaus Musik 📀 100 308 (180' · 4:3 · 2.0 · 2 & 5 · N)
Recorded 1984   Ⓕ❍

This is a 1984 studio re-creation, with the
original cast, of John Copley's ENO production. Mackerras's performing edition is by no
means literally 'authentic'; arias are removed,
including much of Sextus's role, recitatives are
trimmed, and much of Caesar's role is transposed – inevitably, since it was written for the
exceptionally low contralto castrato Senesino.
The result is no travesty, however: it's fast-
moving and dramatically satisfying, and conducted by Mackerras in the same spirit.

Copley also strives to avoid tedium, for instance
backing *da capo* passages with stage activity –
sometimes rather obviously. However, his staging, combining John Pascoe's warm-hued,
vaguely 18th-century designs with more naturalistic acting, translates quite well to the screen –
not least because the singers are so committed.
Janet Baker displays great Handelian affinity. She
not only delivers these difficult, florid arias with
fiery élan and appropriate ornament, but infuses
them with a real emotional intensity that sweeps
one over the credibility gap.

Sarah Walker makes the lachrymose Cornelia
almost as intense, and Valerie Masterson carries
off Cleopatra's gorgeous music with admirable
if slightly self-conscious virtuosity and a kittenish seductiveness reminiscent of Vivien Leigh.
Della Jones is a splendid Sextus, and John Tomlinson a thunderously melodramatic Achillas.
Though James Bowman's hooting tone is rather
obtrusive, he plays Ptolemy as a petulantly
Farouk-ish villain to fine comic effect.

Giulio Cesare   🅟
Sarah Connolly *mez* Giulio Cesare **Danielle de
Niese** *sop* Cleopatra **Patricia Bardon** *mez* Cornelia
Angelika Kirchschlager *mez* Sesto **Christophe
Dumaux** *counterten* Tolomeo **Christopher Maltman**
bar Achillas **Alexander Ashworth** *bass* Curio **Rachid
Ben Abdeslam** *counterten* Nireno **Glyndebourne
Chorus; Orchestra of the Age of Enlightenment /
William Christie**

Stage director **David McVicar**
Video director **Robin Lough**
Opus Arte ③ 📀 OA0950D (3h 46' · NTSC · 16:9 ·
PCM stereo and DTS 5.1 surround · 0). Recorded live
during the Opera Festival, Glyndebourne, in 2005
Ⓕ❍❍❍

David McVicar's 2005 staging, revived the following summer, provoked a deal of contrasting views among the critical fraternity but was adored by the Glyndebourne public. Chief cause of their delight was the overtly sexual, high-hoofing performance of Cleopatra by the irrepressible Danielle de Niese (who is accorded a delightful 22-minute narrative on her Glyndebourne experience among the extras here). Her vocal command and stage presence are spectacular in every sense, and from her first aria she utterly seduces her audience. McVicar took advantage of her attractive skills to build the opera around her personality.

We are here in the high noon of British imperialism and the Ottoman Empire, with Caesar more like a late-19th-century English general than a Roman emperor, and with the Egyptian milieu heavily underlined by milling extras, now always a not-altogether welcome feature of a McVicar production. They clutter the stage and draw attention away from the principals, although one has to admit that the highly disciplined and often captivating choreography is brilliantly executed within Robert Jones's exotic sets. McVicar does at least allow the moments of serious drama to be played out without undue interference – such as the deeply moving duet that closes Act 1 and Cleopatra's 'Piangerò'. Finally it has to be said that only Glyndebourne allows for the rehearsal time to prepare such a complex and ingenious staging.

The musical side of things is equally well prepared and thought-through under William Christie's knowledgeable and commanding direction. He manages to balance with the same finesse and care the light and serious parts of the score, even if his love for Handel leads him to a few self-indulgently slow tempi. The OAE play lovingly and with period skills for him. By the time of this DVD recording, near the end of the run, the whole thing moves with eloquence matched by elegance.

De Niese sings her airy numbers as to the manner born, seconded by expertly erotic dancing. She manages most of the emotional substance of her sadder arias, but they sometimes seem wanting in the tonal weight ideally required. Sarah Connolly's thoroughly believable Caesar is sung with her firm tone and well schooled mastery of Handelian style, including subtle embellishments. This wilful and imperial Caesar manages to change moods as his music demands.

Some of the most accomplished and tender Handelian singing comes from Patricia Bardon's moving Cornelia and Angelika Kirchschlager's concerned Sextus, although the latter does slightly overplay the character's seemingly neurotic state of mind following his father's brutal death. The young countertenor Christophe Dumaux playing

Ptolemy is suitably brat-like and spoilt. He, like most of the cast, fulfils all the stringent demands of this very physical staging. Christopher Maltman makes Achillas as nasty as he should be. The sense of teamwork all round is confirmed in the interviews included in the extras. Robin Lough's DVD direction is faultless.

Giulio Cesare
Graham Pushee counterten Giulio Cesare **Yvonne Kenny** sop Cleopatra **Rosemary Gunn** mez Cornelia **Elizabeth Campbell** mez Sesto **Andrew Dalton** counterten Tolomeo **Stephen Bennett** bass Achillas **Richard Alexander** bass Curio **Rodney Gilchrist** counterten Nireno **Australian Opera and Ballet Orchestra / Richard Hickox**
Stage director **Francisco Negrin**
Video director **Peter Butler**
EuroArts 📀 205 3599 (3h 28' · 4:3 · PCM stereo, 5.1 & DTS 5.1 · 0). Recorded live at the Opera House, Sydney, June 1994   Ⓕ

Francisco Negrin's production of *Giulio Cesare* is remarkably satisfying. Richard Hickox's musical direction is exemplary, with timing, tempi and phrasing that never go awry. The modern-instrument orchestra plays without a trace of soggy over-indulgence. The singing is less uniformly ideal: Yvonne Kenny's gutsy coloratura is undone by wobbly intonation, and Elizabeth Campbell's Sextus inclines towards shrillness. Rosemary Gunn's Cornelia isn't a convincing drop-dead gorgeous icon who could initiate the doom of lusting Egyptians, and her heavy vibrato obscures the melodic beauty of 'Priva son d'ogni conforto'. Stephen Bennett delivers a wonderful 'Tu sei il cor' which suggests that Achillas is capable of greater eloquence and sincerity than we'd suspected. Graham Pushee's lyrical Caesar is consistently marvellous: his superbly acted role as an enlightened ruler perfectly fits Negrin's concept of him as representing ideal kingship, which is how such figures were supposed to be interpreted by Handel's Haymarket audience.

This is by no means a historical Baroque staging, but Negrin ensures that each strand of the plot is faithful to both libretto and Handel's music. He takes some daring risks with staging while doing nothing to subvert the musical rhetoric or the purity of the narrative. He intelligently allows the soliloquy convention to be respected. Unlike so many directors who do not understand Handel's dramatic power, he ensures that Cleopatra sings 'Piangerò' alone; the lack of distractions magnifies an intensely emotional moment. The production nevertheless features plenty of clever stagecraft. The most significant liberty reaps handsome dividends: the role of Nirenus is incidental in the score, yet the director imagines that he pulls all the strings behind the scenes to ensure that all the plot-strands resolve happily. It's common to admire a Handel opera performance for its singing while deploring the staging; here, though, is a precious rare example of a production that's a joy.

Handel Opera

Additional recommendation

Giulio Cesare
Scholl Giulio Cesare **Dam-Jensen** Cleopatra **Stene**
Cornelia **Semmingsen** Sesto **Robson** Tolomeo
Lundgren Curio **Knudsen** Achillas **Maniaci** Nireno
Concerto Copenhagen / Lars Ulrik Mortensen
Stage director **Francisco Negrin**
Video director **Thomas Grimm**
Harmonia Mundi ② 🔲 HMD990 9008/9
(3h 36' · NTSC · 16:9 · PCM stereo and DTS 5.1 · 0)
Recorded live at the Royal Danish Theatre,
Copenhagen, in March 2005   Ⓕ**O**

Francisco Negrin's production (the same
as in Sydney, see above), though not without
judiciously applied humour in a few places, is
essentially of a serious nature. Unsurprisingly,
this sympathetic approach suits Handel's
opera seria to a tee. Andreas Scholl's singing
is consistently astute, and his acting has
advanced considerably in subtlety. However,
this is an excellent team performance. Lars
Ulrik Mortensen's direction of the music from
his harpsichord is well nigh perfect. This is not
the most flamboyant or fancy Giulio Cesare on
DVD, but it is certainly the most insightful and
intelligent for drama, and probably also the best
for all-round musical consistency.

Hercules, HWV60

Hercules
Gidon Saks bass-bar Hercules **Anne Sofie von**   🄿
Otter mez Dejanira **Richard Croft** ten Hyllus **Lynne**
Dawson sop Iole **David Daniels** counterten Lichas
Marcos Pujol bar Priest of Jupiter **Chœur des**
Musiciens du Louvre; Les Musiciens du Louvre /
Marc Minkowski
Archiv ③ 469 532-2AH3 (176' · DDD · T/t)   Ⓕ**O**➡

Hercules has never quite occupied the place it
merits in the Handel canon, even though it
includes some of his most powerfully dramatic
music. This is understood by Marc Minkowski,
whose intentions towards the work are made
clear from the start of the Overture. But he's also
intent on maintaining its dramatic pace and
emphasising its range of feeling. His cast is well
able to share his dramatic vision. Von Otter excels
as Dejanira. This, rather than Hercules himself, is
the central role, carrying the work's chief expressive weight. There's some beautifully shaped
singing as in her opening air she mourns Hercules' absence, and she copes well with
Minkowski's demanding tempo in 'Begone, my
fears'. Lynne Dawson makes a delightful Iole,
crystalline, airy, rhythmic, but able to call on
more intensity where needed. 'My breast with
tender pity swells' is truly lovely. Lichas' music is
done with refinement but also vigour by David
Daniels. Richard Croft, though often hurried by
Minkowski, sings much of Hyllus' music with
elegance, and his delicate sustained pianissimo in
the da capo of 'From celestial seats descending',
one of the most inspired pieces in the score, is
remarkable. The choral singing is strong, secure,

responsive, though the French choir is rather less
euphonious than the best English ones. The
orchestral playing is duly alert. This account benefits from fewer cuts than his rival Gardiner and
superior solo singing.

Orlando, HWV31

Orlando (coupled with Alcina – see page 551)   🄿
Patricia Bardon mez Orlando **Rosemary Joshua** sop
Angelica **Hilary Summers** contr Medoro **Rosa**
Mannion sop Dorinda **Harry van der Kamp** bass
Zoroastro **Les Arts Florissants / William Christie**
Erato ⑥ 2564 69653-2 (6h 59' · DDD · T/t)   Ⓕ

Christie is very much concerned with a smooth
and generally rich texture and with delicacy of
rhythmic shaping. His management of the
recitative could hardly be bettered and moments
of urgency or of other kinds of emotional stress
are tellingly handled. Sometimes he favours a
rather sustained style in the arias, making the
textures seem airless and heavy, and the lines
within them too smooth. However, to set
against it there's his exceptional delicacy of
timing, his careful but always natural-sounding
moulding of cadences and other critical
moments in the score. Not many Handel interpreters show this kind of regard for such matters and it's a delight to hear Handel's music so
lovingly nurtured; it also helps the singers to
convey meaning. The cast is very strong. The
title-role is taken by a mezzo, Patricia Bardon,
who draws a firm and often slender line, with
that gleam in her tone that can so enliven the
impact of a lowish mezzo – the famous Mad
scene is magnificent. The Sleep scene, with
very sweet, soft-toned playing of the violette
marine, is lovely.

Hilary Summers offers a very sensitively sung
Medoro, pure and shapely in line. Harry van der
Kamp makes a finely weighty Zoroastro, with
plenty of resonance in his lower register; the last
aria in particular is done in rousing fashion. As
Angelica, Rosemary Joshua's musicianship
comes through in her attractive phrasing and
timing. Rosa Mannion's Dorinda is no less full
of delights, catching the character to perfection.
Hogwood's lighter orchestral textures are
appealing but the refinement of detail in the
newer set is equally admirable.

Partenope, HWV27

Partenope   🄿
Rosemary Joshua sop Partenope **Kurt Streit** ten
Emilio **Stephen Wallace** counterten Armindo
Andrew Foster-Williams bass-bar Ormonte **Hilary**
Summers contr Rosmira **Lawrence Zazzo** counterten
Arsace **Early Opera Company / Christian Curnyn**
Chandos Chaconne ③ CHAN0719
(3h 10' · DDD · T/t)   Ⓕ➡

Handel composed Partenope for the 1730 London
season, less than a year into the so-called 'Second

Opera **Handel**

Academy' period in which he enjoyed increased artistic control over his productions. *Partenope* was a subject he had long coveted and with a new troupe of singers, less starry than before, he seems to have relished the chance to tone down the rattling virtuosity in favour of a more 'company' feel, and with it a more genuine and subtle mode of expression. He was helped by a strong libretto which is well set-out, humane with a touch of gentle humour, and features characters who are lifelike and credible.

Partenope, Queen of Naples, is wooed by three suitors – the overly proud enemy general Emilio, the mopy but deserving Armindo, and her own favourite, Arsace. Arsace, however, is tormented by the woman he left behind, Rosmira, who is hanging around and making mischief disguised as a man. Eventually, and after much soul-searching, Arsace forces her to reveal her identity by challenging her to a bare-chest duel (which she declines). The couple are reunited, Partenope settles for Armindo, and Emilio accepts his rejection philosophically.

Christian Curnyn conducts a highly competent performance thoroughly in the groove of modern Handelian style, with a cast that has no vocal weaknesses and many dramatic virtues: Rosemary Joshua as Partenope and Hilary Summers as Rosmira have the most technically demanding music, but Joshua's brightly confident singing also effortlessly suggests a woman both regal and desirable, while the dark-voiced Summers sounds like someone not to be messed with. Lawrence Zazzo conveys well the deepening suffering of Arsace, Stephen Wallace shows us the emerging nobility of Armindo, and if Kurt Streit sounds rather like a tenor stepping out of his usual Mozartian realm, then as the pompous Emilio he does need to be a little out of step with the others and his voice and Italian diction are both irresistibly splendid. In general the singing has a warmth to it, and although there are times when the recitatives could make room for more dramatic flexibility and conviction, this is nevertheless a thoroughly recommendable release for Baroque opera fans.

Partenope
Inger Dam-Jensen *sop* Partenope **Andreas Scholl**
counterten Arsace **Tuva Semmingsen** *mez* Rosmira
Christophe Dumaux *counterten* Armindo
Bo Kristian Jensen *ten* Emilio **Palle Knudsen**
bass Ormonte **Concerto Copenhagen /**
Lars Ulrik Mortensen
Stage director **Francisco Negrin**
Video director **Uffe Borgwardt**
Decca ② 074 3348DX2 (3h 7' · NTSC · 16:9 · PCM
stereo and DTS 5.0 · 0). Includes rehearsal footage
and interviews   Ⓕ❍

Partenope is crammed with outstanding arias varying in musical styles and techniques but it is also a beautifully crafted drama in which the different consequences of love upon radically different lovers are examined with warmth, insight and, ultimately, hope. In a sense it is like Handel's counterpart of *Così fan tutte*: a school for conflicting lovers. A few brief moments of outright humour in the libretto have led to *Partenope* being oversimplified as a comedy. Attempts to force the opera into a farce have been catastrophic in the theatre, with profound loss of truthfulness and beauty from the play. Thankfully, Mexican director Francisco Negrin has no trouble in balancing the seriousness of lovers' quarrels with a few moments of hilariously funny staging. The troubled and passionate relationships between all of the main protagonists are understood and conveyed with rare insight and the portrait of each character that emerges from Handel's marvellously crafted music is generally spot on: the adulterous Arsace is initially smug, and his fall from Partenope's favour is followed by some moving soul-searching and a touching reconciliation with his vengeful and tortured ex-fiancée Rosmira; Andreas Scholl copes admirably with the difficult fast coloratura but his finest moment is the heartbroken 'Ch'io parta', in which he begs Rosmira to take him back. Tuva Semmingsen sings and ideally captures Rosmira's conflicting desires for vengeance and to win her man back.

Partenope is beautiful yet mischievous and her eventual realisation that requites the kindly Armindo's love is beautifully portrayed in Negrin's staging.

As in his various productions of *Giulio Cesare*, Negrin uses the servant character (Ormonte) to serve as a silent and wise witness to events, leading the protagonists towards their rightful resolutions. It is an effective idea, even though granting Ormonte 'La gloria in nobil alma' at the beginning of Act 3 (it should be sung by Emilio towards the end) grinds against Handel's musico-dramatic gears. More dubious interventions are placing Partenope's 'Care mura' too early, and Rosmira's gorgeous 'Se non ti sai spiegar' is entirely omitted, which is a crying shame as it portrays her (disguised as a man) giving Armindo advice about how to win Partenope's heart away from Arsace in music of exquisite tenderness and subtlety. However, Lars Ulrik Mortensen's magnificent direction brings out the full measure of excitement, pathos and emotion in Handel's score in a way that few interpreters have quite managed, and Concerto Copenhagen's playing is routinely fantastic.

An inordinate amount of hand-held cameras illustrating close-up details of faces and off-centre shenanigans probably reduces the impact of what must have been a tremendous evening in the theatre. Overall, the production is flawed in theory, but in practice it conveys an enormous amount of what makes *Partenope* very special.

Rinaldo, HWV7

Rinaldo   Ⓟ
David Daniels *counterten* Rinaldo **Cecilia Bartoli**
mez Almirena **Gerald Finley** *bar* Argante **Luba**

559

Orgonášová *sop* Armida **Bejun Mehta** *counterten*
Christian Sorcerer **Mark Padmore** *ten* Herald **Daniel**
Taylor *counterten* Eustazio **Bernarda Fink** *contr*
Goffredo **Catherine Bott** *sop* Siren I **Ana-Maria**
Rincón *sop* Donna, Siren II **Academy of Ancient**
Music / Christopher Hogwood
Decca L'Oiseau-Lyre ③ 467 087-2OHO3
(179' · DDD · T/t)   Ⓕ **ⓄⓄⓄ**▷

In a sense, *Rinaldo* is at once Handel's
most familiar and unfamiliar opera:
familiar because, as his lavish first
stage work for London, it has been much written about both by modern historians and by the
composer's contemporaries; unfamiliar because
the Handel opera revival of recent years has
largely passed it by. Although there are numerous recordings of its two hit slow arias – 'Lascia
ch'io pianga' and 'Cara sposa' – this is its first
complete studio recording for over 20 years. It
may not be Handel's most dramatically effective work (Act 3 marks time rather), and its
magic effects and transformation scenes no
doubt make it a tricky prospect for opera companies, but in many ways its rich orchestration
and impressive set-piece arias make it ideal for
recording. That much makes this release a welcome sight already; add the de luxe cast Decca
has assembled for the purpose and it begins to
look irresistible.

Top of the bill come David Daniels as the
eponymous crusader knight and Cecilia Bartoli as his love Almirena. Daniels's heart-stopping countertenor voice is one of the marvels
of our age. It isn't big, and though he's technically untroubled by the virtuoso runs of the
quicker arias, some may feel it lacks some of
the heroic power expected of a warrior; but
there's an inner strength to it, and in the love
music he's utterly convincing. Bartoli is
equally impressive, though her singing is less
well suited to Handel. She can deliver the
most demanding music with almost frightening ease and force, and, as ever, she throws
herself into her role, but one can't help thinking that a more natural and unaffected style
would have been more appropriate for arias
such as 'Lascia ch'io pianga' and 'Augeletti
che cantate'. The rest of the cast is almost
unwaveringly strong. Daniel Taylor is slightly
less technically secure or forceful than the
others (which is hardly a criticism), but he
does well enough with the opera's least effective role as Goffredo's brother Eustazio.

Christopher Hogwood's direction is typically
neat and well-mannered. He isn't a
natural opera conductor – others may have
found more magic in the enchanted gardens and
more sensuality in the sirens who lure Rinaldo,
and you sometimes get the feeling that he's
rushing the singers at important moments – but
he has an unerring sense of tempo, and the opera
as a whole is well paced. The Academy of
Ancient Music plays to a high standard, backed
up by a startlingly virtuoso performance on the
Drottningholm thunder machine and by some
genuine birdsong at the beginning of Act 2.

This version may not be the last word on the
opera, but for all-round standard of performance and production it currently wins hands
down and it will take some beating.

Rodelinda, regina de' Langobardi, HWV19

Rodelinda   Ⓟ
Simone Kermes *sop* Rodelinda **Marijana Mijanovic**
contr Bertarido **Steve Davislim** *ten* Grimoaldo **Sonia**
Prina *contr* Eduige **Marie-Nicole Lemieux** *contr*
Unulfo **Vito Priante** *bar* Garibaldo **Il Complesso**
Barocco / Alan Curtis
Archiv ③ 477 5391AH3 (3h 12' · DDD · T/t)   Ⓕ **ⓄⓄ**▷

Alan Curtis has done more than most to prove
that many of Handel's 42 operas are first-rate
music dramas – his *Admeto*, from 1979 (see
page 550), was one of the first complete recordings of a Handel opera to feature period instruments and all voices at correct pitch without
transpositions – but it is surprising to note that
this is his first recording of an undisputed
popular masterpiece.

Rodelinda, first performed in February 1725, is
a stunning work dominated by a title-heroine
who remains devoted to her supposedly dead
husband Bertarido and scorns the advances of
his usurper Grimoaldo. The potency of Handel's score was enhanced by the complexity of
the villain, whose lust-driven cruelty gradually
crumbles into a desire to abdicate in order to
find spiritual peace. The scene in which the
penitent tyrant's life is saved from assassination
by the fugitive Bertarido is among Handel's
greatest dramatic moments.

Simone Kermes is full of feisty courage, an
assertive woman for whom Bertarido would
credibly risk death to be reunited with. She
takes no prisoners in some extravagant
cadenzas, and sings 'Morrai, si' with thrillingly
viscous venom. At the other extreme, 'Ritorna
o cara' is simply gorgeous. There are some
weaknesses. Marijana Mijanovic's Bertarido
often slips under pitch on long notes and uses
indiscriminate vibrato instead of singing
through phrases. Her deficiencies with tuning
and idiomatic expression are highlighted in two
duets with Kermes (one not recorded before),
particularly when Handel demands that they
sing sustained notes in unison. There is a good
case for using a fruity female contralto in
castrato roles instead of an angelic countertenor but why Archiv seems keen to record
Mijanovic's inadequate performances of Handel roles for his star castrato, Senesino, is
incomprehensible. A cursory comparison of
Mijanovic's bizarrely unattractive 'Dove sei'
with any of the impressive contributions from
fellow contraltos Marie-Nicole Lemieux or
Sonia Prina indicates that either would have
better suited the role.

Otherwise, this has an abundance of good
things. Il Complesso Barocco have sounded
undernourished on some previous recordings
but here play with admirable vitality and dra-

matic subtlety. Curtis has obviously worked hard to encourage his string players to understand what the singers are communicating: each aria is impeccably interpreted and intelligently paced. On the whole, Curtis's passion and experience ensure another typically persuasive and theatrical vindication of Handel's genius.

Rodrigo, HWV5

Rodrigo   **P**
Gloria Banditelli mez Rodrigo **Sandrine Piau** sop
Esilena **Elena Cecchi Fedi** sop Florinda **Rufus Müller**
ten Giuliano **Roberta Invernizzi** sop Evanco
Caterina Calvi mez Fernando **Il Complesso Barocco
/ Alan Curtis** hpd
Virgin Classics Veritas ② 545897-2 (155' · DDD · T/t)
    Ⓕ

The music of Handel's Italian years has a unique freshness, a boldness of invention, a novelty in textures and lines – characteristics which distinguish his first Italian opera, *Rodrigo*, written in 1707 for the Medici court at Florence. This recording restores all that survives of the lyrical music, with one item composed in a more-or-less Handelian manner by Curtis and other Handel music imported to fit the original text. Curiously, the dances aren't included here, and – presumably in the interest of keeping the set to two CDs – there are many large cuts in the recitative. As a result some quite important sections are omitted and the often very close succession of lyrical numbers gives a slightly misleading impression of the opera. Even so the recording of this fine, often very moving and mostly inspiriting piece is warmly welcome.

Like most Italian operas of its time, it's essentially a succession of arias, mostly shorter ones than those of Handel's mature operas. As so often with Handel, much of the finest music comes in Act 2, with a pair of arias for Esilena (the second a furious outburst), and at the beginning of the next act, with Rodrigo and Esilena apparently facing death, Handel finds that marvellous vein of pathos familiar in his later operas. Alan Curtis, a man of the theatre, keeps the score moving along at a good pace. He conducts, as it were, from a 17th-century standpoint, with a flexibility over accent and metre that allows the music to move unusually freely. Yet he's rather predictable in his use of cadential *rallentandos*, and there are points where the orchestral discipline is a shade loose.

Sandrine Piau sings Esilena's part beautifully, with much attention to detail, to timing and to phrasing, as well as with fluency and with a richness of tone unusual for her. Gloria Banditelli makes a sturdy Rodrigo, direct and accurate, and very controlled in the fast semiquaver passages. Elena Cecchi Fedi perhaps overdoes the characterisation of Florinda as a shrew, singing shrilly at times and with rather

more shouting and pouting than is consistent with musical enjoyment. But the singing is powerful and brilliant in its way. There's competent and spirited playing from Il Complesso Barocco, and excellent notes from Anthony Hicks and Curtis.

Tamerlano, HWV18

Tamerlano   **P**
Nicholas Spanos counterten Tamerlano **Mary-Ellen
Nesi** mez Andronico **Tassis Christoyannis** bar
Bajazet **Mata Katsuli** sop Asteria **Irini Karaianni** mez
Irene **Petros Magoulas** bass Leone
Orchestra of Patras / George Petrou
Dabringhaus und Grimm ③ MDG609 1457-2
(3h 12' · DDD · T/t/N)   Ⓜ

Tamerlano has done quite well on disc but this is the first recording to adopt the version that Handel decided on for the premiere. The story is grim. Tamerlano – Marlowe's Tamburlaine, now generally called Timur – has captured the Ottoman sultan, Bajazet, whose daughter Asteria he proposes to marry. In the end he marries Irene, to whom he was betrothed, and restores Asteria to her lover Andronico, but only after Bajazet has killed himself.

The audience's sympathies lie with the proud father. The part of Bajazet is usually taken by a tenor; but it lies very low, and it is here sensibly given to a baritone. Whereas Marlowe's Bajazeth spectacularly brains himself onstage, in this version the sultan takes poison and is carried off to die. The music moves from defiance to tenderness and back in recitative and arioso, which Tassis Christoyannis handles with consummate skill. He also expresses the character's dignity and resolve in his Act 1 arias with firm, focused tone.

Mata Katsuli is equally impressive as his daughter. Asteria is a strong character who accepts Tamerlano as her husband in order to murder him in bed, but she is desolate when she thinks Andronico has betrayed her. Katsuli sings with a most affecting passion, combined with tenderness.

Mary-Ellen Nesi makes a strong Andronico, the part written for Senesino. She is rich-toned, as at home in powerful accompanied recitative as in the semiquaver runs of 'Più d'una tigre'. Irini Karaianni is attractively smoky in her *siciliano*; lovely clarinets but here, as elsewhere, the continuo is inaudible in places. Nicholas Spanos as Tamerlano, 'Scythian Shephearde' though he be, is properly imperial, and he dispatches the coloratura of his last aria with an appropriately wild brilliance. Petros Magoulas has the right bluffness for Leone.

Apart from the problem of balance, there is nothing but praise for George Petrou and his period-instrument orchestra. Just to hear the swelling on a sustained bass note (in the Overture and in Tamerlano's second aria) is to be reassured that all will be well. All is indeed well, and this recording is a most rewarding surprise.

Tamerlano   **P**
Monica Bacelli *mez* Tamerlano **Thomas Randle** *ten*
Bajazet **Elizabeth Norberg-Schulz** *sop* Asteria
Graham Pushee *counterten* Andronicus **Anna**
Bonitatibus *sop* Irene **Antonio Abete** *bass* Leone
The English Concert / Trevor Pinnock
Stage director **Jonathan Miller**
Video director **Helga Dubnyicsek**
ArtHaus Musik **DVD** 100 702 (323' · 16:9 · 2.0 &
5.1 · 0 · N). Includes documentaries and interviews   (F)

This is an uncommonly interesting examination of how a great Handel opera may be performed without insisting that only Baroque
specialists need apply. Some of the singers
here aren't obvious Handelians: Elizabeth
Norberg-Schulz has something of the attack
and occasionally the cutting edge of a lyric-
dramatic soprano, while Thomas Randle quite
often puts his voice under pressure in response
to the extreme demands of Handel's first and
most intensely dramatic major tenor role. And
yet one hardly ever wishes for more 'authentic'
voices. Both singers are very musical, well
aware of the requirements of Handel's style;
both, especially Randle, are highly accomplished actors – it's a minor but significant
point that when either of them was on screen
I neither watched nor needed the subtitles.
Both, not wholly irrelevantly, are strikingly
handsome.

That they can be so effective is largely due to
Jonathan Miller's very plain but highly intelligent
production, to Trevor Pinnock's alert and sympathetic direction and to the wonderfully intimate theatre at Bad Lauchstadt where the opera
was filmed as part of the 50th Halle Handel Festival in 2001. The set is basic – a few mottled gold
panels – the costumes are sumptuous, but in a
theatre this size everyone in the audience can see
facial expressions and the slightest gestures, and
Miller has concentrated his direction on this. The
result, at such a moment as when Bajazet and his
daughter Asteria resolve on suicide rather than
further humiliation by Tamerlano, is intensely
moving, as is the exquisite duet in which Asteria
and her lover Andronico vow that their love will
even survive her death.

Handelian voices or no, it is in short an utterly
Handelian performance. The orchestra is splendid and Pinnock's pacing of the drama ideal.

Teseo, HWV9

Teseo   **P**
Eirian James *mez* Teseo **Julia Gooding** *sop* Agilea
Della Jones *mez* Medea **Derek Lee Ragin**
counterten Egeo **Catherine Napoli** *sop* Clizia
Jeffrey Gall *counterten* Arcane **François Bazola** *bar*
Sacerdote di Minerva **Les Musiciens du Louvre /**
Marc Minkowski
Erato ② 2292 45806-2 (148' · DDD · T/t)   (M)

Teseo was Handel's third opera for London,
given at the beginning of 1713. Exceptionally,
its libretto was based on a French original,

written by Quinault for Lully; it's a spectacular
piece, in five acts, with Medea (after the events
of *Médée*) and Theseus (before the events of
Hippolyte or the Ariadne operas) as its central
characters. It's Medea who, as slighted lover
and jealous sorceress, provides the principal
musical thrills; but the score is, in any case, an
unusually rich and inventive one, with much
colourful orchestral writing even before she
turns up at the beginning of Act 2. When she
does, she introduces herself with a *Largo* aria,
'Dolce riposo', of a kind unique to Handel in its
depth of poetic feeling, with a vocal line full of
bold leaps above throbbing strings and an oboe
obbligato; but, lest we should think her docile,
Medea hints at her true colours in the ensuing
C minor aria, and by the end of the act she's
singing furious recitative and fiery, incisive
lines – real sorceress music. Her biggest scene
comes at the start of the final act, a *Presto*
vengeance aria, packed with raging rapid semiquavers. Handel scored the opera for a more
varied orchestra than usual; there are recorders, flutes, oboes, bassoons and trumpets called
for. The arias themselves tend to be rather
shorter than usual for Handel. The work needs
first-rate singing, and by and large receives it
here. The role of Medea falls to Della Jones, a
singer with a superb technique and a remarkable ability to identify with the role; she truly
lives Medea's part and brings to it great
resources of spirit and technique. Except when
allowed to play too fast, too loudly or too
coarsely, the Musiciens du Louvre are impressive. Several numbers are accompanied with
only a continuo instrument, to good effect.
The recitative always moves well, and
appoggiaturas are duly observed.

Tolomeo, re di Egitto, HWV25

Tolomeo
Ann Hallenberg *sop* Tolomeo **Karina Gauvin** *sop*
Seleuce **Pietro Spagnoli** *bar* Araspe **Anna**
Bonitatibus *mez* Elisa **Romina Basso** *mez* Alessandro
Il Complesso Barocco / Alan Curtis *hpd*
Archiv ③ 477 7106AH3 (148' · DDD · S/T/t/N)
   (F)OO➔

Tolomeo was the last opera Handel wrote for the
Royal Academy of Music before the opera company dissolved in 1728. It is a fine work that
combines pastoral charm with some powerfully
melodramatic scenes. The best known aria is
'Non lo dirò col labbro' (famous in Somervell's
arrangement 'Silent Worship'), here sung
sweetly by Romina Basso.

There is not a weak link in this superb cast,
with all the singers perfect for the vocal and
dramatic properties of their roles. Ann Hallenberg's supple coloratura is perfectly aligned with
dramatic awareness and melodic sensibility in
numerous accompanied recitatives and arias: the
sleep scene in Act 1 is beautifully judged and the
hedonistic *accompagnato* that precedes 'Stile
amare' is gripping. Anna Bonitatibus's singing is

magnificent, and her ornamentation and cadenza are fabulous. Pietro Spagnoli sings the tyrant Araspe firmly but one also feels a degree of sympathy for his hopeless infatuation with Ptolemy's wife Seleuce. Karina Gauvin's singing is dramatic and colourful: her interplay with two recorders in 'Fonti amiche' is simple yet ravishing and the hushed 'Dite, che fa' (with muted strings and offstage echoes from Ptolemy) is utterly gorgeous.

Alan Curtis's recent Handel opera recordings have been admirable in patches but flawed by inconsistent casts and occasionally weedy instrumental playing. It is a delight to hear the Italian-based American harpsichordist and Il Complesso Barocco back on top-notch form in this delectable performance. The overture oozes with charisma and the orchestral playing is beautifully paced and articulated. Each ritornello shows finesse and a deep-rooted fondness for the subtleties in Handel's writing. Recitatives are never sluggish but Curtis does not force proceedings unnaturally, allowing the language and rhetoric enough space to work their magic. He has all the energy and dynamism necessary but also realises that courtliness and elegance are vital elements of Handel's music. All in all, this is a perfect Handel opera recording.

Howard Hanson   American 1896-1981

Born in Nebraska to Swedish parents, Hanson studied piano, trombone and cello in New York. He became director of the Eastman School at the University of Rochester (1924-64), where he was an influential teacher and founded the Institute of American Music; he also promoted modern American music through his work as a conductor. To celebrate the 50th anniversary of the Boston Symphony Orchestra, Serge Koussevitzky commissioned Hanson's Symphony No 2, the 'Romantic', and premiered it in November 1930. This work was to become Hanson's best known. Among his works are seven symphonies, symphonic poems, choral pieces, chamber and piano music and songs.

Symphonies

Symphony No 1 in E minor, 'Nordic', Op 21. Merry Mount Suite. Pan and the Priest, Op 26. Rhythmic Variations on Two Ancient Hymns
Nashville Symphony Orchestra /
Kenneth Schermerhorn
Naxos 8 559072 (61' · DDD)   ⓈB►

The *Nordic* Symphony was completed when Hanson was in Rome studying with Respighi – stylistically it brings Sibelius south to Italy. The Nashville performance can be compared with the Seattle orchestra under that fine Hanson interpreter, Gerard Schwarz. Schermerhorn is more spacious, taking a good two minutes longer overall – no bad thing in such hyperactive music, as it constantly strives towards the next climax.

Schwarz is faster in the final *Allegro* but both performances are exciting and well recorded: the issue is settled by coupling and price.

There are many attractive features in the *Merry Mount Suite* – Charleston syncopation in the 'Children's Dance' and characteristic Hanson harmony oscillating between two chords at the start of the ecstatic 'Love Duet'. All supremely operatic, but the stage work still remains in limbo. The least-known piece here is the *Rhythmic Variations*, considered lost until recently, and cited as such in the *New American Grove*. This seems distinctly careless of someone, since Hanson recorded this late work himself in 1977. It's serenely spacious, utterly diatonic but no great rediscovery. *Pan and the Priest*, a vivid symphonic poem reaching pagan intensity, completes a bargain Hanson package that's well recorded, too.

Symphony No 2, 'Romantic'. Merry Mount – Suite. Bold Island Suite. Fanfare for the Signal Corps
Cincinnati Pops Orchestra / Erich Kunzel
Telarc CD80649 (66' · DDD)   ⒻB►

Hanson was a skilled conductor and his recordings for Mercury are indispensable documents, though one's listening pleasure is hampered somewhat by the Eastman-Rochester Orchestra's lack of tonal weight and refinement. Hanson's lush, neo-romantic style demands richer, sweeter sounds. Luckily, that's just what the Cincinnati Pops Orchestra offer.

Interpretatively speaking, it seems that Kunzel has made a close study of Hanson's performances, for his approach is similarly incisive. Indeed, Kunzel's *Romantic* Symphony may be tauter and more propulsive than Hanson's own. Even the lyrical pages unfold with a sense of resolve and the conductor's refusal to draw out the rhetorical, brassy outbursts of the Symphony's outer movements mitigates the music's occasional tendency towards pomposity.

Another reason to favour the Telarc disc is that it includes the premiere recording of the *Bold Island* Suite (1961), an atmospheric, tuneful and typically clear-headed tone-poem. Warmly recommended to devotees of orchestral Americana.

Additional recommendation

Symphony No 2
Coupled with **Barber** Violin Concerto
St Louis SO / Slatkin
EMI 747850-2 (68 · DDD)   ⓂB►
  A beautifully shaped performance, played with restrained passion, and coupled with an elegant reading of the Barber (with Elmar Oliveira).

Solo Piano Works

Sonata in A minor, Op 11. Two Yuletide Pieces, Op 19. Poèmes érotiques, Op 9. Three Miniatures,

Op 12. Three Etudes, Op 18. Enchantment.
For the First Time. Slumber Song
Thomas Labé pf
Naxos 8 559047 (76' · DDD)   ⑤🅑➔

Admirers of Hanson's *Romantic* Symphony will surely devour this collection, which includes unknown and unpublished music. A first impression is that the earliest works here, written around 1920, have the sort of ecstatic luxuriance that might be expected of a pupil of Respighi. But this influence came later since Hanson didn't start his three-year residence in Rome until 1921. There's a Nordic, Sibelian intensity about his whole approach, although the fulsome piano style clearly stems from Liszt.

The earliest piece is probably the *Slumber Song*, a pure salon morsel, and the latest is the suite *For the First Time*. The three *Poèmes érotiques* (the fourth has disappeared) are what Hanson called his 'first studied attempt at psychological writing'. They are powerful in a surging melodic style where in several pieces the climaxes stem from an almost Tchaikovskian cathartic need to unburden tensions.

The striking three-movement Sonata (1918) has had to be completed from the composer's shorthand by Thomas Labé since it was never published, although Hanson performed it in 1919. The vivid improvisatory keyboard writing, at times extravagantly rhetorical, causes Labé to hit the piano rather hard in the last two movements. One can understand his enthusiasm, but there are times when a little more *cantabile* might have helped. However, nothing must detract from the real service that this CD does in bringing this music to public attention for the first time.

Karl Amadeus Hartmann

German 1905-1963

Hartmann numbered Hermann Scherchen and Anton Webern among his teachers. After the fall of Hitler, Hartmann was one of the few prominent surviving anti-fascists in Bavaria whom the post-war Allied administration could appoint to a position of responsibility. In 1945 he became a dramaturg at the Bavarian State Opera and there, as one of the few internationally recognised figures who had survived untainted by any collaboration with the Nazi regime, he became a vital figure in the rebuilding of (West) German musical life. He started the Musica Viva festival in Munich to present music that had been banned during the Nazi years, and most of his published works date from after this period. Among his works are a cycle of eight symphonies, several concertos and vocal music including a chamber opera Simplicius Simplicissimus (1949).

Concerto funebre

Concerto funebre[a]. Two Solo Violin Suites.
Two Solo Violin Sonatas

Alina Ibragimova vn [a]**Britten Sinfonia**
Hyperion CDA67547 (81' · DDD)   ⑤🅞🅞🅑➔

It is such an obvious idea to combine Hartmann's *Concerto funebre* (1939, rev 1959) with the four unaccompanied works from 1927 that it's surprising that no company has thought of it before now. The Suites and Sonatas are not well known, not even being performed until the mid-1980s. Hartmann composed them while still a student with his mature style some years away, yet their muscularity, contrapuntal and harmonic élan and the sense of self-belief they exude show them to be products of a formidable, free-thinking creator. Ibragimova proves an ideal exponent, her tempi free and elastic (and mostly quite quick). Her fluency and flexibility pay great dividends time and again, as in the First Suite's central Rondo or concluding Ciaconna or the Second Suite's second span, *Fliessend*. Hyperion's soundpicture is natural.

Ibragimova's fiercely clear-eyed account of the *Concerto funebre* – alive to the music's expressive demands as well as its dynamic markings – faces stiff competition but need not fear comparison with any of the dozen or so rival accounts. Her technique is formidable to say the least and if marginal preferance is for Isabelle Faust (Harmonia Mundi), Ibragimova is on her shoulder, although Hyperion's couplings and recording quality, to say nothing of the excellent Britten Sinfonia, deserve a share in the plaudits. Recommended.

Orchestral works

Symphony No 4. Concerto funebre[a].
Chamber Concerto[b]
[a]**Isabelle Faust** vn [b]**Paul Meyer** cl [b]**Petersen Quartet**
(Conrad Muck, Gernot Sussmuth vns Friedemann Weigle va Hans-Jakob Eschenburg vc)
Munich Chamber Orchestra / Christoph Poppen
ECM New Series 465 779-2 (78' · DDD)   ⑤🅑➔

When Hartmann opted for internal exile during the Nazi era, he took with him some key influences from the free musical world. Beam up around 0'33" into the third movement of the 1939 *Concerto funebre* and you have a virtual quote from the first movement of Bartók's 1934 Fifth String Quartet. Hartmann completed his Chamber Concerto for Clarinet, String Quartet and String Orchestra in 1935, seven years after Bartók wrote his Fourth Quartet – which in turn barges headlong into Hartmann's second movement (an unmistakable reference to the Quartet's finale).

In the Chamber Concerto the melodic and structural profile of the first movement follows the profile of Kodály's 1933 *Dances of Galánta*. The language of the work is Magyar-inspired (even aside from the *Galánta* references) and the scoring lively and luminous.

The *Concerto funebre* opens with a quotation (fully acknowledged this time) of the Hussite chorale 'Ye Who are God's Warriors', best known to Brits for its use in Smetana's *Má vlast*. The reference commemorates the Nazi betrayal of Czechoslovakia, though Hartmann's anger finds controlled expression in the *Allegro di molto* third movement.

The Fourth Symphony is scored for strings, and frames a lively *Allegro di molto* with two profound *Adagios* that, again, draw you in by virtue of their intense arguments. All three performances do Hartmann proud. Isabelle Faust's eloquent playing of the *Concerto funebre* draws maximum effect from extremes in mood and temperature and outplays her rivals. With fine sound and programming, this is the ideal Hartmann primer.

Complete Works with String Quartet
Doelen Quartet (Frank de Groot, Maartje Kraan *vns* Karin Dolman *va* Hans Woudenberg *vc*) with
Arjan Woudenberg *cl* **Wilbert Grootenboer** *perc*
Sinfonia Rotterdam / Conrad van Alphen
Cybele ③ KIG001 (3h 4' · DDD/DSD) Ⓕ▶

Hartmann's music involving string quartet is spread unevenly throughout his career, the *Little Concerto* and First Quartet written during the composition of the Chamber Concerto (1930-35), which is in truth a clarinet concerto, and the Second Quartet following in 1945-46 (revised 1948). The musical novelty here is the bright and vivid single-span *Little Concerto* for quartet and single percussionist (1931-32), receiving – astonishingly – its premiere recording here. The Doelen Quartet and Wilbert Grootenboer do it proud.

The Doelen Quartet also give polished performances of the numbered quartets: their taut, driven approach and their intensity are rewarding, especially in No 2, Hartmann's chamber masterpiece. Yet the First (1933) emerges here truly as a prize-winning work – the title *Carillon* derived from the Belgian competition it won in 1935. The Doelen are relatively minor players in the Chamber Concerto, the focus squarely on the clarinet. Suffice it to say Arjan Woudenberg acquits himself superbly.

The set is the first in a new series, 'Artists in Speech'. For German speakers and scholars of this composer, the spoken extras may be the main attraction here. These account for over half the playing time, comprising Hartmann himself speaking in 1962 about his life, Schoenberg, *Concerto funebre*, opera and 'Art and Politics', plus reminiscences from his wife Elisabeth (recorded privately in 1994) and son Richard. Sadly, no English versions or transcripts are available. Sound quality throughout is very fine, even with the older spoken items. A fascinating issue.

Hamilton Harty   Irish 1879-1941

Best known today for his 'big-band' versions of Handel's music, Hamilton Harty was a prolific composer as well as a conductor of renown (he was conductor of the Hallé Orchestra from 1920). His large output, written in a lush, late-Romantic style, embraces symphonies, tone-poems (including his most popular work, With the Wild Geese), a violin concerto (first performed by Szigeti), a piano concerto, songs and a cantata. Much of his music is available for download from www.chandos.net

---

Orchestral works

Piano Concerto[a]. A Comedy Overture. Fantasy Scenes (from an Eastern Romance)
[a]**Peter Donohoe** *pf*
Ulster Orchestra / Takuo Yuasa
Naxos 8 557731 (55' · DDD) Ⓢ▶

Harty wrote his Piano Concerto in 1922 and gave the first performance the following year with Beecham at the helm of the Hallé Orchestra. Unashamedly indebted to Tchaikovsky and Rachmaninov (the finale even boasts a near-crib from the latter's Second Concerto), it's a thoroughly endearing, red-blooded affair, but not without its occasional longueurs.

Or at least that's how it seemed up until now. Peter Donohoe and Takuo Yuasa drive a truly propulsive (and, it must be said, purposeful) course through both outer movements. The piano sometimes sounds a little tired but Donohoe's bravura is frequently jaw-dropping and there's no lack of enthusiasm or sensitivity about the orchestral support. A refreshing and instructive display.

The Concerto is preceded by a similarly mobile, mostly spick-and-span account of Harty's delightful *A Comedy Overture* of 1906 and what is the first commercial recording of the *Fantasy Scenes (from an Eastern Romance)*. These appeared in 1919 and comprise four fetching vignettes which nod appreciatively towards the likes of Rimsky-Korsakov, Borodin and Balakirev; Yuasa and company do them proud. Nor can there be any major grumbles about the recording, which is commendably truthful. Altogether a most enjoyable release and well worth its modest asking price.

Jonathan Harvey   British b1939

Harvey studied at Cambridge, privately with Erwin Stein and Hans Keller, and with Babbitt at Princeton. He has taught at the universities of Southampton and Sussex. His early music shows enthusiasms ranging from Britten and Messiaen to Stockhausen and Davies, but since the early 1970s he has developed a more integrated style and has emerged as an outstanding composer of electronic music (Mortuos plango, vivos voco, 1980). In the 1980s Harvey produced much music at IRCAM after receiving an invitation from Pierre Boulez to work there. From 2005 to 2008, he held the post of Composer in Association with the BBC Scottish Symphony Orchestra and in 2009 was Composer in Residence at the Huddersfield Contemporary Music Festival.

Death of Light/Light of Death

Death of Light/Light of Death. Advaya. Ricercare una melodia (performed on oboe). Ricercare una melodia (performed on trumpet). Tombeau de Messiaen. Wheel of Emptiness
Ictus / Georges-Elie Octors
Cyprès CYP5604 (77' · DDD)   Ⓕ

Three of the compositions on this disc offer ideal introductions to Jonathan Harvey's work, showing how music centring on a single line, or instrument, can evolve into a potently imaginative discourse when that line or instrument is manipulated electronically. In *Ricercare una melodia* the moment of revelation comes when the electronic material opens out a much wider registral spectrum than that 'naturally' available to the trumpet or oboe. Something similar happens both in the brief *Tombeau de Messiaen*, where the interaction of piano and electronics unleashes a torrential, joyously uninhibited commemoration of the French master, and also in *Advaya*. All three of these works have been recorded before, but Harvey enthusiasts should still find it difficult to resist this new release, not only for its outstanding recording quality, but for the interest and substance of the programme as a whole. The disc ends with the most striking evidence of Harvey's versatility. *Death of Light/Light of Death* is scored for five performers, without electronics, but with the harpist doubling on tam-tam. It offers music of an intensity and, in the end, ceremonial solemnity which few composers today can match. With performances of supreme technical assurance and magnificently lucid sound, this is an outstanding disc in every respect.

Madonna of Winter and Spring

Madonna of Winter and Spring[a].
Percussion Concerto[b]. Song Offerings[c]
[c]**Penelope Walmsley-Clark** sop [b]**Peter Prommel** perc [ab]**Netherlands Radio Philharmonic Orchestra / Peter Eötvös;** [c]**London Sinfonietta / George Benjamin**
Nimbus NI5649 (78' · DDD · T/t)   Ⓕ ⚫⚫

This is an impressive disc indeed: a strong cast, a varied programme, and music of great integrity and beauty. In relation to many British scores that have garnered recent critical praise, Harvey more than holds his own. The three pieces – two of them recorded here for the first time – date from the 1980s and '90s. Each introduces a 'foreign' element to the orchestra in a slightly different way. There are elements of the competitive streak between soloist and orchestra in the Percussion Concerto; in *Song Offerings* relations between the two elements are more symbiotic, as one might expect; but in *Madonna of Winter*

and Spring, the most extended piece here, the 'foreign' element is assumed by synthesisers and electronics. This piece, in particular, sums up Harvey's preoccupations: the interaction of the different media, and the programmatic elements derived from the composer's faith.

At intervals the orchestra recedes, creating electro-acoustic 'windows' reminiscent of similarly mixed-media scores (Birtwistle and Boulez come to mind); at others, individual instruments appear in a quasi-soloistic context, adding an extra dimension to the texture. Moreover, the quality of these interpretations gives this recording a special appeal. The electro-acoustic element is well captured, and conveys something of the spatial imaging mentioned in the composer's booklet-notes.

All three pieces receive committed, dynamic interpretations: if only contemporary music could always enjoy such advocacy.

Body Mandala / Timepieces

Tranquil Abiding[b]. Body Mandala[b]. Timepieces[bc]. White as Jasmine[ab]. …towards a Pure Land[b]
[a]**Anu Komsi** sop **BBC Scottish Symphony Orchestra / [b]Ilan Volkov, [c]Stefan Solymon**
NMC NMCD141 (80' · DDD)   Ⓕ ⚫⚫⚫⚫▷

There is so much to praise about the works on this CD that it's hard to know where to begin. Jonathan Harvey's music juxtaposes moments of disarming simplicity, of naivety almost, with others of considerable sophistication and intricacy. Often these are held in fine balance, the former giving the listener an accessible entry-point or anchor, and allowing the latter considerable scope for development within an audibly logical discourse. The opening premise of both *Tranquil Abiding* and *Body Mandala* are cases in point: in the first, an alternation of two sonorities carries the piece forwards inexorably to its conclusion. By contrast, the arc structure of *…towards a Pure Land* engenders considerable discontinuity. Each piece inhabits its own space. The virtuosity of Harvey's orchestration is breathtaking at times (try the conclusion of the second of the three *Timepieces*, for example), but it is virtuosity in the service of deeply intelligent musical argument; there's nothing merely flashy or self-serving.

Not surprisingly to those familiar with Harvey's concerns, all but one of these pieces explore different facets of spirituality, particularly those drawn from Eastern religions. Perhaps the most immediately involving is *White as Jasmine*, based on texts by a 12th-century Hindu saint. Here, soprano Anu Komsi delivers a superbly controlled performance of great vocal beauty. In her first entry, she is virtually indistinguishable from the surrounding instruments (and it's satisfying, by the way, to hear singing in which each pitch can be clearly discerned, vibrato notwithstanding). But the musicianship here transcends questions of technique: all the participants deserve equal credit for their involvement in a richly rewarding project. A worthy winner of a *Gramophone* Award for Contemporary music.

Passion and Resurrection

Passion and Resurrection
Carolyn Foulkes, Alison Smart sops **Kim Porter** contr **Andrew Mackenzie-Wicks** ten **Stuart Macintyre** bar **BBC Singers; Sinfonia 21 / Martin Neary**
Sargasso ② SCD28052 (85' · DDD · T)
Recorded live 1999   Ⓕ

Were the audience warned that they'd be called on to lend their voices to this performance, recorded by the BBC in 1999? This score is as much a 'liturgical action' as an oratorio (or 'church opera', as it's described in the booklet). It was written for a community celebration at Winchester Cathedral, and most of the text is a translation of extant Passion Plays.

Harvey's ability to combine chant-like idioms (and actual plainchant hymnody) within a predominantly atonal context is quite uncanny. The work opens with a familiar passage from the Book of Common Prayer which gradually morphs into more angular cadences, but there's nothing wilful in the transformation.

The libretto faithfully follows Christ's Passion and Resurrection. In the Passion men's voices and low brass predominate, and the writing is harsher, more angular, the treatment of pacing more earth-bound. The Resurrection sequence points out the greater involvement of women (through their voices); the register is consistently higher, the sense of time more suspended. There's little abstraction in the score – in fact, Harvey allows himself a surprising degree of literal-mindedness: you can even hear the nails being driven in at the Crucifixion.

The action is set in a most direct way, yet never 'talks down' to the congregation or the listener, and the performance is dramatic and well shaped. The BBC Singers and Sinfonia 21 have plenty of body; the strings have much to do; and the brass interventions are most striking. The postlude is quite literally 'recessional', as very low instruments gradually disperse throughout the church of St John's, Smith Square: this spatial element stands in for many of Harvey's preoccupations, and the effect is nicely rendered by the engineers.

Joseph Haydn   Austrian 1732-1809

Haydn's father was a wheelwright and the village sexton. Joseph was the second of his 12 children. His brother Michael, born five years later, also became a composer. Where did the music come from? Haydn's father had taught himself to play the harp by ear but otherwise, like Handel, there was nothing in his ancestry to indicate a musical career. His first lessons were from a cousin, a choral director, and he was only eight when admitted as a chorister to St Stephen's Cathedral in Vienna.

After leaving the choir when his voice broke, he was thrown back on his own resources, borrowing money to rent an attic where he could practise the harpsichord. He made a thorough study of CPE Bach's keyboard works, read as much musical theory as he could absorb and had a few lessons from the then famous Nicolò Porpora, an Italian composer who was living in Vienna. His first compositions began to get noticed and he was engaged as music director and composer to the Austrian Count Maximilian von Morzin at his estate in Lukavec.

In 1760 Haydn married – one of the biggest mistakes of his life. He'd been in love with one of his pupils in Vienna. When she became a nun he married her sister. She had no love of music, no appreciation of her husband's greatness and even used his manuscripts as hair-curlers. He was separated from her for most of his life but still sent her money. It's said that, though he corresponded with her, he never opened her letters.

The turning-point in his life came in 1761 when Prince Anton Esterházy, who'd heard one of Haydn's symphonies at Lukavec, invited him to become second Kapellmeister at his estate in Eisenstadt. Though the Prince died the following year, he was succeeded by his brother Nicholas – the fanatical music-loving 'Nicholas the Magnificent' who entertained on a truly lavish scale and built one of the most splendid castles in Europe, comprising a 400-seat theatre.

Here Haydn remained until 1790 and it was here that he composed most of his 83 string quartets, 80 of his 104 symphonies, nearly all his operas as well as keyboard works – let alone a huge amount of music written for the Prince to play himself. Every week, Haydn and his orchestra had to present two operas and two concerts plus daily chamber music for the Prince. His salary was generous and Haydn was encouraged to compose as he wished. As he himself wrote: 'I was cut off from the world, there was no one to confuse or torment me, and I was forced to become original.' The members of the orchestra loved him (hence his nickname 'Papa Haydn') and Haydn even got on well with the Prince – it must have seemed like a dream.

By 1781 Haydn was acknowledged throughout Europe as a genius, honoured by all. He made only brief annual visits to his beloved Vienna but on one of them he met Mozart for the first time. Mozart was 25, nearly a quarter of a century younger than Haydn. The two became close friends, for Mozart admired Haydn's music (his first six string quartets are dedicated to him) while the ever-generous Haydn described Mozart as 'the greatest composer known to me either in person or by name' and set about promoting Mozart's works rather than his own. The two learnt much from each other.

Prince Nicholas died in 1790 and was succeeded by his son Paul Anton who was more interested in paintings than music. Still, an annuity of 1000 florins kept Haydn as the nominal Kapellmeister to the Esterházys, allowing him to live permanently in Vienna. The same year, the enterprising impresario Johann Peter Salomon invited Haydn to London for a series of concerts. He was feted wherever he went and returned to Vienna 18 months later with a small fortune.

Haydn returned to London for further triumphs in 1794 and later in the year returned to Eszterháza. Paul Anton had died, succeeded by his son (another Prince Nicholas) who planned to revive the Haydn orchestra. As Kapellmeister, Haydn now turned his attention to choral works. From this period come the six late Masses, The Creation and The Seasons.

In his mid-sixties, Haydn's health began to fail and he resigned as Kapellmeister in 1802, though Prince Nicholas II increased his pension to 2300 florins and paid all his medical bills so that Haydn should suffer no financial burden. Haydn made his last public appearance in 1808 at a concert given in his honour conducted by Salieri.

In 1809 Vienna capitulated to Napoleon who ordered a guard of honour to be placed round Haydn's house. When Haydn died, the music at his funeral service was the Requiem by his favourite composer, Mozart.

Cello Concertos

No 1 in C, HobVIIb/1; **No 2** in D, HobVIIb/2

Cello Concertos Nos 1 & 2
Academy of St Martin in the Fields /
Mstislav Rostropovich vc
EMI 567234-2 (49' · ADD). Recorded 1975   Ⓕ **OO**

This deserves a place on any collector's shelf. With Rostropovich directing from the bow the ASMF sounds a little less sturdy than usual, a little more lithe in the First Concerto. The scale of its first movement is little short of perfection: everything a *Moderato* should be, with Rostropovich humming along nonchalantly in its second theme. He's leisurely in the *Adagio*, playing it as an extended meditation which exists almost outside time. Without ever losing the life of the melodic line, Rostropovich progresses as slowly as it's humanly possible to do without total stasis; and, to wonderfully joyful effect, breaks all records for speed in the finale. Every note, every sequential phrase is there in its place, secured by glintingly true intonation and needle-sharp dramatic timing. The almost complete absence of physical stick and finger sound which Rostropovich and his engineers manage between them makes the latter two movements of the Second Concerto a most pleasing experience. Rostropovich takes deep, long breaths: the surface of his slow movement is glassy, every fragment of bowing and phrasing given the microscopic hairpin treatment. For his deep, instinctive understanding of scale, and for Britten's cadenzas, many collectors' preferences in these concertos will remain with Rostropovich.

Cello Concertos – Nos 1 & 2; No 4 in D, HobVIIb/4
(formerly attributed to Haydn)
Gautier Capuçon vc

Mahler Chamber Orchestra / Daniel Harding
Virgin Classics 545560-2 (66' · DDD)   Ⓕ **OOD**➔

Still in his early twenties, Gautier Capuçon plays the cello with the control and wisdom of a much older musician. The lightness of his touch and the consistent clarity of his bow strokes are quite admirable in themselves, but when combined with an uncanny sweetness of tone in the higher registers they're breathtaking. These qualities suit the two Haydn concertos very well indeed and bestow upon the modest little anonymous D major Concerto unexpected dignity and charm.

Daniel Harding, conducting the Mahler Chamber Orchestra, opts for *galant* rather than driven tempi. The scale of his orchestral forces enables him to establish a relationship with the soloist more akin to chamber music than is usually heard in these works. There's lightness of articulation throughout, conveying both intimacy and vitality.

Their reading of the C major Concerto, while not strongly imprinted, is truly Classical in its delicacy and refinement. It's shapely and spirited but never forced. It's the second item, the D major Haydn, which proves the highlight. In the opening movement Capuçon conjures the darting image of a watersprite, who can nevertheless steal time in all the right moments. The double-stops are dizzying and the chords in the poetic cadenza are exquisitely rolled. The *Adagio* takes on the aura of a meditation; Capuçon seems detached while gently supported by the orchestra, in a reverie of his own. When it comes, the elaboration that serves in the place of a cadenza is perfectly attuned to the moment. The final *Allegro* is never allowed to go 'peasant', remaining instead in the aristocrat's drawing room where it sparkles and glows.

Keyboard Concertos

Piano Concertos – in F, HobXVIII/3; in G, HobXVIII/4; in D, HobXVIII/11
Norwegian Chamber Orchestra /
Leif Ove Andsnes pf
EMI 556960-2 (54' · DDD)   Ⓕ **OOO**➔

 Like Emanuel Ax on Sony, Leif Ove Andsnes confines himself to the three concertos that have been fully authenticated. Had the works generally known as 'the Haydn piano concertos' been these three and not a rag-bag of juvenilia and pieces attributed to Haydn, the canon might have been more highly thought. But even the slightest work can dazzle and delight if it's performed as well as these are here. Where Ax's performances have a slightly monochrome feel, everything tapped out (there's much audible fingerwork) with the same well-adjusted mix of energy and sensibility, Andsnes's playing is altogether more various, while perfectly at one with itself stylistically. Ax's Franz Liszt Chamber Orchestra is the more idiomatic of the two ensembles in the

D major Concerto's *Rondo all'Ungarese*, but that's about the only occasion on which it has the edge over Andsnes's stylish and highly articulate Norwegian Chamber Orchestra; and even here Andsnes himself scores points for a less noisy plunge into the interlude in D minor and a more sunlit and finely flighted way with the episode which follows. The Norwegian players are never afraid to play full out, a strategy which the explicit but carefully balanced recording is happy to underwrite. Thus the players make much of the 'look here, young man' chromaticisms in the first movement of the D major Concerto as the piano chatters irrepressibly on; and they contribute decisively to the superbly articulated – nay, revelatory – performance of the G major Concerto with which the disc begins. After a splendidly jaunty account of the first movement, Andsnes pushes this G major Concerto to its limits with a decidedly skilfully shaped account of the glooming C major slow movement and a dashing account of the concluding *Presto*. His playing of the *Largo cantabile* of the F major Concerto – the concerto's centrepiece and its *raison d'être* – is the very embodiment of sweetness and light. This is a simply marvellous disc.

Keyboard Concertos – in G, HobXVIII/4; in F,   P
HobXVIII/6[a]; in D, HobXVIII/11
Andreas Staier *fp* **Freiburg Baroque Orchestra /**
Gottfried von der Goltz [a]*vn*
Harmonia Mundi HMC90 1854 (64' · DDD)   ⒻOO

Many concertos are attributed to Haydn but these three are undisputedly authentic. The keyboard part in No 4 falls in a narrow compass; Andreas Staier introduces variety by ornamenting the slow movement and decorating fermatas in all movements. His embellishments are very good indeed, even if he is ornate in places. (If you dislike ornament, you should choose the Andsnes, who sticks to the letter and does so most artistically.) A rarity is No 6 for violin and keyboard, its outer movements the least interesting with sequential passages. The emotive slow movement (mostly a conversation between the two soloists) redeems matters and gives Gottfried von der Goltz a chance to show his mettle as a sensitive violinist.

In the finest work, No 11, the orchestral exposition is an ideal *Vivace*, the first theme lilting over repeated quavers generating the right degree of forward tension, and the bass line given its full due, oboes and horns colouring the texture tellingly. A similar degree of perception, with Staier's contribution equally telling, is heard throughout. The recording is expertly balanced and tonally truthful. An outstanding disc.

Trumpet Concerto, HobVIIe/1

Haydn Trumpet Concerto
Hummel Trumpet Concerto **Neruda** Trumpet
Concerto **Torelli** Trumpet Concerto, 'Estienne Roger'

Deutsche Kammerphilharmonie, Bremen /
Alison Balsom *tpt*
EMI 216213-0 (53' · DDD)   ⒻOOⒹ▸

Haydn and Hummel composed their concertos for Anton Weidinger's newfangled keyed trumpet, whose timbre was appreciably softer than the natural trumpet (contemporaries likened it to an oboe or clarinet). More than any performance, Alison Balsom brings out the mellow, even veiled, colouring of so much of the writing. Where clarion brilliance is in order she can peal out with the best of them. But what lingers in the memory is the lyrical grace of her phrasing, and her delicacy of shading.

In the entertaining Hummel Concerto, with its palpable Mozart cribs, she mingles tonal subtlety and swagger in the opening movement, spins a refined, beautifully modulated line in the slow movement, and makes the finale's pyrotechnics properly dazzling. The spruce Deutsche Kammerphilharmonie match her all the way in sensitivity and rhythmic verve.

Moving back in time, Balsom savours the bold, bugling fanfares of Torelli's miniature concerto and makes a persuasive case for a pleasant, if hardly distinctive, mid-18th-century concerto by the Czech Johann Baptist Neruda, written for the corno da caccia but forgivably pilfered by trumpeters hard-up for solo concertos. In sum, a stunning recital from a poet of this traditionally martial instrument.

Additional recommendation

Haydn Trumpet Concerto
Coupled with trumpet concertos by **Albinoni,**
Corelli, Hertel, Hummel, JM Molter, Mozart,
FX Richter, J Stamitz plus works by **JS Bach,**
Clarke and **Gounod**
Hardenberger *tpt* **Preston** *org*
ASMF / Marriner; LPO / Howarth; I Musici
Philips Duo ② 464 028-2PM2 (148' · DDD)   ⒶO
    Possibly the finest single collection of trumpet concertos in the catalogue. The trumpet playing on this disc is truly splendid and the accompaniments are distinguished and full of characterful detail.

Symphonies

No 1 in D; **No 2** in C; **No 3** in G; **No 4** in D; **No 5** in A; **No 6** in D, 'Le matin'; **No 7** in C, 'Le midi'; **No 8** in G, 'Le soir'; **No 9** in C; **No 10** in D; **No 11** in E flat; **No 12** in E; **No 13** in D; **No 14** in A; **No 15** in D; **No 16** in B flat; **No 17** in F; **No 18** in G; **No 19** in D; **No 20** in C; **No 21** in A; **No 22** in E flat, 'Philosopher'; **No 23** in G; **No 24** in D; **No 25** in C; **No 26** in D minor, 'Lamentatione'; **No 27** in G; **No 28** in A; **No 29** in E; **No 30** in C, 'Alleluja';

No 31 in D, 'Hornsignal'; **No 32** in C; **No 33** in C; **No 34** in D minor; **No 35** in B flat; **No 36** in E flat; **No 37** in C; **No 38** in C; **No 39** in G minor; **No 40** in F; **No 41** in C; **No 42** in D; **No 43** in E flat, 'Mercury';

No 44 in E minor, 'Irauer'; No 45 in F sharp minor, 'Farewell'; No 46 in B; No 47 in G, 'Palindrome'; No 48 in C, 'Maria Theresia'; No 49 in F minor, 'La Passione'; No 50 in C; No 51 in B flat; No 52 in C minor; No 53 in D, 'Imperiale';

No 54 in G; No 55 in E flat, 'Schoolmaster'; No 56 in C; No 57 in D; No 58 in F; No 59 in A, 'Fire'; No 60 in C, 'Il Distratto'; No 61 in D; No 62 in D; No 63 in C, 'La Roxelane'; No 64 in A, 'Tempora mutantur'; No 65 in A; No 66 in B flat; No 67 in F; No 68 in B flat; No 69 in C, 'Loudon'; No 70 in D; No 71 in B flat; No 72 in D; No 73 in D, 'La chasse'; No 74 in E flat; No 75 in D; No 76 in E flat; No 77 in B flat; No 78 in C minor; No 79 in F; No 80 in D minor; No 81 in G; No 82 in C, 'L'ours'; No 83 in G minor, 'La poule'; No 84 in E flat; No 85 in B flat, 'La Reine'; No 86 in D; No 87 in A; No 88 in G, 'Letter V'; No 89 in F; No 90 in C; No 91 in E flat; No 92 in G, 'Oxford'; No 93 in D; No 94 in G, 'Surprise'; No 95 in C minor; No 96 in D, 'Miracle'; No 97 in C; No 98 in B flat; No 99 in E flat; No 100 in G, 'Military'; No 101 in D, 'Clock'; No 102 in B flat; No 103 in E flat, 'Drumroll'; No 104 in D, 'London'.

Symphonies – box-sets

Symphonies – Nos 1-104; 'A' in B flat; 'B' in B flat.
Sinfonia concertante in B flat, HobI/105
Philharmonia Hungarica / Antál Dorati
Decca 478 1221DX33 (33 discs: ADD)
Recorded 1969-72   Ⓢ❍

Dorati's famous integral recording of all 106 symphonies now returns in a Decca bargain box. It remained for many years in the catalogue as the only complete set to contain everything Haydn wrote in this medium, including the Symphonies 'A' and 'B', omitted from the original numbering scheme because at one time they were not thought to be symphonies at all. The survey also encompasses additional alternative movements for certain works (notably Nos 53 and 103) and alternative complete versions of the *Philosopher* and *Roxelane* Symphonies (Nos 22 & 63), which are fascinating. The remastering confirms the excellence of the vintage Decca sound. No more needs to be said, except that the one minus point in these very convincing modern-instrument performances is Dorati's insistence on measured, often rustic tempi for the minuets. For those who can run to the complete series this is self-recommending – a source of inexhaustible pleasure.

Symphonies, Nos 1-104; 'A' in B flat; 'B' in B flat.
Sinfonia concertante in B flat, HobI/105. Violin
Concertos – in C, HobVIIa/1ª; in G, HobVIIa/4ª.
Overtures – La vera constanza; La fedeltà premiata.
March for the Royal Society of Musicians
ªRainer Küchl *vn* **Austro-Hungarian Haydn**
Orchestra / Adám Fischer
Brilliant Classics 99925 (33 discs: DDD)
From Nimbus originals recorded 1987-2001   Ⓢ❍❍
Also available on eight discs of MP3 files (320kbps)
on Nimbus NI1722

It was little short of tragic that the very last box of symphonies in Adám Fischer's Haydn series for Nimbus, Nos 21 to 39 plus the Symphonies 'A' and 'B', appeared just as the demise of that label was announced in January 2002. The final box was the finest of the series, but all too few copies reached the shops, making this 33-disc box covering all the symphonies very welcome indeed, even if over the 14 years that it took to complete the project, the quality and style varied.

That final box of 20 symphonies was a superb culmination to the project. Not only are they a fascinating sequence of works written in the 1760s when the young Haydn was busy experimenting, the performances are outstanding. They were recorded as recently as 2000 and 2001, and far more than the earliest recordings in the series, they take full note of period practice while staying faithful to modern instruments. More than ever one registers the individual virtuosity of the various soloists in the orchestra, often challenged to the limit by fast speeds. So a movement like the variation finale of No 31, the *Hornsignal*, features a sequence of brilliant soloists such as Haydn might have been writing for in his Esterházy orchestra – violin, cello, horn and so on, even double bass. It's a performance full of panache, with the four horns braying out superbly.

Other striking symphonies in the group include No 22, the *Philosopher*, with its extraordinary parts for two cors anglais. Also the *Alleluia* Symphony, No 30, with trumpets and drums dramatically added to the usual published scoring – brought in later, according to HC Robbins Landon, by Haydn as an option. The minor-key works in this last batch, such as the *Lamentatione*, No 26 in D minor, and best of all, No 39 in G minor, are fine examples of Haydn's *Sturm und Drang* manner, with Fischer heightening dynamic contrasts to good effect. No 39 brings an example of Fischer's mastery when he enhances the tension of the nervy opening and exaggerates the pauses; he's far more effective in that movement than Dorati .

While with those symphonies recorded at the beginning of the project, from 1987 to 1990, comparisons with the Dorati series have the merits of each balanced fairly evenly, the advantage certainly tips in favour of Fischer as the project developed. For the 'London' Symphonies, Nos 93-104, the first to be recorded, the Nimbus engineers – working in the very hall at the Esterházy Palace which Haydn used – produce rather washy sound, whereas the works recorded later benefit from a sharper focus. In those early recordings, too, the slow movements tend to be taken at the sort of broad speeds of tradition, with warmly expressive phrasing.

At that point, no doubt, Fischer was just beginning to woo his select band of Austrian and Hungarian musicians away from their usual Romantic manners. In his notes Fischer makes a point of describing the unfolding development of the project over 14 years. He becomes increasingly aware of historically informed style, notably in faster speeds for both slow movements and Minuets (which increasingly acquire a *scherzo*-like flavour), giving him a clear advantage over Dorati. Also the string playing comes closer to that found in period orchestras, with lighter phrasing and less marked use of vibrato.

That development is noticeable as early as the recordings made in 1994-95, when most of the *Sturm und Drang* symphonies were covered – broadly those in the late 40s and early 50s in the regular Breitkopf numbering. Finales in particular, taken fast, have all the bite and wildness one could want, with pinpoint attack. The very earliest symphonies in numerical order, Nos 1 to 20, were recorded early in the project between 1989 and 1991, with results that are more variable. The finale of No 12, for example, marked *Presto*, is taken surprisingly slowly, almost like a Minuet. No 13, very adventurously for that early period, uses four horns, yet because of the reverberant acoustic they don't ring out as prominently as those used in works such as the *Horn-signal*, recorded later.

Even in these early symphonies, recorded near the beginning of the project, the Trios in Minuets have solo strings, and regularly the vigour and thrust of *Allegros* is exhilarating, with rhythms lifted and admirably crisp ensemble.

This is a set guaranteed to encourage collectors to delve into works which from first to last convey the joy in creation that's the unfailing mark of this ever-welcoming master. Nimbus offers the cycle on eight discs of MP3 files, easily transferred for use with your iPod or computer.

Symphonies – Nos 1-104; 'A' in B flat; 'B' in B flat. Sinfonia concertante in B flat, HobI/105
Stuttgart Chamber Orchestra /
Dennis Russell Davies
Sony 88697 44331-2 (37 discs: DDD)   Ⓢ

Dennis Russell Davies and his Stuttgart musicians performed all 106 symphonies plus the *Sinfonia concertante* throughout Haydn year (2009) and Sony was on hand to record them. Of course, Dorati, Adám Fischer and Naxos's international congregation of musicians offer cycles, each with their advantages and disadvantages, at competitive price-points; so what does this brand new set have to offer?

The Stuttgart band comprises a string section that is compact enough to be wirily athletic when needs be but not so small that the sound becomes scrawny. To this is added a refulgent woodwind section complete with proud horns. The symphonies are presented in something approaching a putative chronological order, which is far removed from their numerical order: thus disc 1 contains Symphonies Nos 1, 37, 18 and 2. The discs are arranged into subgroups: early symphonies, *Sturm und Drang* works, 'London' Symphonies and so on.

The first thing of which one becomes aware is the presence of a harpsichord. This is more noticeable in some symphonies than others but it is there nevertheless, right up to Symphony

No 104. It's especially deleterious in, for example, the beautiful filigree variations of No 75's slow movement, whose muted orchestration is all but shattered by the unsubtle continuo.

The tempo of the opening movement of the First Symphony seems a touch cautious but the slow movement is taken at a brisk *andante* and the finale zips along amiably. In fact it's Davies's preference for careful speeds in opening movements that forms one of the major sticking points. Take Symphony No 69, for example, in which Haydn reimagines the world of the *Maria Theresia* Symphony (No 48) for a more decorous age: this is taken at a four-in-a-bar *allegro* rather than the prescribed two-in-a-bar *vivace*. Odd, as the earlier work is one of the most successful of these performances, played with a palpable sense of vigour and excitement. Interestingly Davies opts in No 48 for the later version with trumpets rather than the original scoring for high horns, whooping joyously in their upper register, a typical Haydn sound in his middle-period symphonies.

This reluctance to catch fire in opening movements afflicts the *Fire* Symphony (No 59) too, although Davies really lets his horns off the leash in the finale. The *Philosopher* Symphony (No 22) also has a sluggish opening movement – slow even by the standards of the marked *Adagio*, making it something of a trudge. The *Mercury* (No 43) is not conspicuously mercurial at the outset, although its finale fares better, and the march rhythms of No 47, the G major work that influenced Mozart so palpably, are too regimented, and the second subject's triplets don't really trip.

There are works, though, where the Stuttgarters really do hit the spot. The *Trauer* Symphony (No 44) receives a truly exciting performance, demonstrating also that Davies is ever alert to a sudden dynamic shift or a surprise accent. And it's not just the better-known works that go with the greatest swing: No 62, an intriguing assemblage of theatrical offcuts, really made me smile, while works such as the sublime No 42 and the outdoor finale of the almost entirely neglected No 71 demonstrate the pedigree of these fine wind-players. By the time they reach the 'Paris' Symphonies and their successors (Nos 88-90 especially) they're in a true purple patch in performances that can hold their own against many on record.

What's often missing, though, is the playfulness essential to Haydn's music, a trait that especially hobbles some of the 'London' Symphonies. While No 95 receives an all-round fine performance, the *London* Symphony itself (No 104) trots along largely humourlessly, and a valiant attempt at the finale of No 98 can't counterbalance its morose first movement. Of course, no one set of Haydn's symphonies is going to tick all of the boxes for all of the people all of the time. Dorati suffers from 40-year-old sound and stodgy tempi in minuets; Fischer's idiosyncrasies are beyond the pale for some; Naxos's set loses the consistency a single group of musicians would have provided. Perhaps Dennis Russell

Davies's Achilles heel is his cautiousness; nevertheless there's much to enjoy here.

Symphonies – No 49, 'La Passione'; No 80.   ☐
Violin Concerto, HobVIIa/1ᵃ
Freiburg Baroque Orchestra /
Gottfried von der Goltz ᵃvn
Harmonia Mundi HMX296 2029 (69' · DDD) Ⓜ ● ● ◗⁺

Symphonies – Nos 41; No 44, 'Trauer';   ☐
No 49, 'La Passione'
Arion Baroque Orchestra / Gary Cooper hpd
early-music.com EMCCD7769 (70' · DDD) Ⓕ ● ● ◗⁺

The Freiburg Baroque Orchestra headline with the C major Violin Concerto but their disc is all the more exciting for offering the first recording on period instruments of Symphony No 80. The Freiburgers are alive to this curious work's contradictions: the vehemence of the *Sturm und Drang* opening, giving way to the lopsided Ländler of the second subject; the wonky opening of the finale that keeps us guessing for ages where the downbeat actually falls. They also play the crucial second repeat in that finale, a musical joke that Mozart might have had in mind at the close of his late E flat Symphony, K543 (they omit the slow movement's second repeat though: a pity).

In *La Passione* the FBO come up against direct competition from Canadian ensemble Arion and British harpsichordist Gary Cooper. The readings are broadly similar: the Freiburg strings are by and large more secure and characterful, while Arion's tempi are brisker, responding well to the fury of the fast movements. The only caveat that may concern some listeners is the use of harpsichord continuo in both recordings (although it's mercifully absent from the FBO's No 80): Cooper's instrument especially makes the finale a most clattery affair.

Gottfried von der Goltz's reading of the C major Violin Concerto extracts maximum characterisation and contrast from this early work, rendering it a pleasing interlude between the two more fiercely individualistic symphonies.

Cooper gives us a decent reading of the *Trauer* Symphony along with the heinously neglected No 41. Cooper wins the day here, not least in the slow movement with Claire Guimond's rapt flute arabesques, and in the opening movement and the Trio with their horns whooping joyously in the top register.

'The Paris Symphonies'   ☐
Symphonies – No 82, 'L'ours'; No 83, 'La poule';
No 84; No 85, 'La Reine'; No 86; No 87
Concentus Musicus, Vienna /
Nikolaus Harnoncourt
Deutsche Harmonia Mundi ③ 82876 60602-2
(3h 6' · DDD) Ⓜ ● ●

When the members of a Parisian concert society commissioned a set of symphonies from Haydn in the mid-1780s they would have looked forward to receiving works of the most up-to-date and sophisticated kind by the genre's acknowledged master. The arrival of a recording of the 'Paris' Symphonies by Nikolaus Harnoncourt and the Vienna Concentus Musicus will have aroused a similar sense of anticipation in some and, just as Haydn must have surpassed expectations with his six superb creations, so the wonders of this three-disc set are surely more than even Harnoncourt fans can have hoped for.

(Three discs? Yes, Harnoncourt takes every repeat going, which means sonata-movement second halves, full sets of repeats for Minuets and Trios and even a repeat for No 85's slow introduction, with the result that most of the performances come in at just over half an hour.) But if this makes for one more disc than the norm, there is certainly no danger of the music outstaying its welcome. For the pre-Revolution Parisians these were grand works of powerful and unrelenting invention, and Harnoncourt's achievement is to remind us of the fact, revealing in these underrated masterpieces a brilliance and muscle that can almost make us forget 200 years of symphonic history.

For that alone we should be thankful, but these are also just about the most enjoyable and involving Paris performances you are likely to come across. The Concentus Musicus are on superb form, serving up a sound both clear and substantial, with horns a more than usually dark flavouring. And Harnoncourt is typically alert to every message the music has for us, drawing drama, humour, tenderness and colour at all turns, leaving the listener nothing to do but gasp, smile or glow in his wake.

There is barely room here to list this set's distinguishing delights, but among the most memorable are the fooling with the placing of the final chords of No 82, the leisured unrolling of the main theme of No 84's first movement, the fiercely stabbing wind chords of No 83's finale, and the gloriously unleashed pedal notes at the climax of No 85. Furthermore, Harnoncourt treats each symphony – indeed each movement, each bar – on its own terms. Harnoncourt has shown here that there is more to the 'Paris' Symphonies than the bluff, rolling bonhomie of some interpreters – so much more, in fact, that you have to wonder if they can ever be the same again.

'The Paris Symphonies'
Symphonies – No 82, 'L'ours'; No 83, 'La poule';
No 84; No 85, 'La Reine'; No 86; No 87
Tonkünstler Orchestra of Lower Austria /
Kristjan Järvi
Preiser ② PR90765 (135' · DDD)
Recorded live at the Musikverein, Vienna, 2005-07 Ⓕ

Pulling no punches, Kristjan Järvi and his crack Viennese band perform Haydn's six 'Paris' Symphonies as if they were playing for Marie Antoinette and her fun-loving entourage. To an unusual extent the performances convey a sense of Haydn using his musical skills to delight, flatter and astound the sophisticated French audiences.

Speeds are on the fast side but the plastic phrasing and subtle, flexible dynamic gradients allow Järvi to give each symphony its own individual character and theatrical dimensions. Of course, Järvi and his crew have lots of fun with the charm and wit of the Trios, but it is the musicians' pacing and structuring of each symphony's fast outer movements that enable their technical precision, rounded phrasing and sheer physical beauty to pay off. Listen to how the superbly played military fanfares at the end of the first movement of Symphony No 82 catch the rest of the orchestra by surprise and take the music to its joyous, triumphant conclusion.

Recorded live in the Musikverein in Vienna, where the wood serves as an organic resonator for the low end, the rich, focused and lively sound has an unusually well defined sweet spot that benefits substantially from increased volume. The antiphonal seating of the first and second violins, combined with wonderful woodwinds and heroic trumpets and drums sitting in the centre of the sound picture, means the full orchestra is always ready to strike quickly, particularly in the potentially heavy-handed Minuets.

'The London Symphonies'
Symphonies Nos 93-104
Stuttgart Radio Symphony Orchestra /
Sir Roger Norrington
Hänssler Classic ④ CD93 252 (4h 57' · DDD)
Recorded live 2009   Ⓜ︎ＯＯ➘

Among Sir Roger Norrington's contributions to the Haydn anniversary year (2009) were these recordings of the 12 'London' Symphonies, made live with his Stuttgart radio orchestra at concerts that took place over a week. Norrington is well known for his almost dogmatic abhorrence of vibrato, and this pays dividends at moments such as the slow introduction to Symphony No 102, although elsewhere it can give rise to occasional spots of sour intonation. Still, ensemble work is generally fine and there are some notably lithe woodwind solos throughout. In fact, the strength of this set lies in its powerful orchestral playing, allied with an avoidance, by and large, of lapsing into mannerism – despite touches of 'local colour' such as the *sul ponticello* passage in the slow movement of Symphony No 97.

Slow movements don't linger (that of the *Clock* Symphony is ear-prickingly swift, that of the *Military* Symphony perhaps a little breathless) and minuets don't lurch to the extremes of tempo favoured by certain period practitioners. The only miscalculation is perhaps the *Allegro* of Symphony No 102, which seems something of an uphill trudge. Virtually everywhere else, though, Norrington is alert to Haydn's effortless wit, his airborne counterpoint and his unerring architecture. These new recordings are thoroughly enjoyable and barely suffer in comparison with the classic rivals.

'The London Symphonies'
Symphonies – Nos 93-94, 97, 99 & 100-101
Concertgebouw Orchestra / Sir Colin Davis
Philips Duo ② 442 614-2PM2 (151 · ADD/DDD)
Recorded 1975-81   Ⓜ︎ＯＯ➘

Symphonies – Nos 95-96, 98 & 102-104
Concertgebouw Orchestra / Sir Colin Davis
Philips Duo ② 442 611-2PM2 (151 · ADD/DDD)
Recorded 1975-81   Ⓜ︎ＯＯ➘

A superb achievement. It's nigh-on impossible to imagine better 'big-band' Haydn than you encounter here on Colin Davis's four well-filled CDs. His direction has exemplary sparkle and sensitivity. Minuets are never allowed to plod, outer movements have an ideal combination of infectious zip and real poise, and the humour is always conveyed with a genial twinkle in the eye. Quite marvellous, wonderfully unanimous playing from the Amsterdam orchestra, too (the woodwind contributions are particularly distinguished), with never a trace of routine to betray the six-year recording span of this acclaimed project. The Philips engineering, whether analogue or digital, is of the very highest quality, offering a natural perspective, gloriously full-bodied tone and sparkling textures within the sumptuous Concertgebouw acoustic. Invest in this set: it will yield enormous rewards for years to come.

Additional recommendations

Symphonies Nos 6-8
Northern Chamber Orchestra / Ward
Naxos 8 550722 (59' · DDD)   Ⓢ➘
A lot to enjoy in the popular Times of Day trilogy, with their colourful and entertaining *concertante* writing. The Northern Chamber Orchestra is a lively, responsive group, and fields a personable bunch of soloists. No one staking a fiver on this disc could possibly be disappointed.

Symphonies Nos 22, 29 & 60
Northern Chamber Orchestra / Ward
Naxos 8 550724 (60' · DDD)   Ⓢ➘
A winning performance that fully captures the composer's infectious wit.

Symphonies Nos 43, 46 & 47
Cologne Chamber Orchestra / Müller-Brühl
Naxos 8 554767 (64' · DDD)   Ⓢ➘
A beefier sound than from many chamber orchestras but with ample detail. Müller-Brühl's speeds can't be faulted, with *Allegros* crisp and alert and slow movements kept flowing. A worthy rival for existing versions, whether on period or modern instruments.

Symphonies Nos 55-69
Austro-Hungarian Haydn Orchestra / Fischer
Nimbus ④ NI5590/4 (317' · DDD)   Ⓢ
A most attractive collection on modern instruments in the helpful acoustic of the Haydnsaal of the Esterházy Palace at Eisenstadt. Fischer's fine

control of dynamics is illustrated in the subtlety of echo phrases, clear but unexaggerated.

Symphonies Nos 49, 52 & 58
Heidelberg SO / Fey
Hänssler Classic CD98 236 (77' · DDD)   Ⓕ⤷

Symphonies Nos 57, 59 & 65
Heidelberg SO / Fey
Hänssler Classic CD98 526 (74' · DDD)   Ⓕ❍❍⤷

Symphonies Nos 69, 86 & 87
Heidelberg SO / Fey
Hänssler Classic CD98 268 (76' · DDD)   Ⓕ❍⤷

   Thomas Fey's series with his Heidelberg SO was one of the musical discoveries of Haydn Year. A pupil of both Bernstein and Harnoncourt, he brings excitement and flair to a sound that owes much to period-instrument practice. Bracing!

Symphonies Nos 41-47, 50-52, 64 & 65, 82-87 (Paris)
& 88-90   🅿
Tafelmusik / Weil
Sony Classical ⑦ 88697 48044-2 (7h 31' · DDD) Ⓢ❍❍
   A very appealing collection of Haydn symphonies performed on period instruments. As well as the 'Paris' Symphonies (Nos 82-87), Bruno Weill includes some of the lesser-known middle-period works. Everything is done with great style, lively attention to rhythm and a generous openness to Haydn's wit and humour. The *Farewell* Symphony (No 45) receives one of the best performances on disc. Competitively priced, this is an excellent single-set Haydn symphony collection.

Symphonies Nos 82-87 (Paris), 88 & 93-104 (London).
The Creation. Harmoniemesse. Paukenmesse.
Nelsonmesse. Theresienmesse.
NYPO / Bernstein
Sony Classical ⑫ 88697 48045-2 (12h 45' · DDD)   Ⓢ
   Leonard Bernstein was an enthusiastic and passionate Haydn conductor. Everything was done on a grand scale but it is never overblown or inflated. Bernstein's innate sense of rhythm ensures dance movements genuinely dance and he responds to Haydn's jokes well. The four Masses make an attractive makeweight with some beautiful singing, both solo and choral.

Symphonies Nos 91 & 92.
Berenice, che fai, HobXXIVa/10ᵇ
ᵃ**Fink; Freiburg Baroque Orch / Jacobs**
Harmonia Mundi HMX296 1849 (69' · DDD)   Ⓕ❍⤷
   Breezy and exuberant performances of two symphonies from 1789. Bernarda Fink is the searingly dramatic soloist in the *Scena di Berenice*.

Symphonies arr Chamber Ensemble

London Symphonies arr Salomon, Volume 1   🅿
Symphonies (arr Salomon) Nos 93ᵃ, No 94ᵇ, 101ᵃ
Florilegium Ensemble
(Ashley Solomon *fl* James Johnstone *fp*
ᵃKati Debretzeni, ᵇRodolfo Richter *vns*
Jane Rogers *va* Jennifer Morsches *vc*)
Channel Classics ⓢ⓪ CCSSA19603 (72' · DDD)   Ⓕ

Johann Peter Salomon, violinist, composer and impresario, was a shrewd businessman. Not only did he organise Haydn's two triumphant visits to London in the 1790s, visits which directly prompted the composition of the 12 'London' Symphonies, but he bought the rights to those masterpieces on Haydn's final return to Vienna in August 1795. Instead of issuing them in full score, in 1798 he published versions for domestic music-making. The basic ensemble is a string quartet and flute, plus a full keyboard part. This music is readily available in its original garb, but these arrangements are worth hearing. Some effects that must have sounded so original to early listeners stand out even more with this chamber ensemble than they do with a full orchestra. The extra transparency generally benefits fast movements. First-movement development sections strike the listener more sharply in their chamber guise, particularly the minor-key darkness of the *Surprise*, which recalls Haydn's *Sturm und Drang* style. The famous 'surprise' itself is intensified by Florilegium's dynamic response. These arrangements, well recorded with stylish if occasionally abrasive period performances and the advantage of an SACD alternative, can be warmly recommended to anyone who's intrigued.

String Quartets

Op 0 in E flat
Op 1: No 1 in B flat, 'La chasse' **No 2**
in E flat **No 3** in D **No 4** in G **No 5** in E flat **No 6** in C
Op 2: No 1 in A **No 2** in E **No 3** (spurious) **No 4** in F
No 5 (spurious) **No 6** in B flat
Op 3 Nos 1-6 (spurious)
Op 9: No 1 in C **No 2** in E flat **No 3** in G
No 4 in D minor **No 5** in B flat **No 6** in A
Op 17: No 1 in E **No 2** in F **No 3** in E flat
No 4 in C minor **No 5** in G **No 6** in D
Op 20, 'Sun': No 1 in E flat **No 2** in C **No 3** in
G minor **No 4** in D **No 5** in F minor **No 6** in A

Op 33 'Gli Scherzi': No 1 in B minor
No 2 in E flat, 'Joke' **No 3** in C, 'Bird'
No 4 in B flat **No 5** in G **No 6** in D
Op 42 in D
Op 50 'Prussian': No 1 in B flat **No 2** in C
No 3 in E flat **No 4** in F sharp minor **No 5** in F, 'Dream'
No 6 in D, 'Frog'
Op 54 'Tost': No 1 in G **No 2** in C **No 3** in E
Op 55 'Tost': No 1 in A **No 2** in F minor, 'Razor'
No 3 in B flat
Op 64 'Tost': No 1 in C **No 2** in B minor **No 3** in B flat
No 4 in G **No 5** in D, 'Lark' **No 6** in E flat

Op 71 'Apponyi': No 1 in B flat **No 2** in D
No 3 in E flat
Op 74 'Apponyi': No 1 in C **No 2** in F **No 3** in
G minor, 'Rider'
Op 76 'Erdödy': No 1 in G **No 2** in D minor, 'Fifths'
No 3 in C, 'Emperor' **No 4** in B flat, 'Sunrise'
No 5 in D **No 6** in E flat
Op 77 'Lobkowitz': No 1 in G **No 2** in F
Op 103 in D minor (unfinished)

Complete String Quartets

Op 0; Op 1 – Nos 1ᵃ, 2, 3, 4ᵃ & 6ᵃ; Op 2 –
Nos 1, 2ᵃ, 4ᵃ & 6; Opp 9, 17, 20, 33, 42ᵃ, 50ᵃ,
54, 55, 64, 71, 74, 76, 77 & 103
Angeles Quartet (Kathleen Lenski, Steven Miller,
ᵃSara Parkins *vns* Brian Dembow *va* Stephen
Erdody *vc*)
Philips 464 650-2PX21 (21 discs: DDD)　　Ⓜ**OO**

The most relevant comparisons for this collection are the Aeolian Quartet on Decca and the
Kodály Quartet on Naxos. The all-digital Naxos
series features performances that are, in the
main, musically reliable and technically proficient. But turn back to the 1973-76 Aeolian
series and every work becomes an event, every
quirk of harmony, rhythm or timing is etched
with maximum relish.

Comparative disc layouts begin to differ from
CD 3, and the Angeles omit *The Seven Last
Words*, a work which, beautiful as it is, wasn't
originally written for string quartet. Recording-
wise, Philips favours a warm, open sound, balanced much as you would hear it from the centre
stalls in a smallish-size concert hall. Decca's
analogue recordings are closer, dryer, more
sensitive to extraneous noise and commonly balanced in favour of Emanuel Hurwitz's first violin. It's a clear and intimate sound frame and the
leader bias actually suits the divertimento-style
early quartets, but Philips's more refined engineering makes for less strenuous listening in
concert-length sessions. A handful of edits are
the only blots on Philips's otherwise immaculate
aural landscape.

The svelte texture of the Angeles' pooled
sound, their consistent evenness in full chords
and the musical like-mindedness of individual
players, whether in excited *prestos* or in shared
rubato is admirable. As to contrasts in playing
styles, think of the relatively smooth-toned Juilliard or Emerson Quartets (Angeles) as compared with the internally differentiated Amadeus
Quartet (Aeolian). The Angeles are generally
lighter, faster and subtler in their use of tone
colouring whereas the Aeolians' roster of virtues
includes strong (even emphatic) characterisation, consistently flexible phrasing and a more
pungent approach to rhythm.

Surfing the set for good sampling-points
brings us, initially, to the early quartets, where
both groups sport some superb first-violin solo
work, tastefully inflected with Lenski, more
candidly expressive with Hurwitz. A particularly telling comparison is provided by the
quietly contrapuntal Minuet of Op 17 No 1,
where the Angeles' seamless *legato* contrasts
against the Aeolians' near *staccato*. The exquisite *Adagio* of Op 20 No 6 is another good place
to compare, the Angeles with their perfectly
timed pauses, warm cello line and overall
restraint set against the more romantic, even
rhapsodic, Aeolian. Listening to the first bars
of Op 33 No 1 is like eavesdropping on a small
gathering mid-conversation, where the cello

line gradually gains in urgency. The Angeles'
sotto voce handling of the *Scherzo* to Op 33 No 3
is wonderful: it's rather more pensive than the
Aeolians and marks much more of a contrast
with the chirping Trio.

Op 50 No 4's *Andante* anticipates the dramatic
interjections that trouble various late Schubert
slow movements. Both groups are effective here,
though when the cello marks an expected change
of key two minutes or so into the movement, it's
the Aeolian's Derek Simpson who makes the biggest impact: you can almost see the rosin erupt
from his strings. In Op 50 No 5 late Beethoven
springs more readily to mind, but there the Angeles' extra speed and restraint is more effective.
Note how beautifully they negotiate the quiet
alternation between upper and lower voices
towards the end of Op 50 No 6's *Poco adagio* and
the sudden blossoming that follows. Then again,
Op 54 No 1's mobile *Allegretto* second movement
harbours the potential to switch from tenseness
to lyrical effusiveness, which the Angeles exploit
to the full, as they do for the rhapsodising *Adagio*
of Op 54 No 2. Late Beethoven is evoked once
more, this time the Cavatina from Op 130.

Beam up around three minutes into the *Adagio*
of the *Lark* Quartet (Op 64 No 5) and you'll note
how skilfully the Angeles cue a *ritardando*, while
the bracing finale to Op 74 No 3 has just the right
bounce to offset all the breathless excitement. The
Sunrise Quartet (Op 76 No 4) opens like a spring
flower (never more so than in the Angeles' ecstatically controlled performance) and Op 77 No 1's
cheeky *Allegro moderato* bounds in with perfectly
modulated high spirits.

Turning to other competition, the Lindsays,
Amadeus, Vienna Konzerthaus, Quatuor
Mosaïques, Pro Arte and Takács, all have added
substantially to the Haydn quartet discography,
and all have their value. However, in this particular context it really is a head-to-head contest
between two 'complete' sets similarly presented.

Richard Wigmore contributes detailed annotation, quite different from Lindsay Kemp's
overview for Decca but just as useful and equally
well written. The Angeles appeal perhaps primarily for their restrained expressiveness and
consistent attention to detail. Philips' superior
recording is another bonus. The Aeolian Quartet generate more immediate heat but, ultimately, the Angeles' intelligence and cooler
blending pay the higher musical dividends.

String Quartets, Op 1

String Quartets – Op 1 No 1; Op 20 Nos 2 & 5;　　Ⓗ
Op 50 No 3; Op 54 Nos 1-3; Op 64 Nos 3 & 4;
Op 74 No 3; Op 76 Nos 3 & 4; Op 77 No 2
Pro Arte Quartet (Alphonse Onnou, Laurent Halleux
vns Germain Prévost *va* Robert Maas *vc*)
Testament mono ③ SBT3055 (3h 49' · ADD)
Recorded 1931-38　　　　　　　　　　　　Ⓕ**O**

Haydn String Quartets – Op 1 No 6; Op 20　　Ⓗ
Nos 1 & 4; Op 33 Nos 2, 3 & 6; Op 50 No 6; Op 55
Nos 1 & 3; Op 64 No 6; Op 71 No 1; Op 74 Nos 1 & 2;

Op 77 No 1 **Hoffstetter** String Quartets, Op 3 –
No 4 in B flat; No 5 in F
Pro Arte Quartet (Alphonse Onnou, Laurent Halleux
vns Germain Prévost va Robert Maas vc)
Testament mono ③ SBT4056 (4h 3' · ADD)
Recorded 1931-38   ⓕ**O**

The Pro Arte Quartet's first London appearance in 1925 prompted *The Times* to declare, 'One has never heard it surpassed, and rarely equalled, in volume and beauty of tone, in accuracy of intonation and in perfection of balance between the parts' – and that could well be the verdict on these sets. The musicians' tempi invariably seem just right and their phrasing has an inner life that's extraordinarily potent. Alphonse Onnou and Laurent Halleux were superbly matched, and Halleux often led in their early days. Such virtuosity as the quartet exhibits is effortless and totally lacking in ostentation. Though the actual sound is dated – the string tone is wanting in bloom and freshness – the ear soon adjusts; but these transfers might have made a little more space between movements.

String Quartets, Op 9

String Quartets, Op 9 – Nos 1, 3 & 4
Kodály Quartet (Attila Falváy, Tamás Szabó vns
Gábor Fias va János Devich vc)
Naxos 8 550786 (52' · DDD)   ⓢ**B**→

String Quartets, Op 9 – Nos 2, 5 & 6
Kodály Quartet
Naxos 8 550787 (58' · DDD)   ⓢ**B**→

Overshadowed by four dozen later masterpieces, Haydn's Op 9 has usually received short shrift from players and commentators. The most familiar is the D minor, No 4, described by Hans Keller as 'the first great string quartet in the history of music'. The minor mode at this period (1769-70) invariably drew something special from Haydn, and this work stands apart from the others for its intensity of expression, its mastery of texture and development and the sheer character of its ideas. The opening *Allegro moderato* could well have been at the back of Mozart's mind when he came to write his own great D minor Quartet, K421. The Kodály Quartet is, as ever, a sympathetic Haydn exponent, impressing with its slightly old-fashioned warmth of sonority, the natural musicality of its phrasing and care for blend, balance and intonation, though the boomy church acoustic hardly helps.

String Quartets – Op 9 No 4; Op 50 No 2;
Op 76 No 1; Op 50 No 1 – Finale
Doric Quartet (Alex Redington, Jonathan Stone vns
Simon Tandree va John Myerscough vc)
Wigmore Hall Live WHLIVE0032 (72' · DDD)   Ⓜ**O**B→

It wasn't all wit and sparkle. Sure, Haydn had a huge capacity for humour but some of his letters to Marianne von Genzinger show another facet of his character, a capacity for depression too – even at 37 when he wrote Op 9 No 4. And the Doric Quartet immediately hones in on its anxious ambience. They convey the resigned melancholy of the opening *Moderato* through subdued attack and tone that remains sombre even when the music moves out of its minor home key into, say, the F major second theme. In fact the Doric's interpretation of the work, including the *Adagio cantabile* in usually bright B flat, has a slightly sunless cast that also permeates the tense drive of the *Presto* finale.

These musicians are different. Not radically different but enough to notice that their style of playing, though highly disciplined, isn't cuttingly concentrated. It's a key to their approach. The *Vivace* first movement of Op 50 No 2 has a relaxed swing that finds time to inflect notes and define modulations. Speed wasn't necessary to express vivacity. Then there is Haydn the musical orator, found in the finale of Op 76 No 1. Listen to how the quartet unfolds its rhetoric, from turbulent G minor to the light-hearted, even flippant G major ending – of wit and sparkle. Want more? Try the encore, the finale from Op 50 No 1, and note how playfully the Doric sign off in this, their very auspicious recording debut.

String Quartets, Op 17   ⓟ

String Quartets, Op 17
London Haydn Quartet (Catherine Manson,
Margaret Faultless vns James Boyd va Jonathan
Cohen vc)
Hyperion ② CDA67722 (148' · DDD) ⓕ

Small works perhaps, not in the same league as the masterpieces of the genre to come, but far from small beer. The London Haydn Quartet certainly see it that way, and they start with a judicious choice of text – an edition by Welcker published in London c1774. It differs in little details from Georg Feder's 1965 version, based on Haydn's autograph and early manuscripts. Some of them include markings in Mozart's hand which suggests that he also took part in performances, playing the viola.

Gut-strung instruments are used here, and the recording very clearly reproduces the subtleties they convey. Watch your volume though because the transfer level is rather high. The violins are antiphonally separated, an arrangement that is particularly important in movements such as the *Adagios* of Nos 1, 3 and 4 where the second violin has a bigger role. Unusually, Haydn places the Minuet and Trio second in all the pieces and, very unusually, he has only one fast first movement.

These musicians arrest attention by the variety of their bowing and articulation. They lean into notes, swelling and contracting the sound (a sort of *messa di voce*) to heighten the potential for expression. The first movement of No 2 (*Moderato*) offers an example of this technique which is allied to discerning part-playing, fine grading of tone and flexible *rubato*. In effect, phrases are shaped to recreate the elements of drama, profundity, elegance and lyricism – and all things in between. A very imaginative interpretation.

String Quartets, Op 20

String Quartets, Op 20 Nos 1-6   **P**
Quatuor Mosaïques (Erich Höbarth, Andrea Bischof *vns* Anita Mitterer *va* Christophe Coin *vc*)
Astrée Naïve ② E8802 (147' · DDD)   Ⓕ**OOO**

G The Op 20 String Quartets date from the composer's so-called *Sturm und Drang* period, though Haydn's increasingly frequent use of the more dramatic and 'serious' minor mode in these pieces can perhaps be attributed just as much to the fruitful influence of the three operatic projects he had been working on just a few years previously. Moreover, these quartets reveal a greater preoccupation with counterpoint than any of his music to that date, and the great fugal finales of Nos 2, 5 and 6 clearly herald the consummate craftsman so overwhelmingly displayed in the mature quartets to come. These wonderfully flexible performances display an altogether breathtaking refinement, sensitivity and illumination. Indeed, in terms of expressive subtlety, imaginative intensity and sheer depth of feeling, the Mosaïques' achievement in these marvellous works is unmatched.

String Quartets, Op 20 – Nos 1, 3 & 4
The Lindsays (Peter Cropper, Ronald Birks *vns* Robin Ireland *va* Bernard Gregor-Smith *vc*)
ASV CDDCA1027 (79' · DDD)   Ⓕ**O**

String Quartets, Op 20 – Nos 2, 5 & 6
The Lindsays
ASV CDDCA1057 (66' · DDD)   Ⓕ**O**

The Lindsays are Haydn interpreters of rare understanding and communicative flair. Their characterisation is bold and decisive, enhanced by a scrupulous observation of the composer's expression and dynamic markings. Faster movements tend to be more urgent, less ruminative, than those from the Quatuor Mosaïques. The *zingarese* cross-rhythms of No 4's Minuet have an abrasive edge, and the *Presto e scherzando* finale is no mere frolic in The Lindsays' hands – its wit can scathe and sting, and the closing theme, with its gypsy *acciaccaturas*, has an almost manic insistence. Elsewhere they bring an ideal warmth and lyricism to the opening movement of No 1, characteristically phrasing in long, eloquent spans, and a quixotic energy to the outer movements of the G minor, No 3, where the Quatuor Mosaïques is broader and tougher. In the Minuet The Lindsays' singing line and flexibility of pulse realise to the full Haydn's searching harmonic progressions; and the lulling E flat Trio is exquisitely floated.

Each of the slow movements reveals dedication and profound identification. The players vindicate their dangerously slow tempo in the sublime *Affettuoso e sostenuto* of No 1 with the breadth and intensity of their phrasing, subtlety of colour and feeling for harmonic flux. As ever, the occasional moment of impure intonation is a small price to pay for performances of such colour, character and spontaneity.

The Lindsays observe all the important marked repeats and the recording is vivid and truthful. Characterisation of the sharply contrasted Nos 2, 5 and 6 is invariably vivid, phrasing is alive and inventive, and the players combine a scrupulous care for Haydn's dynamic and expression markings with a strong feeling for the music's larger contours.

String Quartets, Op 33

String Quartets, Op 33 **P**
Quatuor Mosaïques (Erich Höbarth, Andrea Bischof *vns* Anita Mitterer *va* Christophe Coin *vc*)
Auvidis Naïve ② E8801 (121' · DDD)   Ⓕ**OOO**

G The Mosaïques, at a rather slower tempo than usual, find in the theme-and-variation finale of the G major Quartet, No 5, an unsuspected reflective tenderness. The theme itself is played with a characteristic touch of flexibility and a gentle lift to the dotted rhythms; in the first variation Erich Höbarth shapes his decorative semiquavers *fioritura* with apparently spontaneous fantasy; the luminous, high-lying textures of the second are exquisitely realised; and even the *Presto* send-off has a delicacy and whimsy in keeping with what has gone before. The Mosaïques' readings of the slow movements in the so-called *Joke* (No 2) and *Bird* (No 3) Quartets are again outstanding in their grave tenderness, their sensitivity to harmonic flux and the improvisatory freedom Erich Höbarth brings to his ornamental figuration. The *Bird*, in particular, receives as searching a performance as ever heard: in the first movement the players steal in almost imperceptibly, respond vividly to the music's richness and wit, and bring a spectral *pianissimo* to the mysterious lull in the development. The Slavonic finale, one of several movements to benefit from the lighter, more flexible period bows, goes with terrific fire and panache.

From the teasingly timed initial upbeat of the D major Quartet, No 6, the Mosaïques' performances have all the familiar hallmarks: inventive phrasing, subtly varied colour, a sure sense of organic growth and a spontaneous-sounding delight in Haydn's inspired unpredictability. Tempo and manner in the opening *Vivace assai* of No 6 are, typically, gentler than that of the equally imaginative Lindsays, the articulation lighter and more delicate, as you would expect from period strings. They catch ideally the music's glancing *scherzando* spirit, with a delightfully eager, quick-witted give-and-take between the instruments. Like The Lindsays, the Mosaïques vividly play up the contrast between the perky, high-stepping D major theme and alternating D minor melody. But the Mosaïques flex the tempo more freely and play with the length of Haydn's up-beats, to witty or pathetic effect.

In the *Andante* of the B minor Quartet (No 1) the Mosaïques arguably overdo the whimsical hesitations. However, their unusually reflective way with this movement, and the sense of remoteness they bring to the strange, spare second theme is very appealing. The undervalued B flat Quartet (No 4) is a delight throughout, from the puckish opening movement, with its quasi-improvisatory freedom to the comic exuberance of the finale; the vitality and point of the inner voices' semiquavers in the finale's G minor episode are typical of the character brought to seemingly routine accompanying figuration.

This set has playing that marries uncommon style, technical finesse and re-creative flair. The recording has an attractive ambient warmth.

String Quartets – Op 33; Op 42
Festetics Quartet (István Kertész, Erika Petöfi vns
Péter Ligeti va Rezsö Pertorini vc)
Arcana ② A414 (145' · DDD)   Ⓕ

The veteran Festetics Quartet are uneasy with *presto* finales. But they aren't slack; instead they are tautly metrical so the notes do not flow freely across the bar-lines. It may be an aspect of their style that is direct, sharp in attack and stricter than usual in rhythm, yet far from indifferent. In all the works these musicians meticulously observe phrase indications, choose dynamics where there are none, repeat both parts of a Minuet after its Trio and differentiate between the various accents. Equally meticulously they probe the slow movements of Op 33. Haydn is said to have been in love at the time he wrote this set; and, austerity of approach notwithstanding, it is easy to discern in, say, the *Largo* of No 4 an ardent lyric for the lady, Luigia Polzelli. Not unexpectedly, the *Largo e cantabile* of No 5 is seen in an even more ascetic light, G minor starkly affirmed, the violins (antiphonally separated, as always with this group) contributing to a bare-boned interpretation of the text. Not comfortable. But the Festetics don't buy comfort and the close, 'rosiny' sound brings the results right into the room. No mistaking the message. No mistaking the gauntlets either. Unsettling – but required listening.

String Quartets, Op 33 – Nos 1, 2 & 4
The Lindsays (Peter Cropper, Ronald Birks vns
Robin Ireland va Bernard Gregor-Smith vc)
ASV CDDCA937 (62' · DDD)   ⒻO

The Lindsays' is chamber-music-making of unusual flair, untouched by the faintest hint of routine. In their uncommonly grave, inward

readings of the slow movements of the E flat and B flat Quartets they sustain a daringly slow tempo magnificently, phrasing in long, arching spans, always acutely sensitive to harmonic movement, as in their subtle colouring of Haydn's breathtaking tonal excursions in No 4. Beethoven is evoked in The Lindsays' swift, mordant reading of No 1's epigrammatic *Scherzo*: rarely have the waspish part-writing and the abrupt, disconcerting contrasts in dynamics and articulation been so vividly realised. Typically, it makes the most of the complete change of mood and texture in the major-key Trio, finding an almost Viennese sweetness of tone and phrase, complete with touches of *portamento*. The finale, fast, fierce, utterly uncomical, has a distinct whiff of the Hungarian *puszta* here, both in the wild gypsy figuration and the mounting passion of the sequence in the development. The Lindsays bring an ideal spaciousness and flexibility to the urbane, quietly spoken first movement of the E flat Quartet, No 2, taking due note of Haydn's *cantabile* marking. In the finales of this Quartet and No 4 they bring vital, inventively varied phrasing, palpably relishing Haydn's exuberance and comic sleight of hand.

String Quartets, Op 33 – Nos 3, 5 & 6
The Lindsays (Peter Cropper, Ronald Birks vns
Robin Ireland va Bernard Gregor-Smith vc)
ASV CDDCA938 (61' · DDD)   ⒻOO

The Lindsays eclipse all comers in range of colour, vital, creative phrasing and emotional penetration. They respond gleefully to the subversive comedy that pervades each of the three works – most overtly in the Slavonic-influenced finale of the *Bird* (No 3), and in the outrageous *Scherzo* of No 5, where with explosive *sforzandos* and sly touches of timing they relish to the full Haydn's rhythmic and dynamic mayhem. But time and again in this music wit is suddenly suffused with poetry; and they bring a glancing delicacy and grace of interplay to, say, the startling tonal deflections in the opening *Vivace assai* of No 6. With their slower-than-usual tempo and wonderfully tender, contained *sotto voce*, the second movement of No 3, where Haydn transmutes the Minuet-*scherzo* into a hymn, becomes the expressive core of the quartet. The Lindsays constantly provoke you to respond afresh to Haydn; to his wit, comic exuberance and his often unsuspected profundity.

String Quartet, Op 42

Haydn String Quartet, Op 42
Schumann String Quartet No 3 in A, Op 41 No 3
Shostakovich String Quartet No 3 in F, Op 73
Allegri Quartet (Peter Carter, David Roth vns
Jonathan Barritt va Bruno Schrecker vc)
Naim Audio NAIMCD016 (73' · DDD)   Ⓕ

Haydn's exquisite Op 42 is given an especially

winning rendition, the *Andante ed innocentemente* first movement donning a degree of understatement that reflects its equivocal personality.

Following it with Shostakovich's Op 73 was an inspired idea: the former ends quietly and the latter opens with a sort of distracted innocence, marking time before the real drama starts. The argument suddenly intensifies, playfully, provocatively, though characterisation is cleverly differentiated. In the second movement, Prokofiev is an obvious point of reference and there has rarely been a more delicately pointed account of the weird, tiptoe *staccato* passage that emerges out of the first idea. The third movement is a striking precursor of the Tenth Symphony's violent 'Stalin' *Scherzo*, the slow movement redolent of the Twelfth Symphony's noble opening and the long finale ending in a mood of veiled mystery. Above all, this is profoundly natural playing and the recordings maintain a realistic 'small concert-hall' ambience throughout.

The disc ends with an affectionate, flexible performance of Schumann's loveliest string quartet. The opening *Andante espressivo* sets the mood while the ensuing second set (1'19") is limpid and rapturous, and the finale – which in some hands can seem repetitive – is given precisely the right degree of rhythmic emphasis. Again one senses wholehearted identification between the repertoire and its interpreters – and while one may question the wisdom of mixed-repertory CD programmes, this one is so well planned and well played, that it can be recommended even to those who already own recordings within cycles.

String Quartets, Op 54

String Quartets, Op 54
The Lindsays (Peter Cropper, Ronald Birks *vns* Robin Ireland *va* Bernard Gregor-Smith *vc*)
ASV CDDCA582 (66' · DDD) Ⓕ**OO**

All three quartets are in the usual four-movement form but they contain many surprises: in No 1, the false recapitulation in the first movement, the dark modulations in the following sonata-form *Allegretto* and the Hungarian gypsy flavour (anticipated in the Minuet) and mischievousness of the final rondo. No 2 has a rhapsodic fiddler in its second movement, a nostalgic Minuet with an extraordinarily anguished Trio, and an *Adagio* finale in which a *Presto* section turns out to be no more than an episode.

A notable feature of No 3 is its ternary-form *Largo cantabile*, the centre of which is more like a mini-concerto for the first violin; 'Scotch snaps' pervade the Minuet, and pedal points the finale. The performances and the recording are superb, marked by unanimity, fine tone, suppleness of phrasing, and acute dynamic shaping; in the second movement of No 1 there are hushed passages whose homogeneity and quality of sound are both quite remarkable. Overall, this recording is irresistible.

String Quartets, Op 55

String Quartets, Op 55
The Lindsays (Peter Cropper, Ronald Birks *vns* Robin Ireland *va* Bernard Gregor-Smith *vc*)
ASV CDDCA906 (64' · DDD) Ⓕ**O**

Most immediately striking of the trilogy is the F minor work, No 2, with its searching double variations on related minor and major themes (a favourite form in Haydn's later music), spiky, rebarbative second movement *Allegro* and strangely spare contrapuntal Minuet. The A major, No 1, has much of this key's traditional brilliance, with ample scope for the leader's creative virtuosity in the outer movements and the stratospheric Trio of the Minuet; in contrast the noble, wonderfully scored *Adagio cantabile* prefigures the profound slow movements of Haydn's final years. The more inward-looking No 3 in B flat is specially remarkable for the varied recapitulations in the flanking movements, astonishingly free and inventive even for Haydn, and the subtle chromatic colouring in all four movements which may just owe something to the quartets Mozart had dedicated to Haydn three years earlier. Here and there The Lindsays' intonation is less than true, but as so often with this group, this is a small price to pay for performances of such colour and penetration. The balance, as with many recent quartet recordings, is a shade closer than ideal but the overall sound picture is very acceptable.

String Quartets, Op 64

String Quartets, Op 64 – Nos 1-3
Kodály Quartet (Attila Falvay, Tamás Szabo *vns* Gábor Fias *va* János Devich *vc*)
Naxos 8 550673 (64' · DDD) Ⓢ**B**

String Quartets, Op 64 – Nos 4-6
Kodály Quartet
Naxos 8 550674 (65' · DDD) Ⓢ**B**

The so-called *Lark* (No 5), with its soaring opening melody and *moto perpetuo* finale, is perhaps the most immediately fetching of all Haydn's quartets. But No 6 is at least as fine, with its intimate and intensely argued opening movement, its poignant, exquisitely textured *Andante* and a finale full of instrumental fooling and insouciant contrapuntal virtuosity. Of the other works, No 2 is one of Haydn's most astringent pieces, from its tonally deceptive opening to the mordant, unsettling humour of the finale. Quartets Nos 3 and 4 return to a more familiar vein of sociable wit. Both are endlessly subtle and surprising in their arguments, with *cantabile* slow movements of peculiar candour and eloquence. Quartet No 1, the least favoured of the six, is certainly the plainest in its thematic ideas. But it's an absorbing, immensely sophisticated piece, exploring an astonishing range of textures; the recapitulation of the leisurely first movement opens up marvellous new harmonic vistas, while the central development of the finale is a canonic *tour de force*. The Kodály Quartet has rightly won plaudits for its wonderfully civilised playing; mellow and lyrical, far removed from the highly strung brilliance cultivated by many modern quartets. Ensemble and intonation are first class, tempi generally spacious, with broad, natural and beautifully matched phrasing. It's at its very finest where Haydn is at his most searching; and the Quartets Nos 2, 5 and 6 each receive outstanding, deeply considered performances. In one or two movements the Kodály's penchant for slowish tempi leads to a slight dourness. Against that, it brings a deliciously lazy *Ländler* lilt, enhanced by the first violin's *portamentos*, to the Trio of No 6, and a grave, inward intensity to each of Haydn's slow movements. The recording, made in a Budapest church, is resonant and less intimate than is ideal in this music.

String Quartets, Opp 71 and 74

String Quartets, Op 71 Nos 1-3
Kodály Quartet (Attila Falvay, Tamás Szabo vns
Gábor Fias va János Devich vc)
Naxos 8 550394 (62' · DDD)   Ⓢ🅑▸

String Quartets, Op-74 Nos 1-3
Kodály Quartet
Naxos 8 550396 (63' · DDD)   Ⓢ🅑▸

The Kodály Quartet plays with evident joy and an easy neatness of ensemble. There's never a hint of routine and the inter-communication is matched by enormous care for detail. Just sample the elegant *Andante* with variations which form the slow movement of Op 71 No 3, or the witty Minuet which follows, or any of the consistently inspired Op 74 set. The hushed intensity of playing in the *Largo assai* of Op 74 No 3 is unforgettable. The recordings are wholly natural and balanced within a well-judged acoustic; the sound is of the highest quality and documentation is excellent. At their modest price this pair of CDs is irresistible.

Additional recommendation

String Quartets, Op 71
The Lindsays
ASV Gold GLD4012 (68' · DDD)   Ⓕ

  As we've come to expect from The Lindsays' Haydn, these are deeply considered performances, bringing out the full individuality of each movement. The Lindsays' lively tone quality and robust manner powerfully convey the rhythmic verve that's a mirror of Haydn's extraordinary creative energy.

String Quartets, Op 76

String Quartets, Op 76 – Nos 1-3
The Lindsays (Peter Cropper, Ronald Birks vns

Robin Ireland va Bernard Gregor-Smith vc)
ASV CDDCA1076 (75' · DDD)   Ⓕ⬤

These are among the finest Haydn quartet recordings heard in years, performances which will quickly establish themselves as classics. They are consistently a degree more refined in texture and control of dynamic than the Lindsays' earlier live recordings, and the ensemble is more polished. Yet the feeling of spontaneity is just as intense, with Haydn's witty moments pointed even more infectiously, as in the finale of Op 76 No 2, where in the main theme the little upward *portamentos* at the end of the eighth bar are delectably timed on each occurrence. The studio sound is fuller, too, and far better balanced, so that one can register far more clearly than before the first violin's rapid triplets in the finale of the *Emperor*; it's ideally crisp articulation. Matching the new performances of the *Fifths* and the *Emperor*, The Lindsays' account of Op 76 No 1 is just as strongly characterised. The sense of fun in the opening *Allegro con spirito* is deliciously brought out, leading on to an account of the sublime *Adagio*, both dedicated and refined, which conveys a Beethovenian depth of expression, making most rivals sound superficial.

String Quartets, Op 76 – Nos 4-6
The Lindsays
ASV CDDCA1077 (78' · DDD)   Ⓕ⬤⬤

Here, in the last three Op 76 quartets, you've Haydn interpretations that bring forth the full range of expression in these inspired works of his official retirement. They aren't just polished and refined but communicate with an intensity that simulates live performance. No 5 in D was one of the works which The Lindsays recorded earlier live at the Wigmore Hall, but the extra subtlety this time means that rhythms are a degree more liltingly seductive, in which humour is more delightfully pointed, as in the repeated cadence-figure at the start of the finale, with comic pauses beautifully timed.

The quiet opening of No 4, which gave rise to the nickname *Sunrise*, gently insinuates itself before the full thrust of the *Allegro* takes over; with its heightened contrasts, it could not be more captivating. Most strikingly, too, the slow movements in each of these three quartets are given a visionary intensity, matching The Lindsays' treatment of the slow movement of No 1 in the companion disc.

Here is music from the last years of Haydn's career which in these performances has you thinking forward to middle or late Beethoven and the new world of the 19th century. So the *Adagio* of No 4 brings a hymn-like dedication, not least in the dark E flat minor episode, and the astonishing modulations in the *Fantasia* slow movement of No 6 convey the tingle of new discovery, with magical *pianissimos* for contrast. This was a work which for Donald Tovey marked a tailing-off of inspiration, but one registers the opposite with The Lindsays, when the *adagio* Fantasia gives way to such witty treatment both in the *presto* Minuet (in fact a *scherzo*), with its weird leaps, and the *Allegro spirituoso* finale.

With refined sound that draws out the subtleties of balance between these players, here's another disc of Haydn from The Lindsays that sets the highest standards.

String Quartets, Op 77

String Quartets – Op 77; Op 103   **P**
Quatuor Mosaïques (Erich Höbarth, Andrea Bischof vns Anita Mitterer va Christophe Coin vc)
Astrée Naïve E8800 (62' · DDD)   (F)

Anyone who thinks that period-instrument performance means austerity and coolness should listen to this disc. Here's playing full of expressive warmth and vigour. The opening of Op 77 No 1 is done duly gracefully, but with a sturdy underlying rhythm and the *Scherzo* is crisp and alive. Then the first movement of the F major work is beautifully done, with many sensitive details; and the lovely second movement is ideally leisurely, so that the players have ample room for manoeuvre and the leader makes much of his opportunities for delicate playing in the filigree-like high music. The players show a real grasp of structure and illuminate the key moments with a touch more deliberation or a little additional weight of tone. These performances, clearly recorded, are competitive not merely within the protected world of 'early music' but in the bigger, 'real' world too!

Seven Last Words, Op 51

The Seven Last Words, Op 51, HobIII/50-56
Rosamunde Quartet
ECM New Series 461 780-2 (66' · DDD)   (F)**OOD**

This reading is alert not only to musical texture, but to the modulating phrase and the dramaturgy of key changes between movements. The playing is limpid and subtly coloured, sparing of vibrato (in that respect the Rosamunde are heedful of various period-instrument models) and, at the beginning of the third movement, suspended in a sense of rapture. Another imaginative aspect of this performance is the way it reflects the sense of the text, just as Haydn does in those movements that seem to follow the pattern of the words he set. This feeling of narrative is especially keen in the fourth movement, 'Woman, behold thy son!' and the closing 'Earthquake'.

The list of virtues is fairly simple to enumerate: variety and refinement of tone, internal clarity, historical awareness, imagination and a certain poise that not all its rivals can claim in equal measure. It serves well as a compromise between period-instrument clarity and modern-instrument warmth. Against strong competition its fuller instrumental sonority is marginally to be preferred. A first-rate CD of a wonderful score.

Seven Last Words, Op 51[a] (interspersed with Seven Gregorian Responsories for Holy Week[b])
[a]**Carmina Quartet** (Matthias Enderle, Susanne Frank vns Wendy Champney va Stephan Goerner vc)
[b]**Schola Romana Lucernensis /
Father Roman Bannwart**
Claves 50 2002 (74' · DDD · T/t)   (F)**O**

Haydn's *Seven Last Words* was designed for performance in Holy Week, in the Santa Cueva grotto in Cádiz, with discourses from the bishop on each of the seven utterances followed by Haydn's musical meditation. Originally these were orchestral pieces, not the string quartet versions (arranged by Haydn to widen access to the music) which are more often given today. Haydn was concerned that 'seven *Adagios*' would be exhausting to the listener, and probably wouldn't have favoured performing them without a break. The idea of interspersing them with Holy Week Gregorian responsories is certainly an appropriate solution.

The group singing them here is a mixed choir, although we hear either the men or the women, never the two together. They sing in a carefully moulded style, cadences softly rounded off; ensemble is precise, from the women especially. The Carmina Quartet plays with a remarkably wide range of expression. The Introduction is quite fiercely done, and the 'Terremoto' at the end has a violence and is taken at a pace that almost obscures the pulse of the music.

In between, they play the 'seven *Adagios*' (as Haydn called them – actually three *Largos*, two *Graves*, a *Lento* and an *Adagio*) as they would any other Haydn slow movement. The first is quite relaxed and lyrical, although its accents are well marked, and it has touches of added ornamentation. Refinement and delicacy of line characterise the second, and the third, the E major meditation on 'Mother, behold thy son', is done with much tenderness.

In the fourth their realisation of Haydn's notated ornaments – the appoggiaturas in bars 2 and 4, and at several points later – are oddly perverse and disturbing: one played short, the other long, although the second phrase is a clear echo of the first. No 5 ('I thirst') again draws some very telling soft playing from the quartet, but also pained *forzato* accents, and there's forceful expression of 'Consummatum est', along with moments of tenderness. They play the E flat No 7 with the sense of calm and fulfilment that Haydn surely sought. Their tempi, generally, are well chosen, perhaps faster at times than many quartets take these pieces, but this helps bridge the gulf between Haydn's normal mode of expression and the special significance of this remarkable music.

Additional recommendation

Fitzwilliam Quartet   **P**
Linn CKD153 (62' · DDD)   (F)
   A chaste, inward reading on period instruments, deeply musical, swifter than some but always thoughtfully articulated. A compelling recording.

Piano Trios

HobXV – No 1 in G minor; **No 2** in F; **No 5** in G;
No 6 in F; **No 7** in D; **No 8** in B flat; **No 9** in A;
No 10 in E flat; **No 11** in F minor; **No 12** in E minor;
No 13 in C minor; **No 14** in A flat; **No 15** in G;
No 16 in D; **No 17** in F; **No 18** in A; **No 19** in
G minor; **No 20** in B flat; **No 21** in C; **No 22** in E flat;
No 23 in D minor; **No 24** in D; **No 25** in G, 'Gypsy
Trio'; **No 26** in F sharp minor; **No 27** in C; **No 28** in
E; **No 29** in E flat; **No 30** in E flat; **No 31** in E flat
minor; **No 32** in G; **No 34** in E; **No 35** in A; **No 36** in
E flat; **No 37** in F; **No 38** in B flat; **No 39** in F; **No 40**
in F; **No 41** in G; **No C1** in C; **No f1** in E flat

Complete Piano Trios
Beaux Arts Trio (Menahem Pressler *pf* Isidore Cohen
vn Bernard Greenhouse *vc*)
Philips ⑨ 454 098-2PB9 (10h 34' · DDD)   ⑧❍❍❍➔

This is a remarkable and, indeed,
invaluable box, which is unlikely to be
challenged, let alone surpassed. Nowadays, it is not often possible to hail one set of
records as a 'classic' of the gramophone in quite
the same sense as, say, Schnabel's Beethoven
sonatas or the Busch late Beethoven quartets.
Yet this set can surely be said to enjoy this status.
The playing of the Beaux Arts Trio is of the
highest musical distinction, Menahem Pressler's
contribution is little short of inspired; the set
offers astonishingly lifelike recorded sound, and
the repertoire is unfailingly fresh and inventive.
The performances follow the critical edition
prepared by HC Robbins Landon, whose tireless researches have increased the number of
trios that we know in the standard edition from
31 to 43. These are records to which one returns
with pleasure and profit, for this music is sane
and intelligent, balm to the soul in a troubled
world. Indeed, it is a set that will last a lifetime.

Piano Trios – Nos 18, 24, 25 & 29
Vienna Piano Trio (Wolfgang Redik *vn*
Marcus Trefny *vc* Stefan Mendl *pf*)
Nimbus NI5535 (60' · DDD)   ⑤❍

The *Gypsy* Trio, No 25, may have been written
in and for London, but this ensemble's short,
snappy bowing, stomping piano accents and
instinctive fluctuations of tempo and pulse in the
finale locate the work in the grape-treading,
Romany heart of the Burgenland. The steps of
the dance shape and pervade the E flat Trio, too,
in the jaunty rhythms of the opening *Allegretto*,
and the boisterous and cross-accented *allemande*
of its finale. Among countless delights in these
bold performances is the sensitivity to the power
of silence, and the short, hushed half-tones
within the long-breathed lines of the *Andante* of
the A major Trio. And, not least, the perceptive
understanding and judgement of the shifting
qualities of an *Allegro* which so well supports
the structure of the outer movements of the

D major, as well as enabling many a clearly
articulated yet fanciful variation in the *Gypsy*
Trio. These recordings are close, sometimes
breathy, always thrillingly true.

Piano Trios – Nos 24, 25, 26 & 27
Florestan Trio (Anthony Marwood *vn* Richard Lester
vc Susan Tomes *pf*)
Hyperion CDA67719 (64' · DDD)   ⑤❍❍➔

Tomes and her partners identify themselves fully
with the emotional scale of these works, ostensibly meant for domestic use on small pianos. But
their scope suggests that Haydn structured them
for the powerful English Broadwood instruments
suited to the concert hall. The noise-quelling
opening chord of No 24 would have stopped
rowdy audiences of the day in their tracks.

There is so much from the Florestan to stop us
in our tracks too, not least in their feel for
expressing the content of these sparsely marked
scores, as in the finale of No 24 when *Allegro ma
dolce* in D major changes to a stabbing D minor
before returning to the original key. The musicians intuitively recreate the return even more
sweetly. Their interpretative acumen is unimpeachable. The continuous triplets in the *Adagio*
of No 26, tiresome if badly played, are instead
profoundly yielding. And the *Presto* finale of
No 27 isn't driven on cruise control.

A very special disc, recorded in detailed, front-
row sound.

Piano Trios – Nos 28, 29, 30 & 31
Florestan Trio
Hyperion CDA67757 (60' · DDD)   ⑤❍❍➔

Some of Haydn's most charming and relaxed
music is to be found in his piano trios, many of
them composed for virtuoso lady pianists of his
acquaintance. One such was Therese Jansen-
Bartolozzi, the recipient of the first two works in
the Florestan's second volume of trios (Vol 1 is
reviewed above). Jansen was clearly quite a pianist, and the Florestans display their customary
virtuosity, elegance and caprice in these outwardly easy-going works, once again capturing
the full (and deceptively wide) emotional range
of what may appear on the surface to be merely
domestic entertainment music. The shifting
bass-line of the darkly Baroque *Allegretto* of the
E major Trio (No 28) shows that this music is so
much more than that, and so too does the opening movement of Trio No 31, in the utterly un-
Classical key of E flat minor. A splendid disc.

Piano Trios – Nos 15-17.   ℗
Symphony No 94, 'Surprise'[a]
La Gaia Scienza (Federica Valli *pf* Marco Brolli *fl*
[a]Stefano Barneschi *vn* Paolo Beschi *vc*)
Winter & Winter 910 156-2 (64' · DDD)   ⑤

La Gaia Scienza offer an alternative approach
to Haydn's trios. Nos 15-17 were composed

for the traditional piano trio line-up but eventually published for flute (rather than violin), cello and piano, and that is how they are performed here. The star on this period-instrument recording, though, is the copy of a Ludwig Dulcken (Dresden, 1790s) fortepiano, a clangorous presence in these vivacious performances. The surprise on the disc, though, is the *Surprise* Symphony in a 1793 arrangement for flute and piano trio. The minuet is omitted, as is the gorgeous woodwind variation in the slow movement; and perhaps the skittering string passages don't sit completely comfortably under the fingers of fortepianist Federica Valli. But it's an ingenious arrangement and it's boldly and winningly played.

Keyboard Sonatas

HobXVI: No 1 in C **No 2** in B flat **No 3** in C **No 4** in D **No 5** in A (doubtful) **No 6** in G **No 7** in C **No 8** in G **No 9** in F **No 10** in C **No 11** in G **No 12** in A (doubtful) **No 13** in E (doubtful) **No 14** in D **No 15** (spurious) **No 16** in E flat (doubtful) **No 17** (spurious) **No 18** in B flat **No 19** in D **No 20** in C minor **No 21** in D **No 22** in E **No 23** in F **No 24** in D **No 25** in E flat **No 26** in A **No 27** in G **No 28** in E flat **No 29** in F **No 30** in A **No 31** in E **No 32** in B minor **No 33** in D **No 34** in E minor **No 35** in C **No 36** in C sharp minor **No 37** in D **No 38** in E flat **No 39** in G **No 40** in G **No 41** in B flat **No 42** in D **No 43** in A flat **No 44** in G minor **No 45** E flat **No 46** in A flat **No 47** in F **No 48** in C **No 49** in E flat **No 50** in C **No 51** in D **No 52** in E flat **Deest** E flat (doubtful)

'Unexpected Encounters'
Piano Sonatas, HobXVI – Nos 1, 23, 27 & 50
Tzimon Barto pf
Ondine ODE1154-2 (77' · DDD)   Ⓕ

Piano Sonatas, HobXVI – Nos 34, 40 & 52. Sonata
(un piccolo divertimento: Variations), HobXVII/6
Anne Queffélec pf
Mirare MIR104 (77' · DDD)   Ⓕ

'Unexpected Encounters' is the title of Tzimon Barto's disc, with some unexpected perspectives on Haydn because Barto accepts nothing at face value. The first three sonatas, with minimal expression marks, are written for the harpsichord but Barto doesn't imitate the instrument. Instead he uses the resources of the piano to express what Haydn implied. Ductile sonorities rather than sharp transients fill out the fabric and repeats are varied through changes of touch rather than decoration. No 1's origin is considered doubtful but Barto's interpretation is of a scope that suggests the real thing.

Surface glitter is eschewed. The first movement of No 23, for example, has no tempo marking and Marc-André Hamelin plays it *presto* (see below). Barto prefers *moderato* – and offers a different view. As always, he probes, but goes the wrong way with the Minuet and Trio of No 27. It's finnicky to the point of prissiness. Not so

No 50, written for piano, where depth of feeling takes in the full dramatic force of the work.

Anne Queffélec isn't neglectful of dramatic force either. She too uses the full resources of the piano and her response to the Variations is both thoughtful and richly analytical. The pairs of themes and variations in F minor/F major represent a gamut of feelings, from restrained despair to outright angst. Queffélec expresses these emotions through her pacing and shading of the writing. She is totally involved, and is just as involved in her interpretation of the Sonata traditionally considered Haydn's last but placed third from the end by scholar Georg Feder. Its quirky twists and grand passions are not lost on Queffélec whose dialogue with the composer's voice also extends to a tenderly nuanced slow movement.

Fine rhythm and articulation illuminate her playing. Some of these qualities are apparent in the finale of No 40 but not in the first movement which is comparatively bland. Nor in the outer movements of No 34 where she resorts to a smooth fluency that weakens their shadowy undercurrents. Still, the rest of Queffélec's programme is cherishable; and the sound on both discs is credible.

Piano Sonatas, HobXVI – Nos 20, 32, 34, 37, 40, 42 & 48-52; HobXVII – No 4, Fantasia in C; No 6, Variations in F minor; No 9, Adagio in F
Alfred Brendel pf
Philips ④ 478 1369DOR (3h 25' · ADD/DDD)
          Ⓕ**OOO**ᗹ→

These sonatas are magnificent creations, wonderfully well played by Alfred Brendel. Within the order and scale of these works Haydn explores a rich diversity of musical languages, a wit and broadness of expression that quickly repays attentive listening. It's the capriciousness as much as the poetry that Brendel so perfectly attends to; his playing, ever alive to the vitality and subtleties, makes these discs a delight. The sophistication innate in the simple dance rhythms, the rusticity that emerges, but above all, the sheer *joie de vivre* are gladly embraced. Brendel's continual illumination of the musical ideas through intense study pays huge dividends. The recording quality varies enormously between the different works and though the close acoustic on some of the later discs could be faulted for allowing one to hear too much of the keyboard action, it certainly brings one into vivid contact with the music.

Piano Sonatas, HobXVI – Nos 23, 24, 32, 37, 40, 41, 43, 46, 50 & 52
Marc-André Hamelin pf
Hyperion ② CDA67554 (145' · DDD)   Ⓕ**OOO**ᗹ→

For long confined to the by-ways of the repertoire, the ever-phenomenal Marc-André Hamelin now breaks out into the light with a two-disc set of Haydn sonatas. And unlike Haydn who considered himself less than a wizard of the keyboard, Hamelin is a prodigious virtuoso. Here, he remains one, in a full if not entirely inclusive sense, often susceptible to Haydn's wit, to vertiginous music which can veer to the right just when you expect it to turn left, and vice versa.

He is brilliantly alert to the first Menuetto from No 43, to a dance at once perky and serious, almost as if the composer with his toy fanfares was trying unsuccessfully to keep a straight face. And he can be hauntingly limpid and serene, as in the alternately calm and troubled *Adagio* from No 46. However, in No 23 one longs for Hamelin to relax his virtuoso prowess. Here, there is an unmistakable sense of hurry, of Haydn's riches glimpsed rather than savoured, of a composer's piquancy nearly bustled out of existence. Others, too, have achieved greater grandeur in the final E flat Sonata or made the storm clouds scud more menacingly across the B minor Sonata's finale (Andsnes, Ax and, most of all, Brendel). None the less, these are astonishing performances. Hyperion's sound and presentation are, as always, immaculate.

Piano Sonatas, HobXVI – Nos 26, 31, 33-35, 39, 42, 48 & 49. Sonata (un piccolo divertimento: Variations), HobXVII/6. Fantasia, 'Capriccio', HobXVII/4
Marc-André Hamelin *pf*
Hyperion ② CDA67710 (153' · DDD)　　Ⓜ◗◑◗

Hamelin's second set of Haydn sonatas confirms the adulation that greeted his first. Yet, if anything, it is even more dextrous, magical and enriching. Time and again he reminds you how in the finest pianist's hands technique and musicianship become indivisible considerations. More specifically, Hamelin exhibits a coruscating wit and brilliance known to few pianists. When have you heard dotted rhythms more sprucely articulated than in No 35's finale, or wondered how terms such as *vivace* can take on a whole new meaning given such rapier reflexes and musical sheen?

Hamelin is superbly alive to the Fantasia's fits and starts, to its skittish changes of pace and direction, and the 26th Sonata's finale flashes past in an unbelievable 45 seconds. True, you might take issue with his coolly flowing *Andante* in the F minor Variations but there is no lack of minor-key drama in the final pages, and you may well end up feeling that Hamelin's is a refreshing alternative. Again, the E minor (34th) Sonata's restless patterning is thrown off with never a hair out of place, and the concluding Sonata in C (No 48) is a marvel of precision, grace and fluency. Hyperion's sound and presentation could hardly be more immaculate, leaving one hoping that Hamelin will continue his Haydn series when not effortlessly scaling the heights of cloudier Romantic repertoire.

Piano Sonatas, HobXVI – Nos 26, 32, 36, 37 & 49
Leif Ove Andsnes *pf*

EMI 556756-2 (58' · DDD)　　　Ⓕ◗◑◗

This disc offers delectable performances of five shrewdly contrasted works: two troubled, trenchant minor-key sonatas from the 1770s juxtaposed with a pair of lightweight pieces from the same period and culminating in the great E flat Sonata. Andsnes is responsive to the individual character of these sonatas, to their richness and variety of incident, and their sheer unpredictability. With his wide spectrum of colour and dynamics he makes no apologies for using a modern Steinway. But his playing, founded on a pellucid *cantabile* touch and diamantine passagework, marries classical refinement and clarity with a spontaneous exuberance, a sense that the next phrase is yet to be created. Andsnes is always ready to add stylish and witty touches of embellishment to the repeats. The opening movements of both minor-key sonatas have a lithe, sinewy urgency, above all in the vehement sequences of their developments, together with a rare delicacy of nuance: and here, as elsewhere, you notice how alive and concentrated is his *piano* and *pianissimo* playing. Andsnes brings a bright, buoyant yet lyrical approach to the E flat Sonata's outer movements, to the wonderful *Adagio* a limpid line, a subtly flexed pulse and, in the B flat minor central episode, a true sense of passion. This is just the sort of playing – joyous, imaginative, involving – to win Haydn's sonatas a wider following. The recording of the E flat, made in a church in Oslo, has slightly more ambient warmth than that of the remaining sonatas, recorded at EMI's Abbey Road studios. But throughout, the piano sound is natural and present without being too closely miked.

'Haydn and the Art of Variation'
Keyboard Sonatas, HobXVI – Nos 19, 40, 42 & 48. Sonata (un piccolo divertimento: Variations), HobXVII/6
Carole Cerasi *fp*
Metronome METCD1085 (73' · DDD)　　Ⓕ◗◑◗

'Haydn and the Art of Variation' is Carole Cerasi's title for her latest release; each of its four sonatas contains a variation movement, and the disc culminates predictably (but gloriously) with the famous F minor Variations. It makes an unusual programme, but then Cerasi is never routine. Particularly impressive here is the way she allows her 1790s Schantz piano to shape her interpretations; like many players approaching the instrument from the direction of the harpsichord, she appreciates its special qualities and realises them with a relish and originality that releases this wonderful music from the 'warm-up' status it often endures in 'traditional' piano circles. Quite simply, she restores its colour, expressiveness and grandeur.

Listen to the beautiful other world created by the *una corda* in Sonata No 40, or the big left-hand octaves in the powerful and eloquent No 42. Listen everywhere to the alertness and responsiveness with which she marks out the tiny details of dynamic and timing that make the music really sing and speak. And listen to the utter sensitivity of finger and mind she brings to No 19, for which she switches to a sweet-voiced (and expertly recorded) clavichord. All these attributes find apotheosis in an account of the F minor Variations which is both thought-provoking and affecting. The tearful haze in which the piece usually opens is replaced by a bolder approach, with limping paired quavers in the accompaniment suggesting a more physical level of pain. Only with the final reprise of the main theme does she turn to the *una corda* for emotional effect, now all the better for having been withheld, before unleashing an uncommonly stormy coda. This is fortepiano playing of true distinction.

Piano Sonatas, HobXVI – Nos 24, 32, 36 & 46
Jean-Efflam Bavouzet pf
Chandos CHAN10586 (68' · DDD) Ⓕ ❍❍❍❍ᐅ

Interesting that the most intelligent musicians, the deepest-thinking of them, all maintain Haydn as a private passion. And now Jean-Efflam Bavouzet, acclaimed as a Debussy pianist, has placed himself among their number. His approach to four of Haydn's sonatas from in and around the 1770s is perhaps closer to that of Leif Ove Andsnes than it is to the nonchalant brilliance of Marc-André Hamelin. Clarity of line is paramount in this music and that is what Bavouzet delivers: he views the sonatas with sobriety but by no means dispassionately. While these are not 'difficult' works in terms of breathtaking virtuosity, they require great reserves of control from a pianist. Bavouzet responds vividly to the turbulence of the C sharp minor Sonata and the hieratic unfolding of the B minor, and is equal to the sudden shifts of mood within movements, while the toccata-like writing that features in so much of Haydn's keyboard music never becomes hectoring or hammered-out. Discreet ornamentation adds allure to music that offers both majesty and sweetness, and ranges from the grand gesture to Haydn's trademark high jinks, right down to the disconsolate minuet that draws the C sharp minor Sonata to its downbeat conclusion. A superb start to what we hope will be a long and comprehensive series.

Piano Sonatas, HobXVI – Nos 35-39
Jenö Jandó pf
Naxos 8 553128 (62' · DDD) Ⓢ ❍ᐅ

The exquisite, classical balance evident in these five sonatas makes them rewarding examples of Haydn's exploitation of the piano's broad expressive range and rich textural variety. This volume in Jenö Jandó's complete edition presents these pieces in a compelling, modern-instrument version. For example, there's brilliance and sparkle in the opening movements of the D major and E flat Sonatas; warmth and dramatic intensity in the slow movements (most

notably in the Baroque echoes of the Sonatas in C major and D major), and an appealing blend of wit and elegance in finales such as the third movement of the D major Sonata. Most remarkable, though, is the G major, where Jandó's precision and sensitive balance of linear and harmonic dimensions convey its concerto character and Haydn's imaginative approach to form. Try Jandó's engaging account of the opening *Allegro*, his deft balance of the slow movement's effective blend of major and minor, and his exuberant virtuosity in the finale.

Haydn Keyboard Sonata, HobXVI No 29
Prokofiev Piano Sonatas – No 2, Op 14; No 6, Op 82.
Visions fugitives, Op 22. Legend, Op 12 No 6
Sviatoslav Richter pf
BBC Legends mono BBCL4245-2 (76' · ADD)
Recorded live in 1961 Ⓕ ❍

Sviatoslav Richter is at the top of virtually everybody's short list of great pianists, and the reasons are not hard to find. His range was engulfing, even when he took a personal and surprising dislike to the most exalted repertoire, weeding out, for example, those Beethoven sonatas he considered less than convincing. This added spice to his early status, further enlivened by his first, belated appearances in the West.

On his arrival in New York and London in the '60s, anticipation pulsed at fever pitch and in the first of three London recitals, now blessedly released by BBC Legends, his unique quality was unmistakable. It is no exaggeration to say that his Haydn and Prokofiev recital was among the greatest ever heard on the Southbank. Here, Haydn's mischief is captured with a silken magic and dexterity peculiarly Richter's own, and who else could characterise so acutely the stylised oddity of Prokofiev's *Visions fugitives*? No one has touched Richter's way with the Second Sonata, its self-consciously prickly utterance resolved in a near-classical transparency. Everything is taken by stealth rather than storm with an unforgettably lyrical second subject, though with an unflagging impetus reserved for the *Scherzo* and for the finale's Tom and Jerry-cartoon caperings. The underlying menace of the composer's *inquieto* direction in the Eighth Sonata is frighteningly caught, a dark and introspective journey that leads through the *Andante*'s *faux naïf* charm to a finale of blistering strength and propulsion.

Piano Sonatas, HobXVI – Nos 32, 34 & 50. Fantasia, HobXVII/4. Andante con variazioni, HobXVII/6
Haydn/Sudbin Larking with Haydn
Yevgeny Sudbin pf
BIS Ⓢ BIS-SACD1788 (75' · DDD/DSD) Ⓕ ❍ᐅ

Yevgeny Sudbin becomes the latest star pianist to offer his take on Haydn's sonatas. His selection opens with the austere B minor Sonata, the keyboard counterpart of the later *Fifths* Quartet and something of a favourite among Haydnistas,

585

with recent versions by Marc-André Hamelin, Jean-Efflam Bavouzet and Leif Ove Andsnes. In approach Sudbin seems most similar to Bavouzet or Andsnes, clarity and control being among his foremost concerns, while not eschewing Hamelin's effortless brilliance and an impish delight in Haydn's mischievous rhythmic and harmonic sleight of hand. In fact the other two sonatas here, the lighter-hearted C major and the turbulent E minor, as well as the C major Fantasia and the F minor Variations, also duplicate repertoire from Hamelin's four discs of this music. Keyboard dexterity can naturally be taken as a given from a pianist who excels in the Russian Romantics; but let us not forget that Sudbin opened his account on record with a disc of sonatas by Domenico Scarlatti and he locates in Haydn's piano music the same mercurial shifts of mood and colour that made that debut recital such a delight.

Haydn allowed his fantasy and caprice free rein in the two single-movement works and to close we are treated to the pianist's witty, athletic gloss on the finale of the *Lark* Quartet. Sudbin is always a compelling presence in music ranging from the charming to the demonic, and this disc is another winner.

Piano Sonatas, HobXVI – Nos 49-52
Jenö Jandó pf
Naxos 8 550657 (62' · DDD)   Ⓢ🅑➡

The keyboard sonatas which Haydn originally intended for piano, such as the four considered here, show his exploration of the instrument's capacity for greater dynamic variation. Jandó is sensitive to the relationship between motif and dynamics which is particularly evident in the E flat and D major Sonatas. Aided by clear recorded sound, Jandó's warmth in the lyrical passages provides a dramatic contrast to his crisp, positive approach in the livelier music. Jandó's glittering technique has a high profile in the other two sonatas in the programme. His well-turned readings are uncontroversial, but they lack nothing in excitement. Sample the finale of the E flat Sonata, where the wealth of expressive detail at an extremely fast tempo is breathtaking.

Masses

Masses – in C, Missa in tempore belli (Paukenmesse), HobXXII/9; in B flat, Missa Sancti Bernardi von Offida (Heiligmesse), HobXXII/10. Insanae et vanae curae 🅟
Joanne Lunn sop **Sara Mingardo** contr
Topi Lehtipuu ten **Brindley Sherratt** bass
**Monteverdi Choir; English Baroque Soloists /
Sir John Eliot Gardiner**
Philips 470 819-2PH (79' · DDD · T/t)   Ⓕ🅞➡

This rounds off Gardiner's excellent series of the six late Masses, all supreme masterpieces, which Haydn wrote for the name day each year of the Princess Esterházy. There's also room for a valuable extra in the motet *Insanae et vanae*

curae. Haydn salvaged it from his Italian oratorio *Il ritorno di Tobia*, after he had pruned it, saying that it was 'too good to waste'. With a Latin text replacing the original Italian, it inspires Gardiner and his brilliant team to a searing performance, very different from those you'd get from a cathedral choir.

The Masses also find Gardiner on incisive form. The contrast with Hickox's Chandos cycle is most striking in the *Gloria* of the *Heiligmesse*. Where Hickox makes the music swagger happily, Gardiner directs a biting, crisp reading, with spotlit drums and trumpets and marginally less spring in the rhythm. Contrasts elsewhere are similar, if less marked; Hickox is warmer and more joyful where Gardiner, with some extreme speeds, is consistently crisp and fresh.

Both Masses were written in 1796 and the *Heiligmesse* first performed on the Princess's name day that year. The *Paukenmesse* was held over until 1797, though it had been heard in Vienna the previous December. Not only are both Masses smaller in scale than the succeeding four, the *Paukenmesse* at least is more lyrical, less grandly symphonic that those masterpieces. Haydn is still intent on springing surprises; he characteristically ends each with vigorous, even military settings of the 'Dona nobis pacem' which foreshadow Beethoven's illustration of war in the *Missa solemnis*.

The recording is clear and well balanced, highlighting the pinpoint ensemble of Gardiner's choir and his excellent team of soloists.

Masses – in G, Missa 'Rorate coeli desuper',   🅟
HobXXII/3; in B flat (Schöpfungsmesse), HobXXII/13
(with alternative setting of the Gloria)
Susan Gritton sop **Pamela Helen Stephen** mez
Mark Padmore ten **Stephen Varcoe** bar **Collegium
Musicum 90 Chorus; Collegium Musicum 90 /
Richard Hickox**
Chandos Chaconne CHAN0599 (62' · DDD · T/t)
                                                Ⓕ🅞➡

The *Creation* Mass is no less resplendent or searching than, say, the *Nelson* Mass or the *Harmoniemesse*, a glorious affirmation of Haydn's reverent, optimistic yet by no means naive faith. Even by Haydn's standards, the work is startling in its exploitation of colourful and dramatic key contrasts, as in the sudden swerve from F major to an apocalyptic *fortissimo* D flat at 'Judicare vivos'; the *Benedictus*, characteristically, moves from serene pastoral innocence (shades of 'With verdure clad' from *The Creation*) to urgent intensity in its central development; and the sublime G major *Agnus Dei* has a profound supplicatory fervour extraordinary even among the composer's many memorable settings of this text.

This reading eclipses previous recordings in the quality of its choir and soloists, the subtlety of Hickox's direction and the vividness and transparency of the recorded sound. In faster movements such as the *Kyrie* and the openings of the *Gloria* and *Credo* Hickox strikes just the right balance between dignity and happy, pulsing energy, relishing each of Haydn's dramatic coups; and he brings a marvellous clarity and verve, and a sure sense of climax, to the chromatically inflected fugues in the *Gloria* and at 'Dona nobis pacem'. Abetted by his first-rate orchestra, Hickox is always alive to the felicities of Haydn's scoring, while the 24-strong professional choir is superbly responsive throughout.

We also get the alternative version of the *Gloria*, and the ultra-compressed (6'49") and instantly forgettable *Missa Rorate coeli desuper*, which David Wyn Jones, in his excellent note, wryly describes as 'a reminder of how perfunctory church music in 18th-century Austria could be'. It's neatly dispatched by Hickox and his forces, but inevitably comes as an anticlimax.

Masses – in E flat (Great Organ Mass), HobXXII/4[a]; **P**
in C, Missa Cellensis (Mariazeller), HobXXII/8
Susan Gritton sop **Louise Winter** mez **Mark**
Padmore ten **Stephen Varcoe** bar **Ian Watson** org
Collegium Musicum 90 / Richard Hickox
Chandos Chaconne CHAN0674 (71' · DDD)   Ⓕ**OO**B→

This concluding issue in Richard Hickox's prize-winning Haydn Mass series follows a similar pattern to earlier discs, offering exhilarating performances which wear their period style lightly. Gardiner for Philips is by a fraction the more crisply incisive, with pinpoint attack and clean textures: Hickox generally prefers slightly broader speeds, with full, immediate sound, more clearly bringing out the joy of Haydn's inspiration as well as the drama.

Both of these Masses are relatively neglected, even on disc. The *Great Organ* Mass, dating from 1768-69, seems not to have been composed for a special occasion, but, exceptionally, because Haydn wanted to write it. It's a distinctive work, both in its choice of key, E flat, rare for a Mass of the time, and for replacing oboes in the orchestra with two cor anglais.

The role of the organ is far more important, though; its Baroque figuration attractively decorative, while the *Benedictus* includes a *concertante* organ part, accompanying the quartet of soloists. Choosing light registration, Ian Watson produces delightful sounds throughout, with delicate organ decorations set in contrast with the relatively plain choral writing. As in the rest of the Hickox series, the singing and playing of Collegium Musicum 90 is most stylish.

Hickox has a special relish for Haydn's rhythmic exuberance, as in the syncopated 'Amens' in the *Sanctus* and the robust 6/8 rhythms of the 'Dona nobis pacem' at the very end.

The *Mariazeller* Mass, written much later in 1782, was the last Mass setting that Haydn composed before the final six masterpieces, and already points forward. As in those late Masses, the *Kyrie* is in a compressed sonata form: a slow introduction leads to a vigorous *Allegro*, with the 'Christe eleison' as the development section. Clearly, Haydn was already thinking of his Mass settings in symphonic terms, with striking key-

changes also relating to Haydn's symphonic writing. Even more than in the *Great Organ* Mass, Hickox brings out the vitality of the writing, as in the extraordinary 'Dona nobis pacem' at the end, so wildly syncopated it's almost jazzy. A splendid culmination to an outstanding series.

Masses – in D minor, Missa 'sunt bona mixta   **P**
malis', HobXXII/2; in C, Missa Cellensis
(Cäcilienmesse), HobXXII/5.
Susan Gritton sop **Pamela Helen Stephen** mez
Mark Padmore ten **Stephen Varcoe** bass
Collegium Musicum 90 / Richard Hickox
Chandos CHAN0667 (70' · DDD · T/t)   Ⓕ**O**B→

This is the only current recording of the fragmentary *Missa sunt bona mixta malis*, consisting only of a brief setting of the *Kyrie* followed by a more expansive setting of the *Gloria*, which is cut off after the 'Gratias agimus tibi'. Improbably, the score was discovered as recently as 1983 in a farmhouse in the north of Ireland. Dating from 1768, it's tantalising having only a fragment when the contrapuntal writing presents Haydn at his most striking in this period. It makes a fascinating supplement to Hickox's superb account of the longest setting of the liturgy that Haydn ever composed. The title of the *Missa Cellensis* – referring to the small Austrian town of Mariazell – is misleading in two ways. It's obviously so when there's another, later Mass also entitled *Cellensis*, but equally because it seems highly unlikely that so ambitious a work as this was ever designed for such a place as Mariazell: it was more probably written for a grand occasion in Vienna. So it would surely be less confusing to return to the usual title for this work, 'St Cecilia Mass'.

This is a 'cantata-mass', very different from Haydn's usual settings which involve a single movement for each of the six sections of the liturgy. Here instead, the liturgy is divided into 18 separate movements. Hickox's new version gains over the fine Preston issue from the late 1970s in weight and warmth of expression, helped by the Chandos recording which, while warm, allows ample detail in the many splendid contrapuntal passages. The choir's sopranos are amply bright and boyish and achieve a crisp ensemble. The soloists make an outstanding, responsive team.

Masses – in G, Missa Sancti Nicolai (Nikolaimesse),   **P**
HobXXII/6; in B flat, Missa Sancti Bernardi von Offida
(Heiligmesse), HobXXII/10
Lorna Anderson sop **Pamela Helen Stephen** mez
Mark Padmore ten **Stephen Varcoe** bar
Collegium Musicum 90 / Richard Hickox
Chandos Chaconne CHAN0645 (62' · DDD · T/t) Ⓕ⒟B→

With fresh, inspiriting work from soloists, chorus and orchestra, the performance of the so-called *Heiligmesse* captures the symphonic impetus and the spiritual and physical exhilaration of this gloriously life-affirming music. Hickox opts for Haydn's original scoring, minus the horn parts and the enhanced parts for clarinets that he later added for a performance in Vienna's Court Chapel. Hickox is ever responsive to the drama and colour of Haydn's orchestral writing, while the 24-strong chorus sings with firm, well-nourished tone over a wide dynamic range and a real care for the meaning of the text. The many high-lying entries are always true, never strained or overblown, and the sopranos rise unflinchingly to their frequent high B flats. The soloists have less to do here than in Haydn's other late Masses: but, led by the plangent, beseeching soprano of Lorna Anderson, they sing with a chamber-music grace and intimacy.

The appealing *Missa brevis* is cast in the 'pastoral' key of G major. Again, the soloists make their mark both individually and in ensemble, with Anderson floating a beautiful line in the 'Gratias' and Mark Padmore launching the expressive G minor 'Et incarnatus est' with gently rounded tone and graceful phrasing. The recorded sound is clear, spacious and carefully balanced, combining vivid orchestral detail with plenty of impact from the chorus.

Masses – in B flat, HobXXII/7, Missa brevis
Sancti Johannis de Deo ('Little Organ Mass');
in B flat (Theresienmesse), HobXXII/12
Janice Watson *sop* **Pamela Helen Stephen** *mez*
Mark Padmore *ten* **Stephen Varcoe** *bar*
Collegium Musicum 90 Chorus; Collegium
Musicum 90 / Richard Hickox
Chandos CHAN0592 (60' · DDD · T/t)

Hickox generates the physical and spiritual elation essential to this music, calling to mind Haydn's own much-quoted remark that whenever he praised God his heart leapt with joy. In the glorious *Theresienmesse* of 1799 Hickox's manner is particularly fine in the exultant, springing *Gloria* and the rough-hewn vigour of the *Credo*. He understands, too, the Mass's dramatic and symphonic impetus, bringing a powerful cumulative momentum to the sonata-form 'Dona nobis pacem' and thrillingly tightening the screws in the closing pages. The choir is placed forward, though never at the expense of orchestral detail, keenly observed by Hickox. His uncommonly well-integrated solo quartet framed by the sweet-toned Janice Watson and the gentle, mellifluous Stephen Varcoe, sings with a chamber-musical grace and refinement in the 'Et incarnatus est' and the *Benedictus*. And their supplicatory tenderness in the 'Dona nobis pacem' contrasts arrestingly with the choir's urgent demands for peace.

Hickox also captures the peculiar serenity and innocence of the much earlier *Missa brevis Sancti Johannis de Deo*, or *Little Organ Mass*, its intimacy enhanced here by the use of solo strings. A disc guaranteed to refresh the spirit.

Mass in C, Missa in tempore belli (Paukenmesse),
HobXXII/9. Te Deum in C, HobXXIIIc/1. Te Deum in

C, HobXXIIIc/2. Alfred, König der Angelsachsen,
HobXXX/5 – Aria des Schutzgeistes; Chor der
Dänen
Nancy Argenta *sop* **Catherine Denley** *mez* **Mark**
Padmore *ten* **Stephen Varcoe** *bar* **Jacqueline Fox**
spkr **Collegium Musicum 90 Chorus and**
Orchestra / Richard Hickox
Chandos Chaconne CHAN0633 (64' · DDD · T/t)

Few other conductors on disc convey so happily the drama, symphonic power and spiritual exhilaration of these glorious works than Richard Hickox. He's fully alive to the ominous unease that permeates the great *Mass in Time of War*, but while others strive for maximum dramatic and rhetorical effect, he directs the Mass with a natural, unforced sense of phrase and pace. The playing of Collegium Musicum 90, led by Simon Standage, is polished and athletic, with detail sharply etched, while the chorus sings with fresh tone and incisive attack. The four soloists are well matched in the anxious C minor *Benedictus*; elsewhere Nancy Argenta brings a pure, slender tone, and a graceful sense of phrase to the *Kyrie*, while in the 'Qui tollis' Stephen Varcoe deploys his mellow baritone with real sensitivity.

The fill-ups are imaginatively chosen. The two *Te Deum* settings epitomise the immense distance Haydn travelled during his career, the rococo exuberance and strict species counterpoint of the little-known early work contrasting with the grandeur and massive, rough-hewn energy of the 1799 setting.

The two numbers of incidental music Haydn completed for the play *King Alfred* in 1796, shortly before embarking on the Mass, are a real collectors' item. Argenta sings the first hymn-like E flat aria with chaste elegance, while choir and orchestra palpably enjoy themselves in the following number, a rollicking, brassy celebration of the Danes' victory over the Anglo-Saxons. Invigorating performances and first-class recorded sound, with an ideally judged balance between chorus and orchestra.

Mass in D minor (Nelsonmesse), HobXXII/11.
Te Deum in C, HobXXIIIc/2
Dame Felicity Lott *sop* **Carolyn Watkinson** *contr*
Maldwyn Davies *ten* **David Wilson-Johnson** *bar*
The English Concert and Choir / Trevor Pinnock
Archiv 423 097-2AH (50' · ADD · T/t)

The British Admiral had ousted the Napoleonic fleet at the Battle of the Nile just as Haydn was in the middle of writing his *Nelson* Mass. Although the news could not have reached him until after its completion, Haydn's awareness of the international situation was expressed in the work's subtitle, 'Missa in Augustiis', or 'Mass in times of fear'. With its rattle of timpani, pungent trumpet calls, and highly strung harmonic structure, there's no work of Haydn's which cries out so loudly for recording on period instruments; and it's the distinctive sonority and highly charged tempi of this performance which set it apart. The dry, hard timpani and long trumpets bite into the dissonance of the opening *Kyrie*, and the near vibrato-less string playing is mordant and urgent. The fast-slow-fast triptych of the *Gloria* is set out in nervously contrasted speeds, and the *Credo* bounces with affirmation. Just as the choral singing is meticulously balanced with instrumental inflexion, so the soloists have been chosen to highlight the colours in Pinnock's palette.

Masses – in D minor (Nelsonmesse), HobXXII/11; ℗
in B flat (Theresienmesse), HobXXII/12. Te Deum in C, HobXXIIIc/2
Donna Brown sop **Sally Bruce-Payne** mez
Peter Butterfield ten **Gerald Finley** bass
Monteverdi Choir; English Baroque Soloists /
Sir John Eliot Gardiner
Philips ② 470 286-2PH (89' · DDD · T/t) Ⓜ❶❶❶❶➛

Dating respectively from 1798 and 1799, the *Nelsonmesse* and the *Theresienmesse* are the third and fourth of the six Masses written for the nameday of the Princess Esterházy. That was a period during the Napoleonic wars when Prince Esterházy, Nikolaus II, had economised by dismissing his *Harmonie* or windband. Even so, in 1798 for the *Nelsonmesse*, Haydn, seeking to reflect the mood of the times (hence the official title, *Missa in angustiis* – 'Mass in times of fear'), brought in three trumpets and timpani, and their impact is all the greater when set against strings and organ alone.

That heightened contrast is a point which comes out with thrilling attack in Gardiner's performance at the very opening of the *Kyrie*. This vigorous *Allegro*, typical of Haydn but totally untypical of Mass-settings, introduces martial fanfares, which recur through the whole work. Though Haydn composed the Mass in a mere 53 days in the summer of 1798, just when Nelson was winning the Battle of Aboukir, Haydn knew nothing of that victory till later, and the Nelson association dates from two years later when the admiral visited Eisenstadt, and the Mass was given in his honour.

Gardiner's treatment of the fanfares offers only the first of dozens of examples where his crisp, incisive manner highlights the extraordinary originality of this work. The *Theresienmesse* brings similar revelations. Here, in addition to trumpets and timpani, Haydn scored for two clarinets, and though this is a less sharply dramatic, more lyrical work, a martial flavour is again introduced. There are surprises aplenty, as in the sudden silence of the orchestra in the setting of the word 'miserere' at the end of the 'Gratias agimus tibi', or the setting of 'Et incarnatus' in the *Credo* in the rare key (in this context) of B flat minor, and 'Et vitam venturi' set in a galloping 6/8 time or the bold, square opening of *Agnus Dei* in bare octaves at an unapologetic *forte*. Such points must have startled early listeners, and Gardin-

---

HAYDN NELSON MASS – IN BRIEF

Soloists; The English Concert and Choir / ℗
Trevor Pinnock
Archiv 423 097-2AH Ⓕ❶❶❶❶➛
💎 A thrilling performance from 1989 of Haydn's 'Mass in times of fear'. Pinnock directs with a winning buoyancy that doesn't neglect the work's charged mood. His soloists are superb and The English Concert Choir sing with tremendous power.

Soloists; Monteverdi Choir; English Baroque ℗
Soloists / John Eliot Gardiner
Philips 470 286-2PH Ⓕ❶❶❶➛
Another superb performance characterised by magnificent choral work and thrilling orchestral playing. Gardiner brings his characteristic feel for a work's drama thrillingly to bear on this great work.

Soloists; Collegium Musicum 90 and Choir / ℗
Richard Hickox
Chandos CHAN0640 Ⓕ❶❶➛
Part of Hickox's fine Haydn Mass series, this is well worth hearing, but it's outclassed by the Pinnock and Gardiner for the sheer precision and intensity of their approach. Splendidly recorded, though.

Soloists; London Symphony Chorus; City of
London Sinfonia / Richard Hickox
Decca 448 983-2DEC Ⓑ
If you like Hickox's way with this music but prefer modern instruments, this is well worth acquiring. Excellent solo singing with Barbara Bonney the radiant soprano, and firm, focused choral work from the London Symphony Chorus.

Soloists; Choir of King's College, Cambridge;
London SO / Sir David Willcocks
Decca 458 623-2DM Ⓑ
Sir David Willcocks's 1962 King's College performance of the *Nelson* Mass takes its place alongside the excellent series of Haydn Masses recorded by George Guest at St John's College, Cambridge.

---

er's treatment makes one appreciate that with new ears.

In this respect he even outshines Richard Hickox, whose prize-winning Mass series for Chandos brings equally enjoyable performances of both these works, just as energetic and a degree warmer, thanks in part to the recording acoustic. Gardiner's team, on the other hand, has markedly cleaner separation of textures, with soloists and chorus more sharply defined. Gardiner's Monteverdi Choir as ever sings with passion, brilliance and fine precision, and his soloists are all outstanding, fresh and youthful-sounding with firm clear voices. As a splendid, very apt bonus there's a superb account of the magnificent ceremonial C major *Te Deum*.

Mass in B flat (Harmoniemesse), HobXXII/14.   **P**
Salve regina in E, HobXXIII*b*/1
Nancy Argenta *sop* **Pamela Helen Stephen** *mez*
Mark Padmore *ten* **Stephen Varcoe** *bar* **Collegium**
Musicum 90 Chorus; Collegium Musicum 90 /
Richard Hickox
Chandos Chaconne CHAN0612 (59' · DDD · T/t)
Ⓟ Ⓞ ➔

Haydn's first major work, the *Salve regina* of
1756, is here juxtaposed with his last, the *Harmo-*
niemesse of 1802, so-called because of its exceptionally full scoring for woodwind. The gulf
between the two works, in sophistication, mastery and emotional range, is predictably vast. Yet,
in their very different ways, both reconcile the
formal liturgical conventions of their era with the
expression of Haydn's own life-affirming religious faith. Hickox and his forces ideally capture
this sense of celebratory spiritual energy. Tempi
are lively, rhythms alert and vital. In the Mass
Hickox generates an exhilarating symphonic
momentum in, say, the opening sections of the
Gloria and *Credo*, and, aided by an outstandingly
clear, well-balanced recording, realises to the full
such dramatic coups as the sudden swerve into
A flat in the recapitulation of the 'Benedictus' and
the martial fanfares that slew the music from
D major to B flat at the start of the 'Dona nobis
pacem'. The steely-edged valveless trumpets are
thrilling here; and elsewhere the wind players do
rich justice to Haydn's glorious writing, nicely
balancing rusticity and refinement.
    Nancy Argenta's innocent, bell-like tones and
graceful sense of line are heard to touching
effect in the 'Et incarnatus est' of the Mass. In
the *Salve regina*, she also reveals her deft, fluent
coloratura technique. No great depths in this
youthful work, but Haydn's setting of the Marian antiphon is elegant and affecting, with a
command of shapely, Italianate melody and a
feeling for dramatic contrast. This is certainly
the most memorable work of Haydn's from the
1750s and aptly complements Hickox's fervent,
inspiring reading of the *Harmoniemesse*.

Il ritorno di Tobio, HobXXI/1

Il ritorno di Tobia
Roberta Invernizzi, Sophie Karthäuser *sops*
Ann Hallenberg *mez* **Anders Dahlin** *ten*
Nikolay Borchev *bass* **Cologne Vocal Ensemble;**
Capella Augustina / Andreas Spering
Naxos ③ 8 570300/2 (169' · DDD · T)   Ⓢ ➔

Probably no major Haydn work is harder to 'sell'
today than his Italian oratorio *Il ritorno di Tobia*,
composed for a Viennese benevolent society during winter 1774-75. Far from being a prototype
Creation or *Seasons*, *Tobia* is in effect a sacred *opera*
seria, powered by a succession of gargantuan arias,
with, in its original version, just three choruses for
contrast. For a 1784 revival Haydn spruced it up
with two extra choral numbers, including a cataclysmic 'storm' chorus that has become well
known as the motet *Insanae et vanae curae*.

The prime stumbling-block is the libretto by
Giovanni Gastone Boccherini, brother of the
more famous Luigi. With its murders, monsters
and miracles, the story of Tobias from the Apoc-
rypha could have been a composer's gift.
Instead, Boccherini laboriously observes Classical convention and sets Tobias's adventures
entirely in the past tense. When Tobias and his
new wife, the serially widowed Sara (husbands
one to seven have all been murdered by the
demon Asmodeus), eventually appear, the action
grinds forward with stultifying slowness,
weighed down by reams of sententious moralising. 'Delay could prove fatal', says Tobias to his
mother Anna as he prepares to cure his father
Tobit's cataract with the gall of a sea monster.
He then launches into an eight-minute 'parable'
aria, to which his mother rejoinders, 'A just
sense of urgency spurs him on'.
    Yet while *Tobia* is a virtual non-starter dra-
matically, Haydn's music is carefully and elaborately composed and, provided you can adjust to
the leisurely time-frame, often inspired. The
choruses are all superb, the arias inventive and
vastly challenging. They include spectacular
vocal concertos, enlivened by Haydn's genius
for tone-painting, a dulcet E major love song for
Tobias, and a terrific F minor 'nightmare' scene
for Anna. The oratorio's jewel, though, is Sara's
radiant 'Non parmi essere', with its luxurious
concertante writing for flutes, oboes, cors anglais,
bassoons and horns.
    This new recording is even better than the
old (and long-deleted) Dorati version. The
pacing is generally sharper (crucial in the many
accompanied recitatives), while the period
instruments of the Capella Augustina make for
altogether tangier, more transparent sonorities
than Dorati's smoothly upholstered RPO.
Valveless brass lour and exult in the choral
numbers, while the faintly breathy, bucolic
period woodwind carol enchantingly in "Non
parmi essere". This aria is exquisitely sung by
the pellucid-toned Sophie Karthäuser, a true
classical stylist, who negotiates the coloratura
in her opening aria with grace and panache.
The other female singers match her in virtuosity and vocal allure. The bell-toned Roberta
Invernizzi is properly dazzling in the flamboyant arias for the (disguised) Archangel Raphael,
while mezzo Ann Hallenberg uses the text
imaginatively and brings a ferocious intensity
to her nightmare aria, abetted by Spering's
dangerous energy and the baleful colouring of
brass and cors anglais. In the predominantly
lyrical role of Tobit, Nikolay Borchev impresses
with his warm, soft-grained bass and sympathetic phrasing. Only the pleasant but protein-
deficient tenor of Anders Dahlin, as Tobias,
leaves one wanting more. The choral singing is
fresh and eager, though, as so often, the
recorded balance rather favours the orchestra.
There is also too much pingy harpsichord continuo for some tastes. But these are minor
drawbacks in a stunning performance of some
glorious, under-valued music. Haydn lovers
should snap it up as a matter of urgency.

The Creation (Die Schöpfung), HobXXI/2

Die Schöpfung   P
Sylvia McNair, Donna Brown *sops*
Michael Schade *ten* **Rodney Gilfry,**
Gerald Finley *bars* **Monteverdi Choir;**
English Baroque Soloists /
Sir John Eliot Gardiner
Archiv ② 477 6327AGP2 (101' · DDD · T)   Ⓜ❍❍❍➾

With Gardiner's first down-beat it's obvious that Chaos's days are numbered. Not that 'days' (strictly speaking) are in question till the mighty words have been spoken, and then, in this performance, what an instantaneous blaze! No premonitory intimation (of pre-echo in the old days whereas now even the faintest stirring in the ranks of the choir will do it), but a single-handed switching-on of the cosmic power-grid and a magnificently sustained C major chord to flood the universe with light. This is one of the great characteristics here: the superbly confident, precise attack of choir and orchestra. Enthusiasm, then, in plenty; but how about the mystery of Creation? It's certainly part of the aim to capture this, for the bass soloist's 'Im Anfange' ('In the beginning') with *pianissimo* chorus has rarely been so softly and so spaciously taken: the Spirit that moved upon the face of the waters is a veiled, flesh-creeping presence, felt again in the first sunrise and the 'softer beams with milder light' of the first moon. Even so, others have incorporated this element more naturally.

Gardiner has an excellent Raphael in Gerald Finley, and gains from having extra singers for Adam and Eve, especially as the Eve, Donna Brown, brings a forthright style doubly welcome after the somewhat shrinking-violet manner and breathy tone of Sylvia McNair's Gabriel. On the whole, Gardiner is sound: yet his is a fun *Creation* and a real enrichment of the library. Against others of comparable kind, Gardiner stands firm as an easy first choice: a re-creator of vision, a great invigorator and life-enhancer.

Die Schöpfung
Sally Matthews *sop* **Ian Bostridge** *ten* **Dietrich**
Henschel *bass* **London Symphony Chorus and**
Orchestra / Sir Colin Davis
LSO Live ② 💿 LSO0628 (103' · DDD/DSD)
Recorded live 2007   Ⓑ❍➾

Always an unaffected and inspiriting Haydn conductor, Colin Davis again reveals his profound sympathy for the composer on this LSO Live *Creation*, in German (Haydn would have expected a British performance to be sung in English), recorded at concerts in the Barbican. Encouraging lithe, rhythmically pointed playing from the LSO, he distils an authentically Haydnesque spirit of joyous exhilaration. Yet he is also acutely responsive to the work's majesty and awe, its evocation of what the 18th century termed 'the sublime'. Davis combines an intense feeling for colour and atmosphere with a marvellous breadth and inevitability of phrase.

The LSO Chorus, numbering, at a guess, around 100, cannot, of course, match the focus and incisiveness of the professional choirs used by Harnoncourt, Gardiner et al. Yet from the hushed evocation of the spirit moving upon the face of the waters and the overwhelming cosmic blaze on 'Licht', the choir sings with sensitivity and full-throated enthusiasm; and Davis ensures that each of the choruses that close the three parts builds thrillingly to an incandescent climax.

After a prosaic (and under-the-note) initial entry, Dietrich Henschel is a fiery and imaginative Raphael and an ardent Adam – though the combination of a fast tempo and a lack of true soft singing make for a less-than-poetic 'limpid brook'. Occasionally Ian Bostridge can force his lyric tenor beyond its comfort zone. But his is a subtle, involving performance, minutely attentive to the sound and sense of the German text. In the creation of the first woman he and the LSO's principal cellist Tim Hugh vie with each other in eloquence and tenderness. Sally Matthews, with a darker, creamier voice than most sopranos in this work, makes a sensuous Eve, though she sounds a shade severe and charmless in Gabriel's two arias. 'Nun beut die Flur' (aka 'With verdure clad'), especially, needs more of a smile in the tone.

While the period-instrument versions from Harnoncourt, Gardiner and, for a performance that replicates the grand scale of the 1799 public premiere, McCreesh still top the *Creation* short list, this is certainly a recording to return to: for much of the solo work, for the glorious playing of the LSO and, above all, for Davis's wise, joyous direction.

Die Schöpfung   P
Sunhae Im *sop* **Jan Kobow** *ten*
Hanno Müller-Brachmann *bass* **Cologne Vocal**
Ensemble; Capella Augustina / Andreas Spering
Naxos ② 8 557380/1 (105' · DDD)   Ⓢ❍❍➾

Recorded in Cologne in July 2003 by German Radio, this issue offers a first-rate period performance of Haydn's masterpiece, lively and well sung. Since other issues of *Die Schöpfung* in the super-budget category use modern instruments it fills an important gap, particularly as the digital sound is so clear and transparent. Andreas Spering successfully brings out the composer's eternal freshness.

The prelude representing Chaos is taken slowly, markedly more so than by Gardiner or Brüggen, but that brings out all the more the abrasiveness of Haydn's daring dissonances. After the extreme hush of that opening the choral cry of 'Licht' is shattering in its impact; in the following tenor aria Spering shows his true colours in a crisp, faster-than-usual *andante* that's exhilaratingly carefree, not least

HAYDN'S CREATION – IN BRIEF

Janowitz, Ludwig, Wunderlich, Krenn, Fischer-Dieskau, Berry; Vienna Singerverein; Berlin PO / Herbert von Karajan
DG ② 449 761-2GOR2　Ⓜ ⚫⚫⚫▷

A de luxe line-up for Karajan's *Creation* (Wunderlich's death halfway through the recording meant that Werner Krenn recorded the recitatives). Karajan's feeling for the music is considerable, and he brings drama as well as intimacy to it.

McNair, Brown, Schade, Finley, Gilfry;　Ⓟ
Monteverdi Choir; English Baroque Soloists / Sir John Eliot Gardiner
Archiv ② 449 217-2AH2　Ⓕ ⚫⚫⚫▷

A very fine period-instrument version full of drama and imaginative response to the text. Gardiner's wonderful choir sings superbly and his EBS play thrillingly.

Karthäuser, Kühmeier, Spence, Werba,　Ⓟ
Henschel; Les Arts Florissants / William Christie
Virgin Classics ② 395235-2　Ⓑ

A wonderful entry into the Haydn discography by Christie and his French forces. He characterises vividly and lets the music speak for itself. A fine modern period version.

Kermes, Mields, Davislim, Mannoc, Chung;　Ⓟ
Balthazar-Neumann Choir and Ensemble / Thomas Hengelbrock
Deutsche Harmonia Mundi ② 05472 77537-2　Ⓕ

A swift, exciting period-instrument recording that has a fresh, appealing youthful feel to it. The soloists are delightful and Hengelbrock's chorus is excellent.

Röschmann, Schade, Gerhaher; Arnold　Ⓟ
Schoenberg Choir; Concentus Musicus Wien / Nikolaus Harnoncourt
Deutsche Harmonia Mundi ② 82876 58340-2
Ⓕ⚫⚫

Harnoncourt returns to *The Creation* after 18 years, this time on period instruments, and gives a wise, spiritually satisfying performance. The soloists are superb and the chorus sing magnificently. A period version to rival the Gardiner.

Im, Kobow, Müller-Brachmann;
Cologne Vocal Ensemble;
Capella Augustina / Andreas Spering
Naxos ② 8 557380/1　Ⓢ⚫⚫▷

A splendid bargain-price version which combines power and freshness. Youthful voices and a fine chorus add to its attractions.

Piau, Persson, Massey, Padmore, Harvey,　Ⓟ
Davies; Gabrieli Consort and Players / Paul McCreesh
Archiv ② 477 7361AH2　Ⓕ⚫⚫⚫▷

A superb English language *Creation* done on a grand scale. Magnificent!

at the felicitous passage, marked *sotto voce*, when the chorus sings of 'eine neue Welt'. His speeds are generally on the fast side, but when, as in the prelude, the marking is *largo* as opposed to *andante* or *adagio*, he takes a measured view.

The Cologne Vocal Ensemble is a relatively compact body, incisive in its attack, and set in a helpful but not over-large acoustic. The three soloists are all excellent and youthful-sounding. An outstanding bargain.

The Creation (sung in English)
Sandrine Piau, Miah Persson *sops* **Ruth Massey** *contr* **Mark Padmore** *ten* **Peter Harvey** *bar* **Neal Davies** *bass* **Gabrieli Consort and Players / Paul McCreesh**
Archiv ② 477 7361AH2 (110' · DDD)　Ⓕ⚫⚫▷

Haydn and his librettist Baron van Swieten conceived *The Creation* as the first bilingual oratorio and would surely have been perplexed that Anglophone record-buyers seem to prefer the work in German. The main problem, of course, is that the Baron's command of English failed to match his self-confidence, prompting many attempts to improve on the original.

On this new recording, Paul McCreesh's emendations are less radical than those on the two other available versions in English (from Simon Rattle and Robert Shaw), but on the whole more successful, retaining all the Milton-inspired quaintness of van Swieten's text while rectifying his mistranslations and clumsy Germanic word order.

Language apart, McCreesh's recording differs from its period competitors in scale: where they typically use a smallish professional choir and an orchestra of around 50, McCreesh pits a 113-strong band against a chorus of similar numbers. Abetted by the glowing, spacious acoustics of Watford Town Hall, the big celebratory choruses make a more powerful impact than in any of the rival period versions. Occasionally – say in the rollicking fugue in 'Awake the harp', here done at a constant *fortissimo* – one would have welcomed more nuanced dynamics. But there is no denying the incandescence of the climaxes to 'The heavens are telling' and the final 'Praise the Lord, uplift your voices'.

In all the choruses McCreesh's pacing – eager but never hectic – and rhythmic energy are wonderfully inspiriting. He is acutely responsive, too, to the work's mystery and awe, daring, and vindicating, slower-than-usual tempi for 'Chaos' (launched by the most apocalyptic of timpani rolls), the Sunrise and the first morning in Paradise, celestially evoked by the Gabrieli's trio of flutes. A pity, though, that he allows the cannon-fire timpani to pre-empt Haydn's cosmic blaze at 'light'.

McCreesh's trump card is his solo team, superb both individually and as an exceptionally sensitive ensemble. Has the trio near the close of Part 2, 'On thee each living soul awaits', ever been sung with such radiant inwardness? Other highlights include Sandrine Piau's graceful, smiling 'With verdure clad', here a truly happy song to the spring, Mark Padmore's tender *legato* in Haydn's portrayal of the first woman, and Neal Davies's deep, velvet softness in 'the limpid brook' and his hieratic reverence in the sublime arioso 'Be fruitful all, and multiply'. Peter Harvey, supple and lyrical, and Miah Persson, with a touch of sensuousness in her vernal tone, are beautifully paired as Adam and Eve. For a *Creation* in English, this new version – exhilarating, poetic and marvellously sung – becomes the prime recommendation.

Die Schöpfung
Edith Mathis sop **Christoph Prégardien** ten **René Pape** bass **Lucerne Festival Chorus; Scottish Chamber Orchestra / Peter Schreier**
Video Director **Elisabeth Birke-Malzer**
ArtHaus Musik 🄳🅅🄳 100 040 (109' · PAL/NTSC · 4:3 · PCM stereo · 0)　　　　Ⓕ

This enjoyable performance of Haydn's supreme choral masterpiece was recorded at the Lucerne Festival of 1992. It takes place in the appropriate setting of an evocative Baroque church, which isn't identified either on screen or in the (inadequate) supporting booklet. The small choir sings with attentive enthusiasm, and is weak only in the tenor department. The Scottish Chamber Orchestra players cover themselves in glory both as an ensemble and individually, and they're adept at imposing period practice on modern instruments. Schreier's direction is relaxed and benevolent, yet his keen ear for rhythmic precision and flexibility in phrasing is constantly felt.

The soloists are all Swiss. The veteran Mathis remains a paragon of Classical style, phrasing her arias and contributions to the ensembles with firm tone and finely honed phrasing. Prégardien's liquid, silvery tenor and sensitive way with words is just what the tenor part calls for. The young Pape's sonorous bass and confident delivery are ideal; he and Mathis make an appealing Adam and Eve in Part 3.

The video direction is discreet, and prompt in homing in on the right performer at the right time. The sound picture is as spacious and well defined.

The Seasons (Die Jahreszeiten), HobXXI/3

Die Jahreszeiten　　　　Ⓟ
Marlis Petersen sop **Werner Güra** ten **Dietrich Henschel** bar **RIAS Chamber Choir, Berlin; Freiburg Baroque Orchestra / René Jacobs**
Harmonia Mundi 🔊 ② HMC80 1829/30
(125' · DDD · T/t)　　　　ⒻⓄⓄⓄ➔

It would be hard to imagine a more joyful account of Haydn's culminating masterpiece. Jacobs and his outstanding team perfectly capture the exuberance with

which the composer seemed to be defying the years. Infectious rhythms bring out the fun of *The Seasons* from the start, and when in Simon's first aria Haydn quotes from the slow movement of the *Surprise* Symphony, Jacobs nudges the music persuasively. And in the final chorus of 'Summer', the lowing cattle and quail's cry, and chirping crickets and croaking frogs, sound witty, not naive.

In all this Jacobs is helped by a clear and immediate recording. The RIAS Chamber Choir is a fair match for Gardiner's Monteverdi Choir, and the soloists are first-rate, fresh and youthful-sounding. A final choice is a matter of taste but this newer account's greater sense of relaxation and feeling for the fun in the writing make its claims second to none.

Die Jahreszeiten　　　　Ⓟ
Barbara Bonney sop **Anthony Rolfe Johnson** ten **Andreas Schmidt** bar **Monteverdi Choir; English Baroque Soloists / Sir John Eliot Gardiner**
Archiv ② 431 818-2AH2 (127' · DDD · T/t)　　ⒻⓄⓄ➔

The comparative unpopularity of Haydn's *The Seasons* when considered against *The Creation* is understandable perhaps, but it isn't all that well deserved. Less exalted its subject and libretto may be, but its depiction of the progress of the year amid the scenes and occupations of the Austrian countryside drew from its composer music of unfailing invention, benign warmth and constant musical-pictorial delights. As usual, Gardiner and his forces turn in disciplined, meticulously professional performances, though the orchestra is slightly larger – and consequently a tiny bit less lucid – than the sort you might nowadays find playing a classical symphony. The choir, however, performs with great clarity and accuracy, and brings, too, an enjoyable sense of characterisation to their various corporate roles.

The soloists all perform with notable poise and intelligence: Barbara Bonney's voice is pure and even, Anthony Rolfe Johnson sounds entirely at ease with the music, and Andreas Schmidt is gentle-voiced but certainly not lacking in substance. A first-class recommendation.

Die Jahreszeiten　　　　Ⓟ
Genia Kühmeier sop **Werner Güra** ten **Christian Gerhaher** bar **Arnold Schoenberg Choir; Concentus Musicus Wien / Nikolaus Harnoncourt**
Deutsche Harmonia Mundi ② 88697 28126 2
(137' · DDD)　　　　ⒻⓄⓄ➔

On this, his second recording of *The Seasons*, Nikolaus Harnoncourt's affection for the spirit and teeming detail of Haydn's celebration of an idealised rural world is again manifest. Yet pacing and characterisation now seem that much more natural, with none of the earlier recording's idiosyncratic (usually slow) tempo choices. The opening chorus of 'Spring', for instance, distinctly lethargic in 1987, now has a gentle lilt, with a palpable sense of wonder and delight at nature's rebirth.

Speeds in the choral numbers still tend to be broader than those favoured by Gardiner and the bucolically uninhibited René Jacobs, sometimes, as in the oratorio's majestic finale, with a welcome gain in nobility. One or two of the fugues – say, the ones in the Prayer in 'Spring' and the summer tempest – are again slightly marred by Harnoncourt's trademark exaggerated *staccatos* and fussy, micro-managed dynamics. But the boozy wine harvest rivals Jacobs's in lusty, lurching exuberance. Here and elsewhere – not least in the thrilling account of the autumn chase, with its shifting horn perspectives and vividly whooping grace notes from trombones and bassoons – Harnoncourt and his crack forces relish all the bold and brilliant colours of Haydn's astonishingly inventive score.

Harnoncourt's solo team, too, is a match for any on disc. Fast-rising soprano Genia Kühmeier is an enchanting Hanne, radiant and graceful in her big aria in 'Summer', and singing her song of aristocratic lust outwitted with just the right knowing humour. Werner Güra, as mellifluous and elegant as he was for Jacobs, and the virile, imposing baritone of Christian Gerhaher both bring to their music a Lieder singer's care for precise colouring and character. Abetted by Harnoncourt's atmospheric accompaniments, Güra's description of summer torpor and Gerhaher's sombre and dramatic memento mori in 'Winter' are two highlights of an often inspiring recording. For a prime recommendation in this glorious, life-affirming work of the composer's old age, the choice now lies between Gardiner, Jacobs and this new Harnoncourt.

Die Jahreszeiten
Miriam Meyer sop **James Taylor** ten **Ralf Lukas** bass
Chorgemeinschaft Neubeuern; Klang Verwaltung Orchestra, Munich / Enoch zu Guttenberg
Farao Classics **DVD** B108055
(167' · NTSC · 16:9 · PCM Stereo and 5.0 · 0)　　Ⓕ

This performance comes from the Markgräfliches Opernhaus in Bayreuth, the rococo theatre where Wagner originally thought he might stage *The Ring*. Made for television in 2004, it now appears on DVD for the first time.

What is striking is the way in which Haydn evokes the shade of Mozart. 'Uns speiset Überfluss' and 'Quam olim Abrahae' in the Requiem are perhaps no more than 18th-century common coin; but the slow movement of Mozart's Symphony No 40 can be heard in 'Erblick hier, betörter Mensch', and the last section of the duet for Hanne and Lukas in 'Autumn' recalls Konstanze and Belmonte in *Die Entführung*. Each season includes at least one fugue. Enoch zu Guttenberg claims that Haydn expressed his distaste for having to set a chorus in praise of industry (in the sense of hard work) by writing a 'merciless parody' of a Baroque fugue: unlikely, if only because the fugal last chorus makes use of

the same flattened seventh, and it's addressed to God.

Guttenberg makes this point in one of four optional talks, in which he says much of interest. He and his Bavarian forces give an excellent account of this underrated piece. Well-balanced soloists and orchestra (modern instruments, with natural horns added in the hunting chorus, and a wonderful alphorn in 'Der munt're Hirt'), but the choir could be more forward. The conductor's bizarre liking for quiet endings to loud movements is not enough to spoil enjoyment of this splendid recording.

Folksong arrangements

Scottish Songs for William Whyte
Lorna Anderson sop **Jamie MacDougall** ten
Haydn Trio Eisenstadt
Brilliant Classics ③ 93453 (3h 32' · DDD · T/t)　　Ⓢ

'Up in the morning early' is the title of one of these songs, and we gather from the singer that it's not for her. But if the music of one composer could be guaranteed to cheer the process it would be Haydn's. In whatever mood he writes he carries a wholesome conviction that life is good.

His folksong arrangements are the unexpected, joyous and fairly lucrative work of old age. He came to them through the advances of George Thomson of Edinburgh, and previous volumes in this admirable edition have included the 200-odd written for that enterprising collector and publisher. His contributions were so successful that competitors became interested, and Haydn, on to a good thing, did not turn them down.

His immense output was maintained at an amazingly consistent standard of freshness and apparently effortless invention. Equally consistent is the standard of performance, the singers ideally suited to their task, the instrumentalists unfailingly lively and stylish in their playing.

The distinctive feature of this fourth volume is that these songs were written for one of the rival publishers, William Whyte, and include some of the best-known such as 'John Anderson, my Jo' and 'Auld lang syne', set to a jaunty, light-footed rhythm with no hint of Hogmanay mawkishness. Tales of laddies sent to the wars and lasses left forlorn at home are familiar subject-matter. Some, like 'The braes of Bellenden', come close to the condition of what we call art-song, and several of the melodies require of the singer nimble fluency over a wide range. For ourselves, we are never in danger of forgetting that all are in the Scottish folk tradition, for the texts require frequent recourse to the thoughtfully provided glossary – alas in microscopic type!

Opera, Concert and Oratorio Arias

'L'infedeltà costante'　　Ⓟ
La fedeltà premiata – Sinfonia; Barbaro conte...
È questa la mercè; Dell' amor mio fedele; Placidi

ruscelletti. Orlando Paladino – Sinfonia; Ad un guardo. La vera costanza – Sinfonia; Misera, chi m'aiuta…; Dove fuggo. L'infedeltà delusa – Ho un tumore in un ginocchio; Trinche vaine allegramente. L'isola disabitata – Overtura; Se non piange un infelice. Arianna a Naxos, HobXXVlb/2. Sono Alcina, e sono ancora, HobXXIVb/9 (insertion aria for Gazzaniga's L'isola di Alcina). D'una sposa meschinella, HobXXIVb/2 (insertion aria for Paisiello's La frascatana)
Anna Bonitatibus *mez*
Il Complesso Barocco / Alan Curtis
Deutsche Harmonia Mundi ⏺ 88697 32632-2 (78' · DDD/DSD)   Ⓕ Ⓞ ➔

A captivating, show-stealing Cherubino at Covent Garden, Italian mezzo Anna Bonitatibus quarries arias from Haydn's still rarely aired Eszterháza operas, ranging from a brace of *buffo* songs for the disguised Vespina in *L'infedeltà delusa*, via numbers for the gentle shepherdess Celia and the upwardly mobile Amaranta from *La fedeltà premiata*, to the fisher-girl Rosina's magnificent, despairing outburst from *La vera costanza*.

She also throws in two modestly charming 'insertion' arias Haydn composed for Eszterháza revivals of operas by Paisiello and Gazzaniga, and ends with the great keyboard-accompanied cantata *Arianna a Naxos* that quickly became a favourite in the salons of Vienna and London.

On disc Bonitatibus's quick vibrato, characteristic of singers south of the Alps, may initially faze those accustomed to 'straighter' voices in 18th-century music. Sometimes – as in the opening of Arianna's final aria – she sacrifices a pure *legato* to intensity of expression. That said, Bonitatibus brings to each of these portraits a rich, flavoursome voice and a flair for characterisation, relishing the sound and sense of the words (an Italian always has a head start in this repertoire). She is splendidly imperious in Alcina's fiery entrance aria (*Orlando Paladino*), amusingly over-the-top in Vespina's consumptive old woman act, and catches every shade of the distraught Rosina's fluctuating emotions.

Alan Curtis is not the most poetic of fortepianists in *Arianna*, and as conductor sometimes lets rhythms plod in slower numbers. But in the main he encourages lively, characterful playing from his period band, whether in a rip-roaring account of the 'hunting' overture to *La fedeltà premiata* (which Haydn recycled as the finale to Symphony No 73) or as eager colluders in Vespina's comic play-acting.

Berenice che fai, HobXXIVa/10. Il ritorno di Tobia – Anna, m'ascolta! L'anima del filosofo, ossia Orfeo ed Euridice – Al tuo seno fortunato; Filomena abbandonata; Del mio core il voto estremo. Armida – Parti Rinaldo; Se pietade avete, o Numi. Il mondo della luna – Se la mia stella. Orlando Paladino – Aure chete, verdi allori; Non partir
Simona Šaturová *sop*
North German Radio Philharmonic Orchestra,

Hanover / Alessandro De Marchi
Orfeo C782 091A (62' · DDD)   Ⓕ

Had Haydn been spirited to Hanover in 2008, he would probably have wished for more resonance in Šaturová's lowest notes in his *Scena di Berenice*. That apart, he would surely have appreciated the young Slovakian soprano's clear, expressive voice, shapely line and dramatic intensity as she captures each successive phase of Berenice's disorientation and mounting anguish. In the tremendous final F minor aria Šaturová's tastefully crazy ornamental flourishes enhance the sense of the heroine going out of her mind with grief.

Šaturová is equally impressive in a clutch of operatic arias, including items from three of Haydn's finest soprano roles, Angelica (*Orlando Paladino*), Armida, and Euridice from his London opera *L'anima del filosofo*. She softens her naturally bright tone for a touching, eloquently phrased account of Euridice's death scene. The agility and evenness of her 'divisions' are well displayed in the Genio's showstopper from *L'anima del filosofo* and a gargantuan coloratura aria from the oratorio *Il ritorno di Tobia*. Here and occasionally elsewhere Šaturová's highest notes can acquire an acidic edge. Other provisos include an unnecessary harpsichord continuo in the otherwise spirited orchestral accompaniments and a lack of English translations in the booklet, all the more frustrating when most of the items are little-known. But these should hardly deter Haydn lovers from investigating a splendid recital from a young soprano who rises with skill and flair to the music's varied challenges.

L'anima del filosofo, ossia Orfeo ed Euridice –   Ⓟ
Chi spira e non sprea; Il pensier sta negli aggotti; Mai non sia inulto. Armida – Se dal suo braccio; Teco lo guida al campo. La fedeltà premiata – Sappi, che la bellezza; Mi dica, il mio signore; Di questo audace ferro. L'incontro improvviso – Noi pariamo santarelli. L'infedeltà delusa – Non v'e rimedio. L'isola disabitata – Chi nel cammin d'onore. Il mondo della luna – Non aver di me sospetto[a]; Che mondo amabile. Orlando Paladino – Mille lampi d'accese; Ombre insepolte. La vera costanza – Non sparate… mi disdico. Dice benissimo, HobXXIVb/5. Un cor sì tenero, HobXXIVb/11
Thomas Quasthoff *bass-bar*
[a]Genia Kühmeier *sop* **Freiburg Baroque Orchestra / Gottfried von der Goltz**
DG 477 7469GH (63' · DDD · T/t)   Ⓕ Ⓞ Ⓞ ➔

'These arias are glorious music that give me more pleasure each time I sing them,' enthuses Thomas Quasthoff of his Haydn anniversary recital encompassing 11 roles from nine operas. Judging the arias by Mozartian standards (unfair, but hard to avoid when the idiom is so similar), we might feel that Haydn's response to character and dramatic situation can occasionally seem too amiably non-committal. Far more often, though, Quasthoff's encomium is well justified, whether in the sharp comic portrayals of assorted dolts, lechers and buffoons, the sepulchral solo for the Stygian ferryman Caronte (*Orlando Paladino*), or the graceful *cantabile* arias for Creonte from the London opera *L'anima del filosofo*. If Haydn's operas are alien territory for you, the range and inventiveness of these arias (plus one duet) may come as a surprise.

Quasthoff's performances are vividly imagined and splendidly sung. He characterises each role with relish. As ever, he savours the sound and sense of the words, greedily gobbling up his consonants in the song of the gluttonous monk Calandro (*L'incontro improvviso*). In serious mode, he brings a gravely eloquent *legato* to the numbers for Caronte and Creonte, and commands both the height and the depth for the fine, dignified arias from *Armida* and *L'isola disabitata*.

Once or twice Quasthoff's softer singing sounds unsupported, starved of natural resonance. Nit-pickers might also point to moments where he coarsens his tone in the name of dramatic intensity. But these are minor provisos. Quasthoff has done a still-neglected corner of Haydn's output proud, and the rhythmically lively Freiburg period band match him all the way in colour and gusto.

L'anima del filosofo, ossia Orfeo ed Euridice

L'anima del filosofo, ossia Orfeo et Euridice   Ⓟ
Uwe Heilmann ten Orfeo **Cecilia Bartoli** mez
Euridice, Genio **Ildebrando d'Arcangelo** bass
Creonte **Andrea Silvestrelli** bass Pluto **Angela
Kazimierczuk** sop Baccante **Roberto Scaltriti** bar
First Chorus **Jose Fardilha** bass Second Chorus
Colin Campbell bar Third Chorus **James Oxley** ten
Fourth Chorus **Chorus and Orchestra of the
Academy of Ancient Music /
Christopher Hogwood**
L'Oiseau-Lyre ② 452 668-2OHO2 (124' · DDD · T/t)
                            Ⓕ Ⓞ ➔

Christopher Hogwood builds his band on the model of those prevalent in late 18th-century London theatres. Not only does his phrasing and articulation discover no end of witty and poignant nuances, but the grave austerity of the string playing, and the plangency of the early woodwind instruments are eloquent advocates of an opera whose uncompromisingly tragic ending owes more to Ovid and Milton than to operatic tradition. Hogwood also remembers that Haydn was writing for a Handelian London choral tradition: his chorus, be they cast as Cupids, Shades or Furies, have robust presence, and sculpt their lines with firm muscle.

Cecilia Bartoli takes the role of Euridice. In her very first aria, 'Filomena abbandonata', she understands and eagerly recreates the type of coloratura writing which simultaneously fleshes out the central nightingale simile and incarnates the single word 'crudeltà'. Her unmistakable, melting half-voice comes into its own as emotion first clouds reason, only to create the fatal

emotional extremes to which she gives voice so thrillingly. Uwe Heilmann is just the tenor of rare agility and wide vocal range vital for this particular Orfeo. The minor parts are strongly profiled: d'Arcangelo is a stern, noble Creonte, Silvestrelli a fearsome, stentorian Pluto – and there's even a convincing *strepito ostile* offstage as Euridice's abduction is attempted in Act 2. Beyond the detail, it's the poignancy of the musical drama at the heart of this strange, grave *Orfeo* which Hogwood reveals with such sympathetic and imaginative insight.

Orlando Paladino

Orlando Paladino   Ⓟ
Patricia Petibon sop Angelica **Christian Gerhaher**
bar Rodomonte **Michael Schade** ten Orlando
Werner Güra ten Medoro **Johannes Kalpers** ten
Licone **Malin Hartelius** sop Eurilla **Markus Schäfer**
ten Pasquale **Elisabeth von Magnus** mez Alcina
Florian Boesch bass Caronte
Concentus Musicus Wien / Nikolaus Harnoncourt
Deutsche Harmonia Mundi ② 82876 73370-2
(141' · DDD · S/T/t/N). Recorded live   Ⓕ

Nikolaus Harnoncourt boldly proclaims that *Orlando Paladino* 'is one of the best works in 18th-century music theatre'. Written to commemorate a visit by Russian royalty to Eszterháza that never materialised, *Orlando Paladino* was first performed in 1782, in celebration of Prince Nikolaus's name day.

Sabine Gruber's conversational essay explains how Haydn's musical portraits show an astute affection for Ariosto's epic poem. Although Haydn's *Orlando Paladino* seems part-pantomime, part-fantasy, these characters are never conscious that they are not what they protest to be. Like Ariosto, Haydn lets the audience in on the joke but the characters remain blissfully oblivious to the hypocrisy or naivety of their richly ironic statements to themselves and each other.

Harnoncourt's exemplary team of singers deliver deadpan comedy. For instance, Werner Güra takes on an *opera seria* posture as the romantic 'hero' Medoro in 'Parto, ma, oh Dio': the glorious musical language suggests he suffers from sincere passion, but his real motivation is cowardice. One imagines that Patricia Petibon's Angelica is merely emulating the heroic fidelity and courage of women like Mozart's Konstanze but during 'Non partir, mia bella face' one suspects that there is sincerity in her after all: Angelica is facing possible abandonment and her vulnerability shows through. Michael Schade's voice is smokier than it used to be but his powerful resonant high notes, expressive weight and authority suggest that Orlando is more victim than villain. Only the comic secondary roles sung by Markus Schäfer and Malin Hartelius get hammed up, but they each sing with élan.

There is a vivid sense of dramatic intensity in this live concert recording. It is historically absurd to employ a lute as part of the continuo team in a late-18th-century opera but Harnoncourt leads

Concentus Musicus Wien through a fizzing theatrical performance. This is comfortably among the finest Haydn opera recordings, although the stingy omission of scene numbers and stage directions from the libretto is unhelpful.

Orlando Paladino
Marlis Petersen *sop* Angelica **Pietro Spagnoli** *bass*
Rodomonte **Tom Randle** *ten* Orlando **Magnus**
Staveland *ten* Medoro **Arttu Kataja** *bass* Licone,
Caronte **Sunhae Im** *sop* Eurilla **Victor Torres** *bar*
Pasquale **Alexandrina Pendatchanska** *sop* Alcina
Freiburg Baroque Orchestra / René Jacobs
Stage directors **Nigel Lowery; Amir Hosseinpour**
TV director **Andreas Morell**
EuroArts ② *DVD* 205 7788 (168' · NTSC · 16:9 · PCM
Stereo and DTS 5.1 · 0)
Recorded live at the Staatsoper Unter den Linden,   ·
Berlin in 2009   Ⓕ

Despite serious numbers for Angelica and the mooning Medoro, the opera's prevailing tone is one of chaotic silliness. In this Berlin production, British director Nigel Lowery and Iranian choreographer Amir Hosseinpour heighten the absurdity and artifice with a surreal, cartoonish grotesquerie. Rodomonte, got up as a pantomime pirate, casually slices off the hand of Eurilla's father Licone; Pasquale enters staggering under the weight of an oversized rucksack with a mule perched on the top; Eurilla appears variously as a mini-skirted Madame Mao and gymslip-clad schoolgirl. The sets suggest the Brothers Grimm crossed with Monty Python, with much hurling of Christmas trees and random appearances from hideous shaggy forest denizens of both sexes.

The modern opera producer's abhorrence of stillness means that the action can be cluttered where Haydn's music is at its most heartfelt. Most incongruous and irritating of all is the bearded air hostess who stalks Angelica in her grieving aria 'Aure chete'. But while some of the visual gags fall flat, the staging's zany, over-the-top energy makes an entertaining case for an opera longer on purely musical delights than on subtlety of characterisation, let alone dramatic coherence.

The lively cast is well chosen. Marlis Petersen conveys both Angelica's vulnerability and, in bouts of imperious coloratura, her regal defiance, while Norwegian tenor Magnus Staveland, with a touch of metal in his pleasing lyrical tone, makes the most of the ungrateful part of Medoro. The diminutive Sunhae Im is a charming – vocally and visually – and wily Eurilla, deft in her semaphore routines. Victor Torres, always a vivid comic presence, despatches Pasquale's patter songs with virtuoso flair, while Pietro Spagnoli rants and swaggers vividly as the ludicrous Rodomonte.

In the title-role Tom Randle, with his musky, baritonal tenor, does his fair share of comic ranting too, though he is touching in his final aria as the bemused Orlando emerges from his enchanted sleep. Alexandrina Pendatchanska,

like Im a Jacobs regular, takes her chances brilliantly as a twitchingly neurotic Alcina, singing with darkly flaming tone and rightly bringing the house down in a last-act aria filched from an earlier Haydn comic opera, *Il mondo della luna*. As ever, Jacobs's direction bristles with rhythmic energy and pungent detail. Whatever the provisos, this DVD could well convert those still unconvinced that Haydn's comic operas, for all their musical beauties, can be made to work in the theatre.

Michael Haydn   Austrian 1737–1806

Michael Haydn was Joseph's younger brother and sang with him at St Stephen's Cathedral, Vienna. During 1757-63 he was Kapellmeister to the Bishop of Grosswardein and in 1763 was appointed court musician and Konzertmeister to the Prince-Archbishop of Salzburg. He was a close friend of Mozart and his family, and succeeded Mozart as cathedral organist in 1781. He also taught: Carl Maria von Weber was one of his pupils.

As well as a substantial amount of sacred music, he wrote instrumental works which include about 40 symphonies, 12 string quartets and four duets for violin and viola (Mozart helped an ailing Michael out by composing two to make a set of six). He also composed Singspiels, incidental music, an opera seria (1787), oratorios, cantatas and other secular vocal works.

Masses

Requiem (Missa pro defuncto Archiepiscopo
Sigismundo), MH155 Kl I/8. Missa in honorem
Sanctae Ursulae, MH546 Kl I/18
Carolyn Sampson *sop* **Hilary Summers** *contr* **James**
Gilchrist *ten* **Peter Harvey** *bass* **The King's Consort**
Choir; The King's Consort / Robert King
Hyperion ② CDA67510 (84' · DDD · T/t) Ⓜ●●●Ⓟ→

Robert King suggests that Michael Haydn's Requiem of 1771 for the Prince-Archbishop of Salzburg reflects a personal outpouring of grief for the loss of Haydn's beloved patron and the recent death of his infant daughter. The fervent expressions of grief, consolation and hope must have made some impression on the 15-year-old Mozart. A comparison with Mozart's Requiem setting of 20 years later is inevitable: Haydn didn't give his solo quartet anything that compares with the immediacy of Mozart's 'Tuba mirum', but the older man's masterful choral writing, brilliant orchestral scoring and sensitive use of solo voices created plenty of musical riches and dramatic moods, such as the brooding *Kyrie* and the bursting energy of the 'Dies irae'.

The quartet of soloists is impeccable; the choir and orchestra of The King's Consort prove to be increasingly assured and dynamic with each recording released. Robert King's measured and emphatic direction makes it easy to appreciate why the Requiem was performed at his brother Joseph's funeral in 1809.

His interpretation of the sunnier, extrovert *Missa in honorem Sanctae Ursulae* (1793) helps the music to sound natural and spontaneous. In some respects the Mass is an even finer composition, full of charismatic and inventive musical charms (it's worth buying for Carolyn Sampson's ravishing 'Benedictus' alone).

Anybody who enjoys the choral works of Mozart and Joseph Haydn will be delighted by this double-disc set, and will probably concur that Michael Haydn's neglect in the shadow of his younger friend and older brother is substantially corrected by these exquisite performances.

Johann Heinichen   German 1683-1729

Heinichen studied at the University of Leipzig, qualifying as a lawyer in 1706, and practised law until 1709. During this time he was also composing. In 1709 he moved to Leipzig and put on operas and directed a collegium musicum. During 1710-16 he lived in Italy and he had two operas staged in Venice in 1713. In 1717 Heinichen became a colleague of JS Bach at the court of Leopold, Prince of Anhalt-Cöthen, and subsequently went on to be Kapellmeister to the Elector of Saxony. His pupils included Johann Georg Pisendel. His music has only been rediscovered within the past three decades.

Concertos

Concertos – C, S211; G, S213; G, S214,'Darmstadt';   🅿
S214, Venezia'; G, S215; G, S217; F, S226; F, S231; F, ·
S232; F, S233; F, S234; F, S235. Serenata di Moritzburg
in F, S204. Sonata in A, S208. Movement in C minor,
S240
Musica Antiqua Köln / Reinhard Goebel
Archiv ② 477 6330AGP2 (137' · DDD)   Ⓕ🅞🅞🅞🅒➔

Ⓖ   Johann David Heinichen was a contemporary of Bach and one of an important group of musicians employed by the Dresden court during the 1720s and 1730s. As well as being an inventive composer, Heinichen was also a noted theorist and his treatise on the continuo bass was widely admired. All the music collected here was probably written for the excellent Dresden court orchestra and most of it falls into that rewarding category in which north and central German composers were pre-eminent. Vivaldi had provided effective models but the predilection for drawing upon other influences, too, gives the concertos of the Germans greater diversity. Heinichen admittedly doesn't so readily venture into the Polish regions whose folk-music gives such a piquancy to Telemann's concertos and suites, but the wonderful variety of instrumental colour and deployment of alternating 'choirs' is every bit as skilful. Your attention

will be held from start to finish. Much of the credit for this must go to Reinhard Goebel and his impeccably drilled Musica Antiqua Köln. Some of these pieces might well seem less entertaining in the hands of less imaginative musicians and it would be untruthful to claim that everything is of uniform interest. Each concerto fields its own distinctive wind group drawing variously upon recorders, flutes, oboes, bassoons and horns, the latter always in pairs, in addition to *concertante* parts in many of them for one or more violins and cellos. There's little need to say more. The recorded sound is first-rate, and Goebel's painstaking essay is fascinating to read.

Te Deum

'Christmas at the Court of Dresden'
Heinichen Pastorale in A, 'Per la notte della
Natività Christi'. Te Deum **Ristori** Messa per il
Santissimo Natale di Nostro Signore. Motetto
pastorale **Schürer** Christus natus est nobis. Jesu
redemptor omnium **Seger** Praeludium
Christine Wolff *sop* **Britta Schwarz** *contr* **Martin
Petzold** *ten* **Sebastian Knebel** *org* **Dresden
Körnerscher Singverein; Dresden Instrumental-
Concert / Peter Kopp**
Carus 83 169 (78' · DDD · T/t)   Ⓕ

This charming disc has been lovingly researched and produced: the liturgical model is the Christmas Eve service used at the Dresden Court during the mid-18th century. All the composers were closely associated with Dresden, and the choir, orchestra and conductor are all from that city too.

Peter Kopp is a stylish director, and his youthful choir and orchestra are magnificent. The soloists are capable, although the soprano and alto don't always blend convincingly in Schürer's *Christus natus est*. Heinichen's *Te Deum* is replete with brilliant horns, exhilarating choruses and moments of pastoral tenderness. Giovanni Alberto Ristori, a Bolognese musician who settled in Dresden, composed his *Messa per il Santissimo Natale* in 1744. It's full of glorious and lyrical moments evoking shepherds and the Nativity. The elegant performance of Ristori's *O admirabile mysterium* goes to show what we lost when most of his church music was destroyed during the Second World War. Almost all the works here are receiving their first recordings; Carus deserves credit for its illuminating exploration of the rich Dresden school of Baroque sacred music.

Hans Werner Henze   German b1926

Henze studied at a music school in Braunschweig and, after war service, with Fortner at the Institute for Church Music in Heidelberg. At first his music betrayed a Stravinskian neo-classical style (First Symphony), but soon he was exploring 12-note seri-

alism. He remained open to a more tonal language and his works from the 1950s admitted influences as wide-ranging as neo-classicism, Schoenbergian or Bergian Expressionism and jazz. And he also maintained faith with traditional forms, including symphonies, ballets and operas (such as Boulevard Solitude of 1952).

In 1953 he moved to Italy, where his music became more expansive, sensuous and lyrical and vocal music bercame a dominant mode of expression. He wrote a sequence of operas (König Hirsch, 1956; Elegy for Young Lovers, 1961; The Bassarids, 1966) and cantatas (Kammermusik, 1958; Cantata della fiaba estrema, 1963).

A Second Piano Concerto followed in 1967 and after Henze visited Cuba in 1969 and '70 he became an outspoken advocate of revolutionary socialism. In Cuba he conducted the first performance of his Sixth Symphony, incorporating the tunes of revolutionary songs. Other works from this period that explored a political stance were El Cimarrón (1970) and the opera We Come to the River (1976).

His later works, while arguably less controversial, continued his political and social engagement. His Requiem (1990-93) comprised nine sacred concertos for piano, trumpet and chamber orchestra, and was written in memory of the London Sinfonietta music director Michael Vyner who died young. The choral Ninth Symphony (1997), to a libretto by Hans-Ulrich Treichel based on motifs from the novel The Seventh Cross by Anna Seghers, is a defiant rejection of Nazi barbarism, with which Henze himself lived as a child and teenager. His most recent successes include the 2003 premiere of the opera L'Upupa und der Triumph der Sohnesliebe at the Salzburg Festival, based on a Syrian fairy-tale. Other recent compositions include Sebastian im Traum (2004) for large orchestra, and the opera Phaedra (2007). Elogium Musicum (2008), for large orchestra and chorus singing a text in Latin of Henze's own devising, is an obituary to his partner of more than 40 years, Fausto Moroni.

Concertos

Violin Concertos – No 1; No 2[a]; No 3
Torsten Janicke *vn* [a]**Ulf Dirk Mädler** *bar*
**Magdeburg Philharmonic Orchestra /
Christian Ehwald**
Dabringhaus und Grimm 🎵 MDG601 1242-2
(86' · DDD)   Ⓕ

The concerto has been central to Henze's output throughout his career, even if many works do not bear the title 'concerto' or, as with the Requiem, exist in fusion with other genres. This formal freedom is evident in the three violin concertos. The vibrant First (1948), begun while he was still studying with Fortner, shows his initial, halting attempts at 12-note composition, an ambitious endeavour embarked on with no formal guidance (though the stylistic bedrock is still Hindemith). While a little learning may be a dangerous thing, here it goes a long way indeed. The Concerto teems with magical sounds pointing the way to the operas of the 1950s and '60s.

Concerto and theatre collide in the Second (1971), written at the height of Henze's early period of political engagement. Scored for solo violin (at one point amplified, and whose player is instructed to wear a flowing black tailcoat and plumed tricorn hat), solo baritone, tape and an ensemble of 33 instruments, this Expressionist score is dominated by Hans Magnus Enzensberger's poem *Homage to Gödel* with its central image of the 'liar' Münchhausen extricating himself from a quagmire by pulling at his own pigtail. From it Henze conjures a fascinating sonic tapestry, a most original rethink of the whole notion of the role of the individual that is the Concerto's core concern.

There is a literary connection in No 3 (1997, given here in its 2002 revision), consisting of three character portraits drawn from Thomas Mann's *Doktor Faustus*: Esmeralda, the child 'Echo' and Rudi Schwerdtfeger. The Concerto has common traits with Henze's enchanting Shakespearean Eighth Symphony and is similarly rich in ideas and imagery. The performances by Torsten Janicke are strongly characterised and virtuoso, and Christian Ehwald draws sympathetic accompaniments from the well drilled Magdeburg Philharmonic, recorded somewhat distantly but clearly.

Symphonies

Symphonies Nos 7 & 8
**Berlin Radio Symphony Orchestra /
Marek Janowski**
Wergo WER6721-2 (60' · DDD)   Ⓕ Ⓞ

Inspired by three speeches in *A Midsummer Night's Dream*, Henze's Eighth (1992-93) is the most beguiling and immediately appealing of his symphonies, beautifully written for the orchestra and luminous in tone. Janowski and his Berlin players audibly relish Puck's putting a girdle round the earth (though in under eight minutes, not Shakespeare's 40!), traversing from middle C to the polar extremes of the orchestra's register. There's fun in the *Ballabille scherzo* where Janowski catches the Stravinskian rhythmic undertow.

This is the third outing for the Seventh (1984), making it Henze's most recorded. Sadly, the strongest account – Rattle's, made for EMI while still at Birmingham – is currently unavailable. Despite differences in approach, not least in duration with Rattle three and a half minutes slower (mostly in the sonata-form second movement and finale), Janowski's will do very nicely. True, Janowski does not match Rattle's impulsion in the opening *Tanz* (also in sonata form) but his performance catches fire in the central movements, especially in the *Scherzo's* macabre depiction of the instruments of torture used on the poet Hölderlin. Janowski's finale – much swifter than Rattle's – is wholly convincing. If the symphonies alone are your priority, Janowski's disc is the best option.

Symphony No 8. Adagio, Fuge und Mänadentanz
(Suite from the opera 'The Bassarids'). Nachtstücke
und Arien[a]
[a]**Claudia Barainsky** sop **Gürzenich Orchestra,
Cologne / Markus Stenz**
Phoenix Edition 113 (74' · DDD)   (F)

The three pieces on this disc range across the
majority of Henze's mature career, from 1957 to
2005. Earliest is *Nachtstücke und Arien*, a vocal-
and-orchestral diptych setting poems by Ingeborg Bachmann, perhaps the dearest of Henze's
early collaborators, framed and separated by
three orchestral 'night pieces'. Henze had written to Bachmann two years before about how he
wished 'to write the most beautiful contemporary music' and in this rapt score he took a huge
step towards that aim. So much so, indeed, that
it prompted Boulez, Nono and Stockhausen to
stage a petulant walk-out at the premiere. Claudia Barainsky sings beautifully and Markus
Stenz directs a taut account.

The *Adagio, Fuge und Mänadentanz* is the most
recent item, premiered in 2005 but extracted
from Henze's finest opera, *The Bassarids* (1966).
The opera was premiered under Christoph von
Dohnányi who, 39 years later, requested this 25-
minute suite and conducted its first performance. Drawn from the third of the opera's four
acts (or movements: it is constructed as a two-
hour symphony in four movements), it forms a
compellingly satisfying whole.

So too, though, does the major item here, the
Eighth Symphony, premiered by them in 1993.
Inspired by three scenes in *A Midsummer Night's
Dream*, the Eighth is – like Beethoven's and
Vaughan Williams's – something of a relaxation
between the mightier edifices of the Seventh and
Ninth but an utter delight from first bar to last.
The Gürzenich Orchestra play with real inspira-
tion under Stenz's intelligent direction. Recom-
mended.

Symphony No 10. La selva incantata. Quattro Poemi
**Montpellier National Orchestra /
Friedemann Layer**
Accord 476 7156 (60' · DDD). Recorded live 2004   (F)

After the monumental Ninth, Henze's Tenth
(1997-2000) resumes an engagement with some
of the concerns of its immediate predecessors.
The Seventh and Eighth had literary roots, in
Hölderlin and Shakespeare respectively. There is
no programme as such here, but as the titles of the
four movements – 'A Storm', 'A Hymn', 'A
Dance', 'A Dream' – suggest, there is a large illustrative element in the music. The result is a fascinating orchestral panoply that, when one listens
deeper, is a true symphony. Henze's harmonic
language in his symphonies may not always please
purists, but there is always a clear (if occasionally
halting) flow and, whatever their diverse inspirations, the four movements have a logical and
unified progression.

It is enormously encouraging to see a French
label tackling such a project. And almost as sur-

prising is having a French orchestra tackle so
German a set of pieces. The Montpellier players
emerge with flying colours, giving well drilled,
exciting performances with a real sense of occasion. In the *Quattro Poemi* (1955) they catch at
least as well as their Wergo rivals the 'turbulent
emotionalism and spacious, questing lyricism'
that lies at the heart of the music, while *La selva
incantata* (1991) really buzzes along – as does the
Scherzo of the symphony. Accord's sound is
nicely lucid without being spectacular.

Nachtstücke und Arien

Drei Sinfonische Etüden. Quattro Poemi.
Nachtstücke und Arien[a]. La selva incantata[a]
[a]**Michaela Kaune** sop **North German Radio
Symphony Orchestra / Peter Ruzicka**
Wergo WER6637-2 (61' · DDD)   (F)

This attractive compilation fills significant gaps in
the current discography of Henze's earlier compositions. The main work, *Nachtstücke und Arien*,
dates from 1957, and mortally offended avant-
garde puritans at its premiere by its revival of full-
blooded lyricism, less than 10 years after Strauss's
Four Last Songs was supposed to have said a final
farewell to such self-indulgence. This sumptuous,
at times explosively dramatic music, comes across
well in this performance. Michaela Kaune sings
with poise and, where necessary, an apt operatic
flair. The recorded sound throughout is adequate,
though not especially well defined.

Like the other works on the disc, *Nachtstücke
und Arien* owes far more to the post-Romantic
espressivo of Berg and Schoenberg than it does to
Strauss. It's most directly indebted to Henze's
own opera *König Hirsch*, the major work of the
1950s in which he gave his new-found love of
melody the fullest rein. With *La selva incantata*
('The enchanted forest', 1991) we find Henze
revisiting *König Hirsch* and recasting some of its
most characterful music in purely orchestral
form. *Three Symphonic Studies* and *Four Poems* for
orchestra were both written in the 1950s, and
although less fully rounded than *Nachtstücke und
Arien*, they all have Henze's typical blend of
turbulent emotionalism and spacious, questing
lyricism. In the relatively extended first *Study*
the risk of aimless drifting isn't altogether
avoided. But this lapse is corrected with interest
in the shorter, more tightly controlled *Poems*.
The romantic resonances confirm how fruitful
the experience of composing for the theatre, and
engaging with earlier German traditions, had
become for Henze. Those resonances continue
in most of his finest later works, but the idiomatic performances on this disc let you hear
some of their earliest manifestations.

Operas

Boulevard Solitude
Laura Aikin sop Manon Lescaut **Pär Lindskog** ten
Armand des Grieux **Tom Fox** bass Lescaut **Hubert**

Delamboye *ten* Lilaque père **Pauls Putnins** *bass*
Lilaque fils **Marc Canturri** *bar* Francis
**Cor Vivaldi; Palau de la Música Catalana Chamber
Choir; Liceu Grand Theatre Symphony Orchestra,
Barcelona / Zoltán Peskó**
Stage director **Nikolaus Lehnhoff**
Video director **Xavi Bové**
Euroarts 🟥 205 6358 (102' · NTSC · 16:9 · PCM
stereo, 5.1 and DTS 5.1 · 0). Recorded live at the
Liceu Theatre, Barcelona, in March 2007   Ⓕ🔵

The sceptical voices were disappointingly persistent when the Royal Opera's reopening season in 2000 staged the UK premiere of Henze's
first opera. Could a 90-minute one-acter by a
26-year-old hold attention, and fill seats? That it
did so, and eventually did so triumphantly, was a
measure not only of the composer's precocious
theatrical gifts but of Nikolaus Lehnhoff's production, which held faith with the decision of
Henze and his librettist Grete Weil to update
Prévost's story to the period of its premiere in
1952. The action centres around a grand central
railway station, full of the impersonal grandeur
and busy movement of human flotsam and jet-
sam that are the natural property of such places.
  Billy Wilder and Henri-Georges Clouzot
make their mark on the continual cutting
between scenes; Xavi Bové's direction for video
is unusually subtle, taking full advantage of
Henze's extended intermezzi to watch clocks
and art-deco pillars.
  Bernhard Kontarsky's pacing was tighter in
London, catching more of the clickety-clack of
Henze's percussion writing, but Peskó and the
Liceu band are up to the mark, letting the sly
allusions to jazz and Weill in the intermezzi live
on borrowed time. Henze's Manon is knowingly
self-condemned from the outset, one feels, with
greater self-possession than her literary and
operatic ancestors from Prévost to Puccini. Not
that that makes for static loss of drama or fulfilment, when her story gradually cedes to the
hopeless infatuation of des Grieux. Laura Aikin
is a strong, sluttish Manon, fuller of voice and
more voluptuous of figure than the devastating
femme fatale of Alexandra von der Weth at
Covent Garden. Both steal the show in their
own way, as Lulus deserve to.
  Pär Lindskog reprises his central role, at least
as much Rodolfo as Alwa. Tom Fox as Lescaut
could afford to bluster and shout a little less, but
the smaller roles always bear the composer's
legato lines in mind. Henze takes a bow at the
end, and it must have been moving for him to see
how his forgotten child has grown up and stood
on his own feet.

Der Prinz von Homburg
William Cochran *ten* Elector of Brandenburg **Helga
Dernesch** *sop* Electress of Brandenburg **MariAnne
Häggander** *sop* Princess Natalie **François Le Roux**
bar Prince Friedrich von Homburg **Claes-Håkan
Ahnsjö** *ten* Count Hohenzollern **Hans Günter
Nöcker** *bass-bar* Field Marshal Dörfling **Bavarian
State Orchestra / Wolfgang Sawallisch**

Stage director **Nikolaus Lehnhoff**
Video director **Eckhart Schmidt**
ArtHaus Musik 🟥 100 164 (105' · 16:9 · 2.0 · 2 & 5)
Recorded live 1994   Ⓕ🔵🔵

Der Prinz von Homburg (1958-60) was composed
at a time of burgeoning acclaim for Henze. The
librettist, Ingeborg Bachmann, fashioned a
splendid reduction of Kleist's famous drama of
the dreamy aristocrat who, distracted by love
into disobeying orders in battle, is given the
choice of escaping condemnation if he feels the
verdict unjust. Only when he accepts the inevitability of his sentence, and walks out to face
execution, is he pardoned.
  Henze's crisp and vital music is a remarkable,
natural-sounding fusion (controversially for the
time) of the influences of Schoenberg and
Stravinsky. And Eckhart Schmidt's film is a most
faithful record of Lehnhoff's 1994 production.
Le Roux is almost ideal as the lovestruck
dreamer Prince, alternately distracted and
impetuous. His chemistry with MariAnne Häggander – who sings beautifully – is tangible,
essential for a successful production, though it's
William Cochran, rich-voiced and expressively
stern as the severe but not unbending Elector,
who steals the show. Sawallisch directs the
Bavarian State Orchestra impeccably, the sound
spacious and clear. *Der Prinz von Homburg* may
not be as spectacular as *König Hirsch* or *The Bassarids*, or as directly popular as *Der junge Lord*,
but it remains one of Henze's most completely
achieved and important operas. Its appearance
on DVD (there's no CD equivalent) is unequivocal cause for celebration.

L'Upupa und der Triumph der Sohnesliebe
Laura Aikin *sop* Badi'at **Matthias Goerne** *bar*
al Kasim **John Mark Ainsley** *ten* Demon **Alfred Muff**
bar Old Man **Hanna Schwarz** *mez* Malik **Günther
Missenhardt** *bar* Dijab **Axel Köhler** *counterten*
Adschib **Anton Scharinger** *bass-bar* Gharib
**Vienna State Opera Concert Choir; Vienna
Philharmonic Orchestra / Markus Stenz**
Stage director **Dieter Dorn**
Video director **Brian Large**
EuroArts 🟥 2053929 (143' · NTSC · 16:9 · PCM
stereo, 5.1 & DTS 5.1 · 0). Recorded live at the
Salzburg Festival, August 2003   Ⓕ🔵🔵

The title of Henze's 'German comedy in 11
tableaux based on the Arabic' translates as
'The Hoopoe and the Triumph of Filial Love'.
Setting his own libretto, and regarding the
work as his farewell to the lyric stage, the composer casts a wryly retrospective eye on the
magic and absurdity of the medium. This parable of the good son, al Kasim, who embarks
on a dangerous quest for the beautiful, exotic
hoopoe bird lost and longed for by his father,
follows many time-honoured operatic precedents as the hero undergoes various trials and
tribulations before finding true love and
returning home safely, to be greeted by his
grateful and loving father.

During al Kasim's quest for the hoopoe, his main companion and helper is a gently comic 'demon' who's more a fallen guardian angel than a Mephistopheles. The composer's affection seems centred on this character, portrayed by John Mark Ainsley with a restraint that makes the element of pathos the more effective. During this final 10 minutes the music is purely orchestral, its poetic blend of eloquence and regret as touching in its distinctive way as Strauss's valedictory epilogue for *Capriccio*.

This recording from the Salzburg premiere is in most respects a delight for both eye and ear. It's no great weakness that the young lovers, well sung and acted by Matthias Goerne and Laura Aikin, seem relatively one-dimensional alongside Ainsley's helpful, bewildered demon, and the stage production fits the work's knowingly light-hearted tone without overdoing the comic exoticism. With strong support from such seasoned character-singers as Hanna Schwarz and Alfred Muff, the only weak link is the rather pallid countertenor of Axel Köhler.

Technically, Brian Large is well practised in the art of avoiding excessive nudging of the viewer with obtrusively prolonged close-ups, and Markus Stenz is the ideal conductor to bring out the essential threads of Henze's richly diffuse musical weave.

Louis Hérold
French 1791-1833

'I am going too soon,' Hérold remarked to a friend a few days before his early death. 'I was just beginning to understand the stage.' In his 42 short years, though, he achieved much for he, with Adam and Auber, was responsible for the establishment (and huge popularity) of opéra comique.

His musical genealogy is interesting: he began his career as a pianist, he was taught by his father, his father had been taught by CPE Bach and CPE Bach had been taught by his father, Johann Sebastian – a long musical journey from the single Hérold work that remains in the orchestral repertoire. The opera itself is never performed now – it concerns Zampa, a 16th-century pirate, who is dragged under the sea and drowned by a marble statue – a female one as it happens (but see also Mozart's Don Giovanni). One other piece 'by Hérold' is still popular. In 1960 John Lanchbery rearranged the music Hérold composed for the ballet La fille mal gardée. From that comes the oft-requested Clog Dance. Alas, the music for this particular number is not by Hérold at all, as is generally stated, but by the obscure German composer Peter Ludwig Hertel (1817-99).

La fille mal gardée

La fille mal gardée – excerpts (arr Lanchbery)
Orchestra of the Royal Opera House, Covent Garden / John Lanchbery
Decca Ovation 430 196-2DM (51' · ADD)
Recorded 1962 Ⓜ️Ⓞ☞

The Royal Ballet's *La fille mal gardée* remains a source of perpetual delight, not least for the music that John Lanchbery arranged largely from Hérold's patchwork score for the 1828 version. The Clog Dance is the obvious highlight; but there are felicitous moments throughout, with snatches of Rossini, Donizetti *et al* cropping up all over the place.

This recording is the original one that Lanchbery conducted when the ballet proved such a success in the Royal Ballet's repertoire in 1960. He later recorded the score complete; and ballet lovers will consider this fuller version essential. However, others will find that the complete score rather outstays its welcome by comparison with this constantly uplifting selection. A most compelling recommendation.

Hildegard of Bingen
German 1098-1179

St Hildegard was one of the most remarkable women of the Middle Ages, a visionary, writer, naturalist, poet and composer. She became the abbess of a Benedictine convent and, like some other women of the time, played the part of a sort of prophet among her contemporaries. Her highly coloured 'revelations' were taken most seriously by four popes, various emperors, monarchs and eminent ecclesiastics, while her enemies condemned her as a fraud.

Women composers are a rare breed at any time and Hildegard can hardly be called an important one (indeed, few were aware of her music before the appearance of the cult recording 'A Feather on the Breath of God' by Gothic Voices), but the plainsong melodies she wrote to her own texts are vivid and affecting examples of music in the Christian tradition of 900 years ago.

Vocal Works

'A Feather on the Breath of God'
Columba aspexit. Ave, generosa. O ignis spiritus Paracliti. O Jerusalem. O Euchari, in leta vita. O viridissima virga. O presul vere civitatis. O Ecclesia
Gothic Voices / Christopher Page with **Doreen Muskett** symphony **Robert White** reed drones
Hyperion CDA66039 (44' · DDD)

Here's a collection of choice gems from one of the greatest creative personalities of the Middle Ages. We've limited means of assessing how these inspired pieces were performed in Hildegard's time; but the refreshingly unsophisticated timbre of the four sopranos and the reedy, almost boyish, vocal quality of the contralto are convincing enough to transport the listener right back to the unpolluted atmosphere of her cloister. Most to be savoured are the unaccompanied items, amounting to 50 per cent of the total. Indeed, since the notes make a point of telling us us that 'distractions such as the intrusion of instrumental decorations' were to be avoided, why did the producer go out of his way to introduce symphony and reed drones in the performance of the other 50 per cent? However, this is a delightful recording. When it was first released it sparked new interest in the music of the Middle Ages, and it remains a jewel in Hyperion's crown.

Favus distillans. Et ideo puelle. O tu illustrata. O vos angeli. Studium divinitatis. O ignee Spiritus. O rubor sanguinis. O orzchis Ecclesia. O gloriosissimi lux vivens angeli. Rex noster promptus est. Deus enim in prima muliere. De patria. Sed diabolus in invidia. Nunc gaudeant materna viscera Ecclesia
Sinfonye (Jocelyn West, Vivien Ellis, Stevie Wishart, Emily Levy, Vickie Couper, Julie Murphy)
Members of the Oxford Girls' Choir
Celestial Harmonies 13127-2 (62' · DDD· T/t)   Ⓕ❍

Stevie Wishart succeeds in putting Hildegard's music across chiefly by her imaginative choice of singers, which includes quite young girls. The tuneful, unsophisticated timbre of the youngest voices acts as a foil to the sturdy chest voices of the older women – which have a quality of their own, somewhat akin to that of Hungarian folk-singers. Such contrasts seem typical of the whole Hildegardian picture. Hildegard herself was made up of contrasts: she's both ecstatic and quietly tender; she can be passionate while maintaining a sense of decorum; she's erotic but also chaste.

We could do without the hurdy-gurdy and dispense with the drones and improvised organum. What's left is a penetration of Hildegard's music that rarely comes through in other interpretations. One thinks particularly of the composer's portrayal of the mystery of the Incarnation in *O tu illustrata* and also, particularly, of the remarkably sustained lines of ecstasy in *O vos angeli* – this extraordinary outpouring ranging over two octaves, but which yet has shape and structure for all Hildegard's protestations that she'd never studied her art formally.

Ferdinand Hiller   German 1811-1885

When he was 10 Hiller played a concerto by Mozart at a public concert. Several important artists showed an interest in him, among them Spohr, Speyer, Moscheles and Mendelssohn, who became Hiller's closest friend and on whose recommendation he went to Weimar to become one of Hummel's pupils (1825-27). As a productive, versatile and cultured composer, Hiller occupied a prominent position among his contemporaries; however, Schumann recognised that 'despite mastery of formal techniques' (and occasional originality) his music on the whole 'lacked that triumphant power which we are unable to resist'. His best work is represented by the Piano Concerto Op 69, the songs and some of the piano pieces, in particular

the Sonata Op 47 and the Ghazèles. His opera Die Katakomben also contains many inspired passages.

Piano Concertos

Piano Concertos – No 1, Op 5; No 2, Op 69; No 3, 'Concerto espressivo', Op 170
**Tasmanian Symphony Orchestra /
Howard Shelley** pf
Hyperion CDA67655 (76' · DDD)   Ⓕ❍❍❍ⱂ

History can be a cruel judge, for it is hard to dismiss such a confident, superbly crafted piece as the F sharp minor (Second) Concerto of 1843. It is one of the gems of the genre, the first to be written in that key and with many surprising features such as the soloist kicking off proceedings fiercely and without any introduction, the written-out cadenza opening with a subsidiary rather than principal theme, and the birdsong figuration and unusual left-hand rhythmic accompaniment in the *Andante espressivo*.

Piano Conerto No 1 (1831) is a brilliant display vehicle in the Parisian manner of the day which, however, owes more to Chopin and Moscheles (its dedicatee) than Herz or Kalkbrenner. In No 3 (1874), presumed lost until recently, Hiller again strives to be innovative in terms of structure and handling of material, keeping his soloist fully occupied despite the work's subtitle and dominant character. Inferior they may be to No 2 but, especially in performances like these, well worth hearing.

Once more, one has to take off one's hat to Howard Shelley for leading such exuberant performances while simultaneously tackling demanding keyboard writing with amazing agility, innate elegance and complete stylistic empathy.

Paul Hindemith   German 1895-1963

When it came to a career in music, it seems young Paul ran into parental opposition and, aged 11, ran away from home to make his living playing the violin in theatres and cafés. With the money he made, he was able to put himself through the local music conservatory in Frankfurt aged 13. His self-determination to live life on his own terms never left him: he was leader of the Frankfurt Opera Orchestra by 1919, had his first music published while still a student, co-founded the Amar Quartet (in which he played the viola), renowned for its performances of contemporary music, and by the time he was 30 was regarded as one of the major creative figures in Germany. (Hindemith's status as a viola soloist – and he did as much as anybody to raise the profile of this Cinderella of the strings – led to his giving the first performance of Walton's Viola Concerto in 1929.

Throughout the 1920s, he produced savage, anti-romantic scores, establishing him as the leading musical enfant terrible of the day. Richard Strauss complained to him: 'Why do you write this way? You have talent,' to which the cocky Hindemith replied:

'Herr Professor, you make your music and I'll make mine.'

In 1927 he was offered the influential post of professor of composition at the Hochschule in Berlin. When he moved there, incidentally, three complete rooms of his new home were given over to his electric model railway – not only did he design its elaborate track layout but he also made up detailed timetables. He was fanatical about trains in general and was said to know the complete European train timetable off by heart.

Eventually, his Jewish wife, his many Jewish musical colleagues and, finally, his opera Mathis der Maler (Matthias the Painter) – the theme of which deals with the then overtly sensitive subject of the defeat of German liberalism during the Peasants' Revolt – led to his being denounced by the Nazis as 'musically degenerate'. His music was banned and in 1934 Hindemith left for Turkey and then America. In 1940 he joined the staff at Yale and became an American citizen. After the war he flitted between Europe and the States, eventually settling in Switzerland. The flow of compositions and conducting engagements continued until his health declined in the 1960s.

Orchestral Works

Mathis der Maler Symphony[a]. Symphonia serena[b]. Concert Music[c]. Der Schwanendreher[d]. Symphonic Metamorphosis after Themes by Carl Maria von Weber[d]. Nobilissima visione[d].
[d]**Tabea Zimmermann** va [a]**Berlin Philharmonic Orchestra / Herbert von Karajan,** [b]**Philharmonia Orchestra / Paul Hindemith,** [d]**Bavarian Radio Symphony Orchestra / David Shallon,** [cd]**Philadelphia Orchestra /** [c]**Eugene Ormandy,** [d]**Wolfgang Sawallisch**
EMI 20th Century Classics ② 206863-2 (145' · ADD)
Ⓜ︎Ⓞ➾

An excellent two-disc mid-price Hindemith collection containing some pretty impressive performances. The Philadelphia recordings are very fine: both Ormandy and Sawallisch demonstrating a real feel for this colourful (and much underrated) music. The glorious Philadelphia sound pays huge rewards in these scores. The Karajan *Mathis* also shows off a great orchestra, and the conductor's skill at bringing out the atmosphere of a work is a real plus here.

Tabea Zimmermann isn't as forceful a soloist as the composer in *Der Schwanendreher* but she and David Shallon emphasise the work's lyrical qualities and find an appealing delicacy in the piece. Hindemith himself directs the Philharmonia (then on top form) in the rarely heard *Symphonia serena* and draws some magnificent playing from this outstanding ensemble.

Mathis der Maler Symphony. Symphonic Metamorphosis after Themes by Carl Maria von Weber. Nobilissima visione
Philadelphia Orchestra / Wolfgang Sawallisch
EMI 555230-2 (71' · DDD)
Ⓕ➾

The Philadelphia players for Sawallisch give taut performances that simply outclass the competition. Another plus-point is the unusual running order that achieves a better musical balance, starting with the most brilliant piece, the *Symphonic Metamorphosis*, and increasing in weight to the resounding brass Alleluias at the climax of the *Mathis* Symphony. EMI's sound is relatively recessed. Given the spacious acoustic of Memorial Hall and the conductor's largeness of vision this is entirely apposite, with no loss of detail.

Hindemith Symphonic Metamorphosis after Themes by Carl Maria von Weber **Respighi** Belkis, Queen of Sheba **Schmitt** The Tragedy of Salome
Borusan Istanbul Philharmonic Orchestra / Sascha Goetzel
Onyx ONYX4048 (78' · DDD)
Ⓕ Ⓞ➾

It is good to welcome a Turkish orchestra as strong and refined as the Borusan Istanbul Philharmonic. It is apt that the attractive Hindemith work is included, when Hindemith in the immediate post-war period acted as adviser to the Turkish government on developing Western music in the country.

Despite its cumbersome title, Hindemith's *Symphonic Metamorphosis* is the most immediately attractive of his orchestral works, full of colourful writing enhancing striking themes largely drawn from the incidental music that Weber wrote for a play on the theme of Princess Turandot.

The Hindemith is delightfully refreshing in juxtaposition with both the Respighi and Florent Schmitt works, which in their orientalism regularly suggest Hollywood film music. That especially applies to the Respighi, which was adapted from a cantata into a suite of four movements, and designed to be more manageable.

Florent Schmitt's *The Tragedy of Salome* developed from a dance-mime involving a small orchestra. Four of the six movements in this expansion are dances, skilfully orchestrated, surrounding the evocative 'The Enchantment of the Sea'. The two final movements are both entitled 'Dance of Fear', bringing a spectacular close to the whole work. Drawing polished playing from the orchestra, Vienna-born conductor Sascha Goetzel could hardly be more persuasive in all three works, which are treated to a brilliant, well-balanced recording to match.

Violin Concerto

Violin Concerto[a]. Konzertmusik for Brass and Strings, Op 50. Symphonic Metamorphosis after Themes by Carl Maria von Weber
[a]**Leonidas Kavakos** vn **BBC Philharmonic Orchestra / Yan Pascal Tortelier**
Chandos CHAN9903 (66' · DDD)
Ⓕ Ⓞ➾

Here are top-notch performances and recordings of one of Hindemith's best-loved works and one of his more unaccountably neglected pieces. The benchmark recordings of the *Symphonic Metamorphosis* are those by Blomstedt and Sawallisch. The BBC Philharmonic are not quite in the same league as the San Francisco (at least under Blomstedt) or Philadelphia bands, but provide an invigoratingly energetic performance.

Leonidas Kavakos is the sweet-toned soloist in the unaccountably neglected Violin Concerto, which thankfully is coming into fashion in the studio. Even Oistrakh is worsted in some passages by the fleet-fingered Kavakos, but the Russian's account, directed by the composer, remains essential (though sadly not currently available). Where this cannot compete now with the newcomer is in recording quality. For our money, Kavakos and Tortelier are now the market leaders.

Kammermusik

Kammermusik – No 1, Op 24 No 1; No 2; No 3, Op 36 No 2; No 4, Op 36 No 3; No 5, Op 36 No 4; No 6, Op 46 No 1; No 7, Op 46 No 2. Kleine Kammermusik No 1 for Wind Quintet, Op 24 No 2
Konstanty Kulka *vn* **Kim Kashkashian** *va* **Norbert Blume** *va d'amore* **Lynn Harrell** *vc* **Ronald Brautigam** *pf* **Leo van Doeselaar** *org* **Royal Concertgebouw Orchestra / Riccardo Chailly**
Double Decca download ② 473 722-2DF2
(138' · DDD)   Ⓜ❍❍❍🡢

Hindemith's series of *Kammermusik* ('Chamber Music') began in 1921 as an iconoclastic response to the hyperintense emotionalism of German Expressionist music over the previous 15 years. It continued until 1927, at which point he began to rationalise the harmonic and expressive foundations of his style. This, then, is neo-classicism with a German accent; as such it was to be a vital force in sweeping away the cobwebs of late Romanticism; Walton, Prokofiev, Shostakovich and Britten were among those who, however indirectly, would feel the benefit.

The music is also immensely enjoyable in its own right. Hindemith cheekily throws together disparate idioms and sheer force of personality is all that guards against anarchy. All this is done with more than half an eye on the performers' enjoyment of re-creation, and the fine array of artists assembled by Chailly savour every detail. Recording quality is exemplary.

Additional recommendation

Kammermusik
Coupled with Der Schwanendreher
BPO / Abbado
EMI 397711-2

As the Chailly set appears to have limited distribution, do consider the Abbado discs. While lacking a little of the gem-like incisiveness of his compatriot's Concertgebouw version, it is needless to say magnificently played.

String Quartets

Hindemith String Quartet No 3, Op 22   Ⓗ
Prokofiev String Quartet No 2 in F, Op 92
Walton String Quartet in A minor
Hollywood Quartet (Felix Slatkin, Paul Shure *vns* Paul Robyn *va* Eleanor Aller *vc*)
Testament mono SBT1052 (74' · ADD) Recorded 1951
                                                         Ⓕ

Although many accounts of the Prokofiev have appeared over the years, none has approached, let alone surpassed, the Hollywood version of the Second Quartet. The same would no doubt apply to the Hindemith but for the fact that there have been fewer challengers. What a wonderful feeling for line these players had, what an incredible, perfectly matched and blended ensemble – and how well these transfers sound! That goes for the Walton, too: there's no other account that makes so positive a case for it.

Viola Sonatas

Viola Sonatas – Op 11 No 4; Op 25 No 4; Viola Sonata (1939). Nobilissima visione – Meditation
Lawrence Power *va* **Simon Crawford-Phillips** *pf*
Hyperion CDA67721 (58' · DDD)   Ⓕ❍

Paul Hindemith isn't exactly the first composer you think of when the term 'hit tune' is mentioned but the opening Fantasie of his F major Viola Sonata (Op 11 No 4) of 1919 comes pretty close to providing one, especially as 'sung' by viola-player Lawrence Power. 'Might almost be by Brahms...' says Malcolm MacDonald in a typically persuasive and informative booklet-note, which is surely true. The finale is a fairly assertive mood-breaker, pianist Simon Crawford-Phillips marking a dramatic contrast in tempo and colour (now this really does sound like 'updated' Brahms). The grittier Sonata of 1939 also includes a Phantasie, placed third in the structure rather than first. This is the Hindemith of the *Mathis der Maler* Symphony, purposeful music, square-jawed, angular, confident and assertive, though with more fanciful elements too – especially in the finale, which at times is both playful and delicate.

MacDonald notes the possible influence of Bartók on the Sonata Op 25 No 4 (1922), which seems a justified claim. This is another strong piece, more percussive than the 1939 Sonata, with a desolate but heart-rending slow movement that is savagely interrupted by the finale's aggressive arrival. The CD (Vol 1 of 'The Complete Hindemith Viola Music' is what it's called), which is superbly recorded, is completed with a sensitive performance of the serene Meditation from *Nobilissima visione* in Hindemith's own arrangement for viola and piano. As to the performances, not since the days of William Primrose has Hindemith's viola music been played with such warmth and conviction. A 100 per cent success story.

Sonatas for Solo Viola – Op 11 No 5; Op 25 No 1;
Op 31 No 4. Sonata (1937).
Lawrence Power *va*
Hyperion CDA67769 (64' · DDD)   Ⓕ**O**❿→

Although spread unevenly through his career
(1919, 1922, 1923 and 1937 respectively), Hindemith's solo viola sonatas chart his progress
from late Romanticism through his iconoclastic
and neo-classical stages culminating in the
mature style of the final sonata – written on a
train to Chicago for Hindemith to premiere that
night.

Lawrence Power stands comparison with the
best, his prodigious technical ability – ideally
suited to this repertoire – allied to real musicianship in pieces which, for all their complexities,
should sound grateful to play and hear. His
shaping of Op 11 No 5's passacaglia finale is
particularly impressive. Power relishes the lyricism of the slow movements as much as the
demands of the faster ones, yet is not fazed at all
by Op 25 No 1's notorious fourth movement,
marked 'Raging tempo. Wild. Beauty of tone is
of secondary importance', with its outrageous
metronome marking of crotchet=600.

Power is superb in Op 25 No 1, young man's
music if ever there was any. His firm line and
clear tone, aided by Hyperion's superb recording, are splendid. Excellent notes by Calum
MacDonald, too.

Violin Sonatas

Violin Sonatas – E flat, Op 11 No 1; D, Op 11 No 2;
E (1935); C (1939)
Ulf Wallin *vn* **Roland Pöntinen** *pf*
BIS BIS-CD761 (56' · DDD)   Ⓕ**O**

The E major Sonata of 1935 is brief (under
10 minutes long) and uncomplicated, yet
it's familiar Hindemith from first note to
last. The C major work (1939) is more complex
and grave, and probably the finest of them.
The longest sonata, and most conservative in
idiom, is the D major. Both Op 11 works
were written in 1918 while Hindemith was
on active service, and are remarkable for bearing few traces of either the grimness of the
Great War or the composer's personal
voice. Both deserve wider currency. This issue
is also welcome in including the fragmentary
abandoned finale of Op 11 No 1, a rustic dance
not in keeping with the symmetry of the
whole. The sweet-toned Ulf Wallin is fully
attuned to Hindemith's wavelength, and
Pöntinen provides exemplary support.
The recording is typical BIS (ie excellent).
A splendid disc.

Ludus tonalis

Ludus tonalis. Suite '1922'
Boris Berezovsky *pf*
Warner Classics 2564 63412-2 (75' · DDD)   Ⓕ❿→

It's a long way from music like Chopin/
Godowsky (which Berezovsky has recorded so
superbly) to Hindemith's large-scale cycle of 12
fugues alternating with 11 interludes, the whole
topped and tailed by a Prelude which returns, in
retrograde inversion, as a Postlude. So how does
he fare in *Ludus tonalis* (1942)?

In a word, impressively. There's no attempt to
beef up Hindemith's contrapuntal sobriety with
spurious expressiveness, but a searching sense of
line and a feeling for polyphonic give-and-take
make the quieter fugues absorbing, while the
extrovert ones positively sizzle with attitude. As
for the more freely composed Interludes, dexterity and fantasy combine to project maximum
energy and atmosphere, especially in the cheeky
cross-rhythms of Interlude 4. While Berezovsky
doesn't quite convince that *Ludus tonalis* embodies the white heat of inspiration from beginning
to end, he comes as close as any pianist could, or
should.

Hindemith's early *Suite '1922'* offers the
player more conventional digital rewards, which
Berezovsky clearly relishes, with even the rather
pallid central 'Nachtstück' revealing unexpected
depths. In its riotous 'Shimmy' and 'Ragtime'
movements, 'prodigies of virtuosity' are there in
abundance, helped along by an exceptionally
vivid recording.

Organ music

Kammermusik No 7, Op 46 No 2[ab]. Kleine
Kammermusik, Op 24 No 2[b]. Three Organ Sonatas[a].
Zwei Stücke für Orgel[a]
[a]**Daniel Hyde** *org*
[b]**Britten Sinfonia / Benjamin Bayl**
Signum Classics SIGCD159 (77' · DDD) Ⓕ
[a]Played on the Kuhn organ at Jesus College Chapel,
Cambridge

This disc positively sparkles! With such intelligent and innovative programming, it is the ideal
introduction to Hindemith's organ music. Since
there is insufficient solo organ music to fill a
complete disc, the solution is to add *Kammermusik No 7*, which is effectively the first organ
concerto (albeit with an ensemble of wind
instruments and lower strings).

The novelty on this disc is the premiere
recording of *Zwei Stücke*. Dating from August
1918, these pieces straddle the dying embers of
late Romanticism and the leaner, more contrapuntal aridity of the 1920s. Their shapeliness
and colourfulness are striking and worthy of
repeated hearings. There is plenty of registra-
tional variety, too, in Daniel Hyde's nicely
judged performances of the three solo sonatas.
The seemingly modest new two-manual Swiss
Kuhn organ installed in Jesus College, Cambridge, provides plenty of punch and a wide
dynamic range.

Hindemith's impish characteristics are more
to the fore in the wind quintet *Kleine Kammermusik*. This multifaceted work is a model for all
would-be composers for this combination.

Nicholas Daniel's oboe playing is an especial delight, and the third-movement waltz and folky finale are brought off to perfection.

The chapel acoustic is ideal for all these pieces, which are recorded with maximum fidelity. This is a thoroughly recommendable disc.

Das Unaufhörliche

Das Unaufhörliche
Ulrike Sonntag sop **Robert Wörle** ten **Siegfried Lorenz** bar **Berlin Radio Children's Choir; Berlin Radio Chorus and Symphony Orchestra / Lothar Zagrosek**
Wergo ② WER6603-2 (95' · DDD · T/t)   Ⓕ

The oratorio *Das Unaufhörliche* ('The One Perpetual') was Hindemith's longest concert work. It never established itself in the repertoire (although Boult conducted the UK premiere as early as 1933). It's cast in three parts, the first describing the 'one perpetual' itself, the second its effect on diverse areas of activity (including art, science and love), the third Humankind's reaction away from it and final acquiescence. How closely Hindemith accorded with the poet Gottfried Benn's viewpoint is a matter for conjecture, but his evanescent score matched the poem's expansiveness of theme and nobility of utterance. In this alone it pointed the way to *Mathis der Maler*, for there's nothing here akin to the *Kammermusik* or *Neues vom Tage* (a smash-hit in Berlin at the time).

This is the work's first recording and the performance is a fine one with good sound. Flies in the ointment? Soprano Ulrike Sonntag, who seems too often to be straining for her notes and whose intonation isn't always secure, and Wergo's failure to provide a translation of Benn's spoken introduction, recorded in 1932 and included as the final track. These are quibbles, however, and should not deter anyone from investing in this important release.

Die Harmonie der Welt

Die Harmonie der Welt
Arutiun Kotchinian bass Kaiser Rudolf II, Kaiser Ferdinand II, Sun **François Le Roux** bar Kepler, Imperial Mathematician, Earth **Robert Wörle** ten General Wallenstein, Jupiter **Christian Elsner** ten Ulrich, Kepler's Assistant, Late Soldier, Mars **Michael Burt** bass Pastor in Linz, Mercury **Reinhard Hagen** bass Tansur, Saturn **Michael Kraus** bar Baron Starhemberg **Daniel Kirch** ten Kepler's Brother **Tatiana Korovina** sop Susanna, Venus **Michelle Breedt** contr Kepler's Mother, Luna **Sophia Larson** sop Little Susanna **Berlin Radio Symphony Chorus and Orchestra / Marek Janowski**
Wergo ③ WER6652-2 (161' · DDD · T/t)   Ⓕ

Die Harmonie der Welt is one of Hindemith's major works, perhaps his major post-war work. He first seems to have contemplated an opera on the polymath Johannes Kepler in the late 1930s,

in the wake of *Mathis der Maler*. But it wasn't until 1955 that serious work was started on the libretto, although, as with *Mathis* two decades before, he had already written a symphony using themes reserved for the opera.

There are also superficial similarities in subject treatment between the two stage works. *Die Harmonie* is an opera about an astronomer-cum-philosopher rather than science, just as *Mathis* had been about an artist, not painting. Kepler's career is set in the context of his time, culminating in the tumultuous Thirty Years War, just as Grünewald's had been set against the 16th-century Peasants' Revolt. Yet Kepler isn't as involved in the whirl of events as Mathis; he stands apart from them, concerned increasingly just to resolve his theories about the harmony of the world. In the end his search is in vain and he dies with the word 'Futile' on his lips.

By the time of the premiere, Hindemith's star had waned and some critics regarded the opera also as futile, especially when compared to *Cardillac* and *Mathis*. But in several respects it's just as successful musically: its symphonic coherence and integration are more consistently achieved than in earlier stage works and the composer had grown as an artist. If some of the characterisation is two-dimensional, this is made to serve the symbolic aspects of the whole, most clearly in the final scene as the main characters assume celestial roles in a cosmic passacaglia, the incandescent culmination of which truly raises the roof.

Marek Janowski directs a splendidly paced and committed performance, with some fine singing and playing from the forces of Berlin Radio. François Le Roux turns in a thoughtful and multifaceted account of Kepler, with Robert Wörle's conniving but ultimately doomed Wallenstein and Christian Elsner's Ulrich the pick of the rest. Recorded in the Jesus-Christus-Kirche, Berlin, the sound is clear and spacious, the acoustic and balance serving the music better than in most theatres. A marvellous achievement, strongly recommended.

Das lange Weihnachtsmahl

Das lange Weihnachtsmahl
Ruth Ziesak sop Lucia, Lucia II **Ursula Hesse von den Steinen** contr Mutter Bayard, Ermengarde **Herman Wallén** bar Sam, Roderick **Arutiun Kotchinian** bass Brandon **Christian Elsner** ten Charles **Rebecca Martin** mez Genevieve **Michaela Kaune** sop Leonora **Corby Welch** ten Roderick II **Berlin Radio Symphony Orchestra / Marek Janowski**
Wergo WER6676-2 (48' · DDD · T/t/N)   Ⓕ

Hindemith's final and least-known opera, based on a 1931 play by Thornton Wilder, *Das lange Weihnachtsmahl* ('The Long Christmas Dinner') is – like his earliest essays in the genre – cast in a single act. Unlike them, however, it is a subtle and luminous conception, with none of the provocative and lurid (although undeniably exciting) Expressionism of his twenties. What catches the ear from the start are the limpid scoring and vocal lines, developing the beauty of tone found in the orchestral *Marienleben* songs and more intimate passages in *Die Harmonie der Welt*.

The opera depicts in 50 minutes a remarkable domestic panoply set across 90 years, encapsulated during the Christmas dinners of the Bayard family. Wilder conflates these (culminating in the Great War) into a freely evolving single event, with characters emerging from one side of the stage (denoting birth) and leaving by the other (denoting death).

Hindemith and Wilder blurred the distinctions between several characters and their descendants to underline familial continuity, appearing, being developed and reprised like musical themes. Chief among them is Lucia, sung radiantly by Ruth Ziesak, who dominates the first six scenes until departing, only to reappear briefly as her granddaughter in scene 9. Lucia's husband Roderick – sung solidly by Herman Wallén – eventually returns as his grandson Sam. Ursula Hesse von den Steinen brings great dignity to her portrayals of ageing matriarch Mother Bayard and Cousin Ermengarde, whose last exit through the dark door leaves the old house finally empty.

Janowski directs a superbly paced account, sung well throughout, accompanied by some splendid orchestral playing. Wergo's sound is rich.

Mathis der Maler

Mathis der Maler
Roland Hermann *bar* Mathis **Josef Protschka** *ten*
Albrecht **Gabriele Rossmanith** *sop* Regina **Sabine
Hass** *sop* Ursula **Harald Stamm** *bass* Riedinger
Heinz Kruse *ten* Hans Schwalb **Victor von Halem**
bass Lorenz von Pommersfelden **Hermann Winkler**
ten Wolfgang Capito **Ulrich Hielscher** *bass* Truchsess
von Waldberg **Ulrich Ress** *ten* Sylvester von
Schaumberg **John Cogram** *ten* Der Pfeiffer des
Grafen von Helfenstein **Marilyn Schmiege** *mez*
Helfenstein **North German Radio Chorus;
Cologne Radio Chorus and Symphony Orchestra /
Gerd Albrecht**
Wergo ③ WER6255-2 (166' · DDD · T/t)   Ⓕ

Mathis der Maler is one of the pinnacles of 20th-century German opera. It's become axiomatic to see in it a parable of the times, with Hindemith using the turbulent world of 16th-century Germany to mirror the Nazi Reich and his place in it. But in reality *Mathis* is a spiritual and historical opera, not a political one. Rudolf Stephan in his note plays down the political angle; if Hitler hadn't risen to power until, say, 1936, one doubts that *Mathis* would have turned out much different. Gerd Albrecht's acquaintance with Hindemith's music goes back to the early 1960s, before the composer's death. Hindemith even sanctioned some retouching of the orchestration in *Mathis* made by Albrecht for a festival performance, though it isn't made clear whether Albrecht has applied this here. Rarely have Hindemith's often heavy textures sounded so clear.

As to the music, isn't the brief concluding 'Alleluia' duet that crowns the sixth tableau one of *the* great moments in 20th-century opera? You'll be convinced from your first hearing of it. There are fine moments aplenty in Albrecht's reading, not least where familiar passages from the *Mathis* Symphony surface and precipitate some of the most intense music of the opera.

Roland Hermann is, perhaps, a shade stolid in places as the painter (though his world-weariness in the final scene is just right); Josef Protschka makes a most authoritative Cardinal, acting as a perfect foil to Hermann's Mathis. They head a fine cast, supported by some lusty singing and playing from German radio forces.

Additional recommendation

Sancta Susanna
Coupled with Drei Gesänge, Op 9. Das Nusch-
Nuschi, Op 20 – Dances. Tuttifäntchen – Suite
Bullock Susanna **Jones** Clementia **Gunson** Old Nun
Rowlinson Farmhand **Treedaway** Maid **Leeds
Festival Chorus; BBC PO / Y-P Tortelier**
Chandos CHAN9620 (70' · DDD · T/t)   ⒻⒹ

Sancta Susanna is short, concentrated, highly imaginative and resourceful in its use of sonority; and its Expressionist musical language is so powerful that at the end of its barely 23 minutes you feel you've heard a much longer piece. It's superbly done here. No praise can be too high for the singers and for the delicacy, eloquence and power of the playing Tortelier draws from his orchestra.

Joseph Holbrooke   British 1878-1958

A pupil of Corder at the Royal Academy of Music, Holbrooke was influenced by Wagner and early Strauss. His musical output includes eight symphonies, many tone-poems, two piano concertos, chamber music including string quartets, a piano quintet, a quintet for clarinet and strings and a piano quartet, and much music inspired by Edgar Allan Poe, including choral and orchestral settings for 'The Raven' and 'The Bells', and a ballet score for 'The Masque of the Red Death'. He also wrote a three-part operatic trilogy based on the Welsh epic the Mabinogion.

Piano Concerto No 1

Holbrooke Piano Concerto No 1, Op 52, 'The Song of Gwyn ap Nudd' **Wood** Piano Concerto in D minor
Hamish Milne *pf* **BBC Scottish Symphony
Orchestra / Martyn Brabbins**
Hyperion CDA67127 (69' · DDD · T)   ⒻⓄⓄⒹ

Holbrooke's ambitious First Piano Concerto is by some margin the most impressive orchestral piece of his to appear on disc. Dubbed a symphonic poem by its creator, it follows the narrative of a poem based on a Welsh legend by his patron Lord Howard de Walden entitled The

Song of Gwyn ap Nudd. Yet the work can also be appreciated perfectly well as a red-blooded Romantic concerto in the grand tradition. Holbrooke handles proceedings with deft resourcefulness and a vaulting sweep. It receives outstandingly eloquent and tirelessly committed treatment in this performance.

An altogether more straightforward confection is the D minor Piano Concerto by Haydn Wood (1882-1959), who, before he made his name in the field of light music, was a gifted violinist and composition pupil of Stanford. Indeed, Stanford conducted the Queen's Hall premiere of Wood's big-boned D minor Concerto in July 1909. Grieg's Concerto is the obvious template, and there are stylistic echoes of Tchaikovsky, Rachmaninov and MacDowell. The opening movement is full of effective display, and boasts a ravishing secondary idea. By far the best music comes in the central *Andante* – a haunting, deeply felt essay, boasting some wistfully fragrant orchestral sonorities. Not a great work, by any means, but incurable romantics will devour it.

Heinz Holliger   Swiss b1939

Holliger studied with Sándor Veress in Paris and with Pierre Boulez in Basle. As an oboist he has appeared internationally in a repertory ranging from Baroque concertos to works written for him by Berio, Henze and Lutosławski. His own compositions were initially Boulezian but have drawn nearer to Berio and Kagel. He has also added conducting to his formidable musical armoury. He was composer-in-residence of the Suisse Romande Orchestra in 1993-94 and of the Lucerne Festival in 1998. After the second performance of his opera Schneewittchen (after Robert Walser) at Zürich in October 1998, Holliger received an honorary doctorate from the University of Zürich.

Violin Concerto

Holliger Violin Concerto, 'Hommage à Louis Soutter'[a] **Ysaÿe** Solo Violin Sonata in D minor, 'Ballade', Op 27 No 3
Thomas Zehetmair *vn* [a]**South West German Radio Symphony Orchestra, Baden-Baden and Freiburg / Heinz Holliger**
ECM New Series 476 1941 (54' · DDD)   Ⓕ**ⓄⓄ**▷

During 1993-95 Heinz Holliger composed a three-movement Violin Concerto of about half an hour. Shortly before this recording of 2002 he added a 17-minute Epilogue: 'I want to show that music can age, be sapped of vital energy and end in agony.' The Concerto is inscribed as a homage to Louis Soutter, a Swiss-born violinist and painter (1871-1942) whose troubled images of violence and despair haunted Holliger for many years. The Epilogue is called 'Before the massacre', after one of Souter's macabre paintings from 1939.

The concerto clearly isn't a lighthearted piece, but neither is it emptily depressing or disheartening. Soutter studied with Ysaÿe, so Holliger starts from Ysaÿe's short Third Sonata, played here as a prelude. The first three movements offer a dazzling portrait of virtuosity under strain. The Epilogue is much tougher, but Holliger does not totally renounce all suggestions of compassion for human victims of violence and fanaticism. This may be ageing, agonised music, but its effect is less of futility than of hushed awe in the face of a creative impulse that refuses to lie down and die.

These positive impressions owe much to the artistry of Thomas Zehetmair, who has been associated with the concerto from the beginning. The recording gives a needle-sharp aural image of the progress from bright colours and brittle textures to dark evanescence.

Robin Holloway   British b1943

Holloway studied with Alexander Goehr (from 1960) and at Cambridge, where in 1974 he was appointed lecturer. His large output covers many genres (including numerous songs): some pieces lovingly reinterpret Romanticism (Scenes from Schumann for orchestra and Fantasy-Pieces on the Heine 'Liederkreis' of Schumann). His first opera, Clarissa, a study of rape, was given by English National Opera in London in 1990.

Concertos for Orchestra

Second Concerto for Orchestra, Op 40
BBC Symphony Orchestra / Oliver Knussen
NMC NMCD015M (34' · DDD)   Ⓜ**ⓄⓄⓄ**▷

 A North African holiday was the stimulus for Robin Holloway's Second Concerto for Orchestra. The extremes of contrast, he tells us ('opulence and austerity, richness and drabness, brilliant light and dense shadow…And above all, the noises…the polyphony of hammering, tapping, thudding, tinkling, bashing…'), haunted him and were soon demanding to be turned into music. The experience seems also to have set him off on a more enigmatic, private voyage through his musical past. We hear a few particularly aching bars from Act 2 of *Tristan*, and rather more of Chopin's F sharp major Barcarolle; while a strange, broken tune on muted trombone metamorphoses neatly into Parry's *Jerusalem*. It's bewildering but gripping. Holloway can swerve from lush, late Romanticism to strident modernism and back again with the alarming speed of an opium dream; but as with any really revelatory dream, the more you probe it, the more lucid it seems. When you reach the end, you feel you want to go back and soak in the experience all over again, and then go away somewhere and ponder its riddles.

The members of the BBC Symphony Orchestra play as though each one of them were engaged on his or her own voyage of discovery. Oliver Knussen's triumph in pulling it all together, and then shaping and shading it so lovingly, is just one of the technically miraculous aspects of this disc; another is that the production team have somehow turned BBC Maida Vale Studio No 1 into a fine, spacious acoustic, with details beautifully focused. It all adds up to a quite fascinating disc.

Third Concerto for Orchestra, Op 76
**London Symphony Orchestra /
Michael Tilson Thomas**
NMC NMCD039 (45' · DDD)
Recorded live 1996   ⒻⵔⒹ➛

The first ideas for the Third Concerto for Orchestra came during a trip through South America: there are sound pictures of Lake Titicaca, riotous New Year's Day celebrations in the Bay of Bahia, the slow train-crossing of the Great Brazilian Swamp and the huge, satanic slag heap at the Potosì Silver Mine. Holloway jotted them all down on the spot: then his notebook was stolen, and it took another 13 years to recall them and finish the piece. By then, the alchemical processes of memory had transformed the original musical impressions into something quite different. What might have been simply a descriptive tone-poem finally emerged as a powerful and unusual musical argument – a huge slow movement, with a moderately fast dance-like finale, which evolves from tiny scraps of motifs (there's hardly a 'theme' in sight). And yet much of the original 'illustrative' character of the piece remains.

String and woodwind textures recall dense, overripe rain forest foliage; the dark, 'sluggish' first movement suggests the movement of a vast, slow, muddy river; extravagant sensuousness contrasts with clangorous bells or craggy brass. This recording, based on its 1996 premiere, is quite an achievement. It's rare for a conductor and an orchestra to show such a compelling grasp of the shape and atmosphere of a work at its first performance. Technically the sound has none of the usual problems associated with a live recording – virtually no intrusive noise, good balance, warm tone.

Gilded Goldbergs

Gilded Goldbergs (for two pianos after JS Bach), Op 86
Micallef-Inanga Piano Duo
(Jennifer Micallef, Glen Inanga *pfs*)
Hyperion ② CDA67360 (98' · DDD)   ⓂⵔⵔⵔⵔⒹ

Holloway's initial prompt for these stunning two-piano transcriptions of Bach's *Goldbergs* was his frustration as a single pianist at his 'inability to clarify the close-weave canons or manage the more fiendish hand-crossing numbers so idiomatic on a two-manual harpsichord'. So far, so pleasurable – but then inevitably the full artistic

implication of what he was doing struck home. It was only later, after much agonised self-questioning, that he decided to 'go for the gilding and lose the guilt!' Bach's original is thrown in at the deep centre of a swelling harmonic sea, sometimes as a moment of ineffable calm (Variation 18, a 'canon in sixths'), at other times more like an oncoming tidal wave (Variation 29, 'Toccata with clusters'). The use of modulation is often alarming but always musically effective and never more so than in an ingenious reworking of the closing 'Quodlibet' (Variation 30), which traverses 'all 12 keys', ending in D. Holloway's ear for nuance, and the ingenuity of his invention, will leave you open-mouthed with admiration. Whatever your CD priorities to date, this one surely has to fly straight to the top of your wants list.

Additional recommendation

Fantasy-Pieces on the Heine 'Liederkreis' of Schumann, Op 16
Coupled with Serenade in C. **Schumann** Liederkreis, Op 24
Spence *ten* **Brown** *pf* **Nash Ensemble / Brabbins**
Hyperion CDA66930 (75' · DDD · T/t)   ⒻⵔⒹ➛

> A contemporary composer takes a 19th-century classic, Schumann's Op 24 *Liederkreis*, and sets it in a musical frame of his own devising: a short, astringent 'Praeludium' and four extended movements, the style hovering between pure homage and what the composer calls 'phantasmagorical collage'. Splendid performances from the Nash Ensemble – colourful, precise and sensitive to Holloway's kaleidoscopic shifts in mood.

Vagn Holmboe   Danish 1909-1996

Holmboe studied in Copenhagen and with Toch in Berlin. He then returned to Copenhagen to work as a teacher, critic and composer. He was the leading Danish symphonist after Nielsen (he composed 13 as well as three chamber symphonies and four symphonies for strings), he also wrote 20 string quartets, numerous concertos, one opera and the late series of preludes for chamber orchestra, as well as much choral and other music. His style is influenced by Nielsen, Hindemith and Stravinsky, and is approachable but by no means bland.

Chamber Concertos

Chamber Concertos – No 8, 'Sinfonia concertante', Op 38; No 10, 'Wood, Brass and Gut', Op 40. Concerto giocondo e severo, Op 132. The Ill-Tempered Turk, Op 32b
**Aalborg Symphony Orchestra /
Owain Arwel Hughes**
BIS BIS-CD917 (68' · DDD)   ⒻⒹ➛

Holmboe the concerto writer had a very different agenda from Holmboe the symphonist, and nowhere does that become more apparent than in Chamber Concerto No 8 (1945), subtitled *Sinfonia concertante*, a splendid work that's a direct precursor of the magnificent First Chamber Symphony (1953). Owain Arwel Hughes underscores the music's internal cohesion and plays down the Hindemithian overtones. No 10 (1945-46) is a bracing early example of Holmboe's metamorphosis technique, its nine sections acting like variations within a traditional concerto format: the sections in pairs respectively form an introduction and three 'movements', with the last acting as coda.

Holmboe devotees will be particularly keen on the other two works, both novelties. The *Cheerful and Severe* Concerto is a single (12-minute) movement, though like the Tenth, divided into sections; here, though, they are compressed to form a compellingly fluent design in the composer's late, luminous style. More fascinating still is the suite, made (with some recomposition) in 1969 from the music of the still-unperformed ballet *Den Galsindede Tyrk* (1942-44). The opening 'Dance of the Executioner' has echoes of the contemporaneous Fifth Symphony, while later movements – for instance, the central 'Dance of the Trees' – point towards the Sixth and Seventh (1947-50). But the music also seems eminently danceable, making its neglect all the more astonishing. Heartily recommended.

Chamber Concertos – No 11 for Trumpet and Orchestra, Op 44[a]; No 12 for Trombone and Orchestra, Op 52[b]; Tuba and Orchestra, Op 127[c].
Intermezzo concertante, Op 171[c]
[a]**Håkan Hardenberger** tpt [b]**Christian Lindberg** tbn
[c]**Jens Bjørn-Larsen** tuba **Aalborg Symphony Orchestra / Owain Arwel Hughes**
BIS BIS-CD802 (55' · DDD)　　　Ⓕ➖➔

The Trumpet Concerto has a leanness of texture and a neo-classical air that will surprise those familiar with Holmboe's symphonies. Hardenberger's first entry creates an electricity that's maintained throughout the work – indeed, the disc as a whole. No 11's tripartite design recurs, condensed into a single movement, in No 12: a brief, expressively crucial slow section framed by a large-boned *Allegro* (rather grave in character in the trombone work), and a good-humoured, rollicking finale. The Tuba Concerto (1976), by contrast, requires a full orchestral complement, its one integrated span bearing little semblance of traditional three-movement form. It's the most dramatic and exploratory work here, both in mood and sonority, the demands of which on tuba virtuosos over the years have occasioned it to be played in slightly differing versions, especially with regard to the taxing cadenza. The short *Intermezzo concertante* reaffirms that the tuba really can sing. Wonderful music, wonderfully performed and recorded.

Chamber Concertos – No 1 for Piano and Orchestra, Op 17[a]; No 3 for Clarinet and Orchestra, Op 21[b];

No 7 for Oboe and Orchestra, Op 37[c].
Beatus parvo, Op 117[d]
[c]**Gordon Hunt** ob [b]**Martin Fröst** cl [a]**Noriko Ogawa** pf [d]**Danish National Opera Chorus; Aalborg Symphony Orchestra / Owain Arwel Hughes**
BIS BIS-CD1176 (78' · DDD · T/t)　　　Ⓕ◯➖➔

A word about nomenclature. Holmboe composed 13 chamber concertos between 1939 and 1956 as a series with small-orchestral accompaniment, similar but not so homogeneous a set as Hindemith's *Kammermusik*. Much later he renamed them just concertos, which is how BIS in its continuing series (coupled with other *concertante* works; this is the third issue) refers to them. Dacapo's integral set of the 13 curiously retained the chamber tag.

Irrespective of titles, they make a fine set. The concertos are extremely diverse and may surprise those who know only the symphonies and quartets. Hannu Koivula's nicely paced and well-thought-through interpretations for Dacapo, although a touch studio-bound, set a formidable standard to follow. As with the Brass and Orchestral Concertos, Owain Arwel Hughes more than rises to that challenge with tempi usually a touch swifter and more urgent, and the recorded sound more resonant, giving a warmer sound picture of each work.

This is particularly true in the First Concerto for piano, strings and timpani, where Ogawa is more sympathetically placed and not recessed as was Anne Øland. Ogawa's technique is also the stronger and she shapes Holmboe's neo-romantic lines even more splendidly than her rival.

In the Clarinet and Oboe Concertos honours are more even, though Martin Fröst and Gordon Hunt just shade the decision. There's a 'bigness' to Fröst's tone that Niels Thomsen cannot quite match and Hunt's incisive playing is just about perfect. There's nothing inadequate about the Dacapo issues; but if you're in two minds about buying this newcomer consider the bonus of Holmboe's charming cantata *Beatus parvo*, a kind of concerto for amateur forces full of that marvellous luminosity that characterised so much of his music in his last decades. Strongly recommended.

Symphonies

Symphonies – No 11, Op 144; No 12, Op 175; No 13, Op 192
Aarhus Symphony Orchestra / Owain Arwel Hughes
BIS BIS-CD728 (63' · DDD)　　　Ⓕ◯➖➔

Few who have invested in this series so far can doubt that these are among the most commanding symphonies to have emerged in post-war Europe. Some might even argue that they're *the* finest since Sibelius and Nielsen. All credit to Owain Arwel Hughes and the Aarhus orchestra for their committed advocacy and to BIS for recording them in such vivid, naturally balanced sound. The 11th, composed in 1980, is quintessential Holmboe, and its atmosphere resonates in the mind long after you've heard it. To quote Knud Ketting's notes, 'the symphony's climax in dynamic and emotional terms comes in the second movement and it then slowly retreats within itself…[it] is cast as a strong arch, which impresses at first hearing, and commands increasing admiration on closer acquaintance'. The arabesque that opens the symphony seems to come from another world and the transparent, luminous textures communicate the sense of a spiritual quest that one rarely encounters in modern music. The 12th is a taut, well-argued piece, and is, like its two companions on this disc, in three movements. No one listening to the 13th, written at the instigation of Owain Arwel Hughes, would think that it was the work of an 85-year-old. There have been other octogenarian symphonies, but none that sounds quite so youthful or highly charged as this.

Symphonic Metamorphoses

Symphonic Metamorphoses – No 1, Op 68, 'Epitaph'; No 2, Op 76, 'Monolith'; No 3, Op 80, 'Epilog'; No 4, Op 108, 'Tempo variabile'
Aalborg Symphony Orchestra /
Owain Arwel Hughes
BIS BIS-CD852 (75' · DDD) Ⓕ**O**

In form the symphonic metamorphosis is an off-shoot of the symphonic fantasia (but of a kind radically different from Sibelius's *Pohjola's Daughter*), each of these four very different from its companions. The vigour and luminous orchestration of the symphonies are present, as are many of the internal developmental processes, but not the level of integration. Holmboe's priorities here are unlike those of many others of his pieces, yet the music coheres perfectly on its own terms. Hughes is fully inside Holmboe's idiom, whether in the single-minded determination of *Monolith* or in the visionary *Epilog*, one of the composer's most searching utterances, prefiguring both the Ninth Symphony (1969) and *Requiem for Nietzsche*. This is extraordinary music.

Sinfonias

Sinfonias I-IV, Op 73. Chairos
Danish Radio Sinfonietta / Hannu Koivula
Dacapo ② (two discs for the price of one) 8 226017/8
(114' · DDD) Ⓕ**OＤ**

These four sinfonias for strings (1957-62) can be played either as independent pieces or – in a very particular sequence – as a large meta-symphony, *Chairos*, in which the four movements of Sinfonia IV frame and interlock with the single spans of I-III. Dacapo present, intelligently, both versions, each on its own disc.

Holmboe explained that 'Chairos means "time" in the psychological sense, that is the passage of time as we sense it', in contrast to measured time (Chronos). Sinfonias I-III all embrace the main

elements of traditional symphonism in their unbroken designs, the first two adopting broadly a slow-fast ground plan, III the reverse. If IV's sequence of prelude, interludes and postludes suggests something lightweight, this is misleading, for it's a highly impressive structure; the movement titles are relevant mostly for the larger composition. It's unclear when Holmboe conceived this unusual double-form. The expressive characters and relative brevity of I and III suggest that he may have had a larger design in mind at first, though II, at 19 minutes, the longest by far of the four, hints at a totally separate genesis.

However the music started out, the achievement of *Chairos* is splendid testament to Holmboe's near-unique skill as a composer in the 20th century. In its larger form, it evinces a freedom of line and spontaneity of incident that suggests the tyranny of beat and bar-line had been cast off, yet in reality all is closely argued and achieved by total precision of means. Koivula and the Danish Radio Sinfonietta embrace this dichotomy in the music's soaring lines (which in the highest registers can sound just a touch thin) and multifaceted fantasy. Dacapo's sound is of demonstration quality. Strongly recommended.

Gustav Holst   British 1874-1934

Think of Holst and you think of The Planets. Not much else springs to mind and, indeed, his output is comparatively slender – he was a slow starter and a slow worker – and few of his works were performed in his lifetime. He wrote much else of interest, yet The Planets is such an overwhelming, original work that everything else pales into insignificance in scale and concept.

Gustav von Holst's paternal great-grandfather settled in England from Sweden in 1807. His father was an organist, his mother a piano teacher, but when he went to study at the Royal College of Music in 1893 it was the trombone that became his main instrument (he was a pupil of Stanford for composition). Vaughan Williams was a fellow student and became a lifelong friend. At first he earned his living as a trombonist with various theatre and opera companies before changing course in 1905 and becoming a teacher at St Paul's Girls' School and, two years later, at Morley College, both in London. They were positions he held for the rest of his life.

His early work is dominated by the influence of Wagner, then tempered by his interest in religious philosophy, the mysticism, poetry and spiritualism of the East, and the English folk music to which Vaughan Williams had introduced him. By 1915 he'd 'gone through' these influences, absorbed them and arrived at a voice of his own.

During the First World War, plagued by suspicions of German sympathies because of his German-sounding name, he dropped the 'von' and went out to Salonica and Constantinople to organise concerts for the British troops. The Planets, written between 1914 and 1916, had to wait until 1920 for its first complete public performance but it established his name as a leading composer. In February 1923 he suffered concussion as the result of a fall, causing a rapid deterioration in his health (never robust) which thereafter severely limited all his musical activities except composition. He became more reclusive, declining many honours and taking little interest in public affairs. His daughter Imogen, also a musician, described how 'he sank into a cold region of utter despair...a grey isolation'. Holst himself, summing it all up, pinpointed 'Four chief reasons for gratitude... Music, the Cotswolds, RVW [Vaughan Williams] and having known the impersonality of orchestral playing'.

Egdon Heath

A Somerset Rhapsody, H87. Beni mora, H107. Invocation, H75[a]. A Fugal Overture, H151. Egdon Heath, H172. Hammersmith, H178
[a]**Tim Hugh** vc **Royal Scottish National Orchestra / David Lloyd-Jones**
Naxos 8 553696 (69' · DDD)   ⑤🅑➤

This superb recording was made in the Henry Wood Hall, Glasgow. Lloyd-Jones has as his two weightiest items the Hardy-inspired *Egdon Heath*, arguably Holst's finest work, as well as the prelude and fugue *Hammersmith*, comparably dark and intense. In the latter he chooses the wind-band version, achieving a subtlety of shading in phrasing and dynamic amply to justify that striking choice. The Naxos sound is vividly atmospheric while letting one hear inner detail. Lloyd-Jones generally adopts flowing speeds and is objective in his interpretation while bringing out to the full the tenderness and refinement of the writing. Particularly beautiful is the performance of *A Somerset Rhapsody* which opens the disc, with the cor anglais solo ravishingly played. The six works are neatly balanced, three dating from before the climactic period of *The Planets* and *The Hymn of Jesus*, and three after. Particularly valuable is the atmospheric *Invocation* for cello and orchestra of 1911, rather dismissed by Imogen Holst, but here given a yearningly intense, deeply thoughtful performance with Tim Hugh as soloist. This is a highly recommendable offering, whether for the dedicated Holstian or the newcomer wanting to investigate work outside *The Planets*.

The Perfect Fool

The Perfect Fool, Op 39. The Golden Goose, Op 45 No 1[a]. The Morning of the Year, Op 45 No 2[a]. The Lure
[a]**Joyful Company of Singers;**
BBC National Orchestra of Wales / Richard Hickox
Chandos 🔊 CHSA5069 (68' · DDD)   🄵🅞🅑➤

Though our modern age continues to extol *The Planets* as most archetypal of its composer, this recording of music written and completed during the 1920s serves only to reiterate that Holst's musical purview was much broader, and while he never enjoyed recognition for his ballet music (with the exception perhaps of *The Perfect Fool* as an orchestral suite), his originality rarely faltered. All the works featured here – a 'must' for all Holst fans – reveal how he built steadily on the experimental paradigms of *The Planets* with an orchestral technique second-to-none, 'naked' (as Vaughan Williams once described) in its exposed, gossamer textures.

Holst's distinctive sound is carefully manicured in this recording; the rapid 'mercurial' passages of string- and wind-writing of *The Perfect Fool* are delivered with exemplary crispness and vitality; the superimposed fourth harmonies of the unfamiliar *The Lure*, which develop mysterious bitonal 'saturnine' textures, look forward to the composer's unaccompanied choral masterpiece *The Evening Watch* as well as the desolate landscape of *Egdon Heath*, while the two choral ballets, *The Golden Goose* and *The Morning of the Year* (the former being weaker in quality) ebb and flow between Jovian elation and the more bizarre neo-classicism hinted at in 'Uranus' and the strange modernist textures of the later *Choral Fantasia*. Hickox certainly brings an electric appeal to these little-known, pointillistic scores as does the more finely tuned sense of ensemble between mystical voices and orchestra.

Perhaps the most compelling item on this disc, however, is *The Lure*, which gives us a 'reworking' of *The Perfect Fool* but with a different climactic outcome derived from the warmer timbres and harmonies of the *Ode to Death*.

The Planets

The Planets
Women's voices of the Montreal Symphony Chorus and Orchestra / Charles Dutoit
Decca download 417 553-2DH (53' · DDD)   🄼🅞🅞🅞🅑➤

 The Planets is Holst's most famous work, and its success is surely deserved. The musical characterisation is as striking as its originality of conception: the association of 'Saturn' with old age, for instance, is as unexpected as it's perceptive. Bax introduced Holst to astrology, and while he wrote the music he became fascinated with horoscopes, so it's the astrological associations that are paramount, although the linking of 'Mars' (with its enormously powerful 5/4 rhythms) and war also reflects the time of composition. Throughout, the work's invention is as memorable as its vivid orchestration is full of infinite detail. No recording can reveal it all but this one comes the closest to doing so. Dutoit's individual performance is in a long line of outstanding recordings.

Holst The Planets[a]
(with **C Matthews** Pluto, The Renewer[a]) **Komarov**
Fall **Pintscher** Towards Osiris **Saariaho** Asteroid 4179
'Toutatis' **Turnage** Ceres

HOLST'S THE PLANETS – IN BRIEF

BBC SO / Sir Adrian Boult [H]
Beulah 2PD12 (70' · ADD) (M)
Set down in January 1945, this is the earliest and most exciting of the five recordings under the maestro, who, in the words of the composer, 'first caused *The Planets* to shine'.

London PO / Sir Adrian Boult
EMI 567748-2 (79' · ADD) (M)●●
Dedicatee Boult's final, unerringly paced account of a work with which, perhaps more than any other in his vast repertoire, he was most closely associated.

Montreal SO / Charles Dutoit
Decca download 417 553-2DH (53' · DDD)
(M)●●●●▷
Holst's colourful canvas has rarely been captured with such lustre or transparency by a recording team. Dutoit conducts with infectious bounce and plenty of twinkling affection.

London SO / André Previn
EMI DVD 492399-9 (75' · ADD) (F)
Originally made in quadraphony, Previn's memorable version leaps out of the speakers with startling impact, and is stunningly well played by the LSO at its early-'70s peak. At present only available in DVD-Audio format.

Berlin PO / Sir Simon Rattle
EMI 359382-2 (84' · ADD) (M)●●▷
Rattle's second recording finds the BPO on incandescent form – and with a series of miniature 'asteroids' as a bonus this is a highly recommendable version.

Hallé Orchestra / Mark Elder
Hyperion CDA67270 (75' · DDD) (F)
Like the Rattle recording, this one adds Colin Matthews's 'Pluto' (a Hallé commission), and Elder and his orchestra respond with a performance of idiomatic warmth and enthusiasm. The recording is vivid and surprisingly immediate.

BBC SO / Sir Andrew Davis
Warner Apex 8573 89087-2 (64' · DDD) (S)▷
Davis's admirably prepared account won't break the bank and enjoys sumptuous, stunningly well-defined recording – try 'Saturn' with its devastating climax and floorboard-throbbing organ pedals.

Royal Liverpool Philharmonic Orchestra / Sir Charles Mackerras
Virgin ② 561510-2 (121' · DDD) (S)
Mackerras invariably achieves spontaneous, communicative results on disc and this highly enjoyable 1990 *Planets* is no exception. This is a very satisfying, highly musical performance.

[a]**Berlin Radio Choir; Berlin Philharmonic Orchestra / Sir Simon Rattle**
EMI ② (two discs for the price of one) 359382-2 (84' · DDD) (M)●●▷

Near the beginning of his EMI career Simon Rattle recorded his first *The Planets*. It is excellent, but next to this spectacular new account it rather pales away. That 1982 recording cannot compare with the blazing brilliance, warmth and weight of the new one, which fully brings out the glory of the Berlin sound. Some may find the wide dynamic hard to cope with domestically – too loud at climaxes if the soft passages are to be clearly heard – but the body of sound is most impressive, with string *pianissimos* in 'Venus', 'Saturn' and 'Neptune' of breathtaking beauty.

Rattle's interpretation has intensified over the years. 'Mars' is more menacing and the dance rhythms of 'Jupiter' and 'Uranus' have an extra lift. Clearly the Berlin players have taken to this British work in the way they did for Karajan. Colin Matthews's 'Pluto' is given an exceptionally bold performance which exploits the extremes.

The second disc has four works commissioned by Rattle, dubbed 'Asteroids'. Kaija Saariaho, celebrating the asteroid Toutatis and its complex orbit, uses evocative textures and woodwind repetitions in ostinato patterns, much in line with Holst's technique. Matthias Pintscher's *Osiris* is more individual, featuring a spectacular trumpet solo in celebration of the Egyptian deity who became ruler of the underworld. Again, the piece is reflective rather than dramatic.

Mark-Anthony Turnage's *Ceres* is energetic with jazzy syncopations typical of the composer, while *Komarov's Fall* by Brett Dean, formerly a viola player in the orchestra, builds up to an impressive climax before fading away on evocative trills. Rattle's boldness in offering such unusual couplings is amply justified, even if most purchasers will concentrate on the superb version of a favourite piece.

Additional recommendations

A Somerset Rhapsody
Coupled with Beni mora. A Fugal Overture. Hammersmith. Japanese Suite. Scherzo
London Philharmonic Orchestra; LSO / Boult
Lyrita SRCD222 (62' · ADD) (F)
  Conducted by one of the composer's greatest friends and staunchest advocates, this release is still in the front rank.

Choral works

The Cloud Messenger, H111[aef]. The Hymn of Jesus, H140[ef]. A Choral Fantasia, H177[bdg]. A Dirge for Two Veterans, H144[eg]. Ave Maria, H49[c]. Motets, H159-60[c] – The Evening-Watch. This have I done for my true love, H128[c]. Seven Partsongs, H162[bdg]. O lady, leave that silken thread, H4[c]. Short

Partsongs, H13ᶜ – Soft and gently through my soul.
The autumn is old, H1ᶜ. Winter and the birds,
H *App* I/40ᶜ
ᵃ**Della Jones** *mez* ᵇ**Patricia Rozario** *sop* ᶜ**Finzi
Singers / Paul Spicer;** ᵈ**Joyful Company of Singers;
London Symphony** ᵉ**Chorus and** ᶠ**Orchestra,** ᵍ**City
of London Sinfonia / Richard Hickox**
Chandos Two for One ② CHAN241-6 (147' · DDD)
ⓂⓄ🅑➤

The Cloud Messenger is a 43-minute work of considerable imaginative power. Before its previous
single-issue release it had been virtually forgotten since its disastrous premiere under Holst's
baton in 1913. It shows the composer already
working on an epic scale – something that casts
light on the subsequent eruption of *The Planets*.
It's marvellous to have the work on disc, though,
as you might expect, it's uneven. Those who
admire the ascetic rigour of his later music may
share Imogen Holst's reservations, and find the
score disappointingly 'backward'. There are
certainly echoes of Vaughan Williams's *A Sea
Symphony* and several older models. On the
other hand, the glittering approach to the sacred
city on Mount Kailasa and the stylised orientalism of the climactic dance are new to British
music; another world, that of 'Venus', is fore-
shadowed in the closing pages.

One of the few incontrovertible masterpieces
in Holst's output, the familiar *Hymn of Jesus* has
seldom received a better performance on disc.
The choral singing itself is splendidly crisp, but
the lively acoustic can blunt the impact of
Holst's acerbic harmonies.

Songs

Hymns from the Rig Veda, H90ᶜ. Six Songs, H69ᵃ. Four
Songs, H132ᵃᵈ. 12 Songs, H174ᵇ. Margrete's Cradle
Song, H14 No 2ᵃ. The Heart Worships, H95ᵃ
ᵃ**Susan Gritton** *sop* ᵇ**Philip Langridge** *ten*
ᶜ**Christopher Maltman** *bar* ᵈ**Louisa Fuller** *vn*
Steuart Bedford *pf*
Naxos 8 557117 (76' · DDD · T)
Ⓢ➤

The Four Songs for voice and violin, settings of
medieval texts, were inspired by the composer
hearing one of his pupils singing to herself and
playing her violin in Thaxted Church. They're
singularly moving, especially in this plangently
toned performance by Susan Gritton. She is no
less remarkable in the Six Songs, early pieces in
which Holst perfectly responds to an eclectic
choice of poetry, nowhere more so than in the
opening piece from Tennyson's 'In memoriam'.

Philip Langridge is equally well suited to the
12 Humbert Wolfe settings, to which he brings
his customary gift of an immediate response to
the texts in hand. His empathy with poet and
composer here couldn't be closer. The *Vedic
Hymns* are more rarefied, mystical territory and
not so easy for singer or listener to encompass.
Christopher Maltman does well by them, except
where an incipient beat sometimes spoils pleasure in his singing.

Pianist Steuart Bedford is responsive to all
the varying moods of these groups, and in the
opening group Louisa Fuller is the sensitive
violinist.

Simon Holt
British *b*1955

*Holt was born in Bolton, Lancashire. After completing
a foundation course at Bolton Art College, he went on
to study composition with Anthony Gilbert at the Royal
Northern College of Music in Manchester. The late
Michael Vyner, then artistic director of the London
Sinfonietta, commissioned Kites (1983) from the
young composer. In 1985 he was resident composer of
the Bath International Festival. Holt's relationship
with the London Sinfonietta has continued with a
steady stream of performances and premieres.*

*Holt has found inspiration in, among other things,
the world of Greek myth. His Icarus Trilogy culminated in 1995 with the premiere of his cello concerto
Daedalus Remembers. Holt's recent large-scale pieces
include the violin concerto 'witness to a snow miracle',
performed in London and Bonn by Vivianne Hagner
and the BBC Symphony Orchestra, and judged Best
Orchestral Work at the 2006 British Composer
Awards, and a percussion concerto for Colin Currie
entitled 'a table of noises', premiered by the CBSO in
May 2008. This too won the Orchestral Award at the
British Composer Awards (2009).*

A Book of Colours

Tauromaquia. A Book of Colours. Black Lanterns.
Klop's Last Bite. Nigredo.
Rolf Hind *pf*
NMC NMCD128 (69' · DDD)
Ⓕ

To call a piano composition 'a book of colours'
does rather underline the black-and-white basis
of the instrument and, given the rich textural
imagination of Simon Holt's music for various
ensembles and for orchestra, a disc of nothing
but piano music might leave you feeling that
something essential is missing. Fortunately, this
programme is substantial and varied enough to
prove satisfying – colouristically as well as conceptually – in its own terms.

That's because it gives a good work-out to the
most distinctive aspect of Holt's take on musical
expressionism – the Spanish flavour that results
from allusions to writers and painters like Lorca
and Goya, with Picasso, Miró and others in the
background. Moreover, as is very clear in 'Some
Distant Chimes' from *A Book of Colours*, and also
in *Nigredo*, Holt's Spanishness is never more
seductive than when touches of impressionistic
understatement weave their way into the music's
steadily, subtly evolving forms.

Holt cultivates a surrealistic strain in the concentrated musical comedy of *Klop's Last Bite*,
11 tiny movements chronicling the lethal confrontation between a complacent bedbug and a
mad flea. If the title hints at Beckett-style trag-

edy, the music shows that wit and an abrasive contemporary style are not incompatible. The aura of menace is altogether more disturbing in the other works, however: perhaps too unremittingly so in the early *Tauromaquia* and *Black Lanterns*, but totally gripping and richly nuanced in the 16-minute *Nigredo*. The CD's title links alchemy with Jungian psychology, and it's the importance of transformation to both that gives Holt his musical cue for an absorbing journey from – it would seem – darkness to light. Rolf Hind is the perfect interpreter throughout and the Potton Hall recording is of demonstration quality.

Arthur Honegger

French/Swiss 1892-1955

By far Honegger's best known piece is, ironically, not typical of most of his output. Pacific 231, his musical portrait of a huge steam locomotive, was once considered the last word in adventurousness, dissonance and jarring rhythms. The Concertino for piano and orchestra which appeared the following year on the other hand could have been written by a completely different composer – light (not to say slight), witty and jazzy. It turned out to be Honegger's one concession to 'Les Six', the celebrated group of composers dreamt up by the critic Henri Collet who seemed to think that Honegger, Poulenc, Milhaud, Auric, Tailleferre and Durey had a common musical creed.

Honegger was altogether more serious in his approach than Poulenc and Milhaud. Indeed, Honegger's muse is altogether more Teutonic than Gallic and this became clearer when his style crystallised between the two world wars.

During the Nazi occupation of Paris, Honegger lived as a virtual recluse in the capital but was allowed to continue to compose by the Germans and, by an oversight, act for the French Resistance. After the war, he was invited to America to teach at Tanglewood by Serge Koussevitzky but while there developed angina, the disease from which he eventually died.

Born in France of Swiss parents, Honegger spent most of his life in France and retained dual citizenship throughout his life. Thus he is properly a French composer and not Swiss as is often stated. He composed his first music for the cinema as early as 1923 (La Roue), going on to write the scores for (among many others) Abel Gance's silent masterpiece Napoleon (1927) and the Leslie Howard/Wendy Hiller version of Shaw's Pygmalion (1938).

Cello Concerto

Cello Concerto, H72[a]. Une cantate de Noël, H212[b]. Prélude, fugue et postlude, H71[a]. Horace victorieux, H38
[b]**James Rutherford** *bar* [a]**Alban Gerhardt** *vc*
BBC National Chorus and Orchestra of Wales / Thierry Fischer
Hyperion CDA67688 (76' · DDD · T/t)   Ⓕ**O**

The works collected here cover the full range of Honegger's mature career, from the volatile 'mimed symphony' *Horace victorieux*, his first major orchestral utterance (1920-21), to his final completed work, *Une cantate de Noël* (1952-53). In expressive range, the music alternates from Yuletide light and shade to the Stravinskian high jinks of the Cello Concerto's finale (1929), to the high drama of *Horace victorieux*, not otherwise available.

Horace victorieux was the first real indication of Honegger's natural genius for large-scale orchestral composition. Based on Livy's bloodthirsty tale of Publius Horatius, the score combines vigorous, martial *allegros* depicting the combat and evocative lyrical episodes for the uneasy love of Horatius's sister for his enemy, Curiatius. Heard in abstract, it proves a compelling symphonic poem of elemental power. There is a hint of the same quality in the less intense *Prelude, Fugue and Postlude* Honegger extracted in 1948 from his 1929 score for *Amphion*, although its atmosphere – based on Greek myth – is quite peaceable. There is a real touch of Christmas to the Cantata, one of Honegger's most popular works despite its gloomy, tonally ambiguous opening quarter. It is excellently sung.

Fischer directs controlled but expressive accounts of all four works which would grace any collector's shelves. Gerhardt is excellent in the Concerto, although its delicate, plaintive opening is eclipsed by proximity to *Horace*'s close. Hyperion's superb recording has much to commend it, dealing superbly with some huge dynamic ranges.

Symphonies

No 1 in C; No 2 for Strings and Trumpet obbligato in D, H153; No 3, H186, 'Liturgique'; No 4 in A, H191, 'Deliciae basiliensis' No 5 in D, H202, 'Di tre re'

Symphonies Nos 1-5. Three Symphonic Movements – Pacific 231, H53; Rugby, H67; No 3, H83. Pastorale d'été, H31
Suisse Romande Orchestra / Fabio Luisi
Cascavelle ③ RSR6132 (174' · DDD)   Ⓕ**O**

In most respects this recording is excellent. The textures are clear and sharp, and passages such as the contrapuntal *tour de force* in the last movement of the Fourth Symphony are all the more impressive for it. The Suisse Romande's solo woodwind are fresh and seductive, with a particularly fine first oboe, while, on the other hand, the clarity of the recording can bring with it a certain bleakness, entirely appropriate at the beginning of the Fifth Symphony, which here comes over rather like Sibelius.

In first two symphonies, Luisi's tempi sound just a little heavy. But his penchant for slower speeds brings notable rewards both in the central movement of the Third Symphony and in the final *Adagio* of the third Symphonic Movement. Luisi is alive to the strong element of melancholy and disillusion in this music – strong also in Honegger himself. In the opening of the Second Symphony, Luisi recognises the call of fate, that changeth not. A large measure of Honegger's disillusion came from what he saw as the triumph of the forces of collectivism over the individual human spirit, and in the Third Symphony Luisi brings out the solo cello line in the third movement as the voice of the composer crying out against the waste of war.

Honegger Symphonies Nos 2 & 3, 'Liturgique'
Stravinsky Concerto in D
Berlin Philharmonic Orchestra /
Herbert von Karajan
DG The Originals 447 435-2GOR (72' · ADD)
Recorded 1969   Ⓜ️ⓄⓄⓄ⤇

Ⓖ Karajan's performances of these Honegger symphonies enjoy legendary status – and rightly so. This recording remains in a class of its own for sheer beauty of sound and flawless ensemble. French critic Bernard Gavoty once spoke rather flightily of Karajan 'transcending emotions and imparting to them that furnace heat that makes a work of genius give off light if brought to the desired temperature' – but it's true! There's a luminous quality and an incandescence about these performances.

The Stravinsky Concerto in D was written within a year of the *Symphonie liturgique* and may perhaps be a little too 'cultured' and not spiky enough for some tastes. The lightness of touch, sprightliness of rhythm and flawless ensemble of the Berlin Philharmonic are an absolute joy in themselves.

Jeanne d'Arc au bûcher

Jeanne d'Arc au bûcher
Sylvie Testud, Eric Ruf *spkrs* **Mélanie Boisvert,**
Isabelle Cals *sops* **Marie-Nicole Lemieux** *contr*
Eric Huchet *ten* **Nicolas Testé** *bass* **Soloists and**
Children's Chorus of Opera Junior; Nantes Opera
Chorus; Montpellier Opera Chorus and Orchestra
/ Alain Altinoglu
Stage director **Jean-Paul Scarpitta**
Accord 📀 442 9181 (139' · NTSC ·16:9 · 2.0 · 0)   Ⓕ

Honegger's 'dramatic oratorio' (1938) begins just after Joan's death at the stake, the scenario having her soul guided through the events of her trial by the shade of the founder of the Dominican order, no less. It certainly packs a punch in this vivid staging for Montpellier Opera. Chorus and orchestra are on excellent form throughout and the soloists in the satirical, rather heavy-handed court scene perform with aplomb. Central to the conception, though, are the two spoken roles. Eric Ruf frowns a lot as Joan's familiar, Father Dominic, but his part is less a showcase than the catalyst for Joan herself, on whom everything hinges; and in Sylvie Testud the director found a brilliant advocate.

Elfin in build, Testud catches to a nicety the fragility, childlike innocence and inner steel of the Joan of French literary tradition. From the start, where she stands, left breast exposed, alone onstage, through to her messianic apotheosis clothed in scarlet, she dominates proceedings, her voice strong, her expression rapt when she recalls her inner voices. Her fear at the thought of being burnt is graphically real, as is her aghast realisation at being branded an impious, impure sorceress rather than saviour of France. It is a sensational portrayal that makes Honegger's and Claudel's hybrid form succeed.

Jean-Paul Scarpitta's staging takes some liberties, mostly by omission in streamlining the powerful message. The 'Game of Cards' sequence, in which Dominic exposes the French King's duplicity, does not really come off; the static nature of much of the stage action is not entirely satisfactorily solved. Yet the core expressive message is delivered with skill and power, Don Kent's video presentation capturing it superbly, and the accompanying documentary expands on many of the work's themes with interviews with Scarpitta, Testud and Altinoglu, who conducts with a real feel for Honegger's vivid if idiosyncratically scored music.

Alan Hovhaness   American 1911-2000

Hovhaness was among the most prolific of 20th-century composers, his official catalogue comprising 67 numbered symphonies (surviving manuscripts indicate over 70) and 434 opus numbers. However, the true tally is well over 500 surviving works since many opus numbers comprise two or more distinct works.

He studied with Frederick Converse at the New England Conservatory. In 1932 he won the Conservatory's Samuel Endicott prize for composition, for a symphonic work entitled Sunset Symphony. In July 1934, with his first wife, Martha Mott Davis, he travelled to Finland to meet Sibelius, whose music he had greatly admired since childhood. The two remained in correspondence for the next 20 years. His biggest breakthrough came in 1955, when his Symphony No 2, Mysterious Mountain, was premiered by Leopold Stokowski in his debut with the Houston Symphony. Between 1956 and 1958, at the urging of Howard Hanson (who was an admirer of his music), he taught summers at the Eastman School of Music.

From 1960 he took a keen interest in Japanese and Korean music, which affected his style; only in the 1970s did he return to a more Western style, richer and more spacious. Most of his work is broadly religious in inspiration.

Concertos

Cello Concerto, Op 17[b]. Symphony No 22, 'City of Light', Op 236[b].
[a]**János Starker** *vc* **Seattle Symphony Orchestra /**

[b]**Alan Hovhaness,** [a]**Dennis Russell Davies**
Naxos 8 559158 (61' · DDD)   ⓈＢ➔

City of Light (1970) has some lovely ideas, like the surprisingly sweet and simple string melody in the middle of the 'Angel of Light' movement, and the third movement, *Allegretto grazioso*, which sounds like a minuet in oriental garb. The outer movements, however, outstay their welcome.

On the other hand, the Cello Concerto (1936) is required listening for Hovhaness admirers. The composer destroyed several hundred of his compositions during a period of self-reflection in the early 1940s but the concerto survived the cull, finally receiving its premiere in 1999. The music's modal tinge is pure Hovhaness but there is a spareness to the writing that sets it apart from its successors. Indeed, the tone is unrelievedly elegiac, making the Elgar Concerto seem positively jovial by comparison. János Starker brings sad nobility to the ruminative solo part, and Dennis Russell Davies makes the most of the *Das Lied von der Erde*-like orchestral texture in a warmly recommended disc.

Symphonies

Symphonies – No 2, 'Mysterious Mountain',
Op 132; No 50, 'Mount St Helens', Op 360;
No 66, 'Hymn to Glacier Peak', Op 428.
Storm on Mount Wildcat, Op 2 No 2
**Royal Liverpool Philharmonic Orchestra /
Gerard Schwarz**
Telarc CD80604 (72' · DDD)   Ⓕ

It's easy to dismiss the music of Hovhaness, who was was suspiciously prolific, with opus numbers nearing 500. But despite such sustained productivity over more than seven decades, his work is stylistically consistent – so much so, in fact, that some only half-jokingly claim he wrote the same symphony 67 times. Certainly, the profusion of sing-song fugues and modal, hymn-like tunes throughout his output can give a feeling of predictability.

And yet listening to the opening movement of the *Mount St Helens* Symphony (1982), it's difficult not to be entranced, even awed, by the music's sensuous beauty – those luminous clouds of strings, that majestic rising theme in the horns, then, a little later, the delicate spinning of the harp and a procession of ecstatic, exotic woodwind solos. Perhaps the depiction of the volcano's eruption is a bit primitive, though it's fascinating that Hovhaness seems to view the explosion not only as an elemental event but also as a ritualistic one.

Hymn to Glacier Peak (1992), the composer's penultimate symphony, is also appealing. As the title suggests, it has a preponderance of hymn-like melody, yet there's a touching valedictory quality to the music. The finale is particularly effective, moving from hymn to one of Hovhaness's most tuneful fugues via a darkly atmospheric interlude.

Warmly recommended: this would make an excellent introduction to Hovhaness's music.

Symphony No 63, 'Loon Lake'. Guitar Concerto
No 2ᵃ. Fanfare for the New Atlantis
[a]**Javier Calderón** gtr **Royal Scottish National
Orchestra / Stewart Robertson**
Naxos American Classics 8 559336 (59' · DDD)   ⓈＢ➔

Alan Hovhaness's Second Concerto was commissioned by the great Narciso Yepes in 1985 but wasn't premiered until 1990, shortly before Yepes's death. It's classic Hovhaness, with numerous hymn-like passages for the strings contrasted with lively *pizzicato* sections and fugal textures; the guitar meanwhile rejoices in puckish, modally rich dances enlivened by frequent changes of time signature and broad cantorial utterances. Bolivian-born Javier Calderón's playing is tonally refined and rhythmically supple, qualities which are best savoured in his own third-movement cadenza.

The disc opens with Hovhaness's *Fanfare for the New Atlantis*, in which a slumbering orchestra gradually awakens to the call of a solo trumpet before rushing strings, rumbling timpani and bold brass chords bring the work to a thrilling, Wagnerian climax as the lost city of Atlantis rises anew from the waves. The Symphony No 63, *Loon Lake*, was commissioned by the New Hampshire Music Festival and the Loon Preservation Society in 1987. Here, songs both avian and pastoral for a multitude of wind soloists punctuate a luminous, if occasionally overcast, orchestral skyscape.

The RSNO under Stewart Robertson is excellent throughout; good recorded sound and notes by Hovhaness's widow Hinako Fugihara Hovhaness further enhance what is another excellent release.

Khaldis, Op 91

Khaldis, Op 91ᵃ. Mount Katahdin, Op 405ᵇ.
Fantasy, Op 16ᶜ
[ab]**Martin Berkofsky,** [c]**Alan Hovhaness** pfs [a]**William
Rohdin,** [a]**Dan Cahn,** [a]**Francis Bonny,** [a]**Patrick
Dougherty** tpts [a]**Neal Boyar** perc
Crystal CD814 (52' · ADD)
Recorded [c]1970, [a]1972, [b]1999   Ⓕ

Khaldis (1951) has a connection with Hovhaness's well-known *St Vartan* Symphony (1950) in their common use of a quartet of trumpets: the composer wanted a piece he could play with them and a percussionist alone. It's a striking work – named from the god of the universe of the pre-Armenian Urarduan people – full of apocalyptic visions. The even-movement structure has the feel of a set of studies rather than an integrated concerto, the brass tending to play en bloc and one movement scored as if for some primordial trio of giants.

The sonata *Mount Katahdin* (1986-87) doesn't sound almost a career later than *Khaldis*. The four movements resemble the sequence of a

Bach orchestral suite, with the imposing opening 'Solenne', succeeded by three tiny movements, lighter in character and acting as foils for the first. The central 'Jhala of Larch Trees' is particularly lovely. Berkofsky plays with evident love and conviction, and these are persuasive performances, whether from 1972 or 1999 (*Mount Katahdin*).

Most fascinating of all is Hovhaness's own account of the *Fantasy*, written *c*1936 and also once available on a Poseidon LP. A mesmeric performance of a mesmeric piece, the 10 sections or 'steps' built from Indian ragas utilise Cowellesque devices such as playing the strings inside the instrument with fingers, plectrum, marimba mallet or timpani stick. The sound overall is acceptable but the remastered *Khaldis* and *Fantasy* are a touch lacking in depth.

Herbert Howells   British 1892-1983

Howells studied with Stanford and Wood at the Royal College of Music, where he taught from 1920 almost to his death. He also succeeded Holst at St Paul's Girls' School (1932-62) and was professor of music at London University. His music is within an English diatonic tradition embracing Elgar, Walton and Vaughan Williams. The earlier works include two piano concertos and chamber pieces, but most of his music is choral, including c15 anthems, a concert Requiem (later reused in Hymnus Paradisi, 1938, first performed 1950), Masses and motets, and some fine songs. Deeply tinged by the English choral tradition, Howells's music reflects a subtle and fastidious craftsman who was capable of a restrained, individual eloquence.

Piano Concertos

Piano Concertos[a] – No 1 in C minor, Op 4; No 2 in C, Op 39. Penguinski
[a]**Howard Shelley** pf **BBC Symphony Orchestra / Richard Hickox**
Chandos CHAN9874 (71' · DDD)   (F)**O**B→

An astonishing revelation, especially to anyone who still thinks of Herbert Howells as a nostalgic English rhapsodist, more at home in an organ loft than a concert hall. The First Piano Concerto is very early (1914 – Howells was 22) and hasn't been performed for many years because its last few bars are missing (John Rutter has provided them). It reveals the young Howells as more Russian than English – the dazzlingly flamboyant keyboard writing is strongly reminiscent of Rachmaninov – and with hardly a trace of English reserve as he brandishes theme after theme, intensifying many of them to heights of impassioned eloquence.

One or two lyrical paragraphs suggest the 'real' Herbert Howells. But who, the Second Piano Concerto demands, was he? This work was abused at its premiere (one critic shouted 'Thank God that's over!') and Howells, deeply wounded, withdrew it immediately. Indeed,

although it's a lot closer to 'real' Howells in its rhapsodic lyricism, there's another quality which is angular, sometimes dissonant, tough and determined.

Surely we shall get closer to the real Howells, lifelong admirer of the arch-conservative Stanford, in *Penguinski*, from its title an obvious satire on Stravinsky? But in fact the sidelong glances at him are admiring and affectionate, and the robust humour is Howells's own. There's more to him than we had imagined, and his stature is increased, not diminished, by the realisation that he was once an exuberant Romantic, that his ears were sharp and that he had a sense of humour.

Enthusiastic, virtuoso, very slightly rough-cornered performances and a sumptuously rich recording.

Chamber Works

Howells String Quartet No 3, 'In Gloucestershire'
Dyson Three Rhapsodies
Divertimenti (Paul Barritt, Rachel Isserlis vns Gustav Clarkson va Sebastian Comberti vc)
Hyperion Helios CDH55045 (64' · DDD)   (B)B→

If you don't yet know Howells's masterly *In Gloucestershire* (the last of his three works for string quartet), an exquisitely wrought, hauntingly atmospheric creation, then immediate investigation is recommended.

The coupling, too, is a delight. Completed between 1905 and 1912, Dyson's youthful *Three Rhapsodies* form a most appealing triptych, uncommonly fluent, tightly knit and always evincing an engaging, at times positively Straussian lyrical grace. Divertimenti give a first-rate display brimful of commitment and communicative warmth. The airy, natural sound complements its budget price.

Further listening

Howells Rhapsodic Quintet
Coupled with: **Frankel, Holbrooke, Arnold Cooke**
and **Maconchy** Clarinet Quintets
King cl **Britten Quartet**
Hyperion Helios CDH55105 (66' · DDD)   (B)B→
  Howells's *Rhapsodic Quintet* is a jewel, while no one could fail to be touched by the elegiac last movement of Frankel's eloquent Quintet. Thea King forms a stylish and sensitive partnership with the much-missed Britten Quartet. At budget price, don't miss it.

Organ Sonata No 2

Organ Sonata No 2. Six Pieces (1940-45)
Graham Barber org
Priory PRCD524 (67' · DDD)
Recorded on Hereford Cathedral organ   (F)

These are powerful, authoritative performances which ooze the spirit of Howells – that odd mixture of emotional detachment with a hint of deep personal passion, an undercurrent of tragedy and an almost improvisatory fluidity of structure. The Sonata has a formal structure which makes it easy to follow while the *Six Pieces* give such a kaleidoscopic array of organ colours that the ear is continually enchanted. The Hereford organ is a lovely instrument. Priory has, in focusing the microphones on the organ, expunged much of the building's aural ambience, but the sound is an utter delight to the ear.

Church music

'St John's Magnificat'
A Sequence for St Michael. By the waters of Babylon[a]. A Spotless Rose. Magnificat & Nunc dimittis (Gloucester Service). Psalm 142. A Grace for 10 Downing Street. One thing have I desired. Like as the hart. Magnificat & Nunc dimittis (Collegium Sancti Johannis Cantabrigiense). Salve regina. Te Deum (Collegium Regale)
**Choir of St John's College, Cambridge /
Andrew Nethsingha** with [a]**Paul Whelan** bar
[a]**David Adams** vn [a]**Alice Neary** vc
Chandos CHAN10587 (76' · DDD)　　　Ⓕ◐�____

The sound of the boys at St John's College, Cambridge, has changed considerably since the hard-edged, continental, vibrato-imbued timbre of George Guest's day (a sound all his own), but the new, clear tone under its present director, Andrew Nethsingha, certainly has an impressive vibrancy and conviction. Not since David Willcocks's memorable recording of Howells's church music, made many years ago on Argo, has there been such precise intonation in the challenging *a cappella* works as *One thing have I desired*, the extended *A Sequence for St Michael* or *A Grace for 10 Downing Street* (with Psalm 142, one of two premiere recordings).

On this recording, the numinous, indeed mystical ambience of Howells's lyrical outpourings find an especially apposite voice in the Gloucester and less well known St John's services (the *Nunc dimittis* of the latter is sung with notable power and sonority), the ageless *A Spotless Rose*, the languidly evocative *Like as the hart* and the *Te Deum* written for King's College, the end of which must be among the most affecting pages of church music Howells ever wrote. The *Salve regina* (1915) deserves to be heard more often, while *By the waters of Babylon* (1917), compellingly sung here by Paul Whelan, also reminds us of the prodigious fertility of Howells's early years.

Evening Services – G; Collegium Sancti Johannis Cantabrigiense; New College, Oxford; Collegium Regale; Sarum; York. Magnificat and Nunc dimittis
The Collegiate Singers / Andrew Millinger with
Richard Moorhouse org
Priory PRCD745 (65' · DDD)　　　　　Ⓕ◐

Howells wrote 20 settings of the evening canticles. His first setting (1918), the freshly vigorous

work of the Stanford pupil, sets out on the long life's musical journey with bone and muscle. The gentler passages have a light-footed grace, and in exultation the spirit flares; this is the music of purposeful movement, where the more 'Howells' he becomes the more the firm lines of the Stanford pupil dissolve, and the nearer he draws to a music of mystical stasis. The opening of the Collegium Regale *Magnificat* has something of this, the great thing being that he can still pull out of it (with the strong-boned 'He hath shown strength with his arm', for instance). It's a pity that the series hasn't been arranged chronologically; it would have been good to follow the order of composition, seeing which parts of his musical system he developed and which he left unexercised.

The other slightly faltering element in this welcome release concerns the choice of a choir of mixed voices. The women scrupulously adhere to the tonal ideal but boy trebles and male altos have a distinctive quality, and Howells's own sound is less distinctive without them. It's an extremely good choir, and they're under careful, intelligent direction, yet making a chance comparison with the choir of Bristol Cathedral in the G major setting, one can't help rejoicing in a character (individual as a face) which those trebles possessed and for which the Collegiate sopranos substitute a collective identity somewhat depersonalised.

The recorded sound is fine, balance between choir and the excellent organist is well judged, and the acoustic resonance is sufficient to form an appropriate setting while preserving the clear articulation. The selection here also includes two premiere recordings (the York Service and the 1941 setting for men's voices, performed, as the score suggests, by women).

'Howells from Hereford'
Te Deum & Jubilate (Collegium Regale). Magnificat & Nunc dimittis – Gloucester Service; Hereford Service; Worcester Service; Collegium Regale. Four Anthems
Choir of Hereford Cathedral / Geraint Bowen with **Peter Dyke** org
Regent REGCD316 (74' · DDD) Ⓕ

One sometimes feels Howells must have left the odd *Mag* and *Nunc* behind him like a visiting card almost wherever he went. This recital has four of them: one for each of the three-choir cities and, first and most renowned of the series, that for King's College, Cambridge. Each has its own character though all are unmistakably from the same hand. King's (*Collegium Regale*) is both the most intimate and the most opulent; Gloucester the most mystical; Worcester the most light of heart; Hereford the most angular. Always there comes an exciting injection of vigour at 'He hath shown strength with his arm' and a feeling of inspired breadth at 'And to be the glory of his people Israel'. The *Glorias* themselves are always an occasion for colour and choral enrichment.

The anthems heard here ('Like as the hart', with its yearning 'blues' tone, the most characteristic) exploit choir and organ with similarly exalted effect. The exception is the *Collegium Regale* Morning Service where the manner is more forthright, more distinctly music of the morning.

The choir's performance captures this freshness splendidly, and it gives the recital an invigorating start. Particularly admirable throughout is the finely shaded, sympathetic interchange between choir and organ. As in previous recordings, the choir does credit to its director, Geraint Bowen, singing with keen attentiveness and consistently pleasing tone. The recording conveys a natural, and restful, sense of occupying a customary seat in the Cathedral.

Requiem

Requiem[a]. Choral and Organ Works. Collegium Regale – Communion Service[ab]. St Paul's Service[ab]. Like as the hart[a]. Long, long ago[a]. Take him, earth, for cherishing[a]. Organ Rhapsody No 3[b]. Paean[b]
[b]**Ian Farrington** org [a]**St John's College Choir, Cambridge / Christopher Robinson**
Naxos 8 554659 (76' · DDD · T)   ⑤🅑➤

Howells, probably more than any other composer, extended the cathedral repertoire in the 20th century. Here his music is performed by one of the best choirs. Under Christopher Robinson, St John's has preserved its distinctive character (the bright tone of its trebles a famous part of it) and, as this record demonstrates, has gained in vigour and clarity of purpose. Immediately notable is the choice of relatively quick speeds. Howells sometimes appears to invite a relaxed style of performance which isn't to his advantage.

Robinson's tempi suit the acoustic. This applies to a similar comparison with the Choir of King's College in its more reverberant chapel, singing the Communion Service dedicated to it: the more opulent sound matches the broader tempo, St John's achieving (as in the *Sanctus*) clearer effects within a narrower spectrum. Their discs also have in common the Rhapsody No 3 for organ, and whereas the expansive performance at King's includes a murmurous *pianissimo* nextthing-to-silence, the quicker, more sharply defined one at St John's has a dramatic urgency.

The choice of programme is particularly happy, with one of the lesser-known Evening Services (the St Paul's) and one of the best known of Howells's anthems (*Like as the hart*).

Additional recommendation

Requiem
Coupled with Take him, earth, for cherishing.
Vaughan Williams Mass in G minor. Te Deum
Coxwell, Seers sops **Chance** counterten **Salmon** ten
J Best bass **Corydon Singers / M Best**
Hyperion Helios CDH55220 (67 · DDD)   🅑➤
A fine performance of the Requiem and attractive couplings.

Hymnus paradisi

An English Mass – Hymnus Paradisi
Julie Kennard sop **John Mark Ainsley** ten
Liverpool Philharmonic Choir; Royal Liverpool Philharmonic Orchestra / Vernon Handley
Hyperion CDA66488 (80' · DDD · N/T)   Ⓕ

The *Hymnus paradisi* is music awash with ecstasy, and the listener may resist becoming part of this swimmingly coloured dream. But further listening proves this is not so: that is, the better you know it, the more you see in it of form, energy and pain. The pain is real enough, as biographical facts attest. Howells wrote it as a method of escape from 'the crippling numbness of loss', as he described the effect upon him of his son's death from polio at the age of 10. The work was so full of the emotion of that time that for many years it had to remain private, and it was only with the approach of the 15th anniversary of the death that he showed it to Vaughan Williams and arrangements were made for its inclusion in the Three Choirs Festival of 1950.

A strong performance helps, and Vernon Handley brings real intensity: there is a feeling for the dramatic quality in the score, the crises and relaxations, without losing sight of the essential lyricism. The soloists on the recording sing with sensitivity and pleasing tone.

Jenö Hubay   Hungarian 1858-1937

Violinist and composer, Hubay studied violin with Joachim and later gave concerts with Liszt. He was a close friend and later executor of Vieuxtemps who recommended Hubay to head violin studies at the Brussels Conservatory. His legacy is large, including operas and over 200 works for violin.

Violin Concertos – No 1; No 2. Suite, Op 5
Hagai Shaham vn **BBC Scottish Symphony Orchestra / Martyn Brabbins**
Hyperion CDA67498 (73' · DDD)   Ⓕ🅑➤

Here's a disc to demonstrate what an outstanding melodist Jenö Hubay was, particularly in the first of the concertos, the *Concerto dramatique*, in which one good tune follows another, each of them a candidate for the sort of virtuoso figuration designed to show off the brilliance of the soloist. Hubay himself was a formidable violinist who, to celebrate his 50th birthday in 1908, played this concerto in a concert when his other three violin concertos were played by his pupils Josef Szigeti, Franz von Vecsey and Štefi Geyer, dedicatee of Bartók's early Violin Concerto No 1.

Hubay composed that first concerto in 1884-85 for his former teacher, Joseph Joachim, and much of the writing tends to bring to mind Bruch's concertos, which is no disadvantage. No 2 dates from around 1900 and though the first movement is less distinguished, with a rather rigid main theme like a patriotic song, it too is a tuneful piece. The second and third movements are even more attractive, a charming interlude leading to a sparkling Hungarian dance finale.

The Suite, Op 5 (1877-88), another *concertante* work for violin, starts rather unpromisingly with a gavotte which, with its square main theme and hammered double-stopping, sounds more like a march. The other three movements are freer-running in their lyricism: genre pieces, an 'Idylle' marked *Andantino*, an Intermezzo and a dazzling finale full of virtuoso writing, which misleadingly opens with a brief reminiscence of the opening movement.

Hagai Shaham plays not just with brilliance but with great imagination, avoiding any idea that this is just superficial display music. As in so many of Hyperion's concerto recordings, Martyn Brabbins and the BBC Scottish SO demonstrate what sympathetic accompanists they are, consistently giving an impression of live music-making.

Tobias Hume   English c1570-1645

An officer in the Swedish and Russian armies, Hume played the viol and entered Charterhouse almshouse in London in 1629. His two published lyra viol tablatures (1605, 1607) contain all his known works – dances, descriptive and programmatic pieces, and songs.

Musicall Humors

'Passion and Division'
Captaine Humes Musicall Humors – Loves Pastime; A Jigge; Harke, harke; Now I come; Rossamond; Touch me lightly; The Duke of Holstones Almayne; A Souldiers Resolution; I am melancholy; Tickell, tickell; A French Ayre; Deth; Life; The Spirit of Gambo; Tinckeldum, twinckeldum; Captain Humes Pavan; A Souldiers Galliard; Loves Farewell
Susanne Heinrich *va da gamba*
Hyperion CDA67811 (71' · DDD)   ⓕ**OO**➔

If you enjoyed Susanne Heinrich's solo Abel album (see page 1), you'll want this release. Hume's music stands at the opposite end of the period in which solo viol playing flourished in England but offers a comparable level of technical and musical challenge to the performer. Heinrich raises the stakes by using gut strings without silver or copper winding in the lower register (metal-wound strings post-date Hume) – something many players today would find too risky because they speak grudgingly and produce a slightly gruffer sound than wound strings. The rewards for doing so justify the perils: the lowest notes of bass-lines breathe uncannily and blend seamlessly in chords.

This is not the first time a performer has devoted a disc to 'Captain Humes Musicall Humors' but this one offers listeners selections not previously recorded. Ah, but the music! The melancholy of the opening and closing tracks is bewitching. Here, and elsewhere on the disc, Heinrich dramatically – often poetically – conveys Hume's deeply personal, seemingly reflective musical utterances. Heinrich includes mercurial, conversational pieces that tease the listener and those that evoke the lute (in 'Harke, harke' Hume sought to surpass it with *col legno* effects). Elsewhere she brilliantly captures his military swagger and bravura, evoking trumpets and drums, and a sense of marching into the distance. Bravo!

Additional recommendation

Captaine Humes Pavan; A Souldiers Resolution; Deth; Life; Captaine Humes Galliard; Touch me lightly; A Pavane; My hope is decayed; A Souldiers Galliard; Beccus an Hungarian Lord; The Second part; A Question; An Answere; The new Cut Good againe; The Duke of Holstones Almaine; Hark! Hark!; The Spirit of Gambo: The Lord Dewys favoret Humorous Pavin; Love's Farewell
Jordi Savall *va da gamba*
Alia Vox AV9837 (70' · DDD)   ⓕ**O**

Jordi Savall's cultivated, elegant style is very appropriate for much of the music; occasionally he adopts a more earthy manner to great effect – for example in *A Souldiers Resolution*, with its trumpet and drum imitations. When Captain Hume's *Humors* become more reflective, in a piece like *Beccus an Hungarian Lord*, Savall uses varied bow strokes and dynamic shadings with great artistry to bring out the music's dignified, sombre character.

Johann Hummel   Austrian 1778-1837

You'd have thought that Hummel was assured of immortality: one of the great piano virtuosos of the day, he studied with Mozart (in fact, he lived with Mozart in 1785 for two years), then Salieri, Clementi and Haydn. He toured all over the continent including Russia until, by 1800, he was considered one of the supreme musicians of the age.

He was said to be the equal of Beethoven as a keyboard improviser and the mass of musicians held him as quite the equal of Beethoven as a composer. His compositions had a tremendous influence on the young Romantics. Mendelssohn, Schumann and Liszt all revered him and Chopin was captivated by him – you can hear the influence by comparing Hummel's Piano Concerto in A minor of 1821 with Chopin's E minor Concerto composed in 1830.

Immediately after his death, his music fell out of fashion until one writer at the end of the last century opined: 'quite incapable of humour or passion, but fully equipped with every musical virtue that can be acquired by steady plodding, he appears expressly cut out for the hero of respectable mediocrity.' Yet his music is elegant, superbly crafted, full of memorable tunes, at its best the sort of music you feel Mozart would have written had he lived longer.

Piano Concertos

Piano Concerto No 4 in E, Op 110.
Double Concerto in G, Op 17
Hagai Shaham vn **London Mozart Players /
Howard Shelley** pf
Chandos CHAN9687 (63' · DDD)   Ⓕ◐➔

Shelley is outstanding in this music, blending classical and Romantic elements perfectly. These two concertos are wonderfully infectious. The E major occupies a kind of bridge between Mozart and Chopin, although Mozart's depth and subtlety are in a different vein. Hummel is more of a show-off, and his music almost smiles at you, its charm and sparkle eschewing any pretentiousness. Throughout, Shelley conveys the music's *joie de vivre*, revelling in the figurative passagework. The Double Concerto may have been inspired by Mozart's *Sinfonia concertante*, K364; it doesn't have the same harmonic or lyrical variety as the E major Concerto but it's a charming work, especially when so persuasively played. Shelley's well-proportioned piano part is perfectly complemented by Hagai Shaham's sweet-toned violin. Shelley fulfils his dual role admirably and the London Mozart Players respond well to his playing and conducting. The recorded sound is first-rate. A lovely disc.

Piano Concerto No 5 in A flat, Op 113. Concertino in G, Op 73. Gesellschafts Rondo in D, Op 117
London Mozart Players / Howard Shelley pf
Chandos CHAN9558 (59' · DDD)   Ⓕ🅑➔

These are decorous rarities played with an assured brilliance and affection. Hummel's Mozartian rather than Chopinesque bias declares itself most obviously in his Op 73 Concertino, though even here the figuration has a recognisably Hummelian froth and sparkle. Too charming to be vacuous, such surface brio has little in common with Mozart's depth and subtlety, and for music of greater romantic range and ambition we turn to the A flat major Concerto, with its fuller scoring and lavishly decorated solo part. Lovers of a fine-spun, operatic cantilena will warm to the central 'Romanze'. The *Gesellschafts Rondo* commences in solemn *Adagio* vein before turning to a bustling and ceremonious *Vivace*. It may be that Hummel 'puffed, blew and perspired' when he played but he won the admiration of Chopin (a hard master to please) and his style is infectious when projected with such unfailing expertise by Howard Shelley. The Chandos recordings are exceptionally well balanced.

Additional recommendation

Piano Concertos – A minor, Op 85; B minor, Op 89
Hough; ECO / Thomson
Chandos CHAN8507 (66' · DDD)   Ⓕ🅞🅞🅞➔

The recording that put Stephen Hough on the musical map and won him the recording of the Year at the *Gramophone* Awards. Sparkling playing of sparkling music – glorious!

Trumpet Concerto

Hummel Trumpet Concerto **Haydn** Trumpet Concertos in E flat, HobVIIe/1; in C[a].
Concertos by **Albinoni, Corelli, Hertel, JM Molter, Mozart, FX Richter, J Stamitz.** Works by **JS Bach, Clarke** and **Gounod**
Håkan Hardenberger tpt **Simon Preston** org
Academy of St Martin in the Fields / Sir Neville Marriner; [a]**London Philharmonic Orchestra / Elgar Howarth;** [b]**I Musici**
Philips Duo ② 464 028-2PM2 (148' · DDD)   Ⓜ🅞

This is probably the finest single collection of trumpet concertos in the catalogue. When it first appeared in 1987 (the Hummel and Haydn have since been recoupled with a later set as listed here) it created overnight a new star in the firmament of trumpeters.

The two finest concertos for the trumpet are undoubtedly those of Haydn and Hummel, and Hardenberger plays them here with a combination of sparkling bravura and stylish elegance that are altogether irresistible. Hardenberger opens with the famous Hummel Concerto, played in E major rather than the usual E flat, which makes the work sound bolder and brighter than usual. The finale, with its crisp articulation, fantastic tonguing and tight trills, displays a genial easy bravura, yet overflows with energy and high spirits. Marriner and his Academy accompany with characteristic finesse and warmth, with the lilting dotted rhythms of the first movement of the Hummel seductively jaunty. The lovely *Andante* of the Haydn is no less beguiling, and both finales display a high-spirited exuberance and an easy bravura which make the listener smile with pleasure.

The recording gives him the most vivid realism and presence, but it's a pity that the orchestral backcloth is so reverberant; otherwise the sound is very natural. A superb disc.

Cello Sonata

Hummel Cello Sonata **Moscheles** Cello Sonata No 2.
Melodic-Contrapuntal Studies (after Bach's Well-Tempered Clavier) – No 4 (after Book 2 No 7); No 8 (after Book II No 6); No 9 (after Book 1 No 4)
Jiří Bárta vc **Hamish Milne** pf
Hyperion CDA67521 (65' · DDD)   Ⓕ🅑➔

Hummel and Moscheles make an apt pair: each was a keyboard virtuoso who wrote prolifically. Yet where Hummel has been well represented on disc lately, Moscheles is far more neglected. That makes the new issue specially valuable. Their careers overlapped, but Moscheles lived for 33 years more after Hummel died, actively composing till the last. The works here appeared some three decades apart – not that the stylistic contrast is at all marked, for both adopted an easily lyrical style celebrating the early 19th rather than the 18th century, with Mendelssohn more of an influence than Mozart.

This is particularly so in Moscheles's Cello Sonata of 1850-51, with one or two echoes of the Mendelssohn Octet and with a *Scherzo* marked *ballabile*, sparkling in the way one expects of Mendelssohn. The younger composer, a close friend, also influenced Moscheles in his devotion to Bach, represented here by the three *Melodic-Contrapuntal Studies*, involving flowing melodic writing for the cello neatly fitted to Bach's original keyboard Preludes.

Following tradition, Moscheles gives priority to the piano over the cello in describing the work, not surprising from a pianist-composer, and this recording rather brings that out; the sensitive cellist, Jiří Bárta, is regularly overshadowed. What is more unexpected is how the last two movements echo Czech music, not just in the rhythms and melodic shapes of some of the themes but in the alternation of speeds; that suggests that Moscheles was influenced by the Czech dumka. The Sonata is rounded off with a dashing movement in which Moscheles encourages the pianist to show off in several passages.

Otherwise this is a work designed for intimate music-making, and that is even more clearly so in the Hummel Sonata, which opens with a triple-time *Allegro amabile*. 'Amiable' is an apt description of the piece, not just in that lyrical first movement but the central *Romanze* which is rather like early Beethoven. Here, too, there are echoes of the music of eastern Europe in the finale, maybe influenced by Hummel's tours of Russia and Poland.

Though it is a pity that Bárta is not presented as a full equal to Milne (who plays brilliantly), the recording balance is largely to blame. An attractive disc none the less.

Piano Trios

Piano Trios – No 2; No 5; No 6
Voces Intimae Trio (Richard Cecchetti *fp*
Luigi de Filippi *vn* Sandro Meo *vc*)
Warner Classics 2564 62595-2 (61' · DDD)　　Ⓟ Ⓓ▸

Piano Trios – No 1; No 3; No 4; No 7
Voces Intimae Trio
Warner Classics 2564 62596-2 (70' · DDD)　　Ⓟ Ⓓ▸

Unlike most of Hummel's chamber works the piano trios are relatively well covered on disc – not surprising when they offer such a free flow of attractive ideas. The difference in this new cycle is that the players use period instruments and there is a positive advantage in a having a light and slightly twangy fortepiano in place of a modern concert grand. So in the second-movement *Andante* of the First Trio, the transition from the *pizzicato* arpeggios on the cello at the start to similar figuration from the fortepiano, a restored instrument of 1815, is much more winningly integrated in this lively perfor-

mance. The interplay between the players is a delight. Those who resist period instruments may find that the bright tone of the violin with little vibrato is a shade aggressive but the vigour of the performances is magnetic. The lightness of touch of this antique fortepiano allows Richard Cecchetti to play with phenomenal clarity of articulation even in the fastest movements, such as the *Presto* finale of No 1.

What makes the Voces Intimae performances even more sparkling than the excellent ones from the Beaux Arts Trio from the late 1990s (Philips) is that, playing at speeds generally a shade less extreme in fast movements, they have more room for expressive pointing and phrasing, giving shape to passages that might otherwise seem hectic. That is so in the witty finale of No 3 – in a sort of polka rhythm which sounds like an ancestor of a Gilbert and Sullivan patter song – and in the finale of No 7.

Anyone wanting to sample before investing in the complete cycle should plump for the second disc whose four compact works are likely to quickly charm. The forward recording is admirably clear and full.

Solo Piano Works

Piano Sonatas – No 3 in F minor, Op 20; No 5 in F sharp minor, Op 81; No 6 in D, Op 106
Stephen Hough pf
Hyperion CDA67390 (69' · DDD)　　Ⓟ Ⓞ Ⓓ▸

Stephen Hough's splendid issue is in its way as revelatory as his *Gramophone* Award-winning recordings of the piano concertos. He revels in the element of display which Hummel, one of the leading pianists of his day, must have brought out in his own performances.

These three works are arguably the most interesting of Hummel's nine solo sonatas. The most radical is No 5, with the composer in 1819 enthusiastically throwing himself behind the new Romantic movement. A strikingly angular opening motif leads to an argument which, in a very free rendering of sonata form, brings surges of energy set against moments of reflection; there are many unexpected melodic and harmonic twists and few passages of conventional figuration, such as those that weaken the piano concertos.

The slow movement, too, opens surprisingly, with a heavyweight *fortissimo* gesture, before settling down to a yearning melody, anticipating Chopin's Nocturnes but more bare in texture, with cantilena echoing *bel canto* opera. The finale is a wild Slavonic dance, fierce and energetic in headlong flight, again dotted with unexpectedly angular ideas.

In the Sixth Sonata in 1824 Hummel was rowing back from the Romantic stance of Op 81. The first movement establishes a much lighter tone and is more conventional in structure, exceptionally clear in its presentation of sonata form. The opening theme, for all its lightness of texture, has characteristically quirky twists, and leads to a warmly lyrical second subject, rather like Weber. The second movement *Scherzo*, the most striking of the four, is a fast mazurka, leading to a slow movement rather like a Mendelssohn Song Without Words and a virtuoso finale, light in texture at the start and ending, after all the display, in an unexpected throwaway cadence.

Sonata No 3 in F minor, dating from 1807, again starts gently before developing quirks typical of Hummel. The slow movement then surprisingly has the marking *Maestoso*, majestic, strong and forthright rather than conventionally lyrical, leading to another virtuoso finale, relatively brief, with cross-hand, Scarlatti-like leaps for the left hand.

Masses

Mass in B flat, Op 77. Mass in D, Op 111.
Offertorium, 'Alma Virgo', Op 89aª
ªSusan Gritton *sop* Collegium Musicum 90 /
Richard Hickox
Chandos Chaconne CHAN0681 (76' · DDD · T/t)
Ⓕ❶❶❶➾

 While the glories of Haydn's late Masses have been widely appreciated, it's sad that Hummel's have been so neglected. They are for chorus and orchestra alone, without soloists, which may have deterred potential performers. However, while they can't quite match late Haydn or Beethoven in originality, they're lively, beautifully written and full of striking ideas, inspiring Hickox and his team to performances here just as electrifying as those they have given of Haydn, and just as vividly recorded.

Hummel follows Haydn in both Masses in his fondness for fugues. Similarly, he follows Haydn in offering joyfully energetic settings of 'Dona nobis pacem', only unlike Haydn he doesn't end either Mass on a *fortissimo* cadence, instead fading down the final phrases, maybe for liturgical reasons in the context of a church performance. Hummel, like Haydn and Beethoven before him, fully brings out the drama of the liturgy, though in both settings of 'Et resurrexit' he begins not with a sudden *fortissimo* but with a rising *crescendo*, as though a crowd of bystanders are gradually appreciating the wonder of it.

Another symbolic point is that the Mass in B flat, dating from 1810, the year before Hummel left the Esterházy court, includes a setting of the *Credo* with distinctive unison and octave passages for the chorus, as though to emphasise unity of belief. In both Masses the settings of the *Sanctus* are surprisingly brief, even perfunctory, yet the musical ideas could not be more striking, with a gently flowing 6/8 setting in the D major work and a bold setting in the B flat Mass which crams into the shortest span surprisingly varied ideas.

Thanks to the imagination of Richard Hickox, we're finally able to discover the joys of Hummel's Masses. An extremely fine disc.

Additional recommendations

Mass in E flat, Op 80. Quod quod in orbe, Op 88.
Te Deum in D
Gritton *sop* Murray *mez* Gilchrist *ten* Stephen *bar*
Collegium Musicum 90 / Hickox
Chandos Chaconne CHAN0712 (62' · DDD · T/t)
Ⓕ❶❶➾

The second disc in Richard Hickox's Hummel Mass edition concentrates on works written soon after Hummel was appointed *Konzertmeister* to Prince Esterházy in 1804. The result has a winning freshness. As in the first disc, Hickox captures the joy of Hummel's inspiration, with clean attack and fine diction from chorus and soloists.

Mass in D minor, S67/W13ª. Salve regina, S79/W18ᵇ
ᵃᵇGritton, ªNicholls *sops* ªStephen *mez* ªPadmore
ten ªVarcoe *bar* Collegium Musicum 90 & Chorus /
Hickox
Chandos CHAN0724 (57' · DDD · T/t)   Ⓕ❶➾

The D minor Mass of 1805 was the second of five that Hummel wrote for Prince Esterházy, carrying on from Haydn's late masterpieces. Throughout, Hummel seems intent on taking the listener by surprise. Richard Hickox again proves an ideal interpreter, drawing superb playing and singing.

Missa solemnis in C, W12. Te Deum, W16
Patricia Wright *sop* Zam McKendree-Wright *contr*
Patrick Power *ten* David Griffiths *bar* Tower Voices
New Zealand; New Zealand Symphony Orchestra /
Uwe Grodd
Naxos 8 557193 (57' · DDD)   Ⓢ➾

This, the longest of Hummel's five Masses, is another invigorating example, coupled with an electrifying setting of the *Te Deum*. Both were written in 1806 and feature martial reminders that this was the period of the Napoleonic Wars.

The *Te Deum* opens with a rousing march, and with one or two relaxed passages for contrast – illustrating this long and varied prayer-text – continues in a single span. It ends with a brisk and triumphant fugato, quite different from the sombre close most often heard in Anglican settings. It's a delight. Uwe Grodd draws an exhilarating performance from his forces.

The performance of the Mass is equally successful. The grandeur of the writing is established in the slow introduction to the *Kyrie*, leading to a brisk main *Allegro* (following Haydn's lively practice in *Kyries*) in a rhythmic triple time. The martial flavour of the writing is evident from the *Gloria*'s opening fanfares and continues into the *Credo*, until a sharp change of key to a warm A major brings a relaxed and lyrical setting of 'Et incarnatus', followed by the clashing discords of the 'Crucifixus'. 'Et resurrexit' restores the military mood. One moment to relish comes after the last of the calls of 'Credo' on 'Et vitam venturi' (track 4, 9'09") with two rising scale passages clearly intended to send you up to Heaven in their exhilaration.

Brodd opts to use his admirable soloists throughout the *Benedictus*, even though the autograph suggests otherwise. It works very well, with imitative writing for the soloists set against the four-square tread of the orchestra. With the *Agnus Dei* Hummel at last writes a meditative movement, slow and hushed, which develops into chromatic writing in a minor key, before the 'Dona nobis pacem', as in Haydn's Masses, brings a joyful close. Grodd inspires vigorous playing and singing from his forces, who are freshly and cleanly recorded.

Engelbert Humperdinck
German 1854-1921

Humperdinck, who first studied architecture, won a music prize in 1881 which enabled him to visit France and Italy. In Italy he met Wagner who invited him to his house in Bayreuth. The two got on famously, Humperdinck helping the great man to prepare the score of Parsifal for publication. After professorial spells in Barcelona and Frankfurt, Humperdinck hit the jackpot in 1893 with his fairy-opera Hänsel und Gretel (libretto by his sister Adelheid). The German public had had enough of Wagnerian bombast and to return to a typical German fairy story and music inspired by folk tunes was exactly what they wanted. That was it. Humperdinck could never repeat the success. Neither, it must be said, could a host of would-be Humperdinck imitators who sprang up.

Hänsel und Gretel

Hänsel und Gretel   **H**
Elisabeth Grümmer sop Hänsel **Elisabeth Schwarzkopf** sop Gretel **Maria von Ilosvay** mez Gertrud **Josef Metternich** bar Peter **Anny Felbermayer** sop Sandman, Dew Fairy **Else Schürhoff** mez Witch **Choir of Loughton High School for Girls; Bancroft's School Choir; Philharmonia Orchestra / Herbert von Karajan**
EMI Great Recordings of the Century mono ②
567061-2 or Naxos ② 8 110897/8 (108' · ADD · T/t)
Ⓜ**OO**Ð⇥

The EMI CD transfer has opened up the mono sound, putting air round the voices and instruments, giving presence. Where the earlier transfer of this set sounded disappointingly flat, this one is brighter, clearer, fuller, with textures clarified, the voices better defined and separated.

A full stereo recording would have been better still but it was this recording which Walter Legge would often cite in conversation, when he mounted his curious hobby-horse, questioning the value of stereo over mono. The scene he picked on was where children hear the cuckoo in the forest: there the distancing of the cuckoo-call does indeed simulate stereo atmosphere, but that's far clearer this time than last.

The performance remains a classic, with Karajan plainly in love with the music, and the two principals singing immaculately. This isn't

for those who resist the child-voice inflexion of Schwarzkopf and Grümmer, but everyone else will register the mastery in singing and acting. The thinness of Anny Felbermayer's voice as the Sandman is an unwelcome contrast, but this is otherwise a satisfyingly Germanic team.

Hansel and Gretel (in English)
Jennifer Larmore mez Hansel **Rebecca Evans** sop Gretel **Robert Hayward** bar Peter **Rosalind Plowright** mez Gertrude **Diana Montague** mez Sandman **Sarah Tynan** sop Dew Fairy **Jane Henschel** mez Witch **New London Children's Choir; Philharmonia Orchestra / Sir Charles Mackerras**
Chandos Opera in English ② CHAN3143 (91' · DDD · S/T/N)
Ⓜ**OO**Ð⇥

Following the practice at English National Opera, David Pountney's fresh and idiomatic translation is used, helping the starry cast of soloists, led by Jennifer Larmore and Rebecca Evans, both superb in the title-roles, nicely contrasted while blending well together.

There is strong casting, too, for the Witch, with Jane Henschel refusing to caricature the role in 'funny-voice' singing; Rosalind Plowright, gravitating down to mature mezzo, as the Mother, and Robert Hayward as the Father, don't guy their characterisations, either; while there are good contrasts between the bright Dew Fairy of Sarah Tynan and the warm Sandman of Diana Montague.

All told, this set will clearly stand the test of time as an English version, rivalling even the best of versions in the original German. The exhilaration of the final scene in particular is irresistible, with Mackerras drawing a genuinely Viennese-sounding lilt in the waltz rhythms of the 'Witch is dead' duet, the destruction of the Witch's House powerfully conveyed and the revival of the gingerbread children movingly done. He's wonderfully inspired and imaginative, with pointing and phrasing that readily match Karajan's masterly conducting on the classic mono EMI set. The fresh young voices of the New London Children's Choir are beautifully caught. The recording is clear and beautifully separated yet with an agreeable bloom on voices and instruments.

Hänsel und Gretel
Antigone Papoulkas mez Hansel **Anna Gabler** sop Gretel **Hans-Joachim Ketelsen** bar Peter (Father) **Irmgard Vilsmaier** mez Gertrud (Mother) **Iris Vermillion** mez Witch **Lydia Teuscher** sop Sandman; Dew Fairy **Dresden State Opera Women's and Children's Chorus; Staatskapelle Dresden / Michael Hofstetter**
Stage director **Katharina Thalbach**
Video director **Paul Smaczny**
Euroarts **DVD** 205 5888 (108' · NTSC · 16:9 · PCM stereo, 5.1 and DTS 5.1 · 0)
Recorded live at the Semperoper, Dresden, in December 2006   Ⓕ

This DVD version of *Hänsel und Gretel* starts well with the glorious horns of the Dresden Staatskapelle in the Overture, and Michael Hofstetter draws warmly expressive playing in a work very much central to their repertory. The recording, live in the helpful acoustic of the Semperoper, adds to expectation, with eager children in the large audience.

That said, Katharina Thalbach's production will not please everyone. Grotesquerie rather than charm is the keynote. Hansel and Gretel are portrayed as dolls with crude make-up on spotty faces. Even their movements mimic those of puppets. Costumes are those of German peasants, with the drunken father still more of a caricature, both in costume and acting. The sets and designs by Ezio Toffolutti, minimal and stylised, are undistracting.

Other characters, too, match the grotesque illustrations in traditional German fairy-tale books, which seem strangely old-fashioned to us. The exception is the Witch, characterfully sung by Iris Vermillion, initially glamorous in a form-fitting scarlet gown with shiny high boots but transformed into an old crone when she takes off her wig, revealing a bald head, huge false ears and a hump on her back. Small wonder the children push her into the oven.

The cuckoo is another sort of doll, shooting out from the wings on a spring, with the gigantic sweets of the Witch's house let down from the flies, and with the little house itself made up of gigantic biscuits. The Sandman is another doll, and the Dew Fairy appears wearing ice skates around her neck. The captured children are revealed as sweets, until Hansel with a broom frees them all, and they form a long line to shake hands with Hansel and Gretel in a very Germanic way.

The staging tells the story clearly and believably but the trendy ideas come too thick and fast for comfort. Singing is generally good if not outstanding. Hansel (Antigone Papoulkas) and Gretel (Anna Gabler) are diminutive figures with clear, bright voices, and Hans-Joachim Ketelsen as the Father and Irmgard Vilsmaier as the Mother sing strongly; Lydia Teuscher is jewel-bright as the Sandman and the Dew Fairy. Excellent singing, too, from the chorus of children and women.

Königskinder

Königskinder
Jonas Kaufmann *ten* King's Son **Ofelia Sala** *sop*
Goose Girl **Detlef Roth** *bar* Fiddler **Nora Gubisch**
mez Witch **Jaco Huijpen** *bass* Woodcutter **Henk
Neven** *bass* Landlord **Fabrice Mantegna** *ten* Broom-
maker **Nelly Lawson** *sngr* Broom-maker's Daughter
Hans-Otto Weiss *bar* Senior Councillor **Mareen
Knoth** *mez* Landlord's Daughter **Marc Dostert** *ten*
Tailor **Diana Schmid** *contr* Stable Maid
**Opera Junior Children's Chorus; Latvian Radio
Choir; Montpellier National Orchestra /
Armin Jordan**
Accord ③ 476 9151 (165' · DDD · S/T/t/N) Ⓕ

While it can never match the mastery of the fairy-tale *Hänsel und Gretel*, this seriously neglected opera offers much fine music. The plot is over-complicated and the piece rather long but musically there is much to enjoy, not least the duets and ensembles.

This new version has the advantage of being recorded live, giving it dramatic tautness under the sympathetic direction of Armin Jordan. He draws incisive singing from the multiple choruses, not least the children's, and the excellent cast is superbly led by Jonas Kaufmann, who sings the strenuous role of the King's son with beauty and freedom.

Ofelia Sala as the Princess-Goose Girl has an attractively warm soprano with her vibrato well controlled, well contrasted with the mature-sounding Witch of Nora Gubisch. As the Fiddler, Detlef Roth sings one of the most freely lyrical passages in the opera near the beginning of Act 3 – a memorably simple folk-like melody – in a finely controlled *pianissimo*; but his more outgoing solo leading up to that finds his voice so strained and uneven one would not recognise him as the same singer. Other characters strongly taken include Mareen Knoth as the Landlord's Daughter, and the delightfully fresh-toned child soloist Nelly Lawson as the Broom-maker's Daughter.

The set offers a complete libretto and English translation. Against that there is the minor drawback that the number of tracks in each act – five only for Acts 1 and 3, four for Act 2 – is far too few for so complex a score. Recommended none the less.

Sigismondo d'India   Italian c1582-1629

Most probably born in Sicily, d'India travelled in Italy where he absorbed the musical styles popular at the time. He's known to have been in Florence, the birthplace of opera, as well as Mantua, where Monteverdi was working. In Naples he probably met Gesualdo, and by 1610 he was in Parma and Piacenza. The next year, 1611, he was hired by the Duke of Savoy to direct music in Turin, where he remained until 1623. D'India's output consisted of music in most of the vocal forms of the time, including monodies, madrigals and motets.

Madrigals

Il primo libro de madrigali
La Venexiana (Valentina Coladonato, Nadia Ragni
sops Lucia Sciannimanico *mez* Giuseppe Maletto,
Sandro Naglia *tens* Daniele Carnovich *bass*) /
Claudio Cavina *counterten*
Glossa GCD920908 (49' · DDD · T/t) Ⓕ

The northern and southern Italian madrigal traditions meet in the person of Sigismondo d'India. The date of publication of this, his *First Book of Madrigals* (1606), reveals him to be one of the last of the genre's most significant figures.

By this time the majority of Monteverdi's publications were already in existence, and Gesualdo's too. The influence of both is clearly audible, and not just in the music.

One of the most memorable tracks is *Felice chi ti miro*, although much of the tripartite *Interdette speranze* is equally impressive. Sometimes you feel that a phrase or sentiment might have been more dramatically and elastically projected, or lingered over and savoured. As to tuning, it's generally very accurate, and the slightest slip stands out. But that's the problem with tuning: standards are so high nowadays that critics risk expecting something inhuman, or at least superhuman. This will do just fine. A movingly dramatic account.

Vincent d'Indy
French 1851-1931

French composer, teacher, conductor and editor of early music. His famed veneration for Beethoven and Franck has unfortunately obscured the individual character of his own compositions, particularly his fine orchestral pieces descriptive of southern France. As a teacher his influence was enormous and wide-ranging, with benefits for French music far outweighing the charges of dogmatism and political intolerance. D'Indy's somewhat academic corpus of chamber music (including three completed string quartets) is generally less interesting than his orchestral works which, while always manifesting his concern for the utmost structural coherence, invariably contain important programmatic or symbolic elements; above all, nature painting brought out his full imaginative mastery of orchestral texture.

Orchestral works

Jour d'été à la montagne, Op 61. La forêt enchantée, Op 8. Souvenirs, Op 62
Iceland Symphony Orchestra / Rumon Gamba
Chandos CHAN10464 (63' · DDD)　　　Ⓕ🅱➔

Three of d'Indy's most colourful works show him not only as an impressionist in a Debussian mould but also influenced by Wagner and folk music from his own culture. *La forêt enchantée* (1878) is described as a 'légende-symphonique' and is inspired by an epic ballad by Ludwig Uhland. D'Indy creates a mysteriously expectant opening atmosphere, then Knight Harald and his followers ride out vigorously. Female elves seduce his followers, but Harald loftily resists their enticements and gallops off to reach an enchanted spring, where the elves are waiting for him. This time he yields to their alluring invitation before slipping into a 'centuries-lasting' sleep.

By the time the masterly *Jour d'été à la montagne* was written some 30 years later, d'Indy's style had matured. While the Wagnerian sensuality remains, here the influences from Debussy and even Ravel are very potent: there's a day-break with an orchestral chorus of birds. The sultry central movement, 'Après-midi sous les pins', includes lively folk dancing before the clouds arrive, with thunder in the distance. Twilight transforms the mood for 'Soir' and the work closes in nocturnal bliss.

D'Indy wrote *Souvenirs* almost immediately afterwards (in 1906) in memory of his wife (represented by a leitmotif, Bien-Aimée), recalling the couple's idyllic summers together and again evoking the countryside. This *idée fixe* is continually transformed before the music darkens and 12 harp harmonics set the time of Isabelle's death at midnight; the evocation ends in sad, serene acceptance.

The rich orchestration in all three works is superbly realised by the excellent Iceland Symphony Orchestra under Rumon Gamba and the state-of-the-art Chandos recording; definitely a key record of d'Indy's orchestral output.

Wallenstein, Op 12. Saugefleurie, Op 21. Choral varié, Op 55ª. Lied, Op 19ª
ªLawrence Power va BBC National Orchestra of Wales / Thierry Fischer
Hyperion CDA67690 (74' · DDD)　　　Ⓕ🅾➔

Here's another rewarding d'Indy anthology courtesy of Hyperion, which finds Thierry Fischer obtaining commendably spruce and bright-eyed results from his BBC Welsh forces. The lengthiest (and earliest) offering here is *Wallenstein*. Begun in 1870 but not completed until 1881, it's a highly ambitious 37-minute trilogy based on Schiller's eponymous drama and reveals the budding composer as an unabashed acolyte of Liszt and Wagner. Fortunately the melodic invention (and its cyclical deployment) is as striking as it is satisfying (even on a first hearing the tunes stick in the memory), as is the ripe, unclotted orchestration – d'Indy clearly knew his *Tristan*, *Siegfried* and *Götterdämmerung* inside out.

The 1884 tone-poem *Saugefleurie* distils a most touching, fairy-tale charm (the music depicting the royal hunt readily calls to mind Franck's *Le chasseur maudit* of two years earlier), and once again d'Indy handles his outsize orchestral forces with conspicuous skill. Both the Op 19 *Lied* (written in the same year as *Saugefleurie*) and 1903 *Choral varié* prove very fetching discoveries, especially when Lawrence Power plays with selfless dedication, sense of poetry and lustrous tone.

A toothsome and notably enterprising collection, this, with splendidly ample and atmospheric sound to match.

John Ireland
British 1879-1962

Ireland studied at the Royal College of Music (piano and composition) under Stanford who provided him with a good grounding in the German tradi-

tion, but early encounters with modernist composers such as Debussy, Ravel and Stravinsky offered him new paths along which to explore his musical voice. He served as organist and choirmaster at St Luke's, Chelsea, later returning to the RCM to teach (1923-39). He produced a stream of works, many of which are couched in an English pastoral vein; these include the symphonic rhapsody Mai-Dun (1921), the Piano Concerto (1930), a classic of 20th-century English music, and Legend for piano and orchestra (1933).

Orchestral works

Epic March. The Forgotten Rite. A London Overture. Mai-Dun. The Overlanders. Scherzo and Cortège on Themes from Julius Caesar. Tritons
London Philharmonic Orchestra / Sir Adrian Boult
Lyrita SRCD240 (76' · ADD)   ⓟⓄ➔

Assembled from three of Boult's four Lyrita LPs devoted to Ireland, this generous programme launches with the red-blooded symphonic prelude *Tritons* (a student offering from 1899). Boult and the LPO do not shirk the melodrama and go on to lend equally dedicated advocacy to the magical 1913 prelude *The Forgotten Rite* and glowering 1921 symphonic rhapsody *Mai-Dun*.

The stand-out track remains Boult's wonderfully spry and observant account of *A London Overture* (1936), which is easily a match for Barbirolli's almost exactly contemporaneous LSO version for EMI. The 1942 *Epic March*, too, glints with memorable defiance. The *Julius Caesar* diptych is less immediately gripping, but the five-movement suite compiled by Charles Mackerras from Ireland's 1946 score for Ealing Studios' *The Overlanders* certainly has its moments, not least the touching 'Romance' (which plunders material from *A Downland Suite* of 1932) and infectiously jaunty outer portions of the central 'Intermezzo'.

Considering some of these sessions took place as long ago as December 1965, the judiciously refurbished sound still packs quite a punch. Altogether a very welcome reissue.

A Downland Suite (arr Ireland and Bush). Orchestral Poem in A minor. Concertino pastorale. Two Symphonic Studies (arr Bush)
City of London Sinfonia / Richard Hickox
Chandos CHAN9376 (64' · DDD)   ⓟⓄ

Hickox gives a sensitive account of the *Downland Suite* and extracts great expressive intensity from the glorious second movement 'Elegy'. The *Concertino pastorale* is another fine work, boasting a most eloquent opening 'Eclogue' and tenderly poignant 'Threnody', towards the end of which Ireland seems to allow himself a momentary recollection of the haunting opening phrase of his earlier orchestral prelude, *The Forgotten Rite*. In 1969 Ireland's pupil, Geoffrey Bush, arranged two sections of the score for the 1946 film *The*

Overlanders which were not incorporated into the 1971 concert suite compiled by Sir Charles Mackerras. The resulting, finely wrought *Two Symphonic Studies* were recorded many years ago by Sir Adrian Boult for Lyrita and Hickox proves just as sympathetic an interpreter, whereas the *Orchestral Poem* in A minor is here receiving its recorded debut. This is a youthful essay, completed in 1904, some three years after Ireland's studies with Stanford.

It's a worthy rather than especially inspiring effort, with hardly a glimpse of the mature manner to come, save for some particularly beautiful string writing.

A London Overture. The Forgotten Rite. Mai-Dun. The Overlanders – Suite (arr Mackerras). Satyricon. Epic March
Hallé Orchestra / John Wilson
Hallé CDHLL7523 (68' · DDD)   ⓟⓄ➔

John Wilson directs to the manner born and draws a crisply disciplined response from the Hallé, who seem to be enjoying the experience enormously. The vibrant and purposeful reading of *Mai-Dun* which launches proceedings is surely the finest since Barbirolli's 1949 HMV account with this same band. When it comes to *A London Overture*, Ireland fans will readily attest the very special qualities of both the Boult (Lyrita) and Barbirolli (EMI) performances, but Wilson proves a worthy successor in every way – and the same holds true for *The Forgotten Rite*, which has poetry and atmosphere in abundance. Wilson also makes a terrific splash with the suite that Sir Charles Mackerras compiled from the score for the 1946 film *The Overlanders*, and if the athletic outer portions of *Satyricon* have not quite the snap and familiarity of Boult's benchmark Lyrita version, the Hallé trumpets have a field-day in the rousing *Epic March*. The venue is BBC Manchester's Studio 7, and while the recording falls marginally short in terms of sumptuous glow, it remains superbly detailed and vivid; indeed, the whole disc must be deemed a genuine tonic.

A London Overture. Piano Concerto[a].   **H**
These Things Shall Be[b]. The Forgotten Rite
[b]**Redvers Llewellyn** bar [a]**Eileen Joyce** pf
[b]**Luton Choral Society; London Philharmonic Orchestra / Sir Adrian Boult**
LPO mono LPO0041 (69' · DDD)   Ⓜ
Recorded live at the Royal Albert Hall, London, on September 10, 1949

This release rescues from the BBC vaults Boult's September 1949 Prom celebrating Ireland's 70th birthday. At times the sound calls for a fair degree of tolerance but the ear quickly adjusts – and the actual music-making is a delight. *A London Overture* in particular evinces an entrancing flexibility, playfulness and songful warmth, while Eileen Joyce's partnership with Boult in the Piano Concerto frequently soars to inspirational heights (the slow movement is utterly magical – Boult's sublimely shaped opening paragraph effortlessly matched by Joyce's rapt pianism). The present performance of *The Forgotten Rite* adds nearly two minutes to Boult's Lyrita version, its striking breadth and concentration calling to mind Barbirolli's contemporaneous Hallé recording (last available on Dutton). Boult also directs *These Things Shall Be* with maximum conviction, and the sound here is surprisingly full-bodied; towards the end, listen out for the appearance of the *Internationale* that Ireland subsequently removed from the orchestral score and parts. Don't miss this fascinating restoration of what was obviously a memorable evening.

Violin Sonatas

Violin Sonatas – No 1 in D minor[a]; No 2 in   H
A minor[b]. Phantasie Trio in A minor[c]. The Holy Boy[d]
[ac]**Frederick Grinke,** [b]**Albert Sammons** *vns*
[cd]**Florence Hooton** *vc* [ab]**John Ireland,** [c]**Kendall**
Taylor, [d]**Lawrence Pratt** *pfs*
Dutton Epoch mono CDLX7103 (73' · ADD)
Recorded 1930-45   Ⓜ️ⓄⓄ

Such was the critical acclaim that greeted the March 1917 premiere of Ireland's Second Violin Sonata that the 37-year-old composer's reputation was cemented virtually overnight. The performers on that momentous occasion were the legendary Albert Sammons and pianist William Murdoch. Some 13 years later Sammons finally set down his thoughts on this glorious music with Ireland himself at the piano. Quite why this valuable document never saw the light of day until now is a mystery, so all gratitude to Dutton for granting a long overdue lease of life to a nobly spacious rendering of such palpable feeling and insight.

As for the First Violin Sonata, Frederick Grinke's 1945 Decca recording (again with the composer) continues to strike as, quite simply, the most perceptive interpretation of this early offering ever encountered, possessing a compelling sweep and tingling concentration that grip from first measure to last. The November 1938 recording of the *Phantasie Trio* is yet another cherishable display, the playing wonderfully alive and always radiating a most winning understanding and spontaneity.

Good, if not exceptional transfers. Urgently recommended all the same.

Chamber works

Fantasy Sonata[a]. The Holy Boy[a]. Sextet[b]. Trio[c]
Robert Plane *cl* [b]**David Pyatt** *hn* [c]**Alice Neary** *vc*
[ac]**Sophia Rahman** *pf*
[b]**Maggini Quartet** (Lorraine McAslan, David Angel
vns Martin Outram *va* Michal Kaznowski *vc*)
Naxos 8 570550 (66' · DDD)   Ⓢ️Ⓞ️➡️

This disc is a most welcome addition to the catalogue of recordings of John Ireland's chamber music in that its principal focus is the range of pieces that the composer wrote for clarinet, played here with ravishing lyricism and conviction by Robert Plane, who has surely now fully occupied the shoes of the late Thea King in his championship of British clarinet music. Plane's kinship with this music is clear from the more Brahmsian hues of the Sextet (1898), the limpid lyricism of *The Holy Boy* arrangement (1913), to the extrovert passion of the *Fantasy Sonata* for Clarinet (1943) where he is arguably at his most impressive.

Though the Sextet, a student work, betrays a deference to Brahms, there is a freshness and fluency about the material as well as a flair for the idiom, which compares favourably with those prodigious chamber works of Hurlstone, Coleridge-Taylor (both RCM fellow students) and, later, Frank Bridge. An attractive novelty on this CD is the Clarinet Trio which Ireland composed in 1913 but withdrew after two performances. Left incomplete and in manuscript at Ireland's death, it has been reconstructed skilfully by Stephen Fox. Plane, Alice Neary and Sophia Rahman give a sensitive reading of a style that is much more distinctly 'Irelandesque' in its assimilation of French sonorities and sound-moments, Plane's hushed playing being especially enthralling.

Piano Works

Piano Works, Volume 1
Sarnia. London Pieces. In Those Days. Prelude in
E flat. Ballade. Columbine. Month's Mind
John Lenehan *pf*
Naxos 8 553700 (60' · DDD)   Ⓢ️Ⓞ️➡️

Piano Works, Volume 2
Merry Andrew. The Towing-path. Rhapsody. Two
Pieces (1924-25). Decorations. Leaves from a Child's
Sketchbook. The Darkened Valley. Sonatina. Three
Pastels. Two Pieces (1921). Summer Evening
John Lenehan *pf*
Naxos 8 553889 (71' · DDD)   Ⓢ️Ⓞ️➡️

Piano Works, Volume 3
Piano Sonata. The Almond Tree. Ballade of London
Nights. Equinox. Greenways. On a Birthday Morning.
Two Pieces. Preludes. Soliloquy. Spring will not wait
John Lenehan *pf*
Naxos 8 570461 (73' · DDD)   Ⓢ️Ⓞ️➡️

The pleasures here are many. John Lenehan is a very accomplished performer: not only is his technical address impeccable, but he also has a strikingly wide dynamic range and sophisticated variety of tone colour, both of which he uses to poetic effect throughout. That Lenehan has a real affinity for Ireland's muse is immediately evident from his raptly intimate delivery of the gentle opening diptych, *In Those Days*. Similarly, in the extraordinarily imaginative, harmonically questing *Ballade* of 1929 he rises superbly to the elemental fury of the remarkable central portion, with its brooding echoes of the 'Northern' Bax from the same period. Elsewhere, *Columbine* is a treat, as is the ravishing *Month's Mind* and the haunting Prelude in E flat. Lenehan's supremely affectionate and articulate advocacy will surely win Ireland many friends.

On Volume 2 there's a strong feeling of how purely local influences (Pangbourne and the Thames Valley in *The Towing-path*, Le Fauvic beach, Jersey in 'The Island Spell', to take two examples) are transcended to become statements of wider poetic import.

The large-scale *Rhapsody*, with its powerful Fauréan overtones, is relished by Lenehan, a strong, sympathetic interpreter, and time and again he makes you wonder at works aptly described as 'some of the most appealing English piano music written this century, too long neglected'.

In Volume 3, Lenehan effortlessly maintains the favourable impression left by the first two instalments. With his pellucid, exquisitely variegated tonal palette, he makes a gorgeous thing of *The Almond Trees*, plumbs real depths in *Spring will not wait* and the central "Cypress" from *Greenways*, and masterminds superbly involving accounts of the gale-tossed *Equinox* and mercurial *Ballade of London Nights*. What's more, he has been accorded crystal-clear yet nicely atmospheric engineering.

Complete Piano Works
Alan Rowlands pf
Lyrita mono ③ REAM3112 (3h 45' · ADD)
Recorded 1959-63   Ⓜ

Piano Music by John Ireland, Volume 1
Piano Sonata. Decorations. London Pieces. Ballade. Sonatina
Mark Bebbington pf
Somm SOMMCD074 (69' · DDD)   Ⓕ

Comparative listening to the meaty Sonata that Ireland wrote between 1918 and 1920 (the one work common to all three releases) finds both Rowlands and Bebbington allowing themselves rather greater breathing space than the more urgently propulsive Lenehan (who whips up quite a gale in the first movement's development). Each is a mightily convincing proponent, though Rowlands's interpretation carries particular authority: during the late 1950s he studied intensively with Ireland (the booklet contains a most engaging and fascinating personal reminiscence) and it was Rowlands whom the composer recommended to Richard Itter of Lyrita for its complete recorded edition.

With no editing facilities available, single takes were a necessity in sessions spanning January 1959 to March 1963 which took place in the music room of Itter's Buckinghamshire home. Captured in perfectly acceptable mono sound, Rowlands's memorably intimate performances betoken a very special empathy for this repertoire. Indeed, his playing throughout these three well filled CDs evinces a selfless dedication, recreative wonder and abundant poetic instinct. For first-timers, however, Bebbington's pro-

gramme provides a pretty much ideal introduction, containing two of Ireland's most popular and durable achievements, namely *Decorations* and *London Pieces* – both given with such winning aplomb, scrupulous care and heartwarming sense of new discovery that it's hard not to fall in love with them all over again (the vernally fresh 'Chelsea Reach' positively beams with joy). Elsewhere, Bebbington displays wonderful control in the leaner-textured and economically argued *Sonatina*, just as he is acutely responsive to the fearful undertow of the *Ballade* (close cousin to the riveting *Legend* for piano and orchestra). Somm's sound is clean and true.

Songs

The Bells of San Marie. During Music. Five Poems by Thomas Hardy. Three Songs to Poems by Thomas Hardy. I have twelve oxen. If there were dreams to sell. Marigold – Youth's Spring (Tribute); Penumbra; Spleen. Santa Chiara, 'Palm Sunday, Naples'. Sea Fever. Songs Sacred and Profane – The Salley Gardens. Tryst in Fountain Court. The Vagabond. We'll to the woods no more. When I am dead, my dearest. Tutto è sciulto. Great Things. Two Songs – The Cost
Roderick Williams bar **Iain Burnside** pf
Naxos 8 570467 (66' · DDD)   Ⓢ Ⓞ ➡

Despite the popularity of 'Sea Fever' and (literally) two or three others, the songs of John Ireland are often found oddly inaccessible. Of all the acknowledged masters of English song in the 20th century Ireland is the hardest to pin down, to identify even. It has something to do with an elusiveness about his writing for the voice. When you look at the piano parts you feel contact with a pair of hands (his) touching the keyboard; but (with few exceptions) it's hard to believe that he 'sang' the songs as he wrote. The point here is that Roderick Williams is such a good singer he can make the voice part sound vocal and natural in a way not many have succeeded in doing. The songs are high for baritone, low for tenor, and they are written in a way that seems not to know of the difficulties of passing from one area of the voice to another or returning to a particular region with uncomfortable persistency. For Roderick Williams such difficulties seem hardly to exist. The listener's task eases proportionately.

Before going further, it should be said that the pianist, Iain Burnside, plays with a sureness of touch to match the highly skilled naturalness of Williams's singing. And it has to be added that Williams still does not seem to be a communicator in song in the sense that we can see the images flash before him (Terfel-like) as he sings the words. Sometimes, as in 'The Vagabond' (Masefield, not Stevenson) and 'If there were dreams to sell', he catches the mood extraordinarily well even so. Williams and Burnside find a clearer feeling for Ireland's anxious tenderness and uneasy joy than in any previous recital of his songs.

Charles Ives
American 1874-1954

What an extraordinary man Ives was – and what extraordinary music. One can only sit back and wonder at his stubbornness, the way he expressed his personal vision and refused to be tied to any received wisdom. The devices that he introduced into his music – atonality, polytonality, dissonance, multiple rhythms, jazz, collage – were way in advance of the Stravinskys, Schoenbergs and Debussys of this world. They arrived at their own answers later and their music was widely performed; not so Ives – most of his music was not performed until the 1950s. Only then could it be seen by how much he had been ahead of his time. His stream-of-consciousness technique has been compared with the James Joyce of Ulysses and Finnegans Wake (though Ives anticipated Joyce in this too).

Where did it come from? His father, mostly – a remarkable band-leader who encouraged his son to 'open his ears' and listen to the noise made by two military bands playing different marches simultaneously, to note the out-of-tune singing of hymns in church: in other words to accept natural dissonance, not dismiss it. He even encouraged Ives to sing 'Swanee' in a different key to the one in which it was being played on the piano. The young Ives began to experiment writing in a combination of several keys, first as a spoof, then as a serious proposition. No wonder his teacher at Yale was baffled by someone to whom Chopin was 'soft...with a skirt on', Mozart was merely 'effeminate', Debussy 'should have sold newspapers for a living'. (He had higher opinions only of Bach, Beethoven, Schumann and Brahms.)

After graduating, Ives, with assured unpredictability, went into insurance. In 1907 he established the firm of Ives and Myrick (afterwards Mutual of New York) and he proved an exceptionally able businessman, for he ended up a millionaire. When, in 1918, he suffered a massive heart attack and was no longer able to work (diabetes added to the complications), he was able to publish at his own expense some of the vast amount of music he had written 'out of office hours' and distribute it free to interested parties. Few people were aware of his double life and Ives made no effort to procure performances of his work – he knew he had no hope of commercial success. When his music was performed, he appeared to be indifferent. By 1930 he had all but stopped composing.

He retired to his farm in Connecticut, becoming increasingly reclusive – he never went to concerts and did not have a record player or radio. Slowly, more of his music began to be played (his Third Symphony, written in 1903, won a Pulitzer Prize in 1947) but it was only after his death that his real achievements were recognised and, indeed, he has become something of a cult figure, an example to any composer who feels faint-hearted in following his instincts and developing independent musical thought. 'Ivesian' has entered the language to describe a certain kind of music.

Symphonies

Symphonies – No 1; No 4. Central Park in the Dark
Dallas Symphony Orchestra / Andrew Litton
Hyperion 🔊 SACDA67540 (78' · DDD/DSD)
Recorded live ⓕ⊙◗

Symphonies – No 2; No 3, 'The Camp Meeting'.
General William Booth Enters into Heaven[c]
[c]**Donnie Ray Albert** bar **Dallas Symphony Orchestra / Andrew Litton**
Hyperion 🔊 SACDA67525 (69' · DDD/DSD)
Recorded live ⓕ⊙◗

Ives's symphonies were premiered almost 50 years after they were written – practically nothing was performed when he wrote it – but against all the odds they have achieved classic status. The composer was dismissive about the First Symphony, a student work, but this is now its eighth available recording. Litton has strong climaxes in the first movement, although there's a tendency for the woodwind to get swamped by the strings and brass, and sustains an almost Mahlerian passion in the *Adagio*. There's a magical *pianissimo* at the start of *Central Park in the Dark* with no evidence of the audience at all – apparently they were warned that the performance was being recorded!

Each recording of the Fourth is defined by the inevitably different balance of the dense textures in the second and fourth movements. For example Litton, supported by one associate conductor, rightly has the orchestral piano prominent in the shattering second movement, and in the mystical finale the voices enter with unique effect. It's good to hear a little more than usual of the offstage players both here and in the first movement.

The spacious Second Symphony takes its pervasive popular melodies and makes them symphonic – again a completely convincing performance. The only shock is the dissonant raspberry blown as the final chord – that's what folk fiddlers did to show the evening was over. The Third Symphony is saturated in hymntunes and anyone familiar with earlier recordings will notice the few extra bits in the latest edition of the score. The bonus is a gutsy delivery of Becker's orchestral arrangement of the song *General William Booth Enters into Heaven*.

Overall these two CDs are a winning representation of the Ives symphonies with the fine Dallas Symphony consistently impressive throughout. One might want to look back at certain historic versions of individual symphonies, but as a package this is well recorded, fastidiously presented and deservedly pre-eminent.

Symphony No 2. Robert Browning Overture
Nashville Symphony Orch / Kenneth Schermerhorn
Naxos 8 559076 (67' · DDD) ⓢ◗

Ives's Second Symphony isn't as well served on CD as might be expected. Bernstein gave the premiere in 1951 some 40 years after the work's composition. What's new about this Nashville release is that it uses Jonathan Elkus's edition made for the Charles Ives Society for both works. The main difference for the listener is that the exposition of the second movement of the Symphony is repeated. That this helps the overall balance in this extended, somewhat repetitive movement is debatable. When it comes to Bernstein, he quite unnecessarily cut 16 measures from the last movement. His tempi may be considered slow in the third and fourth movements, but in both his recordings the work luxuriates in a way that nobody else achieves.

The *Robert Browning Overture* is one of Ives's most visionary pieces, with declamatory trumpet parts that make Scriabin's *Poème de l'extase* seem reticent. The mystical calm of the opening is memorably caught in the Nashville performance; the energetic passages are vivid, although some textures inevitably get submerged. It's a great relief to have the obvious errors in the score corrected. This puts earlier recordings such as Stokowski's beyond the pale and it's well worth buying this CD for the *Browning Overture* alone, although both works in these carefully considered editions make a bargain pair.

Additional recommendation

Symphony No 2.
Coupled with The Gong on the Hook and Ladder.
Tone Roads – No 1. A Set of Three Short Pieces –
Largo cantabile, Hymn. Hallowe'en. Central Park in
the Dark. The Unanswered Question
NYPO / Bernstein
DG download *429 220-2GH* (68' · DDD)   Ⓕ**OO**▶

> Although Bernstein thought of Ives as a primitive composer, these recordings reveal that he had a deep understanding of his music. The standard of playing rom the NYPO, both here and in the disc's series of technically demanding shorter pieces, is remarkably high. Essential for any collection.

Symphony No 3, 'The Camp Meeting'. The
Unanswered Question. Central Park in the Dark.
Overture and March, '1776'. Holidays – Washington's
Birthday. Country Band March
Northern Sinfonia / James Sinclair
Naxos 8 559087 (52' · DDD)   Ⓢ▶

James Sinclair has been a dedicated Ives scholar and performer for more than 30 years, which means this CD has to be something special. First on this issue comes the hymn-saturated Third Symphony, where Sinclair uses some of the thinly sketched options in the manuscripts. This means there's a bit extra in the distance at the end of the first two movements and slighty more of the barely audible bells, ingeniously made to sound like an outdoor carillon, at the end of the last movement, compared with Slatkin and the St Louis orchestra. There are more distant effects if you listen carefully.

In *The Unanswered Question* Sinclair uses the version with two flutes and two clarinets rather than four flutes for the attempted answers to the questioning trumpet. Then, in *Central Park in the Dark*, he uses a battered upright piano for the bits taken from the 1899 hit-song 'Hello! ma

Baby' which suggests the tavern scene in Berg's *Wozzeck*. It works, but unfortunately the piano, marked *fff*, almost fades out at the climax.

There are two little-known early pieces which Ives drew on for 'Putnam's Camp', the second of *Three Places in New England*. The *Country Band March* has hilarious junketings as an affectionate reflection of the mistakes of amateur players – Sinclair takes an option without the final chord which leaves the dilatory saxophonist exposed after the end. Then the Overture and March *1776* goes to town with a brass player using the wrong instrument so that quite a lengthy passage comes out in parallel semitones! Vintage Ives, all played with completely idiomatic feeling and adequately recorded.

Symphony No 4 – Fugue[c]. Orchestral Set
No 1, 'Three Places in New England'. Charlie Rutlage[ad]. The Circus Band[bc]. From the Steeples and the
Mountains[c]. General William Booth Enters into Heaven[bc]. In Flanders Fields[ad]. Memories[ad]. The Pond[abc].
Psalm 100[bc]. Serenity[ac]. They are There![abc]. The Things
our Fathers Loved[ad]. Tom Sails Away[ad]. The Unanswered Question[c]
[a]**Thomas Hampson** *bar* [b]**San Francisco Girl's
Chorus; San Francisco Symphony Chorus and**
[c]**Orchestra / Michael Tilson Thomas** [d]*pf*
RCA Red Seal 09026 63703-2 (65' · DDD)
Recorded live 1999   Ⓕ**O**▶

If anyone has a hot-line to the cortex of Ives's imagination, it's Michael Tilson Thomas. The programme he's devised here isn't so much a journey, more a stream of consciousness through the hinterlands of Ives Americana. It's about the things that mattered to Ives: the times, places, events that fashioned the nation and enabled it to find its own way. It's a landscape of ballad songs and snatches, of hymns, marches, tall tales and short orders, assembled exactly as the man remembered them and entirely in keeping with the chaotic comedy of life. But above all, it's about the spirit within us all – great and small.

From the Steeples and the Mountains is classic Ives: a visionary statement fashioned from bare essentials, bells and brass dissonances always just a whisper away from a recognisable hymn tune. Then from the mountains to the back yard – recollections of a very American childhood. Picket fences and parlour songs. Like 'The Things Our Fathers Loved' written 16 years after the craggy bell and brass piece. You can be sure the Ives chronology will constantly wrong-foot you. Thomas Hampson is the man entrusted with these rich pickings from the Ives songbook. He lustily makes a drama out of a crisis in 'Charlie Rutlage', a cowboy song turned operatic *gran scena*. Later he's the Salvation Army's General William Booth banging the drum for all his pimps, floosies, and drunks – his 'saved souls' – as he leads them towards that great courthouse in the sky. Then one of the most heartfelt of all Ives songs, 'Tom Sails Away' – a life in a song from cradle to grave.

Such juxtapositions make this all-live compilation especially affecting. Hard to believe that this is a live recording, so astonishingly lucid and transparent is the multi-layered orchestral sound. Tremendous impact, too.

Finally, a beautiful performance of that little masterpiece *The Unanswered Question*, as close as we get to an understanding of what spirituality actually meant to Ives. A superb disc.

Orchestral Sets

Three Orchestral Sets
Malmö Chamber Chorus; Malmö Symphony Orchestra / James Sinclair
Naxos 8 559353 (63' · DDD) ⓈⒹ▸

This is a fascinating release that offers Ives's three Orchestral Sets for the first time. The curtain is raised with the first of them, *Three Places in New England*, in its original version – this stands somewhere between the *Country Band March* and the later, more familiar *Three Places*. At this stage there's no piano part and the conflicting march rhythm in 'Putnam's Camp' is missing as well as its dissonant opening. Both the First and Second Sets are vintage Ives, with his unforgettable reaction to the sinking of the Lusitania that brought the US into the First World War at the end of the Second Set.

But the novelty here is the Third Set. The first two movements come from sketches edited by David Gray Porter. The opening *Andante* has a structure similar to *Central Park in the Dark* with typical Ives chords and a texture building to a crisis with something left hanging softly at the end. The second movement is called 'During Camp Meetin' Week: One Secular Afternoon'. This again is Ives's idiosyncratic territory with lots of quotations including 'Columbia the Gem of the Ocean' twice and a four-part hymn about the Day of Judgement – not so secular after all?

Completing works by Ives has become an industry that the composer would have welcomed. The perhaps over-extended last movement of this Third Set, realised by Nors Josephson, at times sounds like Varèse, although it begins and ends softly. Well recorded, idiomatic performances all round – a real Ives discovery.

Violin Sonatas

Violin Sonatas – No 1; No 2; No 3; No 4, 'Children's Day at the Camp Meeting'
Curt Thompson vn **Rodney Waters** pf
Naxos 8 559119 (77' · DDD) ⓈⒹ▸

The four violin-and-piano sonatas are at the core of Ives's chamber music output. The style oscillates because Ives was uncertain about his more radical visions and admitted he'd tried to compromise. But this gives all four of them an enlarged frame of reference, saturated with quotations as usual, but relating to European sonata traditions as well. There's everything to savour from these performances on Naxos: lovely soft

textures in the transcendental meditations, well recorded, and everything hectic is under control. Warning: the distant violin in the second movement of No 1 isn't a balance fault – Ives specified that the pianist should overwhelm the defenceless muted violin! This is now the version to choose.

Piano Sonata No 2, 'Concord'

Piano Sonata No 2, 'Concord, Mass: 1840-60'[a]. Ann Street[b]. The Cage[b]. The Circus Band[b]. A farewell to land[b]. The Housatonic at Stockbridge[b]. The Indians[b]. Like a sick eagle[b]. Memories[b]. September[b]. Serenity[b]. Soliloquy[b]. Songs my mother taught me[b]. Swimmers[b]. The things our fathers loved[b]. Thoreau[b]. 1, 2, 3[b]. A sound of distant horn[b]
[b]**Susan Graham** sop [a]**Emmanuel Pahud** fl [a]**Tabea Zimmermann** va **Pierre-Laurent Aimard** pf
Warner Classics 2564 60297-2 (79' · DDD) ⒻⓄⓄⒹ▸

Charles Ives to complaining pianist: 'Is it the composer's fault that man has only 10 fingers?' Listening to Pierre-Laurent Aimard play the *Concord* Sonata it isn't Ives's dry wit but the assertion that man has only 10 fingers that you begin to question. Nothing he wrote was 'reasonable' as in playable, singable. Everything was a stretch, a note or chord or counterpoint too far. Technically optimistic, spiritually aspirational. In a sense Aimard is almost too good, the realisation of everything Ives was striving for in this piece. You can almost hear Ives thinking: 'OK, if that's possible, let's go somewhere else…'

Actually, the *Concord* Sonata goes wherever you want it to go. Its starting-point is American literature but its substance is in ideas. Ives the transcendentalist: beyond the American dream. An amazing stream of consciousness. Concord is a town in Massachusetts; it's where American Independence was bloodily born; but it's also a word for harmony, and for Ives there's harmony in extreme diversity. The big moments in the sonata are all born out of flux. Ideas and notes boil over in the second movement, 'Hawthorne', but at its heart is the basic conflict between the earthly body and its free spirit. The body resists, the spirit meditates. There are moments here where you'd swear two pianists were involved. You'd also swear that the sorrowful song so fleetingly alluded to by solo viola (Tabea Zimmerman) in the first movement or the remnant of solo flute (Emmanuel Pahud) in the last are figments of your imagination.

Ives's imagination – his rampant theatricality – should have made for great operas. Instead he wrote songs: capsule dramas laid out not in scenes or acts but moments in time. Susan Graham inhabits 17 such moments – nostalgic ('Songs my mother taught me'), visionary ('A sound of distant horn'), cryptic ('Soliloquy'), brutal ('1, 2, 3'), expectant ('Thoreau') – and the feminine and masculine qualities of her voice, to say nothing of her musical sensibility, easily encompass the 'expectancy and ecstasy' promised by the song 'Memories' – which appropriately enough recalls her (and others like her) as a little girl 'sitting in the opera house'. Aimard is again a one-man band. Almost literally so in 'The Circus Band'. When Graham shouts 'hear the trombones', you really do.

Additional recommendation

Piano Sonata No 2
Coupled with **Barber** Piano Sonata
Hamelin pf
Hyperion CDA67469 (62' · DDD) Ⓕ🄑➔

A superb recital of two sharply opposed American sonatas. Hamelin subdues his awe-inspiring command to a purely musical end.

Songs

'A Song – For Anything'
A Song – For Anything. Du alte Mutter. Ann Street. Berceuse. The Cage. Charlie Rutlage. Elégie. Feldeinsamkeit. General William Booth Enters into Heaven. The Greatest Man. The Housatonic at Stockbridge. Ich grolle nicht. Like a Sick Eagle. Memories. The New River. Remembrance. Serenity. The Side Show. Slugging a Vampire. Swimmers. 1, 2, 3. The Things Our Fathers Loved. Thoreau. Tom Sails Away. Walking. Weil' auf mir. West London. Where the Eagle. Yellow Leaves. Tolerance. When Stars are in the Quiet Skies
Gerald Finley bar **Julius Drake** pf
Hyperion CDA67516 (71' · DDD · T/t) Ⓕ●●➔

'Romanzo (di Central Park)'
At the river. The Children's Hour. The Circus Band. Down East. Evening. Evidence. Ilmenau. In Flanders Fields. In the Alley. The Last Reader. Mists. My Native Land. A Night Song. On the Counter. Premonitions. Romanzo (di Central Park)[a]. The See'r. Slow march. Songs My Mother Taught Me. They Are There![a]. To Edith. Two Little Flowers. Watchman. Omens and Oracles. A Christmas Carol. The South Wind. The World's Wanderers. Those Evening Bells. Allegro. The Light that is Felt
Gerald Finley bar **Julius Drake** pf with [a]**Magnus Johnston** vn
Hyperion CDA67644 (62' · DDD · T/t) Ⓕ●

These songs, drawn from Ives's 200, can encourage at one extreme a rough declamatory style and at the other an almost voiceless intimacy. Without in any way underplaying, Finlay is always essentially a singer – his tone and command of the singing line are a pleasure in themselves. But he also has the absolute mastery of the composer's idioms and, with Julius Drake, his fearless and totally committed pianist, the technical, virtuoso skills to realise his intentions with (amid all the quirks) complete conviction of naturalness.

'A Song – For Anything' very satisfactorily balances early and late, rumbustious and contemplative. Several of the early German settings are included, always beautiful and always developing with some touch that is entirely personal. Of a quite distinctive beauty are those like 'Remembrance', 'Berceuse', and 'The Housatonic at Stockbridge' where voice and piano work a dreamy, misty spell. And still more characteristic are the settings of his own verses evoking memories of childhood. The 'character' songs (such as 'Charlie Rutlage') and the 'big' numbers ('General William Booth Enters into Heaven') become less prominent than they commonly seem in a recital group where they are programmed as an effective tour de force. The total impression is of an astonishing individuality and, more importantly, of a completely honest, dauntless and increasingly to be valued musical identity.

The mood of the second volume is fairly sedate. In particular some of the early songs in a conventional style are treated with the same seriousness that Finley would apply to Lieder.

An unusual but effective feature here is the provision of violin obbligato both for the jingoistic wartime song 'They Are There!' and the mawkish take-off 'Romanzo (di Central Park)'. Sentimentality is a Victorian characteristic but in 'Songs My Mother Taught Me', as elsewhere in Ives, the emotion is genuine so it invariably convinces.

Many of the songs are transposed down – hard work for the pianist and it makes some of the textures rather dense. The contemplative ones are delivered with an impressive serenity and Finley has his own way of attacking the razzle-dazzle of something like 'The Circus Band' or 'They Are There!'. He's close-miked, which works best in the intimacy of the quieter songs.

Psalms

Psalm 14, The fool hath said. Psalm 24, The Earth is the Lord's. Psalm 25, Unto Thee O God[c]. Psalm 42, As pants the hart[bc]. Psalm 54, Save me, O God, by Thy name. Psalm 67, God be merciful unto us. Psalm 90, Lord, thou hast been our dwelling place[abce]. Psalm 100, Make a joyful noise unto the Lord[e]. Psalm 135, Praise ye the Lord[ce]. Psalm 150, Praise ye the Lord[d]
[a]**Aleksandra Lustig** sop [b]**Julius Pfeiffer** ten [c]**Kay Johannsen** org [d]**Collegium Iuvenum**; **South West German Radio Vokalensemble**; [e]Members of the **Stuttgart Radio Symphony Orchestra / Marcus Creed**
Hänssler Classic CD93 224 (45' · DDD) Ⓕ●●●➔

Ives worked with choirs as a young organist; his father's choir tried out versions of some of these pieces but they wouldn't have got very far. Most of these psalms began life in the 1890s but Ives went on revising them into the 1920s.

The most familiar is Psalm 67, *God be merciful unto us*, with its superimposed gentle bitonal chords – expertly balanced in this performance. Psalm 90 sets a pattern followed in some of the others – there's a low C held in the organ pedal throughout, consonant chords or unison passages erupt into clusters and back, and a generally mystical atmosphere prevails. This is emphasised by three sets of bells and a low gong 'as church bells in distance' that characterise the serene final section. There are more prominent bells in the jubilant Psalm 100. Nobody but Ives could have dreamt up textures like these.

Psalm 135 adds trumpet, trombone, timpani and tenor and bass drums. The percussion creates a subdued march effect against the choir singing in five-time, and there's word-painting for the vapours, lightning and winds. Psalm 25 has extended canons between male and female voices, the whole thing underpinned again by long held pedal notes in the organ. Ives's early Victorian style is represented by Psalm 42, with a lovely solo from Julius Pfeiffer.

These 10 psalms are not first recordings but most of them have dropped out of the catalogue, so this is largely unknown Ives. This fine collection is a revelation in performances like these from the outstanding Stuttgart choir.

Gordon Jacob   English 1895-1984

English composer, teacher and writer. He was educated at Dulwich College and, after active service in the First World War, studied with Stanford, Howells, Boult and Vaughan Williams at the RCM. He was on the teaching staff there from 1924 until his retirement in 1966, and his pupils included Malcolm Arnold, Imogen Holst, Horovitz and Maconchy. Jacob's active career as composer spanned 60 years, during which time the character of his output faithfully reflected the changes in opportunity open to composers of a conservative idiom. In common with other more traditional composers of the time, his music went into eclipse with the rise of the avant garde in the 1960s.

Symphonies

Symphonies – No 1; No 2
London Philharmonic Orchestra / Barry Wordsworth
Lyrita SRCD315 (66' · DDD)   ⒫Ⓓ→

Gordon Jacob's First Symphony (1929) employs sizeable forces (including triple woodwind and two harps) and has five movements: two feisty and purposeful *Allegros* frame the whole edifice, while its dashing central *Scherzo* is flanked by two slow movements, the first of which in particular possesses an elegiac demeanour that accords with the work's inscription to the memory of the composer's favourite brother, Anstey (a victim of the First World War – Jacob, too, served in the trenches). It would make a terrific 'Guess who?' item: on a first encounter the names of Vaughan Williams, Holst, Elgar, Walton, Bliss, Poulenc and Stravinsky might appear. The more you return to it, however, the more individual the voice that emerges. Barry Wordsworth lends this powerful, criminally neglected discovery clear-headed, fervent advocacy, and the LPO are on their toes throughout. Completed in 1945, the Second Symphony was pre-

miered under Boult in a May 1946 broadcast; Rudolf Schwarz gave the first public performance two years later. Cast in the traditional four movements and described by Jacob as 'a meditation on war, suffering and victory', it's tautly argued, full of healthy contrapuntal vigour (at times it calls to mind Nielsen) and concludes with a cleverly crafted passacaglia or 'ground' – perhaps subconsciously influenced by, and yet fascinatingly different from, the finale of Vaughan Williams's roughly contemporaneous Fifth Symphony. These performers bring great tonal heft and intensity (especially in the plangent slow movement), admirably serving this bracing music.

With its agreeably tangible and airy sound in the best Lyrita tradition, this stimulating pairing of two impressive British symphonies merits immediate investigation.

Gabriel Jackson   English b1962

Jackson was born in Bermuda. He was a chorister at Canterbury Cathedral and then studied composition at the Royal College of Music. While at the RCM he was twice awarded the RO Morris Prize for Composition and he also won the Theodore Holland Award. These were followed in 1992 by an Arts Council Bursary. He is best known for his choral works and his liturgical pieces are regularly performed by many of the UK's leading cathedral and collegiate choirs. In 2003 he won the liturgical category at the inaugural British Composer Awards.

Choral Works

'Not No Faceless Angel'
O sacrum convivium. Lux mortuorum. Salve regina. Salve regina 2. To Morning. Song (I gaze upon you). Cecilia Virgo. Orbis patrator optime. Ave Maria. Hymn to the Trinity. Honor, virtus et potestas. Not No Faceless Angel
Polyphony / Stephen Layton
Hyperion CDA67708 (76' · DDD)   ⒻⓄ→

There are many striking features of this ravishing disc, beautifully and imaginatively performed by Polyphony. One is immediately aware of various stylistic resonances – from the musical maelstrom of the 20th century but also from many centuries past. There are hints here and there of Monteverdi, Stravinsky, Poulenc perhaps, yet far stronger is Jackson's profound affinity with English choral music from the time of the Eton Choirbook to the present. There are undoubted allusions to Wylkynson, Browne and other Eton composers in the stylish 'reconstituted' polyphony of *Orbis patrator optime* together with an instinctive feeling for sonority and a craving for a velvet richness in the spacing and 'purring' of extended diatonic combinations in *Salve regina 2* (a truly stunning work) and the 12-part *Cecilia Virgo*. These, after all, have been the materials common to Tallis, Byrd, SS Wesley and the agnostic tradition of Parry, Vaughan Williams, Howells, Britten and so onwards to Jackson himself. Yet these works transcend any simple notion of eclecticism in the new ways that sonority and harmony are reinterpreted. Particularly striking are the numinous strains of the *Ave Maria*, the evocative atmosphere of *Hymn to the Trinity*, the short, more limpid five-part Blake setting *To Morning* and the rapturous world of *Not No Faceless Angel* which seemed to invoke another English tradition – the part-song – but with a refreshing new inventiveness.

Shaped by his Anglican background as a chorister, Jackson possesses, not surprisingly, an instinct for acoustic and vocal texture, but the beauty and sheer appeal of his vocal works, challenging as they are, are sculpted by an energising pragmatism open both to the professional and ambitious amateur choir.

Leos Janáček
Moravian 1854-1928

The ninth of 14 children, Janáček was brought up in the magnificent mountains and forests of north-eastern Moravia on the Polish border. When he was 11, his father, the village schoolmaster, decided to send him to the Augustine monastery in Brno, the Moravian capital, where the choirmaster was a family friend. From there Janáček graduated to the Brno Teachers' Training College (1872-74), the Organ School (College of Music) in Prague (1874-75), thence to the Leipzig and Vienna Conservatories. He returned to Brno, married and settled into teaching and conducting locally.

Like Bartók and Kodály in Hungary, like Vaughan Williams and Holst in England, Janáček became fascinated by his country's folk music and set off with a friend (František Bartos) to collect folk material. Certain elements of this found its way into his early compositions; he evolved a theory that music should follow the rhythms of human speech, of animal and bird noises. For the next 20 years, Janáček continued to live and work in Brno in total obscurity, writing no music of any significance.

It wasn't till his late forties that he found his own distinctive voice in his opera Jenůfa. It was first performed in Brno just before Janáček's 50th birthday. It took another 12 years to reach Prague. In other words, Janáček was 62 when the world of music discovered this unorthodox and original composer. He had 12 more years to live and, though he had not stopped composing after the initial triumph of Jenůfa, an intense period of creative activity ensued including the production of the Glagolitic Mass, the Sinfonietta and two extraordinary string quartets. The foundation of the Czech republic in 1918 further inspired him. Freedom from German domination and his love of Russia and the Russian language provided further spurs to his endeavours. A further catalyst was Janáček's love life. In 1917 he had an affair with one of the singers in the Prague production of Jenůfa and the next year

met Kamila Stösslová, the pretty wife of an antiques dealer. Her husband had been able to provide food for the Janáčeks during the war and Janáček was later in a position to save the Stössls from being expelled as aliens. He became infatuated with Kamila (he'd separated from his wife) and began a voluminous correspondence in the last 16 months of his life amounting to nearly 700 letters. Kamila did not reciprocate his feelings but Janáček transformed her into the heroine of three of his final works – Kát'a Kabanová, The Cunning Little Vixen and The Makropulos Affair. She was also the inspiration for his song-cycle The Diary of One Who Disappeared. His creative urges were undiminished when he caught a cold after a walk in the woods near his home village. This turned into bronchial pneumonia from which he died aged 74.

Orchestral Works

Sinfonietta. The Cunning Little Vixen – Suite.
Taras Bulba. Jealousy. Šárka – Overture.
Kát'a Kabanová – Prelude. Schluk und Jau
Czech Philharmonic Orchestra /
Sir Charles Mackerras
Supraphon ② SU3739-2 (92' · DDD)　Ⓕ**OO**

Issued to celebrate the 150th anniversary of the composer's birth, this two-disc set of orchestral works became one of the last Janáček recordings from our greatest advocate of his work, Sir Charles Mackerras. Where his pioneering Pro Arte recording of the *Sinfonietta* has an earthy quality and Decca's Vienna version is ripe and resonant, the new one is generally lighter and more flexible. The live performance brings dividends in its flow and the build-up of excitement, thrillingly caught when the fanfare theme returns to cap the finale.

Where most versions of the *Cunning Little Vixen* Suite use Václav Talich's reorchestration, Mackerras has gone back to the original. As he says, the orchestral writing may seem unusual, but it certainly isn't amateurish, where Talich's version, for all its beauty, 'rather emasculates the acid sounds produced for the insects'.

Mackerras includes two tiny interludes for *Kát'a Kabanová* which he discovered in Prague, written when the German Theatre needed more time for scene changes. Rightly, he regards them as little jewels, well worth preserving.

The rarity is the incidental music for Gerhardt Hauptmann's play, *Schluck und Jau*, which Janáček was writing at the time of his death. The first of the two completed movements brings intriguing echoes of the fanfares in the *Sinfonietta* and the second in 5/8 time is equally original in its instrumentation, with deep trombones and stratospheric violins.

The helpful acoustic of the Rudolfinum gives a mellow quality to the refined playing of the Czech Philharmonic, with ample space round the sound, without underplaying the contrasts of wind and strings which are so typical of the composer.

Sinfonietta. Taras Bulba.
The Cunning Little Vixen – Suite
Bamberg Symphony Orchestra / Jonathan Nott
Tudor ⦿ TUDOR7135 (62' · DDD)   ⒡❍

Released to mark the Bamberg Symphony
Orchestra's 60th anniversary, this powerful
Janáček triptych reinforces the favourable impression made by these artists both on disc and in
concert. Jonathan Nott's Sinfonietta is something of a 'grower', a thoughtful, defiantly unsensational reading which takes a number of hearings
to reveal its lasting qualities. Aside from a hint of
fluster at the *più mosso* marking in the finale, the
Bambergers respond with striking accomplishment to their British chief, who directs with intelligence, thrusting purpose and a keen eye for
detail. Admittedly, there's greater tenderness in
the initial *Moderato* of the central tableau than
Nott chooses to find (Kubelík and his wonderfully pliable and expressive Bavarian RSO really
do melt the heart every time) but how judiciously
he controls his massed forces in the jubilant panoply towards the close – the cumulative effect is
properly rousing, noble and unflashy. A shame
the sound doesn't quite 'open out' ideally here,
though otherwise there can be nothing but praise
for a vividly truthful co-production between
Tudor and Bavarian Radio.

The suite from *The Cunning Little Vixen* – not
Talich's much-loved overview but an earlier,
16-minute selection by Brno-born František
Jílek (1913-93) – also offers much to enjoy. Only
Taras Bulba slightly disappoints: articulate,
painstakingly prepared and observant, yes, but it
never truly catches fire.

From the House of the Dead – Suite. The Cunning
Little Vixen – Suite (both arr Breiner)
New Zealand Symphony Orchestra / Peter Breiner
Naxos 8 570706 (75' · DDD)   ⓢ♭➤

The suite usually performed from Janáček's *The
Cunning Little Vixen*, arranged by Talich in the
1930s, is a 17-minute diptych using material
from Act 1 only (ie up to the point of the Vixen's
bloody escape from the Forester's yard) and is
based on a reorchestration Talich commissioned
that was easier to play. Breiner's returns to the
original and runs to nearly 40 minutes. Breiner's
first two movements follow the same basic trajectory as Talich's but the suite then takes off
with the Vixen's courtship and eventual marriage to the Fox over the next two spans. The
fifth movement deals with the Vixen's desperate
hunt to feed her cubs and eventual death at the
hand of the poacher and the brief finale ('Vixen
is Running') lights up the orchestra with its
paean to nature.

Hope of a different kind underlies *From the
House of the Dead*, Janáček's final opera. Here
Breiner has started with the Overture and proceeds once again through six highly coloured
movements running to over 35 minutes. The
hard edge of Janáček's scoring, devoid of the
vocal elements, becomes even more telling.

Breiner himself conducts, securing accomplished playing from the New Zealanders, and
Naxos's sound is rich with depth. It might be
said that the two suites here are almost too much
of a good thing, representing significant proportions of the parent works unlike the normal
selection of morsels that are spread through the
repertoire. Those who want to dip more than
their toe into Janáček's sound world should turn
to this fine new disc.

String Quartets

Janáček String Quartets – No 1, 'The Kreutzer
Sonata'; No 2, 'Intimate Letters' **Schulhoff** String
Quartet No 1
Talich Quartet (Jan Talich, Petr Macecek vns Vladimir
Bukac va Petr Prause vc)
Calliope CAL9333 (57' · DDD)   ⒡❍❍

This recording announces itself with a richness
and directness of expression as remarkable as the
previous Talich Quartet's restraint (which, it
has to be said, occasionally registers as mere
circumspection). Sample the last two minutes or
so of *The Kreutzer Sonata* for an abandon that's
almost guaranteed to set the pulse racing. Or,
especially if you have somehow been immune to
Janáček in the past, see if you can resist the eruptive passion in the third movement of *Intimate
Letters*. Given the extraordinary problems with
establishing authoritative texts for these pieces,
there is no question whatsoever of a single recommendation. Perhaps the rather unremitting
sweetness of Jan Talich's tone would be the
nearest thing to a potential drawback. Even so,
this new issue surely has to figure on the shortest
of future short lists.

Schulhoff doesn't even get a billing on the
cover. But his succinct, Bartókian First Quartet
– dazzlingly inventive and light on its feet – significantly enhances the disc's appeal. Thanks to
the Talichs' range of colour and expression, the
Presto first movement fairly leaps off the page,
and the skittish twists and turns of the succeeding *Allegretto* and the upfront peasant pungency
of the *Alla slovacca* third movement are delivered
with equal relish. After which the rhapsodic and,
ultimately, anxiously withdrawn final movement
makes for an unexpected but logical, even
haunting, conclusion. There have been several
highly praised CD recordings of the piece but
these are now variously difficult to acquire; all
the more reason to welcome this new, trenchant
account. The vivid Czech recordings place the
instruments rather further forward than usual
but not inappropriately so in this passionately
communicative repertoire.

String Quartets – No 1, 'The Kreutzer Sonata'[a];
No 2, 'Intimate Letters' (two versions)[a/b]
Quatuor Diotima ([ab]Naaman Sluchin, [ab]Yun-Peng
Zhao vns [a]Franck Chevalier va [ab]Pierre Morlet vc)
[b]**Garth Knox** va da gamba
Alpha ALPHA133 (68' · DDD)   ⒡❍❍

The Diotima Quartet claim the first recording of the new Bärenreiter edition of Janáček's *Intimate Letters* Quartet. And this is no small matter of the odd slur, dot and accidental. Whole phrases come out with startlingly unfamiliar textures and tempo relationships; the floaty five-note downward scale motif in the second movement is no longer in regular whole tones and only has four notes; sundry bowed notes are now plucked, and so on. Performers have always had tough choices to make in this piece; from now on they'll be even tougher.

There's apparently even an option for the end to be played stratospherically on the viola rather than merely high on the violin, which is what the Diotimas do in their reconstruction of how the piece might have sounded with Janáček's programmatically inspired notion of using viola d'amore instead of viola. That conclusion defeats even an exponent as fine as Garth Knox (and curiously the end of the 'straight viola' recording is also unhappy, with unwanted open-string resonance jarring against the D flat major tonic). But elsewhere Knox wields his instrument to wonderfully expressive effect. Its sympathetic strings creating their own magic halo and drawing the ear even when the instrument isn't carrying the main line.

The Kreutzer Sonata is just as carefully prepared and as full-bloodedly executed; however, issues of text and instruments apart, it would be hard to part with the superbly passionate Pavel Haas Quartet's Janáček recordings (see page 519), because by a small but definite margin the young Czechs are more liberated and give a feeling of being more inside the music. That said, the Diotimas' double initiative, on top of their always classy execution, makes this new disc indispensable to the Janáček aficionado.

String Quartets – No 1, 'Kreutzer Sonata'; No 2, 'Intimate Letters'
Skampa Quartet (Pavel Fischer, Jana Lukášová vns Radim Sedmidubský va Peter Jarůšek vc)
Supraphon SU3486-2 (41' · DDD)   ⒻOO

Janáček changed his mind a great deal, especially about the Second Quartet, on the way from composition to performance and even after that. Most records use the scores published in Prague respectively in 1945 and 1949 as 'revised editions'. However, Milan Skampa published further revisions in 1975 and 1979, and these are what are used here by the quartet which studied under him at the time of its formation in 1989.

The differences depend mostly upon dynamic markings and emphases. To these the present players give great attention, stressing the sudden changes of tempo or dynamics and the consequent abrupt changes of mood which mark the music. They also pay particular attention to coloration of tone. In the First Quartet, for instance, where the seducer of the Tolstoy-inspired 'plot' makes his mincing

JANÁČEK STRING QUARTETS – IN BRIEF

Talich Quartet
Calliope CAL9333   ⒻOO
Full of imagination and idiomatic touches, the Talich must top the list of superb interpretations. These are superb performances that really drill to the core of the works.

The Lindsays
ASV CDDCA749   Ⓕ
Another pair of superb performances. The Lindsays play with febrile intensity and minute attention to the numerous shifts of mood and emotional temperature.

New Helsinki Quartet
Warner Apex 0927 40603-2   Ⓢ
A super-budget coupling worth considering: stylish playing and a real sense of the music's variety. Generously coupled with Dvořák's delightful *Cypresses*.

Vlach Quartet
Naxos 8 553895   Ⓢ
Played with passion and imagination, here's another well-filled and competitively priced coupling worth considering.

Skampa Quartet
Supraphon SU3486-2   ⒻO
Tremendous performances that are not afraid to explore some of Janáček's more extreme sonic demands: they almost revel in making sounds that are simply ugly, but they justify it by the intelligence of their overall approach.

Smetana Quartet
Testament ② SBT1074/5   ⒻO
Slightly awkwardly spread over two individual full-price discs, each coupled with Dvořák, the Smetana Quartet really convey the passion and intensity of these two great works. The 1960s sound is outstanding.

Pavel Haas Quartet
Supraphon SU3922-2 (No 1)   ⒻOO
Supraphon SU3877-2 (No 2)   ⒻOOO
Coupled with Pavel Haas's two string quartets (and reviewed on page 519), the Pavel Haas Quartet give searing, intense performances of Janáček's two quartets. There is a glow to the playing here that is revealed by very few groups. These young musicians from the Czech Republic have rightly won awards for their playing.

Quatuor Diotima
Alpha ALPHA133 (68' · DDD)   ⒻOO
A fascinating first recording of the new Bärenreiter edition of the quartets, which also employs the viola da gamba in the Second. A major new Janáček recording.

entrance, the sound is deceptively warm within the delicacy; other quartets play the theme with almost disdainful thinness, but the Skampa allow him his dangerous charm.

In the final movement of the Second Quartet, there's a searing discord marked to be played *fortississimo* but right up near the bridge where string tone is weakest: the outcome is a horrible sound, and the Skampa believe that that's what's meant. In short, these are sharp, considered performances, vivid in detail and excellently judged in structure. They take their place in the catalogue beside the marvellous Talich Quartet (reviewed above) and the Pavel Haas Quartet's discs reviewed on page 519.

Violin Sonata

Janáček Violin Sonata **Nedbal** Violin Sonata, Op 9
Novák Violin Sonata
Ivan Zenatý vn **Martin Kasík** pf
Supraphon SU3978-2 (64' · DDD)   Ⓕ

It is Janáček's Sonata which dominates this recital, standing out from the other two by virtue of its ferocious originality. Yet this was not easily achieved: the work went through numerous revisions before Janáček was able to write modestly to a friend declaring that while he did not regard the work as exceptional, 'the second and third movements have a bit of truth in them'. One of these is the *Balada*, a warm, appealing piece which Zenatý and Kasík play with a quick sensitivity about when to simplify, when to intensify the expression. They are a fine sonata pair, working with a strong instinct for each other and recorded here with a very immediate acoustic. We are sitting in the front row.

The other two sonatas belong very much to the 19th century, both strongly influenced by the composer the loyal insert note studiously avoids mentioning, Brahms. Novák was a gifted pupil of Dvořák, who made him rewrite this sonata no fewer than seven times. It has an unmistakably Brahmsian sweep to the first movement, but escapes from under that shadow into a sunnier and more individual *Andante cantabile* and a finale which is a little forced but does include some charming ideas in dealing with the main subject. It is also excellently written for the instruments, as is the piece by Nedbal, a fellow pupil of Dvořák and once viola in the Czech Quartet. If the first movement is over-extended, it shows the exuberance of talented youth, and there is real charm in the *Andante*.

Piano Sonata 1.X.1905

Piano Sonata 1. X. 1905, 'From the Street'.
On an Overgrown Path. In the Mists. Reminiscence
Charles Owen pf
Somm SOMMCD028 (73' · DDD)   Ⓕ●

It says much for Charles Owen and his understanding of this composer that a young British

pianist should present this music with such a distinctive voice. As is evident from the first of the two movements of the Sonata, he's even more strikingly successful than Rudolf Firkušný (DG), doyen of Czech pianists, at bringing out the quirky side of Janáček's writing. So the jagged little flurries of notes that bite away in contrast to the poetic lyricism of the opening are presented in sharper focus than with either Firkušný or Mikhail Rudy, an effect which directly echoes Janáček's orchestral writing. Here and throughout the disc Owen is helped by the clarity of the recording.

The qualities which distinguish Owen's performance of the sonata recur in the other works. Where Firkušný is regularly faster in a freely expressive style, and Rudy (on EMI) markedly slower, with *rubato* not always so idiomatic, Owen's middle way offers sharper focus and more refined dynamics. So his performances of the two series of miniatures which make up *On an Overgrown Path* reflect the composer's folk influences in their lyrical freshness, both in the songful pieces and the dances. In the four movements of *In the Mists*, Owen matches Firkušný in spontaneity; indeed, he gives an almost improvisatory feel to the suite. The tiny *Reminiscence*, a product from the year Janáček died, makes a moving supplement.

Glagolitic Mass

Glagolitic Mass (original version, ed Wingfield)[a].
Kodály Psalmus Hungaricus, Op. 13[b]
[a]**Tina Kiberg** sop [a]**Randi Stene** contr
Peter Svensson ten [a]**Ulrik Cold** bass
[a]**Per Salo** org [b]**Copenhagen Boys' Choir;**
Danish National Radio Choir and Symphony
Orchestra / Sir Charles Mackerras
Chandos CHAN9310 (63' · DDD · T/t)   Ⓕ[Ⓑ]▸

Mackerras's version is of particular interest as it embodies another of the reconstructions that have been painstakingly made of Janáček's original intentions in different works as his stature has drawn greater scholarly interest. This one has been made by Paul Wingfield. He has gone into the nature of his restorations in great detail in his excellent monograph on the work in the Cambridge Music Handbooks series (CUP: 1992), and summarises them in his note to this recording. Briefly, they involve the playing of the Intrada at the beginning and the end, in the Introduction a very complex rhythmic pattern and in the 'Gospodi pomiluj' ('Kyrie') use of quintuple metre instead of the familiar four-in-a-bar (both far more effective), and fierce timpani interjections in the wild organ solo. There are other points; but in any case, most interested listeners will care less for them in detail than for the heightened force and impact of the music. This it certainly now (or once again) has.

These matters make it regrettable that, despite marvellous handling of the work by Mackerras, there are problems with a quartet of soloists that is less than exciting, and a recording that even with the most modern techniques can obscure the detail of the music and the clarity of the words. This should not detract from the interest of the disc, which every lover of the work must want to hear. Those who acquire it will have the additional benefit of a fine performance of Kodály's *Psalmus Hungaricus*, though the restored Mass is naturally the occasion for recommendation and choice.

Additional recommendation

Glagolitic Mass[a]. Sinfonietta[b]
Palmer *sop* **Gunson** *mez* **Mitchinson** *ten* **King** *bass*
Parker-Smith *org* [a]**CBSO;** [b]**Philharmonia / Rattle**
EMI Great Recordings of the Century 566980-2
(62' · DDD · T/t)   Ⓜ❍❍◗

Rattle's is a full-blooded, urgent view of the work, with particularly fine solo contributions from Felicity Palmer and John Mitchinson. That the language is an unfamiliar one is occasionally evident in the chorus, though they, like the orchestra, give totally committed performances under Rattle's inspired leadership.

The Eternal Gospel

The Eternal Gospel[a]. The Excursions of Mr Brouček –
Orchestral Suite. The Ballad of Blaník. The Fiddler's
Child[b]
[a]**Gweneth-Ann Jeffers** *sop* [a]**Adrian Thompson** *ten*
[b]**Elizabeth Layton** *vn* **Edinburgh Festival Chorus;**
BBC Scottish Symphony Orchestra / Ilan Volkov
Hyperion CDA67517; 💿 SACDA67517
(60' · DDD · T/t)   Ⓕ❍❍

Fans of the *Glagolitic Mass* should definitely make a beeline for Janáček's 1913 cantata *The Eternal Gospel*. Radiating a comparable spiritual and theatrical fervour, it's a setting of a text by Jaroslav Vrchlický inspired by the commentary on the Book of Revelation by the 12th-century mystic Joachim of Fiore, that serves up a seductive brew of rapt lyricism and tingling drama. Much of the solo vocal writing possesses a truly operatic scope and there are some memorably ardent choral interjections. The gifted young Israeli conductor Ilan Volkov masterminds a laudably disciplined and full-throated account of this bracing rarity, and the sound has commendable spread and amplitude (especially in its SACD format).

The rest of the programme is no less enticing. *The Fiddler's Child* (1913) and *The Ballad of Blaník* (1919) are compact and often bewitchingly lovely tone-poems with patriotic leanings; and the disc concludes with an orchestral suite from the satirical two-part opera *The Excursions of Mr Brouček* (1908-17). A thoroughly diverting 21-minute sequence it makes, too: just try the fairground sway of the 'Moon Waltz' or the young lovers' ineffably tender tryst ('Before Dawn') that brings the curtain down on the first half. If it's festive spectacle you're after, the last two movements ('Song of the Hussites' and 'Procession of the Victors') have it by the spadeful.

Performance-wise, there are no real grumbles. Although the music-making has not quite the irresistible tang you get from native interpreters in this repertoire, Volkov (not yet 30 and with talent to spare) directs with considerable flair and sensitivity. If their string section inevitably can't match up to, say, the Czech PO's for sheer heft or tonal lustre, the BBC Scottish SO play with admirable precision and infectious enthusiasm; leader Elizabeth Layton is a warm-hearted, songful presence in *The Fiddler's Child*. Hyperion's glowing natural sound-frame sets the seal on a first-rate anthology.

The Cunning Little Vixen

The Cunning Little Vixen.
The Cunning Little Vixen – orchestral suite (arr Talich)
Lucia Popp *sop* Vixen, Young Vixen **Dalibor Jedlička**
bass Forester **Eva Randová** *mez* Fox **Eva**
Zikmundová *mez* Forester's Wife, Owl **Vladimir**
Krejčik *ten* Schoolmaster, Gnat **Richard Novák** *ten*
Priest, Badger **Václav Zítek** *bar* Harašta **Beno**
Blachut *ten* Pásek **Ivana Mixová** *mez* Pásek's Wife,
Woodpecker, Hen **Libuše Marova** *contr* Dog
Gertrude Jahn *mez* Cock, Jay **Eva Hríbiková** *sop*
Frantik **Zuzana Hudecová** *sop* Pepik **Peter Saray**
treb Frog, Grasshopper **Miriam Ondrášková** *sop*
Cricket **Vienna State Opera Chorus; Bratislava**
Children's Choir; Vienna Philharmonic Orchestra /
Sir Charles Mackerras
Decca ② 417 129-2DH2 (109' · DDD · T/t) Ⓕ❍❍❍◗
Also available in a nine-CD set containing
From the House of the Dead, Jenůfa, Kát'a
Kabanová, The Makropulos Affair, Sinfonietta,
Taras Bulba and the suite from The Cunning
Little Vixen: Decca 475 6872DC9

 Janáček used the most unlikely material for his operas. For *The Cunning Little Vixen* his source was a series of newspaper drawings, with accompanying text, about the adventures of a vixen cub and her escape from the gamekeeper who raised her. The music is a fascinating blend of vocal and orchestral sound – at times ludicrously romantic, at others raw and violent. Mackerras's Czech training has given him a rare insight into Janáček's music, and he presents a version faithful to the composer's individual requirements. In the title-role, Lucia Popp gives full weight to the text while displaying all the richness and beauty of her voice.

There's a well-chosen supporting cast of largely Czech singers, with the Vienna Philharmonic to add the ultimate touch of orchestral refinement. Decca's sound is of demonstration quality.

The Cunning Little Vixen
Eva Jenis *sop* Vixen **Thomas Allen** *bar* Forester
Hana Minutillo *contr* Fox **Libuše Márová** *mez*
Forester's Wife, Owl **Josef Hajna** *ten* Schoolmaster,
Mosquito **Richard Novák** *bass* Parson, Badger **Ivan**
Kusnjer *bar* Harašta **Jean-Philippe Marlière** *bass*
Innkeeper, Dog **Sarah Connolly** *mez* Innkeeper's
Wife, Cock, Jay **Florence Bonnafous** *sop* Hen

François Martinaud *sop* Woodpecker **Châtelet Choir; Hautes-de-Seine Maîtrise; Orchestre de Paris / Sir Charles Mackerras**
Stage director **Nicholas Hytner**
Video director **Brian Large**
ArtHaus Musik ➁ 100 240 (98' · 16:9 · 2.0 · 2 & 5)
Ⓕ**O**

Mackerras conducts with all the vibrancy of his landmark CD recording (reviewed above), plus the immediacy of live performance, and if the Orchestre de Paris has leaner strings and less secure brass than the VPO, it still responds well. Hytner's production was an instant hit at the time, with good reason. The forest scenes rely heavily on dance, as Janáček's notes suggest, so the set is a ballet-style level stage with hanging flats; but within these constraints it comes alive with clever imagery and gaudy colour.

Eva Jenis is a vivacious, characterful Vixen, though not as creamy as Popp on the CD. Janáček's vocal casting isn't observed consistently; Hana Minutillo makes a fine contralto Fox, but there's a case for giving the role to a male voice, as the Dog is here. Richard Novák and Josef Hajna, in the important animal/human roles, and Ivan Kusnjer's roughneck Poacher provide firmly idiomatic support, but Allen's grizzled Forester remains the linchpin. His final paean to the renewing force of Nature, with Mackerras in full lyrical flow, is magical. A strong recommendation.

The Excursions of Mr Brouček

The Excursions of Mr Brouček
Jan Vacík *ten* Brouček **Peter Straka** *ten* Mazal, Blankytný, Petřík **Roman Janál** *bar* Sacristan, Lunigrove, Domšík **Maria Haan** *sop* Málinka, Etherea, Kunka **Zdeněk Plech** *bass* Würfl, Wonderglitter, Councillor **Martina Bauerová** *mez* Young Waiter, Student **Lenka Šmídová** *mez* Housewife, Kedruta **Ivan Kusnjer** *bar* Apparition
BBC Singers; BBC Symphony Orchestra / Jiří Bělohlávek
DG ➁ 477 7387GH2 (123' · DDD · S/T/t/N)
Ⓕ**OOO**▸

Mr Brouček's excursions may have carried him to the moon and the 15th century, but it took him longer to travel beyond his native land into the opera houses and recording studios of the world. But what a lovable work it is. The first excursion in particular is packed with vivid invention; the second dips deeper into wells of Czech history. It all needs the sharp hand and light touch with the agile rhythms which Bělohlávek brings to it. He is not helped by a recording that sets the singers too far back and obscures a good deal of the words, especially in the chorus, though matters improve once the moon is reached. Jan Vacík gives a lively account of poor Brouček, first stranded among the moon aesthetes and then mired in religious controversy, preserving the little man's dignity and allowing him a touching quality that sees him through it all. If he lacks the warmth and the

rounded character of Vilém Přibyl, this is still a fresh and attractive portrayal.

There is, as always, much doubling in the cast. Peter Straka is an elegant Mazal and Petřík, lightly caricaturing his own elegance to send up the posturing Azurean poet. Maria Haan is a lively Málinka, putting on airs and graces for Etherea and returning to a fresh simplicity for Peter's lover Kunka. The many other parts include sturdy contributions from Roman Janál and Zdeněk Plech, though the sense of atmosphere and the depth of feeling which lies under all the satire are richer with Jílek's handling of both singers and orchestra.

House of the Dead / Makropulos Affair

From the House of the Dead[a]. Mládí[b]. Nursery Rhymes[c]
Dalibor Jedlička *bar* Gorjančikov **Jaroslava Janská** *sop* Aljeja **Jiří Zahradníček** *ten* Luka (Morosov) **Vladimir Krejčík** *ten* Tall Prisoner **Richard Novák** *bass* Short Prisoner **Antonín Svorc** *bass-bar* Commandant **Beno Blachut** *ten* Old Prisoner **Ivo Zídek** *ten* Skuratov **Jaroslav Souček** *bar* Čekunov, Prisoner acting Don Juan **Eva Zigmundová** *mez* Whore **Zdeněk Soušek** *ten* Shapkin, Kedril **Václav Zítek** *bar* Shishkov **Zdeněk Svehla** *ten* Cherevin, A Voice **Vienna State Opera Chorus; Vienna Philharmonic Orchestra / Sir Charles Mackerras;** [c]**London Sinfonietta Chorus;** [bc]**London Sinfonietta / David Atherton**
Decca ➁ 430 375-2DH2 (123' · DDD/ADD · T/t)
Ⓕ**OOO**▸

The Makropulos Affair. Lachian Dances[a]
Elisabeth Söderström *sop* Emilia Marty **Peter Dvorský** *ten* Albert Gregor **Vladimir Krejšík** *ten* Vítek **Anna Czaková** *mez* Kristina **Václav Zítek** *bar* Jaroslav Prus **Zdeněk Svehla** *ten* Janek **Dalibor Jedlička** *bass* Kolenatý **Jiří Joran** *bass* Stage Technician **Ivana Mixová** *contr* Cleaning Woman **Beno Blachut** *ten* Hauk-Sendorf **Blanka Vitková** *contr* Chambermaid **Vienna State Opera Chorus; Vienna Philharmonic Orchestra / Sir Charles Mackerras;** [a]**London Philharmonic Orchestra / François Huybrechts**
Decca ➁ 478 1711DOR2 (118' · ADD · T/t)
Recorded 1978 Ⓕ**OOO**▸
Also available in a nine-CD set containing The Cunning Little Vixen, Jenůfa, Kát'a Kabanová, Sinfonietta, Taras Bulba and the suite from The Cunning Little Vixen: Decca 475 6872DC9

Ⓖ *From the House of the Dead* (the 1980 *Gramophone* Record of the Year) was here recorded for the first time in its proper, original version; and this revealed it as even more of a masterpiece – a work, indeed, to count among the handful of masterpieces of 20th-century opera. The loss of the final chorus, a sentimental addition, is but the most striking of the clarifications: throughout, the sound is sharper, the textures are sparer, and this serves to sharpen the effect and to give the singers more clearly differentiated support. The cast is led, nominally, by Goryanchikov, but the character isn't really the hero of an opera that has no heroes, and in which all are heroes, though Dalibor Jedlička sings him warmly and well. The prisoners are skilfully contrasted in Janáček's writing so as to make an apparently random yet actually well-structured group; there isn't a weak performance among them.

The Makropulos Affair does have a heroine, in the tragic figure of Emilia Marty; and here Elisabeth Söderström gives one of her greatest recorded performances. She succeeds amazingly in conveying the complexity of the character, the elegance yet flinty cynicism, the aloofness yet vulnerability, the latent warmth that can flower into such rich expressive phrases and then be reined in with a sense of nervy panic. She's only really alarmed by Prus, the most formidable of the men around her, powerfully sung by Václav Zítek. Mackerras is again masterly. This is a recording to set among great performances of it.

As with *From the House of the Dead*, there's an essay by John Tyrrell that not only gives the listener the best possible introduction to the opera but is also a contribution to scholarship. The fill-ups, *Mládí* and the *Nursery rhyme*, come from David Atherton's splendid 1981 set of five LPs devoted to Janáček; the *Lachian Dances* set is a rather less successful companion to *Makropulos*.

bank scene, here a huge rubbish dump, that opens Act 2) by Peduzzi's trademark steep Italianate high walls. As in all his productions and films, Chéreau's directing turns everyone into such complete and natural actors that the descriptive term 'acting' seems almost redundant. Even in Act 3, where Janáček's dramaturgy calls for perhaps one prisoner story too many, the staging's pulse never falters. Only the plays in Act 2 feel a little too carefully stylised (and Eastern-influenced) for these prisoners to have put on themselves, although they're unfailingly reflective of the characters in the main story.

Boulez once said that he began conducting in order to achieve really good performances of modern works. Now in his 80s, he is still operating at that level in this tricky score (he uses the Mackerras/Tyrrell critical edition), treading the finest balance, as did Janáček, between reported emotion and outright passion. It really is invidious in this ensemble piece to pick out individuals, but Ainsley creates a compellingly dangerous near-ballet out of Skuratov's insanity, and Bär and Stoklossa limn beautifully the growing closeness of the nobleman Gorjančikov and the young Aljeja. The sound picture does justice to Boulez's balances, while the camerawork and editing are a lot happier than the bumpy film of the 2005 Chéreau/Aix *Così*.

From the House of the Dead

Olaf Bär *bar* Gorjančikov **Eric Stoklossa** *ten* Aljeja **Stefan Margita** *ten* Luka **Peter Straka** *ten* Tall Prisoner **Vladimír Chmelo** *bar* Short Prisoner **Jiří Sulženko** *bass* Commandant **Heinz Zednik** *ten* Old Prisoner **John Mark Ainsley** *ten* Skuratov **Jan Galla** *bass* Čekunov **Arnold Schoenberg Choir; Mahler Chamber Orchestra / Pierre Boulez**
Stage director **Patrice Chéreau**
Video director **Stéphane Metge**
DG 🅓 🅓🅥🅓 073 4426GH
(148' · NTSC · 16:9 · PCM stereo and DTS 5.1 · 0)
Includes documentary, 'The Making of The House of the Dead'. Recorded live at the Vienna Festival in 2007   Ⓕ🅞🅞

Nearly 30 years have elapsed since Boulez and Chéreau last created a new production together – the Paris premiere of the Cerha completion of *Lulu*. In the interim the conductor has taken on repertoire he might have blanched at in those days (Bruckner, Janáček, even Richard Strauss) while the director became more involved in the cinema and the plays of his late partner Bernard-Marie Koltès. Their return, in a staging shared by four houses, shows the old fires undiminished, although the heightened realism and visual beauty still practised by Chéreau's team (his designer Richard Peduzzi has worked with him since their schooldays) have changed little over the years and, inevitably, lack the radical edge they had in the 1970s.

Janáček's (and Dostoevsky's) prisoners are modernised painlessly to a non-specific 20th-century gulag surrounded (except in the river

---

The Makropulos Affair (sung in English)

Cheryl Barker *sop* Emilia Marty **Robert Brubaker** *ten* Albert Gregor **John Graham-Hall** *ten* Vítek **Elena Xanthoudakis** *sop* Kristina **John Wegner** *bar* Baron Jaroslav Prus **Thomas Walker** *ten* Janek **Neal Davies** *bass-bar* Kolenatý **Graeme Danby** *bass* Stage Technician **Kathleen Wilkinson** *contr* Cleaning Woman **Graham Clark** *ten* Hauk-Sendorf **Susanna Tudor-Thomas** *contr* Chambermaid **English National Opera Chorus and Orchestra / Sir Charles Mackerras**
Chandos Opera in English ② CHAN3138 (126' · DDD · S/N/T)   Ⓕ🅓→

This is Mackerras's second recording. The first, in 1979, in his series of groundbreaking Janáček recordings for Decca (see above), had the Vienna Philharmonic in radiant form accompanying a fine cast singing in Czech. It says much for the quality of the ENO Orchestra that for this new version in English the playing is equally polished, and often outshines that of the Viennese in its extra dramatic bite.

The recording brings an advantage, too – not as plush as the Viennese version and with extra separation and clarity in a clearly focused acoustic. Those qualities suit the work better, which, as Sir Charles points out, is 'a different kind of music': Janáček emphatically did not want to sound like Strauss or Puccini. That extra clarity and separation means the words are astonishingly clear.

Cheryl Barker rivals Elisabeth Söderström on Decca in dramatic bite and when in Act 3 Emilia is at last given a sustained solo, Barker is even more powerful, aptly abrasive and less moulded. Though the American Robert Brubaker cannot quite match Peter Dvorský on Decca, it is a focused, compelling performance. In some of the smaller roles the Czech singers had an advantage but their counterparts here run them close. On any count both versions have one marvelling at the score's emotional thrust and dramatic compulsion, original in every way and one of Janáček's supreme masterpieces.

Jenůfa

Jenůfa
Elisabeth Söderström sop Jenůfa **Wieslaw Ochman** ten Laca **Eva Randová** mez Kostelnička **Peter Dvorský** ten Števa **Lucia Popp** sop Karolka **Marie Mrazová** contr Stařenka **Václav Zitek** bar Stárek **Dalibor Jedlička** bass Rychtar **Ivana Mixová** mez Rychtarka **Vera Soukopová** mez Pastuchyňa, Tetka **Jindra Pokorná** mez Barena **Jana Janasová** sop Jano
Vienna State Opera Chorus; Vienna Philharmonic Orchestra / Sir Charles Mackerras
Decca ② 414 483-2DH2 (130' · DDD) Ⓕ🅞🅞🅞🅞🅑➔
Also available in a nine-CD set containing From the House of the Dead, The Cunning Little Vixen, Kát'a Kabanová, The Makropulos Affair, Sinfonietta, Taras Bulba and the suite from The Cunning Little Vixen: Decca 475 6872DC9

Ⓖ Janáček's first operatic masterpiece is a towering work, blending searing intensity with heart-stopping lyricism. It tells of Jenůfa and the appalling treatment she receives as she's caught between the man she loves and another who finally comes to love her. But dominating the story is the Kostelnička, a figure of enormous strength, pride and inner resource who rules Jenůfa's life and ultimately kills her baby. Randová's characterisation of the role of the Kostelnička is frightening in its intensity yet has a very human core. The two men are well cast and act as fine foils to Söderström's deeply impressive Jenůfa. The Vienna Philharmonic plays beautifully and Mackerras directs magnificently. The recording is all one could wish for and the booklet is a mine of informed scholarship.

Jenůfa
Roberta Alexander sop Jenůfa **Anja Silja** sop Kostelnička **Philip Langridge** ten Laca **Mark Baker** ten Števa **Menai Davies** contr Grandmother Buryja **Robert Poulton** bar Foreman of the Mill **Gordon Sandison** bar Mayor **Linda Ormiston** mez Mayor's Wife **Alison Hagley** sop Karolka **Sarah Pring** sop Barena **Lynne Davies** sop Jano **Glyndebourne Festival Chorus; London Philharmonic Orchestra / Sir Andrew Davis** Stage director **Nikolaus Lehnhoff** Video director **Derek Bailey**
ArtHaus Musik 📀 100 208 (118' · 4:3 · 2.0 · 2 & 5)
Recorded live 1989 Ⓕ🅞

Nikolaus Lehnhoff's acclaimed 1989 Glyndebourne production makes a welcome appear-

ance on DVD, the picture a touch grainy but still a dramatic improvement over the videotape, the sound still more so. Andrew Davis's conducting emphasises the score's lyricism without diminishing its rhythmic vigour and folk resonances. The staging, in Czech despite its Anglophone cast, is just as idiomatic. If Act 1's mill looks somewhat cramped on the old Glyndebourne stage, the indoor scenes gain a natural, sometimes claustrophobic, intimacy, well captured in Derek Bailey's direction.

The performers display the same naturalness. Roberta Alexander's heroine is sung with a warmth and fervour that exactly captures Jenůfa's open and loving nature. Langridge is a rather mature Laca, but his sinewy tenor and twisted, hungry demeanour render the character's distorting jealousy and inner decency equally credible and sympathetic. Lehnhoff and Silja play the Kostelnička as the traditional black-clad puritan rather than the less sophisticated old peddler woman, pious and desperate, whom Janáček drew from the original play. But her steely tones and incisive diction movingly illuminate the fiercely proud and loving nature, warped (as a restored solo reveals) by marital abuse, which makes her so fanatically protective of Jenůfa; her murderous Act 2 soliloquy and conscience-stricken terror are harrowing.

Additional recommendations

Jenůfa
Mattila Jenůfa **Silvasti** Laca **Silja** Kostelnička **Hadley** Števa **Royal Opera House Orchestra / Haitink**
Erato ② 0927 45330-2 (139' · DDD · T/t) Ⓕ
Recorded live 2001

Haitink may not topple the Mackerras version from its pedestal but it makes a deeply rewarding and valid alternative, especially collectable for Mattila's heroine and Silvasti's superlatively sung Laca.

Jenůfa (sung in English)
Watson Jenůfa **Robson** Laca **Barstow** Kostelnička **Wedd** Števa **Welsh National Opera Chorus and Orchestra / Sir Charles Mackerras**
Chandos Opera in English ② CHAN3106
(120' · DDD · T/t) Ⓜ➔

A superb issue rivalling Mackerras's Award-winning Decca recording. If anything, the intense emotion comes over even more powerfully. For those who prefer opera in translation, this is the one to choose.

Kát'a Kabanová

Kát'a Kabanová. House of the Dead. The Cunning Little Vixen. Jenůfa. The Makropulos Affair. Sinfonietta. Taras Bulba and the suite from The Cunning Little Vixen
Elisabeth Söderström sop Kát'a Kabanová **Peter Dvorský** ten Boris **Naděžda Kniplová** contr Kabanicha **Vladimír Krejčík** ten Tichon **Libuše Márová** mez Varvara **Dalibor Jedlička** bass Dikoj **Zdeněk**

Svehla *ten* Kudrjáš **Jaroslav Souček** *bar* Kuligin **Jitka Pavlová** *sop* Glaša **Gertrude Jahn** *mez* Fekluša
Vienna State Opera Chorus; Vienna Philharmonic Orchestra / Sir Charles Mackerras
Decca ⑨ 475 6872DC9 (ADD · N/T/t)　　　Ⓕ❹❹❹❹➔

Kát'á, a free spirit, is imprisoned by marriage into, and domicile with, a family in a provincial Russian town on the Volga. The family is manipulated by her widowed mother-in-law. The only son (Kát'á's husband) is spineless, and Kát'á looks for escape in love. She finds the love, but true escape only in suicide. Janáček focuses on his heroine, giving her at least two of the most moving scenes in opera: the first where, to music of shimmering, seraphic beauty she describes her childhood imagination given free rein by sunlight streaming through the dome in church; and the second in the last scene where, after confessing her adultery, she concludes that 'not even God's own sunlight' gives her pleasure any more. Söderström has the intelligence and a voice which guarantees total credibility; and of the superb all-Czech supporting cast one might only have wished for a slightly younger-sounding sister-in-law. Mackerras obtains the finest playing from the VPO; and Decca reproduces the whole with clarity, atmosphere, ideal perspectives and discernible stage movement – only a detectable levelling of the score's few extreme *fortissimos* points to the recording's vintage.

At the moment *Kát'á* is only available in a nine-CD box set of all of Mackerras's Janáček recordings but you might be able to find copies of the original set, or download just the opera you require.

Katya Kabanova (sung in English)
Cheryl Barker *sop* Katerina **Jane Henschel** *mez* Marfa Kabanova **Peter Hoare** *ten* Tichon Kabanov **Gwynne Howell** *bass* Dikoi **Robert Brubaker** *ten* Boris Grigoryevich **Victoria Simmonds** *mez* Varvara **Peter Wedd** *ten* Vanya Kudryash **Kathleen Wilkinson** *mez* Glasha **Owen Webb** *bar* Kuligin **Chorus and Orchestra of the Welsh National Opera / Carlo Rizzi**
Chandos Opera in English ② CHAN3145
(92' · DDD · S/N/T)　　　　Ⓜ❷➔

This is the fifth Janáček opera in Chandos's Opera in English series, and with vivid, well separated sound, balancing the voices in front of the orchestra, the first impression is how clear the words are from the singers of the Welsh National Opera production on which the recording is based.

Carlo Rizzi, who conducted the live performances for WNO, is a persuasive Janáček interpreter. It is fascinating to compare this version with Mackerras's Decca recording with the Vienna Philharmonic and an excellent, mainly Czech cast, Elisabeth Söderström taking the title-role. If that recording is marginally richer and weightier than the new Chandos, the strings of WNO play with comparable

refinement. Rizzi's interpretation in all three acts is a degree more urgent, with speeds consistently faster, no doubt reflecting his experience of conducting it live.

As in the English *Makropulos Affair*, the principal singer is Cheryl Barker, fresh, clear and powerful, more girlish-sounding than Söderström. Jane Henschel is outstanding as Marfa Kabanova, the rich widow who persecutes her daughter-in-law, wonderfully rich and firm throughout her range. The three tenor roles are exceptionally well taken, even if the contrasts between Robert Brubaker as Boris, Peter Wedd as Kudryash and Peter Hoare as Tichon, husband of Katya and son of Marfa, are not ideally marked. Gwynne Howell as the merchant Dikoi, uncle of Boris, is also excellent.

The old Norman Tucker translation is used with some minor amendments by Rodney Blumer, *nom de plume* of critic Rodney Milnes, with words admirably clear throughout, adding to the dramatic impact of the piece. Another outstanding issue in the Opera in English series.

Kát'á Kabanová
Nancy Gustafson *sop* Kát'á Kabanová **Barry McCauley** *ten* Boris **Felicity Palmer** *mez* Kabanicha **Donald Adams** *bass* Dikoj **Ryland Davies** *ten* Tichon **John Graham-Hall** *ten* Kudrjáš **Louise Winter** *mez* Varvara **Robert Poulton** *bar* Kuligin **Christine Bunning** *mez* Glaša **Linda Ormiston** *mez* Fekluša **Rachael Hallawell** *mez* Woman **Christopher Ventris** *ten* Bystander **Festival Chorus and Orchestra / Sir Andrew Davis**
Stage director **Nikolaus Lehnhoff**
Video director **Derek Bailey**
ArtHaus Musik ② 100 158 (99' · Regions 2 & 5)
Recorded live in 1988　　　　　　　　Ⓕ

This transfer to DVD of a 1988 Virgin VHS houses an entirely recommendable staging by Lehnhoff for Glyndebourne. He directs his excellent cast with an astonishing ability to delineate their inner feelings, receiving the most positive response from Nancy Gustafson in the title-role. She presents, from her initial entry, an overwrought, highly impressionable girl frustrated beyond endurance by the casual attentions of her husband Tichon, and longing for the erotic charge offered by the attractive Boris. When she finally capitulates to his advances, she mirrors the sense of release tinged with guilt evinced in the music. Her singing is firm, soaring, vibrant. Palmer is the very picture of buttoned-up severity as Kabanicha. Her command over Kát'á and Tichon is terrible to behold. Davies suggests Tichon's lack of backbone. McCauley's Boris conveys the man's ability to infatuate the repressed Kát'á. His tenor is keen, though under strain in the upper register. Andrew Davis brings out all the passion and anguish in the wonderful score. Tobias Hoheisel's sets derive from Russian art of the period of the story's genesis.

John Jenkins English 1592-1678

A lutenist and lyra viol player, Jenkins held the post of court theorbo player in 1660. He performed at various aristocratic houses in East Anglia, though seems not to have held any specific post. After the Restoration he obtained a place as a musician to the Royal Court. The aged Jenkins played the lyra viol for King Charles II, who complimented him that he did 'wonders on an inconsiderable instrument'. He was a prolific composer – predominantly for the viol ands for consorts of viols – and his music displays a remarkable invention and structure. He also fused the Italian style of writing in three parts with the traditional native consort style of England.

Consort music

19 Divisions on a Ground – Division in A. 12 Fantasias in six parts – No 3; No 8; No 5. Two Fantasia-Suites in two parts fantasia-air-corant – A minor. Eight Fantasia-Suites in four parts – No 3. Two In nomines in six parts. Pavan and Galliard, 'Newarke Seidge'. Two Pavans in six parts – No 2. Galliard
Ensemble Jérôme Hantaï (François Fernandez, Simon Heyerick *vns* Jérôme Hantaï, Kaori Uemura, Catherine Arnoux, Alix Verzier *viols* Brian Feehan *lte* Maude Gratton, Pierre Hantaï *orgs*)
Naïve Astrée E8895 (60' · DDD)   Ⓕ

It's common enough to find recordings of Purcell or Byrd from continental ensembles, but to have a distinguished group such as this playing a more insular figure like John Jenkins comes as something of a pleasant surprise. English composers of his generation have something very distinctive to offer, even though they may not score as highly as some of their continental contemporaries in terms of historical eminence.

Jenkins's idiom isn't as angular as that of his contemporary William Lawes, though he can trade in 'those sourest sharps and uncouth flats' along with the best of them, and match Lawes's energy (as in the *Newark Siege*, one of the gems of this collection). The generous tone of Hantaï's ensemble (in which the continuo is an audibly well-nourished presence) lends the gentler pieces a warm glow. And when required, they certainly can play their socks off: the *Newark Siege* sees them switch from swashbuckling truculence to more melancholy repose at the end with barely a hint of changing gear.

This is chamber-music, and chamber music-making, of real distinction.

12 Fantasias in six parts. Two In nomines in six parts. Two Pavans in six parts
Phantasm (Wendy Gillespie, Jonathan Manson, Markku Luolajan-Mikkola *viols*) with **Emilia Benjamin, Mikko Perkola** *viols* / **Laurence Dreyfus** *viol*
Avie AV2099 (66' · DDD)   Ⓕ▶

His discography may not be extensive, perhaps, but in terms of quality John Jenkins has been remarkably well served on disc. His music makes enough demands on players to be more than a match for all but the most intrepid consorts. On that count Phantasm have few worries, though as with the previous recordings, there is the odd moment to remind one that these superlative musicians, too, may find themselves taxed (here, it is especially the top Cs on the treble viol). Never mind; the real interest in this recording lies in the different approach Phantasm bring to this music. The slightly languid, Carolinian reserve one so associates with the repertory is replaced by a more incisive, top-down approach, with sharper attacks and more forthright articulation.

This brings the viol consort nearer to the sound and feel of the string quartet than it has ever been on disc. Whether that reflects what a viol consort is 'about' is a moot point, but to hear music of this refinement and subtlety in a new light is exciting. Of the three available anthologies, Phantasm's is most focused on the six-part consorts and they do their formidable reputation no harm here; if they coax listeners into snapping up more of his music, they will have done right by Jenkins, too.

17 Fantasias in five parts.
Pavans – in G; in G minor; in F
Phantasm (Laurence Dreyfus, Wendy Gillespie, Jonathan Manson, Markku Luolajan-Mikkola *viols*) with **Mikko Perkola** *viol*
Avie AV2120 (73' · DDD)   Ⓕ◉▶

Lawrence Dreyfus's devotion to John Jenkins's cause is little short of messianic. If his booklet-notes don't make the point eloquently enough, consider that the composer is the first to receive not one but two anthologies from Phantasm. The previous disc, devoted to his six-part consorts (see above), departed from previous Jenkins anthologies in forgoing any continuo, and this companion volume follows suit. It's hard not to share Dreyfus's enthusiasm: the playfulness and spontaneity of Jenkins's invention is infectious, and on at least one occasion (the close of Fantasy 15, in which a potentially clichéd downward sequence proliferates almost to the point of absurdity) he had me laughing aloud.

Musically, this new recording is a worthy successor to the six-part disc. Technically speaking, the ensemble is as zestful as ever, and practically flawless in execution. The only possible reservation one might have concerns the programming, which consists almost entirely of Fantasias, with only three Pavans to counterbalance them. As the durations are roughly consistent (three to four minutes for the Fantasias and around five for the Pavans), the effect is less varied than on the previous recording, which included a couple of In nomines as well. The decision to exclude continuo further limits the possibilities for variation. But the whole point of this recording is that a single disc is insufficient to do him justice. On that count, it recommends itself.

Josquin Desprez   French c1440-1521

All other composers of the late 15th century are eclipsed by Josquin. Considering how famous he was, it's strange that no one is sure when or where he was born, although we do know that during his lifetime he was always referred to by his first name, which itself is a pet name for Josse or Joseph; hence reference books always put him under 'J'.

What little is certain about his early life suggests that he may have sung in the French Royal Chapel. In 1459 he moved to Italy and joined the private choir of the Duke Galeazzo Sforza in Milan before service in the Papal Chapel between 1487 and 1494. Why this life devoted to church music? In common with many others at this time, Josquin believed that artistic gifts were a divine loan to be repaid to God in the form of loyal service.

Unlike others, he was fond of the good things in life, liked hunting, fine food and wine and, most unusually, had a sense of fun and humour. This breaks into some of his music, a combination of the formal Italian and the boisterous Flemish; a musician who, in painting terms, could produce a Raphael Madonna with the same ease as a Breughel peasant.

After 1502, Josquin's connections were with the chapels and courts of Duke Hercules I at Ferrara, Louis XII, the Archduchess Margaret of Austria and the Emperor Maximilian I – you can see how in demand he was! – ending his life as Provost (religious overseer) of Notre Dame church in Condé-sur-l'Escaut in Hainault. The epitaph on his tomb is preserved in a manuscript at Lille, though both the tomb itself and his church were destroyed during the French Revolution.

Masses

Missa L'homme armé sexti toni.
Missa L'homme armé super voces musicales
A Sei Voci / Bernard Fabre-Garrus; Maîtrise des Pays de Loire / Bertrand Lemaire
Astrée Naïve E8809 (74' · DDD · T/t)   Ⓕ**OO**

Josquin's Masses on *L'homme armé* have one of the most impressive recording pedigrees of the early Renaissance, but A Sei Voci's is probably the finest so far. There's superlative singing, a compelling, enveloping acoustic presence, and above all an interpretative logic, a sure-footedness of tempo and of phrasing that makes sense of some of Josquin's most prolix and demanding music. First comes *Sexti toni*, which is sung for the first time in the range that the sources' low clefs seem to imply. Where all the previous recordings have women on the top line (in a correspondingly higher tessitura), here it's taken by countertenors, supplemented on occasion by the children of the Maîtrise des Pays de Loire. The sunny, almost genial tone of previous recordings gives way to a quite unsuspected, darker and more interiorised but still luminous sound world.

The contrapuntal intensity of the final *Agnus Dei* is wonderful to hear, especially after the restrained

scoring of much of what precedes it. Still more impressive, perhaps, is the performance of *Super voces musicales*, Josquin's most extended work, and certainly one of his most abstract and intellectually challenging. In the past, its very abstraction bred a suspicion that here was a work easier to admire than to love. Fabre-Garrus and his singers change all that: the intellectual toughness is still there, but in addition they make clear the Mass's rhetorical logic in a way that previous recordings never quite managed. Rarely has Josquin's achievement appeared so compelling. In short, this recording is a revelation.

Missa Malheur me bat. Virgo prudentissima. Liber generationis Jesu Christi. Ave Maria, virgo serena. Baisez moy. Que vous ma dame/In pace in idipsum. Victimae paschali laudes. Comment peult avoir joye
The Clerks' Group / Edward Wickham
ASV Gaudeamus CDGAU306 (71' · DDD · T/t)   Ⓕ

The Clerks' Group once again earn our gratitude by heading straight for the top-class works that lack modern, top-class recordings. The Mass *Malheur me bat* is one of Josquin's most resourceful treatments of received material, taking all three voices of a secular piece and treating each separately, each in different ways; and in the magnificent final movement he follows an almost comical two-voice canon at the second with a broad treatment in six voices with two canons running simultaneously. As a display of contrapuntal techniques, this may well be his most stunning composition.

The Clerks' Group can seem less polished than previously. Intonation isn't always out of the top drawer. And the speeds chosen often seem perplexing, but on further listening, it seems that they're trying to tackle different musical problems; they're going for the music, and that has to be good.

This is particularly the case in the most welcome novelty here, the *Liber generationis*, Josquin's setting of the genealogy from St Matthew's gospel. How wonderful to have this and the other works here in seriously skilled performances.

Missa Pange lingua. Missa La sol fa re mi
The Tallis Scholars / Peter Phillips
Gimell CDGIM009 (62' · DDD · T/t)   Ⓕ**OOO**→

 This is absolutely superb. We must accept that Josquin is unlikely to have heard this music with two women on the top line, but they do it so well that only a fundamentalist would mark the disc down for that. It should also be said that the least successful performance on the entire disc is in the opening *Kyrie* of this Mass where there's a certain brutality in the approach; and although The Tallis Scholars make much of the 'Benedictus' and the last *Agnus Dei*, there may still be better ways of doing it. On the other hand, as just one example among many, these were the first musicians to make the 'Osanna' truly successful and understand why Josquin should have chosen to compose it that way. But they sing even better in the Mass *La sol fa re mi*. Again and again in the singing one has the feeling that Josquin's lines are projected with an understanding and clarity that have rarely been heard before. The *La sol fa re mi* of the title denotes (among other things) the melodic passage which appears over 200 times in the course of the work with its intervals unchanged – which may not seem a recipe for the kind of music one would want to hear. But Josquin treats his material with such astonishing sophistication that you're rarely aware of the melodic fragment as such; and Phillips is scrupulously careful never to emphasise the melody except in places – such as the end of the second 'Osanna' – where it's clearly intended to work as an ostinato. This performance shows that the *La sol fa re mi* belongs with the greatest works of its era.

Missa D'ung aultre amer. Adieu mes amours. Ave Maria, virgo serena. Cela sans plus. De tous biens playne. Fortuna d'un gran tempo. Mille regretz. Planxit autem David. Tu solus qui facis mirabilia. La Bernardina. Qui belles amours. Sanctus 'D'ung aultre amer'. Tu lumen, tu splendor Patris. Victimae paschali laudes/D'ung aultre amer. Ile fantazies de Joskin
Claire Wilkinson sop **Andrew Lawrence-King** hp
Alamire / David Skinner
Obsidian CD701 (68' · DDD)　　　Ⓕ**OO**

This is a most ingeniously devised Josquin recital. Laying emphasis on works of his early maturity, it records the composer's apparent obsession with Ockeghem's rondeau *D'ung aultre amer*. Josquin reworked it several times, including a Mass that generated several minor 'spin-offs', which are also presented here. The Mass is reckoned to be one of his earliest. It is certainly his shortest, and arguably the least well-known (and some scholars in fact dispute Josquin's authorship). But it has an immediate appeal that links it (in attitude, at least) to the songs that make up the rest of the disc. These are engagingly sung by Claire Wilkinson, accompanied on the harp by Andrew Lawrence-King, who gets a few solo spots of his own. The combination of harp and voice works very well and offers a new way of hearing some old favourites: that said, the sound recording seems to make the harp a touch louder than it might be.

The recital is ingenious because alongside this relatively neglected Mass it seamlessly works in a few sacred works that count among Josquin's most popular: the ubiquitous *Ave Maria, virgo serena*, and above all *Planxit autem David*, which receives a particularly moving account. This is the first recording by Alamire, a new ensemble boasting familiar English singers under the guidance of David Skinner. Their approach is direct and unaffected, and to judge by the results they appear to have enjoyed these recording sessions.

Missa Gaudeamus. Recordare virgo Mater.
Regina caeli. Missa Ave maris stella.
Virgo salutiferi/Ave Maria
A Sei Voci; Maîtrise des Pays de Loire / Bernard Fabre-Garrus bass
Auvidis Astrée E8612 (68' · DDD · T/t)　　　Ⓕ

Bernard Fabre-Garrus has long been experimenting with different ways of performing renaissance polyphony. It seems that each of his recordings offers a new sound; and in this particular case his novelty is to use the children of the Maîtrise des Pays de Loire – both boys and girls – to sing the top line of Josquin's Mass *Gaudeamus*. This is one of Josquin's most rhythmically intricate works, so there's a major challenge here; just occasionally the rhythms slip a little. But to compensate for that there's a stirring energy to their singing; and part of the elegance of Fabre-Garrus performances has always been in his fluid, linear approach to polyphony, which works splendidly here. Moreover, with just six singers on the three lower lines, he always manages to produce a beautifully clear and balanced texture. This is a very successful and exciting performance of one of Josquin's most stunning masterpieces. His astonishingly varied treatment of the *Gaudeamus* melody ranges from straight imitation through unusually long-held tenor notes (that have a stunning effect on the work's harmonic rhythm), via bravura exercises in ostinato, to the heart-stopping modulations of the final *Agnus Dei*.

The plainchants are sung with an unusual lucidity and energy. The motets include the rarely heard *Recordare virgo Mater*, which gives a special opportunity for the children to sing in three parts; and they end with a superlatively eloquent and clear performance of one of Josquin's most famous five-voice motets, *Virgo salutiferi*.

Songs and Instrumental Music

'Master of Musicians – Songs and instrumental music by Josquin des Prez, and his pupils and contemporaries'
Includes **Josquin** Adieu mes amours[b]. Bergerotte savoysienne[c]. Comment peult avoir joye. De tous biens pleine – à 3; à 4. Dido – Fama malum à 4[abcd]; Dulces exuviae à 4. El grillo[abcd]. Faulte d'argent[ab]. Je me complains[bc]. Mille regretz[abcd]. Pauper sum ego[d]. Petite camusette[ab]. Pleine de dueil[bc]. Se congié prens[ab] – Recordans de mia segnora; à 6. Si j'avoys Marion. Si j'ay perdu mon amy – à 3; à 4. Le villain. Also includes works by **Agricola, Alonso, Anon, Févin, Gerle, Isaac, Japart, Orto, Le Roy** and **Spinacino**
[a]**Belinda Sykes** contr [b]**John Potter** ten [c]**Jennie Cassidy** mez [d]**Robert Evans** bar **London Musica Antiqua** (John Bryan rec/crumhn/viol Alison Crum rec/crumhn/viol/hp Jacob Heringman viol/lte/gtr Roy Marks crumhn/viol Rebecca Miles rec) /
Philip Thorby
Signum SIGCD025 (68' · DDD · T/t)　　　Ⓕ**O➡**

The secular music of Josquin has not always been very successful in recordings. Many of the pieces are very short – some can seem like exercises for something else, and others make little sense unless they're understood in the wider context of other settings based on the same material. The last problem is solved here by the inclusion of a lot of the related settings alongside those of Josquin. And the recording solves the first problem by unapologetically offering no fewer than 37 tracks, with the pieces grouped together so they flow cleanly from one to the next; it also resists some of the more outgoing pieces, so that the whole disc occupies a consistent sound world.

That sound world is mostly a gentle one, with the lines flowing quite fast in an easy playing style that can occasionally lose a few details but compensates with clarity of design. The musicians also cultivate a sound that favours vivacity and flair over constant attention to all the details of intonation; but that, too, is good, because everything is lively and full of variety. The instruments used range from viols and lutes to an ensemble of recorders and even one of crumhorns (played with an admirable restraint). And the singers offer all the variety of tone-colour one might expect from a group spearheaded by John Potter.

Many pieces here have never been recorded before; and the disc has the twin benefits of being remarkably accessible for easy listening as well as providing a marvellous basis for closer understanding. Most enjoyable.

André Jolivet French 1905-1974

Profoundly impressed at an early age by the music of Debussy, Dukas and Ravel, Jolivet determined on a musical career. He studied with Paul Le Flem who introduced him to Edgard Varèse, who agreed to take him on as a student. A later encounter with Messiaen led to the foundation of 'La Spirale', an avant-garde chamber music society. From 1945 to 1959 Jolivet was musical director of the Comédie Française, writing 14 scores for plays performed there; he later taught composition at the Paris Conservatoire.

Violin Concerto

Jolivet Violin Concerto **Chausson** Poème
Isabelle Faust vn **Deutsches Symphony
Orchestra, Berlin / Marko Letonja**
Harmonia Mundi HMC90 1925 (48' · DDD)   Ⓕ

A new issue of Jolivet's Violin Concerto (1972), the 12th and last of his *concertante* works and held by some to be his musical testament, is long overdue so this splendid account from Isabelle Faust is cause for real celebration.

The Concerto is not immediately easy listening, being a tough late example of Jolivet's primitivist idiom. While outwardly conforming to conventional classical design, internally each movement is a freewheeling, evolving structure. The opening *Appassionato* retains a few traces of sonata form and is volatile and lyrical by turns.

Its ethereal coda is a fine example of the acuity of Jolivet's inner ear as well as Faust's feather-light touch, much in evidence throughout the complex, central *Largo*. Here the steel in Faust's playing is much in evidence in its faster, eruptive episodes. The finale is the most straightforward in manner, centred on the virtuoso cadenza.

It is fascinating to return to Chausson's intensely romantic *Poème* (1894) – with which the disc starts – after Jolivet's richly coloured, piled-up textures. Although stylistically worlds apart, both works share a heady, exotic expression. Faust is equally convincing in both, ably supported by the Deutsches Symphony Orchestra conducted by Marko Letonja and bright, close sound. The playing-time is not generous but the pairing is very effective as it stands and in performances like these self-recommending.

Niccolò Jommelli Italian 1714-1774

Born and educated in Naples, Jommelli established a major reputation as an opera composer and an opera theorist. He lived and worked in Rome and Venice before, in 1753, taking the post of Kapellmeister to the Duke Karl-Eugen at Württemberg, near Stuttgart. It was here, in 1763, that he met the young Mozart who was passing through the city with his father. He wrote over 60 operas, many to libretti by Metastasio.

Armida abbandonata

Armida abbandonata
Ewa Malas-Godlewska sop Armida **Claire Brua** mez
Rinaldo **Gilles Ragon** ten Tancredi **Véronique Gens**
sop Erminia **Laura Polverelli** mez Rambaldo **Patricia
Petibon** sop Ubaldo **Cécile Perrin** sop Dano
Les Talens Lyriques / Christophe Rousset
Ambroisie ③ AMB9983 (3h 1' · DDD · T/t)   ⒻⓄⓄ

The first performance of *Armida abbandonata* was attended by the 14-year-old Mozart, who wrote to his sister that it was 'beautiful, but too serious and old-fashioned for the theatre'. That tells us something about the taste of the Neapolitan audience, which didn't care for the richness and subtlety of the music. And the music is superb.

Jommelli was born in 1714 and, like Gluck, an exact contemporary, he moved away from the conventions of Metastasian *opera seria* to a more flexible style that included choruses and ballets in accordance with the French taste of his ducal employer at the Württemberg court. His accompanied recitatives are particularly fine. One example comes in Act 2: the recitative begins with a descending chromatic phrase in the second violins and includes a weeping figure that is incorporated into the following aria.

Ewa Malas-Godlewska, so touching there, rages impressively in 'Odo, furor, dispetto' ('Hatred, fury, spite'): its *staccato* scales anticipate

Elettra's outburst in *Idomeneo*. That Mozart owed a debt to Jommelli is also suggested by a florid metaphor aria for Tancredi that looks ahead to Idomeneo's 'Fuor del mar'; and although Erminia is no servant, her second aria might well put the listener in mind of Despina in *Così fan tutte*. Gilles Ragon and Véronique Gens are but two in a matchless cast from the rest of which there is space to single out only the gloriously rich-toned Laura Polverelli. Christophe Rousset conducts his fine musicians in a gripping, well-paced performance. A wonderful recording.

Dmitry Kabalevsky

Russian/USSR 1904-1987

No one would claim that Kabalevsky was one of the 20th century's greatest composers but there is a handful of works which are irresistible despite their often derivative nature. Like Khachaturian, a close contemporary and fellow student of Myaskovsky at the Moscow Conservatoire, his music is largely inspired by folk music. He towed the party line more dutifully than most, rising to become a great musical power in the land – director of music for Soviet Radio and the Institute of Arts History – and becoming the regime's leading musical ambassador. One element pervades all of his music – optimism, a rare quality in much recent music and one not to be despised when it's served up with such panache and wit, and in expertly crafted scores. His music for children is especially notable.

Cello Concerto No 2

Kabalevsky Cello Concerto No 2 in G, Op 77
Khachaturian Cello Concerto **Rachmaninov**
(trans Rose) Vocalise, Op 34 No 14
Mats Lidström vc **Gothenburg Symphony Orchestra / Vladimir Ashkenazy** pf
BIS CD719 (65' · DDD) Recorded live 1995   ⒻⒷ►

This coupling offers performances of two works which, if not masterpieces, are still sufficiently rewarding to be in the regular concert repertory. Ashkenazy creates an evocative opening atmosphere for the first movement of the Kabalevsky, when after mysterious string *pizzicatos* the soloist steals in with a gentle, singing tone. The soliloquy continues, for the work's unusual structure, with its three unbroken sections linked by cadenzas, invites an improvisational approach well understood by Mats Lidström.

The Khachaturian Concerto opens with a flamboyantly coloured orchestral declamation before the cello sails off with vigorous animation. This is followed by a sinuous Armenian theme from the wind which the cello takes up ruminatively, with well-judged *espressivo*. Yet it's the energetic main theme that dominates and the soloist is carried along on its impetus, while ardently recalling the secondary material, finally leading to an exciting sequential coda. The

finale offers the busy, rumbustious Khachaturian we know so well from the Violin Concerto. This composer's major works (with the exception of the Violin Concerto) can seem rather inflated, but here the combined concentration of Lidström and Ashkenazy minimises this impression. As an encore we're given a beautiful, restrained account of Rachmaninov's *Vocalise*. The recording is of high quality and well balanced, but a shade over-resonant, though the ear adjusts.

Piano Concertos

Piano Concertos – No 1; No 4, 'Prague'.
Symphony No 2
Kathryn Stott pf
BBC Philharmonic Orchestra / Neeme Järvi
Chandos CHAN10384 (68' · DDD)   ⒻⒷ►

As the work of a 24-year-old seeking to make his mark, Kabalevsky's First Piano Concerto is unsurprisingly replete with references to the Russian concerto tradition. Yet just as one notes the seemingly blatant echoes of Rachmaninov's *Paganini* Rhapsody in the slow movement, one realises that the Rhapsody post-dates the Concerto by six years: evidently Rachmaninov was doing the echoing. Moreover, along with the stylistic affinities comes a less predictable tone of wistful introspection and an urge for symphonic consistency, qualities readily attributable to the influence of Kabalevsky's teacher, Myaskovsky. All this is superbly delineated by Kathryn Stott, completing her outstanding survey of the four Kabalevsky piano concertos with these superbly considered accounts.

Kabalevsky's Second Symphony is again clearly indebted to Myaskovsky. Its relatively conventional layout is capped by a *Scherzo* that mutates rather neatly into a finale and puts the earnestness of the first two movements firmly behind it. Järvi knocks several minutes off the normal timing of the second and third movements by virtue of a robust, no-nonsense approach.

Stott and Järvi steer the Fourth Concerto home in just under 12 minutes, mainly by taking a less drawn-out approach to the slow movement than in the composer's own recording. In most respects they surpass that unsubtle if disciplined version. Beautifully recorded and executed, the new Chandos disc is self-recommending for collectors of Soviet music and/or 20th-century piano concertos.

Mauricio Kagel

German 1931-2008

Composer, film maker and playwright of Argentine birth, Kagel is increasingly regarded as among the most important of late 20th-century European composers, his elaborate imagination, bizarre humour and ability to play with almost any idea or system has brought powerful and unexpected drama to the stage and concert hall.

'The Mauricio Kagel Edition'
Pandorasbox, bandoneonpiece. Tango Alemán.
Bestiarium: Music for Bird Calls. (Hörspiel) Ein Aufnahmezustand
Mauricio Kagel band/voc Alejandro Barletta band
Jorge Risi vn **Carlos Roqué Alsina** pf **Beth Griffith,**
Mesías Maiguashca whistles **Peter Brötzmann**
reeds/voc **Heinz-Georg Thor** bass **Michael Vetter**
rec/voc **Alfred Feussner** voc **Deborah Kagel** voc
William Pearson voc **Christoph Caskel** perc/voc
Film: 'Ludwig van'
Winter & Winter ③ (2 CDs + 1 **DVD**) 910 128-2
(3h 15' · ADD)   Ⓕ❍

Beethoven shows up at Bonn Station in 1970 to survey how the culture industry is marking his bicentenary. That delicious conceit is the basis for *Ludwig van*, Mauricio Kagel's miraculous film now available for the first time on DVD. Beethoven himself holds the wobbly camera during the first section of the film, and we only ever get to see his buckled shoes as he minces through the streets.

There are road works outside the Beethovenhaus as Our Hero visits his erstwhile lodgings and has to hotfoot it over barriers to reach his front door, where he's met by a jobsworth doorman who insists he buy a ticket. Kagel is the composer who made Bach the narrator of his own story in the *St Bach Passion* and he's relishing this historical gibberish. Incongruous historical overlays provoke high comedy while creating weird Philip K Dickian reality-busting narratives. But most importantly this technique licenses Kagel to unravel the trajectory of evolving traditions; and the slapstick over, he gets dark.

Inside the house, Beethoven is confronted by rotting busts of his own form everywhere while sheet music tumbles out of a cavernous cupboard – in his bicentenary year is his music being celebrated or exploited? Ludwig van's most famous scene is next as the camera zooms into Beethoven's music room where every surface is pasted with fragments of his scores. Until now Kagel's music has consisted of jokey arrangements of LvB lollipops for a wheezing wind ensemble, but now musicians follow the direction of the camera as it pans around these haphazardly arranged scores. Musical syntax breaks down and familiar phrases are mulched into a chaotic soundscape that curiously re-energises them as empiric sources of sound.

Another narrative jump and Kagel is featured in an earnest television show discussing Beethoven; one guest puts the boot into Karajan (a particular hate figure for the post-Darmstadt avant-garde) for conducting the orchestra rather than the score. Kagel looks on with gleeful mischief beaming from both eyes.

Alongside the DVD are two CDs of remastered near-contemporary material – the first documents Kagel's own performances of three intriguing works climaxing in *Bestiarium: Music*

for *Bird Calls*, while the second is his seminal, hyperactive radio piece *(Hörspeil) Ein Aufnahmezustand*. Of course, it's a paradox worthy of Kagel himself that this set was released to celebrate his own 75th birthday – geddit?

Imre Kálmán   Hungarian 1882-1953

Kálmán studied, alongside fellow student Bartók and Kodály with Hans Koessler at the Budapest Academy. The success of his first operetta, The Gay Hussars (1908), led him to settle in Vienna, where he produced more such works in Viennese-Hungarian style (Die Csárdásfürstin, 1915; Gräfin Mariza, 1924), and became, with Lehár, one of the leading composers of the so-called 'Silver Age' of Viennese operetta. In 1939 he moved to Paris, and from there in 1940 to the USA.

Die Csárdásfürstin

The Gypsy Princess
Yvonne Kenny sop Sylva Varescu **Michael Roider** ten Edwin Ronald **Mojca Erdmann** sop Countess Stasi **Marko Kathol** ten Count Boni **Karl-Michael Ebner** ten Feri von Kerekes, Notary **Hellmuth Klumpp** spkr Rohnsdorff **Heinz Holecek** bar Prince **Yvonne Kálmán** spkr Princess
Plus orchestral excerpts from Der Zigeunerprimás, Die Faschingsfee, Das Hollandweibchen and Der Teufelsreiter
Slovak Philharmonic Chorus; Slovak Radio Symphony Orchestra / Richard Bonynge
Naxos ② 6 110075-76 (114' · DDD · S/N)   Ⓢ❍❍▷

The English title of Kálmán's most celebrated operetta is a misnomer. The heroine is a princess not of gypsies but (as the German title, *Die Csárdásfürstin*, indicates) of the *csárdás*; she's a Budapest cabaret-singer in love with a young aristocrat. Its score shows Kálmán at his most fluent, with a succession of gloriously tuneful hit numbers that mix spicy Hungarian rhythms with the more graceful strains of the Viennese waltz. Individual numbers have often been committed to disc, but complete recordings have been much less frequent. Yet to appreciate the overall structure of Kálmán's operetta scores you really need to hear his elaborately constructed act finales, in which musical reprises are interspersed with passages of dialogue and melodrama.

Apart from sensibly reducing the opening orchestral flourishes from three to one, Bonynge typically gives us total fidelity to what Kálmán actually wrote. He brings out to the full Kálmán's highly charged rhythms, every detail of the exotic orchestration, and the contrasts of mood between the fiery big numbers and the moments of melancholy and sadness in the Acts 1 and 2 finales. Among a wholly admirable cast, Yvonne Kenny provides the vocal strength, fire and beauty required by the title role. A wonderful bargain.

Giya Kancheli
Georgian b1935

Kancheli studied at the Tbilisi Conservatory (1958-63), where he worked for two decades. Since 1991 he has lived in Western Europe: first in Berlin, and since 1995 in Antwerp, where he is composer-in-residence for the Royal Flemish Philharmonic. He is recognised as one of the most radical thinkers in Georgian music. His works, using folk music, include seven symphonies, jazz pieces and musicals.

Liturgy for Viola and Orchestra

Liturgy for Viola and Orchestra, 'Mourned by the Wind'. Bright Sorrow
Ian Ford, Oliver Hayes *trebs* **France Springuel** *vc*
Cantate Domino Chorus; I Fiamminghi /
Rudolf Werthen
Telarc CD80455 (72' · DDD)　　　　Ⓕ**O**

Givi Ordzhonikidze, the editor of a well-known book on Shostakovich, was one of Kancheli's closest friends and staunchest supporters, and it was the sense of loss after his death in 1984 that prompted the composition of the heart-rendingly beautiful *Liturgy* (subtitled *Mourned by the Wind*). The other inspiration was Yuri Bashmet, for this four-movement lament was originally a Viola Concerto. It goes superbly on the cello too, thanks to France Springuel's passionate advocacy, and in this form it inevitably invites comparisons with Tavener's *The Protecting Veil*.

A common feature of these two pieces is that they can seem almost unbearably moving if they catch you in the right mood and yet almost unbearably protracted if they don't. Yet for all the obvious gestures of lamentation and assuaging, *Liturgy* isn't a tear-jerking piece. In fact the texture is for the most part quite transparent, and Kancheli constantly steers away from potentially manipulative clichés on to stonier paths.

The Flemish orchestra gives a wonderfully controlled performance and Telarc's recording quality is superb. *Bright Sorrow* again draws from the bottomless well of lamentation which is the ex-USSR composer's special curse and privilege. It bears the dedication, 'To children, the victims of war', hence the choice of two boy soloists, symbolising the innocent victims of the last world war addressing themselves to the present-day generation. The soloists sing only slow, fragmented lines, conveying the fragility of innocence. The second half of the work seems to be gaining strength and optimism, but these are soon obliterated, leaving behind only a heart-broken crippled waltz.

Highly recommended, whether or not you already have the Kancheli 'bug'.

Styx

Kancheli Styx[a] **Tavener** The Myrrh-Bearer[b]
[ab]**Maxim Rysanov** *va* [b]**Rihards Zalupe** *perc*

[a]**'Kamer…' Choir;** [b]**Latvia State Choir;**
[a]**Liepaja Symphony Orchestra / Maris Sirmais**
Onyx Classics ONYX4023 (78' · DDD)　Ⓕ**O**

Maxim Rysanov's viola has an inward, lamenting quality. And it feels as though the chorus and orchestra (from Latvia's third city) are living and breathing every note. Crucially, the acoustic of Riga's Dome Cathedral has a rich resonance, wonderfully captured. The sound stage is as wide and deep as the music demands. Expressive extremes register as more abrupt, more startling and more challenging – harder-edged in their ecstasy. The music first transfixes, then scalds, and when consolation intervenes it feels multi-faceted and somehow palpably wise. The texts of *Styx* consist of a succession of names and words, all of profound and intimate significance to the composer. This performance makes one really feel that significance.

The extraordinary qualities of Latvian choral singing – fullness of tone, *legato* and intense stillness – have been often extolled. In *The Myrrh-Bearer* there is the added advantage of the kind of *basso profundo* richness that one would imagine Tavener can only rarely have found in the UK. Whether his piece is perhaps a little too reliant on those subterranean tones, and whether the pairing with Kancheli reveals a slight thinness of invention, are suspicions that may either firm or fade with further acquaintance. In the meantime, all that seems important is to surrender to the urgency and fervour of another extraordinary performance.

In short, here is a disc to blow the mind of anyone already in tune with these composers, and possibly one that may even lead a few sceptics towards a Damascene conversion.

…à la Duduki

…à la Duduki. Trauerfarbenes Land
Vienna Radio Symphony Orchestra /
Dennis Russell Davies
ECM New Series 457 850-2 (57' · DDD)　Ⓕ**O**

…à la Duduki (a 'duduki' is a Georgian folk reed instrument) should prove the ideal introduction to Kancheli's current style. And while a momentary encounter might suggest familiar territories revisited (vast terrains sparsely but dramatically populated), the musical material is more immediately striking, the scoring more texturally variegated, and the time sequences – even the rhetorical uses of silence – quite different from those in Kancheli's other recent work. Furthermore, echoes of modern jazz frequently fall within earshot. *Trauerfarbenes Land* ('Country the Colour of Mourning') employs a large orchestra and is different again, being nearly twice as long as *…à la Duduki* and darker in tone.

The opening has solo piano and *fortissimo* trombones hammer what sounds like a recollection of Carl Ruggles before six significant quavers (which turn up again later, in different hues and keys) mark a dramatic dynamic contrast.

Time and again Kancheli's penchant for 'cliff-hanger' climaxes bring us to the edge of a towering aural precipice. This is the music of personal displacement: desolate, spacious, occasionally cryptic, and with sudden pangs of sweetened nostalgia that flutter across the canvas like torn diary jottings tossed by the wind. Dennis Russell Davies and producer Manfred Eicher conjure between them a precision-tooled sound picture where every grade of nuance is meticulously reported. Performance standards are unusually high throughout, so much so that it's hard to imagine either work being better played. An exceptional release of some extraordinarily powerful music.

Lament

Lament (Music of mourning in memory of Luigi Nono)
Maacha Deubner sop **Gidon Kremer** vn
Tbilisi Symphony Orchestra / Jansug Kakhidze
ECM New Series 465 138-2 (42' · DDD · T/t)   Ⓕ

Music of lamentation has long been Kancheli's preoccupation, and this *Lament*, inscribed to the memory of Luigi Nono, has all the familiar Kanchelian moods: damaged soulfulness, peremptory outbursts and transfigured sadness, invoked aphoristically yet stretched to a hypnotic unbroken 42-minute span. Initial dots of sound on the solo violin grow into painfully sweet bursts of melody, suggesting a context only the composer himself knows and which the listener has to grope towards. Meanwhile a non-vibrato singer intones prayerful fragments. Kremer's violin becomes an eloquent voice; Maacha Deubner's soprano becomes a celestial instrument. Just as you sense the need for new ideas, the orchestra's sculpted orchestral chords gain a pulverising force, and before long all hell breaks loose. The slight residual rawness of the Tbilisi brass is a treasurable authentic feature here, and the entire score is conducted faithfully by the man who knows Kancheli's music better than any musician alive. Eventually the text of Hans Sahl's poem, *Strophen*, reveals the underlying substance. The recording is first-rate.

Nikolai Kapustin   Russian b1937

Kapustin, born in the Ukraine, graduated from the Moscow Conservatoire in 1961 and for some years made a living as a jazz pianist and arranger. His music is nearly all instrumental or orchestral, and is characterised by its use of jazz and rock idioms.

Piano Sonata No 6

Suite in the Old Style, Op 28. Eight Concert Etudes, Op 40. Variations, Op 41. Bagatelle, Op 59 No 9. Piano Sonata No 6, Op 62. Five Etudes in Different Intervals, Op 68. Sonatina, Op 100

Marc-André Hamelin pf
Hyperion CDA67433 (78' · DDD)   ⒻⓄ

'Crossover' is an old rather than recent tradition, whether the jazz elements are peripheral as in Ravel or central as in Kapustin. Jed Distler, writing for Hamelin's disc in a style as witty and engaging as the music itself, speaks of a Chick Corea-based language that lifts a Romantic virtuoso tradition into a beguiling quasi-improvisational style and holds it up to a fun-house mirror. Such high-pitched claims arguably fail to account for too many family likenesses (be they variations, studies or sonatas) or a style that too often suggests composition as a facile rather than arduous process (like Saint-Saëns, Kapustin 'produces music as an apple-tree produces apples'). None the less, there are many scintillating surprises. The Variations' gawky theme blossoms into the sort of elaboration that would have made Bill Evans envious, while the second of the Op 40 Etudes ends with a passing memory of Liszt's *Au bord d'une source*, reminding you of Kapustin's work as a virtuoso pianist with Alexander Goldenweiser. No 6, *Pastoral*, a dream encore, sends a tiny cell-like motif spinning through a variety of guises. The Bagatelle's perky tune would not be out of place 'in a Brazilian Chorino' (Distler) and everything on this remarkable disc is played with a nonchalant aplomb and magical dexterity hard to imagine from any other pianist. Hamelin is in his element, and he's been immaculately recorded.

Mieczysław Karłowicz
Polish 1876-1909

Karłowicz trained as a violinist, and studied in Warsaw and Berlin with Heinrich Urban. From 1906 to 1907 he studied conducting with Arthur Nikisch. He was active in the Warsaw Music Society and a strong supporter of the 'Young Poland' artistic movement. Among his works are symphonic poems using thematic transformation and reflecting pantheism, sorrow and Wagnerian ideas of love and death, including Eternal Songs (1908) and Stanisław i Anna Oświecimowie (1912). Much of his small output was lost during the Second World War.

Orchestral works

Eternal Songs, Op 10. Lithuanian Rhapsody, Op 11. Stanisław and Anna of Oświecim, Op 12
BBC Philharmonic Orchestra / Yan Pascal Tortelier
Chandos CHAN9986 (67' · DDD)   ⒻⓄⓄⓄ�627

What a fine composer Mieczysław Karłowicz might have become, had he not died at the age of 32 in an avalanche in the Tatra mountains. He had already produced a clutch of symphonic poems in a post-Wagnerian style, strongly pantheistic in outlook and, in the case of *Stanisław and Anna of*

Oświecim, with a dash of illicit love thrown in. These luxuriant works set him broadly beside such near-contemporaries as Rachmaninov, Zemlinsky or Suk, and there are even signs in the 'Song of Eternal Being' (third and last of the *Eternal Songs*) of an individuality that might one day have become as powerful as Janáček's. This is, for the most part, sultrily ecstatic music, that hangs fragrantly or ominously in the air and seems to be constantly about to break through to some visionary realm. Even the relatively jaunty *Lithuanian Rhapsody* eventually turns wistful in a rather moving way.

If you've a taste for lush late-Romanticism but haven't yet encountered Karłowicz, you've a treat in store, not least because these are fine performances. His music has never been more than fleetingly represented in the catalogue. Classy playing by the BBC Philharmonic and Yan Pascal Tortelier and the recording by Chandos is correspondingly rich.

Symphony in E minor, 'Rebirth', Op 7. Serenade in C, Op 2. Bianca da Molena, Op 6
BBC Philharmonic Orchestra / Gianandrea Noseda
Chandos CHAN10171 (73' · DDD)　　　Ⓕ**O**▷

This second BBC Philharmonic Karłowicz disc complements the first with three earlier works. Composed in the first two years of the 20th century, Karłowicz's 40-minute *Rebirth* Symphony is very much of its time – not just in its ambitious programmatic span from existential despair to world-saving apotheosis, but in its opulent post-Tchaikovskian idiom. Though he clearly overreached himself, this is a need-to-know piece for anyone interested in the aspirational *Zeitgeist* prevalent before the First World War. Most immediately appealing, perhaps, is the slow movement, which features a tender song-like theme that British listeners may connect with the hymn 'My song is love unknown'.

The symphonic prologue *Bianca da Molena* is extracted from music for a now forgotten Polish play; not surprisingly it contains many echoes of Wagner. The Serenade for String Orchestra is an apprentice piece with a certain charm, notably in the vaguely Parsifalian slow movement, which helps to compensate for the disappointment of the cursory finale. The BBC Philharmonic's playing and Chandos's recording uphold their customary high standards.

Additional recommendation

Episode at a Masquerade. Returning Waves.
The Sorrowful Tale
BBC PO / Noseda
Chandos CHAN10298 (60' · DDD)　　　Ⓕ▷
This instalment is something of a mopping-up exercise, the best of Karłowicz's output being found on the first of the BBC Philharmonic's discs (see above). Noseda has a sure instinct for the music's indulgent textures and

melodramatic effusiveness, and orchestral playing and recording are both of the highest class. Self-recommending, then, to explorers of late-Romantic byways.

Reinhard Keiser　　German 1674-1739

Keiser was a prolific composer of operas (completing over 100). In 1696-97 he was Kapellmeister at Hamburg, and during 1700-1701 also Kapellmeister to the Schwerin court. As joint director of the Hamburg Theater-am-Gänsemarkt, 1702-07, he presented 17 of his own operas. Der Carneval von Venedig, which included local dialect, was especially successful. He remained active in Hamburg until 1718, after which he worked in Stuttgart and Copenhagen, and for the remainder of his live moved between Hamburg and Copenhagen where he held the post of Master of the Danish Royal Chapel.

Croesus

Croesus
Roman Trekel *bar* Croesus **Werner Güra** *ten* Atis
Salomé Haller *sop* Clerida **Brigitte Eisenfeld** *sop*
Trigesta **Johannes Mannov** *bass* Cyrus **Markus
Schäfer** *ten* Eliates **Dorothea Röschmann** *sop*
Elmira **Graham Pushee** *counterten* Halimacus
Johanna Stojković *sop* Nerillus **Klaus Häger** *bass*
Orsanes **Kwangchul Youn** *bass* Solon **Kurt
Azesberger** *ten* Elcius **Hanover Boys' Choir; Berlin
RIAS Chamber Choir; Akademie für Alte Musik
Berlin / René Jacobs**
Harmonia Mundi ③ HMC90 1714/6 (188' · DDD)
　　　Ⓕ**OOO**

Ⓖ　　Reinhard Keiser was principal opera composer at Hamburg's celebrated Theatre on the Goosemarket early in the 18th century, returning intermittently, under Telemann's direction, between 1722 and 1735 when he retired after the death of his wife. During the first of these periods, a young man called Georg Friedrich Händel joined his theatre's orchestra and during his temporary absence composed three operas for the Goosemarket opera house, including *Almira* (1705) to a libretto set by Keiser.

Keiser's opera, given the catchy title *Die Unbeständigkeit weltlicher Ehre und Reichthums der hochmüthige, gestürzte, und wieder erhabene Croesus* ('The inconstancy of earthly glory and riches of the proud, deposed and rehabilitated Croesus') at its first performance in 1711, is called by the *New Grove* one of 'a handful of masterpieces' and René Jacobs concurs in his evangelising essay, 'Why Produce *Croesus* today?' printed in Harmonia Mundi's lavish booklet. The answer to Jacobs's question lies in the quality of the music, which will come as a delightful surprise to Baroque lovers.

The music itself is sheer bliss from first to last, and has a succession of variously characterised arias – the most exquisite are alloted to the heroine Elmira, ravishingly sung by Dorothea Röschmann, the most moving to the deposed Croesus (Roman Trekel) in his prison or facing his death in the flames of a sacrificial fire. The beauties of the work are manifold – the beginning of Act 2 is a pastoral scene in which peasants sing folksongs, and there's a delicious chorus for the peasant children extolling the joys of kissing lips as sweet as nuts. Suffice it so say that anyone who has enjoyed Handel's operas will be delighted by Keiser's.

The solo singing is uniformly first class, with eloquent performances from Trekel as Croesus, and from Werner Güra as his dumb son Atis, whose speech is restored by the shock of an assassination attempt on his father. Klaus Häger as Elmira's villainous, unwanted admirer is first-class, too. There are also vivid contributions from Graham Pushee, Salomé Haller and the performers of the two comic servants, Brigitte Eisenfeld and Kurt Azesberger. This is another outstanding Jacobs resurrection and a great Baroque operatic discovery too.

Albert Ketèlbey
British 1875-1959

At the age of 11 Ketèlbey wrote a piano sonata that won praise from Edward Elgar. He attended Trinity College of Music in London, where he showed his talent for playing various orchestral instruments. At Trinity he beat Gustav Holst in competition for a musical scholarship. He appeared as a solo pianist and conducted internationally. He was a popular composer of light orchestral pieces (In a Monastery Garden, 1915; In a Persian Market, 1920). Although not proven, he is frequently quoted as becoming Britain's first millionaire composer.

In a Persian Market

In a Persian Market[a]. In a Monastery Garden[a]. The Adventurers. Chal Romano. Suite romantique. Caprice pianistique. The Clock and the Dresden Figures. Cockney Suite – No 3, At the Palais de Danse; No 5, Bank Holiday. In the Moonlight. Wedgwood Blue. Bells across the Meadows. Phantom Melody.
[a]**Slovak Philharmonic Male Chorus; Bratislava Radio Symphony Orchestra / Adrian Leaper**
Marco Polo 8 223442 (74' · DDD)   Ⓕ❍

The obvious Ketèlbey favourites (*In a Monastery Garden, In a Persian Market, Bells across the Meadows*) are played with a grace and sensitivity that never invites unfavourable comparison with earlier recordings of the same pieces. If others in the same somewhat maudlin vein (*In the Mystic Land of Egypt, In a Chinese Temple Garden, Sanctuary of the Heart*) are missing, it's to give us the opportunity to hear some of his unjustly overshadowed compositions. And what delights there are! Overexposure to Ketèlbey's more stereotyped, highly perfumed compositions has disguised what varied and inventive music he composed. Once you acquaint yourself with the charms of *The Clock and the Dresden Figures, In the Moonlight* and the invigorating open-air spirit of *Chal Romano*, you'll want to hear them again and again.

Aram Khachaturian
Russian/USSR 1903-1978

Khachaturian was the son of an Armenian bookbinder and was slow to show his talent for composition. His first instrument was the tuba but it was as a biology student that he went to Moscow University. Within a year he had switched to the Gnessin School of Music to study cello, an instrument he'd never played before. (Gnessin himself had been a pupil of Rimsky-Korsakov.) In 1929 Khachaturian went on to the Moscow Conservatoire where his composition teacher was Myaskovsky (another Rimsky pupil), perhaps the strongest influence on him. His arresting First Symphony was written for his graduation 'in honour of the 15th anniversary of Soviet Armenia'.

After the international success of his Piano Concerto, official recognition was quick to follow – the coveted Stalin Prize (three times) and the Order of Lenin (1939) – but in 1948 he was one of the composers (including Prokofiev and Shostakovich) hauled up before the Central Committee of the Communist Party for writing the wrong sort of music, accused of 'decadent formalism'. Interesting because Khachaturian had already been writing the kind of music that was now being requested. Over the next three decades Khachaturian made many visits abroad conducting his own works, as one of the Soviet Union's most eminent musical representatives.

Piano Concerto

Piano Concerto. Dance Suite. Five Pieces for Wind Band – Waltz; Polka
Dora Serviarian-Kuhn pf **Armenian Philharmonic Orchestra / Loris Tjeknavorian**
ASV Platinum PLT8510 (59' · DDD)   Ⓜ❍

In the Piano Concerto Dora Serviarian-Kuhn and her Armenian compatriot, Loris Tjeknavorian, are in every way first-class: both identify naturally with the sinuous oriental flavour of the melodic lines and understand that the outer movements need above all to convey thrusting vitality; here there's plenty of drive and rhythmic lift. But what primarily makes this performance memorable is Serviarian-Kuhn's sense of fantasy, so that her various cadential passages, for all their brilliance, are charismatically quixotic rather than merely bravura displays.

The other works on the disc are small beer. The 'Waltz' for wind band has an engaging carousel flavour; the somewhat vulgar 'Polka' which follows roisterously suggests the circus. The *Dance Suite* goes through the usual Khachaturian routines with which he likes to clothe his agreeable but at times rather insubstantial Armenian folk ideas. Easily the most memorable movement is the first and much the longer of the two Uzbek dances, which opens gently and touchingly.

The performances here are excellent and vividly recorded.

Flute Concerto

Khachaturian Flute Concerto (transcribed from the Violin Concerto by J-P Rampal)[a]
Ibert Flute Concerto[a]. Pièce
Emmanuel Pahud fl
[a]**Tonhalle Orchestra, Zürich / David Zinman**
EMI 557563-2 (64' · DDD)   Ⓟ⊕➤

Most flute concertos are lightweight, so it isn't surprising that flautists are keen to expand the repertory, adapting more ambitious works. That's how, on the suggestion of the composer himself, Jean-Pierre Rampal in 1968 came to prepare a brilliant transcription of Khachaturian's Violin Concerto. In the concert-hall a soft-grained flute can't cut through orchestral textures in the way a violin can, but on disc careful balancing has produced a successful result.

The flute naturally lacks the required incisiveness for the first subject, but there are obvious gains in the lyrical second subject: Emmanuel Pahud's gentle tone and fine shading bring out echoes of Dvořák in *New World* vein, where the violin had more of a gypsy flavour. Rampal and Pahud effectively replace the cadenza's double-stops with little arpeggiated flourishes, and surprisingly little seems changed. Better still is the slow movement, where Pahud's exquisitely hushed playing finds a mystery and tenderness in the hypnotic, Satie-like melody. In place of the finale's brilliant extroversion on the violin, Pahud's flute offers a cheeky lightness.

Ibert's unaccompanied *Pièce* makes an interlude between the concertos: a work which owes its easily improvisatory flow to Debussy's *Syrinx*. The Flute Concerto was written for Marcel Moyse in 1934; the finale's mix of 6/8 and 3/4 metres brings a sharp, jazzy flavour. What sets Pahud's performance apart is the depth of feeling he conveys in the slow movement: poignantly mysterious, with breathtaking *pianissimos* matched by the strings of the Tonhalle Orchestra under David Zinman. The long, slow middle section in the finale, too, has a slinky quality, as in a *valse grise*. The recording is full and clear.

Violin Concerto in D minor

Khachaturian Violin Concerto
Glazunov Violin Concerto
Prokofiev Violin Concerto No 1
Julia Fischer vn **Russian National Orchestra /
Yakov Kreizberg**
Pentatone ⬢ PTC5186 059 (80' · DDD/DSD) Ⓕ⊕⊕

As Julia Fischer explains in the booklet-notes to this, her first CD, she has an abiding love of the Khachaturian Concerto, a work she found impossible to sell to concert-promoters. The freshness of her way with the Khachaturian is immediately striking in the chattering figuration of the opening, and she brings a rare tenderness to the lyrical second subject. The orchestral sound is impressive, too. Though Itzhak Perlman and Lydia Mordkovitch produce a beefier sound, the refinement of Fischer's performance makes it equally compelling. This concerto has claims to be the composer's finest work, claims which the yearning tenderness of the slow movement support. The clarity of Fischer's performance in the finale brings lightness and sparkle.

In the Glazunov, too, it's the clarity and subtlety of Fischer's playing that marks out her reading. She finds the tenderness of the slow middle section of this one-movement work, and gives an easy swing to the bouncy rhythms of the final section. In the Prokofiev she takes a meditative view of the wistful melodies, the element, she says, that most attracts her, even if she does not quite reach the depths of Kyung-Wha Chung's version.

A unique coupling, superbly recorded, that could hardly be more recommendable.

Additional recommendation

Khachaturian Violin Concerto
Sibelius Violin Concerto
Khachatryan vn **Sinfonia Varsovia / Krivine**
Naïve V4959 (70' · DDD)   Ⓕ⊕➤
   The Khachaturian Concerto is given a
   crisp, lightly articulated opening. In the finale
   Khachatryan knows how to coax a workable
   ebb and flow, ease his tone and lighten tension
   to facilitate a change in musical current. Krivine
   and his team are sympathetic collaborators for a
   highly commendable performance.

Gayaneh – Suite No 2

Khachaturian The Widow of Valencia – Suite.
Gayaneh – Suite No 2 **Tjeknavorian** Danses
fantastiques
**Armenian Philharmonic Orchestra /
Loris Tjeknavorian**
ASV CDDCA884 (65' · DDD)   Ⓕ⊕

The Widow of Valencia is an early work (1940), yet already reveals the composer's fund of good tunes. He admitted its lack of authentic Spanishness, and though the 'Introduction' opens with flashing southern Mediterranean gusto, it soon makes way for a sultry Armenian melody of best local vintage. But why worry? Altogether this is a most winning suite, without a dull bar, piquantly scored and brilliantly presented by an orchestra that's completely at home and clearly enjoying themselves. They also give us another suite, comprising six indelible numbers – for the most part little known – from Khachaturian's masterpiece, *Gayaneh*. Tjeknavorian's own

Danses fantastiques frequently burst with energy and the gentler dances have that Armenian flavour so familiar in *Gayaneh*. Brilliant playing in glittering yet spacious sound.

Spartacus

Khachaturian Spartacus: Ballet Suite No 1 – Variations of Aegina and Bacchanalia; Scene and Dance with Crotalums; Dance of the Gaditanian Maidens and Victory of Spa. Spartacus: Ballet Suite No 2 – Adagio of Spartacus and Phrygia Gayaneh – Sabre Dance; Dance of the Rose Maidens; Dance of the Kurds; Lullaby; Lezghinka. Masquerade – Waltz; Nocturne; Mazurka; Romance; Galop **Ippolitov-Ivanov** Caucasian Sketches, Suite 1, Op 10
**Armenian Philharmonic Orchestra /
Loris Tjeknavorian**
ASV CDDCA773 (76' · DDD)   Ⓕ

On this recording the 'Sabre Dance' from *Gayaneh* bursts into the room with explosive impetus and bite. The Sabre dancers are closely followed by the young maidens who come in as if the sabres were being flourished directly behind them, and hard on their heels come the Mountaineers who obviously have the Abominable Snowman in hot pursuit. With the brilliant recording projecting everything in burnished primary colours the effect is exhilarating, yet a shade wearing, so that the haunting 'Lullaby' provides a welcome respite. But not for long, as the 'Lezghinka' immediately develops a similar, almost frenetic thrust (rather more here than in the composer's own recording).

The *Masquerade* Suite has comparable spirit and gusto but some of its charm evaporates in consequence – notably in the 'Waltz', with the ebullient closing 'Galop' suggesting a circus band in an agreeably vulgar manner. The music from *Spartacus* is comparably vibrant and energetic, and although the famous 'Adagio of Spartacus and Phrygia' opens with a beguiling aura of romantic anticipation, the climax develops great Slavonic ardour.

Ippolitov's *Caucasian Sketches* are little more than picture postcards with sinuous sub-Rimsky-Korsakov eastern melodies. Tjeknavorian makes the most of the oriental atmosphere thus generated, but cannot disguise the fact that the hit number, the spectacular closing 'Procession of the Sardar' is head and shoulders above the rest in memorability. It is played with great elan and here Brian Culverhouse's brightly lit recording comes fully into its own.

Zoltán Kodály   Hungarian 1882-1967

The two men who changed the direction of Hungarian music first met in 1900 at the Budapest Conservatory. Bartók and Kodály became lifelong friends, a relationship cemented by a common cause: the vision of an educated Hungary. Together they undertook several expeditions collecting Hungarian folksongs. When you think of the primitive equipment – recording technology had not developed beyond the stage of bulky machines with fragile cylinders – their determination must be wondered at. The results were published jointly, their findings systematically catalogued. Hitherto no one had thought to reap this rich natural harvest and re-invest it in the country's living heritage. (Vaughan Williams and Holst were doing the same thing simultaneously in England.) Together they collected between three and four thousand different tunes. Previously influenced by Brahms and then Debussy, Kodály now found his own voice using Hungarian folksongs and rhythms and his first mature work, the symphonic poem Summer Evening (1906), dates from this period as does his first teaching post at the Academy in Budapest. But teaching was not merely a means of earning money to keep him while he composed. Teaching to Kodály was an essential part of his mission.

He composed diligently without much recognition for the next 15 years and certainly achieved nothing as momentous as Bartók's contemporary works. That changed after 1922 when Kodály, Bartók and Dohnányi were each asked to supply a new work for the 50th anniversary of the unification of Buda and Pest. The result was Kodály's Psalmus Hungaricus which brought him international recognition. His folk opera Háry János followed in 1926 and by the mid-'30s he was a national hero. What makes his music attractive is its directness, its lyrical and melodic appeal and swinging sense of rhythm; Bartók chose another path, preferring to distort the folk-based material, moulding it into something more subjective and obscure.

During the Second World War, Kodály remained in Budapest, surviving under the German puppet government (Bartók, already withdrawing from Hungarian musical life, had left for the States). The Nazis ordered him to divorce his Jewish wife – he refused – and, though threatened by the Gestapo with torture, he was active in the underground movement. Probably it was his reputation that save his life for the Nazis decided in the end to leave him alone. After the war, with Bartók dead, Kodály was acclaimed as the country's greatest living composer. He was certainly the most powerful: his music-teaching system was in use throughout the country and, right up until his death, though latterly he composed little, his influence and decisions dominated the whole of Hungary's musical life.

Dances from Galánta

Dances from Galánta[a]. Dances of Marosszék[a]. Háry János[a] – concert suite; The Flute-Playing Hussar; The Old Woman; The Jewish family; Háry riding Lucifer; The two gipsies. Dancing Song[b]. St Gregory's Day[c]. See the gypsies[b]
[b]**Budapest Children's Choir Magnificat;**
[c]**Kecskemét Children's Choir Miraculum;**
[a]**Budapest Festival Orchestra / Iván Fischer**
Philips 462 824-2PH (66' · DDD · T/t)   ⒻⓄⓄ▷

Iván Fischer and his Hungarian band join the most august company in this wonderful repertoire. As both sets of dances amply demonstrate, Fischer's Budapest Festival Orchestra is no less virtuoso than Ormandy's dazzling Philadelphians or Ferenc Fricsay's exemplary Berlin RSO, and its impassioned playing melds an earthy physicality, tangy exuberance and improvisatory flair to consistently telling effect. Add to the mix Fischer's wittily observant direction (an abundance of affectionate *rubato* in the opening section of the *Marosszék Dances* especially, allied to a generous quotient of 'gypsy' slides from the strings elsewhere), and the results are irresistible. Similarly, their *Háry János* Suite is immensely engaging. After a spectacularly good introductory 'sneeze', Fischer sees to it that Kodály's great arcs of melody are truly *espressivo cantabile* as marked. Napoleon's battlefield antics are hilariously depicted (splendidly bolshy trombones), while Fischer's thrusting 'Intermezzo' has joyous swagger. Moreover, for all the giddy festivities of the brassy 'Entrance of the Emperor and his Court', Fischer still manages to extract plenty of ear-burning detail. Five miniatures from the original *Singspiel* are also included, programmed separately from the suite; in 'The two gypsies' Fischer shares fiddling duties with Gábor Takács-Nagy. Last but not least we get three choral offerings from 1925-9, which are delivered with captivating freshness and charm by the two admirable children's choirs here.

A peach of an issue, complemented by an irrepressibly vivid recording.

Cello Sonatas

Sonata for Solo Cello, Op 8. Sonatina[a]. Nine Epigrams[a]. Romance lyrique[a]. Adagio[a]
Natalie Clein vc [a]**Julius Drake** pf
Hyperion CDA67829 (69' · DDD)　　　Ⓕ**ⓄⓄⓄ**Ⓑ▸

A first hearing of the Kodály Solo Sonata often leaves one amazed at its scope and at the composer's extraordinary resourcefulness. You get something of a renewed sense of wonderment on listening to Natalie Clein's account; she produces an astonishing range of colours and evokes the widest variety of expressive styles. Admirable, too, is how she's able, in the recording studio, to maintain so much of the excitement and directness of live performance. Music of this rhetorical character demands a fine sense of timing; Clein demonstrates this, and her air of conviction is sustained through the first movement's intense declamation, the *Adagio*'s rich, low-range melodies, the finale's dance rhythms and the eerily quiet 'natural' sounds that punctuate the discourse. It must be said that Clein is more concerned with expression than beauty of tone in her effort to capture something of the roughness and raw edges of folk music.

The rest of the programme has a more refined character and Julius Drake's expressive playing is a fine match for Clein's outgoing manner. There's a noble performance of the well known *Adagio* and a sensitive account, stressing its impressionistic features, of the 1922 Sonatina. The *Epigrams* of 1954, intended originally as vocalises, are delightful short pieces with only subtle hints of Kodály's nationalistic style. These, too, are beautifully and simply played. A recording of great immediacy points up the variety of the programme, from the Sonata's grandeur and vividness to the intimacy of the *Epigrams*.

Additional recommendations

Solo Cello Sonata
Coupled with Cello Sonata, Op 4.
Three Chorale Preludes (after Bach)
Kliegel vc **Jandó** pf
Naxos 8 553160 (64' · DDD)　　　ⓈⓄⒹ▸

Maria Kliegel rises to the challenge of Kodály's Solo Sonata with considerable gusto: harmonics, *glissandos, sul ponticello*, fiery arpeggios – all are expertly employed and delivered via a nicely rounded tone. Kliegel's lustrous account of the *Adagio* underlines harmonic similarities with late Liszt and the folky, one-man-band finale has ample panache.

Solo Cello Sonata
Coupled with Cello Sonata, Op 4[a]
Novák Cello Sonata, Op 68[a]
Bárta vc [a]**Cech** pf
Supraphon SU3515-2 (73' · DDD)　　　Ⓕ

Jiří Bárta's command in tackling the most formidable of technical problems means that he's able to keep a steady tempo and clarify textures with clean attack on double-stopping, all seemingly without strain. Yet the intensity of his performance never flags.

Missa brevis

Kodály Laudes organi. Missa brevis
Janáček (ed Wingfield) Mass in E flat
Andrew Reid org **Westminster Cathedral Choir /
James O'Donnell**
Hyperion CDA67147 (73' · DDD · T/t)　　　Ⓕ**ⓄⓄ**Ⓑ▸

Janáček began his Mass around 1908, left it to gather dust for 20 years, then turned it into the first draft of the *Glagolitic Mass*. Paul Wingfield's reconstruction draws substantially on the original draft of the *Glagolitic Mass* to the extent of including a complete movement (the *Sanctus*) from it. Clearly Janáček knew best, and the only distinguishing moments are those bits recognisably from the *Glagolitic Mass*. Unquestionably, though, both the *Missa brevis* and *Laudes organi* are among Kodály's most inspired creations. Yet new recordings of favourite works are prone to disappoint. Not this one. If anything, this stunning performance, crowned by Andrew Reid's masterly organ playing, raises this setting of dog-Latin verses in praise of the organ and commissioned by the American Guild of Organists even higher. About 20 years before *Laudes organi*, the *Missa brevis* was first performed in this version for organ and chorus (it was originally an organ solo) in a bomb shelter during the 1944-45 Siege of Budapest. From such an inauspicious start, the work has fared remarkably well on record and this release represents an undoubted climax. It's a simply glorious performance and, in short, should not be missed.

Charles Koechlin   French 1867-1950

Koechlin studied with Massenet and Fauré at the Paris Conservatoire and was part of a musical circle that included Ravel, Schmitt and Debussy (whose Khamma he largely orchestrated in 1913). His writings on music and his teaching (Milhaud and Poulenc were pupils) tended to eclipse his composing. His output is vast: his opus numbers extend beyond 200, many of them big symphonic, choral or chamber pieces. His best-known works are the symphonic poem Les bandar-log (1939), and the Seven Stars Symphony (1933), a portrait gallery of the contemporary cinema, a work that employs the ondes martenot.

Orchestral Works

La course de printemps, Op 95[a].
Le buisson ardent, Opp 171 & 203[b]
Stuttgart Radio Symphony Orch / Heinz Holliger
Hänssler Classic CD93 045
(73' · DDD) Recorded live [a]2000, [b]2001   Ⓕ**OO**

The influence of Rudyard Kipling's *Jungle Book* on Koechlin was profound and *La course de printemps*, which gestated over a very long period, was the finest of the tone-poems he gathered together under the composite title *Le livre de la jungle*. Although the events depicted are certainly connected with the character and life of Mowgli, the music itself is above all evocative of the jungle itself, its exotically humid atmosphere and unpredictable bursts of violence and animal energy. The underlying sinister ambience is balanced by a Ravelian sensuality (there's even is a hint of *Daphnis* in the dawn evocation of the opening), while the mysteriously gentle but lustrous string monody which closes the work is other-worldly in its vision of a voluptuous moonlit spring night. Koechlin's scoring is headily brilliant and one is engulfed in its rich panoply, so that for all the music's ecclecticism, it has a life and individuality of its own.

Le buisson ardent makes an ideal coupling. An evocation of rebirth – at times passionately intense in the strings, but with the ondes martenot later used to represent the ethereal voice of the reborn spirit. The work climaxes with a lusciously positive affirmation, but closes gently and rapturously. A superb introduction to Koechlin's exotic sound world.

Vers la voûte étoilée. Le Docteur Fabricius
Christine Simonin *onde* **Stuttgart Radio Symphony Orchestra / Heinz Holliger**

Hänssler Classic CD93 106 (64' · DDD)   Ⓕ

Much of Koechlin's highly individual orchestral music remains unexplored: indeed, both works here are premiere recordings. Before he became a composer, Koechlin wanted to be an astronomer and his fascination with the 'starry firmament', and the dream-world it evoked, is sensuously created in the arch-like structure of *Vers la voûte étoilée* ('Towards the vault of stars'). Written in the early 1920s and revised in 1939, this demonstrates the composer's exotic sound world in a nocturnal piece that doesn't outstay its welcome.

The stars in the heavens return in *Le Docteur Fabricius*, written 1941-44, a more ambitious, large-scale symphonic poem with a philosophical underlay, based on a short story by the composer's uncle. The narrative describes a visit to the mysterious house in which the nihilistic Doctor Fabricius has cut himself off from the world. After an austere opening, dolorous chorales symbolise the philosophical disillusion, interrupted by a strident, fugal revolt and interwoven with moments of sadness. A powerfully scored chorale suggests that human hope always re-emerges. The visitor looks out to the starry firmament (the ondes martenot-rich scoring suggests Messiaen) and then, in a passage of radiant exultation, the spirit of Ravel hovers over the music to evoke the consolation of Nature. After an explosion of joy the music returns to the serene, withdrawn evocation of the opening.

Koechlin's powers as an orchestrator ensure his vision is powerfully communicated. Heinz Holliger is very much at home here, and the Stuttgart Radio orchestra play most responsively. The recording is full and atmospheric, though one ideally needs a more voluptuous ambience. But this is well worth trying.

Erich Wolfgang Korngold
Austro/Hungarian 1897-1957

Korngold was the son of the influential music critic Julius Korngold. He studied with Zemlinsky and had spectacular early successes with his ballet Der Schneemann (1910) and operas Violanta (1916) and Die tote Stadt (1920). In 1934 he went to Hollywood at the invitation of Max Reinhardt and wrote some fine film scores. The Adventures of Robin Hood won him an Academy Award for Best Original Score, and he was subsequently nominated for The Private Lives of Elizabeth and Essex (1939) and The Sea Hawk (1940). At the Anchluss, Korngold, as an Austrian Jew, remained in Hollywood for the duration of the war (he became a US citizen in 1943). After the war he wrote orchestral and chamber pieces, including his now hugely popular Violin Concerto.

Violin Concerto

Korngold Violin Concerto[a]. **Rózsa** Violin   Ⓗ
Concerto, Op 24[b]. Tema con variazioni, Op 29a[b].

Korngold Orchestral

Waxman Fantasy on Bizet's 'Carmen'[c]
Jascha Heifetz vn **Gregor Piatigorsky** vc
[b]**Chamber Orchestra;** [a]**Los Angeles Philharmonic
Orchestra / Alfred Wallenstein;** [b]**Dallas Symphony
Orchestra / Walter Hendl;** [c]**RCA Victor Symphony
Orchestra / Donald Voorhees**
RCA Victor Gold Seal [ac]mono/[b]stereo
09026 61752-2 (70' · ADD). Recorded 1946-63 **OOB→**

Heifetz's legendary recording of the Korngold
Concerto serves a double purpose: as an effective introduction to Korngold's seductive musical style, and as the best possible example of
Heifetz's violin artistry. The work itself was
written at the suggestion of Bronisław Huberman, but it was Heifetz who gave the premiere
in 1947. It calls on material that Korngold had
also used in three of his film scores, although the
way he welds the themes into a three-movement
structure is masterly enough to suggest that the
concerto came to him 'of a piece'. The very
opening would be enough to seduce most listeners. Miklós Rózsa's Concerto has its roots in the
composer's Hungarian soil, and echoes of Bartók are rarely absent. But whereas Korngold's
score is taken from movie music, Rózsa's (or
parts of it) became a film score – namely, *The
Private Life of Sherlock Holmes*.

Rózsa's self-possessed, skilfully written *Tema
con variazoni* was taken, in 1962, from a much
larger work then in progress, but Heifetz and
Piatigorsky play it in a reduced orchestration. As
to the *Carmen Fantasy* by Franz Waxman
(another notable film composer), its luscious
tunes and frightening technical challenges were
written with the great violinist in mind. It's a
stunning piece of playing, and wears its years
lightly. The other recordings sound far better,
and the Rózsa items are in stereo.

Korngold Violin Concerto **Brahms** Violin Concerto
Nikolaj Znaider vn
Vienna Philharmonic Orchestra / Valery Gergiev
RCA Red Seal 88697 10336-2 (66' · DDD)   (F)B→

There are readings of the Brahms that take their
time, but the plush grandeur of Znaider and the
VPO seems almost too opulent. The finale, too,
misses an element of dance, of impishness even,
so well caught by Julia Fischer (see page 247).
Instead, we get a wall of sound both terrifying
and awe-inspiring. But tempi apart, there is also
much to celebrate here. Znaider is one of the
greatest artists of his generation, and his consummate musicianship and glorious depth and
range of tone are everywhere apparent, to particular effect in the *Adagio* of the Brahms, where
Znaider's discreet *portamenti* make the most of
the floating lines.

So, unquestionably top-notch playing from all
concerned, even if the interpretation is less convincing. The Korngold is a different matter.
This should have seemed a mere bon-bon after
the Brahms, but such is the commitment from
Znaider, Gergiev and the orchestra that it's a
wonder from start to finish. They relish the

composer's extraordinary ear for orchestral
colour, especially the shattering climax of the
first movement and the work's zany brass-
fuelled ending.

Throughout, there's an ideal marriage of brilliance and warmth. The sound picture places the
soloist very firmly centre stage, but with playing
this scintillating that's not a complaint.

Additional recommendation

Violin Concerto
Coupled with **Korngold** Much Ado about Nothing –
Maiden in the Bridal Chamber; Dogberry and Verges;
Intermezzo; Hornpipe **Barber** Violin Concerto, Op 14
Shaham vn **LSO / Previn** pf
DG 439 886-2GH (71' · DDD)   (F)B→
  Shaham is yearningly warm without being senti-
  mental, and clean and precise in attack, and Previn
  is a superb accompanist. The suite from *Much Ado
  About Nothing* provides a delightful makeweight.

Violin Concerto[a]
Coupled with Gesang der Heliane[b]. Much Ado About
Nothing[b]. Suite, Op 23[c]
[ac]**Schmid,** [b]**Frühwirth** [c]**Weinmeister** vns [c]**Viersen** vc
[c]**Avenhaus,** [b]**Sigfridson** pfs [a]**VPO / Ozawa**
Oehms Classics OC537 (79' · DDD)
Recorded live 2004   (F)O
  Not only does Benjamin Schmid generate a spine-
  tingling rapport with Seiji Ozawa and the Vienna
  Philharmonic but his playing, brimful of elegance,
  affectionate warmth and temperament, betokens a
  very real empathy with this gorgeous score.

Film Music

The Sea Hawk – Suite (ed Gamba)
**Manchester Chamber Choir;
BBC Philharmonic / Rumon Gamba**
Chandos CHAN10438 (77' · DDD)   (F)OB→

Rumon Gamba's 77-minute suite in six parts
from Korngold's towering score for *The Sea
Hawk* (1940) sensibly follows the action and
will leave no listener in any doubt as to the
giddy fecundity of top-flight invention and
awesome architectural sweep of Korngold's
exhilarating canvas. All the big set pieces are
here, not least the unforgettable choral recapitulation of the main title ('Strike for the
shores of Dover!'), while the gorgeous love
music for Thorpe and Dona Maria is always
most touchingly attended to (for a taster try
track 14, 'Rose Garden').

Suffice to say, the orchestral playing under
Gamba's judiciously paced lead has a sophisticated sheen, appropriate sense of spectacle (stellar brass contribution, as ever from this source)
and wholehearted commitment that testify to
the BBC Philharmonic's unimpeachable credentials in this repertoire.

Apart from one jarringly audible page-turn,
Chandos's production values leave nothing to be
desired; indeed, the sound is gloriously wide-

ranging, sumptuous and detailed. Throw in a particularly handsome booklet and it will by now be clear that every true Korngold fan should make haste to this terrific release.

The Sea Wolf. The Sea Wolf – trailer. The Adventures of Robin Hood – Suite
BBC Philharmonic Orchestra / Rumon Gamba
Chandos CHAN10336 (76' · DDD)   Ⓕ Ⓑ→

For Michael Curtiz's 1941 big-screen adaptation of Jack London's *The Sea Wolf* (starring Edward G Robinson as Wolf Larsen, the sadistic captain of the sealer *Ghost*), Korngold produced one of his most searching scores. As Brendan G Carroll observes in his absorbing booklet-notes, anyone coming to this music after the playful, swashbuckling fireworks of, say, *The Sea Hawk*, *Captain Blood* or *The Adventures of Robin Hood* may well be caught unawares by its comparatively uncompromising demeanour.

The ominous 'Main Title' immediately sets the tone and demonstrates Korngold's masterly handling of an extremely large orchestra, which originally included the now defunct Novachord (patented by Hammond as the world's first synthesiser). Perhaps the most striking piece of scoring occurs in the 'Love Music', where a solo harmonica intones one of Korngold's most sweetly poignant melodies against a backcloth of strings. It's a rare moment of tenderness in an otherwise predominantly moody 55-minute sequence.

There's a bonus in the shape of the music for the trailer (the opening measures of which recycle material from Korngold's own score for *The Prince and the Pauper*) and the collection concludes with an irresistible four-movement concert suite from *The Adventures of Robin Hood*. Korngold slimmed down the orchestration and conducted performances in Oakland and San Francisco in 1938.

Needless to say, Rumon Gamba and the BBC Philharmonic are completely at home in this colourful repertoire (the superb brass section has a field day) and the sound is as spectacularly rich and detailed as one could possibly wish. Recommended with enthusiasm.

Complete Piano Music

Sonatas – Nos 1-3. Don Quixote. Der Schneemann. Märchenbilder. Four Waltzes for Piano. Four little caricatures for children. What the woods tell me. Zwischenspiel – Act 3 Intermezzo. Piano Trio. Potpourri from 'Der Ring des Polykrates' (arr Ruffin)ᵃ. Much Ado About Nothing. Geschichten von Strauss. Der Schneemann – Four easy pieces. Schauspiel Overture. Grand Fantasy on 'Die tote Stadt' (arr Rebay)ᵃ
Martin Jones, ᵃ**Richard McMahon** pfs
Nimbus ④ NI5705/8 (5h · DDD)   Ⓢ

A hearty three cheers to this complete Korngold cycle from the indefatigable and inexplicably underrated Martin Jones. The first two discs have those extraordinary works composed

between 1908 and 1910 that put the infant Korngold into the Mozart-Mendelssohn prodigy class – the first two piano sonatas, *Don Quixote*, the ballet-pantomime *Der Schneemann*, *Was der Wald erzählt*, and seven *Märchenbilder*. The final 'Epilog' contains one of his most beautiful melodies, and here Jones captures the *Weltschmerz* of the composer's own treasurable 1951 recording.

The Piano Trio in D major, completed just before Korngold's 13th birthday, is played in the previously unrecorded four-hand version. In this and the 1911 *Schauspiel* Overture, Jones is joined by Richard McMahon. Written in language of pre-nascent maturity that was to develop little over the composer's lifetime, these pieces constitute one of Western music's more noteworthy miracles.

These four well-filled discs are completed by Rebay's substantial (18'31") Grand Fantasy on themes from *Die tote Stadt*, and Korngold's fantasy on Johann Strauss themes. Stylish, lovingly prepared, classily played and with an excellent 10-page booklet from Korngold's biographer Brendan G Carroll, this valuable addition to the catalogue cannot be praised too highly.

Vocal Works

Sonett für Wien, Op 41. Abschiedslieder, Op 14. Drei Lieder, Op 18. Drei Lieder, Op 22. Fünf Lieder, Op 38. Songs of the Clown, Op 29. Four Shakespeare Songs, Op 31. Unvergänglichkeit, Op 27
Sarah Connolly mez **William Dazeley** bar
Iain Burnside pf
Signum Classics SIGCD160 (74' · DDD · T/t)   Ⓕ Ⓞ Ⓑ→

Those for whom Korngold's music is an acquired taste may not feel the need for another CD, but this new collection is exceptionally well performed and recorded. The mixture of songs in German and English works very well, and having two voices sharing them in some groups means that any sense of monotony is avoided.

As in his operas and film scores, one can hear Korngold drawing on different influences – there are a couple of songs that seem like affectionate parodies of Mahler, others in which he is moving away from his Viennese roots and assimilating American and English styles. The *Four Shakespeare Songs*, Op 31, are particularly engaging, William Dazeley really letting go in 'When birds do sing', and Sarah Connolly bringing all her artistry to bear on Desdemona's Willow Song. Both singers are sometimes stretched to the limits of their resources, especially in Korngold's songs composed after the disappointing reception accorded to his 'gargantuan' opera *Das Wunder der Heliane*. The first of the *Drei Lieder*, Op 18, is a setting of a poem by Hans Kaltneker (author of *Heliane*), 'In meine innige Nacht', which Dazeley sings with great intensity. Korngold's last song, 'Sonnett für Wien' (which gives the disc its title) is another, posthumously published, poem by Kaltneker. In this song, one feels that Korngold was bidding farewell not only to Vienna, the city of his youthful success, but to music and life itself. Iain Burnside plays Korngold's often fiercely difficult accompaniments with obvious affection and relish. This is a very beautiful disc, recommended even to those who think they don't care for Korngold's style.

Die Kathrin

Die Kathrin
Melanie Diener sop Kathrin **David Rendall** ten
François **Robert Hayward** bass-bar Malignac **Lilian Watson** sop Chou-Chou **Della Jones** mez Monique
**BBC Singers; BBC Concert Orchestra /
Martyn Brabbins**
CPO ③ CPO999 602-2 (162' · DDD · T/t)   Ⓕ**O**

This is the first modern performance and recording of Korngold's last stage work. *Die Kathrin* is separated by 10 years from its predecessor, *Das Wunder der Heliane*. Between *Heliane* and *Die Kathrin*, Korngold's career had changed. From being the wunderkind of the 1910s, he had developed into the film composer and arranger of large-scale operettas. If *Heliane* is the most grandiose of his operas, *Die Kathrin* is the most unpretentious; Korngold had thought of labelling it a folk-opera. The story is simple. The hero, François, is a singer who has been conscripted into the army. He falls in love with Kathrin, leaving her pregnant. She loses her job, follows him to Marseilles, where in a vaguely *Tosca*-like plot-twist François is implicated in the murder of the villain, who has actually been shot by one of the cabaret girls. Five years pass, François returns to find Kathrin and his child. The opera ends with a rapturous love duet. The music is full of typically lush Korngold scoring. In the night-club scene, obligatory in any 1930s opera, there are two catchy numbers, and Korngold brings in such fashionably jazzy instruments as a trio of saxophones and a banjo. The cast is exceptionally strong. Diener has just the right weight of voice for Kathrin, and Rendall makes François into a very positive hero. Brabbins brings out the essentially Puccinian side of the score; in its structure the opera resembles *La rondine* more than a little: *verismo* didn't die with *Turandot*. Devotees of Korngold's music won't need any encouragement. Those with a taste for tuneful, Romantic opera, sometimes bordering on operetta, should give it a chance.

Die tote Stadt

Die tote Stadt
Torsten Kerl ten Paul **Angela Denoke** sop Marietta
Bo Skovhus bar Frank, Fritz **Daniela Denschlag** mez
Brigitta **Simina Ivan** mez Juliette **Stella Grigorian** sop Lucienne **Lukas Gaudernak** ten Gaston
Eberhard Lorenz ten Victorin **Michael Roider** ten
Count Albert **Salzburg Boys' and Girls' Choir;
Vienna State Opera Chorus; Mozarteum Orchestra Salzburg; Vienna Philharmonic Orchestra /
Donald Runnicles**
Orfeo d'Or ② C634 042I (121' · DDD)
Recorded live 2004   Ⓕ**O**

The production by Willy Decker of Korngold's most famous opera at the 2004 Salzburg Festival created something of a sensation, and now makes its welcome arrival on CD. Georges Rodenbach's 1892 novel *Bruges la morte*, on which the 22-year-old Korngold and his father based the libretto, deals with a man's obsession with his dead lover. In 1920 this struck an immediate spark with audiences recovering from the aftermath of the First World War and, with Korngold's mixture of big, soupy tunes and a sort of post-Wagnerian gloom, it was an immediate hit.

Although there is a good deal of noise from movements on stage, the sound quality here is exceptionally vivid for a live event. Though Denoke is no Jeritza, she has an attractive voice and joins Kerl sweetly in the famous duet 'Glück, das mir verblieb'. They both hurl themselves into the increasingly violent scenes as the fantasy affair progresses. Bo Skovhus is his usual glamorous self, doubling the roles of Fritz and Frank, the faithful guardian of his friend's sanity.

Runnicles and the Vienna Philharmonic play the piece with some fire, bringing out every one of Korngold's ragbag of Puccini, Strauss and Wagner allusions. You have to be in the mood for an overdose of kitsch but when it works, as it does here, *Die tote Stadt* still packs a punch.

Additional recommendation

Kollo Paul **Neblett** Marietta **Prey** Frank **Munich Radio Orch / Leinsdorf**
RCA The Sony Opera House 88697 44660-2 (137' · ADD)   Ⓕ**O**➛

The premiere recording from 1975 and still an outstanding version with Leinsdorf allowing this lush score to unfurl magnificently; some excellent solo contributions, too, with Kollo and Neblett excellent as the lovers.

Fritz Kreisler   Austrian 1875-1962

Best known as a violinist, Kreisler studied at conservatoires in Vienna and Paris. He toured the USA in 1888-89, but real recognition came in 1899, after a concert with the Berlin PO under Nikisch. He made his London debut in 1902 and in 1910 he gave the premiere of Elgar's Violin Concerto. He lived in Berlin, 1924-34, and in 1939 settled in the USA, becoming an American citizen in 1943. His repertory included brief pieces of his own, some of them semi-pastiche pieces which he initially ascribed to composers such as Tartini and Pugnani, some of them sugary Viennese morsels, all beautifully written to show off his stylish violin playing.

Compositions and Arrangements

Original Compositions and Arrangements   Ⓗ
works by Kreisler and arrangements of works by Bach, Brandl, Dvořák, Falla, Glazunov, Heuberger,

Poldini, Rimsky-Korsakov, Schubert, Scott, Tchaikovsky and Weber
Fritz Kreisler vn with various artists
EMI Références mono 764701-2 (78' · ADD)
Recorded 1930-38 ○○○

Kreisler Praeludium and Allegro in the style of Pugnani. Schön Rosmarin. Tambourin chinois, Op 3. Caprice viennois, Op 2. Précieuse in the style of Couperin. Liebesfreud. Liebesleid. La Gitana. Berceuse romantique, Op 9. Polichinelle. Rondino on a theme by Beethoven. Tempo di Menuetto in the style of Pugnani. Toy Soldier's March. Allegretto in the style of Boccherini. Marche miniature viennoise. Aucassin and Nicolette, 'Canzonetta medievale'. Menuet in the style of Porpora. Siciliano and Rigaudon in the style of Francoeur. Syncopation
Joshua Bell vn **Paul Coker** pf
Decca 444 409-2DH (63' · DDD) ⑤🄓➜

Years of encores have guaranteed the cult longevity of Kreisler's music – certainly among violinists. Kreisler's disc consists of his own pieces and a large number of arrangements. Some of the latter are pretty feeble musically, yet the great violinist's unique artistry and magical tone-quality shine through. Sometimes he doesn't land right in the middle of a note, but always plays with the timing and phrasing of a great singer. Nothing is routine or set in his playing, which has a continual feeling of discovery and freshness. The transfers are excellent.

Joshua Bell learnt Kreisler from his teacher, the late Josef Gingold, yet his approach is anything but 'old school'. He habitually avoids the pitfalls of imitation, flashiness and patronising overkill, preferring instead to revisit the music with modern ears. His *Caprice viennois* is light-years removed from the composer's own, a fresh-faced, strongly characterised reading that trades sentimentality for just a hint of jazz. And there's that inseparable twosome, *Liebesfreud* and *Liebesleid*, the latter displaying Bell's tone at its most alluring. The longest piece here is the *Praeludium and Allegro in the style of Pugnani* which he gives the full treatment, deftly pointing the *Allegro*, relishing passagework and double-stopping with impressive accuracy. Some pieces seem indivisible from Kreisler's own very individual tone and phrasing, *Polichinelle*, for example, and *Marche miniature viennoise*, both of which paraded the sort of personalised *rubato*, timing and tone-production that have for so long seemed part of the music's very essence.

Bell's smooth, witty and keenly inflected readings make for elevated entertainment: they may not replace the composer's own, but they do provide a youthful and in many ways illuminating alternative. The recordings are excellent, but Coker's fine accompaniments occasionally seem overprominent.

'Viennese Rhapsody'
Albéniz/Kreisler Tango, Op 165 No 2 **Dvořák/Kreisler** Slavonic Dances – B78: No 2 in E minor; B145: No 2 in E minor **Falla/Kreisler** La vida breve – Danse

espagnole **Granados/Kreisler** Andaluza, Op 37 No 5 **Kreisler** Caprice viennois, Op 2. Tambourin chinois, Op 3. Berceuse romantique, Op 9. Viennese Rhapsodic Fantasietta. Zigeuner-capriccio. La gitana. Polichinelle. Aucassin and Nicolette. Liebesleid. Liebesfreud. Slavonic Fantasie **Scott/Kreisler** Lotus Land, Op 47 No 1 **Wieniawski/Kreisler** Etude-Caprice in A minor, Op 18 No 4
Leonidas Kavakos vn **Péter Nagy** pf
BIS CD1196 (71' · DDD) Ⓕ○○

Leonidas Kavakos's Kreisler is authentic in the best meaning of that term, namely a keen approximation both of the music's spirit and of the composer's inimitable playing style. Few Kreisler recitals have recalled, in so much minute detail, the warmth, elegance and gentlemanly musical manners of the master himself. It was an inspired idea to open the programme with that nostalgic evocation of Old Vienna, the eight-minute *Viennese Rhapsodic Fantasietta*, a Korngold sound-alike that can't waltz without smiling wistfully or even shedding the odd tear. Kavakos has mastered that lilting 3/4 to a T. His tone is uncannily familiar – cooler and less vibrant perhaps than Kreisler's own during the earlier part of his recording career but with a similarly consistent (though never overbearing) vibrato. But don't imagine that these performances are mere imitations: an individual personality does come through, it's just that a Kreislerian accent has become part of the mix – at least for the purposes of this recital. The programme has been very well chosen, ending with what are surely Kreisler's three most famous miniatures – *Liebesleid*, *Liebesfreud* and *Caprice viennois*. The *Slavonic Fantasie* after Dvořák is among the most interesting, incorporating as it does the first of the four *Romantic Pieces*. Cyril Scott's *Lotus Land* is haunting and exotic, while Kreisler's own *Zigeuner-capriccio* provides a fine example of Kavakos's slightly melancholy puckishness. Péter Nagy's stylish accompaniments add yet more flavour to the menu.

György Kurtág Hungarian b1926

Kurtág studied at the Budapest Academy (1946-55) and with Milhaud and Messiaen in Paris (1957). During this time he also discovered the works of Anton Webern and the plays of Samuel Beckett. The String Quartet he composed in 1959 after his return to Budapest marks this crucial turning-point; he refers to this piece as his Opus 1. Between 1960 and 1968 he worked as répétiteur at the National Philharmonia in Budapest. In 1967 he was appointed professor of piano and later also of chamber music at the Franz Liszt Academy, where he taught until 1993.

His works are few and mostly short; most for chamber forces, sometimes with solo voice. Stele, written for Claudio Abbado and the Berlin Philharmonic in 1994, marked a turning-point and found Kurtág working on a much larger canvas. The early 1990s saw a number of orchestral works, but he has since returned to writing for smaller ensembles.

String Quartets

Aus der Ferne III. Officium breve, Op 28. Ligatura,
Op 31*b*. String Quartet, Op 1. Hommage à Mihály
András (12 Microludes), Op 13
Keller Quartet (András Keller, János Pilz vns Zoltán
Gál va Ottó Kertész vc) with **Miklós Perényi** vc
György Kurtág celesta
ECM New Series 453 258-2 (49' · DDD)   Ⓕ

This disc, devoted exclusively to Kurtág's music
for string quartet, is of great significance, and
both performance and recording are equal to the
enterprise. The Keller Quartet have secure
technique as well as emotional commitment,
while ECM has provided a warm yet spacious
acoustic for this expressive music. The journey
begins with Kurtág's Op 1 of 1959, in a world,
dominated by expressionistic fragmentation, of
which he's clearly the master. Eighteen years
later, in the Op 13 *Microludes*, Kurtág has perfected his own personal style, in which small,
separate forms are linked together, and the
music's allusions – to Bartók and Webern, in
particular – are subsumed into a lyrical, dramatic
discourse. The fruits of Kurtág's long apprenticeship are most evident here in the superb
Officium breve of 1988-89, a miracle of textural
imagination and musical thought whose richly
varied language is distilled further into the two
miniatures – *Ligatura* (also 1989) and *Aus der
Ferne* (1991). By now Kurtág's music is characterised by a concentrated homogeneity, and by a
harmony whose tensions, and stability, are the
result of bringing convergence and divergence
into confrontation. The result is memorable,
and these fine recordings provide immensely
rewarding listening.

Játékok

Játékok – excerpts from Books 1-5 & 8. Transcriptions
from Machaut to Bach – No 46, Gottes Zeit ist die
allerbeste Zeit (Bach: BWV106); No 48, Aus tiefer Not
(Bach: BWV687); No 50, Trio Sonata in E flat (Bach:
BWV525/1); No 52, O Lamm Gottes unschuldig
(Bach: BWV*deest*)
György Kurtág, Márta Kurtág pf duet
ECM New Series 453 511-2 (50' · DDD)   Ⓕ

If any contemporary composer can persuade
the musical world that compositions of between
30 seconds and four minutes in length are the
natural vehicle for progressive post-tonal
music, that composer is Kurtág. This sequence
of pieces, the longest of which lasts just over
five minutes, offers a very special experience.
The disc contains a selection from his sequence
of 'games' (*Játékok*) for solo piano and piano
duet. They're a mixture of studies and tributes,
not explicitly pedagogic in *Mikrokosmos* mode,
but ranging widely in technical demands and
style, from fugitive fragments, in which even
the smallest element tells, to the extraordinary
flamboyance of a *perpetuum mobile* containing

nothing but *glissandos*. Most are sombre in
tone, and even the more humorous items have
a bitter side. For access to another musical
world, Kurtág has included four Bach transcriptions, music whose serenity
and confidence speaks immediately of utter
remoteness from the real present. The performances risk overprojection but they're
supremely characterful, and the close-up
recording reinforces the impression of music
that's mesmerically persuasive in its imagination and expressiveness.

Kafka Fragments

Kafka Fragments
Juliane Banse sop **András Keller** vn
ECM New Series 476 3099 (59' · DDD)   Ⓕ▷

Over nearly 50 years, György Kurtág has composed several major song-cycles – *Kafka Fragments* being the biggest in size and scope. Written over an intensive spell in 1985-86, the
selection and editing of texts had actually been
taking place since Kurtág came across Kafka's
writings during his studies in Paris three decades
earlier, and this release of creative energy permeates the music to a degree typical of this most
inscrutable yet fiercely communicative of composers.

The combination of voice and violin should not
be taken to imply emotional restraint, any more
than the brevity of the texts imposes arbitrariness
on the formal trajectory of this hour-long cycle.
The 19 fragments of Part 1 present facets of a
skewed but all-encompassing 'world-view' – set
in relief by the lengthy single setting of Part 2,
'The true path', that is the becalmed centre of
Kafka's (hence Kurtág's) expressive universe. The
12 numbers that comprise Part 3 build in intensity to the authentically Kafkaesque vision of
'Scene on a tram', with its sense of the surreal in
the everyday, then Part 4 reconfigures previous
gestures in a further eight numbers, culminating
in 'The moonlit night dazzled us…', with its aura
of bleak transcendence.

In its vast extremes of elation and despair,
Kafka Fragments is both unnerving and inspiring. Juliane Banse is fully at ease with its myriad
emotional shades and techniques of realising
them. András Keller offers playing of real
insight. Recorded with spacious immediacy and
extensively annotated, this is a fitting commemoration of Kurtág's 80th birthday: no one thus
encountering his music for the first time will be
left unmoved.

Helmut Lachenmann   German b1935

*Lachenmann studied with Johann Nepomuk David
at the Stuttgart Musikhochschule (1955-58) and
with Luigi Nono in Venice (1958-60). In 1966 he
began teaching and he has regularly lectured at*

Darmstadt since 1978; important among his many positions as a teacher was his term as professor of composition at the Stuttgart Musikhochschule from 1981 to 1999. Increasingly he has concentrated on works for the theatre.

Das Mädchen mit den Schwefelhölzern

Das Mädchen mit den Schwefelhölzern
(Tokyo version, 2000)
Nicole Tibbels, Eiko Morikawa sops **Helmut Lachenmann** spkr **Mayumi Miyata** shô **Yukiko Sugawara, Tomoko Hemmi** pfs **Stuttgart Vocal Ensemble; South West German Radio Symphony Orchestra, Baden-Baden and Freiburg / Sylvain Cambreling**
ECM New Series ② 476 1283 (113' · DDD)   Ⓕ

Das Mädchen mit den Schwefelhölzern, the composer's first piece of music theatre, is based on Hans Christian Andersen's *The Little Match Girl*, which he interprets as an attack on a cold and indifferent society. The piece has appeared previously on the Kairos label. There isn't much to choose between the two recordings in terms of performance, but the new ECM version has a pleasing precision that suits Lachenmann's vision well. The chief difference between the two versions lies in a substantial revision undertaken by the composer. The oft-recorded '…zwei Gefühle…' scene is here abridged, subtly altering the work's balance while not quite diminishing the sequence's importance to the whole. Though the work has been shortened only barely, it's possible that a greater concision results, aided perhaps by the slightly tauter sound. Lachenmann's music demands the listener's active engagement, a determined effort at understanding, but here are rewards to be reaped from perseverance.

Edouard Lalo   French 1823-1892

Lalo was over 50 before he had any success as a composer. Indeed, his lack of success had caused him such depression that he abandoned composition and (in the words of one writer) 'turned for precarious solace to matrimony with a contralto'. His Violin Concerto in F, Op 20, was played by the great Spanish violinist Sarasate in Paris in 1874. The same year, Lalo composed the Symphonie espagnole, Op 21, and dedicated it to Sarasate. This one work, a violin concerto in all but name, secured him international fame. Tchaikovsky praised it when he wrote to his patron Madame von Meck: 'It is so fresh and light, and contains piquant rhythms and melodies which are beautifully harmonised...Like Delibes and Bizet, Lalo is careful to avoid all that is routine, seeks new forms without trying to be profound, and is more concerned with musical beauty than with tradition, as are the Germans.'

The work is in five movements though invariably given without the Intermezzo which is felt not to be of *the same quality as the others. His opera Le roi d'Ys was enormously successful in its day but the two other works of Lalo to look out for are his Cello Concerto (1877) and Schumannesque Symphony in G minor (1887), both highly rewarding.*

Lalo, who came from a military family in Lille (his father had been decorated on the battlefied of Lützen by Napoleon), became one of the most distinguished figures in French music. He had 'the appearance of an Austrian diplomat' (according to one source), even after an attack of paralysis in the early 1880s condemned him to walk with a limp. In the later years of his life, the paralysis returned, further aggravating his poor health and deepening mental depression.

Cello Concerto

Lalo Cello Concerto **Massenet** Fantaisie **Saint-Saëns** Cello Concerto No 1 in A minor, Op 33
Sophie Rolland vc **BBC Philharmonic Orchestra / Gilbert Varga**
ASV CDDCA867 (65' · DDD)   ⒻⓄ

Sophie Rolland's performance of the Lalo Concerto is surely as fine as any recorded. It opens with great character, thanks to Gilbert Varga's strong accompaniment, and the solo playing is joyously songful. But Rolland is at her finest as she plays her introduction to the finale with commanding improvisatory spontaneity. The orchestra bursts in splendidly and she shows her technical mettle with some bouncing bowing in the attractive closing Rondo. The Saint-Saëns Concerto brings similar felicities. Massenet's *Fantaisie* opens dramatically and is rhythmically vital, flowing onwards boldly to produce a winningly sentimental yearning melody which the soloist clearly relishes. A cadenza then leads to a charming, very French Gavotte, and the piece ends jubilantly. It really is a find, and it could hardly be presented more persuasively. The recording is near perfect.

Cello Concerto in D minor[a]. Cello Sonata[b]. Chants russes, Op 29[b]
Maria Kliegel vc [b]**Bernd Glemser** pf
[a]**Nicolaus Esterházy Sinfonia / Michael Halász**
Naxos 8 554469 (60' · DDD)   Ⓢ▷

Maria Kliegel views the Concerto as a strong, dramatic work, and she has just the qualities – impressive, powerful tone and brilliant technique – to bring it off. The early exchanges with the orchestra establish her heroic presence, which she then relaxes to give a soft, delicate account of the second theme. The orchestral interruptions sound suitably stern and implacable – although the many loud, *staccato* chords for full orchestra become somewhat wearisome. The finale is excellent; a robust, serious approach allied to energetic, bouncy rhythms. Throughout, the orchestra sounds warmly romantic, the important solo wind parts full of character.

The Sonata, too, is well worth hearing. Written 20 years before the Concerto, it's still a fully mature work, mixing grand Lisztian gestures with classical formal outlines and ingenious, colourful harmony. Kliegel and Glemser play with fine style and intense commitment, encompassing the high Romanticism and, in the outer movement, Lalo's characteristically forceful rhythmic manner. *Chants russes* is an arrangement of the middle movement of the *Concerto russe* for violin – it's very effective as a cello piece. Kliegel's soft, refined sound near the end is especially memorable.

Violin Concerto

Violin Concerto in F, Op 20[a]. Concerto russe, Op 29[a]. Scherzo. Le roi d'Ys – Overture
[a]**Olivier Charlier** vn **BBC Philharmonic Orchestra / Yan Pascal Tortelier**
Chandos CHAN9758 (72' · DDD) Ⓕ🅑➔

This collection opens splendidly with a spankingly good performance of the Overture to *Le roi d'Ys*, with its melodrama, brassy splashes and a rather memorable swooning cello solo. It has all the gusto and panache of a Beecham performance and is certainly the finest account on disc since Paray's old Mercury version. Then come the two *concertante* violin works, both written with Sarasate in mind (separated by the comparatively familiar *Scherzo*, given here with rumbustious zest). Why are they not better known? The Violin Concerto has plenty going for it, a nicely coloured palette, a disarmingly nostalgic lyrical melody to haunt the first movement, followed by a delightful, songful *Andante*, which Olivier Charlier plays with engaging delicacy. But the real surprise is the *Concerto russe*, virtually another *Symphonie espagnole*, but with Slavic rather than Spanish ideas, and very good ones too. Its lovely slow movement, the 'Chant russe', opens with a chorale and the violin steals in with a genuine Russian folk tune, which (with its rhythmic snaps) is astonishingly reminiscent of the Bruch *Scottish Fantasy*. Charlier plays it most tenderly and the result is gently ravishing. The 'Intermezzo', with its off-beat timpani interjections and catchy main theme, is delicious, rhythmically sparkling in Charlier's hands, and there's another luscious secondary theme to come in the middle. The finale opens with a burst of sombre Slavonic passion from the strings, and another folk melody arrives. Soon the music quickens, culminating in a vivacious conclusion, with Charlier's contribution always lightly sparkling. Highly recommended.

Symphonie espagnole

Lalo Symphonie espagnole, Op 21[a] **Vieuxtemps** Violin Concerto No 5 in A minor, Op 37[b]
Sarah Chang vn [a]**Concertgebouw Orchestra,** [b]**Philharmonia Orchestra / Charles Dutoit**
EMI 555292-2 (52' · DDD)
Recorded [a]live 1995, [b]1994 Ⓕ🅑➔

The *Symphonie espagnole* is a more ambitious piece than the Vieuxtemps, and Lalo's inventive Spanishry holds up well throughout the five movements. Dutoit's approach has impetus, so when the *malagueña* secondary theme arrives, it makes a shimmering contrast. The delicious piping woodwind *crescendo* and *decrescendo* which begins the finale sets the scene for scintillating *salterello* fireworks from the soloist. The dash to the home straight brings vociferous applause, which makes one realise that the concentration and spontaneity of the performance has been helped by the presence of an audience, who aren't apparent until this point. Certainly the splendidly resonant Concertgebouw sound and perfect balance would never give the game away.

Vieuxtemps's Fifth Concerto opens disarmingly, but the *tutti* gathers strength in Dutoit's hands before Chang steals in silkily and proceeds to dominate the performance with her warm lyricism and natural, flowing *rubato*. In a performance like this it remains a small-scale work to cherish, for it hasn't a dull bar in it. The recording is warm and full, the balance treating the relationship between the violin and the Philharmonia Orchestra as an equal partnership.

Constant Lambert   British 1905-1951

Educated at Christ's Hospital and the Royal College of Music, Lambert was a prodigy, writing orchestral works from the age of 13, and at 20 received a commission to write a ballet for Serge Diaghilev's Ballets Russes (Romeo and Juliet), the first English composer to do so. Thus started an association with ballet – both as a conductor and composer – that was to stay with him for the remainder of his life. Among his own ballet scores were Pomona (1927) and Horoscope (1938) for the Vic-Wells Ballet, of which he was founder musical director. Among his concert works were the Rio Grande for piano, chorus and orchestra (1927), the Concerto for piano and nonet (1930-31) and the choral orchestral 'masque' Summer's Last Will and Testament (1932-35), held by many to be his greatest score. Lambert was famous in his day as a raconteur and he was also one of the first 'serious' composers to understand fully the importance of jazz and popular culture in the music of his time: this is illustrated by his book Music Ho! (1934). Lambert died in August 1951, two days short of his 46th birthday, of pneumonia and undiagnosed diabetes complicated by acute alcoholism.

Piano Concerto

Concerto for Piano and Chamber Orchestra[a]. Merchant Seamen Suite. Pomona. Prize-Fight
[a]**David Owen Norris** pf **BBC Concert Orchestra / Barry Wordsworth**
ASV White Line CDWHL2122 (66' · DDD) Ⓜ🅞🅞

More gaps in the Lambert discography are enterprisingly plugged by these sensitive and shapely performances, which display most agreeable dash and commitment. The Piano Concerto recorded here isn't that unnervingly bleak 1930-31 creation for soloist and nine players but one from 1924 that remained in short score, never to be heard in the composer's lifetime. Now, thanks to the editorial skills of Giles Easterbrook and Edward Shipley, we can at last savour another astonishingly mature and skilful product of Lambert's youth. Not only is the concerto tightly organised and brimful of striking invention, it also plumbs expressive depths, not least in the *Andante* slow movement which contains music as achingly poignant as any he penned. David Owen Norris does full justice to the glittering solo part, and he receives splendid support from Barry Wordsworth and the BBC Concert Orchestra.

Prize-Fight (Lambert's first ballet score) is earlier still, begun in 1923, completed the following year and overhauled one last time in 1927. It's a veritable romp, pungently scored in the manner of Satie and Milhaud, and with something of the anarchic spirit of Georges Auric's deliciously daft contributions to those glorious Ealing Comedies. In point of fact, Lambert had long been a connoisseur of the silver screen before he finally embarked on his first film score in 1940, for a flag-waving documentary entitled *Merchant Seamen*. Two years later, he compiled the present five-movement suite, and a superior specimen it is. *Pomona* we've had before. Wordsworth's spacious realisation occasionally lacks something in sheer effervescence and dry wit. But this is a most enjoyable and valuable compilation and the recording is vivid and truthfully balanced.

Tiresias

Tiresias. Pomona
English Northern Philharmonia / David Lloyd-Jones
with [a]**Michael Cleaver** pf
Hyperion CDA67049 (72' · DDD)   Ⓕ Ⓞ ➔

Constant Lambert's *Tiresias* was commissioned for the Festival of Britain in 1951 and the subject had been preoccupying the composer for over 20 years. In the event, the ailing Lambert struggled to meet his July deadline and called upon colleagues including Robert Irving, Alan Rawsthorne, Elisabeth Lutyens, Gordon Jacob, Denis Apivor, Humphrey Searle and Christian Darnton to help him finish the orchestration. Lambert directed eight performances in all, but the work was coolly received and he died the following month, just two days before his 46th birthday.

The instrumentation of *Tiresias* calls for neither violins nor violas and features a notably varied battery of percussion as well as an important role for piano obbligato (brilliantly played here by Michael Cleaver). The music has a dark-hued intimacy and at times starkly ritualistic demeanour which probably baffled that glitzy first-night audience. However, Lambert's achievement is ripe for reas-

sessment, and David Lloyd-Jones's meticulously prepared realisation allows us to revel anew in the score's many effective set-pieces. Stravinsky and Ravel are prime influences, but the work is suffused with that distinctive mix of keen brilliance and bleak melancholy so characteristic of its creator. The present account is all one could wish for.

Pomona (1927) is much earlier and altogether lighter in tone. Deftly scored for a chamber orchestra of 34 instrumentalists, *Pomona* comprises eight delightfully inventive numbers whose neo-classical spirit breathes very much the same air as that of Stravinsky and Les Six from the same period. Again, the performance is first-rate and the sound quite admirable.

Romeo and Juliet

The Bird Actors. Pomona. Romeo and Juliet
Victoria State Orchestra / John Lanchbery
Chandos CHAN9865 (56' · DDD)   Ⓕ Ⓞ ➔

The really good news here is the CD debut of *Romeo and Juliet*, one of only two ballet scores that Diaghilev commissioned from British composers for his Ballets Russes. It's a frothy romp firmly in the Stravinsky/Poulenc/Milhaud mould – and a brilliantly confident achievement for a 20-year-old student – but, strange to relate, there's barely a glimpse of the sheer expressive scope of either *Pomona* or *The Rio Grande* (not to mention the remarkable Piano Concerto). We've long needed a worthy successor to Norman Del Mar's affectionate Lyrita version with the ECO (see below); happily, Lanchbery and company have plugged the gap with notable success. Not only does the orchestral playing evince infectious zest and unswerving dedication to the cause, Lanchbery directs with palpable relish throughout.

He also gives us an enjoyably lithe account of *Pomona* and a sparkling curtain-raiser in the guise of *The Bird Actors*, a three-minute overture which originally began life as the finale of an even earlier ballet entitled *Adam and Eve*. The sound throughout is lively and full-bodied, without perhaps being in the very top flight.

Romeo and Juliet[a]. Pomona[a]. Music for Orchestra[b].
Summer's Last Will and Testament – King Pest:
Rondo Burlesca[c]
[a]**English Chamber Orchestra / Norman Del Mar**;
[b]**London Philharmonic Orchestra / Barry
Wordsworth**; [c]**Royal Philharmonic Orchestra /
Simon Joly**
Lyrita SRCD215 (73' · [a]ADD/DDD)   Ⓕ ➔

Norman Del Mar's effervescent pairing of *Romeo and Juliet* (1924-25) and *Pomona* (1926) ranked high on many an enthusiast's Lyrita wish-list and the first thing to say is that the 30-year-old Kingsway Hall production leaps out of the speakers with startling bite and tangibility in its silver-disc reincarnation. Although the intervening years have brought other rewarding versions of these two delicious ballets, Del Mar's vintage performances project with a tangy zest, charisma and infectious rhythmic spring all their own. The ECO's distinguished woodwind roster leave an especially personable impression in both scores.

The fill-ups (recorded in 1989 and 1993 but previously unreleased) are worth having too. *King Pest* (a scary helter-skelter ride fairly grinning with malice) comes from Lambert's towering 1932-35 'masque' *Summer's Last Will and Testament* and Simon Joly's spirited realisation with the RPO makes an enjoyable pendant to the complete work. More valuable still is the long-overdue revival of *Music for Orchestra* (completed in 1927, when Lambert was still only 22). Barry Wordsworth and the LPO strain every sinew in what, amazingly, appears to be this little masterpiece's first stereo recording.

Orlande de Lassus

Franco-Flemish 1532-1594

Lassus was born in Mons (now in modern Belgium), but at the age of 12 he travelled south, spending many years in Italy and Sicily. He was maestro di cappella of St John Lateran, Rome, in 1553. He returned to the Low Countries and in 1556 became a member of he court chapel of Duke Albrecht V of Bavaria in Munich. He took over the court chapel in 1563 and served the duke and his heir, Wilhelm V, for over 30 years, until his death.

He was an enormously prolific composer across most genres – his total output numbers over 2000 works. Most of his Masses are 'parody Masses', using existing motets, chansons or madrigals as the musical germ for the entire work. He published five volumes of sacred music as Patrocinium musices and after his death his sons assembled another (Magnum opus musicum, 1604). He remains one of the most versatile composers of the Renaissance, and one of the greatest.

Masses

Missa Entre vous filles. Missa Susanne un jour.
Infelix ego[a]
Oxford Camerata / Jeremy Summerly
Naxos 8 550842 (68' · DDD · [a]T/t)   ⑤☞

The Masses *Entre vous filles* and *Susanne un jour* show Lassus at his best, full of variety and invention, music of an immediate impact; in fact, they display exactly the same qualities as the better-known motets. The Oxford Camerata has understood this well, taking considerable care with the nuances of the text and really enjoying the music's rich sonorities. Sometimes a slight imprecision in the playing of chords is detectable, but this is more than outweighed by the sense of melodic contour and the powerful, somewhat dark and austere sound which conveys so well the spirit of

the music. With over 68 minutes of some of the finest 16th-century polyphony available at such a low price, no one should hesitate.

William Lawes

British 1602-1645

William Lawes was probably a chorister at Salisbury Cathedral until the patronage of the Earl of Hertford gave him a sound musical education with the Earl's own music master, John Coprario. In 1635 Lawes was appointed 'musician in ordinary for the lute and voices' to Charles I. In 1642 he enlisted in the Royalist army, accompanying the king on campaigns; he was killed during the battle to relieve the garrison at Chester. He was an imaginative and prolific composer whose genius can be best glimpsed in his consort music and in his songs, of which he wrote over 200. His theatrical masques are very fine, and are considered second only to those of Henry Purcell, a generation later.

Consort Setts

Consort Setts a 6 – in G; in C; in F; in B; in C.
Fantazy a 6 in F
Phantasm (Wendy Gillespie, Jonathan Manson, Varpu Haavisto, Susanne Braumann, Markku Luolajan-Mikkola viols) / **Laurence Dreyfus** viol
Channel Classics CCS17498 (60' · DDD)   ⑤**OO**

Dreyfus writes passionately about the music, referring to 'a Dionysian frenzy hell-bent on breaking civilised taboos' and 'jubilant incantations'. So what do we hear? A subtly resonant, particularised landscape: in effect an Elysian soundscape. Gone is the corporate consort sound we learnt to relish in former decades, replaced with rather more democratic textures. With seeming ease, the voice of each viol emerges and withdraws on cue as the music unfolds with sublime logic and unquestionable momentum.

The best setts are perhaps the two in minor keys, which offered Lawes a richer harmonic palette and the players greater expressive possibilities. The harmonically bizarre first Fantazy of the C minor Sett must have excited 17th-century ears, which, if they were lucky, were treated as we are here to an excitingly paced second Fantazy, then an 'Inomine' ('sinewy' and sustained at first, then quicker in the second section, the plainchant exquisitely interwoven and at the same time plain for all to hear), and finally a vibrant Aire, resplendent in its swaggering repeated notes and syncopated dash. Whether it would make so vivid an impression from another ensemble is doubtful. Dreyfus's unselfconscious hyperbolic enthusiasm aside, these are beautifully thought-out, sympathetic performances, worthy of a cultivated monarch and the composer's quatercentenary. A superb disc.

Jean-Marie Leclair French 1697-1764

Leclair, now best known as a violinist and composer, started his career as a dancer. He was based in Paris where his music, primarily for the violin, brought him to the attention of music lovers. In 1733 he became ordinaire de la musique du roi at the French court, and for a period from 1738 he served royals courts in the Netherlands and in the Hague. He then lived mainly in Paris, where he was murdered (probably by his ex-wife) after the breakdown of his second marriage.

The violin features large in Leclair's output with solos, duets and trio sonatas, and he successfully fused the Italian style with that of the French. He also composed concertos, minuets, suites etc, ballet music and an opera (Scylla et Glaucus, 1746). He was also a highly thought-of teacher.

Violin Concertos

Violin Concertos, Op 7 – No 1 in D minor; P
Op 10 – No 3 in D; No 4 in F; No 6 in G minor
Collegium Musicum 90 / Simon Standage vn
Chandos Chaconne CHAN0589 (59' · DDD) (F)O B►

This disc contains Leclair's most vivacious and attractive works, played with great élan, sensitivity and neatness, and recorded with exemplary clarity and balance. The concertos represent a high-water mark in 18th-century violin technique, with extensive double-stopping, an extended range that soars up to heights scarcely ventured previously, rapid scales and flying arpeggios, and elaborate figurations of all kinds. To all of this Standage brings a seasoned virtuosity which he places totally at the service of the music's grace: his bowing in particular commands admiration. From the stylistic viewpoint these concertos are interesting for their mingling of French and Italian elements. There are Vivaldian unisons, but French dance forms for the middle movements – a pair of minuets in the D minor, minuets *en rondeau* in the G minor, a pair of gavottes with unusual interplay between solo and *tutti* in the F major, and an ornate solo line over supporting reiterated chords in the D major. Standage adds spontaneous embellishments of his own on repeats.

Violin Sonatas

Violin Sonatas, Op 1 – No 1 in A minor; P
No 3 in B flat; No 8 in G; No 9 in A
François Fernandez vn **Pierre Hantaï** hpd
Philippe Pierlot va da gamba
Astrée Naïve E8662 (64' · DDD) (F)

Leclair's Op 1 set was so successful when it was first published in 1723 that it had to be reprinted four times. Though it makes considerable technical demands on the violinist, the composer himself was at pains not to employ virtuosity as an end in itself and to condemn the 'trivialisa-

tion' of players who exaggerated the speed of quick movements. Leclair also, like Couperin, was insistent that performers should not add ornamentation of their own – though in the four sonatas here only the initial *Adagio* of No 3 is much decorated. Rather did he place emphasis on 'le beau chant' – expressive *cantabile*, which is well exemplified in the first movements of Nos 1, 8 and 9. The crisp *Allegro*, with its rapid dipping across strings, and the *Largo* of No 3 make play with multiple stopping, including double trills, and there's vigorous cross-string work too in the ebullient Giga of No 1. Leclair shows himself fond of the rondeau form with long episodes, and the Sarabande of No 9 is a set of variations. This last has an athletic gamba line, as does the whole of the G major Sonata; and the alert and positive continuo playing here (from both gamba and harpsichord) is a special pleasure. But naturally the main spotlight falls on François Fernandez, whose lively, pointed bowing, delicate fast movements and graceful slow ones (like the gentle G major Musette) do full justice to Leclair's attractive invention.

Ernesto Lecuona Cuban 1895-1963

Born into a musical family, Lecuona played the piano from an early age. He graduated from the National Conservatory in Havana and soon after was appearing as a composer-pianist. Then, after further studies with Joaquín Nin, he made several tours of Latin America, Europe and the USA as the leader of a dance band, Lecuona's Cuban Boys. For some years he lived in New York, where he wrote for musicals, films and the radio. He was a prolific composer of songs and music for stage and film. His works consisted of zarzuela, Afro-Cuban and Cuban rhythms, suites and many songs which are still very famous (a great deal of Lecuona's music was first introduced to mass American audiences by Desi Arnaz, a fellow Cuban and Lucille Ball's husband).

Songs

'On a Night Like This'
Siempre en mi corazón. Como presiento. Allá en la sierra. Tu no tienes corazón. Mi corazón se fué. Dame de tus rosas. ¡No es por ti! La habanera – ¡Mira! Dame el amor. Que risa me da. La comparsa. Al fin. Se abrieron las flores. Conga Cuba. Amor tardio. En una noche así. Devuélveme el corazón. Primavera de ilusión. Un amor vendrá. Me has dejado. No me engañarás. Rumba mejoral. No me mires ni me hables. Mi amor fue una flor. Canción del amor triste.
Carole Farley sop **John Constable** pf
BIS BIS-CD1374 (70' · DDD · T/t) (F)O

It's curious to think that Paul Hindemith and Ernesto Lecuona were almost exact contemporaries, born a couple of months apart in 1895 and dying within five weeks of each other at the end of 1963. Yet, despite this closeness in time, their music had no real common ground. Hindemith was no mean song-writer, though not especially prolific, unlike the Cuban Lecuona for whom song was a paramount form of expression: he wrote around 400 of them.

For this recording Carole Farley undertook a protracted detective hunt through libraries, publishers, basements and packing cases to arrive at her selection of 25 love songs. Hers is a fine and varied choice, highlighting Lecuona's undeniable gifts as a melodist and word-setter.

Farley sings all the songs with great finesse and warmth of feeling. Very occasionally, as in *Se abrieron las flores* ('The flowers opened'), her vibrato doesn't suit Lecuona's clean lines. She's accompanied sympathetically by the excellent John Constable, whose playing is a model of precision yet catches that feeling of improvisation that is an essential part of these songs. The recording is wonderfully pure and clear.

Franz Lehár   Austro-Hungarian 1870-1948

Lehár was the son of a military bandmaster. He entered the Prague Conservatory to study the violin when he was 12. On showing Dvořák a couple of student sonatas he had written, the great Czech is supposed to have said, 'Hang up your fiddle, my boy. Concentrate on composing.' At 20 he was the youngest bandmaster ever appointed in the Army, but after writing an opera, Kukuschka, the interest of a publisher finally persuaded him to act on Dvořák's advice.

He soon made a name for himself as a composer of operettas with a string of works for Vienna's Theater an der Wien but it wasn't until Die lustige Witwe in 1905 that he hit the jackpot. After a few failures, Lehár tapped into a winning streak again and the space of three months (October 1909 to January 1910) saw the first nights of Das Fürstenkind ('The Prince's Child'), Zigeunerliebe ('Gypsy Love') and The Count of Luxembourg. Rich and famous, he and his wife Sophie moved to the Salzkammergut. With the death of the Emperor Franz Josef and the outbreak of the First World War, Lehár's success subsided. It wasn't until he met the great opera and lieder singer Richard Tauber that his career was revitalised. Lehár wrote a string of operettas tailored to Tauber's magnetic personality and voice and a second string of triumphs followed, including Friederike in 1928, Das Land des Lächelns ('The Land of Smiles') in 1929 – the biggest hit since the Merry Widow – and Giuditta in 1934.

Again, war intervened, this time for good. Tauber was forced to leave for England when the Nazi menace spread. Lehár, though, retired to his villa at Bad Ischl and remained there for the whole war.

Concertino for Violin and Orchestra

Tatjana – Prelude, Act 1; Prelude, Act 2; Prelude, Act 3; Russian Dances. Fieber. Il guado. Concertino for Violin and Orchestra in B flat minor. Eine Vision:

Meine Jugendzeit. Donaulegenden, 'An der grauen Donau'
Robert Gambill *ten* **Latica Honda-Rosenberg** *vn* **Volker Banfield** `pf` **North German Radio Philharmonic Orchestra / Klauspeter Seibel**
CPO CPO999 423-2 (70' · DDD · T/t)   Ⓜ

Lehár's mastery of the orchestra has never been in doubt; and here's further evidence of his technical accomplishment. Such touches of the operetta composer as are here are of the more ambitious operetta scores such as *Zigeunerliebe*. More often it's Wagner, Richard Strauss and Korngold who come to mind. Throughout, the music is tastefully and evocatively written, and with a supreme confidence in the handling of a large orchestra. *Tatjana* was an early operatic attempt of which Lehár was especially fond, and its preludes and dances capture the starkness of its Siberian setting. *Il guado* ('The Ford') and the concert overture *Eine Vision* are works from the *Lustige Witwe* years, when Lehár was still seeking to determine in which direction his future lay. The former is a symphonic poem with some attractively rippling writing for the piano, the latter a recollection of the Bohemian countryside of his youth. The elegant Concertino for violin and orchestra, which has been recorded previously, is a student work that demonstrates his affection for his own instrument. *Fieber* is the starkest piece in the collection – a bitter First World War portrayal of a soldier in the throes of a deadly fever. *Donaulegenden* gives glimpses of the familiar waltz-time Lehár, but a Lehár looking back sadly at a bygone age. What other operetta or waltz composer could have written music as powerful, gripping and spine-tingling as this? Do try it!

Waltzes and Overtures

Gold und Silber, Op 79. Wiener Frauen – overture. Ⓗ Der Graf von Luxemburg – Waltz; Waltz Intermezzo. Zigeunerliebe – overture. Eva – Wär' es auch nichts als ein Traum von Glück; Waltz Scene. Das Land des Lächelns – overture. Die lustige Witwe – concert overture
Tonhalle Orchestra, Zürich / Franz Lehár
Dutton mono CDBP9721 (66' · ADD) Recorded 1947
Ⓢ⊘

These were the 77-year-old composer's last recordings. Most were reissued on LP (latterly on the Eclipse label), but here they're complete for the first time. Mostly the selections represent obvious items from Lehár's melodic output. However, the inclusion of the *Wiener Frauen* overture is an especial joy, representing Lehár at his less familiar but most melodic and inventive. The operetta's principal character was a piano tuner, and the overture includes an ingenious passage where one hears the piano being tuned up before launching into one of Lehár's most luxuriant and beautiful waltzes.

In his excellent notes Malcolm Walker aptly describes these recordings as, in a sense, Lehár's last will and testament. Slower and more indulgent than his earlier recordings they may be; but never for a moment the slightest bit ponderous. Rather they're full of nostalgia, wonder and joyful pride – lovingly caressed performances by a master melodist, master orchestrator and master conductor. The transfers have been excellently done from original shellac discs. Filtering may be required to minimise hiss; but it's more than worth while for uniquely beautiful recordings of some of the most heavenly melodies ever created.

Giuditta

Giuditta (sung in English)
Deborah Riedel sop Giuditta **Jerry Hadley** ten
Octavio **Jeffrey Carl** bar Manuele Biffi, Antonio
Andrew Busher spkr Duke **Naomi Itami** sop Anita
Lynton Atkinson ten Pierrino **William Dieghan** ten
Sebastiano **English Chamber Orchestra /**
Richard Bonynge
Telarc CD80436 (78' · DDD · T)   Ⓕ

Giuditta was Lehár's last stage work and the peak of his compositional development. Written for the Vienna State Opera, it's a highly ambitious score, containing some fiendishly difficult vocal writing and using a large orchestra featuring mandolin and other exotic instruments. For this recording some two hours of music have been compressed into 78 minutes by means of snips here and there and the omission of a couple of subsidiary numbers. The piece has a *Carmen*-like story, about the disenchanted wife of an innkeeper who persuades a soldier to desert, before eventually abandoning and ruining him as she goes from lover to lover. The best-known number is Giuditta's 'On my lips every kiss is like wine', here gloriously sung by Deborah Riedel; the leading male role was written for Tauber, and there are some marvellous and demanding tenor solos, equally superbly sung by the impressive Jerry Hadley. Despite writing for the opera house, Lehár remained faithful to his formula of interspersing the music for the principal couple with sprightly dance numbers for a comedy pair, here in the hands of Naomi Itami and Lynton Atkinson. Assisted by Richard Bonynge's lilting conducting, these contribute richly to the appeal of the recording.

Die lustige Witwe (The Merry Widow)

Die lustige Witwe   Ⓗ
Elisabeth Schwarzkopf sop Hanna **Erich Kunz** bar
Danilo **Anton Niessner** bar Zeta **Nicolai Gedda** ten
Camille **Emmy Loose** sop Valencienne **Josef
Schmidinger** bass Raoul **Ottakar Kraus** bar Cascada
Philharmonia Orchestra and Chorus /
Otto Ackermann
EMI mono 585822-2 (72' · ADD)
Recorded 1953   ⒻⓄⓄⓄ▷

This is a star-studded performance. Emmy Loose has exactly the right appealing kind of voice for

the 'dutiful wife' who plays with fire, and Nicolai Gedda is a superb Camille, sounding extraordinarily like Tito Schipa at his best. His high notes ring out finely and his caressing lyrical tones would upset a far better-balanced woman than the susceptible Valencienne. These two sing their duets beautifully, both excelling in the second act duet, in which Gedda has the lion's share. Nothing in this recording, except Schwarzkopf's 'Vilja', is so ravishing as his soft tone in the second half of the duet ('Love in my heart is waking'), which begins 'Sieh' dort den kleinen Pavillon' ('See over there the little pavilion') which is perhaps the loveliest in the score. Erich Kunz has not the charm but more voice and a perfect command of the style the music requires; and he's very taking in the celebrated Maxim's song. He speaks the middle section of the little song about the Königskinder possibly because the vocal part lies uncomfortably high for him; and perhaps his rich laughter would not be considered quite the thing in the diplomatic service. But his is, in most ways, a very attractive and lively performance. The Baron's part was probably much written up for George Graves but here what little he has to do is done well by Anton Niessner.

Elisabeth Schwarzkopf sings Hanna radiantly and exquisitely. She commands the ensembles in no uncertain manner and makes it clear that the 20-million-francs widow would be a personage even if she had only 20 centimes. It's a grand performance, crowned with the sensuous, tender singing of the celebrated waltz in Act 3. The chorus singing is first-rate and its Viennese abandon sounds absolutely authentic, whatever its address. Otto Ackermann conducts with total understanding, and notable sympathy for the singers, and the members of the Philharmonia Orchestra play like angels for him. The recording is as good as one can reasonably expect and, very important in such a score, the string tone is lovely throughout.

Die lustige Witwe
Cheryl Studer sop Hanna **Boje Skovhus** bar Danilo
Bryn Terfel bass-bar Zeta **Rainer Trost** ten Camille
Barbara Bonney sop Valencienne **Uwe Peper** ten
Raoul **Karl-Magnus Fredriksson** bar Cascada **Heinz
Zednik** ten Njegus **Richard Savage** bar
Bogdanowitsch **Lynette Alcantara** sop Sylviane
Philip Salmon ten Kromow **Constanze Backes** mez
Olga **Julian Clarkson** bass Pritschitsch **Angela
Kazimierczuk** sop Praškowia **Wiener Tschuschen-
kapelle; Vienna Philharmonic Orchestra /**
Sir John Eliot Gardiner
DG 439 911-2GH (80' · DDD · T/t)   ⒻⓄⓄ▷

This is a truly great operetta interpretation. Gardiner's approach is on an altogether more inspired plane than his rivals. In the Viennese rhythms, he shows himself utterly at home – as in the Act 2 Dance scene, where he eases the orchestra irresistibly into the famous waltz. But there are also countless instances where Gardiner provides a deliciously fresh inflexion to the score. The cast of singers is uniformly impressive. If Cheryl Studer's 'Vilja' isn't quite as assured as some others, her captivatingly playful 'Dummer, dummer Reitersmann' is typical of a well-characterised performance. As Danilo, Boje Skovhus acquits himself well with a polished performance and he offers a natural, more human characterisation than his rivals, while Barbara Bonney is superb. Not the least inspired piece of casting comes with Bryn Terfel, who transforms himself outstandingly well into the bluff Pontevedran ambassador. As for Gardiner's personally selected chorus, they make Monteverdi to Montenegro and Pontevedra seem the most natural transition in the world. DG's recorded sound has an astonishing clarity and immediacy, as in the way the piccolos shriek out at the Widow's Act 1 entrance or in the beautiful *pianissimo* accompaniment to the 'Vilja-Lied'.

Additional recommendations

Frühling. Elfentanz. Hungarian Fantasy, Op 45ª
Krahnenfeld Hedwig **Browner** Toni **Wörle** Lorenz
Köhler Ewald ªGothoni vn **Deutsche
Kammerakademie Neuss / Goritzki**
CPO CPO 999 727-2 (78' · DDD · T/t)　　　　Ⓕ

A completely unfamiliar Lehár operetta is a surprise indeed, and an utterly delightful treat it turns out to be. Set against the background of a Viennese housing shortage, it's a 'show-within-a-show' piece, featuring amorous goings-on between a composer, his librettist and two office typists. And it's the composer who gets the girl! CPO has given the piece a winning performance, admirably capturing its lightheartedness in splendidly clear sound. This CD is altogether a sheer delight.

Schön ist die Welt
Mosuc Princess Elisabeth, Mercedes **Todorovich**
Prince Georg, Count Sascha **Bavarian Radio Chorus;
Munich RSO / Schirmer**
CPO CPO777 055-2 (77' · DDD · S/N)　　　　Ⓕ

Two royal intendeds, reluctant to commit to an arranged marriage, come together as strangers. Princess Elisabeth and Crown Prince Georg (incognito as an Alpine guide) walk in the peaks, pick flowers, hear over the radio that there are fears for Her Highness's safety, are stranded overnight by an avalanche – and fall in love. As Lehár's career – and his blood-brotherhood relationship with Tauber – progressed, he demanded increasing virtuosity of his principal singers. Elena Mosuc and Zoran Todorovich are absolutely assured in style, language and technique. Their accomplishment is matched by the affectionate, well-scaled conducting of Ulf Schirmer.

Tatjana
Schubert Sergej **Schellenberger** Tatjana **Lippert**
Alexis **Mewes** Sasha **Sabrowski** Djerid, Nikolajev
Bluth Pimen **Lemme** Punin **Fischer** Raisa **Scholz**
Starost von Uslon **Berlin Radio Chor and SO / M
Jurowski**
CPO ② CPO999 762-2 (122' · DDD · T/t)　　　Ⓕ

The opera opens on the banks of the Volga in the 1840s, moves on to the mines of Siberia, and ends on the Russian steppes. There, in the snow, the lovers Alexis, a soldier, and Tatjana, the daughter of a Volga fisherman, die together. It remains a piece of beautiful lyrical writing, brilliant orchestral colouring and impassioned melody.

Peter Lieberson　　　　American b1946

Son of the legendary president of CBS Records, Goddard Lieberson, Peter Lieberson studied with Milton Babbitt and then at Columbia University with Wuorinen and Sollberger. He worked as an assistant to Leonard Bernstein in 1972 and was an assistant producer of the Young Persons' Concerts for CBS. He also founded and conducted two contemporary music ensembles. His interest in Buddhism started to emerge through his music, intially in his Piano Concerto (1980-83), written for Peter Serkin. In 1997 he wrote his first opera, Ashoka's Dream. He has written concertos for horn and cello. His marriage, in 1999, to mezzo-soprano Lorraine Hunt, led to a number of fine vocal works.

The Neruda Songs

The Neruda Songs
Lorraine Hunt Lieberson mez
Boston Symphony Orchestra / James Levine
Nonesuch 7559 79954-2 (32' · DDD)　　Ⓜ**ⓄⓄ**▷

Not so long ago, 'lush' and 'romantic' were words that would never figure in a description of Peter Lieberson's music. 'Rigorous', perhaps; 'intellectually stimulating', definitely. Of its integrity there was never any question. But deep down, the works were spun with the kind of cool brilliance that commands respect but rarely invites love. Then Lieberson met Lorraine Hunt, and for the next nine years – until her death from breast cancer in July 2006 – the Ice Man of music slowly melted.

Tributes to the mezzo-soprano have come in from all corners of the musical globe but none is more touching than *The Neruda Songs*, jointly commissioned by the Boston Symphony Orchestra and the Los Angeles Philharmonic, and premiered only a year or so before her death. What makes this collaboration particularly poignant is that, like any offspring, one can find traits of both parents: Lieberson's cerebral qualities are warmly humanised, Hunt Lieberson's shimmering vocal sensuality restrained from over-indulgence. These brilliantly crafted songs deserve all the attention they can get; after a respectful period of mourning, other singers need to pick up the mantle.

Clearly this piece is a big advancement for Lieberson. The famously complex Lieberson now has the gift to be simple, and his future works bear watching. That spiritual connection comes around all too rarely and would make it could be repeated. Unfortunately, at slightly more than 30 minutes, this recording is all we've got.

Jón Leifs
Icelandic 1899-1968

Leifs studied in Leipzig (1916-22) and then pursued a career as a conductor and also as a writer. Most of his works are about Icelandic natural phenomena. In the piece Hekla he depicts the eruption of the volcano Hekla which he witnessed. Dettifoss was inspired by the Dettifoss waterfall, the most powerful in Europe. In the Saga Symphony he musically portrays five characters of famous Icelandic sagas.

Edda

Edda, Part 1: The Creation of the World
Gunnar Gudbjörnsson ten **Bjarni Thor Kristinsson** bass-bar **Schola Cantorum; Iceland Symphony Orchestra / Hermann Bäumer**
BIS ⚛ BIS-SACD1350 (76' · DDD · T/t)   Ⓕ**OO**

Jón Leifs was a true original and his *Edda* oratorio cycle was one of his most original inspirations. Planned in the 1920s as a single oratorio on the Völuspá, it grew into an epic tetralogy – though without a hint of Wagnerian Romanticism covering the world's creation, its gods, 'Twilight' and 'Resurrection', setting a patchwork text which reads like a compendium on each subject. Sadly, Leifs only lived to complete the first two parts.

The 13 movements of 'The Creation of the World' (1932-39) tell of the giant Mir and his death at the hands of Odin and his brothers and their fashioning of the Earth, Sea and Heavens – and the first men – from the corpse; the remaining sections then describe its nature.

To relate this epic narrative Leifs deployed a huge orchestra with a large percussion section (including rocks struck with hammers), organ, ocarina, bagpipes and a quartet of lurs, reconstructions of ancient Viking horns. Yet the orchestration – occasionally unleashed to sensational effect – is mostly used with restraint, nowhere more so than in the huge eighth movement, 'Night, Morning', where the dynamics rarely rise above *piano*.

This performance, recorded in the wake of the work's long overdue complete premiere in 2006, sounds thrilling, the BIS engineering catching the huge dynamic range, weight and delicacy of sound. Bäumer holds everything together with finesse and the orchestra play the atmospheric accompaniment marvellously. The main plaudits go, however, to the chorus who sing their extremely difficult parts with compelling conviction. Leifs's slightly ungainly style may not be to everyone's taste but his score is far more varied than first impressions suggest. Like it or loathe it, this is one of the recording events of the year.

Kenneth Leighton
British 1929-1988

Leighton studied at Oxford and with Petrassi in Rome, and following lecturing posts in Deal and in Leeds, in 1970 he was appointed professor at Edinburgh University. His music is in a 12-note but fundamentally diatonic style and demonstrates considerable power and intensity. He left three symphonies as well as a number of works for the Anglican church.

Symphony No 2

Symphony No 2, 'Sinfonia mistica'. Te Deum laudamus
Sarah Fox sop **BBC National Chorus and Orchestra of Wales / Richard Hickox**
Chandos CHAN10495 (57' · DDD · T)   Ⓕ**O**➔

Composed during 1973-74 in direct response to the death of his mother, Leighton's *Sinfonia mistica* is scored for soprano, chorus and orchestra. Described by its creator as 'a requiem or a meditation on the subject of death which usually becomes so more real to us in the second half of life', the symphony has six movements and sets texts by such great metaphysical poets as John Donne, Thomas Traherne and George Herbert, while also making telling use of the 1865 American hymn tune *The Shining River*. The linked 'Meditation' and 'Elegy' at the work's heart manifest an especially potent beauty, serenity and compassion, but, truth to tell, inspiration soars consistently high in this cogently wrought and (above all) profoundly humane utterance. This is music which will amply repay repeated listening. The orchestral version of the glorious 1964 *Te Deum laudamus* makes a rewarding postscript.

Both performances are beyond reproach. Sarah Fox sings with refulgent tone, commendable accuracy and shining intelligence; and Richard Hickox rallies the BBC Welsh forces to the same dizzy heights. Outstandingly vivid sound, too, with a perfectly judged balance throughout. Miss at your peril.

Chamber works

Piano Trio, Op 46[abc]. Partita, Op 35[ac]. Metamorphoses, Op 48[ab]. Elegy, Op 5[ac]
[a]**Michael Dussek** pf [b]**Lorraine McAslan** vn [c]**Andrew Fuller** vc
Dutton Epoch CDLX7118 (77' · DDD)   **O**

Although a fair amount of his music for voices has been recorded, Kenneth Leighton's orchestral and instrumental music is under-represented in the catalogue. This most impressive disc gives a good idea of what we're missing: superbly crafted music of at times overwhelming intensity. The craft and the intensity are inseparable: there's as little here of mere technical cleverness as there is of self-indulgent emotional display; the emotion both needs and is concentrated by tight control.

The Piano Trio is a characteristic example, its first movement building from close working of a broad, sweeping theme and a more subdued and shadowy one to a bitter eloquence slightly reminiscent of Shostakovich before a shadowy, drained conclusion. Calm is eventually achieved, but not serenity. The Partita has similar energy but a less fraught quality; there's even a sort of bony wit, again recalling Shostakovich, to some of the variations of the finale.

Metamorphoses, although ostensibly a single 21-minute movement, could be read as a monothematic sonata, with a quite violent *scherzo* and a slow finale, by turns poignant and ghostly. The very early *Elegy* reveals some of Leighton's English roots: descendants of its sustained lyrical theme can be heard in the later pieces, but there are some harmonic shifts of which John Ireland would have approved. The programme, in short, is an ideal introduction to this important but still underrated composer.

Choral Works

A Sequence for All Saints, Op 75. O God, enfold me in the sun. Morning Canticles. The World's Desire. A Sequence for Epiphany, Op 91. Rockingham
Wells Cathedral Choir; Wells Cathedral School Chapel Choir / Matthew Owens with
David Bednall org
Hyperion CDA67641 (76' · DDD)   Ⓕ Ⓞ ▸

Written in 1978 for the West Riding Cathedrals Festival, *A Sequence for All Saints* is a major score for large choir and organ, its five sections running continuously and containing some of Leighton's more sumptuous passages alongside those characteristic hallmarks: driving, repetitive rhythms, extended sequences and the piling on of harmonic tension. Larger still – weighing in at around half an hour – is *The World's Desire*, a BBC commission for a work reflecting facets of both Western and Eastern liturgy relating to the Feast of the Epiphany. It was premiered by the BBC Northern Singers in 1984. Between these come a typically celebratory anthem with a suitably dazzling organ part, *O God, enfold me in the sun*, a set of three Morning Canticles and an organ piece based on the hymn tune *Rockingham*.

Matthew Owens has certainly brought the Wells Cathedral Choir to the very peak of excellence; it ranks as probably the finest English cathedral choir at the moment. Supplemented by singers from the Wells Cathedral School Chapel Choir, the two large-scale works are delivered with great power and breadth, David Bednall's organ accompaniments as full of colour and pizzazz as one could want. It all adds up to stunning performances of outstanding music, a composer fully in sympathy with the practicalities of performance and musicians who are utterly at home with this distinctive musical idiom. Leighton's memory is well served in this superb release.

Additional recommendation

Crucifixus pro nobis, Op 38. An Easter Sequence, Op 55. Evening Service, 'Collegium Magdalenae Oxoniense'. Evening Service, Op 62. Give me the wings of faith. Rockingham. Veni Creator Spiritus. What love is this of thine?
Oxley ten **Whitton** org **Steele-Perkins** tpt **St John's College Choir, Cambridge / Robinson**
Naxos 8 555795 (67' · DDD)   Ⓢ Ⓑ ▸

Our reviewer summed up: 'In this business of record-reviewing I find, on the positive side, music and performances I like, more that I admire, some that I love, but not much that evokes affirmation from the soul. This does.'

Ruggero Leoncavallo
Italian 1858-1919

Cavalleria rusticana by Mascgani and Pagliacci – 'Cav and Pag' as they're known in the trade, for they're invariably presented together – are both one-act operas which provided their composers with their single successes. Why neither man could produce a further work which equalled these one-off works of indisputable greatness is one of music's curiosities. It certainly was not for lack of trying.

Leoncavallo's first opera, Tommaso Chatterton (about the young English poet) was about to be produced in 1878 when the manager absconded with the funds. Thereafter, Leoncavallo made a living by playing the piano in cafés all over Europe, Egypt and Turkey before settling in Paris. Here he made a thorough study of Wagner's scores and resolved to emulate the great German by writing a trilogy about the Italian Renaissance. The research alone took him six years. After he'd completed the first part and sketched the rest, he couldn't find a publisher.

Enraged at the lack of interest, Leoncavallo turned to Sonzogno, the publisher of Mascagni's Cavalleria rusticana, which had just become a huge success. In five months, Leoncavallo had written the entire libretto, music and orchestration of Pagliacci in a deliberate attempt to emulate the success of Mascagni. He based it on a true incident with which he had some connection: during his childhood in Calabria, a jealous actor had killed his wife after a performance; the magistrate who had tried the case was Leoncavallo's father. Pagliacci ('Clowns') was an instant and international success (Toscanini conducted the first performance in Milan in May 1892). Sonzogno now had under his control the two most popular one-act operas ever written.

Could Leoncavallo hit the jackpot again? He could not. The premieres of the first part of his Italian Renaissance trilogy and Tommaso Chatterton were greeted with indifference and then he had the misfortune to write La bohème – a year after Puccini had tackled the same subject. A light opera Zazà (1900) fared slightly better, but for all intents and purposes that was it. He kept on turning them out without making any impression at all. Just one hour of music for immortality!

'Vesti la giubba' from Act 1 of Pagliacci is among the greatest of tenor arias and was recorded in 1902 by Enrico Caruso. It made him the earliest recorded artist to sell more than a million copies of one record. In 1904 he recorded Leoncavallo's song 'Mattinata' with the composer at the piano and three years later, Pagliacci became the first complete recording of an opera to be issued in the UK.

Miscellaneous

La nuit de mai[a]. Aprile![b]. C'è nel tuo sguardo[b].
Hymne à la lyre[b]. La chanson des yeux[b]. L'addio[b].
Barcarola veneziana[c]. Valse mignonne[c]
[ab]**Plácido Domingo** ten [bc]**Lang Lang** pf
[a]**Orchestra of the Teatro Comunale, Bologna /
Alberto Veronesi**
DG 477 6633GH (60' · DDD)   Ⓕ**OO**🔁

The recording was made in 2007 and the books
give Domingo's date of birth as January 21,
1941: but the voice is firm, rich and resonant,
the high B still in working order, the low notes
somewhat baritonal (as they always have been)
but with no sense that here is a separate register
coming apart from the main body of the voice.
He can still sing with the fervour of youth but
also with its flexibility, its ease and grace of
movement. And, typically, he demonstrates all
of this in something new.

One assumes that the repertoire here is new to
all of us. *La nuit de mai* is a symphonic poem for
tenor and orchestra written in 1886 based on a
long dialogue-poem by de Musset. The tenor
sings the Poet's lines, those of his Muse being
represented orchestrally. The conception is bold,
the execution by no means pusillanimous. Probably most successful in the lighter movements
(there is a waltz, delightfully in the manner of the
French ballet), it aspires to deeper things, both in
happiness and grief, sometimes attaining them.
The composer of *Pagliacci* (1892) emerges with
startling clarity at one point and by shadowy suggestion more frequently. Among the songs, one
('La chanson des yeux') is to become Silvio's
'Decido il mio destin'. The Barcarolle and Waltz
for piano (1885) are joyously inventive, casually
offering something very like one of the best tunes
in *Die lustige Witwe* (1905) before moving on to
something just as catchy. Lang Lang plays them
with (alternately) the lingering fingers of old nostalgia and the headlong impetuosity of youthful
adventure.

I Medici

I Medici
Plácido Domingo ten Giuliano de' Medici **Carlos
Álvarez** ten Lorenzo de' Medici **Daniela Dessì** bar
Simonetta Cattanei **Renata Lamanda** bass Fioretta
de' Gori **Eric Owens** ten Giambattista da
Montesecco **Vitalij Kowaljow** bass Francesco Pazzi
Carlo Bosi ten Bernardo Bandini **Arutjun Kotchinian**
bass L'Arcivescovo Salviati **Fabio Maria Capitanucci**
bass-bar Il Poliziano **Chorus and Orchestra of
Maggio Musicale Fiorentino / Alberto Veronesi**
DG ② 477 7456GH2 (125' · DDD)   Ⓜ

I Medici ('The Medici family', or a seven-year
soap segment of their lives) is nothing less than
the *Walküre* of Leoncavallo's intended Italian
trilogy *Crepusculum*. This *après*-Wagnerian epic
was planned to include Savonarola and Cesare
Borgia. It stopped after the starrily cast Milan

premiere of *I Medici* in 1893 in which Francesco
Tamagno, creator of Verdi's Otello, took the
beau role of Giuliano that Plácido Domingo
records here.

This composer is a master of effects (mostly
Italian Romantic) and forms (mostly Wagnerian), although he is rather short here of the
melodic highlights of *Pagliacci* or even *Zazà*.
The story – 50 per cent political plotting, 50 per
cent sexual frustration, *nul points* for characterisation – is a problem. As in *Rienzi* essential back-
story is omitted (or reduced to footnotes in the
libretto) and the jump cuts replaced with melodramatic declamation. For not the first time in
Leoncavallo's output, one has the impression
that he is acting as an unconscious source of
harmonic and dramatic prompts to Puccini. The
final pages of both *Fanciulla* and *Tosca* are clearly
the work of a man who had read *I Medici*'s short
but crammed Act 4.

This first official recording will please the
(very) curious and add another tenor role, and a
strenuous, difficult one, to Domingo's catalogue. He does well, as do Álvarez as his murdered brother Lorenzo, Dessì and Lamanda (the
lovers he can't decide between) and Veronesi
and his forces in a set which feels like a performance the artists want to give rather than a catalogue duty.

Pagliacci

Pagliacci
Carlo Bergonzi ten Canio **Joan Carlyle** sop Nedda
Giuseppe Taddei bar Tonio **Rolando Panerai** bar
Silvio **Ugo Benelli** ten Beppe **Chorus and Orchestra
of La Scala, Milan / Herbert von Karajan**
DG The Originals 449 727-2GOR (78' · ADD · T/t)
Recorded 1965   **OO**🔁

Conviction and insight instil this *Pagliacci*
with excitement and real drama. A troupe of
actors arrives to give a performance of a *commedia dell'arte* play. The illustration of real
love, life and hatred is portrayed in the interplay of Tonio, Silvio, Nedda and her husband
Canio. As the two rivals, Caro Bergonzi and
Giuseppe Taddei are superb.

Taddei's sinister, hunchbacked clown, gently
forcing the play-within-the-play closer to reality
until it finally bursts out violently, is a masterly
assumption, and Karajan controls the slow
build-up of tension with a grasp that few conductors could equal. The forces of La Scala,
Milan respond wholeheartedly and the 1965
recording sounds well.

Leoncavallo Pagliacci   Ⓗ
Giuseppe di Stefano ten Canio **Maria Callas** sop
Nedda **Tito Gobbi** bar Tonio **Rolando Panerai** bar
Silvio **Nicola Monti** ten Beppe

Mascagni Cavalleria rusticana
Maria Callas sop Santuzza **Giuseppe di Stefano** ten
Turiddu **Rolando Panerai** bar Alfio **Anna Maria**

Canali mez Lola **Ebe Ticozzi** contr Lucia
**Chorus and Orchestra of La Scala, Milan /
Tullio Serafin**
EMI mono ② 586830-2 (141' · ADD · T/t)
Recorded 1954   ⓑⓄⓄ↦

The sound here is much more confined than on
the Karajan set, though more immediate. Serafin conducts swifter-moving performances, yet
ones quite as notable as Karajan's for pointing
up relevant detail. All four interpretations carry
with them a real sense of the theatre and are
quite free from studio routine. It's difficult to
choose between the casts on these two sets. Callas lives the characters more vividly than anyone.
The sadness and anguish she brings to Santuzza's unhappy plight are at their most compelling
at 'io piango' in 'Voi lo sapete' and at 'Turiddu
mi tolse' in her encounter with Alfio, where the
pain in Santuzza's heart is expressed in almost
unbearable terms. As Nedda, she differentiates
marvellously between the pensiveness of her
aria, the passion of her duet with Silvio, and the
playfulness of her *commedia dell'arte* acting.

Her partner in both operas is di Stefano. They
work up a huge lather of passion in the big *Cavalleria* duet, and the tenor is wholly believable as
the caddish Turiddu. In the immediacy of emotion of his Canio, it's the tenor's turn to evoke
pity. Di Stefano does it as well as any Canio on
record without quite having the heroic tone for
the latter part of the opera. Panerai is a strong
Alfio on the Serafin set, but Guelfi, with his
huge voice, is possibly better suited to this
macho part. It's impossible to choose between
the two Tonios, both pertinently cast. Taddei
plays the part a little more comically, Gobbi
more menacingly. Callas or Karajan enthusiasts
will have no difficulty making their choice. Others may be guided by quality of sound. With
either you'll be ensured hours of memorable
listening.

György Ligeti   Hungarian 1923-2006

*After studies at the Budapest Aacdemy, Ligeti began
teaching there in 1950. In 1956 he left Hungary for
Vienna. He worked at the electronic music studio in
Cologne (1957-58) and the work which put him on
the map was Atmosphères (1961). This led to teaching
appointments in Stockholm, Stanford and Hamburg.*

*The Requiem for soprano, mezzo-soprano, five-
voice chorus and orchestra is a four-movement work
in the same totally chromatic style as Atmosphères. It
is a massive, 20-part choral quasi-fugue where the
counterpoint is rethought in terms of the material,
consisting of melismatic masses interpenetrating and
alternating with complex skipping parts. The last
instance of this quoted in the film 2001: A Space
Odyssey. Ligeti confirmed that his parents' experience at Auschwitz is an influence in the piece.*

*From the 1970s, Ligeti turned away from total
chromaticism and began to concentrate on rhythm.
Clocks and Clouds (1972-73) was written before he*

*heard the music of Steve Reich and Terry Riley in
1972, yet the second of his Three Pieces for Two
Pianos, 'Self-portrait with Reich and Riley (and
Chopin in the background)', commemorates this
affirmation and influence. He also became interested
in the rhythmic aspects of African music, specifically
that of the Pygmies. In the mid-'70s, Ligeti wrote his
only opera, Le Grand Macabre. It is a work of absurd
theatre that contains many eschatological references.*

Concertos

Violin Concerto[a]. Cello Concerto[b]. Piano Concerto[c]
[a]**Saschko Gawriloff** vn [b]**Jean-Guihen Queyras** vc
[c]**Pierre-Laurent Aimard** pf **Ensemble
InterContemporain / Pierre Boulez**
DG 439 808-2GH (67' · DDD)   ⒻⓄⓄⓄ↦

The Violin Concerto (1992) is music by
a composer fascinated with Shakespeare's *The Tempest*: indeed, it might
even prove to be a substitute for Ligeti's long-
mooted operatic version of the play. There are
plenty of 'strange noises', the result not just of
Ligeti's latter-day predilection for ocarinas, but
of his remarkable ability to play off natural and
artificial tunings against each other. This work is
superior to the Piano Concerto because the solo
violin is so much more volatile and poetic as a
protagonist, an animator who 'fires up' the
orchestra, functioning as a leader at odds with the
led. Saschko Gawriloff is a brilliantly effective
soloist, and well served by a sharply defined yet
expressive accompaniment – Boulez at his most
incisive – and a totally convincing recording. The
other works are played and recorded with similar
success. The Cello Concerto (1966) is a
particularly powerful reminder of the strengths of
the earlier Ligeti, where simple, basic elements
generate anything but minimal consequences.

Lontano

Lontano[a]. Atmosphères[a]. Apparitions.
San Francisco Polyphony[a]. Concert Românesc
Berlin Philharmonic Orchestra / Jonathan Nott
Teldec 8573 88261-2 (55' · DDD)
[a]Recorded live 2001   ⒻⓄ

Here at last are the scores with which the composer first made his name in the early 1960s
(*Apparitions* and *Atmosphères*); here also is *Lontano*
(1967), one of the finest orchestral scores of the
20th century, and *San Francisco Polyphony* of 1974,
which inaugurates the more self-consciously virtuoso and referential approach that characterises
Ligeti's subsequent works for large forces (*Le
Grand Macabre*, and the concertos for piano, violin
and horn); and, as a postscript of sorts, an early
score from the composer's pre-Western period.
The latter has its first recording here; rather more
incredibly (given its position in Ligeti's output), so
does *Apparitions*. On the last count alone, this
recording is simply a must for anyone interested
in 'new music'.

The two premieres here are studio recordings, whereas *Atmosphères*, *Lontano* and *San Francisco Polyphony* were recorded live. A previous recording of *Atmosphères* and *Lontano* with the Vienna Philharmonic under Claudio Abbado was also live, and unsatisfactory on a number of counts (not least unwanted audience 'participation'). Thankfully there are very few such problems here: the general accuracy is commendable, considering the difficulty of co-ordinating dozens of individual lines (for example, getting 80-odd instruments to attack *pianissimo* together at the beginning of *Atmosphères*: the Berliners just about manage it; at any rate, they're nearer the mark than any of the other recordings). The sound quality has all the requisite impact and delicacy, and the orchestra's shaping of line and continuity (and, when required, their opposites) is equally persuasive.

String Quartets

String Quartets – No 1, 'Métamorphoses nocturnes';
No 2. Andante and Allegretto
Parker Quartet (Daniel Chong, Karen Kim vns
Jessica Bodner va Kee-Hyun Kim vc)
Naxos 8 570781 (56' · DDD)   Ⓢ🔊

Here is another relatively new quartet plunging into the recording fray with 'high end' repertory and reaping the rewards of their apparent fearlessness. Ligeti's two numbered quartets require feats of individual virtuosity to be combined with the kind of effortless coordination that sounds utterly spontaneous. The slightest lapse creates chaos, and perhaps the greatest compliment one can pay the Parker Quartet is that, whatever false starts and shambolic episodes occurred during rehearsals, the recordings have the conviction and character of single takes: these performances might just as well be live.

The disc aims to satisfy completists by including the two movements from 1950 whose polite, occasionally quirky neo-classicism gives little hint of the Ligetian eruptions to come. The *Andante and Allegretto* also steer clear of Bartók, a challenging model for any aspiring Hungarian composer in the Communist era: and the most remarkable aspect of the first quartet 'proper' (1953-54) is its knowing transference of the clichés of Bartókian night-music into the kind of alarmingly comic nightmares that Ligeti would soon make his own.

Fourteen years later, with Hungary abandoned and the full potential of the modern musical West confronted, the nightmares were less comic, more seriously scary. As with much music constructed as a collection of technical studies, it's hard for interpreters of the Second Quartet to get behind the spectacular sound effects to expose ideas of genuine substance. The Parkers manage this as well as any of their more seasoned predecessors and make one eager to hear more contemporary repertory from them, especially when so efficiently recorded and at super-budget price.

Etudes

Etudes Books 1-3. Musica ricercata
Pierre-Laurent Aimard pf
Sony Classical SK62308 (65' · DDD)   Ⓕ🔘🔘🔘🔘▶

 Pierre-Laurent Aimard is not just a modern-music specialist but an artist of phenomenal gifts, and excellently recorded here. First impressions of the music are likely to be of its immediacy. The complexities are a problem only for the pianist – whatever the sources of Ligeti's inspiration, his ideas serve only a musical/poetic purpose. Central to these dazzling pieces is his longstanding interest in composing with layers of material in different metres or different tempi and in producing what he calls 'an illusion of rhythm'; evident, too, are his more recent preoccupations with modern mathematics, in particular the young science of dynamical systems which seeks to explain the precarious balance between pattern and chaos, order and disorder. Ligeti's powerful imagination is fuelled by many things, but there's no question of needing a special key to enter his world. The music is enough. There can be no doubt that Ligeti's *Etudes* belong with the greatest piano music of this or any other century. They are amazing.

Le Grand Macabre

Le Grand Macabre
Sibylle Ehlert sop Venus, Gepopo **Laura Claycomb** sop Amanda **Charlotte Hellekant** mez Amando **Derek Lee Ragin** counterten Prince Go-Go **Jard van Nes** contr Mescalina **Graham Clark** ten Piet the Pot **Willard White** bass Nekrotzar **Frode Olsen** bass Astradamors **Martin Winkler** bar Ruffiak **Marc Campbell-Griffiths** bar Schobiak **Michael Lessiter** bar Schabernack **Steven Cole** ten White Minister **Richard Suart** bass Black Minister **London Sinfonietta Voices; Philharmonia Orchestra / Esa-Pekka Salonen**
Sony Classical Ligeti Edition ② S2K62312 (102' · DDD · T/t). Recorded live 1998   Ⓕ🔘

Le Grand Macabre, a comedy about the end of the world, an elaborate game of musical time-travel, an ambiguous dance on the brink of an abyss, looks more and more like the key opera of the end of the 20th century. Direct comparison between this version and Elgar Howarth's splendid 1987 Wergo performance is difficult, because Ligeti extensively revised the score in 1996, and it's that 'final version', as he calls it, that's recorded here. He's made a number of cuts, a great deal of what was originally spoken dialogue is now sung and there have been many changes to the scoring, making it more practical but also thinning it out. The reduction of spoken dialogue and the lightening of the orchestral texture make life a little easier for the singers (though not for the soprano singing Gepopo, which Ligeti has described as an attempt to out-Zerbinetta Zerbinetta) and for the players. The whole performance is rather more assured than Howarth's and the score's beauties are more lovingly polished. It now sounds rather closer to a 'normal' opera and, perhaps inevitably, lacks a degree of Howarth's alarming impact.

Interestingly enough, it's Salonen's performance, sung in English to a French audience, that draws more laughs at the jokes. Sibylle Ehlert is spectacularly virtuoso and Willard White's gravity is effective in the role of Nekrotzar. Graham Clark is hugely exuberant as Piet the Pot, and Steven Cole and Richard Suart make a splendid double-act of the two Ministers. Jard van Nes and Frode Olsen are perhaps inhibited by the English language from making Mescalina and Astradamors as grotesque as they can be, though both sing well, as does every other member of the cast. The recording, like the performance, is a little more comfortable, rather less in-your-face, than Howarth's. This version is the one to have – Ligeti's revisions are all improvements, and the performance is a fine one – but the older one has a shade more of the quality that Ligeti says he has hoped for in stage productions of the opera, that of 'demoniacal farce'.

Douglas Lilburn   New Zealand 1915-2001

In 1936 Percy Grainger awarded Lilburn the Grainger Prize for Forest, which committed him to music rather than literature, for which he had decided gifts. He studied with Vaughan Williams at the Royal College of Music, returning to his native New Zealand in 1940 to discover he'd won four prizes as part of the centennial celebrations. He later taught at Victoria University in Wellington.

Orchestral Works

Aotearoa Overture. A Birthday Offering. Drysdale Overture. A Song of Islands. Festival Overture. Forest. Processional Fanfare
New Zealand Symphony Orchestra / James Judd
Naxos ② 8 557697 (75' · DDD)   Ⓢ🅑➔

The ardour and sheen displayed by the NZSO, to say nothing of James Judd's elegant and purposeful direction, is deeply impressive. The engineering is beguilingly warm, rich and truthful. Certainly, readers with a fondness for, say, Sibelius, Barber or Vaughan Williams should find plenty to savour.

Both the captivating 1940 overture *Aotearoa* (the Maori name for New Zealand) and 1946 tone-poem *A Song of Islands* pave the way for the first two symphonies (if you like what you hear, make haste to the gloriously lyrical and big-hearted Second). The other stand-out item is *A Birthday Offering*. Written in 1956 for the 10th anniversary of the NZSO, this score explores more astringent expression and affords each section of the orchestra ample opportunity for dis-

play. The music combines a whiff of Tippett with the open-air manner of Copland – and there are even intriguing pre-echoes of James MacMillan's 'keening' string writing.

Sibelius's kindly presence looms over the tone-poem *Forest* (an apprentice effort from 1936) and the following year's infinitely more assured *Drysdale Overture*, whose idyllic beauty reflects the unspoilt North Island landscape in and around the hill farm where Lilburn was raised. This well-filled disc concludes with the bracing 1939 *Festival Overture* and *Processional Fanfare*, a 1961 arrangement for three trumpets and organ of the student song *Gaudeamus igitur*, which the composer reworked 24 years later for small orchestra. Lovely stuff – and a bargain of the first order.

Magnus Lindberg   Finnish b1958

Following piano studies, Lindberg entered the Sibelius Academy where his composition teachers included Rautavaara and Heininen. He was a early member of the informal grouping known as the Ears Open Society, with the aim of encouraging exploration of mainstream modernism. Lindberg's compositional breakthrough came with two large-scale works, Action-Situation-Signification (1982) and Kraft (1983-85). Action was written for and premiered by the new music ensemble Toimii ('It Works' in Finnish), which Lindberg founded during the summer of 1980. Also around the same period, Lindberg co-founded the Ears Open Society with his contemporaries Eero Hämeeniemi, Jouni Kaipainen, Kaija Saariaho and Esa-Pekka Salonen.

During the late 1980s Lindberg's music approached a new modernist classicism, in which many of the communicative ingredients of a vibrant musical language (harmony, rhythm, counterpoint, melody) were reinterpreted. Lindberg became composer-in-residence at the New York Philharmonic with the 2009-10 season, at the invitation of the incoming music director Alan Gilbert. The September 2009 opening night gala of the Philharmonic, which was Gilbert's debut as music director, featured a well-received new work by Lindberg, EXPO.

Concertos

Clarinet Concerto[a]. Gran Duo. Chorale
[a]**Kari Kriikku** *cl*
Finnish Radio Symphony Orchestra / Sakari Oramo
Ondine ODE1038-2 (51' · DDD)   🅟🅞🅞🅞➔

 The clarinet has featured prominently as a solo instrument in Magnus Lindberg's output throughout his career, though it was only in 2002 that he set about writing a concerto for his longtime colleague Kari Kriikku. The finished article, however, is really very different from 1980s pieces such as *Ablauf* and *Linea d'ombra*.

Running for 25 minutes, the work's four sections play continuously, if not seamlessly. Beautifully written for the instrument, there are hints of Debussy in the opening pages and – in the orchestration – of Barber and Copland later on, but the Concerto is in no way derivative. It proceeds with ineluctable momentum through a varied tonal landscape (including some decidedly jazz-like passages) to an ecstatic peroration that is deeply moving and uplifting, before closing out serenely: Rautavaara meeting Gershwin, perhaps.

There is something of Rautavaara's manner in the modest *Chorale* (2001-02), written to precede Berg's Violin Concerto (both use the chorale *Es ist genug*). The larger *Gran Duo* for winds and brass (1999), with its suggestions of Stravinsky's *Symphonies of Wind Instruments*, is utterly different though no less impressive. The duo is between the woodwinds and brass *en masse*, the work a bracing dialogue across some 20 minutes with fascinating incidents along the way, not least where the textures pare down to chamber proportions, though the dark-hued coda has considerable cumulative power. Very strongly recommended.

Lindberg Violin Concerto **Sibelius** Violin Concerto
Lisa Batiashvili vn **Finnish Radio
Symphony Orchestra / Sakari Oramo**
Sony Classical 88697 12936-2 (57' · DDD)   Ⓕ**OO**⯈

It's been said that Magnus Lindberg forges his works more from harmony and rhythm than from unfolding melodic lines, and the celestial acrobatics of this neatly constructed Violin Concerto, a real star-burst of a piece, tend to bear out that theory. It was premiered last year in New York, the soloist, as here, Lisa Batiashvili, whose agility and tonal sweetness serve as an ideal foil for the blinding colours on Lindberg's constantly shifting canvas. The work opens like a bright light descending, the soloist a first among equals who, beyond her brief cadenza, witnesses a gradual darkening of orchestral texture. The harmonic complexion can be either ravishing or dissonant, and the range of musical gesture, from ethereal reverie to Bartókian dance is consistently gripping. The breathless stream of invention recalls Lindberg's similarly hyperactive Clarinet Concerto – anyone who enjoyed that work should relish this one too.

Sibelius's Concerto provides a comforting disc companion, especially as the performance so memorably focuses on the dreamier elements of the first movement. Batiashvili bows a seamless, sensual line, her tone smooth as silk. Sakari Oramo conducts a cleanly detailed and warmly articulated accompaniment, stronger on pulse than on drama, and at times sounding almost like chamber music. Those who like their Sibelius flinty or rough-hewn might find this reading just a little too civilised, though for me the joy of hearing everything so considerately thought through and 'joined up' more than compensates for a lack of elemental drive. In any case it's the Lindberg that makes this disc unmissable.

Orchestral Works

Concerto for Orchestra. Sculpture. Campana in aria[a]
[a]**Esa Tapani** hn
**Finnish Radio Symphony Orchestra /
Sakari Oramo**
Ondine ODE1124-2 (64' · DDD)   Ⓕ**O**⯈

Magnus Lindberg has been dedicated in exploring the potential of the modern orchestra, as this disc confirms. Odd that *Campana in aria* (1998) was unrecorded until now, as its lively investigation of horn sonority makes for the composer's most entertaining *concertante* piece, especially when Esa Tapani is so in control of its virtuosity.

Each decade in his maturity has seen Lindberg pen an orchestral work as a statement of intent: thus the modernist outpouring of *Kraft* (1985), then the reconciliation of innovation and tradition in *Aura* (1994). Fine that the Concerto for Orchestra (2003) is a further step along this path, but quality is simply lacking – whether in the actual ideas or, especially, the interplay of textures such that the harmonies sound derivative of earlier works, while melodic lines are insufficiently defined. Ensemble writing in the latter half fails to sustain momentum, and the apotheosis is perfunctory by Lindberg's standards. Fortunately, *Sculpture* (2005) seems intent on righting its predecessor's wrongs – not least in its skilful mediating between extremes of motion without sacrificing either harmonic or textural intricacy, with a final section that fairly saturates the sound-space.

Quite a piece with which to have opened the Walt Disney Concert Hall in Los Angeles. Sakari Oramo and the Finnish RSO fully appreciate its opportunities for meaningful orchestral display and are accorded spacious sound that lacks nothing in impact. *Sculpture* makes this a mandatory purchase for Lindberg's admirers, many of whom may well find in the Concerto more than incidental pleasures.

Vocal Works

Graffiti. Seht die Sonne
**Helsinki Chamber Choir; Finnish Radio Symphony
Orchestra / Sakari Oramo**
Ondine ODE1157-2 (57' · DDD)   Ⓕ**O**⯈

Two recent large-scale scores by Magnus Lindberg embody one archetypal 21st-century response to 20th-century music: the echoes are all-pervading, but it's probably pointless to try to decide whether they are ironic, serious or a mixture of the two.

Seht die Sonne (2007) alludes to late-Romantic Schoenberg, whose *Gurrelieder* text provides the title, but other memories of magical nature music, from Strauss's *Alpine Symphony* to Henze's *König Hirsch* – and not forgetting Sibelius – can also be sensed. There are considerable risks (as Henze discovered) in opting for expansive orchestral opulence when parody is not the aim, and when densely intertwining rhapsodic lines teeter on the edge of banality. Lindberg's conviction, and technical resourcefulness, in creating this sound world can inspire rapturous enjoyment or alienated bafflement: and wherever on the continuum between these extremes you find yourself, *Graffiti* (2009) might well leave you in a similar location.

A choral work using brief wall texts from Pompeii could be a bracingly austere collage of fragments switching between the mundane and the philosophical, the bawdy and the spiritual: yet Lindberg pursues continuity, and a neo-late-Romantic symphonic idiom, as intensively in *Graffiti* as in *Seht die Sonne*. There are Stravinskian as well as Straussian associations here but the overall result seems to me to have more in common with *Carmina Burana* than *Les noces*, and some of the instrumental writing could be taken as parodying (or celebrating) Hollywood conventions of a Korngoldian Ancient Rome. Whether or not Lindberg is consciously mocking such lush aestheticisation of the primitive and the barbaric is impossible to tell. But the effect is always upbeat, exuberant and laid down with immense panache by the Finnish forces involved, in spectacularly vivid sound.

Franz Liszt
Hungarian 1811-1886

Composer, teacher, Abbé, Casanova, writer, sage, pioneer and champion of new music, philanthropist, philosopher and one of the greatest pianists in history, Liszt was the very embodiment of the Romantic spirit. Yet he remains the most contradictory personality of all the great composers. He was as arrogant and egocentric as he was also humble and generous; he was a profoundly spiritual man yet delighted in the pleasures of the flesh – at least 26 major love affairs and several illegitimate children (Ernest Newman said, 'He collected princesses and countesses as other men collect rare butterflies, or Japanese prints, or first editions'); attracted to the life of a recluse, he loved luxury and the adulation of the public; he practised at the highest level of his art yet could demean himself with meretricious theatrics: all in all, a fascinating man.

By nine Liszt could not only play the difficult B minor Concerto of Hummel in public but was able to extemporise on themes submitted by the audience. Prince Nicholas Esterházy was impressed enough to arrange for a group of Hungarian aristocrats to fund the musical education of the prodigy to the tune of 600 florins a year and Liszt, with his mother and ambitious father, moved to Vienna in 1821. His piano mentor here was the illustrious Carl Czerny, who refused to accept payment for the pleasure of teaching the Hungarian wunderkind. Liszt's composition teacher was Salieri. Soon Liszt was giving concerts. At one, attended by Beethoven and in which Liszt played an arrangement of a Beethoven piano trio from memory, the great master is said to have kissed his brow and exclaimed, 'Devil of a fellow! – such a young rascal!' Liszt also made his bow as a

composer at this time, one of those asked to contribute a variation on a theme by Diabelli.

Still only 12 and a finished pianist, Liszt left Vienna for Paris. A concert at the Opéra in March 1824 established Liszt as one of the finest pianists ever heard. The fashionable salons welcomed him both in the French capital and in London. By the age of 16 Liszt was famous throughout Europe and financially self-sufficient.

Liszt's father died suddenly of typhoid fever enjoining his son to hand over his fortune to his mother in recognition of the person who had made it possible. Liszt, exhausted by constant touring, bowed out of the limelight for a few years, teaching, reading everything he could get his hands on and embarking on the first of his many passionate love affairs. Religion and philosophy for a time replaced music as the dominant force in Liszt's life. Then in 1830 he met three musicians who changed everything: Chopin, Berlioz (then virtually unknown) and Paganini. From Berlioz he learnt about the possible sonorities of the orchestra – Liszt's later orchestral works testify to that; from Chopin he absorbed the poetry and refined, sensitive taste of the Pole's piano style. But it was the electrifying effect of Paganini's stage presence and the spectacular demands of his music that immediately fired Liszt's imagination. Paganini had dramatically extended the possibilities of the instrument with his astounding technical prowess and Liszt consciously set out to emulate on the piano what Paganini had achieved on the violin. To achieve this involved creating a new pianistic technique.

For the next two years, Liszt shut himself away to master his objectives, daily practising assiduously to the point of exhaustion. His re-emergence on the concert platform was a major artistic event and the pianistic artillery he had acquired swept all rivals aside.

In 1834 Liszt met the beautiful Comtesse Marie d'Agoult. The fact that she had a husband and three children was of no importance when it came to such a grand passion. Within a year, she had left her husband and joined Liszt in Geneva where Blandine, the first of their three children, was born. She died in 1867. Their second child was Cosima, born in 1837, destined to become the wife of Richard Wagner. Daniel, their third child, was born in 1839 in Rome but died at the age of only 20. For the next decade Liszt toured all over the continent, from Turkey and Russia to Portugal and Ireland, amassing a fortune along the way, heaped with honours, the intimate of royalty and statesmen wherever he appeared. Then in 1847, at the height of his powers, he changed direction.

The relationship with Marie d'Agoult had gradually disintegrated and, when they finally parted, Liszt took the children to live with his mother in Paris. Here his mistresses included Marie Duplessis (immortalised by Dumas as the Lady of the Camellias and by Verdi in his opera La traviata) and the dancer Lola Montez. While on a concert trip to Kiev in 1847 he met the Polish-born Princess Carolyne Sayn-Wittgenstein, cigar-smoking, unhappily married, intellectual and who suffered from a morbid fear of fresh air. This was Liszt's last great love. The two discovered a mutual interest in religion and mysticism and within a short time the Princess had abandoned her husband and 30,000 serfs to join Liszt in Weimar where he had been appointed Kapellmeister to the Grand Duke.

Here they lived as an unmarried couple for the next 10 years. Liszt's duties were to direct performances of orchestral and operatic works. By the end of the decade, he had transformed Weimar into one of Europe's greatest musical centres, the headquarters of the Music of the Future. Musicians flocked to Weimar. The works Liszt presented and conducted were of the widest variety, from premieres of new and experimental works to high quality revivals of the classic repertoire. Liszt never allowed his personal preferences to dictate what he produced at Weimar. Even composers he personally disliked or whose music he did not care for had a hearing. He was also courageous enough to present a revival of Wagner's Tannhäuser, a work by a political revolutionary sought by the authorities. He then follow it up with the world premiere of Lohengrin. He fought for funds to present other works by Wagner. The Duke's refusal to fund the enterprise was one of the reasons for Liszt's eventual departure. Other avant-garde works of the day, such as Peter Cornelius's The Barber of Baghdad, were hissed by the resentful inhabitants of Weimar and it was the reaction to the premiere of Cornelius's opera that was the final straw.

Two other activities occupied Liszt during his reign at Weimar: teaching and composition. The amount he produced is simply staggering. What we hear today is only the tip of the iceberg. These years include 12 symphonic poems (a form he invented), the Faust and Dante symphonies, two piano concertos and the Totentanz for piano and orchestra, the great B minor Piano Sonata, literally hundreds of other pieces for the piano as well as revisions of all the piano music he had written in the 1830s and '40s.

Although he resigned from his musical duties in 1859, Liszt remained in Weimar till 1861. The religious life again attracted him, however, and in 1865 Pope Pius IX conferred on him the dignity of Abbé. In 1879 he received the tonsure and the four minor orders but was never ordained a priest. Yet he was allowed to discard the cassock and even marry if he so wished.

From now on Liszt divided his time between his religious interests in Rome and teaching piano in Pest and Weimar (he was invited back in 1869). Liszt's influence on the coming generation of music-makers is hard to exaggerate – the likes of Borodin, Balakirev, Rimsky-Korsakov, MacDowell, Smetana, Debussy, Saint-Saëns, Fauré, Grieg and even Brahms (for a time) all benefited from his advice and encouragement; he nurtured a whole school of pianists, giving his time with a generosity that has rarely been matched. He never asked for any fees. Towards the end of his life, one Liszt pupil, the great pianist Moriz Rosenthal (whose recordings attest to his prodigious gifts), summed up Liszt thus: 'He was more wonderful than anybody I have ever known.'

His final triumph was a visit to England in 1886. Though aged and suffering from dropsy, he gave some public concerts again, including a private recital at Windsor Castle for Queen Victoria. He attended a performance of his oratorio St Elizabeth. The reception given to him wherever he went moved him deeply and he stayed on an extra week before travelling to Bayreuth for the festival. During a performance of Tristan and Isolde he had to be taken from the auditorium: pneumonia had set in, swiftly followed by congestion of the lungs. The last word he uttered was 'Tristan'.

Piano Concertos

No 1 in E flat, S124; **No 2** in A, S125; **No 3** in E flat, S125a, Op posth (ed Rosenblatt)

Liszt Piano Concertos[a] Nos 1 & 2.
Beethoven Piano Sonatas Nos 10, 19 & 20
Sviatoslav Richter pf [a]**London Symphony Orchestra / Kyrill Kondrashin**
Philips 50 Great Recordings 464 710-2PM (70' · ADD)
Recorded [a]1961, 1963   Ⓜ ⦿⦿⦿➔

 These were recognised as classic performances virtually from their first appearance. They're characterised not only by the intense expressiveness of Richter's playing, but also by very careful balances of orchestral texture which hitherto hadn't been much apparent in recordings of these works. Throughout, the emphasis is on poetic insight, dramatic impact; these interpretations have in these and other regards exerted a considerable influence. Yet even if sensitive readings of Liszt's concertos are now less rare, this in no way weakens the impression made by Richter's and Kondrashin's. In short, these are among the great Liszt recordings.

Piano Concertos Nos 1 & 2. Totentanz, S126
Krystian Zimerman pf
Boston Symphony Orchestra / Seiji Ozawa
DG 423 571-2GH (56' · DDD)   Ⓕ ⦿➔

This is playing in the grand manner. From the start of First Concerto you're aware of a consciously leonine approach. Zimerman even deliberately takes risks in a few technically perilous places where some of his colleagues, at least in the studio, play safe; and indeed his octaves in the opening cadenza are an example. The result sounds spontaneous and, yes, even brave. Ozawa and the orchestra are behind the soloist in all this. Not only do lyrical sections sing with subtlety, the big passages also are shapely. There's plenty of drive in this Concerto.

In the Second Concerto Zimerman adopts a different approach; he evidently considers it a more poetic piece and the playing style, strong though it is, is to match. Finely though he handles the gentler music, there are odd sniffs and hums in the molto espressivo passage following the D flat major cello solo, and also in the last of the work's quiet sections. In the gorgeously grisly Totentanz, both the music and the playing should make your hair stand on end. The sound has a depth that suits the music and the piano is especially impressive. Zimerman's freshness (he reminds us that this is a young man's music), and the coupling, makes this disc a most desirable one.

Piano Concertos Nos 1 & 2. Totentanz, S126
Eldar Nebolsin pf **Royal Liverpool Philharmonic Orchestra / Vasily Petrenko**
Naxos 8 570517 (54' · DDD)　　　Ⓢ❍❍❍➾

Not only can the performances hold their own with the very best of the same three works but the individual concertos compare with those by the likes of Katchen and Richter. They are that good. And if the opening of *Totentanz* doesn't quite make you jump out of your skin quite like Raymond Lewenthal's, Nebolsin and Petrenko are almost as chillingly shocking. The fugato (Var 5) is attacked with thrilling pace and precision on a par with the very best.

Nebolsin, winner of the first Sviatoslav Richter International Piano Competition in 2005, is a virtuoso of power and poetry. While allowing the music to breathe, he plays in long paragraphs without, as it were, having to come up for air. Try the scintillating final pages of the First Concerto in which Petrenko, always an alert partner, catches the ball and runs with it. Recorded sound is exemplary. At super-budget price, the disc is a real bargain.

Liszt Piano Concerto No 1
Chopin Piano Concerto No 1 in E minor, Op 11
Martha Argerich pf **London Symphony Orchestra / Claudio Abbado**
DG The Originals 449 719-2GOR (56' · ADD)
Recorded 1968　　　❍❍➾

These performances, in DG's beautifully refurbished sound, remain as fanciful and coruscating as the day they were made. Argerich's fluency and recreative spark dazzle and dumbfound to a unique degree but, given her reputation for fire-eating virtuosity, it's perhaps necessary to say that both performances quiver with rare sensitivity as well as drama. Time and again she gives a telling and haunting poetic counterpoint to her, arguably, more familiar way of trailing clouds of virtuoso glory. Abbado partners his mercurial soloist as to the manner born, finding (in the Chopin in particular) a burgeoning sense of wonder where others sound dry and foursquare.

Additional recommendations

Piano Concertos
Coupled with Fantasia on Hungarian Folk Themes, S123 **Chopin** Andante spianato and Grande polonaise in E flat, Op 22
Richter pf **LSO / Kondrashin**
BBC Legends mono BBCL4031-2 (69' · ADD)
Recorded live　　　Ⓜ
Richter's London debut concerts in July 1961 were the sensation of the season, and the Liszt piano concertos at the Royal Albert Hall were the climax. Solos are miked very close by today's standards but

only in this respect do the concertos yield to the famous Philips studio versions, made a little later during the same London visit.

Piano Concertos[a][b]
Coupled with Mephisto Waltz. Transcendental Study, S139 No 1[c]. Grand fantaisie de bravoure sur La clochette de Paganini
Ogdon pf [a]**Bournemouth Symphony Orchestra / Silvestri;** [b]**BBC Symphony Orchestra / C Davis**
BBC Legends [c]mono BBCL4089-2 (73' · ADD)
Recorded live 1967-71　　　Ⓕ
Ogdon plays here with all those characteristics inseparable from his genius: his improvisatory daring, his thrills, spills and poetry. An invaluable issue with excellent sound, he plays as if his life depended upon it.

Piano Concerto No 1
Coupled with **Prokofiev** Piano Concerto No 1 **Shostakovich** Concerto for Piano, Trumpet and Strings
de la Salle pf **Gulbenkian Foundation Orch/ Foster**
Naïve V5053 (60' · DDD)　　　Ⓕ❍❍➾
Nineteen-year-old Lise de la Salle's performances are of the highest quality, her rushes of adrenalin balanced by her precise calibration and control. In the Liszt she is fearless in the face of every treacherous obstacle, but is also romantic and free-wheeling.

A Dante Symphony, S109

A Dante Symphony[a]. Années de pèlerinage – deuxième année, S161, 'Italie' – No 7, Après une lecture du Dante (fantasia quasi sonata)[b]
[a]**Berlin Radio Women's Chorus;** [a]**Berlin Philharmonic Orchestra / Daniel Barenboim** [b]pf
Warner Elatus 2564 61780-2 (67' · DDD)
[a]Recorded live 1992
　　　Ⓜ❍➾

This disc proves conclusively that the *Dante Symphony*, a contemporary of the *Faust Symphony*, no longer needs its apologists. Tone, full and rounded, firm and true, and rock-steady pacing elevate the opening beyond its all too familiar resemblance to a third-rate horror-film soundtrack. As the work progresses, together with the countless examples of Berlin tone and artistry filling out, refining or shaping gestures in often revelatory ways, one becomes aware of Barenboim's skill in maintaining the large-scale tension he's created. As for the final choral *Magnificat*, if Liszt owed Wagner a debt of gratitude for persuading him to conclude the symphony with the 'noble and softly soaring' bars that precede a more noisily affirmative appended coda, in Barenboim's *Magnificat* (and much else in the symphony), it's Wagner's debt to Liszt that's more readily apparent; the Parsifalian radiance of these final pages is unmistakable. More importantly, for once they sound convincingly conclusive. The live recording is spacious, focused and expertly balanced.

The *Dante* Sonata was recorded with the kind of risk-taking abandon and occasionally less than perfect execution that you might expect from a live event. Improvisatory, impulsive and full of extreme contrasts, Barenboim's *Dante* Sonata is vividly pictorial. The instrument itself (closely miked and widely spaced) sounds larger than life. This recording is riveting.

A Faust Symphony, S108

A Faust Symphony
Kenneth Riegel ten **Tanglewood Festival Chorus; Boston Symphony Orchestra / Leonard Bernstein**
DG The Originals 447 449-2GOR (77' · ADD)
Recorded 1976   Ⓜ️ⓄⒺ➔

David Gutman's absorbing booklet-note for the Leonard Bernstein release tells how at a Tanglewood concert in 1941 Bernstein scored a triumph in modern American repertoire and Serge Koussevitzky conducted the first two movements of *A Faust Symphony*. Some 20 years later Bernstein himself made a distinguished recording of the work, faster than this superb 1976 Boston remake by almost five minutes yet ultimately less involving. The passage of time witnessed not only an easing of tempo but a heightened response to individual characters, be it Faust's swings in mood and attitude, Gretchen's tender entreaties or the unpredictable shadow-play of 'Mephistopheles'. Orchestral execution is first-rate, the strings in particular really showing their mettle (such biting incisiveness), while Bernstein's pacing, although often slower than average, invariably fits the mood. The sound too is far warmer and more lifelike than its rather opaque New York predecessor, although when it comes to the tenor soloist in the closing chorus, Kenneth Riegel is rather strident.

A Faust Symphony
András Molnár ten **Hungarian State Choir; Orchestra of the Franz Liszt Academy / András Ligeti**
Naxos 8 553304 (73' · DDD)   Ⓢ➔

There's a lot right with this performance, not least being its outspoken acknowledgement of Faust's stormy character. Liszt's first-movement portrait receives zestful advocacy, less polished than some, perhaps, but fired by immense gusto. The recording, too, is endowed with plenty of body, while András Ligeti's vocal promptings vie with Toscanini's in *La bohème*! Gretchen is quite comely and Ligeti effectively traces both her darker moods and those passages associated with Faust's yearning. Mephistopheles is more angry than 'ironico' and if you want confirmation of Ligeti's Lisztian mettle, then try from 5'49" through the following minute or so: it's quite thrilling. True, woodwind pointing isn't as vivid as under, say, Leonard Bernstein, but there's certainly no lack of enthusiasm. The Orchestra of the Franz Liszt Academy gives its all and the Hungarian State Choir makes noble music of the final chorus, even though András

Molnár's wobbly tenor proves to be something of a distraction. It's a compelling if flawed production, less carefully prepared than its best rivals but more spontaneous than most.

'Symphonic Poems, Vol 2'
A Faust Symphony. Von der Wiege bis zum Grabe
BBC Philharmonic Orchestra / Gianandrea Noseda
Chandos CHAN10375 (80' · DDD)   Ⓕ️ⓄⒺ➔

Volume 2 in Chandos's series of Liszt's orchestral works includes the *Faust Symphony*, his crowning masterpiece, in a performance of supreme clarity and assurance. To achieve such stylistic empathy and lucidity in an hour-long force-of-nature work (the conductor has dropped the choral ending), showing Liszt's transformation of themes and characters at its height, is a daunting achievement. Time and again you are made to realise that accusations (still made in some quarters) of theatricality, of fustian and bombast, are largely the result of inadequate performances that put superficial display before true musicianship. Gianandrea Noseda immediately engages you in Faust's opening and troubled questioning with the promise of epic variations to come. Gretchen's radiance emerges truly *andante soave, dolcissimo e tranquillo e molto*, allowing the music's gently sighing lines and phrases to contrast to maximum effect with Mephistopheles's snapping accentuation and glittering diablerie. Indeed, so precise and articulate is the playing that you are left to wonder if Liszt, like Milton in *Paradise Lost*, was of the Devil's party without realising his ironic bias or inclination. Such a possibility is, however, erased in Liszt's final symphonic poem, *Von der Wiege bis zum Grabe*, where the opening 'Cradle' and closing fade-out suggest the composer's vision at its most ethereal and elevated. Chandos's sound is superb; you could hardly wish for more eloquent advocacy.

Hungarian Rhapsodies, S359

(Orch cpsr/Doppler) – **No 1** in F minor (piano No 14); **No 2** in D minor (piano No 2 in C sharp minor); **No 3** in D (piano No 6 in D flat); **No 4** in D minor (piano No 12 in C sharp minor). **No 5** in E minor (piano No 5); **No 6** in D, 'Carnival in Pest' (piano No 9 in E flat)

Hungarian Rhapsodies Nos 1-6
Budapest Festival Orchestra / Iván Fischer
Philips 456 570-2PH (60' · DDD)   Ⓕ️ⓄⒺ➔

Fischer's idiomatic foray into this well-worn repertoire is distinguished by tonal lustre and high spirits, with the authentic gypsy violin of József 'Csócsi' Lendvay lending a touch of added spice to No 3 (ie the piano No 6) and a tangy cimbalom much in evidence throughout. *Rubato* is legion, though more improvisatory than schmaltzy. Liszt's orchestrations are used for Nos 4-6, with Liszt and Doppler in No 3, and Doppler alone in No 2. Even if you've never particularly liked Doppler's version of the Second, Fischer's performance is so vivid, so imaginative of phrasing, that you may well be won over. Charm abounds. There's plenty of power, too, with meaty brass and growling *crescendos* at the start of No 4, and a riot of colour to close No 6. Fischer's *Hungarian Rhapsodies* are as frisky as foals and as flavoursome as goulash, as dashing and as dancing as anyone might want. They are further aided by excellent, full-bodied sound (especially impressive at high playback levels).

Symphonic Poems

'Symphonic Poems, Vol 1'
Ce qu'on entend sur la montagne, S95. Orpheus,
S98. Les préludes, S97. Tasso, S96
BBC Philharmonic Orchestra / Gianandrea Noseda
Chandos CHAN10341 (79' · DDD)   ℗○❶▷

Volume 1 of Liszt's complete symphonic poems augurs well for the series. Gianandrea Noseda and the BBC Philharmonic remind you at every turn that the days of a lofty critical dismissal of this uneven but pioneering and Romantically audacious music are surely over. Coldly objective complaints about Liszt's lack of craftsmanship or melodic distinction have been echoed in other more stylishly phrased complaints: for Clara Schumann there was 'too much of the tinsel and the drum' while Edward Sackville-West could see little beyond 'the expensive glare and theatricality'. But Liszt was nothing if not ambitious and if there are elements of truth in such accusations, they fail to convey the wider picture. Better an attempt to scale the heights than a safe repose on the lower slopes.

Ce qu'on entend sur la montagne is, indeed, epic in design and intention, seizing on Victor Hugo's obsession with the eternal battle between the forces of good and evil, of light and dark. But if Hugo's poem leaves us with an uneasy resolution, Liszt, a devout Catholic, ends with a radiant state of holiness. *Tasso*, too, celebrates final acclaim after the artist's trials and tribulations, and *Les préludes* attempts to unite four disparate ideas. *Orpheus* also conveys the victory of civilising art over baser forces.

Such music makes huge demands and these are met by Noseda with unfaltering command and lucidity. What could so easily topple into bombast is presented with an enviable clarity and acuteness. Excellent sound and presentation.

'Symphonic Poems, Vol 3'
Festklänge, S101. Héroïde funèbre, S102.
Mazeppa, S100. Prometheus, S99
BBC Philharmonic Orchestra / Gianandrea Noseda
Chandos CHAN10417 (71' · DDD)   ℗○❶▷

No one could accuse Liszt of a lack of largesse. Here, once more, is one dramatic gesture after another to startle and provoke Liszt's contemporaries who, indifferent to such generosity, quibbled over the length of the massive *Héroïde funèbre* and dismissed *Mazeppa* as vulgar and

meretricious. Again, it is possible to see in all these works Liszt's lifelong preoccupation with the triumph of good over evil and, more personally, the recognition due to him long after his death. True, there are times when his reliance on sequence and chromaticism to intensify his themes can seem like so much padding and it says much for the BBC Philharmonic under Gianandrea Noseda that they once more temper drama with discretion.

They achieve a special sense of exultance rather than bombast in *Festklänge*, written to celebrate Liszt's planned marriage to the Princess Carolyne Sayn-Wittgenstein. And they are no less successful in the vast spans of the *Héroïde funèbre*, a still desolating tribute to those who suffered 'throughout the whole spectrum of human carnage' (Liszt). Fluent and eloquent as ever, Noseda and his orchestra have once more been superbly recorded.

'Symphonic Poems, Vol 4'
Hamlet, S104. Hungaria, S103. Hunnenschlacht, S105.
Die Ideale, S106
BBC Philharmonic Orchestra / Gianandrea Noseda
Chandos CHAN10490 (80' · DDD)   ℗○○❶▷

Volume 4 of Chandos's superb cycle of Liszt's symphonic poems takes us through *Hungaria*, *Hamlet* and *Hunnenschlacht* ('The Battle of the Huns') to *Die Ideale*. Liszt's orchestral resources and easy sense of the picturesque still provoke endless debate among avid Lisztians and equally avid detractors. And it is true that his ever-ready susceptibility can involve stock-in-trade gestures and responses, and a wholly 19th-century rhetoric. Yet when performed with such superfine brilliance as here, everything is made irresistibly vital and graphic.

Here you sense how Liszt's first audiences were fired to a renewed sense of nationalism as they listened to *Hungaria*, a glorified Hungarian rhapsody where muted fanfares and foreboding lead to ultimate triumph and freedom from repression. *Hamlet* to an even greater extent achieves its stature through extreme contrasts of violence and introspection, while Hunnenschlacht is alive with a whirling chromaticism and insistent rhythm making terms such as *marziale, eroico* and *trionfante* as central to its theme as in *Hungaria*. Again, *Die Ideale* may commence with a gloomy quote from Schiller but all possible pessimism is resolved by Liszt's preoccupation with duality; with triumph and defeat, good and evil, etc. All these qualities are conveyed by orchestra and conductor in a way that tells you that true virtuosity is achieved through discipline rather than a more generalised and garish drama. This finely recorded disc is a glorious addition to the series.

Vià Crucis

Liszt Via Crucis **Satie/Cage** Socrate
Dezsö Ránki, Edit Klukon pfs

Budapest Music Center BMCCD100 (61' · DDD)   Ⓕ

The way John Cage arranged Erik Satie's *Socrate* for two pianos is simple and quite ingenious. He dovetails Satie's original piano accompaniment between both instruments and generally replicates the vocal line in unison octaves deployed in different registers. As a result, together with the loss of text, we get no sense of the original's dry, declamatory drama. But we do get Satie's ambling gait, pretty harmonies and, especially in the final pages, stark simplicity.

Without choral forces and the organ's sustaining power, Liszt's *Via Crucis* (based on the 14 Stations of the Cross) emerges as a rather severe exercise where bare-bone single lines shuttle between bleak block chords and *tremolos*. Sometimes it sounds static, yet certain moments prove quite effective, such as Station 11's pounded-out opening chords that mirror Christ being nailed to the Cross. The Ránki/Klukon duo make the best case for these arrangements and play with sustained, long-lined concentration and intelligent dynamic scaling that is far more difficult to achieve than it appears to the casual ear. In any event, if you're interested in these works without singers, this excellently engineered release recommends itself.

Piano Sonata in B minor, S178

Liszt Piano Sonata. Hungarian Rhapsody No 6
Brahms Two Rhapsodies, Op 79 **Schumann** Piano Sonata No 2 in G minor, Op 22
Martha Argerich pf
DG Galleria 437 252-2GGA (64' · ADD)
Recorded 1963-72   ⓂⓄⓄⓄⒷ▸

No one could accuse Martha Argerich of unstructured reverie or dalliance and her legendary DG performance of the Liszt Sonata from 1972 suggests a unique level of both technical and musical achievement. Her prodigious fluency unites with a trailblazing temperament, and Valhalla itself never ignited to such effect as at the central *Andante*'s central climax. Both here and in the final *Prestissimo* there are reminders that Argerich has always played octaves like single notes, displaying a technique that few if any could equal. There are times when she becomes virtually engulfed in her own virtuosity yet this is a performance to make other pianists turn pale and ask, how is it possible to play like this?

Argerich's Schumann, too, is among her most meteoric, headlong flights. In terms of sheer brilliance she leaves all others standing yet, amazingly, still allows us fleeting glimpses of Eusebius (the poetic dreamer in Schumann, and one of his most dearly cherished fictions). The Brahms and Liszt Rhapsodies, taken from Argerich's very first 1963 DG disc, are among the most incandescent yet refined on record. The sound, when you bother to notice it, is excellent. (The Liszt and Brahms works are also included in a compilation disc reviewed in the Collections section; refer to the Index.)

LISZT PIANO SONATA – IN BRIEF

Martha Argerich
DG 437 252-2GGA   ⓂⓄⓄⓄⒷ▸
A performance of torrential passion and technical mastery, Argerich's Sonata is a work of huge emotional range. Dating from 1972, this is a roller-coaster ride that still thrills and moves.

Boris Berezovsky
Mirare MIR099   ⒻⒷ▸
The palpable enjoyment Boris Berezovsky conveys of playing this demanding music is not the least attraction of his outstanding performance.

Nikolai Demidenko
Hyperion Helios CDH55184   Ⓜ
An imperious and beautifully conceived performance that veers between playing of terrific weight and fingerwork of a filigree lightness. There's phenomenal authority in Demidenko's approach that some might find daunting, but it's most impressive pianism.

Claudio Arrau
Philips 464 713-2PM   ⓂⒷ▸
Few pianists coveyed the opulence of Liszt's work as did Claudio Arrau, a master of the Olympian stance. This is a towering achievement and a great memento of a major artist.

Paul Lewis
Harmonia Mundi HMC90 1845   ⒻⓄ
A deeply impressive recording by a pianist of the younger generation demonstrating aristocratic playing and a real sense of poetry.

Arnaldo Cohen
BIS BIS-CD1253   Ⓕ
A powerful and technically hugely impressive performance from Cohen which sets this mighty work in an interesting context. Fine recorded sound.

Yundi Li
DG 471 585-2GH   ⒻⒷ▸
A splendid second disc from this impressive young Chinese pianist (a Chopin Piano Concerto winner). He is clearly a Lisztian of serious credentials and draws a host of fabulous colours from his instrument which have been sensitively captured by DG.

'Wild About Liszt'
Earl Wild pf
Ivory Classics ② 🆅🆅🅳 IC77777   ⒻⓄⓄ
No survey of the Liszt sonata would be complete without representation of one of the US's most virtuoso virtuosos. Earl Wild's sonata wasn't commercially recorded for this video but the sound is acceptable. But what playing!

Piano Sonata. Harmonies du soir, S139 No 11.
Mephisto Waltz No 1, 'Der Tanz in der Dorfschenke',
S514. Venezia e Napoli, S162
Chopin Waltz, Op 42
Boris Berezovsky pf
Mirare MIR099 (60' · DDD)   Ⓕ**ⓄⓄ**�´

One gets to hear an awful lot of new recordings
of the Liszt Sonata over the course of a year. Not
surprising: it's a wonderful work, one of the
Everests of the literature and a great showpiece
for any pianist. Not surprising, either, that few
match the finest versions already available –
Horowitz, Argerich, Cohen, Richter and Barere
as *primi inter pares*. Here, though, is another to
join that distinguished company. The palpable
enjoyment Boris Berezovsky conveys of playing
this demanding music is not the least attraction
of his outstanding performance. The technical
challenges are tossed off with aplomb and exhilarating tempi, every detail clearly articulated
within huge, sweeping paragraphs. Liszt's one-
act drama is gripping from beginning to end in
this muscular, unsentimental reading. Berezovsky's preference for recording in front of a
small invited audience pays off here and in the
other three Liszt works which, by the by, remind
one what an inspired melodist he was. This is
Berezovsky's most successful discs: we are hearing a truly great pianist at the top of his game.

Piano Sonata. Fünf Kleine Klavierstücke, S192 – in E;
in A flat; in F sharp; in F sharp. Nuages gris, S199. La
lugubre gondole, S200 (2nd version). RW Venezia,
S201. Schlaflos, Frage und Antwort, S203. En rêve,
S207. Unstern: sinistre, disastro, S208
Paul Lewis pf
Harmonia Mundi HMC90 1845 (60' · DDD)   Ⓕ**Ⓞ**

Once considered musically incomprehensible
and technically unplayable, the Liszt Sonata is
now part of the repertoire of virtually every
pianist of note. Yet even in a crowded market-
place (where Horowitz, Gilels, Richter,
Argerich, Brendel, Pollini and others jostle for
attention), Paul Lewis's recording stands out for
its breadth, mastery and shining musicianship.
Eschewing all obvious display, he concentrates
on the Sonata's monumental weight, grandeur
and ever-elusive inner poetry. His sense of
drama is dark and intense, and his reading of the
central *Andante sostenuto* alone puts his performance in the highest league. Lewis's octaves in the
final *Prestissimo* blaze before the retrospective
coda are of a pulverising strength; with him the
Sonata regains its stature among music's most
formidable milestones.
Moving to the music of Liszt's final years, Lewis
ranges from *Nuages gris*, much admired by
Stravinsky, its language anticipating Debussy,
Bartók and even Schoenberg, to *Unstern* (literally,
and in Shakespearean terms, 'unstarred'), music of
a sinister violence. If there's solace in the relatively
benign world of the four *Little Pieces* and *En rêve*
it's quickly shattered by *La lugubre gondole II*, a
desolate elegy anticipating Wagner's funeral.

This isn't music for late-night listening, more
an invitation to 'sleepless question and answer'.
But these pieces are played with a rapt and
haunting sense of their attenuated beauty, making this one of the finest, most intelligently
planned Liszt recitals for many years. Harmonia
Mundi's sound is of demonstration quality.

Piano Sonata. Vallée d'Obermann. Funérailles.
Rapsodie espagnole
Arnaldo Cohen pf
BIS BIS-CD1253 (73' · DDD)   Ⓕ**ⓄⓄ**�´

Arnaldo Cohen's playing blazes with the risk-
taking, spontaneity and urgency of a live concert.
His *Funérailles* is a truly great performance, perfectly structured, a real sense of angry desolation,
and the central 'cavalry charge' emerging more
logically from its context than in any other
account. In the Rhapsody, he provides the requisite bravura thrills but also does Liszt the honour
of eschewing the vapidity which so many bring to
it. *Vallée d'Obermann* emerges as an inspired dramatic tone-poem, to which Cohen adds the element of white-hot improvisation; in colour and
temperament he yields little to Horowitz's
famous RCA recording (nla). The Liszt Sonata,
Cohen's second recording, mingles narrative and
textual clarity with a musical maturity and heady
virtuosity in the Richter class.

Piano Sonata. Two Légendes, S175. Scherzo and
March, S177
Nikolai Demidenko pf
Helios CDH55184 (67' · DDD)   Ⓕ**Ⓑ**�´

Even in an impossibly competitive field Demidenko's Liszt Sonata stands out among the most
imperious and articulate. His opening is precisely judged and once the Sonata is under its
inflammatory way his virtuosity is of a kind to
which few other pianists could pretend. The
combination of punishing weight and a skittering, light-fingered agility makes for a compulsive vividness yet his economy in the first
cantando espressivo, sung without a trace of luxuriance or indulgence, is no less typical. There
are admittedly times when he holds affection at
arm's length, but just as you're wondering why
he commences the central *Andante* so loudly he
at once withdraws into a wholly apposite
remoteness or reticence. The final climax, too, is
snapped off not only with a stunning sense of
Lisztian drama but also with an even truer sense
and understanding of Liszt's score and instructions. Demidenko's couplings are no less auto-
cratic, with a capacity to make seemingly arbitrary ideas sound unarguable. His *Légendes* are
far from benign, yet his tautness and graphic
sense of their poetic power carry their own
authority. He's in his element in the *Scherzo* and
March's diablerie, music which, coming after
the two *Légendes*, affects one like an upside-
down crucifix, or some dark necromancy. The
recording is outstanding.

'Wild About Liszt'
Includes American, British and Dutch TV broadcast
performances; documentary and performances from
Wynyard in 1986 and a selection of audio-only
interviews
Earl Wild pf
Ivory Classics ② **DVD** IC77777
(6h 1' · NTSC · 4:3 · PCM stereo · 0)   ℉**OO**

Earl Wild (1915-2010) is the last great representative of those pianists directly influenced by the
playing of Rachmaninov and Hoffman: he had
an all-encompassing repertoire; he composed;
he transcribed; he had one of the finest mechanisms in history; he produced some of the most
beautiful sounds you will ever hear from the
piano (as he said himself, he was brought up to
play as though every member of the audience
were blind).

Among history's very greatest Liszt pianists,
he is heard here in no fewer than three full-
length Liszt recitals. They were recorded before
an audience over three evenings in July 1986 at
Wynyard, the ancestral home of the Ninth Marquess of Londonderry, to commemorate the
100th anniversary of the death of Liszt.

'Liszt the Poet' includes the Ballade No 2, a
wonderfully proportioned *Dante* Sonata,
Funérailles and *Mephisto* Waltz No 1 with Wild's
own and (in my opinion) much improved ending; 'Liszt the Transcriber' has 'hyphenated'
Bach, Verdi, Schumann, Chopin, Paganini
(stunning) and the Beethoven-Liszt Symphony
No 1; 'Liszt the Virtuoso' is dominated by the
B minor Sonata. Though not professionally
filmed, the sound recording is quite acceptable
while the picture quality is second-generation
video. There is also an enjoyable, homespun
documentary of Wild's visit to Wynyard, the
tour of the jaw-dropping estate and its immense
house (boasting its own organ and played briefly
by the pianist) conducted by the piano-loving
Marquess himself.

On the second DVD is a 1974 BBC recital/
interview with the much-missed Robin Ray
who elicits the memorable quote that 'the difference between playing a piece like the
d'Albert Scherzo and, say, Beethoven Op 111
is that in the d'Albert you are a decorator; in
the Beethoven you are an architect. A pianist
should be able to be both.' There's an interview on the occasion of Wild's 90th birthday
concert at the Concertgebouw and an additional 124 minutes of audio features: Wild
lecturing (with some wickedly funny anec-
dotes) in 2003, interviewed by John Amis for
the BBC in 1986 and Sharon Eisenhour for
Philadelphia's WUHY station in 1982. What
a cornucopia!

Années de pèlerinage

Années de pèlerinage – Première année: Suisse,
S160. Venezia e Napoli, S162
Sergio Fiorentino pf
APR APR5583 (72' · ADD). Recorded 1962-63   **OO**

The third volume of Sergio Fiorentino's early
Liszt recordings made during the '60s unites the
contemplative (Vol 1) and the virtuoso (Vol 2).
These performances are of a rare virtuosity and
imaginative delicacy, and it's doubtful whether
the sense of bells ringing gently and exultantly
through the crystalline Swiss air in 'Les cloches
de Genève' has often been caught more evocatively. He rightly makes the gloomy and Byronic
'Vallée d'Obermann' the nodal and expressive
centre of the cycle, fully justifying and sustaining
his audaciously slow tempo (after all, it's marked
lento) and, throughout, his performances are alive
with the sort of fantasy and freedom that eluded
Jorge Bolet in his more cautious *Gramophone*
Award-winning Decca recording.

Sadly Fiorentino recorded only one work
from the official Italian *annèe* ('Sposalizio') so
this disc ends with its supplement, *Venezia e
Napoli*, a garland of encores that show off his
poetic resource and, in the 'Tarantella', quicksilver brilliance. His early Saga recordings often
suggested an enviable, if occasionally flippant
facility, but here he's at his finest; even when he
playfully tampers with the score (in 'Les cloches
de Genève') it's usually to Liszt's advantage. The
transfers have come up trumps.

Années de pèlerinage – Deuzième année: Italie, S161
– Sposalizio; Il penseroso; Canzonetta del Salvatore
Rosa; Sonetto 47 del Petrarca; Sonetto 104 del
Petrarca; Sonetto 123 del Petrarca; Après une lecture
du Dante (fantasia quasi sonata). Mephisto Waltz
No 1, 'Der Tanz in der Dorfschenke', S514
Libor Novacek pf
Landor Records LAN278 (73' · DDD)   ℉

Libor Novacek's command of the keyboard is
very impressive and he aspires to the highest
interpretative ideals in this Second Book of
Années de pèlerinage which, like the First, contains some of Liszt's finest music.

This artist takes time to express his views about
these masterpieces. He is not in a hurry, not
even in overtly virtuoso pieces such as the *Dante*
Sonata and the First *Mephisto* Waltz. There is an
expansive dignity to Novacek's playing that
spares them from falling into a trough of banality, as often happens. How a similar approach
works at a slow tempo (basically *lento*) may be
heard in the Petrarch Sonnet No 123 where
Liszt tries to convey its spirit through numerous
marks of expression. Novacek doesn't balk at
observing them. Nor does he balk at emotional
involvement with the music; and both virtues
are duplicated everywhere. An unobtrusively
excellent recording.

Années de pèlerinage – Première année: Suisse, S160;
Deuxième année: Italie, S161; Troisième année, S163
Daniel Grimwood pf
SFZ Music ② SFZM0208 (129' · DDD)   ℉**OO**

Listening to Liszt's musical description of his
travels through Switzerland and Italy affords the

same kind of pleasure as reading a prose journal. Daniel Grimwood, fast making a name for himself as an original and discriminating musician, has chosen to play the cycle on an Érard piano of 1851, an instrument by Liszt's favourite maker built at around the same time as he was radically revising the 16 earlier works that would make up the first two volumes of *Années de pèlerinage*. Tuned to the (unequal) Bach-Lehman temperament (a'=440), the Érard produces the sound Liszt would have heard when composing and playing these works.

This would be just another interesting period-instrument recording were it not for the performances. These are out of the top drawer, for Grimwood is not merely a keyboard colourist (*Au bord d'une source*, for instance, and the two *Thrénodies* from Book 3 emerge as early examples of Impressionism, enhanced by the Érard's harp-like treble register in quieter passages); he throws himself with abandon into the bravura writing of *Vallée d'Obermann* and the *Dante* Sonata, and turns in a delightfully perky *Canzonetta del Salvator Rosa*. It's an enthralling journey that throws new light on these poetic ideals of the Romantic era and, with hardly a pause between each item, leaves the listener, as it would any traveller on the Grand Tour, awed by the wonders of nature, the spectacular scenery and the glories of Italian culture.

Additional recommendation

Années de pèlerinage – Deuxième année: Après une lecture du Dante
Coupled with: Valse oubliée No 4. Mephisto Waltzes Nos 1, 2 and 4. Die Zelle in Nonnenwerth. Ballade No 2. Harmonies poétiques et réligieuses No 9
Andsnes pf
EMI 570022-2 (74' · DDD)   ⓕⒹ→

> Leif Ove Andsnes's *Dante* Sonata is outstandingly well paced and his Ballade excitingly coloured and powerfully projected.

12 Grandes Etudes, S137

'Complete Solo Piano Music, Volume 34'
12 Grandes Etudes, S137.
Morceau de salon, S142
Leslie Howard pf
Hyperion CDA66973 (76' · DDD)   ⓕⒹ→

In this first recording of the concert version of the *Douze Grandes Etudes* (1837), Leslie Howard brings his customary technical wizardry to bear on this outrageously difficult music in an arresting virtuoso display that demonstrates Liszt's consummate skill at transforming musical material. Moreover, despite Liszt's exhortation that only the later revisions of the studies should be played, there's a great deal to recommend the 1837 set, as these performances attest. The extreme technical demands of these pieces have led to critical scorn, but the challenges they contain aren't designed merely for display, but

are the result of the composer's comprehensive exploitation of the piano's expressive capabilities. Saint-Saëns said that 'in Art a difficulty overcome is a thing of beauty' and, in the present instance, Howard's own triumph over the monumental difficulties posed by these pieces reveals the astonishing beauty of Liszt's 'orchestral' use of tone colour and sparkling virtuosity.

19 Hungarian Rhapsodies, S244

No 1 in C sharp minor; No 2 in C sharp minor; No 3 in B flat; No 4 in E flat; No 5 in E minor, 'Héroïde élégiaque'; No 6 in D flat; No 7 in D minor; No 8 in F sharp minor, 'Capriccio'; No 9 in E flat, 'Carnival in Pest'; No 10 in E; No 11 in A minor; No 12 in C sharp minor; No 13 in A minor; No 14 in F minor; No 15 in A minor 'Rákóczy'; No 16 in A minor, 'For the Munkascy festivities in Budapest'; No 17 in D minor; No 18 in F sharp minor, 'On the occasion of the Hungarian Exposition in Budapest'; No 19 in D minor

Hungarian Rhapsodies Nos 1-19. Rhapsodie espagnole, S254
Roberto Szidon pf
DG ② 453 034-2GTA2 (156' · ADD)
Recorded 1972   ⓞⓞⒹ→

This well-known set has been in and out of the catalogue a number of times, always to considerable acclaim. And the performances are every bit as good as everybody has always said. Although individual readings of isolated *Rhapsodies* may surpass Szidon's, taken as a whole this is certainly the most pleasurable set available. Szidon's technique is especially geared towards clarity of passagework and rhythmic precision and he also possesses a convincingly dreamy temperament that enables the slow passages to emerge with a rare distinction. His technical mastery is in no doubt and this is playing of great flair, with a natural feeling for *rubato*. The *Rapsodie espagnole* is a welcome bonus. The sound is sympathetic and vivid.

Harmonies poétiques..., S173

Harmonies poétiques et religieuses, S173
Steven Osborne pf
Hyperion ② (two for the price of one) CDA67445
(84' · DDD)   ⓜⓞⓞⒹ→

Steven Osborne follows his superlative Hyperion recording of Messiaen's *Vingt Regards sur l'Enfant-Jésus* with Liszt's *Harmonies poétiques et religieuses*, surely a precursor of Messiaen's masterpiece. Attuned to the mystic heart at the centre of Liszt's Catholicism, Osborne once more shows the sort of stylistic ease and tonal magic that come to very few young pianists. Sacred and profane love blend with a wholly Lisztian alchemy.

In 'Invocation', the magnificent gateway to the cycle, Osborne offers up its quasi-orchestral rhetoric with immense power but without bombast. The 'Bénédiction' is daringly understated in pages that can all too easily topple into lavish, tear-laden emotionalism. 'Pensées des morts' is a triumph of alternating anguish and exultation. If all conventional pomp and circumstance are erased by the brisk tempo in the opening of 'Funérailles', Osborne's performance is still a marvel of concentrated musicianship and individuality. In the *Andante lagrimoso* he conjures an uncanny stillness in music whose painful climbing looks ahead to the dark, attenuated utterances of Fauré's final years, while the final 'Cantique d'Amour' resolves all past torment in a paean of praise for the union of two traditionally opposed ideas of love.

Few more radiant or deeply considered Liszt recordings have ever been made. Hyperion's sound is immaculate.

Hungarian Themes..., S242

'Complete Solo Piano Music, Volume 29'
Hungarian Themes and Rhapsodies, S242
Leslie Howard pf
Hyperion ② CDA66851/2 (159' · DDD) ⒻⒹ▸

When listening to these 22 pieces, officially entitled *Magyar Dalok* and *Magyar Rapszódiák*, you at once realise you've heard many a snatch of them before. And not surprisingly, for in fact they're the source of most of what eventually emerged as Liszt's worldwide best-sellers, the *Hungarian Rhapsodies*. The composer revels in the lavishly decorative, cimbalom-coloured, improvisational style of the gypsies, in the process making demands on the pianist variously described by Leslie Howard in his insert-notes as 'devil-may-care, frighteningly difficult, frenetic, hand-splitting' and so on. Whether because of Liszt's own waning interest in platform pyrotechnics, or the fact that only he could really bring them off, simplification seems to have been the primary aim when recasting these first flings as *Hungarian Rhapsodies*. But as Howard reveals, there are losses as well as gains in the maturer Liszt. Despite moments of protracted rodomontade there's a vast amount of enjoyment to be had.

Petrarch Sonnets

'Complete Solo Piano Music, Volume 21'
Soirées musicales, S424. Soirées italiennes, S411. Nuits d'été à Pausilippe, S399. Tre sonetti del Petrarca, S158. Venezia e Napoli, S159. La serenata e L'orgia (Grande fantaisie sur des motifs des Soirées musicales), S422. La pastorella dell'Alpi e Li marinari (Deuxième fantaisie sur des motifs des Soirées musicales), S423
Leslie Howard pf
Hyperion ② CDA66661/2 (157' · DDD) ⒻⒹ▸

The two discs comprising Vol 21 of Howard's enormous cycle remind us of the young Liszt's love affair with Italy, the spotlight now falling primarily on frolics with Rossini, Mercadante and Donizetti in lighter, lyrical vein. The special interest of the two original sets of pieces included,

ie the three *Sonetti del Petrarca* and the four *Venezia e Napoli*, is that Howard introduces them as first written (c1839 and 1840 respectively) before Liszt's characteristically painstaking later revisions. There's much to enjoy in the playing itself, especially in simpler contexts when gondolas glide through calm waters, or lovers dream, or shepherds dance. Melody, so important throughout, is nicely sung.

Totentanz

Impromptu in F sharp, S191. Nuages gris, S199. La lugubre gondola, S200 Nos 1 & 2. Unstern: sinistre, disastro, S208. Totentanz, S525. Danse macabre (Saint-Saëns), S555. Réminiscences des Huguenots (Meyerbeer), S412
Arnaldo Cohen pf
Naxos 8 553852 (71' · DDD) ⑤Ⓓ▸

Arnaldo Cohen is as poetically and imaginatively intrepid as he's technically coruscating, and all these performances offer refinement and ferocity in equal proportion. Few pianists could identify or engage so closely with music that hovers on the edge of silence or extinction (*Nuages gris*, *La lugubre gondola* Nos 1 and 2), or that sparks and sports with a truly devilish intent (*Danse macabre*, *Totentanz* and so on). In the *Danse macabre* the music emerges from Cohen's fingers supercharged with malevolence. On the other hand he can send the F sharp *Impromptu* spiralling into a true sense of its ecstasy, or momentarily inflect *Nuages gris* in a manner that accentuates rather than detracts from its abstraction and economy. He makes something frighteningly bleak out of *Unstern* (or 'Evil Star'), with its savagely dissonant climax and its unresolved hymnal solace, yet is no less at home in *Réminiscences des Huguenots*, dismissing ambuscades of treacherous skips, octaves and every other technical terror with a telling mix of verve and nonchalance. These, then, are performances of rare lucidity, virtuoso voltage and trenchancy, and all quite excellently recorded.

Transcendental Etudes, S139

12 Etudes d'exécution transcendante
Jenö Jandó pf
Naxos 8 553119 (64' · DDD) ⑤Ⓓ▸

The 12 *Transcendental Etudes* are the ultimate test of quasi-orchestral virtuosity and of the capacity to achieve nobility and true eloquence. Jandó perhaps lacks diabolic *frisson* in the more ferocious numbers but his performances, overall, aren't disfigured by wilful, sensational attributes or hysteria. No 1 is an impressive, dramatically pointed curtain-raiser, and he can hell-raise with assurance in 'Mazeppa'. His 'Feux follets' hardly sparks with the brilliance of, say, some of the full-blooded accounts of certain Russian artists, but even when it hardly modulates from study to tone-poem it's still more than capable (higher praise than you might think where such intricacy is concerned). He flashes an impressive rapier at the start of 'Eroica' and there's plenty of swagger and facility in the so-called 'Appassionata' Etude. 'Chasse-neige', too, proceeds with a fine sense of its menacing start to a howling, elemental uproar before returning to distant thunder. Jandó is less assured in introspection, yet it has to be said that all-encompassing versions of the *Transcendental Etudes* are hard to come by. Jandó is impressively recorded.

Miscellaneous piano works

'The Pioneering Liszt Recordings, Vol 2'
Soirées de Vienne, S427. La campanella, S141 No 3.
Octaves, S140 No 2. La chasse. Etude de concert
No 2, 'La leggierezza', S144. Gnomenreigen, S145
No 2. Liebestraum, S541 No 3. Transcendental Study,
'Feux follets', S139 No 5. Venezia e Napoli –
Gondoliera, S162 No 1. Tarantella, S162 No 3. RW –
Venezia, S201. En rêve, S207. Csárdás macabre, S224.
Les patineurs (Meyerbeer), S414 No 2
Louis Kentner pf
APR mono APR5614 (77' · ADD)   Ⓜ

Louis Kentner was the most stylish, witty and engaging of all Liszt pianists. Excellently transferred from 78s dating from 1939-59, this selection ranges from Liszt's early exuberance to the grim-faced austerity of his final years, and throughout you will hear playing of a peerless scintillation, patrician command and a poetic engagement known to few pianists.

With the disc subtitled 'The Pioneering Liszt Recordings', APR makes it clear than Kentner was a tireless propagandist for Liszt's genius in the face of lofty scorn and indifference from the musical establishment of the time. Liszt was always at the heart of his vast, all-encompassing repertoire and his affection is evident in his many scintillating flourishes and additions to the score, all gloriously within the style. The *Csárdás macabre*, in particular, crackles with a virtuoso fire and elaboration unknown to the composer, its stark and baleful character generously ornamented and extended. Elsewhere you will have an unalloyed joy in music-making, a Third *Liebestraum* that 'sings' and shimmers with all of Kentner's rich *cantabile*, and *Etudes* as magical as any on record. Finally, the *Les patineurs* paraphrase brings down the curtain on one marvel after another. Here the skaters take to the ice with dazzling aplomb, spinning and pirouetting through one giddy arabesque after another, the only regret being that the performance was marginally cut for accommodation on 78s. Otherwise whatever sparkles and enchants is here in super-abundance together with a reminder of Liszt's prophetic and dark-hued final years.

Christus, S3

Christus
Henriette Bonde-Hansen sop **Iris Vermillion** mez

Michael Schade ten **Andreas Schmidt** bar **Kraków Chamber Choir; Stuttgart Gächinger Kantorei Stuttgart Radio Symphony Orchestra / Helmuth Rilling**
Hänssler Classic Exclusive Series ③ CD98 121
(162' · DDD · T/t). Recorded live 1997   Ⓕ

Christus is essentially a contemplative work and so could really be said to exist in a different time-scale to most music. Much of the opening part, the 'Christmas Oratorio', uses very simple melody and harmony, and is studiously undramatic. Helmuth Rilling does well not to charge it with too much colour, and, if listened to as meditation rather than drama, what can seem static takes on a positive atmosphere as a group of long reflections on the Christmas events. This is a far cry from the sensational Liszt of the early virtuoso years, not yet reaching the terse, inward pieces of the last years. There's greater drama in the middle part, 'After Epiphany', especially in the superb scene of Christ walking on the water. Although there's still the suggestion that a wonder is being contemplated, Liszt stirs up a terrific storm. This part also includes the beautiful setting of the Beatitudes, sung by Andreas Schmidt with a degree of uncertainty which he entirely sheds when he comes to pronounce the sentences in Part 3 ('Passion and Resurrection') for the scene of the Agony in the Garden. The long *Stabat mater* is beautifully controlled by Rilling. His soloists support him well. The recording does excellent justice to Liszt's wide-ranging orchestration.

Songs

'Liszt Abroad'
Blume und Duft, S324. Comment, disaient-ils, S276.
Du bist wie eine Blume, S287. Enfant, si j'étais roi,
S283. Farewell, S299. Ein Fichtenbaum steht einsam,
S309. Gastibelza, S286. Gebet, S331. Go Not, Happy
Day, S335. Im Rhein, im schönen Strome, S272. Die
Loreley, S273. Morgens steh' ich auf und frage, S290.
Oh! Quand je dors, S282. Tre Sonetti di Petrarca,
S270 – Pace non trovo; Benedetto sia 'l giorno; I vidi
in terra angelici costumi. Und wir dachten der Toten,
S338. Über allen Gipfeln ist Ruh, S306. Die Vätergruft,
S281. Wie singt die Lerche schön, S312
Rebecca Evans sop **Andrew Kennedy** ten
Matthew Rose bar **Iain Burnside** pf
Signum Classics SIGCD155 (80' · DDD)   Ⓕ ❶❶➡

'Liszt was here' is a badge of honour that could probably be claimed by most centres of civilisation in 19th-century Europe. The wanderer is here represented by a programme of songs in as many as six different languages. The English selection is an interesting one – Tennyson's 'Go Not, Happy Day', including the 'red man' verse omitted in the better-known setting by Frank Bridge. He treats the words for their sense, which he follows thoughtfully, lingering over the last phrase ('and a rose her mouth') in a manner that reveals its eroticism clearly to Iain Burnside (according to his note). The Russian song, 'Gebet', is a prayer by Lermontov; and the

Hungarian one, gypsy-like in character at the start, is a farewell. The French songs to words by Hugo are comparatively familiar, as are the settings of Goethe and Heine. The Italian is of course Petrarch, with the now-famous Three Sonnets.

These are sung by Rebecca Evans – surprisingly, perhaps (for they are more properly a man's songs, and Andrew Kennedy was at hand), but very beautifully. She has developed in expressive powers, with additional colour in the lower part of her range, and her soft high tones, as in the last phrase of the first sonnet, are magically poised. Kennedy, too, is at his best, masterly indeed in 'Die Loreley'. Matthew Rose, described as 'baritone', sings as a bass the songs clearly written for that voice: most effectively in 'Gastibelza', the song that Iain Burnside distinguishes as the only one he can think of that combines mad scene and bolero. Burnside himself, presiding spirit throughout, accompanies expertly.

Henry Litolff   French 1818-1891

Litolff was highly regarded in his day as a composer and pianist (Liszt dedicated his First Piano Concerto to him). His private life raised a few eyebrows: son of an Alsatian father and English mother, he eloped (aged 17) with his first wife, toured Europe as a pianist and divorced. Imprisoned for debt, he escaped with the help of the daughter of a prison guard, fled to Holland and married the widow of a distinguished music publisher to become one of the pioneers of cheap editions of classical music. His third wife was the Comtesse de Larochefoucauld and when she died in 1870 he married a 15-year-old girl.

Litolff composed five concertos symphoniques (a fancy name for piano concertos). The second movement of No 4 (composed in 1851) is a scintillating presto Scherzo, a rollicking dialogue between piano and orchestra with a mock-solemn chorale in the middle. It's long been a piano lollipop.

Concertos symphoniques

Concertos symphoniques – No 3 in E flat, Op 45; No 5 in C minor, Op 123
Peter Donohoe pf **BBC Scottish Symphony Orchestra / Andrew Litton**
Hyperion CDA67210 (66' · DDD)   Ⓕ**Ⓞ**➔

Litolff's dauntingly ambitious structures accommodate every possible style, looking forwards and backwards Janus-style, yet reaching out in the strange almost Alkanesque oddity of the Fifth Concerto's last two movements towards a more personal and distinctive style. Admired by Tchaikovsky, Liszt and Berlioz (though with some telling reservations), Litolff enjoyed a hectic career which is mirrored in writing of a formidable intricacy. So even if claims that he was 'the English Liszt' and that his development sections

are similar to late Beethoven seem far-fetched, the sheer energy and resource of Litolff's writing are absorbing. Few pianists could approach, let alone top, Peter Donohoe's blistering virtuosity in these works. His performances throughout are as rocksteady as they're dazzling, sweeping aside torrents of notes with both affection and authority. Hear him in the exultant whirl which opens the Third Concerto's finale, and you can only marvel at such unfaltering command, ideally complemented by Andrew Litton and the BBC Scottish orchestra.

Alonso Lobo   Spanish c1555-1617

A choirboy at Seville Cathedral, Lobo later studied at Osuna University. He assisted Guerrero at Seville Cathedral from 1591, becoming maestro de capilla of Toledo Cathedral in 1593 and of Seville in 1604. His output includes Masses and motets. Along with Victoria he is regarded as one of the finest Spanish composers of the Renaissance.

Masses

Lobo Missa Maria Magdalene. O quam suavis est, Domine. Quam pulchri sunt. Ave regina caelorum. Versa est in luctum. Credo quod Redemptor. Vivo ego, dicit Dominus. Ave Maria **Guerrero** Maria Magdalene
The Tallis Scholars / Peter Phillips
Gimell CDGIM031 (63' · DDD · T/t)   Ⓕ**Ⓑ**➔

Alonso Lobo is best known for one work, his setting of the funerary *Versa est in luctum*. This is undoubtedly a masterpiece of its kind but to have it placed alongside other pieces from his 1602 collection affords a welcome chance to assess his composition skills more fully. Lobo's music is sonorous in a manner that's direct and unfussy in effect, though often highly expressive, and always structured with the utmost technical control. Take, for example, the *Ave Maria*, an 8-in-4 canon (in other words, four more voices are generated from the original quartet) which emanates a sense of absolute serenity. In fact, each of the motets explores a different aspect of the compositional techniques brought to the genre, and the Mass is equally fine, Lobo making the spacious textures of the motet *Maria Magdalene* by his teacher Guerrero a distinguishing feature of his own setting of the Ordinary. The Tallis Scholars are on superb form, the overall sound vibrant and immediate with solo sections providing contrast through a more introspective approach. Even if you've never bought a CD of late-Renaissance polyphony, try this one. You'll be bowled over.

Ego flos campi. Lamentations. Missa O rex gloriae. Missa Simile est regnum caelorum
Choir of King's College, London / David Trendell
ASV Gaudeamus CDGAU311 (75' · DDD · T/t)   Ⓕ

This CD confirms the high calibre of Lobo's sacred polyphony: the excellent mixed choir present two Masses (*O rex gloriae* and *Simile est regnum caelorum*, based on motets by Palestrina and Guerrero respectively, and printed in Madrid in 1602), together with a magnificent setting of the *Lamentations* and the motet *Ego flos campi*.

The Masses have carefully honed vocal lines and that sense of vertical spaciousness that characterises the sacred polyphony of 16th-century Iberian composers. The choir sing with absolute conviction and total security, as if they really know the music rather than as if it were a very competent read-through. Trendell paces it all well, the tempo never seeming forced or plodding. The motet is deservedly popular, but the recently discovered six-voice setting of the *Lamentations* is an absolute winner, with meltingly beautiful suspensions, often in the upper voices, in the Hebrew letter sections; the choir again captures just the right degree of intensity without slipping into over-indulgence.

The fresh sound of this student choir combines energy and clarity in a most appealing way. This fine recording will enrich anyone's collection of Renaissance polyphony.

Pietro Locatelli   Italian 1695-1764

Locatelli studied the violin in Rome. He was appointed to the Mantuan court in 1725 but toured extensively (especially Germany), gaining a high reputation; his playing was noted for its virtuosity and sweetness. From 1729 he worked mostly as a teacher and orchestral director in Amsterdam. Locatelli wrote almost exclusively sonatas and concertos; L'arte del violino, printed in Amsterdam in 1733, was one of the most influential musical publications of the early 18th century. It is a collection of 12 concertos, somewhat in the Venetian style of Vivaldi, for solo violin, strings and basso continuo, with a 'capriccio' for unaccompanied violin inserted into the first and last movements of each concerto as a sort of cadenza.

Concerti grossi

12 Concerti grossi, Op 1 – No 2; No 4;
No 7; No 8, 'Christmas'; No 9; No 11
Freiburg Baroque Orchestra /
Gottfried von der Goltz vn
Harmonia Mundi HMC90 1889 (61' · DDD)   Ⓕ

By offering us a single CD of just six of these Op 1 Concerti grossi, published in 1721 when Locatelli was in his mid-twenties, the Freiburg Baroque Orchestra allow us to imagine that they have selected the ones they really believe in. It also enables them to start the disc with its most enchanting music, the first movement of Concerto No 11, in which a glorious solo violin cantilena soars soulfully and searchingly over a

gently chugging orchestral accompaniment. It is a gripping, haunting opening and the promise it offers is duly realised in the superb music-making that follows. Such quality is only what we have come to expect from the Freiburgers, of course. Here they present us with a hearteningly full, satisfyingly fibrous string sound, together with all their usual hallmarks of fine ensemble and naturally lively and intelligent musicianship. First-rate Baroque concertos in first-class performances.

Carl Loewe   German 1796-1869

Loewe began composing songs and instrumental pieces at an early age, also singing his own ballads to great acclaim. Among his finest early solo vocal works are settings of Goethe and Byron. He was a prolific composer in many media, writing five operas, of which only one, Die drei Wünsche, was performed at Berlin in 1834, without much success; 17 oratorios; choral ballads, cantatas, three string quartets and a piano trio; a work for clarinet and piano, published posthumously; and some piano solos. But the genre by which he is remembered is the solo ballad with piano accompaniment. From 1820 to 1865 Loewe worked in Stettin as a conductor, organist and teacher, yet it was through his recital tours that he won international fame; the Viennese called him 'the north German Schubert'.

Lieder

Ballads and Lieder
Dietrich Fischer-Dieskau bar **Jörg Demus** pf
DG ② 449 516-2GX2 (156' · ADD · T/t)
Recorded 1968-79   Ⓜ**ⓞⓞ**

All the best-known ballads are included here, magnificently sung by a great artist at the height of his powers. 'Edward', 'Herr Oluf', 'Heinrich der Vogler', 'Prince Eugen', 'Der Zauberlehrling': these and others are sung with a wonderful sense of the graphic, conveyed through an appreciation of the colour of the words that never descends into overemphasis and that's beautifully attuned to Loewe's illustrative manner. Fischer-Dieskau and Demus are ideal partners, Demus responding quickly and with an ear for the sinister that often marks the piano writing and its subtle use of motive. Not just a composer of ballads, Loewe was also a Lieder writer in the great German tradition, and this is too often overlooked, but not by Fischer-Dieskau.

Two songs alone, from this magisterial collection, are witness to Loewe's stature. They are settings of the wonderful poems from the second part of *Faust* in which Lynceus, the lynx-eyed watcher on the tower, sees the magical appearance, of Helen of Troy herself. He, incarnating the gift of the perception of visual beauty, after a life of watching from his tower can conceive of nothing that could surpass this wonder;

and, in the second song, hymns his gratitude to the gift of sight. Loewe's two settings are beautiful responses to the poetry of a great artist with the gift of an ideal simplicity. These two songs alone should persuade the responsive listener to make the exploration.

Jon Lord
English b1941

Lord's first active contact with music was through the family piano, and he took music lessons from a very early age. In 1963 Lord joined Red Blood and his Bluesicians and acquired his first electric organ. By the next year he occupied the keyboard spot in the seminal Artwoods, led by Art Wood, brother of future Rolling Stone Ronnie Wood. Then came Chris Curtis and Deep Purple. Between 1968 and 1976 Deep Purple was one of the world's most popular and creative bands, with Lord occupying a pivotal role both in the studio and onstage, through every permutation of the band's line-up. He eventually retired from Deep Purple in 2002 to concentrate on his solo work.

To Notice Such Things

To Notice Such Things[a]. Evening Song. For Example. Air on a Blue String. 'Afterwards' by Thomas Hardy[b]
[a]**Cormac Henry** fl [b]**Jeremy Irons** spkr [b]**Jon Lord** pf
Royal Liverpool Philharmonic Orchestra /
Clark Rundell
Avie AV2190 (54' · DDD)   (F)(O)(→)

'He was a man who used to notice such things' is the last line of the Thomas Hardy poem *Afterwards*, in which the poet tried to imagine what people might say about him after his death. It was the poem with which barrister and writer John Mortimer used to close his travelling one-man show in which his friend Jon Lord used to perform. The main work here is a programmatic six-piece suite for solo flute, piano and string orchestra, in which Lord evokes Mortimer's art and wit and aspects of his life and career.

Familiar from Lord's previous concert-hall works is his fluent, enjoyable reimagining of later-19th- and earlier-20th-century symphonic writing and the subject matter of friends pictured within. Lord outlines the 'programme' of 'At Court', the second movement of the Mortimer suite, like something Verdi or Elgar might have set: 'John in his glory in the late '60s, '70s and early '80s…one of the great barristers known for his hugely quick wit and love of debate. He also loved women…' On paper this may sound derivative or even coy, but the result sounds, delightfully, as if Bartók had been enticed to London in the 1930s to work with Eric Coates or Robert Farnon.

The central European feel continues in 'The Stick Dance', an illustration of the dancing-by-proxy which Mortimer, restricted by a stick, still

enjoyed in later life. There are also bleaker moments in which Lord's knowledge of Sibelius and Grieg are good shadows – in the suite itself 'The Winter of a Dormouse' and 'Afterwards', and *For Example*, a development of a piano piece in tribute to the difficult life of the composer's own teacher. The album ends with Lord accompanying Jeremy Irons's reading of the poem *Afterwards*. Performance and recording are both first-class.

Antonio Lotti
Italian c1667-1740

The Venetian Lotti became an organist at St Mark's in 1690, and then maestro di cappella in 1736. He also taught at the Ospedale degli Incurabili (Galuppi was one of his pupils), writing sacred music for both institutions. From 1692 he focused on the composition of operas, presenting about 30, the last four in Dresden. His large output includes oratorios, secular cantatas, duets, madrigals, instrumental pieces and numerous Masses, motets and psalms.

Masses

Lotti Missa Sapientiae
Bach Magnificat in E flat, BWV243a
Balthasar-Neumann Choir and Ensemble /
Thomas Hengelbrock
Deutsche Harmonia Mundi 05472 77534-2
(62' · DDD · T/t)   (F)

Thanks to his only well-known piece, the eight-part *Crucifixus*, Antonio Lotti has a reputation as a Baroque conservative, fuddy-duddily turning out nothing but church music in old-fashioned, Palestrina-inspired counterpoint. Yet, if there were such men in 18th-century Italy, Lotti – singer, organist and later *maestro* at St Mark's in Venice, but also composer of around 20 operas – wasn't one of them. For proof one need only sample this impeccable 18th-century short Mass for soloists, choir and orchestra, a work that Bach and Handel made copies of, and which evidently left its mark on both of them.

Handel actually 'borrowed' two bits of it for oratorios, but further stylistic resemblances are plain to hear. As for Bach, it's hard to believe that the meandering choral chromaticisms and coaxing accompaniment of the 'Qui tollis' weren't in his mind when he fashioned the 'Crucifixus' of the B minor Mass. Furthermore, Lotti must have known Vivaldi personally; we don't know who wrote first, but anyone familiar with the Vivaldi *Gloria* will spot similarities of approach in several movements. This is a fascinating find, and well performed by the pleasingly cohesive Balthasar-Neumann Ensemble, who convey its mood of bright confidence.

The coupling is Bach's *Magnificat* in its original E flat version, which differs from its better-known D major revision in several respects: the most significant are four irresistible extra movements for Christmas. Recordings are rare, though there is recent competition from Philippe Herreweghe. Of the two, Herreweghe's is the more 'traditional' performance, with a polished chorus, fine soloists and brassy trumpets. Hengelbrock achieves greater intimacy, and he's also more urgent.

Lotti Missa a tre cori **Bach** Cantata No 12, Weinen, Klagen, Sorgen, Zagen **Zelenka** Miserere, ZWV57
Balthasar-Neumann Choir; Balthasar-Neumann Ensemble / Thomas Hengelbrock
Deutsche Harmonia Mundi 88697 52684-2
(76' · DDD)   Ⓕ❍❍Ⓓ➤

This trilogy is based loosely on the Dresden connections between the Venetian Antonio Lotti, Bohemian Jan Dismas Zelenka and Thuringian Johann Sebastian Bach. Zelenka's unconventional *Miserere* in C minor (Easter 1738) is a peculiar mixture of archaic music based on a ricercar by Frescobaldi and modern proto-classical movements. Hengelbrock leaps without reticence into the agitated music that opens and dramatically concludes the work. The Balthasar-Neumann Ensemble and Choir perform with full-blooded tension; Hengelbrock makes the fullest possible use of the plangent oboes and pulsating string chords but also ensures that the music-making never loses its focused precision. The abrupt conclusion leads cleverly into the sinfonia of Bach's *Weinen, Klagen, Sorgen, Zagen*. The famous chaconne chorus that conveys weeping is tenderly phrased; solo voices are used for the first entries only and are soon joined by the full complement of 18 singers. This is by no means unpleasant but the sudden change of gears from streamlined intimacy to a larger choral texture feels odd (curiously, Hengelbrock eschews the policy in an entirely 'choral' recapitulation).

The crowning glory is Lotti's *Missa a tre cori*. As Hengelbrock has proved before, the Venetian master's chiaroscuro writing is certainly not run-of-the-mill. The contrapuntal first phrases of the *Kyrie* possess extraordinary expressive quality and accomplishment, whereas the first section of the *Gloria* is an irresistible, dance-like celebration with jaunty rhythms and bold trumpet. Lotti's controlled and sublime setting of 'Et in terra pax' reveals the harmonically adventurous talent and flair for unexpected effects that evidently fascinated Bach and Handel, and some surprising choral harmonies in the ardent 'Qui tollis' lifted me from my chair in astonishment and admiration for both the composer and his modern-day interpreters. This is nothing short of revelatory.

Requiem in F. Credo. Miserere
Balthasar-Neumann Choir and Ensemble / Thomas Hengelbrock
Deutsche Harmonia Mundi 05472 77507-2
(68' · DDD · T/t)   Ⓕ➤

Lotti's Requiem Mass in F major is considered by Thomas Hengelbrock the most important Requiem before Mozart's. It's full of expressive contrast: Lotti has an affection for a quasi-Palestrina style on the one hand and the skill to deploy more up-to-date techniques on the other. This Requiem is essentially in the late Baroque idiom, occasionally recalling certain of Vivaldi's larger sacred vocal pieces. The sections differ from the sequence usually encountered in later 18th-century Requiem Masses. There's neither *Sanctus*, 'Benedictus' nor *Agnus Dei*, but instead a very extended 'Dies irae' as well as a much shorter 'Requiem aeternam', *Kyrie* and Offertory. Full of theatrical gestures, supple polyphony, warmly seductive harmony and some beautiful melodies, the Requiem holds attention from start to finish. The contrasts are often striking, as between the hushed opening section and the awesome introduction to the 'Dies irae'. The *a cappella Miserere* is sung with clarity and finesse. The five-movement *Credo* is a supple piece for choir and strings with affecting, shimmering harmonies in the 'Crucifixus'. As well as full Mass settings, Lotti seems also to have favoured separate autonomous sections such as this, themselves subdivided into short units. The splendid performances bring this highly charged music to life.

Nicholas Ludford   English c1490-1557

He is considered to be one of the most important and innovative composers in early Tudor England. The few contemporary references to Ludford suggest that he was a private and highly religious man. He was not renowned in his own day, and his work cannot be identified with any of the major events of the time. In 1597, the Elizabethan composer Thomas Morley, in his Introduction to Practicall Music, noted Ludford as an 'authority'; but in the 17th century Ludford's music was neglected and finally forgotten. The majority of Ludford's festal settings of the Mass and his Magnificat are copied in the so-called Caius and Lambeth Choirbooks. Of his 17 Masses, Ludford's two six-part works (Missa Videte miraculum and Missa Benedicta et venerabilis) best demonstrate his musical; language at its finest.

Missa Benedicta

Missa Benedicta. Ave cuius conceptio.
Domine Jesu Christe
New College Choir, Oxford / Edward Higginbottom
K617 K617 206 (63' · DDD)   Ⓕ❍❍❍

Though not as showy as Taverner, Ludford's more understated idiom is every bit as persuasive. Repeated listening reveals great subtlety in the handling of texture, an exhilarating sense of confidence in formal planning, and real melodic inspiration. The opening of each movement is identical, and excludes the trebles, whose subsequent appearance in a different context is nicely managed. From the point of view of repertoire this is a major issue.

Here, New College's trebles show how much young singers can achieve in the way of cohesiveness, coherence and sheer persuasiveness of melodic shape. That speaks volumes, considering that, of all the English choral repertory written for trebles, this is perhaps the most difficult for today's youngsters to master. It's difficult to argue that adult female singers are demonstrably better equipped than boys: the advantage of bigger lungs is offset by the careful choice and placement of breaths. For the rest, the tone of these particular trebles is expressive in itself.

Paweł Łukaszewski   Polish b1968

Born in the southern Polish city of Czestochowa, a major destination of pilgrimage for the celebrated Black Madonna icon of the Virgin Mary housed in the Paulist monastery of Jasna Góra, Łukaszewski has an understandable affinity with religious music. Musically he may perhaps be aligned with Górecki, Pärt and Tavener but he feels more drawn to traditional harmonies which he supplements with vocal effects.

Choral Works

Ave Maria. Beatus vir, Sanctus Paulus. Beatus vir, Sanctus Antonius. Beatus vir, Sanctus Martinus. Two Lenten Motets. O Antiphons. Psalm 102. Nunc dimittis
Trinity College Choir, Cambridge / Stephen Layton
Hyperion CDA67639 (66' · DDD · T/t)   Ⓕ**Ⓞ**➔

This is a lovely disc of enchanting choral music. Possibly the Trinity College Choir does not always provide the warmth of tone such unashamedly expressive music demands, but that is more than compensated for by the sheer intensity of Stephen Layton's direction: only the hardest of musical hearts will remain unmelted by such committed interpretations.

It was for Layton that Łukaszewski produced his setting of the *Nunc dimittis*. In its beautifully measured phrases, immaculately tailored textures and ingenious use of light and shade to invoke light shining out of darkness, it is a gem which receives here a beautifully poised account. Effusive reference in the booklet to Łukaszewski's masterful handling of the concluding fade-out – 'a hackneyed effect in the hands of lesser composers' – did get the juices of critical scepticism running for a bit until heard, along with all the other potentially hackneyed choral effects (polytonal clusters in *Memento mei, Domine*, frequently reiterated dynamic contrasts in *Beatus vir, Sanctus Martinus*, continually repeated melodic and rhythmic motifs in *O Sapientia*), and realised that here is a composer who really is a true master of the art of *a cappella* writing and for whom other people's experiments and gimmicks are an essential tool in conveying a profound emotional message.

Once or twice – notably in a saccharine setting of the *Ave Maria* (although the purity of Rebecca Lancelot's voice manages to divert any cloying character) and an over-clichéd *Crucem tuam adoramus* – the musical quality is compromised by emotional effect, but all in all this is a lovely disc. It has been difficult to draw this CD out of the player, so frequently has it been played. There's no higher praise.

Jean-Baptiste Lully
Italian/French 1632-1687

An unusual start, a colourful middle and bizarre end mark out this Italian-born musician who was to become the founder of French opera. He was the son of a poor miller who was taught the elements of music by a Franciscan monk. He could play the guitar, violin and sing, this latter attracting the attention of the Chevalier de Guise who took the 14-year-old boy to Paris to be valet de chambre to Mademoiselle d'Orléans. Lully was in the habit of entertaining the domestic servants in the kitchen with improvisations on the violin; this came to the attention of the Count de Nogent and he was found a place in Mademoiselle's private band and, after losing her favour, entered the service of her young cousin (1652) who happened to be King Louis XIV, the 'Sun King'. Lully was also an excellent dancer, a talent shared with his royal master – the two appeared together in a ballet in 1653, the first of many such occasions.

From then on, Lully's story is one of increasing power and influence, first in royal music circles and latterly as one of the King's secretaires, among his most trusted and important personal advisors. He was a shrewd courtier, ambitious, arrogant, ruthless and determined, a man who knew when to be obsequious and when to flatter. In 1661 he was made official composer to the King, and became music master to the whole royal family the following year, by then earning the enormous sum of £30,000 a year – another factor which, coupled with his avariciousness, failed to endear him to his contemporaries. With the acquisition of the licence to operate the Académie Royale de Musique and various patents from the King, Lully was able to establish a virtual monopoly in the Parisian theatre, depriving any rival from making a reputation. Having said that, the stage works which he now produced over the next 15 or so years were the beginnings of a new school of opera.

During the performance of a Te Deum he had written in celebration of the King's recovery from serious illness, Lully accidentally stabbed his foot with the sharp-pointed cane used to conduct. An abscess developed, he contracted gangrene and died shortly after from blood-poisoning.

Suites

'L'Orchestre du Roi Soleil'   Ⓟ
Première Suite: Le bourgeois gentilhomme.
Deuxième Suite: Le divertissement royal. Troisième Suite: Alceste

Le Concert des Nations / Jordi Savall
Alia Vox AV9807 (64' · DDD)　　　　Ⓕ Ⓞ

Le Concert des Nations offers here a compendium of Lully's music from the heyday of the court of Louis XIV (widely assumed to have been at Versailles, but in fact from before the move from Paris). The pieces, drawn from a variety of Lullian sources to make up three entertainments (or *divertissements*), provide Savall with opportunities to present his musicians in Lully's spectrum of ensemble textures. The players respond to the rhythmic vitality of the music, adding ornamentation with tremendous precision and flair, but the secret of the obvious success of this recording is the rightness of the tempi, whether for a dance, a battle, a gust of wind or a funeral.

Those who saw the film *Tous les matins du monde* will be familiar with Lully's 'March pour la Cérémonie turque' and will immediately hear the difference even a few years has made to Savall: the playing on this new recording more effectively captures the military character without caricaturing the janissary element. The real stars of the recording, however, are the percussion players, Michèle Claude and Pedro Estevan, whose command of the possibilities for accompanying this repertory would have impressed even Lully. Whole evenings of Lully are still an acquired taste, but a recording of highlights as good as this is something anyone who enjoys Baroque music would wish to own.

Grands motets

Miserere. Quare fremuerunt.　　　　Ⓟ
Domine salvum fac regem. Jubilate Deo
Amel Brahim-Djelloul sop **Howard Crook, Damien
Guillon** countertens **Hervé Lamy** ten **Arnaud
Marzorati** bass **Les pages et les chantres de la
Chapelle; Musica Florea / Olivier Schneebeli**
K617 K617 157 (53' · DDD · T/t)　　　　Ⓕ

Grands motets, requiring lavish vocal and instrumental resources, always signalled important occasions at the French court. Until the advent of public concerts in Paris in the 1720s they were performed exclusively by the king's musicians for the court. Olivier Schneebeli has assembled an admirable survey of these large-scale settings of psalm texts, which were excerpted and arranged to convey *doubles entendres* flattering to Louis XIV and his policies. The music employs an orchestra with a full continuo complement, a choir and a *petit choeur* of soloists that relies on high male voices. The only concession to modern times is the use of sopranos instead of castrati in the top part and the inclusion of girls among the pages.

The survey begins with Lully's first *grand motet*, the *Jubilate Deo* (1660), celebrating both the marriage of the king and a peace treaty. The *Miserere* (1663), frequently performed during Lully's lifetime, has remained his best-known work. *Quare fremuerunt* (1685) was composed at a difficult time, when he most needed to please the king. From first to last, one can easily hear the ways in which Lully experimented with his forces, refining the role of the orchestra, the ways in which the soloists relate to the choir, and how he was influenced by his experience of opera.

The singers are attentive to Schneebeli's direction; the five soloists contribute singly, in dialogue with one another and in concert with the choir. Musica Florea's sweet sound suggests a refreshing departure from current ideas of Lullian style.

Miscellaneous works

Ballet de la Raillerie, LWV11 – Overture,　　Ⓟ
Ritournelle & Trio: L'un dell'altro ognun si burla.
Psyché, LWV45 – Air: Deh, piangete al pianto mio.
Ballet d'Alcidiane, LWV9 – Chaconne des
Maures; Ouverture, Ritournelle & Air: Amiam
dunque, infin ch'è lecito; Petite chaconne & Duo:
Cede al vostro valore. Ballet des Nations, LWV43 –
Air: Di rigori armata il seno; Entrée des
Scaramouches; Chaconne; Duo: Bel tempo che vola;
Réjouissance; Chaconne. Ballet de l'Amour malade,
LWV8 – Ritournelle & Air: Que les jaloux sont
importuns; Air: E che sarebbe amor senza cochette?.
Ballet de Flore, LWV40 – Plainte de Vénus: Ah, quelle
cruauté. Ballet des Amours déguisés, LWV21 –
Plainte d'Armide: Ah, Rinaldo, e dove sei?
**Emanuela Galli, Yetzabel Arias Fernández,
Stefanie True** sops **La Risonanza / Fabio Bonizzoni**
hpd
Glossa GCD921509 (72' · DDD · T/t) Ⓕ

Lully is so closely identified with the beginnings of French opera that it's easy to forget that he was Italian. He didn't compose Italian operas but he did make settings of Italian words: this enjoyable disc includes some of them, along with instrumental pieces and a couple of French airs.

Lully's patronage by the young Louis XIV was initially due to his skill as a dancer: all the pieces here are from ballets, composed well before his first opera (including *Psyché*, of which more anon). The *Ballet de l'Amour malade* (1657) was a joint effort with Marco Marazzali, one of the composers imported by Mazarin. 'E che sarebbe amor' alternates a slow refrain with fast passages and, like much else on the disc, would not sound out of place in an opera by Cavalli. The excerpts from the *Ballet d'Alcidiane* of the following year are spread out, for some reason: 'Cede al vostro valore' is a jolly duet, also with a refrain, sung and played with gusto.

Emanuela Galli takes most of the solo numbers, including a full-blown scena from the *Ballet des Amours déguisés*. The duet from the *Ballet des Nations* ends with an exuberant riff for all of the continuo instruments. 'Deh piangete al pianto mio', affectingly sung by Galli, comes from the ballet *Psyché* of 1671.

Acis et Galatée

Acis et Galatée   P
Jean-Paul Fouchécourt ten Acis **Véronique
Gens** sop Galatée **Monique Simon** sop Diane,
Second Naiad **Jean-Louis Meunier** ten Comus
Howard Crook ten Apollon, Télème, Priest of Juno
Françoise Masset sop Scylla, Dryad **Rodrigo del
Pozo** counterten Tircis **Mireille Delunsch** sop
Aminte, Abundance, First Naiad **Laurent Naouri** bar
Polyphème **Thierry Félix** bar Neptune, Sylvan
**Choeur des Musiciens du Louvre;
Les Musiciens du Louvre / Marc Minkowski**
Archiv download 453 497-2AH2 (107' · DDD · T/t)
Ⓕ❍❍🅱

Acis et Galatée was Lully's last completed opera,
and one of his greatest. A *pastoral héroïque* performed in 1686 to entertain the Dauphin during
a hunting party at the Duc de Vendôme's châ-
teau, it employs many features of his *tragédies en
musique* – vocal ensembles, instrumental movements and an enhanced use of the orchestra in
general; and each act contains a *divertissement*
with choruses and dances. One of the glories of
the score is the concluding *passacaille*, which
with instrumental sections builds up from single
voices to chorus. There's also a small but affecting chaconne for Galatea in Act 2; but another
glorious moment is the lengthy scene in which
she discovers the body of her lover and calls on
her father, Neptune, who guarantees Acis
immortality by transforming him into a river.
Marc Minkowski brings out all the drama of the
work by thoughtful treatment of the verbal text,
intelligent pacing and varied instrumental articulation and weight: especially striking are the
rough sonorities of the march in which
Polyphemus first appears, and the intensity of
the lovers' angry confrontation in Act 2. Jean-
Paul Fouchécourt projecting the image of an
ardent youthful lover, and Véronique Gens that
of a passionate goddess, are both excellently
cast, but Laurent Naouri almost steals the scene
from them with his fearsomely powerful
Polyphemus: Howard Crook contributes valua-
bly in various roles, though he's ill at ease in the
very highest register. There's considerable
finesse in the chorus singing, and the theorbo
continuo is admirable. An altogether splendid
performance of a masterpiece.

Cadmus et Hermione

Cadmus et Hermione   P
André Morsch bar Cadmus **Claire Lefilliâtre** sop
Hermione **Arnaud Marzorati** bass Arbas, Pan **Jean-
François Lombard** ten La Nourrice, Dieu champêtre
Isabelle Druet mez Charite, Melisse **Arnaud Richard**
bass Draco, Mars **Camille Poul** sop L'Amour, Palès
Le Poème Harmonique / Vincent Dumestre
Stage director **Benjamin Lazar**
Video director **Martin Fraudreau**
Alpha 📀 ALPHA701 (123' · NTSC · 16:9 · PCM
stereo and 5.1 · 0)   Ⓕ

Lully's *Cadmus et Hermione* (1673) inaugurated
the era of *tragédie lyrique* that held sway until the
Revolution. The performances by both singers
and dancers are first-rate, thanks in no small part
to Vincent Dumestre's clear and zestful conducting and the responsiveness of the orchestra.
André Morsch as Cadmus, Claire Lefilliâtre as
Hermione and Arnaud Marzorati as the cowardly
confidant Arbas deserve particular praise. All are
at ease with the theatrical gestures of the time,
and the choreography by Gudrun Skamletz and
Anne Tournié is stylish and entertaining.
The costumes are exquisitely crafted and so,
too, the masks and the maquillage, bringing to
life the images Berain left us. The giant Draco's
dinosaur coat is a triumph, although some of the
women's costumes seem a trifle short for the
time. Other pleasures include the carefully
researched scene sets with marvellous machin-
ery (transporting gods and operating monsters)
and the striking quality and quantity of light,
originally generated by candles and oil lamps.
Among the musical high-points are the
chaconne that ends Act 1; Cadmus's and Hermione's farewell in Act 2; the divertissement that
ends Act 3; the moment when Cadmus and
Hermione are reunited in Act 4, tellingly in a
minor key; and the divertissement that concludes Act 5. Important, too, are the comic
scenes with servants in Acts 2 and 3 – a holdover
from the *comédies-ballet* of the previous decade,
which Lully avoided in later operas.

Persée

Persée   P
Cyril Auvity ten Persée **Marie Lenormand** sop
Andromède **Stephanie Novacek** mez Cassiope
Monica Whicher sop Mérope **Olivier Laquerre** bass-
bar Céphée, Méduse **Alain Coulombe** bass Phinée
Colin Ainsworth ten Mercure **Vilma Vitols** sop
Vénus **Tafelmusik Chamber Choir and Baroque
Orchestra / Hervé Niquet**
Stage director **Marshall Pynkoski**
Video director **Marc Stone**
Euroarts 📀 205 4178 (127' · NTSC · 16:9 · PCM
stereo, 5.1 and DTS 5.1 · 0)
Recorded live at the Elgin Theatre, Toronto, on April
28, 2004   Ⓕ

A warm welcome to the first opera by Lully to
appear on DVD. Staged performances of his
tragédies lyriques being rare, at least in the UK,
it's good to be able at last to assess one of them
as a drama. *Persée*, to a libretto by Philippe
Quinault, Lully's usual collaborator, was first
performed in 1682, a year before *Phaëton*. As
with all such works the purpose was to flatter,
none too subtly, the person and the reign of
Louis XIV; indeed, the subject was chosen by
the Sun King himself, and the sycophantic composer made an explicit comparison between
Louis and Perseus in the dedication.
The story, taken from Ovid's *Metamorphoses*, is
a conflation of two legends: Perseus' slaying of
Medusa and his rescue of Andromeda. Cassio-

peia has incurred the wrath of Juno, who sends Medusa to terrorise the country. With Medusa dead, Juno causes Cassiopeia's daughter, the princess Andromeda, to be chained to a rock at the mercy of a monster. Perseus swoops from the sky to kill the monster, Venus descends as a *dea ex machina* to take the hero, his beloved and her parents up to heaven, and everybody lives happily ever after. Everybody, that is, except for Merope, fruitlessly in love with Perseus, who dies accidentally; and Phineus, Andromeda's betrothed, whom Perseus turns to stone with Medusa's head.

As a drama, then, there's not much going for *Persée*, especially as Perseus benefits from divine assistance: a sword from Vulcan, a shield from Athena, a helmet from Pluto, not to mention the presence of Mercury, who sends Medusa to sleep. But there's much pleasure to be had from the choral and balletic contributions to the divertissements and from individual scenes.

This production from Toronto is dressed and choreographed in traditional style and the direction is both lively and respectful, the characters encouraged to gesture expressively. Monica Whicher and Alain Coulombe are good as the disappointed lovers; Olivier Laquerre, stentorian as Andromeda's father, has a fine old time camping up the transvestite role of Medusa. Cyril Auvity's Perseus, rather pinched in tone, is outsung by Colin Ainsworth's Mercury, who is nonsensically given a solo belonging to one of the mortals.

Hervé Niquet is a sympathetic conductor, moving seamlessly through recitative, air and ensemble; the orchestra suffers from a recorded balance that favours the theorbo.

A short scene for Medusa's fellow Gorgons is pointlessly cut. The entire allegorical Prologue is omitted, too; no great loss, perhaps, but it should have been mentioned in the booklet. But let's not end on a carping note: this enterprising issue is cause for celebration.

Witold Lutosławski   Polish 1913-1994

Few of the myriad Polish composers following in the footsteps of Szymanowski have made an impact in the West. Andrzej Panufnik and Krzysztof Penderecki have their followers and there has been cult interest in Henryk Górecki, but the most widely known is Lutosławski.

Born into a wealthy family, he studied at the Warsaw Conservatory before becoming a full-time composer. His career was interrupted by the Second World War: he joined the Polish army but was made a German prisoner of war, returning to Warsaw to earn his living by playing piano in cafés and cabarets. Having been halted by the Nazis, the Communists banned his First Symphony as 'formalist' and until the mid-1950s he spent much time writing scores for radio and film, teaching and writing a series of compositions based on Polish folklore. The Overture for Strings (1949), Concerto for Orchestra (1954) and the First Symphony (1947) all use quotations from folk music,

worked in a modern context. In other pieces, such as Muzyka zalobna (1958), funeral music in homage to Bartók, Lutosławski made use of atonalism in a personal manner. He also made forays into aleatory methods (that is, scoring the precise notes but leaving it up to the players to determine the length and placing of the notes). Showered with honours during the Sixties and Seventies, with the fall of Communism he became a global touring musical ambassador of his country, conducting his own music of which he was a fine exponent.

Cello Concerto

Cello Concerto. Livre pour orchestre. Novelette. Chain 3
Andrzej Bauer vc **Polish National Radio Symphony Orchestra / Antoni Wit**
Naxos 8 553625 (73' · DDD)   ⑤Ⓓ

This is an excellent disc; fine music, well played and recorded, and all at the special Naxos price. The earliest composition, *Livre* (1968), was the first work completed by Lutosławski after the Second Symphony, and it shows him at his freshest and boldest, as if relieved to be free (if only temporarily) from the burden of one of music's weightiest traditions. With its well-nigh surreal juxtapositions of strongly contrasted materials, and the unusual ferocity of its tone – the 'book' in question must have been of the blood and thunder variety – *Livre* reveals a Lutosławski quite different from the relatively benign, ironic master of the later works. Coming immediately after *Livre*, the Cello Concerto has an even wider expressive range: indeed, in the balance it achieves between lamenting melodic lines and mercurial *scherzo*-like writing, coupled with a tendency to home in on crucial pitch-centres, it sets out the basic elements of the composer's later style.

This performance owes a great deal to Antoni Wit's skilful shaping of the music's alternations between relatively free and precise notation, and this skill is even more evident in the remaining orchestral scores. *Novelette*, completed in 1979, is Lutosławski's response to his first American commission; it's far more cogent and concentrated than its title might lead you to expect. *Chain 3* (1986) is one of the best later works, let down only by some rather perfunctory quasi-tonal harmony near the end. But this doesn't undermine the impression the disc as a whole conveys of some of the most characterful and individual music of the last 30 years.

Concerto for Orchestra

Concerto for Orchestra. Funeral Music. Mi-parti
BBC Philharmonic Orchestra / Yan Pascal Tortelier
Chandos CHAN9421 (55' · DDD)   ⒻⓄⓄⒹ

Tortelier's virtues as a conductor – expressive warmth allied to a special rhythmic buoyancy –

are apparent in a sizzling account of the Concerto for Orchestra. The musical flow is firmly controlled, yet the effect is never inflexible, and the technical precision and the alertness of the playing is something for the listener to revel in. The sound is bright, well differentiated dynamically, and even if the BBC's Manchester studio lacks some of the depth and atmosphere of Chicago's Orchestra Hall, as caught in Barenboim's version, this recording is generally more vivid, in keeping with a performance which has precisely the kind of bite and energy that the score demands. It's good that Chandos and Tortelier chose *Mi-parti* to complete the disc, since of all Lutosławski's later instrumental works this one makes out the best possible case for his radical change of technique around 1960.

Symphonies

Symphony No 1. Chantefleurs et Chantefables[a].
Jeux vénetiens. Postlude No 1. Silesian Triptych[a]
[a]**Olga Pasiecznik** sop **Polish National Radio
Symphony Orchestra / Antoni Wit**
Naxos 8 554283 (73' · DDD)   Ⓢ

Juxtaposing Lutosławski's early Symphony No 1 with the late *Chantefleurs et Chantefables* reinforces the fundamentally French associations of this composer's very personal musical voice; to contemplate how the symphony's exuberant embrace of a Roussel-like idiom was complemented, more than 40 years later, by the subtle Ravelian overtones of *Chantefleurs et Chantefables* is to recognise that the radical gestures of *Jeux vénetiens* (1961) have worn less well than Lutosławski's more 'conservative' qualities. Indeed, the wild piano cadenza in *Jeux vénetiens* now evokes the high jinks of Ibert's *Divertissement* rather than the liberated avant-garde ethos of more determinedly progressive musical minds. The downbeat ending is far more memorable.

Olga Pasiecznik's singing is outstanding, especially in *Chantefleurs*, where she easily surpasses Dawn Upshaw in subtlety, and Antoni Wit turns in strongly characterised, well-shaped accounts of all the scores. The playing is eloquent as well as energetic, and although, as with earlier Naxos volumes, the recordings are rather glassy and generalised, the music's range of colour and variety of texture is never in doubt. With such a well-filled disc, why did Naxos decide to include the first of the Three Postludes? The composer himself was clearly happy for the piece to appear on its own, but in a series with pretensions to completeness the full set is surely a must.

Symphony No 3. Concerto for Orchestra
Chicago Symphony Orchestra / Daniel Barenboim
Warner Elatus 0927 49015-2 (58' · DDD)
Recorded live 1992   Ⓞ

Lutosławski's Third Symphony was commissioned by the Chicago SO and first performed by them under Sir Georg Solti in 1983, but only nine years later did the orchestra record the work. None of the versions made in the interim can equal Barenboim's blend of refined detail and cumulative power, and the Warner recording is also more faithful to the dynamics marked in the score. The Concerto for Orchestra, completed almost 30 years before the symphony, is comparatively conservative in style, but it possesses ample substance to match its panache. It also remains a formidable challenge to an orchestra. As with the symphony, Barenboim's strength is the large-scale creation and sustaining of tension, and the recording contains the heavy climaxes without draining them of clarity or impact.

Sergey Lyapunov   Russian 1859-1924

On the recommendation of Nikolai Rubinstein, the director of the Moscow Conservatory of Music, Lyapunov enrolled in that institution in 1878. His main teachers were Liszt's former pupil Karl Klindworth (piano) and Tchaikovsky's former pupil and successor at the Conservatory, Sergei Taneyev (composition). He was soon attracted by the nationalism of the New Russian School and became a pupil of Balakirev, who remained the dominant influence in his creative life. He succeeded Rimsky-Korsakov as assistant director of music at the Imperial Chapel, became a director of the Free Music School, then its head, as well as a professor at the St Petersburg Conservatory in 1911. After the Revolution he emigrated to Paris in 1923 and directed a school of music for Russian émigrés. His brilliant technical studies Op 12 recall Liszt's Transcendental Studies. Besides piano showpieces (still in the repertory), he wrote distinctive, lyrical piano miniatures, orchestral works and many songs.

Piano Concertos

Piano Concertos – No 1 in E flat minor, Op 4; No 2 in E, Op 38. Rhapsody on Ukrainian Themes, Op 28
Hamish Milne pf **BBC Scottish Symphony Orchestra / Martyn Brabbins**
Hyperion CDA67326 (59' · DDD)   Ⓕ Ⓞ Ⓞ

Hyperion celebrates the 30th release in its invaluable The Romantic Piano Concerto series with a disc of Lyapunov's works for piano and orchestra as beautiful as it's comprehensive. Whether in Op 4, 28 or 38, you could never fail to guess the composer's nationality, and even when you sense Balakirev's eagle-eyed scrutiny of the First Concerto or Liszt's influence in the Second, Lyapunov's style invariably transcends the sources of his inspiration. Indeed, it's no exaggeration to say, as Edward Garden does in his excellent accompanying essay, that the hushed nocturnal opening to the Second Concerto is among the loveliest in the repertoire, setting the stage for every starry-eyed wonder.

The writing is as lavish and ornate as even the most ardent lover of Russian Romantic music could wish – at 3'35" it's like some richly embroidered cloth winking and glinting with a thousand different lights and colours. More generally, everything is seen through such a personal and committed perspective that all sense of derivation or of a tale twice told is erased.

Such an overall impression wouldn't occur if the performances were less skilful or meticulously prepared. Hamish Milne holds his head high, lucidly and affectionately throughout, commanding cascades of notes; he's stylishly partnered by Martyn Brabbins. There's competition in the Second Concerto from the urbane and scintillating Howard Shelley who is rather more immediately recorded on Chandos. But to have all three works on a single disc is an irresistible bonus.

Symphony No 1

Symphony No 1, Op 12. Polonaise, Op 16.
Piano Concerto No 2, Op 38[a]
[a]**Howard Shelley** pf
BBC Philharmonic Orchestra / Vassily Sinaisky
Chandos CHAN9808 (65' · DDD)　　　　Ⓕ

Sergei Lyapunov has always been a shadowy figure, his derivative yet distinctive voice drowned by his more celebrated compatriots and even by his contemporaries Taneyev, Lyadov and Arensky. Yet hearing the First Symphony in a performance of this calibre you're reminded of the way Lyapunov's melodic appeal is complemented by brilliant craftsmanship.

The opening motif is sufficiently brief to invite elaboration and to play a key role in music as coherent as it's heartfelt. The chromatic undertow as the music eases into the *poco più tranquillo*, its mix of sweetness and unrest looks ahead to Rachmaninov's Second Symphony, and if the themes are less memorable than in that towering Romantic masterpiece they're marshalled and directed with great compositional skill. Vassily Sinaisky and the BBC Philharmonic Orchestra allow the long, sinuous lines of the *Andante sostenuto* to unfold with an unfaltering tact and commitment, and in the balletic *Scherzo*, with its memories of Tchaikovsky, he realises all of the music's captivating grace and charm.

If Borodin is a key influence in the symphony then Liszt is central to the thinking behind the Second Piano Concerto. Lyapunov, after all, paid an eloquent tribute to Liszt in his 12 *Transcendental Etudes* for solo piano, a magnificent if uneven creation, and not surprisingly the lavish and intricate pianism in the Second Concerto is a Romantically inclined pianist's dream. Certainly its succulent themes and star-dust decoration could hardly be spun off more beguilingly than by Howard Shelley. His relaxed mastery and enviably elegant style inform every bar of this most seductive work.

The recordings are magnificent; no lover of Russian Romantic by-ways can afford to be without this.

Edward MacDowell
American 1860-1908

If Gottschalk was the first American-born composer to make use of indigenous American and Latin-American material, MacDowell was the first to be hailed as the equal of his contemporaries in Europe. His training on the continent included study with some of the finest teachers of the day (Ehlert – himself a pupil of Mendelssohn – Joachim Raff, Carl Heymann and, eventually, Liszt). When he returned to the States in 1888 he was feted as a famous composer and pianist. In 1896 'the greatest musical genius America has produced' was offered the position of head of the newly established music department at Columbia University.

Tragedy followed. Relations with the university authorities deteriorated and he resigned his post in 1904. It's debatable whether his periods of deep depression and irritability contributed to the unhappy situation or whether the situation exacerbated his condition. At any rate MacDowell lapsed into total insanity and the last few years he was in an asylum reduced to a childlike state, unaware of his surroundings.

MacDowell was unable to develop any nationalistic trait in his many works (despite some of the fanciful titles: From an Indian Lodge, Of Br'er Rabbit, etc). They are written in the traditional European Romantic manner, pretty, well crafted and tuneful, like the average German composer of his day, which essentially he was.

Piano Concertos

Piano Concertos – No 1 in A minor, Op 15[a];
No 2 in D minor, Op 23[a]. Hexentanz, Op 17 No 2[a].
Romance for Cello and Orchestra, Op 35[b]
[a]**Stephen Prutsman** pf [b]**Aisling Drury Byrne** vc
**National Symphony Orchestra of Ireland /
Arthur Fagen**
Naxos 8 559049 (56' · DDD)　　　　Ⓢ**▷**

Music of another time, another age, the MacDowell piano concertos can, in the right hands, seem more endearing than quaint or overblown. Both may satisfy conventional notions of dark and light, of tragedy and skittishness, but their heart-easing, lavishly decorated themes understandably attracted Liszt. Stephen Prutsman, a brilliant and versatile pianist, plays with ease and fluency, tossing aside the *Presto* movements from both concertos with an enviable sheen, though arguably without a necessarily committed or potent romanticism. Suave and engaging in the Grieg-haunted *Andante tranquillo* from the A minor Concerto, he loses his poise in the deeply welling *più mosso, con passione* from the D minor Concerto's first movement, and it's here, in particular, that one misses Van Cliburn's unforgettable warmth and virtuosity. No pianist has played this concerto with such magisterial command or emotional generosity; indeed, it sounds as if it was written for him. Eugene List, too, shows a higher degree of involvement than Prutsman, though it must be admitted that the latter's occasional reticence results from Naxos's recessed sound, which irons out much sense of dynamic perspective or variety. Too often Prutsman is confined to the shadows when he should be centre stage. The National Symphony Orchestra of Ireland has its uneasy moments, but world-premiere recordings of the *Hexentanz*, in an arrangement for piano and orchestra, and the *Romance* for cello and orchestra make this a tempting issue.

Guillaume de Machaut

French c1300-1377

Machaut entered the service of John of Luxembourg, King of Bohemia, as a royal secretary, in c1323. The king helped him to procure a canonry in Rheims, which was confirmed in 1335; Machaut settled there c1340, although he continued in royal service until the king's death (1346). He then served various members of the French high nobility, including John, Duke of Berry, his later years being dedicated to the manuscript compilation of his works.

With his prolific output of motets and songs, Machaut was the single most important figure of the French Ars Nova. As a composer of the 14th century, Machaut's secular song output includes monophonic lais and virelais, which continue, in updated forms, some of the tradition of the troubadours. He also worked in the polyphonic forms of the ballade and rondeau forms and wrote the first complete setting of the Ordinary of the Mass which can be attributed to a single composer. Machaut fused together contemporary styles and techniques to create a series of masterworks that stand at the summit of 14th-century music.

Machaut survived the Black Death which devastated Europe, and spent his later years living in Rheims composing and supervising the creation of his complete-works manuscripts. His poem 'Le voir dit' is said by some to be autobiographical, recounting a late love affair with a 19-year-old girl, Péronne d'Armentières. When he died in 1377, other composers such as François Andrieu wrote elegies lamenting his death.

Messe de Nostre Dame

Messe de Nostre Dame. Je ne cesse de prier (Lai 'de la fonteinne'). Ma fin est mon commencement
The Hilliard Ensemble / Paul Hillier
Hyperion CDA66358 (54' · DDD · T/t)   Ⓕ➍

Machaut's *Messe de Nostre Dame* is the earliest known setting of the Ordinary Mass by a single composer. Paul Hillier avoids a full reconstruction on this release: his deference to 'authenticity' restricts itself to the usage of 14th century French pronunciation of the Latin. His ensemble sings two to a part, with prominent countertenors. It's arguable whether the musicians sing the chant at too fast a tempo but they're smooth

and flexible, and the performance as a whole is both fluid and light in texture. Also included on this release are two French compositions. The wonderful *Lai 'de la fonteinne'* is admirably sung by three tenors and is pure delight – providing food for the heart as well as for the intellect. The rather more familiar *Ma fin est mon commencement*, with its retrograde canon, completes this admirable disc.

Messe de Nostre Dame. Felix virgo/Inviolata/Ad te suspiramus
Schola Gregoriana, Cambridge / Mary Berry
Herald HAVPCD312 (76' · DDD · T/t)   Ⓕ

This is neither the first recording of Machaut's most famous work to have been made in Rheims Cathedral, where the composer worked, nor the first to present the Mass as part of a 'liturgical reconstruction'. (The first distinction belongs to the Oxford Camerata's recording for Naxos, the second to the Taverner Consort's for EMI.) As a liturgical reconstruction, this is more nearly complete than the Taverner's, to the extent of including the celebrant's *sotto voce* recitation during the Secret.

The plainchant is especially well managed: the beginnings of the longer chant items are sung by a soloist in a rapt, florid style described fairly precisely by contemporary theorists. And as ever in this type of programme, it is most instructive to experience sacred polyphony unfolding in its natural environment (that is, as a literal outgrowth of chant), rather than as the 'bleeding chunks' in which we so often consume it. The Schola Gregoriana recording is currently alone in offering this opportunity.

That said, the polyphony itself doesn't quite have the polish of other recordings. This is felt particularly in the *Gloria* and *Credo*, whose fast-moving 'close harmony' demands a degree of unanimity (both rhythmic and intonational) that these singers do not quite achieve (it's high tenors – as on the Tavener recording – not countertenors who best impart the slightly astringent 'bite' that brings Machaut's dissonances most vividly to life). Whether or not you agree, this stimulating recording is unlikely to be the first choice for the polyphony itself.

Motets

De souspirant cuer, M2. Fine Amour, qui me vint navrer, M3. Puis que la douce rousée, M4. Qui plus aimme, M5. Lasse! Je suis en aventure, M7. Ha! Fortune, M8. O livoris feritas, M9. Helas! Où sera pris confors, M10. Fins cuers dous. Eins que ma dame d'onnur, M13. Faus Samblant m'a deceü, M14. Se j'aim mon loyal ami, M16. Bone pastor, M18. Diligenter inquiramus, M19. Biauté parée de valour, M20. Veni creator spiritus, M21. Plange, regni respublica, M22. Inviolata genitrix, M23
The Hilliard Ensemble (David Gould, David James *countertens* Rogers Covey-Crump, Steven Harrold *tens* Gordon Jones *bar*)

ECM New Series 472 402-2 (63' · DDD · T/t) Ⓕ**OO**Ⓑ➔

This is a landmark recording and a courageous venture. It's probably the first devoted to Machaut's motets, containing no fewer than 18 of the 23 that survive. It's certainly the first to present them in the order in which Machaut himself presented them in his own manuscripts. And the performances are of a truly mandarin refinement. Here are The Hilliard Ensemble with goodness knows how many combined years of experience performing this kind of music in public; they aren't just on the top of their form but also constantly showing the fruits of that experience.

The results of that refinement may surprise some listeners. Tempi tend to be rather slower than on earlier recordings: it's as though they feel no need for lily-gilding, no need to apologise for the music, where earlier performances injected possibly gratuitous energy into Machaut's lines. Dissonances are often made to disappear almost without trace, which will disappoint those who thought the clashes to be the very lifeblood of Machaut's music. (It must be absolutely clear that this was an informed decision by The Hilliards, many of whom have performed this music with other groups over the years.) Diction tends to be clearer than in some recent recordings, and – perhaps most surprising of all – they refrain from adopting current views on the early French pronunciation of Latin. These are all features that could make some listeners find it a touch dull; they might even find that they scarcely recognise old favourites. But they're superbly done, and the performances give the best avenue yet to gaining access to Machaut's still perplexing but always irresistible art.

Sir Alexander Mackenzie

British 1847-1935

Mackenzie studied in Germany and at the Royal Academy of Music, by 1865 becoming known in Edinburgh as a violinist and conductor. In the 1880s he won a reputation as one of England's leading composers, chiefly with the oratorio The Rose of Sharon (1884). From 1885 he lived in London, conducting the Novello Oratorio Concerts and, from 1888, serving as an influential principal of the RAM; he also conducted for the Philharmonic Society (1892-99) and occasionally for the Royal Choral Society, making a tour of Canada in 1903. A popular and generous lecturer with his students, Mackenzie also wrote books on Giuseppe Verdi and Franz Liszt. In his memoirs A Musician's Narrative (1927), he described 'a lifetime spent, boy and man, in the service of British music'.

Scottish Concerto

Mackenzie Scottish Concerto, Op 55
Tovey Piano Concerto in A, Op 15

Steven Osborne *pf* BBC Scottish Symphony Orchestra / Martyn Brabbins
Hyperion CDA67023 (62' · DDD) Ⓕ

From the horns' call to arms at the outset of the piece to the irrepressible merrymaking of the closing pages, Edinburgh-born Sir Alexander Mackenzie's *Scottish Concerto* (1897) spells firm enjoyment, and it's astonishing that this is its first recording. Cast in three movements, each of which employs a traditional Scottish melody, it's a thoroughly endearing and beautifully crafted work which wears its native colours without any hint of stale cliché or cloying sentimentality; indeed, the canny wit, genuine freshness and fertile imagination with which Mackenzie treats his material are in evidence throughout the work.

By contrast, Edinburgh-based Sir Donald Tovey's Piano Concerto (1903) exhibits a rather more formal demeanour, its three movements brimful of youthful ambition and possessing a very Brahmsian solidity and dignity. Tovey's idiomatically assured writing isn't always entirely untouched by a certain academic earnestness, but on the whole any unwanted stuffiness is deftly kept at bay. In fact, repeated hearings only strengthen one's admiration for this work.

No praise can be too high for Steven Osborne's contribution, while the excellent Martyn Brabbins draws a splendidly stylish and alert response from his fine BBC group. Sound and balance are excellent too.

James MacMillan

British b1959

MacMillan studied at Edinburgh University and then with John Casken at Durham University. In 1990 he became affiliate composer of the Scottish Chamber Orchestra; he has since become visiting composer for the Philharmonia and artistic director of its Contemporary Music Series. His music is noted for its energy and emotional power, its religious and political content and its references to Scottish folk music. Major works include The Beserking (1990), a piano concerto for Peter Donohoe; Sinfonietta (1991); and Veni, Veni, Emmanuel (1992), Symphony No 2 (1991) and Symphony No 3 (2002). His 50th birthday saw concerts at the BBC Proms and the Edinburgh Festival, and 2010 saw the US premiere of his St John Passion (2008) under Sir Colin Davis. MacMillan is also working on a Violin Concerto (for Vadim Repin) and a Third Piano Concerto (for Jean-Yves Thibaudet).

Piano Concerto No 2

A Scotch Bestiary[a]. Piano Concerto No 2[b]
Wayne Marshall [a]org/ [b]pf
**BBC Philharmonic Orchestra /
James MacMillan**
Chandos CHAN10377 (64' · DDD) Ⓕ**Ⓑ**➔

James MacMillan's *A Scotch Bestiary* is 'motivated by the great American cartoon makers who represented human characters in animal form,' says the composer, and is 'inspired by human archetypes and personalities encountered in Scottish life over the years'. The work's playful subtitle of 'Enigmatic variations on a zoological carnival at a Caledonian exhibition' acknowledges debts to Elgar, Saint-Saëns and Mussorgsky; indeed, the striding opening theme imitates the metre of (and linking role taken by) 'Promenade' in *Pictures at an Exhibition*. It's a caustic, loopy and exhilarating showpiece for organ and orchestra.

The Second Piano Concerto is scored for piano and strings, and is in three movements, the first of which, 'Cumnock Fair', initially appeared in 1999. This fretful dance fantasy's original title, 'Hoodicraw Peden', refers to a 17th-century Taliban-esque zealot, the subject of an Edwin Muir poem which witheringly refers to 'Burns and Scott, sham bards of a sham nation', thereby providing the titles for the concerto's remaining movements. 'Shambards' mockingly quotes the waltz from the Mad scene in *Lucia di Lammermoor* while the lusty violin reel that launches 'Shamnation' acquires an increasingly desperate energy as it hurtles giddily towards the piano's unhinged, unnerving final flourish.

In both works Wayne Marshall covers himself in glory, as, for that matter, does the BBC Philharmonic under the composer's direction. The sound is superlative to match.

Tryst

Tryst[a]. Adam's Rib[b]. They Saw the Stone had been Rolled Away[a]. Í (A Meditation on Iona)[a]
[b]**Scottish Chamber Orchestra Brass;** [a]**Scottish Chamber Orchestra / Joseph Swensen**
BIS BIS-CD1019 (59' · DDD) Ⓕ▷

This is the third recording of *Tryst* – extraordinary for a contemporary orchestral work. But its individuality is still as striking now as when it first appeared: especially so in this taut, gripping version. MacMillan touches, as warmly and directly as Mahler. The sounds can be violent, acerbic or prickly (as indeed they can in Mahler!); the keening string lament at the heart of the work isn't always easy on the ear, and yet it all speaks – it's plainly the work of someone who urgently wants to tell us something. So too are the performances. Joseph Swensen brings the passionate enthusiasm to *Tryst*, and to *Í*, that has made his concerts with the Scottish Chamber Orchestra such events in Scotland. *Í* (pronounced 'ee') is a quite astonishing work. The subtitle, 'A Meditation on Iona', might suggest something romantically atmospheric, with soft, lilting Celtic accents. In fact this is hard, intense, sometimes eerie music: a tribute to St Columba, the muscular, fiercely contentious monk who brought Christianity to Scotland and founded the monastic college of Iona – perhaps also a reminder of St Paul's words about working out one's salvation with 'fear and trembling'.

Along with this come two short, brooding pieces, which are dominated by the sound of brass: *Adam's Rib* and *They saw the Stone had been Rolled Away*, the latter giving more than a foretaste of MacMillan's Symphony, *Vigil* – the concluding part of the trilogy *Triduum*. As with *Triduum*, the success is total: powerful, concise works, powerfully and understandingly performed, in crisp, clear recordings.

Veni, veni, Emmanuel

Veni, veni, Emmanuel[a]. After the tryst[b]. '... as others see us ...'[c]. Three Dawn Rituals[c]. Untold[c]
[a]**Evelyn Glennie** *perc* [b]**Ruth Crouch** *vn*
[b]**Peter Evans** *pf* [ac]**Scottish Chamber Orchestra /**
[a]**Jukka-Pekka Saraste,** [c]**James MacMillan**
Catalyst 09026 61916-2 (68' · DDD) Ⓕ ⦿⦿

Taking the Advent plainsong of the title as his basis, MacMillan reflects in his continuous 26-minute sequence the theological implications behind the period between Advent and Easter. The five contrasted sections are in a sort of arch form, with the longest and slowest in the middle. That section, 'Gaude, Gaude', expresses not direct joy as the Latin words might suggest but a meditative calm, using the four relevant chords from the plainsong's refrain as a hushed ostinato. Over that the soloist on the marimba plays an elaborate but gentle and intensely poetic cadenza. The main sections on either side are related dances based on hocketing repeated notes and full of jazzy syncopations, with powerful sections for Advent and Easter respectively framing the work as a whole. The plainsong emerges dramatically as a chorale at the climax of the second dance section, a telling moment.

The composer's notes are most helpful, but they deliberately keep quiet about the coda, where MacMillan brings off another dramatic coup. After the soloist has worked through the widest range of percussion in the different sections, there's a gap when players in the orchestra pick up and start playing little jingling bells, and the soloist progresses up to the big chimes set on a platform above the rest of the orchestra. The very close of the work brings a *crescendo* of chimes intended to reflect the joy of Easter in the Catholic service and the celebration of the Resurrection. Disappointingly though, the preparatory jingles are gentle and discreet, and even the final chimes are devotional rather than exuberant. Even so, this is a magnificent representation of one of the most striking and powerful works written by any British composer of MacMillan's generation.

String Quartets

String Quartets – No 1, 'Visions of a November Spring'; No 2, 'Why is this night different?'. Memento. Tuireadh[a]
[a]**Robert Plane** *cl* **Emperor Quartet** (Martin Burgess,

Clare Hayes *vns* Fiona Bonds *va* William Schofield *vc*)
BIS BIS-CD1269 (74' · DDD)   ⒻO

Visions of a November Spring, James MacMillan's First String Quartet, was completed in 1988 and already bears many a stylistic trait of the composer who was to create such a stir two years later with *The Confession of Isobel Gowdie*, not least a mastery of the singing line and the distinctive, 'keening' quality of the string writing itself. The work is cast in two movements, the much lengthier second of which perhaps doesn't quite add up to the sum of its impressive parts.

No such reservations, however, apply to the Second Quartet from 1998, whose title, *Why is this night different?*, comes from the question posed by the youngest member of the family during the Jewish rite of Seder on the first night of Passover. The father answers by telling of the flight of the children of Israel from Egypt. The result is an arrestingly powerful and sure-footed masterwork, ideally proportioned, economically argued and always evincing a riveting narrative and emotional scope. Similarly, *Tuireadh* (Gaelic for 'lament') for clarinet and string quartet packs a wealth of pungent and varied expression into its single-movement frame. MacMillan wrote it in 1991 as a 'musical complement' to Sue Jane Taylor's sculpture in memory of the victims of the Piper Alpha oil rig disaster, having also been greatly moved by a letter from a grieving mother who recalled how, during the memorial service, 'a spontaneous keening sound rose gently from the mourners assembled on the boat'. *Tuireadh* is a deeply compassionate threnody, as is the much briefer, sparer and no less haunting *Memento* for string quartet (1994), which (as so often with this composer) shows the influence of the ancient oral tradition of Gaelic psalmody still practised in the Western Isles today. Performances throughout are as superlatively disciplined as they're tirelessly eloquent; sound, balance and presentation are all beyond reproach. Another MacMillan/BIS triumph.

The Birds of Rhiannon

The Birds of Rhiannon. Magnificat. Exsultet.
Nunc dimittis. Mairi. The Gallant Weaver
**BBC Singers; BBC Philharmonic Orchestra /
James MacMillan**
Chandos CHAN9997 (71' · DDD)   ⒻOᴰ⃗

MacMillan's colours can be garish, his gestures histrionic, but his is an art of passion and commitment: these are the effects of a composer seeking to make you feel and react strongly as well as think deeply. His admixture of Celtic cultural nationalism, leftist politics and Catholicism may be too rich for the blood of some 21st century connoisseurs, but it provides affecting and memorable listening experiences. This CD resolutely demonstrates the point.

The setting of Burns's *Gallant Weaver* (1997) is MacMillan at his gentlest and most intimate, but this only softens you up for *Rhiannon* (2001),

inspired by a tale from the *Mabinogion*, an ancient Welsh collection. *The Times* described its Proms premiere as unwieldy and florid with overworked and impoverished motifs. Maybe the performance has since been refined: here it sounds polymorphous and full of incident. More importantly, there's a cogent musical argument, even if not of the most sophisticated or subtle kind.

The *Magnificat*, a BBC Millennium commission heard here in the version for choir and orchestra, still includes an organ part which powers the violent ensemble interjections in the closing minutes.

He's already handsomely represented on disc, but this is as good an introduction as you'll get.

Choral Works

Seven Last Words from the Cross. Christus vincit.
Nemo te condemnavit. ...here in hiding...
Dmitri Ensemble / Graham Ross
Naxos 8 570719 (71' · DDD)   ⓈOᴰ⃗

Seven Last Words from the Cross is one of James MacMillan's most enduring achievements, a grippingly intense and enviably concentrated setting for double choir and string orchestra of Jesus's final utterances combined with texts from other liturgical sources (most notably the Good Friday Responsories for Tenebrae). Inspiration runs consistently high in this nourishing cantata, not least at the start of the second movement where three times the choir arrestingly cries 'Woman, Behold, Thy Son!' (the tension in the silence between the phrases is mesmeric), the third movement's spellbindingly beautiful treatment of the Good Friday versicle *Ecce lignum Crucis*, those jagged string chords which launch the sixth movement ('It is finished') or, perhaps above all, the achingly expressive Scottish lament that is the orchestral postlude, the string-writing bearing MacMillan's hallmark 'keening' style (Jesus's dying breaths are quite extraordinarily moving).

This is the work's third recording and, on balance, the most compelling and inexorable-sounding yet. Graham Ross secures outstandingly fervent and finely disciplined results from the youthful Dmitri Ensemble, while the remaining three items are just as impressive, especially the radiantly soaring anthem for double choir *Christus vincit*. Plaudits must also go to John Rutter, who is credited with the triple role of producer, engineer and editor: technically speaking the disc is little short of a triumph in its combination of truthful sonority and wholly natural perspective. Richly rewarding listening.

St John Passion
Christopher Maltman *bar*
**London Symphony Chorus and Orchestra /
Sir Colin Davis**
LSO Live ② ⚟ LSO0671 (90' · DDD · T/t)
Recorded live   Ⓑᴰ⃗

An 80th-birthday gift for Sir Colin Davis, James MacMillan's 90-minute setting of the *St John Passion* divides into two parts and is cast in 10 movements, the last of which comprises a deeply affecting and cathartic orchestral elegy (described by the composer as 'a song without words'). A baritone is allotted the sole principal part of Christus, a chamber choir acts as the Narrator/Evangelist and a large chorus is assigned all other duties. In the booklet Mac-Millan relates how some ideas from his 2007 opera *The Sacrifice* have found their way into the score. "I was also aware," he continues, "of the paradoxical tension created between the two highly contrasted musical contexts – liturgical chant and music drama."

In the central role Christopher Maltman gives one of his finest performances to date, sonorous, assured and reassuringly firm of tone. The choral and orchestral contributions are likewise beyond reproach, with the superb LSO brass in particular totally unfazed by MacMillan's at times scarily vertiginous demands. The microphones convey it all with startling immediacy, although, as is customary from this source, there's precious little in the way of ingratiating glow.

Even after a number of hearings, nagging doubts remain as to whether the work as a whole measures up to the exalted level of inspiration or possesses quite the communicative force of *Quickening* but it's valuable to have such an imperious realisation of what is a hugely sincere and often gripping narrative. MacMillan's many admirers will deem it an essential acquisition.

Mass[ab]. A New Song[ab]. Christus vincit[a]. Gaudeamus in loci pace[b]. Seinte Mari moder milde[ab]. A Child's Prayer[a]. Changed[ab]
[a]**Westminster Cathedral Choir / Martin Baker** with [b]**Andrew Reid** org
Hyperion CDA67219 (66' · DDD · T/t)　　Ⓕ**OO**

MacMillan's choral music is more often than not a direct response to his own Christian faith. The Mass recorded here was commissioned by Westminster Cathedral for the 'Glory of God in the Millennium Year of the Jubilee' and unlike MacMillan's two previous Masses, which were composed for congregational use, was specifically written for performance by a professional choir. It's through-composed and this provides a sense of structure, continuity and flow that greatly enhances its accessibility when heard out of context – on disc rather than celebrated. That MacMillan intended the Mass for practical use is apparent by his choice of vernacular rather than the Latin text. His often eclectic style is very much in evidence; the score glimmers with echoes of Howells and Duruflé, especially in the Kyrie and in his often quasi-orchestral organ writing, but in general it's MacMillan's individual voice that shapes this impressive and deeply felt setting. The Gloria contains some particularly effective music, not least some marvellously atmospheric organ writing, and the crepuscular Agnus Dei lingers in the mind long after the

final notes die away. Of the remaining works on the disc, *A New Song* and *A Child's Prayer* (dedicated to the victims of the Dunblane tragedy) stand out as particularly fine examples of Mac-Millan's choral writing. As a bonus we're treated to the wonderfully translucent organ solo *Gaudeamus in loci pace*, beautifully performed by Andrew Reid. Performances throughout are exceptionally fine, the recorded sound radiantly atmospheric. A must.

MacMillan O bone Jesu[a]. Màiri **Vaughan Williams** Mass in G minor[b]. Silence and Music
[a]**Kerstin Steube**, [b]**Aleksandra Lustig** sops [a]**Maria van Eldik**, [b]**Ulrike Becker** contr [a]**Alexander Yudenkov**, [b]**Julius Pfeifer** tens [a]**Achim Jäckel**, [b]**Bernhard Hartmann** basses **South West German Radio Vocal Ensemble, Stuttgart / Marcus Creed**
Hänssler Classic ⓈⒶ CD93 250 (53' · DDD)　Ⓕ**OⒷ**

The SWR Vokalensemble Stuttgart are a tremendously adroit and versatile group whose immaculate polish, scrupulous blend and stylish musicality cannot fail to impress. Certainly it's hard to imagine more luminously textured or jaw-droppingly eloquent renderings of the two pieces by James MacMillan. *O bone Jesu* (2002) was designed as a companion piece to the eponymous 19-part motet by the 16th-century Scot, Robert Carver, and shares that work's exuberant virtuosity and formal design. Creed and company lend it breathtaking advocacy, totally unfazed by the fearsome technical challenges, and it's a similar story in the plaintive glow of *Màiri*, an inspired setting of the 19th-century Gaelic poet Evan MacColl, written for the BBC Singers to mark their 70th anniversary in 1994.

The performance of Vaughan Williams's sublime Mass is an impressively mellifluous display, albeit without disturbing longstanding allegiances to much-loved predecessors like Matthew Best's 1983 Corydon Singers account (Helios). The beautiful part-song *Silence and Music* (VW's contribution to the 1953 Coronation collection *A Garland for the Queen*) comes off very well in Stuttgart. Stunningly natural SACD sound from the SWR production crew.

Quickening[a]. The Sacrifice – Three Orchestral Interludes
[a]**Hilliard Ensemble** (Robin Blaze counterten Rogers Covey-Crump, Steven Harrold tens Gordon Jones bar) [a]**City of Birmingham Symphony Orchestra Chorus and Youth Chorus; BBC Philharmonic Orchestra / James MacMillan**
Chandos ⓈⒶ CHSA5072 (60' · DDD/DSD · T/t)　Ⓕ**OOⒷ**

Quickening is a 45-minute cantata to a text by Michael Symmons Roberts that both celebrates and explores the themes of birth, new life and parenthood. 'The title,' explains MacMillan, 'refers explicitly to the instant of conception – "the quickening of seed that will become ripe grain" – or the moment that a woman first feels her baby kick.' It's a hugely ambitious but never intimidating canvas, the sizeable forces required (four solo voices, children's chorus and chamber organ, mixed chorus and a large orchestra including triple woodwind and a battery of per-cussion) and MacMillan's deployment of them inviting parallels with Britten's *War Requiem*. After the expectant wonder and awe-struck mys-tery of the opening movement ('Incarnadine'), darker images of violence, menace, war and fra-gility occupy the two central tableaux ('Midwife' and 'Poppies'), before the ecstatic apex and magical fade-out of 'Living Water'. There's absolutely no missing this music's visceral impact, spiritual fervour and strength of convic-tion, attributes that should hopefully ensure it a place in the repertoire.

A powerful experience, in sum, and a work well worth getting to know. It's preceded by the Three Interludes that MacMillan has drawn from his second opera, *The Sacrifice* (see below), based upon an ancient Welsh tale (from *The Mabinogion*) of love, warring clans and self-sacri-fice. Inspiration runs high in this communica-tive orchestral triptych, the second and third movements of which owe a not inconsiderable debt to the Passacaglia and Storm from *Peter Grimes*.

Suffice it to say, the composer secures admira-bly disciplined and committed results from all involved. What's more, Stephen Rinker's sound boasts spectacular amplitude, definition and range.

Seven Last Words from the Cross[a].
Te Deum[b]. On the Annunciation of
the Blessed Virgin[b]
Polyphony; [a]**Britten Sinfonia /**
Stephen Layton with [b]**James Vivian** org
Hyperion CDA67460 (69' · DDD)   Ⓕ🅱️

Seven Last Words was commissioned by the BBC in 1993 for Holy Week 1994, when it was broadcast in seven short programmes, a 'word' per day. It remains a highly compelling work. Under Stephen Layton, it certainly receives an impressive performance; an intense, deeply felt interpretation, full of beautiful and affecting singing, with all the elements – string orchestra, featured violin, choir and soloists – nicely balanced.

The other two works, *On the Annunciation of the Blessed Virgin* (1997) and *Te Deum* (2001), receive their premiere recordings. *On the Annunciation* is an intricate but approachable setting for five-part choir and organ of a poem by the 17th-century poet Jeremy Taylor. The luminous lines for voices finally give way to a gradually fading dance for organ. The echoes of Messiaen in this device are matched by some of the organ chords and figures in the dramatic *Te Deum*, written to mark the Queen's Golden Jubilee. From the contemplative opening phrases for male voices, somewhat reminiscent of Mahler's *Urlicht*, a dazzling part emerges for

solo soprano, sung in characteristically stun-ning fashion by Elin Manahan Thomas. As ever, MacMillan incorporates all his allusions, including those to Scottish traditional music, into an utterly individual style. The perform-ance confirms Polyphony's place in the front rank of choirs.

'Bright Orb of Harmony'
MacMillan O bone Jesu. Mitte manum tuam.
A Child's Prayer. Sedebit Dominus Rex
Purcell Jehova quam multi sunt hostes mei.
Miserere mei. Remember not, Lord, our offences.
Beati omnes qui timent Dominum. Let mine eyes
run down with tears. O dive custos. Funeral
Sentences for Queen Mary – First Set. Thou knowest,
Lord, the secrets of our hearts (1695)
The Sixteen / Harry Christophers
Coro COR16069 (66' · DDD · T/t)
Recorded live   Ⓕ🅾️🅱️

These performances were recorded live during the opening concert of The Sixteen's 2009 Cho-ral Pilgrimage to celebrate both Purcell's 350th birthday and Scottish composer James MacMil-lan's 50th. Thus, while the anthems, motets and the first set of *Funeral Sentences* by Purcell pre-sented here definitely tend towards the sombre, and MacMillan's musical language often has recourse to a stark muscularity, the darkness invariably gives way to light in the form of ecstatic melismas and lucent major-mode har-monies.

Throughout, the choral sound is rich yet unfailingly transparent – as obvious in the open-ing *Jehova quam multi sunt hostes mei* of Purcell as in MacMillan's masterly *O bone Jesu*. But the solo work is equally impressive – listen, for example, to tenors Simon Berridge and Mark Dobell and bass Eamonn Dougan in Purcell's *Let mine eyes run down with tears* or sopranos Grace Davidson and Charlotte Mobbs in the same composer's splendid *O dive custos*.

Christophers's direction is, as always, forever alert to the relationship between words and music – especially close with these two com-posers – while ensuring the careful delineation of the overall musical structure and each phrase, period and paragraph within it. Some minor blemishes aside, 'Bright Orb of Har-mony' deserves to be set among that constella-tion of previous dazzling recordings by an ensemble that is less a choir, more an institu-tion.

Opera

The Sacrifice
Christopher Purves *bass* General
Lisa Milne *sop* Sian **Peter Hoare** *ten* Mal
Leigh Melrose *bar* Evan **Sarah Tynan** *sop* Megan
**Chorus and Orchestra of the Welsh National
Opera / Anthony Negus**
Chandos ② CHAN10572 (131' · DDD)
Recorded live 2007   Ⓕ🅾️🅾️🅱️

Commissioned by Welsh National Opera, *The Sacrifice* was premiered in Cardiff in September 2007. The present, enormously involving performance was taped live a couple of weeks into that initial run. The close-set balance ensures that you can positively smell the greasepaint, while every word in Michael Symmons Roberts's libretto is crystal-clear.

The story itself is drawn from the ancient Welsh saga, the *Mabinogion*, specifically 'The Tale of Branwen, daughter of Llŷr', which, as Symmons Roberts explains, 'is about the long-standing emnity between the islands of Britain and island of Ireland, and the attempt to broker a peace deal by arranging a marriage between members of both sides'. The action is transplanted to the present or near future. Act 1 depicts the wedding of Sian and Mal, the ceilidh celebrations abruptly cut short when Evan (Sian's former lover and right-hand man to her father, the General) inflicts a knife wound on Mal. Act 2 opens seven years later just prior to the investiture of Sian and Mal's eldest son, Gwyn; at the ceremony Mal attempts a reconciliation with Evan but the latter pulls a gun on him and then, horrifically, assassinates the boy. Only in the last act is the cycle of violence finally broken by the General's self-sacrifice; disguising himself as Evan, he is killed by Mal. Sian delivers a plea for peace – but it's an uneasy truce.

The narrative is punctuated by seven powerful orchestral interludes, three of which MacMillan subsequently reworked into a symphonic suite – already available on disc as a coupling for the remarkable cantata *Quickening* (see above). In addition, there are plentiful allusions to Strauss's *Elektra* – and there are echoes of Berg, Shostakovich and Sallinen.

At the same time, all of MacMillan's familiar stylistic fingerprints are readily discernable, not least his predilection for pitting ideas of often violently different character against each other ('the more extreme the better', he once told me), the plangently 'keening' quality of the string writing that follows Sian's heartbreaking lament at the start of Act 3 and the judicious employment of a daringly diatonic lyricism.

Invest in this bold set and you'll be rewarded with singing of unflagging stamina from a strong cast (notably Lisa Milne as Sian and Christopher Purves as the General), as well as red-blooded, hugely committed contributions from the WNO Chorus and Orchestra. The audibly spellbound Cardiff audience laps it up – as, indeed, will the composer's many admirers. Enthusiastically recommended.

Stuart MacRae

British b1976

After reading Music at Durham University with Philip Cashian, Sohrab Uduman and Michael Zev Gordon, MacRae studied composition at the Guildhall School of Music and Drama with Simon Bainbridge and Robert Saxton. He was a finalist in the 1996 Lloyd's Bank Young Composer's Workshop

when the BBC Philharmonic gave the first professional performance of Boreraig. From 1999 to 2003 MacRae was Composer in Association with the BBC Scottish Symphony Orchestra. Echo and Narcissus – MacRae's first work for dance – was premiered at the Linbury Studio of the Royal Opera House in May 2007.

Orchestral Works

Violin Concerto[a]. Three Scenes from the Death of Count Ugolino[b]. Motus[c]. Stirling Choruses[d]
[a]**Christian Tetzlaff** vn [c]**Loré Lixenberg** mez
[ad]**BBC Scottish Symphony Orchestra / Ilan Volkov;**
[bc]**Birmingham Contemporary Music Group /
Susanna Mälkki**
NMC NMCD115 (68' · DDD)　　　　Ⓜ ● ➡

A disc devoted to Stuart MacRae is timely, as the composer has built a considerable reputation. As MacRae remarks in his booklet-note, all four pieces (written between 1999 and 2004) outline a journey. Abstractly, in the Birtwistle-like division of brass in the hieratic *Stirling Choruses* and the vividly soloistic sextet of *Motus*, whose progress from the fractured and discursive to the sustained and cumulative recalls that of the fine trumpet concerto *Inter-act*; graphically, as in the Dante texts relating the Infernal afterlife of Count Ugolino, even if the vocal line seems overwrought – at least when delivered with the vehemence of Loré Lixenberg – in the context of instrumental writing itself rich in expressive detail. The Violin Concerto is the most impressive work here: a successful formal recasting of the genre with the emotional emphasis on its finale, a striking amalgam of cadenza and apotheosis that handles the orchestra with considerable finesse. Dedicated playing from Christian Tetzlaff, along with the BCMG and BBC Scottish SO. An important release.

Leevi Madetoja

Finnish 1887-1947

Madetoja studied with Sibelius in Helsinki and with d'Indy in Paris as well as in Vienna and Berlin (1911-12). He then worked in Helsinki as a teacher, critic and composer. His works, often using Ostrobothnian folk music and French techniques, are skilfully orchestrated and include the operas The Ostrobothnians (1923) and Juha (1934), three symphonies and much choral music.

Piano works

Complete Piano Works
Mika Rännäli pf
Alba ② ABCD206 (81' · DDD)　　　　Ⓜ
Recorded live 2004

With Madetoja's operas, symphonies and songs now decently represented in the catalogue, the time is ripe for his even more rarely heard piano music. It consists almost entirely of miniatures (there are 33 tracks on the two CDs) and most of it dates from the 1910s – the first half of his career. Not conspicuously individual and often somewhat four-square in phrasing, the style feels like an organic continuation of Grieg and Tchaikovsky, enlivened by mildly diverting harmonic and melodic turns. Part of its attraction is an underlying melancholy. One readily agrees, too, with Mika Rännäli's identification of its 'childlike charm, a touch of mischief, wild boisterousness'. The minority of more extrovert pieces can be quite pianistically demanding without ever qualifying as virtuoso.

By far the most ambitious work is the three-movement cycle *Garden of Death*. 'One of the best and most poignant works in all Finnish piano literature,' Rännäli calls it, and that proves no overstatement. The austere, elegiac first movement, composed in memory of the composer's brother who was shot by the Red Guard in 1918 during the Finnish Civil War, brings strong echoes of Rachmaninov. It is followed by a volatile and disturbing waltz with an impressive, sombre conclusion, and by a wistful, restless berceuse.

Rännäli has an interesting mixed portfolio. He is not only a composer and pianist but also three-times Finnish champion in Latin American and ballroom dancing – a not irrelevant attribute, perhaps, given Madetoja's penchant for minuets, waltzes and gavottes. Live performances these may be but they are scrupulously clean in execution and engaging in temperament. Everything is flexible and nicely to scale. Beautifully judged recording quality too.

Songs

The Land in our song. Lieder, Op 2 – Since thou didst leave; Alone; Winter morning; Starry night. Dark-hued leaves, Op 19 No 1. Serenade, Op 16 No 1. Folk Songs from Northern Ostrobothnia, Op 18. Songs of Youth, Op 20b. Take up that fair kantele again. A flower is purest when opening. Lieder, Op 25 – From afar I hear them singing; Wintry road; Birth-place; Sometimes weeping in the evening. I would build a hut, Op 26 No 3. Song at the plough, Op 44 No 1. Lieder, Op 49 – Hail, O daylight in the North; Finland's Tree. Lieder, Op 60 – My longing; Evening. Lieder, Op 71 – I want to go home; The word of the Master. Song of the winter wind
Gabriel Suovanen bar **Gustav Djupsjöbacka** pf
Ondine ODE996-2 (79' · DDD · T/t) ⓕⓞ

The 32 songs are chronologically laid out. After the late-Romantic elegiac *lingua franca* of the Op 2 set, the first of Op 9, 'Dark-hued leaves', startles with its affinities with Rachmaninov; this gem of a piece is on the short list for all Finnish song recitals. Composed in 1913, the first of the *Songs of Youth*, Op 20b, couldn't be published until Finland's inde-

pendence from Russia after the First World War, which is no surprise, given that its text is demonstratively nationalistic ('Arise, O young sons of Finland…Saved and cherished shall our homeland soon be!') and its melody strong and catchy. This is an altogether impressive opus, whose concluding 'Christmas song' has become one of Finland's best-loved carols. With Op 25 we're back to the ecstatic tone of the earlier songs. Perhaps most impressive of this set is No 2, 'Wintry Road', with its tolling Brittenish ostinato and air of painful asceticism. Swedish-born baritone Gabriel Suovanen is well attuned both to the late-Romantic manner of Madetoja's early songs and to the ardent national-patriotic tone of his later ones. And his pianist, Gustav Djupsjöbacka, supplies stylish accompaniments. Recording quality is fine, and collectors of Nordic and/or song repertoire should not hesitate.

Albéric Magnard   French 1865-1914

Albéric Magnard was born in Paris to François Magnard, a bestselling author and editor of Le Figaro. Albéric disliked being called 'fils du Figaro' and decided to pursue a career in music based entirely on his talent and without any help from family connections. He entered the Paris Conservatoire, where he studied counterpoint and went to the classes of Jules Massenet. There he met Vincent d'Indy, with whom he studied fugue and orchestration for four years, writing his first two symphonies under d'Indy's tutelage. Many of his 22 works were published by himself. Magnard became a national hero in 1914 when he refused to surrender his property to German invaders and died defending it. His musical language has echoes of both Bruckner and Mahler, though Wagner is probably the most obvious influence.

Symphonies

Symphonies Nos 1-4
**BBC Scottish Symphony Orchestra /
Jean-Yves Ossonce**
Hyperion Helios ② CDD20068 (140' · DDD) Ⓑⓞ▷

The First Symphony (1890) shows the unmistakable influence of Wagner in the *religioso* slow movement. Despite the adoption of the cyclic principle championed by his teacher Vincent d'Indy, under whose watchful eye the work was written and who must have smiled approvingly at his pupil's fluent contrapuntal technique, Magnard's proliferation of ideas threatens structural continuity, especially in the first movement. In contrast to that movement's initial brooding atmosphere, the Second Symphony begins more sunnily and spiritedly, and the following *Scherzo* (which replaced an earlier fugue) is a bucolic 'Danses' tinged with introspection. The emotional core of the symphony is the luxuriant *Chant varié*, and the work ends in an almost light-hearted mood. The Third Symphony's striking organum-like opening leads to an *Allegro* by turns vigorous and contemplative. Next comes a *Scherzo* headed 'Danses' (as in the previous symphony), a mocking soufflé with a wistful central section – an altogether captivating movement that's anything but austere. The movingly tense slow movement's long lines are subverted by menacing outbursts that build to a stormy climax before subsiding; and there's a finale which combines exuberance and lyricism with a return to the symphony's very first theme. This is certainly the work to recommend to newcomers to Magnard.

Several years elapsed before the appearance of his last symphony in 1913, and by then his overall mood had darkened. The turbulent passion that characterises the first movement, presented in dramatically colourful orchestration, is also mirrored in the finale: between them come a highly individual *Scherzo* with strange oriental-type passages and a lengthy, anguished slow movement. The BBC Scottish Symphony Orchestra is on splendid form throughout; their efforts have been recorded in exemplary fashion.

Gustav Mahler
Austrian 1860-1911

'Thin, fidgety, short, with a high, steep forehead, long dark hair and deeply penetrating bespectacled eyes' – that was how the conductor Bruno Walter, Mahler's one-time assistant, described him. He was also sadistic, a manic-depressive, an egomaniac, one of music's great despots, a neurotic with a mother fixation (according to Freud who analysed him) and undoubtedly a genius. As with his music, people either loved him or hated him. 'The dedicated Mahlerians,' wrote Harold Schonberg, 'regard [those who dislike his music] the way St Paul regarded the Heathen. It is hard to think of a composer who arouses equal loyalty. The worship of Mahler amounts almost to a religion...Mahler's [music] stirs something imbedded in the subconscious and his admirers approach him mystically.'

His tragic childhood stalked him for the whole of his life. His grandmother had been a ribbon seller, going from house to house selling her wares; his father had transcended these humble origins and was the owner of a small brandy distillery, married to the daughter of a wealthy soap manufacturer. It was an ill-tempered, badly-matched marriage, one where the young Mahler frequently witnessed the brutality and abuse meted out on a long-suffering mother by an ambitious father. Of their 12 children, five died in infancy of diphtheria; Mahler's beloved younger brother Ernst died from hydrocardia aged 12; his oldest sister died of a brain tumour after a brief, unhappy marriage; another sister was subject to fantasies that she was dying; another brother was a simpleton in his youth and a forger in his adult life while yet another, Otto, a humble musician, committed suicide rather than accept the mediocrity that fate had assigned him.

When he was six, Mahler discovered a piano in the attic of his grandmother's house. Four years later he gave his first solo piano recital and aged 15 he enrolled at the Vienna Conservatoire. Here he not only developed as a pianist but won prizes for his compositions and discovered a talent for conducting. His professors noticed already the diligence and single-minded application that marked his professional career. Within a short space of time, conducting and composition took over his entire life with a totality that left little time for anything else. Realising he could not make a living as a composer writing the sort of music he dreamt of, he took up conducting, first in Bad Hall, Austria, then a permanent position in Laibach (now Ljubljana). In 1882 he moved on to Olmütz and the next year to Vienna and Kassel – the traditional path of the aspiring conductor, moving from opera house to opera house, slowly building a reputation. In 1885 he was in Prague, then got a break in Leipzig working in harness with another brilliant young conductor, Arthur Nikisch. In one season Mahler conducted over 200 performances, apart from editing a Weber opera, falling in love with the wife of Weber's grandson and finishing his First Symphony. One thing that Mahler had in abundance all his life was energy, something he inherited from his mother. From his father came his drive and tenacity. His next step was to take over the Royal Opera House in Budapest from 1886 to 1888. Here he built up a fine company that won the praise of Brahms. When he moved on to Hamburg, Tchaikovsky himself allowed Mahler to conduct Eugene Onegin in his stead. 'The conductor here is not of the usual kind, but a man of genius who would give his life to conduct the first performance,' wrote Tchaikovsky.

Then, in 1897, Mahler quietly converted to Catholicism. Shortly afterwards he got the position he yearned for. With the enthusiastic backing of Brahms, he became artistic director of the Vienna Opera and soon after of the Vienna Philharmonic. He remained at the opera for 10 years and in that decade raised its fortunes to a height which some say has never been equalled since. Here he reigned as king, choosing the repertory, singers, staging many of the productions himself and overseeing every aspect of life in the opera house; he engaged the great stage designer Alfred Roller and experimented with lighting and stage effects: this was Mahler's Wagnerian idealism put into practice – combining all the arts of the music theatre in a single man's vision. Above all he moulded the orchestra into one of the finest in the world. The players respected him as a musician but hated him as a man, for Mahler's quest for perfection and intolerance of anything smacking of second-best was implemented by an uncompromising martinet. He was the sort who'd pick on individual players and reduce them to tears – he even disciplined the audience, forbidding latecomers to enter during the first act. But every work that he laid his hands on came up 'Herrlich wie am ersten Tag', as they say in Vienna – 'Glorious as on the first day' – and he did it all at a profit.

Inevitably, he made enemies. Not just because of his despotic methods and lack of social niceties – he had no small talk and was nervous among people – but because he was a Jew and a genius. He was merciless with his tongue, with his contempt for those who opposed him and with his anger at those who failed to match his standards.

In 1901 he married the step-daughter of the avant-garde Viennese artist Carl Moll, Alma Schindler. She was beautiful, well-read and a composer in her own right, having studied under Zemlinsky, Schoenberg's teacher. It was a remarkable marriage but one in which Mahler demanded complete freedom. His wife was to be mother, wife and amanuensis; she was to give up her composing and be totally subservient to his whims. The first five years of his marriage saw Mahler at the height of his powers and at his happiest. He continued to compose as he had during the previous decade in the one form to which he aspired and (to his austere way of thinking) in the purest, highest form of musical expression – the orchestral symphony. By 1906 he had completed the Fifth, Sixth and Seventh symphonies. Each one was vaster in scale than its predecessor; each one was met with hostility, misunderstandings and vituperation. Mahler was impervious to all around him, convinced that 'my time will come.'

Then personal tragedy hit him. One of his little daughters died from scarlet fever. Mahler went insane with grief and forever after carried around with him the guilt that he had been responsible in part for his child's death, guilt for tempting fate: in 1903 he had composed a set of songs using poems by Rückert entitled Kindertotenlieder – 'Songs on the Death of Children'.

In 1907 he decided to leave Vienna and, the same year, was told he had a serious heart condition. The remaining three years of his life were focused on America. He first went to the Metropolitan Opera for two full seasons. Indifferent performances and the presence of Arturo Toscanini led to friction and more unhappiness. Worse came when he took over the conductorship of the New York Philharmonic in 1909. The audience disliked him, the orchestra loathed him, the critics reached for their poisoned pens. The feeling was entirely mutual. The Philharmonic, in Mahler's words, was 'the true American orchestra – without talent and phlegmatic'. The orchestra board was dominated by 10 wealthy American women. 'You cannot imagine what Mr Mahler has suffered,' Alma Mahler told the press. 'In Vienna my husband was all-powerful. Even the Emperor did not dictate to him, but in New York he had 10 ladies ordering him around like puppet.' In September 1910 he was in Munich to conduct the premiere of his mammoth Eighth Symphony which met with overwhelming success, one of the few triumphs he ever witnessed as a composer. He returned to New York in late 1910 but early the next year collapsed under the strain of 65 rigorous concerts. An infection set in which serum treatments in Paris did nothing to alleviate. In a nursing home in Vienna, he died of pneumonia aged 50.

Symphonies

No 1 in D; No 2 in C minor, 'Resurrection'; No 3 in D minor; No 4 in G; No 5 in C sharp minor; No 6 in A minor; No 7 in E minor; No 8 in E flat, 'Symphony of a Thousand'; No 9 in D; No 10 in F sharp minor

Complete Symphonies

Symphonies – No 1[a]; No 2[b] (with **Cheryl Studer** sop **Waltraud Meier** mez **Arnold Schoenberg Choir**); No 3[b] (**Jessye Norman** sop **Vienna Boys' Choir; Vienna State Opera Chorus**); No 4[b] (**Frederica von Stade** mez); No 5[a]; Nos 6[c] & 7[c]; No 8[a] (**Studer, Sylvia McNair, Andrea Rost** sops **Anne Sofie von Otter** mez **Rosemarie Lang** contr **Peter Seiffert** ten **Bryn Terfel** bass-bar **Jan-Hendrik Rootering** bass **Tölz Boys' Choir; Berlin Radio Chorus; Prague Philharmonic Chorus**); Nos 9[b] & 10[b] – Adagio [a]**Berlin Philharmonic Orchestra**; [b]**Vienna Philharmonic Orchestra**; [c]**Chicago Symphony Orchestra / Claudio Abbado**
DG ⑫ 447 023-2GX12 (11h 58' · ADD/DDD · T/t)
Recorded 1977-94   ⓂⓄⓄ▷

The current pre-eminence of Gustav Mahler in the concert hall and on disc isn't something that could have been anticipated – other than by the composer himself. Hard now to believe that his revival had to wait until the centenary celebrations of his birth in 1960. And yet by 1980 he was more widely esteemed than his longer-lived contemporaries Sibelius and Strauss and could suddenly be seen to tower over 20th-century music much as Beethoven must have done in a previous age. By this time too, a new generation of conductors had come to the fore, further transforming our perceptions of the composer. Claudio Abbado is arguably the most distinguished of this group and, while his interpretations will not satisfy every listener on every occasion, they make an excellent choice for the library shelves, when the price is reasonably competitive and the performances so emblematic (and arguably central to our understanding) of Mahler's place in contemporary musical life.

Of the alternatives, Haitink's package has the fewest expressive distortions while Bernstein's is the most ceaselessly emotive of them all; neither has Abbado's particular combination of qualities. It's probably no accident that Donald Mitchell's notes for this set are focused on the nature of Mahler's 'modernity'. For it's that ironic, inquisitive, preternaturally aware young composer who haunts this conductor's performances. Not for Abbado the heavy, saturated textures of 19th-century Romanticism, nor the chilly rigidity of some of his own 'modernist' peers. Instead an unaffected warmth and elegance of sound allows everything to come through naturally – in so far as the different venues and DG's somewhat variable technology will permit – even in the most searingly intense of climaxes.

Abbado presents Mahler as a fluent classicist, and is less concerned to characterise the surface battle of conflicting emotions than to elucidate the underlying symphonic structure. The lack of Solti's brand of forthright theatricality can bring a feeling of disappointment. But even where he underplays the drama of the moment, sufficient sense of urgency is sustained by a combination of well-judged tempi, marvellously graduated dynamics and precisely balanced, ceaselessly changing textures. The propulsion comes from within.

It was in November 1907 that Mahler famously told Sibelius that 'the symphony must be like the world. It must embrace everything'. And perhaps it's only today that we see this as a strength rather than a weakness in his music. He wrote music that's 'about' its own past while at the same time probing into all our futures, music that's so all-embracing and communicates with such directness that we can make it 'mean' whatever we want it to, confident that we alone have really understood the code. Abbado lacks Bernstein's desire to explore these limitless possibilities, but some will count that as a blessing. These are committed and authoritative performances.

Symphonies – Nos 1 & 2 (**Elly Ameling** sop
Aafje Heynis contr **Netherlands Radio Chorus**);
No 3 (**Maureen Forrester** contr **St Willibrord Church Boys' Choir; Netherlands Radio Chorus**); No 4 (**Ameling**); Nos 5-8 (**Ileana Cotrubas, Heather Harper, Hanneke van Bork** sops **Birgit Finnila** mez **Marianne Dieleman** contr **William Cochran** ten **Hermann Prey** bar **Hans Sotin** bass **St Willibrord and Pius X Children's Choir; Collegium Musicum Amstelodamense; Amsterdam Toonkunst Choir; Amsterdam Stem des Volks Choir**); No 10 – Adagio
Concertgebouw Orchestra / Bernard Haitink
Philips Bernard Haitink Symphony Edition ⑩
442 050-2PB10 (11h 32' · ADD). Recorded 1962-71 Ⓜ**O**

If space is at a premium, this set is undeniably attractive, though the multilingual illustrated booklet dispenses with texts and translations, and several symphonies are awkwardly spread between discs. For a generation of record buyers it was these sane, lucid, sometimes insufficiently demonstrative Concertgebouw readings that represented a way into music previously considered unacceptable in polite society. Haitink's phrasing has an appealing natural simplicity, his rhythmic almost-squareness providing welcome reassurance. The preoccupation with conventional symphonic verities of form and structure doesn't preclude striking beauty of sound and the recordings have come up well in the remastering. There's some residual hiss.

Haitink's early No 1 (1962), his first taping of a Mahler symphony, is usually reckoned the least satisfactory of his career. True, the third movement doesn't quite work: Haitink's attempts at 'Jewishness' are so self-conscious that the results sound rhythmically suspect, not quite together rather than convincingly ethnic. The real problem is the boxed-in sound, uncharacteristically rough and ready, with none of the cool tonal lustre which characterised subsequent LPs from this source.

The Fourth receives a similarly straightforward account with a wonderfully hushed *Poco adagio* and few if any of the aggressive mannerisms which have marred more recent versions. The restraint can border on inflexibility at times. The first movement lacks a certain ele-

---

MAHLER'S SYMPHONIES – IN BRIEF

Various orchs / Claudio Abbado
DG ⑫ 447 023-2GX12 (11h 58' · DDD)   Ⓜ**OOᎏ**
The Italian conductor's dramatic, carefully moulded way with Mahler is best experienced live, but there's no lack of polish or refinement from his de luxe performers.

New York Philharmonic / various
NYP9801/12 ⑫ (15h 3' · ADD)   Ⓕ**OO**
A valuable box for connoisseurs, documenting the orchestra's long Mahler tradition (dating back to when the composer was its music director). Boulez in No 3, Mitropoulos in No 6 and Kubelík in No 7 are highlights.

Concertgebouw Orchestra / Bernard Haitink
Philips ⑩ 442 050-2PB10 (11h 32' · DDD)   Ⓜ**Oᎏ**
Haitink's grasp of the music's many contrasts has sharpened since he made these recordings but their unaffected clarity stands the test of time.

Frankfurt RSO / Eliahu Inbal
Brilliant ⑮ 92005 (14h 40' DDD)   Ⓢ
Denon's fine engineering, the Alte Oper's welcoming acoustic and Inbal's headstrong interpretations are an even more tempting proposition at super-budget price.

NYPO, Israel PO / Leonard Bernstein
Sony ⑫ 88697 45369-2 (11h 53 ' · ADD)   Ⓑ**OO**
The heartfelt passion of possibly the composer's most famous interpreter is well known; his unerring composer's ear for the traffic of Mahler's vast forces and structures is often overlooked. Adds *Das Lied* and a fascinating documentary, 'Gustav Mahler Remembered: Reminiscences by Mahler's Associates and by Musicians Who Played Under His Baton'.

SWR Orchestra Baden-Baden / Michael Gielen
Hänssler ⑬ CD93 130 (12h 31' ADD)   Ⓑ**O**
Age has mellowed and deepened the Mahler interpretations of this one-time colleague of the avant-gardistes. Fine sound shows off Gielen's forensic ear for detail; Mahler's stature as pivotal figure between centuries is clearer than ever.

Bavarian Radio SO / Rafael Kubelík
DG ⑩ 463 738-2 (10 hr 51' · ADD)   Ⓑ**Oᎏ**
The Czech conductor brings an unfussy clarity to Mahler's dance rhythms that can be even more moving than the breast-beating approach. Ideal for those new to Mahler.

West German Radio Symphony Orchestra, Cologne / Gary Bertini
EMI ⑪ 340238-2 (12h 54' · DDD)   Ⓑ**OOOᎏ**
Bertini scores on nearly every count. His lovingly moulded, wonderfully idiomatic performances are enormously satisfying. This is real class at a very affordable price.

ment of fantasy with everything so very accurate and together, and, while Elly Ameling makes a lovely sound in the finale, the orchestra's animal caricatures aren't really vulgar enough, the sense of wonder and awe in the face of heaven rather muted at the close. Though inevitably lacking the gut-wrenching theatricality and hallucinatory colour of Bernstein, the Seventh has none of the staidness and rigidity that occasionally prompts doubts about Haitink's Mahlerian credentials. It emerges here as a high-point of the series, second only to the celebrated Ninth. The opening is deceptively cool and brooding; thereafter the interpretation is unexpectedly driven and intense, even if Mahler's fantastical sonorities are left to fend for themselves. Only those who feel the nth degree of nightmarish 'exaggeration' to be vital to the expression of the whole need have any doubts. The finale is effectively held together but should perhaps sound more hollow than this.

If you must have the Mahler symphonies under a single conductor, Haitink could arguably be the man to go for. His objectivity won't spoil you for alternative readings. Nevertheless you wouldn't want to miss out on Bernstein, unrelenting in his desire to communicate the essentials of these scores, taking his cue from Mahler's remark that 'the symphony must be like the world. It must be all-embracing'. Haitink is more circumspect, the music's vaunting ambition knowingly undersold.

Symphonies Nos 1-9; No 10 – Adagio.
Das Lied von der Erde
Marianne Haggander, Krisztina Laki, Lucia Popp, Julia Varady, Maria Venuti sops **Marjana Lipovšek, Florence Quivar** mezs **Anne Howells, Gwendolyn Killebrew** contrs **Ben Heppner, Paul Frey** tens **Alan Titus** bar **Siegfried Vogel** bass **West German Radio Symphony Orchestra, Cologne / Gary Bertini**
EMI ⑪ 340238-2 (12h 54′ · DDD)   Ⓢ❍❍❍�»

Gary Bertini's 1984-91 Cologne Radio Mahler cycle is the most consistently satisfying on disc, in terms of its lovingly idiomatic and world-class performances, plus robust, realistic engineering that truly replicates the dynamic impact and spatial depth that these scores convey in the best concert halls.

A colleague aptly and accurately likened Bertini's emphasis on the proverbial big picture to Rafael Kubelík's DG Mahler cycle, although Bertini's Cologne musicians operate on an altogether higher level of first-desk refinement and chamber-like sensitivity to the composer's extraordinary palette of orchestral colour. The strands of the Tenth's *Adagio*'s pulverising climactic chords are powerfully yet clearly delineated to the point where you can take dictation from what you hear.

The brass sail through the Fifth's difficult writing with equal aplomb to stare their he-man Solti/Chicago colleagues in the eye, while the soft woodwinds and exposed strings create a haunting atmosphere in the Eighth's second movement to gently joust with Tennstedt or

Nagano for top position. At the same time, Bertini's fervency sometimes gives Leonard Bernstein's magnetism a run for its money, as one readily hears in the First's klezmer tinges, the Seventh's rollicking coda and the most rabble-rousing moments of the Ninth's inner movements. By contrast, Bertini turns in one of the few very slow readings of the finale that rivets your attention in every bar.

Bertini also benefits from terrific singing, highlighted by a tightly knit ensemble in the Eighth (baritone Alan Titus especially stands out as Pater Ecstaticus), plus Ben Heppner and Marjana Lipovšek on ringing, communicative form throughout *Das Lied* (both this and the Eighth stem from live Tokyo performances). And in the Fourth's finale, the late Lucia Popp surpasses her EMI recording under Tennstedt. To be certain, earlier reviews pinpoint weak spots, such as the Sixth's relatively clunky first movement or the Second's finale's fleeting inaccuracies, but these are nitpicks in face of so much excellence elsewhere.

For cost, convenience and quality, there's no better Mahler deal on the planet.

Symphonies Nos 1-9; No 10 – Adagio.
Das Lied von der Erde
Israel Philharmonic Orchestra; London Symphony Orchestra; Vienna Philharmonic Orchestra / Leonard Bernstein
Video directors **Humphrey Burton & Tony Palmer**
DG ⑨ 𝗗𝗩𝗗 073 4088GH9 (13h 24′ · NTSC · 4:3 · PCM stereo and DTS 5.1 · 0). Includes a bonus disc of rehearsals. Recorded 1971-76   Ⓕ❍❍

Between 1971 and 1976 Humphrey Burton directed filmed concerts of Bernstein conducting the nine Mahler symphonies, along with *Das Lied von der Erde* and the *Adagio* from the unfinished Tenth. Previous VHS and laserdisc incarnations suffered from uneven sound and occasional discrepancies of synchronisation between screen image and audio. Happily, DG's new DVD edition not only corrects these problems but also refurbishes the soundtracks in vibrant 5.1 surround sound.

Little can be added to the many words written about Bernstein's intense affinity for and ardent advocacy of Mahler. Indeed, the musicality and specificity of Bernstein's body language often seems to create parallel universes to each score's emotional peaks and dynamic valleys. One doesn't have to turn up the volume to sense the exultation and drive with which Bernstein inspires the huge forces in the Eighth's first part or the Second's final pages, gauging the protracted climaxes as he clenches his baton with both hands in long, agonising downward strokes. Watch, too, how Bernstein's eagle eyes and decisive hands anticipate tricky entries and tempo changes in the Fifth's second movement and the Seventh's first with unshakeable authority, or how he instantaneously adjusts dynamics and aligns rhythmic vagaries (the Fourth's opening bars, the Third's percussion).

Yet for all of Bernstein's podium choreography,

he also knows when to stand back and simply let the musicians play, casually passing the baton back and forth between his hands, as in stretches of the Third's and Ninth's final movements and the Tenth's *Adagio*. And, like a benign sovereign, he frequently shoots his players and singers encouraging glances, with plenty of smiles to reward the Vienna Philharmonic's first-desk soloists, as well as their counterparts in the LSO (No 2) and the Israel Philharmonic (*Das Lied*). Burton's visual style works hand-in-glove with Mahler's orchestration and dynamic game plans, saving close-ups for quiet passages and quick inserts that underline instrumental entrances.

In general, Bernstein's filmed Mahler interpretations represent a centre-point between the raw excitement characterising much of his pioneering 1960s CBS/Sony cycle and his riper, often more expansive late-1980s remakes. On balance, the video Fourth, Fifth and Ninth are Bernstein's finest performances of these works. The Fifth is faster and more incisively shaped than his 1987 traversal and the Vienna players get better as the performance progresses. Edith Mathis looks as radiant as she sings in the Fourth's finale. The Vienna Ninth is notable for the other-worldly stillness and delicacy of the final pages while the central movements bring the sort of abandon he shows in his 1960s Ninth.

A bonus disc provides additional and valuable context. 'Four Ways to Say Farewell' combines rehearsal and performance footage of the Ninth as a backdrop to Bernstein's narration, where he fancifully if plausibly likens the first movement's long-short rhythmic motive to Mahler's irregular heartbeat. Rehearsals of the Fifth reveal an even more balletic, gesticulative conductor than the public usually saw, along with important insights into the music's character (at one point Bernstein cajoles the brass to play 'like in Italian opera', pinpointing the influence of Verdi on Mahler that most critics gloss over).

A *Das Lied* rehearsal shows Christa Ludwig haggling over the breakneck tempo Bernstein sets in the 'Von der Schönheit' central section. Then there is Bernstein at the piano, chain-smoking, giving an informal discourse on the work's symbolism and chamber-like orchestration ('You have to prepare an entire orchestra as if it was a string quartet').

In an age when Mahler's symphonies are ubiquitous, it's fascinating to witness the missionary zeal of Bernstein more than three decades ago, claiming how his 'acting out' the music rather than merely beating time helps him to convince his orchestras of the its greatness. With Bernstein at the helm, one doesn't take Mahler's greatness for granted.

Symphonies – No 1; No 2, 'Resurrection'ᵃ
ᵃ**Sylvia McNair** sop ᵃ**Jard van Nes** contr
ᵃ**Ernst Senff Chorus; Berlin Philharmonic Orchestra / Bernard Haitink**
Video director **Barrie Gavin**
Philips Ⓕ 🎞 074 3131PH
(152' · NTSC · 4:3 · PCM stereo and DTS 5.1 · 0)   Ⓕ

Symphony No 3
Florence Quivar contr **Tölzer Knabenchor; Ernst Senff Women's Chorus; Berlin Philharmonic Orchestra / Bernard Haitink**
Video director **Barrie Gavin**
Philips Ⓕ 🎞 074 3132PH
(106' · NTSC · 4:3 · PCM stereo and DTS 5.1 · 0)   Ⓕ

Symphonies – No 4; No 7
Sylvia McNair sop **Berlin Philharmonic Orchestra / Bernard Haitink**
Video director **Barrie Gavin**
Philips Ⓕ 🎞 074 3133PH
(140' · NTSC · 4:3 · PCM stereo and DTS 5.1 · 0)
All from Philips VHS originals   Ⓕ

Perhaps it's unfair to scrutinise Philips's visual record of Haitink's early-1990s Mahler performances with the BPO so soon after Universal brought out their Bernstein Mahler DVD set (see above). You could scarcely imagine two more disparate Mahler conductors. While Bernstein's charismatic body language often seems to mirror the music, Haitink avoids all flamboyance. The casual viewer might even infer a sense of detachment in his frequently half-shut eyes and all-too-rare smiles. Indeed, there seem to be more close-ups of separate orchestral sections and their first-desk representatives than of the conductor. Still, it looks and sounds as if the Berlin musicians are drawn into the Dutch conductor's fluid stick technique, clear beat, economy of gesture and seasoned awareness of when not to interfere.

Furthermore, the inconsistent sound quality of Bernstein's early-1970s films yields to the present edition's robust, full-bodied digital sonics. Indeed, the Second Symphony finale's offstage brass and the transparent scoring of No 7's two 'night music' movements emerge more atmospherically when experienced via surround sound's multichannel ambience.

Although Haitink's studio Concertgebouw Mahler cycle pretty much outclasses the aborted Berlin studio cycle he began in the late 1980s, the presence of an audience (and camera crew) sometimes elicits more animated, urgent and emotionally three-dimensional music-making on the part of both conductor and orchestra. The Third Symphony is a striking case in point. In contrast to the square and flaccid 1990 Berlin studio version, this live account from a year later features greater tension in the outer movements and a wider degree of colour and inflection within the second and third movements. Florence Quivar's more opulent contralto timbre also contrasts to Jard van Nes's lighter-toned agility.

By contrast, the First and Fourth differ little from their generally excellent studio twins. Both Firsts feature an opening movement whose blended sonorities unfold in a leisurely and organic way, plus an overly languid third movement where the dotted rhythms are stilted and unswinging. However, in the finale, the brass and percussion truly give their all live. The Fourth's bucolic nature absorbs Haitink's relaxed, poetic leadership and astute attention to the composer's specific gradations of soft dynamics. In the finale, Sylvia McNair vividly describes the kingdom of heaven without once dropping her rounded tone's effortless composure.

The Seventh hits and misses; there's little sense of surprise in the first movement's tempo transitions, while the *Scherzo*'s angular, mysterious qualities and chamber-like delicacy only turn up in flashes. Once the adrenalin kicks in for the finale, it stays there, and you're actually happy when Haitink doesn't ease up for the *grazioso* episodes. Similarly, in the *Resurrection*, Haitink saves his most energetic and inspired capabilities for the sprawling finale, where the chorus, organ and myriad percussion make uplifting, joyful noise. If you happened to have cranked up the volume during the soft passages, the subsequent climaxes will pin you to the wall in time for the neighbours to complain. Nothing sexy about the bonus features: a Mahler timeline, a slideshow of photos of the composer, and promos for other Universal Classics DVD releases.

Symphony No 1

Symphony No 1. Lieder eines fahrenden Gesellen
Dietrich Fischer-Dieskau *bar* **Bavarian Radio Symphony Orchestra / Rafael Kubelík**
DG The Originals 449 735-2GOR (67' · ADD · T/t)
Recorded 1967　　　　　　　　　　Ⓜ**O**Ⓑ⁺

Rafael Kubelík is essentially a poetic conductor and he gets more poetry out of this symphony than almost any other conductor who has recorded it. Although he takes the repeat of the first movement's short exposition, it's strange that he should ignore the single repeat sign in the *Ländler* when he seems so at ease with the music. Notwithstanding a fondness for generally brisk tempi in Mahler, Kubelík is never afraid of *rubato* here, above all in his very personally inflected account of the slow movement. This remains a delight. The finale now seems sonically a little thin, with the trumpets made to sound rather hard-pressed and the final climax failing to open out as it can in more modern recordings. The orchestral contribution is very good even if absolute precision isn't guaranteed.

Dietrich Fischer-Dieskau's second recording of the *Lieder eines fahrenden Gesellen* has worn rather less well, the spontaneous ardour of his earlier performance (with Furtwängler and the Philharmonia) here tending to stiffen into melodrama and mannerism. There's much beautiful singing, and he's most attentively accompanied, but the third song, 'Ich hab' ein glühend Messer', is implausibly overwrought, bordering on self-parody. By contrast, Kubelík's unpretentious, Bohemian approach to the symphony remains perfectly valid. A corrective to the grander visions of those who conduct the music with the benefit of hindsight and the advantages of digital technology? Perhaps.

Symphony No 1 (Hamburg 1893 version). Blumine
Netherlands Symphony Orchestra / Jan Willem de Vriend
Challenge Classics Ⓢ CC72355 (56' · DDD) Ⓕ

Don't miss this one. Where mainstream releases of the First Symphony from the likes of Sir Simon Rattle (EMI) have included the discarded *Blumine* movement as a species of makeweight, Jan Willem de Vriend has gone back to the earlier incarnations of the complete score into which *Blumine* slots more naturally as the second segment of what was then a five-movement 'Symphonic Poem in Two Parts'. The smaller sonority isn't primarily the consequence of employing the capable Netherlands SO. Rather it reflects the scoring Mahler required at this earlier stage in what was to prove, even for him, a long compositional process. Whatever the arguments for and against the rehabilitation of Mahler's moonlit serenade, restored to currency only in the 1960s, this is the first recording of the complete 1893 version to acquire international distribution since that of the late Wyn Morris 40 years ago. As such it may be seen as required listening for Mahlerians.

Known principally as an early music specialist, the Dutch conductor's emphasis on clarity of articulation, helped by excellent sound, allows the unusual aspects of the instrumentation to register more clearly than in that older, more romantic reading. In several passages the oddities will bring you up short. Of course, where other composers might have tinkered with their scores to make them less risky in performance, Mahler, the flamboyant composer-conductor, was doing the precise opposite, acquiring more chutzpah over time. In this intermediate incarnation, the work's opening fanfares are given, more traditionally, to muted horns, extra timpani strokes underpin the start of the *Scherzo* and the beginning of the funeral march has a solo cello doubling that famously exposed solo double bass. The very end of the piece would not survive unscathed either.

All fascinating stuff and unlikely to be trumped by a comparable issue. Don't expect the grand manner and you won't be disappointed. The music-making is winningly fresh and vigorous.

Symphony No 2, 'Resurrection'

Symphony No 2
Arleen Auger *sop* **Dame Janet Baker** *mez*
City of Birmingham Symphony Chorus and Orchestra / Sir Simon Rattle
EMI Great Recordings of the Century
② 345794-2 (86' · DDD)　　　　Ⓜ**OOO**Ⓑ⁺

Ⓖ　Where Simon Rattle's interpretation is concerned, we must go into the realm of a giant Mahlerian like Klemperer. For we're dealing here with conducting akin to genius, with insights and instincts that can't be measured with any old yardstick. Rattle's sense of drama, of apocalyptic events, is so strong that at the final chords one is awed. None of this could have been achieved without the CBSO, which here emerges as an orchestra of world class. Such supple and rich string playing, such expressive woodwind and infallibly accurate and mellow-toned brass could be mistaken as belonging to Vienna, Berlin or Chicago. Attention to dynamics is meticulous, and contributes immeasurably to the splendour of the performance. A double *pianissimo* is really that, so when triple *forte* comes along its impact is tremendous. Some outstanding features can be pinpointed: the haunting beauty of the *portamento* horn playing and the strings' sensitive and perfectly graded *glissandos* at fig 23; the magical entry of flute and harps just after fig 3 in the second movement; and the frightening eruption of the two *fortissimo* drum notes just after fig 51 in the same movement. Dame Janet Baker is at her most tender in 'Urlicht', with Arleen Auger as the soul of purity in the finale. The CBSO Chorus is magnificent. Indeed the whole finale is an acoustic triumph. This in a spiritual class of its own and the recording is superb.

Symphony No 2
Elisabeth Schwarzkopf *sop* **Hilde Rössl-Majdan** *mez* **Philharmonia Chorus and Orchestra /**
Otto Klemperer
EMI Great Recordings of the Century 567235-2
(72' · ADD · T/t)   ⓂⓄⓄ🅓➔

You emerge from Klemperer's first movement unharrassed, unsettled in the knowledge that this extraordinary music has something much more to yield. You miss those elements of high risk, the brave rhetorical gestures, the uncompromising extremes, in Klemperer's comparatively comfortable down-the-line response. He knocks minutes off most of the competition (yes, it's a fallacy that Klemperer was always slower), paying little or no heed to Mahler's innumerable expressive markings in passages which have so much to gain from them. Take, for example, the magical shift to remote E major with the *ppp* emergence of the second subject where Klemperer allows himself no latitude whatsoever in the *rubato* despite Mahler's explicit requests to the contrary. Likewise the grisly procession of cellos and basses which begins the approach to the awesome climax of the development. How little Klemperer makes of their cadaverous first entry or Mahler's long backward glance just prior to the coda. But then, come the deceptive second movement minuet, something happens, the performance really begins to find its space. Klemperer's *Scherzo* is ideally big-boned with fine rollicking horns and a lazy Trio with lovely old-world close-harmony trumpets. And the finale, growing more and more momentous with every bar, possesses a unique aura. Not everyone is convinced by Klemperer's very measured treatment of the Judgement Day march. The grim reaper takes his time but the inevitability of what's to come is somehow the more shocking

as a result. Klemperer's trumpets peak thrillingly in the bars immediately prior to the climax itself – and what a seismic upheaval he and his orchestra pull off at this point. The rest is sublime: marvellous spacial effects, offstage brass and so on, an inspirational sense of the music burgeoning from the moment the chorus breathe life into the Resurrection Ode. It's a pity that in those days so many technical blemishes were allowed to make it to the final master, though EMI's digital remastering of this almost legendary reading is superb.

Symphony No 2
Lisa Milne *sop* **Birgit Remmert** *contr*
Hungarian Radio Choir; Budapest Festival
Orchestra / Iván Fischer
Channel Classics ② CCSSA23506
(82' · DDD · T/t)   🅕Ⓞ🅓➔

Stylistically, Fischer is right on the money. He has a keen nose for Mahler's particular brand of the ebb and flow of the music, the way it speaks, or rather sings; the bucolic and melodramatic elements of the score are vividly conflicted; and best of all Fischer really breathes in the atmosphere of Mahler's precipitous flight to eternity. The second theme of the first movement, which Mahler requests enter tentatively, shyly, does exactly that – Fischer's violins are barely audible, a rosy horizon briefly glimpsed through this bleak and forbidding landscape.

Few take this first movement to the edge of possibility that Mahler so clearly envisaged. Fischer does not shirk the often reckless extremes of tempo and dynamics but nor does he throw caution to the four winds in the terrifying stampede to its cliff-hanging climax. Leonard Bernstein is probably still alone in doing just that. But there are many other compensations here: a great sense of logic and line, a second movement whose homespun accenting belongs to a bygone era, likewise the close-harmony trumpets in the trio of the third movement so touchingly redolent of another time, another place.

But the crowning glory is, as it should be, the finale – and it is here that Fischer, his performers and his engineers, really excel. The 'special effects' of Mahler's elaborate Judgement Day fresco have rarely been so magically realised. The offstage horns are so breathtakingly remote as to suggest the world of the living left far behind. Moments of quite extraordinary stasis precede the sounding of the Dies irae and the hushed entry of the chorus. And come the peroration (resplendent with fabulous horns), Fischer knows that it is with that final *crescendo* of the chorus and only then that the heavens really open. Impressive.

Symphony No 2
Miah Persson *sop* **Christianne Stotijn** *mez*
Chicago Symphony Chorus and Orchestra /
Bernard Haitink
CSO Resound ② CSOR901 916 (82' · DDD).
Recorded live in November 2008   🅕ⓄⓄⓄ🅓➔

Haitink's previous recorded *Resurrections* date from the late 1960s and the early 1990s. In this one, captured live, he has drawn back from the dourness and deliberation of his Berlin account to offer a scrupulously prepared mainstream reading that only hardened sceptics will dismiss as merely stolid.

Not that any one incident is allowed to destabilise the organic development of the whole. Those accustomed to Rattle or Bernstein may be underwhelmed by the choir's call to arms at 'Bereite dich' and, as you'd expect, Haitink eschews Solti's ear-grabbing attack at the very start of the work. While the Chicago orchestra retains a corporate sonority of boundless heft, for good or ill some of its edges have been smoothed away. Woodwind detailing is exquisite if invariably rather strait-laced in matters of nuancing. After civilised and articulate accounts of the *Andante moderato* and *Scherzo*, Haitink's 'Urlicht' is notable for the way Christianne Stotijn's rich mezzo is integrated within a silky orchestral texture. The finale is firm and objective, the distancing of offstage brass nicely calibrated and the first choral entry exquisitely hushed (Miah Persson seems initially ill-at-ease).

Those who like more *rubato* in their Mahler – and perhaps a more self-consciously transcendent kind of experience – will look elsewhere. Lacking the ease and subtlety of the finest studio recordings, CSO Resound's sound is immediate and suitably impactful once a higher-than-usual playback level is set. The conductor's many admirers need not hesitate although they may regret that applause has been excised. They will be rewarded with an attractive, well illustrated package containing detailed annotations, texts, translations and performer listings.

Symphony No 3

Symphony No 3. Four Rückert-Lieder.
Kindertotenlieder
Martha Lipton *mez* **Dietrich Fischer-Dieskau** *bar*
Women's Chorus of the Schola Cantorum; Boys'
Choir of the Transfiguration; New York
Philharmonic Orchestra / Leonard Bernstein
Sony Classical ② SM2K61831 (142' · ADD)
Recorded 1962   Ⓜ➨

Few who experienced Bernstein's passionate advocacy of Mahler's musical cause in the 1960s were left untouched by it. These recordings date from those years and the flame of inspiration still burns brightly about them almost 40 years later. The CBS recordings were clearly manipulated, but the sound – at best, big and open but trenchant and analytically clear – suited Mahler's sound world especially well. Bernstein's account of the Third Symphony is as compelling an experience and as desirable a general recommendation now as when it first appeared. The New Yorkers are on scintillating form under the conductor they have most obviously revered in the post-war period. This is a classic account, by any standards. Bernstein himself is a subtle and

self-effacing pianist. Fischer-Dieskau scales the musical heights in several of the *Rückert-Lieder*.

Symphony No 3[a]. Kindertotenlieder[b]
Kathleen Ferrier *contr*
[a]**BBC Symphony Orchestra / Sir Adrian Boult;**
[b]**Concertgebouw Orchestra, Amsterdam /**
Otto Klemperer
Testament mono ② SBT2 1422 (131' · ADD)
Includes interview with Kathleen Ferrier
Recorded [a]November 29, 1947, [b]July 12, 1951   ⒻⓄ

It is difficult, even now, not to be awestruck by the professionalism and unassuming good sense of Sir Adrian Boult. In the winter of 1947-48, the BBC Third Programme took the daring and controversial decision to broadcast the complete Mahler symphonies and Nos 1, 3, 5, 7 and 8 were prepared and conducted by Boult.

His performance of the Third Symphony, a UK premiere, is lucid and unaffected. It is also exceptionally well shaped orchestrally, no mean achievement with a work the players had never seen before. The playing isn't flawless. Post-war raids on London's pool of orchestral players by Beecham and Legge had robbed the BBC SO of some of its former lustre. Passengers are clearly being carried in the horn and trombone sections yet such is Boult's professionalism the wider picture is largely unaffected.

The BBC saved none of the performances. This off-air recording was preserved on a set of acetate discs which Jon Tolansky discovered in a shop in Manchester in 1981. Kathleen Ferrier's presence made the find doubly important. She gives an exceptionally beautiful performance of 'O Mensch!', lovingly accompanied by Boult. What's more, transfer engineer Paul Bailey has done a remarkable job tidying up a patch of badly disintegrating sound near the end of 'O Mensch!'.

Added to the Mahler Third are a noisily recorded live 1951 Amsterdam *Kindertotenlieder* dryly conducted by Klemperer, whom Ferrier disliked, and an interview she gave to CBC in 1950. Hearing Ferrier speak is interesting. Dark-voiced, careful of accent, and not afraid to correct her less than adequate interviewer, she sounds not unlike Margaret Thatcher after her voice had been lowered.

Symphony No 4

Symphony No 4
Juliane Banse *sop*
Staatskapelle Dresden / Giuseppe Sinopoli
Profil PH07047 (60' · DDD)   ⒻⓄ

'Glorious' and 'sublime' were among the epithets applied to the playing of Dresden's 'Royal Chapel' ensemble when Mahler's Fourth Symphony was first performed in the city in 1908. Both epithets could be applied to the playing on this latter-day realisation under Giuseppe Sinopoli. People obsess about the

Berlin and Vienna Philharmonics but under the right leadership the Dresden orchestra, which Sinopoli led from 1992 until his death at the age of 54 nine years later, can surpass either with its flawless ensemble and understated eloquence. There isn't an ugly note or gratuitously unpleasant sound in the *Scherzo* yet no jot of the music's wit, grace and sinister humour is lost. After which, the playing of the slow movement really is a glimpse of musical heaven on earth, the string playing glowing like old gold.

Sinopoli made a studio recording of the Fourth with the Philharmonia Orchestra in the early 1990s. The Dresden reading is essentially unchanged but its realisation is in a different league. The start may seem unduly brisk but a series of exquisitely shaped transitions take us into calmer waters and a succession of ever more enchanted landscapes where the performance reveals its essentially introspective side. Some might think it too introspective in those *espressivo* interludes where the pulse marginally hangs fire.

In the finale's calm opening and meditative close Sinopoli takes a very slow tempo indeed, way below the one Mahler himself adopts on his 1905 piano roll. Lorin Maazel takes a similar tempo in his celebrated 1984 recording with the Vienna Philharmonic. He, though, has Kathleen Battle, a brighter-voiced, less lustrous-sounding soloist than Sinopoli's excellent Juliane Banse. He also guards against somnolence by sharper pointing of the music's barcarolle-like rhythm. Not that straight comparisons are really in order here. Orchestrally, this is archive gold. It is also a happy reminder of a conductor whose prodigious intellect and idiosyncratic ways could never entirely mask the fact that he was a good man and a wonderful musician.

Additional recommendations

Symphony No 4
Battle *sop* **VPO / Maazel**
Sony Classical Digital Masters 07464 44908-2
(75' · DDD)   Ⓑ**OO**🅳➟

The pick of Maazel's 1980s cycle. Throughout it's a very inward-looking performance, and in saying that one merely points to the fact that it is a very, very Viennese performance; in Vienna, Mahler's Vienna or Maazel's, introspection is an unavoidable condition of being. Battle is simply perfect in the last movement.

Symphony No 4
Persson *sop* **Budapest Festival Orch / Fischer**
Channel Classics 🔊 CCSSA26109 (57' · DDD/DSD)
                                          🅵**O**🅳➟

What no one will deny is the amazing unanimity and precision of the playing here and the superlative quality of the sound engineering. But how to read a work that can feel brittle as well as heart-warming and graceful? A performance of countless imaginative touches on an exceptional hybrid SACD.

Symphony No 4 (arr Stein)
Kate Royal *sop* **Manchester Camerata /**
Douglas Boyd
Avie AV2069 (57' · DDD) Recorded live 2004   Ⓢ🅳➟

Erwin Stein's reduction, for solo string quintet (including double bass), flute doubling piccolo, oboe doubling cor anglais, clarinet doubling bass clarinet, piano, harmonium and percussion, was prepared at a time when even the members of Arnold Schoenberg's immediate circle had limited access to the real thing. Even today, some find the transcription focuses the mind wonderfully on the music's contrapuntal essence, others that it is intrinsically a period piece, more redolent of the palm court. Suffice to say that Douglas Boyd and his group offer a performance that is unfailingly fresh and alert.

Andrew Keener's production is the crispest, most immediate the score has received on disc. Out goes evocative distancing. In comes the tangible wheeze of the harmonium, the respiration of sundry woodwind players and the low-level vocalising of Boyd himself.

Douglas Boyd's Mahler may feel overly straightforward but he knows the territory, having directed Schoenberg's reduction of *Das Lied* as well as Mahler's own string quartet arrangements in Manchester. He has further aces up his sleeve: the helpful booklet-notes by Philip Borg Wheeler, the participation of Kate Royal, fresh-voiced soprano winner of the 2004 Kathleen Ferrier competition and, on CD, the highly competitive price.

Symphony No 5

Symphony No 5
Berlin Philharmonic Orchestra / Sir Simon Rattle
EMI 557385-2 (69' · DDD)
Recorded live 2002   🅕**OOO**🅳➟

Mahler's Fifth is a terror to bring off but, brought off, is a joy beyond measure. It made a fine nuptial offering for Rattle and the Berliners on September 7, 2002 – festive yet challenging, a tragi-comic revel and a high-wire act to boot. 'The individual parts are so difficult,' wrote Mahler, 'they call for the most accomplished soloists.' Rattle brought the prodigious first horn to the apron of the stage for his obbligato contribution in the *Scherzo*. Mengelberg's conducting score, which Mahler used for the work's Amsterdam premiere in 1906, has an annotation to this effect, and the practice was followed at the work's English premiere in 1945, but we're left wondering what would have happened if Rattle hadn't brought the player forward. EMI's recording is splendidly explicit, but the horn section, which plays a crucial role at key moments, seems oddly distant on CD.

The *tutti* sound Rattle draws from the orchestra is clean and sharply profiled, not unlike the Mahler sound Rafael Kubelík tended to favour. Rattle's tempo for the *Adagietto* is a good one by modern standards (not too slow) and the string playing has a lovely diaphanous quality, but you may find the playing over-nuanced.

Nowadays it isn't unusual to hear rhythm and line sacrificed to detail and nuance as old-established symphony orchestras are made to rethink their readings by conductors schooled in the arcana of ancient performance practice. Rattle has done his fair share of this. What's interesting about this live Mahler Fifth is the degree to which the detail is absorbed and the line maintained.

Like most latter-day conductors, Rattle tends to underplay the march element in the first movement. Mahler in his 1905 piano roll, Walter, and Haitink in his superb 1969 Concertgebouw recording all preserve this. Some may find the approach too dry-eyed in the long-drawn string threnody at fig 2. But an excess of feeling can damage both opening movements (the second is a mirror of the first) if the larger rhythm is obscured. Rattle, like Barbirolli and Bernstein in his superb Vienna Philharmonic recording, treats the threnody more as a meditation than a march, but the pulse isn't lost and the attendant tempi are good. The frenzied B flat minor Trio is particularly well judged. The second movement is superb (the diminished horn contribution notwithstanding) and none but the most determined sceptic could fail to thrill to the sense of adventure and well-being Rattle and his players bring to the *Scherzo* and finale, even if Barbirolli (studio) and Bernstein (live) both reach the finishing line in rather more eloquent and orderly fashion that this talented but still occasionally fragile-sounding Berlin ensemble.

As a memento, the CD is a triumph of organisation and despatch. As a performance and as a recording, it has rather more character and bite than Abbado's much admired 1993 Berlin version. Indeed, it can safely be ranked among the half dozen or so finest performances on record. It isn't perfect, but do you know of one that is?

Symphony No 5
New Philharmonia Orchestra / Sir John Barbirolli
EMI Great Recordings of the Century 566910-2
(74' · ADD). Recorded 1969   ⓜ🅾🅾➓

Sir John Barbirolli's Fifth occupies a special place in everybody's affections: a performance so big in spirit and warm of heart as to silence any rational discussion of its shortcomings. Some readers may have problems with one or two of his sturdier tempi. He doesn't make life easy for his orchestra in the treacherous second movement, while the exultant finale, though suitably bracing, arguably needs more of a spring in its heels. But against all this, one must weigh a unity and strength of purpose, an entirely idiomatic response to instrumental colour and texture (the dark, craggy hues of the first two movements are especially striking); and most important of all that very special Barbirollian radiance, humanity – call it what you will. One point of interest for collectors – on the

original LP, among minor orchestral mishaps in the *Scherzo*, were four bars of missing horn obbligato (at nine bars before fig 20). Not any more! The original solo horn player, Nicholas Busch, has returned to the scene of this momentary aberration (Watford Town Hall) and the absent bars have been ingeniously reinstated. There's even a timely grunt from Sir John, as if in approval. Something of a classic, then; EMI's remastering is splendid.

Symphony No 5
Vienna Philharmonic Orchestra / Leonard Bernstein
DG 477 6334GGP (75' · DDD). Recorded live 1987   ⓜ🅾🅾➓

Bernstein's tempo for the Funeral March in the first movement of the Fifth Symphony became slower in the 23 years that separated his New York CBS recording from this one, made during a performance in Frankfurt. The strings-only passage at fig 15 in the first movement is exquisitely played, as is the long horn solo in the *Scherzo*. And there's one marvellously exciting moment – the bright gleam of trumpet tone at one bar before fig 29 in the second movement. Best of all is Bernstein himself, here at his exciting best, giving a demonic edge to the music where it's appropriate and building the symphony inexorably to its final triumph.

Thanks to a very clear and well-balanced recording, every subtlety of scoring, especially some of the lower strings' counterpoint, comes through as the conductor intended. One is made aware of the daring novelty of much of the orchestration, of how advanced it must have sounded in the early years of this century. Here we get the structure, the sound and the emotion. The *Adagietto* isn't dragged out, and the scrupulous attention to Mahler's dynamics allows the delightfully silken sound of the Vienna strings to be heard to captivating advantage, with the harp well recorded too. Bernstein is strongest in Mahler when the work itself is one of the more optimistic symphonies with less temptation for him to add a few degrees more of *Angst*.

Symphony No 5
Lucerne Festival Orchestra / Claudio Abbado
Video director **Michael Beyer**
Euroarts 📀 205 4079 (74' · 16:9 · PCM stereo, 5.1 and DTS 5.1 · 0)
Recorded live in Lucerne 2004. Includes multiple viewing angles   Ⓕ🅾🅾🅾

Claudio Abbado's Mahler Fifth is magnificent. It helps that the band is the Lucerne Festival Orchestra, that most exalted of all ad hoc ensembles, rather than the Gustav Mahler Jugendorchester. It does make a difference in Lucerne to have a raft of seasoned players joining the core contingent from the Mahler Chamber Orchestra. The visual dimension is stronger, too, with the option to switch to the so-called 'Conductor Camera' and experience Abbado from a player's perspective. If this strikes some readers as a gimmick I can only say that I welcome it as a natural use of the new medium.

Listen without the images, though, and it quickly becomes apparent that Abbado's previous, audio-only account (DG, subsequently revamped for SACD) is sonically superior, with greater hall ambience and less tendency for wind, brass and percussion to lose themselves in the mix. It's not as if the conductor's conception has changed a great deal. His Fifth has always displayed a tad less inner intensity than some of the great readings of the past but with compensating elegance and grace. Once again the famous *Adagietto* steals in with a magic inevitability that few have matched. Those with limited budgets might do well to consider Leonard Bernstein's Unitel Mahler cycle (though it represents quite a substantial single outlay – see below). That said, Abbado's music-making is as fine as you will find anywhere today and his admirers should be well satisfied.

Symphony No 6

Symphony No 6
San Francisco Symphony Orchestra /
Michael Tilson Thomas
SFS Media/Avie ② ⚛ 821936-0001-2 (87' · DDD)
Recorded live on September 12-15, 2001 Ⓜ️**O**▷

This recording of Mahler's Sixth Symphony was made from performances planned long before the events of September 11 gave the San Francisco Symphony's choice of repertoire extraordinary resonance. And it's a credit to both Michael Tilson Thomas and the orchestra that this ferocious performance is carried out without hysteria or self-indulgence. Tempi are judiciously chosen. In the first movement, for example, Tilson Thomas's *Allegro energico, ma non troppo* is only a hair's breadth slower than Bernstein's in his Vienna Philharmonic recording, yet the difference is enough to give proper weight to the march. Indeed, the SFS strings dig very deep to produce a dark, throaty tone of startling vehemence. Ardently played and generously phrased, the 'Alma' theme provides welcome consolation – and how longingly Tilson Thomas clings to the final peaks of its melody.

Gunshot-like *sforzandos* from the timpani introduce the *Scherzo*, sharply etched here with stinging dotted rhythms. The Trios are similarly pointed – though affectionately *grazioso*, as Mahler requests – and rather deliberately paced, like a long-forgotten dance now remembered in slow motion. The *Andante moderato* is also treated expansively, but the tension never sags. Tilson Thomas mis-steps only once in the sprawling finale, pressing too hard at the end of the introduction so that the orchestra arrives prematurely at the main tempo – a minor flaw and quickly forgiven.

A more impressive start to Tilson Thomas and the SFS's Mahler cycle is difficult to imagine. Less mannered than Bernstein, and more emotionally engaged than Karajan, this is an exceptionally intense and, in the circumstances, remarkably coherent performance that isn't to be missed. Very good sound quality, too, from the orchestra's new in-house label.

Symphony No 6
London Symphony Orchestra / Valery Gergiev
LSO Live ⚛ LSO0661 (77' · DDD/DSD)
Recorded live at the Barbican Hall, London in
November 2007 Ⓑ**O**O▷

Valery Gergiev is one of the most charismatic maestros on the circuit and his Mahler series in London has aroused passionately divergent responses. If you prize the textural elucidation that Claudio Abbado brings to these scores you probably won't care for Gergiev's broader, coarser brush. The raw excitement he engenders may seem beside the point.

This Sixth is dark, sometimes impenetrable, an impression offset only by a raft of sublime *pianissimos*. The silken shimmer of the first movement's central pastoral reverie with cowbells carefully distanced offers surprising relief. Elsewhere Gergiev drives the argument forward with the kind of sullen, monolithic power he applies to Shostakovich at his most barren. While his main tempo is only fractionally faster than Bernstein's, it seems rushed even for this most neurotic of symphonic openers. The exposition repeat is taken. The serene *Andante moderato*, placed second as is now the fashion, is soon being harried towards a climax that blares unmercifully. There's more variety of tone in the *Scherzo*, though it's the finale which really hits home, the orchestra whipped into a frenzy that may or may not be idiomatic but certainly strikes sparks.

If you're looking for a quick-fire, single-disc Sixth with a difference, Gergiev has more gravitas than previous Soviet-trained conductors, even when he's racing. LSO Live backs him up with an impactful, immediate, rather airless sound encoded as a hybrid SACD. The bright-edged, multi-linear treatment favoured by exponents as ostensibly dissimilar as Bernstein and Boulez simply isn't on Gergiev's agenda. Instead, a trail is blazed for a visceral, even thuggish brand of music-making. Yes, these sounds thrilled many in the hall but would you want to revisit them at home? At bargain price you can afford to find out. The enthusiastic applause has been removed.

Symphony No 6
Berlin Philharmonic Orchestra / Claudio Abbado
DG 477 5573GH; ② ⚛ 477 5684GSA2
(80' · DDD/DSD). Recorded live 2004 Ⓕ**O**O O▷

 Whatever the revolution in playing standards since January 1966, when Barbirolli conducted Mahler's Sixth in Berlin, you'd be hard-pressed to encounter a tauter, more refined performance than this, or one that dispenses so completely with the heavy drapes of old-style Mahler interpretation. The work concluded Abbado's first Philharmonie programme since passing the reins to Sir Simon Rattle, an occasion bound to provoke standing ovations and a little myth-making, too. Now, with the music repositioned on the sunny side of the Alps and seen through the prism of the Second Viennese School, an effortless, sometimes breathtaking transparency prevails.

In the first movement, Abbado's sparing use of *rubato* precludes the full (de-)flowering of the 'Alma theme' in the Bernstein manner, and there are some curiously stiff moments in the *Andante moderato*, here an iridescent intermezzo quite unlike Karajan's Brucknerian slow movement. This may not be a Sixth for all seasons and all moods – the Berliners rarely play with the full weight of sonority long thought uniquely theirs – yet reservations soon fall away. For all its fine detailing, Abbado's finale lacks nothing in intensity, with a devastating corporate thrust that may or may not have you ruing DG's decision to include an applause track.

A more serious stumbling block is the maestro's decision to place the *Scherzo* third, following the lead of Del Mar, Barbirolli, Rattle and others. Purchasers of a single disc CD version available in some parts of the world, or indeed the download, can re-programme, of course, but technical constraints for the hybrid SACD disc, available in the UK, have led DG to opt for a pair of discs containing two movements apiece. It must, however, be pointed out that the extra cost is borne by the manufacturer, not the consumer. And, apart from two curious pockets of resonance in the finale (on either side of the 10-minute mark), Christopher Alder's team achieves a much more realistic balance than you'll find in the conductor's previous live Mahler issues. If a little cavernous, the effect is blessedly consistent, allowing us to appreciate that Abbado's sweetly attenuated string sound is just as beautiful as Karajan's more saturated sonority, a testament to the chamber-like imperatives of his latter-day music-making, not to mention the advantage of adequate rehearsal time!

The finale's hammer-blows are clearer and cleaner than ever. Abbado does not include the third of these before the final coda but the hard, dry brutality of his clinching *fortissimo* is guaranteed to take you by surprise. Donald Mitchell provides excellent booklet-notes to cap a remarkable release.

Additional recommendations

Symphony No 6
Coupled with Kindertotenlieder. Rückert-Lieder
Ludwig *mez* **BPO / Karajan**
DG The Originals ② 457 716-2GOR2 (129' · ADD)
Recorded 1974-75   Ⓜ**OO**▷
    Karajan's classic Sixth confirmed his belated arrival as a major Mahler interpreter. His understanding of Mahler's sound world – its links forward to Berg, Schoenberg and Webern as opposed to retrospective links with Wagner – is very acute.

Symphony No 6
LPO / Tennstedt
LPO ② LPO0038 (84' · ADD)
Recorded live   Ⓑ**OO**
    Tennstedt exposes every nerve-ending of the piece from start to finish. Trenchancy is there with a vengeance from the word go – big-boned and punchy with snappy trombone accents. So it's a corker, this performance. It sounds pretty good for 1983, though the BBC fashion then for a more 'open' sound slightly compromises the unflinching immediacy of the reading.

Symphony No 6
LSO / Jansons
LSO Live ② LSO0038 (82' · DDD)   Ⓢ**B**▷

Symphony No 6
Coupled with **Henze** Sebastian im Traum
Royal Concertgebouw Orch / Jansons
RCO Live ② 🔊 RCO06001 (99' · DDD/DSD)   Ⓕ
    Quite a dilemma: two virtually identical performances from Jansons. The acoustic of the Concertgebouw provides better sound and the RCO give a slightly more spacious reading. Otherwise, it's swings and roundabouts: maybe the lush Henze coupling is the clincher.

Symphony No 7

Symphony No 7
Chicago Symphony Orchestra / Claudio Abbado
DG Masters 445 513-2GMA (79' · DDD)   Ⓕ**OO**▷

Abbado's account of Mahler's Seventh was always a highlight of his cycle and remains the ideal choice for collectors requiring a central interpretation in modern sound. Steering a middle course between clear-sightedness and hysteria, and avoiding both the heavy, saturated textures of 19th-century Romanticism and the chilly rigidity of some of his own 'modernist' peers, he is, as the original review reported, 'almost too respectable'. That said, it's all to the good if the forthright theatricality and competitive instincts of the Chicago orchestra are held in check just a little. Even where Abbado underplays the drama of the moment, a sufficient sense of urgency is sustained by a combination of well-judged tempi, marvellously graduated dynamics and precisely balanced, ceaselessly changing textures. For those put off by Mahler's supposed vulgarity, the unhurried classicism of Abbado's reading may well be the most convincing demonstration of the music's integrity. This is a piece Abbado continues to champion in concert with performances at the very highest level.

Symphony No 7
London Symphony Orchestra / Valery Gergiev
LSO Live 🔊 LSO0665 (72' · DDD)
Recorded live 2008   Ⓑ**OO**▷

For some Valery Gergiev's dark, pumped-up Seventh might prove to be the high-point of his

Mahler cycle. True, the over-the-barricades manner precludes much in the way of subtlety but it does hold in tight unity a score that can sprawl into incoherence. Much is paced a notch faster than usual, though not the introduction which is spacious and strong. The playing is consistently assured; the sound powerfully immediate. The reading has a monolithic drive that is nothing if not distinctive.

What Gergiev doesn't deliver is a sense of this music's teeming inner life. No point looking here for either Claudio Abbado's delicate attention to line and colour or Leonard Bernstein's emotive, micro-managed *rubato*. Gergiev's inner movements come across as diligent but brusque. While his idiosyncratic seating arrangements (including antiphonal violins) make for some interesting effects, it's the resilience of the LSO brass at high decibels you're likely to remember, not the meaningful interplay of independent and interdependent strands.

The applause which greeted this performance at London's Barbican Hall has been surgically removed for this hybrid SACD incarnation. The critics will be as divided over its merits as they were following the live performance. Happily, LSO Live's competitive pricing means you can decide for yourself.

Symphony No 7
**New York Philharmonic Orchestra /
Leonard Bernstein**
Sony Classical Bernstein Century Edition SMK60564
(80' · ADD). Recorded 1965　　Ⓜ☐▶

We are often assured that great conductors of an earlier generation interpreted Mahler from within the Austrian tradition, encoding a sense of nostalgia, decay and incipient tragedy as distinct from the in-your-face calamities and neuroses proposed by Leonard Bernstein. Well, this is one Bernstein recording that should convince all but the most determined sceptics. It deserves a place in anyone's collection now that it has been transferred to a single disc at mid-price. The white-hot communicative power is most obvious in the finale which has never sounded more convincing than it does here; the only mildly questionable aspect of the reading is the second *Nachtmusik*, too languid for some. The transfer is satisfactory, albeit dimmer than one might have hoped. It sounds historic, but historic in more ways than one.

Additional recommendation

Symphony No 7[a]
Coupled with **Mozart** Symphony No 41, 'Jupiter'[b]
LPO / Tennstedt
BBC Legends ② BBCL4224-2 (111' · ADD)
Recorded live in [a]1980 and [b]1985　　Ⓕ❍❍

This BBC Legends Seventh comes from a 1980 concert given at the Edinburgh Festival just a few months before Tennstedt and the LPO took the

work into EMI's Abbey Road studios. It's a revelation. Yes, the interpretative outline is similar in both accounts but how fervent the playing is here, and how much more sense Tennstedt's tempo manipulations make. Mozart's *Jupiter* Symphony receives a stylish performance. Treasurable.

Symphony No 8, 'Symphony of a Thousand'

Symphony No 8
Heather Harper, Lucia Popp, Arleen Auger *sops*
Yvonne Minton *mez* **Helen Watts** *contr* **René Kollo** *ten* **John Shirley-Quirk** *bar* **Martti Talvela** *bass*
**Vienna Boys' Choir; Vienna State Opera Chorus; Vienna Singverein; Chicago Symphony Orchestra /
Sir Georg Solti**
Decca 475 7521DOR (80' · ADD · T/t)
Recorded 1971　　Ⓜ❍❍☐▶

Of the so-called classic accounts of the Eighth Symphony, it's Solti's which most conscientiously sets out to convey an impression of large forces in a big performance space, this despite the obvious resort to compression and other forms of gerrymandering. Whatever the inconsistencies of Decca's multi-miking and overdubbing, the overall effect remains powerful even today. The remastering has not eradicated all trace of distortion at the very end and, given the impressive flood of choral tone at the start of the 'Veni Creator Spiritus', it still seems a shame that the soloists and the Chicago brass are quite so prominent in its closing stages. As for the performance itself, Solti's extrovert way with Part 1 works tremendously without quite erasing memories of Bernstein's ecstatic fervour. In Part 2, it may be the patient Wagnerian mysticism of Tennstedt that sticks in the mind. Less inclined to delay, Solti makes the material sound more operatic. Yet for its gut-wrenching theatricality and great solo singing, Solti's version makes a plausible first choice – now more than ever. Also, it has been squeezed onto a single CD.

Symphonies – No 8; No 10 – Adagio
Erin Wall, Elza van den Heever, Laura Claycomb *sops* **Katarina Karnéus, Yvonne Naef** *mezs* **Anthony Dean Griffey** *ten* **Quinn Kelsey** *bar* **James Morris** *bass-bar* **San Francisco Girls Chorus; San Francisco Symphony Chorus and Orchestra /
Michael Tilson Thomas**
Avie/SFS Media ② 821936 00212 (111' · DDD)
Recorded live 2006 and 2008　　Ⓕ❍❍☐▶

First, from a purely sonic standpoint, it's pretty spectacular, most demonstrably in the closing sections of both halves, the 'Glory to the Father' especially, where the sound frame expands with such ease and amplitude that one wonders whether it can possibly carry on building, which it does. Tilson Thomas's reading is always warm and spontaneous-sounding but its real strength lies in the way phrases connect so that what can sometimes seem, on certain versions, merely a series of episodes (specifically in the Symphony's much longer second half) emerges very much 'of a piece'. The rocky soundscape that opens Part 2 is wonderfully atmospheric though never at the expense of detail – again the recording delivers a very believable perspective – and Quinn Kelsey's Pater Ecstaticus is one of the best-sung performances on the set, rather better than James Morris's intense but wobbly Pater Profundis that follows on from it.

There's that unforgettable passage, just before the closing chorus arrives, where, flute, clarinet, harp and celesta set up an ethereal pathway for the resplendent journey's end. And in this context it has been quite a journey, Tilson Thomas drawing more colour and variety (tonal and emotional) from the score than almost any of his rivals, so with wonderful sound, superb playing and generally fine singing (soprano Erin Wall is exceptional) this new version rates among the top two or three.

Attitudes to the Tenth Symphony's infinitely strange and at times deeply unsettling *Adagio* will depend largely on how you view the various performing versions of the whole work. If a completed Tenth is your chosen option, then the *Adagio* on its own won't do. If, however, you view it as a movement that was bequeathed to us more or less intact, and forget about building a context, then Tilson Thomas's probing performance is fairly eventful and deeply haunting, and – again – beautifully recorded.

Additional recommendations

Symphony No 8
Banse, Brewer, Isokoski *sops* **Henschel, Remmert**
contrs **Villars** *ten* **Wilson-Johnson** *bar* **Relyea** *bass*
Toronto Children's Choir; LSC; CBSO Youth
Chorus, Chorus and Orch / Rattle
EMI 557945-2 (74' · DDD · T/t)   Ⓕ❍🅑➔
Recorded live 2004
   Thrilling, euphoric, hair-raising – Rattle holds the score in a perpetual state of wonder.

Symphony No 8
Coupled with Symphony No 4ᵃ
ᵃ**Popp, Connell, Wiens, Lott, Schmidt, Denize,**
Versalle, Hynninen, Sotin Tiffin Boys' School Choir;
LPO & Choir / Tennstedt
EMI download ② 361572-2 (128' · DDD)
Recorded 1986   Ⓜ❍❍❍🅑➔
   Tennstedt's performance leaves no doubt that he believes totally in Mahler's creation. It has a rapt, almost intimate, quality that makes his reading all the more moving. The soloists are on excellent form and the choruses sing with conviction. The reading of the Fourth Symphony too is outstandingly idiomatic and well played (worth tracking down on CD, but a download is available).

Symphony No 9

Symphony No 9. Kindertotenlieder.
Rückert-Lieder

Christa Ludwig *mez* **Berlin Philharmonic Orchestra / Herbert von Karajan**
DG Double ② 453 040-2GTA2 (132' · ADD)
Recorded 1979-80   Ⓜ❍❍❍🅑➔

 Mahler's Ninth is a death-haunted work, but is filled, as Bruno Walter remarked, 'with a sanctified feeling of departure'. Rarely has this symphony been shaped with such understanding and played with such selfless virtuosity as it was by Karajan and the BPO.

For this reissue the tapes have been picked over to open up the sound and do something about the early digital edginess of the strings. There's still some occlusion at climaxes; and if those strings now seem more plasticky than fierce, it's impossible to say whether the conductor would have approved. Karajan came late to Mahler and yet, until the release of his rather more fiercely recorded 1982 concert relay (below), he seemed content to regard this earlier studio performance as perhaps his finest achievement on disc.

The attraction is greatly enhanced by Christa Ludwig's carefully considered Mahler performances of the mid-1970s. The voice may not be as fresh as it was when she recorded the songs in the late 1950s, but there are few readings of comparable nobility. She articulates the text with unrivalled clarity, and 'In diesem Wetter' at least is positively operatic. How much of the grand scale should be attributed to Karajan? It's difficult to say; the voice is sometimes strained by the tempi. This collection isn't to be missed.

Symphony No 9
BPO / Herbert von Karajan
DG ② 439 024-2GHS2 (85' · DDD)
Recorded live 1982   Ⓜ❍❍❍🅑➔

 Choice between the 1982 Karajan classic and the analogue studio recording is by no means easy. Both versions won *Gramophone* Awards in their day. This live performance remains a remarkable one, with a commitment to lucidity of sound and certainty of line. There's nothing dispassionate about the way the Berlin Philharmonic tears into the *Rondo-Burleske*, the agogic touches of the analogue version ironed out without loss of intensity. True, Karajan doesn't seek to emulate the passionate immediacy of a Barbirolli or a Bernstein, but in his broadly conceived, gloriously played *Adagio* the sepulchral hush is as memorable as the eruptive climax. The finesse of the playing is unmatched.

Symphony No 9
Berlin Philharmonic Orchestra / Claudio Abbado
DG 471 624-2GH (81' · DDD)
Recorded live 1999   Ⓕ❍❍🅑➔

Claudio Abbado began his career with Mahler and has been conducting the composer for his entire professional life. The Ninth and, above all, the Seventh, have consistently brought out the best in him.

Abbado's previous recording of No 9, taped live in Vienna, is now only available in his box-set of the complete symphonies (DG, reviewed on page 710). Much acclaimed as an interpretation, its airless sound wasn't to all tastes. This account is another multi-miked extravaganza with sonic shortcomings that are immediately apparent. The opening bars establish a wide open sound stage (complete with hiss) that implodes with the appearance of the harp. That harp is always on the loud side, trumpets are almost always too reticent, the bass feels synthetic and there are troublesome changes of perspective. None of which is enough to nullify the obvious sincerity and conviction of a performance that simply gets better and better as it proceeds. This really is live music-making (the last big first movement climax at 16'54" isn't together), but the inner movements are beyond reproach, ideally paced and characterised and superbly realised. The finale is content to plumb the depths in its own way – as sensitive as any of its celebrated rivals if without the point-scoring you may be used to.

Where some interpreters feel bound to choose between structural imperatives and subjective emotions, proffering either proto-Schoenbergian edginess or late-Romantic excess, Abbado has the confidence to eschew both the heavily saturated textures of his predecessors and the chilly rigidity of some of his own 'modernist' peers. Instead, his unaffected warmth allows everything to come through naturally. There remains something self-effacing about his musical personality. And yet there's sunlight – and a certain tenderness – in this account of the Ninth that you won't find anywhere else, a fluency and ease that's something to marvel at. For those put off even now by the composer's supposed vulgarity, Abbado's readings constitute a convincing demonstration of the music's integrity.

The awed silence that greets the expiration of the Ninth may or may not be stage-managed, but it seems genuine.

Symphony No 9
Berlin Philharmonic Orchestra / Sir Simon Rattle
EMI ② 501228-2 (84' · DDD)   ⒻⓄⓄ🅑➨

In his previous recording of Mahler's Ninth Symphony, made live with the Vienna Philharmonic in 1993, Simon Rattle tapped into the music's emotional extremes to produce a surprisingly volatile reading full of precipitous *accelerandos* and wrenching *ritardandos*. There's some of that volatility in this new account from Berlin, too, though it's certainly less pronounced. There are places, too, where more tenderness wouldn't come amiss: the entrance of the solo violin in the first movement's recapitulation is so much sweeter in Vienna. But Rattle and the Berliners are also capable of taking one's breath away. Listen later in the same movement, as they gather the seemingly chaotic tangle of melodic filaments together, creating a single, gigantic, darkly radiant chord.

The rustic dances in the second movement have a strong, rough-hewn quality, even if they sound slightly dour when compared with the more *gemütlich* charm of, say, Abbado's Berlin recording. Rattle doesn't push hard in the *Rondo-Burleske* until the end; instead, he aims for clarity and articulateness, and scrupulously observes all the dynamic twists and turns. It's an effective approach, though less adrenalin-pumping than Karajan.

It's in the final *Adagio*, however, that Rattle and his orchestra make the most powerful impact. The strings sound gorgeous, of course, yet there's grit as well as radiance in their tone. And it's only in the final pages that the earthy impurities are leeched, leaving a breath-like purity that ebbs into rapt silence.

Symphony No 9
San Francisco Symphony Orchestra / Michael Tilson Thomas
Avie/SFSO ② 821936 00072 (90' · DDD/DSD)
Recorded live 2004   Ⓕ🅑➨

Tilson Thomas immediately establishes a profoundly rapt atmosphere, and the orchestra take what can best be described as a *bel canto* approach, singing their lines with warmth and poised intensity. In keeping with this, the conductor allows the players considerable rhythmic freedom. Yet one always senses a firm hand on the tiller, and the music is never pulled out of shape, as sometimes seems the case in, say, Bernstein's later recording for DG.

Some may feel that there's insufficient grit or angst here, and certainly the second movement Ländler is hearty rather than coarse and the *Rondo-Burleske* could sneer more viciously – though the thrilling *accelerando* in its coda is likely to get one's adrenalin pumping. But, to be fair, Tilson Thomas doesn't entirely neglect the music's darker qualities, and these often creep into one's consciousness rather subtly.

The interpretation's lasting impression, however, is one of lyrical radiance. In the symphony's final pages, Tilson Thomas tenderly holds the melodic shards together so one hears the song continue, even through the silences. And the evanescent glow of the strings at the end – like the last glimmer of light immediately after sunset – is not so much wistful as consolatory. An unusually moving experience, then, and one that marks yet another high point in this continuing cycle.

Symphony No 9
Stuttgart Radio Symphony Orchestra / Sir Roger Norrington
Hänssler Classic CD93 244 (72' · DDD)
Recorded live in September 2009   Ⓕ🅑➨

Sir Roger Norrington thinks this might be the first time since Bruno Walter's famous 1938 Vienna Philharmonic recording that a single live performance has come close to emulating the sound world of Mahler's Ninth Symphony at the time of composition. He means, of course, 'pure' sound where phrasing and characterisation, not vibrato, dictate the expressive palette.

The aural adjustments are perhaps harder to make than in the classical repertoire: Mahler's futuristic sonorities assume a visceral power through contemporary orchestral sound and he would surely have embraced the digital age with a whole heart and open mind. Even so, it is fascinating to set aside sensationalism in favour of re-evaluation and to hear this remarkable piece stripped, as it were, of its veneer and laid bare before us in all its unsettling majesty and humility. From the first faltering opening measures, marking time in harp and stopped horns, the arrival of the first subject in second violins is possessed of a plain-speaking innocence that lends added poignancy. Nothing is glamorised, everything is exposed, and there is no question that Norrington's very open textures give us a clearer picture of the work's harmonic subversiveness. Listen to that extraordinary passage at the heart of the first movement where worming bass clarinet against timpani and fractured *pizzicatos* suddenly leave us marooned in no man's land. Put simply, there is a truthfulness about Norrington's reading from which there is simply no hiding and no escape.

The last movement is honest and beautiful, its aspiration and lust for living intensified by string playing which is about so much more than how grandiloquently the sound can be sustained. Here it sings its way towards the deconstructive valediction with violin *glissandos* so fragile as to suggest life quite literally slipping away.

Interesting, then, to turn back the clock and experience an altogether more fundamental, unvarnished Mahler. You may miss the pure 'theatre' of Bernstein, the inwardness of Abbado and so on – but refresh your ears and your perceptions and prepare to be surprised again.

Additional recommendation

Symphony No 9   **H**
Vienna Philharmonic Orchestra / Walter
Dutton Laboratories mono CDBP9708 (71' · ADD)
Recorded 1938   **⑤OO**
This is a historic document – the Ninth's first commercial recording conducted by its dedicatee. Few modern performances offer more intensity in the first movement (Rattle and Bernstein perhaps excepted). Don't be taken aback by the technical lapses of the VPO; this is music-making in which scrappiness and fervour are indissolubly linked. The original surface noise is filtered to near inaudibility – Dutton's restoration is a must-have.

Symphony No 9
Royal Stockholm PO / Gilbert
BIS ⦿ BIS-SACD1710 (81' · DDD)   **ⒻO▷**
Among familiar and celebrated accounts, Gilbert is aligned with Abbado rather than

Haitink (or Bernstein rather than Giulini). Like Abbado (and very few others), he is exceedingly mindful of Mahler's markings. On a technical level this must, surely, be the finest recording the work has received. This first recording of Gilbert conducting Mahler is rather more than work in progress: it is as exhausting and purifying an experience as any 80 minutes spent in your listening room has the right to be.

Symphony No 10

Symphony No 10 (ed Cooke)
Berlin Philharmonic Orchestra / Sir Simon Rattle
EMI 556972-2 (77' · DDD)   **ⒻOOO▷**

 Over the years, Rattle has performed the work nearly 100 times, far more often than anyone else. Wooed by Berlin, he repeatedly offered them 'Mahler ed Cooke' and was repulsed. He made his Berlin conducting debut with the Sixth. But, after the announcement in June 1999 that he had won the orchestra's vote in a head-to-head with Daniel Barenboim, he celebrated with two concert performances of the Tenth. A composite version is presented here. As always, Rattle obtains some devastatingly quiet string playing, and technical standards are unprecedentedly high in so far as the revised performing version is concerned. Indeed, the danger that clinical precision will result in expressive coolness isn't immediately dispelled by the self-confident meatiness of the violas at the start. We aren't used to hearing the line immaculately tuned with every accent clearly defined. The tempo is broader than before and, despite Rattle's characteristic determination to articulate every detail, the mood is, at first, comparatively serene, even Olympian. Could Rattle be succumbing to the Karajan effect? But no – somehow he squares the circle. The neurotic trills, jabbing dissonances and tortuous counterpoint are relished as never before, within the context of a schizoid *Adagio* in which the Brucknerian string writing is never undersold.

The conductor has not radically changed his approach to the rest of the work. As you might expect, the *scherzos* have greater security and verve. Their strange hallucinatory choppiness is better served, although parts of the fourth movement remain perplexing despite the superb crispness and clarity of inner parts. More than ever, everything leads inexorably to the cathartic finale, brought off with a searing intensity that has you forgetting the relative baldness of the invention.

Berlin's Philharmonie isn't the easiest venue: with everything miked close, climaxes can turn oppressive but the results here are very credible and offer no grounds for hesitation. In short, this new version sweeps the board even more convincingly than his old (Bournemouth) one. Rattle makes the strongest case for an astonishing piece of revivification that only the most die-hard purists will resist. Strongly recommended.

Symphony No 10 (ed Cooke)
**South West German Radio Symphony Orchestra /
Michael Gielen**
Hänssler Classic CD93 124 (77' · DDD) Ⓕ

It has become harder for interpreters to make
their mark in what has become standard fare, yet
Michael Gielen pulls it off. He has reversed his
attitude to the nascent Tenth to present here an
intriguing realisation of Deryck Cooke's performing version.

Gielen's narrative is not invested with Rattle's
passion (see above). He prefers to lay bare its
gaunt, unfinished state, exposing even parts of
the *Adagio* as the harmonic frame over which
Mahler would have stretched more complex
contrapuntal detail. No longer an inexorable
meditation, the movement becomes rather an
unfinished dialogue between arrest and movement. The orchestral sound is lean and light
with some exceptionally hushed playing from
the strings and no lack of exquisite detail. The
transparency means that contested ingredients
such as the deployment of glockenspiel in the
second movement and Cooke's discarded side-
drum and xylophone parts in the fourth really
register. And has there ever been a more perfectly judged *Purgatorio*?

The finale can be achingly tender but only
where necessary. That great flute melody is
almost plain as well as pure, but what care is
lavished on the strings' delicately nuanced
response! Rattle goes for the opposite effect, the
Berlin flautist floating his tone more poignantly,
the strings avoiding the hint of sentimentality.
Under Gielen the upward thrust of the heart-
wrenching sigh concluding the work takes you
by surprise: he has a way of foregrounding emotive detail before retreating to a more expository
Klemperer-like stoicism.

Orchestral Songs

Kindertotenlieder[a]. Rückert-Lieder[b].
Lieder eines fahrenden Gesellen[a]
Dame Janet Baker *mez* [a]**Hallé Orchestra,** [b]**New
Philharmonia Orchestra / Sir John Barbirolli**
EMI 566981-2 (65' · ADD ·T/t) ⒻⓄⒹ➡

The songs of the *Lieder eines fahrenden Gesellen*
('Songs of a Wayfarer') are quoted from Mahler's First Symphony and the fresh, springtime
atmosphere is shared by both works. The
orchestration has great textural clarity and lightness of touch. The *Kindertotenlieder*, more chromatically expressive than the earlier work, tap
into a darker, more complex vein in Mahler's
spiritual and emotional make-up. The *Rückert-
Lieder* aren't a song-cycle as such but gather in
their romantic awareness and response to the
beauties of the poetry a unity and shape that
binds them. Baker and Barbirolli reach a transcendental awareness of Mahler's inner musings. Barbirolli draws from the Hallé playing of
delicacy and precision, establishing a clear case
for having this CD in your collection.

Mahler Rückert-Lieder **Wagner** Wesendonck Lieder.
Tristan und Isolde – Prelude; Mild und leise
(Liebestod)
Felicity Lott *sop* **Schumann Quartet**
(Tedi Papavrami *vn* Christoph Schiller *va*
François Guye *vc* Christian Favre *pf*)
Aeon AECD0858 (53' · DDD) ⒻⓄ

The Schumann Quartet's pianist, Christian
Favre, has made these clear, practical transcriptions (rather than arrangements, the booklet-
note stresses) inspired by Chausson's *Chanson
perpetuelle*, and with a view to adding to the
chamber music literature from the Romantic
world of song. So expect a scaled-down report
on the works concerned rather than Schoenberg's interventionist way with Johann Strauss
or Brahms, or the risk-taking panache of Liszt's
operatic adaptations.

Not the least virtue of the exercise is that we
get Dame Felicity Lott in repertoire she might
otherwise not have attempted. Her performance
of the Liebestod – or 'Verklärung' as we should
call it – is such an object lesson in engagement
with the text, sensuality and controlled power
that one might imagine the late Carlos Kleiber
(whose favourite Marschallin she was) contemplating a further recording of the opera with her.
The *Wesendonck*s have a similar sensual (and
lean) intelligence, devoid of the stuffy Victorian
abstractions that Mathilde's dreadful poetry can
often produce in performance. And, if this is not
the most ideal voice for the darker corners of the
Rückert-Lieder, you'll need to hear what Lott
makes of the poems. The *Tristan* Prelude is fine
too; it's just that it doesn't have a voice part.
Good recordings, and 100 per cent worth it for
the singing.

Kindertotenlieder. Lieder eines fahrenden Gesellen.
Rückert-Lieder. Lieder und Gesänge – No 1,
Frühlingsmorgen; No 3, Hans und Grethe; No 5,
Phantasie aus Don Juan; No 10, Zu Strassburg auf
der Schanz; No 11, Ablösung im Sommer; No 12,
Scheiden und Meiden; No 13, Nicht wiedersehen!
Stephan Genz *bar* **Roger Vignoles** *pf*
Hyperion CDA67392 (73' · DDD · T/t) ⒻⒹ➡

Stephan Genz's voice and style place him above
his many noted contemporaries. His mellifluous
baritone recalls that of a young Thomas Hampson, but his understanding of the Lieder genre is
even more penetrating, as this Mahler recital
reveals. Each song is shaped as a whole yet with
subtleties of phrase and word-painting that seem
inevitable in every respect, especially as the chosen tempi always seem the right ones.

Performing and listening to these songs with
piano is inevitably a more intimate experience
than when they are heard in their orchestral
garb. The pair's rapport is evident throughout.
Memorable are the the poise and stillness of 'Ich
atmet' einen Linden duft' from the *Rückert-
Lieder*, the eloquent sadness of 'Nicht Wiedersehen' and the restrained sorrow of the whole of
Kindertotenlieder. Not a hint of sentimentality,

MAHLER'S DAS LIED VON DER ERDE – IN BRIEF

Urmana, Schade; Vienna PO / Pierre Boulez
DG 469 526-2GH (61' · DDD)　　　　　Ⓕ🅞🅑➔
A real ensemble effort whose guiding light is Boulez. With the help of DG's sound, textures glint with unprecendented clarity; the very end is possibly the most evocative on record.

Ferrier, Patzak; Vienna PO / Bruno Walter　Ⓗ
Decca mono 466 576-2DM (76' · ADD)　Ⓜ🅞🅞🅑➔
This classic meeting of minds in mono now has a better depth of sound than ever before in Decca's latest remastering. The human appeal of Ferrier's 'Farewell' is still magnetic.

Ludwig, Wunderlich; Philharmonia / Otto Klemperer
EMI 566892-2 (64' · ADD)　　　　Ⓜ🅞🅞🅑➔
Another conductor who knew Mahler and worked with him: both singers are in gloriously full voice.

Hodgson, Mitchinson; BBC Northern SO / Jascha Horenstein
BBC Legends BBCL4042-2 (61' · ADD)　　Ⓜ🅞🅞
Horenstein's live legacy of long-breathed Mahler is at last gaining deserved recognition. This is a meditative, deeply felt *Das Lied*. Hodgson eclipses many greater names.

Ferrier, Lewis; Hallé / Sir John Barbirolli　Ⓗ
APR mono APR5579 (77' · ADD)　　　　Ⓕ🅞🅞
Ferrier is in even fuller, finer voice here than for Walter, with a richer, more expansive canvas painted by the Hallé and that most passionate of Mahlerians, Barbirolli. Restricted sound.

Baker, Kmentt; Bavarian RSO / Rafael Kubelík
Audite AUDITE95491 (62' · ADD)　　　　Ⓑ🅞
No survey could be without Janet Baker's sensitive, heartfelt response to the long final 'Farewell': in Kmentt she finally has a partner who is almost her equal, and, in concert, Kubelík finds new expressive heights and depths.

Fischer-Dieskau, King; Vienna PO / Leonard Bernstein
Decca 466 381-2DM (67' · ADD)　　　　Ⓜ🅑➔
If you want Mahler's sanctioned alternative, with a baritone singing the mezzo songs, this is a first choice: Fischer-Dieskau's vast experience in Lieder is telling here, and so are King's credentials as a Wagnerian.

Rigby, Tear; Première Ensemble / Mark Wigglesworth
RCA 09026 68043-2 (69' · ADD)　　　　　Ⓕ
Schoenberg's arrangement reduces the orchestra to a chamber ensemble, and allows the singers to project with more subtlety while exerting an authentic Mahlerian pull.

such a danger in Mahler, spoils the experience of the composer's deeply felt emotions.

Hyperion's recording, beautifully balanced, catches the true quality of Genz's voice and the refinement of Vignoles's playing. This disc is an experience not to be missed by any lover of Mahler and/or of Lieder.

Das klagende Lied

Das klagende Lied
Marina Shaguch *sop* **Michelle DeYoung** *mez*
Thomas Moser *ten* **Sergei Leiferkus** *bar*
San Francisco Symphony Chorus and Orchestra / Michael Tilson Thomas
Avie ♨ 821936 0017-2 (67' · DDD/DSD · T/t)
Recorded live 1996　　　　　　　　Ⓕ🅞🅞🅞

What a glorious prospect Mahler's first major work opens up for us – and how beautifully it is realised here. The original three-part version of this ambitious folkloric cantata is like a musical manifesto of pretty well all Mahler to come. Horn calls in the prelude to 'Waldmärchen' ('Forest Tale') awaken his unique nature-world; elfin woodwind fanfares intimate martial music as far as the Seventh and Eighth symphonies; the First Symphony (third movement) is germinating at the close of part 1, the opening of the Second is already in place with the first bars of 'Der Spielmann' ('The Wandering Musician'); and with 'Hochzeitsstück' ('Wedding Feast') Mahler seems to find himself in Act 2 of Wagner's *Götterdämmerung* contemplating the opera he never wrote. But more startling than anything in *Das klagende Lied* is Mahler's feeling for, and command of, the orchestra – and this from a composer who'd never heard a note of his own orchestration.

Recorded in 1996 (and originally released by RCA), the subtle detailing and nuancing of this performance indicates painstaking preparation but arrives in our living rooms sounding as if the ink is still wet on the page. Each repetition of that madrigal-like choral *ritornello* intensifies the lamentation of the title until release is found in the anguish of the wronged queen and soprano Marina Shaguch hurls out her leaping vocal line to bring down the walls of the castle. That's Mahler's innate theatricality for you. Quite a piece, and quite a performance.

Des Knaben Wunderhorn

Des Knaben Wunderhorn – Revelge[b]. Das irdische Leben[a]. Verlor'ne Müh[ab]. Rheinlegendchen[a]. Der Tamboursg'sell[b]. Der Schildwache Nachtlied[ab]. Wer hat dies Liedlein erdacht?[a]. Lob des hohen Verstandes[b]. Des Antonius von Padua Fischpredigt[b]. Lied des Verfolgten im Turm[ab]. Trost im Unglück[ab]. Wo die schönen Trompeten blasen[a]
[a]**Elisabeth Schwarzkopf** *sop*
[b]**Dietrich Fischer-Dieskau** *bar*
London Symphony Orchestra / George Szell

EMI Great Recordings of the Century 567236-2
(50' · ADD · T/t). Recorded 1968   Ⓜ❍❍❍B➤

EMI's classic recording made in 1968 more or less puts all rivals out of court. Even those who find Schwarzkopf's singing mannered will be hard pressed to find more persuasive versions of the female songs than she gives, while Fischer-Dieskau and Szell are in a class of their own most of the time. Bernstein's CBS version, also from the late 1960s but with less spectacularly improved sound than EMI now provide, is also very fine, but for repeated listening Szell, conducting here with the kind of insight he showed on his famous Cleveland version of the Fourth Symphony, is the more controlled and keen-eared interpreter. Also, few command the musical stage as Fischer-Dieskau does in a song like 'Revelge' where every drop of irony and revulsion from the spectre of war is fiercely, grimly caught. Strongly recommended.

Das Lied von der Erde

Das Lied von der Erde
Christa Ludwig mez **Fritz Wunderlich** ten
**Philharmonia Orchestra, New Philharmonia
Orchestra / Otto Klemperer**
EMI 566892-2 (64' · ADD). Recorded 1964-66 Ⓜ❍❍B➤

In a famous BBC TV interview Klemperer declared that he was the objective one, Walter the romantic, and he knew what he was talking about. Klemperer lays this music before you, even lays bare its soul by his simple method of steady tempos (too slow in the third song) and absolute textural clarity, but he doesn't quite demand your emotional capitulation as does Walter. Ludwig does that. In the tenor songs, Wunderlich can't match Patzak, simply because of the older singer's way with the text; 'fest steh'n' in the opening song, 'Mir ist als wie im Traum', the line plaintive and the tone poignant, are simply unsurpassable.

By any other yardstick, Wunderlich is a prized paragon, musical and vocally free. The sound on the revived EMI is very fresh: with voice and orchestra in perfect relationship and everything sharply defined, the old methods of the 1960s have nothing to fear here from today's competition. These two old recordings will never be thrust aside; the Walter for its authority and intensity, the feeling of being present on an historic occasion, the Klemperer for its insistent strength and beautiful singing.

Das Lied von der Erdeᵃ. Three Rückert-Lieder   Ⓗ
Kathleen Ferrier contr ᵃ**Julius Patzak** ten
Vienna Philharmonic Orchestra / Bruno Walter
Decca 466 5762DM or Naxos 8 110871 (76' · ADD)
Recorded 1952   Ⓜ❍❍❍B➤

The 1952 Walter will never lose its place at the heart of any review of *Das Lied* recordings. Wal-

ter obtains even richer, more impassioned, more pointed playing from the Vienna Philharmonic than in 1936 in, of course, improved sound. With his disciple Ferrier as alto soloist, her songs are richly, warmly voiced, and taken, particularly in the finale, to the limits of emotional involvement. Few have attempted to identify so completely with the work's ethos of farewell and its thoughts of eternity. Ferrier envelops one to the core of one's being. The wholly idiomatic and wonderfully expressive Patzak is the near-ideal tenor.

Pierre de Manchicourt
Franco-Flemish c1510-1564

A choirboy at Arras Cathedral, Manchicourt was director of the choir at Tours Cathedral in 1539, master of the choirboys at Tournai Cathedral in 1545 and maître de chapelle there later that year. By 1556 he was a canon at Arras Cathedral. Later he was master of Philip II's Flemish chapel in Madrid. Similar to many composers of the early to mid-16th century, he predominantly wrote Masses, motets and chansons. His motets are particularly significant as they show the three separate stages of early 16th-century motet development: from Ockeghem via the paired imitation style of Josquin to the stylistic refinement, well-crafted melodic lines and pervasive imitation of Gombert.

Missa Cuidez vous que Dieu nous faille

Regina caeli. Cuidez vous que Dieu nous faille.
Peccantem me quotidie. Missa Cuidez vous que Dieu nous faille. Magnificat secundi toni. Osculetur me.
Ne reminiscaris, Domine
Brabant Ensemble / Stephen Rice
Hyperion CDA67604 (67' · DDD · T/t)   Ⓕ❍B➤

Even in his lifetime, Manchicourt's fame was not what it might have been. There were so many fine composers in the mid-16th century that it's no easy matter to explain what it is that makes certain composers' music stand out. Manchicourt's has something of Gombert's concentration of materials, with textures that are just as full but rather brighter; and his considerable contrapuntal ingenuity is often laced with wit (as in the canonic *Regina caeli*). From the song by Richafort on which he bases his Mass *Cuidez vous que Dieu nous faille*, Manchicourt has a knack of selecting those moments that can be expanded and developed into large-scale passages of considerable rhetorical power. The small-scale as well as the medium-length motets are also worth hearing.

The sound recording is very fine, though the dominance of the trebles slightly obscures the contrapuntal working of the lower voices. All the same, this is a must-have for anybody interested in Renaissance music, marginal or not.

Tigran Mansurian
Lebanese b1939

Since settling in Armenia in 1947 at the age of eight (he was born in Lebanon), Tigran Mansurian has been a leading voice in his adoptive country's contemporary music scene. He found his way towards a fusion of indigenous folk traditions (their spirit more than their letter) and a musical language rooted in East European modernism. More than most, however, he has steered clear of the easy options of minimalism, neo-tonalism and heart-on-sleeve spirituality.

String Quartets – No 1; No 2. Testament
Rosamunde Quartet (Andreas Reiner, Simon
Fordham *vns* Helmut Nicolai *va* Anja Lechner *vc*)
ECM New Series 476 3052 (50' · DDD)   Ⓕ Ⓑ ▸

In the first two string quartets – composed in 1983-84 (there is a third from 1993) – and the short *Testament* of 2004 dedicated to ECM's Manfred Eicher, the influence of Bartók looms large, though Shostakovich is also there in the background. These works join a long and honourable tradition in Russian chamber music as an arena for private memorialisation, for confessions shared between artistic souls. In fact both are in the best sense musicians' music, in that they trace long lines of expressive thought, the ideas ebbing and flowing naturally. In every movement there are memorable ideas that connect and reveal new prespectives on repeated hearings.

In an unsensational way, therefore, this is one of the most satisfying discs of unfamiliar music for a long time. Credit for that impression must go in large part to the sensitivity and musicianly insight of the Rosamunde Quartet and to another beautifully judged recording from ECM.

Marin Marais
French 1656-1728

Marais, the central figure in the French bass viol school, spent his life in Paris, much of it as a court musician. A pupil of Sainte-Colombe and protégé of Lully, he composed four operas that form an important link between Lully and Campra. But his greatest significance lies in his five collections of music for one to three bass viols (1686-1725), comprising over 550 pieces. The Pieces en trio (1692) are recognised as the first appearance of the trio sonata in France.

Pièces de viol

Pièces de viole, Livre 2 – Part 1: Ballet en rondeau;   Ⓟ
Couplets de folies; Prélude; Cloches ou carillon.
Part 2: Prélude lentement; Chaconne en rondeau;
Tombeau pour M de Ste Colombe; Prélude;
Allemande; Courante; Pavan selon de goût des
anciens compositeurs de luth; Gavotte; Rondeau en
vaudeville; Gigue; Chaconne; Fantaisie
Markku Luolajan-Mikkola, Varpu Haavisto *vas da
gamba* **Eero Palviainen** *lte* **Elina Mustonen** *hpd*

BIS BIS-CD909 (73' · DDD)   Ⓕ

The most substantial pieces here are the set of variations of *La folia*, and the *Tombeau pour M de Ste Colombe* in memory of Marais's mentor. His idiom embodies a paradox that's peculiarly French, in that it demands a very high technical standard, yet its proper expression requires the utmost restraint. The young Finnish violist Markku Luolajan-Mikkola is a founder-member of Phantasm. Here he holds his own with elegance and reserve, although in the slower pieces one might have wished for more rhythmic flexibility. The continuo section consists of another violist, and a theorbo or harpsichord (though in the variations on *La folia*, the two are combined). This works well for the most part, though the high partials of the harpsichord tend to drown the viols: the lute is far less obtrusive. The problem of balance also intrudes when the soloist is in the lower range. But as an introduction to Marais's art this is hard to fault – try his Pavan 'in the style of the bygone lute composers': a real treat.

Additional recommendation

Tous les matins du monde (soundtrack)   Ⓟ
Music by **Couperin, Lully, Marais** and **Sainte-Colombe**
Le Concert des Nations / Savall *va da gamba*
Alia Vox AV9821 (76' · DDD)   Ⓕ
This magical disc occupies the more inward world of the solo gamba repertoire, taking in moving and thoughtful compositions such as Marais' *La rêveuse* and Sainte-Colombe's deeply moving *Les pleurs*. Savall shows himself throughout to be a master worthy of these great viol-playing composers.

Luca Marenzio
Italian 1553/54-1599

Marenzio moved to Rome in about 1574 and served cardinals and other wealthy patrons (including Luigi d'Este) until 1586. During these years he published extensively. He briefly served Ferdinando de' Medici in Florence, where in 1589 he composed intermedi for the ducal wedding festivities. He returned to Rome later that year, when he entered Cardinal Cinzio Aldobrandini's service; he held a Vatican apartment in 1594. In 1595-96 he visited the Polish court, returning to Rome in 1598.

Marenzio published over 400 madrigals and villanellas in at least 23 books (1580-99). They long remained popular in Italy and elsewhere, especially England. His motets also feature much verbal imagery and religious symbolism.

Madrigals

Madrigals – Book 1: Così moriro i fortunati amanti;   Ⓟ
Deh rinforzate il vostro pianto; Dolorosi martir, fieri
tormenti; Frenò Tirsi il desio; Liquide perle Amor da

gl'occhi sparse; Per duo coralli ardenti; Tirsi morir volea; Book 2: Là dove sono i pargoletti Amori; E s'io doglio, Amor; Fuggi speme mia, fuggi; Vaghi e lieti fanciulli; Book 4: Caro Aminta pur voi; Donne il celeste lume; Nè fero sdegno mai donna mi mosse; Non può Filli più; Book 5: Basciami mille volte; Consumando mi vo di piaggia in piaggia; Book 6: O-verdi selv'o dolci fonti o rivi; Udite, lagrimosi; Book 7: Cruda Amarilli; Ma grideran per me le piagge; Book-9: Cosí nel mio parlar; Et ella ancide, e-non val c'huom si chiuda **Philips** Tirsi morir volea **Terzi** Intavolatura di liuto, libro primo – Liquide perle Amor, da gl'occhi sparse

Il Concerto Italiano / Rinaldo Alessandrini hpd
Opus111 OP30245 (74' · DDD)   ⓟ**❍❍❍**

Ⓖ Marenzio's music was known throughout Europe during his lifetime; its success was based on what one contemporary identified as its 'new, fresh style, pleasing to the ear, with some simple counterpoint and without excessive artifice', a characterisation that applies more to the earlier books than to the late ones. It's this style which lies at the heart of Rinaldo Alessandrini's selection (though there are plenty of pieces from the later books as well), and the performances nicely capture its essential spirit, its communicability and transparent craftmanship occasionally disturbed (as in 'Dolorosi martir') by more serious intent. These beautifully paced and architecturally controlled performances, many of which make intelligent and appropriate use of added continuo instruments, present the most persuasive argument for understanding the reasons for Marenzio's enormous reputation, throughout Italy and beyond, at the start of the 1580s. Highly recommended.

John Marsh   English 1752-1828

The most important of Marsh's extant compositions, the Eight Favorite Symphonies published between 1784 and 1800, reveal a composer well-versed in the requirements of the mixed professional and amateur provincial orchestras he encountered. Concertante parts for more able players are judiciously juxtaposed with easier tutti writing, and in a work like the Conversation Sinfonie, for two orchestras, composed in 1778, Marsh also shows a keen awareness of orchestral colour, disposing his two groups so as to pit high instruments against low.

Symphonies

Symphonies – No 2; No 6; No 7, 'La Chasse'; No 8. A Conversation Symphony
London Mozart Players / Matthias Bamert
Chandos CHAN10458 (64' · DDD)   ⓟⒽ➔

Though Marsh's invention can be banal and short-breathed, there is an indefinable quality of robust Englishness to many of his melodies. Several movements have a distinct whiff of Han-del, especially the catchy country-dance finale of No 8, with its piquant changes of instrumental colouring (shades here of the *Water Music*). There are rollicking Handelian fanfares, too, in the first movement and minuet of the most ambitious and massively scored symphony, No 6, though Marsh's acknowledged inspiration here was Haydn's late symphonies. The 'London Bach', Johann Christian, is another unmissable influence, above all in the *Conversation Symphony*, an original take on Bach's symphonies for double orchestra.

As ever in their 'Contemporaries of Mozart' series, Matthias Bamert and the LMP give carefully prepared, well-paced performances, rhythmically lively without falling into autopilot, and balancing polish with a down-to-earth directness crucial to Marsh's music. Among a clutch of expert soloists, the horns deserve a tip of the hat for their brave braying in the brief 'hunting' symphony, No 7. The recording has an attractive bloom. A modestly pleasing curio, recommended to anyone who likes to venture down 18th-century symphonic byways.

Frank Martin   Swiss 1890-1974

Martin, the son of a Calvinist minister, studied mathematics and physics at the University of Geneva for two years, working on composition and studying piano on the side. From 1918 to 1926, he lived in Zürich, Rome, and Paris. The compositions of this period show him searching for his own musical language and adopting Schoenbergian serialism while retaining an extended tonal harmony that looked to Debussy. The Petite symphonie concertante (which made Martin's international reputation) is the best known of his orchestral works.

In 1946 he moved to the Netherlands; he also taught at the Cologne Musikhochschule. His later works include the operas Der Sturm and Monsieur de Pourceaugnac, a large-scale Requiem and many concertante pieces.

Cello Concerto

Cello Concerto[a]. Ballade[b]. Eight Preludes[c]
[ab]**Christian Poltéra** vc [bc]**Kathryn Stott** pf
[a]**Malmö Symphony Orchestra /**
Tuomas Ollila-Hannikainen
BIS BIS-CD1637 (66' · DDD)   Ⓕ

Frank Martin's Cello Concerto, so eloquently and sensitively played here, is a real discovery. It is no exaggeration to state that this rapt performance presents this noble concerto with an inspirational intensity to compare with the celebrated Du Pré/Barbirolli recording of the Elgar Concerto. The works share a similar deep, poignant, meditative feeling, although Martin's concerto also has a distinct valedictory character, expressive melancholy which suggests personal loss.

The soloist opens with a gloriously lyrical theme which is to dominate the movement (commentators have likened it to Vaughan Williams). A skittish development is in tarantella rhythm with bolder clashes of angry dissonance but at the close comes the balm of the return of the ravishing opening material. Unexpectedly, the touching central *Adagietto* is in the form of a passacaglia. This sadness is all but dispelled in the brilliantly rhythmic finale, yet the lyricism creeps back and even the tarantella returns briefly before the close.

The (much earlier) *Ballade* is a free fantasia-like dialogue between cello and piano, Kathryn Stott and Christian Poltéra enjoying a perfect partnership. Martin dallied with Schoenberg's 12-note system and he uses it in the Eight Preludes. But he had no intention of giving up tonality, and the result is a stunning set of great variety and resource, thrillingly played by Stott.

This disc, given state-of-the-art recording, makes an ideal introduction to Martin's music.

Mass for Double Choir

Martin Mass for Double Choir. Passaille[a]
Pizzetti Messa di requiem. De profundis
Westminster Cathedral Choir /
James O'Donnell [a]org
Hyperion CDA67017 (71' · DDD · T/t)   Ⓕ❶❶❶

 These are magnificent performances. Written in 1922, the *Agnus Dei* being added four years later, the Mass is one of Martin's most sublime compositions. Surprisingly it gains enormously from using boys' rather than female voices. It's a measure of James O'Donnell's achievement with Westminster Cathedral Choir that the gain in purity and beauty is never at the expense of depth and fervour. This is an altogether moving and eloquent performance, often quite thrilling and always satisfying.

This disc brings us a fine performance by O'Donnell of the *Passacaille* and the Pizzetti *Messa di Requiem*, also composed in 1922. The received wisdom is that it is in his *a cappella* music that Pizzetti is at his finest; in his 1951 monograph Guido Gatti spoke of his setting as 'the most serene and lyrical of all...from Mozart's to Gabriel Fauré's'. Serene and lyrical it most certainly is, and it will come as a revelation to those encountering it for the first time. There is a fervour and a conviction about the Westminster performances of both the Requiem and the 1937 *De profundis*. The luminous tone this choir produce in both these inspired and masterly works will ring in your ears long after you have finished playing this splendidly recorded disc.

Golgotha

Golgotha
Judith Gauthier *sop* **Marianne Beate Kielland** *contr*
Adrian Thompson *ten* **Mattijs van de Woerd** *bar*

Konstantin Wolff *bass* **Cappella Amsterdam;**
Estonian Philharmonic Chamber Choir; Estonian
National Symphony Orchestra / Daniel Reuss
Harmonia Mundi ② HMC90 2056/7
(94' · DDD · T/t)   Ⓕ❶❶Ⓑ

Martin's oratorio *Golgotha* has been well represented on CD recently despite its being a rarity in concert programmes. This splendid new studio recording (made in Tallinn in April 2009) will win many new devotees to one of the most important choral works of the 20th century.

The inspiration for this sturdy music drama was Rembrandt's 1653 etching *The Three Crosses*. Golgotha was composed between 1945 and 1948 after Martin's 1944 oratorio *In terra pax*. It is arranged in 10 musical tableaux lasting an hour and a half. Martin uses text from the Gospels to relate the Biblical narrative, while interweaving selections from the *Meditations of St Augustine* to help reveal the mystery of the Resurrection and to guide the listener's spiritual path. Martin's idiom is overtly post-Romantic and frequently cinematic in its treatment of the Calvary story. The spirit of Bach hovers benignly over the polyphony; Poulenc, too, springs to mind and Martin's word-setting owes much to the lyrical legacy of Debussy, particularly *Pelléas et Mélisande*. Martin's harmonic language is easily assimilated and his orchestration is opaque and luminous.

The quintet of soloists sounds at ease with the demanding roles. Jesus's words are sung with warmth and sensitivity by Mattijs van de Woerd. Konstantin Wolff is on top form. Adrian Thompson's more passionate tenor outbursts can become rather wide of bleat but his French is admirable. Marianne Beate Kielland's intonation suffers at the top of her range and her diction could have been clearer; but these are minor caveats.

The two choirs make light work of Martin's demanding part-writing. Given his long post-war domicile in Holland it is fitting that a Dutch choir should be involved in this recording. The orchestral contribution is polished and nuanced. The organ part is given its rightful prominence and the piano adds punch and a period charm, especially in the *secco* recitatives. Daniel Reuss maintains a tight grip on the unfolding drama. His isn't the quickest performance on record but there is such an obvious intensity and love of this extraordinary piece that it never feels as though it is dragging.

Harmonia Mundi's documentation is excellent and the engineering is top-class. A revelatory recording.

Maria-Triptychon

Passacaglia[ab]. Polyptyque[b]. Maria-Triptychon.
[a]**Juliane Banse** *sop* [b]**Muriel Cantoreggi** *vn*
German Radio Philharmonic Orchestra /
Christoph Poppen
ECM New Series 173 3930 (58' · DDD)   Ⓕ

Polyptyque is one of Martin's most impressive scores, with its impassioned lyricism held, as if in liquid suspension, by the cooler instrumental textures of solo violin and double string orchestra and the inner drama of its sequence of depictions from the Passion story. The alternating fast and slow movements cover by turns Christ's entry into Jerusalem (listen to the seething string textures representing the palm-waving crowd), the Last Supper, Judas, Gethsemane, Christ's scourging and – rather than Calvary – his glorification.

There is a link to the *Maria-Triptychon* (1967-68) through the latter's finale, a setting of the 'Stabat mater dolorosa'. This triptych for soprano, violin and orchestra was written for the husband-and-wife duo of Wolfgang Schneiderhan and Irmgard Seefried, and opens with dovetailed settings of the *Ave Maria* and *Magnificat*, the latter forming an impressive, intense climax (ECM does not provide the texts in the booklet). Unlike *Polyptyque*, however, *Maria-Triptychon* is a work that needs concentrated listening to secure its full impression.

The *Passacaglia* Martin wrote in 1944 for organ and orchestrated richly 18 years later has become one of his better-known works. Here, his devotion to Bach's music is made manifest in sound with organ-like sonorities surviving the transcription and a gripping Busonian power. Poppen directs hugely impressive performances from his excellent soloists and orchestra. ECM's sound is, as usual, crystal clear and superb. A winner.

Le vin herbé

Le vin herbé
Sandrine Piau sop **Steve Davislim** ten **Jutta Böhnert** sop **Berlin RIAS Chamber Choir; Scharoun Ensemble / Daniel Reuss**
Harmonia Mundi Ⓕ ② HMC90 1935/6
(112' · DDD · T/t)   Ⓕ**OO⊞**

Scored for 12 voices, piano and string septet, Frank Martin's setting of the legend of Tristan and Isolde, with its very understated emotions, sparse texture and deliberately limited harmonic vocabulary, has enjoyed a somewhat chequered history on record.

The RIAS Chamber Choir bring rather more than 12 voices to this recording – including the eight principal solo roles, there are a total of 29 singers listed – but, unquestionably, they preserve the intimacy and directness of expression which is so essential in any performance of *Le vin herbé*. It is clearly not to enrich the overall body of sound that Daniel Reuss has brought in so many voices, but he has clearly selected them, both in ensemble and solo, with painstaking care to underline the essential character of each of the individual tableaux, and even at the most climactic moments, there are never more than a handful singing together.

Such an approach pays remarkable dividends in that it allows the three main sections of the work to focus more clearly on their very differ-

ent specific human characteristics. In the first, 'The Love Potion', while their love may have been chemically induced, there is no doubting the sense of mutual affection and respect with which the calm stateliness of Steve Davislim and the unaffected poise of Sandrine Piau portray Tristan and Isolde. The second, 'The Forest of Morois', deals with compassion and forgiveness and Jonathan de la Paz Zaens's portrayal of King Mark exudes profound goodness in a way which sheds a totally new light on the word 'kingly'. The third, 'Death', covers jealousy and reconciliation and Hildegard Wiedemann is utterly convincing in the somewhat difficult role of the vaguely treacherous Isolde of the White Hands.

Alongside all this runs a beautifully crafted instrumental accompaniment, far more involved in the drama than the booklet-notes imply by suggesting that it is 'like the scenery in a play'. There is immense sensitivity in the way the individual members of the Scharoun Ensemble handle the amazingly fluid instrumental textures, the very understatedness of which drives the fundamental message home far more powerfully than a whole plethora of dramatic orchestral gestures. Driven along with a powerful sense of urgency by Reuss, this is an intense and deeply moving performance which, complete with lavish packaging and a superlative recorded sound, brings to the catalogue something which it has never had before; a really first-rate and compelling performance of this most important of Martin's scores.

Bohuslav Martinů   Bohemian 1890-1959

Martinů studied at the Prague Conservatory (1906-10), then worked as an orchestral violinist (in the Czech Philharmonic) before going to Paris in 1923. There he studied with Roussel and developed a neo-classical style, sometimes using jazz. This was also the period of his fantasy opera Julietta (1938) and of numerous concertos. In 1940 he left Paris, and the next year arrived in New York, where he concentrated on orchestral and chamber works, including his first five symphonies. From 1948 his life was divided between Europe and the USA. He was one of the most prolific composers of the 20th century, imaginative in style, with energetic rhythms and powerful, often dissonant harmony, but uneven in quality.

Concertos

Duo concertante for Two Violins and Orchestra, H264[a]. Concerto for Two Violins, H329[b]. Concerto for Flute, Violin and Orchestra, H252[c]
[c]**Janne Thomsen** fl [abc]**Bohuslav Matoušek**, [a]**Régis Pasquier**, [b]**Jennifer Koh** vns **Czech Philharmonic Orchestra / Christopher Hogwood**
Hyperion CDA67671 (55' · DDD)   Ⓕ⊞

Written in Martinů's best 1930s concerto grosso style, the *Duo concertante*'s   three movements (fast-slow-fast) are limpidly scored, allowing the flowing, interweaving lines of the soloists to sound to best advantage; as the excellent booklet-notes say, 'an extraordinary musical experience'.

For this equally vibrant recording, Régis Pasquier partners Bohuslav Matoušek while Jennifer Koh appears with Matoušek in the Concerto in D major (1950). Unlike its predecessor, the later work is in the standard 19th-century concerto format – one reason why Martinů did not number the works – and structurally quite different. For one thing, there is no real slow movement, the central span (dovetailed into the finale) being moderate in pace with a *più vivo* central section. In atmosphere it is one of those fleet-footed yet serene works in which Martinů's inspiration seems just to beam from ear to ear.

This first volume in a series of four devoted to Martinů's *concertante* works for violin is completed by another enchanting early double concerto, for flute and violin, penned in just 10 days in 1936. There is no hint of rush in its fresh and lively invention, the solo roles played with beguiling ease by Janne Thomsen and Matoušek. Accompanied by the Czech Philharmonic – in whose second violin section the composer played in the 1920s – this disc is an utter delight from start to finish.

Concerto for Violin, Piano and Orchestra, H342. Concerto da camera, H285[a]. Czech Rhapsody, H307 (arr Teml)
Bohuslav Matoušek vn [a]**Karel Košárek** pf **Czech Philharmonic Orchestra / Christopher Hogwood**
Hyperion CDA67672 (65' · DDD)   Ⓟ Ⓓ➔

Hogwood and Hyperion here focus on the concertos for violin with piano. In the *Concerto da camera* (1941), the keyboard is part – albeit a prominent one – of the strings-and-percussion accompaniment. Commissioned by Paul Sacher for the leader of his Basle Chamber Orchestra, it was premiered to great success in Switzerland (Martinů having just started his American exile at the time). With its fresh invention and lively demeanour, it remains one of his more popular concertos although it has never received its due on disc. This newcomer sets that omission straight, however, crisply performed and immaculately recorded.

The same applies to its companion pieces. H342 (1952-53) is a true duo concerto, outwardly conventional in format but expressively complex, as Aleš Březina notes in the booklet: 'Enigmatic and highly personal...structurally driven by its emotional nature, [and] probably echoes the crisis in the composer's personal life.' Musically, the work feels like an accompanied sonata for piano and violin with each soloist supporting and occupying the forefront by turns and the orchestra – which enjoys its own 'solo' passages – providing an additional dimension to the discourse.

The disc concludes with Jiří Teml's idiomatic orchestration of the *Czech Rhapsody* (1945), written for Kreisler and intended to be accom-

panied orchestrally; for various reasons the final version was never completed. Premiered by Régis Pasquier in 2001, it is a splendid piece, warm and lyrical and beautifully played. Strongly recommended.

Violin Concertos – No 1, H226a; No 2, H293
Bohuslav Matoušek vn **Czech Philharmonic Orchestra / Christopher Hogwood**
Hyperion CDA67674 (54' · DDD)   Ⓕ Ⓞ Ⓞ ➔

Martinů's two violin concertos have very different histories. The First was created for Dushkin in 1931, much tinkered with over the next few years and then 'lost' until unearthed in 1968. The Second (1943) was written in just two months for Mischa Elman, premiered before the year was out and taken up by several violinists soon afterwards, often being programmed unnumbered until its predecessor came to light.

Josef Suk set the benchmark for both but his recordings, still in the Supraphon catalogue, have been overtaken by this newcomer and, in No 2, by Isabelle Faust's superb recent account (see below). Matoušek and Hogwood certainly have the measure of both scores and in the Second run Faust and Bělohlávek close. Couplings may prove decisive; one recommendation is for the Hyperion set as a whole. Strongly recommended.

Violin Concerto No 2, H293[a]. Toccata e due canzoni, H311[b]. Serenade No 2, H216
[a]**Isabelle Faust** vn [b]**Cédric Tiberghien** pf **Prague Philharmonia / Jiří Bělohlávek**
Harmonia Mundi HMC90 1951 (63' · DDD)   Ⓟ Ⓓ➔

Hot on the heels of Hyperion's series of Martinů's works for violin and orchestra (see above) comes this brilliant new account of the Second Concerto (1943), played with verve and a real feeling for the idiom by Isabelle Faust. What a fine player of the modern repertoire she is and her sweet, precise tone allows Martinů's angular lyricism – or is that lyrical angularity? – to open out for maximum appeal. Superbly supported by the Prague Philharmonia under Bělohlávek, this is as brilliantly played an account as has appeared on disc.

Orchestra and conductor are heard to excellent effect in the other major work, the *Toccata e due canzoni* (1946). Written for Paul Sacher, this invigorating cross between chamber symphony and concerto grosso (though with an extensive piano part, played with nicely suggestive power by Cédric Tiberghien) is both a product of its time – catching the relief, horror and war-weariness in equal measure – and a timeless classic. Yet through its many dramatic moments Martinů's radiant humanism, overtly displayed in the Concerto, shines through. Despite some slight scratchiness of ensemble and tuning in the upper strings in the opening pages, this is a strong performance, taut and purposeful. Sandwiched between the two is the delightful Second

Serenade (1932), scored for string orchestra and inhabiting the joyful folk world of the ballet *Palíček*. Thrown off with élan, music and performance spotlight the splendid engineering that is an unobtrusive delight of this excellent disc. Recommended.

Cello Concertos – No 1, H196; No 2, H304.
Concertino, H143
Raphael Wallfisch vc
Czech Philharmonic Orchestra / Jiří Bělohlávek
Chandos CHAN10547X (76' · DDD)   Ⓜ️Ⓞ🅳➔

The performance history of Martinů's concertos is a chequered affair, with many works not reaching the concert platform in his lifetime. The three cello concertos here provide a typical sample. The neo-Stravinskian Concertino (1924), composed for Maurits Frank, was not played until 1949, ironically in Prague with the composer in exile, while the Second Concerto (1944-45) was not performed until six years after Martinů's death. The First, by contrast, enjoyed three premieres since it went through three separate versions and with what an array of soloists: Gaspar Cassadó (1931), Pierre Fournier (1939) and Miloš Sádlo (1956).

It is perhaps no surprise that the First Concerto has proved to be one of his more popular creations, full of vigorous and attractive music, beautifully poised as the best of his works are. The single-movement Concertino sacrifices poise for energy, perhaps, but proves winning with its combination of vim and lyricism while the Second Concerto, a fine example of his late style, somehow eludes the appeal of its predecessor. Recorded in 1991, Wallfisch's consummate virtuosity and considerable lyrical gifts illuminate Martinů's solo writing like no other. There have been a variety of other recordings of these works, but this – one of Wallfisch's finest discs – remains the best available, especially with Chandos's excellent sound.

Piano Concertos[a] – No 2, H237; No 4, 'Incantation', H358. Overture, H345. Les fresques de Piero della Francesca, H352.
[a]**Robert Kolinsky** pf
Basle Symphony Orchestra / Vladimir Ashkenazy
Ondine ODE1158-2 (66' · DDD)   ⒻⓄ🅳➔

Martinů composed *Les fresques de Piero della Francesca* in 1955 in tribute to the luminous frescoes of the Italian master in the church of San Francesco in Arezzo and responded with a score of impressionist colour and intensity, its sound world utterly different from the Sixth Symphony, *Fantaisies symphoniques*, that preceded it by only a couple of years. Ashkenazy has not previously revealed his hand as a Martinů interpreter, but he responds to its rich and radiant atmosphere with a reading of real verve.

It separates two of the finest Martinů concerto performances to have come along for some time. Robert Kolinsky has the measure of these works

both technically and emotionally, both the Parisian neo-classical chic of No 2 (1934) and the rawer, elemental power of No 4, *Incantation* (1956). In terms of durations, he is not so different from competitors past and present but internally the tempi are often more varied, fresher and more alive – which is just what these new accounts are.

Ashkenazy starts with a bracing, lithe-limbed account of the 1953 Overture, with its *concerto grosso*-style group of soloists. Ondine's recording comes into its own in detailing with superb lightness and precision the nuances of Martinů's scoring, a feature present throughout. The Basle Symphony Orchestra play superbly. Thoroughly recommended.

Piano Concertos – No 3, H316; No 5, 'Fantasia concertante', H366. Piano Concertino, H269
Giorgio Koukl pf **Bohuslav Martinů Philharmonic Orchestra, Zlín / Arthur Fagen**
Naxos 8 572206 (78' · DDD)   Ⓢ Ⓞ🅳➔

Martinů's piano concertos have tended to be overshadowed by those for other instruments, not least for violin and cello. None of the three works here ranks, perhaps, in the top flight of the composer's output but they are all firmly in the next rung down and all should be better known. No 3, with its occasional flashes of Brahmsian or even late-Mozartian sonorities, has never sounded lighter or more vivacious than here. One is constantly thrilled by the sheer vivacity – and virtuosity – of Koukl's playing. In the Fifth, which has often sounded mechanical in previous recordings, the music leaps off the page. The finale in particular is hugely enjoyable.

No less impressive is the account of the bracing Concertino, a product of the composer's full pre-war maturity. Its slighter dimensions perhaps justify the title but not its often serious demeanour; yet the music smiles throughout. Koukl receives splendid support from the Bohuslav Martinů Philharmonic Orchestra of Zlín under Arthur Fagen and Naxos's sound is first rate, clear and bright with the right balance between soloist and orchestra. Warmly recommended.

Additional recommendation

Oboe Concerto
Coupled with **R Strauss** Oboe Concerto
BA Zimmermann Oboe Concerto
Schilli ob **BRSO / Jansons**
Oehms Classics OC737 (55' · DDD)   ⒻⓄ
The almost voluptuously lyrical opening movement of the Martinů's Concerto (1955) immediately demonstrates the folksy undertones of the appealing melodic invention, with the vitality of the rhythmic *tuttis* sharpened by an important piano contribution. All three works are superbly played here by the brilliantly nimble Stefan Schilli, and Mariss Jansons and the Bavarian orchestra give him vivid support.

Symphonies

Symphonies Nos 1 & 2
Bamberg Symphony Orchestra / Neeme Järvi
BIS BIS-CD362 (61' · DDD)   ⓕⒹ⟩

Symphonies Nos 3 & 4
Bamberg Symphony Orchestra / Neeme Järvi
BIS BIS-CD363 (63' · DDD)   ⓕⒹ⟩

Symphonies Nos 5 & 6
Bamberg Symphony Orchestra / Neeme Järvi
BIS BIS-CD402 (59' · DDD)   ⓕⓄⒹ⟩

Despite his travels throughout his formative years as a composer, Martinů remained a quintessentially Czech composer and his music is imbued with the melodic shapes and rhythms of the folk music of his homeland. The six symphonies were written during Martinů's America years and in all of them he uses a large orchestra with distinctive groupings of instruments which give them a very personal and unmistakable timbre. The rhythmic verve of his highly syncopated fast movements is very infectious, indeed unforgettable, and his slow movements are often deeply expressive, most potently, perhaps, in that of the Third Symphony which is imbued with the tragedy of war. The Bamberg orchestra plays marvellously and with great verve for Järvi, whose excellently judged tempi help propel the music forward most effectively. His understanding of the thrust of Martinů's structures is impressive and he projects the music with clarity. The recordings are beautifully clear, with plenty of ambience surrounding the orchestra, a fine sense of scale and effortless handling of the wide dynamic range Martinů calls for. It's enthusiastically recommended.

Symphonies Nos 3 & 4
Czech Philharmonic Orchestra / Jiří Bělohlávek
Supraphon SU3631-2 (63' · DDD)   ⓕⓄⓄⒹ⟩

This is Jiří Bělohlávek's third recording of Martinů's life-enhancing Fourth Symphony (1945) and his second with the Czech Philharmonic. Both those predecessors possess considerable merits but must now yield to this newcomer. Not only is the orchestral playing in the luxury class, but Bělohlávek's reading is as shapely as it's involving. He masterminds a selfless and unforced ccount of the Third (1944), an altogether more troubled work than its successor, and whose homesick undertow is potently realised here (the heart-rending closing pages are precisely that). Bělohlávek's, too, is a meticulously prepared performance of compassion and insight that does justice to a riveting work. Throughout, the inimitable, silvery sonority of this great orchestra has been admirably captured by the Supraphon engineers.

Symphony No 4. Memorial to Lidice. Field Mass[a]
[a]**Ivan Kusnjer** bar **Czech Philharmonic** [a]**Chorus and**

Orchestra / Jiří Bělohlávek
Chandos CHAN9138 (65' · DDD · T/t)   ⓕⓄⒹ⟩

The luscious, intricately scored pages of the big-hearted Fourth Symphony sound opulent in this recording. For the most part, the playing is glorious, intoxicating in its richness and sure-footed poise. But there's some lack of intensity and temperament, so, for a more considered Bělohlávek account, look to his more recent Supraphon disc, reviewed above.

His performance of the *Field Mass*, on the other hand, is an undoubted success. It's wonderfully fervent, boasting a noble-toned, impassioned contribution from the baritone, Ivan Kusnjer, and disciplined, sonorous work from the men of the Czech Philharmonic Chorus. Chandos's recording captures it all to perfection: blend and focus impeccably combined. The moving *Memorial to Lidice* completes this ideally chosen triptych. Bearing a dedication 'To the Memory of the Innocent Victims of Lidice', Martinů's score was written in response to the destruction of that village by the Nazis in June 1942. One of the composer's most deeply felt creations, this is an eight-minute orchestral essay of slumbering power, incorporating at its climax a spine-chilling quotation from Beethoven's Fifth. It, too, receives sensitive advocacy here.

Symphonies Nos 5 and 6, 'Fantaisies symphoniques'
Czech Philharmonic Orchestra / Jiří Bělohlávek
Supraphon SU4007-2 (58' · DDD)   ⓕⓄⓄⒹ⟩

Martinů's final two symphonies inhabit radically different sound worlds to each other, the Fifth more outwardly abstract – although there is no doubting the unalloyed joy achieved at the finale's climax – while the Sixth, as its subtitle suggests, explores deep veins of fantasy. The performances are rather unalike as well, even though both were recorded in Prague's wonderful Rudolfinum, No 5 live at the 2007 Martinů Festival while No 6 followed in 2009 without an audience.

Both works are splendidly rendered with No 5 best of all, a vivid interpretation benefiting from the buzz of a live performance. Bělohlávek gets the balance in the tricky finale just right, letting the mood progression of sadness-joy-determination flow organically and logically. Much as one loves Nos 4 and 6, this is the type of performance that convinces me that the Fifth is the greatest of the symphonies. By comparison, No 6, fantastical though it is, seems a mite deliberate and clinical. A richly rewarding disc.

Chamber Works

Piano Quartet[a]. Quartet for Oboe, Violin, Cello and Piano[b]. Viola Sonata[c]. String Quintet[d]
[b]**Joel Marangella** ob [a]**Isabelle van Keulen,**
[bd]**Charmian Gadd**, [d]**Solomia Soroka** vns
[acd]**Rainer Moog**, [d]**Theodore Kuchar** vas
[ad]**Young-Chang Cho**, [b]**Alexander Ivashkin** vcs
[ac]**Daniel Adni**, [b]**Kathryn Selby** pfs
Naxos 8 553916 (73' · DDD)   ⓈⒹ⟩

The Quartet for oboe, violin, cello and piano is a highly attractive piece in the busy yet unfussy neo-classical style that Martinů made so much his own. Its opening theme is quite captivating, but all three movements have charm. The other music is hardly less delightful. The Viola Sonata is an eloquent work from the mid-1950s, composed three years after the *Rhapsody-Concerto* for the same instrument and orchestra. These were vintage years in Martinů's creativity. The String Quintet is the earliest work, dating from his Paris years, and shows the influence of Roussel. Although the first movement is perhaps not top-drawer Martinů, the slow movement is most imaginative. The performances are often touched with distinction and are never less than eminently serviceable. Adni could perhaps be a little more supple in the Piano Quartet of 1942 though in general he plays with spirit. There's plenty of air round the players and the recording is lifelike and well balanced.

Duo No 2, H371[a]. Piano Quartet[b]. Piano Trio No 3, H332[c]. Oboe Quartet, H315[d]
[b]**Schubert Ensemble** ([ad]Simon Blendis vn
Douglas Paterson va [acd]Jane Salmon vc [cd]William
Howard pf) with [d]**George Caird** ob
Chandos CHAN10551 (67' · DDD)   Ⓕ🄳➔

Martinů was a natural – if often unconventional – chamber composer. One of the few 20th-century composers to tackle the piano trio as a form at all, let alone convincingly or repeatedly, the Third and last (and best) concludes the Schubert Ensemble of London's programme. An even finer work, the Piano Quartet of 1942, opens proceedings, with the lighter, less well known Quartet for oboe, violin, cello and piano (1947) and Second Duo (1958; No 1 had appeared in 1927) more than mere makeweights at the centre.

The 1947 Quartet and Duo are slight only in their dimensions (both under 12 minutes in length). The former's engaging compound-form finale – telescoping slow movement, interlude and finale – offsets the genial opening span to perfection. The Duo is outwardly more traditional in three movements but the liveliness of the composer's relaxed invention (albeit with a touch of sombreness in the central *Adagio*) is never less than quirky. The same stylistic elements recur in the larger public utterances of the Piano Quartet, one of Martinů's finest works, and Trio, but no matter how high-minded their intent, the music still smiles throughout as only Martinů's music does.

The Schubert Ensemble's performances are first-rate, partnered marvellously by George Caird in the 1947 Quartet. Another huge bonus of this new disc is the Chandos sound, typically warm and spacious in the best traditions of the label. Martinů's instrumental writing, being usually quite angular, can often lose its innate lyricism in fierce recordings and acoustics but here it is allowed to bloom with unusual richness.

Piano Trios – No 1, 'Cinq Pièces brèves', H193; No 2, H327; No 3, H332. Bergerettes, H275
Kinsky Trio Prague (Lucie Sedláková Hůlová vn
Martin Sedlák vc Jaroslava Pěchočová pf)
Praga Digitals ⚊. PRD/DSD250 256 (67' · DDD/DSD)
                                                   Ⓕ◐

It is inaccurate to aver that only Ravel and Shostakovich – in his Second – convincingly essayed the piano trio after 1900: Martinů wrote four times for this combination, plus a concerto, works that blithely ignore the technical issues. True, Martinů's grappling with the full 'piano trio' genre did not come until 1950 with the D minor Second, with No 3 following a year later, but the marvellous *Cinq Pièces brèves*, later numbered as Trio No 1, came 20 years before. Why he opted to omit the sparkling *Bergerettes* (1939) from the sequence is unclear; perhaps it was just too illustrative. The Kinsky Trio catch the spirit of both early sets very neatly in performances of great charm and dexterity. In the *Bergerettes* they even manage convincingly to integrate the bold final *Moderato – Trio (poco allegretto)*.

The Second and Third Trios are relatively sombre creations for Martinů, in that there are lengthy passages of serious demeanour in their opening spans without the characteristic smile. This breaks through in good time, however, a feature nicely caught in these well-executed and enthusiastic performances. Praga's sound is spot on, the three instruments carefully but naturally balanced as a satisfying ensemble. Warmly recommended.

'Works for Violin and Piano, Volume 1'
Violin Sonatas – C, H120; D minor, H152; No 1, H182.
Concerto, H13. Elegy, H3. Impromptu, H166. Five
Short Pieces, H184.
Bohuslav Matoušek vn **Petr Adamec** pf
Supraphon ② SU3412-2 (121' · DDD)   Ⓕ◐

Supraphon's decision to present the music in more or less chronological order makes it all the easier to chart a fascinating stylistic journey spanning some 36 years. The 19-year-old Martinů wrote his impassioned *Elegy* in 1909, and the comparatively straightforward violin writing contrasts dramatically with the piano's big-boned, unashamedly dramatic contribution. Strangely, the following year's Concerto proves to be anything but. Indeed, one wonders whether its title was a leg-pull on the young composer's part, for its 27-minute progress totally eschews any ostentatious display in favour of a sunny simplicity and open-hearted playfulness. With the ambitious Sonata in C from 1919, we encounter an increasing confidence and fluency, though there's still little sign of the composer's mature voice. Matoušek and Adamec form a consistently stylish partnership, and the recordings are rich and airy to match. A truly notable achievement.

Cello Sonatas – No 1, H277; No 2, H286;
No 3, H340. Variations on a Slovak Theme, H378.

Variations on a Theme of Rossini, H290
Paul Watkins vc **Huw Watkins** pf
Chandos CHAN10602 (70' · DDD) Ⓕ⮞

The three sonatas (1939; 1941; 1952) and the two sets of variations are the primary works, few performers tackling the clutch of neo-classical pieces from the early 1930s. This new set boasts superior sound quality and – with one small cavil aside – is superb in terms of performance quality. The Watkins duo sound convincingly on Martinů's wavelength from the first bar of the First Sonata. Chandos's sound is wonderfully natural. Each work is projected with fervour, the one glitch being the rushed tempo at the start of No 3. The two sets of variations come off superbly too. An excellent disc and the best of the commercially available sets.

The Greek Passion

The Greek Passion
John Mitchinson ten Manolios **Helen Field** sop
Katerina **John Tomlinson** bass Grigoris **Jeffrey Lawton** ten Panait, Andonis **Arthur Davies** ten
Yannakos **Geoffrey Moses** bass Fotis **Rita Cullis** sop
Lenio **Phillip Joll** ten Kostandis **Catherine Savory** sop Nikolio **John Harris** ten Michelis **Michael Geliot** spkr Ladas **Jana Jonášová** sop Despinio **David Gwynne** bass Patriarcheas Archon **Kühn Children's Chorus; Prague Philharmonic Choir; Brno Philharmonic Orchestra / Sir Charles Mackerras**
Film director **Tomáš Simerda**
Supraphon 📀 SU7014-9
(93' · NTSC · 16:9 · PCM stereo and 5.1 · 0) Ⓕ

The story of Martinů's penultimate opera begins with a priest allotting roles in the local Passion play to various congregation members. When a group of refugees arrive begging land (their village having been sacked by the Turks) the would-be actors begin to assume the roles of their characters. Thus, after the priest rejects the refugees on the pretext that they carry cholera, Manolios, assigned to play Christ, directs them towards Mount Sarakina where there is room to spare, while the pedlar Yannakos, playing Peter, repents of a scheme to deprive the refugees of their valuables in exchange for essentials. Panait, allotted the role of Judas, is incensed by the change of heart of Katerina, playing Mary Magdalene, who is drawn into a close spiritual bond with Manolios, who rejects his fiancée, Lenio, who in turn becomes engaged to another. In the end, Manolios's identification with Christ and sympathy for the plight of the refugees becomes too much for the priest, who excommunicates him. In a confrontation outside the church, Manolios is killed by Panait and the Passion play ended.

Supraphon's film is not of a stage or even studio performance, but was made for Czech Television in 1999 as a kind of outside broadcast, set around a real stone-built village and church. The recording is that made in 1981 in Brno using the local orchestra and Czech choruses by

Sir Charles Mackerras with soloists from Welsh National Opera. The live actors, for the most part Czechs, mouth the English text very well, though differences in mime technique are at times striking.

The outdoor setting works remarkably well, centred on the village square, the church, various cottages and the hillside where the refugees attempt to eke out a new home. The recording still sounds sumptuous, the elision of certain segments has been done expertly and for those unfamiliar with Martinů's radiant score, this film – ending with the iconic image of the dead Manolios on the church steps, should prove a compelling and moving experience.

Julietta

Three Fragments from 'Julietta', H253a[a].
Suite from the opera 'Julietta', H253b
[a]**Michele Lagrange** sop [a]**Magdalena Kožená** mez
[a]**Steve Davislim** ten [a]**Alain Vernhes** bar
[a]**Frédéric Goncalves** bass-bar **Czech Philharmonic Orchestra / Sir Charles Mackerras**
Supraphon SU3994-2 (53' · DDD) Ⓕ🅞🅞⮞

Extracted by the composer in 1939 (two years after completing the opera), these three substantial excerpts were designed as a cantata or *Singspiel* for five singers with orchestra. Martinů hoped to use the cantata to secure a production of the opera in France to which end he set the text in French (unlike the Czech of the opera), thereby returning to the language of Neveux's original play. As it turned out, he was not successful.

At almost 21 and 12 minutes apiece, Martinů's first and last movements seem very substantial for fragments. While showcasing the marvellously lyrical writing for the operatic principals, the extract none the less remains true to the spirit of the original. Thus the surreal fifth scene from Act 2 opens out the expressive landscape after the long patchwork taken from the previous two scenes, while the final extract is essentially the Act 3 finale. Mackerras directs a wonderful performance and while Kožená sings the title-role beautifully she is in excellent company.

The Czech Philharmonic Orchestra play superbly throughout, not least in the sensible coupling of Zbyněk Vostřák's expert arrangement of three of *Julietta*'s orchestral episodes. Given Supraphon's top-notch sound and in the absence of a complete recording from these performers, this scintillating disc cannot be recommended highly enough.

Joseph Marx Austrian 1863-1945

He began composing in earnest at the age of 26 and within four years (1908-12) wrote around 120 songs. His name became known in Vienna, where in

1914 he was offered the post of professor of theory at the music academy (becaming its director). From 1931 to 1938 he was music critic for the Neues Wiener Journal and after the Second World War critic for the Wiener Zeitung. Later he brought out the Weltsprache Musik (Vienna, 1964), which deals with acoustics, tonality, aesthetics and musical philosophy.

Piano Works

Six Pieces for Piano. Herbst-Legende (Adagio). Carneval (Nachstück). Canzone. Die Flur der Engel
Tonya Lemoh pf
Chandos CHAN10479 (55' · DDD)　　　ⒻⓄ🄳

This intriguing recital shows Marx as a defiantly throwback composer often struggling to find his individual voice in a particularly turbulent musical period. Brahms's B minor and E flat Rhapsodies are surely the seeds allowed to germinate in the opening Rhapsody, the first of the Six Pieces (though it is more complex and demanding than either), and the fugue from the Prelude and Fugue is Reger-like, massive, daunting and strenuous. On the other hand, there is something oddly English about the love of fourths in the 'Albumblatt' – almost as if John Ireland had strayed into Vienna – and the Ballade, too, suggests a refugee from English pastoralism. There is something of York Bowen here (the Second Ballade?) though with a sprawling and improvisatory argument and an attempt to accommodate many (too many?) ideas. The 'Humoreske' presents a gnomic though grandly expansive dance.

Just when your ear is longing for less cloyingly rich textures, for greater simplicity and transparency, it is rewarded with four world-premiere recordings where Marx becomes less ambitious and more persuasive and confiding. Sample the 1916 Rhapsody and The Angel's Meadow, music lost in its own archaic world and sidestepping any easy or predictable resolutions. The performances of this very demanding programme by Tonya Lemoh are as powerful and eloquent as you could wish and she has been admirably recorded.

Orchestral Songs

Herbstchor an Pan[bc]. Barkarole[a]. Zigeuner[a]. Der bescheidene Schäfer[a]. Selige Nacht[a]. Sommerlied[a]. Marienlied[a]. Maienblüten[a]. Waldseligkeit[a]. Und gestern hat er mir Rosen gebracht[a]. Piemontesisches Volkslied[a]. Ständchen[a]. Hat dich die Liebe berührt[a]. Morgengesang[c]. Berghymne[c]. Ein Neujahrshymnus[c]
[a]**Christine Brewer** sop [b]**Trinity Boys' Choir**;
[c]**Apollo Voices**; **BBC Symphony** [c]**Chorus and Orchestra / Jiří Bělohlávek**
Chandos CHAN10505 (72' · DDD · T/t)　　Ⓕ🄳

The most substantial work in this selection of Joseph Marx's orchestral songs and choral pieces is the Herbstchor an Pan ('Autumn Hymn to Pan'), his first orchestral work (1911) but one

in which his easy mastery of a rich instrumental palette is already evident. His idiom was formed early and changed little: indeed, he had little sympathy with change, and notoriously failed to mention Schoenberg, Berg or even Hindemith when he brought out Weltsprache Musik, a book of aesthetics and philosophy, in the last year of his life, 1964.

It should be no surprise, then, to find that here is a rich, post-Wagnerian manner, luscious in harmony and sensuous in orchestration. Christine Brewer has the floating purity of voice to soar easily over Marx's beautifully judged textures in, for instance Selige Nacht and Maienblüten, both rapt in manner and unashamedly reflective, the latter suggesting the atmosphere of Strauss's Four Last Songs. Some similarity betwen Marx and Delius suggests that they had both moved away from Wagnerian harmony in comparable directions, influenced by a pantheistic response to nature: lovers of Delius's Sea Drift may appreciate the harmonic flavour and modulatory side-slips of the Herbstchor an Pan. It is in this vein that Marx seems at his most effective; the more exuberant songs sound rather laboured and their jollity contrived. Bělohlávek draws a suitably rich manner from the orchestra and gives Brewer loyal support with textures that are full but always lucid, and served well by the recording.

Pietro Mascagni　　　Italian 1863-1945

Like the composer of 'Pag' (Leoncavallo), the composer of 'Cav' was unable to repeat the success – or come anywhere near the inspiration – of Cavalleria rusticana, this most loved of all one-act operas. It's the epitome of Italian verismo opera, then a new style of opera in which the dramatic development is highly condensed and the action is based on stark realism rather than, say, legends and fairy-tales.

How did its first performance come about? By being one of three winners of a competition for one-act operas, an idea dreamt up by the publisher Sonzogno who would later also publish Leoncavallo's Pagliacci. So great was the opera's success that medals were struck in Mascagni's honour and the King of Italy bestowed upon him the Order of the Crown of Italy, an honour that even Verdi had to wait for until middle-age. His 16 other operas were, with the exception of L'amico Fritz (1891) not merely unsuccessful but in the case of Le Maschere booed off the stage before the final curtain in Genoa.

Latterly, Mascagni became an ardent supporter of Mussolini and Fascism, and most of his friends deserted him. Stripped of all his honours, his last days were spent in comparative poverty in a small hotel in Rome.

Cavalleria rusticana

Cavalleria rusticana
Renata Scotto sop Santuzza **Plácido Domingo** ten

MASCAGNI & LEONCAVALLO: 'CAV & PAG' – IN BRIEF

La Scala Chorus and Orchestra / Herbert von Karajan
DG 457 764-2GOR (Cav)　　　　Ⓜ️Ⓞ
DG 449 727-2GOR (Pag)　　　　Ⓜ️Ⓞ

Karajan and his La Scala forces bring a real feel of the theatre to these two much-loved works. Bergonzi, Panerai, Carlyle and Cossotto are on top form. And the Scala chorus are thrilling in the great choral numbers.

Philharmonia / Riccardo Muti
EMI 763650-2　　　　Ⓜ️

With Carreras at his most intense and Renata Scotto are her most moving, Muti's 'Pag' is very fine. Caballé is a fabulous Santuzza in 'Cav' – and the set has the luxury casting of Astrid Varnay as Mama Lucia.

La Scala Chorus and Orchestra / Tullio Serafin Ⓗ
EMI 556287-2　　　　Ⓜ️Ⓞ

This is Callas's show, though with Di Stefano and Gobbi on stage with her, you can be sure of some high-class drama. Serafin conducts with authority and passion.

National PO / Giuseppe Patanè
Decca 414 590-2DH2　　　　Ⓕ☐➡

Pavarotti and Freni, Varady and Cappuccilli – here's another dream-team. Actually it is Varady who steals the show with her passionate idiomatic singing – enough to make one lament her scarcity on record in Italian repertoire.

La Scala Chorus and Orchestra / Georges Prêtre
Philips 411 484-2PH (Pag)　　　　Ⓕ

Teresa Stratas sings opposite Domingo in a recording made as the soundtrack of a filmed version. But she really has to be seen for maximum effect. Domingo, as always, gives a totally committed performance, but is on better form for Levine.

National PO / James Levine
RCA 74321 39500-2 (Cav)　　　　Ⓕ Ⓞ ➡

Real sparks fly between Domingo's Turiddu and Scotto's Santuzza as they clash and her sense of remorse is palpable. Levine conducts with great sweep and subtlety.

La Scala Chorus and Orchestra / Franco Ghione
Nimbus NI7843/4 (Pag)　　　　Ⓗ
Pearl GEMMVD9288
Naxos 8 110258　　　　Ⓜ️/Ⓢ

Here are three of the numerous incarnations of Benjamino Gigli's 1935 interpretation of Canio. Even if this is not going to be your first choice, it deserves to be heard for the passion and beauty of his singing. The cast has a wonderfully idiomatic approach to this oh-so-Italian opera!

Turiddu **Pablo Elvira** bar Alfio **Isola Jones** mez Lola **Jean Kraft** mez Lucia **Ambrosian Opera Chorus; National Philharmonic Orchestra / James Levine**
RCA Red Seal 74321 39500-2 (71' · ADD · T/t) Recorded 1978　　　　Ⓕ Ⓞ ➡

This was a strong contender in an overcrowded field when it was first released. You'd be hard pressed to find either a more positive or a more intelligent Turiddu or Santuzza than Domingo or Scotto. Scotto manages to steer a precise course between being too lady-like or too melodramatic. She suggests all the remorse and sorrow of Santuzza's situation without resorting to self-pity. Her appeals to Turiddu to reform could hardly be more sincere and heartfelt, her throbbing delivery to Alfio, 'Turiddi mi tolse l'honore', expresses all her desperation when forced to betray her erstwhile lover, and her curse on Turiddu, 'A te la mala pasqua', while not resorting to the lowdown vigour of some of her rivals, is filled with venom. Domingo proved how committed he was to his role when the part was first given to him at Covent Garden in the mid-1970s. He gives an almost Caruso-like bite and attack to Turiddu's defiance and (later) remorse, and finds a more appropriate timbre than Bergonzi (for Karajan, reviewed under Leoncavallo). He also delivers the Brindisi with an appropriately carefree manner, oblivious of the challenge awaiting him. Pablo Elvira's Alfio is no more than adequate, and the other American support is indifferent.

Levine's direction, as positive as Karajan's, is yet quite different. He goes much faster, and time and again catches the passion if not always the delicacy of Mascagni's score. He's well supported by the superb NPO. With a bright and forward recording, this reading of the work is wholly arresting.

Mascagni Cavalleria rusticana (sung in English)　　Ⓗ
May Blyth sop Santuzza **Heddle Nash** ten Turiddu **Marjorie Parry** mez Lola **Justine Griffiths** contr Lucia **Harold Williams** bar Alfio **Chorus and Orchestra of the British National Opera Company / Aylmer Buesst**

Leoncavallo Pagliacci (sung in English)
Miriam Licette sop Nedda **Frank Mullings** ten Canio **Harold Williams** bar Tonio **Heddle Nash** ten Peppe **Dennis Noble** bar Silvio **Chorus and Orchestra of the British National Opera Company / Eugene Goossens**
Divine Art mono ② 27805 (112' · ADD · T) Both recorded in 1927　　　　Ⓜ️

As Andrew Rose, the man responsible for this transfer, points out, there was a period when Columbia records were known for their 'silent surfaces', and happily he has had access to early copies of the originals from this period. The clarity and immediacy of sound reveal performances which at best give pleasure by any standards and, at less than that, are fascinating as period documents.

In *Cav* the violin-playing does credit to nobody, yet this loose, slithery style must then have been acceptable, even 'authentic'. In *Pag* the male chorus sings with unabashed gusto in tones that (inaccurately no doubt) we tend to call 'beery'. Then the pronunciation is very much of its period, every 'r' rolled (as in 'charrm') and the 'I' sounds (Nash was a great one for this) shaded to 'Ae'. The translations represent the kind of thing the current 'Opera in English' series on Chandos is keen to avoid: a favourite is Nedda's beautifully enunciated 'For such a passion / The whip is the fashion'. But there's fine singing, and not only from Nash. Harold Williams, a little shy of the high notes, is splendidly firm and resonant in both operas. Miriam Licette is a very un-Italian Nedda but her 'take' of the high notes is distinctly that of a Marchesi pupil. Similarly, May Blyth is a lightweight Santuzza but still provides much to admire. Of Mullings's Canio, the throatiness and discomfort in the upper range are to some extent offset by a warmly personal timbre and intense dramatic commitment.

The *Pagliacci* also suffers from moments of distortion due to overloading on the originals. The *Cav* suffers from a somewhat hectic rush to get everything on to the 10-inch disc. And it is notable that the orchestra pulls up its metaphorical socks for Eugene Goossens.

MascagniCavalleria rusticana
Violeta Urmana *sop* Santuzza **Vincenzo La Scola** *ten* Turiddu **Dragana Jugovich** *mez* Lola **Viorica Cortez** *contr* Mamma Lucia **Marco Di Felice** *bar* Alfio

Leoncavallo Pagliacci
Vladimir Galouzine *ten* Canio **María Bayo** *sop* Nedda **Carlo Guelfi** *bar* Tonio **Antonio Gandia** *ten* Beppe **Ángel Ódena** *bar* Silvio

Chorus and Orchestra of the Teatro Real, Madrid / Jesús López-Cobos
Stage director **Giancarlo del Monaco**
Video director **Angel Luis Ramírez**
Opus Arte ② **DVD** OA0983D
(3h 21' · NTSC · 2.0 and DTS 5.1 · 0)
Recorded live in February and March 2007   Ⓕ

It is a genuine pleasure to welcome a new production of *Cav and Pag* that presents the contrasting tales of jealousy and infidelity with sincerity and dramatic flair. Giancarlo del Monaco and his designer, Johannes Leiacker, set *Cavalleria* in a stark townscape of white painted buildings and masonry, the black-clad Sicilian women silhouetted under the fierce sunlight. The Easter Hymn is made all the more tense by a parade of penitents dragging a cross. Violeta Urmana and Vincenzo La Scola are well paired as Santuzza and Turridu, their confrontation interrupted by the unusually attractive Lola of Dragana Jugovich. Marco di Felice conveys the terrible pain that Alfio feels on learning of his wife's affair – the fight between him and Turridu is played out onstage, the challenge taken up when a glass of wine is emptied on to the floor.

The great Viorica Cortez is a dignified Mamma Lucia. As Turridu's body is carried away at the end, the scene changes seamlessly into the opening of *Pagliacci* (the Prologue to which is sung from the stalls right at the start of the evening by Carlo Guelfi).

From the 1890s setting of *Cav* we have moved forward 50 years, and the travelling players arrive in a lorry, with posters for the show on the outside – the mood is a bit like Fellini's *La Strada*. From the outset, this *Pagliacci* becomes a really painful story to watch. María Bayo is superb as Nedda, tough and wilful, but trapped by the overbearing Canio of Vladimir Galouzine. His voice is very baritonal in quality, the high notes not always easily achieved, but what tremendous authority and passion he brings to the part; he really has it in him to become the leading dramatic tenor of our time. All the other parts are well cast and the crowd scenes are beautifully handled. Jesús López-Cobos leads the Madrid forces in a performance that could not easily be surpassed anywhere nowadays. Angel Luis Ramírez, deserves high praise for capturing Del Monaco's intense staging so well.

Additional recommendation

Cavalleria rusticana
Cossotto *sop* Santuzza **Bergonzi** *ten* Turiddu **Guelfi** *bar* Alfio **Martino** *mez* Lola **Ellegri** *mez* Lucia **Chorus and Orchestra of La Scala, Milan / Karajan**
DG The Originals 457 764-2GOR   Ⓜ▷▪

A truly red-blooded performance, masterfully controlled by Karajan who draws some fabulous playing from his Milan orchestra.

Jules Massenet   French 1842-1912

'To know Manon is to know Massenet,' said someone and it's true. It is an opera with wonderful melodies, a story that has strong emotions and a frisson of eroticism, and music that combines the sentimental lyricism of the French tradition (exemplified by Gounod) with the dramatic and orchestral advances of Wagner – but not too much. There had to be nothing too demanding to spoil a pleasant night out for the bourgeoisie.

Massenet was called disparagingly both 'la fille de Gounod' and 'Mademoiselle Wagner' by his critics (his music is rather feminine). Massenet was as shrewd a composer as he was an investor (the vast amounts of money he made were handled with the acumen of a sharp businessman). He was not interested in profundity or striking out into uncharted waters but in giving the public what they wanted, and in this he succeeded more than any French opera composer of the last part of the 19th century.

He had studied at the Paris Conservatoire with Ambroise Thomas, who was just about to become famous with his opera Mignon. An able pianist, he also won the coveted Prix de Rome in 1863 which led him to Italy for three years. Here he met Liszt who introduced him to the girl who would became his wife.

His first success as a composer came in 1872 but his methods did not endear him to his colleagues who saw in him a cynical opportunist, all too ready to sacrifice personal and musical ideals for commercial advantage. Rimsky-Korsakov called him 'a crafty fox' and even Massenet admitted to d'Indy that, in spite of the pseudo-religious oratorios and operas he was writing, 'I don't believe in all that creeping Jesus stuff, but the public likes it, and we must always agree with the public'.

Manon, based on the same short story by Abbé Prévost that Puccini would use nine years later for his Manon Lescaut, was an enormous hit (1884). He had to wait until 1892 for a comparable success with his masterpiece Werther. These two, of all the 27 operas that Massenet composed, are the only two survivors in the modern repertory.

Arias

Massenet Le Cid – Ah! tout est bien fini…O souverain. Grisélidis – Je suis l'oiseau. Le Mage – Ah! Parais ! Parais, astre de mon ciel[b]. Manon – Enfin, Manon…En fermant les yeux[a]; Je suis seul!…Ah! fuyez, douce image. Le roi de Lahore – Voix qui me remplissez d'une ineffable ivresse. Roma – Je vais la voir! Tout mon être frémit[b]. Werther – Lorsque l'enfant revient d'un voyage; Ah! bien souvent mon rêve s'envole…Pourquoi me réveiller
Gounod Faust – Quel trouble inconnu me pénètre!; Salut, demeure chaste et pure. Mireille – Mon cœur est plein d'un noir souci!; Anges du paradis. Polyeucte – Stances: Source délicieuse. La reine de Saba – Inspirez-moi, race divine. Roméo et Juliette – L'amour! l'amour; Salut! tombeau sombre
Rolando Villazón ten with [a]**Natalie Dessay** sop French Radio [b]**Chorus and Philharmonic Orchestra / Evelino Pidò**
Virgin Classics 545719-2 (67' · DDD · T/t) Ⓕ**ⓄⓄⓄ**Ɗ

This mostly well-planned and executed recital mixes favourites with extracts from operas that have remained rarities, even with the increased interest in late 19th-century repertory. It begins with Rodrigue's great prayer, 'O souverain' from Act 3 of *Le Cid*. Rolando Villazón sings this with an attractive quiet introspection to start with, but then there is metal and passion in his voice for the climax. Of the other well-known Massenet items, it's good to hear Werther's 'Lorsque l'enfant' as well as the show-stopping 'Pourquoi me réveiller?'. In 'En fermant les yeux' from *Manon*, Natalie Dessay provides Manon's brief phrases, and Villazón makes a really sensitive dreamer. 'Ah, fuyez' goes well too, but it will be the arias from *Roma*, *Grisélidis* and *Le Mage* that will attract most listeners. In all Massenet's output is there a more seductive tune than the one that forms the centre of the *Roma* scene, 'Soir admirable'? This is done very well by Warren Mok in the complete recording, but Villazón outshines him.

Of the Gounod arias, Faust's 'Salut demeure' fares the best, but again it will be the extracts

from *Polyeucte* and *La reine de Saba* that will please immediately.

Villazón has established himself as one of the most promising among the new generation of tenors. His French has improved recently, but there is the odd difficulty still with certain vowels. Accompaniment, recording and presentation are first-rate.

Manon

Massenet Manon[a] **Berlioz** Les nuits d'été, Op 7[b] Ⓗ
Debussy La damoiselle élue[c]
Victoria de los Angeles sop Manon [c]**Carol Smith** mez [a]**Henri Legay** ten Des Grieux [a]**Michel Dens** bar Lescaut [a]**Jean Borthayre** bass Comte des Grieux [a]**Jean Vieuille** bar De Brétigny [a]**René Hérent** ten Guillot [a]**Liliane Berton** sop Poussette [a]**Raymonde Notti** sop Javotte [a]**Marthe Serres** sop Rosette [c]**Radcliffe Choral Society; Boston Symphony Orchestra / Charles Munch;** [a]**Opéra-Comique Choir and Orchestra / Pierre Monteux**
Testament mono ③ SBT3203 (3h 33' · ADD · T/t)
Recorded in 1955 Ⓕ**ⓄⓄ**

Recorded in mono in 1955, the set fell at a unique point in the opera's history on disc. Previous recordings from the 78rpm era had captured the special Opéra-Comique spirit for posterity, but they hold limited sonic appeal to present-day collectors; later recordings have up-to-date sound, but their international casts generally can't claim the same sense of style. Only with this 1955 set do we get the best of both worlds.

Already at the time a practised exponent of Manon on stage, de los Angeles makes a vivid heroine, allowing us to *see* every expression passing across her face, almost as if we were watching a video. Maybe the role lies a little high for her, but de los Angeles surprised herself on the day of recording by hitting the high D in the Cours-la-Reine scene. Monteux's skill in his native French repertoire is second to none, and he brings exemplary sparkle to the music. It would be possible to find fault with various members of the supporting cast, but that's to miss the point. They sing with a grace and wit that nobody from outside the Opéra-Comique tradition can replicate easily. Henri Legay did not have a great tenor voice, but the poetry and the passion of Des Grieux came as second nature to him. Michel Dens's lively Lescaut and Jean Borthayre's serious Comte des Grieux are no less idiomatic; and the delectably perfumed Guillot of René Hérent is a collector's item in the best sense of the term, as he had been singing this role with the company since his debut in 1918.

There's now a clear choice between this reissue and EMI's fine new Pappano set. Opera collectors will probably want both.

Manon
Angela Gheorghiu sop Manon **Roberto Alagna** ten Des Grieux **Earle Patriarco** bar Lescaut **José van Dam** bass-bar Comte des-Grieux **Nicolas Rivenq** bar

De Brétigny **Gilles Ragon** ten Guillot **Anna Maria Panzarella** sop Poussette **Sophie Koch** mez Javotte **Susanne Schimmack** mez Rosette **Nicolas Cavallier** bar Innkeeper **Chorus and Symphony Orchestra of La Monnaie / Antonio Pappano**
EMI ③ 557005-2 (163' · DDD · T/t)   Ⓕ❶❷❸❹

EMI has had the good sense to build this set around Pappano's own company at La Monnaie, a Francophone group of singers who give an authentic flavour that non-French-speakers can't hope to match. The piece is given absolutely complete, including the splendidly played ballet.

Nothing of the myriad character of Massenet's popular work escapes Pappano's eye and ear. He has a near-perfect idea of how to pace the score and he persuades his orchestra and chorus to play and sing with the utmost respect for pertinent detail, so important in Massenet, and to follow, as do the soloists, the many expressive markings demanded by the composer.

Gheorghiu's is a Manon to savour in practically every respect. Suitably coquettish in her first solo, she turns ruminative, plangent for her second, 'Voyons, Manon'. The farewell to her little table is inward and pensive, tone subtly shaded with the 'larmes dans la voix' so admired in native French singers. To the Gavotte and the recitative preceding it, Gheorghiu brings the outward aplomb and, in the second verse, the hint of sadness required. The prayer at St Sulpice has all the urgency and the sense of apprehension as to how Des Grieux, now a servant of the church, will respond to her. Throughout these solos, Gheorghiu prudently follows Massenet's scrupulous instructions as to dynamics and phrasing with unforgettable results, not to mention the sheer glory of her singing, outclassing her compatriot, the sensitive Ileana Cotrubas, who recorded the role for Plasson too late in her career.

If Alagna doesn't quite equal his wife's example, he's an ardent, French-sounding Des Grieux, always suggesting the Chevalier's obsessive love for his 'Sphinx étonnant'. The Dream, finely phrased as it is, hasn't quite the individuality that Ansseau, Heddle Nash (in the famous pre-war broadcast now on Dutton) or Gedda and others, brought to it, mainly because his tone has become a shade occluded. At St Sulpice, it rings out more truly. 'Ah fuyez, douce image' begins in nicely reflective fashion and the B flat climaxes are suitably impassioned. In most respects he surpasses the ageing Kraus for Plasson, even when he isn't quite as elegant.

Earle Patriarco, a young American baritone, proves an excellent Lescaut, keen with the text and properly cynical in manner. Still better is José van Dam as Le Comte (he sang the part for Plasson), words shaped so meaningfully onto tone, his spoken contribution faultlessly timed.

All the smaller parts are enthusiastically taken, small decorations on a masterly interpretation. Given an exemplary recording for balance and presence, this set is about as good as you'll get today (or maybe any day) of this adorable piece.

Manon
Natalie Dessay sop Manon **Rolando Villazón** ten Des Grieux **Manuel Lanza** bar Lescaut **Samuel Ramey** bass Comte des Grieux **Francisco Vas** ten Guillot **Didier Henry** bar De Brétigny **Cristina Obregón** mez Poussette
Chorus and Orchestra of the Gran Teatre del Liceu, Barcelona / Victor Pablo Pérez
Stage director **David McVicar**
Video director **François Roussillon**
Virgin Classics ② 📀 505068-9 (175' · NTSC · 16:9 · PCM stereo, 5.0 and DTS 5.0 · 0)   Ⓕ

David McVicar's production of *Manon* takes a more than usually harsh view of the story, too often softened by Rococo prettiness. Here, everything and everybody is for sale, and behind the façade of 18th-century Paris lurks a world of corruption, disease and perversion. It is thrilling, sometimes even slightly shocking, and throughout the direction of the cast is faultless: every scene bears re-viewing for the amount of detail and dramatic energy that is released.

It is unlikely that Natalie Dessay will ever give a greater performance than this. First glimpsed as a gawky schoolgirl, wearing a travelling-coat two sizes too large, she grows into a coquettish lover, then a manipulative, avaricious courtesan before our eyes. Her singing of each of the great arias is equally fascinating, with delicate embellishments at such moments as 'Profitons de la jeunesse', and a really touching 'Adieu, notre petite table', ending up lying in a foetal position on top of the table. The scene in which she and Rolando Villazón size each other up before speaking is exquisitely managed.

Villazón makes a passionate hero. His interpretation is much more extrovert than Dessay's, and there are moments when one would have wished him to sing yet more softly. This is considerably more subtle, though, than his previous reading of the same part in the modern-dress production in Berlin. Manuel Lanza makes a seductive, sleazy Lescaut, and Francisco Vas is sinister rather than just amusing as the vengeful Guillot. Although his demeanour is suitably dignified as Des Grieux *père*, Samuel Ramey's voice now has such a perilous wobble that 'Épouse quelque brave fille' is rather painful, in the wrong way.

Tanya McCallin's set – a steep amphitheatre from which extras watch the action played out centre-stage – complements her costumes, inspired by the paintings of Chardin rather than the usual sugary Fragonard. The choreography of Michael Keegan-Dolan reaches its height in the elaborate hunting ballet in the Cours-La-Reine scene, one of Massenet's happiest bits of Baroque pastiche. It is hard to imagine that we will see another *Manon* to equal this for a long time: highly recommended.

Thaïs

Thaïs
Renée Fleming sop Thaïs **Thomas Hampson** bar Athanaël **Giuseppe Sabbatini** ten Nicias **Estefano**

Palatchi *bass* Palémon **Marie Devellereau** *sop*
Crobyle **Isabelle Cals** *mez* Myrtale **Enkelejda**
Shkosa *mez* Albine **Elisabeth Vidal** *sop* La
Charmeuse **David Grousset** *bass* Servant
Bordeaux Opera Chorus; Bordeaux-Aquitaine
National Orchestra / Yves Abel
Decca ② 466 766-2DHO2 (147' · DDD · T/t) Ⓕ🅞🅞🅑➔

At last – a modern recording of *Thaïs* with a
soprano who can sing the title-role. All we need is
a soprano with a fabulously beautiful voice, idiomatic French, a sensuous *legato*, pure high notes
up to a stratospheric top D, and the ability to leave
every listener weak at the knees. Where was the
problem? Renée Fleming makes it all sound so
easy. Her earlier success at the Opéra Bastille in
Paris with Massenet's *Manon* showed that she has
an affinity for this composer. As Thaïs, a role with
a similar vocal profile, she proves equally well cast.
Within minutes of her entrance it's clear that
neither of the other sets from the last 25 years will
be able to touch her. Fleming simply has a vocal
class that puts her in a different league and there's
just enough individuality in her singing to give
Fleming's Thaïs a personality of her own, and
vocal loveliness brings a bloom to her every
scene.

The Athanaël she leaves behind is Thomas
Hampson, who is her match in sensitivity and
roundness of tone. Their duet at the oasis in the
desert is beautifully sung, every word clear, every
phrase shaped with feeling. If only Hampson were
equally good at getting beneath the skin of the
operatic characters he plays. In the case of
Athanaël there's plenty of psychological complexity down there to uncover, but Hampson seems
unwilling to engage the character's dark side.

Occasionally, one regrets that Abel doesn't
have the New Philharmonia at his disposal, as
Maazel does, but the subtlety of colour and
accent that he draws from the Orchestre
National Bordeaux-Aquitaine are a world apart
from Maazel's constant up-front aggression.
The famous 'Méditation', elegantly played by
the young French violinist Renaud Capuçon,
and featuring swoony background chorus is a
dream. Add in a first-class Decca recording and
it will be clear that this new *Thaïs* has pretty well
everything going for it.

Werther

Werther
Patricia Petibon *sop* Sophie **Angela Gheorghiu** *mez*
Charlotte **Roberto Alagna** *ten* Werther **Jean-Paul**
Fouchécourt *ten* Schmidt **Thomas Hampson** *bar*
Albert **Jean-Philippe Courtis** *bass* Magistrate
Jean-Marie Frémeau *bass* Johann **London**
Symphony Orchestra / Antonio Pappano
EMI ② 556820-2 (128' · DDD · T/t) Ⓕ🅞🅑➔

Alagna is the first French-speaking tenor to
record the role for a long time and his diction
throughout is clear and full of emotion. At the
climax of his big aria, 'Pourquoi me reveiller?' in
Act 3, he sings 'O souffle du printemps?' with a

beautiful head tone. And he can't resist singing it
full out the second time around – just as Alfredo
Kraus and many others often did.

Whether or not Angela Gheorghiu would be
suitably cast as Charlotte on stage, she makes a
vivid impression on disc. The obvious comparisons with Gheorghiu are two other sopranos
who have recorded the part, Ninon Vallin in the
historic set under Cohen (see below), and Victoria de los Angeles in the Prêtre version, itself
now sounding close to historic. But both Vallin
and de los Angeles were also Carmens – on disc
at least – and both sound more mature as characters than Gheorghiu does.

The sound on this new recording is fine, the
conducting of Pappano taut and passionate. But,
oh dear, what a lot of recordings of *Werther*
there are now to choose from. The historic
Cohen is probably the most completely satisfying version. Not everyone, however, wants to
listen to historic mono. Among the new *Wer-*
thers the Pappano scores mostly because of
Alagna's heroic assumption of the title-role.

Additional recommendation

Werther   Ⓗ
Vallin *sop* Charlotte **Till** *ten* Werther
Paris Orch / Cohen
Naxos mono 8 110061/2   🅜🅞🅞🅑➔
  Recorded in 1931, this is still the most moving and
  idiomatic version around. A classic set.

William Mathias   Welsh 1934-1992

*Mathias is regarded as one of the most significant
Welsh composers of the 20th century and one of the
few to establish an international reputation. He
enjoyed early success with instrumental and orchestral music but eventually composed in virtually all
musical genres. His later popularity in the fields of
choral and particularly church music gave him a high
profile. He often stressed that he did not regard his
church music as peripheral in any way to his main
output, observing no distinction between the sacred
and the secular and viewing his vocation very much
in line with the medieval Welsh 'praise' poets.*

Organ Works

Complete Organ Works
Richard Lea *org*
Priory ② PRCD870 (151' · DDD)
Played on the organ of the Metropolitan Cathedral,
Liverpool   Ⓕ🅞

Here, at last, we have the first truly comprehensive survey of Mathias's organ music, including
pieces very few organists ever knew existed
(notably the *Prelude, Elegy and Toccata* of 1955,
his earliest known foray into writing for the
instrument). It is also useful to have the particu-

larly complex *Antiphonies* prefaced by the two ancient hymns on which it is based – even if treble James Orrell is placed so far distant that you have to strain your ears to hear him intone the *Vexilla regis* – and to hear that remarkably confusing Welsh hymn tune *Braint* given out by the Liverpool Welsh Choral before Mathias's ingenious but, if you don't know the tune, not always coherent Variations.

On top of all this comes really first-rate playing from Richard Lea, organist and assistant director of music at Liverpool Metropolitan Cathedral, and a magnificent, demonstration-quality recording of what is one of the greatest English organs of the 20th century. Lea has real fire in his spirit and Mathias's characteristically angular rhythms and jocular dancing melodies leap out of the pages with almost hypnotic persuasiveness. Everything here is a performance to be reckoned with and while it might be said that, in places, Mathias was inclined to resort to stock devices giving some of these pieces a certain sameness, Lea's masterly handling of the instrument and his understanding of the music ensures that every single note stands out proudly as never a wasted note.

Colin Matthews

British b1946

Matthews collaborated with Deryck Cooke on the performing version of Mahler's Tenth Symphony. He was also assistant at Aldeburgh to Britten (1971-76), with particular involvement in Death in Venice and the Third String Quartet, and he worked with Imogen Holst (1972-84). After Britten's death he edited for publication various works left in manuscript. Matthews's orchestral works demonstrate the archetypal weight and expressive seriousness of a major symphonic composer, an impression reinforced by his ability to generate and sustain musical argument across large structures. Throughout his career Matthews has also maintained a steady output of chamber music including three string quartets, two oboe quartets, songs, piano music (notably the Eleven Studies in Velocity, 1987) and arrangements or adaptions of music by other composers including Britten, Mahler, Dowland, Berlioz, Purcell and Schubert.

Matthews was appointed Associate Composer with the Hallé Orchestra from October 2001, and has written a number of works for them, as well as a project involving the orchestration of all 24 of Debussy's Préludes, completed in May 2007 and recorded by Sir Mark Elder on the Hallé label. Future commissions include works for the Leipzig Gewandhaus and BBC Symphony orchestras, and the London Sinfonietta.

Orchestral Works

Alphabicycle Order[a]. Horn Concerto[b]
[a]Henry Goodman narr **[b]Richard Watkins** hn
[a]children's choir; Hallé Orchestra / [b]Sir Mark Elder,
[a]Edward Gardner
Hallé CDHLL7515 (54' · DDD)

Elemental musical images of sorrow and farewell can be as prominent in contemporary composers as they were in Purcell, Beethoven or Mahler. Ligeti's Horn Trio is a particularly memorable instance, and Colin Matthews's Horn Concerto has a set of comparable associations, including the *Les adieux* Sonata and the 'Abschied' from *Das Lied von der Erde*.

Cast as a sequence of elegies, predominantly lyrical but with occasional outbursts of rage, Matthews's music sustains its dark, questing spirit under the confident control of Sir Mark Elder in this first recording, and soloist Richard Watkins has an unfailingly eloquent presence, even when heard in the distance, offstage. The spatial aspects of the piece benefit from being seen as well as heard, but the drawbacks of a sound-only encounter are minimal, so strong is the character of the music.

In one sense the contrast provided by the companion piece could hardly be more extreme. *Alphabicycle Order*, for children's choir, narrator and orchestra, is a joyously witty musical response to Christopher Reid's brilliantly surreal traversal of the alphabet, and the evident relish with which it is tackled by the Hallé's young singers, backed to the hilt by narrator Henry Goodman and the orchestra under Edward Gardner, shows just how enjoyable it must have been for everyone involved. But Matthews brings an edge and panache to the music – echoing but never merely imitating Britten – which turns what could have been simply a fun piece into something stronger and more durable. These are two excellent recordings of notably substantial 21st-century compositions.

Chamber Works

Divertimento[a]. String Quartet No 2[b]. Oboe Quartet No 1[c]. Triptych[d]. Five Concertinos[e]
[c]Melinda Maxwell ob **[b]Brindisi Quartet;**
[d]Schubert Ensemble; [e]Haffner Wind Ensemble;
[ac]Divertimenti Ensemble / [a]Oliver Knussen
NMC NMCD149 (64' · DDD)

Contemporary composers sink or swim in a sea of perplexingly diverse memories and stimuli – a condition that has been particularly acute since the 1970s. These chamber works from the 1980s show Colin Matthews at his most buoyant, cresting the waves with exuberance and flair. Whether he's reacting to a powerful emblem of late Romanticism, as with the Divertimento's initial quote of chords from Strauss's *Metamorphosen*, or confronting turbulent, Ligeti-like avant-gardisms – the String Quartet No 2 – he is never in danger of being submerged by mighty models. His own voice is unmistakable and, in these pieces, all the more appealing for the compactness and directness of the way the music speaks.

One strategy for ensuring stylistic independence is to lead a source, such as the opening gambit of Strauss's ambivalent, fervent lament, into uncharted waters which are more capricious than grief-stricken, fulfilling the Divertimento's promise to entertain with no hint of triviality. The first Oboe Quartet is another instance of purposeful impetuosity, cast in a form which owes as much to the English Fantasy tradition as to Germanic sonata schemes. While compactness reaches its apogee in the *Triptych* for piano quintet, a study in the very different capacities of piano and strings to sustain as well as to indulge in glittering display, the Five Concertinos for Wind Quintet make witty play with the ensemble's need to resist tendencies to converge into homogenous uniformity. Most powerful of all is the Second Quartet, in a revised version that keeps the balance between fast and slow impulses on a knife-edge throughout. These recordings may be on the dry side acoustically, but the performances fizz and brood to the manner born.

David Matthews
British b1943

Elder brother of Colin Matthews, he studied classics at Nottingham University, took lessons in composition with Milner, and received further advice and encouragement from Maw. He also collaborated with Deryck Cooke on the performing version of Mahler's Tenth Symphony, and during 1966-69 he was music assistant to Britten. Although Matthews began composing at 16, his first acknowledged work dates from the age of 25. He soon found that his affinities led in an alternative direction to the post-Darmstadt trends of the 1960s. Drawing inspiration from the rhythmic vitality and spirited individual approach of Tippett, he has evolved his own deeply expressive sound world – Romantic in character, vibrant in melody and rooted in an expanded tonal harmony – while preserving a classical lucidity and poise, and striving to re-evaluate and breathe fresh life into the traditional 'objective' forms of symphony and string quartet.

Symphonies

Symphonies – No 1, Op 9; No 3, Op 37; No 5, Op 78ᵃ
BBC National Orchestra of Wales /
Martyn Brabbins
Dutton Laboratories CDLX7222 (67' · DDD)　Ⓜ

David Matthews's seven symphonies to date are fine examples of modern British symphonism, true to the heritage of finely crafted, economical, non-gimmicky structures bound together with a strong lyrical threads, yet not offering easy access via programmatic reference, declared or otherwise. His official First succeeded a couple of early efforts, subsequently withdrawn, and was itself cut and recast before finding its final form in 1978. This is wiry music that speaks at times in the accents of Britten, Tippett and Nicholas Maw – an impressive symphonic

debut, certainly, and strong in its control of line and flow at either end, but not ideally focused in between and not entirely convincing in its final gestures.

Also running in a single continuous movement, the Third is for long stretches a good deal sterner in its language, as though now determined to avoid all echoes of other voices, and the 'C major coda' referred to in the composer's own booklet essay keeps its supposed diatonicism fairly well hidden. Like the First, this symphony is open to the criticism of falling between two stools, being neither referential enough to engage at an ethical level nor abstract enough to create an alternative kind of drama (à la Lutosławski, for instance). Yet there is still a strong enough sense of purpose and expressive necessity to encourage and reward repeated listening.

Disconcertingly at first, the Fifth Symphony strides out in confident ceremonial mood, as if appealing to baser audience instincts. But Matthews soon throws some Stravinskian spanners into the works, goading the music to dig deeper, and both *Scherzo* and slow movement ratchet up the intensity effectively. Whether or not the short finale suffices to balance the structure, it's difficult to decide; three hearings haven't yet convinced. And in general one wonders whether Matthews's reticence will halt the progress of his symphonies in the concert hall. But such reservations don't mean that this anything is less than an engrossing disc. And all praise for the efforts of all concerned to preserve and showcase music that is far too good to languish unheard.

Symphonies – No 2, Op 17; No 6, Op 100
BBC National Orchestra of Wales / Jac Van Steen
Dutton CDLX7234 (74' DDD)　ⓂⓄⓄ

It is one thing for Vaughan Williams to have provided a moving meditation on his own hymn-tune *Down Ampney*, as he did (arguably) in the finale of his Fifth Symphony, but the idea, 60 years later, of building an entire 35-minute symphony around the hymn seemed doomed to fail. And yet David Matthews's Symphony No 6 was widely acclaimed as a remarkable success at its BBC Proms premiere in 2007, and similar accolades should attend this recording by the artists who gave that premiere.

After the very different British symphonic cycles, by Robert Simpson and Sir Peter Maxwell Davies, which dominated the later 20th century, David Matthews has emerged as a leading 21st-century exponent of the form. Like his composer-brother Colin, he has acknowledged twin allegiances to Mahler and Britten, but whereas Colin Matthews has responded strongly to the continuation of Mahlerian thinking in (particularly) Berg, David Matthews has ploughed more specifically English furrows. Learning from Tippett, Maw and others that pattern-making must always be purposeful, he shuns rhapsodic rambling and can summon up the kind of creative energy that makes the epic finale of the Second Symphony (completed in 1979) so powerful.

The Sixth Symphony, in keeping with its hymnic source, is more contemplative but no less dramatic, questioning its source (as the agnostic Vaughan Williams would have expected) rather than simply offering a pious pilgrim's progress to some mythic celestial city. These are admirable performances, not always ideally flexible in their approach to changes of tempo but strongly characterised and recorded with immense sonic presence in BBC Wales's new Hoddinott Hall.

Additional recommendation

The Music of Dawn. Concerto in Azzurro[a].
A Vision and a Journey
[a]**Johnston** vc **BBC PO / Gamba**
Chandos CHAN10487 (71' · DDD)   Ⓕ Ⓑ→

These three orchestral works rely on flexibly organised single-movement structures that display strong and positive links with the great 19th-century tradition of the programme symphony and tone-poem. *Concerto in Azzurro* – 'concerto in blue' – is another evocation of light, sky, and an underlying sense of the transcendent. Guy Johnston is a technically immaculate soloist, while Rumon Gamba with the BBC Philharmonic are excellent throughout in first-rate recordings.

Nicholas Maw   British 1935-2009

Maw studied with Lennox Berkeley at the Royal Academy of Music and with Nadia Boulanger in Paris. He taught in England and the USA. His music represents the extension of a solid tonal tradition, traceable back through Britten, Tippett, Bartók and Strauss, all influences on a style of vital imagination. His work embraces all the genres, including operas, the last, Sophie's Choice of 2002, mounted to great acclaim on both sides of the Atlantic.

String Quartet No 3

Maw String Quartet No 3
Britten String Quartet No 3. Three Divertimentos
Coull Quartet (Roger Coull, Philip Gallaway vns
Gustav Clarkson va Nicholas Roberts vc)
Somm Céleste Series SOMMCD065 (60' · DDD)   Ⓕ

The Coull Quartet have often played Nicholas Maw's Third Quartet since giving its premiere in 1995, and this recording – in exceptionally lucid sound – testifies to their mastery of its tricky technical details and their sensitivity to its expressive character.

It begins in a spirit of restless lyricism which builds compellingly, eloquence and drama intensifying in ways which place the music firmly in the tradition of Berg and Bartók without any hint of abject dependency. The work is crowned by a concluding passacaglia which cre-

ates tension from the superimposition of contrasting layers of texture before reaching a climax with a unison line for all four players, a moment of revelation which subsides into a regretful resolution.

The chordal material at the end hints at the opening of Maw's later opera *Sophie's Choice*, and this is one reason why the ideal coupling for the quartet would have been the recent string sextet in which Maw uses material from the opera. The sextet probably wasn't complete when this recording was planned, however, and the Coull have chosen a quartet, Britten's Third, which has certain stylistic and formal features in common with Maw's.

Despite some lack of necessary rawness in the second and fourth movements, this is an admirable account, and particularly successful in projecting the chaconne finale as music constantly on the verge of breakdown. The Britten has been much recorded, and several other performances are as impressive as this one. Even so, its presence does nothing to reduce the feeling that this is an outstanding release.

Opera

Sophie's Choice
Dale Duesing bar Narrator **Gordon Gietz** ten Stingo
Angelika Kirchschlager mez Sophie **Rod Gilfry** bar
Nathan **Adrian Clarke** bar Librarian **Frances McCafferty** sop Yetta Zimmermann **Stafford Dean** bass Zbigniew Bieganski **Stephanie Friede** sop
Wanda **Abigail Browne** sop Eva **Billy Clerkin** bar Jan
**Chorus and Orchestra of the Royal Opera House,
Covent Garden / Sir Simon Rattle**
Stage director **Trevor Nunn**
Opus Arte ② DVD OA1024D
(3h 43' · NTSC · 16:9 · 2.0 and 5.0 · 0). Recorded live at the Royal Opera House, Covent Garden, on December 21, 2002. Also includes Illustrated Synopsis, Cast Gallery and interview with Sir Simon Rattle   Ⓕ Ⓞ Ⓞ →

Any artwork dealing with Auschwitz is certain to arouse strong feelings, and William Styron's novel *Sophie's Choice*, published in 1979, compounded the challenge by placing its tale of a Polish concentration camp survivor in the frame of a lurid after-story. In 1947 New York, Sophie encounters a charismatic, deranged young American, Nathan, who obsesses about her and with whom she eventually commits suicide – choosing her own death as a consequence for having had to select one of her own children for sacrifice in order to save the other child, and herself, from Auschwitz.

The novel, like the film which followed, is nothing if not American in character, and it's not impossible to imagine what a *Sophie's Choice* opera by Leonard Bernstein or John Adams might be like. Though Nicholas Maw was long resident in America, his opera has an undertow of British understatement, especially in the first two acts, which cannot be mistaken for a desire to represent detachment from the subject, even though Maw's reluctance to allow his vocal writing to flower into aria-like melody suggests a determination to shun precisely the kind of sentimental explicitness which Styron embraces so wholeheartedly. However, as the full horror of the story emerges in the later acts, Maw unleashes – mainly in the interludes – the kind of intense and well-nigh expressionistic material that is the crowning glory of his large-scale orchestral masterwork *Odyssey*: and although the vocal writing continues to resist the possibility of Britten-like lyric forms, there is a sense of pathos without mawkishness in the closing scenes which is tellingly represented in this BBC film of the sixth and – to date – final Covent Garden performance.

It's a tribute to the competence and stamina of the cast – Angelika Kirchschlager and Dale Duesing are on stage virtually throughout – that they all survive the ordeal by camera so well. Trevor Nunn's staging, conceived for the large theatre, inevitably appears overwrought in places when the camera creeps in close but it would have been asking a lot for the TV director to have matched the composer's restraint. *Sophie's Choice* might have been more comfortably operatic with a less wordy libretto and with more concentratedly dramatic music. Yet as Maw's last major work it merits the kind of serious attention which this admirable and timely release makes possible.

Billy Mayerl
British 1902-1959

Mayerl studied in the junior department of Trinity College of Music (1914-19) and worked as a pianist for silent films and in hotel bands. In 1921 he joined Bert Ralton's band (later called the Savoy Havana Band) which regularly broadcast in the early years of the BBC. In 1926 he left that band for the music hall and founded his own school of music which pioneered teaching by post, using records. With Nippy (1930) his career moved to music theatre and he composed and directed several musical comedies which were successful at the time. He was a regular broadcaster before the Second World War but the war marked the end of his celebrity. Best known for his syncopated novelty piano solos, he wrote over 300 piano pieces, many of which were named after flowers and trees, including his best known composition, Marigold (1927).

Piano Works

Mayerl Crystal Clear. Orange Blossom. Piano Exaggerations. Pastorale Exotique. Wistaria. Canaries' Serenade. Shy Ballerina. Puppets Suite, Op 77. Piano Transcriptions – Body and Soul; Deep Henderson; Tormented; Sing, you sinners; Cheer up; Have you forgotten?; The object of my affection; Is it true what they say about Dixie?; I need you; Love was born; I'm at your service **Parkin** Mayerl Shots, Sets 1 & 2. A Tribute to Billy Mayerl
Eric Parkin pf

Priory PRCD544 (80' · DDD)　　　　　　　Ⓕ

Nobody since the master himself has come anywhere near Parkin's easy technical mastery and fastidious musicianship in this delightful music. Some pianists hit the more demanding pieces quite hard: Parkin, like Mayerl, knows better and his playing is consistently light and subtle. This has always been his approach, allied to a faultless sense of pace and rhythm. However, Mayerl, apart from perfecting the piano novelty, also contributed to the English pastoral tradition, which Parkin knows equally well. *Shy Ballerina* is charmingly done with *rubato* which would be quite out of place in Mayerl's numbers. The three-movement *Puppets Suite* is a *tour de force*.

As a bonus Parkin adds two sets of his own pieces called *Mayerl Shots*. He explains that, as a result of practising lots of Mayerl, further ideas surfaced spontaneously in a similar idiom. These are all fluent tributes and there are even quotations for the specialists. Essential listening.

Additional recommendations

Scallywag. Jasmine. Oriental. Minuet for Pamela. Fascinating Ditty. Funny Peculiar. Chopsticks. Carminetta. Mignonette. Penny Whistle. Piano Transcriptions – Me and my girl; Blue velvet; Sittin' on the edge of my chair; The pompous gremlin; My heaven in the pines; Alabamy bound; Stardust; Please handle with care; Two lovely people; Two hearts on a tree; You're the reason why. Studies in Syncopation, Op 55 – Nos 7, 10, 14, 15 & 18
Coupled with **Parkin** Mayerl Shots, Set 3
Parkin pf
Priory PRCD565 (76' · DDD)　　　　　　　Ⓕ
This release, 'Scallywag', has its own discoveries, notably the *Studies in Syncopation*, which parallel Bartók's *Mikrokosmos* in this field. And there's real comedy – totally appreciated and effectively realised by Parkin – in *Chopsticks* and *Penny Whistle*. In addition, Eric Parkin gives us his own response to Mayerl in a similar idiom – a third set of his *Mayerl Shots*. The recording is adequate.

April's Fool. Beguine Impromptu. The Big Top – Clowning; Entrance; Trapeze. Three Contrasts, Op 24 – Pastoral. The Forgotten Forest. From a Spanish Lattice. In my Garden: Autumntime – Amber Leaves. In my Garden: Summertime – Alpine Bluebell; Meadowsweet. Four Insect Oddities – Praying Mantis; Ladybird Lullaby. Three Japanese Pictures, Op 25 – The Cherry Dance. Jill All Alone. Leprechaun's Leap. Piano Exaggerations – Antiquary. Postman's Knock. Siberian Lament. Song of the Fir-Tree. Three Syncopated Rambles – 6am: The Milkman (Scherzo). Weeping Willow. Minuet for Pamela
Coupled with **French/Mayerl** Phil the Fluter's Ball
De'Ath pf
Dutton Epoch CDLX7211 (77' · DDD)　　　　Ⓜ
Leslie De'Ath's selection focuses less on the early virtuoso pieces that made Mayerl's name as 'lightning fingers' than on some of the more relaxed lyri-

cal works in the central English tradition of Bridge, Ireland and Scott. This is a personal anthology, well recorded with good notes from De'Ath, and it reminds us that Mayerl's music is an essential part of the British piano repertoire.

John McCabe
British b1939

McCabe studied at the Royal Manchester College and in Munich, then returned to England to work as a pianist, critic and composer; in 1983 he became director of the London College of Music. His works, in an extended tonal style, include five symphonies, much other orchestral music, chamber and keyboard pieces.

Piano Concertos

Arthur Pendragon – Ballet Suite No 1.
Piano Concerto No 1[a]. Pilgrim
[a]**John McCabe** *pf* **BBC Scottish Symphony Orchestra / Christopher Austin**
Dutton Digital Epoch CDLX7179 (73' · DDD)   (F)

It's long been a source of amazement why McCabe's splendid First Piano Concerto, written for the 1967 Southport Centenary Festival, has not been recorded before so Dutton's committed advocacy is unequivocally to be welcomed.

The concerto's rhythmic élan is a feature prominent in most of his output, including *Pilgrim* for double string orchestra (1998, arranged from a string sextet original). Although Bunyan's book was the inspiration, the single-span *Pilgrim* is not illustrative, rather a slow fantasia with two quicker sections, like a *scherzo* and trio in negative. As with the concerto's finale, *Pilgrim* shows how danceable McCabe's concert music is (several works have been successfully choreographed).

The largest item is a suite from his recent ballet diptych, *Arthur* (1998-2001), the four movements deriving from the first part, *Arthur Pendragon*, all but the finale from its first act. The vigour and drive of 'Uther and the Tribes' and 'The Tourney' (in which Arthur draws Excalibur from the Stone) contrast with the poignant beauty of 'Igraine and Uther'. The finale, 'The Lovers', is a complex conflation of two *pas de deux* for Lancelot and Guinevere and the ballet's climax, Arthur's vain and misguided massacre of the innocents (attempting to destroy the infant Mordred). Powerful stuff, the BBC Scottish SO's performance under Christopher Austin is inspired. With excellent sound, this issue is very strongly recommended.

Piano Concerto No 2 (Sinfonia concertante)[a].
Concertante Variations on a Theme of Nicholas Maw.
Six-Minute Symphony. Sonata on a Motet
[a]**Tamami Honma** *pf* **St Christopher Chamber Orchestra / Donatas Katkus**
Dutton Laboratories Epoch CDLX7133 (64' · DDD)   (F)

This is an intriguing orchestral programme of pieces dating mostly from the 1970s. Despite the disparity in dates there's remarkable stylistic consistency, even to the extent of the occasional twang of Tippett in the string writing, as in the delightful *Six-Minute Symphony* (1997) – invigoratingly rattled off in 5'18" – as in the *Concertante Variations* of 1970.

This latter work should be better known: it may lack the exuberance and virtuosity of Britten's *Frank Bridge* Variations but is subtler and more integrated. So, too, is the wonderful *Sonata on a Motet* (1976), McCabe's atmospheric, closely argued fantasia on Tallis's *Spem in alium*. Curiously, it's in the Sonata, rather than the *Concertante Variations*, that he allows his source to be distinctly heard, as for example in the climactic, rip-roaring fugue on the Elizabethan's ground bass. By contrast, the *Six-Minute Symphony* eschews variation form for a real symphonic plan in miniature.

The largest piece, by virtue of its internal cohesion and gravitas rather than mere duration, is the Second Piano Concerto (1970). Subtitled *Sinfonia concertante*, the music plays out on three levels: solo piano, a concertino group of nine instruments and the orchestra. Listen past the dissonance of the opening minute: what emerges, like order from chaos, is one of the finest post-war piano concertos.

Tamami Honma, something of a McCabe expert, plays brilliantly, as do the splendid St Christopher Chamber Orchestra of Vilnius under Donatas Kalkus's smart direction. Excellent sound, too. Very strongly recommended.

Symphony No 4

Symphony No 4, 'Of Time and the River'.
Flute Concerto[a]
[a]**Emily Beynon** *fl*
BBC Symphony Orchestra / Vernon Handley
Hyperion CDA67089 (56' · DDD)   (F)(O)(+)

John McCabe's Fourth Symphony, some half an hour in duration, has something Sibelian about its utterly inevitable, ever-evolving progress. Behind the frequently prodigal surface activity, one is acutely aware of the inexorable tread of a grander scheme – a preoccupation with time mirrored in Thomas Wolfe's novel *Of Time and the River*, from which the work derives its subtitle. The very opening idea is momentarily reminiscent of Britten, and there's a magnificent passage in the second movement that recalls Vaughan Williams at his visionary best. Yet McCabe's score possesses a strong individuality, formal elegance and abundant integrity too. With dedication and scrupulous perception, Handley secures a disciplined and alert response from the BBC SO. The engaging Flute Concerto composed for James Galway in 1989-90 proves both resourceful and communicative. There's much that genuinely haunts here, not least the gently lapping opening idea (inspired by watching the play of waves on a Cornish beach), the ravishing dialogue between the soloist and orchestral flutes and the delightful emergence soon afterwards of an entrancingly naive, folk-like theme. Emily Beynon gives a flawless account of the demanding solo part, and is immaculately partnered by Handley and his BBC forces.

Edward II

Edward II
Royal Ballet Sinfonia / Barry Wordsworth
Hyperion ② CDA67135 (114' · DDD)　　Ⓕ⦿➤

Commissioned by the Stuttgart Ballet, choreographed by David Bintley, *Edward II* is McCabe's third ballet score, and draws its story-line from Christopher Marlowe's eponymous drama and the medieval courtly satire, *Le roman de Fauvel*. Quite apart from the meaty intrigue, complex character relationships and psychological pathos of the plot, McCabe's music communicates with a captivating expressive fervour. It isn't just the superbly judged orchestration (colourful extras include triple woodwind and electric guitar) and wealth of memorable invention that impress. Above all, it's his ability to forge his tightly knit material into a dramatically convincing and organically coherent whole that marks him out as a composer of exceptional gifts. No praise can be too high for Barry Wordsworth's fluent, pungently theatrical direction, not to mention the unstinting application of the excellent Royal Ballet Sinfonia. The excitingly truthful sound allies razor-sharp focus to a most pleasing bloom, too.

Nikolay Medtner　　Russian 1880-1951

Medtner studied the piano at the Moscow Conservatory and had composition lessons with Arensky and Taneyev, though was mostly self-taught. In 1921 he left Russia, settling in Paris (1925-35), but was out of sympathy with musical developments in the 1920s and '30s there and found a more receptive audience in London, where he spent his last 16 years. He belonged in the line of Russian composer-pianists, though his music is close too to the Schumann-Brahms tradition. His works include three piano concertos, much solo piano music, three violin sonatas and songs. In 1949 a Medtner Society was unexpectedly founded in London by the Maharajah of Mysore (an honorary Fellow of Trinity College of Music and also the first president of the Philharmonia Concert Society, London). He founded the society to record all of Medtner's works. Medtner, already in declining health, recorded his three piano poncertos and some sonatas, chamber music, numerous songs and shorter works before his death in London in 1951.

Piano Concertos

No 1 in C minor, Op 33; **No 2** in C minor, Op 50;
No 3 in E minor, Op 60

Piano Concerto No 1. Piano Quintet in C, Op *posth*
Dmitri Alexeev *pf* **New Budapest Quartet; BBC Symphony Orchestra / Alexander Lazarev**
Hyperion CDA66744 (59' · DDD)　　Ⓕ➤

For Dmitri Alexeev the First Concerto is Medtner's masterpiece, an argument he sustains in a performance of superb eloquence and discretion. Even the sort of gestures later vulgarised and traduced by Tinseltown are given with an aristocratic quality, a feel for a love of musical intricacy that takes on an almost symbolic force, but also for Medtner's dislike of display. Time and again Alexeev makes you pause to reconsider Medtner's quality, and his reserve brings distinctive reward. The early *Abbandonamente ma non troppo* has a haunting improvisatory inwardness and later, as the storm clouds gather ominously at 11'55", his playing generates all the necessary electricity. How thankful one is, too, for Alexeev's advocacy of the Piano Quintet where, together with his fully committed colleagues, the New Budapest Quartet, he recreates music of the strangest, most unworldly exultance and introspection. Instructions such as *poco tranquillo (sereno)* and *Quasi Hymn* take us far away from the turbulence of the First Concerto (composed in the shadow of the First World War) and the finale's conclusion is wonderfully uplifting. The recordings are judiciously balanced in both works, and the BBC SO under Lazarev are fully sympathetic.

Medtner Piano Concerto No 1. Aus 'Claudine von Villa-Bella', Op 6 No 5 (arr Sudbin)
Tchaikovsky Piano Concerto No 1, Op 23
Yevgeny Sudbin *pf*
São Paulo Symphony Orchestra / John Neschling
BIS 🎵 BIS-SACD1588 (71' · DDD/DSD)　　Ⓕ⦿⦿⦿➤

Ⓖ　To describe Yevgeny Sudbin as music's brightest young star pianist is in a sense to do him a disservice. For he is above all an artist, and here in his eagerly awaited concerto debut on disc he gives us a Tchaikovsky First of spine-tingling brilliance, poetry and vivacity. This is never the Tchaikovsky you have always known, but an arrestingly novel rethink with the concentration on mercurial changes of mood and direction. Here, amazingly, is one of the most familiar of all concertos rekindled in all its first glory, brimming over with zest and shorn of all the clichés that have adhered to it over the years.

In the first movement Sudbin's octaves ring out like a giant carillon, while the *Andantino*'s central *prestissimo* becomes in such extraordinary hands a true firefly *scherzo*. Not even Cherkassky at his finest possessed a more elfin sense of difference or caprice. And to think that all this and more is accomplished without the lift, or hindrance, of a major competition success.

Medtner's massive First Concerto, too, could hardly be played with a more burning clarity and commitment. Medtner's music remains formidably inaccessible, despite displaying the outward trappings of Romantic rhetoric, yet Sudbin clearly believes in every note and his playing evinces, as on live occasions, a rare sense of affection. Such poetry is confirmed in his encore, his own transcription of Medtner's song 'Liebliches Kind!'. It only remains to add that BIS's balance and sound are of demonstration quality and that the São Paulo SO under John Neschling respond infectiously to their radiant soloist.

Piano Concertos Nos 2 and 3
Nikolai Demidenko pf **BBC Scottish Symphony Orchestra / Jerzy Maksymiuk**
Hyperion CDA66580 (74' · DDD)   ⓕ❶❶❶➜

 This splendid disc is given a fine recording, good orchestral playing from a Scottish orchestra under a Polish conductor and, above all, truly coruscating and poetic playing from the brilliant young Russian pianist Nikolai Demidenko. Medtner was a contemporary and friend of Rachmaninov; he settled in Britain in the 1930s, and like Rachmaninov he was an excellent pianist. But while the other composer became immensely popular, Medtner languished in obscurity, regarded as an inferior imitation of Rachmaninov who wrote gushing music that was strong on gestures but weak on substance. The fact is that he can be diffuse (not to say long-winded) and grandiose, and memorable tunes are in short supply, so that his music needs to be played well to come off. When it is, there's much to enjoy, as here in Demidenko's hypnotically fiery and articulate accounts.

Additional recommendations

Piano Concertos Nos 2 & 3.
Coupled with Arabesque. Fairy Tale in F minor
Medtner pf **Philharmonia / Dobrowen**
Testament mono SBT1027 (77' · ADD)   ⓕ
Listening to the composer himself in the Second's first *molto cantabile a tempo, ma espressivo* or the Third's *dolce cantabile* is to be made doubly aware of his haunting and bittersweet lyricism. The streaming figuration in the Second Concerto's *Romanza* is spun off with deceptive ease, a reminder that while Medtner despised obvious pyrotechnics he was a superb pianist. The 1947 recordings have been superbly remastered.

Piano Concertos Nos 1 & 3
Scherbakov pf **Moscow SO / Ziva**
Naxos 8 553359 (70' · DDD)   ⓢ❶➜
To have such Romantic richness – once the province of specialists – offered on a bargain label is cause for celebration in itself; to have it performed and recorded with such tireless commitment is a double blessing.

Piano Works

Sonata in F minor, Op 5. Two Fairy Tales, Op 8. Sonata Triad, Op 11. Sonata in G minor, Op 22. Sonatas, Op 25 – No 1 in C minor, 'Sonata-Skazka'; No 2 in

E minor, 'The Night Wind'. Sonata-Ballade in F sharp, Op 27. Sonata in A minor, Op 30. Forgotten Melodies – Set I, Op 38; Set II, Op 39. Sonata romantica in B flat minor, Op 53 No 1. Sonata minacciosa in F minor, Op 53 No 2. Sonate-Idylle in G, Op 56
Marc-André Hamelin pf
Hyperion ④ CDA67221/4 (279' · DDD)   Ⓜ❶➜

With this classic recording of the 14 piano sonatas, Medtner's star soared into the ascendant. Superlatively played and presented, it effects a radical and triumphant transition from years of indifference to heady acclaim. True, Medtner was celebrated by Rachmaninov as 'the greatest composer of our time' and championed by pianists such as Moiseiwitsch, Horowitz and Gilels, yet his music fell largely on deaf ears. Such irony and enigma lie in the music itself, in its distinctive character, colour and fragrance. Listeners were understandably suspicious of music that yields up its secrets so unreadily, almost as if Medtner wished it to remain in a private rather than public domain. Moments of a ravishing, heart-stopping allure, and heroics on the grandest of scales are apt to occur within an indigestible, prolix and recondite context. On paper everything is comprehensible, yet the results are never quite what you expect. Much of the writing, too, is formidably complex, with rhythmic intricacies deriving from Brahms and whimsicalities from Schumann supporting a recognisably Slavic yet wholly personal idiom.

Such writing demands a transcendental technique and a burning poetic commitment, a magical amalgam achieved with delicacy, drama and finesse by Marc-André Hamelin. Interspersing the sonatas with miniatures containing some of Medtner's most felicitous ideas, he plays with an authority suggesting that such music is truly his language. Hamelin achieves an unfaltering sense of continuity, a balance of sense and sensibility in music that threatens to become submerged in its own passion. Readers uncertain of Medtner's elusive art should try the *Forgotten Melodies* (and most of all 'Alla reminiscenza'). Such heaven-sent performances will set you journeying far and wide, their eloquence accentuated by Hyperion's sound.

Songs

The Angel, Op 1a. Winter Evening, Op 13 No 1. Songs, Op 28 – No 2, I cannot hear that bird; No 3, Butterfly; No 4, In the Churchyard; No 5, Spring Calm. The Rose, Op 29 No 6. I loved thee well, Op 32 No 4. Night, Op 36 No 5. Sleepless, Op 37 No 1. Songs, Op 52 – No 2, The Raven; No 3, Elegy; No 5, Spanish Romance; No 6, Serenade. Noon, Op 59 No 1. Eight Songs, Op 24
Ludmilla Andrew sop **Geoffrey Tozer** pf
Chandos CHAN9327 (60' · DDD · T/t)
Recorded 1993   ⓕ➜

Musical Opinion, reviewing the newly published Op 52 in 1931, concluded that Medtner could hardly be considered 'a born song-writer'. It says something for the achievement of Ludmilla

Andrew that the 'unvocal' character of Medtner's writing is hardly evident at all, though, to be fair, the first three songs from Op 52 are perhaps the very ones in which the voice is most hard-pressed and in which it's even possible to feel that they might do very well as piano solos. In the 'Serenade' (No 6), the piano part *is* an accompaniment, and the singer brings to it a charm and delicacy worthy of its dedicatee, Nina Koshetz. Geoffrey Tozer is an excellent accompanist. His playing of 'Winter Evening', with its evocative rustling start, is superb; but always, along with the sheer virtuosity, there's a responsive feeling for mood and coloration. There are songs in which the piano takes over. Yet in many the interest is evenly distributed, and these are among the most delightful in the repertoire.

Felix Mendelssohn   German 1809-1847

Mendelssohn's background was wealthy and cultured. Moses Mendelssohn, his grandfather, was a hunchbacked peddler who came to be one of Germany's great intellectual figures of the 18th century, a philosopher whose sobriquet was 'the modern Plato'. The talents of our Mendelssohn's father lay elsewhere. He built up a powerful Hamburg bank and became a man of considerable wealth, while his wife provided the intellectual life of the family – a linguist, musician and gifted painter.

Both Felix and his sister Fanny proved to be exceptionally talented, studying piano, violin, languages and drawing from an early age. By the time he was nine, Felix was a good enough pianist to appear in public; at 10 he joined the Singakademie in Berlin (then under the direction of his teacher Karl Friedrich Zelter) and by 1821 had composed several symphonies, two operas, fugues for string quartet and other works. In all this, he was encouraged by his parents (though not spoilt – Mendelssohn was made to rise at dawn each day for a full period of study) to such an extent that, when it was clear that music was going to be the boy's future, Mendelssohn's father decided to convert from the Jewish faith to Protestantism. He saw how many paths were closed to Jews in the musical world and he took both his children to be converted to Christianity. Later, he and his wife followed suit, adding 'Bartholdy' to their name to distinguish them from other Mendelssohns who were still Jewish.

The Mendelssohn house was always filled with the distinguished and influential. Great musicians would gravitate to there for informal concerts, among them Weber, and when in 1821 Zelter took Felix to Weimar and introduced him to Goethe, the 70-year-old writer and the 12-year-old prodigy became firm friends. All who met the young Mendelssohn and heard him play left with jaws dropped – Spohr, Cherubini, Moscheles, all were incredulous. Here, without a doubt, was a second Mozart.

This was not fanciful, for by the time he was 16 he was composing music of far greater maturity than that which Mozart had written at a similar age: the overture to *A Midsummer Night's Dream*

and his Octet are extraordinarily assured and original.

Mendelssohn was only 20 when he conducted a performance of Bach's St Mathew Passion at the Berlin Singakademie, an event which, more than any other, propelled a general revival of interest in Bach's music. Not long after, he made the first of 10 visits to England, feted as a celebrity and conducting the premiere of his C minor Symphony before travelling to Scotland. This visit inspired his overture Fingal's Cave and the Scottish Symphony, just as his subsequent tour of Italy provided the spark for his Symphony No 4 (Italian).

Established as one of the leading composers, conductors and pianists of the day, he accepted the appointment of musical director of Düsseldorf. This proved one of his few unsuccessful periods (his demands were too high, causing some hostility and resentment, and he left after six months). Within a year, though, and still aged only 26, he was made musical director of the famous Leipzig Gewandhaus Orchestra. During 1835 and the next five years, Mendelssohn turned the orchestra into the finest in the world. The care and concern over preparation and interpretation proved to be an evolutionary point in the history of conducting.

During a stay in Frankfurt he met and fell in love with the 17-year-old daughter of a French Protestant clergyman, Cécile Jeanrenaud. They were married in March 1837 and enjoyed an idyllically happy life together with their five children. In 1840, the King of Prussia appointed Mendelssohn the head of the music department of a projected academy of arts in Berlin. In the end, the idea came to nothing but it gave him the chance to realise one of his dearly held ambitions – to found a conservatory in Leipzig. The King of Saxony gave his permission and the Leipzig Conservatory opened in April 1843 with Mendelssohn and Schumann teaching piano and composition and Ferdinand David in charge of the violin department.

Mendelssohn was now working at a furious pace – conducting, teaching, composing, giving concerts – and his health began to suffer. Pains in the head and abnormal fatigue kept recurring. He was in Birmingham for the premiere of his oratorio Elijah in August 1846 (one of the greatest receptions of his career) before returning to Leipzig, followed by a further visit to England in the spring of 1847. Here he played yet again for Queen Victoria, his longtime and fervent admirer.

In May, news reached him that his beloved sister Fanny had died suddenly. The loss of his lifelong companion had a devastating effect on Mendelssohn. Hearing of her death, he became unconscious, rupturing a blood vessel in the head. He only ever partly recovered, for all the life went out of him; he began suffering terrible depressions and agonising pain. Less than six months later, he too was dead. He was 38.

Piano Concertos

No 1 in G minor, Op 25; **No 2** in D minor, Op 40; **A minor** (piano and strings); **E**; **A flat** (both two pianos)

Piano Concertos – Nos 1 and 2. Capriccio brillant in
B minor, Op 22. Rondo brillant in E flat, Op 29.
Serenade and Allegro giocoso, Op 43
Stephen Hough pf **City of Birmingham Symphony
Orchestra / Lawrence Foster**
Hyperion CDA66969 (75' · DDD) Ⓕ**OO**

With Stephen Hough's Mendelssohn we enter a
new dimension. The soft, stylish arpeggios that
open the first work here, the *Capriccio brillant*,
announce something special. But this is just a
preparation for the First Concerto. Here again,
'stylish' is the word. One can sense the background – especially the operatic background –
against which these works were composed. The
first solo doesn't simply storm away, *fortissimo*;
one hears distinct emotional traits: the imperious, thundering octaves, the agitated semiquavers, the pleading appoggiaturas. The revelation
is the First Concerto's slow movement: not a
trace of stale sentimentality here, rather elegance balanced by depth of feeling. Some of the
praise must go to the CBSO and Foster; after all
it's the CBSO violas and cellos that lead the
singing in that slow movement. Foster and the
orchestra are also effective in the opening of the
Second Concerto – too often dismissed as the
less inspired sequel to No 1. The first bars are
hushed, sombre, a little below the main tempo,
so that it's left to Hough to energise the argument and set the pace – all very effective.

Double Piano Concertos – E; A flat
Benjamin Frith, Hugh Tinney pfs
RTÉ Sinfonietta / Prionnsías O'Duinn
Naxos 8 553416 (74' · DDD) Ⓢ**B**

Mendelssohn was 14 when he completed his
first two-piano Concerto in E major, and still
only 15 when he followed it with a considerably
longer (rather too long) and more ambitious
second in A flat. And it's to the great credit of
Benjamin Frith and Hugh Tinney that without a
score at hand, you would be hard-pressed to
guess who was playing what.

You'll be as impressed by their attunement of
phrasing in lyrical contexts as by their synchronisation in all the brilliant semiquaver passagework in which both works abound. Their uninhibited enjoyment of the imitative audacities of
the later work's finale is a real *tour de force*.

Under Prionnsías O'Duinn the RTÉ Sinfonietta plays with sufficient relish to allow you to
forget that the recording is perhaps just a little too
close. In short, a not-to-be-missed opportunity to
explore the young Mendelssohn at bargain price.

Violin Concerto in E minor

Mendelssohn Violin Concerto
Bruch Violin Concerto No 1 in G minor, Op 26
Schubert Rondo in A, D438
Nigel Kennedy vn
English Chamber Orchestra / Jeffrey Tate

EMI 749663-2 (71' · DDD)   Ⓟ**OB**

These are exceptionally strong and positive performances, vividly recorded. When it comes to
the two main works, Kennedy readily holds his
own against all comers. His view of the Mendelssohn has a positive, masculine quality established at the very start. He may at first seem a
little fierce, but fantasy goes with firm control,
and the transition into the second subject on a
descending arpeggio (marked *tranquillo*) is radiantly beautiful, the more affecting by contrast
with the power of what has gone before.

Kennedy is unerringly helped by Jeffrey Tate's
refreshing and sympathetic support. Though it's
the English Chamber Orchestra accompanying,
there's no diminution of scale. With full and
well-balanced sound, the piece even seems bigger, more symphonic than usual. In the slow
movement Kennedy avoids sentimentality in his
simple, songful view. The coda is always a big
test in this work, and Kennedy's and Tate's
reading is among the most powerful and exciting
on record.

The Bruch brings another warm and positive
performance, consistently sympathetic, with the
orchestra once more adding to the power.
Kennedy's more than a match for rival versions,
again bringing a masculine strength which goes
with a richly expressive yet unsentimental view
of Bruch's exuberant lyricism as in the central
slow movement. Thoroughly recommended.

Violin Concerto[a].
Piano Trios[b] – No 1, Op 49; No 2, Op 66
[b]**Patrick Demenga** vc [b]**Enrico Pace** pf
[a]**Salzburg Camerata / Leonidas Kavakos** vn
Sony Classical ② 88697 43303-2 (83' · DDD)   Ⓜ**OB**

Kavakos offers a compelling, unsugary reading
of the Concerto (where, for a change, you sense
the legacy of Beethoven as much as anyone). But
lack of heart-on-sleeve isn't to suggest in any
way a lack of expression: quite the reverse – how
Kavakos revels in those moments of introspection, the violin looking down from way, way up
in the stratosphere. There's plenty of fine detail,
too, both in the solo part and the orchestra, but
there's always a sense of it arising out of the
music. The Camerata's playing is an additional
delight, creating an intimate rapport with the
soloist.

In lesser hands, Kavakos's moderate tempo for
the slow movement might threaten to drag, but
if the interpretation is sufficiently interesting, it
can still convince. The finale is less an explosion
of exuberance, but Kavakos's filigree lightness
bodes well for the chamber music and the climactic build-up is utterly life-enhancing.

The trios are on a similar level, with Kavakos
joined by two superb musicians. It's striking in
the second movement of the D minor Trio that
they observe Mendelssohn's detached markings
– unlike many who can't resist the temptation to
swoon here. The slow movement is beautifully
poised and the finale justifiably exultant.

MENDELSSOHN'S VIOLIN CONCERTO – IN BRIEF

Yehudi Menuhin; Colonne Concerts Orchestra / George Enescu 🅷
Naxos 8 110967 (75' · ADD) Ⓢ
The youthful Menuhin at his most mercurial and dauntingly accurate. A captivating display, as are its bedfellows, the 17-year-old prodigy's legendary 1933 Lalo *Symphonie espagnole* and Chausson *Poème*.

Josef Suk; Czech PO / Karel Ančerl
Supraphon SU3663-2 (79' · ADD) Ⓢ
Suk at his incomparably eloquent, unaffected best. Ančerl and the Czech PO provide luminous support, and Supraphon's mid-'60s sound has come up very freshly.

Alfredo Campoli; London PO / Sir Adrian Boult 🅷
Beulah 1PD10 (74' · ADD) Ⓜ
This lovely performance dates from May 1958; the slow movement in particular has a homely, fireside glow that's irresistible. Pleasing early stereo. Paired with these artists' underrated account of the Elgar Concerto.

Anne-Sophie Mutter; Leipzig Gewandhaus Orchestra / Kurt Masur
DG 477 8001GH2 (73' · DDD + 📀) 🅕🅑➔
It's impossible not to be impressed by Mutter's playing. Every last detail has been dissected and considered, every phrase is minutely shaded; the subtleties of her bowing could in themselves fill a review.

Nigel Kennedy; English Chamber Orchestra / Jeffrey Tate
EMI 749663-2 (71' · DDD) 🅕🅞🅑➔
One of Kennedy's first forays into mainstream repertory, this 1987 account of the Mendelssohn has not a hint of routine about it. As well as the ubiquitous Bruch G minor, the disc also contains Schubert's little-known Rondo.

Kyung-Wha Chung; Montreal SO / Charles Dutoit
Decca 460 976-2DM (79' · DDD/ADD) 🅕🅑➔
A personable and polished alliance from Chung and Dutoit, glowingly engineered. Now generously coupled with Chung's classic 1971 pairing of Bruch's First Concerto and *Scottish Fantasia* with Kempe.

Joshua Bell; Camerata Academica Salzburg / Sir Roger Norrington
Sony Classical SK89505 (70' · DDD) 🅕🅑➔
Not everyone will go a bundle on Bell's own first-movement cadenza, but this remains a likeable, stimulating account. Perky, clean-limbed playing from the Salzburg chamber orchestra under Norrington, and very realistic sound.

Symphonies

No 1 in C minor, Op 11; **No 2** in B flat, Op 52, 'Hymn of Praise'; **No 3** in A minor, Op 56, 'Scottish'; **No 4** in A, Op 90, 'Italian'; **No 5** in D, Op 107, 'Reformation'.

Symphonies Nos 1-5. Overtures – A Midsummer Night's Dream; Die schöne Melusine; The Hebrides, 'Fingal's Cave'; Ruy Blas; Meerestille und Gückliche Fahrt; Trumpet Overture.
Elisabeth Connell, Karita Mattila *sops* Hans-Peter Blochwitz *ten* London Symphony Chorus and Orchestra / Claudio Abbado
DG ④ 471 467-2GB4 (4h 15' · DDD) 🅑🅞🅞🅞🅑➔

It is in the choral Second Symphony that the advantage of the wide-ranging digital sound comes out most strikingly, in clarifying the big *tuttis* with choir, at the same time providing extra weight of sound, notably in the way the pedal notes on the organ come over in a rich and realistic way. As to interpretation, Abbado in the first instrumental movement conveys a keener sense of joy with a wide expressive range. Again, in the choral finale Abbado's speeds tend to be a degree more relaxed and the sense of joyful release is all the keener. His three soloists are very fine and their tonal beauty and natural feeling for words and phrasing are a delight. So too is the singing of the London Symphony Chorus, particularly beautiful in the chorale, 'Nun danket alle Gott'.

It is that avoidance of Victorian blandness which is striking in Abbado's accounts of Nos 1 and 5. In No 1 he is tough and biting, slower and simpler in the second movement, returning to a tough, dark manner for the Minuet and finale. This is a performance which has one marvelling that Mendelssohn could have ever have countenanced the idea of the Octet *Scherzo* as substitute, a piece so different in mood. The first movement of the *Reformation* finds Abbado in dramatic mood, and crisper and again quicker in the second movement *Allegro vivace*.

In both the *Scottish* and *Italian* Symphonies Abbado's earlier Decca versions clearly come into contention, but where in the *Scottish* the differences of interpretation are relatively unimportant – mainly a question of the slow movement being a little slower and heavier this time – those in the *Italian* are more striking. Here the outer movements are fractionally faster than before, and that difference brings just a hint of breathlessness in the playing of the LSO but whatever my disappointment over those movements, this is now the most centrally recommendable version of the *Italian* on CD.

As for the overtures, they too bring fresh and attractive performances, very fast and fleet in the fairy music of *A Midsummer Night's Dream* and with the contrast between first and second subjects of *The Hebrides* underlined. This was one of Abbado's biggest recording projects with the orchestra of which he was music director, and remains a richly rewarding legacy.

Symphonies Nos 1 and 4, 'Italian'.
Overture, 'Ruy Blas'
Bergen Philharmonic Orchestra / Andrew Litton
BIS ⏤🔊 BIS-SACD1584 (67' · DDD)   Ⓕ🄾🅑→

Symphonies Nos 3, 'Scottish' and 5, 'Reformation'
Bergen Philharmonic Orchestra / Andrew Litton
BIS ⏤🔊 BIS-SACD1604 (70' · DDD)   Ⓕ🅑→

From the hushed polyphony of the slow intro-duction to the *Reformation* – Palestrina refracted through a Mendelssohnian prism – and the combative opening *Allegro* to a truly exultant finale, Litton and his spruce Bergen orchestra (violins lithe rather than rich-toned, basses mobile and articulate) banish any hint of turgid-ity. Tempo and character are acutely judged. The outer movements, which in some perfor-mances can sound like slow music speeded up, have a surging impetus; the *Scherzo* is blithe and airy; the grave G minor *Andante* is eloquently phrased, with a gentle flexibility of pulse. Lit-ton's ear for balance, and the luminous BIS recording, ensure that the (for Mendelssohn) dense textures of the fast movements never sound remotely clogged.

Litton's *Scottish* likewise combines verve, tex-tural clarity and a vivid sense of atmosphere – say, in the whooping *Scherzo*, with its chuckling, cavorting woodwind and horns, and the haunting lull before the finale's 6/8 coda. The slow move-ment, again, is sensitively phrased and timed, with no whiff of sentimentality. And throughout – most obviously in the finale's truculent central *fugato* – the performance gains from the antipho-nal placing of the violins. Only the first move-ment raised doubts. Litton finely catches the mystery and melancholy of the 'Holyrood' intro-duction, oboes and horns rightly dominating in the balance. But the *Allegro un poco agitato* begins steadily, shorn of any *agitato* feeling, at way under Mendelssohn's prescribed metronome marking, accelerates frantically into the first *fortissimo* and then slams the brakes on for the embellished return of the main theme. Other conductors handle the movement's tempo fluctuations more subtly and satisfyingly.

Divisi violins also enhance Litton's fresh, viva-cious performance of the *Italian*, above all in the finale's whirling contrapuntal imbroglios. The athletic Bergen orchestra (articulation superbly crisp and precise) produce marvels of lightness at speed here. Elsewhere the tricky-to-gauge tempi in the middle movements are ideally cho-sen: the modal-flavoured *Andante* solemn and evocative, yet with its *con moto* qualification duly observed, the third movement poised between Classical minuet and Romantic intermezzo, with telling touches of *portamento*. At first the glorious opening movement might beem a shade too driven but the Bergen players vindi-cate Litton's rapid tempo with their deft, poised playing, not least in the development's feathery fugato.

While it's absurd to talk of an outright winner in such a congested field, this is an exhilarating, thoroughly enjoyable *Italian*, superbly played

and recorded. Its attractions are enhanced by the couplings: a trim, elegant and, where apt (as in the Minuet), trenchant performance of the teen-age Mendelssohn's first published Symphony, in part a homage to Mozart's famous G minor Symphony, and a full-blooded reading of the splendid overture to Victor Hugo's melodrama *Ruy Blas*.

Symphony No 3, 'Scottish'. String Symphony No 11
Heidelberg Symphony Orchestra / Thomas Fey
Hänssler Classic CD98 552 (73' · DDD)   Ⓕ🄾🄾🄾🅑→

By all accounts – including those of the hostile Richard Wagner – Mendelssohn favoured urgent tempi when conducting his own and other men's music. His metronome markings for the *Scottish* Symphony bear this out; and Thomas Fey and his eagerly responsive Heidel-berg orchestra cleave closely to the composer's prescribed tempi in all four movements. The upshot, with a lean, athletic 'period' sonority (pared-down string tone, light articulation, hol-lering valveless brass, dry-rattling timpani) and sparing use of *rubato*, is virtually the swiftest, certainly the most abrasive *Scottish* on disc. Mindful of Mendelssohn's original direction *guerriero* ('warlike'), Fey conducts a truly fren-zied, bellicose finale, steely trumpets screaming through the texture.

The pentatonic-flavoured *Scherzo* is a delight: chortling woodwind, gleefully disruptive brass and a crucial Mendelssohnian quality of airy lightness – and thanks both to Fey's ear for pre-cise balance and Hänssler's natural, transparent recording, the wind here compete on equal terms in their spats and sallies with the strings. The *Adagio* is chaste and flowing, with detached phrasing and pungent accents. Any reservations centre on the first movement, where Mendels-sohn's *un poco agitato* tends to emerge as *agitatis-simo*. Fey and his Heidelbergers are certainly viscerally exciting but ultimately just too hectic and unyielding, not least in the evocations of vast, mysterious distances at the start of the development and coda.

As on his recordings of the *Italian* and *Reforma-tion*, Fey pairs a familiar 'named' symphony with one of the delightful string symphonies of Mendelssohn's indecently precocious teens. With its hyperactive, contrapuntally bristling outer movements and lusty *Scherzo* (complete with imported 'Turkish' percussion) based on a traditional Swiss song, No 11 is among the most memorable. If Fey attacks the *Menuetto* fourth movement with a Beethovenian cussedness, he and his expert players vividly catch the music's coursing energy and textural inventiveness, not least the young Mendelssohn's love of viola colour.

Symphony No 3 in A minor, 'Scottish', Op 56. Violin
Concerto in E minor, Op 64[a]. A Midsummer Night's
Dream – Overture; Wedding March
[a]**Frank-Michael Erben** *vn*

MENDELSSOHN'S SYMPHONIES NOS 3, 4 & 5 – IN BRIEF

London SO / Claudio Abbado (Nos 3 & 4)
DG 427 810-2GDC (71' · ADD) ⓂⓄⒹ→

Abbado imparts a winning sense of structural direction and emotional abandon to these works. The myth of Mendelssohn the simple prodigy is satisfyingly exploded.

LCP / Roger Norrington (Nos 3 & 4) Ⓟ
EMI 561735-2 (65' · ADD) ⓂⓄⒹ→

Right from the start of No 4, this offers something different: period instruments and good engineering give a radically altered view of balances and textures without stopping one from revelling in the joy Norrington himself clearly takes in these works.

Berlin PO / James Levine (Nos 3 & 4)
DG 427670-2GH (71' · DDD) ⒻⓄⒹ→

Levine whips up the Berliners in performances of fizzing energy and airborne grace: the edgy dance of the *Italian*'s finale is as exhilarating as any on disc.

Madrid SO / Peter Maag (Nos 3 & 4)
Arts 47506-2 (70' · ADD) ⒷⓄⓄ

The orchestra may not be top-rank but Peter Maag has trained it to give wonderfully wise, humane performances of Mendelssohn and Mozart. A clear budget choice.

Orchestra of the 18th Century / Frans Brüggen (Nos 3, 4 & 5) Ⓟ
Philips 456 267-2PH2 (120' · DDD) ⓂⒹ→

Another period set, with a more reflective approach: Nos 3 & 5 are especially intriguing.

Vienna PO / John Eliot Gardiner (Nos 4 & 5)
459 156-2GH (77' · DDD) ⒷⓄⒹ→

DG's engineering, the VPO at their most twinkle-toed and Gardiner's zeal for contrapuntal clarity combine to offer amazing levels of clarity and rhythmic buoyancy. The revised version of the Fourth is an illuminating bonus.

Leipzig Gewandhaus / Kurt Masur (Nos 3 & 4)
Warner Apex 0927 49817-2 (67' · DDD) Ⓢ

Masur has always been renowned for his joyful, straightforward performances of a composer for whom he has a special affection. Mendelssohn was director of the Leipzig orchestra and they play with an authenticity all their own.

COE / Nikolaus Harnoncourt (Nos 3 & 4) Ⓟ
Warner Classics 2564 69367-4 (69' · DDD) ⓂⒹ→

No speed-merchant, ultra-authentic versions these: the young virtuosos of the Chamber Orchestra of Europe respond zestfully to Harnoncourt's cultured direction, which does much to reveal Mendelssohn's sophisticated sense of symphonic direction.

Leipzig Gewandhaus Orchestra / Kurt Masur
Video director Bob Coles
Arthaus Musik **DVD** 100 030
(82' · NTSC · 4:3 · PCM stereo · 0) Ⓕ

This concert's visual interest rests squarely on the players and conductor; its setting is the anodyne modern Gewandhaus auditorium. Fortunately the director doesn't resort to Karajan-esque gimmickry to compensate. Masur is a pleasure to watch as he shapes his interpretations, underpinned by the orchestra's clear, airy textures, which come over with proper clarity in the Dolby Digital Stereo soundtrack. His *Dream* Overture has plenty of fleet-footed magic, and needs only more of a smile. Erben, the orchestra's leader, is a fluent, committed but unspectacular soloist in the concerto, and is none the worse for that; it's refreshing to hear Mendelssohn speaking for himself. The *Scottish* Symphony is a fine performance, capturing the first movement's melancholy with great grace, and there's plenty of energy in the *Scherzo* and final movement. Only the Wedding March seems rather short of vitality. Visually natural if not especially exciting, it's an engaging programme, and represents a decent body of music for the money.

String Symphonies

String Symphonies Nos 1, 6, 7 and 12
Nieuw Sinfonietta Amsterdam / Lev Markiz
BIS BIS-CD683 (70' · DDD) ⒻⒹ→

Amazing stuff, brilliantly performed. The first of the symphonies fair bursts from the staves, with a chuckling finale that would surely have delighted Rossini. And although the Sixth Symphony's finale harbours hints of miracles to come, Mendelssohn's mature personality is more comprehensively anticipated in the Seventh. Again, the finale suggests the ebullient, life-affirming manner of the orchestral symphonies, albeit sobered by a spot of fugally formal writing later on. The Twelfth Symphony opens with a Handelian sense of ceremony, goes on to incorporate a characteristically tender *Andante* and ends with a finale that, to quote Stig Jacobsson's enthusiastic notes, 'dies away to *pizzicato* and a subsequent *accelerando* which recalls Rossini'. This is truly delightful music, the playing both sensitive and exciting, while BIS's sound is impressively full-bodied.

Octet, Op 20

Octet[a]. Song Without Words, Op 109[b]. Variations concertantes, Op 17[b]. Assai tranquillo[b]
[a]**Ensemble Explorations** (Christine Busch, Lydia Forbes, Zhang Zhang, Francis Reusens *vns* Guus Jeukendrup, Marten Boeken *vas* Geert Debiève *vc*) with **Roel Dieltiens** *vc* [b]**Frank Braley** *pf*
Harmonia Mundi HMC90 1868 (50' · DDD) ⒻⓄⓄⒹ→

It's easy to love the Mendelssohn Octet, and the account from Ensemble Explorations is irresist-

ible. True, the recorded sound is rather too resonant, but the playing has real fire and vitality,
and the more soulful solo passages, violinist
Christine Busch's especially, are truly eloquent;
at the first movement's climactic moments her
tone rings out effortlessly above the texture.
The recent Emerson version is more sharply
recorded, with much finely polished detail, yet
their earnestly projected tone doesn't give the
sense of joyful flight that characterises this new
recording. The *Scherzo* may seem a little tame
after the brilliant, high-speed Emersons, but it
catches the nocturnal atmosphere and leaves
room for an exciting increase in speed for the
Presto finale. The cello and piano items are
played with beautiful expression; Frank Braley
clearly enjoys his 1874 Steinway.

Mendelssohn Octet[b]
Beethoven Piano Trio No 4, Op 11[a]
Nash Ensemble ([a]Ian Brown pf [a]Richard Hosford cl
[b]Marianne Thorsen, [b]Laura Samuel, [b]David Adams,
[b]Malin Broman vns [b]Lawrence Power, [b]Philip Dukes
vas [ab]Paul Watkins, [b]Timothy Hugh vcs)
Wigmore Hall Live WHLIVE0001 (55' · DDD)
Recorded live 2005   Ⓜ▶

This is a recording from a concert given in
March 2005; a very good recording, too, combining intimacy with the warm ambience familiar to Wigmore Hall concertgoers. And the
performances are splendid: there's no doubting
the genuine enthusiasm of the applause at the
end of each work.

The outer movements of the Mendelssohn
have plenty of fire and spirit. The climax of the
first movement's development section is grand
and intense, with the following *pianissimo* full of
romantic mystery and suspense. This performance isn't quite on a level with the account by
Ensemble Explorations (see above), whose
leaner tone and clearer textures (despite a less
attractive, over-resonant acoustic) bring the
work's rhythmic and expressive character into
sharper focus.

The Nash *Scherzo* is beautifully precise and
delicate, but its very fast tempo pre-empts, to
some extent, the effect of the finale. (Ensemble
Explorations, with a gentler but still fantastical
Scherzo, leave room for the *Presto* of the last
movement to increase the level of excitement.)
The Nash's interpretation scores, however,
through the immediacy of the recorded sound,
and a live-performance sense of occasion, of joy
in playing together. The Beethoven is just as
impressive, the players seeming to inspire one
another to make the most of this lively, colourful
music. Particularly appealing is the way they
bring out the character of each of the finale's
variations without compromising the music's
overall impetus.

Octet, Op 20 (arr pf duet). Symphony No 1, Op 11
(arr pf duet, vn & vc)[a]
Yaara Tal, Andreas Groethuysen pf

with [a]**Oliver Wille** vn [a]**Mikayel Hakhnazaryan** vc
Sony Classical 88697 43160-2 (59' · DDD)   Ⓕ

Why record the composer's piano-duet arrangement of the Octet, Mendelssohn's miraculous
teenage masterpiece, when there are numerous
superb versions of the original? The reason is
simple when the musicianship is as fine as on
offer here. Yaara Tal and Andreas Groethuysen
show a keen appreciation of structure, a scintillating range of colours and a compelling lightness of touch. Listen especially to the quicksilver, Goethe-inspired *Scherzo*, the 'greatest hit'
from the work, which Mendelssohn also orchestrated for insertion into his First Symphony. For
this arrangement of the symphony, in which
Mendelssohn channels his inner Beethoven and
Weber, Tal and Groethuysen are joined by *ad
libitum* violin and cello. If an alien landed on
Earth and had his first experience of Mendelssohn via these performances, he'd marvel at the
wonder of the music and never have an inkling it
could have been conceived for anything other
than these forces.

String Quartets

No 1 in E flat, Op 12 **No 2** in A, Op 13
No 3 in D, Op 44 No 1 **No 4** in E minor, Op 44 No 2
No 5 in E flat, Op 44 No 3 **No 6** in F minor, Op 80

String Quartets Nos 1-6. String Quartet (1823).
Four Pieces for String Quartet, Op 81. Octet
Emerson Quartet (Eugene Drucker, Philip Setzer vns
Lawrence Dutton va David Finckel vc)
DG ④ 477 5370GH4 (242' · DDD)   ⒻⓄⓄ▶

Cycles of Mendelssohn's string quartets are no
longer a rarity and now the Emersons issue a full
cycle that includes not only the early E flat work
of 1823 and the Op 81 miscellaneous pieces but
the Octet, which as a recording *tour de force* they
play with themselves, as it were.

The Emersons have much to offer. One of
their outstanding qualities is a sympathy for the
tensions that so often lie within Mendelssohn's
most apparently open music. They are also sensitive to the subtleties in his forms, above all in
the first movements where there can lie a greater
degree of emotional turbulence than is immediately evident. The *Scherzo* of the Fifth Quartet
has a vehemence as well as a vigour, which the
Emersons discover in the fierce figuration, and
which is to some degree realised with the music's
unexpected outcome in a fugue. If the Emersons' response to the finale seems over-
emphatic, this may be heard as the product of a
movement that Mendelssohn marks emphatically, perhaps because the animation in the
music does not seem to come from as deep as it
does elsewhere in the quartets. There is, on the
other hand, a delightful freshness of response to
the whole of the Third Quartet (actually the last
of the Op 44 set of three to have been written).
The final tarantella whirls along brilliantly.

In Quartet No 2, with its questioning motto 'Ist es wahr?' ('Is it true?'), the Emersons handle the opening movement lightly but again with that underlying touch of anxiety; they play the *Adagio* gravely and sense well the disturbance that informs the complexity of the finale. Their flexibility of response suits the opening movement of the First Quartet (they are more direct with the more straightforward opening movement of No 4), and they play the pretty *Canzonetta* quite lightly and briskly.

The last quartet, Op 80, Mendelssohn's masterpiece in the form, at once sums up his preoccupations in the previous quartets and sets them in a more profound context. The modulations within a sonata form movement, which with Mendelssohn are so often colourful or elegant, here take on a darker tinge which the Emersons understand, and they play the closing dozen bars of the *Adagio* with a touching sadness: the composer had recently learnt of the death of his beloved sister Fanny.

String Quartets No 2 & 5. Four Pieces for String Quartet, Op 81 – Capriccio in E minor; Fugue in A flat
New Zealand Quartet (Helene Pohl, Douglas Beilman *vns* Gillian Ansell *va* Rolf Gjelsten *vc*)
Naxos 8 570002 (79' · DDD)   ⓈD→

The New Zealand Quartet clearly love this music, and their strong sense of internal balance allows them to bring out many telling details that often go unnoticed: one example occurs just before the end of the first movement of the Quartet in E flat where a final recall of the second theme is accompanied by double-stopped cello *pizzicatos*; given extra emphasis here, these dark tones cast a deeper shadow over the coda's E flat radiance. In the same quartet's finale, which can seem rather superficial, the New Zealanders' confidence as ensemble players permits a flexible approach; the rhythmic momentum is never destroyed, but bends a little so that the characters of the different motifs can be enhanced.

Whenever Mendelssohn's ardent, Romantic temperament comes to the fore, these players respond. Their passionate finale of Op 13 may not quite have the intensity of some, but the focus here is rather on expressive detail. Conversely, in Op 44 this version may not favour rich tonal variety, but maintains forcefully the music's vigorous impetus, while keeping an essential warmth of expression.

With one more volume to come, this promises to be an outstanding set.

Mendelssohn String Quartets – No 4; No 3 – Andante espressivo **Mozart** String Quartet No 19, 'Dissonance', K465
Schubert String Quartet No 12, 'Quartettsatz', D703
Elias Quartet (Sara Bitlloch, Donald Grant *vns* Martin Saving *va* Marie Bitlloch *vc*)
Wigmore Hall Live Ⓜ WHLIVE0028 (79' · DDD)

Recorded live in 2008   ⒻOD→

Here's an ensemble not in thrall to streamlining to the *n*th degree, but with four personalities still apparent, playing with complete unanimity of purpose. This disc, caught on the wing at Wigmore Hall, offers many delights; and the audience is presumably captivated, as it's remarkably silent.

Along with Mendelssohn, Schubert is clearly another great love of the Elias, and in the *Quartettsatz* they revel in the Viennese charm, an aspect that can sometimes get lost in the sheer drive of some interpretations, and find time to grow the phrases quite beautifully.

In the *Dissonance* the Elias have chosen the most overtly dramatic and groundbreaking of Mozart's quartets, and they relish the emergence of melody from the primeval chromatic swamp. Here there are plentiful examples of their fine musicianship, particularly in the slow movement, where their individuality comes to the fore.

In Mendelssohn's Fourth Quartet, though, we're back to the Elias at their very best, Sara Bitlloch's delectable tone leading the way in the extensive first movement and the piece's underlying unease never underplayed. The Mendelssohn encore is a delightful bonus.

The Elias is one of the most compelling of the younger generation of quartets, and despite minor reservations about the Mozart, this disc offers much pleasure and much promise of a glittering future.

Piano Trios

Piano Trios – No 1 in D minor, Op 49;
No 2 in C minor, Op 66
Florestan Trio (Anthony Marwood *vn* Richard Lester *vc* Susan Tomes *pf*)
Hyperion CDA67485 (54' · DDD)   ⒻD→

With its unforgettable opening cello theme, the D minor First has always been the more favoured of the two. But in a performance as subtle and impassioned as the Florestan's, the C minor Second seems at least as fine. The powerful, almost Brahmsian first movement alone should give the lie to the cliché that Mendelssohn's genius declined irredeemably after the brilliance of youth. While always keeping the potentially dense textures lucid (Susan Tomes's refined, singing tone and articulation a constant pleasure), the Florestan play this with a mingled fire and lyrical tenderness that it's hard to imagine bettered.

The flowing barcarolle slow movement has a crucial quality of innocence, and the flickering nocturnal *Scherzo* is as delicate and pointed as you could wish, at a tempo close to Mendelssohn's optimistically fast marking, while the finale drives impulsively towards its triumphant chorale apotheosis, grandly inevitable rather than bombastic.

From the yearning opening, the great cello melody surging across the bar-lines, the Florestan are equally vivid in the D minor Trio. Scrupulously observant, as ever, of Mendelssohn's detailed dynamic markings, they make you more than usually aware of how much of the music is held down to *piano* and *pianissimo*; and the moment at the start of the recapitulation, where Richard Lester's warm cello is counterpoised with violinist Anthony Marwood's fragile, floated descant, is as magical as you will hear.

Again the Florestan favour an easily flowing tempo for the song-without-words slow movement, phrasing in long spans (uncommonly pure, luminous duetting from Marwood and Lester) and finding a touch of playfulness when the main theme returns. Just as fine are the irresistible airborne *Scherzo* and the finale, where the Florestan, taking note of the qualifying *un poco tranquillo*, make the opening march unusually pensive before sweeping forward with an authentically Mendelssohnian mix of restless agitation, grace and lyrical fervour. Pleasure in these superb performances is enhanced by a beautifully natural recording and Robert Philip's detailed, illuminating notes.

Piano Trios Nos 1 & 2
Julia Fischer *vn* **Daniel Müller-Schott** *vc*
Jonathan Gilad *pf*
Pentatone PTC5186 085 (59' · DDD/DSD)   Ⓕ

Chamber music with star players doesn't always work: lack of rehearsal time or oversized egos can often lead to performances high on surface glitz but low on understanding. Not here though: these young artists, already making waves in their individual careers, give us a recording of Mendelssohn's delectable piano trios that sparkles and fizzes from the outset.

The opening of the D minor Trio No 1 is a touch simpler than the Florestan's recent acclaimed reading (see above) but its urgency sweeps you along. They are particularly fine in the *scherzos* of both trios, with delightful *portamentos* in the D minor which seem to say 'look how easy this is'. In the finale, the new trio set off at a dancing pace; the Florestan are a touch steadier, which makes for an even more explosive contrast as the movement hots up.

The C minor Trio has long lived in the shadow of the D minor. It's darker, slower to reveal its secrets. The new version fully captures its ruggedness, the way that melodies are hewn from the musical material, rather than simply emerging complete as in No 1. The only real quibble is their spacious tempo for the second movement, a Venetian gondola song in all but name. It's played with great tenderness but does seem rather over-extended.

All in all, this new recording is irresistible, with the three players caught in a wholly natural ambience. It's always a good sign when you don't want to stop playing a disc long enough to write about it.

Cello Sonatas

Cello Sonatas – No 1 in B flat, Op 45; No 2 in D, Ⓟ
Op 58. Variations concertantes, Op 17. Assai
tranquillo. Song Without Words, Op 109
Steven Isserlis *vc* **Melvyn Tan** *fp*
RCA Red Seal 09026 62553-2 (62' · DDD)   ⒻⓄ

Isserlis and Tan offer idiomatic, well-turned performances full of freshness and vigour. Try the First Sonata in B flat major (which Mendelssohn wrote for his brother, Paul, in 1838), where the second movement's dual function as *scherzo* and slow movement is convincingly characterised, and the music's passionate outbursts sound arrestingly potent. Isserlis's and Tan's fine blend of subtlety and panache affectingly conveys the nostalgic mood of the *Variations concertantes*, and culminates powerfully in the work's conclusion. In the D major Second Sonata, Isserlis's and Tan's spontaneity and energy in the outer movements, skilfully controlled variety of timbre and touch in the *Scherzo*, and dramatic opposition of chorale (piano) and recitative (cello) in the third movement sound immensely compelling. In the *Assai tranquillo*, as in the charming *Song Without Words*, Op 109, sympathetic tonal balance between cello and fortepiano in the softly lit recording brings out the music's sentiment. Isserlis and Tan effectively draw out the work's inconclusive ending to create a telling analogy of the eternal nature of friendship. Excellent balance and crisp, restrained recording helps vividly to evoke this music's Romantic atmosphere.

Variations sérieuses, Op 54

Variations sérieuses in D minor, Op 54. Piano Sonata
in E, Op 6. Three Preludes, Op 104a. Three Studies,
Op 104b. Kinderstücke, Op 72, 'Christmas Pieces'.
Gondellied in A. Scherzo in B minor
Benjamin Frith *pf*
Naxos 8 550940 (65' · DDD)   ⓈⒹ

The multiplicity of notes in Mendelssohn's piano music sometimes lays him open to the charge of 'note-spinning'. So what higher praise for Benjamin Frith than to say that thanks to his fluency, not a single work outstays its welcome here. The unchallengeable masterpiece is the *Variations sérieuses*, so enthusiastically taken up by Clara Schumann, and still a repertory work today. Frith characterises each variation with telling contrasts of tempo and touch without sacrificing the continuity and unity of the whole. Equally importantly, he never lets us forget the *sérieuses* of the title.

No less impressive is his sensitively varied palette in the early E major Sonata (unmistakable homage to Beethoven's Op 101) so often helped by subtle pedalling. But surely the recitative of the *Adagio* at times needs just a little more intensity and underlying urgency. Of the miniatures the six *Kinderstücke* ('Christmas Pieces' – written for the children of a friend) emerge with an unforced charm. As music they lack the romance of Schumann's ventures into a child's world, just as the *Three Studies* do of Chopin's magical revelations in this sphere. However, Frith's fingers never let him down. In the first B flat Study he even seems to acquire a third hand to sustain its middle melody. For sheer seductive grace, the independent *Gondellied* haunts the memory most of all.

With pleasantly natural sound, too, this disc is quite a bargain.

Songs Without Words

Songs Without Words – Op 19 Nos 1 & 3; Op 30 No 6, 'Venetianisches Gondellied No 2'; Op 38 No 2; Op 53 Nos 2 & 3; Op 67 Nos 3, 4 & 5; Op 85 No 4; Op 102 No 2; in F sharp minor; in F; in E flat. Albumblatt, Op 117. Rondo capriccioso, Op 14. Gondellied in A. Klavierstück in G minor
Sebastian Knauer pf
Berlin Classics 0016372BC (71' · DDD) Ⓕ○○

One of the main reasons for the success of this disc is that instead of doggedly ploughing his way through a chronologically ordered selection of *Songs Without Words*, Sebastian Knauer has chosen only those which appeal to him and about which he feels he has something individual to say. At least, that is the impression one gets from his playing.

For Mendelssohn specialists there are the added bonuses of four world premiere recordings: the Songs in F sharp minor and F major (*sans* opus numbers) are heard here in the first edition of the 2001 Viennese Urtext; the Song in E flat is a completion by Mendelssohn's biographer Larry Todd (who also contributes the booklet here); Op 102 No 2 in D major is a 'recording of the dedicated original score' (no further information is given).

Realistically captured, with strong, sweeping accounts of the *Variations sérieuses* as the programme's centrepiece and the *Andante and Rondo capriccioso* with which Knauer rounds off proceedings, this is a distinguished contribution to the 200th anniversary celebrations.

Mendelssohn Three Caprices, Op 33 – No 2; No 3. Prelude, Op 104*a* No 2. Rondo capriccioso, Op 14. Songs Without Words - selection. Three Studies, Op 104*b*. Variations sérieuses, Op 54. Suleika, Op 34 No 4. A Midsummer Night's Dream – Scherzo (arr Rachmaninov). Scherzo, Op 16 No 2
Liszt Mendelssohn Lieder, S547 – Suleika; Auf Flügeln des Gesanges
Bertrand Chamayou pf
Naïve V5131 (65' · DDD) Ⓕ○

There was a time in the 19th century when Mendelssohn's *Songs Without Words* were regularly regarded as the third great collection of piano music after Beethoven's 32 sonatas and Bach's 48 Preludes and Fugues. While Chopin's piano music is still dominant, Mendelssohn's star as a pianist-composer has faded. It is a splen-

did idea of the young Toulouse-born French pianist Bertrand Chamayou to choose five of the most striking *Songs Without Words* and make them a centrepiece for what he describes as a 'Liederabend without words'.

The *Songs Without Words* are among the least difficult of the pieces here technically, but the other pieces are much more demanding, not just the two bigger pieces, the *Variations sérieuses* and the *Rondo capriccioso*, but such pieces as the *Three Studies*. It says much for Chamayou's virtuosity and artistry that he makes the results so magnetic. He opens with a brief and powerful Prelude in B minor, leading to a sparkling account of the *Rondo capriccioso* bringing out echoes of the *Scherzo* from *A Midsummer Night's Dream*, which right at the end of the recital comes as a tailpiece in Rachmaninov's arrangement.

The articulation in the *Three Studies* is phenomenally clear and light, as it is too in Chamayou's dazzling account of the *Caprices*. There are similar qualities in the longest and most ambitious of the pieces, the *Variations sérieuses*. Along with the *Songs Without Words* it is good too to have Liszt's surprisingly unshowy arrangements of Mendelssohn's most famous Lied, 'On Wings of Song'. Clean, clear sound to match the playing.

Organ works

'Complete Organ Works, Volume 1'
Allegro assai (ed Bate)[b]. Fughetta in A[c]. Two Fugues – in E minor[d]; in D[ae]. Organ Sonata No 1, Op 65[f]. Prelude and Fugue, Op 37 No 1[g]. Six Little Pieces – Prelude in D minor[g]. Four Studies[ce]. Andante and Variations[b]. Chorale Prelude, 'Nim von uns, Herr'[g]
Jennifer Bate with [a]**Martin Stacey** orgs
Somm Céleste Series SOMMCD050 (73' · DDD)
Played on the organs of [b]All Saints Church, Margaret St, London; [c]St Stephen's Church, Bournemouth; [d]Temple Church, Fleet St, London; [e]St John's Church, Upper Norwood, London; [f]St Matthew's Church, Bayswater, London; [g]Wimborne Minster, Wimborne, Dorset Ⓕ

In Jennifer Bate's impressive discography of British organ music she has taken pains to match each individual piece with an appropriate organ. Technically speaking, Mendelssohn may not have been British, but his magnificent Sonatas and Preludes and Fugues were all composed for the British market, so it is entirely fitting that Bate pays the same attention to detail over his music as she does over the genuine, home-grown article.

In this series, which now stretches to five discs, Bate has recorded all 68 pieces contained in a newly published edition of Mendelssohn's complete organ works. It goes without saying that her playing is hugely impressive and impeccably stylish, the virtuoso passagework delivered with almost flawless precision.

The surprise at finding, among the six English organs chosen for this repertoire, Wimborne Minster, with its neo-Baroque organ, is quickly assuaged by Bate's intelligent use of stops included in the 1867 rebuild. Appropriately this instrument is used for the more contrapuntal pieces. For the First Sonata she uses the more opulent-sounding Walker instrument of St Matthew's, Bayswater, while the sumptuous Hill organ of St Stephen's, Bournemouth (here relocated from Dorset to Hampshire, where it was located when the organ was built in 1898), is ideal in the first three of the Four Studies.

Beyond the First Sonata and the Prelude and Fugue, the only piece here to have established itself in the repertory is the lovely *Andante and Variations* which, played with disarming fluidity on the organ of All Saints, Margaret Street, provides a real highlight on a disc which is infinitely more rewarding than an initial glance at the track-listing might imply.

Choruses

Six Choruses, Op 88. Four Choruses, Op 100.
Der Erste Frühlingstag, Op 48. Im Freien zu singen, Op 41. Im Grünen, Op 59
RIAS Chamber Choir, Berlin / Hans-Christoph Rademann
Harmonia Mundi HMC90 1992 (66' · DDD)　Ⓕ**O**▶

But how delightful! Here come Herr Mendelssohn and his choir, walking across the fields making directly for our neck of the woods where we are about to enjoy our own *déjeuner sur l'herbe*. Certainly Mendelssohn liked to take his singers out into the country and particularly to the woods, the 'temple of harmony' as one of his part-songs has it. And if they sang Mendelssohn's pleasant compositions as beautifully as the RIAS choir sing them here, how welcome they would be. Even Wordsworth, listening to the 'still, sad music of humanity', might not have been too put out; for these, on the whole, are Wordsworthian poems, and the settings, however trim and cultivated, are closer to Wordsworth's Nature than to the world of business and 'greetings where no kindness is'.

They are, in fact, kindly works, kindly on the ear and on the voices. Essentially homophonic in their writing for unaccompanied choir, they never leave the individual parts without interest, whether a point of harmony, an imitative phrase or a solo lead. Within the equable sameness of the manner there are many variations and shades of expression. The RIAS Chamber Choir, with their irreproachable homogeneity of tone and flawless intonation, are alive to all the finer points of phrasing and coloration.

Elijah (sung in English)
Renée Fleming, Libby Crabtree sops **Patricia**　Ⓟ
Bardon, Sara Fulgoni mezzos **Matthew Munro** treb
John Mark Ainsley, John Bowen tens **Neal Davies**
bar **Bryn Terfel** bass-bar **Geoffrey Moses** bass
Edinburgh Festival Chorus; Orchestra of the Age of Enlightenment / Paul Daniel
Decca ② 455 688-2DH2 (131' · DDD· T)　Ⓕ▶

Paul Daniel and Bryn Terfel ensure that this is one of the most dramatic performances of the oratorio on disc. The young conductor, with the advantage of an excellent period instrument orchestra, has looked anew at the score and as a reveals much of the rhythmic and dynamic detail not always present in other performances, at least those available in English. His accomplishment in terms of pacing and balance is also praiseworthy, and he earns further marks for using the trio, quartet and double quartet of soloists Mendelssohn asks for in specific pieces, so as to vary the texture of the music.

Bryn Terfel simply gives the most exciting and vivid account of the prophet's part yet heard. His range, in terms of vocal register and dynamics, is huge; his expression, mighty and immediate, befits a man of Elijah's temperament. As the score demands, anguish, anger and sympathy are there in full measure, displayed in exceptional definition of words, and when this Elijah calls on the Lord for the saving rain, the Almighty could hardly resist such a commanding utterance. Yet there's always the inwardness part of the role demands. As far as the other soloists are concerned, for the concerted numbers Daniel has chosen voices that nicely match each other in timbre. The chorus is alert and unanimous in both attack and well thought-through phrasing, but its actual sound can be a little soft-centred, partly because all-important consonants are ignored. The orchestral playing is exemplary.

Elijah (sung in German)
Christine Schäfer sop **Cornelia Kallisch** contr
Michael Schade ten **Wolfgang Schöne** bass-bar
Stuttgart Gächinger Kantorei; Stuttgart Bach Collegium / Helmuth Rilling
Hänssler Classic ② CD98 928 (128' · DDD · T/t)　Ⓕ

Rilling brings out arrestingly the drama of the piece, turning it into a well-varied, exciting quasi-opera, a far from traditional view of the oratorio. The vicissitudes of the prophet's eventful life, his reaction to events, the challenge to Baal, the encounter with Jezebel, have never sounded so electrifying. For that we have to thank Rilling's disciplined chorus, biting in diction, precise and convincing in attack. Yet they can also provide the most sensitive, ethereal tone, as in Nos 28 and 29, trio and chorus, 'Siehe, der Hüter Israels'.

The orchestral playing is no less arresting. Furthermore, as Elijah, Schöne unerringly or authoritatively captures his many moods. Here is the courageous man of action as he confronts Baal's followers and ironically taunts them, the sense of fiery conviction in 'Ist's nichts des Herrn Wort', of doubt in 'Es ist genug', and finally the wonderful Bachian serenity in 'Ja, es sollen wohl Berge weichen', all evoked in the most positive and imaginative delivery of the text. The voice itself, a firm, expressive bassbaritone, is ideal for the role, one on which the singer has obviously lavished much time and consideration – to excellent effect. The same can be said for Schäfer, who brings a Silja-like conviction to all her work. Anyone hearing her declaim 'Weiche nicht' would never be afraid again. The voice itself is interesting, gleaming and yet not without a fair degree of warmth in the tone.

Kallisch is almost as convincing in the mezzo solos and gives us a wonderfully malign portrayal of Jezebel. Schade is a fresh-voiced, communicative Obadiah, and he's another who's vivid with his words. The recording, however, is slightly too reverberant, but the added space around the voices doesn't preclude immediacy of impact.

Gian Carlo Menotti American 1911-2007

An American composer of Italian origin, Menotti studied at the Milan Conservatory and the Curtis Institute, where a co-student was Samuel Barber, later to become his parter and with whom he wrote librettos. His comic one-act opera Amelia al ballo was taken up by the Met in 1938 and led to an NBC commission for a radio opera, The Old Maid and the Thief (1939). His next stage work, The Island God (1942, Met), was a failure; but it was followed after the war by the chamber opera The Medium (1946). Paired with his short comedy The Telephone it notched up a Broadway run of 211 performances, 1947-48. The Consul (1950), in a post-Puccini verismo style, and The Saint of Bleecker Street (1954) both enjoyed much success, as did Amahl and the Night Visitors. It was the first opera ever written for television in America, and first aired on Christmas Eve, 1951. It was such a success that it became an annual Christmas tradition. It remains Menotti's most popular work to this day. His later works include more operas and orchestral pieces, including several works for children. In 1958 he founded the Spoleto Festival of Two Worlds, which he directed until 1967.

Violin Concerto

Violin Concerto[a]. The Death of Orpheus[b].
Muero porque no muero[c]. Oh llama de amor viva[d]
[a]**Jennifer Koh** vn [c]**Julia Melinek** sop
[b]**Jamie MacDougall** ten [d]**Stephen Roberts** bar
[bcd]**Spoleto Festival Choir and Orchestra /
Richard Hickox**
Chandos CHAN9979 (61' · DDD) Ⓕ▶

Gian Carlo Menotti's lyrical Violin Concerto, one of his most popular instrumental works, is here neatly coupled with premiere recordings of three cantatas written since 1982, products of his active old age in his seventies and eighties. Hickox draws from the Festival Orchestra warmly persuasive readings of works which may be unashamedly eclectic, but are powerfully convincing in such committed performances. The young American violinist, Jennifer Koh, is the excellent soloist. The first movement with its sequence of flowing melodies could easily

seem to meander, but Koh and Hickox give it a clear shape, with each new idea emerging seductively. The slow movement, played with hushed dedication, has a tender poignancy here; an intrusive brass motif leads to the central cadenza, technically demanding but not showy. The vigorous finale features a jaunty main theme and ends with virtuoso fireworks, rounding off a piece that deserves resurrecting in the concert hall too.

The two Spanish-language cantatas were written respectively in 1982 and 1991 for the Catholic University in Washington. Menotti confesses to having lost his religious faith, and perhaps understandably here writes sensuous music closer to Puccini's opera, *Suor Angelica*, than to any religious model. Julia Melinek is the vibrant soloist in the St Teresa setting, with her marked vibrato well-controlled. Stephen Roberts, the responsive soloist in the St John of the Cross setting, is caught less happily, his voice ill-focused.

The Death of Orpheus, to an English text by Menotti himself, is even more dramatic, based on the legend of Orpheus being killed by Thracian women in a bacchanalian frenzy. Orpheus's song emerges as a broad diatonic melody, with choral writing of Delian sensuousness and the tenor's part with Britten-like echoes. Jamie MacDougall is the expressive soloist, with the chorus fresh and incisive in all three cantatas.

Operas

Help, Help, the Globolinks!
Edith Mathis sop Emily **Arlene Saunders** sop
Madame Euterpova **Raymond Wolansky** bar
Dr Stone **William Workman** bar Tony
Kurt Marschner ten Timothy
**North German Radio Children's Choir; Hamburg
Philharmonic State Orchestra / Matthias Kuntzsch**
Stage director **Gian Carlo Menotti**
Video director **Joachim Hess**
ArtHaus Musik 🄓🅥🄓 101 281 (71' · NTSC · 4:3 · PCM
mono · 0). Recorded 1969 Ⓕ

Directed by the composer with all the colourful melodrama of an American B-movie, the soloists of Hamburg's late-1960s house ensemble get a real chance to shine in what is virtually the world premiere of Menotti's children's sci-fi opera. In the libretto – a jolly collision between *The War of the Worlds*, the Munchkins from the land of Oz and *Hansel and Gretel* – only (tonal) music and musicians can save the earth from the invading Globolinks and their electronic (ie, non-musical) voices. Nikolas Schöffler (lighting) and Alwin Nikolais (costumes and Globolink choreography) make essential contributions to the visual realisation of the aliens as sinister, flexible lampshades, and the creation of a spooky atmosphere a cut above most contemporary TV series.

The score is an eclectic mix of Menotti's trademark second-generation *verismo* – handy for the tantrums of the principal role, Madame Euterpova, a wacky mid-European music teacher – and Kurt Weill-like recitative and marching rhythms for the children and their driver whose school trip goes astray in the forest. This musical storytelling has a compelling narrative simplicity which, like Benjamin Britten's, never becomes saccharine or patronising. The characters, especially the three supporting teachers, have a pleasing Roald Dahl wackiness, making them natural stage roles.

It's not everyday you get to see Edith Mathis as a violin-playing schoolgirl, or Arlene Saunders (the company's Agathe and Eva) as the eccentric music teacher with a *Bewitched*-style nose. Wolansky too is genuinely funny as the confused, and unmusical, head of the school who becomes the one human sacrifice to the Globolinks. Sterling digital restoration seconds the fine balance of the production between comic and serious, making for an unintended but most effective tribute to Menotti's wide-ranging theatrical creativity.

Aarre Merikanto   Finnish 1893-1958

Aarre Merikanto, son of composer Oskar Merikanto, studied with Reger in Leipzig, and in Moscow. He later taught at the Helsinki Academy (1936-58). His opera Juha (1922) is couched in a language not unlike that of Janáček; other works, in a highly coloured, chromatic style, include three symphonies, three piano concertos and chamber music.

Piano Concertos

Piano Concertos Nos 2 & 3. Two Studies. Two Pieces
Matti Raekallio pf
Tampere Philharmonic Orchestra / Tuomas Ollila
Ondine ODE915-2 (55' · DDD)   Ⓕ

Merikanto's Second and Third Piano Concertos (from 1937-38 and 1955 respectively) are typical of his later output – contrapuntally inventive and impressionistic in scoring. Both have an engaging Prokofievian brio in the brisk outer movements and a Rachmaninovesque Romanticism in the lyrical central *adagios*. Yet Merikanto never entirely forsook his adventurous harmonic writing, and especially in the Second the result – allied to considerable formal latitude – is suggestive of (of all people) Villa-Lobos. Granted it's with a Nordic not a Brazilian accent, but think here of works such as *Momoprecoce* and *Bachiana* No 3 as much as the piano concertos; those who know both will appreciate the similarity.

Matti Raekallio is a pianist of real technical ability and musical sensibility. He has the measure of both concertos, and the Second in particular could well become popular as an alternative to Prokofiev's Third or the *Paganini* Rhapsody. The purely orchestral *Two Studies* and *Two Pieces* (1941), though much slighter affairs, are by no means insignificant trifles. Tuomas Ollila secures more than competent performances

from the Tampere orchestra, matched by excellent sound. A real delight.

Pan, Op 28

Lemminkäinen, Op 10. Pan, Op 28. Four Compositions. Andante religioso. Scherzo
Tampere Philharmonic Orchestra / Tuomas Ollila
Ondine ODE905-2 (54' · DDD)   Ⓕ

Aarre Merikanto's career divided broadly into three phases, those of apprentice, radical and conservative, and there are works from each present on this valuable issue. Critical hindsight accords (quite rightly) that the brief radical phase, roughly corresponding to the 1920s, was the most valuable, though at the time Merikanto's modernistic approach – and that of his like-minded contemporaries, Ernest Pingoud and Väinö Raito – was derided. Only one piece here represents this period, the highly accomplished tone-poem, *Pan* (1924), a wonderful, evocative, yet robust score, possessed of a very Nordic brand of impressionism. *Lemminkäinen* (1916), by contrast, seems immature, and rather parochial. A Sibelian shadow lies heavily across its quarter-hour duration, yet without a trace of the older composer's own *Lemminkäinen* tone-poems. There's little of the latter's emotional and psychological depth – or musical range – but instead a prevailing rollicking good humour broken occasionally by more serious moments. The remaining works all date from the early stages of Merikanto's post-modern period, when he reverted to a simpler, more accessible idiom. The *Four Compositions* (1932) make a very effective and satisfying set, and whereas the *Andante religioso* (1933) seems like a piece out of context, the *Scherzo* (1937) is entirely convincing on its own. The performances are sympathetic and well recorded.

Olivier Messiaen   French 1908-1992

Probably the only classical composer to have a mountain named after him (Mount Messiaen, Utah, 1978), Messiaen is among the most strikingly individual of 20th-century composers. He entered the Paris Conservatoire aged 11, specialising in organ, improvisation and composition (he studied with Dukas fame and with the great French organist Marcel Dupré). When he graduated in 1930, he not only became organist at the Trinity Church in Paris – he played there regularly until the end of his life – but also began a distinguished teaching career and co-founded a group called 'La Jeune France', which had the express intention of promoting modern French music.

He joined the French army at the outbreak of the Second World War but was taken prisoner and spent two years in a German prison camp in Görlitz, Silesia. Here he composed his Quatuor pour la fin du temps. Repatriated in 1942, he resumed his post at Holy Trinity and was appointed to the faculty of the Paris Con-

MESSIAEN TURANGALÎLA-SYMPHONIE – IN BRIEF

Donohoe, Murail; CBSO / Rattle
EMI 586525-2   Ⓜ️Ⓞ➔

Rattle's innate feeling for orchestral colour combined with his skill in negotiating huge and complex scores pays off richly with a fine modern recording. Coupled with the *Quartet for the End of Time* and *La merle*.

Crossley, Murail; Philharmonia / Salonen
Sony Classical SBK89900   Ⓑ➔

Recorded at almost exactly the same time as the Rattle, his contemporary Esa-Pekka Salonen takes a similarly probing approach. Beautiful, silky playing by the Philharmonia and, again, superb soloists.

Aimard, Kim; BPO / Nagano
Teldec 2564 62162-2   ⒻⓄⓄⓄ

Nagano draws playing of quite thrilling excitement from the great Berlin orchestra: maybe they'd never played it before, but they give it 100 per cent. Pierre-Laurent Aimard throws off the piano part with typical aplomb. The top recommendation.

Thibaudet, Harada;
Royal Concertgebouw / Chailly
Decca 436 626-2DH   ⒻⓄ➔

Chailly's driven approach pushes Messiaen's highly charged passions to the point of hysteria. The Concertgebouw Orchestra relish the contrasts and the beautiful acoustic of their hall adds its own magic.

Weigl, Bloch; Polish Nat RSO / Wit
Naxos 8 554478/9   ⓈⓄ➔

A boldy recorded and played performance that makes the most of the work's dynamic and emotional extremes. Wit couples it, more logically, with *L'Ascension*. A fine bargain alternative to the single-CD Salonen.

Shelley, Hartmann-Claverie;
BBC PO / YP Tortelier
Chandos CHAN9678   Ⓕ

Often overlooked by more seemingly glamorous line-ups, this is a fine modern version in typically glorious sound. The BBC Philharmonic sounds really world-class.

Y Loriod, J Loriod; Bastille Opera Orch /
M-W Chung
DG 431 781-2GH   Ⓕ➔

An 'authentic' performance, perhaps, with Messiaen's widow playing the piano. Chung shows himself a natural Messiaen interpreter and draws from his Bastille orchestra some wonderfully idomatic playing.

servatoire. From then, his career as France's leading living composer developed apace and by the early 1950s he had an international standing and a generation of young composers eager to study with him, including Pierre Boulez, Stockhausen and Xenakis.

Messiaen came from a family of literary intellectuals and his breadth of knowledge and interests coloured all his music: he was an expert ornithologist (his *Oiseaux exotiques*, *Catalogue d'oiseaux* and *Réveil des oiseaux* are just some of the complex works which use birdsong as their inspiration); he studied Greek and Indian verse; above all, he was a religious philosopher who knew all the world religions and was himself a devout Roman Catholic. The mystic and celebratory elements are at the root of all his music.

Turangalîla-Symphonie

Turangalîla-Symphonie (1990 revised version)
Pierre-Laurent Aimard pf **Dominique Kim** ondes
Berlin Philharmonic Orchestra / Kent Nagano
Teldec 8573 82043-2 (73' · DDD)   ⒻⓄⓄⓄ

Turangalîla is a difficult score, and to record it live is risky. Even when the orchestra is the Berlin Philharmonic? Yes, since the work is very far from the centre of their repertoire. Whether despite or because of that risk this is a splendidly exciting performance; more surprisingly it's also for the most part a very accurate and detailed one. The textures and colours of the third movement are finely balanced, as they are even in the headlong exuberance of its successor. Although the precision of the seventh seems to understate its balefulness the complex textures and superimposed rhythms of the ninth are outstandingly clear and fascinating. The soloists are admirable; the extremes of the piano part, in particular, are just what Aimard is good at. There are one or two imprecisions of balance, but this is among the two or three best accounts of *Turangalîla* available.

Et exspecto resurrectionem mortuorum

Et exspecto resurrectionem mortuorum.
Chronochromie. La ville d'en-haut
Cleveland Orchestra / Pierre Boulez
DG 445 827-2GH (58' · DDD)   ⒻⓄ➔

Boulez has spoken at his pleasure at performing Messiaen with an orchestra relatively unfamiliar with his music. It sounds as though the Cleveland Orchestra must have enjoyed it too. You would expect them to, perhaps, in such a passage as that in the fourth movement of *Et exspecto*, where the two superimposed plainchant melodies return together with the noble 'theme of the depths' – it has great splendour, as does the chorale melody of the finale, rising at the end to a satisfyingly palpable *fffff*. And in this performance of *Chronochromie* you can hear why Messiaen said that certain pages of it were a double homage to Berlioz and Pierre Schaeffer, the French pioneer of electronic music. In the work's penultimate section, the famous 'Epode' in which 18 string players impersonate different birds, the obvious problems of clarity and precision are expertly negotiated: the players really seem to enjoy their dawn chorus.

Absolute rhythmic precision and the clarity of colour that comes from meticulous balance are among the other pleasures of these performances. They make a most satisfying coupling, too. The recordings are excellent: clean but not clinical and ample in range.

Visions de l'Amen

Visions de l'Amen[a]. Fantaisie burlesque. Pièce pour le tombeau de Paul Dukas. Rondeau
Steven Osborne, [a]**Martin Roscoe** pfs
Hyperion CDA67366 (61' · DDD)   Ⓕ**Ⓞ**▸

It's axiomatic (to use a favourite word of the French) that the Messiaens' own 1962 disc of *Visions* is irreplaceable. At the same time it raises the common interpretative problem when composers play their own music: should we follow what they say in musical and verbal notes, or what they do?

Such problems don't arise with the three early pieces, which hardly show Messiaen at his best, but the metronome mark for the very slow first movement of *Visions*, which literally sets the groundwork for the cycle, dictates a duration of 6'15". He and his wife, Yvonne Loriod, dispatch it in 4'30". Steven Osborne and Martin Roscoe (like the old Regis recording by Peter Hill and Benjamin Frith) prefer to believe the score, and the result is an impressively relentless sweep from the faintest *pppp* to a searing *fff*.

Messiaen's library was full of astonomical picture-books, and his interpretation of the whole work brings out the violence and local disorder involved in the act of creation, even if the ultimate goal (here, a resplendent A major chord) is always in view. This superbly engineered Hyperion disc is true to his Technicolor vision.

Indeed, it's in the rich and immediate piano sound that this version scores most notably over Hill and Frith's, where the playing is no less accurate or intense. Particularly beautiful is a sudden *pianissimo* early in the fourth movement, and there are some decidedly upfront birds from Osborne in the next. (Messiaen always insisted that townspeople, who knew only the sparrow, had no idea how deafening birds in a forest could be.) In the final movement Osborne and Roscoe throw authenticity aside; their *Modéré, joyeux* goes uninhibitedly for the second epithet. And wonderfully exciting it is.

Catalogue d'oiseaux

Catalogue d'oiseaux
Roger Muraro pf
Accord ② 465 768-2 (DDD)   Ⓕ**Ⓞ**

Muraro demonstrates both formidable pianism and an outstandingly imaginative response to

Messiaen's imaginative world. The dynamic range is wide, the colouring often subtly beautiful, the virtuosity quite breathtaking at times. The virtuoso and the poet are in ideal balance here – magnificent rocky landscapes, vivid greens and blues! This is an outstanding reading throughout, and one can only echo the audience's applause after 'The Wood Lark' and their cheers at 'Cetti's Warbler'. Recommended.

Huit préludes

Préludes. Catalogue d'oiseaux – Book 3 No 6, L'Alouette Lulu; Book 5 No 9, La Bouscarle. Quatre études de rythme – Ile de feu 1; Ile de feu 2
Pierre-Laurent Aimard pf
DG 477 7452GH (60' · DDD)   Ⓕ**Ⓞ**▸

Pierre-Laurent Aimard knew Messiaen and studied with Yvonne Loriod, yet these personal associations result in playing of intense sobriety. Indeed, the initial impression, in the first of the early *Préludes*, is of unusual restraint. While pianists anxious to underline the links with Debussy often opt for impressionistic washes of sound, Aimard achieves insight through clarity, a quality aided by superb sound-recording, with a rich range of meticulously graded dynamic levels, and just the right amount of space and resonance around the instrument.

Aimard's technical virtuosity comes through in the evenness of his voicing and the pearly delicacy with which Messiaen's intricate ornamental writing is projected. Nevertheless, when turbulence and incisiveness are required, as in the *Ile de feu* studies, they emerge naturally and inevitably. Aimard never polishes away the rough edges of this music, and one only wishes that the other pair of studies in rhythm had also been included.

Messiaen was at his most ambitious in the grand perspectives of the 13-movement *Catalogue d'oiseaux*, and the two items included here offer a particularly strong contrast. With 'La Bouscarle' – so much more mellifluous a title in French than 'Cetti's Warbler' – diversity is paramount, and although Aimard is characteristically lucid and uncompromising, not least in his timing of the silences near the end, this piece never seems one of the composer's more cogent inspirations. On the other hand, the ravishing alternation of chorales and cadenzas in 'L'Alouette Lulu' ('The Woodlark') is marvellously sustained in this mesmerising account, a miracle of tonal refinement and digital fluency. It caps a disc that promises to give ever more subtle rewards on repeated hearing.

Vingt regards sur l'Enfant Jésus

Vingt regards sur l'Enfant Jésus
Pierre-Laurent Aimard pf
Teldec ③ 3984 26868-2 (116' · DDD)   Ⓕ**Ⓞ**

Any review of the *Vingt regards* should begin by discussing how well the pianist conveys the cycle's visionary awe and builds its disparate sections into a true cycle. But here the virtuosity is so remarkable that even listeners with a profound distaste for Messiaen – for whom the 15th *Regard* ('The kiss of the infant Jesus') is a byword for sentimental religiosity – may listen open-mouthed. Sheer virtuosity is an important part of the cycle's language: one of the functions of *Regard* No 6 ('By Him all was made') is to astonish, and the power and excitement of Aimard's playing are indeed astonishing. Virtuosity is also desirable if Messiaen's demands for a huge palette of colour and orchestral or super-orchestral sonorities are to be met. In No 14 ('The gaze of the angels') his notes evoke 'powerful blasts of immense trombones'; Aimard's prodigious range of timbre and dynamic provide just the sound that Messiaen must have imagined. The penultimate *Regard* makes a more extreme demand: that in the hushed coda the player should recall a passage from the *Fioretti* of St Francis where 'the angel drew his bow across the string and produced a note so sweet that if he had continued I should have died of joy'. Here the effect is suggested not by virtuosity but intense concentration, stillness and purity of colour. Could it have been a little slower? Possibly; Aimard's timing is faster than most and a few of his silences could have been held longer but his dazzling technique and fabulous range of colour make this the most spectacular reading of the *Vingt regards* yet.

Vingt regards sur l'Enfant Jésus
Steven Osborne pf
Hyperion ② CDA67351/2 (127' · DDD) Ⓕ❶❶❶❶Ɗ▸

 There are a number of recordings of *Vingt regards* available, most of them very good indeed. Even the finest, though, provoke very slight reservations: an occasional suspicion of hurry in Pierre-Laurent Aimard's outstanding account, a few misjudgements in Roger Muraro's, and so on. There are no such reservations about the reading by Steven Osborne, who's revealed as a pianist of exceptional gifts.

Messiaen's widow, Yvonne Loriod, invited Osborne to study the work with her after she heard him playing other music by her late husband. One can hear throughout not only her influence but, even more, the qualities in his playing that led her to make the offer. His command of sonority is prodigious: if you've never been able to take Messiaen's talk about the 'colour' of particular chords seriously, then Osborne's playing may change your mind. He also has a remarkable dynamic range. These two qualities combine to provide both clarity and a tremendous climax in the virtuoso quasi-fugal textures of No 6 ('By Him all was made') and, at the other end of the spectrum, to make perfect sense of Messiaen's description of the opening bars of No 17 ('The Gaze of Silence'): 'The music seems to emerge from silence as colours

emerge from the night.' Nor is he insensible to the fact that some of the *Regards* are frankly showy. No 10 ('Gaze of the Spirit of Joy') is dazzling; No 16 ('Gaze of the Prophets, the Shepherds and the Magi') is barbarously colourful. Perhaps most significant of all, he finds in No 15 ('The kiss of the child Jesus') not only the sweet quietness of its opening but the spectacular Lisztian display of its later pages. The recording is ideally responsive to the wide range of sound he draws from the instrument.

Additional recommendation

Complete Keyboard Works
Hill pf
Regis ⑦ RRC7001 (8h 5' · DDD)
Recorded mid-1980s (also available separately)   Ⓑ
  Peter Hill delivers immaculate readings of some of the most technically and philosophically challenging works in the repertoire. The series enjoyed the close support of Messiaen, and you can hear why. The sound in the early volumes occasionally suffers from too close a recording.

Complete Organ Works

Complete Organ Works
Jennifer Bate org
Regis ⑥ RRC6001 (7h 34' · DDD). Recorded on the organs of L'Eglise de la Sainte-Trinité, Paris, and St Pierre de Beauvais Cathedral, 1981, 1983, 1987 Ⓑ❶

Messiaen was of towering importance to the world of 20th-century music, yet the seven and a half hours of his compositions for organ are a salutary reminder of how little time he had for that century's secular and humanistic aspirations. It's therefore only proper that recordings of the organ works should be made in church, not concert hall or studio. Jennifer Bate made the first recording of Messiaen's last and longest cycle, *Livre du Saint Sacrement*, switching from Beauvais to the composer's own Parisian church, Sainte-Trinité. Though hailed as 'a monumental achievement' when new, later judgements have been more critical.

Bate's set stands up well, especially in the *Livre du Saint Sacrement*, where she relishes the extraordinary diversity of material and mood even more intensely than the cooler though never less than commanding Olivier Latry (DG). The other large-scale later cycle, *Méditations sur le mystère de la Sainte Trinité*, reinforces this basic distinction between the two interpreters, and although Latry has the more refined instrument and the more sophisticated recording, his slow tempi (Messiaen never gives metronome marks) can seem too slow, as in the eighth *Méditation*, 'Dieu est simple – les Trois sont Un'. Bate's set makes an excellent bargain-price recommendation.

Livre du Saint Sacrement

Livre du Saint Sacrement
Michael Bonaventure org
Delphian ② DCD34076 (117' · DDD)
Played on the Rieger organ of St Giles's Cathedral,
Edinburgh   Ⓕ

Michael Bonaventure's complete Messiaen project (this is Volume 3) returns to St Giles's Cathedral in Edinburgh and its stunning Rieger organ, which dates from 1992.

Messiaen's farewell to the organ, the *Livre du Saint Sacrement*, was composed in 1984-85 and first performed by Almut Rössler in Detroit in 1986. Messiaen spoke of this *Book of the Blessed Sacrament* as a summation of the experience gained from improvising each Sunday at the Eglise de la Saint-Trinité in Paris, where he was organist for over 60 years. There is no shortage of familiar Messiaenic thumbprints: dislocated ideas, meandering dribbles of plainsong, chirpy birdsong, slow, development-less sudden and spectacular bolts of anger; and those endlessly messy chords that desperately need to resolve.

Playing from memory, Bonaventure takes just under two hours, slightly longer than Olivier Latry at Notre-Dame (DG). Movements 1-4 serve as a prelude or ante-Communion. Movements 5-11 follow events in the life of Jesus, and 12-18 contemplate the mysteries of the Sacrament.

This uneven, over-long piece poses considerable challenges to both player and listener, there being few moments of comfortable repose. The more athletic passages (for example in the Alleluia final – originally entitled 'La Visitation') bounce along with a redeeming joy.

Despite the generous acoustic the Rieger organ is recorded cleanly. It is especially effective in the echo effects in the short fourth movement, 'Acte de Foi'.

La Nativité du Seigneur

La Nativité du Seigneur. Apparition de l'église éternelle. Le banquet céleste.
Gillian Weir org
Priory PRCD921 (75' · DDD). Recorded on the 1928
Frobenius organ of Århus Cathedral, 1994   Ⓜ❍

Remastered, these outstanding recordings made in Århus Cathedral are a model of how to combine atmosphere and clarity in this music, and no other player seems quite to equal Weir's remarkable identification with the reflective and dramatically explosive extremes of Messiaen's idiom. At the risk of being accused of heresy, it's possible to doubt whether *La Nativité du Seigneur* really works as a compositional whole, given the surely undeniable imbalance between meditative and more dynamic music. But Weir evidently has no such doubts, sustaining the long, quiet episodes with particular sensitivity and irresistible conviction: if you're to perform the work complete, this

is how it has to be. So, despite the achievements of both Olivier Latry and Jennifer Bate across the full range of Messiaen's organ works, Gillian Weir's performances again claim the definitive status which they were accorded when they were first released.

Le banquet céleste

Apparition de l'église éternelle. Le banquet céleste. Les corps glorieux
Timothy Byram-Wigfield org
Delphian DCD34024 (65' · DDD). Played on the organ of St George's Chapel, Windsor Castle   Ⓕ

Timothy Byram-Wigfield's programme highlights Messiaen's earlier works, the main emphasis falling on the seven-movement sequence from 1939, *Les corps glorieux*. It's clear from the outset that this will be a strongly delineated reading, with well managed contrasts of registration given added clarity by the superb quality of the recording. It's a very physical sound but the vibrating beats of sustained notes are never oppressive, and the reading has a sense of direction and purpose which even manages to make a compelling experience out of the 15-minute central movement, 'Combat de la Mort et de la Vie'.

The two shorter pieces are well contrasted, with *Le banquet céleste* given a satisfying build-up, and *Apparition de l'église éternelle* magnificently forthright and implacable. This is a highly successful disc and augurs well for Byram-Wigfield's projected survey of Messiaen's early organ music.

Saint François d'Assise

Saint François d'Assise
Dawn Upshaw sop L'Ange **José van Dam** bass-bar
Saint François **Chris Merritt** ten Le Lépreux **Urban Malmberg** bar Frère Léon **John Aler** ten Frère Massée **Guy Renard** ten Frère Élie **Tom Krause** bar Frère Bernard **Akos Banlaky** ten Frère Sylvestre **Dirk d'Ase** bass Frère Rufin **Jeanne Loriod, Valerie Hartmann-Claverie, Dominique Kim** ondes martenots
Arnold Schoenberg Choir; Hallé Orchestra / Kent Nagano
DG 20/21 ④ 445 176-2GH4 (3h 56' · DDD· N/T/t)
                                          Ⓕ❍❍▷

The breakthrough for Messiaen's only opera came with the Salzburg Festival production unveiled in August 1992, Esa-Pekka Salonen conducting. Van Dam and his monks still wore habits, but Peter Sellars's production concept broke with the composer's 'realistic' Umbrian spectacle to put Dawn Upshaw's Angel in a grey business suit, while his trademark video monitors relayed associated imagery. He even invented a second Angel, one that doesn't exist in the score, who dances and mimes.

Nagano took up the reins for the 1998 Salzburg revival as captured here in DG's live recording, and there's no mistaking the remarkable authority and technical self-confidence of the results. Van Dam's definitive Saint François is a remarkable achievement for an artist on the cusp of his sixth decade and his identification with the role is profound. Upshaw too is well cast, with just enough tonal weight to underpin her fresh, ardent, mobile singing. It's mostly plain sailing in the subsidiary roles, although Malmberg's French is still as dodgy as the choir's. The musicians of the Hallé have been drilled to the peak of perfection, closely scrutinised by vivid, upfront sound that doesn't always give their glittering sonorities a natural perspective in which to expand.

All Messiaen's trademarks are here: the birdsong, the modal rigour (especially for the word setting which is crystal clear), the basic triads given new harmonic context and heft, the post-Stravinskian dances. There are also distant echoes of *Boris Godunov* and *Pelléas et Mélisande*. Uninitiated listeners should perhaps try Act 1 scene 3 (the curing of the leper) where the mosaic construction permits a breathtaking conjunction of ideas from timeless chant through 1960s modernism, to childlike eruptions of joy and premonitions of holy minimalism. *Saint François d'Assise* can make *Parsifal* seem like an intermezzo, but it exerts a uniquely hypnotic spell. Strongly recommended.

Saint François d'Assise
Rodney Gilfry bar Saint François **Camilla Tilling** sop L'Ange **Hubert Delamboye** ten Le Lépreux **Henk Neven** bass Frère Léon **Thomas Randle** ten Frère Massée **Donald Kaasch** ten Frère Élie **Armand Arapian** bar Frère Bernard **Jan Willem Baljet** bar Frère Sylvestre **André Morsch** bass Frère Rufin **Chorus of De Nederlandse Opera; The Hague Philharmonic Orchestra / Ingo Metzmacher**
Stage director **Pierre Audi**
Video director **Misjel Vermeiren**
Opus Arte ③ DVD OA1007D (4h 35' · NTSC · 16:9 · PCM stereo and DTS 5.0 · 0)
Recorded live at Het Muziektheater, Amsterdam, in May & June 2008   Ⓕ❂

Set in the small but still adequate confines of Amsterdam's Musiektheater, Pierre Audi's production thoroughly vindicates what may have been a practical decision to accommodate the vast orchestra at the back of the stage, with most of the action on an apron projecting into the stalls, not least by the brilliance of what we hear (thanks also to some superbly balanced engineering). Ingo Metzmacher is typically faithful to Messiaen's markings but he animates lines, clarifies chords and inspires his cohorts to greater feats of stamina and virtuosity than any conductor before him in the opera.

Rodney Gilfry holds the stage as the Saint more by his acting than his singing, which is tireless, and the occasional gruffness betrays the chest infection he was carrying early in the run. It's too bad that the film wasn't made from later performances, but perhaps the producers were mindful of Camilla Tilling's condition: an obvi-

ously pregnant Angel might give rise to unwelcome distraction. In any case she sustains her lines with no obvious strain, swathed in the same robes as the Brothers, who all rise to the challenge of filling out their rather starkly defined characters. Hubert Delamboye's Leper is painfully affecting both to watch and hear. The chorus may be smaller than Messiaen's impractical demands but it is well drilled and deployed with great intelligence.

Giacomo Meyerbeer
German 1791-1864

A century ago Meyerbeer would have merited a long and detailed entry in any book on music. Today his musical worth is viewed differently: his epic grand operas which so delighted the public are now seen as vapid, melodramatic spectacles when compared with, say, Verdi or Wagner (both of whom owed him much). A shame, for though Meyerbeer's melodic invention is limited and his construction flawed, there are many riveting passages of real beauty and excitement.

He was a child piano prodigy born into a prosperous Jewish banking family (the only musician among the Beers) and was only seven when he performed Mozart's Concerto in D minor in public. Two years later he was reckoned to be one of the finest pianists in Berlin. He had lessons from Clementi (a family friend) and went on to study at Darmstadt where one of his fellow students was Weber. Then composition took over and it was Salieri who encouraged him to enliven his heavy German contrapuntal style with the Italian wit of Rossini. Meyerbeer began a long and fruitful association with the librettist Eugène Scribe in 1827 and, having moved to Paris in 1834, rapidly became the leading active composer of opera in France (Rossini was no longer writing by then).

Success after success followed and Meyerbeer became extraordinarily wealthy: star-studded casts, vast crowd scenes, magnificent stage spectacles with elaborate scenery and effects dazzled the audience and he used his money to publicise his work to maximum effect. Yet few composers have been so insecure about their work. Meyerbeer was forever altering, improving and tampering with his scores.

Opera Arias

Il crociato in Egitto – Queste destre l'acciaro di morte[a]; Ah! Non ti son piú cara[b]; Cara mano dell'amore[c]; Sogni, e ridenti[d]. Emma di Resburgo – Di gioja, di pace[e]. L'esule di Granata – Sí, mel credi[f]. Margherita d'Anjou[g] – Pensa e guarda; Amico, all erta! Romilda e Costanza – Che barbaro tormento[h]. Semiramide riconosciuta – Il piacer, la gioja scenda[i]
[eh]**Bronwen Mills**, [d]**Linda Kitchen**, [e]**Maria Bovino**, [bdi]**Yvonne Kenny** sops [h]**Anne Mason**, [bde]**Diana Montague**, [f]**Patricia Spence**, [cd]**Della Jones** mezs [ad]**Bruce Ford**, [h]**Chris Merritt**, [e]**Harry Nicoll**, [e]**Paul Nilon**, [d]**Ugo Benelli** tens [eg]**Geoffrey Dolton**, [d]**Ian Platt**,

[g]Russell Smythe *bars* [fg]Alastair Miles *bass* Geoffrey
Mitchell Choir; [abcd]Royal Philharmonic Orchestra;
[efghi]Philharmonia Orchestra / David Parry
Opera Rara ORR222 (69' · DDD · N) (F)

Meyerbeer, born 1791, was in Italy from 1816 to
1824. On this showing, you're tempted to think
he should have stayed there. He's remembered
for the big Paris operas, such as *Les Huguenots*, *Le
Prophète* and *L'Africaine*, hugely successful in their
time but latterly somewhat buried in their own
grandeur. The Italian period was nearer to the
18th century and Mozart. There was also the
presence of Rossini (almost exactly Meyerbeer's
age); and the music is that of a young man, gifted,
energetic, confident and wealthy. The operas
were admired and, remarkably, he was accepted
by the public, despite being a German and having
an unfashionable interest in orchestration.

These excellent selections include something
of all six operas from the eight years in Italy,
with *Il crociato in Egitto* returning regularly like
the theme in a rondo. All the recordings are
drawn from previous issues in the Opera Rara
catalogue. One of the most attractive numbers is
the semi-comic trio from *Margherita d'Anjou* in
which Margaret's protectors pit their wits
against those of Richard, Duke of Gloucester. In
fact, it seems fairly typical of Meyerbeer at this
stage: his genius seems to lie in the light touch,
the graceful phrase, the felicitous orchestral
scoring; if there's a weakness, it's revealed in the
grandly dramatic moments, for which his music
remains incorrigibly jolly.

The other great delight of the disc is the singing. Meyerbeer's vocal line, like Rossini's, is
written for virtuosos, and that, almost without
exception, is a description to which the soloists
can lay claim. Each has to negotiate passagework
of a kind that half a century ago would have
made everybody shake their head and say it
couldn't be done by 'today's' singers. Bruce
Ford, particularly, performs wonders in the
revised (Trieste) version of *Crociato*; Alistair
Miles is on top form in *L'esule di Granata*; but all
do well, carrying off their respective prizes with
easy competence and no fuss.

L'Africaine

L'Africaine
Shirley Verrett *mez* Sélika **Plácido Domingo** *ten*
Vasco da Gama **Ruth Ann Swenson** *sop* Inès **Justino
Diaz** *bass* Nélusko **Michael Devlin** *bass-bar* Don
Pédro **Philip Skinner** *bass* Don Diégo **Joseph
Rouleau** *bass* Grand Inquisitor **Kevin Anderson** *ten*
Don Alvar **Patricia Spence** *mez* Anna **Mark Delavan**
bar High Priest of Brahma **San Francisco Opera
Ballet, Chorus and Orchestra / Maurizio Arena**
Stage director **Lotfi Mansouri**
Video director **Brian Large**
ArtHaus Musik DVD 100 216 (3h 14' · 4:3 · 2.0 · 2 & 5)
Recorded live 1988 (F)

Handsomely staged and sumptuously costumed,
this famous 1972 production makes good view-

ing; and the DVD sound is a distinct improvement on the original video. The singers benefit
as much as the orchestra; Shirley Verrett in particular is heard to advantage, her high notes
shining out with ease and purity, while Justino
Diaz has body and warmth of tone as well as the
command and panache for his exhilarating role.
Domingo's voice is caught with the metal
revealed rather at the expense of its characteristic richness, but there's a glorious thrust and
passion in his singing and acting. A voice that
sounds equally well in video and DVD is that of
the young Ruth Ann Swenson, whose freshness
and refinement are memorable and touching.
Meyerbeer's last opera exhibits the mastery of a
lifetime in high places. It has the required ingredients in due proportion, with a moving individuality in its quiet ending, where Verrett's
imaginative portrayal makes a strong contribution. Maurizio Arena treats the score appreciatively, with care and precision.

Margherita d'Anjou

Margherita d'Anjou
Annick Massis *sop* Margherita d'Anjou **Bruce Ford**
ten Duke of Lavarenne **Daniela Barcellona** *mez*
Isaura **Alastair Miles** *bass* Carlo Belmonte **Fabio
Previati** *bar* Michele Gamautte **Pauls Putniņš** *ten*
Riccardo **Colin Lee** *ten* Bellapunta **Roland Wood** *bar*
Orner **Geoffrey Mitchell Choir; London
Philharmonic Orchestra / David Parry**
Opera Rara ③ ORC25 (172' · DDD · T/t) (F)

Margaret of Anjou, the widow of Henry VI, is
more familiar to us as the embittered old crone
in Shakespeare's *Richard III*. In the opera she's
relatively young and beautiful, and loved by the
tenor, a married man. The action takes place in
Scotland where Margaret's forces are being pursued by Richard's. The tenor's dilemma is
whether to follow his strong inclination to
remain the Queen's lover or to return to his loving wife, Isaura, who, unknown to him, has followed him to Scotland in disguise.

The opera is called a *melodramma semiseria*,
which is appropriate partly because from the
very first bars of the Overture it's clear that we
can't be expected to take it seriously, and partly
because another principal role is that of the
comical army surgeon, Michele, who in the nick
of time summons a doughty troop of Highland-
ers to thwart Richard, who at that point has the
rest of the cast at his mercy.

The first notes – 'diddly-diddly um-pom-pom'
– may well deter the listener from going further,
especially as the fatuous motif is heard six times
more, plus twice in the minor and several times
referentially in *crescendo*. But that would be a pity.
The singing and orchestration are good, and the
semiseria element stimulates invention and interest: Isaura's plaintive aria and hopeful cabaletta
are combined with a *buffo* subtext for Michele,
and in the cottage scene of Act 2 the tension of
Richard's unsocial visit is partly diffused, partly
increased, by Michele's prevarications, a surreal

situation along the lines of Richard III-meets-Benny Hill. Margherita has a gentle and rather beautiful solo. Particularly charming are the choruses that come just before, slightly suggestive of the villagers in *Cavalleria rusticana*.

Daniela Barcellona as Isaura has a rich contralto that takes flight in the final solo, surprisingly snatched from the eponymous soprano. She, Annick Massis, is a great find, pure and warm in tone, and accomplished in technique. Bruce Ford gives special pleasure in his *cantabile* aria 'Tu, che le vie segrete'. Fabio Previati plays Michele effectively, singing well and keeping the patter on its toes without too much clowning. Alastair Miles's Carlo, potentially the most interesting character, is admirably fluent in passagework but rather lacking in colour and bite. Chorus and orchestra are in good form, David Parry helping to bring out the best in them, as in Meyerbeer, too.

Darius Milhaud   French 1892-1974

His father was a wealthy almond merchant from a old Jewish Provençal family. He was picking out tunes on the piano from the age of three and in 1909 entered the Paris Conservatoire where d'Indy, Widor and Dukas were among his teachers. Early on he became associated with Satie and Cocteau. Another in the circle was his friend the poet Paul Claudel who was made French Ambassador to Brazil in 1917 and who engaged Milhaud as his secretary there. In 1920 he was one of the six young French composers labelled Les Six (Poulenc, Honegger, Auric, Tailleferre and Durey were the others) but, though he flirted briefly with their high-spirited fun, he was always far too independent to belong to any stylistic group.

The onset of crippling rheumatoid arthritis in the late 1920s did nothing to diminish his prolific output in all forms and styles, or his concert appearances as pianist or conductor in his own work. The Second World War forced him to America where he became professor of composition at Mills College, California, a position he retained until 1971 when he retired with his wife to Switzerland.

Le boeuf sur le toit / La création du monde

Milhaud Le boeuf sur le toit. La création du monde
Ibert Divertissement **Poulenc** Les biches – Suite
Ulster Orchestra / Yan Pascal Tortelier
Chandos CHAN9023 (68' · DDD)   Ⓕ B▸

Here is 1920s French music directed by a conductor who's completely in the spirit of it, and plenty of spirit there is, too. Except for Ibert's *Divertissement*, this is ballet music. Poulenc's suite from *Les biches*, written for Diaghilev's ballet company and first heard in Monte Carlo, is fresh and bouncy and stylishly played here, although Chandos's warm recording, good though it is, takes some edge off the trumpet tone; the genial

nature of it all makes us forget that it's a unique mix of 18th-century *galanterie*, Tchaikovskian lilt and Poulenc's own inimitable street-Parisian sophistication and charm. As for Ibert's piece, this is uproariously funny in an unbuttoned way, and the gorgeously vulgar trombone in the Waltz and frantic police whistle in the finale are calculated to make you laugh out loud. Milhaud's *Le boeuf sur le toit* also has Parisian chic and was originally a kind of music-hall piece, composed to a scenario by Cocteau. It was while attending a performance of it in London in 1920 that the composer first heard the American jazz orchestra that, together with a later experience of New Orleans jazzmen playing 'from the darkest corners of the Negro soul' (as he later expressed it), prompted him to compose his masterly ballet *La création du monde*. Tortelier and his orchestra understand this strangely powerful music no less than the other pieces. This is a most desirable disc.

Scaramouche (arr two pianos)

Le boeuf sur le toit, Op 58a (arr cpsr). Scaramouche, Op 165b. La libertadora, Op 236a. Les songes, Op 237. Le bal martiniquais, Op 249. Carnaval à la Nouvelle-Orléans, Op 275. Kentuckiana, Op 287
Stephen Coombs, Artur Pizarro pfs
Hyperion CDA67014 (62' · DDD)   Ⓕ B▸

Milhaud was an inveterate traveller who absorbed influences from many national styles. The music here exudes infectious dance impulses, languid geniality, knockabout humour and *joie de vivre*. It may inhabit a limited expressive sphere, but providing you don't expect introspection or searching profundity you won't be disappointed. There's enjoyment at every turn, whether in the foot-tapping 'Brazileira', the Satie-esque simplicity of the 'Valse' from *Les songes*, or the breezy music-hall atmosphere of *Le boeuf sur le toit*, with its wonderfully imaginative piano writing. The performances are exemplary. Stephen Coombs and Artur Pizarro both enjoy the byways of the piano repertory, and, even if Pizarro is the more starry soloist, they're well matched as a duo. Coombs's top part is suitably bright and sharply lit, and is offset by Pizarro's more subtle colouring. They revel in the protracted playfulness of *Le boeuf sur le toit*, where their feeling for Hispanic exoticism is matched by their virtuosity. The recorded sound is excellent.

Ernest Moeran   British 1894-1950

Moeran studied at the Royal College of Music then, after war service, with Ireland who, with Delius, was a major influence on his early music. In the early 1930s he retired to the Cotswolds, where he wrote his Symphony in G minor (1937), a work of pastoral lyricism drawing on a Sibelian method of thematic development. His other works, all marked by meticulous craftsmanship, include the Sinfonietta (1944) and orchestral Serenade (1948), concertos for violin (1942) and cello (1945), chamber music and songs.

Symphony

Symphony in G minor[a]. Sinfonietta.
Overture for a Masque.
London Philharmonic Orchestra;
[a]New Philharmonia / Sir Adrian Boult
Lyrita SRCD247 (78' · ADD). Recorded 1968-75
Ⓕ**OOO**▷

Boult's affection for the G minor Symphony is evident in every phrase of this rapt and gloriously warm-hearted performance. The New Philharmonia are on blistering form and, thankfully for us, captured in a sumptuous recording of stupendous definition, depth and enticing warmth. In *Gramophone*'s original review in 1975, Edward Greenfield was unequivocal in his praise: 'Anyone who loves English music, and who has never heard this heartwarming music, should go at once to this record.'

String Quartets

String Quartets – No 1 in A minor; No 2 in E flat.
String Trio in G
Maggini Quartet (Laurence Jackson, David Angel *vns* Martin Outram *va* Michal Kaznowski *vc*)
Naxos 8 554079 (59' · DDD)   Ⓢ**O**▷

The A minor Quartet dates from 1921, when Moeran was a pupil of John Ireland at the Royal College of Music. It's an enormously fluent, folksong-inspired creation, full of Ravelian poise; indeed the last movement of the three (an exhilarating rondo) owes much to the finale of the French master's F major Quartet. The Maggini Quartet accords the piece wonderfully assured, flexible advocacy. The E flat Quartet, discovered among Moeran's papers after his death, appears to be another early effort. It's cast in just two movements, the second of which is an ambitious linked slow movement and finale, full of ambition and tender fantasy, and containing some truly magical inspiration along the way. Perhaps this movement's intrepid thematic and emotional diversity engendered sufficient niggling doubts in Moeran's mind for him to suppress the whole work. Certainly, in a performance as convinced and convincing as this, its melodic fecundity and unpretentious, out-of-doors charm will endear it to many.

That leaves the masterly String Trio of 1931, which, in its impeccable craft, rhythmic pungency (the opening *Allegretto giovale* is in 7/8), gentle sense of purpose and unerring concentration (above all in the deeply felt slow movement), represents one of Moeran's finest achievements. The Magginis reveal a relish for Moeran's exquisitely judged part-writing and give an admirably polished, affectionate rendering. Sound and balance are excellent throughout this enterprising, hugely enjoyable collection.

Federico Mompou   Spanish 1893-1987

Mompou studied in Barcelona and in Paris, where he remained until 1941 except for a period in Barcelona in 1914-21; he then returned to his native Barcelona. His output consists almost entirely of small-scale piano pieces and songs in a fresh, naive style indebted to Satie and Debussy; he aimed for maximum expressiveness through minimum means, often achieving a melancholy elegance.

Música callada

Música callada
Herbert Henck *pf*
ECM New Series 445 699-2 (63' · DDD)   Ⓕ

Listening to this disc is rather like entering a retreat. There's a rapt, contemplative atmosphere around these 28 miniatures written between 1959 and 1967 as an attempt to express St John of the Cross's mystic ideal of 'the music of silence'. Practically all slow-moving, using repetition as a structural device but avoiding keyboard virtuosity, and rarely rising even to a *forte*, they seem to acknowledge descent from Erik Satie via the Impressionists, though harmonically much freer and sometimes harsher – even, occasionally, stepping inside the area of atonality. No 3 has a childlike innocence in its folkloric theme: Mompou's fascination with bell sounds finds echoes in Nos 5, 17 and 22. Overall there's a sense of tranquil self-communion which, paradoxically, exerts a strange spell on the listener. Herbert Henck, a specialist in 20th-century music, plays this collection with tender sensitivity and an ideally suited luminosity of tone, and he's finely recorded. An exceptional and haunting issue.

Preludes

Cançons i danses – Nos 1, 3, 5, 7, 8 & 9. Preludes –
Nos 1, 5, 6, 7, 9 & 10. Cants màgics. Charmes.
Variations. Dialogues. Paisajes
Stephen Hough *pf*
Hyperion CDA66963 (77' · DDD)   Ⓕ**OOO**▷

The music of Federico Mompou may appear at first to consist of little more than charming, delicately scented but dilettantish salon near-improvisations with marked overtones of Erik Satie; but it's significant that his earliest works (in the 1920s) are imbued with a sense of mystery and wonder. Later he was to progress from an ingenuous lyricism (in the *Songs and Dances*) to a profounder contemplation and mysticism, to greater harmonic and keyboard complexity (*Dialogues*) and finally, in the 1946-60 *Paisajes* ('Landscapes'), to a more experimental, less tonal idiom. In the hands of an imaginative pianist such as Stephen Hough this other-worldly quality becomes revelatory. Hough's command of tonal nuance throughout is ultra-sensitive, he catches Mompou's wistful moods to perfection, and on the rare occasions when the music lashes out, as in Prelude No 7, he's scintillating. In the more familiar *Songs and Dances* he's tender in the songs and crisp rhythmically in the dances. He treats the 'Testament d'Amelia' in No 8 with a good deal of flexibility, and because Mompou declared (and demonstrated in his own recordings) that 'it's all so free', he takes the fullest advantage of the marking *senza rigore* in No 5, which reflects Mompou's lifelong fascination with bell sounds.

---

12 Preludes. Suburbis. Dialogues. Cants mágics. Chanson de berceau. Fêtes lointaines
Jordi Masó pf
Naxos 8 554448 (79' · DDD)   ⓢ↦

Volume 1 of Jordi Masó's Mompou cycle was given the warmest of welcomes and Vol 2 is no disappointment, either. Everything is presented with crystalline clarity, and if the manner is unusually robust it's never less than musicianly. Directions such as *énergiquement* and *très clair* (Prelude No 2), the *forte* climax of Prelude No 6 or the sudden blaze of anger that erupts in No 7 are arguably more sympathetically conveyed than Mompou's gentler, more characteristic instructions (*con lirica espressione* in No 8 or *un peu plus calme* in the second 'Gitanes' from *Suburbis*). It's almost as if Masó, a vibrant and articulate pianist, wished to draw attention away from sentimental or salon associations, and direct us towards Mompou's underlying fervour and what Wilfrid Mellors calls (in his invaluable book *Le jardin retrouvé*) the 'pre-melodic' nature of Mompou's vocal lines (in *Cants mágics*) or the evocation of a remote, prehistoric world. Masó's boldness is potent and arresting and his comprehensive undertaking makes comparison with Hough (see above) and Martin Jones (Nimbus) a marginal issue. So although he's less tonally subtle than Jones, his playing is vital and idiomatic, qualities highlighted by the bright, immediate sound.

Songs

'Combat del Somni'
Cançó de la fira. Cantar del alma. Combat del Somni – Damunt de tu, només les flors; Aquesta nit un mateix vent; Jo et pressentia com la mar; Fes-me la vida transparent; Ara no sé si et veig encar. Comptines – Margot la pie; Petite fille de Paris; Rossignol joli; Aserrín, aserrán; J'ai vu dans la lune; Pito, pito, colorito; Fréderic tic, tic; D'alt d'un cotxe. Sant Marti. L'hora grisa. Cançoneta incerta. Cuatro melodías
Marisa Martins *mez* **Mac McClure** *pf*
Columna Música 1CM0136 (54' · DDD)   Ⓕ

Wilfred Mellors may have called him 'a minor muse' but Mompou's sense of 'truth', whether expressed in memories of a paradisal childhood or in a mystical Catholicism, results in a unique and instantly recognisable voice. Few composers

have achieved so much so economically; and at his greatest, in, for example, 'Cantar del alma', the final song on this disc, Mompou creates a form of divine monotony, his religious fervour captured with a simplicity that is in a special sense transcendental.

Inspired by the poetry of St John of the Cross, such music, where singer and pianist commune separately rather than together, is vitally related to *Musica callada*, his similarly inspired piano cycle. Indeed, there are many family likenesses between the songs and the piano music where the composer's distinctive world, whether playful or ecstatic, is expressed with a tantalising brevity.

Marisa Martins and Mac McClure make an ardent case for a special corner of the repertoire and they have been well recorded. Unfortunately they have been less well presented. Tomas Marco's note is both assertive and uninformative, only one of the 22 songs on offer is translated into English (inconsiderate for those whose Catalan is, shall we say, a little rusty), the texts do not tally with the index and the last four lines of 'Cantar del alma' are missing. Sadly, gratitude for Columna Música's enterprise is qualified by such lapses in presentation.

Jean-Joseph de Mondonville

French 1711-1772

After a period in Lille, violinist and composer Mondonville settled in Paris, where he won fame. He became sous-maître to the Royal Chapel in 1740 and intendant in 1744. His music is notable for its flair. Best known were his sonatas for harpsichord and violin and his 17 grands motets (among the finest since Lalande's and, like his, much performed at the Concert Spirituel). He wrote 10 works for the stage, all of which were enthusiastically received.

Grands motets

Grands motets – Dominus regnavit;   Ⓟ
In exitu Israel; De profundis
Sophie Daneman, Maryseult Wieczorek *sops* **Paul Agnew, François Piolino** *tens* **Maarten Koningsberger** *bar* **François Bazola** *bass*
Les Arts Florissants / William Christie
Erato 0630 17791-2 (72' · DDD · T/t)   ⒻⓄ

Mondonville's *grands motets* were enormously popular for many years at the Concert Spirituel in Paris. They follow the pattern laid down by Lalande and continued by Rameau, but with more independent instrumental parts and incorporating Italian influences (eg *da capo* arias) and operatic elements. These three on psalm texts are deeply impressive. *Dominus regnavit* (1734) was perhaps the earliest of Mondonville's *grands motets* and, besides its polyphonic opening chorus, is notable for two verses entirely for high-register voices and instruments, an operatic *tempête*, and a stunning complex 'Gloria patri'. *De profundis* (1748), written for the funeral of a Chapel Royal colleague, is by its nature sombre, and ends not with the usual 'Gloria patri' but with 'Requiem aeternam' and a fugue. The initial chorus was praised to the sky by contemporaries: other highlights are a baritone aria over a free chaconne bass, and a chorus illustrating 'morning' and 'night' by high and low voices respectively. There's even more illustrative music in the 1755 *In exitu Israel*: what amounts to a dramatic scena, with agitated strings and rushing voices for the 'fleeing sea', dotted figures for the mountains 'skipping like rams', and tremolos and vocal melismas for the 'trembling earth'. The performances are vivid, with very good soloists, an alertly responsive chorus and a neat orchestra.

Stanisław Moniuszko   Polish 1819-1872

The leading Polish composer of the 19th century, Moniuszko studied in Berlin, encountering works by Weber, Marschner and Lortzing. His opera Halka (1848) was to establish his European reputation. His large output is focused mainly on the voice – operas (of which The Haunted Manor is of importance), songs and choral works – though he did leave some orchestral and chamber works.

Halka

Halka
Tatiana Borodina sop Halka **Oleh Lykhach** ten
Jontek **Aleksandra Buczek** mez Zofia **Mariusz
Godlewski** bar Janusz **Radosław Żukowski** bass
Stolnik **Zbigniew Kryczka** bass Dziemba
Jacek Ryś bar Piper **Rafał Majzner** ten Mountaineer
**Orchestra, Chorus and Ballet of the Wrocław
Opera / Ewa Michnik**
Stage and video director **Laco Adamik**
Dux ⑥ DUX9538 (136' · PAL · 16:9 · 2.0 and 5.0 · 0)
Recorded live at the Wrocław Opera in
September 2005   Ⓕ

Even in its final form from 1858 (the original dates from 10 years earlier), *Halka* is uneven and derivative, but it is precisely its variable quality that makes the work so fascinating. For all the reliance on early-19th-century German and Italian models, one can hear a national operatic language begin to take shape.

The plot is straightforward. The engagement party of the noble Janusz is disturbed by Halka, a peasant girl with whom he had fathered a child, now dead. Halka refuses to accept that Janusz has deserted her despite the promptings of Jontek, whose love for Halka is utterly unrequited. As Halka's despair deepens into madness, she contemplates burning down the church in which the wedding takes place but relents; on forgiving Janusz, she drowns herself.

Wrocław Opera's account, given to mark the 60th anniversary of the company's stage, is full-blooded and vivid. Laco Adamik's sensitive video direction of his own production is a model of clarity, capturing the sweep of the grander passages as well as the more intimate moments. Despite the predominantly monochrome costumes – the aristocrats are mostly in white, the commoners in black – the use of colour throughout is telling, especially in the vivid dance numbers in Acts 1 and 3. The light of the first-act party gradually darkens as Halka's anguish deepens and the action moves back to Janusz's estate. Yet it is in Acts 3 and 4 that Moniuszko's music becomes its most affecting and emotional, in contrast to the superficiality of Stolnik's house.

Tatiana Borodina catches the heroine's fluctuating mental states, from radiant joy to dark desperation, with equal force, her voice rich and powerful although showing some strain in the highest passages. Oleh Lykhach and Mariusz Godlewski are excellent as Jontek and Janusz, the latter especially catching the character's vacillation between cowardice and guilt. The company as a whole is excellent and the orchestra is strongly directed by Ewa Michnik. Recommended.

Stephen Montague   American b1943

Born in New York and educated in Florida, Montague also studied conducting in Salzburg. He is equally active as a performer and as a composer, and has won numerous prizes for his music. He is interested in electronics and has frequently written for a combination of acoustic and electronic instruments.

Southern Lament

Haiku. Southern Lament[a]. Midnight Sun. Chorale for
a Millennium Sunset[c]. Headless Horseman.
Thanksgiving Hymn. A Crippled Ghost at Halloween.
Beyond the Milky Way[c]. Dagger Dance[d]. Paramell Va.
Night Frost Settles on a Pumpkin. Something's in
Grandma's Attic[d]. For Merce C at the Barbican[d].
After Ives…: Four Studies[b]
Philip Mead pf with [a]**Monica Acosta** voc
[b]**Nancy Ruffer** fl [c]**Elysian Quartet**;
[b]**Sousa Band /** [bd]**Stephen Montague** pf/elec
NMC NMCD118 (79' · DDD)   ⒻⒹ

Stephen Montague is an American composer-performer who has lived in the UK for more than 30 years, during which time he has developed an enterprising international career. He honestly admits his sources in Ives, Cowell, Cage and minimalism, and the CD ends with four of his *Studies* 'after Ives'. That wonderful hymn-tune 'What a friend we have in Jesus' (compare Montague's treatment with the third movement of Ives's Piano Sonata No 1) shows the unabated power of diatonic harmony, although there are surprises, and 'Forever JPS' is a spectacular which brings in the voice of Sousa himself as well as the London Sousa Band in *Stars and Stripes*.

Montague points out that when he borrows melodies, unlike Ives he usually quotes them complete. There's plenty of that with the varied settings of the tunes in *Southern Lament*. Then there are several short occasional pieces showing variety and ingenuity, but *Haiku* with live electronics and computer tape is more substantial. This is a subtle, oriental-influenced piece with the live piano gracefully repetitive and the electronics sustaining this mood. When Montague uses electronics the sound is always beguiling; if he's minimalist he gets somewhere rather than being stuck in a groove; and he even manages to use tone-clusters with a light touch.

This is a consistently enjoyable portrait of a composer who knows how to focus his appeal. Terrific performances from Philip Mead, all well recorded.

Claudio Monteverdi Italian 1567-1643

Monteverdi studied with Ingegneri, maestro di cappella at Cremona Cathedral, and published several books of motets and madrigals before going to Mantua in about 1591 to serve as a string player at the court of Duke Vincenzo Gonzaga. There he came under the influence of Giaches de Wert, whom he failed to succeed as maestro di cappella in 1596. In 1599 he married Claudia de Cattaneis, a court singer, who bore him three children, and two years later he was appointed maestro di cappella on Pallavicino's death. Largely as the result of a prolonged controversy with the theorist GM Artusi, Monteverdi became known as a leading exponent of the modern approach to harmony and text expression. In 1607 his first opera, Orfeo, was produced in Mantua, followed in1608 by Arianna. The dedication to Pope Paul V of a grand collection of church music known as the Vespers (1610) indicated an outward-looking ambition, and in 1613 Monteverdi was appointed maestro di cappella at St Mark's, Venice.

There Monteverdi was active in reorganising and improving the cappella as well as writing music for it, but he was also able to accept commissions from elsewhere, including some from Mantua, for example the ballet Tirsi e Clori (1616) and an opera, La finta pazza Licori (1627, not performed, now lost). He seems to have been less active after c1629, but he was again in demand as an opera composer on the opening of public opera houses in Venice from 1637. In 1640 Arianna was revived, and in the following two years Il ritorno d'Ulisse in patria, Le nozze d'Enea con Lavinia (lost) and L'incoronazione di Poppea were given first performances. In 1643 he visited Cremona and died shortly after his return to Venice.

Monteverdi can be justly considered one of the most powerful figures in the history of music. Much of his development as a composer may be observed in the eight books of secular madrigals published between 1587 and 1638. The early books show his indebtedness to Marenzio in particular; the final one, Madrigali guerrieri et amorosi, includes some pieces 'in genere rappresentativo' – Il ballo delle ingrate, Il

Combattimento di Tancredi e Clorinda and the Lamento della ninfa – which draw on Monteverdi's experience as an opera composer. A ninth book was issued posthumously in 1651.

Orfeo was the first opera to reveal the potential of this then novel genre; Arianna (of which only the famous Lament survives) may well have been responsible for its survival. Monteverdi's last opera, L'incoronazione di Poppea, though transmitted in not wholly reliable sources and including music by other men, is his greatest masterpiece and arguably the finest opera of the century. In the 1610 collection of sacred music Monteverdi displayed the multiplicity of styles that characterise this part of his output. The Mass is a monument of the prima prattica or old style. At the other extreme the motets, written for virtuoso singers, are the most thorough-going exhibition of the modern style and the seconda prattica.

Selva morale e spirituale

Selva morale e spirituale   Ⓟ
**Cantus Cölln; Concerto Palatino /
Konrad Junghänel**
Harmonia Mundi ③ HMC90 1718/20
(3h 50' · DDD · T/t)   ⒫❍❍❍

Monteverdi's last publication has always been something of a stepchild in his output, perhaps partly because of its sheer size and variety: there's lots of music in it that's hard to pigeonhole. It's a massive assembly of some 40 pieces, some apparently very early, many from those mysterious years after the 1610 *Vespers*, and a few perhaps very late. In style they range from the purest academic polyphony of the *stile antico* to the most elaborate concerted music with intricate and showy instrumental parts, from the simplest melodic writing to virtuoso floridity with extreme vocal ranges. In this complete recording Konrad Junghänel has effectively made the first and third CDs into approximate Vespers collections, with the second CD containing most of the music that can't be fitted into the others. This works extremely well, not least because those who aren't ready to sit through it all at one sitting can get a satisfying musical unit from any one of the discs.

The 12 singers of Cantus Cölln have among them enough variety of colour to keep the sound lively and interesting. They are always clear, disciplined and balanced; and Junghänel directs the often episodic works with a firm control of their shape. The peerless Johanna Koslowsky leads much of the time in the larger pieces and contributes marvellous solo numbers. For the large-range bass solos Stephan MacLeod makes the impossible lines sound almost effortless. This set is a remarkable achievement.

Vespers of 1610

Vespro della Beata Vergine (with alternative six-voice Magnificat). Missa In illo tempore   Ⓟ
Rebecca Outram, Carolyn Sampson sops **Daniel**

Auchincloss, Charles Daniels, James Gilchrist,
Nicholas Mulroy *tens* Robert Evans, Peter Harvey,
Robert MacDonald *basses* The King's Consort
Choir; The King's Consort / Robert King
Hyperion ② CDA67531/2 (137' · DDD · T/t);
② SACDA67531/2

ⓅⓄⓄ➡

Despite four wonderful volumes of Monteverdi's sacred music from The King's Consort, nothing will prepare you for the ecstatic consequences of taking seriously at least one aspect of Monteverdi's so-called *seconda prattica* – using much freer counterpoint, with an increasing hierarchy of voices: that the word is mistress of the music. And what ecstasy!

Never mind the majestic opening psalm: just listen to the eloquent gestures in the 'Dixit Dominus', which range from the declamatory to the reticent with astonishing flexibility. Or the freedom and delicacy of tenor James Gilchrist in the 'Nigra sum', equally matched by the fragile spaciousness of Caroline Sampson's and Rebecca Outram's 'Pulchra es'.

Spaciousness soon loses its fragility in the propulsive 'Nisi Dominus' and the 'Lauda Jerusalem' with its luxuriant finale. And although the 'Sonata sopra Sancta Maria' is still preferable with a solo soprano line, its instrumental variations are here dispatched with such fluency it's hard not to be won over; the 'Ave maris stella' is similarly eloquent. The second disc includes equally superb performances of the alternative six-voice *Magnificat* and the *Missa In illo tempore*.

The cumulative effect here is of a dazzling chiaroscuro that Monteverdi surely would have recognised. With its use of full choir, King's recording has room to manoeuvre – which gives the imagination more room to take flight.

Vespro della Beata Virgine (ed Parrott/Keyte) Ⓟ
**Taverner Consort; Taverner Choir; Taverner
Players / Andrew Parrott**
Virgin Classics ② 212685-2 (106' · DDD) ⓂⓄ➡

The technical and interpretative problems of the Monteverdi *Vespers* of 1610 are legion. Should the entire volume be performed as an entity, or just the psalms, or perhaps a mixture of psalms and motets? Since the vocal lines in the original are heavily ornamented, does this preclude the addition of further embellishment after the manner of contemporary instruction books? Which portions should be sung chorally (and how large should such a 'choir' be?), and which by the soloists? How should the continuo be realised?

The central controversy concerns five non-liturgical compositions inserted among the Marian psalms, hymn and *Magnificat*. These, the sacred *concerti* described on the title-page as 'suitable for the chapels or private chambers of princes', don't conform textually to any known Marian office but occur in Monteverdi's collection in positions normally occupied by psalm antiphons. Here the *concerti* are performed as

MONTEVERDI'S VESPERS – IN BRIEF

Taverner Consort / Andrew Parrott Ⓟ
EMI ② 212685-2 (148' · DDD) ⓂⓄ➡
The first recording to engage fully with the scholarly debates regarding the form, purpose and pitch of the work, this 1984 version is a comprehensive and radical attempt to reconstruct a festal Vespers service, the music reordered so that it no longer seems to work towards a proto-Wagnerian climax.

Les Arts Florissants / William Christie Ⓟ
Erato ② 3984 23139-2 (100' · DDD) ⒻⓄ
Christie's version, made with relatively large choral and instrumental forces in a resonant venue, conveys the flair, spontaneity and warmth of his live music-making.

Concentus Musicus / Nikolaus Harnoncourt Ⓟ
Teldec ② 2564 69464-8 (105' · DDD) Ⓑ
Harnoncourt in 1986 prefers more rugged sonorities and bigger scoring than those modern rivals who look above all for clarity and simplicity.

Monteverdi Choir / John Eliot Gardiner Ⓟ
Archiv ② 429 565-2AH2 (106' · DDD) Ⓕ
This large-scale live recording (Gardiner's second) was made in Venice's St Mark's Basilica. It captures the drama as well as the ceremonial aspect of the work, despite sometimes cloudy recorded sound (see Archiv 073 035-9AH for the spectacular DVD).

Concerto Italiano / Rinaldo Alessandrini Ⓟ
Naïve ② OP30403 (105' · DDD) ⒻⓄⓄ
A striking and thought-provoking performance from Alessandrini that uses a 'soloistic' approach to impressive effect. Try and hear a little before you buy: it will either repel or entrance. We think the latter…

Concerto Vocale / René Jacobs Ⓟ
Harmonia Mundi ② HMC90 1566/7 (104' · DDD)Ⓕ
More intimate than most, with a dramatic flair that eludes most English versions. Jacobs relates the work to its madrigal inspirations.

Monteverdi Choir, etc / John Eliot Gardiner Ⓟ
Decca ② 443 482-2DF2 (106' · ADD) Ⓜ➡
Gardiner's first version was made with some of the finest English singers of the day and the legendary Philip Jones Brass Ensemble. It may not be as polished, but its vitality stands up well to the later version.

**The King's Consort Choir; The King's Consort /
Robert King** Ⓟ
Hyperion ② CDA67531/2 (137' · DDD) ⒻⓄⓄ
A performance of almost rhapsodic power that finds these assembled musicians on incandescent form. King conducts with glorious flexibility and clearly inspires his colleagues to give of their considerable best.

substitutes for the antiphons missing from Monteverdi's collections. One effect is to make this version feel more unified and monumental.

Both physically and emotionally the *concerti* are presented here as the focal points of the *Vespers*. Certainly they're the occasion for some of the most spectacular singing. The essential ingredient is the performance of Nigel Rogers, surely the most accomplished and convincing singer of the early-17th-century Italian virtuoso repertory. He gives persuasive and seemingly effortless performances in three of the *concerti* in his mellifluous, dramatic yet perfectly controlled manner. In two cases, 'Audi coelum' and 'Duo Seraphim', he's well matched with Andrew King and Joseph Cornwell. 'Pulchra es', sung by Tessa Bonner and Emma Kirkby, seems comparatively rather understated.

One important feature of Andrew Parrott's interpretation is its fundamental conception, historically accurate, of the *Vespers* as chamber work rather than a 'choral' one. Thus only one instrument is used per part, the harpsichord is employed very sparingly, and the basic continuo group is restricted to organ and chitarrone. Following the same principle, one voice per part is taken as the norm. The result is a clarity of texture, evident from the opening bars, which allows correct tempi to be used without stifling often intricate rhythmic features. Another fundamental choice represents something of a novelty. Both 'Lauda Jerusalem' and the *Magnificat* are transposed down a fourth here, as they should be according to the convention relating to the clef combinations in which they were originally notated. This brings all the vocal parts into the tessitura of the rest of the work, and restores the instruments to their normal ranges. Whether or not the result is less 'exciting' than the version we're used to hearing has only partly to do with questions of musicality. For the rest, one of the lasting virtues of this well-balanced, unobtrusive recording is that it allows us to hear the *Vespers* sounding something along the lines that Monteverdi intended.

Madrigals

'La Venexiana – Live in Corsica'
Madrigals from Books 2, 4, 5, 6, 7, 8 and 9.
Lamento d'Arianna
La Venexiana / Claudio Cavina *counterten*
Glossa GCD920015 (64' · DDD). Recorded live 2002 Ⓕ

This live anthology is a clever way of offering a 'sampler' of La Venexiana's survey of Monteverdi's madrigals without resorting to the mere duplication of their existing catalogue. It gives an idea of the ensemble's qualities as performers and of the 'buzz' that a live rendition of these pieces can generate.

The interpretations are not markedly different from their studio counterparts, and since excerpts are included of only those books that have already been issued complete, there are perhaps fewer surprises than one might have liked. An exception is the *Lamento d'Arianna*, published in Monteverdi's lifetime in a collective anthology. Rossana Bertini's rendition is unselfconsciously involving, though its conclusion might have been better paced (it appears to end rather abruptly). The other soloistic pieces (such as *Bel pastor* or *Gira il nemico*) do not quite have the same impact, largely because some of the stage effects get lost in translation. In 'Bel pastor', the shepherd's protestations of love (in response to his lover's repeated demands) seem increasingly forced and tetchy. The comic effect must have been considerable but on the recording it doesn't really 'click'.

The best performances are of the earlier books, particularly Book 2, where La Venexiana's qualities of ensemble are allowed to come to the fore. By Latin standards the audience's response is polite but it stops short of rapture: a verdict with which it's tempting to agree.

Madrigals – Book 2, Il secondo libro de' madrigali
La Venexiana / Claudio Cavina *counterten*
Glossa GCD920922 (70' · DDD · T/t)　　　　Ⓕ

La Venexiana's cast for Book 2 is virtually identical to Concerto Italiano's a decade earlier. Here La Venexiana has the edge. Concerto Italiano zipped through the whole book in just under an hour; given that the same singers take more than 10 minutes longer in the new version it's perhaps surprising that the two approaches don't sound more different. Claudio Cavina doesn't fragment the text in the manner of his rival, but his more leisurely readings generate a more effective charge by lingering over Monteverdi's climactic build-ups (as in the last line of *Mentr'io mirava fiso*, to mention just one instance), and he has the edge on intonation.

Madrigals – Book 3, Il terzo libro de' madrigali
La Venexiana / Claudio Cavina *counterten*
Glossa GCD920910 (63' · DDD · T/t)　　Ⓕ❍❍❍

 The masterly anthology of styles in Book 3 presents very specific challenges in performance precisely because of its variety. La Venexiana have an excellent understanding of the essentially polyphonic nature of such works as *La giovinetta pianta* and are therefore quite superb in the more difficult mixed style of *O dolce anima mia*, *Stracciami pur il core* or *Se per estremo ardore*, whose complicated rhetorical devices are brought off with perfection. Such brief transcendent moments as 'non può morir d'amor alma fedele' in *Stracciami pur il core*, or 'ingiustamente brami' in *O dolce anima mia*, far from seeming isolated jewels, arise here naturally from their context, which is no mean achievement for the uncharted waters that Monteverdi was navigating in these experimental but accomplished works. The singers also have the full measure of the Tasso cycles of Book 3 entering fully into the polychrome, storm-lit intensity of the emotional and musical landscape. La Venexiana's dark hues and dramatic but not histrionic approach sound unbeatable. A very fine disc indeed.

Madrigals – Book 6, Il sesto libro de' madrigali
Concerto Italiano / Rinaldo Alessandrini hpd
Naïve OP30423 (64' · DDD · T/t)   Ⓕ

Monteverdi's Sixth Book of Madrigals (1614) is significant for including both traditional polyphonic and *stile nuove* concerted madrigals. In his booklet-notes, Rinaldo Alessandrini points out that this is also a 'book of partings': many of the madrigals seem to have been written much earlier than the published date, at a time when Monteverdi suffered the loss of his wife Claudia and his live-in pupil, the singer Caterina Martinelli. All the texts deal with loss both temporary or permanent – although it's touching to note that the final madrigal, *Presso un fiume tranquillo*, paints a lovers' reconciliation possibly emblematic of a Heavenly reunion.

When discussing this repertoire it's almost a cliché to say that Concerto Italiano's approach is analytical, La Venexiana's more broadly coalescent (on Glossa). However, this new recording really goes far beyond the supple elegance of line for which La Venexiana are famous, with Alessandrini and his crew employing a tense, edgy rhetoric to reveal an inner psychology while sacrificing neither precision of ensemble nor beauty of sound. Concerto Italiano are now such a sensitive instrument that they respond to the emotional exigencies of the texts like silk to the breeze. Listen to the passionate *terza parte* of the *Lamento d'Arianna*; or the final line of *Zefiro torna*, where the drawn-out dissonances are almost physically painful; or the incredible dynamic and rhythmic control in the Sestina; or the fluid, frighteningly accurate ornamentation in *Qui rise, o Tirsi*. You could find 100 such examples without ever conveying the many excellences of this recording.

Madrigals – Book 7, Il settimo libro de' madrigali
La Venexiana / Claudio Cavina counterten
Glossa ② GCD920927 (137' · DDD · T/t)   Ⓕ

Book 7 (1619) gathers together works that must have been written many years apart. The common denominator is its consistent use of instruments in conjunction with the voices. Recording the complete book is a considerable undertaking, only previously achieved by the Consort of Musicke (Virgin Veritas – nla).

La Venexiana's free approach to rhythm is alive to the spirit of the music. *Ohimè, dov'è il mio ben* manages to be a set of variations on the Romanesca theme, and something else entirely: they convince you that this double-reading is precisely what Monteverdi intended. Though

not everything reflects the multi-faceted Monteverdi aesthetic, the pieces that are recorded less often still shed a useful light on his working process. As the first *intégrale* by a modern Italian ensemble, this is a significant addition to the catalogue.

Madrigals – Book 8, Il ottavo libro di madrigali;
'Madrigali guerrieri et amorosi'
Maria Cristina Kiehr, Salomé Haller sops **Marisa Martins** mez **Bernarda Fink** contr **Christophe Laporte** counterten **John Bowen, Jeremy Ovenden, Mario Zeffiri, Kobie van Rensburg** tens **Victor Torres** bar **Antonio Abete, Renaud Delaigue** basses **Concerto Vocale / René Jacobs**
Harmonia Mundi ③ HMC90 1736/7 (156' · DDD · T/t)   ⒻⓄⓄ

The blurb on the jacket says, 'Indispensable', and this is hardly an exaggeration. A complete Book 8 would be enough to whet any Monteverdian's appetite; but fortunately, completeness isn't the only reason to hail the new arrival. Jacobs's well-rounded team of singers is perhaps most effective in the large ensembles, which have a festive opulence about them, while allowing the necessary shadings to come into play: such things as the opening of *Hor che'l ciel* and *Ardo, avvampo* are admirably done, the one suitably mysterious and opaque, the other happily (but convincingly) chaotic. And with one or two exceptions the soloists acquit themselves handsomely, too: Bernarda Fink's title-role in the *Lamento della ninfa* is very affecting – one of the high-points of the set.

Jacobs's deployment of instruments, even on the continuo, is measured – even sparing, by his standards – but rich enough to evoke the splendid courtly entertainments for which these pieces were conceived. The instrumentalists are perhaps too easily overlooked in this repertoire: they don't draw attention to themselves here, but sound very solid and grounded.

Jacobs's feeling for the music's dramatic qualities is keen, and unsurprisingly encompasses the largest pieces, the 'one-act' operas *Il ballo delle ingrate* and *Combattimento di Tancredi e Clorinda*. For these, some may prefer Concerto Italiano's recording, which includes both pieces on a single disc, but Jacobs's less wilful readings are still most involving. By any objective criteria, Jacobs has pulled it off. So if you're looking for a single recording, this is a natural first choice.

'Banquet of the Senses'
Longe, mi Jesu. Madrigals, Book 4 –
Ah dolente partita; Io mi son giovinetta;
Ohimè, se tanto amate; Piange e sospira;
Quel augellin che canta; Sfogava con le stelle;
Si ch'io vorrei morire. Madrigals, Book 7 –
Parlo, miser'o taccio?
Consort of Musicke (Emma Kirkby, Evelyn Tubb sops Mary Nichols contr Andrew King, Joseph Cornwell tens Simon Grant bass Gabriele Micheli org) /
Anthony Rooley lte

Brilliant Classics **DVD** 99784 (48' · 16:9 · 5.1 · 0) Ⓜ

This programme, released on VHS by the Consort's own label Musica Oscura in 1993, has now reappeared on DVD, and deserves attention both for its fine music-making and adventurous conception.

The performances are recorded in the banqueting apartments of the Gonzaga dukes of Mantua, for whose entertainment many of these madrigals were created. In this intriguing setting, beneath the famously sensuous Mantuan frescoes, the Consort make a brave stab at recreating those original performances, mini-masques almost, with costume and dance. Rooley links them with an amiably informative commentary. The result is a welcome reminder of just how much of this music's magic we lose in the customary stuffed-shirt recital. Nevertheless, it isn't a total success. There's still something ineffably polite about it all, the wholesome 'G&S' jollity that tends to creep in when the English middle-classes aspire to the orgiastic. In the languishing *Parlo, miser'o*, the appearance of Mesdames Kirkby, Tubb and Nichols in diaphanous *deshabillé* could not be less than stirring, but can't quite shed the aura of a merry Roedean dorm party.

All the same, this is an engaging and original programme, and founded on first-rate performances. It isn't long, but it isn't expensive either, and well worth investigating.

Scherzi musicali

Scherzi musicali – Ecco di dolci raggi; Eri già tutta mia; Et è pur dunque vero; Maledetto sia l'aspetto; Quel sguardo sdegnosetto. Lamento d'Arianna. Madrigals, Book 7 – Con che soavita. Ohimè ch'io cado. Si dolce è'l tormento. Voglio di vita uscir. Più lieto il guardo. La mia turca. Perché se m'odiavi
Emanuela Galli sop **La Venexiana / Claudio Cavina**
Glossa GCD920915 (55' · DDD) Ⓕ

Rather than presenting the complete 1632 set of songs entitled *Scherzi musicali* ("musical jokes") – as is implied by Glossa's attractive artwork – La Venexiana instead places just five songs in the centre of music taken from the *Settimo libro dei Madrigali* (1619), the *Quarto scherzo delle ariose vaghezze* (published by Milanuzzi, 1624) and the *Arie di diversi raccolte* (published by Vincenti, 1634), and the song 'Voglio di vita uscir' (edited from a manuscript in Naples). Claudio Cavina takes a flexible approach to what he calls Monteverdi's 'light' music, professing in the booklet note that he 'wanted to have a joke with music… The *pizzicati* from the theorbos and the harp, the melodic lines of the cornetto, the swing of the voice…we present a divertissement for performers and listeners alike'.

The result of La Venexiana's experiment is very subtle; Cavina's 'joke' never condescends into the realms of cocktail lounge jazz-lite, but instead remains closely connected to the composer's chiaroscuro spirit. If there is humour here, it is of a dry type. Emanuela Galli's playful

rendition of 'Ohimè ch'io cado' has a *pizzicato* basso continuo part, but also possesses tangible sincerity. Galli's breathy opening phrase of 'Con que soavità' is exquisitely erotic, even if Glossa's recorded sound becomes uncharacteristically hard when the instrumental ensemble plays (the large continuo group includes three lutes, triple harp and harpsichord). 'Sì dolc'è il tormento' and 'Et è pur dunque vero' both feature the effective combination of Doron David Sherwin's sensitive cornetto playing and Galli's emotive singing. The recital concludes with Cavina's new orchestration of the lament from the lost opera *Arianna* (1608); a sensuous string ensemble gives eloquent support to Galli, whose singing ideally conveys impassioned lamentation without becoming distorted.

Sacred Works

Adoramus te, Christe. Domine, ne in furore. Ⓟ
Exulta, filia Sion. Salve, o regina. Salve regina.
Laetatus sum I. Salve regina I. Beatus vir III.
Dixit Dominus II. Sanctorum meritis II. Magnificat II.
Laudate Dominum III
The King's Consort Choir; The King's Consort / Robert King
Hyperion CDA67519 (70' · DDD · T/t) Ⓕ Ⓑ

The fourth volume of Robert King's exploration of Monteverdi's sacred music continues to mix pieces from different sources: the composer's authorised collection *Selva morale e spirituale*, the posthumous Venetian collection *Messa a quattro voci e salmi*, and various Italian anthologies. The beginning of *Laetatus sum I* instantly establishes the impeccable technical credentials of these stunning performances. The organ and chitarrone continuo is steady and sure-footed, joined a few bars later by a flamboyant violin duel stunningly dispatched by Simon Jones and Andrea Morris, and then crowned with a glorious duet by Carolyn Sampson and Rebecca Outram. The Choir of The King's Consort reinforce *tutti* passages with some splendid contributions and meet the florid, extrovert eight-part writing in *Dixit Dominus II* with colourful commitment. In the motet *Adoramus te, Christe* – not to be confused with the comparably beautiful but better known *Christe adoramus, te* – the choir shows its skill at gentler music, although I wonder if the use of solo voices might have been equally attractive and closer to what Monteverdi would have expected.

Charles Daniels and James Gilchrist beautifully judge several intimate tenor solos; Gilchrist's glorious and heartfelt singing in *Salve regina I* features some wonderful echo contributions from Daniels. Their tender communication of the text and sweet high registers consolidate their status as the finest English tenors of their type. Robert King never rushes the music but cannily treads the fine line between dizzying excitement and authoritative splendour. Even if you already admire seminal recordings of Monteverdi's sacred music by the likes of Andrew

Parrott, Konrad Junghänel and Rinaldo Alessandrini, there are plenty of less familiar gems included that make this series essential.

L'incoronazione di Poppea

L'incoronazione di Poppea   🅟
Sylvia McNair sop Poppea **Dana Hanchard** sop
Nerone **Anne Sofie von Otter** mez Ottavia,
Fortune, Venus **Michael Chance** counterten Ottone
Francesco Ellero d'Artegna bass Seneca **Catherine
Bott** sop Drusilla, Virtue, Pallas, Athene **Roberto
Balcone** counterten Nurse **Bernarda Fink** contr
Arnalta **Mark Tucker** ten Lucano, First Soldier **Julian
Clarkson** bass Lictor, Mercury **Marinella Pennicchi**
sop Love **Constanze Backes** sop Valleto **Nigel
Robson** ten Liberto, Second Soldier **English
Baroque Soloists / Sir John Eliot Gardiner**
Archiv ③ 447 088-2AH3 (3h 11' · DDD · T/t)
Recorded live 1993   Ⓕ

The central question was always about how much needs to be added to the surviving notes in order to make *Poppea* viable on stage. Gardiner and his advisers believe that nothing needs adding and that the 'orchestra' played only when explicitly notated in the score and was a very small group. To some ears this will have a fairly ascetic effect, but it's firmly in line with current scholarly thinking. To compensate, there's a rich group of continuo players who play with wonderful flexibility. And Gardiner's spacious reading of the score bursts with the variety of pace you might expect from a seasoned conductor of early opera. Sylvia McNair is a gloriously sensuous Poppea: from her sleepy first words to the final duet she's always a thoroughly devious character, with her breathy, come-hither tones. Complementing this is Dana Hanchard's angry-brat Nerone, less even in voice than one might hope, but dramatically powerful nevertheless. Whether they quite challenge Helen Donath and Elisabeth Söderström for Harnoncourt is a matter of opinion, but they certainly offer a viable alternative.

The strongest performances here, though, come from Michael Chance and Anne Sofie von Otter as Ottone and Ottavia, both of them offering superbly rounded portrayals. Again they face severe challenges from Harnoncourt's unforgettable Paul Esswood and Cathy Berberian, but here the challenge is more equal. Francesco Ellero d'Artegna is perhaps the most vocally skilled Seneca to date.

The fact that this was recorded at a public concert is noticeable only occasionally.

L'incoronazione di Poppea
Maria Ewing sop Poppea **Dennis Bailey** ten Nerone
Cynthia Clarey sop Ottavia **Dale Duesing** bar
Ottone **Robert Lloyd** bass Seneca **Elizabeth Gale**
sop Drusilla **Glyndebourne Chorus; London
Philharmonic Orchestra / Raymond Leppard**
Stage director **Peter Hall**
Video directors **Peter Hall, Robin Lough**
Warner Music Vision/NVC Arts 📀 0630 16914-2

(155' · NTSC · 4:3 · PCM stereo · 2-6)
Recorded live at the Glyndebourne Festival, 1984 Ⓕ🅞

Raymond Leppard's edition of *Poppea*, first staged at Glyndebourne in 1962, opened many people's eyes and ears to Monteverdi for the first time. By 1984, though, when Glyndebourne mounted this new production, his Respighisation of Monteverdi's sparse original was distinctly old hat. The allegorical prologue was restored; but as well as the lush string textures there remained the downward transposition of castrato roles and the squeezing of three acts into two. Yet only the most fanatical devotee of historically informed performance could fail to respond to this wonderful production with sumptuous designs by John Bury.

Peter Hall's production is, quite properly, dominated by Poppea. Maria Ewing is the personification of sensuousness, singing with rich tone throughout. She brilliantly conveys Poppea's ruthless ambition, her steely determination to become empress at all costs. By the end you feel that Poppea and Nero richly deserve each other, and the empress Ottavia is well shot of her husband. Hall frequently has his singers addressing the camera: a bold move, but one that forces the viewer to become involved in the fate of these mainly rather unappealing characters.

The drawbacks of Leppard's edition notwithstanding, this is a great theatrical experience.

L'Orfeo

L'Orfeo   🅟
Ian Bostridge ten Orfeo **Patrizia Ciofi** ten Euridice
Natalie Dessay sop La Musica **Alice Coote** ten
Messenger **Sonia Prina** ten Speranza **Mario Luperi**
ten Caronte **Véronique Gens** ten Proserpina
Carolyn Sampson ten Nymph **Lorenzo Regazzo** ten
Plutone **Christopher Maltman** ten Apollo Shepherd
III **Paul Agnew** ten Eco Shepherd II **Pascal Bertin** ten
Shepherd I **Richard Burkhard** ten Shepherd IV
**European Voices; Le Concert d'Astrée /
Emmanuelle Haïm**
Virgin Classics Veritas ② 545642-2 (96' · DDD) Ⓕ🅞🅞

Instead of attempting an intellectual reconstruction of *L'Orfeo*, Emmanuelle Haïm presents a full-blooded reinvention of the opera that's firmly modernistic. The cast is primarily composed of world-class opera and recital singers: the overall result is even, cohesive and without vocal blemishes. Some sopranos represent the legacy of 'authenticity' better than others. Natalie Dessay's forthright declamation as La Musica in the exquisite prologue is emotive, but can't eclipse Gardiner's astute Lynne Dawson. In contrast, Carolyn Sampson's fleeting contribution as a Nymph is gorgeously refined and elegantly poised, suggesting that she might make a fine La Musica if given the chance. Véronique Gens is a creamy Proserpina whose tangible pity for Orfeo makes her a very human goddess. Alice Coote's Messenger provides the most compelling moment with a haunted voice full of eloquent pain. The title-role suits Ian Bostridge, and his thoughtfully considered singing effortlessly ranges between smouldering gestures in 'Vi ricorda ò bosch' ombrosi' and shivering disbelief when the messenger tells him Euridice is dead.

European Voices incline towards a full-blooded operatic sound rather than a cool choral blend. Le Concert d'Astrée serve as a linchpin that propels the drama forward with obsessive momentum. The pumping sackbuts during the introductory toccata indicate that the ensuing drama isn't going to be dull, and Les Sacqueboutiers also provide a splendid regal entrance to a vision of Dante's Inferno in Act 3. The strings produce *ritornellos* of magnificent sensitivity and resonating eroticism. Haïm does, though, excessively pepper Monteverdi's score with prominent and improvisational percussion.

Haïm's performance has a much stronger Italianate sense than the comparatively English school that's hitherto dominated the discography, and her compelling perspective possesses a lively spirit that makes the listening hours fly by. Purists will be divided over the liberties she takes, but her performance is a stimulating alternative to the fine pedigree of recordings that has preceded it.

L'Orfeo   Ⓟ

John Mark Ainsley *ten* Orfeo **Juanita Lascarro** *sop* Euridice **Brigitte Balleys** *sop* Messenger **Russell Smythe** *ten* Apollo, Shepherd II **David Cordier** *alto* La Musica **Michael Chance** *counterten* Speranza **Mario Luperi** *bass* Caronte **Bernarda Fink** *mez* Proserpina **Dean Robinson** *bass-bar* Plutone, Shepherd IV **Jean-Paul Fouchécourt** *ten* Shepherd I, Eco **Douglas Nasrawi** *ten* Shepherd III **Suzie Le Blanc** *sop* Nymph **Tragicomedia; Concerto Palatino / Stephen Stubbs**
Stage director **Pierre Audi**
Video director **Hans Hulscher**
Opus Arte ② ᴅᴠᴅ OA0928D (140' · 16:9 · PCM stereo and DTS 5.1 · 0)
Recorded live at Het Muziektheater, Amsterdam, in July 1997. Extra features include Illustrated Synopsis, Cast Gallery, Introduction to the Opera and Interviews   Ⓕ

In a perceptive documentary made during rehearsals, director Pierre Audi comments that *L'Orfeo* is 'an opera about the crisis of an artist: whether art and life are really compatible; what the personal intimate experience of an artist in confronting love and death has to do with his own artistic expression'. Audi's production is starkly conceptual in some ways but the performance has a simplicity and fidelity to the drama. Carefully timed effects, controlled gestures and economical directness have a powerful impact. The action is focused around a circular pool of water set towards the back of the stage, behind a dilapidated wall that is used for different purposes – such as sinking to become the passageway to Hades. The Arcadian frolics of the shepherds and nymphs allow dancing, skipping and splashing in the pool; but later, flames emerge to transform it into the Styx.

Audi weds his own ideas about characters to a faithful reproduction of the libretto. Audi's action shows that the Messenger who brings news of Euridice's death is shunned by the Arcadians, whose society is evidently only superficially pleasant (this reinforces the idea that all earthly pleasure is fleeting, as Orfeo is told by his father Apollo in the opera's conclusion). Plutone's bargain with Orfeo is a vindictive mind game with his wife Proserpina, who desires Orfeo. Likewise, Orfeo seems to yearn for Proserpina despite his quest for Euridice, thus making his moral character tarnished. Audi's skill is to make these ambiguities subtle and paradoxical, for Orfeo's grief and confusion at his permanent loss of Euridice lack nothing in sincerity.

John Mark Ainsley's blend of head and chest voices has beauty and depth, and his acting is equally impressive. Bernarda Fink provides outstanding singing and acting as Proserpina, and Michael Chance delivers a compelling cameo as La Speranza. But it was a bizarre decision to cast David Cordier as an androgynous La Musica who struggles to sing poetically, especially when Suzie Le Blanc – the ideal soprano for this part – steps forward for only a few solo lines.

There are assured contributions from Jean-Paul Fouchécourt, Russell Smythe, Dean Robinson, Brigitte Balleys and Juanita Lascarro. Mario Luperi looks the part as a giant-like Caronte, although his fast vibrato will not please everybody. The trump card is the superb accompaniment from Concerto Palatino and Tragicomedia, expertly directed by Stephen Stubbs.

Il ritorno d'Ulisse in patria

Il ritorno d'Ulisse in patria   Ⓟ

Christoph Prégardien *ten* Ulisse **Bernarda Fink** *contr* Penelope **Christina Högmann** *sop* Telemaco, Siren **Martyn Hill** *ten* Eumete **Jocelyne Taillon** *mez* Ericlea **Dominique Visse** *counterten* Pisandro, Human Fragility **Mark Tucker** *ten* Anfinomo **David Thomas** *bass* Antinoo **Guy de Mey** *ten* Iro **Faridah Subrata** *mez* Melanto **Jörg Dürmüller** *ten* Eurimaco **Lorraine Hunt** *sop* Minerva, Fortune **Michael Schopper** *bass* Nettuno, Time **Olivier Lallouette** *bass* Giove **Claron McFadden** *sop* Giunone **Martina Bovet** *sop* Siren, Love **Concerto Vocale / René Jacobs**
Harmonia Mundi ③ HMC90 1427/9
(179' · DDD · T/t)   ⒻⓄⓄ

The only surviving manuscript score of this major musical drama, preserved in Vienna, presents an incomplete version of three acts. For this recording, René Jacobs has, within the spirit of 17th-century music-making, added more music by Monteverdi and others to expand the work to a satisfying five-act structure suggested by some surviving librettos. He has also considerably expanded the scoring, very much enlivening the instrumental palette that Monteverdi would have had available to him for his original production in Vienna in 1641, and the result is powerful and effective.

The extensive cast, led by Christoph Prégardien in the title-role, is excellently chosen, not only for vocal quality but also for a convincing awareness of Monteverdi's idiom. Without that, the performance could have seemed tame, and that's nowhere better exemplified than in Act 1, Scene 7 where Ulysses awakes, wondering where he is and what's to happen to him. Prégardien here manages to convey as much depth of feeling as a Pagliaccio yet stays clearly within the bounds of Monteverdi's expressive style. The result is a *tour de force*, one of the many within this production. The adept instrumental contribution certainly helps to maintain variety throughout the work, and an accompaniment suited to the sentiments expressed by the vocalists is always possible with these resources. Ultimately, this production is very much one for our time. It's a practical solution to the problems of performing music of another age, and one that turns out to be inspired, moving and totally compelling.

Il ritorno d'Ulisse in patria
Dietrich Henschel *bar* Ulisse, Humana fragilità
Vesselina Kasarova *sop* Penelope **Jonas Kaufmann**
ten Telemaco **Boguslaw Bidzinski** *ten* Eurimaco
Anton Scharinger *ten* Giove **Reinhard Mayr** *bass*
Antinoo **Martin Zysset** *ten* Pisandro **Martin Oro**
counterten Anfinomo **Isabel Rey** *sop* Minerva,
Amore **Thomas Mohr** *ten* Eumete **Pavel Daniluk**
bass Nettuno **Giuseppe Scorsin** *bass* Time **Martina**
Janková *sop* Fortune **Giunone Cornelia Kallisch**
mez Ericlea **Malin Hartelius** *sop* Melanto **Rudolf**
Schasching *ten* Iro **La Scintilla Orchestra, Zürich /**
Nikolaus Harnoncourt
Stage director **Klaus-Michael Grüber**
Video director **Felix Breisach**
ArtHaus Musik **DVD** 100 352 (155' · 16:9 · 2.0 & 5.1 · 0)
Notes included   Ⓕ

The renowned collaborations between Zürich Opera and Nikolaus Harnoncourt in the 1970s and early '80s were crucial milestones in projecting historically aware performance away from historicism-for-its-own-sake, towards vitally conceived productions for contemporary audiences. *Il ritorno* enjoyed great success in 1977 in Jean-Pierre Ponnelle's imaginative staging: Harnoncourt's opulent instrumental palette lifted the hearts of many, though only the eyebrows of the purists. In this musical 'revival' to celebrate 25 years of the swashbuckling original, Harnoncourt allows the nobility of the score to roll unimpeded by the driven intensity of the older recorded account on Teldec from 1971.

The vocal contributions are more eloquent than ever, with outstanding contributions from Vesselina Kasarova and Dietrich Henschel. Can Monteverdi have ever heard this opera sung with such an extraordinary range of vocal beauty and immediacy of expression? This extends to all the characters.

Of the two caveats here, the durability of Harnoncourt's big-band score with its bold instrumental canvas is likely to be a source of debate. Monteverdi left only a shell of his musical genius and, as convention dictated, the performers filled in the rest. The logic of using the greatest array of coloration to suit the context of characterisation and emotional states is highly plausible for all those who value music drama – and Monteverdi, more to the point – in pastels rather than charcoal. Yet there are moments when the spirit of realisation enters the realm of transcription, especially in the richly endowed brass ensembles used for divine intervention. A later Baroque sound world occasionally prevails, and the luminosity of the moment is lost. However, the warm glow of assured fidelity in 'Hor di parlar e tempo' – where Ulysses's *accompagnato* recitative lends authenticity to the composer's primal communicative instincts – is ravishing and persuasive. The DVD production is flawed only by some poor dubbing in Act 2.

Cristóbal de Morales

Spanish c1500-1553

Morales is a towering figure in early-16th-century Spanish sacred music. Educated in Seville, he was appointed maestro de capilla of Avila Cathedral in 1528. In 1531 he resigned and within four years was a singer in the papal chapel in Rome. He left in 1545 and was appointed maestro de capilla at Toledo Cathedral where he stayed until illness forced him to relinquish the post. On returning to Andalusia he became maestro de capilla to the Duke of Arcos at Marchena and in 1551 he took the same post at Málaga Cathedral. His works, almost all liturgical, include over 20 Masses, 16 Magnificats, two sets of Lamentations and over 100 motets.

Masses

Missa Si bona suscepimus **Crecquillon** Andreas
Christi famulus **Verdelot** Si bona suscepimus
The Tallis Scholars / Peter Phillips
Gimell CDGIM033 (56' · DDD · T/t)   Ⓕ ⦿⦿▷

The Tallis Scholars move into new territory for them: Cristóbal de Morales is perhaps the most admired Spanish composer of all time, to judge from the distribution and longevity of his works. But not nearly enough of his music has appeared on disc. In particular, the six-voice Mass *Si bona suscepimus* appears not to have been recorded before. It was printed in his first book of Masses (1544) and undoubtedly comes from his years in the papal chapel. At first listening, there may be something almost too serene about its flawless counterpoint that flows with effortless invention. But there's an abundance of arresting detail in here, and he uses the six voices with an astonishing variety of textures.

The Tallis Scholars are up to their usual standards of magnificent sound colour, nicely judged balance and extremely pure intonation. There's nothing overtly Spanish in the performance: they simply sing what's in the music, without imposing too much externally. They hardly ever rush or slow down severely, preferring to allow the music to unfold at its own flexible pace. That could seem bland until you compare the sound with the introductory five-voice motet of Verdelot on which the Mass is based, or indeed the marvellous Crecquillon motet that ends the disc; these immediately sound quite different.

Sancta Maria, succerre miseris. Beati omnes qui timent Dominum. Lamentations of Jeremiah – Coph: Vocavi; Zai: Candidiores; Nun: Vigilavit. Gaude et laetare, Ferrariensis civitas. Salve regina a 4. Regina caeli a 6. Spem in alium. Magnificat primi toni
Brabant Ensemble / Stephen Rice
Hyperion CDA67694 (73' · DDD · T/t)   Ⓕ**Ⓞ**➤

This recording suggests how central is Morales's position within the High Repertoire. Often spoken of as a precursor of Palestrina, here (as in the Lamentations settings that open the programme) he seems just as clearly to prefigure Lassus's own penitential mode (especially at 'Nun: Vigilavit'). Stephen Rice leaves aside the Mass repertory in favour of the motet. Following the Lamentations set, this selection is mostly of Marian pieces. The single exception is an impressive celebratory piece commemorating the elevation of Ippolito d'Este, brother of the Duke of Ferrara, to the cardinalate. Unlike some of the Marian motets this has not been recorded before, and it shows off a more public side of the composer.

The motets range in scoring from four to six voices, but whatever the number of voices, the counterpoint is always perfectly intelligible. Obviously that's due to the clarity of the composer's textures, but it also reflects well on the Brabant Ensemble, who turn in very solid readings, subdued or serene, as text and music demand. In the *Magnificat*, the intensity steps up a notch, reaching an impressive climax. Indeed, the ensemble quality here belies the fact that only four voices are involved (except at the very end); this is the Brabant Ensemble at their most vigorous and confident. For this reading, Rice opts for the polyphonic setting of all the verses, rather than alternate half of them with plainchant, a common practice of the time. In a fast-growing discography, this is a valuable addition.

'Assumption Mass – Toledo Cathedral, c1580'   Ⓟ
Morales Ave regina caelorum. Exaltata est sancta Dei genitrix. Missa Benedicta est regina caelorum **Cabezón** Beata viscera Mariae Virginis. Tiento sobre el hymno, 'Ave Maris stella' **Ceballos** O pretiosum et admirabile sacramentum **F Guerrero** Ave Maria. Dulcissima Maria **Ribera** Beata mater **Torrentes**

Asperges Mej **Plainchants** – Introitus; Oratio; Graduale and Alleluia; Offertorium; Prefacio; Pater noster; Communio; Postcommunio
Orchestra of the Renaissance / Richard Cheetham and Michael Noone
Glossa GCD921404 (76' · DDD · T/t)   Ⓕ

This is a reconstruction of a Mass for the Assumption as it might have been heard in Toledo Cathedral in about 1580. It follows very much the pattern established by the group's previous discs, with a mixture of musical items that can be pegged, however loosely, to a particular occasion or type of occasion. Here the research into the rich musical repertory and the musico-liturgical practice of Toledo Cathedral by guest conductor Michael Noone makes for a particularly compelling example of the reconstruction genre.

The ways in which instruments and voices are used is well thought out, and the music, including those pieces by the less well-known Toledan maestros Ribera and Torrentes, is of the highest quality. Similar care has been taken over the sources for the plainchant which, as on earlier recordings by the Orchestra of the Renaissance, is performed with just the right inflections and sense of pace by the bass Josep Cabré.

It's clear that Morales's music continued to be performed in Spanish cathedrals throughout the 16th century and beyond, and the superb Mass *Benedicta est regina caelorum* makes it easy to see why. It's performed well by singers and instrumentalists alike, the harp and dulcian adding a distinctive shimmer and depth to the overall sound pool of voices, shawms and sackbuts. Overall, the performances are restrained with a good sense of natural flow, if perhaps occasionally lacking in intensity. An impressive and very attractive CD that grows with repeated listening into one of the most convincing 'occasional' recordings in the catalogue.

Ignaz Moscheles   German 1794-1870

After study in Prague and with Salieri in Vienna, Moscheles became a pianist, travelling throughout Europe. He settled in London, taught at the RAM, established a series of 'historical soirées' (in which he performed Bach and Scarlatti on the harpsichord), wrote fashionable salon music and conducted the Philharmonic Society. He was a friend of Mendelssohn and conducted the London premiere of Beethoven's Missa solemnis (1832). He also translated Schindler's biography as The Life of Beethoven (1841). From 1846 he was professor at the Leipzig Conservatory. He is best known for his piano music.

Piano Concertos

Piano Concertos – No 2 in E flat, Op 56; No 3 in G minor, Op 58. Anticipations of Scotland: A Grand Fantasia, Op 75

Tasmanian Symphony Orchestra /
Howard Shelley pf
Hyperion CDA67276 (76' · DDD)   Ⓕ **OO**

Both the Second and Third Concertos bristle with enough savage jumps and hurdles to throw a less than first-class performer; woe betide the pianist without flawless scales and arpeggios (often twisting into awkward and unpredictable patterns). Moscheles's contemporaries, hungry for heart-stopping acrobatics, surely left the concert hall thrilled and gratified. But there are also many fascinating purely musical surprises.

Most engagingly, Moscheles was highly responsive to local colour, paying tribute to his adopted city of London in his Fourth Concerto by quoting the 'March of the Grenadiers' and, in his *Anticipations of Scotland: A Grand Fantasia*, to folksongs and dances north of the border. Who can resist the assurance of 'Auld Robin Grey' (though even he breaks out into a flash of virtuosity) or a strathspey sufficiently perky to set all true Scotsmen's blood tingling?

The recordings, made in Tasmania, are excellent, and the Tasmanian Symphony Orchestra enter into the spirit of things with verve and affection. In short, a disc of aristocratic brilliance and distinction.

Pierre Moulu   Franco-Flemish c1484-c1550

Not much is known of his life, but he was probably at the French Royal Chapel during the first two decades of the 16th century. He was also associated with the Cathedral in Meaux. He composed music for ceremonial occasions, for example a sombre lament for the death of Queen Anne of Brittany (1514), and he also composed a motet which lists all the composers he considered to be the most celebrated in France, arranged chronologically, and ending with Josquin.

Choral Works

Moulu Mater floreat. Missa Missus est Gabriel angelus. In pace. Missa Alma redemptoris mater
Josquin Desprez Missus est Gabriel angelus
Brabant Ensemble / Stephen Rice
Hyperion CDA67761 (75' · DDD)   Ⓕ **O➤**

Pierre Moulu's claim to fame nowadays rests on two works, his 'singers' motet' *Mater floreat florescat*, which lists most of the famous composers active in his lifetime, and his *Missa Alma redemptoris mater*, which is so devised that it can be performed either as notated or by leaving out all the rests longer than a minim. Both works appear on this, the first recording given over to him entirely. Sensibly, the Brabant Ensemble include both the 'long' and the 'short' versions (that is, with and without the rests) of the 'Kyrie' and 'Agnus Dei', which are brief enough that the attentive listener can, without a score, get some idea of the challenge Moulu set him-

self, and the measure in which he succeeded. Paper music this is not, and as if to dispel any doubt on this point, Stephen Rice has also included another Mass which has no other restriction than the one, usual in this period, of being based on a pre-existing motet, in this case a work by Josquin.

As to the performances, they work very nicely; the feeling that the music of this period comes across better if scored slightly lower is doubtless a personal taste that not all will share, and in any case it suits the transparency of Moulu's textures better than, say, Gombert's thicker ones. As to occasional niggles regarding tuning and approach, they are more easily overlooked when the music itself so clearly deserves to be heard.

Wolfgang Amadeus Mozart
Austrian 1756-1791

There has never been a child prodigy in musical history to rival Mozart. He could compose and play the piano and the violin by the time he was six. His father Leopold was a composer and violinist in the service of the Prince-Archbishop of Salzburg, hoping in due course to become Kapellmeister. Wolfgang and his sister Anna Maria (nicknamed Nannerl) were the only two of Leopold's seven children to survive infancy. Both were musically talented and when, at the age of four, Wolfgang could not only memorise a piece in an hour and play it faultlessly, Leopold realised that he had a prodigy on his hands. There's no doubt that part of Leopold's motive was to make a great musician of his son and let the world know about his God-given gifts, but he exploited these gifts to the full.

Both children set off on their first tour with their father, with the idea of playing at various European courts, first to Munich and the Elector of Bavaria then to Vienna where Nannerl and Wolfgang played in front of the Empress Maria Theresia and the seven-year-old Marie Antoinette. Mozart's first compositions were published in Paris; his first symphonies were written the following year. The family tour continued to London, where audiences flocked to hear the two prodigies, amazed at Wolfgang's powers of improvisation. Johann Christian Bach befriended them; one of the brothers Grimm (of fairy-tale fame) heard Mozart improvise and wrote: 'I cannot be sure that this child will not turn my head if I go on hearing him often; he makes me realise that it is difficult to guard against madness on seeing prodigies. I am no longer surprised that St Paul should have lost his head after a strange vision.'

In 1766 the Mozarts arrived back in Salzburg where Wolfgang applied himself to the serious study of counterpoint under his father's tutelage. The following year, the family were in Vienna where his first opera La finta semplice was begun; his next stage work, the Singspiel Bastien und Bastienne, was produced at the home of Dr Mesmer, the protagonist of the therapy to become known as mesmerism.

Wolfgang and his father spent nearly two years in Italy – the visit when, legend has it, he wrote out the entire score of Allegri's *Miserere* from memory. Here, he benefited from his meetings with the distinguished Italian composer Padre Martini. This was followed by a period in Salzburg in which he composed his first important works including the violin concertos and the popular Haffner Serenade.

Accompanied by his mother, Mozart journeyed to Paris. This tour, unlike previous ones which were financed by expensive gifts from the various courts, had to make money en route. It was during this time that he first fell in love with Aloysia, one of the daughters of the music copyist Fridolin Weber. His mother's death in Paris and Aloysia's rebuttal of his affections persuaded him to return to Salzburg where he spent the next two years composing in the service of the Archbishop. *Idomeneo* (1780), his first important opera was among the commissions he received. Frustrated by the stultifying demands of his employer, Mozart resigned from the Archbishop's service.

Mozart decided to make Vienna his home (it remained his base for the rest of his life), a move which marks the beginning of Mozart's golden years as a mature composer. His first lodgings were with the Weber family and it wasn't long before he had fallen in love with Constanze, the flighty younger sister of his old love (who was now married).

After his wedding in August, a string of fine works appeared (the Haffner and Linz symphonies, a set of six string quartets dedicated to Haydn – the two had become close friends – as well as *The Marriage of Figaro*, 1786). All through this period, the Mozarts' finances were perilously poised, despite many commissions and concert appearances. No court appointment had materialised and, though stories of his poverty at this time are exaggerated, he felt poor enough to write begging letters to his friends. And yet – and in spite of this – between 1784 and 1786 one masterpiece followed another. How could a human being compose nine of the greatest piano concertos in such circumstances? In 1786, three of these concertos were written at the same time as he was working on *The Marriage of Figaro*.

At last, in November 1787, he secured an appointment as Kammermusicus in Vienna in succession to Gluck. But whereas Gluck's stipend was 2000 gulden, Mozart's was a paltry 800. However, this change in his fortunes must have softened the blow of his father's death earlier in the year. It's almost incidental to mention that this was the year that saw the appearance of *Don Giovanni*, his second operatic masterpiece.

The year 1788 was the *annus mirabilis* in which Mozart composed his final three symphonies (Nos 39-41), *Eine kleine Nachtmusik*, the String Quintet in G minor and the exquisite Clarinet Quintet. The following spring, Mozart travelled to Berlin where he played for King Friedrich Wilhelm II and was offered the post of Kapellmeister at a good salary, but Vienna drew him back. He returned to complete *Così fan tutte*, his third collaboration with the librettist da Ponte. Da Ponte had already established himself in London and the opportunity arose for Mozart to go there. Mozart declined.

The Clarinet Concerto and Piano Concerto No 27 in B flat, *The Magic Flute*, the old-fashioned Italian-style opera *La clemenza di Tito* and the Requiem – any one would have been sufficient to make their composer immortal. But all by the same man? In one year (1791)? The achievement is breathtaking.

The circumstances of Mozart's death are well known – the mysterious stranger visiting Mozart to ask for the composition of a Requiem Mass, Mozart thinking the visitor had come from another world and that the Requiem was for his own soul. Mozart did not live long enough to complete it for his terrible death, from a number of bodily failures, occurred a few weeks before his 36th birthday.

Bassoon Concerto, K191

Bassoon Concerto. Flute Concerto No 1, K313.
Horn Concerto No 1, K412. Oboe Concerto, K314
Emily Beynon fl **Alexei Ogrintchouk** ob
Gustavo Nuñez bn **Jacob Slagter** hn
Concertgebouw Chamber Orchestra
Pentatone ⊕ PTC5186 079 (71' · DDD/DSD) Ⓕ🅑➔

This Concertgebouw survey of four wind concertos dates across a fair span of Mozart's adulthood. The First Horn Concerto was composed for Mozart's friend Joseph Leutgeb at Vienna in 1791; modern-day counterpart Jacob Slagter employs a warmly refulgent tone in his lively performance. Next, we have the First Flute Concerto (Paris, 1778). Emily Beynon's neatly executed, charming playing is well suited to the celebratory, sunny first movement. The Concertgebouw strings contribute hushed accompaniment in the *Andante ma non troppo*.

Mozart's Salzburg years are represented by his Bassoon Concerto (1774) and Oboe Concerto (written in 1777 for the Italian oboist Giuseppe Ferlendis, who had joined the Salzburg court only a few months before). Bassoonist Gustavo Nuñez plays with fruity directness, displaying stunning agility in the *Allegro* and poignant playing in the *Andante ma adagio*. Alexei Ogrintchouk's oboe provides a melancholic *Adagio non troppo* and a fluent impression of Mozart's felicitous inventiveness in the gleeful Rondo. All four soloists are principals of the Royal Concertgebouw Orchestra. The chamber incarnation sounds playful yet at ease. Phrases are shaded off and chords often shortened, but there is no self-consciousness or evident struggle in the pervading cheerful spirit.

Clarinet Concerto in A, K622

Clarinet Concerto[a]. Clarinet Quintet in A, K581[b]
Thea King basset cl [b]**Gabrieli String Quartet**
(Kenneth Sillito, Brendan O'Reilly vns Ian Jewel va
Keith Harvey vc) [a]**English Chamber Orchestra /**
Jeffrey Tate
Hyperion CDA66199 (64' · DDD) Ⓕ🅞➔

The two works on this disc represent Mozart's clarinet writing at its most inspired; however, the instrument for which they were written differed in several respects from the modern clarinet, the most important being its extended bass range. Modern editions of both the Clarinet

Concerto and the Quintet have adjusted the solo part to suit today's clarinets, but Thea King reverts as far as possible to the original texts, and her playing is both sensitive and intelligent. Jeffrey Tate and the ECO accompany with subtlety and discretion in the Concerto, and the Gabrieli Quartet achieves a fine rapport with King in the Quintet. Both recordings are clear and naturally balanced.

Clarinet Concerto[a]. Clarinet Quintet[b]
Jack Brymer cl [a]**London Symphony Orchestra / Sir Colin Davis;** [b]**Allegri Quartet**
Philips 442 390-2PM (50' · ADD)
Recorded 1973   Ⓕ**OO**▷▸

From the many recordings of the Concerto Jack Brymer made, this mid-price coupling is well worth looking for. With Davis a master-Mozartian coaxing elegant playing from the LSO, Brymer delivers a performance of poetry and charm. The Clarinet Quintet is no less delightful.

Flute Concertos

No 1 in G, K313; **No 2** in C, K314. **Andante in C major**, K315. **Flute and Harp Concerto** in D, K299

Flute Concertos Nos 1 & 2 (cadenzas by Aho). Andante, K315. Rondo, KAnh184
Sharon Bezaly fl **Ostrobothnian Chamber Orchestra / Juha Kangas**
BIS 🏵 BIS-SACD1539 (56' · DDD)   Ⓕ**OO**

Israeli flautist Sharon Bezaly offers delectable performances of the familiar Mozart concertos. The composer famously protested that he loathed the flute, though he was far too much of a pro to slip from his customary fastidious standards. In the fast movements he is at his most puckish and insouciant, while the slow ones, especially the *Adagio ma non troppo* of the G major, infuse graceful galanterie with exquisite poetry.

To both concertos, plus the two separate movements (of which the D major Rondo is a transcription of the dapper C major Rondo for violin, K373), Bezaly brings pure, delicately coloured tone – beautiful throughout its range – phenomenal agility and breath control, and an impish sense of fun. The *Allegros* have an elegant bounce, with soloist and the ever-alert Ostrobothnian Chamber Orchestra relishing their quickfire interplay. Repeats are always a cue for imaginative new phrasings; and time and again Bezaly provokes a smile with her playfully varied bravura passagework.

Bezaly opts for a lighter tonal palette than usual and favours a cooler, simpler (and arguably more Mozartian) approach in slow movements. Where she steps right out of period is in the cadenzas. Specially written by Kalevi Aho, these refract and fragment Mozart through a 21st-century prism, exploiting the whole compass of the flute and giving Bezaly scope to explore intriguing new colours. Purists may throw up their hands. But if you can adjust to the time-travelling you may find Aho's cadenzas ingenious, entertaining and strangely touching.

Flute and Harp Concerto. Horn Concerto No 3, K447. Concerto for Two Pianos and Orchestra, K365
Frank Theuns fl **Ulrich Hübner** hn
Marjan de Haer hp **Yoko Kaneko** fp
Anima Eterna Orchestra / Jos van Immerseel fp
Zig-Zag Territoires ZZT060201 (67' · DDD)   Ⓕ**OOO**

Director and fortepianist Jos van Immerseel is a veritable pioneer of period Mozart. Belgian period-instrument orchestra Anima Eterna's exuberant performances reveal a natural union of pioneering spirit and refreshing musical flavours. The performers show commendable integrity in their approach to using historical instruments: the characteristics and origins of the solo instruments are each enthusiastically described in the booklet-note but the loving care given to detail in this joyful music means this is never in danger of seeming merely a dour academic exercise.

The invigorating Concerto for two pianos (Salzburg, 1779-80) opens proceedings with a revitalising fix of blazing horns, vibrant woodwind and articulate strings. Anima Eterna's stunning playing in the *tuttis* is perfectly balanced with the fluent playing of Immerseel and Yoko Kaneko. After such *joie de vivre*, the Flute and Harp Concerto (Paris, 1778) features sensitively judged playing from Frank Theuns and Marjan de Haer. Seldom thas there been such an affectionate and warmly stylish performance of the *Allegro*, and the *Andantino* is ravishing.

Ulrich Hübner plays with attractive immediacy in the Third Horn Concerto, composed around 1787: the poetic *Romanze* has a lyrical elegance one seldom hears from even the best natural horn players, and an infectiously sunny performance of the dance-like *Allegro* concludes this magnificent recording with a charismatic flourish. These performances are radiant.

Horn Concertos

No 1 in D, K412; **No 2** in E flat, K417; **No 3** in E flat, K447; **No 4** in E flat, K495

Horn Concertos Nos 1-4.   Ⓗ
Piano Quintet in E flat, K452
Dennis Brain hn **Philharmonia Orchestra / Herbert von Karajan**
EMI mono 566898-2 (55' · ADD)
Recorded 1953   Ⓕ**OOO**▷▸

Ⓖ   Dennis Brain was the finest Mozartian soloist of his generation. Again and again Karajan matches the graceful line of his solo phrasing (the *Romanze* of No 3 is just

MOZART'S HORN CONCERTOS – IN BRIEF

Dennis Brain; Philharmonia Orchestra / Herbert von Karajan   H
EMI mono 566898-2 (77' · ADD)   MOOOO↦

Timelessly neat and elegant orchestral playing under Herbert von Karajan accompanies Dennis Brain's flawless and characterful playing – truly an all-time classic which transcends the mono sound.

Michael Thompson; Bournemouth Sinfonietta
Naxos 8 553592 (76' · DDD)   S↦

Sparkling performances on modern instruments by the Bournemouth Sinfonietta under the direction of the soloist, Michael Thompson, who performs scholarly editions prepared by John Humphries. A top bargain choice.

English Chamber Orchestra / Barry Tuckwell
Decca 458 607-2DM (69' · DDD)   M

Fluent and charming performances by Barry Tuckwell, who also directs the English Chamber Orchestra's idiomatic accompaniment, in his third studio recording of these concertos.

David Pyatt; ASMF / Neville Marriner
Warner Classics 2564 69719-9 (69' · DDD)   MO

Though recorded in 1996, the slightly plush string tone and close-focus miking of David Pyatt's mellow-toned horn makes these accounts sound a tad old-fashioned even next to Karajan and Brain. None the less, these are affectionate performances which will please those wanting modern instrumentation in stereo sound.

Eric Ruske; Scottish CO / Charles Mackerras
Telarc CD80367 (64' · DDD)   F

Attractive performances with golden horn tone complemented by idiomatic orchestral playing in spacious sound. Richard Suart singing Flanders and Swann's 'Ill Wind' makes an unusual encore.

Alan Civil; Philharmonia / Otto Klemperer   H
Testament SBT1102 (72' · ADD)   F

Another historic performance. Alan Civil's tone is more full bodied and his humour more earthy than Brain's. The orchestral accompaniment, however, is not always ideally coordinated with the soloist.

Teunis Van der Zwart hn **Freiburg Baroque**   P
Orchestra / Gottfried von der Goltz
Harmonia Mundi HMC90 1946 (66' · DDD)   F

Though only recorded in Concertos Nos 1 and 4, Teunis Van der Swart gives irresistible performances full of the full-throated joy that natural horns can convey so freely. Gottfried von der Goltz and the Freiburgers provide thrilling support.

---

one ravishing example), while in the *Allegros* the crisply articulated, often witty comments from the Philharmonia violins are a joy. The glorious tone and the richly lyrical phrasing of every note from Brain himself is life-enhancing in its radiant warmth. The Rondos aren't just spirited, buoyant, infectious and smiling, although they're all these things, but they have the kind of natural flow that Beecham gave to Mozart. There's also much dynamic subtlety – Brain doesn't just repeat the main theme the same as the first time, but alters its level and colour. His legacy to future generations of horn players has been to show them that the horn – a notoriously difficult instrument – can be tamed absolutely and that it can yield a lyrical line and a range of colour to match any other solo instrument. He was tragically killed, in his prime, in a car accident while travelling home overnight from the Edinburgh Festival. He left us this supreme Mozartian testament which may be approached by others but rarely, if ever, equalled, for his was uniquely inspirational music-making, with an innocent quality to make it the more endearing. It's a pity to be unable to be equally enthusiastic about the recorded sound. The remastering leaves the horn timbre, with full Kingsway Hall resonance, unimpaired, but has dried out the strings. This, though, remains a classic recording.

Horn Concertos Nos 1-4. Horn Quintet in E flat, K407
David Pyatt hn **Kenneth Sillito** vn **Robert Smissen, Stephen Tees** vas **Stephen Orton** vc **Academy of St Martin in the Fields / Sir Neville Marriner**
Warner Classics 2564 69719-9 (70' · DDD)   MO

David Pyatt, *Gramophone*'s Young Artist of the Year in 1996, provides performances in which calm authority and high imagination fuse; and this disc complements the nobility and urbanity of Dennis Brain. Although there can be no direct comparison with Anthony Halstead, Pyatt's is very much in that mode of supple, understated and often witty playing, accompanied by truly discriminating orchestral forces. Soloist and orchestra create a constantly shifting and lively pattern of dynamic relationships. Pyatt makes the music's song and meditation his own. Compared with the dark, dream-like *cantabile* of Brain, he offers in the Second Concerto an *Andante* of cultivated conversation and, in the Third, a *Romanza* of barely moving breath and light. His finales trip the light fantastic. The Second Concerto's springing rhythms reveal wonderfully clear high notes; the Third is nimble and debonair without being quite as patrician as Brain's; and the Fourth creates real mischief in its effervescent articulation. The cadenzas by Terry Wooding (to the first movements of the Third and Fourth Concertos) epitomise Pyatt's performances as a whole: longer and more daringly imaginative than those of Brain, while remaining sensitively scaled and fancifully idiomatic. The concertos are imaginatively and unusually coupled with a fine performance of the Horn Quintet in E flat.

Oboe Concerto in C, K314

Mozart Oboe Concerto **R Strauss** Oboe Concerto
Douglas Boyd *ob*
Chamber Orchestra of Europe / Paavo Berglund
ASV CDCOE808 (44' · DDD)   Ⓕ

This coupling links two of the most delightful oboe concertos ever written. Mozart's sprightly and buoyant work invests the instrument with a chirpy, bird-like fleetness encouraging the interplay of lively rhythm and elegant poise. Boyd's reading captures this work's freshness and spontaneity beautifully.

If the Mozart portrays the sprightly side of the instrument's make-up the Strauss illustrates its languorous ease and tonal voluptuousness. Again Boyd allows himself the freedom and breadth he needs for his glowing interpretation; he handles the arching melodies of the opening movement and the witty *staccato* of the last with equal skill. Nicely recorded.

Piano Concertos

No 1 in F, K37; **No 2** in B flat, K39; **No 3** in D, K40; **No 4** in G, K41; **No 5** in D, K175; **No 6** in B flat, K238; **No 8** in C, K246; **No 9** in E flat, K271, 'Jeunehomme'; **No 11** in F, K413; **No 12** in A, K414; **No 13** in C, K415; **No 14** in E flat, K449; **No 15** in B flat, K450; **No 16** in D, K451; **No 17** in G, K453; **No 18** in B flat, K456; **No 19** in F, K459; **No 20** in D minor, K466; **No 21** in C, K467; **No 22** in E flat, K482; **No 23** in A, K488; **No 24** in C minor, K491; **No 25** in C, K503; **No 26** in D, K537, 'Coronation'; **No 27** in B flat, K595

Piano Concertos Nos 1-27
English Chamber Orchestra / Murray Perahia *pf*
Sony Classical ⑫ 82876 87230-2 (10h 8' · ADD/DDD)
Recorded 1975-84   ⓂⓄⓄ▸

Mozart concertos from the keyboard are unbeatable. There's a rightness, an effortlessness, about doing them this way that makes for heightened enjoyment. So many of them seem to gain in vividness when the interplay of pianist and orchestra is realised by musicians listening to each other in the manner of chamber music. Provided the musicians are of the finest quality, of course. We now just take for granted that the members of the English Chamber Orchestra will match the sensibility of the soloist. They are on top form here, as is Perahia, and the finesse of detail is breathtaking.

Just occasionally Perahia communicates an 'applied' quality – a refinement which makes some of his statements sound a little too good to be true. But the line of his playing, appropriately vocal in style, is exquisitely moulded; and the only reservations one can have are that a hushed, 'withdrawn' tone of voice, which he's a little too ready to use, can bring an air of self-consciousness to phrases where ordinary, radi-

ant daylight would have been more illuminating; and that here and there a more robust treatment of brilliant passages would have been in place. However, the set is entirely successful on its own terms – whether or not you want to make comparisons with other favourite recordings. Indeed, we now know that records of Mozart piano concertos don't come any better played than here.

Piano Concertos – Nos 6, 15 & 27
Chamber Orchestra of Europe /
Pierre-Laurent Aimard *pf*
Warner Classics 2564 62259-2 (77' · DDD)   Ⓕ▸

There are not many composers for whom one could programme three concertos in the same key. Nevertheless, Mozart allegedly associated B flat major with happiness and with his fecund genius there is little risk of boredom.

A modern grand piano can sound heavy in Mozart's earlier concertos but Pierre-Laurent Aimard handles the solo writing in Concerto No 6 (K238), composed in Salzburg in 1776, with graceful agility. No 15 (K450), composed in Vienna in 1784, shows Mozart's increased emotional complexity and sophisticated use of the orchestra. Aimard encourages orchestral interjections to extend organically from the piano solos; the *Andante* expresses profound yearning in the most civilised manner possible; the last movement bubbles with affection.

In Mozart's last piano concerto, K595, the sunny optimism evident in the other B flat concertos is mingled with melancholic moods in the substantial opening movement (it lasts nearly a quarter of an hour, compared to the seven-minute *Allegro aperto* which opens No 6).

The Chamber Orchestra of Europe produce soft-grained performances in which glossy elegance is favoured over dramatic colour. Woodwind contributions are gently massaged into the texture and the horns seem a little distant and subdued but the orchestra produce lean textures and tight rhythms. Aimard directs from the keyboard, an authentic approach that has been avoided by some of the finest period-instrument Mozartians. In true Glenn Gould style, you can occasionally hear him humming along, this immersion in the music nurturing an admirable sensation of unity and harmony.

Piano Concertos – Nos 9 & 23
Northern Sinfonia / Imogen Cooper *pf*
Avie AV2100 (62' · DDD)   Ⓕ

Imogen Cooper's strongly projected, stylistically sensitive performance stands up even alongside such distinguished modern versions as Uchida, Brendel and Schiff. With crystalline articulation and an exhilarating range of colour and dynamics, Cooper never lets you forget that the so-called *Jeunehomme* (No 9) is a concerto of radical extremes, both within and between movements.

In the opening *Allegro* especially admirable is her vocal lyricism in the second subject, her powerfully directed passagework and the impassioned sweep of the wonderful modulating sequences near the start of the recapitulation. Some may feel she lingers overly in the C minor *Andantino*, though she always balances expressive *rubato* with an eloquent feeling for the long line. She conjures a new forlorn bleakness in the quasi-operatic recitatives towards the end, and rightly makes the cadenza the emotional climax of the movement. Despite odd moments of slack ensemble, the Northern Sinfonia play with style and verve.

Cooper is equally responsive to the radiant, wistful and (in the *Adagio*) elegiac lyricism of K488. Again she illuminates, vividly, affectionately, yet with no hint of sentimentality, the music's shifting moods and colours while maintaining a strong melodic flow. When the main theme of the *Adagio* returns, after the serenading grace of the brief A major episode (beautifully realised here), she enhances its pathos with delicately expressive embellishments. After this, the airborne finale keeps elegance and animal spirits in ideal balance. Anyone who wants this particular coupling will find Cooper and the Northern Sinfonia (wonderfully tangy clarinets, incidentally, in No 23) among the subtlest, liveliest and most probing of Mozartians.

Piano Concertos – Nos 12 & 19
London Mozart Players / Howard Shelley pf
Chandos CHAN9256 (52' · DDD)   Ⓕ

These are clear and stylish readings. The playing of Shelley and the London Mozart Players is assured, relaxed and enjoyable, allowing the music to unfold naturally. Shelley demonstrates his fine judgement of tempo, and textures are well served; the recording gives quite a bold sound to his modern piano, but its overall immediacy and warmth aren't excessive and the balance is just right. Phrasing also deserves praise: Shelley and his expert team shape the music gracefully without falling into the slightly mannered delivery which can affect other artists in this repertory. Finally, cadenzas have the right balance of freedom and formality. Perhaps the two 'slow' movements here – the quotes are because that of No 12 is an *Andante* and No 19's is an *Allegretto* – are richer in style than will suit some tastes: they do not sound authentic in period-performance terms, but then this is another kind of performance and perfectly convincing. The recordings are of high quality.

Piano Concertos – Nos 15ᵃ, 23ᵇ & 24ᵇ   Ⓗ
Solomon pf Philharmonia Orchestra /
ᵃ**Otto Ackermann**, ᵇ**Herbert Menges**
Testament mono SBT1222 (80' · ADD)
Recorded 1953-55   Ⓕ

It was Abram Chasins, the American pianist and critic, who noted in Solomon a 'proportionate grandeur that instead of seeming to lack power

appeared not to desire it'. Others have spoken of his 'matchless austerity', and listening once more to his Mozart is to be reminded of the essential truth of such comments. Mozart may have felt that K450 (No 15) is a concerto 'to make the pianist sweat', but it's difficult to imagine even a single bead of perspiration on Solomon's brow as he tosses off cascades of notes with superlative ease and elegance. In his hands the *Andante*'s set of variations comes as close to Elysium as you could wish, while the finale has a delectable lightness that makes it a true dance of the gods.

In K488 (No 23), Solomon's lucidity, in the canonic interplay, for example, is of a sort granted to very few pianists, and his refinement in the closing pages of the ineffable F sharp minor *Adagio* suggests all his inimitable but lightly worn authority. In K491 (No 24) he shares with Clara Haskil, another supremely prized Mozartian, a characteristic way of taking one of Mozart's two minor-key concertos by stealth rather than by storm, though he compensates for what some may see as undue restraint by giving us Saint-Saëns's storming cadenza. The 1953-55 recordings have been superbly remastered, and his musical partners, Otto Ackermann and Herbert Menges, are as inspired as their soloist.

Piano Concertos – Nos 17 & 20
**Scottish Chamber Orchestra /
Piotr Anderszewski** pf
Virgin Classics 344696-2 (63' · DDD)   Ⓕ➔

Mozart performed his Concerto No 20 at the Mehlgrube Casino on February 11, 1785. It is hard to imagine what the Viennese made of its dark, brooding D minor opening. Piotr Anderszewski superbly captures the uneasy mingling of melancholic passion and revolutionary fervour. This dynamic and impressively balanced performance is full of powerful arguments and emotional pressure.

Anderszewski's well-proportioned playing is in equal partnership with the SCO (perhaps the cohesive blend is a benefit of Anderszewski's directing from the keyboard). The central *Romanze* flows unhindered by saccharine sweetness, and the finale is lean and muscular, though lacking nothing in gracefulness.

In Concerto No 17 Anderszewski's navigation of the piano is articulate, bold and beautiful. His direction is admirably paced, although one imagines that these transparent textures have benefited from the orchestra's lessons in period style from Sir Charles Mackerras: clean-toned strings, precise timpani and brass, and eloquent woodwind flourishes contribute plenty to this attractive disc.

Piano Concertos – Nos 18 & 20
Orpheus Chamber Orchestra / Richard Goode pf
Nonesuch 7559 79439-2 (58' · DDD)   ⒻOO

With a first-rate balance and quality of sound, here's a Mozart concerto record to transcend considerations of style and stance. The excellence of Richard Goode's playing isn't surprising, but the quality of his collaboration with the Orpheus Chamber Orchestra is special: and the beautiful thing about Mozart performance of this calibre is that the two seem inseparable. The freshness and placing of the detail are to be savoured, but it's the long view which holds and persuades. In the D minor Concerto's first movement the brilliant piano writing is so thrilling here because it's projected as being essential to the expression, not just a decoration of it. Goode is particularly impressive in the way he handles the three successive solo statements at the start of the development without slackening pace. They are subtly different in feeling, one from the other, and although he isn't the first player to have noticed this, it's characteristic of his distinction to have kept the detail and the overview in balance. He plays his own cadenza in the finale, in place of Beethoven's. He has some good ideas about dynamics in this last movement, and Mozart's lightening of mood at the turn to the major key towards the end has rarely sounded such an inspiration. The B flat Concerto, K456, is equally enjoyable. The outer movements are brisk and light on their feet, even balletic, but all the colours – and the shadows which pass over the face of the music – are there, just as one wants. At the end, you feel you've had glorious entertainment, and a discourse that has touched on the deepest things. You may well be puzzled as to how Goode achieves so much while appearing to do so little. In this the orchestra matches him, as it also matches his spontaneity.

Piano Concertos – Nos 19 & 27
Orpheus Chamber Orchestra / Richard Goode pf
Nonesuch 7559 79608-2 (55' · DDD)　　Ⓕ**O**

The opening *tutti* of K595 (No 27, which comes first on the disc) makes a striking impact, not only thanks to the crisp, alert playing but to the full, bright, immediate recording. The piano enters with similarly full and immediate sound – very different from the more transparent piano sound on a rival Decca release with András Schiff – but then the orchestra seems to move further off. It's an inconsistency of balance that's disconcerting for no more than a moment or two, but might well make a hypercritical artist or producer have reservations.

What matters is the liveness of the experience that Goode and his partners provide. His approach is more purposeful, more direct than that of Schiff, who favours speeds consistently a shade broader than Goode's. The natural weight and gravity of Goode's playing, reflecting his equivalent mastery as a Beethovenian, emerges clearly in such moments as the hushed B minor opening or the development in the first movement of K595, an extraordinary modulation for a movement in B flat major, or in the opening solo of the *Larghetto* which follows. Not that Goode's Mozart has anything

remotely heavy about it in the wrong way. His lightness and wit in the finales of both concertos is a delight.

In the finale of No 19, Goode, like Schiff, opts for a very fast *Allegro assai*, drawing on his phenomenal agility. Some may prefer a slightly more relaxed tempo, such as Murray Perahia, for example, adopts, with more swagger and fun in it, but Goode's playing is thrilling from first to last.

Piano Concertos – Nos 20 & 24
Alfred Brendel pf **Scottish Chamber Orchestra / Sir Charles Mackerras**
Philips 462 622-2PH (60' · DDD)　　Ⓕ**O**▸

Brendel's conception of Mozart's two minor-key concertos has altered in countless nuances and emphases but little in fundamentals since his 1973 Philips recordings with Marriner. His sensibility, pianistic refinement and sheer questing intelligence remain as compelling as ever. Neither performance will entirely please those who favour a barnstorming approach.

More than in 1973, Brendel is at times concerned to draw out the music's elegiac resignation than to highlight its more obvious passion and turbulence. But more than most pianists he constantly illuminates the smaller and larger shapes of the music with his range of colour and dynamics. In both opening movements, for instance, he brings a speaking eloquence to the piano's initial solo theme and then in the development finds a subtly altered tone of voice, in response to the gradually darkening musical landscape, for each of its reappearances.

Another Brendel hallmark is his variety of tone and articulation in rapid passagework, which is purposefully directed in accordance with its place in the overall scheme. Again he provides apt and spontaneous-sounding embellishments and 'in-filling' at fermatas, this time allowing himself greater freedom in decorating the spare lines of the slow movements; again, he uses his own cadenzas in both concertos, more adventurous in their thematic development than any of Mozart's own surviving examples.

In the opening *tutti* of K491 one can hear the extra character Mackerras brings to the music compared to Marriner – the impact of raw, louring brass (tamed by Marriner) at strategic moments, for instance, or his attentive shaping of inner strands to enhance the tension. The recording has an attractive spaciousness and ambient warmth, though in K491 the keyboard occasionally obscures important thematic ideas on oboes, clarinets and bassoons.

Piano Concertos – Nos 23 & 24
Orpheus Chamber Orchestra / Richard Goode pf
Nonesuch 7559 79489-2 (56' · DDD)　　Ⓕ**O**

This is the third Mozart CD Richard Goode and the Orpheus Chamber Orchestra have made, and collaborations of this kind must necessarily be rare. The demands this sort of music-making imposes on the players are considerable. But so are the potential rewards. They are evident here in the exceptional focus and concentration of the playing. Polished you might expect it to be, but the allure and spontaneity are a joy. First impressions are likely to be of details of scoring in the orchestral expositions of the first movements, details that may not go unnoticed in other performances but which rarely receive such voicing and definition. The pianist doesn't disappoint either. Judge him by his first entry in the C minor Concerto, in the solo theme: there's none more difficult to get right. Goode has the range, the control and the rhetoric. He passes another difficult test in this first movement by supplying an impressive cadenza. It's an outstanding account of this movement, to be returned to again and again. There's no falling off in the other two either.

The A major, K488, equally well illuminated, has light and air from a different world. Indeed, there's an airborne quality to the finale, done here with the utmost vivacity, and a hint of that too in the open textures and the easy, glorious buoyancy of the first movement. The recorded sound is exemplary.

Piano Concertos – Nos 23 & 24
Cleveland Orchestra / Mitsuko Uchida pf
Decca 478 1524DH (60' · DDD)   Ⓕ ❍❍☻

Here Mitsuko Uchida revisits her beloved Mozart, this time conducting from the keyboard, in readings of the greatest poetic poise, empathy and refinement.

Not to put too fine a point on it, here is sublime Mozart-playing whether in C minor turbulence or A major radiance. In K491 (offered before K488) Uchida conveys an ineffable sadness with sudden withdrawals of such subtlety that all the shades of autumn seem with us, though with those shafts of light that can illuminate even Mozart's darkest moments. Her own first-movement cadenza is brilliantly apt and in K488, while nothing is plain sailing, everything is as natural as it is revelatory. When have you heard the central F sharp minor *Siciliano* more gently or lovingly confided, or the *opera buffa* finale more joyfully spun off? Lines are discreetly decorated and the Cleveland Orchestra are entirely at one with their inspired soloist. Balance and sound are ideal and even a few bars will convince you that you are listening to one of the truly great artists of our time.

Piano Concertos – Nos 23 & 24 (plus Nos 20, 26, 27)
Sir Clifford Curzon pf **London Symphony Orchestra / István Kertész**
Decca Legends ② 468 491-2DL2 (ADD)
Recorded 1967   Ⓜ ❍❍

In a list of all-time best recordings of Mozart piano concertos these should have a place. The balances of piano with orchestra are just right, and the sound has clarity and a nicely truthful character. In the No 24 the wind isn't as for-

ward as recordings favour these days, but from the LSO as distinguished soloists and as a wind chorus their contributions tell. Kertész gives Curzon nicely judged support: it sets him off, in a frame, even if it does appear a mite neutral at times and strangely limp in the presentation of the variation theme at the start of the finale of the C minor Concerto. These days, some people might consider the interpretations dated, or unreconstructed. Curzon doesn't decorate the bare, leaping intervals at the close of the slow movement of K488, and he's restrained too in the C minor. But the performances seem to be beyond fashion.

The slow movements are especially fine. In the *Larghetto* of No 24, unfolding at an ideal tempo, Curzon gives the impression of walking while he speaks to us. The gravity of the F sharp minor *Adagio* of No 23 is a different thing; but there, again, he's unaffected and completely unsentimental, direct in manner even while projecting the deepest feeling. He reminds us that the best interpreters do not impose but find a way of letting the music speak through them.

Piano Concertos – Nos 9 & 25
Orpheus Chamber Orchestra / Richard Goode pf
Nonesuch 7559 79454-2 (63' · DDD)   Ⓕ ❍❍

The opening of No 25 sounds tremendous, with a leathery thwack to the kettledrums and the orchestra suitably weighty. Although the acoustic is a bit dry, there's a satisfying depth to the sonority, and the balance and placing of the instruments is absolutely perfect. All the colours are vivid. In contrast to many players of the modern instrument, Goode doesn't pull his punches and makes this first movement a most glorious procession, imposing but never ponderous. His tempo has a propulsive energy and an underlying fitness that makes possible some relaxation of it in the broader paragraphs of the solo part. Wonderful slow movement too, flowing admirably, and it's a tricky one to get right.

This concerto has rarely been recorded so successfully, but the Ninth has been done better. Many of the virtues enjoyed by No 25 apply here also. It needs a different rhetoric, and Goode supplies it, but he waxes and wanes, and there's something a shade impersonal about him. The reservations concern the first movement principally, where it's as if he were saying: 'I do not need to attract your attention, this beautiful thing Mozart has made we are going to lay out before you'. However, this is still a Mozart concerto disc to give exceptional pleasure. And what teamwork! The musical focus sustained here isn't something often encountered outside chamber music.

Mozart Piano Concerto No 27. Concerto for Two Pianos and Orchestra in E flat, K365
Schubert Fantasia, D940
Emil Gilels, Elena Gilels pfs **Vienna Philharmonic Orchestra / Karl Böhm**
DG The Originals 463 652-2GOR (59' · ADD) ❍❍❍☻

This is the most beautiful of Mozart playing, his last piano concerto given here by Emil Gilels with total clarity. This is a classic performance, memorably accompanied by the VPO and Böhm. Suffice it to say that Gilels sees everything and exaggerates nothing, that the performance has an Olympian authority and serenity, and that the *Larghetto* is one of the glories of the gramophone. He's joined by his daughter Elena in the Double Piano Concerto in E flat, and their physical relationship is mirrored in the quality and the mutual understanding of the playing: both works receive marvellous interpretations. We *think* Emil plays first, Elena second, but could be quite wrong. The VPO under Karl Böhm is at its best; and so is the quality of recording, with a good stereo separation of the two solo parts, highly desirable in this work.

Additional recommendation

Piano Concertos – Nos 9, 14, 15, 17 & 18
Coupled with Rondo in D, K382
Uchida pf **English Chamber Orchestra / Tate**
Philips Duo ② 473 313-2PM2 (107' · DDD) **O**↦
 Wonderfully imaginative interpretations that show soloist, orchestra and conductor in perfect rapport.

Violin Concertos

No 1 in B flat, K207; **No 2** in D, K211; **No 3** in G, K216; **No 4** in D, K218; **No 5** in A, K219; **D**, K271a

---

Violin Concertos Nos 1-5[a]. Adagio in E, K261[c]. Rondo in C, K373[a]. Sinfonia concertante in E flat, K364[b]
[a]**Arthur Grumiaux** vn [b]**Arrigo Pelliccia** va
[ab]**London Symphony Orchestra / Sir Colin Davis;**
[c]**New Philharmonia Orchestra / Raymond Leppard**
Philips Duo ② 438 323-2PM2 (153' · ADD)
Recorded 1961-64 **O**

These performances of the five standard violin concertos, the *Sinfonia concertante* and a couple of other pieces were much admired when they came out on LP, and they continue to earn praise for their crispness, lightness and eloquence. Grumiaux was also fortunate in his partner in the *Sinfonia concertante*, for Pelliccia is also an expert Mozartian and they give a performance of this beautiful piece that's expressive but still avoids self-indulgent romanticism. In the solo concertos, too, Grumiaux plays cadenzas that suit the music in length and style. Both Sir Colin Davis and Raymond Leppard are sympathetic partners in this repertory, and since the playing of the two London orchestras is no less satisfying, this issue scores all round artistically. The 1960s recordings do not sound their age, and are pleasing save for a little tape hiss and an excess of bass that hardly suits the style of this translucent music. However, that's a small price to pay when so much else is admirable, and Grumiaux's fine tonal palette is well caught.

Violin Concertos Nos 1-5. Sinfonia concertante, K364[a]
Giuliano Carmignola vn [a]**Danusha Waśkiewicz** va
Orchestra Mozart / Claudio Abbado
Archiv ② 477 7371AH2 (129' · DDD) Ⓕ**OOO**↦

Virtuoso 'violinism' and energising direction notwithstanding, neither Giuliano Carmignola nor Claudio Abbado seems inspired by the B flat Concerto, K207. Nor does slick dispatch do much for the first movement of the D major, K211; but this is not the shape of things to come. Carmignola steps away from neutrality in the succeeding *Andante*. The music breathes a life of its own as he ardently inflects its phrases to shape the tension and relaxation of his line which – as elsewhere – he also embellishes. And pauses are decorated with lead-ins. Here is personal involvement that from now on is present in full flower.

It's a flowering for Abbado too, as he summons a passionate advocacy that takes in the implications of key and time signatures on atmosphere and pacing, uses dynamic markings and intuitive accents to keep rhythm aloft, adjusts the timbres of the wind instruments (oboes are vivid or subdued, horns play *in alto* or *basso*) to suit the colouration he requires, and aerates the orchestral fabric for maximum clarity. Conducting and interpretation are in the realms of greatness – and no mistake.

In the solo concertos, Carmignola is recorded with varying but small changes of volume. His positioning is steadier in the *Sinfonia concertante*; and so is his placement with the artistic, if slightly reticent, Danusha Waśkiewicz. Nevertheless, their skilled dovetailing and intelligent use of tone colour speak of symbiosis. Abbado remains *primus inter pares*, watchful, supportive and fortifying. Pity the sound isn't always clear and detailed. Superlative music-making deserves consistently superlative recording.

Violin Concertos Nos 1-5. Serenade No 7 in D, 'Haffner', K250 – Andante; Menuetto; Rondo
Pamela Frank vn **Zürich Tonhalle Orchestra / David Zinman**
Arte Nova Classics ② 74321 72104-2 (139' · DDD) Ⓢ

What a good idea to include the violin concerto movements from the *Haffner* Serenade as a filler, rather than the more usual group of extra movements for violin and orchestra. The Serenade shows the 20-year-old Mozart with his imagination at full stretch; Frank, Zinman and the Zürich orchestra revel in the wit, the sensuous expressiveness and the melodic fecundity of this still neglected music. Throughout the two discs Pamela Frank gives us violin playing of great technical purity. The music speaks to us without any affectation, yet respecting Mozart's indications and such 18th-century conventions as tailing off the weak beats of the bar. She's given a splendidly positive, well-considered accompaniment. The bouncy rhythms and perfect orchestral balance of the opening *tutti* to K216 establish a sense of *joie de vivre* that carries over into the violin playing.

Zinman's care for detail ensures that nothing of importance is overlooked: on the many occasions where the bass is carried by the second violin or viola these lines are given a bit of extra emphasis to highlight the harmonic movement. The horns deserve special mention; their purity of tone and rhythmic poise give a real sparkle to the outer movements of K207 and to the middle section of the *Haffner* Minuet, spectacularly scored for violin and wind. Zinman also wrote the cadenzas (except in K219, where Frank plays the famous Joachim ones); they're imaginative and stylish, but don't always sound improvisatory enough and occasionally seem too long. Frank is supported by an unusually characterful orchestra and very crisp, clear recording. A fantastic bargain.

Additional recommendations

Violin Concertos Nos 1-5
Coupled with Adagio, K261. Rondos – K269; K373
Mozart Anniversary Orchestra / Ehnes vn
CBC Records ② SMCD5238 (143' · DDD)   Ⓕ
Still barely 30, the Canadian violinist here reinforces his credentials as one of the most brilliant and discerning players of his generation, with a sweet, gleaming tone and a purity of intonation that are second to none. Among classic recordings, Ehnes is closest to the poised, patrician Arthur Grumiaux (see above), though his touch, like the excellent orchestra's (hand-picked from the cream of North American players) is that much lighter.

Violin Concertos Nos 3-5
The English Concert / Manze vn
Harmonia Mundi HMU90 7385 (76' · DDD)   Ⓕ
Andrew Manze's vivid notes point out that 'these concertos verge on the operatic' and, true to his word, gives performances that for inventiveness, impish fun and close, conspiratorial rapport between soloist and orchestra have never been bettered. And a superbly symbiotic partnership with the superb English Concert, beautifully recorded by Harmonia Mundi.

Serenades

No 6 in D, K239, 'Serenata notturna'; **No 7** in D, K250, 'Haffner'; **No 9** in D, K320, 'Posthorn'; **No 10** in B flat for 13 wind instruments, K361, 'Gran Partita'; **No 11** in E flat, K375; **No 12** in C minor, K388; **No 13** in G, K525, 'Eine kleine Nachtmusik'

Serenades Nos 6 & 13. Divertimento in D, K136.
Adagio and Fugue in C minor, K546
Ferenc Liszt Chamber Orchestra / János Rolla
Hungaroton HCD12471 (50' · ADD/DDD)   Ⓕ

The *Eine kleine Nachtmusik* Serenade is a favourite which will never be in any danger of oblivion. The Hungarian Ferenc Liszt Chamber Orchestra plays splendidly with an exceptionally alert style, but with a slightly heavier sound, a slightly solider style, than the Orpheus Chamber Orchestra. Nevertheless, this is to point to minor differences in the two perfectly sensible approaches, not to suggest that either of the performances is in any way materially superior to the other. Another common factor of the two discs is their inclusion, along with the *Nachtmusik*, of Serenade No 6.

The Divertimento here offers a degree of instrumental contrast, adding a few wind players to the basic orchestra of strings. Perhaps rather more of the built-in different sounds of these two groups could have been made in the present recording; but the *Serenade* remains an enchanting one. The Divertimento, also in D, lacks corresponding colour but is nevertheless quite a strong work; and the C minor *Adagio and Fugue* (an arrangement by Mozart himself from a piano duo) offers a very noticeably strong *Adagio*, and a fugue in which Mozart makes one of his few explorations – a successful one – of an earlier contrapuntal idiom.

Serenade No 7, 'Haffner'. March, K249
Netherlands Chamber Orchestra / Gordan Nikolitch vn
Pentatone ⓢ PTC5186 097 (57' · DDD)   ⒻⓄ➔

The *Haffner*, a wedding serenade for the marriage of Elizabeth Haffner in July 1776, was an outdoor summer piece, which was not good for the band, whose members were expected to move around. Thus there are no timpani; and certainly no cellos, because there were aristocratic guests (the bride's father had been burgomaster of Salzburg), so lowly musicians couldn't sit while they stood. When Mozart later shortened this eight-movement work to a five-movement 'symphony', he enhanced the orchestration with cellos and drums.

Gordan Nikolitch goes further. He incorporates these instruments into the original format, thus turning the Serenade into a fuller work. It has a stately expansiveness that only switches to a militaristic snap in the first movement of the Serenade, percussion now lending point both to a regal *Allegro maestoso* and, leading from it, a fiery *alla breve Allegro molto*. In the following *Andante*, the first of three 'violin concerto' movements, Nikolitch shows that he is as superlative a violin soloist as he is a conductor, as unerring in his understanding of lyrical eloquence as he is of dramatic timing. He never puts a foot wrong. Neither does Pentatone's production, which keeps the perspectives steady (for example, the violin is properly balanced with the ensemble and not pulled forward for the cadenzas).

The range, transparency and tonal veracity of the recording offer a total vindication of SACD. This is a tremendous disc.

Serenades – No 10, 'Gran Partita'; No 12
London Winds / Michael Collins cl
Onyx Classics ONYX4012 (73' · DDD)   ⒻⓄ➔

Led with flair and imagination by Michael Collins, London Winds give a vital, refined performance of the *Gran Partita*, exceptionally transparent in texture and full of felicitous detail: the wonderfully veiled *pianissimo* coda of the *Romanze* fifth movement, for instance; or the eloquently phrased oboe cantilena against the dulcet murmurings of clarinets and basset horns in the *adagio* variation.

Outer movements are crisp and athletic, with an easy, quick-witted sense of instrumental interplay; and the two minuets are sharply contrasted, the first done as a stately *menuetto galante*, its G minor Trio more elegiac than agitated, the second as a perky Ländler. Some may raise an eyebrow at the use of contrabassoon instead of Mozart's prescribed double bass (contrabassoons had notoriously unreliable plumbing in the 1780s). But there are gains in overall blend, even if you might miss the double bass's *pizzicato* twangs in the second minuet's beery Trio. The only reservation comes with the *Adagio* third movement, the work's emotional core, where the pulsing accompaniment impinges too prominently on the soaring exchanges of oboe, clarinet and basset horn.

As a fill-up London Winds offer that most undiverting of serenades, K388, in a fine performance, amply powerful and urgent but notable for its poetry and inwardness, whether in the sorrowful, syncopated variant of the second subject in the opening *Allegro*'s recapitulation, or the Trio's exquisite 'mirror canon', celestially floated here by oboes and bassoons.

Mozart Serenade No 13, 'Eine kleine Nachtmusik'. Adagio and Fugue in C minor, K546
Anonymous (arr L Mozart) Cassation in G, 'Toy Symphony' **Pachelbel** Canon and Gigue
Academy of St Martin in the Fields / Sir Neville Marriner
Philips 416 386-2PH (52' · DDD)   Ⓕ🅑➔

Sir Neville Marriner here collects a miscellaneous group of popular classical and Baroque pieces in characteristically polished and elegant performances. The only roughness – and that deliberate – is in the extra toy percussion of Leopold Mozart's *Cassation*, with its long-misattributed *Toy* Symphony. The anonymous extra soloists enjoy themselves as amateurs might, not least on a wind machine, but what's very hard to take is the grotesquely mismatched cuckoo-whistle, an instrument which should readily be tunable.

Eine kleine Nachtmusik brings a performance plainly designed to caress the ear of traditional listeners wearied with period performance. The second-movement *Romanze* is even more honeyed than usual on muted strings. The oddity of the Pachelbel item is that the celebrated Canon – taken unsentimentally if sweetly at a flowing speed – is given a reprise after the Gigue. The recording is warm and well balanced.

Divertimentos

Divertimentos – F, K247; D, K334
Gaudier Ensemble (Jonathan Williams, Christiaan Boers *hns* Marieke Blankestijn, Lesley Hatfield *vns* Iris Juda *va* Stephen Williams *db*)
Hyperion CDA67386 (76' · DDD)   Ⓕ

How lucky the burghers of Salzburg, in Mozart's day, who had such music as this to accompany their family celebrations! Mozart wrote a small group of divertimentos for strings and horns for the local aristocracy during his later years there, to augment his salary and prestige, and he did it with a mastery of technique that enabled him to find exactly the right blend of high spirits, warmth of expression and wit.

When they've been recorded, it's nearly always been with an orchestra rather than a solo group. In Austria in Mozart's time, the word 'divertimento' signified solo performance, and there's a world of difference between what a sensitive solo fiddler and what a galumphing orchestra can do with that top line, in terms of technique, expressiveness and flexibility. And in these performances the bass part is played not by a cello, but, as was preferred in Salzburg, a double bass, which provides a different relationship to the upper voices, and the one that Mozart clearly intended.

The Gaudier Ensemble catch the mood of the music perfectly. The elegant sentiment of the slow movements (there are two in each work) is happily conveyed – listen to the sweetness of violinist Marieke Blankestijn's phrasing in the *Adagio* of K247 and her gentle, unassuming eloquence in that of K334. In the latter work the second violin is called on, too, for some degree of virtuosity, but it's to Blankestijn that most of the rapid and stratospheric music goes, and she copes in style. She also phrases the famous first minuet here gracefully. Mozart's second minuets (each divertimento has six movements) are usually more rumbustious, with the horns prominent, and these too are heartily done. Altogether this is a delectable record.

Mozart Divertimento in D, K334[a]   🅗
Schubert Quintet for Piano and Strings in A, 'Trout', D667[b]
Members of the Vienna Octet (Willi Boskovsky, [a]Philipp Matheis *vns* Günther Breitenbach *va* Nikolaus Hubner *vc* Johann Krump *db* [a]Joseph Velba, [a]Otto Nitsch *hns* [b]Walter Panhoffer *pf*)
Pearl mono GEM0129 (72' · ADD). Recorded 1950   Ⓕ

Mozart's Divertimento for two horns and strings, K334, is one of his ripest and most engaging *pièces d'occasion* and this is a marvellous performance of it. Indeed, some skimping of repeats and a couple of cuts in the finale notwithstanding, this classic, out of the catalogues now for more than 30 years, is still the version to have.

Like the still too little regarded Vienna Konzerthaus Quartet, the Vienna Octet was one of the glories of post-war Viennese musical life. Willi Boskovsky, one of its founders, was a particular inspiration. Boskovsky may not have been every recording producer's dream. A wonderfully inspirational player, he would not necessarily play a take the same way twice. The results, though, are a joy; his playing, and the playing of the ensemble as a whole, is always burnished, idiomatic, intensely alive. The same could be said of this famous 1950 recording of Schubert's *Trout* Quintet, though the Vienna Octet's remake, recorded with Sir Clifford Curzon in 1957 when Boskovsky was still leading, is one of those gramophone classics difficult to knock off its perch. The original Decca LPs of the present performances (Pearl hasn't had access to the original tapes) were often said to be wiry in sound and difficult to reproduce, though this isn't true of the Mozart. Here, it sounds a million dollars. Tracking the latter movements of the *Trout* LP, though, has clearly not been easy. A barely audible amount of surface noise and a tiny amount of incipient distortion persists. That said, the new disc is indispensable.

Symphonies

No 1 in E flat, K16; **No 2** in B flat, K17 (attrib L Mozart); **No 4** in D, K19; **No 5** in B flat, K22; **No 6** in F, K43; **No 7** in D, K45; **No 7a** in G, K45a, 'Alte Lambach'; **No 8** in D, K48; **No 9** in C, K73; **No 10** in G, K74; **No 11** in D, K84; **No 12** in G, K110; **No 13** in F, K112; **No 14** in A, K114; **No 15** in G, K124; **No 16** in C, K128; **No 17** in G, K129; **No 18** in F, K130; **No 19** in E flat, K132; **No 20** in D, K133; **No 21** in A, K134; **No 22** in C, K162; **No 23** in D, K181; **No 24** in B flat, K182; **No 25** in G minor, K183; **No 26** in E flat, K184; **No 27** in G, K199; **No 28** in C, K200; **No 29** in A, K201; **No 30** in D, K202; **No 31** in D, K297, 'Paris'; **No 32** in G, K318; **No 33** in B flat, K319; **No 34** in C, K338; **No 35** in D, K385, 'Haffner'; **No 36** in C, K425, 'Linz'; **No 38** in D, K504, 'Prague'; **No 39** in E flat, K543; **No 40** in G minor, K550; **No 41** in C, K551, 'Jupiter'; **(No 42)** in F, K75; **(No 43)** in F, K76; **(No 44)** in D, K81; **(No 45)** in D, K95; **(No 46)** in C, K96; **(No 47)** in D, K97; **(No 55)** in B flat, K*Anh*214; **F**, K*Anh*223; **B flat**, K74*g*

Complete Symphonies   **P**
The English Concert / Trevor Pinnock
Archiv ⑪ 471 666-2AB11
(13h 36' · DDD)   Ⓑ**O**➔

This set is pure joy. These are period performances, but there's nothing hair-shirt about them. Pinnock caresses the slow movements with great affection, and throughout there's a sense of fun and enjoyment. What's exciting is the sweetness of the period-instrument sound and the suppleness and flexibility The English Concert brings to the music. They play, much of the time, as if it were chamber music, particularly in second subjects – the lyrical passages, that is, where they shape the phrases with a warmth and refinement you hardly expect in orchestral music. Timing is

quietly witty, yet not at all contrived or artificial: it's the sort of expressive refinement that depends on listening to one another, not on the presence of a conductor. There's large-scale playing, too.

The middle symphonies are especially good. The opening of the brilliant K133 (No 20) has a splendid swing, with its prominent trumpets, and a real sense of a big, symphonic piece. K184 (No 26) is duly fiery and its accents are neatly judged. K201 and K202 (Nos 29 and 30) are both very impressively done: an eloquent rather than a fiery account (though something of that too) of the opening movement of K201, with a particularly euphonious and shapely *Andante*. The finales of both are done with exceptional vitality and the rhythmic resilience that's characteristic of these performances.

Pinnock's *Jupiter* (No 41) is truly outstanding. The first movement is duly weighty, but energetically paced, and its critical junctures timed with a keen sense of their role in the shape of the whole. In the *Andante* he draws an extraordinarily beautiful, almost sensuous sound from The English Concert, and the lines are moulded with tenderness. This, above all, is the quality that distinguishes Pinnock's recordings from all others, this natural and musical sound, deriving from the way the players are intently listening to one another; and it's fitting that it reaches its high-point in the *Jupiter*. As for the finale: well, it's decidedly quick, giving the impression of a performance in which the orchestra is pressed to an extent that its ensemble playing is under stress, though it holds together. It's a very bold, outspoken reading, which leaves one gasping afresh at the music's originality.

In short, quite outstanding performances, unfailingly musical, wholly natural and unaffected, often warmly expressive in the slow music and always falling very happily on the ear, with no trace of the harshness that some think is inevitable with period instruments. They are excellently recorded, with the properly prominent wind balance helping to characterise the sound world of each work.

Mozart Symphonies Nos 1, 2, 4 & 5
Abel (formerly attrib Mozart) Symphony, Op 7 No 3
Northern Chamber Orchestra / Nicholas Ward
Naxos 8 550871 (59' · DDD)   Ⓢ➔

Symphonies Nos 6-10
Northern Chamber Orchestra / Nicholas Ward
Naxos 8 550872 (56' · DDD)   Ⓢ➔

These two discs of Mozart's first 10 symphonies offer a unique view of the composer's earliest years of apprenticeship as a symphonist. Ward and his orchestra show a sensitive response to the wealth of stylistic influences apparent in these works. Purists may question the inclusion of two of the symphonies, Nos 2 and 3, since neither work is actually by Mozart. The former is attributed to the composer's father, Leopold, while the latter is Mozart's orchestration of CF Abel's E flat Symphony, Op 7 No 3. However, when they're played with such engaging style and elegance as here, these two works add a further important dimension to Mozart's early symphonic output. Where JC Bach's influence is most powerful (Symphonies Nos 1, 4, 5 and 6), the NCO presents the music's contrasting thematic characters with fine clarity, balancing the music's beautifully transparent textures with appropriate lightness of touch. The inclusion of trumpets and drums in the next three symphonies (Nos 7, 8 and 9) announces the young composer's growing brilliance and stature. In these pieces, the NCO moves into a higher gear, revealing Mozart's potent originality, with powerfully dramatic *tuttis* and expressively sung *andantes*. Mozart made his first trip to Italy in 1770, and the symphony he wrote in Milan that year (No 10) shows his enthusiastic incorporation of Italian stylistic models. Here the NCO's deliciously spacious orchestral playing shows Mozart's ravishing originality, with dramatic opposition of gesture and instrumentation in the exuberant *allegros* and a beguilingly graceful slow movement that winningly displays a keen awareness of the composer's innovative touches. These are indeed splendid performances, admirably complemented by vivid recordings.

Symphonies Nos 15-18
Northern Chamber Orchestra / Nicholas Ward
Naxos 8 550874 (58' · DDD)   ⑤

Nicholas Ward and the NCO bring their customary style and eloquence to this music in performances that evocatively portray its blend of formal unity, radiant vitality and occasionally – as in the rhythmically imaginative finale of the C major Symphony – rustic charm. Opening *allegros* are suitably vivacious, *andantes* are graceful and poignant and the vigorous finales bristle with energy. The first movement of the C major Symphony offers a more potent dramatic formula, with subtly poetic triplets and tense tremolos; however, the highlight of the programme is the F major Symphony (No 18), which Saint-Foix described as 'the first of [Mozart's] great symphonies'. Here, Ward's and the NCO's dramatically compelling account, beautifully presented in a natural, spacious recording, brilliantly highlights the music's operatic qualities.

Symphonies Nos 21-24 & 26
Northern Chamber Orchestra / Nicholas Ward
Naxos 8 550876 (53' · DDD)   ⑤

This is a chance to enjoy Mozart's inexhaustibly imaginative assimilation and transformation of Italian operatic models. Ward's balanced orchestral textures reveal Mozart's fragrant orchestration with great clarity in the A major Symphony. Sample the second movement's deftly handled interplay of strings, woodwind and horns, and buoyantly stately Minuet that culminates effectively in the

finale's restless drive. The complete musical satisfaction provided by the four Italian-overture symphonies that comprise the remainder of the programme is due to the fullness and vigour of the orchestration itself, and to the Northern Chamber Orchestra's lively performances. The opening *allegros* and cheerfully effervescent finales bubble with infectious vitality, while the slow movements give the opportunity for more intimate instrumental ensembles. Most impressive, however, is the E flat major work, which originated as the overture to the play *Lanassa*. Here, Ward and the NCO compellingly portray the dramatic violence of the opening *Presto*, the despair of its minor-key *Andante* and the exuberant rhythms of its finale. The recording is atmospheric.

Symphony No 33. Serenade No 9, 'Posthorn'
Academy of St Martin in the Fields / Iona Brown
Hänssler Classic CD98 129 (59' · DDD)   Ⓕ

Symphony No 35, 'Haffner'. Serenade No 7, 'Haffner'
Academy of St Martin in the Fields / Iona Brown *vn*
Hänssler Classic CD98 173 (72' · DDD)   Ⓕ

Each disc brings together a middle-period symphony and a contemporaneous Serenade. The sound recording has a sharpness of focus and sense of presence more often associated with the finest analogue recordings of the 1960s and '70s. It's surprising to find that the venue was Henry Wood Hall, for this sounds rather more intimate than most recordings made there, with plenty of bloom but no excessive reverberation. This is Mozart sound, using modern instruments but with some concern for the crisper manners encouraged by period performance, that in its freshness and beauty makes one want to go on listening. The finale of the Symphony No 33, for example, brings a hectic speed which doesn't sound at all breathless, with feather-light triplets, and similarly in the finale of the *Posthorn* Serenade with which it's coupled. Exceptionally, in that Serenade, Iona Brown opts for a more relaxed speed and more moulded style in the lovely minor-key *Andantino* of the fifth movement. The posthorn in the Trio of the second Minuet is this time much more brazen and more forwardly balanced than before.

The coupling of the *Haffner* Symphony and *Haffner* Serenade is specially apt. Iona Brown herself is the virtuoso soloist in the Serenade, lighter than ever in the *moto perpetuo* scurryings of the fourth-movement Rondo. For those who continue to resist period performances in this repertory these are very refreshing discs.

Symphony No 38. Piano Concerto No 25, K503[a].
Ch'io mi scordi di te…Non temer, amato bene, K505[b]
[b]**Bernarda Fink** *sop* **Lausanne Chamber Orchestra / Christian Zacharias** [ab]*pf*
Dabringhaus und Grimm MDG340 0967-2
(73' · DDD)   Ⓕ ◯

Here Christian Zacharias successfully experiments with a nicely balanced Mozart group of symphony, aria and concerto. He himself takes multiple roles, conducting a fresh and lively account of the *Prague* Symphony, and acting as piano soloist not only in the Concerto, directing the weighty K503 from the keyboard, but also providing a crisply pointed obbligato in the most taxing of Mozart's concert arias, *Ch'io mi scordi di te*. The sense of freedom and spontaneous enjoyment is enhanced by the clarity of the recording, made in the Metropole, Lausanne. Though *tuttis* are big and weighty, Zacharias finds rare transparency in lighter passages, and a vivid sense of presence throughout. One of Zacharias's great merits as a Mozart pianist is the crispness of his articulation; he defines each note with jewelled clarity.

The Symphony, too, is given a refreshing performance, with due weight in the first movement and light, crisp articulation in the finale. Some may feel that Zacharias underplays the gravity of the central *Andante*, but nowadays few will object to a flowing tempo such as one expects in a period performance.

Most striking of all, though, is the concert aria. Bernarda Fink, officially a mezzo, isn't just untroubled by the soprano tessitura but gives a characterful interpretation, pointing words and phrases with delightful individuality. Using her lovely creamy tone-colours, Fink offers one of the most impressive of all readings since Schwarzkopf's. Her contribution crowns a consistently enjoyable programme.

Symphonies – Nos 38 & 41
Freiburg Baroque Orchestra / René Jacobs
Harmonia Mundi HMC90 1958 (69' · DDD)   Ⓕ❂

Such has been the admiration (if not always affection) for René Jacobs's Mozart operas, and so striking have been the contributions of the period orchestras involved, that it seems only natural that he should try his hand at a couple of the great man's symphonies. The results fascinate in places and infuriate in others, but never lack for talking-points.

The *Jupiter* is the more successful, showing the kind of 'inside-out' rethink with which Roger Norrington used to enrage and delight. The first movement is playful, with Jacobs toning down the Olympian grandeur and mischievously emphasising the *buffo* elements – the chuckling third theme is given the special treatment of a slower tempo and subsequent *accelerando*, with one statement even adorned with an exuberant upward violin slide. The slow movement, luminous and taken at a perfectly judged brisk walking pace, will be less contentious, but not so the Minuet, which races by at an initially disturbing yet ultimately exhilaratingly satisfying one-in-a-bar. After all this creative energy, the surprisingly steady finale seems to lack ideas by comparison, though its contrapuntal panache gains much from the clarity Jacobs draws from the excellent Freiburg band.

Crisp and boisterous orchestral playing likewise characterises the *Prague*, though here Jacobs seems to find it more difficult to find a way into the heart of the music. The first movement has a stricter pulse than in the *Jupiter*, and, while the development emerges as a thrilling battleground, the second subject's beautifully consoling woodwind lines are shown none of the loving tenderness they deserve. The *Andante* seems uncertain of its tempo (Jacobs is not the first conductor to struggle here), and the finale does not quite convince at its supersonic speed. Nevertheless, this is an intriguing and invigorating disc; Jacobs's *Jupiter*, at least, qualifies as among the most thought-provoking of recent years.

Symphonies – Nos 29, 31, 32, 35 & 36
Scottish Chamber Orchestra / Sir Charles Mackerras
Linn ② 💿 CKD350 (117' · DDD/DSD)   Ⓕ❂❂➔

Sir Charles Mackerras and his Scottish players are working backwards through Mozart's symphonies. This second volume follows their acclaimed set of the last four symphonies (see below) with a group of works mainly from the latter part of his Salzburg period along with two he composed following his relocation to Vienna.

These two discs display all the qualities displayed in the later symphonies. There's a clarity to the acoustic as recorded in Glasgow's City Halls, which Mackerras uses to his advantage, instinctively bringing out telling inner lines: listen especially for the ear-tweaking viola 'stabs' in the second subject of No 29's first movement or the clattering horns at climaxes throughout the symphony. This work, surely Mozart's first symphonic miracle, is given added weight and import by Mackerras's decision to take all repeats, demonstrating especially that the fourth movement is far more than a mere *chasse* finale.

The *Paris* is the least convincing of Mozart's later symphonies but Mackerras knows (and shows) that there's plenty to be discovered beyond the French-pleasing special effects and brilliant orchestration. He also offers both slow movements: Mozart wrote a replacement to appease a cloth-eared audience who didn't recognise a genius when he was among them. More fool them, and alleluia that it's all the more Mozart for the rest of us. In fact there's so much to enjoy on these discs – armfuls of the humanity and wisdom displayed in Vol 1, and vivacity aplenty too in the *Haffner* and *Linz*, advanced wayposts on the march towards the unparalleled mastery of the last three symphonies.

Symphonies Nos 38-41
Scottish Chamber Orchestra / Sir Charles Mackerras
Linn ② 💿 CKD308 (139' · DDD)   Ⓕ❂❂➔

There is no need to argue the credentials of Sir Charles Mackerras as a Mozart interpreter, so let us just say that this double CD of the composer's last four symphonies contains no surprises – it is every bit as good as you would expect. Like many modern-instrument performances these days it shows the period-orchestra influence in its lean sound, agile dynamic contrasts, sparing string vibrato, rasping brass, sharp-edged timpani and prominent woodwind, though given Mackerras's long revisionist track-record it seems an insult to suggest that he would not have arrived at such a sound of his own accord. And in any case his handling of it – joyously supported by the playing of the Scottish Chamber Orchestra – is supremely skilled; rarely will you hear such well judged orchestral balance, such effective marrying of textural transparency and substance. The *Jupiter* in particular has a wonderful bright grandeur, yet reveals details in the brilliant contrapuntal kaleidoscope of the finale that too often go unheard.

Seldom, either, will you hear such expertly chosen tempi; generally these performances are on the quick side, but rather than seeming hard-driven they exude forward momentum effortlessly worn. Nowhere is this better shown in the slow movements (even with all their repeats they never flag, yet their shifting expressive moods are still tenderly drawn), but also conspicuously successful are the slow introductions to Symphonies Nos 38 and 39 and the Minuet movements of Nos 40 and 39.

These are not Mozart performances for the romantics out there, but neither are they in the least lacking in humanity. No, this is thoroughly modern-day Mozart, full of wisdom and leaving the listener in no doubt of the music's ineffable greatness.

Symphonies Nos 39-41. Bassoon Concerto   P
Jane Gower bn
Anima Eterna / Jos van Immerseel
Zig-Zag Territoires ② ZZT030501 (104' · DDD)   F

Jos van Immerseel, better known as fortepianist than conductor, sets quickish tempi in almost all the movements of Symphonies Nos 39 and 40. The overall effect is of vitality, brightness and clarity, with contrapuntal interplay much more apparent than usual. There are few of the usual tragic overtones in the gracefully played *Andante* of No 39, or the usual darkness and foreboding in No 40. All this comes partly from the period instruments, and the perceptive way they're handled. Van Immerseel balances them carefully, has little or no string vibrato and clearly requires precise articulation. That's why we hear more of the inner lines.

In the *Jupiter*, however, the approach is less chamber-music-like. This is a trumpets-and-drums symphony, so the manner is more forceful, sometimes rather abrupt; but the first movement is powerfully shaped. Again a quickish *Andante* with Mozart's textures illuminated to fine effect. The dense writing in the Minuet

---

MOZART'S SYMPHONIES NOS 40 & 41 – IN BRIEF

Cleveland Orchestra / George Szell   H
Sony Classical SBK46333 (73' · ADD)   B O
With No 35, the *Haffner*, thrown in, this is great value. Szell's approach is stylish and, obviously, 'big band', but he presents this music with appropriate scale. The late-1950s sound is pretty good.

English Baroque Soloists /   P
Sir John Eliot Gardiner
Philips 426 315-2PH (75' · DDD)   M O O
Vivid, dramatic period-instrument accounts that in no way diminish the reach and ambition of these two masterpieces.

The English Concert / Trevor Pinnock   P
DG 474 229-2 (73' · DDD)   M
Smaller in scale than Gardiner's readings, Pinnock invests these works with great spring and vitality – at times they almost dance along.

Berlin PO / Karl Böhm
DG 439 472-2GCL (73' · ADD)   B
Urbane, autumnal Mozart from one of his greatest interpreters. The BPO are very stylish, and a charming *Eine kleine Nachtmusik* from the VPO adds to the CD's allure.

Vienna PO / Leonard Bernstein
DG 445 548-2GM (69' · DDD)   M O O ▶
Recorded in 1984, Bernstein's Mozart is beautifully conceived: full of light and shade with no sense of overweight or over-dramatising. A charmer of a disc.

Scottish CO / Sir Charles Mackerras
Linn ② ⚏ CKD308 (139' · DDD)   F O O ▶
As part of a set of Mozart's last four symphonies, Mackerras gives the sort of unforced, imaginative and beautifully balanced performance you would except of such a master Mozartian. The SCO plays with a perfect balance of modern-instrumental style and period-infused manners.

Concertgebouw Orchestra /
Nikolaus Harnoncourt
Warner Elatus 0927 49622-2 (74' · DDD)   M
Harnoncourt always has someting fascinating to say in Mozart, but these are somewhat eccentric readings: the *Jupiter* is epic and certainly more succesful than No 40, which never quite settles down.

Anima Eterna / Jos van Immerseel   P
Zig-Zag Territoires ② ZZT030501 (104' · DDD)   F
A delightful, poetic set that seems illuminated by a genuine love for the music. Symphonies Nos 39-41 are supplemented by the Bassoon Concerto: and everything comes up as if newly minted.

profits from a finely balanced texture, and so above all does the finale, where you're constantly aware of all that's going on below the surface. It's passionate, too: listen to those timpani thwacks in the development and the power of the extraordinary recapitulation. The amazing five-part counterpoint of the coda is heard with unprecedented clarity.

These may not be everyone's performances. But they should be treasured: if you think you know these symphonies back to front, these versions will enable you to listen to the music afresh and hear new things in it.

The Bassoon Concerto filler is enjoyably played by Jane Bower on a period bassoon, delightfully uneven in tone but always beautifully tuned and with many neatly imaginative touches.

Clarinet Quintet in A, K581

Mozart Clarinet Quintet
Brahms Clarinet Quintet in B minor, Op 115
Karl Leister *cl* **Berlin Soloists** (Bernd Gellermann, Bernhard Hartog *vns* Wolfram Christ *va* Jörg Baumann *vc*)
Warner Apex 0927 44350-2 (71' · DDD) Ⓑ

This is a familiar and successful coupling of two of the most beautiful works written for clarinet and strings. Karl Leister gives most beautifully easy, charming, relaxed performances of both works, and the recordings are pleasantly fresh and immediate. There's no lack of sparkle in Mozart's final variations, and the Hungarian tinges are beautifully touched upon in the Brahms; the slow music in both works is reflective and tender without any loss of poise. Here are two beautiful performances that can be warmly recommended.

String Quintets

No 1 in B flat, K174 **No 2** in C minor, K406
No 3 in C, K515 **No 4** in G minor, K516
No 5 in D, K593 **No 6** in E flat, K614

String Quintets Nos 1-6
Arthur Grumiaux, Arpad Gérecz *vns* **Georges Janzer, Max Lesueur** *vas* **Eva Czako** *vc*
Philips Trio ③ 470 950-2PTR3 (170' · ADD)
Recorded 1973 Ⓜ**OOO**

Of the six works Mozart wrote for string quintet, that in B flat major, K174, is an early composition, written at the age of 17. It's a well-made, enjoyable work, but not a great deal more than that. The C minor work, K406, is an arrangement by Mozart of his Serenade for six wind instruments, K398. It's difficult not to feel that the original is more effective, since the music seems to sit a little uncomfortably on string instruments. But the remaining four works, written in the last four years of Mozart's life, are a different matter. The last string quintets from

Mozart's pen were extraordinary works, and the addition of the second viola seems to have pulled him to still greater heights. It has been suggested that Mozart wrote K515 and K516 to show King Friedrich Wilhelm II of Prussia that he was a better composer of string quintets than Boccherini, whom the King had retained as chamber music composer to his court. There was no response, so he offered these two quintets for sale with the K406 arrangement to make up the usual set of three. K593 and K614 were written in the last year of his life. Refinement is perhaps the word that first comes to mind in discussing these performances, which are affectionate yet controlled by a cool, intelligent sensitivity. The recordings have been well transferred, and Grumiaux's tone, in particular, is a delight to the ear.

String Quintet No 3.
String Quartet No 16 in E flat, K428
Louise Williams *va* **The Lindsays** (Peter Cropper, Ronald Birks *vn* Robin Ireland *va* Bernard Gregor-Smith *vc*)
ASV CDDCA992 (67' · DDD) Ⓕ

Here's a fine performance of the great C major Quintet. The Lindsays take the first movement at a true *Allegro*, so that it bowls along in top gear, the details vivid and sharply etched. Much of this grandest and most spacious movement in Mozart's chamber output is marked to be played softly: in the Lindsays' hands the wonderful counterpoint in the development section can be heard with exceptional clarity as the tension builds up, but not the dynamic. The *Andante* sounds the more touching for never being overplayed, and it's a special pleasure to hear how the most florid passages for first violin and first viola fit effortlessly into the rhythmic scheme. In the finale, Peter Cropper introduces some beautifully played *portamentos* in the main theme, and the whole movement sounds delightfully witty and happy. The E flat Quartet, K428, is cool and stylish, which suits this enigmatic work rather well. The Lindsays' way of using Mozart's marks of expression and articulation to make the music speak feels absolutely right, especially in their delicate, refined *Andante*, and it's good to hear the quartet played with all its repeats. The recording has a nice intimate quality.

Flute Quartets

Flute Quartets – D, K285; G, K285a; C, K285b;
A, K298
Emmanuel Pahud *fl* **Christoph Poppen** *vn*
Hariolf Schlichtig *va* **Jean-Guihen Queyras** *vc*
EMI 556829-2 (59' · DDD) ⒻⒹ➤

There may be only one movement of any emotional weight, the B minor *Adagio* of the First Quartet, K285, but in that brief cantilena Pahud finds a mystery and subtlety of dynamic shading that outshine almost any rival. For the rest he consistently conveys the fun in the writing here.

The A major work may run the dangerous course of parodying the banalities of the contemporaries whom Mozart despised, but Pahud still finds charm in the invention, helped by the warm, imaginative playing of his string partners. Pahud's lighter, more sparkling playing, with his fresh, clear tone is preferable to Galway's more romantic approach at generally broader speeds, and with phrasing more heavily underlined in characteristically full flute tone. Pahud also observes second-half repeats as well as first in the sonata-form first movements of the first three quartets. Recommended.

Piano Quartets

No 1 in G minor, K478; **No 2** in E flat, K493

Piano Quartets Nos 1 & 2
Isaac Stern vn **Jaime Laredo** va
Yo-Yo Ma vc **Emanuel Ax** pf
Sony Classical Theta SMK89794 (56' · DDD) Ⓜ

This grouping of star names offers performances of imagination and insight. In the E flat Quartet, K493, it isn't just Isaac Stern and Yo-Yo Ma whose solo entries have one sitting up, but also Jaime Laredo in the rare moments when Mozart gives a solo to the viola. Speeds are beautifully chosen, and in both works the performances convey a happy spontaneity. Emanuel Ax shows what a natural, individual Mozartian he is. The G minor work is in many ways parallel to the great piano concertos of the period, with the piano regularly set against the strings in ensemble, and Ax readily establishes the sort of primacy plainly required. He's a shade robust at the start of the central *Andante* but in fast music as in slow his gift of pointing rhythms and moulding phrases is consistently persuasive and imaginative.

The recording, made in the Manhattan Center, New York, is a degree drier than in many of the current rival versions, but there's ample bloom on the sound, fitting very well in a domestic listening room.

Piano Quartets Nos 1 & 2
Paul Lewis pf **Leopold String Trio** (Marianne Thorsen vn Scott Dickinson va Kate Gould vc)
Hyperion CDA67373 (63' · DDD) Ⓟ**OO⮞**

These are unusually expansive works, their first movements each close on 15 minutes' music, prolific in their thematic matter and richly developed. They demand playing that shows a grasp of their scale, playing that makes plain to the listener the shape, the functional character of the large spans of the music.

Paul Lewis and the Leopold String Trio, playing on modern instruments, excel in this, with their feeling for its structure and its tension, particularly in the first movement of the G minor, and especially at its great climax at the end of the development section, which is delivered with a compelling power and a sense of its

logic. This performance is exemplified by its carefully measured tempo, its poise and its subtle handling of the balance between strings and piano. The *Andante* is unhurried, allowing plenty of time for expressive detail; and the darker colours within the finale, for all its G major good cheer, are there too.

The spacious and outgoing E flat work is no less sympathetically done, with plenty of feeling for its special kind of broad lyricism; particularly attractive are the gently springy rhythms and the tenderness of the string phrasing in the first movement, and Lewis's beautifully shaped phrasing in the *Larghetto*. A real winner, this disc: warmly recommended.

String Quartets

No 1 in G, K80 **No 2** in D, K155 **No 3** in G, K156 **No 4** in C, K157 **No 5** in F, K158 **No 6** in B flat, K159 **No 7** in E flat, K160 **No 8** in F, K168 **No 9** in A, K169 **No 10** in C, K170 **No 11** in E flat, K171 **No 12** in B flat, K172 **No 13** in D minor, K173 **No 14** in G, K387 **No 15** in D minor, K421 **No 16** in E flat, K428 **No 17** in B flat, K458, 'Hunt' **No 18** in A, K464 **No 19** in C, K465, 'Dissonance' **No 20** in D, K499, 'Hoffmeister' **No 21** in D, K575 **No 22** in B flat, K589 **No 23** in F, K590

String Quartet No 17. Oboe Quartet. Horn Quintet
Nicholas Daniel ob **Stephen Bell** hn **The Lindsays**
(Peter Cropper vn Ronald Birks vn/va Robin Ireland va Bernard Gregor-Smith vc)
ASV CDDCA968 (68' · DDD) Ⓕ

The Lindsays really make the *Hunt* Quartet sparkle. One could describe their approach as middle-of-the-road; they're as meticulous as many period-instrument groups about details of phrasing, and avoid excessive accents and vibrato, yet their sound is modern, and the care over detail doesn't preclude a very spontaneous approach in which the music's feeling is compellingly communicated. In the Oboe Quartet Nicholas Daniel matches the string players' care over articulation and detailed expression, and plays with exceptional technical polish and brilliance. His gleaming tone is capable of great expressive range. The Horn Quintet is perhaps not quite such an individual or remarkable work as the two quartets. And you may find yourself longing for the extra character and beauty that a fine performance with the natural horn would have had. Yet this is a highly recommendable reading, too. The recording is very lifelike.

String Quartets – Nos 20 & 22 Ⓟ
Quatuor Mosaïques (Erich Höbarth, Andrea Bischof vns Anita Mitterer va Christophe Coin vc)
Astrée Naïve E8834 (63' · DDD) Ⓕ**OO**

This release completes the Mosaïques' recording of the 10 mature Mozart Quartets: an outstanding achievement. Apart from the clear, rich sound of the period instruments and the precise, beautiful tuning, what impresses about this Mozart-playing is the care for detail, the way each phrase is shaped so as to fit perfectly into context while having its own expressive nuances brought out clearly. This often leads the quartet to use more *rubato*, to make more noticeable breathing spaces between sentences than many other groups do.

In the first movements of both these quartets, for instance, the Mosaïques adopt a very similar tempo and tone to the Quartetto Italiano, but the Italians aren't so rhythmically flexible. The Mosaïques make us listen to and appreciate the significance of each detail as it unfolds. With this approach there might be a danger of sounding contrived, but even when adopting a mannered style, as in the *Minuet* of K499, the Mosaïques retain a strong physical connection with the music's natural pulse – by comparison the Italiano here seem a trifle heavy and humourless.

The slow movements of both quartets are taken at a flowing pace, making possible an unusual degree of expressive flexibility. All repeats are made, including those on the Minuet's *da capo* in K499. The longer the better when the playing is as exceptional as this.

Piano Trios

No 1, K496; No 5, K548. Divertimento, K254
Florestan Trio (Susan Tomes *pf* Anthony Marwood *vn* Richard Lester *vc*)
Hyperion CDA67609 (60' · DDD)   Ⓕ Ⓑ➤

So much of Mozart's instrumental music is opera by other means. The Florestan understand this as well as any group, and better than most. At the start of K548's airy finale, Susan Tomes's gracefully demure piano is swiftly countered by Anthony Marwood's raffish *forte* riposte: and this sense of delighted, quick-witted dialogue between quasi-operatic protagonists runs through the whole movement, abetted by touches of sly, subtle timing, from Marwood especially. No performance of this piece brings such a smile to the face.

The Florestan have the knack of bringing alive even apparently neutral figuration, of sensing the possibilities of interplay in what may look like a simple theme-plus-accompaniment texture. Piano and violin dominate in these works, especially in the breezy early Divertimento, K254. But Richard Lester's warm, nutty timbre contributes crucially to the music's colour, here and elsewhere, while he takes his chances when Mozart gives the cello an equal voice in the texture: say, in the first-movement development of K496, where the Florestan typically conjure a vivid operatic imbroglio.

As usual, the Florestan choose flowing speeds in the slow movements, which may initially faze those who know the music from the revered Beaux Arts versions. In in the 6/8 *Andante* of K496 the Florestan show that a graceful dance lilt, even a hint of skittishness, need not preclude an eloquent response to Mozart's extraordinary remote modulations.

Piano Trios – No 3, K502; No 4, K542; No 6, K564
Florestan Trio (Susan Tomes *pf* Anthony Marwood *vn* Richard Lester *vc*)
Hyperion CDA67556 (59' · DDD)   Ⓕ Ⓑ➤

The prolific Florestan here offer three trios, including the two finest, K502 and K542. These are beautifully judged performances, generally fleeter of foot, airier of texture and more intimate in tone than those from Barenboim and colleagues on EMI (see below), with an ideal balance between the instruments (Richard Lester's cello always a telling presence, even when his role is apparently incidental). In K542 the Florestan catch the peculiar Mozartian mix of radiance and passion in the outer movements without any of the excessive lingerings of the EMI performance.

The fast movements of the other two trios – the brilliant, concerto-like K502 and the ingenuous K564 – are just as delightful in their verve, their gleeful, quick-witted repartee and the vitality with which the players invest even routine-looking accompanying figuration. Occasionally, as in the finale of K564, Barenboim and Co are just that much more vivid. But far preferable is the Florestan's flowing tempo and naturally expressive phrasing in K502's *Larghetto*.

For those wanting K502 and K542 on a single disc, the Florestan enchant with their ebullience and spontaneous delight, and find a winning tenderness in the first movement of K542 and choose a sprightly, lilting tempo in same trio's *Andante grazioso*.

Talk of an outright winner is always dangerous, but the Florestan's sparkling, inventive performances make them a top recommendation for the complete Mozart trios, their claims enhanced by the warm, ideally balanced recording.

Piano Trios – No 1, K496[a]; No 2, 'Kegelstatt', K498[b]; No 3, K502[a]; No 4, K542[a]; No 5, K548[a]; No 6, K564[a]
Daniel Barenboim *pf* [b]**Matthias Glander** *cl* [a]**Nikolaj Znaider** *vn* [b]**Felix Schwartz** *va* [a]**Kyril Zlotnikov** *vc*
EMI ② 344643-2 (125' · DDD)   Ⓕ Ⓑ➤

The record companies fell over each other to bring out single discs or sets of piano trios during Mozart year. EMI offers a near-complete cycle, omitting the early Divertimento, K254, but including the wonderful *Kegelstatt* Trio for the (in 1786) unprecedented combination of clarinet, viola and piano.

With Barenboim at the keyboard no Mozart performance is ever dull. And despite a recording that balances the violin too closely, sometimes giving a bright glare to Nikolaj Znaider's normally sweet tone, there is plenty to enjoy in these performances: the bold sweep of K496's opening *Allegro*, for instance, with Barenboim and Kyril Zlotnikov relishing Mozart's spirited dialogues between keyboard and the newly emancipated cello; the mingled grace and swagger of the outer movements in the underestimated K548, full of typically deft touches of shading and timing; or the popular-style finale of the final trio, K564, where Barenboim and his accomplices choose an ideal, relaxed *allegretto* and give a lusty kick to the rhythms in the rustic waltz.

Appealing, too, is the mobile tempo and gentle flexibility of phrase in the not-so-slow movement of K542, perfectly poised between an *ancien régime* gavotte and a Schubertian 'walking' *andante*. In contrast, the central movements of K502 and K548 are taken broadly, with *molto espressivo* phrasing that some will find ideally soulful, others, including me, over-romanticised. The *Andante* first movement of the *Kegelstatt* is also dangerously slow and 'backward-leaning' but, this proviso apart, the performance is warmly sung, with a notably rich, throaty viola.

Violin Sonatas

Violin Sonatas – No 1, K6; No 26, K378/K317d;   **P**
No 27, K379/K373a; No 36, K547
Rachel Podger vn **Gary Cooper** fp
Channel Classics ⚛ CCSSA21804
(77' · DDD/DSD)   🅟**OO**

Violin Sonatas – No 2, K7; No 15, K30; No 18,   **P**
K301; No 20, K303; No 33, K481
Podger vn **Cooper** fp
Channel Classics ⚛ CCSSA22805
(67' · DDD/DSD)   🅕

Violin Sonatas – No 3, K8; No 13, K28; No 28,   **P**
K380; No 32, K454. Andante and Fugue, K402.
Andante and Allegretto, K404
Podger vn **Cooper** fp
Channel Classics ⚛ CCSSA23606
(78' · DDD/DSD)   🅕

Violin Sonatas – No 4, K9; No 14, K29;   **P**
No 19, K302; No 21, K304; No 35, K526
Podger vn **Cooper** pf
Channel Classics ⚛ CCSSA24607
(76' · DDD/DSD)   🅕

Violin Sonatas – No 5, K10; No 6, K11; No 7, K12;   **P**
No 8, K13; No 9, K14; No 10, K15; No 11, K26.
Allegro, K372. Variations on, 'La bergère Célimène',
K359. Variations on an Andantino, 'Hélas, j'ai perdu
mon amant', K360
Podger vn **Cooper** fp with **Alison McGillivray** vc
Channel Classics ② ⚛ CCSSA28109
(115' · DDD)   🅕

Both artists show an impressive command of the rhetorical 18th-century approach to phrasing and expression, giving a very lively air to the music-making – there are no flat, routine moments. The theatrical manner of No 18's first movement inspires a wonderfully bright, colourful performance, and the contrasts inherent in the two-speed opening movement of No 20 are brilliantly realised.

Gary Cooper plays with considerable freedom, often spreading chords to soften their impact or for extra expressiveness, and ornamenting repeated passages most imaginatively. Rachel Podger doesn't generally ornament her part; her accompaniments are unforced and flow easily, and she enjoys taking the lead, playing boldly yet with sensitivity.

Some may find the continually active style of playing a step too far, and there were places, in the first movement of No 33, for example, where a calmer, less eventful approach might have been welcome. But the great *Adagio* of this sonata has a beautiful sense of line and, throughout, the marriage of expertise and stylistic awareness results in truly treasurable performances.

'Duo Sonatas, Vol 1'   **P**
Violin Sonatas – No 18, K301; No 19, K302; No 20,
K303. Variations on, 'La bergère Célimène', K359.
Variations on an Andantino, 'Hélas, j'ai perdu mon
amant', K360
Duo Amadè (Catherine Mackintosh vn Geoffrey
Govier fp)
Chandos Chaconne CHAN0755 (66' · DDD)   🅕🅑➔

For Catherine Mackintosh and Geoffrey Govier the 'rules' of historically informed performance have become second nature; we get the impression they're playing for sheer enjoyment of the music. All the distinctive moments are appreciated and given due emphasis but in a spontaneous way, the interpretative points never going beyond what musicians with good rapport might do on the spur of the moment. Yet it's obvious that Govier and Mackintosh are careful, as well as spirited, interpreters. The recorded sound and balance are excellent, and they artfully control their dynamics so that principal and subsidiary lines are clearly distinguished.

The concluding Rondo of K302 contains many octave passages shared by piano and violin; here, with precise matching of tone colour, articulation and volume, Govier and Mackintosh turn what might seem like a rare lapse of Mozartian imagination into a delightful colouristic device. In the first movement of this sonata they make the most of the quasi-orchestral writing, with its pulsating *crescendos*, horn imitations and *tremolando* effects. Colourful in a different way is the minor section in K301's finale, where the *con sordino* piano's soft quality perfectly supports the poised violin melody.

You may wonder whether to favour Duo Amadè or the impressive Podger/Cooper team (see above). The latter mix into their programmes the juvenile works from the 1760s, but if you are most interested in the great series of works starting with K301, Duo Amadè may suit you better.

Piano Duets

Sonatas for Keyboard Duet – K358; K497. Andante
and Variations, K501. Orgelstück Fantasia für eine
Uhr, K608. Fugue, K401
Andreas Groethuysen, Yaara Tal pf
Sony Classical SK93868 (62' · DDD)   🅕**O**

Sonatas – for Keyboard Duet, K19d; for Two Pianos, K448. Sonata Movements for Keyboard Duet – K357; K500. Adagio and Fugue, K546. Larghetto and Allegro, Kdeest
Andreas Groethuysen, Yaara Tal pf
Sony Classical 82876 78363-2 (65' · DDD)　　Ⓕ●

Yaara Tal and Andreas Groethuysen live and breathe as one on these two wonderful discs in which every performance emerges not merely as 'the best' (if we're talking critical comparisons) but life-affirming. Technically, each fiddly ornament, every phrase shape and every degree of pedalling is miraculously co-ordinated – not that one is ever made aware of such prosaic elements for the music simply flows, newly minted, in joyous, stylish effusion. Here are Wolfgang and Nannerl having a thoroughly enjoyable afternoon, smiling and winking to each other as they negotiate some of the more mischievous twists and turns.

The final movement of the B flat Sonata, K358, has rarely bubbled along like this, while the F major Sonata, K497, confirms its place as a masterpiece with its passages of eerie Schubertian prescience. The playing of this duo marks a clear if subtle distinction between one that comes together occasionally for festivals and recordings, and one that does it every day as a vocation.

Piano Sonatas

No 1 in C, K279 **No 2** in F, K280 **No 3** in B flat, K281 **No 4** in E flat, K282 **No 5** in G, K283 **No 6** in D, K284 **No 7** in C, K309 **No 8** in A minor, K310 **No 9** in D, K311 **No 10** in C, K330 **No 11** in A, K331 **No 12** in F, K332 **No 13** in B flat, K333 **No 14** in C minor, K457 **No 15** in F, K533 **No 16** in C, K545 **No 17** in B flat, K570 **No 18** in D, K576

Piano Sonatas Nos 1-18. Fantasia, K475
Mitsuko Uchida pf
Philips Complete Mozart Edition ⑤ 468 356-2PB5
(5h 25' · DDD)　　Ⓑ❍❍❍❍Ɒ➤

 By common consent, Mitsuko Uchida is among the leading Mozart pianists of today, and her recorded series of the piano sonatas won critical acclaim as it appeared and finally won *Gramophone* Awards in 1989 and 1991. Here are all the sonatas, plus the Fantasia in C minor, K475, which is in some ways a companion piece to the sonata in the same key, K457. This is unfailingly clean, crisp and elegant playing, that avoids anything like a romanticised view of the early sonatas such as the delightfully fresh G major, K283. On the other hand, Uchida responds with the necessary passion to the forceful, not to say *Angst*-ridden, A minor Sonata, K310. Indeed, her complete series is a remarkably fine achievement, comparable with her account of the piano concertos. The recordings were produced in the Henry Wood Hall in London and offer excellent piano sound; thus an

unqualified recommendation is in order for one of the most valuable volumes in Philips's Complete Mozart Edition. Don't be put off by critics who suggest that these sonatas are less interesting than some other Mozart compositions, for they're fine pieces written for an instrument that he himself played and loved.

Mozart Piano Sonata No 6. Rondo, K511.
Variations on 'Ah, vous dirai-je, maman', K265
Prokofiev Piano Sonata No 3. Toccata, Op 11.
Ten Pieces from Romeo and Juliet, Op 75 – excerpts
Lise de la Salle pf
Naïve ② V5080 (91' · DDD). Includes bonus 26-minute DVD documentary, 'Lise de la Salle, majeure!', directed by Jean-Philippe Perrot　　Ⓕ

Young talent does not come more brilliantly or ardently alive than this. Clearly designed to demonstrate this 19-year-old pianist's versatility, Naïve's album showcases her in radically different composers and finds her equally persuasive in both. De la Salle is tremulously expressive in Mozart's A minor Rondo, making every bar pulse and breathe with a special life and prophecy of Romantic things to come. She revels in the bustle and ceremony of the D major Sonata, K284. Hear her enviable *perle* in the last-movement Variations 1 and 3, her change to minor-key contemplation in Variation 7, in the florid musings of Variation 11 – and in her pinpoint definition and character in the K265 Variations – and here you surely have a young pianist born for Mozart.

But then she is no less successful in Prokofiev's diablerie, finding time, despite her headlong tempo, for piquant asides in the Toccata, for a loving romantic dalliance in parts of the Third Sonata and for a reminder in her selection from *Romeo and Juliet* of delicacy and affection beneath Prokofiev's outwardly prickly and intractable nature. This superb album concludes with a short DVD showing De la Salle exclaiming over what she clearly sees as her enchanted life (while acknowledging the hard work involved). All things being equal, she is clearly on the threshold of a major career. Her freshness and vitality are already something very special.

Piano Sonatas – Nos 8 & 15. Courante, K399.
Gigue, K574. Rondo, K511. March, K408/1
Richard Goode pf
Nonesuch 7559 79831-2 (60' · DDD)　　Ⓕ❍❍❍Ɒ➤

 A Mozart programme such as this, which includes two of the greatest sonatas and the A minor Rondo, leaves absolutely no margin for error or insufficiency, nor indeed for anything at all approximate or generalised. It's given to very few to play Mozart as well as Richard Goode, who seems to pitch the rhetoric just right and sustain an ideal balance of strength and refinement.

It's quite big playing, and the range of sonority is appropriate to the A minor Sonata, K310, in particular; no other recent recording realises so well the sharp contrasts, the cross-cut abutments of dynamics, which are such a striking feature in all three movements. Goode has a characteristic touch of urgency that has nothing to do with impetuosity or agitation of the surface, but rather with carrying the discourse forward and making us curious about what will happen next. In the *presto* finale, where Brendel is choppy and rather slow, Goode is exciting and articulate, wonderfully adept at getting from one thing to another.

There's little to choose between these players in the composite F major Sonata, K533. Brendel is at his finest in the dark, far-reaching middle movement; both of them relish the challenge of characterising the multifariousness of the first; Goode is especially convincing in the last movement.

He gives you the overview, too, often powerfully. While admiring the flux of intensities, dynamics, shapes and colours he sets before you in the Rondo, you might wonder three-quarters of the way through whether the totality was going to achieve enough weight. But the coda is to come – passionate and desolate, a close without parallel in Mozart's instrumental music – and at moments such as this you can be assured that Goode will surprise and certainly not disappoint. The shorter pieces, enterprisingly chosen, set off the great works admirably. Exceptional sound throughout – like the playing, quite out of the ordinary run.

Keyboard Sonatas – No 15 & 17. Fantasia, K475. **P**
Variations on 'Unser dummer Pöbel meint', K455
Kristian Bezuidenhout fp
Harmonia Mundi HMU90 7497 (72' · DDD) Ⓕ**OOᗏ**

Written for an Anton Walter fortepiano and played on a 1987 reproduction – by Derek Adlam – of a model similar to one Mozart owned. Does that make these performances authentically Mozartian? Peter Walls (Victoria University, New Zealand) believes that 'getting as near as we can – literally – to the intended sound world of works from the past, is part and parcel of engaging with their essence'. But the essence is only as distilled through the recreative intuition of a performer. Kristian Bezuidenhout offers a personal distillation that is impressively absorbing.

So indeed are the timbre and sonority of the instrument. The hair-trigger transients of a fortepiano, so right for communicating drama, harmonic progressions and abrupt shifts of mood, are as expected. But, perhaps unexpectedly, an expressive singing line is to the fore too because Bezuidenhout is consummately artistic in his use of knee levers for the moderator and sustaining mechanisms that govern tone colour. The *Fantasia*, K475, of varying moods, exemplifies his whole approach.

The sound world may well be as intended but in terms of inspirational reach and gravity towards content, Bezuidenhout is light years removed from a pre-war belief that Mozart's music contained 'the essence of childhood and the fragrance of simplicity' (Alec Rowley). These interpretations – excellent to outstanding – are interpretations of today.

'The Mozart Tapes'
Piano Sonatas – Nos 1-5, 9, 10, 12, 13 & 16
Friedrich Gulda pf
DG ③ 477 6130GM3 (3h 33' · ADD)
Recorded live 1980   Ⓜ

Friedrich Gulda made a series of Mozart sonata recordings shortly before playing all the sonatas in three cycles of concerts during February 1981. They remained unissued during the pianist's lifetime and survived only on cassette dubs from the presumably lost mastertapes. Their first CD appearance adds up to an absorbing listening experience, once you get past the inevitable hiss plus patches of flutter and signal overload.

The close microphone placement shrouds Gulda's Bösendorfer with a harpsichord-like patina that also evokes the fuzzy ping of a vintage Wurlitzer electric piano, yet the pianist's wide dynamic range and hard-hitting accents are anything but emasculating. Indeed, Gulda's Mozart positively rocks, because it's mostly about rhythm. It's not about Gieseking's rippled symmetry, Schiff's ornaments (although Gulda's no slouch in this department), Krauss's angular harmonic stresses or Arrau's operas in miniature. Gulda's unswerving, atomically steady tempi and occasionally downbeat-oriented phrasing never sound mechanical, for two reasons. One, his inner rhythm always conveys a sense of swing in that it's firmly grounded yet forward moving. Two, Gulda's left hand is his trump card. Listen anywhere, really, and notice how much variety the pianist gleans from the composer's endless Alberti basses, how he brings out important melodic elements within the figurations, or how he gets the most dramatic (as opposed to merely theatrical) mileage out of signpost bass octaves without a trace of contrivance or Gouldian exaggeration.

At long last, we have Mozart piano sonata slow movements that you can slow-dance to, if that's your desire. More and more details rise to the surface with each rehearing, although it's best to absorb Gulda's Mozart in small doses – just one or two sonatas at a time. A stimulating release.

Fantasias

Adagio in B minor, K540. Fantasias – C minor, K396; D minor, K397; C minor, K475. Gigue in G, K574. Kleiner Trauermarsch in C minor, K453a. Minuet in D, K355. Rondos – D, K485; F, K494; A minor, K511
Christian Zacharias pf
Dabringhaus und Grimm MDG340 0961-2
(67' · DDD)   Ⓕ

Most of Mozart's single piano pieces are the product of some special stimulus: they aren't the daily bread of music-making, like the sonatas, but something rather more piquant. Christian Zacharias groups the pieces interestingly, starting with a D major-based section: the D minor Fantasia, the D major Rondo, the B minor Adagio and the D major Minuet, as if making a kind of free sonata of them. He omits the *Allegretto* portion of the Fantasia (on the grounds, it seems, that Mozart left it unfinished), and leads directly from the Fantasia into the Rondo. The B minor *Adagio* is one of Mozart's darkest, most inward pieces: written at a difficult moment in his life, it invites autobiographical interpretation with its sense of defeat and protest. Zacharias's sombre, subdued performance underlines such thoughts, and in the very chromatic K355 Minuet, too, his playing is dark and impassioned.

The C minor Fantasia, K396, is a rarity: a completion by Maximilian Stadler of a fragment that Mozart wrote for keyboard and violin. One can't imagine a performance much more persuasive than this; and in the authentic C minor Fantasia Zacharias plays beautifully, again with fire in the turbulent sections and with exquisite gentleness in the coolly reflective music such as the B flat episode. The K494 Rondo – more familiar in its revised version as finale of the K533 Sonata – is played in a more relaxed manner; in the A minor Rondo, K511, Zacharias beautifully captures the 'sentimental' tone and provides a performance of great delicacy and refinement, again drawing the full depth of expression from Mozart's harmonic subtleties.

Masses

Missae breves – G, K49/K47*d*[a]; D minor, K65/K61*a*[b]; **P**
D, K194/K186*h*[a]; C (Spatzenmesse), K220/K196*b*[b]
[a]**Christine Schäfer**, [b]**Angela Maria Blasi** sops
[a]**Ingeborg Danz**, [b]**Elisabeth von Magnus** mezs
[a]**Kurt Azesberger**, [b]**Uwe Heilmann** tens [a]**Oliver Widmer** bar [b]**Franz-Josef Selig** bass **Arnold Schoenberg Choir; Vienna Concentus Musicus / Nikolaus Harnoncourt**
Teldec Das Alte Werk 3984 21818-2 (69' · DDD · T/t) Ⓕ

These youthful Masses, composed between 1768 and 1775, are among Mozart's most concise – K65, in particular, is a *Missa brevis* with a vengeance. Brevity was *de rigueur* in the Salzburg liturgy and we can hardly blame Mozart for rattling unceremoniously through the long texts of the *Gloria* and *Credo*. With minimal scope for musical development, much of the writing in the two earlier works, especially, is perfunctory – the 12-year-old composer dutifully going through the motions. As so often in late-18th-century Masses, the central mystery of the 'Et incarnatus est – Crucifixus' prompts a more individual musical response; and the *Benedictus* of K65 is a touching little duet for soprano and alto soloists based, surprisingly, on a descending chromatic motif, a traditional

trope of lamentation. For all the conventional bustle of their faster movements, the two later Masses are more varied in their textures and more memorable in their ideas. Both the settings of the *Benedictus* have the grace and airiness of 18th-century Austrian churches. But the high-point in each work is the *Agnus Dei*, especially that of K194, with its harmonic poignancy and dramatic alternations of solo and chorus. Occasionally Nikolaus Harnoncourt's direction can sound over-insistent – in, say, the *Kyrie* of K49, with its almost aggressive *marcato* articulation. But for the most part he chooses apt, mobile tempi, keeps the rhythms buoyant and characterises vividly without betraying the music's blitheness and innocence.

Both individually and in consort the soloists make the most of their limited opportunities, with delectable tone and phrasing from the two sopranos, Christine Schäfer and Angela Maria Blasi. The recorded balance is excellent, catching Harnoncourt's sharply etched orchestral detail while giving ample presence to the polished and responsive choir.

Mass in C, 'Coronation', K317. **P**
Vesperae solennes de confessore, K339.
Epistle Sonata in C, K278/K271*e*
Emma Kirkby sop **Catherine Robbin** mez **John Mark Ainsley** ten **Michael George** bass **Winchester Cathedral Choir; Winchester Quiristers Academy of Ancient Music / Christopher Hogwood** with **Alastair Ross** org
L'Oiseau-Lyre 436 585-2OH (54' · DDD · T/t) ⒻⒷ→

It's difficult to think of many recordings of Mozart's church music that so happily capture its character – the particular mixture of confidence, jubilation and contemplation – as Hogwood's. His unfussy direction, broad phrasing, lively but generally unhurried tempi and happy details of timing serve splendidly in the *Coronation* Mass, the finest of Mozart's completed Mass settings; the solemnity of the *Kyrie*, the fine swing of the *Gloria* and the energy of the *Credo*, with due pause for its rapt moment at the 'Et incarnatus', all these come over with due effect. Arguably the 'Osanna' is rather quick, but its jubilation is splendid. And the sweetness of the *Benedictus* is ravishing.

Not more so, however, than the *Agnus*, for there, at a decidedly slow tempo, Hogwood allows Emma Kirkby to make the most of this very sensuous music, which she duly most beautifully does. The soloists are altogether an excellent team, with two refined voices in the middle and Michael George a firm and sturdy bass. The inclusion of the K278 Epistle Sonata is a happy notion. The *Vesperae solennes de confessore* is a setting of the five Vesper psalms and the *Magnificat*, made in 1780, a year after the Mass, for some church feast in Salzburg. With admirable singing from the choir and a spacious recording with exceptionally good stereo separation that properly conveys the ecclesiastical ambience, this is a disc to treasure.

Mass in C minor, 'Great', K427 (ed Maunder)　Ⓟ
Arleen Auger, Lynne Dawson sops **John Mark
Ainsley** ten **David Thomas** bass **Winchester
Cathedral Choir; Winchester Quiristers; Academy
of Ancient Music / Christopher Hogwood**
L'Oiseau-Lyre Florilegium 425 528-2OH
(51' · DDD · T/t)　　　　　　　　　　Ⓕ🔂

Mozart left unfinished the work that ought to
have been the choral masterpiece of his early
Viennese years but there's enough of it to make
up nearly an hour's music – music that's sometimes sombre, sometimes florid, sometimes
jubilant. Hogwood avoids any charge of emotional detachment in his steady and powerful
opening *Kyrie*, monumental in feeling, dark in
tone; and he brings ample energy to the big,
bustling choruses of the *Gloria* – and its long
closing fugue is finely sustained. The clarity and
ring of the boys' voices serve him well in these
numbers. There's a strong solo team, headed by
the late Arleen Auger in radiant, glowing voice
and, as usual, singing with refined taste; Lynne
Dawson joins her in the duets, John Mark Ainsley too in the trio. But this is essentially a
'soprano Mass' – Mozart wrote it, after all, with
the voice of his new wife (and perhaps thoughts
of the much superior one of her sister Aloysia) in
his mind – and Auger, her voice happily stealing
in for the first time in the lovely 'Christe', excels
in the florid and expressive music of the 'Et
incarnatus' (where Richard Maunder has supplied fuller string parts than usual, perhaps fuller
than Mozart would have done had he finished
the work). Hogwood directs with his usual spirit
and clarity.

Mozart Mass in C minor, 'Great', K427[a]　Ⓟ
Beethoven Ah! perfido, Op 65[b]
Haydn Berenice che fai, HobXXIVa/10[c]
[ac]**Sarah Connolly,** [ab]**Camilla Tilling** sops [a]**Timothy
Robinson** ten [a]**Neal Davies** bass **Gabrieli Consort
and Players / Paul McCreesh**
Archiv 477 5744AH (74' · DDD · T/t)　Ⓕ🔂🔂🔂

Discussing the C minor Mass in a booklet interview, Paul McCreesh remarks that 'any attempt
to complete it runs the risk of negating the quality of what survives'. Most editors and performers agree, confining themselves to the sections
Mozart actually composed, and filling out the
missing parts in the *Credo*, 'Et incarnatus est' and
Sanctus-'Osanna'.

Paul McCreesh gives us the familiar torso in a
reading that combines a smallish chorus numbering around 30 with a period-instrument band. At
a fairly urgent tempo, McCreesh's soloists, the
radiant Camilla Tilling and the rich-toned Sarah
Connolly, are excellent, with Connolly unfazed
by her flights into high soprano territory. Elsewhere, Tilling perfectly catches the wondering
pastoral innocence of the 'Et incarnatus est',
taken at a gently lilting two-in-a-bar. In the choral numbers McCreesh is on top form.

There have been excellent period-instrument
recordings from Hogwood and Gardiner, but

McCreesh, sharply responsive both to the Mass's
neo-Baroque monumentality and its Italianate
sensuousness, is at least their match in drama and
colour; and DG's recording is exemplary. The
Gabrieli Consort sing with precision, fresh, firm
tone and marvellous dynamic control, while the
strings play with notable grace and refinement
in the solo numbers. The *Kyrie* unfolds with an
inexorable tread (McCreesh is specially good at
creating and maintaining rhythmic tension), and
the 'Cum Sancto Spiritu' fugue, taken at the
swiftest possible tempo, combines dancing agility
with a thrilling cumulative sweep.

McCreesh's claims as a top recommendation
are enhanced by the additional items, two magnificent, quasi-operatic scenas by Haydn and
Beethoven. Connolly, in the Haydn (again taking the high tessitura, complete with top Cs, in
her stride), and Tilling are both superb, marrying a classical nobility of line with a profound
identification with the plights of these suffering
heroines *in extremis*.

Mass in C minor, 'Great', K427 (ed Schmitt/Gardiner)
Sylvia McNair sop **Diana Montague** mez **Anthony
Rolfe Johnson** ten **Cornelius Hauptmann** bass
**Monteverdi Choir; English Baroque Soloists /
John Eliot Gardiner**
Philips 420 210-2PH (54' · DDD · T/t)　Ⓕ🔂🔂

Writers on Mozart sometimes take him to task for
the alleged mixture of styles in the C minor Mass,
in particular the use of florid, 'operatic' solo writing amid all the severe ecclesiastical counterpoint.
To object is to misunderstand the nature of
Mozart's religion, but it takes a performance as
stylistically accomplished as this one to make the
point in practice. The usual stumbling-block is
the 'Et incarnatus', with its richly embellished solo
line and its wind obbligatos. Sung as it is here, by
Sylvia McNair, beautifully refined in detail, it's
indeed passionate, but passionately devout.
McNair is deeply affecting in the 'Christe', taken
quite spaciously and set in a measured *Kyrie* of
great cumulative power which also has some fine,
clean singing from the Monteverdi Choir.

As with Gardiner's version of the Requiem you
might wish for the sound of a boys' choir (why go
to the trouble of having authentic instruments if
you then use unauthentic voices?) but the bright,
forward tone of his sopranos is very persuasive.
The music is all strongly characterised: the 'Gloria' jubilant, the 'Qui tollis' grandly elegiac with
its solemn, inexorable march rhythm and its
dying phrases echoed between the choirs, the
'Credo' full of vitality. Some of the 'Cum Sancto
Spiritu' fugue is too heavily accented, though.
Nevertheless, a confident recommendation.

Requiem, K626

Requiem. Ave verum corpus, K618　　　　Ⓟ
Anna Maria Panzarella sop **Nathalie Stutzmann**
contr **Christoph Prégardien** ten **Nathan Berg** bass
Les Arts Florissants / William Christie

MOZART'S REQUIEM – IN BRIEF

Schäfer, Fink, Streit, Finley; Arnold Schoenberg Choir; Concentus Musicus Wien / Nikolaus Harnoncourt Ⓟ
DHM 82876 58705-2 (50' · DDD) ⒻⓄⓄ
Strong, sombre and punchy by turns, Harnoncourt's second recording is as idiosyncratic as one expects from him, while benefiting from a stellar line-up of soloists.

McNair, Watkinson, Ataiza, Lloyd; ASMF and Chorus / Sir Neville Marriner
Philips 432 087-2PH (50' · DDD) ⒻⓄⒹ
Consistent and considered, Marriner offers the conventional text with both dignity and polish. Exceptionally fine choral singing.

Panzarella, Stutzmann, Prégardien, Berg; Les Arts Florissants / William Christie Ⓟ
Erato 0630 10697-2 (54' · DDD) ⓂⓄ
Using period instruments, Christie goes none the less for a big-scale, surprisingly emotive rendering. He employs a nicely balanced team of soloists.

Gritton, Rogers, Robinson, Rose; Scottish CO and Chorus / Sir Charles Mackerras
Linn ⓈⒶ CKD211 (55' · DDD) Ⓕ
Susan Gritton leads the soloists in Sir Charles Mackerras's recent rethink. He uses the Robert Levin edition in which the traditional text is retained only in so far as it agrees with 'idiomatic Mozartian practice'.

Della Casa, Malaniuk, Dermota, Siepi; Vienna Philharmonic Orchestra / Bruno Walter Ⓗ
Orfeo C430 961B (76' · ADD) Ⓕ
A taut and powerful account from Walter's final Salzburg Festival concert (1956) with soprano Lisa della Casa in glorious voice and the VPO playing with fierce commitment.

M Price, Schimdt, Schreier, Adam; Staatskapelle Dresden / Peter Schreier
Philips 475 205-2PGR (53' · DDD) ⓂⓄⒹ
Peter Schreier won the *Gramophone* Choral Award in 1984 with this dedicated reading, a little heavy by contemporary standards, yet still compelling thanks to Margaret Price's ravishing singing and the magnificence of the Leipzig Radio Choir.

Rubens, Braun, Davislim, Zeppenfeld; Munich Philharmonic Orchestra / Christian Thielemann
DG 477 5797GH (54' · DDD) ⒻⒹ
A rather old-fashioned approach maybe, with broad tempi and rich tone, but there's no denying the power of Thielemann's conception. He traverses the work with the inexorable build-up that you might expect from a Bruckner symphony interpretation.

Erato 0630 10697-2 (54' · DDD · T/t) ⓂⓄ

Les Arts Florissants provides a substantial, dramatic reading: the tempo for the 'Requiem aeternam' is slow but malleable, and Christie is ready to make the most of the changes in orchestral colour or choral texture and, indeed, to dramatise the music to the utmost. He has little truck with any notion that this is an austere piece: he sees it as operatic, almost Romantic – and the result is very compelling. There are surprising things: 'Quantus tremor', in a very weighty account of the 'Dies irae', for example, is hushed rather than terrifying; the 'Recordare' is slow to the point of stickiness; there are rather mannered *crescendos* in the *Sanctus*; and often cadences are drawn out. The powerful choruses of the Sequence are imposingly done, and the grave 'Lacrimosa' wonderfully catches the special significance not only of the music itself but also of the fact that this is the moment where Mozart's last autograph trails off. The choral singing is sharply etched and generally distinguished. Although the solo singing isn't uniformly outstanding the soprano's melting tone can be very appealing, and Prégardien is an excellent stylist; the *Benedictus* is particularly impressive: shapely and refined. This is a reading full of character and imaginative ideas, very much a conscious modern interpretation of the work and very finely executed. The disc is completed by perhaps the only piece which can reasonably follow the Requiem, the *Ave verum corpus*, in a slow, hushed, rather romantic reading that's undeniably moving.

Requiem Ⓟ
Christine Schäfer, Bernarda Fink *sops* **Kurt Streit** *ten* **Gerald Finley** *bar* **Arnold Schoenberg Choir; Concentus Musicus Wien / Nikolaus Harnoncourt**
Deutsche Harmonia Mundi ⓈⒶ 82876 58705-2 (50' · DDD · T/t) ⒻⓄⓄ

Nikolaus Harnoncourt's recent choral projects seem consciously to be reconciling some of the treasured values of his upbringing, alongside deeply held beliefs as to how a famous score can be illuminated through a 'period' lens. This recording integrates past and present in a way his previous reading from over 20 years ago simply couldn't. The main difference between the two is the interpretative assurance of his latest version; it's far clearer in its message, and articulated with greater rhetorical awareness.

While the 'Dies irae' is a set-piece of graphic, biting and eerie terror, the previous *Kyrie* is treated as a quasi-liturgical introit, unfolding gradually with an understated elegance. The 'Tuba mirum' is also unusual, less statuesque than normal, with a highly charged trombone solo both triumphant and imploring. The solo singers, individually and collectively, are tinged with a glow of deep regret; they sing with a palpable sense of interdependent ensemble and sustained poignancy.

As you'd expect from Harnoncourt, there's a studied punchiness, and the 'Confutatis' leaves us with a series of striking contrasts, with 'salva me' as a gesture of impending loneliness for the 'Recordare': the strings shadow the soloists with questing and characterful figures, belying the restless and unsentimental approach to the 'Lacrimosa'. The Arnold Schoenberg Choir is highly responsive in the modern way, yet unmodish in their soft-edged attack and heterogeneous timbre. Harnoncourt conceives of an almost jocular majesty in the 'Domine Jesu' and *Benedictus*. Of course, there has to be a moment for the iconoclast in him: here it's the 'Hostias', taken at almost twice the usual speed.

This isn't a Requiem that comforts and stirs in the expected ways; instead, a curious and enigmatic undertow of human vulnerability emerges, presenting Mozart's valedictory essay in a striking new light.

Litaniae..., K243

Litaniae de venerabili altaris sacramento, K243. **P**
Mass in C, K257, 'Credo'
Angela Maria Blasi sop **Elisabeth von Magnus**
contr **Deon van der Walt** ten **Alistair Miles** bass
Arnold Schoenberg Choir; Vienna Concentus
Musicus / Nikolaus Harnoncourt
Teldec Das Alte Werk 9031 72304-2
(61 minutes: DDD · T/t) (F)

The *Litaniae de venerabili altaris sacramento* of 1775 has powerful claims to be reckoned the finest of Mozart's church works before the C minor Mass and Requiem; but it's never quite had the recognition it deserves. Or the performance until now. It's a deeply felt work, from the grave, warm opening of the *Kyrie*, through the imposing 'Verbum caro factum' and the graceful 'Hostia' that succeeds it, the 'Tremendum' with its almost Verdian menace and the appealing 'Dulcissum convivium' (a soprano aria with soft textures supplied by flutes and bassoons), the highly original 'Viaticum' and the resourcefully and lengthily developed 'Pignus' to the *Agnus*, a beautiful soprano aria with solo writing for flute, oboe and cello. The performance here under Nikolaus Harnoncourt rightly sees no need to apologise for the stylistic diversity of the work. The issue is made still more attractive by the inclusion of a Mass setting of the same year, one of Mozart's most inventive and original in its textures and its treatment of words. Altogether a very attractive record.

Exsultate, jubilate, K165

Exsultate, jubilate. 'Coronation' Mass, K317 – Agnus Dei. Regina coeli, K108. Regina coeli, K127. Sancta Maria, mater Dei, K273. Sub tuum praesidium, K198. Vesperae de Domenica, K321 – Laudate Dominum. Vesperae solennes de confessore, K339 – Laudate Dominum
Carolyn Sampson sop **Choir of The King's Consort;**
The King's Consort / Robert King
Hyperion CDA67560 (66' · DDD · T) (F)

Though clearly designed as a showcase for a young British singer who seems to be getting better by the minute – the presence of a number of excerpts and a double-tracked duet are evidence of that – it is nevertheless strongly focused on Mozart's Salzburg church music, offering in addition to some of the usual suspects a few relative rarities. It is also a reminder of how, even in works which make no attempts at great depth, the young composer was a marvel of fluency, grace and freshness. There are times in his teenage music when you can really feel the enjoyment he took in his own ability; on this disc you can sense it being transferred to the performances.

Emma Kirkby recorded some of these pieces a few years back (likewise doing *Exsultate, jubilate* in the alternative 'flute' version), and while Carolyn Sampson's singing does not sound like Kirkby's, her rounder voice gives the listener much the same kind of pleasure. What more could you want in these works than a soloist who places every note with joyous precision, moves from one to another so cleanly, and demonstrates at every turn such intelligent but unfussy musicianship? She also has wonderful control of dynamics, beautifully demonstrated in the restrained cadenza of *Exsultate*'s slow middle section, or the hushed reprise of the *Agnus Dei* from the *Coronation* Mass.

The orchestral accompaniments are ably conducted by Robert King, and if the choral singing is not the most polished you will hear, its lusty commitment certainly adds to the honest pleasure of the performances. This is a sunny and unpretentious disc which deserved to be among the successes of the Mozart year.

Concert Arias

Al desio di chi t'adora, K577. Alma grande e nobil core, K578. Ch'io mi scordi di te?, K505a. Vado, ma dove? oh Dei!, K583 La clemenza di Tito – Non più di fiori. Così fan tutte – In uomini, in soldati; Per pietà; È amore un ladroncello. Idomeneo – Padre, germani, addio! Le nozze di Figaro – Non so più; Voi che sapete; Deh vieni non tardar.
Magdalena Kožená mez [a]**Jos van Immerseel** fp
Orchestra of the Age of Enlightenment /
Sir Simon Rattle
Archiv 477 6272AH (64' · DDD · T/t) (F)

'Singing Mozart is second nature to her,' enthuses Rattle of Magdalena Kožená. 'Each woman on each track is a completely distinct personality.' Promotional hype? Well, in hyper-Beckmesserish mode you could say her *legato* in 'Per pietà' is not quite seamless, the tempo for 'Deh vieni' a touch too jaunty. But this is barrel-scraping. If anyone has recorded a lovelier Mozart recital in recent years, we've yet to hear it. In her early thirties, Kožená is consummate mistress of her art. Her liquid high mezzo, with its easy upward extension, combines warmth with the bloom and freshness of youth, while her coloratura, on display in 'Al desio di chi t'adora', is as brilliant and expressive as Bartoli's, yet without the Italian diva's intrusive aspirates.

Beyond this, Rattle's claim is hard to refute. Cherubino (whose 'Voi che sapete' is sung in an embellished version published in 1810) and Dorabella (a blithe, flighty 'È amore un ladroncino') are the only roles here in Kožená's stage repertoire. But she 'lives' each of these wide-ranging characters intensely, from the remorseful Vitellia in *La clemenza di Tito* (sorrow etched into the texture of her voice) via the tenderness and anguish of Ilia in *Idomeneo* to a delightfully sly, knowing Despina. The vivid, tangy accompaniments from Rattle and the OAE go well beyond mere good style, with a classy basset horn obbligato from Anthony Pay in the Vitellia aria. Fortepianist Jos van Immerseel is an equally sympathetic partner in an impassioned yet intimate performance of *Ch'io mi scordi di te*.

Al desio di chi t'adora, K577[a]. Bella mia fiamma... Resta, o cara, K528[a]. Vado, ma dove? oh Dei!, K583[a]. Voi avete un cor fedele, K217[a]. Le nozze di Figaro – Un moto di gioia, K579[a]
[a]**Cecilia Bartoli** *mez* **Vienna Concentus Musicus / Nikolaus Harnoncourt**
Video director **Brian Large**
BBC/Opus Arte **DVD** OA0820D (112' · 16:9 · 2.0, 5.1 & DTS 5.1 · 0) Ⓕ

No doubt this concert, recorded at Graz's elegant Stefaniensaal, is aimed primarily at Bartoli-philes, who will not be disappointed; it's predictably impressive, if a shade short. Mozart's so-called concert arias are formidable pieces, some actually alternatives for his own and other operas, but others, in particular *Bella mia fiamma*, created to challenge ambitious singers such as Josepha Duschek. Bartoli copes with characteristic aplomb, tossing off bravura trills and alarming roulades just effortlessly enough not to be infuriating. The advantage of video, though, is that we can actually see the feeling with which she infuses even the most conventional sentiments, as vivid as her stage interpretations – though with her characteristically earthy twinkle never far off.

What's more, though, this is one of the best-recorded concerts, not just in its excellent picture and first-rate surround sound, but in its video direction. Shooting in a lower, mellower light than usual, Brian Large captures the platform drama in vividly immediate close-up, without Karajan-style excesses. Thoroughly recommended.

Additional recommendation

Lieder and Concert Arias
Schwarzkopf *sop* **Brendel, Gieseking** *pfs*
LSO / Szell
EMI Références 574803-2 (ADD). Recorded 1955, 1968 ⓂⓄ⊕→

A classic disc – the fruitful collaboration of great artists. Schwarzkopf was 39 when she recorded the Lieder, mature in resources but still amazingly capable of the clarity of youth.

Opera arias

La clemenza di Tito – Parto, parto; Deh, per questo; Ecco il punto, o Vitellia...Non piu di fiori. Così fan tutte – E'amore un ladroncello. Don Giovanni – Vedrai, carino Le nozze di Figaro – Non so più; Voi che sapete; Giunse alfin il momento... Deh vieni. Concert Arias – Chi sa, chi sa, qual sia, K582; Alma grande e nobil core, K578; Ch'io mi scordi di te?, K505
Cecilia Bartoli *mez* **András Schiff** *pf* **Peter Schmidtl** *basset cl/basset hn* **Vienna Chamber Orchestra / György Fischer**
Decca 430 513-2DH (58' · DDD · T/t) ⒻⓄ→

Mozart wrote some of his most appealing music for the mezzo-soprano voice with the roles of Cherubino and Susanna in *Le nozze di Figaro*, Dorabella in *Così fan tutte* and Zerlina in *Don Giovanni* each boasting at least one memorable aria. Alongside these this disc includes a handful of concert arias including *Ch'io mi scordi di te?* which was written for the farewell performance of the great mezzo Nancy Storace with Mozart playing the *concertante* piano role. Here with as innate an interpreter of Mozart's piano writing as András Schiff and a voice so remarkably self-assured as Cecilia Bartoli's the electricity of that first, historic performance seems almost to be recreated. And, here as elsewhere, György Fischer directs the splendid Vienna Chamber Orchestra with disarming sensitivity while the recording is wonderfully warm and vibrant.

Cecilia Bartoli boasts a voice of extraordinary charm and unassuming virtuosity: her vocal characterisations would be the envy of the finest actresses and her intuitive singing is in itself a sheer delight. But she also brings to these arias a conviction and understanding of the subtleties of the language which only a native Italian could. Listen to the subtle nuances of 'Voi che sapete', the depth of understanding behind Dorabella's seemingly frivolous 'E'amore un ladroncello'; these aren't mere performances, but interpretations which cut to the very soul of the music. No Mozart lover should be without this CD.

La clemenza di Tito – Deh per questo istante; Ecco il punto...Non più di fiori vaghe catene. Così fan tutte – Temerari...Come scoglio; Ei parte...Per pietà, ben mio. Don Giovanni – Batti, batti; In quali eccessi...Mi tradì. Le nozze di Figaro – Non so più cosa son; Porgi, amor. Concert arias – Oh, temerario Arbace!... Per quel paterno amplesso, K79. Ch'io mi scordi di te...Non temer, amato bene, K505
Véronique Gens *sop* **Orchestra of the Age of Enlightenment / Ivor Bolton** with **Melvyn Tan** *fp*
Virgin Classics Veritas 545319-2 (59' · DDD · T/t) ⒻⓄ→

Véronique Gens is one of the most engaging and stylish Mozart sopranos around, as this sampler of her art confirms. Under the exacting baton of Ivor Bolton, the OAE show sharp and eager teeth to match her own highly strung recitative in 'In quali eccessi'. And this Donna Anna demonstrates more than one-dimensional *Angst* as the orchestra's wind soloists breathe in sympathy with every moment of *palpitando* in Gens's own supple phrasing. There's a similar focus on the emotional potential of breath in a 'Non so più' whose fierce frustration flies out of eloquent consonants. Steady control of breath and tone bring a moving poise to 'Non più di fiori', where Vitellia's horrified introspection finds empathy in the basset horn obbligato. And as Sesto, Gens moulds the moist clay of some of Mozart's most beautiful melodic contours in 'Deh, per questo istante'. There's her Countess and Zerlina to enjoy as well, with the two exquisitely sculpted and sparingly but powerfully ornamented arias from *Così fan tutte*.

Idomeneo – Quando avran; Padre, germani, addio!; Solitudini amiche; Zeffiretti lusinghieri. Il re pastore – Di tante sue procelle. Zaïde – Tiger! wetze nur die Klauen. Die Zauberflöte – Ach, ich fühl's. Concert arias – A Berenice…Sol nascente, K70. Ch'io mi scordi di te…Non temer, amato bene, K505ᵃ
Sophie Karthäuser sop
ᵃ**Inge Spinette** fp **Symphony Orchestra of La Monnaie / Kazushi Ono**
Cyprès CYP8602 (51' · DDD)
Recorded live   Ⓕ

If you can ignore the adulatory – and appallingly translated – booklet-note by Sylvain Fort, there is much to enjoy in the young Belgian soprano's live recital from La Monnaie. Her vernal, finely focused timbre, gleaming top notes and grace of style make her a natural in Mozart, as acclaimed appearances at La Monnaie, Aix and Salzburg have confirmed. For some Karthäuser may sound too doleful in Ilia's rapturous song to the breezes, 'Zeffiretti lusinghieri'. Elsewhere, though, she characterises with feeling and spirit, whether in Ilia's initial grieving recitative and aria, or in Pamina's aria, an intense, 'lived' performance, beautifully shaded, the tricky wide leaps exquisitely negotiated.

With venomously spitting consonants, Karthäuser works up a fine lather in the raging 'Tiger' aria from *Zaïde* and reveals an agile, elegant coloratura technique in two extravagant but vapid early bravura showpieces. Her acute response to shifting mood and harmony in *Ch'io mi scordi di te* is slightly compromised by the misfit between the silvery fortepiano and the solid modern-instrument orchestra. Orchestral accompaniments throughout, in fact, are serviceable but unimaginative, not least in the autopilot handling of repeated notes. Karthäuser, a lovely Mozart singer, deserves a better setting.

La clemenza di Tito – Deh, se piacer mi vuoi. Così fan tutte – Ah, scostati!…Smanie implacabili; Temerari…Come scoglio. La finta giardiniera – Se l'augellin sen fugge; Và pure ad altri in braccio

Concert arias – Alma grande e nobil core, K578. Basta, vincesti…Ah, non lasciarmi, K486a. Chì sà, chi sà, qual sia, K582. Ch'io mi scordi di te…Non temer, amato bene, K505ᵃ. Misero me!…Misero pergoletto, K77.
Elīna Garanča mez ᵃ**Frank Braley** pf
Salzburg Camerata / Louis Langrée
Virgin Classics 332631-2 (62' · DDD · T/t)   Ⓕ🅑➜

Elīna Garanča's voice is warm and ample, its quality enriched in the lower register but still full-bodied, pure and resonant on the top B flats. Her *legato* and fluency are alike well schooled, her intervals exceptionally clean and her feeling for light and shade at any rate aware that it exists. Room for developments lies principally in this area: she is not inexpressive but there is more to be made of the emotions and the part words play in their communication.

The selection of arias, concert and operatic, makes for a satisfying programme. Much is on the grand scale: injured women cry out against malign fate and determine to confront it. This includes, we note, both the mezzo and soprano leads in *Così fan tutte*: essentially sung in the same voice (she does not audibly 'turn soprano' for 'Come scoglio') and, one might well conclude, by the same character. The lighter, more intimate tone used in *Ch'io mi scordi di te* is welcome, and welcome too are some lesser known concert arias, most of all *Ah, non lasciarmi*, which has a melody almost as lovely as the now-famous 'Ruhe sanft' from *Zaide*. The longest is the profoundly set *Misero me!*, where the intricacies of the implied dramatic situation form something of a barrier, but where the sustained powers of the music and the singer impress deeply.

Thinking of comparisons, she is richer and warmer than Teresa Berganza, less imaginative and personally involved than Cecilia Bartoli, but also free of mannerisms. With lively accompaniment by the Salzburg Camerata, this is an exceptionally successful debut recital.

'Tutto Mozart'
Bastien und Bastienne – Diggi, daggi. Così fan tutte – Soave sia il ventoᵃᵇ; Il core vi donòᵇ. Don Giovanni – Madamina, il catalogo è questo; Là ci darem la manoᵃ; Deh! vieni alla finestra. Le nozze di Figaro – Non più andrai; Crudel! perchè finoraᵇ; Aprite un po' quegli occhi. Die Zauberflöte – Der Vogelfänger bin ich ja; Bei Männernᵃ; Ein Mädchen oder Weibchen; Pa-Pa-Pa-Papagenaᵃ. Un bacio di mano, K541. Così dunque tradisci…Aspri rimorsi atroci, K432. Io ti lascio, o cara, addio, KAnh245/K621a. Nun liebes Weibchen, ziehst mit mir, K625/592aᵃ. Männer suchen stets zu naschen, K433/K416c
Bryn Terfel bass-bar with ᵃ**Miah Persson** sop
ᵇ**Christine Rice** mez **Scottish Chamber Orchestra / Sir Charles Mackerras**
DG 477 5886GH (63' · DDD · T/t)   Ⓕ🅞🅞➜

Unlike many showcase CDs for famous singers, this one has been carefully planned to demonstrate Terfel's many-faceted gifts as a Mozartian, boxing the compass of roles and pieces for bass-baritone. Familiar items are interspersed with unfamiliar ones, and the singer, who writes how well Mozart wrote for his kind of voice, is heard in all the roles he has sung on stage (the exceptions include Papageno, for which his figure is unsuited, although in purely vocal terms he proves a lively and sympathetic bird-catcher). His Figaro, which begins and ends the programme, is nicely distinguished from his Count Almaviva, both brought before us by his pointed use of the Italian text. Similarly his suave, insinuating Giovanni is very different from his earthy Leporello, the timbre for each part cleverly differentiated. From *Così fan tutte*, he briefly undertakes Alfonso, another role he hasn't assumed on stage, in the Farewell trio, then switches to Guglielmo for 'Il core vi dono' where he woos the attractive Dorabella of Christine Rice.

Of the rarer operatic items and separate arias he gives a particularly dramatic account of 'Così dunque tradisci' and finds the gentle *Entführung*-like humour of the incomplete 'Männer suchen stets zu naschen' to his liking, with Miah Persson (unfairly not credited on the CD front) as partner to the inauthentic nonsense of 'Nun liebest Weibchen'.

The quality of the disc is confirmed by Sir Charles Mackerras's authoritatively Mozartian direction and fine playing from the SCO. The recording has both space and presence.

Opera Overtures

Bastien und Bastienne – Overture. La clemenza di Tito – Overture; March. Così fan tutte – Overture. Don Giovanni – Overture. Die Entführung aus dem Serail – Overture. Idomeneo – Overture; March, Act 3; Pas seul de Monsieur Legrand. Mitridate, rè di Ponto – Overture; March, Act 1. Le nozze di Figaro – Overture; March, Act 3. Les petits riens – Overture. Der Schauspieldirektor – Overture. Die Zauberflöte – Overture; March of the Priests
Norwegian National Opera Orchestra / Rinaldo Alessandrini
Naïve OP30479 (66' · DDD)   Ⓕ

An album of overtures, shorn of their operas, may seem a curious remnant from the LP era. Who now would put on such a CD and listen through it? That said, the sweep of the programme – running the gamut from the Italianate sinfonia style of the *Mitridate* overture to the late miniature masterpieces – and the zippy performances will win you over. The man pulling the strings is Rinaldo Alessandrini, who has an innate understanding of Mozart's conception of 'sonata form' as concentrated drama. He makes you realise, for instance, why *Figaro* is subtitled *La folle giornata* ('The day of madness'), moving from perky opening statement through increasingly convoluted development to true catharsis as the work draws to its conclusion.

He also has an uncanny ear for sonority. For example, the fetish among practitioners of 'historically aware' performance (and this disc falls into that category, despite the Norwegian

band's use of modern instruments) has been for trumpets to punch out gobbets of punctuation on downbeats. Alessandrini makes the brass an integral part of the woodwind choir: hear how beautifully they are incorporated into the wind chords in *The Magic Flute* – just one of the vivid and thought-provoking details that make this such a delightful disc.

La clemenza di Tito, K621

La clemenza di Tito   Ⓟ
Mark Padmore ten Tito **Bernarda Fink** mez Sesto **Alexandrina Pendatchanska** sop Vitellia **Sunhae Im** sop Servilia **Marie-Claude Chappuis** mez Annio **Sergio Foresti** bass Publio **RIAS Chamber Choir; Freiburg Baroque Orchestra / René Jacobs**
Harmonia Mundi ② HMC90 1923/24;
🎧 HMC80 1923/24 (134' · DDD · T/t)   Ⓕ

La clemenza di Tito
Rainer Trost ten Tito **Magdalena Kožená** mez Sesto **Hillevi Martinpelto** sop Vitellia **Lisa Milne** sop Servilia **Christine Rice** mez Annio **John Relyea** bass Publio **Scottish Chamber Chorus and Orchestra/ Sir Charles Mackerras**
DG ② 477 5972GH2 (128' · DDD · S/T/t/N)   Ⓕ Ⓞ ➔

It is good to read René Jacobs's passionate advocacy for Metastasio's dramaturgy; he openly acknowledges where he has taken some liberties with Mozart's score but it does not guarantee that all of his solutions are convincing, attractive or necessary. Most noteworthy elements in Jacobs's direction could split opinion: the liberal application of pulling back the orchestra in the Overture's opening bars is contrasted with sudden over-accelerations (contrived or revitalising?); elaborately ornamented piano solos or seemingly 'improvised' flourishes from the cello are inserted before some recitatives (intrusive absurdities or imaginative colour?); Mozart's notation of rhythms is frequently interpreted in unpredictable and unconventional ways (reappraisals or mannerisms?); Mozart's magnificent quintet at the end of Act 1 is far too rapid to be a sensible interpretation of the tempo marking *Allegro assai* (fully charged theatricality or losing the music's potential impact?).

There are unequivocally good things on offer: Mark Padmore's smooth-toned Tito has unforced purity, his arias are eminently civilised and his two accompanied recitatives make the Emperor's anguish and inner conflict regarding his treasonous friend's fate transparent. He brings agile coloratura and a sweet top A flat to 'Se all'impero, amici Dei'. Alexandrina Pendatchanska's dark timbre, dramatic conviction and ambitious ornaments in 'Deh se piacer mi vuoi' make her villainous Vitellia formidable (although the stilted shaping of the line 'alletta ad ingannar' seems unnatural). Bernarda Fink's plangent contributions capture Sesto's desperate struggle between honour and love.

There are few Mozartians of Mackerras's standard: every aria, ensemble, march, chorus and recitative is steeped in absorbing Mozartian rhetoric, colour, personality and style. There are no traces of artificiality or idiosyncrasy. Period brass and timpani lend precision and idiomatic colour, and the modern strings and woodwind are stirring, balanced and lyrical. From the first few minutes of the stirring yet immaculately judged overture, he delivers something special.

Rainer Trost's voice has lost its youthful purity since his memorable Ferrando in John Eliot Gardiner's *Così fan tutte* a little over a decade earlier, but the acquisition of darkness and striking authority suits the dignity of his compassionate 'Del più sublime soglio'. His richly textured coloratura and Mackerras's flowing grandeur are marvellous companions in the opera's jubilant final chorus ('Tu, è ver, m'assolvi, Augusto').

Hillevi Martinpelto's seductive Vitellia makes Sesto's obsession thoroughly convincing: 'Deh, se piacer mi vuoi' has the perfect synthesis of power, passion and purity (her ornamentation is every bit as courageous as any of Jacobs's singers, but also fits smoothly with the harmony). She magnificently conveys Vitellia's voyage from vulnerability to penitent heroism in 'Ecco il punto', and follows it with a radiant 'Non più di fiori' (few sopranos manage to get the audience to end up sympathising with Vitellia to this extent).

However, Magdalena Kožená's Sesto steals the show. She is an outstanding Mozart singer; she sings her heart out in the dynamic accompanied recitative 'Oh Dei, che smania è questa' that leads into the quintet at the end of Act I (Mackerras and the SCO strings respond with stunning energy), and her arias are consistently marvellous.

Mackerras and Jacobs both provide fresh impetus to the least-regarded opera of Mozart's maturity. If one must choose between them, the veteran pays richer dividends than the maverick.

Additional recommendation

La clemenza di Tito   Ⓟ
Heilmann Tito **D Jones** Vitellia **Bartoli** Sesto
Montague Annio **Bonney** Servilia **Cachemaille**
Publio **AAM / Hogwood**
L'Oiseau-Lyre Ⓕ 444 131-2OHO2 (137' · DDD · T/t)
                                      Ⓕ➍➤

Hogwood has assembled a remarkable cast, with certainly two, perhaps three, outstanding interpretations. First among them must be Cecilia Bartoli, who rightly establishes Sesto as the central character. Then there's Della Jones's remarkable Vitellia. There are lots of interesting and emotionally suggestive touches in her singing. Uwe Heilmann's Tito is marked by much subtle and finely shaped singing and a keen awareness of how phrasing conveys sense.

La clemenza di Tito
Philip Langridge ten Tito **Ashley Putnam** sop
Vitellia **Diana Montague** mez Sesto **Martine Mahé**
mez Annio **Elzbieta Szmytka** sop Servilia **Peter Rose**
bass Publio **Glyndebourne Festival Chorus; London
Philharmonic Orchestra / Sir Andrew Davis**

Stage director **Nicholas Hytner**
Video director **Robin Lough**
ArtHaus Musik 📀 100 406 (143' · 4:3 · 2.0 · 2 & 5)
Recorded live at Glyndebourne, 1991   Ⓕ○

This performance shows Glyndebourne at its peak in terms of preparatory work and ensemble playing. Add Andrew Davis's superbly taut and perceptive conducting and it's no wonder that here you feel *Tito* to be very near the top of the Mozartian operatic canon, a very different opinion from that which was current for so many years.

At the heart of the performance on stage are Philip Langridge as the clement yet tormented emperor of the title, acting – especially with his eyes – and singing with extreme eloquence, and Diana Montague's equally committed account of Sesto's part, a character so obviously torn, almost fatally, between his erotic love for Vitellia and his deep friendship for Tito. Montague also acts movingly with her eyes, and her singing is noble, warm and technically flawless. As the scheming Vitellia, Ashley Putnam somehow manages to enact both the character's classical origins while suggesting a soap-opera villainess. Vocally she's always willing, but sometimes the flesh is weak, particularly in the higher reaches.

Martine Mahé keeps up the high standard with her urgently sung and acted Annio. So does Peter Rose as the upright and concerned Publio. Only Elzbieta Szmytka, as Servilia, seems to be operating on a more conventional level of operatic expression. The LPO is on its best form. Robin Lough's video direction is spot on. The sound balance is faultless. Even so, main credit for this arresting event goes to Hytner.

Così fan tutte, K588

Così fan tutte
Elisabeth Schwarzkopf sop Fiordiligi **Christa Ludwig**
mez Dorabella **Hanny Steffek** sop Despina **Alfredo
Kraus** ten Ferrando **Giuseppe Taddei** bar Guglielmo
Walter Berry bass Don Alfonso **Philharmonia
Chorus and Orchestra / Karl Böhm**
EMI Great Recordings of the Century ② 567379-2
(165' · ADD · T/t). Recorded 1962   Ⓜ❶❷❸➤

 Così fan tutte is the most balanced and probing of all Mozart's operas, formally faultless, musically inspired from start to finish, emotionally a matter of endless fascination and, in the second act, profoundly moving. It has been very lucky on disc, and besides this delightful set there have been several other memorable recordings. However, Karl Böhm's cast could hardly be bettered, even in one's dreams. The two sisters are gloriously sung – Schwarzkopf and Ludwig bring their immeasurable talents as Lieder singers to this sparkling score and overlay them with a rare comic touch. Add to that the stylish singing of Alfredo Kraus and Giuseppe Taddei and the central quartet is unimpeachable. Walter Berry's Don Alfonso is characterful and Hanny Steffek is quite superb as Despina.

The pacing of this endlessly intriguing work is measured with immaculate judgement. The emotional control of the characterisation is masterly and Böhm's totally idiomatic response to the music is arguably without peer. However, more recent recordings, using period instruments, do offer stimulating alternative views.

Così fan tutte (sung in English) ▣
Janice Watson *sop* Fiordiligi **Diana Montague** *mez* Dorabella **Toby Spence** *ten* Ferrando **Christopher Maltman** *bar* Guglielmo **Lesley Garrett** *sop* Despina **Sir Thomas Allen** *bar* Don Alfonso **Geoffrey Mitchell Choir; Orchestra of the Age of Enlightenment / Sir Charles Mackerras**
Chandos/Peter Moores Foundation Opera in English
③ CHAN3152 (161' · DDD · T) Ⓜ▷

Sir Peter Moores comments that the phrase 'Così fan tutte' is 'almost impossible to translate' into English. Thus it is that the delivery of Ferrando and Guglielmo's pronouncement, under the cynical tutorship of Don Alfonso, is one of the few lines that have not been translated in this volume of the Opera in English series (Alfonso's exclamation 'Misericordia!' is the other one left intact, and rightly so). Sometimes opera in English sounds too close to Gilbert and Sullivan at their cheesiest, but in a sparkling comedy such as *Così fan tutte* that is not necessarily a bad thing: in fact this is tremendously enjoyable because it allows Anglophones to concentrate on exactly what the characters are saying. So if Opera in English brings a wider audience closer to the heart of Mozart's and da Ponte's masterpiece, then it can only be a wonderful thing.

Of course, it helps that the music has seldom sounded as glorious as it does in the hands of Sir Charles Mackerras and the Orchestra of the Age of Enlightenment. Both are consummate Mozartians, and the pacing, ebb and flow of the music is near-perfect. In particular, the OAE's woodwind are on ravishing form. In terms of stylishness, orchestral sound and the sentimental strength of the playing, this *Così* is on a par with the finest period-instrument versions (Ostman and Gardiner), and arguably has more heart than the OAE's previous recording under Sir Simon Rattle (EMI). The three ladies are animated (but not consistently pleasing on the ear), so the three men steal the show vocally: Sir Thomas Allen is, of course, a renowned Don Alfonso of authority and warmth, Christopher Maltman is a suave Guglielmo, and Toby Spence delivers some of the best Mozart tenor-singing in a long time. Although he falls short in softer music, he brings ringing clarity and declamatory emotion to "Tradito! Schernito!" (here "Her ter-reason is poison").

Così fan tutte ▣
Miah Persson *sop* Fiordiligi **Anke Vondung** *mez* Dorabella **Ainhoa Garmendia** *sop* Despina **Topi Lehtipuu** *ten* Ferrando **Luca Pisaroni** *bar* Guglielmo **Nicolas Rivenq** *bass* Don Alfonso

Glyndebourne Chorus; Orchestra of the Age of Enlightenment / Iván Fischer
Stage director **Nicholas Hytner**
Video director **Francesca Kemp**
Opus Arte ② *DVD* OA0970D (3h 30' · NTSC · 16:9 · PCM stereo & DTS 5.1 · 0)
Recorded live at the Opera House, Glyndebourne, on June 26 and July 1, 2006. Extra features include Insights with Iván Fischer, Nicholas Hytner and members of the cast Ⓕ**○○○**

Since 1934 when Glyndebourne revived this then-neglected work and began its run of success it has presented a succession of exemplary stagings all within the parameters of da Ponte's libretto. When this, the latest, was produced it was universally hailed: as faithful a representation of the equivocal comedy as one could wish. That's confirmed by this DVD.

Both Despina and Alfonso are played traditionally and with notable brio by Garmendia and Rivenq. The delightful Persson and Vondung make a wholly believable and vocally attractive Fiordiligi and Dorabella, and deliver their music in ideal Mozartian tone and style. Similarly Lehtipuu is a charming and wide-eyed Ferrando and Pisaroni a warm-voiced and personal Guglielmo. They both woo with seductive charm.

As reviews at the time reported, Fischer conducts with an unassumingly correct sense of timing and has the inestimable advantage of the OAE's period instruments.

Additional recommendations

Così fan tutte
Wall Fiordiligi **Garanča** Dorabella **Bonney** Despina **Mathey** Ferrando **Degout** Guglielmo **Raimondi** Don Alfonso **Mahler CO / Harding** *Stage director* **Chéreau** *Video director* **Metge**
Virgin Classics ② *DVD* 344716-9 (179' · NTSC · 16:9 · PCM stereo, 5.0 and DTS 5.0 · 0). Ⓕ
Patrice Chéreau's production is full of strokes of near-genius from old (Chéreau, his regular set designer Richard Peduzzi, his photogenic Don Alfonso, Ruggero Raimondi), not so old (Barbara Bonney's unhackneyed Despina) and new (Daniel Harding – a thrilling Mozart conductor on the wing – Elīna Garanča's Dorabella, and the men) but, at least as filmed here, is often less than the sum of its parts. Musically, things are also mixed. The best of Harding's *Così* is as earthily thrilling; elsewhere this is work-in-progress

Così fan tutte ▣
Roocroft Fiordiligi **Mannion** Dorabella **James** Despina **Trost** Ferrando **Gilfry** Guglielmo **Nicolai** Don Alfonso **Monteverdi Choir; EBS / Gardiner** *Stage director* **Gardiner** *Video director* **Mumford**
Archiv *DVD* 073 026-9AH2 (3h 13' · 16:9 · 5.1 · 0) Ⓕ
Gardiner decided to be his own director because he didn't trust any available alternative to be faithful to da Ponte's and Mozart's original. In the circumstances this was a sensible decision because his deeply discerning stage interpretation perfectly seconds his own musically perceptive reading.

Amanda Roocroft's Fiordiligi is intrepidly sung. She's partnered, as originally intended, by a soprano Dorabella. Rosa Mannion proves an apt foil for her sister. Rainer Trost is the young, fluent, eager Ferrando and his vulnerable portrayal is a nice contrast to Rodney Gilfry's macho Guglielmo. The four voices blend well in the many ensembles. In the pit, Gardiner's direct, big-scale yet sensitive conducting is the engine-room of the performance, superbly sustained by his period-instrument band.

Don Giovanni, K527

Don Giovanni   **H**
Eberhard Waechter bar Don Giovanni **Joan Sutherland** sop Donna Anna **Elisabeth Schwarzkopf** sop Donna Elvira **Graziella Sciutti** sop Zerlina **Luigi Alva** ten Don Ottavio **Giuseppe Taddei** bar Leporello **Piero Cappuccilli** bar Masetto **Gottlob Frick** bass Commendatore **Philharmonia Chorus and Orchestra / Carlo Maria Giulini**
EMI Great Recordings of the Century ③ 567869-2 (162' · ADD · T/t). Recorded 1959   **Ⓜ❍❍➔**

Although this set is over 50 years old, none of its successors is as skilled in capturing the piece's drama so unerringly. It has always been most recommendable and Giulini captures all the work's most dramatic characteristics, faithfully supported by the superb Philharmonia forces of that time. At this stage of Giulini's career, he was a direct, lithe conductor, alert to every turn in the story and he projects the nervous tension of the piece ideally while never forcing the pace, as can so easily happen. Then he had one of the most apt casts ever assembled for the piece. Waechter's Giovanni combines the demonic with the seductive in just the right proportions, Taddei is a high-profile Leporello, who relishes the text and sings with lots of 'face'. Elvira was always one of Schwarzkopf's most successful roles: here she delivers the role with tremendous intensity. Sutherland's Anna isn't quite so full of character but is magnificently sung. Alva is a graceful Ottavio. Sciutti's charming Zerlina, Cappuccilli's strong and Italianate Masetto and Frick's granite Commendatore are all very much in the picture. The sound is so good, the set might have been recorded yesterday.

Don Giovanni   **P**
Rodney Gilfry bar Don Giovanni **Luba Orgonášová** sop Donna Anna **Charlotte Margiono** sop Donna Elvira **Eirian James** mez Zerlina **Christoph Prégardien** ten Don Ottavio **Ildebrando d'Arcangelo** bass Leporello **Julian Clarkson** bass Masetto **Andrea Silvestrelli** bass Commendatore **Monteverdi Choir; English Baroque Soloists / Sir John Eliot Gardiner**
Archiv ③ 445 870-2AH3 (176' · DDD · T/t) Recorded live 1994   **Ⓕ➔**

Gardiner's set has a great deal to commend it. The recitative is sung with exemplary care over pacing so that it sounds as it should, like height-ened and vivid conversation, often to electrifying effect. Ensembles, the Act 1 quartet particularly, are also treated conversationally, as if one were overhearing four people giving their opinions on a situation in the street. The orchestra, perfectly balanced with the singers in a very immediate acoustic, supports them, as it were 'sings' with them. That contrasts with, and complements, Gardiner's expected ability to empathise with the demonic aspects of the score, as in Giovanni's drinking song and the final moments of Act 1, which fairly bristle with rhythmic energy without ever becoming rushed. The arrival of the statue at Giovanni's dinner-table is tremendous, the period trombones and timpani achieving an appropriately brusque, fearsome attack. Throughout this scene, Gardiner's penchant for sharp accents is wholly appropriate; elsewhere he's sometimes rather too insistent. As a whole, tempi not only seem right on their own account but also, all-importantly, carry conviction in relation to each other. Where so many conductors today are given to rushing 'Mi tradì', Gardiner prefers a more meditative approach, which allows his soft-grained Elvira to make the most of the aria's expressive possibilities.

Rodney Gilfry's Giovanni is lithe, ebullient, keen to exert his sexual prowess; an obvious charmer, at times surprisingly tender yet with the iron will only just below the surface. Suave and appealing, delivered in a real baritone timbre, his Giovanni is as accomplished as any on disc. Ildebrando d'Arcangelo was the discovery of these performances: this young bass is a lively foil to his master and on his own a real showman, as 'Madamina' indicates, a number all the better for a brisk speed. Orgonášová once more reveals herself a paragon as regards steady tone and deft technique – there's no need here to slow down for the coloratura at the end of 'Non mi dir' – and she brings to her recounting of the attempted seduction a real feeling of immediacy. As Anna, Margiono sometimes sounds a shade stretched technically, but consoles us with the luminous, inward quality of her voice and her reading of the role, something innate that can't be learnt.

Nobody in their right senses is ever going to suggest that there's one, ideal version of *Don Giovanni*; the work has far too many facets for that, but for sheer theatrical élan complemented by the live recording, Gardiner is among the best, particularly given a recording that's wonderfully truthful and lifelike.

Don Giovanni   **P**
Johannes Weisser bar Don Giovanni **Olga Pasichnyk** sop Donna Anna **Alexandrina Pendatchanska** sop Donna Elvira **Sunhae Im** sop Zerlina **Kenneth Tarver** ten Don Ottavio **Lorenzo Regazzo** bass Leporello **Nikolay Borchev** bass Masetto **Alessandro Guerzoni** bass Commendatore **Berlin RIAS Chamber Choir; Freiburg Baroque Orchestra / René Jacobs**
Harmonia Mundi ③ HMC90 1964/6 (170' · DDD · S/T/t/N)   **Ⓕ❍**

MOZART DON GIOVANNI – IN BRIEF

Eberhard Waechter *Don Giovanni* **Joan** [H]
Sutherland *Donna Anna* **Elisabeth Schwarzkopf**
Donna Elvira **Philharmonia Chorus & Orchestra /**
Carlo Maria Giulini
EMI ③ 567869-2 (163' · ADD) Ⓜ❂❂➾
Among an increasingly vast choice this
remains a prime recommendation, both for
its rich-voiced, characterful singers and
Giulini's mercurial conducting.

Rodney Gilfry *Don Giovanni* **Luba Orgonášová**
Donna Anna **Charlotte Margiono** *Donna Elvira*
Monteverdi Choir; English Baroque Soloists /
Sir John Eliot Gardiner [P]
Archiv ③ 445 870-2AH3 (176' · DDD) Ⓕ➾
An immensely dynamic, theatrical perfor-
mance recorded live, with a magnetic young
Don heading a splendidly fresh cast. Original
instruments; but this is a field leader by any
standards.

Bo Skovhus *Don Giovanni* **Christine Brewer**
Donna Anna **Felicity Lott** *Donna Elvira* **Scottish**
Chamber Chorus & Orchestra / Sir Charles
Mackerras
Telarc ③ CD80420 (3h 3' · DDD) Ⓕ
Mackerras conducts the excellent Scottish
players with characteristically theatrical
energy, uniting a fine cast in an unusual
sense of ensemble.

Johannes Weisser *Don Giovanni* **Olga Pasichnyk**
Donna Anna **Alexandrina Pendatchanska** *Donna*
Elvira **Freiburg Baroque Orchestra /**
René Jacobs [P]
Harmonia Mundi ③ HMC90 1964/6 (170' · DDD)
Ⓕ❂
A younger Giovanni than we're used to is at
the centre of Jacobs's thrillingly dramatic
reading. Love it or hate it, you're unlikely to
remain unmoved by this great score.

Thomas Allen *Don Giovanni* **Carol Vaness** *Donna*
Anna **Maria Ewing** *Donna Elvira* **Glyndebourne**
Festival Chorus, London PO / Bernard Haitink
EMI ③ 747037-8 (172' · DDD) Ⓕ❂
Derived from Glyndebourne's legendary
Peter Hall production, this has a fine dra-
matic atmosphere, with Thomas Allen's
silken, sinister Giovanni confronting Carol
Vaness under Haitink's urbane direction.

Thomas Allen *Don Giovanni* **Carolyn James**
Donna Anna **Carol Vaness** *Donna Elvira* **Cologne**
Opera Chorus; Cologne Gürzenich Orchestra /
James Conlon
ArtHaus Musik 🎥 100 020 (173') Ⓕ
A straightforward staging, visually accept-
able, if not thrilling, but with a fine cast, even
if Thomas Allen's Don has aged a little since
Glyndebourne. Ferruccio Furlanetto is a live-
wire Leporello; Conlon conducts with brio.

If Jacobs is hardly the first modern conductor to
present the opera in its 'original colours', his
Don Giovanni is among the liveliest and most
enjoyable on offer. It is certainly one of the most
brilliantly played. The Freiburg band, forwardly
balanced, are eager, involved participants in the
drama. Mozart's wonderful woodwind commentaries are as pungent as you will hear, while
rasping, minatory valveless brass and gunfire
period timpani create a properly terrifying frisson in the Commendatore's retribution scene.

Jacobs being Jacobs, there are controversial
things here. Tempi can suddenly spurt forward
or slow down, usually – as in the opening scene
– with dramatically exciting results. Both finales
hurtle forward with thrilling impetus. Elsewhere
speeds can sound a shade frenetic: in the Act 1
Quartet, for instance, or in Zerlina's two arias.
As in Jacobs's *Figaro*, the recitatives are done in
a natural, conversational style, with fortepiano
and cello adding their creative 'commentaries',
like the instruments in the arias.

For Jacobs, Donna Elvira is the opera's central female character. Accordingly, he casts
Anna with the relatively light-toned Olga Pasichnyk, who sings 'Non mi dir' tenderly and
gracefully, and sounds more sorrowful than
vengeful in 'Or sai chi l'onore' – a more vulnerable and more likeable figure than usual. Conversely, Alexandrina Pendatchanska's Elvira is
as hysterically obsessive as any on disc, with a
mingled desperation and tragic grandeur in her
big Act 2 recitative: it's an exciting performance, certainly, though her phrasing can be
disconcertingly gusty.

Smooth *legato* is hardly a priority for Johannes
Weisser either. His Giovanni is less the sinister,
demonic anti-hero, more an over-sexed, heedless
young bounder with a taste for danger and a penchant for cruelty. He is casually seductive with
Sunhae Im's coquettish, sweet-toned Zerlina,
rapier-sharp in his exchanges with Leporello,
where his youthful, tenorish timbre contrasts
strongly with Lorenzo Regazzo's bass-baritone.
Regazzo's is a charismatic performance, never
descending to caricature; his lubricious relish in
the Catalogue aria does not preclude a hint of
elegance. The mellifluous-toned Kenneth Tarver
makes a sympathetic, concerned Ottavio, the
Masetto is aptly sullen, the Commendatore amply
imposing. But few could deny the zest, sweep and
sheer theatrical charge of this recording.

Additional recommendations

Don Giovanni [H]
Siepi Don Giovanni **Jurinac** Donna Elvira **Gencer**
Donna Anna **Lewis** Don Ottavio **Evans** Leporello
Freni Zerlina **Savoie** Masetto **Ward** Commendatore
Royal Opera House Chor & Orch / Solti
Royal Opera House Heritage Series mono ③
ROHS007 (173' · ADD). Recorded live 1962 Ⓜ
  If we buy these archive recordings it's usually not so
  much for the opera itself as for something specific
  about the performance. Here, what we might call
  the connoisseur-interest centres on the Donna

Anna of Leyla Gencer. She proves an excellent Mozartian stylist, singing both arias with exemplary cleanness and precision, and characterising with warmth and nobility. Her Ottavio is Richard Lewis. No connoisseur-interest there yet, his was the performance which gave the most pleasure. The others do more or less as expected, Jurinac with sturdy tone and ever-dependable technique, Freni with crystalline purity, Siepi with generous sonority, Evans with broad humour and a degree of vocal opulence in reserve. The Solti touch is specially evident at certain points.

Don Giovanni
Simon Keenlyside bar Don Giovanni **Joyce DiDonato** mez Donna Elvira **Marina Poplavskaya** sop Donna Anna **Ramón Vargas** ten Don Ottavio **Kyle Ketelsen** bass Leporello **Miah Persson** sop Zerlina **Robert Gleadow** bar Masetto **Eric Halfvarson** bass Commendatore
Chorus and Orchestra of the Royal Opera House, Covent Garden / Sir Charles Mackerras
Stage director **Francesca Zambello**
Video director **Robin Lough**
Opus Arte ② 💿 OA1009D (3h 22' · NTSC · 16:9 · PCM stereo and DTS 5.1 · 0). Recorded live   Ⓕ**OO**

This is eminently listenable and surprisingly viewable – 'surprisingly' because complaints were commonly heard concerning the production. It's not particularly edifying to see so much of Simon Keenlyside's torso or to have Giovanni taking his last supper in shorts, but by modern standards it's almost tasteful. And the singing is almost uniformly fine. If one of the cast is to be named above the rest, that should be Joyce DiDonato, an outstandingly accomplished Elvira, brilliantly projected, interestingly conceived, her singing concentrated in tone. Marina Poplavskaya's Anna is both dignified and sympathetic, and she too has remarkable command of the necessary technique. Yet the voice itself doesn't serve quite as well as one might have hoped, wanting more heft in 'Or sai chi l'onore' and more ease of passage in 'Non mi dir'. Miah Persson is an adorable Zerlina, and one liked what she and others were encouraged to do by way of vocal ornamentation.

Of the men, Giovanni is the least tested vocally though it's all to the good if he can turn a serenade as ingratiatingly as Keenlyside does. Ramón Vargas hardly looks a suitable lover for this Donna Anna but he sings both arias like the admirably reliable and gifted artist he is and has been for a good many years now. The Masetto looks rather too like the Leporello but that hardly matters and both deserve their applause. The Commendatore's uneven voice production does matter in spite of his sonorous bass notes and imposing stage presence. Mackerras at the helm is such a reassuringly familiar and well loved figure that we may be tempted to take him for granted. Happily the Covent Garden audience shows every sign of appreciation and the final curtain-call is deservedly his.

Additional recommendations

Don Giovanni
Drabowicz Don Giovanni **Schorg** Donna Anna **Gens** Donna Elvira **Martins** Zerlina **Reijans** Don Ottavio **Youn** Leporello **Bou** Masetto **Kocherga** Commendatore **Palau de la Música Catalana Chbr Ch; Gran Teatre del Liceu Orch / de Billy** Stage director **Bieito** Video director **Bargalló**
Opus Arte Ⓕ ② 💿 OA0921D
(156' · NTSC · PCM stereo and DTS 5.1 · 0)   Ⓕ

Calixto Bieito's staging of Mozart's *dramma giocoso* caused something close to apoplexy among the more conservative daily newspapers. Was this because, like da Ponte's libretto, the Catalan director's vision of the last hours in the life of the 'extremely licentious', not-very-noble man is set in a contemporary world of sex, violence, remorse and social and psychological breakdown? The crises that bind these characters' lives together are explored with unflinching directness. and there are any number of illuminations – the Giovanni/Leporello hierarchy of control/exploitation/need; the tabloid, Ibiza clubworld of Masetto and Zerlina; Gens's terrifyingly complete portrait of a woman who loves too much. The musical performance has its own distinction, as well as complete integration with the staging concept.

Don Giovanni
Álvarez Don Giovanni **Bayo** Donna Anna **Ganassi** Donna Elvira **Moreno** Zerlina **Bros** Don Ottavio **Regazzo** Leporello **Lopez** Masetto **Reiter** Commendatore **Madrid SO & Chor / Pérez** Stage director **Pasquel** Video director **Lough**
Opus Arte ② OA0958D (3h 28' · NTSC · 16:9 · PCM stereo and DTS 5.1 · 0)   Ⓕ

Updating is more or less de rigueur in today's operatic circles and Madrid once again comes up with the goods in a wholly plausible re-siting of *Giovanni* to 1940s Spain. The transfer of the various scenes is by and large convincing and Lluis Pasquel's perceptive ideas about the characters illuminate afresh the familiar story, with the opera's saturnine side very much to the fore. Carlos Álvarez, a Giovanni recalling in voice George London in the part, wholly dominates this opera with a nasty, driven reading of the lecher and bully. By his side is Lorenzo Regazzo as Leporello: he proves a wonderfully resourceful actor and singer, and a proper alter ego to his master. José Bros is a concerned Ottavio, whose long-breathed 'Il mio tesoro' is a wonder. Much the most exciting of the female singers is Sonia Ganassi's deeply felt, urgently sung Elvira.

Die Entführung aus dem Serail, K384

Die Entführung aus dem Serail   Ⓟ
Christine Schäfer sop Konstanze **Patricia Petibon** sop Blonde **Ian Bostridge** ten Belmonte **Iain Paton** ten Pedrillo **Alan Ewing** bass Osmin **Jürg Löw** spkr Pasha Selim **Les Arts Florissants / William Christie**
Erato ② 3984 25490-2 (127' · DDD · T/t)   Ⓕ

Reviewing the Strasbourg production of which this recording is based, *Opera*'s Andrew Clark commented that Christie sets 'brisk but flexible tempi, and builds the ensembles into a fever of musical jubilation'. That is all amply confirmed in this finely balanced, intimate recording. In the Overture and some of the early numbers, Christie is inclined to clip his rhythms with almost brusque accents, but once the Pasha and Konstanze appear on the scene, he settles into an interpretation that evinces the elevated sensibility that informs his Rameau and Handel on disc, strong on detail but never at the expense of the whole picture.

But then he has by his side a Konstanze to stop all hearts. Having delivered herself of a fleet, easy 'Ach, ich liebte', Schäfer (who wasn't in the original cast) pierces further than does any other interpreter into the soul of the woman who is both physically and emotionally imprisoned. From the deeply felt, vulnerable recitative leading into 'Traurigkeit' she pours out Konstanze's woes in that pure, plaintive, highly individual tone of hers and, above all, offers a wonderfully fresh and inward execution of the text. With Christie going all the way with her, musically speaking, 'Traurigkeit' itself is heart-rending in its G minor sorrowing, 'Martern aller Arten' the epitome of determined defiance and resolution. Try the final section from 'Doch du bist entschlossen' – have you ever heard it sound so resolute, so detailed?

In the great Act 2 Quartet and the last-act duet, where Mozart peers into his musical future, she is just as moving and inspires Bostridge to equal heights of tender inflexion. At first you may find Bostridge lightweight for Belmonte, but in the context of this period-instrument performance, with a small band, his silvery voice and Mozartian know-how carry the day, though his voice sometimes sounds disconcertingly similar to the nimble, ingratiating tenor of the Pedrillo, Iain Paton.

Like her mistress in her role, Petibon gives us a Blonde to make us forget just about every other soprano in the part on disc. She plays with and smiles through her opening aria with a delightful freedom of technique and expression, nothing daunted by its tessitura, even adding decorations to the already-demanding vocal line (the whole recording is literally adorned by small embellishments, naturally delivered). She maintains this high standard throughout in a winning performance.

As Osmin, Ewing's vibrant, individual bass-baritone is attractive on its own account but, as on the other period-instrument performances, one does rather miss a true bass voice in such a low-lying part, and Ewing proves a benevolent, homely Osmin rather than a threatening one. But, like all the other singers and the keenly spoken Pasha of Löw, he fits easily into the performance's overall and likeable concept, so I am not inclined to labour this slight drawback.

Christie includes all the recently rediscovered music, but opts for a shorter amount of dialogue than many. Its delivery is easy and idiomatic. And the recording is excellent.

Additional recommendations

Die Entführung aus dem Serail
Aikin Konstanze **Montvidas** Belmonte **Rydl** Osmin
Erdmann Blonde **Smallwood** Pedrillo van
Watermeulen Pasha Selim **Netherlands Opera Chor
& Chamber Orchestra / Constantinos Carydis**
Stage director **Simons** *Video director* **Vermeiren**
Opus Arte ② 📀 OA1003D (3h 34' · NTSC · 16:9 ·
PCM stereo and DTS 5.1 · 0)   Ⓕ

Director Johan Simons's take on *Die Entführung* is summed up by a remark in one of the accompanying interviews: 'At the end people see that the Pasha is a much better match for Konstanze than Belmonte is.' Other productions have suggested a mutual attraction between the heroine and her oriental captor. Simons carries this to extremes. His staging is dominated by Konstanze's inner struggle between her loyalty to her betrothed and her disturbing feelings for the man who, we sense, has awakened her sexually. Constantinos Carydis conducts the excellent Netherlands CO with zest and a fair sense of period style. While many will prefer a more comically straightforward staging, Simons's production certainly makes you think afresh about Mozart's ostensibly innocent, happily-ever-after harem Singspiel.

Die Entführung aus dem Serail   Ⓟ
Hartelius Konstanze **Léger** Blonde **Klink** Belmonte
Felix Pedrillo **Smilek** Osmin **Moshkin-Ghalam** Pasha
Selim **Europa Academy Chorus; Les Musiciens du
Louvre / Minkowski** *Stage directors* **Deschamps** &
Makeïeff *Video director* **Kent**
Bel Air Classiques 📀 BAC028 (128' · NTSC · 16:9 ·
PCM stereo, 5.0 and DTS 5.1 · 0)   Ⓕ

Marc Minkowski is the moving spirit of the performance and 'moving' is the right epithet, as most of his speeds are on the fast side. He assembled a fine young cast, all of whom are up to their taxing parts, headed by Malin Hartelius as Konstanze, who is at once a visually attractive performer, absolutely tireless in her three arias, and at the same time projects a very moving portrayal. She is partnered by a promising young tenor in Matthias Klink as Belmonte. But in a way the star of the cast is Shahrokh Moshkin-Ghalam, who makes the Pasha Selim both sympathetic and believable. The stage direction and sets are simple and quite effective.

Die Entführung aus dem Serail
Mei Konstanze **Ciofi** Blonde **Trost** Belmonte
Montazeri Pedrillo **Rydl** Osmin **John** Pasha Selim
**Chor & Orch of Maggio Musicale Fiorentino /
Mehta** *Stage director* **Gramss** *Video director* **Blume**
TDK Mediactive 📀 DV-OPEADS (136' · 16:9 · 2.0,
5.1 & DTS 5.1 · 0)   ⒻⓄ

What a pleasure it is to come upon this *Seraglio*, freshly recorded in Florence's beautiful Teatro della Pergola. It's straightforward without being staid, a crisp, witty, fast-moving production – and in Christoph Wagenknecht's colourful set, a seascape fronted with swiftly sliding panels in Turkish patterns, visually delightful as well. Musically, too, it holds its end up. Zubin Mehta isn't an ideal Mozartian, but he conducts with affectionate warmth and theatrical verve, and he has a first-rate cast. This performance is very satisfying – and entirely recommendable.

Idomeneo, re di Creta, K366

Idomeneo   P
Anthony Rolfe Johnson ten Idomeneo **Anne Sofie von Otter** mez Idamante **Sylvia McNair** sop Ilia **Hillevi Martinpelto** sop Elettra **Nigel Robson** ten Arbace **Glenn Winslade** ten High Priest **Cornelius Hauptmann** bass Oracle **Monteverdi Choir; English Baroque Soloists / Sir John Eliot Gardiner**
Archiv ③ 431 674-2AH3 (3h 31' · DDD · T/t)
Ⓕ❍❍❍❍▷

This is unquestionably the most vital and authentic account of *Idomeneo* to date on disc (though see the more recent review of the Mackerras set below). We have here what was given at the work's first performance in Munich plus, in appendices, what Mozart wanted, or was forced, to cut before that premiere and the alternative versions of certain passages, so that various combinations of the piece can be programmed by the listener. Gardiner's direct, dramatic conducting catches ideally the agony of Idomeneo's terrible predicament – forced to sacrifice his son because of an unwise row. This torment of the soul is also entirely conveyed by Anthony Rolfe Johnson in the title-role to which Anne Sofie von Otter's moving Idamante is an apt foil. Sylvia McNair is a diaphanous, pure-voiced Ilia, Hillevi Martinpelto a properly fiery, sharp-edged Elettra. With dedicated support from his own choir and orchestra, who obviously benefited from a long period of preparation, Gardiner matches the stature of this noble *opera seria*. The recording catches the excitement which all who heard the live performances will recall.

Idomeneo
Ian Bostridge ten Idomeneo **Lorraine Hunt Lieberson** mez Idamante **Lisa Milne** sop Ilia **Barbara Frittoli** sop Elettra **Anthony Rolfe Johnson** ten Arbace **Paul Charles Clarke** ten High Priest **John Relyea** bass Oracle **Dunedin Consort; Edinburgh Festival Chorus; Scottish Chamber Orchestra / Sir Charles Mackerras**
EMI ③ 557260-2 (3h 23' · DDD · T/t)   Ⓕ❍❍

There were golden opinions for the *Idomeneo* given at 2001's Edinburgh Festival by these performers, and here it is on CD. The work is given complete, at the marvellously extravagant length at which Mozart initially planned it, bar some small (and authentic) cuts in the *secco* recitative. And it works. It works triumphantly, in fact. That's partly due to Mackerras's truly inspired reading of the score, and his insights into the meaning of its musical gestures. This is a score full of gestures, heavy with emotional significance, not only in the arias and the ensembles but perhaps above all in the orchestral recitative that

abounds in this score as in no other of Mozart's. It's partly the expressiveness of Mackerras's handling of what's, in effect, Mozart's emotional commentary on the unfolding of the plot that makes this performance so powerful. He has a clear vision of the expressive messages that Mozart transmits through texture or harmony or dynamic or rhythmic refinement.

The performance is also full of dramatic energy. During the Overture you experience that tingle in your spine that comes of the expectation of a curtain about to rise. Never mind that this isn't a 'period instrument' performance: the textures are as lucid as one could wish, the articulation as light and precise, the balance as just. Tempi are unhurried.

Ian Bostridge makes a strong Idomeneo. His opening aria, 'Vedrommi intorno', is exquisitely done, smoothly and lovingly phrased. Mozart wrote it in a traditional style to flatter the voice of his original singer, Anton Raaff. Just here and there, and especially in the closing aria, one might perhaps have liked more variety of tone and in particular more soft and lyrical colouring. Idamante, originally a castrato part, is sung by a mezzo, and one can't imagine one much better than Lorraine Hunt Lieberson: it's a lovely, focused sound, with the firm centre that a male part needs, and there are many happy details of phrasing. Lisa Milne provides a sympathetic yet not frail Ilia, with a clear and warm ring to the voice. The singing of Barbara Frittoli as Elettra has properly a bit more edge to it and there's plenty of tension and power to her first aria and especially her stormy final one, 'D'Oreste, d'Ajace'. With Anthony Rolfe Johnson to sing Arbace, both of that character's arias (as well as his important accompanied recitatives) are given, understandably, although the second in particular isn't on the level of most of the score – Mozart probably excluded both of them in his own performances. It's a joy to hear them so beautifully sung; the *legato* line and the smooth large leaps in the first are a delight.

The chorus is first-rate, and there's excellent orchestral playing. This set, enshrining Mackerras's profound and mature understanding of the music, is deeply moving; readers are urged to buy it.

Idomeneo
Philip Langridge ten Idomeneo **Jerry Hadley** ten Idamante **Yvonne Kenny** sop Ilia **Carol Vaness** sop Elettra **Thomas Hemsley** bar Arbace **Anthony Roden** ten High Priest **Roderick Kennedy** bass Oracle **Glyndebourne Chorus; London Philharmonic Orchestra / Bernard Haitink**
Stage director **Trevor Nunn**
Video director **Christopher Swann**
Warner Music Vision/NVC Arts ▩ 5050467 3922-2-9 (3h 1' · NTSC · 4:3 · 2.0 · 2-6). Recorded live   Ⓢ

Trevor Nunn produced his first opera, *Idomeneo*, Glyndebourne in 1983, with felicitous results. John Napier's designs imaginatively evoke the Cretan milieu, supported by restrained, dignified costumes and lighting. The spare setting now seems a model beside what usually passes for decor today. Within it Nunn directs his principals and chorus with economic yet pointed care.

Philip Langridge is a compellingly distraught and haunted Idomeneo, singing with his customary feeling for word-painting. He easily encompasses the longer version of 'Fuor del mar'. Carol Vaness offers a fiery, richly contoured Elettra. Yvonne Kenny's beautifully sung Ilia is more conventional and Jerry Hadley is a fresh, pleasing Idamante. Bernard Haitink conducts a lithe, forward-moving account of the score, though you'll need a high volume setting to get the best out of the sound.

Additional recommendation

Idomeneo
Croft Idomeneo **Fink** Idamante **Sunhae Im** Ilia
Pendatchanska Elettra **Tarver** Arbace **Rivenq** High
Priest **Tittoto** Oracle **RIAS Chamber Choir; Freiburg
Baroque Orch / Jacobs**
Harmonia Mundi ③ HMC90 2036/8
(3h 11' · DDD' · S/T/t/N)   ⒻⒹ→
Like Gardiner and Mackerras, René Jacobs treats the work as an urgent, desperate human drama. He goes even further than they do in presenting every note of the opera as it was originally conceived, including by far the longest version of the Oracle's speech, willingly jettisoned by Mozart. Jacobs's cast is not quite ideal. Yet if you can take his interventionist continuo and occasional eccentricities of tempo, this new version, beautifully recorded, at its best eclipses all comers in dramatic tension, not least in the magnificent, anguished account of the great Act 3 quartet.

Lucio Silla, K135

Lucio Silla
Lothar Odinius ten Lucio Silla **Simone Nold** sop
Giunia **Kristina Hammarström** mez Cecilio
Henriette Bonde-Hansen sop Cinna **Susanne
Elmark** sop Celia **Jakob Naeslund Madsen** ten
Aufidio **Ars Nova Copenhagen; Danish Radio
Sinfonietta / Adám Fischer**
Dacapo ③ 8 226069/71 (170' · DDD)   Ⓕ

The Milan premiere of *Lucio Silla*, on Boxing Day 1772, was a near-fiasco: ham acting from the last-minute tenor and the prima donna in a sulk. But from the second performance Mozart's second *opera seria* was an unalloyed triumph. The libretto is lumbering, sententious and dubiously motivated, culminating in an astonishing volte-face in which the sadistically ruthless Emperor suddenly morphs into a paragon of Enlightenment clemency. Not that this would have bothered 16-year-old Mozart's audiences one iota. What they came for – and got in spades – were varied and inventive arias that showcased the star singers.

The central roles of Giunia and her betrothed, the banished senator Cecilio (written for the castrato Rauzzini), inspired Mozart to his most powerful operatic music to date: darkly coloured accompanied recitatives that look forward to *Idomeneo*, Cecilio's anguished aria of parting, 'Ah, se a morir', a Gluckian *ombra* aria for Giunia as she prepares for death, and a dramatic trio that pits the two lovers against the raging Emperor.

This 2001-02 recording from Danish Radio archives is well sung and excitingly conducted. Adám Fischer encourages playing of quivering energy from the trim, lean-toned Danish orchestra. In the accompanied recitatives the players grieve and rage as vividly as the singers. Only Fischer's jerky tempo fluctuations, à la Harnoncourt, in the trio fail to convince.

While there are no big names among the soloists, they have fresh, youthful-sounding voices, and cope elegantly with Mozart's coloratura demands. As the put-upon heroine Giunia, Simone Nold sings with grace and agility, and fiery intensity, too – try the agitated Act 2 aria 'Parto, m'affretto'. Kristina Hammarström impresses especially in Cecilio's sombre memento mori scene in Act 1 and the spectacular vengeance aria 'Quest' improvviso tremito'. The secondary pair of lovers, Cecilio's friend Cinna and the Emperor's blithely innocent sister Celia, are equally well cast, Susanne Elmark dispatching high *staccato* passages with delightful insouciance.

The recording gives the orchestra plenty of presence without short-changing the singers. This is now the version to have of an ambitious, over-long but often richly expressive opera.

Mitridate, re di Ponto, K87

Mitridate, re di Ponto
Mathias Zachariassen ten Mitridate **Henriette
Bonde-Hansen** sop Aspasia **Maria Fontosh** sop
Sifare **Kristina Hammarström** mez Farnace **Lisa
Larsson** sop Ismene **Anders J Dahlin** ten Marzio
Sine Bundgaard sop Arbate **Ars Nova
Copenhagen; Danish Radio Sinfonietta /
Adam Fischer**
Dacapo ③ 🎵 6 220580/82 (168' · DDD)   Ⓕ❶❷❸❹Ⓓ→

 Adam Fischer's interpretation of the 14-year-old Mozart's first attempt at an *opera seria*, recorded by Danish Radio in March 2002, now makes its belated appearance on CD. The Danish Radio Sinfonietta play with an ideal balance between lean rhythmic articulation and shapely melodic phrasing. Fischer conducts with a sure sense of pacing; dramatic details in the orchestral ritornellos of each aria are astutely brought out. His versatile shading of the orchestra during the contrasting slow and fast sections of Sifare's 'Parto, nel gran cimento' is sensitively attuned to Maria Fontosh's switches between tender melodic outpourings and flowing coloratura. The emergence of vigorous orchestral nuances in Farnace's defiant outburst 'Venga pur, minacci e frema' is exemplary because the marvellous Kristina

Hammarström is never forced to compete for attention. Mathias Zachariassen navigates notoriously wide leaps with unusual assurance in his entrance cavata 'Se di lauri il crine adorno'; Zachariassen also copes better than most with the fiendish technical gauntlet thrown down at him in the furious 'Quel ribelle e quell'ingrato'.

Most impressively, this performance captures the full theatrical potency of the unfurling plot. At the heart of Act 3, Henriette Bonde-Hansen's solemn characterisation of Aspasia coming to terms with being forced to drink poison is showstopping. The lighter voices of Sine Bundgaard and Lisa Larsson suit the roles of Arbate and Ismene perfectly, and Anders J Dahlin neatly dispatches the small role of the Roman tribune Marzio. Harpsichordist Richard Lewis prepared the performing edition by abridging the original recitative, adding trumpets and timpani to four numbers with military overtones (some may doubt that this was necessary), and providing a cadenza for the horn obbligato in Sifare's 'Lungi da te' (beautifully played by Thomas Kjelldén). It's hard to imagine a more satisfying Mozart opera recording.

Le nozze di Figaro, K492

Le nozze di Figaro   **P**
Lorenzo Regazzo bass Figaro **Patrizia Ciofi** sop Susanna **Simon Keenlyside** bar Count Almaviva **Véronique Gens** sop Countess Almaviva **Angelika Kirchschlager** mez Cherubino **Marie McLaughlin** sop Marcellina **Antonio Abete** bass Bartolo, Antonio **Kobie van Rensburg** ten Don Basilio, Don Curzio **Nuria Rial** sop Barbarina **Ghent Collegium Vocale; Concerto Köln / René Jacobs**
Harmonia Mundi ③ HMC90 1818/20 (172' · DDD · T/t)
Ⓕ **OOO**➼

Ⓖ René Jacobs always brings new ideas to the operas he conducts, and even to a work as familiar as *Figaro* he adds something of his own. First of all he offers an orchestral balance quite unlike what we are used to. Those who specially relish a Karajan or a Solti will hardly recognise the work, with its strongly wind-biased orchestral balance: you simply don't hear the violins as the 'main line' of the music. An excellent corrective to a tradition that was untrue to Mozart, to be sure, but possibly the pendulum has swung a little too far.

Jacobs is freer over tempo than most conductors. The Count's authoritarian pronouncements are given further weight by a faster tempo: it gives them extra decisiveness, though the music then has to slow down. There are other examples of such flexibility, sometimes a shade disconcerting, but always with good dramatic point. The Count's Act 3 duet with Susanna is one example: the little hesitancies enhanced and pointed up, if perhaps with some loss in energy and momentum. Tempi are generally on the quick side of normal, notably in the earlier parts of the Act 2 finale; but Jacobs is willing to hold back, too, for example in the

MOZART LE NOZZE DI FIGARO – IN BRIEF

Lorenzo Regazzo Figaro **Simon Keenlyside**   **P** Count Almaviva **Véronique Gens** Countess Almaviva **Collegium Vocale; Concerto Köln / René Jacobs** Ⓜ**OOO**
Harmonia Mundi ③ HMC90 1818/20 (172' · DDD)
A new contender in a crowded field, Jacobs's performance is idiosyncratic but both finely detailed and entertaining, with a particularly strong cast.

Bryn Terfel Figaro **Rodney Gilfry** Count   **P** Almaviva **Hillevi Martinpelto** Countess Almaviva **Monteverdi Choir; English Baroque Soloists / Sir John Eliot Gardiner**
Archiv ③ 439 871-2AH3 (179' · DDD)   Ⓕ**O**
A brilliant period-instrument set recorded live. Brisker and lighter-hued than the old school, with a superior cast but a rather obtrusive audience.

Cesare Siepi Figaro **Alfred Poell** Count Almaviva **Lisa della Casa** Countess Almaviva **Vienna State Opera Chorus; Vienna PO / Erich Kleiber**   Ⓗ
Decca ③ 478 1720DC (172' · ADD)   Ⓢ**OO**
In the great Viennese tradition, conducted with fleet-footed dramatic energy, with a cast of rather heavyweight but exceptionally beautiful voices, albeit on a recording that is showing its age.

Samuel Ramey Figaro **Thomas Allen** Count Almaviva **Kiri Te Kanawa** Countess Almaviva **London Opera Chorus, London PO / Sir Georg Solti**
Decca ③ 410 150-2DH3 (169' · DDD)   Ⓕ**O**➼
Large-scale Mozart, but conducted with irresistible verve and wit, and an outstanding ensemble, all in a brilliant modern recording.

Hermann Prey Figaro **Dietrich Fischer-Dieskau** Count Almaviva **Gundula Janowitz** Countess Almaviva **Deutsche Oper Chor & Orch / Karl Böhm**
DG ③ 449 728-2GOR3 (173' · ADD)   Ⓜ
Strongly cast with Janowitz as a fiery Countess; Troyanos is a sparky Cherubino and Mathis enchanting as Susanna. Fischer-Dieskau and Prey spar splendidly. And over everything, Böhm presides magnificently. The sound is still immediate and impressive.

Heinz Blankenburg Figaro **Gabriel Bacquier**   Ⓗ Count Almaviva **Leyla Gencer** Countess **Royal Philharmonic Orchestra / Silvio Varviso**
Glyndebourne ③ GFOCD001-62 (162' · ADD)   Ⓕ
A 1962 night at Glyndebourne that enshrines the best Mozartian style of the old house. The young Silvio Varviso conducts with wonderful panache and the cast includes Mirella Freni's enchanting Susanna and Gencer's world-weary Countess. Blankenburg and Bacquier spar splendidly.

Susanna-Marcellina duet, in the fandango, and in the G major music at the denouement where the Count begs forgiveness.

The cast is excellent. Véronique Gens offers a beautifully natural, shapely 'Porgi amor' and a passionate and spirited 'Dove sono'. The laughter in Patrizia Ciofi's voice is delightful when she's dressing up Cherubino, and she has space in 'Deh vieni' for a touchingly expressive performance. Then there's Angelika Kirchschlager's Cherubino, alive and urgent in 'Non so più', every little phrase neatly moulded. Lorenzo Regazzo offers a strong Figaro, with a wide range of voice – angry and determined in 'Se vuol ballare', nicely rhythmic with some softer colours in 'Non più andrai', and pain and bitterness in 'Aprite'. The Count of Simon Keenlyside is powerful, menacing, lean and dark in tone. Marie McLaughlin sings Marcellina with unusual distinction.

Strongly cast, imaginatively directed: it's a *Figaro* well worth hearing.

Le nozze di Figaro   🄿
Bryn Terfel *bass-bar* Figaro **Alison Hagley** *sop* Susanna **Rodney Gilfry** *bar* Count Almaviva **Hillevi Martinpelto** *sop* Countess Almaviva **Pamela Helen Stephen** *mez* Cherubino **Susan McCulloch** *sop* Marcellina **Carlos Feller** *bass* Bartolo **Francis Egerton** *ten* Don Basilio, Don Curzio **Julian Clarkson** *bass* Antonio **Constanze Backes** *sop* Barbarina **Monteverdi Choir; English Baroque Soloists /
Sir John Eliot Gardiner**
Archiv Produktion ③ 439 871-2AH3 (179' · DDD · T/t)
Recorded live 1993   Ⓕ🅞🅑➤

The catalogue of *Figaro* recordings is long, and the cast lists are full of famous names. In this version only one principal had more than half a dozen recordings behind him, and some had none at all. Yet this version can stand comparison with any, not only for its grasp of the drama but also for the quality of its singing. It's more evidently a period-instrument recording than many under Gardiner. The string tone is pared down and makes modest use of vibrato, the woodwind is soft-toned. The voices are generally lighter and fresher-sounding than those on most recordings, and the balance permits more than usual to be heard of Mozart's instrumental commentary on the action and the characters. The recitative is done with exceptional life and feeling for its meaning and dramatic import, with a real sense of lively, urgent conversation.

Bryn Terfel and Alison Hagley make an outstanding Figaro and Susanna. Terfel has enough darkness in his voice to sound menacing in 'Se vuol ballare' as well as bitter in 'Aprite un po' quegli occhi'; it's an alert, mettlesome performance – and he also brings off a superlative 'Non più andrai'. Hagley offers a reading of spirit and allure. The interplay between her and the woodwind in 'Venite inginocchiatevi' is a delight, and her cool but heartfelt 'Deh vieni' is very beautiful. Once or twice her intonation seems marginally under stress but that's the small price you pay for

singing with so little vibrato. Hillevi Martinpelto's unaffected, youthful-sounding Countess is enjoyable; both arias are quite lightly done, with a very lovely, warm, natural sound in 'Dove sono' especially. Some may prefer a more polished, sophisticated reading, of the traditional kind, but this is closer to what Mozart would have wanted and expected.

Rodney Gilfry provides a Count with plenty of fire and authority, firmly focused in tone; the outburst at the *Allegro assai* in 'Vedrò mentr'io sospiro' is formidable. Pamela Helen Stephen's Cherubino sounds charmingly youthful and impetuous. There's no want of dramatic life in Gardiner's direction. His tempi are marginally quicker than most, and the orchestra often speaks eloquently of the drama.

Additional recommendations

Le nozze di Figaro   Ⓗ
Siepi Figaro **Gueden** Susanna **Poell** Count Almaviva **della Casa** Countess Almaviva **Danco** Cherubino **Rössl-Majdan** Marcellina **Corena** Bartolo **Dickie** Don Basilio **Meyer-Welfing** Don Curzio **Pröglhöf** Antonio **Felbermayer** Barbarina **Vienna State Opera Chor;
VPO / E Kleiber**
Decca Legends ③ 478 1720DC (172' · ADD)
Recorded 1955   Ⓢ🅞🅞

Kleiber's *Figaro* is a classic of the classics of the gramophone: beautifully played by the Vienna Philharmonic, conducted with poise and vitality and a real sense of the drama unfolding through the music. It's very much a Viennese performance, not perhaps as graceful or as effervescent as some but warm, sensuous and alive to the interplay of character. The true star is Erich Kleiber. The beginning of the opera sets your spine tingling with theatrical expectation. Act 1 goes at pretty smart tempi, but all through he insists on full musical value. There's no rushing in the confrontations at the end of Act 2 – all is measured and properly argued through. The sound is satisfactory, for a set of this vintage, and no lover of this opera should be without it.

Le nozze di Figaro   Ⓗ
Blankenburg Figaro **Freni** Susanna **Bacquier** *bar* Count Almaviva **Gencer** Countess **Mathis** Cherubino **Cava** Bartolo **Peters** Marcellina **Cuénod** Don Basilio **Kentish** Don Curzio **Davies** Antonio **Zeri** Barbarina **McCarry** Bridesmaid **Glyndebourne Chorus;
RPO / Varviso**
Glyndebourne ③ GFOCD001-62 (162' · ADD)
Recorded live 1962   Ⓕ

The young Silvio Varviso made his Glyndebourne debut as conductor of *Figaro*. Count (Gabriel Bacquier) and Countess (Leyla Gencer) were other newcomers and Mirella Freni was singing Susanna for the first time anywhere. As heard here, everything takes its place with a delightful combination of freshness and assurance, and the audience clearly (and more audibly after the interval) responds appreciatively. The recording seems to catch the stage action almost as well as if it were a DVD, though the women's voices are apt to acquire that bright hard edge which is the accursed associate of digital remastering: still, not as badly as some. Gencer's vibrant, almost tragic tone distinguishes her Countess, and as (nearly) always at Glyndebourne the ensemble work is a model of stylish efficiency.

Le nozze di Figaro
Knut Skram bass Figaro **Ileana Cotrubas** sop
Susanna **Benjamin Luxon** bar Count Almaviva **Kiri Te
Kanawa** sop Countess Almaviva **Frederica von
Stade** mez Cherubino **Nucci Condò** sop Marcellina
Marius Rintzler bass Bartolo **Glyndebourne Chorus;
London Philharmonic Orchestra / John Pritchard**
Stage director **Peter Hall**
Video director **Dave Heather**
ArtHaus Musik 🎬 101 089 (3h 5' · NTSC · 4:3 · PCM
stereo · 0). Recorded live   Ⓕ

Peter Hall's Glyndebourne *Figaro* of 1973 was his memorable first effort at staging Mozart, and was much praised at the time. His unfussy production is set in John Bury's lived-in, warmly coloured decor and combines well with John Pritchard's unassumingly stylish conducting. Dave Heather's TV direction is worthy of the original, and the picture looks as if it might have been filmed yesterday. The sound, however, lacks a little in clarity and range.

The cast that season was choice. Kiri Te Kanawa, youthful of mien, glowing of voice, sings the Countess. It is a wonderful memento of her great promise and appreciable achievement at the time. Her admirably priapic Count is Benjamin Luxon, singing with firm, velvet tone and a fine line. The participants below stairs are of equal stature. Ileana Cotrubas is an alert, cool-headed and warm-hearted Susanna, and she sings faultlessly. Knut Skram, her Figaro, isn't such a definite character, but is unobtrusively right. The young Frederica von Stade's Cherubino is sparky and wide-eyed if vocally a little thin. It's a cast welded into a true and rewarding ensemble.

Die Zauberflöte, K620

Die Zauberflöte   Ⓟ
Rosa Mannion sop Pamina **Natalie Dessay** sop
Queen of the Night **Hans-Peter Blochwitz** ten Tamino
Anton Scharinger bass Papageno **Reinhard Hagen**
bass Sarastro **Willard White** bass Speaker **Steven
Cole** ten Monostatos **Linda Kitchen** sop Papagena
Anna Maria Panzarella sop Doris **Lamprecht** mez
Delphine Haidan contr First, Second and Third Ladies
**Damien Colin, Patrick Olivier Croset, Stéphane
Dutournier** trebs First, Second and Third Boys
Christopher Josey ten First Armed Man, First Priest
Laurent Naouri bass Second Armed Man, Second
Priest **Les Arts Florissants / William Christie**
Erato ③ 0630 12705-2 (150' · DDD · T/t)   Ⓜ

With a background primarily in the French Baroque, William Christie comes to *Die Zauber-*

flöte from an angle quite unlike anyone else's; yet this is as idiomatic and as deeply Mozartian a reading as any. In the booklet-note Christie remarks on the unforced singing that's one of his objectives, much more manageable with the gentler sound of period instruments. All this is borne out by the performance itself, which falls sweetly and lovingly on the ear.

Overall the performance is quick and light-textured – and often quite dramatic. Some may find Christie less responsive than many more traditional interpreters to the quicksilver changes in mood, yet this is a part of his essentially broad and gentle view of *Die Zauberflöte*. His cast has few famous names, though there's Hans-Peter Blochwitz, probably the finest Tamino around these days. As Pamina, Rosa Mannion has much charm and a hint of girlish vivacity, but blossoms into maturity and passion in 'Ach, ich fühl's', whose final phrases, as the wind instruments fall away, leaving her alone and desolate, are very moving. Natalie Dessay's Queen of the Night is forthright, clean and well tuned, with ample weight and tonal glitter.

The orchestral playing from Les Arts Florissants is polished, and the translucent sound is a joy. In short, Christie offers a very satisfying, acutely musical view of the work.

Die Zauberflöte
Dorothea Röschmann sop Pamina **Erika Miklósa**
sop Queen of the Night **Christoph Strehl** ten Tamino
Hanno Müller-Brachmann bass-bar Papageno **René
Pape** bass Sarastro **Kurt Azesberger** ten Monostatos
Julia Kleiter sop Papagena **George Zeppenfeld**
bass Speaker **Arnold Schoenberg Choir; Mahler
Chamber Orchestra / Claudio Abbado**
DG ② 477 5789GH2 (149' · DDD · T/t)
Recorded live 2005   ⒻⒹ

This is certainly the most desirable version using modern instruments to appear since Solti's second recording in 1990. That said, its characteristics are rather nearer William Christie's 1995 period performance (reviewed above). Abbado undertook the opera for the first time in performances in Italy in 2005, directed by his son (the production was seen at the 2006 Edinburgh Festival). On this occasion, he conducts a direct, keenly articulated, inspiriting account of the score, obviously aware of what has been achieved in recent times by the authenticists, yet when he reaches the work at its most Masonic – the Act 2 trio and the scene with the Armed Men, Tamino and Pamina – Abbado, directing his beloved Mahler Chamber Orchestra, gives the music its true and wondrous import. The playing throughout is alert and scrupulously articulated.

Casts varied between performances; here Abbado assembled one predominantly chosen from a youngish generation of German-speaking singers, each of whom approaches his or her role with fresh sound and interprets it in impeccably Mozartian style. The Tamino and Pamina are well nigh faultless. Tamino has been taken by

MOZART DIE ZAUBERFLÖTE – IN BRIEF

Ruth Ziesak *Pamina* **Uwe Heilmann** *Tamino*
Kurt Moll *Sarastro* **Vienna State Opera Choir;**
Vienna PO / Sir Georg Solti
Decca ② 433 210-2DH2 (152' · DDD)   Ⓕ ⚫⚫Ɗ
Crisply brilliant yet warm and well-paced
conducting, with a superlative cast, clear-
voiced and refreshingly youthful – except for
Kurt Moll's appropriately grave Sarastro –
drawn from a stage production, and vividly
recorded. Solti's Mozart at its freshest.

Rosa Mannion *Pamina* **Hans-Peter Blochwitz** Ⓟ
Tamino **Reinhard Hagen** *Sarastro* **Les Arts**
Florissants / William Christie
Erato ③ 0630 12705-2 (150' · DDD)   Ⓜ
The best original-instrument version and
among the best ever, a graceful, well-paced
reading with plenty of magic and a memora-
ble cast including Rosa Mannion's passionate
Pamina, Natalie Dessay's cut-glass Queen
and Willard White the Speaker.

Tiana Lemnitz *Pamina* **Helge Rosvaenge** Ⓗ
Tamino **Wilhelm Strienz** *Sarastro* **Favres Solisten**
Vereinigung; Berlin PO / Sir Thomas Beecham
Naxos mono ② 8 110127/8 (130' · AAD)   Ⓜ⚫⚫
A pre-war classic in very reasonable sound,
albeit dialogue-free, vibrantly conducted by
Beecham with a memorable cast including
Tiana Lemnitz and the great Gerhard Hüsch
as Papageno.

Gundula Janowitz *Pamina* **Nicolai Gedda**
Tamino **Gottlob Frick** *Sarastro* **Philharmonia**
Chorus and Orchestra / Otto Klemperer
EMI ② 567388-2 (134' · ADD)   Ⓜ Ɗ
Old-fashioned, grave and monumental, omit-
ting dialogue, but enshrining some glorious
singing from Nicolai Gedda, the young
Lucia Popp and Gundula Janowitz, and
Elisabeth Schwarzkopf and Christa Ludwig
among the Ladies.

Rebecca Evans *Pamina* **Barry Banks** *Tamino*
John Tomlinson *Sarastro* **London Philharmonic**
Orchestra / Sir Charles Mackerras
Chandos/Peter Moores Foundation Opera in
English ② CHAN3121 (137' · DDD)   Ⓜ⚫⚫Ɗ
A superb English-language version that is not
only beautifully cast (Keenlyside, Garrett and
Tomlinson all ideal), but magisterially con-
ducted by a great Mozartian.

Elizabeth Norberg-Schulz *Pamina* **Herbert**
Lippert *Tamino* **Georg Tichy** *Papageno* **Failoni**
Orchestra, Budapest / Michael Halász
Naxos ② 8 660030/1 (149' · DDD)   Ⓢ Ɗ
A fine bargain-price introduction, a satisfyingly theatrical performance with a cast
including rising stars such as Herbert Lippert
and Hellen Kwon, and Halász's lively conducting, very well recorded.

many outstanding tenors on disc but Christoph
Strehl sings with a Wunderlich-like strength and
beauty, and rather more light and shade than his
famous predecessor brought to the role. His is a
wonderfully virile, vital reading that gives pleasure to the ear, as much in ensemble as in aria. He
is partnered by Dorothea Röschmann, who has
already appeared as Pamina at Covent Garden,
and in many other houses. Her full-throated,
positive singing, finely shaped, cleanly articulated, is a true match for Strehl's.

Hanno Müller-Brachmann is a properly lively
and amusing Papageno, and delivers the role in
a richer bass-baritone than many interpreters
provide. He doesn't attempt a Viennese accent
in the dialogue (a fairly full version), but brings
plenty of simple humour to the part. The high
and low roles are well catered for. The Hungarian coloratura Erika Miklósa has been making a
speciality of the Queen of the Night over the
past few years and shows just why in a technically secure and fiery account of her two arias.
René Pape sings Sarastro: now at the peak of his
career, he conveys all the role's gravity and dignity in a gloriously sung performance. Kurt
Azesberger is a suitably nasty Monostatos.

Abbado allows a few neatly executed decorations. The extensive dialogue, spoken in a manner suitable for the theatre, sometimes sounds
over-emphatic in the home, with the Papagena
as an old woman the worst culprit. The recording is reasonably well balanced. As a whole the
performance conveys a welcome immediacy and
spontaneity and the daring of Abbado's way with
the score is very alluring.

The Magic Flute (sung in English)
Rebecca Evans *sop* Pamina **Elizabeth Vidal** *sop*
Queen of Night **Barry Banks** *ten* Tamino **Simon**
Keenlyside *bar* Papageno **John Tomlinson** *bass*
Sarastro **Christopher Purves** *bass* Speaker **John**
Graham-Hall *ten* Monostatos **Lesley Garrett** *sop*
Papagena **Majella Cullagh** *sop* First Lady **Sarah Fox**
sop Second Lady **Diana Montague** *mez* Third Lady
Geoffrey Mitchell Choir; London Philharmonic
Orchestra / Sir Charles Mackerras
Chandos/Peter Moores Foundation Opera in English
② CHAN3121 (137' · DDD · S/T/N)   Ⓕ ⚫⚫Ɗ

No work makes better sense in the vernacular
than Mozart's concluding masterpiece. The composer and, assuredly, Schikaneder would have
approved of giving the work in the language of
the listeners, and when you have to hand such a
witty, well-worded translation as that of Jeremy
Sams, it makes even better sense. Sir Charles
Mackerras has always been an advocate of opera
in English when the circumstances are right.

As ever, he proves himself a loving and perceptive Mozartian. Throughout he wonderfully
contrasts the warmth and sensuousness of the
music for the good characters with the fire and
fury of the baddies, and he persuades the LPO to
play with a lightness and promptness that's
wholly enchanting, quite the equal of most
bands on the other available versions.

In no way is his interpretation here inferior to his German one on Telarc; indeed, in the central roles of Tamino and Pamina the casting for Chandos is an improvement, and Keenlyside is fully the equal of Thomas Allen on the Telarc set. Keenlyside's loveable, slightly sad, very human and perfectly sung Papageno is at the centre of things. Rebecca Evans's voice has taken on a new richness without losing any of its focus or delicacy of utterance. Everything she does has sincerity and poise, although her diction might, with advantage, be clearer.

The recording is fine apart from an over-use of thunder and lightning as sound effects. Anyone wanting the work in English needn't hesitate to acquire this set, the first ever on CD.

Die Zauberflöte
Ulrike Sonntag sop Pamina **Deon van der Walt** ten Tamino **Cornelius Hauptmann** bass Sarastro **Andrea Frei** sop Queen of Night **Thomas Mohr** bar Papageno **Patricia Rozario** sop Papagena **Sebastian Holecek** bass-bar Speaker **Kevin Connors** ten Monostatos **Elizabeth Whitehouse** sop First Lady **Helene Schneiderman** mez Second Lady **Renée Morloc** mez Third Lady **Ludwigsburg Festival Choir and Orchestra / Wolfgang Gönnenwein**
Stage director **Axel Manthey**
Video director **Ruth Kärch**
ArtHaus Musik 💿 100 188 (147' · 4:3 · 2:0 · 0) Ⓕ●

This is one of the most wondrous and simple stagings of Mozart's elevated Singspiel yet. As its musical attributes are almost as excellent, it's a DVD experience no one should miss. The action is choreographed in a manner precisely fitting the mood of the moment, serious or comic. Details, such as the dragon, animals responding to Tamino's flute, the arrival of the three Boys, the evocation of fire and water and several others, often invitations to director's *bêtises*, all march here with the thought-through and pleasing-to-look-at concept. How happy that it should be preserved on video, though a pity it's in 4:3 rather than in widescreen format.

Gönnenwein conducts a reading that fits perfectly with what's happening on stage in terms of unaffected, rhythmically firm and keenly articulated playing from his fine orchestra. Deon van der Walt's Tamino is a well-known quantity but he surpasses himself here in strong tone and finely moulded phrasing. He has a fit partner in Ulrike Sonntag's pure-voiced, moving Pamina. Thomas Mohr, though unflatteringly attired, is a nicely unfussy and gently amusing Papageno. Good and evil, at bottom and top of the range, aren't so happily done. Hauptmann's visually impressive Sarastro lacks vocal presence and tends to unsteadiness. Similarly Frei's formidable figure as the Queen of the Night produces an edgy, uncontrolled sound. Ladies and Boys are all admirable.

The video direction is sensitive; the sound, for the most part clear and well balanced, suffers from occasional moments of distortion. But that shouldn't detract from your enjoyment of this life-enhancing experience.

Thea Musgrave Scottish-American b1928

Born in Edinburgh, Musgrave studied first at the University of Edinburgh and later at the Conservatoire in Paris, where she spent four years as a pupil of Nadia Boulanger, before establishing herself back in London as a prominent member of British musical life with her orchestral, choral, operatic and chamber works. In 1970 she became guest professor at the University of California, Santa Barbara, which anchored her increasing involvement with the musical life of the United States. In 1971 she married the American viola player and opera conductor Peter Mark, and has lived in the US since 1972. In 1974 she received the Koussevitzky Award, resulting in the composition of Space Play, which after its London premiere was performed in New York by the Lincoln Center Chamber Players.

Musgrave has consistently explored new means of projecting essentially dramatic situations in her music, frequently altering and extending the conventional boundaries of instrumental performance by physicalising their musical and dramatic impact. As she once put it, she wanted to explore dramatic musical forms: some works are dramatic-abstract, that is without programmatic content, and others project specific programmatic ideas – all extensions of concerto principles.

It was therefore not surprising that her focus on the lyric and dramatic potential of music should have led to Musgrave's fluency in the field of opera, and it is interesting to see that her large-scale operas of the past 40 years (The Voice of Ariadne, 1972, Mary, Queen of Scots, 1977, A Christmas Carol, 1979, and Harriet, The Woman Called Moses, 1984), are in every sense the true successors to the instrumental concertos. These have been followd by Simón Bolívar (1993) and Pontalba (2003).

Turbulent Landscapes

Turbulent Landscapes[a]. Songs for a Winter's Evening[b]. Two's Company[c]
[b]**Lisa Milne** sop [c]**Nicholas Daniel** ob [c]**Evelyn Glennie** perc [b]**BBC Scottish Symphony Orchestra /** [ab]**Osmo Vänskä**; [ac]**BBC Symphony Orchestra /** [c]**Jiří Bělohlávek**
NMC NMCD153 (69' · DDD). Recorded live Ⓕ●➔

After studies in Edinburgh and Paris which encouraged rejection of radicalism for its own sake, Thea Musgrave has spent most of her time in America, and it is with a degree of affectionate distancing that she alludes to things Scottish and British in two of these compositions from the last 15 years.

Songs for a Winter's Evening sets seven Burns lyrics, including such familiar items as 'Ca' the yowes' and 'Ye banks and braes', in ways which acknowledge their folky associations while opening them out to a more opulent, romanticised idiom. The result has a very positive, personal perspective, yet the blend isn't entirely convincing despite an excellent performance. By contrast, Musgrave's no less individual response to a group of Turner's paintings in *Turbulent Landscapes* is a triumph: cogently structured yet uninhibitedly pictorial encapsulations of these canvases which manage to be economical, witty and distinctively expressive all at the same time.

Two's Company adds to Musgrave's sequence of concertos in which the obvious contrast between soloist(s) and orchestra is enhanced by allowing the soloists to move around the performance space, challenging and responding to different groups of supporting (or opposing) instruments. Here the unusual pairing of oboe and percussion suggests a progression from initial disparity to eventual unanimity. The later stages of this are engaging, the earlier music more diffuse, less focused. All three live performances come across well in recordings that bring out Musgrave's myriad instrumental felicities: but *Turbulent Landscapes* is the stand-out success.

Modest Mussorgsky

Russian 1839-1881

Mussorgsky's musical talent was nurtured by his mother (he was good enough to play a John Field concerto by the age of nine) and as a 13-year-old cadet at the military academy he began writing an opera, though he had had no formal musical training. In 1856 he took a commission in the élite Preobrajensky Regiment. Borodin was then a medical army officer and remembered him as something of a fop with signs of pretentiousness: 'He spoke through his teeth and his carefully chosen words were interspersed with French phrases…he showed quite unmistakably perfect breeding and education.' The following year he was introduced to Balakirev and Cui, and he also became friendly with the critic Stasov, the main champion of Russian national music. Already a heavy drinker, Mussorgsky abandoned his military career forthwith.

In 1861, when the serfs were emancipated, his family went bankrupt, forcing him into paid work as a clerk in the Ministry of Communications. During the next four years he composed continuously, though his lack of a formal musical education led him to abandon most of the works he began. He resigned from his job in 1865 and when, two years later, Stasov made his famous declaration about the 'mighty handful of Russian musicians', Mussorgsky was ready to take up the challenge with his comrades-in-arms Balakirev, Borodin, Cui and Rimsky-Korsakov: 'The Mighty Five'.

By this time, Mussorgsky was living in abject poverty and well on the way to becoming an alcoholic, struggling to get his thoughts down on paper. In 1869 he entered Government service again, this time in the forestry department. Simultaneously he worked on what was to become his greatest masterpiece, the opera Boris Godunov, which eventually (after many revisions) saw the light of day in St Petersburg in 1874. Its success was tempered by strong criticism by Mussorgsky's fellow musicians and this upset him greatly. Cui attacked the work for its immaturity and 'lack of technique'. Now a dipsomaniac, Mussorgsky began a second opera, Khovanshchina (left incomplete at his death), still managing to

write some fine music, but his concentration and lifestyle had disintegrated. The artist Rapin recalled how often Stasov 'on his return from abroad was hardly able to get him out of some basement dive, nearly in rags, swollen with alcohol'. Intermittently, Mussorgsky appeared as a pianist and accompanist but he was now hopelessly ill, suffering from delirium tremens and epileptic fits. He died following one such fit just a week after his 42nd birthday.

Pictures at an Exhibition (orch Ravel)

Mussorgsky (orch Ravel) Pictures at an Exhibition
Tchaikovsky Symphony No 4
Orchestre National du Capitole de Toulouse / Tugan Sokhiev
Naïve V5068 (76' · DDD) Ⓕ**OO**

Every so often a disc comes along that really makes you sit up. This is such a disc. Tugan Sokhiev is back in his element dispensing star quality with almost every bar of this coupling. If the ability to create atmosphere, to transport, to excite, to provoke reassessment of a piece, are the first signs of greatness then Sokhiev's beautifully heard and richly imagined account of Mussorgsky's *Pictures* is very much the promise of things to come. It is the case throughout that the subtlety, the piquancy, the Frenchness of Ravel's colorations appear disarmingly pristine – as in 'why have I never noticed that before?' One quibble amid everything that is so well judged (and so well played) is the increasing of tempo as 'The Great Gate of Kiev' is finally flung wide. Why?

No quibbles at all about the Tchaikovsky, though. Seriously, this is one of the most impressive accounts since the days of Markevitch and Mravinsky. Sokhiev makes real musical and emotional sense of the notoriously hazardous first movement. The listless, febrile nature of it reaches great heights in the development and coda where the hair-raising *tremolando* restatement of the first subject achieves real catharsis. Indeed, Sokhiev's songful Toulouse woodwinds – so poetic in the *Andantino* – cannot for long disguise an air of desperation. The whizz-bang finale delivers that in spades.

Pictures at an Exhibition[a] (orch Ravel).
Night on the Bare Mountain (arr Rimsky-Korsakov).
Khovanshchina – Prelude (orch Shostakovich).
Sorotchintsy Fair – Gopak (orch Liadov)
Vienna Philharmonic Orchestra / Valery Gergiev
Philips 468 526-2PH (52' · DDD)
[a]Recorded live 2000 Ⓕ**O**▸

This is a larger-than-life reading of *Pictures*, which underplays the subtleties of colouring introduced by Ravel in favour of more earthily Russian flavours. The coupling is an all-Mussorgsky one, surprisingly rare in the many versions of this work.

This live account brings some superb playing, with fast, brilliant movements dazzlingly well played, and with the speed bringing an edge-of-seat feeling from perils just avoided, something not usually conveyed in a studio performance. The opening 'Promenade', taken squarely, establishes the monumental Russian quality, enhanced by the immediacy of the sound. Even the 'Hut on Fowl's Legs' seems larger than life, and the performance culminates in an account of the 'Great Gate of Kiev' shattering in its weight and thrust.

That and the all-Mussorgsky coupling establish a clear place for this new issue in an overstocked market, even though the coupling isn't generous. The regular Rimsky version of *Night on the Bare Mountain*, though not recorded live, brings a performance to compare in power with *Pictures*, with very weighty brass, while Shostakovich's orchestration of the *Khovanshchina* Prelude, though less evocative than it can be, is warm and refined, with the Gopak added as a lively encore.

Additional recommendations

Mussorgsky (orch Ravel) Pictures at an Exhibition
Coupled with **Rachmaninov** The Isle of the Dead.
Etudes-tableaux (orch Respighi) – Op 33 No 4; Op 39 No 2
BBC SO / Svetlanov
BBC Legends BBCL4259-2 (71' · DDD)   Ⓕ
Recorded live in October 1999
  Evgeny Svetlanov had a firm dramatic grip,
  evoking potent atmosphere and harnessing the
  BBC SO's spectrum of instrumental colour in
  giving a performance that both chills and thrills.
  In the Mussorgsky/Ravel *Pictures* he masterfully
  combines precise characterisation of the individual
  images with clear structural cohesion.

Pictures at an Exhibition (orch Ravel)
Coupled with Night on the Bare Mountain – two versions: orch Mussorgsky; orch Rimsky-Korsakov. Sorotchintsy Fair – Gopak. Khovanshchina – The Departure of Prince Golitsïn
Ukraine National SO / Kuchar
Naxos 8 555924 (63' · DDD)   ⓈⒹ▸
  This is a quite remarkable CD on all counts – outstandingly fine orchestral playing, vividly exciting and very Russian music-making, and a very tangible sound picture, consistently in the demonstration bracket.

Pictures at an Exhibition (orch Ravel)
Coupled with Night on the Bare Mountain (arr Rimsky-Korsakov). Khovanshchina – Prelude, Act 1, 'Dawn over the Moscow River'
Atlanta SO / Levi
Telarc CD80296 (50' · DDD). Recorded 1991   Ⓕ
  When this was released, Telarc established a position for it as sonically the most spectacular set of *Pictures* among the many in the current catalogue. The characterisation is no less successful, although it's an essentially mellower view. Levi's is a performance where the conductor makes the most of the colour and brilliant orchestral effects of Ravel's inspired score, revealing much that often goes unheard. A first choice if state-of-the-art recording is your prime consideration.

MUSSORGSKY/RAVEL PICTURES AT AN EXHIBITION – IN BRIEF

Chicago SO / Fritz Reiner   Ⓗ
RCA 09026 61958-2 (71' · ADD)   Ⓜ⒪Ⓑ▸
An all-time classic from Reiner's legendary days at the helm of the Chicago Symphony. Bold characterisation and orchestral playing of tremendous conviction. The astonishingly vivid stereo dates from 1957.

Boston SO / Serge Koussevitzky   Ⓗ
RCA mono 09026 61392-2 (75' · ADD)   Ⓜ
It was Koussevitzky who commissioned and premiered Ravel's orchestration in 1922. This electrifying first recording from eight years later shows off the phenomenal articulation and tonal breadth of his fabulous Boston orchestra.

Cleveland Orchestra / George Szell
Sony SBK48162 (74' · ADD)   ⒷⓄⓄ
Dazzling stuff from Szell and his immaculate Clevelanders. This partnership's irresistibly swaggering suites from Kodály's *Háry János* and Prokofiev's *Lieutenant Kijé* make up an unbeatable bargain triptych.

Berlin PO / Claudio Abbado
DG 445 238-2GH (65' · DDD)   ⒻⓄⒷ▸
Abbado has long been a doughty Mussorgsky conductor. These live *Pictures* from 1993 are studded with newly minted detail, outstandingly well played by the Berliners.

Atlanta SO / Yoel Levi
Telarc CD80296 (50' · DDD)   Ⓕ
Levi's is a thoughtful interpretation, but by no means lacking in sheer personality or heady excitement. The Telarc engineering astonishes in its sheer weight of sonority and X-ray-like transparency.

Oslo Philharmonic / Mariss Jansons
EMI Encore ② 350824-2 (127' · ADD)   ⓈⓄ
Sitting alongside Rimsky-Korsakov favourites, Jansons's *Pictures* are typically full of colour and imagination. And the fine Oslo orchestra plays with tremendous flair.

National SO of Ukraine / Theodore Kuchar
Naxos 8 555924 (63' · DDD)   ⓈⒹ▸
Kuchar conducts with palpable relish and secures an enthusiastic response from his hard-working band. A super bargain all round from Naxos.

Vienna PO / Valery Gergiev
Philips 468 526-2PH (52' · DDD)   ⒻⓄⒷ▸
Assembled from a series of live concerts in Vienna's Musikverein during April 2000. Gergiev takes the listener on an illuminating journey, culminating in a simply majestic evocation of 'The Great Gate of Kiev'.

Pictures at an Exhibition (orch Stokowski)

Mussorgsky Pictures at an Exhibition (orch
Stokowski). Night on the Bare Mountain. Boris
Godunov – Symphonic Synthesis (arr/orch Stokowski)
Khovanshchina – Entr'acte (Act 4) **Stokowski**
Traditional Slavic Christmas Music **Tchaikovsky** Two
Morceaux, Op 10 – Humoresque. Six Songs, Op 73 –
No 6, Again, as before, alone
**Bournemouth Symphony Orchestra /
José Serebrier**
Naxos 8 557645 (77' : DDD)   ⓈⓄ⮞

Stokowski's orchestrations, as flamboyant and
full of flair as his interpretations as a conductor,
have increasingly been accepted and welcomed
on disc, a good sign that rigidly purist attitudes
have nowadays softened. This Naxos collection
of Stokowski's arrangements offers outstanding
performances by the Bournemouth Symphony
Orchestra, brilliantly recorded.

Few would claim that Stokowski's arrangement
of *Pictures at an Exhibition* matches, let alone outshines, that of Ravel. But with its weighty brass it
is certainly more Russian. In fact – one of the
most serious shortcomings – Stokowski omits
two of the movements, 'Tuileries' and the 'Market Place at Limoges' on the grounds that they
are too French. Yet Serebrier's new performance
makes it very convincing with speeds well chosen
and the brass wonderfully incisive.

The atmospheric qualities of the *Boris Godunov*
Symphonic Synthesis come over superbly too,
starting with a hauntingly rarefied bassoon solo,
even if the recording catches the clicking of the
keys. The mystery of the chimes in the Coronation
scene as well as the Death scene are more evocatively handled. If *Night on the Bare Mountain* finds
the Naxos recording rather less immediate than in
the other items, the weight of the arrangement
comes over well, and the *Khovanshchina* Entr'acte
has impressive weight and clarity.

The extra items also weigh in Serebrier's
favour: an arrangement of a Tchaikovsky song
that explores an astonishingly wide emotional
range within a tiny span and the jolly *Humoresque*, a piano piece that Stravinsky memorably
used in his ballet *The Fairy's Kiss*. Finally, a
baldly effective piece, attributed to Stokowski
himself, based not just on a Christmas hymn but
on Ippolitov-Ivanov's *In a Manger*.

Pictures at an Exhibition (piano)

'Pictures Reframed'
Mussorgsky Pictures at an Exhibition. Souvenirs
d'enfance. Duma (Rêverie) on a Theme of VA
Loginov. On the Southern Shore of the Crimea
Schumann Kinderszenen, Op 15
Leif Ove Andsnes *pf*
EMI 698360-2 (62' · DDD)   ⒫ⓄⓄⓄ⮞

You don't need to know the title of the
disc or to have seen Leif Ove Andsnes's
fascinating collaboration with visual/

performance artist Robin Rhode (on DVD as
part of a deluxe edition) to feel the impact of his
Pictures. For a start, there's an audacious degree
of addition and alteration to the score itself.
Anyone who has ever tried to play *Pictures* will
know that in many ways it's frustratingly unpianistic. Horowitz famously remodelled it, the
ends justifying the means. And many others have
indulged in the odd spot of octave filling-out
and so on. Andsnes goes further than most, not
only filling out harmonies but also transposing
up or down an octave and generally tinkering
with the score. Some of the effects may begin to
pall after a while but so far the effect is thrilling.
What comes across most strongly is the work's
iconoclasm: Andsnes isn't as violent or visceral,
or as raw, as Richter in his various readings – but
then no one is. Instead, he constantly reminds us
of the human element in Mussorgsky's reimagining of Hartmann's images.

The disc is filled out with miniatures by Mussorgsky, including two intended as part of a suite
of childhood reflections, plus Schumann's
greatest work of nostalgia, *Kinderszenen*. Capturing its apparent simplicity and doing full justice to the swiftly shifting vignettes takes pianism of the first order, but Andsnes has long been
a superb interpreter of Schumann, and that
holds true here. In Andsnes's hands, both these
great cycles, utterly different though they are,
feel like first-hand, vital and highly personal
experiences, and it's these qualities that make
this disc so compelling.

Additional recommendation

Mussorgsky Pictures at an Exhibition
Coupled with **Balakirev** Islamey
Ravel Gaspard de la nuit
Kempf *pf*
BIS ⚫ BIS-SACD1580 (65' · DDD)   Ⓕ

Freddy Kempf's immense energy and facility
allows him an unusual degree of freedom with
a brisk opening Promenade followed by an
unleashing of his virtuoso credentials in
'Gnomus'. He takes a uniformly *forte* view of
'Bydlo' (though his final fading of the vision is
masterly). And so, too, is his enviable verve in
both 'Ballet of the Unhatched Chicks' and
'Limoges'. 'Baba Yaga' is boldly characterised,
and there is a dramatic splash of colour, a sudden
pedal haze at 1'12" in 'The Great Gate of Kiev'.
In Ravel's *Gaspard* every teeming complexity is
resolved with the coolest of mind and hands. and
in Balakirev's *Islamey* Kempf relishes everything
the composer throws at him.

Boris Godunov

Boris Godunov (1874 version)
Nikolai Putilin *bar* Boris Godunov **Viktor Lutsiuk** *ten*
Grigory **Nikolai Okhotnikov** *bass* Pimen
Fyodor Kuznetsov *bass* Varlaam **Konstantin
Pluzhnikov** *ten* Shuisky **Nikolai Gassiev** *ten* Missail

Zlata Bulycheva *mez* Fyodor **Olga Trifonova** *sop*
Xenia **Yevgenia Gorokhovskaya** *mez* Nurse **Liubov**
Sokolova *mez* Hostess **Evgeny Akimov** *ten*
Simpleton **Vassily Gerello** *bar* Shchelkalov **Grigory**
Karassev *bass* Nikitich **Evgeny Nikitin** *bass* Mityukha
Yuri Schikalov *ten* Krushchov

Boris Godunov (1896 version)
Vladimir Vaneyev *bass* Boris Godunov **Vladimir**
Galusin *ten* Grigory **Olga Borodina** *mez* Marina
Nikolai Okhotnikov *bass* Pimen **Fyodor Kuznetsov**
bass Varlaam **Konstantin Pluzhnikov** *ten* Shuisky
Nikolai Gassiev *ten* Missail **Evgeny Nikitin** *bass*
Rangoni, Mityukha **Zlata Bulycheva** *mez* Fyodor
Olga Trifonova *sop* Xenia **Yevgenia Gorokhovskaya**
mez Nurse **Liubov Sokolova** *mez* Hostess **Evgeny**
Akimov *ten* Simpleton **Vassily Gerello** *bar*
Shchelkalov **Grigory Karassev** *bass* Nikitich **Yuri**
Schikalov *ten* Krushchov **Andrei Karabanov** *bar*
Lavitsky **Yuri Laptev** *ten* Chernikovsky **Chorus and**
Orchestra of the Kirov Opera / Valery Gergiev
Philips ⑤ 462 230-2PH5 (5h 6' · DDD · T/t) ⓜⓄⓄ⤳

What we have here is, literally, two operas for
the price of one. That's to say, the two discs
containing Mussorgsky's first *Boris Godunov* and
the three containing his second are available at
five discs for the normal cost of three. And, in a
real sense, what we're dealing with is two operas.
First, a brief résumé of the facts. In 1868-69
Mussorgsky composed seven scenes: outside the
Novedevichy Monastery, Coronation outside
the Kremlin, Pimen's Cell, the Inn, the Tsar's
rooms in the Kremlin, outside St Basil's Cathedral, Boris's Death in the Kremlin. When these
were rejected by the Imperial Theatres in 1872,
he made various revisions. To meet objections
about the lack of female roles, Mussorgsky
added the two scenes with the Polish princess
Marina Mniszek; he also substituted the final
Kromy Forest scene for the St Basil's scene. He
made a large number of adjustments, some of a
minor nature, some rather more significant
(such as dropping Pimen's narration of the murder of the young Tsarevich), and one huge, the
complete rewriting of the original fifth scene, in
the Kremlin, sometimes known as the Terem
scene. This was the work that he resubmitted,
and which was first performed in St Petersburg
in 1874. Rimsky-Korsakov's famous version
(which does much more than reorchestrate) was
first heard in 1896, and for many years superseded its predecessors.

However, it has increasingly been recognised
that *Boris* II isn't a revision of *Boris* I but a different
work, both as regards the view of the central character and his place in the historical narrative, and
also as regards the rethought musical technique
and sometimes change of idiom which this has
brought about. Therefore the present set makes a
real contribution to our understanding and enjoyment of Russia's greatest opera. It follows that
there have to be two singers of the central role.
Putilin (*Boris* I) is in general more capacious in
tone, more brooding and lofty, in the Terem
scene more embittered and harsh, willing to act
with the voice. Vaneyev is a decidedly more

immediate and human Boris, tender with his son
Fyodor (a touching, engaging performance from
Zlata Bulycheva) both in the Terem and at the
end, not always as dominating as this Tsar should
be but sympathetic, allowing his voice to blanch as
death approaches, and especially responsive to the
melodic essence of Mussorgsky's speech-
delivered lines. This enables him to be rather freer
with the actual note values. It doesn't necessarily
matter that much: Mussorgsky changed his mind
over various details, and the important thing is to
use his notes to create character rather than be too
literal with what the different versions propose.
Pimen, strongly sung with a hint of the youthful
passions that he claims to have abjured, is sung by
Nikolai Okhotnikov more or less identically in
both performances.

The only character, apart from Boris, to be
accorded two singers is Grigory, the False
Dmitri. Viktor Lutsiuk (*Boris* I) is strenuous,
obsessed, vital; Vladimir Galusin (*Boris* II) can
sound more frenzied, and has the opportunity
with the addition of the Polish acts to give a convincing portrayal of a weak man assuming
strength but being undermined by the wiles of a
determined woman. Here, she's none other than
Olga Borodina, moodily toying with her polonaise rhythms and then in full sensuous call.
Yevgenia Gorokhovskaya is a jolly old Nurse in
the *Boris* II Terem scene. The rest of the cast do
not really change their interpretations from one
Boris to another, and indeed scarcely need to do
so: it isn't really upon that which the differences
depend. Liubov Sokolova sings a fruity Hostess,
welcoming in Fyodor Kuznetsov a Varlaam who
can really sing his Kazan song rather than merely
bawling it. Konstantin Pluzhnikov makes Shuisky
move from the rather sinister force confronting
Boris in the Terem to a more oily complacency in
the Death scene: many Shuiskys make less of the
part. Evgeny Nikitin is a creepy, fanatical
Rangoni, Vassily Gerello a Shchelkalov of hypo-
critical elegance, Evgeny Akimov a sad-toned
Simpleton. Gergiev directs strong, incisive performances, accompanying sympathetically and
controlling the marvellous crowd scenes well.

However, it's a pity that he allows fierce whistles to drown the speeding violins opening the
Kromy Forest scene (the music can be heard
only when it returns), and he hasn't been given
sufficient clarity of recording with the chorus.
The words are often obscure, even with the
boyars in the Death scene, and far too much is
lost in the crowd exchanges. This is regrettable
for a work that, in either incarnation, draws
so much on realistic detail of articulation.
Nevertheless, these five discs form a fascinating
set, one no admirer of this extraordinary
creative achievement can afford to ignore.

Additional recommendation

Boris Godunov (1874 version)
Kotcherga Boris **Larin** Grigory **Lipovšek** Marina
Ramey Pimen **Nikolsky** Varlaam **Langridge** Shuisky
Wildhaber Missail **Leiferkus** Rangoni **Nichiteanu**

Fyodor **Valente** Xenia **Gorokhovskaya** Nurse
Zaremba Hostess **Fedin** Simpleton **Shagidullin**
Shchelkalov **Drabowicz** Mitukha, Krushchov
**Slovak Philh Chor; Berlin Radio Chor; Tölz Boys'
Choir; BPO / Abbado**
The Sony Opera House ③ 88697 52728-2
(3h 20' · DDD · T/t)　　　　　　　　　　Ⓑ⊙

> Few conductors have been more diligent than
> Claudio Abbado in seeking the truth about this vast
> canvas. He chooses the definitive 1872-74 version,
> adding scenes, including the complete one in
> Pimen's cell and the St Basil's scene from 1869. His
> is a taut, tense reading – grand, virtuoso, at times
> hard-driven, favouring extremes of speed and
> dynamics. Kotcherga is a Boris avoiding conven-
> tional melodrama and concerned to show the lov-
> ing father. The ambitious lovers are well repre-
> sented. Indeed, Larin is quite the best Grigory yet
> recorded on disc, sounding at once youthful, heroic
> and ardent, and quite free of any tenor manner-
> isms. Lipovšek characterises Marina forcefully.

Nesterenko Boris **Atlantov** Grigory **Obraztsova**
Marina **Ognivtsiev** Pimen **Eizen** Varlaam **Lissovski**
Shuisky **Baskov** Missail **Mazurok** Rangoni **Bolshoi
Theatre Chorus and Orchestra / Mark Ermler**
Regis ③ RRC3006 (3h 10' · ADD · S/N)　　　Ⓢ

> A performance in the old Bolshoi style using the
> Rimsky-Korsakov edition. At its super-budget
> price, this magnificent 1982 set is an easy recom-
> mendation.

Boris Godunov (1874 version)
Robert Lloyd bass Boris Godunov **Alexei Steblianko**
ten Grigory **Olga Borodina** mez Marina **Alexander
Morosov** bass Pimen **Vladimir Ognovenko** bass
Varlaam **Yevgeny Boitsov** ten Shuisky **Igor Yan** ten
Missail **Sergei Leiferkus** bass Rangoni **Larissa
Dyadkova** mez Fyodor **Olga Kondina** sop Xenia
Yevgenia Perlassova mez Nurse **Ludmila Filatova**
mez Hostess **Vladimir Solodovnikov** ten Simpleton
Mikhail Kit bar Shchelkalov **Yevgeny Fedotov** bass
Nikitich **Grigory Karasyov** bass Mityukha **Kirov
Opera Chorus and Orchestra / Valery Gergiev**
Stage directors **Andrei Tarkovsky, Stephen Lawless**
Video director **Humphrey Burton**
Philips 📀 075 089-9PH2 (3h 41' · NTSC · 4:3 · 2.0,
DTS 5.1 · 0). Recorded live at the Mariinsky Theatre,
St Petersburg 1990　　　　　　　　　　　Ⓕ

Film director Andrei Tarkovsky, famous for
science-fiction classics *Solaris* and *Stalker* and the
historical epic *Andrei Rublev*, was a master of symbolic effect – the gigantic pendulum, the grotesquely faceless Idiot, living statuary, the angelic
murdered child amid falling snow. But against
such stylisation the action, vividly captured by
video director Humphrey Burton, comes correspondingly alive, no stiff Bolshoi pageant; chorus
and soloists act their hearts out.

Borodina is an ideal Marina, beautiful and burnished of tone but chillingly self-absorbed; perhaps rightly, she strikes more sparks with Leiferkus's vampiric, honey-toned Rangoni than with
Steblianko's stolid but lyrical Pretender. Ognovenko's Varlaam is somewhat young and bari-

tonal, but foreshadows stardom, as does Dyadkova's superbly touching, plangent Fyodor.
Boitsov's Shuisky, Morosov's noble Pimen and
Solodovnikov's Idiot are less outstanding but still
excellent. The only outsider is at the centre. Robert Lloyd's Boris first appears (reflecting contemporary portraits) moustached but beardless; the
customary hedge appears in later acts, neatly
marking the passing years. His finely shaded *basso
cantante* has been criticised for being too light, but
such doubts fade before his idiomatic-sounding
Russian and magnificent characterisation, culminating in a truly harrowing death scene.

Gergiev's reading is less brilliant than his dual
recording, often rather soft-centred; but he still
brings out the sheer anguished beauty of the score.
The excellent stereo soundtrack has also been
remastered into DTS surround sound, and very
airy and ambient this sounds, from the opening
wave of applause sweeping across the auditorium.

Khovanshchina

Khovanshchina
Aage Haugland bass Ivan Khovansky **Vladimir
Atlantov** ten Andrey Khovansky **Vladimir Popov** ten
Golitsin **Anatolij Kotscherga** bar Shaklovity **Paata
Burchuladze** bass Dosifey **Marjana Lipovšek** contr
Marfa **Brigitte Poschner-Klebel** sop Susanna **Heinz
Zednik** ten Scribe **Joanna Borowska** sop Emma
Wilfried Gahmlich ten Kouzka **Vienna Boys' Choir;
Slovak Philharmonic Choir; Vienna State Opera
Chorus and Orchestra / Claudio Abbado**
DG ③ 429 758-2GH3 (171' · DDD · T/t)
Recorded live 1989　　　　　　　　　　Ⓕ⊙⊙▷

The booklet-essay suggests that Mussorgsky's
music constantly poses a question to his Russian
compatriots: 'What are the causes of our country's continuing calamities, and why does the
state crush all that is good?' Anyone who follows
today's news from Russia and then experiences
this opera will understand what's meant, and
while we observe with sympathy we seem no
nearer than the citizens of that great, tormented
country to finding solutions for its endemic problems. However, Mussorgsky was not the least of
those Russian musicians who found lasting
beauty in her history and he expressed it in a powerfully dramatic idiom that drew on folk music
and had both epic qualities and deep humanity as
well as an occasional gentleness. There's also an
element here of Russian church music, since
Khovanshchina has a political and religious theme
and is set in the 1680s at the time of Peter the
Great's accession. Since the work was unfinished
when Mussorgsky died, performances always
involve conjectural work, and the version here –
which works convincingly – is mostly that of
Shostakovich with the choral ending that Stravinsky devised using Mussorgsky's music.

The cast in this live recording isn't one of star
opera singers, but they're fully immersed in the
drama and the music, as is the chorus and the
orchestra under Abbado, and the result is deeply
atmospheric.

Nikolay Myaskovsky

Russian 1881-1950

Myaskovsky studied for a military career but entered the St Petersburg Conservatory where his teachers included Lyadov and Rimsky-Korsakov. He served in the war, and from 1921 taught at the Moscow Conservatory. He was not an innovator but was an influential, individual figure working within the Russian tradition. Despite his personal feelings about the Stalinist regime Myaskovsky did his best not to engage in overt confrontation with the Soviet state, and while some of his works refer to contemporary themes, they do not do so in a programmatic or propagandistic way. His large output is dominated by the cycle of 27 symphonies (1908-50), highly regarded in and outside Russia in his lifetime. He also wrote 13 string quartets, choral and chamber music.

Violin Concerto in D minor, Op 44

Myaskovsky Violin Concerto
Tchaikovsky Violin Concerto in D, Op 35
Vadim Repin vn
Kirov Orchestra / Valery Gergiev
Philips 473 343-2PH (72' · DDD)　　　Ⓕ**OOO**▷

It's the Myaskovsky that really makes this disc a 'must-have'. His Violin Concerto was premiered by David Oistrakh in Leningrad in 1939. As with Tchaikovsky's Concerto, the opening *tutti* plays for less than a minute and the slow movement is touchingly lyrical. The rather melancholy first movement is built on a grand scale and includes an expansive cadenza where Repin's mastery is virtually the equal of Oistrakh's. It's forceful music, epic in scale and earnestly argued, the sort of piece that Gergiev thrives on.

Listening to Repin's Tchaikovsky Concerto (his second recording of the work) confirms just how far he's journeyed in a few years. Tone projection is stronger, attack more aggressive and his solo demeanour seems better focused than before, far more confident and spontaneous. Mixed in with these improvements are one or two affectations, but it's a cracking performance, one of the best from the younger generation. The recording sounds like a digital update of the sort of blowsy in-your-face sonics typical of the first stereo recordings of the late 1950s. Nevertheless, a fabulous disc.

Symphonies

Symphonies – No 17, Op 41; No 21, Op 51.
Salutatory Overture, Op 48
Russian Federation Academic Symphony Orchestra / Evgeni Svetlanov
Alto ALC1023 (77' · DDD)　　　　Ⓢ

Complete Symphonies. Orchestral Works
USSR State Symphony Orchestra; Russian

Federation Academic Symphony Orchestra / Evgeni Svetlanov
Warner Classics ⑯ 2564 69689-8 (20h 38' · DDD)
　　　　　　　　　　　　　　　Ⓢ**OOO**

Though presumably similarly sourced, the transfers on these two issues are not always identical in matters of balance and equalisation. The main drawback of the Warner set is the skimpiness of its annotations. Alto remains committed to giving us the contextual material such unfamiliar scores can scarcely do without. Its makeweight here is a case in point. A seemingly innocuous overture, it turns out to have been the composer's contribution to Stalin's 60th birthday celebrations in 1939. In which case its avoidance of vulgarity may even be considered quietly heroic.

Of the two symphonies in the Alto instalment, the 17th (1936-37) is indubitably a large statement. Composed at the height of the Great Terror, its idiom seems a little more extroverted than usual, Rachmaninov crossed with Khachaturian perhaps. The epic slow movement will be a must for listeners with a sweet tooth even if things could, with advantage, move on a little faster! Liadov meets Korngold in the Trio of the third. You may well have come across this performance in an earlier Melodiya incarnation.

The 21st (1940) was long Myaskovsky's calling-card. It was commissioned by the Chicago SO and there are vintage recordings originating from both sides of the Iron Curtain. None is as long-breathed as this one. Perhaps one can forgive the blaring confusion of Svetlanov's climaxes for the nobility of his take on the elevated, Roy Harris-style opening section. The score's most memorable idea, referencing Rimsky's *Antar* Symphony, has that authentic Myaskovsky lyricism in spades and of course Svetlanov milks it for all it's worth. Glorious heartfelt stuff although those brought up on more tautly controlled readings may cry self-indulgence. As usual the playing ranges from the inspired to the sketchy, the results compellingly 'noble' even where manifestly flawed.

For anyone coming fresh to the composer and his world, the Warner set provides an extraordinarily economical, if potentially mystifying, entrée.

Conlon Nancarrow

Mexican 1912-1997

Nancarrow studied with Slonimsky, Piston and Sessions in Boston (1933-36), but made his home in Mexico from 1940. There he composed exclusively for player piano. His music first received serious attention only in the 1970s. The composer György Ligeti described the music of Conlon Nancarrow thus: 'This music is the greatest discovery since Webern and Ives...something great and important for all music history! His music is so utterly original, enjoyable, perfectly constructed, but at the same time emotional...for me it's the best music of any composer living today.'

Instrumental works

Studies and Solos

Studies for Player Piano – Nos 3b[h], 3c[e], 3[d], 4[f], 6[f], 9[d], 14[d], 15[g], 18[f], 19[d], 26[d]. Prelude[e]. Sonatina[ag]. Three Canons for Ursula[b]. Blues[b]. Three Two-Part Studies[c]. Tango?[c]
(trans [d]Helena Bugallo; [e]Bugallo-Williams; [f]Erik Ona; [g]Yvar Mikhashoff; [h]Amy Williams)
[a]**Bugallo-Williams Piano Duo**
([b]Helena Bugallo, [c]Amy Williams pfs)
Wergo WER6670-2 (63' · DDD)   (F)

Conlon Nancarrow moved from the US to Mexico City in 1940 largely because of his communist affiliations. He spent the rest of his life there in almost total isolation, composing for player-pianos because he knew performers would never cope with his complex rhythms. Times have changed, and pianists and ensembles have been taking up the challenge by using transcriptions of some of his studies. Those used here are by composers Yvar Mikhashoff and Erik Ona and the Bugallo-Williams duo themselves. The results are simply stunning.

Nancarrow's experience as a jazz trumpeter and knowledge of *The Rite of Spring* were catalysts for a distinctive contrapuntal idiom, in which separate voices are superimposed at different speeds leading to acoustic overcrowding and apparent chaos. But it's all finely controlled: several pieces stop dead on a unison or a major chord.

By the late 1970s Nancarrow was beginning to be rediscovered and, in a more appreciative context, wrote for live performers again, including *Tango?* and *Three Canons for Ursula* (Oppens). The studies work just as well with live pianists as with the twangy sound of Nancarrow's own player-pianos. Obviously some of the very fast studies will never be playable, but, since he allowed some transcription, there's no harm when performers of this calibre can rise to the occasion so brilliantly. This wonderfully affirmative music not only questions conventional notions about rhythm but provides a uniquely exhilarating experience for the listener – well recorded and really attractive in every way.

Studies for Player Piano, Vol 2
Dabringhaus und Grimm MDG645 1403-2
(68' · DDD)   (F)

Why release yet another set of Nancarrow studies, given that these mechanical masterpieces merely replicate themselves every time a roll is activated inside the player piano? First, the well-known Wergo recording made in Nancarrow's Mexico City home in 1988 was flawed in certain respects. Of the two pianos equipped to play these studies, Nancarrow's preferred instrument – possessing a softer, warmer tone – was in need of reconditioning. It was decided to record the whole set on a piano normally reserved for more dense rhythmic studies. Its tinny honky-tonk timbre thus created a skewed impression of

Nancarrow's studies. They sounded even more strange and eccentric than intended.

Second, after the Wergo release other player piano pieces have come to light, including *For Yoko* and the Study No 51 (aka *#3750*). Jürgen Hocker's new recording for MDG therefore plugs some gaps and restores the studies to their original state. And what a difference it makes to hear these works afresh, but also in sequential (though not necessarily chronological) order. Like a well-oiled machine, the Bösendorfer grand plays out Nancarrow's highly inventive studies with surprising ease and dexterity, almost as if it had been designed to do nothing else.

This second volume in a projected five-part series, consisting of Nos 13-32, contains arguably some of Nancarrow's best music. The first seven or so studies explore a number of related canonic conundrums and proportional puzzles, playfully resolving onto a tonic chord or octave unison with Escher-like logic. Study No 20 sees Nancarrow relax mathematical processes for a more controlled improvisatory approach, but No 21 – the famous *Canon X* – is surely one of the disc's highlights. An extraordinary example of controlled chaos, two parts are made to pound out obsessively the same cyclical 54-note row while simultaneously speeding up and slowing down, their rhythmic trajectories momentarily coinciding.

José de Nebra   Spanish 1702-1768

José de Nebra was principal organist of the Spanish Royal Chapel and the Descalzas Reales convent at Madrid from 1724. In 1751 he was promoted to deputy director of the chapel and head of the choir school. A gifted dramatic composer, he saw 57 stage works performed in Madrid and Lisbon between 1723 and 1751. They are strong works, usually employing spoken dialogue, which embrace a wide emotional palette.

Tempestad grande amigo

'Napoli/Madrid'
Nebra Tempestad grande amigo[acd]
Petrini Graziello e Nella[ac] **Vinci** Erighetta e Don Chilone[ad]. Sinfonia per archi. Adónde fugitivo[b]. Triste, ausente, en esta selva[a]. Cuando infeliz destino[b]
[a]**Roberta Invernizzi**, [b]**Cristina Calzolari** sops
[c]**Giuseppe de Vittorio** ten [d]**Giuseppe Naviglio** bar
Capella della Pietà de' Turchini / Antonio Florio
Naïve OP30274 (72' · DDD · T/t)   (F)

For more than two centuries Naples was a province of Spain, and after this ended in 1707 the remarkable cross-fertilisation of culture between them did not stop. Much of the Italian music featured here has been edited from sources in Spanish collections. The vast bulk of it is devoted to Leonardo Vinci (one of the most celebrated Italian opera composers of the 1720s). Only one short piece tacked onto the end is actually Spanish: a colourful fandango from José de Nebra's zarzuela *Vendado es amor, no es ciego* (1744) in which three singers mockingly compare the squabbling goddesses of classical antiquity to bickering mothers-in-law.

Antonio Florio and Cappella della Pietà de' Turchini have already given unstinting service to the cause of music from Naples, but this is one of their best recordings so far. The playing and singing are theatrically charged without ever becoming crass or forced, and there is a lean articulacy evident throughout. This is no mean feat in two cliché-ridden intermezzos in which the comedy relies largely on long recitatives, but the programme has been intelligently chosen: Vinci's *Erighetta e Don Chilone* (in which a young widow hoodwinks a wealthy old hypochondriac into marrying her by posing as a doctor) is entirely different in tone and style to Giuseppe Petrini's *Graziello e Nella* (in which a young man – sung by a woman – heaps ridicule upon an old woman – sung by a man – who thinks she is still young and gorgeous). If these are fascinating and mildly amusing rather than magnificent, three *cantate con strumenti* by Vinci (sung in contemporary Spanish versions) offer ample musical rewards. *Triste, ausente, en esta selva* is superbly sung by Roberta Invernizzi – the central accompanied recitative is spectacular and highly dramatic. Cristina Calzolari is equally impressive in the other two cantatas. These cantatas give us a precious insight into why Vinci was reputedly one of Handel's favourite composers.

Carl Nielsen
Danish 1865-1931

Anyone seeking a gentle introduction to 20th-century music could do worse than listen to the six symphonies by this remarkable composer, neglected by the musical world (apart from Scandinavia) during his lifetime and only in the 1950s internationally recognised for what he was – Denmark's most important composer. In his charming autobiography, My Childhood, Nielsen tells of his life on the Island of Fyn (or Funen) where his father was a labourer. The Danish soil and character (though not so much its folk music) pervades all his work; there's an attractive, unsentimental directness about it and, though it has its bleak moments, a life-affirming spirit abounds, in music of clear-cut colours and structures.

Nielsen received his first rudimentary music lessons from his father, a keen fiddle player, and then took up the trumpet in the local band. (His first job was as a shepherd.) Apart from his elementary musical education at school, that was all the tuition he had before composing a string quartet, one which qualified him for admission to the Royal Conservatory in Copenhagen. Among his teachers was the esteemed Niels Gade, friend of Mendelssohn and Schumann and the founding father of the Scandinavian school of composition. Nielsen's career after this was devoted to playing the violin (in the Royal Chapel Orchestra), con-

ducting all over Denmark and Europe – and composing. He died of a heart attack shortly after being made director of the Copenhagen Conservatory, a national hero.

Clarinet Concerto

Nielsen Clarinet Concerto **Lutosławski** Dance Preludes **Prokofiev** Flute Sonata in D, Op 94 (arr Kennan)
Richard Stoltzman *cl* **Warsaw Philharmonic Orchestra / Lawrence Leighton Smith**
RCA Red Seal 09026 63836-2 (66' · DDD) (F)

Richard Stoltzman's Nielsen, Prokofiev and Lutosławski compilation is a fine achievement. He brings to the Nielsen Concerto both virtuosity and depth of characterisation. There may be other ways of presenting this complex musical character-study but his fluency and broad expressive range are as impressive as any modern recorded account. The Warsaw Philharmonic under Lawrence Leighton Smith sound exceptionally well prepared. They lend a natural idiomatic pliancy to the Lutosławski *Dance Preludes*, where Stoltzman is perkiness personified, and make a fine foil for him in the Concerto.

Kent Kennan's orchestration of the Prokofiev Flute Sonata is also well worth hearing – indeed, well worth taking up by other clarinettists. This is a tactful and adroit arrangement for chamber orchestra. Stoltzman lavishes care on the solo part, making a persuasive case for the *Scherzo* as an *allegretto scherzando* rather than Prokofiev's suggested *presto*. His romanticised approach to the slow movement is less convincing, but his earthy characterisation of the finale is admirable. RCA's recording quality is outstanding.

Violin Concerto

Nielsen Violin Concerto[a].
Sibelius Violin Concerto in D minor, Op 47[b]
Cho-Liang Lin vn
[a]**Swedish Radio Symphony Orchestra,**
[b]**Philharmonia Orchestra / Esa-Pekka Salonen**
Sony Classical SMK89748 (69' · DDD)
Recorded 1987-88 (M)**OOO**

At the time it was first issued, this was the best recording of the Sibelius Concerto to have appeared for over a decade, and probably the best ever of the Nielsen. It remains one of the classic concerto recordings of the century. Cho-Liang Lin brings an apparently effortless virtuosity to both concertos. He produces a wonderfully clean and silvery sonority, and there's no lack of aristocratic finesse.

Only half a dozen years separate the two concertos, yet they breathe a totally different air. Lin's perfect intonation and tonal purity excite admiration and throughout them both there's a strong sense of line from beginning to end. Esa-Pekka Salonen gets excellent playing from the Philharmonia Orchestra in the Sibelius and almost equally good results from the Swedish Radio Symphony Orchestra.

Flute Concerto

Clarinet Concerto. Flute Concerto. Violin Concerto.
Gareth Davies *fl* **Kevin Banks** *cl* **Jonathan Carney**
vn **Bournemouth Symphony Orchestra /**
Kees Bakels
Naxos 8 554189 (79' · DDD)   ⓢ☞

For those on a limited budget, this outstandingly generous Naxos anthology will prove a pretty irresistible purchase. In the glorious Violin Concerto, Jonathan Carney turns out to be a thoroughly musical soloist, his sweet-toned contribution at once unforced and affectionate. Tempi are unfailingly well-judged, and Kees Bakels and the Bournemouth orchestra accompany with admirable spirit. Deftly as Carney plays, however, he doesn't possess quite the noble poise and silk-spun purity of Cho-Liang Lin, whose irreproachably eloquent 1988 version (above) with Esa-Pekka Salonen and the Swedish RSO continues to dominate the digital stakes. The Clarinet Concerto brings another capable, committed display. Bournemouth SO principal Kevin Banks copes manfully with the taxingly virtuoso solo part. Gareth Davies is a shapely, nimble advocate of the delectable Flute Concerto. Memories of dedicatee Holger Gilbert-Jespersen are not banished, but this remains a likeable reading all the same. Reasonable value overall, then, and a pretty decent recording too.

Overtures

Helios. Pan and Syrinx. Rhapsody Overture: An imaginary trip to the Faroe Islands. Amor and the Poet – Overture. Maskarade – Overture; Dance of the Cockerels. Master Oluf Rides – Prelude. Saul and David – Prelude. Snefrid. Willemoes – Prelude, Act 3
Danish National Symphony Orchestra /
Thomas Dausgaard
Dacapo ⏺ 6 220518 (72' · DDD)   ⒡❶❶❶❶☞

This is outstanding, and unmissable for Nielsen collectors – and not only for the less familiar items, all of which have been recorded before (not badly, either). The Danish Radio Symphony must have played the *Saul and David* and *Maskarade* excerpts and the *Helios* Overture more times than they can count. But for Dausgaard they relish every detail, without ever sounding self-conscious. To call the balance in the 'Cockerels' Dance' felicitous would be an understatement; it is revelatory. Nor is affectionate an adequate word for Dausgaard's interpretations of all the music on this disc; there is love here, and a sense of crusading mission.

The praises of the *Rhapsody Overture* and *Pan and Syrinx* could be sung just as extravagantly. As could those over the theatre music excerpts,

all of which lead to or from the world of Nielsen's symphonies. Given playing of such finesse and bite (one virtually takes idiomatic understanding for granted) they all feel like gems in their own right.

Here's a Nielsen disc that comes about as close to the ideal as one could hope to hear, and it eclipses almost all others in its field. Dacapo's recording quality is top-drawer, and there is an exemplary essay from Jørgen I Jensen.

Symphonies

No 1 in G minor, FS16; **No 2**, FS29, 'The Four Temperaments'; **No 3**, FS60, 'Sinfonia espansiva'; **No 4**, FS76, 'The Inextinguishable'; **No 5**, FS97; **No 6**, FS116, 'Sinfonia semplice'

Symphonies Nos 1, 2 & 3ᵃ. Maskarade – Overture.
Aladdin – Suite, FS89
ᵃ**Nancy Wait Fromm** *sop* ᵃ**Kevin McMillan** *bar*
San Francisco Symphony Orchestra /
Herbert Blomstedt
Double Decca 460 985-2DF2 (134' · DDD)   Ⓜ❶❶❶☞

Ⓖ Nielsen always nurtured a special affection for his First Symphony – and rightly so, for its language is natural and unaffected. It has great spontaneity of feeling and a Dvořákian warmth and freshness. Blomstedt's recording is vital, beautifully shaped and generally faithful to both the spirit and the letter of the score. The recording is very fine: the sound has plenty of room to expand, there's a very good relationship between the various sections of the orchestra and a realistic perspective. The Second and Third are two of Nielsen's most genial symphonies, both of which come from the earliest part of the century, in performances of the very first order.

The Second (1902), inspired by the portrayal of *The Four Temperaments* (Choleric, Phlegmatic, Melancholic, Sanguine) that he had seen in a country inn, has splendid concentration and fire and, as always, from the right pace stems the right character. Moreover the orchestra sounds inspired, for there's a genuine excitement about its playing. Indeed Blomstedt's accounts are by far the most satisfying available. The Third, *Espansiva* (1910-11) is even more personal in utterance than *The Four Temperaments*, for during the intervening years Nielsen had come much further along the road of self-discovery. His melodic lines are bolder, the musical paragraphs longer and his handling of form more assured. It's a glorious and richly inventive score whose pastoral slow movement includes a part for two wordless voices. Blomstedt gives us an affirmative, powerful reading and in the slow movement, the soprano produces the required ethereal effect.

The sound is very detailed and full bodied, and in the best traditions of the company. Blomstedt's *Espansiva* has greater depth than most accounts; the actual sound has that glowing radiance that characterises Nielsen, and the tempo, the underlying current on which this music is borne, is expertly judged – and nowhere better than in the finale.

Symphony No 1. Flute Concerto. Rhapsody Overture: An imaginary trip to the Faroe Islands, FS123
Patrick Gallois *fl* **Gothenburg Symphony Orchestra / Myung-Whun Chung**
BIS BIS-CD454 (63' · DDD)   Ⓕ

This recording of the First Symphony is hardly less fine than that of Blomstedt. Tempi are generally well judged and there's a good feeling for the overall architecture of the piece. It gets off to a splendid start and Chung shapes the second group affectionately. He doesn't put a foot wrong in the slow movement, which has a splendid sense of line, and phrasing which is attentive but never overemphatic. The finale is exhilaratingly played. Throughout the work Chung knows how to build up to a climax and keep detail in the right perspective. As always, the Gothenburg Symphony plays with enthusiasm and spirit, as if it has always lived with this music and yet, paradoxically, is discovering it for the first time.

The Rhapsody Overture *An imaginary trip to the Faroe Islands* begins most imaginatively but inspiration undoubtedly flags. The performance of the Flute Concerto is rather special. It's most strongly characterised by Patrick Gallois who plays with effortless virtuosity and an expressive eloquence that's never over- or understated. His purity of line in the first movement is quite striking and he has the measure of the poignant coda. His dynamic range is wide, the tone free from excessive vibrato and his approach fresh.

Symphonies Nos 2 & 3
National Symphony Orchestra of Ireland / Adrian Leaper
Naxos 8 550825 (68' · DDD)   Ⓢ▶

The vital current on which every phrase must be borne in Nielsen needs to flow at higher voltage. This is music which needs to be played at white heat. Well, there's certainly no lack of electricity in Leaper's reading of the Second. He sets a cracking pace for the first movement, the choleric temperament, and hardly puts a foot wrong in its three companions. His tempi in the *Sinfonia espansiva* are well judged and sensible throughout all four of the movements. The finale, where many conductors get it wrong, seems to be just right. These are more than just serviceable performances: they're very good indeed and the Irish orchestra sounds well rehearsed and inside the idiom. You can pay more and do worse although some collectors will think the additional polish one gets from Blomstedt or Myung-Whun Chung is worth the extra outlay. These latter performances continue to grow in stature, and it's no mean compliment to the Naxos versions to say that they

give them a very good run for their money. Naxos doesn't identify the singers in the slow movement of the *Espansiva*.

No one investing in this issue and then going on to either of the Blomstedt accounts is going to feel that they have been let down. The recording team secures a very decent balance: well laid-back wind and brass, with good front-to-back perspective and transparency of texture.

Additional recommendation

Nielsen Symphony No 4, 'The Inextinguishable'
Coupled with **Sibelius** Symphony No 3, Op 52
Hallé / Barbirolli
BBC Legends BBCL4223-2 (65' · ADD)   Ⓕ
Each of these performances, recorded live in the Royal Albert Hall, makes a heavier entrance than in any modern recording. But not many bars have gone by before it is clear that the emphatic playing is a sign not of lethargy but of significant things being imparted. No one in the UK was making a more passionate case for Nielsen in 1965 than Barbirolli. And the Sibelius four years later also gets right to the heart of the matter, moving towards its blazing conclusion with a fantastic sense of inevitability – a classic single-breath performance.

Symphonies Nos 4-6. Little Suite in A minor, FS6[a].
Hymnus Amoris[b]
[b]**Barbara Bonney** *sop* [b]**John Mark Ainsley**, [b]**Lars Pedersen** *tens* [b]**Michael W Hansen, Bo Anker Hansen** *bars* **San Francisco Symphony Orchestra / Herbert Blomstedt;** [a]**Danish National Radio Symphony Orchestra /** [a]**Ulf Schirmer**
Double Decca 460 988-2DF2 (142' · DDD)   Ⓜ Ⓞ▶

The Fourth and Fifth are two of Nielsen's most popular and deeply characteristic symphonies. Blomstedt's are splendid performances. The Fourth occupied Nielsen between 1914 and early 1916 and reveals a level of violence new to his art. The landscape is harsher; the melodic lines soar in a more anguished and intense fashion (in the case of the remarkable slow movement, 'like the eagle riding on the wind', to use Nielsen's own simile). Blomstedt's opening has splendid fire and he isn't frightened of letting things rip. The finale with its exhilarating dialogue between the two timpanists comes off splendidly.

The Fifth Symphony of 1922 is impressive, too: it starts perfectly and has just the right glacial atmosphere. The climax and the desolate clarinet peroration into which it dissolves are well handled. The recording balance couldn't be improved upon: the woodwind are well recessed (though clarinet keys are audible at times), there's an almost ideal relationship between the various sections of the orchestra and a thoroughly realistic overall perspective.

Blomstedt's account of the Sixth Symphony is a powerful one, with plenty of intensity and an appreciation of its extraordinary vision. It's by far the most challenging of the cycle and inhabits a very different world from early Nielsen. The intervening years had seen the cataclysmic events of the First World War and Nielsen was suffering increasingly from ill health. Blomstedt and the fine San Francisco orchestra convey the powerful nervous tension of the first movement and the depth of the third, the *Proposta seria*.

Complete Symphonies
Danish National Symphony Orchestra / Michael Schønwandt
Video director **Pia Borgwardt**
'The Light and the Darkness' – A documentary written and directed by **Karl Aage Rasmussen**
Dacapo ③ ⏺ 2 110403/5 (5h 26' · NTSC · 16:9 · 2.0 and DTS 5.1 · 0)   Ⓕ

The number of Nielsen symphony cycles has grown steadily, with more than a dozen available. For this new DVD cycle, Schønwandt took orchestra and works back into the concert hall in November 2004, coming out with leaner, fitter accounts than his CD versions, well prepared and played with undeniable enthusiasm. Timings overall are swifter compared with the CD set but while there is more fire in the collective belly the performances do not consistently raise the roof or possess the electricity that Bernstein, Blomstedt or Vänskä found in this repertoire.

There are some reservations about the orchestral sound, particularly in Nos 1 and 2 where it occasionally lacks weight – the climax of the Second's opening *Allegro collerico*, for instance. However, from the outset of the *Sinfonia espansiva* (No 3) the textures are fuller-bodied; perhaps the slightly cavernous acoustic of the Danish Radio Concert Hall was a factor, perhaps the orchestra were pacing themselves knowing the task ahead. The recorded balance is good throughout.

The video direction is of fairly standard concert broadcasting type, mixing orchestral panoramas with interesting details. The latter are overused and long before the Fifth one begins to wonder whether there were more than two pretty violinists in the first section, if the tuba was alone in having an engraving or only the trombonists could see their reflections in the bells of their instruments. The direction hits the spot, however, in the finale of No 4, *The Inextinguishable*, where the camera angles along both sets of rampaging timpani, with the brass caught between as if in crossfire.

The set is augmented by an extra disc with a useful documentary by composer Karl Aage Rasmussen setting the music in the context of Nielsen's turbulent personal life. The English translation is read in curiously stilted fashion by Paul Hillier. Make sure that your DVD player is NTSC-capable - or everything in colour will appear a rather unhealthy shade of pink (the sound is unaffected). On Disc 1, when playing movements individually, the menu irritatingly reverts to the First Symphony, whereas on Disc 2 it remembers where you were. All in all, though, a very worthwhile issue.

Wind Quintet, FS100

Nielsen Wind Quintet **Fernström** Wind Quintet, Op 59 **Kvandal** Wind Quintet, Op 34. Three Sacred Folktunes, Op 23*b*
Oslo Wind Quintet (Tom Ottar Andreasson *fl* Lars Peter Berg *ob* Arild Stav *cl* Hans Peter Aasen *bn* Jan Olav Marthinsen *hn*)
Naxos 8 553050 (70' · DDD)   ⓈⒹ

This thoroughly entertaining CD combines three very different and unfamiliar works with what's probably the finest wind quintet ever penned. The major item here is the Nielsen: a glorious work which achieves the rare combination of seriousness of expression as well as being utterly relaxed in tone. The Oslo ensemble is a little slower than usual, but its measured tempi are most convincing; indeed, in the finale they highlight musical connections with Nielsen's Fifth and Sixth Symphonies in ways rarely heard. The Swede John Axel Fernström was undeniably a minor composer. If his music doesn't possess many visionary qualities it's certainly well crafted and his 1943 Quintet is an engaging concert opener. Johan Kvandal from Norway is a weightier proposition and better-known outside of his native country than is Fernström. Kvandal's Quintet, Op 34 (1971), was written for the Oslo ensemble and is serious and high-minded in tone, contrasting effectively with both the Fernström and Kvandal's own *Sacred Folktunes* of 1963. In the Quintet's fast second movement Kvandal adopts a rather Shostakovian manner, even alluding to the Soviet master's 12th Symphony, though to what purpose is unexplained. The idiomatic playing is reproduced in a slightly flat recording, although the Naxos sound has great immediacy.

String Quartets

No 1 in G minor, FS4; **No 2** in F minor, FS11; **No 3** in E flat, FS23; **No 4** in F, FS36

String Quartets Nos 1 & 2
Oslo Quartet (Geir Inge Lotsberg, Per Kristian Skalstad *vns* Are Sandbakken *va* Oystein Sonstad *vc*)
Naxos 8 553908 (62' · DDD)   ⓈⓄⒹ

Nielsen wrote five quartets in all between 1882 and 1919, although two exist in different versions, and the opus numbering is contradictory. This may explain why Naxos gets itself into such a pickle over the numbering of the G minor and F minor Quartets here, the second and third he composed. (The early D minor of 1882-3 remains unnumbered.) The G minor, Op 13 (FS4; 1887-88 but thoroughly rewritten in 1898) is No 1 and the F minor, Op 5 (FS11; 1890) is No 2. The front cover cites the works correctly as 'Quartets No 1, Op 13. No 2, Op 5', but the back cover has 'Quartet No 1 in F minor,

Op 5 (rev 1898)' and 'No 2 in G minor, Op 13 (1890)', managing thus to confuse both dates and numbering. Although in his notes Keith Anderson lays out the composition history quite simply, he refers only to the opus numbers, which should be consigned to oblivion and replaced by the more accurate Fog-Schousboe numbers.

The performances are as clear-sighted as the labelling is a mess. As with the first volume, the Oslo are sympathetic exponents, and do not over-lay any extraneous expression on the music as the disappointing Zapolski for Chandos did. Like the almost exactly contemporaneous early Sibelius quartets, there's barely a hint of the familiar, mature Nielsen in either work, but both are well crafted and beautifully written for the instru-ments. The Oslo seem completely at home in the style, more so than either the Kontra for BIS (who, like the Zapolski, have the benefit of top-quality sound) or Danish (Kontrapunkt) Quartets, making them come alive as none of their rivals manage. The recording is, like Volume 1, a touch confined but not constricted; that aside, this disc can be unreservedly recommended.

String Quartets Nos 3 & 4
Oslo Quartet (Geir Inge Lotsberg, Per Kristian Skalstad vns Are Sandbakken va Øystein Sonstad vc)
Naxos 8 553907 (57' · DDD)   Ⓢ

Why is it that quartets of international standing have not taken up the Nielsen quartets (or the Berwald or Stenhammar for that matter)? They are marvellous pieces and their neglect outside Scandinavia seems quite unaccountable. This release by the Oslo Quartet is refreshingly straightforward, full of vitality and spirit. Both scores are played with evident feeling but without any intrusive expressive exaggeration. The recordings are a little closely balanced, and as a result *fortissimo* passages can sound a touch fierce and wiry, for example in the closing page or so of the first movement of the F major (seven minutes into track 5). A pity the Oslo doesn't have as well-balanced a recording as Chandos and the Danish engineers provide for the Zapolski. The quartet is scrupulous in observing dynamic markings and gives totally dedicated, idiomatic performances. Artistically it's the finest at any price point.

String Quartets Nos 1-4. Movements for String Quartet, FS3c
Danish Quartet (Tim Frederiksen, Arne Balk-Møller vns Claus Myrup va H Brendstrup vc)
Kontrapunkt ② 32150/1 (138' · DDD)   Ⓕ

Nielsen composed two quartets and a string quintet during his student years. There was a gap of eight years between the F minor Quartet and the Third, in E flat, Op 14 (FS23) during which Nielsen had written his First Symphony, and another eight before the F major, Op 44 (FS36) saw the light of day. By this time he had written his opera *Saul and David* and the best

part of *Maskarade* as well as the Second Symphony.

The Danish Quartet is very sensitive to dynamic nuance and phrases imaginatively. The F major Quartet goes deeper than the Third. There's a grace, an effortless fluency and a marvellous con-trol of pace. Ideas come and go just when you feel they should; yet its learning and mastery is worn lightly. Though the earlier quartets aren't such perfect works of art, they're always endearing. The Danish Quartet is completely inside this music and is totally persuasive. In spite of the closely balanced recording this set gives real pleasure and can be recommended with enthusiasm.

Piano Works

Complete Piano Works
Martin Roscoe pf
Hyperion ② CDA67591/2 (114' · DDD)   Ⓕⓞ

Roscoe is famed for his touch and his playing's delicacy and finesse is evident throughout, from the early Five Pieces (1887-90) to the *Piano Music for Young and Old* (1930). In the Op 45 Suite *Det Luciferiske* (1919-20), he emphasises the lighter side – Lucifer was the bringer of Fire and Light after all – while in the Three Pieces (1928) he gets the balance between expression and experimentation just right (as does Leif Ove Andsnes in his selection).

However, there is more to Nielsen in his key-board works than subtlety: the bigger pieces need power and at times Roscoe seems reticent compared to his rivals. He is on record as finding *Det Luciferiske*'s finale expressively 'terrifying' yet that quality is absent from his playing.

This applies elsewhere, whether the trifling *Festival Prelude for the New Century* which Mina Miller (Danacord) makes more substantial, or the *Humoresk-Bagatelles'* electrifying 'The Jump-ing Jack'. Miller is generally livelier (some may argue over-characterised) but is let down by a somewhat clattery instrument; hers remain an impressive achievement. Roscoe's need more time to make their full impression as he lets the music make its own mark. While it may be invidious to judge a set on a single work, perhaps it is the treatment of the wonderful *Chaconne* (1916) that provides the truest benchmark: Ros-coe is at his best here, showing a clear grasp of its structure and momentum.

Joaquín Nin   Spanish-Cuban 1874-1949

Joaquín Nin y Castellanos was a Spanish-Cuban pianist and composer. Nin studied piano with Moritz Moszkowski and composition at the Schola Canto-rum (where he taught from 1906 to 1908). He toured as a pianist and was known as a composer and arranger of popular Spanish folk music. Nin was a member of the Spanish Academy and the French Legion of Honour. He was the father of the writer Anaïs Nin.

Piano Works

Cadena de valses. Canto de cuna para los huérfanos de España. '1830' variaciones sobre un tema frivolo. Danza ibérica. Segunda Danza ibérica. Danza andaluza. Danza murciana. Mensaje a Claudio Debussy
Martin Jones pf
Nimbus NI5851 (67' · DDD)   Ⓕ

With this endlessly fascinating disc the indefatigable Martin Jones adds another milestone to his towering Spanish discography. As Calum MacDonald tells us in his excellent accompanying essay, Nin wrote in a militantly Spanish style despite his sojourn in Paris and his birth and death in Cuba. Throughout all these works, familiar ideas gleaned from other Spanish composers, most notably Falla, are given with a witty and acidic twist. Anyone looking for picture-postcard Spain will be disappointed, while others with keener ears will be astonished by Nin's endlessly surprising idiom, his 'tangily Spanish' (MacDonald) vibrancy and colour.

Mensaje a Claude Debussy remembers a composer who prompted Falla to exclaim 'I wish I could write something as Spanish as that' (he was referring to *La soirée dans Grenade*). *Cadena de valses* is characteristically more sour than sweet and *Canto de cuna para los huerfános de España* is a moving reminder of those made orphans by the civil war. Nin's *Variations* incorporate an affectionate mockery of convention and, finally, in the *Danza murciana*, dark colouring gives way to a seductive, syncopated charm. All this music, much of it of an intricate virtuosity, is played with unflagging brio and complete poetic empathy by Martin Jones, whose missionary zeal of behalf of Spanish music deserves every honour Spain can offer. A crowning touch is provided by Nimbus's excellent sound.

Luigi Nono   *Italian 1924-1990*

A leading figure in the post-war European avant garde, he asserted his independence from that circle in the late 1950s, exploring a passionate social and political commitment through the most advanced technical means, electronics especially. While political messages are less explicit in his works from the late 1970s onwards, he sought in his last decade, through an extreme concentration of musical material and a meticulous attention to sound itself, modes of listening and performing which would embody on a more intimate level the same ethical concerns with perception, communication and human interaction.

Miscellaneous Works

No hay caminos, hay que caminar...Andrei Tarkovsky[a]. 'Hay que caminar' sognando[b].
Caminates...Ayacucho[c]
[c]**Susanne Otto** *contr* [c]**Roberto Fabbriciani** *fl* [b]**Irvine Arditti**, [b]**Graeme Jennings** *vns* [c]**Freiburg Soloists**

Choir; [c]**Freiburg (im Breisgau) Experimental Studio**; [c]**Cologne Radio Chorus and** [a]**Symphony Orchestra / Emilio Pomarico**
Kairos ② 0012512KAI (86' · DDD)   Ⓕ

Prometeo
Monika Bair-Ivenz, Petra Hoffmann *sops* **Susanne Otto** *contr* **Noa Frenkel** *counterten* **Sigrun Schell, Gregor Dalal** *spkrs* **Freiburg Soloists Choir; Recherche Ensemble; Members of the Freiburg Philharmonic Orchestra; Members of the South West German Radio Symphony Orchestra, Baden-Baden and Freiburg / Peter Hirsch, Kwamé Ryan**
Col Legno ② ⌨ WWE2SACD20605
(135' · DDD · T/N)   Ⓕ

These two splendid sets between them contain a substantial proportion of Luigi Nono's output in the last decade of his life: a complete studio recording of his stage work *Prometeo* (subtitled 'a tragedy of listening'), and the first complete recording of his *Caminantes* trilogy. Common to all of late Nono is a concern with sound events stripped to bare essentials: usually built on held notes and localised clusters punctuated by more discrete gestures, the music moves slowly – sometimes very slowly. Occasionally, disconcerting, more consonant sonorities are sketched, especially in *Prometeo*, which incorporates materials from earlier music. Not infrequently, near-silence prevails over a span of minutes. The demands made of the listener are considerable, but so, arguably, are the rewards.

The music makes considerable demands of the performers as well, both practically and interpretatively: with the exception of the two-violin piece *'Hay que caminar' sognando*, all these pieces mobilise large forces, including voices, with or without live electronics. The role of the latter, incidentally, is underlined by the use of SACD technology: Nono, who was born and died in Venice, was fond of invoking the spatial, polychoral effects of the Gabrielis. Finally, the role of silence or near-silence is such that the risk involved in live recordings is very great, any extraneous noise the potential 'killer' of an otherwise great performance. So in both these recordings there is a real sense of achievement, and one comes away, apart from anything else, with a profound gratitude to all concerned!

Of the two sets, the more immediately accessible is the one from Kairos, due to the greater variety of media: apart from the two-violin piece, Nono's last completed work, it includes *No hay caminos, hay que caminar...Andrei Tarkovsky*, scored for seven instrumental groups, and the still longer *Caminates...Ayacucho*, for three orchestral groups, choir, soloists (both vocal and instrumental), organ, electronics and percussion. The sense of scale is not markedly different in these works from that of the opera, though the spans of stillness are necessarily shorter, as a rule. In *Prometeo*, the avoidance of narrative doesn't exclude some impressive build-ups: the first *tre voci* episode consists of single voices very gradually evolving into much louder, complex sounds. It's a particularly moving climax, its effectiveness inversely proportional to Nono's use of the strategy. Both sets are essential listening and both are lovingly produced: *Prometeo* is accompanied by two booklets, including a 'listening score' in which the different text sources are colour-coded.

Vítězslav Novák   Bohemian 1870-1949

Novák studied with Jiránek and Dvořák at the Prague Conservatory (1889-92). He was strongly influenced by the folk music of Moravia and Slovakia, which he began to collect and study in the last decade of the 19th century. His output was substantial, with a focus on the symphonic poem as a form. He also wrote dramatic cantatas. His music is characterised by a rich melodic language and a fine sense of form and technique, in a plush late-Romantic vocabulary.

De profundis

Toman and the Wood Nymph, Op 40.
Lady Godiva, Op 41. De profundis, Op 67
BBC Philharmonic Orchestra / Libor Pešek
Chandos CHAN9821 (66' · DDD)   Ⓕ Ⓞ➸

Vítězslav Novák was a keen walker and each piece on this absorbing CD testifies to his vivid sense of outdoors. He was also fascinated by the female psyche and two of the works programmed bring rival viragos to mind: Smetana's Šárka (in the opening pages of *Lady Godiva*) and Strauss's Salome (the close of *Toman and the Wood Nymph*).

Yet for all their lustre, excitement and charm, even *Godiva* and *Toman* can't rival the oppressive power of Novák's wartime masterpiece *De profundis*, a work that surely levels with Martinů's *Lidice* as being among the most poignant musical memorials of the period. Composed during the Nazi occupation of Czechoslovakia, *De profundis* finds Novák employing a significantly darkened palette, though the exultant closing section (track 7) bears little resemblance to the various politically motivated 'happy endings' that were surfacing elsewhere. Novák's use of the organ runs parallel with Scriabin's in *The Poem of Ecstasy* (albeit to very different effect).

Libor Pešek shows obvious sympathy for this repertoire and the playing of the BBC Philharmonic reaches formidable heights of passion, notably at the close of *De profundis*. Alternative discs of Novák's music are few and far between, and hard to come by.

Jacob Obrecht   Netherlands c1450-1505

Obrecht's early life can be traced from Utrecht, c1476-78, then choirmaster for the Corporation of Bergen op Zoom, Cambrai – where he held the post of singing master – to Bruges. After a visit to Italy he was appointed maître de chapelle at Bruges in 1490. In his later years he alternated between Antwerp and Bergen op Zoom. He died of the plague while on a visit to Ferrara. An outstanding composer of sacred music, Obrecht's reputation during his life was considerable and widespread.

Missa Sub tuum praesidium

Missa Sub tuum praesidium. Salve regina. Ave regina caelorum. Ave maris stella. Alma redemptoris mater. Magnificat. Beata es Maria
Ars Nova / Paul Hillier
Ars Nova VANCD02 (63' · DDD · T/t)   Ⓕ

Missa Sub tuum praesidium. Factor orbis. Salve crux. Salve regina a 3. Beata es Maria. Benedicamus in laude. Mille quingentis
The Clerks' Group / Edward Wickham
ASV Gaudeamus CDGAU341 (70' · DDD · T/t)   Ⓕ

Back in the days of LPs, *Sub tuum praesidium* was one of the first of Obrecht's Masses to appear, and a second recording followed soon after. But 30 years have elapsed since then, so these two CDs are long overdue.

The scholar Birgit Lodes recently suggested that *Sub tuum praesidium* may be one of Obrecht's last Mass settings. It's concise, both in terms of length and economy of means; at the same time its rich scoring packs a real punch. Its premise is typical of Obrecht at his most rational, but also visionary. The *Kyrie* begins with three voices; each movement adds another, culminating in the seven-voice *Agnus Dei*. The *cantus firmus* recurs virtually unchanged in each movement, a fixed point; but as new voices and new chants (all of them Marian) are progressively added, the identity of the original plainchant is increasingly obscured as the texture thickens.

The tension between these two complementary processes generates a peculiar magic, and Ars Nova's performance captures this crucial feature. There's a certain lack of security in matters of detail, that may be put down to the recording venue: the church acoustic seems to dull the rhythmic angularity that characterises much of the Mass: bursts of rapid runs often seem to lose crispness and direction, and Hillier's brisk tempi at the start of sections have a tendency to slacken.

Though Hillier sets more consistent tempi (and in this work consistency is surely a virtue: the contrasts in tempo in The Clerks' *Kyrie* are a bit forced), Wickham makes his decisions tell more meaningfully. Where Ars Nova occasionally sound rushed, The Clerks hold every rhythmic detail, every imitative flourish in place.

The role of the title *cantus firmus* is nicely contrasted in the two versions: with Hillier (who has more than one soprano on each line, even when the music divides into several top lines) the additional voices superimpose themselves on the main chant, as though actively obscuring it; Wickham splits his two sopranos once occasion demands it, so that the plainsong gives the impression of receding gradually, as though of its own accord, into the distance. In the *Sanctus* and *Agnus Dei* Wickham takes his foot off the throttle: that's one solution to the score's increasing complexity, and though Hillier maintains the tension, it's Wickham and his singers who defend their conception more persuasively.

The Clerks' recording, a return to form for the group, is one of the strongest and well-rounded introductions to Obrecht in the catalogue. *Salve crux* and *Factor orbis* rank among his most impressive statements. The Clerks don't eclipse memories of the Orlando Consort in *Salve crux*, but their reading offers a most effective contrast. Even a slender-looking piece such as the three-voice *Salve regina* is handled with a sure-footedness that signals regained confidence; the astonishing conclusion has a delicacy one mightn't readily associate with its composer. Every piece contains similarly striking insights, where music and musicians are perfectly in sync. *Beata es, Maria* has been recorded many times but never more lucidly than here. This seems to be the first recording of *Mille quingentis*, Obrecht's memorial to his father, a work whose hieratic structure doesn't inhibit depth of feeling.

Johannes Ockeghem
Flanders c1410-1497

The earliest reference to Ockeghem as a singer shows that he was a vicaire-chanteur at Notre Dame, Antwerp, for a year from June 24, 1443. His déploration on Binchois's death (1460) suggests a connection with the Burgundian ducal chapel where Busnois and Dufay worked. He entered the service of Charles I, Duke of Bourbon, in Moulins in the mid-1440s and was a member of the chapel in 1446-48. In the year ending September 30, 1453, he is cited in the French court archives 'nouveau en 1451'. This service continued during Louis XI's reign, though he held other offices, including a canonry at Notre Dame, Paris (1463-70). In 1470 he visited Spain, in 1484 Bruges and Dammes. After Louis's death he remained premier chapelain and was still on the payroll in 1488. He enjoyed an enviable personal and professional reputation. His most imposing works are his Mass settings. Several are based on pre-existing material, sacred or secular. The level of contrapuntal skill and artistic excellence of his music laid a foundation for the achievements of Josquin's generation.

Masses

Missa Cuiusvis toni (four versions: Dorian, Phrygian, Lydian and Mixolydian). Intemerata Dei mater
Ensemble Musica Nova / Lucien Kandel
Aeon ② AECD0753 (115' · DDD)   Ⓕ

This is a recording that was waiting to happen: to do full justice to Ockeghem's famous Mass

designed for performance 'on whatever tone you choose', you really need to hear several complete versions side by side, and this is the first to present it that way. What's more, Ensemble Musica Nova's performances are technically superior to any that have been committed to disc so far.

The precise number of possible versions intended by Ockeghem has long been a matter of conjecture, but recently scholars have come back round to the idea that there may have been no more than three (starting on re, mi, and fa). Here, there are four, comprising the Dorian, Phrygian, Lydian and Mixolydian modes. For what it's worth, the last two are so close as to be virtually indistinguishable (which supports the view that the Mixolydian version is superfluous). Inevitably, given the uncertainties attending modal usage in medieval polyphony, one can take issue with certain decisions affecting the 'colour' of each mode. The decision, for instance, to interpret many Bs as flat in the Phrygian is slightly confusing.

In each version, the modal final (roughly equivalent to the home key in tonal music) is sung on the same absolute pitch. As well as being sound from a historical standpoint, this eliminates at a stroke any problems of range and tessitura: the singers deliver each version with the same ease. In addition, each version is sung at precisely the same tempo. Though this decision is less self-evident, it has at least the virtue of consistency.

Ensemble Musica Nova are a mixed choir singing two-to-a-part in a sympathetic acoustic that allows for contrapuntal clarity and a sound image at once warm and bright. Just occasionally one detects signs of tiredness, at the beginning of the Mixolydian *Sanctus* for instance, where there is also an inexplicable 'gain'. But these really are quibbles in the face of such an enterprising project: the music is glorious!

Ockeghem Missa L'homme armé. Ave Maria. Alma redemptoris mater **Josquin Desprez** Memor esto verbi tui **Plainchant** Alma redemptoris mater. Immittet angelus Domini **Anonymous** L'homme armé
Oxford Camerata / Jeremy Summerly
Naxos 8 554297 (57' · DDD · T/t)   ⓈⒹ▸

The centrepiece here is Ockeghem's *L'homme armé* Mass. It may be one of his earliest Masses, dating perhaps from the early 1450s. It's also one of his most curious. For the most part it lies in a relatively high register, belying his usual predilection for low bass ranges; but every now and again the basses descend in spectacular fashion. In the third *Agnus* they hold down the tune in very long notes, while the other voices seem to float above them. Seldom before in the history of music can the articulation of time have been so clear a feature of a piece's design: it seems almost to have been suspended altogether. It's an extraordinary moment, difficult to pull off in performance, but here the singers seem to have got it right. Elsewhere, Summerly's approach is nicely varied, but on the whole more meditative than emphatic. The performance grows in stature with each movement, as though keeping pace with the cycle's ambition. The reading isn't without the odd glitch, but taken as a whole it's a fine achievement. The accompanying motets work very well, but it's a shame that the choir's richness of sound isn't quite matched by the acoustic. But the overall impression is resoundingly positive: those new to Ockeghem should find this disc too good an opportunity to pass up.

Ockeghem Requiem. Fors seulement. Missa Fors seulement **Brumel** Du tout plongiet/Fors seulement **De la Rue** Fors seulement
The Clerks' Group / Edward Wickham
ASV Gaudeamus CDGAU168 (71' · DDD · T/t)
Ⓕ🅞🅞🅞

 Top billing goes to the Requiem, Ockeghem's most widely recorded work, and perhaps his most enigmatic piece, stylistically very wide-ranging and diverse. Aesthetic judgement is hard to pass, since it may well be incomplete; but the surviving movements contain some of his most arresting inspirations. This is the first version of any quality to feature sopranos on the top lines. Incidentally, no recording of the Requiem is uniformly excellent; on the other hand, the words of the Mass for the dead conjure up many associations, and The Clerks deserve praise for the verve and imagination with which they respond to the work's interpretative challenges.

The fillers are the works built on Ockeghem's song *Fors seulement* (which includes Antoine Brumel's *Du tout plongiet*). It's difficult to decide which to praise more highly: the pieces themselves, which are incomparable, or the singing, which represents The Clerks' finest achievement to date. *Fors seulement* inspired a flowering of astonishing pieces scored for very low voices (initiated, it appears, by the composer himself): in both the Mass and in *Du tout plongiet*, the basses descend to written low Cs. In addition, these pieces are exceptionally richly scored (the Mass and the De la Rue song are five-voice works), creating polyphony as dense and as dark as a strong Trappist ale. The Clerks achieve almost miraculous linear definition here, without losing an iota of the music's sensuous appeal: that's quite a feat, given the low pitch and awesome contrapuntal complexity involved. This must be counted as a major achievement.

Jacques Offenbach

German/French 1819-1880

Ironically, the composer who came to epitomise the gay frivolity of the Second Empire, 'the King of the Paris Boulevards', was a German, born Jakob Eberst, the son of a Jewish cantor and bookbinder. 'Jakob' became

'Jacques' and his father, known as Isaac der Offenbacher (after Offenbach-am-Main where he lived), decided to change the family name to 'Offenbach'. By the age of 14 Jacques was in the Paris Conservatoire studying the cello and Paris remained his base for the rest of his life. After that he was a cellist in the orchestra of the Opéra-Comique and started to compose both operettas and pieces for his instrument. In 1850 he was engaged as the conductor at the Théâtre Français. By the mid-1850s he was well versed in every aspect of operetta production from start to finish.

An eccentric, wiry-looking man, Offenbach had little success as a composer until his forties when he took the bold step of opening his own theatre in order to mount the work that had been consistently been turned down by others. In 1855 the former Théâtre Comte was renamed Bouffes-Parisiens and for the next decade, under Offenbach's direction, it was the fashionable place to be.

During this time, Offenbach elevated burlesque opera into an art form all his own. His melodic invention and skill as a composer and orchestrator won him immense respect but it was the subjects of his operettas that made him incredibly popular – he satirised other composers such as Wagner and Meyerbeer, the army, the social order, the present government, Greek mythology – you name it. Wagner wrote that Offenbach's music was 'a dung heap in which all the swine of Europe wallowed'.

For 20 years, Offenbach reigned supreme as the master of his particular art. By the mid-1870s, the public had begun to tire of him: a series of spectacular productions failed, leaving him bankrupt and (irony of ironies) Johann Strauss, whom he'd encouraged to write operettas, came and conquered Paris with Die Fledermaus. Offenbach took off for America where he was offered $1000 a night for a minimum of 30 nights. When he returned home in 1876 to write what was to prove his masterpiece, The Tales of Hoffmann, it was to show a more serious side. He never lived to finish the work. It was his 102nd piece for the stage.

Gaîté parisienne

Gaîté parisienne. Offenbachiana (both arr Rosenthal)
**Monte Carlo Philharmonic Orchestra /
Manuel Rosenthal**
Naxos 8 554005 (68' · DDD) Ⓢ🄳►

Manuel Rosenthal was 92 when he made this recording – his third – of *Gaîté parisienne*, his ballet for Massine that had produced such a storm of applause in Monte Carlo back in 1938. He made very clear why he was anxious to do so: not only had there been poor recordings, cut versions and mauled arrangements of his score by others, but in his own previous recordings he had felt obliged to accommodate the dancers' wishes as regards tempi, and now he wanted to treat his work symphonically, with more spacious speeds that would enable details of the orchestration to emerge fully for the first time. So we can now accept this 45-minute version as authentic, and the more deliberate pace adopted in some places (beautifully and expressively so in the Barcarolle) in no way diminishes the brilliant impact of his treatment of Offenbach's heady tunes. The Monte Carlo orchestra, long familiar with the work, give their all to the aged maestro, with voluptuous string playing in lyrical sections; and the recording is exceptionally vivid. But the real joy of this disc is *Offenbachiana*, music drawn from a handful of the stage works arranged by Rosenthal. This is a subtler, wittier and, if anything, even more scintillating score. Absolutely not to be missed!

Operetta and Opera Arias

'Entre Nous – Celebrating Offenbach'
Artists include **Cassandre Berthon, Mark le Brocq,
Laura Claycomb, André Cognet, Loïc Félix, Yvonne
Kenny, Jennifer Larmore, Colin Lee, Alastair Miles,
Diana Montague, Alexandra Sherman, Mark
Stone, Elizabeth Vidal, Mark Wilde; London
Philharmonic Orchestra / David Parry**
Opera Rara ② ORR243 (154' · DDD · T/t)   ⓕ**OO**

Offenbach composed over 100 works for the stage, only a few of which have been recorded complete. This groundbreaking set offers 41 extracts from two dozen comic operas from the master of irony and melody, ranging from the early *Une nuit blanche* – which was on the bill at the opening night of Les Bouffes-Parisiens in 1855 – to elaborate spectacles such as *Les bergers*, an essay in time travel from ancient Greece to modern France, *Vert-Vert*, which features a dead parrot, and *Le voyage dans la lune*, in which the Moonfolk catch that dirty disease from Earth – love.

Offenbach tailored all his operas to particular performers, and it is a challenge to modern singers to find their own way of suggesting the outsize personalities of such stars as Hortense Schneider and Zulmar Bouffar. Colin Lee is splendid in an aria written for Etienne Pradeau in *La rose de Saint-Flour*, in which a stuttering coppersmith brings a cooking-pot as a gift to his beloved. Yvonne Kenny and Alexandra Sherman offer the contrasting personalities of the two heroines of *La Créole*, while Jennifer Larmore takes on the shade of Schneider in *La Diva*, with an outrageous parody of the Act 2 finale of *La traviata*. From *Geneviève de Brabant* comes a nifty little rondo about a pâté, sung by Cassandre Berthon, and Offenbach's first opera based on a story by ETA Hoffmann, *Le roi carotte*, gives us a 'Ronde de chemins de fer', one of the earliest operatic train journeys. *Le fifre enchanté* has a giddy coloratura marching song which Laura Claycomb negotiates with panache. Even from the extracts it's easy to gauge the thin line Offenbach and his librettists were treading vis-à-vis the censors with works like *La jolie parfumeuse* (hear Mark Stone sing 'Pardieu!'), *Les Braconniers* – Diana Montague in a typical Bouffar moment celebrating her lover's 'grosse frimousse' – and *L'île de Tulipatan*, a satire on the folly of emperors, as Loïc Félix as King Cacatois sings about gossip columns. Entrancing and highly recommended.

Barbe-Bleue – Y'a des bergères dans le village.
La belle Hélène – C'est le devoir des jeunes lilies;
Amours divins! ardentes flammes! Les contes
d'Hoffmann – Belle nuit, ô nuit d'amour[b]. Fantasio[a] –
Voyez dans la nuit brune; Quel murmure charmant
soudain viens-je d'entendre? La fille du tambour-
major – Que m'importe on titre éclatant. La Grande-
Duchesse de Gerolstein[c] – Portez armes…Ah, que
j'aime les militaires; Oui, General, quelqu'un vous
aime…Dites-lui qu'on l'a remarque; Ah! C'est on
fameux regiment. Lischen et Fritzchen – Je suis
alsacienne[f]. Madame l'archiduc[cdef] – Sextuor de
l'Alphabet. La Périchole – Ah! quel diner je viens de
faire. La vie parisienne – Nous entrons dans cette
demeure[cef]. Le carnaval des Revues – Le symphonie
de l'avenir; Marche de fiancés. Ouverture à grand
orchestre
Anne Sofie von Otter *mez*
[a]**Magali Léger,** [b]**Stephanie d'Oustrac** *sops* [c]**Gilles
Ragon,** [d]**Jean-Christophe Keck,** [e]**Jean-Christophe
Henry** *tens* [f]**Laurent Naouri** *bar* [d]**Christophe
Grapperon** *bass* **Choeur des Musiciens du Louvre;
Les Musiciens du Louvre / Marc Minkowski**
DG 471 501-2GH (70' · DDD)
Recorded live 2001   ⓕ**OOO**▷

Anne Sofie von Otter immediately stamps her brilliance on this fascinating collection as Offenbach's voluptuous Grand-Duchess. Her commanding projection and phrasing in 'Ah, que j'aime les militaires' are followed by tender lyricism in 'Dites-lui'. Gilles Ragon trills irresistibly as a youthful and virile Lieutenant Fritz in the 'Chanson militaire', and there's a refreshing spring in the step of Minkowski's conducting, with just the sort of lightweight orchestra that Offenbach favoured. There follow two glorious numbers from *Fantasio*, a virtually forgotten pre-*Hoffmann* serious work. And then – wonder of wonders! – we get the oft-cited Wagner spoof Le symphonie de l'avenir. Modest in scope it is, but fascinating to hear at last.

We scarcely needed another *Hoffmann* Barcarolle, and yet the image of the gondola floating along the Grand Canal has seldom been created as gracefully as here. The rest is conceived with intelligence and imagination, and performed with equal brilliance, with the range of supporting performers heightening the variety.

The programme encompasses all that is fascinating in Offenbach's output – tender and sparkling by turns, engaging throughout – and all quite wonderfully performed. Irresistible!

La belle Hélène

La belle Hélène   Ⓟ
Felicity Lott *sop* Hélène **Yann Beuron** *ten* Pâris
Michel Sénéchal *ten* Ménélas **Laurent Naouri** *bar*
Agamemnon **François Le Roux** *bar* Calchas **Marie-
Ange Todorovitch** *mez* Oreste **Eric Huchet** *bar*
Achille **Alain Gabriel** *ten* Ajax I **Laurent Alvaro** *bar*
Ajax II **Hjördis Thébault** *sop* Bacchis
Choeur et Musiciens du Louvre / Marc Minkowski
Virgin Classics ② 545477-2 (118' · DDD · T/t)   ⓕ**OO**▷

From its very first bars, this recording strikes a chord of authenticity. Too often Offenbach's works are recorded with large orchestra, huge chorus and swimming-bath acoustics. Offenbach himself was perfectly happy to accept larger forces when available, but they do rather swamp the gossamer lightness and piquancy of what he actually composed.

The feeling of a stage production pervades the recording in its integration of dialogue and music, as also in the uninhibited singing and playing of Orestes' opening couplets. Marie-Ange Todorovitch performs with appropriately boyish high spirits throughout, and Michel Sénéchal as Ménélas, Laurent Naouri as Agamemnon and François Le Roux as Calchas ensure this recording is cast from strength. Although Felicity Lott's Hélène lacks that distinctive French way of wrapping the voice round the words in her great arias, she succeeded in capturing Paris (the city as well as the Trojan prince). What appeals especially is her lightness of voice compared with the mezzo tones of many other interpreters. Yet the voice and interpretation that captivate the ear most here are those of Yann Beuron as Pâris. His hon-eyed tones are heard to absolute perfection throughout, but his *pianissimo* singing of the final verse of the 'Judgement of Paris' makes it an especially model interpretation. Moreover, Beuron has music to sing that isn't in any previous recording – a lullaby, complete with dove cooing, preceding the Dream Duet. There's more, too. In the 1865 German version, the scene of the Game of Goose was longer than in the 1864 French original, and here it's longer still. But most importantly, this is a sparkling, beautifully paced recording and is now a clear first choice for what's surely Offenbach's most captivating operetta.

Additional recommendation

La belle Hélène
Kasarova Hélène **Davislim** Achille **van der Walt** Pâris **Widmer** Agamemnon **Amoretti** Ajax I
Davidson Ajax II **Rohner** Bacchis **Chausson** Calchas
Vogel Ménélas **Nichiteanu** Oreste **Baumann** Slave
Zürich Opera House Chor & Orch / **Harnoncourt**
Stage director **Lohner** *Video director* **Schottler**
ArtHaus Musik 🟥 100 086 (124' · 16:9 · PCM stereo ·
2, 5). Recorded live 1997   🄵🔵

This Zürich production fully enters into the spirit of Offenbach's satirical romp, hardly ever stepping over into farce. Everything is at once disciplined, contained and at the same time appropriately zany under the observant stage direction of Helmut Lohner. In the pit is Harnoncourt to ensure that the musical values are as exemplary as the visual ones. The polyglot cast, speaking and singing excellent French, enjoys its collective self, headed by Kasarova's languidly erotic Helen.

Les contes d'Hoffmann

Les contes d'Hoffmann
Plácido Domingo *ten* Hoffmann **Dame Joan**

Sutherland *sop* Olympia, Giulietta, Antonia, Stella
Gabriel Bacquier *bar* Lindorf, Coppélius,
Dapertutto, Dr Miracle **Huguette Tourangeau** *mez*
La Muse, Nicklausse **Jacques Charon** *ten* Spalanzani
Hugues Cuénod *ten* Andrès, Cochenille,
Pitichinaccio, Frantz **André Neury** *bar* Schlemil **Paul
Plishka** *bass* Crespel **Margarita Lilowa** *mez* Voice of
Antonia's Mother **Roland Jacques** *bar* Luther
Lausanne Pro Arte Chorus; Du Brassus Chorus;
Suisse Romande Chorus and Orchestra /
Richard Bonynge
Decca ② 417 363-2DH2 (143' · ADD · T/t)
Recorded 1968   🄵🔵🔵🔾➤

This is a wonderfully refreshing set. The story emerges crystal-clear, even the black ending to the Giulietta scene in Venice, which in Bonynge's text restores the original idea of the heroine dying from a draught of poison, while the dwarf Pitichinaccio shrieks in delight. One also has to applaud his rather more controversial decision to put the Giulietta scene in the middle and leave the dramatically weighty Antonia scene till last. That also makes the role of Stella the more significant, giving extra point to the decision to have the same singer take all four heroine roles. With Dame Joan available it was a natural decision, and though in spoken dialogue she's less comfortable in the Giulietta scene than the rest, the contrasting portraits in each scene are all very convincing, with the voice brilliant in the Doll scene, warmly sensuous in the Giulietta scene and powerfully dramatic as well as tender in the Antonia scene. Gabriel Bacquier gives sharply intense performances, firm and dark vocally, in the four villain roles, Hugues Cuénod contributes delightful vignettes in the four *comprimario* tenor roles, while Domingo establishes at the very start the distinctive bite in his portrait of Hoffmann; a powerful and a perceptive interpretation. The recording is vivid, and the listener is treated to some first-class playing from the Suisse Romande Orchestra.

Les contes d'Hoffmann
Raoul Jobin *ten* Hoffmann **Renée Doria** *sop*   🄷
Olympia **Vina Bovy** *sop* Giulietta **Géori Boué** *sop*
Antonia **Fanély Revoil** *mez* Nicklausse **Louis Musy**
bar Lindorf **André Pernet** *bass* Coppélius **Charles
Soix** *bass* Dapertutto **Roger Bourdin** *bar* Dr Miracle
René Lapelletrie *ten* Spalanzani **Camille Maurane**
bar Hermann **Chorus and Orchestra of the Opéra-
Comique, Paris / André Cluytens**
Naxos Historical ② 8 110214/5 (130' · ADD · T)
Recorded 1948   🅂🔵

In the 1930s in Paris, Raoul Jobin and José Luccioni were the two great opera matinée-idols. Jobin, a French Canadian, made his debut in 1930 and was soon singing at both the Opéra, as Faust, Lohengrin and Raoul in *Les Huguenots*, and at the Opéra-Comique, where he was a favourite Hoffmann and Don José. This recording may perhaps find him just a little late in his career. His years at the Metropolitan (throughout the German occupation) obviously took their toll, when he sang roles that were too heavy for him in such a huge theatre. However, the splendour of this set is the authenticity of the vocal style and the diction of such stalwarts of the Opéra-Comique ensemble as Louis Musy, Roger Bourdin, Fanély Revoil (better known as an operetta singer) and, luxurious casting, Camille Maurane in the small part of Hermann.

The three heroines are well inside their roles, but they're afflicted with a little strain in the higher-lying passages. Renée Doria sang all these parts later in her career – when this recording was made she was just at the outset, having made her debut in Paris in 1944. Her Olympia is strong on the *staccato* notes but a bit fragile in the long phrases – this doll broke quite easily, one imagines. In the same act, André Pernet, a great figure from pre-war Paris, is a superb Coppélius. In the Venice act, Vina Bovy is dramatically convincing as Giulietta, but hasn't much vocal sheen left (she made her debut in 1919). Géori Boué, the Antonia, is one of the great figures from French post-war opera, but one feels that Giulietta would have been her role ideally. As for Jobin, despite some strain, he makes a convincing poet. Although there's such strong competition on CD where *Hoffmann* is concerned, this historic version is without doubt essential listening for a sense of style if the work absorbs you.

Orphée aux enfers

Orphée aux enfers
Yann Beuron ten Orphée **Natalie Dessay** sop Eurydice **Jean-Paul Fouchécourt** ten Aristeus-Pluto **Laurent Naouri** bar Jupiter **Lydie Pruvot** sop Juno **Ewa Podles** mez Public Opinion **Steven Cole** ten John Styx **Véronique Gens** sop Vénus **Patricia Petibon** sop Cupid **Jennifer Smith** sop Diane **Etienne Lescroart** ten Mercury **Virginie Pochon** sop Minerva **Grenoble Chamber Orchestra; Chorus and Orchestra of the Opéra National de Lyon / Marc Minkowski**
EMI ② 556725-2 (110' · DDD · T/t)   Ⓕ**Ⓞ🅑➔**

Orphée aux enfers may be Offenbach's best-known operetta, but it's had limited attention on disc. The lightly scored original 1858 version was in two acts and four scenes. The spectacular 1874 version had lots of extra songs and ballet numbers. Since this latter demands huge forces, it's scarcely viable on stage today. The usual solution in the theatre is thus to add selected numbers from the 1874 version to the 1858 text, and this is what was done for the performances at Geneva, Lyons and Grenoble that formed the basis of this recording. Home listeners may prefer to make their own selections of numbers, and musicologically questionable decisions such as the rescoring of 1874 pieces for 1858 orchestral resources become more exposed. What matters most, though, is the quality of performance, and the pleasures of this one are formidable.

Above all, Natalie Dessay's exchanges in the first act with her despised violinist husband (the admirable Yann Beuron) are superbly done. So is her sighing over Jean-Paul Fouchécourt's Aristeus, whose two big solos show equal elegance. Later come Laurent Naouri's formidable Jupiter and cameos such as Etienne Lescroart's agile performance of Mercury's song and Patricia Petibon's deliciously winning account of Cupid's 'Couplets des baisers'. Ensemble numbers are extremely well done and throughout, Marc Minkowski provides thoughtful, lively direction.

What causes doubt is the tendency towards overstatement, from the opening monologue of Ewa Podles's Public Opinion, where almost every word seems to be given exaggerated emphasis, through Aristeus's crude falsetto in his opening solo, to a curiously mechanical version of John Styx's 'Quand j'étais roi de Béotie' and some gratuitous vocal gymnastics in the 'Hymne à Bacchus'. Ultimately, however, those doubts are banished by the virtues.

Minkowski's is a consistently imaginative performance, and at its best a superbly musical version of Offenbach's sparkling creation.

Orphée aux enfers
Yann Beuron ten Orpheus **Natalie Dessay** sop Eurydice **Jean-Paul Fouchécourt** ten Aristeus-Pluto **Laurent Naouri** bar Jupiter **Lydie Pruvot** mez Juno **Martine Olmeda** mez Public Opinion **Steven Cole** ten John Styx **Maryline Fallot** sop Venus **Cassandre Berthon** sop Cupid **Virginie Pochon** sop Diane **Etienne Lescroart** ten Mercury **Alketa Cela** sop Minerva **Grenoble Chamber Orchestra; Chorus and Orchestra of the Opéra National de Lyon / Marc Minkowski**
Stage director **Laurent Pelly**
Video director **Jean-Pierre Brossmann**
TDK Mediactive ② 🅓🅥🅓 DV-OPOAE (123' · 16:9 · PCM stereo, 5.1 & DTS 5.1 · 0)   Ⓕ

Before their acclaimed *La belle Hélène*, Laurent Pelly and Marc Minkowski staged Offenbach's first great success for Lyon Opéra in the same pleasantly outrageous manner. Minkowski's conducting again recalls Leibowitz's classic recordings – bone-dry, sprightly and slightly manic. Certain quirks in the CD version, in particular the destructive speed of Eurydice's sensuous 'Bacchus Hymn', are explained if not excused by Pelly's production – as manic and as refreshing, in his clever use of dancers, surreal sight gags, and cheerfully unfettered sex. His 'backstage' settings make less sense than *Hélène*'s, but the Cloud-Cushion-Land Olympus is inspired.

The hard-worked cast respond superbly, notably Natalie Dessay's modern Parisienne Eurydice, dressy, leggy, and neurotic, delivering zinging coloratura while bouncing on a sofa or perched high on a stage lift.

Minkowski occasionally forces the pace, and Pelly's high camp sometimes tips over into shrill vulgarity. The remastered surround-sound is rather stagey, occasionally losing voices in unfriendly perspectives. It's still treasurable, and vastly superior to its only DVD rival, a dismal Brussels staging. Avoid that; buy this; rejoice.

La vie parisienne

La vie parisienne
Laurent Naouri bar Baron de Gondremark **Marie
Devellereau** sop Gabrielle **Jean-Sébastien Bou** bar
Raoul de Gardefeu **Marc Callahan** bar Bobinet **Maria
Riccarda Wesseling** mez Métella **Michelle
anniccioni** sop La Baronne **Jean-Paul Fouchécourt**
ten Frick **Lyon National Opera Chorus and
Orchestra / Sébastien Rouland**
Stage director **Laurent Pelly**
Video director **François Roussillon**
Virgin Classics 📀 519301-9 (135' · NTSC · 16:9 ·
PCM stereo, 5.0 and DTS 5.1 · 0)
Recorded live in December 2007   Ⓕ**O**

La belle Hélène
Felicity Lott sop Hélène **Yann Beuron** ten Pâris
Michel Sénéchal ten Ménélas **Laurent Naouri** bar
Agamennon **François Le Roux** bar Calchas
Les Musiciens du Louvre / Marc Minkowski
Stage director **Laurent Pelly**
Video director **Ross MacGibbon**
ArtHaus Musik 📀 107 000 (153' · 16:9 · PCM stereo,
5.1 and DTS 5.1 · 2). Recorded live at the Théâtre du
Châtelet, Paris, in 2000   Ⓕ**OO**

Both these productions by Laurent Pelly of classic Offenbach opéras-bouffes are somewhat radical in their staging. Neither of them presents the works in a way one would choose to see very often, but they are performed with such vigour and vaudevillian élan that it's hard to resist their appeal.

La vie parisienne was conceived by Offenbach's librettists, Henri Meilhac and Ludovic Halévy, as an entertainment for and about the hordes of tourists visiting Paris for the 1867 Exposition Universelle. Pelly and his designer Chantal Thomas update it to the present, so that instead of waiting for the train in Act 1, the two heroes, Bobinet and Raoul de Gardefeu, are in the arrivals section of an international airport. This scene is punctuated by many irritating announcements over the loudspeakers. To a large extent this spoils the scene, so it's a relief when it changes to Raoul's exquisitely minimalist apartment. Here the action perks up with the arrival of Marie Devellereau as the glove-seller, Gabrielle, and Jean-Paul Fouchécourt as Frick, the bootmaker. The riotous finale, as the table-d'hôte guests are summoned to dinner, really goes with a swing. Best of all is Act 3, when all the girls, impersonating aristocrats, arrive in haute-couture black gowns and march around like catwalk mannequins. In particular, Brigitte Hool as Pauline joins Laurent Naouri as the duped Swedish baron in a splendid account of 'O, beau nuage'. The finale, culminating in the ensemble 'Tout tourne, tout danse' really won me over. The last act is in a somewhat sleazy disco, but again the sheer energy of the dancing and the whole spirit of irreverence is so well caught that one feels like joining in the applause. Sébastien Rouland leads the orchestra and chorus of the Lyon Opéra in a performance that is

true to the spirit, if not the letter, of the work. Jean-Sébastien Bou and Marc Callahan as Raoul and Bobinet make a terrific pair of womanising socialites, Jesus Garcia a vigorous Brésilien, and in her few moments Michelle Canniccioni is suitably eager as the Baroness out to savour the delights of Paris.

Musically, La belle Hélène from the Châtelet is a stronger proposition. The production is even more extreme, everything happening as if in the dream of a suburban housewife, played by Dame Felicity Lott with her usual mixture of restraint and comic irony. Everyone is consequently in pyjamas and night attire a lot of the time. (The same recording has been issued on CD from Virgin). Yann Beuron is a salty Paris, and the presence of Michel Sénéchal, François Le Roux and again Laurent Naouri ensures that vocal values triumph over some of the excesses of the production.

Tarik O'Regan   British b1978

After studying at both Oxford and Cambridge, O'Regan divides his time between New York City and Trinity College, Cambridge, where he is Fellow Commoner in the Creative Arts. He has held the Fulbright Chester Schirmer Fellowship in Music Composition at Columbia University and a Radcliffe Institute Fellowship at Harvard. He has also served on the Visiting Faculty of Yale University's Institute of Sacred Music. His music has been performed by the BBC Symphony Orchestra, London Sinfonietta, Estonian Philharmonic Chamber Choir and Los Angeles Master Chorale. An opera based on Joseph Conrad's Heart of Darkness is scheduled to be premiered late in 2011.

Vocal Works

Threshold of Night. Care Charminge Sleepe. Had
I not seen the sun. The Ecstasies Above. Tal vez
tenemos tiempo. Triptych. I had no time to hate
**Company of Voices; Conspirare /
Craig Hella Johnson**
Harmonia Mundi 💿 HMU80 7490
(60' · DDD/DSD)   Ⓕ**O⊕**

Tarik O'Regan can justifiably stake a claim as one of the leading British choral composers of his generation. This is supported to an extent by the seven choral compositions contained on this recording.

At the basis of O'Regan's style lies a thoroughgoing understanding of both the English choral tradition and medieval music, a knowledge gained from studies at Oxford and Cambridge. But recent works suggest that he casts his creative net much wider these days. Post-minimal and pop features can be detected in the use of straightforward harmonic progressions and melodic repetitions in the final sections of both The Ecstasies Above and Triptych, where O'Regan

ORFF CARMINA BURANA – IN BRIEF

Janowitz, Stolze, Fischer-Dieskau; Deutsche Oper Chorus and Orchestra / Eugen Jochum
DG 447 437-2GOR (56' · DDD) Ⓜ❶❶❶❷

Recorded in the presence of the composer back in 1968. The soloists are very vivid, with Janowitz quite ravishing in her restraint and purity of tone. The chorus is superb.

Armstrong, English, Allen; London Symphony Chorus and Orchestra / André Previn
EMI 566899-2 (63' · ADD) Ⓜ❶❶❷

Still one of the great recordings of the work, full of excitement, event and above all good humour. Allen is magnificent, and the sound, from 1975, still sounds amazingly vivid.

Walmsley-Clark, Graham-Hall, Maxwell; London Symphony Chorus and Orchestra / Richard Hickox
Regis RRC1136 (64' · DDD) Ⓢ❶

Hickox the choral trainer is shown off here to great effect in an exciting and vivid performance reissued at budget price. The solo singing is good too, so definitely worth considering if you're on a budget.

Matthews, Brownlee, Gerhaher; Berlin Radio Chorus; Berlin PO / Sir Simon Rattle
EMI 557888-2 (60' · DDD) Ⓟ❶❷

An invigorating revisiting of an ever-popular score: Rattle has stripped it down and rebuilt it in a way that will either entrance or annoy. Thrillingly alive and superbly recorded.

Rutter, Randle, Eiche; Bournemouth Choruses and SO / Marin Alsop
Naxos 8 570033 (62' · DDD) Ⓢ❷

A performance that has divided the critics. On the positive side are Alsop's innate sense of rhythm and the characterful singing of the male soloists. But some have found it all a little underpowered. Try and sample before you purchase – but it is a bargain!

Hendricks, Aler, Hagegård; London Symphony Chorus and Orchestra / Eduardo Mata
RCA 74321 53657-2 (60' · DDD) Ⓑ❶❷

Another stunning LSO *Carmina Burana* that employs Mata's rhythmic virtuosity to spectacular effect. Full of character and beautifully sung. A superb budget version.

Popp, Van Kesteren, Prey; Bavarian Radio Chorus; Munich Radio Orchestra / Kurt Eichhorn
RCA *DVD* 74321 85285-9 (78') Ⓕ

Jean-Pierre Ponnelle's racy video interpretation takes Eichhorn's fine 1975 performance as its soundtrack. It's all a lot of fun and gives the work a dramatic outlet that in concert it often so desperately seems to aspire too.

---

dispenses with contrapuntal complexity for a direct and unadorned approach. If this suggests an American influence then it is also evident in his choice of text settings, with Edgar Allan Poe and Emily Dickinson's poetry framing the collection.

However, it is sometimes difficult not to draw comparisons between the often static, sometimes propulsive, polymodal layers incorporated throughout O'Regan's music (especially effective in *Care Charming Sleepe*) and similar processes at work in the choral writing of John Adams. In contrast, Adams has effected a fine timbral and textural balance between voices and instruments in his music – homogeneity rather than hierarchy – but one senses that the string instruments contained on this recording struggle to find their place in and among the dense choral web.

Carl Orff
German 1895-1982

Coming from a musical family in Munich with strong army associations, the young Orff had his first works published when he was 16 and in just six months of 1911 wrote over 50 songs; he flirted with the ideas of Schoenberg and the works of Richard Strauss but by the early 1920s he still hadn't found his own voice. It was, of all things, a school for gymnastic dancing which opened the door. He met Dorothee Günther in 1924 and they founded the Günther Schule with the aim of 'reviving the natural unity of music and movement' to children. The Orff methods were widely adopted in schools all over Germany, England, Russia and America. From his teaching, his interest in primitive rhythms and simple, monodic melodies led him to stage presentations of Monteverdi and Bach and from there sprung his masterpiece.

Carmina Burana was first performed in June 1937. Orff described it as a 'scenic cantata', for the orchestra, chorus and soloists should be accompanied by dance and mime. The words, in Latin and German, are from 13th-century student poems found in the monastery of Benediktbeuern in Bavaria, bawdy celebrations of drinking, love-making and other earthy delights. Its wide appeal comes from its rhythmic vivacity, its raw, direct energy and its fusion of traditional, jazz and modern compositional techniques.

Carmina Burana

Carmina Burana
Gundula Janowitz sop **Gerhard Stolze** ten **Dietrich Fischer-Dieskau** bar **Schönberg Boys' Choir; Chorus and Orchestra of the Deutsche Oper, Berlin / Eugen Jochum**
DG The Originals 447 437-2GOR (56' · ADD · T/t)
Recorded 1967 Ⓜ❶❶❶❷

Since its original release, Jochum's performance has been consistently a prime recommendation for this much-recorded piece. Listening to it again in the superbly remastered sound, one can easily hear why. He pays great attention to detail – particularly with regard to tempo and articulation – yet the performance as a whole has a tremendous cogent sweep and the choruses have terrific power. The more reflective sections aren't neglected, however, and movements such as 'Stetit puella', with Janowitz sounding alluring and fey, have surely never been more sensitively handled. Stolze is ideal as the roasted swan and Fischer-Dieskau encompasses the very varied requirements of the baritone's music with ease. This distinguished performance, authorised by the composer, retains its place at the head of the queue.

Johann Pachelbel   German 1653-1706

What is actually the first part of the Canon and Gigue in D major for three violins and basso continuo has become a 'pop' classic, used in umpteen television commercials. It takes the form of a series of variations over the repeated short bass phrase of the Introduction. Pachelbel was a German whose main claim to fame during his lifetime was as an organist and composer – he wrote dozens of chorales for organ, 95 Magnificat fugues, as well as books full of non-liturgical toccatas, preludes, keyboards suites and so on; the list of his motets is a long one indeed. As a friend of the Bach family, he taught Johann Christoph Bach, who in turn taught Johann Sebastian. More importantly, he pioneered musical symbolism by using such devices in his sacred music as repeated notes to illustrate steadfastness, minor keys for sorrowful moods, major keys for joy and, to portray evil, a broken diminished seventh chord.

Canon

Pachelbel Canon and Gigue **Mozart** Serenade No 13. Adagio and Fugue in C minor, K546 **Anonymous** (arr L Mozart) Cassation in G, 'Toy Symphony'
Academy of St Martin in the Fields / Sir Neville Marriner
Philips 416 386-2PH (52' · DDD)   Ⓕ Ⓓ◆

Sir Neville Marriner here collects a miscellaneous group of popular classical and Baroque pieces in characteristically polished and elegant performances. Pachelbel's celebrated Canon – taken unsentimentally if sweetly at a flowing speed – is given a reprise after the Gigue; unusual but why not? Warm, well-balanced recording.

Keyboard Suites

Keyboard Suites – C, S25; D minor, S26; E minor, S28; E minor, S29; F, S32; G minor, S33; G minor, S33b; G, S34; A, S36
Joseph Payne hpd
BIS BIS-CD809 (74 minutes: DDD)   Ⓕ
First-class recordings of fine organ music and

motets by Pachelbel seem to have been unable to plant his name in the minds of the general musical public other than as the composer of that attractive but over-recorded canon. These suites (definitely for harpsichord, not organ) are all printed in the *Denkmaler der Tonkunst in Bayern* series, but except for Nos 29, 32 and 33*b* their authorship is questionable. Whoever wrote them, however, they contain some very impressive movements, and Pachelbel displays some intriguing rhythmic quirks on occasion.

Each of the suites consists of an allemand, courant and saraband, plus a 'gyque' [*sic*] in all but two cases. Playing on a copy of a bright-toned early Flemish instrument, Joseph Payne offers clean and vital performances, with neat ornaments. In general his playing is most appealing and he's recorded with total fidelity.

Choral Works

'Vespers'
Pachelbel Ingressus – P88; P92; P96; P97; P98. Magnificats – P250; P253 **Kerll** Sonata a 5 in G minor **Krieger** Sonata a 5 in A minor
· **The King's Singers** (David Hurley, Timothy Wayne-Wright *countertens* Paul Phoenix *ten* Philip Lawson, Christopher Gabbitas *bars* Stephen Connolly *bass*); **Charivari Agréable / Kah-Ming Ng**
Signum SIGCD198 (72' · DDD) Ⓕ

The title is a misnomer. This is not the Vespers from soup to nuts but a selection of five settings of the 'Ingressus' – the opening versicle and response 'Deus in adjutorium meum' plus the *Gloria* – and two of the *Magnificat*. They were composed for the church of St Sebald in Nuremberg, where Pachelbel was organist from 1695 until his death 11 years later. They are attractive pieces, full of euphonious writing in thirds: a result, presumably, of Pachelbel's exposure to Italianate music during his time as deputy organist of St Stephen's Cathedral in Vienna.

The King's Singers are hardly to be equated with Pachelbel's choir of men and boys, and even with downward transposition the upper voices sound rather strained. If not all the members of the group perform well as soloists, in the *tuttis* their brisk cheerfulness is infectious; and there's nothing wrong with the solo work in the most memorable section, the slow, thoughtful *Gloria* of the *Magnificat* in E flat. The strings of Charivari Agréable complement the singers admirably and offer more delight in sonatas by Krieger and Kerll.

Giovanni Pacini   Italian 1796-1867

Pacini studied singing in Bologna, then turned to composition. Between 1813 and 1867 he wrote nearly 90 operas, first very much in the style of Rossini and later, after contact with Bellini's works, focusing more on orchestral colour. A fine melodist, he was perfectly equipped for the showstopping aria and cabaletta approach then popular. In 1833 he halted stage compositons for four years and established a music school in Viareggio, and composed sacred works for the ducal chapel in Lucca, of which he was director from 1837. His return to operatic compositon was marked in 1840 by Saffo, considered his masterpiece. His reputation didn't cross the border, but within Italy his operas were well received and were couched in a style that appealed to contemporary tastes.

Carlo di Borgogna

Carlo di Borgogna
Bruce Ford ten Carlo **Elizabeth Futral** sop Leonora di Jork **Roberto Frontali** bar Arnoldo **Jennifer Larmore** mez Estella **Helen Williams** sop Amelia **Dominic Natoli** ten Lord Athol **Gary Magee** bar Gugliemo d'Erlach **Geoffrey Mitchell Choir; Academy of St Martin in the Fields / David Parry**
Opera Rara ③ ORC21 (3h 4' · DDD · T/t)   Ⓕ●

First, a word to enthusiasts, to those with a special interest in early 19th-century opera, who may, perhaps, have acquired and enjoyed other operas of Giovanni Pacini that have appeared on records in recent years for the first time and who may look with some eagerness at this review. Don't read it! To borrow a well-known slogan of our time: just do it!

The one point that's well known about Pacini's career is that it divides in two, with a four-year period of retirement for further thought and study. From this he emerged with his masterpiece *Saffo* (1840), and the general assumption has been that the operas from before the divide are inferior. In particular, it's understood that Pacini himself recognised this, his shortcomings being brought home to him by the relative failure of the last opera he wrote before 'resting'. That opera was *Carlo di Borgogna*. It's an opera well set-up with characters and situations; more importantly, one in which the forms themselves almost guarantee satisfaction if they're handled by such a master as Pacini was. We aren't necessarily looking here for originality but (in no debased sense) for entertainment. As a matter of fact, originality is to be found as well: it's a curious feature of Pacini's writing that, while he can at one moment follow his stated theme with a sequential phrase of disheartening banality, he may also at any moment provide a harmonic or rhythmic lift that delights as it surprises.

The dominant character is Estella, Charles's true love who turns savage on being dropped in favour of an arranged marriage but changes tack again as she tries to warn him that he's going to his death. Jennifer Larmore takes full advantage of her opportunities, sings the difficult role with some depth of vocal colour, is the assured mistress of technique and gives her words a vivid intensity of expression. The lower men's voices are strongly cast, with Gary Magee wasted in a role with little to sing. Bruce Ford takes the name-part, his tone virile, runs and *gruppetti* delivered with fluency we used to be told had disappeared with singers of the golden age.

As ever, David Parry conducts with a conviction to which his players respond, and the Mitchell Choir sing with precision and fresh tone. As to recorded sound, slightly closer contact with the soloists might be preferable, but for many this will be just about the right balance.

Maria, regina d'Inghilterra

Maria, regina d'Inghilterra
Nelly Miricioiu sop Mary Tudor **Bruce Ford** ten Riccardo Fenimoore **José Fardilha** bass Ernesto Malcolm **Mary Plazas** sop Clotilde Talbot **Alastair Miles** bass Gualtiero Churchill **Susan Bickley** mez Page **Benjamin Bland** bass Raoul **Geoffrey Mitchell Choir; Philharmonia Orchestra / David Parry**
Opera Rara ③ ORC15 (172' · DDD · T/t)   Ⓕ

Pacini wrote happily within the formal conventions of Italian opera in his time. Opening chorus, aria and cabaletta, duet likewise in two 'movements', big ensemble as finale of the middle act, 'brilliant' solo for prima donna just before the final curtain. A great point about the plot is the scope it provides for duets, which are both plentiful and good. There are choruses of merrymakers, soldiers and Londoners out for blood. The ensemble, an excellent example of its kind, comes at the point when Fenimoore is cornered and feelings run high. So do the voices. We're lucky to have Bruce Ford: at a *fortissimo* he may sound underpowered, and he doesn't play imaginatively with *mezza voce* effects, but in florid passages he moves swiftly and gracefully, he appears to be comfortable with the tessitura, and in the prison scene, which provided Ivanov with his greatest success, he sings with feeling and style.

The women have suitably contrasting voices, Mary Plazas's fresh and high, Nelly Miricioiu's older in tone, more dramatic in timbre. Both are expressive singers, and though Miricioiu too habitually resorts to the imperious glottal emphasis associated with Callas and Caballé, she brings conviction to all she does. The baritone, José Fardilha, has a touch of the flicker-vibrato that can give distinctive character, and Alastair Miles confers nobility of utterance upon the vindictive Chancellor. The cast, in fact, is worthy of the opera, which in this recording has probably its most important performance since the premiere of 1843. There's fine work from the Philharmonia under Parry. Recorded sound is well balanced, and the production handles the drama well. You are likely to play it straight through from start to finish, chafing at any interruption; and that says something for both the music and the drama.

Juan Gutiérrez de Padilla
Spanish c1590-1664

Born in Málaga, Padilla became maestro di capilla in Cádiz – he is also known to have been a ordained priest. In 1622 he was named cantor and assistant maestro at Puebla Cathedral in Mexico. The cathedral at that time boasted one of the finest musical establishments in Spanish America, on a par with the best in Europe. As well as Latin sacred music, Padilla wrote numerous vernacular villancicos. Written in, or based on, a popular style, they were intended for the large and enthusiastic crowds attracted to services at Puebla Cathedral partly by the special music composed for feast days.

'Streams of Tears'
Missa Ave regina caelorum. Deus in adiutorium. Mirabilia testimonia tua. Stabat mater. Transfige, dulcissime Domine. Lamentations. Tristis est anima mea. Versa est in luctum. Pater peccavi. Salve regina. Ave regina caelorum
The Sixteen / Harry Christophers
Coro COR16059 (67' · DDD)   Ⓕ Ⓞ ➔

Padilla's music has been awaiting a recording such as this for some time: the earliest of the transcriptions on this recording date from the mid-1980s, when, at the prompting of Bruno Turner, British choirs were persuaded to take an interest in the music of early Spanish America. A number of publications, concerts and recordings resulted from this initiative, and the music entered to some degree into the repertoire. It is good, therefore, to see it revisited by a choir of the calibre of The Sixteen at this distance in time.

The music, much of which is fully scored – Padilla, a Spaniard who emigrated to Mexico, was particularly deft at double-choir writing – and richly sonorous, is just the kind of fare that The Sixteen excel at – the two-choir *Mirabilia testimonia tua* and the most extensive work on the disc, the *Missa Ave regina*, are fine examples. But another aspect of Padilla's style, delicate and crystalline, is seen in smaller-scale motets such as *Pater peccavi*, *Versa est in luctum* (a significant contribution to the Iberian tradition of settings of that text) and the intense, dissonant *Stabat mater*, as well as the remarkable devotional motet *Transfige, dulcissime Domine*, for two sopranos, alto and bass; these more intimate works also receive fine readings. In many ways, the *Salve regina* reconciles both styles to perfection, just as it does the 'old' polyphony and the new Italianate style, alternating between them and building into a positively incandescent work. The odd rather heavy-handed entry from the men apart, these works bring out the very best in The Sixteen, supple, powerful and full of colour.

Nicolò Paganini   Italian 1782-1840

Paganini's father taught him the mandolin and the violin (Paganini would also become a virtuoso on the guitar and viola) and he made his first public appearance when he was 11. He was only 16 when he wrote his famous 24 Caprices, the ne plus ultra of violin playing to this day, a compendium of fiddle technique. They are so in advance of anything written before that they seem to have arrived out of the ether. In fact Paganini was greatly influenced by a now-forgotten violinist called Duranowski from whom he later admitted 'many of my most brilliant and popular effects were derived to a considerable extent'; another influence was the French violinist Rodolphe Kreutzer and also, from a century earlier, the 24 Caprices by Locatelli. (Paganini quotes Locatelli's Caprice No 7 in his own Caprice No 1 as a tribute).

From 1805 he became violinist to Napoleon's sister, Princess Elise, in Lucca (Paganini was rumoured to be her lover) and here he developed some of the violinistic 'tricks' which so captivated the audiences and led to his unwarranted reputation (in some quarters) as a charlatan. He would enter the stage with just two strings on his violin – the E string representing a lady and the G string representing a man – and play 'an amorous scene' between the two. At other times he would cut three strings of the violin 'by accident' and continue to play on just the G string, a musical feat that demands incredible athleticism and accuracy.

The most enduring relationship in Paganini's life was the four-year liaison with the singer Antonia Bianchi whom he met on tour in northern Italy in 1824. Their son Achille was born in 1825 and though the relationship foundered four years later, Paganini was a devoted father. Achille accompanied him on his travels wherever he went.

Paganini began his conquest of Vienna, Berlin, Paris and London in 1828. In three years he became the most famous musician alive. People flocked to hear (and see) him though ticket prices were doubled, among them the young Liszt who vowed to become the 'Paganini of the piano'. On the way he amassed a fortune – enough to give Berlioz 20,000 francs after hearing him conduct a concert of his work and to leave Achille 'nearly half a million dollars'.

By 1834 his health was broken and there was a gradual decline in his powers. He had had all his teeth removed in 1828 (and two operations on his jawbone). In 1837 he suffered from a paralysed larynx which robbed him of his speech. Eventually he could barely swallow. Condemned as a heretic, the church denied him a burial. Unbelievably his body was stored in a cellar for several years. In 1845 the Grand Duchess of Parma authorised the removal of his remains to the Villa Gaione; they were reinterred in Parma cemetery in 1876 and yet again in 1896 in a new cemetery.

Violin Concertos

No 1 in E flat, Op 6; **No 2** in B minor, Op 7, 'La campanella'

Violin Concertos Nos 1 & 2
Ilya Kaler vn **Polish National Radio Symphony Orchestra / Stephen Gunzenhauser**
Naxos 8 550649 (67' · DDD)   Ⓢ ➔

Ilya Kaler is a Russian virtuoso, a pupil of Leonid Kogan. He's a first-rate fiddler and an excellent musician. Paganini's once fiendish pyrotechnics hold no terrors for him, not even the whistling harmonics, and how nicely he can turn an Italianate lyrical phrase, as in the secondary theme of the first movement of the First Concerto. Then he can set off with panache into a flying *staccato*, bouncing his bow neatly on the strings when articulating the delicious *spiccato* finales of both works. Stephen Gunzenhauser launches into the opening movements with plenty of energy and aplomb and is a sympathetic accompanist throughout. How nicely the violins shape the lyrical ritornello introducing the first movement of the Second, and there's some sensitive horn playing in the *Adagio*. Kaler's intonation is above suspicion and he's naturally balanced: there's none of the scratchiness that can ruin your pleasure in Paganinian pyrotechnics. With excellent notes, this is a superior product at super-bargain price. The recordings were made in the Concert Hall of Polish Radio in Katowice. It has an ideal ambience for this music: nicely warm, not clouded. Great value on all counts.

Paganini Violin Concerto No 1 **Spohr** Violin
Concerto No 8, 'In modo di scena cantante'
Hilary Hahn vn **Swedish Radio Symphony
Orchestra / Eiji Oue**
DG 477 6232GH (58' · DDD)

After nearly 200 years Paganini still poses considerable challenges but Hilary Hahn's superior technique surmounts them easily, the highest and fastest passages accomplished with clarity, excellent intonation and no compromise on tonal quality. The notorious double-harmonics episode in the finale sounds wonderfully secure and beautiful.

And Hahn's musicianship is of a high order; we hear the Concerto not as the patchwork of showy tricks and memorable tunes it often seems, but as a well crafted, unified work. Other violinists may have produced performances with more edge-of-the-seat excitement but few have excelled Hahn for finesse. Rather than striving to present the soloist as a heroic figure, she's content, with sympathetic orchestral support, to let us hear the concerto as a beautiful, enthralling piece.

In the Spohr, Hahn plays the recitative sections with splendid, bold expressiveness, and in the brilliant final movement shows a winning combination of strength, delicacy and lyricism. Her very slow speed in the first aria, though, doesn't work: the music appears to stand still, with a complete change of mood for the contrasting episode. It's an outstanding disc, however, and can only enhance Hahn's reputation.

Cantabile in D, Op 17[a]. Violin Concerto Nos 1[b]
& 2 (arr vn/pf)[a]. Introduction and Variations on 'Nel
cor più non mi sento' from Paisiello's 'La Molinara',
Op 38. Moses-Fantasie[a]
Ilya Gringolts vn [a]**Irina Ryumina** pf
[b]**Lahti Symphony Orchestra / Osmo Vänskä**
BIS BIS-CD999 (72' · DDD)

Ilya Gringolts is an outstanding young Russian violinist; with this Paganini programme he began his recording career at the deep end. He's able to surmount the ferocious technical demands, and has, too, a notably rich, beautiful, unforced tone. In the unaccompanied *Nel cor più non mi sento* Variations, he seems rather careful – missing the passionate directness that some bring to this piece. But Gringolts's more expansive and delicate account is equally valid, the theme, with its freely expressive ornamentation, especially appealing. The other shorter items work well, too, in particular the elegant *Cantabile* – originally for violin and guitar. Only *La campanella* is a bit disappointing: one feels the need for a more vigorous approach, and despite the finesse of the playing it's difficult not to regret the absence of the orchestra.

The First Concerto benefits from a truly outstanding accompaniment, performed (and recorded) with a wonderful sense of space and balance. Even the bass drum and cymbal parts are played with sensitivity – what can sound like a crudely overloaded score emerges here full of colour and grandeur. With such fine orchestral sonority, one might wonder what the concerto would sound like in its original key. Paganini played it in E flat, by tuning his strings a semitone higher, and wrote the orchestral parts in the higher key; his aim was to produce a more brilliant, penetrating sound. Present-day soloists, understandably, prefer the standard tuning for such a demanding work.

Gringolts plays with sweetness or brilliance as required, though perhaps the first movement didn't need so many extreme tempo changes and perhaps the *Adagio* should have had a more dramatic tone, to match the darkly romantic orchestration. But the finale is terrific, with all the verve and high spirits you could want.

Violin and Guitar Duos

Centone di sonate Nos 7-12
Moshe Hammer vn **Norbert Kraft** gtr
Naxos 8 553142 (72' · DDD)

The *Centone di sonate* (a 'hotchpotch of sonatas') consists of 18 'sonatas' which are really salon works with a variety of movements – none of them in sonata form. Whether Paganini, who wrote them sometime after 1828, intended these pieces for public performance or merely for the use of the then abundant amateur musicians isn't known. As usual in his works of this genre, it's the violin that hogs the limelight while the guitar remains a humble bag-carrier. The guitar parts are indeed so simple that they would have been within the reach of any amateur who was capable of keeping his end up with another musician; Segovia considered them beneath his dignity and refused many invitations to play them with famous partners! Nothing is harder than to be 'simple': Mozart managed it, while at the same time being deceptively complex; Paganini did it at a far less sublime level, with sentimental, cheerful and pert tunes. Truth to tell, they aren't the kind of works which impel one to listen to them at one sitting except for the most devoted *aficionado* of Paganini's violinistic voice or of hearing the guitar in an unremittingly subservient but genuinely complementary role.

These splendid performances on modern instruments make no claim to 'authentic' status, but they're no less appealing for that. They squeeze every last drop from the music with (inauthentically) full sound, and a Siamese-twin tightness of ensemble that was probably rare among those who played these works in Paganini's own time. In the end, these works have a charm that's hard for any but the most straitlaced to resist. It's unlikely that the *Centone* will ever be better played and/or recorded.

Additional recommendations

Six Sonatas for Guitar and Violin, Op 2. Cantabile e Valtz, Op 19. Variazioni di bravura on Caprice No 24. Duetto amoroso. Sonata per le gran viola e chitarra
St John *vn* **Wynberg** *gtr*
Naxos 8 550759 (59' · DDD) Ⓢ🅑➔

Six Sonatas for Guitar and Violin, Op 3. Sonata concertata in A, Op 61. 60 Variations on 'Barucabà', Op 14. Cantabile in D, Op 17
St John *vn* **Wynberg** *gtr*
Naxos 8 550690 (54' · DDD) Ⓢ🅑➔

Collectively, these works present the full range of Paganini's technical armoury – left-hand *pizzicatos*, high harmonics, double-stopping, 'sneaky' chromatic runs and the rest, and Scott St John betrays no difficulty in dealing with every googly that comes his way. Simon Wynberg proves as well matched a partner as St John could have wished for. Violinists, guitarists and lovers of winsomeness for its own sake should revel in these very well-recorded discs.

---

24 Caprices, Op 1

24 Caprices
Itzhak Perlman *vn*
EMI Great Recordings of the Century 567237-2 (72' · ADD) Ⓜ🅞🅑➔

This electrifying music with its daredevil virtuosity has long remained the pinnacle of violin technique, and the Caprices encapsulate the essence of the composer's style. For a long time it was considered virtually unthinkable that a violinist should be able to play the complete set; even in recent years only a handful have produced truly successful results. Itzhak Perlman has one strength in this music that's all-important, other than a sovereign technique – he's incapable of playing with an ugly tone. He has such variety in his bowing that the timbre of the instrument is never monotonous. The notes of the music are dispatched with a forthright confidence and fearless abandon. The frequent double-stopping passages hold no fear for him. Listen to the fire of No 5 in A minor and the way in which Perlman

copes with the extremely difficult turns in No 14 in E flat: this is a master at work.

The set rounds off with the famous A minor Caprice, which inspired Liszt, Brahms and Rachmaninov, among others, to adapt it in various guises for the piano.

Additional recommendations

24 Caprices
Becker-Bender *vn*
Hyperion CDA67763 (80' · DDD) Ⓕ🅓➔

Adopting generally slower speeds, Tanja Becker-Bender has time to turn the music gracefully, articulate cleanly, achieve remarkable purity of tuning, and use variations of tone-colour to open up the music's expressive potential. This results in a sparkling, cleaned-up version of Paganini, sounding the more amazing for its polish and clarity, and bringing into focus the poetic, Romantic sensibility that enthralled the composer's contemporaries.

24 Caprices
Ehnes *vn*
Onyx ONYX4044 (78' · DDD) Ⓕ🅛➔

Ehnes has recorded the Caprices before, in 1995, at the age of 19. Since then his view of the music hasn't changed a great deal. There's the same daring, bold approach, relying on exceptional technique to deliver an inner vision of each piece – no pauses or stretching of the rhythm to make awkward corners more manageable. What has changed is that Ehnes's technique has got even better, the intonation more precise, the bow control more sensitive. And the new recording adds an extra degree of clarity so that the playing makes a more vivid impact.

Giovanni Palestrina Italian c1525/26-1594

Beginning as a boy chorister in Santa Maria Maggiore in Rome, Palestrina's first job was as organist at the Cathedral in Palestrina. In 1551 he was back in Rome as maestro di cappella of the Julian Chapel, having married and produced two sons in the meantime. After dedicating a book of Masses (the first of over 100) to Pope Julian III, Palestrina was rewarded with a place in the papal choir – without having to take the usual audition. This caused some annoyance to his fellow choristers as he was said not to have a good voice. Shortly afterwards under the new Pope, Paul V, he was dismissed on the grounds that he was a married man. After a string of appointments, he found himself back in the Julian Chapel as maestro under Pope Gregory XIII where he remained until his death. In 1580 the plague took Palestrina's wife and sons and, in despair, he took the first steps to enter the priesthood. He was persuaded to do otherwise by the wealthy widow of a furrier and, combining music with his new wife's business and a new-found talent for real estate, prospered.

Palestrina is acknowledged as the greatest composer of the Catholic Church and one of the finest masters of classical polyphonic writing. He is still held up as a model for students. He was working for the Vatican at the time of the Counter-Reformation when the Roman Church was doing all in its power to strike back at the Protestant movement. This called for music which avoided elaborate contrapuntal settings (these tended to obscure the words) and Palestrina knew exactly what was wanted – an ethereal cloud of sound to fill St Peter's.

Masses

Missa Dum complerentur. Dum complerentur. Magnificat VI toni. Motets, Book 3 – Alleluia: Veni Sancte Spiritus. Veni Sancte Spiritus (plainchant). Spiritus sanctus replevit totam domum. Veni Creator Spiritus
Westminster Cathedral Choir / Martin Baker
Hyperion CDA67353 (71' · DDD · T/t)   Ⓕ**ⓄⒹ**

The opening six-part motet, *Dum complerentur*, a vivid description of the coming of the Holy Spirit as a 'mighty rushing wind', has a text calculated to stimulate any composer. Palestrina's stirring motet reappears completely transformed in his Mass, quiet and pleading in the *Kyrie*, exuberant in the *Gloria*. The choir catches the spirit of each movement with remarkable flexibility .

The choir's renowned, so-called Continental, vocal quality has persisted throughout its existence, even with a succession of very different choir directors. Due in part to the building's acoustic, this factor almost certainly affects their singing of the chant. The beautiful Carolingian *Alleluia: Veni Sancte Spiritus*, with its melisma on the word 'amoris', is an excellent illustration of the trebles in full flight, singing with enormous confidence in the vast cathedral. In alternation with the low voices in the sequence *Veni Sancte Spiritus*, they have the edge over the men who sound a trifle strained on their top notes.

Palestrina's double-choir version of this text shows the whole choir in top form, revelling in the composer's exciting rhythmic acrobatics: while never departing from the noble majesty of his style, Palestrina describes with thrilling realism the many-voiced confusion when 'they all began to speak in a multitude of different tongues'. Highly recommended.

Missa Ecce ego Johannes. Cantantibus organis. Laudate pueri. Magnificat IV toni. Peccantem me quotidie. Tribulationes civitatum. Tu es Petrus
Westminster Cathedral Choir / James O'Donnell
Hyperion CDA67099 (65' · DDD · T/t)   Ⓕ**ⓄⒹ**

For sheer beauty of sound, this recording is unsurpassed. The choice of a programme of music by Palestrina, the one composer ever to have been honoured by official ecclesiastical recognition, was inspired. This CD represents several high-points of solemn liturgy; a six-part polyphonic Mass, *Ecce ego Johannes*, and two groups of motets, including a festal psalm, two penitential pieces, antiphons for the feasts of St Peter and St Cecilia and a solemn *alternatim*

Magnificat. What's very admirable about the whole performance is the excellent integration of the choir. Ivan Moody underlines in his notes Palestrina's skill in the seamless interweaving of homophony and flowing counterpoint; the choir, in its turn, moves from one to the other with the utmost ease and art. In particular, the give-and-take of dovetailing produces a perfect balance. In this respect, top praise for the trebles, with a firm, mature tone and assured flexibility.

Missa Assumpta est Maria. Missa Sicut lilium inter spinas. Motets – Assumpta est Maria a 6; Sicut lilium inter spinas I. Plainchant: Assumpta est Maria
The Tallis Scholars / Peter Phillips
Gimell CDGIM020 (72' · DDD · T/t)   Ⓕ**Ⓓ**

In this recording of *Missa Assumpta est Maria* Peter Phillips has included the motet on which the work is based, together with another parody Mass, the *Sicut lilium* with its corresponding motet. It's illuminating to hear how the larger-scale compositions unfold with reference to the original motets: close study reveals much about the compositional processes of the High Renaissance, but any listener will be able to appreciate the organic relationship between motet and Mass.

In addition, Phillips has deliberately paired two sharply contrasted parody Masses: *Assumpta est Maria*, the better known, is thought to be one of Palestrina's last Masses, while *Sicut lilium* dates from relatively early in his career. The former, with its major tonality and *divisi* high voices, is marvellously bright and open, and is given an outgoing performance; the latter, inflected with chromaticism and melodic intervals that constantly fall back on themselves, is darker-hued and more plaintive, a mood well captured here in the intensity of the singing. But what's perhaps most striking is the difference in compositional technique between the two works: *Sicut lilium* relies largely on imitative textures for the unfolding of its structure (though there are the customary block chords on phrases such as 'et homo factus est', performed here with magical effect), while *Assumpta est Maria* makes far greater use of vocal scoring as a formal device, and thus looks forward to the contrast principle of the Baroque. The Tallis Scholars make the most of the contrasted blocks of sound here, achieving an impressive vocal blend and balance. The phrasing, particularly in the *Kyrie*, is perhaps a little too mannered and the very beautiful *Agnus Dei* verges on the narcissistic and therefore becomes too static. The flow in the *Missa Sicut lilium*, though, is excellent throughout.

Palestrina Missa Te Deum laudamus. Missa Tu es Petrus. **Victoria** Te Deum laudamus
Choir of Westminster Cathedral / Martin Baker
Hyperion CDA67785 (78' · DDD)   Ⓕ**ⓄⒹ**

Any recording of Renaissance polyphony by the Choir of Westminster Cathedral made in its resplendent home acoustic tends to be a special event. The passionate articulation of texts and richness of sonority is allied with immaculate tuning and ideal shaping of long arching lines. As the choir has demonstrated often before, these attributes are ideally suited to Palestrina.

On this occasion, Martin Baker directs two fine and contrasting examples chosen from the composer's 104 polished essays in the genre. The *Missa Te Deum laudamus* is a fine example of Palestrina's perfection at counterpoint (on this occasion in the Phrygian mode). The 20 boy choristers possess seemingly faultless techniques and exquisite harmonies ring with clarity and precision in the *Kyrie*, maximising the climactic effect of surprising harmonies as they rise and fall from the polyphony. Some performances of Palestrina's music can be merely ethereal and lovely but there is nothing perfunctory here about the eloquent singing of the flowing suspensions and resolutions in a magnificent setting of the *Gloria*, and the devout and communicative use of words in the *Credo* is marvellous: Baker seems to have taken care for his choir to convey fully the sense of mystery and wonder ('Et incarnatus est'), and the lay clerks convey pathos and tenderness ('Crucifixus'). The *Missa Te Deum laudamus* is preceded by a *Te Deum* canticle by Tomás Luis de Victoria, whereas the more extrovert *Missa Tu es Petrus* follows a glorious performance of Palestrina's own splendid antiphonal motet upon which his Mass is parodied. This is manna from heaven.

Music for Holy Week

Music for Holy Saturday　　　　　　　Ⓟ
Lamentations, Book III – I-III. Stabat mater.
Benedictus for Holy Week. Sicut cervus.
Responsories and Antiphons
Musica Contexta / Simon Ravens
Chandos Chaconne CHAN0679 (60' · DDD · T/t)
　　　　　　　　　　　　　　　　　　Ⓕ❶❸➔

This outstanding recording of music for Holy Saturday opens with two lessons from the third of Palestrina's four settings of texts from *Lamentations*, passages chanted during the Office of Tenebrae on the last three days of Holy Week. The third lesson is Palestrina's superb setting of the *Prayer of Jeremiah*.

The performance is objectively straightforward, allowing the music, in its utter poignancy expressed with marked restraint, to speak for itself. The clarity of the individual voices is remarkable and the acoustic clear, yet warm: even the six-part final cry, 'Jerusalem...convertere ad Dominum Deum tuum', comes across with perfect intelligibility. In the chanted liturgy each lesson is followed by a florid reponsory, and full marks should go to Musica Contexta for transcribing these chants from Giovanni Guidetti's edition of 1587, which naturally comes from the right place and is of the right date.

Though the responsories might have been better in a slower, more determinedly solemn style, these singers are well on the way to achieving

perfection here. It's particularly interesting to hear them sing Palestrina's wonderful *Sicut cervus*, with its surging phrases, and also his famous *Stabat mater* for double choir, displaying that dramatic alternation between antiphonal choir and combined choral sections. For maximum effect, more antiphonal distinction might have helped in the choir-versus-choir sections; but overall this is a well-thought-out and moving performance.

Giovanni Antonio Pandolfi
Italian fl1660-1669

Italian composer and violinist Pandolfi is a shadowy figure known only for handful of violin sonatas. He was among the instrumentalists of Archduke Ferdinand of Austria at Innsbruck when his Opp 3 and 4 violin sonatas were published in 1660.

Violin Sonatas

Six Sonatas per chiesa e camera, Op 3.　　Ⓟ
Six Sonatas for Violin and Continuo, Op 4
Andrew Manze vn **Richard Egarr** hpd
Harmonia Mundi HMG50 7241 (80' · DDD)　Ⓜ❶❸❸

These are virtuoso performances of some quite extraordinary music. Each sonata has its own descriptive subtitle and a movement layout which seems reluctant to conform to any set pattern. Presumably the sections have their own tempo indications, though these aren't disclosed either in the booklet or in the listing on the reverse side of the box. A pity, since there are lots of interesting and unusual juxtapositions of a strikingly nonconformist nature. Much of the writing is characterised by virtuoso figurations which, especially in faster movements, might become a little wearisome in the hands of a lesser player. But Manze seems to sense this danger and averts it with panache and a highly developed sense of fantasy. Slow movements, on balance, are more interesting. There's an especially memorable one in *La Clemente*, the fifth sonata of Op 3, with a pathos-laden aria-like character. Manze plays it sensitively and the result is touching. Several movements have a strong ostinato element and, in *La Monella Romanesca*, the third piece from Op 4, we have a set of variations on a melody contained in the bass.

Harpsichordist Richard Egarr is a lively and an imaginative accompanist throughout. In short, an exhilarating recital of music whose exoticism, melancholy and wild, passionate outbursts resist categorisation and convenient definition. Strongly recommended.

Andrzej Panufnik　Polish/British 1914-1991

He began his formal musical training in 1932 at the Warsaw Conservatory, taking classes in percussion before transferring to theory and composition. His first acknowledged work, the Piano Trio, was composed in 1934. After graduating in 1936, he studied conducting with Felix Weingartner in Vienna (1937-38). During the Second World War Panufnik stayed in Warsaw and participated in its severely restricted musical life, notably as a duo-pianist with Lutosławski.

In 1944-45 all his manuscripts were inadvertently destroyed by an occupant of a friend's Warsaw apartment. After the war, Panufnik reconstructed several of these lost scores. Between 1945 and 1947 he worked mainly as a conductor, firstly of the Kraków PO and then of the Warsaw PO. Panufnik was soon acknowledged as an innovatory composer thanks largely to Circle of Fifths and the orchestral Lullaby and Nocturne (1947). That year he was awarded the Szymanowski Prize for the Nocturne, while in 1949 his Sinfonia rustica took the Chopin Prize.

In 1954 he emigrated to England where he received financial support from fellow composers including Vaughan Williams and Arthur Benjamin. For two years (1957-59) Panufnik's financial situation eased slightly when he was appointed principal conductor of the City of Birmingham Symphony Orchestra, but it took him away from composition for too long. Late in life his works were in demand by such major figures as Leopold Stokowski, Yehudi Menuhin who commissioned a violin concerto, and Mstislav Rostropovich who commissioned a cello concerto.

Symphonies

Symphonies – No 3, 'Sinfonia sacra'; No 5, 'Sinfonia di sfere'. Heroic Overture. Landscape
Tampere Philharmonic Orchestra / John Storgårds
Ondine ODE1101-5 (75' · DDD)   Ⓕ

Panufnik's music has always seemed more elusive than its demonstrable surface suggests. Even the wartime *Heroic Overture* – a work that plays to the gallery and knows it – has a more sober subtext as the Polish patriotic song on which it's based is secreted in the background. Is its relegation a symbol of repression? Could be, but Panufnik's driving optimism simultaneously transforms his source into a beacon of hope, something to be aspired to at a time of uncertainty.

The Tampere Philharmonic deliver a rhythmically propulsive and dramatically epic performance. Throughout the disc, the Tampere brass sound has the swank and punch of a big band, while the string playing is fastidiously nuanced – power-house sheets of sound rain down as required, and *pianissimos* are acutely hushed. This honed orchestral playing makes for a *Sinfonia sacra* that's a revelation. Probably Panufnik's most popular symphony, the work begins with brass fanfares embedded with tart harmonic ambiguities that Storgårds has primed with snarling clarity. His sense of pace, as Panufnik strips the orchestra down to strings alone and rebuilds it again over a 30-minute duration, has the precision of sonar and supreme dramatic flair.

Panufnik's increasing interest in geometry governed much of the music he wrote in the

1970s, the *Sinfonia di sfere* included. The beauty of the music became highly objectified, just as his ear for piquant harmonies and idiosyncratic orchestration intensified. A potent combination, equally powerfully in the execution.

Roxanna Panufnik   British b1968

Roxanna Panufnik, the daughter of Andrzej Panufnik (see above), studied composition at the Royal Academy of Music. She has written opera, ballet, music theatre, choral works, chamber music and music for film and television. Among her most widely given works is Westminster Mass, commissioned for Westminster Cathedral Choir on the occasion of Cardinal Hume's 75th birthday. She wrote a violin concerto commissioned by the Savannah Music Festival for Daniel Hope, incorporating Christian, Islamic and Jewish music. This was converted into an overture, commissioned by the World Orchestra for Peace and premiered in Jerusalem under the baton of Valery Gergiev.

Westminster Mass

Westminster Mass. Angel Sing!. Kyrie cum jubilo. The Spirit of the Saints. Ave Maria. All in Tune
London Oratory School Schola / Lee Ward with **David Terry** org
Regent REGCD293 (54' · DDD)   ⒻⓄⓄ

One might well ask whether there is a need for another recording of the *Westminster Mass* (there are currently three in the catalogue) but listening to this disc will make it clear that it was a very good idea. Not only do we hear the work in a new version for choir, bells, harp and organ, but it is sung by a Roman Catholic boys' choir quite different in sound from that of Westminster Cathedral, for whom the work was originally written. In addition, it is performed as part of a liturgically ordered sequence, troped, as it were, with other works by Panufnik, three of which have not previously been recorded. These three include a very fine *Kyrie cum jubilo* for organ, performed by the Schola's conductor, Lee Ward, which makes one long to hear what else the composer might do with the instrument.

There are moments in the Mass – in the *Gloria*, for example – that stretch the choir's technique; but its sound is so warm, the sense that the liturgical nature of the music is clearly understood and appreciated so palpable, that they are really minor details. Challenges are present, too, in some of the carols recorded here: 'Sleep little Jesus' abounds in impressive choral effects aimed at suggesting 'a psychedelic effect of angels looking down from heaven upon the sleeping Jesus' that certainly distances it from more conventional Christmas fare. Impressive indeed.

Hubert Parry
British 1848-1918

The son of an English country gentleman, Eton-educated Parry became director of the Royal College of Music in 1894, professor of music at Oxford in 1897, was knighted the following year and created a baronet five years later. It comes, therefore, as a surprise to learn from one acquaintance that 'he was prominent in almost every branch of athletics and constantly ran into every kind of danger that land and water could afford, suffering almost every possible injury short of the immediately fatal'. More importantly, the writer goes on: 'His geniality, generosity, moral character and artistic ideals had an influence which those who received it hope they may be enabled in some measure to pass on to future generations; indeed, he was everything that one would like the world to consider as implied by the description "English gentleman".'

The English choral tradition, if nothing else, was safe in Parry's hands, passed from Tallis to Byrd, from Byrd to Gibbons, Gibbons to Purcell, Purcell to Battishall and Greene, on through the Wesleys to Parry, from Parry to Vaughan Williams and Holst – and Parry deserves greater recognition for his role in the renaissance of English music. It's ironic that Jerusalem, not only Parry's shortest work but also one which he allegedly threw into the fire in dissatisfaction (it was rescued by a friend from the flames), should be the only piece by which he is now remembered. It quickly caught on after its first performance at the Queen's Hall, London, in 1916. It became the song for the 'Votes for Women' campaign in 1918 and was subsequently taken up by the National Federation of Women's Institutes – besides being an indispensable finale to the BBC Proms season.

Complete Organ Works

Fantasia and Fugue in G (1882 & 1913 vers). Three Chorale Fantasias. Chorale Preludes, Sets 1 & 2. Elegy in A flat. Toccata and Fugue in G. Elégie **Various** A Little Organ Book in Memory of Sir Hubert Parry
James Lancelot org
Priory ② PRCD682AB (135' · DDD)   Ⓕ❶❶❶
Played on the organ of Durham Cathedral

It's all too easy to dismiss Parry's music as being workmanlike and living in the shadow of Bach and Brahms. Yet there's real beauty and passion here, and at his best Parry can match the intensity of his contemporary Max Reger.

The appeal of this recording is enhanced by the inclusion of both the published and unpublished versions of the C major Fantasia and Fugue, and also by *A Little Organ Book*. This latter collection is an intensely moving tribute to Parry by 13 of his friends, colleagues and pupils (including Stanford, Bridge and Thalben-Ball).

This recording presents the best possible advocacy for Parry, and the combination of Lancelot and the Durham Willis/Harrison organ is, to coin a phrase, a 'dream ticket'. The greatness of Lance-lot's playing lies in the perfect fusion of meticulously honed detail with an effortless flow to the whole performance. He fully exploits the beauty and grandeur of Durham's magical organ, and of all the available CDs, this one is the finest showcase for this most charismatic of cathedral instruments. The excellence of the playing is matched by the recording. Quite simply, this is a definitive, outstanding, glorious recording.

I was glad / Jerusalem

I was glad when they said unto me. Evening Service in D, 'Great'. Songs of Farewell. Hear my words, ye people. Jerusalem
Timothy Woodford, Richard Murray-Bruce trebs **Andrew Wickens, Colin Cartwright** countertens **David Lowe, Martin Pickering** tens **Bruce Russell, Paul Rickard** bars **John Heighway** bass **Roger Judd** org **Choir of St George's Chapel, Windsor / Christopher Robinson**
Hyperion CDA66273 (58' · DDD · T)   Ⓕ Ⓓ➤

The more of Parry's music one comes to know, the more apparent it becomes that the received opinion of him is askew. Take the 1882 settings of the *Magnificat* and *Nunc dimittis*, for instance. These, amazingly, were not published until 1982. This recording – another example of Hyperion's courageous policy – shows how un-Victorian in the accepted sense they are. In other words, they're bold, unconventional and unsanctimonious – like quite a lot of Victorian church music, one may add. Perhaps the big anthem, *Hear my words* (1894), shows more signs of conventionality, but it has an attractive part for solo soprano (treble here) and ends with the hymn 'O praise ye the Lord'. The St George's Chapel Choir, conducted by Christopher Robinson, sings these works with more ease than it can muster for the famous and magnificent Coronation anthem *I was glad*, ceremonial music that not even Elgar surpassed. A sense of strain among the trebles is always evident. Although a wholly adult choir in the *Songs of Farewell* might be preferable, these are assured and often beautiful performances – excellent diction – of these extraordinarily affecting motets. English music doesn't possess much that's more perfect in the matching of words and music than the settings of 'There is an old belief' and 'Lord, let me know mine end', invidious as it is to select only two for mention. A stirring *Jerusalem* completes this enterprising recording, which brings the sound of a great building into our homes with absolute fidelity.

Arvo Pärt
Estonian b1935

Until 1980, Pärt's music was unknown in the West. Now he is something of a cult. By the time he emigrated to Vienna and thence to Berlin in 1980, Pärt had already had two careers as a composer, composing in the 12-tone system and experimenting with collage techniques; while working as a technician for Estonian Radio (1958-67) he wrote over 50 film scores.

He finally abandoned these methods and underwent a voluntary period of compositional silence, during which he meditated and studied religion. His music emerged quite differently: 'I have discovered it is enough when a single note is beautifully played,' he has said. 'This one note, or a moment of silence comforts me. I work with very few elements – with one voice, with two voices. I build with primitive materials – with the triad, with one specific tonality. The three notes of a triad are like bells. And that is why I call it tintinnabulation.' The result is music of undramatic, uneventful, monk-like simplicity.

Symphony No 3

Symphony No 3. Summa. Trisagion. Fratres. Silouans. Festina lente. Cantus in memoriam Benjamin Britten
Estonian National Symphony Orchestra / Paavo Järvi
Virgin Classics 545501-2 (73' · DDD)　　Ⓕ Ⓞ ➔

With Arvo Pärt the terms of comparison normally used for focusing differences between this or that recording tend to fall redundant. Pärt's mature music responds most readily to luminous textures, carefully timed silences and mastery of line, and only rarely to the more subjective impulses of dramatic conducting.

Järvi's performance of the first movement suggests urgent parallels with the fraught confrontations in Nielsen's Fifth. And there's more than a hint of 'the spring water purity of Sibelius's Sixth Symphony' in the finale. Everywhere one senses the hovering spectre of early music, but this Third Symphony is the ideal stepping stone for first-timers who wish to journey from standard symphonic fare to Pärt's cloistered tintinnabulation.

The more familiar tintinnabulation pieces work very well, with Järvi opting in the *Cantus* and *Festina lente* for warmer textures than some rivals, which usefully underlines Pärt's quietly cascading harmonies. There are those who will still prefer a more chaste sonority, the sort favoured on virtually all the ECM productions. But Paavo Järvi's more central approach will appeal to those who until now have heard in Pärt's music ascetic denial rather than quiet affirmation. Recommended.

Additional recommendation

Symphony No 3
Coupled with Tabula rasa[a]. Collage on B-A-C-H.
[a]**Hatfield,** [a]**Hirsch** *vns* **Ulster Orchestra / Yuasa**
Naxos 8 554591 (52' · DDD)　　Ⓢ ➔
　Yuasa's reading is somewhat akin to Järvi's first (BIS) recording – certainly for tempo. The Ulster brass are excellent and if the orchestra's strings aren't quite on a par with those in Bamberg and Gothenburg, they're still pretty good. Quality samplings of Pärt don't come any cheaper.

Fratres / Summa

Fratres (seven versions). Summa. Festina lente.
Cantus in memoriam Benjamin Britten

Peter Manning *vn* **France Springuel** *vc*
Mireille Gleizes *pf* I **Fiamminghi**
Telarc CD80387 (79' · DDD)　　Ⓕ

Telarc's *Fratres-Fest* proves beyond doubt that good basic material can be reworked almost *ad infinitum* if the manner of its arrangement is sufficiently colourful. This sequence is particularly imaginative in that it alternates two varied pairs of *Fratres* with atmospheric original string pieces, then separates the last two versions with the sombre pealing of *Festina lente*. The first *Fratres* opens to a low bass drone and chaste, ethereal strings: the suggested image is of a slow oncoming processional – mourners, perhaps, or members of some ancient religious sect – with drum and xylophone gradually intensifying until the percussive element is so loud that it resembles Copland's *Fanfare for the Common Man*. One envisages aged figures who have been treading the same ground since time immemorial, whereas the frantically propelled, arpeggiated opening to the version for violin, strings and percussion leaves a quite different impression. Still, even here the music does eventually calm and Peter Manning provides an expressive solo commentary.

Next comes the gentle cascading of Pärt's *Cantus in memoriam Benjamin Britten*, with its weeping sequences and lone, tolling bell. The eight-cello *Fratres* uses eerie harmonics (as does the cello and piano version that ends the programme), whereas *Fratres* for wind octet and percussion is cold, baleful, notably Slavonic-sounding and occasionally reminiscent of Stravinsky. The alternation of *Summa* (for strings) and the quartet version of *Fratres* works nicely, the former more animated than anything else on the disc; the latter, more intimate. The performances are consistently sympathetic, and the recordings are excellent.

Lamentate

Lamentate[a]. Da pacem Domine[b]
[a]**Alexei Lubimov** *pf* [b]**Hilliard Ensemble;** [a]**Stuttgart Radio Symphony Orchestra / Andrey Boreyko**
ECM New Series 476 3048 (43' · DDD · T)　　Ⓕ ➔

The main piece on this latest release has passages of visceral power unheard in Pärt's work for almost three decades. *Lamentate* was inspired by Anish Kapoor's gigantic sculpture *Marsyas*, which filled the Turbine Hall at Tate Modern in London. Confronted with this monumental work, Pärt felt he was standing before his own body after death. 'I had a strong sense of not being ready to die,' he says, 'and was moved to ask myself what I could still accomplish in the time left to me.' *Lamentate* is intended as a lament for the living, 'struggling with the pain and hopelessness of this world'. The solo piano part can be seen as the first-person narrative of an individual, beset by challenges represented by the orchestra, which uses sharper textures, more dramatic gestures and a broader range of colours than we usually expect from this most controlled and ascetic of composers. It makes one eager to know what his next step will be. In *Da pacem Domine* (2004), for which Sarah Leonard extends the Hilliard's range, Pärt takes a ninth-century antiphon as his starting-point, floating the serene, radiant lines of this prayer for peace with characteristic airy grace, slowly opening up the textures and exploring some tart harmonies before returning to a final consoling chord.

Berliner Messe

Berliner Messe. Magnificat. Seven Magnificat Antiphons. The Beatitudes. Annum per annum. De profundis
Polyphony / **Stephen Layton** with **Andrew Lucas** org
Hyperion CDA66960 (74' · DDD · T/t)   Ⓕ Ⓑ➤

Pärt's music is about equilibrium and balance – balance between consonance and dissonance, between converging voices and, in the context of a CD such as this, between the individual works programmed. Stephen Layton has chosen well, starting with the variegated *Berliner Messe* and closing with the starkly ritualistic *De profundis*, a memorable and ultimately dramatic setting of Psalm 130 for male voices, organ, bass drum and tam-tam, dedicated to Gottfried von Einem. The Mass features two of Pärt's most powerful individual movements, a gently rocking 'Veni Sancte Spiritus' and a *Credo* which, as Meurig Bowen's unusually perceptive notes remind us, is in essence a major-key transformation of the better-known – and more frequently recorded – *Summa*. Everything here chimes to Pärt's tintinnabulation style, even the brief but fetching organ suite *Annum per annum*, where the opening movement thunders an alarm then tapers to a gradual *diminuendo*, while the closing coda shoulders an equally well-calculated *crescendo*. The five movements in between are mostly quiet, whereas *The Beatitudes* flies back to its opening tonality on 'a flurry of quintuplet broken chords'. It's also the one place that witnesses a momentary – and minor – blemish on the vocal line, but otherwise Layton directs a fine sequence of warmly blended performances. Polyphony employs what one might roughly term an 'early music' singing style, being remarkably even in tone, largely free of vibrato and alive to phrasal inflexions.

If you're new to Pärt's music, then this disc would provide an excellent starting-point. Maybe the individually shaded *Seven Magnificat Antiphons* first, then tackle the *Berliner Messe*, followed, perhaps, by the *Magnificat*.

Como cierva sedienta

'Orient and Occident'
Como cierva sedienta[a]. Orient and Occident. Ein Wallfahrtslied[a]
Swedish Radio [a]**Choir and Symphony Orchestra / Tõnu Kaljuste**
ECM New Series 472 080-2 (47' · DDD)   Ⓕ ❶❷❸➤

This programme represents a retreat from the remote cloister where for so long Arvo Pärt invited us to join him, a definite shift from the aerated tintinnabuli. The purity remains, so do the spare textures and, to a limited extent, earlier stylistic traits. Pärt's voice is always recognisable. And yet who, years ago, could have anticipated the tempered tumult that erupts in the third movement of *Como cierva sedienta*, a half-hour choral drama commissioned by the Festival de Música de Canarias?

This recording subscribes to ECM's well-tried aesthetic, in which clarity, fine-tipped detail and carefully gauged perspectives are familiar priorities. The texts come from Psalms 42 and 43, opening with 'As the hart panteth…' (Psalm 42). Even in the first few seconds, after chorus and bell have registered, vivid instrumental colour signals a fresh departure. It's almost as if Pärt is relishing textures previously denied him, like a penitent released from fasting. Take the second movement, 'Why art thou cast down, my soul?', which opens among lower strings then switches to tactile *pizzicati* and woodwinds that are almost Tchaikovskian in their post-Classical delicacy. The long closing section is pensive but conclusive: a dramatic opening, drum taps that recall Shostakovich's Eleventh Symphony, expressively varied instrumental commentary, quiet string chords later on and a closing episode filled with equivocal tranquillity.

The two shorter works are also significant. *Wallfahrtslied* (1984, 'Song of Pilgrimage'), a memorial to a friend, is presented in the revised version for strings and men's choir. Again Pärt engages a lyrical muse, particularly for the emotionally weighted prelude and postlude whereas the accompaniment to the main text (Psalm 121, 'I lift up mine eyes unto the hills…'), a combination of *pizzicato* and shuddering bowed phrases suggests a lament tinged with anger.

The seven-minute string piece *Orient and Occident* has 'a monophonic line which runs resolutely through [it]', to quote Pärt's wife. Snake-like oriental gestures, coiled with prominent *portamentos* (the sort used by Indian orchestras) sound like an Eastern variant of Pärt's earlier string works. The choral pieces, though, are the prime reasons for investing in this exceptional and musically important release.

Da pacem Domine

'Da pacem'
An den Wassern zu Babel. Magnificat. Nunc dimittis. Dopo la vittoria. Da pacem Domine. Two Slavic Psalms. Salve regina. Littlemore Tractus
Estonian Philharmonic Chamber Choir / Paul Hillier with **Christopher Bowers-Broadbent** org
Harmonia Mundi HMU90 7401 (65' · DDD · T/t)   Ⓕ Ⓑ➤

This collection showcases four compositions from the last decade alongside some earlier works, most of which have been revised, as is

Pärt's habit, within the past 15 years. While his methodology has remained much the same, Pärt admitted a greater harmonic and textural richness over that period, and this relative lushness is superbly realised by the EPC Choir without ever betraying the fundamental asceticism of Pärt's sound.

The album opens with the most recent piece, *Da pacem Domine* (2004), a typical work not least because of its slow harmonic speed coupled with increasingly intense light and colour. It contrasts with *Salve regina* (2001-02) which, as Hillier comments, could almost be 'a dream sequence from a film about a peasant community' in the early passages. Indeed, at first hearing one could almost confuse it with something Preisner might have written for Kieslowski, although there are enough characteristic chords and intervals to mark it out as Pärt. The Psalms (1984), with their unusually strong Slavonic tinge, again show the variety Pärt can achieve within restricted means. As always, Hillier and his colleagues have done Pärt proud. This beautiful release is another compelling illustration of the emotional and textural intensity central to the composer's art.

Mein Weg hat Gipfel und Wellentäler[c].
Da pacem Domine[ac]. In principio[ab]. La Sindone[ab].
Cecilia, vergine romana[ab]. Für Lennart in memoriam[c]
[a]**Estonian Philharmonic Chamber Choir;**
[b]**Estonian National Symphony Orchestra;**
[c]**Tallinn Chamber Orchestra / Tõnu Kaljuste**
ECM New Series 476 6990 (71' · DDD)   Ⓕ Ⓞ Ⓓ⁺

These recent works demonstrate a certain expansion in Pärt's horizons. They still dwell in the niche of lapidary minimalism, but while they keep faith with his trademark 'tintinnabulatory' style, they now use it with flexibility and flow. The dramatic directness of *In principio*, at 20 minutes the longest work on this CD, has one thinking of Janáček or even the Icelander Jón Leifs, not to speak of its candidly neo-Bachian progressions; exhilaration emanates from this score, along with piety and lamentation. Of the other works for chorus and orchestra, *Cecilia, vergine romana* commemorates in more restrained terms the martyrdom of the third-century Roman noblewoman adopted 1200 years later as the patron saint of music, while the five-minute *Da pacem Domine* is a statuesque tribute to the victims of the 2004 Madrid terrorist bombings.

La Sindone ('The Shroud'), for trumpet, trombone, four percussionists and strings, leaves more room for listeners to find their own symbolic meaning in its frequent silences. *Mein Weg* ('My Path'), for 14 strings and percussion, is nothing to do with autobiography but a response to an extract from the French-Jewish poet Edmond Jabès's *Livre des questions* concerning the vicissitudes of life, and the disc ends with an austere memorial to Lennart Meri, president of Estonia from 1992 to 2001. Superbly performed and recorded.

Passio

Passio Domini nostri Jesu Christi secundum Johannem
Mark Anderson ten **Robert Macdonald** bass
Tonus Peregrinus / Antony Pitts
Naxos 8 555860 (62' · DDD)   Ⓢ Ⓞ Ⓓ⁺

Arvo Pärt's *Passio* is a shining beacon among countless late-20th-century religious works that confronted the formidable prospect of a new millennium. Put briefly, *Passio* sets St John's Gospel to a simple but powerful triadic musical language, its prescribed forces limited to a small chorus, a handful of solo voices and a chamber-size instrumental line-up consisting of organ, violin, oboe, cello and bassoon. Pärt treats the text as paramount and yet there's scarcely a hint of word-painting in the accepted sense of the term. Spiritual underlining, yes, with telling support from the solo instruments. There are no written dynamics save for the opening, marked *Langsam* and *forte*, and the close, a *Largo* that blossoms from *pianissimo* to triple *forte*. Which doesn't mean that the singers are expected to deliver monotonously uninflected lines. Thankfully, none of them does.

Tonus Peregrinus shape phrases with a certain degree of freedom, just as choirs on rival versions have done before them. And Antony Pitts comes up trumps in his ability to keep lines lively and fluid, blending or clarifying as the text dictates. His is an excellent reading, always alert to Pärt's shifting harmonic plane and with consistently fresh voices, the women especially. Robert Macdonald's 'inward' portrayal of Jesus is nicely judged and Pitts's instrumental group is more than adequate.

Viewed overall, Tonus Peregrinus and Naxos have done Pärt proud. If this is your first *Passio*, rest assured that all the essentials are there. And if you want a top-grade specimen of quality music from the past 40 years, you won't find better. *Passio* truly is a wonderful work.

Nunc dimittis

'Triodion'
Dopo la vittoria. Nunc dimittis. ...which was the son of.... I am the true vine. Littlemore Tractus[a]. Triodion.
My Heart's in the Highlands[ab]. Salve regina
[b]**David Jones** counterten [a]**Christopher Bowers Broadbent** org **Polyphony / Stephen Layton**
Hyperion CDA67375 (77' · DDD · T/t)   Ⓕ Ⓞ Ⓓ⁺

Meurig Bowen's notes observe that choral pieces composed in the 1990s suggested Pärt was moving into 'more complex, exotic harmonic territory'. Some of his music began to give a glimpse of what was described as 'an attractively post-minimalist aspect' of the composer's recent work. All rather premature, perhaps, since, as Bowen acknowledges, Pärt subsequently returned to a more strictly diatonic, triadic approach.

Even so, the *staccato*, carol-like episodes bracketing *Dopo la vittoria*, commissioned in 1991 and delivered in 1997, come as a shock, but the bulk of the piece is more recognisably by Pärt, and the *Nunc dimittis*, with its lovely, lambent solo part for soprano Elin Thomas, evoking Allegri's *Miserere*, assuages all doubts.

The idea of Pärt setting Burns might surprise, but *My Heart's in the Highlands*, with its serene, Pachelbel-like organ line and pellucid vocal by countertenor David James, is a triumph. In the hymn-like *Littlemore Tractus* and *Salve regina*, warm melodies and bursts of colourful chords mellow Pärt's sound without detracting from its sublime, ethereal beauty. Polyphony's performance is gorgeous.

Anthony Payne
British b1936

Best known as the man who gave us Elgar's Third Symphony, Anthony Payne came to professional composition quite late in life. His very distinct musical voice has blossomed through his numerous works for chamber forces, the medium in which he excels. Initially he developed a technique loosely derived from various numerical systems that were increasingly linked to the more musical concept of interval size. Many of his vocal works were written for his wife, Jane Manning.

Miscellaneous Works

Empty Landscape – Heart's Ease. Scenes from The Woodlanders[a]. Of Knots and Skeins. Poems of Edward Thomas[a]. The Stones and Lonely Places Sing
[a]**Jane Manning** sop **Jane's Minstrels / Roger Montgomery**
NMC NMCD130 (79' · DDD) Ⓜ️Ⓑ➔

Anthony Payne's musical response to English pastoral is wide-ranging, welcoming challenges and shunning easy options. This programme, with two vocal and three instrumental works composed over a period of nearly a quarter of a century, gives a good sense of his scope, and also of his strengths.

The three *Poems of Edward Thomas* for soprano and piano quartet respond imaginatively to some fine poetry, as Payne matches the rhythmic economy and energy of 'Words' as effectively as the juxtaposition of images normally kept separate – steam trains and birdsong – in 'Adlestrop'. Thomas Hardy's prose in his novel *The Woodlanders* is no less evocative, but setting prose is always more difficult. Payne's solution is to invest particular poetic force in the instrumental representations of seasonal flux, underlining the obvious analogies between nature and humanity, and leading to a strong climax with the memorable final sentence 'the funereal trees rocked and chanted their dirges unceasingly'.

Of the three purely instrumental works, it's good to be reminded of the sustained expressive power and inventiveness of Payne's relatively early tone-poem for mixed sextet *The Stones* and *Lonely Places Sing*. The raw intensity which is so striking here is more muted in the later pieces, though comparable issues are at stake. *Empty Landscape – Heart's Ease* just manages to keep moves into bleakness at bay, while *Of Knots and Skeins* offers a more abstract interpretation of comparable concerns in its poised interactions of harmonic and melodic forces. With accomplished performances and spacious recording, this disc does Payne proud.

Krzysztof Penderecki
Polish b1933

Penderecki studied at the Kraków Conservatory, where he has also taught. He gained international fame with such works as Threnody for the Victims of Hiroshima for 52 strings (1960), exploiting the fierce expressive effects of new sonorities. Central to his work is the St Luke Passion (1965), with its combination of intense expressive force with a severe style with archaic elements alluding to Bach, and its sequel Utrenia, in which Orthodox chant provides musical material and at the same time a sense of mystery. His compositions also include four operas, eight symphonies and other orchestral pieces, a variety of instrumental concertos, choral settings of mainly religious texts, as well as chamber and instrumental works.

A Polish Requiem

A Polish Requiem
Izabella Kłosinska sop **Jadwiga Rappé** contr
Ryszard Minkiewicz ten **Piotr Nowacki** bass
Warsaw National Philharmonic Choir and Orchestra / Antoni Wit
Naxos ② 8 557386/7 (99' · DDD · T/t) Ⓢ➔

The *Polish Requiem* had its origins in a setting of the *Lacrimosa* dedicated to Gdańsk shipyard workers who died during clashes with the Communist authorities in 1970. Though the work's tendency to swing between bombast and sentimentality may make you long for the austerity of an Arvo Pärt, if you approach it as a valid attempt to continue the tradition of 19th-century concert Requiems – Verdi's, above all – then you may well feel it has much to offer.

This performance is well played and conducted, Antoni Wit ensuring that the big climaxes make their effect without labouring the less eventful episodes. The choral singing is robust, though the sustained high writing is demanding enough to give the Polish Philharmonic Choir some anxious moments. Of the vocal soloists, both Jadwiga Rappé and Piotr Nowacki are excellent, but the normally reliable Izabella Kłosinska was clearly under strain, and Ryszard Minkiewicz also sounds out of sorts in places. The sound is typical of Naxos's Polish recordings in being rather too bright and generalised for music that depends for its effect on such strong contrasts between the very quiet and the extremely loud.

Additional recommendation

St Luke Passion
Kłosinska sop **Kruszewski** bar **Tesarowicz** bass
Kolberger spkr **Malanowicz** org **Warsaw Boys' Ch;**
Warsaw Philh Ch; Warsaw Nat PO / Wit
Naxos 8 557149 (76' · DDD) ⓈⒹ▶

The relatively brief moments of almost
expressionistic drama come off best, aided by a
pungently immediate recording, complete with
rasping organ and blazing brass. The soloists are
all excellent.

Giovanni Pergolesi   Italian 1710-1736

*Pergolesi studied in Naples and worked as a violinist.
He became maestro di cappella to the Prince of
Stigliano in 1732 and to the Duke of Maddaloni in
1734. He wrote a number of stage works for Naples
and an opera seria, L'Olimpiade (1735), for Rome.
His other works include sacred music (notably a Stabat mater of 1736, possibly his most performed
work), chamber cantatas and duets, and a few
instrumental pieces. His reputation has grown posthumously as he didn't enjoy a great deal of fame
during his lifetime.*

Stabat mater

Stabat mater.' Salve regina in C minor   Ⓟ
Emma Kirkby sop **James Bowman** counterten
Academy of Ancient Music /
Christopher Hogwood
L'Oiseau-Lyre Florilegium 425 692-2OH
(52' · DDD · T/t)   ⒻⒹ▶

Pergolesi's *Stabat mater*, written in the last few
months of his brief life, enjoyed a huge popularity throughout the 18th century. But modern
performances often misrepresent its nature,
either through over-romanticising it or by transforming it into a choral work. None of these are
qualities overlooked in this affecting performance, for Emma Kirkby and James Bowman are
well versed in the stylistic conventions of
Baroque and early Classical music – and their
voices afford a pleasing partnership. Both revel
in Pergolesi's sensuous vocal writing, phrasing
the music effectively and executing the ornaments with an easy grace. Singers and instrumentalists alike attach importance to sonority,
discovering a wealth of beguiling effects in Pergolesi's part-writing. In the *Salve regina* in
C minor Emma Kirkby gives a compelling performance, pure in tone, expressive and poignant,
and she's sympathetically supported by the string
ensemble. The recording is pleasantly resonant.

Messa di S Emidio

Pergolesi Messa di S Emidio ª   Ⓟ
A Scarlatti Messa per il Santissimo Natale

Concerto Italiano / Rinaldo Alessandrini
Naïve OP30461 (58' · DDD)   ⒻⓄⒹ▶

 These two Masses were performed in
Rome almost 30 years apart by composers both strongly associated with
Naples. The *Messa di S Emidio* is one of only two
works that are accepted as authentic Pergolesi
Mass settings, although different versions survive. It was apparently composed for a service in
the Neapolitan church of S Maria della Stella
de' PP Minimi in 1732, but Pergolesi later
revised it for several choirs and two orchestras
(the version recorded here). Concerto Italiano's
10 singers and 19 instrumentalists (including
two horns and two trumpets) make an extraordinary noise in the stacking chords that commence
the volatile *Kyrie*. Some of Alessandrini's singers
suffer from dodgy tuning at first, but things soon
settle down, and reflective moments are particularly well performed.

The disc concludes with an impressive account
of Alessandro Scarlatti's magnificent *Messa per il
Santissimo Natale*. Written in 1707 for the
Roman Basilica S Maria Maggiore, it shows
Scarlatti's mastery at fusing Renaissance *stile
antico* for two choirs (with very little doubling)
with solo voice passages and imaginative instrumental parts for two violins. Concerto Italiano
are on especially good form in Scarlatti's finely
woven counterpoint (*Agnus Dei* is exquisite),
though both neglected Masses benefit from
Alessandrini's articulately shaped interpretations.

Missa S Emidioª. Manca la guida al pièᶜ.
Laudate pueri Dominumᵈ. Salve regina in F minorᵇ
ᵃᶜ**Veronica Cangemi,** ᵈ**Rachel Harnisch** sops
ᵃᵇ**Sara Mingardo** contr ᶜ**Teresa Romano** mez
Coro della Radiotelevisione Svizzera;
Orchestra Mozart / Claudio Abbado
Archiv 477 8463AH (64' · DDD)   ⒻⒹ▶

Claudio Abbado and the Bolognese Orchestra
Mozart present a fine *Missa brevis* that seems to
have been composed for the feast of St Emidius,
protector against earthquakes and patron saint
of Naples, on December 31, 1732. It contains
ample evidence of Pergolesi's mastery of late-
Baroque double-choir techniques and the new
galant style of writing for virtuoso solo voices.
There are some striking features, such as an
astonishing second 'Kyrie' that has some
extraordinary harmonic twists packed into its
brief duration, and magnificent double-choir
passages in the first part of 'Qui tollis' that bring
to mind Mozart's counterpart in the Mass in
C minor (written half a century later).

Diego Fasolis's Swiss-Italian choir is on good
form, settling down after the unbridled opening
of the 'Gloria in excelsis Deo' threatens to
become undisciplined. Sara Mingardo and
Veronica Cangemi combine to good effect in
the duet 'Domine Deus': the latter gives a vivid
account of a soliloquy from the oratorio *La con-
versione e morte di San Guglielmo duca d'Aquitania*

(1731); the former gives an emotive, some might say exaggerated, performance of the F minor version of the *Salve regina* composed near the end of Pergolesi's life. A spectacular *Laudate pueri* featuring Rachel Harnisch's fluent coloratura, incisive choral singing and colourful orchestration concludes the disc brightly. Those who found Abbado's *Stabat mater* to be nondescript will be delighted to discover a surer sense of purpose and stylistic articulation in this rewarding collection.

Pérotin   French c1155/60-c1225

Pérotin was the most celebrated musician involved in the revision and re-notation of the Magnus liber (attributed to Léonin). He is one of very few composers of his day whose name has been preserved and can be reliably attached to individual compositions; this is due to the testimony of an anonymous English student at Notre Dame known as Anonymous IV, who wrote about him and his predecessor Léonin. Anonymous IV called him 'Pérotin the master or expert'. The name Pérotin is itself derived from 'Perotinus', the Latin diminutive of Petrus, the Latin version of the French name Pierre.

Viderunt omnes / Sederunt principes

Pérotin Viderunt omnes. Alleluia, posui adiutorium. Dum sigillum summi Patris. Alleluia, Nativitas. Beata viscera. Sederunt principes **Anonymous** Veni Creator Spiritus. O Maria virginei. Isias cecinit
Hilliard Ensemble (David James *counterten* John Potter, Rogers Covey-Crump, Mark Padmore, Charles Daniels *tens* Gordon Jones *bar*) / **Paul Hillier** *bar*
ECM New Series 837 751-2 (68' · DDD · T)   Ⓕ**O**➔

This is a superb and original recording. It gives musical individuality to a group of works that have hitherto tended to sound much the same. Moreover, as a special attraction for those wanting to see artistic individuality in early composers, it includes all but one of the identifiable works of Pérotin. Inevitably his two grand four-voice *organa* take up much of the record. At nearly 12 minutes each they may have been the most ambitious polyphonic works composed up to the end of the 12th century. The Hilliard Ensemble adopts a suave and supple approach to both *Viderunt* and *Sederunt*, softening the pervasive rhythms that can make them a shade oppressive and showing a clear view of the entire architecture of each piece. They surge irrepressibly from one section to another, creating a musical momentum that belies the admirably slow speeds they generally adopt. They also beautifully underline the musical differences between the two works, producing a sound which seems a credible reflection of what one might have heard at Notre Dame in the late 12th century. Particularly exciting is the way in which the musicians grasp at the individual dynamic of each work: the huge open spaces they create to project the text

of the magical *O Maria virginei*; the breakneck virtuosity in their swirling performance of *Dum sigillum*, the gently modulated rhythms in the strophic *Veni Creator*; the harder edge in their tone for *Alleluia Nativitas*; and so on. This is a recording of the highest distinction.

Allan Pettersson   Swedish 1911-1980

Pettersson studied at the Stockholm Conservatory (1930-39), played the viola in the Stockholm PO (1939-51), then went to Paris for further study with Honegger and Leibowitz. Back in Sweden he concentrated on composition, in particular on large-scale, single-movement symphonies in an impassioned diatonic style (there were eventually 16). Most of his symphonies are written in a single movement, making them all the more demanding. Overwhelmingly serious in tone, often dissonant, his music rises to ferocious climaxes, relieved, especially in his later works, by lyrical oases. Most of his music has now been recorded. He also wrote concertos, songs and chamber pieces. Pettersson's writing is tonal but very strenuous and often has many simultaneous polyphonic lines.

Symphonies

Symphonies Nos 5 & 16
John-Edward Kelly *sax* **Saarbrücken Radio Symphony Orchestra / Alun Francis**
CPO CPO999 284-2 (65' · DDD)   Ⓜ

The orchestral playing is full of commitment, the account of the 40-minute Fifth (1960-62) sounding tremendously vivid; Francis has the edge over rival versions where it counts, in his overall view of this magnificent work. Yet the coupling – the last symphony the Swede completed – is better still. No 16 was written in 1979 for the American saxophonist Frederik Hemke. Here Kelly, who has made some minor modifications to the solo part for reasons explained in the booklet (the ailing composer appears to have been uncertain of the instrument's range), glides through the hair-raising virtuosity with breathtaking ease. This is the kind of advocacy Pettersson, who never heard the work, can only have dreamed of. An excellent disc.

Symphonies Nos 7 & 11
Norrköping Symphony Orchestra / Leif Segerstam
BIS BIS-CD580 (70' · DDD)   Ⓕ

Most of Pettersson's major works are constructed as large, unified movements (although he was an accomplished miniaturist) and Nos 7 and 11, respectively 46 and 24 minutes in length, are no exceptions. The former in some ways is unrepresentative of the composer; the obsessiveness of mood and hectoring tone are present, especially in the *Angst*-ridden first and third spans, but the range of expression is much wider than in most of his other works. Composed in 1967-68, it has a unique atmosphere, both haunting and haunted, which will stay with you for a long time. His melodic genius is confirmed in the long and heart-felt central threnody, as well as by the beautiful quiet coda, truly music to 'soften the crying of a child'; its delivery by the Norrköping players has just the right amount of detachment. Segerstam's tempi permit the work to breathe and resonate not unlike Mahler. The Eleventh Symphony (1974) is less combative in tone, although it has its moments, and isn't on the same elevated plane as the Seventh. The recording quality is first-rate, allowing both the devastating power and delicate fine detail of these scores to emerge equally well.

Hans Pfitzner
German 1869-1949

Pfitzner, after study at the Hoch Conservatory, Frankfurt, was a teacher in Berlin, Strasbourg and Munich until 1934, when he was relieved of his post. In his opera Palestrina (1917) he produced a powerful and still often-performed reflection on the juxtaposition of the everyday demands of life with the spiritual inner life of the creative artist. Increasingly nationalistic in his middle and old age, Pfitzner was at first regarded sympathetically by important figures in the Third Reich (in particular by Hans Frank, with whom he remained on good terms). But he soon fell out with chief Nazis, who were unimpressed by his long musical association with the conductor Bruno Walter, who was Jewish. He also wrote three symphonies, concertos for the piano, violin and two for the cello, chamber music (including three string quartets) and over 100 songs.

Piano Trio

Violin Sonata in E minor, Op 27. Piano Trio in F, Op 8ª
Benjamin Schmid *vn* ª**Clemens Hagen** *vc*
Claudius Tanski *pf*
Dabringhaus und Grimm MDG312 0934-2
(70' · DDD)   Ⓕ**O**

The Sonata is a fine piece from Pfitzner's maturity, while the much earlier Piano Trio is one of the most extraordinary works for the medium you're likely to have ever heard. To be sure, enterprising chamber players hunting for neglected repertory may well have come across early critical reactions to both these pieces, and references to (for example, in the case of the Trio) Pfitzner's 'sick imagination' and the work's 'monstrous length' might put anyone off. When he wrote it Pfitzner was in despair at his financial and other problems; he told a friend that after finishing it all he wanted was to die. It does at times suggest a man at the end of his tether, but also a composer chronicling such a state when at the height of his powers.

It's long, extremely tense, at times weirdly obsessive, even hysterical, but all this takes place within a cunningly plotted ground plan. After the

strange and powerful contrasts of the first movement, with its wild coda, the noble but perilously assaulted main theme of the slow movement, the dance-like but fraught and nervous *Scherzo*, Pfitzner begins his finale with a choleric gesture which soon fades to pathos and pallor. After 10 minutes of desperate attempts to climb out of this pit, a positive coda seems possible, but when the music turns instead to utterly euphonious calm the listener is likely to be moved by what seems in context heroic as well as wonderfully beautiful.

The Sonata, from 1918, sounds like a demonstration – with various modernisms obvious – that Pfitzner's late-Romantic style and prodigious craft still had abundant life in them. Its inexhaustible inventiveness and the beauty of its themes are accompanied by a considerable enjoyment of virtuosity: Pfitzner, you realise, is having a high old time. Both works are vastly welcome, in short, but that they should be so superbly played goes beyond all reasonable expectations.

Palestrina

Palestrina
Christopher Ventris *ten* Palestrina **Peter Rose** *bass*
Pope Pius IV **Michael Volle** *bar* Giovanni Morone
John Daszak *ten* Bernardo Novagerio **Roland Bracht** *bass* Christoph Madruscht **Falk Struckmann** *bar* Carlo Borromeo **Christiane Karg** *sop* Ighino
Bavarian State Opera / Simone Young
Stage director **Christian Stückl**
Video director **Karina Fibich**
EuroArts ② **DVD** 207 2528 (3h 17' · NTSC · 16:9 · PCM Stereo and DTS 5.0 · 0)
Recorded live at the National Theatre, Munich, on July 10 and 14, 2009   Ⓕ**OO**

'*Palestrina* will remain. The work has all the elements of immortality.' So declared Bruno Walter who conducted the world premiere in Munich in the war-weary Germany of 1917. Fischer-Dieskau declared it one of the 'most special' 20th-century German operas, alongside *Doktor Faust* and *Mathis der Maler*.

Palestrina's legendary status is ironically founded on myths and unlikelihoods. The scenario is rooted in the romantic premise that the eponymous composer created the *Missa Papae Marcelli* to save polyphony from an attempt to return to Gregorian chant. Nor did Palestrina have composer's block at the time (c1563) due to his wife's death – she would not expire until 1580, yet in the opera is the only female character and a dead one at that. She it is who finally inspires him to compose the Mass in a single night. Unlikely!

Christian Stückl's fine staging is fully worthy of Pfitzner's conception, though the composer would probably have loathed it. The use of colour is striking, from the monochromes of the opening to the pinks and greens of later scenes, all nicely caught by Karina Fibich's filming. Simone Young directs a flowing and nicely paced account. Christopher Ventris is sensitive, achieving exhausted nobility as the composer, and Falk Struckmann provides a rounded portrayal of the subtle Borromeo, albeit not to rival Fischer-Dieskau. Michael Volle's Morone is fine. Christiane Karg provides much needed textural contrast in what is a very male-voice dominated opera.

Montague Phillips · British 1885-1969

Philips studied organ and composition at the Royal Academy of Music. He first made a name with popular ballads composed for his wife, soprano Clara Butterworth, who also starred in his finest work, The Rebel Maid (1921). For the centenary of the RAM in 1922 he composed The Song of Rosamund and he was for many years professor of harmony and composition there. He composed many works for orchestra, but only the lighter pieces, which showed off his talents to greater advantage, made any real mark.

Piano Concertos

M Phillips Piano Concertos – No 1; No 2
Hely-Hutchinson The Young Idea
David Owen Norris pf
BBC Concert Orchestra / Gavin Sutherland
Dutton Epoch CDLX7206 (69' · DDD)   Ⓜ

Purely for sound quality, this disc is a winner. It is a sumptuous, full-blooded recording with a richly resonant bass matched by the soloist's powerful Fazioli. Both concertos are real finds. The F sharp minor First Concerto (1907) has not been played for more than 95 years; the E major (1919) especially, once a favourite of conductor Vilém Tausky, is tremendously effective. It would bring the house down were it played at the Proms again (it received its premiere there in 1920) if only for the last movement's big tune which simultaneously combines Celtic lament, Elgarian *nobilmente* and a (prescient) celluloid weepie. True, the orchestra has the best of this, but the soloist, by the time of its final full statement, has earned a few bars' rest. Talking of whom, Norris gives the performance of his life in these two works, handling the bravura writing with aplomb and total conviction. He also has a marvellous repose at the keyboard – in the slow movement of the First Concerto, for example, before it builds to its shattering climax. Less, he knows, is more.

The final (eight-minute) work, aptly subtitled 'Cum grano salis' is, as the composer noted only three years after its publication in 1931, 'hopelessly out of date' and a somewhat bathetic appendage to the grand romance of Phillips's concertos.

Orchestral Works

A Surrey Suite, Op 59. Moorland Idyll, Op 61. Revelry Overture, Op 62. A Spring Rondo. A Summer

Nocturne. A Shakespearean Scherzo: Titania and her Elvish Court. Sinfonietta in C, Op 70. Arabesque, Op 43 No 2. The Rebel Maid – Jig; Gavotte; Graceful Dance; Villagers' Dance
BBC Concert Orchestra / Gavin Sutherland
Dutton Epoch CDLX7140 (76' · DDD)   ⓂⵔO

Montague Phillips's music, like that of Arthur Sullivan, Edward German and Samuel Coleridge-Taylor, was on the more serious side of 'light'. He had a thorough technical musical grounding at the Royal Academy of Music, where he was later professor of composition, and he was also a church organist and accompanist. These are emphatically not radio jingles but concert items of genuine symphonic status. If the sparkling *Revelry* Overture, with which the programme opens, evokes Eric Coates's *Merrymakers* Overture, much of the rest is Elgarian in its grandeur. The orchestration is bold and accomplished, with a use of brass that sometimes suggests Phillips's Royal Academy contemporary Bax.

The once widely popular dances from *The Rebel Maid* (a light opera whose entire score merits rediscovery) may recall German's dance sets in their concept, but they're made of sturdier stuff. The moving *Moorland Idyll*, the picturesque and varied *Surrey Suite*, the sparkling *Titania and her Elvish Court* and the charming *Arabesque* all constitute music to be treasured. Phillips's voice, so eloquently served here by fine performances and recording, deserves to be heard not just as light music but in a wider British music context.

Astor Piazzolla · Argentinian 1921-1992

A child prodigy on the bandoneón, Piazzolla emigrated with his family to New York in 1924. In 1954 he won a scholarship to study with Nadia Boulanger, who encouraged him in the composition of tangos. Piazzolla's unique version of the tango, which initially met with opposition, included dissonance, jazz elements and chromaticism. By the 1980s his work had finally become accepted in Argentina and had begun to be taken into the 'classical' repertoire.

Tangos

Piazzolla Libertango (arr Calandrelli). Tango Suite (arr S Assad) – Andante; Allegro. Le Grand Tango (arr Calandrelli). Sur – Regreso al amor. Fugata. Mumuki. Tres minutos con la realidad. Milonga del ángel. Histoire du Tango – Café 1930 (all arr Calandrelli)
Calandrelli Tango Remembrances
Yo-Yo Ma vc **Antonio Agri** vn **Nestor Marconi,**
Astor Piazzolla bandoneón **Horacio Malvicino,**
Odair Assad, Sérgio Assad, Oscar Castro-Neves
gtrs **Edwin Barker, Héctor Console** db **Kathryn**
Stott, Gerardo Gandini, Leonardo Marconi,
Frank Corliss pfs
Sony Classical SK63122 (64' · DDD)   ⒻⒹ▶

Yo-Yo Ma is the latest international artist to surrender to the spell of the Argentinian dance: he can also be heard on the soundtrack of the film *The Tango Lesson*. Here, surrounded by a brilliant group of experts in the genre, he presents with wholehearted commitment a well-varied programme of Piazzolla pieces. They range from the melancholy or sultry to the energetic or fiery. Among the latter, *Fugata* is ingenious, *Mumuki* richly eloquent, and *Tres minutos con la realidad* nervily edgy: in this last, Kathryn Stott understandably earned the admiration of her Argentinian colleagues. She also shines with Yo-Yo Ma in an exciting performance of *Le Grand Tango*: his playing in the *Milonga del ángel* is outstandingly beautiful. Special mention must also be made of some spectacular virtuosity by the Assad brothers in the *Tango Suite*. The characteristic bandoneón is featured with the cellist in *Café 1930*; and by technological trickery Yo-Yo Ma partners Piazzolla himself (recorded in 1987) in a confection called *Tango Remembrances*. Those who are already fans of this genre will be in no need of encouragement.

Concerto for Bandoneón

Concerto for Bandoneón, Strings and Percussion[a].
Las cuatro estaciones porteñas (arr Franzetti).
Mar del Plata 70 (arr Carli). Sinfonía Buenos Aires
[a]**Juan José Mosalini** *band*
**Württemberg Philharmonic Orchestra /
Gabriel Castagna**
Chandos CHAN10419 (71' · DDD)　　　Ⓕ🅓➔

Gabriel Castagna gives us the first recording of the *Sinfonía Buenos Aires*. Composed in 1951, it is far more ambitious in scope than the Sinfonietta – and more daring, as well. The music's tightly coiled rhythms are typical of the composer, certainly, but there's an edgy grandeur and harmonic pungency here that's like nothing else in his output. Indeed, with its onslaught of percussion and blazing brass, the wailing climax of the slow movement calls to mind Shostakovich's Eighth Symphony. Castagna inspires some ferocious playing from his German orchestra.

The Concerto for bandoneón, strings and percussion (1979) is played with verve, too. Juan José Mosalini puts a jaunty spring in the rhythms of the solo part, a delectable reminder of the score's dance-music roots. José Carli's full-orchestra arrangement of *Mar del Plata 70* retains the tango's acerbic character. Less appealing is Carlos Franzetti's transcription of *Cuatro estaciones porteñas*: Franzetti is a marvellous composer himself, and this suite is expertly scored, but the results are overly lush.

John Pickard　　　British b1963

Pickard read for his BMus degree at the University of Wales, Bangor, where his composition teacher was

William Mathias. Between 1984 and 1985 he studied with Louis Andriessen at the Royal Conservatory in The Hague on a Dutch Ministry of Culture Scholarship. He was awarded a PhD in composition in 1989 and, from 1993, has been senior lecturer in music and later professor of composition and applied musicology at the University of Bristol. Pickard is best known for a series of powerful orchestral and instrumental works.

The Flight of Icarus

The Flight of Icarus. The Spindle of Necessity[a].
Channel Firing
[a]**Christian Lindberg** *tbn* **Norrköping Symphony Orchestra / Martyn Brabbins**
BIS BIS-CD1578 (66' · DDD)　　　Ⓕ❍❍❍❍➔

In many respects, *The Flight of Icarus* (1990) was John Pickard's breakthrough work, at least into the wider national consciousness, partly thanks to its London premiere at the 1996 Proms but also due to its clear structure, accessible (though not unchallenging) musical language and the sheer élan of its orchestral writing. Playing continuously, its three compelling sections are indicative of the ascent of Icarus and Daedalus from their Minoan confinement, their exhilarating albeit turbulent flight and Icarus's catastrophic fall, prompting a wonderfully direct, emotive elegy (all the more remarkable for a composer then just 27).

Icarus remains Pickard's best-known orchestral work, unjustly since three years later he trumped it with *Channel Firing*, written in memory of his teacher, William Mathias. Inspired by Thomas Hardy's dark pre-Great War poem where the dead in a churchyard are woken by naval gunnery practice and assume it is the Day of Judgement, Pickard constructs a gripping symphonic poem redolent of not-quite-apocalypse: it is not time for the dead to be judged, Europe is not yet in the grip of war; but both are coming.

Separating these full-orchestral conceptions is a concerto for trombone, strings and percussion showing a quite different side to his musical character. Like *Icarus*, *The Spindle of Necessity* (1998) derives from Greek myth via Plato's *Republic*. Here the textures are often gossamer-thin, with light percussion interweaving with natural string overtones and translucent harmonies. Lindberg plays the emotionally detached solo part with consummate skill while Brabbins draws sensational playing from the Norrköping orchestra in what must have been *terra incognita*. BIS's sound as always is first rate. Highly recommended.

Walter Piston　　　American 1894-1976

Piston trained as a draughtsman before studying composition at Harvard and, after a period in the US Navy, with Paul Dukas and Nadia Boulanger in

Paris; he then returned to Harvard (1926-60), becoming a renowned theory teacher (among his illustrious students were Leroy Anderson, Leonard Bernstein and Elliott Carter). Piston wrote four books on the technical aspects of music theory which are considered to be classics in their respective fields: Principles of Harmonic Analysis, Counterpoint, Orchestration and Harmony. They are still widely used by teachers and students of harmony. His music is in a tonal style with, perhaps, a nod to his French contemporaries. The main works include eight symphonies, five string quartets and the ballet The Incredible Flutist (1938).

Violin Concertos

Violin Concertos Nos 1 & 2.
Fantasia for Violin and Orchestra
James Buswell *vn* **National Symphony Orchestra of Ukraine / Theodore Kuchar**
Naxos 8 559003 (61' · DDD)   Ⓢ**O**🅓➔

Piston's First Violin Concerto, written in 1939, has much in common with the Barber, including a similar abundance of individual melody. The heart of the work is in the moving, pensive central *Andantino molto tranquillo*. With just a hint of Gershwin in its bluesy opening, the movement is essentially searching and ruminative. This is a masterpiece, as will be confirmed when other violinists take it up.

The Second Concerto, written two decades later, is less obviously 'popular', its atmosphere more elusive. But its opening is similarly haunting and the more one hears it the more one is drawn by its depth of inner feeling. The extended, pensive *Adagio* introduces a serene and very beautiful theme, which later forms a canonic duet with the flute. The finale is another sparkling, jaunty rondo. The *Fantasia* is a late work, first performed in 1973. In five intricately related sections, its language more dissonant with almost feverish, bravura *allegros* framed by troubled, lonely *adagio* passages, dominated by the soloist, which have been described as 'painfully aware and transcendentally serene'. The closing section is profoundly gentle.

It may seem remarkable that these works should make their CD debut played by a Russian orchestra, but it plays the music with splendid commitment, much subtlety of expression and fine ensemble too. The sure idiomatic feeling is explained by the fact its conductor, Theodore Kuchar, moved to the Ukraine from Cleveland, Ohio. James Buswell is a superbly accomplished and spontaneous soloist, and the recording is first class.

Symphony No 4

Symphony No 4. Capriccio.
Three New England Sketches
Seattle Symphony Orchestra / Gerard Schwarz
Naxos American Classics 8 559162 (52' · DDD) Ⓢ**O**🅓➔

Those unfamiliar with Piston's work should investigate this Naxos disc that repackages performances originally issued on Delos. This one is arguably the best of the lot as it features the Fourth Symphony (1951) and the *Three New England Sketches* (1959), two of the composer's greatest and most attractive scores.

The Fourth's rollicking syncopations show that Piston had been listening closely to Copland's ballets. This is a symphony in the true sense, though, and its musical ideas are as lucidly argued, profoundly uttered and strongly structured as any in the classical repertoire. Perhaps the surface dissonance of 'Seaside', the first of the *Sketches*, might be off-putting to some, but how could anyone resist the exquisite colours Piston conjures up. 'Summer Evening', with its flitting, twittering evocation of insect activity, is as vivid as the best of Mendelssohn's *scherzo*s, and the craggy majesty of 'Mountains' is truly awesome.

We also get the delightfully atmospheric *Capriccio* for harp and strings, and the quality of both the performances and recorded sound is as impressive as ever. At budget price, this disc should prove utterly irresistible.

Fantasy

The Incredible Flutist – Suite. Fantasy for English Horn, Harp and Strings. Suite for Orchestra. Concerto for String Quartet, Wind Instruments and Percussion. Psalm and Prayer of David
Scott Goff *fl* **Glen Danielson** *hn* **Theresa Elder Wunrow** *hp* **Juilliard Quartet** (Robert Mann, Joel Smirnoff *vns* Samuel Rhodes *va* Joel Krosnick *vc*)
Seattle Symphony Chorale and Orchestra / Gerard Schwarz
Delos DE3126 (68' · DDD)   Ⓕ

Gerard Schwarz's flutist fixes you with his limpid tone. However, it will always be known as the score with the Tango. Schwarz goes with the flow, the sway of the melody, but it can never linger long enough. The Fantasy enters darkened Elysian fields – Piston's lyricism sits well with this distinctive voice of sorrow and regret. We can trace their kinship right back to the composer's first published work – the orchestral Suite of 1929. At its heart is a long and intense pastorale: the cor anglais is there at the inception. Framing it, motoric syncopations carry us first to a kind of drive-by blues with bar-room piano and Grappelli violin. The finale is essentially a fugal work-out: high-tech Hindemith. Piston's very last work, the Concerto, is 10 eventful minutes where the imperative is once again pitted against the contemplative. The mixing of timbres is masterly, a fleck of woodwind or a brush of tambourine or antique cymbal speaking volumes. But at the centre of gravity is the Juilliard Quartet, moving in mysterious ways. In fact, the last words uttered here are those of the *Psalm and Prayer of David* – a rare vocal setting for Piston, and as such, refreshingly open, unhackneyed, unhieratical. Performance and recording are superb.

861

Ignaz Pleyel
French 1757-1831

Born in Lower Austria, Pleyel studied initially with Haydn thanks to aristocratic patronage. After working for Count Erdödy, Pleyel moved to Strasbourg and then to Paris where he narrowly escaped the Terror during the Revolution. In 1797 he set up a business as a music publisher ('Maison Pleyel'); it lasted for 39 years and published about 4000 works during this time, including compositions by Adam, Boccherini, Beethoven, Clementi, Dussek, Hummel and Onslow. In 1807 Pleyel became a manufacturer of pianos. He was a prolific composer, writing 41 symphonies, 70 string quartets and several operas, all in Classical, Haydnesque language.

Concertante Works

Symphonie concertantes – Ben 112[a]; Ben 114[b].
Violin Concerto, Ben 103/103[ac]
David Perry, [b]**Isabella Lippi** vns [a]**Victoria Chiang** va
Baltimore Chamber Orchestra / Markand Thakar
Naxos 8 570320 (71' · DDD)   ⑤🅳➔

Pleyel's concertos, symphonies and, especially, his *symphonies concertantes*, were hugely popular in Paris and London during the 1780s and early 1790s. The two *concertantes* recorded here – the B flat for the Mozartian pairing of violin and viola, the A major for two violins – reveal a polished technique and a vein of amiable, on occasion ear-tickling, melodic invention. The A major, composed for London in 1792, is the more attractive of the two, with its plaintive *siciliano* slow movement and chic rondo finale. There is also a touching minor-key *Adagio*, like a wordless aria, in the D major Violin Concerto, played here with the jaunty replacement finale Pleyel supplied for a performance in Strasbourg.

In the first movements of both the Violin Concerto and the B flat *Symphonie concertante*, Pleyel can amble and chatter to no great purpose. Certainly it would be futile in these leisurely, undemanding works to seek the inventiveness and tight formal control of Haydn, who composed his own 1792 *Sinfonia concertante* in a spirit of friendly rivalry with his onetime pupil. Still, if none of these concertos is as interesting as the best of Pleyel's symphonies, explorers of the Haydn-Mozart hinterland should find plenty of innocent enjoyment here. Performances are more than acceptable, with trim playing from the (modern-instrument) Baltimore band, and assured solo contributions from David Perry (stylish and sweet-toned in the solo concerto) and his violin and viola partners.

Amilcare Ponchielli
Italian 1834-1886

Poor Ponchielli. His lifetime coincided with Verdi's creative career and shortly after his death one of his

pupils, Puccini, made quite a name for himself. He had a tough life, brought up in poverty near Cremona, the son of a shopkeeper, and not achieving any real success until 10 years before the end of his life. One work of his remains in the repertoire, his 1876 opera La Gioconda. It's an important work because Ponchielli, inspired by Wagner, aimed to make the music more continuous, more suited to the action and with a richer orchestral texture than had been heard previously in Italian opera. It's a marvellous work and singers have been attracted to its dramatic and lyrical bel canto roles. It contains the celebrated tenor aria 'Cielo e mar!' (Act 2) and the impassioned 'Suicidio!' from Act 4 for the soprano heroine. Yet the one bit that everyone knows is the ballet from Act 3.

La Gioconda

La Gioconda   🅗
Maria Callas sop La Gioconda **Fiorenza Cossotto**
mez Laura Adorno **Pier Miranda Ferraro** ten Enzo
Grimaldo **Piero Cappuccilli** bar Barnaba **Ivo Vinco**
bass Alvise Badoero **Irene Companeez** contr La
Cieca **Leonardo Monreale** bass Zuane **Carlo Forte**
bass A Singer, Pilot **Renato Ercolani** ten Isepo, First
Distant Voice **Aldo Biffi** bass Second Distant Voice
Bonaldo Giaiotti bass Barnabotto **Chorus and
Orchestra of La Scala, Milan / Antonio Votto**
EMI mono ③ 556291-2 (167' · DDD)
Recorded 1959   Ⓜ🅞

Ponchielli's old warhorse has had a bad press in recent times, which seems strange in view of its melodic profusion, his unerring adumbration of Gioconda's unhappy predicament and of the sensual relationship between Enzo and Laura. But it does need large-scale and involved singing – just what it receives here on this now historic set. Nobody could fail to be caught up in its conviction. Callas was in good and fearless voice when it was made, with the role's emotions perhaps enhanced by the traumas of her own life at the time. Here her strengths in declaiming recitative, her moulding of line, her response to the text are all at their most arresting. Indeed she turns what can be a maudlin act into true tragedy. Ferraro's stentorian ebullience is most welcome. Cossotto is a vital, seductive Laura. Cappuccilli gives the odious spy and lecher Barnaba a threatening, sinister profile, while Vinco is a suitably implacable Alvise. Votto did nothing better than this set, bringing out the subtlety of the Verdi-inspired scoring and the charm of the 'Dance of the Hours' ballet. The recording sounds excellent for its age.

Additional recommendation

La Gioconda
Coupled with arias by Bellini, Donizetti and Rossini 🅗
Arangi-Lombardi La Gioconda **Granda** Enzo
Grimaldi **Viviani** Barnaba **Rota** La Cieca **Zambelli**
Alvise Badoero **Stignani** Laura Adorno **Baracchi**
Zuàne **Nessi** Isèpo [a]**Chorus and Orchestra of La
Scala, Milan / Molajoli**

Naxos Historical mono ③ 8 110112/4 (169' · ADD)
Recorded 1926-33   ⑤O▣▸

Outstanding among Italian operatic sets of the inter-war years, this was also the first complete recording of Ponchielli's masterpiece. Inevitably the sound quality of 1931 is at some disadvantage; the carefully orchestrated score, large-scale ensembles and off-stage effects need more space and clarity to do them full justice. Yet, to compensate, the voices have the vivid immediacy of their period and the transfers are excellent. Arangi-Lombardi, the heroine of the recording, is one of the main reasons for acquiring this set, which also includes a selection of her solo recordings, giving a fuller portrait of a highly distinguished artist.

Francis Pott   British b1957

A chorister as a child, Pott latter sang with choirs at New College, Oxford, Temple Church, London, and Winchester Cathedral. An academic, Pott is currently working on a study of Nikolay Medtner. He has composed for various forces, but the main focus is on organ and choral music. His most ambitious work to date is an oratorio A Song on the End of the World, composed for the 1999 Three Choirs Festival.

'Meditations and Remembrances'
Jesu dulcis memoria – 'Jesu, the very thought of thee'. Mass in Five Parts. A Meditation. A Remembrance. O Lord, support us all the day long. Introduction, Toccata and Fugue. Turn our Captivity (Psalm 126)
**Christ Church Cathedral Choir, Dublin /
Judy Martin** with **Tristan Russcher** org
Signum Classics SIGCD080 (71' · DDD · T/t)   ⓕ▣▸

Some composers are difficult to pigeonhole. The unsuspecting listener really can't help it if other composers' stylistic thumbprints spring to mind. In the case of Francis Pott he readily acknowledges the abiding influence of Byrd, 'that venerable, artistically transcendent and yet vulnerably human face of enduring Englishness'. True, they share a sense of long-limbed phrases and eschew saccharinity. Couple this to the astringency of Kenneth Leighton and the contrapuntal rigour of Rubbra and you have part of the picture.

For poets Pott favours Traherne (*A Meditation* and *A Remembrance*), Newman (*O Lord, support us*), the Psalmists and St Bernard of Clairvaux. The unaccompanied Mass in Five Parts arches and glows, rolling along unhurriedly, the few lively passages being the climaxes in the *Gloria* and the bouncy 'Osanna' conclusion to the *Sanctus* and *Benedictus*. Wisely, the Mass sequence is interrupted by the motet *Jesu dulcis memoria* (with its beautiful alto solo sung by Áine Mulvey), and the *Introduction, Toccata and Fugue*, played with clarity and aplomb by the young Australian-born organist Tristan Russcher.

The disc's programme is perfectly balanced. The performances are authoritative, passionate and convincing. The two dozen mixed voices of the Christ Church Cathedral Choir are more than a match for their English counterparts. The organ accompaniments are unobtrusive (unlike an occasional whoosh from the Dublin traffic) and, under Judy Martin's expert direction, everything flows seamlessly. A beautiful disc in every sense.

Francis Poulenc   French 1899-1963

One of Poulenc's friends described him as 'moitié moine, moitié voyou' ('half monk, half guttersnipe'), which suits his physical appearance perfectly and goes halfway to describing his music. His face resembled that of the great French clown Fernandel and, especially in his early work, Poulenc does seem to revel in the role of the clown of French music. This was balanced by the Catholic faith he was born into, lost and then rediscovered in 1935.

His father was a wealthy pharmaceutist, his mother was the music lover and gave Francis his first piano lessons. In 1916, when he was 17, he continued these with one of the most respected pianists of the day, the Spaniard Ricardo Viñes, who gave the premieres of many of Ravel's and Debussy's piano music. Years later, Poulenc admitted 'I owe him everything...it's really to Viñes that I owe my first flights in music and everything I know about the piano'. The same year he was introduced to the father-figure of the young, irreverent group of French composers of the day, Eric Satie. Shortly afterwards, Poulenc had his first composition published, Rhapsodie nègre. Overnight he was at the centre of the avant-garde circle in Paris and befriended the group of composers who came to be known as 'Les Six' - Auric, Durey, Honegger, Milhaud and Tailleferre.

After service in the French army (1918-21) – he composed his popular Trois mouvements perpétuels while on the Vosges front – he decided to take his musical education a little more seriously, but not too seriously: one of the charms of Poulenc's music is that it is untainted by preconceived ideas and an academic conservatory outlook.

He embraced the gay social life of 1920s Paris, producing a string of expertly crafted, witty, tuneful scores 'sometimes verging on triviality but never falling into vulgarity' (as the critic Roland-Manuel neatly put it). Ballet commissions from Diaghilev, piano pieces of charm and elegance and, especially, songs, flowed from his pen. In this latter field, he found his ideal interpreter in the gifted baritone Pierre Bernac. The two men became lifelong companions and provided inspiration for each other.

In 1935 Poulenc's religious faith, which had diminished after his father's death, was revived after a visit to the shrine of Notre Dame de Rocamadour. From here on, while never abandoning his role as the worldly, chic jester, a religious vein recurs through the remainder of his music. His final works were two sonatas: the Oboe Sonata written in memory of Prokofiev and the Clarinet Sonata written in memory of Honegger. He himself died suddenly in Paris.

Organ Concerto

Concerto for Organ, Strings and Timpani in G minor.
Suite française, d'après Claude Gervaise. Concert
champêtre
Elisabeth Chojnacka hpd **Philippe Lefebvre** org
Lille Symphony Orchestra / Jean-Claude Casadesus
Naxos 8 554241 (59' · DDD)   ⓈⒹ┼

Elisabeth Chojnacka gets off to a head start
against most others who have recorded the
Concert champêtre by using the right kind of
instrument: she understands that it's much sil-
lier to play newish music on a period instrument
than old music on a modern one. The effective
proportions secured here between her deft playing and the orchestra also owe much to Jean-
Claude Casadesus's nice sense of judgement and
to the work of an excellent recording team.

It was particularly perverse of Poulenc to ask a
harpsichord to contend with large brass and
percussion sections and then, a decade later,
employ only strings and timpani in his concerto
for the intrinsically far more powerful organ;
and that perversity is underlined here by using
the massive organ of Notre Dame, Paris –
though once again the recording technicians
have skilfully succeeded in producing a string
sonority that doesn't suffer beside the organ's
awesome thunders. You can't help wondering
whether Poulenc really had such a giant sound
in mind, but it's undeniably thrilling; and the
quieter moments are captured with commendable clarity and calm. From the interpretative
point of view, it's quite a performance. The wind
and percussion of the Lille orchestra get a
chance to demonstrate their quality in accomplished playing of the spry dances of the *Suite
française*. This is an eminently recommendable
disc.

Additional recommendation

Organ Concerto
Coupled with **Saint-Saëns** Symphony No 3, 'Organ'
Barber Toccata festiva
Latry org **Philadelphia Orch / Eschenbach**
Ondine ⊕. ODE1094-5 (79' · DDD/DSD)
Recorded live   ⒻⓄⓄ
  Eschenbach's Poulenc is heavily romanticised,
  squeezing every last drop of pathos from the score
  and finding many moments of ravishing beauty.
  Latry is, for the most part, a willing accomplice and
  he clearly relishes Eschenbach's slow tempi in
  reaching the work's two powerful climaxes. The
  organ shows its stature with palpable depth in the
  first movement and majestic presence in the finale;
  but the real star of the show here is the Philadelphia Orchestra itself.

Piano Concertos

Piano Concerto. Concerto for Two Pianos[a]. Aubade
François René Duchâble, [a]**Jean-Philippe Collard** pfs

Rotterdam Philharmonic Orchestra / James Conlon
Warner Apex 2564 62552-2 (55' · DDD)   Ⓑ

An appealing bargain collection of Poulenc's
concertante piano music. Duchâble is a stylish
player in the Piano Concerto and is joined by
Collard for the sparkling Double Piano Concerto – and they find a glorious sense of poise in
the languid slow movement. Conlon and his
Rotterdam orchestra accompany with panache.
The stylistic inconsistency of the various sections of the *Aubade* (appreciation of which really
depends on a knowledge of the story of the ballet
for which it was intended) is perhaps the reason
for its comparative lack of popularity – it
includes Poulenc's characteristic pianistic
helter-skelter, ingenuous wistful lyricism, *gamin*
pertness and Stravinskian angularity, ending
with a typical Stravinskian repetition of a single
phrase.

Concert champêtre

Les animaux modèles[b]. Concert champêtre[ab].
Improvisations[a] – No 13; No 15
[a]**Stefano Bollani** pf
[ab]**Filarmonia '900 del Teatro Regio di Torino /
Jan Latham-Koenig**
Avie AV2135 (74' · DDD)   ⒻⓄ

Poulenc's third and final ballet, *Les animaux
modèles*, was begun, he wrote, 'in the darkest
days of the summer of 1940, and one way or
another I wanted to find a reason for hope in
the future of my country'. The fables of La
Fontaine provided him with the plot and it
was first performed on August 8, 1942, in
occupied Paris (in the penultimate section,
'Les deux coqs', Poulenc mischievously quotes
the song 'Non, non, vous n'aurez pas notre
Alsace-Lorraine' for an audience made up
mainly of German officials).

Why we don't hear this delicious score more
often is a mystery. Too many good tunes,
probably. Its eight movements are quintessential Poulenc with the characteristic mélange
of harmonic and stylistic influences that make
their composer's voice so unmistakable. There
is also a good deal of self-plagiarising (spot the
quotes from the Organ Concerto and the contemporaneous *Babar the Elephant*). Only one
other recording is currently available, apart
from the abbreviated version recorded by
Georges Prêtre from 1966. The Turin players
match the Parisians every step of the way with
their incision, sure-footedness and sheer
panache.

Stefano Bollini, whose career has been mainly
in jazz, makes a good fist of the *Concert champêtre*
(commissioned by the harpsichordist Wanda
Landowska, of course, but sanctioned by the
composer to be played on the piano as well),
rounding off the disc with his own 'elaborations'
of two of Poulenc's late Improvisations, No 13
from 1958 and No 15 ('Hommage à Edith Piaf'),
from 1959, the last of the cycle.

Chamber works

Complete Chamber Works
Sextet for Piano and Wind Quintet[a]. Trio for Oboe, Bassoon and Piano[b]. Flute Sonata[c]. Oboe Sonata[d]. Clarinet Sonata[e]. Violin Sonata[f]. Cello Sonata[g]. Sonata for Two Clarinets[h]. Sonata for Clarinet and Bassoon[i]. Sonata for Horn, Trumpet and Trombone[j]. Villanelle[k]. Elégie[l]. Sarabande[m]
Nash Ensemble (Philippa Davies [a-c]fl/[k]picc [abd]Gareth Hulse ob [aehl]Richard Hosford, [h]Michael Harris cls [abl]Ursula Leveaux bn [aij]Richard Watkins hn [j]John Wallace tpt [j]David Purser tbn [f]Leo Phillips vn [g]Paul Watkins vc [m]Craig Ogden gtr) [a-g/kl]**Ian Brown** pf
Hyperion ② CDA672556 (146' · DDD)   Ⓕ Ⓓ→

Invidious as it may seem to pick out just one of these excellent artists, special mention must be made of Ian Brown, who plays in nine of the 13 works included and confirms his standing as one of the most admired and musicianly chamber pianists of our day. He knows, for example, how to control Poulenc's boisterous piano writing in the Sextet without sacrificing the sparkle, and as a result the work coheres better than ever before. Like the Trio (whose opening reveals Stravinskian influence), it's a mixture of the composer's madcap *gamin* mood and his predominantly melancholy bittersweet lyricism. The latter characteristic is most in evidence in his most enduring chamber works: the solo wind sonatas with piano, all three of which were in the nature of *tombeaux*, the Flute Sonata for the American patron Mrs Sprague Coolidge, that for clarinet for Honegger, and that for oboe for Prokofiev. All are given idiomatic, sensitive and satisfying performances by the Nash artists.

The *Elégie* for Dennis Brain was a not altogether convincing experiment in dodecaphony: Poulenc had earlier dabbled in atonality and polytonality in the little sonatas (really sonatinas) for, respectively, two clarinets and for clarinet and bassoon. There's a touching reading of the little *Sarabande* for guitar. A hint of the guitar's tuning at the start of the second movement is almost the only Spanish reference in the Violin Sonata, which was composed *in memoriam* the poet Lorca, whose loss is bitterly suggested in the angry finale. In this work Poulenc allotted to the piano (his own instrument) rather more than equal status in the duo – a situation rather paralleled in the lighthearted Cello Sonata, over which the composer dallied longer than any other of his works – but balance in both is finely judged by the performers and the recording team.

The whole issue wins enthusiastic recommendation: it bids fair to become the undisputed yardstick for the future.

Gloria

Gloria. Stabat mater
Janice Watson sop **BBC Singers; BBC Philharmonic Orchestra / Yan Pascal Tortelier**

Chandos CHAN9341 (56' · DDD · T/t)   Ⓕ Ⓞ Ⓑ→

We are immediately struck, at the start of the *Gloria*, by the radiantly warm but clean orchestral sonority: only later does an uneasy suspicion arise that, apparently seduced by the sound, the recording engineers may be favouring it at the expense of the chorus, especially at orchestral *fortes*. But it's committed and thoroughly secure choral singing, perhaps most easily appreciated in some of the unaccompanied passages – tender in the almost mystic 'O quam tristis' and firm-toned at 'Fac ut ardeat' (both in the *Stabat mater*); it gives real attack at 'Quis est homo' (just holding its own against the orchestra); the sopranos can produce a bright, ringing tone; and only the very first line of the 'Stabat mater', lying low in the basses, needed to be a bit stronger (as in most performances). Janice Watson is a sweet-voiced soloist with very pure intonation; but she could with advantage have strengthened her consonants throughout.

Tortelier gives intensely felt readings of both works – the murmurous ending of the *Stabat mater* and the thrilling *fortissimo* chords at 'Quoniam' in the *Gloria* spring to mind – and fortunately he keeps the vocal 'Domine Deus' entry moving at the same pace as at its introduction. He takes the Stravinskian 'Laudamus te' fast and lightly; the only questionable speed is of 'Quae moerebat', which sounds too cheerful for the words ('mourning and lamenting'). These are performances of undoubted quality.

Gloria[a]. Exultate Deo. Quatre Motets pour le temps de Noël. Quatre Motets pour un temps de pénitence. Salve regina
[a]**Susan Gritton** sop **Polyphony;** [a]**Trinity College Choir, Cambridge;** [a]**Britten Sinfonia / Stephen Layton**
Hyperion CDA67623 (56' · DDD)   Ⓕ Ⓞ Ⓞ Ⓞ Ⓑ→

From the very outset of the *Gloria* it's clear that this is a performance of real distinction. The gloriously pompous opening orchestral fanfare has a swagger and a self-satisfied strut which is one of those rare moments on disc where you would wish it were tracked separately so that you could just play it over and over again. But to do that would miss the scintillating choral entry, the basses starting the ball rolling with the kind of pent-up energy which you just know is going to explode in the most spectacular way. Other recordings have a pleasant, smiley quality here; Stephen Layton's crew has an almost piratical swagger, buoyantly breasting Poulenc's turbulent waves of barely restrained exuberance.

The 38 voices of Polyphony are augmented by 31 from Trinity College, Cambridge, while an unusually hefty contingent of orchestral players makes up the Britten Sinfonia on the disc. What results is not only music-making of immense power and vibrancy – take the riveting declamation 'Qui sedes ad dexteram Patris', hardly subtle or even particularly refined (the men shout and the brass blares) but unbelievably spine-tingling – but also an ability, brilliantly directed by Layton, to capture Poulenc's 'half hooligan, half monk' musical persona (in Claude Rostand's oft-quoted aphorism). Thus, in the final chorus of the *Gloria*, after the boisterous start, we have a moment of profound sanctity and another, crowned with incredible delicacy by Susan Gritton, of mouth-watering enchantment.

Not everything is quite so enticing: Gritton wallows a little too much perhaps in the 'Domine Deus', mischievously abetted by Layton's almost kitsch romanticism. But it is the vivid sense of unfettered joy in the *Gloria* and the matchless intensity of feeling revealed in the motets that make this such a gloriously distinguished disc.

Unaccompanied Choral Works

Mass in G. Quatre Motets pour un temps de pénitence. Quatre Motets pour le temps de Noël. Exultate Deo. Salve regina
Berlin RIAS Chamber Choir / Marcus Creed
Harmonia Mundi HMC90 1588 (52' · DDD · T/t)   Ⓕ

There has never been a more beautiful performance of the *Salve regina*. And elsewhere this virtuoso choir displays, beyond impeccably pure intonation and chording (chorus-masters everywhere will note with envy the sopranos' clean, dead-sure attacks on high notes), a sensitivity to verbal meaning, dynamics and vocal colour that argues not only skilful direction but a complete ease and absorption into the music's often chromatic nature by all the singers. They bring a bright-eyed tone to the *Exultate Deo*, awe to 'O magnum mysterium' (in the Christmas motets), and a striking diversity of timbre to 'Tristis est anima mea' (in the penitential motets); in the Mass they interpret to perfection the *doucement joyeux* indication of the *Sanctus*. They appear to have been recorded in some large church, but without any problems of resonance and the words are extremely clear throughout. In all, this is a first-class disc.

Chanson à boire. Sept Chansons. Figure humaine. Quatre Petites prières de Saint François d'Assise. Un soir de neige
RIAS Chamber Choir, Berlin / Daniel Reuss
Harmonia Mundi HMC90 1872 (54' · DDD · T/t)   Ⓕ

Poulenc's earliest work for unaccompanied chorus is the 1922 *Chanson à boire* that concludes this disc. It was a commission from the Harvard Glee Club, composed while Poulenc was in the middle of trying to finish *Les biches*. It has some of the same uninhibited *joie de vivre* that distinguishes the ballet (which also has choral movements, seldom heard now). The male voices of the RIAS Chamber Choir give it a good, robust performance. It is typically mischievous of Poulenc to have chosen this 17th-century drinking song (from the same collec-

tion as his later *Chanson gaillardes*), to be sung while America was in the early years of Prohibition.

There could be no greater contrast than the *Quatre Petites prières*, to words by St Francis of Assisi. Poulenc composed this at the request of his nephew, Frère Jérome Poulenc, for the choir at the abbey of Carrières-sous-Poissy. The direct simplicity of St Francis's verse is reflected in the music, which does not try to add any extra emotion.

Pierre Bernac wrote that 'from their first meeting, Poulenc felt an immediate bond of sympathy' with the poet Paul Eluard. All but two of the *Sept Chansons* of 1935 are settings of Eluard. This was one of Poulenc's first large-scale choral pieces and the poems, at turns surreal and erotic, inspired him to a work of glittering sophistication. *Figure humaine*, from 1943, is considered by many to be one of Poulenc's most perfect compositions. Eluard's poems were circulated anonymously during the Occupation and the climactic 'Liberté' is the single most affecting work to have come from Poulenc's reaction to the Second World War and its atrocities. *Un soir de neige*, composed in December 1944, during the first winter after the Liberation, while the war in Europe was still raging, is in contrast a quietly reflective chamber cantata. It is indicative of Poulenc's often-cited dual personality that he should have composed this while he was at work on *Les mamelles de Tirésias*.

Although there are no French names listed among the members of the RIAS Chamber Choir, the clarity of diction achieved here is first-rate. The balance and the acoustic of the Jesus-Christus-Kirche in Berlin are sympathetic. A beautiful disc, which is a fine introduction to Poulenc's choral music.

Additional recommendation

Figure humaine. Sept Chansons. Un soir de neige
Accentus / Equilbey
Naïve Classique V4883 (39' · DDD · T/t)   Ⓕ Ⓞ ➔
Accentus's phrasing is unfailingly sensitive to the verbal shifts of the poems and no less to the harmonic and textural shifts of Poulenc's music. It's unlikely that a non-French choir would be able to achieve these standards. Tuning and ensemble are impeccable, tone quality excellent and the varied textures sharply characterised within a spacious acoustic and with slightly distant recording.

Mélodies

Banalités. Bleuet. Chansons gaillardes. Chansons villageoises. Dernier poème. Quatre Poèmes. Métamorphoses – C'est ainsi que tu es. Montparnasse. Poèmes – C. Priez pour paix. Rosemonde. Tel jour, telle nuit – Bonne journée; Une ruine coquille vide; Une herbe pauvre; Je n'ai envie que de t'aimer; Nous avons fait la nuit
Michel Piquemal bar **Christine Lajarrige** pf
Naxos 8 553642 (67' · DDD)   Ⓢ Ⓞ Ⓞ ➔

The first time Michel Piquemal met Pierre Bernac, for whom most of these songs were written, Piquemal recalls that Bernac said: 'I am very moved, because what you're doing is exactly what Francis Poulenc was hoping for. He would have been happy.' Afterwards Piquemal studied both with Bernac and Denise Duval, the two singers who were closest to the composer, so this recital is part of a real, authentic tradition. The greatest challenge for a singer comes in the best-known songs, for instance 'Montparnasse' and 'C'. Piquemal doesn't disappoint. He hasn't got the luxurious voice for the lyrical climax of the first, at the words 'Vous êtes en réalité un poète lyrique d'Allemagne / Qui voulez connaître Paris,' but he delivers all the complicated Apollinaire verse in this and the cycle *Banalités* with a complete understanding of the necessary balance between stressing the irony and maintaining the strict forward-moving musical line.

The one group that wasn't composed for a light baritone is *Chansons villageoises*, which, although sung and recorded by Bernac, was intended for a Verdi baritone; 'Un tour de chant symphonique' Poulenc called it. Like Bernac, Piquemal doesn't have the opulent vocal quality here that Poulenc was looking for, but instead he has an actor's way with the words that brings personality and humour to a text such as the opening 'Chanson du clair tamis' – *très gai et très vite* in Poulenc's marking. All the brilliance of Maurice Fombeure's poetry gains clarity from Piquemal's diction and sense of fun, while the ensuing sadness of 'C'est le joli printemps' and the macabre parable of 'Le mendiant' are sharply contrasted.

If you want to sample this disc, try 'Bleuet', and the 'sensitive lyricism' that Bernac wrote of. It's one of the saddest songs Poulenc composed, with its image of the young soldier, the blue referring to the uniform of the conscript who has seen such terrible things while he's still almost a child. It has to be sung 'intimately', wrote Poulenc; Bernac, however, thought that it should also be 'virile and serious'. The penultimate line in which the boy faces the reality – he knows death better than life – is sung by Piquemal with a natural feel for the simplicity of the poem, never overdoing the emphasis, and never becoming arch.

At Naxos's low price this is a first-rate introduction to Poulenc's songs, but more than that it's an example of the best kind of French singing. Christine Lajarrige is a sensitive accompanist, for Poulenc always acknowledged that his songs are duets, for voice and piano.

Dialogues des Carmélites

Dialogues des Carmélites   H
Denise Duval *sop* Blanche de La Force **Régine Crespin** *sop* Madame Lidoine **Denise Scharley** *mez* Madame de Croissy **Liliane Berton** *sop* Soeur Constance **Rita Gorr** *mez* Mère Marie **Xavier Depraz** *bass* Marquis de La Force **Paul Finel** *ten* Chevalier de La Force **Janine Fourrier** *sop* Mère Jeanne **Gisèle Desmoutiers** *sop* Soeur Mathilde **Louis Rialland** *ten* L'Aumônier **René Bianco** *bar* Le Geôlier **Jacques Mars** *bar* L'Officier **Raphael Romagnoni** *ten* First Commissaire **Charles Paul** *bar* Second Commissaire **Michel Forel** *ten* Thierry **Max Conti** *bar* Javelinot **Chorus and Orchestra of the Opéra, Paris / Pierre Dervaux**
EMI Great Recordings of the Century mono ②
562751-2 (144' · ADD · T). Recorded 1958   ⓂⓄⓄ▷

In the history of French opera *Dialogues des Carmélites* is a worthy successor to Debussy's *Pelléas*, and indeed its touching heroine Blanche shares much of the troubling, troubled, out-of-this-world, fey personality of her predecessor. Poulenc is as accomplished a master at setting the French language in a melodic yet at the same quasi-*parlando* style as Massenet, and his use of a large orchestra is at once fastidious and convincing, conservative but never derivative, though inevitably there are influences, mostly beneficial ones.

It is evident from this recording that the singers were inspired by the piece to give of their considerable best. With the benefit of hindsight we can judge that this was a final flowering of the authentic school of French singing. Denise Duval is part of the long line of clear-voiced, incisive sopranos in the Heldy mould. She catches here all the conflicting facets of Blanche's personality, girlish, wilful, frightened, elated as the role requires. Crespin, even though at this early stage of her career she was already not altogether happy above a high G, is a moving, authoritative Madame Lidoine. Still better is Rita Gorr's commanding yet sympathetic Mother Marie and Denise Scharley's haunted and haunting Old Prioress, quite devastatingly desparate in her death scene. Liliane Berton is a charming Sister Constance, and the smaller roles are finely taken, not least Louis Rialland as the hapless, helpless Chaplain.

Pierre Dervaux conducts an inspired, inspiriting account of the work, attentive to both its smaller detail and to its grander, elevated passages, raising the final scene of martyrdom to a proper degree of intensity as some inner strength and group-fervour grips the nuns. As compared with the vocal score, there are a few cuts and changes in the voice parts, both sanctioned by Poulenc. The mono recording is more than adequate. For anyone interested in 20th-century opera, this is a 'must': we are unlikely to have another recording and certainly not one so authentic as this.

Dialogues des Carmélites
Catherine Dubosc *sop* Blanche de la Force **Rachel Yakar** *sop* Madame Lidoine **Rita Gorr** *mez* Madame de Croissy **Brigitte Fournier** *sop* Soeur Constance **Martine Dupuy** *mez* Mère Marie **José van Dam** *bass-bar* Marquis de la Force **Jean-Luc Viala** *ten* Chevalier de la Force **Michel Sénéchal** *ten* L'Aumônier **François Le Roux** *bar* Le Geôlier **Lyon Opéra Chorus and Orchestra / Kent Nagano**
Virgin Classics ② 358657-2 (152' · DDD · T/t)
ⒻⓄⓄⓄ▷

Poulenc's *chef d'oeuvre* is one of the few operas written since *Wozzeck* that has survived in the repertory – and deservedly so. It's written from, and goes to, the heart, not in any extrovert or openly histrionic way but by virtue of its ability to explore the world of a troubled band of Carmelite nuns at the height of the terrors caused by the French Revolution, and do so in an utterly individual manner. Poulenc unerringly enters into their psyches as they face their fatal destiny. Nagano responds with perceptible keenness to the sombre, elevated mood and intensity of the writing and unfailingly delineates the characters of the principals as they face their everyday martyrdom. The magisterial authority of Martine Dupuy's Mère Marie, the agony of Rita Gorr's Old Prioress, the inner torment of Catherine Dubosc's Sister Blanche, the restraint of Rachel Yakar's Madame Lidoine, the eager charm of Brigitte Fournier's Sister Constance are only the leading players in a distribution that's admirable in almost every respect. The score is for once given complete. The atmospheric recording suggests stage action without exaggeration.

Additional recommendation

The Carmelites (sung in English)
Wyn-Davies Blanche de la Force **Holland** Marquis de la Force **Wedd** Chevalier de la Force **Davies** Chaplain **Stephenson** Jailor **Palmer** Madame de Croissy **Boylan** Madame Lidoine **Barstow** Mother Marie **Tynan** Sister Constance **Powell** Mother Jeanne **Gibbons** Sister Mathilde
ENO Chor and Orch / Daniel
Chandos ② CHAN3134 (144' · DDD · S/T/N)   ⒻⒷ➨
Poulenc's *Carmelites* had its definitive recording with the original cast in 1958 under Dervaux (EMI – see above) but a performance in the vernacular recorded in the studio following stage performances has its own relevance, especially when it is conducted with such conviction as by Paul Daniel. The first third of the performance is commanded by Felicity Palmer's lacerating performance as the Old Prioress. This is a gift of a role for a mezzo of a certain age and Palmer makes the most of it as she conveys the old woman's seeming loss of faith and fear of death. As Sister Constance, Sarah Tynan sings with charm and ease. As the new Prioress, Orla Boylan provides an admirable line; her final solo before the executions is most moving. Smaller parts are taken variably.

Les dialogues des Carmélites
Didier Henry bar Marquis de la Force **Anne Sophie Schmidt** sop Blanche de la Force **Laurence Dale** ten Chevalier de la Force **Léonard Pezzino** ten L'Aumônier **Christophe Fel** bass Le Geôlier **Nadine Denize** mez Madame de Croissy **Valérie Millot** sop Madame Lidoine **Hedwig Fassbender** mez Mère Marie **Patricia Petibon** sop Soeur Constance **Michèle Besse** contr Mère Jeanne **Allison Elaine Cook** mez Soeur Mathilde **Ivan Ludlow** ten L'Officier **Vincent de Rooster** ten First Commissaire **Merih Kazbek** bass Second Commissaire **Yves Ernst** bar Thierry **Jenz Kiertzner** bar Javelinot
Rhine National Opera Chorus; Strasbourg

Philharmonic Orchestra / Jan Latham-König
Stage director **Marthe Keller**
Video director **Don Kent**
ArtHaus Musik 🎦 100 004 (149' · Region 0)   Ⓕⵔ

Marthe Keller's staging of Poulenc's austere, deeply eloquent opera was produced at the Opéra du Rhin early in 1999. Keller's simple ideas match precisely with the intentions of the original, the plain sets and economy of movement mirroring the direct simplicity of Poulenc's beautiful score.

Every artist here performs in a wholly dedicated fashion as part of a well-tutored ensemble, no one more so than Anne Sophie Schmidt in depicting the psychological struggle and vulnerability of the central character, Blanche de la Force. With her greatly expressive features and her refined voice, Schmidt's portrayal is starkly moving. In complete contrast is Petibon's bright, radiant, perfectly sung Constance. Among the older members of the Convent community, Nadine Denize plays her two scenes as the Old Prioress with the authority and concentration they call for, going to her death as she loses her faith in an agonising bout of self-understanding. Hedwig Fassbender is all stern authority as Mother Marie, although one senses sympathy behind the harsh exterior, which is how this part should be. Valérie Millot is outwardly more sympathetic and warm as the new Prioress, Madame Lidoine, who instils courage in her charges when it comes to the crunch and, one by one, they go to the guillotine.

Video direction, sound and picture quality are admirable. This is one of the most worthwhile opera performances yet to appear on DVD.

La voix humaine

La voix humaine. La dame de Monte-Carlo
Felicity Lott sop **Suisse Romande Orchestra / Armin Jordan**
Harmonia Mundi HMC90 1759 (51' · DDD)   Ⓕ

Poulenc was certainly in close touch with his *anima*. His heroines, often suffering, as in these two works, readily take upon themselves his own depressive and even hysterical character. But not only is the rejected woman in *La voix humaine* Poulenc himself (he admitted as much), she's also Denise Duval, the first interpreter of the work, for whom it was written. Duval said that both she and the composer were in what the tabloids call 'love tangles' at the time and that the work spoke for both of them. So it's a brave act for any other soprano to compete with her 1959 recording, let alone someone who isn't French.

Felicity Lott is one of the few British sopranos who could hope to come close. And she does. The voice is in excellent shape, the French likewise. The recording doesn't place her so firmly in the limelight as Duval's, while Jordan draws fine playing from the orchestra – maybe not quite as explosive as Prêtre in the emotional outbursts, but if anything with more of the *sen-*

sualité orchestrale that Poulenc asked for. And if she doesn't quite get the necessary hysteria and vulgarity, she very nearly does. She seems more at home in *La dame de Monte-Carlo*, also on a Cocteau text but this time in verse. The top of the voice is radiant where Mady Mesplé's is sometimes shrill and marred by heavy vibrato, and throughout she captures exactly the right tone of outraged dignity.

André Previn   German/American b1929

American conductor, pianist and composer of German birth, Previn studied in Berlin and at the Paris Conservatoire, and moved to Los Angeles in 1939. His early career was in the film industry and as a jazz pianist. He adapted and conducted the music for several films, some of them stage-to-film adaptations, such as My Fair Lady, Kismet, Porgy and Bess and Paint Your Wagon. But several scores were written especially for film, including the Academy Award-winning Gigi. He made his conducting debut in 1963 and was conductor in chief of the Houston SO, 1967-70. From 1965 he headed the LSO (principal conductor, 1969-79), and recorded extensively. He conducted the Pittsburgh SO, 1976-86, and headed the RPO and the Los Angeles and Oslo Philharmonics. He has composed operas and orchestral and chamber works.

A Streetcar Named Desire

A Streetcar Named Desire
Renée Fleming *sop* Blanche Dubois **Elizabeth Futral** *sop* Stella Kowalski **Rodney Gilfry** *bar* Stanley Kowalski **Anthony Dean Griffey** *ten* Mitch **Judith Forst** *mez* Eunice Hubbell **San Francisco Opera Orchestra / André Previn**
Stage director **Colin Graham**
Video director **Kirk Browning**
ArtHaus Musik 📀 100 138 (167' · 16:9 · 2.0 · 2, 5) Ⓕ

Perhaps the most convincing portrayal is that of Rodney Gilfry as the rough worker Stanley, perpetually chewing, smoking or drinking, periodically exploding into violence, but with beefy baritone always beautifully produced. Anthony Dean Griffey is almost equally good as the naive, mother-loving Mitch, so cruelly deceived by Blanche; while Elizabeth Futral does quite wonderfully well as the tender Stella. For all the beauty of her arias and her high notes throughout, perhaps the least convincing is Renée Fleming herself. Partly, this is because Previn too often pushes the voice into its higher reaches irrespective of natural speech patterns. It's almost as though he was determined to emphasise that this is opera, not musical theatre. In addition, though, Fleming's starry presence requires some suspension of belief to accept the full extent of Blanche's mental deterioration. But overall the work makes gripping listening and viewing, and the DVD is a marvellous memento of what was surely a significant landmark in operatic history.

Sergey Prokofiev   Russian 1891-1953

Prokofiev died on the same day as Stalin. Apart from the final years of his life, he managed more successfully than any other great Russian composer living under the dictatorship to maintain his musical ideals.

He was a brilliant student. By the age of 13 when he entered the St Petersburg Conservatoire he was already a good pianist and had produced an opera (aged nine), an overture and other works. He had the best teachers including, Glière, Liadov and Rimsky-Korsakov, and Anna Essipova – who had been married to one of the greatest piano teachers of the 19th century, Theodor Leschetizky – taught Prokofiev piano. Such a precocious, blazing talent inevitably rebelled against the stifling conservatism that confronted him.

Like Shostakovich and Britten, his style seemed to be pre-formed, completely original and one which remained constant for his entire creative life. Even before graduation, he caused a stir in musical circles with some of his compositions – the First Piano Concerto caused a furore when it was first played with its violent keyboard gymnastics, unexpected harmonic and melodic twists and angular rhythms. Before he was 20, he was famous. But Prokofiev was no wunderkind who burns out after initial brilliance.

In 1918 he left Russia and travelled through Siberia to Japan and America giving concerts of his own music and in 1920 arrived in Paris. Here, he met another expatriate, Sergei Diaghilev, who commissioned three ballets, Chout, Le pas d'acier and L'enfant prodigue. Further commissions came from his publisher Koussevitzky and in 1921 he visited America again for the premiere of his opera The Love for Three Oranges.

After returning to Russia in 1927, where he was greeted as a celebrity, he flitted between his mother country, Paris and other European cities before deciding in 1932 to settle in Russia for good. Quite why he did this is open to question. Surely he knew to what political pressures artists were subjected. Stravinsky stated that it was because Prokofiev was politically naive, also because he had not met with all that much success in America: Prokofiev's return to Russia, he said, was 'a sacrifice to the bitch goddess'. Why did he not live and work abroad in peace like Stravinsky and Rachmaninov? Perhaps he thought he was famous enough to be treated differently by the authorities. In this he was sadly mistaken and, after an initial period of co-habitation, the authorities and Prokofiev were at loggerheads. Nevertheless, some of his finest music was written in the 1930s and during the war years, despite increasing ill-health and the break up in 1941 of his marriage after an affair with a 25-year old student, Mira Mendelson.

When the Central Committee of the Communist Party denounced Prokofiev, Shostakovich and others for 'formalism' – music that had no immediate function and did not extol the virtues of the wonderful Stalinist regime – a humiliating public apology appeared: 'We are tremendously grateful to the Central Committee of the All-Union Communist Party and personally to you, dear Comrade Stalin, for the severe but profoundly just criticism of the present state of Soviet music...We shall bend every effort to apply our knowledge and our artistic mastery to produce vivid realistic music reflecting the life and struggles of the Soviet people.'

Thereafter, in the few years left to him, Prokofiev churned out inconsequential scores, the equivalent of the paintings of tractors and chemical works that Soviet artists were producing.

Piano Concertos

No 1 in D flat, Op 10; **No 2** in G minor, Op 16; **No 3** in C, Op 26; **No 4** in B flat, Op 53 (left-hand); **No 5** in G, Op 55

Piano Concertos Nos 1-5
Vladimir Ashkenazy pf
London Symphony Orchestra / André Previn
Decca ② 452 588-2DF2 (126' · ADD)
Recorded 1974-75   Ⓜ❍❍➲

While it's true that the Prokofiev piano concertos are an uneven body of work, there's enough imaginative fire and pianistic brilliance to hold the attention even in the weakest of them; the best, by common consent Nos 1, 3 and 4, have stood the test of time very well. As indeed have these Decca recordings. The set first appeared in 1975, but the sound is fresher than many contemporary digital issues, and Ashkenazy has rarely played better. Other pianists have matched his brilliance and energy in, say, the Third Concerto, but very few have kept up such a sure balance of fire and poetry. The astonishingly inflated bravura of the Second Concerto's opening movement is kept shapely and purposeful and even the out-of-tune piano doesn't spoil the effect too much. And the youthful First has the insouciance and zest its 22-year-old composer plainly intended.

Newcomers to the concertos should start with No 3: so many facets of Prokofiev's genius are here, and Ashkenazy shows how they all take their place as part of a kind of fantastic story. But there are rewards everywhere, and the effort involved in finding them is small.

Piano Concertos Nos 1-5
Boris Berman (Nos 1, 4 & 5), **Horacio Gutiérrez** (Nos 2 & 3) pfs **Royal Concertgebouw Orchestra, Amsterdam / Neeme Järvi**
Chandos Classics ② CHAN10522X (123' · DDD)
Recorded in 1989 and 1990   Ⓜ❍❍➲

Here, in brilliantly refreshed sound, is a reissue of Prokofiev's five piano concertos. The performances with the Royal Concertgebouw Orchestra under the superb direction of Neeme Järvi are shared between Horacio Gutiérrez (Nos 2 and 3) and Boris Berman (Nos 1, 4 and 5). And while honours are not quite evenly divided, both pianists show themselves gloriously in sympathy with Prokofiev's idiom. Cuban-American

Gutiérrez unleashes some of the most thrilling virtuosity on record, storming the Second Concerto's first movement development/cadenza in a manner that will make lesser pianists tremble. He is no less stunning in the less obviously demanding Third Concerto where once again his ebullience is complemented by flawless technique and musicianship.

Berman may offer less supercharged vitality but all three of his performances alternate poise and exuberance to a most stylish and musical degree. Again, his way with the Fourth Concerto is so finely tuned that it makes what is arguably the weakest of the concertos a scintillating success. He is fully alive to the First Concerto's rampant mischief-making (never more so than in the central *Andante*'s satirical romance) and is more than equal to the Fifth Concerto's grotesquerie. Järvi works hand in glove with his soloists and the result is a triumph.

Prokofiev Piano Concertos Nos 1 & 3
Bartók Piano Concerto No 3, Sz119
Martha Argerich pf
Montreal Symphony Orchestra / Charles Dutoit
EMI 556654-2 (70' · DDD)   Ⓟ❍❍➲

Martha Argerich's return to the studios in two concertos she has not previously recorded is an uplifting moment. As always with this most mercurial of virtuosos, her playing is generated very much by the mood of the moment, but you may well be surprised at her relative geniality with Dutoit here. Her entire reading is less hard-driven, her opening arguably more authentically *brioso* than ferocious, her overall view a refreshingly fanciful view of Prokofiev's youthful iconoclasm. The central *Andante assai* is inflected with an improvisatory freedom she would probably not have risked earlier in her career and in the *Allegro scherzando* she trips the light fantastic, reserving a suitably tigerish attack for the final octave bravura display.

Again, while her performance of the Third Concerto is less fleet or nimble-fingered than in her early legendary disc for DG with Abbado; it's more delectably alive to passing caprice. Part-writing and expressive detail interest her more than in the past and there's no lack of virtuoso *frisson* in the first movement's concluding quasi-fugal *più mosso* chase. Once more Argerich is unusually sensitive in the central *Andantino*, to the fourth variation's plunge into Slavic melancholy and introspection. Personal and vivacious throughout, she always allows the composer his own voice.

This is true to an even greater extent in Bartók's Third Concerto where her rich experience in chamber music makes her often *primus inter pares*, a virtuoso who listens to her partners with the greatest care. Dutoit and his orchestra achieve a fine unity throughout. The recordings are clear and naturally balanced and only those in search of metallic thrills and rushes of blood to the head will feel disappointed.

Piano Concertos No 2 & 3. Piano Sonata No 2
Freddy Kempf pf
Bergen Philharmonic Orchestra / Andrew Litton
BIS 🎵 BIS-SACD1820 (81' · DDD/DSD) Ⓕ**OOO**B+

There have been several complete surveys of the piano concertos from Prokofiev specialists but relatively few pair the Second and Third alone. While Freddy Kempf's remarkably generous 80-minute programme is unique, in his chosen concertos he goes head to head with Evgeny Kissin, forceful and dazzling in live performance. Kempf's contained sonority and generally thoughtful approach make for a less oppressive, more variegated effect which may or may not be authentic. Prokofiev himself was often described as a brutal pianist yet his own 78rpm set of the Third Concerto has a softer grain than the legend suggests.

In the Second Concerto the composer presents us with a first subject in the style of Rachmaninov and Kempf treats it with greater intimacy than many. Of the various accompanists Andrew Litton and his Bergen forces seem the most attentive and detailed, even if it's BIS's impressively translucent sound engineering that really makes the difference. For once you can hear the orchestra interacting with the soloist. The first movement's elaborately hazardous cadenza strikes out into a brand of grotesquerie that at least one early critic found 'unbearable…such a musical mess that one might think [it] created by capriciously emptying an inkwell on the paper.' Here Kempf is less flamboyant than some, perhaps seeking to make musical sense of the argument. The second movement is as lithe and scintillating as one might wish. Though somehow less 'Russian' than usual, the rendition as a whole is finely honed, suitably mercurial and certain to impress. Yes, the Third Piano Concerto has boasted even greater individuality but the rarely recorded Second Sonata, centrally placed on the disc, is a considerable bonus.

With good design, full recording information and a useful booklet-note from Andrew Huth, here is a dazzling successor to the pianist's earlier Prokofiev recital.

Prokofiev Piano Concerto No 5 **Ravel** Piano Concerto in G **Schlimé** Three Improvisations
Francesco Tristano Schlimé pf
Russian National Orchestra / Mikhail Pletnev
Pentatone 🎵 PTC5186 080 (65' · DDD)   Ⓕ

Here is music-making to wonder at. Rarely in their history can the two concertos have been performed with such meticulous care and affection. The Luxembourg-born, 25-year-old pianist includes Pletnev – his more-than-distinguished partner on this disc – among his teachers and has won first prize in one of the less celebrated competitions (so often venues of true musical discovery).

What sadness and introspection he conveys beneath Ravel's clowning surface, shadowed, as it were, by the Left Hand Concerto, by an inwardness mirrored in his own haunting *Three Improvisations*. The central *Adagio* emerges as a timeless reverie, making it hard to recall a performance of greater magic or tonal translucency, a far cry indeed from a more superficial tradition emanating from Marguerite Long, the work's dedicatee. In the Prokofiev Schlimé and Pletnev take an almost chamber music-like view of the grotesquerie and acrobatics, and the result is lyrical and musicianly in a wholly fresh and unsuspected way. Nothing sounds bleak or conventionally percussive and a mysterious, winter fairy-tale aura hangs over the entire work (never more so than in the *Larghetto*).

Schlimé confesses that he has always felt impelled to play what he calls his 'other' music, in this case improvised reflections on the two concertos. Recorded late one night in the Moscow Conservatoire, they were added with Pletnev's blessing, and the concluding mournful, jazzman's chime is very much music that registers 'long after it was heard no more'. Pentatone's sound and balance are exemplary.

Violin Concertos

No 1 in D, Op 19; **No 2** in G minor, Op 63

Prokofiev Violin Concerto No 1
Shostakovich Violin Concerto No 1
Maxim Vengerov vn **London Symphony Orchestra / Mstislav Rostropovich**
Teldec 4509 98143-2 (62 minutes: DDD)   Ⓕ**OOO**B+

Ⓖ Vengerov uses Heifetz's bow but it is to David Oistrakh that he is often compared. His vibrato is wider, his manners less consistently refined, and yet the comparison – we can now see – is well-founded. One would guess that Vengerov has been listening to those earlier Oistrakh renditions of the Shostakovich as there is nothing radically novel about his interpretation. It is possible that some will find Vengerov's impassioned climaxes a shade forced by comparison. Yet he achieves a nobility and poise worlds away from the superficial accomplishment of most modern rivals.

He can fine down his tone to the barest whisper; nor is he afraid to make a scorching, ugly sound. While his sometimes slashing quality of articulation is particularly appropriate to the faster movements, the brooding, silver-grey Nocturne comes off superbly too, though it seems perverse that the engineers mute the low tam-tam strokes. Rostropovich has the lower strings dig into the third movement's passacaglia theme with his usual enthusiasm. There are some expressive swellings in accompanimental detail. Indeed the orchestral playing is very nearly beyond reproach.

Vengerov and Rostropovich take an unashamedly epic, wide-open-steppes view of the Prokofiev concerto. Closely observed digital recording (Vengerov sounds sweeter in reality) uncovers a wealth of detail, most of it welcome, with the conductor's erstwhile clumsy tendency barely noticeable. Towards the end of the first movement, the approach to the reprise of the opening melody on solo flute (*pp dolcissimo*) with harp, muted strings and lightly running tracery from the soloist is very deliberately taken, and the long-breathed finale builds to a passionate, proto-Soviet climax. The central *Scherzo* is predictably breathtaking in its virtuosity.

If you're looking for a recording of the Shostakovich, Vengerov's coupling may be less logical than a disc of the two together, but no one should be deterred from investigating *Gramophone*'s 1995 Recording of the Year. Lacking Oistrakh's authenticity of experience, Vengerov displays similarly boundless technical assurance plus an extra edge of youthful adrenalin and excitement. His Prokofiev is scarcely less fine, the tone gloriously rich, every note hit dead centre. However committed you are to alternative interpretations, these demand to be heard.

Prokofiev Violin Concerto No 2
Glazunov Violin Concerto in A minor, Op 82
Tchaikovsky Souvenir d'un lieu cher, Op 42 – No 1, Méditation (orch Glazunov)
Nikolaj Znaider *vn* **Bavarian Radio Symphony Orchestra / Mariss Jansons**
RCA Red Seal 74321 87454-2 (57' · DDD)   Ⓕ Ⓞ ▷

Znaider's confident, abundantly characterful account of the Prokofiev is probably the finest since Vadim Repin's similarly stimulating 1995 version with Nagano and the Hallé. Znaider brings an extra lyrical ardour and tender intimacy to Prokofiev's soaring melodies, not to mention a greater rhythmic swagger in the finale. But what really lifts this account to special heights is the chamber-like rapport and concentration Znaider generates with Mariss Jansons and the Bavarian Radio SO, whose playing is a model of scrupulous observation and profound musicality. Time and again, these intelligent artists will have you gasping anew at the giddy beauty and wondrous fantasy of Prokofiev's stunningly inventive inspiration, and theirs is a strongly communicative performance which grips from first measure to last.

The Glazunov receives a reading notable for its refreshing thoughtfulness and unforced, 'old world' charm. By the side of the dazzlingly slick Vengerov, Znaider emerges as an altogether more personable and imaginative story-teller, yet there's heaps of panache and twinkling affection when needed, and his playing has none of the slight technical shortcomings that take the shine off Shaham's less distinctive account.

A slight niggle concerns the slightly up-front solo balance, which imparts a certain nasal wiriness to Znaider's tone in the upper reaches.

Symphony-Concerto (for cello)

Symphony-Concerto[a]. Cello Sonata in C, Op 119[b]
Han-Na Chang *vc* [a]**London Symphony Orchestra / Antonio Pappano** [b]*pf*

EMI 557438-2 (62' · DDD)   Ⓕ Ⓞ Ⓞ Ⓞ ▷

Ⓖ Chang and Pappano offer a fiercely communicative Symphony-Concerto (EMI has reverted to the outmoded nomenclature of *Sinfonia concertante*) and an equally distinctive, though more conventionally ruminative account of the Sonata.

It's fair to assume that the Korean cellist is the youngest exponent of these pieces on disc, and it shows in the best possible way as her youthful vivacity meets Prokofiev's mature style. Although still in her teens, she's an experienced, even mature recording artist with several fine discs under her belt. Her taut, ardent conception of the main work here, music that can often come across as rambling and discursive, is the most radical thing she has done, knocking minutes off the timings of almost every previous recording. The first movement is perfectly pitched, never self-indulgent, and it's easy to forgive any momentary lack of unanimity when editing might have impaired the forward thrust of the music-making. Chang's authoritative style reaps huge rewards from 7'25", where the theme sings out in the very highest register.

The central *Scherzo* is sensationally swift and articulate but deeply felt too, with more emotional as well as physical precision than in previous performances barring Rostropovich's own. Prokofiev's sometimes wan lyricism is revivified by Chang's refined sensibility; her phrasing truly breathes with the music and the vulnerable, confessional quality she reveals may well bring a tear to the eye. Autumnal half-lights are usually more potent for being strictly rationed, and Pappano is forthright as well as 'sensitive', giving us some minatory, Soviet-sounding brass interventions amid the hustle and bustle.

It's not only the refined direction that brings new colour, clarity and lustre to Prokofiev's orchestral fabric. EMI's sound is top-notch, and you may be taken aback to discover just how terrific this orchestra can sound in a sympathetic recording studio. The cellist is placed closer than would be the case in live concert, but such technically invulnerable playing can take it. Han-Na Chang's disc is quite superb.

Additional recommendations

Prokofiev Symphony-Concerto
Coupled with **Tchaikovsky** Variations on a Rococo Theme, Op 33
Capuçon *vc* **Mariinsky Orch / Gergiev**
Virgin Classics 694486-0 (61' · DDD)   Ⓕ ▷
Recorded live 2008
Gautier Capuçon stands out as exceptional, majoring in elegant, pure, singing tone and long lyrical phrasing rather than waspish attack. His collaboration with Valery Gergiev, a very different artist, was bound to strike sparks. Capuçon isn't a natural for Prokofiev but, that said, there are grand and glorious things here. And the live recording has impressive transparency.

Symphony-Concerto
Coupled with Cello Concerto
Gerhardt *vc* **Bergen PO / Litton**
Hyperion CDA67705 (73' · DDD)　　　ⒻⒹ➼

Hearing either work in isolation is unsettling, compared to the wholeness of the finest of Prokofiev's concertos and symphonies. Yet experiencing both versions side by side is a revelation – even more disturbing, in many ways, yet also endlessly thought-provoking – as it shows one of the most brilliantly gifted composers in history beset by irreconcilable conflicts between instinct and culture. With the best will in the world, neither the orchestral playing here nor the recording are of the richest. But Alban Gerhardt's playing, appropriately spotlit, is top-drawer stuff. This important, if troubling, disc is nothing if not a triumph for him.

Symphonies

No 1 in D, Op 25, 'Classical'; **No 2** in D minor, Op 40; **No 3** in C minor, Op 44; **No 4** in C, Op 47 **(original 1930 version)**; **No 4** in C̆, Op 112 **(revised 1947 version)**; **No 5** in B flat, Op 100; **No 6** in E flat minor, Op 111; **No 7** in C sharp minor, Op 131

Symphonies Nos 1-7 (including two versions of No 4)
London Symphony Orchestra / Valery Gergiev
Philips ④ 475 7655PM4 (4h 20' · DDD)
Recorded live 2004　　　Ⓜ❶❶❶❶➼

Ⓖ In comparison with Shostakovich, Sergey Sergeyevich Prokofiev's less caring personality, lack of social and political engagement and frequent failure to consider what a symphony might be (beyond a mould to be filled with wonderful tunes and short-term effects) need not alter the fact that there is some tremendous music here which deserves to be on every collector's shelf. For all its protean variety it's an idiom that responds well, perhaps better than Shostakovich's, to Valery Gergiev's extrovert, sometimes brusque approach.

The new performances of the Second, Sixth and Seventh are probably the finest on CD. While the Third packs a supercharged punch, it may be found too raw and driven for its subtleties to register. The familiar *Classical* No 1 gets the most destabilising treatment with a stodgy opening movement and a whirlwind finale.

The cycle was taped live during Gergiev's Barbican series in May 2004 and emerges now not on the orchestra's own label but in Philips livery. Given the venue's acoustic problems, sound quality is better than one dared hope – bold, immediate and lacking only the last ounce of depth and allure. As those who attended will recall, the maestro directed with a toothpick and a gestural armoury all his own. Whatever the difficulties, the players deliver the goods with a hefty, if not overly refined, sonority. A pity that there was no space for the optimistic

PROKOFIEV SYMPHONY NO 5 – IN BRIEF

Berlin PO / Herbert von Karajan
DG 463 613-2GOR (78' · ADD)　　Ⓜ❶❶❶❶➼
DG 437 253-2GGA (71' · ADD)　　Ⓜ❶❶❶❶➼

Ⓖ Recorded in 1968, Karajan's interpretation remains a classic. (The first listed CD couples it with his rather soft-grained Stravinsky *Rite of Spring*; the second, more appropriately, with the *Classical* Symphony, No 1.) Karajan's is a rich, long-breathed conception with full-blooded Berlin sonority.

Leningrad PO / Mariss Jansons
Chandos CHAN8576 (38' · DDD)　　　ⒻⒹ➼
Short on playing time but heavy on temperament. Jansons gives a very fine performance and draws some superb playing from the St Petersburg orchestra, but he does force the work at times, over-pressuring lines that really don't need it.

City of Birmingham SO / Sir Simon Rattle
EMI 388694-2 (64' · DDD)　　　Ⓑ❶❶Ⓓ➼
Coupled with Prokofiev's ear-shattering *Scythian* Suite, Rattle's Fifth is a tremendous performance, lighter on its toes than either Jansons or Karajan, and sounding magnificent. This Rattle at his most recreatively imaginative.

Royal Scottish National Orchestra / Neeme Järvi
Chandos CHAN8450 (57' · DDD)　　　ⒻⒹ➼
A wonderful natural, unfussy reading with the RSNO on fine form and Chandos's recording is nicely handled – but for a modern version Rattle does have the edge. The coupling is a delightful *Waltz Suite*.

Paris Conservatoire Orchestra / Jean MartinonⒽ
Testament SBT1296 (72' · ADD)　　　Ⓜ
Coupled with the gorgeous No 7, Martinon's Fifth is a strong performance, muscular and imaginative. Obviously the 1959 sound leaves a little to be desired, but for those interested in fine conductors of yore this is well worth considering.

Slovak PO / Stephen Gunzenhauser
Naxos 8 550237 (61' · DDD)　　　ⒻⒹ➼
Coupled with a rather lacklustre No 1, Gunzenhauser offers a very fine reading full of incident and nice detail. The Slovak band play superbly and the recording quality is very fine. An excellent budget price alternative.

London SO / Valery Gergiev
Philips ④ 475 7655PM4 (4h 20' · DDD)　　Ⓜ❶Ⓓ➼
Only available as part of Gergiev's complete Prokofiev symphony cycle, this is a fine, romantic Fifth with rich, dark playing from a clearly inspired LSO.

final flourish Prokofiev tacked onto his Seventh Symphony in pursuit of Stalin Prize winnings. Both alternatives were given in concert. That said, there's enough toughness and disquiet in what has gone before to make its omission feel right. We do get both editions of the Fourth, not always the case in previous recorded *intégrales*. Any sense of disappointment there may be associated with the music's relative poverty of invention, though there is more charm in the material than the conducting allows.

Swallowed whole as it must be, the set none the less confirms Gergiev as Prokofiev's most ardent contemporary advocate. The visceral thrust and passion of the LSO's playing knocks the likes of Ozawa's Berlin Philharmonic into a cocked hat. Strongly recommended.

Prokofiev Symphony No 5[a]
Stravinsky The Rite of Spring[b]
Berlin Philharmonic Orchestra /
Herbert von Karajan
DG The Originals 463 613-2GOR (78' · ADD)
Recorded [a]1968, [b]1977 Ⓜ❍❍❍▷

Karajan's 1968 Prokofiev Fifth is a great performance. Whenever one compares it with later versions inevitably the DG account holds its place at the top of the list. The analogue recording was uncommonly good for its time. With the advantage of the Jesus-Christus-Kirche acoustics, the sound is full and spacious, naturally defined and balanced; there's a slightly leonine quality to the strings and a natural bloom on woodwind and brass. Karajan lived with the work for a decade before he recorded it and this is immediately apparent in the way the first movement unfolds so inevitably. The ironic opening of the *Scherzo* with its flawless BPO articulation brings a splendid but unexaggerated bite, and in the more lyrical central section every subtle detail of colour comes over. The passionate string threnody of the *Adagio* (what playing, what intensity!) is superbly underpinned by darker wind murmurings; the tangibly hushed close leads naturally to the mellower opening of the essentially upbeat finale with its throbbing horns and instant echoes of *Romeo and Juliet*.

Karajan's *Rite of Spring* came a decade later and is more controversial. Stravinsky had been sarcastically scathing about the conductor's earlier 1964 account, even describing one section as 'tempo di hoochie-koochie'. So, Karajan let the work rest, and when he re-recorded it in January 1977 it was done in one single uninterrupted take. The result has less visceral excitement than some but it's still very rewarding, combining both the symphonic and balletic aspects of this extraordinary score, with the BPO providing much sheer beauty of sound, as in the ravishing melancholy of the opening of Part 2 and the haunting 'Evocation des ancêtres', although other versions find more pungent drama when the horns enter later. The Philharmonie sound is excellent and both

CD transfers are expertly managed to retain the full character of the originals.

Romeo and Juliet, Op 64

Romeo and Juliet
London Symphony Orchestra / Valery Gergiev
LSO Live ② 💿 LSO0682 (139' · DDD)
Recorded live 2008 Ⓜ❍❍❍▷

Although Prokofiev's *Romeo and Juliet* is not through-composed in the manner of Stravinsky, it gains in stature when heard in its entirety. These days you can acquire the complete work in multifarious dramatico-musical presentations on DVD but if anyone can prove the continuing viability of the uncut score as a concert piece, even to the extent of threatening to displace those distinguished predecessors, it has to be Valery Gergiev. This new account stems from concerts given in London's Barbican Centre.

Gergiev is in his element and not just in moments of gritty angularity or romantic excess. The lighter numbers, sometimes taken more spaciously than usual, are equally memorable. Sample if you can the maximally colourful 'Dance with mandolins' or the subtle shadings of the 'Dance of the young girls with lilies'. We are reminded that Prokofiev's ear for original instrumental combinations could be as acute as his flair for melodic invention. Only the Gavotte, a late addition forced out of a reluctant composer, sounds clunky: this is music Gergiev tends to overstate even in its original *Classical Symphony* context. Elsewhere the playing is eloquent, the timbres dark, without the coarseness some of us hear in the team's Mahler. Applause is excluded.

With the blunting effect of the wide-but-shallow Barbican stage ameliorated somewhat by SACD formatting, the sound is thoroughly acceptable, the performance a good deal more than that. Unusually detailed booklet-notes from David Nice and Andrew Huth enhance the claims of a well priced issue. A winner.

Peter and the Wolf, Op 67

Peter and the Wolf[a]. Symphony No 1. March in
B flat minor, Op 99. Overture on Hebrew Themes,
Op 34bis[b]
[a]**Sting** narr [b]**Stefan Vladar** pf **Chamber Orchestra of**
Europe / Claudio Abbado
DG 429 396-2GH (50' · DDD) Ⓕ❍▷

Abbado and the multi-talented Sting offer a lively and beautifully crafted account of Prokofiev's ever popular *Peter and the Wolf*. Any fears that the original freshness of Prokofiev's creation may be lost in favour of a less formal approach are soon dispelled – Sting is an effective and intelligent storyteller capable of capturing the imagination of adults and children alike, and there's never a feeling of contrivance or mere gimmickry.

Cello Works

Cello Concertino in G minor, Op 132 – Andante. Cello Sonata in C, Op 119. Solo Cello Sonata in C sharp minor, Op 134 (ed Giovale). Adagio in C, Op 97b No 10. Ballade in C minor, Op 15. Chout, Op 21a (arr Sapozhnikov) – The Buffoon and his Wife; Dance of the Buffoons' Wives; Dance of the Buffoons' Daughters; In the Merchant's Bedroom; Quarrel of the Buffoon and the Merchant
Alexander Ivashkin vc **Tatyana Lazareva** pf
Chandos CHAN10045 (68' · DDD)   ⓕⒹ→

Captured in the Maly Hall of the Moscow Conservatory where much of Prokofiev's work was first heard, it's surprising to find so many aspects of the composer's style represented, from the Romanticism of the early *Ballade* through the spiky dissonances of *Chout* to the elegiac, unfinished Solo Sonata. Aided by characterful piano playing by Tatyana Lazareva, Ivashkin's recital compares most favourably with his similar programme on Ode for which he was accompanied by a more reticent pianist; although the earlier disc includes the Concertino movement in the guise of Rostropovich's cello quintet arrangement, the absence of the *Chout* transmogrification makes the Chandos collection appear better value.

We start with the familiar Cello (and piano) Sonata, a highly polished and deeply felt account with Lazareva providing a weighty, authentically Russian accompaniment. The *Ballade* is surely the best version yet of this increasingly popular work. Good though Wallfisch's expansive reading is, Ivashkin surpasses him in his juxtaposition of the 19th-century style of the opening and the ghostly second idea, hushed to a real *pianissimo*. Instead of Wallfisch's 'March' from *The Love for Three Oranges*, we get a *Chout* selection arranged by the Russian cellist Roman Sapozhnikov; again the rendition is technically spotless. Finally comes the Sonata for cello alone, its nostalgic opening brought off perfectly. Ivashkin's playful treatment of the central gavotte-like section reminds us that he can do humour as well.

Violin Sonatas

Violin Sonatas – No 1, Op 80; No 2, Op 94a. March, Op 12 No 1. Cinq Mélodies, Op 35b. The Love for Three Oranges, Op 33 – Marche. Romeo and Juliet, Op 64 – Masks
Gil Shaham vn **Orli Shaham** pf
Canary Classics CC02 (73' · DDD)   ⓕ

The Shahams, brother and sister, make a formidable team. It's obvious throughout that they're entirely comfortable playing together, effortlessly accommodating any freedoms in timing and matching each other's tone and dynamics. Granted that the Shahams' insistence on clearly separating each phrase sometimes results in a loss of momentum (in the opening *Moderato* of the Op 94 Sonata, for instance), these still

emerge as brilliant, highly expressive performances. The particularly wide dynamic range – of the recording as well as of the playing – here works decisively to the music's advantage. And, especially in the *Cinq Mélodies*, we hear some wonderfully subtle shades of expression: both players have clearly entered right into Prokofiev's distinctive idiom. They show the divergent natures of the two sonatas exceptionally vividly – Op 80 sombre and concentrated, Op 94 full of ebullient fantasy.

Additional recommendation

Prokofiev Violin Sonata No 2   Ⓗ
Coupled with **K Khachaturian** Violin Sonata
Szymanowski Violin Sonata in D minor, Op 9
D Oistrakh vn **Yampolsky** pf
Testament mono SBT1113 (65' · ADD)
Recorded 1955   ⓕ
　David Oistrakh's playing is, at its best, a calming force in an agitated world – intelligent, considered (just occasionally overcalculated), invariably poised, big-toned and confident. This is a quite superb disc, expertly annotated and very well presented. The Prokofiev Second Sonata is as near definitive as anyone has a right to expect, while the remainder is typical of a violinist whose aristocratic playing and artistic diplomacy remain an inspiration to us all.

String Quartets

String Quartets – No 1, Op 50; No 2, Op 92. Sonata for Two Violins, Op 56
Pavel Haas Quartet (Veronika Jarůšková, Eva Karová vns Pavel Nikl va Peter Jarůšek vc)
Supraphon SU3957-2 (61' · DDD)   ⓕⓄⓄⓄⒹ→

Prokofiev's chamber music is at last making an impact in concert yet remains curiously under-represented on disc given the ubiquity of a certain Soviet Russian contemporary. Fortunately this is just the kind of collection to challenge preconceptions. The logical and useful coupling has been tried before but the Emerson Quartet's unyielding, high-powered projection for DG was not much liked. There's almost too much light and shade with the Pavel Haas Quartet, whose emotional engagement, youthful ardour and occasional penchant for extreme *pianissimo* will be familiar from a brace of award-winning Czech programmes.

Based, like Myaskovsky's 23rd Symphony, on ideologically vetted Kabardinian folk materials, Prokofiev's Second Quartet is one of the most immediately attractive quartets in the repertoire. It dates from 1941 when the two men were evacuated to the relative stability of the Caucasus and points east. That Prokofiev's young companion Mira Mendelson was in tow might explain the jollity of the outer movements although their music can be tough as well as witty. In the wondrous *Adagio* the cello line rises high, ghostly melodic statements in octaves can expose the smallest tuning difficulties and *pizzicati* needs must sparkle like ice. The young players pass every test before dispatching the inventive finale with equal aplomb, differentiating a wide variety of moods and timbres within a swiftish frame.

The strenuously wrought First Quartet comes off just as well. It's a pre-Soviet score and hence formally heretical as well as rather more advanced harmonically. After the sometimes Bartókian vehemence of the *Vivace* element at its core, the work winds down to end slowly on a note of sustained expressive intensity. The concluding *Andante* is rarely tackled with the passion you find here.

The Sonata for Two Violins, written to Parisian order in 1932, takes in a variety of manners, rhapsodic and intimate as well as brusque, without always persuading us that it is more than the compositional exercise adumbrated in the booklet-notes.

Of the small clutch of 'classic' performances of the component pieces, none is more usefully programmed than the present disc, nor so naturally recorded. Why hesitate?

Piano Sonatas

No 1 in F minor, Op 1; **No 2** in D minor, Op 14; **No 3** in A minor, Op 28; **No 4** in C minor, Op 29; **No 5** in C, Opp 38/135; **No 6** in A, Op 82; **No 7** in B flat, Op 83; **No 8** in B flat, Op 84; **No 9** in C, Op 103; **No 10** in E minor, Op 137

Piano Sonatas Nos 1-10. Sarcasms, Op 17
Anne-Marie McDermott pf
Bridge ③ BRIDGE9298A/C (3h 3' · DDD) Ⓜ❍❍❍

You will search high and low for a more meticulously prepared set of the Prokofiev piano sonatas than Anne-Marie McDermott's, which also includes the early, outrageous *Sarcasms* for good measure. With technique to burn and a fierce commitment to every note, she offers highly individual performances which none the less remain scrupulously true to the composer.

In her accompanying notes McDermott speaks of Prokofiev's 'intense and dramatic musical voice', for her a 'visceral and stimulating challenge'. Such eloquence is reflected in all these performances where no stone is left unturned; where every 'i' is perfectly dotted and every 't' no less perfectly crossed. And just when you feel, in the Seventh Sonata's 7/8 *precipitato* finale that her tempo is perhaps more judicious than thrilling, she whirls you away with a vengeance in the Sixth Sonata's opening, discarding Prokofiev's *allegro moderato* in favour of something more racy. She is smartly on the move again in the following, sardonically dancing *Allegretto*, yet is at the same time glowingly alert to the fourth movement's *Romance*, to its expressive weight and intensity. Here, in particular, you are made aware of her rich tonal resource, big-scaled but never confusing strength with violence. In the second movement of the quirky Ninth Sonata (dedicated to

Sviatoslav Richter) McDermott's command is as breathtaking as her ethereal resolution of Prokofiev's elfin capering at the close of the finale.

Just occasionally (in, for example, the '*scherzoishness*' – the composer's own term – of the Second Sonata's second movement) you might wish she had indulged herself in a little more fantasy and freedom, let the music off the lead, so to speak. Yet all in all you could hardly wish for playing of a greater integrity than from Anne-Marie McDermott. Hers is a formidable achievement, reminding us that we have waited a long time for an American pianist of this stature.

Prokofiev Piano Sonata No 4 in C minor, Op 29 **Rachmaninov** Etudes-tableaux, Op 39 – No 3 in F sharp minor; No 4 in B minor **Scriabin** Piano Sonata No 9, 'Black Mass', Op 68 **Tchaikovsky** The Seasons, Op 37a – January; May; June; November
Sviatoslav Richter pf
BBC Legends BBCL4082-2 (67' · ADD)
Recorded live 1966 Ⓕ❍❍

Recorded live at Richter's beloved Aldeburgh in 1966, this issue shows an incomparable pianist at the height of his powers. Indeed, it would be difficult to imagine a more authentic yet personal voice in Prokofiev's Fourth and Scriabin's Ninth Sonatas. Richter carved out a special niche in Prokofiev's Fourth Sonata, the most cryptic and ambiguous of the series, written in a language that can seem oddly exclusive and inaccessible to those born outside Russia. No other pianist has approached Richter in this work, in his capacity to clarify so much awkward writing while at the same time (in the central *Andante assai*) acknowledging a wholly individual utterance full of dark confidences and, in the finale, a forced gaiety alive with stiff virtuoso challenges resolved in a mock-triumphant coda.

Few performances of the Scriabin have been more stealthily mobile or breathed a more satanic menace. For once, directions such as *avec une douceur de plus en plus caressante et empoisonnée* are made meaningful rather than merely idiosyncratic or eccentric. Yet, in more amiable territory Richter is enviably poised, less remote or enigmatic in Mozart's G major Sonata, K283, than one might have expected. His opening *Allegro* is gently flowing and is memorably contrasted with his brilliantly vivacious finale.

The recordings have come up excellently, allowing us to appreciate Richter's range, unique empathy in Russian music and endlessly thought-provoking musicianship in all their glory.

Alexander Nevsky, Op 78

Alexander Nevsky. Scythian Suite, Op 20
Linda Finnie sop **Scottish National Chorus and Orchestra / Neeme Järvi**
Chandos CHAN8584 (60' · DDD · T/t) Ⓕ

At the chill opening of Järvi's fine version of *Alexander Nevsky* one can really feel the bitter wind of the Russian winter. The acoustics of the Caird Hall in Dundee where these Chandos recordings were made adds an extra atmospheric dimension to this splendidly recorded performance. The choral entry has an affecting poised melancholy, yet their geniality in the call to 'Arise ye Russian people' has a ring of peasantry. The 'Battle on the Ice' is the enormously spectacular climax, with the bizarre dissonance of the orchestral *scherzando* effects given tremendous pungency capped by the exhilarating shouts of fervour from the singers. Linda Finnie's contribution is most eloquent too and Järvi's apotheosis very moving. The *fortissimo* force of Chandos's recording is especially telling. As a coupling, Järvi chooses the ballet *Ala and Lolly*, originally written for Diaghilev which, when rejected by him, became the *Scythian Suite*. Its aggressive motoric rhythms are as powerful as anything Prokofiev wrote (indeed, their primitive force has an element of almost brutal ugliness to which you may not wholly respond) but the lyrical music is top-quality Prokofiev. 'It remains one of his most richly imaginative, harmonically sophisticated and wonderfully atmospheric scores', suggests Robert Layton in the notes. Certainly Järvi has its measure and so do the Chandos engineers, but it's not music for a small flat.

Ivan the Terrible, Op 116

Ivan the Terrible – complete film music
Irina Chistyakova contr **Dmitry Stepanovich** bass
Vesna Children's Choir; Yurlov State Capella;
Tchaikovsky Symphony Orchestra /
Vladimir Fedoseyev
Nimbus ② NI5662/3 (99' · DDD)   Ⓕ●

This is a must for completists, in that it's produced in association with a new edition of the score (1997), collating all that survives of the composer's contribution to the project. Indeed, Fedoseyev goes so far as to include music from the Russian Orthodox Liturgy that occurs in the completed films but isn't actually by Prokofiev.

Confused? Let's recap. Part 1 of Eisenstein's masterpiece was released in 1946 to worldwide acclaim, though Stravinsky for one did not care for its mix of iconography and melodrama. In poor health, Prokofiev recommended that Gavriil Popov take over as composer for Part 2. Later he did after all resume work – only to find the film withheld from distribution. Soviet officials found its portrayal of Ivan's psychological decline too negative and, no doubt, too close to home. Which isn't to say that Prokofiev intended to encode any criticism of Stalin in the notes. The film was released in the USSR in 1958, by which time plans to complete the trilogy had been abandoned, its prime movers long dead.

We know Prokofiev thought highly enough of the score to re-use sections of it, but he left no guidelines for presenting it in the concert hall. The oratorio we always used to hear was fashioned in 1962 by Abram Stasevich; it provided

the missing element of continuity by reshaping the cues to fit a chronological narrative. Muti recorded this to superb effect. Christopher Palmer's solution for Järvi was to dispense with Stasevich's interpolated speaker, whereas Rostropovich revived the melodramatic element in an edition by Michael Lankester with English-language narration (Sony Classical). Gergiev's forceful version left the music to fend for itself, but was still based on Stasevich.

By cutting out the middleman, Fedoseyev now goes to the top of the heap as the most scholarly option. He produces a more convincing, well-prepared performance than many that have come out of Russia of late. Not all of what he presents is familiar even from the films, and there's a certain amount of crudely illustrative material. His orchestra, the present-day manifestation of the USSR broadcasting band with which Rozhdestvensky was associated in the 1960s and '70s, acquits itself well: crude primary colours predominate, and the brass players avoid inauthentic finesse. Gergiev has only the mock-Soviets of the Rotterdam Philharmonic, though his Kirov chorus aren't outclassed by the Yurlov State Capella deployed here. Admittedly, Fedoseyev's contralto is extremely Russian, which you may find difficult in 'The Song of the Beaver'. Nor does he race in with quite Gergiev's irresistible flair. That said, Nimbus's Moscow-made recording is technically much better than you might expect.

The two-disc package includes a helpful account of the working methods of Prokofiev and Eisenstein, while key episodes are discussed in more depth and cross-referenced to the relevant tracks.

The Fiery Angel, Op 37

The Fiery Angel
Galina Gorchakova sop Renata **Sergei Leiferkus** bar
Ruprecht **Vladimir Galusin** ten Agrippa **Konstantin**
Pluzhnikov ten Mephistopheles **Sergei Alexashkin**
bass Faust **Vladimir Ognovanko** bass Inquisitor
Evgeni Boitsov ten Jakob Glock **Valery Lebed** bass
Doctor **Yuri Laptev** ten Mathias **Mikhail Kit** bar
Servant **Evgenia Perlasova** mez Landlady **Larissa**
Diadkova mez Fortune teller **Olga Markova-**
Mikhailenko contr Mother Superior **Yevgeny**
Fedotov bass Innkeeper **Mikhail Chernozhukov**
bass First Neighbour **Andrei Karabanov** bar Second
Neighbour **Gennadi Bezzubenkov** bass Third
Neighbour **Tatiana Kravtsova** sop First Nun **Tatiana**
Filimoniva sop Second Nun **Chorus and Orchestra**
of the Kirov Opera / Valery Gergiev
Philips ② download 446 078-2PH2 (119' · DDD · T/t)
Recorded live 1993   Ⓜ❶❶❶❶ⱽ

The opera is no blameless masterpiece – Prokofiev's indulgence in lurid sensationalism sometimes gets the better of his artistic judgement. But that sounds a pretty po-faced judgement in the face of the overwhelming power which so much of this score exudes. This Mariinsky performance comes live from what's clearly a highly charged occasion in one of the world's great opera houses. That brings with it the disadvantage of a constrained opera-pit acoustic, which makes some of Prokofiev's over-the-top scoring seem pretty congested. But the immediacy and clarity of the sound, plus the orchestra's rhythmic grasp, ensures that the effect is still blood-curdling. If Leiferkus's distinctive rich baritone at first sounds a touch microphoney, the ear can soon adjust to that too, and Gorchakova brings intense beauty as well as intensity to Renata's hysterics, taking us right inside the psychological drama. The supporting roles are filled with distinction and this makes a huge difference to the sustaining of dramatic tension, the *crescendo* which Prokofiev aimed to build through his five acts. Considering the extent of the stage goings-on there's remarkably little audience distraction on the recording.

anticipates this geometric theme as the audience settles down for the show. The milling crowds of extras in baseball caps, designer gear and/or mafia specs won't please everyone but the approach makes more sense of the hyperactive plot and the interaction of the protagonists than any production seems possible. Kristine Opolais as Polina and especially Misha Didyk as Alexei both look and sound well: their closing scene is superbly directed and brought off with an emotional intelligence not necessarily apparent in the score.

Perhaps the biggest surprise comes in the pit. Barenboim is here at his most obviously committed: he has found in the piece a depth and expressionist power that brings us close to the world of *Wozzeck*. A certain brittle capriciousness is sacrificed but the pertinence of Prokofiev's brutal take on Dostoyevsky emerges more strongly than ever. All the subsidiary roles are well served and the sound is good, too. Strongly recommended.

The Gambler, Op 24

The Gambler
Misha Didyk *ten* Alexei **Kristine Opolais** *sop* Polina
Vladimir Ognovenko *bass* General **Stefania**
Toczyska *mez* Babulenka **Stephan Rügamer** *ten*
Marquis **Sylvia De La Muela** *contr* Blanche **Viktor**
Rud *bar* Mr Astley **Gian-Luca Pasolini** *ten* Prince
Nilsky **Alessandro Paliaga** *bar* Baron Wurmerhelm
Plamen Kumpikov *bass* Potapych **Gleb Nikolsky**
bass Casino Director **Orchestra and Chorus of the**
Staatsoper, Berlin / Daniel Barenboim
Stage director **Dmitri Tcherniakov**
C major 🎥 701708; 💿 701804 (135' · NTSC · 16:9 ·
PCM Stereo and DTS-HD 5.1 · 0). Recorded at the
Staatsoper Unter den Linden, Berlin in 2008
Ⓕ❍❍❍

Daniel Barenboim and Sergey Prokofiev might seem like an odd couple but then *The Gambler*, composed during the First World War and revamped during the '20s, is not what we expect from Prokofiev. There is more lyrical invention in the opera than its reputation allows – still, it comes rather late in the day and is mainly associated with the elderly Babulenka's return to Mother Russia rather than the central love interest. More problematic to Prokofiev's admirers, given the cinematic specificity of his later work, is the frequent disconnect between the *scherzo*-ish furore in the orchestra and the detailed developments on stage.

Dmitri Tcherniakov in Berlin has chosen to mirror the capitalist excesses of our own day and does so with tireless attention to detail, playing everything in the naturalistic style of a TV movie located in hotel lobbies and gaming rooms. This suits the conversational and/or declamatory vocal writing given here in the original Russian. One is reminded of Janáček and not just in the avoidance of set-piece arias. The designs, also credited to Tcherniakov, are unfussy, with modular stage spaces neatly dovetailed to echo the mutual dependencies of the cast and colour-coordinated in cobalt blue. The filming itself rather neatly

The Love for Three Oranges, Op 33

The Love for Three Oranges (sung in English)
Bruce Martin *bass* King of Clubs **John Mac Master**
ten Prince **Deborah Humble** *contr* Princess Clarissa
Teddy Tahu Rhodes *bar* Leandro **William Ferguson**
ten Truffaldino **Warwick Fyfe** *bar* Pantaloon **Jed**
Arthur *bass* Tchelio **Elizabeth Whitehouse** *sop* Fata
Morgana **Wendy Dawn Thompson** *contr* Linetta
Sally-Anne Russell *mez* Nicoletta **Alison MacGregor**
sop Ninetta **Arend Baumann** *bass* Cook **Richard**
Alexander *bass* Farfarello **Catherine Carby** *mez*
Smeraldina **Opera Australia Chorus; Australian**
Opera and Ballet Orchestra / Richard Hickox
Chandos ② CHAN10347 (99' · DDD · T/t)
Recorded live 2005
ⒻⒹ➔

It has been noted that with Prokofiev's sole operatic success the original Russian is perhaps less vital than with most of his operas, and in many ways the very best way to experience the work is in the vernacular. Well, now here's the chance for English speakers to prove that pudding. Prokofiev's sense of humour (or rather Carlo Gozzi's, filtered through adapter-producer Vsevolod Meyerhold and colleagues to Prokofiev, who then wrote his own libretto) has kept something of its edge, thanks to its mixture of mild cruelty and pantomime sauciness – it is the sight of Fata Morgana accidentally showing her knickers that cures the Prince of his melancholic hypochondria and draws upon him the curse of loving three oranges. Tom Stoppard's translation comes nicely off the page and seems relatively congenial to the voices.

Hickox and his Australians have a ball throughout, and the recording somehow captures all the sparkiness of live performance without the usual excessive dryness of an opera-house acoustic. Crucially, the chorus and orchestra sound as fully engaged as the soloists themselves. All we lack is the additional fun of the curtain calls, which – authenticity or otherwise – extend an all but irresistible invitation to reuse the famous

March. Without that the ending inevitably feels a bit of a let-down.

In a sense the serious collector has to have Gergiev for the original Russian text (Philips, available to download) but also Nagano's (in French), because Prokofiev was involved in the French adaptation of the text which featured in the first performances. But for the most instant enjoyment, the new issue will surely score highest for native English speakers. The Chandos documentation is fine, though why it has bothered to print the French text alongside the English is a mystery.

The Love for Three Oranges (sung in French)
Gabriel Bacquier bar King of Clubs **Jean-Luc Viala** ten Prince **Hélène Perraguin** mez Princess Clarissa **Vincent le Texier** bass-bar Leandro **Georges Gautier** ten Truffaldino **Didier Henry** bar Pantaloon Farfarello **Gregory Reinhart** bass Tchelio **Michèle Lagrange** sop Fata Morgana **Consuelo Caroli** mez Linetta **Brigitte Fournier** sop Nicoletta **Catherine Dubosc** sop Ninetta **Jules Bastin** bass Cook **Béatrice Uria-Monzon** mez Smeraldina **Lyon Opera Orchestra and Chorus / Kent Nagano**
Stage director **Louis Erlo**
Video director **Jean-François Jung**
ArtHaus Musik **DVD** 100 404 (106' · 16:9 · 2.0 · 2 & 5)
Recorded live 1989   Ⓕ◐

Yet another classic opera video reappears refreshed. The DVD, though, metaphorically flicks a light-switch to reveal that the fresh, fluent conducting and singing are only elements in a splendidly lively, witty and thoroughly integrated production.

As the production's pace demands, the singers are mostly young, although old stagers Jules Bastin and Gabriel Bacquier provide resonant ballast. Jean-Luc Viala's chubby, light-toned Prince, Georges Gautier's amiable wide-boy Truffaldino, Vincent le Texier's reptilian Leandro, Michèle Lagrange's Wagnerian Fata Morgana, Catherine Dubosc's delicate Ninetta – they're all excellent, but the real star is the ensemble, with no weak links and the benefit of natural French. Whether or not this is the 'original' language, Prokofiev approved it; more viewers will understand it; and it fits the vocal line at least as well as the Russian. The DVD transfer refreshes the original recording but also reveals its limitations: slightly thin sound and some grain in the picture. But you'll enjoy yourself too much to care.

Semyon Kotko, Op 81

Semyon Kotko
Tatiana Pavlovskaya sop Sofya **Ekaterina Solovieva** sop Lyubka **Lyudmila Filatova** mez Semyon's Mother **Olga Markova-Mikhailenko** mez Khivrya **Olga Savova** mez Frosya **Evgeny Akimov** ten Mikola **Nikolai Gassiev** ten Klembovsky, Workman **Viktor Lutsiuk** ten Semyon Kotko **Vladimir Zhivopistev** ten German Interpreter **Viktor Chernomortsev** bar

Tsaryov **Yuri Laptev** bar Von Wierhof **Gennady Bezzubenkov** bass Tkachenko **Grigory Karasev** bass Ivasenko **Andrei Khramtsov** bass German NCO, German sergeant **Yevgeny Nikitin** bass Remeniuk **Kirov Opera Chorus and Orchestra / Valery Gergiev**
Philips ② 464 605-2PH2 (137' · DDD · T/t)   Ⓕ

Valentin Katayev's tale of a local hero getting his girl despite strife with a prospective in-law is the kind of thing an opera lover would normally take in their stride. What makes Semyon Kotko hard to live with isn't the fact that the soldier-boy returning to his village in the Ukraine at the end of the First World War is so unimpeachably virtuous, nor even that the Germans who break up the wedding preparations and lay waste to the village are so one-dimensionally villainous – it's rather that the reactionary-collaborator father-in-law-to-be, Tkachenko, is so obviously a token of Soviet propaganda. Prokofiev would probably never have considered such subject-matter at all had it not been for the political climate of the late 1930s and he did his best to make a working compromise between the order of the day and the kind of melodious simplicity he wanted to cultivate. He took Katayev's prose-draft as it stood and sought to minimise its schematic and propagandist elements. In Act 3 he came up with two of his most effective 'dramatic crescendos', first for the arrival of the reactionary Ukrainian cavalry, then for the burning of Semyon's cottage.

There are more fine moments in Act 4, where the oppositional writing for Soviets and Germans has something of the power of Alexander Nevsky, composed just before the opera. There's also some attractively pungent folk-imitation writing in the second tableau of Act 1. Some less distinguished scenes suggest a rummaging through Prokofiev's cast-off ideas for all-purpose filler material, but such passages aren't so extensive or so deadly as to destroy all enjoyment. This splendid recording plugs another major gap in the discography of opera. Gergiev's interpretation is ardent and well paced, his orchestra is in fine fettle, and his soloists are of high quality. Prokofiev gives little or no opportunity for star turns, but Viktor Lutsiuk's Semyon is passionate and youthful-sounding, and Tatiana Pavlovskaya as his beloved Sofya is radiant. The recording is free from the dryness and sudden shifts of perspective that have dogged some previous issues in this Mariinsky series.

Giacomo Puccini   Italian 1858-1924

The fifth of seven children, he was christened Giacomo Antonio Domenico Michele Secondo Maria, the fifth (and as it turned out the last) generation of a dynasty of Italian musicians: his great-great grandfather Giacomo, his great-grandfather Antonio, his grandfather Domenico and father Michele all had positions as (mainly) organists and church composers in Lucca. Puccini's mother was determined that her son should follow in the family tradition and sent him to the Istituto Musicale in Lucca where his teacher, Carlo Angeloni, fired the boy's enthusiasm for music. Before long he was playing the piano and organ like a good Puccini was expected to. But it was a visit to Pisa in 1876 to see a production of Aida that had a revelatory effect on him: from that time forward he was determined to follow in Verdi's footsteps.

First, though, he rounded off his studies in Lucca with a Mass. Then he went to the Conservatory in Milan for serious study with Antonio Bazzini and with Amilcare Ponchielli, famed as the composer of the opera La Gioconda. In 1883 the publishers Edoardo Sonzogno announced the first of a series of competitions for a one-act opera (Mascagni's Cavalleria rusticana was to win the 1889 competition). Puccini, encouraged by Ponchielli, wrote a work with a young journalist named Fontana. This was Le Villi, written within a few weeks. It was not even mentioned when the prizes were announced in 1884. However, Puccini was at a party soon afterwards where Boito and other influential people in the musical world were present and he was asked to sing extracts from Le Villi. The direct result was a production of the work at the Theatro dal Verme in May 1884. It was an immediate triumph, the great Italian publishing house of Ricordi snapped up the rights and commissioned Puccini to write another. He remained with the firm for the rest of his career.

Five years passed before he completed his next opera, Edgar. It was a failure, one of only two that he experienced. Puccini admitted it was 'a blunder' but during this time he began his affair with Elvira Gemignani. Being married in Catholic Italy meant divorce from Elvira's merchant husband was impossible. Nevertheless, she bore Puccini an only son in 1886 – it was not until 1904, after Elvira's husband died, that the couple could marry. Meanwhile, Puccini was searching for a good librettist. His next choice was a potential disaster. The subject he had selected was a cheeky and daring one in the circumstances, for Puccini decided on writing an opera based on the same story, Manon Lescaut, as that with which Massenet had had a huge success only nine years earlier (Manon, 1884). The original libretto by Domenico Oliva was entirely rewritten by Puccini and Ricordi with contributions along the way from Leoncavallo, Marco Praga, Luigi Illica and Giuseppe Giacosa. In the final score of Manon Lescaut, no librettist is credited, a unique curiosity in the annals of opera. Paradoxically, Manon Lescaut provided Puccini with an unprecedented success. It is the work in which he discovered his own musical voice and overnight it made his name internationally famous.

With his next opera, La bohème, Puccini confirmed that prediction, though initial reaction was far cooler than the enthusiastic welcome accorded Manon Lescaut. It was more conversational in style, more grittily real and the orchestral score was more impressionistic. The conductor for the premiere was the young Arturo Toscanini, just beginning to make a name for himself (he recorded the work many years later). Within a short time La bohème had been produced all over the world; it's still regarded by many as Puccini's supreme masterpiece.

With fame came wealth and in 1900 he built a fabulous villa in the simple village of Torre del Lago by

the lake of Massaciuccoli near Florence – he'd been living in the place since 1892 – and began work on his next project. It was based on Victorien Sardou's 1887 play La Tosca. Using the same team as La bohème (librettists Luigi Illica and Giuseppe Giacosa) Puccini completed the work in 1893. Now one of the best loved of all operas with some of the most famous of arias, Tosca divided the critics. Shaw referred to Sardou's melodramas as 'Sardoodledom', describing the original play as 'a cheap shocker'. The remark was copied 50 years later by the American critic Joseph Kerman when he described Puccini's opera as 'that shabby little shocker'.

Four years after the premiere of Tosca came the third of this remarkable trilogy written by the same three men, Madam Butterfly. Puccini once more went to great pains not to repeat himself musically and created an exotic atmosphere for his Japanese setting, using authentic Japanese folk tunes in the score. The first performance was a fiasco orchestrated by Puccini's rivals, but after many cuts and revisions it was represented two months later at Brescia (May 1904) where it triumphed.

Another Belasco play, The Girl of the Golden West, furnished Puccini with his next venture in the unlikely operatic setting of the 1849 California gold rush. It had an American premiere (1910, Toscanini conducting, Caruso starring as the hero Dick Johnson) and, though it has many fine moments and was liked by the public, it has never caught on in the same way as the previous three. His next work, La rondine, was Puccini's second professional failure (it's an uneasy mix of opera and operetta). Challenging himself once more, Puccini then conceived the idea of an evening of three one-act operas: Il trittico ('The Triptych') is made up of Il tabarro ('The cloak'), Suor Angelica ('Sister Angelica') and Gianni Schicchi - the latter by far the best of the three.

Puccini's final opera presented even greater self-imposed challenges. He was a shrewd operator and kept abreast of all the latest musical developments, so that Turandot, with its exotic setting of Peking in ancient times, incorporates some contemporary music techniques we don't normally associate with Puccini. It was adventurous stuff, the last opera to be written that has entered the standard repertoire and remain beloved by the public at large. The composer himself never finished the score – the last two scenes were completed from sketches by one Franco Alfano. Puccini died aged 65 from a heart attack while undergoing treatment for cancer of the larynx.

Messa di Gloria

Messa di Gloria[a]. Preludio sinfonico. Crisantemi
[a]**Antonello Palombi** ten [a]**Gunnar Lundberg** bar
Hungarian Radio Orchestra and [a]Choir /
Pier Giorgio Morandi
Naxos 8 555304 (60' · DDD · T/t)   ⓈⓄ⮞

This recording is to be preferred to Antonio Pappano's very fine account on EMI – and it's not just a question of price. If the recorded sound isn't as opulent as EMI's, it's very clear and lets in the light. If the dynamic contrasts aren't so big, they're also rather more refined.

Generally Giorgio Morandi prefers slightly faster speeds, though not so fast as Pappano when he really gets up some steam in the last sections of the *Gloria*. But in context Morandi brings out the inherent excitement very effectively and naturally whereas Pappano underlines it. With Pappano the majestic Verdian unisons of the 'Qui tollis' broaden like a great smile across a large face: it's grand fun but tends towards vulgarity. Of the work as a whole, Morandi and his forces give a more youthful performance. There's an easy lightness of step (the *Gloria* sets off with a dance). The chorus is particularly fresh in tone and response, and the tenor soloist, Antonello Palombi, is more gracefully lyrical and Italianate in timbre than either Alagna (with Pappano) or his predecessor Carreras (with Scimone). The baritone is less apt and certainly no match for Hampson (Pappano) or Prey (Scimone); musical nevertheless, and blending well with his colleague in the *Agnus Dei*. In the string piece, *Crisantemi*, Morandi's somewhat quicker tempo, still answering to the marking *andante mesto*, is welcome, keeping mawkishness at bay and limiting the over-exposure of rather thin material.

Opera Arias

La bohème – Sì, mi chiamano Mimì; Donde lieta usci. Gianni Schicchi – O mio babbino caro. Madama Butterfly – Un bel dì vedremo; Che tua madre; Tu, tu, piccolo iddio. Manon Lescaut – In quelle trine morbide; Sola, perduta, abbandonata. La rondine – Chi il bel sogno di Doretta. Suor Angelica – Senza mamma, O bimbo. Tosca – Vissi d'arte. Turandot – Signore, ascolta!; In questa reggia; Tu, che di gel sei cinta
Julia Varady *sop*
Berlin Radio Symphony Orchestra / Marcello Viotti
Orfeo C323 941A (52' · DDD)   Ⓕ**OO**

A lovely and somewhat surprising record by the most fascinating and patrician lyric soprano of the age: 'surprising' because, though Varady is associated closely enough with Verdi, the Puccini connection is less readily made, 'lovely' because the voice is still so pure, the style so musical and the response so intelligent, immediate and full-hearted. She adjusts wonderfully well to the Italian idiom, lightening the vowels, freeing the upper range, allowing more *portamento* than she would probably do in other music, yet employing in its use the finest technical skill and artistic judgement.

Her singing of Magda's song in *La rondine* opens the record and introduces a singer who sounds (give or take a little) half her actual age: Varady's debut dates back to 1962. In Mimì's narrative she sings with so fine a perception of the character – the hesitancies, the joy in 'mi piaccion quelle cose' – that Schwarzkopf's exquisite recording comes to mind, just as, from time to time, and especially in the *Madama Butterfly* excerpts, the finely concentrated, tragic restraint of Meta Seinemeyer is recalled. It's good to hear,

too, how sensitively Varady differentiates between characters, Manon Lescaut having that essential degree of additional sophistication in tone and manner. What runs as a thread through all these characterisations is a feeling for their dignity. Mimì doesn't simper. Sister Angelica doesn't sob. Lauretta has resolution in her pleading. Butterfly, Liù and Tosca are what they should be: women whose pathos lies not in their weakness but in a passionate, single-minded fidelity. That leaves Turandot, which is a mistake. That is, she's outside the singer's scope and should remain so: it isn't merely a matter of vocal thrust, weight and stamina, but also of voice-character, although the performance of her aria has clear merits. None of which should deter purchase; overall this is singing to treasure.

'Ritrovato'
La rondine – Ed ora bevo all'amor[a]; Parigi è la città dei desideri. Madama Butterfly – Con onor muore. Edgar – Act 1, Prelude; Sia benedetto il giorno; Evviva le coppe colmate!...La coppa è simbol della vita. Manon Lescaut – Sola perduta, Act 3, Prelude (original version, Part 1). La fanciulla del West – Oh, se qualcuno vuol quell' oro[b]. Suor Angelica – Amici fiori. Preludio a Orchestra. Adagietto
Plácido Domingo *ten* **Violeta Urmana** *mez*
with [a]**Anna Maria dell'Oste** *sop* [b]**Alfredo Nigro**,
[a]**Stefano Secco** *tens* **Vienna State Opera Chorus;**
Vienna Philharmonic Orchestra / Alberto Veronesi
DG 477 7455GH (63' · DDD · T/t)   Ⓕ**OOᐅ**

No *Bohème*, no *Tosca*, no *Turandot* – this is definitely not another disc of Puccini's greatest hits, but a fascinating delve into mostly unfamiliar second thoughts or earlier versions of some key moments in the composer's output.

The earliest item here is the charming orchestral Prelude from 1876, when Puccini was a student in Lucca. Even then, when he was only 18 years old, the style is recognisable. We then leap forward 44 years to the second version of *La rondine*, altered by Puccini for the work's first performance in Vienna. Here the second tenor, Prunier, was re-cast as a baritone. The gorgeous melody of the Act 2 quartet, possibly the best ensemble in all his oeuvre, in this version (reconstructed by Michael Kaye) gives even more prominence to the soprano line. Then Butterfly's death from the 1904 La Scala premiere. This is more drawn-out than the familiar solo, unbearable, surely, for the soprano after such a gruelling evening; Pinkerton's voice is not heard. The longest item, and the biggest surprise, is the duet from *Edgar* in its 1889 original form. Here a pre-echo of Act 3 of *Tosca* is vividly heard.

The beautiful Prelude to Act 1 of *Edgar* precedes two earlier versions of passages from *Manon Lescaut*: the Prelude to the original Act 3, really lovely, using the melody of Manon's 'L'ora, o Tirsi', and then 'Sola, perduta', substantially different in form, although the main theme is as usual.

The two arias that will be familiar to many listeners are 'Parigi è la città dei desideri' from the

1920 *La rondine*, and Suor Angelica's "Amici fiori". Although Plácido Domingo's name is, naturally, given equal billing with that of Violeta Urmana, he only sings on three of the tracks (*La rondine* and *Edgar*). Urmana concludes the recital with the exhilarating aria with chorus from *Edgar*, 'Evviva le coppe colmate!'. The Vienna forces under Alberto Veronesi accompany with gusto. A most enterprising and scholarly issue, which is also a great pleasure to listen to.

Madama Butterfly – Un bel dì vedremo; Tu, tu piccolo iddio[a]. La bohème – Mi chiamano Mimì; Quando m'en vo; Donde lieta usci. Edgar – Addio, addio mio dolce amor?; Nel villaggio d'Edgar. Gianni Schicchi – O mio babbino caro. La fanciulla del West – Laggiù nel Soledad. Manon Lescaut – In quelle trine morbide; Sola, perduta, abbandonata. La rondine – Chi il bel sogno di Doretta? Suor Angelica – Senza mamma. Turandot – Signore, ascolta!; Tu che di gel sei cinta; In questa reggia[a]. Le Villi – Se come voi piccina
Angela Gheorghiu sop [a]**Roberto Alagna** ten
Giuseppe Verdi Symphony Chorus and Orchestra, Milan / Anton Coppola
EMI 557955-2 (70' · DDD)   ⓕ**OOO▸**

This is a considerable addition to this ever-enterprising artist's growing discography. Just when many of us were declaring there would never be anyone to take on Renata Tebaldi's mantle in *spinto* roles, here's Angela Gheorghiu doing just that. There is a similar strength of tone, breadth of phrasing and attention to musical and verbal detail. Everything she achieves here is technically assured, thought through and emotionally rewarding.

Her Mimì in Decca's *La bohème* was an appealing, cleanly articulated reading, and it still is, even if the youthful bloom isn't quite so much in evidence. Musetta, though, is now very much her role, her Waltz Song sung with zest adding to the fullness only a few others have brought to the piece. One can hear why EMI wanted 'Un bel dì vedremo' at its top: Gheorghiu's account is overwhelming, as is the death scene. She's almost as moving in *Suor Angelica*'s 'Senza mamma'. Magda's solo and 'O mio babbino caro' are as smiling and therefore as winning as they should be. From *Turandot*, Liù's pains and sorrows are encompassed with ease and an apt *morbidezza*, with finely poised *pianissimo* high notes.

This is a deeply satisfying traversal of the Puccini canon, well supported by the Milan orchestra and Anton Coppola, artistic director of Florida's Opera Tampa.

La bohème

La bohème   Ⓗ
Victoria de los Angeles sop Mimì **Jussi Björling** ten Rodolfo **Lucine Amara** sop Musetta **Robert Merrill** bar Marcello **John Reardon** bar Schaunard

Giorgio Tozzi bass Colline **Fernando Corena** bass Benoit, Alcindoro **William Nahr** ten Parpignol **Thomas Powell** bar Customs Official **George del Monte** bar Sergeant **Columbus Boychoir; RCA Victor Chorus and Orchestra / Sir Thomas Beecham**
EMI Great Recordings of the Century mono ②
567750-2 (108' · ADD · T/t) or Naxos 8 111249/50
Recorded 1956   Ⓜ**OOO▸**

 The disadvantages of this famous Beecham *Bohème* are obvious. It's a mono recording and restricted in dynamic range. The sense of space for the complex crowd scene of Act 2 is to emerge with the maximum impact is inevitably lacking; the climaxes here and elsewhere are somewhat constricted; no less important, it's sometimes harder to focus on the subtleties of Puccini's orchestration. It was also made in a great hurry, and this shows in a number of patches of slightly insecure ensemble, even a couple of wrong entries. But there's no other important respect in which it doesn't stand at least half a head (often head and shoulders) above its more recent rivals. Nobody has ever been so predestinately right for the role of Mimì than Victoria de los Angeles: right both in vocal quality and in sheer involvement with every word and every musical phrase that Mimì utters. Beyond a certain point (usually a certain dynamic level) most sopranos stop being Mimì and simply produce the same sound that they would if they were singing Aida or Tosca. De los Angeles rarely does this; even under pressure (and Beecham's unhurried tempi do put her under pressure at times), the very difficulties themselves are used as an expressive and interpretative resource. Hers is the most moving and involving Mimì ever recorded. And Björling's is the most musical Rodolfo. He has the reputation of having been a bit of a dry stick, dramatically (on stage he looked like the other Bohemians' elderly, portly uncle), but on record he's the one exponent of the role to be credible both as a lover and as a poet. His voice is fine silver rather than brass, it can caress as well as weep, and his love for Mimì is more often confided than it is bellowed for all Paris to hear. This, indeed, is one of the most conspicuous differences between Beecham's account and most others: its simple belief that when Puccini wrote *pp* he meant it. Beecham (whose spell over his entire cast – in which there's no weak link – extends as far as teaching his Schaunard, John Reardon, an irresistibly funny, cut-glass English accent for the parrot-fancying milord) makes one realise what an intimate opera this is, how much of it is quiet, how many of its exchanges are *sotto voce*, and he thus enables his singers to use the full range of their voices and to employ subtleties of colour, phrasing and diction that are simply not available to a voice at full stretch (and in the process he largely cancels out the disadvantage of his recording's restricted dynamic range). It's the same with his handling of the orchestra: one would expect Beecham to seem understated, but again and again one turns back to his reading and discovers nothing missing – he has achieved as much or more with less. This is as complete a distillation of Puccini's drama as you're likely to hear. (The Naxos set is not available in the United States, Australia and Singapore due to possible copyright restrictions.)

La bohème
Mirella Freni sop Mimì **Luciano Pavarotti** ten
Rodolfo **Elizabeth Harwood** sop Musetta **Rolando Panerai** bar Marcello **Gianni Maffeo** bar Schaunard
Nicolai Ghiaurov bass Colline **Michel Sénéchal** bass
Benoit, Alcindoro **Gernot Pietsch** ten Parpignol
**Schoenberg Boys' Choir; Berlin German Opera Chorus; Berlin Philharmonic Orchestra /
Herbert von Karajan**
Decca ② 421 049-2DH2 (110' · ADD · T/t)   ⓕ❶❶➔

Pavarotti's Rodolfo is perhaps the best thing he has ever done: not only the finest recorded account of the role since Björling's on the Beecham set, but adding the honeyed Italianate warmth that even Björling lacked. He can't quite match Björling's poetic refinement, and he's less willing to sing really quietly, but Pavarotti's sincerity counts for a great deal: his pride as he declares his vocation as a poet, the desperate feigning of his 'Mimì è una civetta' are points that most tenors miss or treat as mere opportunities for a big sing. His latter-day image may tend to hide it, but this recording is a reminder that Pavarotti was an artist of intelligence and delicacy as well as splendour of voice.

His Mimì, Freni, sings beautifully and sensitively. Panerai is a strong, vividly acted Marcello. Harwood is an interesting Musetta: her tiny narration, in Act 4, of her meeting with the stricken Mimì is a gripping moment, and her waltz-song in Act 2 is a passionate (and irresistible) avowal to Marcello. Karajan is a great Puccini conductor who can linger over the beauties of orchestration without losing his grip on the drama or relaxing his support of the singers. There aren't many operas of which a better case can be made for having more than one account in your collection. For a modern *La bohème* to supplement the Beecham this Karajan set must go to the top of the list.

La bohème
Anna Netrebko sop Mimì **Rolando Villazón** ten
Rodolfo **Nicole Cabell** sop Musetta **Boaz Daniel** bar
Marcello **Stéphane Degout** bar Schaunard **Vitalij Kowaljow** bass Colline **Tiziano Bracci** bass Alcindoro
Kevin Connors ten Parpignol
**Bavarian Radio Symphony Chorus and Orchestra /
Bertrand de Billy**
DG ② 477 6600GH2 (105' · DDD · S/T/t/N)
Recorded live at the Philharmonie am Gasteig,
Munich, in April 2007   ⓕ❶➔

Vividly recorded, vigorously conducted and sung by a distinguished cast still in their relatively youthful prime, it presents the score with an appeal that will be readily felt by newcomers

and with a freshness that will make those of riper years feel…well, feel young again.

Act 1 moves quickly up to Mimì's entry. The vigour is not brash or wearing; there are moments of respite, but it is conducted as a symphonic unit, a first-movement *allegro giocoso*. The love music takes its natural pace, though it adds a silent beat immediately following Mimì's solo and another before the start of 'O soave fanciulla'. The second act registers clearly as a symphonic *scherzo*, or, in this arrangement where you play the first CD without a break, as an extended Mozartian finale. The various elements – the main solo group, the Christmas Eve crowd, the children (in splendidly disciplined high spirits), the stage band – are all well defined and the great ensemble runs its joyful course so that we can almost feel ourselves to be part of it.

Among the singers, it is important that Marcello has the presence and gaiety to be the life and soul and Boaz Daniel has all of that. Stéphane Degout as Schaunard may be a little too like him for the purposes of the recording but is lively and stylish. The Colline, Vitalij Kowaljow, is less effective. The lovers Anna Netrebko and Rolando Villazón are a famous pair and deservedly so. His voice is richly distinctive, his style genial and ardent. Netrebko is pure-toned and ample in climaxes. As Musetta, Nicole Cabell shows many of the qualities of a well cast Mimì – might Netrebko (a little solid and sturdy in vocal character for the Mimì of these acts) not have made a brilliant Musetta, as Welitsch did?

In the remaining acts no such qualms arise. Netrebko sings with feeling and imagination and Villazón is an inspired, golden-voiced Rodolfo. In fact, these are as finely performed as in any recording. The orchestra play almost as though reading a supplementary libretto, so vivid is their commentary. This is a recording which takes its place alongside the acknowledged 'classics'.

La bohème
Mirella Freni sop Mimì **Gianni Raimondi** ten Rodolfo
Adriana Martino sop Musetta **Rolando Panerai** bar
Marcello **Gianni Maffeo** bar Schaunard **Ivo Vinco** bass Colline **Carlo Badioli** bass Benoit **Carlo Badioli** bass Alcindoro **Franco Ricciardi** ten Parpignol
Giuseppe Morresi bass Sergeant **Carlo Forti** bass
Customs Official **Chorus and Orchestra of La Scala, Milan / Herbert von Karajan**
Stage director **Franco Zeffirelli**
Video director **Wilhelm Semmelroth**
DG 📀 073 027-9GH (111' · 4:3 · 2.0 · 0)
Recorded 1965   ⓕ❶❶

Dating from 1965, this is a thoroughly old-fashioned opera film. As was often Karajan's practice, the singers mime to their own pre-recording, not always in perfect synchronisation, and to see an ample *fortissimo* phrase launched with apparently no effort at all is disconcerting. Zeffirelli's La Scala sets have been reproduced but amplified for the purpose of filming, and the joins between 'real' and painted fence in the Bar-

PUCCINI'S LA BOHÈME – IN BRIEF

Victoria de los Angeles *Mimì* **Jussi Björling**
Rodolfo **Lucine Amara** *Musetta* **Columbus
Boychoir; RCA Victor Chorus & Orchestra /
Sir Thomas Beecham**
EMI mono ② 567750-2 (107' · AAD)   Ⓜ❶❷❸
A classic, with extra electricity derived from
the hasty recording, with Beecham's living,
vivid conducting and a superb cast, both stel-
lar and supporting, even though the mono
sound is less kind to the orchestra.

Mirella Freni *Mimì* **Luciano Pavarotti** *Rodolfo*
Elizabeth Harwood *Musetta* **Schoenberg Boys'
Choir; Berlin Deutsche Oper Chorus; Berlin PO
/ Herbert von Karajan**
Decca ② 421 049-2DH2 (110' · ADD)   ⒻⒶ➤
Karajan's lush but eloquent Puccini, with
top-notch voices, Pavarotti in particular, that
at least equal Beecham's. Magnificent orches-
tral playing in an equally fine recording.

(In English) **Cynthia Haymon** *Mimì* **Dennis
O'Neill** *Rodolfo* **Marie McLaughlin** *Musetta*
**Peter Kay Children's Choir; Geoffrey Mitchell
Choir; Philharmonia Orchestra / David Parry**
Chandos ② CHAN3008 (111' · DDD)   Ⓕ
Despite the stilted old translation a highly
enjoyable recording, warmly conducted and
sung by a cast of international standing, and
very directly communicative.

Anna Netrebko *Mimì* **Rolando Villazón** *Rodolfo*
Nicole Cabell *Musetta* **Bavarian RSO and
Chorus / Bertrand de Billy**
DG ② 477 6600GH2 (105' · DDD)   ⒻⒶ➤
A terrific new *Bohème* with the operatic duo
of the moment in the lead roles. And both
Netrebko and Villazón acquit themselves
with honours. The Bohemians are a lively
bunch and the whole thing has the whiff of
the stage about it. De Billy conducts with
great verve and poetry. Worthy to stand
alongside the 'classics'.

Ileana Cotrubas *Mimì* **Neil Schicoff** *Rodolfo*
Marilyn Zschau *Musetta* **Royal Opera House
Chorus and Orchestra / Lamberto Gardelli**
NVC Arts 🎦 4509 99222-2 (118')   Ⓕ
Of several DVD *Bohèmes*, this is the most
convincing: an immensely vital production in
richly atmospheric sets. Cotrubas, Allen and
a vivid supporting cast are affectionately
conducted by Gardelli.

Cheryl Barker *Mimì* **David Hobson** *Rodolfo*
Christine Douglas *Musetta* **Australian Opera
Chorus and Orchestra / Julian Smith**
ArtHaus Musik 🎦 100 954 (113')   ⒻⒶ
The famous stage production by Baz Luhr-
man in its original and genuinely operatic
approach. It's engaging, heartfelt and may
well captivate opera newcomers with its
1950s Paris setting and youngish cast.

rière d'Enfer scene, for example, are very obvious. The lighting is often most unconvincing
when the action is so would-be naturalistic: a
single candle can fill the stage with light, and the
proverbial blind man with half an eye would have
no difficulty in finding Mimì's dropped key.

And yet it's as near an ideal *Bohème* as you could
hope to find. Firstly because there are no 'guest
artists' – this is La Scala's *Bohème* cast of the
period; all are at home in this production and with
each other – and all are believably young or
youngish Bohemians. Mirella Freni was near the
beginning of her international career, her voice at
its freshest, and her acting is all the more affecting
for its restraint: a downcast glance, a shy smile.
Gianni Raimondi partners her very well and sings
with elegance and ardour. Rolando Panerai is an
immensely likeable and finely sung Marcello,
Gianni Maffeo hardly his inferior as Schaunard
and Ivo Vinco is a tow-haired, cheroot-smoking
young philosopher. Adriana Martino's Musetta
is, if you like, conventionally tarty in her vivid
scarlet décolleté gown, but she sings charmingly.
Karajan sounds as though he's enjoying himself
thoroughly, never pressing the music or his singers too hard, quite often indulging both with a
rubato that encourages long and eloquent line.
The recorded balance is at times peculiar: Rodolfo's friends are evidently in the street below when
they urge him to hurry, but they must have
climbed the fire escape to comment ironically
that he has 'found his poetry' in Mimì. The lovers
sound properly off-stage at the end of Act 1 but
they're quite visibly on it, in the doorway. But
even these little flaws are oddly endearing; this is
definitely a *Bohème* to live with.

Additional recommendations

La bohème
Carreras *Rodolfo* **Ricciarelli** *Mimì* **Putnam** *Musetta*
Wixell *Marcello* **Royal Opera House Chorus and
Orchestra / C Davis**
Philips ② 442 260-2PM2 (106' · ADD)   Ⓜ➤
Carreras and Ricciarelli make a wonderful pair of
lovers – totally credible, their fresh, supple voices
totally suited to the roles – while Davis conducts
somewhat coolly.

La bohème
Freni *Mimì* **Pavarotti** *Rodolfo* **Pacetti** *Musetta*
Quilico *Marcello* **Ghiaurov** *Colline* **Dickson**
Schaunard **Tajo** *Benoit, Alcindoro* **Chorus and
Orchestra of the San Francisco Opera / Severini**
Stage director **Zambello** *Video director* **Large**
ArtHaus Musik 🎦 100 046 (116' · Region 0)
Recorded live 1988   ⒻⒶ
The staging is traditional in the best sense, even if it
can't rival the great Zeffirelli/La Scala production,
also with Freni (reviewed above). Brian Large has
his cameras in the right place at the right time, with
a fine balance of distant and close-up shots. One can
share John Steane's enthusiasm for the restraint
and experience of Freni and Pavarotti, who (even
in 1988, when the performance took place) didn't
look like the young lovers predicated by the

libretto, but who made up for it with the 'rich humanity' (JBS's words) of their portrayals. Ghiaurov, at 59, remains a tower of strength as Colline, although his voice sounds a shade rusty.

La bohème

Mula Mimì **Machado** Rodolfo **Giordano** Musetta **Capitanucci** Marcello **Menéndez** Schaunard **Bou** Colline **Martínez** Benoit **Mariotti** Alcindoro **de Terán** Parpignol **Gallar** Sergeant **Villoria** Customs Official **Madrid SO / López-Cobos**
Stage director **G Del Monaco** *Video director* **Lough**
Opus Arte ② 🔴 OA0961D; 🔵 OABD7007D (149' · NTSC · 16:9 · PCM stereo and DTS 5.1 · 0)
Recorded live at the Teatro Real, Madrid, in March 2006   Ⓕ❂❂

This *Bohème* is a glorious vindication of traditional staging at its imaginative, recreative best. Giancarlo Del Monaco here turns his attention to the work and comes up with a humdinger of a production. In the pit López-Cobos's experienced hand is at all times in evidence. Centre stage is Inva Mula's appealing, vulnerable and intensely sung Mimì (justly given a tremendous ovation at the close). At first glance, Aquiles Machado hardly fits one's idea of a romantic poet but he lives Rodolfo with so much feeling and identification with the role that doubts are banished, and there is much sensitivity and passion in his singing.

La bohème

Gallardo-Domàs *sop* Mimì **Álvarez** *ten* Rodolfo **Hong** *sop* Musetta **Servile** *bar* Marcello **de Carolis** *bar* Schaunard **Parodi** *bass* Colline **Peirone** *bass* Benoit
Giuseppe Verdi Chorus, Milan; Children's Choir, Chorus and Orchestra of La Scala, Milan / Bruno Bartoletti
Stage director **Franco Zeffirelli**
Video director **Carlo Battistoni**
TDK 🔴 DV-OPBOH (134' · 16:9 · PCM stereo, 5.1 & DTS 5.1 · 0)
Recorded live February 2003   Ⓕ❂

This La Scala production is particularly good at capturing the Christmas spirit in the Latin Quarter and the snows of a wintry dawn at the Barrière d'Enfer. But that's Zeffirelli. It's beautiful to look at, meticulous in detail, and true to the score and the book. Vocally we're, let's say, a little lower than the angels. But nothing seriously spoils the joy of this. The sound is fine, team-working among the Bohemians has the combination of precision and apparent spontaneity which betokens inspired and thorough rehearsal. The orchestral playing under Bruno Bartoletti carries an assurance that never lapses into mere routine.

Edgar

Edgar
Adriana Damato *sop* Fidelia **Plácido Domingo** *ten* Edgar **Marianne Cornetti** *mez* Tigrana **Juan Pons** *bar* Frank **Rafal Siwek** *bass* Gualtiero **Santa Cecilia Academy Chorus, Rome; Santa Cecilia Academy Orchestra, Rome / Alberto Veronesi**

DG 477 6102GH2 (85' · DDD · T/t)   Ⓜ❂❂▸

Edgar, Puccini's second opera, composed in 1888 and first given the following year at La Scala, has never really caught on. The title-role is the only Puccini tenor lead role that Plácido Domingo has never sung until now. In his 65th year (the recording was made in 2005, just after his Covent Garden Siegmund), it is a tribute to his tenacity and vigour that he should have learnt it, and gone on to give such a convincing performance. There is no hint of strain, and throughout an arduous three acts he uses his voice with all his accustomed commitment and fervour.

The music is full of pre-echoes of Puccini's later works and the orchestra is constantly employed in a remarkably confident and innovative way for a beginner in his late twenties. What no one can do is to rescue the opera from its libretto. Fernando Fontana based it on a story by Alfred de Musset, in which the hero burns down his own house to show his contempt for his fellow countrymen. He makes off with the hysterical and sacrilegious gypsy Tigrana, but then grows tired of their illicit liaison and yearns for Fidelia, the girl next door back in the Tyrol. After a victorious battle, he has his armour sent home, and in disguise as a monk, watches his own funeral. At the last moment, as he prepares to escape with Fidelia, the seductress Tigrana stabs her to death.

The finale of Act 1, in which Edgar defends Tigrana against the townspeople, builds up to a spectacular ensemble. The opening of Act 2, with a mournful woodwind solo which looks forward to the prelude to 'E lucevan le stelle' in *Tosca*, has Edgar's big aria, 'L'orgia, chimera dall'occhio ardente'. There is a passionate duet, in which he rejects Tigrana. The final act, the most confusing dramatically, has a pair of beautiful arias for Fidelia.

Domingo is well partnered by Marianne Cornetti as Tigrana and Adriana Damato as Fidelia. Juan Pons takes the rather ungrateful role of Frank, Fidelia's brother, and a rival for Tigrana's affections. The emotional turmoil in which Edgar finds himself is not unlike that of Don José in Carmen – a man torn between the lure of raw sex and the ideal of virtuous simplicity. Edgar tries to take advantage of both, with tragic consequences. Alberto Veronesi conducts an often exciting performance, the first studio-made set and an easy recommendation.

La fanciulla del West

La fanciulla del West
Carol Neblett *sop* Minnie **Plácido Domingo** *ten* Dick Johnson **Sherrill Milnes** *bar* Jack Rance **Francis Egerton** *ten* Nick **Robert Lloyd** *bass* Ashby **Gwynne Howell** *bass* Jake Wallace **Paul Hudson** *bass* Billy Jackrabbit **Anne Wilkens** *sop* Wowkle **Chorus and Orchestra of the Royal Opera House, Covent Garden / Zubin Mehta**
DG ② 474 840-2GOR2 (130' · ADD · T/t)
Recorded 1977   Ⓜ❂❂❂▸

This opera depicts the triangular relationship between Minnie, the saloon owner and 'mother' to the entire town of gold miners, Jack Rance, the sheriff, and Dick Johnson (alias Ramerrez), a bandit leader. The music is highly developed in Puccini's seamless lyrical style, the arias for the main characters emerge from the texture and return to it effortlessly. The vocal colours are strongly polarised with the cast being all male except for one *travesti* role and Minnie herself. The score bristles with robust melody as well as delicate scoring, betraying a masterly hand at work. Carol Neblett is a strong Minnie, vocally distinctive and well characterised, while Plácido Domingo and Sherrill Milnes make a good pair of suitors for the spunky little lady. Zubin Mehta conducts with real sympathy for the idiom.

La fanciulla del West
Mara Zampieri sop Minnie **Plácido Domingo** ten Dick Johnson **Juan Pons** bar Jack Rance **Sergio Bertocchi** ten Nick **Luigi Roni** bass Ashby **Mario Chingari** bar Jake Wallace **Aldo Bramante** bass Billy Jackrabbit **Nella Verri** mez Wowkle **Antonio Salvadori** bar Sonora **Ernesto Gavazzi** ten Trin **Giovanni Savoiardo** bar Sid **Orazio Mori** bar Bello **Francesco Memeo** ten Harry **Aldo Bottion** ten Joe **Ernesto Panariello** bar Happy **Pietro Spagnoli** bass Larkens **Claudio Giombi** bass José Castro **La Scala Chorus and Orchestra, Milan / Lorin Maazel**
Stage director **Jonathan Miller**
Video director **John Michael Phillips**
Opus Arte 📀 OALS3004D (144' · 4:3 · 2.0 · 0 · N/T/t)
Recorded live at Teatro alla Scala, Milan, 1991

This DVD of *La fanciulla del West* presents Jonathan Miller's atmospheric production for La Scala, with sets by Stefanos Lazaridis and costumes by Sue Blane. The cast is strong, and Lorin Maazel proves a warmer, more idiomatic Puccinian here than he generally was in his audio recordings for CBS/Sony. His direction makes one marvel afresh at the imagination and colour in this score, distinct from other Puccini operas in its obsession with the whole-tone scale.

Miller's production takes the melodrama seriously, with realistic sets and period costumes. It even manages to bring off the improbable scene in Act 2 when Sherriff Rance finds Dick Johnson's blood dripping down from the loft of Minnie's cabin, leading to the game of poker when Minnie blatantly cheats. Though at the end Dick and Minnie get no further than the back of the stage instead of riding off into the sunset, the authentic gulp of emotion is well caught in this rare Puccini happy ending.

Plácido Domingo is in superb voice, and wins ovations for each of his big solos. Juan Pons is wonderfully firm and dark of tone as Jack Rance. Though Mara Zampieri as Minnie sings with clear focus and no suspicion of a wobble, the result is often near to hooting – a strong performance, none the less.

Camerawork is a little fussy but not too distracting. Not only is the documentation fuller than usual in DVD booklets, with a facsimile of the opera house's cast-list on the back, it also contains a complete (if minuscule) libretto and translation.

Madama Butterfly

Madama Butterfly
Renata Scotto sop Madama Butterfly **Carlo Bergonzi** ten Pinkerton **Rolando Panerai** bar Sharpless **Anna di Stasio** mez Suzuki **Piero De Palma** ten Goro **Giuseppe Morresi** ten Prince Yamadori **Silvana Padoan** mez Kate Pinkerton **Paolo Montarsolo** bass The Bonze **Mario Rinaudo** bass Commissioner **Rome Opera House Chorus and Orchestra / Sir John Barbirolli**
EMI Great Recordings of the Century ② 567885-2 (142' · ADD · T/t). Recorded 1966   Ⓜ❶➟

This is Barbirolli's *Butterfly*; despite Scotto's expressiveness and Bergonzi's elegance it's the conductor's contribution that gives this set its durability and its hold on the affections. The Rome Opera Orchestra isn't the equal of the Vienna Philharmonic for Karajan. However, the rapport between conductor and orchestra and their mutual affection for Puccini are evident throughout, and they make this the most Italianate of all readings. It's hugely enjoyable, not just in the big emotional outpourings (like the Act 2 interlude, where Barbirolli's passionate gasps and groans spur the orchestra to great eloquence) but in many tiny moments where you can almost see the conductor and his players lovingly and absorbedly concentrating on subtleties of phrasing and texture.

There's a lot of good singing, too. Scotto's voice won't always take the pressure she puts on it, but her portrayal is a touching and finely detailed one. The ever stylish Bergonzi sings with immaculate phrasing and perfect taste, Panerai is an outstanding Sharpless (beautifully sung, the embodiment of anxious, pitying concern) and di Stasio's Suzuki is attractively light-voiced and young-sounding.

The recording, however, is a bit narrow in perspective, rather close (really quiet singing and playing rarely register as such) and some of the voices are edged or slightly tarnished in loud passages. Barbirolli's set is perhaps for those who find the meticulously refined detail of Karajan studied (also ravishing and stunningly recorded); those, in short, for whom Latin warmth and impulsive open-heartedness are indispensable in this opera. They will find those qualities here, with singing to match, and won't mind the occasional strident patch.

Madama Butterfly
Mirella Freni sop Madama Butterfly **Luciano Pavarotti** ten Pinkerton **Robert Kerns** bar Sharpless **Christa Ludwig** mez Suzuki **Michel Sénéchal** ten Goro **Giorgio Stendoro** bar Prince Yamadori **Elke Schary** mez Kate Pinkerton **Marius Rintzler** bass The Bonze **Hans Helm** bass Commissioner **Vienna State**

Opera Chorus; Vienna Philharmonic Orchestra /
Herbert von Karajan
Decca ③ 417 577-2DH3 (145' · ADD · T/t)
Recorded 1974   Ⓕ❍▷

In every way except one the transfer of Karajan's
radiant Vienna recording for Decca could hardly
provide a firmer recommendation. The reservation is one of price – this Karajan is on three discs,
not two, at full price. However it does allow each
act to be self-contained on a single disc, and for
such a performance as this no extravagance is too
much. Movingly dramatic as Renata Scotto is on
the Barbirolli set, Mirella Freni is even more compelling. The voice is fresher, firmer and more
girlish, with more light and shade at such points as
'Un bel dì', and there's an element of vulnerability
that intensifies the communication. In that, one
imagines Karajan played a big part, just as he must
have done in presenting Pavarotti – not quite the
superstar he became but already with a will of his
own in the recording studio – as a Pinkerton of
exceptional subtlety, not just a roistering cad but
in his way an endearing figure in the first act.

Significantly CD brings out the delicacy of the
vocal balances in Act 1 with the voices deliberately distanced for much of the time, making
such passages as 'Vienna la sera' and 'Bimba
dagli occhi' the more magical in their delicacy.
Karajan, in that duet and later in the Flower duet
of Act 2, draws ravishing playing from the
Vienna Philharmonic strings, getting them to
imitate the *portamento* of the singers in an *echt*-
Viennese manner, which is ravishing to the ear.
Christa Ludwig is by far the richest and most
compelling of Suzukis.

Madama Butterfly
Angela Gheorghiu sop Madama Butterfly **Jonas
Kaufmann** ten Pinkerton **Enkelejda Shkosa** mez
Suzuki **Fabio Capitanucci** bar Sharpless **Gregory
Bonfatti** ten Goro **Raymond Aceto** bass Bonze
**Chorus and Orchestra of the Accademia Nazionale
di Santa Cecilia / Antonio Pappano**
EMI ② 264187-2 (135' · DDD · T/t)   Ⓕ❍❍▷

Approaching such a familiar work one waits for
something individual, a clue to the artist's vision
of the role. This came at the beginning of Act 2,
in the scene between Suzuki and Butterfly when
she describes Pinkerton's departing words,
'Quell'ultima mattina'. Gheorghiu somehow
conveys not only the depth of Butterfly's love
but also her inner knowledge that, in fact, her
belief in Pinkerton's devotion is hopeless. This
is a mature interpretation which suggests
strength above all, so that the touches of vulnerability are added with subtlety; this performance
could be her best Puccini role since Magda in *La
rondine* more than a decade ago. The rest of the
cast live up to her standard: Jonas Kaufmann is
an ardent Pinkerton although he cannot suggest
a touch of youthful charm, the only possible
redeeming feature for this anti-hero. Enkelejda
Shkosa is a vivid Suzuki and Fabio Capitanucci
the sympathetic Sharpless.

**PUCCINI MADAMA BUTTERFLY –
IN BRIEF**

Renata Scotto Madama Butterfly **Carlo Bergonzi**
Pinkerton **Rolando Panerai** Sharpless **Rome
Opera Chorus & Orch / Sir John Barbirolli**
EMI ② 567885-2 (142' · ADD)   Ⓜ❍▷
In one of his rare operatic showings Barbirolli created a warmly idiomatic, Italianate
performance, fluent, detailed and superlatively sung by a distinguished cast, even if
the recorded sound is not up to the very
best.

Mirella Freni Madama Butterfly **Luciano
Pavarotti** Pinkerton **Robert Kerns** Sharpless
**Rome Vienna State Opera Chorus, Vienna PO /
Herbert von Karajan**
Decca ③ 417 577-2DH3 (145' · ADD)   Ⓕ❍▷
A stunningly beautiful performance, Karajan's conducting measured and luxuriant
yet still dramatic, with two thrilling central
performances sounding younger than Barbirolli's, a fine supporting cast and an outstanding recording.

Victoria de los Angeles Madama Butterfly **John
Lanigan** Pinkerton **Covent Garden Chorus and
Orchestra / Rudolf Kempe**   Ⓗ
Royal Opera House Heritage Series ② ROHS006
(122' · ADD)   Ⓢ❍❍
An astounding central performance that
won't leave a dry eye in the house takes its
place in a real company performance.

Maria Callas Madama Butterfly **Nicolai Gedda**
Pinkerton **Chorus & Orchestra of La Scala, Milan
/ Herbert von Karajan**   Ⓗ
EMI ② 556298-2 (139' · AAD)   Ⓕ❍▷
Magnificently compelling despite the mono
sound, with Maria Callas a heartbreaking
Butterfly, Nicolai Gedda an intensely roman-
tic Pinkerton and Karajan more vividly thea-
trical than in his much later recording.

Angela Gheorghiu Madama Butterfly **Jonas
Kaufmann** Pinkerton **Santa Cecilia Chorus and
Orchestra / Antonio Pappano**
EMI ② 264187-2 (135' · DDD)   Ⓕ❍❍▷
Possibly Gheorghiu's finest Puccini role to
date: a wonderfully rounded, considered performance. Kaufmann is an ardent Pinkerton
and Pappano conducts with his customary
style and passion. A very fine modern set.

Ying Huang Madama Butterfly **Richard Troxell**
Pinkerton **Orchestre de Paris / James Conlon**
Columbia 📀 CDR24673 (128')   Ⓕ
A cinematic version, somewhat indulgently
directed by Frédéric Mitterand, with reasonable lip-sync. The very young Ying Huang is
a light-voiced but deeply touching Butterfly,
and though Richard Troxell is only serviceable as Pinkerton, this is still unusual and
enjoyable.

Conducting the orchestra and chorus of the Santa Cecilia Academy, Antonio Pappano takes a less driven and melodramatic way with the score than Karajan in his three recordings; it's nearer in mood to Barbirolli (a favourite), though there is no lack of passion at the great climaxes – just listen to the spine-tingling moment of the sighting of the ship. So, a fine new *Butterfly*, unlikely to topple some of the great recordings of the past but worthy to set beside them.

Madama Butterfly   H
Victoria de los Angeles sop Madama Butterfly **John Lanigan** ten Pinkerton **Geraint Evans** bar Sharpless **Barbara Howitt** mez Suzuki **David Tree** ten Goro **David Allen** bar Prince Yamadori **Joyce Livingstone** mez Kate Pinkerton **Michael Langdon** bass The Bonze **Ronald Firmager** bar Imperial Commissioner **Harry Gawler** bass Registrar **Chorus and Orchestra of the Royal Opera House, Covent Garden / Rudolf Kempe**
Royal Opera House Heritage Series mono ②
ROHS006 (122' · ADD). Recorded live 1957   Ⓜ**OO**

This quite overwhelming performance has the advantage of Victoria de los Angeles's unique Cio-Cio-San, fulfilling every aspect of the taxing but rewarding title-role. She made two commercial recordings of the work, but here heard live she surpasses both with a reading that, as far as singing and acting with the voice are concerned, is shattering, every emotion, every phrase ideally presented. It comes across the years with such heartfelt feeling and at the close such tragedy that it goes to the top of *Butterflies* on disc.

As Alexandra Wilson points out in her well researched notes, de los Angeles was 33 at the time and at the apex of her career. She's never fazed either by the intimate solos of Act 2 or the strength needed for 'Un bel dì', and her final dying solo is as moving as I have ever heard it.

No less remarkable is Kempe's conducting – taut, immediate and, when needed, loving. His Covent Garden orchestra plays its heart out for him. Both in small and big things, the work could hardly sound more deeply felt than here. The large climaxes are shattering, the many moments of intimacy so touching.

Another reason why we are unlikely to hear the work so well done again is the overall sense of a company and ensemble, each member of it a dedicated singer. Today such a thing has ceased to exist. John Lanigan never had a truly Italianate tenor, but his keen voice and articulation and his commitment to the role of Pinkerton are satisfying enough on their own terms. The young Geraint Evans, singing Sharpless for the first time, is as warm and sympathetic as he should be in this tricky role. Barbara Hewitt is a natural, clear-voiced Suzuki. Michael Langdon roars loudly as the threatening Bonze. Only David Tree's dry-voiced Goro is a bit of a trial.

Of course, de los Angeles's studio-made sets have better sound, and the versions with Callas and Scotto, in a different vein, remain remark-

able; but at this moment it is hard to imagine hearing a more soulful, dramatic traversal of the work than we have here.

Manon Lescaut

Manon Lescaut
Mirella Freni sop Manon Lescaut **Luciano Pavarotti** ten Des Grieux **Dwayne Croft** bar Lescaut **Giuseppe Taddei** bar Geronte **Ramon Vargas** ten Edmondo **Cecilia Bartoli** mez Singer **Federico Davia** bass Innkeeper, Captain **Anthony Laciura** ten Dancing Master **Paul Groves** ten Lamplighter **James Courtney** bass Sergeant **Chorus and Orchestra of the Metropolitan Opera / James Levine**
Decca ② 440 200-2DHO2 (120' · DDD · T/t)   Ⓕ

With Luciano Pavarotti a powerful Des Grieux, James Levine conducts a comparably big-boned performance of *Manon Lescaut*, bringing out the red-blooded drama of Puccini's first big success, while not ignoring its warmth and tender poetry in exceptionally full, vivid sound with the voices well in front of the orchestra. In the title-role Freni's performance culminates in an account of the big Act 4 aria, more involving and passionate than any of the others on rival versions, with the voice showing no signs of wear, and with her sudden change of face at the words 'terra di pace' ('a land of peace') bringing a magical lightening of tone. That aria makes a thrilling climax, when too often this act can seem a let-down. In this as in so much else, Levine conveys the tensions and atmosphere of a stage performance in a way that owes much to his experience at the Met.

More completely than other versions, it avoids the feeling of a studio performance. Reactions to Pavarotti as Des Grieux will differ widely. The closeness of balance means that in volume his singing rarely drops below *mezzo-forte*, but there's little harm in having so passionate a portrait of Des Grieux as Pavarotti's. Needless to say, the hero's big emotional climaxes in each of the first three acts come over at full force. The rest of the cast is strong too, with Dwayne Croft a magnificent Lescaut. Many collectors will count this a clear first choice among current versions.

Manon Lescaut   H
Maria Callas sop Manon Lescaut **Giuseppe di Stefano** ten Des Grieux **Giulio Fioraventi** bar Lescaut **Franco Calabrese** bass Geronte **Dino Formachini** ten Edmondo **Fiorenza Cossotto** mez Singer **Chorus and Orchestra of La Scala, Milan / Tullio Serafin**
Naxos Ⓢ ② 8 112031/2 (135' · ADD) or
EMI ② 556301-2 (120' · ADD · T/t)
Recorded 1957   ⒻO**➡**

Manon Lescaut   H
Licia Albanese sop Manon Lescaut **Jussi Björling** ten Des Grieux **Robert Merrill** bar Lescaut **Franco Calabrese** bass Geronte **Mario Carlin** ten

Edmondo **Anna Maria Rota** *mez* Singer
Chorus and Orchestra of Rome Opera /
Jonel Perlea
RCA Red Seal mono ② 88697 57906-2 (119' · ADD)
Recorded 1954 ⓢ❶❶❷ⓑ

The sets reissued here were recorded in Italy in
the 1950s by top-line producers Walter Legge
(EMI) and Richard Mohr (RCA) when there had
only been three previous competitors regularly
in the catalogues. A flood of subsequent versions
followed but none have matched the charisma
provided here by the central pairs. For EMI, di
Stefano is at his most rhapsodic and sensual, rising to great heights of melodramatic agony on
the Act 3 quayside at Le Havre or the Act 4 desert. If you want all that a degree or two more
cultivated, more within the bar-lines but not a
whit less exciting, Björling is in excellent voice
on the rival set.

The Manons are similarly difficult to separate.
Simply put, Albanese gives a more conventional
frivolous girly portrait of Acts 1 and 2 (she'd
performed the role onstage, Callas hadn't) but
doesn't disappoint either in terms of tessitura or
emotion in the turn-to-the-tragic of the final
acts. Callas thinks herself well into what
becomes, to begin with, a more serious, calculating Manon – and a very accurate Manon, too.
Then, dying in the wilderness in Act 4, she produces a performance so harrowing that it should
surely claim a prime spot on any fantasy best-of-
Callas single disc.

Elsewhere, Perlea's conducting is more impassioned than Serafin's (compare the famous
Intermezzo) and Naxos's new transfer of the
EMI set (from LPs, of course, not the original
tapes) smooths out some of the spatial inconsistencies and 'boxiness' of earlier issues but is not
as present as EMI's last (1997) transfer. The
RCA wins overall, but that Callas last scene is
unmissable.

La rondine

La rondine.
Le Villi – Prelude; L'Abbandono; La Tregenda;
Ecco la casa…Torna ai felice dì. Morire!
Angela Gheorghiu *sop* Magda **Roberto Alagna** *ten*
Ruggero **Inva Mula-Tchako** *sop* Lisetta **William**
Matteuzzi *ten* Prunier **Alberto Rinaldi** *bar* Rambaldo
Patricia Biccire *sop* Yvette **Patrizia Ciofi** *sop* Bianca
Monica Bacelli *mez* Suzy **Riccardo Simonetti** *bar*
Périchaud **Toby Spence** *ten* Gobin **Enrico Fissore**
bar Crébillon **London Voices; LSO /**
Antonio Pappano *pf*
EMI ② 556338-2 (131' · DDD· T/t) ⓟ❶❶❶ⓑ

 It couldn't be more welcome when a
recording transforms a work, as this
one does, setting it on a new plane. *La
rondine* ('The Swallow'), Puccini's ill-timed
attempt to emulate Lehár in the world of operetta, was completed during the First World
War. It's long been counted his most serious
failure. Puccini's cunning has never been in

doubt either, for he and his librettists interweave
elements not just of *La traviata* but of *The Merry
Widow* and *Die Fledermaus*, not to mention earlier Puccini operas. His melodic style may be
simpler than before, but one striking theme follows another with a profusion that any other
composer might envy. What Pappano reveals
far more than before is the subtlety with which
Puccini interweaves his themes and motifs, with
conversational passages made spontaneous-
sounding in their flexibility. Above all, Pappano
brings out the poetry, drawing on emotions far
deeper than are suggested by this operetta-like
subject, thanks also to Gheorghiu's superb performance, translating her mastery as Violetta to
this comparable character. Magda's first big
solo, 'Chi il bel sogno di Doretta', finds Gheorghiu at her most ravishing, tenderly expressive
in her soaring phrases, opening out only at the
final climax. From first to last, often with a throb
in the voice, her vocal acting convinces you that
Magda's are genuine, deep emotions, painful at
the end, intensified by the ravishing beauty of
her voice.

As Ruggero, Alagna has a far less complex role,
winningly characterising the ardent young student. What will specially delight Puccinians in
this set is that he's given an entrance aria about
Paris, 'Parigi è una città', which transforms his
otherwise minimal contribution to Act 1. The
partnership of Gheorghiu and Alagna highlights
the way that Puccini in the melodic lines for
each of his central characters makes Ruggero's
more forthright, Magda's more complex. Among
much else, the role of the poet, Prunier, is transformed by the clear-toned William Matteuzzi in
what's normally a *comprimario* role. Not only is
his relationship with Magda beautifully drawn,
his improbable affair with the skittish maid,
Lisetta, is made totally convincing too, mirroring Magda's affair. For the fill-ups, the excerpts
from *Le Villi*, warm and dramatic, make one
wish that Pappano could go on to record that
first of Puccini's operas, with Alagna giving a
ringing account of Roberto's aria, as he does of
the song, 'Morire!' – with Pappano at the piano.
Originally an album-piece written for a wartime
charity, Puccini used it, transposed up a semitone, with different words, as the entrance aria
for Ruggero. Altogether a set to treasure.

Tosca

Tosca
Maria Callas *sop* Tosca **Giuseppe di Stefano** *ten* Ⓗ
Cavaradossi **Tito Gobbi** *bar* Scarpia **Franco**
Calabrese *bass* Angelotti **Melchiorre Luise** *bass*
Sacristan **Angelo Mercuriali** *ten* Spoletta **Alvaro**
Cordova *treb* Shepherd Boy **Dario Caselli** *bass*
Sciarrone **Dario Caselli** *bass* Gaoler
Chorus and Orchestra of La Scala, Milan /
Victor de Sabata
EMI 562890-2 (108' · ADD · N/T/t) Ⓜ❶❶❶ⓑ
EMI 585644-2 (108' · ADD · N/S) Ⓑ❶❶❶ⓑ
Naxos 8 110256-2 (108' · ADD · N/S) ⓢ❶❶❶ⓑ
Regis RRC2065 (108' · ADD · N/S) ⓢ❶❶❶

PUCCINI TOSCA – IN BRIEF

Angela Gheorghiu *Tosca* **Roberto Alagna**
Cavaradossi **Ruggero Raimondi** *Scarpia*
**Tiffin Children's Choir, Chorus and Orchestra of
the Royal Opera House / Antonio Pappano**
EMI ② 557173-2 (114' · ADD) Ⓕ🔵▷
An excellent modern recording, distinguished
by Gheorghiu's passionate, nervy Tosca
and Pappano's dramatic conducting, with
Alagna's lyrical Cavaradossi and Ruggero
Raimondi's veteran Scarpia.

Monserrat Caballé *Tosca* **José Carreras**
Cavaradossi **Ingvar Wixell** *Scarpia*
**Chorus and Orchestra of the Royal Opera
House / Sir Colin Davis**
Philips ② 438 359-2PM2 (118' · DDD) Ⓜ
Richly theatrical conducting by Davis, with
Montserrat Caballé a compelling heroine
and José Carreras at his ardent best, although
Ingvar Wixell is an uncompelling Scarpia.

Leontyne Price *Tosca* **Giuseppe di Stefano**
Cavaradossi **Giuseppe Taddei** *Scarpia*
**Vienna State Opera Chorus, Vienna PO /
Herbert von Karajan**
Decca ② 466 384-2DM2 (114' · DDD) Ⓜ🔵🔵▷
Much finer than Karajan's later recording.
Leontyne Price and Giuseppe di Stefano
are wonderfully rich-voiced and passionate,
Taddei a hellishly charismatic Scarpia, with
Karajan balancing detail and drama superbly.

Maria Callas *Tosca* **Giuseppe di Stefano** Ⓗ
Cavaradossi **Tito Gobbi** *Scarpia* **Chorus and
Orchestra of La Scala, Milan / Victor de Sabata**
EMI ② 562890-2 (110' · AAD) Ⓜ🔵🔵🔵▷
EMI ② 585644 2 (110' · AAD) Ⓑ🔵🔵🔵
Naxos ② 8 110256/57 (110' · AAD) Ⓢ🔵🔵🔵
This could still be called a definitive *Tosca*,
with Callas, di Stefano and Gobbi striking
sparks off the score and each other, sup-
ported by de Sabata's masterly conducting
and a still impressive recording.

(In English) **Jane Eaglen** *Tosca* **Dennis O'Neill**
Cavaradossi **Gregory Yurisitch** *Scarpia* **Geoffrey
Mitchell Choir, Philharmonia Orchestra /
David Parry**
Chandos ② CHAN3000 (118' · DDD) Ⓕ🔵
Exceptionally competitive English-language
recording, with idiomatic performances from
Jane Eaglen, Dennis O'Neill and Gregory
Yurisitch, ripely conducted by David Parry.

Maria Callas *Tosca* **Renato Cioni** *Cavaradossi*
Tito Gobbi *Scarpia* **Chorus and Orchestra of the
Royal Opera House / Carlo Felice Cillario**
EMI ② 562675-2 (109' · AAD) Ⓜ
A historic 1964 live broadcast from Covent
Garden, with Callas and Gobbi splendidly
fierce antagonists, Renato Cioni a fine Cavara-
dossi and well conducted by Cillario, although
the mono sound is clear but rather lean.

 In this remastering of one of the classic
performances of the gramophone, one
of Walter Legge's masterpieces as a
creative recording producer, you barely miss
stereo recording. With offstage effects for example – so important in Puccini – precisely placed,
there is a sense of presence normally reserved for
twin-channel reproduction. In the long duet
between Tosca and Cavaradossi in Act 3 you can
even detect a difference of placing between the
two singers, Callas set at a slight distance, though
whether or not to offset a microphone problem
with so biting a voice one can only guess. The
immediacy is astonishing, and the great moment
of the execution with trombones rasping and the
fusillade reproduced at a true *fortissimo* has never
been represented on record with greater impact.
The contrasts of timbre are beautifully brought
out – amazingly wide with Gobbi as with Callas
and with di Stefano producing his most honeyed
tones. Though there is less space in the Milan
acoustic than we have grown used to in the age of
stereo, the separation of voices and orchestra is
excellent, with the strands of the accompaniment
to 'Vissi d'arte', for example, finely clarified. Only
in the big *Te Deum* scene at the end of Act 1 is
there a hint of overloading.

Wonderful as Gobbi's and di Stefano's performances are, and superbly dramatic as de Sabata's
conducting is, it is the performance of the unique
Callas in the title-role that provides the greatest
marvel, and here more than ever one registers the
facial changes implied in each phrase, with occasional hints of a chuckle (usually ironic) more
apparent than on LP. A truly Great Recording of
the last Century which is available in numerous
guises. Naxos's transfer is particularly impressive,
but if you want top-class supporting material, the
mid-price EMI is the one to go for.

Tosca
Angela Gheorghiu *sop* Tosca **Roberto Alagna** *ten*
Cavaradossi **Ruggero Raimondi** *bar* Scarpia
Maurizio Muraro *bass* Angelotti **Enrico Fissore** *bass*
Sacristan **David Cangelosi** *ten* Spoletta **Sorin
Coliban** *bass* Sciarrone **Gwynne Howell** *bass* Gaoler
James Savage-Hanford *treb* Shepherd Boy **Tiffin
Children's Choir; Royal Opera House Chorus and
Orchestra / Antonio Pappano**
EMI ② 557173-2 (114' · DDD) Ⓕ🔵▷

Antonio Pappano's conducting alone would make
this a *Tosca* of distinction, whether in big matters
(the voicing of those snarling opening chords) or
tiny ones: the carefully measured pause after
Tosca asks Cavaradossi whether he's happy at the
prospect of stealing away to their villa: he's preoccupied and hasn't really been listening. The
orchestral sound is splendidly full whenever it
needs to be, but never at the expense of fine detail,
and Pappano's pacing is admirable: the Act 2 dialogue between Tosca and Scarpia, for example,
inexorably builds in tension instead of being feverish from the outset, as is too often the case.

Gheorghiu's Tosca responds to this. She's
impetuous, nervously intense, but capable also

of a lovely, quiet purity). She's a very complete Tosca, indeed, and intelligently capable of bringing her own perceptions to the role. After the killing of Scarpia, her 'And before him all Rome trembled!' is neither triumphant nor melodramatic but wondering and fearful: she's aghast at what she has done and already suspects that this isn't the end of the matter. Her 'Vissi d'arte' is most beautiful, her intimacy in the first scene with Cavaradossi tender and touching.

In that passage Alagna responds to her delicacy, and in Act 3 he receives her acting lesson with a touch of humour. Elsewhere he's in fine, mostly full voice, nowhere near as subtle as Gheorghiu. His tone hardens under pressure once or twice, and his *mezza voce* can sound thin, but he's never short of vocal glamour: a creditable but not especially interesting Cavaradossi.

Raimondi's Scarpia, on the other hand, is very interesting. The quieter shades of his voice now need careful management (and besides, it's darker and softer-grained than a true dramatic baritone), but although he may initially seem to lack authority his reading is full of finesse.

A very fine *Tosca*, in short, not quite in the same league as the celebrated Callas/di Stefano/Gobbi/de Sabata (see above), but giving all the others an exciting run for their money. The recording is all that could be wished.

Tosca
Montserrat Caballé sop Tosca **José Carreras** ten Cavaradossi **Ingvar Wixell** bar Scarpia **Samuel Ramey** bass Angelotti **Piero De Palma** ten Spoletta **Domenico Trimarchi** bar Sacristan **William Elvin** bar Sciarrone, Gaoler **Ann Murray** mez Shepherd Boy **Chorus and Orchestra of the Royal Opera House, Covent Garden / Sir Colin Davis**
Philips Duo ② 438 359-2PM2 (118' · ADD · S)
Recorded 1976   Ⓜ

Caballé's Tosca is one of the most ravishingly on record, with scarcely a less than beautiful note throughout, save where an occasional phrase lies a touch low for her. She doesn't quite have the 'prima donna' (in quotes, mind) temperament for the part (the coquettish malice of 'but make her eyes black!', as Tosca forgives Cavaradossi for using a blonde stranger as model for his altarpiece of the Magdalen, isn't in Caballé's armoury; either that or she knows that her voice would sound arch attempting it), but her portrayal is much more than a display of lovely sounds. She's precise with words, takes minute care over phrasing, and she knows to a split second where dead-centre precise pitching becomes crucial. Carreras's Cavaradossi is one of his best recorded performances: the voice untarnished, the line ample, and if he's tempted at times to over-sing one forgives the fault for the sake of his poetic ardour. Wixell is the fly in the ointment: a capable actor and an intelligent artist, but his gritty timbre lacks centre and thus the necessary dangerous suavity.

Davis's direction is flexible but dramatic and finely detailed, and the secondary singers are all

very good. The recording, despite some rather unconvincing sound effects, still sounds very well, with space around the voices and a natural balance between them and the orchestra. It's pity Philips should have saved space by omitting the libretto.

Tosca
Leontyne Price sop Tosca **Giuseppe di Stefano** ten Cavaradossi **Giuseppe Taddei** bar Scarpia **Carlo Cava** bass Angelotti **Piero De Palma** ten Spoletta **Fernando Corena** bass Sacristan **Leonardo Monreale** bass Sciarrone **Alfredo Mariotti** bass Gaoler **Herbert Weiss** treb Shepherd Boy **Vienna State Opera Chorus; Vienna Philharmonic Orchestra / Herbert von Karajan**
Decca Legends ② 475 7522DOR2 (114' · ADD · T/t)
Recorded 1962   Ⓜ**OO**

Karajan's classic version of *Tosca* was originally issued on the RCA label, but produced by John Culshaw of Decca at a vintage period. The first surprise is to find the sound satisfying in almost every way, with a firm sense of presence and with each voice and each section of the orchestra cleanly focused within the stereo spectrum. Less surprising is the superiority of this version as an interpretation. Karajan was always a master Puccinian, and this set was a prime example. A typical instance comes at the end of Act 1, where Scarpia's *Te Deum* is taken daringly slowly, and conveys a quiver of menace that no other version begins to match. An extra nicety is the way that in the instrumental introduction to Cavaradossi's first aria, 'Recondita armonia', he treats it as the musical equivalent of a painter mixing his colours, the very point Puccini no doubt had in mind. Karajan, though individual, and regularly challenging his singers, is most solicitous in following the voices. It's fascinating to note what expressive freedom he allows his tenor, Giuseppe di Stefano, and he makes Leontyne Price relax, giving a superb assumption of the role, big and rich of tone; the voice is the more beautiful for not being recorded too closely.

Tosca
Catherine Malfitano sop Tosca **Richard Margison** ten Cavaradossi **Bryn Terfel** bar Scarpia **Mario Luperi** bass Angelotti **John Graham-Hall** ten Spoletta **Enrico Fissore** bass Sacristan **Jef van Wersch** bass Sciarrone **Ton Kemperman** bass Gaoler **Andreas Burkhart** treb Shepherd Boy **Royal Concertgebouw Orchestra, Amsterdam / Riccardo Chailly**
Stage director **Nikolaus Lehnhoff**
Video director **Misjel Vermeiren**
Decca 📀 074 3201DH
(137' · NTSC · 16:9 · PCM stereo and DTS 5.1 · 0)
Recorded live at Het Muziektheater, Amsterdam
Includes bonus documentary, 'Tosca – Behind the Scenes'   Ⓕ

This is a 'strong' *Tosca*, using the adjective in the sense in which it is sometimes applied to language (meaning 'thoroughly disgusting'). But then, you might say, that's *Tosca* being true to itself: it tells of a thoroughly disgusting state of affairs, when a man can be arrested by party thugs, taken off to headquarters for torture and summary execution, and a woman is at the mercy of a dictator's lust. Its official description is 'a melodrama in three acts', and a melodrama this is, with jeering villain, manly hero and distraught heroine. And as though to drive the point home, Tosca acts and is costumed and made up to look like an old-time star of the silent screen. To that extent we know it's make-believe. There are also scenery and props to persuade us to take it for real. And the sets are heavy with symbols suggesting 'significance'. But yes, it's 'strong': a good *Tosca*, one might have to concede.

Certainly it has a good, no, a magnificent Scarpia. Terfel is in fine voice, and his acting and singing are as one. In both, his style is forceful without exaggeration or over-emphasis. Richard Margison is a likeable Cavaradossi, his well placed tenor reliably meeting the challenges of the role, and he himself, never a conventionally romantic figure, gaining sympathy notwithstanding. And Malfitano, a Tosca without any special vocal allure, exercises her personality and compels attention. A gaunt, sonorous Angelotti, a Sacristan who huffs and puffs effectively, and a Spoletta even nastier than his master, help to fill in the background. The Concertgebouw, subordinated in balance to the singers, play well under Riccardo Chailly's enlightened direction.

Tosca
Maria Guleghina *sop* Tosca **Salvatore Licitra** *ten* Cavaradossi **Leo Nucci** *bar* Scarpia **Giovanni Battista Parodi** *bass* Angelotti **Ernesto Gavazzi** *ten* Spoletta **Alfredo Mariotti** *bass* Sacristan **Silvestro Sammaritano** *bass* Sciarrone **Ernesto Panariello** *bass* Gaoler **Virginia Barchi** *treb* Shepherd Boy **Chorus and Orchestra of La Scala, Milan / Riccardo Muti**
Stage director **Luca Ronconi**
Video director **Pierre Cavasillas**
TDK Mediactive 🅓🅥🅓 DV-OPTOS (121' · 16:9 · 2.0, 5.1 & DTS 5.1 · 0 · N)   Ⓕ

In March 2000 Muti conducted a staged performance of *Tosca* for the first time, only the second Puccini opera he'd conducted at La Scala. As this live-recorded DVD powerfully reveals, he emerged as the hero of a great occasion. The high-voltage electricity is unflagging, with the drama timed to perfection, the whole magnetically compelling from first to last. It makes one regret that he's so rarely turned to Puccini. But as the music director at La Scala since 1986, he knows unerringly how to pace his singers, letting them phrase expansively where needed, yet holding the structure firmly together.

Maria Guleghina makes a formidable Tosca, very believable in her jealousy, using a rich

tonal range, with just a touch of vinegar at the top. She's at her finest in the great scene with Scarpia in Act 2, leading up to a radiant account of 'Vissi d'arte' and a chilling murder, even though the very ordinary dinner-knife she uses looks an unlikely weapon. The veteran Leo Nucci, tall, thin and mean, is most compelling as the police chief, at times a smiling villain, though the voice has its occasional roughness. As Cavaradossi, Salvatore Licitra may be an unromantic figure, and he's heavy-handed at the start in 'Recondita armonia', but he develops from there, and in Act 3 he sings superbly with fine shading of tone for 'E lucevan le stelle' and the duet with Tosca.

Luca Ronconi's production, well-directed for television by Pierre Cavasillas, consistently heightens the dramatic conflicts. The sets of Margherita Palli, as redesigned by Lorenza Cantini, bring a surreal contradiction between realism and fantasy, looking like conventional sets that have been hit by an earthquake, with uprights at all angles. Sections of scenery are retained from act to act, with an increasing pile of debris left behind. That makes the battlements of the Castel Sant'Angelo look like a bombsite, which Tosca has to climb before flinging herself to her death. The idea, presumably, is to reflect the distorted mind of Scarpia, though in this *verismo* opera pure realism might be said to work best of all.

Tosca
Renata Tebaldi *sop* Tosca **Eugene Tobin** *ten* Cavaradossi **George London** *bar* Scarpia **Gustav Grefe** *bass* Angelotti **Hubert Buchta** *ten* Spoletta **Heinz Cramer** *bass* Sacristan **Siegfried Fischer-Sandt** *bass* Sciarrone **Wilhelm Baur** *bass* Gaoler **Claudia Hellmann** *treb* Shepherd Boy **Stuttgart State Opera Chorus and Orchestra / Franco Patanè** *Stage and Film directors* Uncredited
Video Artists International 🅓🅥🅓 VAIDVD4217 (126' · 4:3 Black & White · 1.0 · 0)
Recorded live at the Stuttgart Staatsoper, 1961   Ⓕ

Coming to this historic video recording after Muti's La Scala version is to register a quite different operatic world. Recorded in black and white at a performance in the Stuttgart Staatsoper in June 1961, it offers a sound, conventional production with in-period costumes and realistic if symmetrical sets by Max Fritzsche. The film direction too is highly conventional.

This DVD is specially valuable for Renata Tebaldi's assumption of the title-role. So dominant in our memories has Maria Callas's characterisation become, that we tend to forget that the role of Tosca was just as central in the repertory of her great rival of the time, Tebaldi, whose firm, creamy tones, perfectly controlled, could hardly be more sharply contrasted with the thrillingly individual, if at times flawed, singing of Callas. Tebaldi seemed to represent the essence of the prima donna, grand in a traditional way, and who better to play the role of Tosca?

There's ample evidence here of that commanding security in the role, with Tebaldi in 1961 still at her peak. Yet as recorded in limited mono sound, with voices well forward of the orchestra, at times there's an untypical edge on the creamy tone at the top. True to form, Tebaldi rises magnificently to the challenge of 'Vissi d'arte' in Act 2, with fine shading of tone and flawless *legato* in that moment of repose. That said, one has to note that in her acting this Tosca isn't so much passionate as stately.

Eugene Tobin as Cavaradossi, like many tenors, starts lustily, and then gets more expressive as he goes along, never betraying signs of strain. George London makes a handsome Scarpia, imperious and vehement both in his acting and in his singing. Yet as so often in recordings, his pitching is often vague. Franco Patanè as conductor is at times over-emphatic, again presenting a conventional view, and rarely conveying the sort of magnetism that makes the Muti performance so gripping.

Worth buying to hear Tebaldi in her prime.

Tosca
Magda Olivero sop Tosca **Alvinio Misciano** ten Cavaradossi **Giulio Fioravanti** bar Scarpia **Giovanni Foiani** bass Angelotti **RAI Chorus and Orchestra, Turin / Fulvio Vernizzi**
Stage director **Mario Lanfranchini**
With documentary, 'A tu per tu con Magda Olivero, artista e donna', including arias by Alfano, Cilea, Franck, Gounod, Handel, Mascagni, Puccini and Verdi
Hardy Classic Video DVD HCD4011
(3h 28' · NTSC · 4:3 · 1.0 · 0)   Ⓕ

The production of *Tosca* dates from 1960. Ah, those naïve times when people believed it was set in Scarpia's Rome (not in Mussolini's, for example). The date is 1800 and the Battle of Marengo is news. And the scenery is for real. You could nose your way around Sant'Andrea della Valle, and feel quite at home in the Palazzo Farnese.

As for the prima donna, Magda Olivero (born 1910, debut 1932) has thought out every move, every expression, creating the conviction of living the whole role afresh here and now. She also sings with distinction. Try her in phrases like 'le voce delle cose' for delicacy and the great two-octave lunge of 'Io quella lama piantai nel cor' for power. Her Scarpia isn't so very far inferior to Gobbi: suave and brutal by turns, with fine resonance. Cavaradossi is likeable, both vocally and dramatically; Angelotti, for his brief operatic life, is outstanding.

The documentary of 2003 puts 1960 in perspective. It includes glimpses of Olivero singing in Milan the previous year, marking the 25th anniversary of Callas's death. It's a weirdly ethereal sound, sometimes very flat, but flat in a beautiful way. She sings *Panis angelicus*, and at a late stage is joined by her tenor pupil Danilo Formaggio. In interviews Olivero tells of the tenors in her career, from Schipa to Domingo,

including a long story about appeasing Gigli. But the best things are three excerpts filmed in 1965: a delicately acted scene from *Iris*, authentic voice and style for Alfano's *Risurrezione*, and the great solo from Act 1 of *La traviata*. The last is astonishing in every way: the 'Ah, fors' è lui' muses privately; the 'Follies' are sudden, impetuous; the 'vortici' brilliant with nervous energy; top Cs that swell and diminish as you thought they did only in text-books; and a top E flat which you hadn't thought would be in her voice at all. And this is a youngster of 55.

It's a pity we don't get a taste of her pre-war recordings: that would have deepened the perspective. Seeing her at 92 leaves us with admiration and wonder for this extraordinary woman and her unquenchable devotion to her art.

Il trittico

Il tabarro
Carlo Guelfi bar Michele **Maria Guleghina** sop Giorgetta **Neil Shicoff** ten Luigi **Riccardo Cassinelli** ten Tinca **Enrico Fissore** bass Talpa **Elena Zilio** mez Frugola **Barry Banks** ten Ballad-seller **Angela Gheorghiu** sop Lover **Roberto Alagna** ten Lover **London Voices; London Symphony Orchestra / Antonio Pappano**

Suor Angelica
Cristina Gallardo-Domâs sop Suor Angelica **Bernadette Manca di Nissa** contr Princess **Felicity Palmer** mez Abbess **Elena Zilio** mez Monitoress **Sara Fulgoni** mez Mistress of the Novices **Dorothea Röschmann** sop Sister Genovieffa **Judith Rees** sop Sister Osmina **Rachele Stanisci** sop Sister Dolcina **Francesca Pedaci** sop Nursing Sister **Anna Maria Panzarella** sop First Almoner Sister, First Lay Sister **Susan Mackenzie-Park** sop Second Almoner Sister **Deborah Miles-Johnson** contr Second Lay Sister **Rosalind Waters** sop Novice **London Voices; Tiffin Boys' School Choir; Philharmonia Orchestra / Antonio Pappano**

Gianni Schicchi
José van Dam bass-bar Gianni Schicchi **Angela Gheorghiu** sop Lauretta **Roberto Alagna** ten Rinuccio **Felicity Palmer** mez Zita **Paolo Barbacini** ten Gherardo **Patrizia Ciofi** sop Nella **James Savage-Hanford** treb Gherardino **Carlos Chausson** bass Betto di Signa **Luigi Roni** bass Simone **Roberto Scaltriti** bar Marco **Elena Zilio** mez La Ciesca **Enrico Fissore** bass Spinelloccio **Simon Preece** bar Pinellino **Noel Mann** bass Guccio

London Symphony Orchestra / Antonio Pappano
EMI ③ 556587-2 (162' · DDD · T/t)   ⒻⒹ▸

No previous recordings bring such warmth or beauty or so powerful a drawing of the contrasts between each of the three one-acters in Puccini's triptych as these. It's Pappano above all, with his gift for pacing Puccini subtly, who draws the set together. In each opera he heightens emotions fearlessly to produce unerringly at key moments the authentic gulp-in-throat, whether for the cuckolded bargemaster, Michele, for Sister Angelica in her agonised suicide and heavenly absolution, or for the resolution of young love at the end of *Gianni Schicchi*. It will disappoint some that the starry couple of Angela Gheorghiu and Roberto Alagna don't take centre stage, but quite apart from their radiant singing as Lauretta and Rinuccio in *Gianni Schicchi* – not least in that happy ending, most tenderly done – they make a tiny cameo appearance in *Il tabarro* as the off-stage departing lovers, a heady 45 seconds. It's the sort of luxury touch that Walter Legge would have relished. No doubt Gheorghiu would have been just as persuasive as Giorgetta in *Il tabarro* and as Sister Angelica, but having different sopranos in each opera sharpens the contrasts. Maria Guleghina makes a warm, vibrant Giorgetta, and the touch of acid at the top of the voice adds character, pointing to the frustration of the bargemaster's wife.

Even more remarkable is the singing of the young Chilean soprano Cristina Gallardo-Domàs as Sister Angelica. Hers is a younger, more vulnerable Angelica than usual. Her vocal subtlety and commanding technique go with a fully mature portrayal of the nun's agony, her defiance of the implacable Princess as well as her grief over her dead son. As with Gheorghiu, the dynamic shading brings *pianissimos* of breathtaking delicacy. The Princess is powerfully sung by Bernadette Manca di Nissa, her tone firm and even throughout. Felicity Palmer, with her tangy mezzo tone, is well contrasted as the Abbess, and she's just as characterful as the crabby Zita in *Gianni Schicchi*. The casting in *Suor Angelica* is as near flawless as could be, with Elena Zilio and Dorothea Röschmann outstanding in smaller roles. Zilio is the only singer who appears in all three operas, just as effective as Frugola in *Il tabarro*, though there her full, clear voice isn't always distinguishable from Guleghina as Giorgetta. Among the men Carlo Guelfi makes a superb Michele, incisive, dark and virile. He brings out not just the anger but the poignancy of the bargemaster's emotions, as in the duet with Giorgetta, when they lament what might have been. Neil Shicoff makes a fine Luigi, the nerviness in his tenor tone aptly bringing out a hysterical quality in the character. The male *comprimarios* are vocally more variable, if always characterful, as they are too in *Gianni Schicchi*. As Schicchi himself José van Dam's voice perfectly conveys the sardonic side of the character, and the top Gs he has to negotiate are wonderfully strong and steady. Maybe the full voice he uses for the name 'Gianni Schicchi', when in impersonation of old Buoso he's dictating the new will, makes too obvious a contrast with the quavering old man imitation, but it's what Puccini asked for.

Also worthy of praise is the sumptuous and atmospheric sound. Off-stage effects are magical, and always thanks to Pappano and fine playing from both the LSO and Philharmonia, the beauty and originality of the carefully textured instrumentation can be appreciated with

new vividness. This is a set to renew your appreciation of operas that represent Puccini still at his peak.

Il trittico
Il tabarro
Piero Cappuccilli *bar* Michele **Sylvia Sass** *sop* Giorgetta **Nicola Martinucci** *ten* Luigi **Sergio Bertocchi** *ten* Tinca **Aldo Bramante** *bass* Talpa **Eleonora Jankovic** *mez* Frugola **Ernesto Gavazzi** *ten* Ballad-seller **Anna Baldasserini** *sngr* Lover I **Bruno Brando** *sngr* Lover II

Suor Angelica
Rosalind Plowright *sop* Suor Angelica **Dunja Vejzovic** *contr* Princess **Maria Garcia Allegri** *mez* Abbess **Nella Verri** *mez* Mistress of the Novices **Giovanna Santelli** *sop* Sister Genovieffa **Maria Dalla Spezia** *sop* Sister Osmina **Midela d'Amico** *sop* Sister Dolcina

Gianni Schicchi
Juan Pons *bar* Gianni Schicchi **Cecilia Gasdia** *sop* Lauretta **Yuri Marusin** *ten* Rinuccio **Eleonora Jankovic** *contr* Zita **Ferrero Poggi** *ten* Gherardo **Anna Baldasserini** *sop* Nella **Alessandra Cesareo** *contr* Gherardino **Franco Boscolo** *bass* Betto di Signa **Mario Luperi** *bass* Simone **Giorgio Taddeo** *bar* Marco **Nella Verri** *mez* La Ciesca **Claudio Giombi** *bass* Spinelloccio **Virgilio Carbonari** *bar* Notary **Pio Bonfanti** *bass* Pinellino **Ruggero Altavilla** *bass* Guccio
Orchestra and Chorus of La Scala, Milan / Gianandrea Gavazzeni
Stage director **Sylvano Bussotti**
Video director **Brian Large**
Warner Music Vison/NVC Arts 🄳🅅🄳 5050467-0943-2-1
(161' · NTSC · 4:3· PCM stereo · 2-6)
Recorded at La Scala, Milan, 1983   Ⓕ

This Warner DVD offers idiomatic performances from La Scala of Puccini's trilogy. The productions are broadly traditional, with an ultra-realistic set for the grand guignol of *Il tabarro* and rather more stylised settings for *Suor Angelica* and *Gianni Schicchi*.

Casting is strong in *Il tabarro*, with Piero Cappuccilli in his prime as Michele, the cuckolded bargemaster. His appeal to Giorgetta, his estranged wife, is so passionate and tender that his climactic solo has your total sympathy. Sylvia Sass as Giorgetta tends to overact; the steely edge in her voice helps keep your sympathies with Michele. As Luigi, Nicola Martinucci is powerful and unstrained. Outstanding among the others is Eleonora Jankovic as La Frugola, firm of voice and characterful without overacting. The staging of the murder and Michele's revealing of the body under his cloak, always tricky to bring off, is neatly managed.

The stylised set for *Suor Angelica* is unobjectionable. What dominates, as it should, is Rosalind Plowright's moving performance of the title role. Next to her, Dunja Vejzovic is disappointing, not so much vocally as in appearance and personality; she seems too young and lightweight; hardly the unforgiving Princess. The nuns are nicely touched in, and the chorus is impressive. Brian Large's direction sidesteps the final and sentimental vision of Angelica's dead child.

Gianni Schicchi is placed in an enormous apartment with a panoramic view over Florence. The claustrophobia that can add point to the comic story is entirely absent, but the set is undistracting. Eleonora Jankovic again stands out among the incidental characters as the old woman, Zita, and Yuri Marusin as Rinuccio copes well with his big aria. Lauretta, his lover, is strongly cast, with Cecilia Gasdia luxuriantly drawing out 'O mio babbino caro' in finely shaded phrases, to the delight of the Scala audience. Juan Pons is a firm and commanding Schicchi, taking centre stage from his first entry.

Turandot

Turandot·
Dame Joan Sutherland *sop* Princess Turandot
Luciano Pavarotti *ten* Calaf **Montserrat Caballé** *sop*
Liù **Tom Krause** *bar* Ping **Pier Francesco Poli** *ten*
Pang, Prince of Persia **Piero De Palma** *ten* Pong
Nicolai Ghiaurov *bass* Timur **Sir Peter Pears** *ten*
Emperor Altoum **Sabin Markov** *bar* Mandarin
Wandsworth School Boys' Choir;
John Alldis Choir; London Philharmonic
Orchestra / Zubin Mehta
Decca ② 414 274-2DH2 (117' · ADD · T/t)
Recorded 1972   Ⓕ❶❶➾

Turandot is a psychologically complex work fusing appalling sadism with self-sacrificing devotion. The icy Princess of China has agreed to marry any man of royal blood who can solve three riddles she has posed. If he fails his head will roll. Calaf, the son of the exiled Tartar king Timur, answers all the questions easily and when Turandot hesitates to accept him, magnanimously offers her a riddle in return – 'What is his name?'. Liù, Calaf's faithful slave-girl, is tortured but rather than reveal his identity kills herself. Turandot finally capitulates, announcing that his name is Love. Dame Joan Sutherland's assumption of the title-role is statuesque, combining regal poise with a more human warmth, while Montserrat Caballé is a touchingly sympathetic Liù, skilfully steering the character away from any hint of the mawkish. Pavarotti's Calaf is a heroic figure in splendid voice and the chorus is handled with great power, baying for blood at one minute, enraptured with Liù's nobility at the next. Mehta conducts with great passion and a natural feel for Puccini's wonderfully tempestuous drama. Well recorded.

Turandot   Ⓗ
Maria Callas *sop* Princess Turandot **Eugenio**
Fernandi *ten* Calaf **Dame Elisabeth Schwarzkopf**
sop Liù **Mario Borriello** *bar* Ping **Renato Ercolani**
ten Pang **Piero De Palma** *ten* Pong **Nicola Zaccaria**
bass Timur **Giuseppe Nessi** *ten* Emperor Altoum
Giulio Mauri *bass* Mandarin **Chorus and Orchestra**
of La Scala, Milan / Tullio Serafin

PUCCINI TURANDOT – IN BRIEF

Joan Sutherland Turandot **Luciano Pavarotti**
Calaf **Montserrat Caballé** Liù John Alldis Choir;
London PO / Zubin Mehta
Decca ② 414 274-2DH2 (117' · ADD)   Ⓕ❶❶➾
Slightly unexpected casting pays dividends in this exciting set, with Mehta luxuriating in the exotic textures, and all three principals bringing out the sheer beauty of the vocal writing.

Maria Callas Turandot **Eugenio Fernandi**   Ⓗ
Calaf **Elisabeth Schwarzkopf** Liù Chorus and
Orchestra of La Scala, Milan / Tullio Serafin
EMI ② 556307-2 (118' · AAD)   Ⓜ❶❶➾
In this mono recording Callas is a less powerful ice-princess than many, but more compelling, despite an unexciting Calaf. With Serafin's vigorous support she and Schwarzkopf infuse the performance with memorable feeling.

Katia Ricciarelli Turandot **Plácido**
Domingo Calaf **Barbara Hendricks** Liù
Vienna State Opera Chorus, Vienna PO /
Herbert von Karajan
DG ② 423 855-2GH2 (132' · DDD)   Ⓕ
Flawed by the casting of Katia Ricciarelli, game but overparted, this is still a very exciting set, with Plácido Domingo's thrilling Calaf, Barbara Hendricks's appealing Liù, and Karajan's monumentally lustrous reading.

Birgit Nilsson Turandot **Jussi Björling** Calaf
Renata Tebaldi Liù Rome Opera Chorus and
Orchestra / Erich Leinsdorf
RCA ② RD85932 (115' · ADD)   Ⓕ
With Molinari-Pradelli's more likeable version unavailable, this is the only way to enjoy Birgit Nilsson's spectacular Turandot, here alongside Jussi Björling's ardent Calaf, with Renata Tebaldi's creamy Liù and a good supporting cast.

Eva Marton Turandot **Michael Sylvester** Calaf
Lucia Mazzaria Liù San Francisco Opera Chorus
and Orchestra / Donald Runnicles
ArtHaus Musik 🆅🅳 100 089 (123')   Ⓕ
Marton is unsteady, Michael Sylvester a strong but unphotogenic Calaf, but with Runnicles's theatrical conducting and David Hockney's glowingly original sets, this is an enjoyable production, well worth considering.

Giovanna Casolla Turandot **Sergei Larin** Calaf
Barbara Frittoli Liù Maggio Musicale Chorus
and Orchestra, Florence / Zubin Mehta
RCA 🆅🅳 74321 60917-2   Ⓕ
The famous staging in Beijing's Forbidden City is robustly conducted by Mehta and well worth a look, even if Sergei Larin's Calaf and Barbara Frittoli's Liù outshine Gianna Casolla's serviceable Turandot.

EMI mono ② 556307-2 (118' · ADD · T/t)
Recorded 1957   Ⓜ❍❍▷

To have Callas, the most flashing-eyed of all sopranos as Turandot, is – on record at least – the most natural piece of casting. Other sopranos may be comparably icy in their command, but Callas with her totally distinctive tonal range was able to give the fullest possible characterisation. With her, Turandot was not just an implacable man-hater but a highly provocative female. One quickly reads something of Callas's own underlying vulnerability into such a portrait, its tensions, the element of brittleness. With her the character seems so much more believably complex than with others. It was sad that, except at the very beginning of her career, she felt unable to sing the role in the opera house, but this recording is far more valuable than any memory of the past, one of the most thrillingly magnetic of all her recorded performances, the more so when Schwarzkopf as Liù provides a comparably characterful and distinctive portrait, far more than a Puccinian 'little woman', sweet and wilting.

Next to such supreme singers it was perhaps cruel of Walter Legge to choose so relatively uncharacterful a tenor as Eugenio Fernandi as Calaf, but at least his timbre is pleasingly distinctive. What fully matches the positive character of the singing of Callas and Schwarzkopf is Serafin's conducting, which is sometimes surprisingly free, but in its pacing invariably captures colour, atmosphere and mood, as well as dramatic point. The Ping, Pang and Pong episode has rarely sparkled so naturally, the work of a conductor who has known and loved the music in the theatre over a long career.

The conducting is so vivid that the limitations of the mono sound hardly seem to matter. As the very opening will reveal, the CD transfer makes it satisfyingly full-bodied. Though with its rich, atmospheric stereo the Mehta set remains the best general recommendation, it's thrilling to have this historic document so vividly restored.

Turandot
Birgit Nilsson sop Turandot **Giuseppe di Stefano** ten Calaf **Leontyne Price** sop Liù **Nicola Zaccaria** bass Timur **Kostas Paskalis** bass-bar Ping **Ermanno Lorenzi** ten Pang **Murray Dickie** ten Pong **Peter Klein** ten Altoum **Alois Pernerstorfer** bass-bar Mandarin **Vienna State Opera Chorus and Orchestra / Francesco Molinari-Pradelli**
Orfeo d'Or mono ② C757 082I (113' · ADD)
Recorded live on June 22, 1961   Ⓕ❍

It's not so hard to think oneself present, especially when the recording is as vivid as this and the performance so compelling. It was a special night in Vienna. Karl Löbl wrote it up (and partly down) for his paper at the time, and now, contributing the notes for this issue, says of his generation that they didn't know how lucky they were. He is clearly convinced that, whatever the shortcomings then, they were great times compared with the pallid present.

And it's true we have no Birgit Nilsson now. She is in magnificent form here. Though she is singing much of the time from some way back on stage, the sound is still immensely powerful, and when she does come down front for the final duet we mentally take a step or two back. Much of the special interest, however, lies with the Calaf and the Liù. Di Stefano wins through by the conviction of all he sings: blazing, for instance, in the enigmas. Leontyne Price, too, brings unusual intensity to her role. Vibrant and warm in tone, she shades her phrases sensitively, disappointing only in that she does not resist the temptation to make an effect by investing the B flat of "Signore, ascolta" with a *crescendo*. The others – the aged Emperor, the deposed King and the three quaint Ministers – are strongly cast, and the chorus make a grand contribution. Molinari-Pradelli conducts with more character than in the famous studio set, and the recording picks out details of orchestration we may well have missed in other, technically better balanced, versions.

Additional recommendation

Turandot (sung in English)
Eaglen Turandot **O'Neill** Calaf **Plazas** Liù **Bayley** Timur **New London Children's Choir; Geoffrey Mitchell Choir; Philharmonia Orchestra / Parry**
Chandos Opera in English ② CHAN3086
(135' · DDD · T)   Ⓜ▷

The great glory of this set is Jane Eaglen's Turandot. There's no strain even in the most taxing passages, a firmness and a clarity that hasn't always marked her recordings. O'Neill gives a strong, heroic reading, but with the occasional moment of strain. Thoroughly recommended.

Le Villi

Le Villi
Sylvie David Narrator **Melanie Diener** sop Anna **Aquiles Machado** ten Roberto **Ludovic Tezier** bar Guglielmo **Radio France Chorus; French Radio Philharmonic Orchestra / Marco Guidarini**
Naïve V4958 (71' · ADD · N/T/t)   Ⓕ❍

Puccini's first two operas may have been written before he came to full maturity, but they do not deserve the neglect that they have suffered on disc. If the complications of *Edgar* detract from its impact, *Le Villi* might almost suffer from the opposite problem, when the story – very similar to that of Adam's ballet, *Giselle*, with the Willies (*Le Villi*) destroying the faithless lover, Roberto – is so severely telescoped. After Act 1, when Roberto leaves swearing loyalty to Anna, a narrator has to be introduced, to explain first that Roberto has been led astray and then that Anna has died of a broken heart. Where the CBS/Sony set had Tito Gobbi as narrator, the new one has Sylvie David, lighter and more conversational. The telescoping of the story also involves two striking interludes, The Abandonment and The Witches' Sabbath, a superb showpiece, which Pappano also recorded as fill-ups for his set of *La rondine*.

Marco Guidarini proves a convincing Puccinian, bringing out the dramatic bite of such passages as these, as well as moulding the big melodies affectionately. The Sony set had Lorin Maazel conducting, but he was not helped by the closeness of the Sony sound, which at times makes him sound too aggressive. Equally Renata Scotto is not flattered by the closeness, and though both she and Plácido Domingo as Roberto are more characterful than Melanie Diener and Aquiles Machado on the new disc, the refinement of sound helps to make the fresh, sensitive singing of the newcomers just as enjoyable. Equally Ludovic Tezier is clear and direct as Anna's father Guglielmo. Very welcome indeed.

Henry Purcell   British 1659-1695

Many regard Purcell as the greatest English composer of all time. That is arguable, but considering his importance in the history of British music, it's ironic that so little is known about his short life. (He died when he was only 36.) There's even some dispute as to who his father was – either Henry or his brother Thomas Purcell. We know that both were singers in the Chapel Royal and thus in the musical service of King Charles II.

Young Purcell's rise to fame was precocious: at 15 he was a mere 'organ tuner' (in other words, he pumped the bellows), at 18 he was composer to the King's private band, at 20 he was organist of Westminster Abbey. Thereafter he was one of the busiest men in England – and one of the best known for he composed music of such variety and for so many different occasions that wherever there was music there was also the name Purcell, everything from lewd drinking songs to ceremonial odes, from opera and incidental theatre music to chamber works, dances and anthems.

Five days after his death he was buried in Westminster Abbey. The music he had composed the previous year for Queen Mary's funeral was played at his own service. His epitaph reads: 'Here lies Henry Purcell Esquire, who left life and is gone to that blessed place where only his harmony can be exceeded'.

Complete Ayres for the Theatre

The History of Dioclesian, or The Prophetess, Z627[b]. King Arthur, Z628[b]. The Fairy Queen, Z629[b]. The Indian Queen, Z630[b]. The Married Beau, Z603[a]. The Old Bachelor, Z607[b]. Amphitryon, Z572[a]. The Double Dealer, Z592[a]. Distressed Innocence, Z577[a]. The Gordian Knot Unty'd, Z597[a]. Abdelazer, Z570[a]. Bonduca, Z574[a]. The Virtuous Wife, Z611[a]. Sonata While the Sun Rises in 'The Indian Queen'[b]. Overture in G minor[a]. Sir Anthony Love, Z588 – Overture[a]. Timon of Athens, Z632[a]. The Indian Queen, Z630 – Symphony[b]
[a]The Parley of Instruments; [b]The Parley of Instruments Baroque Orchestra / Roy Goodman

Helios ③ CDS44381/3 (209' · DDD)   ⑧▷

All these works were published within 18 months of Purcell's death. The 13 suites of choice movements from plays and semi-operas, entitled *A Collection of Ayres, compos'd for the Theatre, and upon other occasions*, may well have been the editing work of Purcell's brother, Daniel. Whoever it was had a rare combination of musical integrity and commercial flair: the pieces lifted from Purcell's interpolations to plays are often reordered and arranged with a deftness and charm which conveys the spirit of the theatre as well as heightening the loss and poignancy of Purcell's passing. How moving the Rondeau Minuet from *The Gordian Knot Unty'd* must have seemed to those who knew and loved Purcell.

As a major retrospective of Purcell's life in the theatre, the *Ayres for the Theatre* mainly comprise instrumental dances from their original sources, though there are several movements readapted from sung airs, such as 'Fairest isle' from *King Arthur* and 'If love's a sweet passion' from *The Fairy Queen*. The tunes are wonderful and varied, the inner part-writing skilful and the rhythmic imagination knows no bounds. Even so, this isn't music where more than a suite at a time can be recommended for ultimate satisfaction: stop while you still want more. And more you'll most certainly want with Roy Goodman's alert and distinctive direction. If a few of the movements sound a touch mundane and lack dynamism as one follows on from another, the positive side is that the performances are never forced and rarely mannered. For the semi-opera 'suites', Goodman employs a full orchestra. What The Parley of Instruments has in abundance is a cordiality of expression which seems so absolutely right, especially in the slower airs.

Fantasias

Fantasias – three part, Z732-34; four part, Z735-43; five part, 'upon one note', Z745. In nomines – G minor, Z746; G minor, 'Dorian', Z747
Joanna Levine, Susanna Pell, Catherine Finnis *viols*
Phantasm (Laurence Dreyfus, Wendy Gillespie, Jonathan Manson, Markku Luolajan-Mikkola *viols*)
Simax PSC1124 (51' · DDD)   Ⓕ❍❍❍

Purcell's contrapuntal mastery is dazzling, with the points of imitation in the various sections of each fantasia treated in double or triple counterpoint, inversion, augmentation and all other technical devices – for instance, the initial subjects of fantasias Z739, 742 and 743 at once appear in mirror images of themselves – but the music's deep expressiveness and the dramatic tension created by its chromaticisms and unpredictable harmonies make it clear that he certainly had performance in mind (a matter of some dispute), even if, because of the king's dislike of such intellectual pursuits, only privately by conservative-minded music-lovers. It's this expressiveness which Phantasm emphasises in this recording, both in their varied dynamics and in their use of vibrato. Speeds here are in general fast and there's great variety of bowing and hence of articulation.

Complete Fantasias
Fretwork (Wendy Gillespie, Asako Morikawa, Susanna Pell, Richard Boothby, Richard Campbell, Richard Tunnicliffe *viols*)
Harmonia Mundi HMU90 7502 (50' · DDD)
Ⓕ❶❷❸❹➤

Most of the finest viol consorts of our day recorded the Fantasias to celebrate Purcell's bicentenary in 1995. Fretwork were no exception but they've recorded the Fantasias again, with slightly different personnel (in the interim Asako Morikawa and Richard Tunnicliffe have joined the ensemble), and omitting Purcell's afterthought (the incomplete four-part Fantazia in A minor).

Time has passed and interpretations have evolved. Fretwork have grown in confidence and flair; they've listened, experimented and rethought their interpretations. In this new recording they bring a stronger sense of the linear progression of the music, helped by slightly quicker tempi. They are less introspective, more engaging: they have mellowed. If you already own the 1995 version, make room on your shelf for another. Purcell's remarkable Fantasias – out of sync with their time, never widely circulated or acknowledged in his day, yet works of true genius – are definitely worth revisiting.

Ten Sonatas in Four Parts

Ten Sonatas in Four Parts, Z802-11
Retrospect Trio (Matthew Truscott, Sophie Gent *vns* Jonathan Manson *bass viol*) with **Matthew Halls** *org*
Linn ⦿ CKD332 (73' · DDD/DSD)   Ⓕ

The newly founded Retrospect Ensemble has been created by members and trustees of the King's Consort who wish to continue under the artistic direction of Matthew Halls. Retrospect intends to apply historically informed principles and inquisitive musicianship to a wide variety of repertoire, from large-scale works to intimate trio sonatas. It is in the latter sphere that the rebranded group makes its debut on disc, with the first of a two-disc series exploring Purcell's sonatas in four parts.

Although not among Purcell's most familiar works, there have been some fine recordings of these sonatas. Retrospect's performances comfortably rank alongside the most stylish. Matthew Truscott and Sophie Gent take turns as first violinist in five of the sonatas each, and the quality of conversational playing between them is deeply eloquent. Halls and Jonathan Manson contribute polished and heartfelt continuo-playing. Slow music such as the central *Grave* movement in Sonata X is ideally melancholic,

and there is ripe emotional tension in the ascending chromaticism of the short *Adagio* that concludes Sonata V. The quicker music is played with impeccable technique and taste (such as the playful yet unforced *Canzona Allegro* in Sonata IX). Moreover, Linn producer Philip Hobbs has captured all of these musical virtues in a beautiful audiophile recording.

Keyboard works

Eight Keyboard Suites, Z660-69. Chaconne, ZT680. Ground, ZT681. A New Ground, ZT682. Ground in Gamut, Z645. Ground ZD221. Round O, ZT684. Ground, ZD222
Richard Egarr *hpd*
Harmonia Mundi HMU90 7428 (75' · DDD)   Ⓕ❶❷❸➤

While the eight posthumously published suites (with judiciously selected miscellany to create some elbow-room between each) are woefully unknown, they are beautifully crafted. Purcell's keyboard style rarely reverts to French luxuriance, rather more questing in its unpredictable steers, deliberately wrong-footed harmonic inflections, often quite tough textures and extended lyrical journeys.

Richard Egarr's devotion to these pieces comes in the form of studied spaciousness which allows these rich strains to become gently infused into our listening habits. This is no background *tafelmusik*, which is why it requires our indulgence, to stop and follow the thread – especially in the sustained narrative of the minor-key suites.

If the Almand of the G major Suite offers homage to the exquisite character-piece Almans of Gibbons, the A minor work is prescient of 18th-century models in its directed figuration and the grandiloquence of its easy conflation of French and Italian styles. Indeed, one of Egarr's greatest achievements is to challenge the homespun perception of this repertoire and present it as great keyboard music. The C major Suite is a wonderful demonstration of this, as is the gamey tuning of the D major work with its burly final hornpipe. The harpsichord by Joel Katzman (after Ruckers) covers all the bases with its disarming colour, clarity and resonance. An outstanding recital.

Anthems and Services

Complete Anthems and Services, Volume 7   Ⓟ
I was glad when they said unto me[b]. I was glad when they said unto me, Z19[a]. O consider my adversity, Z32[b]. Beati omnes qui timent Dominum, Z131. In the black dismal dungeon of despair, Z190. Save me, O God, Z51[b]. Morning and Evening Service in B flat, Z230 – Te Deum; Jubilate. Thy Way, O God, is Holy, Z60. Funeral Sentences for the death of Queen Mary II[b] – Drum Processional; March and Canzona in C minor, Z860; Man that is born of Woman, Z27; In the midst of Life, Z17[b]; Thou know'st Lord, Z58[b]; Thou know'st Lord, Z58[c]

Mark Kennedy, Eamonn O'Dwyer, James
Goodman *trebs* Susan Gritton *sop* James Bowman,
Nigel Short *countertens* Rogers Covey-Crump,
Charles Daniels, Mark Milhofer *tens* Michael
George, Robert Evans *basses* [a]New College Choir,
Oxford; [b]The King's Consort Choir; The King's
Consort / Robert King
Hyperion CDA66677 (70' · DDD · T/t) ⓕⒹ➤
Also available on Hyperion CDS44141/51 (11 discs) Ⓑ

This CD is made up predominantly of anthems,
devotional songs and a morning service (a functional, though not perfunctory, setting of the *Te
Deum* and *Jubilate*), most of which disclose the
range and quality of the composer's sacred oeuvre near its best. Of the two settings of *I was glad*,
the first was, until not long ago, thought to be
the work of John Blow. This full anthem more
than whets our appetite with its agreeable tonal
and melodic twists; when the *Gloria* arrives,
we're assured that this is vintage Purcell by the
sensitive pacing as much as an exquisite contrapuntal denouement. The earlier setting is more
poignant. Opening with a string symphony in
the spirit of a Locke consort, the music blossoms
into a deliciously Elysian melodic fabric. Good
sense is made of the overall shape and the soloists are, as ever, excellent. *Beati omnes* is a positive gem; this may well have been written for the
composer's wedding. Of the small-scale pieces,
In the black dismal dungeon is the real masterpiece; it's delivered astutely by the secure and
musicianly voice of Susan Gritton.

Finally to the funeral pieces. Here we have an
ominous procession from the Guild of Ancient
Fifes and Drums and the first appearance of four
'flatt' trumpets – as opposed to two plus two sackbuts; the effect of this subtle timbral change makes
extraordinary sense of the music, engendering a
new grandeur and uncompromising clarity as
would have befitted such an occasion. The vocal
performances are earthy and impassioned.

Odes & Welcome Songs

Odes for St Cecilia's Day – 'Hail, bright Cecilia', Z328;
'Welcome to all the pleasures', Z339
Susan Hamilton, Siri Thornhill *sops* Robin Blaze,
Martin van der Zeijst *countertens* Mark Padmore
ten Jonathan Arnold, Peter Harvey, Jonathan
Brown *basses* Collegium Vocale /
Philippe Herreweghe
Harmonia Mundi HMC90 1643 (73' · DDD ·T) Ⓕ

The two famous St Cecilian Odes reflect a
remarkable polarity in the composer's creative
priorities: the shorter of the two, *Welcome to all
the pleasures*, is a supreme amalgamation of Fish-
burn's words and Purcell's music, bursting with
contained subtlety and enchantment. There's
also a unique sense of conveying something
novel, in this case an inaugural tribute on
November 22, 1683, to the patron saint of
music, henceforth annually celebrating 'this
divine Science'. *Hail, bright Cecilia* from 1692 is
three times longer and explores all the startling

orchestral sounds which changed English music
towards something approaching a Handelian
palette. It's also truly *fin de siècle* (some might say
Newtonian) in ambition and the imagery is as
breathtakingly splendid now as it was when the
Victorians first revered it for its boldness and
scale. Such qualities clearly animate Herreweghe and he shapes this music with rapture
and precision.

The whole is infectiously fresh and never
rushed. Herreweghe is sensitive to the nuances
which irradiate from Purcell's colouring of
words. He largely uses English voices. 'Hark!
hark! each tree' boasts the versatile and effortless alto of Robin Blaze who, with the assured
Peter Harvey, achieves a delightfully naturalistic
lilt. One blip here is the piping soprano in 'Thou
tun'st this world' (Susan Hamilton) where the
voice seems technically and expressively limited.
But for beauty of sound Herreweghe is your
man.

Songs

She loves, and she confesses, Z413. Amintas, to my Ⓗ
grief I see, Z356. Corinna is divinely fair, Z365.
Amintor, heedless of his flocks, Z357. He himself
courts his own ruin, Z372. No, to what purpose, Z468.
Sylvia, 'tis true you're fair, Z512. Lovely Albina's come
ashore, Z394. Spite of the godhead, pow'rful love,
Z417. If music be the food of love, Z379/3. Phyllis,
I can ne'er forgive it, Z408. Bacchus is a pow'r divine,
Z360. Bess of Bedlam, Z370, 'From silent shades'. Let
formal lovers still pursue, Z391. I came, I saw, and was
undone, Z375. Who can behold Florella's charms?,
Z441. Cupid, the slyest rogue alive, Z367. If prayers
and tears, Z380. In Chloris all soft charms agree,
Z384. Let us, kind Lesbia, give away, Z466. Love is
now become a trade, Z393. Ask me to love no more,
Z358. O Solitude! my sweetest choice, Z406. Olinda
in the shades unseen, Z404. Pious Celinda goes to
prayers, Z410. When Strephon found his passion vain,
Z435. The fatal hour comes on apace, Z421. Sawney
is a bonny lad, Z412. Young Thirsis' fate, ye hills and
groves, deplore, Z473
Barbara Bonney, Susan Gritton *sops* James
Bowman *counterten* Rogers Covey-Crump, Charles
Daniels *tens* Michael George *bass* Mark Caudle,
Susanna Pell *vas da gamba* David Miller *lte/theorbo*
/ Robert King *org/hpd*
Hyperion CDA66730 (76' · DDD · T) ⓕⒹ➤

This third and last volume of Purcell's non-
theatrical secular songs consummates a most
rewarding survey of 87 songs with more of the
same: a vocal palette of six singers who are by
now so steeped in the nuances of Purcell's strains
that even the slightest offering sparkles with
something memorable. The treasure is shared
between Barbara Bonney and Susan Gritton who
complement each other superbly. Gritton,
becoming more refined in characterisation and
tonal colour by the day, is allotted the free-style
and dramatic pieces while to Bonney's fluid and
sensual melisma are designated the more
strophic or *cantabile* settings. *Lovely Albina's come*

ashore is one of the composer's most mature creations, tantalisingly hinting at a new, tautly designed and classically balanced type of song. This work, *If music be the food of love* (the best of the three versions) and *I came, I saw* are striking examples of how exceptionally Bonney negotiates Purcell's skipping and curling contours and makes these songs sound even finer creations than we previously thought. *From silent shades* ('Bess of Bedlam') is Purcell's quintessential mad-song and Gritton has the measure of it all the way; packed full of incident, imagery and musical detail, her narration is clear and finely judged, reporting the tale with irony and change of colour. The CD is beautifully documented.

'Music of Henry Purcell'
Includes performances by **John Whitworth** *counterten* **Granville Jones, Neville Marriner, Peter Gibbs** *vns* **George Malcolm** *hpd* **Oriana Concert Choir and Orchestra; Kalmar Chamber Orchestra of London / Michael Tippett; Concentus Musicus, Vienna / Nikolaus Harnoncourt; Leonhardt Baroque Ensemble / Gustav Leonhardt** *hpd* **Deller Consort / Alfred Deller** *counterten*
Musical Concepts ⑦ MC194 (6h 19' · ADD)   Ⓢ

This second volume of Vanguard's reissued recordings of Alfred Deller and his consort comprises works by Purcell, the composer most closely associated with Deller, and consists of six CDs, well packaged and with a CD-Rom giving access to more detailed information. The first two present a mixed programme of songs, duets and instrumental pieces. The third has a complete performance of *Dido and Aeneas* conducted by Deller and recorded in 1965. The remaining discs include the *Odes to St Cecilia*, *Come, ye Sons of Art* and music for the Masque in *Dioclesian*, the whole collection ending with Blow's *Ode on the Death of Mr Henry Purcell*.

In his middle and later years Deller habitually lightened notes above the centre of his range, so that his style became somewhat predictable and the evenness of his production somewhat impaired. That accounts for main differences between these later performances of such 'signature' pieces as 'Music for a while' and 'Sweeter than roses': the purity of tone, the extraordinary resonance of lower and middle notes, the technical skill and sensitivity of his singing all remain. As a conductor, he had difficulties, and it cannot be claimed that the *Dido* is a success. Some stodgy speeds and sluggish rhythms, a pantomime coven of witches, a Dido lacking nobility of tone and an Aeneas out of oratorio make it hard for other contributions (most notably Helen Watts's sorceress) to have their due effect. Still, no doubt the best way of avoiding disappointment is to be prepared for it.

That Deller could conduct well, holding his place along with the highly professional Harnoncourt in his *Dioclesian* and the very personally involved Tippett in *Hail, bright Cecilia*, is evident in the Odes. Stylish playing by George Malcolm and other instrumentalists (including

the young violinist Neville Marriner) gives further pleasure. The album celebrated not only Deller himself but his generation who did so much to bring Purcell out of the text books, the full range of his genius revealed.

'The Food of Love'
Corbette Caprice de chacone in C major **Purcell** If Music be the Food of Love, Z379c. Corinna is divinely fair, Z365. Ah, how sweet it is to love, Z613. What a sad fate is mine, Z428a. I see she flies me ev'rywhere. O solitude, my sweetest choice, Z406. Music for a while, Z583. Ground in C minor, ZD221. O! Fair Cedaria, hide those eyes, Z402. Man is for the woman made. Not all my torments can your pity move, Z400. On the brow of Richmond Hill, Z405. Pious Celinda goes to prayers, Z410. When first I saw Aurelia's eyes, Z627a/1. The cares of lovers. The fatal hour comes on apace, Z421. I loved fair Celia, Z381. When her languishing eyes said 'Love!', Z432. Thou wakeful shepherd that dost Israel keep (A Morning Hymn), Z198. The earth trembled, Z197. An Evening Hymn, 'Now that the sun hath veiled his light', Z193. If music be the food of love Z379a **C Simpson** Preludes – in D; (in E) Visée Prelude D minor
Paul Agnew *ten* **Anne-Marie Lasla** *bass viol*
Elizabeth Kenny *theo/gtr* **Blandine Rannou** *hpd*
Ambroisie AM185 (74' · DDD)   Ⓕ

Paul Agnew is perhaps most readily associated with the French Baroque, but he is equally at home in English music. Here he presents a marvellous anthology of songs by Purcell. They are divided into groups which are separated by short instrumental pieces by other composers, giving well deserved solo spots to Anne-Marie Lasla and Elizabeth Kenny.

The programme – and it is a programme, which can be enjoyed at a sitting – begins with one version of 'If music be the food of love' and ends with another: not Shakespeare, but Colonel Henry Heveningham. As you might expect, several songs employ a favourite device of Purcell's, the ground bass. 'O solitude', exquisitely shaded though it is, comes across as rather too austere with nothing between the bass viol and the voice; but in the introduction to 'Music for a while', the viol starts and is joined in turn by theorbo and harpsichord, to excellent effect.

If the tone is predominantly sombre, there's relief in 'Man is for the woman made', Agnew's cheerful delivery perfectly complemented by a strumming guitar. The *Evening Hymn* ends with a string of 'Hallelujahs' that Agnew sings with an appropriate inwardness; it's aptly preceded by the lesser-known and very different *Morning Hymn*. In a word: magnificent.

Dido and Aeneas

Dido and Aeneas   Ⓟ
Stephen Wallace *counterten* Second Witch **Gerald Finley** *bar* Aeneas **Rosemary Joshua** *sop* Belinda **Lynne Dawson** *sop* Dido **John Bowen** *ten* First Sailor **Dominique Visse** *counterten* First Witch

Maria Cristina Kiehr *sop* Second Woman **Susan
Bickley** *mez* Sorceress **Robin Blaze** *counterten* Spirit
**Clare College Choir, Cambridge; Orchestra of the
Age of Enlightenment / René Jacobs**
Harmonia Mundi HMX290 1683 (60' · DDD · T)　Ⓜ︎Ⓞ

René Jacobs was one of the very few luminaries
of the current Baroque dramatic scene not to
have tackled this singular masterpiece. He does
so, like Hogwood, with a gaggle of top-class
singers; when you can casually call on Maria
Cristina Kiehr to sing her tuppenceworth of
Second Woman, not to mention Robin Blaze as
Spirit and Dominique Visse as First Witch, it
augurs well for a new benchmark recording.
Rosemary Joshua's Belinda is a straightforward,
dramatically unobtrusive but essential presence,
never manipulated to be more of an influence in
Dido's life than Purcell clearly relates in the
lady-in-waiting's offerings of advice, revealed in
'Pursue thy conquest love'. Act 2 is where things
really get going, after the fairly perfunctory
introduction to the solid hunk that is Aeneas.
Whether you choose to cast your Sorceress as
male or as a crooning hag, the part is crucial to
the temperament of a performance, made neither to be too camp nor too earnest in delivery.
Susan Bickley is a fine Sorceress of the old
school, precise, yet retaining an authority
through quality of tone rather than pantomine.
Jacobs's richly paletted, pacy and boldly theatrical reading will prove a breath of fresh air to those
who feel that Purcell's music in general can withstand being 'un-Englished' for want of new
approaches to colour, characterisation and the
composer's inimitable lyrical undercurrent. The
odd instrumental dance seems a touch lacking in
native roughage, but the finely proportioned
Orchestra of the Age of Enlightenment bound
through the Grove's Dance and are even more
purposeful in the First Sailor's song that opens
Act 3. Lynne Dawson will disappoint few in her
devastated, long-breathed and honest Lament,
elegantly turned (if not vocally peerless) and,
crucially, consequential of so much that has
passed before. The last chorus is more beautifully
sung than you've ever heard: a true funeral rite.
These are the elusive ingredients of a compelling
and truly involved reading. Imaginative and
invigorating, Jacobs has revitalised *Dido*.

Dido and Aeneas
Sarah Connolly *mez* Dido **Gerald Finley** *bar* Aeneas
Lucy Crowe *sop* Belinda **Patricia Bardon** *mez*
Sorcerer **William Purefoy** *counterten* Spirit **Sarah
Tynan** *sop* Second Woman **John Mark Ainsley** *ten*
Sailor **Carys Lane** *sop* First Witch, Chorus **Rebecca
Outram** *sop* Second Witch, Chorus **Choir and
Orchestra of the Age of Enlightenment / Elizabeth
Kenny, Stephen Devine**
Chandos Chaconne CHAN0757 (70' · DDD · T/t) Ⓕ︎Ⓞ︎Ⓓ➛

Here is England's first great opera presented
with a truly cohesive sense of theatrical purpose,
one which unusually allows the drama to unfold
in a close identification with each of the cameo

characters. That said, Sarah Connolly is the
driving force from the start; she's a singer who,
on her own admission, is obsessed with Dido.
Consequently we have a supremely wide-ranging,
tragic and experienced queen from the start,
inhabiting the shadows of 'Ah! Belinda' with
early signs of deplorable fate, which are accentuated by an extended symphony luxuriating poignantly on this resonating conceit.

Lucy Crowe's Belinda is a splendid foil for
Connolly's self-absorption, with her astute and
increasingly desperate buoying up. The Sorceress of Patricia Bardon oozes class with an implacable display of vocal authority over cheap cliché, joined by two witches who gossip like a
couple of housewives in the launderette. And
then there's that single-tracked Aeneas, whom
Purcell gives nothing of great moment. Gerald
Finley parades the conventional Trojan Prince
with generic regret and a smattering of hubris.

The textural lightness of the OAE, for whom a
certain emotional reserve ultimately appears all
the more powerful, is another feature of this
excellent recording, as is the outstandingly deft
co-direction of Elizabeth Kenny and Steven
Devine.

Dido and Aeneas　Ⓟ
Véronique Gens *sop* Dido **Nathan Berg** *bass-bar*
Aeneas **Sophie Marin-Degor** *sop* Belinda **Claire
Brua** *sop* Sorceress **Sophie Daneman** *sop* Second
Woman, First Witch **Gaëlle Mechaly** *sop* Second
Witch **Jean-Paul Fouchécourt** *ten* Spirit, Sailor
Les Arts Florissants / William Christie
Erato 4509 98477-2 (52' · DDD · N/T)　Ⓕ︎Ⓓ➛

William Christie's reading of *Dido* is very much
in terms of the reputed French influence on
Purcell. Overdotting, reverse dotting and *inégal-
ité* are used throughout; the lines are often heavily embellished in the manner of Lully. This is a
perfectly justifiable approach to the music, since
there's little direct evidence to say exactly how
much the French style dominated in England.
This version, with single strings, an excellent
small choir and a slightly obtrusive harpsichord,
stands well alongside what's available. Apart
from a few moments' inattention in Belinda's
'Haste, haste to town', you'd hardly notice that
most of the cast are Francophone, except in that
Nathan Berg's imposing bass-baritone finds it
slightly easier to exploit the colour and the
meaning of Aeneas's words. Véronique Gens is a
lucid and sensible Dido, partnered by a sprightly
Belinda from Sophie Marin-Degor and a good
Second Woman from Sophie Daneman. Claire
Brua's Sorceress is a splendidly insinuating conception, with a slithering melodic style.

Perhaps the main musical distinction of this version is the way Christie presents the final paragraphs. Up to this point he's taken generally quick
speeds, and he runs the final confrontation of Dido
and Aeneas at a headlong tempo, which works
well. Then he comes almost to a standstill at the
moment when Aeneas leaves the stage, choosing
an unusually slow speed for the chorus 'Great

minds against themselves conspire'. This makes way for a dangerously slow Lament, which is heart-stopping, and the final chorus, which is not.

Dido and Aeneas
Sarah Connolly mez Dido **Lucas Meachem** bar Aeneas **Lucy Crowe** sop Belinda **Sara Fulgoni** mez Sorceress **Anita Watson** mez Second Woman **Eri Nakamura** sop First Witch **Pumeza Matshikiza** sop Second Witch **Iestyn Davies** counterten Spirit **Ji-Min Park** ten Sailor **Royal Opera House Chorus, Covent Garden; Orchestra of the Age of Enlightenment / Christopher Hogwood**
Stage director **Wayne McGregor**
Opus Arte 🅓🅥🅓 OA1018D (72' · NTSC · 16:9 PCM stereo and DTS 5.1 · 0). Recorded live at the Royal Opera House, Covent Garden, London, on April 3 & 8, 2009. Bonus features include cast gallery and interview with Wayne McGregor ⒻOO

For Purcell's 350th birthday celebrations, the ROH mounted *Dido and Aeneas*, directed by choreographer Wayne McGregor: a respectable attempt at a difficult task. Difficult because it's an intimate piece, not suited to the vast acreage of Covent Garden; in fact, thanks to the film director Jonathan Haswell it works better here than in the theatre. Another difficulty is the under-drawn character of Aeneas, who usually comes across with all the vigour of a stuffed owl. *Les Troyens* it is not.

The plainness of Hildegard Bechtler's set design – a bare stage, with a few trees for the grove scene and a token boat in Act 3 – is matched by Fotini Dimou's monochrome costumes. This rightly focuses the attention on the singers – and the dancers, of course. Generally speaking, the latter don't obtrude, except for the synchronised PT that illustrates 'Oft she visits this lone mountain': the singlets and shorts don't help. McGregor handles the chorus well: nowhere better than at the end, where his arrangement of the group standing and kneeling by Dido's body is mesmerisingly beautiful. He gets natural, unexaggerated acting from the principals, too; his rare miscalculations are to have the Spirit utter his command to Aeneas offstage and to spoil the postlude to 'When I am laid in earth' with Belinda trying to revive her mistress. Sara Fulgoni admirably refrains from camping up the Sorceress; her attendant witches, conjoined with one arm apiece, are sung and acted with gusto by Eri Nakamura and Pumeza Matshikiza. It's a surprise to learn that Lucas Meachem is American: he doesn't sound at home in English, making diphthongs out of 'stay' and 'obey'. Belinda is unaffectedly played by Lucy Crowe, her bright tones and precise articulation all one could desire. Sarah Connolly, whether tormented by love or grief, makes an equally ideal Dido.

Christopher Hogwood conducts with sensitivity, the languorous 'Thanks to these lonesome vales' being a high-point, and the musicians of the OAE respond to his direction with a spring in their step. Definitely worth investigating.

Dido and Aeneas
Malena Ernman mez Dido **Christopher Maltman** bar Aeneas **Judith van Wanroij** sop Belinda **Hilary Summers** mez Sorceress **Lina Markeby** mez Second Woman **Céline Ricci** sop First Witch **Ana Quintans** sop Second Witch **Marc Mauillon** counterten Spirit **Damian Whiteley** bass Sailor **Fiona Shaw** spkr Prologue **Les Arts Florissants / William Christie**
Stage director **Deborah Warner**
FRA Musica 🅓🅥🅓 EDV1610 (66' · 16:9 · DTS 5.1 · 0)
Ⓕ🅞

This recent, much-travelled production takes a straight view of Purcell's unfinished masterpiece – pastel 18th-century clothes for the soloists and scenery (Chloe Obolensky), naturalistic but emotional direction. The chorus, in black casuals of today and positioned on the edges of the set, support these images of Stuart beauty. A mini-army of modern-dress schoolgirls (a sly reference to the 1689 Josias Priest London school performance), and a part music-hall/part Elizabethan styling of the Sorceress and Witches' acting poke disruptive fun at this Arcadia. And all begins with actress (and now opera director) Fiona Shaw in a Prologue compiled from texts by Ted Hughes, TS Eliot and Yeats about frustrated love – their contemporariness both clever and relevant.

Purcell, and this opera, have been special to William Christie's repertoire. He presents the score here in lyrical mode, avoiding the harsh edges and digging rhythms of many another modern period interpretation. Vocal ornamentation likewise is present but discreet, illustrating stage emotion instead of provoking it.

The dramatic performance is at its most fully realised in the scenes for which we have all Purcell's music, that is for the court and the royal lovers. Agonisingly in love, the central impersonations of Malena Ernman and Christopher Maltman are unmissably realised and directed. The camera likes them, they know how to work in close-up, and their final farewell (in silence) is heartbreaking. Less finished is the punky work of the experienced Hilary Summers and her Witches. The stylistic break, the choreographic difference of movement, the mocking feel so right for the piece – but cannot quite decide here whether to upfront anarchy or comedy. The schoolgirls, frankly, are a one-hit wonder (their first appearance); the nouveau St Trinian's routines have become boring by the time they run in and out of the Witch scenes. The sailors are jolly and casual and don't seem to have fired up the production team much. But for the special commitment of Ernman and Maltman, and the conductor's and director's working out of the opera in performance, this is worth acquiring.

Additional recommendation

Dido and Aeneas
Baker Dido **Herincx** Aeneas **Clark** Belinda **English Chamber Orchestra / A Lewis**
Decca 466 387-2DM (53' · ADD). Recorded 1961   Ⓜ

A very early recording by Janet Baker in a role she was to make her own. Lewis directs a traditional but sensitive account of the score.

The Fairy Queen

The Fairy Queen   P
Gillian Fisher, Lorna Anderson sops **Ann Murray** mez **Michael Chance** counterten **John Mark Ainsley, Ian Partridge** tens **Richard Suart, Michael George** basses **The Sixteen Choir and Orchestra / Harry Christophers**
Coro ② COR16005 (133' · DDD · N/T)   ⓂO🅑➔

The Fairy Queen is hardly an 'opera' in the conventional sense: its musical virtues lie in the composer's uncanny ability to summon a discrete, potent atmosphere whose capacity to move the listener lies outside a sustained dramatic context. The masques draw heavily on vernacular situations and a form of tragicomedy which requires a crafty hand in performance.

Harry Christophers allows the music to breathe with a warm spontaneity, encouraged by a strong and diverse vocal cast. Gillian Fisher is a touch disappointing, but the likes of Ann Murray (who's both radiant and a misfit in one), Michael Chance, John Mark Ainsley, Ian Partridge, Richard Suart and Michael George present a greater array of characterisation than any other extant reading. Just sample the wonderful slapstick between Mopsa and Coridon. Christophers strikes most imploringly at the heart of Purcell's native sensibilities (Partridge's Phoebus sums it up) for a satisfying performance capturing the indigenous humour, grandeur and poignancy of Purcell's exquisite score.

The Indian Queen

The Indian Queen   P
Tessa Bonner, Catherine Bott sops **Rogers Covey-Crump** ten **Peter Harvey** bass **Purcell Simfony Voices; Purcell Simfony / Catherine Mackintosh** vn
Linn CKD035 (60' · DDD)   Ⓕ

If *The Indian Queen* is less ambitious than the other three 'operas' there's the sure touch here of the composer at his most mature and adept. The Prologue, in which he had the rare opportunity to set an extended dialogue, is beautifully balanced, and the music in Act 3 – when Zempoalla's ill-fated love is prophesied by Ismeron the magician in 'Ye twice 10,000 deities' – ranks alongside the finest moments in Purcell's output. The small-scale character of the work, compared to its siblings, is taken a stage further by the Purcell Simfony, which employs a minute chamber-size group of four strings, doubling oboe and recorder, single trumpet and drums. The soloists sing with airy restraint but each responds to these Hilliard-esque proportions with a rhythmic buoyancy and direct intimacy which projects a finely gauged overall conception of the work.

If the expressive power of the music is at times rather glazed, there's a sure atmosphere which is captured by recorded sound that's both warm and yet never imposing. The ensemble isn't always first-rate but there's nothing too worrisome and the instrumental numbers are elegantly shaped. Tessa Bonner gets the lion's share of the solo soprano numbers, ahead of the more colourful Catherine Bott, though the former's comparatively brittle sound has a crystalline quality which suits Catherine Mackintosh's consistent, if austere strategy.

In short, this release is consistently touching, one which in a paradoxical way gets under the skin despite the recessed emotional climate it conveys.

King Arthur

King Arthur   P
Véronique Gens, Claron McFadden, Sandrine Piau, Susannah Waters sops **Mark Padmore, Iain Paton** tens **Jonathan Best, Petteri Salomaa, François Bazola-Minori** basses **Les Arts Florissants Chorus and Orchestra / William Christie**
Erato ② 4509 98535-2 (90' · DDD · N/T)   Ⓕ❶❷❸

If the co-operation with John Dryden led to a unity of vision in terms of music's expressive role in the overall drama, Purcell was limited to a historical patriotic fantasy with little room for the magic and pathos of, say, the superior *Fairy Queen*. Yet in the context of a stage presentation, Purcell's music shines through strongly. On disc though, with just the music, not even the dramatic powers of William Christie can restore its place in the overall scheme. But never mind, this is a score with some magnificent creations and Christie is evidently enchanted by it. The choral singing is richly textured, sensual and long-breathed, yet always alert to a nuance which can irradiate a passage at a stroke, as Christie does in the bittersweet close of 'Honour prizing' – easily the best moment in Act 1. The instrumental movements are finely moulded so that sinewy counterpoint and rhythmic profile are always strongly relayed. The songs, too, have been acutely prepared and are keenly characterised without resorting to excess. All the basses deliver their fine music with aplomb.

If there's one drawback to extracting the musical numbers from the 'opera' when they've so clearly been delivered in a theatrical context, it's that the contextual characterisations lend themselves less well to the musical continuity of a CD. *King Arthur* without the play is dramatically a nonsense, so why try to pretend? Christie doesn't, but makes the strongest case yet for this music.

Additional recommendation

King Arthur
Gens, Bayodi, Jarrige, Auvity, Cornwell, Harvey; Le Concert Spirituel / Hervé Niquet

Glossa GCD921608 (76' · DDD · N/T) Ⓕ

The triumph of this reading is its joy and vigour. Unlike other non-British Purcellians, Niquet doesn't fall foul of projecting an excessively Frenchified view at the cost of the composer's indigenous and expressive language.

The Tempest

The Tempest[a]. Suite in G minor, Z770 –
Overture[b]. Chaconne for Strings in G minor, Z730[c].
Sonata for Trumpet and Strings No 2 in D, Z850[d].
If ever I more riches did desire, Z544[e].
The Indian Queen – Trumpet Overture[f]
[a]**Michael Colvin** ten Aeolus [ae]**Meredith Hall** sop
Amphitrite [a]**Rosemarie van der Hooft** mez Ariel
[ae]**Gillian Keith** sop Dorinda [a]**Brett Polegato** bar
Neptune, First Devil [ae]**Paul Grindlay** bass-bar
Second Devil [a]**Robert Stewart** voc Third Devil
[e]**Nils Brown** ten [d.f]**Norman Engel** tpt Aradia
Baroque Ensemble / Kevin Mallon vn
Naxos 8 554262 (76' · DDD · T) Ⓢ

There's so much pleasure to be had from Purcell's semi-operas that it's easy to wish we had more of them. Much of *The Tempest* is thought to have been written by other hands, but that's no reason for refusing to give it shelf-room. The score is cast in the same mould as Purcell's fully accredited dramatic works and offers a similar range of music. Director Kevin Mallon doesn't fuss over shaping the slower music, and the fast numbers go with plenty of zest. The ensemble includes oboes, recorders and bassoons, quite sparingly used, and bells for the setting of Ariel's 'Full fathom five'. The line-up of solo singers has no weak links and a few real strengths. Brett Polegato may lack authority in the role of Neptune, but sings with a fine, warm, well-rounded tone. Meredith Hall brings a winning sensitivity to the long solo 'Halcyon days' and finds an ideal soprano partner in the young Gillian Keith. Purcell's setting of 'If ever I more riches did desire' and his Trumpet Sonata No 2 are substantial makeweights. The recording acoustic is more church than theatre, but lively enough. Recommended.

Miscellaneous

Bess of Bedlam, 'From silent shades', Z370. The Blessed Virgin's Expostulation, Z196. An Evening Hymn on a Ground, 'Now that the sun hath veil'd his light', Z193. The Fatal hour comes on apace, Z421. O! fair Cederia, hide those eyes, Z402. O Solitude! my sweetest choice, Z406. When first Amintas sued for a kiss, Z430. Yorkshire Feast Song, Z333 – The Bashful Thames. The Fairy Queen, Z629 – If love's a sweet passion; Now the night is chased away; Thrice happy lovers (Epithalamium); O let me weep (The Plaint). The Indian Queen, Z630 – I attempt from love's sickness; They tell us that your mighty powers. King Arthur, Z628 – Fairest isle. The Mock Marriage, Z605 – Man is for woman made. Oedipus, Z583 – Music for a while. Pausanias, Z585 – Sweeter than roses. If music be the food of love

Carolyn Sampson sop with
Andrea Morris, Sarah Sexton vns **Jane Rogers** va
Anne-Marie Lasla va da gamba **Elizabeth Kenny**
arch lute/theo **Laurence Cummings** hpd/spin
BIS ⏺ BIS-SACD1536 (72' · DDD/DSD · T) ⒻＯＯ

It is immediately obvious from the first few songs that this disc is truly special. Carolyn Sampson's singing is deliciously enjoyable for its sweet tuning, flawless intonation, impeccable stylishness, shapely phrasing of melodic lines and textual awareness. Each of these 19 songs, mostly taken from Purcell's operas and music for theatre plays, are given judicious performances. The programme admirably shows the variety of characteristics and styles in Purcell's writing, and Sampson achieves the perfect degree of joyful radiance, seductiveness, witty comment or bittersweet melancholy in each song. 'Sweeter than roses' is an old warhorse for early music singers, but the poetry has seldom seemed so personal as it does in Sampson's heart-rending rendition. The Plaint from *The Fairy Queen* is beautifully done and the line 'he's gone and I shall never see him more' is remarkable for its stylish precision and emotional truthfulness (the performance is also notable for Sarah Sexton's superb solo violin-playing).

The supporting players always sound as if they are fully interested in the subtle nuances of the music. Well known favourites such as 'Music for a while', 'Fairest isle' and 'I attempt from love's sickness to fly' are excellently done, but several of the relatively obscure songs ('The fatal hour' and 'From silent shades') are shown to be equally rewarding and engaging. First-class new recordings of Purcell's music are much too rare, and this one deserves to be an enormous success.

Sergey Rachmaninov
Russian/American 1873-1943

Few musicians have successfully followed two musical disciplines with equal success, but Rachmaninov managed three: composer, conductor and pianist. The music came from his father, its nurture from his mother. Grandfather had been a good amateur pianist and a pupil of John Field; Rachmaninov's aristocratic father Vassili was also a good pianist. Like many land-owning families at the time, times were hard in the 1870s and, when Rachmaninov was nine, the estate was sold, his parents separated, and he went with his mother and five siblings to live in St Petersburg. As an aristocrat, music would have been closed to him as a profession. Now, without property or income, he was free to embark seriously on the study of music, for he had clearly inherited the family talent for the piano.

After a couple of years at the St Petersburg Conservatory, Rachmaninov entered the Moscow Conservatory in 1885 on the advice of his cousin, the pianist Alexander Siloti. Under the strict regime of Zverev, Rachmaninov quickly developed into a formidable player. He studied composition with Taneyev

and Arensky, Tchaikovsky took an interest in the young man's work and by the age of 19 he had written his First Piano Concerto and the group of Five Pieces, Op 3 (dedicated to Arensky) which include the celebrated Prelude in C sharp minor, one of the most popular of all piano compositions. He found a publisher, his one-act opera Aleko made a considerable impression at its premiere in 1893 and he won the Great Gold Medal for the piano when he graduated – altogether an impressive start to a career.

Then came a profound setback. For two years he worked on the composition of his First Symphony. The premiere was a disaster: the music was derided by the critics and the performance a fiasco, poorly conducted by a drunken Glazunov. This humiliation prompted a period of severe self-doubt and depression. His confidence was boosted by an invitation to appear in London as conductor, composer and soloist (his tone-poem The Rock was given and the by now inevitable C sharp minor Prelude) but when he returned to Moscow and tried to complete a Second Piano Concerto, his depression returned. Rachmaninov went to consult a psychologist, Dr Dahl, and after a course of hypnosis, during which Dahl insisted that Rachmaninov would 'start writing, and the work will be excellent', the composer indeed was able to complete the Second Piano Concerto. It has become one of the most popular of the genre.

Rachmaninov married his cousin Natalie Satina in 1902. For the next few years he managed to conduct at the Bolshoi (1904-06), compose (if not prolifically) and appear as a soloist. He and his family moved to Dresden for two years to concentrate on composition, then back to Moscow in 1909, then over to America for his first tour of the country. For this he wrote his Third Piano Concerto, playing it twice in New York, the second time under the baton of Mahler. His fame and the success of this visit led to his being offered the conductorship of the Boston Symphony Orchestra. He turned it down (the offer was repeated in 1918 and again declined). Then it was back to Moscow.

From 1910 to 1917 he remained there conducting the Moscow Philharmonic concerts and composing – as well as making many foreign tours, by now world-famous. When the Revolution came, it changed his life for ever. In November 1917 he and his family left Russia for a Scandinavian tour, the catalyst that decided him to make the break rather than live under the new regime. Rachmaninov never returned to Russia again.

When he eventually settled on America as his base, he arrived with very little money. He changed career and turned himself into a full-time concert pianist. This involved an extraordinary amount of work – he had a small repertoire compared with most pianists – but by specialising in the sort of music the public wanted to hear (Chopin, Schumann, Liszt and, of course, his own compositions) he made a sensational success. His career as a conductor evaporated (although he carried out many engagements) and he wrote comparatively little music after he left Russia. Instead, he became known as one of the greatest pianists in history.

He bought a house on Lake Lucerne in Switzerland – his grandmother's house on the banks of the River Volchov had engendered a lifelong love of rivers and boats – making annual tours of Europe. In 1935 he decided to make New York his home, later settling in Los Angeles. His home there was an exact replica, down to the food and drink, of the home he had left in Moscow. Composition gradually became more and more difficult for him but he continued to play in public until a month before his death from cancer, a few weeks after becoming an American citizen. He was buried in the Kensico Cemetery in New York.

Piano Concertos

No 1 in F sharp minor, Op 1; No 2 in C minor, Op 18; No 3 in D minor, Op 30; No 4 in G minor, Op 40. Rhapsody on a Theme of Paganini, Op 43

Piano Concertos Nos 1-4. Paganini Rhapsody
Earl Wild pf **Royal Philharmonic Orchestra / Jascha Horenstein**
Chandos ② CHAN10078 (134' · ADD)
Recorded 1965   Ⓜ️Ⓞ▶️

Such is the luxuriance of sound revealed in these remasterings, it's difficult to believe the recording date; and such is the quality of the piano playing that it's easy to understand why Chandos should have wanted to go to such trouble. There aren't so many Rachmaninov pianists who dare to throw caution to the wind to the extent that Earl Wild does in the outer movements of the First Concerto, fewer still who can keep their technical poise in the process. The improvisatory feel to the lyricism of the slow movement is no less remarkable. Wild's panache is every bit as seductive in No 4, and the *Paganini* Rhapsody is a rare example of a performance faster than the composer's own – devilishly driven in the early variations and with tension maintained through the following slower ones so that the famous 18th can register as a release from a suffocating grip, rather than an overblown, out-of-context exercise in grandiosity. Because of his lightness and touch Wild's tempi never seem excessive. Undoubtedly he shifts the balance from languishing pathos and overwhelming grandeur towards straightforward exuberance; but that may be no bad thing for refreshing our view of the composer. It keeps us in touch with an earlier tradition. The RPO appears to be revelling in the whole affair, in a way one wouldn't have immediately associated with Horenstein. To pick on the very few weaknesses, the very relaxed clarinet tone in the slow movement of Concerto No 2 rather misses the character, and elsewhere in this work the balance engineers rather crudely stick a microphone under the cello section's nostrils. But then the solo playing in this concerto is generally a little disappointing too, as though Wild had actually played the piece rather too often. In No 3 there are the hateful cuts to contend with, and one senses that the performance has been rather thoughtlessly modelled on the composer's own, idiosyncrasies and all. None the less, for the sake of the outstanding performances of Nos 1 and 4 and the Rhapsody, and for the unique combination of old-style bravura and modern sound, this issue earns a strong recommendation.

RACHMANINOV
PIANO CONCERTOS – IN BRIEF

Krystian Zimerman
Boston PO / Seiji Ozawa
DG 459 643-2GH (62' · DDD)   ⓕ❶❷❸❹▸

Zimerman's incendiary pianism trounces all comers in the First Concerto, not excluding the composer himself. The Second, more ruminative in mood, comes over less well, thanks in part to a recording balance that attenuates the orchestral sound.

Stephen Hough
Dallas SO / Andrew Litton
Hyperion ② CDA67501/2; ⦿ SACDA67501/2
(146' · ADD)   ⓕ❶❷❸
A stunning new set of the four concertos and *Paganini* Rhapsody played with towering virtuosity by Hough. A real winner.

Leif Ove Andsnes
Berlin Philharmonic Orchestra / Antonio Pappano
EMI 474813-2 (59' · DDD)   ⓕ❶❷❸❹▸
Powerful yet poetic accounts of the first two concertos. Pappano matches Andsnes with accompaniments of uncommon sympathy and style.

Arturo Benedetti Michelangeli
Philharmonia Orchestra / Ettore Gracis
EMI 567238-2 (47' · ADD)   Ⓜ❶❷
Less surgingly romantic than some, Michelangeli's transcendent pianism and refined sensibility come together in this classic coupling of the Fourth Concerto and the Ravel G major, available continuously since the late 1950s.

Sergey Rachmaninov
Philadelphia Orchestra / Leopold Stokowski, Eugene Ormandy   Ⓗ
Nos 2 & 3: Naxos 8 110601 (65' · ADD)   Ⓢ▸
Nos 1 & 4: Naxos 8 110602 (71' · ADD)   Ⓢ▸
Rachmaninov's own fastidious, never lugubrious 78rpm performances remain indispensable, more than just historical documents despite their primitive recording technology.

Vladimir Ashkenazy
London SO / André Previn
Decca ② 444 839-2DF2 (135' · ADD)   Ⓜ❶▸
Vladimir Ashkenazy
Concertgebouw / Bernard Haitink
Decca ② 421 590-2DH2 (142' · ADD)   Ⓜ❶❷▸
At mid-price, Vladimir Ashkenazy's fresh and involving analogue stereo set with André Previn and the LSO stands up amazingly well. The pianist demonstrates great poetic imagination and lightning reflexes as well as his formidable bravura and characteristic weight of sonority. His later set with Haitink is mellower and slightly more inward: neither would disappoint.

Piano Concertos Nos 1-4
Vladimir Ashkenazy pf **London Symphony Orchestra / André Previn**
Double Decca ② 444 839-2DF2 (135' · ADD)
Recorded 1970-72   Ⓜ❶❷▸

 Despite the recording dates, the sound and balance are superb, and there's nothing to cloud your sense of Ashkenazy's greatness in all these works. From him every page declares Rachmaninov's nationality, his indelibly Russian nature. What nobility of feeling and what dark regions of the imagination he relishes and explores in page after page of the Third Concerto. Significantly his opening is a very moderate *Allegro ma non tanto*, later allowing him an expansiveness and imaginative scope hard to find in other more 'driven' or hectic performances. His *rubato* is as natural as it's distinctive, and his way of easing from one idea to another shows him at his most intimately and romantically responsive. There are no cuts, and his choice of the bigger of the two cadenzas is entirely apt, given the breadth of his conception. Even the skittering figurations and volleys of repeated notes just before the close of the central *Intermezzo* can't tempt Ashkenazy into display and he's quicker than any other pianist to find a touch of wistfulness beneath Rachmaninov's occasional outer playfulness (the *scherzando* episode in the finale).

Such imaginative fervour and delicacy are just as central to Ashkenazy's other performances. His steep unmarked *decrescendo* at the close of the First Concerto's opening rhetorical gesture is symptomatic of his Romantic bias, his love of the music's interior glow. And despite his prodigious command in, say, the final pages of both the First and Fourth Concertos, there's never a hint of bombast or a more superficial brand of fire-and-brimstone virtuosity. Previn works hand in glove with his soloist. Clearly, this is no one-night partnership but the product of the greatest musical sympathy. The opening of the Third Concerto's *Intermezzo* could hardly be given with a more idiomatic, brooding melancholy, a perfect introduction for all that's to follow. If you want playing which captures Rachmaninov's always elusive, opalescent centre then Ashkenazy is hard to beat.

Piano Concertos Nos 1-4. Paganini Rhapsody
Stephen Hough pf **Dallas Symphony Orchestra / Andrew Litton**
Hyperion ③ CDA67501/2; ⦿ SACDA67501/2
(146' · DDD)   ⓕ❶❷❸❹▸
Concertos recorded live at the Morton H Meyerson Symphony Center, Dallas, April-May 2004

Hough. Litton. Rachmaninov concertos. Hyperion. Already a mouth-watering prospect, isn't it? So, like the old Fry's Five Boys chocolate advert, does Anticipation match Realisation in these five much-recorded confections?

The answer is 'yes' on almost every level. Culled from one or more live performances the concertos may be, but they manifest a real sense of occasion. Hough has clearly been burning to record these pieces for years. Litton is one of the world's most adept accompanists. He and his Dallas players offer exemplary support, with bright precision, purring strings and a judiciously blended brass section. A handsomely voiced piano brings a near-perfect balance; only in the final pages of the studio-made *Paganini* Rhapsody does Hough struggle to make himself heard.

Unlike most of his peers, he takes the composer at his word (scores and recordings) in matters of tempo, dynamics and the performance practice of Rachmaninov's musical language, as he makes clear in a trenchant apologia in the superb booklet-note (by David Fanning).

Where Wild and Argerich seem glib in the cadenzas of the First and Third Concertos respectively, Hough imparts the right sense of heroic struggle; not even Rachmaninov caresses the second subject of the First Concerto's finale so beguilingly; the notoriously tricky opening pages of the Second Concerto's finale are dispatched with breathtaking élan, as is the last movement of the Third Concerto.

It's quite an achievement when each of Hough's five performances rivals the greatest versions recorded individually by other pianists (the younger Horowitz in the Third, for example, Michelangeli in the Fourth). As a competitive set, that from the much-lamented Rafael Orozco comes close to matching Hough's fleet-fingered ardour, but is less impressively recorded; Howard Shelley offers a convincing, slower alternative with powerful, weighty tone. Overall, though, only Earl Wild (see above) and, before that, Rachmaninov himself truly convey the composer's intentions with such miraculous fluency, passion and stylistic integrity.

Piano Concertos Nos 1 & 2
Krystian Zimerman pf
Boston Symphony Orchestra / Seiji Ozawa
DG 459 643-2GH (62' · DDD)　　　Ⓟ❶❷❸❹▷

Ⓖ The catalogue may bulge with recordings of these two concertos, yet the verve and poetry of these performances somehow forbid comparison, even at the most exalted level. Zimerman claims that Rachmaninov says everything there is to say about the First Concerto in his own performance. But had Rachmaninov heard Zimerman he might have been envious. Zimerman opens in a blaze of rhetorical glory before skittering through the first *Vivace* with the sort of winged brilliance that will reduce lesser pianists to despair. The cadenza is overwhelming, and at 4'36" in the central *Andante*'s starry ascent his *rubato* tugs painfully at the heartstrings. In the finale, despite a dizzying tempo, every one of the teeming notes is pinpointed with shining clarity.

The Second Concerto also burns and coruscates in all its first heat. A romantic to his fingertips, Zimerman inflects one familiar theme after another with a yearning, bittersweet intensity that he equates in his interview with first love. Every page is alive with a sense of wonder at Rachmaninov's genius. Seiji Ozawa and the Boston orchestra are ideal partners, and DG's sound and balance are fully worthy of this memorable release.

Piano Concertos Nos 1 & 2ª
Leif Ove Andsnes pf
Berlin Philharmonic Orchestra / Antonio Pappano
EMI 474813-2 (59' · DDD)
ªRecorded live 2005　　　　Ⓟ❶❷❸❹▷

Ⓖ With no shortage of fine versions of this pairing from which to choose, EMI must rely on the undoubted selling power of its Norwegian star to make this release stand out from the rest. It is certainly a worthy contender for the Top Ten when aided by the world-class Berlin Phil, a conductor who is in the Barbirolli class of adroit accompanists, superb recorded sound and a beautifully voiced piano.

With judicious tempi (though, as is now customary, slightly slower than the composer's) and a well-nigh ideal balance between piano and orchestra, instrumental detail is tellingly observed, such as the bassoon and clarinet counterpoint at the beginning of the second movement of the First Concerto and the triangle in its finale, both well integrated into the sound picture, even if there is a hint of the engineer's hand.

Nor is there anything mannered about the soloist, though some may wish he was slightly less well mannered. Andsnes here gives the lie to those who find his playing on the cool side of emotional but he is always the reliable guest who never gets drunk, no matter how much alcohol he has consumed. The fiery section of the cadenza in the First Concerto, for example, runs out of steam in the final bars to which Byron Janis, for instance, brings a despairing vehemence.

The Second Concerto (live, as opposed to the studio First, but without any appreciable difference in acoustic and balance) is, similarly, given a Rolls-Royce reading with which only the pickiest could find fault. The last movement, though, is something special and the final appearance of its glorious second subject, greeted with a mighty timpani wallop and braying brass, is heart-stopping. The audience rightly roar their approval.

Piano Concerto No 3ª. Cello Sonata in G minor, Op 19 – Andante (arr Volodos). Morceaux de fantaisie, Op 3 – No 5, Sérénade in B flat minor. Morceaux de salon, Op 10 – No 6, Romance in F minor. Preludes – F minor, Op 32 No 6. Prelude in D minor. Etudes-tableaux, Op 33 – No 9 in C sharp minor
Arcadi Volodos pf

[a]Berlin Philharmonic Orchestra / James Levine
Sony Classical SK64384 (61' · DDD)   Ⓕ

Straight into the top flight of Rachmaninov Thirds goes Arcadi Volodos's recording, made live at the Berlin Philharmonie. So many things about it are distinguished and thrilling. Volodos's phrasing is consummately tasteful, all the way through to the cadenza. There his textures are superbly graded, his tone never glaring, even under the pressure of torrents of notes. All's well, in fact, until mid-way in the first-movement cadenza, where he inserts a hiatus before the *Allegro molto*. It sounds terribly calculated, as does the way he steers the cadenza towards its main climax. Just a whiff of self-consciousness can be enough to cancel out a host of poetic or virtuoso touches.

Though this isn't a world-beater, it's certainly one to assess at the highest level. Nothing but praise can be showered upon the BPO for their wonderfully cushioned accompaniment, and upon Levine for his avoidance of all the usual pitfalls. The piano is quite forwardly balanced, so that every tiniest note emerges bright as a new pin; and, given how wonderfully Volodos shapes everything, it's fine, although you do occasionally feel that you aren't hearing the orchestra in its full glory.

As for the solo pieces, the Cello Sonata arrangement is a marvel. It floats ecstatically, with air seemingly blowing through the textures as if through a Chekhovian country house on a cool summer evening. It's heavenly, and the other solos are little short of that.

Piano Concerto No 3[a].
Suite No 2 for Two Pianos, Op 17[b]
Martha Argerich, [b]Nelson Freire pfs **[a]Berlin Radio Symphony Orchestra / Riccardo Chailly**
Philips 50 Great Recordings 464 732-2PM (62' · DDD)
Recorded live 1982   Ⓜ

Rarely in her extraordinary career has Argerich sounded more exhaustingly restless and quixotic, her mind and fingers flashing with reflexes merely dreamt of by other less phenomenally endowed pianists. Yet her Rachmaninov is full of surprises, her opening *Allegro* almost convivial until she meets directions such as *più vivo* or *veloce*, where the tigress in her shows her claws and the music is made to seethe and boil. The cadenza (the finer and more transparent of the two) rises to the sort of climax that will make all pianists' hearts beat faster and her first entry in the 'Intermezzo' interrupts the orchestra's musing with the impatience of a hurricane. But throughout these pages it's almost as if she's searching for music that will allow her virtuosity its fullest scope. In the finale she finds it, accelerating out of the second movement with a sky-rocketing propulsion. Here the music races like wildfire, with a death-defying turn of speed at 7'21" and an explosive energy throughout that must have left audience, conductor and orchestra feeling as if hit by some seismic shock-wave.

Rachmaninov Piano Concerto No 3   ⊞
Tchaikovsky Piano Concerto No 1, Op 23
Kabalevsky Rondo, Op 59
Van Cliburn pf
**Moscow Philharmonic Orchestra /
Kyrill Kondrashin**
Testament mono SBT1440 (80' · ADD)   Ⓕ
Recorded 1958

Here, published for the first time, are the performances that sealed the Texan's first prize in the inaugural International Tchaikovsky Piano Competition, earning him a ticker-tape welcome back home and the Soviet bureaucrats red faces. The strings are acidic, the solo cello sounds like an alto sax, the piano is frequently clunky-toned, the Moscow coughers are out in force and Cliburn has his fair share of fluffs and fudges – but none of this matters. There is a palpable sense of occasion, one in which all concerned sense they are witnessing history in the making as Cliburn gives the performances of his life. No wonder the audience erupts after the first movement of the Tchaikovsky. The *allegro vivace assai* section of the slow movement is taken at a daring pace, while the final pages are as thrilling as any on disc. The second item on the programme was the Rondo by Kabalevsky, a *pièce imposé* written especially for the occasion. On this disc, Testament places it as the final work after the Rachmaninov. It's hardly a masterpiece but Cliburn dignifies it by treating it like one. And then Rach Three. Despite the sonic imperfections and some scarily uncoordinated moments, this one punches a hardly less emotional impact than Cliburn's astounding RCA recording. The first-movement cadenza (Cliburn plays the bigger of the two) will make the hairs stand up on the back of your neck; the finale's peroration will sweep you away. Whatever that magical, indefinable gift is, Cliburn had it in 1958, his *annus mirabilis*.

Rachmaninov Piano Concerto No 3   ⊞
Tchaikovsky Piano Concerto No 1
Vladimir Horowitz pf **New York Philharmonic
Symphony Orchestra / Sir John Barbirolli**
APR mono APR5519 (66' · ADD)
Recorded live 1940-41   Ⓕ

This is the Rachmaninov Third to end all Rachmaninov Thirds, a performance of such super-human pianistic aplomb, pace and virtuosity that it makes all comparisons, save with Horowitz himself, a study in irrelevance. Horowitz's 1930 recording with Albert Coates made Arthur Rubinstein pale with envy; goodness knows how he'd have reacted had he heard Horowitz and Barbirolli! Taken from a 1941 New York broadcast (with apologies from the producer for snaps, crackles, pops and the like) Horowitz's tumultuous, near-apocalyptic brilliance includes all his unique and tirelessly debated attributes; his swooning *rubato*, thundering bass and splintering treble, his explosive attack, his super-erotic inflexions and turns of phrase. Try the skittering *scherzando* variation just before the close of the central *Intermezzo* and note how the pianist's velocity eclipses even his legendary recording with Fritz Reiner. This ultimate wizard of the keyboard is in expansive mood in the Tchaikovsky. There are ample rewards, too, for those who rejoice in Horowitz at his most clamorous, for the thunder and lightning of this 'Tornado from the Steppes'. The performance ends in what can only be described as a scream of octaves and an outburst by an audience driven near to hysteria. Barbirolli and the New York Philharmonic Symphony Orchestra are equal to just about every twist and turn of their volatile soloist's argument and so these performances (and most notably the finale of the Rachmaninov) are simply beyond price.

Rachmaninov Piano Concerto No 4.
Floods of Spring, Op 14 No 11
Medtner Piano Concerto No 2, Op 50
Yevgeny Sudbin pf **North Carolina Symphony
Orchestra / Grant Llewellyn**
BIS ⚏ BIS-SACD1728 (74' · DDD)   Ⓕ

This richly enterprising programme couples Rachmaninov's 1926 version of his Fourth Piano Concerto with Medtner's Second, works which both composers lovingly dedicated to each other. For good measure Sudbin adds his own transcription of Rachmaninov's *Floods of Spring*, to say nothing of lively accompanying notes. By 1941 Rachmaninov presented a drastically pruned version of his Fourth Concerto, reducing it by 192 bars, and it is this version, much to Sudbin's chagrin, that is generally played today. But here he makes a strong case for Rachmaninov's early length and elaboration both verbally and in playing which captures a special sense of the chill wind that blows across its surface, the fast fading of the emotional warmth of the first three concertos. Here, former sweetness is very much on the turn and there are many moments when this dazzling and unsettling work sounds like a parody of Rachmaninov's first rhetoric and grandiloquence. Sudbin's relatively low-key playing never leaves you in doubt of his musicianship and dexterity. For him both Rachmaninov and Medtner are too serious for overt display so that even when you miss the brilliance of a Michelangeli or a Demidenko you may well warm to a gentler, more accommodating view. Sudbin's poetic quality shines through every bar of his encore. BIS's sound and balance emphasise their pianist's reserve and occasional self-effacement.

Rachmaninov Piano Concerto No 4   Ⓗ
Ravel Piano Concerto in G
Arturo Benedetti Michelangeli pf
Philharmonia Orchestra / Ettore Gracis
EMI Great Recordings of the Century 567238-2
(47' · ADD). Recorded 1957   Ⓜ︎ⒶⒶⒶⒹ︎

 In crude and subjective terms Michelangeli makes the spine tingle in a way no others can approach. How does he do

it? This is the secret every pianist would love to know, and which no writer can ever pin down. But it's possible to give some general indications. It isn't a question of technique, at least not directly, because Ashkenazy, for example (on Decca) can match their most virtuoso feats; indirectly, yes, it's relevant, in that there are dimensions in Michelangeli's pianism which allow musical conceptions to materialise which might not dawn on others. Nor is it a question of structure, in the narrow sense of the awareness of overall proportions, judicious shaping of paragraphs, continuity of thought; but the way structure is projected and the way it's transmuted into emotional drama; these things are critical.

In one way or another most of the recordings in this section respond vividly to the excitement of Rachmaninov's dramatic climaxes; but with Michelangeli these climaxes seem to burst through the music of their own volition, as though an irresistible force of nature has been released. It's this crowning of a structure by release, rather than by extra pressure, which gives the performance a sense of exaltation and which more than anything else sets it on a different level. It enables him to be freer in many details, yet seem more inevitable as a whole.

The impact of all this would be negligible without a sympathetically attuned conductor and orchestra. Fortunately that's exactly what Michelangeli has. Michelangeli's Ravel is open to criticism, partly because many listeners feel uncomfortable with his persistent left-before-right mannerism in the slow movement and with his unwarranted textual tinkerings (like changing the last note). But he's as finely attuned to this aloof idiom as to its temperamental opposite in the Rachmaninov.

And although the recording can't entirely belie its vintage, it does justice to one of the finest concerto records ever made.

Symphonies

No 1 in D minor, Op 13; **No 2** in E minor, Op 27;
No 3 in A minor, Op 44

Symphonies Nos 1-3. Symphonic Dances,
Op 45. The Isle of the Dead, Op 29. Vocalise
(arr cpsr). Aleko – Intermezzo; Gipsy Girls' Dance
London Symphony Orchestra / André Previn
EMI ③ 764530-2 (3h 47' · ADD)
Recorded 1974-76   Ⓜ︎ⒶⒶⒹ︎

Rachmaninov's three symphonies reflect three very different phases in his creative development: the First (1895) is a stormy synthesis of contemporary trends in Russian symphonic music, the Second (1906-07), an epic study in Tchaikovskian opulence, and the Third (1935-36) a seemingly unstoppable stream of original ideas and impressions. The Second was the first to gain wide acceptance, and with good reason. It shares both the key and general mood of Tchaikovsky's Fifth. Cast in E minor, its initial

RACHMANINOV SYMPHONY NO 2 – IN BRIEF

Philadelphia Orchestra / Eugene Ormandy
Sony ② SB2K63257 (137' · ADD)   Ⓜ
Ormandy and the Philadelphians gave us the first stereo Rachmaninov symphony cycle, and their account of the Second generates a heady sweep that makes it easy to forgive some niggling cuts.

Russian National Orchestra / Mikhail Pletnev
DG 439 888-2GH (64' · DDD)   Ⓕ❍❍Ⓓ
Pletnev's is a superbly controlled and enviably sure-footed performance, if a bit too cool and calculated for some tastes. Full-bodied, though not ideally clear recording.

LSO / André Previn
EMI 566982-2 (74' · ADD)   Ⓜ❍❍Ⓓ
Many collectors maintain an unswerving allegiance to Previn's famous account from 1973, now sounding more refulgent than ever in its latest remastering.

Concertgebouw Orchestra / Vladimir Ashkenazy
Decca ② 448 116-2DF2 (139' · DDD)   Ⓜ❍Ⓓ
An enjoyably red-blooded account with bags of temperament and athleticism. Ripe Decca engineering, albeit not quite as resplendent as on the two other instalments in Ashkenazy's Rachmaninov symphony cycle.

Berlin PO / Lorin Maazel
DG 457 913-2GGA (75' · DDD)   Ⓜ
Maazel's is an urgently intense conception, and accordingly he drives an unusually swift course through the first movments. High-powered orchestral playing, but the sound is just a tad fierce and unglowing.

National SO of Ireland / Alexander Anissimov
Naxos 8 554230 (58' · DDD)   ⓈⒹ
The Dublin orchestra may not be world-beaters but there's absolutely nothing slipshod about their contribution. Anissimov's deeply felt, keenly pondered conception enjoys realistic sound.

Budapest Festival Orchestra / Iván Fischer
Channel Classics CCSSA21698 (65' · DDD)   Ⓕ❍
More musical alchemy from Iván Fischer and his Budapest orchestra. A real sense of dialogue permeates this malleable, joyous performance, whose textual revelations are legion. The sound, not surprisingly from this source, is superb.

LSO / Valery Gergiev
LSO Live LSO0677 (65' · DDD)   Ⓕ❍Ⓓ
This finds the LSO warm and irresistibly propulsive. Gergiev has a feel for the romantic urgency of the music as well as its lyrical impulse and the LSO responds at white heat.

gloom ultimately turns to triumph, and the symphony includes enough glorious melodies to keep Hollywood happy for decades.

The First Symphony had a difficult birth, largely through the incompetent musical midwifery of Alexander Glazunov whose conducting of the work's premiere apparently left much to be desired. However, it's an immensely promising piece and, although undeniably the product of its times, prophetic not only of the mature Rachmaninov, but of other Northern voices, including – occasionally – the mature Sibelius. Both the Third Symphony and its near-contemporary, the *Symphonic Dances* find Rachmaninov indulging a fruitful stream of musical consciousness, recalling motifs and ideas from earlier compositions, yet allowing gusts of fresh air to enliven and rejuvenate his style. Both works have yet to receive their full due in the concert hall, although the strongly evocative *Isle of the Dead* is more securely embedded in the repertory.

What with these and a trio of warming shorter pieces, André Previn's mid-1970s LSO package is an excellent bargain. The performances are entirely sympathetic, avoiding familiar interpretative extremes such as slickness, bombast and emotional indulgence. Previn shows particular understanding of the Third Symphony, the *Symphonic Dances* and *The Isle of the Dead*, works that represent Rachmaninov at his most innovative and assured. The Second Symphony is played without cuts (not invariably the case, even today) and the recordings are generous in tone and revealing of detail.

Symphonies Nos 1-3
Concertgebouw Orchestra / Vladimir Ashkenazy
Double Decca ② 448 116-2DF2 (140' · DDD) Ⓜ❍❍Ⓓ

Ashkenazy has made few more distinguished discs as conductor than his Rachmaninov symphony recordings of the early 1980s. The downside of the repackaging in this two-CD format is that you have to put up with a change of disc half-way through the Second Symphony and lose the shorter orchestral works included in the Previn set. Previn is the most natural but not always the most electrifying of Rachmaninov interpreters and many will find Ashkenazy preferable, particularly in No 1. Although some of Ashkenazy's speeds seem unnaturally pressed – he fairly tips us into the first movement reprise having declined to cap the climax with unvalidated bells – the excitement is infectious. Previn's LSO isn't at its best in the *Larghetto*, but in the corresponding movement of the Second Symphony the boot is on the other foot. Not that Ashkenazy isn't convincing too – so long as you can forget the Previn. Ashkenazy's volatile approach is at its most extreme in the Third, the mood much less autumnal than it usually is, with the fruity Concertgebouw brass unconstrained. Such an unashamedly episodic rendering of the score has its drawbacks, but the virtuoso energy and Romantic gush are hard to resist. The recordings sound very well indeed.

Symphony No 2. Vocalise, Op 34 No 14.
Budapest Festival Orchestra / Iván Fischer
Channel Classics ⊕ CCSSA21698 (65' · DDD) Ⓕ↩

A new century brings a fresh start – at least,
that's the feeling that Iván Fischer engenders
here. He conducts the piece as Rachmaninov
might have played it: with a free and malleable
sense of spontaneity. It's the romantic more
than the epic that Fischer emphasises. Words
like ardent, fleet, airborne appear in my listening notes. In short, a narrative imperative.

The first movement quickly shakes off the
lugubriousness of its introduction. It's a low-
cholesterol sound that Fischer produces as
layer upon layer of string texture and finally
flutes carry us towards the first subject. Channel
Classics has complemented his reading with a
lovely, open and natural production. The blend
is all Fischer's, though.

Nothing shy about the second subject of the
Scherzo, though. Rachmaninov's written *portamento* can sound horribly contrived here – pasted
dutifully between notes rather than evolving
effortlessly from the rise and fall of the phrase.
But then Fischer's Budapest strings aren't about
imitating the Rachmaninov style; they inhabit it.

Fischer's musical story-telling is exceptional.
What do those sombre brass shadings tells us at
the close of the *Scherzo*? Rarely have they ever
sounded quite so unsettling. Nor has the opening of the slow movement – arriving as it does
mid-sentence – sounded more like Rachmaninov abruptly changing the subject. Anything but
confront the demons. The eternal clarinet solo
(ravishingly played here) may be sad but it's
songful (in a way that the melancholic *Vocalise*,
the filler here, is songful). You don't need words
to feel the regret.

Fresh and engaging, then and well worth your
attention – guaranteed to clear your head of
preconceptions.

Symphony No 3. Morceaux de fantaisie, Op 3 – No 3,
Mélodie in E; No 4, Polichinelle in F sharp minor
(both orch anon)
**National Symphony Orchestra of Ireland /
Alexander Anissimov**
Naxos 8 550808 (52' · DDD) Ⓢ↩

Barely represented on disc a generation ago,
Rachmaninov's orchestral works are firm favourites these days, and it's no surprise Naxos has
entered the lists. Can Anissimov hope to compete in a field that includes Ashkenazy's high-
octane digital accounts in sundry bargain formats? Perhaps surprisingly the answer is yes, for
the conductor produces a highly distinctive performance of the Third, inspiring his orchestra to
playing of considerable warmth and flair. Sound
quality is excellent, too. String tone is crucially
important with this composer, and here again
any worries prove unfounded. Not for Anissimov the 'neurotic' Russianness of Ashkenazy's
Rachmaninov. Like Jansons, he disregards the
first-movement exposition repeat, but he makes

the orchestral voices speak with a gentler tone.
There are shattering climaxes when the music
calls for them, and the symphony ends in rousing style; elsewhere the sophisticated languor
and careful phrasing recall Previn's famous
recording. Although some will be disappointed
with the generally slow tempi, there's an unusual
wholeness of musical vision and pacing which
never sacrifices the needs of the larger structure
to the lure of momentary thrills. Despite the
short measure, this is thoroughly recommendable at the price.

The Isle of the Dead / Symphonic Dances

The Isle of the Dead. Symphonic Dances
**London Philharmonic Orchestra /
Vladimir Jurowski**
LPO LPO0004 (51' · DDD)
Recorded live 2003-04 Ⓜ○○

The electricity Jurowski can generate is clearly
established in the *Symphonic Dances*, leading up
to a thrilling close, and if the hushed sequence of
The Isle of the Dead is not a work to bring such a
rush of adrenalin, the mystery of this piece
inspired by Böcklin's great painting is perfectly
caught. These are fine performances that gain in
tension from being recorded live. Even if this
involves some odd balances the definition of
detail is good and one can readily rectify the
rather low level of the CD transfer.

What for many might give pause is that, by the
standards of rival versions (both Previn and
Jansons pair Symphony No 1 with *The Isle of the
Dead* and Symphony No 3 with the *Symphonic
Dances*), this is an ungenerous coupling, even
when you take into account the fact that
Jurowski's speeds are broader. Yet these LPO
performances are both recommendable and will
delight anyone wanting a disc from this exciting
conductor.

The Isle of the Dead. The Rock, Op 7.
Symphonic Dances
**Royal Liverpool Philharmonic Orchestra /
Vasily Petrenko**
Avie AV2188 (70' · DDD) Ⓕ●↩

This first disc in the RLPO's series of Rachmaninov expediently brings together three
works from different eras of his life, presenting
them in reverse order of composition. The *Symphonic Dances* (1940), *The Isle of the Dead* (1909)
and *The Rock* (1893) all have a distinctive Rachmaninov stamp, for which Petrenko has a sure
ear, coupled with a stylistic acuity that enables
him to point out the differences between the
later and the earlier music. In the *Symphonic
Dances* he and his finely honed, malleable RLPO
lucidly characterise the tangy instrumental timbres and crisp, syncopated rhythms, while nursing (but not over-pampering) the passages of
nostalgia and the sinister allusions to the 'Dies
irae'. In the brooding world of *The Isle of the*

Dead, the shrouded imagery of the opening and ending is both sombre and tender. In rising to the music's first anguished climax, Petrenko identifies the drooping chromatic woodwind motifs that render the picture all the more chillingly ominous, and the approach to the second is fraught with foreboding.

Deft orchestral equilibrium and supple *rubato* give *The Rock* the helping hand it needs. In fact the detail and emotional substance are so sympathetically handled that this early piece, which is by no means unskilled but lacks Rachmaninov's later finesse, is invested with a passion, lustre and sensitivity that fully justify its being placed alongside two masterpieces of his maturity.

Piano Trios

Rachmaninov Trio élégiaque No 1
Tchaikovsky Piano Trio, Op 50
Vadim Repin *vn* **Mischa Maisky** *vc* **Lang Lang** *pf*
DG 477 8099GH (64' · DDD)   Ⓕ**OOⒹ**

Temperaments don't come much bigger than Lang Lang, Repin and Maisky. But what impresses most of all about these performances is their single-mindedness. Nowhere is there even a suggestion of conflicting temperaments with their own agenda. What shines through here is the give and take, the kinship, of outstanding chamber music playing.

Of course, the great advantage of 'celebrity' partnerships such as this is the strength of the musical personalities. From out of the whispered oscillations (barely perceptible) at the start of the Rachmaninov come three distinct voices. And while a shared experience (and blend) is immediately apparent there is also added intrigue in the way they each in turn personalise the melody. And as it burgeons into something bigger and more voluble than the word *appassionato* can possibly convey one is also reassured that none of these wonderful musicians thinks himself bigger than the music.

The Tchaikovsky successfully balances the intimate against the symphonic nature of the piece – and while it is quite clearly a Piano Trio there is no sense in which Lang Lang is the dominant force. All three players display a palpable sense of empathy, as in knowing at any given moment what their leading or supporting role is. The theme and variations of the second movement display a fantastic range of character. Lang Lang, far from 'taking centre stage' at the outset, simply presents the unremarkable theme as if at all costs to preserve its folksy naivety – a nice touch.

But then come the transformations. There's the tinkling 'troika' variation, the balletic salon waltz of Variation 6, the imperial splendour and big chordal opulence of No 7, or No 9 wistfully adorned with Lang Lang's watery figurations. Repin is a perfect complement to Maisky's soulful outpourings and collective virtuosity is certainly felt in the 'finale and coda' where the tri-

umvirate really goes into overdrive – nimble, articulate, uplifting. The big return of the work's opening lament has Lang Lang thrillingly invoking the B flat minor Piano Concerto while Repin and Maisky soar heavenward. Repin is quoted as saying that Lang Lang's playing shines as though full of light – and that's the overriding spirit here, even in darkness.

Additional recommendation

Trio élégiaque No 2, Op 9
Coupled with **Shostakovich** Piano Trio No 2
Makhtin *vn* **Kniazev** *vc* **Berezovsky** *pf*
Warner Classics 2564 61937-2 (79' · DDD)   Ⓕ**Ⓓ**

This reading comes closer than most to concealing the work's flaws. The opening movement is wonderfully realised. And the second couldn't be more musically played. It's a highly piano-centric work, but you never feel that Berezovsky is hogging the limelight, superbly matched as he is by his compatriots. By contrast, the finale, despite its portentous, Brahmsian opening, is over all too soon, as if Rachmaninov simply ran out of steam. The recording is warm and convincingly balanced and complements the superb performances.

Complete Piano Music

Variations on a Theme of Chopin, Op 22. Variations on a Theme of Corelli, Op 42. Mélodie in E, Op 3 No 3. Piano Sonatas – No 1 in D minor, Op 28; No 2 in B flat minor, Op 36 (orig version); No 2 in B flat minor, Op 36 (rev version). 10 Preludes, Op 23. 13 Preludes, Op 32. Prelude in D minor. Prelude in F. Morceaux de fantaisie, Op 3. Morceau de fantaisie in G minor. Song Without Words in D minor. Pièce in D minor. Fughetta in F. Moments musicaux, Op 16. Fragments in A flat. Oriental Sketch in B flat. Three Nocturnes – No 1 in F sharp minor; No 2 in F; No 3 in C minor. Quatre Pièces – Romance in F sharp minor; Prélude in E flat minor; Mélodie in E; Gavotte in D. 17 Etudes-tableaux, Opp 33 & 39.
Transcriptions – **Bach** Solo Violin Partita No 3 in E, BWV1006 – Preludio, Gavotte, Gigue **Behr** Lachtäubchen, Op 303 (pubd as Polka de VR) **Bizet** L'arlésienne Suite No 1 – Menuet **Kreisler** Liebesleid. Liebesfreud **Mendelssohn** A Midsummer Night's Dream, Op 61 – Scherzo **Mussorgsky** Sorotchinsy Fair – Gopak **Rachmaninov** Daisies, Op 38 No 3. Lilacs, Op 21 No 5. Vocalise, Op 34 No 14 (arr Kocsis) **Rimsky-Korsakov** The Tale of Tsar Saltan – The Flight of the Bumble-bee **Schubert** Die schöne Müllerin, D957 – Wohin? **Tchaikovsky** Cradle Song, Op 16 No 1
Howard Shelley *pf*
Hyperion ⑧ CDS44041/8 (7h 29' · DDD)   Ⓜ**OⒹ**

This Hyperion set is a significant testament to Howard Shelley's artistry. Pianistically impeccable, he understands what Rachmaninov was about. The original piano works span 45 years of the composer's life. The earliest pieces here, the Nocturnes, strangely owe allegiance neither to Field nor Chopin, but are very much in the mid- to late-19th-century Russian salon style. The Third, in

C minor, has nothing whatever to do with its title. Nicely written too, but still uncharacteristic, are four pieces from 1888, which amply demonstrate that from his early teens the composer had something individual to say. The *Mélodie* in E major is memorable for its hypnotic use of piano tone. Hyperion's recording quality can be heard at its very best here; there's real bloom and colour. Written shortly after his First Piano Concerto in the early 1890s, the *Morceaux de fantaisie*, Op 3, bring us to familiar Rachmaninov. The ubiquitous Prelude in C sharp minor is the second number but Shelley tries to do too much with it; he's more effective in the *Sérénade* with its Spanish overtones. In the E flat minor *Moment musical*, Op 16 one feels that he's able to master Rachmaninov's swirling accompaniments idiomatically. In Variation 15 of the *Variations on a Theme of Chopin* he succeeds in bringing the notes to life, getting his fingers around the fleet *scherzando* writing.

The first set of Preludes is mainstream repertoire. In the warmly expressive D major Prelude he lends the piece a strong Brahmsian feel and it emerges as very well focused. He transforms the C minor into a restless mood picture. The First Sonata is often dismissed as being unwieldy but Shelley gives it a symphonic stature and allows it to be seen in conjunction more with the composer's orchestral writing. Shortly after the Third Concerto Rachmaninov wrote the Op 32 Preludes. Shelley conjures up an exquisite moonlit scene for the G major, but he's not as impressive in the B minor. However, with him it's always the music that dictates the course of the interpretation. In the two sets of *Etudes-tableaux* he excels, as he does too in the Second Sonata. He draws together the disparate elements of the finale with terrific mastery and is the equal of the 'Horowitz clones' for technique. In the *Corelli* Variations he's not quite in tune with the scope of the work but is outstanding in the transcriptions, if a little straight-faced. The recorded sound is never less than serviceable and is sometimes excellent.

Piano Sonata No 2

Piano Sonata No 2. Variations on a Theme of Corelli. Cinq Morceaux de fantaisie
Bernd Glemser pf
Oehms Classics OC558 (75' · DDD)   Ⓕ

Bernd Glemser is described in the booklet as having 'a particular affinity for the works of Sergey Rachmaninov'. And judging by this CD, that's not something to quibble with. This is a recording which allows you to concentrate purely on the music and the artist's interpretation, and not be distracted by any worrying deficiencies in recorded sound, piano tone or pianistic technique: it's all there. Glemser's golden, burnished sound is a treat for the ears in the *Corelli* Variations and, indeed, throughout. The Piano Sonata No 2 is heard in its original version with a few references to and additions from the revised version. Glemser's impas-

sioned reading is as tempestuous as it is heartfelt, among the most magnificent on disc. It is also a pleasure to hear the complete *Morceaux* – the famous C sharp minor Prelude is the second of the set (and a fine, fiery account it is, too) – the highlight of which is the *Mélodie*, No 3. A fleeting magical moment at 1'39" makes you catch your breath. The revised version of this and the *Sérénade*, No 5, concludes the disc, the former amounting to Rachmaninov's transcription of his own work. All in all, then, a disc to relish.

Rachmaninov Piano Sonata No 2.
Variations on a Theme of Chopin. Daisies. Lilacs
Kreisler (arr Rachmaninov) Liebesfreud. Liebesleid
Yevgeny Sudbin pf
BIS 🔊 BIS-SACD1518 (64' · DDD/DSD)   ⒫➔

After the richly deserved acclaim that greeted his debut disc of Scarlatti, Yevgeny Sudbin moves onto home ground. And here, surely, is a young virtuoso in the widest, most encompassing sense. Sudbin makes an unforgettable case for the *Chopin* Variations, a florid and uneven work, though at its finest (in, say, Variation 21) as memorable as anything in Rachmaninov. Omitting the quickly aborted fugue of Variation 12 and choosing the quiet rather than rumbustious coda, he is breathtakingly fleet in Variations 7-8 and goes through Variations 9-10 with all guns firing. Hear him in the whirling measures of Variation 20 (complete with sky-rocketing *ossia*) in page after page of dark, lyrical introspection and you will be hard-pressed to recall a more talented or deeply engaged young artist.

The Second Sonata, played here in Sudbin's own Horowitz-based conflation, is equally inspired, going out in a spine-tingling final blaze of glory. In the two song transcriptions he sounds warmly committed to their floral enchantment. Again, whether in love's joys or sorrows, Sudbin evinces a deft and super-sensitive virtuosity; and even though competition in both the Variations and the Sonata is intense he creates an entirely individual aura. His own personal and informative notes provide a crowning touch to this well recorded, deeply heartfelt recital.

'Unknown Rachmaninov'
Piano Sonata No 2, Op 36. Etudes-tableaux, Op 39 – No 2; No 6; No 9. Preludes – Op 23 No 5; Op 32 No 12. Fugue. Suite
Denis Matsuev pf
RCA Red Seal 88697 15591-2 (60' · DDD)   Ⓕ

Denis Matsuev is a virtuoso in the grandest of grand Russian traditions who returns us to the great days of Emil Gilels. He possesses the sort of technique which begins where others end, and here in Rachmaninov his playing is truly 'stewed in Russian juices'.

His recital, entitled 'Unknown Rachmaninov', is in fact a mix of the familiar and newly discovered. And while the piano version of the

D minor orchestral Suite is hardly characteristic, let alone vintage Rachmaninov, it is played up to the hilt by Matsuev. The D minor Fugue is a more convincing discovery with its prophecy of the E minor *Moment musical* demanding and receiving a red-hot virtuosity. Again, Matsuev may have you longing for the fuller 1913 version of the Second Sonata but his playing blazes with such towering strength and conviction that he leaves you with virtually no grounds for complaint. His pace in the 'Red Riding Hood' A minor *Etude-tableau* is hair-raising and the earlier *Etude* in the same key is given with a scale and romantic turbulence that declare the pianist's nationality in every bar. The G minor Prelude can scarcely have been played more stunningly in its entire history. This excellently recorded disc presents the most trenchant and commanding Rachmaninov recital in years.

Corelli Variations, Op 42

Rachmaninov Variations on a Theme of Corelli
Tchaikovsky The Seasons, Op 37*b*
Hideyo Harada *pf*
Audite ⊕ AUDITE92 569 (68' · DDD) ⑤❶

What a compelling coupling this is, and how good to hear Tchaikovsky's still-underrated cycle given a reading which conveys its grit and grandeur as well as its beauty. The cycle was commissioned by the editor of a St Petersburg journal, *Le Nouvelliste*, and the pieces were published as a kind of musical part-work. When the set was published complete, each piece was headed by lines of verse by a Russian poet, Tolstoy and Pushkin among them, though such is the vividness of Tchaikovsky's writing that the music needs no explanation.

Tchaikovsky's flitting lark (March) and his irresistible walzes for April and December are a particular delight in Hideyo Harada's hands. She's not afraid of full-blooded climaxes either, as witness the choppier waters of June's initially lilting barcarolle. And her 'Autumn Song' (October) is desolate enough to soften the hardest of hearts.

Harada is also up against some very fine recordings of Rachmaninov's *Corelli* Variations, that solo masterpiece just one opus number apart from his more popular *Paganini* Variations. The subtlety with which Harada approaches the theme itself sets the scene for a reading that thrills as much for its nuance as for its brilliance – especially the extrovert Variationss 11, 16 and 18. The wonderfully warm recording sets the seal on a highly recommendable disc.

Etudes-tableaux, Opp 33 & 39

Etudes-tableaux – Opp 33 & 39
Rustem Hayroudinoff *pf*
Chandos CHAN10391 (62' · DDD) ⑤❶

These are meticulously prepared and observed readings – if Rachmaninov asks for *ppp legatissimo* or sharply contrasted dynamics from one bar to the next, then Hayroudinoff takes the composer at his word, a courtesy to Rachmaninov not granted by every pianist.

But Hayroudinoff goes much further than mere accuracy. If he cannot quite equal the composer's breathtaking nonchalance in the three he recorded (Op 33 Nos 2 and 7 in 1940, and Op 39 No 6 in 1925), he comes close. His rich tone and beefy attack serve him well in such passages as the ecstatic climax to the Op 39 E flat minor study (superbly paced and structured) and the pealing bells of Op 39 No 9; he sings with a touching simplicity in the C major and first of the A minor Op 39 studies.

Temperamentally he is right inside the music. This is powerful Rachmaninov playing that transcends the artificial constraints of the recording studio.

Preludes

Preludes – Op 3 No 2; Op 23; Op 32
Steven Osborne *pf*
Hyperion CDA67700 (79' · DDD) ⑤❶❶❶❶▷

It's all too easy to coarsen Rachmaninov's melodic genius with an overtly applied emotionalism, its clearly drawn lines becoming smudged. But Osborne conveys both the monumentality of these pieces, even the most fleeting, and their very human qualities. It's rare to find the balance so acutely achieved. The composer himself, of course, knew how to achieve that equilibrium, but then he had a head start.

Yet this is only a starting-point – the detail is equally delectable: the way that Osborne shapes the tear-stained melody of Op 23 No 4, for instance, and picks out the line from the dark, bustling figuration of Op 23 No 7 or the left-hand countermelody of Op 23 No 8. Then, in the Op 32 set, there's the simplicity of the second, with its incessant tolling around the note C, through to the meditative quality of No 10, the line rising out of the depths as sonorously as Debussy's cathedral. Another fascination is the way Osborne's range of touch puts the Preludes into such a clear historical context.

Osborne throws down the gauntlet with a towering C sharp minor Prelude: it's arguably too slow but makes an apt curtain-raiser on a set that glories in the magnificence of this music. And while there's no empty barnstorming on display here, that's not to say the technical challenges are shirked or underplayed in any way. There are few pianists who offer such range and depth of palette.

Additional recommendation

Rachmaninov Preludes, Op 23 – Nos 1, 2, 4, 5, 8;
Op 32 – Nos 1, 2, 6, 7, 10, 12

Coupled with **Beethoven** Piano Sonata No 11.
Variations and Fugue on an Original Theme, 'Eroica'
Chopin Nocturnes – Op 72 No 1; Op 15 No 1
Haydn Piano Sonata in E, HobXVI/22
Schumann Symphonic Etudes
Richter *pf*
BBC Legends ② BBCL4090-2 (144' · ADD)
Recorded live 1967-69   Ⓜ●

These performances took place when Richter was
as his height, his early insecurity resolved in playing of imperious mastery. Richter's empathy for
his great compatriot is overwhelming and the
sound is excellent. This is phenomenal playing.

Liturgy of St John Chrystostom, Op 31

Liturgy of St John Chrysostom
King's College Choir, Cambridge /
Stephen Cleobury
EMI 557677-2 (75' · DDD · T/t)   Ⓕ●●●▷

This recording may well consolidate its place in
the repertoire, for it's a triumph. Compared with
the Vigil the writing is generally sober, though
there are unforgettable moments such as the
opening of the Second Antiphon, which allows
the boys' crystalline tone to shine. In fact, the
King's choir make a virtue of an apparent limitation, producing an astounding choral blend in the
simple responses of the litanies that punctuate the
Liturgy.

The most famous section of the work is the
lovely Lord's Prayer, movingly sung with fine
attention to detail. Other sections, such as the
Beatitudes, ought also to attract the attention of
any discerning choir director. Only in the Creed
do the choir slightly lose the spring in their step;
perhaps inevitable with such a lengthy setting in
an unfamiliar language.

The great majority of the priest's and deacon's
intonations have been included. This makes sense
of the whole, and proves, if it needed proving, that
Rachmaninov knew all about liturgical pacing.
This aspect of the recording benefits from the
magnificent bass and fluent Slavonic of Protodea-
con Peter Scorer, who has the lion's share. If
Deacon Tobias Sims, singing the celebrant's
parts, can't entirely disguise his English origins,
the contrast between the two voices also helps
convey the liturgical feeling. There are excellent
booklet-notes by Archimandrite Kyril Jenner.

Liturgy of St John Chrysostom
Flemish Radio Choir / Kaspars Putnins
Glossa 🔊 GCDSA922203 (65' · DDD/DSD)   Ⓕ●

Rachmaninov's Liturgy is less well known than
his *All-Night Vigil* ('Vespers'), but has nevertheless gained in popularity with Western choirs as
a concert item in recent years, though the double-choir setting of the Lord's Prayer has always
enjoyed a certain renown, often being sung in an
English paraphrase. It is far more than a mere
sketch for the more famous work, too, though
the links are clear – anyone hearing the opening

psalm, 'Blagoslovi, dushe moya', for the first
time will immediately make the connection.

The Flemish Radio Choir's rendition is very fine
indeed, reverent, well paced and at the same time
electrically atmospheric (and also including sufficient of the celebrant's petitions that it comes
across neither as an artificial celebration nor a
concert suite) and the magnificent SACD sound is
just what such a riveting performance merits. The
only criticism is of their very light 'l' sound, which
truly gives them away as non-Russians.

There is strong competition but, curiously,
none is Russian; indeed, the King's College
recording is as unrepentantly and beautifully
English as you could wish for. In an ideal world
one would have to have all of them, and if you
have room on your shelves for one more, do add
this new recording to your collection. There is
one aspect in which the others score, however –
they include full texts and translations, while for
the new disc they must be downloaded.

Further listening

All-Night Vigil ('Vespers')
National Academic Choir of Ukraine 'Dumka' /
Savchuk
Regis RRC1043 (62' · DDD)   Ⓢ

A first-rate bargain issue to compete with the very
best. The Ukrainian choir is a superb body of
singers, producing a beautifully warm, dark-hued
sound and with an extraordinary sense of pacing.
Their *piano* singing is unrivalled on disc.

Songs

12 Songs, Op 21. 15 Songs, Op 26.
Were you hiccoughing?. Night
Joan Rodgers *sop* **Maria Popescu** *mez*
Alexandre Naoumenko *ten* **Sergei Leiferkus** *bar*
Howard Shelley *pf*
Chandos CHAN9451 (72' · DDD · T/t)   Ⓕ●▷

Two figures in particular haunt this second volume of Chandos's survey of Rachmaninov's songs
– Feodor Chaliapin and Rachmaninov himself.
They had become friends in the years when they
worked together in an opera company and when
Rachmaninov was concentrating on developing
his piano virtuosity. As a result the Op 21 songs are
dominated by an almost operatic declamatory
manner coupled with formidably difficult accompaniments. Leiferkus rises splendidly to the occasion, above all in 'Fate' (Op 21 No 1), and so
throughout the songs does Howard Shelley. He's
unbowed by the technical problems and he understands the novel proportions of songs in which the
piano's participation has an unprecedented role.
He also enjoys himself in the roisterous exchanges
with Leiferkus in what's really Rachmaninov's
only lighthearted song, 'Were you hiccoughing?'.

The songs for the other voices are less powerful, in general more lyrical and intimate.
Alexandre Naoumenko only has five songs, and
they aren't, on the whole, among the more

striking examples, but he responds elegantly to 'The fountain' (Op 26 No 11). Maria Popescu gives a beautiful account of one of the most deservedly popular of them all, 'To the children' (Op 26 No 7), and of the remarkable Merezhkovsky setting, 'Christ is risen' (Op 26 No 6). Joan Rodgers is enchanting in 'The Lilacs' (Op 21 No 5) and moving in the song acknowledging that love is slipping away, 'Again I am alone' (Op 26 No 9). She has complete mastery of the style, and nothing here is finer than her arching phrase ending 'How peaceful' (Op 21 No 7) – 'da ty, mechta moya' ('and you, my dream') – with Shelley gently articulating Rachmaninov's reflective piano postlude from the world of Schumann.

Additional recommendation

14 Songs, Op 34. Letter to KS Stanislavsky. From the Gospel of St John. Six Songs, Op 38. A prayer. All wish to sing
J Rodgers sop **Popescu** mez **Naoumenko** ten **Leiferkus** bar **Shelley** pf
Chandos CHAN9477 (68' · DDD · T/t) Ⓕ**ⓄⒹ➔**

Some of Rachmaninov's greatest songs are here, coloured in their invention by the four great singers whose hovering presence makes the disposition of this recital between four similar voices a highly successful idea. The Chaliapin songs go to Sergei Leiferkus, occasionally a little overshadowed by his mighty example but more often his own man. Alexandre Naoumenko inherits the mantle of Leonid Sobinov, and though he sometimes resorts to a near-falsetto for soft high notes, he appears to have listened to that fine tenor's elegance of line and no less subtle feeling for poetry. Maria Popescu has only two songs, but she has a light tone and bright manner. Joan Rodgers is exquisite in the most rapturous and inward of the songs.

The Miserly Knight

The Miserly Knight
Ildar Abdrazakov bass The Baron **Misha Didyk** ten Albert **Sergey Murzaev** bar The Duke **Peter Bronder** ten The Moneylender **Gennady Bezzubenkov** bass Servant **BBC Philharmonic Orchestra / Gianandrea Noseda**
Chandos CHAN10544 (59' · DDD · S/T/t/N) Ⓕ**ⓄⓄⒹ➔**

This fine, fiery, brooding performance of *The Miserly Knight* is an indispensable companion to the recording of Rachmaninov's other mature opera, *Francesca da Rimini*, with which the same team (with some differences in soloists) launched this survey. Gianandrea Noseda leads the BBC Philharmonic and a cast from St Petersburg's Mariinsky Theatre in delving deep into the score's substance. Both operas might have their dramaturgical difficulties when done on stage, but in concert or on disc they are powerful examples of Rachmaninov's capacity to tap the expressive potential of the voice and to charge emotional situations with energy and poignancy.

Whereas *Francesca da Rimini* has a fairly workmanlike libretto by Tchaikovsky's brother, Modest, Rachmaninov decided in *The Miserly Knight* to set almost exactly word-for-word a prose poem-cum-play by Pushkin. Its central panel is a long monologue for the Baron (the Miserly Knight of the title), a role conceived with Chaliapin in mind and here sung with commanding presence and rich, malleable tone by Ildar Abdrazakov as he drools over his wealth and the cruel ways in which it has been amassed. He is well matched by, and contrasted with, the passionate tenor of Misha Didyk as his resentful son, Albert, and by the sly, ingratiating characterisation of the Moneylender by tenor Peter Bronder. Orchestral atmosphere, backed by a spectrum of colour comparable to that of the Second Symphony, is compellingly established by Noseda, whose theatrical instincts also reflect and enhance the opera's dramatic thrust.

Jean-Philippe Rameau
French 1683-1764

Although revered as being among the most influential and important French composers of the 18th century, little of Rameau's music is heard today. Yet his theories on music continue to exert an influence.

He had a strangely disjointed career. At seven he could sight-read anything put in front of him on the harpsichord (his father was an organist) and for the first 40 years of his career, he was merely a provincial organist, moving around from Avignon to Clermont-Ferrand to Paris, Dijon, Lyons and back to Clermont again. In 1722 he returned to Paris and published a controversial and revolutionary textbook on harmony (Traité de l'harmonie) which, with his reputation as one of the country's leading organists, helped make his name. Then he changed course and, backed by the wealthy tax gatherer and arts patron Le Riche de la Poupelinière, devoted himself to writing opera. From 1733 for the next 30 years, Rameau produced some 30 pieces for the theatre in one form or another. Though he was no judge of librettos, he raised the musical side of opera to a new level and in his ballets introduced many novel descriptive effects – the French loved these – such as the earthquake in Les Indes galantes. Audiences found them deafening and musicians complex and demanding. In fact, Wagner came in for much the same criticism for much the same reason a century later.

Suites

Naïs; Zoroastre – Orchestral Suites Ⓟ
Orchestra of the Eighteenth Century / Frans Brüggen
Glossa GCD921106 (64' · DDD) Ⓕ
Recorded live

No corner of the operatic repertory offers a greater wealth of freestanding orchestral dances than the French Baroque, and no composer wrote such a rich and enjoyable array of them as

Rameau, that master blender of melodic inspiration, rhythmic irresistibility and orchestral colour. While Rameau's dances tend to be integrated into the action more than most, you do not really need to study the plots of these operas too much to enjoy the music they deliver. In the end the music is just there to be enjoyed, and in any case Rameau himself was not always that particular; those familiar with his harpsichord pieces will recognise a few old friends wearing hastily chosen new clothes.

As for the performances, little needs to be said about them save that they meet the Orchestra of the Eighteenth Century's normal high standards – impressively weighted sound, tight ensemble and excellent style – and are all the more admirable for being recorded live in concert, as usual.

Pièces de clavecin en concerts

Pièces de clavecin en concerts   Ⓟ
Trevor Pinnock hpd **Rachel Podger** vn
Jonathan Manson va da gamba
Channel Classics CCS19098 (67' · DDD)   ⒻⓄⓄ

Rameau's 1741 collection represents a major and entirely logical departure from the trio sonata and suite traditions that had held sway in western European chamber music since the beginning of the 17th century. Rameau's textures are uniquely complex, demanding of the players a heightened awareness of their role in the musical texture at hand.

These are balanced and refreshingly musical performances that will draw you back again and again to savour the gracefulness and the kaleidoscopic blending of instrumental colours they bring to the music. Pinnock's playing is lively and engaging, inspiring and inspired. His accuracy is breathtaking, his ornamentation jewel-like. Podger and Manson respond with clarity and shapely phrasing, even in the hair-raising 'Tambourins' (Troisième Concert).

A movement such as 'La Boucon' (Deuxième Concert) is made wonderfully languid, 'La Timide' (Troisième Concert) sinuous but never oppressively so; and 'La Pantomime' (Quatrième Concert) is altogether civilised. And 'La Marais' (Cinquième Concert), which concludes the CD, reminds us how well the tone of a violin and viol can blend when produced by players of this calibre.

Pièces de clavecin

Premier Livre de pièces de clavecin (1706) – Suite   Ⓟ
in A minor. Pièces de clavecin (1724, rev 1731) – Suite
in E minor, Suite in D
Sophie Yates hpd
Chandos Chaconne CHAN0659 (71' · DDD)   ⒻⓄⓄⒹ⇥

The release of a CD devoted to Rameau's harpsichord music is relatively rare. But it's less Rameau, and much more French keyboard music in general, that suffers neglect from an over-cultivated image. However, if Rameau's music is highly allusive, it's also possessed of an immediacy that makes it approachable today. Sophie Yates's firmly grounded yet sensitive and spirited playing will quickly dispel any lingering reservations, and she writes with authority and charm in the accompanying booklet (and plays here a copy of a 1749 Goujon harpsichord made by Andrew Garlick).

Yates's astute selection from Rameau's output is bound to please. The first suite, in A minor, is from the book of *Pièces de clavecin* published shortly after Rameau arrived in Paris in 1706, and displays a youthful brilliance that relies heavily on ornamentation (as, for example, in the Allemande 1 and the Courante) and, delightfully, occasionally reveals a certain provincialism – although Rameau never travelled to Italy, he clearly made certain assumptions about life there: his 'La Vénitienne' makes particular allusion to the beggars' bagpipe and hurdy-gurdy.

The second and third suites, from his later book of 1724 (rev 1731), are altogether more stylish and sophisticated. The E minor Suite begins sedately and with the gravitas befitting an Allemande, but is otherwise shot through with fashionable, pastoral *rondeaux*, and includes two of Rameau's best-known party pieces, 'Le rappel des oiseaux' and 'Tambourin'. The D minor Suite amuses with *pièces de caractère* (the flirtatious 'La Follette', the devious 'Le Lardon' and the pathetic 'La Boiteuse') and amazes with the virtuosity of 'Les Tourbillons' and 'Les Cyclopes'. But only a player of Yates's calibre can address the musical subtleties of 'Les Soupirs', the deceptive 'Les niais de Sologne' and the sensuous 'L'entretien des Muses'. A *tour de force* in every sense.

'La Pantomime'
Pièces de clavecin – in G major-minor; in A major-minor; in D minor. Pièces de clavecin en concert[a] – La Coulicam; La Livri; Air pour les esclaves africains; La Forqueray; La Cupis; La Pantomime
Skip Sempé with [a]**Olivier Fortin** hpds
Paradizo PA0005 (58' · DDD). Includes bonus DVD   Ⓕ

Skip Sempé is known for a love of spontaneity, which informs his solo performances and enlivens the duos. Technically demanding if idiomatic, Rameau's music has the power to impress and amuse. Asked what he thought was most important to Rameau, Sempé replied 'nobility and humour'. Both can be found in abundance on this CD (the former in the Sarabande, the latter in 'Le Triomphe' and 'Les Cyclopes', which together with 'La Dauphine' epitomise extrovert virtuosity) – but further delights await in 'L'Inharmonique' and 'L'entretien des Muses', where we hear – thanks to Sempé's formidable command of 'rhetorical syntax' – Rameau seemingly conducting an inner dialogue with himself.

In the tradition begun by Couperin, Sempé and Fortin perform five duo arrangements of single *Pièces de clavecin en concert* and one air from

Les Indes galantes. The luxuriant textures that result are perfect for 'La Forqueray', evoking as it does a viol player known for his excesses, but they're less successful in other pieces where details are blurred and subtlety compromised, if nevertheless their phrasing is beautifully judged.

Several of the duo tracks from the CD are duplicated on the accompanying DVD, allowing us to glimpse the recording process. Commenting on the challenge of performing with another harpsichordist, Sempé concedes that it is almost impossible to achieve 'razor-edged' vertical precision, and that instead the guiding principle is 'touch-oriented horizontality'. He's too modest. With a minimum of eye contact, their timing is perfection.

Les Indes galantes   **P**
Christophe Rousset hpd
Ambroisie AM152 (63' · DDD)   ⓕ**➔**

Here Christophe Rousset extends his Rameau discography by recording what are said to be the composer's own reductions of orchestral numbers from his 1735 opéra-ballet *Les Indes galantes*. 'Reductions' seems a better word than 'transcriptions' for these 32 pieces, some of which are more idiomatically rendered for harpsichord than others. Did Rameau really do them all himself? And are the pieces that are more successful as harpsichord pieces the works which, like many of his operatic instrumental numbers, actually started out life as harpsichord works? Inconveniently, the one piece here for which we know that to be true, 'Les sauvages', is in a less satisfying version here than in the 1728 *Nouvelles Suites*.

All rather unclear then. But there are certainly pieces here to make this collection a worthy appendix to the Rameau harpsichord canon, such as the rich *Airs pour les esclaves africains*, the exquisite *Air tender pour la rose* or the soft-spoken *Air gracieux pour les amours*.

The *Airs pour les bostangis* and *Gavotte pour les fleurs* show Rameau in all his exotic harmonic strength, the *Tambourins* his earthy rhythmic excitement. Rousset's decision to persevere with a handful of pieces of unfeasible difficulty also pays dividends, above all in the 'ecstatic beauty' of *Adoration au soleil*. Rousset's virtuosity, fine touch and tightly executed ornamentation in both hands ensure that the music sounds idiomatic, yet at the same can be rattled off with suitably orchestral aplomb when required. An enticing Rameau bonus.

Motets

Deus noster refugium. In convertendo.   **P**
Quam dilecta
Sophie Daneman, Noémi Rime sops **Paul Agnew** ten **Nicolas Rivenq** bar **Nicolas Cavallier** bass
Les Arts Florissants / William Christie
Erato 4509 96967-2 (70' · DDD · T/t)   ⓕ**OOO**

 All three motets date from relatively early in Rameau's career, before he had really made a name for himself, yet all show to a certain extent some of the characteristics that 20 years or so later would so thrillingly illuminate his operas. *Deus noster refugium*, for instance, features impressive depictions of nature in turmoil that would not sound out of place in *Hippolyte et Aricie*, and all three begin with long, expressive solos not unlike the opening of an act from a *tragédie-lyrique*. *Quam dilecta* does sound a little more 'churchy' than the others, with its impressive, rather Handelian double fugue, but *In convertendo* – a work which Rameau heavily revised well into his operatic Indian summer in 1751 – absolutely reeks of the theatre.

Drop anyone familiar with the composer's operas into the middle of this piece, and surely only its Latin text would give away that this is church music. It comes as no surprise to find Christie going to town on this dramatic element. The slightly dry acoustic of the Radio France studio is a help, as are the forceful, penetrating qualities of the solo and choral singers. But it's Christie's command of gesture, pacing and contrast which really gives these performances such an invigorating character.

Castor et Pollux

Castor et Pollux   **P**
Howard Crook ten Castor **Jérôme Corréas** bass Pollux **Agnès Mellon** sop Télaïre **Véronique Gens** sop Phebe **René Schirrer** bar Mars, Jupiter **Sandrine Piau** sop Venus, Happy Spirit, Planet **Mark Padmore** ten Love, High Priest **Claire Brua** sop Minerve **Sophie Daneman** sop Follower of Hebe, Celestial Pleasure **Adrian Brand** ten First Athlete **Jean-Claude Sarragosse** bass Second Athlete
Les Arts Florissants / William Christie
Harmonia Mundi ③ HMC90 1435/7 (173' · DDD · T/t)   ⓕ**O**

Castor et Pollux was Rameau's second *tragédie en musique*. Its first performance was in October 1737, but the opera was greeted with only moderate enthusiasm. It was only with the composer's thoroughly revised version of 1754 that it enjoyed the popularity that it deserved. The revision tautened a drama which had never been weak, but it dispensed with a very beautiful Prologue. Christie and Les Arts Florissants perform Rameau's first version, complete with Prologue. The librettist, Pierre-Joseph Bernard, was one of the ablest writers with whom Rameau collaborated and his text for *Castor et Pollux* has been regarded by some as the best of 18th-century French opera. Bernard focuses on the fraternal love of the 'heavenly twins' and specifically on the generosity with which Pollux renounces his immortality so that Castor may be restored to life. Christie's production was staged at Aix-en-Provence in the summer of 1991 and recorded by Harmonia Mundi a year later. This performance realises the element of tragedy, and Christie's singers sound very much at home with French declamation. A very beautiful score, affectionately and perceptively interpreted.

Hippolyte et Aricie

Hippolyte et Aricie   **P**
Mark Padmore ten Hippolyte **Anne-Maria Panzarella** sop Aricie **Lorraine Hunt** sop Phèdre **Laurent Naouri** bass Thésée **Eirian James** mez Diane **Gaëlle Mechaly** sop L'Amour, Female Sailor **Nathan Berg** bass Jupiter, Pluton, Neptune **Katalin Károlyi** mez Oenone **Yann Beuron** ten Arcas Mercure **François Piolino** ten Tisiphone **Christopher Josey** ten Fate I **Matthieu Lécroart** bar Fate II **Bertrand Bontoux** bass Fate III **Mireille Delunsch** sop High Priestess **Patricia Petibon** sop Priestess, Shepherdess **Les Arts Florissants / William Christie**
Erato ③ 0630 15517-2 (3h 2' · DDD · T/t)   Ⓕ**OOO**

G William Christie adheres throughout to the 1733 original (Rameau revised the start of Act 2 in 1757), in so doing opening up some passages previously omitted. He uses an orchestra with a good string weight and it plays with security both of ensemble and intonation, and with splendidly crisp rhythms. Despite the opera's title, the main characters are Theseus and his queen Phaedra, whose guilty passion for his son Hippolytus precipitates the tragedy. Phaedra is strongly cast with a passionate Lorraine Hunt who's particularly impressive in the superb aria, 'Cruelle mère des amours', which begins Act 3. Throughout the opera, one is also struck by the profusion of invention, the unobtrusive contrapuntal skill, the charm and colour of the instrumentation and the freedom allotted to the orchestra. The work's final scene, for example, set in a woodland, is filled with an enchanting atmosphere, ending, after the customary chaconne, with 'Rossignols amoureux' (delightfully sung by Patricia Petibon). Anna-Maria Panzarella makes an appealingly youthful Aricia, and Mark Padmore is easily the best Hippolytus on record. Pains have been taken with the whole cast over the expressive delivery of words and neatness of ornamentation; and production values such as the proper perspective for the entry of the crowd rejoicing at Theseus's return have been well considered.

Zoroastre

Zoroastre   **P**
Mark Padmore ten Zoroastre **Nathan Berg** bar Abramane **Gaëlle Méchaly** sop Amélite **Anna Maria Panzarella** mez Erinice **Matthieu Lécroart** bar Zopire, God of Revenge **François Bazola** bass Narbanor **Eric Martin-Bonnet** bass Oramasès Ariman **Stéphanie Revidat** sop Céphie **Les Arts Florissants / William Christie**
Erato ② 0927 43182-2 (157' · DDD · T/t)   Ⓕ**OO**

To describe Zoroastre as one of Rameau's most uncompromising music-dramas may seem strange when you consider that when it was revived in 1756, seven years after its premiere

had met a rather lukewarm reception, it was in a heavily revised version in which the love interest had been stepped up. The story is of the endless struggle between good and evil which dominates the religion Zoroastre himself has founded.

Rameau's prime concern isn't with Zoroastrianism, but the elemental magic scenes and the intensely human emotions of love, jealousy, vengeance and rage thrown up by the story. Even so, there's a concentrated seriousness of intent about this work which sets it apart from standard *tragédie lyrique*. The French practice of blurring the distinction between recitatives and arias is intensified, so that choruses and snatches of melody fly past in a breathless, flexible flow of incident. And Rameau's music conjures massive dramatic contrasts, ranging from ineffably tender love scenes for Zoroastre and Amélite in Acts 3 and 5 to the almost oppressive demonic power of the subterranean incantations of Act 4, led by the strongly drawn characters of Abramane and Erinice.

The cast is in the best Les Arts Florissants tradition of dramatic commitment and intelligent treatment of text. Mark Padmore has the perfect high tenor for Zoroastre, able to charm in tender moments yet rage in the confrontational scenes without losing any of its essential sweetness, while Nathan Berg makes a strong and fearsome-sounding Abramane. Even more impressive, however, are the two principal sopranos: Anna Maria Panzarella gives her all as the tormented Erinice, while Gaëlle Méchaly is wonderfully bright and clear as Amélite. There are odd moments of vocal weakness among some of the other roles, but they cause no serious damage. The chorus and orchestra both perform for Christie with great vigour, the former contributing memorably to the underworld scenes, and the latter performing delightfully in the opera's many dances.

Einojuhani Rautavaara   Finnish b1928

Rautavaara studied with Merikanto at the Helsinki Academy (1948-52), where from 1966 he taught, and with Persichetti at the Juilliard School (1955-56); he also took lessons from Roger Sessions and Aaron Copland at Tanglewood. Rautavaara is a prolific composer and has written in a variety of forms and styles. He experimented with serial techniques in his early career but left them behind in the 1960s and even his serial works are not obviously serial. His Third Symphony, for example, uses such techniques, but sounds more like Anton Bruckner than it does a more traditional serialist. His later works often have a mystical element. A characteristic 'Rautavaara sound' might be a rhapsodic string theme of austere beauty, with whirling flute lines, gently dissonant bells, and perhaps the suggestion of a pastoral horn.

His output includes eight symphonies, several concertos, choral works (several for unaccompanied choir), sonatas for various instruments, string quartets and other chamber music, and a number of bio-

graphical operas including *Vincent (1986-87, based on the life of Vincent van Gogh), Aleksis Kivi (1995-96)* and *Rasputin (2001-03)*.

Flute Concerto, Op 63

Flute Concerto, 'Dances with the Winds'[a].
Anadyomene. On the Last Frontier[b]
[a]Patrick Gallois *fl* [b]Finnish Philharmonic Choir;
Helsinki Philharmonic Orchestra / Leif Segerstam
Ondine ODE921-2 (59' · DDD)   (F)(O)►

Anadyomene (1968) suggests a Turner canvas recast in sound. It opens restlessly among undulating pastels, the tone darkens further, there are brief comments from flute and bass clarinet, the brass prompts a swelling climax, then the mood gradually becomes more animated before we're ferried back whence we came. It's 'a homage to Aphrodite, born of the sea foam, the goddess of love', and a very appealing one at that. The colourful Flute Concerto *Dances with the Winds* is a more extrovert piece with Nielsen as a fairly certain forebear. It shares its material between ordinary flute, bass flute, alto flute and piccolo. The action-packed opening movement withstands some fairly aggressive interjections from the brass, the brief second movement recalls the shrill sound world of fifes and drums; the elegiac *Andante moderato* offers plenty of jam for the alto flute, and the finale's striking mood-swings have just a hint of Bernsteinian exuberance.

Rautavaara's prompt for *On the Last Frontier* (1997) was an early encounter with *The Narrative of Arthur Gordon Pym* by Edgar Allan Poe. He calls it 'a seafaring yarn in the typical boys' reading mould' and responds accordingly with a 24-minute slice of descriptive musical reportage, not of Poe's exact 'narrative', but of an imagined *Last Frontier* based on ideas from the story's closing section. It's an eventful, majestic, slow-burning tone-poem, nourished further by some distinctive instrumental solos and with telling use of a full-blown chorus.

No texts are provided, and yet the aura of unexplored maritime depths and a sense of mystery associated with them carry their own wordless narrative. All three works are expertly performed and exceptionally well recorded.

Piano Concerto No 3

Piano Concerto No 3, 'Gift of Dreams'[a].
Autumn Gardens
Helsinki Philharmonic Orchestra /
Vladimir Ashkenazy [a]*pf*
Ondine ODE950-2 (68' · DDD)   (F)(O)►

Autumn Gardens extends the Rautavaarian experience at least one step beyond the Seventh Symphony. You sense it especially in the animated finale, which begins *giocoso e leggiero* before a Baroque-style, four-note figure slowly makes its presence felt. The figure is first heard

on the bassoon, then shifts timbre and focus (timpani and bells play a crucial role later on), inspiring the strings to lyrical heights. The piquantly scored first movement conjures a gentle beating of wings, with glowing modulations that sometimes darken, though they never cloud the issue. The reflective central movement follows without a break.

The Third Piano Concerto (1998) is stronger meat. More meditative than its predecessors though visited by some cluster-like dissonances, it seems to take its principal stylistic cue from the middle movement of Bartók's Second Piano Concerto. The opening string chord motif is simple, austere, the piano writing bold or decorative rather than overtly pianistic. As a whole, it's cast vaguely in the manner of Delius or Debussy, more an orchestral tone-poem with piano than a display piece. The most striking movement is the second, which incorporates some fairly harsh brass writing and memorably beautiful closing pages. The *Energico* finale calls in the big guns and is well served by Ondine's recording team, but one could imagine a more forceful performance. Otherwise, things go well. The disc closes with an interview, a disarmingly natural slice of dialogue where the composer relates to Ashkenazy how he views his works as received phenomena. That, for the most part, is precisely how his music sounds – like audible episodes drawn from nature, messages that, in a world seduced by banal artifice, are all too easily ignored.

Cantus arcticus, Op 61

Cantus arcticus (Concerto for Birds and Orchestra)
with taped birdsong. Piano Concerto No 1, Op 45[a].
Symphony No 3, Op 20
[a]Laura Mikkola *pf* Royal Scottish National
Orchestra / Hannu Lintu
Naxos 8 554147 (74' · DDD)   (S)(O)►

No other new music stands to benefit more from extensive exposure, not so much because of its quality (which is beyond question), as because of an almost tangible connection with nature, than that by Rautavaara. One constantly senses the joy of a man alone with the elements: awe-struck, contented, inspired. Birdsong comes from all directions, literally in the 'Concerto for birds and orchestra' or *Cantus arcticus*, which sets taped birdsong against a rustic orchestral backdrop. The tape blends well with the music and is very atmospheric. The young Finnish conductor Hannu Lintu directs a fine performance. The First Piano Concerto and Third Symphony (out of seven) receive good performances, most notably the Brucknerian Symphony, an impressive and often dramatic work that begins and ends in the key of D minor. The orchestration incorporates four Wagner tubas, though some of the finest material is also the quietest. The slow movement is sullen but haunting, the *Scherzo* occasionally suggestive of Nielsen or Martinů and the finale brings the parallels with Bruckner fully within earshot. The First Piano Concerto has a brilliance and immediacy that should please orchestral adventurers and piano aficionados. The solo writing employs clusters and much filigree fingerwork, but it's the noble, chorale-like second movement that leaves the strongest impression. Laura Mikkola gives a good performance. Naxos gives a full sound picture and overall, this is an excellent CD, concisely annotated by the composer.

Manhattan Trilogy

Manhattan Trilogy. Symphony No 3
Helsinki Philharmonic Orchestra / Leif Segerstam
Ondine ⊛ ODE1090-5 (54' · DDD/DSD)　　　Ⓕ🅑➔

Manhattan Trilogy. Symphony No 8,
'The Journey'. Symphony No 6, 'Vincentiana' –
IV: Apotheosis (revised version)
**New Zealand Symphony Orchestra /
Pietari Inkinen**
Naxos 8 570069 (56' · DDD)　　　Ⓢ🅑➔

Rautavaara studied at the Juilliard School in 1955-56 and *Manhattan Trilogy* (2004) was commissioned to celebrate its centennial. In recalling his youthful sojourn in the Big Apple, the composer deployed the full panoply of his late orchestral manner in a hugely engaging triptych describing his 'hopeful Daydreams', 'sudden Nightmares of doubt' and 'slowly breaking Dawn of the personality'. Where Segerstam's vivid interpretation, allied to Ondine's sumptuous recording, glows through its 20 minutes, Inkinen provides a beautifully focused reading, nearly two minutes swifter, with every detail brought out to telling effect.

Not the most gripping of Rautavaara's recent orchestral essays, *Manhattan Trilogy* is none the less accomplished. What connects it to the Third Symphony (1959-61) is the treatment of the past. The symphony – one of the finest of the post-war period, serially organised within a vibrant tonal framework – recreates the idiom of Bruckner from a late-1950s sensibility and, ironically, remains the more progressive.

Rautavaara's most recent symphony, the Eighth (1999), was memorably recorded by Segerstam (Ondine). Inkinen once again produces a refined interpretation with crystal-clear detail although Segerstam achieved more grandeur in the peroration. Choice here really will depend on couplings (the Harp Concerto on Ondine). The revision of the Sixth Symphony's finale as a – presumably – stand-alone concert piece shorn of its part for synthesiser works well enough, though it is no substitute for the whole work, for which turn to Max Pommer's bracing account (also with the Helsinki Philharmonic) for Ondine. In context, though, the Naxos programme works most effectively and is a near-perfect introduction to Rautavaara's late manner. Both discs are highly recommendable; at its price, the Naxos is hard to beat but Ondine has the Third. Buy both!

Symphonies

Symphony No 1. Book of Visions. Adagio celeste
National Orchestra of Belgium / Mikko Franck
Ondine ⊛ ODE1064-5 (76' · DDD)　　　Ⓕ🅑➔

Rautavaara's First Symphony, written in 1955 in four movements, was recast in 1988 – not wholly convincingly – as a diptych. In 2003 Rautavaara added a new slow movement based on a song composed in the 1950s. The result is better balanced and Mikko Franck's account has considerable poise.

Rautavaara's euphonious late style is perfectly adapted for visionary slow movements, so it may surprise that *Adagio celeste* (1997, given here in its 2000 version) is based on a 12-note row. More relevantly, it is derived from a sensuous romantic poem by Lassi Nummi: it is broadly languorous in tone with a strong undertow.

Wonderfully subtle is an apt description for the four-movement *Book of Visions* (2003, rev 2005). Running to a full 40 minutes, the work superficially has a Henzean ground plan with its succession of four tales of 'Night', 'Fire', 'Love' and 'Fate'. However, its internal processes, while organic, have goals other than the symphonic and it calls to mind Lutosławski's *Livre pour orchestre* (however stylistically remote). Its emotional vision is the most intense of the works here, much of it autobiographical in essence. Franck proves a most sympathetic interpreter and draws fine playing from the Belgian orchestra. Excellent sound.

Symphony No 7, 'Angel of Light'. Annunciations
Kari Jussila org **Helsinki Philharmonic Orchestra /
Leif Segerstam**
Ondine ODE869-2 (65' · DDD)　　　Ⓕ🅞🅑➔

The Seventh Symphony's opening *Tranquillo* evokes a calm though powerful atmosphere, with many Sibelian points of reference, especially in recognisable echoes of the *Largo* fourth movement from Sibelius's Fourth Symphony, whereas the closing *Pesante-cantabile* is more in line with the symphonic world of Hovhaness. The Angel idea originates in a series of works (*Angels and Visitations* and *Angel of Dusk*, for instance), the reference being to 'an archetype, one of mankind's oldest traditions and perennial companions'. This Jungian axis is reflected in monolithic chords, ethereal harmonic computations (invariably broad and high-reaching) and an unselfconscious mode of musical development. Readers schooled in the more contemplative works of Górecki, Pärt and Tavener will likely respond to this spatially generous essay, though Rautavaara's language is more a celebration of nature than any specific religious ritual.

Comparisons with the *Annunciations* (for organ, brass quintet, wind orchestra and percussion) find the earlier work far harsher in tone, much more demanding technically (it calls for a formidable organ virtuoso) and more radical in its musical language. The style ranges from the primeval drone that opens the work through canon, 'bird forest' activity and the novel effect of having the 'notes of a dense chord weirdly circulating in the room' when the organ motor is switched off. Kari Jussila rises to the various challenges with what sounds like genuine enthusiasm (his fast finger-work is amazing) while Leif Segerstam and his orchestra exploit the tonal drama of both works. The recordings are warm and spacious.

Additional recommendation

Symphonies Nos 1-7
Nat Orch of Belgium / Franck[1]; Leipzig RSO / Pommer[2-5]; Helsinki PO / Pommer[6]; Helsinki PO / Segerstam[7,8]
Ondine ④ ODE1145-2 (3h 56' DDD)   ⒷOOⒹ
A wonderful conspectus of a fascinating musical voice unfolded over 44 years. Beautifully engaged and engaging performances by some of Rautavaara's greatest champions.

String Quartets

String Quartets Nos 1 & 2.
String Quintet, 'Unknown Heavens'
Jan-Erik Gustafsson vc **Jean Sibelius Quartet**
(Yoshiko Arai-Kimanen, Jukka Pohjola vns Matti Hirvikangas va Seppo Kimanen vc)
Ondine ODE909-2 (62' · DDD)   Ⓕ

Here we encounter not one Rautavaara, but three: the fledgling student captivated by folk-lore; the dodecaphonic zealot stretching the expressive potential of 'the system'; and the triumphant melodist basking in his own unique brand of harmonic complexity. The stylistic leap from the Second Quartet to the Quintet, or Unknown Heavens is more a matter of tone than temperament. All three works are ceaselessly active, the First (1952) being perhaps the leanest, and the last (1997) the richest in texture. Unknown Heavens takes its name from an earlier work for male chorus, which Rautavaara quotes, initially in the second bar of the first movement ('when the second violin answers the question posed by the first,' as Rautavaara writes), many times thereafter, and then significantly revised at the start of the fourth movement. The third begins as a cello duet, sure justification for why five players are employed where the Kuhmo Music Festival originally commissioned a piece for four. 'The work seemed to acquire a will of its own,' writes Rautavaara. The equally well-performed string quartets are stylistically rather more challenging. The First Quartet plays for just over 11 minutes and inhabits a mildly rustic world roughly akin to Kodály. Best here is the Andante's haunting coda, whereas the 1958 Second Quartet is at its most inventive for the faster second and fourth movements. The current Rautavaara is more relaxed,

more contemplative, wiser and softer-grained than his former self. He seems happier reflecting nature than organising abstract patterns: you sense that the Quintet is authentically self-expressive, whereas the quartets speak interestingly about nothing in particular. The recordings are full-bodied and well balanced.

Piano Works

Etudes, Op 42. Icons, Op 6. Partita, Op 34. Piano Sonatas – No 1, 'Christus und die Fischer', Op 50; No 2, 'The Fire Sermon', Op 64. Seven Preludes, Op 7
Laura Mikkola pf
Naxos 8 554292 (61' · DDD)   ⒻⒹ

The most interesting aspect of hearing piano music by a composer known primarily for his orchestral work is in spotting those inimitable harmonic fingerprints that help define his musical personality. Rautavaara's piano music is full of tell-tale signs, even in an early work like the Op 7 Preludes, where he indulged a sort of clandestine protest against the 'neo-classical' confines he experienced in Helsinki and America. Rautavaara was studying with Copland at the time but chose to keep his Preludes to himself. And yet it's Copland's Piano Sonata that spontaneously comes to mind during the austere opening of his 'The Black Madonna of Blakernaya' from Icons, perhaps the most striking of all his solo piano works. The translucent colours in 'The Baptism of Christ' make a profound effect, as does the serenity of 'The Holy Women at the Sepulchre'. Aspects of 'angels' seem prophetically prevalent – whether consciously or not – in the Etudes of 1969. Each piece tackles a different interval: thirds in the first, sevenths in the second, then tritones, fourths, seconds and fifths. The third is reminiscent of Messiaen, and the fifth of Bartók, but Rautavaara's guiding hand is everywhere in evidence. Spirituality is an invariable presence, especially in the two piano sonatas, though the Second ends with an unexpected bout of contrapuntal brutality. Perhaps the most instantly appealing track is the brief but touching central movement of the three and a half-minute Partita, Op 34, with its gentle whiffs of Bartók. Laura Mikkola plays all 28 movements with obvious conviction. Naxos's recorded sound is excellent.

Choral works

Complete Works for Male Choir
Tuomas Katajala ten **Talla Vocal Ensemble / Pasi Hyökki; YL Male Voice Choir / Matti Hyökki**
Ondine ② ODE1125-2D (99' · DDD · T/t)   Ⓜ

YL divide up the works between the main body and their 10-man offshoot, the Talla Vocal Ensemble – the latter, incidentally, are superb in the two TS Eliot Preludes (1956, rev 1967). Ondine's recording is rich, with great presence, matched by singing of urgency and vividness.

And YL and Talla's interpretations have impetus and power, as in the half-hour-long *A Book of Life* (1972), which is split between the two groups (as are the *Four Serenades*, 1978), setting 11 poems – including texts by Rilke, Rimbaud, Goethe, Emily Dickinson and Whitman – in five languages.

The greater textural palette attained through using two differently sized choirs is more akin to that found in some early-music recordings. Perhaps there's a loss of intimacy and a certain dreamy quality – for instance in the Psalms (1968-71) or some of the folksong arrangements. But this is a small price to pay for the gains which, for collectors of Rautavaara, will chiefly be the quartets of songs to poems by Aleksis Kivi (arr 2005) or from the opera *Rasputin* (arr 2006), not otherwise issued.

Aleksis Kivi

Aleksis Kivi
Jorma Hynninen bar Aleksis Kivi **Lasse Pöysti** spkr
August Ahlqvist **Eeva-Liisa Saarinen** mez Charlotta
Helena Juntunen sop Hilda **Gabriel Suovanen** bar
Young Aleksis **Marcus Groth** buffo JL Runeberg **Lassi
Virtanen** ten Mikko Vilkastus **Jaako Kietikko** bass
Uncle Sakeri **Jyväskylä Sinfonia / Markus Lehtinen**
Ondine ② ODE1000-2D (98' · DDD · T/t)   Ⓕ

Idyll turned to nightmare, optimism to disillusionment, creative fruitfulness to barren schizophrenia and premature death. The tragic fate of the founder of Finnish-language literature has haunted Rautavaara ever since his youth. The opera *Aleksis Kivi* (1995-96) was the melodious crystallisation of a lifetime's pondering. Kivi (1834-72) was active while Swedish words still predominated in Finnish literature, the Finnish poet Johan Ludvig Runeberg having been the best-known Swedish-language exponent of the genre. Kivi's descent from lyrical flights of pastoral fancy to mental derangement was caused in part by damning assessments of his work from the poet and aesthetician August Ahlqvist, the only speaking role in the opera. Ahlqvist is portrayed here by the actor Lasse Pöysti, whose rhythmically inflected recitation is utterly bewitching. Musically *Aleksis Kivi* calls on a varied array of styles. The Prologue depicts Kivi as despondent, despairing and deranged, the music dark and grainy, with a reptilian clarinet in the foreground and a skilfully deployed synthesiser. The scoring is economical throughout (strings, clarinets, percussion) but those who gravitate most readily to his 'angel' orchestral works will likely respond best to the first act, music filled with mellow light which reflects, in its rich, constantly shifting hues, the protagonist's inspirational flights. The performance is consistently good, the mezzo Eeva-Liisa Saarinen excelling as Charlotta. Confidently conducted, keenly played and vividly recorded, *Aleksis Kivi* is a powerful narrative written with the kind of descriptive facility that Bartók employed for *Bluebeard's Castle*.

Maurice Ravel   French 1875-1937

Ravel's family moved to Paris when Maurice was three months old and his talent was encouraged. His music lessons began in 1882 when he was seven; in 1889 he entered the Paris Conservatoire where Fauré was among his teachers and he remained a student for a further 16 years, an unusually long time. One reason for this was his strenuous attempts to win the coveted Prix de Rome, which Berlioz, Bizet and Debussy before him had won. He was placed second in 1901, tried and failed in 1902 and 1903, and then was eliminated, humiliatingly, in 1905 before the final stage of the competition. But by this time he was already established as a respected composer: the lovely Pavane pour une infante défunte, his piano piece Jeux d'eau, his String Quartet and the three songs with orchestra called Shéhérazade had been well received. The jury's decision became a cause célèbre, amid charges of favouritism, and it led to the resignation of the director of the Conservatoire, Théodore Dubois (Fauré took his place). When the scandal had died down, Ravel was famous. Over the next decade or so, he wrote some of his finest work (Rapsodie espagnole, Gaspard de la nuit, Daphnis et Chloé).

The First World War had a decisive and ultimately fatal effect on Ravel: he volunteered his services for the army and the air force, but neither could use him because of his very light weight (about seven stones) and frail physique. Instead he became an ambulance driver at the front in Verdun. Although short in stature (a little over five feet) and sensitive by nature, his health up to that time had been good. However, the war broke him physically and emotionally. After being released from his driving duties with dysentery, he was compelled to recuperate in hospital. His mother's death followed closely afterwards, deeply affecting him, and he began to suffer from insomnia and what he called 'nervous debility'. Thereafter, despite producing a number of masterpieces, inspiration came less frequently. Nevertheless, his career continued smoothly.

Ravel never married. Soon after the war he moved to a small villa called Belvédère about 30 miles to the south-west of Paris in Montfort-l'Amaury, living in semi-seclusion. All his affection was lavished on his beautiful home which, according to his biographer Madeleine Goss, 'became his mother, wife and children...the only real expression of his entire life'. There he lived with his housekeeper, a collection of mechanical and clockwork toys and a family of Siamese cats (a passion he shared with Debussy). He accepted few pupils but gave friendly advice to many (including Vaughan Williams); he never taught in any conservatory. In fact Ravel comes across as an isolated, reserved and coolly aloof individual, 'more courteous than cordial...and more ingenuous than anything else,' as his lifelong friend Roland-Manuel put it. After Debussy's death in 1918 he was hailed as France's greatest living composer and honours were heaped upon him, though (perhaps in retaliation for the Prix de Rome débâcle) he vehemently turned down the Légion d'honneur in 1920. Invitations poured in for him to conduct his music all over Europe (in this and as a piano soloist he was only adequate, and then only in his own works).

RAVEL PIANO CONCERTOS – IN BRIEF

Krystian Zimerman; London SO, Cleveland Orchestra / Pierre Boulez
DG 449 213-2GH (56' · DDD) Ⓕ❍❍❍➓

Ⓖ A *Gramophone* Award winner in 1999, this truly magnificent achievement enshrines musicianship of the highest calibre. Zimerman is on top form, his pianism quite astonishingly clear and precise, and Boulez is a superb accompanist.

Louis Lortie; London SO / Frühbeck de Burgos
Chandos CHAN8773 (57' · DDD) Ⓕ❍➓

Fine playing and rich, idiomatic accompaniment makes this a fine CD (the coupling is Fauré's *Ballade*). Lortie is best in the G major – his Left-Hand Concerto is slightly eccentric – but the sound he makes, as captured by Chandos, is most appealing.

Jean-Philippe Collard; French National Orchestra / Lorin Maazel
EMI 574749-2 (64' · DDD) Ⓑ❍➓

Another *Gramophone* Award winner – and the version to get if you're watching the pennies. Collard is on sparkling form, and Maazel is in his element in this music. There's real fizz here, and there are some generous solo piano works as coupling.

Alicia de Larrocha; LPO / Lawrence Foster, Rafael Frühbeck de Burgos
Decca Australian Eloquence 4762351 (78' · ADD) Ⓜ➓

Sparkling musicianship from the doyenne of Spanish pianists – she brings a glorious range of colours to these two scores as well as her characteristic attention to detail. Where others sparkle she goes for poetry and magic. Generously coupled with the Fauré *Fantaisie* and the Franck *Symphonic Variations*.

PIANO CONCERTO IN G

Martha Argerich; Berlin PO / Claudio Abbado
DG 447 438-2GGA (71' · ADD) Ⓕ❍➓

Coupled with a fiery Prokofiev Third Concerto, Argerich's G major Concerto is outstanding, with filigree-textured fingerwork, rhythmic vitality of crystal and a wonderful identification with the work's idiom. A magnificent performance.

Arturo Benedetti Michelangeli; Philharmonia / Ettore Gracis
EMI 567238-2 (47' · ADD) Ⓜ❍❍➓

Simply the classic recording. Michelangeli demonstrates his total sympathy for the work. The Philharmonia are on top form in this great disc from 1957. Coupled with Rachmaninov No 4, this is one of EMI's Great Recordings of the Century – and no one would surely question that accolade!

In the autumn of 1932 he had a road accident in a Paris taxi from which he never fully recovered. Gradually, his memory went. Eventually, suspecting a brain tumour, an operation was decided upon. No tumour was found. Nine days later, having briefly regained consciousness and calling for his brother, Ravel passed away. Shortly before, he had heard a performance of his own Daphnis et Chloé and is reported to have said, in tears, 'I still have so much music in my head. I have said nothing. I have so much more to say.'

Piano Concertos

Piano Concerto in G[ab]. Piano Concerto for the Left Hand[ac]. Valses nobles et sentimentales (orch cpsr)[b]
[a]**Krystian Zimerman** pf [b]**Cleveland Orchestra,** [c]**London Symphony Orchestra / Pierre Boulez**
DG 449 213-2GH (56' · DDD) Ⓕ❍❍❍➓

Ⓖ Krystian Zimerman's pianism is self-recommending. His trills in the first movement of the G major Concerto are to die for, his passagework in the finale crystal-clear, never hectic, always stylish. For their part Boulez and the Clevelanders are immaculate and responsive; they relish Ravel's neon-lit artificiality and moments of deliberate gaudiness. That goes equally for the *Valses nobles*, which have just about every nuance you'd want, and none you wouldn't. The recording is generous with ambience, to the point where some orchestral entries after big climaxes are blurred. Otherwise detail is razor-sharp and one of the biggest selling-points of the disc. Zimerman's humming may be a slight distraction for some listeners, especially in the Left-Hand Concerto, where you may not be always convinced that the LSO knew quite what it was supposed to do with the long notes of the main theme, and where there's a slight lack of tension in exchanges between piano and orchestra. There again, had the G major Concerto not been so wonderful those points might not have registered at all, for this is playing of no mean distinction. In the Left-Hand Concerto, Zimerman's phenomenal pianism sets its own agenda and brings its own rich rewards.

Orchestral Works

Boléro. Pavane pour une infante défunte. Daphnis et Chloé – Suite No 2. Ma Mère l'Oye – Pavane de la Belle au bois dormant; Les entretiens de la Belle et la Bête; Petit Poucet; Laideronnette, Impératrice des Pagodes; Apothéose: Le jardin féerique
Cincinnati Symphony Orchestra / Paavo Järvi
Telarc CD80601 (63' · DDD) Ⓕ❍❍❍➓

Ⓖ Most of this disc is very enjoyable. Järvi is always in absolute control, and one or two moments of unscheduled *rubato* in *La valse* can be forgiven, such was the tact and intelligence with which they were managed. Any conductor must balance the impulse to lilt *à la viennoise* against what appears to be Ravel's implicit instruction not to vary the tempo until around halfway. Järvi does it well and, notably, his speed for the return of the opening is spot on the original, not faster as so often happens.

His *Boléro* is on the quick side, but there's no feeling of scramble, and the only things to miss are the extra trombone slides from Ravel's disc, which unfortunately have never found their way into the score. The *Pavane* is lovely in all respects – steady but not stodgy – and the *Daphnis* suite has all the colour and warmth one could ask for. Just occasionally in *Ma Mère l'Oye* the balance isn't ideal: in the first movement the cor anglais momentarily obscures the clarinet, and in 'Laideronnette' the piccolo, too, is lost in its lower reaches. The only moment where Järvi's identification with the music seems to falter is with his handling of the *retenu/a tempo* marking leading into the final peroration of 'Le jardin féerique'. But these are small points to set against the quality of the whole.

La valse. Daphis et Chloé – Suite No 2. Ma Mère l'Oye – Suite. Valses nobles et sentimentales
Rotterdam Philharmonic Orchestra / Yannick Nézet-Séguin
EMI 966342-2 (62' · DDD)   ℗**OOOO**▶

One of the toughest tests for any conductor of Ravel comes towards the close of *Ma Mère l'Oye*'s climactic 'Le jardin féerique' where as the last lap approaches the opening theme returns freshly cushioned on some of Ravel's most sumptuous string writing. If you want the suite rather than the whole ballet then Yannick Nézet-Séguin in Rotterdam achieves layered textures that are as warm and as flowing as any. The 'happy ending' *crescendo* is especially joyous, and there's a gorgeous blend of woodwind timbres in 'Impératrice au bois'. Knitting together the *Valses nobles et sentimentales*, charting their many contrasts in mood and colour, is always a challenge, and again Nézet-Séguin reveals himself to be not only a fine conductor but an expert listener too, the slow epilogue with its wafting motifs like so many stray letters blowing in the early hours charged with a very special atmosphere.

Not everyone brings this music off as well whereas the challenges of *La valse* are quite different and here Nézet-Séguin and his players don't quite achieve the same level of expressive continuity. The closing pages, too, need to sound more riotous and disruptive. However the *Daphnis et Chloé* Second Suite is given a gem of a performance, the opening dawn sequence unravelling like a luxuriant carpet, the principal climax truly momentous. This is a sultry, insinuating *Daphnis*, stronger on seduction than on translucency, a performance steeped in a sense of theatre, very dynamically recorded. It's the crowning glory of a fine and compelling programme.

Daphnis et Chloé

Daphnis et Chloé. La valse
Berlin Radio Chorus; Berlin Philharmonic Orchestra / Pierre Boulez
DG 447 057-2GH (71' · DDD)   ℗**O**▶

Increasingly, for considering modern recordings of *Daphnis*, it seems you must banish memories of 1959 Monteux; put behind you the most playful, mobile, texturally diaphanous, rhythmically supple account of the score ever recorded; one that's uniquely informed by history and selfless conductorial wisdom. For some, Monteux's view may remain a rather moderate one – certainly in terms of basic tempo and basic dynamic range; and Ravel's score suggests tempi and dynamics which modern performances, and especially recordings, have more faithfully reproduced.

Boulez has acquired a wealth of experience of conductorial wisdom since his first New York recording of *Daphnis*. Here he has the Berlin Philharmonic Orchestra on top form to sustain and shape melody within some of his strikingly slow tempi (such as the opening, and Part 3's famous 'Daybreak'), and who remain 'composed' in his daringly fast ones (the 'Dance of the young girls around Daphnis' and the 'Danse guerrière' – one of the most exciting on disc). Just occasionally, you feel that there are parts of the work that interest him less than others. But anyone who doubts Boulez's ability to achieve, first, a sense of ecstasy should hear this 'Daybreak'; secondly, a refined radiance, should try the first embrace (track 5, 2'49"; at this point, this is also one of the very few recordings where you can hear the chorus); or, thirdly, to characterise properly the supernatural, listen to the 'flickering' accents he gives the string *tremolo* chords in the 'Nocturne'.

The chorus work, not least in the 'Interlude', is outstanding; the harmonic boldness of this passage was just as startling in New York, but the Berlin chorus, unlike the New York one, is here properly set back.

In general, DG's recording strikes exactly the right compromise between clarity and spaciousness, much as Decca's did for Dutoit. With the added lure of an expansive and often massively powerful *La valse* (spectacular timpani), this is now the most recommendable modern *Daphnis* available.

Daphnis et Chloé[a]. Shéhérazade – Ouverture
[a]**MDR Rundfunkchor, Leipzig; Lyon National Orchestra / Jun Märkl**
Naxos 8 570992 (71' · DDD)   ⑤**OO**▶

This Naxos disc, in dazzling sound, demonstrates that under its latest music director, Jun Märkl, the Lyon National Orchestra's standards remains high. This is one of the most spectacular of showpieces among ballet scores, and the Lyon orchestra gives a powerful and

RAVEL'S STRING QUARTET – IN BRIEF

Quartetto Italiano
Philips 464 699-2PM (52' · ADD)   Ⓜ️Ⓓ➤
One of the cornerstones of the chamber catalogue. The Italians perform with a nimble grace and sense of wonder that never pall. The 1965 recording still sounds good to modern ears.

Vlach Quartet
Supraphon SU3461-2 (56' · ADD)   Ⓜ️
An interpretation of uncommon recreative eagerness and genuine staying power. This distinguished Czech ensemble respond with all the freshness of new discovery. Admirably remastered 1959 sound.

Melos Quartet
DG Galleria 463 082-2GGA (53' · ADD)   Ⓜ️Ⓓ➤
The Melos always put the music first and have both consumate artistic flair and impeccable technical address to commend them. DG's production-team strike a most natural balance.

Juilliard Quartet
Testament SBT1375 (74' · DDD)   ⒻⓄⓄ
The Juilliards bring a wealth of experience and enviable sense of purpose to Ravel's masterly quartet. A heartfelt, concentrated reading, beautifully recorded.

Ebène Quartet
Virgin Classics 519045-2 (80' · DDD)   ⒻⓄⓄⓄⒹ➤
Ⓖ A stunning new recording that approaches perfection. These players are completely inside this miraculous score and play like four angels. Magnificent!

Ad Libitum Quartet
Naxos 8 554722 (57' · DDD)   ⓈⒹ➤
An arresting, sparkily individual rendering from this gifted young Romanian group, winners of the 1997 Evian String Quartet Competition. Coupled with a highly perceptive account of Fauré's elusive but alluring Quartet.

Petersen Quartet
Capriccio 10 860 (68' · DDD)   Ⓕ
Exceptionally refreshing and articulate music-making. Part of a hugely rewarding programme including Milhaud's First Quartet and attractive works by Chausson and Lekeu.

Belcea Quartet
EMI 574020-2 (71' · DDD)   ⓈⓄⓄⓄⒹ➤
Ⓖ An auspicious start to what promises to be a stellar career. Uncommonly well-integrated quartet playing and winner of the Best Debut Recording Prize at the 2001 *Gramophone* Awards.

subtle performance, with the wind and brass soloists outstanding.

The Leipzig Radio Choir, which comes from where Märkl was last in charge, adds to the glow of the performance, which can match almost any version in the catalogue. Naxos has again demonstrated its rare ability to produce excellent discs at bargain price. The shimmering sounds of the 'Daybreak' movement are perfectly caught, with the wind nicely defined, and the final 'Danse générale' rounds the performance off thrillingly.

To add to the attractions a substantial fill-up is offered. The Ouverture *Shéhérazade* is a student work but already demonstrates Ravel's gift for creating magical orchestral textures, very reminiscent of Debussy but not entirely derivative with its climactic fanfares leading to a hushed close. It provides a delightful makeweight to an outstanding disc.

Additional recommendation

Daphnis et Chloé
Coupled with Complete Works for Orchestra
London Symphony Orchestra and Chorus / Abbado
DG Trio ③ 469 354-2GTR3 (3h 20' · DDD)   Ⓜ️Ⓓ➤
A very desirable set, with the LSO putting on its best, totally convincing, French accent. Abbado's *Daphnis et Chloé* is reminiscent of that from Monteux. The sophistication and power of these performances is something to marvel at.

String Quartet in F

Ravel String Quartet **Debussy** String Quartet, Op 10
Fauré String Quartet, Op 121
Quatuor Ebène (Pierre Colombet, Gabriel Le Magadure vns Mathieu Herzog va Raphaël Merlin vc)
Virgin Classics 519045-2 (80' · DDD)   ⒻⓄⓄⓄⒹ➤

Ⓖ Among the many breathtaking moments on the Ebène Quartet's CD, there is one in particular that keeps calling one back. It occurs at around 1'14" into the Ravel's slow movement, the second set, which enters like a bittersweet memory before a literal recollection of the Quartet's opening motif. Other subtle details of interpretation include the chord at 2'03" that underpins a transformation of the first subject before the same chord leads directly into the second subject – and when it does, utterly changing in character, turning warmer, more openly inviting. The ebb and flow of the passage at 5'29" where the second subject rides above an arpeggiated accompaniment, music that looks both forwards to Debussy's own *La mer* and backwards to Rimsky's *Sheherazade* (or so it seems). There's a fluidity to the Ebène's playing of both works that suits the music's character, a mood of wistfulness too that the Ravel especially benefits from. This improvisatory approach is hardly surprising from an ensemble that is also celebrated for its jazz performances.

It was a brilliant idea to include Fauré's late Quartet which, in a sense, provides the linchpin for all three works, the Ravel having been composed in Fauré's class to mark the 10th anniversary of Debussy's quartet, and which is dedicated to Fauré. An extraordinary work by any standards, ethereal and other-worldly with themes that seem constantly to be drawn skywards, Fauré's Quartet responds well to the Ebène's sensitised approach.

Anyone requiring this particular trio of works won't be disappointed, which makes the various pairings of the Ravel and Debussy quartets on their own seem somewhat less enticing.

Complete Piano Works

Complete Solo Piano Works
Angela Hewitt pf
Hyperion ② CDA67341/2 (138' · DDD)　　Ⓕ**O**▷

Angela Hewitt's set of Ravel's piano music is a remarkable feat of the most concentrated imaginative delicacy, wit and style. Fresh from her success in Bach she shows how such prowess – namely a scrupulous regard for the score, an acute ear for part-writing, for polyphony, and for meticulous clarity and refinement – can bring extensive rewards. Everything in her performances betokens the greatest care and a special empathy for Ravel's neo-classicism, for his way of paying affectionate tribute to the past while spicing its conventions with a wholly modern sensibility. Everything in the *Pavane* is subtly graded and textured, the pedalling light and discreet, with a special sense of luminous poetry when the theme makes its final and magical reappearance. No distorting idiosyncrasy is allowed within distance of *Le tombeau de Couperin*, yet nothing is taken for granted.

Her *Gaspard* is a marvel of evocation through precision. Gone are old-fashioned vagueness and approximation: her 'Le gibet' is surely among the most exquisitely controlled on record. Again, her opening to 'Scarbo' is alive with menace because all four of Ravel's directions are so precisely observed; and if she's too sensible to yearn for, say, Martha Argerich's chilling virtuoso *frisson* she makes no concessions to wildness, impetuosity or telescoped phrasing. Nothing is done in the heat of the moment; she keeps Ravel's nightmare under control rather than allowing it to engulf her.

Yet Hewitt can be as romantically yielding as she's exact. In the return of the principal idea from 'Oiseaux tristes' (*Miroirs*) she achieves an extraordinary sense of stillness, of 'birds lost in the sombre torpor of a tropical forest'.

Hyperion's sound is of demonstration quality. Hewitt joins Gieseking, Rogé, Thibaudet and Lortie among the most distinguished if entirely different Ravel cycles on record, and easily withstands comparison.

Gaspard de la nuit

Ravel Gaspard de la nuit
Carter Night Fantasies. Two Diversions. 90+
Pierre-Laurent Aimard pf
Warner Classics ② 2564 62160-2 (59' · DDD)
Includes bonus CD with illustrated talk by
Pierre-Laurent Aimard　　　　　Ⓕ**OOO**▷

One could expect Pierre-Laurent Aimard's account of *Gaspard de la nuit* to have pleased the composer mightily: totally focused and attentive to the text, scrupulously controlled in sound and movement, the articulation of the continuity as Ravel insisted it should be, that's to say with the unity of time preserved, in all three pieces. No otiose slowings. Nothing imposed, only revealed. Be expressive, be dazzling, be magical, be a virtuoso story-teller, but get on with it (as Ravel might have said), and above all play in time.

With the composer looking over his shoulder, the pianist might murmur that there's also the little matter of taking care of every note, intellectually and technically, and of being able not only to play them but to conjure a range of sonority and a rhythmic context in which everything happens at the right time. Aimard might agree that *Gaspard de la nuit*, consisting as it does of three highly contrasted pieces, is not just hugely demanding but an encyclopedic work, in the sense that the performance of it is the measure of all the artistic and technical qualities of the mature player. Difficult to overpraise his achievement here for its freshness and authority and the impeccable pianistic address, and the only reservation, a very small one, has to do with the lack of a touch of fury, or frenzy, in his characterisation of 'Scarbo': the dwarf is a hideous little devil, not just a mischievous one…

The conjunction of Ravel and Elliott Carter may not be attractive to everyone but Aimard sees a commitment to new music as part of his job; would that there were more artists like him. On a bonus disc Aimard talks well about how the Carter pieces are made, and for people unfamiliar with them this could be a way in. How Carter's pieces are made is very much their raison d'être: his is predominantly a music of lines, of contrapuntal voices highly differentiated in character and movement and in their stability one against another, and how these may be built into structures rich in polyrhythmic effects.

Night Fantasies is the major work for piano of Carter's maturity, and it has a lot going on. It's admirable but unmemorable, masterly music which offers much to the mind but not enough refreshment to the spirit, as if a dimension were missing. The three shorter pieces, in which the play of invention is delightful in itself, raise expectations less and satisfy them more. But in Carter, as in Ravel, Aimard's advocacy is wonderful. The excellent recording derives from the large hall of the Konzerthaus in Vienna; the acoustic has character and the sound is at an apt distance.

RAVEL GASPARD DE LA NUIT – IN BRIEF

Martha Argerich
EMI 557101-2 (52' · ADD)   Ⓕ ⦿Ⓞ⮞
A wildly exciting concert performance from 1978, with Argerich live in Amsterdam shaving four minutes off the timing of her previous LP version (see below).

Martha Argerich
DG 447 438-2GOR (71' · ADD)   Ⓜ�Ⓞ⮞
For those who prefer studio recordings, Argerich's highly regarded 1974 taping has been added to her famous pairing of the Ravel G major and Prokofiev Third Piano Concertos. This one has both raw passion and wonderfully controlled gradations of touch and tone.

Pierre-Laurent Aimard
Warner Classics ② 2564 62160-2 (59' · DDD)
                                      Ⓕ ⦿ⓄⓄ⮞
Intriguingly coupled with music by Elliott Carter, this disc aligns Ravel with some of the most visionary of 20th composers.

Ivo Pogorelich
DG 463 678-2GOR (73' · ADD)   Ⓜ⮞
The unpredictable Pogorelich at his very best, accomplishing miracles of tone colour, refinement   and   control,   with   a coruscating final 'Scarbo'. The couplings are both piano sonatas: Prokofiev No 6 and the Chopin B flat minor.

Arturo Benedetti Michelangeli
BBC Legends BBCL4064-2 (78' · ADD)   Ⓕ
A scintillating BBC studio performance of 1959 in which Michelangeli seeks to convey the details of the score with what some hear as inhuman exactitude.

Pascal Rogé
Decca ② 440 836-2DF2 (142' · DDD)   Ⓜ⦿ⓄⓄ⮞
Rogé eschews sensationalism in his elegantly achieved Ravel complete solo piano music. The set includes a *Gaspard* whose relative restraint and Gallic economy won't spoil you for other readings.

Angela Hewitt
Hyperion ② CDA67341/2 (138' · DDD)   Ⓕ⮞
The pellucid qualities of Hewitt's Bach-playing are applied to the French master with compelling results in this set. An initially cool, slow-burn *Gaspard* with very clear textures in luminous sound.

Jean-Yves Thibaudet
Decca ② 433 515-2DH2 (130' · DDD)   ⒻⓄ⮞
The complete Ravel piano music as pianistic *tour de force*. Thibaudet's high-flying *Gaspard* is given greater impact by the vigour and immediacy of Decca's recording.

Gaspard de la nuit. Valses nobles et sentimentales. Jeux d'eau. Miroirs. Sonatine. Le tombeau de Couperin. Prélude. Menuet sur le nom de Haydn. A la manière de Borodine. Menuet antique. Pavane pour une infante défunte. A la manière de Chabrier. Ma Mère l'Oye[a]
Pascal Rogé, [a]**Denise-Françoise Rogé** pfs
Double Decca ② 440 836-2DF2 (142' · ADD)
Recorded 1973-94   Ⓜ⦿ⓄⓄ⮞

Everything is expressed with a classic restraint, elegance and economy, an ideal absence of artifice or idiosyncrasy. Rogé knows precisely where to allow asperity to relax into lyricism and vice versa, and time and again he finds that elusive, cool centre at the heart of Ravel's teeming and luxuriant vision. True, those used to more Lisztian but less authentic Ravel may occasionally find Rogé diffident or *laissez-faire*. But lovers of subtlety will see him as illuminating and enchanting. How often do you hear *Ma Mère l'Oye* given without a trace of brittleness or archness, or find *Jeux d'eau* presented with such stylish ease and tonal radiance? Rogé may lack something of Thibaudet's menace and high-flying virtuosity in 'Scarbo' (also on Decca) but how memorably he recreates Ravel's nocturnal mystery. Even if one misses a touch of cruelty behind Ondine's entreaty, few pianists can have evoked her watery realm with greater transparency. Arguably one of the finest Ravel recordings available.

Miroirs

Ravel Miroirs **Schumann** Kreisleriana
Herbert Schuch pf
Oehms Classics OC541 (64' · DDD)   Ⓕ ⓄⓄ

Herbert Schuch is a 27-year-old Romanian whose recording debut is of an intimidating mastery and stylistic assurance. Wherever you turn in the intricate mosaic of Schumann's *Kreisleriana* you will hear playing impossible to fault and easy to praise. The opening upsurge is truly *agitatissimo*, as boldly coloured and inflected as the magically chiming central section is spun off with a special inwardness and insight. The *sehr langsam* and its following, flowing *bewegter* could hardly be phrased more eloquently; and if the pace of No 7 is wild, the control is absolute. Schuch is no less immaculate in Ravel's *Miroirs*. Never for an instant do you hear the sort of diffidence or non-chalance that often passes for an authentic French style. 'Alborada del gracioso' is thrown off with the most concentrated verve and brilliance and the final ascent in 'Noctuelles' is a marvel of *pianissimo* delicacy and precision. Every chord in 'La vallée des cloches' is weighted and textured to perfection. Such playing has been faultlessly groomed for competition success (Schuch has won three international events in a year) and if there is an occasional suspicion that one is listening to an overly calculating if superlative pianist rather than a more spontaneous and acute artist, this is never less than a magnificent album. Oehms's sound is admirable.

Songs

Ravel Shéhérazade[b]. Menuet antique. Pavane pour
une infante défunte. Le tombeau de Couperin.
Debussy Danse sacrée et danse profane. Trois
Ballades de François Villon[a]. Cinq Poèmes de Charles
Baudelaire – Le jet d'eau[a]
[a]**Alison Hagley** sop [b]**Anne Sofie von Otter** mez
Cleveland Orchestra / Pierre Boulez
DG 471 614-2GH (76' · DDD · T/t)   Ⓕ❶❷🔁

Anne Sofie von Otter is really exploiting the
French repertory nowadays. After her Mélisande
and Carmen, and Chaminade and Offenbach
recitals, here she tackles Ravel's *Shéhérazade*
with total success. From the first cry of 'Asie' in
the opening song, von Otter beguiles using a
hushed yet expectant quality. Throughout her
soft singing is exquisite. The balance between
voice and orchestra has all the subtlety this
extended prologue requires. At the sinister line,
'Je voudrais voir des assassins', she employs a
harsh edge to the voice that's immediately echoed in the orchestral climax. As the poet
describes the story telling, Boulez brings the
song to its end with a perfect *diminuendo*, leading
into the mysterious 'Flute enchantée'. Here
again von Otter's control of dynamics pays off
with a gorgeous 'mysterieux baiser'.

The final song is also the most difficult. In its
ambiguity, 'L'indifférent' mustn't be overstressed, and yet that ironic remark at the end,
'Ta démarche feminine et lasse' needs to be not
so much regretful as a sigh of half-amused resignation. *Le tombeau de Couperin*, in its orchestral
version, is an equally difficult challenge which
Boulez and the Cleveland orchestra bring off
with precision. With the other two orchestral
arrangements of piano pieces, the *Pavane* and the
Menuet antique, again Boulez achieves such clarity
that even these over-familiar works sound surprising and fresh.

The Debussy *Danses*, for harp and strings,
serve as a sort of interlude, leading into the other
three-song event, the *Trois Ballades de François
Villon*. These are so often sung by a baritone;
indeed, they were premiered by Jean Périer, the
first Pelléas, so it's a slight jolt to hear them done
by a soprano. Alison Hagley deals well enough
with what Jane Bathori used to call the 'rough
and quite choppy' vocal lines of the first song,
'Ballade de Villon à s'amye', but the fuller,
darker tones of a baritone might be more appropriate in the central prayer. The account of the
chattering wives of Paris brings the programme
to a merry conclusion. The disc is a most enjoyable combination of orchestral music and song.
The sound throughout is exceptionally vivid,
and Boulez, the orchestra and his soloists provide exemplary performances at almost every
turn: heartily recommended.

Chants populaires – Chanson française; Chanson
italienne; Chanson hébraïque; Chanson écossaise.
Don Quichotte à Dulcinée. Deux Epigrammes de

RAVEL SHÉHÉRAZADE – IN BRIEF

Régine Crespin
Suisse Romande Orchestra / Ernest Ansermet
Decca 460 973-2DM   Ⓕ❶❷❸🔁
Sultry, languorous yet sung with a richness of
tone, this is a classic version of this ravishing
work. Ansermet accompanies exquisitely.

Susan Graham
BBC Symphony Orchestra / Yan Pascal Tortelier
Warner Classics 2564 61938-2   Ⓕ❶❷🔁
Coupled with Chausson's delicious *Poème de
la mer et de l'amour*, here's a *Shéhérazade* to
cherish with a wonderful range of colours
and emotions.

Anne Sofie von Otter
Cleveland Orchestra / Pierre Boulez
DG 471 614-2GH   Ⓕ❷🔁
Von Otter is making quite reputation in
French music and this glorious disc merely
enhances that reknown. Her singing is mag-
nificently controlled and coloured and Boulez
is a superb partner.

Felicity Lott
Suisse Romande Orchestra / Armin Jordan
Aeon AECD0314   Ⓕ
A lighter voiced *Shéhérazade* than usual, but
the delicacy of Lott's approach is very
attractive and Armin Jordan accompanies
with typical style; the Geneva orchestra
recalls the Crespin version with its full tone.
The couplings are Chausson and Duparc.

Elisabeth Söderström
BBC Symphony Orchestra / Pierre Boulez
BBC Legends BBCL4153-2   Ⓜ❶
Caught live in London's Royal Albert Hall,
Söderström gives a performance to rival the
best, letting her voice soar from smokey
mezzo to translucent soprano. Boulez makes
the orchestral accompaniment shimmer with
colour. A fascinating and mesmerising performance.

Kiri Te Kanawa
**Brussels National Opera Orchestra /
Jeffrey Tate**
EMI 586652-2   Ⓑ
It's hard not to warm to Te Kanawa's rich,
luxurious soprano and she rides the orches-
tral line with glorious ease. She doesn't dig as
deep into the text as many other sopranos.

Victoria de los Angeles
**Orchestre de la Société des Concerts du
Conservatoire / Georges Prêtre**
EMI Great Recordings of the Century 345821-2
                                        Ⓜ❶🔁
De Los Angeles brings all the languor, poetry
and irony to this entrancing cycle, her Span-
ish passion bringing something special.

Clément Marot. Un grand sommeil noir. Les grands vents venus d'outre-mer. Histoires naturelles. Deux Mélodies hébraïques. Cinq Mélodies populaires grecques. Noël des jouets. Ronsard à son âme. Sur l'herbe
Gerald Finley bar **Julius Drake** pf
Hyperion CDA67728 (71' · DDD · T/t)   Ⓕ**O**▶

There is a vast gulf between the bibulous bravado of the 'Chanson à boire' that Ravel included in his *Don Quichotte à Dulcinée* songs and the bleak, dark despair of his Verlaine setting 'Un grand sommeil noir'. Placing them next to one another in this fine selection of over two dozen songs emphasises the broad expressive range that Ravel was able to embrace. It also throws into focus the way that Gerald Finley and Julius Drake can so evocatively tap their emotional substance.

These exquisitely crafted miniatures, whether in the folk-inspired *Chants populaires* and *Cinq Mélodies populaires grecques* or in the tender *Noëls des jouets* to a text of Ravel's own, show his creative fastidiousness in a consistently positive light: the mood might be robust or rarefied, but Ravel's sense of colour and atmosphere is infallible. The imagery of the *Histoires naturelles*, for example, testifies to Ravel's intuitive response to poetry and to his precise placing of the tonal brushstrokes. In this respect, the piano is an essential collaborator, etching in the background for the gliding grace of the swan or the chirping of the cricket.

Drake draws the ear ineluctably into Ravel's imaginative world, as he does elsewhere in the cool restraint of 'Ronsard à son âme' or the turbulence and shifting currents of 'Les grands vents venus d'outre-mer'. Finley's mellifluous, malleable baritone is similarly an ideal match for this repertoire, with lines eloquently floated, nuances subtly voiced and character sensitively defined. This is a beguiling programme, beautifully performed.

Operas

L'enfant et les sortilèges
Magdalena Kožená mez L'Enfant **Annick Massis** sop Le Feu, La Princesse, La Rossignol **Nathalie Stutzmann** contr Maman, La Tasse Chinoise, La Libellule **Sophie Koch** mez La Bergère, La Chatte, L'Écurieul, Un Pâtre **José van Dam** bar La Fauteuil, Un Arbre **François Le Roux** bar L'Horloge Comtoise, Le Chat **Jean-Paul Fouchécourt** ten La Théière, Le Petit Viellard, La Rainette **Mojca Erdmann** sop Une Pastorelle, La Chauve-souris, La Chouette

Ma Mère l'Oye
Berlin Philharmonic Orchestra / Sir Simon Rattle
EMI 264197-2 (73' · DDD)   O▶

L'enfant et les sortilèges[a]
Julie Boulianne mez L'Enfant **Geneviève Després** mez Maman, La Libellule, L'Écureuil **Kirsten Gunlogson** mez La Tasse Chinoise, Un Pâtre, La

Chatte **Philippe Castagner** ten La Théière, La Petit Viellard, La Rainette **Ian Greenlaw** bar L'Horloge Comtoise, Le Chat **Kevin Short** bass-bar Le Fauteuil, Un Arbre **Agathe Martel** sop La Princesse, La Chauve-souris **Cassandre Prévost** sop Le Feu, Le Rossignol **Julie Cox** sop La Bergère, Une Pastourelle, La Chouette

Shéhérazade
Julie Boulianne mez [a]**Chattanooga Boys Choir**; [a]**Chicago Symphony Chorus**; **Nashville Symphony** [a]**Chorus and Orchestra / Alastair Willis**
Naxos 8 660215 (64' · DDD)   Ⓢ▶

In many ways *L'enfant et les sortilèges* is an ideal opera for recording. The imagination can create stage pictures of the fire, the shepherds, the trees and the animals, and a balance between orchestra and voice is possible that will do justice to Ravel's orchestral effects – what Ned Rorem once called 'lusciously carefree, with its daft blues and dizzy foxtrots'. These two new additions to the catalogue will not displace three classic recordings that have held the field for decades – those conducted by Ernest Bour (Testament), Ernest Ansermet (Decca) and Lorin Maazel (DG).

However, both have strong casts and are very well recorded. Simon Rattle has long held the work in affection. In the new recording his approach is somewhat more symphonic, especially compared with the Naxos CD, taken from a live performance in Nashville, which has a slightly earthier feel to it. The line-up of soloists in Berlin could hardly be starrier but the American group does not lose face in comparison. The roles are shared out differently. Ravel stipulated that the same singer ought to sing the Fire, the Princess and the Nightingale – as Annick Massis does for Rattle, whereas in Nashville these are shared between Cassandre Prévost and Agathe Martel. As the child, Magdalena Kožená manages to seem suitably boyish and wilful, Julie Boulianne has a more mature sound. The fill-up items are well chosen: *Ma Mère l'Oye*, lusciously played by the Berlin Philharmonic for Rattle, *Shéhérazade* done with feeling by Boulianne for Alastair Willis and the Nashville Symphony.

L'enfant et les sortilèges[a]
Cynthia Buchan mez L'Enfant **Fiona Kimm** mez Maman **Malcolm Walker** bar L'Horloge Comtoise **François Loup** bass Le Fauteuil **Hyacinth Nicholls** mez La Bergère **Thierry Dran** ten La Rainette **Louise Winter** mez La Chatte **Nan Christie** sop Le Feu **Carol Smith** mez La Libellule **Harolyn Blackwell** sop La Princesse **Anna Steiger** sop L'Écureuil **Alison Hagley** sop Le Chouette

L'heure espagnole[b]
Anna Steiger sop Concepcion **François Le Roux** bar Ramiro **Rémy Corazza** ten Torquemada **Thierry Dran** ten Gonzalve **François Loup** bass Don Inigo Gomez
Glyndebourne Festival Opera Choir; London Philharmonic Orchestra / [b]**Sian Edwards,** [a]**Simon Rattle**

Stage director **Frank Corsaro**
Set designer **Maurice Sendak**
NVC Arts Ⓕ 🔗 5186 54314-2
(100' · NTSC · 4:3 · PCM stereo · 2-5)

Frank Corsaro's 1987 productions of Ravel's one-act operas met with a somewhat mixed critical reception. Maurice Sendak's pop-up children's-book-style sets may have seemed somewhat simplistic then but they have survived the years successfully and now have a charming period feel. *L'heure espagnole* boasts two singing actors who understand the limitations of camera close-ups. As Concepcion, Anna Steiger is wonderfully deadpan, and she sings her aria, 'Oh! la pitoyable aventure' with a nice combination of sensuality and tension. François Le Roux is the muleteer with little conversation but unquenchable energy, and when he realises that the clockmaker's young wife is interested in him as a lover rather than a furniture-remover, his look of eager anticipation leaves one in no doubt that he is going to be equal to his new task. Rémy Corazza as Torquemada directs the action from the clock tower, and this includes three dancers who mime some clockwork figures. Sian Edwards conducts, with keen attention to all Ravel's use of Spanish dance rhythms.

L'enfant et les sortilèges is the greater challenge, and the camera is not always kind to Cynthia Buchan's attempts to impersonate a little boy. Corsaro has added a silent prologue, in which we see what a tiresome brat this one is. Once the action gets going, though, there are many amusing details, such as the leapfrog antics of Thierry Dran and his crew, François Loup and Hyacinth Nicholls as quite aggressive armchairs, and Anna Steiger again, now as the Squirrel, who sings one of Ravel's most enchanting melodies.

Some of it may seem a little too literal, and the wonderful moment when the child goes out into the garden doesn't have the air of mystery that was so well caught in the famous Hockney-Dexter production at the Met a few years earlier. The fireflies portrayed by small children waving sparklers are an inspired touch. Simon Rattle conducts a performance somewhat freer in spirit than his more recent effort with the Berlin Philharmonic.

Alan Rawsthorne   British 1905-1971

Rawsthorne studied as a pianist at the Royal College of Music and with Egon Petri. Influenced by Hindemith, he developed a highly crafted and abstract style, chiefly in concertos and other orchestral works, but recognition was slow coming. He wrote three symphonies, two piano concertos, two violin concertos, three string quartets and sonatas for viola, cello and violin.

Piano Concertos

Piano Concertos – No 1; No 2. Improvisations on a
Theme by Constant Lambert

Peter Donohoe *pf* Ulster Orchestra / Takuo Yuasa
Naxos 8 555959 (57' · DDD)   Ⓢ🔴▸

Rawsthorne's First Piano Concerto, originally written with just strings and percussion accompaniment, was introduced in its later full orchestral form at a 1942 Promenade Concert by Louis Kentner. The Second was commissioned by the Arts Council for the 1951 Festival of Britain and premiered by Clifford Curzon in the then-new Royal Festival Hall. He later recorded it with Sargent and the LSO on a 10-inch LP for Decca. *The Record Guide*'s review commented on the 'open air tune in the finale with an instant appeal' and suggested the work would achieve the 'wide popularity it certainly deserves'. Alas that never came about. Peter Donohoe plays the First with an effervescent lightness of touch that emphasises the *scherzando* element of the first movement. Yuasa provides witty orchestral detail – there's an engaging contribution from the bassoon – and yet still finds the underlying lyrical melancholy. He opens the Chaconne hauntingly, and the following dialogue with the piano has a compelling delicacy. The Tarantella finale brings an infectious élan and splendid momentum. Donohoe's brilliant solo contribution has all the sparkle you could want, and the gentle pay-off of the brief coda is neatly managed.

In the Second Concerto the fluidity of Donohoe's playing is particularly appealing, and the overall balance – though the opening flute solo is perhaps a little recessive – is mostly admirable. Donohoe and Yuasa deftly manage the quixotic changes of mood of the initally 'rather violent' *Scherzo* (the composer's description) and lead naturally into the wistful *Adagio semplice*, with its nostagic clarinet cantilena answered so exquisitely by the piano.

The *Improvisations* are based on a seven-note theme from Lambert's last ballet, *Tiresias*. They are widely varied in mood and style, and, even though Rawsthorne flirts with serialism, the variations are friendly and easy to follow, and the listener's attention is always fully engaged. Certainly this Naxos disc can be strongly recommended, especially to those who have not yet before encountered Rawsthorne's always rewarding music.

Cello Concerto

Symphonic Studies. Oboe Concerto[a].
Cello Concerto[b]
[a]**Stéphane Rancourt** *ob* [b]**Alexander Baillie** *vc*
**Royal Scottish National Orchestra /
David Lloyd-Jones**
Naxos 8 554763 (72' · DDD)   Ⓢ🔴🔴▸

David Lloyd-Jones directs a swaggering, affectionate and ideally clear-headed account of Rawsthorne's masterly *Symphonic Studies* (1939), one of the most stylish and exuberantly inventive products of British music from the first half of the last century. The work's formal elegance, impeccable craftsmanship and healthy concision are exhilarating. It's an impressively assured orchestral debut, its tightly knit 20-minute span evincing a remarkable emotional scope. The present performance is a great success.

First heard at the 1947 Cheltenham Festival, the Concerto for Oboe and String Orchestra was composed for Evelyn Rothwell. Brimful of gentle melancholy, it's another delectably clean-cut creation, whose touchingly eloquent first movement is succeeded by a wistfully swaying, at times cryptic *Allegretto con morbidezza* and a spirited, though never entirely untroubled *Vivace* finale. Impeccable solo work from RSNO principal oboe Stéphane Rancourt and a spick-and-span accompaniment to match.

There's another first recording in the guise of the Cello Concerto (1965). This is a major achievement, a work to rank beside Rawsthorne's superb Third Symphony and Third String Quartet of the previous year in its unremitting concentration and nobility of expression. A strongly lyrical vein runs through the notably eventful, ever-evolving opening movement, whereas the central *Mesto* mixes dark introspection with outbursts of real anguish. The clouds lift for the rumbustious finale. A substantial, deeply felt utterance, in short, which will surely repay closer study. Soloist Alexander Baillie gives a stunningly idiomatic rendering; Lloyd-Jones and the RSNO offer big-hearted, confident support. Apart from a hint of harshness in the very loudest *tuttis* of the *Symphonic Studies*, Tim Handley's engineering is immensely vivid and always musically balanced. Overall, a wonderfully enterprising triptych.

Violin Concertos

Violin Concertos Nos 1 & 2.
Cortèges – fantasy overture
Rebecca Hirsch vn **BBC Scottish Symphony Orchestra / Lionel Friend**
Naxos 8 554240 (64' · DDD)   ⓈⓄ➔

Rawsthorne enthusiasts should waste no time in snapping up this disc, containing music-making of perceptive dedication and impressive polish. He completed his First Violin Concerto in 1947, dedicating the score to Walton (there's a quotation from *Belshazzar's Feast* just before the end). Cast in just two movements, it's a lyrically affecting creation that weaves a spell, especially in a performance as dignified and consistently purposeful as this. However, the revelation comes with the Second Concerto of 1956. Rebecca Hirsch and Lionel Friend locate a deceptive urgency and symphonic thrust in the opening *Allegretto* that genuinely compel. If anything, the succeeding *Poco lento* wears an even more anguished, nervy demeanour, the music's questing mood very well conveyed. By contrast, the finale proceeds in serene, almost carefree fashion, its witty coda forming a delightfully unbuttoned conclusion to a striking, much-underrated work. As a curtain-raiser Naxos gives us the fantasy overture *Cortèges*. Commissioned by the BBC and premiered at the 1945 Proms by the LSO under Basil Cameron, it's a well-wrought essay, pitting an eloquent *Adagio* processional as against an irrepressible *Allegro molto vivace* tarantella. The composer develops his material with customary skill, and Friend draws a committed and alert response from the BBC Scottish SO. Boasting a spacious, bright and admirably balanced sound picture (no attempt to spotlight the soloist), here's an enormously rewarding issue and a bargain of the first order.

Concerto for String Orchestra

Concertante pastorale[a]. Concerto for String Orchestra. Divertimento. Elegiac Rhapsody. Light Music. Suite for Recorder and String Orchestra[b] (orch McCabe)
[a]**Conrad Marshall** fl [a]**Rebecca Goldberg** hn
[b]**John Turner** rec **Northern Chamber Orchestra / David Lloyd-Jones**
Naxos 8 553567 (64' · DDD)   ⓈⓄ➔

The most substantial offering here, the resourceful and magnificently crafted Concerto for String Orchestra, dates from 1949. David Lloyd-Jones and his admirably prepared group give a performance which, in its emotional scope and keen vigour, outshines Boult's 1966 recording with the BBC Symphony Orchestra (nla). Not only does Lloyd-Jones achieve a more thrusting urgency in the outer movements, he also locates an extra sense of slumbering tragedy in the *Lento e mesto*. He gives a sparkling account of the immensely engaging Divertimento, written for Harry Blech and the London Mozart Players in 1962; the rumbustious concluding 'Jig' is as good a place as any to sample the spick-and-span response of the Northern Chamber Orchestra. The *Concertante pastorale*, written for the Hampton Court Orangery Concerts, is an atmospheric, beautifully wrought 10-minute essay for solo flute, horn and strings. It's succeeded by the perky *Light Music* for strings, composed in 1938 for the Workers' Music Association and based on Catalan folk-tunes. Then there's McCabe's expert orchestration of the miniature Suite for recorder and strings, the second of whose four linked movements is a reworking of a ballad from the *Fitzwilliam Virginal Book*. But the most exciting discovery has to be the 1963-64 *Elegiac Rhapsody*, a deeply felt threnody for string orchestra written in memory of Rawsthorne's friend, the poet Louis MacNeice. Not only does it pack a wealth of first-rate invention and incident into its 10-minute duration, it attains a pitch of anguished expression possibly unrivalled in this figure's entire output.

Symphonies

Symphonies – No 1; No 2, 'A Pastoral Symphony'[a]; No 3
[a]**Charlotte Ellett** sop **Bournemouth Symphony Orchestra / David Lloyd-Jones**

Naxos 8 557480 (75' · DDD · T)   Ⓢ🅓➔

David Lloyd-Jones directs Rawsthorne's three symphonies with evident conviction, and secures a consistently enthusiastic and spruce response from the Bournemouth SO. He improves on Sir John Pritchard's 1975 Lyrita account of the terse, immaculately scored First Symphony (1950), bringing elegant proportion and thrusting purpose. As for its luminous and poignant successor, *A Pastoral Symphony* (1959), honours are more equally divided. Lloyd-Jones distils rather more in the way of gentle melancholy, whereas Nicholas Braithwaite and the LPO on Lyrita achieve the greater poise.

Norman Del Mar's BBC SO version of the imposing Third (1964) has done sterling service down the years, but Lloyd-Jones fully matches its blazing commitment, tying up the symphonic threads to even more clinching effect in the finale (whose peaceful coda recalls material from the opening movement), while distilling every ounce of brooding atmosphere and forceful emotion from the stately tread of the second movement 'Alla Sarabanda'.

A touch of rawness aside, the recording is hugely vivid, offering a pretty much ideal combination of bite and amplitude. The disc represents irresistible value for money.

Additional recommendation

Film Music
The Captive Heart – Suite. Lease of Life – Main Titles and Emergency. Burma Victory – Suite. Saraband for Dead Lovers – Saraband and Carnival (all arr Schurmann). West of Zanzibar – Main Titles. The Cruel Sea – Main Titles and Nocturne. Where No Vultures Fly – Suite. Uncle Silas – Suite. The Dancing Fleece – Three Dances (all arr and orch Lane)
BBC PO / Gamba
Chandos CHAN9749 (73' · DDD)   Ⓟ🅞➔

Rawsthorne brought a professional integrity, great clarity of expression and unerring economy of thought to every field of music in which he worked, not least the 27 film scores he penned between 1937 and 1964. Here are selections from nine scores in all, the arranging and orchestrating duties being shared by the indefatigable Philip Lane and Gerard Schurmann. Gamba draws playing of panache and infectious enthusiasm from the BBC Philharmonic, with spectacularly wide-ranging Chandos sound. Not to be missed!

Chamber Works

Piano Quintet[a]. Concertante for Violin and Piano[b]. Piano Trio[c]. Viola Sonata[d]. Cello Sonata[e]
[abc]**Nadia Myerscough**, [a]**Mark Messenger** *vns* [a]**Helen Roberts**, [d]**Martin Outram** *vas* [ace]**Peter Adams** *vc* [a]**John McCabe**, [bce]**Yoshiko Endo**, [d]**Julian Rolton** *pfs*
Naxos 8 554352 (70' · DDD)   Ⓢ🅞🅞➔

Here's a disc brimming with high-quality music and superlative performances. The Piano Quin-

tet, from 1968, is cast in a single continuous movement divided into four contrasting sections. Although only 15 minutes long, it abounds with musical ideas and interest. Much of the material is vigorous, powerful and concisely presented, but there's much poetry, too, particularly in the *Lento non troppo* section and the brief epilogue that closes the energetic opening section. The *Concertante* for violin and piano is a much earlier work dating from the mid-1930s and, although early influences such as Shostakovich and even Busoni in 'Faustian' mood can be detected, it's perhaps among the earliest of Rawsthorne's works in which his own voice begins to emerge. First performed by the distinguished Menuhin-Cassadó-Kentner Trio, the Piano Trio of 1963 contains much impressive and finely crafted material, as well as a good deal of colourful soloistic writing. The Viola Sonata dates from 1937, but the score was lost shortly after its premiere only to be rediscovered in a Hampstead bookshop and revised in 1954. The Sonata is something of a watershed in Rawsthorne's early output, and shows a considerable advance in style and technique from the *Concertante* of only a few years earlier, and both this and the equally fine Cello Sonata of 1948 are particularly valuable additions to the catalogue. Performances throughout are first class, although John McCabe's commanding reading of the Piano Quintet (he played for the work's premiere) stands out as exceptionally authoritative and compelling.

Jean-Fery Rebel   French 1661-1747

After serving the Count of Ayen in Spain, Rebel became a leading member of the French king's 24 Violons and the Académie Royale de Musique orchestra. He later held court posts including that of chamber composer and was active as a harpsichordist and conductor. Many of his compositions are marked by striking originality that includes complex counter-rhythms and audacious harmonies that were not fully appreciated by listeners of his time. He wrote various vocal works, string sonatas, and 'symphonies' for the Académie Royale dancers including Les caractères de la danse (1715), Terpsichore (1720) and the much admired Les elemens (1737), which begins with a startling dissonance to represent chaos – six decades before Haydn's comparably inspired portrayal.

Violin Sonatas

Violin Sonatas, Op 2 – B minor; D major. Recueil de douze sonates à II et III parties – Le tombeau de Monsieur de Lully; La Pallas; L'Apollon; La Brillante
L'Assemblée des Honnestes Curieux (Alba Roca *vn* Baldomero Barciela *bar vio* Ronaldo Lopes *theo* Chiao-Pin Kuo *hpd*) / **Amandine Beyer** *vn*
Zig-Zag Territoires ZZT051102 (56' · DDD)   Ⓟ🅞

For many people, if Jean-Fery Rebel is known as anything more than a name, it is for one chord

– the spectacular dissonance which conjures primeval chaos at the opening of his ballet suite *Les elemens*. Yet, as the members of L'Assemblée des Honnestes Curieux maintain here, he should perhaps be better remembered for his chamber works, which include some of the earliest duo and trio sonatas to be composed in France (they probably date from the 1690s), and which were noted in their day for successfully combining 'Italian genius and fire' with 'French wisdom and tenderness'.

It seems a reasonable claim, too: the sonatas on this disc – taken from sets Rebel published in 1712 and 1713 – intermingle *lentement* and *gracieusement* movements of great Gallic sweetness and melodic refinement with *vistes* and *gays* whose violinistic flair and vigour call to mind the ever-influential Corelli. And if that 'Chaos' crush-chord suggests that Rebel had a taste for harmonic adventure, then that is backed up by these pieces, which contain a number of bold moves.

All of the works on this disc are available elsewhere, but this new release scores a hit by mixing works, and therefore textures, from both publications. That is not the only thing that makes the disc worth your money, however, for the performances are first-rate, with impeccable and vigorous ensemble playing put at the service of rich and intelligent expression – note how when the achingly sad opening movement of *Le tombeau de Monsieur de Lully* returns at the end the intensity is cranked up by leaving out the harpsichord. Well recorded, too, this disc is all pleasure.

Max Reger   German 1873-1916

Reger studied in Munich and Wiesbaden; in 1901 he settled in Munich and in 1907 he moved to Leipzig to take a post as professor of composition at the university, though he was also active internationally as a conductor and pianist. He was appointed conductor of the court orchestra at Meiningen in 1911 and in 1915 moved to Jena. During a relatively short composing life, he produced a large output in all genres, nearly always in abstract forms. Many of his works are fugues or in variation form, including what is probably his best known orchestral work, the Variations and Fugue on a Theme by Mozart. He also wrote a large amount of music for organ, including the Fantasy and Fugue on BACH (considered one of the most difficult and demanding in organ literature). He was particularly attracted to the fugal form his entire life. He created music in almost every genre, opera and the symphony being the two exceptions.

Four Symphonic Poems, Op 128

Four Symphonic Poems after Arnold Böcklin. Variations and Fugue on a Theme of JA Hiller
Royal Concertgebouw Orchestra / Neeme Järvi
Chandos CHAN8794 (67' · DDD)   Ⓟ Ⓞ➤

Mention of Reger's name in 'informed' circles is likely to produce a conditioned reflex: 'Fugue!' In his day he was the central figure of the 'Back to Bach' movement, but he was also a Romantic who relished all the expressive potential of the enormous post-Wagnerian orchestra. Chandos exploits the open spaces of the Concertgebouw, forsaking some healthy transparency for an extra spatial dimension; a more sumptuous glow.

With Järvi's instinct for pacing in late-Romantic music, and his great orchestra's evident delight in the copious riches of the discovery, for the *Hiller* Variations, this disc is very tempting. Anyone who warms to Vaughan Williams's *Tallis Fantasia* will immediately respond to the 'Hermit playing the violin', the first of the four *Böcklin* tone-poems; Debussy's 'Jeux de vagues' from *La mer* was obviously in Reger's mind for the second poem 'At play in the waves'; and the 'Isle of the dead' is Reger's no less doom- and gloom-laden response to the painting that so captured Rachmaninov's imagination. The final painting, 'Bacchanal', was described as a Munich beer festival in Roman costume – an entirely fitting description for Reger's setting of it!

Clarinet Quintet in A, Op 146

Clarinet Quintet[a]. String Quartet in E flat, Op 109.
[a]**Karl Leister** *cl* **Vogler Quartet** (Tim Vogler, Frank Reinecke *vns* Stefan Fehlandt *va* Stephan Forck *vc*)
Nimbus NI5644 (72' · DDD)   Ⓕ

Who could fail to smile at the winding lyricism that opens both these works, or at the self-possessed fugue that potters gleefully at the end of the Op 109 String Quartet? This is music that simply had to be written, complex music maybe, but with so much to say at so many levels that once you enter its world, you're hooked. Previous recordings of the gorgeous Clarinet Quintet have included two with Karl Leister, though for sheer naturalness, musicality and team spirit, this new production will be hard to beat. Reger's frequent allusions to early musical modes inspire playing of rare sensitivity. Humour surfaces in the *Scherzo*'s rough and tumble, a downward scale idea backed by lively *pizzicatos*, teasingly discursive and with a sunny, song-like Trio. The slow movement recalls Brahms's Quintet but without the gypsy element, while the theme-and-variation finale reminds us that Reger's homage to Mozart extends beyond the chosen key of A major. The String Quartet is more openly argumentative, especially in the first movement. Hints of Taranto inform the tarantella-like *Scherzo*, whereas the slow movement combines hymn-like nobility with more echoes of Brahms. The closing fugue is the work of a joyful creator drunk on counterpoint, though there's plenty to engage the heart as well as the mind. The Vogler commands a wide range of tonal colour and is ideal for all doubting Thomases who'd have you believe that Reger is a bore.

Piano Trios

Piano Trios – B minor, Op 2; E minor, Op 102
Gunter Teuffel *va* **Parnassus Trio** (Wolfgang
Schröder *vn* Michael Gross *vc* Chia Chou *pf*)
Dabringhaus und Grimm MDG303 0751-2
(67' · DDD)   Ⓕ〇

It was very wise to programme Reger's masterly
Op 102 E minor Trio before its B minor
predecessor. Unsuspecting listeners who jump
straight in at Op 2 will discover a pleasing if
discursive piece, forged in the shadow of
Brahms, with an opening *Allegro appassionato*
which, although half the length of its disc-
companion's first movement, seems twice as
long. The *Scherzo* is frumpish, the closing *Adagio
con variazioni* sombre and somewhat long-
winded. And yet the use of viola in place of a
cello has its attractions, and there are numerous
telling glimpses of the mature Reger.

The E minor Trio is something else again, a
rugged masterpiece, with a finely structured
opening *Allegro moderato, ma con passione* (the
three stages of its argument are divided equally
within a 15-minute framework), a mysterious
Allegretto that opens in the manner of later
Brahms then suddenly lets in the sunlight, and a
noble, hymn-like *Largo* that recalls 'The Hermit
playing the violin' from the *Böcklin* Portraits.
Reger's Second Trio is full of audacious modulations and striking dramatic gestures; it *is* long
(something in excess of 40 minutes), but never
outstays its welcome. No one could reasonably
ask for more than the Parnassus Trio offers,
either in terms of drama or of interpretative
subtlety. If you love Brahms, and fancy diving in
among a plethora of stimulating musical complexities, invest without delay. If you love melody, there's plenty of that, too.

Violin Works

Solo Violin Sonata No 7 in A minor, Op 91ᵃ.
Three Solo Viola Suites, Op 131dᵇ
Luigi Alberto Bianchi ᵃ*vn*/ᵇ*va*
Dynamic CDS383 (56' · ᵇADD/ᵃDDD)
Recorded ᵃ1992, ᵇ1977   Ⓕ

Violin Sonata in C, Op 72. Little Sonata in A, Op 103ᵇ
No 2. Tarantella in G minor. Albumblatt in E flat
Ulf Wallin *vn* **Roland Pöntinen** *pf*
CPO CPO999 857-2 (60' · DDD)   Ⓕ〇〇〇

The variety of Reger's music could hardly be
better suggested than by this pair of discs. Reger
the wild modernist (by the standards of 1903) s
vividly before us in the headlong, turbulent,
disconcertingly chromatic outer movements of
the Op 72 Sonata, with their huge variety of
moods and frequent abrupt changes of direction. But the *Little Sonata* of only six years later
is almost classical by comparison; it's much
more direct, economically worked and tightly
argued. And in all the unaccompanied music in

Luigi Alberto Bianchi's recital we meet Reger
paying sincere and often touching homage to
Bach.

Bianchi's disc is beautiful but poignant. The
three Suites for viola were recorded in 1977 on a
large and sumptuously rich-toned viola by the
brothers Amati, the Medicea. It was stolen three
years later; Bianchi began playing the violin
instead and eventually acquired a fine Stradivari,
the Colossus, upon which in 1992 he recorded the
unaccompanied Violin Sonata. That too was stolen six years thereafter, and apart from the interest
of the music and the eloquence of the playing this
disc has the sad value of being perhaps the last that
we shall hear of two exceptional instruments.
Reger's love for the violin is as evident in the
Op 91 Sonata as is his reverence for Bach. All
the movements are like Bach in late-Romantic
dress, and the finale is a magnificent chaconne.

Ulf Wallin plays with a slightly narrower tone
than Bianchi, which works well in the
tumultuous gestures of Op 72. But he and
Roland Pöntinen are just as alive to Reger's
moments of withdrawn pensiveness and long
lines, which need care if their chromatic shifts
aren't to make them seem diffuse; they never
do here. The recordings are excellent.

Cello Sonatas

Cello Sonatas – No 1, Op 5; No 2, Op 28; No 3,
Op 78; No 4, Op 116. Three Suites, Op 131c
Alban Gerhardt *vc* **Markus Becker** *pf*
Hyperion ② CDA67581/2 (138' · DDD)   Ⓕ〇➔

Max Reger is often blamed for thickness of musical texture, but although the piano writing here is
certainly prolix, the first two sonatas are imbued
with a Brahmsian/classical Romanticism and a
virility which keeps the music thoroughly alive.
The First Sonata surges passionately and heroically at the opening yet the touching second
subject sighs very personally, the *Adagio 'con gran
affetto'* is gently lyrical and the finale is skittish.
The Second Sonata also sails off *agitato* and has a
brilliant but more muted *Scherzo* and an engaging Trio. An Intermezzo replaces the slow movement and the finale is a graceful *grazioso*.

The last two sonatas are more mature, major
works in which Reger has left Brahms behind
and found his own voice. The highlight of No 3
is a substantial set of variations, Busoni's speciality, and the final sonata is even more impressive,
with the cello introducing a kind of motto
theme; the melodic writing in the secondary
material is characteristically chromatic. There
follows a whimsical, tarantella-like *Scherzo*, a
warmly expressive slow movement and an
engaging *Allegretto con grazia* finale.

The Cello Suites are in a direct line from Bach,
although not collections of Baroque dances but
three- or four-movement works. No 1 ends with
a jolly fugue and No 2 includes both a Gavotte
and a Gigue. Easily the finest is the Third with
its richly sustained, intensely melodic Prelude, a

brilliantly contrasted *Scherzo* and another appealing set of variations for its finale.

This is a stimulating package, very well played: both artists produce the passionate response demanded of them. Alban Gerhardt has a warm, resonant middle register and Markus Becker is well able to undertake the music's considerable virtuosity. The recording is vivid and clear.

Viola Sonatas

Reger Solo Viola Suites, Op 131d
Coupled with **Bach** Solo Cello Suites Nos 1 & 2
Tabea Zimmermann va
Myrios Classics ⊙ MYR003 (66' · DDD/DSD)
Ⓕ❶❷❸❹▶

Despite the scarcity of repertoire for solo viola, Reger's three suites have never achieved widespread circulation. It's not the most original, distinctive music, perhaps, yet it's beautifully conceived for the instrument, and the balance between neo-Baroque features and a more up-to-date *étude* style is cleverly maintained. And in Tabea Zimmermann the suites have an interpreter able to bring out every facet of the music, from the introspective, melancholy opening movement of the First Suite to the spirit and verve of the First and Third Suites' finales.

Her beautiful tone, constantly varied, and lively musical intelligence are, of course, ideal assets in Bach as well as Reger. Transposed up an octave, Bach's cello writing is equally apt for viola, and though the viola can't match the dark sonority of the cello in the Prelude and Sarabande of the Second Suite, there are compensations. The G major Suite's Prelude may lack the gravitas a cellist can bring to it, but Zimmermann imparts an airy quality that's just as appealing. And her vivacious accounts of the concluding Gigues of both suites entirely banish the lugubrious impression the larger instrument can sometimes leave.

Zimmermann has an excellent appreciation of Baroque style, but her modern equipment can lead to the creation of general rather than particular effects. It's a magnificent recital, however, with Zimmermann proving a true fairy godmother to the viola's Cinderella image.

Organ Works

Chorale Fantasias, Op 52 – Wachet auf, ruft uns die Stimme. Pieces, Op 145 – Weihnachten. Organ Sonata No 2 in D minor, Op 60. Symphonic Fantasia and Fugue, Op 57
Franz Hauk org
Guild GMCD7192 (73' · DDD)
Played on the Klais organ of Ingolstadt Minster Ⓕ❶

Opinions about Reger's music are polarised between admirers and detractors. The latter group would say of him, as Emperor Joseph II did of Mozart, that he wrote too many notes.

Even in this new century the complexity of his scores still presents an awesome challenge to performers and listeners alike. Yet the rewards are immense; Reger is arguably even as great a composer as Liszt. His radical, eclectic approach took organ music to new dimensions, and he fully deserves a whole CD to himself. He's well served here by an inspired choice of player, instrument and venue. Hauk's performances are amazingly virtuoso; he brings clarity of rhythm and articulation to the faster passages and a serene poetry to the quieter moments. He plays the spectacular Klais organ of Ingolstadt Minster, which must be one of the best instruments in Europe. Its brilliant *tutti*, combined with a 12-second reverberation, does full justice to Reger's epic climaxes, and there are some ravishing colours in the softer sections. As resident organist, Hauk knows this instrument intimately, and exploits all the available colours and dynamics. Guild's fine recording stops the reverberation from becoming excessive, and captures the organ's full dynamic range. Whatever your views on Reger, this disc can be unreservedly recommended as an overwhelming and uplifting experience.

Choral Works

Drei geistliche Gesänge, Op 110. Drei Gesänge, Op 39
Danish National Radio Choir / Stefan Parkman
Chandos CHAN9298 (56' · DDD · T/t) Ⓕ▶

Mere mentions of Reger's *a cappella* music will send sensitive souls scurrying to the nearest karaoke lounge. Visions of myriad notes covering the page would frighten most choirs away, but these singers are made of sterner stuff. They're undaunted by complex contrapuntal structures, devious chromatic harmonies and textures so thick you need a forage knife to get through them. They not only weave their way through Reger's characteristically tangled scores without a moment's doubt, but illuminate the paths so clearly one hardly notices the dense musical undergrowth all around. Parkman has a clear-sighted view of what's wanted, and, aided by singers whose pure, perfectly blended tone is a joy to hear, he follows his vision unfalteringly: everything falls neatly into place, making real musical sense. The hefty Op 110 Motets (ostensibly in five, but often diverging into as many as nine independent parts) can sound oppressively heavy, but here offer some of the most sublimely beautiful moments yet captured on CD. A triumph of skill over adversity if ever there was one.

Johannes Regis Franco-Flemish c1425-96

In contrast to the peripatetic careers of many of his contemporaries, there is no record of Regis ever having worked or travelled outside the diocese of Cambrai, and his ties both to Dufay and to Cambrai Cathedral apparently remained strong. Regis's most innovative and influential works are his cantus-firmus motets in five voices. These represent one of the earliest sustained attempts to compose in five parts and appear to have been models for younger musicians such as Obrecht, Compère, Weerbeke and Josquin.

Complete Works

Complete Works
The Clerks' Group / Edward Wickham
Musique en Wallonie ② MEW0848/9 (127' · DDD)   Ⓕ

Johannes Regis is certainly not a household name, mainly because very little of his music survives, far less than for the two figureheads of his generation, Ockeghem and Busnois. Scholars have rated him for many years, but for lovers of early polyphony, the chance to hear his output in the round will be indeed be a treat, because this is a master of the first rank who sounds quite unlike either of his more famous colleagues. Listen to his marvellous *Puisque ma dame*, not only one of the most unusual songs of its time, but also an instantly seductive one.

The best-known part of his output, and the one that proved the most influential, is his motets. Most are on texts that were rarely set, or even specially written. The Christmas motet *O admirabile commercium* is at once boldly conceived and playful, intricately detailed but punctuated by well staged, memorable gestures; and his *Ave Maria…Virgo serena* probably inspired Josquin's earliest surviving masterpiece. Then there are the Masses: the one on *L'homme armé* is perhaps the more immediately outgoing, a worthy contribution to an illustrious tradition; but the more reflective *Ecce ancilla/Ne timeas* Mass grows in stature with repeated listening. However little music survives, one senses that with Regis, as with Ockeghem, each work explores, and resolves, its own set of challenges.

Much of this has been recorded once before in performances of real value, but the cumulative effect of hearing it all done by a single group yields a different level of insight. That the group in question is on top form is more than a bonus. Edward Wickham's choice of tempi is sure-footed, as a result of which most details simply fall into place. The close recording captures the energy and zest with which they tackle the music. Add the stylish presentation and an informative text, and the project makes the leap from self-recommending to essential listening: wonderful.

Steve Reich   American *b*1936

Reich studied drumming when he was 14 with the New York Philharmonic Orchestra timpanist; later he took a degree in philosophy at Cornell (1953-57) and studied composition at the Juilliard School (1958-61) and at Mills College (1962-63) with Milhaud and Berio, also becoming interested in Balinese and African music. In 1966 he began performing with his own ensemble, chiefly of percussionists, developing a music of gradually changing ostinato patterns that move out of phase, creating an effect of shimmering surfaces; this culminated in Drumming (1971), a 90-minute elaboration of a single rhythmic cell. From c1972 he added harmonic change to his music, and later (Tehillim, 1981) melody. He has also worked with larger orchestral and choral forces (The Desert Music, 1983). Different Trains (1988), for string quartet and tape, won a Grammy for best new composition. Reich often cites Pérotin, JS Bach, Debussy and Stravinsky as composers he admires, whose tradition he wished as a young composer to become part of. Jazz is a major part of the formation of Reich's musical style, and two of the earliest influences on his work were vocalists Ella Fitzgerald and Alfred Deller, whose emphasis on the artistic capabilities of the voice alone with little vibrato or other alteration was an inspiration to his earliest works.

Different Trains

Different Trains. Triple Quartet. The Four Sections.
Lyon National Orchestra / David Robertson
Naïve Montaigne MO782167 (65' · DDD)   Ⓕ�O

This version of *Different Trains*, a reworking of the original string quartet version, impresses immediately by the richness of its vastly expanded sound palette. It reveals that inside that frenetic chamber work was a much larger piece trying to get out, and here it is, fully realised, as it were, in glorious technicolor. Some of the writing has an almost Beethovenian quality. It's a hugely impressive performance of a work that has, quite literally, grown in stature. And, of course, if you're going to record Reich with 48 strings, you may as well include the largest version of *Triple Quartet* from 1999, scored for 36 of them.

If in going back to *The Four Sections* for orchestra from 1986 one has the feeling that much is inchoate, it's also true that all the elemental power of the more recent works is there, too, and the Lyon musicians react to it with fantastic energy and precision. A major addition to the Reich discography.

Drumming

Drumming
Synergy Vocals; Ictus / Georges-Elie Octors
Cyprès CYP5608 (55' · DDD)   Ⓕ

Drumming is from 1971, but it has lost none of its strength. The players of Ictus here put their hearts and souls into a work that demands ferocious concentration (though other approaches are possible – a composer friend once said that it was quite the best music for building bookcases), and which rewards accordingly. Now, we know that nobody likes the label 'minimalist' any more, but with music of this quality it's very hard to find that description insulting. This performance is quite the equal of, and possibly more colourful than, Reich's second version, on Nonesuch, and clearly outstrips the original, less trim DG version.

Daniel Variations

Daniel Variations[a].
Variations for Vibes, Pianos & Strings[b]
[a]**Los Angeles Master Chorale / Grant Gershon;**
[b]**London Sinfonietta / Alan Pierson**
Nonesuch 7559 79949-4 (52' · DDD)   Ⓕ Ⓞ

Reich's interest in variation has not been confined to music alone; he also employs linguistic variation to examine the relationship between sound and sense, and even uses language to frame wider moral, philosophical and religious concerns. This is heard in the *Daniel Variations*. Composed in response to the futile killing of the American reporter Daniel Pearl in 2002, and premiered in October 2006 at the highly successful 'Phases' retrospective at London's Barbican Centre, the work combines short biblical excerpts with contemporary textual commentary to create a dark and often unsettling sound world. Much of this is derived from Reich's juxtaposition of block-like structures with a set of harmonic axes which emphasise the most traditionally unstable of all intervals – the augmented fourth (or tritone).

In contrast, the *Variations for Vibes, Piano & Strings* displays Reich's musical inventiveness at its ebullient and infectious best. Given a top-notch workout by Alan Pierson and members of the London Sinfonietta, the *Variations* alternately powers and glides throughout a tautly structured three-movement design – by way of a series of simultaneously unfolding canonic layers – which zigzag their way inexorably towards a quite thrilling close. Critics often lament Reich's shift away from the strict processes of his early minimalist style but all the techniques discovered along the way are still present here: rhythmic goal-orientation, harmonic clusters rich in overtones and upper partials, and a complex but audible polyphonic weave. And all underpinned by those variations, no less.

Music for 18 Musicians

Music for 18 Musicians
Anonymous Ensemble / Steve Reich pf
ECM New Series 821 417-2 (57' · ADD)
Recorded 1978   Ⓕ Ⓞ

Reich's first recording of *Music for 18 Musicians* was a landmark release in the history of new music on record and showed what a towering masterpiece it is. The recording was produced by Rudolf Werner for DG, following the release of a three-LP set of *Drumming, Six Pianos* and *Music for Mallet Instruments, Voice and Organ*. Legend

has it that Roland Kommerell, at that time head of German PolyGram, foresaw the commercial potential of Reich's piece but realised that DG was not the best vehicle to market the recording. Kommerell therefore offered the recording instead to Manfred Eicher of ECM, a company which had hitherto only released jazz and rock. The ECM release sold well over 100,000 copies, around 10 times higher than might be expected of a new music disc.

The 1978 recording still sounds beguilingly fresh. When Steve Reich and Musicians came to re-record *Music for 18 Musicians* for Nonesuch's 10-CD box set in 1996, their performance was amazingly 11 minutes longer than the ECM version. Normally, you would expect such a big difference to come from a slower tempo, but in fact the underlying pulse of both recordings is virtually identical. This is because of the unusual structure of *Music for 18 Musicians*, where the gradual fading-in and fading-out of different elements aren't given a fixed number of repetitions but are played simply as long as it takes for this process to happen. In the 1996 version these fade-ins and fade-outs are more finely graded and require more repetitions than in the 1978 version.

Electric Guitar Phase

Electric Guitar Phase (arr Frasca)[a]. Music for Large Ensemble[b]. Tokyo/Vermont Counterpoint (arr Yoshida)[c]. Triple Quartet[d]
[a]**Dominic Frasca** gtr [c]**Mika Yoshida** mari
[d]**Kronos Quartet** (David Harrington, John Sherba vns Hank Dutt va Jennifer Culp vc)
[b]**Alarm Will Sound;** [b]**Ossia / Alan Pierson**
Nonesuch 7559 79546-2 (54' · DDD)   Ⓕ Ⓞ

Triple Quartet is Reich's first new work for the Kronos Quartet since writing his masterpiece *Different Trains* in 1988. It may disappoint – there doesn't appear to be anything particularly new or different happening here. *Electric Guitar Phase*, on the other hand, shows precisely what's missing in *Triple Quartet*. The American guitarist Dominic Frasca has arranged *Violin Phase*, originally composed for four violins in the heady days of 1967, for four overdubbed guitars, and the result is sheer joy. Such is Frasca's sensitivity to every nuance of phrasing between the four lines that this recording is a classic for the minimalist genre, easily eclipsing the violin original in terms of intensity and tonal variety.

Up to now performances of Reich's music have been dominated by the composer's participative presence, even in larger concert works such as *The Desert Music*. His predilection for earthy, well-grounded tempi set the norm for performances of his music throughout the 1970s and '80s. Two recordings here are fascinating because they were made without Reich's active participation. In this recording of *Music For Large Ensemble*, the melodic invention at this jazzy, vibrant tempo sounds almost as if Reich had been listening to Ghanaian and Scottish folk music. Yet this is nothing compared to *Tokyo/Vermont Counterpoint*, where Mika Yoshida's articulation is so fast that at times you feel helium had escaped in the studio. This is compulsory listening for anyone who appreciates a little perversity now and again.

Piano Phase

Sextet. Piano Phase. Eight Lines
The London Steve Reich Ensemble /
Kevin Griffiths
CPO CPO777 337-2 (57' · DDD)   Ⓕ

Time was when Steve Reich's music was the exclusive domain of his own ensemble: then he was signed to Boosey & Hawkes and his scores were eagerly picked up by a second generation of interpreters. The result has done nothing but good for Reich's music as 'outsider' groups inevitably bring fresh nuance to works designed for a specific pool of musicians. The London Steve Reich Ensemble – who trade under the great man's name with his blessing – was formed by students from the Royal Academy of Music in 2005 and they quickly demonstrate that Reich's booklet-note claim that 'these performances pulse with life' is more than puffery. *Eight Lines* – a 1983 rewrite of the Octet – is less sour than the Reich Ensemble's own recording, and sits comfortably in a conversational slipstream that is highly rewarding. *Piano Phase* is monumental and steely, again a point of departure from the original.

But most intriguing is the Sextet from 1984, a work that has been unfairly neglected on disc since Reich's recording. Scored for a trademark ensemble of keyboards and mallet percussion, Reich focuses on how he might make the ensemble sound more instrument-heavy than it actually is. Curvaceous bowed vibraphone strokes are a beautiful counterpoint to the inherently brittle ensemble attack and are judiciously highlighted. The cleanness of the recording certainly helps: low-register piano figurations have a throbbing clarity that creates telling perspective against the rest of the ensemble.

You Are (Variations)

You Are (Variations)[a]. Cello Counterpoint[b]
[b]**Maya Beiser** vc [a]**Los Angeles Master Chorale;**
[a]**Ensemble Modern / Grant Gershon**
Nonesuch 7559 79891-2 (39' · DDD)   Ⓕ

With *You Are (Variations)*, Reich has consciously moved sideways from recent works such as *The Cave* and *Three Tales* and returned to the earlier sound worlds of *Tehillim* and *The Desert Music*. Scored, like those works, for vocal ensemble and instruments, it also follows their lead in dealing in a more meditative fashion than the decidedly interrogative *Three Tales*, say, intended to do, with fundamental questions of existence (hence, of course the title's 'You Are'). The texts, all very short, in English and Hebrew, are drawn from an 18th-century Jewish mystic, the Psalms,

Wittgenstein and the Talmud. While this bare list may sound highly improbable and even contradictory, Reich himself has said that he spent six months looking for the right texts, and they do indeed have a forceful logic and cohesion.

The shortness of the texts means that Reich has gone back to the techniques of *Tehillim*, in which very short ideas are also varied, rather than to the longer-breathed constructions of *The Desert Music*, and there is no doubt that it's the aphoristic nature of the texts and their accompanying musical ideas that gives the work its power. The performance positively glitters; it seems quite clear that the Los Angeles Master Chorale under Grant Gershon are responding to the work's intrinsic glow, the sense of spontaneity – the swing – in the music that Reich has rediscovered. And that swing is a fundamental element in *Cello Counterpoint*, which rounds off the disc. It is performed in this version by the remarkable Maya Beiser (formerly of the Bang On A Can All Stars) with seven pre-recorded parts – it may also be performed by eight live cellists. Beiser manages to make the eight parts sound very often as though they were one gigantic humming, strumming instrument, and while at times Reich's contrapuntal chugging seems a little worthy, there's no doubt that this is a work of real substance.

City Life

Proverb. Nagoya Marimbas. City Life
Bob Becker, James Preiss *maris* **Theatre of Voices**
(Andrea Fullington, Sonja Rasmussen, Allison Zelles *sops* Alan Bennett, Paul Elliott *tens*) **Steve Reich Ensemble / Paul Hillier; Bradley Lubman**
Nonesuch 7559 79430-2 (42' ·DDD)   ⒻⓄ

The Wittgenstein quotation 'How small a thought it takes to fill a whole life' serves as the basis of *Proverb* for three sopranos, two tenors, vibraphones and two electric organs, a composition that was premiered as a partial work 'in progress' at a 1995 Prom. The complete piece (it plays for some 14 minutes) holds together very well. Three sopranos 'sing the original melody of the text in canons that gradually augment, or get longer', whereas Pérotin's influence can be heard in the tenor parts.

Reich's skill at inverting, augmenting and transforming his material has rarely sounded with such immediacy. After a virtuoso, pleasantly upbeat *Nagoya Marimbas* lasting four and a half minutes, comes *City Life*, probably Reich's best piece since *Different Trains*. The sound frame includes air brakes, pile drivers, car alarms, boat horns and police sirens, all of which are loaded into a pair of sampling keyboards and played alongside the instrumental parts. The first movement opens with what sounds like a distant relation of Stravinsky's *Symphonies of Wind Instruments* then kicks into action on the back of a Manhattan street vendor shouting 'Check it out'. The second and fourth movements witness gradual acceleration – the second to a pile driver, the fourth to a heartbeat – and the third has the two sampling keyboards engaging in top-speed crossfire based on speech samples. The last and most dissonant movement utilises material taped when the World Trade Centre was bombed in 1993.

City Life is a tightly crafted montage, formed like an arch (A-B-C-B-A), lean, clever, catchy and consistently gripping. In fact the whole disc should thrill dyed-in-the-wool Reichians and preach convincingly to the as-yet unconverted. The sound is excellent.

Ottorino Respighi   Italian 1879-1936

Respighi began his career as a violinist and viola player and in 1900 went to Russia where he played first viola in the Imperial Opera orchestra in St Petersburg. Here he took lessons from Rimsky-Korsakov who proved to be a decisive influence on his compositional style for Respighi became one of the century's most masterly orchestrators, fond of splashy, flamboyant effects. All his scores are notable for their imaginative, luscious harmonies and 'sound colour'. In 1902 he spent some time in Berlin studying with Max Bruch and he continued his career as a violin soloist and as viola player with the Mugellini Quartet of Bologna. He was made a professor of composition at the Santa Cecilia Academy in Rome in 1913 and appointed its director 10 years later. He remained in the post for only two years so as to concentrate on composition full-time. Respighi's works may lack the ultimate in individuality but it was he and Busoni who revived the Italian instrumental tradition after the domination of the country's great opera composers.

Piano Concerto in A minor

Piano Concerto. Toccata. Fantasia slava
Konstantin Scherbakov pf **Slovak Radio Symphony Orchestra / Howard Griffiths**
Naxos 8 553207 (51' · DDD)   ⓈⒹ▸

All these pieces are otherwise available in decent performances, but at this price how could anyone with the slightest weakness for Respighi hesitate? Scherbakov and Griffiths do a good deal more than dutifully go through the motions, the soloist in particular playing with delicacy and affection, grateful for the opportunities to demonstrate how well he would play Liszt or Rachmaninov, but in the *Toccata* he's interested as well in Respighi's more characteristic modal vein; as a Russian, he demonstrates that this too, like so much in Respighi, was influenced by the time he spent in Russia.

Russian soloist, English conductor and Slovak orchestra all enjoy the moment in the *Fantasia slava* where Respighi presents a morsel of Smetana in the evident belief that it's a Russian folk-dance, but the Concerto and the *Fantasia*, both very early works, aren't patronised in the slightest.

The *Toccata* isn't so much an exercise in the neo-Baroque, often though its dotted and florid figures promise it, more of an essay on how far one can be neo-Baroque without giving up a post-Lisztian keyboard style and comfortable orchestral upholstery. But in a slow and florid central section, a rather melancholy aria that passes from the soloist to the oboe, to the strings and back again, there's a real quality of Bachian utterance translated not unrecognisably into a late-Romantic language. Scherbakov sounds touched by it, and obviously wants us to like it. The recordings are more than serviceable, but each work is given only a single track.

Roman Trilogy

Pines of Rome; Fountains of Rome; Roman Festivals

Roman Triology. Il tramonto[a]
[a]**Christine Rice** mez **Santa Cecilia Academy Orchestra, Rome / Antonio Pappano**
EMI 394429-2 (81' · DDD)   Ⓕ●Ⓑ▸

What more appropriate orchestra to record the three Roman colour-scapes of Respighi than Rome's greatest orchestra under its music director, Antonio Pappano? In every way this new version is more than a match for the fine Dutoit version of the trilogy (Decca). As in Italian opera, Pappano has a natural feeling for flexible phrasing without exaggeration, and here he has even more resilience in his springing of rhythms than Dutoit, while the fine EMI recording offers clean separation and a wide dynamic range to match even the brilliant Decca.

It adds to the attractions of the disc that as a bonus Pappano offers the lovely setting of Shelley in translation for mezzo and strings, *Il tramonto* ('The Sunset'), beautifully sung with clear, firm tone by Christine Rice. Dutoit puts the trilogy pieces in his chosen order while Pappano presents them in chronological order, ending with the noisiest – and least inspired – *Roman Festivals*. None the less, Pappano conducts that, as he does the earlier two pieces, with all the flamboyance needed for such boldly extrovert music.

These are unashamed picture-postcards in music, and the images they evoke are always exceptionally vivid. One slight reservation is that the recording of a nightingale that the adventurous Respighi includes towards the close of 'The Pines of the Janiculum' is so faint you can barely hear it. Pappano's trilogy now stands as a model for a colourful and ideal coupling, particularly with such an apt fill-up as *Il tramonto*.

Roman Trilogy
Royal Philharmonic Orchestra / Enrique Bátiz
Naxos 8 550539 (61' · DDD)   Ⓢ●Ⓑ▸

This Naxos disc is an extraordinary bargain; it would be recommendable at full price; in the super-budget area it's unbeatable. It has such excitement and verve that you can accept an extra degree of brazen extroversion, indeed revel in it. In *Roman Festivals* the opening 'Circuses' is immensely spectacular, its character in the unfettered gladiatorial tradition of the Coliseum: the trumpets and drums are quite thrilling. The gossamer opening of 'The Jubilee' leads to the most dramatic climax. In the 'October Festival' the strings play their Latin soliloquy very exotically for Bátiz. The closing section brings a gentle mandolin serenade. The great clamour of the Epiphany celebrations which follow unleashes a riotous *mêlée* from the RPO, which sounds as if it's enjoying itself hugely, and the obvious affinity with the final fairground scene of *Petrushka* is all the more striking when the strings have that bit more bite. The *Pines* and *Fountains* are also very fine. When the unison horns signal the turning on of the Triton Fountain, and the cascade splashes through the orchestra, the RPO unleashes a real flood. Yet the lovely, radiant evocation of the central movements of *The Pines*, and the sensuous Italian light of the sunset at the Villa Medici, are most sensitively realised by the RPO, and at the very beginning of the finale, 'The Pines of the Appian Way', the ever present sound, with its growling bass clarinet, gives a sinister implication of the advancing Roman might.

Brazilian Impressions

Brazilian Impressions. Church Windows. Rossiniana.
Buffalo Philharmonic Orchestra / JoAnn Falletta
Naxos 8 557711 (65' · DDD)   ⑤ⲇ➤

Naxos offers another group of rich and exotic Respighi works which demonstrate his extraordinary gift for brilliant orchestrations. The longest and most ambitious is *Church Windows*, though curiously the idea of linking the four pieces with great paintings only came after the work was finished. He chose The Flight into Egypt for the gentle opening piece, St Michael the Archangel for the vigorous second, The Matins of St Clare for the third and St Gregory the Great for the grandest piece, described by Edward Johnson as like a papal coronation in sound.

Brazilian Impressions stemmed from a visit that the composer made to Brazil. He planned a sequence of five pieces, but by 1928 he had completed only three, and left it at that for the first performance in 1928 in Rio. The first is a nocturne, 'Tropical Night', with fragments of dance rhythms hinted at in the sensuous textures. The second piece is a sinister picture of a snake farm Respighi visited, with hints of birdsong, while the final movement is a vigorous and colourful dance.

Rossiniana of 1925 is Respighi's attempt to follow up the enormous success of *La boutique fantasque*. It's also based on pieces by Rossini, this time using some of his piano trifles, *Les riens*. The first is a sort of barcarolle, the second a lament and the third an intermezzo featuring the celesta. In the finale he comes nearest to the

ebullience of *La boutique fantasque* in a tarantella, but colourful as these pieces are, they hardly rival those in the earlier suite. Well worth hearing, though. The Buffalo Philharmonic under music director JoAnn Falletta is treated to warm and spectacular recording, apt for such exotica.

Church Windows

Church Windows. Brazilian Impressions.
Roman Festivals
**Cincinnati Symphony Orchestra /
Jesús López-Cobos**
Telarc CD80356 (71' · DDD)   Ⓕ◐

You might easily argue that neither *Church Windows* nor *Brazilian Impressions* is quite as successful as the 'essential' Respighi of the Roman Trilogy. The only answer to that, López-Cobos seems to suggest, is to take the music perfectly seriously and pay scrupulous attention not just to its potential for sonorous spectacle but to its wealth of beautifully crafted detail. The gong at the end of the second movement of *Church Windows* is magnificently resonant, as is the organ in the finale, and the work is given an extra inch or two of stature by sensitive handling of those moments that need but don't always get delicacy. He pays such care to character and detail in 'Butantan', that creepy depiction of a snakefarm in *Brazilian Impressions*, that you can not only recapture the real, crawling horror that Respighi experienced there, but discover in the music also a queer sort of Debussian grace as well. And as for *Roman Festivals*, well, what's wrong with 20-odd minutes of wide-screen spectacular once in a while? But if every colour is precisely rendered, the quiet passages as affectionately turned as they are here, what skill is to be found in it, what a gift for immaculately precise instrumental detail. With that sort of handling all three pieces sound quite worthy of sharing shelf space with *Pines* and *Fountains*. The recording is spectacular.

La boutique fantasque

Respighi La boutique fantasque. La pentola magica
Bach Prelude and Fugue in D, BWV532
(orch Respighi)
BBC Philharmonic Orchestra / Gianandrea Noseda
Chandos CHAN10081 (80' · DDD)   Ⓕⲇ➤

Noseda's vigorous account of *La boutique fantasque* makes a fine coupling with two rarities which similarly show off Respighi's brilliance as an orchestrator of others' music. *La pentola magica* ('The magic pot') is a ballet score from 1920 whose scenario has been lost, though the titles of the 10 brief movements give an idea of the Russian story behind it. Respighi drew on relatively neglected Russian composers such as Grechaninov, Arensky and Rubinstein, and Polish-born Pachulski, as well as including his arrangements of Russian folk themes. Slow music and a relaxed mood predominate in evocative orchestration. His joy in orchestral sound is even more striking in the exuberant account of his arrangement of Bach's D major Prelude and Fugue, with rich, weighty brass and dramatic contrasts of timbre and dynamic. The performance of *La boutique fantasque* has similar zest. The playing of the BBC Philharmonic is expressive, with *rubato* that dancers wouldn't welcome on stage. The speeds tend to be a trifle extreme, bringing an apt and enjoyable sense of danger in the pointing of the tricky woodwind flurries dotted through the score. The Chandos sound, satisfyingly full and bright, matches the performance.

Additional recommendation

La sensitiva[b]. Deità silvane[a]. Nebbie[b]. Aretusa[b]
[a]**Attrot** sop [b]**Finnie** mez **BBC PO / Hickox**
Chandos CHAN9453 (60' · DDD · T/t) ⒻⓄ➸

Once or twice in *Deità silvane*, one wishes that the poems' classical imagery would lead him towards an evocation or even a direct quotation from Italian music's 'classical' past of the kind that so often renders his better-known music so memorable. In *La sensitiva*, however, his care for the imagery and prosody of Shelley's poem (in Italian translation) was so responsive that striking melodic invention was the result. The orchestral colour of the piece is exquisite. Everything here is played with a real care for Respighi's line as well as his sumptuous but never muddy colours. First-class recording.

Silvestre Revueltas   Mexican 1899-1940

Revueltas studied in Mexico City, Austin and Chicago, his teachers including Tella and Borowski. From 1929 to 1935 he was assistant conductor of the Mexico SO, for which he composed rhythmically vigorous, boldly coloured pieces. He wrote film music, chamber music, songs and a number of other works. Among his orchestral music are a number of symphonic poems with Sensemayá (1938), based on a poem by Nicolás Guillén, the most famous. His music is often vigorous, rhythmically vital, and frequently has a distinctly Mexican flavour.

Orchestral Works

Revueltas Homenaje a Lorca. Planos. Ocho x radio. El renacuajo paseador. Pieza para doce instrumentos. Sensemayá. Caminando. Este era un rey. Hora de Junio **J Pomar** Preludio y Fuga ritmicos
Juan Carlos Tajes spkr
Ebony Band, Amsterdam / Werner Herbers
Channel Classics 🅂🄰🄲🄳 CCSSA21104 (67' · DDD)
Recorded live Ⓕ

The sheer verve and power of his music leads one to think of Revueltas as primarily an orchestral composer, but many of his works are written for relatively modest forces (or started out that way, like *Sensemayá*, given a spirited performance here). Often, it's the ferocity of his sound – and liberal use of percussion – that gives the music a bigger texture than its actual layout might suggest. Even so relatively modest a piece as the playful octet *Ocho x radio* (1933) feels like a small orchestral score. Curiously, the early *Pieza para doce instrumentos* (1929; left untitled by Revueltas) seems much smaller in scale despite being longer. The four movements chart a gentle course in increasing tempi from *lento* to *allegro*. Here the burlesque and grotesque strains in his musical psyche were yet to be allowed full rein, but were unleashed in *El renacuajo paseador* ('The Wandering Tadpole', 1933), with its quotations and teasing allusions. The tiny suite describes how a tadpole meets an untimely end after going out for a drink with a mouse, the moral of which did not deter the composer from terminal alcoholism. *Caminando* (1937) is a real find.

One of the final projects Revueltas worked on was Luis Córdova's 'caustic satire on fascism', *Este era un rey* ('Once there was a king', 1940). The *Preludio y Fuga ritmicos* by his close friend José Pomar completes a splendid disc – derived from concert performances – that deserves every success. Highly recommended.

Nikolay Rimsky-Korsakov
Russian 1844-1908

Compared with the music of Tchaikovsky and Rachmaninov, a meagre amount of Rimsky's music is ever played. And his operas, the works which Rimsky believed to be his finest achievements, are all but unknown. Yet his place in the development of Russian music cannot be overstated for, apart from his own work, he was an important teacher, numbering among his pupils Glazunov, Liadov, Arensky, Ippolitov-Ivanov, Grechaninov, Myaskovsky, Prokofiev and (privately) Stravinsky.

From a wealthy, aristocratic landed family where music was part of the fabric, Rimsky was discovered to have a natural talent for the piano at an early age but all his ambitions were focused on joining the navy like his elder brother. Instead of a conservatory, he entered the Naval School in St Petersburg in 1856 but took piano lessons and began to form ideas for composition while he was there, enthused by performances of various operas – especially Glinka's A Life for the Tsar and Ruslan and Lyudmila. He was introduced to Balakirev and, like many another, fell under his charismatic influence, cajoled into attempting a symphony. In time, Rimsky would become the fifth (and youngest) member of the group known as 'The Mighty Handful' – Cui, Mussorgsky, Borodin and Balakirev himself – who were to shape the force of Russian nationalism in music.

In the meantime, the call of the sea was more powerful and on graduating in 1862 he joined the clipper Almaz for a voyage that kept him from St Petersburg for two and a half years. On his return, Balakirev conducted a performance of Rimsky's First Sym-

phony in December 1865 which, as much as anything, finally determined him to make music his life. He was still considered as a gifted musical amateur by the circle in which he moved – and he was certainly musically under-educated – when Cui asked him to help to orchestrate an unfinished opera by Dargomïzhsky (The Stone Guest). This proved to be a formative experience, one which provided a vivid and intense lesson in the arts of dramatic construction and orchestration.

His astonishment can be imagined then, when, at the age of 27, he was offered the post of professor of composition at the St Petersburg Conservatory. He remained on the faculty from 1870 until his death. As he himself said, 'I did not know at that time how to harmonise a chorale properly,' confessing that he had 'never written a single contrapuntal exercise in my life, and had only the haziest understanding of strict fugue; I didn't even know the names of the augmented and diminished intervals or chords' – irrelevant terms for the layman, perhaps, but basic considerations for a teacher of composition. Instinct alone had got him thus far.

From here on, Rimsky-Korsakov's history is one of increasing influence as a teacher and administrator, parallel with his development as one of Russia's most celebrated composers. For, by the mid-1870s, the basic characteristics in all his music had flowered – a love of fantasies and fairy-tales and a dedication to nationalistic music coloured, like the work of the other four of 'The Mighty Handful', by orientalism. Overwork brought him to the verge of a nervous breakdown in 1889, to be followed, after a relapse of two years, by a creative outburst which established him firmly as the most famous of The Five, whose power in the musical world of St Petersburg was absolute.

Rimsky, though, was no dictator. Indeed, when the conservatory students rebelled against the authorities in 1905, Rimsky took the side not of the establishment but of the students and was dismissed from his post for his pains. It made him something of a hero. Glazunov resigned in protest. When he was recalled and made director, Glazunov immediately reinstated Rimsky. His last appearance abroad was in 1907 – in Paris where he conducted two concerts of Russian music put on by Diaghilev. His last work, the opera Le coq d'or, was banned by the censor – it dealt with the bungling administrators of Russia and a stupid Tsar – but he died of angina pectoris before the situation was resolved.

Fantasy on Russian Themes, Op 33

Rimsky-Korsakov Fantasy on Russian Themes
Taneyev Concert Suite, Op 28
Lydia Mordkovitch vn
Royal Scottish National Orchestra / Neeme Järvi
Chandos CHAN10491 (65' · DDD) Ⓟ Ⓞ Ⓑ

There's Russian and there's Russian. The St Petersburg and Moscow schools of composition are typified with this coupling. Rimsky-Korsakov's *Fantasy on Russian Themes* is self-evidently home-grown with the real magic conjured through the composer's elegant sleight of hand. The first of Rimsky's pair of themes – the

reflective one – is alluded to and even elaborated upon before emerging in its entirety. It's almost as if the sultana Sheherazade is spinning her tall tales once more. Lydia Mordkovitch does so alluringly, making much of the moment when all is finally revealed. The ensuing *Lento* is beautiful and evocative, achieving transfiguration in rapt harmonics over impressionistic *tremolandos*.

Mordkovitch has mellowed. She has refined her intonation, curbed her edgy dynamism. She is seeking and finding more tenderness. The heat of the moment, though, is still there and she dispatches Rimsky's not inconsiderable pyrotechnics, his double- and triple-stopped passagework, with fiery determination. On the threshold of Taneyev's splendid *Concert Suite* she flashes her pride in the opening declamation suggesting some kind of curious pact between Paganini and Wagner. Mordkovitch gives the piece its Russian accent, though, and Neeme Järvi's Royal Scottish National Orchestra fully exploit its visionary aspects – nowhere more so than in the 'finale e coda' of the *Theme with Variations* where the whole work achieves sublimation. Mordkovitch's intonation is truly tested here but there's no denying the intensity she culls from a chromaticism that is right on the edge of reason.

Sheherazade, Op 35

Rimsky-Korsakov Sheherazade **Balakirev** Islamey (arr Lyapunov) **Borodin** In the Steppes of Central Asia
Kirov Orchestra / Valery Gergiev
Philips 470 840-2PH (63' · DDD) Ⓟ Ⓞ Ⓞ Ⓑ

Recorded under live conditions but without an audience in St Petersburg's Mariinsky Theatre, this *Sheherazade* is the most red-blooded, exciting account of Rimsky-Korsakov's orchestral warhorse currently available, helped by full, immediate sound of a richness rare in Russian recordings. The magnetism is established from the start, with Gergiev completely dispelling the feeling that this is a work which keeps stopping and starting too often for its own good. Consistently you register that these are players who have the music in their blood, with *rubato* naturally inflected. In expressive freedom Gergiev is often less extreme than Reiner or Karajan, as in the *quasi recitando* bassoon solo near the start of the second movement or the *espressivo* oboe solo which follows, in which Gergiev notes also the *a tempo* marking, keeping it steady. The virtuosity of the St Petersburg soloists conveys an edge-of-seat tension, particularly when Gergiev opts for challengingly fast speeds in the climactic passages of the second and fourth movements.

This is a work written over only a few weeks, and far more than usual this is a performance that, defying the many changes of tempo, conveys that urgency of inspiration. Yet Gergiev brings out points of detail in the brilliant instrumentation normally bypassed, as in the upward *glissando* for the cellos in the opening section of the third movement, either ignored or merely hinted at by others.

Two points might be counted controversial. The tempo for that opening section of the third movement, 'The Young Prince and Princess', is markedly slower than with the others. Yet in context Gergiev conjures extra contrast with the other movements. The other point is that, though the recorded sound has spectacular weight and power over the widest range, it's clear that reverberation has been added to a recording made in a relatively dry theatre acoustic. Happily, it doesn't get in the way of orchestral detail. Both performance and recording, whatever the acoustic juggling, have a power that pins you back in your seat.

Additional recommendations

Sheherazade
Coupled with The Tale of Tsar Saltan, Op 57 –
Tsar's farewell and departure; Tsarina in a barrel at sea; The three wonders
Philharmonia / Bátiz
Naxos 8 550726 (61' · DDD)   ⓈO☞

Bátiz proves an impulsive, purposeful interpreter. This budget issue is at least as compelling and just as exciting as its full-price rivals, and rather better recorded than many. The fill-up can be warmly recommended too.

Sheherazade
Coupled with Capriccio espagnol
LSO / Mackerras
Telarc CD80208 (60' · DDD). Recorded 1990   ⒻO

Sir Charles Mackerras, a vibrant interpreter of Russian music, throws himself into this music with expressive abandon, but allies it to control so that every effect is realised, and the London Symphony Orchestra plays these familiar works as if it was discovering them afresh. Together they produce performances that are both vivid and thoughtful, while the solo violin in *Sheherazade* is seductively and elegantly played by Kees Hulsmann.

Joaquín Rodrigo   Spanish 1901-1999

Rodrigo and his wife, the Turkish pianist Victoria Kamhi, moved to the little town of Aranjuez just outside Madrid in 1939, having spent much of the previous decade in Paris. Here he put the finishing touches to a guitar concerto that has firmly planted itself in the affection of music lovers as have few 20th-century works. Has there ever been a more vivid musical picture of Spain than this, the work of a man who has been blind since the age of three? (All his works are notated and played through by his wife.) The sunshine and sangria is there but also nostalgia in its wistful and beautiful Adagio.

*It's something of a surprise to learn that not only is Rodrigo not a guitarist himself (the writing is so convincing) but that he was a pupil of Paul Dukas. Not surprisingly, the success of the Concierto de Aranjuez inspired Rodrigo to write other works for guitar and orchestra (a notoriously difficult combina-*tion *when scoring the weak-toned guitar against a full orchestra) – his Fantasia para un gentilhobre, the Concierto madrigal (for two guitars and orchestra) and the Concierto Andaluz (for four guitars).*

Concertos (including 'de Aranjuez')

Concierto de Aranjuez[a]. Concierto andaluz[a]. Fantasía para un gentilhombre[b]
[a]**Ricardo Gallén** *gtr* [b]**EntreQuatre Quitar Quartet** (Jesús Prieto, Roberto Martínez, Carlos Cuanda, Manuel Paz *gtrs*) **Asturias Symphony Orchestra / Maximiano Valdes**
Naxos 8 555841 (68' · DDD)   Ⓢ☞

Concierto en modo galante[b]. Canconeta[a]. Concierto como un Divertimento[b]. Concierto de estío[a]
[a]**Mikhail Ovrutsky** *vn* [b]**Asier Polo** *vc* **Castille and León Symphony Orchestra / Max Bragado-Darman**
Naxos 8 555840 (78' · DDD)   Ⓢ☞

Piano Concerto (Concierto heroico – ed Achúcarro)[a]. Juglares. Homenaje a la Tempranica. Música para un jardín
[a]**Daniel Ligorio Ferrándiz** *pf* **Castille and León Symphony Orchestra / Max Bragado-Darman**
Naxos 8 557101 (60' · DDD)   Ⓢ☞

The focus of these three volumes is on concertos, the most popular and arguably the best segment of Rodrigo's orchestral music. The best known are those for guitar and orchestra, of the very numerous recordings of which these are 'good enough to keep'. Lest anyone might think that the *Concierto para piano y orquesta* listed on Volume 4 is a previously overlooked work, it's in fact the *Concierto heroico* in modestly repackaged form. Achúcarro revised it with the composer's consent to make the work 'slightly more dynamic'. This is now the definitive form and performance of the concerto. The 'symphonic essay' *Juglares* (1923) was Rodrigo's first orchestral work, brief but characteristic of the music of Valencia, where he lived before going to Paris to study. It has no other current recording. All the remaining works on these three discs have alternative recordings but though one may prefer the warmer-sounding version of the *Concierto de estío* by Agustín León Ara, the composer's son-in-law, on the EMI set, these recordings are in every respect comparable with the 'opposition'.

Concierto de Aranjuez[a]. Three Piezas españolas[b]. Invocacíon y danza[c]. Fantasía para un gentilhombre[d]
Julian Bream *gtr* [a]**Chamber Orchestra of Europe / Sir John Eliot Gardiner;** [d]**RCA Victor Chamber Orchestra / Leo Brouwer**
RCA Victor 09026 61611-2 (69' · DDD)
Recorded [abc]1982-83, [d]1987   ⓂOOO

 In the early 1980s Bream had entered a phase when his musical and technical powers were at their height, which he too recognised and celebrated in this remarkable album. With it he confirmed that he's Segovia's truest and best successor, though in no sense his imitator, and established a benchmark in the history of the guitar on record. Everything he touched turns to music, and is here recorded with the utmost reality. If anyone is wondering why he should here have taken his third bite at *Aranjuez*'s cherry, it was in order to 'go digital' but in the event this proved a subsidiary *raison d'être*. At the time the COE was no casual band assembled for a session, but a newly formed orchestra of young players from several countries, greeting the concerto as a fresh experience and playing it with splendid precision and vitality. John Eliot Gardiner's conducting is unfailingly idiomatic. Who catalysed whom is hard to say, but Bream certainly responded with the *Aranjuez* of his life, eloquently phrased and passionate; nothing is lost in the recording and the guitar is 'prestidigitalised' into unfailing audibility. This version of the concerto must remain the touchstone for a very long time, reaffirming the thoroughbred character of a warhorse that often sounds tired and overworked.

Fantasía para un gentilhombre has its own merits and demerits, with Bream stressing the musical rather than the virtuoso elements, adopting somewhat slower tempi than other interpreters in most of the movements – that of the final 'Canarios' is more in keeping with the character of the dance itself. Brouwer's splendid control of the orchestra reflects his experience of both sides of the concerto 'fence'. This disc is a must.

Rodrigo Concierto de Aranjuez **Castelnuovo-Tedesco** Guitar Concerto No 1 in D, Op 99
Villa-Lobos Guitar Concerto
Norbert Kraft gtr **Northern Chamber Orchestra / Nicholas Ward**
Naxos 8 550729 (60' · DDD)   Ⓢ**ⓞ**➔

The time has long passed when it was possible to point to any one recording of any of these concertos (the Rodrigo in particular) as 'The Best'; as with players, one can only discern a 'top bracket' within which choice depends finally on personal preference – or allegiance to your favourite performer, or indeed with the other works on the disc. Norbert Kraft's accounts of these concertos takes its place therein. In this recording Kraft is placed forwardly enough for every detail to be heard, but not to create an impression of artificiality. The Northern Chamber Orchestra plays with freshness and is alert to every detail and the beautifully clear recording catches it faithfully. A bargain.

Concierto madrigal

Concierto madrigal. Danza de la Amapola[a].
Evocaciones – Mañana en Trianae[a]. Gran marcha de los subsecretarios[a]. Piezas – Fandango del ventorrillo[a]. Serenata española[a]. Sonada de adiós, 'Hommage à Paul Dukas'[a]. Tonadilla ([a]arr Peter Katona, Zoltán Katona)
Peter Katona, Zoltán Katona gtrs **Rotterdam**

Chamber Orchestra / Conrad van Alphen
Channel Classics CCS16698 (62' · DDD)   Ⓕ**ⓞ**

The best of the established guitar duos have consisted of players who are/were either married or blood-related – favourable conditions for in-built empathy. Presti-Lagoya set the pace in the 1960s, one which has still to be fully matched. Now we have the Hungarian duo of the Katona twins, possessed of a technique most others can only dream of. Their needle-sharp unanimity of thought and attack is such that listening 'blind' you might wonder how a player could possibly have so many digits. Rodrigo wrote only two works for two guitars, the *Tonadilla* and (with orchestra) the *Concierto madrigal*. Neither has been better recorded than here. In the latter the recorded balance often tips slightly in favour of the orchestra, but this is a minor quibble. In order to flesh out the programme the Katonas have made admirable arrangements of six piano pieces written between 1931 and 1981, and these magnificently played versions for two guitars should keep Rodrigo aficionados happy enough. The Katonas have yet to parallel the emotional depth and warmth of Presti-Lagoya, but they have youth on their side and, being in total command of every other necessary 'tools', they may well become world-beaters. This is a stunning disc, to which the orchestra and recording engineers have made fitting contributions.

Additional recommendation

Concierto madrigal
Coupled with Concierto para una fiesta
Gallén, Clerch gtrs **Asturias SO / Valdés**
Naxos 8 555842 (62' · DDD)   Ⓢ➔

This recording of the *Concierto madrigal* can hold its own with any of its rivals – finely played with good sound from all concerned, excellently balanced and faithfully recorded. The *Concierto para una fiesta* isn't the most riveting of Rodrigo's concertos for solo guitar but it's notable for its slow movement, a clear souvenir of that of the *Concierto de Aranjuez*, and Gallén's performance certainly does it justice.

Per la flor del lliri blau

Per la flor del lliri blau. A la busca del más allá. Palillos y Panderetas. Dos Danzas españolas[a]. Tres Viejos aires de danza
[a]**Lucero Tena** castanets **Castilla y León Symphony Orchestra / Max Bragado Darman**
Naxos 8 555962 (69' · DDD)   Ⓢ➔

At the heart of this volume are two of Rodrigo's finest orchestral works – *Per la flor del lliri blau* (1934) and *A la busca del más allá* (1976). The former is a symphonic poem based on a Valencian legend in which the three sons of a dying king go in search of a blue lily whose magic powers can save their father. The outcome is successful but tragic, as clearly depicted as that of the eponym of Elgar's *Falstaff*. *A la busca del más allá* was commissioned by the Houston Symphony for the bicentennial celebrations in the US. Their choice of composer may seem curious, but it proved a wise one. Its title ('In search of what lies beyond') reflected Houston's status as the centre of space exploration. How would Rodrigo, who had until then devoted his attention to all things Spanish and was then 75, deal with such an unfamiliar demand? The answer was that he did so with skill and imagination, leaving little or no trace of Spanishry. The curtain rises and falls with a long roll on an undamped cymbal, and the principal motif of what separates these events contains a 'questioning' tritone. The performances of all the 'fillers' are exemplary but it's the two large works that make this recording indispensable to Rodrigo lovers.

Solo Piano Works

Piano Music, Volume 1
Al'ombre de Torre Bermeja. Air de Ballet sur le nom d'une Jeune Fille. Bagatela. Berceuse de Otoño. Berceuse de primavera. Cuatro Estampas andaluzas. Pastorale. Cincos Piezas del siglio XVI. Cuatro Piezas. Preludio de Añoranza. Serenata española. Sonada de adiós, 'Hommage à Paul Dukas'. Zarabanda lejana. Fantasía que contrahace la harpa de Ludovico
Artur Pizarro pf
Naxos 8 557272 (70' · DDD)   ⓈⓄⓄ⟿

Here's a first-class collection from the perceptive and sympathetic Artur Pizarro, who opens brilliantly with Rodrigo's evocation of Albéniz, *A l'ombre de Torre Bermeja*, here, as elsewhere, bringing out its affinities with the guitar. *Cuatro Piezas* include a glittering 'Fandango' and a touchingly pensive 'Prayer of the Princess of Castille', while among the *Andalusian Pictures* (*Cuatro Estampas andaluzas*), 'Twilight over the Guadalquivir River' makes a reflective contrast with the quirky bravura of the devilish 'Seguidillas'. Among the simpler items, the nostalgic *Preludio* and delicate *Pastorale*, the rippling *Serenata española* and charming *Air de Ballet* are all highly beguiling. Pizarro captures the varying moods of this music very well. This generous collection is vividly recorded and has excellent booklet-notes by Graham Wade.

Philippe Rogier   Flemish 1561-1596

Born in Arras (now in France), Rogier became a chorister at Philip II of Spain's chapel. He was ordained and become vice-maestro in 1584 and maestro de capilla in 1586. He was a prolific composer of sacred music but only 16 motets, five Masses and some shorter works survive (most of it was destroyed in 1755 when the library of John IV was destroyed during the Lisbon earthquake).

Missa Ego sum qui sum

Rogier Missa Ego sum qui sum. Laboravi in gemitu meo. Heu mihi Domine. Vias tuas. Taedet animam meam. Peccavi quid faciam tibi. Dominus regit me
Gombert Ego sum qui sum
Magnificat / Philip Cave
Linn CKD109 (75' · DDD · T/t)   ⒻⓄ⟿

So much first-rate 16th-century music still remains unrecorded, but here's a welcome addition. Philippe Rogier's death at the age of 35 in 1596 cut short a prolific stream of music. Worse was to come. In 1734 a fire destroyed the library of the Spanish royal chapel, which must have held a large number of his compositions (at the time of his death he was chief court musician to Philip II). How large a number can be gauged from the terrible earthquake that struck Lisbon in 1755, swallowing up the royal library along with 243 works. Today we're left with only 51, of which the present recital represents a sizeable proportion.

Rogier's music has Palestrina's imposing solidity and classical feel, but is more florid and freer in its use of dissonance. In this sense it looks forward to later Iberian music of the 17th century, achieving a sustained intensity in the motets. The Mass is a consummate demonstration, the skilful working out of a motet by Gombert, whose influence is very audible. The booklet-note rightly points out how Rogier develops his model in very different directions: the sequences that conclude most movements are persuasively managed, but sound utterly unlike Gombert.

Rogier's Mass *Domine Dominus noster* appears in a fine recording on Ricercar. But Magnificat's interpretation is of a different order. This is singing in the English tradition, but with greater warmth and richness than we're used to from mixed choirs of this kind. Given Rogier's predilection for fully scored writing, that richness pays dividends, as does the relatively large cast of 18 singers. Interpretation and music are well matched in more ways than one. Neither are strikingly original, but both make a striking impression.

Guy Ropartz   French 1864-1955

Ropartz read law but on graduating moved to Paris to study at the Conservatoire, and took lessons with Franck and Massenet. He became director of the conservatoire in Nancy where he made a huge impact, establishing classes in viola in 1894, trumpet in 1895, harp and organ in 1897, then trombone in 1900. His musical voice is conservative, with Franck a dominant influence.

Orchestral Works

Rhapsodie[a]. Pêcheur d'Islande. Oedipe à Colone
[a]**Henri Demarquette** vc **Orchestre de Bretagne / Kirill Karabits**

Timpani 1C1095 (57' · DDD)   Ⓕ

Literature, the sea and Brittany were recurrent sources of inspiration throughout the life of Joseph-Guy Ropartz. Like Bax, he had been a poet in his twenties but for *Pêcheur d'Islande* ('Iceland Fisherman', 1890-91) and *Oedipe à Colone* (1914) he turned to Pierre Loti and Sophocles respectively. Although never a seaman like Roussel, the marine influence is strong in *Pêcheur d'Islande* and the *Rhapsodie* for cello and orchestra (1928), both of which make use of folksongs from Brittany, and in his best known work, the huge Third Symphony.

For those unfamiliar with Ropartz's style – and there are quite a few discs devoted to his music – he was much influenced by Franck and Fauré. There are Magnard resonances, too, though Ropartz was the more intuitive, less rigorous creator. In *Pêcheur d'Islande*, for example, the opening 'La mer d'Islande' ('Iceland's Sea') is subtitled 'Symphony' but there is little genuinely symphonic in the music. Rather, as in the central 'Scène d'amour', the music is evocative in a fantasia-like way. The lively finale, 'Les danses', however, does illustrate the protagonists' wedding. There is more of the descriptive in the suite from his incidental music to *Oedipe à Colone*. In places the music even hints that Brittany's shores are lapped by the Aegean!

The Orchestre de Bretagne's performances are full of verve and sound well prepared, and they and Karabits accompany the lyrical and smooth-toned Henri Demarquette nicely in the *Rhapsodie*. Timpani's sound is spacious and warm.

Cipriano de Rore   Flemish 1515/16-1565

Born in Flanders, not much is known of Rore's early life. By the 1540s he was in Italy and it has been suggested that was a student of Willaert and others in Venice. He was established as a composer by 1547, when he was maestro di cappella at the Ferrarese court, and embarked on a hugely productive period of his life. From 1559 he held various posts in Brussels, Parma and Venice, returning to Parma in 1564. Rore is best known for his Italian madrigals; he was also a prolific composer of sacred music, both Masses and motets.

Missa Praeter rerum seriem

Missa Praeter rerum seriem. Calami sonum ferentes. Mon petit cueur. Plange quasi virgo. Dissimulare etiam sperasti. Il secondo libro de madrigali – Mia benigna fortuna; Schiet'arbuscel. Il quarto libro de madrigali – Se ben il duol
Huelgas Ensemble / Paul van Nevel
Harmonia Mundi HMC90 1760 (65' · DDD · T/t)   Ⓕ

The Huelgas Ensemble have recorded a masterly recital of works by Cipriano de Rore, subtitled 'Music, Mirror of the Text'. That's an apt description of much of Rore's output, but the inspired and truly brilliant way in which he achieves his goal is what has left his mark upon future generations of composers. The major work of the collection is Rore's seven-part 'parody-cum-*cantus-firmus*' *Missa Praeter rerum seriem*, with its flowing melody and showers of taut little imitations. Based on a motet by Josquin and dedicated to Duke Ercole d'Este, in whose service Rore was enrolled in 1547, the composer hails his master by name in the tenor part of every movement. The remainder of the programme includes such widely different pieces as the charming little eight-part love-song *Mon petit cueur*, with its full canonic imitation and wonderful final cadence, and the slow-moving five-part responsory for Holy Saturday *Plange quasi virgo*. Another striking piece is the four-part madrigal *Calami sonum ferentes*, which exploits the lowest range of the basses in slowly rising chromatic scales. But possibly the most original and forward-looking of all are the last two pieces, in which Rore promotes his own, very personal, technique of chordal homophony. The anguished experimental *Se ben il duol* is a small masterpiece, and so is the fully developed motet on a text from Virgil, *Dissimulare etiam sperasti*. Huelgas rises to the challenge of interpreting, with colour and genius, this amazing music describing Dido's despair.

Ned Rorem   American b1923

Rorem studied in Chicago (1938-39) and with Virgil Thomson (1944) and David Diamond in New York, also attending the Curtis Institute and the Juilliard School. From 1949 to 1958 he was based in Paris, though he spent two of those years in Morocco: his published diaries of this and later periods are flamboyantly candid (his most recent is Wings of Friendship: Selected Letters 1944-2003). His large output includes eight operas (of which Miss Julie is the best known), three symphonies (all from the 1950s), instrumental pieces and choral music, though he has been most productive and successful as a composer of songs.

Concertos

Piano Concerto No 2[a]. Cello Concerto[b]
[a]**Simon Mulligan** pf [b]**Wen-Sinn Yang** vc
Royal Scottish National Orchestra / José Serebrier
Naxos 8 559315 (59' · DDD)   Ⓢ▶

How remarkable that two such delectable concertos should be receiving their world premieres on disc. Unapologetically romantic and accessible, those qualities may well have mitigated against acceptance among the industry's fashion-mongers. The Second Piano Concerto (1951) was written for Julius Katchen and was given its first performance by that superb pianist in 1954.

Since then it has lain dormant until its present revival by Simon Mulligan whose brilliance, ideally matched by José Serebrier, is worthy of Katchen himself. Here, the ghosts of Ravel, Françaix, Gershwin, Stravinsky and, most of all, Poulenc jostle for attention. Yet Rorem's idiom is as personal as it is chic. The final pages of the central 'Quiet and Sad' movement, where the piano weaves intricate tracery round the orchestral theme, may owe much to the *Adagio assai* from Ravel's G major Concerto but it maintains its own character. The finale, 'Real Fast', is an irresistible *tour de force* played up to the hilt by Mulligan.

In the Cello Concerto Rorem happily eschews a conventional form, giving programmatic subtitles to each section. These range from 'Curtain Raise' to 'Adrift', offering Wen-Sinn Yang a rich opportunity, whether playing *primus inter pares* or revelling in Rorem's alternating nostalgia and effervescence. Finely recorded, it's a clear winner.

Chamber Works

Book of Hours[a]. Bright Music[b]. End of Summer[c]
The Fibonacci Sequence ([ab]Anna Noakes *fl* [c]Julian Farrell *cl* [a]Gillian Tingay *hp* [bc]Kathron Sturrock *pf* [bc]Jonathan Carney, [b]Ursula Gough *vns* [b]Michael Stirling *vc*)
Naxos American Classics 8 559128 (60' · DDD)
Ⓢ**OOᴰ**

In Ned Rorem's *End of Summer* (1985) for clarinet, violin and piano, dramatic juxtapositions seem to be the work's organising principle. Without postmodern trickery, Rorem shows us that seemingly disparate elements can co-exist quite happily. One hears a similar kind of musical détente going on in parts of *Bright Music* (1987) for flute, two violins, cello and piano – particularly in the opening Fandango, inspired by the image of a rat inside a rubbish bin. This is a substantial, delightful suite, centred on a brilliant *scherzo* movement ('Dance-Song-Dance') that enfolds one of Rorem's loveliest tunes. The slow movement (entitled 'Another Dance') is an expansive, aching song without words, and the whirlwind finale a clever and ultimately unsettling take on the last movement of Chopin's *Funeral March* Sonata.

Book of Hours (1975), for flute and harp, is structured on the timetable of monastic prayer, beginning with Matins and continuing through Lauds all the way to Vespers and Compline. There are few sweet melodies here, though Rorem's language is always expressive. 'Sext (Noon)' is especially touching, with the flute's shakuhachi-like *glissandi* sighing over the harp's exquisitely fragile song.

The performances by the Fibonacci Sequence are consistently polished and persuasive. Clear recording, too, though the instruments are placed very close to the microphones. Very strongly recommended.

Songs

Santa Fé – No 2, Opus 101; No 4, Sonnet; No 8, The wintry mind; No 12, The sowers. Clouds. Early in the morning. The serpent. Now sleeps the crimson petal. I strolled across an open field. To a young girl. Jeanie with the light brown hair. Ode. For Poulenc. Little elegy. Alleluia. Look down, fair moon. O you whom I often and silently come. I will always love you. The tulip tree. I am rose. The Lordly Hudson. O do not love too long. Far far away. For Susan. A journey. Sometimes with one I love. Love. Orchids. Stopping by woods on a snowy evening. Do I love you more than a day? Ferry me across the water. That shadow, my likeness
Susan Graham *sop* **Malcolm Martineau** *pf* with
Ensemble Oriol (Christiane Plath *vn* Sebastian Gottschick *va* Friedeman Ludwig *vc*)
Erato 8573 80222-2 (61' · DDD · T)   Ⓕ**OOᴰ**

If Rorem's songs aren't as well known as those of Copland or Cole Porter it's probably because they're more difficult to sing. The earliest here is from 1947 ('The Lordly Hudson', on a poem by Paul Goodman), the latest from 1983 ('That shadow, my likeness', one of several Walt Whitman settings). Most of the others, though, were composed in the 1950s when Rorem was living in France. One could look for obvious French influences – Rorem was a close friend of Auric and Poulenc – but strangely it's the later songs, from the cycle *Santa Fé* on poems by Witter Bynner, that have a more Gallic sound, having that aching, nostalgic mood which Rorem himself describes as 'a period removed from Time and, like the act of love, [it] has no limits, no beginning nor end.' The only song in French is a poem by Ronsard, an ode to peace, but two songs are about Paris. 'Early in the morning', a poem by Robert Hillyer, is an evocation of a young poet in love in and with Paris, its accompaniment a homage to all the sad waltzes that murmur their recollections of the city from Satie to Kosma. 'For Poulenc', written especially by Frank O'Hara for Rorem to set as part of an album of songs in memory of Poulenc, describes all the city in mourning.

Rorem called his autobiography *Knowing when to Stop*, and it's a wonderful description of his own songs. The strength and beauty of his settings lies in their directness and candour. He doesn't linger, the poem and song are one, the melody growing from the accompaniment into the vocal line, but just as you seem able to grasp it, it's gone. Martineau plays with an unfailing sensitivity, giving the tiny shifts of mood from exuberance to elegiac melancholy their exact weight.

Alleluia. Are you the new person?. As Adam early in the morning. Ask me no more. Early in the morning. Far Far Away. Full of life now. I am Rose. I strolled across an open field. Little Elegy. Love in a Life. Lullaby of the Woman of the Mountain. Memory. My Papa's Waltz. Nantucket. Night Crow. The

Nightingale. Now sleeps the crimson petal. O you to whom I often and silently come. Orchids. Root Cellar. Sally's Smile. See how they love me. The Serpent. Snake. Spring. Stopping by Woods on a Snowy Evening. Such beauty as hurts to behold. Visits to St Elizabeth's. The Waking. What if some little pain… Youth, Day, Old Age and Night
Carole Farley sop **Ned Rorem** pf
Naxos 8 559084 (58' · DDD)   ⑤B→

These 32 include some of Rorem's finest and most haunting. The utter simplicity that weaves a magic spell in 'Nantucket', the beautiful paralleling of Gerard Manley Hopkins's ecstatic imagery in 'Spring', the bare but deeply eloquent 'Such beauty as hurts to behold', the amiable contemplation of old age and possible immortality in 'Full of life now' – all these are warmly welcome, and it's good to have for the first time a complete recording of Rorem's nine settings of Theodore Roethke. Carole Farley's diction is so immaculate that you'll hardly need the booklet of texts, and her acute response to words must be one reason why Rorem so willingly collaborated with her on this recording. About the voice itself some might have a reservation. Although Farley fines her tone down for the most part effectively her sound is basically operatic. But rejecting this disc on that account would mean foregoing the infectious lilt of 'The Nightingale', the amply lyrical, movingly expressive 'Love in a life', the beautiful long lines of 'Ask me no more' and all the others mentioned. No, admirers of Rorem's unique talent will simply have to have this collection. His piano playing is beautifully supportive.

'On an Echoing Road'
Early in the morning. Are you the new person drawn toward me?. Rain in Spring. For Susan. Stopping by Woods on a Snowy Evening. Jeanie with the light brown hair. To a Young Girl. Catullus: on the burial of his brother. Requiescat. I will always love you. That shadow, my likeness. On an echoing road. I strolled across an open field. Alleluia. Little Elegy. Sometimes with one I love. Hymn for Evening. Orchids. On a Singing Girl. Now sleeps the crimson petal. What if some little pain. Look down, fair moon. The Rainbow. Do I love you more than a day?. Their lonely betters. Do not love too long. Comment on War. The Serpent. Full of life now
The Prince Consort (Anna Leese sop Jennifer Johnston mez Tim Mead counterten Andrew Staples ten Jacques Imbrailo bar) / **Alisdair Hogarth** pf
Linn ⌖ CKD342 (57' · DDD)   ⑤O B→

A first thought here is that the poems would make an excellent anthology in themselves – and that is not to disparage the music. Armin Zanner's introductory essay on the composer and his songs makes much of the echo motif (the phrase adopted for the subtitle is from a poem, well translated by Rorem, by Colette). Rorem is quoted as saying: 'I set words to music as I talk them'. He also says that the germ, 'the spark that's lit in the night', usually goes into the

accompaniment. Does that explain a second thought – that these songs are characteristically just a little too delicate?

Certainly – certainty at last – this is a most attractive disc. The Prince Consort comprises five singers still young, clear and intelligent in their way with words, and their pianist-director, Alisdair Hogarth. Unusually they have a countertenor in their midst, the excellent Tim Mead, who shares the title-song, a duet, with Anna Leese, and has two of the best solos. South African baritone Jacques Imbrailo is also noteworthy: the recording brings out the individual timbre of his voice, and to him goes what is perhaps best of the songs, 'Early in the morning'.

Gioachino Rossini   Italian 1792-1868

His father was the town trumpeter for Pesaro and played brass instruments in various theatres as well as doubling as a municipal inspector of slaughterhouses; his mother was a small-time opera singer. Rossini's gifts showed themselves at an early age so that by the time he reached his teens he could not only play the piano, the viola and the horn but was much in demand as a boy soprano.

By the time he had left the Liceo Musicale in Bologna he had composed a large amount of music including five string quartets. He wrote his first opera, Demetrio e Polibio, in 1808 and this led to his first commission – La cambiale di matrimonio, a one-act opera which in turn prompted further commissions. From here Rossini's career snowballed rapidly. His first full-length opera, Tancredi, was an enormous success (the aria 'Di tanti palpiti' was the equivalent of one of today's pop hits) and less than three months later he had an even greater triumph with his comic opera L'italiana in Algeri. By 21 he was famous throughout Italy.

Venice had been the stage for his early work. Rossini then moved on to Naples and temporarily to Rome where he'd been asked to write an opera for the Teatro Argentina. Desperate for a story, he decided to use Beaumarchais's play Le barbier de Séville. It was an audacious choice for any composer, but Rossini composed the 600 pages of his The Barber of Seville in 13 days (according to Rossini – his biographer says 19). Though he borrowed from some of his previous work, it remains one of the most astonishing feats of sustained, instant musical creation. The premiere was a fiasco but the second performance was a triumph and Rossini's Il barbiere di Siviglia has continued to delight audiences throughout the world on a regular basis ever since.

Based in Naples, Rossini began an affair with the prima donna Isabella Colbran and continued his triumphant progress with La Cenerentola (1817), Mosè in Egitto (1818), La gazza ladra (1817) and Zelmira (1822). In fact, between 1808 and 1829 he produced no less than 40 operas. Now married to Colbran, Rossini moved to Vienna where he met Beethoven and composed Semiramide (1823), his next big hit. Then on to London where he was feted by public and royalty alike (George IV sang duets with him) and treated as the greatest living composer. In 1824 he headed for Paris where he adapted his style to French tastes with Le comte Ory (1828), following it with his grand opera masterpiece William Tell. That was in 1829.

Rossini was by now immensely wealthy and at the height of his creative powers. Then his life took a completely unexpected course. He simply stopped composing. Except for his Stabat mater and Petite Messe solennelle of 1863, he wrote nothing else of importance. No one has yet come up with a completely convincing explanation why he made this decision – lack of inspiration? Worn out? His neurasthenia? Inability to find good singers? Afraid of competition? It could be none or any of these reasons.

In 1832 Rossini met Olympe Pélissier, a celebrated Parisian beauty, who became his mistress. They left Paris for Bologna in 1836 and, when Isabella Colbran died in 1845, the two were married. From 1848 to 1855 they lived in Florence and then returned to Paris. Like many Italians, Rossini was extremely superstitious and was terrified of Friday 13th, He died on November 13, 1868 – a Friday. There were 6000 mourners in his funeral procession, four military bands and a chorus of 399 which sang the Prayer from his Mosè in Egitto. His estate, when he died, was valued at about one million pounds.

Overtures etc

'Discoveries'
Robert Bruce – Overture (arr Niedermeyer). Péchés de vieillesse, Book 3, 'Morceaux réservés' – Le chant des Titans. Grande Fanfare (Le rendez-vous de chasse). Guillaume Tell – Final du Divertissement; Pas de deux. Ermione – Sinfonia. Moïse et Pharaon – Ouverture et Introduction[b]. La siège de Corinthe – Ballabile-Galop. Inno alla pace, 'È foriera la pace'[cd]. Hymne, 'De l'Italie et de la France'[ac]. Hymne à Napoléon III et à son vaillant peuple[b]
[a]Laura Giordano sop [b]Ildar Abdrazakov, [c]Michele Pertusi bars [d]Nelson Calzi fp Giuseppe Verdi Chorus and Symphony Orchestra, Milan / Riccardo Chailly
Decca 470 298-2DH (69' · DDD · T/t)   Ⓕ**OO**▸

Philip Gossett calls this 'a Rossinian curio cabinet'. 'A banquet made with leftovers from the Rossini kitchen' would do as well. Whatever the analogy, the art is as much in the assembling of the materials as in the materials themselves. The most familiar music – gleanings from *Zelmira*, *Armida* and *La donna del lago* – is to be found in the very first item, the overture to the Rossinian pastiche *Robert Bruce*, assembled for the Paris Opéra in 1846 by the composer Louis Niedermeyer. The other orchestral items are all *echt*-Rossini. The splendid *Le rendez-vous de chasse* for four hunting horns and orchestra dates from the time of the composition of *Guillaume Tell* and could almost be a pendant to it. But the pillars of the anthology are the splendid *Le chant des Titans* and three of Rossini's grand but little-known occasional hymns. The earliest of these is *De l'Italie et de la France*, written in 1825 for Charles X's

coronation; the latest, written in 1867 when Rossini was 75, is the grandiose *Hymne à Napoléon III et à son vaillant peuple*. It all goes with a tremendous swing and the cannon-and-church-bells end is spectacular. The voltage of Chailly's performances is unremitting high, as is the attention to shading and fine detail. This is conducting Toscanini or De Sabata would have been hard-pressed to better. The recordings, in Milan's new Auditorium di Milano, are also spectacularly good, vivid yet sensitive to the smallest detail.

Songs

Songs – Il Salotto, Vol 13
Danse sibérienne. Le Sylvain (Romance). Les amants de Séville. Le dodo des enfants. La chanson du bébé. Soupirs et sourire. Le chant des Titans. Au chevet d'un mourant. Ariette villageoise. L'esule. À Grenade. Ridiamo, cantiamo che tutto sen va. Preghiera. Addio ai viennesi. Le départ des promis. Chanson de Zora. La notte del Santo Natale. Toast pour le nouvel an.
Mireille Delunsch sop **Jennifer Larmore, Catherine Wyn-Rogers** mez **Lawrence Brownlee, Mark Wilde** ten **Geoffrey Mitchell Choir / Nicholas Bosworth harm; Malcolm Martineau** pf
Opera Rara ORR 247 (78' · DDD)   Ⓕ**OOO**

For its 13th volume the series comes home to sup with the master of the musical salon himself. From the *Soirées musicales* of the 1830s to the *Péchés de vieillesse*, Rossini exercised the light touch with the firm hand, and his villa in the Bois de Boulogne, shown in a fine introductory illustration to the booklet, became the centre of civilised Saturday night entertainment in Paris. The songs heard here preserve the flavour of those evenings much as potpourri may the scent of past summers.

Presiding at the piano is Malcolm Martineau, and with sufficient (and not excessive) play of light and shade in both tempo and touch, he opens the proceedings with his single solo, the *Danse sibérienne*. First of the singers is the twice-welcome Lawrence Brownlee – the double accolade accounted for by the ideal suitability of his vibrant, clear-cut tenor voice, elegance of style and technical accomplishment. When Jennifer Larmore joins him for the duet 'Les amants de Séville', we are treated to some of the most delightful singing of the whole soirée.

Larmore herself is in splendid form: her 'Chanson du bébé' with the dear little horror's artless cries of 'Pipi, maman, papa, caca' is a winner among party-pieces. At the far end of the programme there are a number of choral items performed immaculately by the Geoffrey Mitchell Choir. Particularly charming is the last of all, *Toast pour le nouvel an*, a 'dapper brindisi' as Richard Osborne describes it in his notes – notes which manage to be economical but tell you what you want to know and are clearly drawn from an immense reservoir of background knowledge.

'Soirées musicales'

Soirées musicales – La promessa[a]; Il rimprovero[b]; La partenza[c]; L'orgia[c]; L'invito[b]; La pastorella dell'Alpi[a]; La gita in gondola[c]; La danza[c]; La regata veneziana[ab]; La pesca[ab]; La serenata[ac]. Mi lagnerò tacendo II[b]. Péchés de vieillesse – Book 2, Album français: Les Adieux à la vie[a]; L'Orpheline du Tyrol[b]; Book 3, Morceaux réservés: L'esule[c]; Les amants de Séville[bc]; Book 11, Miscellanée de musique vocale: La chanson du bébé[a]. La regata veneziana[b]

[a]**Miah Persson** sop [b]**Stella Doufexis** mez [c]**Bruce Ford** ten **Roger Vignoles** pf

Hyperion CDA67647 (79' · DDD · T/t) ⓕⒹ➜

This is a classic case of 'spoiling the ship for a ha'porth of tar', as well as further evidence of Hyperion's uncharacteristically uncertain touch with Rossini. Having taken the trouble to engage three distinguished singers to record the *Soirées musicales*, they have drawn the line at employing a fourth, the bass required for the final duet 'Li marinari'. The disc cannot therefore be the 'library' recording of *Les soirées* we currently need. After the 11 numbers from *Soirées musicales*, we are given a further nine songs plucked somewhat randomly from the later *Péchés de vieillesse*.

That said, there is much to enjoy on the record. The ordering and voice allocation of *Les soirées* is open to variation. The eight solo songs are generally sung by a soprano or a mezzo, 'La danza' by the tenor. Here the tenor has three of the songs. In 'La danza' memories of singers from Caruso to Pavarotti are perhaps a shade too insistent. Elsewhere in *Les soirées*, Bruce Ford shows every sign of shifting from opera to chanson with skill and imagination; the duet 'Les amants de Séville' from *Péchés* in which he partners mezzo Stella Doufexis is one of the disc's highlights. The two women barely put a foot wrong, though Miah Persson's Alpine shepherdess is preferable to her somewhat over-indulged *bébé*.

The real star of the record is pianist Roger Vignoles. Rossini's writing for the piano is highly idiosyncratic. It requires a first-rate technique, a sure sense of style and an ability to bring off with insouciance all manner of hair's-breadth effects. Vignoles has the measure of all this and more.

Petite Messe solennelle

Petite Messe solennelle
Daniella Dessì sop **Gloria Scalchi** mez **Giuseppe Sabbatini** ten **Michele Pertusi** bass **Chorus and Orchestra of the Teatro Comunale, Bologna / Riccardo Chailly**
Decca ② 444 134-2DX2 (82' · DDD · T/t) Ⓜ●

A proper representative of the orchestrated version of the *Petite Messe* has been long overdue. Chailly's performance is a glorious, heart-warming affair. Not that you're likely to be convinced right away. To ears accustomed to the *Kyrie* in its original form, the texturing

here is pure suet. Nor does the sound of the largish and here rather distantly placed choir seem especially well focused in the 'Christe eleison'. Gradually, though, the ear adjusts, the musicians warm to their task, the performance gets into its stride. The Bologna Chorus sings the *Gloria* and *Credo* with passion, clarity and love. The tenor is adequate, the bass superb, the two girls absolutely fabulous. If the 'Crucifixus' can never be as painful as it's in the sparer original version, this is amply offset by the sheer beauty of Daniella Dessì's singing and by the hair-raising force of the 'Et resurrexit' (superbly recorded) as Chailly and his choir realise it.

By the end, after Gloria Scalchi's deeply affecting account of the *Agnus Dei*, you begin to wonder whether the orchestral version wasn't more than a match for the original. It isn't, but it's an indication of the cumulative eloquence of this utterly inspired performance that it comes to seem so.

Stabat mater

Stabat mater Ⓟ
Krassimira Stoyanova sop **Petra Lang** mez **Bruce Fowler** ten **Daniel Borowski** bass **RIAS Chamber Choir, Berlin; Akademie für Alte Musik, Berlin / Marcus Creed**
Harmonia Mundi HMC90 1693 (57' · DDD · T/t) ⓕ●

One of the first, and best, recordings of this splendid but interpretatively elusive work was made in Berlin in 1954 under the direction of Ferenc Fricsay. Like the present recording, it featured the RIAS (Berlin Radio) Chamber Choir, though in those days the fledgling choir was supplemented in the full choruses by the famous St Hedwig's Cathedral Choir. Now on its own, it acquits itself superbly in all movements and dimensions with its own conductor, the English-born Marcus Creed. That this recording uses period instruments might seem in so obviously 'vocal' a piece to be of no particular moment. In practice, the work's prevailingly dark orchestral colours are memorably realised by the instrumentalists of Berlin's Academy for Ancient Music. In the grand opening movement, the four soloists are recorded uncomfortably far forward; but if you can establish an agreeable level for this movement, the rest of the performance sounds very well indeed. Choir and orchestra are themselves unfailingly well balanced.

Creed's reading is full of character: immensely strong but always sensitively paced. Rossini might have raised an eyebrow at Creed's fondness for romantically protracted codas; equally, he would have applauded his sensitive moulding of the accompaniments, matched shrewdly but never indulgently to the singers' (and the music's) needs. The soloists, highly talented, are excellent, more than a match for most rival teams.

Opera Arias

La donna del lago – Tanti affetti in tal momento.
Elisabetta, Regina d'Inghilterra – Quant' è grato
all'alma mia; Fellon, la penna avrai. Maometto II –
Ah! che invan su questo ciglio; Giusto ciel, in tal
periglio. Le nozze di Teti e di Peleo – Ah, non potrian
reistere. Semiramide – Serenai vaghirai … Bel raggio
lusinghier. Zelmira – Riedi al soglio
Cecilia Bartoli mez
**Chorus and Orchestra of the Teatro La Fenice,
Venice / Ion Marin**
Decca 436 075-2DH (59' · DDD · T/t)   ⓕⓄ➔

This sparkling disc brings together a collection of arias Rossini composed for one of the
great prima donnas of the 19th century, his
wife, Isabella Colbran. It's tempting to wonder
whether even she could match Cecilia Bartoli,
one of the most luscious, most exciting voices
in opera. All those dazzling chromatic runs,
leaps, cadenzas and cascading coloraturas are
handled with consummate ease. Throughout
she sounds as if she's enjoying the music;
there's always an engaging smile in the voice,
although she's properly imperious in the
extracts from *Elisabetta* and disarmingly
simple in the prayerful 'Giusto ciel, in tal periglio' from *Maometto II*. The orchestral and
choral forces provide a delightful intimacy,
with some cheeky woodwind solos and fruity
brass passages.

The recording, produced at the Teatro La
Fenice by Decca veteran Christopher Raeburn,
favours the voices but gives just enough distance to accommodate high Cs and astounding
A flats at the bottom of the range. The
orchestral perspective is changeable but
satisfactory. For Rossini and Bartoli fans, this
disc is a must.

Aureliano in Palmira – Overture; Perché mai le luci
apprimo. Tancredi – Overture; Oh patria! Dolce e
ingrate patria. Semiramide – Overture; Eccomi…Ah,
quel giorno; In si barbara sciagura. La donna del lago
– Mura felici; Quelle spietate…Ah si pera
Max Emmanuel Cencic counterten
**Le Motet de Genève Vocal Ensemble; Geneva
Chamber Orchestra / Michael Hofstetter**
Virgin Classics 385788-2 (74' · DDD)   ⓕ

If countertenors can sing Handel, why not Rossini? Among the many fine singers Rossini heard
during his student days in Bologna, two were
especially important: the castrato Giovan Battista Velluti and the young Spanish soprano Isabella Colbran. Hearing both on the same stage
must have been an astonishing experience: the
old order of the castrati, doomed to extinction,
side by side with the new order of singing
actresses whose brilliantly developed coloratura
techniques were in some sense a bequest from
the castrati. Purity of tone, flexibility of technique and a 'profoundly penetrating accent'
were what most impressed Rossini about the

castrati. It was a different sound from that of the
modern countertenor but the stylistic principles
are not a hundred miles removed.

The singing of Viennese countertenor Max
Emmanuel Cencic is distinguished by good
rhythm, crisp divisions and clear, expressive
word use. The range these roles require sits
comfortably on his voice. The G below the stave
is rounded and full, the two octaves beyond are
clear and bright, albeit with a marked vibrato in
places. Cencic's musicianship is generally impeccable: a tribute to the values instilled in him
during his time in the Vienna Boys' Choir which
he left in 1992, nine years before his decision to
'recreate' himself as a countertenor.

Rossini created one operatic role for Velluti, in
Aureliano in Palmira. Having antagonised the
company with his self-regarding antics, Velluti
is said to have made next to no impact onstage.
Cencic does not disappoint in the opera's celebrated pastoral plaint or in Tancredi's cabaletta
'Di tanti palpiti'. However, it is the scene from
Act 2 of *Semiramide* which provides the recital's
high-point. Hamlet-like, Arsace recognises his
mother's guilt (in an expressive transition finely
realised by Cencic) alongside his duty to avenge
his father's death, as music familiar from the
overture anticipates the crises to come.

With three overtures, Cencic's contributions
add up to just 49 minutes. Short measure, you
might think, but more than enough to give one a
sense of what a talented countertenor can bring
to Rossini.

'Rossini Mezzo'
La Cenerentola – Nacqui all'affanno. La donna del
lago – Mura felici; Elena! o tu, che chiamo!; Ah! Si
pera; Douglas! Douglas! Ti salva!. L'italiana in Algeri
– Cruda sorte! Amor tiranno!; Pensa alla patria.
Semiramide – Eccomi alfine in Babilonia; Ah! quel
giorno ognor rammento. Tancredi – Oh patria! dolce,
e ingrata patri!
Silvia Tro Santafé mez
**Lluis Vich Vocalis; Navarra Symphony Orchestra /
Julian Reynolds**
Signum Classics SIGCD170 (61' · DDD)   ⓕⓂ➔

Silvia Tro Santafé began her professional career
at the Rossini festival at Pesaro, and has made
something of a speciality of the three main
comic roles in his operas (Rosina, Cenerentola,
Isabella). She begins with two extracts from
L'italiana in Algeri, and although there are only a
couple of moments here where she can demonstrate her comic skills, there is a definite twinkle
in 'Cruda sorte!'. Where necessary all the other
characters are present for their brief interjections, and the Lluis Vich Vocalis chorus provide
the essential support in the big moments from
the final scenes of *L'italiana* and *La Cenerentola*.
Of course, one cannot help comparing Santafé
in these with her illustrious predecessors, Super-
via and Berganza. As yet she hasn't quite their
facility at investing the lyrics, or the coloratura,
with a completely individual quality. Her diction is exemplary, and she negotiates all the

rapid runs, trills and leaps without any apparent difficulty.

The other inevitable name for comparison is that of Marilyn Horne, and the trouser roles of Malcolm in *La donna del lago* and Arsace in *Semiramide* seemed almost Horne's exclusive property 30 years ago. It is in these parts that Santafé provides her most confident singing. The jaunty cabaletta to 'Mura felice' has an engaging swagger to it, especially at the words 'Tutto è imperfetto, tutto detesto'. As for 'Ah, quell giorno', if a suitable Semiramide could be found to partner Santafé's Arsace, this opera might prove viable again. The Navarra orchestra under Julian Reynolds provide sensitive accompaniments throughout. This is a most impressive recital.

'Colbran the Muse'
Armida – D'amor al dolce impero; Se al mio crudel tormento. La donna del lago – Oh mattutini albori!; Tanti affetti…Fra il padre. Maometto II – Giusto ciel, in tal periglio. Elisabetta, regina d'Inghliterra – Quant'è grato all'alma mia. Semiramide – Derina i vaghi rai…Bel raggio lusinghier. Otello – Ah! Dagli affanni oppressa…Assisa appiè d'un salice
Joyce DiDonato *mez*
Lawrence Brownlee *ten* **Banda Musicale della Guardia di Finanza; Chorus and Orchestra of the Accademia Nazionale di Santa Cecilia, Rome / Edoardo Müller**
Virgin Classics 694579-0 (72' · DDD)   Ⓕ❶❷❸❹➔

Joyce DiDonato is proving herself one of the most delightful artists of our time. She sings with a rare purity of tone, ease on the high Bs, an impressive degree of technical skill and lively powers of characterisation. She is invigoratingly precise in her placement, fluent in scale work and well furnished with *staccatos* and trills. Ideally one would prefer the well-articulated triplets (Berganza, for instance, managed this) to be sung *legato* rather than with the notes lightly separated as they are here; and perhaps one could wish for a greater range of colouration in the lower register. But the difficult repertoire is sung with charm and mastery, and from all we read, their original exponent, to whom the recital is dedicated, is worthily honoured. Choral and orchestral work are equally stylish, and the short tenor solos by Lawrence Brownlee are a treat.

Armida – Dove son io!ᵍ. Aureliano in Palmira – Se tu m'ami, o mia reginaᵇ. Bianca e Falliero – Cielo, il mio labbro ispiraᶜ. Elisabetta, Regina d'Inghilterra – Qant'è grato all'alma miaᵃ. Mosè in Egitto – Mi manca la voceᵉ; Porgi la destra amataʰ. Semiramide – Se la vitaᶠ. Vallace – Viva Vallace! Vallace Vivaⁱ. Zelmira – Riedi al soglioᵈ
Nelly Miricioiu with ᵉʰⁱ**Patrizia Biccire** *sops* ᵇᶜ**Enkelejda Shkosa** *mez* ⁱ**Antonia Sotgiù** *voc* ᶜᵉᵍ**Bruce Ford,** ᵈᵉʰⁱ**Barry Banks,** ʰ**Dominic Natoli** *tens* ᶜᵈʰⁱ**Gary Magee,** ʰ**Dean Robinson** *bars* ᶠ**Alastair Miles** *bass* ⁱ**Simon Bailey** *voc* ᵃᶜᵈʰⁱ**Geoffrey Mitchell Choir; Academy of St Martin in the Fields / David Parry**
Opera Rara ORR211 (67' · DDD · T/t)   Ⓕ❶

Rossini is a difficult composer to anthologise. Callas and Walter Legge or Sutherland and Bonynge might have come up with something fascinating and fabulous had they been so minded. Caballé did: the eminently collectable 'Rossini Rarities' disc she produced for the Rossini centenary in 1968. For the rest, successful recitals have been few and far between, indifferent singing or poor planning principally to blame. Not so Opera Rara's Rossini gala. Patric Schmid's inventive programme focuses on Rossini's Naples period and the extraordinary array of roles he created for the great Spanish soprano Isabella Colbran. What distinguishes this recital is that it doesn't only anthologise set-piece arias. Rossini gave Colbran some grand entrances and some even grander exits, and there are examples of both here: Queen Elizabeth's arrival and Zelmira's final florid song of thanksgiving. But there are also two wonderful quartets, two exquisite duets, a famous *coup de théâtre* (the Act 2 finale of *Mosè in Egitto* with its terrific lightning-strike), and one of Rossini's finest pieces of music-theatre: the scene near the start of Act 2 of *Semiramide* where the Queen and her lover, the adulterous regicide Assur, have rows worthy of the Macbeths over events which are beginning to overshadow them.

Miricioiu isn't a *bel canto* specialist; Santuzza is as much her territory as Semiramide. In neither role is the technique perfectly honed, but the effect is rarely less than compelling. Every one of the heroines presented here is vividly depicted, with a distinguished supporting cast helping to etch each scene into the imagination.

The gala ends with an intriguing rarity which has nothing to do with Colbran or Miricioiu. *Vallace* is a shortened, revised and relocated version of *Guillaume Tell* prepared for La Scala, Milan, in 1836-37. Austrian tyranny being an uncongenial subject to Milan's Austrian rulers, the libretto was recast to show English tyranny instead: Edward I's bloody crusade against the Scots, with William Wallace as a Scottish Tell. Rossini wasn't much involved in the adaptation, though he did agree to recast the finale scene so that the opera could end with a reprise of the overture's famous *pas redoublé*. It's that revised finale we have here, a travesty of Schiller (and Rossini), but great fun.

Playing, choral work and conducting for this Rossini gala are all of a high order of excellence. As is the engineering (the lightning strike in *Mosè in Egitto* isn't for the faint-hearted). As always with Opera Rara, the accompanying 116-page booklet is superlatively informative. At the price of a single full-price CD, the disc is a terrific bargain, not least for the splendid hawk's-eye view the programme provides of 'serious' Rossini.

Il barbiere di Siviglia

Il barbiere di Siviglia
Roberto Servile *bar* Figaro **Sonia Ganassi** *mez* Rosina **Ramón Vargas** *ten* Count Almaviva **Angelo Romero** *bar* Bartolo **Franco de Grandis** *bass* Don

ROSSINI IL BARBIERE DI SIVIGLIA – IN BRIEF

Roberto Servile Figaro **Sonia Ganassi** Rosina
Ramón Vargas Almaviva **Hungarian Radio
Chorus; Failoni Chamber Orchestra /
Will Humburg**
Naxos ③ 8 660027/9 (158′ · DDD)   ⑤●●🄑▸
Happily one of the best is also among
the cheapest; fresh, full and brilliantly con-
ducted, with a ripely Italianate cast including
star-in-the-making Ramón Vargas.

Thomas Allen Figaro **Agnes Baltsa** Rosina
Francisco Araiza Almaviva **Ambrosian Opera
Chorus; ASMF / Sir Neville Marriner**
Decca ② 470 434-2DOC2 (148′ · DDD)   Ⓜ●●🄑▸
None the worse for international star quality.
Marriner conducts a superlative, characterful
cast with infectious sparkle and warmth, and
first-rate recording.

Sesto Bruscantini Figaro **Victoria de los Angeles**
Rosina **Luigi Alva** Almaviva **Glyndebourne
Festival Chorus; Royal PO / Vittorio Gui**
EMI ② 567762-2 (141′ · ADD)   Ⓜ●●●🄑▸
A magical performance, not least
because it derives from a much-loved
Glyndebourne production. Gui's conducting
is warm and affectionate, his stars more light-
hearted and witty than brashly comic.

Nathan Gunn Figaro **Elīna Garanča** Rosina
Lawrence Brownlee Almaviva **Bavarian Radio
Chorus; Munich Radio Orchestra / Miguel
Angel Gómez-Martínez**
Sony Classical ② 82876 80429-2 (152′ · DDD)
Recorded at concert performances, this is a
Barber with a lot of spirit. Nathan Gunn is an
energetic, bouncy Figaro and if Garanča
could afford to smile a little more, she sings
with a lovely tone. Gómez-Martínez keeps
everything bubbling along elegantly.

Tito Gobbi Figaro **Maria Callas** Rosina **Luigi Alva** 🄗
Almaviva **Philharmonia Orchestra / Alceo Galliera**
EMI ② 556310-2 (132′ · ADD)   🄕🄑▸
An inauthentic soprano Rosina is still a gain
when it's Callas, with Gobbi's warmly robust
Figaro as foil; she makes an enchanting spitfire, with some showy ornamentation. The
experienced cast are splendid and Galliera's
conducting wonderfully theatrical. One of
the most thoroughly comic sets.

Hermann Prey Figaro **Teresa Berganza** Rosina
Luigi Alva Almaviva **Chorus and Orchestra of
La Scala, Milan / Claudio Abbado**
DG 📀 073 021-9GH (142′)   🄕
A rather old-fashioned cinematic version in
lip-sync, but still enjoyable and well worth
considering for Abbado's rich but lively
conducting and a very strong cast, even if
Prey, though excellent, seems insufficiently
Italianate, and Berganza is a shade mature.

Basilio **Ingrid Kertesi** sop Berta **Kázmér Sarkany**
bass Fiorello **Hungarian Radio Chorus; Failoni
Chamber Orchestra, Budapest / Will Humburg**
Naxos ③ 8 660027/9 (158′ · DDD · N/T)   ⑤●●🄑▸

Not everyone will approve, but there are ways in
which this super-budget set of Il barbiere di
Siviglia puts to shame just about every other version of the opera there has been. Those it may
not please are specialist vocal collectors for
whom Il barbiere is primarily a repository of
vocal test pieces. If, however, you regard Il barbiere (Rossini, ex-Beaumarchais) as a gloriously
subversive music drama – vibrant, scurrilous,
vital – then this recording is guaranteed to give a
great deal of pleasure.

'Performance' is the key word here. Humburg
is described in the Naxos booklet as 'Conductor
and Recitative Director', and for once the recitatives really are part of the larger drama. The
result is a meticulously produced, often very
funny, brilliantly integrated performance that
you'll almost certainly find yourself listening to
as a stage play. With a virtually all-Italian cast,
the results are a revelation. The erotic allure of
the duet 'Dunque io son' is striking. Similarly,
Don Basilio's Calumny aria, superbly sung by
Franco de Grandis, a black-browed bass from
Turin who was singing for Karajan, Muti and
Abbado while still in his twenties. This takes on
added character and colour from the massive
sense of panic created by de Grandis and the
admirable Dr Bartolo of Angelo Romero when
Basilio comes in with news of Almaviva's arrival
in town.

The Overture is done with evident relish: the
playing of the Failoni Chamber Orchestra is
nothing if not articulate. Aided by a clear, forward recording, a sine qua non with musical
comedy, the cast communicates the Rossini/
Sterbini text with tremendous relish. They're
never hustled by Humburg, nor are they spared:
the stretta of the Act 1 finale is a model of hyper-
tension and clarity. This Il barbiere jumps to the
top of the pile.

Il barbiere di Siviglia
Sesto Bruscantini bar Figaro **Victoria de los
Angeles** sop Rosina **Luigi Alva** ten Count Almaviva
Ian Wallace bass Dr Bartolo **Carlo Cava** bass Don
Basilio **Duncan Robertson** ten Fiorello **Laura Sarti**
mez Berta **Glyndebourne Festival Chorus; Royal
Philharmonic Orchestra / Vittorio Gui**
EMI Great Recordings of the Century mono ②
567762-2 (141′ · ADD · T/t). Recorded 1962   Ⓜ●●●🄑▸

Perhaps it's a shade misleading to refer
to this classic EMI recording as a
'Glyndebourne' set. It has all the ingredients of a Glyndebourne production: notably
the cast, the orchestra and chorus, and that
doyen of Rossini conductors, Vittorio Gui. But
as far as can be ascertained, there was no actual
stage production of Il barbiere in 1962. Nor was
the recording, for all its dryness and sharp-

edged immediacy, actually made at Glynde-bourne. It's a well-honed, conservatively staged stereophonic studio recording made by EMI in its Abbey Road Studio No 1. Gui's performance is so astutely paced that, while the music bubbles and boils, every word is crystal-clear. This is a wonderfully declaimed reading of the score, but also a beautifully timed one. Gui's steady tempi allow the music to show its underlying tough-ness, and he secures characterful playing from the RPO, the wind players in particular. Where Victoria de los Angeles is so memorable is in the beauty of her singing and the originality of the reading. There has never been a Rosina who manages to be both as guileful and as charming as she. Team her up with the incomparable Sesto Bruscantini and, in something like the nodal Act 1 duet, 'Dunque io son', you have musical and dramatic perfection. Ian Wallace is a fine character actor, given plenty of space by Gui, allowing his portrait of Dr Bartolo to emerge as a classic compromise between the let-ter and the spirit of the part.

Il barbiere di Siviglia
Nathan Gunn bar Figaro **Elīna Garanča** mez Rosina
Lawrence Brownlee ten Almaviva **Bruno de Simone**
bar Doctor Bartolo **Kristinn Sigmundsson** bass Don
Basilio **Giovanna Donadini** mez Berta **Roberto**
Accurso bass Fiorello
Bavarian Radio Chorus; Munich Radio Orchestra /
Miguel Angel Gómez-Martínez
Sony Classical ② 82876 80429-2 (152' · DDD · S/N).
Recorded live. Enhanced CD features libretto with
translations in PDF format   Ⓕ

Here's a *Barbiere* light of heart and light of touch, graceful in style, with fresh, young-sounding voices (where appropriate), well schooled so as to make those forbiddingly diffi-cult vocal flights sound like flights of fancy, quick as thought and natural as intuition.

It's a concert performance and carries with it a real sense of enjoyment. The Overture moves with relish as from one good thing to another, and movement is the motto for most of the first act. Fiorello and the chorus are no clod-hoppers and the Count is no show-off. 'Ecco ridente' has the assurance of a young aristocrat who has practised his scales and scorns the use of aspi-rates. Figaro likewise wears his skills and his energy lightly, the brag and bounce of his intro-ductory solo kept within civilised limits. Their duet is a ball-game of high velocity neatly played in time to an inexhaustible supply of rhythm and melody.

The Rosina is Elīna Garanča who is not very liberal with her smiles. The possibility of fun is admitted with 'farò giocar' but the keynote is determination ('vincerò'). Later the characteri-sation warms, but right from the start we have been won by the beauty of her tone and the accomplishment of her florid work, never going hard or shrill at the top and keeping the voice whole and even throughout its range. Her guardian, Doctor Bartolo, in this version is a

lightweight *buffo* baritone rather than the usual bumbling fatty, and it's left to the Basilio to play the traditional tricks.

At times during this first act, one may wish for a moment here and there to linger over phrases or merely to savour the sound of a fine voice. In compensation, the conductor offers a clear view in which everything has its place. In Act 2 he makes room for more expansion. In both, the clarity of ensemble is a delight, as is the elegant playing of the Munich orchestra.

Il barbiere di Siviglia
Hermann Prey bar Figaro **Teresa Berganza** mez
Rosina **Luigi Alva** ten Almaviva **Enzo Dara** bar
Doctor Bartolo **Paolo Montarsolo** bass Don Basilio
Stefania Malagù mez Berta **Renato Cesari** bass
Fiorello **Luigi Roni** bar Officer **Hans Kraemmer** bass
Ambrogio **Milan La Scala Orchestra and Chorus /**
Claudio Abbado
Stage director **Jean-Pierre Ponnelle**
Video director **Ernst Wild**
DG 🔘 073 021-9GH (142' · 4:3 ·2.0 · 0)   Ⓕ

Claudio Abbado's youthful Beatle-cut marks the age of this film, still one of the better screen *Barbiere*s if not absolutely the best. Jean-Pierre Ponnelle based it on his Scala stagings, but filmed it, as he always preferred, in studio with lip-sync, more successfully than most. As a result, it looks and sounds very much fresher on DVD than contemporary videotapes.

The strong cast reproduces that of Abbado's 1972 CD recording, but with La Scala forces. Teresa Berganza, often rather unexciting in sound alone, reveals a charming presence here, only a shade mature for a role she'd sung since the 1950s. In the manner of that era her Rosina is coquette rather than minx, but her slightly resinous tone and sensuous delivery makes 'Contro il cor' irresistible. You'd never guess Luigi Alva had been singing Almaviva for just as long, still youthful-looking, honeyed and ele-gant, even if his heavily aspirated ornament – the 'ha-ha' effect – wouldn't be acceptable today. Hermann Prey has everything a good Figaro needs, but despite his warmly incisive baritone and cheerfully egocentric, athletic characterisa-tion he simply isn't idiomatic enough. Enzo Dara's pompous, foppish Bartolo is amusingly observed and richly sung, but he suffers unduly from the film's major drawback, the direction.

Ponnelle feels obliged to reinforce the comedy with a barrage of ingenious but spurious business, such as Basilio's alchemical explosions, and choppy editing. The effect is enjoyable but overdone.

Il barbiere di Siviglia
David Malis bar Figaro **Jennifer Larmore** mez
Rosina **Richard Croft** ten Almaviva **Renato Capecchi**
bar Doctor Bartolo **Simone Alaimo** bass Don Basilio
Leonie Schoon mez Berta **Roger Smeets** bass
Fiorello, Officer **Netherlands Opera Chorus;**
Netherlands Chamber Orchestra / Alberto Zedda
Stage director **Dario Fo**

Video director **Hans Hulscher**
ArtHaus Musik 📀 100 412 (154' · 4:3 · PCM stereo · 2 & 5). Recorded 1991 ⓕ❍❍❍

We've cursed modern producers and their productions often enough, but here's a delight. The conductor, working with his own edition of the opera, is Alberto Zedda. But when the director and designer, Dario Fo, takes the last, climatic bow, he deserves every cheer he gets.

The performance was filmed at the Netherlands Opera in 1991, but the production dates back to 1987, and was Fo's first for the operatic stage. Employing a group of mime artists, he places the action in a *commedia dell'arte* setting and opens with a brilliant pantomime-accompaniment to the overture. The ideas match the music, and the visual style suits the elegance of Zedda's orchestral players. Throughout the opening solos, chorus and duet, a delightful ingenuity of movement plays along with the singers, who have the youth and elasticity of voice, limb and spirit to cope with the thousand-and-one tasks thrown at them. There's very little sense of distraction or overloading; just a feast of melody, wit and energy.

The tenor Robert Croft impresses most: his tone is clear; his scales are fluent and evenly articulated, and he can apply vocal decoration with panache and delicacy. The Figaro, another American, David Malis, has personality and bright high notes. Jennifer Larmore's Rosina, better when seen than merely heard, is strong-voiced and technically accomplished. Renato Capecchi is a memorable Bartolo, distinct from the potbellied bumbler of convention.

In the theatre the production might be found too restless; but, expertly filmed, it's just about the most enjoyable comic opera production available on DVD.

Il barbiere di Siviglia
Manuel Lanza *bar* Figaro **Vesselina Kasarova** *mez*
Rosina **Reinaldo Macias** *ten* Count Almaviva
Elizabeth Magnuson *mez* Berta **Carlos Chausson**
bar Doctor Bartolo **Valery Murga** *bar* Officer **Nicolai
Ghiaurov** *bass* Don Basilio **Kenneth Roberson** *bass*
Ambrogio **Zurich Opera House Chorus and
Orchestra / Nello Santi**
Stage director **Grischa Asagaroff**
Video director **Felix Breisach**
TDK Euro Arts ② 📀 DV-OPBDS (161' · 16:9 · DTS
5.1 & 2.0 · 0) ⓕ

This set offers a novel but never outlandish view of a familiar work. It's most distinguished by Luigi Perego's utterly delightful décor, which places the action in the art deco period. The gimmicky first scene has Almaviva arriving on a motorcycle with sidecar and Figaro on a bicycle, but once indoors Asagaroff's direction proves witty, eschewing slapstick, making the characters larger than life, as perhaps they should be, but never to the point of exaggeration. He's helped by a youthful cast. Although rather young-looking, Carlos Chausson's fine observation of Bartolo's quirks are in the best tradition of the role, and his singing

of his virtuoso aria is masterly. Manuel Lanza's slightly too laid-back and modern Figaro, and Reinaldo Macias's subtly acted, adequately sung Almaviva form part of a true ensemble. At its centre is Vesselina Kasarova's Rosina; she gives a typically individual performance, full in tone, clean in *fioriture*, but a bit too dramatically calculated. Nicolai Ghiaurov, though his voice is a shadow of its former self, makes a genial Basilio. Veteran conductor Nello Santi's reading of the score is clean-cut, never drawing attention to itself, always aware of Rossini's irresistible orchestration. A thoroughly enjoyable performance.

La Cenerentola

La Cenerentola
Teresa Berganza *mez* Angelina **Luigi Alva** *ten* Don
Ramiro **Renato Capecchi** *bar* Dandini **Paolo
Montarsolo** *bar* Don Magnifico **Margherita
Guglielmi** *sop* Clorinda **Laura Zannini** *contr* Tisbe
Ugo Trama *bass* Alidoro **Scottish Opera Chorus;
London Symphony Orchestra / Claudio Abbado**
DG Double ② 459 448-2GTA2 (144' · ADD · T/t)
Recorded 1971 Ⓜ❍❍❍▸

Rossini's Cinderella is a fairy-tale without a fairy, but no less bewitching for that. In fact the replacement of the winged godmother with the philanthropic Alidoro, a close friend and adviser of our prince, Don Ramiro, plus the lack of any glass slippers and the presence of a particularly unsympathetic father character, makes the whole story more plausible. La Cenerentola, Angelina, is more spunky than the average pantomime Cinders. She herself gives Don Ramiro one of her pair of bracelets, charging him to find the owner of the matching ornament, and thus taking control of her own destiny. Along the way, Don Ramiro and his valet Dandini change places, leading to plenty of satisfyingly operatic confusion and difficult situations.

This recording, when originally transferred to CD, was spread across three discs, but has now been comfortably fitted into two at mid-price. It gives a sparkling rendition of the score with a lovely light touch and well-judged tempi from Abbado and the LSO. Virtuoso vocal requirements are fully met by the cast. The chief delight is Teresa Berganza's Angelina, creamy in tone and as warm as she's precise. The supporting cast is full of character, with Luigi Alva a princely Don Ramiro, Margherita Guglielmi and Laura Zannini an affected and fussy pair of sisters, and Renato Capecchi, gleeful and mischievous as he takes on being prince for a day. The recording sounds more than usually well for its age.

Additional recommendation

Bartoli Angelina **Matteuzzi** Don Ramiro **Corbelli**
Dandini **Bologna Teatro Comunale Chorus and
Orchestra / Chailly**
Decca ② 436 902-2DHO2 (148' · DDD) ⓕ▸
For Bartoli fans, a cherishable set that doesn't quite

match the sparkle of the Abbado. Matteuzzi sings well and there are some nicely drawn characters. Chailly directs with spirit.

Le comte Ory

Le comte Ory
Juan Diego Flórez ten Comte Ory **Stefania Bonfadelli** sop Adèle **Alastair Miles** bar Gouverneur **Marie-Ange** Todorovitch mez Isolier **Bruno Praticò** bar Raimbaud **Marina De Liso** mez Ragonde **Rossella Bevacqua** sop Alice **Prague Chamber Choir; Teatro Comunale Orchestra, Bologna / Jesús López-Cobos**
DG ② 477 5020GH2 (130' · DDD · T/t)
Recorded live 2003   ⓕ**OO**▣

Le comte Ory is the first great French-language comic opera. A late work (Paris, 1828), sensuous, witty and exquisitely crafted, it's always been something of a connoisseur's piece.

The selling-point here is the Ory, Juan Diego Flórez, and very striking he is, too. He has terrific presence, a well-nigh flawless technique, and a keen sense of the French vocal style. Jesús López-Cobos, an old Rossini hand, conducts robustly but with style. He overdrives the Act 1 ensemble in which the villagers come to Ory with their requests but paces to perfection the action within the celebrated nocturnal Trio in Act 2.

It would be nice to have a French Raimbaud, but Bruno Praticò, an old hand, knows how to ring the changes in a strophic patter-song. The only problematic *comprimario* role is that of Ory's Tutor. His Act 1 aria, a bespoke commission for the great French *basse chantante* Nicolas Levasseur, is a devil of a piece to bring off; López-Cobos races through the aria in a vain attempt to disguise the fact that Alastair Miles isn't entirely at ease with it.

The recording has colour, life, dash, brio, and a measure of wit. It also has Juan Diego Flórez. Enough to be going on with? Absolutely. An *Ory* for the connoisseur? Not entirely.

La donna del lago

La donna del lago
Carmen Giannattasio sop Elena **Kenneth Tarver** ten Uberto/Giacomo **Patricia Bardon** mez Malcolm **Gregory Kunde** ten Rodrigo di Dhu **Robert Gleadow** bass Douglas d'Angus **Francesca Sassu** sop Albina **Mark Wilde** ten Bertram; Serano **Edinburgh Festival Chorus; Scottish Chamber Orchestra / Maurizio Benini**
Opera Rara ③ ORC34 (160' · DDD · S/T/t/N)
Recorded live 2006   ⓕ**O**

One of Rossini's most attractive scores, *La donna del lago* is both bold and delicate, at one moment looking ahead to Verdi, at several others suggesting a Mozartian affinity. The orchestral writing offers colour, adornment and a steady supply of additional interest. For the voice, opportunities for brilliance are matched by passages of sustained lyrical elegance. Dramatically, the construction is effective, the tension well contrived, with characters and situations that can touch the heart.

Live in Edinburgh's Usher Hall, Gregory Kunde, in the fearsome role of Rodrigo, sounded at times foggy, almost as though singing through a cold, his tone breaking free with startling clarity on the high notes. The recording is more evenly voiced, the low notes clearer, the top not quite so exciting. And whereas the memory of Carmen Giannattasio as Elena is of something very special, the recorded sound seems not quite to catch the distinctive beauty of her tone throughout the range. Also the recording is without applause: and there was much.

It was an evening of general rejoicing in the singers' art. Perhaps the greatest enthusiasm of all greeted Kenneth Tarver, especially after his solo at the beginning of Act 2: and that comes out on record exactly as remembered, a model of *legato* singing from the start and blissfully even and precise in florid work later on.

Though this was a concert performance, all was fully expressive and, if one couldn't claim a high degree of dramatic involvement, at least as a member of the audience one felt interest and sympathy. The orchestra is well to the fore, and its playing is certainly a main strength, Maurizio Benini conducting with spirit and finesse. Offstage band and chorus are also effectively recorded, and a well-chosen version of the text is presented. Opera Rara also brings its habitual generosity and scholarship to the accompanying booklet, with a handsome box and stylish packaging.

La donna del lago
Sonia Ganassi mez Elena **Maxim Mironov** ten Uberto/Giacomo **Marianna Pizzolato** mez Malcolm **Ferdinand von Bothmer** ten Rodrigo di Dhu **Wojtek Gierlach** bass Douglas d'Angus **Olga Peretyatko** sop Albina **Stefan Cifolelli** ten Serano **Prague Chamber Choir; Tübingen Festival Band; Kaiserslautern Radio Orchestra / Alberto Zedda**
Naxos ② 8 660235/6 (147' · DDD · S/N)   ⓢ▣

Like the excellent Opera Rara recording (reviewed above), this new Naxos set was also made live in 2006. An excess of mid-act applause notwithstanding, it offers yet another distinguished account of the score. Key to the set's success is the cast of rising young stars of the Rossini circuit which veteran conductor and Rossini editor Alberto Zedda has assembled. Maxim Mironov is memorable as the King and there are equally compelling performances by Sonia Ganassi, Marianna Pizzolato and Ferdinand von Bothmer. A more than useful addition to the *La donna del lago* discography.

Elisabetta, regina d'Inghilterra

Elisabetta, regina d'Inghilterra
Jennifer Larmore mez Elisabetta **Bruce Ford** ten

Leicester **Majella Cullagh** sop Matilde **Manuela Custer** mez Enrico **Colin Lee** ten Guglielmo **Antonio Siragusa** ten Norfolk **Geoffrey Mitchell Choir; London Philharmonic Orchestra / Giuliano Carella**
Opera Rara ② ORC22 (147' · DDD · T/t)　　　Ⓕ

Rossini wrote *Elizabeth, Queen of England* for the star-studded San Carlo Opera in Naples in 1815. The plot is a verse reduction of a half-remembered drama by an Italian advocate out of an entertaining but historically implausible English romance. Larmore makes a formidable Elizabeth; beautifully sung, her performance has presence, character, and a real sense of ingrained authority. The lovely *cantabile* duet for Elizabeth and Matilde at the start of Act 2 is sung to perfection by Caballé and Masterson on Philips' rival set but there's a greater depth of emotion, a grainier, gutsier feel to Larmore's performance with Majella Cullagh's equally characterful, if not at every point inch-perfect, Matilde. There's little to choose between Bruce Ford's Leicester and Carreras's for Philips – Carreras perhaps wins on points with a certain added youthful allure – but Opera Rara's Antonio Siragusa is a more compelling Norfolk than Ugo Benelli, who sings splendidly but without much menace. Siragusa is very fine. With such strong casting, it goes without saying that the great confrontations in the opera – Elizabeth and Norfolk, Leicester and Norfolk, and so on – all come vividly to life. The Opera Rara performance has a lovely rich, dark feel to it. This is partly to do with Carella's conducting and the London Philharmonic's playing; partly to do with the fact that orchestration is clearly different in places. For first-time buyers, this is the set to go for.

La gazza ladra

La gazza ladra
Carlos Feller bass Fabrizio Vingradito **Nucci Condò** mez Lucia **David Kuebler** ten Giannetto **Ileana Cotrubas** sop Ninetta **Brent Ellis** bar Fernando Villabella **Alberto Rinaldi** bass-bar Gottardo (Il Podestà) **Elena Zilio** mez Pippo **Erlingur Vigfússon** ten Isacco **Eberhard Katz** ten Antonio **Klaus Bruch** bass Giorgio **Ulrich Hielscher** bass Ernesto **Cologne Opera Chorus; Gürzenich Orchestra, Cologne / Bruno Bartoletti**
Stage director **Michael Hampe**
Video director **José Montes Pagano**
ArtHaus Musik 🖭 102 203 (3h 2' · NTSC · 4:3 · PCM stereo · 0). Recorded live at the Cologne Opera in 1987　　　Ⓕ

In an odd way, *La gazza ladra* is as disorientating as Shakespeare's *Measure for Measure*, which answers the old definition of tragi-comedy as a form of drama bringing characters near to death 'which maketh it no comedy', yet ends happily so that it is no tragedy either. On first acquaintance Rossini's *opera semiseria* can have you seriously worried. The title, overture and opening scenes induce the sure expectation of a comedy of nothing more serious than errors. The Mayor's das-

tardly designs upon Ninetta give the framework for a plot and the father's return as a deserter from the wars thickens it; but it still comes as quite a profound shock when Ninetta is sent to prison.

When the court sentences her to death we rub our eyes. They strike up the funeral march and we say 'Oh no!' But Rossini and his librettist risk a stage further towards tragedy as Ninetta sings her last prayer and is led off to execution out of our sight. Of course other developments are in hand and the musical conventions assure us that what seems now inevitable must take a turn for the better. But there is a distinct element of touch-and-go, which makes the opera a remarkable piece for its time, and for its composer. It also presents a challenge to the producer and the whole company, a challenge well met here, with the right balance struck, and no undermining of one half by the other.

Sets, costumes and acting are all under sensible direction and there are none of those silly diversionary indulgences that have become so habitual in recent years. There are four good vocal performances: by Elena Zilio and Nucci Condò, both sturdy mezzos; by David Kuebler, an accomplished lyric tenor; and by the grand veteran Carlos Feller, looking rather like Bertrand Russell but endowing the old croaker with a full-bodied and still resonant bass voice. The baritones are sonorous but uneven, while Ileana Cotrubas as the heroine sometimes touches the heart but at this stage in her career rarely delights the ear. Bartoletti and his players do justice to Rossini's score, as do the video director and his crew to the events onstage.

Guglielmo Tell

Guglielmo Tell
Sherrill Milnes bar Guglielmo Tell **Luciano Pavarotti** ten Arnoldo **Mirella Freni** sop Matilde **Della Jones** mez Jemmy **Elizabeth Connell** mez Edwige **Ferruccio Mazzoli** bass Gessler **Nicolai Ghiaurov** bass Gualtiero **John Tomlinson** bass Melchthal **Cesar Antonio Suarez** ten Un Pescatore **Piero De Palma** ten Rodolfo **Richard Van Allan** bass Leutoldo **Ambrosian Opera Chorus; National Philharmonic Orchestra / Riccardo Chailly**
Decca ④ 417 154-2DH4 (235' · ADD · T/t)　　　Ⓕ⬤🔲▸

If ever there was a case for armchair opera it's Rossini's *Guglielmo Tell*. The very limitations which have made it, so far, a non-repertory work, give space for the imagination to redress the balance: the short, Rousseau-esque scenes of life by Lake Lucerne, the distant entrances and exits of shepherds and huntsmen, the leisurely but perfectly balanced side-vignettes of fisherman, hunter, child.

Thanks to the clarity and liveliness of the recording itself and, above all, the shrewd casting, this set creates a vivid charivari of fathers, sons, lovers and patriots, all played out against some of Rossini's most delicately painted pastoral cameos. Chailly keeps up the undercurrent of tension between private love and public loyalty, as well as working hard the rustic jollity of the score. Tell himself could hardly have a better advocate than Sherrill Milnes. Arnoldo and Matilde, too, are cleverly cast. Pavarotti contains the coarse, direct impulsiveness of Arnoldo's shepherd stock with the tenderness of love, in his characteristic charcoal *cantabile* and the numbness of his remorse.

Mirella Freni, singing opposite Pavarotti as the forbidden Princess Matilde, phrases with aristocratic poise, folding into every fragment of embryonic *bel canto* the fragile ardour of a young girl's love. The vocal chemistry between them in their Act 2 declaration of love is a lively incarnation of their roles. A similarly interesting patterning of vocal timbres is produced by the casting of Elizabeth Connell as Edwige, Tell's wife, and of Della Jones as Jemmy, their son. Their last-act trio with Matilde is matched by the contrasting colours of the basses of Ghiaurov, Tomlinson and Van Allan: their roles may be small, but their characters are vividly stamped on an excellent ensemble performance.

L'italiana in Algeri

L'italiana in Algeri
Jennifer Larmore *mez* Isabella **Raúl Giménez** *ten* Lindoro **Alessandro Corbelli** *bar* Taddeo **John del Carlo** *bass* Mustafà **Darina Takova** *sop* Elvira **Laura Polverelli** *mez* Zulma **Carlos Chausson** *bass-bar* Haly
Geneva Grand Theatre Chorus; Lausanne Chamber Orchestra / Jésus López-Cobos
Teldec ② 0630 17130-2 (147' · DDD · T/t) Ⓕ**O**

This recording is hard to fault on any count. López-Cobos revels in all aspects of this dotty comedy, timing everything to perfection, enthusing his accomplished orchestra and cast to enjoy their collective self. First there's a magic moment as Isabella and Lindoro espy each other for the first time, and comment on the joy of reunion; then the main section gets under way to a perfectly sprung rhythm from the conductor, with all the passage's detail made manifest; finally the *stretta* is released with the kind of vitality that sets the feet tapping.

Larmore obviously thoroughly enjoys the role and conveys that enjoyment in singing that matches warm, smiling tone to bravura execution of her *fioriture*. She's a mettlesome Isabella, who knows how to tease, then defy her would-be lover, Mustafà, and charm her real *amour*, Lindoro, her 'Per lui che adoro' sung with an immaculate line and sensuous tone, its repetition deftly embellished. Finally 'Pensa alla patria' evinces a touch of true élan.

Lindoro is taken by that paragon among Rossini tenors, Raúl Giménez, who presents his credentials in 'Languir per una bella', honeyed tone succeeded by fleet runs. He's no less successful in his more heroic Cavatina in Act 2. Corbelli, another master-Rossinian, is witty as the put-upon Taddeo, his textual facility a marvel.

The American bass-baritone John del Carlo is a characterful Mustafà, managing to suggest, as Rossini surely intended, a paradox of lovesick tyrant and ludicrous posturing without ever overstepping the mark into farce, and rolling Italian and his rotund roulades off his tongue with idiomatic assurance. The recording is up to Teldec's impeccably high standard.

L'italiana in Algeri
Marilyn Horne *mez* Isabella **Ernesto Palacio** *ten* Lindoro **Domenico Trimarchi** *bar* Taddeo **Samuel Ramey** *bass* Mustafà **Kathleen Battle** *sop* Elvira **Clara Foti** *mez* Zulma **Nicola Zaccaria** *bass* Haly
Prague Philharmonic Chorus; I Solisti Veneti / Claudio Scimone
Erato Libretto ② 2292 45404-2 (140' · ADD · N/T) Recorded 1980 Ⓜ

Written within the space of a month during the spring of 1813, and with help from another anonymous hand, Rossini's *L'italiana in Algeri* was an early success, and one which went on to receive many performances during the 19th century, with an increasingly corrupt text. A complete reconstruction was undertaken by Azio Corghi and published in 1981; this recording uses this edition which corresponds most closely to what was actually performed in Venice in 1813. *L'italiana* is one of Rossini's wittiest operas, featuring as did a number of his most successful works a bewitching central character, in this case Isabella, who makes fun of her various suitors, with the opera ending with a happy escape with her beloved, Lindoro, a typical *tenorino* role. This fine recording has plenty of vocal polish. Scimone's biggest asset is Marilyn Horne as Isabella: possibly the finest Rossini singer of her generation and a veteran in this role, she sings Rossini's demanding music with great virtuosity and polish. Her liquid tone and artful phrasing ensure that she's a continuous pleasure to listen to. She's strongly supported by the rest of the cast: Kathleen Battle is a beguiling Elvira, Domenico Trimarchi a most humorous Taddeo, and Samuel Ramey a sonorous Bey of Algiers. Ernesto Palacio's Lindoro, however, has patches of white tone and is correct rather than inspiring. Scimone's conducting is guaranteed to give considerable pleasure.

The Italian Girl in Algiers (highlights in English)
Jennifer Larmore *mez* Isabella **Barry Banks** *ten* Lindoro **Alan Opie** *bar* Taddeo **Alastair Miles** *bass* Mustafà **Sarah Tynan** *sop* Elvira **David Soar** *bass* Haly **Anne Marie Gibbons** *mez* Zulma
Geoffrey Mitchell Choir; Philharmonia Orchestra / Brad Cohen
Chandos Opera in English CHAN3160 (77' · DDD)

Rossini's *The Italian Girl* distils readily on to a single CD. The first act is substantially there and the second can survive without the Quintet.

The only gripe concerns the decision to end with Isabella's Rondo. Rossini finished serious and mixed-mode operas this way but not the out-and-out comedies. The final vaudeville runs for around 2'20" and should have been included.

With opera in English, translation is key. Arthur Jacobs's translation in the vocal score of the Ricordi Critical Edition is a workmanlike affair but it isn't a patch on David Parry's brilliant new version. Lines from Isabella's cavatina are typically felicitous: "Through years of practising / I have perfected / The gesture languishing / The sigh affected".

Jennifer Larmore has recorded the opera in Italian (reviewed above) but her English Isabella, superbly articulated and projected, is both formidable and funny. Her Act 2 cavatina, played with the original cello obbligato, is the lyric highlight. Happily, the three men in her life are equally vividly characterised: Alan Opie as her hang-dog admirer Taddeo, Barry Banks a most eloquent Lindoro, and Alastair Miles as the lascivious Mustafà. Fifty years ago there was barely a bass in Europe who could find his way around Mustafà's bumbling coloratura, let alone project the text as Miles does here.

Brad Cohen conducts superbly, bringing out the strength and expressive range of music that revels in the thrill of sexual confrontation and the speed and power of the vortex into which so-called civilised society can all too rapidly vanish.

L'italiana in Algeri
Christianne Stotijn *mez* Isabella **Maxim Mironov** *ten* Lindoro **Marco Vinco** *bass* Mustafà **Ruben Drole** *bar* Haly **Giorgio Caoduro** *bar* Taddeo **Elisaveta Martirosyan** *sop* Elvira **Sabina Willeit** *mez* Zulma **Arnold Schoenberg Choir; Mahler Chamber Orchestra / Riccardo Frizza**
Stage director **Toni Servillo**
Video director **Vincent Bataillon**
Bel Air Classiques 🔲 BAC025 (135' · NTSC · 16:9 · PCM stereo, 5.1 and DTS 5.1 · 0). Recorded live at the Aix-en-Provence Festival in June 2006 Ⓕ

Aix-en-Provence is generally a guarantor of musical excellence and this performance is no exception. Maxim Mironov may not be as well known as Flórez but he is rightly the *tenore di grazia* of choice for leading Rossini houses much as Nicolai Gedda and Luigi Alva were a generation or so ago. In those days, no bass was capable of singing Mustafà properly, without cuts and with all the notes in place. Marco Vinco, one of a new breed of Rossini basses, is exemplary. Christianne Stotijn is not the most fetching or dynamic of Isabellas but she will 'do'.

Conductor Riccardo Frizza makes the most of his eight minutes on camera in the overture, play-acting like a fantasy conductor in front of his gramophone before bringing the orchestra to its feet for time-consuming bows and solo plaudits. What follows, however, is taut and well drilled. Space is given for the comedy to flower,

though Frizza's tempo is too quick in the wonderful duet between Isabella and Taddeo 'Ai capricci' (the marking is *Allegro* not *Allegro molto*) where he appears oblivious to the fact that Rossini's use of musical form is a key contributor to the comedy (Isabella flattening Taddeo with a rejoinder which also happens to be a sonata-form recapitulation). The duet barely raises a smile from the audience.

A single set does service throughout: an empty stage dominated by a three-story ziggurat that can be transformed into the prow of a three-deck ocean liner at the drop of a painted cloth. For much of the evening there is movement in and around the ziggurat but no production to speak of – unless you count Haly being sent into the audience to sing his chirpy sorbet aria 'Le femmine d'Italia'. It is in effect a colourfully costumed concert. That said, director Toni Servillo's minimalist approach works well in the pivotal Act 2 quintet and climactic Act 2 trio. As stage comedy *L'italiana* must seem pretty thin stuff to modern audiences, yet the various elements in the Rossini cuisine come together most agreeably in the closing scenes of this Aix production.

Matilde di Shabran

Matilde di Shabran
Juan Diego Flórez *ten* Corradino **Annick Massis** *sop* Matilde di Shabran **Hadar Halevy** *mez* Edoardo **Bruno de Simone** *bass* Isidoro **Chiara Chialli** *mez* Contessa d'Arco **Gregory Bonfatti** *ten* Egoldo **Lubomír Moravec** *ten* Rodrigo **Bruno Taddia** *bass* Raimondo Lopez
Prague Chamber Choir; Galicia Symphony Orchestra / Riccardo Frizza
Decca ③ 475 7688DHO3 (3h 9' · DDD). Recorded at the Teatro Rossini, Pesaro, in August 2004 Ⓕ ●●●▷

Here is treasure indeed: a memorable recording of Rossini's grand, exhilarating, yet down the years too-little-noticed *Matilde di Shabran*. A comic-heroic romp written for the 1821 Roman Carnival but substantially revised for Naples later that same year, the opera is an important staging-post between Rossini's two earlier Roman entertainments, *Il barbiere di Siviglia* and *La Cenerentola*, and their Parisian successors *Il viaggio a Reims* and *Le comte Ory*. The opera soon dropped from the repertory, dogged by travellers' tales of a bizarre plot (a raving misogynist, a mad poet, damsels being thrown off cliffs) and an impossible-to-sing leading role.

This 2004 Pesaro production, based on Jürgen Selk's new Critical Edition, catches Flórez at the peak of his powers. Spectacular as the role of Corradino is, there are no solo arias. This is ensemble opera *par excellence*. His spectacular entry – pure Errol Flynn – turns into a quartet. His first meeting with Matilde takes place in the latter half of the Act 1 Quintet. Later, despite Corradino's best efforts to silence young Edoardo, their Act 2 duet remains just that: a duet. The joke fails, of course, if the singer playing

Corradino lacks the wherewithal to drive a coach and horses through Rossini's cunningly contrived maze. Flórez is terrific, literally so at times.

Matilde is sister to Isabella and Rosina, albeit a soprano brandishing high C sharps and the occasional top F. Unlike Corradino, she does have a solo aria, the opera's showpiece finale, vividly thrown off by Annick Massis, who is well matched to Flórez histrionically and vocally. The two other leading players are Isidoro, a down-at-heel poet who ends up running the show, and the androgynously charming Edoardo, captive son of Corradino's arch-enemy Don Raimondo. Rossini conceived the roles for the Neapolitan *buffo* Antonio Parlamagni and his daughter, Annetta, then refined them in the rewrite. In Naples, Isidoro was played (as here, in Neapolitan dialect) by the legendary *buffo* Carlo Casaccia. Decca's Bruno de Simone is the gamest of Isidoros, Hadar Halevy a mellifluous-sounding Edoardo.

Isidoro bears the brunt of the stretches of *secco* recitative: eight minutes before the Act 1 finale, a further stretch as the plot thickens midway through Act 2. None of this hangs heavy. This being a distillation of five live theatre performances, the entire cast and fortepiano player Rosetta Cucchi are fully engaged with the drama.

Riccardo Frizza's conducting is fierce and sharp-edged in the modern style. Occasionally one misses that Gui-like turn of the wrist which distinguishes the musician from the martinet but Frizza's marshalling of the all-important ensembles is rarely less than masterly. The recording has the voices well forward, the orchestra a little too much to the rear. If the stereo placings are to be believed, Flórez was always centre stage: understandable but oddly wearisome.

La pietra del paragone

La pietra del paragone
Sonia Prina *mez* Clarice **Jennifer Holloway** *sop* Aspasia **Laura Giordano** *sop* Fulvia **François Lis** *bass* Asdrubale **José Manuel Zapata** *ten* Giocondo **Joan Martín-Royo** *bass* Macrobio **Christian Senn** *bass-bar* Pacuvio **Filippo Polinelli** *bass* Fabrizio
Ensemble Matheus / Jean-Christophe Spinosi
Stage directors **Giorgio Barbiero Corsetti** and **Pierrick Sorin**
Video director **Philippe Béziat**
Naïve ② 💿 V5089 (3h 51' · NTSC · 16:9 · 2.0 · 0)
Ⓕ❍❍❍

This is an utterly remarkable and fantastically enjoyable theatre-cum-video staging of Rossini's *La pietra del paragone*. Philippe Béziat, who has described the production as 'the most original I have seen for a long time on the operatic stage', created his own filmic realisation during live performances in Paris's Théâtre du Châtelet. His breathtakingly precise and witty filming adds a further dimension to the experience.

So how, precisely, does it work? Watched by three video cameras that stand centre stage, the performers play out the action in a blue virtual reality space devoid of scenery. On the edge of the stage are a series of miniature sets, equipped with their own bespoke cameras. Behind and above the singers is a bank of six video screens on to which the images of the players and the set designs are mixed and superimposed. To take just one example (there are hundreds as the performance unfolds), a tennis ball placed by the lovelorn Giocondo on the miniaturised set appears on screen as large yellow garden seat on which he appears to perch to sing his aria.

This aspect of the production – Rossini meets Magritte – is the work of the celebrated video artist and specialist in comic burlesque, Pierrick Sorin. As in a Magritte painting, the interplay of image and reality blurs our perceptions sufficiently to make us wonder whether what we thought to be reality is merely a construction of the mind. This is itself pure Rossini. At some point in a Rossini *commedia* the characters will question their grasp of reality. In more abstract pieces such as *Il turco in Italia* or *La pietra* itself the sense of the drama being played out in a world that is not entirely real is all the more marked.

Stage director Giorgio Barberio Corsetti directs a gem of production. The video set designs, which have a chic minimalist 1920s feel to them, are the work of Sorin and Corsetti in collaboration with Cristian Taraborrelli whose vivid modern-dress costuming works brilliantly both on the all-blue virtual reality set and in the vibrantly coloured video show above.

The singers, a richly talented ensemble of rising young stars, are superb, not only in their delivery of Rossini's text but in their mastery of the hugely difficult task of playing simultaneously to camera and to the audience. Film close-ups can be cruel to singers but they turn this to their advantage, building facial movements into a larger ensemble of gesture and mime. Jean-Christophe Spinosi's conducting of his period band Ensemble Matheus is a *tour de force*, funny in its own right. This is Rossini conducting of real point, colour, vibrancy and drive.

The DVD comes in a stylishly produced 100-page hardback rich in background information, including two superb essays by Rossini scholar Damien Colas. The show runs for two hours 40 minutes but since its ingenuity appears to know no bounds there are no longueurs. In the annals of Rossini performance, this is an important and entertaining landmark creation.

Semiramide

Semiramide
Dame Joan Sutherland *sop* Semiramide
Marilyn Horne *mez* Arsace **Joseph Rouleau** *bass* Assur **John Serge** *ten* Idreno **Patricia Clark** *sop* Azema **Spiro Malas** *bass* Oroe **Michael Langdon** *bass* Ghost of Nino **Leslie Fryson** *ten* Mitrane
Ambrosian Opera Chorus; London Symphony Orchestra / Richard Bonynge
Decca ③ 475 7918DM3 (168' · ADD · T/t)

Recorded 1966 Ⓜ**OO**

Wagner thought it represented all that was bad about Italian opera, and Kobbé's *Complete Opera Book* proclaimed that it had had its day – but then added that 'were a soprano and contralto to appear in conjunction in the firmament the opera might be successfully revived'. That was exactly what happened in the 1960s, when both Sutherland and Horne were in superlative voice and, with Richard Bonynge, were prominent in the reintroduction of so many 19th-century operas that the world thought it had outgrown. This recording brought a good deal of enlightenment in its time. For one thing, here was vocal music of such 'impossible' difficulty being sung with brilliance by the two principal women and with considerable skill by the men. Then it brought to many listeners the discovery that, so far from being a mere showpiece, the opera contained ensembles of quite compelling dramatic intensity. People who had heard of the duet 'Giorno d'orrore' were surprised to find it remarkably unshowy and even expressive of the ambiguous feelings of mother and son in their extraordinary predicament. It will probably be a long time before this recording is superseded.

Tancredi

Tancredi
Ewa Podles *contr* Tancredi **Sumi Jo** *sop* Amenaide
Stanford Olsen *ten* Argirio **Pietro Spagnoli** *bar*
Orbazzano **Anna Maria di Micco** *sop* Isaura **Lucretia
Lendi** *mez* Roggiero **Capella Brugensis; Collegium
Instrumentale Brugense / Alberto Zedda**
Naxos ② 8 660037/8 (147′ · DDD) Ⓢ**OD**

Tancredi is a seminal work in the Rossini canon, mingling a new-found reach in the musical architecture with vocal and instrumental writing of rare wonderment and beauty. The singing is splendid throughout, with a cast that's unusually starry. Podles has sung the role of Tancredi to acclaim at La Scala, Milan; the Amenaide, Sumi Jo, is a touch cool at first, too much the pert coloratura but this isn't an impression that persists. Hers is a performance of wonderful vocal control and flowering sensibility.

Podles likes to go her own way at times. In the event, though, she and Sumi Jo work well together, and they sound marvellous. Podles also manages, chameleon-like, to adjust to the purer, more obviously stylish Rossini manner of a singer who's very unlike herself, the American tenor Stanford Olsen. His portrait of the conscience-stricken father Argirio matches singing of grace and impetus with great fineness of dramatic sensibility. As a result, something like the scene of the signing of his daughter's death-warrant emerges here as the remarkable thing it is.

Alberto Zedda is lucky to have at his disposal another of those wonderfully stylish chamber orchestras and chamber choirs that Naxos seem able to conjure at will. The aqueously lovely preface to Tancredi's first entrance is a repre-

sentative example of the players' ear for Rossini's delicately limned tone-painting. The recording itself is beautifully scaled.

Il turco in Italia

Il turco in Italia
Michele Pertusi *bass* Selim **Cecilia Bartoli** *mez*
Fiorilla **Alessandro Corbelli** *bar* Don Geronio **Ramón
Vargas** *ten* Don Narciso **Laura Polverelli** *mez* Zaida
Francesco Piccoli *ten* Albazar **Roberto de Candia** *bar*
Prosdocimo **Chorus and Orchestra of
La Scala, Milan / Riccardo Chailly**
Decca ② 458 924-2DHO2 (142′ · DDD · T/t)
Ⓕ**OOOD**

Ⓖ Chailly has recorded the work before, but in the years since he's matured as a Rossini conductor, and the Scala orchestra has this music under its fingers; there's an energy and vitality to this playing that's infectious. For his earlier recording, Montserrat Caballé was an underpowered Fiorilla; but Cecilia Bartoli is full of fire and mettle here (her 'Sqallido veste bruna' is sensational). Michele Pertusi is a fine Selim whose performance seems to breathe stage experience – it's a characterisation that's as vocally fine as it's theatrically adept. Alessandro Corbelli, reinforcing his credentials as a Rossini singer of flair and panache, is a strongly characterised Geronio. This is a recording that smacks of the theatre, and unlike so many so-called comic operas, has lost nothing in its transfer to disc. Under Chailly's baton it fizzes and crackles like few other sets – recitatives are dispatched with the assurance of native Italian speakers, and with a genuine feeling for the meaning of the text. Decca's recording is beautifully judged and the set makes a fine modern alternative to the now classic (but cut) 1954 recording under Gavazzeni with Maria Callas.

Il turco in Italia
Simone Alaimo *bass* Selim **Myrtò Papatanasiu** *sop*
Donna Fiorilla **Bruno de Simone** *bass* Don Geronio
Antonino Siragusa *ten* Don Narciso **Vincenzo
Taormina** *bass* Prosdocimo **Antonella Nappa** *sop*
Zaida **Federico Lepre** *ten* Albazar
**Chorus and Orchestra of Teatro Carlo Felice,
Genoa / Jonathan Webb**
Stage director **Egisto Marcucci**
Video director **Andrea Dorigo**
ArtHaus Musik 🎦 101 391; 📀 101 392 (162′ · NTSC
· 16:9 · PCM Stereo, DTS 5.1 and DTS-HD Master
Audio 7.1 · 0). Recorded live in 2009 Ⓕ**OO**

This beautifully shot television film of a live Genoese performance is a memorial tribute to the great Genoese stage designer, book illustrator and film-maker Emanuele 'Lele' Luzzati who died in 2007 at the age of 85. His designs, and the stunningly beautiful costumes by his longtime collaborator Santuzza Calì, were originally seen at the 1983 Pesaro Festival. Luzzati was a master of pre-Romantic theatre design.

He also loved 'the play within the play'. *Così fan tutte* and *Il turco in Italia* were particular favourites, as was Stoppard's *Rosencrantz and Guildenstern are Dead*, which he once designed to Stoppard's personal delight.

In this pleasingly stylish and urbane *Il turco in Italia* we look through the proscenium arch to a stage that has on either side opera boxes with painted masked figures. Such backdrops as do descend are two-dimensional flats in the Baroque style. And yet the drama that is played out within this painted space is intensely human. The puppet-master Poet (Vincenzo Taormina) has rarely been more pointedly or more humanely played; and there is a similarly credible and touching bond between Don Geronio the cuckolded husband, superbly played by Bruno de Simone, and his flighty wife who fancies herself in love with the eponymous Turk. Myrtò Papatanasiu follows her compatriot Maria Callas in playing Fiorilla with a fine mix of wit and kittenish allure.

Simone Alaimo has presence and plausible technique as Selim; Antonino Siragusa is an agile, bright-toned Don Narciso. Jonathan Webb's conducting is as spruce and stylish as the production itself. There is even pleasure to be had from the Overture, with Erica Vitellozzi's brilliantly precise and insightful camerawork helping point up every last detail of Rossini's irrepressible wit.

effective backdrop to the primary colours of Mireille Dessingy's haute couture costumes. Events, such as they are, are mainly played out along the front of the stage and on a T-shaped catwalk that extends into the auditorium. Since this is not a full-blown theatre staging, there is no grand visual display in the closing scene.

The opening sequence is unpromising. The staging is aimless and the words of the hotel housekeeper, delivered from a stage box, are inaudible because the sound engineer has omitted to provide her with a microphone. Things improve as the cast warms to its task and individual singers begin to catch the eye and the ear. The staging, however, continues to be variable. Don Profondo's catalogue aria manages to be both messy and dull, yet the duet between Count Libenskof and Belfiore is a delight. Corinna and her harp are awkwardly separated but the idea of having the solo flautist playing alongside the diffident Lord Sidney dressed as a silver-clad Rosenkavalier is an inspired one. Gergiev conducts in a brown racing trilby. The reading is exquisitely paced, the ensemble work often stunningly good, remarkably so given the fact that conductor and orchestra are behind the singers.

There is no attempt here to adapt the tributes to Charles X to latter-day political concerns, let alone rewrite the end as Dario Fo did – cruelly, wittily, timelessly – in his famous Helsinki production. The Russians play the score as written, a number of small cuts notwithstanding.

Il viaggio a Reims

Il viaggio a Reims
Anastasia Belyaeva *sop* Madame Cortese **Larisa Youdina** *sop* Contessa di Folleville **Anna Kiknadze** *mez* Marchesa Melibea **Irma Guigolachvili** *sop* Corinna **Alexei Safiouline** *bar* Don Alvaro **Dmitri Voropaev** *ten* Cavalier Belfiore **Daniil Shtoda** *ten* Conte di Libenskof **Edouard Tsanga** *bass* Lord Sidney **Nikolaï Kamenski** *bass* Don Profondo **Vladislav Ouspenski** *bass* Barone di Trombonok **Alexeï Tannovistski** *bass* Don Prudenzio **Mariinsky Theatre Orchestra / Valery Gergiev**
Stage director **Alain Maratrat**
Video director **Vincent Bataillon**
Opus Arte ![DVD] OA0967D (135' · NTSC · 16:9 · PCM stereo and DTS 5.1 · 0)
Recorded live at the Théâtre du Châtelet, Paris in 2005. Extra features include Illustrated Synopsis and Cast Gallery Ⓕ

Il viaggio a Reims was the Théâtre Italien's offering to the celebrations surrounding the coronation of Charles X in the summer of 1825, a showcase for Italian music-making in Paris. Since the Russians later supplanted the Italians as purveyors of high-class art to the French, there is something apt about this Russian revival of *Il viaggio* in Paris's Théâtre du Châtelet.

A stylishly designed concert in costume, it is a latter-day showcase for the rising stars of the Mariinsky Theatre. The orchestral players are seated at the rear of the stage. Decked out in cream-coloured evening attire, they make an

---

Nino Rota
Italian 1911-1979

Rota studied at the Milan Conservatory, privately with Pizzetti (1925-26), with Casella in Rome, and at the Curtis Institute (1931-32) where he was taught conducting by Fritz Reiner and had Rosario Scalero as an instructor in composition. In 1939 he joined the staff at the Liceo Musicale in Bari (where he was director from 1950). He wrote fluently in a cool, direct style: his output includes operas (notably The Italian Straw Hat, 1955), three symphonies, concertos and instrumental pieces. He wrote more than 150 scores for Italian and international productions (many for Fellini, Visconti and Zeffirelli) from the 1930s until his death – an average of three scores each year over a 46-year period.

Piano Concertos

Piano Concertos – E minor; C
Massimo Palumbo *pf* I Virtuosi Italiani / **Marco Boni**
Chandos CHAN9681 (64' · DDD) ⒻⓄ▸

Both these works are unashamedly Romantic and nostalgic in style. The E minor Piano Concerto was composed in 1960, at the same time as Rota's music for Fellini's film *La dolce vita*. As if in answer to the extreme cynicism of that and much of his other film music, the concerto seems to be a questioning exploration of the remaining possibilities in a modern, Romantic form. The opening *Allegro-tranquillo* movement begins with a dreamlike theme on the piano which is then taken up by the orchestra and developed as a sort of conversation – the orchestra insisting on a heroic, almost martial sound, while the piano and woodwind reiterate the original soft mood. The first movement is over 16 minutes: away from the rule of the film-editor's stopwatch Rota felt free to indulge himself. The same four-note figure that runs through the opening is taken up in the second movement, a quiet, slow section with a haunting intensity. The finale continues the awake-in-a-dream contrasts.

Rota composed four piano concertos, but the date of the one in C major seems to be in doubt. It's earlier than 1960, and is a sparer, jauntier work, in mood more reminiscent of the 1920s. It, too, presents a dialogue between the quest-like piano part and the orchestra asserting a darker mood.

Both concertos are played by Massimo Palumbo with brilliant technique; the recorded sound is excellent.

Symphonies

Symphonies Nos 1 & 2
Filarmonica '900 del Teatro Regio, Turin /
Marzio Conti
Chandos CHAN10546 (62' · DDD)　　Ⓟ**O**➔

As with Miklós Rózsa, Nino Rota is so well known as a film composer (of over 100 scores) that his concert music has all but been eclipsed. One will look in vain for the familiar Rota-cinematic style in the first two symphonies. The First (1935-39) is a largely pastoral affair, full of sunlit harmonies and quietly lush textures in denial of the nervous political times in which it was written, except in the grave *Largo* introduction to the finale. Otherwise, this is a relaxed and genial work, stylistically slightly anachronistic, with bright and breezy quick movements and a lilting *Adagio*: the type of piece one might expect from a master symphonist in between two weightier masterworks.

The Second (1937-39) is unsurprisingly very close in manner and spirit to No 1. A little more varied in profile, it is less individual but still makes a rewarding listen, especially in these lovingly prepared accounts. Conti gets to the heart of both symphonies. The Italian orchestra (who have made several film music recordings) play Rota's lines with great fervour and understanding and with sumptuous Chandos sound this is the version to have.

Orchestral Works

Il Gattopardo – Dances. La Strada – Orchestral Suite.
Concerto soirée[a]
[a]**Benedetto Lupo** pf **Granada City Orchestra /**
Josep Pons
Harmonia Mundi HMC90 1846 (64' · DDD)　　Ⓕ

This lavishly packaged CD brings together two suites from Rota's most famous film scores plus a *concertante* piece for piano and orchestra which quotes from his film work.

There's a seven-movement suite from *La Strada* (1954) directed by Fellini, with whom Rota collaborated frequently. The brilliant opening sets the scene for the raffish charms of the film's circus folk, depicted in colourful orchestration and with vibrant, tuneful music that conveys the atmosphere of life under the big top. His themes, both romantic and rhythmically infectious, are skilfully interwoven between movements.

Rota wrote the music for Visconti's *Il Gattopardo* ('The Leopard', 1963), before the film was shot. He probably knew that the set-piece was to be a lavish ballroom sequence lasting over an hour in the original print. The sequence begins with a previously unpublished waltz by Verdi (in Visconti's private collection) and continues in a manner akin to Verdi's own ballet music. The intention was to give the impression of 'a modest ensemble hired for the occasion' and this is just the treatment it receives from the Granada orchestra under Josep Pons. Nothing is inflated or allowed to disturb the seamless flow of this delightful dance music.

Proportion and balance are just right, too, for the modest and endearing *Concerto soirée* in which the fetching piano writing, very much the centre of attention, is brilliantly performed by Benedetto Lupo and wittily executed by the orchestra. A most attractive disc.

Alec Roth　　British b1948

After reading music at Durham University, Roth studied at the Academy of Indonesian Performing Arts (ASKI) in Surakarta. Posts he has held include founder and artistic director of the Royal Festival Hall Gamelan Programme, music director of the Baylis Programme, English National Opera; Composer in Association, Opera North; Composer in Residence, Wellington College; and lecturer in music, University of Edinburgh. His collaborations with Indian writer Vikram Seth include two song-cycles.

Songs

Songs in Time of War. Chinese Gardens
Mark Padmore ten **Philippe Honoré** vn
Alison Nicholls hp **Morgan Szymanski** gtr
Signum Classics SIGCD124 (62' · DDD)　　Ⓟ**O**➔

Alec Roth the composer and Vikram Seth the poet become so much of a unit during the course of these song-cycles that one feels it would be quite natural to ask Roth for a personal background to the poems and query Seth about the whistling-tune or some other feature of the music. The style (of both) is idiosyncratic – a carefully versified informality of talk, a structural development of musical motifs that sounds like free recitative. The *Chinese Garden* songs (Roth's is the Dr Sun Yat Sen Classical garden in Vancouver) are modern, while the *Songs in Time of War* derive from eighth-century China, but there is modernity in that too, just as the themes of the others might have found recognition and a response in ages of the past.

These are attractive works, the *Songs in Time of War* probably striking deepest though in an utterly non-ponderous, unpretentious way. The music takes interesting turns, as when a cynical blues passage emerges from the timeless observation that 'the great are always paid in disuse and neglect'. The resources of voice and instruments are imaginatively exploited. And the performances (by the 'creator' artists) are excellent. If the disc constitutes an introduction to this composer, it is one you won't regret following up.

Albert Roussel French 1869-1937

After embarking on a naval career, in 1894 Roussel began studies with Gigout, going on to train with d'Indy and others at the Schola Cantorum (1898-1908) where in 1902 he began teaching (his students included Satie, Varèse and Martinů). In 1909 he made a tour of India and Indo-China (an experience that bore fruit in his Hindu opera-ballet Padmâvatî of 1923). Roussel was by temperament a classicist. While his early work is strongly influenced by Impressionism, he eventually found a personal style which was more formal in design, with a strong rhythmic drive, and with a more distinct liking for functional tonality. Roussel's most important works are the ballets Le festin de l'araignée, Bacchus et Ariane and Aeneas, and the four symphonies (of which the Third and the Fourth epitomise his mature neo-classical style). His other works include numerous ballets, orchestral suites, a piano concerto, much chamber music, solo piano music and songs.

Symphonies

Symphonies – No 1, 'Le poème de la forêt'; No 4
Orchestre de Paris / Christoph Eschenbach
Ondine ODE1092-2 (67' · DDD) Ⓕ🅑➔

For a work composed originally as independent items, Roussel's impressionist First Symphony (1904-06) works surprisingly well. True, its structure is unorthodox, each of the four movements – which form a seasonal cycle from winter to autumn – larger than its predecessor, but it all flows together remarkably well, adding up to rather more than a picturesque set of tone-poems or suite. Small wonder it so impressed early audiences.

Roussel refined his symphonic style considerably over time, so comparing the First with the Fourth of three decades later shows just how far he had travelled. The Fourth is an abstract masterpiece, typically mixing up compositional

rigour, lyrical intensity and rhythmic élan. If the Fourth does not quite match the Apollonian drive of No 3, this is because it is a very different type of work to its celebrated forebear.

As with his recording of No 2, Eschenbach's accounts are highly evocative and beautifully phrased. Tempi are again broad, working well in *Le poème de la forêt* where he relishes the poetry of this quietly sumptuous score. In the Fourth, however, after finely shaped readings of the first two movements, the third and fourth are dispatched with a lightness bordering on the throwaway. What makes this newcomer recommendable is the superb playing and Ondine's first-rate sound.

Symphony No 2. Bacchus et Ariane – Suites Nos 1 and 2
Orchestre de Paris / Christoph Eschenbach
Ondine ODE1065-2 (78' · DDD) Ⓕ🅞🅑➔

The familiar exuberant Roussel style, a synthesis of Busoni-esque Young Classicality and impressionism heard here in the two suites from *Bacchus et Ariane*, did not come easily. His move away from a successful early manner was accelerated by the Great War and was somewhat directionless when he began his Second Symphony in the summer of 1919. When completed two years later, the score showed both a leap in the dark and the crucial step towards the manner of his best known music.

Yet the Second Symphony remains deep in eclipse from its two magnificent successors, despite its shimmering, multi-textured instrumentation, its moments of rapt beauty and illustrative nature. Partly constructed in places from episodes from his abandoned opera *Le roi Tobol*, the symphony – Roussel's longest – is also the most complex and elusive. Here and there are tantalising foretastes of the sound world of the Third, yet its structure lacks the latter's clean lines, seeming more a hybrid with the symphonic fantasia: prophetic of post-Second World War symphonism.

Eschenbach's account is strong on both atmosphere and clarity of line and he takes broad tempi. Ondine's sound is superb. The juxtaposition with the two *Bacchus et Ariane* concert suites makes for a rich programme, all brilliantly played by the Orchestre de Paris. Roussel's symphony has lived far too long in the shadows; this disc should help bring it out into the light.

Symphony No 3. Bacchus et Ariane
Royal Scottish National Orchestra /
Stéphane Denève
Naxos 8 570245 (63' · DDD) Ⓢ🅑➔

The Third is the most sheerly exciting of Roussel's four symphonies. The pounding, soaring opening *Allegro vivo* has become iconic but there is far more to the symphony than that, with an *Adagio* of great emotional range, two *scherzos* (one embedded in the slow movement) and a whirlwind finale that fuses all the expressive elements together by its close.

The RSNO's performance is fully alive to the music's sweep and irrepressible *joie de vivre* as well as its more lyrical aspects. There is an edge-of-the-seat quality to the interpretation that is winning. In the third span, *Vivace*, Denève pushes on and here, as in the *Allegro con spirito* finale, he outpaces his rivals. But it is with its sound and orchestral balance that this newcomer scores, making audible a wealth of detail often submerged.

The woodwinds in particular benefit and their superb playing illuminates *Bacchus et Ariane*. The cover states that the complete ballet is being presented whereas the track listings show Suites Nos 1 and 2. There is little appreciable difference, the suites mirroring the two acts and published this way after the lacklustre premiere. Suite No 2 has become a warhorse for Francophile conductors but there is much to enjoy in the First. If you are coming new to Roussel, this is the perfect introduction. Highly recommended.

Orchestral Works

Concerto for Small Orchestra, Op 34. Petite Suite, Op 39. Rapsodie flamande, Op 56. Sinfonietta, Op 52. Symphony No 4, Op 53
Royal Scottish National Orchestra /
Stéphane Denève
Naxos 8 572135 (69' · DDD)   ⓈⓄⓄⒷ

Although often cited with the Third Symphony as one of Roussel's major utterances, the Fourth (1934) has never enjoyed the same popular acclaim. True, it does not have the Third's visceral impact but its classical limpidity, ebullient good humour, especially in the final two movements, and the beauty and profundity of the *Lento molto* (surely Roussel's greatest slow movement) should more than compensate – and do in this vibrant and compelling reading. Denève catches the mood of the music to a tee, confirming his deep-seated sympathy with Roussel. Naxos's sound is perfectly fine and the RSNO's performance is well paced.

The fillers make a fascinating collection, from the delicacy of the Concerto for Small Orchestra (1926) to the formal clarity of the invigorating Sinfonietta (1934). The less well-known *Petite Suite* (1929) is full of imaginative writing, illustrative in a non-specific way and full of the gentle good humour Roussel shared with his most famous pupil, Martinů. Overall, then, an excellent disc, splendidly and idiomatically performed and a superb advertisement for composer, conductor and orchestra. Highly recommended.

Bacchus et Ariane

Bacchus et Ariane, Op 43.
Le festin de l'araignée, Op 17
BBC Philharmonic Orchestra / Yan Pascal Tortelier
Chandos CHAN9494 (68' · DDD)   ⒻⓄⓄⒷ

Unlike his contemporary Dukas, Roussel has been somewhat sidelined as a 'connoisseur's composer'. That presumably means that he didn't write fat, lush tunes that could be exploited in television commercials, but produced works of vigorous ideas and more subtle quality. Record companies used to fight shy of his music – the Third and Fourth Symphonies have indeed maintained a foothold, but with the ballet *Bacchus et Ariane*, which is closely linked with the Third, we've mostly been given only its second half. Here are alert, rhythmically vital performances of Roussel's two most famous ballets, which even at the most exuberantly excited moments (like the 'Bacchanale' in *Bacchus*) preserve a truly Gallic lucidity, and which Tortelier marks by a captivating lightness of touch; and when it comes to quiet passages one could not ask for greater tenderness than in the beautiful end of Act 1 of *Bacchus*, when Bacchus puts Ariadne to sleep.

Le festin de l'araignée, written 18 years earlier, is in a quite different style. Where *Bacchus*'s trenchant idiom at times makes one think of Stravinsky's *Apollon musagète*, *Le festin* (which had the misfortune to be overshadowed by *The Rite of Spring*, produced only eight weeks later) is atmospheric and more impressionistic (in the same vein as Roussel's First Symphony). It's a score full of delicate invention, whose one weakness is that for its full appreciation a knowledge of its detailed programme is needed – and that's provided here in the booklet.

The BBC Philharmonic play it beautifully. If this is 'connoisseur's music', then be happy to be called a connoisseur: you'll find it delectable.

Pancrace Royer   French 1705-1755

French composer, harpsichordist, organist and administrator. His father was sent by Louis XIV to be the intendant of gardens and fountains at the court of Savoy. Royer acquired a great reputation for playing the harpsichord and organ, and as a composer was a brilliant and influential contemporary of Rameau through much of the latter's career.

Harpsichord Works

Pièces de clavecin – La Majestueuse: Courante;
La Zaïde: Rondeau; Les matelots: Modérément;
L'Incertaine: Marqué; L'Aimable: Gracieux;
La Bagatelle; Suitte de la Bagatelle; La Remouleuse:
Rondeau; Les tendres sentiments: Rondeau; Le
vertigo: Rondeau; Allemande; La Sensible: Rondeau;
La marche des scythes: Fièrement
Christophe Rousset hpd
Ambroisie AM151 (59' · DDD)   ⒻⓄ

Pancrace Royer's one book of *Pièces de clavecin*, published in 1746, is full of spark and variety, ranging from the dulcet 'La Zaïde' to the robust jollity of 'Les matelots', and from the eloquence of 'La Sensible' to the dizzyingly quirky virtuosity of 'Le vertigo'. And while it is Rameau who rightly dominates our knowledge of the musical times in which Royer lived as harpsichord teacher to Louis XV's daughters, composer of operas and director of Paris's prestigious Concert Spirituel, as a keyboard composer in the imaginative, full-bodied mould of someone like Forqueray, Royer need not be considered as totally blotted out by the more famous composer's shadow.

Yet this disc is one of only a handful devoted to Royer's harpsichord music. Remarkably, it is also the second by Christophe Rousset, his first having been 15 years ago for L'Oiseau-Lyre. The first noticeable difference is in the harpsichords themselves; first time around Rousset had an easy-toned 1751 Hemsch, but this time he uses a composite 18th-century instrument, more aggressive in sound, more 'zingy' at the top end and with less of the Hemsch's mellow resonance. This is not without knock-on effect; whereas before there was a stylish elegance and easy grace of line in the way Rousset dispatched these demanding pieces, now there is a sense that, while his technique remains as enviable as ever, he has to work harder at the music, draw things out more, become more mannered. Harpsichord enthusiasts unfamiliar with Royer's generous musical personality should take this opportunity to make his acquaintance now.

Miklós Rózsa

Hungarian/American 1907-1995

Rózsa studied piano with his mother (who was at the Budapest Academy with Bartók) and violin and viola with his uncle, a musician with the Royal Hungrian Opera. He had written his first works by the age of eight. In 1926 he was a student at the Leipzig Conservatory and his music (mainly for chamber groups) was being widely performed. In 1931 he moved to Paris where he finished his Theme, Variations and Finale, a work that soon gained international recognition. He was introduced to the film music genre by Honegger and during 1935-39 wrote film scores for London Films under Hungarian-born producer Alexander Korda. In 1940 he travelled with Korda to Hollywood to complete the score of The Thief of Baghdad and was soon in great demand as a freelance film composer and conductor. As a staff member at MGM (1948-62), he became one of the most highly regarded composers in the industry, writing music for over 100 films. Rózsa was a three-time Oscar winner, and was nominated a total of 16 times, making him one of the most nominated composers in Oscar history.

Concertos

Viola Concerto, Op 37a. Hungarian Serenade, Op 25
ªGilad Karni va Budapest Concert Orchestra MÁV / Mariusz Smolij

Naxos 8 570925 (61' · DDD) ⓢⒹ⟶

The recording industry's sustained interest in Rózsa's concert music is heartening and this new disc from Naxos is its latest manifestation. Both works exhibit fully the strengths and appeal of the composer's output as a whole, from its impeccable craftsmanship to its lilting Hungarian accent. The personal voice – close stylistically at times to Kodály and Bartók – is recognisably that of the film composer whose music graced the silver screen for so long.

The *Hungarian Serenade* started life in the early 1930s as his Op 10 for strings but Ernö von Dohnányi persuaded the young composer to recast it for a larger orchestra with a punchier finale. The work underwent several further revisions before emerging as the work given here. It's is high-quality light music and is superbly played here.

Gilad Karni's ardent interpretation of the Viola Concerto is especially welcome. A fine player and former Lionel Tertis Competition prize-winner, Karni audibly relishes the work's dark colours and rich writing. The Concerto had a difficult genesis (for Rózsa), taking four years to complete with several interruptions by film work which the composer later claimed ruined the flow. Yet the finished result does not betray this, its four movements holding together as if written in a single burst of inspiration. Karni proves a fine advocate and the Budapest orchestra provide excellent support.

'Three Choral Suites'
Ben-Hur. King of Kings. Quo Vadis
Mormon Tabernacle Choir; Cincinnati Pops Orchestra / Erich Kunzel
Telarc CD80631 (62' · DDD) Ⓕ

At the time of his death in 1995, the Hungarian-born composer and Hollywood veteran Miklós Rózsa had been planning to turn three of his famous epic film scores – *Ben-Hur*, *Quo Vadis* and *King of Kings* – into concert works of equally biblical proportions. These completed choral suites owe their existence to Rózsa's associates and pupils (most notably Daniel Robbins), but there's no doubt that their essence is strictly that of Rózsa himself.

What's so striking about hearing these works in close proximity is the paradox of having essentially the same musical forces and a similarly focused musical language yield such diverse results. The Overture to *Ben-Hur* sets an imposing tone, historically speaking, yet this loosens up a bit in *Quo Vadis* with the choral text changing midway through from Latin to English (as well as including an English narration). Seeing how every great historical figure in Hollywood speaks English regardless of era or ethnicity, I suppose one shouldn't expect too much here in the way of linguistic consistency.

Once again, Erich Kunzel and the Cincinnati Pops display the very qualities, including attention to orchestral colour and full commitment to unabashedly emotional sentiment, that keep performances of this type from either pandering or slumming. The clarity of the orchestra is something of a strange fit with the 360-voice Mormon Tabernacle Choir, which relies less on musical precision than overwheming the listener through sheer force of sound, but one would have to think hard to conceive of a more memorable performance of these works.

Anton Rubinstein   Russian 1829-1894

In the last half of the 19th century, Anton Rubinstein – the first great Russian pianist, the first really great international pianist, a teacher, conductor, man of vision and a prolific composer – was a giant in the musical firmament. Hans von Bülow called him 'the Michelangelo of Music'. Today his reputation has dwindled to nothing.

His family were prosperous Jewish merchants who were baptised in 1831. They moved to Moscow when Anton was five and he began piano studies at the age of eight with Alexander Villoing. 'By my 13th year,' wrote Rubinstein in his autobiography, 'I had no other teacher.'

He made concert tours all over Europe before going to Berlin with his talented brother Nicholas to study composition, returning in 1848 to St Petersburg where, in 1862, he founded the Imperial Conservatory. In the first 20 years of the conservatory's existence Tchaikovsky, Rachmaninov, Siloti, Essipov, Gabrilowitsch and a host of other important artists and composers passed though its doors. Rubinstein left the running of the Conservatory to others for two decades from 1867 while he toured, conducted and composed. He made a triumphant tour of America during 1872-73, giving 215 recitals all over the country, amassing a small fortune on the way. He created a sensation by playing without music in his concerts, a virtually unheard-of practice, and presented a famous cycle of concerts surveying keyboard literature from Byrd to the present day.

Much of his music has a depressing anonymity about it for, like many fluent composers, Rubinstein suffered from being too unselfcritical. Chopin, Schumann and Mendelssohn look over his shoulder, but 'moderns' such as Liszt and Berlioz are rarely in his company. The music simply poured out in every form: six symphonies, five piano concertos, songs, chamber music, choral works, operas, ballets, cantatas and 13 operas.

Piano Concerto No 4

'The Romantic Piano Concerto, Volume 38'
Rubinstein Piano Concerto No 4
Scharwenka Piano Concerto No 1
Marc-André Hamelin pf
BBC Scottish Symphony Orchestra / Michael Stern
Hyperion CDA67508 (60' · DDD)   Ⓕ

Described by one respected critic as the greatest living pianist, Marc-André Hamelin soars to ever new heights of virtuosity. His phenomenal if non-chalantly deployed dexterity is matched by a cool, lyrical insight, making these performances virtually unsurpassable. Earl Wild's account of the Scharwenka, aptly described in America as 'a wing-ding of a romp', is a hard act to follow but there are few pianists of world class more adept at trumping other people's aces than Hamelin. Here it is possible to see his Scharwenka as equally dashing and razor-sharp as Wild's but with a subtler, more inclusive sense of poetry. There is never a question of virtuosity for its own sake.

Writing of Rubinstein's Fourth – and best – Piano Concerto, the august authors of *The Record Guide* once claimed that if the swelling introduction promises great things, all that emerges is a rather large mouse. But such words were written long before the advent of Hamelin, whose brilliance sets every potentially tired page alive with a truly blazing conviction. His concentrated force in the finale sweeps all before it, and he pulls out all the stops in the gloriously over-the-top conclusion. He is superbly partnered and recorded, and lovers of lush, Romantic melody embellished with hundreds and thousands of winking sequins need look no further.

Edmund Rubbra   British 1901-1986

Rubbra, a pupil at the Royal College of Music (1921-25), worked as a pianist, teacher and critic before his appointment as lecturer at Oxford (1947-68). His early works owe much to the language of Bax, Holst and Ireland but his independent and unique voice began to emerge with his First Symphony (1937). His works include 11 symphonies, concertos for viola, piano and violin, four string quartets, Masses and motets (reflecting his conversion to Roman Catholicism in 1948).

Violin Concerto

Violin Concerto. Improvisations on Virginal Pieces by Giles Farnaby. Improvisation
Krysia Osostowicz vn
Ulster Orchestra / Takuo Yuasa
Naxos 8 557591 (57' · DDD)   ⑤🅑→

Composed in 1959, the Violin Concerto is one of Rubbra's most compelling large-scale offerings, comprising a masterly opening *Allegro* that finds lyrical intensity and organic growth in blissful accord, a ravishing central 'Poema' (whose gentle rapture harks back to the 'Canto' slow movement of the Sixth Symphony from 1954) and a wonderfully earthy finale, full of bracing vigour and rhythmic élan. The 1956 *Improvisation* for violin and orchestra also repays close inspection, a 12-and-a-half-minute essay of notable economy of thought and expressive variety that salvages material from an earlier *Fantasia* for violin and orchestra from the mid-1930s.

Not only is Krysia Osostowicz thoroughly steeped in the idiom but she plays with great spirit and beauty of tone and is unfazed by any technical hurdles. No grumbles with the sensitive reading of the *Improvisation*, in which Osostowicz generates a stimulating rapport with Takuo Yuasa and the Ulster Orchestra. However, in the Concerto one might have preferred a touch less reserve and more in the way of songful joy from her collaborators – not to mention a greater sense of impetus in the first movement. Explicit, if slightly clinical sound.

Fortunately, the 1946 *Improvisations on Virginal Pieces by Giles Farnaby* show conductor and orchestra in more spontaneous, personable form. It's a most beguiling, concise score. In all a very likeable and useful disc.

Symphonies

Symphony No 3, Op 49. Symphony No 7 in C, Op 88
BBC National Orchestra of Wales / Richard Hickox
Chandos CHAN9634 (71' · DDD)   Ⓕ**OO**
All 11 symphonies also available as a box-set,
Chandos CHAN9944 (five discs for the price of four)

Commentators have noticed a certain Sibelian cut to the Third Symphony's opening idea (with woodwind in thirds) but everything else strikes you as completely personal. There's a whiff of Elgarian fantasy in the fourth variation of the finale. It's been called the most genial and relaxed of Rubbra's symphonies but there's a pastoral feel to many of the ideas, bucolic even, in the same way that there is about the Brahms Second Symphony. Brahms springs to mind in the masterly variations and fugue of the finale, for not long before, Rubbra had orchestrated the Brahms *Handel* Variations.

Hickox and his players give a persuasive and totally convincing account of the symphony. Anyone coming to the Seventh for the first time, particularly in this performance, will surely not fail to sense the elevated quality of its musical thought. Its opening paragraphs are among the most beautiful Rubbra ever penned, and it's evident throughout that this is music that speaks of deep and serious things. This performance speaks with great directness and power. The horn playing in the opening is eloquent and the orchestral playing throughout is of a uniformly high standard. These are magnificent and impressive accounts, and the recording is truthful and splendidly balanced.

Additional recommendations

Symphonies Nos 3 & 4
Couplings. A Tribute for Ralph Vaughan Williams on his 70th Birthday. Resurgam Overture
Philharmonia Orchestra / Del Mar
Lyrita SRCD202 (73' · DDD)   Ⓕ**D**
Dedicated performances of these superb symphonies under Norman Del Mar. The coupling, *Resurgam*, is a late work of great beauty.

Symphony Nos 5 & 8, 'Hommage à Teilhard de Chardin'. Ode to the Queen[a]

[a]**Bickley** *mez* **BBC Nat Orch of Wales / Hickox**
Chandos CHAN9714 (64' · DDD · T)   Ⓕ**D**
This is the finest account of the Fifth ever. Part of the success of Hickox's series is his instinctive feeling for the tempo at which this music best comes to life and his scrupulous adherence to dynamic markings. Find the right tempo and everything falls into place. The Eighth Symphony (1966-68), subtitled *Hommage à Teilhard de Chardin*, has a mystical feel and luminous texture at times reminiscent of Holst. The Eighth speaks of deep and serious things and in this performance proves a powerful musical experience.

Symphony No 9, 'Sinfonia sacra'.
The Morning Watch, Op 55
Dawson *sop* **D Jones** *mez* **Roberts** *bar* **BBC Nat Chor & Orch of Wales / Hickox**
Chandos CHAN9441 (57' · DDD · T)   Ⓕ**OD**
The Ninth (1973) is Rubbra's most visionary utterance, and its stature has so far gone unrecognised. Its subtitle, *Sinfonia sacra*, gives a good idea of its character. It tells the story of the Resurrection very much as do the Bach Passions. This is music of an inspired breadth and serenity and everyone connected with this magnificent performance conveys a sense of profound conviction.

Sinfonia concertante, Op 38

Sinfonia concertante[a]. A Tribute, Op 56[d]. The Morning Watch, Op 55[b]. Ode to the Queen, Op 83[c]
[c]**Susan Bickley** *mez* [a]**Howard Shelley** *pf*
BBC National [b]**Chorus and Orchestra of Wales / Richard Hickox**
Chandos CHAN9966 (62' · DDD)   Ⓕ**D**

A mouth-watering reissue comprising four outstandingly eloquent performances. The stand-out item here has to be Howard Shelley's imperious traversal of the big-boned *Sinfonia concertante* for piano and orchestra. Certainly, the opening 'Fantasia' exhibits an exhilarating thematic resource and craggy, almost Bartókian resilience. It's the finale, however, which contains the work's most rewarding, deeply felt inspiration: this is a prelude and fugue of grave nobility, economy and poise, whose elegiac countenance reflects Rubbra's sense of loss at the death of his teacher and good friend, Gustav Holst.

Next comes an affectionate account of *A Tribute* (Rubbra's 70th-birthday tribute to Vaughan Williams), followed by *The Morning Watch*, a noble choral setting of Henry Vaughan's mystic poem which possesses a power and radiance that can't fail to impress. Last, but not least, there's *Ode to the Queen* (1953); employing texts by three Tudor poets (Crashaw, D'Avenant and Campion), it's a charming, 13-minute creation, the two extrovert outer songs framing a *Poco adagio e tranquillo* setting of chaste beauty. Mezzo Susan Bickley is ideally cast, and Hickox tenders bright-eyed support. Superb sound throughout, enormously ripe and wide-ranging.

String Quartets

String Quartets – No 1 in F minor, Op 35; No 3, Op 112.
Cello Sonata, Op 60[a]. Improvisation for
Unaccompanied Cello, Op 124[b]
[a]**Michael Dussek** pf **Dante Quartet** (Krysia
Osostowicz, Matthew Truscott vns Judith Busbridge
va [ab]Pierre Doumenge vc)
Dutton Epoch CDLX7123 (72' · DDD)   Ⓜ ⦿⦿

Rubbra originally conceived the first of his four
string quartets in 1933. Thirteen years later, he
overhauled his thoughts and added a new finale.
Dedicated to Vaughan Williams and beautifully
laid out for the medium, it's an invigorating and
purposeful work, boasting a particularly memorable slow movement. The Third Quartet of
1963 is even finer; its seamlessly evolving structure demonstrates Rubbra's sebtle ear for harmony and counterpoint. The three movements
play without a break, and once again the *Adagio*
centrepiece plumbs great depths.

It's good that the Dante Quartet have lost no
time in completing their Rubbra cycle for Dutton. The previous coupling of Quartets Nos 2
and 4 (see below) was shortlisted for a *Gramophone* Award, and if anything this disc attains an
even greater level of accomplishment and perception. These are eloquent readings that strike
a perfect equilibrium between communication
and rigour. Bouquets, too, for the Dante's young
French cellist, Pierre Doumenge, who teams up
with pianist Michael Dussek for a cogent and
impassioned account of the 1946 Cello Sonata
(more convincing than either comparative rival).
Doumenge also shines in the unaccompanied
Improvisation from 1964. The production values
are exemplary. This is a most rewarding release.

String Quartets – No 2, Op 73[a]; No 4, Op 150[b].
Lyric Movement, Op 24[c]. Meditations on a
Byzantine Hymn, 'O Quando in Cruce', Op 117[ad]
[c]**Michael Dussek** pf [abc]**Dante Quartet** (Krysia
Osostowicz vn/[d]va Declan Daly vn Judith Busbridge
[d]va Alastair Blayden vc)
Dutton Epoch CDLX7114 (59' · DDD)
                                              Ⓜ ⦿

Completed in 1951, the Second Quartet is a
marvellously inventive piece, beautifully scored
for the medium, unfailingly purposeful and full
of beguilingly subtle rhythmic and harmonic
resource. Bearing a dedication to Robert Simpson, the two-movement Fourth Quartet of
1975-77 was one of Rubbra's last major works.
Probing and intensely poignant, it's another
hugely eloquent, seamlessly evolving affair
which repays repeated hearings. The Dante
Quartet prove outstandingly sympathetic pro-
ponents of Rubbra's noble inspiration, their
playing urgently expressive and tonally ingratiating. Pianist Michael Dussek joins proceedings
for a stylish and delectably unforced account of
the *Lyric Movement* of 1929, an expertly wrought
essay for piano quintet which itself grew out of

an earlier, discarded string quartet. Tony
Faulkner's Maltings sound is excellent on the
whole, if just a fraction too closely balanced. No
matter, a wonderful disc.

Violin Sonatas

Violin Sonatas[a] – No 1, Op 11; No 2, Op 31;
No 3, Op 133. Four Pieces, Op 29[a].
Variations on a Phrygian Theme, Op 105
Krysia Osostowicz vn [a]**Michael Dussek** pf
Dutton Epoch CDLX7101 (59' · DDD)   Ⓜ ⦿

Rubbra's First Violin Sonata is a notable
achievement all round: its first two movements
exhibit a bittersweet lyricism that will strike a
chord with anyone who has ever responded to,
say, John Ireland's glorious Second Violin
Sonata or the chamber music of Howells. By
contrast, the 'Fugal Rondo' finale intriguingly
pursues an altogether more sturdy, determinedly
neo-classical mode of expression.

Written six years later in 1931, the Second
Sonata already reveals a wider emotional scope, as
well as a striking use of progressive tonality that at
least one contemporary critic found 'disturbing
and unnecessary'. Championed by Albert Sammons, it will come as a substantial discovery to
many: comprising an eventful, ever-evolving first
movement, a strong, but never sentimental
'Lament' centrepiece, and a quasi-Bartókian
finale, its wild exuberance seems to look forward
across the decades to the last movement of this
same figure's Violin Concerto of 1959.

Framing that are the Four Pieces for beginners
and the unaccompanied *Variations on a Phrygian
Theme*, a work of compact resourcefulness. But
even finer is the Third Sonata. It's a wondrous
piece, its sense of purpose, rapt intuition and
profound serenity irresistibly calling to mind
Rubbra's Eighth Symphony, and it fully deserves
the exalted advocacy it receives here. Indeed,
Osostowicz and Dussek form an outstandingly
sympathetic partnership.

Piano Works

Prelude and Fugue on a Theme of Cyril Scott, Op 69.
Sonatina, Op 19. Introduction, Aria and Fugue, Op
104. Preludes, Op 131. Nemo Fugue. Studies, Op
139. Invention on the Name of Haydn, Op 160.
Fantasy Fugue, Op 161. Teaching Pieces, Op 74[a]
Traditional (arr Rubbra) Fukagawa
Michael Dussek, [a]**Rachel Dussek** pfs
Dutton Epoch CDLX7112 (62' · DDD)   Ⓕ

Rubbra was an excellent pianist, and his output
for the instrument spans pretty much his entire
career. It's the earliest work here, the Sonatina
of 1928-29, that proves by far the most technically demanding. Whereas the raptly lyrical first
two movements have something of the outdoor
tang of Vaughan Williams and Howells, the
finale seems to stand apart, its timeless, intuitive
spirit and bracing contrapuntal mastery the hall-

marks of Rubbra's mature voice. Other stand-out items include the noble *Introduction, Aria and Fugue*, the pithy Four Studies of 1970-71 and the Eight Preludes, Rubbra's most substantial piano offering, completed in 1966. The latter comprise a hugely rewarding sequence, the organic wholeness of Rubbra's luminous inspiration often calling to mind his masterly Eighth Symphony. Suffice it to say, Michael Dussek acquits himself extremely well throughout, and he has been sympathetically recorded.

Vocal Works

Missa Cantauariensis, Op 59[ab]. Magnificat and Nunc dimittis in A flat, Op 65[ab]. Missa in honorem Sancti Dominici, Op 66[a]. Prelude and Fugue on a Theme of Cyril Scott, Op 69 (arr Rose)[b]. Tenebrae, Op 72[a]. Meditation, Op 79[b]
[a]**St John's College Choir, Cambridge / Christopher Robinson** [b]org
Naxos 8 555255 (71' · DDD · T/t) ⑤❍❍▷

Christopher Robinson and his St John's College Choir prove especially eloquent, humane advocates of the eight-part *Missa Cantuariensis*. We've long needed a top-notch digital recording of this, the first of Rubbra's five Mass settings. Robinson and company rise to the challenge admirably, not least in the exuberant concluding *Gloria* with its lung-burstingly high tessitura. We also get a thoroughly idiomatic rendering of the taut and imposing *Magnificat* and *Nunc dimittis* in A flat that Rubbra wrote two years later.

In the glorious *Missa in honorem Sancti Dominici* from 1949 (inspired by Rubbra's own conversion to Roman Catholicism the previous year, on the feast day of St Dominic) our Cambridge group doesn't quite match the sumptuous blend, miraculous unanimity or spine-tingling fervour displayed by James O'Donnell's Westminster Cathedral Choir. On the other hand, these newcomers sound wholly captivated by the nine motets that make up the remarkable Op 72 *Tenebrae*. Boasting an infinitely subtle harmonic and contrapuntal resource, these timeless, wonderfully compassionate settings of the responsories used during Matins on Maundy Thursday show Rubbra very much at the height of his powers, encompassing an extraordinarily wide dramatic and expressive range. Robinson also gives us two instrumental bonuses in the rapt *Meditation* for organ, Op 79, and Bernard Rose's transcription of the more substantial *Prelude and Fugue on a Theme of Cyril Scott* (originally written for piano in 1950 to celebrate Scott's 70th birthday). Throw in Naxos's praiseworthy production, and you've a bargain of the first order.

Additional recommendation

Missa Cantuariensis
Coupled with Missa in honorem Sancti Dominici, Op 66. St Non's (That Virgin's Child Most Meek), Op 114 No 2. Dormi Jesu, 'The Virgin's Cradle Song', Op 3

St Margaret's Westminster Singers / Hickox
Chandos CHAN10423 (47' · ADD) Ⓜ▷

How good it is to have these deeply sympathetic performances (which were recorded in the presence of the composer at St Alban's Church, Holborn, over one December day in 1975) restored to the catalogue. Richard Hickox and the St Margaret's Westminster Singers bring to both these rapt and timeless Mass settings an unhurried, intuitive understanding and devotional glow.

Poul Ruders   Danish b1949

Ruders – who studied piano and organ at the Odense Conservatory and graduated from the Royal Danish Conservatory in 1975 – is widely recognised as the leading Danish composer of his generation. The greater proportion of his works are for orchestra or large chamber ensemble; some of his scores use electronic keyboards and samplers. Ruders has created a large body of music ranging from opera and orchestral works through chamber, vocal and solo music in a variety of styles, from the Vivaldi pastiche of his First Violin Concerto (1981) to the explosive modernism of Manhattan Abstraction (1982). Other works include the operas Tycho *(1986),* The Handmaid's Tale *(1990) and* Kafka's Trial *(2005), four symphonies, three string quartets and two piano sonatas.*

Violin Concerto No 1

Violin Concerto No 1[a]. Etude and Ricercare[b]. The Bells[c]. The Christmas Gospel[d]
[c]**Lucy Shelton** sop [ab]**Rolf Schulte** vn [c]**Speculum Musicae / David Starobin** gtr [a]**Riverside Symphony Orchestra / George Rothman;** [d]**Malmö Symphony Orchestra / Ola Rudner**
Bridge BCD9057 (62' · DDD · T) Ⓕ❍

Ruders' First Violin Concerto (1981) begins as routine minimalist auto-hypnosis. But it develops some wonderfully inventive ways of disrupting and reassembling itself. Admittedly the last movement, with its chaconne based on Vivaldi and Schubert, tiptoes on the border of sensationalism. Otherwise the work could join Schnittke's Fourth as one of the few contemporary violin concertos with a strong claim to standard-repertoire status. Schulte gives an intense account of the solo part; the Riverside orchestra is tight in discipline, the recording close. All these factors help to make the overall musical impression extremely vivid. Less persuasive is Ruders's vocal writing in *The Bells* (the same Edgar Allen Poe texts set by Rachmaninov), and there's something not quite convincing about the instrumental setting too – perhaps too uniform an intensity, too much frantic heterophony. *The Christmas Gospel*, tossed off in two weeks for a mixed animation and live-action film, is darkly impressive – necessarily simple and direct, but still rewarding, even when divorced from the visual images.

The Handmaid's Tale

The Handmaid's Tale
Marianne Rørholm *mez* Offred **Hanne Fischer** *mez*
Double **Poul Elming** *ten* Luke **Ulla Kudsk Jensen**
mez Offred's Mother **Anne Margrethe Dahl** *sop*
Aunt Lydia **Dijna Mai-Mai** *sop* Moira **Lise-Lotte**
Nielsen *sop* Janine **Annita Wadsholt** *contr* Moira's
Aunt **Susanne Resmark** *contr* Serena Joy **Kari**
Hamnøy *contr* Rita **Aage Haugland** *bass*
Commander **Gert Henning-Jensen** *ten* Nick
Elsebeth Lund *sop* Ofglen **Pia Hansen** *mez* New
Ofglen **Bengl-Ola Morgny** *ten* Doctor **Elisabeth**
Halling *mez* Warren's Wife **John Laursen** *ten*
Commander X **Uffe Henriksen** *bass* First Eye and
Guard **Morten Kramp** *bass* Second Eye and Guard
Royal Danish Opera Chorus and Orchestra /
Michael Schønwandt
Dacapo ② 8 224165/6 (144' · DDD · T/t)
Recorded live 2000   Ⓕ**OO**

Ruders says of his vividly imaginative opera,
based on Margaret Atwood's novel, that he composed it as though he were directing a film.
Precisely: it's divided into 44 scenes, some very
short, several incorporating flashbacks in which
present and past sometimes appear simultaneously. The opera's 'present' is the not-too-distant
future, a hideous fundamentalist autocracy in
which women have no rights, not even to read
and write, and those of them convicted of
'gender-treachery' (adultery, second marriage,
contraception, abortion) are compelled to
become 'Handmaids', ritually impregnated by
the husbands of childess women. The central
character, Offred (Of Fred – the name of the
man whose property she now is), is portrayed by
two singers: her present, brainwashed and
imperfectly remembering self, and Offred as she
was in 'Time Before', happily married (though
as her husband's second wife a 'gender traitor' to
the new order) with a five-year-old daughter.
The opera depicts the brutal totalitarianism of
'Time Now', Offred's relationship with the
Commander (Fred) and his alarming wife, her
longing for her dimly remembered husband and
child and her enlistment in a sort of resistance
group. But it's in the very nature of the plot that
we never learn her ultimate fate.

It's also in the plot's nature that it needs a great
variety of types of music, as we move from past to
present, from the grim rituals of Time Now to
Offred's memories of Time Before. Ambiguous
music, too, since in this shadowy, threatening
world things are often not what they seem. Ruders's great achievement is to provide that variety
and ambiguity from within the resources of his
own style; in particular, he balances on the tight-
rope from tonality to atonality with great skill.
The rituals of the Handmaids are accompanied
by simple, chorale-like chants with 'minimalist'
accompaniment. The most striking passage to
emerge from the score is a duet for the two
Offreds in which both voices seem to be yearning
for a tonal resolution, but can no more achieve it
than two people 20 years apart in time can meet.

Ruders has been best known for his prodigiously
resourceful orchestral writing, and he surpasses
himself here: electronic keyboards, samplers and
additional percussion are added to the large
orchestra, but many of the strangest, most nightmarish or most radiant sounds are produced by
normal instruments used with brilliant originality.
Some of the more monstrous inhabitants of this
nightmare world are portrayed in vocal lines that
go to extremes, but far more often the writing for
voices is idiomatically singable. The cast, among
whom there isn't one single weak link, sing their
hearts out, and Schønwandt conveys the kaleidoscopic colours of Ruder's score with a remarkable
degree of clarity. The recording is first class.

Additional recommendation

Kafka's Trial
Van Hal Josef K **Stille** Miss Bürstner; Felice Bauer
Rørholm Miss Montag; Greta Bloch; Leni
Henning-Jensen Inspector; Court Recorder; Titorelli
Kristensen Deputy Manager; Businessman Block
Reuter Interrogator; **Royal Danish Opera Chor &**
Orch / Søndergård
Dacapo ② 8 226042/3 (125' · DDD · T/t)   Ⓕ**B➔**

The enigmatic, nightmarish *The Trial* is probably
Franz Kafka's most celebrated tale. Poul Ruders's
opera to Paul Bentley's intelligent libretto, premiered in March 2005, is at least the seventh such
treatment but where theirs differs from previous
versions is in the attempt to link directly the creation of the story to events in Kafka's life. Ruders's
setting is nervous and mostly fast-paced, the music
incorporating tonal and modern expressionist elements, splashes of klezmer colouring (particularly for
Kafka himself) but little that might be called comic.
Yet the score abounds in moments where the orchestral accompaniment seems to be mocking the hapless
K/Kafka. In the end, *Kafka's Trial* is an unsettling
rather than disturbing work, fascinating without
being insightful, but undeniably entertaining.

John Rutter   British b1945

One of the most popular and widely performed com-
posers of his generation, Rutter studied at Clare Col-
lege, Cambridge, then taught at Southampton Uni-
versity, returning to Clare College as director of
music in 1975. He left in 1979 to devote himself to
composition and founded the Cambridge Singers
with whom he has made many recordings of both his
own and others' music. His works are predominately
vocal; his musical style draws upon the British choral
tradition but also late-19th-/early-20th-century
European music, especially Fauré and Duruflé.

Mass of the Children

Mass of the Children[a]. Shadows[b]. Wedding Canticle[c]
[a]**Angharad Gruffydd Jones** *sop* [ab]**Jeremy Huw**
Williams *bar* [c]**Daniel Pailthorpe** *fl* [bc]**Stewart French**

gtr [a]James McVinnie org [a]Farnham Youth Choir; Clare College [ac]Choir and [a]Chamber Ensemble, Cambridge / Timothy Brown
Naxos 8 557922 (67' · DDD · T/t)   Ⓢ⯮

Choirs love to sing Rutter's music, audiences love to hear it and, if reviewers are lukewarm, the record/ticket-buying public compensates with effective demonstrations of its enthusiasm.

Rutter believes the seed of the Mass, premiered at Carnegie Hall in 2003, was planted when, as a member of the Highgate School choir, he performed on the original 1963 recording of Britten's *War Requiem*. This inspiration is nowhere more clear than in the introduction to the *Gloria*, which recalls Britten's use of brass, woodwind and percussion.

Rutter re-imagines Britten's brilliant juxtaposition of adult and children's voices in a joyful context. Like his model, he mixes Latin liturgy with poetry: here, the texts include poems by Archbishop Ken and William Blake. The *Kyrie* opens vividly with a sunny, breezy setting of Ken's 'Awake my soul', the *Domine Deus* begins effectively with a bassoon ostinato against mysterious long notes, but his openings often raise expectations which, for me, are seldom fulfilled. The *Sanctus* evokes Fauré at best, Lloyd Webber at worst, and early in the *Agnus Dei* some phrases, startlingly, recall Penderecki's *St Luke Passion*. But fear not, this is mostly unmistakably Rutter.

The shades of Britten and Pears hover over *Shadows* (1979), a cycle of pleasant settings of 16th- and 17th-century poems, paying tribute to the lute-song tradition. The *Wedding Canticle* is sweet, airy and graceful. Rutter's many fans will not be disappointed.

Requiem

Requiem[a]. Hymn to the Creator of Light. God be in my head. A Gaelic Blessing. Psalmfest – No 5, Cantate Domino. Open thou mine eyes[b]. A Prayer of St Patrick. A Choral Fanfare. Birthday Madrigals – No 2, Draw on, sweet night; No 4, My true love hath my heart. The Lord bless you and keep you
[a]Rosa Mannion, [b]Libby Crabtree sops Polyphony; Bournemouth Sinfonietta / Stephen Layton
Hyperion CDA66947 (69' · DDD · T/t)   Ⓕ⬤

Here is music finely crafted, written with love for the art and an especial care for choral sound. It's melodious without being commonplace, harmonically rich without being sticky, modern in the graceful way of a child who grows up responsive to newness but not wanting to kick his elders in the teeth. He gives us the heart's desire. But he's on too familiar terms with our heart's desires, he doesn't extend them, or surprise us into realising that they were deeper and subtler than we thought. This is by way of cautiously savouring a remembered taste, which could readily be indulged without perceived need for an interval: one item leads to another and before we know it the pleasurable hour is over. The Requiem is the longest work; the

other pieces vary from two to just over six minutes. Most are unaccompanied and show the choir of 25 voices as another of those expert groups of assured and gifted professionals that are among the principal adornments of modern musical life. Their capacity as a virtuoso choir is tested in the *Cantate Domino* and *Choral Fanfare*, but Rutter writes for real singers (not just singer-musicians) and their tone is unfailingly beautiful. The two soloists are excellent.

Additional recommendation

Requiem
Coupled with Advent anthem, 'Arise, shine'. Go forth into the world in peace. Toccata in seven. Variations on an Easter theme for organ duet. A Clare Benediction. Musica Dei donum. Come down, O Love divine.
Thomas sop **Jones** fl **Hooker** ob **Rimmer, Collon** org **Dorey** vc **Clare College Choir, Cambridge; City of London Sinfonia / Brown**
Naxos 8 557130 (69' · DDD · T/t)   Ⓢ⬤⬤⯮

A fine selection of Rutter's work, recorded with the choir of Rutter's own Cambridge college. They're fresh and natural, thoroughly musical in feeling and professional in care. The version of the *Requiem* is the scoring for solo instruments and organ, rather than the full orchestral score heard on Hyperion.

Gloria

Gloria[abc]. Come down, O Love divine. Lord, make me an instrument of thy peace[b]. To everything there is a season. I my best-beloved's am. Praise the Lord, O my soul[ac]. I will lift up mine eyes[b]. As the bridegroom to his chosen[b]. A Clare Benediction. The Lord is my light and my salvation. Go forth into the world in peace. Thy perfect love[b]. Te Deum[ac]
Polyphony, [a]The Wallace Collection; [b]City of London Sinfonia / Stephen Layton with [c]**Andrew Lumsden** org
Hyperion CDA67259 (79' · DDD · T/t)   Ⓕ

This superb disc contains a balanced cross-section of Rutter's sacred choral music, spanning over a quarter century and featuring several first recordings. Rutter's stylistic hallmarks are all here: an unfailing knack to get to the root of the text, exquisitely balanced vocal writing, melting harmonies, intensely sweet turns of phrase, short ecstatic climaxes, but also a willingness to be astringent, and rhythmically powerful. There are nods to pageantry, for example in the conclusion of the *Gloria* with its Waltonian swagger, some decliously *echt* Sullivan at the end of the *Te Deum* and, in *I my best-beloved's am*, an occasional vision of the neo-Byzantine sound world of his fellow Highgate School pupil, John Tavener.

The artistry of the 25 full-bodied voices of Polyphony is beyond reproach, only suffering a deficit in sheer volume when pitted against the full fury of The Wallace Collection. Sumptuously recorded, all the forces involved play to perfection. Greatly enjoyable.

Carl Rütti
Swiss b1949

Carl Rütti studied music at the Zürich Conservatoire, graduating in 1975 with a Solisten-diploma in both piano and organ. During the following year, studying in London, he became fascinated by English choral singing, which inspired him to write several pieces for a cappella choir. Rütti's music blends the English choral tradition with other genres including jazz and the blues in rich colourful textures, and has been performed all over the world. He teaches piano at the Zürich Conservatoire.

Requiem

Requiem
Olivia Robinson sop **Edward Price** bar
**The Bach Choir; Southern Sinfonia /
David Hill** with **Jane Watts** org
Naxos 8 572317 (55' · DDD)   ⓈO➔

The Swiss composer Carl Rütti has a gift for finding a memorable 'hook' to trigger a section – and, in this case, the entire work, which begins with a haunting soprano solo, beautifully sung by Olivia Robinson – and a clear connection to the English choral tradition (he studied in London, in fact). The orchestration is the same as that of the Fauré Requiem, and that is not the only resemblance between the two works: there is frequently a wistful gentleness here that any admirer of the French composer's work will respond to. Rütti also does not, of course, include the 'Dies irae', but does set the 'In paradisum'.

While gentleness is far from being the end of the story, however, as the Elgar-meets-John Adams style of the opening of the *Kyrie*, for example, or the Nymanesque moments of the 'In Paradisum' demonstrate, the tone is definitely predominantly elegiac and consoling. The Bach Choir under David Hill respond to this with warmth and passion, and soloists Olivia Robinson and Edward Price are outstanding. The recording, made in St John's, Smith Square, is wonderful, responding to the wide sonic and dynamic range of the music in every detail.

Kaija Saariaho
Finnish b1952

After studying with Paavo Haininen at the Sibelius Academy, Helsinki, she worked for Brian Ferneyhough and Klaus Huber at the Musikhochschule in Freiburg (1981-82) and attended a computer music course at IRCAM in Paris in 1982. Although much of her output is chamber works, she has turned increasingly to larger forces and broader structures, such as the opera L'amour de loin, premiered at the 2000 Salzburg Festival, and Oltra mar for chorus and orchestra, commissioned by the NYPO. Her second opera, Adriana Mater, was commissioned for the Opéra National de Paris's 2006 season. Her second string quartet, Terra memoria, was commissioned for the Emerson Quartet by Carnegie Hall. The third opera, Émilie, has the life and death of Émilie du Châtelet as its subject.

Orchestral works

Orion. Notes on Light[a]. Mirage[ab]
[b]**Karita Mattila** sop [a]**Anssi Karttunen** vc
Orchestre de Paris / Christoph Eschenbach
Ondine ODE1130-2 (63' · DDD)
Recorded live 2008   ⒻO➔

Light is the element that allies Kaija Saariaho to so many of her Nordic peers; that, plus related things such as fire, sky, eclipse and mirage, all of which feature as titles or subtitles in the three pieces recorded here. Musical textures that shimmer, scintillate, explode, darken and extinguish are her bridge between modernism and tradition, and potentially also the listener's path from familiar modes of listening into her fascinating, never vulgarly gratifying, realm of sonic imagination.

These performances from the '100% Finland' festival in Paris are just about ideal as introductions to Saariaho, and self-recommendable for anyone already initiated. Two out of three are world premieres, and it will surely not be long before other soloists take up the crusade begun so valiantly by Anssi Karttunen and Karita Mattila. The two combine to magical effect in *Mirage*, where they jointly interpret the transformations of the woman in Mexican shamanhealer María Sabina's ecstatic text (set in English). By comparison *Notes on Light* feels just a fraction long for its material; whereas *Orion* – inspired by the mortal and cosmic aspects of the mythological hunter – deserves to figure on any short list for orchestral masterpiece of the new millennium.

Kaleidoscopic orchestral colour, remote from human gesture and drama but rich in intellectual imagination, is a dimension in which Christoph Eschenbach excels, and demonstration recording quality of the kind Ondine supplies is the other notable ingredient in this compelling programme.

L'amour de loin

L'amour de loin
Daniel Belcher bar Jaufré Rudel **Marie-Ange Todorovitch** mez Pèlerin **Ekaterina Lekhina** sop Clémence **Berlin Radio Chorus; Deutsches Symphonie-Orchester Berlin / Kent Nagano**
Harmonia Mundi ② 🎬 HMC80 1937/8
(121' · DDD)   ⒻOO➔

Kaija Saariaho's first work for the lyric stage (Salzburg, 2000) looks set to establish itself as one of the most significant and successful operas of recent decades. Premiered in a Peter Sellars production (under the baton of this recording's conductor, Kent Nagano) that travelled quite widely, it has survived the crucial test of other stagings. It's easy to understand its appeal, even if *L'amour de loin* does sometimes seem to resemble *Pelléas et Mélisande* without the jokes.

Saariaho's hypnotic score combines with a poetic libretto by Lebanese-born writer Armin Maalouf to exquisite effect. The result is not, it must be said, the most dramatic opera, but then neither is *Pelléas* or *Tristan und Isolde*, pieces in which music works powerfully on the imagination. And there is a sense in which the Saariaho-Maalouf work, which translates as 'Love from afar', also belongs to the tradition of Debussy's opera. The five connected acts are inspired by the tale of a medieval Provençal troubadour named Jaufré, who visualises the Countess Clémence of Tripoli as the epitome of chaste love. A Pilgrim criss-crosses the Mediterranean carrying messages between the two distant lovers but when Jaufré finally summons up the courage to sail to Tripoli he is taken ill while at sea and dies on arrival in the arms of Clémence.

Saariaho has declared herself uninterested in the concept of courtly love and prefers to see her work as a more modern, wider meditation on love. Her delicate music, superbly realised here by the Deutsches Symphonie-Orchester Berlin under Nagano, reflects this in the same way that Maalouf is able to look beyond the clichés of Orientalism. The fine cast features American baritone Daniel Belcher as a lithe, musical Jaufré and Russian soprano Ekaterina Lekhina as a delicate and languid Clémence. Not surprisingly, the Montpellier-born Marie-Ange Todorovitch boasts the best French as the Pilgrim, yet the cast works very well together in a perfumed piece so meditative and purely musical in its essence that this CD is preferable to the earlier DVD based on Sellars's staging.

Camille Saint-Saëns

French 1835-1921

Saint-Saëns was one of the most remarkable prodigies in the history of music – indeed, he had an altogether remarkable mind: organist, pianist, conductor, caricaturist, dabbler in science, mathematics and astronomy, critic, traveller, archaeologist, writer of plays, poetry, philosophy, essayist on botany and ancient music, editor of music and the composer of more than 300 works touching every area of music.

Saint-Saëns began playing the piano at two and a half (taught by his great-aunt), gave a performance in a Paris salon at five, began to compose at six and made his official debut aged 10. As an encore he offered to play any one of Beethoven's 32 sonatas from memory. After the Paris Conservatoire he competed unsuccessfully for the Prix de Rome and again in 1864 when he was an established composer. His First Symphony appeared in 1853: Gounod was present and sent an admiring note of encouragement. As a pianist and organist of exceptional ability he was much in demand and at the age of 22 he secured the most prestigious organ post in France at the Madeleine. Here he developed his legendary gifts for

improvisation – Liszt called him the greatest organist in the world – and soon famous musicians visiting Paris would make a point of stopping off at the Madeleine to hear him play – Clara Schumann, Anton Rubinstein and Sarasate among them. Hans von Bülow rated Saint-Saëns as a score reader and all-round musician greater than Liszt.

Saint-Saëns toured extensively as a pianist, both in solo concerts and in performances of his own piano concertos – his technique was apparently effortless. He became a professor of piano at the École Niedermeyer in 1861 and 10 years later helped found the Société Nationale dedicated to the performance of music by French composers. He composed at tremendous speed: his Op 12, the Oratorio de Noël, was completed in 12 days; a commission he had forgotten about produced 21 pages of full score in two hours; the popular Second Piano Concerto took three weeks from start to finish.

By the late 1860s Saint-Saëns was numbered among the top few great living composers, awarded the Légion d'Honneur at only 33, befriended by the leading musicians of the day and a habitué of the salon of Princesse Mathilde. His private life was not so fortunate. He was 40 when he married the 19-year-old Marie Truffot, sister of one of his pupils. The couple had two children but Saint-Saëns had little time for family life and in the first three years of his marriage he completed his opera Samson et Dalila, his Piano Concerto No 4, the oratorio Le Déluge, a suite for orchestra and a symphonic poem, made a visit to Russia (where he became close friends with Tchaikovsky), composed numerous other short works, gave concerts and, in the spring of 1878, returned from Switzerland after writing a Requiem Mass. His arrival coincided with a terrible tragedy: his two-and-a-half year old son André had fallen out of a fourth-floor window; barely six weeks later his second son died suddenly of an infant malady. Three years after that, Saint-Saëns and his wife were on holiday and the composer one day, without warning, disappeared. Marie Saint-Saëns never saw her husband again (the couple never divorced) and she died aged nearly 95 in January 1950.

After 1890, he wrote very little of consequence and began to indulge in his passion for foreign travel – frequent visits to the Canary Islands and Algeria, and as far afield as Colombo and Saigon where, it's said, he developed a close interest in the natives (usually young boys). As his music became less and less appreciated by the coming generation, he became proportionately more irritable, more outspoken in his condemnation of new music. He was still giving recitals three months before his death (he went on a concert tour of Algiers and Greece at the age of 85). When he announced his retirement in August 1921, he had been before the public for 75 years.

Cello Concertos

No 1 in A minor, Op 33; **No 2** in D minor, Op 119

Cello Concerto No 1. Le carnaval des animaux – The Swan[a]. Romance in F, Op 36[b]. Romance in D, Op 51[b]. Cello Sonata No 1 in C minor, Op 32[b]. Chant saphique in D, Op 91[b]. Gavotte in G minor,

Op *posth*[b]. Allegro appassionato in B minor, Op 43[b].
Prière, Op 158
Steven Isserlis *vc* [a]**Dudley Moore**, [b]**Pascal Devoyon**
pfs [c]**Francis Grier** *org* **London Symphony Orchestra**
/ Michael Tilson Thomas [a]*pf*
RCA Victor Red Seal 09026 61678-2 (67' · DDD)
Recorded 1992   Ⓕ

This disc is recommendable not so much for
Steven Isserlis's Cello Concerto – smooth and
intelligent as that is – as for the fill-ups. *The
Swan* has Moore and Tilson Thomas as joint
accompanists, elegantly executed, but the items
with Pascal Devoyon are especially valuable, the
First Cello Sonata full of elegantly tailored
drama, the two *Romances*, *Chant saphique* and
Gavotte palpable charmers, tastefully played; and
the headstrong, thematically memorable *Allegro
appassionato*, one of the finest shorter pieces in
the cellist's repertory. The disc is enhanced by
the opportunity of hearing the rather affecting
but relatively unfamiliar *Prière*, composed for
André Hekking just two years before Saint-
Saëns's death.

Cello Concerto No 2 in D minor, Op 119[c]. La muse et
le poète, Op 132[ac]. Romance in E flat, Op 67[c] (orch
cpsr). Cello Sonata No 2 in F, Op 123[b]
Steven Isserlis *vc* [a]**Joshua Bell** *vn* [b]**Pascal Devoyon**
pf [c]**North German Radio Symphony Orchestra /
Christoph Eschenbach**
RCA Red Seal 09026 63518-2 (76' · DDD)   Ⓕ

Steven Isserlis follows up his earlier outstanding
release of Saint-Saëns's cello music with another
that's even more revelatory. This disc concentrates on the more neglected cello works that
Saint-Saëns wrote towards the end of his long
career. It's true that neither Concerto nor
Sonata quite matches its predecessor in memorable melody, but Isserlis, in powerful, imaginative performances, brings out other qualities to
show how unjust their neglect is. That's particularly true of the Sonata, which, vividly supported
by Pascal Devoyon, rivals Brahms's magnificent
Second Cello Sonata in heroic power and scale.
At 33 minutes, this is easily the longest of Saint-
Saëns's cello works, its ambitious tone of voice
instantly established (as it is in the Brahms) and
then masterfully sustained throughout the first
movement. The second-movement *scherzo*,
almost as long and far more than just an interlude, is a sharply original set of variations, leading to a songful slow movement which in turn
leads up to a passionate climax. Then in the
surgingly energetic finale, both Isserlis and
Devoyon articulate the rapid passagework with
thrilling clarity.
   The cello writing in the Second Concerto is
rather less grateful, with its thorny passages of
double-stopping, but the two-movement structure characteristic of Saint-Saëns works well,
with each divided clearly in two, *Allegro* into
Andante, *Scherzo* into cadenza and reprise of
Allegro. Making light of technical problems,
Isserlis is persuasive both in the bravura *Alle-*

gros and in the hushed meditation of the slow
section. Yet neither he nor Eschenbach can
quite overcome the truncated feeling at the
end, when the reprise of the opening material is
so short.
   The *Romance* is an adaptation of the slow
fourth movement of the Cello Suite, Op 16, a
charming piece which Saint-Saëns reworked
several times. Yet best of all is the lyrical dialogue of *La muse et le poète*. Inspired by Alfred de
Musset's poem, *La nuit de mai*, it opens with
Saint-Saëns at his most luscious, reflecting de
Musset's role as a hothouse romantic among
French poets. It then moves seamlessly through
contrasted episodes, with the violin (superbly
played by Joshua Bell) representing the muse
and the cello as the poet himself. A generous
collection, warmly recorded.

Additional recommendation

Cello Concertos Nos 1 and 2
Coupled with Suite, Op 16 (arr vc/orch). Allegro
appassionato in B minor, Op 43. Le carnaval des
animaux – The Swan
Kliegel *vc* **Bournemouth Sinfonietta / Monnard**
Naxos 8 553039 (62' · DDD)   Ⓢ Ⓑ ▸
   Maria Kliegel performs the Second Cello
   Concerto with impressive panache and precision.
   The First, too, is well played, though not a first
   choice for the work.

Piano Concertos

No 1 in D, Op 17; No 2 in G minor, Op 22;
No 3 in E flat Op 29; No 4 in C minor, Op 44;
No 5 in F, Op 103, 'Egyptian'

Piano Concertos Nos 1-5. Wedding Cake, Op 76.
Rapsodie d'Auvergne, Op 73. Africa, Op 89.
Allegro appassionato, Op 70
Stephen Hough *pf* **City of Birmingham Symphony
Orchestra / Sakari Oramo**
Hyperion ② CDA67331/2 (155' · DDD)   Ⓕ ❶❶❶ ▸

If Saint-Saëns's idiom once answered – and
maybe still does – to qualities fundamental to the
French musical character, it must be said
straight away that Hough sounds the complete
insider. He commands the range of the big statements, whatever their character, as well as sparkle and panache, a sense of drama and seemingly
inexhaustible stamina; and he can charm. Yet
perhaps most delightful is the lightness and clarity of his decorative playing. It's a bonus for the
virtuoso passages not to sound hectic or overblown – for Saint-Saëns, virtuosity always had
an expressive potential. There's an air of manufacture about the writing sometimes, certainly,
but as Hough knows, there must be nothing
mechanical in its delivery. Sweeping across the
keyboard, dipping and soaring through the
teeming notes, he flies like a bird. He manages
to convey what makes these pieces tick: fine
workmanship, fantasy, colour, and the various

ways Saint-Saëns was so good at combining piano and orchestra. The orchestra has plenty to do. These scores are textbooks of lean but firm orchestration from which at least one major French composer learnt (Ravel, another eclectic, who must have seen the 'old bear' as a kindred spirit). The days are past when the CBSO under Louis Frémaux was considered Britain's 'French' orchestra, but with Sakari Oramo it does splendidly here, playing alertly with its inspiring soloist as he does with it (another plus). The recording balances are fine, with lovely piano sound and plenty of orchestral detail in natural-sounding perspectives.

Saint-Saëns Piano Concerto No 2   ⊞
Rachmaninov Piano Concerto No 3 in D minor, Op 30
Shostakovich Prelude and Fugue in D, Op 87 No 5
Emil Gilels pf **Paris Conservatoire Orchestra /
André Cluytens**
Testament mono SBT1029 (65' · ADD)
Recorded 1954-56   Ⓕ🔵🔵

Gilels was a true king of pianists, and these Paris- and New York-based recordings only confirm his legendary status. Here, again, is that superlative musicianship, that magisterial technique and, above all, that unforgettable sonority. What breadth and distinction he brings to the first movement of the Saint-Saëns, from his fulmination in the central octave uproar to his uncanny stillness in the final pages. High jinks are reserved for the second and third movements, the former tossed off with a teasing lightness, the latter's whirling measures with infinite brio. An approximate swipe at the *Scherzo*'s flashing double-note flourish, a false entry and a wrong turning five minutes into the finale offer amusing evidence of Gilels's high-wire act. No performance of this concerto is more 'live', and it's small wonder that Claudio Arrau included it among his desert island favourites.

Gilels's Rachmaninov is altogether more temperate yet, once more, this is among the few truly great performances of this work. His tempo is cool and rapid, and maintained with scintillating ease through even the most formidable intricacy. The cadenza – the finer and more transparent of the two – billows and recedes in superbly musical style and the climax is of awe-inspiring grandeur, and the central *scherzando* in the finale is as luminous as it's vivacious. The finale's *meno mosso* variation is excluded and, it has to be said, Cluytens's partnership is distant and run of the mill. But the recordings hardly show their age in such admirably smooth transfers. Gilels's 'encore', Shostakovich's Prelude and Fugue No 5, is like a brilliant shaft of light after the Rachmaninov. The performance is perfection.

Saint-Saëns Piano Concerto No 4ᶜ. Etude en   ⊞
forme de valse, Op 52 No 6ᵈ **Franck** Symphonic
Variationsᵃ **Ravel** Piano Concerto for the Left Handᵇ
Alfred Cortot pf ᵃ**London Philharmonic Orchestra /**

Landon Ronald; ᵇorchestra, ᶜParis Conservatoire
Orchestra / ᵇᶜCharles Munch
Naxos Historical 8 110613 (60' · ADD)   Ⓢ🔵🔵

Here are performances of a timeless vitality and validity. The exception is the Ravel Concerto, which is wildly approximate and confused. Elsewhere, though, there's a super-abundance of wit and charm – of Cortot at his most beguiling. His capacity to be free and ecstatic yet bracingly unsentimental was one of his most exhilarating qualities, and his *rubato* at the start of the Saint-Saëns makes modern rivals such as Rogé (Decca), Collard (EMI) and Hough (Hyperion) pale in comparison. At 8'12" (*dolce tranquillo legato*) there's a classic instance of the *cantabile* for which he was celebrated, and in the final pages of the same movement an inimitably limpid and delicate poetry. Again, in the central *Allegro vivace*, his famous or infamous scrambles and skirmishes are never at the expense of the music's innate elegance and style, and who else has spun off the Concerto's closing cascades with such glitter and aplomb? Cortot's playing may not have been note-perfect but there's no doubt that he was every inch the virtuoso. As an encore, there's Saint-Saëns's *Etude en forme de valse*, and while the 1931 recording is by no means the equal of the legendary 1919 disc, a performance that prompted Horowitz's envy, it's gloriously alive with Cortot's verve and magic. Mark Obert-Thorn's transfers are exceptional and all lovers of past but ever-present greatness will want this second and final Naxos volume of Cortot's sadly few concerto recordings.

Violin Concertos

No 1 in A, Op 20; No 2 in C, Op 58;
No 3 in B minor, Op 61
Philippe Graffin vn **BBC Scottish Symphony
Orchestra / Martyn Brabbins**
Hyperion CDA67074 (76' · DDD)   Ⓕ🔵

The first two violin concertos of Saint-Saëns were composed in reverse order. The Second is the longer and lesser-known of the two, but the First Concerto more resembles the thematic charm and concise design of the First Cello Concerto. Cast in a single short movement that falls into three distinct sections, it launches the soloist on his way right from the start, and features a delightful central section with some felicitous woodwind writing. Hyperion holds a trump card in Philippe Graffin, whose elegant, emotionally charged playing is strongly reminiscent of the young Menuhin, and whose understanding of the idiom is second to none – certainly among modern players.

Saint-Saëns's First Violin Concerto was composed in 1859, whereas his Second preceded it by a year. Unexpectedly, the first movement's thematic material has an almost Weberian slant. The orchestration is heavier than in the First, and the musical arguments are both more

SAINT-SAËNS, SYMPHONY NO 3, 'ORGAN' – IN BRIEF

Peter Hurford; Montreal SO / Charles Dutoit
Decca 475 7728DOR (58' · DDD)　　Ⓜ❍❍🅓
A thrilling performance (and recording) of this highly coloured work. Dutoit draws some ravishing playing from his superb Canadian orchestra and Peter Hurford, who must have played it dozens of times, brings his characteristic imagination to the score. Coupled with Poulenc's Organ Concerto.

Olivier Latry; Philadelphia Orchestra /
Christoph Eschenbach
Ondine ODE1094-5 (79' · DDD)　　Ⓕ❍❍🅓
Another performance that matches top-notch musicianship with a first-rate recording. Eschenbach directs a vivid performance with Olivier Latry supplying some truly dazzling playing. The couplings are the Poulenc Organ Concerto and Samuel Barber's *Toccata festiva*.

Simon Preston; Berlin Philharmonic /
James Levine
DG 419 617-2GH (46' · DDD)　　Ⓕ❍🅓
The mighty Berlin Philharmonic are on top form here and combined with the might of the organ virtually pin one to the seat. Levine relishes the score's variety and whips up a veritable whirlwind of sound. The coupling is a witty and affectionate performance of Dukas's *Sorcerer's Apprentice*.

Gaston Litaize; Orchestre de Paris /
Daniel Barenboim
DG 474 612-2GOR (56' · DDD)　　Ⓕ🅓
Another mid-price alternative for this favourite score. Barenboim draws some thrilling playing from the Paris orchestra and the sound – slightly fierce – merely adds to the sense of drama. Generously coupled with three orchestral excerpts from *Samson et Dalila* and the *Danse macabre*.

Gillian Weir; Ulster Orchestra /
Yan Pascal Tortelier
Chandos CHAN8822 (53' · DDD)　　Ⓕ❍🅓
The beautifully judged Chandos recording makes this a joy for the ears: recorded with the organ *in situ* rather than grafted on, the balance is very skilfully managed. And Tortelier makes it sound more French than many other performances. The coupling is a lovely performance of the Second Symphony.

Noel Rawsthorne; RLPO / Loris Tjeknavorian
Regis RRC1262 (62' · ADD)　　Ⓢ
Recorded in Liverpool Cathedral, with its vast acoustic, this performance takes a little getting used to, but it's full of spectacle and makes an excellent budget-price alternative. Coupled with *Carnival* and the *Danse macabre*.

formal and more forcefully stated. It's a more overtly virtuoso work than the First Concerto, and perhaps rather less memorable, but again Graffin weaves a winsome solo line and Martyn Brabbins directs a strong account of the orchestral score, with prominently projected woodwinds. The relatively well-known Third Concerto (1880) is roughly the same length as the Second (around half an hour), but is more consistently interesting. The basic material is of higher quality, the key relations more telling and orchestration infinitely more delicate. No other recording liberates so much of the score's instrumental detail, probably because most of Graffin's predecessors have been balanced way in front of the orchestra.

Symphony No 3, 'Organ'

Symphony No 3[a]. Le carnaval des animaux[b]
Peter Hurford org [a]**Montreal Symphony Orchestra;**
[b]**London Sinfonietta / Charles Dutoit**
Decca 475 7728DOR (58' · DDD)　　Ⓜ❍❍🅓

In 1886 Saint-Saëns poured his considerable experience as an unequalled virtuoso of the organ, piano and practitioner of Lisztian unifying techniques into his *Organ* Symphony; it instantly put the French Symphony on the map, and provided a model for Franck and others. With its capacity for grand spectacle (aside from the organ and a large orchestra, its scoring includes two pianos) it has suffered inflationary tendencies from both conductors and recording engineers. Dutoit's (and Decca's) achievement is the restoration of its energy and vitality. Poulenc's wonderful Gothic Organ Concerto receives a terrific performance, the drama and intensity unleashed with amazing power. As with the Saint-Saëns, the Decca recording is superbly handled.

Orchestral Works

Danse macabre in G minor, Op 40. Phaéton in C, Op 39. Le rouet d'Omphale in A, Op 31. La jeunesse d'Hercule in E flat, Op 50. Marche héroïque in E flat, Op 34. Introduction and Rondo capriccioso in A minor, Op 28[a]. Havanaise in E, Op 83[a]
[a]**Kyung-Wha Chung** vn [a]**Royal Philharmonic Orchestra; Philharmonia Orch / Charles Dutoit**
Decca 425 021-2DM (66' · ADD)　　Ⓜ❍🅓

It's enough to make you weep – Saint-Saëns wrote his first tune at the age of three, analysed Mozart's *Don Giovanni* from the full score when he was five, and at 10 claimed he could play all Beethoven's 32 piano sonatas from memory. There's some consolation that, according to a contemporary, physically 'he strangely resembled a parrot', and perhaps even his early brilliance was a curse rather than a blessing, as he regressed from being a bold innovator to a dusty reactionary. In his thirties (in the 1870s) he was at the forefront of the Lisztian avant-garde. He was the first Frenchman to attempt Liszt's new genre, the 'symphonic poem', bringing to it a typically French concision, elegance and grace. Charles Dutoit has few peers in this kind of music; here's playing of dramatic flair and classical refinement that exactly matches Saint-Saëns's intention and invention. Decca's sound has depth, brilliance and richness.

The Carnival of the Animals

Le carnaval des animaux[a]. Fantaisie, Op 124[b]. Prière, Op 158[c]. Romance, Op 36[d]. Septet, Op 65[e]. Samson et Dalî'la – Mon cœur s'ouvre à ta voix[f]
[a]**Emmanuel Pahud** fl [a]**Paul Meyer** cl [e]**David Guerrier** tpt [a]**Florent Jodelet** perc [acdef]**Frank Braley**, [a]**Michel Dalberto** pfs [abe]**Renaud Capuçon**, [ae]**Béatrice Muthelet**, [ae]**Esther Hoppe** vns [acdef]**Gautier Capuçon** vc [ae]**Janne Saksala** db [b]**Marie-Pierre Langlamet** hp
Virgin Classics 545603-2 (63' · DDD)   Ⓕ **OO**▶

'What hard things,' wrote Saint-Saëns, 'have been said against virtuosity!…The fact must be proclaimed from the house-tops – in art a difficulty overcome is a thing of beauty.' There are many such beauties in *Le carnaval des animaux*, and their difficulties aren't for the faint-hearted or the technically challenged, especially where the two pianists are concerned. On this disc not only are the difficulties overcome, but dispatched with tremendous verve and wit.

In the Septet the players rightly refuse to make more of the music than is really there. This light touch allows us to relish Saint-Saëns's professionalism: every part in the texture has its own shape and colour and, if there were compositional difficulties to be overcome, you'd never know. The four shorter pieces on this splendid disc include the delicious *Fantaisie* for violin and harp, and three arrangements for cello and piano taken from the horn, organ and operatic repertoires.

Chamber Works

Bassoon Sonata, Op 168[a]. Caprice sur des airs danois et russes, Op 79[b]. Clarinet Sonata, Op 167[c]. Oboe Sonata, Op 166[d]. Piano Quartet, Op 41[e]. Piano Quintet, Op 14[f]. Septet, Op 65[g]. Tarantelle, Op 6[h]
Nash Ensemble ([bh]Philippa Davies fl [bd]Gareth Hulse ob [bch]Richard Hosford cl [a]Ursula Leveaux bn [g]Mark David tpt [efg]Marianne Thorsen, [g]David Adams, [f]Benjamin Nabarro vns [efg]Lawrence Power va [efg]Paul Watkins vc [g]Duncan McTier db Ian Brown pf)
Hyperion ② CDA67431/2 (134' · DDD)   Ⓕ **OO**▶

Saint-Saëns's chamber music fares better in the concert hall than the recording studio, perhaps because musicians tend to listen less to academic name-calling than to the music itself. The three late wind sonatas in particular have received far fewer recordings than their status as repertoire staples deserves. Try the kinky-Baroque first movement of the Oboe Sonata, jauntily phrased by Gareth Hulse, or the *animato* second of the Clarinet Sonata, garbed in

rich Mozartian cloth by Richard Hosford. Or, particularly, the Bassoon Sonata, for its fresh and gentle wit and skirting of cliché: Ursula Leveaux does it proud, with especially luscious tone in the opening *Allegretto*.

Surprises are thinner on the ground in the earlier works but none is less than, to echo Ravel's assessment, 'finely put together'. Hummability quotient is high in the Piano Quartet and Quintet, and off the scale in the Septet. The late Lionel Salter used to complain that recordings of the Septet tend to sound like a trumpet concerto; not this one. If you employ hit artists like Maurice André they will tend to hog the microphone but, happily, Mark David is a more sensitive soul who has fully imbibed the Nash's joyous spirit of corporate music-making, and Hyperion's engineers have placed him at a respectable distance.

If anything it is Ian Brown's piano that takes centre stage, and that's no bad thing except in the extensive fugal finales to the Piano Quartet and Quintet where Saint-Saëns, most unusually, seems to over-run himself. Sheer delight.

Cello Sonatas

Cello Sonatas – No 1, Op 32; No 2, Op 123. Prière, Op 158. Le carnaval des animaux – The Swan. Romance, Op 36
Christian Poltéra vc **Kathryn Stott** pf
Chandos CHAN10552 (65' · DDD)   Ⓕ **O**▶

Inevitably, 'The Swan' from *The Carnival of the Animals* features on this disc of Saint-Saëns's cello music – and it is played with gliding, liquid lyricism by Swiss cellist Christian Poltéra across the smooth surface of Kathryn Stott's arpeggios. But the chief interest lies in the two sonatas.

The First in C minor is, within the context of Saint-Saëns's long life, a fairly early work, written in 1872 when he was in his mid-30s. It combines passion, energy and rigour in the two outer movements, with a central one that envelops a chorale-like theme in a mood of solemn reflectiveness. Saint-Saëns certainly knew how to tap the technical resources of his soloists and Poltéra and Stott are as one in playing some fleet, taxing passagework with fluency and power, Poltéra's mellow tone adding a dimension of poignancy and shapely phrasing that traces and defines the music's surging contours.

Some three decades after the First Sonata, Saint-Saëns wrote the Second in F (1905), again a piece that fuses beguilingly melodic, restrained touches with a good deal of urgent, athletic activity in the outer movements. The slow *Romanza* is one of Saint-Saëns's most seductive inventions and in the set of variations forming the second movement his ingenuity in terms of texture, contrapuntal workings and lively instrumental interplay is finely honed. The disc is invaluable for these two works alone, but 'The Swan' and two other miniatures – a *Prière* and a *Romance* – show how acute Saint-Saëns was in matching musical ideas to instrumental timbre.

Piano Trios

Piano Trios – Nos 1 & 2
Florestan Trio (Anthony Marwood vn Richard Lester
vc Susan Tomes pf)
Hyperion CDA67538 (60' · DDD)   Ⓕ❍❍❍❍▷

Well, the Florestan Trio have done it again – a
sure-fire *Gramophone* Award nominee. Indeed,
such is the cumulative emotional impact of these
performances that tears welled up during the
wonderful *fortissimo* climax of the E minor
Trio's first movement – even before the astonishing intensity of the final, precipitous *Allegro*.
'Cumulative' because most of the time the Florestan prefer stealth and suggestion; they don't
wear their hearts on their sleeves. Instead they
offer, like Saint-Saëns's art, a filigree lightness
and clarity that somehow twists itself into an
ever-deepening pattern of turmoil.
  Listen to the underlying wistfulness in the
F major Trio: how the élan of the first movement's final chords provides a springboard into
a cheerful bucolic landscape that is nevertheless
crossed with clouds – this brought about by a
web of delicate rhythmic and tonal shading in
the string-playing stretched over Susan Tomes's
dancing, pellucid framework.
  Or the maturity and self-confidence in the
E minor: nothing is forced, everything flows –
from the stormy first movement through the
lighter central movements (and here the languid
descending phrases of the *Andante con moto* are
beautifully sculpted by both Marwood and Lester) to the complex yet never turgid imitative
writing of the last. Recorded sound and accompanying notes are, of course, impeccable. No
argument: just buy it.

Piano Quartets

Piano Quartets – Op 41; in E. Barcarolle, Op 108
Mozart Piano Quartet (Mark Gothoni vn
Hartmut Rohde va Peter Hörr vc Paul Rivinius pf)
Dabringhaus und Grimm 💿 MDG943 1519-6
(58' · DDD)   Ⓕ

Saint-Saëns is so well known nowadays for his
symphonies, concertos and orchestral works
that it is easy to overlook his substantial chamber output. Instrumental music was his main
love, much against the grain of French musical
life in the mid-19th century. Listen to the sparkling *Scherzo (Poco allegro più tosto moderato)* of
the Op 41 Piano Quartet (1875), or the lilting
central *Andante* of the earlier E major piece, a
three-movement student quartet of considerable imagination completed in 1853 when he
was just 18.
  It is unclear whether this early Quartet was
played in its composer's lifetime; by the time
chamber music became more fashionable in
French music-making in the 1880s, it might
have seemed too old-fashioned to programme.
Yet it is not an immature work except by the

standards of Saint-Saëns's later works, not least
the Op 41 Quartet, which has a power and brilliance of execution that make it worthy of comparison with Schumann's Op 47.
  The Mozart Piano Quartet play both quartets
with considerable élan, evoking the spirit of
their namesake in Saint-Saëns's beautifully balanced, often gossamer textures. Where power is
required, though, as in the outer movements of
Op 41, they respond with assurance. The
delightful makeweight of the *Barcarolle* completes a splendid disc.

Organ works

Three Preludes et Fugues, Op 99. Cyprès, Op 156a.
Fantaisie, Op 101. Fantaisie No 3, Op 157. Fantaisie
(1857). Bénédiction nuptiale, Op 9. Marche
religieuse, Op 107
Andrew-John Smith org
Hyperion CDA67713 (78' · DDD)
Played on the Cavaillé-Coll organ of
La Madeleine, Paris   Ⓕ

Andrew-John Smith's clever programming
alternates the Three Preludes and Fugues,
Op 99, with the three Fantaisies and other
works. Wisely, he begins and ends the CD with
the loudest and most extrovert pieces, namely
the E flat major Prelude and Fugue and the
E flat Fantaisie. In between there are long
stretches of quiet, introspective music, and listeners may long for the more dramatic compositions of Franck, Vierne or Widor. However, at
his best Saint-Saëns has an originality and charm
all his own; possibly no other French organist-
composer could have produced the delicate
beauty of the B major Prelude or the *Bénédiction
nuptiale*.
  It's clear from his highly detailed booklet-
notes plus his polished and stylish performances
that Smith is an enthusiastic advocate of Saint-
Saëns. What prevents this CD achieving its fullest impact is a cautious approach by player and
sound engineers to the cavernous acoustic of the
church of La Madeleine. The potential loss of
detail leads Smith to adopt tempi which are
sometimes slower than the composer's moderato and *sans lenteur* markings. Meanwhile the
1846 four-manual 58-stop Cavaillé-Coll organ
is recorded close-up, and although we gain clarity we lose the sense of grandeur with a large
instrument ringing around a massive edifice.
  On the plus side, Smith's warm and sympathetic *rubato* is a constant delight, and his
inspired choice to make the recording on an
instrument played regularly by Saint-Saëns
means that listeners can relish the authentic
Gallic tones of the splendid La Madeleine
organ.

Mélodies

Chanson (Nouvelle chanson sur un vieil air). Guitare.
Rêverie. L'attente. Le chant de ceux qui s'en vont sur

la mer. Le pas d'armes du Roi Jean. La coccinelle. A quoi bon entendre. Si vous n'avez rien à me dire. Dans ton cœur. Danse macabre. Mélodies persanes, Op 26 – La brise; Sabre en main; Au cimetière; Tournoiement. Marquise, vous souvenez-vous?. La Cigale et la Fourmi. Chanson à boire du vieux temps. Nocturne. Violons dans le soir. Guitares et mandolines. Une flûte invisible. Suzette et Suzon. Aimons-nous. Temps nouveau. Le vent dans la plaine. Grasselette et Maigrelette
François Le Roux *bar* **Krysia Osostowicz** *vn* **Philippa Davies** *fl* **Graham Johnson** *pf*
Hyperion CDA66856 (78' · DDD · T/t)   Ⓕ**O**▷

This is the most resounding blow yet to be struck for the *mélodies* of Saint-Saëns. François Le Roux, with his incisive diction and ability to characterise each song, is a real champion for the man, once so successful, who became, as Graham Johnson puts it in the booklet, 'a footnote' rather than a chapter in the history of French music.

Many of the poems that Saint-Saëns set were used by other composers, for instance 'Dans ton cœur', which became Duparc's *Chanson triste*, by 'Jean Lahor' (Henri Cazalis). The first song of the *Mélodies persanes*, 'La brise', is full of eastern promise, the second, 'Sabre en main' a rollicking bit of toy-soldier galloping away, but just as you're beginning to think that Johnson is shooting himself in the foot by being so ironic about the music they're performing, along comes the hauntingly beautiful fifth song, 'Au cimetière', with its quietly rippling accompaniment and the languorous poem about the lovers sitting on a marble tomb and picking the flowers. Le Roux sings this with controlled, quiet intensity.

Johnson makes the point that it's of little importance from which part of the composer's life the songs come. He embodies that totally French 19th-century style, sometimes anticipating Hahn and Massenet, sometimes harking back to Boïeldieu. If a setting of La Fontaine's fable about the cicada and the ant is pure salon charm, then the final 'Grasselette et Maigrelette' Ronsard *chanson*, composed when Saint-Saëns was 85 in 1920, is a vivacious *café-concert*-style evocation of old Paris.

Samson et Dalila

Samson et Dalila
Plácido Domingo *ten* Samson **Waltraud Meier** *mez* Dalila **Alain Fondary** *bar* Priest **Jean-Philippe Courtis** *bass* Abimelech **Samuel Ramey** *bass* Old Hebrew **Christian Papis** *ten* Messenger **Daniel Galvez-Vallejo** *ten* First Philistine **François Harismendy** *bass* Second Philistine **Chorus and Orchestra of the Bastille Opera, Paris / Myung-Whun Chung**
EMI ② 754470-2 (124' · DDD · T/t)   Ⓕ**OO**▷

This is the most subtly and expertly conducted performance of this work to appear on CD, excellent as others have been in this respect, and also the best played and sung. Chung's

achievement is to have welded the elements of pagan ruthlessness, erotic stimulation and Wagnerian harmony that comprise Saint-Saëns's masterpiece into a convincing whole. His success is based on the essentials of a firm sense of rhythm and timing allied to a realisation of the sensuousness and delicacy of the scoring. Whether in the lamenting of the Hebrews, the forceful music written for the High Priest, the heroics of Samson, the sensual outpourings of Dalila, or the empty rejoicing of the Bacchanale, he and his orchestra strike to the heart of the matter – and that orchestra plays with Gallic finesse, augmented by a dedicated discipline.

The choral singing, though too distantly recorded, is no less alert and refined, with a full range of dynamic contrast. Meier's Dalila is a fascinating portrayal of this equivocal anti-heroine, seductive, wheedling, exerting her female wiles with the twin objects of sexual dominance and political command. All her sense of purpose comes out in her early greeting to the High Priest, 'Salut à mon père'; then she's meditative and expectant as Dalila ponders on her power at 'Se pourrait-il'. The set numbers are all sung with the vocal ease and long phrase of a singer at the zenith of her powers. She makes more of the text than Domingo who sings in his familiar, all-purpose style, admirable in itself, somewhat missing the particular accents brought to this music by the great French tenors of the past. They exist no more and one must salute the sterling and often eloquent tones of Domingo.

Alain Fondary is superb as the High Priest, firm and rich in tone, commanding and vengeful in delivery: the most compelling interpreter of the part on disc, *tout court*. Ramey is luxury casting as the Old Hebrew, but as this is a part once sung by Pinza, Ramey probably felt he wasn't slumming it. After an unsteady start, he sings the small but important role with breadth and dignity. As Abimelech, Jean-Philippe Courtis makes much of little. Apart from the two reservations already made, the recording is admirable, with a wide and spacious sound, and the soloists forward, but well integrated. This must now be the outright recommendation for this work.

Additional recommendation

Vickers Samson **Gorr** Dalila **Paris Opéra Orchestra / Prêtre**
EMI Great Recordings of the Century ② 567598-2 (121' · ADD)   Ⓜ**O**▷
A classic recording with Rita Gorr's magnificent Dalila towering over the performance. Vickers, too, is superb. The sound isn't perfect but don't let that deter you.

King Samson **Ludwig** Dalila **Munich RSO / Patanè**
RCA Red Seal 88697 45118-2 (134' · ADD)   Ⓑ
Not the most idiomatic of recordings but there's some classy singing here, though one would have liked Ludwig to take a few more risks. Patanè presides over everything with passion.

Antonio Salieri
Italian 1750-1825

Salieri studied with Gassmann and others in Vienna, and also knew Gluck (who became his patron) and Metastasio. In 1774 he succeeded Gassmann as court composer and conductor of the Italian opera and from 1788 he was also court Kapellmeister. He made his reputation as a stage composer, writing operas for Vienna from 1768 and presenting several in Italy, 1778-80. Later he dominated Parisian opera with three works of 1784-87; Tarare (1787), his greatest success, established him as Gluck's heir. In 1790 he gave up his duties at the Italian opera. As his style became old-fashioned his works lost favour, and he composed relatively little after 1804, but he remained a central and influential figure in Viennese musical life. His many pupils included Beethoven, Schubert and Liszt.

Overtures

'Overtures & Stage Music'
Overtures and incidental music from Il mondo alla rovescia, Tarare, Axue, re d'Ormus, Palmira, regina di Persia, Die Neger, La grotta di Trofonio, La calamita de' cuori, Daliso e Delmita, Die Hussiten vor Naumburg and L'Angiolina, ossia Il matrimonio per sussurro
Mannheim Mozart Orchestra / Thomas Fey
Hänssler Classic CD98 554 (51' · DDD)　Ⓕ❶❶❶🔁

Poor Antonio Salieri. Once he was a hugely influential musical figure in Vienna, but his reputation waned steeply after 1800; and, inexplicably, he was implicated in the whispered poison theories surrounding Mozart's death.

Rivalry between the two composers may have been due to Salieri's eminence as an opera composer in 1780s Vienna: in all he wrote over 40 works. Thomas Fey's selection of orchestral pieces from 10 of them shows that Salieri was no pushover. Neither is Fey who, as usual, couples individuality in interpretation to dynamic, sizzling conducting and whiplash precision of ensemble. His graphic feel for drama at the heart of music is here sharpened to accommodate the expressive power of the operatic medium. From the rasping blaze of trumpets, high horns and timpani in *Il mondo alla rovescia* to the beautifully shaped *Adagio* from the Sinfonia to *La calamita de' cuori*, Fey's grasp of extremes is a fearless re-creation of Salieri's creative invention. Bravo!

Opera Arias

Armida – E non degg'io seguirla…Vieni a me. La grotta di Trofonio – La ra la. Il ricco d'un giorno – Dopo pranzo addormentata; Eccomi piu che mai. La scuola de' gelosi – Che dunque! La secchia rapita – Questo guajo mancava. Palmira, Regina di Persia – Voi luingate invano; Lungi da me. La fiera di Venezia – Vi sono sposa e amante. La Cifra – E voi da buon marito; Alfin son sola. La finta scema – Se lo

dovessi vendere
Cecilia Bartoli *mez* **Orchestra of the Age of Enlightenment / Adám Fischer**
Decca 475 100-2DH (68' · DDD)　Ⓕ🔁

As the leading figure in Viennese operatic life for some three decades, and successful too in Venice and Paris, Antonio Salieri occupies no inconsiderable position in operatic history. This is a well-chosen selection of music from his Italian operas, in serious, comic and mixed genres. The purely comic pieces are perhaps the least interesting: his conception of comedy is, in the Italian tradition, quite literal and direct. But among the lighter items are a delightfully spirited little 'rustic' piece from *La finta scema* and a charming minuet from *La grotta di Trofonio*, very sharply and neatly characterised here.

That piece was written for Nancy Storace, the English soprano who created Mozart's Susanna. So is the beautiful slow aria from *La scuola de' gelosi*, preceded by a recitative sung with much feeling by Bartoli; the aria itself is a lament for lost love, deeply felt and affecting. So, too, is the rondo from *La cifra*, written for another Mozart singer, Adriana Ferrarese, the first Fiordiligi, again preceded by a forceful recitative, which is reminiscent of Mozart's 'Per pietà', written for Ferrarese shortly after, and which it surely influenced. This is a noble and powerful piece.

Others that demand to be mentioned here include a couple with spectacular orchestral writing: one from *La fiera di Venezia* with solo parts for flute and oboe, a real virtuoso piece, with lots of top Ds, and another from *La secchia rapita* with its dialogues with oboe and its arresting trumpet interventions.

Bartoli is an enormously accomplished artist: every note plumb in the middle, the words always carefully placed, naturally musical phrasing, and beauty and variety of tone. Musicianly and finely modulated playing from the OAE sets off the voice perfectly.

Aulis Sallinen
Finnish b1935

Sallinen studied at the Helsinki Academy (1955-60), where he returned to teach in 1970. After early experimentation with serialism, he adopted a clear, diatonic style that often evokes the cold expanse of Finnish landscapes. With a strong sense of national identity, Finnish traditional melodies often appear in Sallinen's works, and the subject matter of several of his six operas draws on the history and folklore of that country. He has also written eight symphonies, concertos for violin, cello, flute and horn and any number of chamber works.

Orchestral Works

Variations for Orchestra, Op 8. Violin Concerto, Op 18ᵃ. Some aspects of Peltoniemi Hintrik's funeral march, Op 19. The nocturnal dances of Don

Juanquixote, Op 58[b]
[a]Eeva Koskinen vn [b]Torleif Thedéen vc
Tapiola Sinfonietta / Osmo Vänskä
BIS BIS-CD560 (63' · DDD)   (F)

Sallinen's operas and symphonies have stolen the limelight in recent years at the expense of other works fully worthy of attention, as this well-played and well-recorded disc proves. Whereas the Variations (1963) are somewhat anonymous if deftly written, the Violin Concerto (1968) is an altogether maturer work, unusually sombre for so bright a solo instrument, and perhaps the first piece to point to his later stature. His next published work was the Third String Quartet (1969), subtitled *Some aspects of Peltoniemi Hintrik's funeral march*, which, thanks to the Kronos Quartet's advocacy has become one of Sallinen's most heard works This arrangement for string orchestra dates from 1981. *The nocturnal dances of Don Juanquixote* is an extended fantasia for cello and strings, the title being the only parody of Strauss (although a solo violin enters late as Sancho Panza-Leporello!). Sallinen is fond of playing games and all is never as it seems: one can almost hear the collective thud of critics' jaws falling open at this Arnold-like spoof.

The King Goes Forth to France

The King Goes Forth to France
Tommi Hakala *bar* Prince Jyrki Korhonen *bass* Prime Minister Riikka Rantanen *sop* Nice Caroline Lilli Paasikivi *mez* Caroline with the Thick Mane Mari Palo *sop* Anne who Steals Laura Nykänen *contr* Anne who Strips Jyrki Anttila *ten* Guide Herman Wallén *bar* English Archer Kirsi Thum *sop* Queen Santeri Kinnunen *spkr* Froissart Tapiola Chamber Choir; Finnish Philharmonic Choir; Helsinki Philharmonic Orchestra / Okko Kamu
Ondine ② ODE1066-2D (128' · DDD · S/T/t/N)   (F)

The King Goes Forth to France (1980-83) was Sallinen's third opera and is regarded by many commentators as the composer's most problematic. On the contrary, it is the best and most profound, and its impact on Sallinen's subsequent music is incalculable. Subtitled 'Chronicle for the Music Theatre of the Coming Ice Age', *The King Goes Forth* is a bitingly satirical musical allegory. Sallinen has referred to it as a 'fairy-tale for adults' and there are undoubtedly fantastical elements in the storyline, which blends the past, present and one possible future into a dark yet vivid vision of the corruptibility of absolute power.

The premise of the opera, to Paavo Haavikko's libretto based on his own radio play, is this: at some point in the near future, England will be overwhelmed by the advance of a new ice sheet. The Prince, whom the Prime Minister is urging to take a wife (even providing a quartet of nubile candidates: the two Carolines and two Annes), decides instead that the only safe course is to abandon England (and, presumably, the old King) and cross the Channel on a bridge of ice to

resettle in France – where he is declared King. Along the way, however, the events of the Hundred Years War unfold again with the Battle of Crécy and Siege of Calais refought to the same result. In the meantime, the King has married, for political reasons, a German Princess and immediately pawned her (and his crown) to raise funds for his campaign. As Calais falls once more – the tale recorded by a new Froissart – and a storm signals the advance to Paris and the onset of spring, the King instructs his chronicler to omit him from history, abrogating all responsibility, claiming to have been made by Time.

Those familiar with Sallinen's Fourth Symphony, Fifth Quartet or, especially, the orchestral prelude *Shadows* will recognise several strands in the music. Brilliantly scored, the orchestral contribution is crucial, underpinning the foreground action – often with emotional correctives, such as the chirpy march that accompanies the flaying of the Archer – and the word-setting and dramaturgy have the effectiveness of Britten or Henze. The cast is uniformly good, although Tommi Hakala as the King cannot banish memories of Jorma Hynninen in the premiere productions, while Lilli Paasikivi shines as the mentally fragile Caroline with the Thick Mane. Ondine's spectacular sound catches both the quietest ruminations of the four women and the explosive eruptions of the King's great cannon, Parliament. Highly recommended.

Esa-Pekka Salonen   Finnish b1935

Well known as a conductor – he is currently principal conductor of the Philharmonia, after 17 years at the helm of the LAPO – Salonen is also a highly regarded composer. His music is imaginative and approachable with a strong rhythmic sense and a keen ear for colour. Salonen has progressed through a number of stylistic phases during his career as a composer. In the late 1970s when he was studying with Rautavaara at the Sibelius Academy, he wrote in a lyrical, neo-Romantic style; a few years later, after studying in Italy with Donatoni and Castiglioni, he adopted strict serial principals, notably in his Yta series of solo pieces. For a number of years after his conducting career took off in 1983, he had little time for composition, but he began to write once again in the mid-1990s, mostly in larger forms, with a new sense of energy, joie de vivre and orchestral brilliance.

Orchestral works

Foreign Bodies. Insomnia. Wing on Wing[a]
[a]Anu Komsi, [a]Piia Komsi *sops* Finnish Radio Symphony Orchestra / Esa-Pekka Salonen
DG 477 5375GH (67' · DDD)   (F)(B)
The download, available from iTunes, contains a bonus piece, Dichotomie, played by Yefim Bronfman

The immediate sensory impact of these three scores, written between 2001 and 2004, bears out the booklet's claim that for Salonen 'sound first and foremost leads a physical, rather than an intellectual or mental existence'. Would that the densely orchestrated sound and fury which predominates signified something substantial, something truly memorable.

Foreign Bodies, with its governing image of nature under threat, is too amorphous to create a genuinely visceral excitement. The short finale – 'Dance' – works best, with some effective rhythmic cross-cutting, but even this grows clotted in texture: it's too reluctant to expose, juxtapose or superimpose its mechanisms in ways which would bring much-needed light and air to the music.

The 21-minute, single-movement work *Insomnia* displays a similar lack of differentiation, the great washes of sound more effective in keeping a large orchestra busy than in promoting a persuasive musical argument. Finally there's the 26-minute *Wing on Wing*, written for the opening of the LAPO's new base, the Walt Disney Concert Hall, in June 2004. Understatement was clearly not an option, and Salonen's overblown hymn of praise aims to celebrate 'a fusion between instrument and body, nature and technology'. The voice of architect Frank Gehry is electronically treated to produce mysterious, oracular sounds, and a pair of wordless sopranos soar ecstatically above saturated post-Messiaen chorales, in tribute to the imagery of wings and sails which links Gehry's building to the nearby Pacific Ocean.

It seems more than a little ironic that this technically imposing recording should have been made in Helsinki rather than Los Angeles. But the Finnish RSO play magnificently. If you like your music to be 'first and foremost physical', this disc will not disappoint.

Helixª. Piano Concertoᵇ. Dichotomieᶜ
ᵇᶜ**Yefim Bronfman** pf ªᵇ**Los Angeles Philharmonic Orchestra / Esa-Pekka Salonen**
DG 477 8103GH (60' · DDD). Recorded live   Ⓕ**O**▷

Esa-Pekka Salonen's Piano Concerto runs for more than half an hour, barely pausing for breath. The turbulence and energy of the music give it a surreal quality, as if the whole history of the Romantic concerto were being feverishly revisited and reshaped in 2007 with a matter-of-life-and-death urgency. You may hear echoes of any number of august historical figures – Scriabin, Rachmaninov, even Respighi – but the aura is always contemporary. While those composers might recognise Salonen's rhythmic vocabulary and the flamboyant rhetoric of his piano writing, his harmonic palette is something else.

Recorded live in Los Angeles's Walt Disney Concert Hall, this performance has virtuosity and no-holds-barred exuberance in abundance. On early acquaintance it was hard to find enough shape or sense of purpose within the welter of notes, the sheer density of the solo-orchestra mix. But Salonen the composer certainly has the courage of his convictions. *Helix*, written two years before the concerto and less

than a third of its length, is an even more uncompromising demonstration of textural overload, a noisy, relentlessly forceful response to the image of a spiral revolving at increasing speed. Performance and recording are stunning, the audience reaction at the end ecstatic.

Dichotomie (2000) for solo piano provides a useful digest of Salonen's current compositional preoccupations. Its first movement deploys aggressive but constantly shifting rhythmic mechanisms whose origins lie in Prokofiev, while its second seems closer to the flowing spontaneity of the Ligeti *Etudes*. Bronfman's authority in this music is phenomenal and here, at last, you sense a genuine match between medium and message.

Erik Satie   French 1866-1925

The extreme simplicity of many of Satie's pieces, their thin textures and strange, unprepared harmonies coupled with his idiosyncratic sense of humour have led many to view him as the clown (or the madman) of French music. Certainly some of his jokes are as banal as some of his compositions – he holds the dubious distinction of being the world record holder for the longest duration of any piece of music: his Vexations, played in New York in 1963, is a 180-note piano piece with instructions for it to be played 840 times. It took five pianists working in relays overnight to get through it. His colleagues were puzzled by him, a man who worked as a cabaret pianist in Montmartre, wrote popular songs and gave his (mainly piano) compositions titles like Flabby Preludes for a Dog, Bureaucratic Sonata, Desiccated Embryos and Three Pieces in the Shape of a Pear (the last written in response to a critic who said his music had no form). Some are witty, concise, satirical, effervescent; other pieces are more lyrical and reflect his spiritual interests (he was involved with the Rosicrucians).

Listen to his Sarabandes (1887) and you will hear harmonies that anticipate those for which Debussy would later become famous; he rebelled against the excessive emotionalism of the Romantics and the dominating influence of Wagner, and was instrumental in returning music to simpler, sparser textures. Whimsical, unorthodox and musically undereducated, he was 40 when he decided to become a pupil of D'Indy and Roussel. This period of study led him to become more ambitious, resulting in his most famous work, the Cubist ballet Parade, a collaboration with Picasso and Cocteau, commissioned by Diaghilev (the score calls for a siren, a typewriter and a revolver). Revered by the younger French composers, he became the father figure of Les Six, mocking Debussy and the excesses of Impressionism. He died in poverty aged 59 from cirrhosis of the liver.

Piano Works

Six Gnossiennes. Ogives. Petite ouverture à danser. Sarabandes. Trois Gymnopédies
Reinbert de Leeuw pf

Philips 446 672-2PH (67' · DDD)   ℗◉➔

Tender, solemn, droll, silly and occasionally plain boring, Satie's piano music has certainly proved its appeal for performers and record collectors, judging from the number of recitals devoted to it. But this one is out of the ordinary, for unlike the majority of artists, who offer a mixed bag of pieces, Reinbert de Leeuw has chosen music that's entirely solemn and even hieratic in utterance. He begins with the archaically beautiful *Gnossiennes*, taking the first of them unusually slowly but with compelling concentration. The composer's devotees will be thrilled, though you have to surrender completely to get the message of this repetitive, proto-minimalist music. The four *Ogives* derive their name from church architecture, and their unbarred, diatonically simple music has clear affinities with plainchant although, unlike chant, it's richly harmonised. Monotonous it may be, but that's part of its charm, if that term can apply to such a contemplative style. The very brief *Petite ouverture à danser* is a mere meandering sketch in lazy waltz-time, but all Satie is sacred to the converted and the writer of the booklet-essay accords it four lines, finding in it (as translated here) 'a suggestion of indifference, vacillating between a melancholy melody and indecisive harmony'. (Not exactly Beethoven, one might say.) The two pensively sad triptychs of *Sarabandes* and *Gymnopédies* – here very slow yet tonally most refined – complete this finely played and recorded disc, which offers nothing whatsoever of the bouncier *café-concert* Satie.

Alessandro Scarlatti   Italian 1660-1725

As a boy Scarlatti may have studied with Carissimi in Rome. In 1678 he was appointed maestro di cappella of S Giacomo degli Incurabili (now 'in Augusta'). A precocious composer, he wrote two operas during his teens and his second – Gli equivoci nel sembiante – was a huge success. Thereafter opera compositon became the centre of his musical life. It also brought him to the attention of Queen Christina of Sweden, who made him her maestro di cappella.

The 1680s and '90s saw him in Naples where he dominated the opera scene. In 1702 he left with his family for Florence, hoping to secure a position in the household of Prince Ferdinando de' Medici. When this failed to bear fruit, he retruned to Rome as assistant music director at S Maria Maggiore. Opera was banned by the Pope so Scarlatti turned his hand to oratorio and cantatas. In 1706 he was elected to the Arcadian Academy, along with Pasquini and Corelli. A failed attempt to establish himself in Venice, then an important centre for opera, led him back to Rome where he secured a more senior post at S Maria Maggiore. However, composing for the church did not satisfy him and he moved to Naples to work for the Austrian viceroy. He continued to maintain his links with Rome and his important patrons there, and his final opera, La Griselda, was written for Rome in 1721.

Davidis pugna et victoria

Davidis pugna et victoria
Roberta Invernizzi, Robin Johannsen sops
Martin Oro counterten **Fredrik Akselberg** ten
Antonio Abete bass **Academia Montis Regalis /**
Alessandro de Marchi
Hyperion CDA67714 (65' · DDD · T/t)   ℗◉➔

Davidis pugna et victoria is the only one of Alessandro Scarlatti's Latin oratorios now extant, and research suggests very strongly that it was composed about 1680. Its 17th-century musical vocabulary certainly places it closer to Stradella than Vivaldi or Italian Handel.

The oratorio, a learned dramatisation of the story of David and Goliath, is given a crisp performance by Academia Montis Regalis. The full strings are vivid yet supportive in their sporadic contributions, and in numerous short continuo arias the instrumentalists are impressively alert. Alessandro de Marchi does a neat job of conveying Scarlatti's fluent and imaginative writing. The opposing attitudes of the courageous Jonathan and melancholic Saul in the face of impending defeat to the Philistines are sung sensitively by Robin Johannsen and Martin Oro. Roberta Invernizzi's sparkling singing is both heroic and ideally youthful as the boy David, whose spirited confrontation with Antonio Abete's bullying bass Goliath is marvellously enacted. De Marchi avoids overplaying the drama too soon, which allows Scarlatti's astutely constructed climactic scene to peak with contrasts between the bloodthirsty Philistines' massed call to arms and the solitary David's reflective prayer. The choir is full-blooded yet also disciplined; the double chorus 'Heu sodales' cleverly juxtaposes the Philistines' lament for Goliath with Israelite jubilation. A fine addition to the elder Scarlatti's discography.

Dixit Dominus

Dixit Dominus I. Arsi un tempo e l'ardore. Mori, mi dici. O morte, agli altri fosca, a me serena. O selci, o tigre, o ninfa. Sdegno la fiamma estinse. Magnificat a 5 voci
Concerto Italiano / Rinaldo Alessandrini
Naïve OP30350 (59' · DDD · T/t)   ℗

For this setting of *Dixit Dominus* Alessandro Scarlatti harked back to the early 17th century (if not earlier) with some wilfully old-fashioned *stile antico*. Likewise, the *Magnificat* is an exquisite polyphonic composition: it opens with long sustained contrapuntal lines and closes with a flowing 'Amen'. All of the music featured here is simply scored for voices and continuo; choral passages are superbly sung by Concerto Italiano's five singers, and some intimate passages for solo voice accompanied only by theorbo ('Quia respexit humilitatem') require excellent coloratura. Scarlatti's genius as a word-painter and composer for voices is obvious in five superb madrigals.

The two sopranos are infrequently guilty of loose intonation but on the whole Concerto Italiano perform with a commendable juxtaposition of colour and restraint. The close-knit ensemble finely judges sweetly balanced suspensions during *Sdegno la fiamma estinse*. The glorious harmonic unfurling during the opening bars of *O morte, agli altri fosca, a me serena* is worth the price of the disc alone.

Vespers

The Cecilian Vespers. Salve regina. Audi filia, et inclina aurem. Nisi Dominus
Dominique Labelle, Susanne Rydén sops **Ryland Angel** counterten **Michael Slattery** ten **Neal Davies** bass **Philharmonia Chorale and Baroque Orchestra / Nicholas McGegan**
Avie ② AV0048 (131' · DDD/DSD · T/t)
Recorded live Ⓕᐅ

Scarlatti's *Vespers* were composed for a service at the Roman church of Santa Cecilia in Trastevere in 1721. He was in his sixties by then, his music out of fashion, and one can sense that with this friendly commission he was relishing the freedom to be himself, revisiting all his old skills in vocal brilliance, melodic charm, graceful counterpoint and succinctly effective word-setting. There are echoes of Handel and Vivaldi, though given Scarlatti's eminence in his own time it might be more appropriate to think of things the other way round. And if in the end it lacks either Handel's grandeur or Vivaldi's spark, it's palpably the work of a master. The performance is expertly shaped and paced by Nicholas McGegan.

Cain, overo Il primo omicidio

Cain, overo Il primo omicidio Ⓟ
Graciela Oddone, Dorothea Röschmann sops **Bernarda Fink** contr **Richard Croft** ten **Antonio Abete** bass **Academy for Ancient Music, Berlin / René Jacobs** counterten
Harmonia Mundi ② HMC90 1649/50
(138' · DDD · T/t) ⒻOOO

 This is a stunning performance of a remarkable work. It was classified at the time not as an oratorio but as a *trattenimento sacro* ('sacred entertainment'), which suggests that its first performance, in 1707 in Venice, took place in a private palace rather than a church. But Scarlatti brought to the work, besides his seemingly inexhaustible invention, all the dramatic instinct that had made him famous as a composer of operas (of which he had already written about 40). Anyone charged with extracting a 'highlights' selection from this would find themselves in a quandary, since almost every number could be considered a highlight, from the brilliant opening aria for Adam, to two remorseful arias, with affecting chromaticisms, for Eve, and Lucifer (with excited violins) tempting Cain.

Jacobs has assembled an absolutely outstanding cast whose technical accomplishment, dramatic commitment and stylish ornamentation could scarcely be bettered. Furthermore, the instrumental playing is first class.

Stabat mater

Stabat mater[a]. Flute Concerto No 21[b]
[a]**Emma Kirkby** sop [a]**Daniel Taylor** counterten **Theatre of Early Music** ([b]Francis Colpron rec [b]Oliver Brault, [a]Adrian Butterfield, [ab]Hélène Plouffe vns [ab]Susie Napper vc [a]Peter Buckoke, [b]Pierre Cartier, [a]Jeremy Gordon vcs [a]Sylvain Bergeron lte [a]Nicholas Kraemer, [b]Alexander Weimann orgs)
ATMA Baroque ACD2 2237 (51' · DDD · T/t) Ⓕ

Alessandro Scarlatti's celebrated *Stabat mater* was commissioned by a confraternity of aristocrats, the Cavalieri della Vergine dei Dolori, for its annual Lenten service at the Franciscan church of San Luigi in Naples. It remained in use until the confraternity commissioned Pergolesi to compose his famous setting to supplant Scarlatti's old-fashioned music. Both Pergolesi and Scarlatti composed for limited resources, each using two solo voices, two violins and basso continuo. Scarlatti's setting is by no means inferior to Pergolesi's but remains much less familiar, despite several excellent recordings.

This ATMA recording boasts a beautifully captured atmospheric sound, with the perfect amount of reverberation. Daniel Taylor gives an understated and gentle performance. His solos, especially the longest movement, 'Iuxta crucem tecum stare', are the best elements of a performance that is spiritually contemplative rather than dramatic, although the final 'Amen' duet contains dynamic energy.

Although Emma Kirkby's attention to text and style is as admirable as ever, she does not sound at ease and compensates for the loss of clarity by under-singing. Her voice is pinched and vulnerable in some of the divisions during 'Fac ut ardeat'. The Theatre of Early Music excellently capture the contrasts and subtleties in Scarlatti's instrumental parts.

La Griselda

La Griselda
Dorothea Röschmann sop Griselda **Lawrence Zazzo** counterten Gualtiero **Veronica Cangemi** sop Costanza **Bernarda Fink** mez Roberto **Silvia Tro Santafé** mez Ottone **Kobie van Rensburg** ten Corrado **Akademie für Alte Musik Berlin / René Jacobs**
Harmonia Mundi ③ HMC90 1805/7
(3h 2' · DDD · N/T/t) ⒻO

The opera *Griselda* was performed only once at Rome's Teatro Capranica in 1721, towards the end of Alessandro Scarlatti's career. It was probably sponsored by Prince Ruspoli, who'd been Handel's major Roman patron 15 years earlier.

The libretto, adapted from the *Decameron*, portrays Gualtiero, King of Sicily, relentlessly testing his wife Griselda's fidelity. There's a lot of recitative among the irony, deceptions and intense passions, but the action progresses at a compelling pace, and the concise arias are consistently inventive, unpredictable and attractive. Dorothea Röschmann brings dignified integrity to a dangerously subservient title-role, and Lawrence Zazzo's lyrical singing is both sweet and theatrical as the complex Gualtiero. Veronica Cangemi's steely voice is judiciously cast as Griselda's daughter Costanza, and Bernarda Fink is strong and stylish as her lover Roberto. Silvia Tro Santafé is arrogant and dislikable as Ottone, which is entirely right for the King's malcontent villainous servant. Kobie van Rensburg displays marvellous assured coloratura that flows smoothly, and it's good to hear a tenor of such quality in this repertoire.

If *Griselda* represents one of Scarlatti's finest artistic achievements, it's apt that this recording accordingly shares a similarly privileged status within René Jacobs's discography. The conductor is helped by the alert brilliance of the Akademie für Alte Musik Berlin, which clearly relishes the splendid score. Jacobs paces the drama sensitively, and characterises the arias with intelligence. His only sin is overly fussy decisions about restless recitatives in which the continuo is historically implausible and artistically intrusive. Yet whether you love or loathe Jacobs, this is an immensely important achievement. Handel wasn't the only talented opera composer working in the early 18th century, but at long last we've a genuinely credible comparison on disc.

Domenico Scarlatti   Italian 1685-1757

Domenico was the son of Alessandro Scarlatti (see above) and while his father served as maestro di cappella to the viceroy's court in Naples, Domenico was organist and composer. A trip to Venice to seek employment there may have been his first contact with Handel – the two men became long-term friends. He moved to Rome with his father and worked as his assistant at S Maria Maggiore. He worked in Rome for 12 years serving a number of royal and aristicratic employers.

He left Rome in 1719 and, after a period of some years in Palermo, he was employed by the Portuguese Court in Lisbon. Among his many tasks was the musical education of the royal children. When Princess Maria Barbara married the crown prince of Spain in 1733, Scarlatti followed her there and lived first in Seville and then in Madrid for the rest of his life. It was during this peiod that produced the vast body of instrumental music for which he's best known, and in particular the keyboard sonatas. These works extended the genre immeasurably, introducing a virtuosity and brilliance that broke new ground. He was also the author of seven operas (from his Roman period).

Keyboard Sonatas

Keyboard Sonatas Kk1, 3, 8, 9, 11, 17, 24, 25, 27, 29, 87, 96, 113, 141, 146, 173, 213, 214, 247, 259, 268, 283, 284, 380, 386, 387, 404, 443, 519, 520 & 523
Mikhail Pletnev pf
Virgin Classics ② 561961-2 (140' · DDD)   Ⓑ❍❍❍▶

 Every so often a major pianist reclaims Scarlatti for the piano with an outstanding recording. As Ralph Kirkpatrick put it, Scarlatti's harpsichord, while supremely itself, is continually menacing a transformation into something else. True, the relation of the music to harpsichord sound could hardly be closer, and it wouldn't have been composed the way it is for a different instrument. Scarlatti is marvellous at suggesting imaginary orchestrations and stimulating the imagination. He makes us aware of different vantage points as the music passes before us, of the different tones of voice and rhetorical inflexions – as various in these sonatas as the events in them are unpredictable. There are dances, fiestas and processions here, serenades, laments, and evocations of everything from the rudest folk music to courtly entertainments and churchly polyphony; and as the kaleidoscope turns you marvel at the composer who could embrace such diversity, shape it and put it all on to the keyboard.

Pletnev's playing is strongly individual, and his free-ranging poetic licence may not be to your taste. Not that his spectacular virtuosity is likely to be controversial: this really is *hors de catégorie* and enormously enjoyable. And the evocations of the harpsichord are often very witty, but he doesn't shrink from using the full resources of the piano, sustaining pedal included, and if you baulk at the prospect, he may not be for you. The sustaining pedal is certainly dangerous in music that's almost wholly to do with lines, not washes of colour; it can make us see Scarlatti as if through Mendelssohn's eyes. Yet moments of such falsification are rare. Characterisation is everything, and though he can be coy in the reflective sonatas, he generally goes straight to the heart of the matter. The vigorous, full tone in the quick numbers is a joy, and most admirable is the way he makes sound immediately command character. Superb recorded sound.

Keyboard Sonatas Kk3, 54, 141, 145, 175, 162, 177, 185, 199, 208, 248, 249, 299, 310, 484, 492, 531 & 535
Pierre Hantaï hpd
Mirare MIR9918 (68' · DDD)   Ⓕ❍❍

The first track (Kk535) is typical of the quick-moving sonatas that abound in this programme – an astonishing display of dexterity in which the harpsichord he uses (a 1999 copy of an anonymous Thuringian instrument of 1720) and the acoustic help in preserving total clarity. Even at maximum velocity (did Scarlatti and his pupil reach such speeds?) he manages to shape his phrases with microsecond dwellings.

It isn't only the speedy sonatas that are impressive; Kk208 exemplifies his skilful shifts to either side of the pulse in giving the lines a natural 'vocal' quality. It also illuminates Kk185, 310, 199 and 162, in the last of which it's more evident in the playful quicker 'interludes'. The irresistible disc is splendidly annotated by Hantaï and beautifully packaged.

Keyboard Sonatas Kk443, 444, 448, 450, 462, 466, 469, 474, 503, 504, 508, 516, 517, 526, 527, 531, 540, 541, 545 & 548
Frédérick Haas hpd
Calliope CAL9330 (78' · DDD)   Ⓕ

This is a stunning recording. There are some tough nuts here but Haas cracks them with ease and a sense of surging virtuosity. He plays on the warmly resonant but clear-sounding French harpsichord last used by Scott Ross. If you want to introduce Scarlatti to someone you couldn't do it better than by playing this disc. This appears to be a one-off recording but it offers strong temptation as a 'supplement' to anyone already embarked on an integral sonata collection.

Keyboard Sonatas Kk3, 14, 20, 27, 32, 33, 39, 98, 109, 141, 146, 208, 209, 213, 322, 436, 481, 492 & 517
Michael Lewin pf
Naxos 8 553067 (76' · DDD)   ⓈⓄ🔁

Michael Lewin is an American pianist as dexterous and assured as he's audacious. Here there's no sense of 'studio' caution but only of liberating and dazzling music-making, live and on the wing. Kk492 in D could hardly provide a more brilliant curtain-raiser, and in Kk3 in A minor (the one where Scarlatti's impish humour offers the musical equivalent of someone slipping on a banana skin) Lewin's playing positively brims over with high spirits. The D major Sonata, Kk33, is all thrumming guitars and bursts of sunlight and in Kk141, with its cascades of repeated notes, Lewin even gives Martha Argerich a run for her money. There's a no less appealing balm and musical quality in the more restrained numbers such as Kk32 in D minor and Kk208 in A, though the recital comes to a suitably ebullient conclusion with Kk517 in D minor which is here like a river in full spate.

The New York-based recordings are suitably lively. Not even the most persistent lover of Scarlatti on the harpsichord could accuse Michael Lewin of an absence of the necessary glitter, panache and stylistic awareness.

Keyboard Sonatas Kk20, 24, 27, 30, 87, 197, 365, 426, 427, 429, 435, 448, 455, 466, 487, 492 & 545
Yevgeny Sudbin pf
BIS BIS-CD1508 (76' · DDD)   Ⓕ🔁🔁

This generously packed CD is sheer delight from start to finish. Even with recorded selections available from the likes of Horowitz, Pletnev, Schiff and Pogorelich, the 25-year-old Russian pianist Yevgeny Sudbin makes his solo debut on disc with performances of a superlative vitality and super-fine sensitivity.

His choice of sonatas is richly enterprising, pinpointing their infinite variety, their abrupt changes of mood and direction, so that whether familiar or unfamiliar (and there are many unfamiliar numbers), each offering is a delectable surprise. Free from the nervous tension that can sometimes plague him in the concert hall, Sudbin relishes the way Scarlatti turns convention topsy-turvy, presenting him in both performance and his affectionate accompanying essay as one of music's most ardent and life-affirming adventurers. He's brilliant and incisive in Kk545, and makes every bar of the reflective Kk57 glisten with poetry. What thrumming guitars he evokes in Kk435 and 487, reminding us that Scarlatti forsook his native Italy and later Portugal for a heady addiction to all things Spanish.

There are spicy and witty imitations of changing registrations and some notably rumbustious closes to make every facet of these diamond-like sonatas spark and scintillate as if new-minted. This is, arguably, among the finest, certainly most enjoyable of all Scarlatti recitals. As a crowning touch Sudbin is heard in a beautifully warm and natural acoustic.

Giacinto Scelsi   Italian 1905-1988

Of aristocratic birth, Scelsi had no formal training and ranged over many styles in his earlier works while remaining constant to an ideal of music as a link with the transcendental. That remained his conviction in works after the 1950s, in which he often used microtones, thin textures and extremely slow movement.

Choral Music

Complete Choral Works
Three Latin Prayers. Sauh – III; IV. Yliam.
TKRDGª. Antifona sul nome Jesu.
Tre Canti populari. Tre Canti sacri
ªAlan Thomas gtr New London Chamber Choir;
ªPercussive Rotterdam (Wilbert Grootenboer,
Hans Leenders, Norman van Dartel perc) /
James Wood
Accord 465 401-2 (72' · DDD)   Ⓜ

The best known music here is the *Tre Canti sacri*, but just about everything is on a very high level of virtuosity and inspiration. The *Tre Canti populari* are scarcely less inventive.

Scelsi's mysticism encompasses a fair degree of stylistic variety, but repeated listening tends to bring out what unites rather than the opposite.

At the same time, he was capable of assuming strikingly different idioms more or less contemporaneously. The chant-inspired *Three Latin Prayers* and *Antifona* (the former seem like preparatory studies for the latter) both date from 1970, only two years after the *Canti sacri*. The year 1968 also saw the composition of *TKRDG*, which incorporates the strongest Eastern influences, the only instrumental interventions (ably supplied by Percussive Rotterdam and guitarist Alan Thomas), and arguably the most radical aesthetic of this collection. The slightly earlier *Yliam* is marginally reminiscent of the choral music of Ligeti (and indeed Xenakis) from the same period: the treatment of the super-high register is very effective, and admirably dispatched by the sopranos. That adjective describes these performances in the round (with perhaps the exception of the *Three Latin Prayers*, which sound a little tentative).

Scelsi's stature has grown steadily since his death in 1988 and this reissue only adds to his reputation. Within the contemporary choral repertory, it ought to be required listening.

warmth in the third movement *Lento*, and pulses with the most nonchalant glitter in the finale; one guaranteed to strike down less intrepid and fluent spirits with St Vitus's dance.

Emil von Sauer's First Concerto has a style and content to make even the least susceptible listeners' heads nod and feet tap. The Cavatina is as luscious and enchanting as the finale is teasingly brief and light-hearted. Throughout, haunting melodies are embroidered with the finest pianistic tracery. Once again the performance is bewitching. In the Cavatina Hough's caressing, fine-spun tone and long-breathed phrasing are a model for singers as well as pianists, and in the finale there's a lightly deployed virtuosity that epitomises his aristocratic style.

Though the spotlight falls unashamedly on the soloist in such music, the orchestra has no small part in the proceedings, and Lawrence Foster and the CBSO are superbly resilient and enthusiastic, with strings that sing their hearts out. Sound and balance are exemplary. Stephen Heliotis's accompanying notes deserve separate publication for their wit and perspicacity.

Franz Xaver Scharwenka
Polish-German 1850-1924

Scharwenka studied in Berlin. A well-known touring pianist (celebrated as a Chopin interpreter), he became increasingly active as a concert organiser and teacher in Berlin, founding his own conservatory in 1881 (the Klindworth-Scharwenka, with a New York offshoot in 1891).

Piano Concerto No 4

Scharwenka Piano Concerto No 4 in F minor, Op 82
Sauer Piano Concerto No 1 in E minor
Stephen Hough pf **City of Birmingham Symphony Orchestra / Lawrence Foster**
Hyperion CDA66790 (70' · DDD)   Ⓕ**ⓞⓞⓞ**▷

This jewel in the crown in Hyperion's Romantic Piano Concerto series marries flawlessly composer, performance, recording and presentation. Scharwenka's Piano Concerto No 4 is a far cry from his early, ubiquitous success, the E flat minor *Polish Dance*. Grand, Lisztian ambitions are fulfilled and embellished in writing of the most ferocious intricacy; the tarantella finale in particular throws everything at the pianist, seemingly simultaneously. It's therefore hardly surprising that after early triumphs the Fourth Concerto fell into neglect. At its second performance, given in 1910 with Scharwenka as soloist and Mahler as conductor, it was described as being of a 'truly Dionysian and bewildering brilliancy', a phrase that encapsulates Stephen Hough's astonishing performance. For here is scintillating wit and ebullience. As magisterial as it's ear-tickling and affectionate, his playing glows with

Samuel Scheidt
German 1587-1654

Scheidt studied with Sweelinck in Amsterdam before becoming Halle court organist in 1609. In 1619-20 he was also court Kapellmeister. Between 1627 and 1630 he was director of music in Halle, also composing for the Marktkirche. Scheidt was active as an organ expert and a teacher and knew both Schütz and Schein. Scheidt distinguished himself in both keyboard and sacred vocal music, in which he combined traditional counterpoint with the new Italian concerto style. Contrapuntal chorale settings are important among his c150 keyboard pieces and he left some 160 sacred vocal works.

Ludi musici

Ludi musici – Alamande a 4; Canzon ad   Ⓟ
imitationem Bergamas angl a 5; Canzon super
Cantionem Gallicam a 5; Canzon super O Nachbar
Roland a 5; Five Courants a 4; Courant dolorosa a 4;
Two Galliards a 4; Galliard a 5; Galliard battaglia a 5;
Three Paduanas a 4
Hespèrion XX / Jordi Savall viol
Astrée Naïve ES9980 (62' · DDD)   Ⓜ

Scheidt's *Ludi musici* reflects the fusion of English and German traditions in the emergent world of instrumental music in early-17th-century Germany and is a mouth-wateringly diverse and inventive mixture of dance, canzona and variation. These are works which brim over with character and nonchalantly brilliant craftsmanship. Scheidt has that rare knack, for the 1620s and '30s, of sustaining an instrumental piece for more than two minutes without bombarding us with a new idea every

10 bars; the longer pieces such as the Paduanas and the brilliant Canzon a 5 *ad imitationem Bergamas angl*, with its thrilling close, convey admirable long-term direction amid a concentrated love of ephemeral effect. This is a cocktail which Hespèrion XX relishes.

The Pavans are, as you would expect from Jordi Savall, eventful. There are moments when an indulgence from Savall's treble viol stifles the potential for a more reflective allusion, but the overriding effect is of a performer striving to find a meaningful discourse, not content just to 'let the music play itself'; the colour and shape he brings to line and texture is often beguiling (disarmingly poignant in the stillness of the final Paduana), at times too much of a good thing but always engaging.

Johann Heinrich Schmelzer
Austrian c1620/23-1680

Schmelzer was trained in Vienna and served in the court chapel from the mid-1630s, becoming a member of the orchestra in 1649, vice-Kapellmeister in 1671 and Kapellmeister in 1679. The leading Austrian composer of instrumental music before Biber, he wrote 150 ballet suites for court dramatic productions and over 100 sonatas. Schmelzer's prolific output also includes sepolcri and other dramatic pieces, nearly 200 sacred works and some secular vocal music.

Sonatae unarum fidium

Schmelzer Sonatae unarum fidium[b] **Anonymous** [P]
Scordatura Violin Sonata[a] **Bertali** Chiaconna
John Holloway vn [ab]**Aloysia Assenbaum** org
[a]**Lars Ulrik Mortensen** hpd/org
ECM New Series 465 066-2 (63' · DDD)   [F]**OO**[D→]

Johann Heinrich Schmelzer was the first home-grown Kapellmeister to be appointed at the Habsburg Court in Vienna in 1679, following generations of Italians hired for their *oltremontani* flair and easy command of prevailing fashion. Schmelzer's six sonatas from 1664 are certainly Italianate, and not without freewheeling virtuosity, but they also contain a type of extended lyricism and, as in the opening of the Fourth Sonata, a sense of no-nonsense progression of comforting expectation. In fact, this work, and that by his dynamic forebear, Antonio Bertali (whose own *Chiaconna* is quite a party-piece) are typical 17th-century showcases for the violin where intricate and fantastical divisions unfold above a recurring bass pattern. The playing in this technically demanding repertoire is dazzling, and the intonation faultless. Yet equally impressive is John Holloway's measured classicism and subtle poetical restraint. Not every bar of Schmelzer's set is compelling and he opts for a consistent clarity of sound rather than milking every note as if it's of earth-shattering importance; he uses *rubato* discerningly, as in the

introspective musings in the Fifth Sonata where the narrative is beautifully and elegantly articulated. The idea of a double continuo of organ and harpsichord is highly effective throughout. The sense of a rich consort-like texture can only bring a much-needed breadth to music which might otherwise test the concentration over the course of an hour. Holloway and his excellent keyboardists are less extrovert than some, softer-grained and more inclined to hover with sweet and restrained decorum.

Franz Schmidt
Austrian 1874-1939

He first performed as an infant prodigy on the piano and continued his studies with Leschetizky. In 1888 he moved to Vienna, and in 1890 began attending the conservatory of the Gesellschaft der Musikfreunde, where he studied theory and cello. From 1896 to 1911 he was a cellist in the Vienna PO, playing also in the orchestra of the Hofoper from 1896 until 1914. In 1901 he began teaching at the conservatory. After it had been renamed the Hochschule, Schmidt served as both its director (1925-27) and its rector (1927-31). His compositions, which include four symphonies, chamber and organ music and the oratorio Das Buch mit sieben Siegeln (composed 1935-37), show sensitive melodic invention and reveal the influence of Bruckner, Mahler, Reger, Schoenberg and Debussy. Romanticism, Expressionism and atonality can all be found in his music.

Concerto for Piano Left-Hand

Concerto for Piano Left-Hand. Konzertante Variationen über ein Thema von Beethoven
Carlo Grante pf
MDR Symphony Orchestra / Fabio Luisi
Querstand VKJK0611 (79' · DDD)   [F]

Franz Schmidt's works for piano left-hand and orchestra have merited even less coverage than his symphonies. Yet of all his commissions, Paul Wittgenstein valued them the most highly; not least because the balance between soloist and orchestra is so painstakingly achieved. Ironic, then, that both works have long been available only in two-hand editions: expertly prepared, but no match for the poise and subtlety of the originals – as Carlo Grante's performances so eloquently attest.

The *Beethoven* Variations (1922) demonstrate Schmidt's innovative approach to a form too frequently dogged by its inherent limitations. The variations (on the *Scherzo* from the *Spring* Sonata), are grouped in sequences whose contrast of pace and variety of mood ensure a cumulative momentum from the slow introduction to the fugal finale – both of which are an active part of the process. Cast in the familiar three movements, the Piano Concerto (1934) might seem defiantly conventional, and Schmidt's ingenuity in building the work from the unassuming melody heard in the initial *tutti* only gradually becomes clear; notably when the finale's lengthy cadenza recalls the opening material as if setting the seal on the concerto's evolution as a whole.

Grante sets new standards in both works: a noted Busonian, one would expect so keen a response to the elusive coherence of the Variations and revivified classicism of the Concerto. Fabio Luisi displays great conviction and the sound is up to Querstand's high standards. Newcomers are in for a real treat.

Symphonies

Symphony No 1. Notre Dame – Introduction;
Carnival Music; Intermezzo
Malmö Symphony Orchestra / Vassily Sinaisky
Naxos 8 570828 (61' · DDD)　　　　Ⓢ➔

Despite some celebrated past recordings, Franz Schmidt's symphonies have never quite made it into the musical premier league. It is not through lack of championship nor the quality of the works themselves, which is of the highest order.

The quality of Schmidt's music is demonstrated here by the least of his four symphonies, the prize-winning First (1899). Its four expansive movements play for some 45 minutes, the essential qualities of Schmidt's style evident in every bar: attractive melodies in appealing late-Romantic (but not overdone) harmonies with plentiful contrapuntal interest. If not possessing its successors' structural subtleties, the First is a well made and more satisfying whole than many better-known works. True, there are traces of Brahms, Bruckner and Wagner (and even foreshadowings of Elgarian *nobilmente* in the finale), but Schmidt's own voice shines through.

So it does in the splendid extracts from the first act of his opera *Notre Dame* (1902-04), of which the Intermezzo shows the lyrical Hungarian side of Schmidt's musical personality to radiant effect. Sinaisky directs searching accounts of the works here and the Malmö players relish the task of tackling this repertoire. For those unfamiliar with Schmidt this newcomer makes a fine introduction.

Symphony No 2. Fuga solemnis[a]
[a]**Anders Johnsson** org **Malmö Symphony Orchestra / Vassily Sinaisky**
Naxos 8 570589 (63' · DDD) Ⓢ➔

Composed in 1911-13, Schmidt's Second Symphony remains that rare combination, a work of tremendous immediate appeal and a compositional *tour de force*. Its three movements share thematic links reinforcing the impression of craftsmanship about this score, but the exuberance of the melodic invention and rich orchestration sweep such academic considerations aside through its sheer physical impact.

It is this physicality that makes such a lasting impression, such that once heard it is not forgot-

ten. Thus the beguiling opening paragraph draws one into what seems a benign and peaceful musical environment only for this to be swept away by the invigorating developments that ensue.

Sinaisky and the Malmö Symphony get into the swing of Schmidt's freewheeling invention and with a splendid recording from Naxos at super-budget price this is self-recommending. And there is the added bonus of the late, celebratory *Fuga solemnis* for organ, brass and percussion (1937), written to inaugurate a new instrument in Vienna. Even if one has the symphony already, do try this newcomer.

Das Buch mit sieben Siegeln

Das Buch mit sieben Siegeln
Johannes Chum ten St John **Robert Holl** bass-bar
Voice of the Lord **Sandra Trattnigg** sop **Michelle Breedt** mez **Nikolai Schukoff** ten Manfred Hemm bass **Robert Kovács** org **Wiener Singverein; North Austrian Tonkünstler Orchestra / Kristjan Järvi**
Chandos ② ＿＿ CHSA5061 (114' · DDD · T/t)
Recorded live 2005　　　　Ⓜ➔

Best known for his work with the left-field Absolute Ensemble, Kristjan Järvi might not be thought a natural exponent but there can be no doubting his conviction. He is abetted by a strong vocal line-up: Johannes Chum is a youthful and forthright St John who, though a little strained in his initial entry, exudes the right impulsiveness and awe; Robert Holl is eloquently authoritative as the Voice of the Lord; and with the remaining quartet well contrasted as soloists and finely balanced in ensemble. The Wiener Singverein lack nothing in either incisiveness or sensitivity, while the Tonkünstler Orchestra, if a mite undernourished in string sound, are more than equal to Schmidt's surprisingly wide-ranging demands.

Surprising in that this is a piece which marks a culmination within the Austro-German choral tradition and yet looks defiantly to its future – an aspect Järvi pointedly emphasises – whether in the stark expressive contrasts as the Seven Seals are opened, the powerful momentum unleashed by the Seven Trumpets, or the climactic 'Hallelujah' chorus whose grandeur is charged with a keen fervency.

More evocative than Franz Welser-Möst (EMI) but less theatrical than Nikolaus Harnoncourt (BMG), Järvi makes it the concert-drama Schmidt surely intended. SACD sound maximises its textural and dynamic extremes, but a pity that applause was retained at the end of disc 1. Even so, this could well be first choice for those new to the work.

Alfred Schnittke　　　　USSR 1934-1998

Schnittke was a pupil of Rakov and Golubev at the Moscow Conservatory (1953-61), where he taught until 1972. Thereafter, he supported himself mainly by composing film scores and composed nearly 70 scores in 30 years. Schnittke converted to Christianity and possessed deeply held mystic beliefs which influenced his music. He was often the target of the Soviet bureaucracy. His First Symphony was effectively banned by the Composers' Union, and after he abstained from a Composers' Union vote in 1980, he was banned from travelling outside of the USSR. In 1985 Schnittke suffered a stroke. In 1990 he left Russia and settled in Hamburg where he died in 1998. His works often use quotations, parodies and stylistic imitations. His output includes nine symphonies, various stage works, five concerti grossi, four violin concertos, two violin sonatas and much chamber music.

Cello Concertos

Cello Concertos – No 1[a]; No 2[b]. Concerto grosso No 2[c]. Cello Sonatas[d] – No 1; No 2
Alexander Ivashkin vc
[c]**Tatjana Grindenko** vn [d]**Irina Schnittke** pf
[ab]**Russian State Symphony Orchestra /**
Valéri Polyansky
Chandos ② CHAN241-39 (153' · DDD)   Ⓜ🠒

Schnittke's Cello Concerto No 1 was written in the months after his first devastating stroke in 1985 and gives a grim portrayal of the composer's psychological terror and disorientation, to the point where you start to empathise. Polystylistic jump-cuts, once the result of political repression, flip inwards as mournful intoning slams against feral, expressionistic orchestral screams. Schnittke lays it on with a trowel, but his genius for building dialectic tension between competing harmonies raises his argument above the vanilla juxtapositions of lesser composers. When Schnittke returned home from hospital he had no memory of sketches he'd already made for his concerto – these narrative disjoints are painfully authentic.

The Concerto No 1 is one of Schnittke's most recorded works, but it would be difficult to imagine a more physically committed performance than Alexander Ivashkin's. The Cello Concerto No 2 was written in 1990 and is less in-your-face. A Viennese waltz that sounds like it's been reharmonized by Berg briefly wanders into focus, hinting at Schnittke's earlier compositional techniques. But 'borrowed' reference-points are now more distilled, and the work spends 40 minutes amplifying and reinvestigating the implications of its opening moments, as the orchestra sits on the soloist's attempts to generate more extended gestures.

Chandos has added Schnittke's two cello sonatas to this reissued pairing of the concertos. The First is archetypal Schnittke, with grave slow opening and closing movements interrupted by the black humour of an intervening *Scherzo*, in this case characterised by dense tone clusters and bizarre *pizzicato* cello figurations. Impetus is turned on its head – progress gets increasingly staggered to create a kind of anti-momentum, a paradox that Ivashkin exploits keenly. The apho-

ristic Second Sonata is less imposing, and the 'wrong-note' humour of the *Concerto grosso* No 2 is a brand of Schnittke that may be something of an acquired taste, but that's neither here nor there – here's the definitive document of Schnittke's relationship with the cello.

Piano Quintet

Schnittke Piano Quintet[a] **Shostakovich** String Quartet No 15 in E flat minor, Op 144
[a]**Alexei Lubimov** pf **Keller Quartet** (András Keller, János Pilz vns Zoltán Gál va Judit Szabó vc)
ECM New Series 461 815-2 (65' · DDD)   Ⓕ

Just as Schnittke's First Symphony picks up the threads from Shostakovich's last, so his Piano Quintet feels like the natural successor to Shostakovich's last string quartet; that makes ECM's coupling of the two chamber works an effective and thought-provoking one, the more so since both performances are of the highest quality.

This music is a good deal harder to bring off than it looks. The textures are emaciated, and the pain of emotional starvation needs to register with unremitting intensity. In Schnittke's solo piano opening, Alexei Lubimov shows the requisite temperament and control of sonority, and both he and the Kellers keep us inside the Quintet's world through the first movement's obsessive, quarter-tone-inflected bell-tolling, through the ghost-train-ride of the film-derived *Tempo di valse*, through the catatonic laments of the two succeeding slow movements, all the way to the anxious transfigurations of the finale. Curiously, Lubimov goes against the score in the final phrase, where Schnittke asks for pitched notes to fade into the noise of fingertips tapping on the keys, echoing the pedal-knocking at the end of the first movement. But his carefully graded *diminuendo* is effective enough in its own way.

Single-disc versions of Shostakovich's valedictory quartet are surprisingly thin on the ground. Here, too, the Kellers can stand comparison with the very finest. Shostakovich's parched and starved textures can be made to sound even more discomforting, but the Kellers' tonal control brings out its own range of nuance. Recording quality is nicely judged, the players being set in a nicely unobtrusive perspective.

Violin Sonatas

Violin Sonatas – No 1; No 2, 'Quasi una Sonata'; No 3. Gratulations rondo. Stille Nacht. Suite in the Old Style
Francesco d'Orazio vn **Giampaolo Nuti** pf
Stradivarius STR33675 (75' · DDD)   Ⓕ

Schnittke's music for violin and piano spans most of his composing career, from the early 1960s, when Shostakovich's genius and Soviet ideology both loomed large, to the mid-1990s, a time of freedom and desperate illness. The three sonatas and three other works chart

Schnittke's sad but heroic decline, as he confronted head-on the special 20th-century challenge of composing from the heart as well as from a sense of history.

The First Sonata (1963) is probably the best of the six compositions. There's already plenty of that sardonic, to-hell-with-it manner he made his own, but his willingness to grapple with the possibilities of well-made instrumental design and to admit a sense of pathos that didn't exclude touches of understatement make for a memorable 15 minutes. By comparison, the Second Sonata (1968) is more slapdash, not polystylistic enough to engineer the surreal confrontations of his most powerful exercises in bringing old and new into collision, its climactic bashings-out of a minor triad as dated as they are annoying. In the Third Sonata (1994) the earlier energy hasn't totally drained away, and the poignancy of a musical voice facing its own imminent extinction still gets through. Hearing this after the winsome pastiche of the *Suite in Old Style*, the po-faced Mozartisms of the *Gratulations rondo*, and the crude but unfailingly shudder-making deconstruction of *Stille Nacht* is moving, with its hints of what might have been had Schnittke lived in more stable times. Francesco d'Orazio, as recorded here, doesn't have the full-bodied tone and blazingly forthright rhetoric of a Russian violinist like Mark Lubotsky, for whom Schnittke composed. But he shapes the sonatas well, and has strong support from Giampaolo Nuti.

Concerto for Choir

Concerto for Choir. Requiem[a]
Prague Philharmonic Choir; [a]members of the
Prague Philharmonia / Jaroslav Brych
Praga Digitals PRD350 044 (66' · DDD)　　　Ⓕ

Had Alfred Schnittke's Concerto for Choir been written in 1975 rather than '85, it would have necessarily been a different piece. Mikhail Gorbachev took office in 1985 and Schnittke, perhaps sniffing the profound change that was about to sweep his country, thought it was timely to reaffirm a core Russian identity. Consequently his Concerto is that rarest of beasts – a Schnittke work that is unequivocally sincere, and evolves organically rather than through a dialogue of competing styles.

With the Prague Philharmonic Choir you get authentic east European enunciation and those boomy, sonorous low male voices raise the emotional temperature to at least the power 10. Getting the 'right' sound for the Concerto is vital. Schnittke's basic melodic contours and modal harmonies are rooted in his deep understanding of the Orthodox choral tradition, but he loads his piece with intricate complexities and ambiguous shadings: the occasional tart dissonance tells of now, and ebbing-and-flowing chromatic tumbles are strategically balanced against authentic open 'perfect' intervals. The second movement's conclusion may feel like an antici-

pation of Holy Minimalism, but this bountiful score makes John Tavener and his like sound like intellectual cowards.

Schnittke's Requiem was indeed written in 1975 and is full of trademark incongruous clashes and grotesque theatricals. Rockist electric guitars and, in the *Credo*, a brief input of kit drumming symbolise a spirit of defiance. It's another powerful performance on an unfailingly top-notch disc.

12 Penitential Psalms

12 Penitential Psalms
Swedish Radio Choir / Tõnu Kaljuste
ECM New Series 453 513-2 (53' · DDD · T/t)　　Ⓕ Ⓞ

Schnittke's 12 *Penitential Psalms* (1988) aren't biblical: Nos 1-11 use 16th-century Russian texts and No 12 is a wordless meditation which encapsulates the spirit and style of what precedes it. Though at times dark and despairing in tone, this is in no sense liturgical music. It's too expansive, and reaches towards the ecstatic too consistently, to qualify as ascetic or austere. Indeed, the warmly euphonious chorale-like textures with which several of the movements end are sumptuous enough for one to imagine a soulful saxophone weaving its way through them. As this suggests, the recording is extremely, and not inappropriately, resonant, and the performance is polished to a fault, the individual lines superbly controlled and the textures balanced with a fine feeling for their weight and diversity. Although some may find this issue a little too refined, it realises the work's expressive world with imposing and irresistible authenticity. In these works, Schnittke seems to be doing penance for the extravagant indulgences of pieces such as *Stille Nacht* and the Viola Concerto, abandoning modernism in general and Expressionism in particular. The music nevertheless retains strong links with the images of lament and spiritual aspiration, and there's nothing in the least artificial or contrived about its emotional aura. It's difficult to imagine a more convincing or better recorded account of it than this one.

Othmar Schoeck　　Swiss 1886-1957

One of the leading Swiss composers of his time, Schoeck studied at the Zürich Conservatory and with Max Reger in Leipzig (1907-08). His appointment as conductor of the St Gall Symphony Orchestra (with special permission to remain resident in Zürich), combined with an annuity from his patron Werner Reinhart, allowed Schoeck to give up his jobs as chorus director and to compose more or less undisturbed. His numerous songs, usually setting German Romantic poetry, establish him among the foremost Lieder composers, but he also wrote important operas: the dense and richly scored Penthesilea (1927) and

Vom Fischer und syner Fru (1930). The rest of his output includes choral and orchestral scores, and a few chamber pieces.

Cello Concerto, Op 61

Cello Concerto[a]. Cello Sonata[b]. Song Transcriptions[b] – Der Reisebecher, Op 60 No 19; Epigramm, Op 31 No 5; 12 Lieder, Op 30 – Nachklang; Winternacht; Nacht. In der Herberge, Op 7 No 3
Christian Poltéra vc [b]**Julius Drake** pf
[a]**Malmö Symphony Orchestra / Tuomas Ollila**
BIS BIS-CD1597 (62' · DDD)   Ⓕ Ⓞ

Of Schoeck's three concertos, that for cello (1947) is among his last pieces and exudes an autumnal spirit. Its opening *Allegro* is among the composer's most successful sonata movements, generating no mean rhythmic momentum in spite of its predilection for long-breathed melodic lines, and purposefully sustaining its considerable length. The slow movement is the emotional heart – a luminous threnody in which the interplay of cello and strings is particularly felicitous. A brief but animated *Scherzo* and a finale that recalls earlier themes, while maintaining impetus on the way to a decisive conclusion, complete a work that ought to find its way into the still-limited cello canon now the Schumann Concerto has become firmly established.

Christian Poltéra taps its ruminative depths unerringly and receives sensitive support from the Malmö Symphony strings under the direction of Tuomas Ollila. Julius Drake is equally responsive in the remaining pieces. The Cello Sonata remained incomplete at Schoeck's death: if its first movement evinces a certain weariness, the pert *Scherzo* and songful *Andantino* suggest a work likely to become more than the sum of its parts. The song transcriptions (presumably by Poltéra) are idiomatically done; that of the winsome 'Nachklang' deserves to be an encore in every cellist's repertoire. Warmly spacious sound and informative booklet-notes round out this desirable debut from a highly promising cellist.

Notturno, Op 47

Notturno
Christian Gerhaher bar **Rosamunde Quartet**
(Andreas Reiner, Diane Pascal vns Helmut Nicolai va Anja Lechner vc)
ECM New Series 476 6995 (44' · DDD)   Ⓕ Ⓞ ➔

Notturno is described not as a song-cycle but as 'Five movements for string quartet and voice'. All but one of the poems are by Nikolaus Lenau (1802-50); the last is a prose poem by Gottfried Keller (1819-90).

One doesn't hear much of Othmar Schoeck these days, though he was championed by Fischer-Dieskau, who recorded *Notturno* and the earlier work for baritone and orchestra, *Lebendig begraben*. And it's Fischer-Dieskau who

comes to mind, uncannily so, in the opening phrases of this performance. *Notturno*, completed in 1933, was inspired by a love affair between Schoeck and a woman called Mary de Senger that had ended 10 years previously. A triplet phrase associated with Mary recurs throughout the piece; the word-setting is syllabic, the style Expressionist, like Berg on an off-day, with a dash of Debussy in the first of two interludes for the strings alone.

It's all pretty unlovable at first, but parts of it grow on you. 'Blick in den Strom', the fourth poem in the long opening movement, is anchored by a pedal C on the cello while the restless second violin and viola depict the stream of the title. And Schoeck's setting of the Keller prose poem is a real surprise: pure C major (with a few chromatic inflexions), the strings sustaining chords over a simple ground bass. It makes a haunting contrast to the prevailing gloom.

The performance is admirable, the intensity and beauty of Christian Gerhaher's singing matched by the quartet. The booklet-note is indispensable for the background but the analysis is a bit of a muddle.

Penthesilea

Penthesilea
Helga Dernesch sop Penthesilea **Jane Marsh** sop Prothoe **Mechtild Gessendorf** sop Meroe **Marjana Lipovšek** mez High Priestess **Gabriele Sima** sop Priestess **Theo Adam** bass-bar Achilles **Horst Hiestermann** ten Diomede **Peter Weber** bass Herold **Austrian Radio Chorus and Symphony Orchestra / Gerd Albrecht**
Orfeo C364 941B (80' · ADD · N/T)
Recorded live 1982   Ⓕ

Schoeck's one-act opera *Penthesilea* is an astonishing and masterly score. It seems barely credible that a work so gripping in its dramatic intensity, and so powerful in atmosphere, should be so little known. It has the listener on the edge of the seat throughout its 80 short minutes and, like any great opera, it continues to cast a spell long after the music has ended. In the *Grove Dictionary of Opera*, Ronald Crichton wrote that 'at its most intense, the language of *Penthesilea* surpasses in ferocity Strauss's *Elektra*, a work with which it invites comparison'. In so far as it's a one-act work, set in the Ancient World, highly concentrated in feeling and with strongly delineated characters, it's difficult not to think of Strauss's masterpiece. Yet its sound world is quite distinctive. Though he's a lesser figure, Schoeck similarly renders the familiar language of Straussian opera entirely his own. The vocabulary isn't dissimilar yet the world is different. We are immediately plunged into a vivid and completely individual world, packed with dramatic incident: off-stage war cries and exciting, dissonant trumpet calls. There's an almost symphonic handling of pace, but the sonorities are unusual: for example, there's a strong wind section, some 10 clarinets at various pitches, while there are only a handful of violins; much use is made of two pianos in a way that at times almost anticipates Britten.

This performance emanates from the 1982 Salzburg Festival; Helga Dernesch in the title-role commands the appropriate range of emotions as Penthesilea and the remainder of the cast, including the Achilles of Theo Adam, rise to the occasion. The important choral role and the orchestral playing under Gerd Albrecht are eminently committed and the recording is good. There's a useful essay and libretto, though in German, not English.

Arnold Schoenberg
Austro/Hungarian 1874-1951

The events in the life of this brave giant can be briefly sketched; his music and his ideas need a book to themselves. His father Samuel, who ran a shoe shop and sang in local choral societies, died when Schoenberg was 16, forcing him to take a job in a bank to support his mother and sister. For the man who was to become the most revered musical theoretician of the age and a great teacher, Schoenberg had remarkably little formal training, mainly gained from counterpoint lessons with Alexander Zemlinsky, who became his brother-in-law in 1901.

To those who think of Schoenberg as a purveyor of 'squeaky-gate' music, it comes as a surprise to hear his first two undoubted masterpieces, Verklärte Nacht ('Transfigured Night') (1899) and the mammoth Gurrelieder (1911), for they are lusciously scored, richly Romantic works in the traditions of Brahms and Wagner. From the early 1900s onwards he became increasingly adventurous and his compositions provoked a furore whenever they were played. Why? Schoenberg was frustrated by what he saw as the limitations of current musical language. What Wagner and others had been hinting at, he now openly embraced: music that, for the first time, had no key – atonal music. The sounds that emerged were greeted with incomprehension; it seemed to those listening as though they were being subjected to an assault of cacophonous, random, improvised notes. This wasn't music as they understood it – and indeed Schoenberg was writing in a new language, so how could they understand? This was meaningless gibberish.

After a spell in Berlin where he conducted a kind of intellectual cabaret called Überbrettl, he moved back to Vienna, devoting himself to composition and teaching, gradually assimilating a reputation as a formidable musical thinker and attracting a group of devoted disciples who shared his experimental aims, among them Alban Berg and Anton von Webern, a group that musical history now refers to as the Second Viennese School (as opposed to the school of Haydn and Mozart). Critical hostility to his music in Vienna extended to anti-Semitic smears and violent abuse. But Schoenberg pugnaciously held his ground.

*During the First World War he served sporadically in the Austrian Army. Once the conflict had ceased, discouraged by the lack of performances of his work, he formed the Society for Private Perform-*ances. *Here his music and that of his followers could be heard in ideal conditions – critics were not invited. In 1922, about the time the Society was disbanded, he began work on the Suite for Piano, Op 25, the first formal 12-tone piece to be composed.*

Three years later he was made a professor at the Prussian Academy of Arts in Berlin. The rise of the Nazis ensured that he was dismissed from his post. Although born a Jew, he had converted to the Christian faith in 1898; moving to Paris in 1933, confronted with the German persecution of Jews, he reconverted to Judaism and left Europe for America.

The first year he spent in Boston, but in 1935 he was made a professor at the University of Southern California, moving on to UCLA in 1936. Here he taught until 1944 when he reached the mandatory retirement age of 70. In April 1941 he became an American citizen; he died in Los Angeles.

Piano Concerto, Op 42

Schoenberg Piano Concerto[a]. Drei Klavierstücke, Op 11. Sechs Klavierstücke, Op 19 **Berg** Sonata for Piano, Op 1 **Webern** Variations, Op 27
Mitsuko Uchida pf
[a]**Cleveland Orchestra / Pierre Boulez**
Philips 468 033-2PH (63' · DDD)　Ⓕ❍❍❍▷

Uchida's distinctive musical personality and outstanding technique make her Schoenberg, Berg and Webern well worth hearing, however many other version of these works you have in your collection. She brings a marvellous spontaneity and sense of drama to the more overtly Romantic compositions here – Berg's Sonata and Schoenberg's Op 11 *Pieces*. This certainly isn't one of those accounts of the Berg where you question the composer's wisdom in marking the first section for repeat. As for the Schoenberg, never has one been more aware of this music's closeness in time and spirit to the cataclysmic world of the monodrama *Erwartung*. Uchida's earlier recording of Op 11 was warmly praised, and this one is no less accomplished. Elsewhere, her relish for strongly juxtaposed contrast risks occasional over-emphasis, as in the third of the Op 19 pieces, and the virtues of more sharply articulated playing in this repertory are demonstrated on Peter Hill's admirable super-bargain-price Naxos disc. His account of Webern's *Variations* is exemplary in its clarity and feeling for line; yet Uchida manages to suggest deeper links with more Romantic perspectives without in any way traducing the music's inherent radicalism.

Links with Romanticism are even more explicit in the texture and thematic character of Schoenberg's Concerto, and this performance places the work firmly in the tradition of Liszt and Brahms. Not even Pierre Boulez can bring ideal lucidity to the occasionally lumpy orchestral writing, but the performance as a whole, with excellent sound, has an attractive sweep and directness of utterance.

Violin Concerto, Op 36

Schoenberg Violin Concerto
Sibelius Violin Concerto
Hilary Hahn *vn* **Swedish Radio Symphony Orchestra / Esa-Pekka Salonen**
DG 477 7346GH (63' · DDD) Ⓕ❍❍❍❍▷

Hilary Hahn's performance of Schoenberg's Concerto is magnificent recording. When the last chord sounds its full stop, the sense of satisfied finality is exhilarating. Hahn has the full of measure of the piece, its gawky lyricism, ethereal filigree and cripplingly difficult cadenzas (awkward chords galore), all rendered seemingly effortless. Wisps of old-world Vienna echo from the *Andante*, whereas in a performance of this calibre the finale's complex acrobatics suddenly have musical meaning. Of course, having a first-rate orchestra and conductor helps: Esa-Pekka Salonen's direction is in the very best sense of the term 'slick', a perfect example of musical badinage, alert, crystal-clear and superbly recorded. Which makes the CD mandatory listening both for lovers of the work who crave an appreciative performance and for doubters who still await conversion.

The Sibelius performance is fascinating but less wholly convincing, although as with the Schoenberg Hahn weaves a seductive, evenly deployed tone and her technique is impeccable. But while in the Schoenberg you sense a palpable level of emotional engagement, Hahn's approach to Sibelius is cool, sphinx-like one might say, the first movement's many solo passages broadly drawn but somehow remote. No violinist currently performing makes a lovelier sound and although time and again one notes some illuminating phrase (not to mention Salonen's immaculately groomed accompaniment) the sum effect is of a strangely cold beauty. But the Schoenberg performance is magnificent.

Violin Concerto, Op 36[a]. Dreimal tausend Jahre, Op 50[ab]. Psalm 130, 'De profundis', Op 50[b]. Ode to Napoleon, Op 41[c]. A Survivor from Warsaw, Op 46[d]. Prelude to Genesis, Op 44[e]
[cd]**David Wilson-Johnson** *spkr*
[a]**Rolf Schulte** *vn* [c]**Jeremy Denk** *pf*
[c]**Fred Sherry Quartet**; [bde]**Simon Joly Chorale**; [ade]**Philharmonia Orchestra / Robert Craft**
Naxos 8 557528 (71' · DDD) ⓈⒹ▷

Hilary Hahn's recording of Schoenberg's Violin Concerto (see above) paraded cool beauty where others could find only sweat and tears. Yes, an overstatement perhaps – Louis Krasner and Israel Baker, for example, are among a few honourable exceptions.

Rolf Schulte and Robert Craft credibly project a work that sounds like an extension of Brahms's language in terms of Schoenberg's treatment of the orchestra and his melodic structures. Schulte's performance reminds one of Huberman's *bon mot* about Brahms setting the violin against the orchestra: it's a gutsy, fiercely intense inter-

pretation with next to nothing of Hahn's centredness about it, though Craft's sane but enthusiastic conducting assures a workable temperature beyond the solo line. It's attractive but the sensation of Hahn holding her poise in the eye of a storm is preferable.

Most of Craft's programme is fervid stuff. Both *A Survivor from Warsaw* and *Ode to Napoleon* are fired-up reactions to the Second World War, the former – a concise and startling music drama magnificently scored for full orchestra – is a chilling slice of narrative about Nazi brutality; the latter – a 15-minute chamber work that waves a clenched fist for the duration – is a bold indictment of totalitarianism, based on a poem by Byron. Both works place English recitations centre stage, declaimed with clarity and dramatic zeal by David Wilson-Johnson.

Craft's direction is very much 'straight from the hip', and the results are at the very least humbling. The *Genesis Prelude* is terse and powerful, and the two choral works, both at times starkly beautiful, take their prompts from Schoenberg's Jewish roots.

This is not an easy programme to take in at a single sitting, but it's a valuable one; an essential addition to Craft's invaluable Schoenberg series.

Chamber Symphony No 2, Op 38

Chamber Symphony No 2[a].
Wind Quintet, Op 26[b]. Die glückliche Hand, Op 18[c]
[c]**Mark Beesley** *bar* [b]**New York Woodwind Quintet**;
[ac]**Philharmonia Orchestra / Robert Craft**
Naxos 8 557526 (79' · DDD) Ⓢ

This eighth instalment of Robert Craft's Naxos cycle touches the polar opposites of Schoenberg's output. The radiant Chamber Symphony No 2 might be a beloved classic if Schoenberg hadn't so comprehensively queered his pitch elsewhere, while the Wind Quintet represents darkest deepest 'elsewhere', a work to challenge even the most devoted Schoenbergian.

This magisterial recording of the Quintet from the New York Woodwind Quintet marks a new plateau in our understanding of the work. As Craft's notes testify, performances during Schoenberg's life were normally conducted and lasted around an hour. This lithe, quicksilver version clocks in at 38 minutes and, with the right tempi restored, Schoenberg's contrapuntal labyrinth sparks into life. Melodic motifs evolve and morph into new terrain with profound inevitability, while his harmonic daring and recherché timbres now feel holistically connected.

The Chamber Symphony No 2 is another work where intellectual energy equates to a virtuoso instrumental showdown. The Philharmonia are fully engaged and Craft's fastidious approach makes every little detail count: but, as the cumulative impact of the second movement demonstrates, his ear is also focused on the larger picture. The 20-minute melodrama *Die glückliche Hand* sits in the stylistic overlap between Quintet and Symphony. Mark Beesley's small but anchoring role is powerfully executed, while Craft's artful unpicking of the prickly orchestral and choral writing places the listener at the core of Schoenberg's dream-world.

Verklärte Nacht, Op 4

Verklärte Nacht. Pelleas und Melisande, Op 5
Berlin Philharmonic Orchestra /
Herbert von Karajan
DG The Originals 457 721-2GOR (74' · ADD)
Recorded 1973-74   ⓂⓄⓄⓄ⯈

This is a very distinguished coupling, superbly played by the BPO – a truly 'legendary' reissue, quite unsurpassed on record. Karajan never approached contemporary music with the innate radicalism and inside knowledge of a composer-conductor like Boulez; yet he can't be accused of distorting reality by casting a pall of late-Romantic opulence and languor over these works. He's understandably most at home in the expansive and often openly tragic atmosphere of Schoenberg's early tone-poems *Verklärte Nacht* and *Pelleas und Melisande*. The richly blended playing of the BPO provides the ideal medium for Karajan's seamless projection of structure and expression. He remains especially sensitive to the music's lyricism, to the connections that to his ears override the contrasts. Although *Verklärte Nacht* has certainly been heard in performances less redolent of 19th-century tradition, as well as less calculated in its recorded acoustic, this remains a powerfully dramatic reading. One man's view, then: but, given the man, a notably fascinating one.

Schoenberg Verklärte Nacht (original version)   Ⓗ
Schubert String Quintet in C, D956
Alvin Dinkin va **Kurt Reher** vc **Hollywood Quartet**
(Felix Slatkin, Paul Shure vns Paul Robyn va
Eleanor Aller vc)
Testament mono SBT1031 (73' · ADD)
Recorded 1950-51   ⒻⓄⓄⓄ

This was the first ever recording of *Verklärte Nacht* in its original sextet form and it remains unsurpassed. When it was first reviewed in *Gramophone*, the late Lionel Salter wrote of it as being 'beautifully played with the most careful attention to details of dynamics and phrasing, with unfailing finesse, with consistently sympathetic tone, and, most important, with a firm sense of the basic structure'. The Schubert too fully deserves its classic status. The tranquillity of the slow movement has never been conveyed with greater nobility or more perfect control.

The Hollywood Quartet made music for the sheer love of it and as a relaxation from their duties in the film-studio orchestras, for which they were conspicuously over-qualified. They have incomparable ensemble and blend; and their impeccable technical address and consummate tonal refinement silence criticism. To add to the pleasure, the transfers could not be better.

Variations for Orchestra, Op 31

Variations for Orchestra. Pelleas und Melisande
Chicago Symphony Orchestra / Pierre Boulez
Erato 2292 45827-2 (62' · DDD)   ⒻⓄⓄ

The two faces of Schoenberg could scarcely be more starkly juxtaposed than they are on this superbly performed and magnificently recorded disc – Boulez and the CSO at their formidable best. *Pelleas und Melisande* can be taken not only as Schoenberg's 'answer' to Debussy's opera (also based on Maeterlinck's play), but as his challenge to Richard Strauss's supremacy as a composer of symphonic poems. It's an intensely symphonic score in Schoenberg's early, late-Romantic vein, with an elaborate single-movement structure and a subtle network of thematic cross-references. Yet none of this is an end in itself, and the music is as gripping and immediate a representation of a tragic love story as anything in the German Romantic tradition.

To move from this to the abstraction of the 12-note Variations, Op 31, may threaten extreme anticlimax. Yet from the delicate introduction of the work's shapely theme to the turbulent good humour of the extended finale Schoenberg proves that his new compositional method did not drain his musical language of expressive vitality. The elaborate counterpoint may not make for easy listening, but the combination of exuberance and emotion is irresistible – at least in a performance like this.

String Quartets

No 1 in D minor, Op 7; No 2 in F sharp minor, Op 10;
No 3 Op 30; No 4 Op 37

String Quartets Nos 1-4
ᵃ**Dawn Upshaw** sop **Arditti Quartet** (Irvine Arditti,
David Alberman vns Garth Knox va Rohan de Saram
vc)
Auvidis Montaigne ② MO782135 (139' · DDD)   ⓂⓄ

These recordings were made in London, in collaboration with the BBC, and the sound is consistently spacious, with a natural clarity and an even balance; the details of Schoenberg's complex counterpoint, as evident in No 1 as in No 4, can be heard with a minimum of stress and strain. Though one occasionally gets the impression that the Arditti is relatively cool in its response to this often fervent music, the mood they create is far from anti-Romantic, and they call on a wide range of dynamics and tone colours. Even if every nuance in Schoenberg's markings isn't followed, this is warmly expressive playing. Dawn Upshaw's contribution to the Second Quartet helps to heighten the drama, although she misses some of that mysterious, ecstatic quality which makes this music so haunting. It's in the Third and Fourth Quartets that the superior sound quality of the Auvidis Montaigne issue pays greatest dividends. Textural clarity is vital here, and although even the Arditti struggles to sustain the necessary lightness in the long second movement of No 4, their wider dynamic range brings you close to the toughly argued, emotionally expansive essence of this music. Yet the performance of No 3 is the finest achievement of the set: clarity of form and emotional conviction combine to create an absorbing account of a modern masterwork. It sets the seal on a most distinguished enterprise.

Gurrelieder

Gurrelieder
Karita Mattila sop **Anne Sofie von Otter** mez
Thomas Moser ten **Philip Langridge** ten **Thomas
Quasthoff** bass-bar **Berlin Radio Chorus; MDR
Radio Chorus, Leipzig; Ernst Senff Choir; Berlin
Philharmonic Orchestra / Sir Simon Rattle**
EMI ② 557303-2 (110' · DDD · T/t) Ⓕ**❍❍❍**Ⓑ➔

Apparently Rattle told the Berlin Philharmonic to play *Gurrelieder* 'as though it were *Daphnis et Chloé*', which sounds crazy until you listen to the result: indeed, the sonorities do rather often sound subtly and delicately French. It also seems obvious from this performance that he means it when he says that *Gurrelieder* is 'the world's largest string quartet'. It's only rarely that the full resources of Schoenberg's gargantuan orchestra are called for (all the more satisfyingly vast when they are). This has an effect on the soloists: none is required to force. Karita Mattila gains from this intimate approach, floating over exquisite orchestral textures in her first song and touching the second very lightly, though in the fourth she can manage both a splendid opening out and an ethereal close. Anne Sofie von Otter has a brighter voice than many exponents of the Wood Dove, better at quieter expressiveness than the wild, gutturally expressed grief of Brigitte Fassbaender, still unrivalled in this role in Riccardo Chailly's recording. Langridge is vividly characterful as Klaus-Narr, Thomas Quasthoff a fine Peasant and a vehement Speaker. The choral singing is first class, the orchestral playing superfine and the recording – a mixture of live and studio performances – both detailed and spacious. There are several fine accounts of *Gurrelieder* in the current catalogue, of which Chailly's has for a long while been a favourite; his soloists are at least as fine as Rattle's, but Rattle's control of *rubato*, his readiness to adopt more relaxed tempi and to allow silences to register are all tangible advantages. He now replaces Chailly at the head of the list.

Gurrelieder
Susan Dunn sop **Brigitte Fassbaender** mez
Siegfried Jerusalem, Peter Haage tens **Hermann
Becht** bass **Hans Hotter** narr **St Hedwig's Cathedral**

**Choir, Berlin; Dusseldorf Musikverin Chorus; Berlin
Radio Symphony Orchestra / Riccardo Chailly**
Decca ② 473 728-2DF2 (101' · DDD · T/t) Ⓜ**❍**Ⓑ➔

This vast cantata, a direct descendant of Wagnerian music-drama, was for the turn-of-the-century musical scene the ultimate gorgeous sunset. Schoenberg's forces are, to put it mildly, extravagant. As well as the six soloists and two choruses, the orchestra sports such luxuries as four piccolos, 10 horns and a percussion battery that includes iron chains; and so complex are some of the textures that, to achieve a satisfactory balance, a near miracle is required of conductor and recording engineers. Decca has never been mean with miracles where large-scale forces are concerned and this set is no exception.

Chailly gives us a superbly theatrical presentation of the score. The casting of the soloists is near ideal. Susan Dunn's Tove has youth, freshness and purity on her side. So exquisitely does she float her lines that you readily sympathise with King Waldemar's rage at her demise. Siegfried Jerusalem has the occasional rough moment, but few previous Waldemars on disc have possessed his heroic ringing tones and range of expression. And Decca makes sure that its trump card, the inimitable Hans Hotter as the speaker in 'The wild hunt of the summer wind', is so tangibly projected that we miss not one vowel or consonant of his increasing animation and excitement at that final approaching sunrise.

Gurrelieder
Melanie Diener sop **Jennifer Lane** mez **Stephen
O'Mara, Martyn Hill** tens **David Wilson-Johnson**
bass **Ernst Haefliger** spkr **Simon Joly Chorale;
Philharmonia Orchestra / Robert Craft**
Naxos ② 8 557518/9 (118' · DDD · N) Ⓢ**❍**Ⓑ➔

On the evidence of this superb performance we've quite clearly been underestimating Robert Craft. Precision and finely moulded detail are evident throughout, at least as clearly as in Chailly's and Rattle's accounts, but in Craft's case one is no less often aware of sumptuous richness, passionate eloquence and satisfying orchestral weight. He's also more prepared than rivals to adopt broad tempi and expressive *rubato*. Despite a few tiny reservations it is a more thrilling account than either of the rivals mentioned above, and carries something of the excitement of a live performance.

Stephen O'Mara has the sort of voice you associate with Wagner's Siegmund, but with a fine sense of line and sufficient variety of dynamic to open out stirringly at climaxes. There have been more expressive Toves than Melanie Diener, but not many who are so firm-voiced and steady. Jennifer Lane is an excellent Wood Dove, dramatic and expressive, David Wilson-Johnson a grippingly vehement Peasant, while anyone who thinks of Martyn Hill as a typically understated English tenor will be astonished by his Klaus-Narr, which is vividly acted and firm of voice. In his 83rd year Ernst Haefliger is an extraordinarily lively, urgent Speaker. The chorus are inspiritingly full-voiced, singing out like heroes.

Yet most of the memorable moments of this performance are Craft's and the Philharmonia's: the wonderfully glittering chamber textures of the penultimate scene, the passion and savagery of the orchestral interlude that heralds the death of Tove, the tumultuous power of the 'wild hunt'. *Gurrelieder* has been exceptionally fortunate on disc in recent years, but this recording (whose sound is often magnificently full and spacious) need fear none of its rivals.

Pierrot lunaire

Pierrot lunaire, Op 21. Herzgewächse, Op 20.
Ode to Napoleon, Op 41
Christine Schäfer sop **David Pittman-Jennings** narr
Ensemble InterContemporain / Pierre Boulez
DG 457 630-2GH (53' · DDD · T/t) Ⓕ**Ⓞ**➛

Pierre Boulez's third recording of *Pierrot lunaire* is an intense yet intimate reading, in a recording that's positively anti-resonant, and which veers, like the music itself, between harshness and reticence. Boulez's second recording (for Sony), with Yvonne Minton, has long been notorious as the 'sung' *Pierrot*, flouting the composer's specific instructions about recitation. This time Christine Schäfer is more speech-orientated, the few fully sung notes perfectly pitched, and although slidings-away from sustained sounds are on the whole avoided, the effect is superbly dramatic in the work's more expressionistic movements. The work's strange world, halfway between cabaret and concert hall, is admirably caught.

In the *Ode to Napoleon* David Pittman-Jennings has a heavy voice, but he skilfully inflects the sketchily notated dynamics of the vocal part, and the instrumental backing is forceful and well nuanced. The sound may be clinically dry, but this is scarcely a serious drawback when the performance has such expressive immediacy. The disc is completed by the brief, exotic Maeterlinck setting from 1911, whose hugely demanding vocal line deters all but the hardiest. Christine Schäfer copes, while the accompaniment for celesta, harmonium and harp weaves its usual spell. A thoroughly memorable disc.

Moses und Aron

Moses und Aron
David Pittman-Jennings narr Moses **Chris Merritt**
ten Aron **László Polgár** bass Priest **Gabriele Fontana**
sop Young Girl, First Naked Woman **Yvonne Naef**
mez Invalid Woman **John Graham Hall** ten Young
Man, Naked Youth **Per Lindskog** ten Youth **Henk de**
Vries bar Young Man **Siegfried Lorenz** bar Another
Young Man **Chorus of the Netherlands Opera;**
Royal Concertgebouw Orchestra / Pierre Boulez
DG ② 449 174-2GH2 (106' · DDD · T/t) Ⓕ**Ⓞ**➛

Moses und Aron is respected rather than loved, with the reputation of being a tough assignment for all concerned. One of the essays in the booklet accompanying this recording calls it a didactic opera. Pierre Boulez, however, is a conductor in whom didacticism is close to a passion, and he's obviously passionate about this opera. We take it for granted that, in any work to which he feels close, every detail will be both accurate and audible. But for Schoenberg *Moses und Aron* was a warning as well as a homily, and as much a confession of faith as either. Boulez, often himself a Moses preaching against anti-modern backsliding, is at one with Schoenberg here.

Some such reason, surely, has led to this being not only a performance of immaculate clarity, but of intense and eloquent beauty and powerful drama. The recording was made during a run of stage performances, but in the Concertgebouw in Amsterdam, not in the theatre. In the beautiful acoustic of their own hall, the orchestra plays with ample richness and precision, and the sometimes complex textures benefit enormously from a perceptible space around them.

The choral singing matches the orchestral playing in quality: beautiful in tone, eloquently urgent, vividly precise in the difficult spoken passages. The soloists are all admirable, with no weak links. Merritt in particular seems to have all that the hugely taxing role of Aron demands: a fine control of long line, intelligently expressive use of words, where necessary the dangerous demagogue's glamour. Pittman-Jennings is a properly prophetic Moses, grand of voice. This is one of Boulez's finest achievements.

Moses und Aron
Franz Grundheber bar Moses **Thomas Moser** ten
Aron **Ildikó Raimondi** sop Young Girl, Second Naked
Woman **Janina Baechle** sop Invalid Woman **Peter**
Jelosits ten Young Man, Youth **Johann Reinprecht**
ten Naked Youth **Morten Frank Larsen** bar Another
Man **Georg Tichy** bass Ephraimite **Alexandru Moisiuc**
bass Priest **Ileana Tonca** sop First Naked Woman
Slovak Philharmonic Chorus; Vienna State Opera
Chorus; Vienna State Opera Orchestra /
Daniele Gatti
Stage director **Reto Nickler**
Video director **Claus Viller**
ArtHaus Musik 🎥 101 259 (134' · NTSC · 16:9 ·
PCM stereo, 5.1 and DTS 5.1 · 0)
Recorded live at the Staatsoper, Vienna, 2006 Ⓕ

A student recently asked Milton Babbitt what he made of the plot of *Moses und Aron*. 'Oh I don't know, I'm not really a plot person,' he replied. 'Boy meets Girl, Moses meets Aron...' Of course, there's more than a grain of truth to Babbitt's quip.

The bonus to this appearance of Schoenberg's 'opera fragment' on DVD is a discussion which does not attempt to explain what the piece is 'about' (dread phrase) but throws up some arresting images along the way, not least the suggestion that Moses is a 'Führer des Jüdischen Volks'. It certainly accords with the director

Reto Nickler's conception of the work as 'a highly topical psychodrama that represents the thorny path between theory and practice'. Indeed, Schoenberg's absurdly unrealisable stage directions make the last scene of *Les Troyens* pale into insignificance.

Nickler takes an effectively practical tack, abstract but straightforward. Three-dimensional video conjures the miracles of the first act, staff into serpent and so forth, while in Act 2 it becomes the focus of consumer materialism. Aron dons a natty gold jacket while the chorus wave hankies of the same material, economically symbolising the banality of their demands and theology. The Golden Calf is revealed as a set of letters spelling out ICH BIN GOTT, the counterpart of Moses's tablets of stone.

Such intelligent, dramatic pragmatism lends equal lustre to the musical values. It's good to hear a conductor who is steeped in *verismo* conveying the underestimated sweep of these Biblical declamations, even if it is inevitably at the expense of many of the notes. Both Grundheber and Moser seize every cue for lyrical expression, and the super-size chorus is every bit the collective hero/anti-hero of the piece. The prologue to Act 2 is typically stark and precise, with harsh lighting and tenebrous murk reflecting the *sotto voce* polyphony of abandonment as the Jewish people sit motionless. Their grim suitcases, their raised clenched fists and mob behaviour, all allude to fresher horrors in Jewish history, until they whip out gold party-frocks and dinner-jackets for the orgy. The Ephraimites become Scaramangas, murdering the true believers to a backdrop of clicking cameraphones and rolling TV coverage – then Z-list celebs totter on as alter egos of the Four Naked Virgins, copulating with the God-letters while Buñuel-esque images of cruelty dominate the giant TV screens. No wonder the Viennese loved it.

Franz Schreker
Austrian 1878-1934

Schreker studied with Fuchs at the Vienna Conservatory (1892-1900). His first score to attract attention was the ballet Der Geburtstag der Infantin (1908) and this was followed, with even more enthusiasm, by the opera Der ferne Klang (1912). It unveiled Schreker's lush late-Romantic musical voice, its harmonies teetering on the edge of atonality. In 1908 he founded the Philharmonic Choir and in 1912 was invited to teach at the Music Academy in Vienna. In 1920 he moved to Berlin as director of the Musikhochschule: during the 1920s he enjoyed his greatest success as a composer with a number of operas and a handful of orchestral works and songs.

Overtures and Preludes

Prelude to a Drama. Symphonic Interlude. Nachtstück. Valse lente. Ekkehard, Op 12. Fantastic Overture, Op 15

BBC Philharmonic Orchestra / Vassily Sinaisky
Chandos CHAN9797 (78' · DDD)　　　　Ⓕ●Ⓑ▸

Sumptuously performed and unflinchingly recorded, this collection will be seized on by Schreker enthusiasts, who will enjoy every massively scored climax, every gorgeously coloured, embroidered and encrusted texture. Those who are only Schreker enthusiasts north-north-west may need to be warned that the climaxes are pretty frequent and that the textures are in constant flux. Listening to this programme uninterrupted is recommended only to addicts; others may wonder whether Schreker isn't repeating himself. The Prelude, Interlude and *Nachtstück* come from *Die Gezeichneten*, *Der Schatzgräber* and *Der ferne Klang* respectively, and all serve similar functions: to represent in a darkened auditorium erotic acts or emotions that could scarcely be represented on a stage. The *Valse lente* is balletic light music, softly and delicately scored. *Ekkehard* is a tone-poem about a monk who falls in love with a Duchess and goes to war to defend her: each of these aspects has its own theme, and they're turbulently developed before a peaceful conclusion on Ekkehard's 'monastic' melody over a palpable organ pedal. No programme is stated for the *Fantastic Overture*, but it approaches the three big dramatic pieces in richness. Not many composers demand quite so much of a vast orchestra as Schreker, and Sinaisky and his orchestra amply fulfil those demands.

Der Gerburtstag der Infantin

Der Gerburtstag der Infantin. Die drei Tänze der Zwerges. Die Rose. Der Spiegel. In leichter Bewegung. In wiegender, walzserähn Bewegung. Wie am Anfäng. Valse lente. Festwalzer und Walzerintermezzo. Der Wind. Ein Tanzspiel
Lucerne Symphony Orchestra / John Axelrod
Nimbus NI5753 (71' · DDD)　　　　Ⓕ●Ⓑ▸

Bürger Zwei Lieder[a]. Legende. Stille der Nacht.
Krenek Symphony No 1, Op 7
Schreker Intermezzo, Scherzo, Op 8
[a]**Dietrich Henschel** bar
Lucerne Symphony Orchestra / John Axelrod
Nimbus NI5808 (72' · DDD)　　　　Ⓕ●Ⓑ▸

The main work by Franz Schreker on these discs is *The Birthday of the Infanta* (1908), a dance score inspired by an Oscar Wilde novel which later provided the subject for Zemlinsky's engrossing opera *Der Zwerg* ('The Dwarf', 1922). There are only a few anticipations of Schreker's later, hyper-Romantic operatic style: most strikingly in a movement called 'The Mirror'. But much of the music here has a lighter touch. *Festwalzer und Walzerintermezzo* is closer to Johann Strauss than to Richard, and the two string pieces on the second disc are accomplished, undemanding trifles. Most characterful is *Der Wind* (1909), a dance score which sounds like music for a silent film, responding with entertaining flexibility to an economical scenario.

The second disc couples Schreker's two string pieces, written in 1900 when he was just 22, with music by two of the many young composers he taught, later on, in Vienna and Berlin. The *Two Songs* (1919) by Julius Bürger have an extravagant Schrekerian opulence in places, and these performances wring every last drop of intensity from their often rather solemn music, Dietrich Henschel coping admirably with Bürger's high-lying phrases. (Nimbus unaccountably fail to provide the texts: a pity, though at least Christopher Hailey's booklet-notes are detailed and informative.)

The main work on the second disc is the very un-Schreker-like Symphony No 1 (1921) by Ernst Krenek. Written when he was 21, it's unashamedly youthful, often sounding like a self-conscious gesture of disrespect to most of what then passed as Germanic tradition. There are signs of the anti-Romanticism which was becoming increasingly fashionable, and a wealth of quirky, brash materials which almost manage to sustain one's interest throughout its not inconsiderable length.

On both CDs, the Lucerne Symphony Orchestra perform with energy and spontaneity, and the recordings are particularly effective in revealing the many felicities of Schreker's expert orchestration.

Franz Schubert   Austrian 1797-1828

When Schubert's musical talent began to emerge, though it was encouraged, there were no higher ambitions than that he should grow up to be a respectful, hard-working teacher like his father whose diligence and thrift had allowed him to buy the schoolhouse where the family lived. His early lessons were with his father and brother but Schubert was soon far beyond their modest accomplishments. By the age of 10, Schubert could play the piano, organ, violin and viola.

He became a member of the Imperial Court chapel choir in Vienna where among his teachers was Salieri. 'You can do everything,' he announced to this timid, diffident little boy, 'for you are a genius.' Schubert began composing while at school. When his voice broke, he decided to leave and return to his father's house to follow in his footsteps and become a teacher. (One added bonus of the profession was that it meant avoiding military service.) Schubert was singularly unsuited to the task – he could not keep discipline; all he wanted to do was to write music. And write it he did. There has probably been no one in the history of music with such a prodigious facility as Schubert. In this period he composed five symphonies, four Masses, several string quartets, stage music, an opera and some of his most famous Lieder (in 1815 alone he composed no fewer than 140 songs.

Taking the plunge, he finally abandoned the teaching career and took his chances as a full-time composer. He befriended the poets Johann Mayrhofer and Franz von Schober, and it was through the latter that he met the great baritone Johann Vogel, who was to

champion so many of Schubert's songs (he gave the first performance of 'Erlkönig'). His self-discipline allowed him to produce an enormous amount of music (he wrote as much in 20 years as Brahms wrote in 50). His evenings were given over to music at the homes of his friends where Schubert presided as the life and soul of the party – the gatherings came to be known as 'Schubertiads'. Unlike Beethoven, he felt uncomfortable in aristocratic circles, preferring the Bohemian, intellectual, art-loving circle of Vienna.

The meagre income Schubert earned was supplemented by teaching music to the daughters of Count Esterházy at his summer estate in Zelésk, Hungary. Unlike Haydn before him, there was no permanent post for him there; and unlike Beethoven, Schubert never found a rich (and permanent) patron.

By 1820 he had composed over 500 works embracing every branch of composition. Yet only two of them had ever been heard in public – the Mass in F (in 1814) and one single solitary song (in 1819). The music commissioned for a play and an opera were both critical flops and it wasn't until 1821 that his first works (a volume of songs) were published.

Failure and lack of recognition now began to bite hard. Poverty and having to live on the charity of friends made him increasingly despondent. Added to this, he had to cope with the effects of venereal disease. Yet in the midst of this, he wrote the Unfinished Symphony. The death of his idol Beethoven came as a terrible blow to him and his ambition from then on was to be buried next to him. And still, amid his awful personal predicament, some of the most divine music ever written continued to flow – the String Quintet, the last three great piano sonatas, the Mass in E flat and the song-cycle Schwanengesang.

On March 26, 1828, in the Musikverein of Vienna, there was given for the first time a programme entirely devoted to Schubert's music. It was put on by his friends, of course, but though successful, was never even reviewed. Less than eight months later, Schubert died of typhoid, delirious, babbling of Beethoven. He was 31 and was buried as near to him as was practicable with the epitaph 'Here lie rich treasure and still fairer hopes'. Schubert left no estate at all, absolutely nothing – except his manuscripts.

It was only by chance and the diligence of a few musicians that some of it came to light – in 1838 Schumann happened to visit Schubert's brother and came across the great Symphony in C (the Ninth) and urged its publication; the Unfinished Symphony was not heard until 1865 after the score was found in a chest; it was George Grove (of Grove's Dictionary fame) and the young Arthur Sullivan (of Gilbert and Sullivan fame) who unearthed in a publisher's house in Vienna Schubert's Symphonies Nos 1, 2, 3, 4 and 6, 60 songs and the music for Rosamunde. That was in 1867. Over a century later, in 1978, the sketches for a tenth symphony were unearthed in another Viennese archive.

Symphonies

No 1 in D, D82; **No 2** in B flat, D125; **No 3** in D, D200; **No 4** in C minor, D417, 'Tragic'; **No 5** in B flat, D485; **No 6** in C, D589; **No 8** in B minor, D759, 'Unfinished'; **No 9** in C, D944, 'Great'

Symphonies Nos 1-6, 8 & 9
Berlin Philharmonic Orchestra / Karl Böhm
DG Collectors Edition ④ 471 307-2GB4 (4h 10' · ADD)
Recorded 1963-71   ⑧

These are marvellous performances: vibrant, clear, characterful and effortlessly well played. The recordings, too, still seem new-minted, even the Ninth, the first of the symphonies to be recorded. The Berliners' art is the art that disguises art. Böhm never feels the need to do anything clever but just quietly sees to it that this superb orchestra plays at its best. His way with the two late symphonies is, in fact, highly sophisticated. The *Unfinished* begins in what seems to be a leisurely fashion but his performance of the first movement catches Schubert's mix of lyricism and high drama with extraordinary acuity. Conversely, the second movement seems swift but brings the work full circle with an equally extraordinary sense of calm and catharsis in the final pages. The celebrated 1963 Ninth out-Furtwänglers Furtwängler in the myriad means it uses within a single grand design to capture the symphony's sense of danger and derring-do in addition to its lyricism, nobility and earthy Austrian charm.

In the early symphonies, Böhm's approach is simpler-seeming and more direct. Rhythms are so finely propelled, the pulse so effortlessly sustained, the music always lands on its feet. The zest comes from the stylish Berlin string playing; melodically, it's the woodwinds (every one a Lieder singer) who catch the beauty of Schubert's melodies and the skirl of the attendant descants. You won't find yourself tiring of Böhm's approach; he doesn't give in to irritating idiosyncrasies (à la Harnoncourt), but ensures that the Schubertian stream is always clear to the ear and sweet to the taste.

Additional recommendations

Symphonies Nos 1-6, 8 & 9. Rosamunde Overture. Grand Duo (orch Joachim)
COE / Abbado
DG ⑤ 423 651-2GH5 (5h 20' · DDD)   Ⓜ️Ⓞ➡️
With wonderfully vivacious playing from the youthful Chamber Orchestra of Europe, Abbado presents a lively and fresh cycle of the Schubert symphonies (plus a couple of extras). The early symphonies (Nos 1-6) benefit from this approach, but the later, greater works are by no means lightweight. Fine, warm sound, too.

Symphonies Nos 1-6, 8 & 9
Royal Concertgebouw Orch / Harnoncourt
Teldec ④ 2564 62323-2 (4h 44' · DDD)
Recorded live   Ⓜ️Ⓞ
The differences between Harnoncourt's interpretative Schubert and Abbado's are startling. The Ninth's finale, unlike Abbado's a whirling, spinning *vivace*, is borne aloft on astonishingly precise articulation of its rhythms and accents and a springy delivery of the triplets, characteristics one has come to expect from a Harnoncourt perform-

ance. Harnoncourt doesn't set apart the first six symphonies as merely diverting, unlike Abbado: their bittersweet ambiguities and apparent affectations of anxiety here acquire a greater significance, and the cycle, as a whole, a greater continuity.

Symphonies Nos 3, 5 & 6   Ⓗ
**Royal Philharmonic Orchestra /
Sir Thomas Beecham**
EMI Great Recordings of the Century 566984-2
(78' · ADD). Recorded 1955-59   Ⓜ️ⓄⓄⓄ➡️

Beecham was well into his seventies when he made these recordings with the Royal Philharmonic, the orchestra he had founded in 1946. His lightness of touch, his delight in the beauty of the sound he was summoning, the directness of his approach to melody, and his general high spirits will all dominate our memory of these performances. But listening again, we may be reminded that Beecham could equally well dig deep into the darker moments of these works. Schubert's elation was rarely untroubled and the joy is often compounded by its contrast with pathos – Beecham had that balance off to a tee. It should be noted that he doesn't take all the marked repeats and he doctored some passages he considered over-repetitive. However, these recordings may also serve as a reminder of the wonderful heights of musicianship that his players achieved, as in the Trio of the Third.

Symphonies – No 4, 'Tragic', & No 5
**Netherlands Chamber Orchestra /
Gordan Nikolitch**
Pentatone 🔊 PTC5186 340 (68' · DDD)   ⒻⓄⓄⓄ➡️

Both these works date from 1816, when Schubert was still in his teens, and the freshness of the invention, particularly in No 5, is irresistible. The very opening demonstrates the young Schubert's originality, when it seems to start in mid-sentence on a phrase that is off-hand, almost as though the music has just emerged into human hearing. Nikolitch and his fine team phrase it beautifully with a convincing degree of *rubato*, and very quickly the advantages of a performance on chamber scale become apparent when the woodwind have extra clarity as well as prominence, even while the strings, relatively thin, are clear and fresh.

The same is true of the *Allegro vivace* finale, which is light and fast with good contrasts. The flowing *Andante* slow movement, much the longest of the four, is neat and nicely scaled, while the third movement (labelled Menuetto despite the *Allegro molto* indication) is well sprung with sharp accents leading to a more relaxed Trio.

Symphony No 4 is traditionally entitled the *Tragic* because of its key of C minor and the Beethovenian gravity of the very opening with its big timpani roll, all the more prominent in a performance on this scale. The slow introduction leads to an athletic *Allegro molto* with leaping triplets, crisply played here.

The slow movement – as in No 5 much the longest of the four – flows with gentle lyricism, while the third movement has accents so placed that initially there is a hint of quadruple time, leading to a *Ländler*-like Trio. The minor key of the finale and the light clarity of the textures make it sound like an anticipation of Mendelssohn, all well achieved in this performance. An excellent issue of distinctive performances in a relatively rare coupling. Vivid recording.

Symphony No 9, 'Great'
Bamberg Symphony Orchestra / Jonathan Nott
Tudor ⊛ TUDOR7144 (62' · DDD)   Ⓕ❶❶Ⓑ➤

Relatively unfamiliar conductor, very familiar symphony. But don't let the unfamiliarity of Jonathan Nott allow you to believe that this is yet another version of a much-recorded work. It isn't. On the contrary, Nott offers a performance that hews close to the text (all repeats are also observed) yet is replete with the touches of a thoughtfully considered interpretation. And consideration begins at the beginning: the solo horn theme broadly stated, hairpin accents strong, the tempo picking up almost imperceptibly afterwards but no speeding up to the main *Allegro ma non troppo*, no slowing down for the second subject and no dissipation of tension in the coda. Nott keeps the momentum going to the end.

This literal account may suggest rigidity – which isn't the case. What cannot actually be described is Nott's malleable control of rhythm, the subtle distensions and contractions of phrases, and a feel for orchestral colour and balance that is particularly noticeable in the second movement. The bass here is firmly delineated, wind writing is finely clarified, *fortissimos* don't degenerate into noise. The texture remains clean. Sound and perspective are natural. Though SACD playback could offer improvements in audio quality, it couldn't sharpen Nott's subjective immersion in the many facets of the music, one of which is a lilting impulse that he senses in the finale. Yet the line doesn't go slack. Nott, as always, keeps a tight hold on the reins while expressing his convictions with a conviction that is sure to win you over.

Symphony No 9, 'Great'
Berlin Philharmonic Orchestra / Sir Simon Rattle
EMI 339382-2 (58' · DDD). Recorded live 2005   Ⓕ Ⓑ➤

Knowing Sir Simon Rattle has regularly conducted period-instrument orchestras, it may come as a surprise that with his Berlin Philharmonic he takes a relatively free and romantic view of this massive symphony, maybe reflecting that this is a live recording. Not only are his speeds on the broad side, but he allows marked *rallentandos* at the ends of sections, as at the end of the development sections of both the first and last movements.

His moulding of phrases, too, seems to reflect the older traditions of this great orchestra rather

---

SCHUBERT SYMPHONY NO 8, 'UNFINISHED' – IN BRIEF

COE / Claudio Abbado
DG 423 655-2GH   Ⓕ❶❶Ⓑ➤
Available coupled with Joachim's orchestration of the *Grand Duo*, Abbado's *Unfinished* combines elegance and energy in equal measure. Stunningly alive playing from the young COE.

Royal Concertgebouw Orchestra / Nikolaus Harnoncourt
Warner Classsics 0927 49813-2   Ⓜ❶Ⓑ➤
Drawn from his complete symphony cycle, Harnoncourt offers an *Unfinished* of dark, rich colours. The opening movement is emotionally draining, and everything is done with immense skill.

Cologne Gürzenich Orchestra / Günter Wand Ⓗ
Testament SBT1364   Ⓕ❶
A master conductor at work early in his career. The sound is good for its age but the performance it contains is touched with greatness. Try and sample first.

Philharmonia Orchestra / Giuseppe Sinopoli
DG 445 514-2GMA   Ⓕ
The recording that put Sinopoli on the musical map. Controversial perhaps, but it's a reading vividly alive to the move from dark to light. The playing of the Philharmonia does him proud.

Hallé Orchestra / Sir John Barbirolli
BBC Legends BBCL4120-2   Ⓜ
Recorded in the BBC's London studios, Barbirolli's *Unfinished* is a wonderfully humane performance drawing on a lifetime's experience of the work. Good sound.

Vienna PO / Carlos Kleiber
DG 449 745-2GOR   Ⓜ❶Ⓑ➤
Kleiber's Schubert is not on a level with his Beethoven but it is still worth hearing. Taken quite swiftly, this is an *Unfinished* slightly short on poetry but high on drama.

London Classical Players / Sir Roger Norrington
Virgin Classics 562227-2   Ⓜ Ⓑ➤
It may not get off to the most auspicious start but once in its stride, Norrington's is a swift, lively affair with an almost jaunty gait. The second movement achieves appealing levels of serenity.

Berlin PO / Karl Böhm
DG 453 664-2GFS   Ⓜ Ⓑ➤
Karl Böhm's Schubert is elegant, unforced and beautifully played by a large-sounding Berlin Philharmonic. He doesn't overplay the drama but at the same time he captures the work's darker currents.

than those of Karajan. One key passage comes in the middle of the *Andante con moto* slow movement, where on repeated phrases in *crescendo* Schubert builds up the movement's biggest climax, resolved after a sudden pause on an affectionate cello melody. What emerges from this relatively relaxed approach is an extra sense of joy in Schubert's inspiration, with rhythms lifted infectiously.

Not that Rattle's interpretation lacks bite or precision – quite the opposite: one of its great qualities is the way he brings out the many counter-motifs, notably on cellos or second violins, that in many performances are hidden. That transparency of texture is outstanding: Rattle persuades the orchestra to produce extreme *pianissimos*, as at the start of the recapitulation in the first movement, where far more than usually one is aware of the score markings.

With full, warm sound, this is a first-rate recommendation. The only slight reservation is that it comes without a coupling, though at 58 minutes for the symphony (even with one of the repeats in the *Scherzo* and that of the exposition in the finale omitted), one cannot really complain of short measure.

Schubert Symphony No 9, 'Great'^c   Ⓗ
Cherubini Anacréon – Overture^a
Cornelius The Barber of Baghdad – Overture^b
^aRoyal Philharmonic Orchestra; ^bcBBC Symphony
Orchestra / Sir Adrian Boult
BBC Legends ^bmono BBCL4072-2 (72' · ADD)
Recorded live ^a1963; ^b1954, ^c1969   Ⓕ

Schubert's *Great* C major Symphony was a work close to Boult's heart. He recorded it for the first time in 1934, for the last in 1972, and in between came countless performances. This one was at rather a noisy Prom in 1969, when he returned to the BBC SO from which he had been severed by the mercilessness of BBC bureaucracy.

Among much else, he was a supreme master of the orchestra, attentive to his players without ever losing sight of a work's architecture. In this performance there's his absolute security of tempo, which doesn't mean stiffness. The finale is steady without inflexibility; the *Scherzo* drives along brightly; and the *Andante* moves inexorably towards its terrifying climax, with a movingly sad cello aftermath. This is vintage Boult. So, in their own ways, are the two overtures.

Symphony No 10 in D, D936a (realised Newbould).
Symphonic fragments – D, D615; D, D708a (orch
Newbould)
Scottish Chamber Orchestra / Sir Charles Mackerras
Hyperion CDA67000 (54' · DDD)   Ⓕ

Someone will have to find another name for Schubert's *Unfinished* Symphony (the B minor) before long. In fact there are six unfinished Schubert symphonies: there are two whole movement expositions for D615, torsos of three movements and a nearly complete *Scherzo* for D708a, and enough sketch material for Brian Newbould to attempt a complete conjectural reconstruction of D936a, the symphony Schubert began writing in the last weeks of his life. Inevitably some will ask, why bother? Well, apart from the increase in the sense of wonder at Schubert's sheer productivity, there's some wonderful music here, especially the slow movement of D936a, desolate and warmly consoling by turns. As a whole, D936a suggests that, even at this late stage, Schubert was still thinking in terms of new developments. The concluding third movement, contrapuntally fusing elements of *scherzo* and finale, is like nothing else in Schubert – or any other composer of the classical period. Newbould has had to do some guessing here, but the results are mostly strikingly authoritative. The performances carry conviction and the recordings are atmospheric yet detailed. Altogether a fascinating disc.

String Quintet in C, D956

Schubert String Quintet
Beethoven Grosse Fuge in B flat, Op 133
Hagen Quartet (Lukas Hagen, Rainer Schmidt vns
Veronika Hagen va Clemens Hagen vc) with
Heinrich Schiff vc
DG 439 774-2GH (68' · DDD)   ⒻⓄⓄⒷ

By following Boccherini in using two cellos instead of two violas for his String Quintet, Schubert increased the potential for greater textural contrast. Moreover, the dichotomy between the tragic perspective and Viennese gaiety in the Quintet, so evident in much of Schubert's greatest music, generates an especially potent dramatic force.

The Hagen Quartet's performance of the first movement, which presents remarkably clear textural detail, is broad and expansive. The Hagen include the exposition repeat in a movement that lasts almost 20 minutes. Perhaps as a consequence, they play the *Adagio* second movement at an unusually fast tempo. However, through breathtaking dynamic control in the first section, passionate intensity in the second, and engaging spontaneity of the ornamentation in the final section, the Hagen achieve an expression that's powerfully compelling.

The second half of the Quintet is often treated as a period of emotional relief from the profound concentration of the first two movements. Startlingly, the Hagen maintain the tension with violent textural and dynamic contrast in the *Scherzo*, and distinctively varied registral sonority in the Trio. The finale, in which the Hagen effectively balance the music's charming Hungarian flavour with its more sinister touches, provides an arresting conclusion.

The Hagen's account of Beethoven's *Grosse Fuge* is polished and sensitive and it vividly conveys the difference between Beethoven's and

Schubert's compositional means. The Hagen's is an outstanding disc, in which exceptional performances, that challenge the finest alternatives, are complemented by superb recording.

String Quintet[a]. Symphony No 5[b]   H
[a]Isaac Stern, [a]Alexander Schneider vns [a]Milton Katims va [a]Paul Tortelier vc [b]Prades Festival Orchestra / Pablo Casals [a]vc
Sony Classical Casals Edition mono SMK58992 (76' · ADD). Recorded 1952-53   Ⓜ❍❍❍

This should have an in-built fail-safe against hasty consumption, in that the interpretative ingredients are so rich, varied and unpredictable that to experience it all at once is to invite mental and emotional exhaustion. Casals is the linchpin. A charismatic presence, he embraces everything with the passion of a devoted horticulturist tending his most precious flowers, and that his love extended beyond the realms of music to mankind itself surely enriched his art even further. The most celebrated Prades recording ever is still the Stern/Casals/Tortelier reading of the C major Quintet, a masterful traversal graced with elastic tempi, songful phrasing, appropriate rhetorical emphases (especially in the first and second movements) and fabulous string playing. The coupling is a 'first release' of Schubert's Fifth Symphony, recorded in 1953 – a warm, keenly inflected performance, jaunty in the outer movements and with an adoring, broadly paced *Adagio*. One presumes that it has been held from previous view only because of a few minor executant mishaps. It's certainly well worth hearing. The transfer of the Quintet reveals itself as marginally warmer but occasionally less well-focused than previous incarnations. Still, the original was no sonic blockbuster to start with but this shouldn't deter you from hearing this disc.

Piano Quintet in A, 'Trout', D667

Piano Quintet, 'Trout'[a]. Litanei, D343.
Variations on 'Trockne Blumen', D802
Renaud Capuçon vn [a]**Gérard Caussé** va [a]**Gautier Capuçon** vc [a]**Alois Posch** db **Frank Braley** pf
Virgin Classics 545563-2 (59' · DDD)   Ⓕ❍❍❍❍➤

A memorable account of the *Trout* Quintet. This group may not project the warmth and bonhomie of the famous Curzon/Boskovsky recording, nor does it have the searching quality of the performance led by Alfred Brendel, but for verve and refinement it's hard to beat. The happy, carefree nature of the music is captured perfectly on a beautifully clear recording; it's especially notable how every detail of the double bass's very spirited contribution is clearly heard yet with no sense that Alois Posch is 'bringing out' his part. Especially enjoyable is the *Scherzo* – a fast tempo, but finely poised, and with a subtle, effective relaxation of the trio – and the Variations. In Variation 2 Renaud Capuçon's

---

SCHUBERT STRING QUINTET – IN BRIEF

Heinrich Schiff; Hagen Quartet
DG 439 774-2GH (68' ·DDD)   Ⓕ❍❍➤
Coupled with the *Grosse Fuge*, the Hagen Quartet and Heinrich Schiff give a very fine reading, full of detail and sensitivity to texture. It's a performance that maintains a high level of intensity throughout. Very impresive.

Stern; Schneider; Katims; Tortelier; Casals   H
Sony Classical mono SMK58992 (76' · ADD)
Ⓜ❍❍❍
Recorded in 1952 at Casals's Prades Festival, this is one of the great Schubert Quintets, human, rich, varied and totally spontaneous. The sound is good for the age but the sheer quality of playing soon sweeps any sonic reservations to one side. (Coupled with Schubert's Fifth Symphony conducted with charm by Casals.)

Douglas Cummings; Lindsay Quartet
ASV CDDCA537 (58' · DDD)   Ⓕ
A fine, natural performance with an appealingly intimate sense of scale. There are some truly heavenly moments in this reading which fills the disc thanks to the first-movement repeat.

Heinrich Schiff; Alban Berg Quartet
EMI 566890-2 (48' · DDD)   Ⓜ❍❍➤
Another recording featuring Heinrich Schiff and something of a modern classic. There is a wonderful ease about the playing that's very appealing. Rather short value though.

Kurt Reher; Hollywood Quartet   H
Testament mono SBT1031 (73' · ADD)   Ⓕ❍
A glorious and civilised reading from the 1950s. These musicians really get under the skin of the music and search out its passionate, beating heart. Generously coupled with Schoenberg's *Verklärte Nacht*.

Villa Musica Ensemble
Naxos 8 550388 (77' · DDD)   Ⓜ❍➤
A fine, super-budget-price performance coupled with the B flat String Trio that offers some very classy chamber musicianship. Theirs is quite a dramatic reading with plenty of passion.

Valentin Erben; Belcea Quartet
EMI ② 967025-2 (130' · DDD)   Ⓑ❍❍➤
Take it for granted that the playing is on the loftiest level, ensemble always transparently clean; and the ability to think, listen and prepare as a coordinated team results in an extraordinarily cogent performance sure in its grasp of phraseology, structure and dynamics. Available coupled with Schubert's last two string quartets.

SCHUBERT PIANO QUINTET, 'TROUT' – IN BRIEF

Christian Zacharias; Leipzig Quartet
Dabringhaus und Grimm MDG307 0625-2
(66' · DDD)   ⓕ🔵🔵
Beautiful string tone and glistening piano work are just the surface trappings of a fine, musicianly account of Schubert's evergreen masterpiece, caught in excellent sound.

Capuçon; Caussé; Capuçon; Posch; Braley
Virgin Classics 545563-2 (59' · DDD)   ⓕ🔵🔵🔵🔵▷
A joyful, youthful Trout from these superb chamber musicians. There's a delightful sense of interplay as they toss the tunes around. The variations themselves are quite enchanting.

Clifford Curzon; members of the Vienna Octet 🅷
Decca download 467 417-2DEQ (71' · ADD) Ⓑ🔵▷
Curzon's genial piano playing and the sweet-toned playing of Willi Boskovsky and his colleagues ideally complement each other in this classic recording. The dryish mono sound adds to the intimate charm.

Baertsen; Tetzlaff; Tamestit; Hecker; Posch; Helmchen
Pentatone PTC5186 334 (69' · DDD)   ⓕ🔵🔵🔵▷
A beautifully recorded, well-filled disc from some of the finest younger musicians of today with pianist Martin Helmchen giving a stylish lead in touching the work's poetic heart.

András Schiff; Hagen Quartet
Decca Ovation 458 608-2DM (75' · DDD)   Ⓜ
After a tension-filled opening, this proves to be another fresh reading, most delightful in the bouncing lightness of the *Scherzo*.

Brendel; Zehetmair; Zimmermann; Duven; Riegelbauer
Philips 446 001-2PH (75' · DDD)   ⓕ🔵🔵🔵▷
Despite a rather languid start, the performance becomes quite forthright – serious rather than relaxed – yet it's also persuasive and engaging.

Jenö Jandó; Kodaly Quartet; Istvan Toth
Naxos 8 550658 (53' · DDD)   Ⓢ🔵▷
Though the sound is not quite in the same class as the full-price versions, with the piano a touch prominent at the expense of the strings, this is a charming performance and excellent value at the price.

Clifford Curzon; Amadeus Quartet; James Edward Merrett
BBC Legends BBCL4009-2 (82' · ADD)   Ⓜ
A joyous live performance which, despite one or two slightly rough spots and a moment of premature applause, rises to truly memorable heights. Coupled with an inspired account of the Brahms Piano Quintet.

figuration is so delicate that the viola melody can create a particularly strong expressive effect, and the following variation is just as magical – Frank Braley's demisemiquavers are quite brilliant, with a lovely, silvery tone, and the bass melody has, for once, nothing elephantine about it.

The elaborate, showy set of variations on 'Trockne Blumen' from *Die schöne Müllerin*, dating from 1824, is an unhackneyed choice of filler. It's curious that the current catalogue lists only two recordings, and one of these, like the present version, substitutes violin for the original flute. It certainly makes a virtuoso violin and piano piece, and played with the precision and delicacy that Capuçon and Braley bring to it is highly effective, though with only occasional touches of the melancholy we expect in late Schubert. After this extravagant music, the touching simplicity of the song arrangement is the more striking.

Piano Quintet, 'Trout'[a].
String Trios – B flat, D581; B flat, D111a
Members of the **Leipzig Quartet** (Andreas Seidel *vn* Ivo Bauer *va* Matthias Moosdorf *vc*) [a]**Christian Zacharias** *pf* [a]**Christian Ockert** *db*
Dabringhaus und Grimm MDG307 0625-2
(66' · DDD)   ⓕ🔵🔵

This *Trout* must surely be one of the very best versions of this much-recorded work – the sound is wonderfully natural, and so is the performance. You get the impression that here was an occasion when everything 'clicked', giving the playing a friendly, relaxed feeling that's just right for this carefree piece. Zacharias has the knack of making even the simplest phrase sound expressive, and the strings, without any exaggeration, produce the most beautiful tonal shadings. All five players, too, have an impressive sense of line; the phrasing and points of emphasis are balanced so that Schubert's expansive designs are projected compellingly. If the *Trout* shows a Schubertian spaciousness, his one completed String Trio is unusually compact. Another distinguished feature is the florid, Spohr-like elegance of much of the violin writing – Andreas Seidel is splendidly stylish and confident. This is another very fine performance, emphasising the predominating gentle lyricism, but with plenty of vigour and panache when required. The String Trio fragment, less than two minutes, continues the same 'let's hear everything' approach; it's a sketch for what subsequently became the comparatively familiar B flat Quartet, D112.

Piano Quintet, 'Trout'[a]. Notturno, D897[b].
Variations on 'Trockne Blumen', D802[c]
[c]**Aldo Baerten** *fl* [ab]**Christian Tetzlaff** *vn*
[a]**Antoine Tamestit** *va* [ab]**Marie Elisabeth Hecker** *vc*
[a]**Alois Posch** *db* **Martin Helmchen** *pf*
Pentatone 🔊 PTC5186 334 (69' · DDD/DSD)
                              ⓕ🔵🔵▷

Recorded in Berlin in excellent sound, this version of the much-recorded *Trout* Quintet earns its place, imaginatively coupled with the sublime *Notturno* for piano trio and the Variations for flute and piano on the song 'Trockne Blumen' from *Die schöne Müllerin*.

The clarity of separation between the instruments in the *Trout* is owed in part to the recording but also to the performers themselves, a well attuned group. Helmchen ensures that the opening of the variation movement quoting the song, *Die Forelle*, is far gentler than usual, obeying the score, and the climax brings wonderfully bouncy playing, leading to a jaunty account of the finale.

Aldo Baerten plays the variations on 'Trockne Blumen' on a wooden Baroque flute, adding to the delicacy and agility of the playing. Yet in some ways the most striking performance of all comes in the *Notturno*, tenderly affectionate in its flowing *adagio*. Though the *pianissimos* are extreme, every note can be clearly heard. A distinctive disc.

Additional recommendations

Schubert Piano Quintet, 'Trout'ᵃ
Coupled with **Mozart** Piano Quartet in G minor, K478
Zehetmair *vn* **Zimmermann** *va* **Duven** *vc*
ᵃ**Riegelbauer** *db* **Brendel** *pf*
Philips 446 001-2PH (75' · DDD)   ℗⊙⊙⊙⊳

Brendel is the linchpin here, and, as ever, balances heart and mind with innate good taste. Time and again you find yourself overhearing detail that might otherwise have passed for nothing. And yet it *is* a dialogue, with the loose-limbed Thomas Zehetmair leading his supremely accomplished colleagues through Schubert's delightful five-tier structure. Mozart's G minor Quartet makes for an unexpected, though instructive, coupling. Both works include their respective first movement repeats.

Piano Quintet, 'Trout'ᵃ.
Coupled with Adagio and Rondo concertante in F, D487
Kodály Qt; ᵃ**I Tóth** *db* **Jandó** *pf*
Naxos 8 550658 (53' · DDD)   Ⓢ⊙⊳

Jenö Jandó's recording of the *Trout* Quintet, in a version which is based on the first edition of 1829, is buoyant and vigorous. The string support from members of the Kodály Quartet and István Tóth, despite some rough edges, is generally sonorous and appropriate. Balance is good, with the piano agreeably highlighted. The result is a performance which is a most desirable acquisition.

String Quartets

D18 in B flat; **D32** in C; **D36** in B flat; **D46** in C; **D68** in B flat; **D74** in D; **D87** in E flat; **D94** in D; **D103** in C minor (fragment); **D112** in B flat; **D173** in G minor; **D353** in E; **D703** in C minor (Quartettsatz); **D804** in A minor (Rosamunde); **D810** in D minor (Death and the Maiden); **D887** in G

String Quartets, D87, D703 & D804
Belcea Quartet (Corina Belcea, Laura Samuel *vns* Krzysztof Chorzelski *va* Alasdair Tait *vc*)
EMI 557419-2 (73' · DDD)   ℗⊙⊙⊙⊳

 'Schubert's Quartet has been performed, rather slowly in his opinion, but very purely and tenderly,' wrote Moritz von Schwind on the day D804 was premiered by the Schuppanzigh Quartet. The composer may well have reacted similarly on hearing the Belcea's first movement. It's a spacious tempo, certainly, causing some of the more energetic music – the last four bars for instance – to sound slightly ponderous. But purity and tenderness are certainly in evidence. Internal balance and intonation are exemplary, and in the songful melodic writing that dominates the whole work, Corina Belcea and her colleagues seem to have the knack of shaping each long phrase to perfection, knowing just when to intensify the vibrato or give a note extra emphasis, and when to allow the music to flow effortlessly onwards.

These fine qualities persist throughout. There may be more dramatic accounts of D703, but no other group presents its *cantabile* music in a more affecting way. The lesser work, D87, gets a charming, persuasive interpretation, but the profound and subtle way these young players engage with the later, greater music is the most impressive thing this group has done so far.

String Quartets D703ᵃ, D804ᵇ, D810, 'Death and the Maiden'ᵃ & D887ᵇ
Quartetto Italiano (Paolo Borciani, Elisa Pegreffi *vns* Piero Farulli *va* Franco Rossi *vc*)
Philips Duo ② 446 163-2PM2 (142' · ADD)
Recorded ᵃ1965, ᵇ1976-77   Ⓜ

The Italians' playing has freshness, affection, firm control and above all authority to a degree that no relative newcomer can match. It's notable not only for the highest standards of ensemble, intonation and blend, but also for its imaginative insights; these attributes readily apply to the music-making on this Duo reissue, particularly in the slow movements. Indeed, the players' progress through the wonderful set of variations in the *Andante con moto*, which reveals the *Death and the Maiden* Quartet's association with the famous Schubert song of that name, has unforgettable intensity.

The comparable *Andante* of No 13, with its lovely *Rosamunde* theme – which is approached here in a relaxed, leisurely manner – is held together with a similar (almost imperceptible) sureness of touch. When this work was originally issued, the first-movement exposition repeat was cut in order to get the quartet complete on to a single LP side. Here it has been restored.

Finest of all is the great No 15, a work of epic scale. The first movement alone runs to nearly 23 minutes, and the players' masterly grip over the many incidents that make up the *Allegro molto moderato* is effortless. For an encore we're given No 12, a piece on a smaller scale, but here presented with a comparable hushed intensity of feeling. This, like No 14, was recorded in 1965 and the textures are leaner than on the others, with a fractional edge on *fortissimos*. Nevertheless, the ear soon adjusts when the playing is as remarkable as this. The other recordings have more body, and a fine presence. The CD transfers throughout are excellent.

String Quartets – D804 & D810, 'Death and the Maiden'
Takács Quartet (Edward Dusinberre, Károly Schranz *vns* Geraldine Walther *va* András Fejér *vc*)
Hyperion CDA67585 (69' · DDD)　　　Ⓜ❍❍❍❿

With their Decca Beethoven cycle, the Takács Quartet set a modern-day benchmark. Now, with a new record company and a replacement viola player, things look set for them to do the same for Schubert's two most popular string quartets. These works were written in 1824, a year of despondency for Schubert who was ill and clearly felt he was living under the shadow of death. Whereas in the *Rosamunde*, the underlying feeling is a tearful nostalgia, in *Death and the Maiden*, there's a black despair that at times gives way to anger.

The Takács have the ability to make you believe that there's no other possible way the music should go, and the strength to overturn preconceptions that comes only with the greatest performers. Tempi are invariably apt – the opening of the *Rosamunde* is wonderfully judged. They also have a way of revealing detail that you'd never previously noticed – in the *Allegro* of D810, Schubert's sighing figure in the viola is here poignantly brought out.

But though there's plenty of humanity in these recordings, there's nothing sentimental about the playing; they make Schubert sound symphonic, and a sense of drama and tensile strength underlines everything, even a movement as luscious as the *Andante* of the *Rosamunde* Quartet, which is based on the theme that gives this quartet its name.

The recording captures the quartets vividly and realistically and Misha Donat's notes are erudite and stylish.

String Quartets – No 14, 'Death and the Maiden', D810; No 15, D887. String Quintet, D956ª
Belcea Quartet with ªValentin Erben *vc*
EMI ② 967025-2 (130' · DDD)　　　Ⓟ❍❍❍❿

The traditionally ceremonial key of C major takes on a different hue in Schubert's Quintet. Its demands, ranging from the pensive to the passionate, don't ruffle the Belcea Quartet and Valentin Erben. Take it for granted that the playing is on the loftiest level, ensemble always transparently clean; and the ability to think, listen and prepare as a coordinated team results in an extraordinarily cogent performance sure in its grasp of phraseology, structure and dynamics.

Schubert spatters the music, virtually all his music, with filigree sounds, *p* to *ppp*, throwing in sudden changes of *f* to *p* from one note to another. Such details are always obeyed. Nothing is generalised, as can be heard at the last close of the slow movement where absolute mastery over hushed tone, diaphanous texture and instrumental balance produces an awed stillness of time-stopping beauty. Here is technique fully subservient to emotional force not only in this movement, with its charged F minor middle section, but throughout the whole work.

Throughout the other works too. The Belcea's response to Schubert's kaleidoscopic moods, from anguished tempestuousness to poetic felicity, centres round their superfine sensitivity to all his markings. The very wide arc through which their softest dynamic layer swings across to its loudest is a critical factor in recreating the dramatic impact of D810; and D887 where the depiction of raw nerve ends and explosions of wrath also incur the most daunting challenges to performers. The Belceas don't flinch from any of them. Nor do they slacken the tension inherent in the lines. Yet they punctuate the music with a yielding freedom of expression that allows phases to breathe; and Schubert's last quartet, in scope probably his greatest and most disquieting, ends in an *Allegro assai* finale where the Belceas underline its message of discomfiture in a *tour de force* of icy intensity. Their executive aplomb and penetrating intelligence (both clearly conveyed in the recording) place the interpretation of this work, and indeed the whole set, on a pinnacle.

Octet in F, D803

Octet
Gaudier Ensemble (Richard Hosford *cl* Robin O'Neill *bn* Jonathan Williams *hn* Marieke Blankestijn, Lesley Hatfield *vns* Iris Juda *va* Christoph Marks *vc* Stephen Williams *db*)
Hyperion CDA67339 (60' · DDD)　　　Ⓟ❍❍❿

An intriguing point arises in the second movement. It's meant to be *Adagio* but the Gaudier pace it fairly swiftly, offering a reminder that one edition marks it *Andante un poco mosso*. The Vienna Octet of 1957 followed this instruction, but its 1990 counterpart preferred something slower. The Gaudier, though, are anything but perfunctory. Their line is curvaceous and malleable with a dynamic range that contains many shades of softness. Engineer Tony Faulkner has helped by using the ambience of the Henry Wood Hall to create both a blend and a distinctiveness of timbre. There's a glow to the sound that other versions don't have.

The Gaudier's control over the grading of tonal intensity draws attention to the many passages in this work that are written *piano* or *pianissimo*; and where leavened by hairpin accents, stabbing *sforzandos* and even *fortissimos* they supply necessary impact without being crude. If there's one movement that encapsulates all that's striking about this performance, then it's the fourth – an *Andante* with seven variations. Here's an example of how these musicians balance themselves, and how they've thought about the different facets of the music. Were he alive today, this recording might even persuade Schubert scholar Maurice JE Brown to change his mind about the seventh variation, which he described as 'a distasteful episode'.

Additional recommendations

Octet[a]
Coupled with Der Hirt auf dem Felsen, D965[b]
[b]**Tynan** *sop* [ab]**Collins** *cl* [a]**O'Neill** *bn* [a]**Owen** *hn* [a]**van Keulen**, [a]**Brunt** *vns* [a]**Tomter** *va* [a]**Müller-Schott** *vc*
[a]**Riegelbauer** *db* [b]**Martineau** *pf*
Wigmore Hall Live WHLIVE0017 (74' · DDD)
Recorded live in 2006 ⓟ**OO**

A hugely enjoyable account of Schubert's Octet. It is a work lasting an hour, which with its many repeats can easily outstay its welcome despite the freshness of Schubert's invention. But Michael Collins and friends give a performance that is wonderfully resilient and imaginative. The sense of a live performance in both Octet and song is beautifully caught.

Octet
Mullova Ens
Onyx ONYX4006 (64' · DDD) ⓟ**O**

A spacious performance, enthralling and poetic: it leaves behind the world of happy Viennese music-making. Instead, we have a view of the Octet as one of Schubert's major achievements. The *Adagio* is taken unusually slowly, but without any feeling of the rhythm sagging. The thoughtful shaping of phrases isn't confined to the *Scherzo*; it's present throughout, keeping us constantly aware of the music's expressive power. Even when these inflections seem slightly contentious – in the finale's main theme, for example – they contribute to a constant feeling of lively communication.

Piano Trios

Piano Trios[a] – B flat, D28 (Sonatensatz);
B flat, D898; E flat, D929. Notturno in E flat, D897[b].
String Trios[b] – B flat, D471; B flat, D581
[a]**Beaux Arts Trio** (Menahem Pressler *pf* Daniel Guilet *vn* Bernard Greenhouse *vc*); [b]**Grumiaux Trio** (Arthur Grumiaux *vn* Georges Janzer *va* Eva Czako *vc*)
Philips Duo ② 438 700-2PM2 (127' · ADD)
Recorded 1966-69 Ⓜ**O**

These performances are polished, yet the many solo contributions from each of the players emerge with a strong personality. The Beaux Arts cellist brings lovely phrasing and a true simplicity of line, so right for Schubert – memorably in the lovely slow movement melody of the Trio No 2 in E flat. In addition to the great piano trios (B flat, D898 and E flat, D929) the set includes the extremely personable, very early Sonata in B flat, D28, where the lyrical line already has the

unmistakable character of its young composer. Also included is the *Notturno*, D897, a raptly emotive short piece played here with a remarkable depth of feeling that recalls the gentle intensity of the glorious slow movement of the String Quintet. The recording is naturally balanced, although a little dry in the treble. Of the two rarer string trios, also early works, the four-movement Trio, D581, is totally infectious, with that quality of innocence that makes Schubert's music stand apart. Such persuasive advocacy and vivid recording can't fail to give the listener great pleasure.

Piano Trio in E flat, D929
Florestan Trio (Anthony Marwood *vn*
Richard Lester *vc* Susan Tomes *pf*)
Hyperion CDA67347 (58' · DDD) ⓟ**OO**

This profound, yet still often light-hearted, E flat Trio was written in the same month (November) that Schubert completed *Winterreise*. We are instantly reminded of this in the Florestan's eloquent and aptly paced account of the C minor *Andante con moto*, with what Richard Wigmore describes as its 'stoical trudging gait'. Its essential melancholy is gently caught, first by the cellist, Richard Lester, and then equally touchingly by the pianist, Susan Tomes. The dramatically rhythmic opening of the first movement could almost be by Beethoven, but once again these players show themselves to be completely within the Schubertian sensibility and catch perfectly the atmosphere of the more important lyrical motif, first heard on the cello (in bars 15 and 16), which is to dominate the movement alongside the engaging repeated-note figure (so delicately articulated by the piano).

They set a winningly jaunty mood for the finale, which is maintained whenever the main theme reappears, even though, as always with late Schubert, much happens to vary the music's mood and atmosphere. Another superb performance then from the Florestans, penetrating, yet full of spirited spontaneity, and in spite of the moments of sadness, much Schubertian bonhomie. The recording is completely lifelike and very well balanced.

Piano Trios – Sonatensatz, D28; E flat, D929
Kungsbacka Trio (Malin Broman *vn* Jesper Svedberg *vc* Simon Crawford Phillips *pf*)
Naxos 8 555700 (61' · DDD) Ⓢ**O**

The opening to this trio appears to take up the gauntlet thrown down by Beethoven's mature piano trios – but how very different a path Schubert takes. It's easy to sound strenuous at the beginning of this movement but it's not a mistake the Kungsbacka Trio make, sounding strong yet never belligerent, and finding almost as many colours as the miraculous Florestan recording (see above). What is particularly impressive is their confidence and sweep: more extrovert than the soul-searching Florestan Trio, they relish the outgoing E flat major (surely Schubert was inspired by the fact that for Beethoven this was the ultimate heroic key). For the second movement, the Kungsbacka choose their trudging tempo carefully, vividly reminding us that this work dates from the same year as *Winterreise*. The remaining movements are similarly impressive: the minuet/*scherzo* hybrid, a tail-chasing canon, is great fun, the Trio stomping but never coarse. Unusually, the Kungsbacka choose the composer's uncut original finale (also offered by the Florestan Trio as an additional track alongside the shorter version). It's one of those extraordinary Schubert movements that starts unassumingly and yet stretches out to the horizon, seemingly unstoppable. In the hands of the Kungsbacka, there are no longueurs.

The Kungsbacka fill out their disc with the early *Sonatensatz*, D28, a delightful little *petit four* to complete the feast, elegantly played. This is certainly impressive playing, and a bargain at the price.

Arpeggione Sonata

Schubert Arpeggione Sonata, D821
Schumann Adagio and Allegro, Op 70.
Drei Fantasiestücke, Op 73. Fünf Stücke
im Volkston, Op 102. Märchenbilder, Op 113
Antonio Meneses *vc* **Gérard Wyss** *pf*
Avie AV2112 (78' · DDD)   Ⓕ🅑➔

Meneses negotiates the Arpeggione Sonata's dauntingly high tessitura with no sense of strain, and the Schumann sets, designed respectively for horn, clarinet and viola, sound like idiomatic cello music. He's a true virtuoso, as the fast passages in the Arpeggione and the third of the *Märchenbilder* amply demonstrate, but one never feels that he's presenting himself. The impression is rather that he's inviting us into Schumann's or Schubert's inner world, urbanely drawing attention, by means of subtle emphasis or change of colour, to all the music's incidental beauties.

Gérard Wyss, as an experienced Lieder accompanist, has a similar eye for illustrative detail; his touch is unusually sensitive, with chords always beautifully balanced, and his left hand gives exceptional vitality to the bass-lines. The finale's minor-key episode in Hungarian style bubbles with vitality. Similarly, all the Schumann pieces are performed in an outgoing, friendly way; especially enjoyable is the first of the *Stücke im Volkston*, progressing from a light, playful start to sweeping Romantic gestures, and the last of the *Märchenbilder*, sweet and tender, with an almost Mahlerian sense of regret and loss.

Arpeggione Sonata, D821. Violin Sonata, D574.   🅟
Fantasie, D934
Pieter Wispelwey *vc* **Paolo Giacometti** *fp*
Onyx Classics ONYX4046 (65' · DDD)   Ⓕ🅑➔

Back in 1996 Wispelwey and Giacometti recorded transcriptions of Schubert's three 'little' violin sonatas (D384, 385, 408): the change

of instrument didn't seem to bring any gains to compensate for inevitable losses. The same question arises here; but, against expectations, the *Fantasie*, especially, is remarkably convincing in its new guise. The transposition to cello increases the difficulties of what is already a demanding work, and enhances the sense of virtuosity as Wispelwey triumphantly surmounts each hurdle. Only twice – in the *Andante*'s third variation and in the fast arpeggios in the finale – does the change of instrument create problems of clarity or balance.

Giacometti matches his partner in projecting the *Fantasie*'s glittering surface, and in the first movement of D574 he coaxes an inspiring range of expressive sonorities from his Viennese fortepiano. This movement sounds as though it could have been written for cello but there are a few problems in the following movements, especially where Schubert writes a low-lying violin accompaniment. Here the cello can't play at a lower octave and, however much Wispelwey reduces his sound, the cello still penetrates too keenly.

As expected from these artists, the performance of the Arpeggione Sonata is most accomplished: the last two movements are enormously enjoyable but in the first *Allegro* Wispelwey and Giacometti are afflicted by an excessive tendency to hold back the rhythm. Performers who are able to break free of metronomic regularity are to be admired; but where the freedom comes almost exclusively in taking extra time, it can induce impatience.

Violin and Piano Works

Violin Sonata, D574. Fantasie, D934.
Rondo brillant, D895
Isabelle Faust *vn* **Alexander Melnikov** *pf*
Harmonia Mundi HMC90 1870 (58' · DDD)   Ⓕ

In nearly every respect this is outstanding. The *Rondo* and the *Fantasie*, both written for the virtuoso duo of Karl von Bocklet and Josef Slawik, can sound as if Schubert were striving for a brilliant, flashy style, foreign to his nature. Both are in places uncomfortable to play (when first published, the *Fantasie*'s violin part was simplified), but you would never guess this from Faust's and Melnikov's performance; they both nonchalantly toss off any problem passages as though child's play.

The *Fantasie*'s finale and the *Rondo brillant* are irresistibly lively and spirited, and this duo's technical finesse extends to more poetic episodes – Melnikov's *tremolo* at the start of the *Fantasie* shimmers delicately, while the filigree passage-work in the last of the variations that form the *Fantasie*'s centrepiece have a delightful poise and sense of ease.

The Sonata's more intimate style is captured just as convincingly; in all three performances Faust and Melnikov observe Schubert's often very detailed, careful expression marks, not as a matter of duty, but as a stimulus to the imagination, as a way of entering more deeply into the music.

The one slight reservation concerns Isabelle Faust's manner of expression. She makes the most of any passionate phrases and is equally convincing at cool, mysterious or dreamlike moments. But the lyrical phrases in the Rondo's introduction surely demand a more heartfelt utterance. In the Sonata, too, there are places where one longs for more warmth. This quibble aside, it's a lovely disc, one to listen to over and over again.

Works for Piano Duet

Allegro, 'Lebensstürme', D947. Divertissement à la hongroise, D818. Divertissement, D823. Fantasie, D940. German Dance with Two Trios and Two Ländler, D618. Grande marche funèbre, D859. Grande marche héroïque, D885. Vier Ländler, D814. Two Marches caractéristiques, D968b. Six Grandes marches, D819. Trois Marches héroïques, D602. Trois Marches militaires, D733. Rondo, D951. Piano Sonata, 'Grand Duo', D812. March, D928
Christoph Eschenbach, Justus Frantz pf
Brilliant Classics ④ 92858 (4h 31' · ADD)
From HMV originals, recorded 1970-79   ⑨

In the late 1970s Christoph Eschenbach and Justus Frantz recorded around half of Schubert's four-hand output. Their performances were always unsurpassed for refinement of touch and hyper-sensitive balancing of voices. Reincarnated in a slimline four-CD set they make a terrific bargain.

Even they cannot do much for dull utility pieces like the three *Marches héroïques*. But with playing that mingles fire, grace and a vast range of colour and dynamics (finely caught by the engineers), they rekindle the appetite for the *Marches militaires*, so much more appealing as piano duets than in their more familiar brash orchestral guise. The magnificent *Grand Duo* is dangerously leisurely and flexible in its opening movement. Both rival performances listed strike a better balance between epic sweep and ravishing detail and give the *Scherzo* more of Schubert's prescribed *vivace* – though Eschenbach and Frantz yield to no one in pace and temperament in the Hungarian-tinged finale.

Among the other masterpieces, the A minor *Lebensstürme* receives a thrilling, richly imagined performance, with *pp* and *ppp* playing of ethereal tenderness, while the F minor *Fantasie* has drama, colour and intense, aching *cantabile*, and surpasses rivals in the élan and *delicatezza* of the *Scherzo*. A spellbinding performance, crowning a feast of memorable Schubert playing from one of the great duo partnerships.

Sonata for Piano Duet, 'Grand Duo', D812. Allegro, 'Lebensstürme', D947. Fantasie, D940. Marche militaire, D733 No 1. Marche caractéristique, D968b No 1
Evgeny Kissin, James Levine pfs
RCA Red Seal ② 82876 69283-2 (85' · DDD)
Recorded live in 2005   Ⓜ🅾🅾➡

On paper it seems an unlikely pairing. On disc, however, it is something of a triumph, a recording that is far more than a mere *souvenir d'occasion* of a memorable night in Carnegie Hall. Intriguingly, it is difficult to detect purely aurally which is the world-famous pianist and which the world-famous conductor. From his familiar sometimes over-insistent tone, we guess it is Kissin who takes the *primo* part in the F minor *Fantasie* (he plays to the back of the hall, not to the microphone) but elsewhere it is impossible to tell them apart, so well do they blend dynamics, phrasing and ensemble. This is even more remarkable given that the music, written for four hands at one piano, is played on two (beautifully balanced) Hamburg Steinways – less of a squeeze on the piano stool but trickier to coordinate.

The *Fantasie* is the least successful item. Its dramatic elements are energetically characterised but its introspective, questioning discourse goes by the board, leaving the emotions untouched. *Lebensstürme* ('Storms of Life'), written a month after the *Fantasie*, is given a terrific whirlwind of a performance and completes the first short disc (34'05").

The second half features the *Grand Duo* (40'49"), a symphony for piano in all but name. Here Kissin and Levine come into their own with a fiercely argued, compelling account some way removed from the intimacy of a Schubertiad, and the best reason for buying this release. They close with two fast and furious crowd-pleasers bringing as much pleasure to the audience as they so obviously do to the players.

Piano Sonatas

D157 in E; **D279** in C; **D459** in E; **D537** in A minor; **D557** in A flat; **D566** in E minor; **D568** in E flat; **D571** in F sharp minor; **D575** in B; **D613** in C; **D625** in F minor; **D664** in A; **D784** in A minor; **D840** in C (Relique); **D845** in A minor; **D850** in D; **D894** in G; **D958** in C minor; **D959** in A; **D960** in B flat

Piano Sonatas – A minor, D537; E flat, D568; B, D575; A, D664; A minor, D784; C, D840; A minor, D845; D, D850; G, D894; C minor, D958; A, D959; B flat, D960. Moments musicaux, D780. German Dances, D790 & D820. Klavierstücke, D946. Impromptus, D899 & D935.
Mitsuko Uchida pf
Philips 475 628-2PB8 (7h 56' · DDD)   Ⓜ🅾🅾➡

While the deletions axe may have removed individual volumes in Uchida's cycle, this collection, competitively priced, is a highly tempting proposition. This is a set that celebrates the music first and foremost: her Schubert is never less than wonderfully finished in pianistic terms. With her exceptional finger technique Uchida takes everything in her stride, yet she never allows physical excitement to become the be-all-and-end-all. She is also extremely good at exposing the light-filled dream world that Schubert so often inhabits as well as guiding us into stark waking reality. The sound throughout the set is very fine indeed.

Piano Sonatas – E, D157; G, D894. Die schöne Müllerin – Der Müller und der Bach (arr Liszt, S565)
Arcadi Volodos pf
Sony Classical SK89647 (64' · DDD)   Ⓕ○

Here is irrefutable proof of Arcadi Volodos's genius and versatility. Naturally, lovers of long-cherished recordings by Schubertians of the stature of Schnabel, Kempff, Pollini and Brendel will hesitate, equating Volodos's sheen and perfection with an external glory rather than an interior poetic truth. But such witnesses for the prosecution will find themselves silenced by an empathy with Schubert's spirit so total that it would be extraordinary in a pianist of any age, let alone one still in his twenties.

The jubilant burst of scales and arpeggios that launch the E major Sonata, D157, are given with a deftness and unforced eloquence that are pure Volodos, while the *Andante*'s sighing chromaticism and surprise modulations have a tonal translucence that will make lesser mortals weep with envy. But it's in the G major Sonata, D894, that epitome of Schubertian lyricism, that Volodos erases all possible doubts. His opening has an unforgettable stillness and mystery, his velvet-tipped sonority and seamless *legato* a reminder that Schubert's vocal and instrumental inspiration were for the most part one and the same. For Volodos and for his listeners this is a true dance of the gods. The recordings are as flawless as the playing.

Piano Sonatas – B, D575; F minor, D625; A, D664. Moment musical in C, D780 No 1
Sviatoslav Richter pf
BBC Legends BBCL4010-2 (78' · ADD)
Recorded live 1979   Ⓜ○○

Richter's Schubert is simply in a class of its own. No pianist did more to overturn the traditional view of the composer as a blithe, unreflecting child of nature. And in this Festival Hall recital three sonatas from 1817-19 unfold with a grandeur of conception, a spirituality and a stoical timelessness that were unique to Richter. The first two movements of the A major Sonata are, on the face of it, implausibly slow: but with his mesmeric, self-communing intensity Richter convinces you for the duration of the performance that no other way is admissible. Phrases, paragraphs are shaped with calm inevitability, underpinned by the sublime, luminous simplicity of Richter's *cantabile*; and no pianist is more sensitive to Schubert's magical harmonic strokes or understands more surely their place in the larger scheme. As Richter conceives them, the first two movements of the A major, D664, foreshadow the rapt, philosophical contemplation of the late G major and B flat Sonatas, D894 and D960; and even the finale, projected with Richter's

characteristic mastery and subtlety of rhythm, has something rarefied in its playfulness. Richter is equally lofty and far-sighted in the two lesser-known sonatas.

The BBC recording, while perhaps a shade bass-light, is warm, and does ample justice to Richter's vast dynamic and tonal palette. A bronchial March audience can intrude at the start of tracks, especially in finales. But no matter. All but those terminally resistant to Richter's uniquely introspective, long-spanned view of the composer should acquire as a matter of urgency these visionary performances by one of the greatest Schubertians of the 20th century.

Piano Sonatas – C, D613; A minor, D784; B flat, D960
Stephen Hough pf
Hyperion CDA67027 (76' · DDD)   Ⓕ○Ⓑ→

Stephen Hough's moving performance of D960 is marked throughout by refined, discerning pianism and an uncommonly subtle ear for texture. In all four movements, he seeks out the music's inwardness and fragility, its ethereal, self-communing remoteness. The opening *Molto moderato*, unfolding in vast, calm spans, has a hypnotic inevitability; there are countless felicities of timing and colour, but always a vital sense of forward motion. Hough adopts a dangerously slow tempo in the *Andante* but sustains it through the breadth and concentration of his line, the subtlety of his tonal palette and his pointing of rhythmic detail. His rarefied grace and delicacy, his gentle probing of the music's vulnerability, are of a piece with his conception of the sonata as a whole.

As usual, Hyperion doesn't stint over playing time, offering another complete sonata in addition to the two-movement fragment, D613. D784, perhaps Schubert's most depressive instrumental work, is magnificently done. Hough distils an immense weight of suffering from the pervasive two-note motif that dominates the first movement like some massive, Wagnerian pendulum; but, typically, the lyrical music is limpidly coloured and poignantly inflected, with an unusually precise observation of Schubert's accents. The *Andante* is flowing and long-arched, with some ravishing soft playing, and he a brings a superb rhythmic impulse to the eerily scudding counterpoint of the main subject and a piercing tenderness to the contrasting F major theme. The fragmentary C major Sonata, D613, one of numerous Schubert torsos from the years 1817-22, is no great shakes: two pleasant but uneventful movements, both incomplete. The recording is of exemplary clarity, warmth and truthfulness.

Piano Sonatas – A minor, D784; C, 'Relique', D840; B flat, D960. 12 Deutsche (Ländler), D790. Ungarische Melodie, D817. Four Impromptus, D899. Allegretto, D915
Imogen Cooper pf
Avie ② AV2158 (134' · DDD). Recorded live   Ⓕ○Ⓑ→

Imogen Cooper offers a near-perfect balance of head and heart in Schubert, her expressive technique and musical personality wholly in the service of the composer. Plaudits are due, too, to recording producer Adam Gatehouse and engineers Simon Hancock and Neil Pemberton for capturing the piano sound so faithfully – and also to the (unnamed) piano technician for such a beautifully voiced instrument.

These live performances raised the perhaps contentious thought that this is how recordings should ideally be made now: music-making for an audience (rather than a microphone) without the safety blanket of six, seven or possibly eight takes, but just a patch session if necessary (Cooper, needless to say, is note-perfect). Why should we listen any longer to performances that are the results of hundreds of edits?

There is a caveat to this volume, however. It is not Cooper's fault but by happenstance rather than intention the programme, with few exceptions, is too consistently melancholic and introspective to be enjoyed in one sitting. This is most pronounced in the 15 minutes of the A minor Sonata's first movement where Schubert lays on the self-pity with a trowel; but in the 12 German Dances and even in the second and fourth Impromptus and the B flat Sonata's *Scherzo* one senses the surface jollity is forced. Having said that, this performance of the G flat Impromptu is treasurable, a miracle of heartfelt *cantabile* playing. Likewise, the radiant pessimism of the opening movement of the B flat Sonata, played without the exposition repeat. The one criticism is the coda of D960 where one wished Cooper had, instead of politely concluding the work, wrapped it up more precipitately, leaving us with the impression that Schubert had suddenly realised that he had revealed more of his troubled soul than he intended to.

Piano Sonatas – A minor, D784; D, D850
Alfred Brendel pf
Philips 422 063-2PH (63' · DDD)

There's an extraordinary amount of highly experimental writing in Schubert's piano sonatas. The essence of their structure is the contrasting of big heroic ideas with tender and inner thoughts; the first impresses the listener, the second woos him. The two works on this CD are in some ways on a varying scale. The D major, D850, lasts for 40 minutes, the A minor, D784, for around 23. However, it's the latter that contains the most symphonically inspired writing – it sounds as if it could easily be transposed for orchestra. Alfred Brendel presents the composer not so much as the master of Lieder-writing, but more as a man thinking in large forms. Although there are wonderful quiet moments when intimate asides are conveyed with an imaginative sensitivity one remembers more the urgency and the power behind the notes. The A minor, with its frequently recurring themes, is almost obsessive in character, while the big D major Sonata is rather lighter in its mood, especially in

the outer movements. The recorded sound is very faithful to the pianist's tone, while generally avoiding that insistent quality that can mar his loudest playing.

'The Russian Piano Tradition: The Neuhaus School'
Schubert Piano Sonatas – A minor, D845; D, D850.
Impromptu, D899 No 2
Sviatoslav Richter pf
APR mono APR5669 (78' · ADD)
Recorded 1956-57

Sviatoslav Richter's Schubert has always provoked controversy and APR's reissue of recordings dating from 1956-57 is a savage reminder of a pianist of uncompromising vision. Rhythms are held in a vice-like grip and there can rarely have been a more radical shift of simple-minded notions of Viennese charm and gentility. Certainly there is little sweetness from Richter, though his remorseless tread is unforgettably countered in the Trio of the A minor Sonata's *Scherzo* which is played with such poise and lucidity that it soars to ultimate heights of poetry. A suitably icy wind blows across the finale and even in the exultant, less despairing pages of the D major Sonata Richter's adamantine strength and rhythm are paramount. You may miss Kempff's beguiling lilt in the sing-a-song-of-sixpence finale or Gilels's emotionalism in the *con moto* but you can never be less than awed by such consummate if chilling mastery.

Piano Sonatas – A minor, D845; D, D850; No 20,
D959. 11 Ecossaises, D781. Drei Klavierstücke, D946
Imogen Cooper pf
Avie ② AV2516 (149' · DDD)
Recorded live 2008

Imogen Cooper's astonishing achievement is the fruit of her tireless devotion to a composer very much at the heart of her richly varied repertoire. Now she returns to Schubert, though this time with a vital difference. These performances were recorded live at a Queen Elizabeth Hall recital. Free from the confines of the studio, Cooper rises to the occasion with performances that show a courageous advance on her already distinguished work.

This is true, most strikingly, in the great penultimate A major Sonata, D959. The catalogue may be filled to the brim with oustanding discs of this epic work (Schnabel, Kempff, Brendel, Kovacevich, Lupu and Paul Lewis to name but six) yet few seem more deeply charged or felt performances now exist on record. Everything is weighted with greater drama and significance than before. Cooper wrings every expressive ounce from the massive opening *Allegro* and the result is movingly personal rather than overbearing or idiosyncratic. Time and again she makes you sense the dark undertow beneath Schubert's outward geniality, the pain as well as the fullness of his tragically brief life. Here, the dramatic and poetic parameters are stretched

SCHUBERT PIANO SONATA IN B FLAT, D960 – IN BRIEF

Mitsuko Uchida
Philips 456 572-2PH (71' · DDD)   ⒻⓄⓄ➟
There is a sense of wariness, even apprehension from the start, as if anticipating the
ominous bass trill. This is a beautifully
nuanced performance, with poignant lyricism and baleful menace revealed as complementary traits. Excellently recorded.

Alfred Brendel
Philips ② 456 573-2PM2 (138' · DDD)   Ⓜ
Although in this live recording the listener is
initially aware of Brendel's audience (in this
respect the sound on the coupled works is
better), such is the concentration of his playing that you're quickly absorbed. A truly
dramatic account not to be missed.

Stephen Hough
Hyperion CDA67027 (76' · DDD)   ⒻⓄ
Hough takes relatively slow speeds in his
thoughtful and concentrated performance,
his sensitivity to phrasing and pianistic colour
compelling attention throughout.

Andras Staier   Ⓟ
Teldec ② 0630 13143-2 (119' · DDD)   Ⓕ
A masterful performance on a fortepiano,
whose different registers translate into quasi-
orchestral contrasts in colour, so adding a
further dimension to Schubert's masterpiece.

Imogen Cooper pf
Avie ② AV2158 (134' · DDD)   ⒻⓄ➟
Imogen Cooper offers a near-perfect balance
of head and heart in Schubert, her expressive
technique and musical personality wholly in
the service of the composer. The radiant pessimism of the opening movement of the
sonata, played without the exposition repeat,
is breathtaking.

Clifford Curzon   Ⓗ
Decca ④ 475 084-2DC4 (304' · ADD)   ⓂⓄ➟
A musicianly account which cuts to the core
of Schubert's inspiration, yet overstates
nothing: details are in place, but never at the
expense of the overall musical structure.

Wilhelm Kempff
DG ② 459 412-2GTA2 (150' · ADD)   ⓂⓄⓄ➟
A ravishingly beautiful account, though the
sound is quite dated, and can often seem
rather shallow. But nothing stands in the way
of appreciating such a master at work.

Leif Ove Andsnes
EMI 557901-2 (71' · DDD)   ⒻⓄ➟
A beautifully judged performance that
emphasises Schubert's poetry – something
highlighted by the coupling of a group of
songs in which Andsnes accompanies Ian
Bostridge. Nicely recorded, too.

close to the edge, and in the second movement
Cooper's numbingly slow and intense view of
Schubert's *Andantino* makes you feel as if the
protagonist from *Winterreise* had returned to
haunt you with his world-weary despair.

Elsewhere nothing is taken for granted and
every musical shadow, whether passing or
engulfing, is acutely registered, whether in the
magical close to Variation 3 in D845, the subtle
inflections of a true artist in the following flow
of ideas and the fluency and tonal finesse in the
windswept finale. Her desire to avoid an undue
or cloying romanticism sees her moving swiftly
through the *con moto* of the D major Sonata.

Always you sense how the influences of her
fellow musicians, of Brendel and Holzmair in
particular, have now been subsumed into a
vision entirely her own. Finely recorded.

Piano Sonatas – G, D894; C minor, D958. Moments
musicaux, D780. Deutsche Tänze, D783. Impromptus,
D935
Imogen Cooper pf
Avie ② AV2157 (150' · DDD)
Recorded live   ⓂⓄ➟

For the duration of these two CDs, not only
does Cooper not put a foot (or rather finger)
wrong, but she holds one spellbound, as much as
the audiences in the Queen Elizabeth Hall
clearly were. Mercifully unobtrusive and cough-
free, they reward her with generous and well
earned applause. They know they have been
present at a very special recital. The BBC
sound, too, is exemplary.

Imogen Cooper writes in the booklet of her
love of Lieder, and one thing she can do is make
the piano sing, whether it be the lovely third
subject of the G major's second movement
floated over rippling 32nd-notes, the *molto
espressivo dolente* melody in the final *Allegretto* or
the lullaby opening of the second (A flat)
Moment musical. Songs without words. Colours
are gracefully shaded, dynamics are artfully controlled and contained; there are no intrusive
idiosyncrasies (à la Richter, say) to detract from
the enchantment. In the tarantella finale of the
great C minor Sonata which, in some hands, can
become relentless and outstay its welcome,
Cooper somehow leaves you wanting more. The
heartbreaking theme of the F minor *Moment
musical* (No 5) is allowed to speak for itself without the addition of over-egged sentiment. Perhaps above all, there is throughout a serenity and
poise to the playing which is pure balm for the
soul. Here is a great artist of taste and integrity.

Piano Sonata in G, D894. Impromptus, D935   Ⓟ
Andreas Staier fp
Harmonia Mundi HMC90 2021 (71' · DDD)   Ⓕ

Andreas Staier promises much in his hushed yet
sonorous opening of D984, grounding us in
G major as evocatively as does Beethoven in his
Fourth Piano Concerto. It's evident throughout

that Staier has the full measure of this quietly remarkable work, from its *Molto moderato* opening movement onwards. He also understands well that the momentum of this drama comes not from extreme contrast but from organic growth, and that when Schubert does hurl the listener into stormier realms – at the start of the development of the first movement, for instance – Staier shows us how it relates to what has gone before. Similarly, while the martial dotted figures and *fz* outbreaks in the slow movement in no way lack drama, they don't – as in some readings – sound as if they've landed from a different piece entirely.

He has the advantage of a superb instrument, a modern copy of an 1827 Graf fortepiano by Christopher Clarke. Not only does it offer the ideal degree of mellowness, but the sounds Staier coaxes from it at the quieter end of the spectrum (fading almost to inaudibility in the winsome Trio) are a joy indeed. The upper registers, too, have enough transparency to allow the burnished lower octaves to be heard to full effect. The Impromptus are equally persuasive, in their sense of journeying within each work, in their beauty of sound in the poignancy of No 2, and in finding an unbridled approach to the Hungarian inflections of No 4.

Regardless of your attitude to fortepianos, if you love this music, you'll want this interpretation. Staier is unquestionably one of the most probing and thoughtful of musicians around today.

Piano Sonata in A, D959. Moments musicaux, D780
Martin Helmchen pf
Pentatone ⦿ PTC5186 329 (67' · DDD)   ⓕⓞⒷ›

Here is musical gold indeed. Martin Helmchen is a 27-year-old German pianist who won the Clara Haskil Competition in 2001 and whose playing in its mastery and unadorned quality has much in common with that great artist. Memorable recordings of Schubert's D959 Sonata and the six *Moments musicaux* are hardly thin on the ground yet such is the strength and poetic commitment of Helmchen's playing that he already makes comparison irrelevant. And if one was to single out one awe-inspiring moment it would be the *Andantino* from the Sonata, naturally paced, enviably poised and focused with a stealthy approach to the central elemental uproar that suggests a young pianist of rare maturity and vision.

All possible longueur, too, in the finale is banished in playing that makes for heavenly rather than interminable length. Again, the last of the *Moments musicaux*, an epic in miniature, is given with an unforgettable inwardness and quite without recourse to sub-normal timing or false sophistication. Just occasionally you could say that Helmchen's tempi are insufficiently integrated with a tendency to relax into lyricism and accelerate into drama. But given his overall command this is little more than a spot on the sun. Pentatone's sound is both clear and natural.

Piano Sonata in B flat, D960. Drei Klavierstücke, D946
Mitsuko Uchida pf
Philips 456 572-2PH (71' · DDD)   ⓕⓞⓞⒷ›

Uchida's concentration and inwardness are of a rare order in her absorbed, deeply poetic reading of the B flat Sonata. No pianist makes you so aware how much of the first two movements is marked *pp* or even *ppp*; and none conjures such subtlety of colour in the softest dynamics: listen, for instance, to her playing of the three unearthly C sharp minor chords that usher in the first-movement development, or her timing and colouring of the breathtaking sideslip from C sharp minor to C major in the *Andante*. Other pianists may find a stronger undercurrent of foreboding or desperation in these two movements – though Uchida builds the development of the initial *Molto moderato* superbly to its dramatic climax. But none probes more hauntingly the music's mysterious contemplative ecstasy or creates such a sense of inspired improvisation. And her limpid *cantabile* sonorities are always ravishing on the ear. She's equally attuned to the less rarefied world of the *Scherzo* and finale, the former a glistening, mercurial dance, *con delicatezza* indeed, the latter graceful and quixotic, with a hint of emotional ambiguity even in its ostensibly cheerful main theme and a tigerish ferocity in its sudden Beethovenian eruptions.

The coupling is generous: to the three *Klavierstücke*, D946, she brings a wonderfully impassioned sweep, with razor-sharp rhythms. The recording finely captures Uchida's subtle, pellucid sound world. A revealing disc from a Schubertian of rare insight and spirituality.

Wandererfantasie, D760

Fantasie in C, D934[a]. Fantasy in C, 'Wandererfantasie', D760
[a]**Yuuko Shiokawa** vn **András Schiff** pf
ECM New Series 464 320-2 (50' · DDD)   ⓕⒷ›

Nearly all Schubert's great instrumental works maintain the Classical four-movement layout: but he did turn occasionally to the fashionable, looser, fantasia-style forms – in the case of the *Wandererfantasie*, one of his most disturbing works, he seems to be using his structural know-how in order to subvert the expectations of Classical form. András Schiff vividly brings out the switches between Classical poise, intensely Romantic mood-painting and near-expressionistic disruption; the key lies in the way he doesn't exaggerate any range of contrast, but makes each detail tell, so that the full range of the piece can be heard. One shouldn't underestimate the technical achievement – the lead-in to the *adagio* section is a perfect demonstration of a gradual *diminuendo*, of energy falling away, and when the *Adagio* arrives the chordal playing is superb – the melodic line perfectly balanced by the dark, melancholic colours in the bass.

Balance and lack of exaggeration inform the D934 *Fantasie*, too. From the start, when

Shiokawa steals in above the piano *tremolando*, there's an air of magic. Her fine, silvery tone only rarely expands to a richer or more dramatic utterance, but her care not to overplay actually adds to the rich impression the performance gives. Whereas Kremer and Afanassiev present the central variation set as a brilliant showpiece, Schiff and Shiokawa paint a noticeably more varied picture – drama and virtuosity alternating with delicacy and touches of lyrical tenderness. In short, these are interpretations of rare penetration and individuality.

Schubert Fantasy in C, 'Wandererfantasie', D760
Schumann Fantasie in C, Op 17
Maurizio Pollini pf
DG The Originals 447 451-2GOR (52' · ADD)
Recorded 1973   Ⓜ❍❍❍❍▷

Ⓖ The cover shows Caspar David Friedrich's familiar *The Wanderer above the Sea of Fog*. Pollini, on the other hand, is a wanderer in a transparent ether of crystalline light, and both these legendary performances, recorded in 1973 and beautifully remastered, are of a transcendental vision and integrity. In the Schubert his magisterial, resolutely un-virtuoso approach allows everything its time and place. Listen to his flawlessly graded triple-*piano* approach to the central *Adagio*, to his rock-steady octaves at 5'23" (where Schubert's merciless demand is so often the cause of confusion) or to the way the decorations in the *Adagio* are spun off with such rare finesse, and you may well wonder when you've heard playing of such an unadorned, unalloyed glory. Pollini's Schumann is no less memorable. Doubting Thomases on the alert for alternating touches of imperiousness and sobriety will be disappointed, for, again, Pollini's poise is unfaltering. The opening *Moderato* is *sempre energico*, indeed, its central *Etwas langsamer* is so sensitively and precisely gauged that all possible criticism is silenced. The coda of the central march (that *locus classicus* of the wrong note) is immaculate and in what someone once called the finale's 'shifting sunset vapour' Pollini takes us gently but firmly to the shores of Elysium. Here is a record that should grace every musician's shelf.

Impromptus

Impromptus – D899; D935. Drei Klavierstücke, D946
Allegretto in C minor, D915
Maria João Pires pf
DG ② 457 550-2GH2 (108' · DDD)   Ⓕ❍❍❍❍▷

Ⓖ This is something very special. Pires's characteristic impassioned absorption in all she plays – that concentration which makes the listener appear to be eavesdropping on secrets shared between friends – could hardly find a truer soul mate than Schubert. Each Impromptu has a rare sense of integrity and entirety, born of acute observation and long-pondered responses.

Pires's instinct for tempo and pacing brings a sense of constant restraint, a true *molto moderato* to the *Allegro* of the C minor work from D899, created by a fusion of right-hand *tenuto* here with momentary left-hand *rubato* there. Then there's the clarity of contour within the most subtly graded undertones of the G flat major of D899 which recreates it as a seemingly endless song. Or an *Andante* just slow, just nonchalant enough for the *Rosamunde* theme of the D935 B flat major to give each variation space and breath enough to sing out its own sharply defined character.

The *Allegretto*, D915, acts as a *Pause* between the two discs, a resting place, as it were, for reflection and inner assessment on this long journey. Its end – which could as well be its beginning – is in the *Drei Klavierstücke*, D946, of 1828. The first draws back from the fiery impetuousness within the *Allegro assai*'s tautly controlled rhythms, to an inner world with its own time scale; the second, more transpired than played, has an almost unbearable poignancy of simplicity. The paradox of these unselfregarding performances is how unmistakably they speak and sing out Pires and her unique musicianship. To draw comparisons here would be not so much odious as to miss the point.

Impromptus, D899. Allegretto, D915.
Six Moments musicaux, D780
David Fray pf
Virgin Classics 694489-0 (73' · DDD)   Ⓕ❍❍❍❍▷

French pianist David Fray, 28 years old at the time of this disc and already acclaimed for an intensive and dazzling career, offers a Schubert disc of the rarest distinction. Indeed, it is no exaggeration to say that few pianists have been more acutely sensitive to Schubert's complex inner world, one where an often pained and world-weary quality is thinly disguised by outward geniality.

Crystalline and precise in every detail, Fray leaves an unforgettable impression in the six *Moments musicaux*. Time and again you are made conscious of music where every note is worth its weight in gold. In the four Impromptus, D899, a similar quality of introspection and concentrated vitality obtains. Such artistry even rivals that of Radu Lupu, a pianist once aptly described as 'a lyricist in a thousand'. Virgin's sound is immaculate and it can surely only be a matter of time before this consummate young artist gives us the second book of Impromptus and, hopefully, many of the Schubert sonatas.

Piano Transcriptions

Schubert/Godowsky Passacaglia. Die schöne Müllerin, D795 – No 8, Morgengruss. Winterreise, D911 – No 1, Gute Nacht **Schubert/Prokofiev** Waltzes Suite **Schubert/Busoni** Overture in the Italian style, D590 **Schubert/Liszt** Erlkönig, D328. Winterreise – No 5, Der Lindenbaum; No 17, Im Dorfe; No 18, Der stürmische Morgen

Antti Siirala *pf*
Naxos 8 555997 (63' · DDD) ⓈⓄ🅓➤

This young Finnish prize-winning pianist makes his recorded debut with a challenging and enterprising a programme of Schubert transcriptions by Liszt, Godowsky, Prokofiev and Busoni.

Schubert takes less kindly to arrangement than most; his profound simplicity is easily compromised. True Schubertians might well have winced at what Godowsky does to 'Morgengruss' from *Die schöne Müllerin*, where innocence is turned into experience and a tropical efflorescence. Yet if to some this is sacrilegious, others will celebrate an act of engaging decadence. Liszt, for all his theatricality, is much more an ardent devotee than mischief-maker, often memorably true to both his own and Schubert's sharply opposed natures, whereas Prokofiev and Busoni's offerings are disappointingly more deferential than genuinely recreative.

Siirala's performances are masterly and warmly sympathetic throughout, and never more so than in Godowsky's horrendously demanding Passacaglia on Schubert's *Unfinished Symphony*. Even Horowitz balked before this challenge, complaining that you needed six hands to encompass such fearsome difficulties.

Masses

Mass No 6, D950
Susan Gritton *sop* **Pamela Helen Stephen** *mez*
James Gilchrist, Mark Padmore *tens* **Matthew Rose** *bar* **Collegium Musicum 90 / Richard Hickox**
Chandos Chaconne ② CHAN0750 (53' · DDD · T/t)
Ⓕ🅞➤

Long the Cinderella work of Schubert's miraculous final year, the E flat Mass is now acknowledged as a powerful masterpiece that mingles liturgical grandeur with the composer's own subjective Romanticism. The apocalyptic *Sanctus*, with its daring harmonic shifts and heaven-storming *crescendos*, is a musical counterpart to Turner's molten canvases, while the *Agnus Dei* has a violent, contorted anguish unmatched in a setting of this text. The least personal, and most problematic, sections of the Mass are the monumental set-piece fugues at the end of the *Gloria* and *Credo*, where Schubert ostentatiously displays his contrapuntal credentials, probably with an eye on an official church appointment. At the worthy tempi prevalent 20 and more years ago, these could seem interminable, and were often cut.

Hickox chooses broad tempi, balancing dignity and vitality, and building thrillingly to the climaxes. In the *Kyrie*, at a mobile tempo, he combines gravitas with a Schubertian lyrical ease, and later he manages the tempo fluctuations far more naturally. You hear how this heavenly music should sound, with the three soloists (Mark Padmore, James Gilchrist – an ideally matched tenor pairing – and soprano Susan Gritton) singing with pure tone and wondering tenderness.

Hickox scores over most rivals with his extra choral firepower at climaxes, and the wonderfully pungent sonorities of Collegium Musicum 90, whether in the dry, fearful rattle of period timpani in the *Credo*, the lovely 'woody' oboe and clarinet in the 'Et incarnatus est' or the steely, scything trumpets in the *Agnus Dei*.

Part-songs

Psalm 23, D706. Im Gegenwärtigen Vergangenes, D710. Gesang der Geister über den Wassern, D714. Gondelfahrer, D809. Coronach, D836. Nachthelle, D892. Grab und Mond, D893. Nachtgesang im Walde, D913. Ständchen, D920. Die Nacht, D983c. Gott im Ungewitter, D985
Birgit Remmert *contr* **Werner Güra** *ten* **Philip Mayers** *pf* **Scharoun Ensemble; RIAS Chamber Choir, Berlin / Marcus Creed**
Harmonia Mundi HMC90 1669 (59' · DDD · T/t) Ⓕ🅞

Most of the part-songs here evoke some aspect of night, whether benevolent, romantic, transfigured or sinister. Between them they give a fair conspectus of Schubert's achievement in the part-song genre, ranging from the mellifluous, Biedermeier *Die Nacht*, forerunner of many a Victorian glee, and the gently sensuous *Gondelfahrer* to the eerie, harmonically visionary *Grab und Mond* and the brooding *Gesang der Geister über den Wassern*. Other highlights here include the alfresco *Nachtgesang*, with its quartet of echoing horns, *Ständchen*, a delicious nocturnal serenade, the austere, bardic Scott setting *Coronach* and the serenely luminous *Nachthelle*.

The RIAS Chamber Choir confirms its credentials as one of Europe's finest, most virtuoso ensembles. It sings with rounded, homogeneous tone, well-nigh perfect intonation and an excitingly wide dynamic range. Characterisation tends to be very vivid, whether in the ecstatic central climax in *Nachthelle*, sharp contrasts in *Gesang der Geister über den Wassern* or the great sense of awe – and palpable feeling for Schubert's strange modulations – in *Grab und Mond*.

Birgit Remmert, the alto soloist in *Ständchen* (sung, incidentally, in the version with women's voices), sings well enough but with insufficient lightness and sense of fun. But Werner Güra negotiates what one of Schubert's friends called 'the damnably high' tenor solo in *Nachthelle* gracefully and with no sense of strain. Philip Mayers is a serviceable rather than specially imaginative pianist, though the delicate, silvery treble of the early 19th-century instrument is enchantingly heard in *Psalm 23*. The recorded sound is clear and warm, with a well-judged vocal-instrumental balance.

Lieder

Abendstern, D806[a]. Amalia, D195[a]. Atys, D585[a]. Auf dem See, D543[b]. Auflösung, D807[a]. Augenlied, D297[a]. Blumenlied, D431[b]. Die Entzückung an Laura,

D390ª. Gondelfahrer, D808ᵇ. Die Götter
Griechenlands, D677 – Stropheᵇ. Die junge Nonne,
D828ᵇ. Der Jüngling am Bache, D30ª. Der Jüngling
und der Tod, D545ᶜ. Memnon, D541ª. Der
Musensohn, D764ª. Das Rosenband, D280ᵇ.
Schwestergruss, D762ᶜ. Sehnsucht, D636ª. Der Sieg,
D805ª
Dame Janet Baker mez ªGeoffrey Parsons,
ᵇGraham Johnson, ᶜMartin Isepp pfs
BBC Legends BBCL4070-2 (73' · ADD)
Live broadcasts from ᶜ1970, ᵇ1977, ª1980   Ⓕ**O**

The interpretation of Schubert's Lieder comes
no better than this, a recital taken from three
different broadcast sources, catching Dame
Janet at the absolute peak of her powers. Most of
the songs are by poets who moved the composer
to his most noble inspiration. As several Schubert specialists have commented, for each he
reserved a particular style, in response to their
very different manner, and Baker catches the
precise meaning of each.

Of the Schiller settings, the operatic expression
of 'Amalia' and the dreamy rapture of the praise
of 'Laura' (here the singer achieves one miraculous *pianissimo* effect) are perfectly caught. Best of
all is that wonderful song, 'Die Götter Griechenlands', where longing is so movingly expressed.
All seven Mayrhofer settings find Baker truly at
one with the poet's high-minded self-communing on the meaning of life, and with his underlying fatalism. Most notable are the calm assurance
and serenity she brings to 'Der Sieg', the resigned
isolation found in 'Abendstern', and the holy fire
of 'Auflösung', the last two masterpieces that the
singer did so much to make popular.

As Gerald Moore once pointed out, Baker
liked the stimulus of the different ideas she
received from different pianists. Here Isepp,
Parsons and the young Graham Johnson provide just that, completing pleasure in a recital
that goes to the heart of the chosen material: as
ever one realises that Baker was, above all, a
singer of conviction. The absence of any texts or
translations is the only blot on a superb issue.

'Lieder, Vol 1'
Fahrt zum Hades, D526. Freiwilliges Versinken, D700.
Das Weinen, D926. Das Fischers Liebesglück, D933.
Der Winterabend, D938. Memnon, D541. Lied eines
Schiffers an die Dioskuren, D360. Der Schiffer, D536.
Sehnsucht, D636. Der Jüngling am Bache, D638. An
Emma, D113. Der Pilger, D794. Gruppe aus dem
Tartarus, D583. Hoffnung, D295. Grenzen der
Menschenheit, D716
Matthias Goerne bar **Elisabeth Leonskaja** pf
Harmonia Mundi HMC90 1988 (65' · DDD · T/t)   Ⓕ**O**

'Do you know of any happy music?' Schubert
once asked a friend. 'I don't.' Those words could
stand as an epigraph to Matthias Goerne's opening salvo in a projected 11- or 12-disc survey of
Schubert Lieder. Evanescence, elegy and yearning for a transcendent otherness are the keynotes of a programme that encompasses the
Attic majesty and *terribilità* of 'Memnon' and

'Gruppe aus dem Tartarus', the disillusioned
fatalism of 'Der Pilgrim' and the philosophical
grandeur of 'Grenzen der Menschenheit'. In
these songs Goerne, with his distinctive dark,
velvet timbre, is in his element. An intense,
almost tortured concentration of thought and
feeling has always been his hallmark, as has an
unblemished *legato*. The way he bows Schubert's
long lines like a cellist is reminiscent of the great
Hans Hotter.

Goerne's rich bass resonances are heard to
advantage in a performance of 'Grenzen der
Menschenheit' that embraces aching tenderness
as well as deep, rolling gravitas. 'Memnon' – a
typical Mayrhofer allegory of the artist as tragic
outsider – is equally spellbinding, illuminated by
telling details like the lingering *portamento* on
'liebend' – 'lovingly' – as dawn's rays break
through the mists. And when have the hazardous leaps of another allegorical Mayrhofer song,
'Freiwilliges Versinken', been negotiated with
such smoothness and hypnotic eloquence?

Where doubts creep in is in the handful of
songs where, *pace* Schubert's own words, a certain lightness of tone and spirit is implied, but
Goerne's involvement is so palpable and his
style so scrupulous. For two-thirds and more of
this recital the interpretative rewards are
uncommonly rich, with the baritone well complemented by Elisabeth Leonskaja's deep-toned
(if on occasion over-pedalled), often orchestrally
conceived accompaniments.

'Heliopolis'
Die Götter Griechenlands, D677. Philoktet, D540.
Fragment aus dem Aischylos, D450b. Der entsühnte
Orest, D699. Aus Heliopolis, D753. Heliopolis, D754.
An die Leier, D737. Atys, *Nachlass* Lfg22.
Meeresstille, D216. Der König in Thule, D367.
Blondel zu Marien, D626. Die Gebüsche, D646. Der
Hirt, D490. Pilgerweise, D789. Wandrers Nachtlied,
D224. Frühlingsglaube, D686. Das Heimweh, D851.
Der Kreuzzug, D932. Abschied, D475
Matthias Goerne bar **Ingo Metzmacher** pf
Harmonia Mundi ② (CD + 𝗗𝗩𝗗)
HMC90 2035 (72' · DDD)
Bonus DVD: 'The Making of the Recording' Ⓕ**OO**▶

The Schubert shelves bend and groan and are
full to overflowing, but they'll have to find room
for one more. This is a simply unmissable
recital, and for two prime reasons – the grave
beauty of its programme and the corresponding
beauty of the singer's voice. Here's an artist who
clearly takes his art very seriously and marries it
to a loveliness of an even-voiced tone and a sensitivity of response to all that he has to sing
here.

And the selection and collocation of songs are
wonderfully made so as to define a particular
frame of mind and sustain and develop it. The
haunting Schiller setting 'Die Götter Griechenlands', with its ghostly evocation of the *Rosamunde* Quartet, is seminal. Throughout the
recital, an occasional harmony or melodic
sequence recalls it to mind, and the horns of

'Griechenland' are heard faintly blowing in the last song of all, the Mayrhofer 'Abschied'. These are *ernste Gesänge*, every one of them, yet there is nothing meanly austere or ponderously sententious. These songs of yearning, essentially spiritual, are very personal, and the imagination never shuts down.

The pianist, Ingo Metzmacher, is fully responsive to this, and the recorded sound, of both voice and piano, is warm and vivid. Regrettable, but unavoidable, are the audible intakes of breath. Less interesting is the 'bonus' DVD called 'The Making of the Recording'. Highly interesting are the notes, by Christophe Ghristi, which start as an uncommonly thoughtful engagement with the concept of the recital and are diverted into a commentary on the 19th-century tenors Nourrit and Duprez.

Abendstern, D806. Abschied von der Harfe, D406. Am Bach im Frühling, D361. Am Flusse (first version), D160. An die Laute, D905. An die Musik, D547. An eine Quelle, D530. Am mein Herz, D860. An Mignon, D161. Auf dem See, D543. Auf der Donau, D553. Auflosung, D807. Augenlied, D297. Drang in die Ferne, D770. Du bist die Ruh, D776. Der Fischer, D225. Geheimnis An Franz Schubert, D491. Gondelfahrer, D808. Das Heimweh, D456. Heiss mich nicht reden Mignon I (second version), D877/2. Der Herbstabend, D405. Der Herbstnacht, D404. Der Jüngling und der Tod, D545. Klage, D371. Liebeslauschen, D698. Lied, 'Ins stille Land', D403. Das Lied im Grünen, D917. Liedesend, D473. Nachtstück, D672. Nähe des Geliebten, D162. Nur wer die Sehnsucht kennt (fourth version), D877/4. Rückweg, D476. Der Sänger am Felsen, D482. Der Sieg, D805. Die Sternennächte, D670. Über Wildemann, D884. Der Wanderer, D649. Wer sich der Einsamkeit ergibt Harfenspieler I, D478. Wie Ulfru fischt, D525. Willkommen und Abschied, D767. Wonne der Wehmut, D260
Matthias Goerne bar
Eric Schneider, Helmut Deutsch pfs
Harmonia Mundi ② HMC90 2004/5
(124' · DDD · T/t)   ⓅⓄ🅑➔

Here elegy, fatalism and death-longing predominate and in such repertoire Goerne's mellow, darkly rounded timbre, expressive diction and care – rare in Lieder singers today – for a true, 'bound' line are well nigh ideal. Even at the most anguished *fortissimo*, his tone never grows harsh or hectoring. Perfectionism like Goerne's has inevitably provoked charges of over-calculation. Some might protest at the ultra-slow tempo for 'Du bist die Ruh'. Yet Goerne's beauty of tone and phrasing (founded on seemingly superhuman reserves of breath), and a rapt intensity that rises to spiritual radiance in the final verse are mesmerising. At a more conventional tempo, he sings 'An die Musik' as a simple, sincere confession of faith, with affectionate touches of *rubato* (and how eloquently Helmut Deutsch's left hand duets with the voice). Elsewhere Goerne's unsentimental tenderness can illuminate little-known songs that seem ordinary on the printed page –

'Abschied von der Harfe', say, or the quasi-operatic lament 'Der Sänger am Felsen'. He even appropriates, successfully, two of Mignon's songs, giving one of the most desolate and – in the central section – disturbed performances of 'Nur wer die Sehnsucht kennt' you will hear.

True to form, Goerne makes an uncommonly melancholy serenader in 'An die Laute' and 'Des Mädchens Liebeslauschen', which never smiles. Yet he can lighten up, as in the story-telling of 'Der Fischer' and 'Wie Ulfru fischt'. Like Deutsch on the first disc, Eric Schneider fully matches Goerne in acumen and command of colour, not least in a performance of 'Nachtstück' of mingled grandeur, mystery and compassionate gentleness.

Lied eines Schiffers an die Dioskuren, D360. Nachtstück, D672. Auf der Donau, D553. Abendstern, D806. Auflösung, D807. Geheimes, D719. Versunken, D715. Schäfers Klagelied, D121. An die Entfernte, D765. Am Flusse, D766. Willkommen und Abschied, D767. Die Götter Griechenlands, D677. An die Leier, D737. Am See, D746. Alinde, D904. Wehmut, D772. Über Wildemann, D884. Auf der Riesenkoppe, D611. Sei mir gegrüsst, D741. Dass sie hier gewesen, D775. Der Geistertanz, D116
Ian Bostridge ten **Julius Drake** pf
EMI 557141-2 (68' · DDD)   ⒫ⓄⓄ🅑➔

A truly memorable experience. The first half of the programme is divided between settings of Mayrhofer and Goethe, two poets who drew the very best out of Schubert. Bostridge responds to this inspiration with singing that's worthy of the pieces both in terms of silvery, poised tone and inflection of the text. Such musing songs as 'Nachtstück', 'Abendstern', 'Geheimes', 'Versunken' and 'An die Entfernte' are delivered in that peculiarly plangent tone of the tenor's which causes his audiences to tremble in admiration.

Using vibrato, verbal emphases, *pianissimos* and floated touches to quite magical yet seemingly spontaneous effect, these songs, and many others receive near-ideal performances. Only in the rough-hewn 'Willkommen und Abschied' would perhaps a heavier voice, a baritone rather than a tenor, be preferable. Bostridge enthusiasts will lap up this wonderful issue; so ought all lovers of Schubert Lieder. Bostridge need fear no comparison with other great interpreters of these songs. The admirable recording catches voice and piano in ideal balance.

An den Mond, D193. Wandrers Nachtlied I, D224. Der Fischer, D225. Erster Verlust, D226. Heidenröslein, D257. Erlkönig, D328. Litanei auf das Fest Allerseelen, D343. Seligkeit, D433. Ganymed, D544. An die Musik, D547. Die Forelle, D550. Frühlingsglaube, D686. Im Haine, D738. Der Musensohn, D764. Wandrers Nachtlied II, D768. Der Zwerg, D771. Auf dem Wasser zu singen, D774. Du bist die Ruh, D776. Nacht und Träume, D827. Fischerweise, D881. Im Frühling, D882. An Silvia, D891

Ian Bostridge ten **Julius Drake** pf
EMI 556347-2 (69' · DDD · T/t)　　　Ⓕ**ⓄⓄⒹ▶**

Bostridge's devoted admirers will once more
wonder at his famed engagement with the text in
hand and his innate ability both to sing each piece
in an entirely natural manner and at the same
time to search out its inner meaning, everything
achieved without a vocal or technical mishap
within hearing. His gift for finding the right manner for each song is exemplified in the contrast
between the easy simplicity he brings to such
apparently artless pieces as 'Fischerweise', 'Frühlingsglaube' and the less familiar 'Im Haine' (this
a wondrous performance of a song that's the very
epitome of Schubert the melodist) and the depth
of feeling found in 'Erster Verlust' (a properly
intense reading), 'Nacht und Traüme', 'Wandrers Nachtlied' I and II, 'Du bist die Ruh' (so elevated in tone and style) and 'Litanei'.

Bostridge also characterises spine-chillingly
the intense, immediate drama of 'Erlkönig' and
'Der Zwerg', though here some may prefer the
weight of a baritone. In the latter piece Drake is
particularly successful at bringing out the originality of the piano part, and in a much simpler
song, 'An Sylvia', he gives to the accompaniment
a specific lift and lilt that usually goes unheard.
In these songs, as in everything else, the ear
responds eagerly to the tenor's fresh, silvery
tone and his ever-eager response to words. The
recording and notes are faultless.

An die Entfernte, D765. Auf dem Wasser zu singen,
D774. Du bist die Ruh, D776. Erlkönig, D328.
Die Forelle, D550. Heidenröslein, D257. Das
Heimweh, D456. Der Jüngling an der Quelle, D300.
Der Jüngling und der Tod, D545. Das Lied im
Grünen, D917. Litanei auf das Fest aller Seelen,
D343. Nachtgesang, D314. Der Schiffer, D536.
Sei mir gegrüsst, D741. Ständchen, 'Horch! Horch!
die Lerch', D889. Der Strom, D565. Der Tod und
das Mädchen, D531. Der Wanderer, D649. Der
Winterabend, D938. Das Zügenglöcklein, D871.
Der zürnende Barde, D785
Dietrich Fischer-Dieskau bar **Gerald Moore** pf
EMI 574754-2 (69' · ADD). Recorded 1960/66　　Ⓢ

Almost 70 minutes of Fischer-Dieskau singing
Schubert in his absolute prime at super-bargain
price can't be bad, in spite of the absence of
texts. The songs chosen – some outright
favourites, others fine pieces the baritone
helped to rescue from obscurity – make up a
most desirable programme. As regards interpretation, Fischer-Dieskau is at his most soft-
grained and persuasive in the lyrical pieces,
notably the rarely heard but most beautiful
'Nachtgesang', at his most melodramatic in the
more forceful Lieder, culminating in a hair-
raising account of 'Erlkönig'.

Moore is both sensitive and positive as the
great baritone's partner, and contributes meaningfully to all the performances. EMI's recording of the period was wholly successful in catching the full tone of its singers.

'Abendbilder'
Abendbilder, 'Nocturne', D650. Alinde, D904. Am
Fenster, D878. Auf der Bruck, D853. Bei dir allein,
D866 No 2. Dass sie hier gewesen, D775. Drang in
die Ferne, D770. Du bist die Ruh, D776. Des Fischers
Liebesglück, D933. Fischerweise, D881.
Greisengesang, D778. Himmelsfunken, D651. Im
Abendrot, D799. Der Musensohn, D764. Willkommen
und Abschied, D767. Der Winterabend, D938. Das
Zügenglöcklein, D871
Christian Gerhaher bar **Gerold Huber** pf
RCA Red Seal 82876 77716-2 (70' · DDD · T/t)
　　Ⓕ**ⓄⓄⒹ▶**

Eschewing the eccentricities and exaggerations
of some of his contemporaries, Gerhaher wonderfully exhibits the verities of Schubert interpretation in this well-planned and absorbing
programme. Everything he does evolves from
the song in hand and so accords with all that is
needed in performing some of the composer's
greatest Lieder.

The title, 'Abendbilder', is interpreted freely
but almost all the pieces have some relevance to
the dreams and moods of evening. Gerhaher
enters into these nocturnal moods with unerring
artistry where line, tone and word-painting are
concerned. He is at his very best in the three settings of Rückert. That quirky, equivocal piece
'Dass sie hier gewesen', prophesying the style
and harmony of Hugo Wolf, is sung with a full
understanding of its inner meaning. 'Du bist die
Ruh' is delivered with the fine line and intense
concentration such a great song deserves, and
the thoughts of an elderly man in 'Greisengesang' are as meaningful as they should be.

Highly appealing throughout is the mellifluousness and breath control, a feature prominent
throughout the recital, of the quietly contemplative 'Im Abendrot', and the appropriate dreaminess brought to the hypnotic barcarolle that is
'Des Fischers Liebesglück'. As a nice contrast,
Gerhaher brings virile energy to the fierce riding
of 'Auf der Bruck' – and here Gerold Huber
deserves as much praise as his partner for portraying the insistent beat of horse's hooves in the
piano part so vividly – and the familiar 'Der
Musensohn' has just the right verve as does
another Goethe setting, the ecstatic 'Willkommen und Abschied', that brings a rewarding recital
to an exhilarating close with Huber – as throughout – seconding the singer with his discerning
contribution. The recording is ideally balanced.

'Poets of Sensibility, Volume 3'　　　　Ⓟ
Abendlied, D499. An den Mond, D193. An die
Apfelbäume, D197. An eine Quelle, D530. Auf dem
Wasser zu singen, D774. Auf den Tod einer
Nachtigall, D201. Auf den Tod einer Nachtigall, D399.
Die Frühe Liebe, D430. Klage an den Mond, D436.
Klage, D371. Der Leidende (two versions), D432,
D432b. Der Liebende, D207. Lied in der
Abwesenheit, D416. Minnelied, D429. Die Mutter
Erde, D788. Die Nonne (first version), D208. Seligkeit,
D433. Seufzer, D198. Stimme der Liebe, D412.
Täglich zu singen, D533. Der Tod und das Mädchen,

D531. Totengräberlied, D44. Der Traum, D213
Wolfgang Holzmair bar **Ulrich Eisenlohr** fp
Naxos 8 557568 (61' · DDD)　　　　　Ⓢ⮕

The pre-Romantic poets of *Empfindsamkeit* ('sensibility'), represented here by Hölty, Claudius and Stolberg, inspired a handful of famous Schubert settings alongside dozens of songs that are still too little known. 'Die Mutter Erde', for instance, written when the composer was suffering from the first symptoms of syphilis, is quintessentially Schubertian in its mingled grandeur, serenity and yearning; 'Stimme der Liebe', dating from 1816 but sounding 10 years later, is one of his most poignant and intense love songs (a reflection of his failed affair with Therese Grob?); 'An die Apfelbäume' is a *bel canto* melody of delicious sensuous grace. Elsewhere we have what must be the jolliest song ever about death ('Totengräberlied'), a pair of solemnly archaic hymns, and charming Haydnesque settings of poems in that faintly risqué (and, to us, impossibly coy) vein beloved of the 18th century.

As ever, Wolfgang Holzmair, with his plangent, tenorish (and distinctly Viennese) timbre, is a highly sympathetic Schubertian, scrupulous in enunciation, always sensitive to mood and nuance yet never prone to exaggeration. Where darker, deeper voices make Death in 'Der Tod und das Mädchen' a solemn, hieratic figure, Holzmair intones Death's chant with a gentle beneficence. The many songs of pathos or wistful longing – say, 'Der Leidende' or the exquisite 'Seufzer' – suit Holzmair to perfection. He brings an unforced variety to the successive verses of strophic settings like 'Abendlied' (another little-known gem), finds the vocal equivalent of a twinkle in the eye for 'Der Traum' (marked to be sung 'flirtatiously'), and even compels you to listen in the potentially absurd ballad 'Die Nonne', in which a nun of fiery Latin temperament turns murderess. Holzmair understands, too, the virtue of simplicity in early Schubert.

Reservations? Well, these days Holzmair sounds a touch strained at high-lying climaxes; and while he can spin a true *legato*, his line can on occasion be slightly bumpy, as in an otherwise touching (and unusually reflective) 'Auf dem Wasser zu singen'. But there is nothing to detract seriously from enjoyment of a shrewdly planned recital that begins in the grip of Death and ends with an exuberant affirmation of life's pleasures ('Seligkeit'). Ulrich Eisenlohr is a discerning partner, drawing an array of delicate, evocative sonorities from his 1820s fortepiano, including (in, for instance, 'An den Mond') a hazy *con sordino* (muted) resonance impossible to conjure on a modern grand. Naxos provide texts and translations via their website.

'Lieder, Volume 27'
Lob der Tränen, D711. Lebensmelodien, D395.
Sprache der Liebe, D410. Wiedersehn, D855.
Sonett I, D628. Sonett II, D629. Sonett III, D630.
Abendröte, D690. Die Berge, D634. Die Vögel, D691.
Der Fluss, D693. Der Knabe, D692. Die Rose, D745.
Der Schmetterling, D633. Der Wanderer, D649. Das Mädchen, D652. Die Sterne, D684. Die Gebüsche, D646. Blanka, D631. Der Schiffer, D694. Fülle der Liebe, D854. Im Walde, D708
Matthias Goerne bar **Christine Schäfer** sop
Graham Johnson pf
Hyperion CDJ33027 (78' · DDD · T/t)　　Ⓕ⮕

Goerne's brief is Schubert's settings of the brothers Schlegel, whose volatile character and life are amply and fascinatingly described in Johnson's introduction to the booklet. As ever in this series, there are songs that we should curse ourselves for neglecting for so long. Among the few settings of August von Schlegel is the interesting 'Lebensmelodien', where the Swan and the Eagle engage in a colloquy – the one all tranquil, the other all disturbed – and are observed by doves on whom Schubert lavishes his most beautiful music. In the formal 'Wiedersehn', as Johnson avers, Schubert imitates the style of a Handelian aria. The second of three Petrarch translations prefigures, arrestingly, the mood of *Winterreise*.

When we come to brother Friedrich and the quasi-cycle *Abendröte* we're in an even more exalted world where 'Der Fluss', another of Schubert's miraculous water songs, 'Der Knabe', above all 'Die Rose', where the fading of the rose is a metaphor for lost virginity (this, movingly done by Schäfer), and 'Der Wanderer' show just how willingly Schubert responded to Schlegel's imagery. About Goerne's singing as such, ably assisted by Johnson's playing, there are no reservations, particularly in the visionary 'Die Sterne', but as the CD progresses his interpretations can seem a shade soporific; one wonders if he has lived long enough with these songs to penetrate to their heart. His easily produced, slightly vibrant and mellifluous baritone and sense of Schubertian style make him a largely rewarding interpreter. The recording is superb.

Schubert Atys, D585. Einsamkeit, D620. Der Fluss, D693. Im Freien, D880. Die Gebüsche, D646.
Die-Götter Griechenlands, D677. Sehnsucht, D516
Hüttenbrenner Frühlingsliedchen. Der Hügel.
Lerchenlied. Die Seefart. Seegras. Spinnerlied. Die Sterne
Gundula Janowitz sop **Irwin Gage** pf
Orfeo C592 021B (72' · DDD). Recorded live 1972 Ⓜ●

This is an unusual and wholly absorbing recital by a soprano often, mistakenly, considered no more than a singer with a lovely voice. In 1972, at the height of her appreciable powers, Janowitz impressed her Salzburg audience with this, her first recital at the Festival. Her discerning choice comprises some notable songs by Schubert rarely heard in recital and ones by his contemporary Hüttenbrenner, which Janowitz sang from manuscript copies, seldom performed since the composer's day. These are surely their first recordings.

Has there ever been such a lovely, poised account of the great Schiller-inspired song, 'Die

Götter Griechenlands' or such an ingratiating one of 'Sehnsucht', the Mayrhofer setting? The first offering, 'Im Freien', has its winning cantilena filled with gloriously sustained, long-breathed tone. The programme ends with 'Einsamkeit'. This grandly imaginative if slightly impersonal quasi-cantata, to a Mayrhofer text, a composition that Schubert himself thought so highly of, is a kind of a panorama of a life, ending in a wonderfully reposeful final section. Janowitz and her impressive partner perform it with total conviction, sustaining interest throughout.

Although not in Schubert's class, Hüttenbrenner reveals a talent apparently well able to encompass the meaning of poems in fluent and often imaginative writing. Orfeo provide no texts, let alone translations, but the delightful 'Spinnerlied' must be about spinning: it's an artlessly charming song. 'Der Hügel' is obviously about more serious matters, and in its sad course comes closes to Schubert in depth of feeling. 'Frühlingsliedchen' has a simple, spring-like joy to it, and an appealingly varied, strophic form. Janowitz takes the measure of them all, and adds to a gently vibrant tone many tints and touches of half-voice. They could not have a better advocate.

The recording catches the full glow of the singer's voice. The only drawback, that absence of texts, isn't serious enough to stop acquiring this issue, given that Janowitz virtually tells you in her utterance what the songs are about.

'Lieder, Volume 23'
Der Tod Oscars, D375. Das Grab, D377ª. Der Entfernten, D350. Pflügerlied, D392. Abschied von der Harfe, D406. Der Jüngling an der Quelle, D300. Abendlied, D382. Stimme der Liebe, D412. Romanze, D144. Geist der Liebe, D414. Klage, D415. Julius an Theone, D419. Der Leidende, D432. Der Leidende (second version), D432b. Die frühe Liebe, D430. Die Knabenzeit, D400. Edone, D445. Die Liebes-götter, D446. An Chloen, D363. Freude der Kinderjahre, D455. Wer sich der Einsamkeit ergibt, D478. Wer nie sein Brot mit Tränen ass, D480. an die Türen, D479. Der Hirt, D490. Am ersten Maimorgen, D344. Bei dem Grabe meines Vaters, D496. Mailied, D503. Zufriedenheit, D362. Skolie, D507
Christoph Prégardien ten ªLondon Schubert Chorale; Graham Johnson pf
Hyperion CDJ33023 (78' · DDD · T/t)   Ⓕ Ⓓ➤

When the Hyperion Schubert Edition is completed, this latest wondrous offering will rank among its most precious jewels. Prégardien is a prince among tenor interpreters of Lieder at present, on a par with Blochwitz in instinctive, natural and inevitably phrased readings. Johnson, besides finding exactly the right performers for these songs, surpasses even his own high standard of playing in this series. Then there's Schubert himself, the Schubert of 1816 by and large, who was, Johnson tentatively suggests in his notes, going through a phase of 'bringing himself under control'. That means, largely but far from entirely, writing gently lyrical strophic songs, most of them of ineffable beauty and

simplicity, starkly contrasting with the *Harfenspieler* settings from *Wilhelm Meister*, two of which were written in 1816, the other in 1822.

In such an outright masterpiece as 'Der Jüngling an der Quelle', Prégardien and Johnson confirm the latter's view that this piece 'makes time stand still'. They emphasise, in 'Stimme der Liebe', how Schubert uses shifting harmonies to indicate romantic obsession. They show in the two similar but subtly different versions of 'Der Leidende' ('The suffering one') what Johnson calls 'two sides of the same coin', with the tenor's plangent, tender singing, line and text held in perfect balance. The two Hölty songs that follow, 'Die frühe Liebe' and 'Die Knabenzeit', evince a wonderful affinity with thoughts of childhood on the part of poet and composer, again ideally captured here. So is the 'chaste and wistful' mood of Klopstock's 'Edone'. The recording is ideally balanced .

Gruppe aus dem Tartarus, D583. Litanei auf das Fest Allerseelen, D343. Die Forelle, D550. An die Leier, D737. Lachen und Weinen, D777. Schwanengesang, D957 – Ständchen; Das Fischermädchen; Die Taubenpost. Meeresstille, D216. Der Wanderer, D489 (formerly D493). Erlkönig, D328. Der Tod und das Mädchen, D531. Heidenröslein, D257. Wandrers Nachtlied II, D768. An die Musik, D547. Auf der Bruck, D853. Schäfers Klagelied, D121. An Silvia, D891. Du bist die Ruh', D776. An die Laute, D905. Rastlose Liebe, D138. Ganymed, D544. Der Musensohn, D764
Bryn Terfel bass-bar **Malcolm Martineau** pf
DG 445 294-2GH (69' · DDD · T/t)   Ⓕ ⓄⓄⓄ➤

Terfel's gift is a generous, individual voice, a natural feeling for German and an inborn ability to go to the heart of what he attempts. His singing here is grand in scale – listen to any of the dramatic songs and the point is made – but like Hotter, whom he so often resembles, he's able to reduce his large voice to the needs of a sustained, quiet line, as in 'Meeresstille'. When the two come together as in 'Der Wanderer', the effect can be truly electrifying, even more so, perhaps, in 'Erlkönig' where the four participants are superbly contrasted. Yet this is a voice that can also smile, as in 'An die Laute' and 'Die Taubenpost' or express wonder, as in 'Ganymed', a most exhilarating interpretation, or again explode in sheer anger as in the very first song, the strenuous 'Gruppe aus dem Tartarus'. Terfel isn't afraid to employ *rubato* and vibrato to make his points and above all to take us right into his interpretations rather than leave us admiring them, as it were, from afar. Throughout, Martineau's at once vigorous and subtle playing is an apt support: his accompaniment in 'Erlkönig' is arrestingly clear and precise.

'Lieder, Volume 24'
Schäfers Klagelied, D121. An Mignon, D161. Geistes-Gruss, D142 (two versions). Rastlose Liebe, D138. Der Gott und die Bajadere, D254. Tischlied, D234. Der

Schatzgräber, D256. Der Rattenfänger, D255.
Bundeslied, D258. Erlkönig, D328. Jägers Abendlied,
D215. Jägers Abendlied, D368. Wer nie sein Brot mit
Tränen ass, D480 (two versions). Nur wer die
Sehnsucht kennt, D359. So lasst mich scheinen,
D469a & D469b (two fragments). Nur wer die
Sehnsucht kennt, D481. Nur wer die Sehnsucht
kennt, D656. An Schwager Kronos, D369. Hoffnung,
D295. Mahomets Gesang, D549 (cptd R Van
Hoorickx). Ganymed, D544. Der Goldschmiedsgesell,
D560. Gesang der Geister über den Wassern, D484
(cptd R Van Hoorickx). Gesang der Geister über den
Wassern, D705 (cptd E Asti).
Christine Schäfer sop **John Mark Ainsley** ten **Simon
Keenlyside** bar **Michael George** bass **Graham
Johnson** pf **London Schubert Chorale /
Stephen Layton**
Hyperion CDJ33024 (79' · DDD · T/t)   Ⓕ Ⓑ➔

Renewed praise first of all for Graham Johnson.
This volume is as cogent an example as any of his
method, a masterly exposition, in written words
and musical performance, of the crucial relationship between Goethe and Schubert upon
which Johnson throws a good deal of new light.
Not all here is notable Schubert, but the lesser
songs serve to place in perspective the greater
ones.

The CD begins with one of the latter, 'Schäfers
Klagelied', in a finely honed, dramatic performance by Ainsley, who's heard later on the disc
always to advantage. Good as Christine Schäfer
is in the first version of 'An Mignon', she's better
in the sadly neglected 'Der Gott und die
Bajadere', as Johnson avers. This is the only
song in the genre about prostitution, and a
haunting one too, even though, throughout its
appreciable length, it relies on just one melody,
and Schäfer precisely catches its haunting
atmosphere. But the climax of her contribution
comes in 'Ganymed' – with Johnson providing
exactly the right rhythmic lilt at the piano, her
voice conveys all the elation of poem and music.

Schäfer is the child in a three-voice rendering
of 'Erlkönig', a manner of performing the piece
that has the composer's blessing. Johnson has
surely never surpassed his account here of
the hair-raisingly difficult piano part. George,
who perhaps has the least ingratiating songs to
perform, sings with feeling and style but sometimes an excess of vibrato. An invaluable addition to the series.

'Lieder, Volume 26'
Der Einsame, D800. Des Sängers Habe, D832. Lied
der Delphine, D857 No 1. Lied des Florio, D857 No 2.
Mondenschein, D875. Nur wer die Sehnsucht kennt,
D877 No 1. Heiss mich nicht reden, D877 No 2. So
lasst mich scheinen, D877 No 3. Nur wer die
Sehnsucht kennt, D877 No 4. Totengräberweise,
D869. Das Echo, D990C. An Silvia, D891. Horch,
horch! die Lerch', D889. Trinklied, D888. Wiegenlied,
D867. Widerspruch, D865. Der Wanderer an den
Mond, D870. Grab und Mond, D893. Nachthelle,
D892. Abschied von der Erde, D829
Christine Schäfer sop **John Mark Ainsley** ten

Richard Jackson bar **London Schubert Chorale;
Graham Johnson** pf
Hyperion CDJ33026 (76' · DDD · T/t)   Ⓕ ⊙⊙

It's hard to know where to begin in praise of this
disc. It has several centres of excellence, the first
being Schäfer's beseeching, urgent account of
the Mignon settings from Goethe's *Wilhelm
Meister* that make plain her pre-eminence today
among sopranos in Lieder. Next comes Ainsley's
winningly fresh account of 'An Silvia'. You may
be surprised at how wholly new-minted Ainsley's
ardent tones and Johnson's elating piano manage
to make of such a hackneyed song. Schäfer and
Johnson do the same service for 'Horch, horch!
die Lerch''. Then comes the extraordinary discovery of this volume. As a rule, Johnson has
excluded unaccompanied vocal pieces from his
project; happily, he has made an exception in the
case of the astonishingly original Seidl setting
'Grab und Mond', which touches on eternal matters, or rather the permanence of death, a message starkly expressed in typically daring harmony. The London Schubert Chorale gives it a
spellbinding interpretation and also contributes
positively to a performance of another Seidl setting, the better-known 'Nachthelle', where the
high-lying tenor lead provides no problems for
Ainsley. There have to be reservations over the
work of Richard Jackson; his tone is inadequate
to the demands of 'Der Einsame', the unjustly
neglected 'Totengräberweise' and 'Der Wanderer an den Mond', which call for a richer
sound-palette. Throughout, Johnson's playing is
a source of pleasure and enlightenment. The
recording is well-nigh faultless.

An den Mond, D193. Suleika I, D720. Im Abendrot,
D799. Sei mir gegrüsst, D741. Die Forelle, D550.
Heimliches Lieben, D922. Der Sänger am Felsen,
D482. Thekla, D595. An die Sonne, D270. Aus Diego
Manzanares, D458. Nacht und Träume, D827.
Frühlingsglaube, D686. Die Blumensprache, D519.
Nähe des Geliebten, D162. An die Nachtigall, D497.
Liane, D298. Des Mädchens Klage, D191.
Nachtviolen, D752. Marie, D658. Lambertine, D301.
Die Männer sind méchant, D866/3
Elizabeth Watts sop **Roger Vignoles** pf
RCA Red Seal 88697 32932-2 (70' · DDD)   Ⓕ Ⓑ➔

Hailed as a singer to watch after winning the 2006
Kathleen Ferrier Award and the 2007 Cardiff
Song Prize, Elizabeth Watts makes her CD debut
with this refreshingly unhackneyed Schubert
programme. Perennial soprano favourites – 'Die
Forelle', 'Nacht und Träume', 'Frühlingsglaube',
'Suleika' – are not shunned. But Watts has
alighted on some rarely aired gems. How often in
recital do we hear the agitated scena-in-miniature
'Aus Diego Manzanares'; or the playfully charming paean to spring 'Die Blumensprache'; or the
Novalis setting 'Marie', where sacred and profane
blur in a song of exquisite, rarefied grace?

A voice in its first, radiant freshness is always to
be cherished in Schubert. Watts is a thoughtful
interpreter, too, alive to mood and atmosphere,

colouring her tone in response to a darkening of the harmony in, say, 'Sei mir gegrüsst'. Crucially, she also brings a measure of innocence and simplicity – not quite the same thing as artlessness – to many of these songs, allied to a technical mastery that allows her to spin a rapt, unblemished line in 'Nacht und Träume'. Encouraged by Vignoles's buoyant accompaniment, she makes an engaging story-teller in 'Die Forelle', with an unexaggerated touch of indignation at the angler's treachery; and she sings the mildly salacious refrain song 'Die Männer sind méchant' with just the right wide-eyed mock-pathos.

Quibbles? Well, in one or two songs, including the opening 'An den Mond', Watts struck me as overly languid. She treats 'Nähe des Geliebten' as an elegiac litany, where, say, Janet Baker, choosing a more mobile tempo and finding greater variety from verse to verse, sings it as a passionate avowal of love. Watts also emphasises melancholy over excited anticipation in 'Frühlingsglaube' and 'Suleika'. Here and elsewhere, Watts under-exploits the expressive potential of German consonants. That said, highlights are lovely performances of 'Nachtviolen' – the high tessitura effortlessly negotiated – or the Mozartian barcarolle 'Liane': just two songs among many where the vernal purity of Watts's tone and the grace of her phrasing are priceless assets.

'Lieder, Volume 32'
An die Sonne, D439. Beitrag zur fünfzigjährigen Jubelfeier des Herrn von Salieri, D407. Das war ich, D174a/D450a. Didone Abbandonata, D510a (both cptd Hoorickx). Der Entfernten, D331. Entzückung, D413. Der Geistertanz, D494. Gott der Weltschöpfer, D986. Gott im Ungewitter, D985. Grablied auf einen Soldaten, D454. Das Grosse Halleluja, D442. Des Mädchens Klage, D389. Licht und Liebe, D352. Naturgenuss, D422. Ritter Toggenburg, D397. Schlachtgesang, D443. Die verfehlte Stunde, D409. Der Wanderer, D489. Zufriedenheit, D501. Zum Punsche, D492
Lynne Dawson, Patricia Rozario, Christine Schäfer sops **Ann Murray, Catherine Wyn-Rogers** mezzos **Paul Agnew, John Mark Ainsley, Philip Langridge, Jamie MacDougall, Daniel Norman, Christoph Prégardien, Michael Schade, Toby Spence** tens **Simon Keenlyside, Maarten Koningsberger, Stephan Loges, Christopher Maltman, Stephen Varcoe** bars **Neal Davies, Michael George** basses **Graham Johnson** pf **London Schubert Chorale / Stephen Layton**
Hyperion CDJ33032 (78' · DDD · T/t)   Ⓕ⊙➔

Like the previous Schubertiads in the Edition, this disc mixes solo songs and part-songs, familiar and unfamiliar. The only really famous work here is 'Der Wanderer', that archetypal expression of Romantic alienation whose popularity in Schubert's lifetime was eclipsed only by that of 'Erlkönig'. Some of the part-songs – *Zum Punsche*, *Naturgenuss* and *Schlachtgesang* – cultivate a vein of Biedermeier heartiness that wears a bit thin today. Nor will Schubert's consciously archaic tribute to his teacher Salieri have you

itching for the repeat button – though, like several other numbers, it shows the 19-year-old composer rivalling Mozart in his gift for musical mimicry. To compensate, though, there are part-songs like the sensual *Der Entfernten*, with its delicious languid chromaticisms, and the colourful setting of *Gott im Ungewitter*. The slight but charming setting of 'Das war ich' is appealingly done by the light-voiced Daniel Norman, and Ann Murray brings her usual charisma and dramatic conviction to the pathetic Italian scena *Didone Abbandonata*.

Christine Schäfer is equally charismatic in the neglected 'Die verfehlte Stunde' (recorded here for the first time), catching perfectly the song's mingled yearning and ecstasy and negotiating the mercilessly high tessitura with ease. Other happy discoveries include Schubert's third setting of 'Des Mädchens Klage', with its soaring lines, a melancholy tale of courtly love, sung by Christoph Prégardien with as much drama and variety as the music allows; and the surging 'Entzückung' ('music for an infant Lohengrin', as Graham Johnson puts it), for which Toby Spence has both the flexibility and the necessary touch of metal in the tone. Doubts were fleetingly raised by Lynne Dawson's slight tremulousness in 'Des Mädchens Klage', and by Christopher Maltman's prominent vibrato at *forte* and above in an otherwise involving performance of 'Der Wanderer'. But, these cavils apart, no complaints about the singing or the vivid accompaniments.

'Lieder, Volume 34'
La pastorella al prato, D513[f]pt. Frohsinn, D520[q]. Der Alpenjäger, D524[r]. Die Einsiedelei, D563[l]. Das Grab, D569[u]. Atys, D585[o]. Der Kampf, D594[s]. Das Dörfchen, D598[f]pt. Die Gesellschaft, D609[cdgt]. Sing-Übungen, D619[ac] (ed Roblou). Das Abendrot, D627[s]. Abend, D645[h] (ed Brown). Das Mädchen, D652[e]. Cantate zum Geburtstag des Sängers Michael Vogl, D666[blm]. Prometheus, D674[p]. Über allen Zauber Liebe, D682[k] (ed Hoorickx). Die gefangenen Sänger, D712[n]. Grenzen der Menschheit, D716[e]. Wandrers Nachtlied II, D768[r]
[a]**Lorna Anderson**, [b]**Lynne Dawson**, [c]**Patricia Rozario** sops [d]**Catherine Denley**, [e]**Marjana Lipovšek** mezzos [f]**John Mark Ainsley**, [g]**Ian Bostridge**, [h]**Martyn Hill**, [i]**Philip Langridge**, [j]**Jamie MacDougall**, [k]**Daniel Norman**, [l]**Michael Schade** tens [m]**Gerald Finley**, [n]**Matthias Goerne**, [o]**Thomas Hampson**, [p]**Simon Keenlyside**, [q]**Stephan Loges**, [r]**Christopher Maltman** bars [s]**Neal Davies** bass-bar [t]**Michael George** bass [u]**London Schubert Chorale / Stephen Layton**; **Graham Johnson** pf
Hyperion Schubert Edition CDJ33034 (79' · DDD · T/t)   Ⓕ⊙➔

In his guise as a wizard of an impresario, Graham Johnson has gathered together four baritones and one bass-baritone (Neil Davies) to give us a feast of finely wrought, intelligent interpretations. Hampson's rendering of that outsider's lament, 'Atys', is at once an object-lesson in refined singing and a deeply felt outpouring of sorrow. Keenlyside, singing with as much firm, mellow tone and feeling as his American coeval, gives a properly intense, agonised account of the great, Zeus-defying 'Prometheus', magnificently supported by Johnson. Goerne is assigned the seldom-heard Schlegel setting, 'Die gefangenen Sänger', and brings his gently vibrant tone, reminiscent of his noted predecessor Herbert Janssen, and his natural gift for phrasing to bear on this strange but captivating piece. Maltman, growing in stature as a Lieder artist, begins the programme with the extrovert 'Der Alpenjäger' and ends it with the introverted 'Wandrers Nachtlied' on which he lavishes the hushed concentration due to a page of rapt utterance, a suitable conclusion to the performance of Goethe settings in the whole edition.

Neil Davies erupts into the series with three absorbing interpretations: the declamatory Schiller setting 'Der Kampf', the flowing, glowing 'Das Abendrot' and the awe-inspiring 'Grenzen der Menschheit'. All three evince his real affinity for the German language and the world of Schubert. He also has the low notes the pieces call for. The one female solo brings back Lipovšek at her most beguiling in the poignant and unforgettable Schlegel setting 'Das Mädchen', already performed just as movingly by Christine Schäfer in Vol 27. This wonderful fare is interspersed with lighter, less demanding material, all done with pleasure by varying groups of singers, plus three tenor solos. Langridge is predictably charming in 'Die Einsiedelei'. Hill isn't quite at his best, and Norman's style is etiolated in their offerings. Piano playing both maintain Hyperion's usual high standard.

'Lieder, Volume 37'
Auf dem Strom, D943[cd]. Herbst, D945[a]. Bei dir allein, D866/2[c]. Irdisches Glück, D866/4[c]. Lebensmut, D937[c]. Schwanengesang, D957 – No 1, Liebesbotschaft; No 2, Kriegers Ahnung[a]; No 3, Frühlingssehnsucht[a]; No 4, Ständchen[a]; No 5, Aufenthalt[a]; No 6, In der Ferne[a]; No 7, Abschied[a]; No 8, Der Atlas[b]; No 9, Ihr Bild[b]; No 10, Das Fischermädchen[b]; No 11, Die Stadt[b]; No 12, Am Meer[b]; No 13, Der Doppelgänger[b]. Die Taubenpost, D965A[b]. Glaube, Hoffnung und Liebe, D955[abc]
[a]**John Mark Ainsley,** [b]**Anthony Rolfe Johnson,** [c]**Michael Schade** tens [d]**David Pyatt** hn
Graham Johnson pf
Hyperion Schubert Edition CDJ33037
(80' · DDD · T/t)   Ⓕ**O➜**

This disc, the last in Hyperion's Schubert Edition, is in large part devoted to the performance of the non-cycle *Schwanengesang*, that extraordinary collection in which Schubert seems more original and more inclined even than in earlier Lieder to peer into the future. We usually encounter the work transposed for a baritone, though Schreier and Schiff have recorded it memorably for Decca. Johnson has astutely divided the songs between two voices. Ainsley is given the Rellstab settings, Rolfe Johnson the Heine, plus Seidl's 'Die Taubenpost', which so poignantly and airily closes the set.

Ainsley interprets his songs with the tonal beauty, fine-grained phrasing and care for words that are the hallmarks of his appreciable art, even if his voice sometimes lacks a difficult-to-define individuality of timbre. The over-exposed 'Ständchen' is given a new spontaneity of utterance by both the singer and Graham Johnson. Anthony Rolfe Johnson brings all the appropriate intensity one would expect from him to the tremendous Heine settings. Sometimes his tone hardens when he's depicting the deserted lover present in so many of these pieces, but that's hardly inappropriate to the depth of feeling being expressed. Most of the other songs of 1828, which open the recital, are assigned to Schade, who sings them with refined tone and an innate feeling for sharing his enjoyment in performing them, nowhere more so than in the opening 'Auf dem Strom'. Ainsley reads his sole offering here, 'Bei dir allein', with just the fiery passion it calls for.

This is a worthy, often inspired conclusion to the series, once more enhanced by Johnson's copious notes. It also has a complete index to the Edition. The recording is faultless.

Song-cycles

Die schöne Müllerin, D795. **Schwanengesang**, D957. **Winterreise**, D911

Die schöne Müllerin[a]. Nacht und Träume, D827[b]. Ständchen, D889[b]. Du bist die Ruh, D776[b]. Erlkönig, D328[c]
Dietrich Fischer-Dieskau bar
[a]**Jörg Demus,** [bc]**Gerald Moore** pfs
DG 463 502-2GFD (75' · ADD)
Recorded 1968, [bc]1970

Ⓜ**OO➜**

Die schöne Müllerin, D795

You wouldn't think that a recording by Fischer-Dieskau, given his huge Schubert discography, could still offer an exciting revelation – but that's what the 'new' *Die schöne Müllerin* recording offers. Explanations for its suppression vary. The singer seems to think it has something to do with its technical quality; the booklet-note, slightly more credibly, tells us that it was planned before DG decided to include the cycle in its 'complete' Schubert with the baritone and Gerald Moore, which caused this performance to be put on the back burner. Now we can enjoy a reading that's absolutely spontaneous, daring in its dramatic effects – bold extremes of dynamics, for instance – and full of even more subtle detail than in Fischer-Dieskau's other recordings.

This approach owes not a little to Demus's piano. As Alan Newcombe says in his notes: 'Aided by Demus's lightly pedalled, often almost brusque *staccato* articulation, the result is starker, more elemental, less comfortable [than the reading with Moore], conceived on a larger scale.' To that one should add that the singer is at the absolute height of his powers; tone, line, breath control and intuitive imagination are most remarkable in the strophic songs that, in lesser hands, can seem over-long. Another feature of this is the significant underlining he gives to pertinent words. For instance, in 'Pause' note how 'gehängt', 'durchschauert' and 'Nachklang' receive this treatment. It's this unique vision of the German language in music that still marks out this baritone from his many successors. Immediate, unvarnished sound heightens the value of this extraordinary performance.

Die schöne Müllerin
Jochen Kupfer bar **Susanne Giesa** pf
Channel Classics CCS18898 (66' · DDD · T/t)   Ⓕ**OO**

This reading of Schubert's cycle is confirmation, as if that were needed, of Jochen Kupfer's beautiful singing, and even more of his gifts as a Lieder interpreter. Kupfer's voice and style is highly reminiscent of Wolfgang Holzmair's, but his technique is just that shade firmer and his voice more youthful than the older baritone's with Imogen Cooper, recalling rather Holzmair's first (1983) recording on Preiser. Both artists have a tenor-like quality to their voices, coming near to some ideal for the work. Kupfer begins with the basic verities of immaculate line and imaginative phrasing, to which he adds a complete identification with the youthful lover's aspirations and eventual disappointment and tragedy.

This lad sets out with a spring in his heels and a smile in his voice, quite avoiding any sense of despondency from the outset. All is going to be well in his wooing. That's conveyed in the first few songs with fresh immediacy as though the poetic emotions and their setting were new-minted. The arrival of the unwanted and aggressive hunter provokes an almost breathless jealousy and, in that arresting song, 'Die liebe Farbe', an appropriately mesmeric, plaintive approach. From there on the downward curve of emotional feeling, so arrestingly depicted in the words and music, finds in Kupfer and his alert partner an answering mood of despair, the raw and anguished passion in those final three songs fully achieved. All the while you feel the disillusionment and pathos in the texture and verbal acuity of the interpretation.

With a finely balanced recording to add to one's pleasure, this is a performance among baritones to place very near the top of the pile, if not at its apex, and it challenges even the prevailing tenor recommendations, the versions by Ian Bostridge and Werner Güra.

Die schöne Müllerin
Werner Güra ten **Jan Schultsz** pf
Harmonia Mundi HMC90 1708 (63' · DDD · T/t)
Ⓕ**OOOↁ**

Ⓖ An enthralling account of the cycle on virtually every count that seriously challenges the hegemony of the many desirable versions already available. In the first place

Güra must have about the most beautiful voice ever to have recorded the work in the original keys (and that's not to overlook Wunderlich, a far less perceptive interpreter). Its owner has a technique second to none, able to vary his tone, sing a lovely *pianissimo* and/or a long-breathed phrase with perfect control. Then no musical or verbal subtlety seems to escape him at any stage of the young man's disillusioning journey from happiness to misery and death.

The plaintive quality of his voice and its youthful sap are precisely right for conveying the protagonist's vulnerability and, where needed, his self-pity. That great song 'Der Neugierige' encapsulates these virtues, with the final couplet of questioning the brook immaculately done, just as the *pp* at the close of the previous song is given a curious sense of uncertainty on the boy's part. The three strophic songs are finely varied: here, as throughout, the use of *rubato* is natural and inevitable and the integration of singer and pianist, who's happily playing a Bechstein, are at their most compelling. 'Mein' is properly eager, expectant, 'Pause' as plangent as it should be, especially at its end. The frenetic anger of the 14th and 15th songs is as over-heated as it should be, 'Die liebe Farbe' rightly hypnotic. In those great songs, 'Trockne Blumen' and 'Der Müller und der Bach', both artists go to the heart of the matter, and the final lullaby is soft-grained and consoling. Schultsz's contributions are sometimes controversial, always challenging. Güra surpasses even the *Gramophone* Award-winning Bostridge, simply because his voice is under even better control and because his German is more idiomatic. The Harmonia Mundi sound, in spite of some reverberance, catches voice and piano in ideal balance.

Die schöne Müllerin, with a reading of six poems not set by Schubert
Ian Bostridge ten **Dietrich Fischer-Dieskau** narr
Graham Johnson pf
Hyperion CDJ33025 (73' · DDD · T/t)   Ⓕ**OOOↁ**

 The 20 songs of *Die schöne Müllerin* portray a Wordsworthian world of heightened emotion in the pantheistic riverside setting of the miller. The poet, Wilhelm Müller, tells of solitary longings, jealousies, fears and hopes as the river rushes by, driving the mill-wheel and refreshing the natural world. Ian Bostridge and Graham Johnson go to the heart of the matter, the young tenor in his aching tones and naturally affecting interpretation, the pianist in his perceptive, wholly apposite playing. The sum of their joint efforts is a deeply satisfying experience.

Bostridge has the right timbre for the protagonist and a straightforward approach, with an instinctive rightness of phrasing. His peculiarly beseeching voice enshrines the vulnerability, tender feeling and obsessive love of the youthful miller, projecting in turn the young lover's thwarted passions, self-delusions and, finally, inner tragedy. Nowhere does he stretch beyond the bounds of the possible, everything expressed in eager then doleful tones. Johnson suggests that 'Ungeduld' mustn't be 'masterful and insistent' or the youth would have won the girl, so that even in this superficially buoyant song the sense of a sensitive, sad, introverted youth is maintained. The day-dreaming strophic songs have the smiling, inno-cent, intimate sound that suits them to perfection, the angry ones the touch of stronger metal that Bostridge can now add to his silver, the tragic ones, before the neutral 'Baches Wiegenlied', an inner intensity that rends the heart as it should. An occasional moment of faulty German accent-ing matters not at all when the sense of every word is perceived.

As a bonus we have here a recitation of the Prologue and Epilogue and of the Müller poems not set by Schubert: Fischer-Dieskau graces it with his speaking voice. The ideal Hyperion recording catches everything in very present terms. In all musical matters, everything John-son writes only enhances one's enjoyment, if that's the right word, of a soul-searching inter-pretation.

Die schöne Müllerin
James Gilchrist ten **Anna Tilbrook** pf
Orchid ORC100006 (66' · DDD) Ⓕ**OO**▷

James Gilchrist's Wanderer has been around a bit. Not enough to make him weary or wary, far from it – a first-kindled enthusiasm only burns itself out a little in the fourth song, 'Danksagung an den Bach' – but in place of youthful impetu-osity is the anxiety of a man to seize what he can while he can. His jealousy – 'Eifersucht und Stolz' – gains thereby a specially manic edge, and leaves him almost shouting at the end of 'Die Böse Farbe' before he takes his leave of love and life in both sorrow and anger over the ever-more-painful course of the last triptych.

If that brief account, and the timings, often very quick or slow, suggest exaggeration or melodrama, then they mislead: one was never aware of a word being presented for particular attention, and in some songs Gilchrist can barely get the words out in time, but line and sense never falter.

How aptly Anna Tilbrook's pedalling poses the question to the brook at the beginning of 'Die Neugierige', and how graciously Gilchrist waits until the last verse before slowing down to ask himself. That his mix of chest and head reg-isters tends more towards the latter than is usual may disconcert some, but it allows for the most intimate and touching of quarter-voices at the end of his confession to the flowers, 'Des Mül-lers Blumen', and brings uneasy rest indeed to the final lullaby. Gilchrist and Tilbrook offer one of the very finest of modern versions.

Die schöne Müllerin
Dietrich Fischer-Dieskau bar **András Schiff** pf
Video director **Fritz Jurmann**
TDK ☐ **DVD** DV-CODSM (83' · 4:3 · PCM stereo · 0).

Recorded live at the Montforthaus, Feldkirch, on June 20, 1991. Includes 1985 interview with Dietrich Fischer-Dieskau Ⓕ**OO**

To celebrate Fischer-Dieskau's 80th birthday Austrian Television issued this film made at the 1991 Schubertiade. It marked the return, after a 20-year break, of the great baritone, aged 66, to Schubert's first cycle. In restudying the work, the singer comments that he tried, really for the first time, to sing these songs 'not so much by feeling as by narrative, not so much concentrat-ing on the vocal line as responding with curios-ity and openness to the wealth of colour and expression in the piano part – which calls for a pianist as sensitive as Schiff'.

He's as good as his word, singing the cycle even more off the words than he had in the past, giving his audience a kind of mini-drama, underlined by some movement on the platform and a wealth of facial expression. At this late stage in his career his voice inevitably shows some decline in tonal body, but in almost every other respect he retains the famed qualities of his prime: astonishing breath-control, an arrest-ing command of wide-ranging dynamics and total control in putting his ideas into action. The hypnotic reading reaches its proper moment of epiphany in the two penultimate, tragic songs, delivered with all the varied resources the per-formers can offer them.

As a bonus there's a 20-minute portrait of the singer, assembled at the 1985 Schubertiade. It includes a couple more valuable examples of his singing and a fascinating interview, in which he tells us a lot about himself and his approach to his art, something invaluable in years to come.

Schwanengesang, D957

Schubert Schwanengesang
Beethoven An die ferne Geliebte
Matthias Goerne bar **Alfred Brendel** pf
Decca 475 6011DH (72' · DDD · T/t)
Recorded live 2003 Ⓕ**OOO**▷

 As Misha Donat reminds us in out-standing booklet essays, *Schwanengesang* divides clearly into eight Rellstab and six Heine settings; 'Herbst' is here added to the Rellstab group, while the Seidl 'Die Taubenpost' is made into the encore of a wonderful recital.

Goerne and Brendel form one of the great Lieder partnerships of the day. The sympathy between them goes beyond skilful ensemble and shared enjoyment of the wealth of illustration in Schubert, into a deep understanding of the poetry as he composed it. It's no surprise that they should produce powerful performances of the most inward-looking Heine songs – the suf-fering power of 'Der Atlas', the misery from which the harmony allows no escape in 'Die Stadt', the terror of 'Der Doppelgänger'. But the lighter ones are scarcely less affecting. And their mutual understanding completely solves such a difficult song as 'Kriegers Ahnung'.

The Beethoven cycle moves in a steady progress not into the usual triumphant assertion but into a warmth of belief that song may truly join the parted lovers. This is music-making of genius.

Schwanengesang. Wer sich der Einsamkeit ergibt (Harfenspieler I), D478. An die Türen (Harfenspieler III), D479. Ganymed, D544. Geheimes, D719. Der Musensohn, D764. Rastlose Liebe, D138. Schäfers Klagelied, D121. Wandrers Nachtlied II, D768. Wer nie sein Brot mit Tränen ass, D480
Peter Schreier ten **András Schiff** pf
Wigmore Hall Live WHLIVE0006 (79' · DDD · T/t)
Recorded live 1991   Ⓜ ⊙⊙

The 1991 recital by Peter Schreier and András Schiff is highly desirable, though the sound is not quite on the same level. Schreier was never the most honeyed of tenors; but in the lighter songs of *Schwanengesang* he compensates for a touch of reediness and a tendency to harden on high notes with the supple grace of his phrasing and his ultra-keen response to the text. 'Liebesbotschaft' is eager and volatile, enhanced by Schiff's wonderfully limpid touch and his care to make the piano's singing left hand match the voice in eloquence (Schubert's original, high, key an advantage, here and elsewhere).

On the downside, 'Aufenthalt' is surely too slow and life-weary, weighed down by recurrent submissive *rallentandos*. But 'Das Fischermädchen' has a lilting tenderness, Schiff again singing in dulcet partnership with the voice, while in the remaining Heine songs singer and pianist unflinchingly probe the extremes of anguish and bitterness. 'Die Stadt' (the swirling, impressionistic arpeggios eerily insubstantial from Schiff) and 'Der Doppelgänger' are as desolate and disturbing as any performances on disc, the suggestion of a whine, even a sneer, in Schreier's timbre extraordinarily apt here.

After this we get a sharply characterised Goethe group that encompasses the bleakness of the three Harper's Songs (done with characteristic intense immediacy) and ends with an impulsive, dancing 'Der Musensohn' that rightly brings the house down.

Schwanengesang. Abschied, D475.
An Schwager Kronos, D369. Geheimnis, D491.
Widerschein (second version), D949.
Ian Bostridge ten **Antonio Pappano** pf
EMI 242639-2 (61' · DDD)   Ⓕ⊕⊃

Schwanengesang is really no such thing, and there is nothing to prevent a singer omitting a song or changing the order. Bostridge follows the publisher's order and does not flinch before 'Aufenthalt'; and if momentarily he goes under, perhaps it is part of the musical-verbal picture that he should. In any case, all of this is a diversion, almost a frivolity. At the heart of the matter are 'Der Doppelgänger', 'Die Stadt', 'Ihr Bild', 'Am Meer' and, from the Rellstab settings, 'In der

Ferne'. Bostridge has, in the pallor of voice and expression, the haunting that pervades these songs. In the first mentioned (the last sung) he is one of the few who can create unease without anticipating the horror, still making those open-mouthed vowels ('starret', 'Schmerzensgewalt', 'so manche Nacht') call out into the night like a wounded animal.

Such rare moments are the singer's own; elsewhere the performance is equally the pianist's. Pappano plays with imagination as verbally attuned as Bostridge's. The rightness of touch is evident in the first additional song, 'Geheimnis', and in the last, the very simple and aptly chosen 'Abschied'. He is also graceful and interesting in the happier songs. There's one misgiving – Bostridge makes so much of the German words, rather as though anxious to communicate with the back rows of a concert hall full of non-German-speakers. Whatever the justification *in situ*, it nags a little on records.

Schwanengesang. Herbst, D945. Die Taubenpost, Ⓟ D965a. Sehnsucht, D879. Am Fenster, D878. Bei Dir allein, D866. Der Wanderer an den Mond, D870. Das Zückenglöcklein, D871. Im Freien, D880
Christoph Prégardien ten **Andreas Staier** fp
Challenge Classics ⊞ CC72302 (72' · DDD · T/t)
                                                     Ⓕ⊙⊙⊃

Planning a CD programme around *Schwanengesang* is always tricky. The vastly experienced duo of Christoph Prégardien and Andreas Staier here come up with a solution as satisfying as any. They preface the quasi-cycle with the bleak, windswept Rellstab setting 'Herbst', which Schubert unaccountably omitted from the Rellstab sequence that opens *Schwanengesang*. Then, at the end, they follow 'Die Taubenpost' – always in danger of jarring after the *Weltschmerz* of the Heine group – with other, complementary, Seidl settings, ending with the blissful nocturnal homecoming of 'Im Freien'.

Prégardien's dulcet tenor, subtly and gracefully deployed, is heard to advantage both in these Seidl songs and in *Schwanengesang*. Where so many singers seem to 'think' the whole collection in the minor key, as it were, Prégardien is eagerly expectant in 'Liebesbotschaft' and sings a smiling, seductive 'Fischermädchen'. His 'Ständchen', taken at an easy, mobile tempo, is likewise all caressing charm, while 'Abschied' is blithely insouciant, the wistfulness of the final verse lightly touched – and how well the delicate, slightly veiled sonorities of Staier's fortepiano complement the voice, here and elsewhere.

In the anguished Heine songs Prégardien's less extreme style than, say, Peter Schreier, is scarcely less moving, whether in the rhythmically incisive 'Der Atlas' (where the fortepiano's percussive resonance brings uncommon clarity to Schubert's quasi-orchestral textures), or an 'Am Meer' of aching tenderness, the final stab of pain all the more affecting for being understated. 'Die Stadt', taken at an unusually urgent tempo, emerges in a single grim sweep, with the fortepiano's sustaining pedal creating a mysterious haze impossible to replicate on a modern grand. Prégardien occasionally adds discreet, graceful embellishments to his lines, especially apt in 'Ständchen'. While it is absurd to speak of an outright 'winner' in such a crowded field, Prégardien and the ever-illuminating Staier join the roster of indispensable *Schwanengesang* recordings.

Winterreise, D911

Winterreise
Mark Padmore ten **Paul Lewis** pf
Harmonia Mundi HMU90 7484 (74' · DDD · T/t)
Ⓜ❶❶❶➔

Ah, this journey! How many have made it, sincerely and imaginatively, two setting out as nearly as possible as one! So many on records too, following the elusive track as with torchlight concentrated upon it. Yet, of all, it's hard to think of one that leads more faithfully to the cold comfort of its end. And when we get there in this performance, what an end it is!

The journey begins with ever such a slight whine high in the voice, as with a calm acceptance of pain. The piano abstains from jabbing *sforzandi* to underline what the chords make plain enough, instead insisting calmly on its left-hand *legato*. The melting major-key modulation is all affection: no hint of bitterness in the sentiment that his passing footsteps should not disturb the faithless beloved's sleep. But outside in the open, stillness and turbulence alternate like the moods of the weather-vane. And so throughout much of the trek the self-confiding of the loner holds in check the utterance of emotion as the icy surface of the river conceals the running water beneath. Even so the pain will out, as it does in the last phrase, 'ihr Bild dahin', of 'Erstarrung'.

On we go, lulled and tormented by the magic music-box of 'Frühlingstraum', till the tragic chord before 'so elend nicht' in 'Einsamkeit' brings a dreadful reality into focus. The deceptive sweetness of 'Die Krähe', the giddy disorientation of 'Letzte Hoffnung', the subdued feverish excitements of 'Täuschung' find an almost holy stability in 'Das Wirtshaus', but still the external world exists, felt as almost an intrusion in 'Mut'. And soon we meet the organ-grinder. And his secrets must on no account be revealed by reviewer or arts-gossip. And the listener must wait, out of respect to this marvellous partnership of Mark Padmore and Paul Lewis, until time can be taken for it, alone and uninterrupted, to accompany them on the journey through to its unearthly end.

has a decision to make along lines which probably never even presented themselves to his predecessors of perhaps 20 years ago. Then, it was assumed that you were singing Schubert's masterpiece for, and as, yourself or Everyman. Now the question is whether (or to what extent) you are singing as a character – the *Winterreise*-man, an objective creation, an operatic role confined to dramatic monologue. Werner Güra appears to have gone as far in that direction as any.

This *Winterreise*-man is, if not 'mad' then seriously 'disturbed' or unhinged. He is given to secretive, wild-eyed confidings, to sudden changes of mood (singing softly one moment, desperately loud the next). His enunciation may be deadpan, almost expressionless, or it may stab emphatically – and the pianist will do the same. But after the pause before 'Die Post' comes a gradual change: the fever subsides, the voice qualities suggesting a partly self-dramatised wildness are no longer heard, and the desolation of reality becomes a fact to be recognised and accepted. At the point where others grow into madness, Güra's calm is, in this context, still more terrible.

One says 'Güra', but mean to include the pianist, Christoph Berner, whose playing is the very enactment of the man, his apprehensions and his setting. Güra himself has probably the most elegantly ingratiating voice of all the present-day Lieder-singing tenors and it has often seemed that he prefers to use it for any purpose rather than elegant ingratiation; but this is certainly a performance to take to heart.

Winterreise
Dietrich Fischer-Dieskau bar **Jörg Demus** pf
DG The Originals 447 421-2GOR (71' · ADD · T/t)
Recorded 1965
Ⓜ❶❶➔

On the verge of his fifth decade, Fischer-Dieskau was in his absolute prime. Listening to his interpretation is like coming home to base after many interesting encounters away from the familiar. Indeed, it's possibly the finest of all in terms of beauty of tone and ease of technique – and how beautiful, how smooth and velvety was the baritone's voice at that time. This is the most interior, unadorned and undemonstrative of his readings, perhaps because Demus, a discerning musician and sure accompanist, is the most reflective of all the singer's many partners in the cycle. Demus never strikes out on his own, is always there unobtrusively and subtly supportive, with the right colour and phrasing, literally in hand.

Given an intimate, slightly dry recording, finely remastered, the whole effect is of a pair communing with each other and stating the sad, distraught message of Schubert's bleak work in terms of a personal message to the listener in the home. A deeply rewarding performance.

Winterreise
Werner Güra ten **Christoph Berner** pf
Harmonia Mundi HMC90 2066 (73' · DDD)
Ⓟ❶❶❶➔
The modern singer preparing his *Winterreise*

Winterreise
Ian Bostridge ten **Julius Drake** pf
Stage director **David Alden** Video director **Peter West**

NVC Arts **DVD** 8573 83780-2 (124' · Regions 2-6)
Includes documentary on the making of the film Ⓕ Ⓞ

Winterreise lives on its own without any staging. The initially dubious Bostridge and Drake make that point at the start of the feature, their faces filling with dismay as Alden describes his seemingly hare-brained ideas to turn it into a melodrama about a crazed protagonist. It's implied in what follows that singer and pianist gained confidence in what Alden had in mind, while the director came to respect Bostridge's intelligence and dramatic gifts. Indeed, the project would have collapsed had not the tenor the ability to sear the soul as much visually as aurally. His piercing eyes, striking looks and age make him an ideal candidate for such an experiment.

Inspired by a disused mental asylum in north London, Alden and his designer create a huge, empty space, as desolate as the abandoned asylum itself, in which the beginning and end of the cycle are enacted. In between, Bostridge is projected on to a white background, arrestingly so in the case of 'Die Krähe', where the singer is viewed from above by the crow with Bostridge spread-eagled on the floor below, an astonishing image, mirroring the bird's menace. Among the unforgettable shots are the picture of the forlorn shattered figure in 'Die Nebensonnen', which Alden and Bostridge agree has a mystic, religious aura to it, the lone protagonist seen at a distance in 'Das Wirtshaus', the singer seated back to back with the pianist in 'Mut'. Doubts arise only with the introduction during two songs of the unfaithful girl and her family, disturbing the vision of the lonely sufferer.

At the heart of the video lies Bostridge's silvery tone, special, highly individual intensity of utterance and identification with the man's desperate plight. Drake supports him with playing of equal insight. The sound, fairly closely miked, is excellent; the camerawork highly imaginative.

Winterreise
Thomas Quasthoff *bar* **Daniel Barenboim** *pf*
Video director **Michael Beyer**
DG **DVD** 073 4049GH (83' · NTSC · 16:9 ·
PCM stereo, 5.1 and DTS 5.1 · 0) Ⓕ

As we know from his fine CD version, Thomas Quasthoff is a master of this cycle, his command of word and music consistently true and compelling. His interpretation here is once more imbued with sincere empathy with the suffering traveller, suggesting, as he says in the accompanying interview, a man at once at the end of his tether and yet defiant. He is also keen to show that each song could not exist without its being part of the whole, just one aspect of Schubert's genius. The cohesion of his reading is supported with deep acumen by Barenboim's thoughtfully felicitous playing. Some 30 years ago he recorded the cycle with Fischer-Dieskau, and again he manages to underpin his singer's intentions while managing to add his own mite of individuality. So why do the results rather

underwhelm? The direction is too restless and in close-up Quasthoff constantly rocks from side to side; the effect becomes dizzying. For a DVD version Bostridge offers rich rewards, but for those allergic to any visual dimension outside the music as such, this DVD has much to offer purely in musical terms.

Ervín Schulhoff   Bohemian 1894-1942

Schulhoff, of German-Jewish ancestry, was a pupil of Max Reger in Leipzig; later in Germany he associated with Paul Klee and the Dadaists. In Prague he was active as a pianist, in jazz and as an exponent of Hába's quarter-tone music. When the Nazis invaded Czechoslovakia in 1939, he had to resort to performing under a pseudonym. In 1941 the Soviet Union approved his petition for citizenship but he was arrested and imprisoned before he could leave Czechoslovakia. In June 1941 Schulhoff was deported to the Wülzburg concentration camp, near Weissenburg, Bavaria. He died in August 1942 from tuberculosis. His works include stage pieces, six symphonies and two piano sonatas, displaying diverse styles.

Sextet

Sextet. String Quartet in G, Op 25. Duo[a].
Solo Violin Sonata[b]
Rainer Johannes Kimstedt *va* **Michael Sanderling**
vc **Petersen Quartet** ([b]Conrad Muck, [a]Gernot
Sussmuth *vns* Friedemann Weigle *va* [a]Hans-Jakob
Eschenburg *vc*)
Capriccio 10 539 (77' · DDD) Ⓕ Ⓞ

As Schulhoff enthusiasts will have come to expect, the works represented aren't at all uniform in style. The early quartet is prematurely neo-classical. It was conceived in 1918 when the composer was still serving in the Austrian Army. The German group certainly gives it their all. Taut and tough, they seem intent on radicalising the discourse whether through a heightened response to its finer points or a profound understanding of the Beethovenian models that lurk beneath the surface invention. As a result, the Quartet emerges as a witty, substantial piece.

The string Sextet was completed six years later but sounds quite different, its Schoenbergian first movement well integrated with the more eclectic idiom of the rest. Whatever the outward manner, Schulhoff's rhythmic phraseology is metrically conceived. Even if you already know the Sextet the Petersen makes a plausible first choice. The aggressive communication of their playing is emphasised by the bright, not quite top-heavy sound balance.

The Janáček-Bartók-Ravel axis of the *Duo* is equally well served. The Sonata for solo violin (1927) is at least as interesting as similar works by Hindemith. A thoroughly distinguished issue by an ensemble seemingly incapable of giving a dull performance.

William Schuman   American 1910-1992

Schuman studied at Columbia University and under Roy Harris at the Juilliard School. He taught at Sarah Lawrence College from 1935 to 1945, then became president of the Juilliard School, which he extensively reorganised. He was president of Lincoln Center, 1962-69. He received many honours and awards. His symphonies (10 in all, though the first two were withdrawn) are central to his output; they embody vigorous drive, febrile rhythms and expansive musical and orchestral gestures, with a broad melodic line and a generally tonal idiom. His chamber music includes four string quartets; he also composed, mainly after the mid-1970s, large-scale vocal pieces.

Violin Concerto

Schuman Violin Concerto[a]. New England Triptych
Ives Variations on 'America' (orch Schuman)
[a]**Philippe Quint** vn **Bournemouth Symphony Orchestra / José Serebrier**
Naxos 8 559083 (57' · DDD)   ⓈⒶⒹ

The rediscovery here is the William Schuman Violin Concerto. The work is in two substantial movements both showing Schuman's own kind of exuberant energy with brass and percussion as well as a special mystical stillness in soft music. The soloist plunges in right at the start of the first movement; there's an oasis of calm at and then a sprawling cadenza of nearly three minutes. The second movement has an aggressive start which clears the way for the delayed entry of the soloist. Again there's lyrical rapture as well as fireworks and – another Schuman fingerprint – a fugato. Philippe Quint, the Russian-born American violinist, make his recorded debut here. It's a very capable performance in every way – look out for him again.

Schuman's *New England Triptych*, based on three hymns by the first prominent American pioneer-composer, William Billings, is one of his most familiar pieces, well represented on CD. The *Variations on 'America'* – sending up the USA, royalty or both – ensures that this useful Schuman package ends with a good laugh.

Clara Schumann   German 1819-1896

Taught by her father, Friedrich Wieck, Clara became one of the greatest pianists of the 19th century, an artist of consummate skill. She maintained a highly successful touring career both before and after she married Robert Schumann (1840). She was a great champion of music by her contemporaries (Chopin, Schumann and Brahms). She also taught extensively, both privately and at the conservatories in Leipzig and Frankfurt. As a composer she showed imagination and flair, but her ambitions were not directed in that direction (she ceased composing in

1854, the year of Robert's collapse). She prepared a complete edition of Robert's music, raised a large family and maintained a close relationship with Brahms to the end of her life.

Piano Concerto in A minor, Op 7

Piano Concerto. Piano Trio, Op 17.
Francesco Nicolosi pf
Rodolfo Bonucci vn **Andrea Noferini** vc
Alma Mahler Sinfonietta / Stefania Rinaldi
Naxos 8 557552 (54' · DDD)   ⓈⒹ

The autograph manuscript of Robert Schumann's Piano Concerto (1845) revealed not only the toil but also the hand of Clara, particularly in the last movement. Eleven years earlier, Robert had orchestrated a *Concertsatz* by the 14-year-old Clara and this became the corresponding movement of her concerto which she soon completed on her own.

The *Concertsatz* is as long as the other movements put together and a shorter finale might have been beneficial. Yet the complete, though imperfect, work is a notable achievement for so young a composer; and the piano part could be seen as a vehicle for virtuosity. All credit therefore to Francesco Nicolosi for not succumbing to temptation. His playing is deep-toned and tractable and, in conjunction with Stefania Rinaldi who eschews strident orchestral attack, finds a vein of melancholy in the music. He also ably balances the implied duality of the *Romanze* in which the marking *con grazia* conflicts somewhat with the additional *La melodia ben marcato e legato*.

'Not a gifted melodist but skilful handling of other elements compensates' is one of biographer Nancy B Reich's verdicts on Clara Schumann. And an element is the assured way modulations are treated in the Piano Trio (1846). Nicolosi adapts his playing to the demands of the genre, and he interacts sympathetically with his fine partners. Perhaps the *Scherzo* (to be played *Tempo di menuetto*) ought to have been bucolic rather than gracious but this doesn't detract from a very communicative performance. The orchestra's cellos and basses are lightweight and the solo violin occasionally squeaky but the sound is otherwise good.

Piano Works

Complete Works for Piano Solo
Susanne Grützmann pf
Profil ④ PH07065 (3h 55' · DDD)   Ⓜ

This four-CD album redresses a faulty or at least misunderstood balance. Superbly played and recorded, it prompts a sharp and necessary awareness of the full range of Clara Schumann's gifts. A deeply courageous woman who juggled her roles of wife, mother (to eight children), pianist and composer, she also bore the tragedy of her beloved Robert's collapse into insanity and the added complication of her relationship with Brahms with rare strength and fortitude. Certainly her Op 1 (composed when she was 11) suggests a startling precocity before her skill deepened over the years into music where outward conventions thinly disguise a highly personal and poetic nature. True, she pays loving tribute to her husband's work, but the listener should not be misled. Theirs was clearly a symbiotic relationship, and composing side by side during the early days of their legendary romance, Schumann both marvelled at and feared her gifts. Indeed, there is evidence to show that Clara felt over-shadowed ('I compose, too,' she asserted as she pushed her compositions under Robert's door) while Robert felt threatened by his wife's celebrity as a pianist (the Tsar of Russia politely enquired of Clara, 'and is your husband also musical?').

Yet Clara always remained true to her own lights. And even when her veneration for others (to Chopin in the exquisite Nocturne from Op 6) is clear she always maintains her own voice. There are some strange prophecies (Alkan's *En rhythme molassique*, for example, in her *Le ballet des revenants* from Op 5) as well as a capacity to wear her cap and gown with the best of them (the Op 16 Preludes and Fugues) or play her virtuoso trump cards with aplomb (Op 14 and the *Agitato* from Op 21). But whether you turn to the chirpy *Scherzo* from her single Piano Sonata or to the scintillating *volante* close to the Op 8 Variations you will be brilliantly surprised and subtly challenged. This issue is an invaluable addition to the catalogue.

Robert Schumann   German 1810-1856

Mendelssohn, Chopin, Schumann, Liszt, Verdi and Wagner were born within four years of one another; composers were still writing music under their influence 100 years later.

Schumann's father was a Saxon bookseller and publisher, well-to-do and cultured. Robert was his fifth child and though he and his wife were not musical, they encouraged their son's musical talents and at the age of 10 he began piano lessons. For a career, however, he was persuaded to study law and Schumann dutifully travelled to nearby Leipzig where, at the same time, he began piano lessons with his future father-in-law, Friedrich Wieck.

On the early death of his father, he persuaded his mother and guardian to allow him to study music and the same Friedrich Wieck was recommended. So he returned to the Wiecks' house where he lodged and boarded, determined to become a world-famous virtuoso like Wieck's talented young daughter Clara. Schumann's mature career as a composer dates from about this time. In 1832 he developed some sort of ailment in the index and middle fingers of his right hand. He tried all the fashionable remedies available including, fatally, a mechanical device which purported to help strengthen and lift the middle finger. It left his right hand permanently crippled, so much so

that it exempted him from military service – but it also put an end of his ambitions as a concert pianist.

Throughout the 1830s, Schumann's career as a composer slowly grew while he also developed his literary activities. In 1834 he co-founded a progressive journal, the Neue Zeitschrift für Musik, which fulminated against the vapid salon music of the period. His sharp and perceptive writing made him one of the foremost critics of the day, the first German critic to recognise Chopin, among the first to champion Berlioz and predict Brahms' greatness. Sometimes his judgements have proved to be askew but by and large, Schumann's musical criticism was as fine as the style and objectivity with which he wrote.

He also translated his journalistic and musical convictions into real life, as it were. He formed an association of intimate friends which he named Davidsbündler: David against the Philistines, a group that would oppose philistinism in the arts and support passionately all that was new and imaginative. (Schumann immortalised this in his piano work Davidsbündlertänze.)

Perhaps surmising that Schumann was an unstable character, Friedrich Wieck violently opposed the relationship between Robert and Clara and his actions over the following seven years won him a place in music history, not as the obscure teacher of a great composer or as the father of a great pianist (which Clara would become) but as the disagreeable father-in-law who thwarted Young Love. He forced the couple to separate, opened their love letters and initiated a campaign of personal vilification against his former pupil, so set was he against his daughter's marriage.

The affair ended in court, judgment went against Wieck and the happy couple were married the day before Clara's 21st birthday. Schumann's career as a composer clearly entered a new stage: in 1840 alone he wrote over 100 songs and in 1841, during the space of only four days, he sketched out his Symphony No 1, the 'Spring' Symphony. Many other masterful works followed rapidly but, though Clara was intensely ambitious for her husband, the two of them found it hard to balance the need for a pianist to practise and a composer to work in silence. On tour, he found it galling to be introduced at times as 'the husband of Clara Schumann' and returned home before her from a concert tour of Russia in 1844. His mental health began to fail, he resigned from the teaching post Mendelssohn had created for him at his new conservatory in Leipzig, and in 1844 the Schumanns moved to Dresden. The great Piano Concerto was composed here, the Second Symphony, more songs, but from the late 1840s it was clear that Schumann was becoming increasingly unstable.

In 1850 he accepted the post of director of music in Düsseldorf. It proved to be a disaster. Schumann was no conductor, a talent which the position pre-eminently demanded, and together with his natural reserve (Liszt and Wagner found him boring) now exaggerated by his inability to communicate and, at times being unaware of his surroundings, he was forced to resign.

Aural hallucinations were now accompanied by visions of demons and angels and on February 27, 1854, he tried to kill himself by drowning in the

Rhine. He was rescued and placed at his own request in an asylum at Endenich near Bonn. Here, Brahms was one of the few welcome visitors. Schumann lived on in this unhappy state for a further two years. He died in Clara's arms and was buried the next day in Bonn. Opinions vary as to whether the cause of his final illness was tertiary syphilis, sclerosis of the brain (his own doctor's verdict) or dementia praecox.

Piano Concerto in A minor, Op 54

Piano Concerto[a]. Cello Concerto[b]. Introduction and Allegro appassionato, Op 92[a].
[a]**Daniel Barenboim** pf [b]**Jacqueline du Pré** vc
[a]**London Philharmonic Orchestra / Dietrich Fischer-Dieskau;** [b]**New Philharmonia Orchestra / Daniel Barenboim**
EMI Encore 574755-2 (74' · ADD)
Recorded [a]1974, [b]1968   Ⓑ⚫

If ever a performance of Schumann's Piano Concerto stressed the principle of dialogue between soloist and conductor, then this is it. True, the Philharmonia's string ensemble isn't as watertight under Fischer-Dieskau as it might have been under some other conductors; and poetry is invested at the premium of relatively low-level drama. Orchestral textures are absolutely right for Schumann – warm yet transparent, full-bodied yet never stodgy – and poetry is a major priority. Add Barenboim's compatible vision and keyboard finesse, and you indeed have a memorable reading. Despite the extensive competition, both Stephen Kovacevich and Leif Ove Andsnes remain the top recommendations for this work (reviewed under Grieg) though.

The more discursive *Introduction and Allegro appassionato* has plenty of interest, but remembering that this isn't exactly top-drawer Schumann, the performance could be more arresting. The coupling is du Pré's Schumann Cello Concerto, the tear-laden quality in the slow movement more than matching that in her famous Elgar account. A rewarding disc.

Violin Concerto, Op posth

Schumann Violin Concerto **Wieniawski** Légende, Op 17. Violin Concerto No 2 in D minor, Op 22
Juliette Kang vn **Vancouver Symphony Orchestra / Sergiu Comissiona**
CBC Records SMCD5197 (63' · DDD)   Ⓕ⚫

Juliette Kang here plays with quicksilver brilliance not only in the virtuoso Wieniawski concerto but in the rugged Schumann work, less grateful for the player. Yet, though she plays brilliantly, with dazzlingly clean articulation in bravura passages, these are comparatively small-scale readings. Where those virtuosos in the grand Romantic tradition are balanced relatively close, Kang is more naturally balanced in a slightly recessed acoustic. The impression is of a sweet, silvery violin tone that can't expand so fully; the orchestral strings, too, sound relatively

small-scale. What matters is that the performances are all very persuasive. The Schumann, with its bravura double-stopping at the start, finds Kang fiery and impetuous, making up for barnstorming power, and when it comes to lyrical passages the poetry is beautifully caught. So too in the slow movement – introduced in a tender account of the brief opening cello solo – while the finale is taken at a speed which allows a delicious lilt in the dance-rhythms.

Similarly, in the Wieniawski concerto, Kang is light and volatile in the rapid passagework, and relaxes sweetly into the songful beauty of the motto theme, playing with a natural, unexaggerated lyricism.

Those who insist on display as the first essential may not be completely satisfied, but deeper qualities amply make up for that. For those who want this unique coupling, this is a first-class recommendation.

Symphonies

No 1 in B flat, Op 38, 'Spring' **No 2** in C, Op 61 **No 3** in E flat, Op 97, 'Rhenish' **No 4** in D minor, Op 120

Symphonies Nos 1-4.
Overture, Scherzo and Finale, Op 52
Staatskapelle Dresden / Wolfgang Sawallisch
EMI Great Recordings of the Century ② 567768-2 (148' · ADD). Recorded 1972   Ⓜ⚫⚫↦

Schumann's symphonies come in for criticism because of his supposed cloudy textures and unsubtle scoring, but in the hands of a conductor who's both skilful and sympathetic they're most engaging works. Sawallisch's recordings, brightly transferred, are a much admired set. His style, fresh and unforced, isn't as high powered as some other conductors but it's sensible, alert and very pleasing. He achieves great lightness in the First and Fourth Symphonies – there's always a sense of classical poise and control but never at the expense of the overall architecture of the pieces. The Second and Third Symphonies, larger and more far-reaching in their scope, again benefit from Sawallisch's approach. The playing of the Staatskapelle Dresden is superlative in every department, with a lovely veiled string sound and a real sense of ensemble. With the *Overture, Scherzo and Finale* thrown in for good measure, this isn't to be missed.

Symphonies Nos 1 & 2
Bavarian Radio Symphony Orchestra / Rafael Kubelík
Sony Classical Essential Classics SBK48269 (74' · ADD)   Ⓑ⚫

Symphonies Nos 3 & 4. Manfred, Op 115 – Overture
Bavarian Radio Symphony Orchestra / Rafael Kubelík
Sony Classical Essential Classics SBK48270 (76' · ADD)
Recorded 1978-79   Ⓑ

It's hard to understand why Kubelík's wonderful cycle failed to make an impact when it was first issued. His sensitivity to detail, his refusal to bully Schumann's vulnerable structures and his ability to penetrate occasional thickets of orchestration make these especially memorable. Just listen to the cheeky bassoon backing clarinet 1'44" into the *Spring* Symphony's fourth movement or the to-ing and fro-ing between first and second violins in the last movement of the Second. Only the first movement of the Fourth seems a little heavy-handed, but then the poetry of the *Romanze* and the exuberance of the finale more than make amends. First-movement repeats are observed and the playing throughout is rich in felicitous turns of phrase. The sound, though, is a minor stumbling block: violins are thin, brass a little fuzzy and the whole production less focused than Sawallisch's set. But Kubelík's insights are too varied and meaningful to miss, and there's much pleasure to be derived from them. What with a stirring *Manfred* Overture added for good measure, they also constitute exceptional value for money.

Symphonies Nos 1-3; No 4 (1841 & 1851 versions); P
in G minor, WoO29, 'Zwickauer'. Overture, Scherzo
and Finale, Op 52. Konzertstück in F, Op 86
Roger Montgomery, Gavin Edwards, Susan Dent,
Robert Maskell hns **Orchestre Révolutionnaire et**
Romantique / Sir John Eliot Gardiner
Archiv ③ 457 591-2AH3 (3h 22' · DDD)   Ⓕ Ⓞ ⤷

The first point to note is how much more comprehensive this is than previous cycles, even the outstanding RCA set of period performances from Roy Goodman and the Hanover Band. Gardiner offers both versions of Symphony No 4, 1841 and 1851, and his performances of them are very well geared to bringing out the contrasts. Still more fascinating is the inclusion of both the early, incomplete Symphony in G minor, and the *Konzertstück* of 1849 for four horns, with the ORR soloists breathtaking in their virtuosity in the outer movements, using horns with rotary valves crooked in F. Otherwise, except in three specified movements, natural horns are used, braying clearly through orchestration which always used to be condemned as too thick. In his note, Gardiner fairly points out the merits of the 1841 version of the Fourth in transparency and other qualities, suggesting, as others have, that the doublings in the later version make it safer and more commonplace. Paradoxically in performance, Gardiner is if anything even more electrifying in the later, more thickly upholstered version, as ever clarifying textures and building up to a thrilling conclusion. Even the *Zwickauer* Symphony of 1832 emerges as very distinctive of Schumann.

The contrasts between Gardiner and Goodman in their approaches to the numbered works aren't as marked as expected, often as much a question of scale and recording quality as of interpretative differences, with Goodman's orchestra more intimate, and with the RCA sound a degree less brightly analytical. Both prefer fast speeds, with Goodman a shade more relaxed and Gardiner more incisive, pressing ahead harder, with syncopations – so important in Schumann – more sharply dramatic. One advantage that Gardiner has in his slightly bigger scale is that he brings out more light and shade, offering a wider dynamic range. Hence the solemn fourth movement of the *Rhenish* Symphony inspired by Cologne Cathedral – as with Goodman taken at a flowing speed – builds up more gradually in a bigger, far longer *crescendo*, in the end the more powerful for being held back at the start. Though the Goodman set still holds its place, Gardiner offers a conspectus of Schumann as symphonist that's all the richer and more illuminating for the inclusion of the extra rarities.

Additional recommendations

Symphonies Nos 1-4   Ⓗ
Coupled with Manfred Overture
Cleveland Orch / Szell
Sony Classical Masterworks Heritage ② 5160272
(135' · ADD). Recorded 1958-60   Ⓜ Ⓞ ⤷
This famous set gives us the heart of George Szell, his feeling for style, for line and for Schumann's warming but fragile symphonic structures. He sometimes takes *crescendo* to imply *accelerando*, but his insistence on watertight exchanges facilitates a snug fit between various instrumental choirs, the strings especially. Playing standards are very high, but the close-set recordings occasionally undermine Szell's painstaking efforts to clarify Schumann's orchestration, the *Rhenish* being the worst offender.

Symphonies Nos 1-4 / **Zinman**
Tonhalle Orch, Zürich / Zinman
Arte Nova ② 82876 57743-2 (123' · DDD)   Ⓢ
This Swiss return to the Schumann symphonies involves a radical change of orchestral sonority, more grainy, notably lighter, with the sort of sharpened dynamic profile and fine-tipped attenuation more associated with period-instrument orchestras. Zinman uses period brass and timpani: note the stopped horns for the pivotal four-note motif in the *Spring* Symphony's *Allegro molto vivace*. Tempi are in general swifter than before. Think of this as a sort of Schumann slimming kit, useful for those who find the symphonies turgid and who crave more air between and around the notes.

Symphony No 1, 'Spring', Op 38. 'Zwickau'
Symphony, WoO29 – I. Overture, Scherzo and Finale,
Op 52. Die Braut von Messina, Op 100. Genoveva,
Op 81 – Overture
Swedish Chamber Orchestra / Thomas Dausgaard
BIS ⌖ BIS-SACD1569 (78' · DDD/DSD)   Ⓕ

To call a performance 'well made' might seem like a half-hearted compliment but in the case of

Thomas Dausgaard's account of the *Spring Symphony* it's only part of the story, albeit a very important part. Clarity is a given with this particular band and here the same impressions of transparency, watertight ensemble, dovetailed phrasing and buoyant rhythms pertain. The first movement is kept on its toes and 'in tempo', and likewise the *Scherzo* where the Trios are skilfully integrated into the rest of the movement, the first of them opening, unusually, to a gently brushed *legato*. The *Larghetto* is streamlined without sounding cold, the important horn and *pizzicato* string parts always crystal-clear, whereas the finale's prime virtue is its judicious pacing, especially the idyllic horn passage just after the halfway point, and the symphony's closing pages, which are thrillingly played.

Dausgaard's understanding of tempo relations is even better demonstrated in the *Zwickau* movement of an early G minor symphony. There are reminders of early Schubert and Bruckner in that rays of light are crossed with moments of darkness, for example the unresolved bassoon motif that closes the exposition, very imaginative (and unsettling), and so is the return of the stern introduction towards the end of the movement.

The Mendelssohnian *Overture, Scherzo and Finale* is again beautifully shaped, the introduction unusually pensive, the ensuing *Allegro* full of life, the *Scherzo* crisp but unhurried. The two relatively late overtures again benefit from smaller-than-usual orchestral forces and perceptive direction, Dausgaard generating bags of energy while allowing textures to breathe. The recorded sound is superb.

Symphonies – No 2, Op 61; No 4, Op 120 (original version, 1841). Szenen aus Goethes Faust – Overture. Julius Cäsar, Op 128
Swedish Chamber Orchestra / Thomas Dausgaard
BIS 🔊 BIS-SACD1519 (76' · DDD/DSD)　　　　Ⓕ

All this talk of Schumann's stodgy orchestral writing…Rubbish! Evidence for the defence is simple: keep the orchestra slim and well balanced, the tempi lively and the textures clear and the calories positively fall away. Thomas Dausgaard, with just 38 players, turns the symphonic Schumann into a thoughtful athlete who burns energy while his mind spins.

Dausgaard opts for the 1841 original version of the Fourth Symphony, with its faltering, even abrupt, transition from an opening *Andante* to a fleet *Allegro*. It leaves a very different impression to the revision. The transition from *Scherzo* to finale is much as it is in the familiar 1851 version but the finale itself contains 'new' material and neither of the outer movements has repeats. All in all, it is less thick-set than its successor: Brahms preferred it.

The Second Symphony is similarly revealing with keen accents and prominent inner voices, the latter half of the slow introduction biting and muscular, the main *Allegro* superbly built. In the *Scherzo* Dausgaard slows and softens the

bridge passage appealingly, accentuating the dizzy flight back to the main subject. In the achingly beautiful *Adagio*, top line and accompaniment seem to lean on each other to ease the pain, and in speeding for the finale's second set Dausgaard intensifies the argument, making fresh sense of it.

BIS's realistic sound quality helps the clarifying process and the timps (with hard sticks) have tremendous presence. A good idea, too, to include Schumann's *Julius Caesar* and *Faust* overtures: strange, relatively late essays, equivocal music, slightly unhinged and played – appropriately enough – with a restless, slightly nervous edge.

Piano Quintet in E flat major, Op 44

Piano Quintet. Andante and Variations, Op 46. Fantasiestücke, Op 73. Märchenbilder, Op 113.
Marie-Luise Neunecker hn **Dora Schwarzberg, Lucy Hall** vns **Nobuko Imai** va **Natalia Gutman, Mischa Maisky** vcs **Martha Argerich, Alexandre Rabinovitch** pf
EMI 557308-2 (75' · DDD)
Recorded live 1994　　　　　　Ⓕ**ⒶⒶ**▶

After 'one memorable day of rehearsal', as the introductory note puts it, Martha Argerich and a group of friends recorded this programme at a public concert in Holland 'with the enthusiasm and intimate inspiration of a house-party'. The rarity is the Andante and Variations, Op 46, here brought up with all the spontaneous freshness of new discovery in a performance as enjoyable for its self-generating continuity as its diversity. Argerich and her fellow pianist, Rabinovitch, divide keyboard responsibilities in the remainder of the programme. Her own major triumph comes in the Quintet (with truly inspirational help from Maisky's cello). Every note tingles with life and colour in an arrestingly imaginative reading of exemplary textural transparency. In none of the more familiar works in the concert is that little extra stimulus of live as opposed to studio recording combined with more finesse and finish than here.

In the smaller pieces Argerich reaffirms herself as an artist of 'temperament', much given to the impulse of the moment. The recording itself is pleasingly natural. And there's heartening audience applause as a further reminder that we're at a live performance.

Piano Quintet[a]. String Quartet No 3, Op 41 No 3.
[a]**Marc-André Hamelin** pf
Takács Quartet (Edward Dusinberre, Károly Schranz vns Geraldine Walther va András Fejér vc)
Hyperion CDA67631 (57' · DDD)　　　　Ⓕ**ⒶⒶ**▶

Marc-André Hamelin and the Takács Quartet toured with Schumann's Piano Quintet and this shows in the deep rapport they demonstrate in this recording of the work. Not that Hamelin isn't centre stage, with the Quartet deployed widely across the stereo spectrum; but the sense is of true chamber interplay between five equals. Hamelin scampers and thunders by turns but not once does he upstage the string players. The direct comparison is with Leif Ove Andsnes and the Artemis Quartet (reviewed under its coupling, the Brahms Piano Quintet), winners of a *Gramophone* Chamber Award, and the new recording runs them close. Hamelin and the Takács take a more rhapsodic approach to tempo and *rubato* but, like their rivals, keep clear sight of the work's large-scale structure. While no one will topple Andsnes from pole position, Hamelin and the Takács will remain within easy reach for some time.

The Takács also come up against an Award-winner (the Zehetmair Quartet's Disc of the Year in 2003, reviewed below) with their performance of the A major Quartet, and once again acquit themselves admirably. The Hyperion recorded sound is the more spacious – ECM might well have stuck microphones up the noses of the Zehetmairs, so visceral is their sound world – and once again the Takács revel in the classical logic of Schumann's vision, in contrast to the German group's mercurial response to the composer's blazing inspiration. That this disc simply gets better and better on repeated listening is ample recommendation.

String Quartets, Op 41

No 1 in A minor No 2 in F No 3 in A

String Quartets Nos 1 & 3
Zehetmair Quartet (Thomas Zehetmair, Matthias Metzger *vns* Ruth Killius *va* Françoise Groben *vc*)
ECM New Series 472 169-2 (50' · DDD) Ⓕ**OOO**Ⓓ➔

Ⓖ The Zehetmair Quartet's coupling focuses the music's alternating wildness and fragility with altogether unique perception. Theirs is an agitated, combustible and loving view of Schumann, a credible trip into his troubled world that reflects older playing styles not by exaggerating or abandoning vibrato but by constantly varying tone, tempo, bow pressure and modes of attack. Aspects of this trend are usefully exemplified by their handling of the pensive second section of the Third Quartet's third movement, and by the way they negotiate the sudden, bloodless *moderato* passage that forms the coda of the First Quartet's finale. In the less consistent but more challenging First Quartet, minute variations in pulse and emphasis are consistently engaging – they enjoy maximum freedom within the law of the page. Contrapuntal passages that other quartets present as dry or self-conscious – at 2'36" into the first movement of No 1, for example, where the viola takes the initial lead – assume new-found meaning.

These aren't comfortable performances. They pass on cosmetic appeal and would rather grate and rail than pander to surface 'gloss'. So be warned. But they're profoundly beautiful in

their truthful appropriation of music that can be both poignant and aggressive. Delicate, too, in places (Mendelssohn with added fibre); in fact more comprehensive as musical statements than most of us had previously suspected. That realisation is due almost entirely to the persuasive powers of these supremely accomplished, and realistically recorded, performances.

Piano Trios

No 1 in D minor, Op 63; **No 2** in F, Op 80; No 3 in G minor, Op 110

Piano Trios Nos 1 & 2
Florestan Trio (Anthony Marwood *vn* Richard Lester *vc* Susan Tomes *pf*)
Hyperion CDA67063 (57' · DDD) Ⓕ**OOO**

Ⓖ For those who have always thought of Schumann's First Piano Trio as his finest chamber work after the Piano Quintet, the Florestan Trio may encourage you to think again about the Second Trio – a wonderful piece, full of poetic ideas. The artists make vigorous work of the first movement's urgent thematic interrelations but the real surprise is the third movement, a lilting barcarolle awash with significant counterpoint, although the heart of the Trio is its slow and deeply personal second movement. The differences in the trios are more marked than their similarities. The Second Trio is mellow, loving and conversational, but the First is troubled, tense, even tragic – save, perhaps, for its Mendelssohnian finale. The Florestan Trio realises the music's myriad perspectives, coaxing its arguments rather than confusing them. Marwood employs some subtle *portamento* and varies his use of vibrato, whereas Susan Tomes never forces her tone. Real teamwork, equally in evidence for the gently cantering *Scherzo* and the fine, elegiac slow movement.

Piano Trio No 3. Fantasiestücke, Op 88.
Piano Quartet in E flat, Op 47[a]
[a]**Thomas Riebl** *va* **Florestan Trio** (Anthony Marwood *vn* Richard Lester *vc* Susan Tomes *pf*)
Hyperion CDA67175 (71' · DDD) Ⓕ**O**Ⓓ➔

After their 1999 *Gramophone* Award-winning disc of the first two piano trios (reviewed above), these players champion three works which are less frequently encountered in concert, proving once again how a revelatory interpretation can make us all think again.

The G minor Piano Trio (No 3) of 1851 suffers from over-repetitive, at times perfunctory rhythmic patterning. But thanks to the mercurial vitality and the spontaneous response to every passing innuendo from all three interwoven voices, not a note here sounds unmotivated. The three fanciful 1842 miniatures for piano trio (revised under the title of *Fantasiestücke* in

1849) have long been criticised for the dominance of the keyboard in all but the third, entitled 'Duet'. Susan Tomes makes no attempt to disguise this.

Last but not least, the Piano Quartet of 1842, long overshadowed by the much-loved Piano Quintet. Misha Donat's appreciative note reminds us that even the loyal Clara waited some seven years before taking it into her repertory. The piano is rarely silent, and mustn't be allowed to dominate; so praise goes to Susan Tomes for a keen ear for balance. The *Scherzo* has a Mendelssohnian, elfin fleetness, and the finale (surely Schumann's *ne plus ultra* in exhilarating contrapuntal ingenuity) an exemplary textural clarity. The slow movement, played with touching simplicity, speaks as eloquently as any of the composer's Clara-inspired love-songs. Excellently recorded, this welcome disc should win all three works a new lease of life.

Additional recommendation

Schumann Piano Trio No 1[b]   **H**
Coupled with **Mendelssohn** Piano Trio in D minor, Op 94[a]
Cortot pf **Thibaud** vn **Casals** vc
Naxos Historical mono 8 110185 (59' · ADD)
Recorded 1928/29   ⓈⒹ▸

It's difficult to evaluate the playing in technical terms such as minute attention to expressive detail without loss of flow, impeccable ensemble, and last but not least, choice of tempo. The impression is more of intimately shared awareness of, and response to, the music's inner secrets – as if personally communicated to them by the composer himself. Ward Marston's skilful engineering is at its truest and best here.

Cello and Piano works

Drei Fantasiestücke, Op 73. Adagio and Allegro, Op 70. Violin Sonata No 3, Op 121 (arr Isserlis). Abendlied, Op 85 No 12 (arr Joachim). Drei Romanzen, Op 94. Fünf Stücke im Volkston, Op 102
Steven Isserlis vc **Dénes Várjon** pf
Hyperion CDA67661 (70' · DDD)   ⒻⓄⓄ▸

Steven Isserlis has long been a stalwart champion of Schumann, through his advocacy of not only the often-maligned Concerto but also the chamber works. For this disc he has had to beg, borrow and steal but the results absolutely justify the means.

In the wrong hands, a work such as the *Fantasiestücke*, Op 73 (which Isserlis plays in its earliest incarnation), can sound a touch seasick, with too much swelling through every phrase, and a loss of the overall shape as a result. But how well Isserlis paces everything; some of his tempi are quite spacious but this gives the music a wonderfully considered and luxuriant aspect; the results never ever sound contrived. That's partly to do with Isserlis's sound (extravagantly he uses not one but two Strads on this recording), which has

a very focused centre to it, but also his utterly innate relationship with pianist Dénes Várjon. Perhaps the most ravishing item on the disc is the poignant *Abendlied*, arranged by Joachim from its piano duet form but then further borrowed by Isserlis, playing it down an octave. In his hands it's as moving a wordless Lied as anything you could imagine.

The substantial work here, though, is the Third Violin Sonata. Two of its movements – the Intermezzo and finale – originated in the multi-composer 'FAE' Sonata written for Joachim (for which Brahms famously wrote the *Scherzo*). Schumann later added two more movements to form his last large-scale work. It decisively refutes the theory that he had – metaphorically and literally – lost the plot by this stage. While it certainly doesn't conform to standard 19th-century sonata form, in Isserlis's hands it's a work of compelling power, whether in the terrifying *scherzo* sections of the second movement or the dreamy Intermezzo, a much-needed point of repose in a work of great tumult.

The disc ends with the *Fünf Stücke im Volkston*, and finds Schumann in a more folky idiom. Too often these pieces can sound like an awkward amalgam of styles, but Isserlis again is utterly inside them, revealing Schumann's innovation even at this late stage, from the edginess of the first, via the tender, Brahmsian second one to the spirited fifth piece, where Mendelssohn collides with Bartók.

For all that Isserlis has made many wonderful recordings, not least his seminal Bach Suites, this might just be his finest yet, with warmly detailed sound and a typically acute note from the cellist himself.

Violin Sonatas

No 1 in A minor, Op 105 No 2 in D minor, Op 121
No 3 in A minor

Violin Sonatas Nos 1-3
Carolin Widmann vn **Dénes Várjon** pf
ECM New Series ② 476 6744 (72' · DDD)   ⒻⓄⓄ▸

Schumann's violin-and-piano sonatas have never become favourite staples of the repertoire. Full textures, with the violin mainly confined to its middle and lower registers, often continue uninterrupted for many bars, and a somewhat grey, monotonous effect can be compounded by the composer's obsessive repetition of certain rhythms and motifs. But is this a fair description? You wouldn't think so after hearing Carolin Widmann and Dénes Várjon; their imaginative, wide-ranging variations of tone colour unlock the music's Romantic, atmospheric potential, and their command of genuine *rubato* – passionate, unimpeded forward motion followed by lingering backward glances – gives the sonatas an expressive flexibility that's surely authentic.

'With sorrowful expression', writes Schumann at the start of the First Sonata, and the surges of painful emotion in this performance, while sounding quite spontaneous, are rigorously based on the printed expression marks. Similarly, the gripping account of the Second Sonata's slow introduction starts from meticulous observance of Schumann's dynamics, slurs and *staccatos*, adding to this an entirely convincing rhythmic freedom. The opening page of this sonata's third movement, which creates a remote, almost chilling effect, isn't quite so convincing. Back in 1952, George Enescu, playing with Celiny Chailley-Richez (Opus Kura), gently arpeggiated his plucked chords and, on taking up the bow, found a beautifully intimate, confiding tone – this mood may well be closer to what Schumann intended. Overall, however, Várjon and Widmann are entirely persuasive. Whether or not you know the music well, you'll be enthralled and delighted.

Violin Sonatas Nos 1 & 2; No 3 – Intermezzo
Ilya Kaler vn **Boris Slutsky** pf
Naxos 8 550870 (51' · DDD)   ⑤⊞

These performances, powerfully recorded in Indiana by these two young Russian artists, are most enjoyable. The passion of their playing is perhaps not wholly Germanic, but every artist legitimately brings something of himself to the music he performs, and nothing here takes us out of touch with Schumann's world. There's an impressive intensity to this playing, although refinement and tenderness are rightly also present. Kaler and Slutsky mould these melodies well; it's a matter of timing as well as tone and dynamics, as the *Allegretto* of the A minor Sonata shows. The same moment also demonstrates how they follow Schumann naturally through his characteristically rapid changes of mood, while the finale that follows has power and purpose. The single movement from the composite 'FAE' Sonata dedicated to Joseph Joachim, in which Schumann collaborated with the young Brahms and Albert Dietrich, makes a useful bonus in a disc which would otherwise last under 50 minutes. The Naxos disc at super-bargain price represents fine value.

Davidsbündlertänze, Op 6

Davidsbündlertänze. Etudes symphoniques, Op 13 (1852 version). Arabeske in C, Op 18. Blumenstück in D flat, Op 19
András Schiff pf
Warner Elatus 0927 49612-2 (76' · DDD)   Ⓜ

Schumann was a great rethinker, in Schiff's opinion not always for the better in later life – hence his choice of Schumann's original (1837) conception of the *Davidsbündlertänze* rather than its more usually heard 1851 revision. Except for a touch of mischief (subsequently removed) at the end of No 9, textual differences are slight. But Schiff prefers the fewer repeat markings in the first edition, so that ideas never

lose their freshness. More importantly, the exceptional immediacy and vividness of his characterisation reminds us that Schumann initially signed nearly all these 18 'bridal thoughts' with an F (the impetuous Florestan) or an E (the introspective, visionary Eusebius) – or sometimes both – as well as including literary inscriptions (and one or two more colourful expression marks) as a clue to the mood of the moment.

Schiff laughs and teases, storms and yearns, as if the hopes and dreams of the youthful Robert, forbidden all contact with his distant beloved, were wholly his own – there and then. The impatient Florestan fares particularly well. For the much metamorphosed *Etudes symphoniques* Schiff chooses the generally used late version of 1852 with its admirably tautened finale. Here, his bold, firmly contoured approach reaffirms it as the most magisterially 'classical' work the young Schumann ever wrote. Schiff emphasises its continuity and unity as a whole. Even the five so-called supplementary variations emerge as more purposeful, less ruminative, than often heard. These Schiff wisely offers as an independent group at the end. The recital is completed by the *Arabeske* and *Blumenstück*, again played with a very strong sense of direction, even if Schiff isn't yet Richter's equal in disguising the repetitiveness of the latter. Nothing but praise for the naturalness of the reproduction.

Davidsbündlertänze. Papillons, Op 2. Carnaval, Op 9. Etudes symphoniques, Op 13. Kinderszenen, Op 15. Kreisleriana, Op 16. Fantasie in C, Op 17. Arabeske in C, Op 18. Humoreske in B flat, Op 20. Piano Sonata No 2 in G minor, Op 22. Vier Nachtstücke, Op 23. Drei Romanzen, Op 28. Waldszenen, Op 82. Bunte Blätter, Op 99 – No 9, Novelette
Wilhelm Kempff pf
DG Collectors Edition ④ 471 312-2GB4 (4h 57' · ADD)
Recorded 1967-75   ⓂⓄⓄ⊞

A collection that will give great pleasure. Sample it anywhere and there can be no mistaking who this is – you know great pianists by their sound. Kempff was one of the most distinguished German pianists of the last century, blossoming through two decades in the Austro-German repertory after the death of Schnabel and Edwin Fischer, but he never carried the flame quite as they did. Performing bravura pieces didn't interest him, so the Toccata, the *Concert-Studies after Paganini*, Op 10, and the *Abegg* Variations aren't here. Nevertheless it's a good selection, lacking only the Fantasy Pieces, Op 12, to give a rounded picture of the phenomenal explosion of Schumann's creativity for the piano that took place between the ages of 20 and 29.

Kempff's special quality seems to be a songfulness and *cantabile* style which is in danger of becoming a forgotten art nowadays. Listening to him in Schumann, it's as if a wind is blowing through, rising and falling, sweeping incident along and carrying everything forward: song, dance, stories, poems, moods, portraits, parades of characters, visions of landscape, recollections.

Few players have matched his infallible touch with the way the music holds together.

As pianism his *Carnaval* may not leave you astonished, but it's immaculately characterised: festive, buoyant, irresistible in movement, the comings and goings of the masked personages and the guest appearances of 'Chopin' and 'Paganini' all spot on. There's no single right way to play this masterpiece, but his is vivid.

When he made the earliest of these recordings he was already 71; the last are from his 78th year. In the later ones you notice more weight on the keys and perhaps a reduced inclination to be volatile; but he has kept his technique in trim, and continues to sound at ease with the instrument. The difficult numbers in the *Davidsbündlertänze* are hard for every pianist, but Kempff doesn't see them as virtuoso challenges to be confronted and dispatched. Always the music is paramount, and beautiful sound, and a control of voices under the fingers that seem to be following Schumann instinctively in the exploration of the piano's potential. The opening of *Kreisleriana* hangs fire as if he were feeling his way into it but the rest is magnificent and thrillingly projected.

When at his best you have the impression his insights aren't only musical but brought to bear on every area of Schumann's imagination. All the big works have this definition and can be counted among the best on record. The *Fantasy* comes high on the list, perhaps top, as does the undervalued *Humoreske*. He's a guide to Schumann you should not be without, authoritative and companionable, balanced and most human.

Additional recommendation

Davidsbündlertänze
Coupled with Fantasiestücke, Op 12
Frith pf
Naxos 8 550493 (63' · DDD)　　　　　ⓈⒹ➔

Frith summons his excellent technique here for some exciting pianism. Recommended not just for the budget-conscious but for those who enjoy youthful pianistic exuberance.

Etudes symphoniques, Op 13

'The Complete Works for Piano, Volume 3'
Etudes symphoniques. Abegg Variations, Op 1.
Intermezzi, Op 4. Nachtstücke, Op 23.
Faschingsschwank aus Wien, Op 26.
Bunte Blätter, Op 99
Finghin Collins pf
Claves ② 50 2806/7 (146' · DDD)　　　　Ⓕ**OO**

Finghin Collins, the Irish pianist who won the Clara Haskil International Piano Competition in 1999, plays Schumann in a refreshingly direct, unfussy manner, with a warm-hearted tone full of telling touches and refined *rubato*. Listen, for instance, to the way he subtly shapes the melody of the first of the 'Three Little Pieces' of *Bunte Blätter* (the whole set is a joy, not least the concluding 'Quick March') and sings his way over

the energetic semiquaver accompaniment in the Intermezzo from *Faschingsschwank aus Wien*.

The only quibble is with the *Etudes symphoniques* into which Collins inserts the five posthumous variations that Schumann suppressed on the grounds that the work would be too long with their inclusion (they were not published till 1873). Most pianists take the composer's advice and play the revised 1852 version, though admittedly it means missing out the exquisite posthumous variation No 5. Collins presents them in numerical order in a performance that lasts 40 minutes, as opposed to 25 without the extras. This is, after all, 'The Complete Schumann'.

Fantasiestücke, Op 12

Fantasiestücke. Kinderszenen, Op 15.
Humoreske, Op 20
Philippe Cassard pf
Ambroisie AMB9961 (74' · DDD)　　　　Ⓕ**O**

Here's a disc of fine Schumann-playing, superbly recorded and on a beautifully voiced piano. To undertake a critical nit-pick of each of the 27 short pieces that make up these three works would seem invidious and, besides, not reflect the spirit in which the music is offered. In the *Fantasiestücke* some might feel that Cassard uses too much pedal here, or takes such-and-such too fast or too slow there; others might justifiably counter by saying that Richter in his famous 1956 selection uses too little pedal, and strives for effect, compared with Cassard's more relaxed approach in infinitely better sound.

Kinderszenen, likewise, is distinguished by its simplicity, its tenderness and unexaggerated *rubato*, nowhere more apparent than in the final 'Der Dichter spricht'. Perhaps Argerich finds more impish delight in the extrovert titles, but that again must be a matter of personal preference.

Humoreske – 42 pages almost all in B flat major or G minor – is one of Schumann's works that might have been more satisfactory had he let it mature in the cellar for a while before drinking. It's difficult to overcome the problems presented by a continuous flow of fragments of such varying musical interest. Cassard almost succeeds if only because his mellifluous tone and subtle phrasing are such a pleasure to hear. Both Ashkenazy (1972) and Horowitz (1979) in their very different ways find more character in the details, the latter's pacing of Schumann's meandering 'Conclusion' more convincing than Cassard. But that's quite the wrong note on which to conclude a review of a recital that merits the highest praise.

Kreisleriana, Op 16

Kreisleriana. Humoreske in B flat, Op 20
Kinderszenen, Op 15.
Radu Lupu pf
Decca 440 496-2DH (75' · DDD)　　　　Ⓕ**OO**➔

SCHUMANN KINDERSZENEN & KREISLERIANA – IN BRIEF

Radu Lupu
Decca 440 496-2DH (75' · DDD) Ⓕ**OO**▶
Lupu's characteristically limpid and purposeful playing effortlessly holds attention, revealing the character and charm of each vignette in *Kinderszenen*. Just as effortlessly, he hurls his listener into the quite different world of *Kreisleriana*, capturing its emotional turmoil and its dazzling contrasts.

Vladimir Horowitz
Sony SMK90443 (61' · ADD) Ⓜ**O**
A classic account of *Kreisleriana*, demonstrating profound understanding of Schumann's idiom and projected with extraordinary clarity, most impressively in the final movement where several themes weave together symphonically.

Alfred Cortot Ⓗ
Music & Arts ② CD858 (131' · ADD) Ⓕ
Here's a style of piano playing all but non-existent today, yet one which still compels attention with its combination of rhetoric and limpid musicality. Both as narrator and protagonist, Cortot is an engaging artist, fully identifying with the emotional tenor of Schumann's music.

Martha Argerich
DG 410 653-2GH (52' · DDD) Ⓕ**O**▶
By turns affectionate and vigorous, these are never tame performances. Argerich's vivid characterisations in *Kinderszenen* may be a bit extreme for some but will delight those who dislike more salon-friendly performances.

Wilhelm Kempff
DG ④ 471 312-2GB4 (317' · ADD) Ⓜ▶
Kempff made these recordings in his seventies; though he doesn't, or possibly can't, play up the virtuosity of *Kreisleriana*, he projects the music compellingly. His laconic style, however, is perhaps not ideal for Schumann's fervid Romanticism.

Maurizio Pollini (*Kreisleriana* only)
DG 471 370-2GH (48' · DDD) Ⓕ**OO**▶
Despite rather close and clangorous sound, Pollini's artistry shines through in a performance which may seen a touch detached from the emotional drama, but has a steady burn that becomes irresistible.

Mitsuko Uchida (*Kreisleriana* only)
Philips 442 777-2PH (67' · DDD) Ⓕ▶
A virtuoso and brilliantly executed account that may yet strike some as rather detached from Schumann's drama. None the less the music's sometimes quite strange beauty shines through.

As piano playing this disc has an aristocratic distinction reminiscent of Lipatti. As music-making it's underpinned by unselfconscious intuition, making you feel you're discovering the truth of the matter for the first time. It's difficult to recall a more revealing performance of Schumann's *Humoreske*. Lupu captures all the unpredictability of its swift-changing moods while at the same time imparting a sense of inevitability to the sequence as a whole. Florestan's caprice is as piquant as Eusebius's tenderness is melting. Yet there's an underlying unity in the diversity from Lupu, enhanced by most beautifully timed and shaded 'links'. Goodness knows how long this work has been in his repertory. But here it emerges with the keen edge of new love.

Next, *Kinderszenen*: simplicity is its keynote. To begin with (as notably in the opening 'Von fremden Ländern und Menschen') you wonder if, in rejection of sentimentality, he might not be allowing himself enough time for wide-eyed wonderment. But you're soon over by his limpid tonal palette and the sheer purity of his phrasing. Each piece tells its own magical little tale without the slightest trace of special pleading. Such pristine grace will never pall, however often heard.

Kreisleriana in its turn offers rich contrasts of desperation, dedication and Hoffmannesque drollery. And except, perhaps, in the impetuous No 7 (taken dangerously fast), it brings further reminders that we're in the presence of a master pianist – among so much else able to rejoice in this work's endless dialogues between left hand and right with his opulent bass and gleaming treble. Reproduction is totally faithful throughout.

Kreisleriana. Arabeske, Op 18. Davidsbündlertänze, Op 6. Fantasiestücke, Op 12. Frühlingsnacht (arr Liszt). Papillons, Op 2. Waldszenen, Op 82. Widmung (arr Liszt)
Leon McCawley pf
Avie ② AV0029 (143' · DDD) Ⓜ▶

This two-CD album celebrates a richly inclusive cross-section ranging from Schumann's Op 2 to Op 82, from early ardour to later introspection, and vice versa. For whatever the opus, Schumann's ultra-Romantic genius – his rapid shifts from pain to solace, from tears to laughter – is paramount. Above all, it's in his wide-eyed wonder, his naivety, that Leon McCawley shines and makes his mark.

True, a certain politeness inhibits him from relishing to the full every shift of the kaleidoscopic imagination in, say, *Papillons*, but elsewhere – in the closing, enchanted reminiscence of *Davidsbündlertänze* or in the 'exquisite bird song in an ominous setting' (the 'Prophet Bird' from Op 82) – he's at his very best. In the *Fantasiestücke* he delights in the cross-accentuation, kittenish by-play of 'Fabel' and provides an attractive alternative to more hectic performances of 'Träumes Wirren'.

The *Arabeske* is another notable success (particularly in the glowing retrospective coda).

Most of all, he's finely sensitive to the inner promptings and recesses of *Kreisleriana*: the *sehr langsam* and *Bewegt* of No 4, the central mock-polyphonic whirl of No 7 or the alternately gentle and explosive whimsy of No 8 all testify to his winning ease and sensitivity. Excellent recording, first-class accompanying essay and lavish presentation.

Fantasie in C, Op 17

Fantasie in C. Faschingsschwank aus Wien, Op 26.
Papillons, Op 2
Sviatoslav Richter pf
EMI Encore 575233-2 (67' · ADD
Recorded 1961-62   Ⓢ❍❍❍

G There can surely be no doubt as to Richter's status as a giant of the piano world. And collectors now have a bewildering array of his concert performances and reissues to choose from. Richter's Schumann is unequalled. The *Fantasia* is arguably Schumann's keyboard masterpiece. And Richter plays it better than other pianists. Nobody can phrase as beautifully as he can, or produce those marvellously soft accompaniments beneath quietly singing tunes or toss off the middle movement with such speed and brilliance. There's astonishing poetry in his playing. It almost amounts to a rediscovery of the work.

And the same could be said of *Faschingsschwank aus Wien* and *Papillons*. (The way he plays the main theme of the latter should make you buy this disc if nothing else does – he seems to add stature to the work.) His assets in all these works are, first, an unusually musical sense of phrasing. Secondly, he can reduce an accompaniment to a mere murmur without any loss of evenness so that a tune above it can sing even when it's soft. Thirdly, he uses a great deal of *rubato*, but always with impeccable taste; his *rubato* in slow passages has a mesmeric quality only partly due to the fact that he usually plays such passages much slower than other pianists. Fourthly, he has faultless technique. His superiority is apparent throughout. The recording is magnificent for its date. Classic performances which no pianophile should be without.

Piano Sonatas

No 1 in F sharp minor, Op 11; **No 2** in G minor, Op 22
No 3 in F minor, Op 14

Piano Sonatas Nos 1 & 3
Bernd Glemser pf
Naxos 8 554275 (65' · DDD)   Ⓢ❍❍▷

Bernd Glemser's playing here is an exceptionally arresting experience in its graphic immediacy and freshness. With his prodigious technique, underpinned by exuberant imaginative vitality, it was no surprise to learn that in a wide-ranging repertory, he feels particularly drawn to the later Romantic virtuoso school. Some listeners might well think his approach to Schumann's F sharp minor Sonata (written at the age of 25) too overtly Lisztian in expression to be truly stylish. Sure, the more classically disciplined Clara, for example, would never have allowed herself such extreme changes of tempo in contrasting Florestan's turbulence with Eusebius's idyllic lyricism in the two spacious outer movements. Yet with his innate musicality Glemser somehow allows the argument to cohere. His challenging rhythm in the *Scherzo* (and the richly savoured burlesque of its Trio), like the *senza passione ma espressivo* of the slow movement's intimate song, are all finely judged. The F minor Sonata comes in Schumann's 1853 revision, restoring the second of the two *Scherzo*s omitted when the work was first published 17 years earlier, as a three-movement *Concert sans orchestre*. With Naxos's tonal reproduction at its best, this disc comes recommended as a true 'super-bargain' not to be missed.

Piano Works

Allegro, Op 8. Arabeske, Op 18. Blumenstück, Op 19. Acht Fantasiestücke, Op 12. Drei Fantasiestücke, Op 111. Fantasiestücke (additional movement). Humoreske, Op 20. Kinderszenen, Op 15. Drei Romanzen, Op 28. Waldszenen, Op 82
Finghin Collins pf
Claves ② 50 2601/2 (149' · DDD)   Ⓕ

In this young Irish pianist we have an artist of rare poetic empathy, one with an uncanny and moving capacity to arrive at the still centre, the very heart, of Schumann's teeming and frenzied imagination.

Winner of the 1999 Clara Haskil Competition, Collins is here to stay. Indeed, it is no exaggeration to say that he plays in the spirit of Haskil herself, a great artist who while appearing to do so little ended by doing everything. At his finest his playing is enviably clear and transparent yet touched with a subtle and distinctive eloquence, allowing Schumann's voice to shine through. Hear him in the *Waldszenen*, capturing the quizzical melancholy in 'Vogel als Prophet' and the dark and lighter sides of Schumann's schizophrenic nature in the sinister 'Verrufene Stelle' and 'Freundliche Landschaft'.

The storm clouds scud across the sky in the first of the *Fantasiestücke*, Op 111, and the B minor *Allegro*, a souvenir of Schumann's early ambitions as a virtuoso pianist, takes on a new poetic quality and dimension, and never more so than in the glorious sunset coda. *Kinderszenen* glows with an inner warmth and radiance, 'Träumerei' displaying rare musical honesty and 'Rocking Horse' set in realistic cantering rather than jet-propelled motion.

Humoreske, a notably elusive challenge, is again a marvel of interior light, grace and energy, and if Collins's *Fantasiestücke*, Op 12, are less illuminating they include a fascinating final addition, a

'Feurigst' normally excluded. Claves's sound is as natural as the playing.

Additional recommendation

Schumann Papillons. Arabeske. Humoreske
Coupled with **Haydn** Piano Sonata HobXVI/20
A Schiff
Dal Segno DSPRCD044 (72 · DDD)   Ⓑ

Youthful Schiff from his Denon days, but already demonstrating the poetry and imagination that make him an artist of the top rank.

Szenen aus Goethes Faust

Szenen aus Goethes Faust
Karita Mattila, Barbara Bonney, Brigitte Poschner-Klebel, Susan Graham sops **Iris Vermillion** mez **Endrik Wottrich, Hans-Peter Blochwitz** tens **Bryn Terfel** bass-bar **Jan-Hendrik Rootering, Harry Peeters** basses **Tölz Boys' Choir; Swedish Radio Chorus; Berlin Philharmonic Orch / Claudio Abbado**
Sony Classical ② S2K66308 (115' · DDD · T/t)
Recorded live 1994   ⒻⓄⓄ

No one before Schumann had ever attempted to set Goethe's mystical closing scene, which he finished in time for the Goethe centenary in 1849. What eventually emerged as his own Parts 1 and 2 (in turn portraits of Gretchen and the by now repentant Faust) followed later, after his move from a Mendelssohn-dominated Leipzig to a Wagner-ruled Dresden, hence the striking difference in style. Nothing Schumann ever wrote is more dramatic than Faust's blinding and death in the course of Part 2.

The Berlin Philharmonic is very forwardly recorded – occasionally perhaps a little too much so for certain voices. But never in the case of Bryn Terfel in the title-role. Any advance fears that he might disappoint were immediately banished not only by the generosity and flow of his warm, round tone but also the total commitment and conviction of his characterisation. Moreover as Dr Marianus in Part 3 he offers some wonderfully sustained *mezza* and *sotto voce*. Karita Mattila's Gretchen is always sympathetically pure-toned, clean-lined and assured. At times, as positioned, the other male soloists seem a little outweighed by the orchestra.

No praise can be too high for the Four Grey Sisters (so tellingly contrasted in vocal colour) led by Barbara Bonney: their midnight encounter with Faust and his eventual blinding is brilliantly done. And there's splendidly characterful choral singing throughout from both adult and youthful choirs. In the more operatically conceived Parts 1 and 2 and the visionary Part 3, Abbado himself takes the music to heart and what he draws from his orchestra makes nonsense of the charge that Schumann was an inept scorer. This is worth every penny of its full price.

Szenen aus Goethes Faust
Mojca Erdmann sop **Christiane Iven** mez **Elisabeth von Magnus, Birgit Remmert** contrs **Werner Güra** ten **Christian Gerhaher** bar **Alastair Miles, Franz-Josef Selig** basses **Netherlands Children's Choir; Netherlands Radio Choir; Royal Concertgebouw Orchestra, Amsterdam / Nikolaus Harnoncourt**
RCO Live ② ⚏ RCO09001 (119' · DDD/DSD)
Recorded live 2008   ⓂⓄⒹ

Nikolaus Harnoncourt never ceases to surprise with his enthusiasms. Compared to Gershwin's *Porgy and Bess*, this is perhaps a less unexpected venture: a live recording with the Concertgebouw and a first-rate soloistic line-up of Schumann's choral masterpiece, *Szenen aus Goethes Faust*.

For years Schumann had contemplated Faust as the subject of a possible opera, and perhaps if he'd produced such a work it would have gained a more certain place in the repertoire. What has hampered *Szenen*'s progress is certainly not musical quality, which is brilliantly sustained, the final part arguably one of the composer's most moving achievements. But in this postmodern world, we're as suspicious of grand literary cantatas as we are of the oratorios of Mendelssohn and Liszt. A pity, for this particular piece deserves to be up there with the Faust-inspired works of Berlioz and Gounod.

What Harnoncourt does particularly superbly is steer away from the slightest hint of anything saccharine: the chorus of blessed boys being a case in point. He's aided by the outstanding Christian Gerhaher, who is moving not only as Faust but in the Dr Marianus music too. Franz-Josef Selig and Alastair Miles are also great assets to the set, though Christiane Iven is not quite in the same class.

You're aware that Harnoncourt's version is live not only from the occasional noises off, but also (inevitably) the odd moment that would have been retaken in a studio. But he's never less than compelling, and his vision of this great work is consistently enlightening.

Das Paradies und die Peri, Op 50

Das Paradies und die Peri, Op 50
Dorothea Röschmann, Malin Hartelius sops **Rebecca Martin, Bernarda Fink** mez **Christoph Strehl, Werner Güra** tens **Christian Gerhaher** bar **Bavarian Radio Chorus and Symphony Orchestra / Nikolaus Harnoncourt**
RCA Red Seal ② ⚏ 88697 27155-2
(101' · DDD/DSD)   ⒻⓄⓄⒹ

Initially envisaged as an opera, Schumann's haunting 1843 oratorio *Das Paradies und die Peri* tells of how a Peri – according to Persian mythology, the 'impure' child of a fallen angel and a human female – can enter Paradise only if she arrives at Heaven's gates with a worthy offering. Her first two offerings (a hero's blood and a vision of selfless love) fail the test whereas a third (abstinence inspired by a child at prayer) wins her Heavenly access.

Clara Schumann thought *Das Paradies* her husband's finest work and Nikolaus Harnoncourt calls it a 'splendid' score. So why the neglect? Partly negative political memory, maybe (Goebbels commissioned an arrangement that emphasised sacrificial death), and partly the work's hybrid nature. But it contains music that is at once dramatic, lyrical, ethereal, deeply personal and shot through with sincere human feeling. Mendelssohn's influence is discernible more or less throughout, especially in the choral writing which is very lightly dispatched on this superb 2005 performance from Munich's 'shoebox' Herkulessaal. The dramatic core is vividly exemplified by the chorus 'Doch seine Ströme sind jetzt rot', which reports rivers of human blood, whereas the transition to the tenor solo about the felled hero is meltingly beautiful, Christoph Strehl on excellent form.

Bach is another obvious point of reference, particularly at the point where the mezzo (Bernarda Fink) sings of a plague-inflected youth facing death, 'Verlassner Jüngling', music that's unmistakably reminiscent of Bach's Passion music and where Harnoncourt leans meaningfully on every fourth note of the strings' accompaniment. His Bavarian RSO sound warm, though period awareness on the conductor's part ensures sonorities that are light and pointedly attenuated.

Der Rose Pilgerfahrt, Op 112

Der Rose Pilgerfahrt
Inga Nielsen, Helle Hinz *sops* **Annemarie Møller, Elizabeth Halling** *mezzos* **Deon van der Walt** *ten* **Guido Päevatalu** *bar* **Christian Christiansen** *bass* **Danish National Radio Choir and Symphony Orchestra / Gustav Kuhn**
Chandos CHAN9350 (62' · DDD · T) Ⓕ⚫

Amid today's great upsurgence of interest in Schumann's later choral undertakings, the work's long neglect is no doubt due to its all-too-naive tale of a rose who, after an eagerly sought transformation into a maiden to experience human love, chooses to sacrifice herself for her baby. Schumann's own ready response to Moritz Horn's poem can best be explained by its underlying moral message together with a strain of German rusticity then equally close to the composer's heart. Having said that, how grateful Schumann lovers should be to Chandos for at last introducing the work to the English catalogue in so sympathetic yet discreet a performance from this predominantly Danish cast. All credit to the conductor, Gustav Kuhn, for revealing so much fancy in fairyland, so much brio in peasant merriment, and so much charm in more tender lyricism without ever making heavy weather of this essentially *gemütlich* little score.

No praise can be too high for the Danish National Radio Choir: such immediacy of response leaves no doubt as to their professional status. Nor do the soloists or orchestra disappoint. Tonal reproduction is agreeably natural.

Liederkreis, Op 24

Liederkreis. Myrthen, Op 25 – No 7, Die Lotosblume; No 21, Was will die einsame Träne?; No 24, Du bist wie eine Blume. Romanzen und Balladen – Op 45: No 3, Abends am Strand; Op 49: No 1, Die beiden Grenadiere; No 2, Die feindlichen Brüder; Op 53: No 3, Der arme Peter; Op 64: No 3, Tragödie. Belsatzar, Op 57. Lieder und Gesänge, Op 127 – No 2, Dein Angesicht; No 3, Es leuchtet meine Liebe. Gesänge, Op 142 – No 2, Lehn deine Wang; No 4, Mein Wagen rollet langsam
Stephan Genz *bar* **Christoph Genz** *ten* **Claar ter Horst** *pf*
Claves CD50 9708 (59' · DDD · T/t) Ⓕ⚫

This is a recital of promise and fulfilment. Stephan Genz's voice and style are as wide-ranging as his mode of expression. He lives every moment of Op 24, entering into all aspects of Schumann's settings and Heine's originals yet never overstepping the mark in his verbal painting. The other Heine settings receive no less than their due. The sensuous and plaintive qualities in Genz's tone are well suited to the three Heine poems in *Myrthen*. In contrast he rises to the histrionic challenges of 'Die beiden Grenadiere', 'Belsatzar' and the rarely encountered 'Die feindlichen Brüder', performances that are felt as immediately as if at the moment of composition. In 'Abends am Strand' the voice follows to the full the song's romantic import. In the third song of Op 64, 'Tragödie', the baritone is joined by his talented tenor brother: their voices naturally blend well. Finally, Genz is inspired by that amazingly original song, 'Mein Wagen rollet langsam', to give of his absolute best. Here, as throughout, Claar ter Horst matches the perceptions of her partner, and both are caught in an amenable acoustic.

Frauenliebe und -leben, Op 42

Frauenliebe und -leben. Sieben Lieder, Op 104. Gedichte der Königen Maria Stuart, Op 135. Lieder und Gesänge – I, Op 27: No 1, Sag an, o lieber Vogel; No 4, Jasminenstrauch; III, Op 77: No 3, Geisternähe; No 4, Stiller Vorwurf; IV, Op 96: No 4, Gesungen!; No 5, Himmel und Erde. Romanzen und Balladen – III, Op 53: No 1, Blondels Lied; No 2, Loreley; IV, Op 64: No 1, Die Soldatenbraut. Die Kartenlegerin, Op 31 No 2
Juliane Banse *sop* **Graham Johnson** *pf*
Hyperion CDJ33103 (74' · DDD · T/t)
Includes readings of 'Traum der eignen Tage' and 'Nachschrift'. Ⓕ⚫

This offering places Banse and Johnson among the most thoughtful and convincing of Schumann interpreters in the history of recording the composer's Lieder. From start to finish, in well-loved pieces and in others that will be new discoveries to many, the pair at once work in close concord and get to the heart of Schumann's very particular genius. The pair wholly dispel the oft-repeated view that Schumann's later songs are by and large failures: it's simply that the older man wrote differently from his younger, Romantically exuberant self. Thus the 1852 settings of Mary Stuart unerringly capture the soul of the troubled Queen's predicaments through the most concise means. Not a florid or untoward gesture is allowed to destroy the mood of sustained concentration and intimate musings. Banse brings to the songs just the right sense of a person sharing her innermost thoughts with us, the mezzo-like warmth of her lower voice gainfully employed, Johnson's piano communing in consort with the voice.

Schumann showed himself equally in sympathy with the poems of Elisabeth Kulmann (Op 104), a susceptible girl who died at the age of 17, his writing here simple and apparently artless. The composer, amazingly, thinks himself into the thoughts of the imaginative, fanciful young poetess; so does his interpreter, Banse, here using a lighter, more palpitating tone. The faultless recording completes one's pleasure in a very special issue.

Frauenliebe und -leben, Op 42. Myrthen, Op 25 – No 3, Der Nussbaum; No 7, Die Lotosblume. Die Kartenlegerin, Op 31 No 2. Ständchen, Op 36 No 2. Das verlassne Mägdlein, Op 64 No 2. Aufträge, Op 77 No 5. Lieder-album für die Jugend, Op 79 – No 13, Der Sandmann; No 29, Mignon. Lieder, Op 90. Nachtlied, Op 96 No 1
Bernarda Fink mez **Roger Vignoles** pf
Harmonia Mundi HMC90 1753 (60' · DDD · T/t) Ⓕ**O**

Bernarda Fink proves conclusively here that she can be just as compelling in German song as she is in Baroque works. For a start few accounts of any of these pieces have been quite so beautifully and effortlessly sung. Not a note in this recital is ugly or mishandled; everything is projected on a stream of perfectly produced, mellow mezzo tone. In itself, that's almost enough to recommend the disc. But Fink has so much more to offer. Her interpretation of the oft-recorded *Frauenliebe* cycle isn't one with the kind of overwhelming emotional tug evinced by Baker and von Otter, yet in her slightly more reticent way Fink conveys just as much feeling as her rivals. Her sweet, reflective, slightly vibrant tone very much calls to mind Seefried's and Isokoski's equally artless style among soprano versions. With Roger Vignoles as a sympathetic and positive partner, Fink's version deserves to be equated with those of her distinguished predecessors. There's no anti-climax in the other performances.

The very familiar 'Nussbaum' and 'Aufträge' are as delightfully eager and spontaneous as they ought to be. Those ineffably Schumannesque pieces, 'Die Lotosblume' and, in the Op 90 set-

tings of Lenau, 'Meine Rose', receive treatment in timbre and line and verbal assurance that would be hard to better. The recording has the singer blessedly forward so one catches the true flavour of her voice and words. A joy from start to finish.

Dichterliebe, Op 48

Dichterliebe. Liederkreis, Op 24. Belsatzar, Op 57. Abends am Strand, Op 45 No 3. Die beiden Grenadiere, Op 49 No 1. Lieder und Gesänge, Op 127 – No 2, Dein Angesicht; No 3, Es leuchtet meine Liebe. Vier Gesänge, Op 142 – No 2, Lehn deine Wang; No 4, Mein Wagen rollet langsam
Ian Bostridge ten **Julius Drake** pf
EMI 556575-2 (69' · DDD · T/t) Ⓟ**OOO**▶

Ⓖ Bostridge makes you think anew about the music in hand, interpreting all these songs as much through the mind of the poet as that of the composer, and, being youthful himself, getting inside the head of the vulnerable poet in his many moods. Quite apart from his obvious gifts as a singer and musician, that's what raises Bostridge above most of his contemporaries, who so often fail to live the words they're singing. Every one of the magnificent Op 24 songs has some moment of illumination, whether it's the terror conveyed so immediately in 'Schöne Wiege', the breathtaking beauty and sorrow of 'Anfang wollt ich' or the breadth and intensity of 'Mit Myrten und Rosen'. In between the two cycles comes a group of the 1840 Leipzig settings that adumbrates every aspect of Bostridge's attributes, as well as those of his equally perceptive partner.

The vivid word-painting in 'Belsatzar' brings the Old Testament scene arrestingly before us. Perhaps best of all is the unjustly neglected 'Es leuchtet meine Liebe', a melodrama here perfectly enacted by both performers. 'Mein Wagen rollet langsam' forms a perfect introduction, in its lyrical freedom, to *Dichterliebe*, an interpretation to rank with the best available in terms of the sheer beauty of the singing and acute response to its sustained inspiration. Listen to the wonder brought to the discovery of the flowers and angels in 'Im Rhein', the contained anger of 'Ich grolle nicht', the sense of bereavement in 'Hör ist das Liedchen' and you'll judge this is an interpretation of profundity and emotional identification, the whole cycle crowned by the sensitivity of Drake's playing of the summarising postlude. To complete one's pleasure EMI has provided an exemplary and forward recording balance.

Dichterliebe. Liederkreis, Op 39
Werner Güra ten **Jan Schultsz** pf
Harmonia Mundi HMC90 1766 (56' · DDD · T/t) Ⓕ**OO**

Güra delivers *Dichterliebe* with impeccable line and tone, and in a style following the best traditions of German tenors in the work. Only in 'Ich will meine Seele tauchen' does he stray from grace, choosing an oddly dragging tempo, slower than any other singers in this song. Although Bostridge's singing for EMI is slightly softer-grained, he opts for a more dramatic approach than Güra, distinctly underlining certain words, even syllables, to press home the import of Heine's and Schumann's inspiration. This may be found a shade mannered on repeated hearing. The contrast is most marked in 'Ich hab' im Traum geweinet'. Güra sings this in a dreamy *legato*, as if in a trance; Bostridge often breaks the shape of a phrase in order to give it a more histrionic edge. His very personal approach is underlined by a more intimate recording than Güra receives. Both pianists seem wholly in consort with their respective singer.

Bostridge adds to his disc more Heine, Op 24, and separate songs to texts by the same poet, a consistent policy, and it also has more music over all; but Güra's choice of Op 39 is entirely justified by his quite beautiful rendering of this haunting work. His classically wrought, plangent-voiced reading goes, without too much interpretative intervention, to the heart of Eichendorff, and to Schumann's imaginative response to the poems. Listen to such masterpieces as 'Die Stille', 'Mondnacht' (a perfect *legato* here again) and 'Wehmut' and you'll hear him at his most eloquent, pianist Jan Schultsz adding his own insights to the tenor's reading. This simpler, unsophisticated version goes to the heart of the matter, and deserves a place among the élite.

Dichterliebe. Die Lotosblume, Op 25 No 7. Die Minnesänger, Op 33 No 2. Romanzen und Balladen – II, Op 49: No 1, Die beiden Grenadiere; III, Op 53: No 3, Der arme Peter; IV, Op 64: No 3, Tragödie. Belsatzar, Op 57. Lieder und Gesänge – Op 127: No 2, Dein Angesicht; No 3, Es leuchtet meine Liebe. Gesänge, Op 142 – No 2, Lehn deine Wang; No 4, Mein Wagen rollet langsam **C Schumann** Lieder, Op 13 – No 1, Ich stand in dunklen Träumen; No 2, Sie liebten sich beide. Loreley. Volkslied
Christopher Maltman *bar* **Graham Johnson** *pf*
Hyperion CDJ33105 (77' · DDD · T/t)   Ⓟ**OO**

With this superbly executed recital Maltman leaps in a single bound into the front rank of Lieder interpreters today. Seemingly inspired by the wonderful programme, he executes it with bitingly intense tone and an innate feeling for the German language, his high baritone easily encompassing every test placed on it. There are so many deeply satisfying performances here of mostly familiar songs that it's difficult to know which to alight on for special praise, but the last two groups – the sad, frightening tale of the near-deranged Peter and the great *Dichterliebe* cycle – undoubtedly form the climax of the recital.

Maltman's and Johnson's account of the cycle is reminiscent of the underrated version made long ago by Waechter and Brendel: it has the same immediacy, the same perceptions, with the singer's voice on each occasion being of the ideal weight and tessitura, and in its absolute prime. All the inner melancholy of words and notes, all their

variety of texture are adumbrated. And here we have the added advantage of Johnson's inspired exegesis of the work in his accompanying notes.

Johnson also points out the foretaste of Mahler in the third of the Peter songs, a piece Maltman sings with just the right touch of vulnerability. He's just as sensitive in such well-known pieces as 'Die Lotosblume' and 'Dein Angesicht', and brings tremendous impulse of drama to the familiar 'Die beiden Grenadiere', here sounding new-minted. The songs by Clara are a pleasing bonus, but the difference between talent and genius is apparent in comparing her setting of 'Es fiel ein Reif' (from Heine's *Volkslied*) with Schumann's. A perfectly balanced recording adds to one's pleasure in listening to this generously filled CD, which is up to the high standard of this series to date.

Dichterliebe. Sechs Gedichte und Requiem. Belsatzar. Die Löwenbraut. Der arme Peter
Christian Gerhaher *bar* **Gerold Huber** *pf*
RCA Red Seal 82876 58995-2 (66' · DDD · T/t)   Ⓟ**OO**►

With this recital Christian Gerhaher confirms his pre-eminence in Lieder, and bids fair to equal or surpass his fellow baritones by dint of his attractively warm, firm tone and his complete understanding of the songs. In *Dichterliebe* he fully enters into the melancholic, romantic world of the rejected lover, projecting the love and sorrow in a committed yet unexaggerated manner. It's hard to imagine a reading by a voice of his kind that could possibly surpass his inspired performance – and that includes even the legendary Fischer-Dieskau.

He makes as good a case as possible for the *Six Poems* and *Requiem*, though it's hard to breathe life into the broken-backed ballad that is *Die Löwenbraut*. On the other hand, Gerhaher arrestingly enacts the melodrama of *Belsatzar*, biting consonants to the fore; the sadness of *Der arme Peter* benefits from the same thoughtful approach as *Dichterliebe*. Huber supports his partner with finely honed playing. The recording could not be better balanced or more immediate. This is, in every respect, a winner.

Dichterliebe, Op 48. Belsatzar, Op 57. Vier Gesänge, Op 142 – No 2, Lehn' deine Wang'; No 4, Mein Wagen rollet langsam. Fünf Lieder und Gesänge, Op 127 – No 2, Dein Angesicht; No 3, Es leuchtet meine Liebe. Myrthen, Op 25 – No 7, Die Lotosblume; No 21, Was will die einsame Träne?; No 24, Du bist wie eine Blume. Abends am Strand, Op 45 No 3. Romanzen und Balladen II, Op 49 – No 1, Die beiden Grenadiere; No 2, Die feindlichen Brüder. Der arme Peter, Op 53 No 3. Tragödie, Op 64 No 3
Gerald Finley *bar* **Julius Drake** *pf*
Hyperion CDA67676 (69' · DDD)   Ⓟ**OOO**►

In close collusion with the ever-sentient Julius Drake, Gerald Finley gives one of the most beautifully sung and intensely experienced performances on disc of Schumann's cycle of rapture, disillusion and tender regret. This is a *Dichterliebe* firmly in the past tense, the poet-lover achingly resigned from the outset. Finley sings the second song, 'Aus meinen Tränen', as if in a trance, and lingers luxuriantly, even masochistically, over the remembered 'Ich liebe dich' in 'Wenn ich' in deine Augen seh". Yet here and elsewhere some dangerously slow tempi are vindicated by the acuity of his verbal and musical responses. Where most singers end 'Im Rhein' in wistful tenderness, Finley infuses his final words with a wry bitterness. The disenchantment of 'Ich grolle nicht' is already glimpsed. In the cycle's latter stages Finley veers between numb reverie and acerbic self-dramatisation. The birds' assuaging response in 'Am leuchtenden Sommermorgen' is magical, barely breathed, the mounting trauma of the funereal dream-song 'Ich hab' im Traum geweinet' chillingly conveyed, the dissolving vision of the penultimate 'Aus alten Märchen' relived with ineffable sadness. Adding a cutting edge to his warm, mahogany baritone, Finley imbues the final song with savage irony, before the rueful, healing close. Throughout, Drake's playing is a model of clarity and acutely observed detail (he is more attentive than most to bass-lines), epitomised in his fluid, exquisitely voiced epilogue.

Singer and pianist are just as compelling in the other Heine settings here. The church acoustic is more resonant than is ideal for Lieder, though that hardly detracts from a glorious Schumann recital.

Schumann Dichterliebe[a] **Schoenberg** Pierrot lunaire[b]
Christine Schäfer sop [a]**Natascha Osterkorn** pf
[b]**Ensemble Intercontemporain, Paris / Pierre Boulez** Film director **Oliver Herrmann**
ArtHaus Musik **DVD** 100 330 (126' · 16:9 · 2.0 · 0)   Ⓕ**O**

Schäfer's virtuosity as a singing actress is exploited to the full in this highly imaginative double-bill. In the Schumann, work and artists are placed in a new and controversial context, with the production of the film intermingled with the performance of the cycle. In an intimate, sparsely lit nightclub in Berlin-Mitte, re-creating the salon atmosphere of a performance in the composer's time, the cycle is sung by the soprano in a tight-fitting black outfit while moving around the room in sympathy with evocations of each song's mood. The idea is to make the emotions of the work part of everyday life. Schäfer's reading of the songs is at once simple and intense, devoid entirely of sentimentality. She's supported in the performance and rehearsal by the equally fascinating personality of the pianist Natascha Osterkorn.

As far as one can tell, the singer isn't dubbed here. But in the 'staging' of *Pierrot lunaire*, she's undoubtedly miming to her own *Sprechgesang*. With clown-like make-up, Schäfer wanders, Kafka-like, through a kaleidoscopic range of situations and venues – including an abattoir, railway station and a medical lecture theatre –

vaguely appropriate to the texts. In this, one of the soprano's best-known roles, she excels in declaiming the text with meaning, assisted by that past master of the genre, Pierre Boulez.

As a bonus, there's a 45-minute interview with the singer. This whole issue extends the boundaries of interpreting vocal works on DVD. A riveting experience.

Lieder Recitals

'Melancholie'
Sechs Gedichte, Op 36. Der Einsiedler, Op 83 No 3. Gesänge des Harfners, Op 98a. Liederkreis, Op 39. Spanische Liebeslieder – Tief im Herzen trag ich Pein, Op 138 No 2. Spanisches Liederspiel, Op 74 – No 6 Melancholie
Christian Gerhaher bar **Gerold Huber** pf
RCA Red Seal 88697 16817-2 (73' · DDD)   Ⓕ

Though the catch-all title 'Melancholie' is slightly misleading, Christian Gerhaher's enterprisingly planned programme provides a conspectus of Schumann's art as a Lieder composer. With his bright, burnished high baritone, expressive diction and alert, unexaggerated response to mood and nuance, Gerhaher confirms his credentials as one of the most probing Lieder singers of the younger generation. While it is virtually impossible for a single voice to do equal justice to all 12 songs of the *Liederkreis*, he succeeds better than most. He beautifully suggests the melancholy and mystery of the opening 'In der Fremde', singing with fine *legato* and a subtly judged use of *rubato*, and brings an impetuous urgency and a chilling final frisson to the Lorelei scene 'Waldesgespräch'. 'Die Stille', a difficult song for a man to bring off, is delicate and wondering without archness; the bardic 'Auf einer Burg' is hypnotically sustained in a numb, blanched tone, devoid of all nuances, while the final 'Frühlingsnacht', which can easily sound flustered, here has an ecstatic sense of finality. Perhaps Gerhaher and the discerning if sometimes over-discreet Gerold Huber slightly miss the tremulous expectation of 'Intermezzo'; and there have been more magical performances of 'Mondnacht', here taken dangerously slowly. But for imaginative depth in the *Liederkreis* Gerhaher can certainly stand alongside the best.

Gerhaher and Huber choose unusually slow tempi for one or two of the other songs, most questionably in the Andersen song 'Der Spielmann', where the village wedding music should surely suggest more feverish wildness than here. Far more often, though, Gerhaher impresses with his unselfconscious eloquence, whether in the anguished life-weariness of the Harpers' songs, a chillingly timed and coloured 'Der Soldat' or in the potentially mawkish 'Liebesbotschaft', sung with a rapt, *echt* Schumann-esque inwardness. Not for the only time in these Reinick songs, Gerhaher makes you 'upgrade' music that can look distinctly homely, even bland, on the printed page. The baritone provides his own thoughtful note, though frustratingly you'll have to go to his website for English translations of the song texts.

'Complete Lieder, Volume 1'
Das verlassene Mägdlein, Op 64 No 2. Melancholie,
Op 74 No 6. Aufträge, Op 77 No 5. Op 79 – No 7a,
Zigeunerliedchen I; No 7b, Zigeunerliedchen II; No 23,
Er ist's!. Die Blume der Ergebung, Op 83 No 2.
Röslein, Röslein!, Op 89 No 6. Sechs Gedichte und
Requiem, Op 90. Op 96 – No 1, Nachtlied; No 3 Ihre
Stimme. Lieder und Gesänge aus Wilhelm Meister,
Op 98a – No 1, Kennst du das Land?; No 3, Nur wer
die Sehnsucht kennt; No 5, Heiss' mich nicht reden;
No 7, Singet nicht in Trauertönen; No 9, So lasst mich
scheinen. Sechs Gesänge, Op 107. Warnung, Op 119
No 2. Die Meerfee, Op 125 No 1. Sängers Trost,
Op 127 No 1. Mädchen-Schwermut, Op 142 No 3
Christine Schäfer sop **Graham Johnson** pf
Hyperion CDJ33101 (75' · DDD · T/t)   Ⓕ**ⓄⓄⓄ**▸

Ⓖ This disc launches Hyperion's Schumann Lieder project as auspiciously as Dame Janet Baker's recital opened their Complete Schubert Edition. As ever, Graham Johnson shows an unerring gift for matching singer and song. These are almost all late pieces, written between 1849 and 1852 under the shadow of depression and sickness; and their intense chromaticism can all too easily seem tortuous. However, imaginatively supported by Johnson, Christine Schäfer illuminates each of these songs with her pure, lucent timbre, her grace and breadth of phrase and her unselfconscious feeling for verbal meaning and nuance. The voice is an expressive, flexible lyric-coloratura; she can spin a scrupulously even *legato*, integrates the high notes of, say, 'Er ist's' perfectly within the melodic line, and has the breath control to sustain the long phrases of 'Requiem' with apparent ease.

Aided by Johnson's lucid textures and subtle feel for *rubato* and harmonic direction, Schäfer avoids any hint of mawkishness in songs such as 'Meine Rose', Op 90 No 2, 'Mädchen-Schwermut' and 'Abendlied'. Several songs here have been overshadowed or eclipsed by the settings by Schubert, Wolf or Brahms, and Schäfer and Johnson do much to rehabilitate them.

Schäfer brings an exquisite wondering stillness to the Goethe 'Nachtlied', more disturbed and earthbound than Schubert's sublime setting, but here, at least, scarcely less poignant. She also has the dramatic flair to bring off the difficult Mignon songs, especially the volatile, quasi-operatic 'Heiss' mich nicht reden' and 'Kennst du das Land', where the final verse, evoking Mignon's terrifying passage across the Alps, builds to a climax of desperate, almost demented yearning. At the other end of the emotional spectrum, Schäfer brings a guileful, knowing touch to the first of the *Zigeunerliedchen*; the Mendelssohnian 'Die Meerfee' glistens and glances and 'Aufträge' has a winning eagerness and charm, with a delicious sense of flirtation between voice and keyboard. A delectable, often revelatory recital. The recording is natural and

well balanced, while Graham Johnson provides typically searching commentaries.

'Complete Lieder, Volume 2'
Drei Gedichte, Op 30. Die Löwenbraut, Op 31 No 1.
12 Gedichte, Op 35. Lieder und Gesänge aus
Wilhelm Meister, Op 98a – No 2, Ballade des
Harfners; No 4, Wer nie sein Brot mit Tränen ass;
No 6, Wer sich der Einsamkeit ergibt; No 8, An die
Türen will ich schleichen. Vier Husarenlieder, Op 117
Simon Keenlyside bar **Graham Johnson** pf
Hyperion CDJ33102 (70' · DDD · N/T/t)   Ⓕ**ⓄⓄ**▸

In his notes Graham Johnson says that what we have always lacked is a convincing way of performing late Schumann songs, often spare in texture and elusive in style. Well, he and Keenlyside seem to have found one here in their wholly admirable versions of the very different Opp 98a and 117. The Op 98a settings of the Harper's outpourings from *Wilhelm Meister* have always stood in the shade of those by Schubert and Wolf. This pair show incontrovertibly that there's much to be said for Schumann's versions, capturing the essence of the old man's sad musings, as set by the composer in an imaginative, free way, alert to every nuance in the texts.

The extroverted Lenau *Husarenlieder* could hardly be more different. Keenlyside identifies in turn with the bravado of the first, the cynicism of the second, and the eerie, death-dominated mood of the fourth. The pair enter into the open-hearted mood called for by the *Knabenhorn* settings, most of all in the irresistible 'Der Hidalgo'. Keenlyside is just as forthright in *Die Löwenbraut* and in those of Op 35, the well-known Kerner settings, and he brings impressive control to the Eusebius ones, not least the all-enveloping 'Stille Tränen'. The interpretation of this quasi-cycle is convincing and unerringly paced. The recording and Johnson's persuasive playing are superb.

'Complete Lieder, Volume 6 '
Lieder, Op 40ᵃ. Spanisches Liederspiel, Op 74ᵇ.
Spanische Liebeslieder, Op 138ᶜ
C Schumann Lieder aus Jucunde, Op 23ᵈ
ᵇᶜᵈ**Geraldine McGreevy** sop ᵇᶜ**Stella Doufexis** mez
ᵇᶜ**Adrian Thompson** ten ᵃᵇᶜ**Stephan Loges** bar
Graham Johnson, ᶜ**Stephen Hough** pfs
Hyperion CDJ33106 (76' · DDD · N/T/t)   Ⓕ**Ⓞ**▸

This disc is a delight from start to finish. Songs and interpretations are on a high level of achievement, in this case all the more welcome as these groups, for various reasons, don't figure that often in recitals. Both the Spanish sets are of the highest order of composition, though not often acknowledged as such. The Op 74 set is notable for many mood changes and its touches of fantasy, melded with a typically Schumann-esque pull on the emotions. Alone or together, all four singers revel in their chances for expressive singing, none more than McGreevy, now a Lieder singer of major calibre, in 'Melancholie'. McGreevy also stands out in the wistful duet 'In der Nacht' with the sensitive Thompson, a poem set quite differently, as are some others, by Wolf later in the century. Loges contributes to concerted pieces with his expected artistry and has fun with 'Die Contrabandiste'.

The Op 138 set is even fuller of variety of mood and composition. All four singers seize their chances eagerly, with faultlessly sculpted readings under the tutelage of Johnson, who's joined here by no less a pianist than Stephen Hough in the two-piano accompaniments. The Andersen settings (Op 40) are fascinating songs delivered by Stephan Loges with refined tone and diction to which he adds a sure insight into their meaning in performances that compel one to place the set among Schumann's masterpieces in the genre. Add the naturally balanced recording and Johnson's extensive notes and this issue is treasure indeed.

'Complete Lieder, Volume 7'
Myrthen, Op 25ᵃ. Four Duets, Op 34ᵃ.
Four Duets, Op 78ᵃ. John Anderson, Op 145 No 4ᵇ
ᵃ**Dorothea Röschmann** sop ᵃ**Ian Bostridge** ten
Graham Johnson pf ᵇ**Polyphony / Stephen Layton**
Hyperion CDJ33107 (78' · DDD)　　Ⓕ🅞🅞➔

Hyperion's Schumann song series has already produced some profoundly satisfying discs, but none quite to equal the pleasures found on this volume. Its centrepiece, *Myrthen* – the cycle of love songs celebrating the union of Clara and Robert – is framed by eight duets to form a wonderfully balanced offering, and one that could hardly be surpassed in execution, through the understanding and skills of the three participants.

If one has to be singled out for particular praise, it must be Dorothea Röschmann. In tones at once fresh, warm and communicative, she sings all her contributions with an ideal balance between word and note. To such a familiar and lovely song as 'Der Nussbaum' she brings a heartfelt sense of anticipated pleasure that bears comparison with any of the heap of noted performances from the past, occasional vibrato used to arresting effect, as in all her readings. And 'Lied der Suleika' has its intensity underlined by the palpitating intimacy of her singing.

Not to be outdone, Bostridge presents deeply considered accounts of all his songs, combining his silvery, lightly tremulous tone with his customary feeling for words, most notably in the song 'Aus den hebräischen Gesängen' and the two Venetian Songs. Even better is his sensitive enactment of the marvellous setting of Heine, 'Was will die einsame Träne', which reveals his complete understanding of the idiom, and of the popular 'Du bist wie eine Blume', where his half-voice is skilfully deployed.

Johnson is on his most alert and empathetic form at the piano throughout. In the two sets of duets, full of Schumann at his most easeful, the voices intertwine effortlessly. Some oldsters will recall the famous, endearingly romantic Lehmann/Melchior recordings of some of these: Röschmann and Bostridge are just as persuasive.

With one of Hyperion's best recordings to complement the performances, voices nicely forward, this disc is definitely one to have.

'Complete Lieder, Volume 10'
Liederkreis, Op 39ᵃ. Schön Hedwig, Op 106ᵇ. Zwei Balladen für Deklamation, Op 122ᵇ. Drei Gedichte nach Emanuel Geibel, Op 29ᵇ. Die Nonne, Op 49 No 3ᵈ. Was soll ich sagen, Op 27 No 3ᵉ. Frühlingsgrüsseᶠ. Drei Duette, Op 43ᵍ. Mein Garten, Op 77 No 2ʰ. Sommerruh, WoO 7ⁱ. Mädchenlieder, Op 103ʲ. Bei Schenkung eines Flügels, WoO 26 No 4ᵏ
ᵃ**Kate Royal**, ᵍʰⁱʲ**Felicity Lott**, ᶜᵈᶠᵏ**Lydia Teuscher** sops
ᵍⁱʲ**Ann Murray**, ᶜᵏ**Daniela Lehner** mezzos
ᶜᵉᵏ**Stephan Loges** bar ᵇ**Christoph Bantzer** spkr
Graham Johnson pf with ᶜ**Edith Barlow** sop
ᶜ**Melanie Lang** mez ᶜᵏ**Adrian Ward**, ᶜ**Nicky Spence**
tens ᶜ**Lucas Kargl** bar ᶜ**Marcus Gruett** perc
Hyperion CDJ33110 (76' · DDD · N · T/t)　　Ⓟ🄳➔

The prime attraction for many here will be English soprano-of-the-moment Kate Royal in the popular Eichendorff *Liederkreis*. Royal's pure, pellucid tone, free-soaring top notes (gloriously heard in, say, 'Schöne Fremde') and refined musicianship give constant pleasure. In this cycle of dusk and shadows there are two or three songs that always seem to elude a bright, lyric soprano; and for all her beauty of voice and care for phrasing, Royal doesn't quite catch the fear and eeriness of 'Zwielicht' (which here sounds merely melancholy) or the sudden sense of isolation and dread at the end of 'Im Walde'. Other singers, too, have made 'Waldesgespräch' more scary, though Royal does touchingly suggest a human sadness in the spooky woodland drama.

But these are minor quibbles. Abetted by Johnson's ever-sentient keyboard-playing, Royal reveals a true understanding of Schumann's *Innigkeit*, whether in the suppressed passion of the opening 'In der Fremde' (the notorious phrase beginning 'Und über mir rauscht' taken effortlessly in a single breath) and 'Die Stille' (where she avoids the trap of ingénue coyness), the exquisite poise of 'Die Mondnacht' or the tremulous excitement and sense of imminent revelation in 'Schöne Fremde'. In the final 'Frühlingsnacht', often rushed off its feet, she and Johnson catch the elusive mix of secretiveness and ecstasy to perfection.

The remainder of the disc is given over to curiosities and rarities. Despite the eloquent declamation of actor Christoph Bantzer, it's hard to work up much enthusiasm for three 'melodramas' which too easily suggest silent-movie music. But there are innocent, Biedermeier delights in assorted duets, sung with bright-eyed eagerness by Felicity Lott and Ann Murray, and in three settings of Emanuel Geibel, beginning with a duet in Schumann's most cosy-comfy vein and ending with a mildly exotic ensemble evoking the gypsy life.

Among a clutch of young singers making cameo appearances, the virginal-toned Lydia Teuscher is true and touching in 'Die Nonne' and in the virtually unknown 'Frühlingsgrüsse', whose shy, halting lyricism is so typical of late Schumann. Collectors of this revelatory series will need no reminder that Johnson writes about the music as discerningly and eloquently as he plays.

'Complete Lieder, Volume 11'
Sechs Gesänge, Op 89[a] – No 1, Es stürmet am Abendhimmel; No 2, Heimliches Verschwinden; No 3, Herbstlied; No 4, Abschied vom Walde; No 5, Ins Freie. Drei Gesänge, Op 83[a] – No 1, Resignation; No 3, Der Einsiedler. Fünf Lieder und Gesänge, Op 127 – No 4, Mein altes Ross[a]. Drei Gesänge, Op 95[b]. Minnespiel, Op 101[cd]. Sechs Gedichte aus dem Liederbuch eines Malers, Op 36[a]. Des Sängers Fluch, Op 139 – No 4, Provenzalisches Lied[d]; No 7, Ballade[a]. Der Handschuh, Op 87[a]
[b]**Katherine Broderick**, [c]**Geraldine McGreevy** sops [c]**Stella Doufexis** mez [d]**Adrian Thompson** ten [a]**Hanno Müller-Brachmann**, [c]**Stephan Loges** bars **Graham Johnson** pf
Hyperion CDJ33111 (78' · DDD)   Ⓕ**Ⓞ**Ⓓ➤

Hyperion's Schumann Song Edition ends, as it began 12 years earlier, with a recital devoted largely to the problematic late songs of 1849-52. With the odd exception, these have often been castigated, not least by Eric Sams in *The Songs of Robert Schumann*, as the products of a torpid and increasingly sick mind. But though most of the songs on this disc tend to be more understated, less Romantically subjective than those of Schumann's great song year, 1840, the best of them are not necessarily inferior to their predecessors, just different.

There are undeniable duds, usually when Schumann is in hearty or heroic vein, alongside touching lyrics like the fragile 'Heimliches Verschwinden', the rapturous 'Liebster, deine Worte stehlen', or 'Provenzalisches Lied', a piquant celebration of courtly love.

The lion's share of the programme, including the six Reinick Songs falls to baritone Hanno Müller-Brachmann, whose singing is more notable for robust directness than subtlety. He exploits his deep bass resonances to good effect in 'Sonntags am Rhein', that quintessential song of pious Biedermeier contentment. In 'Liebesbotschaft', Müller-Brachmann sounds lugubrious, despite the flowing tempo, rather than tenderly devoted. He is at his best in declamatory, dramatic mode, recounting a minstrel's bloody revenge in 'Ballade', or in a powerful and atmospheric performance of another chivalrous ballad, 'Der Handschuh'.

Elsewhere there are welcome cameo appearances from Adrian Thompson (graceful and smiling in 'Provenzalisches Lied'), Geraldine McGreevy and Stella Doufexis, who combine with baritone Stefan Loges in two attractive quartets from the Rückert *Minnespiel*. Katherine Broderick, a Wagnerian soprano of the future, impresses with her vibrant intensity in the three Op 95 songs, though even she and Johnson cannot disguise the bombastic tawdriness of 'Dem Helden'. Whatever the provisos, this disc goes

far to vindicating some of Schumann's least-favoured late songs, not least due to Graham Johnson's eloquent advocacy, in print and in performance.

Gedicht der Königin Maria Stuart, Op 135. Liederkreis, Op 39. Myrthen, Op 25. Rückert-Lieder
Bernarda Fink mez **Anthony Spiri** pf
Harmonia Mundi HMC90 2031 (63' · DDD)   Ⓕ**Ⓞ**Ⓓ➤

Schumann was by no means the only composer obsessed with Robert Burns but no one caught the Scot's sentiments more vividly, even via German translation. Bernarda Fink's selection of six highly evocative songs from *Myrthen* immediately grabs the ear, from the drama of 'Hauptmanns Weib' to the widow's terror in 'Die Hochlander-Witwe'. Fink's readings are wonderfully detailed and wide-ranging.

The *Maria Stuart* songs came out of an otherwise disastrous year for Schumann, and were his extraordinary farewell to the song-cycle; and Fink lays bare the pain of both poet and composer, sensitively supported by Anthony Spiri. Rare glimpses of warmth, such as in 'Abschied von der Welt', where the poet seems to have made peace with her fate, are beautifully conveyed, even if it's a fleeting comfort, overcome by the cry of 'O Gott' that opens the final song. Here Fink leaves the listener unnerved.

After such emotional pain, balm is needed, and Fink shows her experience in programme-building by offering precisely that in the Rückert settings, ending with the rapturous 'Mein schöner Stern!'. In *Liederkreis*, Fink's 'Mondnacht' is compelling and in 'Zwielicht' she grasps your attention as only the greatest of Lieder singers can do.

There is just one niggle about Harmonia Mundi's otherwise flawless production: a CD sleeve design that leaves no space for the booklet. It's an irritating trend.

Genoveva, Op 81

Genoveva
Ruth Ziesak sop Genoveva **Deon van der Walt** ten Golo **Rodney Gilfry** bar Hidulfus **Oliver Widmer** bar Siegfried **Marjana Lipovšek** mez Margaretha **Thomas Quasthoff** bar Drago **Hiroyuki Ijichi** bass Balthasar **Josef Krenmair** bar Caspar **Arnold Schoenberg Choir; Chamber Orchestra of Europe / Nikolaus Harnoncourt**
Teldec ② 0630 13144-2 (129' · DDD · T/t)
Recorded live 1996   Ⓕ**Ⓞ**

For most listeners Schumann's only opera is still a relatively unknown quantity, but lovers of his music will celebrate a work that's intimate, thought-provoking and melodious. The libretto (by Schumann himself, after Tieck and Hebbel) deals with secret passion and suspected adultery, while the music mirrors emotional turmoil with great subtlety, and sometimes with astonishing imagination. Copious foretastes are provided in the familiar overture, and thereafter, discoveries abound. Sample, for example, the jagged counter-motif that shudders as Genoveva's husband Siegfried entreats Golo (his own *alter ego*) to guard his wife while he's away at war; or the off-stage forces representing drunken servants; or the almost expressionist writing at 4'00" into track 10, where Golo responds with seething hatred to Genoveva's vengeance. The entreaties of Drago's ghost (track 4, 6'10") aren't too far removed from Siegmund's 'Nothung!' in Act 1 of *Die Walküre*, and Genoveva's singing from 'a desolate, rocky place' (track 5, first minute or so), sounds prophetic of Isolde (who was as yet unborn, so to speak). Harnoncourt suspects that *Genoveva* was a 'counterblast' to Wagner, and though Wagner apparently thought the opera 'bizarre', there remains a vague suspicion of sneaking regard, even a smidgen of influence.

Teldec's balancing is mostly judicious, and the musical direction suggestive of burning conviction. The worthy though relatively conventional Gerd Albrecht (in Orfeo's mellow 1992 recording) only serves to underline the leaner, more inflected and more urgently voiced profile of Harnoncourt's interpretation. As to the two sets of singers, most preferences rest with the latter's line-up. Stage effects are well handled; the sum effect is of a top-drawer Schumann set within an unexpected structural context.

Heinrich Schütz   German 1585-1672

In 1598 Schütz was taken to Kassel where he served as a choirboy and studied music with the court Kapellmeister, Georg Otto. The University of Marburg followed where he studied law, but his patron, Landgrave Moritz, advised him to abandon his university studies and to go to Venice as a pupil of Giovanni Gabrieli; Schütz remained in Venice for over three years. The following year he was seconded to serve for two months at the electoral court in Dresden, and in 1615 the Elector Johann Georg I requested his services for a further two years – this was again extended and Schütz remained in his permanent employ. There his responsibilities included providing music for major court ceremonies, whether religious or political. In 1619 Schütz published his first collection of sacred music, the Psalmen Davids, dedicated to the elector. Towards the end of the 1620s economic pressures of the Thirty Years War began to affect the electoral court and in 1628 Schütz decided on a second visit to Venice, where he was able to study developments in dramatic music under Monteverdi's guidance. He returned to Dresden in 1629, but two years later Saxony entered the war and in the folowing Schütz worked in Copenhagen, Dresden, Copenhagen again, Brunswick and (in semi-retirement) Weissenfels. He was far from inactive during his remaining 15 years.

Schütz was the greatest German composer of the 17th century and the first of international stature. His output was almost exclusively sacred.

Lukas-Passion

Lukas-Passion, SWV480
Johan Linderoth ten **Jakob Bloch Jespersen** bass-bar **Ars Nova Copenhagen / Paul Hillier**
Dacapo 8 226019 (53' · DDD)   Ⓕ

The 14 singers in this performance of Heinrich Schütz's *St Luke Passion* sing with superb diction, poise, intonation, blend and expressiveness. This is no mean feat because Schütz's solemn setting is entirely *a cappella*, in accordance with the Dresden court's tradition that during Holy Week all musical instruments were silenced. Apart from the short opening and concluding choruses, the music is a narration of the Passion as it is related in the Gospel of Luke, intoned by solo voices as narrative plainchant with occasional choral passages (such as the crowd of onlookers at the Crucifixion wondering if Christ will save himself).

The excellent sound recording has an attractive amount of reverberation, which is shrewdly manipulated by Johan Linderoth and Jakob Bloch Jespersen, who never slip under pitch or lose lustre during their intoning, and are careful to remain sensitive and alive to the text. Half of the 12 chorus singers chip in with occasional solo turns (for example, lines for Peter, Pilate and the Centurion). Choral interjections, though few and far between, and the marvellous introductory and concluding choruses, are immaculately sung by Ars Nova Copenhagen.

Psalms of David

Psalmen Davids sampt etlichen Moteten und Concerten, SWV22-47
Cantus Cölln; Concerto Palatino / Konrad Junghänel
Harmonia Mundi ② HMC90 1652/3
(143' · DDD · T/t)   Ⓕ●

Here's something to get excited about: a new recording, at last, of Schütz's first monumental publication of sacred music. Whether anything can be worth waiting for that long is a moot point, but Cantus Cölln and Concerto Palatino give us an interpretation that's unlikely to be surpassed. With eight singers and no fewer than two dozen instrumentalists, the scale is little short of symphonic. For sheer splendour, who can top *Danket dem Herren* (SWV45) or the next piece in the collection, *Zion spricht*?

It's easy enough to single out the most opulent pieces, but as Peter Wollny remarks in his admirable booklet-notes, the whole point of the *Psalmen Davids* is its variety in the treatment of a medium whose potential for cliché is very great. The musicians respond to Schütz's demands with verve and perception and the sort of confidence that would carry any music aloft in triumph. The sound recording does them full justice. You'll almost certainly listen, enthralled, to the entire collection – nearly two-and-a-half hours – in one sitting.

Symphoniae sacrae

Symphoniae sacrae, tertia pars
**Cantus Cölln; Concerto Palatino /
Konrad Junghänel**
Harmonia Mundi ② HMC90 1850/1
(126' · DDD · T/t)   Ⓕ

This is the third offering from Konrad Junghän-el's ensemble, who team up once again with Concerto Palatino; the result is bound to impress even the casual listener, and will certainly delight those already well acquainted with Schütz's music. The third and final volume of the *Symphoniae sacrae* was issued in 1650 when Schütz was 65. One of the pieces in the collection had originally been composed more than 30 years earlier, which suggests a concern to bring together his life's work: he could hardly have foreseen that he would live some 20 years more.

As ever, Schütz puts the biblical texts right at the heart of the music. It is striking just how many of the texts you will be able to recall instantly, such is his knack for their acute characterisation. The same applies to the performances, which capture the aura of the grand statement, juxtaposed with an intimate feeling for detail and psychological observation. This comes across particularly in *Mein Sohn, warum hast Du uns das getan*, the 'dialogue' between the child Jesus and his parents. The parable of the sower is evoked in *Es ging ein Sämann aus*, and Psalm 127 ('Except the Lord build the house') in *Wo der Herr nicht das Haus bauet.*

These count among the most impressive pieces in the collection, alongside the most famous one, *Saul, Saul, was verfolgst du mich*. So persuasive is the architecture of these readings that local niggles are easily dismissed: at times the sound recording favours the voices at the expense of detailed instrumental passagework, and just occasionally intonation goes off the straight and narrow. But never do such details detract from a project whose high ambitions are so consistently realised.

Opus ultimum (Schwanengesang)

Opus ultimum (Schwanengesang), SWV482-94
**Ghent Collegium Vocale; Concerto Palatino /
Philippe Herreweghe**
Harmonia Mundi ② HMC90 1895/6 (89' · DDD · T/t) Ⓕ

The beauty of this remarkable performance of Schütz's last work resides principally in Collegium Vocale's blooming cradle of sound and how it unassumingly stakes its claim – with no subtext – on the unique ambitions of Schütz's 'Swansong'. These are founded on the composer's distilled and often austere contemplation of Psalm 119 in 11 double-choir motets, joined by Psalm 150 and the impressive *Deutsches Magnificat.*

If not texturally pared down, this is a journey where the 86-year-old Schütz withdraws from the world in a lexicon of finely drawn plainchants, antique modes, taut contrapuntal and antiphonal exchanges, melodic swathes and quicksilver declamations. Herreweghe illuminates each verse with a considered and gentle ear for the progression from the 'statutes' of faith towards a sense of hope and salvation as we move towards a new Covenant, revealed in the final motet with its assuaging supplications and rock-like assurance. Here we sense, above all, Schütz's mix of defiance and resignation for the gradual passing of a self-contained sacred tradition threatened by radical worldly things (like operas).

Collegium Vocale relish Schütz's introspection and easy exchange between solo and *tutti* sections, which allow the inspired rhetorical mood-changes to reveal each marked-out image ('when thou shalt enlarge my heart' at the end in the second motet is dealt a moment of special attention as it moves towards a conclusion in rapt homage to Monteverdi). Herreweghe's performances are generally outstanding in their attention to detail: some might quibble that the inner *tutti* voices occasionally lack focus and energy, but this is a performance where Schütz's seasoned harmonic shifts are treated as pure music and not over-accentuated by rhetorical zeal: the music doesn't need it. Can a greater work have been completed by an octogenarian? This recording urges us, very persuasively, to think perhaps not.

Weihnachtshistorie

Weihnachtshistorie. Auferstehungshistorie, SWV50
Else Torp sop **Johan Linderoth, Adam Riis** tens
Jakob Bloch Jespersen bass **Sirius Viols; Concerto
Copenhagen / Paul Hillier**
Dacapo 8 226058 (78' · DDD) Ⓕ

In 1664 the 79-year-old Schütz published the *Christmas Story*. This recording by Paul Hillier and Ars Nova Copenhagen couples it with the much earlier *Resurrection Story*, written in about 1623, only a few years after the composer was appointed Kapellmeister at Dresden. Schütz may be rightly regarded as the genius who bridges the gap between Monteverdi's madrigals and Bach's cantatas but several artists and labels have admitted that recording his music is commercial suicide. This is a crying shame. If any reminder were necessary, these Danish performances provide ample and conclusive proof that Schütz is a phenomenal master of his chosen idioms: his harmonic imagination, fantastic word-painting and profound expressivity are intensely rewarding for those willing to devote a little time and attention to his music.

The beginning of the *Christmas Story* immediately establishes that the instrumental playing of the dozen-strong Concerto Copenhagen is of the very highest quality: the tasteful continuo playing and sympathetic violin ritornellos are a pleasure to hear. The pastoral effect of the recorders accompanying the shepherds' trio is gorgeous and the soft sackbuts give magnificent support to the quartet of Herod's chief priests and scribes.

Ars Nova Copenhagen reaffirms its status as an outstanding vocal ensemble with luminous and pure choral singing. Its members also provide excellent solos: Adam Riis's soothing Evangelist perfectly narrates the nativity tale, Else Torp radiantly proclaims the good news to the shepherds and Jakob Bloch Jespersen's regal Herod is frighteningly persuasive and plausible. The different groups of shepherds and wise men perform their contrapuntal trios with clarity and eloquence. Hillier paces and shapes Schütz's music to perfection, allying flawless performance practice to distinctively warm-hearted story-telling. These qualities are also fully to the fore in an immaculately poised performance of the *Resurrection Story*, during which Johan Linderoth's compassionate Evangelist is emotively partnered with Hille Perl's consort Sirius Viols. Schütz recordings of such ardent beauty are much too rare, so this is not to be missed.

Secular Works

Freue dich des Weibes deiner Jugend, SWV453. Liebster, sagt in süssem Schmerzen, SWV441. Nachdem ich lag in meinem öder Bette, SWV451. Glück zu dem Helikon, SWV96. Haus und Güter erbat man von Eltern, SWV21. Tugend ist der beste Freund, SWV442. Teutoniam dudum belli atra pericla, SWV338. Wie wenn der Adler, SWV434. Siehe, wie fein und lieblich ists, SWV48. Vier Hirtinnen, gleich jung, gleich schön, SWVAnh1. Lässt Salomon sein Bette nicht umgeben, SWV452. Die Erde trinkt für sich, SWV438. Wohl dem, der ein Tugendsam Weib hat, SWV20. Itzt blicken durch des Himmels Saal, SWV460. Syncharma musicum, SWV49
Weser-Renaissance Bremen / Manfred Cordes
CPO CPO999 518-2 (71' · DDD · T/t)   Ⓜ️Ⓞ

Here's a discovery of several unrecorded byways of Schütz's miscellaneous secular music. The 17th century being what it is, secular and sacred are deliberately dovetailed into a cultural pea soup: these works are embedded in the literary morality of the age and aren't entirely profane. There's a pleasing lightness of touch from the soloists (especially the soprano) and the instrumental consort doesn't attempt, as is so mistakenly regarded these days as the ideal, to ape the vocal lines at every turn in a wash of homogeneity; there are many distinctive virtuoso commentaries, as in *Tugend ist der beste Freund*, which Cordes (enhanced by the excellent recorded sound) allows to breathe naturally.

Noble intensity and harmonious accord are the order of the day in the splendidly uplifting concerto *Teutoniam dudum*, which through its extraordinary structural clarity immediately delights the listener with a celebration of the cessation of hostilities after the miserable Thirty Years War. Most impressive, though, is the sympathetic and gentle treatment of the words from Weser-Renaissance, beautifully complemented by the soft articulation of the winds, especially in *Siehe, wie fein* and the domestic charm of *Wohl dem, der ein Tugendsam*. This is chamber music-making from the heart, tempered convincingly by the intellect and affectionately delivered.

Cyril Scott   British 1879-1970

Early musical promise led to study at the Frankfurt Conservatoire, where he encountered 'The Frankfurt Group', Norman O'Neill, Roger Quilter, Balfour Gardiner and Percy Grainger. His early orchestral works received performances in Germany and his Second Symphony was conducted by Henry Wood. A prolific composer, Scott wrote some 400 works including four symphonies, three operas, four oratorios, two piano concertos, concertos for violin, cello, oboe and harpsichord, many chamber works and innumerable songs.

Orchestral Works

Cello Concerto[a]. Symphony No 1
[a]**Paul Watkins** vc
BBC Philharmonic Orchestra / Martyn Brabbins
Chandos CHAN10452 (58' · DDD)   Ⓟ️Ⓞ️▶️

This fourth volume in the Chandos Scott series opens not only with a first recording, but a first performance of the Cello Concerto from 1937. By then Scott had become so unfashionable that, along with at least two unperformed operas, this concerto got forgotten. That would be an unjust final judgement. It opens with a 16-minute movement that is virtually a concerto on its own. Right at the start the sustained strings with superimposed celesta create a magical atmosphere. The cello soloist enters with a distinctive rising figure and then Scott's improvisatory instinct takes over. The continuity is close to Delius and some of the scoring is as rich as Ravel.

The second movement is largely an accompanied cadenza, leading to the final rondo where a perky solo bassoon kicks off. There's plenty for the soloist to do but it takes a few hearings for the distinctive qualities of Scott's idiom to sink in. Unlike the Elgar Concerto there's little thematic repetition. Paul Watkins sounds superb and, as before, Martyn Brabbins is an admirable exponent.

The Symphony No 1 (1899) is another curiosity – this is probably only its second performance since the composer withdrew it after the premiere. The first movement is labelled *Allegro frivolo* and it's not far from Sullivan; the *Andante* has a baleful cor anglais solo; and, because the first two pages of the score were missing, the *Allegretto* has been completed by Leslie De'Ath, the pianist who has recorded Scott's complete piano works. The finale starts with a modal trombone theme followed by a series of variations and a tentative fugue. A weird touch is the minor-key ending.

Symphony No 4. Piano Concerto No 1ª.
Early One Morning
ªHoward Shelley pf BBC Philharmonic Orchestra /
Martyn Brabbins
Chandos CHAN10376 (73' · DDD) Ⓕ🅳►

Cyril Scott was born in 1879, the same year as
Ireland and Bridge, and with CDs like this he can
be heard alongside their contributions in both
piano and orchestral music. The First Piano
Concerto (the Second is on a previous Chandos
CD) was premiered by the composer under Beecham in 1915, by which time Scott's reputation in
Germany had taken a terminal blow. Lewis Foreman, in the CD booklet, remembers seeing Scott
at his 90th birthday concert at the Queen Elizabeth Hall in 1969 when Moura Lympany played
the concerto. Reviews were generally condescending – and wrong. This is a wonderfully
inventive work, completely imagined in every
detail: the core of this music, like that of Delius, is
the present sensual moment. If the actual sound is
seductive enough it satisfies the ear. Both Scott
and Delius, like Messiaen, were fixated on chords
decked in luxuriant orchestral textures.

The extraordinary thing about this CD is that
both *Early One Morning* (1931) and the Fourth
Symphony (1952) are not just first recordings
but first performances, too. Scott, neglected to
the point of ostracism, continued to compose
when anyone else would have succumbed to
clinical depression long before. As his psychic
writings show, he was supported by higher powers. The symphony, however courageous, is not
as original as either of the piano concertos and
the exuberant finale falls somewhere between
Debussy's *La mer* and Ravel's *Daphnis*.

Chamber works

Sonata lirica. Elégie, Op 73 No 1. Romance, Op 73
No 2. Valse triste, Op 73 No 3. Tallahassee Suite,
Op 73 No 4. Three Little Waltzes, Op 58 W178 –
Andante languido. Danse nègre, Op 58 No 5 W89.
Two Pieces, Op 47 – Lotus Land. Lullaby, Op 57 No 2.
Four Pieces, Op 67 – Intermezzo, W161. Two
Preludes. Fantasie Orientale
Clare Howick vn Sophia Rahman pf
Dutton Epoch CDLX7200 (76' · DDD) Ⓕ

The Scott revival marches on! The *Sonata lirica*
(1937) was lost for years and this seems to be its
first performance. Hearing it without knowing
the composer, one might have guessed Delius.
There's the same rhapsodic improvisational
approach, if less subtle, where attractive melody
is qualified by sumptuous chords. But Scott has
his own way of doing this and the violin-and-
piano medium exploits his gift for melody.

The disc contains five transcriptions, of which
the most famous is *Lotus Land* (1905), arranged by
Kreisler in 1922. It was always a mesmeric piano
solo with its oriental inflections but the violin version is ecstatic. Walter Kramer's arrangement of
another evergreen, *Danse nègre*, creates some odd
exchanges but is catchy and vivid. The lovely

melodies of the *Intermezzo* and the *Lullaby*, also a
haunting song, work beautifully in this arrangement. The *Tallahassee Suite* (1911) is presumably
evocative of the Florida landscape and the final
'Danse nègre' boasts ragtime syncopations.

The whole collection is a most attractive
expression of Scott's highly characteristic style,
all wonderfully played by Howick and Rahman.

'Complete Piano Music, Volume 1 – Ⓗ
Suites and Miniatures'
Leslie De'Ath pf
Dutton Epoch ② CDLX7150 (146' · DDD)
Includes bonus historical recordings performed by
the composer Ⓜ

This admirable recording inaugurates Cyril
Scott's complete solo piano music on disc. Scott
was a pianist-composer – and he was a capable
player, as the bonus historic performances show.
The instrument's Romantic associations, inherited from Chopin, Scriabin and Debussy, permeate Scott's earlier works. And he was fascinated by harmony, which he employed
sensuously to define his idiom: Grainger aptly
called him a 'perpendicular' composer.

Like Bridge and Ireland, Scott wrote miniatures
for the amateur market but he also made history
with the experimental rhythmic and harmonic
features of his Piano Sonata No 1 in 1908 and the
expansive Suite No 2, dedicated to Debussy, who
much admired him. The five movements of this
half-hour Suite range from a two-minute Caprice
to a substantial theme and variations with a concluding 10-minute Introduction and Fugue.
Some of this is rhapsodic and the charm of the
salon miniatures, at which De'Ath excels, is not so
easily extended. But Scott has his own kind of
rhetoric, as the oddly titled *Handelian Rhapsody*,
dedicated to Grainger, also shows.

Absolutely fascinating, in clean transfers, are
the eight pieces Scott recorded between 1928
and 1930. He plays *Water Wagtail* delicately, a
perfect counterpart to the airy skipping motions
of these birds. But the perennial favourite *Lotus
Land* is played eccentrically, the rapid notes inexplicably rushed to cut almost half a beat at times.
There are informative notes from De'Ath but
little about the pieces Scott plays. The piano
sound is clean but slightly close.

'Complete Piano Music, Volume 3 –
Music for two pianos and piano duet'
Leslie De'Ath with Anya Alexeyev pfs
Dutton Epoch ② CDLX7166 (153' · DDD) Ⓜ

The first disc contains works for two pianos or
piano duet. In the 1930s Scott had a recital partnership with the pianist Esther Fisher and provided works for them to play. He also made
arrangements of Bach, five of which are included
here. These are really re-compositions, attractively and sometimes amusingly done – you
can't kill Bach – and should be a hit in these
sparkling performances.

The first CD opens with one of Scott's catchiest tunes, *Russian Fair*, in its two-piano version, followed by the extended but impressive Theme and Variations (1935). The Three Symphonic Dances from the turn of the century were arranged by Percy Grainger in 1920. He and Scott were students together at Frankfurt; Scott often dedicated pieces to him, and this is a thoroughly idiomatic exploitation of the two-piano medium.

The piano solo CD contains four unpublished pieces, all worth having, although the Ballade is a Brahmsian student work. There's evidence to support the description of early Scott as 'the English Debussy' and the *Inclination à la danse* (1922) is enticingly Scriabinesque; but Scott developed his own way with melody and harmony that we can now appreciate in more detail than ever before. The two picturesque suites, *Egypt* and *Karma*, are piano solo versions of ballet scores, both with occult connections. Good recording and presentation again: nobody could do better for Scott.

Alexander Scriabin   Russian 1872-1915

You can divide Scriabin's career into two halves: before about 1900 he was a latter-day Russian Chopin, writing the sort of piano pieces that Chopin might have written had he lived longer; after that, Scriabin increasingly came to believe that he was God. This makes him and his music not uninteresting. His music broke with all previous forms and traditions. It has enormous originality and the ideas and theories he had were truly messianic but he did not have Wagner's determined pragmatism or a long enough life to see his grandiose schemes come to fruition.

The teachers who developed Scriabin's prodigious gifts were the best in Moscow – men like Conus, Zverev, Taneyev and Safonov. Scriabin was a fellow student with Rachmaninov at the Moscow Conservatory and destined to be a great pianist like him, until he damaged his right hand trying to outdo the pianistic feats of another Safonov pupil, Josef Lhévinne (thereafter, Scriabin never quite regained the keyboard fluency he had enjoyed and played only his own works in public). He stayed on at the Conservatory to study fugue with Arensky but never completed the course. By this time he was writing his first pieces in the manner of Chopin and was taken up by the publisher Belaieff who offered him a contract. A successful European tour ensued and by the late 1890s he was giving concerts devoted entirely to his own music.

In 1897 he married a fellow pianist, Vera Isakovich, with whom he had three children; and from 1898 to 1903 he taught piano at the Moscow Conservatory. So far, so conventional.

About 1898 a shift in style emerged. The classical outlines became blurred, the harmonies cryptic and unusual; he turned out two huge symphonies incorporating the germs of his new creative thoughts, and started reading Nietzsche and the mystic musings of Helena Blavatsky. He devised the so-called 'mystic chord' (C, F sharp, B flat, E, A, D) and worked out entire pieces based on this. He abandoned key signatures and the music became more dissonant.

In 1908 Scriabin acquired another wealthy patron in the person of conductor Serge Koussevitzky. His publishing house was devoted to Russian composers and Russian music. Scriabin, controversial and provocative, was exactly what Koussevitzky needed and Scriabin, in turn, needed money and a publisher. They toured together as soloist and conductor and, though the relationship did not last long, Koussevitzky continued to support the Scriabin cause, including giving the first performance of his last major work for orchestra, Prometheus.

In March 1914 he was in London for a concert conducted by the adventurous Sir Henry Wood (the Piano Concerto and Prometheus were included) and he gave his last recital in Petrograd just over a year later in April 1915. In London a boil had developed on his upper lip but healed without medical attention. Back in Moscow after the Petrograd recital, Scriabin developed a fever and before long gangrene covered his entire face. Within a few days he was dead.

Piano Concerto in F sharp minor, Op 20

Scriabin Piano Concerto **Tchaikovsky** Piano Concerto No 1 in B flat minor, Op 23
Nikolai Demidenko pf BBC Symphony Orchestra / Alexander Lazarev
Hyperion Helios CDH55304 (65' · DDD)   Ⓕ

The chief attraction here is the unusual coupling which pairs two sharply opposed examples of Russian Romanticism, and although the reasons for the neglect of Scriabin's Piano Concerto aren't hard to fathom (its lyrical and decorative flights are essentially inward-looking), its haunting, bittersweet beauty, particularly in the central *Andante*, is hard to resist. Demidenko's own comments, quoted in the accompanying booklet, are scarcely less intense and individual than his performance: 'in the ambience, phrasing and cadence of his music we meet with a world almost without skin, a world of nerve-ends where the slightest contact can bring pain'. His playing soars quickly to meet the music's early passion head on, and in the first *più mosso scherzando* he accelerates to produce a brilliant lightening of mood. His flashing *fortes* in the *Andante*'s second variation are as volatile as his *pianissimos* are starry and refined in the finale's period reminiscence, and although he might seem more tight-lipped, less expansive than Ashkenazy on Decca, he's arguably more dramatic and characterful.

Demidenko's Tchaikovsky, too, finds him ferreting out and sifting through every texture, forever aiming at optimum clarity. While this is hardly among the greatest Tchaikovsky Firsts on record, it's often gripping and mesmeric. The recorded balance isn't always ideal and the piano sound is sometimes uncomfortably taut.

Symphonies / Prometheus

No 1 in E, Op 26; **No 2** in C minor, Op 29; **No 3** in C minor, Op 43 'Divin poème'.

Symphonies – Nos 1[a], 2 & 3. Le poème de l'extase,
Op 54[b]. Prometheus, Op 60, 'Le poème du feu'[c]
[a]Stefania Toczyska *mez* [a]Michael Myers *ten* [c]Dmitri
Alexeev *pf* [b]Frank Kaderabek *tpt* [a]Westminster
Choir; [c]Philadelphia Choral Arts Society;
Philadelphia Orchestra / Riccardo Muti
Brilliant Classics ③ 92744 (3h 8' · DDD) ⓈOO

There can be few more thrilling sounds on disc
(and no more compelling reason for a totally
sound-proofed listening room) than the climax
to Muti's *Poème de l'extase*. The clamour of bells
here (both literal and imitative) reveals an
essentially Russian heart at the core of this
most cosmopolitan of Russian composers, and
the *maestoso* proclamation of the theme of self-
assertion has the raised Philadelphia horns in
crucially sharp focus. As in the corresponding
climax in *Prometheus* (at 18'21"), this 'éclat
sublime' is filled out with a floor-shaking contribution from the organ. Like the organ, the
wordless chorus at this point in *Prometheus*
registers more as a device for enriching and
exalting the texture, rather than as a striking
new presence.

Muti's *Prometheus* is, arguably, the most
complete realisation of the mind-boggling
demands of this score ever to have been
recorded. The inert opening ('Original chaos'
– lovely *pp* bass drum!) and mysterious awakening have rarely sounded so atmospheric.
Alexeev's first entry isn't as strong willed as
some, but he seems to be saving a more imperious attack for the same point in the recapitulation. Muti builds the work superbly: the
imposing clash of states in the development
(and the changes of tempo) charted with
mighty assurance. And thereafter *Prometheus* is
airborne, with Alexeev both agile and articulate in the 'Dance of Life'.

Throughout the cycle, the tonal allure of the
Philadelphia Orchestra is fully in evidence.
Only in the Third Symphony, *Divin poème*, do
Muti and the recording team seem to be on less
than their indomitable form. Compared with
some versions, the tempo relationships in the
first movement don't fully convince. However,
this cycle is unlikely to be seriously challenged
for many a year. As a whole it immeasurably
enhances Scriabin's stature as a symphonist and
offers the kind of playing and recording which,
as recently as two decades ago, Scriabin enthusiasts could only have imagined in their dreams
– and its ridiculously low new price makes it a
real bargain!

Etudes

Etude in C sharp minor, Op 2 No 1. 12 Etudes, Op 8.
Eight Etudes, Op 42. Etude in E flat, Op 49 No 1.
Etude, Op 56 No 4. Three Etudes, Op 65
Piers Lane *pf*
Hyperion CDA66607 (56' · DDD) ⒻO

Although Scriabin's Etudes do not fall into two
neatly packaged sets in the same way as Chopin's

celebrated contributions, nevertheless there's a
strong feeling of continuity and development
running throughout the 26 examples produced
between the years 1887 and 1912. This is admirably demonstrated in this excellent issue from
Hyperion, which, far from being an indigestible
anthology proves to be an intriguing and pleasurable hour's worth of listening charting Scriabin's progression from late-Romantic adoles-
cence to harmonically advanced mystical poet.
Indeed, although these studies can be counted as
among the most digitally taxing and hazardous
of their kind, Scriabin also saw them as important sketches and studies for his larger works,
and as experiments in his gradually evolving
harmonic language and mystical vision.

Piers Lane attains the perfect balance of virtuoso display and poetic interpretation. Expressive
detail and subtle nuance are finely brought out,
and he's more than receptive to Scriabin's sometimes highly idiosyncratic sound world; rarely,
for instance, has the famous 'Mosquito' Etude
(Op 42 No 3) been captured with such delicate
fragility as here, and in No 1 of the three fiendishly difficult Etudes, Op 65, the tremulous,
ghostly flutterings are tellingly delivered with a
gossamer-light touch and a sense of eerie mystery. The clear, spacious recording is exemplary.

Preludes

Complete Preludes – Op 2 No 2; Op 9 No 1;
Opp 11, 13, 15-17, 22, 27, 31, 33, 35, 37 & 39;
Op 45 No 3; Op 48; Op 49 No 2; Op 51 No 2;
Op 56 No 1; Op 59 No 2; Opp 67 & 74
Piers Lane *pf*
Hyperion ② CDA67057/8 (127' · DDD) ⒻOO▸

Everything about this two-disc set is ideal.
Beautifully packaged and recorded, superbly
played, there's the added bonus of an outstanding essay by Simon Nicholls, in which acute
musical analysis is presented within the wider
context of Scriabin's bewildering genius.
Nicholls sees Scriabin as 'a musical Fabergé', a
composer who contrasted his love of the ambitious epic with an even greater love of miniatures
that could be 'short as a sparrow's beak or a
bear's tail'. And throughout the extraordinary
journey from Op 2 No 2 to Op 74, where the
memories of Chopin are subdued by 'scarifying
documents of individual and social catastrophe',
you're tossed abruptly from a serene or bitter
introspection to a crazed violence and exuberance, encouraged by idiosyncratic directions
such as *patetico, con stravaganza, vagamente, irato
impetuoso, sauvage belliqueux*.

The demands on the pianist are fierce, but it
would be hard to imagine a more focused or
immaculate reading than that offered by Piers
Lane. Few pianists could show more sympathy
and affection for such volatile Romanticism,
or display greater stylistic consistency. He
underlines the despondency of the left-hand
Prelude, Op 9 No 1 (here separated from its
celebrated Nocturne companion); and in, for

example, Op 11 No 3 the fleeting melodic outline is always kept intact amid so much whirling activity. The turbulence of No 14 is caught just as surely, and as an instance of how his scrupulousness is combined with the most vivid imagination, he gives us No 16 in an agitated and freely expressive style rather than opting for a more conventional, stricter tempo, creating a novel and nightmarish dimension. He takes No 2 at a true *allegro* (as marked) and is never tempted into the sort of virtuoso skirmish offered by lesser players. Indeed, his gift for clarifying even the most tortuous utterances with an exemplary poise and assurance is among his finest qualities. The machine-gun fire of Op 31 No 3 and the menacing tread of Op 33 No 4 are fully realised, and Lane ably taps the darkest regions of the imagination in the final Op 74 Preludes.

These discs complement Piers Lane's earlier recording of the complete Etudes (see above), and should be in any serious record collection.

Preludes – Opp 22, 27, 31, 33, 35, 37, 39, 48, 67 & 74. Prelude in E flat, Op 45 No 3. Prelude in F, Op 49 No 2. Prelude in A minor, Op 51 No 2. Prelude in E flat minor, Op 56 No 1. Prelude, Op 59 No 2
J Scriabin Prelude in C, Op 2. Preludes, Op 3 – No 1 in B; No 2. Prelude in D flat
Evgeny Zarafiants *pf*
Naxos 8 554145 (65' · DDD)   ⓈⒶ➤

With this second volume Evgeny Zarafiants completes his superb survey of Scriabin's 86 Preludes, adding four Preludes by Julian Scriabin, the composer's precociously gifted son, as encores. Listening to music of such morbid and refined intricacy played with the finest musical poise and commitment returns us to Stravinsky's bemused question, 'Scriabin, where does he come from, and who are his followers?' Is the angst and angry convolution of, say, Op 27 No 1 a Slavonic memory of Brahms's Op 118 No 1? Does the explosive whimsy of Op 35 No 3 take its cue from the *Scherzo* of Beethoven's Op 26 Sonata? The hair-raising *presto* of Op 67 No 2 recalls the menace and enigma of the finale from Chopin's Op 35 Sonata, while the terse and belligerent Op 33 No 3 looks ahead to Stravinsky's sharpest modernist utterances. Yet if there are countless examples of reflection and prophecy, there are still more of the most startling originality. Scriabin is always Scriabin, and as he journeys from Op 22 to Op 74 into the darkest reaches of the imagination you're reminded that this is hardly music for the faint-hearted.

Once again, Zarafiants is equal to each and every vivid occasion. Whether in the fragrant *grazioso* of Op 22 No 2, where the line twists and turns like so much honeysuckle, in the toppling argument of Op 31 No 3, or in the *sauvage belliqueux* of Op 59 No 2, he's richly responsive, his playing alive with a rare pianistic skill and imaginative brio. The Brandon Hill recordings are resonant and full-blooded.

Piano Sonatas

No 1 in F minor, Op 6 No 2 in G sharp minor (Sonata-fantasy), Op 19 No 3 in F sharp minor, Op 23 No 4 in F sharp, Op 30 No 5 in F sharp, Op 53 No 6 in G, Op 62; No 7 in F sharp (White Mass), Op 64 No 8 in A, Op 66 No 9 in F (Black Mass), Op 68 No 10 in C, Op 70

Piano Sonatas Nos 1-10. Fantasie in B minor, Op 28. Sonata-fantaisie in G sharp minor
Marc-André Hamelin *pf*
Hyperion ② CDA67131/2 (146' · DDD)   ⒻⓄⒶ➤

Scriabin was an ambitious composer. A Romantic alchemist, he saw his music as a transmuting agent. Through its influence pain would become happiness and hate become love, culminating in a phoenix-like rebirth of the universe. With Shakespearean agility he would change the world's dross into 'something rich and strange'. Not surprisingly, given Scriabin's early prowess as a pianist, the 10 sonatas resonate with exoticism, ranging through the First Sonata's cries of despair to the Second Sonata's Baltic Sea inspiration, the Third Sonata's 'states of being', the 'flight to a distant star' (No 4) and 'the emergence of mysterious forces' (No 5). Nos 7 and 9 are *White* and *Black Mass* Sonatas respectively, and the final sonatas blaze with trills symbolising an extra-terrestrial joy and incandescence.

Such music makes ferocious demands on the pianist's physical stamina and imaginative resource. However, Marc-André Hamelin takes everything in his stride. Blessed with rapier reflexes he nonchalantly resolves even the most outlandish difficulties. He launches the First Sonata's opening outcry like some gleaming trajectory and, throughout, his whistle-stop virtuosity is seemingly infallible.

You might, however, miss a greater sense of the music's Slavonic intensity, its colour and character; a finer awareness, for example, of the delirious poetry at the heart of the Second Sonata's whirling finale. Hamelin's sonority is most elegantly and precisely gauged but time and again his fluency (admittedly breathtaking) erases too much of the work's originality and regenerative force. However, he shows a greater sense of freedom in the Fifth Sonata, and in the opalescent fantasy of the later sonatas he responds with more evocative skill to subjective terms, as well as to moments where Scriabin's brooding introspection is lit by sudden flashes of summer lightning.

The recordings are a little tight and airless in the bass and middle register, but the set does includes a superb essay on Scriabin.

Piano Sonatas – Nos 2, 5 & 9. Etude, Op 2 No 1. Four Pieces, Op 56 – Nuances. Two Pieces, Op 59 – Poème. Etude, Op 8 No 12. Mazurkas, Op 3 – Nos 1, 3, 4 & 6. Valse, Op 38

Yevgeny Sudbin pf
BIS ⊛ BIS-SACD1568 (57' · DDD/DSD) Ⓕ**OOOO**B+

Writing in prose as delirious as his playing, Yevgeny Sudbin speaks in his accompanying nine-page essay of the incomprehension that greeted Scriabin's half-crazed genius in both Russia and the West. This is entirely apt and no pianist of any generation has surely captured Scriabin's volatility so vividly as Sudbin.

In his choice of sonatas (ranging through Scriabin's early, middle and late periods), his mix of drama and introspection are positively alchemic and entirely his own. It is as if the music's very nerve-ends are exposed to view and rarely has a pianist been prepared to take such risks on record. He takes virtuosity to the very edge at the end of the Fifth Sonata and his dare-devil aplomb is at its height in the Ninth, suitably named *Black Mass* Sonata.

How he varies the colour, light and shade in the early D sharp minor Etude so that its familiar heroic octaves sound newly minted and never merely frenetic! His selection of Mazurkas is given with a breathtaking subtlety, making you long to hear him in Chopin, while his response to Scriabin's command in the Fifth Sonata, *presto tumultuoso esaltato*, is like the vortex of a whirlwind. All these performances are flecked with personal touches and brilliances above and beyond even Scriabin's wildest demands.

Finally, BIS captures Sudbin's astonishing range of colours and sonorities, ranging from the utmost delicacy to an enraged uproar, in crystalline demonstration sound. This, put suitably euphorically, is a disc in a million.

Piano Sonatas – Nos 4, 5, 8 & 9.
Deux Poèmes – Op 32; Op 69; Op 71.
Vers la flamme, Op 72
Andrei Korobeinikov pf
Mirare MIR061 (64' · DDD) Ⓕ**OO**

Andrei Korobeinikov's recital of music taken from Scriabin's middle and late periods, alternating light and darkness, exultation and desolation, will surely become a compulsory addition to all lovers of his neurotic and compulsive genius.

At 22 this Russian pianist already ranks among his foremost interpreters. He offers playing of an unswerving musical honesty backed by a gargantuan technical command. His tempo for the Fourth Sonata's opening *Andante* may be exceptionally slow but it is sustained with rare poise and concentration; and if the following *Prestissimo volando* is less mercurial than from others it is once again totally convincing in its own ultra-Russian terms.

Korobeinikov goes through the second of the *Deux Poèmes*, Op 32, and the Fifth Sonata's final outburst in a blaze of elemental thunder and lightning. And his authority is no less unarguable in the Eighth Sonata's extra-territorial wanderings and in *Vers la flamme* where Scri-

abin's obsessive patterning receives its ultimate nemesis. Such playing, finely recorded and presented, makes further recordings by this phenomenally gifted young pianist a necessity rather than a probability.

'The Early Scriabin'
Piano Sonata in E flat minor. Sonate-fantaisie. Allegro appassionato, Op 4. Canon in D minor. Etude No 12 in D sharp minor, Op 8. Fugue. Nocturne in A flat. Two Nocturnes, Op 5. Two Pieces for the Left Hand, Op 9. Mazurkas – in B minor; in F. Valses – Op 1; Op 6, No 1; No 2. Variations on a Theme by Mlle Egorova
Stephen Coombs pf
Hyperion CDA67149 (74' · DDD) Ⓕ B+

Stephen Coombs's 'The Early Scriabin' is a programme of fascinating rarities played with touching sensitivity and affection. Coombs's booklet essay, a mine of information and research, tells the history of such oddities as the sombre D minor Canon and E minor Fugue (their titles essentially alien to Scriabin's precociously Romantic and far-reaching sensibility) or the complex provenance of the masterly E flat minor Sonata. He also tells us that Scriabin's genius received short shrift from the academic *ancien régime*; allowing him to graduate in piano but not in composition.

Coombs's performances are, for the most part, what painters call 'low in tone', and even when you wish for greater voltage in, say, the nightmarish equestrian finale of the Sonata you can hardly wish for more gently persuasive accounts of the Waltzes or the A flat Nocturne. He's much less dazzling and rhetorical than, for example, Leon Fleisher in the Prelude and Nocturne for the left hand but, conversely, his playing suggests a subtly characterful and communing alternative. He does, though, make a full-blooded but finely graded assault on the cadenza just before the return of the principle idea in the *Allegro appassionato*. This record is a most impressive achievement, as beautiful in sound as it's endlessly thought-provoking.

Piano works

Complete Solo Piano Works
Maria Lettberg pf
Capriccio 49 586 (8h 9' · DDD)
Includes bonus DVD, 'Mysterium: The Multimedia Projects' Ⓢ

Here is a virtually complete recording of Scriabin's piano music (works without opus numbers are omitted). Each disc allows you to journey from his early Romanticism to middle-period idiosyncrasy and finally to the hallucinatory magic of his last years. Reactions to Scriabin's 'creative laboratory' have fluctuated wildly. For some such music was a reminder that 'there are those who think that the air is filled with green monkeys with crimson eyes and sparkling tails, a kind of ecstasy that is sold in Russia at two roubles a bottle,' while Stravinsky wondered: 'Scriabin, where does he come from and who are his followers?'

What is not controversial is the immensity of the challenge facing even the most intrepid pianist compelled on a journey of discovery as fraught as it is dazzling. And while Maria Lettberg, a Swedish pianist who has found fame outside the competition circuit, is not in the same league as, say Horowitz, Richter or Ashkenazy, she is for the most part warmly fluent and sympathetic.

How she relishes the violent mood-swings of the Op 11 Preludes, music alternately lost in its own delirium or ablaze with pianistic heroics. She understands ideally the Mazurkas where Chopin is made to speak with an increasingly strong Russian accent and she casts a shimmering haze across the necromancy of the late sonatas where we are ushered into a painfully self-absorbed world. Here obsessive patterns, harmonies and intervals seem to spin in interstellar space, but Lettberg manages to make sense of an instruction such as *très doux et pur* (the Tenth Sonata's opening) when the mood is cloudy and malignant.

An accompanying DVD shows the pianist once more fully attuned to Scriabin's demand in the Fourth Sonata to 'fly towards the blue star', to imply 'the creation of the world' in the Fifth Sonata and, finally, to realise the composer's assumption that he was God. This is an invaluable issue and a formidable achievement finely recorded.

Waltzes – Op 1; Op 38; in D flat major. Polonaise, Op 21. Fantasy, Op 28. Deux Poèmes, Op 32. Poème tragique, Op 34. Poème satanique, Op 36. Poème, Op 41. Trois Morceaux, Op 52. Albumblatt, Op 58. Vers la flamme, Op 72. Deux Danses, Op 73
Xiayin Wang pf
Naxos 8 570412 (65' · DDD)   ⓈⓄⓄ▷

Xiayin Wang offers a Scriabin recital with a difference. Avoiding large-scale works (the sonatas), she takes us on a carefully planned journey offering a bird's-eye view of the composer's restless, meteoric career. An exception is provided by the Fantasy where Wang's scintillating technique makes light of every virtuoso challenge and where her commitment makes you wonder why such starry, ultra-Romantic poetry is not in the repertoire of many more pianists. Here, as Wang puts it in her excellent notes, Scriabin 'abandons Chopinesque poise for abandonment'. Already a far cry from her curtain-raiser, two waltzes composed when Scriabin was 14 are clearly besotted with Chopin. The single Polonaise, too, while teetering on the edge of experimental horizons, is a fierce memory of Chopin and it is only when you arrive at the later works that you meet the composer's more obsessive, opalescent and fragmented style. On the other hand, the Op 38 Waltz unites all aspects of Scriabin's multifaceted genius, a

magical and dazzling memory of Liszt's *Valses oubliées*.

Wang plays all this music with a special brilliance and refinement, and if you occasionally doubt her musical range in the darker regions of Scriabin's personality, she comes up with a performance of *Vers la flamme* that moves superbly from a brooding menace to a final apocalyptic blaze. Finely recorded, Wang's recital provides an unusually perceptive introduction to Scriabin's piano music.

Deux Poèmes: Op 32; Op 44; Op 63; Op 69; Op 71. Poème tragique, Op 34. Poème satanique, Op 36. Poèmes – Op 41; Op 52 No 1; Op 59 No 1. Poème ailé, Op 51 No 2. Poème languide, Op 52 No 3. Poème-nocturne, Op 61. Poème 'Vers la flamme', Op 72. Feuillet d'album, Op 45 No 1. Poème fantasque, Op 45 No 2. Quasi valse, Op 47. Valse, Op 38
Pascal Amoyel pf
Calliope CAL9353 (75' · DDD)   Ⓕ

Pascal Amoyel admits he was driven close to neurosis when preparing his Scriabin recording and found it difficult to re-emerge into the world of other composers. Aphoristic or endlessly protracted, seemingly lost in a harmonic limbo or fiercely to the point, such music is indeed challenging to both listener and performer. For Amoyel the tirelessly extended *Poème-nocturne* is 'phantasmagorical, ill-defined and confused' (terms he intends as the greatest compliment) and his playing on what he describes as a 'rather sombre-sounding Steinway' amply conveys his enthusiasm.

He is acutely sensitive to the dark mystery at the heart of the Op 41 *Poème*, its final section a decadent memory of Chopin's Op 10 No 6 Etude, and responds with refinement as well as energy to the *Poème tragique* with its demands of *festivamente*, *fastoso*, *irato* and *fiero*. In the *Poème satanique* (music indelibly associated with Sofronitsky), light is stalked by darkness in a menacing game of tag, while the enchanting Op 38 *Valse* is an all-Russian extension of the world of Liszt's *Valses oubliées*. The Op 69 No 2 *Poème* is a notably grotesque *danse macabre* and in the final *Vers la flamme* Amoyel takes us on a mesmeric journey from threatening shadows to searing brilliance.

Yet even here he resists virtuoso temptations, making it odd that he should be described in France as one of Cziffra's 'spiritual heirs'. Confidentiality and insinuation are his hallmarks rather than wildness or flamboyance. Calliope's sound, like Amoyel's instrument, is subdued but it hardly detracts from an experience that is stifling or exhilarating, according to taste.

Peter Sculthorpe   Australian b1929

Sculthorpe studied at Melbourne University and with Rubbra and Wellesz at Oxford, and in 1963 he began teaching at Sydney University. Much of his music has resulted from an interest in the music of Australia's neighbours as well as from the impulse to bring together aspects of native Australian music with that of the heritage of the West. He is known primarily for his orchestral and chamber music, such as Kakadu (1988) and Earth Cry (1986), which evoke the sounds and feeling of the Australian bushland and outback. He has also written 17 string quartets, using unusual timbral effects, works for piano, and two operas.

Piano Concerto

Piano Concerto. Little Nourlangie.
Music for Japan. The Song of Tailitnama
Kirsti Harms mez **Mark Atkins** dijeridu **Tamara Anna Cislowska** pf **David Drury** org **Sydney Symphony Orchestra / Edo de Waart**
ABC Classics 8 770030 (53' · DDD · T) Ⓕ

Sculthorpe has long been preoccupied with the music from other countries situated in and around the Pacific – and Japanese music in particular, elements of which he has incorporated into other works such as the present Piano Concerto of 1983. Sculthorpe's Piano Concerto is an imposing creation, less indigenous-sounding and 'pictorial' than many of his other compositions, including *The song of Tailitnama* (1974). Conceived for high voice, six cellos and percussion, this haunting piece was in fact written for a TV documentary.

Little Nourlangie dates from 1990. It takes its name from a small outcrop of rocks in Australia's Kakadu National Park on which can be found the Aboriginal Blue Paintings, depicting fish, boats and ancestral figures and which inspired the composer. *Little Nourlangie* is a characteristically striking creation, scored with much imaginative flair. It shares its diatonic main theme with that of Sculthorpe's 1989 guitar concerto, *Nourlangie*, and comprises four and a half minutes of 'straightforward, joyful music' (to quote the composer). By contrast, *Music for Japan* exhibits a much more uncompromising demeanour, and according to annotator Graeme Skinner, is at once 'his most abstract and modernist orchestral score'.

Edo de Waart presides over a set of performances that exhibit great commitment and exemplary finish. The recording is excellent too.

Cello Dreaming

Irkanda Iª. Irkanda IVᵃᶜ. Lament for Stringsᶜ. Sonata for Strings No 2ᶜ. Cello Dreamingᵇᶜ. Djilileᶜ
ᵇ**Emma-Jane Murphy** vc ᶜ**Australian Chamber Orchestra / Richard Tognetti** ᵃvn
Chandos CHAN10063 (66' · DDD) Ⓕ🅑➛

The Australian Chamber Orchestra has consistently championed the music of its countryman Peter Sculthorpe. *Cello Dreaming*, premiered by Steven Isserlis and the BBC Philharmonic dur-

ing the 1998 Manchester Cello Festival, is inspired by the sights, sounds and diverse cultural mix of Australia's northern coastline. It's a beguiling evocation, boasting nature music of imagination and local colour; Emma-Jane Murphy is an impressive soloist. The Aboriginal melody known as 'Djilile' was first used by Sculthorpe as far back as 1950 in his Fourth String Quartet. This transcription for strings is one in a series of reworkings of a tune that has haunted the composer for over 50 years. No less appealing is the substantial Second String Sonata (1988), an arrangement of the Ninth Quartet of 1975.

Shrewd programming frames the threnodic *Irkanda IV* for solo violin, strings and percussion (Sculthorpe's first real breakthrough from 1961, named after the Aboriginal word for a remote and lonely place) between *Irkanda I* for solo violin from 1955 (a beautifully proportioned essay which provides the first glimpse of the mature composer in its rapt identification with Australia's landscape and wildlife) and the moving 1976 *Lament* for strings. It isn't hard to detect a kinship, so naturally does each piece emerge from its predecessor.

Three tracks here (*Irkanda IV*, *Lament* and the Second Sonata) overlap with a rival ABC Classics release featuring these same artists. There's little to choose between the two in terms of performance (those earlier accounts are a degree more restrained), but Chandos's sound has the edge, possessing breathtaking definition and range. A very fine issue.

Earth Cry

Earth Cryª. Kakadu. Piano Concertoᵇ. Memento mori. From Oceania
ª**William Barton** dijeridu ᵇ**Tamara Anna Cislowska** pf
New Zealand Symphony Orchestra / James Judd
Naxos 8 557382 (71' · DDD) Ⓢ🅑➛

Earth Cry. Kakadu. Mangrove. Songs of Sea and Sky.
From Ubirr
William Barton dijeridu **Queensland Orchestra / Michael Christie**
ABC Classics ABC476 1921 (71' · DDD) Ⓕ

Earth Cry (1986), previously recorded in 1989 by Stuart Challender, is one of Sculthorpe's major utterances, music at once approachable and elusive. These aspects are extraordinarily heightened by a recently added dijeridu part. The two recordings here sound quite different. Judd revels in a harsher orchestral sound, spotlighting each detail, while Christie conjures a more rounded tone, though edgy and laden with menace. William Barton's haunting dijeridu playing is quite different on each.

Kakadu (1988), another shared item, finds both Judd and Christie alive to every nervy detail, though Christie responds more naturally to its mercurial changes. It's Challender, however, who finds the sheer joy: his interpretation is unsurpassed. He's also unbeatable in *Mangrove*, another heavyweight score that repays further investigation, though Christie summons a shining performance and shows a fine understanding of every nuance of the intricate orchestration.

Christie's disc includes another work revised to include dijeridu: *From Ubirr*, which is conceptually and audibly related to *Earth Cry*. Sculthorpe wrote it for Kronos, and Christie has arranged it for larger forces. The orchestra finds greater sonic depth and the dijeridu emphasises the earthy quality of the music. *Songs of Sea and Sky*, originally for clarinet and piano, also benefits from expansion from its original chamber format.

The mesmerising Piano Concerto, dating from 1983, is one of Sculthorpe's finest creations. Tamara Anna Cislowska has already recorded it with Edo de Waart, a relaxed performance with 'impressionistic' orchestral sound; this Naxos recording is sharper. Judd also includes a work from Sculthorpe's 'sun music' period, *From Oceania* (1970/2003), more ostentatiously bright and more 'foreign' than later works, as well as the affecting and straightforward *Memento mori* (1993).

Sculthorpe lovers will want both these recordings, but for a one-disc showcase of his work the programme and performances of the Queensland Orchestra have the edge.

Rodion Shchedrin   Russian b1932

Shchedrin studied at the Moscow Choir School and in 1955 he graduated from the Moscow Conservatory, and later (1965-69) taught there too. In 1958 he married ballerina Mayya Plisetskaya. From 1973 to 1990 he was Shostakovich's successor as Chairman of the Composers' Union of the Russian Federation. Since 1992 he has divided his time between Moscow and Munich. Among his works are the ballets The Little Humpbacked Horse (1955), Carmen Suite (1967), based on the opera Carmen by Georges Bizet, Anna Karenina (1971), and Lady with a Lapdog (1985); the operas Not Only Love (1961), Dead Souls (1976) and The Enchanted Wanderer (2002); piano concertos, symphonies, chamber and piano music. He has written five concertos for orchestra: the first, often translated as Naughty Limericks, is by far the best known, and was the work which first established him on the international stage.

Concertos for Orchestra

Concertos for Orchestra – No 4, 'Khorovody';
No 5 'Four Russian Songs'. Crystal Psaltery
**Bournemouth Symphony Orchestra /
Kirill Karabits**
Naxos 8 572405 (59' · DDD)   Ⓢ❍❍◗

Rodion Shchedrin's long and varied work-list includes five concertos for orchestra, a form (if it can be called that) which suits much in his manner. It is above all his ear for orchestral colour

that dominates, as he himself has pointed out in connection with the Fifth, subtitled *Four Russian Songs*, a piece written for the entertainment of Proms audiences in 1989. The suggestion is that a troika speeds between four Russian cities, 'collecting' a different song from each. The progress is vivid and lively, and the songs (three of them, of Shchedrin's own invention) are really an excuse for a dazzling display of orchestral invention. Much the same is true of the Fourth Concerto, *Khorovody*, a khorovod being the Russian version of the round dance common in most Eastern European folklores. Some of the sounds are faintly weird – a recorder against flute players blowing into their mouthpieces – but Shchedrin's gift ensures that the ear is constantly beguiled. How much lies beneath his somewhat minimalist approach, with long strings of ostinatos or simply repeated notes introducing or underpinning the magical sounds, is questionable. But the idea is recognisably Russian, not so much thematic development as melodies circling over varied repetition, as Russians have enjoyed in many different ways ever since Glinka.

Crystal Psaltery applies this delicacy of ear to the more avant-garde kind of music characteristic of Shchedrin's friend Takemitsu, something that can come to seem to be refined almost out of existence. Kirill Karabits and the Bournemouth orchestra do brilliantly with it all, and so, crucially, do the recording engineers in capturing all the delicate and original sounds.

Operas

The Sealed Angel
Marie Macklin, Emma Walshe *sops* **Nina Canter** *contr* **Benedict Hymas** *ten* **Clare Wills** *ob* **Gonville and Caius College Choir, Cambridge / Geoffrey Webber; King's College Choir, London / David Trendell**
Delphian DCD34067 (55' · DDD)   Ⓕ❍

The allegorical resonances of *The Sealed Angel* – in which a rural community protects a religious icon – seem obvious and the text is purely religious, the equivalent of a cinematic treatment featuring the icon alone. The nine movements play continuously, the first three a flowing evocation of angels before the atmosphere changes in the freely dissonant fourth, depicting Judas's betrayal. After the great choral screech at its climax, the music calms down with the choir *tacet* in the fifth; the halting, static sixth is a chordal prayer of repentance and salvation. The vertical and horizontal elements then fuse in a powerful setting of the Lord's Prayer (section eight) before the quiet reprise of the opening.

Shchedrin provides a detached counterpoint to the voices with a series of oboe solos, free variations not so much on a theme as a way of writing. These top and tail the main choral blocks, punctuating rather than accompanying, nicely played by Clare Wills. The choirs sing splendidly, without producing a Russian sound, yet the composer is aware of the English choral tradition so his music's translation here is fascinating. So is his avoidance of the holy minimalism of many of his compatriots or the consonance of Rautavaara's larger choral works. Caught here in fine sound, this is a splendid disc of a multifaceted, many-layered modern masterpiece.

The Enchanted Wanderer[a]. The Little Humpbacked Horse – Four Fragments. Concerto for Orchestra No 1, 'Naughty Limericks'
[a]**Sergei Aleksashkin** bass Ivan Severyanovich Flyagin, Story-teller [a]**Kristina Kapustinskaya** mez Grusha the Gypsy, Story-teller [a]**Evgeny Akimov** ten The Flogged Monk, Prince, Magnetiser, Old Man in the Forest, Story-teller
Mariinsky [a]**Chorus and Orchestra / Valery Gergiev**
Mariinsky ② _⑨_ MAR0504 (111' · DDD)   Ⓕ Ⓑ►

Shchedrin's 2002 'opera for the concert stage' tells, in highly condensed form, Leskov's story of the archetypal Russian life of a horse-driver who accidentally kills a monk, and after episodes of captivity, sins of the flesh and heroic deeds eventually fulfils the prophecy that he will become a penitent monk himself.

Acclaimed at its St Petersburg premiere, *The Enchanted Wanderer*'s reception at its 2002 New York premiere, as at the 2008 Edinburgh Festival performance, was, shall we say, more mixed, reviewers finding it for the most part unmemorable and tedious. It is easy to understand both points of view. Shchedrin only has to underscore the scenes of contrition, temptation and lament with fairly obvious musical imagery in order to tap a Russian audience's hunger for lost national identity; while for Western audiences, used to more concentrated doses of modernism and sharper dramatic focus, there is little to compensate for the lack of musical incident. Nobly as Sergei Aleksashkin takes the role of the Wanderer, Shchedrin gives the listener a lot of rather anonymous music to wade through.

The second disc is bulked out with excerpts from the ballet *The Little Humpbacked Horse* and with the familiar *Naughty Limericks* mini-Concerto for Orchestra. Both are talented examples of the interest in indigenous Russian culture that binds together the apparently polarised worldly and spiritual aspects of Shchedrin's output. Whatever the intrinsic strengths or weaknesses of his music, his loyalty to those values represents a significant strand in late-Soviet and post-Soviet culture. On that basis, and notwithstanding its verbose and hagiographical booklet essays, these finely executed and recorded CDs can be counted an important document.

John Sheppard   British c1515-1559/60

Sheppard was at Magdalen College, Oxford, between 1543 and 1548, and by 1552 was a Gentle-

man *of the Chapel Royal. Most of his extant music for the Latin rite probably dates from Mary's reign. Among his more modern works are the four-voice* Magnificat *and the* Cantante *and* Western Wynde Masses. *The English works, which include 15 anthems and service music, seem to date from Edward's reign.*

Western Wynde Mass

Western Wynde Mass. Gaude, gaude, gaude Maria; Dum transisset Sabbatum I; Spiritus Sanctus procedens II; In manus tuas II; Audivi vocem de coelo; Libera nos, salva nos II; Beata nobis gaudia; Impetum fecerunt unanimes; Sancte Dei preciose; Sacris solemniis; Aeterne Rex altissime; Dum transisset sabbatum II; Hostes Herodes impie; In manus tuas III; Te Deum laudamus. Second Service
The Sixteen / Harry Christophers
Hyperion Dyad ② CDD22022 (125' · DDD · T/t)
                                         Ⓜ Ⓞ ►

This set centres round one of Sheppard's best-known four-part Masses, *The Western Wynde*. Though largely syllabic in style, in accordance with liturgical prescriptions at a time when taste in church music was turning towards ever greater emphasis on the text, this Mass still has moments that recapture the earlier visionary style in all its wonder. The section 'Et incarnatus est', coming after an amazing cadence at 'descendit de coelis' in the *Credo*, is a case in point. 'Pleni sunt coeli' is another, and also the opening of the *Benedictus*, where the melody unfolds unhurriedly over the delicate counterpoint of the mean and the bass. In such passages The Sixteen is in its element, each singer relating to the others with the intimacy and mutual understanding of performers of chamber music.

The supporting programme includes *alternatim* hymn settings, responsories and a *Te Deum*. In all these the chant is sung with excellent phrasing and a smooth *legato*. Some subtle repercussions in the intonation to *Dum transisset Sabbatum* are particularly pleasing.

In all five pieces, though, the tempo of the chant sections bore little relationship to the polyphony – the least far removed being that of the hymn *Aeterne Rex altissime*, where the individual chant notes had roughly the duration of a half-beat of the polyphony. The English *Magnificat* and *Nunc dimittis* reveal Sheppard fully conforming to the later syllabic style in a rich and joyful texture. Here and in the Latin *Te Deum* The Sixteen display to the full their glowing vocal qualities. This is wonderful singing, with a sense of freedom and flow that's almost overpowering.

Choral works

Media vita. Gaude, gaude, gaude Maria. Te Deum laudamus. The Lord's Prayer. Christ rising again. Haste thee, Oh God. I give you a new commandment

Stile Antico
Harmonia Mundi HMU80 7509 (70' · DDD)
ⓕⓞⓞⓞ➔

This recording by the 14-strong Stile Antico offers three extensive Latin pieces by Sheppard leavened by shorter English anthems composed during the reign of Edward VI. It opens with the responsory *Gaude, gaude, gaude Maria*. The outer sections are for six voices, the lowest but one being a cantus firmus. These frame simpler 'gymel' passages, where the sopranos and altos, each divided in two, are combined with the bass. Then there is plainchant, some of it consisting of a melisma on the last syllable of the preceding polyphony. It is a most attractive piece, with clashes of harmony duly relished by the choir.

Even more elaborate is the 25-minute antiphon that gives the disc its title. Here the *Nunc dimittis* is chanted, its simplicity an affecting contrast to the intensity of the counterpoint. Stile Antico take the beginning quietly, as befits the words – 'In the midst of life we are in death' – and work up to a powerful conclusion. The *Te Deum* is an *alternatim* setting, probably composed earlier than the other two works.

Of the English anthems, *I give you a new commandment* is constructed like, for instance, Tallis's *If ye love me*, where the second part is repeated. Whether the music be simple or complex, Stile Antico have the measure of it. Excellent!

'Audivi vocem'
Sheppard Gaudete celicole omnes. Beati omnes.
Laudate pueri Dominum. Eterne rex, altissime **Tallis**
In ieiunio et fletu. Te lucis ante terminum. Audivi
vocem. Salvator mundi **Tye** Omnes gentes. Missa
sine nomine
The Hilliard Ensemble (David James *counterten*
Rogers Covey-Crump, Steven Harrold *tens* Gordon
Jones *bar* Robert Macdonald *bass*)
ECM New Series 476 6353 (72' · DDD)　　ⓕ

The Hilliards here return to familiar territory with a programme of Tallis, Tye and Sheppard. While the territory may be familiar, however, not all of its landmarks are, and neither is their disposition – this is an extremely well organised disc, surveying the impact that the musical aspects of the Reformation had in the first instance on English composers (what David Skinner aptly describes as 'that musicologically grey period in the last decades of Henry VIII's reign'). Thus, while all the works by Tallis (*In ieiunio et fletu*, *Te lucis ante terminum*, *Audivi vocem* and *Salvator mundi*, the latter given a particularly beautiful performance) are well known, they are set in the context of much more recondite material.

The rarities from Sheppard include the early *Gaudete celicole omnes*, whose constant flow almost suggests at times a kind of English Gombert, and later, clearly Henrician works, such as the marvellously luminous hymn *Eterne rex, altissime*. The music by Tye includes *Omnes*

gentes plaudite, which may perhaps be considered relatively known, but the four sections of the *Missa sine nomine* from the Peterhouse part-books will probably be unknown even to most connoisseurs of this period, precisely on account of the missing voice. Hopefully these beautifully blended performances will help to change this state of affairs, for it is an extremely impressive work, heralding the new, compact and more declamatory style with consummate skill. An outstanding release.

Dmitri Shostakovich
Russian/USSR 1906-1975

After his death, the government of the USSR issued the following summary of Shostakovich's work, drawing attention to a 'remarkable example of fidelity to the traditions of musical classicism, and above all, to the Russian traditions, finding his inspiration in the reality of Soviet life, reasserting and developing in his creative innovations the art of socialist realism and, in so doing, contributing to universal progressive musical culture'.

It wasn't always like that, despite his three Orders of Lenin and other Soviet honours, for Shostakovich's life happened to run in tandem with the Communist regime and he frequently fell foul of the authorities for not writing the right type of music. Nevertheless, while Prokofiev and Stravinsky had grown up under the Tsars, Shostakovich was the first and arguably the greatest composer to emerge from Communism.

His first music lessons (on the piano) came from his mother, a professional pianist, but it was Glazunov who took him under his wing when he entered the St Petersburg Conservatory when he was 13. His graduation composition was his First Symphony which made him internationally known at the age of 20 and has subsequently proved to be one of his most popular works. His Second Symphony, To October, was less successful despite its rousing choral finale and revolutionary sentiments.

Shostakovich, child of the revolution, believed it was the duty of an artist to serve the state. Yet his next venture, the satirical opera The Nose, was attacked by the arbiters of Soviet musical taste as 'bourgeois decadence'. The same year, his Third Symphony, subtitled The First of May, its finale saluting the 'International Workers' Day' was criticised as being no more than 'a formal gesture of proletarian solidarity'. This was nothing compared to the reaction to his opera The Lady Macbeth of the Mtsensk District (1934). Soviet musicians generally welcomed it as a significant work, as good as anything being produced in the West. But its scenes of adultery, murder and suicide shocked puritan officialdom and, after the opera's Moscow production, Pravda (the official Communist party newspaper) published an article headed 'Chaos instead of Music', accusing Shostakovich of creating 'a bedlam of noise', 'a confused stream of sounds' and 'petty bourgeois sensationalism'.

Shostakovich, when he apologised for his errors, said he would try to do better and would henceforth write, even though he thought he had been, music that fell in line with 'socialist realism'. After his next stage work, the tepid ballet *The Limpid Brook, was also condemned by Pravda as being insufficiently dignified on the subject of Soviet life, Shostakovich abandoned the theatre and from 1938 to 1955 wrote chiefly symphonies and string quartets.*

His Fourth Symphony fared no better as far as musical officialdom went and it was withdrawn before its first performance. With the Fifth Symphony (1937) Shostakovich was allowed in from the cold, as it were. It's certainly a magnificent work by anybody's standards. The miracle is that the Soviet regime agreed, hailing it as 'a model of true Soviet art'. During the war, he volunteered for active service but was turned down because of his poor eyesight; but in the 1941 siege of Leningrad by the Nazis, Shostakovich served in the fire brigade before flying to the temporary Soviet capital Kuibishev to complete his Seventh Symphony, the Leningrad (the ever-mindful authorities feared for the safety of their valuable Peoples' Artist). Its theme, the rampant German army being overcome by the victorious Russians, led to performances in every Allied country and its composer became a kind of artistic war hero.

Even this esteem was not enough to save him from being denounced in the famous edict of 1948 when he, Prokofiev and other prominent Russian composers were accused of 'formalism' and 'anti-people art'. He defended himself with some dignity, while accepting the political dogma behind the criticism, but was still dismissed from his professorship at the Moscow Conservatory and wrote only film scores and patriotic music until after Stalin's death in 1953. Symphonies Nos 9, 10 and 11 created little interest, No 12 (dedicated to the memory of Lenin) a little more, but with his Symphony No 13, Shostakovich again met with official criticism, this time from the Communist Party chairman Nikita Khruschev who complained that the text of the choral part referring to the massacre of the Jews in Kiev during the war did not pay sufficient attention to the others who were slaughtered. The text was altered to meet the chairman's objections. Shostakovich's final two symphonies passed the political quality test without controversy.

His first wife died in 1954 (he remarried two years later). Meanwhile, his son Maxim, born in 1938, was progressing with his musical studies and has since become one of his father's most distinguished interpreters. In the 1960s restrictions on the arts were slackened somewhat. Shostakovich was left more or less in peace to compose as he wished and many of the works previously condemned by the regime were given a clean bill of health. At the time of his death, The Times wrote of him in its obituary that he was beyond doubt 'the last great symphonist'.

Cello Concertos

No 1 in E flat, Op 107; **No 2** in G, Op 126

Cello Concertos Nos 1 & 2
Daniel Müller-Schott vc **Bavarian Radio Symphony Orchestra / Yakov Kreizberg**
Orfeo C659 081A (67' · DDD)   Ⓕ**ⓄⒹ**➔

With roughly a dozen single-disc couplings of the two Shostakovich cello concertos available on CD, a new one needs a sharp profile in order to gain visibility. Müller-Schott and his sup-

porting team have most of the obvious credentials: technique and temperament in abundance, finely judged tempi, and excellent recorded balance and perspective, the soloist placed a little further forward than in some versions, but not distractingly so. They bring dash, drive and discipline to the fast movements, and soulfulness to the slow ones. But the trick with Shostakovich is to combine those things with weight of tone and flashes of personal expression, so that the drama of the individual caught up in the machinations of larger forces gains life-or-death significance.

How that is achieved is a matter for debate and legitimate disagreement. For all Mischa Maisky's special touches of romantic eloquence, he comes up with some bizarre technical fudges in the big cadenzas, while Heinrich Schiff is far more direct but so fast and furious in the first movement of the E flat First Concerto that it loses as much in stoical defiance as it gains in physical excitement. Müller-Schott's tempi and characterisation are more central, and as a modern alternative to Rostropovich they take the lead, also because there are a number of telling passages in Kreizberg's accompaniments.

Cello Concerto No 1ᵃ. Cello Sonataᵇ
Han-Na Chang vc ᵃ**London Symphony Orchestra / Antonio Pappano** ᵇpf
EMI 332422-2 (57' · DDD)   Ⓕ**Ⓓ**➔

Antonio Pappano belies his reputation for carefully prepared, soft-grained music-making, encouraging the LSO winds to emulate the edginess of Soviet Russian playing styles. True, his cellist has a smaller sound than Rostropovich, something only partly disguised by close miking, yet she plays with such conviction that you feel she too could have been the inspiration for those great composers.

Chang's intense and aggressive style carries its own risks. Adopting in fast music speeds a notch swifter than the norm, Chang combines raw emotion with a structural grip that, in its way, is even more remarkable in one so young. No doubt some will find her playing OTT, her tone too lean, her approach inelegant. And the LSO is right there with her, as deeply attentive in the slow movement as in the composer's astringent, nagging brand of fireworks elsewhere in the piece.

The Cello Sonata is a less passionate utterance, though it too has its (quieter) attractions. This is Shostakovich trying his hand at a purer, relatively neutral idiom even before Stalin's direct intervention in his creative life. With Pappano at the keyboard the performance is sympathetic if less extraordinary than that of the main work, Chang's projection at times unduly vehement. Still in her early twenties, she is none the less a phenomenon.

Piano Concertos

No 1 in C minor for Piano, Trumpet and Strings, Op 35; **No 2** in F, Op 102

Piano Concertos Nos 1 & 2. The Unforgettable Year
1919, Op 89 – The assault on beautiful Gorky
Dmitri Alexeev pf **Philip Jones** tpt **English
Chamber Orchestra / Jerzy Maksymiuk**
Classics for Pleasure 382234-2 (48' · DDD)   ⒷⓄ

Shostakovich's piano concertos were written in
very different circumstances, yet together they
contain some of the composer's most cheerful and
enlivening music. The First, with its wealth of
perky, memorable tunes, has the addition of a brilliantly conceived solo trumpet part (delightfully
done here by Philip Jones) that also contributes to
the work's characteristic stamp. The Second Concerto was written not long after Shostakovich had
released a number of the intense works he had
concealed during the depths of the Stalin era. It
came as a sharp contrast, reflecting as it did the
optimism and sense of freedom that followed the
death of the Russian dictator. The beauty of the
slow movement is ideally balanced by the vigour
of the first, and the madcap high spirits of the last.
The poignant movement for piano and orchestra
from the Suite from the 1951 film *The Unforgettable Year 1919*, 'The assault on beautiful Gorky',
provides an excellent addition to this disc of perceptive and zestful performances by Alexeev. He's
most capably supported by the ECO under Maksymiuk, and the engineers have done them proud
with a recording of great clarity and finesse. A joyous issue.

Piano Concerto No 1ᵃ. Concertino, Op 94ᵇ.
Piano Quintet, Op 57ᶜ
Martha Argerich pf with ᵃ**Sergei Nakariakov** tpt
ᶜ**Renaud Capuçon,** ᶜ**Alissa Margulis** vns
ᶜ**Lida Chen** va ᶜ**Mischa Maisky** vc
ᵇ**Lilya Zilberstein** pf ᵃ**Orchestra della
Svizzera Italiana / Alexander Vedernikov**
EMI 504504-2 (66' · DDD)   ⒻⓄⓄⓄ▷
Recorded live 2006

Argerich's 1994 DG reading of the Concerto for
Piano, Trumpet and Strings is already a benchmark version among modern recordings, complementing the composer's own technically fallible yet still indispensable 1958 account. But
now there is a more natural flow in the slow
movement, some previously slightly forced
rubatos are smoother, and although the textures
are a fraction more richly pedalled, as often
needs to be the case for projection to a big audience rather than the microphone, there is no
more than an infinitesimal loss of clarity. So if
anything Argerich's playing has the tiniest of
edges even over her former self. More decisively, Sergei Nakariakov brings an extra dash of
wit and soloistic presence to the trumpet part,
not to mention an astonishing feat of (circular?)
breathing in the slow movement. There is a
fraction more flair from orchestra and conductor too, while the recording brings everything
further forward, so that the electricity of the
playing crackles around the room.

The two-piano Concertino is a little piece of
high-quality *Gebrauchsmusik* for the then

16-year-old Maxim Shostakovich to romp
around with; Argerich and Zilberstein give it a
wonderfully characterful rendition.

Much of the Piano Quintet also emerges as
one has always only dreamt of hearing it – vivid
from moment to moment, yet with a long musical line and dramatic overall conception. Occasionally the nervous energy of the playing is too
much of a good thing, as in the tricky bridge
from Intermezzo to finale – from darkest profundity to deceptive easy-going cheeriness – and
as in the piano's first statement of the fugue
theme in the second movement. So, recommended alongside the safer Ashkenazy/Fitzwil-
liam recording rather than above it. As for the
disc as a whole: a sure-fire winner.

Violin Concertos

No 1 in A minor, Op 99;
No 2 in C sharp minor, Op 129

Violin Concertos Nos 1 & 2
Lydia Mordkovitch vn
Scottish National Orchestra / Neeme Järvi
Chandos CHAN8820 (69' · DDD)   ⒻⓄⓄ▷

This coupling completely explodes the idea of
the Second Violin Concerto being a disappointment after the dramatic originality of No 1.
Certainly No 2, completed in 1967, a year after
the very comparable Cello Concerto No 2, has
never won the allegiance of violin virtuosos as
the earlier work has done, but here Lydia Mordkovitch confirms what has become increasingly
clear, that the spareness of late Shostakovich
marks no diminution of his creative spark,
maybe even the opposite. In that she's greatly
helped by the equal commitment of Neeme
Järvi in drawing such purposeful, warmly
expressive playing from the SNO. With such
spare textures the first two movements can be
difficult to hold together, but here from the
start, where Mordkovitch plays the lyrical first
theme in a hushed, beautifully withdrawn way,
the concentration is consistent.

It isn't just that Mordkovitch has the benefit
of far fuller recording and a less close recording
balance, but that her playing has an even wider
range of colouring and dynamic than Oistrakh's. She conveys more of the mystery of the
work and is perfectly matched by the orchestra.
As in the First Concerto the principal horn has
a vital role, here crowning each of the first two
movements with a solo of ecstatic beauty in the
coda. The range of the recording helps in the
finale, where the *Allegro* has a satisfyingly barbaric bite, while the *scherzando* element is
delectably pointed, as it is in the first movement too.

In the First Concerto Mordkovitch is hardly
less impressive. As in Concerto No 2 one of her
strengths lies in the meditative intensity which
she brings to the darkly lyrical writing of the first
and third movements. Here, too, she has never
sounded quite so full and warm of tone on

record before. In the brilliant second and fourth movements she may not play with quite the demonic bravura of Oistrakh, but again there's no lack of power, and in place of demonry she gives rustic jollity to the dance rhythms, faithfully reflecting the title of the finale, *Burlesque*. She's helped by recorded sound far fuller than Oistrakh's. This is a superb disc.

Violin Concertos Nos 1 & 2
Maxim Vengerov *vn*; **London Symphony Orchestra / Mstislav Rostropovich**
Warner Apex 2564 68039-7 (73' · DDD)   ⑤❍❍❍❍▶

There's an astonishing emotional maturity in Vengerov's Shostakovich. He uses Heifetz's bow, but it's to David Oistrakh that he's often compared. His vibrato is wider, his manners less consistently refined, and yet the comparison is well founded. Oistrakh made three commercial recordings of the Shostakovich and one can guess that Vengerov has been listening to those earlier Oistrakh renditions, as there's nothing radically novel about his interpretation. Some may find Vengerov's impassioned climaxes a shade forced by comparison. Yet he achieves a nobility and poise worlds away from the superficial accomplishment of most modern rivals. He can fine down his tone to the barest whisper; nor is he afraid to make a scorching, ugly sound. While his sometimes slashing quality of articulation is particularly appropriate to the faster movements, the brooding, silver-grey 'Nocturne' comes off superbly too, though it seems perverse that the engineers mute the low tam-tam strokes. Rostropovich has the lower strings dig into the third movement's passacaglia theme with his usual enthusiasm. Indeed the orchestral playing is very nearly beyond reproach.

This is an exceptionally fine peformance of the Second, the desperate bleakness perfectly realised. There has been no finer account since that of the dedicatee, David Oistrakh (Chant du Monde). With Rostropovich rather than Kondrashin on the podium, tempi are comparatively deliberate in the first two movements, but there's no lack of intensity in the solo playing and rather more in the way of light and shade. In the stratospheric writing of the *Adagio*, Vengerov is technically superb, while the all-pervading atmosphere of desolation has never been more potently conveyed. The finale is more extrovert than some will like, the fireworks irresistible, and yet you do not lose the disquieting sense of a composer at the end of his tether, seemingly contemptuous of his own material. This is an extraordinary disc – and it's now at super-budget price!

Additional recommendations

Violin Concertos Nos 1 & 2
Khachatryan; French Nat Orch / Masur

Naïve V5025 (70' · DDD)   ⓜ❍❍

Sergey Khachatryan is a real rival to Maxim Vengerov in this repertoire: the Shostakovich No 1 is his party piece as well. Interpreting it with a less unyielding intensity, he too satisfies its demands as few have done since the great David Oistrakh. Rock-solid intonation is combined with wonderfully sweet tone. Kurt Masur's accompaniment is characteristic of him. His lack of theatricality puts the focus on the way the music is put together.

Shostakovich Violin Concerto No 1
Coupled with **Prokofiev** Violin Concerto No 1
S Chang; **BPO / Rattle**
EMI 346053-2 (60' · DDD)   Ⓕ❍❍▶
In making the transition from wunderkind to mature artist, Sarah Chang is fortunate to be partnered by Sir Simon Rattle and his Berliners and this is a reminder of his unambiguous excellence as a concerto accompanist. What you might miss is that indefinable factor 'authenticity of experience'. Not that Sarah Chang lacks heart, courage or individuality. She plunges excitedly into climactic passages, determined to give her big, dark sound a scorching edge. The technical control is mightily impressive.

Shostakovich Violin Concerto No 2[b]
Coupled with **Bliss** Fanfare[a]
Tchaikovsky Violin Concerto[c]
[bc]**D Oistrakh** *vn* [ab]**LSO / Ormandy**;
[c]**LPO / M Shostakovich**
BBC Legends BBCL4267-2 (64' · ADD)
Recorded live [ab]1967; [c]1972   Ⓕ❍❍
Oistrakh had played the new concerto three times in Russia before this Western premiere in London. Barring a few insignificant moments of imprecision, there's no need to make allowances for its being a new work for conductor and orchestra; it's a splendid performance, and very well recorded. Oistrakh appears to command the stage effortlessly and to catch the mood exactly. (And how could anyone become tired of Oistrakh's Tchaikovsky?)

Symphonies

No 1 in F minor, Op 10; **No 2** in B, Op 14, 'To October'; **No 3** in E flat, Op 20, 'The First of May'; **No 4** in C minor, Op 43; **No 5** in D minor, Op 47; **No 6** in B minor, Op 54; **No 7** in C, Op 60, 'Leningrad'; **No 8** in C minor, Op 65; **No 9** in E flat, Op 70; **No 10** in E minor, Op 93; **No 11** in G minor, Op 103, 'The Year 1905'; **No 12** in D minor, Op 112, 'The Year 1917'; **No 13** in B flat minor, Op 113, 'Babi Yar'; **No 14**, Op 135; **No 15** in A, Op 141

Symphonies Nos 1-15. October, Op 131. Violin Concerto No 2. The Execution of Stepan Razin, Op 119. The Sun Shines on our Motherland, Op 90
Evgenia Tselovalnik *sop* **Evgeny Nesterenko, Vitaly Gromadsky, Artur Eizen** *basses* **David Oistrakh** *vn*
Russian State Polyphonic Cappella; Moscow Choral Academy Boys Chorus; Moscow Philharmonic Symphony Orchestra / Kyrill Kondrashin
Melodiya MELCD1001065 (12h 1' · ADD)   Ⓕ❍❍

If Kondrashin's name isn't the first listeners associate with the composer these days that has more to do with the spotty availability of his recordings than with their intrinsic quality. Of course the sound is not state-of-the-art, the mid-range tending to be rather crowded and shouty, but the transfers are more than listenable. The Fourth in particular is an enormous improvement on its mono-only predecessor, the Ninth disappointing only in the way the sound cuts out abruptly at the close, probably to disguise wear on the master tape. Both these readings are usually judged 'definitive' and the Russians have added to the attractions of the cycle with extras occupying the same high ground. You'll not find a more compelling account of *The Execution of Stepan Razin* than the one by its onlie begetters and this would seem to be the most 'official' transfer of David Oistrakh's Second Violin Concerto currently doing the rounds.

Black marks, and there had to be some, are earned by the flimsiness of the box containing the 11 sturdy individual cardboard folders and the lack of adequate annotations, texts and translations. This is the textually bowdlerised version of the Thirteenth which weakens the author's personal identification with the fate of the Jewish people. Here the indictment of anti-Semitism becomes less specific to Mother Russia and we are reminded of the latter's 'heroic deed in blocking the way to Fascism'. Not that you'd know it. Neither this nor the Fourteenth make much sense without the words in front of us.

Whatever the case, the Melodiya set is a compulsory purchase for all true lovers of Shostakovich, especially those who feel that most recent recordings speak with a foreign accent or are simply too damn slow! The first complete Shostakovich cycle from one interpreter can still startle with its resilience and panache, and the raw tone of the Moscow Philharmonic is part and parcel of the appeal. Over to you.

Additional recommendation

Symphonies Nos 1-15.
Coupled with: Six Poems of Marina Tsvetayeva.
From Jewish Folk Poetry
Soloists; Concertgebouw; LPO / Haitink
Decca ⑪ 475 7413DC11 (12h 49 · DDD)   ⑧〇▶
   The first Western complete Shostakovich cycle
   and a very fine achievement indeed. Competitively
   priced and stunningly recorded, this is well worth
   considering.

Symphony No 1

Symphonies Nos 1 & 6
Russian National Orchestra / Vladimir Jurowski
Pentatone ⑨ PTC5186 068 (67' · DDD/DSD)   Ⓕ

The Russian National Orchestra's relatively lean, frosty sonority, only partly a product of divided violins, is presented with outstanding fidelity in a spacious acoustic. While both performances are excellent, the Sixth receives the more remarkable interpretation. Here Shostakovich can be Beethovenian in his allocation of seemingly unworkable metronome marks and most conductors blunt his excesses. Leonard Bernstein, one of the few to give credence to the *Largo*'s broad opening indication of quaver=72, makes the *Scherzo* into something ambivalent and dogged, a more 'logical' transition to the *Presto* finale than the composer seems to intend. Yevgeny Mravinsky, altogether brisker in that *Scherzo*, attempts to articulate its substance at dotted crochet=144 (the dot missing from my score can reasonably be inferred). Only this comes after a first movement incontrovertibly more fluid than quaver=72.

It's Jurowski who proves the most faithful, almost too dour as the argument gets under way, yet potently conveying the near-paralysis at its heart. The second movement is a fierce whirlwind outpacing even Mravinsky, a gambit that only occasionally sounds like a gabble. Perhaps there have been more exhilarating finales but this one has grace as well as the necessary vulgarity. All in all a remarkable achievement.

Symphony No 1
**Schleswig-Holstein Music Festival Orchestra /
Leonard Bernstein**
Medici Arts 📀 207 2158
(85' · NTSC · 4:3 · PCM stereo and DTS 5.1 · 0)
Recorded live on July 16, 1988   Ⓕ

This ties up nicely – Leonard Bernstein performing Shostakovich's First Symphony, written when he was 19, with an orchestra of young music students at the 1988 Schleswig-Holstein Music Festival. Bernstein was a first-rate Shostakovich interpreter and here's the clearest available insight into his concept of how the pathologically enigmatic Russian composer ticked. The DVD opens with a 40-minute rehearsal in which Bernstein cogently describes Shostakovich's 'naughty boy' attitude – 'would you really want to start your first symphony like this?' he asks his amused orchestra, as he sings the jaunty, deadpan introductory bars.

Shostakovich's First was written only two years into Stalin's dictatorship, but Bernstein is right to locate an emerging, self-defensive satirical approach in these opening bars – if Ian MacDonald's *The New Shostakovich* is to be believed, he didn't think much of Lenin either. His description of how the work gradually fills the dimensions of a 'proper' symphony and arrives, symbolically, at a middle section filled with references to Wagner is persuasive. The complete performance, too, accumulates expressive weight as Bernstein holds the satire of the opening at a distance, letting the material tell its own story, before unlocking the magisterial depth of the symphony's middle section and finale.

This version was cut only a month after his 'official' reading with the Chicago SO. Hearing the two versions together demonstrates that this was Bernstein's settled view. And watching him gently coax his young charges – especially an obviously petrified clarinettist – is unexpectedly touching.

Symphony No 4

Shostakovich Symphony No 4
Britten Russian Funeral
**City of Birmingham Symphony Orchestra /
Sir Simon Rattle**
EMI 555476-2 (68' · DDD)   Ⓕ●

This could just be the most important Western recording of the Fourth since the long-deleted Ormandy and Previn versions. Naturally, it complements rather than replaces Kondrashin's reading (Melodiya), taped shortly after the work's belated unveiling in December 1961. In his recording, Rattle's approach is more obviously calculated, supremely brilliant but just a little cold. A certain firmness and self-confidence is obvious from the first. The restrained Hindemithian episode is relatively square, the first climax superbly built. The second group unfolds seamlessly with the glorious *espressivo* of the strings not much threatened by the not very mysterious intrusions of harp and bass clarinet. Tension builds again, some way into the development, with the lacerating intensity of the strings' *moto perpetuo fugato* passage.

Six miraculously terraced discords herald the two-faced recapitulation. Kondrashin and Järvi (Chandos) find more emotional inevitability in Shostakovich's destabilising tactics hereabouts. Rattle doesn't quite locate a compensating irony, although his closing bars are convincingly icy, with nicely audible gong. Even in Rattle's experienced hands, the finale isn't all plain sailing. The initial quasi-Mahlerian march is underpinned by disappointingly fuzzy timpani strokes which lose the point of their own lopsidedness. But then the section's mock-solemn climax is simply tremendous (and tremendously loud). The incisive *Allegro* is launched with (deliberate?) abruptness at an unbelievably fast tempo and, even if the music doesn't always make sense at this pace, the results are breathtaking. The denouement is approached with real flair. A superbly characterised trombone solo, hushed expectant strings and the most ambiguous of all Shostakovich perorations is unleashed with devastating force. The coda is mightily impressive too.

Rattle does give us a thrilling example of what a relatively objective, thoroughly 'modern' approach has to offer today. With its huge dynamic range and uncompromising, analytical style, EMI's recording pulls no punches, and the awesome precision of the CBSO's playing makes for an unforgettable experience. After this, the Britten encore risks seeming beside the point; this really is emotional play-acting.

Symphony No 4ᵃ. Katarina Izmaylova,
Op 114a – selectionᵃ. Festive Overture, Op 96ᵇ

ᵃ**Philharmonia Orchestra;** ᵇ**London Symphony Orchestra / Gennady Rozhdestvensky**
BBC Legends BBCL4220-2 (74' · ADD)
Recorded live in ᵃ1962, ᵇ1985   Ⓕ●●

A genuine BBC Legend this. We tend to think of Kyrill Kondrashin as the most 'authentic' pioneer of Shostakovich's long-suppressed Fourth Symphony, except that the recordings of this work by Gennady Rozhdestvensky are no less fine. Where Kondrashin offers total commitment and unremitting intensity, Rozhdestvensky proves peculiarly adept at teasing out the score's strange, subversive elements.

Here, giving the work its first hearing outside the Soviet bloc during a large-scale Shostakovich retrospective at the 1962 Edinburgh Festival, Rozhdestvensky conducts with greater urgency than usual, galvanising the Philharmonia into a coruscating display. Small wonder the piece so wowed contemporary critics. The inclusion of an edited and reordered *Katerina Izmaylova* Suite, performed a few days earlier, reminds us that this was also the period in which Shostakovich at last secured official acceptance of his opera *The Lady Macbeth of Mtsensk*, albeit in bowdlerised form. Western commentators were understandably less kind about the Twelfth Symphony which featured on the same programme.

BBC Legends' festive filler is an LSO relay from 1985, dangerously like a non sequitur in this context. It also betrays a more worrying aspect of the Rozhdestvensky phenomenon. While the rendition has more than enough verve and spirit to delight the audience at London's Barbican Hall, you may find it too sloppy for repeated listening. Applause is retained.

Symphony No 5

Symphonies Nos 5 & 9
**Royal Liverpool Philharmonic Orchestra /
Vasily Petrenko**
Naxos 8 572167 (78' · DDD)   Ⓢ●●▶

Petrenko's Fifth is remarkable for the tight discipline and detailed characterisation of musicians plainly on the up. At full cry, the strings seek to emulate the weighty tone of the old Soviet ensembles without quite getting there; the hushed intensity of their *pianissimo* is already quite something. Tempi are broad while eschewing too much point-scoring. The great *Largo* has Leonard Bernstein's breadth without his sometimes intrusive breast-beating. The finale sounds more 'negative' than it did in the 1960s, in part because the sort of fiery, finally hell-for-leather interpretation with which Bernstein and the New York Philharmonic impressed the composer on their groundbreaking Soviet tour took its cue from a misprinted metronome mark. Petrenko drags himself towards the final climax with weary deliberation, transforming what might be construed as an active Soviet archetype into a heavier-footed dirge of dissent.

SHOSTAKOVICH SYMPHONY NO 5 – IN BRIEF

Philadelphia Orchestra / Leopold Stokowski Ⓗ
Dutton CDAX8017 (79' · ADD)   Ⓜ
Stokowski's 1939 world premiere recording continues to thrill to the marrow in its searing intensity and overwhelming emotional clout.

Czech PO / Karel Ančerl
Supraphon SU3699-2 (71' · ADD)   Ⓜ
There's no missing the tingle-factor in this vintage display from Prague. Ančerl's lucid conception has tremendous sweep and ardour, while the playing of the Czech PO is predictably superb.

Concertgebouw Orchestra / Bernard Haitink
Decca 467 478-2GH (76' · DDD)   ⒷⓄ
In sheer sonic splendour, Haitink's 1981 Decca recording has no equals. The performance unfolds in typically noble, unmannered fashion and won't disappoint this maestro's many admirers.

RLPO / Vasily Petrenko
Naxos 8 572167 (78' · DDD)   ⓈⓄⓄ➔
A very impressive contribution to this Liverpool cycle: Petrenko draws some thrilling playing from his orchestra and characterises both works (the coupling is No 9) with terrific flair and imagination. A genuine bargain.

Royal Scottish National Orchestra / Neeme Järvi
Chandos CHAN8650 (76' · DDD)   ⒻⓄ
Interpretatively, Järvi doesn't put a foot wrong. Although the RSNO's hard-working strings are not always absolutely secure, this account replicates the buzz of Järvi's Shostakovich in the concert hall.

New York PO / Leonard Bernstein
Sony SMK66937 (77' · DDD)   Ⓜ
An no-holds-barred performance from Lenny and his beloved New Yorkers, recorded live on tour in Japan during the summer of 1979.

Vienna PO / Mariss Jansons
EMI 556442-2 (71' · DDD)   Ⓕ
Another live recording, this time from January 1997, and Jansons's second recording of the Fifth for EMI. Although not entirely free of self-regarding gesture, it's a painstakingly prepared performance that communicates urgently.

BBC NOW / Mark Wigglesworth
BIS ② BIS-CD973/4 (140' · DDD)   ⒻⓄ
Wigglesworth is nothing if not individual. Often daringly broad and pungently characterised, this Fifth serves up plenty of ear-tickling observation and sumptuous food for thought.

The anti-cathartic treatment, quite orthodox nowadays, will disappoint some listeners.

The five-movement Ninth has sufficient energy and muscle to make it more than a mere divertissement. As seems to be his wont Petrenko takes his time with the second movement, imparting almost too much aching reflectiveness, notwithstanding the loveliness of the playing. This *Moderato*, so-called, is succeeded by a whizzing *Presto*, demonstrating just how far the RLPO's corporate virtuosity has developed in a relatively short time. The finale puts on a cartoonish burst of speed at its pompous apex. Though you may not like this or that effect, the performance as a whole is deft and undeniably persuasive. If things continue like this Petrenko may well prove himself an orchestra builder of distinction in the Koussevitzky mould. Recommended.

Symphony No 5. Chamber Symphony, Op 110*a*
Vienna Philharmonic Orchestra / Mariss Jansons
EMI 556442-2 (71' · DDD)   Ⓕ➔

Jansons exercises tight technical control, imparting rather less in the way of inner character. As usual he goes for maximal rhythmic clarity, smooth *legato* lines and extreme dynamic contrasts. Inevitably, some will feel that the luscious string sound only gets in the way and there are a few agogic touches. Isn't there something unnatural about the shift up a gear in the first-movement development (around 8'00"), the cliff-edge dynamics of the slow movement, the self-conscious pacing of the start of the finale?

More positively, there are some wonderfully sustained *pianissimos* from both strings and winds – try the return of the first movement's second subject (from 12'26"). EMI's recording isn't quite ideal, cavernous and a little occluded in the bass; the presence of an audience is never betrayed, and doesn't seem to have influenced the character of the music-making. The Chamber Symphony is distinguished by its unique atmosphere.

Symphony No 7

Symphonies Nos 1 & 7, 'Leningrad'
Chicago Symphony Orchestra / Leonard Bernstein
DG ② 427 632-2GH2 (120' · DDD)
Recorded live 1988   ⒻⓄⓄ➔

The *Leningrad* Symphony was composed in haste as the Nazis sieged and bombarded the city (in 1941). It caused an immediate sensation, but posterity has been less enthusiastic. What business has the first movement's unrelated long central 'invasion' episode doing in a symphonic movement? Is the material of the finale really distinctive enough for its protracted treatment? Michael Oliver, in his original *Gramophone* review, wrote that in this performance 'the symphony sounds most convincingly like a symphony, and one needing no programme to justify it'. Added to which the work's epic and cinematic manner has surely never been more powerfully realised. These are live recordings, with occasional noise from the audience (and the conductor), but the Chicago Orchestra has rarely sounded more polished or committed. The strings are superb in the First Symphony, full and weightily present, and Bernstein's manner here is comparably bold and theatrical of gesture. A word of caution: set your volume control carefully for the *Leningrad* Symphony's start; it's scored for six of both trumpets and trombones and no other recording has reproduced them so clearly, and to such devastating effect.

Symphony No 7, 'Leningrad'
Cologne Radio Symphony Orchestra /
Rudolf Barshai
Regis RRC1074 (72' · DDD)
Recorded live 1992   ⒷO

It's idle to pretend that the players of Bernstein's Chicago Symphony need look to their laurels. Nor does Barshai feel the need to go for broke (and bombast?) in the Bernstein manner. That said, his first movement is both 'felt' and fluent, the main material presented with convincing elegance and lucidity at a flowing pace. Barshai's slow movement glows with (rather than oozes) compassion, and it's principally in the finale that the conducting doesn't always succeed in disguising the fact that Shostakovich was, of necessity, composing on automatic pilot. Even here, timps are well tuned, and Barshai's diligence is always readily apparent in the detailed phrasing of his strings. The recorded sound has been well managed too, the crystalline textures obtained by the conductor and the attractively spacious acoustic compensating for a relatively constricted dynamic range and limited bass response.

This disc is a clear winner in its price-range. Expect a few fluffs and some audience noise and you won't be disappointed.

Symphony No 8

Shostakovich Symphony No 8
Mozart Symphony No 33 in B flat, K319
Leningrad Philharmonic Orchestra /
Evgeny Mravinsky
BBC Legends ② BBCL4002-2 (82' · ADD)
Recorded live 1960   ⓂO

There was a time when Mravinsky's greatness had to be taken on trust, such was the paucity of his representation in the record catalogues. The situation has been transformed in recent years; hence this version of the Shostakovich has to find its niche in a market-place documenting the orchestra's prowess in the piece from the 1940s to the 1980s. In a variety of different transfers (and at a variety of different pitches) Mravinsky's March 1982 concert performance is widely known. But in 1960, when the orchestra made an epochal visit to these

shores with Rostropovich, Rozhdestvensky and Shostakovich himself in tow, the work had never been heard here and was unavailable on disc. Small wonder the event was such a sensation, with the November 1960 *Gramophone* leading the call for new recordings of the Soviet repertoire played on the tour.

Mravinsky was a conductor in the Karajan mould both in his undemonstrative, albeit politically ratified, exercise of authority and the way in which his interpretations remained broadly consistent from one decade to the next. The authentic timbre of the Leningrad Philharmonic is there for all to hear – the winds tearing into their phrases like scalded cats, the string sound huge and inimitable, dominating the sound stage and yet never fat or complacent. In almost every respect, Mravinsky's London performance lives up to its legendary status, and the sound has been reprocessed to yield excellent results. Unfortunately the listeners in the hall are surprisingly restless. The first movement is patiently built, stoic, even bleaker than usual from this source, and with only minor technical imperfections: the problem is the barrage of coughing. The power and control of the second and third movements are awesome by any standards and here the audience is less intrusive. In the finale, Mravinsky keeps a tight rein on his players, adopting marginally slower tempi and securing finer results than he did in 1982. The climax is cataclysmic with the paying public at last stunned into silence during the magical coda. Shostakovich dedicated the symphony to Mravinsky, and it's for this work that most people will want to acquire the set.

Symphony No 8
London Symphony Orchestra / André Previn
EMI Encore 509024-2 (61' · DDD)   ⒷOO

André Previn's first, 1973 version of the Eighth sneaks back into contention at budget price. More than a decade after Mravinsky introduced what is now perhaps an over-familiar score to London audiences, EMI undertook this, the first commercial recording to be made in the West. It stands up remarkably well. The first and fourth movements are long-breathed, as deeply felt as any, while the reckless tempo of the second *Scherzo* is probably modelled on early US accounts by Koussevitzky and Rodzinski. Rhythmic flair is a hallmark of the LSO's work in this period and the freshness, colour and spontaneity of the playing cannot be gainsaid. One curious oddity comes with the violin solo leading into the finale's mysterious C-D-C coda. The aberrant ascending line there is also to be found in earlier studio sessions by Haitink *et al*.

Gloomy and spiritless it may be at times, yet this is also young man's music, something that rarely comes across in recent, apparently more idiomatic (and, dare one suggest, more boring?) performances. Shostakovich sceptics in particular should give it a listen.

Symphony No 10

Symphony No 10
Berlin Philharmonic Orchestra /
Herbert von Karajan
DG 477 5909GOR (52' · DDD)   Ⓜ️Ⓞ🅑

Few works give a deeper insight into the interior landscape of the Russian soul than Shostakovich's Tenth, and this is a powerful and gripping account of what's, by general consent, his masterpiece. Karajan has the measure of its dramatic sweep and brooding atmosphere, as well as its desolation and sense of tragedy. Haitink's is nowhere near so intense or, for that matter, so well played, though the recording has impressive transparency of detail. There are many things here (the opening of the finale, for example) which are even more succesful than in Karajan's 1966 recording, though the main body of the finale still feels too fast – however, at crotchet=176, it's what the composer asked for. His earlier account of the first movement is for some more moving – particularly the poignant coda. However, the differences aren't significant and this is hardly less impressive. The CD deserves a strong recommendation.

Symphony No 10
London Philharmonic Orchestra / Bernard Haitink
LPO LPO0034 (55' · ADD). Recorded live at the Royal
Albert Hall, London, on August 28, 1986   Ⓜ️Ⓞ

The Tenth has never seemed dependent on performers steeped in the Russian tradition and the only drawback of Haitink's well played, expertly recorded studio account (1977) was its over-confident tone in the enigmatic third movement. Attempts to decode that *Allegretto* have gone through several phases since but it remains desirable to convey a mood of wistfulness and frustrated self-assertion.

There's no lack of subtlety in this 1986 Prom relay which also has the advantage of a true sense of euphoria at the end. The applause is earned, frenzied rather than merely respectful though rather abruptly faded. In other respects little has changed. The inexorability and stoicism of the big opening *Moderato* is predictably impressive and there is no hint of restraint in the *Scherzo* which some, Kurt Sanderling among them, have been prepared to accept as a portrait of Stalin himself.

Whatever the truth of this, Haitink's musical priorities always deliver the goods and his admirers will welcome this unexpected reclamation from the archives of BBC Radio 3. The famously resonant acoustic of the Royal Albert Hall gives us the sound from the bottom up, with great weight in the cellos and basses. The booklet-note by Geoffrey Norris appropriately eschews speculative revisionist comment. Is the Tenth Shostakovich's greatest single achievement? Haitink may make you think so.

Symphony No 11

Symphony No 11, 'The Year 1905'
West German Radio Symphony Orchestra,
Cologne / Semyon Bychkov
Avie 🎙️ AV2062 (59' · DDD/DSD)   ⒻⓄ🅞🅞🅑

Half a century on from its composition and a full century from the events it ostensibly commemorates, the Eleventh Symphony remains a problematic work for conductors, not least because very few of them or their players have direct memories to draw on. Whatever view they take, nothing is going to come across unless the balance between atmosphere and flow is convincingly struck, and in this respect Bychkov has sure instincts.

Now that he has been principal conductor in Cologne for nearly 10 years, it seems that matters of texture, colour and line in Shostakovich have become second nature for his players: Bychkov gives onward momentum its due, and urgency and inevitability are his reward.

Quibbles could be entered. In the second movement, from 12'45" (the scene of the attack of the Tsarist police), the trombone *glissandi* may disappoint those who have heard them given full power. At the heart of the following 'In memoriam' more poignancy would not have gone amiss. But then the climax of that movement is magnificently denunciatory, and the WDR cor anglais laments with eloquence and depth but not a trace of sentimentality. The *attacca* into the finale is ideal in its sudden spit of venom.

Symphony No 11, 'The Year 1905'
Royal Liverpool Philharmonic Orchestra /
Vasily Petrenko
Naxos 8 572082 (58' · DDD)   ⓈⓄ🅑

Vasily Petrenko has galvanised Liverpool music-making to such an extent that his contract was very soon extended, with a fair chance that the Rattle/Birmingham phenomenon will be replicated on Merseyside. That said, who made the decision to start the new series with No 11? This is a piece which, viewed variously as a conformist artefact of socialist realism, a coded indictment of Soviet tyranny, 'a film score without the film' and/or something more complex, tends to divide the composer's admirers. Mstislav Rostropovich was one of its most individualistic interpreters, extending its playing time to more than 72 minutes in his epic 2002 account (see above). Petrenko has no truck with that kind of self-indulgence, if self-indulgence it be, looking instead to the furious 54-minute precedent of Kyrill Kondrashin in 1973. There's never any feeling of ploughing dutifully through the notes at this kind of lick, although the Naxos recording is not quite ideal. Timps and bells could be more sympathetically miked and more carefully pitched, while brass and upper strings lack the extraordinary weight of Rostropovich's LSO. Still, there's no mistaking the rapid transformation of the RLPO's corporate profile, no want of character, attack or rhythmic definition.

Symphony No 13

Symphony No 13, 'Babi Yar'
Sergei Aleksashkin bass **St Petersburg Philharmonic Choir and Orchestra / Yuri Temirkanov**
RCA Red Seal 88697 02163-2 (58' · DDD) ⒻOO

Of the many recent versions of Shostakovich's finest vocal symphony, surprisingly few employ a Russian chorus. And for all that Western choirs can now draw on superb language coaches and emulate the darkness of Slavonic voices, the difference is still decisive. Temirkanov's Petersburg basses speak and speak about their words, unencumbered by the basic need to get them right, and without having to take their expressive cue solely from the conductor. This helps the episodes in the 'Babi Yar' first movement to unfold with an inevitability that few Western recordings can match. Some may even find that the *bel canto* mellifluousness the chorus brings to Yevtushenko's verses compromises the poet's moralising tone, by comparison with the raw passion of performances from nearer the time of composition.

This is Sergei Aleksashkin's fourth CD appearance as soloist in this work, and he has never done it better than here. Apart from his familiar nobility of line, there are many fresh nuances, of a piece with Temirkanov's subtle interpretation. Temirkanov's most conspicuous intervention is to dash through the second movement in record time: pretty disconcerting at first, but he puts across the scalding quality of Shostakovich's take on 'Humour'. And although communicative urgency is again the watchword in the slower surrounding movements, Temirkanov actually finds a happy medium between Kondrashin (conductor of the fraught 1962 premiere) and broader modern accounts. Recording quality is straightforward and well balanced. Overall then, this is the preferred modern studio version.

Symphony No 13, 'Babi Yar'
Marius Rintzler bass **Concertgebouw Orchestra Choir** (male voices); **Concertgebouw Orchestra / Bernard Haitink**
Decca 425 073-2DM (64' · DDD · T/t) ⓂO

With one single reservation Haitink's account of *Babi Yar* is superb. The reservation is that Marius Rintzler, although he has all the necessary blackness and gravity and is in amply sonorous voice, responds to the anger and the irony and the flaming denunciations of Yevtushenko's text with scarcely a trace of the histrionic fervour they cry out for. The excellent chorus, though, is very expressive and it makes up for a lot, as does the powerful and sustained drama of Haitink's direction. He has solved the difficult problems

of pacing a symphony with three slow movements (one is gripped throughout) and the atmosphere of each movement is vividly evoked, with a particular care for the subtleties of Shostakovich's orchestration. The orchestral sound, indeed, is magnificent: one can readily believe that the huge forces called for in the score were actually provided, but this doesn't necessitate any unnatural focusing on (say) the celesta in order that it shall register. The perspective is very natural throughout, and there's an excellent sense of the performance taking place in a believable space.

Additional recommendation

Symphony No 13, 'Babi Yar'
Rootering bass
Netherlands Radio Ch and PO / Wigglesworth
BIS ⊕ BIS-SACD1543 (62' · DDD/DSD) Ⓕ
 Wigglesworth has plenty of ideas about timing and articulation, and they are of a piece with a powerful overall view. This is a performance in which you feel the presence of a lyrical commentator throughout, rather than being in the grip of some overwhelming larger force. Soft-grained but marvellously spacious recording.

Symphony No 14

Symphony No 14.
Two Pieces for String Quartet (arr Sikorski)
Margareta Haverinen sop **Petteri Salomaa** bass
Tapiola Sinfonietta / Joseph Swensen
Ondine ODE845-2 (59' · DDD · T/t) ⒻO

The multilingual version of the Fourteenth Symphony was sanctioned by the composer but it remains a rarity on disc; some vital and specific tone colour is lost along with the original note values, and the 'three lilies' adorn the grave of 'The Suicide' more elegantly in the Russian. Haitink may not agree. He elected to use the multilingual text in his 1980 recording and now Joseph Swensen presents this compelling alternative. We tend to take sonic excellence for granted these days but this is a true state-of-the-art recording with the soloists more naturally placed than in the rival Decca issue and an orchestral sound combining great clarity with just enough hall resonance. The performance has character too, if lacking the pervasive chill of the earliest Soviet accounts. The conductor secures excellent results from the Tapiola Sinfonietta.

Of the soloists, the bass-baritone Petteri Salomaa is particularly impressive: his is a voice of rare tonal beauty, a Billy Budd rather than a Boris. His pronunciation is a little odd at times, but you may not see this as a problem. Tempi are perceptibly more 'extreme' than Haitink's, with the opening 'De profundis' dangerously slow in the modern manner and a strikingly well-characterised instrumental contribution to 'A la Santé' ('In the Santé Prison'). The fillers, larger than life, brilliantly dispatched and curiously inappropriate, are based on original quartet pieces which only came to light in the mid-1980s. The first shares material with *The Lady Macbeth of Mtsensk*; the second appears as the polka from *The Age of Gold*! This is nevertheless a more rewarding, more probingly conducted disc than much of the current Shostakovich crop.

Symphony No 15

Symphonies Nos 1 & 15
**Cincinnati Symphony Orchestra /
Jesús López-Cobos**
Telarc CD80572 (77' · DDD)　　　　　　　(F)

These are extremely well played and cleanly recorded performances, and in a field surprisingly lacking in strong contenders they deserve serious consideration. By dint of careful preparation López-Cobos brings exceptional clarity to the First Symphony, forcing you to admire afresh the sheer inventiveness of the teenage Shostakovich's counterpoint. His Cincinnati players are suave, without ever sounding emotionally complacent, and they seem to appreciate better than most Western orchestras the extraordinary depth of feeling at the heart of the finale. That said, there's little of the bite and sheer recklessness that make Kondrashin's interpretation so special, though sadly that classic version is hampered by poor recording quality, and the Moscow Philharmonic's first oboe in the slow movement is excruciating.

López-Cobos's account of Symphony No 15 lacks a fanatical edge in the fast movements, a sense of mystery in the slow ones and of strangeness throughout, but this Cincinnati version is as good as anything currently available, and certainly better than the over-praised Haitink, Rostropovich or Sanderling. López-Cobos plays the symphony straight and keeps the stylistically competing elements in balance. He negotiates the treacherous finale successfully, building the passacaglia to a properly passionate climax.

The Golden Age, Op 22

The Golden Age
**Royal Stockholm Philharmonic Orchestra /
Gennadi Rozhdestvensky**
Chandos ② CHAN9251/2 (134' · DDD)　　(F)(B)

The ballet *The Golden Age* (1930) depicts an industrial exhibition organised in a capitalist country, at which a group of Soviet sportsmen have been invited to compete. The general idea of the music is to differentiate between goodies and baddies by assigning them respectively healthy-folk and decadent-bourgeois idioms. The trouble was that Shostakovich couldn't stop himself enjoying being decadent.

Not all the 37 movements stand up independently of the stage-action. But the finales and the whole of Act 3 are top-notch stuff, at times surprisingly threatening in tone and symphonic in

continuity; and there are several movements which could undoubtedly be promoted alongside the four in the familiar concert suite (the Tap Dance of Act 2 is especially appealing, for instance). Those who know their Shostakovich will be constantly intrigued by foretastes of *Lady Macbeth*, Symphony No 4 and the *Hamlet* music, and by the appearance of Shostakovich's 'Tea for Two' arrangement as an Interlude in Act 2.

This first complete recording is a major coup for Chandos. Admittedly not even their flattering engineering can disguise a certain lack of confidence and idiomatic flair on the part of the Royal Stockholm Philharmonic Orchestra. But don't let that deter anyone with the least interest in Shostakovich, or ballet music, or Soviet music, or indeed Soviet culture as a whole, from investigating this weird and intermittently wonderful score. A really fascinating disc.

Film Music

Odna, Op 26 – complete film score
Irina Mataeva sop **Anna Kiknadze** mez
Dmitri Voropaev ten **Mark van Tongeren** voc
Barbara Buchholz theremin **Frankfurt University of
Music and Performing Arts Vocal Ensemble;
Frankfurt Radio Symphony Orchestra /
Mark Fitz-Gerald**
Naxos 8 570316 (80' · DDD)　　　　　　(S)(B)

Although long known through various selections, Shostakovich's second film score *Odna* ('Alone') is only now available complete. This 1931 Kozintsev/Trauberg collaboration – in which a young teacher finds herself transferred to the remote Altai region, incurs the wrath of the local peasantry and is left to die in a snowstorm, only to be rescued by a Soviet plane – emerged on the cusp of 'silent' and 'sound' cinema. Lack of suitable venues meant the film received few showings with its soundtrack and, while it received considerable acclaim abroad, it was allowed to fall into obscurity until the 1960s.

Even now, the film – reconstructed after the master was destroyed in wartime Leningrad – is missing its 'snowstorm' reel. Luckily, the score has now been reclaimed in full – due in no small part to Mark Fitz-Gerald, who has assembled it from numerous sources and presented it in live showings around Western Europe. The result is one of Shostakovich's most innovative scores: the ebullience of his early theatre music being combined with music anticipating the emotional intensity of *The Lady Macbeth of Mtsensk*, alongside some of his most startling experiments – with cues for overtone singing and a contribution from the theremin (an early electronic instrument).

The brief vocal items are attractively done, and Fitz-Gerald secures playing of exceptional vitality from the Frankfurt orchestra. Vividly recorded, with a detailed note from Russian film expert John Riley, *Odna* is engrossing and pleasurable in purely musical terms. Those wishing to investigate Shostakovich's film music should start here.

Light Music

'The Dance Album'
Moscow-Cheryomushki, Op 105 – concert suite (ed Cornall). The Bolt – ballet suite, Op 27a (1934 version). The Gadfly, Op 97 – Overture; The Cliff; Youth; Box on the Ear; Barrel Organ; Contredanse; Galop; At the Market Place; The Rout; The Passage of Montanelli; Finale; The Austrians; Gemma's Room
Philadelphia Orchestra / Riccardo Chailly
Decca 452 597-2DH (73' · DDD)   ⓕⓞ�'

Although entitled 'The Dance Album', interestingly only one of the items on this disc (*The Bolt*) is actually derived from music conceived specifically for dance. However, what the disc reveals is that Shostakovich's fondness for dance forms frequently found expression in his other theatrical/film projects.

The world premiere recording of a suite of four episodes from the 1959 operetta *Moscow-Cheryomushki* will be of particular interest to Shostakovich devotees. Despite the somewhat mundane plot, the score produces some surprisingly attractive and entertaining numbers, most notably perhaps the invigorating 'A spin through Moscow' and the 'Waltz'. For the suite from the ballet *The Bolt* Chailly brings us the less frequently heard 1934 version in which the composer dropped two of the eight numbers and changed some of the titles in order to deflect from the story-line of the ballet. Lots of parody and plenty of Shostakovich with his tongue planted firmly in his cheek is what we get, and if this aspect of the composer's output appeals then you'll certainly enjoy Chailly's and his players' spirited and colourfully buoyant performances of this energetic score.

Less familiar light is also shed on the music from the film *The Gadfly* which is heard here in a version which brings together 13 of the score's episodes and preserves Shostakovich's original orchestration, as opposed to the suite prepared and reorchestrated by Levin Atovmyan. All the performances on the disc are superbly delivered and the recorded sound is excellent.

'The Jazz Album'
Jazz Suites Nos 1 & 2. Tahiti Trot, Op 16. Piano Concerto No 1.
ᵃ**Peter Masseurs** tpt ᵃ**Ronald Brautigam** pf
Royal Concertgebouw Orchestra / Riccardo Chailly
Decca 433 702-2DH (59' · DDD)   ⓕⓞⓞ�'

Shostakovich's lively and endearing forays into the popular music of his time were just that, and light years away from the work of real jazz masters such as, say Jelly Roll Morton or Duke Ellington. And yet they do say something significant about Shostakovich's experience of jazz, as a comparison of these colourful, Chaplinesque Jazz Suites with roughly

contemporaneous music by Gershwin, Milhaud, Martinůq, Roussel and others will prove. Shostakovich engaged in a particularly brittle, almost Mahlerian form of parody – his concert works are full of it – and that's what comes across most powerfully here. Besides, and as annotator Elizabeth Wilson rightly observes, 'real' jazz was treated with suspicion in Soviet Russia and Shostakovich's exposure to it was therefore limited.

The two Jazz Suites were composed in the 1930s. The First will make you chuckle, but it's the Second (subtitled 'Suite for Promenade Orchestra') that contains the best music, especially its achingly nostalgic second Waltz. The instrumentation is light (the saxophone and accordion add a touch of spice to a generally bland recipe), while the playing is quite superb. In fact, there's little to be said about Chailly's direction other than that it's good-humoured, affectionate and utterly professional, his Royal Concertgebouw players sound at home in every bar and the recording (Grotezaal, Concertgebouw) is both clean and ambient.

Tahiti Trot came to life when Nikolai Malko challenged Shostakovich to score Vincent Youmans's *Tea for Two* in an hour, or less – which he did, as a sort of mini-concerto for orchestra, each refrain being dealt to different instrumental forces. Fun that it is, its charm is terminal. Which leaves the Piano Concerto, music that for sophistication and inventive ingenuity is actually closer to what we now think of as jazz than the Jazz Suites. (Sample the free-wheeling, improvisatory opening to the last movement, on track 7.)

Ronald Brautigam's instrument is twangy at the bass end, which mightn't seem too inappropriate, but as it was recorded two years before the other items on the disc (1988), I doubt that that was the intention. Still, it's a lively and fairly intense reading, neatly supported by Chailly and trumpeter Peter Masseurs.

Piano Quintet in G minor, Op 57

Piano Quintetᵃ. String Quartets – No 1; No 12
ᵃ**Martin Roscoe** pf **Sorrel Quartet**
(Gina McCormack, Catherine Yates vns Sarah-Jane Bradley va Helen Thatcher vc)
Chandos CHAN10329 (77' · DDD)   ⓕ

Volume 6 of the Sorrel Quartet's Shostakovich series gives us two of his outwardly formulaic works framing one of his most audacious, the Twelfth Quartet. It's a rather peculiar programme, not that this need bother anyone collecting this particular *intégrale*.

The playing is as idiomatic as you might expect from an ensemble once coached by Rostislav Dubinsky, founder member and first leader of the Borodin Quartet. True, the almost casual opening of the First Quartet is not ideally euphonious and, in the first movement of the Twelfth, there's a momentary lapse of concentration from the viola, whose expressive swoops elsewhere may not be to all tastes. What matters more is the palpable, very human sense of engagement, something you don't always get from glitzier groups.

Given that the best recordings of the Piano Quintet are 20 years old and either tucked away or buried altogether, the present account is not unwelcome, though it is relatively small-scale. It's the subtle intimacy of the final pay-off one remembers, the warmth of the Maltings acoustic masking any thinness of tone.

String Quartets

No 1 in C, Op 49 **No 2** in A, Op 68 **No 3** in F, Op 73 **No 4** in D, Op 83 **No 5** in B flat, Op 92 **No 6** in G, Op 101 **No 7** in F sharp minor, Op 108 **No 8** in C minor, Op 110 **No 9** in E flat, Op 117 **No 10** in A flat, Op 118 **No 11** in F minor, Op 122 **No 12** in D flat, Op 133 **No 13** in B flat minor, Op 138 **No 14** in F sharp minor, Op 142 **No 15** in E flat minor, Op 144

String Quartets Nos 1-15. Two Pieces
Emerson Quartet (Eugene Drucker, Philip Setzer vns
Lawrence Dutton va David Finckel vc)
DG ⑤ 475 7407DC5 (6h' · DDD)   Ⓕ❶❷❸❹➔

The Emersons have played Shostakovich all over the world, and this long-
pondered *intégrale* sets the seal on a
process that has brought the quartets to the very
centre of the repertoire – the ensemble's and
ours. While some listeners will miss the intangi-
ble element of emotional specificity and sheer
Russianness that once lurked behind the notes,
the playing is undeniably committed in its coolness, exposing nerve-endings with cruel clarity.
The hard, diamond-like timbre of the two violins (the leader's role is shared democratically) is
far removed from the breadth of tone one might
associate with a David Oistrakh, just as cellist
David Finckel is no Rostropovich. But these
recordings reveal surprising new facets of a body
of work that isn't going to stand still. The
Fourth Quartet is a case in point, more delicate
than most rivals with the finale relatively
pressed, less insistently Jewish. The Fifth sometimes seems closer to Ustvolskaya or American
minimalism than the mid-century Soviet symphonic utterance we're used to; the Emerson's
almost hectoring mode of address and unfluctu-
ating tempo are maintained for as long as
(in)humanly possible. The very vehemence of,
say, the finale of the Ninth tends to blunt the
harmonic sense of the music, leaving something
more visceral and rosiny than the argument can
stand. To get the unique feel of this set, sample
one of the encore pieces, the 'Polka' from *The
Age of Gold*. Little humanity and wit, but can you
resist the explosive brilliance of the technique?

DG's recording is exceptionally vivid if somewhat airless, the separation of the instruments
being achieved at the expense of tonal blend.
Given that all the quartets were taped live with
only remedial patching, the audience is commendably silent: their enthusiastic applause is

retained for Nos 1, 2, 9 and 12 only. This is a Shostakovich cycle for the 21st century.

String Quartets Nos 1-15
Danel Quartet (Marc Danel, Gilles Millet vns Tony
Nys va Guy Danel vc)
Fuga Libera ⑤ FUG512 (6h 16' · DDD)   Ⓑ

This is a remarkable set which sells for less than
£30 in the UK or around $50 in the States. The
recordings, made by Bavarian Radio between
2001 and 2005, are, if anything, classier still,
with equally classy annotations by Shostakovich
scholars Frans Lemaire and David Fanning.
Since fact and speculation are for once carefully
defined, you won't see here the incautious revi-
sionism of so much Shostakovich commentary.

After securing first prize at the 1993 International Dmitri Shostakovich Competition, the
Brussels-based Danel Quartet started their on-
disc explorations with rarities, mainly French and
Belgian, Modernist and Romantic. Meanwhile,
Quartet colleagues have worked with members of
both the Borodin and Beethoven Quartets,
enjoying cordial relations with the composer's
widow, Irina. Fascinating then to find that their
approach is often unlike that of recent exponents.
While many of those groups have brought the
quartets to the very centre of the repertoire, they
have tended to make them into big, declamatory
statements, public property if you will. This
development may have begun gloriously with the
post-Dubinsky, Soviet State-sanctioned Borodin
line-up, but a quartet like the Emerson (see
above) displays a forceful technocratic sensibility
that precludes much sense of four musicians playing together for pleasure.

With consistently sweet sounds, pronounced
yet carefully matched vibrato and lithe, intimately drawn interpretations, the Danel offer
something else again. Though old hands may
take a while to adjust, their Gallic wit and finesse
add a new dimension to familiar music. You're
never hit with anything more visceral and rosiny
than the argument (and the tuning) can stand,
but neither is there is any lack of commitment
and fire. There is, however, some close-miked
sniffing and at times the recorded sound takes
on a wiry quality (especially in No 5). In the
conventional *intégrale* we would certainly rate
them above many bigger names.

Shostakovich String Quartet No 5
Beethoven String Quartet No 10, 'Harp', Op 74
Atrium Quartet (Alexey Naumenko, Anton Ilyunin
vns Dimitri Pitulko va Anna Gorelova vc)
Zig-Zag Territoires ZZT080702 (60' · DDD)   Ⓕ

The Atrium Quartet won first prize in the 2003
London International String Quartet Competition with a gripping account of Shostakovich's
Fifth Quartet – along with the Twelfth, the
most wide ranging and powerfully wrought of
the cycle, though among the least performed.
On their disc, unfazed by its demands, the

Atrium steer a propulsive course through the *Allegro* – easily the most persuasively argued of Shostakovich's sonata-form movements – and effect a suspenseful transition into the *Andante*, whose otherworldliness is underlined by the sparing but varied use of vibrato. Nor does the finale disappoint – its initial animation and violent culmination leading to a coda whose bittersweet oblivion is unerringly captured.

This is undoubtedly the finest recording of the Fifth Quartet to have appeared during recent years and if that of Beethoven's *Harp* Quartet is not of the same stature, then the smouldering pathos and visceral excitement that the Atrium draw from its slow movement and *Scherzo* respectively suggest that the Beethoven quartets are territory hardly less ripe for further exploration. The Atrium's Shostakovich, however, is a performance to treasure. Decently recorded, too.

String Quartets Nos 6 & 11
Jerusalem Quartet (Alexander Pavlovsky, Sergei Bresler *vns* Amichai Grosz *va* Kyril Zlotnikov *vc*)
Harmonia Mundi HMC90 1953 (63' · DDD) Ⓕ❍

The Sixth Quartet is by no means all sweetness and light, yet the Jerusalem are rather too vehement in the first movement development and a touch coy in the ensuing intermezzo. They catch the pathos of the passacaglia third movement to perfection, but the finale is again overwrought. In the Eighth Quartet, the Jerusalem are right not to point up extra-musical associations, but the opening *Largo* is too passive, the *Allegro* too relentless and expressive nuance in the *Allegretto* awkwardly inflected. In the fourth movement they strike the right balance between formal control and expressive candour but the finale fails to clinch the design with real conviction.

It is with the Eleventh Quartet that this disc really comes into its own. A tribute to Vasily Shirinsky (second violin of the Beethoven Quartet), the contrasts between its seven brief movements are less remarkable than the motivic unity evident by the close. A quality fully borne out in a reading that is fully aware of the music's elusive spirit, and wonderfully successful in seeing the work whole. Spacious if neutral sound, and a release that certainly confirms the Jerusalem as one of the most technically assured and tonally responsive quartets of today.

Piano Trios

No 1 in C minor, Op 8 **No 2** in E minor, Op 67

Shostakovich Piano Trios Nos 1 & 2
Schnittke Trio
Vienna Piano Trio (Wolfgang Redik *vn*
Marcus Trefny Stefan Mendl *pf*)
Nimbus NI5572 (69' · DDD) Ⓕ❍

Shostakovich's adolescent First Trio's ramshackle structure seems to matter less than its

surprisingly Gallic-sounding, passionately late-Romantic invention. The Vienna Piano Trio offers a rich-toned and meticulously prepared account. The tricky cello opening to the Second Trio is wonderfully ethereal here, and the even more tricky accumulating tempo over the entire movement is steady and logical, though this and the main tempo for the *Scherzo* are both more reined-in than in the composer's own account (once available on Supraphon). The passacaglia and finale are properly intense and none the worse for being kept within the bounds of euphony, though the ideal performance, yet to be realised on CD, would be one which drained bitterer dregs of sorrow and took excitement closer to the point of hyperventilation.

Schnittke's Trio is more than an interesting makeweight. The String Trio original dates from 1985, the fateful year of the composer's first stroke and a period when he seemed to have a direct line to a kind of other-worldly inspiration. True, the two longish movements occasionally seem at a loss, but overall this is one of Schnittke's most economical and restrained scores, and one of his finest. At every turn the Vienna Piano Trio is sensitive to the character and flow of this haunting music. A fine disc, then – imaginative programming, accomplished performances, and rich, well-balanced recording.

---

24 Preludes and Fugues, Op 87

No 1 in C **No 2** in A minor **No 3** in G **No 4** in E minor **No 5** in D **No 6** in B minor **No 7** in A **No 8** in F sharp minor **No 9** in E **No 10** in C sharp minor **No 11** in B **No 12** in G sharp minor **No 13** in F sharp **No 14** in E flat minor **No 15** in D flat **No 16** in B flat minor **No 17** in A flat **No 18** in F minor **No 19** in E flat **No 20** in C minor **No 21** in B flat **No 22** in G minor **No 23** in F **No 24** in D minor

---

Preludes and Fugues Nos 1-24
Vladimir Ashkenazy *pf*
Decca ② 466 066-2DH2 (142' · DDD) Ⓕ▷

Here's a Shostakovich Preludes and Fugues cycle to be reckoned with. It starts none too promisingly, with (by the highest standards) a rhythmically stiff, tonally lumpy C major Prelude and some overpedalling in the fugue. However, the neo-Baroque figuration of the A minor Prelude and its spiky Fugue, on the other hand, presents his true credentials. On form and well prepared, as here, Ashkenazy remains a formidably fluent pianist, and the clarity and energy he brings to the faster, denser pieces is surpassed only by Richter (Philips). The sound itself is quite 'pingy', with a generous ambience behind it. That serves to heighten the impact of the more demonstrative pieces, but makes it difficult for Ashkenazy to sustain the atmosphere of the more meditative ones. Or maybe he simply doesn't feel the music that way. In the final D minor Fugue (No 24), where you can almost hear Shostakovich's Tenth Symphony being born, Ashkenazy fails to build the texture as mightily as the early stages lead you to expect. Nikolaieva surpasses him here, and in general she reveals both subtler and grander perspectives, especially in her tauter, more drily recorded 1987 Melodiya set. Even so the balance-sheet for Ashkenazy comes out comfortably in the black. For consistency of pianism, straightforward integrity of interpretation and high quality of recording, his set can be warmly recommended.

Preludes and Fugues, Op 87
Alexander Melnikov pf
Harmonia Mundi ③ (includes 📀) HMC90 2019/20
(151' · DDD)
DVD includes interview with Alexander Melnikov and
Andreas Staier   Ⓜ🅞🅑▸

Even Tatiana Nikolaieva, who inspired this work – most generous and warm-hearted of artists – would surely have been the first to salute Alexander Melnikov's superlative achievement. Few pianists have shown themselves so sensitive to music which is the response of a complex visionary to the corrosive banality of Soviet life at the time. Whether terse, playful, enigmatic or profoundly expressive, the Preludes and Fugues are a testimony to Shostakovich's strength in the face of endlessly depressing and undermining circumstances.

Melnikov, who has written his own brilliantly informed notes and who offers a moving interview on an accompanying DVD, responds to all this with an impeccable all-Russian mastery and with a poetic commitment few could equal. Hear him in the delightfully piquant Fifth Prelude, its melody set against thrumming 'guitar strokes', or in the Sixth Fugue where so much is said in a distant murmur, and you are clearly listening to a master pianist. He achieves a marvel of imaginative delicacy in the Seventh Prelude and Fugue where one carillon of bells replies to another, and he is acutely aware of the whimsy behind the dialogue of growling bass and piping treble in No 9. He is more characterful than Richter in the galumphing Fifteenth Prelude with its crazy-paving fugue and his virtuosity in the *moto perpetuo* whirl of No 21 is astonishing. In short, whether Shostakovich's utterance is fiercely driven or mystical and remote, Melnikov's poise in this finely recorded album is unfaltering.

From Jewish Folk Poetry, Op 79

From Jewish Folk Poetry. The New Babylon – suite
(arr Rozhdestvensky)
Tatyana Sharova sop **Ludmila Kuznetsova** mez
Alexei Martynov ten **Russian State Symphony**
Orchestra / Valéry Polyansky
Chandos CHAN9600 (70' · DDD · T/t)   Ⓕ🅞

This recording of Shostakovich's song-cycle *From Jewish Folk Poetry* is first-rate. For a start Polyansky's three vocal soloists are uncommonly well chosen: the light, youthful, slightly

vulnerable soprano, the rich, world-weary mezzo and the ardent but unheroic tenor are ideally suited to the texts Shostakovich cunningly chose to convey his solidarity with mass suffering. Polyansky sets spacious tempi which allow every nuance of that suffering to register, and his orchestra is responsive and idiomatic in colouring. The recording, by Russian engineers, feels almost too good to be true in its excessive warmth; otherwise this version is preferable to the rival Rozhdestvensky on RCA.

Polyansky's choice of the first of Shostakovich's 35 or so film scores makes for a more than welcome coupling. Polyansky offers an admirably idiomatic version of the Suite. He's especially adept at choosing timbres to reflect mood and situation. Even if you don't know the storyline the music was designed to accompany, this performance is so vividly characterised it can hardly fail to engage you.

Songs

Four Verses of Captain Lebyadkin, Op 146[a]. Five
Satires, Op 109[a]. Five Romances, Op 121[a] (all orch
Tishchenko). Suite of Eight Waltzes (from the films
The Gadfly, The Golden Hills, The Human Comedy,
The Return of Maxim, Michurin, Pirogov, The First
Echelon, Unity, 'Song of the Great Rivers'). Preface to
the complete edition of my works and a brief
reflection apropos of this preface, Op 123 (orch
Desyatnikov)[ab].
[a]**Sergei Leiferkus** bar [b]**Moscow State Chamber**
Choir; Russian Philharmonic Orchestra /
Thomas Sanderling
DG 477 6111GH (71' · DDD)   Ⓕ🅑▸

Satire of various hues is the running theme on this disc devoted mainly to songs from Shostakovich's embittered last 15 years. These have been orchestrated with a faultless grasp of the idiom by Boris Tishchenko, the composer's favourite pupil from the early 1960s, and in the case of the self-pillorying *Preface*, by Leonid Desyatnikov (a nice touch on his part to bring in the chorus just to sing the composer's name). In all of these Sergei Leiferkus bends and shapes his voice to the words and to the musical line so as to administer a double dose of causticity, and Sanderling makes the orchestra spit and curse to properly alarming effect. Recording quality is absolutely outstanding.

Cheryomushki

Cheryomushki (Cherry Town)
Olga Zabotkina sop Lidochka **Vladimir Vasilyev** bar
Boris **Marina Khotuntseva** mez Masha **Grigori**
Bortnikov bar Sasha **Svetlana Zhivankova** sop
Lyusya **Vladimir Zemlyanikin** ten Sergei **Marina**
Polbentseva mez Vava **Leningrad Philharmonic**
Orchestra / Nikolai Rabinovich
Film director **Gerbert Rappaport**
Decca 📀 074 3138DH (87' · NTSC · 4:3 · PCM
enhanced mono · 0)   Ⓕ

Like *The Lady Macbeth of Mtsensk* a quarter of a century earlier, Shostakovich's one and only musical was a hit. Other similarities are hard to find. Unlike its bloody predecessor, *Cheryomushki* did not fall from official grace. In fact such was the breadth of esteem it enjoyed that it was reworked as a feature-film in 1963 – four years after its first staging – and broadcast on Soviet television at intervals for the rest of the composer's life. It was even, as Andrew Huth's helpful essay recalls, released in the US, under the title *Song over Moscow*, albeit it to rather less acclaim than in its homeland.

This anodyne little comedy about rehousing (to Moscow's 'Cherry-trees' suburbs) and petty corruption had enormous resonance for Russians in the Khrushchev and Brezhnev eras. Both the musical and the film were brilliantly engineered pieces of socialist realist spin, encouraging good-humoured acceptance of dire social conditions and continued belief in a 'bright future'. There is satire here, but only of the most cautious variety: with a smile, but no teeth.

Of its kind the film is admirably put together, and both audio and video scrub up well in its remastering for DVD. A good deal of innocuous fun is had on the part of the singer-actors, many of whom would have been familiar to Soviet audiences. The squally sopranos and boomy baritones may be an acquired taste, but the direction – both musical and visual – has the sharpness of pacing crucial to the genre.

Yet the film version is in no way a substitute for the musical itself. For one thing, probably little more than a third of the music Shostakovich 'composed' survives the translation of media (though completists should note that he actually added bits for the film as well). For another thing, the re-jigging of the scenario is extensive (but then so it would most likely have been in stage productions). For a full picture of Shostakovich's score we really need also a reissue of the sparky Melodiya LP recording conducted by Grigory Stolyarov. Meanwhile this DVD provides us with a fine document of Soviet culture in the late-Thaw years and some modest entertainment value over and above that.

The Lady Macbeth of Mtsensk, Op 29

The Lady Macbeth of the Mtsensk District
Galina Vishnevskaya *sop* Katerina Izmailova **Nicolai Gedda** *ten* Sergey Dubrovin **Dimiter Petkov** *bass* Boris Izmailov **Werner Krenn** *ten* Zinovy Borisovich Izmailov **Robert Tear** *ten* Russian Peasant **Taru Valjakka** *sop* Aksinya **Martyn Hill** *ten* Teacher **Leonard Mroz** *bass* Priest **Aage Haugland** *bass* Police Sergeant **Birgit Finnila** *mez* Sonyetka **Alexander Malta** *bass* Old Convict **Leslie Fyson** *ten* Milhand, Officer **Steven Emmerson** *bass* Porter **John Noble** *bar* Steward **Colin Appleton** *ten* Coachman, First Foreman **Alan Byers** *bar* Second Foreman **James Lewington** *ten* Third Foreman **Oliver Broome** *bass* Policeman **Edgar Fleet** *ten* Drunken Guest **David Beaven** *bass* Sentry **Lynda Richardson** *mez* Female Convict **Ambrosian Opera Chorus; London**

Philharmonic Orchestra / **Mstislav Rostropovich**
EMI Great Recordings of the Century ③ 567776-2 (155' · ADD · T/t) Ⓜ●Ⓞ↦

Rostropovich's cast has no weak links to it. More importantly, he gives a full-blooded projection of the poignant lyricism that underlies the opera's brutality. Vishnevskaya's portrayal of Katerina is at times a bit too three-dimensional, you might think, especially when the recording, which favours the singers in any case, seems (because of her bright and forceful tone) to place her rather closer to you than the rest of the cast. But there's no doubt in her performance that Katerina is the opera's heroine, not just its focal character, and in any case Gedda's genially rapacious Sergey, Petkov's grippingly acted Boris, Krenn's weedy Zinovy, Mroz's sonorous Priest, and even Valjakka in the tiny role of Aksinya, all refuse to be upstaged.

The 'minor' parts are luxuriously cast from artists who may not have had the advantage of singing their roles on stage but have clearly relished building them into vivid portraits. The close focusing on the voices and the relative distancing of the orchestra into a warmer, more ample acoustic is a bit more noticeable on CD.

The Lady Macbeth of the Mtsensk District
Galina Vishnevskaya *sop* Katerina Izmailova **Nicolai Gedda** *ten* Sergey Dubrovin **Dimiter Petkov** *bass* Boris Izmailov **Werner Krenn** *ten* Zinovy Borisovich Izmailov **Robert Tear** *ten* Russian Peasant **Taru Valjakka** *sop* Aksinya **Martyn Hill** *ten* Teacher **Leonard Mroz** *bass* Priest **Aage Haugland** *bass* Police Sergeant **Birgit Finnila** *mez* Sonyetka **Alexander Malta** *bass* Old Convict **Leslie Fyson** *ten* Milhand, Officer **Steven Emmerson** *bass* Porter **John Noble** *bar* Steward **Colin Appleton** *ten* Coachman, First Foreman **Alan Byers** *bar* Second Foreman **James Lewington** *ten* Third Foreman **Oliver Broome** *bass* Policeman **Edgar Fleet** *ten* Drunken Guest **David Beaven** *bass* Sentry **Lynda Richardson** *mez* Female Convict **Ambrosian Opera Chorus; London Philharmonic Orchestra / Mstislav Rostropovich** *Film director* **Petr Weigl**
Carlton Entertainment 📀 ID5655CLDVD (100' · Region 1) Ⓕ●

Petr Weigl returns to form with this remarkable realisation of Shostakovich's scarifying drama. Filming in his native Czech Republic, as usual with actors lip-synching singers, he nevertheless brings its nasty and brutish setting to vivid life. Only the Siberian trek looks a little milder than traditional depictions, but it's accurate enough. The atmospheric photography of the Izmailov farm's barren, lamplit rooms and bathhouse adds a *verismo* dimension to the music's quasi-expressionist force. You really feel a place like this would breed adultery and impulsive murder. The soundtrack is the classic Rostropovich recording (reviewed above).

Its splendid pace and vivid playing suit the film, as do its lively effects, though it's substantially cut. The generally excellent actors do their best with the limitations of lip-sync, no doubt assisted by Czech's kinship with Russian. The Katerina is youngish, nervy and intense, tragically ripe pickings for Sergey's – and indeed her own – passion, but Vishnevskaya's maturely resonant dramatic soprano sits uneasily on her. The Sergey melds better with Gedda's bright tones to suggest the ruthless predator beneath the boyish charm, and Aksinya, old Izmailov and the Old Convict are splendidly portrayed.

The studio acoustic is too evident to make the outdoor scenes convincing. But they achieve their effect through the music none the less. Highly recommended.

The Lady Macbeth of the Mtsensk District
Eva-Maria Westbroek sop Katerina Izmailova
Christopher Ventris ten Sergey **Vladimir Vaneev** bass Boris Izmailov **Ludovít Ludha** ten Zinovy Izmailov **Alexander Kravets** ten Shabby Peasant **Carole Wilson** sop Aksinya, Female Convict **Valentin Jar** ten Teacher **Alexandre Vassiliev** bass Priest, Old Convict **Nikita Storojev** bar Police Sergeant **Lani Poulson** contr Sonyetka **Harry Teeuwen** bar Millhand
Netherlands Opera Chorus; Royal Concertgebouw Orchestra, Amsterdam / Mariss Jansons
Stage director **Martin Kušej**
Opus Arte ⒻⓋ **DVD** OA0965D (3h 56' · NTSC · 16:9 · PCM stereo and DTS 5.1 · 0)
Recorded live at Het Muziektheater, Amsterdam, in June 2006
Extra features include 'The Tragedy of Katerina Izmailova' – a documentary film by Reiner E Moritz, Illustrated Synopsis and Cast Gallery

Katerina Izmailova
Galina Vishnevskaya sop Katerina Izmailova
V Tretyak ten Sergey **Alexander Vedernikov** bass Boris Izmailov **V Radziyevsky** ten Zinovy Izmailov **S Strezhnev** ten Shabby Peasant **V Reka** contr Sonyetka
Kiev Opera Chorus and Orchestra / Konstantin Simeonov
Film director **Mikhail Shapiro**
Decca Ⓕ **DVD** 074 3137DH
(112' · NTSC · 2.35:1 · PCM mono · 0)
Filmed in 1966. Extra features include excerpts from 'Cheryomushki' and 'Shostakovich Against Stalin', and Shostakovich Chronology

Shostakovich's operatic masterpiece is notoriously problematic to stage, especially if directors go back to the 1932 score and try to present the action realistically, as these days they almost all seem hell-bent on doing. In fact a whole book has been written (in Russian) about the absurdities that result, with suggestions offered for combining all three principal versions (the 1935 first published score was already substantially different from the original).

For Netherlands Opera, Martin Kušej comes up with at least one effective ploy, which is to show the seduction scene through stroboscopic lighting. That really does solve a problem and add theatrical frisson, all in one go. Otherwise he produces a dreary, concept-driven, vaguely

updated mish-mash. His declared aim is to present 'the entire complex of Eros and sexuality when it is put under pressure from power and dependency structures', as if that theme is not already blindingly and deafeningly obvious. This he does through indulging an apparent obsession with underpants (even the police station scene features them) and by adding absurdities of his own, such as having the Shabby Peasant drag Zinovy's body to the police and telling them that said body is in the Izmailovs' cellar, while we can all see it on his back. Worst of all, having Katerina ultimately lynched by her fellow convicts destroys the glimmer of compassion that is essential to the final scene, as well as making another mockery of the sung text.

There is some good singing and Jansons obtains classy orchestral playing. Visually the casting is poor. The 'documentary film' is nothing more than a tedious retelling of the story through paraphrases from the director and his principal singers, intercut with illustrations from the production.

Mikhail Shapiro's 1966 film uses a cut version of Shostakovich's heavily revised score, prepared over several years but only finalised in 1963 and generally known as *Katerina Izmailova*. This excises the adult-rating sex and violence but otherwise has far more to be said in its favour than most people are inclined to these days. In its own early Brezhnev-era terms, the film itself is really rather fine. Vishnevskaya sings passionately, if unsubtly, and also acts well (her reminiscences of the whole filming process in her autobiography, *Galina*, make for compelling reading). For all the other roles the singing and acting are split, but in every case with superb results. Konstantin Simeonov paces the score with an acuity that many other conductors, including Jansons, could learn from.

Even given the extra cuts that reduce the opera to feature-film length, and the painfully close miking of Vishnevskaya's in any case somewhat raucous voice, the sense of dramatic truthfulness is more overwhelming than in any staging with the exception of David Pountney's at English National Opera. Oh, for a DVD of that...

Jean Sibelius   Finnish 1865-1957

To most people Sibelius is the composer of Finlandia and the Karelia Suite; to others he is one of the great symphony composers; to the people of Finland he is these things and a national hero. While he was still alive the Finnish government issued stamps with his portrait and would have erected a statue to him as well had not Sibelius himself discouraged the project. Probably no composer in history has meant so much to his native country as did Sibelius. He still does. 'He is Finland in music; and he is Finnish music,' observed one critic.

Sibelius was born in a small town in south central Finland, the son of a regimental doctor who died during the cholera epidemic of 1867-68, and was brought up by his mother and grandmother. (He adopted the name Jean after coming across a set of visiting cards used by his sea-faring uncle who had gallicised his name from Johan to Jean.)

The usual early music lessons (piano and violin were his chosen instruments) led to his first composition effort aged 10, followed by a series of juvenilia, influenced by the likes of Mozart and Grieg. The law drew him briefly at Helsinki University but music quickly took over. Busoni was on the staff of the Music Academy and a lifelong friendship developed between the two. In 1889 Sibelius went off to Berlin for further study, then to Vienna as a pupil of Karl Goldmark. On his return to Finland in 1891 he produced his first major composition, the Kullervo Symphony, based on an episode from the great Finnish epic poem Kalevala. Overnight, this ambitious score established him as the country's most important composer.

Finnish mythology had a profound effect on him and he formed the ideal of creating music that resonated with these ancient legends and so reflected the spirit and unique culture of his people and country. Works like En saga, The Swan of Tuonela and his First Symphony had a tremendous impact. Above all, it was Finlandia, an overtly patriotic orchestral work, that identified him with the growing nationalist movement.

A grant from the enlightened Finnish Senate enabled him to give up all other work so that he could concentrate entirely on composing. This was not enough to keep him out of debt and he and his wife (Aino Järnefelt, whom he'd married in 1892) were beset with money worries all through the 1890s to the end of the First World War. Ironically, he sold one of his most popular compositions, the little salon Valse triste, to his publishers for 300 marks – it made them a fortune. He was also a heavy drinker with a fondness for beer and cognac as well as fine cigars, none of which helped his problems. In 1901 a disease of the ear threatened to make him totally deaf – it was successfully treated – but seven years later he had to undergo 13 throat operations to remove a malignant growth, at first diagnosed as cancer. His music during this period (including the Valse triste and the melancholy Fourth Symphony) reflected his morbid frame of mind at the time.

By the outbreak of the First World War, honours were being heaped upon him as he travelled all over Europe and even to America to conduct his music. The war not only cut off his foreign visits and royalties but heralded the complete stop to all creative activity. Apart from some trivial piano music, only the Fifth Symphony was composed during the conflict, completed in time for his 50th birthday celebrations. Finland proclaimed its independence after the October Revolution and was plunged into a civil war after a coup d'état by the Red Guards. Sibelius's brother was murdered and he himself was forced to flee the Villa Ainola, which since 1904 had been his home in Järvenpää, to the north of Helsinki.

After the war he composed his Sixth and Seventh Symphonies, the symphonic poem Tapiola and the incidental music to a production of The Tempest. He travelled, he toured, he conducted, but his last known work was completed in 1929. After that, all was silence. Rossini amused himself in his old age by

writing little jeux d'esprits; for the last 31 years of his life Sibelius didn't put pen to paper. He was 91 when he died of a cerebral haemorrhage.

Violin Concerto in D minor, Op 47

Violin Concerto (original 1903-04 version and final 1905 version)
Leonidas Kavakos *vn*
Lahti Symphony Orchestra / Osmo Vänskä
BIS BIS-CD500 (75' · DDD)

It's difficult to conceive of a masterpiece in any other form than it is. The impression the listener receives from Sibelius's Fifth Symphony – or *The Rite of Spring* or *La mer* – must convey what Schoenberg called the illusion of spontaneous vision. It's as if the artist had caught a glimpse of something that's been going on all the time, and has stretched out and effortlessly captured it. One of Sibelius's letters written to his friend Axel Carpelan in the autumn of 1914 puts it perfectly: 'God opens his door for a moment, and his orchestra is playing Sym 5'. But life isn't like that, and Sibelius worked for seven years (1912-19) before the Fifth Symphony reached its final form. He was nothing if not self-critical, and a number of his works underwent their birth pangs in public. The main theme of the Violin Concerto came to him much earlier than 1903, and he recognised it for what it was, an inspired idea which remained unchanged. After its first performance in Helsinki in 1904 Sibelius decided to overhaul it. He realised the necessity to purify it, to remove unnecessary detail that impedes the realisation of a cogent structure. In its finished form, it was given in Berlin with Karl Halir as soloist and Richard Strauss conducting.

Listening to Sibelius's first thoughts played with great virtuosity and excellent taste by Leonidas Kavakos and the superb Lahti orchestra is an absorbing experience. Although it's a great pity that many interesting details had to go, there's no doubt that the movement gains structural coherence. The fewest changes are in the slow movement, which remains at the same length. As in the case of the Fifth Symphony, where the revision is far more extensive than it is here, the finished work tells us a great deal about the quality of Sibelius's artistic judgement, which is what makes him such a great composer.

This disc offers an invaluable insight ino the workings of Sibelius's mind. Kavakos and the Lahti orchestra play splendidly throughout, and the familiar concerto which was struggling to get out of the 1903-04 version emerges equally safely in their hands. Invaluable.

Sibelius Violin Concerto
Tchaikovsky Violin Concerto in D, Op 35
Kyung-Wha Chung *vn* **London Symphony Orchestra / André Previn**

SIBELIUS VIOLIN CONCERTO – IN BRIEF

Ginette Neveu; Philharmonia Orchestra / Walter Susskind
Dutton CDEA5016 (71' · ADD) Ⓢ ⭕⭕
Among the pantheon of great fiddlers who have recorded Sibelius's Concerto, the tragically short-lived Ginette Neveu continues to occupy a special place of honour.

Jascha Heifetz; Chicago SO / Walter Haendl Ⓗ
RCA 09026 61744-2 (69' · ADD) Ⓜ⭕
As jaw-droppingly brilliant a display as you would expect from this giant of the violin. Heifetz's pioneering 1935 mono recording with Beecham is also definitely worth seeking out.

David Oistrakh; Stockholm PO / Sixten Ehrling
Testament SBT1032 (75' · ADD) Ⓜ
The composer himself professed admiration for Oistrakh's wonderfully poised and serene interpretation. Sibelians and violin fanciers alike needn't hesitate.

Salvatore Accardo; London SO / Sir Colin Davis
Philips ② 446 160-2PM2 (146' · ADD) Ⓜ
Accardo plays with great taste and assurance. Part of an all-Sibelius twofer which includes Sir Colin Davis's magnificent Boston accounts of Symphonies Nos 3, 6 and 7.

Kyung-Wha Chung; London SO / André Previn
Decca download 477 7734DOR (66' · ADD) Ⓜ⭕🅳➔
Chung was at the outset of her career when she set down this touching, spontaneous-sounding recording, which is balanced to perfection by Decca's Kenneth Wilkinson.

Cho-Liang Lin; Philharmonia Orchestra / Esa-Pekka Salonen
Sony 07464 44548-2 (65' · DDD) Ⓜ⭕⭕
Lin's immaculate, silk-spun version is second to none, and Salonen conducts with great sympathy both here and in the Nielsen Concerto which acts as a coupling.

Sergey Khachatryan; Sinfonia Varsovia / Emmanuel Krivine
Naïve V4959 (70' · DDD) Ⓕ
Armenian Sergey Khachatryan was just 15 when, in 2000, he became the youngest ever winner of the Sibelius Competition. He's already an exceptionally gifted musician, and this, his debut concerto recording, has to be be heard.

Lisa Batiashvili; Finnish Radio Symphony Orchestra / Jukka Pekka Saraste
Sony Classical 88697 12936-2 (57' · DDD) Ⓕ🅳➔
Enterprisingly coupled with Lindberg's new concerto, here's a Sibelius that emphasises the work's dreamier qualities, elegantly done.

Decca download 475 7734DOR (66' · ADD)   Ⓕ🅞🅳➔

If the vital test for a recording is that a performance should establish itself as a genuine one, not a mere studio run-through, Chung's remains a disc where both works leap out at you for their concentration and vitality, not just through the soloist's weight and gravity, expressed as though spontaneously, but through the playing of the LSO under Previn at a vintage period. The great melodies of the first two movements of the Sibelius are given an inner heartfelt intensity rarely matched, and with the finale skirting danger with thrilling abandon.

Chung's later Montreal version of the Tchaikovsky (also Decca) is rather fuller-toned with the tiny statutory cuts restored in the finale. Yet the very hint of vulnerability amid daring, a key element in Chung's magnetic, volatile personality, here adds an extra sense of spontaneity. This remains breathtaking playing, and the central slow movement, made to flow without a hint of sentimentality, has an extra poignancy. The Kingsway Hall sound, full and sharply focused, gives a sense of presence to match or outshine today's digital recordings.

Violin Concerto[a]. Symphony No 2[b]   Ⓗ
[a]Ginette Neveu vn **[a]Philharmonia Orchestra / Walter Susskind; [b]New York Philharmonic Symphony Orchestra / Sir John Barbirolli**
Dutton mono CDBP9733 (71' · ADD)
Recorded 1940-46   Ⓢ⭕⭕

In Ginette Neveu's fêted account of Sibelius's Violin Concerto, the strength, passion and stamina of the solo playing is particularly admirable, though Walter Susskind's Philharmonia accompaniment is rather foursquare, especially in the finale. Heifetz and Beecham triumph every time. Still, EMI's famous recording is a fine memento of a fiery interpretation, and the solo line comes across with miraculous immediacy in this Dutton transfer – better, in fact, than the orchestra, which tends to retreat under a veil whenever the music quietens.

Barbirolli's impulsive New York recording of the Second Symphony burns bright and fast, but there are countless minor imprecisions that may irritate on repetition. A handful of slow but distant swishes suggests that Dutton's generally excellent refurbishment might have been based on an early LP transfer.

Symphonies

No 1 in E minor, Op 39 **No 2** in D, Op 43 **No 3** in C, Op 52 **No 4** in A minor, Op 63 **No 5** in E flat, Op 82 **No 6** in D minor, Op 104 **No 7** in C, Op 105

Symphonies Nos 1-7. The Oceanides. Kuolema – Scene with Cranes. Nightride and Sunrise[a]
City of Birmingham Symphony Orchestra, [a]Philharmonia Orchestra / Sir Simon Rattle

EMI ⑤ 764118-2 (267' · DDD) Ⓜ︎Ⓞ︎➔

Simon Rattle's reissued Sibelius cycle is now accommodated on four mid-price CDs (as opposed to five full-price ones), losing among the fill-ups only Kennedy's well-played account of the Concerto. The first movement of Symphony No 1 is impressive; its epic quality is splendidly conveyed. You may be less taken with the slow movement: the rather mannered closing bars, not particularly acceptable in the concert hall, are distinctly worrying on disc. The measured tempo of the *Scherzo* is also a problem: it's slower than the metronome marking and the movement lacks fire. However, *The Oceanides* is the finest on disc. In the Second Symphony, Rattle's first movement is again on the slow side and the Trio section of the *Scherzo* is pulled about. The Fourth and Seventh find him at his finest and the magnificent EMI recording is very richly detailed and well defined. The Fourth distils a powerful atmosphere in its opening pages; one is completely transported to its dark landscape with its seemingly limitless horizons. Only Beecham has surpassed Rattle in the slow movement.

Rattle's version of the Sixth is still among the best around, with tremendous grip and concentration. In both the Third and the Fifth he's equally impressive, although his handling of the celebrated transition in the first movement of the Fifth in his Philharmonia version is preferable (reviewed further on).

However, the inducement of *The Oceanides*, *Nightride and Sunrise* and an evocative account of the 'Scene with Cranes' from *Kuolema* tips the scales in Rattle's favour.

Symphonies Nos 1-7
Philharmonia Orchestra / Vladimir Ashkenazy
Double Decca ② 455 402-2DF2 &
② 455 405-2DF2 (144' & 150' · ADD/DDD)
Recorded 1980-86 Ⓜ︎Ⓞ︎Ⓞ︎

Of all the cycles of Sibelius's symphonies recorded in recent years this is one of the most consistently successful. Ashkenazy so well understands the thought processes that lie behind Sibelius's symphonic composition just as he's aware, and makes us aware, of the development between the Second and Third Symphonies. His attention to tempo is particularly acute and invariably he strikes just the right balance between romantic languor and urgency. The Philharmonia plays for all it's worth and possesses a fine body of sound. The recordings are remarkably consistent in quality and effectively complement the composer's original sound world.

Symphony Nos 1 & 7
Helsinki Philharmonic Orchestra / Leif Segerstam
Ondine ODE1007-2 (59' · DDD) Ⓕ︎Ⓞ︎

This is an issue to rank alongside Segerstam's outstanding Helsinki PO coupling of the *Leg-*

ends and *Tapiola* in its pungent character and recreative spark. Segerstam's Seventh is well paced and keenly phrased, hitting real heights in the darkly boiling maelstrom beginning at 13 bars before fig L (9'53") and awe-inspiring culmination at fig Z (18'06"). His orchestra responds with zest and no mean poise. In fact, despite what sounds suspiciously like an edit at 15'50", this Seventh is one of the most imposing and highly charged of recent years. Bracing drama and a bold emotional scope are the keynotes to Segerstam's deeply pondered reading of the First Symphony. Assisted by alert and enthusiastic playing from his Helsinki band, he uncovers much illuminating detail within Sibelius' meticulous canvas, yet seldom to the detriment of the grander scheme. You may not agree with every interpretative decision, but Segerstam never sells the music short, revelling in its passion and often daring originality (sample the untamed fury of the *Allegro molto* material in the finale – nature red in tooth and claw). If Segerstam's strikingly pliable account lacks the thrust of, say, Vänskä's exhilarating Lahti SO performance, his Helsinki strings generate greater lyrical breadth.

True, the recording is very good rather than exceptional, but Segerstam is never dull and makes you listen.

Symphonies Nos 1 & 3[a]
Hallé Orchestra / Mark Elder
Hallé CDHLL7514 (69' · DDD) Ⓟ︎Ⓞ︎➔
[a]Recorded live 2007

The rhetorical thrust Sibelius inherited from the music of Tchaikovsky is downplayed in Sir Mark Elder's studio recording of the First Symphony so as to expose those compositional details which make the invention inescapably Sibelian. Throughout Elder looks for significant detail, heightening string sawings more often viewed as accompanimental and even reintroducing touches of *portamento* redolent of the Barbirolli era. He seems fascinated by the way Sibelius can make his music appear to move at different speeds at different levels of an orchestral texture. What's missing is the adrenalin rush of a speed merchant like Anthony Collins or the über-Romantic throb of Leonard Bernstein.

With the Third Symphony (taped live) Elder is on firmer ground. Sibelius seems to have intended to give the music a self-consciously cool attitude anticipating that defined in 1920 by his friend Ferruccio Busoni as *Junge Klassizität* or the 'New Classicality'. Its freshness has a studied air but who's to say it shouldn't have? The overall pacing is spacious with the finale fusing its various sections into a convincing proto-minimalist chug.

The back inlay quotes the claim by an unnamed *Guardian* critic (actually Tim Ashley) that the Hallé sound captures the composer's 'quintessential mix of frost and fire better than any other UK orchestra'. That may be pushing it. Still this is a thought-provoking pairing, finely recorded.

Symphonies Nos 1 & 4
London Symphony Orchestra / Sir Colin Davis
LSO Live 🅢 LSO0601 (78' · DDD/DSD)
Recorded live 2006 & 2008   ⒷＯ➳

Sir Colin Davis and the LSO pair the First and
Fourth Symphonies as once they did for RCA.
Davis cleaves to the heavier sound and interpretative subjectivity of an earlier age, fiercely
engaged and, to some, a tad over-dressed. The
First is archetypal latter-day Davis, vehemently
alive and unafraid to slam on the brakes in the
interests of heightened expressivity. Sir Colin's
third commercial recording of this work is taken
from live concerts, with the maestro caught
humming along to the second movement's languishing Tchaikovskian melody.

The Fourth is even more impressive in its
muscular directness, contemplating barren
wastelands without the sugar-coating of Romanticism. Sir Colin's slow movement redefines
slow, here with an awesome Brucknerian weight
and dignity. His finale solves the dilemma posed
by Sibelius's ambiguous request for *glocken* by
doubling up on glockenspiel and tubular bells,
an unusual effect that will catch the ears of
ardent Sibelians. Davis's Boston version of No 4
for Philips was always highly regarded and,
although LSO Live's SACD encoding cannot
transform the impactful if rather shallow sound
stage of the orchestra's home base, this second
remake preserves an extraordinary evening.
There are full notes as throughout what has
been a distinguished series, well worth its modest asking price.

Symphony No 2ª. Pohjola's Daughterᵇ
London Symphony Orchestra / Sir Colin Davis
LSO Live 🅢 LSO0605 (59' · DDD/DSD)
Recorded live 2005/06   ⓂＯＯ➳

What Sir Colin Davis has to say about Sibelius's
Second Symphony hasn't changed in substance
since his first recording with the Boston Symphony (Philips), but the paragraphs now flow
with ever more assured cadences. The life-and-
death struggle of the second movement is
underlined by two alternating tempi which
Davis has not contrasted so dramatically before.
Strong rhythmic underpinnings in the *Scherzo*,
the highly contrasted Trio and their eventual
assimilation into the mighty onrush towards the
finale: these all have a distinctively Beethovenian
cast. The finale's jubilations justify their length
and splendour, just about, with some generous
portamento and care over the recitatives of the
central, quieter section.

Pohjola's Daughter is an unusual but logical
coupling, having its origins in the same Italian
trip that brought the birth pangs of the Second
Symphony. The tone-poem only saw the light
five years after the symphony, however, and you
could see it as the Yin to the finale's Yang, moving from the interrupted sonata-form processes
of the symphony's first movement into still
darker regions of creative despair – the Fourth

Symphony looms on the horizon. You can sense
this in Davis's conception, which prizes coherence over local colour.

Symphonies Nos 2 & 3
Lahti Symphony Orchestra / Osmo Vänskä
BIS BIS-CD862 (76' · DDD)   ⒻＢ➳

The first issue in the Sibelius cycle by Osmo
Vänskä and the Lahti orchestra (Symphonies
Nos 1 and 4) made a strong impression. Indeed
it holds its own against the most exalted competition. The present set doesn't disappoint either:
these artists are right inside this music.

First, the Second Symphony where competition is stiffest, with Karajan, Barbirolli and
Colin Davis leading a field that includes Szell
(Philips), Kletzki (EMI) and Ormandy (Sony).
Admittedly it would have been preferable if
Vänskä had set a slightly brisker tempo at the
very opening, though he's not alone in the pace
he adopts. Karajan and Sir Colin are equally
measured. Kajanus took 8'14" over this movement and Sibelius's first biographer, the scholar-
critic Erik Furuhjelm, records that the composer took it even faster! Perhaps the briskest of
all modern performances is Neeme Järvi and the
Gothenburg Symphony Orchestra. Vänskä's
reading is both powerfully wrought and well
thought-out though there are some self-
conscious touches. He pulls back a little too
much at the *tranquillo* marking in the first movement (track 1, 4'31"), of which one becomes too
aware. Elsewhere he makes one think afresh
about the score. The F sharp major tune on the
strings in the slow movement marked *ppp* is
played as a barely audible whisper (track 2,
4'40") and so exaggerated does it seem that the
wind four bars later sound (and are) much louder
than the marked *pianissimo*. But these are minor
matters in a performance marked by feeling and
eloquence.

It's good to see the Third Symphony doing so
well on record. Vänskä sets the right tempo for
the first movement and gets the right atmosphere. The opening bars do not build up as
powerfully as they do in the hands of the LSO
and Sir Colin, and it's possible to feel a certain
want of momentum in the slow movement by
their side and in comparison with Kajanus's
pioneering set. On the whole, however, this is a
very good performance, well paced and full of
perceptive touches. The sound is excellent and,
exceptionally wide-ranging.

Symphonies Nos 2ª & 5ᵇ
ª**Royal Philharmonic Orchestra;**
ᵇ**Hallé Orchestra / Sir John Barbirolli**
Testament SBT1418 (77' · ADD)
ᵇRecorded live at the Royal Albert Hall, London, on
August 9, 1968   ⒻＯＯ

In the pantheon of essential Sibelius recordings,
Barbirolli's October 1962 account of the Second
Symphony with the RPO deservedly occupies a

place of honour. Recorded at Walthamstow for Reader's Digest with Charles Gerhardt producing and Decca's legendary Kenneth Wilkinson as balance engineer, it finds Sir John at his inspirational best in a reading which marries outsize but never wilful temperament to edge-of-seat spontaneity and keen poetic instinct. The experience is very much akin to attending a live concert of one's dreams.

The deceptively tricky slow movement is particularly remarkable for its daring flexibility of pulse and line yet never threatens to run aground, while the stirring finale (its big string tune so fervently sung both times round) will have you on your feet long before the end. If you haven't yet made this famous performance's acquaintance, don't hesitate for an instant.

The coupling is a Fifth Symphony with Barbirolli's beloved Hallé from the 1968 Proms which, in strength of personality and palpable depth of feeling, has a lot going for it. As on this team's 1966 EMI recording, the opening pages have exactly the right sense of awe-struck wonder and pregnant growth, and in the second movement it's a joy to hear Sibelius's delicious *pizzicato* writing "speak" with such clarity and eloquence. The first half of the finale has vitality and atmosphere in abundance, but you might crave a greater nobility of utterance in the towering epilogue. A commendably unbronchial audience roars its approval. Despite any minor quibbles, JB's many fans should be well pleased that Testament has salvaged such a typically vibrant display from the BBC vaults.

Symphonies Nos 4 & 7. Kuolema – Valse triste
Berlin Philharmonic Orchestra /
Herbert von Karajan
DG Galleria 439 527-2GGA-(66' · ADD)
Recorded 1965-67 　　　　　　　　Ⓜ◐◑▷

Karajan recorded the Fourth Symphony three times, once in the 1950s with the Philharmonia and twice with the Berlin Philharmonic. The work obviously meant a great deal to him. He insisted on its inclusion in his very first concert on his appointment at the Berlin Philharmonic in the mid-1950s at a time when Sibelius's cause had few champions in Germany, so keen was he to stake its claim as one of the great symphonies of the day. Karajan's account has withstood the test of time as one of the most searching, profound and concentrated performances of this masterpiece, and its reappearance at mid-price was very welcome. The Seventh is finer than his earlier Philharmonia version but doesn't enjoy quite the same classic status. Karajan's *Valse triste* is wonderfully seductive. Indispensable!

Symphonies Nos 4 & 7ª.　　　　　　　　Ⓗ
Pelleas and Melisande, Op 46. Swanwhite, Op 54.
The Tempest – Dance of the Nymphs. Tapiola, Op 112
Royal Philharmonic Orchestra /
Sir Thomas Beecham

BBC Legends/IMG Artists ② BBCL4041-2 (139' · ADD)
Recorded live ª1954, 1955. Includes Beecham on
Sibelius, broadcast 1955　　　　　　　Ⓜ◐

In a broadcast concert to mark Sibelius's 90th birthday on December 8, 1955, the RPO under Sir Thomas Beecham (one of his doughtiest champions) played to a capacity Royal Festival Hall. The inclusion here of the British and Finnish national anthems, both stirringly done, recreates the necessary sense of occasion. In the delightful, too rarely encountered *Swanwhite* suite, from which Beecham omits the powerfully sombre fifth movement ('The Prince alone'), one may at first miss his characteristic concentration and charisma, but his leisurely, affectionate rendering grows on one. Orchestral discipline takes a dip with the Fourth Symphony, but far more disconcerting is the all-pervading air of loose-limbed impatience: the opening *Tempo molto moderato, quasi adagio* is wayward and fussy. There are glimpses of greatness in the third movement, as well as some effective dynamic emendations in the finale, but overall it's a curiously uninvolving display.

Only in the concert's second half does this legendary partnership really begin to show what it's capable of. The *Pelleas* suite distils a poetic enchantment (try the ineffably touching 'Melisande') and tingling sense of atmosphere that not only make you forget about the maddeningly bronchial audience, but also act as a timely reminder that these artists' glorious studio recording dates from exactly the same period (EMI – unavailable at present). *Tapiola* is even finer, a performance of giant authority, devastating emotional candour and towering humanity – indeed Beecham's most powerful *Tapiola* currently available. As an encore, the fetching 'Dance of the Nymphs' from *The Tempest* is delectably done. As a substantial bonus there's a radiantly moving Sibelius Seventh from the 1954 Proms, and a personable, at times entertainingly scatty talk on Sibelius and his music by the inimitable maestro recorded for the BBC's Third Programme two weeks before that 90th-birthday concert. A mandatory purchase for the frequently spellbinding contents of disc 2 alone.

Symphony No 5 (original 1915 version).
En saga (original 1892 version)
Lahti Symphony Orchestra / Osmo Vänskä
BIS BISCD800 (58' · DDD)　　　　　　Ⓕ◐◐◐

Every so often a CD appears which, by means of some interpretative insight, changes our view of a piece of music. This disc changes our whole perspective in a wholly different sense, for it gives us a glimpse of two familiar masterpieces in the making. Sibelius struggled with the Fifth Symphony for almost seven years from about 1912 until it reached its definitive form in 1919. Although the finished score of the first version doesn't survive, the orchestral material does, so it was not difficult to reconstruct the score. To study how the two scores differ is to learn some-

SIBELIUS'S SYMPHONY NO 5 – IN BRIEF

London SO / Robert Kajanus [H]
Koch Historic 37133-2 (62' · ADD) (M)(O)
Kajanus was one of the composer's favourite interpreters of his music. What this pioneering 1932 recording may lack in refinement is more than made up for by the subtlety and electric charge of the conductor's purposeful direction.

Boston SO / Serge Koussevitzky [H]
Naxos Historical 8 110170 (71' · ADD) (S)⊞→
A performance of boundless integrity and pedigree, notable for its painstaking attention to detail and astonishing depth of string tone. The 1936 recording has impressive body and bloom in this new transfer.

Berlin PO / Herbert von Karajan
DG ② 457 748-2GOR2 (149' · ADD) (M)(O)(O)⊞→
Karajan always had the measure of this great symphony and this famous 1965 recording for DG is by common consent one of the pinnacles of his recorded legacy.

Philharmonia Orchestra / Vladimir Ashkenazy
Decca ② 455 405-2DF2 (150' · DDD) (M)
By no means a first choice artistically, but Decca's Kingsway Hall sound is just stunning. Excellently played, Ashkenazy's fresh-faced performance gives little cause for complaint.

City of Birmingham SO / Sir Simon Rattle
EMI 749717-2 (62' · DDD) (F)⊞→
Rattle's Birmingham remake is fascinatingly different from his 1982 Philharmonia predecessor in its fleeter, more animated manners. Coupled with Rattle's invigorating 1987 account of the Sibelius Concerto with Nigel Kennedy.

Lahti SO / Osmo Vänskä
BIS BIS-CD800 (58' · DDD) (F)(O)(O)(O)⊞→
This BIS issue is a model of rewarding enterprise, coupling the Fifth in the second of its three versions from 1915 with *En saga* in its original 1892 guise. Exemplary performances and production values.

Iceland SO / Petri Sakari
Naxos 8 554377 (69' · DDD) (S)⊞→
If the pennies are in short supply, then this likeable account from Reykjavík should prove just the ticket. Alert and enthusiastic playing from the Iceland SO under Petri Sakari, and very good sound to boot.

Swedish RSO / Sergiu Celibidache
DG ④ 469 070-2GH4 (278' · ADD) (M)⊞→
Celibidache conducts an astounding account from 1971, full of fascinating detail. It comes as part of a four-CD Swedish RSO collection, but you can download selectively.

thing important about the creative process and it's this mystery that makes this disc imperative listening – and not just for Sibelians. The four-movement 1915 score has a more complex harmonic language than the final score and so it provides a missing link, as it were, between the Fourth Symphony and the definitive Fifth. The opening horn motif has yet to emerge, and the finale's coda has yet to acquire its hammer-blow chords. And in between you'll find that the various themes, some distinctly recognisable, others taking off in totally unexpected directions and charting unknown regions.

The version of *En saga* with we're familiar with doesn't come between the *Kullervo* Symphony and the *Karelia* music, but from 1901, between the First and Second Symphonies, and was made for Busoni.

The original offers fascinating material for comparison: there's a brief glimpse of Bruckner, whose work he had encountered in Vienna a year or two earlier, and the orchestral writing, though not always as polished as in the later version, still has flair. Praise to the Lahti orchestra and their fine conductor, and the excellent and natural balance.

Symphonies Nos 6 & 7. Tapiola, Op 112
Lahti Symphony Orchestra / Osmo Vänskä
BIS BIS-CD864 (68' · DDD) (F)(O)(O)

The Lahti orchestra bring total dedication to these great scores, and Osmo Vänskä is a Sibelian of substance. With this account of the Sixth and Seventh he brings his survey to a triumphant conclusion. Indeed this is every bit as impressive as the First and Fourth. To the Sixth Symphony he brings total concentration: a serene slow movement but a very fast *Scherzo* and tautly held-together finale. The Seventh is finely conceived and paced and though the Lahti orchestra aren't the equal of the Finnish RSO for Saraste or the Helsinki PO for Berglund (both conductors fine Sibelians), directed by Vänskä they give the more compelling and convincing performances. The *Tapiola* is thrilling: atmospheric and powerfully built up and though it doesn't displace Karajan, Koussevitzky or Beecham, it's a measure of its splendour and power – and the terror it evokes – that it invites only the most exalted comparisons. In the Sixth Symphony one wouldn't want to be without either Sir Colin Davis, the Beecham or any of the Karajan versions, and for the Seventh the roll-call must certainly include Koussevitzky's seminal account, as well as both Sir Colin's Boston and LSO accounts.

This is an impressive issue. The recorded sound is in the first flight, and there are excellent notes by Andrew Barnett.

Symphonies Nos 6 & 7.
The Tempest – Suite No 2, Op 109
Iceland Symphony Orchestra / Petri Sakari

Naxos 8 554387 (71' · DDD) ⑤☞

A most enjoyable conclusion to Petri Sakari's Sibelius symphony cycle. Sakari's Sixth impresses by dint of its unpretentious honesty and quiet cogency. As on previous instalments within this series, the Icelanders respond with a keen fervour as contagious as it's heartwarming. Their woodwind roster comprises an especially personable bunch, and if the strings inevitably lack that very last ounce of tonal clout and sheer composure provided by, say, Karajan's Berlin Philharmonic or the San Francisco Symphony under Blomstedt – to name but two of the strongest rivals – there's no missing the touching expressive warmth they bring to the work's transcendental closing pages. In Sakari's hands both outer movements develop real fire and purpose, and he uncovers plenty of happy detail along the way – the distinctive colouring of the bass clarinet being one of this performance's chief pleasures.

Sakari's Seventh, too, is very good indeed, patient and imaginative in the manner of Vänskä, or Sanderling's much underrated, irresistibly sinewy 1974 recording with the Berlin Symphony Orchestra. Perhaps the Iceland Symphony's principal trombonist could have been just a touch more assertive for that heroic initial solo six bars after fig C, and the timpanist appears to enter a bar late just before fig E, but the only sizeable niggle concerns Sakari's not-quite-seamless handling of that tricky *Poco a poco affrettando* transition passage into the *Vivacissimo* section beginning at fig J, itself not entirely free of a certain breathless fluster. All this means that Sakari's conception as a whole isn't as thrillingly inevitable an experience as Koussevitzky's, Maazel's or Boult's masterly 1963 concert relay with the RPO. That said, Sakari builds the shattering *Largamente* climax at fig Z superbly, and the closing bars are exceptionally fine. Not a front-runner, perhaps, but no mean achievement all the same. Well worth investigating at Naxos price.

Additional recommendations

Sibelius Symphony No 7
Coupled with **Schubert** Symphony No 8. **Bizet** Jeux d'enfants – excerpts. **Ravel** Daphnis et Chloé
RPO / Boult
BBC Music Legends BBCL4039-2 (75' · ADD)   Ⓜ
Boult isn't a conductor you'd immediately associate with Sibelius but this honest reading forms part of a highly enticing concert.

Symphonies Nos 1, 2, 4 & 5
Boston SO / C Davis
Philips Duo ② 446 157-2PM2 (154' · ADD)   Ⓜ☞
Davis's late-1970s Boston Sibelius cycle has many admirers and should entrance a new generation of music lovers in this competitive reissue.

Symphonies Nos 3, 6 & 7
Coupled with Violin Concerto. Finlandia. Tapiola.
Legends, 'Lemminkaïnen Suite', Op 22
Accardo *vn* **Boston SO; LSO / C Davis**

Philips Duo ② 446 160-2PM2 (146' · ADD)   Ⓜ☞
The second half of the cycle. The symphonies have a wonderful sheen and the couplings are particularly generous.

Symphony No 2
Coupled with Romance for Strings
Gothenburg SO / Järvi
BIS BIS-CD252 (DDD)   Ⓕ☞
This is a performance full of sinew and fire. Fast and vigorous in the first movement, the orchestra play with tremendous commitment.

Symphonies Nos 4-7
Coupled with The Swan of Tuonela. Tapiola
BPO / Karajan
DG The Originals ② 457 748-2GOR2 (ADD)   Ⓜ☞

Symphonies Nos 5 & 6
Coupled with Legends, 'Lemminkaïnen Suite', Op 22
BPO / Karajan
DG Galleria 439 982-2GGA (69' · ADD)   Ⓜ☞
Karajan's Sibelius is very compelling and the BPO have the full measure of the music.

Symphonies Nos 1 & 3
Iceland SO / Sakari
Naxos 8 554102 (68' · DDD)   ⑤☞
Well worth considering for those on a budget. Good, committed playing from the Iceland SO.

Symphonies Nos 6 & 7
Coupled with Nightride and Sunrise
Berlin SO / Sanderling
Berlin Classics 0092812BC (70' · DDD)   Ⓜ
A coupling that enjoys quite a following among informed Sibelians. By no means mainstream but worth exploring.

En saga, Op 9

En saga. Nightride and Sunrise, Op 55.
The Dryad, Op 45 No 1. Dance Intermezzo,
Op 45 No 2. Pohjola's Daughter, Op 49.
The Bard, Op 64. The Oceanides, Op 73
Lahti Symphony Orchestra / Osmo Vänskä
BIS BIS-CD1225 (76' · DDD)   Ⓕ〇〇〇

Anyone who has already encountered the Lahti/Vänskä partnership in Sibelius will know to expect performances of great vitality and freshness. And the expectation is fully met – perhaps even surpassed; in these tone-poems he simply allows his profound grasp of musical inner workings to dictate the course of events. The trenchant Lahti strings, the ecstatically floating woodwind and the rasping brass all play their part. But while their contributions are gripping in their own right, they're the more impressive for being so precisely placed at the service of the music's larger-scale unfolding.

Each of the longer works feels as though composer and performers alike have imagined them in one huge mental breath. Vänskä knows exactly when and how much to hold back, when to push on, and, crucially, when simply to stand back and let the music tick over to the beat of some higher rhythm. The same sense of inevitability informs the more compact masterpieces – *The Dryad* and the extraordinarily cryptic *The Bard*. Only the *Dance-Intermezzo*, companion piece to *The Dryad*, is in any way negligible.

All the other tone-poems have been recorded many times over, but rarely with such a consistent feeling of idiomatic rightness. (Vänskä himself has recorded the 1892 original version of *En saga* as well – coupled with the original Fifth Symphony on a *Gramophone* Award-winning set, reviewed under Symphony No 5 – and a fascinating contrast it makes with the more compact 1902 revision offered here.) BIS's recording is of demonstration quality. An outstanding release.

Additional recommendations

En saga
Coupled with Tapiola. The Bard. The Oceanides. Pohjola's Daughter
Iceland Symphony Orchestra / Sakari
Naxos 8 555299 (70' · DDD)　　　　ⓢⒹ►

En saga unfolds with enviable naturalness and vigour, yet the dusky mystery of the coda is also very well conveyed. *Tapiola*, too, receives a stimulating interpretation, with a gripping climax to its famous storm.

Karelia Suite, Op 11

Karelia Suite. Incidental music – King Christian II; Pelleas and Melisande (all original versions)
Anna-Lisa Jakobsson *mez* **Raimo Laukka** *bar*
Lahti Symphony Orchestra / Osmo Vänskä
BIS BIS-CD918 (78' · DDD · T/t)　　　　Ⓕ

Sibelius supplied four numbers for the February 1898 Helsinki premiere of Adolf Paul's historical drama *King Christian II* – 'Minuet', 'The Fool's Song', 'Elegy' and 'Musette' – and these eventually took their place in the five-movement concert suite alongside the 'Nocturne', 'Serenade' and 'Ballade' which the composer completed the same summer. The street music of the 'Musette' is simply delightful in its original garb without added strings, and in both the 'Serenade' and 'Ballade' Vänskä uncovers strong thematic and stylistic links with the almost exactly contemporaneous First Symphony. The defiant quality these fine artists bring to 'The Fool's Song' (eloquently delivered by Raimo Laukka) is also very likeable. Music-making of refreshing perception and meticulous sensitivity similarly illuminates this first complete recording of Sibelius's original incidental music for a 1905 production of Maeterlinck's symbolist play (the venue was again Helsinki's Swedish Theatre). There are 10 numbers in all.

The performance of the *Karelia Suite* in its original scoring (which acts as a splendid

curtain-raiser here) has been compiled from Vänskä's complete recording of the original *Karelia* music. Both outer movements have a real sense of pageantry about them (Vänskä directs with exhilaratingly clean-limbed swagger), though there are certain reservations about his occasional predilection for exaggerated and affected *pianopianissimos*. Thus, at around 3'30" in the central 'Ballade' (track 2), the dynamic level drops almost below the threshold of audibility and has you rushing to boost the volume control (Vänskä repeats this trick twice in the *King Christian II* 'Elegy', and towards the end of the final number in *Pelleas*). For optimum results, therefore, playback needs to be higher than many listeners may think reasonable. That said, the engineering is quite spectacularly truthful throughout and there's no doubt that this is an unusually absorbing collection.

Legends (Lemminkäinen Suite), Op 22

Legends. En saga
Swedish Radio Symphony Orchestra / Mikko Franck
Ondine ODE953-2 (74' · DDD)　　　　ⒻⓄⓄⒹ►

Mikko Franck presides over the most intrepidly individual and pungently characterful performance of the Lemminkäinen *Legends* since Leif Segerstam's 1995 Helsinki PO account for this same label. Clocking in at an eyebrow-raising 53'48" overall, Franck's conception evinces an unhurried authority, a generous expressive scope and a richly stocked imagination remarkable in one so young.

Lemminkäinen and the Maidens of the Island unfolds in especially gripping fashion here. Even more than Segerstam, Franck takes an extraordinarily long-breathed, flexible view of this heady tableau, imparting an unashamedly sensual voluptuousness to the secondary material in particular. It's a risky, impulsive approach, but one that pays high dividends in terms of intoxicating sweep, brazen ardour and, well, sheer daring. Both *The Swan of Tuonela* (which, in a refreshing change from the norm these days, Franck places second, according to Sibelius's final wishes) and *Lemminkäinen in Tuonela* combine dark-hued grandeur with tingling atmosphere, the latter's haunting A minor central episode handled with particular perception. True, *Lemminkäinen's Return* lacks something in animal excitement, but its unruffled sense of purpose, rhythmic spring and sinewy, clean-cut textures serve up plenty of food for thought none the less.

The *Legends* are preceded by an uncommonly fresh *En saga*, brimming with watchful sensitivity and interpretative flair, and once again studded with revelatory detail. Throughout, the Swedish RSO responds with heartwarming application and genuine enthusiasm, audibly galvanised by Franck's fervent, always invigorating direction. The engineering, too, is very good, without perhaps being absolutely in the top flight.

An auspicious recording debut, then, from a young artist of clearly prodigious potential.

Lemminkäinen in Tuonela, Op 22 No 3 (reconstructed 1896 version, ed Davis). Humoresque, Op 87 No 1 (first version)[a]. In memoriam, Op 59 (two versions). Two Serious Melodies, Op 77[b]. Three Pieces, Op 96. Presto for Strings
[a]**Jaakko Kuusisto** vn [b]**Marko Ylönen** vc
Lahti Symphony Orchestra / Osmo Vänskä
BIS BIS-CD1485 (78' · DDD)   Ⓕ🔊

The centrepiece of this fine collection is a reconstruction of *Lemminkäinen in Tuonela* as it sounded at the April 1896 Helsinki premiere. When Sibelius reworked the score in 1939, he excised at least 108 bars, including an impressive 32-bar introduction and a hefty chunk of the ghostly A minor central episode.

Annotator Andrew Barnett tells us that the Op 77 *Two Serious Melodies*, for violin and orchestra, were first heard in March 1916 in Sibelius's arrangement for cello. Soloist Marko Ylönen is a rapt proponent of this headily lovely diptych, while the Lahti SO's leader Jaakko Kuusisto is a model of sensitive agility in the first version (from 1917) of the enchanting *Humoresque* No 1 in D minor.

The *Three Pieces* contain a fetching 18th-century pastiche, 'Autrefois', which incorporates a setting for soprano and contralto of a poem by Hjalmar Procopé. Bookending the programme are the original and revised versions (from 1909 and 1910 respectively) of the funeral march *In memoriam*, a stark yet noble (and at times intriguingly Mahlerian) processional to remind us that the uncompromising Fourth Symphony was not far off.

Vänskä and his bright-eyed Lahti band are on irreproachable form, and the BIS production crews have come up trumps once again with resplendently natural sound.

Legends. Karelia Suite, Op 11. Finlandia, Op 26
Iceland Symphony Orchestra / Petri Sakari
Naxos 8 554265 (73' · DDD)   Ⓢ🔊➔

Most impressive. In its keen intelligence, fiery snap and thrust, Petri Sakari's account of the four *Legends* proves more than a match for the finest. The Iceland SO may not be world-beaters, but they respond to their thoughtful young Finnish maestro's illuminating direction with clean-limbed zest and commitment to the cause (their winds are an especially personable bunch).

Perhaps the highlight of the new set is *Lemminkäinen in Tuonela*, which, like Segerstam and Salonen before him, Sakari places second (reverting to the composer's original scheme), and where he distils a relentless concentration and pin-sharp focus (only Segerstam is more gripping in this brooding essay). No one should miss out on the heady opulence of Ormandy's magnificent Philadelphia strings in those glorious

singing lines of *Lemminkäinen and the Maidens of the Island*, but the Icelanders play their hearts out, and anyway Sakari gives a dramatic reading of bold contrasts and strong symphonic cohesion. No grumbles, either, about *The Swan of Tuonela* or *Lemminkäinen's Homeward Journey* which is firmly controlled, dashingly detailed and genuinely exciting (as opposed to merely excitable).

Sakari's rewarding *Legends* comes very near the top of the heap alongside (though, ultimately, not ahead of) Segerstam, Saraste and Ormandy. In the popular couplings, Sakari's unhackneyed approach once again pays dividends, though his unusually brisk (and ever-so-slightly hectic) tempo for the main portion of the *Karelia Suite*'s opening Intermezzo isn't always convincing . None the less, this is quite a bargain. Eminently pleasing sound, too: free of gimmickry and tonally very true.

Legends. Tapiola, Op 112
Helsinki Philharmonic Orchestra / Leif Segerstam
Ondine ODE852-2 (70' · DDD)   Ⓕ🔊

The four *Legends* first began to surface in Sibelius's mind in 1893, at the same time as he was working on his *Kalevala* opera, *The Building of the Boat*, the prelude to which became *The Swan of Tuonela*. It isn't the only thing from the opera that found its way into the *Legends*. The lovely A minor idea for muted strings in the middle section of *Lemminkäinen in Tuonela* is also among the sketches, where Sibelius scribbled over it the words, 'the Maiden of Death'. In the opera she would have rowed Väinämöinen across the river to Tuonela. In the tone-poem she symbolises the very opposite, the loving mother whose ministrations return Lemminkäinen to life. In 1954 Sibelius reversed the order of the inner movements so that *The Swan* preceded *Lemminkäinen in Tuonela*. Segerstam disregards the composer's wishes and places them in the old order; there's a case for this – you otherwise have two highly dramatic pieces (*Lemminkäinen in Tuonela* and *Lemminkäinen's Homeward Journey*) placed alongside each other. Segerstam gets very good results from the Helsinki orchestra, which responds with a keen enthusiasm that's inspiriting. The performance is free from excessive mannerisms, and his account of *Tapiola* is very impressive. He tellingly evokes the chilling terrors and awesome majesty of the Nordic forest.

Finlandia, Op 26

Finlandia[a]. Karelia Suite, Op 11[a]. Tapiola, Op 112[a]. En saga[a]. Luonnotar, Op 70[a]. Pohjola's Daughter, Op 49[b]. Nightride and Sunrise, Op 55[b]. Legends, 'Lemminkäinen Suite', Op 22[b]
[a]**Philharmonia Orchestra / Vladimir Ashkenazy;**
[b]**Orchestra de la Suisse Romande / Horst Stein**
Double Decca ② 452 576-2DF2 (DDD/ADD)
[a]Recorded 1980-85   Ⓜ🔊➔

SIBELIUS TAPIOLA – IN BRIEF

Helsinki PO / Leif Segerstam
Ondine ODE852-2   Ⓕ●

The Helsinki orchestra have just the perfect sound for Sibelius, and naturally they play with a total grasp of the idiom. Segerstam can be a wilful Sibelian, but he unfurls this glorious piece with a winning simplicity.

Royal Philharmonic Orchestra / Sir Thomas Beecham   Ⓗ
BBC Legends BBCL4041-2   Ⓕ●

Recorded in 1955, this shows what a great Sibelian Beecham was: this is his finest version of *Tapiola*, an interpretation of colossal emotional weight and scope.

Lahti Symphony Orchestra / Osmo Vänskä
BIS BIS-CD864   Ⓕ●●

Joining the Sixth and Seventh Symphonies, Vanska's *Tapiola* receives an extraordinarily intense performance with fine playing from his loyal Lahti band. Top-class BIS sound.

Philharmonia Orchestra / Vladimir Ashkenazy
Decca 452 576-2DF2   Ⓜ●Ⓓ→

A really tremendous performance that gives this atmospheric work a colossal emotional charge. Ashkenazy has clearly absorbed much of the Finnish spirit oin his many visits to the country and it certainy shows in this powerful vision of *Tapiola*.

Boston SO / Sir Colin Davis
Philips 446 160-2PM2   Ⓜ Ⓓ→

Paired with Symphonies Nos 5 and 6, this is Sibelius-playing with a strong and loyal following: the Boston orchestra have a really alluring sound in this music and Davis is totally in his element.

Berlin Philharmonic Orchestra / Herbert von Karajan
DG 457 748-2GOR2   Ⓜ●●Ⓓ→

Coupled with Symphonies Nos 4-7 (including a magnificent No 6), this *Tapiola* from the mid-1960s remains for many unsurpassed, evoking the mood of the Nordic forests. Glorious, rich tone from the BPO.

Gothenburg SO / Neeme Järvi
DG ③ 477 552-2GTR3   Ⓕ Ⓓ→

Neeme Järvi is an excellent guide in the music of Sibelius, and with his superb Gothenburg orchestra on fine form, this is an impressive performance.

Iceland Symphony Orchestra / Petri Sakari
Naxos 8 555299   Ⓢ Ⓓ→

A fine collection of shorter Sibelius works contains this excellent performance of *Tapiola*, with a particularly gripping account as the storm reaches its powerful climax.

Ashkenazy makes a superb job of *Finlandia*, which boasts some of the most vibrant, powerful brass sounds on disc.

More than 30 years separate *En saga* and *Tapiola*, yet both works are quintessential Sibelius. The latter is often praised for the way Sibelius avoided 'exotic' instruments, preferring instead to draw new and inhuman sounds from the more standard ones; and the former is, in many ways, just as striking in the way the orchestration evokes wind, strange lights, vast expanses and solitude. Both works suggest a dream-like journey: *En saga* non-specific, though derived from Nordic legend; *Tapiola* more of an airborne nightmare in, above and around the mighty giants of the Northern forests inhabited by the Green Man of the Kalevala, the forest god Tapio (the final amen of slow, bright major chords brings a blessed release!). Ashkenazy's judgement of long-term pacing is very acute; the silences and shadows are as potent here as the wildest hurricane. And Decca's sound allows you to visualise both the wood and the trees; every detail of Sibelius's sound world is caught with uncanny presence, yet the overall orchestral image is coherent and natural.

Nightride and Sunrise, Op 55

Nightride and Sunrise, Op 55. Pan and Echo, Op 53. Two Pieces, Op 45. Kuolema – Valse triste, Op 44 No 1; Scenes with Cranes, Op 44 No 2. Canzonetta, Op 62a; Valse romantique, Op 62b. Belshazzar's Feast, Op 51 – Oriental Procession; Solitude; Night Music; Khadra's Dance
New Zealand Symphony Orchestra / Pietari Inkinen
Naxos 8 570763 (65' · DDD)   Ⓢ Ⓓ→

As on this partnership's previous Sibelius anthology (see below) the New Zealand Symphony Orchestra respond with conspicuous poise and application for their Finnish chief. Inkinen's readings, too, show a real feeling for the idiom: phrases are shaped – and textures sifted – with fastidiousness and imagination, and he brings an abundant recreative flair and cogent grip to the task in hand, not least in *Nightride and Sunrise*, whose elusive structure he binds together with a sure-footed skill that belies his tender years. Moreover, Inkinen's luminous account of the suite from *Belshazzar's Feast* will have you questioning why such an appealing and highly evocative score is so seldom performed.

Elsewhere, rarities such as *Pan and Echo* and *The Dryad* emerge with a dewy freshness and ear-pricking sophistication that prompt a radical reappraisal. Inkinen even manages to breathe new life into the Op 44 diptych from the 1903 incidental music for *Kuolema* (the ubiquitous 'Valse triste' and bleakly beautiful 'Scene with Cranes'), and his alchemy extends to the two altogether more mundane numbers that Sibelius added for a 1911 revival of the play. A disc, then, guaranteed to give pretty much unbridled pleasure. Naxos's sound combines helpful transparency with plenty of ambient glow.

Humoresques, Opp 87 and 89

Humoresques Nos 1-6, Opp 87 & 89. Two Serenades, Op 69. Two Pieces, Op 77. Overture in E. Ballet scene
Dong-Suk Kang vn **Gothenburg Symphony Orchestra / Neeme Järvi**
BIS BIS-CD472 (62' · DDD)   Ⓕ●

The music for violin and orchestra here is marvellously rewarding and gloriously played. The six *Humoresques*, Opp 87 and 89, come from the same period as the Fifth Symphony, at a time when Sibelius was toying with the idea of a second violin concerto, and some of the material of the *Humoresques* was possibly conceived with a concerto in mind. Sibelius wrote that these radiant pieces convey something of 'the anguish of existence, fitfully lit up by the sun', and behind their outward elegance and charm, there's an all-pervasive sadness. This is even more intense in the Serenades, which are glorious pieces and quintessential Sibelius. Dong-Suk Kang is an outstanding player. His impeccable technique and natural musical instinct serve this repertoire well and he seems to have established an excellent rapport with Järvi and the Gothenburg orchestra. The two fill-ups are juvenilia and are only intermittently characteristic. The Overture is very much in his *Karelia* idiom, though they're of undoubted interest to all Sibelians. The recording is up to BIS's usual high quality.

Pelleas and Melisande, Op 46

Pelleas and Melisande. Cassazione, Op 6. Suite mignonne, Op 98a. Suite champêtre, Op 98b.
Suite caractéristique, Op 100. Presto
Tapiola Sinfonietta / Tuomas Ollila
Ondine ODE952-2 (56' · DDD)   Ⓕ

Don't let the low opus number hoodwink you: *Cassazione* dates from 1904 and was first given under Sibelius's baton at the same Helsinki concert as the premiere of the first version of the Violin Concerto. Revised the following year but never published, it's well worth hearing, containing as it does echoes of both *Pelleas and Melisande* and the Second Symphony's finale. The dashing *Presto* began life as the third movement of Sibelius's Op 4 String Quartet in B flat of 1889-90, and was subsequently transcribed for string orchestra in 1894. The three suites date from 1921-22. True, the *Suite caractéristique* serves up a pretty thin brew, but both the *Suite mignonne* and *Suite champêtre* contain their fair share of felicities and are delightfully scored.

These performances from Tuomas Ollila and the Tapiola Sinfonietta evince a bracing, unsentimental thrust and high degree of technical finish, though some will crave more in the way of affectionate charm and tingling atmosphere.

However, it's in the *Pelleas and Melisande* incidental music that these newcomers truly throw down the gauntlet. There's no hint of the customary portentous grandeur in Ollila's 'At the Castle Gate', a nervy urgency that resurfaces with a vengeance in 'Melisande at the Spinning Wheel' and the ensuing 'Entr'acte'. Elsewhere, those screaming winds and *sul ponticello* strings at the heart of 'At the Seashore' set one's teeth on edge, while textures throughout are uncommonly transparent. What's missing is any real sense of poignancy or pathos: 'The Death of Melisande' is very cool, the characteristically bleached string timbre emphasising the disconcertingly pristine, self-conscious mood. An intriguing and intelligent re-think, then, but not to all tastes (anyone brought up on, say, Beecham will be in for a shock). Crystal-clear, slightly clinical sound.

Scènes historiques – I, Op 25; II, Op 66. King Christian II, Op 27 – Nocturne; Elegie; Musette; Serenade; Ballade; Menuetto
New Zealand Symphony Orchestra / Pietari Inkinen
Naxos 8 570068 (63' · DDD)   Ⓢ●Ⓓ➤

Recordings of this entrancing repertoire are always welcome, particularly when they are as polished and involving as this. Pietari Inkinen (*b*1980) has recently taken up the reins as the NZSO's music director and, on this showing, is a talent to watch. Not only does he draw some high-quality, notably zestful playing from his new charges, he directs both sets of *Scènes historiques* with such keen temperament, abundant character and sensitivity to texture and nuance that they come up sounding strikingly new-minted. Indeed, his generously expressive and pliable shaping of the ravishing secondary material in 'Festivo' manages to stoke memories of Beecham's indelible RPO rendering from the early 1950s – and that's saying something!

In the *King Christian II* suite, Inkinen and his responsive band easily hold their own against some stiff competition. There's some particularly eloquent string playing in the achingly wistful 'Elegy' (where Inkinen distils a hushed intimacy that is deeply touching), while the dashing helter-skelter ride of the concluding 'Ballade' has both invigorating spring and bite to commend it.

Boasting handsomely true and atmospheric sound, this collection certainly merits the attention of all Sibelians and represents enticing value at bargain price.

Chamber Works

String Quartet, 'Voces intimae', Op 56.
Piano Quintet, JS159ᵃ
Coull Quartet (Roger Coull, Philip Gallaway vns Rose Redgrave va Nicholas Roberts vc) with ᵃ**Martin Roscoe** pf
Somm SOMMCD096 (69' · DDD)   Ⓜ○○

The Coull Quartet prove unflashy, dedicated and profoundly humane interpreters of the great D minor Quartet, scrupulously faithful to both the letter and spirit of the score, and their pacing throughout seems pretty much spot-on, especially in the deeply felt *Adagio di molto* centrepiece. In fact, the sole tiny quibble concerns the overlong gap between the first and second movements, which surely scuppers the intended impact of Sibelius's *attacca* marking. Otherwise, nothing but praise for a display so full of wisdom and musicality.

Completed in 1890 during Sibelius's period of study in Berlin, the early Piano Quintet is likewise cast in five movements and already displays a sense of scale and raw ambition that point the way forward to *Kullervo*. If no forgotten masterpiece, it does constitute a most agreeable discovery and contains more than its fair share of endearing invention (it's not hard to detect Dvořák's kindly presence in the slow movement, for example). Roscoe and the Coulls well disguise the work's tendency to sprawl. No grumbles with Somm's flatteringly ripe sound and judicious balance. Acquire with confidence!

Five Pieces, Op 81. Novelette, Op 102.
Five Danses champêtres, Op 106.
Four Pieces, Op 115. Three Pieces, Op 116
Nils-Erik Sparf vn **Bengt Forsberg** pf
BIS BIS-CD625 (57' · DDD)   ⓕⓄ➔

No one listening to this music would doubt that Sibelius had a special feeling for the violin, whether he's composing lighter music such as the captivating 'Rondino' from the Op 81 set or the more substantial later pieces, such as the first of the *Danses champêtres*, which comes close to the world of *The Tempest*. Neither the Op 115 nor the Op 116 set contains great music but they're much finer than they have been given credit for. Both 'On the heath' and the 'Ballade', Nos 1 and 2 of Op 115, have an innocence that calls to mind the wonderful *Humoresques* for violin and orchestra. In particular 'The Bells', Op 115 No 4, is a rather cryptic miniature and the 'Scène de danse' of Op 116, with its striking tonal juxtapositions, is a kind of Finnish equivalent of the Bartók *Romanian Dances*. Nils-Erik Sparf and Bengt Forsberg are dedicated and sensitive exponents who make the most of the opportunities this repertoire provides. One small reservation: the piano tone sounds a little thick at the bottom end, and the violin is by no means the dominant partner. Enthusiastically recommended.

Kullervo, Op 7

Kullervo
Lilli Paasikivi mez **Raimo Laukka** bar Helsinki
University Chorus; Lahti Symphony Orchestra /
Osmo Vänskä
BIS BIS-CD1215 (81' · DDD · T/t)   ⓕⓄⓄ

Vänskä is undoubtedly a Sibelian of strong instinct, and his *Kullervo* enshrines an interpretation of extraordinary grandeur and slumbering, runic mystery. After an ideally paced opening *Allegro moderato* (the Lahti strings lacking just a touch in sheer muscle), 'Kullervo's Youth' lasts an eyebrow-raising 19'18", well over three minutes longer than any predecessor. Courageously, Vänskä sticks to his guns, the music's unnervingly tragic portents distilled with mournful gravity. It's in the big central *scena* that BIS's sumptuously realistic and wide-ranging production really comes into its own. Vänskä directs with keen observation and tingling narrative flair, not missing the wondrous poetry of the nature music accompanying the lament of Kullervo's sister. What's more, his soloists and chorus are first-rate, though baritone Raimo Laukka isn't quite as fresh-voiced here as he was for Segerstam's in 1994. Following a splendidly lusty 'Kullervo goes to war', Vänskä crowns proceedings with a thrillingly grim and inevitable 'Kullervo's death', with eloquent contributions from the men of the Helsinki University Chorus. As should be clear by now, this recording must feature high on any short list.

Kullervo
Soile Isokoski sop **Tommi Hakala** bar
YL Male Voice Choir; Helsinki Philharmonic
Orchestra / Leif Segerstam
Ondine ⯑ ODE1122-5 (78' · DDD)   ⓕⓄ➔

As a fine Wagner conductor Leif Segerstam knows something about pacing and maintaining a strong rhythmic profile over the longest spans of musical narrative, and for all the composer's vaunted debt to Bruckner in the instrumental movements, a grander, operatic sweep seems more germane to this always intriguing, *sui generis* hybrid of symphonic poem, symphony and cantata. Segerstam's second cycle of the numbered symphonies has at points such as the Seventh come a cropper with such largesse of gesture and tempo, but like his first recording (Chandos – now available as a download only), this is refreshingly straightforward with sound and well chosen tempi. Perhaps partly due to a superbly contoured recording, but also the more keenly expressive responses of the Helsinki orchestra, especially its woodwind, the many transitions in the work seem to count for more, and in 'Kullervo's youth' achieve a Mussorgskian abruptness and intensity.

That first recording was also graced by Soile Isokoski in the part of Kullervo's raped sister, but here she surpasses herself in creating a self-contained scena for her third-movement lament, vibrant and enticing before turning bitterly eloquent over her shame. Tommi Hakala and the YL Choir bring a complementary, sappy youthfulness. If the finale rather goes off the boil, the composer must take some of the blame; Isokoski too, for stealing the show with a contribution to this over-recorded work which deserves to win currency outside connoisseurs of early Sibelius.

Karelia

Incidental Music – Karelia; Kuolema. Valse triste,
Op 44 No 1 (1904 versions)
Heikki Laitinen, Taito Hoffren sngrs **Kirsi Tiihonen**
sop **Raimo Laukka** bar **Lahti Symphony Orchestra /
Osmo Vänskä**
BIS BIS-CD915 (76' · DDD · T/t)   (F)

This is a disc which will be of great interest to
Sibelians. The original score of the *Karelia*
music was discovered in the conductor Kajanus's
library after his death in 1933 and his widow
returned it to Sibelius three years later. The
music extended to eight tableaux which portrayed various episodes in Karelian history. In
the 1940s Sibelius destroyed the score, about
which he had had second thoughts since its premiere in 1893, sparing only the Overture, the
movements familiar from the suite and the first
number, 'A Karelian Home – News of War'.
Fortunately for posterity, a set of orchestral
parts came to light, albeit incomplete, and were
put into shape by Kalevi Kuoso. It was these that
the composer Kalevi Aho used in preparing the
edition on which this recording is based.

In all there are some 40 minutes of music, over
half of which is new. Those familiar with the 'Ballade' from the Op 11 Suite will no doubt be
slightly disconcerted to hear the familiar cor
anglais melody taken by a baritone and will find
the piece too long in its original form. The opening of the fifth tableau, 'Pontus de la Gardie at the
gates of Käkisalmi [Kexholm Castle] in 1580', is
highly effective and leads into the famous 'Alla
marcia'. It's fascinating to hear what the piece is
like, and what Sibelius was prepared to lose. Listening to this reaffirms and illumines both the
sureness of his artistic judgement and the vitality
of his creative imagination.

Sibelius's incidental music to *Kuolema*, the play
by his brother-in-law, Arvid Järnefelt, dates from
1903. The most familiar music from it is the *Valse
triste*, which Sibelius revised the following year,
adding flute, clarinet, horns and timpani and
making it altogether more sophisticated harmonically and melodically. Osmo Vänskä and his
Lahti players prove reliable and responsive guides
in this atmospheric music and it's hard to imagine
their performances being improved on. Wide-
ranging and expertly balanced recorded sound.

Songs

King Christian II, Op 27 – Fool's Song of the Spider.
Five Christmas Songs, Op 1. Eight Songs, Op 57.
Hymn to Thaïs. Six Songs, Op 72 – No 3, The Kiss;
No 4, The Echo Nymph; No 5, Der Wanderer und der
Bach; No 6, A Hundred Ways. Six Songs, Op 86. The
Small Girls
Monica Groop mez **Love Derwinger** pf
BIS BIS-CD657 (66' · DDD · T/t)   (F)(B)

Monica Groop, following her success in the Cardiff Singer of the World Competition, has built

up a busy career. Communication is her strength,
and unevenness of line a relative weakness. Sibelius's songs are a rich and still undervalued part of
the song repertoire. Still only four or five are
really well known, and none of those is included
here. Not all are of very special quality: the title is
probably the best thing about the 'Fool's Song of
the Spider' (from *King Christian II*), and the *Hymn
to Thaïs* gains interest through being Sibelius's
only song in English rather than through intrinsic merit. Yet there are many delights here,
including the closing waltz-song, 'The Small
Girls'. The acoustic is perhaps somewhat too
reverberant but has plenty of presence.

'Songs, Volume 3'
Seven Songs, Op 13. Six Songs, Op 50. Six Songs,
Op 90. The Wood Nymph. Belshazzar's Feast – The
Jewish Girl's Song. Resemblance. A Song. Serenade.
The Thought[a]
Anne Sofie von Otter, [a]**Monica Groop** mezzos
Bengt Forsberg pf
BIS BIS-CD757 (67' · DDD · T/t)   (F)(O)(B)

Most of Sibelius's songs are in Swedish, the language with which he grew up as a child, and here
they're given by a distinguished native Swedish
partnership. The *Seven Songs*, Op 13, are all
Runeberg settings and come from the composer's early years (1891-92). Best known, perhaps,
are 'Spring is flying' and 'The Dream', but there
are others, such as 'The Young Hunter', that are
no less delightful and characterful. The other
Runeberg settings here, the *Six Songs*, Op 90,
come towards the end of Sibelius's career as a
song composer (1917-18). 'The north', as in all
the nature poetry of Runeberg, touches a very
special vein of inspiration. Along with 'Die stille
Nacht', Op 50 No 5, which is equally affectingly
given by these two artists – it's among his finest
songs. Interest naturally focuses on the rarities.

'The Wood Nymph', not to be confused with
the melodrama or the tone-poem, is recorded
here for the first time. As well as 'A Song', there
are two other early Runeberg settings, the 1888
'Serenade' and 'Resemblance', both of them also
premiere recordings. 'The Jewish Girl's Song'
will be familiar from the incidental music to
Belshazzar's Feast, and is affecting in this form –
particularly sung as it is here. Given the artistry
and insight of this splendid partnership, and the
interest and beauty of the repertoire, this is a
self-recommending issue.

To Evening, Op 17 No 6. Six Songs, Op 36. Five
Songs, Op 37. Six Songs, Op 50. Belshazzar's Feast,
Op 51 – The Jewish Girl's Song. I am a Tree, Op 57
No 5. The Elf-King, Op 57 No 8. The North, Op 90
No 1. Who has brought you here?, Op 90 No 6. Under
the fir-trees, Op 13 No 1. Spring is flying, Op 13 No 4
Katarina Karnéus mez **Julius Drake** pf
Hyperion CDA67318 (65' · DDD· T/t)   (F)(O)(B)

Sibelius's songs have taken a long time to come
in from the cold. After all, the few that are rela-

tively well-known ('Black roses' and Op 37 No 5, 'The Tryst') are passionate enough to have come from Italian opera, and others which over the years have found a place in the repertoire have a span of phrase and a melodic surge that encourage the voice to rise thrillingly, as in 'The Tryst's' predecessor, 'Was it a dream?'. The tingle of a Nordic chill in among this is in fact a further excitement of the blood. Given a voice that can combine the sparkle of sunlight on snow with the dark splendour which lies at the heart of those black roses, an entire programme of Sibelius's songs offers not an austere pleasure but almost a rich indulgence.

But from both singer and pianist there must also be a ready supply of imagination. Katarina Karnéus and Julius Drake answer these calls magnificently. The voice is firm and resonant, purest in quality in the upper D-to-F region and of ample range. In Julius Drake she has a pianist who extends the normal field of vision, and the two work together to great effect.

In the opening song, 'To evening' ('Illalle'), Karnéus and Drake 'build' the verses with such effective graduations of power and intensity that everything is enhanced – the vocal line, the piano's *tremolando*s, words, mood, the poem-as-painting, the song as miniature epic. In some others – 'Little Lasse' in Op 37 and the remarkable 'Tennis in Trianon' of Op 36 are examples – von Otter and Bengt Forsberg bring a further sophistication, more rightfully placed in the second example than the first. But if you want a single disc of 25 to to represent Sibelius's output of roughly 100 songs then this disc must take first choice.

Luonnotar, Op 70. Arioso, Op 3. Seven Songs, Op 13 – Neath the fir trees; Spring is flying. Seven Songs, Op 17 – And I questioned them no further; The Dragonfly; To Evening; Driftwood. Six Songs, Op 36 – But my Bird; Sigh, Sedges, Sigh; The Diamond on the March Snow. Five Songs, Op 37 – The First Kiss; Sunrise; Was it a Dream?. Five Songs, Op 38 – Autumn Evening; On a balcony by the sea. Eight Songs, Op 57 – Duke Magnus. Six Songs, Op 72 – The Echo Nymph. Swim, Duck, Swim
Soile Isokoski sop
Helsinki Philharmonic Orchestra / Leif Segerstam
Ondine ⦿ ODE1080-5 (62' · DDD/DSD ·T/t)   Ⓕ⯈

Sibelius wrote his songs originally for voice and piano and in that form they are most often recorded. Some he later orchestrated, while others were arranged by Jussi Jalas (his son-in-law), Ernest Pingoud, Ivan Hellman and Nils-Eric Forgstadt. All produce good results and none of the songs appear over-dressed. On the contrary, they are, as it were, fulfilled: orchestral textures are so strongly implicit that the full range of instruments brings out their coloration and renders them complete.

Soile Isokoski has recorded a number of the songs previously with piano, part of a fine recital on Finlandia in 1989, which was about the time we first learnt of the radiant Finnish soprano

who five or six years later would receive the international acclaim she deserved. The voice then sounded fuller and was entirely pure in tone: today it is a little more worn but still lovely, firm and ample in range. Above all, she has a rare command of the *legato* style which makes her singing a delight to the ears when others, more subtle and expressive, may frustrate the full satisfaction their efforts would otherwise offer. There are limitations even so, some of them technical. 'The Dragonfly' ('En slända') cannot really be sung without a genuine trill, and Isokoski's trill is a very sketchy, rudimentary one compared with, say, Elisabeth Söderström's. The popular 'Was it a Dream?' ('Var det en dröm?') sounds well enough until Schwarzkopf is produced for comparison, her voice emerging magically out of the dreamy, murmurous introduction and minting afresh developments that are too nearly predictable and routine in Isokoski.

Yet the recital always gives pleasure, and the challenge of *Luonnotar* itself is joyfully met. The orchestra play with full appreciation of the richly coloured scores, and since Flagstad in the 1950s there have been few recordings which provide these genuinely enhancing accompaniments as an alternative to the piano.

Valentin Silvestrov   Ukrainian b1937

Silvestrov studied at the Kiev Conservatory (1958-64). Influenced at first by his teacher, Borys Lyatoshynsky, and by Shostakovich, he came in the early 1960s to use serialism, aleatory forms and other avant-garde techniques and in the 1970s to work with a plurality of styles, new and old. Silvestrov's Symphony No 5 (1980-82), considered by some to be his masterpiece, may be viewed as an epilogue or coda inspired by the music of late-Romantic composers such as Gustav Mahler. His works include eight symphonies, chamber music, piano pieces, songs, characterized by an individual, expressive lyricism.

Orchestral works

Bagatellen[a]. Der Bote[b]. Zwei Dialoge mit Nachwort[b]. Elegie. Stille Musik. Abschiedsserenade
[a]**Valentin Silvestrov**, [b]**Alexei Lubimov** pfs
Munich Chamber Orchestra / Christoph Poppen
ECM New Series 476 6178 (75' · DDD)   Ⓕ

ECM marks Valentin Silvestrov's 70th birthday with a disc that assembles smaller pieces and collections written over the past decade. A disc, moreover, of two distinct halves – the first of which features the composer in his *Bagatelles*: 13 miniatures that do not so much succeed as 'bleed' into each other in a half-hour sequence whose spectral allusions to Romantic pianism and consistently attenuated dynamics (the damper pedal sustained throughout) go some way to defining the essence of Silvestrov's music. Even then, the dissonance on which the final piece evanesces hints at those darker ambiguities which are present in even his seemingly most unequivocal statements.

The second half focuses on music for strings, sensitively rendered by the Munich Chamber Orchestra and Christoph Poppen. If the trio of ethereal dances comprising *Stille Musik* and distanced elegance of the two-part *Abschiedsserenade* are all of a piece with what came before, *Elegie* evinces a more anguished expression. Pianist Alexei Lubimov makes a fastidious contribution to *Der Bote* – a Mozartian rondo of deceptive tranquillity – and the oblique recollections of Wagner and Schubert that inform the serene *Zwei Dialoge mit Nachtwort*. Recording and annotations reflect ECM's customary high standards.

Requiem for Larissa

Requiem for Larissa
National Choir of Ukraine, 'Dumka'; National Symphony Orchestra of Ukraine / Volodymyr Sirenko
ECM New Series 472 112-2 (53' · DDD · T) Ⓕ Ⓞ Ⓑ

Much of Silvestrov's music since the mid-1970s has been a Requiem in all but name – a rite of regret and consolation for music and for the hopes and dreams of modern consciousness. So it's no surprise that he should join Schnittke, Denisov, Tishchenko and others of the post-Shostakovich generation in composing a work of that name. The external stimulus was the sudden death in 1996 of his musicologist wife Larissa Bondarenko, his staunch supporter through trials of the kind virtually all modernist composers in the former USSR had to face.

He completed the work three years later, having built into the 'Tuba mirum' section the fractured but passionate textures of his First Symphony of 1963, and having arranged the second *Agnus Dei* around his Mozartian piano piece, *The Messenger*. At the heart of the Requiem is his Taras Shevchenko setting, 'The Dream', as breathtakingly moving here as in its original place in the cycle *Silent Songs*. Otherwise he fragments the Requiem text and disposes its incomplete phrases across seven mostly slow movements; only the 'Lacrimosa' survives intact. The choir features a *basso profundo* section and three soloists who gently ease in and out of the texture. The classical-size orchestra is augmented by synthesiser, first heard in the celestial harmonies succeeding the first *Agnus Dei*.

Whether or not you know the fragile, haunting sound world of Ukraine's senior composer, this is a disc you should try.

Robert Simpson   British 1921-1997

Simpson, a pupil of Herbert Howells, worked for the BBC from 1951 to 1980. His main achievement was his cycles of nine symphonies and eight string quartets, both begun in 1951 and both displaying a dynamic tonality quite individual in its energy and purposefulness, encouraged more than influenced by his admiration for Beethoven, Bruckner and Nielsen (on whom he published studies).

Symphonies

Symphonies Nos 3 & 5
Royal Philharmonic Orchestra / Vernon Handley
Hyperion CDA66728 (71' · DDD) Ⓕ Ⓞ Ⓞ Ⓑ

The Third Symphony is Simpson's best-known work and Vernon Handley plays the symphony like the repertoire piece it deserves to be, and Hyperion's recording reveals a wealth of unsuspected detail and beauty. The Beethovenian impulse still comes across, and the abrasive edge is only slightly softened. But what has been gained is clarity, blend and perspective, plus a sense of dialogue (Simpson's polyphony never ceases to amaze) and an altogether subtler realisation of the luminosity of Simpson's scoring. The long accumulating second movement is absorbingly poetic, witty in its dialogue, and inevitable in its conclusion.

The Fifth Symphony is surely one of Simpson's most vivid pieces. Moods of terror, anger, anxious probing and fierce determination are right on the surface, and there's a feeling of terrific will-power being exerted to transmute those moods into a symphonic experience. This is one of the great symphonies of the post-war era, magnificently realised by all concerned.

Symphonies Nos 6 & 7
Royal Liverpool Philharmonic Orchestra / Vernon Handley
Hyperion CDA66280 (60' · DDD) Ⓕ Ⓑ

The first performances of these symphonies had shown many characteristic and admirable qualities, but there was a suspicion of some tentativeness a lowering of sights even, after the explosive Fifth Symphony. One should have guessed that closer acquaintance and more expert performance would show this to be more a matter of concentration of ideas and of conscious change of direction. The RLPO and Vernon Handley show the Sixth to be a work of immense inner power, and if the Seventh is a more cryptic statement, this recording certainly brings it into a clearer focus than previously.

Whereas Tippett (in the same year) wrote a birth-to-death symphony (No 4), Simpson's Sixth shifts the process one stage back – from conception to prime of life. Intense expectancy gives way to a memorable downward-stalking unison figure, the fertilised seed which becomes the most active force in the early stages of the work. From here to the irresistible energy of the final pages Simpson's control of musical momentum can only be marvelled at; and if you don't marvel at it, that may be because you're worrying about the apparent restriction on colour and lyricism, and thus missing the point.

As yet the final D major outcome still refuses to register as a natural outcome, although presumably there's any amount of logical justification for it. The neutral, non-triadic conclusion to the Seventh rings truer, though in this work the processes before it are more inscrutable – not in the technical sense, but simply in terms of what the techniques are driving at. But anyone who has puzzled over, and then clicked with, say, Sibelius's Fourth or Shostakovich's Fifteenth, will know how dangerous it is to jump to conclusions. And even if the click never happens, one probable masterpiece is surely enough to be getting on with.

Symphony No 9
Bournemouth Symphony Orchestra /
Vernon Handley
Hyperion CDA66299 (68' · DDD)
Includes an illustrated talk by the composer

Ⓕ OOOÐ

If you know that feeling of expectancy, of vast potential energy, at the outset of a great symphony, you'll surely respond to the opening of Simpson's Ninth – and be wholly engrossed. You'll be led through shifting pedal-points and wedge-shaped themes encompassing a specific harmonic universe; through waves of energy pulsating fit to burst, until burst they do into a titanic *scherzo*; through slow, disembodied traceries of string lines, through awe-inspiring climaxes to a no less awe-inspiring hushed coda. And as rising scales pass through the coda's pedal-points into the final glacial sonority you'll know that you've heard one of the finest symphonies of the post-war era.

A totally absorbing symphony and the performance and recording are surely the best possible tribute to all concerned. The composer adds an explanatory 18-minute talk. Here are laid bare some of the salient constructional features of the work.

String Quartets

String Quartets Nos 7 & 8
Delme Quartet (Galina Solodchin, Jeremy Williams vns John Underwood va Stephen Orton vc)
Hyperion CDA66117 (51' · AAD)
Recorded 1983   Ⓕ OOÐ

String Quartet No 9
Delme Quartet
Hyperion CDA66127 (58' · AAD) Recorded 1984   ⒻÐ

Quiet music with a sense of purpose and forward-looking destiny; slow music which bears the promise of a controlled release of energy, these are rare and treasurable qualities in music of our time, and they make their presence felt at the beginnings of Simpson's Seventh and Eighth Quartets. How he progresses through subdued

scherzo to vehement climax is something to reflect on at length, and with further acquaintance comes the Beethovenian thrill of hearing the music think. But at first these things just steal up on you and take the breath away.

The Seventh Quartet is dedicated to Susi Jeans, widow of astronomer and mathematidan Sir James Jeans; the Eighth is dedicated to entomologist David Gillett and his wife. Both works draw on the kind of motion suggested by those areas of scientific enquiry. On the other hand the Ninth calls up what would seem to be the bitterest enemy of forward movement – the palindrome; 32 variations and a fugue, in fact, on the minuet from Haydn's Symphony No 47 and all of them, like the original theme, palindromic. If Simpson's powers of invention falter at any stage in this hour-long *tour de force* you would be hard pushed to discover where. But then this music so completely absorbing that the necessary critical detachment is difficult to achieve. The only reservation that did register was over recording quality, which for the Ninth Quartet is disappointingly boxy – sensuous appeal isn't what this music is about, but a more ingratiating acoustic wouldn't do it any harm – and to hear the Seventh without the distraction, however faint, of traffic noise would be preferable.

The Delme Quartet's performances are outstandingly dedicated. The Ninth Quartet was composed for their 20th anniversary and they prove themselves entirely worthy of the honour.

Vocal Works

Canzona[a]. Media morte in vita sumus[b].
Tempi[c]. Eppur si muove[d]
[d]**Iain Quinn** org [ab]**Corydon Brass Ensemble;**
[bc]**Corydon Singers / Matthew Best**
Hyperion CDA67016 (68' · DDD · T)   Ⓕ●

Simpson would never have claimed that choral music was his *métier*. Yet for lovers of his music there's something especially revealing about the two pieces recorded here. In *Media morte in vita sumus* ('In the midst of death we are in life') he deliberately reverses the scriptural motto in order to articulate his personal 'anti-pessimist' creed. The musical setting for chorus, brass and timpani is appropriately austere, and Simpson's words are translated into Latin for the sake of universality. *Tempi* for *a cappella* chorus is a *jeu d'esprit*, the text consisting entirely of Italian tempo and character markings. The Corydon Singers offers superbly confident performances, as does the Corydon Brass Ensemble which also shines in the comparatively well-known *Canzona*. It's impossible to avoid comparisons with Nielsen when it comes to the 31-minute *Eppur si muove* ('But it does move') for organ. This 12-minute *ricercare* followed by a 19-minute passacaglia sets its jaw squarely against conventional organ-loft grandiosity. Its intellectual monumentality is clearly in the *Commotio* mould, though it's considerably tougher going than Nielsen's late masterpiece. Iain Quinn joins the long line of dedicated performers who have made Hyperion's Simpson series such a consistent triumph. Recording quality leaves nothing to be desired.

Nikos Skalkottas   Greek 1904-1949

*Skalkottas studied as a violinist at the Athens Con-
servatory and as a composer in Berlin with, among
others, Weill and Schoenberg. In 1933 he returned
to Athens, where he worked as a back-desk violinist.
His Berlin works are relatively compact and high-
spirited but the bulk of his music dates from 1935-
45, when the genres remained traditional but the
forms were greatly expanded to contain a deep complexity of serial thematic working.*

Piano Concerto No 1, AK16

Piano Concerto No 1ª. The Maiden and Death –
Ballet Suite, AK12. Ouvertüre concertante, AK46
ªGeoffrey Douglas Madge *pf* Iceland Symphony
Orchestra / Nikos Christodoulou
BIS BIS-CD1014 (56' · DDD)   ⓕⓞ➔

BIS's Skalkottas cycle started very well and gets better with each release. The First Piano Concerto's characteristic use of a family of note-rows, rather than just one, may have ignited the rift between the apprentice composer and his teacher, Schoenberg. The neo-classical elements can't have been to the latter's liking, either. Geoffrey Douglas Madge gives a barnstorming perform-ance and the accompaniment is electrifying. The orchestra is heard at its best and in its own right in the suite from the folk-ballet *The Maiden and Death* (1938). Here Skalkottas's brilliant orches-tration shines through in what's much more than a pre-run of *The Mayday Spell*. The idiom is less fragmentary than the latter; indeed, it suggests a Greek *Miraculous Mandarin*, if less overtly spec-tacular in sound or scandalous in plot.

The disc concludes with a further movement from the unfinished Second Symphonic Suite (1944-45; compare the *Largo sinfonico*, reviewed below). This *Ouvertüre concertante* is pretty much what the title leads you to expect it to be, a superbly scored sonata-derivative, employing the composer's note-row-complex manner in a most attractive fashion.

Violin Concerto, AK22

Violin Concertoª. Largo sinfonico, AK4a.
Greek Dances, AK11 – Epirotikos; Kretikos; Tsamikos;
Thessalikos; Mariori mou-Mariori mou; Arkadikos;
Kleftikos (arr cpsr)
ªGeorgios Demertzis *vn* Malmö Symphony
Orchestra / Nikos Christodoulou
BIS BIS-CD904 (78' · DDD)   ⓕⓞ➔

From Skalkottas's earliest works, a personal idiom was clearly in evidence, combining Euro-pean modernism with the rhythmic dynamism of Greek traditional music, and characterised by a tensile strength and translucency of sound. Like Bartók, Skalkottas wrote 'popular' music without compromise. The *Greek Dances* are ideal encore pieces, not least in these suave arrangements for strings.

The Violin Concerto of 1937 is among his major works, with a solo part that's demanding yet integral to the symphonic nature of the score – something that Georgios Demertzis's vital account readily conveys here. The close of the *Andante* possesses true lyrical repose, before the finale provides fireworks as well as clinching the musical design.

The *Largo sinfonico*, completed in 1944, embodies some of Skalkottas's most personal music; a seamless fusion of variation and sonata forms, it's as satisfying formally as it is emotion-ally. Nikos Christodoulou's accompanying notes speak of a private musical universe, yet the plan-gency of the cello theme and the remorseless tread of the central climaxes betray an unease that must surely be inseparable from the time of com-position. The final bars, with the thematic mate-rial recast as a series of unearthly chords, feel as much a stoic acceptance of reality as they are a 'harmony of the spheres'. With the Malmö orchestra fully attuned to the idiom, Christo-doulou's powerfully shaped reading makes for a compelling experience.

Violin Sonatinas

Violin Sonatinasª – No 1, AK46; No 2, AK47; No 3,
AK48; No 4, AK49. March of the Little Soldiers, AK53ª.
Rondo, AK54ª. Nocturne, AK55ª. Little Chorale and
Fugue, AK56ª. Gavotte, AK57ª. Scherzo and Menuetto
Cantato, AK58ª. Solo Violin Sonata, AK69
Georgios Demertzis *vn* ªMaria Asteriadou *pf*
BIS BIS-CD1024 (66' · DDD)   ⓕⓞ➔

Here's a window onto Skalkottas's music for his own instrument, itself a microcosm of his development. There's nothing stylistically ten-tative about the early Solo Violin Sonata (1925). Written with a Bachian economy of manner, the composer draws in references to jazz and popu-lar music; the finale serves notice of his technical skill with an arching four-part fugue, reaching maximum intensity at the point where it returns to the prelude. The sense of a still-emerging personality is reinforced by the first two Sona-tinas (both 1929, the *Andantino* is all that sur-vives from No 1). Skalkottas's rhythmic incisiveness owes something to Stravinsky and even Bartók, but the tang of the harmonic writ-ing is his alone. With the Third and Fourth Sonatinas (both 1935), the Skalkottas idiom, sinuous and expressive, is in place. The thematic integration of No 3 is breathtaking, as is the variety of tone with which the violin sustains continuity in the *Andante*. If the Fourth Sona-tina is almost too diverse in mood, its *Adagio* is one of Skalkottas's finest: a threnody unfolding in three waves of mounting intensity, it looks forward to the expansive slow movements of the composer's last decade.

The miniatures are anything but trifles. *March of the Little Soldiers* is a savage take on militarism, while *Nocturne* reinterprets the expressive vocabulary of the 'song without words' for the 20th century. There could be no more sympathetic advocate than Georgios Demertzis. As in his recording of the Violin Concerto (see above), he gets to the heart of Skalkottas's demanding but deeply felt music, with Maria Asteriadou an attentive partner. Inquiring listeners shouldn't hesitate to acquire this disc.

Piano Works

Musik für Klavier: 32 Piano Pieces, AK70.
Suite No 1, AK71. Four Etudes, AK74
Nikolaos Samaltanos pf
BIS ② BIS-CD1133/4 (119' · DDD)　　　　Ⓕ Ⓞ

Over 60 years after its completion, Skalkottas's *Musik für Klavier* – the overall title of his 32 Piano Pieces – can assume its place among the major piano cycles of the 20th century. Formidably difficult technically, its apparently disparate content – there isn't the conceptual focus of, say, Messiaen's *Vingt regards sur l'Enfant Jésus* – may have militated against its wider recognition. So it's a tribute to Nikolaos Samaltanos, in this first complete recording, that he projects the work as an integral entity, and as the compendium of mid-century pianism that the composer intended.

Achieving equal conviction across such diversity is a tall order, given the absence of a performing tradition against which to assess an interpretation. His playing of individual pieces may be open to question but Samaltanos has the measure of the cycle and the way that its groupings of pieces interconnect. The powerful rhetoric of the 'Passacaglia' and sombre poetry of 'Nachtstück', a double-apex on all levels, are impressively wrought, while the relative nonchalance of the closing *divertissement* is dispatched with élan. Other recordings will surely follow but rivals will be hard pressed to match the scintillating virtuosity of Samaltanos in 'Katastrophe' or the 'Etüde phantastique'.

Wide-ranging sound, lacking only the last degree of clarity in the more heavily chorded pieces.

Howard Skempton　　　　British b1947

Skempton was associated from the outset of his career with the English school of experimental music which evolved in the late 1960s out of Satie, Cage, Feldman and others, in which he, in common with Cardew, played a significant part. Webern and La Monte Young, as well as Feldman, were strong formative influences on the development of Skempton's style. Landmarks in what can also be identified as a response to the wider audience his music has gained

during this period include Lento for orchestra (1990) and the series of concertos composed during the 1990s. The latter includes a pair of double concertos in which Skempton bestows his characteristic favours on some of the less-favoured members of the Western instrumental pantheon, the hurdy-gurdy in one, the accordion in the other.

Choral Works

'The Cloths of Heaven'
Missa brevis. Magnificat and Nunc dimittis
(Edinburgh Service). Upon my lap my sovereign sits.
Locus iste. O Saviour of the World. The Song of
Songs. Adam lay y-bounden. Lamentations: How sits
this city?; I am the man; The anointed Lord; For
oughtest Thou, O Lord. He Wishes for the Cloths of
Heaven. Beati quorum via. Emerson Songs. Ave
Virgo sanctissima. Ostende nobis Domine. O Life!;
Nature's Fire. Recessional.
Exon Singers / Matthew Owens org
Delphian DCD34056 (70' · DDD)　　　　Ⓕ Ⓞ

Music for piano and accordion may be the 'central nervous system' of his work but recent discs suggest Howard Skempton's chamber and vocal output is hardly less significant. This new disc gives an inclusive overview of his choral music and songs. The former ranges from the austerity of the *Magnificat* and *Nunc dimittis*, through the rhythmic repetition and harmonic accretion of *Locus iste* and *The Song of Songs*, to the subtle intricacy of *Ostende nobis Domine* and luminous ecstasy found in Yeats's *He Wishes for the Cloths of Heaven* – a miniature masterpiece to be sure. The *Missa brevis* is a composite of these approaches – whether in the inward anxiousness of its *Gloria*, the surging ardour of its *Sanctus* or the plaintive supplication of its *Agnus Dei*. Highlights from among the songs include the formal yet fervent treatment of Burns in *O Life!*, methodical settings from Donne's versification of *Lamentations*, and the harmonic/melodic interplay of the *Emerson Songs*. Two organ pieces round out the programme, with the artless *Recessional* being an apt conclusion.

Music such as this is easy to kill with overstatement or dull with caution, neither of which is true of these performers: notably the mellifluous Bartholomew Lawrence in the *Lamentations*, and the Exon Singers, whose responsiveness is a tribute to Matthew Owens, whether as director or organist. The sound provides an ideal ambience and presentation is on a par with earlier Delphian issues, making for a release in which Skempton admirers and newcomers alike will find much to savour.

Bedřich Smetana　　　　Bohemian 1824-1884

Czechoslovakia as such did not exist in Smetana's day. The lands of Bohemia merely constituted part of the Austrian Empire. During the 19th century, nationalist movements developed all over Europe, culminating in the 'Year of Revolution', 1848. It was the Prague uprising, during which the previously apolitical Smetana helped man the barricades, that helped in his development as the first composer to give a voice to Czech music. It took him some time to realise his ambition.

'With God's help and grace, I will be a Mozart in composition and a Liszt in technique,' Smetana wrote ambitiously in his diary in 1843. Prodigiously gifted as a child, he was able enough to play first violin in a Haydn quartet at the age of five and make his public debut as a pianist a year later. But because of parental opposition, his talent was not allowed to flourish immediately. At 19 he had had little formal training and his aim to become a great piano virtuoso like Liszt had spectacularly failed. Then luck started to play a part: his girlfriend Katerina Kolárová persuaded her own music professor to give him lessons and simultaneously he became the piano teacher to the family of Count Leopold Thun, enabling him to write his first compositions. However, for eight years after the Prague uprising, Smetana made little progress (he married Katerina but tragedy coloured their relationship – of their four daughters only one, Zofie, survived and Katerina showed signs of tuberculosis from 1855).

In 1856, encouraged by Liszt, he made the bold step of moving to Gothenburg in Sweden and his life started to take shape – he attracted an enthusiastic band of pupils, he at last established himself as a pianist and he composed three symphonic poems (Richard III, Wallenstein's Camp and Hakon Jarl) which attracted much attention.

Katerina died in 1859 and Smetana returned to Prague, having married the sister-in-law of his brother Karl the previous year. The political situation had improved and Smetana was now a mature composer with a reputation to reckon with. He knew Glinka's nationalistic operas, with their Russian melodies and Russian librettos, and determined to do the same for Bohemia. He was given the important job of music director of the Prague Provisional Theatre and his first opera, The Brandenburgers in Bohemia (1863), made use of his new credo. Three years later he wrote his masterpiece, The Bartered Bride. His six other operas show a remarkable versatility in their different styles and content but The Bartered Bride remains the only one in the general repertoire outside Prague today. The 1870s saw Smetana at the height of his creative powers with such original and remarkable works as his cycle of symphonic poems Má vlast (My Country) and his wonderful E minor String Quartet inspired by reflections of his youth.

Smetana ended his days suffering from the effects of syphilis. He had become totally deaf, suffered from headaches and hallucinations and frequently lost the power of speech. Having ceased to appear in public, he lived with his daughter Zofie and her husband in the country, before being confined to an asylum.

Má vlast

Má vlast
Czech Philharmonic Orchestra / Rafael Kubelík
Supraphon SU1910-2 (78' · DDD)

Recorded live 1990   Ⓕ ⊙⊙

Smetana's great cycle of six tone-poems, Má vlast, celebrates the countryside and legendary heroes and heroines of Bohemia. It's a work of immense national significance encapsulating many of the ideals and hopes of that country. What a triumphant occasion it was when Rafael Kubelík returned to his native Czechoslovakia and to his old orchestra after an absence of 42 years and conducted Má vlast at the 1990 Prague Spring Festival. Supraphon's disc captures that live performance – not perfectly, since the sound is efficient rather than opulent – but well enough to show off what's arguably the finest performance on record since Talich's early LP set.

You'd never imagine that Kubelík had emerged from five years of retirement and a recent serious illness, such is the power and eloquence of his conducting. He takes a lyrical rather than a dramatic view of the cycle, and if there's strength enough in more heroic sections there's also a refreshing lack of bombast. Kubelík's intimate knowledge of the score shows time and time again in the most subtle touches. Even the weakest parts of the work are most artfully brought to life, and seem of much greater stature than is usually the case. 'Vltava' flows beautifully, with the most imaginative flecks of detail, and in 'From Bohemia's Woods and Fields' there are vivid visions of wide, open spaces. The orchestra rewards its former director with superb playing.

Má vlast   Ⓗ
Czech Philharmonic Orchestra / Václav Talich
Supraphon mono SU3826-2 (74' · AAD)
Recorded 1954   Ⓕ ⊙⊙⊙

 Try listening from just before six minutes into 'From Bohemia's Woods and Fields' and you reach the very heart of this great performance. The CPO brass lunges towards the main melody with unconstrained eagerness, their impact much aided by smiling glissandos. And as Talich and his players climb aboard Smetana's homespun melody, everything assumes a sunny glow: it's almost as if the entire work thus far had prepared for that one magical moment. But there are countless additional splendours: the luminous mobility of 'Vltava', the grimness of 'Šárka' (so different here to the excitable Kubelík), the sense of foreboding in 'Tábor' and the chest-swelling patriotism of 'Blaník'. The strings retain more than a hint of the portamentos that were such a distinctive feature of Talich's 1929 recording, but the woodwinds are notably superior and the basically excellent sound releases more of the music's dynamism than was easily audible on 78s.

The transfer makes a warmer case for the original tapes than did the old LPs, and generally serves Talich well – except in one maddening respect. A couple of bars have dropped from 'Tábor', thus utterly ruining the contour of a major climax. The offending cut was not present

SMETANA MÁ VLAST – IN BRIEF

Czech PO / Václav Talich ⊞
Supraphon SU3826-2 (74' · ADD) Ⓜ❍❍❍
Infinitely flexible, warm-hearted and full of chest-swelling pride, the great Václav Talich's third and final recording from 1954 has the very stamp of greatness in every bar. This is the Real Thing – totally inside the idiom.

Czech PO / Karel Ančerl
Supraphon SU3661-2 (75' · ADD) Ⓜ
Ančerl's 1961 recording sounds far richer on CD than it ever did on LP. It's an exciting, always purposeful account, marvellously well played.

Czech PO / Rafael Kubelík
Supraphon 11 1208-2 (78' · DDD) Ⓕ❍❍❒➻
Returning to his homeland after an absence of nearly 42 years, Rafael Kubelík launched the 1990 Prague Spring Festival with this unforgettable performance of Smetana's patriotic cycle.

Bavarian RSO / Rafael Kubelík
Orfeo C115 842A (77' · DDD) Ⓕ❍❍
Kubelík again, this time at the helm of his beloved Munich band in arguably the most spellbinding, subtly moulded version of all.

London Classical Players / Roger Norrington �Ⓟ
Virgin 5453012-2 (76' · DDD) Ⓜ❒➻
An enjoyable *Má vlast* give period-instrument garb courtesy of one of today's most questing musicians. Worth hearing.

Vienna Philharmonic / James Levine
DG download 474 565-2GEN (60' · DDD) Ⓜ❒➻
For sensationally beautiful orchestral playing, Levine's VPO recording is most appealing. It may not have the authentic bite of Czech PO versions, but it's full of detail, and the couplings are generous.

Polish National RSO / Antoni Wit
Naxos 8 550931 (80' · DDD) Ⓢ❒➻
A distinctive account from Katowice. Wit opts for unusually lesiurely tempi but there's no lack of momentum or atmosphere. Worth snapping up as a supplement to Talich and Kubelík.

Czech PO / Sir Charles Mackerras
Supraphon SU3465-2 (74' · DDD) Ⓕ
Another memorable Prague Spring Festival concert, this time from May 1999 and featuring a maestro whose lifelong experience and wisdom in Slavonic repertoire require no further comment. As always the Czech Philharmonic play with an understanding of the idiom possessed by no other orchestra.

on the original recording. If you can write off the missing bars as 'historical wear and tear', then expect a *Má vlast* that's way above average, an inspired affirmation of national pride by a wonderful people who had only recently escaped one form of tyranny, and would subsequently fall prey to another.

Symphonic Poems

'Orchestral Works, Vol 1'
Der Fischer, 'Rybář', T103/B138. Hakon Jarl, B118. Jubel-Ouverture, T46/B63. March for Shakespeare Festival, T93/B129. Richard III, B106. Venkovanka, 'The Peasant Woman', T123. Wallenstein's Camp, B111
BBC Philharmonic / Gianandrea Noseda
Chandos CHAN10413 (76' · DDD) Ⓕ❍❍➻

This is a superb disc. There have been distinguished collections of Smetana's symphonic poems but none quite to compare with this in excitement, richness of detail and, in the case of *Wallenstein's Camp*, sonic spectacle – how well Smetana writes for the brass! Indeed this, *Richard III* and especially *Hakon Jarl* emerge afresh as symphonic poems every bit the equal of those of Liszt. The early *Jubel-Ouverture* (1848) with its thundering, frantic opening timpani and energetic folksy flavour is a real find. So, too, is the beautiful watery tableau *The Fisherman*, which has a Wagnerian evocation gently reminding one of the moonlight sequence in 'Vltava'.

But the key works are the first three mentioned above, *Wallenstein's Camp* full of vivid military invention, *Richard III* with its atmospheric, doom-laden portrait, including a memorable dominating theme, gently lurching to represent the king's gait. The orchestration is highly evocative, as it is in the even more ambitiously dramatic *Hakon Jarl*. Here the central lyrical section with its falling scalic main theme, introduced by harp and bass clarinet, is all but Tchaikovskian and leads to a superb climax. The *Shakespeare* March closes the programme boisterously.

Gianandrea Noseda draws wonderfully characterful and spontaneous playing from the BBC Philharmonic, and the Chandos engineers surpass themselves with the realistic vividness of the sound and the naturalness of the balance. Not to be missed.

'Orchestral Works, Vol 2'
The Bartered Bride – Overture; Polka; Furiant; Dance of the Comedians (Skočná). The Brandenburgers in Bohemia, T90/B124 – Prelude; Ballet, Act 1. Dalibor, T96 – Entr'acte. The Devil's Wall, T129 – Overture; Infernal Dance. The Kiss, T115 – Overture. Libuše, T107 – Prelude. The Two Widows, T109 – Overture; Prelude, Act 2; Polka. The Secret, T118 – Overture
BBC Philharmonic Orchestra / Gianandrea Noseda
Chandos CHAN10518 (73' · DDD) Ⓕ❍❍➻

Brilliant, picturesque and nationalistic, all the music on this superb disc pays colourful tribute to 'the father of Bohemian music'. Even the most familiar pages from *The Bartered Bride* come up fresh as paint, the BBC Philharmonic's immaculate virtuosity as musicianly and refined as it is sparkling. However rapid and propulsive the tempo, nothing is pushed or over-driven. The Polka's grandiose opening leads to music of a courtly charm, enough to set even the least susceptible heads nodding and feet tapping. The Furiant's catchy cross-rhythms lead to a suavely romantic melody and in the Overture to *The Secret* there is a typical Smetana progression from sobriety to lightness and exultance.

The Prelude to *Libuše* was written to celebrate the coronation of the Emperor Franz Josef. But even if Smetana was left in the lurch (the event never took place) his ceremonial fanfares carry all the importance of a promised state occasion. The Entr'acte from *Dalibor* is a special delight, a magical dream-like interlude before a return in *The Two Widows* to hyperactivity. Everything is permeated with a sense of Czech pride and ideals, a mood memorably captured by Noseda. Chandos's sound is exceptional.

String Quartets

String Quartets – No 1, 'From my Life'; No 2.
Škampa Quartet (Pavel Fischer, Jana Lukášová *vns* Radim Sedmidubský *va* Lukas Polak *vc*)
Supraphon SU3740-2 (47' · DDD)   Ⓕ

This is music that these Czech players have in their blood, and the variations of tempo which are an essential part of Smetana's idiom seem genuinely improvisatory. Yet the ensemble could not be more polished, with wonderfully clear textures, helped by an excellent, cleanly balanced recording made in Prague's Dvořák Hall.

The Skampa players fully bring out the drama of the First's finale and its spine-chilling tinnitus whistle which the deaf composer included from experience. No 2 finds them in more relaxed mood, with extreme tempo changes in the first movement, infectious 'oompah' rhythms in the second, and high contrasts in the finale.

The Bartered Bride

The Bartered Bride   Ⓗ
Ada Nordenová *sop* Mařenka **Otta Horáková** *sop* Esmeralda **Marie Pixová** *sop* Ludmila **Marta Krásová** *mez* Háta **Valdimir Toms** *ten* Jeník **Jaroslav Gleich** *ten* Vašek **Karel Hruska** *ten* Circus Master **Jan Konstantin** *bar* Krušina **Emil Pollert** *bass* Kecal **Zdenek Otava** *bass* Mícha **Václav Marek** *bass* Indian **Prague National Opera Company Chorus; Prague National Opera Company Orchestra / Otakar Ostrčil**
Naxos mono ② 8 110098/9 (118' · ADD)
Recorded 1933   Ⓢ🅓➔

This is the first ever recording of Smetana's most popular opera, performed by a team steeped in the tradition of interpreting the work in Prague. Otakar Ostrčil gives a rhythmically

exhilarating, suitably expectant account of the overture, directs the dances with just the right amount of brio tempered by lightness, and gives thoughtful support to his singers. The whole cast is Czech, so the recitative flows with a natural feeling for speech rhythms and accentuation. Nordenová as Mařenka has a sweet, unaffected timbre that's exactly right for her part, and she employs *portamento* in a way that would not be tolerated today; so much the worse for today. Her Jeník has a plangent tone and intimate delivery near-ideal for the role, though some may be surprised at hearing such a light voice in a part now assigned to heavier tenors. The somewhat confined recording has been miraculously restored to obviate most of the drawbacks of the original. At the asking price, anyone interested in the early traditions of interpreting this work will enjoy a welcome bargain.

The Bartered Bride (sung in English)
Susan Gritton *sop* Mařenka **Paul Charles Clarke** *ten* Jeník **Timothy Robinson** *ten* Vašek **Peter Rose** *bass* Kecal **Neal Davies** *bar* Krušina **Diana Montague** *mez* Háta **Geoffrey Moses** *bass* Mícha **Yvette Bonner** *sop* Ludmila, Esmeralda **Robin Leggate** *ten* Circus Master **Kit Hesketh-Harvey** *bass* Indian **Royal Opera House Chorus, Covent Garden; Philharmonia Orchestra / Sir Charles Mackerras**
Chandos Opera in English ② CHAN3128 (148' · DDD)   Ⓜ

By almost any reckoning, this is the most popular of Czech operas, in the repertory of almost every opera house, so it is astonishing how few recordings have appeared in recent years; Košler's Supraphon set of 1981 is the only other digital recording hitherto. That well-cast version is in the original Czech; this one comes in a crisp translation by Kit Hesketh-Harvey of cabaret duo Kit and the Widow. Hesketh-Harvey, sporting a cheeky cockney accent, also takes the tiny role of the Indian in the Act 3 Circus scene.

What makes this version so successful? The brilliant conducting of Sir Charles Mackerras, of course, plus the scintillating playing of the Philharmonia; an exceptionally strong team of soloists, too. But it's the extra impact of having the comedy delivered in the vernacular that makes this stand out.

Kecal, the marriage-broker, for example, has many patter numbers, and Peter Rose is agile and crystal clear, establishing himself as the key character in the story. Hesketh-Harvey gives the chorus some rapid tongue-twisters to cope with: the Covent Garden Chorus does so admirably.

The sparkling mood is set at the start, with Mackerras taking the Overture at headlong speed and the Philharmonia strings responding with perfect clarity and precision, vividly caught in the warm, clear, well-balanced Chandos recording. The chorus reinforces the mood, and the duet between the heroine Mařenka and her beloved Jeník instantly has you involved in the complicated story.

Susan Gritton is radiant, producing golden tone and rising superbly to the challenge of the poignant numbers when it seems that Jeník has betrayed her. Paul Charles Clarke as her suitor is less successful: the voice becomes strangulated and uneven under pressure though the characterisation is first-rate. Timothy Robinson as the stuttering simpleton Vašek and Robin Leggate as the Circus Master are superb. Peter Rose as Kecal is wonderfully fluent, matched by the excellent Esmeralda of Yvette Bonner, both defying the tradition of having actors in the roles of the circus artists. Strong casting, too, means the two sets of parents make a considerable impact.

Above all, thanks are due to Mackerras for the emotional warmth as well as highlighting the colour and energy of Smetana's masterpiece.

The Bartered Bride
Gabriela Beňačková sop Mařenka **Peter Dvorský** ten Jeník ten Vašek **Richard Novák** bass Kecal **Jindřich Jindrák** bar Krušina **Marie Mrázová** mez Háta **Jaroslav Horáček** bass Mícha **Marie Veselá** sop Ludmila **Jana Jonášová** sop Esmeralda **Alfréd Hampel** ten Circus Master **Prague Philharmonic Chorus; Prague National Theatre Chorus and Ballet; Czech Philharmonic Orchestra / Zdeněk Košler**
Film director **František Filip**
Supraphon *DVD* SU7011-9 (138' · NTSC · 4:3 · 2.0 and 5.1 · 0)　　　　　　　Ⓕ

Košler's *Bride* remains a benchmark for a modern recording of Smetana's epochal Czech comedy. Supraphon now makes available on DVD the TV film from which that audio derived. The overture is given in concert, then, via stock footage of Prague and the Vltava, we fade into a touristy museum/studio set of a 19th-century Czech village. Yes, Czech festivals are a riot of colour and movement – but the clothes don't look as if they're fresh off the costume rail. There's no real production as such, just the soloists giving a concert in costume, with movement and 'action' being provided by the dancers and actors. The result is relentlessly pretty, undramatic and dull.

The vocal performances are almost all distinguished. In camera, Richard Novák's light, laid-back Kecal makes more sense than it did without pictures. Peter Dvorský's passionate, Italianate Jeník does itself justice in acting terms. Film close-ups are not overkind to the two 'young' girls of the cast but both Beňačková and Jonášová's Esmeralda know their business. Košler's fluent conducting avoids what one might call the 'German' side of Smetana, heard clearly on Ostrčil's nonpareil set and Mackerras's recent English version (see above). The sound is fine; the picture quality misty.

Fernando Sor　　　　Spanish 1778-1839

After leaving Spain, composer and guitarist Fern-

ando Sor lived in Paris and London and visited Russia. He was a famous concert performer and wrote over 60 guitar works (sonatas, studies, variations etc) and an important method (1830). His guitar music is notable for its part-writing. He was also admired for his songs and eight ballets (1821-28); other works include an opera and chamber and keyboard pieces.

Guitar Works

Fantaisies – No 12, Op 58; No 13, Op 59, 'Fantaisie élégiaque'. Studies, Op 60
Nicholas Goluses gtr
Naxos 8 553342 (65' · DDD)　　　　　　　Ⓢ▶

Sor's guitar music forms a body of work that's perhaps the most consistent in quality and most manageable in quantity of any major guitar composer of the period. While he was born and died later than Beethoven Sor's language was closer to that of Mozart, barely on the edge of Romanticism.

He was a polished, elegant composer, whose works have more quiet emotional content and expressiveness than those of his contemporaries, and though he often calls for technical virtuosity he doesn't lean too heavily on it. The *Fantaisie*, Op 58 isn't one of Sor's more riveting works. Goluses plays it in a somewhat matter-of-fact way. The *Fantaisie élégiaque*, arguably Sor's finest single work, elicits a very different response, a deeply sensitive and dignified reading in which the moments of silent grief are given the breathing-space they call for. Sor devoted five opus numbers to his 97 studies, of which Op 60 was the last. Each has a clear technical and/or musical purpose and even the simplest is lovingly crafted music – which is how Goluses treats it, with lots of care lavished on it.

The guitar of Sor's time differed from today's in construction, stringing and sound, and Sor played without using the right-hand nails. Goluses uses a modern instrument and plays with nails, which inevitably leads to differences in sound and, to some extent, interpretation. Accepting the differences, Goluses sets a benchmark for present-day guitarists.

Minuets, Op 11 – No 4; No 5; No 6; No 7; No 8. Ⓟ
Menuets – Op 3; Op 5 No 3; Op 24 No 1.
Introduction and Variations on a Theme by Mozart, Op 9. Andante largo, Op 5 No 5. 12 Studies, Op 6 – No 2; No 8; No 9; No 11; No 12. Grand Solo, Op 14
William Carter bq gtr
Linn ⊕ CKD343 (62' · DDD)　　Ⓕ●●●▶

Here, period-instrument specialist William Carter turns his attention to the early solo works of Sor via a guitar built by Tony Johnson after various 19th-century instruments. And while there are other recordings available of Sor's music on period instruments, this is a first in that Carter also plays, as did Sor, with the flesh of the fingertips rather than the nails.

The use of an instrument which is lighter and smaller than a modern classical instrument and the fingertips of the right hand results in a delicate yet surprisingly broad range of tones and colours that perfectly evokes the period-instrument sound world in a chamber or orchestral context. This, combined with Carter's refined musicianship and trademark dynamic shading shows the selection of Sor's minuets, the famous *Variations on a Theme of Mozart*, the beautiful Mozartian *Andante largo*, some of the better-known studies from Op 6 and the masterful *Grand Solo* to be so much more than merely well crafted salon music. Superb.

Grand Sonatas – C, Op 22; C, Op 25. Divertissement, Op 23. Eight Short Pieces, Op 24
Adam Holzman gtr
Naxos 8 553340 (75' · DDD)　　　　　Ⓢ↪

The major works in Holzman's programme are the two sonatas, each with four movements. Of these Op 25 is by far the finer – and the best work of its kind from the period; the last movement is a Minuet, a final lightening of atmosphere that was not then uncommon. The *Divertissement*, Op 23 contains 10 pieces – *valses, allegrettos, andantes*, a *minuetto* and an *allemande*. With a few exceptions they're more likely to be of interest to guitarists than to the general listener.

Holzman plays very well, with a softer sound than Goluses (see above), and in a tighter acoustic. At slower tempi he exercises a pleasing degree of *rubato* and commendable dynamic shading; one wishes he had done likewise in the quicker ones, which incline to the metronomic. These are two discs that should, both in their own right and at super-budget price, be irresistible to guitarists.

Introduction and Variations on 'Que ne suis-je la fougère!', Op 26. Introduction and Variations on 'Gentil Housard', Op 27. Introduction and Variations on 'Malbroug', Op 28. 12 Studies, Op 29. Fantaisie et Variations brillantes, Op 30
Jeffrey McFadden gtr
Naxos 8 553451 (62' · DDD)　　　　　ⓈⓄⓄ↪

This contribution to Naxos's integral archive of Sor's guitar music consists neatly of the last works he published with Meissonnier, before transferring to Pacini. Sets of variations, whether *per se* or framed in the *Fantaisie*, Op 30, abound. The *12 Studies*, Op 29 are described as 'Book 2', those of Op 6 being 'Book 1', and are here given as Nos 13-24, as they were in the original edition of 1827. Jeffrey McFadden is a very musical player, with the clear and three-dimensional tone for which his fingers are admirably suited. No composer for the guitar of the time wrote studies that were more truly expressive than those of Sor; McFadden plays them, and everything else here, with humanity and respect. An outstanding disc.

Kaikhosru Sorabji　English 1892–1988

Sorabji was of Spanish-Sicilian-Parsi parentage. Largely self-taught, he occupies a curious place in the repertoire. Several of his works are of extraordinary length and difficulty, making them inaccessible to many pianists. His works were influenced by Alkan, Busoni (to whom his Second Piano Sonata is dedicated), Godowsky, Reger, Szymanowski, Scriabin and Delius. He was friends with Philip Heseltine (aka Peter Warlock) and became a music journalist in part because of their friendship. He was a perceptive and often venomous critic. He was equally notorious for refusing permission for his works to be publicly performed.

Piano Works

'Legendary Works for Piano'
Fantaisie espagnole. Fantasiettina. Gulistān. Le jardin parfumé. Nocturne. Three Pastiches. Opus clavicembalisticum – Introito and Preludio-Corale. Prelude, Interlude and Fugue. Quaere reliqua hujus materiei inter secretiora. St Bertrand de Comminges, 'He was laughing in the tower'. Two Pieces. Valse-Fantaisie. Fragment for Harold Rutland **Habermann** A la manière de Sorabji: 'Au clair de la lune'
Michael Habermann pf
British Music Society ③ (three discs for the price of two) BMS427/9CD (3h 17' · ADD/DDD)　　　Ⓕ

The music of Sorabji acquired mythic status long before his death in 1988, not least through the ban on public performances imposed by him in 1938. When the ban was lifted in 1976 Michael Habermann was among the first pianists to take up Sorabji in earnest. The fruits of his devotion – technically and conceptually – to some of the most demanding music yet conceived for piano can be heard on these recordings, made over a 15-year period.

Spanning mainly the period 1918-41, the set covers the first half of Sorabji's career, dominated by the vast *Opus clavicembalisticum*, later championed by John Ogdon and Geoffrey Douglas Madge, and represented here by a swift and eventful rendition of its first two sections. 'In the Hothouse' and *Fantaisie espagnole* will appeal to anyone who enjoys the more demonstrative output of Scriabin or Szymanowski, while the pastiches show that Sorabji's music wasn't without humour.

The second disc comprises a trio of nocturnes: pieces whose rhapsodic unfolding belies their intricacy of construction. If the harmonic profile of *Le jardin parfumé* draws in resonances of Delius and pre-echoes of Messiaen, that of *Djâmî* represents a sublimation of means to wholly original ends – and is the undoubted masterpiece of this collection. Aficionados would no doubt make even greater claims for *Gulistān*, but here the very complexity of texture seems designed to conceal rather than intensify expression.

As to the performances, there can be no doubting the extent of Michael Habermann's sympathies, nor his depth of insight. The release comes with informative notes by Habermann, and can be cordially recommended to those keen to immerse themselves in a composer whose singularity of expression is sometimes matched by the conviction of his achievement.

100 Transcendental Studies

100 Transcendental Studies – Nos 1-25
Fredrik Ullén pf
BIS BIS-CD1373 (71' · DDD)   Ⓕ

Given the number of recordings now appearing, it was inevitable that Kaikhosru Sorabji's 100 *Transcendental Studies* be tackled, and Swedish pianist Fredrik Ullén has taken up the challenge. Composed in 1940-44, the cycle constitutes the largest known collection of its kind – encompassing brief studies in piano technique and extended pieces amply illuminating the 'parallel universe' that is Sorabji's creativity.

Right from No 1 it is clear that Sorabji's conception of the study is all-embracing. No 3 scatters its melodic content over layers of intricate polyphony, while No 6 is a scintillating study in seconds (with studies for each interval to follow). The febrile whole-tone volleys of No 10 and the delicate interplay of melodic patterns in No 14 touch on different but equally characteristic aspects of Sorabji's pianism – less so the Messiaen-like rhythmic unison writing of No 17. The liquid chains of fifths that inform No 18 and the coolly iridescent textures of No 20 confirm these studies as among the highlights of the cycle so far, with the cumulative rhythmic overlaying of No 23 likely to remain among the most technically demanding. The striding *staccato* chords of No 25 bring this first quarter of the cycle to a typically quizzical conclusion.

Ullén has the dexterity and finesse to do this music justice without making light of either its innate difficulty or its protean imagination.

Louis Spohr   German 1784-1859

After work as a chamber player at the Brunswick court, Spohr become a virtuoso violinist, touring throughout Germany. As Konzertmeister in Gotha (1805-12) he took up conducting (with a baton) and had some of his own works performed. Operatic conducting posts at Vienna (1813-15) and Frankfurt (1817-19) coincided with significant bursts of composing activity, yielding chamber music and the successful operas Faust (1813) and Zemire und Azor (1819).

He settled as Kapellmeister at Kassel in 1822, and embarked on a hugely creative period which saw the premieres of the operas Jessonda, the oratorio Die letzten Dinge and the Symphony No 4. A favourite in England, he received international honours and became Generalmusikdirektor at Kassel (1847). By the 1850s he had been somewhat sidelined as his

music was rather traditional when compared with the younger generation of Romantic composers. Among his works are 15 violin and 10 other concertos, 10 symphonies, virtuoso solo works, scores of chamber works, four clarinet concertos, string quartets, and the Octet and Nonet for wind and strings.

Clarinet Concertos

Clarinet Concertos – No 1; No 2. Potpourri on Two Themes from Winter's 'Das Unterbrochene'. Variations on a Theme from 'Alruna'
Michael Collins cl
Swedish Chamber Orchestra / Robin O'Neill
Hyperion CDA67509 (62' · DDD)   ⒻⓄⓄ↦

The memorable opening C minor theme of the First Clarinet Concerto (1809) has a Beethovenian contour, yet the solo roulades which follow suggest the minor key is not to be taken too seriously. The work, like its companion, was commissioned by the clarinet virtuoso Johann Hermstedt, who adapted his instrument for the music, adding five extra keys! It is a fine piece with a lovely *Adagio* to remind us that Mozart's Quintet was Spohr's inspiration. The charming finale lollops along engagingly.

The Second Concerto, written a year later, is distinctly galant in the jaunty Hummelian march theme which dominates the first movement. The eloquent *Adagio* is unashamedly operatic, with characteristic turns in the melodic line, but the highlight is the *Polacca* finale, opening neatly with a solo timpani flourish answered by the horns. This gives Michael Collins wonderful opportunities for a spirited bravura display that invites a smile of pleasure, as do his fluid, lyrical line and lovely tone and phrasing throughout.

The *Potpourri* opens invitingly on the horns but is no medley. Instead it centres on two themes, the second with a set of variations, offering more bravura fireworks, clearly relished here. The Variations are very much in the same vein. An outstanding disc, excellently recorded.

Symphonies

Symphonies Nos 3, Op 78, & 6, 'Historical Symphony', Op 116. Der Fall Babylons, WoO63
Orchestra della Svizzera Italiana / Howard Shelley
Hyperion CDA67788 (64' · DDD)   ⒻⓄ↦

Howard Shelley has a strong feeling for the varieties and subtleties of Spohr's symphonic style, and here continues his cycle of the 10 symphonies with two more works making different demands. No 3 was first performed in 1828, the year after Beethoven's death, and the early reviews suggest relief that the German symphony had not died with him. The stormy opening *Allegro* bursts with energy and Shelley makes the most of a fine *Larghetto* (though one that is not free from cliché) and of a *Scherzo* with echoes of Mendelssohn as well as of Beethoven. Spohr's finale is given its full strength with thematic material that receives imaginative handling.

This includes some excellent fugal writing, something which Mendelssohn respected in Spohr and which returns in the opening movement of the Sixth Symphony, of 1839. This is the strange *Historical Symphony* in which Spohr sought to invoke different historical periods. So we have a '1720' movement with Bach (the fugue) and Handel (a pastorale, as in *Messiah*), then a '1780' movement in which first Haydn and then Mozart are recomposed as if in the 19th century, to which suitably expanded scoring is further added for Beethoven in '1810' (though it is perhaps the earlier *Eroica* that most comes to mind). The finale, '1840' or 'The very latest period', runs riot among various composers, with strange French devices, mostly operatic. Shelley steers the necessary course between parody and genuine appreciation, and as a fill-up includes a first recording of the vigorous overture *The Fall of Babylon*.

Sir John Stainer
British 1840-1901

Stainer, after posts in Tenbury and Oxford, became organist at St Paul's Cathedral (1872-88), reforming the musical service there. He soon became a pre-eminent church musician, scholar and composer, helping found the Musical Association, and becoming professor at Oxford University. He was knighted in 1888. As a scholar he made valuable editions of music before Palestrina and Tallis. His services and anthems were fashionable during his lifetime and his hymn-tunes are still used; his oratorio The Crucifixion (1887) is probably his best-known work.

The Crucifixion

The Crucifixion
Martyn Hill ten **Michael George** bass **BBC Singers;**
Leith Hill Festival Singers / Brian Kay with
Margaret Phillips org
Chandos CHAN9551 (71' · DDD · T)   Ⓕ**O**Ⓓ▸

Stainer's *Crucifixion* unfolds with a seamless ease, never jolting the listener with gratuitous theatricality or the type of rhetorical intensity which the English find mildly embarrassing. The emotional engagement here is about an unintrusive sobriety, affected by a glowing sentimental identification with the Saviour's plight. One has to admire Stainer for writing a challenging work of sensible length which, without an orchestra, is achievable and satisfying for a capable parish choir: Stainer's *Crucifixion* is a celebration of amateurism, that cherished English virtue. Brian Kay has worked a great deal with committed amateurs, in this case the Leith Hill Festival Singers, the festival of which he's director. There's an underlying freshness of expression here, of singers with eyes and ears on stalks and a real sense of purpose. They are fortified by the excellent BBC Singers. Margaret Phillips's imaginative, genial registrations, not to mention her skilful accompaniment, provide notable support to the fine contributions of the soloists. An unselfregarding and genuine performance.

The Crucifixion
Andrew Kennedy ten **Neal Davies** bass
Huddersfield Choral Society / Joseph Cullen with
Darius Battiwalla org
Signum SIGCD176 (62' · DDD)   Ⓕ**Ⓑ**▸

Executed as it is here with fervour, in the passionate solos by Andrew Kennedy and Neal Davies (the best on disc), the bold organ accompaniments (often underplayed) provided by Darius Battiwalla, and expressive choruses such as 'O come unto me', the work has considerable expressive power. This comes through vividly in the 'Processional to Calvary' where, besides the clarity of the text, the dynamic shades give the interpretation life and vivacity. Similarly, the *a cappella* gem of the work, 'God so loved the world', has a moving poignancy. Just occasionally there is a slightly flat edge to the soprano and tenor lines but this by no means detracts from the impassioned Romanticism of this performance which other 'cathedral type' recordings, beautiful as they are, sometimes lack.

Sir Charles Villiers Stanford
Irish/British 1852-1924

After education at Cambridge and then in Leipzig, and teaching posts at Trinity College and the Royal College of Music in London, Stanford became one of the most influental eductors in late-19th-century England. He was appointed professor of composition at the Royal College of Music in 1883; was conductor of the Bach Choir from 1886 to 1902; was professor of music at Cambridge; and conductor of the Leeds Philharmonic Society from 1897 to 1909, and of the Leeds Festival from 1901 to 1910. He was an exacting but respected teacher whose pupils included Samuel Coleridge-Taylor, Gustav Holst, Ralph Vaughan Williams, John Ireland, Frank Bridge, Charles Wood, Ivor Gurney and Herbert Howells. Apart from his Anglican cathedral music, little of his large output (nearly 200 opus numbers) has remained in performance, though he has been luckier on record. His works include 10 operas, a quantity of choral music and songs (his B flat Service of 1879 is still used, and some of his sensitive part-songs are remembered, particularly The Blue Bird), seven symphonies and other orchestral scores (Clarinet Concerto, 1902, and a series of Irish Rhapsodies), eight string quartets, and organ and piano music.

Concertos

Violin Concerto. Suite for Violin and Orchestra, Op 32
Anthony Marwood vn **BBC Scottish Symphony**

Orchestra / Martyn Brabbins
Hyperion CDA67208 (67' · DDD)   Ⓟ Ⓞ ▶

This is a discovery of major importance. Hubert Parry (no mean critic) regarded Stanford's Violin Concerto as one of his finest works, yet it has been played rarely, if at all, since his death in 1924. One preliminary word of warning though: despite Stanford's reputation as a disciple of Brahms, don't listen to this concerto expecting it to sound Brahmsian. Often enough it does, but when it doesn't it isn't because Stanford has failed to match the quality of his 'model'; far more often it's because he's going his own way, speaking with his own and not a derivative voice.

The very opening of the concerto is a case in point: the soloist's melody is accompanied by a beautifully delicate texture of plucked strings and rippling woodwind. There's nothing quite like it in Brahms; nor is Brahms always so generous with his thematic material as Stanford is in this movement. After that 'first subject' and an extensive and varied 'second subject group', a big and dramatic orchestral *tutti* leads not to the expected development but to a new and quite splendid theme. There's plenty of room for virtuosity, but very often the display is modified by a pensive quality, a reticence, that's seemingly Stanford's own, and most attractive.

The slow movement is also notable for its individual scoring (very spare at the outset; a magical return of the melancholy opening melody at the end over murmuring *tremolando* strings) and for its melodic distinction. The sadness of the first theme is again reticent, adding greatly to the eloquence of the heartfelt *tutti* that leads to the finest theme in the entire work, upon which Stanford lavishes rhapsodic figuration of great beauty.

There's not a player better suited to bringing this concerto back to life than Anthony Marwood. He easily surmounts its technical demands, but his distinction as a chamber musician enables him to seek out all its quieter subtleties and pensive asides. The Suite is a lesser but still highly entertaining work, an exercise in neo-Baroque designed as a warmly affectionate tribute to Joseph Joachim. Its sheer ingenuity (the first movement, for example, is a combination of sonata form and two sets of interlocked variations) saves it from being a mere exercise, and its melodic freshness from being a mere makeweight to the masterly concerto. First-class orchestral playing, sympathetically conducted, and a recording that's both clean and spacious.

Cello Concerto[a]. Piano Concerto No 3, Op 171 (orch G Bush)[b]
[a]**Alexander Baillie** vc [b]**Malcolm Binns** pf **Royal Philharmonic Orchestra / Nicholas Braithwaite**
Lyrita SRCD321 (65' · DDD)   Ⓟ Ⓓ ▶

Stanford composed nine concertos, only four of which made it into print. The Cello Concerto in D minor is an early work dating from 1879-80. Apart from the slow movement, the concerto was never performed and soon consigned to dusty oblivion by its creator. An endearing effort it proves, too, the solo writing always grateful and assured (the central *Adagio* displays a winsome lyrical charm reminiscent of Dvořák and Sullivan) and deftly scored, above all in the finale which trips along most engagingly. Alexander Baillie's impassioned and stylish advocacy could hardly be improved upon (he also supplies the first-movement cadenza); Nicholas Braithwaite and the RPO provide alert support, though string tone is not as sweet as it might be.

Completed four decades later, the Third Piano Concerto survives in just a two-piano score and was orchestrated for this recording by Geoffrey Bush. Perhaps the imposing opening *Allegro moderato*, like the performance itself, takes a while to get into its stride, but the slow movement has one or two unexpected twists and the exuberant finale is a joy. Malcolm Binns gives an accomplished rendering, but his chosen instrument sounds in less than first-class condition and there's little of the enticing bloom evident on his splendid 1976 Lyrita recording of Stanford's Second Concerto. Musically, however, there's plenty to savour.

Symphonies

Symphony No 1. Clarinet Concerto, Op 80a
[a]**Robert Plane** cl **Bournemouth Symphony Orchestra / David Lloyd-Jones**
Naxos 8 570356 (71' · DDD)   Ⓢ Ⓞ ▶

This is the final recording in the Naxos series of Stanford symphonies, featuring an unusual coupling of the early (but by no means juvenile) First Symphony (1876), without an opus number, and the much later Clarinet Concerto (1903). The sound of these Naxos recordings with an on-form Bournemouth SO has a nice forward quality which, for the rather luminous chamber quality of Stanford's second and third movements (especially the solo string and wind writing), gives great clarity to the pointillistic, almost Mendelssohnian orchestration.

As with the other three recordings, Lloyd-Jones shows a real flair for the classical architecture of Stanford's art but at the same time he responds to the underlying and inescapable passion that exudes from the scores. The first movement retains a spaciousness and verve, while the finale has an infectious rhythmical élan reminding us of its foremost influence, Schumann's *Spring* Symphony (in the same key).

Stanford's first (though unpublished) foray into symphonic music deserves to be better known but his Clarinet Concerto, here played by Robert Plane, is frequently given an airing. A fine work in one continuous movement, written for Robert Mühlfeld (who never played it), it makes masterly use of the instrument's wide register and variety of timbres. Plane's interpretation of the composer's long lyrical lines (in particular the central *Andante*), the climactic peaks, dramatic interjections and tender *pianissimos*, are nothing short of exceptional in their careful grading; clearly, he has a special affinity for this music.

Symphonies – No 2, 'Elegiac'; No 5, 'L'Allegro ed il Penseroso'
Bournemouth Symphony Orchestra /
David Lloyd-Jones
Naxos 8 570289 (75' · DDD)　　　　　Ⓢ🅑➔

Although labelled *Elegiac* and prefaced with lines from Tennyson's *In memoriam*, Stanford's Second Symphony (1880) wears a largely untroubled demeanour. In fact, it's a thoroughly congenial, skilfully scored creation, with frequent glances of approval towards Mendelssohn, Schumann, Brahms and Dvořák, yet it received just two performances in 1882 and 1883 before falling into oblivion. Vernon Handley revived it with the Ulster Orchestra in 1990 and went on to record it a year later as part of his pioneering Stanford symphony cycle (Chandos). Like Handley, David Lloyd-Jones proves an undisruptive, clear-headed guide, while the playing of the Bournemouth SO has an extra finish, buoyancy and lustre that tip the scales in his favour.

Honours are more evenly divided in the altogether meatier Fifth Symphony of 1894, which derives its subtitle and inspiration from Milton's twinned poems *L'Allegro* and *Il Penseroso*. Lloyd-Jones's bright-eyed approach is especially effective in the first two movements (the rustic *Scherzo* gambols along most winningly), whereas it's Handley who better captures the more thoughtfully restrained character and inexorable grandeur of the work's second half. Moreover, Chandos's 1987 Ulster Hall production has the estimable advantage of an organ *in situ* for the symphony's heady apotheosis (its initial entry on the Naxos disc is too discreet – the sound is otherwise very pleasing). Tiny grumbles aside, Lloyd-Jones's remains a strongly recommendable pairing and should be snapped up without delay.

Symphonies – No 3, 'Irish', Op 28;
No 6, 'In memoriam GF Watts', Op 94
Bournemouth Symphony Orchestra /
David Lloyd-Jones
Naxos 8 570355 (80' · DDD)　　　　　Ⓢ🅑➔

Completed in 1887, the *Irish* Symphony enjoyed considerable acclaim both at home and abroad (von Bülow and Richter were early champions, and in 1910 Mahler conducted two performances in New York). After a solidly constructed opening *Allegro moderato*, the Irish flavour comes to the fore with a disarming hop, skip and jig of a *scherzo*, followed by a nobly beautiful lament (of markedly Brahmsian hue and framed by some gorgeous harp writing) and a finale which deploys

two folk tunes and ties up the threads in rousingly effective fashion. Lloyd-Jones's is, in fact, the second recording of this lovable creation we've had from Bournemouth and represents a more dynamic and luminous voyage of discovery than its sturdier 1982 predecessor under Del Mar (EMI). Handley's sprightly 1986 Ulster account (Chandos) is arguably more cogent than either but now sounds a little raw next to this judiciously balanced newcomer.

Written very quickly in the spring of 1905 as a personal response to the recent death and legacy of the esteemed Victorian artist George Frederick Watts (1817-1904), the Sixth Symphony has fared less happily, receiving a mere two performances until its Belfast revival under Handley some 80 years later. A looser-limbed affair than its lengthier bedfellow here, it still affords a sizeable quotient of incidental pleasures (the glowingly sincere slow movement and consolatory closing pages stand out from their garrulous surroundings). Lloyd-Jones masterminds an affectionate, finely disciplined reading, with tensions kept agreeably on the boil throughout, though again it's Handley (Chandos) who better disguises any architectural shortcomings. No matter, it all adds up to another thoroughly desirable (and, at just over 80 minutes, generous) coupling in this useful series.

Additional recommendation

Symphonies Nos 1-7
Ulster Orchestra / Vernon Handley
Chandos ④ CHAN9279/82　　　　　Ⓜ🅞➔
　　Wonderfully rich and imaginative late-romantic creations – melodically long-breathed and harmonically engaging. Handley conducts superbly paced and splendidly idiomatic performances. Also available to download singly.

Clarinet Sonata

Clarinet Sonata[a]. Piano Trio No 3, Op 158[b].
Fantasies[c] Nos 1 & 2. Three Intermezzi, Op 13[a]
[a]**Robert Plane** *cl* [a]**Mia Cooper** *vn*
[a]**David Adams** *va* [b]**Gould Piano Trio**
(Lucy Gould *vn* Alice Neary *vc* [a]Benjamin Frith *pf*)
Naxos 8 570416 (74' · DDD)　　　　　Ⓢ🅞➔

The Clarinet Sonata is one of Stanford's strongest achievements from his later years, boasting at its heart a powerful *Adagio* ('Caoine' – an Irish lament) which finds Plane wonderfully responsive to the music's raw emotion. Ravishing in tone and exploiting an excitingly wide range of dynamic, Plane forges a commandingly articulate alliance with pianist Benjamin Frith. Indeed, it's hard to imagine more sympathetic music-making – a statement which also holds true for the *Three Intermezzi* (an exceedingly attractive trilogy dating from 1879) and the two substantial, utterly disarming *Fantasies* for clarinet and string quartet, written in 1921-22 for use by students towards the end of Stanford's 40-year stint as professor of composition at the Royal College of Music. As if all that were not enough, we're also treated to the world premiere recording of the last of Stanford's three piano trios. Completed in 1918, it's a tautly constructed, urgently communicative piece dedicated to the memory of the two sons of Alan Gray, Stanford's successor as organist of Trinity College and conductor of the Cambridge University Music Society. Again, the performance is absolutely first-class and, with sound that is at once intimate and true, this valuable anthology can be welcomed with open arms. Naxos's absurdly modest asking-price is the icing on the cake!

String Quartets

String Quartets – No 1; No 2. Fantasy[a]
RTÉ Vanbrugh Quartet (Gregory Ellis, Keith Pascoe vns Simon Aspell va Christopher Marwood vc) with
[a]**Stephen Stirling** hn
Hyperion CDA67434 (68' · DDD)   Ⓕ Ⓑ➤

Stanford wrote the first two of his eight string quartets within just six weeks during the summer of 1891. Cast in four movements and impeccably laid out for the medium, the G major First Quartet launches with an impressive *Allegro assai*, whose considerable intellectual and expressive resource is quarried to the full by the Vanbrughs. Both the *Scherzo* and finale smile as they should, while these fine players bring a rare eloquence to the deeply felt slow movement. Superior craftsmanship is also a trademark of its A minor companion. The first movement's ruminative main theme is developed further still in the *Andante espressivo* slow movement. In between comes a dashing *Prestissimo scherzo*. The work concludes with an irresistible *Allegro molto* (whose cheeky initial idea brings with it more than a whiff of Hungarian paprika).

The A minor Fantasy for horn and string quartet (1922), a companion piece to the Two Fantasy Pieces for clarinet quintet completed not long before, shares that diptych's formal integration (its four sections are interlinked) and technical flair. Stephen Stirling audibly relishes the superbly judged horn writing and generates a most satisfying rapport with the Vanbrughs.

These exemplary first recordings make the best possible case for all this rare material; sound and balance are first-class, too.

Piano Quintet in D minor

Piano Quintet[a]. String Quintet No 1[b]
Vanbrugh Quartet (Gregory Ellis, Keith Pascoe vns Simon Aspell va Christopher Marwood vc) with
[b]**Garth Knox** va [a]**Piers Lane** pf
Hyperion CDA67505 (65' · DDD)   Ⓕ Ⓑ➤

Boosted by the warm reception afforded to his early sonatas for violin and cello and First Piano Quartet, the 33-year-old Stanford penned what would prove to be his biggest chamber work in the spring of 1886. Lasting some 37 minutes and

dedicated to Joseph Joachim, the Piano Quintet in D minor owes much to the example of the Schumann and Brahms quintets (one also wonders whether Elgar ever heard it). In its vaulting ambition, consummate polish and wealth of strong ideas, it's a mightily impressive achievement all round; indeed, such is the music's epic sweep, there are pages in the first and third movements especially which seem to cry out for orchestral garb. It's also full of good tunes, not least in the playful scamper of the *Scherzo* and surgingly energetic and confident finale. A considerable discovery, in sum, which Piers Lane and the Vanbrugh Quartet do absolutely proud.

For the First String Quintet of 1903 the Vanbrughs are joined by viola player Garth Knox (formerly of the Arditti Quartet) to give a passionate and stylish rendering of a piece of such beguiling facility and songful grace that one is amazed that it has lain neglected for so long. Of its three movements, the most individual and compelling is the extended concluding *Allegretto*, an entrancing theme-and-variations which not only manages to fuse elements of both *scherzo* and sonata-form finale but also effectively incorporates material from the work's central *Andante* (an Irish lament in all but name).

The booklet essay by Jeremy Dibble is a model of scholarly research and enthusiasm. Flawless sound and balance, too.

Requiem, Op 63

Requiem. The Veiled Prophet of Khorassan – Overture; Ballet music No 1; There's a bower of roses; Ballet music No 2
Virginia Kerr, Frances Lucey sops **Colette McGahon** mez **Peter Kerr** ten **Nigel Leeson-Williams** bass-bar **RTÉ Philharmonic Choir and National Symphony Orchestra of Ireland / Adrian Leaper, Colman Pearce**
Naxos ② 8 555201/2 (105' · DDD · T)   Ⓢ Ⓑ➤

This resissue of a late-Victorian masterpiece gains the well-deserved chance of wider circulation on the popular Naxos label. The Requiem was written in 1896 in memory of Lord Leighton. Scored for the usual forces of solo quartet, chorus and orchestra, it strikes a familiar balance between grief and condolence; its manner is essentially lyrical, its form determined by that of the Mass and by its well-defined musical climaxes. Yet the composer's individuality is everywhere unobtrusively evident, as is the warmth of his feeling. If these things were indeed too unobtrusive to gain recognition in their own time and the largely unsympathetic century that followed, they should win it now.

The performance is admirable, with good work by all four soloists. A special word of appreciation is due to the delightful soprano, Frances Lucey. The choir needs more presence in the recorded sound, which in general is none too sharply defined. The excerpts from *The Veiled Prophet*, another rarity, provide a well-chosen bonus.

Stabat mater, Op 96

Stabat mater. Te Deum. Six Bible Songs
Ingrid Attrot sop **Pamela Helen Stephen** mez **Nigel Robson** ten **Stephen Varcoe** bar **Ian Watson** org
Leeds Philharmonic Chorus; BBC Philharmonic Orchestra / Richard Hickox
Chandos CHAN9548 (74' · DDD · T/t)　　　　Ⓕ●

Writing of his old teacher in 1952, Vaughan Williams foretold that his time would come round again: 'With the next generation the inevitable reaction will set in and Stanford will come into his own.' It has taken more than a generation, but at last it does begin to look as though he was right. This recording of a 'symphonic cantata', the *Stabat mater*, strong in ideas, deeply felt and structurally assured, will certainly strengthen the steadily growing appreciation of his worth. The Prelude, impressive as it is, is almost *too* soundly constructed, and the first choral movement, rich in its Verdi-like foreground of soloists, signs off with a slightly self-conscious repetition of the opening words by the soprano. Stanford is never abashed by the prospect of melodic commitment, and the orchestral Intermezzo comes out boldly with what promises to be a good, old-fashioned Grand Tune; but then he seems to remember where he is, and the piece ends with murky explorations that seem not quite to find what they may be seeking. The work itself ends, as Lewis Foreman suggests in his useful notes, in Eternity: 'we seem to reach the crest of a hill only to find the path stretching onward and upward to another.' The performance carries conviction, with Hickox exercising that natural rightness of his so that in a work such as this, without predecessors on record, a listener will feel that this is how it should 'go'.

Fine orchestral playing and choral singing give pleasure throughout. The solo quartet is led by Ingrid Attrot's colourful but none too evenly produced soprano, and in the *Bible Songs* Stephen Varcoe sings sensitively to the judiciously registered organ accompaniment of Ian Watson. The most tuneful of *Te Deums* follows, blithe and buoyant in its orchestrated version.

Morning and Evening Services

Morning and Evening Services in B flat, Op 10[a].
Evening Services – A, Op 12[a]; F, Op 36[a]; E flat[b]. Two Anthems, Op 37[b]. Three Motets, Op 38. Pater noster. The Lord is my Shepherd[a]
Winchester Cathedral Choir / David Hill with
[a]**Stephen Farr,** [b]**Christopher Monks** org
Hyperion CDA66964 (78' · DDD · T)　　　　Ⓕ●

The *Magnificat and Nunc dimittis* in E flat major dates back to 1873 isn't with any certainty known even to have been performed. Perhaps this is because both settings are almost indecently tuneful: an apocalyptic 'scattered the proud', a broadly melodious 'to be a light' and a 'Gloria' as catchy as a comic opera. As for the B flat major settings written six years later, these

(both Morning and Evening Services) have long owed their popularity to a melodic gift that's almost Schubertian and a correspondingly deft mastery of construction.

Winchester Cathedral Choir is surely one of the best in the UK. Under David Hill, the trebles have a bright, distinctive tone. The men are excellent, and all sound as though they're singing for the joy of it. Several of these works involve more than the customary four parts, and the eight-part *Pater noster*, recorded for the first time, has splendid richness, with the choir forming massive pillars of sound in the powerful climax. Stanford's writing for the organ is also a delight, and at times we might wish that the fine playing of both organists had been brought into sharper focus. The choir we hear with rare clarity.

Evening Service in G, Op 81. Services in C, Op 115.
Six Short Preludes and Postludes: Set 2, Op 105 –
No 3, Prelude in G; No 6, Postlude in D minor.
For lo, I raise up, Op 145. Three Motets, Op-38.
St John's College Choir, Cambridge / Christopher Robinson org
Naxos 8 555794 (72' · DDD)　　　　Ⓢ●⇥

The mean old saying, 'Those who can, do, and those who can't, teach', would have withered in the presence of Stanford; and no doubt one of the reasons why he was such a great teacher is that he could and did, and so set an example. His C major Services (Morning, Evening and Communion, all included in this programme) are so eminently the works of a master who knows how to get from here to there in one move, to keep always something in reserve for later use but never to write without a good clear melodic idea in the first place. Everything in this programme has freshness and well-founded assurance. It's music with clarity of purpose: it knows where it's going and doesn't put a foot wrong.

Under Christopher Robinson, the St John's choir has enjoyed a period in which the distinguishing mark has been a renewed vitality of style. It's well caught in this CD. The start of the first track, the C major *Te Deum*, has it straightaway – the praise carries spirit and conviction. The final track opens still more strikingly. This is *For lo, I will raise up*, for which Stanford, writing in 1914, set his imagination free to bestir the choir stalls into an almost fiercely dramatic life. The St John's choir bite into the words with relish, while the acoustic and their well-judged tempo reinforce the rhythmic energy of the passage.

Even in the best-stocked collection this would prove a welcome addition, and for those who have as yet nothing of the master, it should provide a lively introduction.

Songs

Tragödie, Op 14 No 5. Op 19 – No 2, A Lullaby; No 5, To the Rose. Windy Nights, Op 30 No 4. Clown's Songs from 'Twelfth Night', Op 65. The Fairy Lough,

Op 77 No 2. Songs of the Sea, Op 91. Songs of Faith, Op 97 No 4, 'To the Soul'; No 6, 'Joy, Shipmate, Joy'. Phoebe, Op 125. A Fire of Turf, Op 139. The Pibroch, Op 157 No 1. For Ever Mine. Tom Lemmin
Stephen Varcoe bar **Clifford Benson** pf
Hyperion CDA67124 (77' · DDD · T/t)　　Ⓕ**O**▶

Stanford's *Songs of the Sea* have kept the British baritone afloat for the best part of a century. Drake's hammock and the barnacles of The Old Superb used to be familiar in parlours and drawing-rooms throughout the land. The cries of Captain Keats and his crew ('"Ship ahoy!" a hundred times a day'), the alliterative mysteries of 'Fetter and Faith…Faggot and Father' and the assurance that Drake even now was 'ware and waking' were assimilated almost as the words of folksongs, while the music seemed part of our flesh and blood. They are splendid songs, and the set of five constitutes a small masterpiece. Sceptical readers should try them again in this new recording. Stephen Varcoe and Clifford Benson give a most sensitive performance, not emasculated but treating them thoughtfully. The two quieter songs, 'Outward Bound' and 'Homeward Bound', become more central, better integrated, than usual, and the very fact that this is the solo version, without the male-voice chorus added later, makes it easier to hear them (the whole set) as a personal utterance. With 'Drake's Drum', for instance, Varcoe is very intent upon seeing sense, where others have often sought for little beyond a generalised patriotic earnestness. These, perhaps, are *The Songs of the Sea* as Captain Edward Fairfax Vere might have sung them.

In reviewing the first volume, Michael Oliver wrote of the difficulty of reconciling the Irishman and the Brahmsian in Stanford: the melodic vein of the one seemed at odds with the harmonic language of the other. The occasions here when a dichotomy of style does cause trouble are found in the *Songs of Faith*. Whitman's auto-intoxication incites Stanford to indulge in grandiose gestures that aren't natural to him at all. He's much more at home with Shakespeare and Dekker, or, for that matter, with Quiller-Couch and Winifred M Letts, whose *A Fire of Turf* provides him with poems for some masterly settings. All are beautifully performed by these excellent artists.

Songs of the Fleet. Songs of the Sea. The Revenge: a Ballad of the Fleet
Gerald Finley bar **BBC National Chorus and Orchestra of Wales / Richard Hickox**
Chandos 🔊 CHSA5043 (70' · DDD · T)　　Ⓕ**OOO**▶

Ⓖ　Two of Stanford's catchiest and most popular settings frame his 1904 *Songs of the Sea* for baritone, male chorus and orchestra: both 'Drake's Drum' and 'The Old Superb' are instantly memorable and have alone justly secured the work's survival. But there's some terrific music tucked away in the three remaining numbers, not least the marvellously serene 'Homeward Bound' with its burnished

orchestral palette (Stanford's skilful scoring gives enormous pleasure throughout, in fact), rapt eloquence (nowhere more potent than at the line 'Swiftly the great ship glides') and adventurous harmonic scope.

Six years later, Stanford returned to Henry Newbolt's maritime verse to pen a more reflective sequel entitled *Songs of the Fleet*. Its spacious centrepiece, 'The Middle Watch', evokes a dusky mystery and sense of awe, while the opening 'Sailing at Dawn' is a gloriously assured and noble essay worthy of Elgar himself. In both sets, Gerald Finley's firmly focused, ringing tone is a joy. He doens't possess the salty tang of Benjamin Luxon (a true sea-dog if ever there was one), but the voice is steadier and he sings with unfailing ardour, intelligence and sensitivity. Hickox and his BBC Welsh forces provide exemplary support.

Not so immediately appealing is the 1886 choral ballad *The Revenge*, one of the composer's biggest early successes. Tennyson's poem depicts how Sir Richard Grenville and his Devonian crew aboard *Revenge* took on – and inflicted terrible damage upon – the Spanish fleet off the Azores in 1591 (one ship against 53 – believe it or not!). Stanford's breezy setting proved a hit with Victorian choral societies up and down the land. Though no forgotten masterpiece, it's most ably served by Hickox and company. Throw in an admirable booklet-essay by Jeremy Dibble and ripe, airy sound from Chandos, and it certainly adds up to a hearty recommendation.

Wilhelm Stenhammar
Swedish 1871-1929

Raised in a musical family, Stenhammar composed from childhood though had little formal training. His earlier music is in a late-Romantic style showing influences from Wagner, Liszt and Brahms. Stenhammar himself described the style of his First Symphony in F major as 'idyllic Bruckner'. He subsequently sought to emancipate himself and write in a more 'Nordic' style, looking to Nielsen and Sibelius for guidance. His works include two symphonies, two piano concertos, cantatas, six string quartets (1894-1916) and songs. An admired pianist (he recorded five piano rolls for Welte-Mignon in 1905), he was also conductor of the Gothenburg Symphony Orchestra from 1906 to 1922.

Piano Concertos

Piano Concertos – No 1, Op 1; No 2, Op 23
Seta Tanyel pf **Helsingborg Symphony Orchestra / Andrew Manze**
Hyperion CDA67750 (75' · DDD)　　Ⓕ**OO**▶

Stenhammar was the soloist for the premiere of his First Piano Concerto in March 1893. He subsequently played it under Nikisch, Weingartner, Muck, Richard Strauss and Hans Richter. Andrew Manze, in the informative booklet, points up the work's indebtedness to Brahms (structure, key sequence, keyboard style) with the elfin touch of Saint-Saëns in the *Scherzo*. Stenhammar, though, is very much his own man, not least in the folk-style finale in which, halfway through, he changes direction and quotes his own song 'Lutad mot gärdet' before bravely ending his 46-minute work on a *pianissimo* chord.

The Second Concerto (1904-07) also has four movements with the *Scherzo* placed second, though these are played without pause, resulting in a 'novel, some have said "improvised", structure' (Manze). Few will be able to resist the tumultuous finale. Manze was a shrewd choice of conductor, as was Seta Tanyel as soloist, a pianist whose lyrical grace is matched by a no-holds-barred bravura and an innate sparkle that makes her the preferred choice. The recorded sound is of Hyperion's usual high standard.

Symphony No 2, Op 34

Excelsior!. Symphony No 2
Royal Scottish National Orchestra / Petter Sundkvist
Naxos 8 553888 (58' · DDD)

This is the first recording of Stenhammar's G minor Symphony to be made by a non-Swedish orchestra; Petter Sundkvist, a young Swedish conductor, draws very good results from the RSNO and conducts with evident feeling. This symphony grows more glorious with every hearing and this time is no exception. Sundkvist realises its moments of poetry with a natural ardour and eloquence and without the slightest expressive self-indulgence. He builds up the architecture of the symphony impressively.

The exhilarating *Excelsior!* overture can more than hold its own with any rival, even if the recording doesn't. The acoustic is a shade on the dryish side. Notwithstanding this caveat, the quality of the performance is such as to deserve a strong recommendation.

Piano Sonatas

Piano Sonatas – in G minor (1890); Op 12. Nights of Late Summer, Op 33. Three Fantasies, Op 11
Martin Sturfält pf
Hyperion CDA67689 (76' · DDD)

Although Stenhammar's orchestral and *concertante* works are now quite well known, the music he wrote for the piano has, until recently, been unfamiliar. As a recitalist he seemed to value the music of others more than his own. He gave his splendid G minor Sonata (composed at 19) its premiere in May 1891 and then never played it again! Yet it is an ambitious, Romantic work with an unforgettable main theme dominating its first movement, and in many ways it is an equivalent in its youthful ardour of the Brahms F minor work.

Stenhammar did, however, take the Three Fantasies, Op 11, of 1895 into his repertoire. They are Brahms-influenced, the first again boldly passionate, but the composer's own personality comes through, notably so in the ingenious *Dolce scherzando* and the closing *Molto espressivo*. The five pieces which make up *Nights of Late Summer* are certainly atmospheric but not overtly descriptive: their feeling is personal and introspective, although the exception is the closing charming *Poco allegretto*, which has almost a whiff of Grieg. But the late A major Sonata (composed in the same year) is a highly individual work balancing serious, even sombre, lyricism with drama and closing with a vibrant unpredictable finale. Martin Sturfält suggests it has an affinity with Beethoven.

He plays all this music with powerful feeling and understanding, and great spontaneity – as at a live recital – and the recording is very real indeed. Well worth exploring.

Rudi Stephan   German 1887-1915

Rudi Stephan remains one of 20th-century music's most tantalising 'might have beens'. Before his death aged just 28 in the trenches on the Eastern Front, the young German composer had produced an opera, Die ersten Menschen (1910), as well as a clutch of single-movement essays which display a highly developed grasp of organic thought and serve up a heady stylistic cocktail. Die ersten Menschen was eventually premiered in Frankfurt five years after his death from a bullet in the brain fired by a Russian sharpshooter on the Galician Front.

Orchestral works

Music for Violin and Orchestra[a]. Music for Orchestra (1910). Music for Orchestra (1912)
[a]**Sergey Stadler** vn **Melbourne Symphony Orchestra / Oleg Caetani**
Chandos CHSA5040 (63' · DDD)

The main interest here surrounds the first commercial recording of the 1910 *Music for Orchestra*. Premiered in Munich in January 1911, it's an ambitious and frequently arresting creation. Caetani secures a polished and shapely rendering, though a touch more thrusting purpose might not have come amiss. That observation also holds true for the performance of its eponymous and altogether more tightly knit bedfellow from two years later (both pieces share some thematic material).

In the *Music for Violin and Orchestra* Sergey Stadler plays with admirable precision and sensitivity, though rather greater passion and tonal warmth wouldn't come amiss. This is fascinating and frequently intoxicating repertoire – do try it. Play 'spot the influence' and you might come up with names as diverse as Wagner, Mahler, Richard Strauss, Debussy, Berg, Reger,

Schreker, Hindemith and Szymanowski. The sound is spacious and true.

Die ersten Menschen

Die ersten Menschen
Gabriele Maria Ronge sop Chawa **Hans Aschenbach** ten Chabel **Florian Cerny** bar Kajihn **Siegmund Nimsgern** bass Adahm
Berlin Radio Symphony Orchestra / Karl Anton Rickenbacher
CPO ② CPO999 980-2 (112' · DDD · T/t)   Ⓕ

Die ersten Menschen ('The first humans'), the Bible story of Cain and Abel given an erotic, early-20th-century psychological spin by playwright Otto Borngräber, was Stephan's first and only completed opera. The musical language is most akin to that of Richard Strauss, yet, when you start making detailed comparisons with individual works, it's more often the case that the younger composer is anticipating or paralleling the progress of his famous contemporary. The quasi-recitative setting of dialogues recalls strongly Barak and his brothers in *Die Frau ohne Schatten*, while Chawa's (Eve's) big opening number in Act 2, 'Allmachtiger', feels like a first run for Helena's 'Zweite Brautnacht' more than a decade in the future. Occasionally, too, a certain folky tang or Oriental lushness (Stephan invoking the world just post-Garden of Eden) reminds us that *Duke Bluebeard's Castle* was on Bartók's desk at the same period.

The four-handed, two-act drama runs its course excitingly until Abel's murder. If Stephan sometimes is over-faithful to Borngräber's play in the sheer amount of soliloquising he gives his characters (especially Kajihn, his Cain), and is rather too fond of *tremolando* effects, it's a significant and obviously stageable achievement for a first go at the medium. This performance is blessed by fluent, stylish singing, especially from Gabriele Maria Ronge as the (literally) much put-upon Chawa/Eve, but lacks that extra degree of dramatic insight that an interpretation taken from the stage would have brought. Karl Anton Rickenbacher, an expert in rare Strauss, is careful to allow Stephan's often Pfitzner-like lyricism its say alongside more purple passages. The 1998 recording (Deutschland Radio) is clean and true. So far, so good – but once again the wholly incompetent English translations used by CPO render booklet-note and libretto both risible and annoying to non-German readers.

Karlheinz Stockhausen
German 1928-2007

Stockhausen was widely acknowledged as one of the most important but also controversial composers of the 20th and early 21st centuries. He is known for his groundbreaking work in electronic music, alea- *tory (controlled chance) in serial composition, and musical spatialisation. He was educated in Cologne and later studied in Paris (with Olivier Messiaen) and in Bonn.*

One of the leading figures of the Darmstadt School, his compositions and theories were and remain widely influential, not only on composers of art music but also on jazz and popular-music artists. His works, composed over a period of nearly 60 years, break new ground and turn their back on traditional methods. In addition to electronic music – both with and without live performers – they range from miniatures for musical boxes through works for solo instruments, songs, chamber music, choral and orchestral music, to a cycle of seven full-length operas: his seven-part operatic cycle Licht is possibly the most ambitious project ever undertaken by a major composer. His theoretical and other writings comprise 10 large volumes. He received numerous prizes and distinctions for his compositions and recordings, and for the scores produced by his publishing company.

Stimmung

Stimmung
Theatre of Voices / Paul Hillier
Harmonia Mundi 🔊 HMU80 7408 (78' · DDD/DSD)
Ⓕ🅾🅾▷

Paul Hillier sang bass in the famous performances of Stockhausen's psychedelic *Stimmung* that Gregory Rose's Singcircle vocal troupe toured during the mid-1980s. Two decades on and Hillier's understanding of this unique piece might even have been greater than the composer's own. He has objectivity on his side – a quality that Stockhausen himself squandered long before.

Stimmung is structured around an electronically sustained drone that is sounded throughout the work's duration. Anchored around B flat, the drone contains the complex harmonic overtone series around which Stockhausen constructs his constantly generating sound world of rarefied timbres and ethereal melodies. He provides embryonic melodic cells and fragments of text, arranged in 51 'Models', leaving the singers to embellish this given material during the performance. It's probably more accurate to say that *Stimmung* is 'realised' than 'performed'.

If this all sounds rather academic then the result is actually one of the most gorgeous vocal soundscapes in all 20th-century music. Hillier's Theatre of Voices operate at such a refined level of specialised technique that radically new expressive territory emerges. Standard vocal delivery feels superseded by loops of vocalised harmonics, tactile humming and, as the piece nears its conclusion, a catchy whistled refrain that calmly draws threads together. Stockhausen's flexi-notation blurs the supply-and-demand chain that usually defines composer and performer relationships. The musicians are licensed to define the micro as they transform and deliberate over the material. They converse and explore, and an enigmatic piece-specific discipline is created. A thrilling and important performance.

Helicopter String Quartet

Helicopter String Quartet
Arditti Quartet (Irvine Arditti, Graeme Jennings vns Garth Knox va Rohan de Saram vc)
Video director **Frank Scheffer**
Medici Arts 💿 307 7508 (77' · DDD)   Ⓕ

When word went round the contemporary music community that Stockhausen was sending the Arditti Quartet up in helicopters there were some who said he was touched by genius. Others reckoned he was just touched. A decade on, how does Stockhausen's *Helicopter Quartet* really stand up?

Frank Scheffer's gripping documentary follows Stockhausen and the Ardittis as they prepare for the premiere, and his film ends with the complete performance. Stockhausen is on hand throughout to explain himself. If the concept of sending each member of a string quartet up in their own helicopter, where what they play is beamed back into the concert hall and mixed electronically with the sounds of the 'copters seems eccentric, then Stockhausen explains he is simply following the directions of his dreams. From *Gruppen* – his 1957 piece for three spatially distributed orchestras – onwards he was always interested in the idea of sound flying around the heads of his listeners. And here is a supreme realisation of that fantasy.

You could argue that Stockhausen had long since lost touch with reality by the time he conceived and executed this piece. But that's missing the point: although Stockhausen's rock-star ego did lead him to produce some tedious late pieces that relied on the unquestioning faith of his groupies, the *Helicopter String Quartet* has a charm and fascination of its own. As Stockhausen deconstructs his material during rehearsal, singing bits to the players, it becomes clear there is real harmonic depth and melodic direction. Shame about the carbon footprint though.

Johann Strauss II   Austrian 1825-1899

Johann II's grandfather was a humble innkeeper on the outskirts of Vienna and committed suicide after his second marriage; Johann I (1804-49) picked up a love of music from the itinerant musicians who played at his father's inn. His ambition was to play the kind of entertainment music he had grown up with and he set about learning the violin with a will. Within a year he was playing the viola in an orchestra. Here he befriended the charming Josef Lanner (1801-43) and joined him when Lanner started up his own orchestra. So successful was the venture that they decided to run two bands – Lanner conducting one, Strauss the other, and although they soon went their

separate ways, Strauss the composer and conductor was firmly established with the Vienna public. Before long they were touring all over Europe and were the official dance orchestra for Austrian court balls, and when Queen Victoria was crowned, it was the Strauss orchestra that came over to play at the coronation ball. That's how the dynasty began. (It died out in 1939 with the death of Johann Strauss III, son of Eduard, one of Johann II's brothers.)

Johann I had six children by his wife Anna – Johann, Josef, Nelli, Therese, Eduard and Ferdinand (who died after a few months). He also had five illegitimate children by his mistress Emilie Trampusch and eventually left his family in order to live with her. The opposition that he had put in the way of Johann II's musical ambitions thus disappeared. Johann II assembled his first orchestra at the age of 19, making his debut in October 1844. His success was instantaneous. 'Good night, Lanner. Good evening, Father Strauss. Good morning, Son Strauss', ran the headline in a Viennese paper. The two Strauss family orchestras ran in open rivalry with one another until 1849 when the elder Strauss contracted scarlet fever from one of his illegitimate children and was found dead in his apartment.

Johann Strauss II now combined both orchestras and for the rest of his life enjoyed a career of fabulous success, composing and conducting all over Europe. Eventually he ran six orchestras running simultaneously. With his assistant conductors, copyists, librarians, publicists and booking agents, the Strauss music business was a highly lucrative concern. In 1872 he was invited to America to conduct his Blue Danube for the colossal fee of $100,000 for 14 performances (at one concert he conducted a choir of 20,000 in front of an audience of 100,000). He then went on a short tour, doubled his money and returned to Europe, by which time he was a millionaire.

Johann's brother Eduard took over as conductor of the court balls after 1871 so that Johann could concentrate more on composition. And that might have been that, turning out waltz after polka after march after galop from an inexhaustible gold mine of melody. But in 1863 he met Offenbach, then at the height of his fame as the composer of French operettas (he came to Vienna for a production of Orpheus in the Underworld). They became involved in a competition to write the best waltz for a ball – and Offenbach won. This, as much as Offenbach's suggestion that Strauss should try his hand at operetta, was the spur to writing something for the stage. After a few flops, Strauss came up with one of the most perfect examples of the genre, Die Fledermaus (1874), followed in 1885 by another – Der Zigeunerbaron.

His flair, energy and creativity never left him until the last few years of his life. His third wife, Adele, had introduced him to Brahms and the two became close friends.

Dance Music

'Ein Straussfest II'
E Strauss Ohne Aufenthalt, Op 112 **Josef Strauss** Plappermäulchen, Op 245. Sphären-Klänge, Op 235. Jockey, Op 278 **J Strauss I** Chinese Galop, Op 20 **J Strauss II** Ägyptischer Marsch, Op 335a. Künstler-

Quadrille, Op 71. Kaiser-Walzer, Op 437. Freikugeln, Op 326. Jubelfest-Marsch, Op 396. Tritsch-Tratsch-Polka, Op 214. Geisselhiebe, Op 60. Klipp Klapp, Op 466. Wein, Weib und Gesang, Op 333. Perpetuum mobile, Op 257
Cincinnati Pops Chorale and Orchestra / Erich Kunzel
Telarc CD80314 (68' · DDD)   Ⓕ**○**

This collection sets out to adorn popular Strauss pieces with sound effects to outdo anything one hears at a Vienna New Year Concert. It starts with Eduard Strauss's *Ohne Aufenthalt*, which is accompanied by steam railway effects, has bullets flying mercilessly in the *Freikugeln* Polka, and includes neighing nags and swishing whips in the *Jockey* Polka. The fun is increased by the inclusion of the *Künstler-Quadrille*, a sort of 1850s 'Hooked on Classics' that begins with Mendelssohn's 'Wedding March' and continues through the likes of Mozart's Symphony No 40 and Chopin's 'Funeral March' Sonata to Beethoven's *Ruins of Athens* and *Kreutzer* Sonata. If the Viennese lilt is just a shade lacking in the waltzes, the playing is nevertheless excellent throughout. The Strausses themselves would have approved.

J Strauss II An der schönen, blauen Donau.   Ⓟ
Furioso. Egyptischer Marsch. Eljen a Magyar! Frühlingsstimmen. Im Sturmschritt. Neue Pizzicato. Nordseebilder. Perpetuum mobile. Tritsch-Tratsch. Die Fledermaus – Overture; Csárdás. Der Zigeunerbaron – Overture
Anima Eterna / Jos van Immerseel
Zig-Zag Territoires ZZT020601 (71' · DDD)   Ⓕ

Most of us have got used to period instruments playing Beethoven but 'early music' groups tackling later repertoire still raise eyebrows. Similarly, the suggestion that there is a good composer named Strauss whose first name is not Richard usually invokes derision.

Both of these sniffy attitudes are bravely challenged by Jos van Immerseel, who penitently writes that 'like many musicians I found Strauss's music a bit cheap. This wasn't the case when I began studying music as a 10-year-old and sight-read Strauss waltzes...I liked the music, but the pleasure was short-lived. In the music school where I next studied, it was forbidden to play music by Strauss (or to enjoy anything); Bach and Czerny replaced Strauss on the music desk. The prejudice against Strauss's "unworthy" music made it impossible for me to appreciate even his orchestral scores'.

Aided by a new critical edition published by Bärenreiter, Immerseel's vibrant and ostentatious revisionist approach allows no wilting pretentiousness, but instead the superb Anima Eterna use their period instruments to deliver full-on, gutsy, direct performances that are an unaffected joy.

'New Year's Concert, 2002'
Hellmesberger II Danse diabolique **J Strauss**

Beliebte Annen-Polka, Op 137. Radetzky March, Op 228 **J Strauss II** Zivio!, Op 456. Carnevals-botschafter, Op 270. Künsterleben, Op 316. Die Fledermaus – Overture. Perpetuum mobile, Op 257. Elisen-Polka, Op 151. Wiener Blut, Op 354. Tik-Tak Polka, Op 365. An der schönen blauen Donau, Op 314 **Josef Strauss** Die Schwätzerin, Op 144. Vorwärts!, Op 127. Arm in Arm, Op 215. Aquarellen-Polka, Op 258. Die Libelle, Op 204. Plapper-mäulchen, op 245. Im Fluge, Op 230
Vienna Philharmonic Orchestra / Seiji Ozawa
Video director **Brian Large**
TDK Mediactive 🄳🅅🄳 DV-WPNK02 (141' · 16:9 · 2.0, 5.0 & DTS 5.0 · 0)   Ⓕ

What an advantage DVD provides in comparison with the Philips CD of this concert. Quite apart from the bonus of visual presentation, the DVD offers five numbers omitted from the CD – two of them by Josef Strauss celebrating his 175th anniversary, the polkas *Arm in Arm* and *Im Pfluge*, and three Johann Strauss numbers, the *Carnevalsbotschafter* waltz, the *Beliebte Annen* polka and *Perpetuum mobile*.

Ozawa is at his most relaxed, naturally idiomatic in his often extreme use of idiomatic pauses and of warm *rubato*, reflected in his decision not to use a baton, relying instead on the inborn expressiveness of the Viennese players to mould in perfect time. In the *Fledermaus* Overture, for example, the switches of tempo and rhythm and the affectionate phrasing are immaculately achieved with a mere flutter of the fingers from the conductor.

Even by the standards of this celebratory occasion this was an unusually warm and happy event thanks to Ozawa. And more than anyone since Karajan in his one New Year concert, Ozawa controls the clapping of the audience, limiting it to the proper passages in the final *Radetzky* March. The direction can't be faulted.

Additional recommendations

New Year's Concert in Vienna 1987
Battle; VPO / Karajan
DG 477 6336GGP (80' · DDD)   Ⓕ**○○**▷
Karajan and the great Vienna Phil on superb form – relaxed, stylish and wonderfully elegant in music by three of the Strauss family. The frail elderly conductor, totally inside the idiom, lets the years slip away and draws deep on his Austrian roots. And Kathleen Battle in *Frühlingsstimmen* is a total delight. One of the classic New Year concerts.

New Year's Concert in Vienna 1989
VPO / C Kleiber
DG 🄳🅅🄳 073 4014GH (80' · DDD)   Ⓕ**○○**
One can share in a more carefree expression of joy here. Many fine conductors have presided over these traditional Strauss tributes, but none with such élan as the late Carlos Kleiber. The music swings and sways in terpsichorean ecstasy. Kleiber appears blissful as he inscribes elegant arcs with his baton, and the players beam.

Die Fledermaus

Die Fledermaus
Julia Varady sop Rosalinde **Lucia Popp** sop Adele
Hermann Prey ten Eisenstein **René Kollo** ten Alfred
Bernd Weikl bar Doctor Falke **Ivan Rebroff** bass/mez
Prince Orlofsky **Benno Kusche** bar Frank **Ferry
Gruber** ten Blind **Evi List** sop Ida **Franz Muzeneder**
bass Frosch **Bavarian State Opera Chorus and
Orchestra / Carlos Kleiber**
DG The Originals ② 457 765-2GOR2 (107' · ADD · T/t)
Recorded 1975   Ⓜ❍❍▶

Twenty-five years after its original release
there's still no recording of *Die Fledermaus* that,
for many collectors, matches this one for the
compelling freshness of its conductor's interpretation – the attention to every nuance of the
score and the ability to bring out some new
detail, all allied to extreme precision of vocal and
instrumental ensemble. The ladies, too, as so
often seems to be the case in recordings of *Die
Fledermaus*, are quite superlatively good, with
ideally characterised and projected singing. If
the men are generally less outstandingly good,
one can have no more than minor quibbles with
the Eisenstein of Hermann Prey or the Alfred of
René Kollo. But it's less easy to accept Ivan
Rebroff singing the role of Orlofsky falsetto.
Some collectors find that his contribution quite
ruins the whole set, but most will find it tolerable enough for the glories to be found elsewhere
on the recording.

DG remastered the set to make it sound as
though it were recorded only yesterday; but it
continues to provoke puzzlement by the break
between discs, which occurs during the Act 2
finale. If a split into such uneven lengths is to
be made, why not have it between Acts 1 and
2? Enough of minor quibbles – this set is a
'must buy'.

Die Fledermaus[a]
[a]**Nancy Gustafson** sop Rosalinde [a]**Judith Howarth**
sop Adele [a]**Louis Otey** bar Eisenstein [a]**Bonaventura
Bottone** ten Alfred [a]**Anthony Michaels-Moore** bar
Doctor Falke [a]**Jochen Kowalski** counterten Prince
Orlofsky [a]**Eric Garrett** bar Frank [a]**John Dobson** ten
Doctor Blind [a]**Glenys Groves** sop Ida [a]**John Sessions**
spkr Frosch [a]**Peter Archer** spkr Ivan

including Joan Sutherland's farewell to the stage
Bishop Home, sweet home[b]. **Cilea** L'arlesiana[c] – E la
solita storia. **Rossini** Semiramide[d] – Serbami ognor sì
fido. **Saint-Saëns** Samson et Dalila[e] – Mon coeur
s'ouvre à ta voix **Verdi** La traviata[f] – Parigi, o cara
[bdf]**Dame Joan Sutherland** sop [cf]**Luciano Pavarotti**
ten [de]**Marilyn Horne** mez

**Royal Opera House Chorus and Orchestra,
Covent Garden / Richard Bonynge**
Stage director **John Cox**
Video director **Humphrey Burton**
ArtHaus Musik ② 📀 100 134 (197' · Region 2 & 5)
Recorded live 1990   Ⓕ❍

JOHANN STRAUSS II
DIE FLEDERMAUS – IN BRIEF

Julia Varady Rosalinde **Lucia Popp** Adele
Hermann Prey Eisenstein **Bavarian State Opera
Chorus and Orchestra / Carlos Kleiber**
DG ② 457 765-2GOR (107' · ADD)   Ⓜ❍❍▶
Kleiber's mercurial, translucent conducting
and a superb cast make this a marvellous per-
formance – except, sadly, for popular singer
Ivan Rebroff's weird falsetto Orlofsky.

Elisabeth Schwarzkopf Rosalinde **Rita Streich** Ⓗ
Adele **Nicolai Gedda** Eisenstein **Philharmonia
Chorus and Orchestra / Herbert von Karajan**
EMI ② 966844-2 (110' · AAD)   Ⓜ❍❍
A 1955 mono recording with a wonderfully
idiomatic cast and Karajan's urbane conduct-
ing it still sounds engaging.

Hilde Gueden Rosalinde **Erika Köth** Adele
Waldemar Kmentt Eisenstein **Vienna State
Opera Chorus, Vienna PO /
Herbert von Karajan**
Decca ② 421 046-2DH2 (143' · ADD)   Ⓕ❍▶
A 1960 stereo classic, with one of the most
characterfully Viennese casts and Karajan in
almost as fine form. A huge star-studded gala
scene featuring the likes of Del Monaco,
Nilsson and Sutherland will appeal to many.

Anny Schlemm Rosalinde **Rita Streich** Adele
Peter Anders Eisenstein **RIAS Chamber Choir
and SO / Ferenc Fricsay**
Audite mono ② AUDITE23 411 (114' · ADD) Ⓜ❍
Recorded in 1949, this shows what a wonder-
ful Strauss conductor Fricsay was, idiomatic
and totally alive to the work's give and take.
Anders is a very stylish Eisenstien and
Schlemm a glorious Rosalinde, the rest of the
cast elegant and charming.

Kiri Te Kanawa Rosalinde **Hildegard Heichele**
Adele **Hermann Prey** Eisenstein **Chorus and
Orchestra of the Royal Opera House /
Plácido Domingo**
NVC Arts 📀 4509 99216-2 (177')   Ⓕ
Domingo on the podium can't match Kleiber's *Schwung*, but remains lively and serviceable for Covent Garden's splendidly batty
multilingual production, in richly authentic
sets with fine principals, including Dennis
O'Neill's hilariously Italianate Alfred, and
authentic Viennoiserie from Josef Meinrad's
beanpole Frosch.

Lucia Popp Rosalinde **Edita Gruberová** Adele
Bernd Weikl Eisenstein **Chorus and Orchestra
of the Vienna State Opera /
Theodor Guschlbauer**
ArtHaus Musik 📀 107 153 (169')   Ⓕ
Otto Schenk's wonderfully Viennese produc-
tion, gloriously cast (Fassbaender a perfect
Orlofsky) is sheer delight, and the orchestra
has this music in its bones. Charming.

'Oh, what a night!' sings everybody on stage as Prince Orlofsky's ballroom takes leave of its earthly confines and sails for the happy isles borne on a tide of waltzes and a sea of champagne. It's always a good moment in *Die Fledermaus*, and this particular night was special. Most of those present at Covent Garden had seen a few New Year's Eves in their time, but never a one like this on December 31, 1990. And never, surely, has a *prima donna* been treated to such a stage party for her farewell. Dame Joan Sutherland sang that night for the last time in the house where she had made her debut in 1952. Somebody had a brainwave when they thought of this as the occasion for what might otherwise have been a rather tearful event: Joan and two of her most illustrious partners of many performances would themselves be guests at Orlofsky's party in Act 2. Husband Richard Bonynge would conduct, so the party would therefore be complete. The guests slot in nicely at the moment when the revels are at their height. And there was New Year's Eve to celebrate. If the plan had a drawback it was one that concerned the opera itself. Act 3 of *Fledermaus* is always something of an anticlimax, and, with a celebrity recital thrown in, the middle act could seem to end with chords that cried 'Follow that!'. Happily, the production has a good move in store when, for the Finale, the backdrop for the prison scene goes up to reveal Orlofsky's ballroom aglow and once more ready to receive its guests.

Without in the least dominating, the orchestra here are present with a quite remarkable immediacy and naturalness. The outstanding voices among the cast were (in respect of pure tone) those of Judith Howarth and Anthony Michaels-Moore. Among the three celebrities, gallantly as both ladies sang, it was (and is on the film) Pavarotti whose voice had retained its quality. There's also plenty to watch, and with enjoyment. All on stage, including the chorus, act well. Humphrey Burton has supervised the filming so that the home viewer has the most privileged seat of all.

Der Zigeunerbaron

Der Zigeunerbaron
Pamela Coburn *sop* Saffi **Herbert Lippert** *ten*
Barinkay **Wolfgang Holzmair** *bar* Homonay **Rudolf
Schasching** *ten* Zsupán **Christiane Oelze** *sop* Arsena
Júlia Hamari *mez* Czipra **Elisabeth von Magnus**
contr Mirabella **Jürgen Flimm** *bar* Carnero **Robert
Florianschutz** *bass* Pali **Hans-Jürgen Lazar** *ten*
Ottokar **Arnold Schoenberg Choir; Vienna
Symphony Orchestra / Nikolaus Harnoncourt**
Teldec ② 4509 94555-2 (150' · DDD · T/t)   Ⓕ●

This is an uncommonly interesting and enjoyable release. The extra music comes because Harnoncourt and Johann Strauss specialist Norbert Linke have sought to restore *Der Zigeunerbaron* to the form it had before Strauss made various cuts. The real merits of the set lie elsewhere. Not

least, Harnoncourt has stripped away generations of Viennese schmaltz and performing tradition.

This is the first recording to include every number of the published score, and for once the music is sung at its original pitch, without the usual downward transpositions for Zsupán and Homonay. Most particularly Harnoncourt has completely rethought the style of the performance. *Der Zigeunerbaron* is a long work, described as 'komische Oper' rather than 'Operette', and much of its music is unusually solid for Strauss. Harnoncourt gives the major numbers their full weight, phrasing them beautifully, and drawing refined singing from the soloists, among whom Herbert Lippert and Pamela Coburn combine beautifully in the duet 'Wer uns getraut?', and Christiane Oelze is a delectably sweet Arsena.

The necessary light relief comes not only from Zsupán (Rudolf Schasching in fine voice) but from usually omitted subsidiary numbers. Elisabeth von Magnus sings Mirabella's 'Just sind es vierundzwanzig Jahre' with exhilarating comic zest, and joins with Jürgen Flimm (more actor than singer) to make the trio 'Nur keusch und rein' an irresistible delight. The live recording comes with some audience laughter and coughs but with the applause suppressed. This deserves to win new admirers both for Harnoncourt and for Strauss's masterly score.

Richard Strauss   German 1864-1949

Richard Strauss's father, Franz, was the leading horn player in Munich. Though Wagner entrusted to him the important horn solos in the premieres of Tristan, Meistersinger and Parsifal, he was openly scathing about Wagner's music. He lived till 1905, long enough to see, paradoxically, his son become the most passionate advocate of Wagner's music and among its most brilliant interpreters.

Richard's formal academic schooling ran parallel to his musical studies. He very quickly made a name for himself, his technical assurance (if not his style) seemingly pre-formed. It's not everyone that has his first symphony, a violin concerto and a second symphony all premiered and under his belt by the age of 20. The influential pianist, composer and conductor Hans von Bülow took a shine to the young Strauss. When he left his orchestra at Meiningen in 1885, Struass took over for a year. Von Bülow was an ardent Wagnerite, despite having been cuckolded by the great man; Strauss now also met the poet and musician Alexander Ritter (married to Wagner's niece). Between them they convinced Strauss of the musical aesthetics of Liszt and Wagner, the concept of 'music as expression', to abandon the classical, restricting forms of the German Romantic style. Wagner's music dramas and Liszt's symphonic tone-poems were to be his models. From that point on, all Strauss's music would have a literary or philosophic outline.

His first venture in which he parted company from his traditional past was the symphonic fantasy Aus

Italien. It caused a furore. The audience hissed it, considering it ugly and confusing, bewildered by its occasional dissonance. Strauss was undeterred, now convinced of his destiny and, to be sure, never averse to a little controversy. The next decade from 1887, in which he wrote a succession of tone-poems, made his name throughout the musical word: Don Juan, Till Eulenspiegel, Ein Heldenleben and Also sprach Zarathustra.

By the turn of the century Strauss was recognised not only among the most important and provocative composers of the time but in the front rank of great conductors. In 1898 he was given one of the most important musical posts in the world – the conductorship of the Berlin Philharmonic, which he retained for a dozen years. Using his immense influence he introduced a system by which, for the first time, German composers would receive a royalty from every performance of their work by a major orchestra or opera house.

Concurrent with the tone-poems were his operas. Guntram (1894) and Feuersnot (1901) were failures. (The soprano lead in Guntram was Pauline de Abna; she married Strauss in September 1894, remaining with him, despite a stormy relationship, until the end of his life, dying only months after him.) In 1900 he met the poet Hugo von Hofmannsthal, a librettist who was to have a profound effect on his career in the theatre. Their collaboration began with Salome, premiered in 1905, followed by Elektra in 1909. He managed to provoke the same hearty opprobrium as the tone-poems: 'There is a vast deal of ugly music in Salome – music that offends the ear and rasps the nerves like fiddlestrings played on by a coarse file…' (New York Tribune). As if by way of concession Hofmannsthal's and Strauss's next venture could not have been more different, evoking the graceful world of 18th-century Vienna in their charming comedy Der Rosenkavalier. It remains among the most cherished of all operas.

Indisputably the leading German composer of the day, Strauss had already become something of a legend in his own lifetime. Music lovers would make pilgrimages to his beautiful villa in Garmisch in the Bavarian Alps to pay their respects. He continued composing for the rest of his life – and writing good music too – but the truth is that he wrote nothing after the First World War that compared with his early tone-poems and operas. Although an immensely cultured man and congenial company, there was a darker side to him: conceited, jealous of rivals and notoriously, even psychopathically mean, Strauss was anything but the munificent Great Composer. His wife, who ruled him with a of iron, held the purse strings and gave him a small allowance to live on.

It is not easy to excuse his behaviour in Germany during the 1930s. He accepted the position of President of the Third Reich Music Chamber, supported the boycott of Jewish music in Germany, and when Bruno Walter was removed from his post as head of the Leipzig Gewandhaus Orchestra, promptly substituted for him. Toscanini refused to conduct at Bayreuth; Strauss accepted. True, he resigned his official post in 1935 and spoke out against the regime when he insisted on working with the Jewish librettist Stefan Zweig on his opera Die schweigsame Frau (The Silent Woman). But when he was asked why he

did not leave the country, Strauss reportedly replied: 'Germany had 56 opera houses; the United States had two. It would have reduced my income.'

He and his wife went to live in Switzerland for most of the Second World War but returned to their villa in the Bavarian Alps after the conflict. He was allowed to remain there composing by the American Army, and cleared of Nazi affiliations in 1948, after facing a special court in Munich. His last year witnessed a creative Indian summer that brought us, inter alia, Capriccio, the Oboe Concerto, the Second Horn Concerto and the Four Last Songs.

Despite all this, so revered was he by the musical world that he was feted during his visit to London in 1947 and his 85th birthday was celebrated worldwide, just a few months before he died.

Horn Concertos

Horn Concertos Nos 1 & 2. Duett-Concertino, AV147. Serenade, Op 7
David Pyatt hn **Joy Farrall** cl **Julie Andrews** bn
Britten Sinfonia / Nicholas Cleobury
Classics for Pleasure 573513-2 (66' · DDD)   Ⓑ**ⓞⓞⓞ**

 David Pyatt won the BBC's Young Musician of the Year Competition back in 1988. Since then the fledgling has well and truly flown. This is sensationally good horn playing, with a noble *legato* and a beautiful sound, full, even and unclouded. He's sparing with the brassy timbres, holding them in reserve for dramatic effect, for such times as the instrument's well-rounded jocularity must take on a brazen, huntsmen-like air, or rise to shining heroics – like the challenging motto theme of the First Concerto. He shapes the big phrases with ease and authority, but his personality is equally conveyed in the rhythmic articulation: a dashing, Jack-be-nimble mischievousness in Strauss's athletic *allegros*. Most of all, though – and this is rare – he loves to play really quietly. He's a master of those dreamy, far-away departures – twilit forest-murmurings: mysterious, unreal.

The recording helps with a beautifully integrated balance. The sound of the early Serenade, Op 7, is particularly fine with ripe, euphonious *tuttis* and room enough for individual personalities to open up. And that's the most remarkable aspect of the piece, the utterly natural way it blends and contrasts across the whole spectrum of wind voices. Two of them take centre stage in the delightful *Duett-Concertino*. Joy Farrall's clarinet and Julie Andrews's bassoon are like Octavian and the Baron Ochs in this gentle but spirited opus. This is a spendid disc, then, and sympathetically directed, too.

Additional recommendation

R Strauss Horn Concertos[a]   Ⓗ
Coupled with **Hindemith** Horn Concerto[b]. Concert Music for Brass and Strings[c]
Brain hn **Philharmonia Orchestra /** [a]**Sawallisch,** [bc]**Hindemith**

EMI Great Recordings of the Century [b]mono 567782-2 (65' · ADD). Recorded 1957-59   Ⓜ❍❍🅑➔

Brain relishes the Straussian bravura in the First Concerto, and the coda is stunning – wonderfully nimble. The frolicking *Rondo* finale of the Second is another highlight, played with a deliciously light *spiccato* by Brain. Sawallisch proves himself a natural Straussian, and his account of the *Concert Music for Brass* is marvellously played – an outstanding bonus.

Eine Alpensinfonie (An Alpine Symphony)

Eine Alpensinfonie
Staatskapelle Weimar / Antoni Wit
Naxos 8 557811 (54' · DDD)   Ⓢ❍❍🅑➔

This is a magnificent record. The Weimar Staatskapelle are rare visitors to disc, but they are a top-class orchestra, with superb strings which sound overwhelmingly, sensuously beautiful in the opening 'Night' and 'Sunrise' sequences.

The warm and spacious acoustic of the Weimarhalle helps; reminiscent of the Lukaskirche in Dresden, where the Staatskapelle there made their famous analogue Strauss recordings under Kempe. This disc is in that same league of excellence. Indeed, conductor Antoni Wit must take a lion's share of the credit for the success of this mountain-climb.

His tempi are spacious but his pacing is not consistently slow. It is during the vistas that Wit takes his time to overwhelm us with the beauty of what his orchestra are describing, the 'Entry into the Forest', dallying a little 'On the Alpine Pasture' and, most telling of all, the burst of radiance on reaching the summit. Then on the way down there is a storm, thunderously captured, but in the calm before it breaks, Wit creates an almost sinister atmosphere of apprehension. As Strauss's descent nears its end and the music winds down, Wit manages a wonderful feeling of triste, a consciousness of danger experienced and triumphed over, and in that 'Ausklang' the organ steals in magically.

Eine Alpensinfonie
**Berlin Philharmonic Orchestra /
Herbert von Karajan**
DG Karajan Gold 439 017-2GHS (51' · DDD) Ⓕ❍❍🅑➔

The *Alpensinfonie* is no longer a rarity on disc, but there are still grounds for preferring the famous Karajan version to subsequent digital rivals, especially in this successful remastering. Karajan's sureness of line is always impressive in Strauss and, while the Berlin Philharmonic Orchestra isn't at its immaculate best, some playing is magnificent here. The sound remains rather fierce, but several passages have been substantially remixed, and the effect is certainly less constricted overall.

Perhaps it doesn't matter that the horn theme that floats in with the (still blinding) 'Sonnenaufgang' isn't quite aligned with the strings. More worrying is the subtle transformation of the opening phrase of 'Der Ansteig': whereas we used to experience it 'from the bottom up' with the balance favouring the basses, we hear more cellos now – and most of them fluff the B flat! That said, the breadth and majesty of Karajan's conception is indisputable.

Additional recommendation

Eine Alpensinfonie
Coupled with Don Juan
Royal Concertgebouw Orch / Jansons
RCO Live 🎙️ RCO08006 (70' · DDD/DSD)
Recorded live   Ⓜ❍🅑➔

Jansons structures the work unerringly and the Concertgebouw sound picture, with extraordinary vividness of detail at every stage of the journey, is remarkable. The Concertgebouw string playing has, of course, an eloquent sweep, and if the violins are less sensuously ravishing than at Weimar (partly the effect of closer microphone placing in Amsterdam), they play particularly beautifully in the score's gentler moments.

Symphonia domestica, Op 53

Symphonia domestica. Josephslegende – Suite
Seattle Symphony Orchestra / Gerard Schwarz
Delos DE3082 (77' · DDD)   Ⓕ

Schwarz and his orchestra give an extremely fine account of the *Symphonia domestica*. The Seattle Symphony sound to be enjoying themselves and to be appreciating the wit, fun and sentiment of the music. Schwarz's achievement is that the work becomes a real symphony under his baton. The playing is relaxed and warm and often very tender. At strenuous moments, though, the sound inclines to be a little unflattering to the strings but otherwise it's clear and spacious.

Why don't more orchestras include *Josephslegende* – such a tuneful, colourful score – in their repertoires? Schwarz clearly believes in it, and his excellent orchestra, with a pliant string section and lively woodwind, respond enthusiastically to his lead. Recommended.

Symphonia domestica[c]. Burleske, AV85[ac].   🅷
Till Eulenspiegels lustige Streiche, Op 28[b].
Don Juan, Op 20[c].
[a]**Alfred Blumen** pf [b]**BBC Symphony Orchestra**;
[c]**Philharmonia Orchestra / Richard Strauss**
Testament mono ② SBT2 1441 (100' · ADD)
Broadcast performances from the Royal Albert Hall,
London, on October 19 and [b]29, 1947   Ⓜ❍

'One of my chief pleasures is to hear *Till* and *Don Juan* on the wireless, conducted by yourself. What a difference!' So wrote the 91-year-old George Bernard Shaw to the 83-year-old Richard Strauss shortly before Christmas 1947. Shaw was referring to the two concerts broadcast from the Royal Albert Hall that autumn by the BBC Third Programme during the festival of

Strauss's music which the BBC, Sir Thomas Beecham and Strauss's London publishers had jointly sponsored.

In *Till* and briefly in *Domestica* there is audible interference from an adjacent station. The transfers of Leech's flawed acetates are by Testament's miracle-worker-in-chief Paul Baily. Examples of what the acetates sounded like before treatment are cheekily offered as an addendum to disc 2. The transformation is astonishing. Perhaps Baily should have a go at Strauss's 1929 Berlin Staatskapelle recording of *Don Juan*. Until he does, we are bound to conclude that this live Philharmonia performance is not only fierier and more expressive but far better played.

Strauss had a famously economical beat. Even so, for a man of 83 to conduct a concert of this length at this pitch of intensity – after the three principal works he threw in the *Rosenkavalier* waltzes for good measure – is astonishing. In the opening of *Don Juan* he yields to no one, not even Toscanini, in the brilliance of his attack, yet in the lyric sections there is a yearning loveliness that put me in mind of the fact that in October 1947 the *Four Last Songs* were already gestating. What a crossing of the years is here!

What is true of *Don Juan* is doubly true of this startlingly wonderful performance of *Symphonia domestica*, a work Strauss loved more than most of his public did. This London account communicates fervently his tender and passionate belief in the piece.

The *Till Eulenspiegel*, which he conducted 10 days later during one of Sir Adrian Boult's BBC SO concerts, is less remarkable, too slow and careful. Why, one asks, was the fledgling Philharmonia the more empathetic ensemble, conjuring forth phrasing and nuances the Vienna Philharmonic would have been proud to own? Beecham may be the answer. Many of the Philharmonia's players had worked for the old wizard whose mastery of Strauss's music went back four decades.

The hiring of the gifted and witty but barely remembered Austrian-born Jewish pianist Alfred Blumen was both personal and political. An acquaintance of Strauss, Blumen had spent the war in an internment camp in the north of England. There were reports of disagreements in rehearsal, Strauss telling Blumen to slow down, Blumen muttering how Strauss used to speed through *Burleske*. Neither man hangs about.

Also sprach Zarathustra, Op 30

Also sprach Zarathustra. Ein Heldenleben, Op 40 **H**
Chicago Symphony Orchestra / Fritz Reiner
RCA Living Stereo 82876 61389-2 (76' · ADD)
Recorded 1954 Ⓜ❶❶❷

It's astonishing that this recording of *Also sprach Zarathustra* was made in 1954, in stereo when Toscanini was still (just) recording in lo-fi in New York's Carnegie Hall. The sound may be

RICHARD STRAUSS'S ALSO SPRACH ZARATHUSTRA – IN BRIEF

Chicago SO / Fritz Reiner
RCA 82876 61389-2 (76' · ADD) Ⓜ❶❶❷
Reiner's incandescent 1954 account is the stuff of which legends are made. Impossible to believe that the stereo tapes are half a century old. And Reiner draws from his crack Chicago ensemble playing of incredible intensity and concentration.

Berlin PO / Herbert von Karajan
DG 447 441-2GOR (79' · ADD) Ⓜ❶❶❶❷
Arguably the most imposing of Karajan's three recordings. An interpretation of tremendous stature and aplomb; fabulous playing from the Berliners who had a uniquely dense sound when they played the music of Richard Strauss under Karajan.

Concertgebouw Orchestra / Bernard Haitink
Philips ② 442 281-2PM2 (152' · ADD/DDD) Ⓜ
Bernard Haitink's distinguished 1973 account appeared at roughly the same time as the above-mentioned Karajan. Some might even prefer it for its extra nobility and opulence.

Boston SO / Serge Koussevitzky
Biddulph WHL054 (65' · ADD) Ⓜ
Koussevitzky was an exciting and dedicated Straussian, and his pioneering 1935 recording of *Zarathustra* remains a 'must hear'.

Vienna PO / Clemens Krauss
Testament SBT1183 (76' · ADD) Ⓕ
Once you've adjusted to the rather acidulous string timbre, Clemens Krauss's authoritative 1950 reading with the VPO displays a glowing perception that never loosens its hold on the listener.

Staatskapelle Dresden / Rudolf Kempe
EMI 574590-2 (79' · ADD) Ⓢ❶❷
A somewhat lightweight introduction apart, Kempe secures a performance of treasurable flexibility and comprehensive understanding. What a great Straussian he was!

Zürich Tonhalle Orchestra / David Zinman
Arte Nova 74321 87071-2 (76' · DDD) Ⓢ
Anyone wanting a bargain-basement *Zarathustra* in realistic, up-to-date sound could do a lot worse than invest in this characterful and sympathetic account from Zürich.

Berlin PO / Karl Böhm
DG ③ 463 190-2GB3 (176' · ADD) Ⓢ
Housed in a collection of Strauss tone-poems, Böhm's *Zarathustra* is beautifully shaped and tremendously well played by the BPO. Böhm knew Strauss well so there's added authentic element brought into play.

tonally fierce by current standards, but the balance is fully acceptable, with the first and second violins set close to the listener on either side of the podium, and the basses hard left.

Reiner's *Also sprach* is intense and extrovert. In his second year with the Chicago Symphony Orchestra, the conductor was already getting a thrilling response from the strings, though woodwind intonation could be a problem. Confident and well played as it is, the spectacular opening sunrise inevitably lacks the impact of modern recordings. Instead there's a measure of raw passion and forward thrust unequalled on disc. In the reflective passages, conductor and engineers display some reluctance to achieve a real *pianissimo*, but as the tempo builds Reiner invariably creates great excitement. His reading of *Ein Heldenleben* has humanity as well as virtuosity.

Also sprach Zarathustra. Don Juan, Op 20
Berlin Philharmonic Orchestra /
Herbert von Karajan
DG 439 016-2GHS (54' · DDD). Recorded 1983 Ⓕ**O**Ⓑ→

Also sprach Zarathustra. Don Juan, Op 20.
Till Eulenspiegels lustige Streiche, Op 28.
Salome – Dance of the Seven Veils
Berlin Philharmonic Orchestra /
Herbert von Karajan
DG The Originals 447 441-2GOR (79' · ADD)
Recorded 1973 Ⓜ**OOO**Ⓑ→

The playing of the Berlin Philharmonic on both sets is as glorious as ever; its virtuosity can be taken for granted along with its sumptuous tonal refinement, and in Strauss Karajan has no peer. As a recording the 1983 disc is very good indeed. The famous opening has greater intensity in the 1973 version, and you may prefer its marginally greater warmth and glow of the strings.

The DG engineers adopt a slightly closer balance on this newcomer, which has greater range and impressive detail, particularly in the bass. Both *Don Juans* are fine performances, too. To sum up, Karajan's classic 1973 account holds sway.

Don Quixote, Op 35

Don Quixote.
Lieder – Morgen, Op 27 No 4;-Der Rosenband, Op 36
No 1; Wiegenlied, Op 41 No 1; Freundliche Vision,
Op 48 No 1; Waldseligkeit, Op 49 No 1; Die heiligen
drei Könige, Op 56 No 6
Dame Felicity Lott *sop* **André Vauquet** *va* **François**
Guye *vc* **Suisse Romande Orchestra / Armin Jordan**
Mediaphon MED72 165 (69' · DDD) Ⓜ**O**

This disc is notable for taking advantage of the superlative acoustic of the Victoria Hall in Geneva, home of the Suisse Romande Orchestra, thus giving us the most impressively recorded *Don Quixote* yet, in sound terms. The detail of the brilliant scoring is

clearly delineated, while the whole picture is one of amazing warmth and resplendence. Jordan and his orchestra offer a performance worthy of both the place and the production. Guye brings out all Quixote's endearing and aggravating qualities without a hint of exaggeration, his tone always full and poised.

The songs are more than a makeweight. Lott, the leading Straussian soprano of the day, knows how to make the most of six of the composer's best-loved songs with ethereal, fine-grained tone and line. Jordan presents the music without any excess of sentiment. So what a great pity, then, that texts and translations aren't provided, the only blot on a disc that's certain to give much pleasure and satisfaction.

R Strauss Don Quixote[a] **Haydn** Cello Concerto
No 2, HobVIIb/2[b]
Mstislav Rostropovich *vc* [a]**Harry Danks** *va*
[a]**BBC Symphony Orchestra / Sir Malcolm Sargent,**
[b]**London Symphony Orchestra**
BBC Legends mono BBCL4240-2 (66' · ADD)
Recorded live in [a]1964 and [b]1965 Ⓕ

This BBC Legends issue celebrates the playing of Mstislav Rostropovich relatively early in his career. The disc also provides a welcome reminder that, at a time when his reputation has rather fallen back, Malcolm Sargent always produced his best performances at the Proms and that he was always at his best in late-Romantic music such as that of Strauss.

Rostropovich's playing is masterly, dominating each performance with its magnetism as well as its resonance. Harry Danks, principal viola in the BBC SO for many years, makes a colourful character out of the faithful Sancho Panza, bringing out the wit of the writing even if his tone is no match for the resonant cello of the principal soloist. Each of the 10 variations is presented in clean separation, with the orchestral players relishing the often spectacular orchestral effects, like the imitation of the bleating of sheep in the second variation, the brilliant percussion-writing in the 'Ride through the Air' and the powerful brass and ominous timpani beats in 'Defeat of Don Quixote'.

That leads up to the most glorious playing of all from Rostropovich in the long epilogue marking the Don's death. He uses a very free vibrato, and yet in the close of his solo his *pianissimo* is breathtaking. For radio recordings of the mid-1960s the sound is excellent and Tully Potter's notes are exemplary.

Ein Heldenleben, Op 40

R Strauss Ein Heldenleben
Beethoven Symphony No 4
Berlin Philharmonic Orchestra /
Herbert von Karajan
Testament SBT1430 (80' · ADD)
Recorded live at the Royal Festival Hall, London,
in April 1985 Ⓕ**OO**

For anyone lucky enough to have secured a ticket few orchestral concerts have remained so vividly in the memory as the one given by Karajan's incomparable Berlin Philharmonic in London's Royal Festival Hall on April 27, 1985. The surprises began with the conductor's own physical frailty. Edging unsteadily towards the rostrum and propping himself up against the railing, he adopted the peculiar posture that enabled him to remain upright and in command notwithstanding a debilitating spinal condition.

In truth the Beethoven was and is a gift to his many detractors. With the maestro unwilling or unable to lift his arms, the band turns in its patented imitation of a gramophone record. Surfaces are immaculate but it's like being trapped in a pudding without air in the texture. Phrases, even whole sections glide by with no intake of breath and the first two movements in particular may induce feelings of claustrophobia in younger listeners. They should persevere.

No superlatives can convey the inevitability, conviction and sweep of Karajan's *Heldenleben* which makes even this notoriously shrill-sounding venue resound in glory. The original BBC sound team of producer Misha Donat and balance engineer John McCulloch capture a paradoxical sonority, rich yet transparent, 'lambent in its beauty, never cloying or opaque' as described by Richard Osborne in his characteristically generous booklet-notes. The battle scene may be slow but was it ever more incisively chronicled? The Strauss at least is indispensable.

Ein Heldenleben. Metamorphosen
West German Radio Symphony Orchestra,
Cologne / Semyon Bychkov
Avie AV0017 (75' · DDD)   Ⓕ Ⓞ Ⓓ➔

Semyon Bychkov's Op 40 'Hero' is the sort you could happily live with: he knows his worth but doesn't thrust his exploits in your face. The opening self-portrait more or less says it all, a confident exposition (warm strings, strong brass, crystal-clear timps), well paced, sonorous but never over-forceful. Strauss's cackling adversaries are more chuckled over than caricatured, and violinist Kyoko Shikata makes for an affectionately playful companion, thankfully not the manic cadenza that's sometimes visited on us.

In *Metamorphosen* the line remains fluid but constant, urged on (though never hampered) by genuine warmth of feeling. You sense that the notes and their emotional subtext are being granted an equal footing. Avie's recording has impressive amplitude and, in *Heldenleben*, credible presence. Any rival would need to do a lot to upstage this sympathetic production. Recommended.

Ein Heldenleben, Op 40. Metamorphosen
Staatskapelle Dresden / Fabio Luisi
Sony Classical 🔊 88697 08471-2 (73' · DDD)   Ⓕ Ⓞ

Ein Heldenleben and *Metamorphosen*, though written at opposite ends of Strauss's long career, make an ideal coupling, as both were directly inspired by Beethoven's *Eroica* Symphony. The warm strength of the key of E flat is at the root of *Heldenleben* too, while *Metamorphosen*, reflecting Strauss's pain over the wartime destruction of so much he loved in Germany, repeatedly and movingly quotes the *Eroica*'s Funeral March. Aptly too, the orchestra is the Staatskapelle Dresden, Strauss's favourite, responsible for many Strauss performances.

In this new version of *Heldenleben*, Fabio Luisi has opted to go back to what he describes as the original ending. This was Strauss's first idea, never published, of ending the piece *pianissimo*. It was only later, realising that the response of audiences would be greater from a loud ending, that he was persuaded to append the now usual ending, adding some two dozen bars with fanfares and a final *fortissimo* chord.

Luisi proves an outstanding Straussian, drawing passionate playing from the orchestra, as flamboyant in *Heldenleben* as anyone would want, and darkly intense in the valedictory paragraphs and complex counterpoint of *Metamorphosen*, though the recording makes it sound as though more than 23 strings are playing. In *Heldenleben* Luisi is excellent in bringing out the massive structure of the work like a gigantic sonata form, quite apart from the programmatic element. Kai Vogler proves an outstanding violin soloist in the role of the Hero's partner, a clear portrait of the volatile Frau Strauss, here played with just the right degree of spontaneous flexibility. The recording is exceptionally full and brilliant, to match the resonant beauty of the playing.

Additional recommendation

Ein Heldenleben[a]
Coupled with Le bourgeois gentilhomme
BPO / Rattle
EMI 339339-2 (82' · DDD) [a]Recorded live   Ⓕ Ⓓ➔
It says much for Rattle's achievement in Berlin that the result in this live recording offers the keenest rivalry to the finest versions already in the catalogue. The heroic opening section already establishes Rattle's approach as a degree more flexible, more warmly expressive than Karajan's. Karajan is certainly warm, but he generally keeps his expressiveness within steady speeds, where Rattle is a degree freer, with rhythms subtly pointed. The fill-up is a generous one, bringing the overall timing of the disc to an exceptional 82 minutes.

R Strauss Ein Heldenleben
Coupled with **Debussy** Prélude à L'après-midi d'un faune **Schumann** Piano Concerto, Op 54[a]
[a]**Frager; Staatskapelle Dresden / Kempe**
Profil ② PH08053 (87' · ADD)   Ⓜ
Recorded live in March 1974
The lower strings at the opening of *Ein Heldenle-ben* make one catch one's breath, as does the rich-

ness of sonority of the full string patina for which the orchestra under Kempe was famous. The playing is deeply felt, glows with life and provides a vividly detailed scenario. This is the key work in the concert but the performance of the *Prélude à L'après-midi d'un faune* is also totally memorable. Kempe also found a natural partner in Malcom Frager in Schumann's Piano Concerto, a performance full of freshness and vitality.

R Strauss Ein Heldenleben   **H**
Coupled with Don Juan **Wagenaar** Cyrano de Bergerac
Concertgebouw Orch; NYPO / Mengelberg
Pearl mono GEMMCD0008 (71' · ADD)
Recorded 1928-42   **Ⓜ O**

The perfect set for anyone remotely interested in Strauss or in the history of recording. By the time this disc was made Mengelberg had nearly three decades of the piece under his belt – this is the definitive *Heldenleben*. Given its age, the transfer is little short of miraculous.

Metamorphosen

Metamorphosen. Tod und Verklärung. Four Last Songs[a]
[a]**Gundula Janowitz** *sop* **Berlin Philharmonic Orchestra / Herbert von Karajan**
DG The Originals 447 422-2GOR (77' · ADD)
      Ⓜ O O O �田

These are a clear first-choice in all three works. Karajan's *Metamorphosen* has almost unbearable intensity and great emotional urgency – it's a gripping and involving account. The sound is marginally more forward and cleaner than is ideal, though the rich ambience is very appealing. *Tod und Verklärung* isn't as spectacularly recorded as some more modern versions, but it's a greater performance that just about any other. It's electrifying, with superb playing and a life-and-death intensity to the climaxes. It's more vividly recorded than his most recent previous version, and the performance is tauter and more powerful. The quality of the recording gives no cause for reproach. See page 1123 for comments about the Janowitz *Four Last Songs* (in an alternative coupling).

Josephslegende, Op 63

Josephslegende
Budapest Festival Orchestra / Iván Fischer
Channel Classics 🅢 CCSSA24507
(65' · DDD/DSD)   **Ⓕ O O O ⟦**

Richard Strauss's *Josephslegende* (1914) is a truly extraordinary work. It was written for Diaghilev, who wanted something sensational to follow *The Rite of Spring*. But Nijinsky was unable to take the title-role planned for him, and it was the young Massine as substitute who had to dance what Nijinsky later described as 'undanceable music'. But

Nijinsky also had an eccentric hand in the extraordinary scenario which tells of the attempted and unsuccessful seduction of Joseph by Potiphar's wife, her suicide after her failure, the attempt by the suspicious Potiphar to torture the innocent Joseph, and his celestial rescue by an angel who frees him from his bonds.

All this drew from Strauss a richly sensuous score, in many ways an amalgam of his previous successes, predominantly *Salome*, in the voluptuous dances of the veiled and unveiled women near the begining, climaxed by 'Sulamith's dance' of burning desire. But the spectacle of the *Alpine Symphony*, the passion of *Don Juan*, the hyperbole of *Ein Heldenleben*, to say nothing of a touch of *Death and Transfiguration*, are all mixed in. The booklet offers an elaborate cued synopsis of the narrative, so that one can relate Strauss's extraordinary score to what is being described.

Iván Fischer and the enlarged Budapest Festival Orchestra give a magnificent account of the work, readily going over the sensual top when Strauss demands it, but with Fischer ensuring that Strauss's underlying lyrical flow moves seamlessly but erotically onwards to the final climax. This is surely a work for sumptuous surround sound, which is exactly what the Channel Classics recording team provide, and very impressively, too.

Der Rosenkavalier – Suite

Ein Heldenleben, Op 40. Der Rosenkavalier – Suite
City of Birmingham Symphony Orchestra / Andris Nelsons
Orfeo C803 091A (73' · DDD). Recorded live **Ⓕ O O O**

The voltage count in Symphony Hall on May 28, 2009, when Andris Nelsons took the CBSO through Artur Rodzinski's 25-minute *Rosenkavalier* Suite, must have been pretty high. At one level, the suite is an unabashed piece of musical kitsch, at another it is an effective and affecting if occasionally rambunctious overview of this glorious work. Nelsons has yet to conduct the opera itself but he directs Rodzinski's suite as if he was Karajan and both Kleibers rolled into one, with a touch of André Kostelanetz thrown in for good measure. The CBSO play superbly for their new young principal conductor.

The *Rosenkavalier* Suite was recorded at a single performance, *Ein Heldenleben* taken from three performances the following month. The CBSO is some way from acquiring the full range and blend of colours and sonorities Strauss ideally needs. As Beecham proved, this doesn't have to be a specifically Austro-German sound but Beecham's Strauss was rarely less than sensuous and always finely nuanced. In this new *Ein Heldenleben* the more energetic music can be a bit of a free-for-all. The troops need shrewder marshalling in the battle scene if the hero's routing of them is to carry its full weight and glory. As to the hero's works of peace, it probably needs more experience of Strauss's music than Nelsons currently possesses for their significance to be fully savoured. That said, Nelsons and his musicians bring sensitivity and style to many of the score's more reflective passages. The Symphony Hall recording is very fine.

Works for Winds

Complete Works for Wind Ensemble
Academy Symphonic Wind / Keith Bragg
Royal Academy of Music ② RAM034 (97' · DDD)　Ⓕ

Strauss wrote his Serenade in E flat for 13 instruments in 1881, when he was only 17. It is essentially Mozartian in derivation, yet immediately the ear registers the Romantic swing of the melodies and the lusher textures which make the Straussian imprint. Already the young composer's textural blending is masterly, while the sonorities anticipate the future.

The four-movement Suite in B flat (also for 13 instruments) is more diverse and further removed from Mozart, with a tender *Romanze* (with rich horns), a good-natured Gavotte and a finale which begins in mock darkness before setting off into a jolly, robust fugue.

The two major works date from his last years and show him in full maturity. Extra instruments were added to the Symphony in F – a C clarinet, basset-horn and bass clarinet – and the full sonority is quite luscious, the lines even more melodically complex. The Symphony in E flat dates from 1945 and seems to take off from where the previous symphony finished, the opening glowingly animated and vivacious and – as played here – with exuberant forward thrust. The finale quotes from *Götterdämerung* but spirits soon lift; the *allegro* sets off with light-hearted lyricism, with swiftly intertwining woodwind, and the music gathers force and momentum to reach its spectacular, life-asserting coda.

It's a magnificent performance, but all four works here are superbly and spontaneously played by eager musicians from the Royal Academy of Music who provide wonderful blending and a splendidly polished, professional ensemble under their fine conductor, Keith Bragg. This new set certainly trumps its rivals.

Piano Quartet

Metamorphosen (version for string septet)[b].
Piano Quartet[a]. Prelude to Capriccio
Nash Ensemble ([a]Marianne Thorsen, Malin Broman vns [a]Lawrence Power, Philip Dukes vas [a]Paul Watkins, Pierre Doumenge vcs [b]Duncan McTier db
[a]Ian Brown pf)
Hyperion CDA67574 (78' · DDD)　Ⓕ Ⓓ▶

The early and late Strauss on this finely recorded disc are separated by some 60 years: the Piano Quartet was completed in 1884, the year after Wagner's death, while *Metamorphosen* dates from the early months of 1945. Strauss at 20 had abundant promise: Strauss at 80 had managed to avoid lapsing into self-parody. The result is full of interest.

The Piano Quartet is invariably labelled 'Brahmsian' and the opening makes that association clear. Yet the piece is too loosely put together, too focused on small-scale harmonic effects, to sound like Brahms for long. Anyone looking for evidence that Strauss's true métier would be programme music and opera need look no further. It's an enjoyable piece for all that, expansively dramatic and genuinely expressive with that touch of spontaneity which signals Strauss at his best.

The Nash Ensemble bring affectionate fervour to the Quartet, without lingering excessively over its creakier transitions. A cooler touch might have been preferable with the *Capriccio* Prelude and *Metamorphosen* – the latter in particular risks overheating, with uniformly high dynamic levels. The status of this version of *Metamorphosen* is ambiguous, since it derives from a draft discovered in 1990. This preceded the final scoring for 23 solo strings, and one wonders if Strauss might not have revised the former in light of the latter as he wished to preserve it – especially the very awkward harmonic switch at the end, which the final version eliminates. A curiosity, then, which inevitably sounds more like a dilution of the familiar score than a genuine alternative.

Violin Sonata in E flat, Op 18

R Strauss Violin Sonata **Bartók** (arr Székely)
Six Romanian Folkdances, Sz56 **Stravinsky** (arr Stravinsky/Dushkin) Divertimento
Vadim Repin vn **Boris Berezovsky** pf
Erato 8573 85769-2 (53' · DDD)　Ⓕ Ⓞ

Stylistically, Strauss's lyrical Op 18 (1887) sits poised somewhere between Brahms's chivalrous song-cycle *Die schöne Magelone* and Strauss's own *Don Juan* of the following year. The finale is rich in heroics though not before a seductive 'Improvisation' and the appearance of one of Strauss's loveliest melodies. Anyone familiar with Heifetz's three recordings – his second, the first of two with the late Brooks Smith, is probably the most comprehensively expressive – will have a job adapting to anyone else. No one draws a sweeter, more tender opening phrase, though Vadim Repin more or less matches Heifetz in terms of repose.

Repin's feline violin faces leonine support from Boris Berezovsky, whose outsize musical personality draws maximum mileage from Strauss's virtuoso piano writing, though he too is capable of relaxing. His elegant fingerwork is nicely demonstrated in the decorative figurations that dominate the third section of second movement. Kremer and Oleg Maisenberg are also excellent, but Repin's engagement with the music's lyrical element just about gives him the edge. Heifetz is more 'accompanied' by Brooks Smith than partnered by him.

Echoes of Strauss return for the *Adagio* from Stravinsky's *Fairy's Kiss* re-run, a witty *Diverti-*

mento prepared in collaboration with violinist Samuel Dushkin. Repin's strongest current rival is Perlman, though his reading is perhaps less subtly characterised and, again, Berezovsky's strong-arm pianism strengthens the frame. Bartók's ubiquitous *Romanian Folk-dances* are rather less spicy here than you would expect from someone who has fiddled in gypsy style with Lakatos, but Repin's harmonics in the 'Pe loc' third movement are admirably clean and the final dances are suitably dashing. The sound is very well balanced.

Enoch Arden

Enoch Arden, Op 38[a].
Piano Pieces, Op 3 – No 1; No 4
[a]**Patrick Stewart** *spkr* **Emanuel Ax** *pf*
Sony Clasical 88697 09056-2 (62' · DDD)   Ⓕ

The genius of *Enoch Arden* lies in Strauss's positioning of the actually rather small amount of music: he introduces, interludes and comments on the narrative, but only rarely underpins it. The actor has to take much of the initiative in style and pacing. He must decide whether to remain glowingly neutral, as the veteran Claude Rains does with Glenn Gould (Sony) or pitch in and characterise both the *ménage à trois* at the centre of the tale and the dramatic locations of the story as does Fischer-Dieskau (DG).

Patrick Stewart has a naturally compelling voice. He opts for a soft Northern burr for Enoch, friend Philip and their girl Annie, and a cunning use of volume and pace for the story's dramatic peaks. Ax, whose spacious, fluent control and use of colours as if lit from behind often remind one of Schnabel, partners perfectly, taking deliberately a more neutral line. The recording is natural and free of trickery. Whoever's idea it was to follow the melodrama with two of the Op 3 piano pieces has provided the ideal wind-down after Strauss's (intentionally) short and unmelodramatic postlude. Hugely recommended.

Choral Works

Deutsche Motette, Op 62[a]. Gesänge, Op 34.
An den Baum Daphne (epilogue to 'Daphne'),
AV137[b]. Die Göttin im Putzzimmer, AV120
[a]**Tina Kiberg,** [b]**Marianne Lund** *sops* [b]**Christian Lisdorf** *treb* [a]**Randi Stene** *contr* [a]**Gert Henning-Jensen** *ten* [a]**Ulrik Cold** *bass* [b]**Copenhagen Boys' Choir; Danish National Radio Choir / Stefan Parkman**
Chandos CHAN9223 (57' · DDD · T/t)   ⒻⓄ

Under Stefan Parkman the Danish National Radio Choir has established a reputation second to none. Parkman handles his singers as if they were a fully fledged symphony orchestra; which isn't at all inappropriate in this programme by the supreme master of orchestral colour. From the heart of the 16 chorus parts of

the *Deutsche Motette* a further seven are projected by solo voices emerging imperceptibly from the midst of a dense, luxuriant texture. The depth of colour and range of emotions are every bit as extensive in these works as in the great orchestral tone-poems; indeed few orchestral tone-poems evoke dusk and sunset so vividly as 'Der Abend', the first of the 1897 *Zwei Gesänge*. There's a wonderfully luminous soundscape here; a combination of superb compositional skill, sensitive musical direction, superlative choral singing and a warm, full-bodied recording.

Deutsche Motette. Zwei Gesänge, Op 34.
Traumlicht, AV123 No 2
Jane Archibald *sop* **Dagmar Pecková** *contr* **Eric Soklossa** *ten* **Robert Gleadow** *bass-bar* **Accentus; Latvian Radio Choir / Laurence Equilbey**
Naïve V5194 (48' · DDD)   Ⓕ

'Formal orgies' was Strauss's phrase – only it's better in German, *Gestaltungsorgien*. In the whole choral repertoire, it's hard to think of anything that more luxuriates in sheer sound. That is the sensual, the orgiastic part. The formality lies in the controlling hand, the strong consciousness of textual demands and of musical themes and motifs to be stated, developed and brought into relationship. All is wonderfully well accomplished in each of these works but with surpassing mastery in the *Deutsche Motette* to words, from the Persian, by Rückert. The programme opens with this – which may be a mistake, as it often is to put the best first.

The Latvian performance's distinction is in blend, or rather the natural weighting of the various elements so that the sound is as you would hope to hear it from an advantageous seat (not too near the front) in the concert hall. One feels the blessing of repose and reintegration, grateful nevertheless for having been through the more analytical processes involved in listening to the others.

This a fine choir – or combination of choirs – tone both gentle and firm, and with a sensitivity to the shadings and modulations so richly characteristic of Strauss's choral writing. It's rather short measure, that is the main fault, and the excellence of the men's voices in *Traumlicht* makes one wish all the more that the programme had been extended to include, at least, the other two choruses from the group for male-voice choir.

Four Last Songs

Four Last Songs. Das Rosenband, Op 36 No 1. Lieder, Op 68 – Ich wollt ein Sträusslein binden; Säusle, liebe Myrte; Als mir dein Lied erklang. Befreit, Op 39 No 4. Lieder, Op 27 – Ruhe, meine Seele!; Morgen. Wiegenlied, Op 41 No 1. Meinem Kinde, Op 37 No 3. Zueignung, Op 10 No 1. Die heiligen drei Könige aus Morgenland, Op 56 No 6
Soile Isokoski *sop* **Berlin Radio Symphony**

Orchestra / Marek Janowski
Ondine ODE982-2 (64' · DDD · T/t)   Ⓕ**OOO**

 Strauss-singing doesn't come much better than this. No doubt the composer himself, with his love of the soprano voice, would have been enthralled by Isokoski's glorious singing. He might also have approved of Janowski's straightforward, quite brisk conducting as he was never one to sentimentalise his own music. With a combination of free, unfettered tone, not a hint of strain in high-lying passages, a fine *legato* and an amazingly long breath, Isokoski fulfils every demand of her chosen songs. To those attributes she adds just a hint of quick vibrato, which she uses unerringly to expressive purpose throughout. Add the depth of feeling she brings to inwardly emotional pieces such as 'Befreit', 'Ruhe meine Seele!' and, above all, 'Morgen!', a perfect realisation of this oft-recorded piece, and you have performances to rival any of the greats of the past.

She reminds one most of Lisa della Casa, the first soprano to record the *Four Last Songs*, and Sena Jurinac. She has the same smiling timbre, the same natural style, the same avoidance of wallowing in music that contains its own proportion of sentiment. Try the ecstatic execution of the final verse of 'Beim Schlafengehen' and you'll understand. If, on the other hand, you prefer a more leisurely approach, there are always Janowitz and Karajan.

Janowski is obviously at one with his soprano, not only here but also in *Zueignung*. Refined playing from the Berlin Radio Symphony and an open recording complete the pleasure.

Four Last Songs[a]. Capriccio – Morgen mittag um elf!
… Kein andres[b]. Tod und Verklärung[c]
[ab]**Gundula Janowitz** *sop* [a]**Berlin Philharmonic Orchestra / Herbert von Karajan;** [b]**Bavarian Radio Symphony Orchestra,** [c]**Staatskapelle Dresden / Karl Böhm**
DG Classikon 439 467-2GCL (65' · ADD)
Recorded 1971-72   Ⓜ**OO**▸

Here's a feast of glorious Strauss at bargain price, though the performances are anything but bargain in quality. In spite of strong challenges from far and wide, the singing of them by Gundula Janowitz has, arguably, still not been surpassed for Straussian opulence and tenderness – we emphasise 'arguably', for people feel passionately about interpretations of this work! – and Karajan conducts a near-ideal account of the orchestral score. Janowitz, in glorious voice, sings the *Four Last Songs* flowingly. The recording is more hazy than on the other two exemplary performances. The fashion of the moment to denigrate Böhm is incomprehensible when you encounter readings as splendid as his two contributions here, in which he again proves himself an ideal Straussian.

The live account of *Tod und Verklärung* caught at the 1972 Salzburg Festival but not released

RICHARD STRAUSS'S FOUR LAST SONGS IN BRIEF

Soile Isokoski; Berlin RSO / Marek Janowski
Ondine ODE982-2 (64' · DDD)   Ⓕ**OOO**
 Perfectly realised interpretations with which Isokoski proves herself a radiant Straussian yet avoids any trace of sentimentality with relatively brisk tempi. Ideally clean and luminous recording helps.

Gundula Janowitz;
Berlin PO / Herbert von Karajan
DG 439 467-2GCL (65' · ADD)   Ⓜ**OO**▸
A more measured, rich-textured approach from a soprano and conductor at one in their pursuit of tonal beauty and sureness of line in 1973. Janowitz's way with the poetry creates an almost liquid stream of sound.

Renée Fleming;
Houston SO / Christoph Eschenbach
RCA 82876 59408-2 (69' · DDD)   Ⓜ
Munich Philharmonic Orchestra /
Christian Thielemann
Decca 478 0647DH (56' · DDD · T/t)   Ⓜ**O**▸
Fleming in 1995 and 2008. While both performances take their time, Fleming's richer, burnished tone on the later, Decca version, plus its more interesting couplings, make it the one to go for. Both conductors are sensitive to their singer but the Munich orchestra has a more *echt*-Straussian sound and the live Decca recording is very well managed.

Jessye Norman;
Leipzig Gewandhaus / Kurt Masur
Philips 475 8507PB (48' · DDD)   Ⓢ**O**▸
As set down in 1982, the most commanding of all recordings, and probably the slowest. The original disc won the solo vocal category of the 1984 *Gramophone* Record Awards, and the *Last Songs* are now available with a choice of couplings. Simply glorious.

Elisabeth Schwarzkopf;
Berlin RSO / George Szell
EMI 566908-2 (65' · ADD)   Ⓜ**OOO**▸
Elisabeth Schwarzkopf's several recordings combine beauty of sound with unequalled feeling for the words. This final version under George Szell, with its very special autumnal quality, has acquired classic status.

Lisa della Casa;   Ⓗ
Vienna Philharmonic Orchestra / Karl Böhm
Regis mono RRC1192 (65' · ADD)   Ⓢ**OO**
Della Casa's early-1950s version is still full of exquisite singing – coupled with some fascinating *Capriccio* excerpts from 1953. This was the work's first commercial recording and, as so often is the case, has a special magic all of its own.

until 1988 (*in memoriam*) builds naturally to its various incandescent climaxes, and the music is never allowed to drag or descend into sentimentality. The playing of the Dresden orchestra is lithe and warm. The final scene of *Capriccio* comes from the complete set recorded in Munich in 1971. Once more Böhm judges tempos and texture to a nicety, the music always moving forward in perfect balance to its end.

Four Last Songs. Capriccio – Interlude (Moonlight Music); Morgen mittag um elf!^b Salome – Ach, du wolltest mich nicht deinen Mund küssen lassen^a
Nina Stemme *sop*
^a**Liora Grodnikaite** *mez* ^a**Gerhard Siegel** *ten*
^b**Jeremy White** *bass* **Royal Opera House Orchestra, Covent Garden / Antonio Pappano**
EMI Ⓕ 378797-2 (56' · DDD)   Ⓜ❶➤

To borrow a phrase from Richard Osborne, mighty tents are already pitched on these fields – for the *Four Last Songs* Schwarzkopf/Szell, Della Casa/Böhm, Norman/Masur; for the *Salome* finale Krauss/Cebotari, Welitsch/Reiner and so on. But the conductor who has already got onto record a newly thought-through *Bohème*, a *Tosca* that can hold its own with de Sabata's, and a modern *Tristan* with Domingo need fear no competition. All the hounds of hell are let loose by the ROH's percussion section to launch a wild, but always intricately shaped and detailed, account of young Princess Salome's sickly Liebestod. Being already a searching, grown-up Isolde, Stemme, like her 1950s forerunners, now really manages to cut a teenage Isolde too, by turns sweet, spooky and growing up.

The discs's running order is cunning and effective, and both conductor and soprano are in command of the switch to Madeleine's music-or-words dilemma. In *Capriccio*'s Moonlight Interlude, as in the *Songs*, Pappano achieves richness without overweighting; his *rubato* lingers rather than indulges (like…but let's not compare). Stemme is a more torn and dramatic Countess than, say, Janowitz, Schwarzkopf or Della Casa; this performance harks back to Clemens Krauss and Viorica Ursuleac, emotion shaping the (fine) text, rather than vice versa.

As if to create a valedictory survey of Strauss, the soprano voice and the orchestra, the start of 'Frühling' aptly seconds the Countess's mood. Michael Tanner's note for the new remastering of Flagstad's creator's performance (see above) remarks how tempi in this work have got slower over the past 50 years. Pappano and his orchestra (what solo playing!), while never hurrying, keep the forward pace of an attentive Lied accompanist – emotional points are made without milking, matching the cool beauty of the soloist's timbre. Stemme has vocal height and weight in equal measure and (again) really uses her text. Finally, the record is produced and engineered with sensitivity to the layout of Strauss's instrumental and vocal textures.

Additional recommendation

R Strauss Four Last Songs
Coupled with **Wagner** Götterdämmerung – Siegfried's Rhine Journey; Brünnhildes's Immolation. Tristan und Isolde – Prelude; Liebestod
Flagstad; Philharmonia / Furtwängler
Testament mono SBT1410 (67' · ADD)
Recorded live in 1950   Ⓕ❶❶

Here's a live recording of the concert in 1950 when Flagstad gave the premiere of Strauss's *Four Last Songs*, followed by some truly unforgettable Wagner. The performance of the Strauss is now heard in improved sound; but Flagstad, for all the richness of her singing, gives a fairly generalised interpretation compared with many that were to follow, and the conductor was never the greatest of Straussians. Still, as a historic document this is an important issue. The whole disc, carefully remastered, is a treasure.

Songs

Don Juan. Macbeth. Lieder^a – Morgen, Op 27 No 4; Der Rosenband, Op 36 No 1; Meinem Kinde, Op 37 No 3; Befreit, Op 39 No 4; Wiegenlied, Op 41 No 1; Waldseligkeit, Op 49 No 1; Die heiligen drei Könige aus Morgenland, Op 56 No 6
^a**Anne Schwanewilms** *sop*
Hallé Orchestra / Mark Elder
Hallé CDHLL7508 (68' · DDD)   Ⓜ❶

Anne Schwanewilms, already well-known as an interpreter of Arabella and other Strauss heroines, challenges the likes of Della Casa, Schwarzkopf and Janowitz, and isn't put in the shade by the comparison. Her silvery tone soars easily into the grateful lines of these warm, glowing songs, and she has the gift to fine down her tone to ravishing *pianissimi*. She catches the rich-hued character of *Waldseligkeit*, the intimacy of *Wiegenlied* and *Meinem Kinde*, the sad serenity of *Morgen* and the inner intensity of *Befreit*, one of Strauss's most profound settings. Just once or twice her approach seems a shade self-regarding but, by and large, these are near-ideal readings, securely supported by Mark Elder and his orchestra.

This is the latest in the series of recordings emanating from the Hallé and does much to confirm their high place in this country's orchestral hierarchy today. There are many masterly accounts of *Don Juan* in the catalogue but this one, nicely timed and richly played, is up among the best. By comparison *Macbeth*, Strauss's first tone-poem and written a year earlier, seems rather an empty piece, successful neither as an evocation of the play nor as a piece in its own right. Elder and the Hallé make as good a case as they can for it and – as a whole – the programme works well, the Lieder sandwiched between the two orchestral works.

'The Complete Songs – 1'
Acht Gedichte aus Letzte Blätter, Op 10 – No 1, Zueignung; No 4, Die Georgine; No 8, Allerseelen.

Sechs Lieder aus Lotusblätter, Op 19 – No 2, Breit über mein Haupt dein schwarzes Haar; No 4, Wie sollten wir geheim sie halten. Sechs Lieder, Op 37 – No 1, Glückes genug; No 2, Ich liebe dich; No 6, Hochzeitlich Lied. Fünf Lieder, Op 39 – No 1, Leises Lied; No 4, Befreit. Fünf Lieder, Op 41 – No 1, Wiegenlied; No 2, In der Campagna. Sechs Lieder, Op 56 – No 5, Frühlingsfeier; No 6, Die heiligen drei Könige aus Morgenland. Gesänge des Orients, Op 77

Christine Brewer sop **Roger Vignoles** pf
Hyperion CDA67488 (61' · DDD · T/t) Ⓕ ❶❷❸➛

This is the first volume in Hyperion's Richard Strauss edition, something to be devoutly hoped for: he was a great Lieder composer but only a small fraction of his 200-plus songs are at all well known. Admittedly, his taste in poetry wasn't always as elevated as that of his fellow composers, yet his music can transform rather ordinary verses. And the major poets do get a look-in. This disc includes two Heine settings, one of which, 'Frühlingsfeier', came a year after *Salome* and echoes the operatic score. This is where Christine Brewer, whose repertory includes the title-roles in *Ariadne auf Naxos* and *Die ägyptische Helena*, might be expected to be most comfortable: her big, gleaming soprano sweeps through impressively. If at first her voice seems less than ideally flexible as a Lieder instrument, especially in the earlier songs, it would be ungrateful not to marvel at what she does ultimately bring to these performances.

Opening with 'Zueignung', which Strauss never intended to be relegated to encore status, Brewer sounds glorious if a little staid. But she quickly lightens up, catching the palpitations of 'Wie sollten wir geheim sie halten' and the gem-like intimacy of 'Leises Lied'. She positively blazes in the sunlight-evoking 'In der Campagna', where Vignoles's piano captures the splash of a Straussian orchestra. Both artists bring something fresh to the chestnuts 'Allerseelen' and 'Wiegenlied', in which Brewer floats a beautiful line over the rippling accompaniment. Having the high tessitura demanded in the rarely heard *Gesänge des Orients*, she clinches any remaining argument magnificently.

'The Complete Songs – 2'
Acht Lieder aus Letzte Blätter, Op 10 – No 3, Die Nacht; No 5, Geduld. Mein Herz ist stumm, Op 19 No 6. Schlichte Weisen, Op 21 – No 1, All' mein Gedanken, mein Herz und mein Sinn; No 2, Du meines Herzens Krönelein; No 3, Ach Lieb, ich muss nun scheiden. O wärst du mein, Op 26 No 2. Ruhe, meine Seele, Op 27 No 1. Drei Lieder, Op 29. Vier Lieder, Op 31 – No 1, Blauer Sommer; No 3, Weisser Jasmin. Das Rosenband, Op 36 No 1. Acht Lieder, Op 49 – No 1, Waldseligkeit; No 2, In goldener Fülle; No 3, Wiegenliedchen; No 7, Wer Lieben will; No 8, Ach, was Kummer, Qual und Schmerzen. Drei Lieder der Ophelia, Op 67. Blindenklage, Op 56 No 2

Anne Schwanewilms sop **Roger Vignoles** pf
Hyperion CDA67588 (66' · DDD · T/t) Ⓕ❷➛

Not just for *Salome* did Strauss demand several voices in one: here he ranges from the ditzy skitterings of the *Ophelia* Songs via the full-on operatic scena that is the Schwarzkopf favourite 'Blindenklage' to the wandering tonalities of 'O wärst du mein!', not to mention the tricky characterisation of 'Ach, was Kummer' (with its repeated 'hm, hm') and the naive playfulness of 'Schlagende Herzen'.

It's hard to dispute Roger Vignoles's claim that Anne Schwanewilms is 'a great singing actress'. That's clear in every song, where both the overall *tinta* and the text have not just been scrupulously attended to in the head but are excitingly delivered with the heart. The occasional price to pay is in pitching (coming onto a note from above) and in vocal agility – this is a large voice and it can move through its gears quite slowly – but it's of little significance given the repertoire, the live nature of the takes for which Hyperion opted, and the sheer intensity of the singing.

Schwanewilms achieves the full compass of the testing items noted, finds an appropriately rich skein of tone for 'In goldener Fulle' and manages real affection – and a degree of playfulness – in 'Wiegenliedchen'. There's a real experience here, knowingly and profoundly communicated. Vignoles is, as always, an equal and fully 'worked-in' team member. As well as being an impressive achievement in itself, this recital is a timely addition to a catalogue currently rather short of female competition in these songs.

'The Complete Songs – 3'
Acht Lieder aus Letzte Blätter, Op 10 – No 2, Nichts; No 6, Die Verschwiegenen; No 7, Die Zeitlose. Sechs Lieder, Op 17. Sechs Lieder aus Lotusblättern, Op 19 – No 1, Wozu noch, Mädchen, soll es Frommen; No 3, Schönsind, doch kalt die Himmelssterne; No 5, Hoffen und wieder verzagen. Schlichte Weisen, Op 21 – No 4, Ach weh, mir unglückhaften Mann; No 5, Die Frauen sind oft fromm und still. Heimliche Aufforderung, Op 27 No 3. Fünf Lieder, Op 32. Vier Lieder, Op 36 – No 2, Für fünfzehn Pfennige; No 4, Anbetung. Fünf Lieder, Op 48 – No 1, Freundliche Vision; No 4, Winterweihe; No 5, Winterliebe

Andrew Kennedy ten **Roger Vignoles** pf
Hyperion CDA67602 (63' · DDD · T/t) Ⓕ➛

Hyperion is an old hand at programming attractively playable discs that make up complete Lied editions. Kennedy's selection has the earlier material, with the Opp 17 and 32 groups given complete. Strauss's choice of poets at this stage in his Lied career may not have been as sophisticated as it became but he never chose a text that didn't inspire a clear musical portrait. Especially well pointed are two *Des Knaben Wunderhorn* songs ('Himmelsboten' and the droll love-on-the-cheap story of 'Für fünfzehn Pfennige') and the dark, serious 'Sehnsucht'. The better-known 'Ständchen' and what Roger Vignoles's notes call the 'ebullient barnstormer' 'Heimliche Aufforderung' are placed cunningly within the recital order.

Vignoles's playing continues to achieve a maximum of freshness and invention and a chameleon-like closeness to his singer's tone and line. Kennedy's voice is young, sweet, fluent and has what some commentators call 'sap'. Greater naturalness (and especially inwardness) will come in his live and later performances of this repertoire. In the meantime, a lot of work and study has gone into this disc and the readings attain a consistently high standard of beautiful music-making.

'The Complete Songs – 4'
Fünf Lieder, Op 15ᵃ. Stiller Gang, Op 31 No 4ᵃ.
Fünf Lieder, Op 39ᵃ – No 3, Der Arbeitsmann;
No 5, Lied an meinen Sohn. Fünf Lieder, Op 41ᵃ –
No 3, Am Ufer; No 5, Leise Lieder. Des Dichters
Abendgang, Op 47 No 2ᵃ. Das Lied des
Steinklopfers, Op 49 No 4ᵃ. Sechs Lieder, Op 56 –
No 1, Gefundena; No 3, Im Spätbootᵇ; No 4, Mit
deinen blauen Augenᵃ. Vom künftigen Alter, AV115
Op 87 No 1ᵇ. Erschaffen und Beleben, Op 87 No 2ᵇ.
Und dann nicht mehr, AV114 Op 87 No 3ᵇ.
Im Sonnenschein, AV121 Op 87 No 4ᵇ
ᵃ**Christopher Maltman** bar ᵇ**Alastair Miles** bass
Roger Vignoles pf
Hyperion CDA67667 (59' · DDD · T/t)   Ⓕ**O**▶

With one possible exception, these are all among Strauss's more rarely performed songs, and quite undeservedly so. Most are highly characteristic and clearly written with affection, while those that may not immediately proclaim the composer's identity ('Das Lied des Steinklopfers' for instance) are among the most interesting. Perhaps that sense of a structured improvisation may (as in the Rückert setting 'Und dann nicht mehr') call for a restraining hand, but more often it is such an appealing personal quality that complaint would be sourly puritanical. Indeed some of the joy arises in just those moments, such as the inspired passage between verses in 'Des Dichters Abendgang', when Strauss the pianist takes over and claims his composer's freedom.

Roger Vignoles captures well the expansiveness and generosity of the writing for piano. He is also a sensitive accompanist in songs where the piano part is relatively simple. "Heimkehr", the last song of Op 15, is one of these, and this is also the exception to the songs' general unfamiliarity. It is well sung, with finely controlled high *pianissimi*, by Christopher Maltman, who has all but the last five songs (mostly Op 81), which are written specifically for bass. It must be said that with the first sound of Alastair Miles, one is immediately aware of a change, not merely in the quality and nature of the voice, but in its production too. Maltman is a valuable artist in many respects, but recording exposes an unevenness of emission which his art is usually able to render inconspicuous 'in the flesh'. Miles impresses deeply, down indeed to the depths of his low D flat.

Opera Arias

Der Rosenkavalierᵃ – Da geht er hin; Ach, du bist wieder da!; Die Zeit, die ist ein sonderbar Ding; Ich hab ihn nicht einmal geküsst; Marie Theres!...Hab' mir's gelobt; Ist ein Traum. Arabellaᵇ – Ich danke, Fräulein. Capriccioᶜ – Interlude; Wo ist mein Bruder?
Renée Fleming sop with ᵃᵇ**Barbara Bonney** sop
ᵃ**Susan Graham** mez ᵃ**Johannes Chum** ten ᵃᶜ**Walter Berry** bass-bar **Vienna Philharmonic Orchestra / Christoph Eschenbach**
Decca 466 314-2DH (78' · DDD · T/t)   Ⓕ**OO**▶

This is a happily chosen Strauss showcase for Fleming. Her creamy, full-toned, vibrant voice is about the ideal instrument not only for the Marschallin but also for the other parts she attempts here. She has mastered the phraseology and verbal inflexions needed for all three roles, and imparts to them a quick intelligence to second the vocal glories. Sometimes her performance as the Marschallin or Countess Madeleine recalls, almost uncannily, those of Schwarzkopf, leaving one in no doubt that she has studied the readings of her distinguished predecessor. If Schwarzkopf with a slightly slimmer tone has the finer line and quicker responses, her successor provides the richer tone. Fleming need fear no comparisons with more recent interpreters such as Te Kanawa, Tomowa-Sintow and, as Madeleine only, Janowitz. Indeed, Fleming's account of the closing scene of *Capriccio* is just about ideal. Her deluxe team of co-stars includes Susan Graham, who makes an ardent suitor in *Rosenkavalier*'s Act 1 duets; her timbre is so similar to Fleming's that it's hard to tell them apart, though she isn't so verbally acute as her partner. And Barbara Bonney finally commits an extract of her enchanting Sophie, the best since Lucia Popp's; she also joins Fleming in the Arabella-Zdenka duet. Even the cameo appearances of a lackey at the close of Act 1 of *Der Rosenkavalier*, of Faninal after the Act 3 trio, and the major-domo in the closing scene from *Capriccio*, are filled by the veteran Walter Berry. Under Eschenbach, the VPO plays immaculately – the horn solo in the Moonlight music is pure magic – and the sound quality is outstandingly life-like. A treat for Straussians.

Salome – Ach! du wolltest mich nicht deinen Mund küssen lassen. Ariadne auf Naxos – Overture; Ein Schönes war; Es gibt ein Reich. Die Liebe der Danae – Wie umgibst du mich mit Frieden; Interlude, Act 3. Capriccio – Interlude; Wo ist mein Bruder?; Kein andres, das mir so im Herzen loht▪
Julia Varady sop **Bamberg Symphony Orchestra / Dietrich Fischer-Dieskau** ᵃbar
Orfeo C511 991A (62' · DDD)   Ⓕ**O**

After giving choice recitals of Verdi and Wagner, Varady turned her attention to Strauss, and once again the results are for the most part rewarding. The final scene of *Salome*, under the watchful eye of Varady's husband, Fischer-Dieskau, has the perfection of pitch and phrase one expects of this singer, as well as an expected acuity for the meaning of the text. Perhaps, away from the theatre in a part she never undertook on stage, the absolute conviction of such great interpreters as Cebotari, Welitsch and Rysanek is absent, but not by much. The two almost consecutive solos of *Ariadne* benefit from shapely, poised singing, ever obedient to the score, although occasionally one misses the creamier tones that Lisa della Casa (DG) and Gundula Janowitz (DG video, and EMI) brought to the part. As Danae, Varady seems a shade tentative and vocally out of sorts. There need be no reservations about the final scene of *Capriccio*, in which she catches ideally Countess Madeleine's emotional perplexity as she tries (unsuccessfully) to choose between her poet and musician admirers. Both her identification with the role and her execution of Strauss's operatic farewell to his beloved soprano voice are near-ideal. Fischer-Dieskau, endearingly, sings the short part of the Haushofmeister. However, his conducting, although sensibly paced, sometimes errs on the side of caution. As a whole, this CD nicely complements Fleming's Strauss concert on Decca, the two discs offering a compendium of the composer's writing for the soprano voice he loved so much.

Arabella

Arabella
Julia Varady *sop* Arabella **Helen Donath** *sop* Zdenka
Dietrich Fischer-Dieskau *bar* Mandryka **Walter
Berry** *bass* Waldner **Helga Schmidt** *mez* Adelaide
Elfriede Höbarth *sop* Fiakermilli **Adolf Dallapozza**
ten Matteo **Hermann Winkler** *ten* Elemer **Klaus-
Jürgen Küper** *bar* Dominik **Hermann Becht** *bar*
Lamoral **Doris Soffel** *mez* Fortune Teller **Arno
Lemberg** *spkr* Welko **Bavarian State Opera Chorus;
Bavarian State Orchestra / Wolfgang Sawallisch**
Orfeo ② C169 882H (144' · DDD · T/t) R Ⓟ⒐

Complete except for a brief cut in Matteo's part in Act 3, Sawallisch's 1981 Orfeo recording of *Arabella* has been easily fitted onto two CDs. Sawallisch is the most experienced conductor of Strauss's operas alive today and at his best in this one, his tempi exactly right, his appreciation of its flavour (sometimes sentimental, at others gently ironic and detached) unequalled. Helen Donath's delightful Zdenka is a perfect foil for Varady's Arabella. Varady's singing of the title-role is characterful and intelligent. One should be left with ambivalent feelings about this heroine; is she lovable or a chilling opportunist? Or both? And while Fischer-Dieskau's singing of Mandryka has not the total security of his earlier DG recording of the role with Keilberth, he remains the best Mandryka heard since the war.

Arabella Ⓗ
Lisa Della Casa *sop* Arabella **Elfride Trötschel** *sop*
Zdenka **Hermann Uhde** *bar* Mandryka **Max Proebstl**
bass Count Waldner **Ira Malaniuk** *mez* Adelaide
Lorenz Fehenberger *ten* Matteo **Franz Klarwein** *ten*

Count Elemer **Karl Hoppe** *bar* Count Dominik
Albrecht Peter *bass* Count Lamoral **Käthe Nentwig**
sop Fiakermilli **Chorus and Orchestra of the
Bavarian State Opera / Rudolf Kempe**
Testament mono ② SBT2 1367 (147' · ADD)
Broadcast by the BBC from the Royal Opera House,
Covent Garden, London, 1953 ⓂⓄⓄ

You'd be hard pressed to find a more elating and satisfying interpretation of this work than this live recording, which derives from a BBC Third Programme broadcast, privately taped. Kempe more or less made his name in London with the visit of the Munich company to the Royal Opera House; it alerted everyone to his great merits as a conductor and particularly as an interpreter of Richard Strauss.

Della Casa, in one of the earliest of her many assumptions of the title-part, is in ravishing voice and wholly spontaneous in her immaculately phrased and sung performance. She catches every aspect of the heroine's character, at once firm, warm and positive, and she treats the text with loving care. Here, as throughout, Uhde proves himself the most convincing Mandryka on disc. Not only is he the only baritone who seems quite unfazed by the role's high-lying tessitura but he sings it with an exemplary line and tonal breadth. As far as characterisation is concerned he is to the life the wilful country landowner, unused to city ways, and he makes us believe successively in the man's sincerity, jealousy and profound love, while never overdoing the histrionics.

At that time, there was a strong, experienced ensemble in Munich from which Max Proebstl's endearingly Viennese Waldner, Ira Malaniuk's fussy Adelaide and Lorenz Fehenberger's impassioned Matteo stand out.

Mike Ashman puts the performance in its historical perspective in his booklet-note, but you have to go to the web to get a libretto. The remastering of the sound by Paul Baily allows us to hear this historic performance in more-than-tolerable sound. At two for the price of one, this is an issue worth any Straussian's attention.

Additional recommendation

Arabella Ⓗ
Coupled with Four Last Songs[b]
[b]**Della Casa** Arabella **Rothenberger** Zdenka **Fischer-
Dieskau** Mandryka **Edelmann** Count Waldner
Vienna State Opera Chor; VPO / Keilberth, [b]**Böhm**
Orfeo d'Or mono ③ C651 053D (178' · ADD · S/N)
Recorded live July 1958 ⓂⓄⓄ

> This is a broadcast of the auspicious first night of the 1958 Salzburg production and it appears here for the first time on disc. The part of Arabella might have been written for Della Casa. Excellent as some of her successors may have been, she remains supreme. In 1958 she was at her vocal and interpretative peak. Fischer-Dieskau on stage was the rough-hewn, impulsive Mandryka to the life. His performance has enormous presence and vitality but he is rather inclined to go into his hectoring

mode. The Adelaide and Waldner are both admirable in depicting the Viennese bourgeoisie. A clinching factor may be the inclusion of the *Four Last Songs*, recorded at Salzburg the night after the *Arabella*. Here Della Casa, Böhm and the VPO renew their famous alliance in this work.

Ariadne auf Naxos

Ariadne auf Naxos   **H**
Elisabeth Schwarzkopf *sop* Ariadne **Irmgard Seefried** *sop* Composer **Rita Streich** *sop* Zerbinetta **Rudolf Schock** *ten* Bacchus **Karl Dönch** *bar* Music-Master **Hermann Prey** *bar* Harlequin **Fritz Ollendorff** *bass* Truffaldino **Helmut Krebs** *ten* Brighella **Gerhard Unger** *ten* Scaramuccio **Lisa Otto** *sop* Naiad **Grace Hoffman** *mez* Dryad **Anny Felbermayer** *sop* Echo **Hugues Cuénod** *ten* Dancing Master **Alfred Neugebauer** *spkr* Major-Domo **Philharmonia Orchestra / Herbert von Karajan**
EMI Great Recordings of the Century mono ②
567077-2 (128' · ADD). Recorded 1954   Ⓜ**OOO**B⃗

Karajan's *Ariadne* is perfectly cast, magnificently performed, and very well recorded. The scoring, for a small orchestra, demands virtuoso playing from what, in effect, is a group of soloists; the members of the Philharmonia Orchestra rise brilliantly to the occasion. There's a warmth and beauty of tone, a sweep of phrase, that gives lively promise of the wonderful playing we hear throughout the opera. Karajan's genius has never been more apparent than in his treatment of the Bacchus-Ariadne scene, where he makes the score glow with a Dionysiac ardour and in which, at the tremendous climax when Bacchus enters and is greeted by Ariadne as the herald of Death, he gets an ample volume of tone from his players.

Every character is vividly brought to life – Karl Dönch's harassed Music-Master is offset by the cynical Dancing Master of Hugues Cuénod, and Alfred Neugebauer, in his speaking role, conveys with a superbly calm pomposity his contempt for both sets of artists. The way he enunciates his words is superb. The other small parts, all sung by experienced artists, are wholly in the picture. Rita Streich sings the lyrical phrases of Zerbinetta beautifully. Technical difficulties do not appear to exist for her and all she does is musical. Irmgard Seefried, as the Composer, has less beauty of tone but more variety. The ineffably lovely trio for the Naiad, Dryad and Echo is exquisitely sung by Lisa Otto, Grace Hoffman and Anny Felbermayer, paralleled by the equally beautiful singing of the other trios. They are simply ravishing and, like all the concerted music, have a perfect ensemble. The *commedia dell'arte* characters are all very good, especially Hermann Prey: and their ensembles between themselves and with Zerbinetta are a great delight. After an awkward start, Elisabeth Schwarzkopf, as Ariadne, brings the dark tone that's needed, to Ariadne's sorrows, and gives us much lovely singing thereafter, and also all the rapture called for at the end of her great address to the herald of Death and in her greeting to Bacchus. Rudolf Schock sings the latter with

heroic tone and sufficient nuance to make one believe in the youthful god.

The general impression is of a truly magnificent performance and recording in which all concerned have, under Karajan's superb direction, been inspired to give of their best.

Ariadne auf Naxos
Emily Magee *sop* Ariadne **Michelle Breedt** *mez* Composer **Elena Mosuc** *sop* Zerbinetta **Roberto Saccà** *ten* Bacchus **Michael Volle** *bar* Music-Master **Sandra Trattnigg** *sop* Echo **Eva Liebau** *sop* Naiad **Irène Friedli** *contr* Dryad **Blagoj Nacoski** *ten* Brighella **Guy de Mey** *ten* Dancing Master **Martin Zysset** *ten* Scaramuccio **Randall Ball** *ten* Officer **Gabriel Bermúdez** *bar* Harlequin **Andrew Ashwin** *bar* Wigmaker **Reinhard Mayr** *bass* Truffaldino **Alexander Pereira** *spkr* Major-Domo **Zürich Opera Chorus and Orchestra / Christoph von Dohnányi**
Stage director **Claus Guth**
Video director **Thomas Grimm**
TDK Ⓕ 📀 DVWW-OPAAN (127' · NTSC · 16:9 · LPCM stereo, 5.1 and DTS 5.1 · 0)
Recorded live at the Opernhaus, Zürich, in December 2006   **O**B⃗

If many productions of this fascinating, but awkward, Strauss/Hofmannsthal hybrid have erred towards the story's comic side – the interruptions of Zerbinetta and her Harlequin troupe – Claus Guth's brave Zürich staging centres markedly on the fate of Ariadne herself. The 'backstage' Prologue plays scenery-less in front of tall curtains which work, of course, as dressing-room doors but also focus on the Composer's frustration at having his opera mounted in such chaos. All the character's despair is played for real here and, despite an obvious attraction to Zerbinetta, the Composer shoots himself, reappearing as a ghost in the opera proper to dance with Zerbinetta or approve Ariadne's dilemma.

The opera proper plays in a smart restaurant where Ariadne, *Brief Encounter*-like with a touch of Joan Crawford, mourns her loss of Theseus. The Harlequins and Nymphs are other diners and waitresses. Ariadne's despair, then her frustrated hope that Bacchus is Theseus, leads her to suicide by overdose. She spends the duet with Bacchus dying. It's amazing how well this concept fits the text sung by the opera's serious pair.

Emily Magee has recently been seen on DVD as Elsa and Ellen Orford, superb in two widely differing operas. This performance (her debut in the role) tops both of those, beginning with the prelude to the opera where her sitting, grieving, at table is the entire action. She can also sing the part gloriously. Roberto Saccà manages this tricky target for his affections well – he becomes a sympathetic assistant to a patient's demise – and has the vocal demands well in control. Michele Breedt is the ultra-intense suicidal Composer, Michael Volle her enigmatic, blind Music-Master. Dohnányi, as always (one may truly say), is a master of Straussian balance and climax. The (very) close-up filming seems to tell

Guth's story to perfection. Magee's towering performance must be seen and heard.

Capriccio

Capriccio
Elisabeth Schwarzkopf sop The Countess **Eberhard Waechter** bar The Count **Nicolai Gedda** ten
Flamand **Dietrich Fischer-Dieskau** bar Olivier **Hans Hotter** bass-bar La Roche **Christa Ludwig** mez
Clairon **Ruldolf Christ** ten Monsieur Taupe **Anna Moffo** sop Italian Soprano **Dermot Troy** ten Italian
Tenor **Karl Schmitt-Walter** bar Major-domo
Philharmonia Orchestra / Wolfgang Sawallisch
EMI Great Recordings of the Century mono
② 567394-2 (135' · ADD · T/t)
Recorded 1957   Ⓜ❍❍❍❍➔

Not only is *Capriccio* a source of constant and none-too-demanding delight but its performance and recording, especially in this CD reincarnation, are well-nigh faultless. Walter Legge assembled for the recording in 1957 what was almost his house cast, each singer virtually ideal for his or her part. Some might say that no role she recorded suited Schwarzkopf's particular talents more snugly than Countess Madeleine. Her ability to mould words and music into one can be heard here to absolute advantage. The charming, flirtatious, sophisticated, slightly artificial character, with the surface attraction hiding deeper feelings revealed in the closing scene (quite beautifully sung), suits her to the life. She, like her colleagues, is superbly adept at the quick repartee so important as an element in this work.

As her brother, the light-hearted, libidinous Count, the young Eberhard Waechter is in his element. So are the equally young Nicolai Gedda as the composer Flamand, the Sonnet so gently yet ardently delivered, and Fischer-Dieskau as the more fiery poet Olivier. Christa Ludwig is nicely intimate, conversational and cynical as the actress Clairon, handling her affairs, waning with Olivier, waxing with the Count, expertly. Above all towers the dominating presence of Hotter as the theatre director La Roche, impassioned in his defence of the theatre's conventions, dismissive of new and untried methods, yet himself not above a trivial flirtation – and how delicately Hotter manages his remarks about his latest protegee as she dances for the assembled company.

Even with so many distinguished singers gathered together, it's the closeness of the ensemble, the sense of a real as distinct from a manufactured performance that's so strongly conveyed. And Legge did not neglect the smaller roles: Rudolf Christ makes an endearingly eccentric Monsieur Taupe, the veteran Schmitt-Walter a concerned Major-domo. Anna Moffo and Dermot Troy sing the music of the Italian soprano and tenor with almost too much sensitivity.

Crowning the performance is the musical direction of Wolfgang Sawallisch, always keeping the score on the move, yet fully aware of its sensuous and its witty qualities: Krauss's amusing libretto has much to do with the work's fascination. Both the extended Prelude and the interludes are gloriously played by the vintage Philharmonia, who are throughout alert to the old wizard's deft scoring, as refined here as in any of his earlier operas. The recording might possibly have given a little more prominence to the instruments; in every other respect, although it's in mono, it hardly shows its age.

Elektra

Elektra
Birgit Nilsson sop Elektra **Regina Resnik** mez
Klytemnestra **Marie Collier** sop Chrysothemis
Gerhard Stolze ten Aegisthus **Tom Krause** bar
Orestes **Pauline Tinsley** sop Overseer **Helen Watts**
contr **Maureen Lehane, Yvonne Minton** mezs
Jane Cook, Felicia Weathers sops First, Second,
Third, Fourth and Fifth Maidservants **Tugomir
Franc** bass Tutor **Vienna Philharmonic Orchestra /
Sir Georg Solti**
Decca ② 475 8231DOR2 (108' · ADD)
Recorded 1966-67   Ⓑ❍❍❍➔

Elektra is the most consistently inspired of all Strauss's operas and derives from Greek mythology, with the ghost of Agamemnon, so unerringly delineated in the opening bars, hovering over the whole work. The invention and the intensity of mood are sustained throughout the opera's one-act length, and the characterisation is both subtle and pointed. It's a work peculiarly well suited to Solti's gifts and it's his best recording in the studios. He successfully maintains the nervous tension throughout the unbroken drama and conveys all the power and tension in Strauss's enormously complex score which is, for once, given complete. The recording captures the excellent singers and the Vienna Philharmonic in a warm, spacious acoustic marred only by some questionable electronic effects. Notwithstanding the latter, this is undoubtedly one of the greatest performances on record and sounds even more terrifyingly realistic on this magnificent transfer.

Elektra   Ⓗ
Inge Borkh sop Elektra **Jean Madeira** mez
Klytemnestra **Lisa della Casa** sop Chrysothemis **Max
Lorenz** ten Aegisthus **Kurt Böhme** bass Orestes
Alois Pernerstorfer bass-bar Tutor **Anny
Felbermayer** sop Confidante **Karol Loraine** mez
Trainbearer **Erich Majkut** ten Young Servant **György
Littasy** bass Old Servant **Audrey Gerber** sop
Overseer **Kerstin Meyer, Sonja Draksler, Sieglinde
Wagner, Marilyn Horne** sop First,
Second, Third, Fourth and Fifth Maidservants **Vienna
State Opera Chorus; Vienna Philharmonic
Orchestra / Dimitri Mitropoulos**
Orfeo mono ② C456 972I (107' · ADD)
Recorded live 1957   Ⓜ❍❍

This is an enthralling performance. Mitropoulos made a speciality of the score, his most important contribution to opera interpretation. Souvenirs exist of his performances at the Met in 1949 and at the Maggio Musicale in Florence in 1950, but his Salzburg reading is the one to have. No other conductor, not even Böhm or Solti in the studio, quite matches the *frisson* of this overwhelming account. And it confirms that Inge Borkh is indeed the most comprehensively equipped soprano for the title-role, vocally secure – high C apart – and emotionally capable of fulfilling every demand of the strenuous part. In the great scene with Orestes she first expresses ineffably the sorrow at his supposed death, the 'tausendmal' and 'nie wiederkommt' passage done with such a searing sense of loss; then comes the great release of recognition – sung with immense warmth – followed by another almost silvery voice as Elektra recalls her lost beauty. It's a passage of singing to return to repeatedly for its many insights. Chrysothemis finds in della Casa an unusual interpreter, wonderfully ecstatic and pure of voice if not as emotionally involving as some. Madeira is a formidable Klytemnestra, her nightmarish thoughts expressed in a firm voice, accurately deployed. Böhme, a real bass, presents an implacable, angry Orestes, not as subtle or as sympathetic as Krause for Solti. Lorenz's fading *Heldentenor* is ideal to express Aegisthus's fatuity. And the maids have never, surely, been cast with such secure voices.

Inevitably, cuts are made as is almost always the case in the theatre where, otherwise, Elektra might be left voiceless by the end. If you want the complete score, the famous Solti set will do very nicely. If you want Borkh, you must choose between the Böhm in stereo (DG) or this unique experience.

Elektra
Eva Marton *sop* Elektra **Brigitte Fassbaender** *mez* Klytemnestra **Cheryl Studer** *sop* Chrysothemis **Franz Grundheber** *bar* Orestes **James King** *ten* Aegisthus **Goran Simic** *bass* Tutor **Waltraud Winsauer** *mez* Confidante **Noriko Sasaki** *sop* Trainbearer **Wilfried Gahmlich** *ten* Young Servant **Claudio Otelli** *bass-bar* Old Servant **Gabriele Lechner** *sop* Overseer **Margarita Lilowa, Gabriele Sima, Margareta Hintermeier, Brigitte Poschner-Klebel, Joanna Borowska** Maidservants **Vienna State Opera Chorus and Orchestra / Claudio Abbado**
Stage director **Harry Kupfer**
Video director **Brian Large**
ArtHaus Musik 🔵 100 048 (109' · DDD)
Recorded live 1989   Ⓕ🔵🔵

This is an enjoyable performance, if that's the right word for *Elektra*'s gruesome drama, of Strauss's opera (taken from the first night of a new production at the Vienna State Opera in 1989), still one of the most sensational scores of the last century. Harry Kupfer may have conceived the work in even more lurid terms than its creators Hofmannsthal and Strauss intended, but the principals' psychotic behaviour is so convincingly enacted that we're carried into

the soul of all their personal tortures of the mind. Elektra herself is a determined, raddled, single-minded harridan, lording it over sister and mother, a portrayal Eva Marton carries out with a deal of conviction, once one accepts the judder in her voice. Chrysothemis becomes a writhing, overwrought, frustrated figure, at one stage seeming to fake an orgasm, all of which Studer conveys with much emphasis on physical contact with her sister. She sings the taxing role with opulent tone and soaring phraseology.

Physicality is also of the essence in Fassbaender's study of guilt and inner disintegration as a Klytemnestra of intriguing complexity, yet she still somehow manages to suggest the character's feminine attraction. This portrayal alone makes this DVD essential viewing. Grundheber is the avenging Orestes to the life, with savagely piercing eyes and implacable tone. King is a properly futile paramour. In the activity of the extras, and such episodes as the butchering of Aegisthus and Chrysothemis wallowing in his blood-stained cloak, very little is left to the imagination. This is an enclosed world where licence and human sacrifices, unbridled in their ferocity, have taken over from order and humanity, and that was surely Kupfer's intention, so that Orestes' arrival has even more of a cleansing effect than usual.

In the pit, Abbado conducts with a single-minded intensity, constantly aware of the score's brutal and tragic aspects, and he procures playing of tremendous concentration from the Vienna Philharmonic. Although the staging takes place in Stygian gloom, you can discern more of its detail in this reincarnation on DVD, which has the added advantage of containing the whole opera on a single disc.

This is a version to buy for its absorbing, fully integrated view of Strauss's masterpiece.

Additional recommendation

Elektra
Johansson Elektra **Lipovšek** Klytemnestra **Diener** Chrysothemis **Schasching** Aegisthus **Muff** Orestes **Zürich Opera House Chor & Orch / Dohnányi**
Stage director **Kušej** *Video director* **Breisach**
TDK Ⓕ 🔵 DVWW-OPELEK (102' · NTSC · 16:9 · PCM stereo, 5.1 and DTS 5.1 · 0)
Recorded live in 2005   Ⓕ🔵

Martin Kušej directs people well, and since *Elektra* is largely an opera of dialogues, his work demands attention. Eva Johansson's Elektra is a hooded tomboy with definite Asbo leanings; she has to be on full throttle for this role but both Dohnányi's orchestra and TDK's engineers are kind to her. Melanie Diener locates the hard, hard role of Chrysothemis somewhere between Victoria Beckham and Brechtian alienation: every entry, every new event is as surprising to her as a goldfish going round its bowl. Marjana Lipovšek presents their mother as a complex of confused identities, eschewing both in voice and acting any melodramatic harridan tendencies. As their brother, Alfred Muff presents a revenger of quiet, un-neurotic determination. Equally original is Rudolf Schasching's lecherous groper of an Aegisthus, convincingly deceived when Elektra plays up to his libido.

Die Frau ohne Schatten

Die Frau ohne Schatten
Julia Varady sop Empress **Plácido Domingo** ten
Emperor **Hildegard Behrens** sop Dyer's Wife **José
van Dam** bar Barak the Dyer **Reinhild Runkel** contr
Nurse **Albert Dohmen** bar Spirit-Messenger **Sumi Jo**
sop Voice of the Falcon **Robert Gambill** ten
Apparition of a Young Man **Elzbieta Ardam** mez
Voice from Above **Eva Lind** sop Guardian of the
Threshold **Gottfried Hornik** bar One-eyed Brother
Hans Franzen bass One-armed Brother **Wilfried
Gahmlich** ten Hunchback Brother **Vienna Boys'
Choir; Vienna State Opera Chorus; Vienna
Philharmonic Orchestra / Sir Georg Solti**
Decca ③ 436 243-2DHO3 (3h 15' · DDD · T/t)
Ⓕ❶❷❸❹▷

This was the most ambitious project on which Strauss and his librettist Hugo von Hofmannsthal collaborated. It's both fairy-tale and allegory with a score that's Wagnerian in its scale and breadth. This Solti version presents the score absolutely complete in an opulent recording that encompasses every detail of the work's multifaceted orchestration. Nothing escapes his keen eye and ear or that of the Decca engineers. The cast boasts splendid exponents of the two soprano roles. Behrens's vocal acting suggests complete identification with the unsatisfied plight of the Dyer's Wife and her singing has a depth of character to compensate for some tonal wear. Varady gives an intense, poignant account of the Empress's taxing music. The others, though never less than adequate, leave something to be desired. Domingo sings the Emperor with vigour and strength but evinces little sense of the music's idiom. José van Dam is likewise a vocally impeccable Barak but never penetrates the Dyer's soul. Runkel is a mean, malign Nurse as she should be, though she could be a little more interesting in this part. It benefits from glorious, dedicated playing by the VPO.

Guntram

Guntram
Alan Woodrow ten Guntram **Andrea Martin** bar The
Old Duke **Elisabeth Wachutka** sop Freihild **Ivan
Konsulov** bar Robert **Hans-Peter Scheidegger** bar
Freihold **Enrico Facini** ten The Duke's Fool **Thomas
Kaluzny** bar Messenger, Young Man, Minnesinger
Jin-Ho Choi bar Old Man, Minnesinger **Ute Trekel-
Burkhardt** mez Old Woman **Manfred Bittner** ten
Young Man, Minnesinger **Matthias Heubusch** voc
Minnesinger **Werdenfelser Male Chorus;
Marchigiana Philharmonic Orchestra /
Gustav Kuhn**

Arte Nova Classics ② 74321 61339-2 (100' · DDD · T)
Recorded live 1998   Ⓢ

However much influenced by Wagner this, Strauss's first opera, may have been, it already shows him moving off in his own melodic and harmonic direction. It contains much attractive, well-crafted music, but from the start it was lamed by the composer's own prolix libretto and hesitant dramaturgy. The story of the brave, libertarian knight Guntram's adventures in 13th-century Germany and his love for the heroine Freihild, daughter of the local ruler, whose husband Duke Robert is a sort of villain and opponent of peace, is really one about individual responsibility being more important than religious orthodoxy, something that offended Strauss's strict Catholic mentor, Alexander Ritter. This live performance under the experienced Straussian Gustav Kuhn gives a fair idea of its virtues and defects. His direction is vigorous, forward-moving, strongly limned with a proper advocacy of the score's more original features, with resplendent playing from his orchestra. The performance is well served by its two principals. In the title-role, the ENO tenor Alan Woodrow here makes a more-than-passable Heldentenor in the first of many roles for that voice calling for strong, virile, penetrative tone. Woodrow produces just that, plus much of the romantic fervour Guntram's role calls for. Elisabeth Wachutka is reasonably successful as the object of Guntram's desires. Though her tone can be edgy, she rises finely to the challenge of her extended monologue in Act 2. The rest, who don't have much to do, are so-so. The recording is clear and well balanced. At the price, this is worth sampling to hear Strauss's apprentice effort in the operatic field he was so soon to grace with many masterpieces.

Der Rosenkavalier

Der Rosenkavalier   Ⓗ
Elisabeth Schwarzkopf sop Die Feldmarschallin
Christa Ludwig mez Octavian **Otto Edelmann** bass
Baron Ochs **Teresa Stich-Randall** sop Sophie
Eberhard Waechter bar Faninal **Nicolai Gedda** ten
Italian Tenor **Kerstin Meyer** contr Annina **Paul Kuen**
ten Valzacchi **Ljuba Welitsch** sop Duenna **Anny
Felbermayer** sop Milliner **Harald Pröghlöf** bar
Notary **Franz Bierbach** bass Police Commissioner
Erich Majkut ten Feldmarschallin's Major-domo
Gerhard Unger ten Faninal's Major-domo, Animal
Seller **Karl Friedrich** ten Landlord **Loughton High
School for Girls and Bancroft's School Choirs;
Philharmonia Chorus and Orchestra /
Herbert von Karajan**
EMI ③ 3773572 (3h 11' · ADD · T/t)
Recorded 1956   Ⓑ❶❷❸❹▷

Der Rosenkavalier concerns the transferring of love of the young headstrong aristocrat Octavian from the older Marschallin (with whom he's having an affair) to the young Sophie, a girl of *nouveau riche* origins who's of his generation. The portrayal of the different levels of passion is masterly and the Marschallin's resigned surrender of her young lover gives opera one of its most cherishable scenes. The comic side of the plot concerns the vulgar machinations of the rustic Baron Ochs and his attempts to seduce the disguised Octavian (girl playing boy playing girl!). The musical richness of the score is almost indescribable, with streams of endless melody, and the final trio which brings the three soprano roles together is the crowning glory of a masterpiece of the 20th century.

This magnificent recording, conducted with genius by Karajan, and with a dream cast, is unlikely to be challenged for many a year. The Philharmonia play like angels, and Schwarzkopf as the Marschallin gives one of her greatest performances. The recording, lovingly remastered, is outstanding.

Der Rosenkavalier
Claire Watson *sop* Die Feldmarschallin **Brigitte Fassbaender** *sop* Octavian **Lucia Popp** *sop* Sophie **Karl Ridderbusch** *bass* Baron Ochs **Benno Kusche** *bar* Faninal **Annelie Waas** *sop* Marianne **David Thaw** *ten* Valzacchi **Margarethe Bence** *mez* Annina **Albrecht Peter** *bass* Police Commissioner **Gerhard Unger** *ten* Italian Tenor **Bavarian State Opera Chorus and Orchestra / Carlos Kleiber**
Orfeo d'Or ③ ♫ C581 083D (178' · ADD)
Recorded live at the Nationaltheater, Bavarian State Opera, Munich, on July 13, 1973 Ⓕ**OO**

It's taken over 35 years but at last we have a professional audio transfer of Kleiber leading the opera that probably meant more to him than all others. If you're not yet a convert, or a doubter, cut to the chase: go from track 18 of disc 3 (the great Trio) and you'll hear why the Munich Festival audience cannot wait to start clapping some of the most attentively sculpted Strauss conducting, traditional romance mixed with savouring of those still ear-bending harmonies, since, well, Clemens Krauss and a certain Erich Kleiber.

So what is especially magical? The energy, the attention to the stage drama in the music (not least its wit), the pacing – 'fast' compared with Karajan but with a wonderful *rubato* that allows for real pointing and emotion but owes more to Kleiber's natural instincts (and his father's) than Viennese so-called tradition – and the slim textures. Under Kleiber the opera sounds like what its creators sought to do – follow *Elektra* in a different vein, not retreat from it, either musically or dramatically.

In retrospect we might call this Kleiber's first favoured *Rosenkavalier* cast which, like the second (Lott, van Otter, Bonney – DG), was led by its ladies. Long-term Munich resident Claire Watson has done little finer on disc and is well 'aged' in relationship to Fassbaender's *tour de force* Octavian (she makes a good youth throughout and a laugh-aloud Mariandel) and Popp's sweet but never vacant Sophie. But did Kleiber ever find an Ochs to match his girls? As with Ridderbusch here, he tended to trim their traditional excesses but never quite put enough in its place. The so-called 'supporting' roles are energetically taken by an evidently fired-up house ensemble.

Der Rosenkavalier
Gwyneth Jones *sop* Die Feldmarschallin **Brigitte Fassbaender** *sop* Octavian **Manfred Jungwirth** *bass* Baron Ochs **Lucia Popp** *sop* Sophie **Benno Kusche** *bar* Faninal **Francisco Araiza** *ten* Italian Tenor **Gudrun Wewezow** *contr* Annina **David Thaw** *ten* Valzacchi **Anneliese Waas** *sop* Duenna **Susanne Sonnenschein** *sop* Milliner **Hans Wilbrink** *bass* Notary **Albrecht Peter** *bass* Police Commissioner **Georg Paskuda** *ten* Major-domo **Friedrich Lenz** *ten* Faninal's Major-domo **Norbert Orth** *ten* Landlord **Osamu Kobayashi** *ten* Animal Seller **Bavarian State Opera Chorus; Bavarian State Orchestra / Carlos Kleiber**
Stage and video director **Otto Schenk**
DG ② 🎬 073 4072GH2 (3h 6' · NTSC · 4:3 · PCM stereo and DTS 5.1 · 0) Ⓕ**OOO**

More than three decades on, this unforgettable performance has lost nothing of its power to delight eye and ear, and is in almost every way superior to Carlos Kleiber's 1994 remake in Vienna. Schenk's direction is finely judged, strong in detail, in Jürgen Rose's handsome, traditional sets. Eschewing fashionable modernities, its has stood the test of time.

Kleiber's reading has that essential mix of warmth and élan the score demands, and a lightness of touch allied to controlled but never effusive sentiment. The Bavarian State Opera Orchestra plays with the brio and confidence gained from long experience of Kleiber's impulsive ways. The shots of the conductor in the pit during the preludes to Acts 1 and 3 show how incisive his beat can be and how much he actually enjoyed conducting the piece.

The instinctive interaction of the principal singers is another indication of the rapport achieved in this wonderful staging. The intimacy of the Act 2 dialogues between the Marschallin and Octavian and between Sophie and Octavian, and the interplay among the three in the closing scene of Act 3, is rewarding and deeply moving. In the name part, Fassbaender acts the ardent, impetuous youth to the life, sensual with the Marschallin in Act 1, lovestruck with Sophie in Act 2 and wittily amusing in the Mariandel disguise, the eyes conveying all the character's changes of mood. Nothing is exaggerated, everything rings true in an ideal assumption.

Popp conveys all the shy charm called for in the Silver Rose scene, indignation at Ochs's boorish behaviour, and in Act 3 confusion as her emotions are torn apart; she sings with the right blend of purity and sensuousness. Dame Gwyneth, in one of her best roles, looks appealing and girlish in Act 1, and then becomes all dignified authority and resignation in Act 3. She is right inside the role, and suggests all the heartbreak at the end, adapting her large voice throughout to the work's conversational style. Jungwirth is a ripely experienced, *echt* Viennese Ochs, for the most part avoiding excessive boorishness. Kusche is a tetchy old Faninal, Araiza a mellifluous Italian Tenor. The smaller parts are taken by long-serving members of the Munich company.

The picture comes up fresh on DVD and the sound is mostly first-rate, as is the video direction. This is a must-buy.

Additional recommendation

Der Rosenkavalier
Crespin Marschallin **Minton** Octavian **Jungwirth** Ochs **Donath** Sophie **VPO / Solti**
Decca 475 9988DOR3 (3h 20' · DDD)　　Ⓜ❻❻❾➔

For those craving good sound and a reading of great charm – Crespin's rather Gallic Marschallin is wondrously sung – Solti's 1968 set is worth considering. Many collectors rate this even more highly than the classic Karajan.

Der Rosenkavalier
Stemme Marschallin **Kasarova** sop Octavian **Muff** Zürich Opera House Chor & Orch / Welser-Möst
Stage director **Bechtolf** Video director **Duplat**
EMI 📀 544258-9 (3h 25' · NTSC · 16:9 · PCM stereo, 5.1 and DTS 5.1 · 0). Recorded live at the Opernhaus, Zürich, in July 2004　　Ⓕ

This version creates a dilemma. So much that the director does as regards the interplay between the characters is original and interesting, which makes one deeply regret that the settings and much of the detail are so irritating. That is all the more trying given the fact that Bechtolf enlivens the relations between the principals with perceptive insight, helped by an intelligent cast. Vesselina Kasarova's highly impulsive, youthfully impetuous Octavian is a wholly credible lover in Act 1, then falls in love with Sophie in a truly precipitate, love-at-first-sight manner. Nina Stemme's Marschallin seems almost to be feeling what is to follow from the first. Malin Hartelius's Sophie is all eager anxiety, as she prepares to meet her bridegroom, making her shocked recognition of his true nature that much more arresting. Alfred Muff's Baron Ochs is much more traditional in his responses but always a believable character, the role reasonably sung. Welser-Möst's reading is fleet and buoyant, avoiding sentimentality, more lithe and accurate than warm in a Viennese manner. The traditional cuts are observed.

Salome

Salome
Birgit Nilsson sop Salome **Eberhard Waechter** bar Jokanaan **Gerhard Stolze** ten Herod **Grace Hoffman** mez Herodias **Waldemar Kmentt** ten Narraboth **Josephine Veasey** mez Page **Tom Krause** bar First Nazarene **Nigel Douglas** ten Second Nazarene **Zenon Koznowski** bass First Soldier **Heinz Holecek**

RICHARD STRAUSS'S DER ROSENKAVALIER – IN BRIEF

Elisabeth Schwarzkopf Marschallin　　　　Ⓗ
Christa Ludwig Octavian **Otto Edelmann** Baron Ochs **Philharmonia Chorus and Orchestra / Herbert von Karajan**
EMI ③ 567605-2 (3h 2' · ADD)　　Ⓜ❻❻❻❾➔

Taped as long ago as 1956, Karajan tends to linger over the work's purple passages, but, for most commentators, this is *the* classic, thanks not least to the casting of Schwarzkopf, Ludwig and Stich-Randall. Polished yet passionate and often intensely beautiful.

Maria Reining Marschallin **Sena Jurinac**　　Ⓗ
Octavian **Ludwig Weber** Baron Ochs **Vienna State Opera Chorus; Vienna PO / Erich Kleiber**
Decca ③ 478 1396DC3 (3h 17' · ADD)　　Ⓜ❻❻

Recorded in 1954 in mono only, Kleiber's *echt* Viennese set is still top-rated by connoisseurs who welcome its opening out of the small stage cuts sanctioned by the composer and followed by Karajan.

Yvonne Kenny Marschallin **Diana Montague** Octavian **John Tomlinson** Baron Ochs **London PO / David Parry**
Chandos CHAN3022 (80' · DDD)　　Ⓜ❻➔

A delightful highlights disc with several principals familiar from English-language ENO productions, who are at least as distinguished as their counterparts on the more recent original-language recordings.

Kiri Te Kanawa Marschallin **Anne Sofie von Otter** Octavian **Kurt Rydl** Baron Ochs **Dresden State Opera Chorus; Staatskapelle Dresden / Bernard Haitink**
EMI ③ 754259-2 (3h 43' · DDD)　　Ⓕ➔

Warmly played and sung, Haitink's Dresden recording is the finest audio-only account of the digital era. Te Kanawa's Marschallin is the most beautiful of recent years.

Régine Crespin Marschallin **Yvonne Minton** Octavian **Manfred Jungwirth** Baron Ochs **Vienna State Opera Chorus; Vienna PO / Sir Georg Solti**
Decca ③ 475 9988DOR3 (3h 20' · ADD)　　Ⓜ❻➔

Solti's 1968 set has high production values and an all-star casting of minor roles. He avoids the over-affectionate approach, but takes the climactic moments very broadly.

Claire Watson Marschallin **Brigitte Fassbaender** Octavian **Lucia Popp** Sophie **Bavarian State Opera Chorus and Orchestra / Carlos Kleiber**
Orfeo d'Or ③ 🔊 C581 083D (178' · ADD)　　Ⓕ❻❻

The only available audio *Rosenkavalier* from Carlos Kleiber to put alongside his two magnificent videos. This is top-class Strauss singing and conducting!

bass Second Soldier **Theodore Kirschbichler** *bass*
Cappadocian **Vienna Philharmonic Orchestra /
Sir Georg Solti**
Decca The Originals ② 475 7528DOR2 (99' · ADD · T/t)
Recorded 1961   Ⓜ❍❍❍➼

Solti's *Salome* was one of Decca's notable Sonic Stage successes and still beats
most of its competitors in terms of
sound alone. There's a real sense here of a theatrical performance, as produced by John Culshaw,
with an imaginative use of movement. The
vivid, nervous energy of Strauss has always been
Solti's territory, and this is an overwhelming
account of Strauss's sensual piece, sometimes a
little too hard-hitting: there are places where the
tension might be relaxed just a shade, but
throughout, the VPO answers Solti's extreme
demands with its most aristocratic playing. With
only a single break, the sense of mounting fever
is felt all the more. Birgit Nilsson's account of
the title-role is another towering monument to
her tireless singing. Here, more even than as
Brünnhilde, one notices just how she could fine
away her tone to a sweet and fully supported
pianissimo, and her whole interpretation wants
nothing of the erotic suggestiveness of sopranos
more familiar with the role on stage. Gerhard
Stolze's Herod is properly wheedling, worried
and, in the final resort, crazed, but there are
times, particularly towards the end of his contribution, when exaggeration takes over from
characterisation. Other interpretations show
how effects can be created without distortion of
the vocal line. Eberhard Waechter is an aggressive rather than a visionary Jokanaan. Grace
Hoffman is a suitably gloating Herodias. Much
better than any of these, Nilsson apart, is Waldemar Kmentt's wonderfully ardent Narraboth.
Hardly any of the rivals since 1961 has managed
a true challenge to this simply outstanding
recording.

Salome
Cheryl Studer *sop* Salome **Bryn Terfel** *bar* Jokanaan
Horst Hiestermann *ten* Herod **Leonie Rysanek** *sop*
Herodias **Clemens Bieber** *ten* Narraboth **Marianne
Rørholm** *contr* Page **Friedrich Molsberger** *bass* First
Nazarene **Ralf Lukas** *bass* Second Nazarene **William
Murray** *bass* First Soldier **Bengt Rundgren** *bass*
Second Soldier **Klaus Lang** *bar* Cappadocian
**Orchestra of the Deutsche Oper, Berlin /
Giuseppe Sinopoli**
DG ② 431 810-2GH2 (102' · DDD)   Ⓕ❍❍❍➼

Strauss's setting of a German translation of
Oscar Wilde's play is original and erotically
explicit. It caused a sensation in its day and even
now stimulates controversy. Sinopoli's recording is a magnificent achievement, mainly
because of Cheryl Studer's representation of the
spoilt Princess who demands and eventually gets
the head of John (John the Baptist) on a
platter as a reward for her striptease ('Dance of
the Seven Veils'). Studer, her voice fresh, vibrant
and sensuous, conveys exactly Salome's growing

fascination, infatuation and eventual obsession
with Jokanaan, which ends in the arresting nec-
rophilia of the final scene. She expresses
Salome's wheedling, spoilt nature, strong will
and ecstasy in tones that are apt for every aspect
of the strenuous role.
  She's supported to the hilt by Sinopoli's incandescent conducting and by Bryn Terfel's convincing Jokanaan, unflaggingly delivered, by
Hiestermann, who makes a suitably fevered,
unhinged sound as the near-crazed Herod, and
Rysanek's wilful Herodias. The playing is excellent and the recording has breadth and warmth.
This is eminently recommendable. For a newcomer to the work, Studer's superb portrayal
may just tip the balance in favour of Sinopoli,
though Solti's famous version is in a class of its
own, with a gloriously sung Salome and the ravishingly beautiful playing of the Vienna Phil.

Salome
Nadja Michael *sop* Salome **Michaela Schuster** *mez*
Herodias **Thomas Moser** *ten* Herod **Joseph Kaiser**
ten Narraboth **Michael Volle** *bar* Jokanaan
**Royal Opera House Orchestra, Covent Garden /
Philippe Jordan**
Stage director **David McVicar**
Video director **Jonathan Haswell**
Opus Arte ② 📀 OA0996D (168' · NTSC · 16:9 ·
PCM stereo and DTS 5.1 · 0). Extra features include
documentary 'David McVicar: A work in process'
                                           Ⓕ❍❍

For all its nudity and gore Salome ends the evening in a white petticoat red with blood (mostly
from the executioner) – this is a conventional
production which lays out the story straightforwardly. It is based on Pasolini's film *Salo* which
gives us the 1930s setting and 'decadent' extras
(who could be much more animated) standing
around watching an everyday story of the
Herods. Es Devlin's handsome set shows us
Herod's banquet in progress upstairs in addition
to the main area of the basement, and becomes
nicely mobile during a Dance in Seven Rooms
(which, according to the accompanying documentary, depicts Salome's abused upbringing).
Nadja Michael has become in short order
Europe's Number One not-quite-*hochdramatische*
choice for physically demanding productions.
She is an attractive Salome, moving like a
dancer, as physically unafraid as she is vocally –
and this tricky sing, with its ferocious tuning,
suits her. Michael Volle is an imposing, rich-
toned Narraboth, given little to do but emote
about Jesus. Both these German artists make a
considerable impact through their own voices
and physicality – but it is Thomas Moser's
weakly human Herod who emerges as the most
truly lived-in character. Philippe Jordan seems
to have balanced his orchestra extremely well for
both house and cast and is especially alert to the
most modern twists of Strauss's harmonies. The
filming (Jonathan Haswell) is sensitive to David
McVicar's work while being much more than
merely a static record.

Additional recommendations

Salome

Nielsen Salome **Hale** Jokanaan **Goldberg** Herod
Silja Herodias **Danish National RSO / Schønwandt**
Chandos ② CHAN9611 (99' · DDD · T/t)   Ⓕ🅾

Inga Nielsen is a Salome of quite exceptional talent, even inspiration. Better than any of her predecessors she creates a princess who sounds credibly teenaged with surely just the pearl-like yet needle-sharp tone Strauss intended. She fashions her reading with supreme intelligence in her response to words and notes. Happily Nielsen's riveting interpretation receives suitable support. Schønwandt yields to none of his illustrious predecessors in impressing on us the still-extraordinary originality, fascination and tense horror of Strauss's score. Hale is a noble-sounding, resolute Jokanaan of long experience. Goldberg is just right as the degraded, superstitious, lecherous Herod, vocally astute and characterful. Silja is a well-routined, if sometimes over-the-top Herodias.

Die schweigsame Frau

Die schweigsame Frau
Kurt Böhme bass Sir Morosus **Martha Mödl** mez
Housekeeper **Barry McDaniel** bar Barber **Donald
Grobe** ten Henry Morosus **Reri Grist** sop Aminta
Lotte Schädle sop Isotta **Glenys Loulis** mez Carlotta
Albrecht Peter bar Morbio **Benno Kusche** bar
Vanuzzi **Max Proebstl** bass Farfallo **Bavarian State
Opera Chorus and Orchestra / Wolfgang Sawallisch**
Orfeo d'Or ② C516 992I (126' · ADD)
Recorded 1971   Ⓕ

That ardent and devoted Straussian, William Mann, slated this production (in *Opera*) when he saw it at its premiere in Munich in 1971 because the score was 'cut to ribbons', declaring that it was therefore, in Strauss's home city, 'a national disgrace'. Notwithstanding this objection, all the liveliness and spirit of the Munich event is conveyed in this recording from the archives of Bavarian Radio to the extent that you hear a lot of stage noises. Sawallisch wholly enters into the spirit of the Ben Jonson comedy as adapted for his libretto by Stefan Zweig.

The cast, excellent all round, easily get their collective tongues around the profusion of words. Kurt Böhme, near the end of his long career, is, as he was in the flesh, a magnificently rotund Morosus, with real 'face' in his singing. The then-young American singers, who all spent most of their careers in Germany, cast as Aminta, Henry and the Barber, all possess good German. Grist is a delightfully fresh and pleasing Aminta and Barry McDaniel an inventive Barber, though his rivals on the other sets are even better. As Henry, Grobe isn't quite the equal of Wunderlich – who can be? Mödl enjoys herself hugely as the Housekeeper.

Sawallisch, in 1971 newly appointed Music Director in Munich and destined to do so much there for the cause of Strauss, manages to keep clear all the many strands in Strauss's score.

Further listening

Daphne

Gueden Daphne **King** Apollo **Schoeffler** Peneios
Wunderlich Leukippos
Vienna State Opera Chorus; VSO / Bohm
DG ② 445 322-2GX2 (94' · ADD)   Ⓜ
Recorded live

Daphne isn't perhaps as involving as Strauss's later operas, but it contains some typically beautiful writing for the soprano voice in the title-role. A fine performance.

Die Liebe der Danae

Kupper Danae **Schöffler** Jupiter **Traxel** Mercury   Ⓗ
Vienna State Opera Chorus, VPO / Krauss
Orfeo mono ③ C292 923D (164' · ADD)
Recorded live at the Salzburg Festival   Ⓕ

Despite a number of pages in Strauss's most appealing, late autumnal vein, this is a deeply flawed work, not least because of the wordy and rather empty libretto. For Strauss completists, though, this 1952 recording is the one to have.

Igor Stravinsky
Russian/French/American 1882-1971

Stravinsky's father sent him to study criminal law and legal philosophy at St Petersburg University in 1901. Through his friendship with Vladimir and Andrei Rimsky-Korsakov, two sons of the great composer, Stravinsky became a family friend and a frequent visitor to Rimsky's house. With Feodor Stravinsky's death in 1902, Igor began taking lessons (free of charge) in orchestration from Rimsky who became something of a father figure to the young man. These lessons and his own study of counterpoint were the only formal musical studies Stravinsky undertook – he never went to a music conservatory or graduated with a degree in music. His early progress as a composer was unusually slow and Rimsky-Korsakov was hesitant in encouraging his young friend to become a full-time composer. To celebrate the wedding of Rimsky-Korsakov's daughter, Stravinsky wrote an orchestral fantasy called Feu d'artifice (Fireworks). His adored teacher died a few days after the wedding.

If Stravinsky believed in Fate then he was well rewarded, for in 1909 his Feu d'artifice together with his Scherzo fantastique were given in a concert in St Petersburg. In the audience happened to be Serge Diaghilev, the ballet impresario, founder of the Paris-based Ballets Russes and one of the great talent-spotters of musical history. He commissioned Stravinsky to write a ballet score for him. The result was The Firebird. It was presented at the Paris Opéra in 1910 and it made Stravinsky famous overnight. Almost immediately, Diaghilev persuaded him to write a second score, another ballet, another work for the musical theatre – the world in which Stravinsky had been brought up. Petrushka provided him with a second triumph. It also marked a turning-point in 20th-century music with its electric rhythms, novel instrumental textures and daring polytonality. These innovations marked an extraordinary development in a composer who only four years earlier had produced such inexperienced and technically deficient works as the Symphony in E flat. Now he was hailed as among the most significant of living composers, a fashionable icon in the avant-garde of Paris.

This success, this revolution, was as nothing compared with the third masterpiece commissioned by Diaghilev. The premiere of The Rite of Spring at the Théâtre des Champs-Elysées in Paris on May 29, 1913, created possibly the biggest scandal in musical history. Exotically choreographed by Nijinsky with bizarre settings and costumes (by Roerich), the first night ended in a riot, so violent was the reaction to the music. Catcalls and stamping feet from detractors threatened to drown out the music while musicians like Ravel and Debussy were on their feet yelling their support. The reception of The Rite of Spring at its London premiere in July 1913 was better mannered but savaged by the critics. Acceptance of the sound world of The Rite came slowly but inevitably. By 1940 it was so much part of the standard repertoire that it was included in Walt Disney's Fantasia – along with Beethoven's Pastoral Symphony and Tchaikovsky's The Nutcracker.

Two more ballets followed The Rite (Le rossignol and Les noces) in which he used smaller orchestral forces. Then came the revolution of 1917 and Stravinsky's life changed irrevocably. He and his wife (he'd married his cousin Catherine Nossenko in 1906) had moved to Switzerland for health reasons but when it was clear that his property in Russia would be confiscated and that his royalties would dry up, Stravinsky opted for voluntary exile in Paris.

After the war, Diaghilev once again prevailed upon Stravinsky to produce another ballet. Pulcinella (1920) marked the beginning of a second stage in his musical development. The themes on which the music was based were from the 18th-century composer Pergolesi and other Italian contemporaries. Not only was the material 'classical' but the form in which this and future works were conceived relied on old structures which had fallen out of fashion - the Piano Concerto followed, and the Octet for wind instruments. These are far removed from the luxuriantly orchestrated, ferocious pre-war scores which he now abandoned in favour of what we now call 'neo-classicism'.

Parallel with his career as a composer, Stravinsky, obsessed with earning enough money, produced a number of keyboard works in which he could be a capable soloist, and travelled all over Europe, North America and South America in the two decades after the First World War. This was the period of Oedipus Rex (1927), an opera/oratorio, the Symphony of Psalms (1930) and the ballet Perséphone (1933). In 1934 he became a French citizen but by the end of the decade Stravinsky was tiring of Europe. With the Second World War inevitable, Stravinsky accepted an invitation from Harvard University to take a professorship and in 1939 he moved to America, joined shortly after by his longtime mistress Vera de Bosset – he'd been in love with her since 1922. They were married in 1940 and became American citizens shortly after the end of the war.

In 1948 he agreed to return to the theatre by writing a full-scale opera. With a libretto by WH Auden and Chester Kallman based on a series of paintings by Hogarth called The Rake's Progress, the composition took Stravinsky three years. It was premiered in Venice in 1951, the composer conducting. This proved to be almost the last work in the neo-classical style he had made his own for the previous 30 years for, while working on The Rake's Progress, he was introduced to a young man named Robert Craft, a young American musician in his early twenties. Craft became his musical factotum and also introduced Stravinsky to recordings of the works of Schoenberg and the Second Viennese School. Stravinsky had always opposed Serialism - in fact, though he and Schoenberg were near neighbours in Hollywood, they never met. Now he began cautiously to experiment with the technique. Thus began the third period of his development, producing his first composition in the new form at the age of 75 (Agon, 1957). It must be said that little of the music from this last period has found any favour with the public.

With Craft's help, Stravinsky was able to resume worldwide touring and in 1962, just before his 80th birthday, he made a triumphant return to Russia. Soon after, his music, long denounced by the authorities, began to be played there. His last major work was the Requiem canticles (1966) after which ill-health slowed him down, but throughout the decade he was feted as few other musicians in history, universally acknowledged as the greatest living composer. In 1966 he moved from Hollywood to New York where he died in 1971. A few weeks later his body was flown to Venice where he was buried on the island of San Michele, near the resting place of Serge Diaghilev.

Apollon musagète

Apollon musagète (1947 version). [a]The Rite of Spring. The Firebird – Suite. Jeu de cartes. Petrushka.
Royal Concertgebouw Orchestra, [a]Cleveland Orchestra / Riccardo Chailly
Double Decca ② 473 731-2DF2 (149' · DDD) ⓂⓄⓄ▶

This is a great little set, coupling a ravishing Apollon musagète with a truly stunning Rite of Spring. The Petrushka is equally fine. The fact that Stravinsky's revision of Apollon dispensed with half the woodwind, two of the three harps, glockenspiel and celesta from the original scoring hardly constitutes the bleaching process that a less colour-sensitive performance might have allowed. Part of the effect comes from a remarkably fine recording where clarity and tonal bloom are complementary, but Chailly must take the credit for laying all Stravinsky's cards on the table rather than holding this or that detail to his chest. Everything tells, much as it does in the Scherzo fantastique – whether the euphonious winds and brass at 3'52", the motorised repeated notes later on or the ornamental swirlings that, in stylistic terms, dance us all the way from Rimsky's Arabian Nights to the unmistakably Russian world of The Firebird.

Apollon musagète is something else again, and Chailly takes the lyrical line, pointing without punching and allowing his excellent strings their head. The coda is jaunty, the 'Apothéose' suitably mysterious, and 'Variation d'Apollon' features fine solo work from the orchestra's leader, Jaap van Zweden. Viable alternatives include leaner, more ascetic readings, but Chailly balances gracefulness with tonal substance and the sound is glorious.

Apollon musagète. Pulcinella – Suite
**Chamber Orchestra of Europe /
Alexander Janiczek**
Linn CKD330 (54' · DDD/DSD)   Ⓕ🅞➡

These two classic ballet scores, composed eight years apart, could hardly be more different. The *Pulcinella* Suite (1920) comes from the ballet suggested by Diaghilev and is based on existing music by Pergolesi and some 18th-century Italian contemporaries. Stravinsky was sceptical about the idea to start with but soon went through everything of Pergolesi he could find and 'fell in love'. He regarded *Pulcinella* as 'to some extent a satire' but found he had to change or add very little to make the music his own.

Apollo (1928) was written for Balanchine and represents pure ballet unencumbered by a narrative although the nine dances are related to episodes in the life of the Greek god. As in *Pulcinella* Stravinsky distorts Classical and Baroque idioms to his own idiosyncratic ends in a technique of masterly restraint. Less became more.

What comes over in these new recordings by the justly lauded Chamber Orchestra of Europe is the lyricism of *Apollo*. Stravinsky as a melodist? It's a claim rarely made for him but this impeccable and stylish performance radiates melodic appeal devoid of sentimentality. Overall this is a most attractive release, an imaginative coupling and an excellent recording.

The Firebird – Ballet & Suite

The Firebird (1910 version). Song of the Nightingale.
Flemish Radio Orchestra / Yoel Levi
Glossa GCDSA922001 (71' · DDD/DSD)   Ⓕ🅞

This striking SACD provides remarkably high-calibre recordings: both works sound pretty marvellous played back through normal CD equipment. But if you have a good four-speaker system and set the rear volume level gently and judiciously, the sound is almost unbelievably realistic. Indeed, this Flemish performance of *The Firebird* is one of the finest orchestral recordings of recent years. Stravinsky's vivid scoring lends itself to demonstration sound. Moreover, the music is miraculously well played.

Yoel Levi's totally idiomatic and involving reading, though not lacking drama, is warmly relaxed and evocatively atmospheric, with the Flemish orchestra playing with ravishing sensitivity. Orchestral textures are delectably diaphonous and transluscent: everything seems to be in a magical haze, with iridescent colouring at the 'Appearance of the Firebird', while the music for the 'Enchanted Princesses' is exquisitely tender. Arguably the *piano-pianissimo* opening is a little too quiet but the ear soon revels in the wide range of playing and sound: the whole progres-

sion of infernal music for Kashchei brings some quite astounding sounds. For the great closing rejoicing, the lovely horn melody seemingly appears out of the mist, and the climax builds slowly and magically until the brass enter. Then Levi pulls back a little, creating a spacious, no less involving, climax.

In *Song of the Nightingale*, the orchestra again play with refinement and beauty, especially at the close. The extra dimension of the Glossa recording makes one feel the orchestra really is out there, beyond the speakers.

Petrushka

Petrushka. The Firebird – Suite. Scherzo à la russe
Cincinnati Symphony Orchestra / Paavo Järvi
Telarc CD80587 (60' · DDD)   Ⓕ🅞

Paavo Järvi's Telarc coupling of *Petrushka* and *The Firebird* Suite is outstanding in every way. *Petrushka* is so arresting that it invites comparison with the famous pioneering Ansermet account. It should be noted that Ansermet uses the original 1911 score, and Järvi the 1947 version. Switching between the two accounts, the surprise is the closeness of the two interpretations, with Ansermet pressing forward at one moment, Järvi the next, each relishing every detail of Stravinsky's sparkling orchestral palette, yet each completely individual. The more natural concert hall-balance in the superb acoustics of Cincinnati's Music Hall, adds ambient warmth and atmosphere, giving a translucent glow to the woodwind (yet still achieving wonderful detail), a rich patina to the strings, and filling out the brass sonorities without loss of bite. The important piano roulades, too, brilliantly played by Michael Chertock, glitter irridescently. Järvi's reading certainly doesn't lack histrionic qualities, yet it has added pathos, particularly the scene in the Moor's Room, and at the very end of the ballet. With Ansermet, Petrushka's ghost reappears fiercely, even demonically; Järvi chooses a distanced effect and creates a haunting atmosphere of desolate melancholy.

The Firebird Suite is equally memorable. Again the wonderful Rimskyan colouring is conveyed in lusciously translucent detail, but the spectacular entry of Kashchei will surely make you jump, and the finale expands gloriously. Jack Renner, Telarc's outstanding chief recording engineer, produces the best bass drum in the business, and those thwacks as Järvi builds his final climax are riveting, as is the amplitude of the overall sound.

So this CD not only offers truly memorable performances, splendidly played, but demonstration sound that audiophiles will relish.

Pulcinella

Pulcinella[a]. Symphony in Three Movements.
Four Etudes
[a]**Roxana Constantinescu** mez [a]**Nicholas Phan** ten
[a]**Kyle Ketelsen** bass-bar **Chicago Symphony**

Orchestra / Pierre Boulez
CSO Resound ⊚ CSOR901 920 (71' · DDD/DSD)
Recorded live 2009   Ⓕ❶❷➡

Boulez seems to 'get' the Symphony, whether stamping (though never pounding) through the neanderthal opening or maintaining tension in that wonderful passage near the close of the first movement where the flute meanders to a weirdly offbeat strings-and-piano accompaniment. On this new Chicago recording the piano is rather too close, the strings just a little tentative: a small detail, maybe, and in general the Chicago performance is very fine, the second movement sharing with its Berlin predecessor (DG) many delicate textures though the actual sound of the two orchestras provides an interesting study in tonal contrasts, the Berlin band yielding a typically golden body of tone, albeit slimmed down under Boulez's calorie-conscious direction, the Chicago Symphony more steel and velvet than gold, though polished and mostly precise.

The third of the *Studies* provides another sort of comparison, Chicago with Chicago this time – 1992 for DG versus 2009 – this newer performance suggesting a stark sense of ritual whereas in 1992 the same music sounds more homogeneous but has less of an 'edge' to it. *Pulcinella* is mostly quite relaxed and affectionately played though with no lack of drama where needed, such as in the tellingly invasive *Allegro assai*. There's a measured but pointed Tarantella and a very nicely played Gavotte with variations which leads back to territory where ballet and suite coincide, most memorably for the famous *Vivo*, where those fabulous Chicago trombones really have a chance to show off. Good singing throughout and many felicitous instrumental solos keep one hooked, which means an unhesitating recommendation unless your main interest is the Symphony in which case the Berlin recording remains, by a small margin, my overall preference.

The Rite of Spring

Stravinsky The Rite of Spring
Scriabin Le poème de l'extase
Kirov Orchestra / Valery Gergiev
Philips 468 035-2PH (55' · DDD)   Ⓕ❶❷➡

This is probably the most extraordinary *Rite of Spring* to have been dreamt up since Stravinsky's own final (and finest) 1960 recording. Stravinsky himself said, in so many words, that *The Rite* was born from his unconscious. And although now isn't the time or place to ponder to what extent his – and our – unconscious minds are capable (if at all) of harbouring any memories of pre-Christian ritual, suffice it so say that an exceptional performance of *The Rite* should at least have us thinking about it as a possibility…and about why we respond to *The Rite* in the way that we do.

Among modern interpreters, there isn't anyone better than Gergiev at the important dual roles of showman and shaman. So many of the score's darker workings have a striking profile here – tubas bellowing strange moans, the bass drum sending shock waves around the performance space, the lower strings in 'Spring Rounds' almost 'exhaling' their notes, and, for once, giving a proper foundation to that most significant of quiet chords – the one where the Sage kisses the earth. Indeed, 'Earth' and the 'elemental' seem not so much cultivated in this performance as an inherent part of it.

Either Gergiev has really pondered the 'sound stuff' of the *Rite*, or it just comes naturally to him and his players. Though whether nature or nurture, the end results make for a marginally more compelling overall listen than all the finest recorded *Rite*s of the last four decades. More controversial is some of the timing of 'events', especially the delay of the ascent to the final chord, though when it arrives, you wonder if its shocking make-up has ever been as effectively exposed. The delaying tactics – theatrical pauses and suspensions – proved a little more problematic in the second half of Scriabin's *Poem of Ecstasy* – along with Gergiev's extremes of tempo in the piece. But should one even be thinking these thoughts when offered a *Poem* which openly embraces the extravagant wonders of the piece as this one does? Better to marvel at all the mysterious curves, the fabulous dark rushes of sound, the celebratory splendours, and the final resolution (dissolution?) into an uncomplicated glory of C major. Here, as in *The Rite*, the recording is superb.

The Rite of Spring (two versions)   Ⓗ
Philharmonia Orchestra / Igor Markevitch
Testament mono/stereo SBT1076 (67' · ADD)
Mono version recorded 1951, stereo 1959   Ⓕ❷❷

Markevitch's 1959 stereo *Rite* is in a league of its own. This is a model of how to balance the score (and of how to create the illusion of a wide dynamic range within more restricted parameters). Markevitch would have been totally familiar with every note of the piece (in 1949 he sent Stravinsky a list of mistakes he had noticed in the recently revised edition), and by 1959 he clearly knew what it needed in performance, including how to keep its shock-value alive. There are 'improprieties' here, such as the slowing for the 'Evocation of the Ancestors' (making the most of those timpani volleys), but nothing serious. As it happens, Markevitch's 'Introduction' to Part 2 is unusually fast, but he's able to take in the following small marked variations of tempo, providing valuable contrasts. And in any case, the playing is so alive, alert and reactive, whatever the dynamic levels: listen to the incisive clarinets' entry in the 'Mystic Circles' and the *frisson* imparted to the following *pianissimo tremolando* from the strings.

We could fill the rest of the page with similar highlights and other features unique to the performance, but that would be to spoil the fun of discovery (or rediscovery – and what a transfer of the original!). This is a great *Rite* for many reasons, not the least of which is that the sessions were obviously electric. As a fascinating bonus, Testament also offers a 1951 mono recording of a great *Rite* in the making. The differences aren't radical, but enough to justify the idea.

The Rite of Spring. Apollon musagète
**City of Birmingham Symphony Orchestra /
Sir Simon Rattle**
EMI 749636-2 (65' · DDD)   Ⓕ🅞🅞🅓➤

Recordings of *The Rite of Spring* are legion, but it's rare to find Stravinsky's most explosive ballet score coupled with *Apollon musagète*, his most serene. The result is a lesson in creative versatility, confirming that Stravinsky could be equally convincing as Expressionist and neo-classicist. Yet talk of lessons might suggest that sheer enjoyment is of lesser importance, and it's perfectly possible to relish this disc simply for that personal blend of the authoritative and the enlivening that Simon Rattle's CBSO recordings for EMI so consistently achieve. Rattle never rushes things, and the apparent deliberation of *The Rite*'s concluding 'Sacrificial Dance' may initially surprise, but in this context it proves an entirely appropriate, absolutely convincing conclusion. Rattle sees the work as a whole, without striving for a spurious symphonic integration, and there's never for a moment any hint of a routine reading of what's now a classic of the modern orchestral repertoire.

The account of *Apollon* has comparable depth, with elegance transformed into eloquence and the CBSO strings confirming that they have nothing to fear from comparison with the best in Europe or America. The recordings are faithful to the intensity and expressiveness of Rattle's Stravinsky, interpretations fit to set beside those of the composer himself.

Symphonies

Symphony in Three Movements. Symphony of Psalms[a]. Symphony in C
**[a]Berlin Radio Choir; Berlin Philharmonic Orchestra
/ Sir Simon Rattle**
EMI 207630-0 (76' · DDD)   🅜🅞🅞🅓➤
Recorded live in 2007

The *Symphony in Three Movements* doesn't so much start as erupt and Sir Simon Rattle's second recording of it has impressive immediacy, richer tonally than his rougher-edged 1980s recording with the CBSO, but textually warmer and with more refined solos. Interesting points of comparison arise at around 4'00" into the first movement (chamber-like textures involving strings and winds) and the serene passage for strings and harp at 2'08" into the second movement, the relative earnestness of the earlier version replaced here by a true but 'terrible beauty'. In comparison with conductors like Boulez and Gielen, Rattle offers the most polished option,

---

STRAVINSKY'S THE RITE OF SPRING – IN BRIEF

Columbia SO / Igor Stravinsky
Sony download 88888 02047-5 (65' · ADD)   🅜🅓➤
Stravinsky's own interpretation exhibits an innate musicality, rhythmic bounce and satisfying transparency that really hits the mark. The 1960 recording still packs a pleasing wallop.

Cleveland Orchestra / Pierre Boulez
Sony SMK64109 (69' · ADD)   🅜🅞🅓➤
Boulez's 1969 performance remains intensely compelling in its cumulative drive, seismic power and irreproachable precision. Very fine sound, too.

CBSO / Sir Simon Rattle
EMI 749636-2 (65' · DDD)   Ⓕ🅞🅞🅓➤
A refreshingly thoughtful, immaculately honed *Rite* from Rattle. Rhythm and ensemble are consistently tight; nor is there any lack of primitivistic fervour.

**Concertgebouw Orchestra /
Sir Colin Davis**
Philips ② 464 744-2PM2 (142' · ADD)   🅜🅓➤
Davis's *Rite* has an irresistible poise, choreographic flair and giddy sense of drama, all captured with unflinching splendour by the Philips engineers.

San Francisco SO / Michael Tilson Thomas
RCA ③ 09026 68898-2 (119' · DDD)   🅜🅓➤
A superbly balanced live recording from Davies Symphony Hall in San Francisco. Tilson Thomas's *Rite* is as copiously detailed and exhilarating as any that have appeared in many a moon.

Philadelphia Orchestra / Riccardo Muti
EMI 574581-2 (64' · ADD)   🅢🅓➤
Muti puts his virtuoso Philadelphia band through their paces to flamboyant, often startling effect. As bargain-basement *Rites* go, you won't do better than this.

Philharmonia Orchestra / Igor Markevitch   🄷
Testament SBT1076 (67' · ADD)   Ⓕ🅞🅞
Testament allows us the opportunity to compare and contrast Markevitch's 1951 recording and his stereo remake of eight years later. Both are little short of stunning in their immaculate co-ordination and volcanic force.

Kirov Orchestra / Valery Gergiev
Philips 468 035-2PH (55' · DDD)   Ⓕ🅞🅞🅓➤
Gergiev has the happy knack of making you listen with fresh ears. Here's a searingly powerful *Rite*, full of elemental fury and fierce abandon.

mindful of both mood and structure and beautifully engineered, but don't forget Stravinsky's own 1946 (New York Philharmonic) version, which reflects a new-born masterpiece in the heat of its creation.

Rattle's *Symphony of Psalms* is very sensitively traced, with a rowdy account of the reveille-style 'Laudate Dominum' passage in the last movement. However, the real highlight of this CD is Rattle's pressing but never impatient account of what in my view is Stravinsky's greatest symphony, the terse and poignant Symphony in C, music forged in the wake of illness and death but that only ever suggests anguish, never confesses it. Tchaikovsky's spirit looms large, especially in the first movement, at the onset of the angry central climax where Rattle and his Berliners achieve considerable intensity. Rattle focuses each episode without sounding episodic and shapes the *Larghetto*'s opening most poetically. Stravinsky himself is faster and lighter (especially on his second, stereo, recording) but Rattle gives us both urgency and tonal body. Henceforth, his is a digital front-runner. (And if purchased as a download, a finely observed account of the *Symphonies of Wind Instruments* is thrown in as a generous bonus.)

Symphony in C[c]. Symphony in Three Movements[d]
Octet[a]. Concerto in E flat, 'Dumbarton Oaks'[b]
[a]**Twentieth Century Classics Ensemble;**
[b]**Orchestra of St Luke's;** [cd]**Philharmonia
Orchestra / Robert Craft**
Naxos 8 557507 (76' · DDD)   Ⓢ

Robert Craft's best rostrum work involves relatively small forces and transparent textures, such as the Octet, which is here given a crisp, dapper performance, biting where needs be and bursting with life. Musical line and clear projection are invariable Craft priorities and both in the Octet and in the post-Baroque *Dumbarton Oaks* Concerto the pulse is kept moving and the musical journey is always clearly directed with generally superb execution from the New York players. All these selections were previously available. An earlier Craft-led version of the *Symphony in Three Movements* (from 1991) is marginally swifter than this 1999 Philharmonia remake, leaner too with a sharper edge (notably from the brass) but the finale on the new version is very appealing, with the incisive snap of woodwinds against eerily winding strings. The tighter, more astringent language of the Symphony in C suits Craft better, though the outer movements occasionally sound rushed.

In the Symphony in C Craft's approach is all animation and nervous energy. As ever with him, there's the feeling that the mind in charge knows exactly what this music is about, and with generally excellent sound makes for a thoroughly reliable programme, while in the case of the two chamber works the effect is decidedly impressive. Needless to say, Craft's own programme-notes are a mine of relevant information.

L'histoire du soldat

L'histoire du soldat (in English)[a]. Concerto in E flat,
'Dumbarton Oaks'
[a]**David Timson,** [a]**Benjamin Soames,** [a]**Jonathan
Keeble** spkrs **Northern Chamber Orchestra /
Nicholas Ward**
Naxos 8 553662 (76' · DDD)   Ⓢ▷

In this full-length *The Soldier's Tale* (the English translation by Michael Flanders and Kitty Black), the actors have the full measure of their parts, and the musicians, taken as a group, about two-thirds the measure of theirs. The notes are there, but not always the will to make something of them. Perhaps one shouldn't expect violin and trumpet playing of the flair and feature of Manoug Parikian and Maurice André in the classic 1962 Markevitch recording (now part of a two-disc set on Philips, and spoken in the original French). On the other hand Nicholas Cox's always fully responsive clarinet playing on the Naxos recording is a vast improvement on Markevitch's narrow-toned and quavery clarinettist. If Nicholas Cox seems to do a little better out of the Naxos balance than some of his musical colleagues, it's probably because of his more consistent projection of character.

In general, it's a very natural balance that welds the years and miles between the separately recorded actors and musicians into a reasonably convincing illusion of a single-stage whole (with the actors placed in front of the musicians), though it's less convincing than the Markevitch, where the same acoustic was used by both actors and musicians (and where Jean Cocteau's narrator can become almost submerged). The generous bonus here is Stravinsky's modernised 'Brandenburg Concerto', *Dumbarton Oaks*, marginally more presently recorded than the musical contributions to the main work, but with the same mixture of determination to put it across (a wonderful strutting *marcato* at the start of the finale) and lapses into a competent neutral. So, should you be interested at the price? If you only know *The Soldier's Tale* through the Concert Suite (most of the music; none of the words), and can sample before purchasing this complete recording, try two 'low points' – the very opening ('The soldier's march'), and the close ('The devil's triumphal dance') – and if the proceedings don't strike you as tame and lacking vitality, this could be a very rewarding purchase.

Shorter Works and Ballets

Jeu de cartes[a]. Danses concertantes[b].
Scènes de ballet[c]. Variations[d]. Capriccio[e]
[e]**Mark Wait** pf [b]**Twentieth Century Classics
Ensemble;** [ce]**Orchestra of St Luke's;** [d]**London
Philharmonic Orchestra;** [a]**Philharmonia Orchestra /
Robert Craft**
Naxos 8 557506 (79' · DDD)   Ⓢ▷

This collection of Stravinsky's later ballets represents the composer in lighter mood, making a delightful sequence, very well played and recorded under the authoritative direction of the composer's principal amanuensis. *Jeux de cartes* ('The Card Game') of 1936 points directly forward to Stravinsky's style in his opera *The Rake's Progress*, the piece reflecting his love of the game of poker: the three main sections of the ballet represent first, second and third deals, with the Joker figuring in each. The piece was written for the great choreographer Georges Balanchine. Craft's performance with the Philharmonia has an aptly clean attack, with the chugging rhythms well lifted, very suitable for ballet.

Danses concertantes represents Stravinsky in even lighter mood, the first major work he wrote after his arrival in the United States. It's fun music full of playfulness, ending with a jolly galloping theme in compound time. *Scènes de ballet* of 1944 was commissioned for a Broadway show, but sadly, the bars in 5/4 time were too difficult for the theatre orchestra to play, and it had to be abandoned for its original purpose, only to emerge later as a full concert piece and ballet.

Variations, much the shortest item on the disc, represents Stravinsky using 12-tone technique, an uncompromising, densely packed five minutes which makes for difficult listening, while the *Capriccio* for piano and orchestra of 1929 returns to his jolly and light-hearted mood, the popular rhythms jauntily presented. Mark Wait is an outstanding soloist. Altogether, a delightful collection brilliantly played and recorded.

Agon. Jeu de cartes. Orpheus
BBC Scottish Symphony Orchestra / Ilan Volkov
Hyperion CDA67698 (73' · DDD)　　　　Ⓕ**O**🔁

Three ballet scores that Stravinsky wrote for New York – *Jeu de cartes* (staged in 1937), *Orpheus* (1948) and *Agon* (1957) – are given virile, cogent performances by the BBC Scottish Symphony Orchestra under Ilan Volkov. Questions of style are closely observed, so that, while there are certain traits common to all three works, the individuality of each one is clearly delineated and, in the process, the progression of Stravinsky's musical character is rendered all the more perceptible. *Jeu de cartes*, the most classically 'neo-classical' of the three, is crisply sculpted and propulsive, the rhythmic sleights of hand diamond-sharp, the instrumental colours bold, the impact exhilarating.

With *Orpheus* Stravinsky achieves a 'new austerity and intensity that might suggest a breaking away from the more mechanical aspects of neo-classicism' (Stephen Walsh). And this performance is one that, while alert to neo-classicism's incisive facets in, for example, the Furies' dance of the second scene, also hauntingly summons up the darker, softer, more mysterious and intimate atmosphere that the music emanates. *Agon*, even with some fleet, rhythmically cross-cut numbers that hark back to razor-like neo-classicism, enters even stranger worlds in its refraction of

such ancient dances as the sarabande, galliard and branle through a 20th-century prism and in its piquant combination of instruments, with mandolin and harp eerily deployed and Stravinsky's ability to surprise at its most alert. The statuesque quality of these ballets is ever-present, but these performances also bring them vividly to life in the mind's eye.

The Fairy's Kiss. Scènes de ballet
BBC Scottish Symphony Orchestra / Ilan Volkov
Hyperion CDA67697 (59' · DDD)　　　　Ⓕ**OOO**🔁

Recordings of Stravinsky continue to pour out: and what's immediately apparent when playing Stravinsky's own recordings followed by the new ones is – obviously – the great improvement in recorded sound since the mid-1960s. Further, there is little scope for conductors to diverge from the master's interpretations because his instructions were always so precise.

The welcome curiosity here is *Scènes de ballet*, with few recordings. Stravinsky called it "a period piece, a portrait of Broadway in the last years of the war" and he found the $5000 fee very acceptable. The show ran for 183 performances but Stravinsky was annoyed that there were cuts and he famously refused any reorchestrations by Robert Russell Bennett. The score is attractive American-period Stravinsky before he moved towards serial techniques. Apart from the vivid sound quality, the balance in the new recording is better with details such as the piano much clearer.

The Fairy's Kiss goes back to 1928, with Stravinsky's neo-classical borrowing techniques firmly entrenched, and this time it's Tchaikovsky. Stravinsky adapted songs and piano pieces and composed some numbers himself. This passionate liaison is so integrated that it's impossible to tell which was which, and Stravinsky couldn't always remember himself. Without the dance, *The Fairy's Kiss* is at times fairly low density and the ending seems drawn out. But overall this is an attractive coupling in Hyperion's admirable ballet series, produced with its usual finesse.

Scherzo à la russe[a]. Song of the Volga Boatmen[b]. Pastorale, Op 5[c]. Three Pieces for Solo Clarinet[d]. Two Poems of Konstantin Bal'mont[e]. Cats' Cradle Songs[f]. Three Japanese Lyrics[g]. Pribaoutki[h]. L'histoire du soldat – Suite[i]. Renard[j]. Pour Picasso[d]
[e,g]**Susan Narucki** sop [f,h]**Catherine Ciesinski** mez [j]**John Aler,** [j]**Paul Spears** tens [j]**David Evitts** bar [j]**Wilbur Pauley** bass [j]**Tara O'Connor** picc/fl [d]**Stephen Taylor** ob/cor ang [c]**Melanie Feld** cor ang [j]**Alan Kay,** [c,d]**Charles Neidich,** [j]**William Blount** cls [c]**Frank Morelli** bn [j]**Daniel Grabois,** [j]**William Purvis** hns [j]**Chris Gekker,** [j]**Louis Hanzlik** tpts [j]**Michael Powell** tbn [j]**Chris Deane** cimb [j]**Gordon Gottlieb** timp [j]**Danny Druckman, Thomas Kolor** perc [c]**Rolf Schulte, Jennifer Frautschi,** [j]**David Bowlin** vns [j]**Richard O'Neill** va [j]**Fred Sherry** vc [j]**John Feeney,** [j]**Kurt Muroki** dbs [b]**Philharmonia Orchestra;**

ᵃʰOrchestra of St Luke's; ᵉᵍTwentieth Century
Classics Ensemble / Robert Craft
Naxos 8 557505 (74' · DDD)   Ⓢ▶

Wistful is not a word one expects to use to describe a composition of Stravinsky but the *Pastorale* which opens this collection has just that kind of charm. Written originally as a vocal piece in 1908, it introduces Robert Craft's collection of early works dating from 1911 to 1918, the exception being the audacious arrangement of the *Scherzo à la russe* that Stravinsky made for Paul Whiteman's Band in 1944. The most familiar work here is the *Histoire du soldat* Suite, given a sharply characterised performance. But the opening of *Renard* establishes a similarly dynamic instrumental character, while the dramatic vocal participation is exuberantly full of bawdy wit. It is presented with great accuracy and élan, laced with weird barnyard noises from the orchestra, and is great fun even if one cannot hear all the words (no text is provided).

The two Bal'mont songs are beautiful and the *Three Japanese Lyrics* are sinuously seductive, all exquisitely sung by Susan Narucki. Both sets are provided with translations, but the four *Pribaoutki* are not. Here Catherine Ciesinski brings out their primitive, often robust Russian folk derivation. The four *Cats' Cradle Songs* are equally memorable, slinky morsels with stealthy clarinet colouring. The programme ends with the *Song of the Volga Boatmen*, vulgarly scored but played roisterously by the Philharmonia Orchestra.

All these performances offer superb ensemble playing and spirited, crisply detailed direction from Craft who also provides excellent notes.

Chamber Works for Violin and Piano

Complete Works for Violin and Piano
Anthony Marwood vn **Thomas Adès** pf
Hyperion ② CDA67723 (86' · DDD)   Ⓜ❍❍❍▶

At the 2005 Aldeburgh Festival Marwood and Adès gave a recital of Stravinsky's violin and piano works and it was immediately apparent that theirs was a remarkable partnership, confirmed when Marwood gave the premiere of Adès's Violin Concerto later that year.

If Stravinsky didn't feel like writing tunes himself – and there are plenty here – he just swiped them from somebody else: Pergolesi in *Pulcinella*, Tchaikovsky in *The Fairy's Kiss*. But he made the violin and piano versions himself, except the *Tango*, for his recitals with Samuel Dushkin in the 1930s, and they are recompositions rather than just arrangements.

There are old friends. Three numbers from *The Firebird*, with a mesmeric *Berceuse*; the exhilarating *Danse russe* from *Petrushka* stunningly delivered; and a reworked aria from the chamber opera *Mavra*. The Tango was written in America in 1940 as a pop song but not used and the version here was made by Dushkin. The opening improbably recalls Schubert's *Death and the Maiden* and Marwood gets the insidi-

ously erotic inflections of the Trio just right. The only original work here is the *Duo concertant*, vintage neo-classical Stravinsky with styles ranging from coolly lyrical to busy. All these demands are superbly met by Marwood and Adès with immaculate rhythmic precision. The piano is sometimes aggressive but the engineers usually cope.

Les noces

Les noces[a]. Mass. Cantata on Old English Texts[b]
[ab]**Carolyn Sampson** sop [a]**Susan Parry** mez [a]**Vsevolod Grivnov**, [b]**Jan Kobow** tens [a]**Maxim Mikhailov** bass
Berlin Radio Chamber Choir; musikFabrik / Daniel Reuss
Harmonia Mundi ⚬ HMC80 1913(67' · DDD · T/t)
                                                Ⓕ❍❍▶

Stravinsky's recording of *Les noces* is famous for its ruthlessness, yet the piece is about a folk wedding, and one feature of most weddings is joy. That, a feeling of rhythmic joy, is what makes this new performance so exhilarating. The rhythms are unrelenting, spellbinding, only pausing for the blessing, the two mothers' lament, and the moment the mother lets her daughter go. The performance is terrific, directed with superb exuberance by Daniel Reuss.

Why is the Mass not better known? Stravinsky, an ardent believer, wrote it for himself and for liturgical use, but it is only really known from recordings. It too has an archaic feeling but it is wonderfully lyrical and inspired. The pungent harmonies give it bite, especially in the thrilling *Sanctus*, and the *Agnus Dei* is haunting in the same way that the 'alleluias' at the end of the *Symphony of Psalms* are unforgettable. The Cantata, too, opens gloriously and is lyrically inspired throughout, using four verses from the *Lyke-Wake Dirge* interspersed with polyphonic Ricercari allotted to solo voices accompanied by celestial flutes, oboe, cor anglais and cello. The music is extraordinarily beautiful – and here is another surprise: it is possible to write serial music worth listening to! The performances are all marvellous: who would have expected to hear Carolyn Sampson singing Stravinsky? This record is not to be missed.

Perséphone

Stravinsky Perséphone[a] Dukas Polyeucte[b]
[a]**Nicole Tibbels** sop [a]**Paul Groves** ten [a]**Trinity Boys' Choir**; [a]**Cantate Youth Choir**; **BBC Symphony** [a]**Chorus and Orchestra** / [a]**Sir Andrew Davis**, [b]**Yan Pascal Tortelier**
Warner Classics 2564 61548-2 (67' · DDD · T/t)
Recorded live 2003   Ⓜ

Stravinsky's recordings of his own music always have a certain indispensable something. But it's surprising what performers under his baton were sometimes allowed to get away with. In his recording of *Perséphone* it's the French language that suffers, notably at the hands of Vera Zorina in the title-role, whose French was probably close to Stravinsky's own.

Happily, Nicole Tibbels, Paul Groves and the three choruses employed here have changed all that. Tibbels's narration is particularly impressive. Her French diction is full of variety in speed and tone, and always alive to the drama. Her placing of the narrative in relation to the music is also intelligent. Groves is quite simply one of the best tenors around, and his singing here is clean, powerful and practically faultless in pitching the sometimes awkward melodic lines. The orchestra and choruses live up to these high standards in every respect to produce a treasurable recording of this extraordinarily haunting piece.

The Dukas overture makes an odd coupling, but it's one of the best things he ever wrote, with its Wagnerisms surprisingly well digested for a 26-year-old. Yan Pascal Tortelier produces a more sinewy, contrapuntally aware reading than David Zinman, but also one that breathes more expansively.

Requiem Canticles

Canticum sacrum[a]. Agon. Requiem Canticles[b]
[c]**Stella Doufexis** mez [a]**Christian Elsner** ten
[ac]**Rudolf Rosen** bar **South West German Radio**
[ab]**Vocal Ensemble and Symphony Orchestra,**
Baden-Baden and Freiburg / Michael Gielen
Hänssler Classic CD93 226 (58' · DDD)

Rarely has the late, gnomic *Requiem Canticles* sounded so fluent, from the extraordinary prelude (a fast, nervous pulsing with string lines crossing each other), through the taut drama of the 'Dies irae' to the second interlude (so reminiscent of the *Symphonies of Wind Instruments*) and the chiming finale, where ritual bells are enacted by celesta, glockenspiel and vibraphone, a distant recollection of *Les noces*. This was Stravinsky's last major composition and although it plays for barely a quarter of an hour it seems fully to justify that dodecaphonic route that so many at the time had criticised him for taking.

The marginally more expansive and noticeably more austere *Canticum sacrum* marked the composer's return to the Russian Orthodox faith and calls on the unique combination (unique to Stravinsky that is) of flute, three oboes and bassoons, four trumpets and trombones, harp, violas, basses and organ, in addition to the voices. Again Michael Gielen drives a confident course through a work that brooks no compromise and culminates in a harshly oratorical 'Illi autem profectae', one of the most striking episodes in all late Stravinsky.

The ballet *Agon* post-dates *Canticum sacrum*, just, and employs an even wider array of instruments, all of them used with the greatest economy and expressive force, the distinctive and rhythmically alluring interlude/prelude, a recurring motif, connecting a series of brief but terse and mostly outspoken dance movements. *Agon* is pure aural sculpture, angular and uncompro-

mising (with a short-lived fugue in the finale), but in a performance such as this that focuses its every pungent detail makes for an alluring and stimulating listen. The recordings are both airy and admirably clear.

Symphony of Psalms

Symphony of Psalms[a]. Cantata on Old English Texts[b]. Mass[c]. Babel[d]. Credo[e]. Pater noster[e]. Ave Maria[e]
[b]**Mary Ann Hart** mez [b]**Thomas Bogdan** ten
[d]**David Wilson-Johnson** spkr [b]**Michael Parloff**,
[b]**Bart Feller** fls [b]**Stephen Taylor** ob [b]**Melanie Feld** cora [b]**Fred Sherry** vc [bce]**Gregg Smith Singers;**
[ad]**Simon Joly Chorale;** [ad]**Philharmonia Orchestra;**
[c]**St Luke's Orchestra / Robert Craft**
Naxos 8 557504 (73' · DDD)

This superb collection partly duplicates the aurally fascinating Harmonia Mundi disc (see opposite) in the Cantata and the superb Mass in fine, authoritative performances from Robert Craft. He does not have the advantage of Carolyn Sampson among his soloists but he does have excellent choral singing, and in the glorious *Symphony of Psalms* the Philharmonia Orchestra on top form. This is the highlight of the programme, a superbly structured account, rich in lyrical feeling, building to the frisson-creating 'Alleluias' of the closing section. The Cantata is finely sung and played, with characteristically clear instrumental detail, and the mini-cantata *Babel*, with its spoken narration and choral responses, is also a success.

The programme opens with three brief Russian sacred chorales which are immediately appealing and as idiomatic as one can expect from non-Russian singers. The recordings were made over a decade between 1992 and 2002 and are of good quality, with the *Symphony of Psalms* (2001) – made at Abbey Road – standing out on all counts. Craft is obviously uplifted by the music of the composer's supreme vocal masterpiece. As always with Naxos, excellent documentation, with the detailed notes provided by Craft himself. A bargain!

Oedipus Rex

Oedipus Rex. Symphony of Psalms
Ivo Zídek ten Oedipus **Věra Soukupová** mez Jocasta
Karel Berman bass Créon **Eduard Haken** bass
Tiresias **Antonin Zlesák** ten Shepherd **Zdeněk Kroupa** bar Messenger **Jean Desailly** narr **Czech Philharmonic Chorus and Orchestra / Karel Ančerl**
Supraphon Historical SU3674-2 (73' · AAD)
Recorded 1964-66

Oedipus Rex, to words by Jean Cocteau, is one of Stravinsky's most compelling theatre pieces, a powerful drama that re-enacts the full force of a glorious high spot in ancient culture. The fusion of words and music in *Oedipus* is masterly, and arrests the attention consistently, from the animated severity of the opening narration, through the calculated tension of its musical argument, to the tragic restraint of its closing pages. Karel Ančerl was one of Stravinsky's most committed exponents.

This particular recording was taped in the Dvořák Hall of the House of Artists, Prague, and earned itself at least three major awards. Ančerl traces and intensifies salient points in the tragedy yet maintains a precise, sensitive touch. His vocal collaborators include the noble Karel Berman (Créon) who, like Ančerl himself, suffered considerably during the Nazi occupation of Czechoslovakia. Věra Soukupová is a fine Jocasta and the convincing but occasionally unsteady Ivo Zídek sings the part of Oedipus. Both here and in the *Symphony of Psalms* – one of the most serenely perceptive recorded performances of the work – the Czech Philharmonic Chorus excel, while Supraphon's 1960s engineering (not the DDD suggested on the box) has an appealing brightness.

Le rossignol

Le rossignol
Natalie Dessay sop Nightingale **Hugo Simcic** Child
Marie McLaughlin sop Cook **Violeta Urmana** mez
Death **Vsevolod Grivnov** ten Fisherman **Albert
Schagidullin** bar Emperor **Laurent Naouri** bass
Chamberlain **Maxime Mikhailov** bass Bonze
**Paris National Opera Chorus and Orchestra /
James Conlon**
A film by **Christian Chaudet**
Virgin Classics *DVD* 544242-9 (50' · NTSC · 16:9 · PCM
Stereo and 5.1 · 0). Extras include a 'making of'
documentary, post-production and audio recording
session footage   Ⓕ

Too many mediocre stage productions are being preserved for vocal, not visual, reasons. All the more important, then, is a release like this where a skilled (and musically literate) film director uses state-of-the-art computer technology to sculpt a multi-dimensional portrait of Stravinsky's gorgeous pre-First World War opera-pantomime.

Christian Chaudet bases it on the well-received EMI recording of 1999, reuniting the major soloists in front of blank blue- and green-screens to act their hearts out to imaginary scenery, effects and people that the computer will supply later. This technique, long used in feature films, has a range and flexibility that might have been created for 20th-century opera.

The film begins with a fairly traditional dream frame: a little boy 'sees' his father's pottery turn into a Chinese landscape introducing all the story's characters and events. Later, the Emperor who so desires the Nightingale's singing is seen to live in a forbidden city made of chinaware. This image of communication via images coming to life is developed to include the presence of mobile phones (with the Nightingale's image and song), webcams and computer screens – a modernisation that works through seamless integration with more traditional references. Relevant instruments of the orchestra are also frequently dropped into view as part of the digital landscape.

Wearing a selection of T-shirts that almost suggest a 1960s Bond girl, Natalie Dessay gives a mesmerising but never indulgent or twee performance as the Nightingale, sometimes with a real bird in the hand. Marie McLaughlin's Cook (who steers the Child through the dream) is equally comfortable and subtle on close-up camera, while Schagidullin, Mikhailov and Naouri exhibit much presence and facial dexterity. From all his players Chaudet has secured that deliberately unemotional and real acting that so distinguishes French (and American) cinema and is such an asset in music-theatre of this genre.

The DVD is of a high visual and sonic quality and (another rarity in opera releases) there are some worthwhile 'extras' not devoted to company promotion. These 'making of' features really show you something of how the film was technically achieved.

On the soundtrack (as we may now call it) James Conlon goes all out for a colour and bite that binds Stravinsky's 1908-09 Debussian Act 1 more closely to the 1913-14, post-*Rite of Spring* final acts than a trenchant, Boulezian approach might have done, although it is not the only way. The singing is first-rate (as was the language-coaching), seeming almost to have been achieved in anticipation of this outstanding film.

The Rake's Progress

The Rake's Progress
Ian Bostridge ten Tom Rakewell **Deborah York** sop
Anne **Bryn Terfel** bass-bar Nick Shadow **Anne Sofie
von Otter** mez Baba the Turk **Peter Bronder** ten
Sellem **Anne Howells** mez Mother Goose **Martin
Robson** bass Trulove **Julian Clarkson** bass Keeper of
the Madhouse **Monteverdi Choir; London
Symphony Orchestra / Sir John Eliot Gardiner**
DG ② 459 648-2GH2 (134' · DDD · T/t)   Ⓕ ⓄⓄ↦

Gardiner's *Rake's Progress*, in all but one respect, easily withstands comparison with its five rivals, and in several it surpasses them; if you're happy with Terfel's Nick Shadow, it can be set alongside Stravinsky's own 1964 recording as the finest available. Gardiner is conscious throughout that this is a chamber opera, and the orchestral textures are outstandingly clean and transparent, the rhythmic pointing crisp but airy. This enables his cast to give a fast-moving, conversational account of the text, with every word crystal-clear (including those from the chorus) and no need for any voice to force.

This benefits the soprano and tenor especially. Deborah York sounds a very young and touchingly vulnerable Anne; her voice may seem a little pale, but there's pathos as well as brilliance in her Act 1 aria, and the desolation of her reaction to Tom's marriage to Baba the Turk ('I see, then: it was I who was unworthy') is moving. Ian Bostridge is the best Tom Rakewell since Alexander Young in Stravinsky's recording: he too sounds likeably youthful, sings with intelligence and sweetness of tone and acts very well.

Howells is an unexaggerated Mother Goose, and von Otter's economy of comic gesture is a marvel. 'Finish, if you please, whatever business is detaining you with this person' receives the full Lady Bracknell treatment from most mezzos; von Otter gives it the vocal equivalent of a nose wrinkled in well-bred disdain. Terfel often demonstrates that he can fine his big voice down to the subtlety of the other principals, and when he does he's a formidably dangerous, insinuating Shadow. But almost as often he not only lets the voice rip but indulges in histrionics quite uncharacteristic of the performance as a whole. You may not mind: why after all should the Devil restrainedly under-act? At times, though, he sounds bigger than the orchestra. The recording is close but theatrically atmospheric. There are a few sound effects, though some may find the raucous owl in the graveyard scene distracting.

The Rake's Progress
Laura Claycomb sop Anne **Andrew Kennedy** ten
Tom Rakewell **William Shimell** bar Nick Shadow
Julianne Young mez Mother Goose **Dagmar**
Pecková mez Baba the Turk **Darren Jeffery** bass
Trulove **Donald J Byrne** ten Sellem **Shadi Torbey**
bass Keeper of the Madhouse
Chorus and Symphony Orchestra of La Monnaie –
De Bunt, Brussels / Kazushi Ono
Stage director **Robert Lepage**
Video director **Benoît Vlietinck**
Opus Arte ② *DVD* OA0991D (174' · NTSC · 16:9 ·
PCM stereo and DTS 5.1 · 0). Recorded live at the
Théâtre Royal de la Monnaie, Brussels, in April 2007.
Extra features include Illustrated Synopsis, Cast
Gallery, Interview with Robert Lepage, Insight into
rehearsals, costumes and make-up   Ⓕ**OO**

Auden first met Stravinsky to discuss the libretto of *The Rake's Progress* in Hollywood in 1947, and Robert Lepage winds forward his 'clock of fashion' to the time and place of the opera's composition. Hogarth's Gin Alley runs into Easy Street, populated by Vegas hookers, dancers and chancers. The composer-sanctioned division into two halves rather than three acts is a complementary move from the conventions of the opera house to the theatre, and what a show we have. Madam, or rather Mother Goose (Julianne Young, bearing a disconcerting resemblance to Julianne Moore), lures the naive Tom onto a heart-shaped satin bed, and the pair literally sink into its folds – before our hero re-emerges, worldly wise and weary, in front of a blow-up Winnebago, and banishes ennui not with mother's ruin but a line or two of Colombia's finest.

Andrew Kennedy takes all this in his stride, and his always fresh, appealing tenor ensures we retain our sympathy through Tom's piteous downfall from indolence to insanity, far more so than we are likely to for his operatic model, Ferrando. From Nick Shadow's first entrance under the shade of a Dallas derrick to his flame-capped

Broadway nemesis, the parallels are not with Dons Alfonso or Giovanni but rather Alberich. This is largely thanks to William Shimell's iron-black baritone and rasping wit, though lines such as 'That man alone is free who chooses what to will and wills his choice as destiny' certainly strike a Wagnerian ring of mania.

The recorded balance is slightly unfavourable to Laura Claycomb in 'I go to him': this is her 'Abscheulicher', but she is no Leonora, and is happiest vocally when she is dramatically downcast. The two crucial scenes, either side of the interval, between her, Tom and Dagmar Pecková's show-stealing Baba are models of ensemble writing and direction, pulling between operatic naturalism and Stravinsky's preferred realism just as Tom is torn between one woman and the other – and all in front of a chorus who change from waltz-time party guests to painfully well observed inhabitants of Bedlam with phenomenal assurance.

Doubtless Kazushi Ono must take credit for some slickly cinematic pacing. This is a show to be seen and, down to the witty, period and silent menu screens, a model of its kind.

Additional recommendation

The Rake's Progress   Ⓗ
Gueden Anne **Conley** Tom Rakewell **Harrell** Nick
Shadow **Thebom** Baba the Turk **Lipton** Mother
Goose **Scott** Trulove **Franke** Sellem **Metropolitan**
Opera Chor & Orch / Stravinsky
Naxos ② 8 111266/7 (146' · ADD · S/N)
Recorded 1953   Ⓢ**O**⚡

In February 1953, 17 months after the world premiere in Venice, *The Rake's Progress* received its first American production, conducted by Fritz Reiner. Less than a month later, this studio recording was made, with the smaller orchestra that Stravinsky envisaged. The cast is strong, though with more conventionally operatic qualities than would be favoured today. As Tom, Eugene Conley suggests ease in Verdi and Puccini rather than in Monteverdi, Mozart or Britten. But he brings much more than mere fecklessness to the character. It takes Baba the Turk and Sellem the Auctioneer to bring the opera back to life, and both performances here are admirable in avoiding excessive caricature. As Nick Shadow, Mack Harrell is almost too benign. Hilda Gueden, also on unfamiliar territory, manages the lullaby with touching simplicity.

Josef Suk   Bohemian 1874-1935

Suk studied at the Prague Conservatory with Dvořák (whose daughter he was to marry). Dvořák was a major influence on his early music but in his later works – above all in the vast symphony Asrael (1906), written under the impact of the deaths of his wife and his father-in-law – he developed a more personal style akin to Mahler's in structural mastery and emotional force. Other works include two published quartets (he was second violinist in the Czech Quartet for most of his life and played in over 4000 concerts), piano pieces and a group of symphonic poems, A Summer's Tale (1909), The Ripening (1917) and the choral-orchestral Epilog (1929). From 1922 he taught at the Prague Conservatory where his pupils included Bohuslav Martinů and Rudolf Firkušný.

Asrael, Op 27

Asrael
**Helsinki Philharmonic Orchestra /
Vladimir Ashkenazy**
Ondine ⑨ ODE1132-5 (62' · DDD/DSD) Ⓕ🅑➔

As Rafael Kubelík's uniquely powerful (and idiomatic) Bavarian Radio tape (see below) is currently elusive, there's certainly room for Ashkenazy's marginally fleeter, cleaner, texturally airier conception. He holds together the sometimes disjunct finale with skill, avoiding any hint of lassitude or bombast; the understated optimism and luminosity of the coda is most moving.

This hybrid SACD, a live recording from which applause has been excised, comes with helpful booklet-notes by Jan Smaczny. Helsinki's Finlandia Hall may look better than it sounds but its acoustic presents no problems to this production team.

Asrael
**Bavarian Radio Symphony Orchestra /
Rafael Kubelík**
Panton 81 1101-2 (64' · ADD). Recorded 1981 Ⓕ🅞🅞

To use large-scale symphonic form for the purging of deep personal grief carries the danger that the result will seriously lack discipline. In 1904-05 Suk's world was shattered by two visits from Asrael (the Angel of Death in Muslim mythology): he lost his father-in-law (and revered teacher) Dvořák, and his beloved wife, Otylka. Forgivably, Suk does perhaps linger a little too long in the fourth movement's gentle, mainly lyrical portrait of Otylka, but elsewhere the progress is as satisfying psychologically as it is symphonically. Much of the music has a concentrated dream-like quality; at the extremes, spectral nightmare visions merge with compensatory surges of lyrical ardour. Set Kubelík's reading alongside any of the other modern versions and one is immediately aware of a wholly compelling imaginative intensity and interpretative flair that betoken a true poet of the rostrum. Kubelík's control throughout is awesome and he conjures up playing of enormous expressive subtlety from his fine Munich orchestra. No other recorded performance – not even Václav Talich's legendary 1952 Supraphon account – succeeds in conveying the intensely personal nature of this music with such devastating emotional candour. Technically, too, one need have no qualms about this Panton disc – the Bavarian Radio engineers secure most truthful results.

Sir Arthur Sullivan   British 1842-1900

If ever a composer was born with a musical silver spoon in his mouth it was Sullivan, the son of an Irish bandmaster. By eight he could play every instrument in the band and became a chorister in the Chapel Royal when he was 12. His first composition was published the following year and aged 14 he won the newly established Mendelssohn Scholarship against stiff competition. This won him three years' study in Leipzig – his piano teacher was Moscheles, he met Liszt and Grieg – and when he returned to London his incidental music for The Tempest made him famous overnight. By the time his cantata Kenilworth had been performed at the 1864 Birmingham Festival, Sullivan had been marked out as a composer of the first rank. He looked set to become the first English composer of any importance since Purcell.

It didn't happen for, as the world knows, he was introduced to a writer and librettist called William Schwenk Gilbert, and his name is indissolubly linked with his as surely as Rolls with Royce and Fortnum with Mason. The first operetta Sullivan wrote was Box and Cox – not with Gilbert but with FC Burnand – and the famous team's first collaboration in 1871 was not a success (the score of Thespis has disappeared off the face of the earth). The impresario Richard D'Oyly Carte brought them together again four years later and the result was Trial By Jury, a one-act skit on the legal system (and the only one of their operettas with no spoken dialogue). From there the run of successes was extraordinary, comic operettas which retain their freshness and popularity to this day. They made Gilbert and Sullivan very famous and very rich, each earning an income of over £10,000 a year, twice as much as the Prime Minister, Mr Gladstone. Only Princess Ida (1884) Utopia Limited (1893) and The Grand Duke (1896) were less than box-office hits but, by the end, the two had lost their will to work together – or rather put up with each other. Though they had much mutual respect for each other's gifts, the two men were as different as chalk and cheese – Sullivan the charming and elegant society man, befriended by royalty, and Gilbert the acerbic, gruff egotistical man of the theatre, never happier when there was a visit to the law courts in the offing.

Sullivan's health was never good. In 1892 he was reported to be dying while holidaying in Cannes and was brought back to convalesce at Sandringham with his friends the Prince and Princess of Wales. When he died of pneumonia in the last weeks of 1900 he was only 58. He was buried in St Paul's Cathedral.

Symphony in E, 'Irish'

Symphony in E, 'Irish'. The Tempest – Suite.
Overture in C, 'In memoriam'
BBC Philharmonic Orchestra / Richard Hickox
Chandos CHAN9859 (75' · DDD) Ⓕ🅑➔

Plaudits all round to Richard Hickox and his excellent Manchester band (and the Chandos production team) for at last granting Sullivan's

Irish Symphony the first wholly recommendable digital recording it so richly deserves. And what a charmer of a work it is! Mendelssohn (and his *Reformation* Symphony above all) provides the dominant stylistic template, but the work is soundly constructed, effectively scored, and the *Scherzo*'s irresistibly perky oboe tune, in particular, already reveals a very real melodic gift. Hickox observes the first-movement repeat, but his direction is highly imaginative and he never allows tensions to sag. What's more, the playing of the BBC Philharmonic ideally combines bright-eyed affection, keen vigour and nimble polish.

The sudden death of his father just a few weeks before the symphony's successful March 1866 premiere jolted Sullivan into penning the likeable overture, *In memoriam*. In terms of inventive freshness and orchestral scope it's rather trumped by the astonishingly confident incidental music for Shakespeare's *The Tempest* that Sullivan had written while still a student at the Leipzig Conservatory. Again, Hickox and company do plentiful justice to Sullivan's precocious inspiration.

Overtures

Overtures – Cox and Box; The Sorcerer; HMS Pinafore; The Pirates of Penzance; Patience; Iolanthe; Princess Ida; The Mikado; Ruddigore (arr Toye); The Yeomen of the Guard; The Gondoliers; The Grand Duke
Royal Ballet Sinfonia / Andrew Penny
Naxos 8 554165 (70' · DDD)

The first thing that sets this apart from other collections of Sullivan overtures is that – for the first time – it covers the entire Gilbert and Sullivan output. The only works that are missing are *Thespis*, *Trial by Jury* and *Utopia Limited*, none of which had overtures as such. The sensible addition of the overture to *Cox and Box* means that all the Sullivan comic operas likely to be of interest to the general collector are here. An even more intelligent feature is that they're presented in chronological order, so that one can chart the progression of Sullivan's comic opera style from the very French-sounding ending of *Cox and Box* and the equally French-sounding opening of *The Sorcerer* through to more distinctively Sullivanesque sounds of the later pieces.

None of this would count for much if the performances weren't up to scratch. Happily they're models of their kind. Andrew Penny has an agreeably light touch, alternatively reflective and sparkling, and gets graceful phrasing from the Royal Ballet Sinfonia – ideal performers of light music. Nobody wanting a collection of Sullivan's comic opera overtures need look elsewhere.

Pineapple Poll

Pineapple Poll (arr Mackerras). 'Irish' Symphony
Royal Liverpool Philharmonic Orchestra / David Lloyd-Jones

Naxos 8 570351 (78' · DDD)

A coupling of these works has never appeared before. Yet Mackerras's medley of Savoy melodies provides an ideal appetiser for Sullivan's *Irish* Symphony, distinguished by delightfully easy-going charm and lightness of touch. Mackerras recorded *Pineapple Poll* complete three times, the versions marked more by progressive improvements in sound quality than by changes in interpretation. If Lloyd-Jones shaves the odd second or two off Mackerras's timings for individual movements, it's due as much as anything to the latter's greater flexibility in allowing the score to unfold. Lloyd-Jones is less successful, too, in drawing out the individual themes of the elaborately woven score.

The Symphony is a different matter. This new version is an improvement both interpretatively and sonically on the pioneering Groves version, one that also lacks the first movement's exposition repeat. More particularly, Lloyd-Jones has the edge on Hickox and the BBC Philharmonic (Chandos – above) in the natural unfolding and emotional contrasts of the work. There's a more inherent urgency to the outer movements and greater attention to instrumental detail throughout. The second movement is especially beautifully done. Even for those who have an earlier version there's a strong case for this inexpensive newcomer. For those who don't, the recommendation is a clear one.

Ivanhoe

Ivanhoe
Toby Spence ten Wilfred, Knight of Ivanhoe
Geraldine McGreevy sop Rebecca **James Rutherford** bar Sir Brian de Bois-Guilbert **Janice Watson** sop The Lady Rowena **Catherine Wyn-Rogers** mez Ulrica **Peter Wedd** ten Maurice de Bracy **Andrew Staples** ten Locksley, The Squire **Peter Rose** bass Cedric the Saxon **Neal Davies** bar Richard Coeur-de-Lion **Matthew Brook** bass-bar Friar Tuck **Stephen Gadd** bar Prince John, Lucas de Beaumanoir **Leigh Melrose** bar Isaac, the Jew of York **Adrian Partington Singers / BBC National Orchestra of Wales / David Lloyd-Jones**
Chandos ② CHAN10578 (165' · DDD)

Sullivan's take on Scott's epic historical novel was his bid to escape the shackles of popular musical theatre and Gilbertian librettos. No more than Britten 60 years later did Sullivan strive to be at the cutting edge of operatic form – rather to extend the English Romantic opera tradition. More particularly, he had to achieve commercial success for Richard D'Oyly Carte's new opera house at London's Cambridge Circus – today's Palace Theatre. So brilliantly did Sullivan succeed that the opera achieved a remarkable 155 consecutive performances – though it failed in Berlin and was staged nowhere else outside Britain.

That this first fully professional recording so clearly outclasses two previous semi-professional efforts is due above all to David Lloyd-Jones's dramatic pacing. The three key roles are well cast. Toby Spence admirably balances heroic and lyrical demands, culminating in a fine Act 3 solo 'Come gentle sleep'. James Rutherford as Sir Brian de Bois-Guilbert and Geraldine McGreevy as Rebecca combine to bring the most out of Act 2 scene 3 – the opera's musical high-point. There is writing of a greater emotional intensity than Sullivan ever produced elsewhere, with two fine solos – the Templar's 'Woo thou thy snowflake' and Rebecca's 'Lord of our chosen race'.

The opera has its shortcomings. Armed combat takes place off-stage to a running commentary on-stage, and the ending is contrived. Altogether, the action moves quickly, and prior knowledge of Scott's novel is advantageous – even if gained through Hollywood or television adaptation. Yet, as an operatic representation of the novel it is a remarkable achievement, with striking vocal writing, rousing choruses and superb orchestration for forces undreamt of for the Savoy Operas. Chandos's recording has the orchestra at times a shade backward. However, nobody interested in British opera should miss this opportunity to hear a work that represents a milestone in British operatic history.

Operettas written with WS Gilbert

The Gondoliers. Overture di ballo (1870 version)
Richard Suart bar Duke of Plaza-Toro **Philip Creasey** ten Luiz **John Rath** bass Don Alhambra **David Fieldsend** ten Marco **Alan Oke** bar Giuseppe **Tim Morgan** bar Antonio **David Cavendish** ten Francesco **Toby Barrett** bass Giorgio **Jill Pert** contr Duchess of Plaza-Toro **Elizabeth Woollett** sop Casilda **Lesley Echo Ross** sop Gianetta **Regina Hanley** mez Tessa **Yvonne Patrick** sop Fiametta **Pamela Baxter** mez Vittoria **Elizabeth Elliott** sop Giulia **Claire Kelly** contr Inez **D'Oyly Carte Opera Chorus and Orchestra / John Pryce-Jones**
TER ② CDTER2 1187 (109' · DDD)   Ⓕ

This is one of a series of recordings by the new D'Oyly Carte Opera Company that offers a vastly better quality of sound than any of its ageing competitors. Orchestral detail is the most immediate beneficiary, and the overture serves to demonstrate John Pryce-Jones's lively tempi and lightness of touch. Outstanding among the singers are perhaps John Rath, who gives Don Alhambra's 'I stole the prince' and 'There lived a king' real presence, and Jill Pert, a formidable Duchess of Plaza-Toro. Richard Suart not only provides the leading comedy roles with exceptionally clear articulation and musicality, but also adds considerable character to his portrayals. David Fieldsend and Alan Oke provide attractive portrayals of the two gondoliers, and Lesley Echo Ross and Regina Hanley are also most agreeable.

Seasoned listeners may note numerous changes of detail as a result of the purging of the performance material of changes made to the parts around the time of the 1920s Savoy Theatre revivals. There's no dialogue, but added value is provided by Sullivan's sunniest comic opera score being accompanied by the sparkling *Overture di ballo*, played in its original version with some traditional cuts opened up.

HMS Pinafore
Richard Suart bass Sir Joseph Porter **Felicity Palmer** mez Little Buttercup **Rebecca Evans** sop Josephine **Thomas Allen** bar Captain Corcoran **Michael Schade** ten Ralph Rackstraw **Donald Adams** bass Dick Deadeye **Valerie Seymour** sop Hebe **Richard Van Allan** bass Bill Bobstay **John King, Philip Lloyd-Evans** bars Bob Becket **Welsh National Opera Chorus and Orchestra / Sir Charles Mackerras**
Telarc CD80374 (74' · DDD · N/T)   Ⓕ ❂❂

As always, Mackerras keeps the livelier numbers moving along comfortably without ever a hint of rushing, while giving full weight to the tender moments and, above all, caressing all the details of Sullivan's delicious orchestration.

Right from the Overture, with its beautifully shaped *Andante* section, this is music-making to perfection. Of the singers, Felicity Palmer's Buttercup truly oozes plumpness and pleasure, while Thomas Allen's Captain doesn't just do the crew of the *Pinafore* proud, but all of us. If Rebecca Evans's Josephine is a shade lacking in colour, Mackerras has found in Michael Schade's Ralph Rackstraw a most elegant addition to his G&S team. As for Richard Suart's Sir Joseph Porter, this is surely as stylish a demonstration of patter singing as one can find anywhere on disc, while Donald Adams's Dick Deadeye is no worse for his 40-odd years singing the role.

Add orchestral playing of refinement, choral work whose perfection extends from the formal numbers to the varied inflexions of 'What nevers?', plus a recording that brings out the instrumental detail to perfection, and one has a *Pinafore* that's unadulterated delight from first note to last.

The Mikado
John Holmes bass The Mikado **John Wakefield** ten Nanki-Poo **Clive Revill** bar Ko-Ko **Denis Dowling** bar Pooh-Bah **John Heddle Nash** bar Pish-Tush **Marion Studholme** sop Yum-Yum **Patricia Kern** mez Pitti-Sing **Dorothy Nash** sop Peep-Bo **Jean Allister** mez Katisha.
Iolanthe – excerpts **Elizabeth Harwood, Elizabeth Robson, Cynthia Morey** sops **Heather Begg, Patricia Kern** mezzos **Stanley Bevan** ten **Eric Shilling, Denis Dowling, Julian Moyle** bars **Leon Greene** bass **Sadler's Wells Opera Chorus and Orchestra / Alexander Faris**
Classics for Pleasure ② 575990-2 (135' · ADD)
Recorded 1962   Ⓑ ❂❂

At the core of these performances are some of the finest British singers of the time, who were all chosen not just for their singing but for their sense of the theatricality and humour of Gilbert and Sullivan. Just listen, for instance, to how John Heddle Nash gives full expression to every word of Pish-Tush's 'Our great Mikado'. Here, too, is Marion Studholme's delicious Yum-Yum and Elizabeth Harwood's joyous Phyllis.

If one singles out Clive Revill for special mention, it's because his Ko-Ko is uniquely well judged and imaginative, combining superb comic timing, verbal clarity and vocal dexterity. His 'little list' is hilarious, and you can almost feel your hand gripped at the words 'shake hands with you *like that*'. At the helm in both works is Alexander Faris who knew supremely well how to capture the lightness and sparkle of operetta. The new Overture put together for *The Mikado* may come as a surprise, but it's apt and cleverly done. The sound is inevitably dated when compared with more recent recordings, but it scarcely mars the enjoyment.

Additional recommendation

Adams The Mikado **Rolfe Johnson** Nanki-Poo **Suart** Ko-Ko **Van Allen** Pooh-Bah **McLaughlin** Yum-Yum **Howells** Pitti-Sing **Palmer** Katisha **Welsh National Opera Chorus and Orchestra / Mackerras**
Telarc CD80284 (79' · ADD)   Ⓕ
   A delicious Nanki-Poo and a magnificent Katisha.

The Pirates of Penzance
Eric Roberts bar Major-General Stanley **Malcolm Rivers** bar Pirate King **Gareth Jones** bar Samuel **Philip Creasy** ten Frederic **Simon Masterton-Smith** bass Sergeant of Police **Marilyn Hill Smith** sop Mabel **Patricia Cameron** sop Edith **Pauline Birchall** mez Kate **Susan Gorton** contr Ruth **D'Oyly Carte Opera Chorus and Orchestra / John Pryce-Jones**
TER ② CDTER2 1177 (85' · DDD)   Ⓕ

The revival of the D'Oyly Carte Opera Company produced the first digital recordings of complete Gilbert and Sullivan scores, and this TER set is a very happy example. Philip Creasy is an engaging and vocally secure Frederic, and Marilyn Hill Smith trips through 'Poor wandering one' with a delectable display of vocal ability and agility. The couple's interplay with the chorus in 'How beautifully blue the sky' is quite enchanting, and their exchanges in 'Stay, Frederic, stay' splendidly convincing. Eric Roberts makes the Major-General a thoroughly engaging personality, and the dotty exchanges between Simon Masterson-Smith's Sargeant of Police and his police force are sheer joy. Even such details as the girls' screams at the appearance of the pirates in Act 1 have a rare effectiveness. John Pryce-Jones keeps the score dancing along. Those who want the dialogue as well as the music must look elsewhere, but this is certainly to be recommended.

The Yeomen of the Guard
Peter Savidge bar Sir Richard Cholmondeley **Neill Archer** ten Colonel Fairfax **Donald Adams** bass Sergeant Meryll **Peter Hoare** ten Leonard **Richard Suart** bar Jack Point **Donald Maxwell** bar Shadbolt **Alwyn Mellor** sop Elsie **Pamela Helen Stephen** mez Phoebe **Felicity Palmer** mez Dame Carruthers **Clare O'Neill** sop Kate **Ralph Mason** ten First Yeoman **Peter Lloyd Evans** bar Second Yeoman

Trial by Jury
Rebecca Evans sop Plaintiff **Barry Banks** ten Defendant **Richard Suart** bar Judge **Peter Savidge** bar Counsel **Donald Adams** bass Usher **Gareth Rhys-Davies** bar Foreman **Welsh National Opera Chorus and Orchestra / Sir Charles Mackerras**
Telarc ② CD80404 (121' · DDD · N/T)   Ⓕ●

Between them, *The Yeomen of the Guard* and *Trial by Jury* contain all that's best in Sullivan's music for the theatre. In the former there's some of his more serious and ambitious writing, in the latter some of his most consistently light-hearted and engaging. All of this is brought out in Telarc's series of recordings with Welsh National Opera. As always, Sir Charles Mackerras paces the music impeccably, and he has assured contributions from such stalwarts as Donald Adams, Felicity Palmer and Richard Suart. The last-named may be a shade light-voiced compared with some of the more comic performers of Jack Point and the Learned Judge; but in *The Yeomen* it's surely his performance that stands out. His handling of the dialogue after 'Here's a man of jollity' is masterly, and his 'Oh, a private buffoon' is as winning as any, with impeccable clarity of diction and a perfectly judged French accent for 'jests… imported from France'.

Neill Archer and Alwyn Mellor are admirable as Fairfax and Elsie; but Pamela Helen Stephen could have displayed more of the minx in Phoebe Meryll's personality, while in *Trial by Jury* Barry Banks has too small a voice to convince as the Defendant. Recommended, especially if you want both works on the same set.

Giles Swayne   British b1946

Swayne, with encouragement from his cousin Elizabeth Maconchy, started composing at an early age. At Cambridge he studied with Nicholas Maw; he then won a scholarship to the Royal Academy of Music. He was on the staff at Glyndebourne – working as a répétiteur – in the early 1970s before embarking full-time as a composer. His huge choral work CRY was premiered in 1980 and has been performed the world over. Since then he has produced a steady stream of work accross all genres to considerable acclaim.

Chamber Works

Cello Sonata, Op 103ᵃ. Four Lyrical Pieces, Op 6ᵃ. Suite No 1, Op 111. Canto, Op 31

Robert Irvine vc [a]**Fali Pavrí** pf
Delphian DCD34073 (70' · DDD)　　　　　Ⓕ

Superbly played by the Glasgow-based duo of
Robert Irvine and Fali Pavrí, this survey of Giles
Swayne's compositions for solo cello and cello
and piano is recorded with trademark spaciousness and clarity, and has the added appeal of
including two of Swayne's most recent large-
scale compositions.

The Cello Sonata (2006) proclaims its ambitions with a 15-minute first movement called
'Turbulence', which challenges the listener's
sense of stylistic stability as it explores a welter of
conflicting ideas. At once beholden to and
resisting tradition, its tone of rhapsodic spontaneity – ironic? celebratory? – involves a protracted tussle with conventional ideas of coherence. But the three remaining movements
imaginatively complement all this agitation, and
the finale – 'Threnody' – is a richly conceived set
of variations that somehow manages to balance
out the earlier conflicts without any risk of
dumbing down.

Your response to the solo Suite No 1 (2007),
will depend on your attitude to its way with historical allusion. It's as if Swayne's response to
the august opus number involved prompted him
to opt for a whimsical embrace of those musical
memories which can never be entirely eliminated, especially in solo cello music: but the
piece's jokey scenario seems more than a touch
complacent.

Set against this very recent work we have one
of Swayne's earliest. *Four Lyrical Pieces* (1970) is
a resourceful student effort, occasionally diffuse
but showing purposeful engagement with the
most potent trends of the time. Finally, *Canto*
for solo cello (1981) is a full-on response to
Swayne's experience of African musics. Minimalist in some ways, quite complex in others, it
projects that positive tone and enquiring spirit
which represent this composer at his considerable best.

Choral Works

Magnificat, Op 33[e]. Missa Tiburtina[e]. The Coming
of Saskia Hawkins, Op 51[c]. The Tiglet, Op 68[ad].
Four Passiontide Motets – Vidit suum dulcem
natum[e]; Eia, mater![d]; Fac me cruce custodiri[e];
Dona nobis pacem[e]. A Convocation of Worms[ac].
Winter Solstice Carol[bd]. Midwinter[d]
[a]**Stephen Wallace** counterten [b]**Philippa Davies** fl
[c]**Michael Bonaventure** org [d]**Laudibus**; [e]**National
Youth Choir of Great Britain / Michael Brewer**
Delphian DCD34033 (79' · DDD · T/t)　　　　Ⓕ

Giles Swayne's *A Convocation of Worms* (1995) is
a 20-minute cantata for countertenor and organ
setting a thoroughly alarming 15th-century text,
adapted from the Coventry miracle plays, in
which Death, appearing at Herod's court after
the massacre of the innocents, effects instant
retribution, declaring that 'where I smite, there
is no grace'. This stark mixture of menace and

lament is a gift for a composer with Swayne's
propensity for questioning received social and
religious conventions from the inside, and even
if the austerity of the work's central stages risks
some loss of impact, the effect of the whole is
powerful and memorable. Stephen Wallace and
Michael Bonaventure do it proud, and it's
recorded, like everything on the disc, in a spacious acoustic which doesn't compromise clarity
of texture.

One short, bold organ piece apart, the rest of
the music is choral, and includes three of
Swayne's most attractive successes: *Magnificat*,
The Tiglet (that is, Blake's 'The Tyger'), and
Missa Tiburtina. The National Youth Choir of
Great Britain and its offshoot Laudibus tackle
this music with enormous energy and skill.
There is less to enjoy in *Midwinter* – setting
Christina Rossetti's cringingly sentimental verse
in 2003 might be thought a touch eccentric – but
the *Four Passiontide Motets* include some of
Swayne's most cogent musical imagery and
abound in imaginative textures. A highly com-
mendable enterprise.

Jan Pieterszoon Sweelinck
Dutch 1562-1621

*Sweelinck studied with his father, organist of the
Oude Kerk, Amsterdam, succeeding him in about
1580. He remained in this post all his life, with a few
excursions to inspect new organs in other cities.
Among the most influential and sought-after teachers of his time, he included Germans among his
pupils, notably Scheidt, Jacob Praetorius and Schei-
demann. He wrote over 250 vocal works but he is best
known for his c70 keyboard works, which include
monumental fugal fantasias, concise toccatas and
well-ordered variation sets. He represents the highest
development of the Dutch keyboard school, and indeed
represented a pinnacle in keyboard contrapuntal
complexity and refinement before JS Bach.*

Keyboard Works

Complete Keyboard Works
**Freddy Eichelberger, Liuwe Tamminga, Leo van
Doeselaar, Pieter van Dijk, Bernard Winsemius,
Reinhard Jaud, Stef Tuinstra, Bert Matter, Vincent
van de Laar** orgs **Glen Wilson, Siebe Henstra,
Menno van Delft, Pieter Dirksen, Bob van
Asperen, Pieter-Jan Belder** hpds
NM Classics ⑨ NM92119 (10h 29' · DDD)　　　Ⓑ

The fact that no fewer than 15 musicians
(nearly all Sweelinck's countrymen) have contributed to this complete keyboard project in
no way lessens the impressiveness of what has
been achieved here. Led by Pieter Dirksen and
Pieter van Dijk, they get through nearly 90
pieces (some of which are heard more than
once on organ and on harpsichord). This complete edition rests on sound and fresh scholar-

ship, and is laid out in an engaging and informative manner. Each artist contributes a recital intended to stand on its own, usually on the same instrument.

Fourteen organs from the 16th and 17th centuries, and three harpsichords, are heard over the course of 10 and a half hours. The harpsichords are an original by Johannes Ruckers, and two recent copies of other instruments also by him. But it's the organs that steal the show: spread across three countries, several still close to original condition, their individual characteristics and the acoustics of their respective churches make for endlessly absorbing listening. As an anthology of great early organs this set would be worth recommending. The fact that here they're pressed into serving music of such sustained quality only increases their impact. For there's no doubting Sweelinck's variety, charm and infinite resource. He touched all the significant genres of the keyboard repertory of his day (toccatas, fantasias, dance movements, variation sets, ricercars).

Sweelinck needs no advocacy beyond the performances themselves; rather, it's the consistency of these performances that concerns us here. That consistency would be impressive had it originated with a single interpreter, but given the number of participants it's equally remarkable. It's all very impressive. What more could one want?

Esce mars, Sw3 No 3. Fantasia crommatica. Mein junges Leben hat ein Endt. Unter der Linden grune. Pavana lachrimae. Pavana Philippi. Die flichtig Nimphae. Allemand (Gratie). Toccata noni toni, SwWV297. Toccata, C2. Toccata primi toni, d2, SwWV286. Toccata a 3, SwWV289. Toccata secundi toni, g1, SwWV292. Von der Fortuna werd ich getrieben, Sw3 No 2.
Robert Woolley hpd/virg
Chandos CHAN0758 (64' · DDD)

What a fine composer Sweelinck was! This volume drives the point home by presenting several of his best compositions, including the imaginatively patterned variations on *Esce mars* and *Unter der Linden grune*, the weighty and implacable *Fantasia crommatica* (how Bach would surely have admired this piece) and the hauntingly beautiful variations on *Mein junges Leben hat ein Endt*. Other works here include a take on Peter Philips's *Pavana dolorosa*, a lovingly plumped-up version of Dowland's *Lachrymae*, and a handful of improvisatory toccatas. Sweelinck brings together in his music many of the influences current in the first years of the 17th century – Italian flair, north European seriousness, English resonance and melodic grace – and makes of them a rich and rewarding brew, maintaining coherence by the force of his own good taste and sound compositional judgement.

Robert Woolley switches between two marvellous harpsichords – Malcolm Rose's currently much-in-demand copy of the Victoria and Albert Museum's 1579 Theewes claviorganum,

and a deep and mellow copy by Derek Adlam of a 1611 Ruckers virginals. His playing, too, covers most bases. Without forcing the pace, he shows brilliant fingerwork in *Esce mars* or a piece like the Toccata C2, and achieves clarity and composure in the more melodically driven works. The toccatas occupy a convincing middle ground between the improvisatory and the written-out in feel, and tempi are for the most part expertly judged. In other words, these are pleasingly natural performances. There is not much competition in the world of Sweelinck recordings, but this stands out as an excellent harpsichord release in its own right.

Organ Works

Toccata in C. Ballo del granduca. Ricercar. Malle Sijmen. Mein junges Leben hat ein Endt. Aeolian Echo Fantasia. Onder een linde groen. Toccata in A minor I. Erbarm dich mein, o Herre Gott. Poolsche dans
James David Christie org
Naxos 8 550904 (64' · DDD). Played on the CB Fisk Organ, Houghton Chapel, Wellesley College, USA

The Houghton Chapel is nowhere near as resonantly spacious as the Oude Kerk in Amsterdam, but its relative intimacy doesn't rob the organ of its natural resonance and tonal beauty. James David Christie presents what's in effect a most satisfactory re-creation of one of Sweelinck's organ recitals, given daily between 1580 and 1621, for the burghers of Amsterdam. One hopes they were appreciative of the most consistently witty and generous-spirited keyboard music before the era of Buxtehude, Couperin and Bach.

While Christie may not possess the lyricism of a Leonhardt, the humane warmth of a Piet Kee or the mercurial whimsy of a Koopman, he is, in his own right, a bold, stylish, unhasty player, clearly thoroughly versed in early performance practice, with an incisive technique disclosing musical intelligence and common sense. He's particularly successful in the five major variation sets here, relishing the variety of decorative motifs but still conveying an impression of structural coherence and unity. Just occasionally his articulation might have worked better in a somewhat larger acoustic: at times a more obviously singing touch might have suggested greater tenderness in quieter moments and more ample majesty in louder ones.

Nevertheless, with appealing registrations, an almost ideal choice of programme and undistractingly natural recording this is recommended.

Karol Szymanowski   Polish 1882-1937

Szymanowski was born into a wealthy land-owning Polish gentry family in Tymoszówka, then in the Russian Empire, now in Ukraine. He studied music privately with his father before going to Gustav Neu-

haus's Elizavetgrad School of Music from 1892. From 1901 he attended the State Conservatory in Warsaw, of which he was later director (1926-30). He travelled widely throughout Europe, North Africa, the Middle East and the USA. These travels, especially those to the Mediterranean area, provided much inspiration. The fruits of these trips included not only musical works (notably the opera King Roger), but poetry and his novel on Greek love Efebos, parts of which were subsequently lost in a fire in 1939.

Szymanowski was influenced by the music of Wagner, Richard Strauss, Reger, Scriabin and the impressionism of Debussy and Ravel. He also drew much influence from his countryman Chopin and from Polish folk music. He died in a sanatorium in Lausanne from tuberculosis.

Violin Concertos

No 1 Op 35; **No 2** Op 61

Violin Concertos Nos 1 & 2. Three Paganini Caprices, Op 40. Romance in D, Op 23
Thomas Zehetmair vn **Silke Avenhaus** pf
**City of Birmingham Symphony Orchestra /
Sir Simon Rattle**
EMI 503429-2 (65' · DDD)   Ⓕ**ОOOⒹ**

They make an admirable coupling, the two Szymanowski violin concertos, but a demanding one for the soloist. They are both so beautiful that it must be tempting to embellish both with a similarly glowing tone. They inhabit quite different worlds (they were written 16 years apart) and Zehetmair shows how well they respond to quite different approaches.

In the First, after a rapt solo entry, he uses for the most part a lovely but delicate tone, expanding to athletic incisiveness but not often to lushness. It all fits very well with Rattle's handling of the orchestra: occasionally full and rich but mostly a sequence of exquisitely balanced chamber ensembles. Generous but finely controlled *rubato* from both soloist and conductor allows the concerto's improvisatory fantasy to flower; and the quiet close even has a touch of wit to it.

Zehetmair's sound even is immediately less ethereal, more robust, for the opening melody of the Second Concerto. This is the sort of tone, you suspect, that he would use in Bartók's Second Concerto, and it points up a vein of Bartókian strength to this work's longer and firmer lines. Rattle, too, seeks out bolder and more dense colours.

The *Paganini Caprices* were equipped by Szymanowski not with deferential accompaniments but with independent and quite freely composed piano parts. They change Paganini, even where the violin part is unmodified, into a late-Romantic virtuoso, with a hint of Lisztian poetry alongside the expertly pointed-up fireworks of the 24th Caprice; even here Zehetmair is a listening violinist, not one to upstage his excellent pianist. The *Romance*, the warmest and most luscious piece here, is beautifully done but

with a touch of restraint to prevent it cloying. A first-class coupling, and a recording that makes the most of the superb acoustic of Symphony Hall in Birmingham.

Violin Concertos Nos 1 & 2. Nocturne and Tarantella, Op 28 (orch Fitelberg)
Ilya Kaler vn
Warsaw Philharmonic Orchestra / Antoni Wit
Naxos 8 557981 (60' · DDD)   Ⓢ**ОⒹ**

Naxos offers an exceptionally clear recording of these three *concertante* works by Szymanowski, not just the two violin concertos but an orchestrated version of the *Nocturne and Tarantella*. Ilya Kaler, as on his other Naxos discs, gives pure, clear readings with flawless intonation and careful use of vibrato. Having a Polish conductor and orchestra as his accompanists adds to the idiomatic feel of each, with the magical orchestral sounds beautifully conjured up, particularly in No 1, the more radical of the two works.

Kaler is a degree warmer with a shade more vibrato than some interpreters, and the Naxos recording brings out the fantasy of the composer's orchestration, particularly in No 1, with wonderful clarity. In the more openly lyrical Second Concerto, Kaler adopts more flowing speeds with lighter results.

Kaler then plays the relatively brief *Nocturne and Tarantella* just as sympathetically, with the *Tarantella* a flamboyant virtuoso vehicle making a splendid climax to an excellent disc.

Szymanowski Violin Concertos Nos 1 & 2[a]
Britten Violin Concerto, Op 15[b]
Frank Peter Zimmermann vn [a]**Warsaw Philharmonic Orchestra / Antoni Wit;** [b]**Swedish Radio Symphony Orchestra / Manfred Honeck**
Sony Classical 88697 43999-2 (76' · DDD)   Ⓕ**ОOⒹ**

Frank Peter Zimmermann's coupling of the Szymanowski concertos enters what is fast becoming a highly competitive field. Fortunately these urgently expressive, cogent and polished performances more than hold their own. Backed by a notably willing Warsaw Philharmonic under Antoni Wit's watchful lead, Zimmermann plays with flawless technique, ravishing poise and subtle range of colour. These are readings of strong personality, gutsy temperament and full-throated ardour. The captivating First Concerto is as passionate, sensuous and poetic as one could wish, and Wit conducts with even greater freedom and insight than on his admirable Naxos recording with Ilya Kaler (see above). Zimmermann displays a comparable empathy for the altogether earthier Second Concerto, comprehensively attuned to the ruddy vigour, yearning lyricism and raw emotion of this exhilarating score. Biggest climaxes bring a hint of glare; otherwise, the solo balance is most cannily judged.

The Britten is scarcely less impressive, at just under half an hour the swiftest rendering since

Ida Haendel's outstanding 1977 version with Berglund and the Bournemouth SO (EMI) – and, it must be said, more convincingly held together than many. Once again, Zimmermann is fortunate indeed in receiving such sympathetic support as that provided by Manfred Honeck and the Swedish RSO. The full-bodied sound here gives little cause for complaint. All told, an absorbing and thoroughly commendable release.

Symphonies

No 1 in F minor, Op 15; **No 2** in B flat, Op 19; **No 3** (The Song of the Night), Op 27; **No 4** (Symphonie concertante), Op 60

Symphonies – Nos 1 & 4[a]. Etude, Op 4 No 3 (orch Fitelberg). Concert Overture, Op 12
[a]**Jan Krzysztof Broja** pf **Warsaw Philharmonic Orchestra / Antoni Wit**
Naxos 8 570722 (67' · DDD)

The early *Concert Overture*, son of *Rosenkavalier* and proud of it, is resplendently played here, only at rare moments craving a more glamorous sound stage. And the over-heated two-movement First Symphony, which the composer himself described as a 'contrapuntal-harmonic-orchestral monstrosity' and withdrew after its premiere, emerges as far more purposeful and less rebarbative than any of the admittedly few rival versions that have come and gone over the years.

As a listening experience the Fourth Symphony is initially somewhat more problematic, in that the opening pages (surely the model for Bartók's Third Piano Concerto) suffer from slight intonation problems between the *concertante* piano and the orchestra. But with a bit of acclimatisation, helped by the firm and affectionate shaping of the performance, this proves to be liveable with. Jan Krzysztof Broda seems to grow in stature through the rhapsodic slow movement, and he never loses the thread in the finale's Ravelian and Prokofievian deviations.

All in all, it would take significantly greater financial outlay to find anything better than this, and even then the differences would be marginal.

Symphonies – Nos 2 & 3[a]
[a]**Ryszard Minkiewicz** ten **Warsaw Philharmonic Choir and Orchestra / Antoni Wit**
Naxos 8 570721 (61' · DDD)

Antoni Wit conducts his Warsaw forces in exceptionally warm and idiomatic performances of these two exotic symphonies, vividly recorded. They make an important addition to the Naxos catalogue. The more immediately attractive is No 3, subtitled *Song of the Night*, with its tenor solo and chorus adding to its impact. The poem which the tenor sings has the refrain 'Do not sleep friend' and builds to the most powerful climax with Szymanowski's love of exotic orchestral colours exploited to the full. The

thrust and passion of Wit's performance, splendidly supported by the clear-voiced tenor and the chorus, is impossible to resist, and leads to a second movement with hints of birdsong followed by a slow finale, a deep meditation.

The performance of No 2 in two movements, an opening *Allegro* followed by an extended set of variations, is equally persuasive. Again the first movement is passionate and thrustful and the variations bring some fascinating contrasts, ending with a powerful fugue. Antoni Wit's performance could not be more idiomatic, with singers and players totally inside the music. An outstanding issue.

String Quartets

Szymanowski String Quartets – No 1, Op 37; No 2, Op 56 **Rózycki** String Quartet, Op 49
Royal Quartet (Izabella Szałaj-Zimak, Elwira Przybyłowska vns Marek Czech va Michał Pepol vc)
Hyperion CDA67684 (70' · DDD)

This is what Szymanowski needs: firm, full-bodied playing, with a wide range of dynamic, colour and attack, and with all the unexpected twists and turns confidently negotiated. The Royal Quartet are as finely tuned to his quirkiness as to his trademark voluptuous post-Impressionism and moments of mystic withdrawal or volatile transition. In every way this makes a persuasive bid for best available version.

Ludomir Rózycki was two years younger than Szymanowski, with whom he co-founded the group that came to be known as Young Poland, and he was prominent enough as composer and teacher in Lwów, Warsaw and Katowice to have at least two books written about him. Most highly regarded for his symphonic poems and songs, he wrote his sole string quartet in 1916 during a stay in Paris.

It moves confidently enough within its somewhat impersonal Romantic idiom, occasionally giving off a perfume of Debussy and Ravel, and in the finale even some moments of Bartók. This is a not dissimilar mixture to Szymanowski, in fact, but in far less concentrated form, and at nearly 33 minutes the prospect of a concert-hall breakthrough is rather remote. On CD, however, the piece is more than welcome as a coupling to the Royal's outstanding Szymanowski.

Szymanowski can take a degree more atmosphere in the acoustic than we get here; but the clarity of the recording certainly lets the myriad details speak eloquently.

Piano Works

Piano Sonata No 3. Masques. Métopes
Piotr Anderszewski pf
Virgin Classics 545730-2 (68' · DDD)

Here Anderszewski turns his attention away from well-tried classics of the repertoire to Szymanowski and to 'an aura of extreme *fin de siècle* opulence' (John Ogdon). Szymanowski's neurotically questing imagination was fired by his travels in Africa and the Mediterranean; and leaving earlier influences of Chopin (the Op 1 Preludes) and a lengthy dalliance with Reger and Richard Strauss (the Second Piano Sonata) far behind, he turned to Impressionism, to Debussy and the glittering, mosaic-like structures he inherited from Scriabin.

Yet despite such influences his music achieves a unique fragrance and character and both *Masques* and *Métopes* shed a new and scintillating light on the myths of ancient Greece. Such music calls for a pianist of unlimited, superfine virtuosity and a complete temperamental affinity for such exoticism, and in Anderszewski it has surely found its ideal champion. Under his astonishing mind and fingers the chains of trills at the climax of 'Schéhérazade' take on an incandescence that transcends their Scriabinesque origins and Anderszewski's razor-sharp clarity and stylistic assurance make you hang on every one of the composer's teeming notes.

Here and in *Métopes* every hyper-nervous fluctuation of mood is judged to an uncanny perfection and in the Third Sonata, where Szymanowski returns from his richly programmatic sources to a more objective if no less intricate utterance, every aspect of the music's refined and energetic life is held in a blazing light from which it is impossible to escape. Visceral and superhuman, all these performances have been superbly recorded.

Piano Sonata No 1 in C minor, Op 8. Mazurkas, Op 50 – No 13, Moderato; No 14, Animato; No 15, Allegretto dolce; No 16, Allegramente – Vigoroso. Etudes, Op 33. Four Polish Dances, Op 47. Prelude and Fugue in C sharp minor
Martin Roscoe pf
Naxos 8 553867 (69' · DDD)   Ⓢ❶▷

This CD offers a cross-section of Szymanowski's styles as a composer for the keyboard, from the early First Sonata to the pungent Mazurkas, with their flavour of Bartók as well as of late Grieg. The Prelude and Fugue is an interesting link between that early Sonata and the Op 33 Etudes which are usually referred to as representing Szymanowski's 'Impressionist' phase. Again, Roscoe makes you question this conventional description: yes, the harmonies look rather Debussian but they don't often sound that way. These very brief pieces (just over a minute on average) are studies in the conventional sense, written by one fine pianist for another, Alfred Cortot, but they're also exercises in harmonic subtlety and rich in Szymanowski's personal fantasy. The *Four Polish Dances* inhabit the same world as the Mazurkas, and it's obvious that Roscoe enjoys open fifths and flat sevenths as much as Szymanowski did.

Stabat mater, Op 53

Stabat mater. Litany to the Virgin Mary, Op 59. Symphony No 3'
Elzbieta Szmytka sop **Florence Quivar** contr

Jon Garrison ten John Connell bass City of Birmingham Symphony Orchestra and Chorus / Sir Simon Rattle
EMI 555121-2 (56' · DDD · T/t)   Ⓕ❶❶❶❶▷

 The first impression here is that Rattle is relatively new to Szymanowski. There's a huge enthusiasm here, a missionary quality that bespeaks the recent convert. On the other hand the care over matters of balance, the knowledge of just those points where Szymanowski's complexity needs very careful handling if it isn't simply to blur into opacity, suggest a conductor who has been there before and knows the dangers. You get the feeling that a conscious decision was made to delay recording this music until the circumstances were right.

The CBSO Chorus sound thoroughly at home not only in the music but in the language too. In Elzbieta Szmytka, Rattle has a soprano who might have been born to sing Szymanowski's pure, floated and very high-lying soprano lines. The result is very fine: one of the most beautiful Szymanowski recordings ever made. And yet 'beautiful Szymanowski' isn't all that hard if the orchestra's good enough and the conductor capable. Rattle's insistence that all the music be heard, its urgency and passion as well as its deliquescent loveliness, makes for uncommonly gripping Szymanowski as well. He reminds one of how much more there is to the Third Symphony than voluptuous yearning.

The choice of soloists for the *Stabat mater* is interesting: alongside Szmytka's radiant purity are Quivar's throaty vibrancy and Connell's weighty darkness. Not a matching trio, but the contrast is appealing. Garrison in the symphony is a touch hard and strenuous, less enraptured than one or two of the Polish tenors (and sopranos) who've recorded it, but he's a musicianly and likeable singer. The recording is outstanding: lucid, rich and spacious.

Songs

Complete Songs for Voice and Piano
Juliana Gondek, Iwona Sobotka sops **Urszula Kryger** mez **Piotr Beczala** ten **Reinild Mees** pf
Channel Classics ④ CCS19398 (264' · DDD · T/t)   Ⓜ

This set proposes a kind of luxury musical package-tour for the jet-set age – today Expressionist Austria, tomorrow Slavic fantasy, the day after high-Romanticism in Germany, and then away for a weekend in the exotic realms of the Near East. The different locales materialise out of thin air, colourful, fully formed, without a moment for the traveller to get bored on the way. Szymanowski's song output is doubly intriguing – first, for those far-flung contrasts of style; second, because it's so little known. Though the Polish language is an issue, this admirable set reminds us that there are also songs in German and even a James Joyce cycle in English.

Four singers take part, one to each disc. Piotr Beczala is a light, poetic young tenor with some passion up his sleeve. He's dreamily captivating in the early Six Songs of Op 2, where Fauré and Rachmaninov seem to be whispering ideas alternately over Szymanowski's shoulders; catches well the change of tone to religious concentration in the *Three Fragments by Jan Kasprowicz*; and brings lyric beauty to the Schoenberg-inspired Op 13 settings.

The voice of soprano Juliana Gondek is a touch brittle for the sultry mood Szymanowski must have had in mind for the *Songs of the Infatuated Muezzin*, and a bit more could be made of the words in the Joyce cycle; yet there's still much to enjoy. The sensitive singing of mezzo Urszula Kryger plunges straight into the swirling *Tristan*-esque ecstasy of the Wagnerian Op 20 set. The glinting lights of the Orient return in *Des Hafis Liebeslieder*, another set of paraphrases by Hans Bethge to place beside *Das Lied von der Erde*, and the four songs of Op 41 take us forward into more ambiguous and experimental terrain.

The familiar *Songs of the Fairy Princess* promise a magical opening to the fourth disc in a winning performance by young Iwona Sobotka. Here's a pure, steady, light soprano who can flit up into the leger lines without a hint of shrillness. She's also interesting in the antique Polish songs of the *Słopiewnie*, Op 46, and makes a lively job of the miniature *Children's Rhymes* of Op 49, even if a few go rather a long way.

The pianist, Reinild Mees, exhibits a faultless sense of atmosphere throughout, whether delicately conjuring Oriental mystery or thundering up and down Lisztian octaves. The adventurous traveller need look no further.

Songs of a Fairy-tale Princess[a].
Eight Love Songs of Hafiz[b]. Harnasie[c]
[a]**Iwona Sobotka** *sop* [b]**Katarina Karnéus** *mez*
[c]**Timothy Robinson** *ten*
City of Birmingham Symphony [c]**Chorus and Orchestra / Sir Simon Rattle**
EMI 364435-2 (65' · DDD)　　　Ⓕ**ⓞⓞ▷**

Here's another sumptuous instalment of Sir Simon Rattle's Szymanowski cycle, showing that his rapport with his former Birmingham colleagues is as productive as ever. The main item is *Harnasie*, a 'ballet-pantomime' which loses nothing in concert performance, at least when that performance is as exciting as this one. It occupied the composer on and off for eight years (1923-31), bridging the gap between the exotic late-Romanticism that reached its apogee in the opera *King Roger* and his final pair of concertos. *Harnasie* has long been acclaimed for demonstrating Szymanowski's ability to move with the times but its use of folk music doesn't mean that it challenges mid-1920s Bartók or Janáček in progressiveness. This tale of romance and mayhem in bandit country is kitschy in the extreme. Yet even when the music evokes Borodin more vividly than Stravinsky it is utterly irresistible.

Timothy Robinson makes a strong contribution to *Harnasie* but it's the solo singing of Katarina Karnéus and Iwona Sobotka in the two song sets that confirms the disc's special appeal. In the *Eight Love Songs of Hafiz* Szymanowski conjures up a sound world of almost Bergian concentration and opulence, with the richly eloquent final lament the crown in this superbly refined account. *The Songs of a Fairy-tale Princess* is a slighter piece and Iwona Sobotka is not ideally flexible in its taxingly florid lines. But Rattle ensures, as he does throughout, that the mesmerising allure and elaborate textural fantasy of the music are always tinglingly immediate. With a recording that projects the often dense orchestral fabric without undue constraint or loss of clarity, this disc is undoubtedly a winner.

Harnasie

Harnasie, Op 55[a]. Mandragora, Op 43[b].
Prince Potemkin, Op 51[c]
[a]**Wiesław Ochman**, [b]**Alexander Pinderak** *tens*
[c]**Ewa Marciniec** *mez* [a]**Ewa Marczyk** *vn* [b]**Kazimierz Koslacz** *vc* **Warsaw Philharmonic** [a]**Choir and Orchestra / Antoni Wit**
Naxos 8 570723 (73' · DDD)　　　Ⓢ**ⓞⓞ▷**

The ballet *Harnasie* is a powerful complement to the opera *King Roger*, giving similarly Dionysian subject-matter a very different dramatic setting. Szymanowski's joyous embrace of folk idioms in *Harnasie*, and his relish for exploring them in ways which retain certain points of contact with his earlier late-Romantic opulence, invites comparisons with Bartók and Janáček in the years after the First World War. But *Harnasie* has a very personal, Polish aura to it, well projected in this robust yet technically secure account by Antoni Wit and his Warsaw forces, including brief contributions from the veteran yet still strong-voiced Wiesław Ochman.

The other examples of Szymanowski's theatre music are rarities, and neither quite convinces as a concert work. *Mandragora* was designed for a 1920 Warsaw production of Molière's *Le bourgeois gentilhomme* and depicts, all too episodically, the mugging and mayhem of various attempts to entertain the assembled company – a scenario best known from Strauss's *Ariadne auf Naxos*. The incidental music Szymanowski provided in 1925 for the final act of *Prince Potemkin*, a Polish play about Russian history, was left in manuscript during the composer's lifetime, and he might well have been surprised to learn of its revival apart from its original function. While not entirely lacking in character, it comes across as rather dull, even in a performance as accomplished, committed and decently recorded as this one.

King Roger, Op 46

King Roger
Thomas Hampson *bar* Roger II **Elzbieta Szmytka** *sop* Roxana **Ryszard Minkiewicz** *ten* Shepherd **Robert Gierlach** *bar* Archbishop **Jadwiga Rappé** *contr* Deaconess **Philip Langridge** *ten* Edrisi
City of Birmingham Symphony Youth Chorus;

City of Birmingham Symphony Chorus

Symphony No 4, 'Symphonie concertante'
Leif Ove Andsnes pf **City of Birmingham
Symphony Orchestra / Sir Simon Rattle**
EMI ② 556823-2 (112' · DDD · T/t)   Ⓕ**OOO**Đ

 King Roger is a ravishingly beautiful opera, but a very fragile one. With a shrill soprano or a less than ideally cast tenor it would be fatally flawed. Minkiewicz's Dionysiac Shepherd betrays a slight hardness and a touch of stress in full voice, but he has both the allure and the mystery that the role imperatively demands. Almost his first words are 'My God is as beautiful as I', and he should vocally suggest that he is indeed radiantly beautiful. His voice shades to a croon at times, but he never sounds epicene.

Szmytka is a wonderful Roxana, with beautifully pure high notes and bell-like coloratura. At the end of Act 2 her florid aria is repeated (in Szymanowski's concert version), at just the point where you might well have replayed the earlier track for the pleasure of listening to her again. The use of distinguished singers in the smaller roles is no extravagance: Langridge evokes the exotic strangeness of the Arab sage Edrisi, while Rappé and Gierlach add to the hieratic gravity of the opening scene. Hampson in the central role is in fine voice, easily conveying Roger's authority, his angry but bewildered rejection of the Shepherd's new religion. He's even finer, however, in Act 5, where the King is painfully torn between Dionysus and Apollo. The ambiguity of the final scene remains, as it must. Is Roger accepting the Shepherd in place of Roxana? Or, since Roxana herself immediately succumbs to the Shepherd's glamour, is Roger achieving wholeness by at last acknowledging feminine intuitions within himself?

That these questions remain resonant and provoking at the end of the performance is a tribute both to the work itself, and also to Rattle's handling of it. The orchestral textures are voluptuously rich and subtly coloured, aided by a spacious recording (the vast Byzantine basilica of the opening scene is magnificently evoked) and orchestral playing of a very high order indeed. This is the finest recording of *King Roger* that has so far appeared.

The Fourth Symphony, in Szymanowski's later, folk-derived and harder-edged style, is a huge contrast: quite a shock after the opera's radiant conclusion. Andsnes's powerfully athletic playing points up the music's affinities with Prokofiev, and both he and Rattle emphasise the new vigour that Szymanowski was drawing from the fiddle music of the Tatra region.

Further recommendation

King Roger
Drabowicz Roger ‖ **Olga Pasiecznik** Roxana **Polish
National Opera Chorus and Orchestra / Kaspszyk**
CD Accord ACD131-2 (80' · DDD · T/t)   Ⓕ

The sound is more vivid than the EMI, allowing these completely idiomatic performers maximum impact. Where Rattle was characteristically high-gloss, Jacek Kaspszyk uses the experience of live performance to dig deep into this ambiguous work.

Tōru Takemitsu   Japanese 1930-1996

Influenced by Webern, Debussy and Messiaen, Takemitsu always drew out what is most oriental in these composers: a concern with timbre and elegant sound and with the precision of the moment rather than with pattern and development. His music often gives the impression of spatial experience and of materials evolving freely of their own accord; silence is fully organised. In 1958 he received international attention for his Requiem for strings (1957), which settled his reputation as the leading Japanese composer of the 20th century. He was the recipient of numerous awards, commissions and honours; he composed over 100 film scores and about 130 concert works for ensembles of various sizes and combinations. He also found time to write a detective novel and appeared frequently on Japanese television as a celebrity chef. Some of his works use Japanese instruments, but most are for Western orchestral and chamber media. Among the best known are November Steps for biwa, shakuhachi and orchestra (1967), A Flock Descends into the Pentagonal Garden (1977), and From me flows what you call Time (1990) for percussion quintet and orchestra.

I Hear the Water Dreaming

I Hear the Water Dreaming[a]. riverrun[b]. A String around Autumn[c]. A Way A Lone II
[a]**Sharon Bezaly** fl [c]**Philip Dukes** va [b]**Noriko Ogawa** pf
BBC National Orchestra of Wales / Tadaaki Otaka
BIS BIS-CD1300 (60' · DDD)   Ⓕ**OOO**Đ

 Since Takemitsu's evolution into self-confessed Romantic, virtually every major label has released something by him, so Otaka has stiff competition, notably Patrick Gallois's fine reading of *Water Dreaming*. *A Way A Lone II* is included in Rudolf Werthen's admirable survey of Takemitsu's film and concert music. Aided effectively by the soloists, Otaka's interpretations compare well.

In *riverrun* Takemitsu approached closer to the conventional soloist-ensemble than usual. Noriko Ogawa, who has recorded the complete piano solos for BIS, judges the balance sensitively, preparing the ground for that moment when the orchestra leaves the piano to decorate the silence with a few farewell notes.

riverrun and *A Way A Lone* draw inspiration from *Finnegans Wake*. Leif Hasselgren notes a parallel between the circular structure of Joyce's novel and the way Takemitsu's music seems to 'start from nowhere and disappear into the same nowhere'. For all his acknowledged debt to French Impressionism, and to

Japanese traditions, his early interest in electronic music – where sounds appear and fade like headlights on the horizon or plants flowering in a time-lapse film – has undoubtedly had a strong influence.

Sharon Bezaly's flute playing intensifies the feeling that *Water Dreaming* is a perfect crash-course in later Takemitsu, full of references to his influences yet identifiable at any moment as pure, individual and personal Takemitsu, and always bewitching.

A Flock Descends into the Pentagonal Garden

Dreamtime. A Flock Descends into the Pentagonal Garden. Solitude sonore. Spirit Garden. Three Film Scores for String Orchestra
Bournemouth Symphony Orchestra / Marin Alsop
Naxos 8 557760 (63' · DDD) Ⓢ Ⓞ ▶

Discs of Takemitsu's orchestral music have been numerous these past two decades but this Naxos release has the advantage of providing a chronological overview. What comes through, above all, is the consistency of his musical development during that time. The sound world of *Solitude sonore* (1958) might evoke an Asiatic Messiaen, yet the translucent sonorities and suspended – never merely static – sense of motion denote an already personal voice.

Moving to *A Flock Descends into the Pentagonal Garden* (1977) is to reach the point where all the elements of Takemitsu's mature idiom are in place: the music unfolding as waves of diaphonous textures in which melodies and harmonies are ceaselessly changing. Less sensuous in manner, *Dreamtime* (1981) is possibly the finer piece – its interplay of motifs effortlessly evoking an atmosphere remote yet ethereal. From the output of the composer's last decade, *Spirit Garden* (1994) stands out for its clarity and subtlety of thought – a 'concerto for orchestra' that is emphatically no display piece.

The Bournemouth orchestra are on fine form in what is probably their finest collaboration yet with Marin Alsop. She also includes three pieces for strings drawn from film scores – of which 'Funeral Music' has a baleful intensity rare in Takemitsu's concert music. First rate sound, not too close in perspective, and detailed notes from Andrew Burn complete a worthwhile introduction to this singular composer.

Air

Airª. And then I knew 'twas Windᵇ. Bryceᶜ. Itinerantᵈ. Rain Spellᵉ. Rain Treeᶠ. Toward the Seaᵍ. Voiceʰ.
New Music Concerts Ensemble (ᵉJoaquin Valdepenas *cl* ᵉDavid Swan *pf* ᶜᵉRobin Engelman *mari/ vib* ᶜJohn Wyre, ᶠBob Becker, ᶠRussell Hartenberger, ᶠRyan Scott *percs* ᵍNorbert Kraft *gtr* ᵇᶜᵉErica Goodman, ᶜSanya Eng *hps* ᵇSteven Dann *va*) /
ᵃᵇᶜᵈᵉᵍʰ**Robert Aitken** *fl*
Naxos 8 555859 (72' · DDD) Ⓢ Ⓞ ▶

Takemitsu's work in the final decade of his life was gentle, full of tenderness, sentiment and sighs. But he never entirely discarded the starker beauty of his earlier work. *Air* distills much of the spirit of his music, evoking the French Impressionists, modernist asceticism and the pared-down elegance of Japanese traditional music and gardens. It was written for flautist Aurèle Nicolet and first played in public by Yasukazu Uemura, but it's hard to imagine Robert Aitken's performance being bettered.

Aitken invited Takemitsu to Canada in 1975 and 1983. From these visits grew a special relationship with the musicians featured on this outstanding album. They performed most of these works for the composer, so we can assume that the interpretations bear the hallmark of authenticity: they sound utterly convincing, with their perfect balance of the technical and the emotional. *Itinerant* (1989) is a case in point: Takemitsu pictures a garden where vegetable and mineral, motion and stability mingle in precisely designed harmony, yet each visitor's perspective discovers a fresh view.

The programming is as admirable as the playing, surveying Takemitsu's music for small forces from 1971 (*Voice*, with its references to Noh theatre) to 1995 (*Air*). From the pastoral, slightly eerie trio for flute, viola and harp *And then I knew* – devised as a companion-piece to Debussy's 1915 Sonata for the same instruments – and the shimmering, celestial *Rain Tree*, to *Rain Spell*, brooding and turbulent in turns, this is yet another excellent 20th-century showcase from Naxos.

Thomas Tallis
British c1505-1585

Tallis can fairly be said to be the first important English composer, though little is known of his life. He held a succession of posts as organist, most notably at Waltham Abbey in Essex (until the dissolution of the monasteries in 1540) before joining the Gentlemen of the Chapel Royal from about 1543. He remained there for the rest of his life, serving under Henry VIII, Edward VI, Mary and Elizabeth I. In 1572 William Byrd (40 years his junior) joined Tallis in the Chapel Royal, forming one of music's earliest great partnerships: they became joint organists of the Chapel and, in 1575, were granted the sole right to print music in England. Their first publication was a joint venture – a volume of Cantiones sacrae to which each contributed 17 motets. Tallis spent the last years of his life in Greenwich, described in 1577 as 'verie aged'. His epitaph reads: 'As he did live, so also did he die, in mild and happy sort (O! happy man)'.

Most of Tallis's music is, not surprisingly, for the church and his historic importance is in being one of the first composers to write for the Anglican service, the composer who bridged the transition from the Roman rite. Why important? Because the English church-music tradition is among the richest in music history. Though most of the texts Tallis chose to set are in Latin, as a Catholic one may guess that after Queen Mary's reign pragmatism took precedence over belief as he adapted to Thomas Cranmer's English and his requirement of a 'playn and distincte note for every sillable'.

Tallis composed in the whole range of styles and forms then in use. We can marvel at his handling of choral sonority, his technical assurance of grand polyphonic textures as well as in the simplicity of four-part hymn tunes. 'Tallis in D' is still in use today (No 78 in Hymns Ancient & Modern Revised). This first appeared in Archbishop Parker's Psalter of 1567 in which can also be found the tune on which Vaughan Williams based his Fantasia on a Theme of Thomas Tallis.

Lamentations of Jeremiah

Lamentations of Jeremiah. Motets – Absterge Domine; Derelinquat impius; Mihi autem nimis; O sacrum convivium; In jejunio et fletu; O salutaris hostia; In manus tuas; O nata lux de lumine. Salve intemerata Virgo
Tallis Scholars / Peter Phillips
Gimell CDGIM025 (68' · DDD · T/t)   Ⓕ Ⓞ🔁

This, the third volume of the survey by the Tallis Scholars of the music of the Tudor composer, Thomas Tallis, contains the well-known *Lamentations*, eight motets, and the extended motet *Salve intemerata Virgo*. The *Lamentations* and motets are typical of the style of late-Renaissance English composers. The overall mood is one of considerable austerity and their simplicity is indicative of the probability of their having been written for the private use of loyal Catholics rather than for formal ritual. *Salve intemerata Virgo*, on the other hand, looks back to the glories of the late 15th century. In particular, Tallis's use of the phrygian mode gives the work as a whole a strong sense of the medieval. Despite this disparity of styles the Tallis Scholars acquit themselves, as always, with great distinction. In the *Lamentations* and motets they achieve an appropriate sense of intimacy, while in *Salve intermerata Virgo* they rise fully to the challenges of one of the more extended and demanding examples of Tudor choral composition. In addition the formidable challenges which this latter work sets for the conductor, such as the sense of pace, variation of dynamics, and overall architecture of the work, are all extremely well handled by Peter Phillips. The recording is very fine.

'Complete Works – 8,
Lamentations and Contrafacta'
Sing and glorify heaven's high majesty. Lamentations of Jeremiah – I; II. Blessed are those that be undefiled. I call and cry to thee. Wipe away my sins. Forgive me, Lord, my sin. Arise, O Lord, and hear. With all our hearts. O sacred and holy banquet. When Jesus went into Simon the Pharisee's house. Blessed be thy name. O praise the Lord (2nd version)
Chapelle du Roi / Alistair Dixon

Signum SIGCD036 (64' · DDD · T/t)   Ⓕ🔁

Two of the Biblical lessons for Maundy Thursday show Tallis at his most creative and imaginative. 'Incipit lamentatio...', the rising fourth, followed by a descending minor scale, imitated in turn by each of the other voices, sets the tone of sorrowful lamenting. Chapelle du Roi capture this mood with calm perfection. The flowing melodies of the introductory Hebrew letters, the clear articulation of the homophonic sections, each element is performed with understanding, due restraint, and never overdone.

The Latin motets that lie behind the English *contrafacta* have been recorded on Volume 7 of this series. It's remarkable how well the English texts, not necessarily translations or paraphrases, are made to fit the originals. Much interesting research lies behind the notes to Volumes 7 and 8: the identification of the original sources throws additional light on the religious and political struggles of Tallis's working life, and offers glimpses of domesticity. Dixon's choice between two possible groupings of five voices, the lower male-voice group and a higher one to include the ladies of the house, makes perfect sense.

Sing and glorify is a *contrafactum* of Tallis's monumental *Spem in alium*, intended for a joyful royal investiture a quarter of a century after his death. The motet was recast in an entirely different mould: to wish long life to the young Prince of Wales was a far cry from a desperate appeal to God for mercy: even Dixon's faster tempo can't alter that, but what a fine performance his singers give of it.

Additional recommendation

Tallis Lamentations of Jeremiah
Coupled with **Brumel** Lamentations **A Ferrabosco I**
De lamentatione Ieremiae prophetae **Palestrina**
Lamentations for Holy Saturday **Tallis** Lamentations of Jeremiah **White** Lamentations of Jeremiah
Tallis Scholars / Phillips
Gimell CDGIM996 (73' · DDD · T/t)   Ⓕ🔁

A compilation of 16th-century Tenebrae music for Holy Week. The Lamentations texts set are quite different, but all show an intensity and a devotional power that work cumulatively to produce a remarkably satisfying disc.

Spem in alium

Te lucis ante terminum. Salvator mundi. Spem in alium. In jejunio et fletu. O salutaris hostia. Lamentations I & II. Miserere. Mass for four voices
Magnificat / Philip Cave
Linn CKD233 (67' · DDD · T/t)   Ⓕ ⓄⓄⓄ🔁

Ⓖ This is quite simply the best performance of Tallis's 40-part *Spem in alium* to date. Sung by a constellation of singers, many of them familiar names from other well-established choral groups, it's a gripping realisation. The effect of the slowly moving harmonies is enhanced by a well-conceived and very positive use of dynamics. Precise entries, gently undulating rhythms that are wonderfully supple, and then those firm antiphonal phrases – one group of choirs answered by another at 'Creator coeli et terra' – raise the tension, until we twice almost miss a heartbeat at the well-placed rest before 'Respice…'.

That great motet, so central to the whole programme, is well supported by the four-part Mass and the delightful group of other pieces for various combinations of voices. The hymn *Te lucis* with its alternating chant strophes sounding so very English (almost too perfect for what was, after all, just run-of-the-mill everyday chant!) has the tempo relationship of the chant to the polyphony just right, which is a tremendous plus, rarely achieved.

Spem in alium. Salvator mundi (I, II). Sancte Deus, sancte fortis. Gaude gloriosa Dei mater. Miserere nostri. Loquebantur variis linguis
Tallis Scholars / Peter Phillips
Gimell CDGIM006 (43' · DDD)   ⒡**OO**B

For the 1985 quatercentenary of Tallis's death, Peter Phillips and the Tallis Scholars produced this version of *Spem in alium*; in many respects it's clearly the most successful ever recorded. Not only is the choir superb and the interpretation an intelligent one; this is also the only recording in which the eight choirs seem genuinely to sing from different positions in the stereo spread, a technical achievement that leads to some thrilling antiphonal exchanges. Above all, Phillips's reading is a confident and assertive one. The effect is more that of a plea than a prayer, and the overall shaping is most characterful. Inevitably there are problems of balance, both at the top of the texture (several of the trebles are given rather too much prominence) and in the middle, where in full sections the music of the inner voices sometimes blends too readily into rich chords rather than emerging as a complex web of counterpoint. But these are relatively small complaints to be made against an outstanding achievement. This is a *Spem in alium* to be cherished.

'Complete Works – 7, Music for Queen Elizabeth'
Spem in alium. Absterge Domine. Derelinquat impius. Domine quis habitat. In ieiunio et fletu. In manus tuas. Laudate Dominum. Mihi autem nimis. Miserere nostri. O nata lux de lumine. O sacrum convivium. O salutaris hostia. Salvator mundi, salva nos – I & II
Chapelle du Roi / Alistair Dixon
Signum SIGCD029 (63' · DDD · T/t)   ⒡**OO**B

Volume 7 of Chapelle du Roi's complete series of Tallis recordings is a further witness to the composer's consummate command of his art, in whatever religious or political situation he found himself at each changing period of his life. It might seem puzzling that Elizabeth, in 1575, should sanction the publication of Tallis's and

TALLIS SPEM IN ALIUM IN BRIEF

Tallis Scholars / Peter Phillips
Gimell ② CDGIM203 (159' · DDD)   Ⓜ**OO**B
Gimell CDGIM006 (43' · DDD)   ⒡**OO**B
The punchy, no-holds-barred sonorities and spot-on tuning of The Tallis Scholars make for exhilarating listening. The recording – crucial when it comes to delineating 40 separate lines – doesn't wrap around the listener, but offers a tightly focused experience. It's available both with the original couplings of Latin motets or as the starter for the Scholars' complete recordings of Tallis.

Magnificat / Philip Cave
Linn CKD075 (67' · DDD)   ⒡**OOO**
Demonstration-quality openness and balance make this quite spacious version one to treasure. Lots of young British voices bring an unchurchy, dynamic panorama to Tallis's elaborate testament of faith – *My hope is founded in the Lord* – and demonstration of compositional skill.

Clerkes of Oxenford / David Wulstan
Classics for Pleasure 575982-2 (69' · ADD)   Ⓑ
A pioneering 'new' early-music choir in the 1970s combining modern scholarship (and female voices) with roots in the English choral tradition. The result is unhurried and effortlessly conveys the scale of Tallis's conception. Fine couplings of church music.

Chapelle du Roi / Alistair Dixon
Signum SIGCD047 (20' · DDD)   Ⓑ
If you only want *Spem*, this is the one to have. The second track is the first recording of the English version of the motet, *Sing and glorify*. Carefully sung and balanced.

The Sixteen / Harry Christophers
Coro ⦿ CORSACD16016 / ⮩ CO5RDVD1 (72' · DDD)   ⒡
Spem is literally a surround-sound piece, so this recording, the first to use the latest technology in new audio formats, gets closer than most. The Sixteen (enlarged to the requisite 40) have a suitably festive air for this, their 25th anniversary recording.

Choir of Winchester Cathedral / David Hill
Hyperion CDA66400 (59' · DDD)   ⒡
A definite first choice for those who want to hear the boys' voices that Tallis would have composed for. A wide, open recording within Winchester's vast space still captures all the intricate detail to touching effect.

Kronos Quartet
Nonesuch 7559 79242-2 (62' · DDD)   ⒡
For something a bit different: the avant-garde string quartet, multitracked with sometimes revelatory clarity.

Byrd's *Cantiones sacrae*, but she apparently enjoyed hearing Latin-texted music in her private chapel, and many of the prayers would have been familiar from her childhood.

Dixon makes a number of interesting points. He demonstrates Tallis's use of older material: for example, the Latin *Absterge Domine*, side by side with its later English contrafactum *Discomfort them, O Lord*. He shows how five-voice scoring might be used for an all-male ensemble, or privately in, say, a recusant family situation, with ladies on the top line (*In ieiunio et fletu*). Tallis's craftsmanship is further revealed in his two through-composed psalms, *Domine, quis habitabit* and *Laudate Dominum*, which, while adhering to 16th-century principles of syllabic word-setting, are varied enough to relieve the inevitable tedium. We hear finally, Dixon's masterly interpretation of *Spem in alium* 'in the round' – or 'in horseshoe formation' – possibly the Chapelle's highest achievement to date.

Tan Dun   Chinese/American b1957

Growing up during the Cutural Revolution, Tan Dun received no early musical training. After working as a violinist, at the age of 19 he entered the composition department of Beijing's reopened Central Conservatory of Music. There he encountered Western music and was stimulated by visits of guest composers Goehr, Crumb and Takemitsu. He moved to New York in 1986.

The Map

Concerto for Cello, Video and Orchestra, 'The Map' – A multimedia event in rural China[a]. Includes the documentary, 'Rediscovering the Map'[b]
Anssi Karttunen vc **Shanghai Symphony Orchestra / Tan Dun** [a]Aural and visual imaging **Davey Frankel** Video directors [a]**Sheng Boji,** [a]**Wang Ping,** [b]**Uri Gal-Ed**
DG 20/21 **DVD** 073 4009GH (73' · NTSC · 4:3 · PCM stereo, 5.1 & DTS 5.1 · 0)   Ⓕ**O**

The Map is Tan Dun's quest to find the shamanistic 'stone man' he once heard in his youth. Armed with a commission from Yo-Yo Ma and the Boston Symphony Orchestra, he returned to Hunan with a camera crew to document village musical life and the non-Han minority peoples in particular. Once back in New York, he became a sort of Bartók for the media age, spinning ethnic traditional material into an abstract modernism while simultaneously preserving its roots on screen. The results are sprawling, to say the least. At times, such as the polyphonic tongue-singing of a group of Dong women, the orchestra merely frames the film footage. Elsewhere Tan's orchestral writing cheekily adapts the techniques of the village practitioners on a grand scale, such as having the entire percussion sec-

tion enter into a dialogue with a group of Tujia cymbal players, or the winds and brass playing their reeds and mouthpieces in response to a village leaf-blower. The most creative touch comes in a *feige*, traditionally an antiphonal courtship song sung across mountains and valleys, but here featuring a Miao girl on screen performing with a live cello soloist, transcending entirely new boundaries of time and space.

Grasping the dimensions of this piece in a home format obviously requires a video recording; fortunately Hunan television was on hand when Tan brought the *The Map* to the village that inspired it. That broadcast, carefully edited and remixed here, is paired with a short film documenting that production, as well as Tan's original writing process.

Much of these musical traditions, it must be said, remain as exotic to most Chinese listeners as a Navajo chant would in the West. The most obvious weakness of *The Map* is that sometimes Tan seems all too content to play tourist, filming music that villagers play for outsiders rather than what they perform for themselves. Still, since his stated goal was not to document those cultures but to bring their rustic vitality into counterpoint with the slick urban world, *The Map* succeeds not in spite of its messiness but because of it.

Sergey Taneyev   Russian 1856-1915

Taneyev studied with the best and taught the best. At the Moscow Conservatory his teachers were Nikolai Rubinstein (piano) and Tchaikovsky (composition). He became a close friend of Tchaikovsky and gave the Moscow premiere of Tchaikovsky's Piano Concerto No 1 (1875); he succeeded him as teacher at the conservatory (1878), and eventually became director (1885-89). Among his pupils were Scriabin, Rachmaninov and Glière.

A musical traditionalist, his study of Bach and the Renaissance contrapuntists gave him a compositional craftsmanship unsurpassed by his Russian contemporaries. He may not be a great melodist but his works are all superbly put together and unfold with a satisfying logic. He wrote some important chamber works (including the very fine Piano Quintet and 11 string quartets), symphonies and many works for chorus.

Piano Concerto

Piano Concerto[c]. Andante semplice. Prelude. Lullaby. Theme and Variations. Allegro. Repose Elegy. March. Four Improvisations. The Composer's Birthday (two versions)[a/ab]
Joseph Banowetz, [a]**Adam Wodnicki** pfs [b]**Vladimir Ashkenazy** narr [c]**Russian Philharmonic of Moscow / Thomas Sanderling**
Toccata Classics TOCC0042 (77' · DDD)   Ⓕ**D➜**

How can it be that the only piano concerto by a pianist-composer of the standing of Taneyev has never previously been recorded? True, it was left incomplete – Taneyev was a harsh self-critic, and adverse comment from Anton Rubinstein, Cui and Rimsky-Korsakov can hardly have helped. True, it was only published in 1957. True, there are times in the 25-minute first movement when it's hard not to wish that the 19-year-old recent graduate from Tchaikovsky's class might have drawn the threads of the structure a little tighter. Yet the very opening bars bring a characteristic touch of nobility, gravitas and subdued enthusiasm. And while it's unlikely that anyone would rank the two movements beside the finest of Taneyev's mature symphonic or chamber works, the fact that the Concerto remained unfinished and unrevised surely robbed us of a work worthy of a place in the great Russian tradition.

The performance never gives off the whiff of dutiful generality that so often accompanies such ventures. Banowetz plays with a natural eloquence and heart, as well as a fine technical address, qualities which ennoble the frankly less distinguished solo pieces too. The rather rambling *Theme and Variations* cannot entirely disguise its origins as a composition exercise, and there are no regrets that the *Allegro* never grew into a complete sonata.

But the end of the disc is a delight. The *Four Improvisations* are a cataloguer's nightmare, since they were jointly composed with Arensky, Glazunov and Rachmaninov, passing round sheets of manuscript paper in a game of musical 'consequences'. Just as quirky is Taneyev's greeting for Tchaikovsky's 52nd birthday, whose whimsical scenario is built around quotations of nine of the latter's major works. The piece is helpfully recorded here once with the accompanying text declaimed (by Ashkenazy, no less), once without.

Less than one fifth of the music on the disc has been previously recorded. All of it is excellently recorded, and serious collectors should flock to snap it up.

Symphonies

Symphonies Nos 1 & 3
Russian State Symphony Orchestra /
Valery Polyansky
Chandos CHAN10390 (64' · DDD)   Ⓟ Ⓓ➔

Taneyev's first composed symphony, in E minor, was the work of a 17-year-old student, dutifully ticking the prescribed boxes for his graduation from Moscow Conservatoire. As so often in the academic Russian tradition, the *Scherzo* is the most striking movement; the finale, by contrast, puts its folksong material through so many harmonic and contrapuntal routines that one almost imagines it crying for mercy.

The Third Symphony, in D minor and dedicated to Arensky, drew Tchaikovsky's praise for its musical content but also his reservations about the 'abstract' (ie non-orchestral) nature of the material. That seems a just assessment. The first movement, like Beethoven's *Eroica*, Schumann's *Rhenish* and Nielsen's *Espansiva*,

moves in a liberally cross-accented triple metre (a useful aide-mémoire that these should all be third symphonies). It is in many ways no less ingenious than those works but never achieves lift-off in the way they do; the same goes for the *Scherzo*, whose strategy for integrating the Trio is resourceful but hardly revelatory. The modest Intermezzo is easy to like as a pleasantly relaxing episode, but would be more effective placed in more dramatic surroundings.

Polyansky and the Russian State Symphony have done Taneyev a superb service with these thoroughly prepared, expertly recorded performances. The music itself may be too firmly tied to academic apron-strings to be viable in the concert hall, and the composer's verdict in not releasing them was surely the right one. But these are still need-to-know pieces for anyone interested in the Russian symphonic repertoire.

Symphonies No 2 & 4
Russian State Symphony Orchestra /
Valery Polyansky
Chandos CHAN9998 (75' · DDD)   Ⓟ Ⓓ➔

Polyansky provides a splendidly passionate and invigorating introduction to music that we really should know better in the West. The Fourth Symphony has always been the most popular of Taneyev's symphonies, and with good reason. He writes a powerful opening *Allegro* and a well-built finale, but for all his symphonic skills here, it's in the middle two movements that the most personal music is to be found. The *Scherzo* dances along with the vitality that many a Russian composer has brought to comparable movements, and with the rhythmic quirks that he liked so much; but it's in the *Adagio* that something more is discovered. Taneyev has routinely been reproached for lacking melodic distinction, sometimes with reason, but this superb movement comes close to the manner of Bruckner, or sometimes Mahler. For English ears, the sense of 'stately sorrow' serves as a reminder that the phrase was coined of his own music by Elgar.

Conductor and players make of this fine music a tragic statement, and it's here that they're at their most intense. Polyansky also produces a strong case for the Second Symphony, his sense of structure holding the rather oddly organised opening movement together, as a powerful chorale passage has to be integrated with a sonata *Allegro*. He doesn't play down the suggestions of Dvořák, whom Taneyev clearly found sympathetic. This is a striking, and very well-recorded, pair of performances, well worth the attention of lovers of Russian music.

Chamber works

Piano Quintet[a]. Piano Trio, Op 22
Vadim Repin, [a]**Ilya Gringolts** *vns* [a]**Nobuko Imai** *va*
Lynn Harrell *vc* **Mikhail Pletnev** *pf*
DG 477 5419GH (83' · DDD)   Ⓟ ⓄⓄⓄ Ⓓ➔

Piano Quartet, Op 20ª. Piano Trio, Op 22
Barbican Piano Trio (James Kirby *pf* Gaby Lester *vn*
Robert Max *vc*) with ªJames Boyd *va*
Dutton CDSA6882 (74' · DDD)   (F)

Sergey Taneyev composed his three piano chamber works in the years 1902-11, on either side of his 50th birthday, when his days as director of the Moscow Conservatoire were well behind him but when he still commanded nationwide respect for his gifts as pianist, administrator and craftsman-composer. These pieces were in the first instance vehicles for his own concert performances, and the piano parts are accordingly massive. Compositionally the writing is unfailingly well wrought and resourceful: by no means entirely confined to middle-of-the-road tastefulness, yet rarely, if ever, touched by the kind of distinction evinced by his great pupils, Rachmaninov and Scriabin.

The Piano Quintet is the latest and grandest of the three works, its structural layout and textures being indebted in just about equal measure to Tchaikovsky and César Franck. The initially consoling second subject is destined for heroic things in a grandstand résumé at the end of the finale, and on repeated hearings it's a pleasure to discover its unassuming beginnings. In between, the *Scherzo* has that touch of fairy-tale magic that came so naturally to most of the great Russians while the slow movement daringly strips down to a passacaglia theme on the cello before dressing up impressively again. Pletnev and his dream-team string colleagues are passionate advocates, as they are for the more classically conceived Trio.

The strings are placed rather far forward, and the acoustic is a fraction too dry for comfort. It's a tribute to the Barbican Piano Trio that they hardly ever find themselves outdone in crusading passion, or indeed outplayed technically, by their bigger-name rivals. James Kirkby is as sensitive as Pletnev to the oases of calm in the slow movement of the Trio, where the piano holds the stage in moments of quiet rapture. By contrast, the Piano Quartet launches immediately into its ecstatic stride, risking anticlimax but rescuing itself by constant renewed initiatives. Violist James Boyd makes his presence strongly felt in the dark-hued slow movement. The Dutton recording strays a fraction the other side of the ideal from DG by giving us a little too much of the room acoustic of St George's, Brandon Hill, Bristol; but once again it is perfectly serviceable.

String Trios – in E flat, Op 31; in B minor; in D
Leopold String Trio (Isabelle Van Keulen *vn*
Lawrence Power *va* Kate Gould *vc*)
Hyperion CDA67573 (67' · DDD)   (F)O●▸

Given the scarcity of Russian contributions to this traditionally most demanding of chamber media, there is all the more reason to investigate what Russia's greatest master of counterpoint (according to Tchaikovsky and others well placed to comment) does with it.

Hyperion has wisely placed the finest of the three first. The E flat Trio (1910-11) is chronologically second, and apart from Taneyev's usual craftsmanly values, there is a winning freedom of invention. The first movement has the confidence to go down inviting sidetracks, confident that there will be marvels to bring back. One of Taneyev's trademark quick-witted *scherzos* follows – irresistibly charming – then a gorgeously warm-hearted slow movement, with plentiful florid yet never tasteless elaboration, and a jocund finale. Given that the lowest part of the E flat Trio was conceived and published for the tenor viola (tuned a fourth higher than the cello) there is some justification for Kate Gould's occasional redistribution of the texture; though if anyone can dig out an example of the original instrument it would be fun to compare.

After this the unfinished B minor Trio (1913), partially reconstructed from sketches for its posthumous first publication, is a tougher nut, grainier in its texture and more heavily shadowed in its moods – a sober and impressive footnote to one of the great chamber music composing careers. The D major Trio (1879-80) is a perfectly respectable debut in the medium, checking every step of the way before boldly going where no major Russian composer had gone before.

It would be hard to over-praise the Leopold Trio's performances. Agility and all-round aplomb? Check. Warmth and colour? Check. Structural and idiomatic awareness? Check. Fine recording quality and helpful annotation (Calum MacDonald) too; so no reason not to invest.

Alexandre Tansman   Polish 1897-1986

Tansman spent his early years in his native Poland but lived in France for most of his life. His music is primarily neo-classical, drawing on his Polish and Jewish heritage as well as his French musical influences. Tansman always described himself as a Polish composer, though he spoke French at home and married a French pianist, Colette Cras. In 1941, fleeing Europe as his Jewish background put him in danger with Hitler's rise to power, he moved to Los Angeles where he made the acquaintance of Arnold Schoenberg. Tansman composed the score for two Hollywood movies and six films in all. He was nominated for an Academy Award in 1946 for Paris Underground. He also wrote jazz under the name Stan Alson.

Orchestal Works

Sinfoniettas – No 1; No 2. Sinfonia piccola.
Symphonie de chambre
Orchestra della Svizzera Italiana / Oleg Caetani
Chandos CHAN10574 (61' · DDD)   (F)▸

Four small-scale but by no means trivial works neatly sum up different phases of Tansman's output. Stravinsky, Ravel and Poulenc are joint godfathers to the Sinfonietta No 1 (1924), the acid tones of whose Mazurka second movement refract musical images from the homeland Tansman had left for Paris four years earlier. In 1951-52 the *Sinfonia piccola* shows him productively mining the seams of Stravinsky's *Dumbarton Oaks*, while in 1960 he was comfortably bedded down in the neo-neo-classical world of the likes of Jean Françaix in the *Symphonie de chambre*. The Second Sinfonietta of 1978 proves that he could 'do' 12-note music (albeit of a simplistic and complaisant kind) as well as smuggling in popular Polish melodies and rounding everything off in neo-romantic consolatory tones.

Oleg Caetani and the Orchestra della Svizzera Italiana have their work cut out with some of Tansman's exposed and unrelenting fugues and *perpetuum mobiles*. But they emerge with great credit; as does the music itself. First-rate recording quality and authoritative documentation support a more than worthwhile issue.

Piano Works

Sonata rustica. Sonatina No 3. Trois Préludes en forme de blues. Mazurkas Vol 1, 'Recueil de Mazurkas'. Quatre Nocturnes. Album d'amis
Margaret Fingerhut pf
Chandos CHAN10527 (74' · DDD)　　　Ⓕ B→

Tansman lived from 1897 to 1986, and this selection of his compositions for solo piano spans the years 1915 to 1980. From carefree youthfulness to elderly melancholia? Such an extreme progression was not Tansman's style: but there is a clear shift from early sparkle to later wistfulness. This is not music to storm the barricades, whether in defence or defiance of modernism. What it has, in these well judged, well recorded performances, is charm, and a refusal to spin things out which are best left concise and understated.

The initial collection of Mazurkas establishes Tansman's favoured stylistic territory for piano music, in which echoes of Paderewski and Rachmaninov co-exist contentedly with hints of Szymanowski and Prokofiev. In the relatively expansive *Sonata rustica* (1925) dedicated to Ravel, that meticulous master is a presence, but so too is Poulenc and (up to a point) Stravinsky. The mélange is refreshing but studiously unprofound, even in the relatively rhapsodic and showy gestures of the sonata's first movement, and Margaret Fingerhut has an unerring sense of when to indulge the flamboyance, as well as of how to introduce a poetic quality without becoming unduly sentimental.

The later pieces, all collections of miniatures, include the rather soft-centred *Trois Préludes en forme de blues*, and the very late *Album d'amis*, whose friends pictured within include pianists and publishers. Most of these are little more than casual doodles, though elements of vigour and harmonic 'bite' pop up when you least expect them.

Giuseppe Tartini　　Italian 1692-1770

Tartini studied in Assisi and by 1714 had joined the orchestra at Ancona. He later spent time in Venice and Padua, where in 1721 he was principal violinist at the Basilica of S Antonio. He worked there until 1765 except for a period in Prague (1723-26). Besides performing with success, he founded a 'school' of violin instruction. He was one of the foremost Italian instrumental composers, writing over 400 works: these include violin concertos and sonatas (many with virtuoso solo parts), trio sonatas and sonatas for string ensemble. He also composed some sacred music. Noteworthy among his writings are a work on violin playing and ornamentation and two treatises on the acoustical foundations of harmony.

Violin Concertos

Violin Concertos – C, D4[a]; E minor, D56[b]; 　Ⓟ
F, D63[c]; G, D75[d]
[ad]**Federico Guglielmo**, [c]**Carlo Lazari** vns
L'Arte dell'Arco / [b]**Giovanni Guglielmo** vn
Dynamic CDS220 (64' · DDD)　　　　　Ⓕ

The works in this fourth volume of Tartini's violin concertos all supposedly belong to the composer's earliest period, the years between *c*1720 and 1735. One of them, in E minor, has long been popular with soloists and has often been recorded. The remaining three, however, are less familiar and, it's claimed, here make their first appearance on disc. The C major piece sounds as if it might be the earliest concerto here, though many of the distinctive hallmarks of Tartini's style are firmly in place – little chromaticisms and short-lived, playful melodic patterns in the outer movements, and wistfully lyrical solo cantilenas in the tenderly expressive slow one. The author of the accompanying note erroneously claims the tonal plan is more imaginative than in Vivaldi's concertos. Tartini simply avails himself of a more advanced pool of stylistic knowledge, in no sense improving on the art of his forebears – especially Vivaldi.

An enjoyable programme with engaging solo contributions from Guglielmo. Listeners will notice the acid quality of the *tutti* playing, and a recorded sound that does little to ameliorate it, though they will quickly adjust to both.

Violin Sonatas

Violin Sonatas – G minor, 'Devil's Trill', B:g5; 　Ⓟ
A minor, B:a3. Variations on a Gavotte by Corelli, B:F11 – excerpts. Pastorale in A, B:A16 (all arr Manze)
Andrew Manze vn
Harmonia Mundi HMU90 7213 (69' · DDD)　　Ⓕ ●

The romantic connotations of Tartini's Violin Sonata in G minor, the *Devil's Trill*, deriving from the composer's account of an appearance by the devil in a dream, have contributed towards making it one of the great *morceaux favoris* of the 19th and 20th centuries. Furthermore, it's just about the only remaining piece of Baroque music where a piano accompaniment can still be countenanced without raised eyebrows. Some traditions die hard. But Tartini never intended anything of the kind; in fact, he probably never envisaged a keyboard continuo part at all, since none of his surviving autographs contains a figured bass for keyboard realisation. Most include unfigured bass parts, though these were often provided as an afterthought, for reasons of convention. Andrew Manze sees this as a justification for playing all the pieces in his programme without bass accompaniment. On the whole the experiment works well, since the expressive content and structural power of the music lies foremost in Tartini's melodic line. There are moments, however, where harmonic support from the bass is required, and at such times, above all in the *Devil's Trill* Sonata, Manze has had to introduce chords in the violin part to compensate for the absence of a cello. His athletic technique, his musical sensibility and perhaps, too, his engaging sense of fun, ensure fascination and entertainment in equal measure. None will regret the passing of the piano in this context. A stimulating release, beautifully recorded, and rich in fantasy.

Tartini Solo Violin Sonatas – No 2; No 13; No 14; No 17; in A minor, Brainard A3. Solitario bosco ombroso **Rolli** Solitario bosco ombroso[a] **Anonymous** Lieto ti prendo e poi[a]. Depon Clorinda la sue spoglie inteste[a]. Intanto Erminia fra l'ombrose piante **Chiara Banchini** vn with [a]**Patrizia Bovi** voc Zig-Zag Territoires ZZT080502 (67' · DDD)　Ⓕ Ⓞ ➔

Tartini often prefaced movements of his later sonatas with short poetic quotations (usually from Metastasio or Tasso) indicating his expressive intent. An adherent of the fashionable theory that the role of art is to imitate nature, he showed a keen interest in folksong (perceived as closer to nature than art music). In several pieces he quotes the melody of the celebrated 'Aria di Tasso', an anonymous setting of verses from *La Gerusalemme liberata*, sung by Venetian gondoliers, and this forms the starting-point for Banchini's disc, which alternates solo sonatas with some of the popular melodies that inspired the composer.

Patrizia Bovi sings these most convincingly, combining stylish ornamentation with strong projection of line and text. There's a handsome booklet too, with texts of the songs and the poems quoted by Tartini, a little selection of 18th-century writings and paintings, and an interesting essay (by Stefano Aresi).

It's the violin, however, that's the main focus of attention, and Banchini plays elegantly, with great expressive freedom and, in the quicker movements, with considerable force and panache. She also ornaments liberally and imaginatively, obviously inspired by Tartini's own examples and instructions concerning embellishment. Listeners can be assured, however, that the startling dissonances in the open-

ing *Siciliana* of Sonata No 2 (in D minor, not B minor as printed) stem from Tartini's own pen. In the way it allows us to appreciate fully the aesthetic ideals of a bygone age, this is an exceptional issue.

Sir John Tavener　British b1944

Tavener studied with Berkeley and Lumsdaine at the Royal Academy of Music. Most of his music is explicitly religious, some influenced by late Stravinsky. His biblical cantata The Whale (1966) enjoyed popularity. An early leaning towards Catholic devotion reached a consummation in the Crucifixion meditation Ultimos ritos (1972) and the opera Thérèse (1979). In 1976 he converted to the Russian Orthodox faith, composing in a simpler, luminous style. Works from this period are often extremely long. His best known works are his cello concerto The Protecting Veil (1989) and his simple Song for Athene (heard by millions at the funeral of Princess Diana).

The Protecting Veil

The Protecting Veil. Wake Up...And Die. **Yo-Yo Ma** vc **Baltimore Symphony Orchestra / David Zinman** Sony Classical SK62821 (67' · DDD)　Ⓕ Ⓞ ➔

This was the third recording of *The Protecting Veil* to appear since Steven Isserlis's *Gramophone* Award-winning premiere recording on Virgin Classics (see below). As expected, Yo-Yo Ma brings us a reading of tremendous stature and technical refinement which is a serious rival to Isserlis's equally remarkable account. However, whether Isserlis is preferable to Ma or vice versa seems irrelevant; what is essential is that the work continues to live and grow through performance, and with a piece such as *The Protecting Veil* the interpretative scope for the soloist is wide indeed. Ma's version is quite different from Isserlis's in many ways. Isserlis takes the opening of the work ('The Protecting Veil' section) slightly faster and certainly with more passionate phrasing than Ma, whose pacing in the corresponding bars is altogether more static, though he still matches Isserlis in intensity. He is complemented by the strings of the Baltimore Symphony Orchestra under David Zinman. Tavener's comment that 'the strings should act as a vast resonating chamber for the solo cello' is fully realised and the effect is at times quite awesome. Particularly beautiful is Ma's reading of 'The Dormition of the Mother of God' section.

Wake up … And Die, for cello solo and orchestral cello section, is a 20-minute work in two parts. The Byzantine, chant-like opening section for solo cello has great beauty and the second half of the work, with cello section harmonically supporting the solo cello with its hypnotic repeating episodes, is quite spellbinding. This is a piece that will quickly find admirers who are familiar with

Tavener's unique sound world. The recording is vivid and well balanced.

Additional recommendation

The Protecting Veil
Coupled with The Last Sleep of the Virgin. Choral Music
Isserlis; LSO / Rozhdestvensky
EMI 20th Century Classics ② 237691-2   Ⓜ ❍❍❍🄳⇥
The premiere recording and one that has a magic all of its own. Isserlis brings huge amounts of passion and intensity to this now very popular work for cello and orchestra.

Lalishri

Tavener Song for Athene. Dhyana. Lalishri
Vaughan Williams The Lark Ascending
Nicola Benedetti *vn* **London Philharmonic Orchestra / Andrew Litton**
DG 476 6198GH (64' · DDD)   Ⓟ❍🄳⇥

The third disc of DG's deal with the former BBC Young Musician amply justifies the company's confidence in this wonderfully pure-toned young violinist. It is an imaginative coupling of three Tavener works – two inspired by Benedetti and a third arranged for her – and the VW work voted the nation's most popular classic.

The choral *Song for Athene* crowned the music at Princess Diana's funeral. This arrangement cannot match that haunting quality although it's beautifully played. Tavener has described Benedetti's playing as 'like a voice…you feel her breathing a line,' and the brief *Dhyana* (Sanskrit for 'meditation') is meant to reflect her contemplative style. *Lalishri* is much more ambitious, almost 40 minutes long, and is inspired by the 14th-century Hindu poet and saint Lalia Yogishwari. The solo violin represents the songs of the poet while the music reflects Tavener's devotion to the Indian raga, meditational depths punctuated by sharp, even frenetic, changes of mood in dance rhythms. Benedetti's fine performance sustains its length well with much double-stopping, *pizzicato* effects, trills and quarter tones. Unlike much of Tavener's music, the work has great vigour with a powerful rather than meditative close.

The Lark Ascending receives a spacious performance, reflective and pure-toned in the fluttering evocations of the lark and powerful in the *tuttis*, thanks to the weighty accompaniment of Andrew Litton and the LPO, with far bigger dynamic contrasts than usual.

Lament for Jerusalem

Lament for Jerusalem
Angharad Gruffydd Jones *sop* **Peter Crawford** *counterten* **Choir of London; London Orchestra / Jeremy Summerly**
Naxos 8 557826 (55' · DDD)   Ⓢ🄳⇥

Lament for Jerusalem was premiered in Australia in 2003 but this disc features a revised version Tavener prepared for the Choir of London's visit to Jerusalem, Ramallah and Bethlehem in December 2004.

Tavener insists that *Lament* should be seen less as a statement about the current plight of Jerusalem and its inhabitants than as an elegy for humankind's exile from the soul's home, and seeks to remind us what Judaism, Christianity and Islam have in common. Through the purity of his musical gestures he achieves an intensity that can affect listeners regardless of their own religious convictions.

This revision radically reduces the forces needed, both in numbers and range of instrumentation. While some weight is lost, along with the variety of sounds (the brass section comprises just three trumpets, the woodwind two flutes, two bassoons and oboe), this is amply compensated for by increased radiance and clarity.

The premiere recording of the full-scale *Lament* was recorded under Thomas Woods for ABC Classics; and even though it is almost impossible to find in the UK, to a large extent this more transparent version is preferable. The soprano part was originally taken by the marvellous Patricia Rozario but even on this count Summerly's recording need not fear comparison: Angharad Gruffydd Jones has a less distinctive voice but uses it to beautiful effect. Peter Crawford sings well too, less passionate but sweeter in tone than Christopher Josey, the countertenor on the first recording.

Svyati

God is With Us. Song for Athene. The Lamb. The Tiger. Magnificat and Nunc dimittis. Funeral Ikos. Two Hymns to the Mother of God. Love Bade Me Welcome. As One Who Has Slept. The Lord's Prayer. Svyati[a]
[a]**Tim Hugh** *vc* **St John's College Choir, Cambridge / Christopher Robinson**
Naxos 8 555256 (70' · DDD)   Ⓢ❍❍🄳⇥

If John Tavener's reputation were to rest solely on his unaccompanied choral music and nothing else, then his stature as one of the most striking and original composers working today would be just as high. Much of Tavener's creativity is founded on the traditions of his Orthodox faith and of Orthodox chant, and yet curiously, intentionally or unintentionally, he has also, through works such as those presented here, extended the tradition of English choral music. Through their popularity *The Lamb*, *The Tiger* and *Song for Athene* have become immovably imbedded in our choral tradition, but one need only listen to the splendid *Magnificat and Nunc dimittis*, for instance, to find a unique symbiosis of Eastern and Western traditions at work.

Many of the works presented on this CD have enjoyed wide circulation on numerous Tavener-only and compilation discs, but the performances here from the Choir of St John's College,

Cambridge, under the direction of Christopher Robinson, have much to recommend them and the super-budget price makes this issue especially desirable for those seeking a survey of Tavener's choral music for the first time.

Svyati for solo cello and choir, with echoes of *The Protecting Veil*, opens a window on Tavener's more overtly Eastern/Orthodox-inspired music. Tim Hugh's serenely beautiful account of the solo cello part is a winner from beginning to end. The recording, made in St John's College Chapel, is resplendently atmospheric.

Choral Works

As One Who Has Slept. The Bridegroom. Birthday Sleep. Butterfly Dreams. The Second Cominga. Schuon Hymnen. Shûnya. Exhortation and Kohima
Polyphony / Stephen Layton with ªChristopher **Bowers-Broadbent** org
Hyperion CDA67475 (75' · DDD · T/t)   Ⓕ**OOO**▷

As One Who Has Slept, the earliest work here, represents Tavener's most musically ascetic period, which by 1996 was drawing to a close. The mesmeric use of drone-like chords behind and beyond the melodic lines reassures and comforts the listener during this portrait of Christ's harrowing of hell. He soon returned to a warmer palette and a wider range of techniques. In *Birthday Sleep* and *The Bridal Chamber* (1999) hymn-like tunes still predominate, but the voices move more independently, the harmonies are richer.

The 2001 setting of Yeats's *The Second Coming* is full of skilfully realised, dramatically startling gestures, but the mood is quizzical where it should describe fear-threaded apprehension, bombastic where it should be aghast with dismay. Finally, a group of pieces completed in 2003. In *Butterfly Dreams*, a set of miniatures, form and content are better matched. Parts of *Schuon Hymnen*, especially the writing for solo soprano (a glittering, heart-lifting performance by Amy Haworth) suggests music from 1950s sci-fi films: as with those films, it's easy to see how the effects are achieved, yet somehow the magic survives. *Exhortation and Kohima* achieves a Tudoresque splendour, while *Shûnya* adds elements of Buddhist ritual to the mix.

John Taverner   English c1490-1545

*Little is known about the life of Taverner. In 1524-25 he was a lay clerk at the collegiate church of Tatershall. In 1526 he accepted the post of instructor of the choristers at Cardinal College (now Christ Church), Oxford, and in about 1530 he became a lay clerk (and probably instructor of the choristers) at the parish church of St Botolph, Boston. By 1537 he had retired from full-time employment as a church musician. Most of his extant works, which include eight Masses, three Magnificats, numerous motets and votive anti-*phons and a few consort pieces and fragmentary secular partsongs, probably date from the 1520s. His Western Wynde Mass is based on a secular tune and is in a less expansive, more Lutheran style. His four-voice In nomine, the prototype of this English genre, is simply a transcription of the 'In nomine Domine' section of his Missa Gloria tibi Trinitas. It created something of a vogue among English composers of Taverner's and later generations.*

Missa Gloria tibi Trinitas

Taverner Missa Gloria tibi Trinitas. Dum transisset Sabbatum I. Mater Christi sanctissima. O Wilhelme, pastor bone **Anonymous** Cantus firmus: Gloria tibi trinitas. Kyrie, 'Deus creator omnium'
Christ Church Cathedral Choir, Oxford / Stephen Darlington
Avie AV2123 (63' · DDD · T/t)   Ⓕ**OO**▷

The Choir of Christ Church could hardly have made a more ambitious return to recording after their valuable but variable series of Nimbus discs. Taverner's Mass is the *chef d'oeuvre* of the greatest composer of his time, yet it has never before been recorded by the kind of liturgical choir which he had in mind; this is a courageous and significant act of reclamation. Courageous, because Taverner's demands of phrase and melodic continuity are more subtle, but no less daunting in their own way, than those presented by Palestrina and Gombert. Performing at written pitch helps.

Stephen Darlington and his choir aren't afraid of a few dirty edges around the sound; this is a world away from the hygienic surfaces of the Gabrieli Consort or from the shapely halo of King's, Cambridge. The Christ Church trebles have a full-frontal attack to a phrase that is more commonly heard from middle-European choirs. That makes it more susceptible to the glare of the microphone, but the recording itself dares to go in closer than Nimbus ever did. The risk largely pays off in *tutti* passages of startling immediacy, contrasted with more solo verse sections than is usual (to rest tired voices?). Some distended cadences leave you wondering whether they can possibly have the puff to sustain them. Sometimes they can't (at the end of the first paragraph of the *Sanctus*); often they can (the 'Hosanna' at the end of the famous *Benedictus*). The motets are no less individual in concept and execution, including a cheeky but winning slide in *Mater Christi*; like the rest of the disc it will divide opinion, but it demands to be taken seriously.

Missa Mater Christi sanctissima

Hodie nobis caelorum Rex. Mater Christi   Ⓟ
sanctissima. Magnificat sexti toni. Nesciens mater. Quemadmodum a 6. Missa Mater Christi sanctissima. In nomine a 4
Fretwork (Wendy Gillespie, Richard Campbell *treble* viols Susanna Pell, Julia Hodgson, Richard Boothby

bass viols William Hunt great bass viol)
The Sixteen / Harry Christophers
Hyperion Helios CDH55053 (65' · DDD · T/t) Ⓑ Ⓞ ➔

The Sixteen offer an impressive account of Taverner's five-part *Missa Mater Christi sanctissima*, based on his votive anthem of the same name. It's a lively and vigorous work, beautifully crafted, and this performance amply matches its craftsmanship. Harry Christophers attempts no liturgical reconstruction, concentrating instead upon sheer musical quality. Three female sopranos replace the boy trebles. The music is pitched up a tone, which has the effect of adding brilliance to every climax. He demonstrates the good acoustic of St Jude's in Hampstead – an acoustic of space and definition, ideal for the interweaving of the strands of early Tudor polyphony; indeed, clarity and a sense of space are hallmarks of the recording. The supporting programme of the Christmas responsory, *Hodie*, the votive anthem *Mater Christi* and a four-part *Magnificat* is completed – unexpectedly but most delightfully – by two pieces for viols.

Pyotr Ilyich Tchaikovsky
Russian 1840-1893

His father was a successful mining engineer while his mother was the artistic, sensitive one, French by birth, and a good linguist. Pyotr was the second of her six children. He had a good education, a French governess and a stable beginning to his life. As early as eight, though, signs of neurosis manifested themselves, often brought on by listening to music. In 1848 his father resigned his government post hoping for a better position in Moscow. This did not materialise and Pyotr and his elder brother were packed off to boarding school. This second period of relative security ended in 1854 when his mother died of cholera. His relationship with her was profound to the point of obsession and it can be argued that he never recovered from this blow.

His period at the St Petersburg School of Jurisprudence led to a job as a clerk in the Ministry of Justice, a job for which he was singularly unsuited. The decisive factor was the founding of what would become the St Petersburg Conservatory in 1862 by Anton Rubinstein. Tchaikovsky followed his teacher Nicholas Zaremba to the Conservatory and the following year resigned his post to become a full-time musician. Only two years later, Rubinstein's brother Nikolai had invited Tchaikovsky to teach harmony at the Moscow Conservatory.

For a time, he lived in Nikolai Rubinstein's house in Moscow while his first large-scale compositions began to emerge (Symphony No 1, *Winter Dreams*, among them). His nervous disorder began to manifest itself again in the forms of colitis, hypochondria, hallucinations and numbness in his hands and feet.

In 1868 a Belgian soprano, Désirée Artôt, part of an opera company visiting St Petersburg, became attached to Tchaikovsky and for a while he contem-

plated marriage. She, however, was as celebrated for her sexual peccadilloes as her singing and soon after married a Spanish singer. Tchaikovsky accepted it all philosophically (on the surface at least). The music that followed the affair was the first version of his famous Romeo and Juliet Fantasy Overture, one of his most popular works, containing the most radiant love music he ever wrote.

Tchaikovsky's career progressed in an untroubled way for the next few years. He contributed music criticism to Moscow newspapers, made many trips abroad, taught and continued composing. Then came a series of crises. Late in 1874 he finished his Piano Concerto No 1 and played it through to Nikolai Rubinstein to whom he had dedicated the work. Rubinstein denounced it as ugly and unplayable. Tchaikovsky was stunned. Rubinstein eventually relented and became a fervent champion of the concerto but Tchaikowsky was flung into a morbid depression by Rubinstein's reaction to the concerto and the initial failure of his ballet Swan Lake. He tired of his work at the Conservatory, he had financial problems and, above all, nagging away at the back of his mind, was the guilt attached to his homosexuality.

At exactly the right time a guardian angel appeared in his life. Through the violinist Kotek, an affluent and cultured widow, Nadezhda von Meck, heard about Tchaikovsky and engaged him to write some music for large fees. She was a remarkable woman aged 45, the mother of 11 children and passionately fond of music. But shortly after his introduction to Mme von Meck another crisis hit Tchaikovsky. A pretty blonde, a 28-year old music student named Antonina Milyukova, became obsessed with him. Without disclosing to Antonina his true sexual preference, without loving her, thinking that marriage would scotch the current rumours of his 'deviancy', Tchaikovsky nevertheless married her in July 1877. It was a disaster. He was 'ready to scream' (he admitted) the first time they were alone together. Five days later, he was going out of his mind and fled to his sister's estate at Kamenka. Later he attempted to kill himself by standing in the freezing Moscow River. He next went to St Petersburg where his brother Anatol, a lawyer, made suitable arrangements for a separation. The couple were never divorced and never met again.

Nadezhda von Meck was kept informed of this relationship by Tchaikovsky (though never of the real cause of its failure) and the same year (1877) settled an annual allowance of 6000 roubles on him. His Fourth Symphony (dedicated to Mme von Meck), the opera Eugene Onegin and the great Violin Concerto were but three of the works written shortly after Tchaikovsky had been given financial security. For the next 13 years, this extraordinary relationship continued, one of the most curious and moving in musical history. It was the perfect relationship for the composer, a replacement for his lost mother, a woman who had no personal or sexual interest in him, yet who supported him financially and emotionally. In all the period of their touching friendship they never met. One of the conditions for her generous subsidy was that they should never become involved on a personal level.

The initial burst of unqualified masterpieces was followed by an uneven period (his opera Joan of Arc,

Tchaikovsky

the Second Piano Concerto, Capriccio italien and the Serenade for Strings, the Piano Sonata and Piano Trio). By 1880 he was famous and respected. Then, between 1881 and 1888, he dried up.

Inspiration returned in 1888 with the Fifth Symphony. The government settled an annual pension on him and he made an extensive tour of Europe conducting his works to enormous acclaim. Then in 1890 came a letter from Nadezhda von Meck saying that, due to financial reversals, she was no longer able to subsidise Tchaikovsky. The composer replied expressing sympathy for her changed fortunes, pointed out that he was now financially self sufficient and hoped their friendship would continue. The letter went unanswered. So did many more. Then he learnt that in fact Mme von Meck was not financially embarrassed and had used it merely as an excuse to discontinue the friendship. After 13 years, his trusted confidante and mother-figure had abruptly terminated their relationship. Perhaps she had discovered the truth about his homosexuality, perhaps she had become bored with Tchaikovsky's letters; more likely, her family had put pressure on her to terminate the friendship and put an end to all the society gossip about its nature. It was a shattering blow to Tchaikovsky's confidence and initiated a period of morbid depression.

In 1893 he completed his great Sixth Symphony, the Pathétique, and in June travelled to Cambridge to receive an Honorary Doctorate of Music. In October he conducted the premiere of the Pathétique (it was coolly received). On November 2, after an agreeable evening meal, he drank a glass of tap water. His friends were appalled. Didn't he know it was the cholera season in St Petersburg, that no water should be drunk without first boiling it? Tchaikovsky, it seems, was unconcerned.

There are many stories surrounding his death. The question of 'Was it suicide or not?' has fascinated scholars for over a century and provided the material for plays, novels, doctorates and romantic biographers. The most likely theory is the simplest one, that Tchaikovsky was a fatalist: someone who makes little effort in the face of threatened disaster and believes that all events are subject to fate. The fact is that Tchaikovsky died from cholera four days after drinking the water. One troubling piece of evidence confuses the cholera-suicide theories. Tchaikovsky's body lay in state in his brother's bedroom. It was then taken to Kazan Cathedral where mourners filed passed his hundreds to pay their respects and touch the body. Not one of them contracted the highly contagious disease.

Piano Concertos

No 1 in B flat minor; **No 2** in G, Op 44;
No 3 in E flat, Op 75

Piano Concertos Nos 1, 2 & 3. Concert Fantasia.
Andante non troppo (from Concerto No 2, ed Siloti)
Andante non troppo (from Concerto No 2, ed Hough).
Solitude, Op 73 No 6 (arr Hough). None but the lonely heart, Op 6 No 6 (arr Hough)
Stephen Hough pf
Minnesota Orchestra / Osmo Vänskä

Hyperion ② CDA67711/2 (141' · DDD)   Ⓕ OOⒹ→

Stephen Hough's contribution to the Romantic piano concertos series has been one of its outstanding successes and it is to him that Hyperion gives the honour of the milestone Vol 50 containing, as it does, the quintessence of this series: Tchaikovsky's First Concerto.

All four *concertante* works were recorded live in America. These, you can hear, are not performances made with the safety net of a studio but ones with a sense of occasion, purpose and risk-taking. Osmo Vänskä, particularly attuned to the sensibilities of Russian music, is an ideal partner for his inspired soloist. The old warhorse comes up as fresh as paint. Even with 130 alternatives on the market, this is an exceptional reading with brisk tempi and subtle nuances. The electrifying pace Hough injects into the codas of No 1 and the *Concert Fantasia* are suitably exciting, though these are nothing compared to the tumultuous final pages of No 2 (a tremendous performance). The audience whoops in amazement.

The best comparable set is Pletnev with the Philharmonia and Fedoseyev (Virgin Classics) in their identical programme. Hough plays with a weightier tone, however, and the Minnesota players are more forwardly focused and evenly balanced (Andrew Keener is the producer common to both sets). Hyperion also includes as extra tracks Siloti's brutally cut version of No 2's *Andante*, followed by Hough's own solution to the movement's structure (how Tchaikovsky must be kicking himself not to have thought of this) as well as two delectable Tchaikovsky song transcriptions by Hough. This is a great recording, no doubt about it.

Piano Concerto No 1[a]. The Nutcracker – Suite, Op 71a (arr Economou)[b]
Martha Argerich, [b]**Nicolas Economou** pfs [a]**Berlin Philharmonic Orchestra / Claudio Abbado**
DG 449 816-2GH (53' · DDD)
Recorded live [b]1983   Ⓕ OⒹ→

Tchaikovsky's First Concerto has already appeared twice on disc from Martha Argerich in complementary performances: live and helter-skelter on Philips with Kondrashin, studio and magisterial with Dutoit on DG. Now, finely recorded, here's a third, live recording with the BPO and Claudio Abbado surpassing even those earlier and legendary performances. Argerich has never sounded on better terms with the piano, more virtuoso yet engagingly human. Lyrical and insinuating, to a degree her performance seems to be made of the tumultuous elements themselves, of fire and ice, rain and sunshine. The Russians may claim this concerto for themselves, but even they will surely listen in disbelief, awed and – dare one say it – a trifle piqued. Listen to Argerich's *Allegro con spirito*, as the concerto gets under way, where her darting *crescendos* and *diminuendos* make the triplet rhythm speak with the rarest vitality and caprice. Her nervous reaching out towards further pianistic frays in the heart-easing second subject is pure Argerich and so are the octave storms in both the first and third movements that will have everyone, particularly her partners, tightening their seat belts. The cadenza is spun off with a hypnotic brilliance, the central *Prestissimo* from the *Andantino* becomes a true '*scherzo* of fireflies', and the finale seems to dance off the page; a far cry from more emphatic Ukranian point-making and brutality.

For encores DG has reissued Argerich's 1983 performance of *The Nutcracker* where she's partnered by Nicolas Economou in his own arrangement, a marvel of scintillating pianistic prowess, imagination and finesse.

Violin Concerto in D, Op 35

Tchaikovsky Violin Concerto **Brahms** (arr Joachim) Hungarian Dances – No 1 in G minor; No 2 in D minor; No 4 in B minor; No 7 in A
Sarah Chang vn **Jonathan Feldman** pf **London Symphony Orchestra / Sir Colin Davis**
EMI 503433-2 (49' · DDD)   Ⓕ🅞🅑➤

The range of dynamic truthfulness conveyed in Sarah Chang's performance, helped by a clear, full, naturally balanced recording, brings not just momentary delight in individual phrases but cumulative gain, in a reading that strongly hangs together. Not only does she play with exceptionally pure tone, avoiding heavy coloration, but her individual artistry doesn't demand the wayward pulling-about often found in this work. She's enormously helped by the fresh, bright and dramatic accompaniment of the LSO under Sir Colin Davis. In the outer movements she conveys wit along with the power and poetry, and the intonation is immaculate. Brahms's *Hungarian Dances* are delectable, marked by the sort of naughty pointing of phrase and rhythm that tickles your musical funny-bone just as Kreisler always did. Here's a young artist who really does live up to the claims of the publicists.

Violin Concerto. Piano Concerto No 1
ªChristian Tetzlaff vn ᵇNikolai Lugansky pf
Russian National Orchestra / Kent Nagano
Pentatone 🄬 PTC5186 022 (68' · DDD)   Ⓕ

These are stimulating versions of two favourite concertos, which take a fresh interpretative approach. Nikolai Lugansky's conception is spacious, with pianist and conductor taking time to relish the music's puissance. The opening is broad and weighty. Then, although the first subject of the *Allegro* has a vividly Russian rhythmic character, in both the exposition and recapitulation much is made of the beauty of lyrical secondary material and the Romantic link with Tchaikovsky's *Romeo and Juliet*. The exquisitely delicate central *Andantino* is followed by a scin-

---

TCHAIKOVSKY PIANO CONCERTO NO 1 – IN BRIEF

Vladimir Horowitz; NBC SO / Arturo Toscanini Ⓗ
Naxos 8 110671 (74' · ADD)   Ⓢ🅞
Horowitz's celebrated live 1941 Carnegie Hall recording with his father-in-law Toscanini serves up a potent mix of adrenalin-fuelled vigour and jaw-dropping virtuosity.

Solomon; Philharmonia Orch / Issay Dobrowen Ⓗ
Testament SBT1232 (60' · ADD)   Ⓕ
A high-voltage yet nourishing reading from this incomparable British pianist. Definitely one to hear, as is Solomon's earlier 1929 recording with Harty and the Hallé (now refurbished on Naxos 8 110680).

Emil Gilels; Chicago SO / Fritz Reiner Ⓗ
RCA 09026 68530-2 (74' · ADD)   Ⓜ
The work with which Gilels made his belated American debut in October 1955. Later that same month, RCA shrewdly took the opportunity to preserve his by turns dazzling and poetic interpretation for posterity.

Yevgeny Sudbin; São Paulo Symphony Orchestra / John Neschling Ⓕ🅞🅑➤
BIS 🄬 BIS-SACD1588 (71' · DDD/DSD)
An astounding new account from the 26-year-old Sudbin who brings a freshness and power to this warhorse. He is particularly good at the mercurial changes of mood.

Martha Argerich; Berlin PO / Claudio Abbado
DG 449 816-2GH (53' · DDD)   Ⓕ🅞🅑➤
Martha Argerich's smouldering pianism silences criticism and sparks off a hugely eloquent reponse from the Berliners under Claudio Abbado.

Mikhail Pletnev; Philharmonia Orchestra / Vladimir Fedoseyev
Virgin Classics ② 561463-2 (112' · DDD)   Ⓢ
Pletnev's imperious account represents tempting value, coming as it does with this same team's laudable survey of all of Tchaikovsky's output for piano and orchestra.

Stephen Hough; Minnesota Orchestra / Osmo Vänskä
Hyperion ② CDA67711/2 (141' · DDD)   Ⓕ🅞🅞🅑➤
The old warhorse comes up as fresh as paint. Even with 130 alternatives on the market, this is an exceptional reading with brisk tempi and subtle nuances.

Nikolai Lugansky; Russian National Orchestra / Kent Nagano
Pentatone 🄬 PTC5186 022 (68' · DDD)   Ⓕ
Lugansky, winner of the 1994 Tchaikovsky Competition, possesses quicksilver reflexes and a dark, burnished tone. A thoughtful performance, but with a passionate edge, too.

TCHAIKOVSKY VIOLIN CONCERTO – IN BRIEF

Jascha Heifetz; Chicago SO / Fritz Reiner Ⓗ
RCA 09026 61495-2 (64' · ADD) ⓂⒶ
A performance of outsize personality from Heifetz and Reiner. Coupled with this same partnership's sovereign account of the Brahms Concerto.

David Oistrakh; Staatskapelle Dresden / Ⓗ
Franz Konwitschny
DG ② 447 427-2GOR2 (142' · ADD) ⓂⒶ
Oistrakh at his sublimely musical and involving best in a work that stood at the centre of his extensive concerto repertoire. DG's 1954 mono recording retains its remarkable sense of presence.

Leonid Kogan; Paris Conservatoire Orchestra /
Constantin Silvestri
EMI Encore 574757-2 (69' · ADD) Ⓢ
Yet another fabulous Russian fiddler, this time Leonid Kogan, who plays with a muscular panache and unruffled security that rivet the attention. Silvestri lends splendidly feisty support.

Julia Fischer; Russian National Orchestra /
Yakov Kreizberg
Pentatone ⊚ PTC5186 095 (68' · DDD) ⓂⒶⒷ
A splendid recording from the hugely impressive young Julia Fischer. There's power and poetry in spades and the orchestra accompany with thrilling commitment.

Kyung-Wha Chung; London SO / André Previn
Decca 425 080-2DCS (66' · ADD) ⓂⒶ
Chung's engagingly svelte and warm-hearted account has barely aged at all. A long-standing favourite, this, with Previn and the LSO also on top form.

Sarah Chang; London SO / Sir Colin Davis
EMI 754753-2 (49' · DDD) ⒻⒶⒷ
For once the hype didn't mislead: soloist Sarah Chang was only 11 when she made this recording, and her vibrant tone and absolute technical security betoken a very special talent.

Vadim Repin; Kirov Orchestra / Valery Gergiev
Philips 473 343-2PM (72' · DDD) ⒻⒷ
Enterprisingly coupled with Myaskovsky's lovely Concerto, Repin's remake of the Tchaikovsky proves even more masterly and engrossing than his Erato predecessor.

Christian Tetzlaff; Russian National Orchestra /
Kent Nagano
Pentatone ⊚ PTC5186 022 (68' · DDD) Ⓕ
Tetzlaff and Nagano take a gentler, more restrained approach than is customary, but there's no want of brilliance or brazen intensity.

tillating *Scherzando*. The finale bursts forth with irrepressible dash and virtuosity. When, near the close, the tempo broadens massively to make a hugely positive climax some forward impetus is lost, but Lugansky's bravura is thrilling.

Tchaikovsky's friendly opening for his Violin Concerto is shaped by Nagano in a mood of disarming simplicity, and the two main themes are invested with lyrical warmth. Tetzlaff bounces his bow with engaging lightness in the key passage (7'03") that Hanslick described as 'beating the violin black and blue', while the cadenza is played with such affectionate detail that it becomes a highlight of the work. Tetzlaff's playing throughout is polished and secure.

In both concertos the recording has the orchestra placed naturally within a warm concert hall acoustic.

Violin Concerto. Souvenir d'un lieu cher, Op 42
(arr Lascae)
Janine Jansen vn
Mahler Chamber Orchestra / Daniel Harding
Decca 478 0651DH (53' · DDD) ⒻⒷ

You can anticipate something individual and special from the way that Janine Jansen insinuates herself into the first subject of the Concerto – shyly confidential at first, building assertiveness with the double-stopped reprise. Everything here is vital, un-hackneyed. And yet Jansen is very much the old-fashioned romantic. Her way with *rubato* and with dynamic contrasts is unashamedly free. She spins sound like an excellent singer, taking it away *subito pianissimo* in true *bel canto* fashion. She does so quite demurely, suggestively, with the second subject of the first movement and again with the second movement canzonetta, which is lovely – and natural.

There's an intimacy about her playing which sits well with the Mahler Chamber Orchestra; not that the introverted elements of the concerto in any way upstage the extrovert. In many ways it's the Cossack-dancing finale that sends this version spinning into the orbit of the very best available. The partnership with Daniel Harding could hardly be tighter. No rhetorical slacking of tempo as Jansen responds to the fiery orchestral introduction – she presses forward with a will. The gritty second theme is very much a coarse folksy baritone against hang-dog bassoon, and come the second round of dancing, Harding has the orchestral *pizzicati* really kicking up dust.

A smashing performance, then, with only marginal disappointment concerning the recorded sound – crisp and immediate, but of a dry ambience without much atmosphere. The supporting piece – *Souvenir d'un lieu cher* – gives us the chance to hear the concerto's original slow movement in a lovely arrangement for violin and strings by the Romanian-Dutch conductor Alexandru Lascae. Again, the sense of Jansen as the first among equals makes for especially telling interplay with her colleagues.

Symphonies

No 1 in G minor (Winter Daydreams), Op 13; **No 2** in C minor (Little Russian), Op 17; **No 3** in D (Polish), Op 29; **No 4** in F minor, Op 36; **No 5** in E minor, Op 64; **No 6** in B minor (Pathétique), Op 74

Complete Symphonies

Symphonies Nos 1-6. Violin Concerto in D, Op 35ª. Piano Concerto No 1 in B flat minor, Op 23ᵈᵉ. 1812 Overture, Op 49. Capriccio italien, Op 45. Eugene Onegin – Polonaise; Waltz. Marche slave, Op 31. The Nutcracker – Suite, Op 71ª. Romeo and Juliet Fantasy Overture. Serenade in C, Op 48. The Sleeping Beauty – Suite. Swan Lake – Suite. Variations on a Rococo Theme, Op 33ᶜ
ªChristian Ferras, ᵇMichel Schwalbé vns ᶜMstislav Rostropovich vc ᵈSviatoslav Richter pf Berlin Philharmonic Orchestra, ᵉVienna Symphony Orchestra / Herbert von Karajan
DG ⑧ 463 774-2GB8 (8h 51' · ADD/DDD)
Recorded 1962-80   Ⓑ**OO**

Karajan was unquestionably a great Tchaikovsky conductor. Yet although he recorded the last three symphonies many times, he did not turn to the first three until the end of the 1970s, and then proved an outstanding advocate. In the Mendelssohnian opening movement of the First, the tempo may be brisk, but the music's full charm is displayed and the melancholy of the *Andante* is touchingly caught. Again at the opening of the *Little Russian* (No 2), horn and bassoon capture that special Russian colouring, as they do in the engaging *Andantino marziale*, and the crisp articulation in the first-movement *Allegro* is bracing. The sheer refinement of the orchestral playing in the *scherzos* of all three symphonies is a delight, and finales have great zest with splendid bite and precision in the fugato passages and a convincing closing peroration.

The so-called *Polish* Symphony (No 3) is the least tractable of the canon, but again Karajan's apt tempi and the precision of ensemble makes the first movement a resounding success. The *Alla tedesca* brings a hint of Brahms, but the Slavic dolour of the *Andante elegiaco* is unmistakeable and its climax blooms rapturously. No doubt the reason these early symphonies sound so fresh is because the Berlin orchestra was not over-familiar with them, and clearly enjoyed playing them. The sound throughout is excellent. It gets noticeably fiercer in the Fourth Symphony, recorded a decade earlier, but is still well balanced. The first movement has a compulsive forward thrust, and the breakneck finale is viscerally thrilling. The slow movement is beautifully played but just a trifle bland. Overall, though, this is impressive and satisfying, especially the riveting close.

DG has chosen the 1965 recording of the Fifth, rather than the mid-'70s version, and they were right to do so. It's marvellously recorded (in the Jesus-Christus-Kirche): the sound has all the richness and depth one could ask and the performance too is one of Karajan's very finest. There's some indulgence of the second-subject string melody of the first movement. But the slow movement is gloriously played from the horn solo onwards, and the second re-entry of the Fate theme is so dramatic that it almost makes one jump. The delightful Waltz brings the kind of elegant warmth and detail from the violins that's a BPO speciality, and the finale, while not rushed Mravinsky fashion, still carries all before it and has power and dignity at the close.

The *Pathétique* was a very special work for Karajan (as it was for the Berlin Philharmonic) and his 1964 performance is one of his greatest recordings. The reading as a whole avoids hysteria, yet the resolution of the passionate climax of the first movement sends shivers down the spine, while the finale has a comparable eloquence, and the March/*Scherzo*, with ensemble wonderfully crisp and biting, brings an almost demonic power to the coda. Again the sound is excellent, full-bodied in the strings and with plenty of sonority for the trombones.

The String Serenade is digital, brightly recorded in the Philharmonie in 1980, but naturally balanced. Marvellous playing. The Waltz, with a most felicitous control of *rubato*, is the highlight, and the *Elégie* is certainly ardent; and if the first movement could have been more neatly articulated, the finale has tremendous bustle and energy. As for the *concertante* works, the account of the glorious *Rococo* Variations with Rostropovich is another classic of the gramophone, even though it uses the truncated score. The First Piano Concerto is a disappointment, with Richter and Karajan failing to strike sparks as a partnership. In spite of brilliant solo playing, the first movement lacks supporting tension in the orchestra, and in the finale you can sense Richter wanting to press forward, while Karajan seems to hold back: the coda itself hangs fire in the orchestra. Similarly Ferras was not an ideal choice for the Violin Concerto. Not all will take to his somewhat febrile timbre, with its touches of near-schmaltz. But the performance as a whole works better than the Piano Concerto.

Romeo and Juliet is finely done, passionate and dramatic, if not quite so spontaneously inspired as Karajan's early VPO version for Decca, especially at the opening. But *Marche slave*, ideally paced, is very successful, sombre and exciting by turns. *Capriccio italien* and *1812* are both brilliantly played, and the triptych of ballet suites can be recommended almost without reservation, with the *Sleeping Beauty* suite memorable for some very exciting climaxes.

Even with the reservations about the two concertos, this bargain box is a fine investment, and certainly value for money. The documentation is excellent.

Symphonies – Nos 1-6. Manfred Symphony, Op 58. Capriccio Italien, Op 45. Serenade in C, Op 48. The Tempest, Op 18. Romeo and Juliet. Eugene

Onegin – Polonaise
Bournemouth Symphony Orchestra /
Andrew Litton
Virgin Classics ⑥ 561893-2 (7h' · DDD)   ⑤**○○▷**

Here's another of those extraordinary Virgin bargain boxes, offered at an astonishingly low price. These Tchaikovsky performances would be highly recommendable if they cost twice as much, while the recordings – realistically set back in a concert hall acoustic – are superb, full-bodied, and wide ranging and brilliant. The playing of the Bournemouth orchestra may not always be quite as polished as, say, the BPO for Karajan, but it's still very, very good indeed: ensemble is as keen as it's passionately responsive. Moreover Litton has a natural ear for Tchaikovskian detail – time and again he draws the listener to revel in those delightful orchestral touches with which Tchaikovsky embroiders his melodies.

Litton gets off to an outstanding start with Nos 1 and 2, where the atmosphere is imbued with bonhomie and high spirits; he readily disguises the structural flaws of the *Polish* Symphony with his geniality and a clever ebb and flow of tempi; in No 4 you're more aware of the slight distancing of the sound, which he matches by his spacious tempo in the first movement; the same broad approach works less well in No 5, where you need more impetus in the outer movements; but he's back on form in No 6. There the phrasing of the first movement's secondary theme is ravishing, and the climax is as powerful as the cumulative peak of the *Scherzo*/March. In *Manfred* his emphasis is on its programmatic basis, with tenderly delicate and splendidly dramatic moments.

The extra items are all enjoyably spontaneous. The *Capriccio italien* has visceral thrills and panache, the *String Serenade* is warmly romantic; and both *Romeo and Juliet*, matching romantic pathos with passion, and the underrated but masterly Shakespearean *Tempest* are among the highlights. Even if you have much of this repertoire already, this set remains very enticing.

Symphonies – selected

Symphony No 1, 'Winter Daydreams'
Oslo Philharmonic Orchestra / Mariss Jansons
Chandos CHAN8402 (44' · DDD)   ⑤**○▷**

Symphony No 2' Little Russian'. Capriccio italien
Oslo Philharmonic Orchestra / Mariss Jansons
Chandos CHAN8460 (48' · DDD)   ⑤**○▷**

The composer gave the First Symphony the title *Winter Daydreams*, and also named the first two movements. The opening *Allegro tranquillo* he subtitled 'Dreams of a winter journey', while the *Adagio* bears the inscription 'Land of desolation, land of mists'. A *Scherzo* and finale round off a conventional four-movement symphonic structure. In the slow movement Jansons inspires a performance of expressive warmth and tenderness, while the *Scherzo* is managed with great delicacy and sensitivity. Both the opening movement and finale are invested with vigour and passion, and everywhere the orchestral playing is marvellously confident and disciplined.

Jansons also has the full measure of the Second Symphony. It's a direct performance – the first movement *allegro* is relatively steady, but never sounds too slow, because of crisp rhythmic pointing – and the second movement goes for charm and felicity of colour. The finale is properly exuberant, with the secondary theme full of character, and there's a fine surge of adrenalin at the end. The *Capriccio italien*, a holiday piece in which the composer set out to be entertaining, is also played with great flair and the hint of vulgarity in the Neapolitan tune isn't shirked. Again the closing pages produce a sudden spurt of excitement which is particularly satisfying. The recording here is just short of Chandos's finest – the massed violins could be sweeter on top, but the hall resonance is right for this music.

Symphonies Nos 1, 'Winter Daydreams', and 6, 'Pathétique'
London Philharmonic Orchestra /
Vladimir Jurowski
LPO ② LPO0039 (89' · DDD)
Recorded live   ⑧**○▷**

Of the two performances, it's that of *Winter Daydreams* which conveys the greater imaginative spark and spontaneity. Jurowski steers a marvellously lithe and clear-sighted course through this youthful canvas, with springy basslines, luminous textures and bracing contrapuntal vigour the keynotes (the antiphonally divided first and second fiddles are a boon, as is the LPO's personable woodwind roster). There's genuine affection, too, nowhere more evident than in the third movement's radiant Trio melody which is allowed to blossom fully yet with no unwanted loss of momentum. The finale can sometimes outstay its welcome, but not here.

Jurowski's *Pathétique*, too, has much to commend it, not least a keen sense of architecture, scrupulous observation and total eschewal of histrionics. Everything is exquisitely nuanced, and Jurowski exploits an intrepidly wide range of dynamic, but his tasteful handling of the great second subject only intermittently tugs at the heart-strings. The orchestral playing positively sizzles in the first movement development (which goes off like a rocket) but tends to a steely, excitable slickness towards the end of the *Scherzo*. The towering finale is strong, thoughtful and full of freshly minted detail but it's not, in all honesty, terribly moving. Hugely impressive in parts, then, and well worth hearing, but think of it as a bonus: this LPO release merits immediate investigation for the First Symphony alone.

Symphony No 2, 'Little Russian'. Festival Overture on the Danish National Hymn. The Storm. Overture in F
Gothenburg Symphony Orchestra / Neeme Järvi
BIS ⚖ BIS-SACD1418 (72'· DDD/DSD)   ⑤**○○▷**

The Gothenburg Symphony Orchestra, under their longtime music director Neeme Järvi, give an outstanding performance of the *Little Russian* Symphony, beautifully played and paced and immaculately recorded, though it lacks a little on felicitous detail.

Järvi's flowing tempo for the long opening *Andante* is reassuring and his free expressiveness is most persuasive, the crisp attack of the *Allegro*, with its Ukrainian themes, bringing echoes of Tchaikovsky's ballet music. Though the *Andantino marziale* is on the brisk side, the rhythmic lift again is most persuasive. The *Scherzo* is fresh and light and the opening of the finale has ample weight to contrast with the lightness of the second subject, its cross-rhythms suggesting Cuban rhythms. The way Järvi presses forward as the climaxes build adds to the excitement.

The overture inspired by Ostrovsky's play *The Storm* is by far the most inspired of the three and is given a powerful performance. The Overture in F is a student work whose deft orchestration points to the mature Tchaikovsky while the one on the Danish national anthem suffers from its relatively uninteresting theme. It's not nearly as striking as the Russian national anthem, with which it is entwined – rather as the *Marseillaise* is in the *1812*. Tchaikovsky thought it a much more successful piece though it is hard to justify the pompous final repeat of the Danish theme, *fortissimo*, even in a performance as well judged as Järvi's.

Symphony No 3, 'Polish'. Serenade for Nikolai Rubinstein's Name Day. Eugene Onegin – Waltz; Polonaise. The Voyevoda, Op 3 – Entr'acte; Dance of the Chambermaids. Dmitri the Pretender and Vassily Shuisky – Act I, Introduction; Mazurka
Gothenburg Symphony Orchestra / Neeme Järvi
BIS 🔊 BIS-SACD1468 (77' · DDD/DSD) Ⓕ Ⓞ ➤

Neeme Järvi's understated cycle of the Tchaikovsky symphonies has certainly accentuated the innate classicism of this music and, within that, its need to dance. What really excites this performance of the so-called *Polish* is an approach to rhythm and articulation which keeps the textures open (the BIS sound engineers of course play their part in this) and the phrasing fluid.

Järvi's reading of the symphony may sometimes lack temperament and that last degree of swagger but at tempi that would indeed keep Tchaikovsky's imaginary dancers on their toes it exhibits great vitality and, more importantly, an abiding warmth and affection for what one can safely say is Tchaikovsky's most lyric symphonic creation. The middle movements especially repay Järvi's lightness of touch, spontaneous and luminous.

We remain 'on stage' for the rest of the disc – a selection of sweetmeats from Tchaikovsky's theatre music, familiar or not, incidental or otherwise. The most interesting morsels come from the 'dramatic chronicle' *Dmitri the Pretender and Vassily Shuisky*: a darkly contemplative and fleet-

ingly tormented Introduction and a rather graceful Mazurka.

But the most touching item has to be the tiny Serenade that Tchaikovsky wrote for the name day of his friend and champion Nikolai Rubinstein, the man who first conducted the Third Symphony. It's amazing what can be revealed in three minutes and in this very personal charmer we graduate from wistful introspection to hymnic admiration in less time than it takes to realise that Tchaikovsky has fleetingly and so very discreetly opened his heart to his friend.

Symphony No 4
Oslo Philharmonic Orchestra / Mariss Jansons
Chandos CHAN8361 (42' · DDD) Ⓕ Ⓞ ➤

A high emotional charge runs through Jansons's performance of the Fourth, yet this rarely seems to be an end in itself. There's always a balancing concern for the superb craftsmanship of Tchaikovsky's writing: the shapeliness of the phrasing; the superb orchestration, scintillating and subtle by turns; and most of all Tchaikovsky's marvellous sense of dramatic pace. Rarely has the first movement possessed such a strong sense of tragic inevitability, or the return of the 'fate' theme in the finale sounded so logical. The playing of the Oslo Philharmonic Orchestra is first rate: there are some gorgeous woodwind solos and the brass achieve a truly Tchaikovskian intensity. Recordings are excellent.

Symphonies Nos 4-6
Leningrad Philharmonic Orchestra /
Evgeny Mravinsky
DG ② 477 5911GOR2 (129' · ADD)
Recorded 1960 Ⓕ Ⓞ Ⓞ ➤

Ⓖ These recordings are landmarks not just of Tchaikovsky interpretation but of recorded orchestral performances in general. The Leningrad Philharmonic plays like a wild stallion only just held in check by the willpower of its master. Every smallest movement is placed with fierce pride; at any moment it may break into such a frenzied gallop that you hardly know whether to feel exhilarated or terrified. The whipping up of excitement towards the fateful outbursts in Symphony No 4 is astonishing – not just for the discipline of the *stringendos* themselves, but for the pull of psychological forces within them. Symphony No 5 is also mercilessly driven, and pre-echoes of Shostakovian hysteria are particularly strong in the coda's knife-edge of triumph and despair. No less powerfully evoked is the stricken tragedy of the *Pathétique*. Rarely, if ever, can the prodigious rhythmical inventiveness of these scores have been so brilliantly demonstrated.

The fanatical discipline isn't something one would want to see casually emulated but it's applied in a way which sees far into the soul of the music and never violates its spirit. Strictly speaking there's no real comparison with

Mariss Jansons's Chandos issues, despite the fact that Jansons had for long been Mravinsky's assistant in Leningrad. His approach is warmer, less detailed, more classical, and in its way very satisfying. Not surprisingly there are deeper perspectives in the Chandos recordings, but DG's refurbishing has been most successful, enhancing the immediacy of sound so appropriate to the lacerating intensity of the interpretations.

Symphony No 5
Oslo Philharmonic Orchestra / Mariss Jansons
Chandos CHAN8351 (43' · DDD)   (F)**O**(B)

With speeds which are fast but never breathless and with the most vivid recording imaginable, this is as exciting an account as we have had of this symphony. In no way does this performance suggest anything but a metropolitan orchestra, and Jansons keeps reminding one of his background in Leningrad in the great years of Mravinsky and the Philharmonic. Nowhere does the link with Mravinsky emerge more clearly than in the finale, where he adopts a tempo very nearly as hectic as Mravinsky's on his classic DG recording. In the first movement he resists any temptation to linger, preferring to press the music on, and the result sounds totally idiomatic. In the slow movement Jansons again prefers a steady tempo, but treats the second theme with delicate *rubato* and builds the climaxes steadily, not rushing his fences, building the final one even bigger than the first. In the finale it's striking that he follows Tchaikovsky's notated slowings rather than allowing extra *rallentandos* – the bravura of the performance finds its natural culmination.

The Oslo string ensemble is fresh, bright and superbly disciplined, while the wind soloists are generally excellent. The Chandos sound is very specific and well focused despite a warm reverberation, real-sounding and three-dimensional with more clarity in *tuttis* than the rivals.

Symphony No 5. Romeo and Juliet
Royal Philharmonic Orchestra / Daniele Gatti
Harmonia Mundi HMU90 7381 (66' · DDD)   (F)**O**

In Daniele Gatti's performance of Tchaikovsky's Fifth the detail of the wind scoring is continually and vividly revealed, helped by some superb playing from the RPO's soloists. Tempi are close to the composer's metronome markings, somewhat faster than usually heard. The result in the first movement is invigorating, the forward thrust carrying from beginning to end. The primary secondary theme is graceful and romantic, rather than ardently passionate in a Slavic manner. The great climaxes of the slow movement are spacious but not viscerally overwhelming, and the powerful interruptions of the motto theme are less theatrical than usual. The Abbey Road recording is first class, full-bodied, with resplendent brass, and glow-

ing woodwind and horns. Perhaps the massed violins lack a little weight, but the overall sonority has the necessary depth and amplitude for Tchaikovsky.

Gatti's acount of *Romeo and Juliet* is superbly characterised. It opens chillingly, then introduces the great love theme very gently, followed by the most delicate moonlight sequence. The central climax, with the reintroduction of the Friar Lawrence theme, is terrific, and the love theme blooms gloriously in a great curving sweep of violins. What more can you ask?

Symphony No 5, Op 64. Francesca da Rimini, Op 32
Simón Bolívar Youth Orchestra of Venezuela / Gustavo Dudamel
DG 477 8022GH (74' · DDD)
Recorded live 2008   (F)**OO**(B)

A sinewy, uninhibited Tchaikovsky Fifth – you'd expect nothing less from this source. Dudamel and his young players feed on one another; the exchange of energy is extraordinary. Tchaikovsky's impulsive changes of tempo feel more naturally impetuous while the phrasing is directly reflected in the sound: just listen to the yearning second theme of the *Allegro con anima* and the way that the sheen on the violin sound intensifies with the release.

But as with their famous Prom a few years back, it's not just the fireworks but the inwardness of this performance that brings the biggest surprises. The great *Andante cantabile* horn theme (so soft and consoling) emerges almost imperceptibly from the somnolent harmonies of the lower strings at the start of the movement. It's like discovering Romeo and Juliet before the unwelcome dawn – the atmosphere is extraordinarily charged. And what sweep the Simón Bolívar string players lend the second theme, not least in the climactic return. As for the finale – well, there's nothing like headstrong youngsters to reignite an old favourite: the *Allegro vivace* comes off the starting-blocks at such a blistering pace as to register a nanosecond of disbelief that such a tempo is even possible.

But the real disbelief is still to come. To better this account of *Francesca da Rimini* you need to go back to Stokowski or Bernstein. As if the descent into Dante's inferno isn't intense enough – Dudamel's pacing of this lengthy introduction is quite masterly – the whirlwind at its core glows white hot with astonishing virtuosity displayed from every department. And though Dudamel's *rubato* in the string-led approach to the climax may not be as abandoned as Bernstein's, it's still pretty brave. Hearing is believing in the coda as the trombones and trumpets tumble into the abyss. Exciting? Deliriously so.

Symphony No 6. Marche slave, Op 31. The Seasons, Op 37b. Six morceaux composés sur un seul thème, Op 21. The Sleeping Beauty (arr Pletnev) – excerpts
Russian National Orchestra / Mikhail Pletnev pf

Virgin Classics ② 561636-2 (138' · DDD)   ⒷOOOᐅ

 There's no denying that Russian orchestras bring a special intensity to Tchaikovsky, and to this Symphony in particular. But, in the past, we have had to contend with lethal, vibrato-laden brass and variable Soviet engineering. Not any more. Pianist Mikhail Pletnev formed this orchestra in 1990 from the front ranks of the major Soviet orchestras, and the result here is now regarded as a classic. The brass still retain their penetrating power, and an extraordinary richness and solemnity before the Symphony's coda; the woodwind make a very melancholy choir; and the strings possess not only the agility to cope with Pletnev's aptly death-defying speed for the third movement march, but beauty of tone for Tchaikovsky's yearning *cantabiles*. Pletnev exerts the same control over his players as he does over his fingers, to superb effect. The dynamic range is huge and comfortably reproduced with clarity, natural perspectives, a sense of instruments playing in a believable acoustic space, and a necessarily higher volume setting than usual. *Marche slave*'s final blaze of triumph, in the circumstances, seems apt.

Pletnev finds colours and depths in *The Seasons* that few others have found even intermittently. Schumann is revealed as a major influence, not only on the outward features of the style but on the whole expressive mood and manner. And as a display of pianism the whole set is outstanding, all the more so because his brilliance isn't purely egotistic. Even when he does something unmarked – like attaching the hunting fanfares of 'September' to the final unison of 'August' – he's so persuasive that you could believe that this is somehow inherent in the material. This is all exceptional playing, and the recording is ideally attuned to all its moods and colours.

Manfred Symphony, Op 58

Manfred Symphony. The Voyevoda
**Royal Liverpool Philharmonic Orchestra /
Vasily Petrenko**
Naxos 8 570568 (69' · DDD)   ⓈOOOᐅ

 Petrenko's *Manfred* emerges from the gothic greys of the opening wind chorale to vent his heartache in an emotive surge of string sound. And to ensure that we've grasped the measure of his despair, he repeats himself. Petrenko's Byronic petulance makes something really stirring of the self-loathing – Tchaikovsky's as much as that of Byron's anti-hero. But the real miracle of this first movement is the vision of idealised love emerging so tenderly in what one might normally call the development. The palest clarinet against muted *tremolando* strings takes us directly to the heart of the matter, and Petrenko and his orchestra don't disappoint. Likewise in the epic coda, where anguish is again writ large in overreaching horns and trumpets. No superfluous tam-tam, thankfully.

TCHAIKOVSKY'S SYMPHONIES NOS 4-6 – IN BRIEF

Berlin PO / Herbert von Karajan
DG ② 453 088-2GD2 (139' · ADD)   ⓂOᐅ
Of Karajan's countless recordings of Tchaikovsky's three last symphonies, this set from the mid-1970s is possibly the finest. With excellent playing by the BPO it certainly makes a safe recommendation, neither over-emotional nor cool. (His 1960s set is also available on a budget-price DG set, but it's worth going for this one at much the same price.)

Philharmonia / Vladimir Ashkenazy
Decca ② 443 844-2DF2 (136' · DDD)   Ⓜᐅ
Among Ashkenazy's earliest recordings as a conductor, this trilogy demonstrates his effectiveness of the podium. There's a really refreshing feeling here, with the Philharmonia playing superbly.

**Leningrad PO / Kurt Sanderling (No 4),
Evgeny Mravinsky**
DG mono ② 447 423-2GDO2 (133' · ADD) ⓂOOᐅ
Staggering performances from the great St Petersburg orchestra. Everything is held on a very tight rein, but the passion and intensity come through with incredible force. The *Pathétique* leaves you absolutely shattered.

Leningrad PO / Evgeny Mravinsky
DG ② 477 5911GOR2 (129' · DDD)   ⓂOOOᐅ
 Mravinsky re-recorded Nos 5 and 6 when on tour in the UK, and also set down No 4 – in stereo. It may lack the visceral thrill of the mono set but here we're talking high-intensity performances, way above the norm. These are stunning, with playing of astounding virtuosity.

Oslo PO / Mariss Jansons
Chandos CHAN8361, CHAN8351, CHAN8446 (42', 43' & 44' · DDD)   ⓂOOᐅ
The three individual Chandos CDs from Jansons's cycle are included here simply because they are so fine, and deserve to be considered in any discussion of the last three Tchaikovsky symphonies. The Fifth is earth-shattering; the other two scarcely less involving. And, given the extraordinarily high standard of sound Chandos achieved here, these are major performances – also available in a super-budget six-disc set of the complete symphonies.

Orchestra dell'Accademia Nazionale di Santa Cecilia (Rome) / Antonio Pappano
EMI ② 353258-2 (127' · DDD)   ⒻOᐅ
Recorded live in front of a very quiet Roman audience, these are wonderfully fresh readings, with a nice feeling for Tchaikovsky's *legato*. If they lean towards the vocal rather than the symphonic that's no hardship.

The dazzling apparitions of the second movement's light-catching waterfall are sharply etched, and if Petrenko has a rather leisurely idea of what constitutes *Andante con moto* in the third movement, he can't be blamed for loving this vintage Tchaikovsky melody too much. The playing, again, is lovely. Petrenko also keeps his head in the inferno of the finale, emphasising Tchaikovsky the classicist in the hard-working fugue. The 'phantom' organ, though impressively caught here, gets no better, but is quickly forgotten amid the serenity of the final pages.

The opening pages of *The Voyevoda* seem to suggest a psychological summit meeting between Manfred and Hermann from *The Queen of Spades*. Its galloping obsessiveness ratchets up the torment again. The bass clarinet gives everyone the evil eye; no wonder Tchaikovsky tried to destroy it. This is impressive – and, at Naxos's pricing, not to be missed.

Manfred Symphony
London Philharmonic Orchestra /
Vladimir Jurowski
LPO LPO0009 (59' · DDD). Recorded live 2004   Ⓜ▶

With a work as episodic as the *Manfred Symphony*, particularly in the long first movement, there is much to be said for a live recording, with dramatic tension more readily sustained. Vladimir Jurowski directs a powerful performance in which the tension never flags. Recorded live, the sound is clear and well balanced.

In his characteristic manner, Jurowski presses the music hard, generally to impressive effect, except that he goes too far in the second-movement *Scherzo*. At his hectic speed it loses much of its sparkle and gives little idea of the programme the composer was illustrating – the Alpine Fairy appearing to Byron's hero Manfred. Compared with some the ensemble is not as crisp though more than acceptable by general standards. The 'live-ness' offers ample compensation, though, making this a strong recommendation at mid-price and a welcome addition to the orchestra's own label.

Ballets

Sleeping Beauty
Orchestra of the Royal Opera House, Covent
Garden / Mark Ermler
Sony Classical ③ 88697 57530-2 (173' · DDD)   Ⓢ▶

Tchaikovsky The Nutcracker
Arensky Variations on a Theme of Tchaikovsky
Orchestra of the Royal Opera House, Covent
Garden / Mark Ermler
Sony Classical ② 88697 58124-2 (91' · DDD)   ⓈⓄ▶

Swan Lake
Orchestra of the Royal Opera House, Covent
Garden / Mark Ermler
Sony Classical ② 88697 57534-2 (153' · DDD)   Ⓢ▶

Sleeping Beauty
London Symphony Orchestra / André Previn
EMI ② 967689-2 (157' · ADD)   ⓈⓄⓄ▶

Tchaikovsky The Nutcracker
Løvenskiold La Sylphide
London Symphony Orchestra / André Previn
EMI ② 967694-2 (147' · ADD)   ⓈⓄ▶

Swan Lake
London Symphony Orchestra / André Previn
EMI ② 967684-2 (147' · ADD)   Ⓢ▶

It is striking, in the comparative approaches of André Previn and Mark Ermler on these reissued sets of the ballets, that in general Previn, with minimal experience of ballet conducting, reponds to the colour and animation of the music, whereas Ermler, with long experience at the Bolshoi and then as principal guest conductor with the Royal Ballet at Covent Garden, seems almost to relish being liberated from the constraint of accompanying dancers.

Ermler, then, is more 'symphonic' with the scores, which he seems to feel can gain from being detached from tempi imposed by Petipa's choreography and treated as masterpieces in their own right. In general, he favours broader tempi than Previn, almost immediately in *Swan Lake* handling the famous waltz subtly and flexibly, where Previn gives it a lively forward thrust. Perhaps a few of Ermler's tempi are more expansive than some dancers might have cared for. He also gets the Covent Garden orchestra's brass to produce a firm, strong, 'Russian' sound which is likely to have been in Tchaikovsky's ears. Previn benefits from the excellent brass and wind players of the LSO, and in the *Andante* of the *Pas de deux* he plays an ace by having Ida Haendel as soloist, making something of a concerto with the violin solo. John Brown's gentle, sensitive playing for Ermler is quieter, more personal.

Ermler is also excellent at the distinction which Tchaikovsky's 'symphonic' approach makes between the tragedy of the main characters, who have a central key structure, and the lighter divertissements that lie dramatically and harmonically outside it. So his handling of the crucial moment when, the score tells us, Odette's gestures are asking the Prince and his hunting party, 'Why do you persecute me?', is strong and eloquent. Previn, who also benefits from rather better orchestral balance in the recording, is more in his element with the lighter moments: the national dances, the baby swans bobbing and skipping.

Several early reviews of *The Sleeping Beauty* repeated, as newspapers will, the old charge about the music being 'too symphonic'. It is a symphonic score in that Tchaikovsky had now mastered more completely the art of finding a central structure around which there is plenty of room for the wonderful array of lighter dances that mark a score of genius. The two themes that characterise the bad fairy Carabosse and the good Lilac Fairy are skilfully worked throughout by both conductors, though neither is given a clear recording for the furious 'Carabosse' opening. Preparing the scene for the christening, Ermler produces more grandeur, with gathering tension underlying the situation and with skilful inflections in the waltz, while Previn settles for exhilaration, bustle and elegance. In the rich profusion of incidental dances, there is really little to choose between them: the aristocratic ladies perform well for both, with dainty baronesses and more heavy-footed countesses; at the wedding, Ermler's wolf snarls more alarmingly at Red Riding Hood, Previn's cats spit and mew with more feline fury. The wonderful Panorama and Sleep interludes are beautifully played by both conductors, though Ermler is more rapturous in the love duet *Adagio* towards which he builds the drama. EMI, incidentally, quite sensibly fits the whole ballet onto two discs by dropping the *Pas Berrichon* and the *Sarabande*, less than five minutes of music.

With *The Nutcracker* there is little difference between the two performances in the latter part of the ballet, when old-fashioned convention takes over and Tchaikovsky produces the famously pretty dances. Previn has a lighter touch, on the whole, especially with a graceful Waltz of the Flowers and a Trepak that is nimble where Ermler is terrifyingly fast. The first act is a very different matter, shot with the ambiguities of Hoffmann's weird *Novelle* that are abandoned half-way through the ballet. Previn makes Drosselmeyer grotesque but still comic, where Ermler finds him sinister and alarming; he is of course all of these. Ermler's Grandfather – in the dance marked *Tempo di Grossvater* – is more arthritic than Previn's. In the battle, Previn makes the contest more exciting and sharp-edged than Ermler, who is less precise but more menacing. In short, Ermler takes the dark side of the ballet more seriously, where Previn is happy with the lighter elements of fairy-tale.

Swan Lake, Op 20

Swan Lake
Montreal Symphony Orchestra / Charles Dutoit
Decca ② 436 212-2DH2 (154' · DDD)   Ⓕ Ⓞ🔁

No one wrote more beautiful and danceable ballet music than Tchaikovsky, and this account of *Swan Lake* is a delight throughout. This isn't only because of the quality of the music, which is here played including additions the composer made after the premiere, but also thanks to the richly idiomatic playing of Charles Dutoit and his Montreal orchestra in the superb and celebrated location of St Eustache's Church in that city. Maybe some conductors have made the music even more earthily Russian, but the Russian ballet tradition in Tchaikovsky's time was chiefly French and the most influential early production of this ballet, in 1895, was choreographed by the Frenchman Marius Petipa. Indeed, the symbiosis of French and Russian elements in this music (and story) is one of its great strengths, the refinement of

the one being superbly allied to the vigour of the other, notably in such music as the 'Russian Dance' with its expressive violin solo. This is a profoundly romantic reading of the score, and the great set pieces such as the Waltz in Act 1 and the marvellous scene of the swans on a moonlit lake that opens Act 2 are wonderfully evocative; yet they do not overshadow the other music, which supports them as gentler hills and valleys might surround and enhance magnificent, awe-inspiring peaks, the one being indispensable to the other. You do not have to be a ballet aficionado to fall under the spell of this wonderful music, which here receives a performance that blends passion with an aristocratic refinement and is glowingly recorded.

The Sleeping Beauty, Op 66

The Sleeping Beauty
Czecho-Slovak State Philharmonic Orchestra /
Andrew Mogrelia
Naxos ③ 8 550490/92 (174' · DDD)   Ⓢ Ⓞ🔁

Andrew Mogrelia is clearly a ballet conductor to his fingertips. His account of *The Sleeping Beauty* isn't only dramatic, when called for, but graceful and full of that affectionate warmth and detail which readily conjure up the stage imagery. Moreover, the House of Arts in Košice seems to have just the right acoustics for this work. If the sound is too brilliant the louder passages of Tchaikovsky's score can easily hector the ear; if the effect is too mellow, the result can become bland. Neither happens here – the ear is seduced throughout and Mogrelia leads the listener on from number to number with an easy spontaneity. The woodwind playing is delightful (try track 9 with its 'singing canaries' – so like Delibes in its scoring). At the end of Act 1 the Lilac Fairy's tune is given a spacious, *frisson*-creating apotheosis. The alert Introduction to Acts 2 and 3 brings crisp brass and busy strings on the one hand, arresting hunting horns on the other, and what sparkling zest there is in the strings for the following 'Blind-man's buff' sequence, while the famous Act 2 Waltz has splendid rhythmic lift. Act 3 is essentially a great extended *Divertissement*, with Tchaikovsky's imagination at full stretch through some two dozen characterful dance numbers of every balletic flavour, all played here with fine style.

The Sleeping Beauty
BBC Symphony Orchestra /
Gennadi Rozhdestvensky
BBC Legends ② BBCL4091-2 (141' · ADD)
Recorded live 1979   Ⓜ Ⓞ🔁

David Brown, Tchaikovsky's eminent biographer, thought that on balance *The Sleeping Beauty* was the finest of the three great ballet scores. But as Diaghilev found to his cost when he mounted it in London in 1921, it's a very extended work and suffers from a storyline in which not a great deal happens. Performing it as a complete orchestral work in the concert hall is probably not the best way to approach the work but, if it's to be performed in this way, Rozhdestvensky is just the man for it. In this recording he shows just how to hold together Tchaikovsky's remarkably diverse score as a symphonic entity by creating a consistent narrative momentum without ever over-driving.

The very opening is enormously dramatic and arresting, and then the petite Lilac Fairy appears in her delectably delicate orchestral apparel. Rozhdestvensky is a master of this kind of contrast. Sample the daintiness of string texture at the opening of the 'Pas de six' (track 3), the delicious piccolo and *pizzicatos* for the 'Singing canary' (track 8), so reminiscent of Delibes, followed by the sheer energy of track 9 ('Violente').

The ballet ends grandiloquently, but with great majesty, and one is left in wonder: there isn't a single number in which Tchaikovsky's imagination fails him.

Several fine versions of this ballet are available on CD, but Rozhdestvensky is even finer, and the BBC recording is remarkably good, with plenty of amplitude, a warm string patina, glowing woodwind and a natural concert-hall balance. Highly recommended.

The Sleeping Beauty – excerpts. The Nutcracker – excerpts. Swan Lake – excerpts
Royal Liverpool Philharmonic Orchestra / Vasily Petrenko
Avie AV2139 (58' · DDD)　　　Ⓕ**OO**

Vasily Petrenko was a shrewd choice of principal conductor for the Royal Liverpool Philharmonic Orchestra. His promise is clear, his reputation growing. These bonbons from the Tchaikovsky ballets don't offer too many surprises in terms of choice (except perhaps the exclusion of the *Rose Adagio* from *Sleeping Beauty*) but they do clearly demonstrate the difference Petrenko is already making to the quality of the RLPO playing.

Essentially it's a personalisation process where the articulation of the wind voices (listen, for instance, to the 'Entrée' from the *Bluebird Pas de quatre* in *Sleeping Beauty*) takes on a really idiomatic colour and cast and the string playing sounds freer and fuller. Petrenko's watchwords are shape and purpose and clarity; there is an elegance and inner life to the playing making everything sound freshly minted. The three great waltzes are pivotal, of course, and they glide across Tchaikovsky's imperial ballroom with all due suavity and opulence.

The *Swan Lake* highlights wipe the floor with Gergiev's pale showing in the complete ballet (Decca): the nobility of the horns emblazoned across the opening Scene, the swagger and sophistication of the national dances with a brilliant trumpet solo in the *Danse napolitaine* and a

delightfully folksy lilt to the contrasting Trio of the Mazurka.

The climactic modulation of the Lilac Fairy's spellbinding pronouncement that love will redeem all is nailed with all the assurance of a young master, but what is thus far missing if you compare someone like Rostropovich in this music (his *Sleeping Beauty* highlights with the Berlin Philharmonic on DG are simply sensational) is the stamp of real temperament, a daring born of long and intimate familiarity. Give him time. All the signs are favourable.

1812 Overture, Op 49

Tchaikovsky 1812 Overture[a]. Capriccio italien,　Ⓗ
Op 45[b] **Beethoven** Wellingtons Sieg, 'Die Schlacht bei Vittoria', Op 91[c]
[a]**University of Minnesota Brass Band;** [ab]**Minneapolis Symphony Orchestra;** [c]**London Symphony Orchestra / Antál Dorati**
Mercury Living Presence 434 360-2MM (66' · ADD)
Recorded 1955-60. Includes commentary on making the recordings　　Ⓜ**OO**

Both battle pieces incorporate cannon fire recorded at West Point, with *Wellington's Victory* adding antiphonal muskets and *1812*, the University of Minnesota Brass Band and the bells of the Laura Spelman Rockefeller carillon. In a recorded commentary on the *1812* sessions, Deems Taylor explains how, prior to 'battle', roads were blocked and an ambulance crew put on standby. The actual weapons used were chosen both for their historical authenticity (period instruments of mass destruction) and their sonic impact, the latter proving formidable even today. In fact, the crackle and thunder of *Wellington's Victory* could easily carry a DDD endorsement; perhaps we should, for the occasion, invent a legend of Daring, Deafening and potentially Deadly. Dorati's conducting is brisk, incisive and dramatic. The *1812* in particular suggests a rare spontaneity, with a fiery account of the main 'conflict' and a tub-thumping peroration where bells, band, guns and orchestra conspire to produce one of the most riotous key-clashes in gramophone history.

Capriccio italien was recorded some three years earlier (1955, would you believe) and sounds virtually as impressive. Again, the approach is crisp and balletic, whereas the 1960 LSO Beethoven recording triumphs by dint of its energy and orchestral discipline. As 'fun' CDs go, this must be one of the best – provided you can divorce Mercury's aural militia from the terrifying spectre of real conflict. Wilma Cozart Fine has masterminded an astonishingly effective refurbishment, while the documentation – both written and recorded – is very comprehensive.

1812 Overture. Marche slave, Op 31. Festival Coronation March. Festival Overture on the Danish National Hymn. Moscow Cantata[a]
[a]**Lyubov Sokolova** *mez* [a]**Alexey Markov** *bar*

Mariinsky [a]Chorus and Orchestra / Valery Gergiev
Mariinsky ⏺ MAR0503 (64' · DDD/DSD)
Recorded live   Ⓕ🅑➔

However disparaging Tchaikovsky might have been about the *Festival Coronation March*, who but he could have turned such an obvious show-stopper into something quite so exhilarating? But there you have it – state commissions meant something to Tchaikovsky (staunch monarchist and traditionalist that he was) and though he may have laboured with the means of delivery, the message was loud and clear.

Valery Gergiev clearly shares those sentiments wholeheartedly but perhaps the most notable feature of these performances is their refusal to undermine the character[ful] in pursuit of the sensational. The *Marche slave*, for instance, is resonant and resolute but what you really come away humming are the fife and drum effects and brilliant trumpetings of the orchestration. The *Festival Overture on the Danish National Hymn* (celebrating the future Tsar Alexander III's marriage to the Danish Princess Dagmar) wears its classical craftsmanship with pride with the Russian national anthem – in minor mode humility – showing deference to the celebratory mood of the Danish anthem.

The *1812* catches one off-guard straight away with its unusually 'vocal' phrasing of the old Russian prayer at the outset and throughout the performance the song quotations sound 'sung'. Tempo (blistering) rather than trenchancy defines the main *Allegro* with the *Marseillaise* sounding unusually corny (deliberate?) in the trumpets. You might want a bit more 'crunch' from the canons in that most ubiquitous peroration but the peeling cascades of strings chime tellingly with the panoply of bells.

Tchaikovsky, though, is most evidently (and gloriously) Tchaikovsky in the *Moscow Cantata*. A vintage melody turns the first page of Russian history, illuminating it in that inimitable Tchaikovskian way. The baritone monologue in praise of Moscow culminates in a marvellously stirring idea and in the second mezzo-soprano arioso honouring the women of Russian we find a heroine worthy of any Tchaikovsky opera. No doubt about it, Tchaikovsky had a gift for personalising even his most official duties. The word 'dutiful' was not really in his vocabulary.

Francesca da Rimini. Romeo and Juliet. 1812
Overture[a]. Eugene Onegin – Waltz[a]; Polonaise
**Santa Cecilia Academy [a]Chorus and Orchestra,
Rome / Antonio Pappano**
EMI 370065-2 (71' · DDD)   Ⓕ🅞➔

With chorus added in the *1812* as well as the Waltz from *Eugene Onegin*, this is an exceptional Tchaikovsky collection, a fine start for Antonio Pappano's recordings with his Italian orchestra. What is very striking is how refreshing the *1812* is when played with such incisiveness and care for detail, with textures clearly defined. It starts with the chorus singing the opening hymn,

expanding thrillingly from an extreme *pianissimo* to a full-throated *fortissimo*.

A women's chorus then comes in very effectively, twice over, for one of the folk-themes, and at the end the full chorus sings the Tsar's Hymn amid the usual percussion and bells, though Pappano avoids extraneous effects, leaving everything in the hands of the orchestral instruments. It is equally refreshing to have the Waltz from *Eugene Onegin* in the full vocal version from the opera, again wonderfully pointed, as is the Polonaise which follows.

What comes out in all the items is the way that Pappano, in his control of flexible *rubato*, is just as persuasive here as he is in Puccini, demonstrating what links there are between these two supreme melodists. So he builds the big melodies into richly emotional climaxes without any hint of vulgarity, strikingly so in both *Francesca da Rimini* and *Romeo and Juliet*. Pappano is impressive in bringing out the fantasy element in *Francesca*, and in *Romeo* the high dynamic contrasts add to the impact of the performance. There have been many Tchaikovsky collections like this, but with well balanced sound, outstandingly rich and ripe in the brass section, this is among the finest.

Fantasy Overtures

Hamlet, Op 67. The Tempest, Op 18.
Romeo and Juliet
Bamberg Symphony Orchestra / José Serebrier
BIS BIS-CD1073 (62' · DDD)   Ⓕ🅞🅞➔

What a good idea to couple Tchaikovsky's three fantasy overtures inspired by Shakespeare. José Serebrier writes an illuminating note on the genesis of each of the three, together with an analysis of their structure. He notes that once Tchaikovsky had established his concept of the fantasy overture in the first version of *Romeo and Juliet* in 1869 – slow introduction leading to alternating fast and slow sections, with slow coda – he used it again both in the *1812* Overture and *Hamlet*. *The Tempest* (1873) has similarly contrasting sections, but begins and ends with a gently evocative seascape, with shimmering arpeggios from strings divided in 13 parts.

It's typical of Serebrier's performance that he makes that effect sound so fresh and original. In many ways, early as it is, this is stylistically the most radical of the three overtures here, with sharp echoes of Berlioz in some of the woodwind effects. The clarity of Serebrier's performance, both in texture and in structure, helps to bring that out, as does a warm and analytical BIS recording.

Hamlet, dating from much later, is treated to a similarly fresh and dramatic reading, with Serebrier bringing out the yearningly Russian flavour of the lovely oboe theme representing Ophelia. He may not quite match the thrusting power of his mentor, Stokowski, but he's not far short, and brings out far more detail.

Serebrier is also meticulous in seeking to observe the dynamic markings in each score. Those in *The Tempest* are nothing if not extravagant – up to a *fortissimo* of five *f*s in the final statement of the love theme – yet Serebrier graduates the extremes with great care. Highly recommended.

Hamlet, Op 67*a* – Overture and Incidental Music[a].
Romeo and Juliet – Fantasy Overture
[a]**Tatiana Monogarova** *sop* [a]**Maxim Mikhailov** *bass*
Russian National Orchestra / Vladimir Jurowski
Pentatone ⚅ PTC5186 330 (60' · DDD/DSD) Ⓕ**O**▶

At first glance this might look like the traditional pairing of Tchaikovsky's two fantasy overtures – but you might have known that Vladimir Jurowski was likely to be more inquisitive than that. In 1891 a complete stage performance of Shakespeare's *Hamlet* took place in St Petersburg with music by Tchaikovsky. His fantasy overture, written for a charity event three years earlier, was heard again, this time filleted to roughly half its original length and reduced in scoring to the requirements of a theatre orchestra. The results are fascinating, not least for the ingenuity of Tchaikovsky's cut-and-paste job, jump-cutting now with renewed urgency. Of course, one misses the symphonic weight of the original. The effect is more muted here, the scale diminished so as not to pre-empt that moment in the actual drama. But Ophelia is more than ever at the heart of the piece, her plaintive oboe melody very much dominating this version and exquisitely played – as is everything – by the Russian National Orchestra, whose refinement has opened a new chapter in Russian orchestral playing. Ophelia's first entrance, incidentally, is none other than the graceful 'Alla tedesca' second movement of Tchaikovsky's Third Symphony, the *Polish*. How's that for recycling? And there's more with the Prelude to Act 4 scene 1, a poignant string elegy turned on wistful arabesques. That is one of the more substantial of the 16 clips and touchingly foreshadows Ophelia's tragedy. She – the lovely Tatiana Monogarova – has a two-part Mad Scene or 'melodrama' where the spoken lines lend a stark reality to her delusions.

Those who know the original 1869 version of the *Romeo and Juliet* Fantasy Overture will be aware that it's another example of how much more interesting, though not necessarily better, a composer's first thoughts can be. Fascinating is the earlier premonition of the great love theme and the way Tchaikovsky quite literally tosses it about in the more radical and certainly more violent development of the fight music: all gone in the revision!

Jurowski savours the differences and makes capital of the anomalies. Very exciting.

Variations on a Rococo Theme, Op 33

Variations on a Rococo Theme. Nocturne No 4, Op 19. (arr Tchaikovsky). Pezzo capriccioso, Op 62. When Jesus Christ was but a child Op 54 No 5. Was I not a little blade of grass?, Op 47 No 7

(both orch Tchaikovsky). Andante cantabile, Op 11 (arr Tchaikovsky)
Raphael Wallfisch *vc*
English Chamber Orchestra / Geoffrey Simon
Chandos CHAN8347 (48' · DDD) Ⓢ**O**▶

This account of the *Rococo* Variations is the one to have: it presents Tchaikovsky's variations as he wrote them, in the order he devised, and including the *allegretto moderato con anima* that the work's first interpreter, 'loathsome Fitzenhagen', so high-handedly jettisoned. (See also the review under Dvořák where Rostropovich uses the published score rather than the original version.) The first advantage is as great as the second: how necessary the brief cadenza and the *andante* that it introduces now seem, as an up-beat to the central sequence of quick variations (Fitzenhagen moved both cadenza and *andante* to the end). And the other, shorter cadenza now makes a satisfying transition from that sequence to the balancing *andante sostenuto*, from which the long-suppressed eighth variation is an obvious build-up to the coda – why, the piece has a form, after all! Raphael Wallfisch's fine performance keeps the qualifying adjective 'rococo' in mind – it isn't indulgently over-romantic – but it has warmth and beauty of tone in abundance. The shorter pieces are well worth having: the baritone voice of the cello suits the *Andante cantabile* and the Tatyana-like melody of the *Nocturne* surprisingly aptly. The sound is first-class.

Serenade in C, Op 48

Serenade in C. Souvenir de Florence, Op 70
Vienna Chamber Orchestra / Philippe Entremont
Naxos 8 550404 (65' · DDD) Ⓢ**OO**▶

This is one of the many CDs now on the market that dispel the myth once and for all that only full-price recordings contain really outstanding performances. The Naxos label is just about as 'bargain' as you can get, and here they have given us superlative performances of two of Tchaikovsky's most endearing works. The Serenade in C contains a wealth of memorable and haunting music, beautifully and inventively scored and guaranteed to bring immense pleasure and delight to those dipping their toes in to the world of classical music for the first time. Philippe Entremont and the Vienna Chamber Orchestra give a marvellously polished and finely poised performance full of warmth, affection and high spirits, and the famous second-movement Waltz in particular is played with much elegance and grace. The *Souvenir de Florence*, originally written for string sextet, makes a welcome appearance here in Tchaikovsky's own arrangement for string orchestra. This is a delightfully sunny performance, full of suavity, exuberance and romantic dash, but always alert to the subtleties of Tchaikovsky's skilful, intricate part-writing. The *Adagio cantabile* is particularly notable for some extremely fine and poetic solo playing from the violin and cello principals of the VPO. The beautifully spacious recording does ample justice to the performances.

Suites

Suite No 2. The Tempest
Detroit Symphony Orchestra / Neeme Järvi
Chandos CHAN9454 (64' · DDD) ⒻⒹ⮞

Tchaikovsky's elusive blend of instrumental precision and free-flowing thematic fantasy in the Second Suite meets its match in the Detroit/ Järvi partnership: the conductor's imagination works alongside the lean, clean Detroit sound with interesting results. The strings aren't always the ideal: the lush chordings and central fugal energy of the opening movement, 'Jeu de sons', cry out for a richer, Russian tone. But the semiquaver patter is beautifully done, the lower lines clear and personable. Keen articulation and driving force go hand-in-glove as Järvi prepares for the entry of the four accordions in the virile 'Rondo-Burlesque', sweeping on to the folk-song of the central section with characteristic aplomb. It's in the Schumannesque phrases and the subtly shifting moods of the most poetic movement, 'Rêves d'enfant', that Järvi really comes into his own; the short-lived, otherworldly radiance at the heart of the movement seems more than ever like a preliminary study for the transformation scenes of *The Nutcracker*, just as the woodwind choruses look forward to that and *Sleeping Beauty*.

The magical haze surrounding Prospero's island in *The Tempest* doesn't quite come off; here it's Pletnev (reviewed above) who surprises us with the true magician's touch, but then his Russian horns, and later his trumpeter, cast their incantations more impressively. Järvi is no more successful than any other conductor in stitching together Tchaikovsky's strong impressions of the play, though a little more forward movement in the love-music might have helped.

Tchaikovsky Suite No 3
Stravinsky Divertimento from 'La baiser de la fée'
Russian National Orchestra / Vladimir Jurowski
Pentatone ☸ PTC5186 061 (64' · DDD/DSD) Ⓕ

Vladimir Jurowski here offers performances that are as near-ideal as one can imagine, the electric tension giving the illusion of live music-making. We have had some impressive recordings from this Moscow-based orchestra in the past but this one is among the finest.

Tchaikovsky's Third Suite, with its final extended set of variations, can seem rather square under some conductors but Jurowski, maybe influenced by conducting opera and ballet, brings out the surging lyricism. So the opening 'Elegie' is warmly moulded without sounding fussy, the phrasing totally idiomatic. The rhythmic second-movement Waltz leads to a

dazzling account of the *Scherzo*, taken at a genuine *presto* yet with no feeling of breathlessness, while the Variations have rarely seemed so attractive in their breadth of ideas, with a thrilling build-up and conclusion.

Stravinsky's Divertimento, its four movements taken from the ballet *The Fairy's Kiss*, may make an unexpected coupling, but it is apt and illuminating. Jurowski steers a nice course between the Romantic warmth of the Tchaikovsky sources from which Stravinsky took his material (songs and piano pieces) and his 1920s neo-classicism. The delicate and refined account of the slow first section leads to sharp syncopations in the *Vivace agitato* which follows, and the chugging rhythms on horns in the most memorable section of the second movement show jollity in their springing step, while the pointing of contrasts in the final 'Pas de deux' brings yearning warmth in the big lyrical moments and wit in the faster sections. With exceptionally vivid sound, recorded by Pentatone's engineers in Moscow, this disc cannot be recommended too highly.

Souvenir de Florence, Op 70

Tchaikovsky Souvenir de Florence.
Dvořák String Sextet in A, B80
Sarah Chang, Bernhard Hartog vns **Wolfram Christ, Tanjia Christ** vas **Georg Faust, Olaf Maninger** vcs
EMI 557243-2 (68' · DDD) ⒻⓄⓄⒹ⮞

 Two of the finest string sextets ever written by Slavonic composers make an excellent coupling, particularly with such a starry line-up of musicians. Sarah Chang's warmly individual artistry is superbly matched by players drawn from the Berlin Philharmonic, past and present. These are players who not only respond to each other's artistry, but do so with the most polished ensemble and a rare clarity of inner texture, not easy with a sextet.

Souvenir de Florence is given the most exuberantly joyful performance. Written just after he had left Florence, having completed his opera *The Queen of Spades*, Tchaikovsky was prompted to compose one of his happiest works, one which for once gave him enormous pleasure. The opening movement's bouncy rhythms in compound time set the pattern, with the second subject hauntingly seductive in its winning relaxation, a magic moment here (track 1, 1'28").

The *Adagio cantabile* second movement is tenderly beautiful, with the central section sharply contrasted, while the folk-dance rhythms of the last two movements are sprung with sparkling lightness. There are now dozens of versions of this winning work in the catalogue, both for sextet and string orchestra, but none is more delectable than this.

Equally, the subtlety as well as the energy of Dvořák's Sextet is consistently brought out by Chang and her partners, with the players using a huge dynamic range down to the gentlest *pianissimo*. Here, too, it just outshines the competition.

String Quartets

No 1 in D, Op 11; **No 2** in F, Op 22;
No 3 in E flat minor, Op 30

String Quartets Nos 1-3. Quartet Movement in B flat.
Souvenir de Florence, Op 70
Yuri Yurov va **Mikhail Milman** vc **Borodin Quartet**
(Mikhail Kopelman, Andrei Abramenkov vns Dmitri
Shebalin va Valentin Berlinsky vc)
Teldec ② 4509 90422-2 (151' · DDD)   Ⓕ**OOO**

Who could fail to recognise the highly characteristic urgency and thematic strength of the
F major Quartet's first movement development
section, or miss premonitions of later masterpieces in the Third Quartet's *Andante funèbre*?
None of these works is 'late' (the last of them predates the Fourth Symphony by a couple of years),
yet their rigorous arguments and sweeping melodies anticipate the orchestral masterpieces of
Tchaikovsky's full maturity. So why the neglect
of all but the First Quartet? The most likely reason is our habitual expectation of orchestral colour in Tchaikovsky, a situation that doesn't really
affect our appreciation of the early, almost Schubertian D major Quartet (the one with the
Andante cantabile that moved Tolstoy to tears).
The Second and Third Quartets are noticeably
more symphonic and particularly rich in the
kinds of harmonic clashes and sequences that
Tchaikovsky normally gave to the orchestra.
Even minor details, like the quick-fire exchanges
near the beginning of No 3's *Allegretto*, instantly
suggest 'woodwinds' (you can almost hear oboes,
flutes and clarinets jostle in play), while both
finales could quite easily have been transposed
among the pages of the early symphonies. But if
these and other parallels are to register with any
conviction, then performers need to locate them,
and that's a challenge the Borodins meet with the
ease of seasoned Tchaikovskians.

They are natural and spontaneous, most noticeably in the first movement of the exuberant *Souvenir de Florence* sextet, and in that wonderful
passage from the Second Quartet's first movement where the lead violin calms from agitated
virtuosity to a magical recapitulation of the principal theme – an unforgettable moment, superbly
paced here. Additionally we get a 15-minute
B flat Quartet movement – an appealing torso
imbued with the spirit of Russian folksong.

Piano Trio

Tchaikovsky Piano Trio **Smetana** Piano Trio, Op 15
Vienna Piano Trio (Wolfgang Redik vn Matthias
Gredler vc Stefan Mendl pf)
Dabringhaus und Grimm Ⓕ ⑲ MDG942 1512-6
(74' · DDD)   Ⓕ**OO**

This version of the Tchaikovsky measures up
extremely well against its competition; moreover
it is (like all chamber recordings from this source)

very well balanced. Pianist Stefan Mendl is able to
dominate yet become a full member of the partnership throughout. The second movement's
variations open gently but soon develop the widest range of style, moving through Tchaikovsky's
kaleidoscopic mood-changes like quicksilver and
often with elegiac lyrical feeling.

But what makes this disc especially recommendable is the inclusion of Smetana's G minor
Piano Trio, which the composer himself premiered in 1855. All three movements are in the
home key and thematically linked yet are enticingly diverse, the first with strong contrasts of
dynamic and tempo, the second a most engaging
scherzo (marked *non agitato* and with slower
interludes), while the rondo finale bursts with
energy (especially as presented here). All in all a
real winner of a disc that can be highly recommended on all counts.

Additional recommendation

Tchaikovsky Piano Trio
Coupled with **Rachmaninov** Trio élégiaque
Kempf Trio
BIS BIS-CD1302 (69' · DDD)   Ⓕ**O**▸

　Freddy Kempf leads with great conviction, yet can
　pull back whenever his colleagues are in the ascend-
　ant. The very opening is lyrically seductive, and the
　closing pages, with a moving reprise of the opening
　theme at the *Lugubre* finale, are most sensitively
　managed. The recording is very well balanced, and
　the acoustic seems equally suitable for both works.
　Altogether this is a splendid disc.

Piano Works

Tchaikovsky 18 Morceaux, Op 72
Chopin Nocturne No 20 in C sharp minor, Op posth
Mikhail Pletnev pf
DG 477 5378GH (70' · DDD)
Recorded live 2004   Ⓕ**OOO**▸

Mikhail Pletnev's persuasive 1986 recording of
Tchaikovsky's *18 Morceaux* for Melodiya was
unfortunately hampered by strident sound and
an ill-tuned piano. Happily, a state-of-the-art
situation prevails in this new live recording for
Deutsche Grammophon, extending, of course,
to Pletnev's own contributions. His caring, characterful and technically transcendent way with
this cycle casts each piece in a three-dimensional
perspective that honours the composer's letter
and spirit beyond the music's 'salon' reputation,
while making the most of its pianistic potential.
The results are revelatory, akin to, say, Ignaz
Friedman's illuminating re-creations of Mendelssohn's *Songs Without Words*.

The Fifth *Morceau*, 'Meditation', demonstrates the Pletnev-Tchaikovsky chemistry at
its most sublime. The melodies are firmly projected yet flexibly arched over the bar-lines, as
if emerging from different instruments,
culminating in a febrile central climax that

gently dissipates into some of the most ravishing trills on record. In No 8, 'Dialogue', Pletnev elevates Tchaikovsky's *quasi parlando* with the type of off-hand skill and pinpoint timing of a master actor who knows just which lines to throw away.

Note, too, the deliciously pointed scales and music-box colorations in No 13, 'Echo rustique'. Shades of Liszt's Third *Liebestraum* seep into No 14, 'Chant élégiaque', in what amounts to a masterclass in how to sustain long melodies against sweeping accompaniments. A stricter basic pulse throughout No 9, 'Un poco di Schumann', might have made the dotted rhythms and two strategically placed *ritenutos* more obviously Schumannesque, yet there's no denying the inner logic the looser treatment communicates.

There's extraordinary virtuosity behind the musical insights. For example, the interlocking octaves in the coda to No 7, 'Polacca de concert', are unleashed with Horowitz-like ferocity and not a trace of banging. The rapid, vertigo-inducing triplet runs in No 10, 'Scherzo-fantaisie', could scarcely be more even and controlled. Pletnev is all over the final, unbuttoned *trepak* in grand style, and he certainly makes the *glissandos* swing. A fresh, unfettered account of Chopin's C sharp minor Nocturne is offered as an encore to this urgently recommended recital.

Liturgy of St John Chrysostom, Op 41

Liturgy of St John Chrysostom. Nine Sacred Pieces. An Angel Crying
Corydon Singers / Matthew Best
Hyperion CDA66948 (75' · DDD · T/t)   ⓕⓄ▸

Tchaikovsky's liturgical settings have never quite caught the popular imagination which has followed Rachmaninov's (his *All-Night Vigil*, at any rate). They are generally more inward, less concerned with the drama that marks Orthodox celebration than with the reflective centre which is another aspect. Rachmaninov can invite worship with a blaze of delight, setting 'Pridite'; Tchaikovsky approaches the mystery more quietly. Yet there's a range of emotion which emerges vividly in this admirable record of the Liturgy together with a group of the minor liturgical settings which he made at various times in his life. His ear for timbre never fails him. It's at its most appealing, perhaps, in the lovely 'Da ispravitsya' for female trio and answering choir, beautifully sung here; he can also respond to the Orthodox tradition of rapid vocalisation, as in the Liturgy's Creed and in the final 'Blagosloven grady' (in the West, the Benedictus). Anyone who still supposes that irregular, rapidly shifting rhythms were invented by Stravinsky should give an ear to his Russian sources, in folk poetry and music but also in the music of the Church.

Matthew Best's Corydon Singers are old hands at Orthodox music, and present these beautiful settings with a keen ear for their texture and 'orchestration'. The recording was made in an (unnamed) ecclesiastical acoustic of suitable resonance, and sounds well.

Songs

'Romances'
My genius, my angel, my friend. Six Songs, Op 6 – No 1, Do not believe, my friend; No 2, Not a word, O my friend; No 5, Why?; No 6, None but the lonely heart. Cradle Song, Op 16 No 1. Six Songs, Op 25 – No 1, Reconciliation; No 2, Over burning ashes. The Fearful Moment, Op 28 No 6. Six Songs, Op 38 – No 2, It was in the early spring; No 3, At the Ball. Seven Songs, Op 47 – No 1, Had I only known; No 6, Can it be day?; No 7, The Bride's Lament. Children's Songs, Op 54 – Cuckoo. Twelve Songs, Op 60 – No 7, Gypsy Song; No 12, The mild stars looked down. The lights were being dimmed, Op 63 No 5. Six Songs, Op 73 – No 4, The sun has set; No 6, Again, as before, alone
Christianne Stotijn *mez* **Julius Drake** *pf*
Onyx Classics ONYX4034 (63' · DDD)   ⓕⓄ▸

For the most part these are angst-ridden stories of death and lost love. The two best-known songs open proceedings: 'At the Ball', with its reminiscence of unrequited passion to the lilt of a sad waltz, and then 'None but the lonely heart'. Everyone conceivable from Rosa Ponselle to Frank Sinatra has recorded this, but Stotijn loses nothing in comparison with ghosts from the past. Her voice is a full-blooded mezzo but steady and true, without a hint of that vibrato that can often disturb the line in Slavonic singers (Stotijn is from the Netherlands).

The emotional climax of the selection comes with 'The Bride's Lament'. This outpouring of grief can seem over melodramatic but Stotijn and Drake find exactly the right mood. The piano parts are superbly done: in every sense these songs are duets. There are a couple of other light moments – 'Cuckoo', one of 16 children's songs composed in the 1880s, and a 'Gypsy Song' from around the same time. Tchaikovsky's songs are not nearly well enough known and this superb recital should encourage more interest in them. Highly recommended.

The Snow Maiden

The Snow Maiden
Irina Mishura-Lekhtman *mez* **Vladimir Grishko** *ten*
**Michigan University Musical Society Choral Union;
Detroit Symphony Orchestra / Neeme Järvi**
Chandos CHAN9324 (79' · ADD · T/t)   ⓕ▸

Tchaikovsky wrote his incidental music for Ostrovsky's *Snow Maiden* in 1873, and though he accepted it was not his best, he retained an affection for it and was upset when Rimsky-Korsakov came along with his full-length opera on the subject. The tale of love frustrated had its appeal for Tchaikovsky, even

Dmitri Hvorostovsky Eugene Onegin
Nuccia Focile Tatyana **Neil Shicoff** Lensky
**St Petersburg Chamber Choir; Orchestre de
Paris / Semyon Bychkov**
Philips ② 475 7017PM2 (141' · DDD)   Ⓑ❍❍▷
A fleet-footed, vividly conducted perform-
ance with two highly convincing stars in
Dmitri Hvorostovsky's warm-voiced Onegin
and Nuccia Focile's Tatyana, fresh and
youthful. Neil Shicoff's plangent Lensky
heads a fine supporting cast, and the record-
ing is excellent.

Bernd Weikl Eugene Onegin **Teresa Kubiak**
Tatyana **Stuart Burrows** Lensky
**John Alldis Choir; Orchestra of the Royal
Opera House / Sir Georg Solti**
Decca ② 417 413-2DH2 (143' · ADD)   Ⓕ▷
A polished old warhorse, conducted by Solti
with superlative warmth, and international
principals. The theatrical energy is there
but, despite orchestral gloss and some
superb singing, especially Stuart Burrows's
Lensky, it never quite attains the idiomatic
feeling of more Slavic versions.

(In English) **Thomas Hampson** Eugene Onegin
Kiri Te Kanawa Tatyana **Neil Rosenshein** Lensky
**WNO Chorus and Orchestra / Sir Charles
Mackerras**
Chandos ② CHAN3042 (142' · DDD)   Ⓕ▷
This English-language recording is not the
best, but with Thomas Hampson's strong
Onegin and Mackerras's propulsive, atmos-
pheric conducting it's still enjoyable; and for
non-Russian listeners the English does make
this intimate drama much more immediate.

Panteleimon Nortsov Eugene Onegin **Yelena** Ⓗ
Kruglikova Tatyana **Ivan Kozlovsky** Lensky
**Bolshoi Theatre Chorus and Orchestra /
Alexander Orlov**
Naxos ② 8 110216/7 (136' · AAD)   Ⓢ❍
The first Bolshoi version of 1937, in early
but reasonable sound and still fascinating,
particularly for its principals, Nortsov's resonant Onegin, Kruglikova's sensitive, touching Tatyana, and the great Ivan Koslovsky's
plangent Lensky.

Bernd Weikl Eugene Onegin **Teresa Kubiak**
Tatyana **Stuart Burrows** Lensky
**John Alldis Choir; Orchestra of the Royal
Opera House / Sir Georg Solti**
Decca 📀 071 124-9DH (117')   Ⓕ
Enterprising director Petr Weigl has created
this cinematic version, using, as he often does,
actors miming to a recording, in this case
Solti's (see above). It looks marvellous, with
lustrous production values; but chunks are cut,
especially half the opening scene, and though
the actors convince, the lip-sync may not.

though he was not to make as much as Rimsky
did of the failed marriage between Man and
Nature. But though he did not normally interest himself much in descriptions of the natural
world, there are charming pieces that any lover
of Tchaikovsky's music will surely be delighted
to encounter. A strong sense of a Russian folk
celebration, and of the interaction of the natural and supernatural worlds, also comes
through, especially in the earlier part of the
work. There's a delightful dance and chorus
for the birds, and a powerful monologue for
Winter; Vladimir Grishko, placed further
back, sounds magical.

Natalia Erassova (for Chistiakov's recording
on CdM) gets round the rapid enunciation of
Lel's second song without much difficulty, but
doesn't quite bring the character to life;
Mishura-Lekhtman has a brighter sparkle.
Chistiakov's Shrove Tuesday procession goes at
a much steadier pace than Järvi's, and is thus the
more celebratory and ritual where the other is a
straightforward piece of merriment. Both performances have much to recommend them, and
it isn't by a great deal that Järvi's is preferable.
Chandos provides transliteration and an English
translation.

Additional recommendation

Arias from The Enchantress, Eugene Onegin, The
Maid of Orleans, Mazeppa and Queen of Spades
Varady sop **Evangelatos** mez
Munich Radio Orchestra / Kofman
Orfeo C540 011A (78' · DDD)   Ⓕ
Varady is truly a phenomenon; recording in her
59th year she shows no signs of age and brings to
these arias her innate gift for going to the heart of
the matter.

Eugene Onegin, Op 24

Dmitri Hvorostovsky bar Eugene Onegin **Nuccia
Focile** sop Tatyana **Neil Shicoff** ten Lensky **Sarah
Walker** mez Larina **Irina Arkhipova** mez Filipyevna
Olga Borodina contr Olga **Francis Egerton** ten
Triquet **Alexander Anisimov** bass Prince Gremin
Hervé Hennequin bass Captain **Sergei Zadvorny**
bass Zaretsky **Orchestre de Paris; St Petersburg
Chamber Choir / Semyon Bychkov**
Philips ② 475 7017PM2 (141' · DDD · N/t)   Ⓑ❍❍▷

This is a magnificent achievement on all sides.
In a recording that is wide in range, the work
comes to arresting life under Bychkov's vital
direction. Too often of late, on disc and in
the theatre, the score has been treated self-
indulgently and on too large a scale. Bychkov
makes neither mistake, emphasising the unity of
its various scenes, never lingering at slower
tempi than Tchaikovsky predicates, yet never
moving too fast for his singers.

Focile and Hvorostovsky prove almost ideal
interpreters of the central roles. Focile offers
keen-edged yet warm tone and total immersion

in Tatyana's character. Aware throughout of the part's dynamic demands, she phrases with complete confidence, eagerly catching the girl's dreamy vulnerability and heightened imagination in the Letter scene, which has that sense of awakened love so essential to it. Then she exhibits Tatyana's new-found dignity on Gremin's arm and finally her desperation when Onegin reappears to rekindle her romantic feelings.

Hvorostovsky is here wholly in his element. His singing has at once the warmth, elegance and refinement Tchaikovsky demands from his anti-hero. He suggests all Onegin's initial disdain, phrasing his address to the distraught and humiliated Tatyana – Focile so touching here – with distinction, and brings to it just the correct *bon ton*, a kind of detached humanity. He fires to anger with a touch of the heroic in his tone when challenged by Lensky, becomes transformed and single-minded when he catches sight of the 'new' Tatyana at the St Petersburg Ball. Together he, Focile and Bychkov make the finale the tragic climax it should be: indeed here this passage is almost unbearably moving in this reading.

Shicoff has refined and expanded his Lensky since he recorded it for Levine. His somewhat lachrymose delivery suits the character of the lovelorn poet, and he gives his big aria a sensitive, Russian profile, full of much subtlety of accent, the voice sounding in excellent shape, but there is a shade too much self-regard when he opens the ensemble at Larin's party with 'Yes, in your house'. Anisimov is a model Gremin, singing his aria with generous tone and phrasing while not making a meal of it. Olga Borodina is a perfect Olga, spirited, a touch sensual, wholly idiomatic with the text – as, of course, is the revered veteran Russian mezzo Arkhipova as Filipyevna, an inspired piece of casting. Sarah Walker, Covent Garden's Filipyevna, is here a sympathetic Larina. Also from the Royal Opera comes Egerton's lovable Triquet, but whereas Gergiev, in the theatre, dragged out his couplets inordinately, Bychkov once more strikes precisely the right tempo.

There will also be a very special place in the discography of the opera for the vintage Russian versions, but as a recording they are naturally outclassed by the Philips, which now becomes the outright recommendation.

Iolanta, Op 69

Iolanta
Galina Gorchakova *sop* Iolanta **Gegam Grigorian** *ten* Vaudémont **Dmitri Hvorostovsky** *bar* Robert **Sergei Alexashkin** *bass* King René **Nikolai Putilin** *bar* Ibn-Hakia **Larissa Diadkova** *mez* Martha **Nikolai Gassiev** *ten* Alméric **Tatiana Kravtsova** *sop* Brigitta **Olga Korzhenskaya** *mez* Laura **Gennadi Bezzubenkov** *bar* Bertrand **Chorus and Orchestra of the Kirov Opera, St Petersburg / Valery Gergiev**
Philips ② 442 796-2PH2 (96' · DDD · N/T/t)　　　Ⓕ

Iolanta, the touching little princess, blind and virginal, into whose darkness and isolation there

eventually shines the 'bright angel' of Duke Robert, is delightfully sung by Galina Gorchakova. There's a freshness and sense of vulnerability here, especially in the opening scenes with Martha in the garden as she sings wistfully of something that appears to be lacking in her life: the *Arioso* is done charmingly and without sentimentality. Gegam Grigorian sometimes sounds pinched and under strain, even in the Romance. He's also overshadowed by Hvorostovsky who's at his best here: warm and with a somewhat dusky tone. The King, Provence's 'bon roi René', is benignly if a little throatily sung by Sergei Alexashkin, and he has at hand a sturdy-voiced Ibn-Hakia in Nikolai Putilin. Valery Gergiev conducts a sensitive performance, responding constructively to the unusual scoring, and not overplaying the more demonstrative elements in a score that gains most through some understatement.

The Queen of Spades

The Queen of Spades
Gegam Grigorian *ten* Herman **Maria Gulegina** *sop* Lisa **Irina Arkhipova** *mez* Countess **Nikolai Putilin** *bar* Count Tomsky **Vladimir Chernov** *bar* Prince Yeletsky **Olga Borodina** *mez* Pauline **Vladimir Solodovnikov** *ten* Chekalinsky **Sergei Alexashkin** *bass* Surin **Evgeni Boitsov** *ten* Chaplitsky **Nikolai Gassiev** *ten* Major-domo **Gennadi Bezzubenkov** *bass* Narumov **Ludmila Filatova** *mez* Governess **Tatiana Filimonova** *sop* Masha **Kirov Theatre Chorus and Orchestra / Valery Gergiev**
Philips ③ 438 141-2PH3 (166' · DDD · N/T/t)　　Ⓕ**O**➔

There are major problems with all the current sets of *The Queen of Spades*, but Valery Gergiev, one of the outstanding Tchaikovskians of the day, here coaxes from a thoroughly Western-sounding Kirov Theatre Orchestra what's surely the most refined account of the score yet recorded, and one that's never lacking energy or full-blooded attack. His isn't so much a compromise approach as one which stresses fatalism and underlying sadness. The recording was made in the Kirov Theatre itself, and there's admittedly some constriction to the orchestral sound picture; but for many the atmosphere of a real stage venue will be a plus, and the all-important balance between voices and orchestra is just right. If the spine still fails to tingle as often as it should, that's mainly a reflection of the respectable but unexciting singing.

The Queen of Spades
Yuri Marusin *ten* Herman **Nancy Gustafson** *sop* Lisa **Felicity Palmer** *mez* Countess **Sergei Leiferkus** *bar* Count Tomsky **Dimitri Kharitonov** *bar* Prince Yeletsky **Marie-Ange Todorovitch** *contr* Pauline **Graeme Matheson-Bruce** *ten* Chekalinsky **Andrew Slater** *bass* Surin **Robert Burt** *ten* Chaplitsky **Geoffrey Pogson** *ten* Major Domo **Christopher Thornton-Holmes** *bass* Narumov **Enid Hartle** *mez* Governess **Rachel Tovey** *sop* Masha **Glyndebourne**

Festival Chorus; London Philharmonic Orchestra /
Sir Andrew Davis
Stage director **Graham Vick**
Video director **Peter Maniura**
ArtHaus Musik 🎦 100 272 (170' · 4:3 · 2.0 · 0) Ⓕ🅾

Graham Vick's 1992 staging is worthy of this extraordinary score. He reflects exactly the highly charged emotions and sense of brooding menace pervading the composer's re-enactment of Pushkin's story, thus creating a compelling psychodrama that compels both eye and ear. Davis catches most, if not all, of the score's romantic sweep and inner, dislocating turbulence, although the impassioned undercurrents are better achieved in the Kirov video, conducted by Gergiev (below). Yuri Marusin is the crazed Herman incarnate. Whether or not you can accept his often off-pitch singing is a personal matter. As his Lisa, Nancy Gustafson, offers a portrayal of an impressionable girl driven to distraction and suicide by the unhinged behaviour of her lover. She sings the part in warm, passionate tones.

Peter Maniura's video direction catches every facial expression of both characters and of Felicity Palmer's electrifying Countess. Sergei Leiferkus is elegant and commanding as the free-loving Tomsky. Dimitri Kharitonov is the soul of rectitude as Yeletsky and brings a bronzed tone to his lovely aria. Marie-Ange Todorovitch is an attractively palpitating Pauline. Picture and sound are exemplary.

Additional recommendation

The Queen of Spades
Grigorian ten Hermann **Guleghina** sop Lisa **Filatova** mez Countess **Leiferkus** bar Count Tomsky **Gergalov** bar Prince Yeletsky **Borodina** contr Pauline **Kirov Opera Chorus and Orchestra / Gergiev**
Stage director **Temirkanov** Video director **Large**
Philips 🎦 070 434-9PH (179' · NTSC · 16:9 · 2.0 & DTS 5.1 · 0) Ⓕ🅾

This production from St Petersburg, contemporaneous with the Glyndebourne production reviewed above, is a much more conventional but equally valid approach. The staging is always apt, and in terms of cast, the Kirov holds the edge over its rival. The young Guleghina is the intense, vibrant Lisa to the life. The video direction is exemplary, though the sound leaves something to be desired.

Georg Philipp Telemann
German 1681-1767

The son of a clergyman, Telemann was a virtually self-taught musician – he had an uncanny ability to soak up knowledge and from a variety of disciplines. Science, languages and jurisprudence seem to have been his subjects at the University of Leipzig. By then he had picked up the violin, the zither and the oboe as well as having a reputation as a brilliant organist.

Most of his music theory was gained by studying the scores of the older masters such as Lully.

He wrote operas and cantatas for the Collegium Musicum he founded while still a student in Leipzig and thereafter held a succession of posts – as organist and kapellmeister in Sorau (Poland), and as music director in Eisenach and Frankfurt. In 1721 he was offered the prestigious job of music director of St Thomas's Church in Leipzig. He turned it down to become city musical director in Hamburg, where he stayed for the rest of his life. The third choice for the post in Leipzig was JS Bach. (Telemann, incidentally, was godfather to Bach's son Carl Philipp Emanuel.)

He was a popular figure – his lively mind and genial high spirits are caught in his music – but his private life was not so happy: his first wife died in childbirth; by his second wife he had eight sons and two daughters, few of whom survived infancy, but she later abandoned him for a Swedish army officer. Like Bach and Handel, Telemann suffered from failing eyesight as he grew older.

It was Handel who said, famously, 'Telemann could write a motet for eight voices more quickly than one could write a letter'. Music, Telemann thought, 'ought not to be an effort' and disarmingly asserted that 'a good composer should be able to set public notices to music'.

Telemann was probably the most prolific composer in musical history. He wrote almost as much as Bach and Handel put together (and each of them wrote a perplexing amount) including 600 French overtures or orchestral suites, 200 concertos, 40 operas and more than 1000 pieces of church music.

All of Telemann's music is extremely well fashioned and elegant; his technique is sophisticated, combining the operatic elements of Italian Baroque, the German contrapuntal style and the French school of dance-based suites.

Flute Concertos

Concerto for Flute, Strings and Continuo in D, TWV51:D2. Concerto for Flute, Strings and Continuo in G, TWV51:G2. Concerto for Two Flutes, Violone, Strings and Continuo in A minor, TWV53:A1[a]. Concerto for Flute, Violin, Cello, Strings and Continuo in A, TWV53:A2. Concerto for Flute, Oboe d'amore, Viola d'amore, Strings and Continuo in E, TWV53:E1
Emmanuel Pahud, [a]**Jacques Zoon** fls
Berlin Baroque Soloists (Wolfram Christ va d'amore Georg Faust vc Klaus Stoll violone Albrecht Mayer ob d'amore) / **Rainer Kussmaul** vn
EMI 557397-2 (66' · DDD) Ⓕ🅾➔

You'll rarely hear such personality in a Baroque-concerto soloist as the extraordinary Emmanuel Pahud exhibits here. The Berlin Baroque Soloists acclimatise effortlessly to an 18th-century palette, and distinguished colleagues they make for Pahud. The flautist sets out his stall from the *Andante* of the succinct G major concerto (completed from a damaged source and therefore making its recording debut) whose startling resemblance to the slow movement of Bach's F minor Concerto, BWV1056, seems to inspire Pahud to a lyricism of understated elegance which one often hears in the best performances of the Bach work. Indeed, it's his sensitivity to Telemann's gestural implications and ability to colour the music at every turn which makes Pahud's playing so enchanting in all five concertos.

Telemann performance on a modern flute will inevitably lead to some recoiling, but one never feels deprived of the gentle and beguiling articulation of a 'period' instrument or its capacity for soft dynamic and purity of sound. One only has to hear the lithe performance of the A major Triple Concerto, from Part 1 of Telemann's famous banquet publication of 1733, *Tafelmusik*, where character abounds through Pahud's concern with first principles. Joyous exchange and textural delights abound in the Triple Concerto in E major, where Wolfram Christ's viola d'amore and Albrecht Mayer's oboe d'amore combine with the flautist in a ravishingly blended montage. The Flute Concerto in D confirms everything about Pahud's exquisite taste and mesmerising sound. A winner.

Horn Concertos

Concerto for Three Horns, Violin and Orchestra **P**
in D major. Overture-Suites – C, TWV55:C5, 'La bouffonne'; F, TWV55:F11, 'Alster Echo'. Concerto in G, 'Grillen-Symphonie'
Anthony Halstead, Christian Rutherford, Raul Diaz hns **Collegium Musicum 90 / Simon Standage** vn
Chandos Chaconne CHAN0547 (70' · DDD). Ⓟ**O**Ⓑ➔

This release shows Telemann at his most irrepressibly good-humoured and imaginative. There's a concerto for three rattling horns and a solo violin (a splendid sound, with the horns recorded at what seems like the ideal distance), and an elegant suite for strings which sounds like Handel, Bach and a few French composers all thrown in together. More striking, though, is the most substantial piece on the disc, the *Alster Echo* Overture-Suite, a nine-movement work for strings, oboes and horns full of tricks and surprises occasioned by a host of representative titles. Thus 'Hamburg Carillons' brings us horns imitating bells, 'Concerto of Frogs and Crows' has some mischievously scrunchy wrong notes, and in 'Alster Echo' there's a complex network of echoes between oboes and horns. But the showstealer is the *Grillen-Symphonie* ('Cricket Symphony'). This is a work for the gloriously silly scoring of piccolo, alto chalumeau, oboe, violins, viola, and two double basses, a somewhat Stravinskian combination that you're unlikely to encounter every day. But it's not just the instrumentation that's irresistibly odd. There's a slow movement with curious, melancholy woodwind interventions a little reminiscent of *Harold in Italy*, and a finale which is quite a hoot.

Overture-Suites

Overture-Suite in G, 'Burlesque de Don Quichotte', TWV55:G10. Overture-Suite in D minor, WV55:d3.

Overture-Suite in E flat, 'La lyra', TWV55: Es3
Northern Chamber Orchestra / Nicholas Ward
Naxos 8 554019 (57' · DDD) Ⓢ Ⓑ➔

Overture-Suite in G, 'Burlesque de Don Quichotte',.
TWV55:G10. Overture-Suite in B minor, TWV55:h1.
Concerto for Two Violins, Bassoon and Strings in D.
Overture-Suite in G. **P**
Collegium Musicum 90 / Simon Standage
Chandos Chaconne CHAN0700 (66' · DDD) Ⓟ Ⓑ➔

Telemann is never more irresistible than when he's in light-hearted pictorial mode, and both these new releases feature one of the most entertainingly evocative of all his overture-suites for strings, the *Burlesque de Don Quichotte*. Taking episodes from the Cervantes novel as its inspiration, it provides us with a memorable sequence of cameos, from the deluded Don tilting at windmills and sighing with love, to Sancho Panza tossed high in a blanket, to portrayals of the pair's respective steeds. Telemann achieves all this with such humour and descriptive precision that, when you hear it, you'll surely laugh in delighted recognition. What a good film composer he would have been!

Both performances strike an appropriate tongue-in-cheek attitude. Northern Chamber Orchestra show good style and a pleasingly light and clear texture, unclouded by excessive vibrato or over-egged string tone. Only at the bass end does the sound occasionally become a little thick, but this is really quibbling when what we actually have is a good demonstration of how to perform Baroque music on modern strings. It still makes quite a contrast with Collegium Musicum 90, however, whose period instruments, recorded more intimately, sound slighter and sparkier. Having already recorded so much of Telemann's music, they sound more at home and have that extra ounce of freedom to enjoy themselves.

The couplings of the Chandos disc are more interesting. For all that the NCO offer another attractive string suite, *La lyra*, containing a typically realistic and beguiling hurdy-gurdy impersonation, the D major Overture isn't especially memorable; CM90 have found more colourful stuff in the strikingly French-accented G major Overture and a thoroughly charming Concerto for two violins, bassoon and strings. A pair of bassoons also makes a delightful appearance in the second Minuet of the Overture in B minor.

Musique de Table / Tafelmusik

Musique de Table, 'Tafelmusik', Part 3 – Concerto **P**
for Two Horns and Strings in E flat; Overture in B flat; Quartet in E minor; Sonata for Oboe and Continuo in G minor; Trio in D; Conclusion in B flat
Orchestra of the Golden Age
Naxos 8 553732 (73' · DDD) Ⓢ Ⓑ➔

The Orchestra of the Golden Age bring expressive warmth to this evergreen repertoire. The present disc contains the third of the three 'Productions' that make up Telemann's most comprehensive orchestral/instrumental publication. It's the shortest of the three and so can be accommodated comfortably on a single disc. Like its predecessors, the Third consists of an orchestral Suite, Quartet, Concerto, Trio, Sonata for melody instrument with figured bass and an orchestral 'Conclusion'. Telemann had already generously provided for transverse flute, trumpet and solo violins in the previous 'Productions' while maintaining the flute profile (Quartet and Trio) in the third anthology; he gives pride of place to oboe(s) in the Suite, Sonata and Conclusion, and a pair of horns in the Concerto.

One might feel that a slightly augmented string section would have been justified for the orchestral suites and concertos. But, in this instance the players realise the innate nobility of the French overture character with a justly 'occasional' tempo. In the Concerto, which comes over well, if perhaps a shade rigidly in its rhythm, the horn players Roger Montgomery and Gavin Edwards sustain an evenly balanced and tonally secure partnership. That also goes for the lightly articulated flute partnership of Edwina Smith and Felicity Bryson in the Trio. The lovely G minor Oboe Sonata is played with warmth and expressive intimacy by Heather Foxwell. Telemann brings all to a vigorous close with a little three-section orchestral coda, marked *Furioso*. This is a set which makes rather more of Telemann's inflective *délicatesse* than others at twice or even three times the price.

Chamber Works

Sonata Corellisante No 1 in F, TWV42:F2.   **P**
Paris Quartets, 'Nouveaux quatuors en Six Suites' –
No 6 in E minor, TWV43:e4. Essercizii musici – Trio No
8 in B flat, TWV42:B4. Quartets – A minor, TWV43:a3;
G minor, TWV43:g4
Florilegium Ensemble
Channel Classics CCS5093 (53' · DDD)   Ⓕ**OO**

The rarity here is the *Sonata Corellisante* for two violins and continuo in which Telemann pays tribute to Corelli. The remaining works are the sixth and perhaps finest of the 1738 *Nouveaux quatuors* or 'Paris' Quartets as they have become known, a little Quartet (or *Quadro*) in G minor, a B flat Trio from the *Essercizii musici* collection (c1739) and a fine *Concerto da camera* (Quartet) in A minor, very much along the lines of Vivaldi's pieces of the same kind in which each instrument other than the continuo has an obbligato role. The finest work is the 'Paris' Quartet, which consists of a Prelude, a sequence of dance-orientated movements and an elegiac Chaconne that lingers long in the memory. The performance is full of vitality and probes beneath the music's superficialities. Throughout the programme there's an intensity and a youthful spontaneity about this playing which has considerable appeal.

'Paris Quartets, Volume 2'   **P**
Quartets – in D, TWV43:D3; in A minor, TWV43:a2;

in G, TWV43:G4. Six Concerts and Six Suites –
Suite No 1 in G, TWV42:G4
Florilegium (Ashley Solomon *fl* Kati Debretzini *vn*
Reiko Ichise *viol* Jennifer Morsches *vc* James
Johnstone *hpd*)
Channel Classics ⬜ CCSSA20604 (71' · DDD)   Ⓕ

'Paris Quartets, Volume 2'   **P**
Paris Quartets, 'Nouveaux quatuors en Six Suites',
TWV43 – No 2; No 3; No 4. Six Concerts et Six Suites
– Suite No 3
Florilegium Ensemble (Ashley Solomon *fl* Kati
Debretzeni *vn* Reiko Ichise *viol* Jennifer Morsches *vc*
James Johnstone *hpd*)
Channel Classics ⬜ CCSSA21005 (74' · DDD)   Ⓕ

The quartets have become among the most popular pieces in the Baroque chamber repertoire, so there is no need to rehearse their qualities here, save to reiterate that their beguiling, convivial style is about as comfortably civilised as it gets. Florilegium's performances mix technical and musical finesse in equal measure and observe every expressive and rhetorical nuance with a delicious light touch. Theirs is not the chiselled precision and upfront high energy of some modern-day Baroque chamber groups, but their playing is unfailingly alive and the details of their elegant conversation are well captured in a recorded balance in which no instrument is allowed undue dominance. The chaconne which ends the sixth quartet, TWV43:e4, is exquisitely drawn out, there are some charming drone effects here and there, and overall it is difficult to know what else to add – only, perhaps, that in their mutual refinement and good taste, Florilegium and Telemann could have been made for each other.

12 Fantaisies for Violin without Continuo,   **P**
TWV40:14-25. Der getreue Music-Meister –
'Gulliver' Suite in D, TWV40:108
Andrew Manze, Caroline Balding *vns*
Harmonia Mundi HMU90 7137 (78' · DDD)   Ⓕ

Andrew Manze brings a very distinctive angle to the 12 *Fantaisies*. We have learnt to take virtuosity for granted with Manze – his remarkable feats allow the most prejudiced to forget that he's playing a Baroque fiddle. But without such an instrument he could barely create such a biting astringency in the more self-effacing and tortured moments (*Fantaisie* No 6) or a cultivated assurance and definition in articulation to the recognisably regular sections, such as *Fantaisie* No 10, where Telemann is working in established forms – particularly in the latter works in the set where dance forms predominate. If characterisation is the key, Manze is arguably more persuasive than any of his rivals. He grows through phrases in the Gigue of the Fourth *Fantaisie* in a fashion which gives the work a peculiarly stoical strength, purrs through the contrapuntally conceived *Fantaisies* with nonchalant disdain for their extreme technical demands and leaves sighs and pauses hanging with supreme eloquence. With sheer lucidity, imagination and colour, he most acutely captures the sense of a famous public figure ensconced in a private world against the backdrop of a musical world in a state of flux. To add spice to an already outstanding release, we have the short and delightful *Gulliver* Suite for two violins.

Die Donner-Ode, TWV6:3

Der Herr ist König, TWV8:6. Die Donner-Ode   ℙ
Ann Monoyios, Barbara Schlick *sops* **Axel Köhler**
counterten **Wilfried Jochens** *ten* **Harry van der**
Kamp, Hans-Georg Wimmer, Stephan
Schreckenberger *basses* **Rheinische Kantorei;**
Das Kleine Konzert / Hermann Max
Capriccio 10 556 (65' · DDD · T/t)   Ⓕ

The *Donner-Ode* was one of Telemann's biggest public successes during his lifetime and is a striking piece in its own right, a vivid reaction to the Lisbon earthquake of 1755. The shock caused to the international community by this dreadful event (in which some 60,000 people were killed) was enormous, and in Hamburg a special day of penitence was the occasion for this 'Thunder Ode', though it does perhaps suggest a rather smug satisfaction that such a disaster didn't befall northern Germany. 'The voice of God makes the proud mountains collapse', the text proclaims, 'Give thanks to Him in His temple!' The music, too, both in its mood and in that extraordinarily up-to-date style of Telemann's later years, frequently conjures the benign, entertainingly song-like pictorial mood of a Haydn Mass or oratorio. Entertaining is the word, though, especially in this energetic performance under Hermann Max. He's fleet-footed and buoyantly athletic, benefiting from what's becoming his customary excellent team of German soloists.

For the coupling Max chooses another German work, the cheerful cantata *Der Herr ist König*, written much earlier in the composer's life and more Bach-like in character and form (though it's worth pointing out that since it survives partly in Bach's hand, we ought perhaps to conclude that Telemann was the one wielding the influence here). As in the *Ode*, choir, soloists and orchestra are bright, tight-knit and well recorded, making this release an enjoyable one.

Brockes Passion

Brockes Passion, TVWV5:1   ℙ
Lydia Teuscher, Birgit Christensen *sops* **Marie-**
Claude Chappuis *mez* **Donát Havár, Daniel Behle**
tens **Johannes Weisser** *bar* **RIAS Chamber Choir,**
Berlin; Akademie für Alte Musik Berlin /
René Jacobs
Harmonia Mundi ② HMC90 2013/14
(140' · DDD)   ⒻⓄ➤

The Hamburg poet Barthold Heinrich Brockes wrote the Passion oratorio libretto *Der für die Sünde der Welt gemarterte und sterbende Jesus* for Reinhard Keiser to set to music in 1712. Handel composed a setting in London about four years later (probably for Hamburg), and in April 1716 Telemann's version was first performed in Frankfurt. The broody opening Sinfonia makes one think of Haydn's late orchestral writing at its most daring. The Berlin AAM's playing is lean and angular but the 35-strong RIAS Chamber Choir seems overpowering at times, and it would be good to hear this work performed by smaller and more integrated forces.

René Jacobs divides the soprano arias for the Daughter of Zion and the Faithful Soul between Birgitte Christensen and Lydia Teuscher (the booklet fails to indicate what singer performs which arias): 'Was Bärentatzen, Löwenklauen' has snappy percussive horn fanfares, and several contrasting arias during the scene of Christ's scourging are among the highest points of the oratorio. Marie-Claude Chappuis's singing of Judas's guilt-wracked scene, in which the betrayer resolves to commit suicide, is extraordinary. The trio 'O Donnerwort!' crackles with theatrical velocity. Johannes Weisser is a grainy Jesus, but his declamatory singing in the volatile 'Erwäg, ergrimmte Natterbrut' is impressive. Donát Havár does not have a mellifluous timbre but is a good communicator of Peter's texts. Jacobs paces the oratorio as if it is a vivid religious opera: he omits six arias and two recitatives 'for reasons of dramatic coherence'. There are moments of brittle intensity that could have afforded more gentleness, but Jacobs's committed vision provides us with a valuable glimpse of Telemann's brilliant imagination.

Die Hirten an der Krippe zu Bethlehem

Die Hirten an der Krippe zu Bethlehem.   ℙ
Siehe, ich verkündige Euch, TWV1:1334. Der Herr hat
offenbaret, TWV1:262
Constanze Backes *sop* **Mechthild Georg** *contr*
Andreas Post *ten* **Klaus Mertens** *bass* **Michaelstein**
Chamber Choir; Telemann Chamber Orchestra /
Ludger Rémy
CPO CPO999 419-2 (65' · DDD · T/t)   ⒻⓄ

The tenderly expressive and ingenuous character of German Protestant Christmas music of the Baroque seldom fails to exert its magic. Though the greatest achievements in this tradition greatly diminished after Bach, there were exceptions. One of them is Telemann's intimate and imaginative oratorio *Die Hirten an der Krippe zu Bethlehem* ('The Shepherds at the Crib in Bethlehem'). The text is by the Berlin poet Ramler, and though Ramler's taste for classical forms sometimes makes his work stiff and austere, nothing could be further removed from this than his intimate account and celebration of Christ's birth. Certainly, it touched a chord in Telemann, who responded with music of expressive warmth and irresistible charm.

This isn't at all the world of Bach's *Christmas Oratorio*. Indeed, it's only approximately a sixth of the length of Bach's masterpiece. Telemann's concept is one rather of noble simplicity, a sought-after goal in post-Bach church music which, in this respect, at least, provided a perfect foil to Ramler's text. Every reader will recognise the melody of the opening number as belonging to the Latin carol *In dulci jubilo*. Telemann's harmonisation of the 16th-century tune sets the scene concisely and intimately. Thereafter follows one delight after another. Of outstanding beauty are the 'Shepherd's Song' and the bass aria, 'Hirten aus den goldnen Zeiten'. This is an extremely pleasurable, well-filled disc with a pervasive charm. The remaining two items are both Christmas cantatas, of 1761 and 1762 respectively, and contain music of enormous appeal. Performances are excellent, with outstanding singing by Klaus Mertens and Mechthild Georg. Both choir and orchestra rise to the occasion under the sensitive and stylish direction of Ludger Rémy. Three hitherto unrecorded pieces in performances of such vitality make this a very strong issue.

Cantatas

Lobet den Herrn, alle seine Heerscharen, TWV1:061.
Wer nur den lieben Gott lässt walten, TWV1:593.
Der Tod ist verschlungen in den Sieg, TWV1:320
Dorothee Fries *sop* **Mechthild Georg** *contr*
Andreas Post *ten* **Albert Pöhl** *bass* **Friedemann
Immer Trumpet Consort** (Friedemann Immer, Klaus Osterloh, Ute Hübner *tpts* Stefan Gawlik *timp*)
**Bach Collegium Vocale, Siegen;
Hanover Hofkapelle / Ulrich Stötzel**
Hänssler Classic CD98 179 (56' · DDD · T/t)   Ⓕ

While Telemann's concertos, suites, instrumental chamber music and oratorios have been well explored by performers, his large-scale cantatas, comparatively speaking, have not. Part of the problem is that there's a truly daunting number of them. And, it need hardly be said, the quality is variable. But few are utterly devoid of inspiration and the three pieces contained in this programme rise well beyond that category. Until now they have remained very possibly unperformed, but certainly unrecorded. These aren't domestic pieces of the kind which characterise his well-known Hamburg anthology, *Der harmonische Gottes-dienst*, but generously, sometimes colourfully orchestrated works with choruses, recitatives, arias and chorales. The format, in short, is Bach-like, though with nothing remotely comparable to the great opening choral fantasies of which Bach was the master. Telemann usually treats his hymn melodies simply, this approach lending them a distinctive, ingenuous charm.

The three cantatas offer strong contrasts of colour and of mood. The New Year piece *Lobet den Herrn* has glittering trumpet parts with timpani and Telemann's deployment of them is deft

and effective. The Neumeister setting, on the other hand, with an orchestra confined to strings and woodwind, is quietly spoken and more reflective. Performances are stylish, and the director, Ulrich Stötzel, has a lively feeling for Telemann's frequent use of dance rhythms. The soloists are expressive, notably Mechthild Georg, who offers a lyrical account of her aria with oboe in the Easter cantata *Der Tod ist verschlungen in den Sieg*. In short, this is a release which should interest and delight all readers with a taste for the music of this imaginative, prolific and seemingly indefatigable composer.

Domingo Terradellas Catalan 1711-1751

Domingo Terradellas was Catalan by birth but moved to Italy in 1732, and studied with the celebrated master Francesco Durante at the conservatory Poveri di Gesù Cristo in Naples. His first major operatic triumph was Merope (Rome, 1743); a Neapolitan envoy wrote of its success, 'the like of which no one can remember for many years'. Terradellas worked mainly in Rome, but his setting of Metastasio's Artaserse was performed at Venice in 1744. A year later, Terradellas went to London, where he composed for the King's Theatre. By 1750 he was back in Italy, and his last opera, Sesostri, was a huge hit at the Rome Carnival in 1751. Highly esteemed and innovative (Burney claimed that he pioneered the use of woodwind instruments in accompanied recitative), he was embroiled in a bitter rivalry with Nicolò Jommelli – although the legend that Jommelli had a hand in Terradellas's body being dumped in the Tiber has been discredited.

Artaserse

Artaserse
Anna Maria Panzarella *sop* Artaserse **Céline Ricci**
sop Arbace **Marina Comparato** *mez* Mandane
Sunhae Im *sop* Semira **Augustín Prunell-Friend** *ten*
Artabano **Mariví Blasco** *sop* Megabise **La Real
Compañía Ópera de Cámara / Juan Bautista Otero**
RCOC Records ③ RCOC0800-3 (175' · DDD · S/T/N)
                                                   Ⓕⵔ

Those wanting to sample Terradellas's music will find much to enjoy in Juan Bautista Otero's accomplished performance of *Artaserse*, recorded in Barcelona in 2008. Those who find Hasse, pre-reform Gluck or even early Mozart impenetrable and dulled by *da capo* conventions won't be easily dissuaded from that opinion, but others – including those who admire Metastasio's tense political dramas – will enthuse that Terradellas's setting is varied, imaginative, melodically assured and dramatically astute. It is true that the plot is complicated, but the best thrillers always are. There are irresistible moments of dramatic tension, such as Arbace's intense 'Fra cento affanni e cento', as he reels in shock that his father has murdered the king (the deed which ignites the ensuing drama, as Arbace is torn between filial and political senses of duty).

La Real Compañía Ópera de Cámara plays with energy and refinement; the string section is just big enough to bring the varied sonorities to proceedings; warmly illustrative woodwind and confident brass playing feature in numerous arias. All of the singers are fully immersed in the dramatic action, and most of them dispatch astonishing arias to good effect. In the two leading male roles, Anna Maria Panzarella and Céline Ricci are both totally committed to their characters. The closing part of Act 1, during which Arbace is disowned or rejected by everyone else (in superb short arias), concludes with him led to prison as he boldly declares the heroic 'Quando freme altera l'onda' (with two splendid trumpets fully to the fore). At the conclusion to Act 2, Arbace's father Artabano (the real murderer) envisages being accused by the ghost of his innocent son in a vivid accompanied recitative and aria ('Ombre, o dei perchè tornate?', feverishly sung by tenor Augustín Prunell-Friend). Sunhae Im aptly conveys the anguished predicaments of Semira, the daughter of the murderer, brother of the accused, but also lover of the victim's son and heir; her sweetly sung 'Torna innocente' and 'L'augellin ch'è in lacci stretto' are spellbinding. Mariví Blasco delivers ornamentation in 'Allor che irato freme' that manages to be both stratospheric and tasteful. In such scenes there is little doubt of Terradellas's great talent as a musical dramatist. Nowadays our appreciation of serious operas performed in Italy during the first half of the 18th century is embarrassingly narrow, but this magnificent recording goes some way towards showing how the imbalance can be redressed.

Ambroise Thomas   French 1811-1896

Born into a musical family – his father had played in the theatre orchestras of Metz – Thomas was groomed for a career in music and by the age of 10 was accomplished both as a pianist and as a violinist. He subsequently became a respected teacher and published pedagogical works. After years of neglect, Thomas's music has seen a considerable revival, with major performances of his two greatest works, the operas Mignon and Hamlet. Though not hugely prolific, in the context of French opera of the late 19th century Thomas was a figure of considerable importance.

La cour de Célimène

La cour de Célimène
Laura Claycomb *sop* La Comtesse **Joan Rodgers**
sop La Baronne **Alastair Miles** *bass-bar* Le
Commandeur **Sébastien Droy** *ten* Le Chevalier
Nicole Tibbels *sop* Bretonne **Geoffrey Mitchell**
Choir; Philharmonia Orchestra / Andrew Litton

Opera Rara ② ORC37 (73' · DDD · S/T/t/N)   Ⓟ ⬤

La cour de Célimène was introduced at the Opéra Comique in 1855, a time of mass-production of new operas in Paris, and was dropped after 19 performances. It was probably not so robust in tunefulness or dramatic situation as to make its way through in these circumstances. It was also tagged with the old-fashioned characteristic of an ornate vocal style. Presumably, with its courtly setting in the *ancien régime* it would have appeared to the more serious-minded and left-inclined of Parisians to be reactionary in its nostalgic appeal and trivial in every other respect.

Today the first reaction is likely to be gratitude and delight in the discovery of a score which, if not coming up with 'big' tunes, is unfailingly melodious. We may also be more inclined to credit the comedy with a certain sophistication, the light irony of a raised eyebrow surveying the human scene, as in *Così fan tutte*. The title, with its implied reference to Molière, possibly adds a suggestion or two, for the countess, the central character here, is like Célimène in *Le misantrope* representative of the maddeningly beautiful, frivolous and privileged, and here too the world arranges itself to suit its convenience rather than its virtuous principles.

At least if time rejects it yet again it will not be the fault of this performance. Both sopranos manage the florid work with apparent ease, Laura Claycomb soaring aloft gracefully, Joan Rodgers having the additional warmth to suit the Baroness's more thoughtful nature. Alastair Miles enjoys himself in his role of worldly aristocrat with the attributes of a virtuoso and a *buffo* bass. Sébastien Droy has the right lightness and youth of voice and manner, and, as the only Frenchman, does not show up the efforts of the English in his language. Chorus and orchestra contribute splendidly; Andrew Litton conducts with stylish zest; recorded sound is clear and well balanced.

Sir Michael Tippett   British 1905-1998

Nice to think that a man who was born the year after the death of Dvořák (Grieg had another two years to live, Rimsky-Korsakov three) was still writing music three years before the new millennium. He was a comparatively slow starter for, after a period at the Royal College of Music, then teaching and composing, he returned to the college for further study, frustrated with what he was writing. It wasn't until 1934 that he allowed his first pieces to be performed publicly. His First String Quartet attracted little attention and the (now well-known) Concerto for Double String Orchestra gained little more.

It was his oratorio A Child of Our Time that finally made his name, inspired by the case of a Jewish boy who assassinated a member of the German embassy in Paris in 1938. During the war itself, Tippett, a confirmed pacifist, served two months in Wormwood Scrubs in 1943 for his beliefs but man-

Tippett

aged to regain the respect of his fellow citizens after the war. Even so, it wasn't until after the peace was regained, by which time Tippett was 40, that any of his music was readily available. As director of music at Morley College in London (1940-51) and as director of the Bath Festival (1969-74) together with other appointments, Tippett established himself firmly at the centre of British musical life, resulting in a CBE in 1959 and a knighthood in 1966.

His music is hard to categorise, unmistakably English but quite dissimilar in aim and content from his contemporaries Walton and Britten. He has nothing to do with atonalism or minimalism yet writes resolutely complex music which takes time to appreciate and absorb; his lyrical neo-romantic impulses are obscured by his individual expression of harmony and rhythm. Tippett was never a prolific composer, and his works, completed slowly, comprise five string quartets, four concertos, four symphonies, five operas and a number of vocal and choral works.

Concerto for Double String Orchestra

Concerto for Double String Orchestra. Fantasia concertante on a Theme of Corelli. The Midsummer Marriage – Ritual Dances
BBC Symphony Chorus and Orchestra /
Sir Andrew Davis
Warner Apex 8573 89098-2 (64' · DDD)   ⓢ☛

Sir Andrew Davis's formidable Tippettian credentials shine through in every bar of this outstanding anthology. Aided by realistic, firmly focused sound, the Concerto for Double String Orchestra sounds glorious here. Davis directs a performance of enormous humanity, intelligence and dedication – even Sir Neville Marriner's excellent EMI remake now seems a little matter-of-fact by comparison. In the slow movement Davis secures a rapt response from his BBC strings (the exquisite closing bars are drawn with ineffable tenderness), while the finale bounds along with irrepressible vigour and fine rhythmic panache. Davis's *Fantasia concertante* is an even more remarkable achievement. This is another inspirational display: sensitive and fervent, yet marvellously lucid and concentrated too. Once again, the BBC strings are on radiant form, and the lyrical intensity of their playing during the central climax has to be heard to be believed. Davis's identification with this sublime music is total. Much the same applies, for that matter, to the committed and incisive account of the Ritual Dances from *The Midsummer Marriage*, a veritable *tour de force* to which the BBC Symphony Chorus contributes thrillingly in the final dance.

Piano Concerto

Piano Concerto[a]. Fantasia on a Theme of Handel[a]. Four Piano Sonatas
Steven Osborne pf
[a]**BBC Scottish Symphony Orchestra /**
Martyn Brabbins
Hyperion ② CDA67461/2 (141' · DDD)   Ⓕ❍❍❍☛

The young Tippett – magpie and maverick – sought maximum intensity of feeling while shunning what he felt to be the sentimental fervour of Elgar, Bax and Walton. Equally abhorrent were the pastoral pieties of Vaughan Williams. Tippett took his stand with Blake and Yeats rather than Bunyan, and a Blake whose 'bow of burning gold' required something altogether less complacent than Parry's well upholstered jingoism.

The results are plain to hear in Tippett's earliest works for piano, the First Sonata and the *Handel* Fantasia. The slow movement of the sonata may flirt briefly with Hindemith-style counterpoint but the predominant spirit is fiery and spontaneous, with a reinvigorated romanticism embracing those aspects of popular music which Tippett believed to have 'classical' potential.

The road ahead was bumpy and he occasionally lost his way, as in the very long slow movement of the Third Sonata, aspiring to Beethovenian depth but bogged down in overly dense textures. There are also several repetitions too many in the Fourth Sonata, though the final movement's gently poetic sense of resignation more than compensates.

Most powerful of all is the mighty Concerto, starkly and confidently poised between Tippett's still richly potent earlier style and the brave new possibilities explored in its visionary central movement. This recording blends the piano in with the orchestra, acknowledging the work's symphonic attributes, and there is a certain recessed quality to the sound of the piece throughout. Nevertheless, the eloquence and fantasy of what is undoubtedly one of the major works of the 1950s is superbly projected in a performance which need fear no comparison with the best earlier recordings. As for the sonatas, Steven Osborne is at least the equal of Paul Crossley (CRD) in interpretative empathy, and has the advantage of superlative modern recording. There's a further advantage: perceptive and lucid booklet-notes by Ian Kemp, Tippett's friend and biographer, and one of Osborne's mentors. The set is dedicated to him.

Symphonies

Symphonies Nos 1-4. New Year – Suite
Faye Robinson sop
Bournemouth Symphony / Richard Hickox
Chandos ③ CHAN10330 (193' · DDD)   Ⓜ❍❍☛

The riot of proliferating counterpoint that is Tippett's Symphony No 1 presents enough problems of orchestral balance to give recording teams nightmares. Chandos has managed creditable degrees of containment and clarity, without loss of realism, and the impact, when the last movement finally settles on to its long-prepared harmonic goal, is powerful and convincing. Doubts as to whether initial impetus is sufficient to keep the complex structures on course prove groundless. This is a fine account, well balanced between lively rhythmic articulation and broad melodic sweep.

The balance Hickox achieves between attention to detail and large-scale symphonic sweep is exemplary, and especially impressive in the tricky finale of Symphony No 2, where he conveys the essential ambiguity of an ending which strives to recapture the optimistic *élan* of the work's opening without ever quite managing it. The recording, too, gives us much more of the symphony's contrapuntal detail. The first recording of music from Tippett's opera *New Year*, premiered in 1989, is thoroughly welcome. The music of this suite may seem over-emphatic to anyone who hasn't experienced the opera in the theatre, and the recording relishes the booming electric guitars and wailing saxophones, as well as the taped spaceship effects.

The Third Symphony (1972) is one of Tippett's most complex and highly charged attempts to create a convincing structure from the collision between strongly contrasted musical characteristics. The first two movements (Part 1, as Tippett calls it) remain a considerable technical challenge, especially to the strings, but this performance manages to sustain an appropriate level of tension without sounding merely effortful, and without skimping on the opportunities for eloquence of phrasing. It could well be that Tippett has over-indulged the percussion in the slow movement, but this vivid and well-balanced Chandos recording lets us hear ample detail without exaggerating the bright colours and hyper-resonant textures. The later stages have the advantage of a superbly characterful singer in Faye Robinson who has the power, the edge, and also the radiance, to make Tippett's progression from idiosyncratic blues to Beethoven-quoting peroration utterly convincing.

It is good to find Richard Hickox and the Bournemouth SO taking on some imposing competition and holding their own so well. Hickox's Fourth Symphony is more broadly conceived than Solti's for Decca, and it's a considerable success, for despite giving even more weight to the work's strong contrasts, as is evident especially in the final stages, Hickox avoids any impression that the work is merely a succession of separate episodes. This well-integrated reading receives a well-rounded recording, and playing which needn't fear comparison with the best Chicago has to offer. (The individual works are also available as downloads.)

String Quartets

String Quartets – Nos 1-5
The Lindsays (Peter Cropper, Ronald Birks *vns* Roger Bigley/Robin Ireland *va* Bernard Gregor-Smith *vc*)
ASV ② CDDCS231 (123' · ADD/DDD)
Recorded 1975-92   ⒻⓄ

Tippett coached the The Lindsays for these recordings of his first three quartets, and wrote the other two for the quartet. In a note written for their 25th anniversary in 1992 he said that in these recordings they were 'concerned to estab-

lish good precedents in matters of style, so that succeeding generations of interpreters start at an advantage'. In fact one of the most enjoyable things about these readings is that they're so very characteristic of the The Lindsays. A number of the qualities you might call 'characteristic' are uncommonly well suited to Tippett's earlier quartets: big tone, vigour of attack and an infectious enjoyment of his lithe sprung rhythms. These performances are excellent precedents for later interpreters. They establish a style – big-scaled, urgently communicative – that's presumably 'authentic' and yet they challenge listeners as well as other performers to imagine how else they might be done. They also affirm the aching absence of a quartet between the Third and the Fourth (Tippett intended to write one in the late 1940s or early 1950s but got side-tracked by *The Midsummer Marriage*) and make one wonder what the rejected two movements of the First Quartet might be like. It's wonderful, though, to hear the five as a sequence in such authoritative readings. The recordings sound very well, but have been transferred at an exceptionally high level.

String Quartets – Nos 3 and 5
Tippett Quartet (John Mills, Jeremy Isaac *vns* Maxine Moore *va* Bozidar Vukotic *vc*)
Naxos 8 570497 (60' · DDD)   ⓈⓄⓄ▷

Tippett in 1946 was entering his most visionary phase but the Tippett Quartet's approach to the Third Quartet emphasises weight and earthiness rather than the transcendent lightness of spirit that would emerge most fully in *The Midsummer Marriage*. There's a sense of the piece's formidable technical challenges being bravely confronted rather than triumphantly overcome; but this is certainly a performance full of drama and excitement, a feature enhanced by the closely focused recording.

Tippett was 85 when he began work on his Fifth Quartet in 1990, and the best music comes in a first movement whose sustained spontaneity is admirably conveyed in this performance. The Tippett Quartet can also be commended for not rushing or over-dramatising the more diffuse and repetitive second movement, even though it now seems a pity that the composer wasn't persuaded to prune some of its more extended duplications. The Tippett Quartet's well integrated sound is a pleasure throughout.

Piano Sonatas

Piano Sonatas Nos 1-3
Peter Donohoe *pf*
Naxos 8 557611 (54' · DDD)   ⒻⓄ▷

It's a pity that, at 35 minutes-plus, Tippett's Fourth and last piano sonata is too long to join the others on a single CD. Be that as it may, it's good Naxos is opening up this repertoire, and Peter Donohoe is recorded with pleasing immediacy.

The First Sonata is especially successful – imaginatively characterised, the music's tendency to sprawl in the outer movements kept firmly in check. Despite the derivative aspects of its style, the piece has many distinctive qualities and – at least in Donohoe's performance – it stands up rather better than its successors.

No 2, a single-movement mosaic closely linked to *King Priam* and the Concerto for Orchestra, is in most respects the absolute antithesis of No 1, and the sheer number of repetitions of small thematic units creates a degree of stasis at odds with the free-flowing aspirations of the overall design.

Donohoe is acutely responsive to the broad contrasts and insistent rhythmic patterns of the Third Sonata but his tempo for the first movement is distinctly slower than Paul Crossley's (the Third Sonata's commissioner and first performer).

Choral Works

The Windhover. The Source. Magnificat and Nunc dimittis, 'Collegium Sancti Johannis Cantabrigiense'. Lullaby. Four Songs from the British Isles. Dance, Clarion Air. Five Negro Spirituals from 'A Child of Our Time'. Plebs angelica. The Weeping Babe
Finzi Singers / Paul Spicer
with **Andrew Lumsden** org
Chandos CHAN9265 (55' · DDD · T)　　　Ⓕ Ⓞ 🅑➔

The Finzi Singers are eloquent in the Spirituals, and polished in the *British Isles* Songs (especially the beguiling 'Early One Morning'). However, it's especially good to have the works which represent early sightings of Tippett's later, less lusciously lyrical style – the *Lullaby* (with countertenor, reminding us that it was written for the Deller Consort) and the *Magnificat* and *Nunc dimittis*: here not only are the intonation and phrasing of the tricky lines supremely confident, but the accompanying organ is recorded with exemplary naturalness. The vocal sound throughout is generally no less successful. There may be almost too full and rich a texture for the linear intricacies of *Plebs angelica* and *The Weeping Babe* to make their maximum effect, but there's no lack of exuberance in *Dance, Clarion Air* and the other secular pieces.

Four Songs from the British Isles. Dance, Clarion Air. Lullaby. Two Madrigals. Magnificat and Nunc dimittis, 'Collegium Sancti Johannis Cantabrigiense'. Five Negro Spirituals from 'A Child of Our Time'. Plebs angelica. The Weeping Babe. Unto the Hills. Over the Sea to Skye
BBC Singers / Stephen Cleobury
with **Ian Farrington** org
Signum SIGCD092 (63' · DDD · T/t)　　　Ⓕ 🅑➔

Tippett's choral music makes for a heterogeneous collection on disc: just the sort of programme you would never expect to encounter at a live concert. Signum underlines the heteroge-

neity by cramming the 19 items together with only a few brief seconds between them. This makes for several jarring shifts of tonality, and seems especially careless since the disc plays for under 63 minutes anyway. Constant use of the pause button is the only solution.

Fortunately, the performances compensate. The polish and professionalism of the BBC Singers are everywhere apparent, and they bring an imposing tonal weight to such familiar items as the Spirituals from *A Child of Our Time*. This is a fine account, aided by the lively acoustic of the Temple Church: for once one hardly misses the orchestra in 'Go down, Moses'. For the same reason the absence of boys' voices in the *Magnificat* and *Nunc dimittis* for St John's College, Cambridge, and of a plangent solo countertenor in *Lullaby*, for the Deller Consort, are less troubling than they might otherwise be.

Stephen Cleobury and the BBC Singers are especially impressive in the weaving lines and dancing rhythms of the madrigals and motets from the 1940s. Even they can do little to clarify the congested textures of the *Songs from the British Isles*, but there are two previously unrecorded items: an arrangement of 'Over the Sea to Skye' weaves the familiar tune in some appealingly offbeat counterpoints, and a hymn-tune written by the atheist Tippett for the Salvation Army proves to be touchingly sincere.

A Child of our Time

A Child of Our Time
Indra Thomas sop **Mihoko Fujimura** contr
Steve Davislim ten **Matthew Rose** bass
**London Symphony Chorus and Orchestra /
Sir Colin Davis**
LSO Live ⚏ LSO0670 (64' · DDD · T)
Recorded live 2007　　　Ⓑ Ⓞ 🅑➔

Having recorded *A Child of Our Time* twice before (Philips and live for Profil), Sir Colin Davis returned to the work in the very different environment of London's Barbican Hall. On this occasion the Classic Sound engineers and editors have managed a good blend of the intimate and the intense. Now and again a soloist may seem unduly reticent – perhaps a vocal problem on the day rather than a matter of recorded balance. But is there another recording that surpasses this one in the expressive power with which choral singing and orchestral playing combine to reinforce the timeless message of this most history-conscious work, rooted as it is in events just prior to the years of its composition (1939-41)?

The formidable discipline and sensitivity of the London Symphony Chorus are immediately clear in the well defined dynamic contrasts of Part 1's first movement. While an imposing weight of sonority, as in the Spiritual 'Go down, Moses', can be guaranteed, there is a rare lightness of articulation in the passage beginning 'We are as seed before the wind', which returns in 'Nobody knows the trouble I see'.

Of the soloists, soprano Indra Thomas struggles with foggy vibrato while still managing to float some beautifully unstrained high notes in the final ensemble. Mihoko Fujimura, Steve Davislim and Matthew Rose are all excellent, and it's especially good to have a tenor who sounds young enough to embody the character of Herschel Grynszpan convincingly. Of course, some collectors will not be persuaded that Sir Colin could ever match, let alone outdo, his first, 1975 Philips recording of the work. Nevertheless, the enduring significance of the piece for him is palpable right through to the superbly shaped account of the final Spiritual, 'Deep River'. There are emotional depths here which turn this recording into something very special.

Additional recommendation

A Child of Our Time
Robinson sop **Walker** mez **Garrison** ten **Cheek** bass
CBSO & Chor / Tippett
Naxos 8 557570 (70' · DDD)   ⑤❿

'Tippett was 87 when this recording was made, and neither its rhythmic momentum nor its textural clarity are ideal. But the composer's own lovingly crafted reading has a special place in the discography of this still-modern masterpiece.

Songs

Tippett Music. Songs for Ariel. Songs for Achilles. Boyhood's End. The Heart's Assurance. **Purcell** If music be the food of love, Z379/2. The Fairy Queen – Thrice happy lovers. The fatal hour comes on apace, Z421. Bess of Bedlam, Z370. Pausanias – Sweeter than roses
Martyn Hill ten **Craig Ogden** gtr **Andrew Ball** pf
Hyperion CDA66749 (70' · DDD · T)   ⒻⓄ

The two longest works – the cantata *Boyhood's End* and song cycle *The Heart's Assurance* – challenge the musicianship and sensitivity of both singer and pianist alike. *Boyhood's End* (1943), a setting of prose that's never prosaic, shows the ecstasy of *The Midsummer Marriage* to be already within the system, and the profusion of notes has to be mastered so that the dance shall seem as delicate and natural as graceful improvisation. In *The Heart's Assurance* (1951) the spirit's similar, although the technical accomplishment of all concerned, composer and performers, is heightened. For the singer, in addition to the quite fearsome difficulties of pitch and rhythm, there's also likely to be some problem of tessitura, particularly in the third of the songs, 'Compassion'. For the pianist, concentration has to be divided between the virtuoso writing of his own part and responsiveness to the singer, his notes, words and expression. Martyn Hill and Andrew Ball are wonderfully at one in all this, and the balancing of voice and piano has been finely achieved. The *Songs for Achilles*, with guitar, also convey a real sense of ardent improvisation, and the voice rings out freely. The *Songs for Ariel* here work their natural magic. Tippett's affinities with Purcell are felt at one time or another in most of these compositions, starting with the opening of the programme, the setting of Shelley's 'Sleep'. The disc was issued to mark the composer's 90th birthday, and serves as a touching and eloquent tribute.

'Remember Your Lovers'
Tippett Boyhood's End. The Heart's Assurance. Music. Songs for Ariel. **Britten** Canticle No 1, 'My beloved is mine' **Humfrey** A Hymn to God the Father **Purcell** (arr Tippett/Bergmann) An Evening Hymn on a Ground, 'Now that the sun hath veil'd his light'. If music be the food of love. The Fairy Queen – Thrice happy lovers (Epithalamium). The Indian Queen – I attempt from love's sickness. The Mock Marriage – 'Twas within a furlong. Oedipus – Music for a while. Pausanias – Sweeter than roses. Tyrannic Love – Ah! how sweet it is to love. The History of Dioclesian – What shall I do?
John Mark Ainsley ten **Iain Burnside** pf
Signum Classics SIGCD066 (73' · DDD · T)   Ⓕ❿

John Mark Ainsley and Iain Burnside make a formidable combination and they are matched here with a formidable programme. Tippett's writing for voice and piano is unremitting in its demands and much less certain in its rewards. The performers' concentration must be absolute: that is fact. Whether the listener will be proportionately moved is a matter for doubtful speculation.

It goes against the grain to say this, because the Tippett of youthful ecstasy (as in *The Midsummer Marriage* and the Concerto for Double String Orchestra) exerts a strong allure. But there's no escaping the fact that *Boyhood's End* and *The Heart's Assurance* exert a slim hold on the memory – only a few specific phrases, particularly of the singer's music, having stuck. That is extraordinary, and it is reinforced by the inclusion here of the Canticle by Britten which the mind retains, both in feeling and specific detail.

That work, the setting of Francis Quarles's 'So I my best-beloved's am', presumably has been chosen, as the one item in which Tippett is neither composer nor arranger, because it accords with the line 'Remember your lovers', taken as the title-phrase. I'm not sure it was a good idea, as Britten's mastery suggests just what is so often wanting in Tippett: economy and repose.

The other composer present in force is Purcell and here, curiously, Tippett's self-discipline is impressive, even as against Britten's in his comparable arrangements. Burnside writes in his introductory notes: 'While Britten's dense pianistic approach now jars on ears that have undergone the Early Music revolution, Tippett and [Walter] Bergmann stay light on their feet.' The recording is fine with excellent presence.

King Priam

King Priam
Rodney Macann bass Priam **Sarah Walker** mez
Andromache **Howard Haskin** ten Paris **Anne Mason**
sop Helen **Janet Price** sop Hecuba **Neil Jenkins** ten
Achilles **Omar Ebrahim** bar Hector **Kent Opera**
Chorus and Orchestra / **Roger Norrington**
Stage director **Nicholas Hytner**
Video director **Robin Lough**
ArtHaus Musik ⏺ 102 087
(138' · NTSC · 4:3 · PCM stereo · 0)   Ⓕ🔴🔴

Many listeners – even or especially those who
had been beguiled by *The Midsummer Marriage*
– could once take refuge in the harsh assessment
of Tippett's biographer, Ian Kemp, that *King
Priam* was 'the most didactic and theoretical of
his works'. This Kent Opera production proved
them wrong. The Royal Opera premiere at Coventry had been overshadowed by the acclaim for
Britten's *War Requiem*, first heard the following
night, and the big voices and grand, clangorous
manner of the fine Decca recording (based on a
later Covent Garden production) are fully operatic in scale and projection.

By contrast, Roger Norrington and the young
Nicholas Hytner push right into the claustrophobic citadel of the drama to find out, in the
composer's words, 'what happens when the
psychological balance symbolised by marriage
is knocked awry by responsibilities, war and
fate'. Acoustic, camera and microphones are
close, oppressively and rightly so. We are but a
few feet from Rodney Macann's piercing blue
eyes as his Priam rebels against the choices that
Tippett so relentlessly adumbrates: to smother
Paris or love him, to sacrifice Helen or Troy, to
confront Achilles or retain his royal dignity –
how different from the hopeless determinism
of Britten and Owen, where men are 'the foolish toys of time', to quote Eric Crozier for
St Nicolas.

Robin Lough's direction for TV uses the tricks
of the medium sparingly, and to most telling
effect in the blood-lust of the Trojans' vengeance trio at the end of Act 2, answered by
Achilles' war-cry with Verdian immediacy. All
the principals have the measure of their roles. If
Sarah Walker's Andromache, Neil Jenkins's
Achilles and Macann's Priam do most to stop us
in our tracks, perhaps it is their painfully human
heroism that Tippett was most interested in
himself. In the brief but demanding role of the
boy Paris, Nani Antwi-Nyanin also deserves a
special mention: Tippett was not in the habit of
writing down for younger performers.

Boris Tishchenko   Russian b1939

*Tishchenko studied at the Leningrad Conservatory
and with Shostakovich (1962-65). He is an outstanding representative of a generation that reinvigorated Russian music in the 1960s. His richly inventive works include symphonies, concertos, string
quartets, piano sonatas and children's stage pieces.*

Symphony No 7, Op 119

Symphony No 7
Moscow Philharmonic Orchestra /
Dmitry Yablonsky
Naxos 8 557013 (53' · DDD)   Ⓢ⏵

Not very much of Boris Tishchenko's substantial list of works has so far appeared on record. It
includes 10 piano sonatas, five string quartets
and a cello concerto for Rostropovich, which
Shostakovich himself took the trouble to rescore
for more conventional forces than the original.
Like so many composers of his generation he's
been much influenced by Shostakovich, with
whom he studied for a while. The influence
shows in this symphony, even though it's for the
most part thoroughly absorbed and makes for a
quirky but fascinating work.

Tishchenko doesn't give his movements titles
or even tempo indications. The first is an unusual but convincing symphonic exposition,
based on an obsessive use of a simple figure. The
second makes much play with ragtime clichés,
merry enough on the face of it though with a
deliberately forced atmosphere creeping in. The
third is a forlorn, dirge-like piece, with a bleak
climax. The fourth begins gracefully enough
with what one may perhaps describe as a frightened waltz. Like the other movements, including the finale, it has a restrained lyricism that
seems vulnerable to attack, and indeed is
attacked by dissonant and alarming orchestral
climaxes, after which the music ends on an
equivocal note.

Tishchenko scores imaginatively, with chamber music textures and single instruments unusually handled – xylophone, bass clarinet, piano,
tom-toms. The Moscow players respond skilfully, and though the recording is sometimes
over-anxious to single out individual instrumental contributions, it seems to give a fair representation of the imaginative scoring. This is a piece
well worth hearing.

Thomas Tomkins   English 1572-1656

*Tomkins divided his time between Worcester Cathe-
dral (organist from 1596) and London, becoming a
Gentleman in Ordinary of the Chapel Royal by 1620
rising to the rank of senior organist in 1625; that
year he wrote music for Charles I's coronation. He
left Worcester in 1654. His career straddled several
reigns as well as the Cromwell era and this had an
impact on his music, which otherwise reflects the
influence of his mentor, William Byrd. A prolific and
respected successor of Byrd, he composed church music,
including over 100 anthems, madrigals, over 50
keyboard pieces and a few highly original fantasias,*

pavans and galliards for viol consort. His half-brothers John, Giles and Robert and his son Nathaniel were also musicians.

Keyboard Works

Barafostus' Dream. Fantasia. Fancy. Fancy for two to play. Fortune my foe. A Ground. A Grounde. In nomine, 'Gloria tibi Trinitas'. The Lady Folliott's Galliard. Miserere. Pavan. Pavan and Galliard, 'Earl Strafford'. Pavan and Galliard of Three Parts. A sad pavan for these distracted times. Toy, 'Made at Poole Court'. What if a day. Worster Braules
Carole Cerasi hpd **James Johnstone** virg/bhpd
Metronome METCD1049 (74' · DDD)   Ⓕ**OO**

Forming a mental picture of Thomas Tomkins isn't difficult. Most of the pieces here were composed in the 1640s and '50s, yet adopt the style of three or four decades earlier, when composers like Gibbons, Bull and Tomkins's own teacher Byrd were alive. A contemporary of these men, Tomkins had survived them through the execution of Charles I and the destruction during the Civil War of the organ at Worcester Cathedral, where he had presided since 1596. Now, in later life, he had retired to live with his family and quietly compose plainsong settings, variation sets, fancies, grounds and pavans 'for these distracted times'. But though about as fashionable as a 'Welcome home, Walter Raleigh' hat, these pieces have a quality to them – showing by turns something of the exuberance of Bull and the eloquence of Byrd – that's more than enough to maintain their currency today. This disillusioned early version of a *Daily Telegraph* reader was nothing less than the last representative of that great school of keyboard composers known as the English virginalists, and more than 350 years on, it matters not a bean to the listener which decade he was writing in.

Cerasi's selection of about a third of Tomkins's extant keyboard pieces showcases all the genres in which he composed, as well as demonstrating the excellence and range of her own technique. Few listeners will fail to be impressed by the fearless accuracy and panache with which she throws off Tomkins's torrential passage-work and finger-breaking double thirds, but she's sensitive, too, in the slower pavans and fancies. Like Leonhardt, she achieves a supreme eloquence in such pieces by the sheer precision and control with which she places each note, and it's a pleasure just to hear her playing. An outstanding disc.

Choral Works

'These Distracted Times'
A Fancy. A sad pavan for these distracted times. Almighty God, the fountain of all wisdom. When David heard. The Fifth Service – Te Deum; Jubilate; Magnificat; Nunc dimittis. The heavens declare. Pavan I (a 4); Pavan VII; Pavan VIII. Hear my prayer, O Lord. O Lord, how manifold. Remember me, O Lord.

My help cometh from the Lord
Fretwork; Alamire; Choir of Sidney Sussex College, Cambridge / David Skinner with **Jamal Sutton** org
Obsidian CD702 (67' · DDD)   Ⓕ**OOO**

Vocal textures are varied, clear and satisfying; the instrumental works, too, exude sanity in what were turbulent times. Tomkins favoured the solo bass voice, which introduces four of the sacred choral works here, though others contain ravishing, if brief, duets for tenors and sopranos. Best known is the lament on the death of Absalom, which with the verse anthem *My help cometh from the Lord* crowns the disc.

In the choral works David Skinner has drawn a beautifully blended sound from his Sidney Sussex Chapel Choir of mixed voices; the solo parts are taken by members of both Alamire (the polished male vocal quartet Skinner founded in 2005) and the choir. Although the organ is present as a solo instrument in the title-track and in *A Fancy* as well as accompanying Alamire in *The heavens declare*, Skinner transcribed the organ parts for the Fifth Service and the closing anthem for viol quartet – a liberty he defends in his engaging booklet-notes and which are so sensitively played by members of the renowned Fretwork.

The viol music and much of the church music date from Tomkins's time as organist of Worcester Cathedral, which came to an abrupt end in 1647; he composed the 'Sad Pavan' for organ just two weeks after the execution of Charles I in 1649. Once also a Gentleman of the King's Chapel Royal, Tomkins had good reason to feel 'distracted'. Cromwell happens to have been a member of Sidney Sussex College.

The college chapel provides a clear and sympathetic acoustic. It's difficult to know whether Tomkins or Cromwell would have been the more surprised. Tomkins would most certainly have been delighted.

Veljo **Tormis**.   Estonian b1930

Tormis is considered by Estonians to be one of their most important composers of the 20th century. He has taught at the Tallinn Music School and the Tallinn Music High School, and served as a consultant at the Estonian Union of Composers. From 1969 he supported himself through the purchase of his manuscripts by the Ministry of Culture, by frequent prizes for his choral works, and by numerous sojourns at 'houses of creativity' in the Soviet Union. Although Tormis has written a well-crafted opera and various instrumental pieces (including film scores), his special voice is heard in his choral works.

Choral works

An Aboriginal Song[a]. The Bishop and the Pagan. Curse upon Iron[a]. Forging the Sampo[ab]. Double

Dedication. Crosswind. Our Shadows. Incantation for a Stormy Sea. Men's Songs – Men's Song; Bundling Song; Betrothal Visiting Song; Song of the Turkish War; Serf's Song; Dancing Song
Svanholm Singers / Sofia Söderberg Eberhard with ªVeljo Tormis, ᵇStefan Engström perc
Toccata Classics TOCC0073 (68' · DDD · T/t) Ⓕ🅾️🄳►

Livonian Heritage. Singing Aboard Ship. Two Songs to Words by Ernst Enno. Three Estonian Game Songs. Three Songs from the Epic 'Kalev's Son'. Autumn Landscapes. Four Estonian Lullabies. Childhood Memory Herding Calls.
Holst Singers / Stephen Layton
Hyperion CDA67601 (72' · DDD · T/t)   Ⓕ🅾️🅾️🄳►

The quality of choral singing in the Baltic region is legendary, and with the 20 male voices of the Svanholm singers – most of them apparently students at Lund University – the legend lives on. Tormis writes that any of his doubts about the 2006 concert they organised in his honour melted with just a few phrases from his *Double Dedication*. No wonder. Both music and performance of this celebration of two poets who emigrated from Soviet Estonia to Sweden immediately seize the attention, even without knowledge of the poems, the cultural role of the poets or the nature of the composer's tribute to them – all of which only serve to reinforce and deepen the initial impact.

So, which to single out? The phenomenal precision of intonation, tonal focus and communicative urgency in the singing, the high-mindedness and vividness of the poetry, or the music's sheer range of appeal and refusal to recognise boundaries between different kinds of audience? There are rich pickings here, the programme covering a gamut of expression from folk-comic-macho through saga-epic to wondrous-romantic.

Tormis himself gives the disc a symbolic imprimatur by playing the shaman drum in *An Aboriginal Song* and *Curse upon Iron*. Whistling, sighing, tongue-clicking, falsetto and log drumming add to the tonal palette but the music and singing are seductive enough even without them. Documentation is exemplary, recording quality perfectly judged. Irresistible!

Hard on its heels comes another beautifully prepared and executed compilation. Stephen Layton and his Holst Singers have a well deserved reputation as bold explorers, and their intelligence and dedication are evident here. It seems that the language barrier has not proved greatly inhibiting: they've thrown down the gauntlet to others outside the Baltic region to investigate this superb repertoire.

By comparison with the crack Nordic teams, the English voices are admittedly a degree softer-focused in tone and not quite so high-pressure in expression. The composer's compatriots bring even more electricity to the five marvellous songs that make up *Livonian Heritage*, for example, though the Holst Singers find a subtlety and affection that certainly compensates. In any case, given that there is little very

duplication of repertoire with available CDs (and none at all with the superb Svanholmers), and that the quality of Tormis's output is wonderfully consistent, there is really no reason not to invest in both new issues.

Charles Tournemire French 1870-1939

Tournemire was a pupil of Widor at the Paris Conservatoire and of Franck, whose post as organist at Ste Clotilde he inherited in 1898; from 1919 he also taught at the Conservatoire. His works include operas, oratorios and eight symphonies. But he is remembered for the monumental L'orgue mystique (1932), 51 organ Masses using plainsong melodies appropriate to a particular Sunday, for the liturgical year, in a mystical style between Franck and Messiaen.

L'orgue mystique

L'orgue mystique – Office 2, Postlude; Office 3, Paraphrase; Office 7, Fantaisie; Office 11, Diptyque; Office 27, Fantaisie paraphrase; Office 29, Alleluia No 1; Office 30, Alleluia No 2; Office 31, Alleluia No 3; Office 32, Alleluia No 4; Office 33, Alleluia No 5; Office 35, Paraphrase and Carillon; Office 43, Choral alleluiatique No 1; Office 51, Fantaisie sur le Te Deum et Guirlandes Alleluiatiques Office 44, Choral alleluiatique No 2; Office 45, Choral alleluiatique No 3; Office 46, Choral alleluiatique No 4; Office 47, Choral alleluiatique No 5
Marie-Bernadette Dufourcet-Hakim org
Priory ② PRCD669 (134' · DDD)
Played on the organs of La Sainte Trinité and La Basilique du Sacré-Cœur de Montmartre, Paris   Ⓕ

This two-CD set makes an excellent introduction to the sprawling, theatrical, sometimes hysterically neo-Gothic and spontaneous world of *L'orgue mystique*, the magnum opus of Charles Tournemire. Until 1927 his compositional output was directed mostly at secular music, orchestral symphonies, string quartets and opera. Over the next five years he renewed French liturgical organ music, writing 51 suites (one for each Sunday of the year) based on 300 Gregorian plainchants. Dufourcet-Hakim's 17-track selection consists of postludes, 11 of them drawn from the 13 suites for Sundays during Pentecost.

She captures brilliantly the improvisatory fleetingness and impressionistic mysticism inherent in Tournemire's music. She steers committedly and seemingly effortlessly around this often turbulent organistic assault course, helped by the generous acoustics of La Sainte Trinité (Messiaen's church), and, in two tracks, the Basilica of Sacré-Coeur in Montmartre, the latter more out of tune than the former. For anyone intrigued by the roots of Messiaen's radical organ writing these recordings will provide clear answers. Strongly recommended.

Suite évocatrice, Op 74

Tournemire Suite évocatrice, Op 74
Vierne Symphony No 3, Op 28
Widor Symphonie gothique, Op 70
Jeremy Filsell org
Herald HAVPCD145 (71' · DDD). Played on the
Harrison & Harrison organ of Ely Cathedral Ⓕ**OO**

Compared with, say, the symphonies of Tchaikovsky or Sibelius the organ symphonies of Widor and his pupil Vierne aren't particularly long. But in terms of organ music they're among the longest single works in the repertory. Within their five-movement form the composers set out to exploit the full expressive range of the organ, and it was no coincidence that the organ symphony developed in turn-of-the-century France. The great French organ builder Aristide Cavaillé-Coll was then producing instruments capable of hitherto undreamt-of colour and expression. Both Widor at St Sulpice and Vierne at Notre Dame had at their disposal the finest instruments in Paris and they indulged themselves fully in their symphonies.

The subtitle of Widor's Ninth (*Gothic*) says it all. The structure is vast, intricately detailed, and almost forbidding in its grandeur. Vierne's Third also presents an awesome spectacle, full of complex music and technically demanding writing, while Tournemire's neo-classical Suite gives a moment almost of light relief in such heavyweight company. Jeremy Filsell is an outstanding virtuoso player with a gift for musical communication, and the Ely Cathedral organ produces the range of the great French instruments, but within an altogether clearer acoustic. These are performances and recordings of exceptional quality.

Donald Tovey.   British 1875-1940

Longtime Reid Professor of Music at Edinburgh University, Sir Donald Francis Tovey remains best known for his magnificently readable and insightful Essays in Musical Analysis *(OUP: 1935-44). He was also a gifted pianist and composer, completing a Piano Concerto in 1903 and, 10 years later, this earnest and admirably ambitious Symphony in D.*

Orchestral Works

Cello Concerto, Op 40ᵃᶜ. Elegiac Variations, Op 25ᵃᵇ. Aria and Variations, Op 11 – Aria (arr P Shore)ᶜ
ᵃ**Alice Neary** vc ᵇ**Gretel Dowdeswell** pf
ᶜ**Ulster Orchestra / George Vass**
Toccata Classics TOCC0038 (67' · DDD) Ⓕ**D➔**

With a playing time of nearly 55 minutes, Sir Donald Tovey's Cello Concerto (composed in 1932-33 for Pablo Casals) is almost certainly the longest ever written. Casals gave the world premiere in Edinburgh's Usher Hall in November 1934, with the composer conducting. Two London performances by the dedicatee followed in 1935 and 1937. Plans for a modern recording fell through a decade or so ago; now Toccata Classics has at last delivered the goods.

Readers who know and love their Brahms and Elgar will recognise many a stylistic and temperamental bond in this painstakingly plotted music. However, the protracted opening *Allegro moderato* constitutes something of a stumbling block. Both middle movements do little to dispel the obstinately somnolent mood – although the finale's jocular yet cleverly manipulated antics nearly save the day. If you've enjoyed grappling with Tovey's large-scale Symphony in D, it's worth persevering. Alice Neary performs valiantly, with sympathetic (if at times rather under-energised) support from George Vass and the Ulster Orchestra. Throw in the engaging fill-ups, decent sound and assiduously detailed booklet-notes, and it adds up to yet another intriguing release from this young label.

Symphony, Op 32. The Bride of Dionysus – Prelude
Malmö Opera Orchestra / George Vass
Toccata Classics TOCC0033 (64' · DDD) Ⓕ**D➔**

Although lasting the best part of an hour and occasionally over-thickly scored, Tovey's Symphony holds the attention, not least due to his keen sense of long-term dialogue and harmonic adventure, allied to a felicitous mastery of counterpoint. Brahms and Reger are the most obvious stylistic templates (the symphony's arrestingly pregnant *pianissimo* opening idea even hints at Nielsen), yet a quiet individuality emerges from the radiant *Canzonetta* slow movement in particular, and the scampering *Scherzo* has a pleasingly mischievous twinkle in its eye.

A very creditable performance, too, from the Malmö Opera Orchestra under George Vass, who also acquit themselves most ably in the noble Prelude to Tovey's 1918 opera *The Bride of Dionysus* which launches proceedings. Good if not perhaps ideally ventilated sound.

Piano Trios

Piano Trios – Op 1; Op 8, 'Style tragique'
London Piano Trio (Robert Atchison vn
Bozidar Vukotic vc Olga Dudnik pf)
Toccata Classics TOCC0068 (65' · DDD) Ⓕ**D➔**

Having already given us useful modern recordings of Donald Francis Tovey's Symphony in D and vast Cello Concerto (see above), Toccata Classics now presents this first volume in a series devoted to his chamber music. Both works were composed in 1895, during Tovey's first full calendar year at Balliol College, Oxford.

Inscribed to Parry 'as the first work of a grateful pupil', Tovey's Op 1 is as sizeable as it is thoughtful – a patiently argued creation of remarkable fluency, organisational skill and imagination for one so young. The influence of Brahms dominates, and the German master's kindly presence can also be felt in Op 8 in C minor, which was originally conceived for clarinet, horn and piano. The version performed here was eventually published by Schott in 1912, by which time the trio had also acquired the title *Style tragique*. At its heart is a particularly appealing *Largo* in A flat (thus following the key scheme of Beethoven's Fifth Symphony and *Pathétique* Sonata), which leads without a break into the confidently striding finale.

The London Piano Trio audibly believe in every note, and their dedicated performances are set within a bold sound frame that's somewhat tiring on the ear. The presentation is copiously detailed, as ever from this source. Inquisitive collectors can safely investigate.

Eduard Tubin   Estonian 1905-1982

Tubin was a pupil of Eller at the Tartu Academy (1924-30). After the Soviet Union invaded Estonia in 1944, Tubin fled to Stockholm, where he remained for the rest of his life, although he did return to Estonia on occasions. After a while Tubin moved to a suburb of Stockholm where he could devote himself entirely to composition. Here he wrote some of his greatest works, including much music for choir and his last five of his 10 symphonies. Towards the end of his life, Tubin slowly began to gain recognition, particularly after the conductor Neeme Järvi, also an Estonian, moved to the USA in 1980. In the last year of his life his Tenth Symphony was performed by the Boston Symphony Orchestra.

Symphonies

Symphonies – No 1 in C minor[a]; No 2, 'The Legendary'[b]; No 3 in D minor[c]; No 4 in A, 'Sinfonia lirica'[d]; No 5 in B minor[e]; No 6[b]; No 7[f]; No 8[c]; No 9, 'Sinfonia semplice'[g]; No 10[h]. Kratt – Ballet Suite[e]. Toccata[g]

[abc]Swedish Radio Symphony Orchestra; [d]Bergen Philharmonic Orchestra; [e]Bamberg Symphony Orchestra; [fgh]Gothenburg Symphony Orchestra / Neeme Järvi

BIS ⑤ BIS-CD1402/04 (5h 31' · DDD)   Ⓜ●O⮞

Vividly scored and dynamically expressive, Tubin's symphonies span almost his entire creative career. The First, only his third orchestral score, dates from 1931-34, and the single-movement Tenth from 1973, while at his death nine years later an Eleventh lay unfinished on his desk. Even without the Eleventh, the BIS set has much to commend it. The performances, variable in acoustic, are remarkably consistent in approach and quality of execution.

Järvi's commitment to and understanding of the music is total and its quality shines through in every bar, whether in the early symphonies

where Tubin was still moving towards his mature style, or Nos 5 to 8 with their absolute mastery of form. OK, even Järvi can't avoid the Third's peroration sounding like *The Pines of Tallinn*, but there's no doubt of the work's or its creator's stature. Although repackaged from the original issues, BIS avoids laying out the symphonies in chronological sequence. The recordings still sound wonderful, though occasionally perhaps too spacious. Järvi never sounds rushed, allowing the Eighth's opening *Andante quasi Adagio* to build into an impressive-sounding edifice. He's unmatched in the deeply felt finale.

Joaquín Turina   Spanish 1882-1949

Turina studied in Seville, Madrid and Paris (at the Schola Cantorum), and was associated with Falla, with whom he returned to Spain in 1914; he remained there, working as a teacher, critic and composer. His works include operas, orchestral works, chamber music, guitar music, songs and numerous piano pieces, including many colourful and effective character and genre pieces as well as some larger-scale works.

Orchestral Works

Sinfonía sevillana. Danzas fantásticas. Ritmos (Fantasía coreográfica). La procesión del Rocío
Castilla y León Symphony Orchestra / Max Bragado Darman
Naxos Spanish Classics 8 555955 (62' · DDD)   ⑤●O⮞

Turina was a gentle man who, like Segovia, placed high value on beauty and clarity of thought, and responded to 'programmatic' images; the portrayal of profound tragedy had no place in his music. Although he tried harder than his contemporaries to write in the conventional musical forms, his *Sinfonía sevillana* is a poetic and colourful tone-poem rather than a symphony, a French-influenced depiction of aspects of the city of his birth.

Ritmos was conceived as a ballet but was never performed as such – present-day choreographers please note! The *Danzas fantásticas* range from the quietly poetic to the energetic, and relate to quotations from José Más's novel *La orgía*. Two dances, the Aragonese *jota* and the Andalusian *farruca*, frame a dream-like evocation of elements of Andalusian melody and dance rhythms of the Basque *zortziko*. More specifically focused is *La procesión del Rocío*, a charming picture of the annual festival procession in the village of El Rocío.

Turina's skill and sensitivity in the art of orchestration shines throughout this programme, as does that of the Castilla y Léon Symphony Orchestra in extracting every good feature the music offers. The recording is clear, with a believably spacious acoustic. There are other recordings of these works, but none that brings them all together – or exceeds the quality of these performances. An outstanding issue.

Mark-Anthony Turnage British b1960

Mark-Anthony Turnage is one of the most admired and widely performed composers of his generation. He studied with Oliver Knussen and John Lambert in London and Gunther Schuller at Tanglewood. His works skilfully blend classical and jazz idioms, modernism and tradition. He has worked as Composer in Association with the City of Birmingham Symphony Orchestra, English National Opera and the BBC Symphony Orchestra, and holds current residencies with London Philharmonic Orchestra and Chicago Symphony Orchestra. Turnage has composed numerous orchestral and chamber works, and two widely performed operas: Greek (1988) is based on Steven Berkoff's adaptation of Oedipus the King; The Silver Tassie (2000) is based on the play by Seán O'Casey. Other works include Three Screaming Popes (after the paintings by Francis Bacon) and Your Rockaby, a concerto for saxophone and orchestra, and a concerto for trombone and orchestra, Yet Another Set To, dedicated to Christian Lindberg. Turnage's 50th-birthday celebrations in 2010 featured performances at the Cabrillo Festival; the world premiere of Hammered Out at the BBC Proms conducted by David Robertson and its US premiere by the Los Angeles Philharmonic and Susanna Mälkki; and the US premiere of Texan Tenebrae by the Chicago Symphony and Andrew Davis. Anna Nicole, a new opera for the Royal Opera House, Covent Garden, is to be premiered in February 2011.

Orchestral Works

Yet Another Set To[a]. Scherzoid[b].
Evening Songs[c]. When I Woke[d]
[d]**Gerald Finley** bar [a]**Christian Lindberg** tbn
London Philharmonic Orchestra / [a]**Marin Alsop,**
[cd]**Vladimir Jurowski,** [b]**Jonathan Nott**
LPO 🔊 LPO0007 (66' · DDD) Ⓜ➔

Mark-Anthony Turnage has enjoyed associations with the CBSO, BBC SO and now the London Philharmonic, each resulting in a wealth of new music and, fortunately for us, a CD for home listening. A number of ensembles had a hand in commissioning *Scherzoid*, the first work on this latest collection, and its particular propulsive character would seem to have been influenced by the involvement of the New York Philharmonic. Though rhythmically complex and changing its mood as rapidly as the title punningly suggests, the music is easy to assimilate. Its urban bustle and swagger take in minimalist influences alongside the usual Stravinsky-meets-Miles Davis mélange. As if to secure transatlantic approval, at one point there's a distinct whiff of *On the Waterfront*, although, in the event, Lorin Maazel elected not to conduct

the first performance. Jonathan Nott does the honours here – and splendidly.

Turnage's subtler, shell-shocked lyricism is more in evidence in the purely orchestral *Evening Songs*. Originating in lullabies for his sons, the calm outer panels enclose an interlude with a more troubled, expressionist melodic line, typically Brittenish at the outset. The Dylan Thomas settings, *When I Woke*, were written for a celebrated singer who did not take them up but it's difficult to feel them in any way problematic in this ardent account. Certainly, the spare accompanying textures create no difficulties for the soloist. *Yet Another Set To* brings back the more boisterous, head-banging Turnage. All is not plain sailing in that the composer here shows us his Boulez-like propensity to reshape and recycle existing music.

Cheekily, the score incorporates not only 2000's *Another Set To* – itself a reworking, previously recorded by Christian Lindberg for Chandos – but also a movement derived from *Blood on the Floor*. It's exhilarating, explosive stuff, even more fun in live performance. Here alone concluding applause is (not inappropriately) retained.

All credit to the LPO for compiling a whole evening of Turnage. You may not always like what he does or how he does it but his instantly recognisable voice is well served by the blunt immediacy of the sound and the obvious flair of the performances.

Chamber Works

Two Memorials[a]. An Invention on Solitude[b]. Sleep On[c]. Cortège for Chris[d]. Two Elegies Framing a Shout[e]. Three Farewells[f]. Tune for Toru[g]
Nash Ensemble ([f]**Philippa Davies** fl [bdf]**Richard Hosford** cl [bf]**Marianne Thorsen,** [bf]**Elizabeth Wexler** vns [bdf]**Lawrence Power** va [bcdf]**Paul Watkins** vc [f]**Skaila Kanga** hp [cdeg]**Ian Brown** pf [ce]**Richard Hosford** cl [ae]**Martin Robertson** sop sax)
Black Box BBM1065 (58' · DDD) Ⓕ

An effective showcase for the composer's small-ensemble music of the 1990s, this album might have been entitled 'Another Side of... Mark-Anthony Turnage'. Where, in some of his major orchestral works, Turnage's idiom has seemed quintessentially urban, indebted (via Tippett and Britten) to Stravinsky and Berg, here we come surprisingly close to the much-derided English pastoral tradition. The jazz element is evident too, as you might expect, but there's little trace of the composer's penchant for rock and raunch; the mood is more wistful than confrontational. Anyone who thinks that contemporary music and memorable melodic writing are somehow incompatible should audition this disc without delay. From the plangent solo sax of the *Two Memorials* to the intensely evocative solo piano version of *Tune for Toru*, there's little to frighten the horses and much that touches the heart. The biggest utterance is the clarinet quintet, *An Invention on Solitude*, composed, like much of this music, during Turnage's work on the score of his opera *The Silver Tassie*. The Nash Ensemble are no strangers to Turnage and their unsentimental playing is well served by the boldly immediate recording.

This Silence[a]. True Life Stories[b]. Slide Stride[c]. Two Baudelaire Songs[d]. Eulogy[e]. Two Vocalises[f]. Cantilena[g]
[d]**Sally Matthews** sop **Nash Ensemble** ([d]Philippa Davies fl Gareth Hulse [g]ob/[e]cora [ade]Michael Collins cl [a]Ursula Leveaux bn [ae]Richard Watkins hn [acdeg]Marianne Thorsen, [acdg]Benjamin Nabarro vns [acdeg]Lawrence Power va [acdfg]Paul Watkins vc [ae]Duncan McTier db [e]Lucy Wakeford hp [bcdef]Ian Brown pf) / [d]**Lionel Friend**
Onyx Classics ONYX4005 (79' · DDD · T/t)   Ⓕ🅑➔

Here's yet another disc from the Nash Ensemble devoted to the music of Mark-Anthony Turnage and it is, in a sense, the most representative because it gives a fine indication of his range.

Favourites come from opposite tendencies. *Slide Stride* (2002) is a noisily affirmative piano quintet based on James P Johnson's style of jazz piano and dedicated to Richard Rodney Bennett, whereas *True Life Stories*, unveiled as a group by Leif Ove Andsnes in 2000, are cool piano miniatures. As is usual with Turnage these days, not all the core material is new and the last in the sequence, the haunting tribute to Takemitsu, cheekily reprises the final item on that Black Box anthology. Ian Brown plays it with more restraint and less pedal this time around – or it could be simply that the sound is not as resonant.

While Turnage demonstrates a continuing ability to straddle disparate musical worlds, his startling fluency begins to look as much a problem as an asset. In *Two Baudelaire Songs* (2004) he sets poems already transmogrified by Debussy and Henri Duparc. Only here *L'invitation au voyage* is deconstructed rather than indulged, a peculiarly dissonant close undercutting the 'Luxe, calme et volupté' of the text. As mixed, the soloist Sally Matthews is very much one of the band. Lawrence Power's viola seems rather forwardly placed in the autumnal *Eulogy* (2003), an immediately convincing composition that doesn't strive for novelty.

Turnage's world has dark, claustrophobic qualities, underlined here by the immediate, focused recording masterminded by Chris Craker. Barry Witherden's copious notes are helpful. Not perhaps a disc you would want to digest at one sitting though this generous selection of definitive performances is well worth sampling.

Twice Through the Heart[a]. Hidden Love Song[b]. The Torn Fields[c]
[a]**Sarah Connolly** mez [c]**Gerald Finley** bar [b]**Martin Robertson** sax **London Philharmonic Orchestra / Marin Alsop**
LPO LPO0031 (66' · DDD). [b]Recorded live   Ⓜ

Twice Through the Heart is a revival of a dramatic song-cycle-cum-scena from as long ago as 1997. The text is drawn from a series of poems originally written for a television film about a woman who stabs her abusive husband. As might be expected it's a pretty bleak affair. Sarah Connolly is a distinguished protagonist, and if listeners feel uncomfortable with the mix of artful delivery and documentary realism, that may be part of the intended effect.

Hidden Love Song, featuring saxophonist Martin Robertson, derives from a live concert with applause retained. This first new composition associated with Turnage's LPO tenure is a wordless offering built from musical ciphers associated with the composer's partner. The characteristic attempts to disrupt the lyrical line are thus carefully rationed and there's no mistaking the professional gleam and twinkle of the results.

Confirming a certain softening of idiom, *The Torn Fields* is equally accessible though weightier thematically. Here Turnage eschews Jackie Kay's down-to-earth phraseology in *Twice Through the Heart*, preferring the sort of poetry that attracted composers of a previous anti-war generation. The music still draws on vernacular bluesy elements but they lie within a smoother, more melodic, high-culture mix. It's difficult to imagine a more ardent exponent than Gerald Finley. While the orchestral writing is spare, Finley's diction is second to none, allied to exceptional beauty of tone. Particularly haunting is the Wilfred Owen setting, the narrative of a soldier who, like the protagonist of *The Silver Tassie*, survives severely maimed only to experience physical and emotional rejection. The gentle treatment of the familiar final poem by Siegfried Sassoon provides a glimpse of the transcendent. Excellent contextual notes plus full texts (including passages not set by the composer).

Blood on the Floor

Blood on the Floor
Martin Robertson sax **Peter Erskine** drums **John Scofield** elec gtr **Ensemble Modern / Peter Rundel**
Video director **Barrie Gavin**
ArtHaus Musik 🆅🅓 100 430 (92' · NTSC · 4:3 · PCM stereo · 2 & 5)   Ⓕ

The title comes from a painting by Francis Bacon, while the music ranges widely in its references and allusions. A decade on, *Blood on the Floor* remains Turnage's magnum 'fusion' opus. With a raw expressive energy fuelled by the loss of his brother to a drugs overdose, the composer's gift for sour melody and guttural sonority has never been deployed to better effect.

The body of this DVD release is a live performance taped in Frankfurt's Alte Oper during the same 1996 premiere tour that yielded a CD recording. The concert was presumably intended for lo-fi TV broadcast and consists of the usual series of close-ups of instrumentalists edited to the music. The technique is less irksome here than in many such outings; it highlights the breathtaking artistry of the multifarious musicians involved, genuinely conveying a charged atmosphere.

Sound quality is good if not quite up to the standard of the audio equivalent; there are some perplexing moments when the camera focuses on an instrument barely audible in the mix. More happily, John Scofield is shown creating something wonderful from the simple melody of 'Elegy for Andy', while Peter Erskine's *sotto voce* drum solos in 'Crackdown' are astonishing.

Extras include an unrevealing introduction shot during rehearsals and the more welcome inclusion of two encores, arrangements of pieces by Erskine and Scofield which prefigure Turnage's recent *Scorched* project.

Greek

Greek
Quentin Hayes bar Eddy **Richard Suart** bar Dad, Cafe Manager, Police Chief **Fiona Kimm** mez Wife, Doreen, Waitress 1, Sphinx 2 **Helen Charnock** sop Mum, Waitress 2, Sphinx 1
Almeida Ensemble
Video directors **Peter Maniura, Jonathan Moore**
ArtHaus Musik ⏵ 102 105
(81' · NTSC · 4:3 · PCM stereo · 0)
Recorded at the Liverpool Warehouse in 1990   Ⓕ

Mark-Anthony Turnage's first opera, his Steven Berkoff treatment *Greek* (1988), packs quite a punch, reminding us of the vehemently oppositional mood of so much cultural production in the Thatcher years. Even if you attribute some of its pugnacious energy to the text's radical mix of the highfalutin and the scatological, Turnage's musical treatment imparts an edginess of its own. There is lyricism of a kind but more late Stravinsky than Britten, Tippett or Vaughan Williams, a balance neatly reversed in *The Silver Tassie* (2000), a less economical, more stylistically conformist successor.

While an audio recording of *Greek* was a jewel in the crown of the Argo label, the ultra-stylised retelling of the Oedipus myth works better in the context of this vintage BBC film chock-full of memorably revolting scenes. Greater chronological distance may be required to give the piece's indictment of 1980s Britain the timeless quality of great art. That may seem a pretentious comment but Berkoff is nothing if not ambitious: '...this is not simply an adaptation of Sophocles but a recreation of the various Oedipus myths which seemed to apply, particularly to a play about what I saw London had become. London equals Thebes and is full of riots, filth, decay, bombings, football mania, mobs at the palace gates, plague madness and post-pub depression.'

The singers are close-miked but opting into the subtitles (available in several languages) helps focus the sense and the warped poetry of the whole. Light entertainment it ain't. The direction by Jonathan Moore and Peter Maniura certainly avoids the cosy naturalism of conventional TV drama. And you may not feel like

eating toast for a long time after witnessing the Act 1 breakfast scene. Unusually helpful booklet-notes provide extra context. Strongly recommended.

Erkki-Sven Tüür   Estonia b1959

Tüür studied flute and percussion at the Tallinn Music School, and composition at the Tallinn Academy of Music and privately with Lepo Sumera from 1980 to 1984. From 1979 to 1984 he headed the rock group In Spe, which quickly became one of the most popular in Estonia. Tüür left In Spe to concentrate on composition. Drawing on both his immediate classical heritage and aspects of jazz and rock, he came to prominence with the Architectonic series of nine ensemble pieces (1990-93), each with an atmospheric and open-minded approach to instrumental writing. This timbrel sensitivity has been continued in later works as the Third Symphony (1997).

Symphonies

Symphony No 3. Cello Concerto[a]. Lighthouse
[a]**David Geringas** vc **Vienna Radio Symphony Orchestra / Dennis Russell Davies**
ECM New Series 465 134-2 (64' · DDD)   Ⓕ◉⊕

Among the younger generation of would-be symphonists, Erkki-Sven Tüür is one of the most hope-inspiring. The first movement of his Third Symphony builds impressive momentum from the contrast of two types of music: one dogged and metronomic, the other free and apparently tempo-less. These eventually collide, producing an electrifying climax. The second movement has wildly diffuse elements – from Lutosławskian modernism to quasi-Bachian chorale tune and lush tonal Romanticism. This is music of strong personality, integrity and confidence, with warmth as well as acerbity, directness as well as ingenuity. The same could equally be said for the string fantasy *Lighthouse*, and still more for the Cello Concerto, though here the transition from modernism to Romantic lyricism is easier to follow and harder to resist. Also appealing is the vigour of much of the writing, especially for the strings, occasionally recalling the great string works of Tippett. Like the Finnish symphonist Kalevi Aho, Tüür is plainly worth taking very seriously, and it's good to report that the performers on this disc do just that. Excellent recordings too.

Symphony No 4, 'Magma'[a]. Inquiétude du fini[b]. Igavik[c]. The Path and the Traces
[bc]**Estonian Philharmonic Chamber Choir;** [c]**Estonian National Male Choir;** [a]**Evelyn Glennie** perc **Estonian National Symphony Orchestra / Paavo Järvi**
Virgin Classics 385785-2 (66' · DDD)   Ⓕ◉◉⊕

Estonia's best-known internationally orientated modernist has composed six symphonies, among which the 30-minute single-movement Fourth, dating from 2002 and subtitled *Magma*, is outstanding. Tüür's style is essentially mobile-sculptural: which is to say that shifting sound-masses count for more than expressivity. Sibelius is a distant yet clear affinity, and Lutosławski and the sonorism of the Polish school of the 1960s and '70s supply something of the technical means. At its gentlest – as in the tinkling early stages of *Magma* – the effect resembles Oliver Knussen; at its toughest, Elliott Carter. Impersonal yet irresistible forces seem to guide the structure, while the orchestra builds up a succession of analogies to unpopulated landscapes and natural forces. Behind the sonic richness and the dazzling surfaces there is an ascetic instinct at work: a refusal to take easy, opportunistic paths and an immensely impressive traversal of craggier ones.

Though written for Evelyn Glennie, who takes the solo percussion part with superb aplomb, this really is a symphony rather than a flashy, beefed-up concerto. It stays just on that side of the divide everywhere except in the brief cadenza at approximately the half-way mark.

The other three works on this disc feel similarly substantial and born of inner necessity. *The Path and the Traces* is simply the finest recently composed piece for string orchestra, and each of the choral items is memorable, without sacrificing complexity. Tüür is currently well represented on CD, but this new disc is probably the most rewarding devoted to his music, no doubt partly because performances and recordings are first-class. If the prospect of challenging, granite-hewn musical invention has any appeal, then this is a must.

Crystallisatio

Architectonics VI. Passion. Illusion.
Crystallisatio. Requiem
Estonian Philharmonic Chamber Choir;
Tallinn Chamber Orchestra / Tõnu Kaljuste
ECM New Series 449 459-2 (64' · DDD · T/t) Ⓕ Ⓑ▸

Architectonics VI (1992) sounds like one of those titles that are too good to resist, and it's to the credit of Erkki-Sven Tüür that he admits as much in the brief interview in the booklet to this beguiling disc. Tüür's piece isn't especially architectonic in construction, but it's well put together and effective on its own terms. *Passion* and *Illusion*, both for string orchestra and composed in 1993, are closer in spirit to the prevailing 'New Simplicity' of current east Baltic composition. *Passion*, indeed, is occasionally reminiscent of Tüür's better-known compatriot, Arvo Pärt, although the brief *Illusion* has a curiously English feel to it. The title track, *Crystallisatio* (1995), is scored for three flutes, bells, string orchestra and live electronics and is somewhat more demanding in scope. It's here that Tüür's synthesis of minimalism with serial tech-

niques is heard most eloquently; not wholly achieved, perhaps, but fascinating in application. By far the biggest piece is the Requiem (1992-93), in memory of the conductor Peeter Lilje. It's a deeply felt, half-hour-long setting of the Mass for the Dead, and is of markedly different character to the other pieces here. This is a handsomely produced, thought-provoking release. If you want to hear up-to-the-minute new music that won't sear the ears off your head, do try it.

Geirr Tveitt   Norwegian 1908-1981

Tveitt studied at the Leipzig Conservatory and in Paris. Here he obtained lessons from some of the greatest and most well-known composers of the times: Arthur Honegger and Heitor Villa-Lobos both agreed to see Tveitt. He further managed to enrol in the classes of Nadia Boulanger. Tveitt also made a visit to Vienna, where he was able to study for some time with Austrian composer Egon Wellesz, a pupil of Arnold Schoenberg. His often rhythmic, dynamic music derives from Norwegian folk music and he wrote two concertos for the Hardanger fiddle. He was heard as the soloist in his six piano concertos.

Hardanger Fiddle Concertos

Hardanger Fiddle Concertos[a] – No 1, Op 163; No 2, 'Three Fjords', Op 252. The Water Sprite, Op 187
[a]**Arve Moen Bergset** *hardanger fiddle* **Stavanger Symphony Orchestra / Ole Kristian Ruud**
BIS BIS-CD1207 (65' · DDD)   Ⓕ

The Hardanger fiddle of western Norway probably originated in the mid-17th century, possibly – as Reidar Storaas suggests in his notes – as a hybrid of earlier folk fiddles and the viola d'amore. Its tone is smaller than the violin and, with its four sympathetic strings, sounds not unlike a treble viol. Local boy Geirr Tveitt has produced these two marvellous concertos for the instrument. The First dates from 1955, and its premiere at the Bergen Festival the following year was a triumph for the composer. It isn't hard to hear why: the idiom is Tveitt's best folksy manner, the orchestration expert and bright, with a virtuoso solo part. The opening movement is relatively gentle, succeeded by a wonderfully atmospheric if wistful *Andante* and a lively finale reminiscent of Malcolm Arnold. The Second followed 10 years later, and replicates the same basic design, yet is a more personal utterance, the structure more concisely realised, the inspiration drawn from the three fjords of his native region. Arve Moen Bergset is a prize-winning folk player and plays with commendable feeling and technical assurance. He's ably supported by Ruud and the splendid Stavanger orchestra, who also provide an excellent performance of *The Water Sprite* ('Nykken',

1956), a tone-poem relating how the sprite snares a boy by disguising itself as a horse. Beautifully clear as usual from BIS.

Piano Concerto No 4

Piano Concerto No 4, 'Aurora Borealis'. Variations on a Folksong from Hardanger[a]
Håvard Gimse, [a]**Gunilla Süssmann** pfs **Royal Scottish National Orchestra / Bjarte Engeset**
Naxos 8 555761 (61' · DDD) ⓈⓄⓄ🄳

There are many musical depictions of the Northern Lights, but few if any on quite so lush and expansive a scale as Tveitt's Fourth Piano Concerto (1947). A paean to this extraordinary natural phenomenon, it's conceived on a Baxian scale following a seasonal cycle with its kaleidoscopic first movement, 'The Northern Lights awakening above the autumn colours', running to almost 31 of the whole 51-minute length. The slower central span, 'Glittering in the winter heavens, and…' is more straightforward and the swifter final movement ('Fading away in the bright night of spring') acts as an epilogue. The manuscript of the Fourth Concerto was lost in the calamitous 1970 fire that destroyed Tveitt's home and 80 per cent of his output. Christian Eggen was able to reconstruct it from the orchestral parts and a two-piano reduction, leaving the Third to be issued (Nos 2 and 6 are irretrievably lost). The coupling here is the delightful *Variations on a Folksong from Hardanger* for two pianos and orchestra, written in 1939 for Tveitt to play with his first wife, a highly diverse late-Romantic effusion and a real winner. The performances are superb, Gimse totally in the Tveitt style with exemplary support from the RSNO and Bjarte Engeset; Gunilla Süssmann makes a splendid second soloist in the *Variations*. Excellent sound and a marvellous disc.

A Hundred Hardanger Tunes

A Hundred Hardanger Tunes, Op 151 – Suite No 2, 'Fifteen Mountain Songs'; Suite No 5, 'Troll-tunes'
Royal Scottish National Orchestra / Bjarte Engeset
Naxos 8 555770 (72' · DDD) Ⓢ🄳

Only four of Geirr Tveitt's suites from his unique, folk-inspired collection, *A Hundred Hardanger Tunes*, survive. The two presented here exhibit the same principal characteristics as Nos 1 and 4 (also on Naxos), although without the quasi-narrative structure of No 4, *Wedding Suite*. The Second Suite is largely a pastoral affair, though with moments of rugged grandeur befitting its subject, the mountains of Hardanger in western Norway. They are brilliantly orchestrated, as one now expects from Tveitt, the final six exceptionally so. The scoring of the Fifth Suite is richer still, like a kind of concerto for orchestra. The trolls here aren't the moronic ogres of *Harry Potter* or *The Fellowship of the Ring*, nor even the subterra-

nean imps of *Peer Gynt*, but rather all the 'netherworld' peoples, whose music is as dazzling as they were legendarily beguiling.

The Royal Scottish orchestra sound as if they thoroughly enjoyed themselves in this music, as well they should have. A splendid and enjoyable disc, beautifully played and recorded. Strongly recommended.

Edgard Varèse French/American 1883-1965

Varèse studied with d'Indy at the Schola Cantorum and with Widor at the Paris Conservatoire, then moved to Berlin, where he met Strauss and Busoni. In 1915 he emigrated to New York; nearly all his early compositions disappeared at this stage. His creative output therefore effectively begins with Amériques *for large orchestra (1921), which sets out to discover new worlds of sound.*

In 1921 he and Carlos Salzedo founded the International Composers' Guild, who gave the first performances of several of his works for small ensemble, these prominently featuring wind and percussion. They include Hyperprism *(1923),* Octandre *(1923) and* Intégrales *(1925).* Arcana *(1927), which returns to the large orchestra and extended form with perfected technique, brought this most productive period to an end.*

There followed a five-year stay in Paris (1928-33), during which he wrote Ionisation *for percussion orchestra (1931), the first European work to dispense almost entirely with pitched sounds. The flute solo* Densité 21.5 *(1936) was then his last completed work for nearly two decades.*

During this time he taught sporadically and also made plans for Espace, *which was to have involved simultaneous radio broadcasts from around the globe. Then, with electronic music at last a real possibility owing to the development of the tape recorder, he produced* Déserts *for wind, percussion and tape (1954). Le Corbusier was commissioned by Philips to present a pavilion at the 1958 World Fair and insisted (against the sponsors' resistance) on working with Varèse, who developed his* Poème électronique *for the venue, where it was heard by an estimated two million people. Using 400 speakers dispersed throughout the interior, Varèse created a sound and space installation geared towards experiencing sound as it moves through space. Received with mixed reviews, this piece challenged audience expectations and traditional means of composing, breathing life into electronic synthesis and presentation. His last years were devoted to projects on themes of night and death, including the unfinished* Nocturnal *for voices and chamber orchestra (1961).*

Complete Works

Tuning Up. Amériques. Poème électronique. Arcana. Nocturnal. Un grand sommeil noir (orig version/orch Beaumont). Offrandes. Hyperprism. Octandre. Intégrales. Ecuatorial. Ionisation. Densité 21.5. Déserts. Dance for Burgess

Sarah Leonard, Mireille Delunsch *sops* Kevin Deas *bass* Jacques Zoon *fl* François Kerdoncuff *pf* Edgard Varèse *electronics* Prague Philharmonic Choir; ASKO Ensemble; Royal Concertgebouw Orchestra / Riccardo Chailly
Decca ② 460 208-2DH2 (151' · DDD · T/t) Ⓜ❍❍❍❸➡

Naxos 8 557882 (67' · DDD) ❍❍❸➡

Works such as *Octandre* and *Intégrales* require scrupulous attention to balance if they're to sound more than crudely aggressive: Chailly secures this without sacrificing physical impact – witness the explosive *Hyperprism*. He brings out some exquisite harmonic subtleties in *Offrandes*, Sarah Leonard projecting the surreal imagery of the texts with admirable poise. The fugitive opening bars of *Ionisation* sound slightly muted in the recorded ambience, though not the cascading tuned percussion towards the close.

The instrumentational problems of *Ecuatorial* are at last vindicated, allowing Varèse's inspired mix of brass and electronic keyboards to register with awesome power. Chailly opts for the solo bass, but a unison chorus would have heightened the dramatic impact still further. *Amériques*, the true intersection of Romanticism and modernism, is performed in the original 1921 version, with its even more extravagant orchestral demands and bizarre reminiscences of *The Rite of Spring* and Schoenberg's *Five Orchestral Pieces*, understandably replaced in the revision. *Arcana* was recorded in 1992, Chailly probing beyond the work's vast dynamic contours more deeply than any other rival on disc.

No one but Varèse has drawn such sustained eloquence from an ensemble of wind and percussion, or invested such emotional power in the primitive electronic medium of the early 1950s. *Déserts* juxtaposes them in a score which marks the culmination of his search for new means of expression. The opening now seems a poignant evocation of humanity in the atomic age, the ending is resigned but not bitter. The tape interludes in Chailly's performance have a startling clarity, as does the *Poème électronique*, Varèse's untypical but exhilarating contribution to the 1958 Brussels World Fair. The unfinished *Nocturnal*, with its vocal stylisations and belated return of string timbre, demonstrates a continuing vitality that only time could extinguish. Varèse has had a significant impact on post-war musical culture, with figures as diverse as Stockhausen, Charlie Parker and Frank Zappa acknowledging his influence. Chailly's recordings demonstrate, in unequivocal terms, why this music will continue to provoke and inspire future generations.

Orchestral Works

Amériques. Ecuatorial[a]. Nocturnal[b]. Ionisation. Hyperprism. Densité 21.5[c]. Un grand sommeil noir[d]. Dance for Burgess. Tuning Up
[bd]Elizabeth Watts *sop* [c]Maria Grochowska *fl* [a]Thomas Bloch *onde* [ab]Camerata Silesia; Polish National Radio Symphony Orchestra / Christopher Lyndon-Gee [d]*pf*

With Varèse fans still revelling in Riccardo Chailly's groundbreaking 1998 Decca cycle, anybody else approaching this provocative and inflammable music better have something profound to say: Christopher Lyndon-Gee and the Polish National Radio Symphony Orchestra don't let the side down. These Polish musicians are well used to the rough-and-tumble of performing the early textural works of Penderecki and Górecki and that visceral rawness, inherent in their own culture, transmutes powerfully to these seminal Varèse scores.

The stand-out performance for sure is the original 1921 version of *Amériques*, scored for an orchestra of over 150 musicians and an offstage 'banda'. Lyndon-Gee marshals his charges with a careful ear to balancing this monolithic ensemble: Varèse's emphatically reiterated rhythmic mantras are daintily articulated, but the musicians never sound browbeaten by his attention to detail. The elemental power of the closing moments is feral way beyond the call of duty.

Performances of the trailblazing percussion ensemble work *Ionisation*, and other classics like *Hyperprism*, *Densité 21.5* and *Ecuatorial*, are cut from the same devoted cloth. And the rest of the album is devoted to curios like *Dance for Burgess* and *Tuning Up*, reconstructed by Varèse's pupil Chou Wen-Chung and recorded for the first time by Chailly. *Tuning Up* was conceived for a 1947 film about Carnegie Hall and incorporates Ives-like illusions to Varèse's own and borrowed music, all ricocheting against repeated As. Inevitably he came to blows with the film-makers, but Lyndon-Gee makes one think the by-product of their collaboration might be a minor masterpiece.

Pēteris Vasks
Latvian b1952

Pēteris Vasks trained as a double-bass player. In 1970 he joined the Latvian National Opera orchestra, the Latvian Symphony Orchestra and Chamber Orchestra. In 1978, after graduating from the Latvian State Conservatory's Composition Class, Vasks began his teaching career, and many of his pupils are now noted Latvian composers. Vasks's early style owed much to the aleatoric experiments of Witold Lutosławski, Krzysztof Penderecki and George Crumb. Later works included elements of Latvian folk music. His works are generally extremely clear and communicative, with a solid and muscular sense of harmony.

Violin Concerto

Vasks Violin Concerto, 'Distant Light'
Weill Violin Concerto
Academy of St Martin in the Fields / Anthony Marwood *vn*
Hyperion CDA67496 (57' · DDD) ⒻⓈ➡

This new account of Vasks's *Distant Light* swells the number of recordings it has garnered to five, an amazing statistic for a work premiered as recently as August 1997. Then again, perhaps we shouldn't be too surprised: the Latvian's music speaks without artifice and offers an enticing blend of unspoilt beauty, compassionate heartache and superior compositional craft. Of all the competing versions, Gidon Kremer's pioneering Teldec reading has a charisma, intensity and concentration that are wholly arresting. More's the pity it has been deleted, so head-of-the-pack status must now pass to this excellently engineered newcomer. Anthony Marwood keeps a tight grip on the structural tiller and plays with exquisite polish and intimacy of feeling; he also secures an exceptionally alert and involving contribution from his Academy forces.

Winds, percussion and double basses assemble for the coupling, Kurt Weill's ambitious early Violin Concerto of 1923-24, which receives as persuasive and vital a performance as any. Marwood and company quarry every ounce of bony lyricism and spooky burlesque from what can initially seem a rather dry, unyielding creation. Again, the sound is vividly realistic (if lacking just a whisker in bite and focus), and the disc as a whole certainly bodes well for Marwood's tenure as artistic director of the Irish CO.

Symphony No 2

Symphony No 2[a]. Violin Concerto, 'Distant Light'[b]
[a]**Tampere Philharmonic Orchestra** / [b]**John Storgårds** vn [b]**Ostrobothnian Chamber Orchestra / Juha Kangas**
Ondine ODE1005-2 (73' · DDD)　　Ⓕ**O🔊**

Pēteris Vasks has been winning himself something of a cult following over the past decade. On the evidence of this blistering premiere recording, his Second Symphony of 1998-99 seems set to repeat the popular and critical success of *Voices*, its hugely effective 1991 predecessor for string orchestra.

A single-movement canvas of nearly 40 minutes' duration, it traverses emotions from bare-faced rage and serene contemplation to icy despair, achieving a vast, uneasy quietude at the close ('a sense of light-filled sorrow,' in the composer's words). Stylistic echoes are plentiful: Shostakovich, Kancheli, Górecki and Pärt; folk-music, birdsong and hymnody are further ingredients in this approachable cocktail. Fortunately, Vasks's compassionate inspiration eschews any hint of New Age pretentiousness or designer chic, conveying instead a strength of conviction, unflinching honesty and profound sense of wonder that easily hold the listener in its thrall. All of which is also testament to the formidable interpretative skills of conductor John Storgårds, who secures exemplary results from the Tampere Philharmonic. The sound is splendidly ample and detailed to match.

For the coupling, Storgårds gives a heartfelt performance of Vasks's Violin Concerto (*Dis-*

tant Light). Written in 1996-97 at the behest of Gidon Kremer and his then recently formed Kremerata Baltica, it is another single-movement, readily assimilable essay, though its at times enigmatically disparate elements are here perhaps less convincingly fused into a satisfying whole. Nevertheless, this enterprising release deserves every success.

Choral works

Dona nobis pacem. Pater noster. Missa
Latvian Radio Choir; Riga Sinfonietta / Sigvards Klava
Ondine ODE1106-2 (58' · DDD)　　Ⓕ🔊

In the booklet interview, Pēteris Vasks notes that during the Soviet rule in Latvia composition of sacred choral music was heavily discouraged. Personal necessity as well, it seems, also put him off writing the *Pater noster* his Protestant minister father kept asking for. Instrumental music was of greater importance.

When he did write a *Pater noster* (1991), it was in a simpler, more consonant style than much of his earlier work, expressively close to the 'holy minimalism' common to a number of Baltic composers, but Vasks's triadic style – which he feels essential for sacred music – shares little with them. A short, peaceful meditation, it is reverentially performed by the Latvian Radio Choir. So, too, is *Dona nobis pacem* (1996), inhabiting the same evocative sound world.

The *Missa* (2000, rev 2000-05) is a different matter. True, the expressive idiom is the same, but Vasks here invests his ideas in more musically satisfying forms. The use of string orchestral accompaniment is reminiscent in places, the *Sanctus* especially, of English music and sounds a touch like what an early Mass setting by Tippett might have sounded like. There are sympathetic echoes (no doubt coincidental) of Howells in the *Benedictus* and overlong *Agnus Dei*, too.

Ralph Vaughan Williams
British 1872-1958

Down Ampney, the picturesque Cotswold village of his birth, is also the hymn-tune to which we sing 'Come down, O Love divine'. With or without the words, it provides a perfect evocation of a village church in the tranquil English countryside. That, the tune Sine nomine ('For all the saints'), Monks Gate (the folk tune he named after the place near Horsham, Sussex, where he first heard it, to which he set the words 'Who would true valour see') and his arrangement of the Old 100th Psalm Tune ('All people that on earth do dwell') may be his most performed music. They define the 'English' part of the Church of England.

He was related to a distinguished family of lawyers on his father's side and to both Charles Darwin and Josiah Wedgewood on his mother's. He was brought up in the home of his maternal grandfather in Surrey, after his clergyman father died young. Music studies began at an early age with piano and violin, and continued through his schooling at Charterhouse. Indeed, his studies were nothing if not protracted – he was fortunate in having a private income – for, after the Royal College of Music, he took a MusB and BA at Trinity, Cambridge, returned to the Royal College for lessons with Stanford, took off for Berlin for further study with Max Bruch and in 1908 at the age of 35 – still dissatisfied with what he was doing – went to Ravel in Paris for (as he put it) 'a little French polish'.

After all this – conservative English and German instruction, plus modern French orchestral technique – Vaughan Williams emerged as an adventurous, unmistakably English composer with a distinct voice of his own. His discovery in the early 1900s of English folksong, through the recently formed English Folk Music Society, focused his style. VW and Gustav Holst, his lifelong friend whom he'd met at the Royal College, went out seeking the source of their country's folksongs; many had never been written down before and the cataloguing and research that VW and Holst undertook in this area was of considerable cultural significance. His music now took on a different character. Apart from war service (for which he volunteered, although over 40), Vaughan Williams devoted the rest of his long life to composition, teaching and conducting.

Vaughan Williams worked on into old age with undiminished creative powers – his Eighth Symphony appeared in 1955 (the score includes parts for vibraphone and xylophone) while his Ninth, composed at the age of 85, uses a trio of saxophones. After his wife's death in 1951, he married the poet and librettist Ursula Wood at the age of 80 and moved from his home of many years (The White Gates, near Dorking in Surrey) to a house in London's Regent Park. He was a familiar sight at the capital's concert halls and opera houses, his bulky figure, snowy white hair and old-fashioned hearing aid doing nothing to detract from his role as the Grand Old Man of English music.

Piano Concerto

Vaughan Williams Piano Concerto.
Foulds Dynamic Triptych, Op 88
Howard Shelley pf **Royal Philharmonic Orchestra / Vernon Handley**
Lyrita SRCD211 (57' · DDD) Ⓕ Ⓞ

There are four unequivocal masterpieces for piano and orchestra in English 20th-century music: Bax's *Winter Legends*, Frank Bridge's *Phantasm* and the two works recorded here. Until the appearance of this recording the VW Concerto had been more frequently presented in its revised 1946 version for two pianos and orchestra – one that did no favours in revealing the masterpiece of his original inspiration. The exceptionally taxing solo part, and the power required by the soloist to project over an extremely large orchestra, almost certainly inhibited the original version's ingress into the repertoire. However, when heard under the guiding hand of a

pianist of Howard Shelley's calibre, we're allowed once more to discover the work in its true glory.

It's easy to see why the piece was so admired by Bartók when it received its German premiere under Hermann Scherchen and the concerto's dedicatee Harriet Cohen, for this is surely one of the most cogent and tautly constructed examples of its genre to have emerged from English music of the period. John Fould's *Dynamic Triptych* is scarcely less impressive. Though it lacks the conciseness of the VW, this is a work and a performance to treasure.

Piano Concerto (original version)[a].
The Wasps – Suite. English Folk Song Suite (orch Jacob). The Running Set
[a]**Ashley Wass** pf **Royal Liverpool Philharmonic Orchestra / James Judd**
Naxos 8 572304 (70' · DDD) Ⓢ Ⓞ Ⓞ ↦

Written in the mid-1920s, Vaughan Williams's Piano Concerto looks forward in many ways to the radical developments in the composer's style which erupted in the ballet music for *Job* and above all in the abrasive Fourth Symphony. Early critics complained about its dissonance but that is hardly likely to worry anyone today; and a performance as fine as this one from Ashley Wass will simply have one marvelling at the originality of the piece and its distinctive slant on the idea of a piano concerto.

This fine performance, superbly recorded in clean, perfectly balanced sound, brings up some strange, unexpected echoes, as for example in the finale where there is a hint of Ravel's *La valse*. One point that may help to explain the work's failure to be appreciated is that instead of ending with a bang, as most piano concertos do, it fades down to nothing, surprising one that it has finished. None the less Wass, James Judd and the RLPO carry that off most effectively.

The other works on the disc make an attractive programme, with the five movements of the suite from VW's incidental music to *The Wasps*, introduced by its superb overture, crisply presented. Gordon Jacob's arrangement of the brief *English Folk Song Suite* makes a colourful filler, rounded off with a piece in a similar folky vein, *The Running Set*. Naxos again offers a disc of the highest quality at super-budget price.

Symphonies

No 1, 'A Sea Symphony'; **No 2**, 'A London Symphony'; **No 3**, 'A Pastoral Symphony'; **No 4** in F minor; **No 5** in D; **No 6** in E minor; **No 7**, 'Sinfonia antartica'; **No 8** in D minor; **No 9** in E minor

---

Complete Symphonies

Symphonies Nos 1-9 Ⓗ
Baillie, Ritchie sops **Cameron** bar **Gielgud** narr
LPO & Choir / Boult

Decca British Music Collection ⑤ 473 241-2DC5
(5h 53' · ADD). Recorded 1952-58 Ⓜ
Music-making of the highest calibre throughout.
The mono engineering is always vivid, often
stunningly so – especially in *A Sea Symphony* and
Sinfonia antartica.

Symphonies Nos 1-9
Coupled with Fantasia on a Theme by Thomas Tallis.
The Wasps. Serenade to Music. In the Fen Country.
Norfolk Rhapsody No 1. The Lark Ascending.
English Folk Song Suite. Fantasia on 'Greensleeves'.
Concerto for Two Pianos and Orchestra. Job
Armstrong, Burrowes, Price *sops* **Case** *bar*
London Philharmonic Choir and Orchestra;
New Philharmonia / Boult; various artists
EMI ⑤ 573924-2 (5h 34' · ADD) Ⓑ
An ideal supplement to Boult's mono VW cycle
for Decca.

Symphonies No 1-9
Coupled with Tallis Fantasia. In the Fen Country.
The Lark Ascending. Norfolk Rhapsody No 1.
On Wenlock Edge
Soloists; LPO & Choir / Haitink
EMI ⑦ 586026-2 (7h 35' · DDD · T) ⓈⓄ➔
Haitink's majestic VW symphony cycle was
recorded with the LPO over 13 years. His eloquent
and illuminatingly intense interpretations serve up
a feast of stimulating listening. The fill-ups are
mostly marvellous, too; both *On Wenlock Edge*
(with Ian Bostridge) and *In the Fen Country* receive
sublime advocacy. An outstanding bargain.

Symphonies No 1-9
Coupled with Flos campi. Serenade to Music. Job
Soloists; RLPO & Choir / Handley
Classics for Pleasure ⑦ 575760-2 (7h 54' · DDD · T)
ⓈⓄ➔
Handley's performances can withstand comparison
with the very best. These consistently idiomatic
readings will provide many hours of pleasurable listening. This is VW from the heart conducted by a
man, like Boult, who'd lived with these scores for
decades. A wonderful set, also available singly.

Symphonies – selected

Vaughan Williams Symphony No 2 (original version,
1913) **Butterworth** The Banks of Green Willow
London Symphony Orchestra / Richard Hickox
Chandos CHAN9902 (68' · DDD) ⒻⓄⓄ➔

 It was during the summer of 1911 that
George Butterworth, whose enchanting 1913 idyll, *The Banks of Green Willow*, comprises the achingly poignant curtain-
raiser here, first suggested to Vaughan Williams
that he should write a purely orchestral symphony. VW dug out some sketches he'd made
for a symphonic poem about London, while at
the same time deriving fruitful inspiration from
HG Wells's 1908 novel, *Tono-Bungay*. Geoffrey Toye gave the successful Queen's Hall
premiere in March 1914, and VW subsequently
dedicated the score to Butterworth's memory.

Over the next two decades or so, the work
underwent three revisions (including much
judicious pruning) and was published twice (in
1920 and 1936). In his compelling 1941 recording with the Cincinnati SO, Eugene Goossens
employed the 1920 version, which adds about
three minutes of music to that definitive 1936
'revised edition'. Now Richard Hickox at long
last gives us the chance to hear VW's original,
hour-long canvas – and riveting listening it
makes too!

Whereas the opening movement is as we
know it today, the ensuing, expanded *Lento*
acquires an intriguingly mournful, even world-
weary demeanour. Unnervingly, the ecstatic
full flowering of that glorious E major *Largamente* idea, first heard at fig F in the final revision, never materialises, and the skies glower
menacingly thereafter. Towards the end of the
Scherzo comes a haunting episode that Arnold
Bax was particularly sad to see cut ('a mysterious passage of strange and fascinating cacoph-
ony' was how he described it). The finale, too,
contains a wealth of additional material, most
strikingly a liturgical theme of wondrous lyrical
beauty, and, in the epilogue, a gripping paragraph that looks back to the work's introduction as well as forward to the first movement of
A Pastoral Symphony. Sprawling it may be, but
this epic conception evinces a prodigal inventiveness, poetry, mystery and vitality that do
not pall with repeated hearings. Hickox and the
LSO respond with an unquenchable spirit,
generous flexibility and tender affection that
suit VW's ambitious inspiration to a T, and
Chandos's sound is big and bold to match. An
essential purchase for anyone remotely interested in British music.

Symphonies Nos 4ᵃ & 5ᵇ Ⓗ
ᵃ**BBC Symphony Orchestra / Ralph Vaughan**
Williams; ᵇ**Hallé Orchestra / Sir John Barbirolli**
Dutton mono CDBP9731 (66' · ADD)
Recorded ᵃ1937, ᵇ1944 ⓈⓄⓄⓄ

No performance on record of Vaughan
Williams's Fourth Symphony has ever
quite matched this very first one,
recorded under the composer's baton in October 1937. As Michael Kennedy says in his note
for this reissue, it's 'taken at a daredevil pace',
and more importantly has a bite and energy
beyond any rival. If early listeners to this violent
work were shocked by the composer's new
boldness, here his conducting demonstrates the
passionate emotion behind the piece. The
remastered sound is so vivid and immediate, so
full of presence, that in places one almost has the
illusion of stereo before its time.

Barbirolli's premiere recording of the Fifth
Symphony, made in February 1944 eight
months after the first performance, is hardly less
remarkable. This, too, has never been matched
since for the stirring passion of the great climaxes in the first and third movements, with
Barbirolli in each carefully grading the intensity

between exposition and recapitulation. It's also a revelation to find him taking the triple-time of the Passacaglia finale much faster than latter-day rivals, relating it more closely than usual to the great example of the finale of Brahms's Fourth Symphony, making it no pastoral amble but a searing argument. Here again hiss has been virtually eliminated, but that has left the high violins sounding rather papery. Even so, there's no lack of weight in the big climaxes, with brass and wind atmospherically caught.

An outstanding issue for all lovers of this composer's music, not just those who specialise in historic recordings.

Symphony No 5ᵃ. Valiant-for-truthᵇ. The Pilgrim Pavementᶜ. Psalm 23 (arr Churchill)ᵇ. Hymn-tune Prelude on 'Song 13' by Orlando Gibbons (arr Glatz)ᵃ. Prelude and Fugue in C minorᵃ
ᶜIan Watson org ᵇᶜRichard Hickox Singers;
ᵃLondon Symphony Orchestra / Richard Hickox
Chandos CHAN9666 (71' · DDD · T)   Ⓕ**OO**➔

This is an exceptionally powerful yet deeply moving account of the Fifth. Aided by glowing, wide-ranging engineering, Hickox's is an urgently communicative reading. The first and third movements in particular emerge with an effortless architectural splendour and rapt authority, the climaxes built and resolved with mastery. The *Scherzo* is as good a place as any to sample the lustrous refinement of the LSO's response. Hickox ensures that the symphony's concluding bars positively glow with gentle ecstasy: here's a Fifth that can surely hold its own in the most exalted company.

Material from *The Pilgrim's Progress* made its way into the Fifth Symphony and two of the five enterprising couplings here provide further links with John Bunyan's timeless allegory: the 1940 motet for mixed voices with organ, *Valiant-for-truth* and John Churchill's 1953 arrangement for soprano and mixed chorus of Psalm 23 (originally sung by The Voice of a Bird in Act 4 of *The Pilgrim's Progress*). The latter receives its finely prepared recorded debut on this occasion, as do both *The Pilgrim Pavement* (a 1934 processional for soprano, chorus and organ) and Helen Glatz's string-orchestra arrangement of the solo-piano *Hymn-tune Prelude on 'Song 13' by Gibbons*. Which just leaves the Prelude and Fugue, originally written for organ in 1921, but heard here in a sumptuous orchestration.

Symphony No 6 in E minorᵃ. The Lark Ascendingᵇ. A Song of Thanksgivingᶜ
ᶜBetty Dolemore sop ᶜRobert Speaight narr ᶜHarry Grab org ᵇJean Pougnet vn ᶜLuton Choral Society;
ᵃLondon Symphony Orchestra, ᵇᶜLondon Philharmonic Orchestra / Sir Adrian Boult
Dutton mono CDBP9703 (69' · ADD)
Recorded 1949-52   Ⓑ**OO**

Although it was Boult who premiered VW's awesome Sixth Symphony, his white-hot February

1949 account with the LSO wasn't in fact the work's debut recording – that honour fell to Stokowski and the New York Philharmonic (who pipped their British counterparts to the post by just two days). The return to the catalogue of Boult's legendary version – last available on an identically programmed Great Recordings of the Century anthology (EMI) – is a cause for celebration, especially in such a vivid transfer (if fractionally hollow in the bass), and so modestly priced to boot. Like Stokowski's scarcely less thrilling realisation, the performance offers us the opportunity to hear VW's original *Scherzo*. This has been allotted a separate track at the end of the symphony, its place taken by the same team's February 1950 recording of the composer's revision (not an ideal arrangement, perhaps). Whether the performance as a whole entirely displaces Sir Adrian's marvellous 1953 Decca version with the LPO (available in a disappointingly rough transfer on Belart) is open to debate, but both interpretations comprehensively outflank Sir Adrian's New Philharmonia stereo remake for EMI in terms of fiery concentration and sheer guts.

Written in response to a commission from the BBC in 1943 for a work to celebrate the defeat of Hitler's Germany, *A Song of Thanksgiving* was first broadcast shortly after VE Day. This commercial recording followed in December 1951. The work (which is scored for soprano, narrator, chorus and orchestra) has a smattering of decent invention (including, from around 4'30", fleeting echoes of the Sixth's second movement), but overall it's hardly representative of VW at his most inspired.

Last, and certainly not least, comes a wholly cherishable account (from October 1952) of *The Lark Ascending*, with Jean Pougnet a wonderfully silky toned, humane soloist. Boult's accompaniment, too, is a model of selfless dedication and intuitive rapture. For some, it remains, quite simply, the most tenderly unaffected and profoundly moving *Lark* on disc, though the string timbre on that earlier EMI restoration is much preferable to this over-processed newcomer. None the less, a most valuable VW reissue.

Symphony No 6. Fantasia on a Theme by Thomas Tallis. The Lark Ascending
Tasmin Little vn BBC Symphony Orchestra / Sir Andrew Davis
Warner Apex 0927 49584-2 (62' · DDD)   Ⓢ**O**➔

Sir Andrew Davis clearly thought long and hard before committing this enigmatic and tragic symphony to disc, and the result is one of the most spontaneous and electrifying accounts of the Sixth Symphony available. The urgency and vigour of the first and third movements is astonishing, leaving one with the impression that the work might have been recorded in one take. His treatment of the second subject's reprise in the closing pages of the first movement is more underplayed and remote than the beautifully sheened approach of some recordings, but is arguably more nostalgic for being so. The feverish, nightmare world of the *Scherzo* is a real *tour de force* in the hands of an inspired BBC Symphony Orchestra, and the desolate wasteland of the eerie final movement has rarely achieved such quiescence and nadir as here. Davis's searchingly intense *Tallis Fantasia* is finely poised with a beautifully spacious acoustic. The disc concludes on a quietly elevated note with Tasmin Little's serene and gently introspective reading of *The Lark Ascending*. The recording is excellent.

Film Music

'The Film Music of Ralph Vaughan Williams, Volume 2'
49th Parallel – Suite[a]. The Dim Little Island[b]. The England of Elizabeth – Suite[c]. (all ed Hogger)
[a]**Emily Gray** sop [b]**Martin Hindmarsh** ten [c]**Chetham's Chamber Choir; BBC Philharmonic Orchestra / Rumon Gamba**
Chandos CHAN10244 (71' · DDD) Ⓕ ⦿ ➔

Directed by Michael Powell and written by Emeric Pressburger and Rodney Ackland, *49th Parallel* (1941) was the Ministry of Information's only feature film, its plot – of five stranded Nazi U-boat crewmen journeying through Canada to the haven of the then neutral United States – designed, in Powell's words, 'to scare the pants off the Americans and bring them into the war'. Vaughan Williams's film score was the first of 11 he wrote between 1941 and 1958.

It was a challenge that evidently stoked his imagination, for inspiration runs high throughout this 39-minute sequence fashioned by Stephen Hogger. The unforgettable, nobly flowing 'Prelude' accompanies both the opening and closing titles, and enthusiasts will enjoy spotting thematic and stylistic links with masterworks to come (including Symphonies Nos 5-7 and the Second String Quartet).

The present suite from *The England of Elizabeth* (written in the autumn of 1955 for a British Transport Commission documentary) adds eight minutes to Mathieson's three-movement adaptation (familiar to many from Previn's 1968 LSO account). It is, as annotator Michael Kennedy observes, a splendidly vital and inventive achievement. In the section depicting Tintern Vaughan Williams quotes a theme from his unpublished tone-poem of 1906, *The Solent* (the tune also crops up in his first and last symphonies), and it's soon followed by a haunting passage for choir alone.

Sandwiched between these two is a partial reconstruction of VW's amiable 1949 score for *The Dim Little Island*, a 10-minute short commissioned by the Central Office of Information (which also featured the composer in the role of narrator). It borrows heavily from VW's own *Five Variants of Dives and Lazarus* and even incorporates a verse of that self-same melody sung by a solo tenor.

Rumon Gamba draws a polished and wholehearted response from all involved. The Chan-

dos recording has striking body and lustre; exemplary presentation, too. Very strongly recommended.

String Quartets

String Quartets – No 1 in G minor; No 2 in A minor. Phantasy Quintet[a]
[a]**Garfield Jackson** va **Maggini Quartet**
Naxos 8 555300 (66' · DDD) Ⓢ ⦿⦿⦿⦿ ➔

 Why isn't Vaughan Williams's Second Quartet part of the international chamber repertory? Played as eloquently as this it seems unarguably a masterpiece, one specifically of its time: 1942-43. Its first movement and deeply fraught *Scherzo* are as troubled as Shostakovich (whose music at moments, like a sudden stab of violence in that first *Allegro*, it passingly resembles), while the misleadingly titled slow *Romance* is haunted and haunting. It's tranquil but not at peace. It achieves an impassioned nobility and approaches serenity at the end, but something ghostly (it walks again in the Epilogue to the Sixth Symphony) refuses to be exorcised until the beautiful calm finale.

What these players do with the two much earlier pieces is no less remarkable. In them Vaughan Williams's style is audibly emerging from the influences (notably Ravel, briefly his teacher) that helped form it. In the First Quartet's opening movement an arching, lyrical melody that sounds like Vaughan Williams speaking with a French accent (and is it a French lark that ascends a little later?) has shed the accent by its return; something similar happens in the finale. But it was not an immature composer (he was 36, after all) who in the slow movement recognised a kinship with Fauré. And the *Phantasy Quintet* is audibly by the composer of the *Tallis Fantasia*, grateful to Ravel for giving him access to a deft rhythmic flexibility, but exploring his own unmistakable territory in the serenity tinged with poignancy of the slow movement. The Magginis and Garfield Jackson clearly love this music deeply; they play it with great beauty of tone and variety of colour and with passionate expressiveness. The ample recording allows both grand gestures and quiet intimacy.

Dona nobis pacem

Dona nobis pacem[a]. Sancta Civitas[b]
[a]**Yvonne Kenny** sop [b]**Philip Langridge** ten **Bryn Terfel** bass-bar [b]**St Paul's Cathedral Choir; London Symphony Chorus and Orchestra / Richard Hickox**
EMI British Composers 754788-2 (63' · DDD · T) Ⓑ ⦿⦿

This is a generous and inspiring coupling of two of Vaughan Williams's most important choral utterances. Hickox coaxes magnificent sounds from the LSO throughout: in *Dona nobis pacem*, for example, the sense of orchestral spectacle during 'Beat! Beat! drums!' is riveting in its physical impact. The London Symphony Chorus combines full-throated discipline and sensitivity to nuance, and Hickox's trio of soloists is excellent, with Terfel outstandingly eloquent. *Sancta Civitas* is a work whose multi-layered scoring places great demands on both conductor and production team alike: suffice it to report, it's difficult to see Hickox's inspirational account of this still-underrated score being surpassed for years to come. EMI's clean, wide-ranging sound is admirable.

Dona nobis pacem[a]. Sancta Civitas[b]
[a]**Christina Pier** sop [b]**Andrew Staples** ten **Matthew Brook** bar **Bach Choir; Winchester Cathedral Choristers**[b]; **Winchester College Quiristers**[b]; **Bournemouth Symphony Orchestra / David Hill**
Naxos 8 572424 (65' · DDD)   Ⓢ🅾️🄳➔

Though a period of 10 years separates the two works in date of composition, they have such affinity that it is as natural to think of them together as it is for them to be paired in recording. That *Sancta Civitas* is called an oratorio and *Dona nobis pacem* a cantata must be something of a technicality: the distinction between a wholly biblical text and one which incorporates words by a poet and a politician. Whitman's verses inspired by the American Civil War and John Bright's 'angel of death' referring to the Crimea have also in common the harrowing disturbance of what seemed to so many a settled time of peace. Invoked in the mid-1930s, they have – particularly in retrospect – a dreadful prescience about them. And it is not fanciful to hear in the awed and sometimes fearful tones of *Sancta Civitas* the echoes of that other war which so haunted Vaughan Williams's generation and of which they so rarely spoke.

These performances under David Hill are fine, responsive to the beauty and the terror. *Dona nobis pacem* has a strong initial impact, with the timpani's sudden *fortissimo* striking like the first bomb over a sleeping city. The forward orchestral presence places the chorus at a slight disadvantage. Bryn Terfel's singing of the baritone part for Hickox (above) is warmer in humanity as well as tone than Matthew Brook's. Hill's other soloists, Christina Pier and Andrew Staples, do well. These performances under David Hill impress as impassioned and the recorded sound has a keener range and depth of perspective.

Mass in G minor

Vaughan Williams Mass in G minor. Te Deum in G
Howells Requiem. Take him, earth, for cherishing
Mary Seers sop **Michael Chance** counterten **Philip Salmon** ten **Jonathan Best** bass **Corydon Singers / Matthew Best** with **Thomas Trotter** org
Hyperion CDA66076 (60' · ADD · T)   Ⓕ🅾️🅾️

Vaughan Williams's unaccompanied Mass in G minor manages to combine the common manner of Elizabethan liturgical music with those

elements of his own folk-music heritage that make his music so distinctive, and in so doing arrives at something individual and new. The work falls into five movements and its mood is one of heartfelt, if restrained, rejoicing. Howells's Requiem dates from 1936, a year after the death of his only son. The work was not released in his lifetime but was reconstructed and published in 1980 from his manuscripts. It's a most hauntingly beautiful work of an intensely personal nature. *Take him, earth, for cherishing* was composed to commemorate the assassination of JF Kennedy. The text is an English translation of Prudentius's 4th-century poem, *Hymnus circa Exsequias Defuncti*. Again it shows the great strength of Howells's choral writing, with a clear outline and affecting yet unimposing harmonic twists. The Corydon Singers give marvellous performances and the sound is very fine.

Mass in G minor. Lord, thou hast been our refuge. Prayer to the Father of Heaven. O vos omnes. O clap your hands. O taste and see. O how amiable. The Christian Year. Come down, O Love divine
Thomas Fitches org **Elora Festival Singers / Noel Edison**
Naxos 8 554826 (57' · DDD)   Ⓢ🅾️🄳➔

This fine Canadian choir perform very beautifully in a style which seems natural and right. The Elora Festival Singers have much in common with King's College, Cambridge, under Willcocks; relaxed and habituated, they offer the welcome loveliness of a choral tone where the blend and match of voices produce a sound that's eminently 'at unity with itself'. There's no shortage of good recordings of the Mass in G minor, the one that stands out as being open-eyed and adventurous in spirit being the version on Meridian by the Choir of New College, Oxford. They favour a sharper tone, a quicker tempo in the *Credo* and a brighter acoustic. The choice between women's and boys' voices may prove the deciding factor when it comes to which version; the Elora Singers' female voices seem to give this music precisely what's required. Yet more decisive may be the coupling. The two recordings by the college choirs couple music by other composers. The Canadians stay with Vaughan Williams, in a mood which assorts well with the Mass. Particularly apt is *O vos omnes*, also written for Sir Richard Terry and the Choir of Westminster Cathedral. The Skelton setting, *Prayer to the Father of Heaven*, from 1948 – a comparative rarity and sensitively performed – has a chill which is partly medieval, partly perhaps from the Antarctica of VW's Seventh Symphony. *Down Ampney* ('Come down, O Love divine') brings the warmth and cheer of a settled major tonality at the close.

Serenade to Music

Serenade to Music. Flos campi. Five Mystical Songs[a]. Fantasia on Christmas Carols[a]

Elizabeth Connell, Linda Kitchen, Anne Dawson,
Amanda Roocroft *sops* Sarah Walker, Jean Rigby,
Diana Montague *mezzos* Catherine Wyn-Rogers
contr John Mark Ainsley, Martyn Hill, Arthur
Davies, Maldwyn Davies *tens* ᵃThomas Allen, Alan
Opie *bars* Gwynne Howell, John Connell *basses*
Nobuko Imai *va* Corydon Singers; English
Chamber Orchestra / Matthew Best
Hyperion CDA66420 (68' · DDD · T)   Ⓕ**O**➔

In 1938 Sir Henry Wood celebrated his 50 years
as a professional conductor with a concert.
Vaughan Williams composed a work for the
occasion, the *Serenade to Music*, in which he set
words by Shakespeare from Act 5 of *The Merchant of Venice*. Sixteen star vocalists of the age
were gathered together for the performance and
Vaughan Williams customised the vocal parts to
show off the best qualities of the singers. The
work turned out to be one of the composer's
most sybaritic creations, turning each of its subsequent performances into a special event.
Hyperion has gathered stars of our own age for
this outstanding issue and Best has perceptively
managed to give each their head, while melding
them into a cohesive ensemble. A mellow, spacious recording has allowed the work to emerge
on disc with a veracity never achieved before.

The coupled vocal pieces are given to equal
effect and the disc is completed by Nobuko
Imai's tautly poignant account of *Flos campi*, in
which the disturbing tension between solo viola
and wordless chorus heightens the cryptic
nature of the work.

Additional recommendations

Serenade to Music   Ⓗ
Coupled with The Wasps – Overture.
Symphony No 2. Fantasia on 'Greensleeves'
Sols inc **Baillie, Suddaby** *sops* **Nash** *ten* **Henderson**
bar **BBC Symphony Orchestra; Queen's Hall
Orchestra / Wood**
Dutton CDBP9707 (63' · ADD)   Ⓜ

This performance with the 16 original soloists
possesses a very special beauty and atmosphere.

Five Tudor Portraits

Five Tudor Portraits. Five Variants of 'Dives and
Lazarus'
Jean Rigby *mez* **John Shirley-Quirk** *bar* **London
Symphony Chorus and Orchestra / Richard Hickox**
Chandos CHAN9593 (55' · DDD · T)   Ⓕ**O**➔

First heard at the 1936 Norwich Festival,
Vaughan Williams's *Five Tudor Portraits* find the
composer at his most dazzlingly inventive, the
resourceful and witty writing fitting Skelton's
words like a glove. Moreover, an irresistible
humanity illuminates the most ambitious of the
settings, 'Jane Scroop (Her Lament for Philip
Sparrow)', which contains music as compassionate as Vaughan Williams ever conceived. It's a
life-enhancing creation and well deserving of

this first-rate recording. Aided by disciplined
orchestral support, the London Symphony
Chorus launches itself in lusty fashion into the
ale-soaked narrative of 'The Tunning of Elinor
Rumming', though the resonant acoustic rather
precludes ideal clarity of diction. Hickox is exuberant in this sparkling tableau, while Jean Rigby's characterful contribution should raise a
smile. John Shirley-Quirk's is a touching presence in 'My Pretty Bess', and the mordant, black
humour of 'Epitaph of John Jayberd of Diss' is
effectively captured. Jane Scroop's lament in the
fourth (and surely best) movement finds these
fine artists at their most perceptive. How ravishingly Hickox moulds his strings in the hushed
passage following 'It was proper and prest!'
where the music movingly anticipates the
poignancy of the closing section. Listen out,
too, for the wealth of exquisitely observed
woodwind detail in the enchanting funeral processional. The concluding 'Jolly Rutterkin' goes
with a swing, though Shirley-Quirk is a mite
unsteady at the top of his range.

The coupling is a heart-warming *Dives and
Lazarus*, with the LSO strings producing their
most lustrous tone.

A Cotswold Romance

A Cotswold Romance. Death of Tintagiles
Rosa Mannion *sop* **Thomas Randle** *ten* **Matthew
Brook** *bar* **London Philharmonic Choir; London
Symphony Orchestra / Richard Hickox**
Chandos CHAN9646 (54' · DDD · T)   Ⓕ➔

A Cotswold Romance is a gift from Vaughan Williams to those who hold the music of *Hugh the
Drover* in deep affection but who, under
torture, would probably have to admit that the
opera itself is less than perfect. *Hugh*, first produced in 1924, enjoyed sufficient immediate
success for a set of records to be produced with
the original cast. It then had to wait till 1979 for
a complete recording on LP (reissued on EMI),
and till 1994 for a new one on CD. The adaptation as a dramatic cantata came out in 1951,
reducing the two-act opera to 10 numbers and
rescoring some of the music to allow a larger
part for the chorus. The addition of wordless
chorus is delightful, not least when the chorus
sings the first part of Hugh's song of the road
and re-enters with delicious harmonies at 'All
the scented night'. Thomas Randle, who has the
voice of a man of the road and a lover, is admirably cast. Rosa Mannion, with a slight hint of
turning tremulous under pressure, is otherwise
an ideal Mary, and the chorus is excellent.
Hickox conducts with brio and with due feeling
for the romance.

Death of Tintagiles is incidental music written
for a play by Maeterlinck, performed without
much success in 1913. In his interesting notes,
Stephen Connock associates it with *Riders to the
Sea* and the *Sinfonia antartica*; and it's true that
there are sternly impressive moments of menace
and darkness. Though it hardly seems viable as

an orchestral suite, it's good to have on this disc, nevertheless.

On Wenlock Edge

On Wenlock Edge. Merciless Beauty. Two English Folksongs. Ten Blake Songs. Along the Field
John Mark Ainsley ten **Nash Ensemble** (Gareth Hulse ob Leo Phillips, Elizabeth Wexler vns Roger Chase va Paul Watkins vc Ian Brown pf)
Hyperion CDA67168 (69' · DDD · T) Ⓕ**Ⓞ**➔

The programme here has an identity of its own and as such is without competitors. Its 'theme' is to collect those of Vaughan Williams's songs which have something other than piano accompaniment. *On Wenlock Edge* (1909) is for voice, piano and string quartet, *Merciless Beauty* (1921) with string trio, *Along the Field* (1927) and *Two English Folksongs* (published 1935 but of earlier date) voice and violin, and the Blake songs (1957) with oboe. Eligible for inclusion might have been *Four Hymns* (1914) with piano and viola, and perhaps *The Willow Whistle* (1939) for voice and pipe. The *Three Vocalises* of 1958, with clarinet, are specifically for soprano, but show the composer's continuing taste for such combinations right into the last year of his life. John Mark Ainsley sings with the sense of a civilised personal utterance, refined and restrained, yet capable of full-bodied tone and a ringing *forte* when needed: the cry 'O noisy bells, be dumb' is as emotional as an operatic climax and all the more effective for the exceptional frankness of its release. These are highly demanding pieces, the voice unremittingly exposed. He brings to them a fine poise, in breathing, phrasing, expression and the even emission of quite beautiful tone. He has also the considerable advantage of exceptional players to work with. Individually admirable, they combine in *On Wenlock Edge* to give an unusually imaginative performance.

Songs of Travel

Vaughan Williams Songs of Travel **Butterworth** Bredon Hill and other songs. A Shropshire Lad **Finzi** Let us garlands bring, Op 18 **Ireland** Sea Fever. The Vagabond. The Bells of San Marie
Bryn Terfel bass-bar **Malcolm Martineau** pf
DG 445 946-2GH (77' · DDD · T) Ⓕ**ⓄⓄ**➔

There's a touch of genius about Bryn Terfel. To those who've known most of these songs since childhood and heard them well performed innumerable times, it will come not quite as a revelation but more as the fulfilment of a deeply felt wish, instinctive rather than consciously formed. As in all the best Lieder singing, everything is specific: 'Fly away, breath' we recite, thinking nothing of it, but with this singer it's visual – we see it in flight, just as in *Sea Fever* we know in the very tiniest of gaps that in that second he has *heard* 'the

seagulls crying'. As in all the best singing of songs, whatever the nationality, there's strong, vivid communication: he'll sometimes sing so softly that if he'd secured anything less than total involvement he'd lose us. There's breadth of phrase, variety of tone, alertness of rhythm. All the musical virtues are there; and yet that seems to go only a little way towards accounting for what's special. One after another, these songs are brought to full life. There's a boldness about Terfel's art that could be perilous, but which, as exercised here, is marvellously well guided by musicianship, intelligence and the genuine flash of inspiration. Malcolm Martineau's playing is also a delight: his touch is as sure and illuminating as the singer's.

Songs

Seven Songs from 'The Pilgrim's Progress'. Ten Songs from 'Hugh the Drover'. Sir John in Love – Greensleeves; See the chariot at hand
Sarah Fox sop **Juliette Pochin** mez
Andrew Staples ten **Roderick Williams** bar
Iain Burnside pf
Albion ALBCD001 (60' · DDD) Ⓕ

According to the booklet, no fewer than 11 world premieres adorn this first release from Albion Records, the RVW Society's own label. The 10 songs from *Hugh the Drover* (the first of VW's six operas, 1911-14) were arranged by the composer in 1924, the same year as its belated first performance under Malcolm Sargent, and make doubly absorbing listening as they offer us a glimpse into the composer's initial thoughts. Particularly heartwarming here are the two extended love duets for Hugh and Mary ('Ah! Love I've found you' and 'Hugh my lover'), the latter a cunning conflation of the most tenderly lyrical music to be found in Act 2 (culminating in the ecstatic 'O the sky shall be our roof').

Next come two numbers from *Sir John in Love*, including the sublime setting of Ben Jonson's 'See the chariot at hand' from Act 4. Seven songs from *The Pilgrim's Progress* make up the remainder and find Roderick Williams and Sarah Fox both ingratiating in tone and pleasingly articulate. In fact, all four singers acquit themselves with credit, while Iain Burnside's accompaniments are past praise in their scrupulous sensitivity.

Beautifully produced and attractively presented, this likeable anthology deserves to do well – and if it fosters further exploration of VW's operatic output, so much the better!

The Pilgrim's Progress

The Pilgrim's Progress
Gerald Finley bar Pilgrim **Peter Coleman-Wright** bar John Bunyan **Jeremy White** bass Evangelist, Envy, Third Shepherd **Donaldson Bell** bar Pontius Pilate **Gidon Saks** bass Apollyon, Lord Hate-Good,

Mistrust **Richard Coxon** *ten* Pliable, Mister By-Ends
Francis Egerton *ten* Timorous, Usher **Roderick
Williams** *bar* Obstinate, Watchful, First Shepherd
Adrian Thompson *ten* Lord Lechery, Celestial
Messenger **Rebecca Evans** *sop* Madam Wanton,
Shining One **Pamela Helen Stephen** *mez* Madam
Bubble, Shining One, Heavenly Being II **Anne-Marie
Owens** *mez* Madam By-Ends, Pickthank **Christopher
Keyte** *bass* Simon Magus **John Kerr** *bass* Judas
Iscariot **Susan Gritton** *sop* Malice, Bird, Shining One,
Heavenly Being I **Neil Gillespie** *ten* Worldly Glory
Jonathan Fisher *bar* Demas **Mark Padmore** *ten*
Interpreter, Superstition, Second Shepherd **Robert
Hayward** *bar* Herald **Mica Penniman** *sop*
Woodcutter's Boy **Chorus and Orchestra of the
Royal Opera House, Covent Garden /
Richard Hickox**
Chandos ② CHAN9625 (130' · DDD · N/T)   Ⓕ Ⓞ ➔

John Noble was a fine Pilgrim on the old Boult
recording, but Gerald Finley brings not only a
voice that's as good and well suited but also a
dramatic quality that is more colourful and
intense. But Boult's cast is very strong, with
several of the short parts, such as the Herald
('Terence Sharpe') better sung than as here (Robert Hayward). In the Valley of Humiliation the
voice of Apollyon comes as an amplified sound
from off-stage, but on record the trick is to catch
an overpowering terror, and this they managed
better on EMI, partly by virtue of having Robert
Lloyd to strike it, and also by the producer's
decision to bring it closer. Nor, in the comparison, is there any sense of a confrontation of
'bright young feller' and 'grand old fuddy-
duddy'. Boult doesn't *sound* like an old man, any
more than Hickox sounds like a youngster.

Hickox has a big canvas for the recorded
sound, and achieves a clearer texture from
Chandos. The newer version also has Gerald
Finley, and is a fine performance anyway.

The Poisoned Kiss

The Poisoned Kiss
Neal Davies *bar* Dipsacus **Janice Watson** *sop*
Tormentilla **Pamela Helen Stephen** *mez* Angelica
James Gilchrist *ten* Amaryllus **Roderick Williams**
bar Gallanthus **Gail Pearson** *sop* First Medium
Helen Williams *sop* Second Medium **Emer
McGilloway** *sop* Third Medium **Anne Collins**
contr Empress Persicaria **John Graham-Hall** *ten*
Hob **Richard Suart** *bar* Gob **Mark Richardson**
bass Lob **Adrian Partington Singers; BBC
National Orchestra of Wales / Richard Hickox**
Chandos ② CHAN10120; ⊕ CHSA5020
(116' · DDD · N/T)   Ⓕ Ⓞ ➔

Written in the late 1920s when he was at the
height of his powers, *The Poisoned Kiss* is Vaughan
Williams's forgotten opera: this is the first complete recording. The composer chose his friend
Evelyn Sharp to write a libretto based on a short
story by Richard Garnett about a beautiful princess who lives on poison. But the verse treatment
is deplorable. Though the pair had in mind the

operettas of Gilbert and Sullivan, the result is coy
and self-conscious, never witty or pointed in a
Gilbertian way. Vaughan Williams made revisions in 1936 and 1955, but there are still too
many embarrassingly unfunny lines. This recording helps to rehabilitate the opera by eliminating
virtually all the spoken dialogue.

Neither Vaughan Williams nor Sharp could
work out the right balance between comedy and
the central romance – the love between Prince
Amaryllus and Tormentilla, brought up on poison by her magician father, Dipsacus.

Though planned as a light opera, the music has
substance. The score is rich in ideas; each
number is beautifully tailored, never outstaying
its welcome. At almost two hours of music, it has
to be said that the opera is too long (and it would
be even longer with dialogue), but the inspiration never flags.

Charm predominates, with tender melodies
like that in the Act 1 duet of Amaryllus and Tormentilla, 'Blue larkspur in a garden', and a surging emotional climax in the ensemble which
crowns Act 2, when their love leads to the passionate poisoned kiss. There are direct echoes of
Sullivan in the multi-layered ensembles and patter numbers, which come closest to achieving
the lightness aimed at.

Whatever the shortcomings of the piece, no
lover of Vaughan Williams's music should miss
hearing this wonderful set, with a strong and
characterful cast superbly led by Richard Hickox,
and with atmospheric sound enhancing the musical delights. Janice Watson as Tormentilla sings
with sweetness and warmth, while giving point to
the poisonous side of the character, and James
Gilchrist makes an ardent Amaryllus. Pamela
Helen Stephen and Roderick Williams are totally
affecting in their love music, and Neal Davies is
firm and strong as the magician Dipsacus.

Sir John in Love

Sir John in Love
Adrian Thompson *ten* Shallow, Dr Caius **Stephan
Loges** *bar* Shallow, Host **Stephen Varcoe** *bass* Sir
Hugh Evans **Daniel Norman** *ten* Slender **Henry Moss**
ten Peter Simple **Roderick Williams** *bar* Page **Don-
ald Maxwell** *bar* Sir John Falstaff **John Bowen** *ten*
Bardolph **Richard Lloyd-Morgan** *bass* Nym **Brian
Bannatyne-Scott** *bass* Pistol **Susan Gritton** *sop*
Anne Page **Laura Claycomb** *sop* Mrs Page **Sarah
Connolly** *mez* Mrs Ford **Mark Padmore** *ten* Fenton
Mark Richardson *bass* Rugby **Anne-Marie Owens**
mez Mrs Quickly **Matthew Best** *bass* Ford
**The Sinfonia Chorus; Northern Sinfonia /
Richard Hickox**
Chandos ② CHAN9928 (137' · DDD · N/T)   Ⓕ Ⓞ ➔

There's no lack of glorious melody in *Sir John
in Love*, and not just folksong cunningly interwoven. Musically, what comes over strongly, more
richly than ever before in this magnificent recording from Richard Hickox, is the way
that the writing anticipates later Vaughan Williams, not just the radiant composer of the Fifth

Symphony and *Serenade to Music*, with key-changes of heartstopping beauty, but the composer's darker side, with sharply rhythmic writing.

The work's title, *Sir John in Love*, points to Vaughan Williams's different approach to the central character. With him Shakespeare's fat knight isn't just comic but a believable lover, more genial and expansive than in Boito's portrait, yet hardly a noble figure such as Elgar portrayed in his big symphonic study. Donald Maxwell makes a splendid Falstaff, relishing the comedy without making it a caricature. Above all, his full, dark voice is satisfyingly fat-sounding. On the only previous recording, the vintage EMI set of 1974, Raimund Herincx gave a finely detailed performance, but lacked that important quality. The 1974 set certainly stands the test of time remarkably well, but the extra fullness and richness of the Chandos sound coupled with as keen a concern for the atmospheric beauties of the score, notably in offstage effects, gives the new set an obvious advantage. Interpretatively, Hickox is just as incisive as Meredith Davies on EMI in bringing out the sharper side of the score, though he's more warmly expressive, a degree more affectionate in drawing out the glowing lyricism.

Chandos's casting is satisfyingly consistent, with no weak link. Matthew Best may be rather gruff at times as Ford, but that's very much in character, when, if anything, he's more venomous here than in Verdi, until at the start of Act 3 Vaughan Williams allows a wonderful duet of reconciliation with Mrs Ford, 'Pardon me, wife'.

As Ursula Vaughan Williams reported, her husband wrote *Sir John in Love* 'entirely for his own enjoyment', because he was in love with the subject. And from first to last this new set reflects that.

Giuseppe Verdi   Italian 1813-1901

The greatest of Italian opera composers was the son of a village inn-keeper and began his long musical career as an organist, taking over the duties at the local church when still a small child. His father sent him off to Busseto for formal music studies, thence (1821) to the home of Antonio Barezzi, a local merchant and patron of music. Barezzi supplied the funds for the young Verdi to progress to the Milan Conservatory where his protégé failed the entrance examination due to 'lack of piano technique and technical knowledge' according to some sources, 'over age and insufficiently gifted' according to others.

Verdi persevered in his ambitions by taking private lessons. After his studies with one Vincenzo Lavigna, from whom he acquired a thorough mastery of counterpoint, fugue and canon, Verdi applied for the post of maestro di musica in Busseto. He was turned down but instead appointed director of the Philharmonic Society.

In 1836 he married Margherita Barezzi, the daughter of his patron, but tragedy intervened: their two infant children died and in 1840 his beloved young wife died of encephalitis. During these four

years he had completed his first opera, Oberto, conte di San Bonifacio, and moved to Milan; La Scala mounted the work with some success and Verdi was given a contract to write more for the opera house. He was 27. His last opera, Falstaff, would be mounted at the same theatre in 1893 when he was 80.

Un giorno di regno, a comic opera, completed in the face of personal tragedy, was produced in 1840 but was a fiasco. Its failure convinced Verdi he should abandon his operatic ambitions but the impresario Merelli persuaded him to undertake a third work, this time using the biblical subject of Nabucodonosor – or Nebuchadnezzar – later shortened to Nabucco. It was a turning point in Verdi's career and also for Italian opera. Here, for the first time, he found his own individual voice (though still much influenced by Rossini and Donizetti); here was the successor to Bellini and Donizetti, and Verdi's fame spread throughout Italy. His next success, again a historical subject, came with I Lombardi alla prima Crociata, followed by another based on Victor Hugo's drama Ernani. This time the subject was more overtly political, the life of a revolutionary outlaw, and the work was acclaimed.

For the next eight years from 1851, one opera followed another with varied success. During a stay in Paris where a French production of I Lombardi was being given (renamed Jérusalem), Verdi renewed his acquaintance with the soprano Giuseppina Strepponi who had created the role of Abigaille in the original production of Nabucco. After living together for several years, the couple were married in Savoy in 1859. By then, Verdi had written the three masterpieces that were to make him famous throughout the civilised world. The fact is that none of the subsequent operas had come close to the successes of Nabucco and Ernani. Then, using another drama by Victor Hugo, Le roi s'amuse, he composed Rigoletto. Soon every barrel organ in Europe was playing 'La donna è mobile', the teasing aria of the lecherous Duke. Neither this number (which Verdi kept under wraps until the dress rehearsal for fear that someone would steal what he knew to be a hit tune!) or, indeed, the whole opera show any sign of diminishing in popularity 150 years later.

Rigoletto alone would have been enough to perpetuate his name as a fine composer of operas and Verdi would have ended up as another Mascagni or Leoncavallo. But to follow that with two more masterpieces (and within the space of a couple of years) and still have some of his greatest works ahead of him guaranteed him a place among the immortals of music. Il trovatore received its first performance in Rome in January 1853; La traviata followed less than two months later in Venice. By the age of 40 he had eclipsed Meyerbeer as the most acclaimed living composer of opera.

Two years elapsed before his next work, his first opera in French, Les Vêpres siciliennes, which was given a rousing reception at its premiere in Paris in 1855, despite the fact that it dealt with the slaughter in medieval times of the French army of occupation in Sicily. Another two years, another triumph: Simon Boccanegra (1857). The pattern was repeated by the first performance in 1859 of Un ballo in maschera.

Verdi was a fervent supporter of the Risorgimento, the reorganisation of the numerous small Italian states into one country. The theme of resurgent nationalism in his early operas, the frequent clashes with the censor (who suspected him of revolutionary tendencies), his political career in the 1860s when he sat for five years as a deputy in that part of Italy already unified – all these things endeared him to the general public. The symbol of the nationalist movement was Vittorio Emmanuel, the future King of Italy. By coincidence, the initials V-E-R-D-I stood for 'Vittorio Emmanuel, Re D'Italia' and everywhere, all over Italy, the composer's name / political slogan was to be seen. The cries of 'Viva Verdi' could be heard as vociferously in the opera house as in the street. Verdi, however, disliked direct involvement with politics and withdrew from the first Italian parliament. (He was made a Senator in 1874, an honorary office which made no demands on him.)

During the summers, he and Giuseppina lived on a huge farm in Sant' Agata, enjoying a simple peasant existence. The winters were spent in their palatial home in Genoa. His frequent foreign travels included a special trip to St Petersburg to see the first performance of his latest creation, La forza del destino, which the Imperial Opera had commissioned.

The next milestone in Verdi's grand procession was his flawed masterpiece Don Carlos (1867), a huge, sprawling affair subject to revisions and cuts (it was not given in its original version until a century after the premiere) which many opera lovers cite as the zenith of grand opera. In most people's minds, though, it is his next creation that embodies all that Grand Opera should be.

Verdi was commissioned by the Khedive (Viceroy) of Egypt to write a piece for the new opera house in Cairo. He requested a fee of $20,000, an enormous amount in those days, and received it without a murmur. Though the score of Aida was completed by 1870, the premiere had to wait until Christmas Eve 1871. The first performance was an international event but Verdi, who hated such glitzy occasions and loathed travelling by sea even more, refused to attend the first performance. Instead, he stayed in Milan to rehearse the singers for the forthcoming Italian premiere of Aida. The Khedive's assistant wired him from Cairo that the reaction had been one of 'total fanaticism…we have had success beyond belief'.

The death of the Italian poet and patriot Manzoni in 1873 prompted Verdi to write his great Messa da Requiem. Then, for the next 13 years, he retired to the country and wrote nothing. It would have been reasonable to expect no more but, using a fine adaptation by Arrigo Boito of Shakespeare's Othello, he entered a notable Indian summer.

Verdi was 79 when he completed his final opera, Falstaff, using material from The Merry Wives of Windsor and Henry IV, another collaboration with Boito. These two works constitute the high-points of Italian opera, showing that Verdi's creative powers, far from waning, had increased. After the premiere of Falstaff, the King of Italy offered to ennoble him and make him Marchese di Busseto but Verdi declined. 'Io son un paesano,' he told Victor Emmanuel.

Giuseppina died from pneumonia in November 1897. Verdi was desolate and gradually lost the will to live, his sight and hearing deteriorated and he suffered paralysis but, setting aside 2,500,000 lire,

he founded the Casa di Riposa per Musicisti in Milan, a home for aged musicians. It is still in operation, supported by his royalties. In 1898 he composed his last work, the Four Sacred Songs. He spent the Christmas of 1900 visiting his adopted daughter in Milan. It was here, at the Grand Hotel, that he died from a sudden stroke. He was 87. A quarter of a million people followed his funeral cortège on the way to his final resting place in the grounds of the Casa di Riposa.

Overtures and Preludes

Overtures and Preludes – Oberto; Un giorno di regno; Nabucco; Ernani; Giovanna d'Arco; Alzira; Attila; I Masnadieri; Macbeth; Il corsaro; La battaglia di Legnano; Luisa Miller; Rigoletto; La traviata; I Vespri siciliani; Un ballo in maschera; La forza del destino; Aida
Berlin Philharmonic Orchestra / Herbert von Karajan
DG ② 453 058-2GTA2 (113' · ADD)
Recorded 1975   Ⓜ Ⓞ➔

Karajan was one of the most adaptable and sensitive of dramatic conductors. His repertoire in the theatre is extraordinarily wide, and he's at home equally in Verdi, Wagner, Richard Strauss and Puccini. In this celebrated 1975 collection of all Verdi's overtures, he gives us some fine insights into the composer's skill as an orchestrator, dramatist and poet. Though Karajan had only recorded Aida complete his dramatic instincts bring some fine performances of the lesser-known preludes. The earliest, Nabucco from 1842 (the collection is arranged chronologically), already shows a master craftsman at work, with a slow introduction promising much. La traviata shows a quite different skill – the delicate creation of a sensitive poet working in filigree. The final four preludes are great works fully worthy of this individual presentation. Even the lesser-known preludes are enhanced by Karajan's dramatic instincts. Good recordings, though less than outstanding.

Messa da Requiem

Messa da Requiem
Anja Harteros sop **Sonia Ganassi** mez **Rolando Villazón** ten **René Pape** bass **Chorus and Orchestra of the Accademia Nazionale di Santa Cecilia / Antonio Pappano**
EMI ② 698936-2 (84' · DDD · T/t)
Recorded live 2009   Ⓕ ⓄⓄⓄ➔

Ⓖ Three recordings stand out as landmark achievements: Toscanini's live 1951 Carnegie Hall performance, Giulini's 1963-64 studio recording, and the 1992 John Eliot Gardiner. To which we can now add, as a superbly realised garnering of these accumulated insights, this exceptionally fine new Pappano set.

Toscanini's performance represented the old authenticity. Toscanini played for Verdi and knew the tradition from within. He conducted the Requiem with Italian singers and an unremitting intensity, born in part of a desire to honour the often surprisingly brisk metronome marks. It was Giulini who forged another way, more Catholic and more considered, in a reading that opened out the work's meditative aspect, marrying broad tempi in the lyric sections to a powerfully argued dramatic continuum organically evolved.

So concentrated an approach places great demands on the solo quartet and here Giulini set the bar high in terms of both the quality of the voices needed and their blend. Without these qualities – Gardiner's soloists have them and so in remarkable measure do Pappano's – the Holy Grail of a near-perfect Verdi Requiem will always be a distant dream.

Gardiner further developed our sense of the multi-layered skill of Verdi's vocal writing. His expert shaping of the vocal lines – tempi finely judged, often broad, never metronomically driven – revealed the work occupying spaces which Bruckner or Fauré might have been pleased to inhabit. And now Pappano follows suit. The Monteverdi Choir, you might think, would have a head start over Rome's Santa Cecilia Chorus; yet it is a sign of how far choral singing has come in recent years that nowadays even an Italian opera chorus is not easily outmanoeuvred. The Santa Cecilia *Sanctus*, defter than Giulini's, is almost as dancingly precise as Gardiner's. Moulding vocal and instrumental lines with an authentically Italianate feel is important to any performance of the Requiem. Second nature to Toscanini and Giulini, it is a quality that contributes hugely to the eloquence and allure of Pappano's performance. You hear this early in the sense of a live narrative unfolding which mezzo-soprano Sonia Ganassi brings to the 'Liber scriptus'. Fine as Gardiner's Anne Sofie von Otter is at this point, the manner is a degree or two less Italianate.

Ganassi's soprano partner is Anja Harteros. Where Giulini sought fuller voices – Elisabeth Schwarzkopf and Christa Ludwig, both flawless and richly involving – Harteros's lighter yet similarly accomplished singing, radiant and sympathetic, suits Pappano's reading to perfection: part and parcel of the wonderful blend within the quartet. It was Giulini's Nicolai Gedda who showed how the tenor is more an inspiring presence than an egregious showstopper. Rolando Villazón is similarly discreet in the self-abasing loveliness of his 'Ingemisco' and the proffered quiet of the 'Hostias'. Meanwhile, the bass René Pape is as fine as any on record, strong yet discreet, with a mastery of the subtly inflected *cantabile* line that is profoundly satisfying. As with Alastair Miles's not dissimilar performance under Gardiner, this is markedly different from the Commendatore-like manner of Giulini's Nicolai Ghiaurov.

Where London's Kingsway Hall barely contained the might of Giulini's reading, Rome's superb new Parco della Musica auditorium is all clarity and ease, as sympathetic to the Lieder-like musings of the *Agnus Dei* as it is to the decibel-fuelled fires of the 'Dies irae'. Pappano's all-inclusive reading needs both.

The sole reservation concerns the opening. The composer Ildebrando Pizzetti spoke of the Requiem beginning 'like the murmur of an invisible crowd'. Even so, you will have difficulty hearing anything on the new set much before bar 6. What one misses here is the old Italian way of suggesting intense quiet with a *pianissimo* that truly sounds. Pappano's tempo for the first 77 bars is not, by post-Toscanini standards, unduly slow yet on this occasion it is only with the arrival of the tenor's cry of 'Kyrie' that the great musical journey really begins.

That apart, it is wonderful to hear the Requiem so memorably revealed as the dramatic and meditative masterpiece it clearly is.

Verdi Messa da Requiem[b]. I Vespri siciliani – Overture[c] **Schubert** Mass No 6 in E flat, D950[a]
[a]**Anne Pashley**, [b]**Amy Shuard** sops [a]**Sybil Michelow**, [b]**Anna Reynolds** mezs [a]**David Hughes**, [b]**Richard Lewis**, [a]**Duncan Robertson** tens [a]**William McCue**, [b]**David Ward** basses [a]**Scottish Festival Chorus**, [a]**New Philharmonia Orchestra; Philharmonia** [b]**Chorus and** [b,c]**Orchestra / Carlo Maria Giulini**
BBC Legends BBCL4029-2 (153' · ADD)
Recorded live [b,c]1963, [a]1968   Ⓜ❍❍❍

In Great Britain in the 1960s, the art of large-scale choral singing reached what was arguably its apogee with the work of the two choruses featured here: the Philharmonia Chorus, directed by Wilhelm Pitz, and the Edinburgh Festival Chorus, directed by Arthur Oldham. Even allowing for the fact that this Prom performance of the Verdi Requiem was given around the time of an intensive period of rehearsal during which the EMI studio recording was also being made, the Philharmonia Chorus's singing is stunningly good: first-rate diction, impeccable intonation, fine dynamic control and absolute involvement in the music as Giulini relays it to them.

In the Schubert Mass the Edinburgh Festival Chorus acquits itself magnificently. Giulini's reading is powerful and reverential, one in which the chorus comes to speak with the single voice of an individual believer.

The Verdi is superbly recorded. The unnamed BBC team working live in the Royal Albert Hall produce sound that's focused yet open, clear but warm. Giulini's reading of the Requiem, thrilling yet humane, is precisely the one we hear on EMI's recording, with the Philharmonia Chorus and Orchestra as expert live as they are on record (the orchestral playing is well-nigh flawless). Of the solo singers, the youngest, Anna Reynolds, could have gone straight into the EMI recording, so well does she sing. Richard Lewis, nearing the end of his career, is less gorgeous of voice than EMI's Nicolai Gedda, but the bass, David Ward, here at the height of his powers, is more than a match for the younger Nicolai Ghiaurov. Amy

Shuard and EMI's Elisabeth Schwarzkopf are complementary. Shuard is technically fine; very much the real thing dramatically and absolutely right for the live performance. In short, this is an indispensable set.

Messa da Requiem
Angela Gheorghiu *sop* **Daniela Barcellona** *mez*
Roberto Alagna *ten* **Julian Konstantinov** *bass*
Swedish Radio Chorus; Berlin Philharmonic Orchestra / Claudio Abbado
Video director **Bob Coles**
EMI **DVD** 492693-9 (89' · 16:9 · 2.0, 5.1 & DTS 5.1 · 0)   Ⓕ**O**

Seeing makes a deal of difference here. Though the CD issue of this performance at the Philharmonie, Berlin, in January 2001 was hugely enjoyable, this DVD enables one actually to see how the recently sick Abbado conducts the work as if it might be the last thing he does (happily not the case). He looks gaunt and tense: that translates into a heaven-seeking, searing account of the work, one to which everyone taking part readily responds. All the singers and players perform as though their lives depended on the outcome, and the results are simply electrifying.

Praise can't be too high for the two professional choirs or for the Berlin Philharmonic who, technically and emotionally, give their all. The soloists also seem on a devotional high, singing with appropriately spiritual fervour so that incidental criticisms seem of no importance. Bob Coles's video direction is always in the right place at the right time, and the sound perspective is as excellent as on the CD.

Messa da Requiem
Leontyne Price *sop* **Fiorenza Cossotto** *mez* **Luciano Pavarotti** *ten* **Nicolai Ghiaurov** *bass* **Chorus and Orchestra of La Scala, Milan / Herbert von Karajan**
Video director **Henri-Georges Clouzot**
DG **DVD** 073 4055GH (83' · NTSC · 4:3 · PCM stereo and DTS 5.1 · 0)   Ⓕ**OO**

This film of the Verdi Requiem was made under studio conditions, in an empty La Scala before a concert in 1967 in memory of Toscanini's death a decade earlier. In his vision of this work, Henri-Georges Clouzot sees ranks of choristers – from heaven or hell – with Price and Cossotto framed by the sopranos' hands and grey silk wraps beneath like angels' wings, double basses angled heavenwards, Karajan's quiff with a life of its own, his profile at home among all those Roman (and Milanese) noses.

Price is simply magnificent but Karajan colludes with Cossotto (in a lovely black empire-line number) in letting her steal the show, as the two of them warm every line with intimate little touches: the 'Recordare' and 'Lux aeterna' are rapt highlights. Pavarotti, clutching a score like a votive offering, looks out of his depth in such company but he shades the opening phrase of 'Hostias' with all the subtlety at his disposal.

VERDI MESSA DA REQUIEM – IN BRIEF

Santa Cecilia Chor & Orch / Antonio Pappano
EMI ② 698936-2 (84' · DDD · T/t)   Ⓕ**OOO**▶
A magnificent achievement that leaps straight to the top of the best modern versions.

Philharmonia Orchestra / Carlo Maria Giulini
BBC Legends ② BBCL4029-2 (153' · ADD)   Ⓜ**OOO**
Of the several performances by Giulini currently in circulation, this one arguably has the most atmosphere and the best sound. It's a live relay of a concert he gave at the Royal Albert Hall with British soloists in the run up to his starrier studio recording.

Berlin PO / Claudio Abbado
EMI ② 557168-2 (84' · DDD)   Ⓕ**O**▶
A live recording, also available on DVD, to mark the occasion of the 100th anniversary of the composer's death. The conductor's searing intensity reflects his own recent brush with mortality. The soloists, Angela Gheorghiu in particular, are excellent too.

La Scala Chorus and Orchestra / Riccardo Muti
EMI ② 749390-2 (88' · DDD)   Ⓕ**O**▶
Muti's second recording is an authentically Italian affair on a big operatic scale, with sometimes histrionic extremes of tempo and Pavarotti in the line-up of soloists. The recorded sound conveys the spaciousness of the venue at some expense of detail.

Orchestre Révolutionnaire et Romantique / Sir John Eliot Gardiner
Philips ② 442 142-2PH2 (120' · DDD)   Ⓕ**OO**▶
Gardiner's historically aware set has many assets: uncommonly accurate choral singing, a cleaned-up text, the widest dynamic range and traditionally broad tempi. The makeweight is an unbeatable *Four Sacred Pieces*.

Hungarian State Opera / Pier Giorgio Morandi
Naxos ② 8 550944/5 (126' · DDD)   Ⓢ**O**▶
A super-budget account with youthful sounding soloists and effective, if not ideally focused choral forces.

Cologne RSO / Semyon Bychkov
Profil ② PH08036 (81' · DDD)   Ⓜ**OO**▶
A supremely well directed Requiem, scrupulously observed, meticulously prepared, vivid, lucid, forward-moving.

NBC SO / Arturo Toscanini
RCA mono ⑫ 82876 67893-2 (141' · ADD)   Ⓢ**O**
Toscanini's searingly intense RCA version of 1951 is considered a classic of the gramophone; his singers are Nelli, Barbieri, di Stefano and Siepi. Available in an 12-CD set of all of Toscanini's Verdi recordings, but also on a variety of other labels.

Ragged choral work and occasional dead spots notwithstanding – the 'Quam olim' and *Sanctus* seem handled rather than shaped – Clouzot's and Karajan's achievement has the authentic sniff of pathos. Even Toscanini might have given grudging approval.

Additional recommendations

Milanov *sop* Thorborg *mez* Rosvaenge *ten* Ⓗ
Moscona *bass* **BBC Symphony Chorus and Orchestra / Arturo Toscanini**
Testament mono ② SBT21362 (89' · ADD · N/T/t).
Recorded live at the Queen's Hall, London,
on May 27, 1938   Ⓜ

Skilfully remastered from BBC originals, this is a superior performance to Toscanini's familiar RCA version of 1951 simply because he gives the music more time to breathe. He imposes a unified and beseeching style on all his charges, impressing on them his own awe before Verdi's score.

Opera Choruses

Un ballo in maschera – Posa in pace. Don Carlos – Spuntato ecco vi di. Aida – Gloria all' Egitto. I Lombardi – Gerusalem!; O Signore, dal tetto natio. Macbeth – Tre volte miagola; Patria oppressa. I masnadieri – Le rube, gli stupri. Nabucco – Gli arredi festivi giù cadano infranti; Va, pensiero, sull'ali dorate. Otello – Fuoco di gioia. Rigoletto – Zitti zitti. La traviata[a] – Noi siamo zingarelle…Di Madride nio siam mattadori. Il trovatore – Vedi! Le fosche notturne spoglie; Squilli, echeggi la tromba guerriera. Requiem – Sanctus
[a]**Marsha Waxman** *mez* [a]**David Huneryager**, [a]**Richard Cohn** *basses* **Chicago Symphony Chorus and Orchestra / Sir Georg Solti**
Decca 430 226-2DH (70' · DDD · T)   ⒻⓄ➔

Verdi's opera choruses are invariably red-blooded and usually make a simple dramatic statement with great impact. The arresting Chorus of the Hebrew Slaves from *Nabucco* is probably the best-known and most popular chorus in the entire operatic repertoire, immediately tugging at the heart-strings with its gentle opening cantilena, soon swelling out to a great climax. Solti shows just how to shape the noble melodic line, which soars with firm control, yet retaining the urgency and electricity in every bar. The dramatic contrasts at the opening of 'Gerusalem!' from *I Lombardi* are equally powerfully projected, and the brass again makes a riveting effect in 'Patria oppressa' from *Macbeth*. But not all Verdi choruses offer blood and thunder: the volatile Fire chorus from *Otello* flickers with an almost visual fantasy, while the wicked robbers in *I Masnadieri* celebrate their excesses gleefully, and with such rhythmic jauntiness that you can't quite take them seriously. The Gypsies' chorus from *La traviata* has a nice touch of elegance, and the *scherzo*-like *Sanctus* from the Requiem is full of joy. But it's the impact of the

dramatic moments that's most memorable, not least the big triumphal scene from *Aida*, complete with the ballet music, to provide a diverse interlude in the middle. The recording is in the demonstration class.

Opera Duets

Aida[a] – La fatal pietra; Morir si pura e bella; O terra addio[b]. Don Carlo – E dessa!…Un detto, un sol; Vago sogno m'arrise; Ma lassù vi cedremo. I Lombardi[a] – Oh belle, a questa misera; All' armi! I Masnadieri – Qual mare, qual terra; Qui nel bosco?; Lassù risplendere. Otello – Già nella notte densa; Venga la morte!. Rigoletto – Ah! veglia, o donna; Signor ne principe; T'amo! T'amo; E il sol dell' anima; Addio, addio[c]. Simon Boccanegra – Cielo di stelle orbato; Vieni a mirar la cerula. La traviata[a] – Libiamo, ne' lieti calici. Il trovatore[a] – Miserere…Ah, che la morte ognora. I Vespri siciliani – Pensando a me!
Angela Gheorghiu *sop* **Roberto Alagna** *ten*
[bc]**Sara Mingardo** *mez* [c]**Brian Parsons**, [c]**Rodney Gibson** *tens* [ab]**London Voices; Berlin Philharmonic Orchestra / Claudio Abbado**
EMI 556656-2 (70' · DDD)   ⒻⓄⓄ➔

This long, fascinating, highly ambitious recital is nothing less than a conspectus of Verdi's soprano-tenor duets, and is executed with distinction on all sides. Gheorghiu deserves particular plaudits. It seems that nothing in Verdi (and indeed in much else) is beyond her capabilities. Her singing here, especially as Gilda, Aida and Desdemona, is so exquisite, the tone so warm and limpid, the phrasing so shapely as surely to melt any heart. Take, for example, Gilda's touching exchanges with Giovanna, herself sung by the superb mezzo Sara Mingardo, the whole of Aida's solo beginning 'Presago il core', with the soprano's warm lower register coming into play and that ultimate test, Desdemona's poised 'Amen'. Throughout, both musically and interpretatively, she simply can't be faulted.

Neither she nor her husband is backward in coming forward with less hackneyed pieces, those from the early operas – try the section starting 'Ma un' iri di pace' in the *Masnadieri* duet, the two voices in ideal blend, phrases and tone sweetly shaded with the following cabaletta all light eagerness on both sides. Then there's plangent singing on both sides in the sad little piece from *Vespri*, though it's a pity they did not attempt this in the original French. Here and throughout Alagna is his customary self, assured (a few over-pressed high notes, some unwritten, apart), impassioned, thoughtful and accurate in his phraseology, nowhere more so than in the parts he's unlikely as yet to take on stage – Radames and Otello. Even more important in so many passages, Alagna finds the right *mezzo-piano*, where heavier tenors have to sing *forte*, notably in the closing phrases where Otello wafts his love of Desdemona on to the night air – a moment of sheer magic.

Abbado and the Berlin Philharmonic Orchestra are at their peak of achievement and the recording catches these voices in their full glory, making this a most desirable issue.

Opera Arias

Un ballo in maschera – Ecco l'orrido campo…Ma dall'arido stelo divulsa…Morrò, ma prima in grazia. La forza del destino – Pace, pace, mio Dio. Nabucco – Ben io t'invenni…Anch'io dischiuso un giorno. La traviata – E strano!…Ah, fors'è lui…Follie! Sempre libera[a]; Teneste la promessa…Addio del passato. Il trovatore – Tacea la notte placida…Di tale amor; Timor di me?…D'amor sull'ali rosee
Julia Varady sop [a]**Lothar Odinius** ten **Bavarian State Orchestra / Dietrich Fischer-Dieskau**
Orfeo C186 951 (51' · DDD)　　　　　Ⓕ🔾

Varady endows these arias we have heard hundreds of times, and of which we all have our favourite memories and recordings, with renewed life through an art which is fully responsive, highly fastidious, lovely in the quality of its sound and individual in its timbre and inflection. The beauty of tone is evident first of all in its well-preserved purity (and Varady, born in 1941, is of an age when normally allowances have to be made). Hers isn't a full-bodied, rich Ponselle-like voice, but she makes wonderfully effective use of her resources, which include a surprisingly strong lower register and an upward range that (as we hear) easily encompasses the high D flat and has an E flat available. She's dramatic in style yet also thoroughly accomplished in her scales, trills and other *fioriture*. Her first *Trovatore* aria, for instance, includes the cabaletta with its full complement of technical brilliances. The musical instinct seems almost infallible – a 'wrong' *portamento* or *rubato* always irritates and here everything seems just right. A remarkable sensitivity is at work throughout.

The orchestra is conducted by Fischer-Dieskau, Varady's husband, and here too is a fine example of a positive, non-routine collaboration, the pacing and shading of the orchestral parts so frequently having something specific to offer (for example, in the Letter passage from *La traviata*). The recording is well balanced.

Aida

Aida　　　　　　　　　　　　　　　Ⓗ
Maria Callas sop Aida **Fedora Barbieri** mez Amneris **Richard Tucker** ten Radames **Tito Gobbi** bar Amonasro **Giuseppe Modesti** bass Ramphis **Nicola Zaccaria** bass King of Egypt **Elvira Galassi** sop Priestess **Franco Ricciardi** ten Messenger **Chorus and Orchestra of La Scala, Milan / Tullio Serafin**
EMI mono ② 562678-2 or Regis RRC2074
(144' · ADD · T/t). Recorded 1955　Ⓕ/Ⓢ🔾🔾🔾➔

Callas's Aida is an assumption of total understanding and conviction; the growth from a slave-girl torn between love for her homeland and Radames, to a woman whose feelings tran-

scend life itself represents one of the greatest operatic undertakings ever committed to disc. Alongside her is Fedora Barbieri, an Amneris palpable in her agonised mixture of love and jealousy – proud yet human. Tucker's Radames is powerful and Gobbi's Amonasro quite superb – a portrayal of comparable understanding to set alongside Callas's Aida.

Tullio Serafin's reading is in the central Italian tradition of 50 years ago. That's to say, it's unobtrusively right in matters of tempo, emphasis and phrasing, while occasionally passing indifferent ensemble in the choral and orchestral contribution. Although the recording can't compete with modern versions (it was never, in fact, a model of clarity), nowhere can it dim the brilliance of the creations conjured up by this classic cast.

Aida
Birgit Nilsson sop Aida **Grace Bumbry** mez Amneris **Franco Corelli** ten Radames **Mario Sereni** bar Amonasro **Bonaldo Giaiotti** bass Ramfis **Ferruccio Mazzoli** bass King **Piero de Palma** ten Messenger **Mirella Fiorentini** mez Priestess **Chorus and Orchestra of Rome Opera / Zubin Mehta**
EMI ② 358645-2. Recorded 1966　　　Ⓜ➔

In the 1950s and '60s EMI made a series of what have become classics with Rome Opera forces that have Verdi in their blood. This *Aida*, greeted with reservations then, now seems like manna from heaven in a world starved of true Verdian voices. Above all there's Corelli's truly *spinto* tenor, a thrilling sound in itself, and used, as Radames (one of the most exciting on disc), with far more sensitivity than is usually allowed for. Nilsson matches Corelli in vocal bite and gets inside the character, even if she's a touch unwieldy at times. As on stage, Bumbry is an imposing, spirited Amneris, Sereni makes an above-average Amonasro and Giaiotti sounds like Pinza as Ramfis – praise can't be higher. The young Zubin Mehta conducts with a deal of dramatic verve. The recording is excellent.

Aida
Anna Tomowa-Sintow sop Aida **Brigitte Fassbaender** mez Amneris **Plácido Domingo** ten Radames **Siegmund Nimsgern** bar Amonasro **Robert Lloyd** bass Ramfis **Nikolaus Hillebrand** bass King **Norbert Orth** ten Messenger **Marianne Seibel** sop Priestess; **Bavarian State Opera Chorus and Orchestra / Riccardo Muti**
Orfeo d'Or ② C583 022I (143' · ADD · N)
Recorded live 1979　　　　　　　　Ⓕ🔾

Riccardo Muti's 1974 studio recording on EMI, with Caballé, Cossotto and Domingo, has been one of the steady recommendations for this work on CD. This live account from 1979 in many but not all ways surpasses the studio performance. In the first place, Muti's reading has matured to the extent of being less wilful – for

VERDI AIDA – IN BRIEF

Anna Tomowa-Sintow *Aida* **Brigitte Fassbaender** *Amneris* **Siegmund Nimsgern** *Amonasro* **Bavarian State Opera Chorus and Orchestra / Riccardo Muti**
Orfeo ② C583 022I (143' · ADD)　　Ⓜ❍

Under Riccardo Muti's vivid direction an already special cast gains greatly from the excitement of a live recording, worth the very few flaws in voice and recording.

Maria Callas *Aida* **Fedora Barbieri** *Amneris* **Ⓗ Tito Gobbi** *Amonasro* **Chorus and Orchestra of La Scala, Milan / Tulio Serafin**
EMI ② 556316-2 (144' · AAD)　　Ⓕ❍❍▷

Maria Callas's blazing yet vulnerable Aida heads a cast of great names, conducted with real grandeur by Serafin. Only the mono recording is any drawback.

Birgit Nilsson *Aida* **Grace Bumbry** *Amneris* **Mario Sereni** *Amonasro* **Rome Opera Chorus and Orchestra / Zubin Mehta**
EMI ② 358645-2 (141' · ADD)　　Ⓑ❍▷

Nilsson and Corelli are a vocally towering pair of lovers, along with Bumbry's rich Amneris the main attractions of a cast that otherwise ranges from excellent to acceptable.

Leontyne Price *Aida* **Rita Gorr** *Amneris* **Robert Merrill** *Amonasro* **Rome Opera Chorus and Orchestra / Sir Georg Solti**
Decca ② 460 765-2DF2 (152' · ADD)　　Ⓜ▷

Two superlative voices, Leontyne Price a sensuous, dark-toned Aida, and Vickers a steely yet tormented Radames, with strong support from Rita Gorr's Amneris and Robert Merrill's bluff Amonasro. Solti's conducting is electrifyingly dramatic.

Adina Aaron *Aida* **Kate Aldrich** *Amneris* **Giuseppe Garra** *Amonasro* **Arturo Toscanini Foundation Chorus and Orchestra / Massimiliano Stefaneli**
TDK ▦ DV-AIDDB (188')　　Ⓕ

Aida works unexpectedly well in the smaller scale, in a good-looking 'traditional' staging by Franco Zeffirelli with a non-starry but immensely vital young cast, in the theatre at Verdi's birthplace Busseto.

Aprile Millo *Aida* **Dolora Zajick** *Amneris* **Sherrill Milnes** *Amonasro* **Metropolitan Opera Chorus and Orchestra / James Levine**
DG ▦ 073 001-9GH (158')　　Ⓕ

The Met's staging is on a suitably Pharaonic scale, although the spectacularly authentic sets aren't matched by the rather silly costumes. Domingo, though below his best, is a splendid Radames, and, while local girl Millo isn't as expressive as some, she's still involving. Levine conducts with epic grandeur but too little *brio*.

instance, his tempo for the closing scene's 'O terra addio' is the better for being more orthodox – and even more persuasive in terms of fulfilling Verdi's exacting demands on all concerned. Seldom can the full panoply and subtlety of the composer's scoring, especially the wonderful wind writing, have been so clearly expounded. The chorus is also commendable in every respect.

Domingo, fine enough on EMI, here gives possibly his most responsive and exciting Radames on disc and that's saying something. In tremendous voice, he produces magic towards the end of 'Celeste Aida' with the triple *pianissimo* Verdi asks for but seldom gets, and throughout he makes every effort to fulfil Verdi's demand for *dolce* and *pp* effects. It hardly needs saying that he was at the time at the peak of his amazing powers.

Tomowa-Sintow provides most of the heft combined with sensibility that the title-part calls for. Although she can't manage Caballé's many exquisite moments when she floats her tone on high, she has the firmer, stronger voice to ride the orchestra at climactic moments. You don't quite feel the strong identification with the part that Fassbaender undoubtedly gives to her first Amneris. Fassbaender is very much her idiosyncratic, wholly compelling self, rising to heights of music-drama in Amneris's great Act 4 scene, the repeated 'io stessa…lo getta' rending the heart. This is an interpretation to savour.

The recording, although the voices are sometimes a little distanced, catches the high excitement of a first night in the opera house. Applause is never intrusive, scenery change only once so. This is as gripping an account of the piece of any on disc.

Aida
Adina Aaron *sop* Aida **Kate Aldrich** *mez* Amneris **Scott Piper** *ten* Radames **Giuseppe Garra** *bar* Amonasro **Enrico Giuseppe Iori** *bass* Ramfis **Paolo Pecchioli** *bass* King **Stefano Pisani** *ten* Messenger **Micaela Patriarca** *sop* Priestess **Arturo Toscanini Foundation Chorus and Orchestra / Massimiliano Stefanelli**
Stage and video director **Franco Zeffirelli**
TDK ② DVD DV-AIDDB (3h 8' · 4:3 · 2.0 & 5.1 · 0)
Includes documentary, 'The Making of Aida'　　Ⓕ❍

Who would have imagined that this performance, which took place at Verdi's birthplace, Busseto, in January 2001 to mark the centenary of the composer's death, would carry such an emotional charge and evince such dramatic truthfulness? The performers are young singers gathered together under the auspices of the Toscanini Foundation and under the artistic direction of tenor Carlo Bergonzi, and of Franco Zeffirelli who directs the performance. It took place in the small gem of a 19th-century theatre at Busseto, not the most likely venue for such a grand opera, yet the very confinement of the surroundings forces everyone to rethink the work on a more intimate scale and in doing so they manage to go to the heart of the matter.

Adina Aaron is already a complete Aida. Every gesture, every movement, every note seems to come from the very soul of her being and her naturally shaped singing and sheer beauty of tone bespeak an auspicious future. As moving an Aida in fact since the young Leontyne Price.

Kate Aldrich as Amneris is very nearly as impressive. Possessor of a strikingly beautiful mezzo and the wherewithal to project it, she conveys every facet of the tormented Princess's predicament with total conviction. As Amonasro, Giuseppe Garra discloses a strong, vibrant baritone in the best traditions of his kind and he, like everyone else, acts with complete conviction. If the Radames, Scott Piper, another singer keen to obey Verdi's markings – witness a *pp* high B flat at the end of 'Celeste Aida' – was slightly less impressive, it's only because his voice is at present one size too small for the role. The orchestra plays with every fibre of its collective being for its committed conductor. Zeffirelli directs stage and film alike with all the experience at his command. The sound is a shade boxy, surely due to the small size of the venue. But that shouldn't be enough to stop anyone enjoying this riveting occasion.

Aida
Nina Stemme sop Aida **Salvatore Licitra** ten Radames **Luciana d'Intino** mez Amneris **Juan Pons** bar Amonasro **Matti Salminen** bass Ramfis **Günther Groissböck** bass King **Christiane Kohl** sop Priestess **Miroslav Christoff** ten Messenger **Zürich Opera House Chorus and Orchestra / Adám Fischer** Stage director **Nicolas Joël** Video director **Andy Sommer** Bel Air Classiques ② **DVD** BAC022 (3h 37' · NTSC · 16:9 · PCM stereo, 5.1 and DTS 5.1 · 0). Extra features include 'The Story of Aida' – a film by Louis Wallecan and an interview with Andy Sommer ⓕ**OO**

This 2006 production from the Zürich Opera is a traditional one by Nicolas Joël in veteran Ezio Frigerio's wonderfully evocative, highly coloured sets. Then Adám Fischer in the pit leads a remarkably strong yet subtle account of the score, which – when played and sung like this – is once more revealed as one of Verdi's greatest masterpieces.

Four of the principals easily surpass their DVD rivals. Stemme offers a deeply considered, expressive and superbly sung Aida, one for whom the work's vocal perils do not seem to exist. Add to that acting that goes to the heart of the matter, and one is left breathless in admiration after so many sopranos not truly fitted to the part. Licitra has done nothing better than his Radames here. At last fulfilling his potential, he sings the role with an open-hearted sincerity and a heroic voice up to the part's exigent demands. He and Stemme make their Act 3 duet the highlight it should be.

D'Intino, an experienced Amneris, sings her role with intense feeling allied to a mezzo of generous proportions. The demands of her Act 4 scena are

fully met, and she storms off to a well earned burst of applause. Stemme and Licitra give the final scene with the utmost sensibility. Salminen remains a force to be reckoned with, but Pons – as Amonasro – no longer is the baritone he once was, although dramatically he is up to the part.

The showpiece close to Act 2 is the one comparative disappointment, not offering the frisson it ought to. And here Andy Sommer's video direction is uncertain, too often dividing the screen into three for no discernible purpose, but he directs the principals with a deal of sensitivity. So this is the DVD *Aida* we have long awaited.

Additional recommendation

Aida
Caballé Aida **Domingo** Radames **Cossotto** Amneris **Chorus of the Royal Opera House, Covent Garden; New Philharmonia Orchestra; Trumpeters of the Royal Military School of Music, Kneller Hall / Muti** EMI Great Recordings of the Century ② 567613-2 (148' · ADD) Ⓜ**▶**

Montserrat Caballé gives her most successful Verdi performance on record, full of those vocal subtleties and beauties that inform her best singing, while Muti gives an impassioned account of the score.

Attila

Attila
Samuel Ramey bass Attila **Cheryl Studer** sop Odabella **Giorgio Zancanaro** bar Ezio **Kaludi Kaludov** ten Foresto **Ernesto Gavazzi** ten Uldino **Mario Luperi** bass Leone **Chorus and Orchestra of La Scala, Milan / Riccardo Muti** Stage director **Jerome Savary** Video director **Christopher Swann** Opus Arte **DVD** OALS3010D (118' · NTSC · 4:3 · 2.0 · 0) Recorded live 1991 Ⓕ

Spectacular and pacy, *Attila* fills the stage with barbarians, gives them good tunes to sing and places them in a busy world where every moment may bring a reversal of fortune. Moreover, the four leading characters are fired with passionate determination which in turn fires their magnificent voices. There is sure to be something to write home about after a good *Attila*. And this is a La Scala performance fully worthy of the great house and its best traditions. It is very much the kind of opera that thrives in Muti's care.

A hard, percussive energy plays off against long elegiac phrases, and the resulting tension, very Italian with its sense of personal suffering in the midst of great public events, permeates the whole performance. The singers match up to the challenge wonderfully well. Samuel Ramey's iron-fisted voice is the perfect vocal image of the man, a voice with no flab, trained as by an athlete. The limitations are of tonal variety, in the dream sequence; but this is still a triumphant *Attila*. The soprano role of Odabella is as formidable as any in the Verdi canon, and Cheryl Studer masters it with astonishing assurance, and without the usual register-breaks and smudged scales. The tenor Kaludi Kaludov brings a clean, incisive tone and a well-schooled *legato*, and among all these foreigners Giorgio Zancanaro represents his country in its leading national opera house with a welcome infusion of Italian resonance and a reminder (intrusive aspirates apart) of the true vocal method of which Italy was for so long the fount. Moreover, these individual talents come together as a well-disciplined ensemble, and the concerted numbers have the authentic thrill of Italian opera in best working order.

Un ballo in maschera

Un ballo in maschera   ⓗ
Maria Callas *sop* Amelia **Giuseppe di Stefano** *ten* Riccardo **Ettore Bastianini** *bar* Renato **Eugenia Ratti** *sop* Oscar **Giulietta Simionato** *contr* Ulrica **Antonio Cassinelli** *bass* Sam **Marco Stefanoni** *bass* Tom **Giuseppe Morresi** *bar* Silvano **Angelo Mercuriali** *ten* Judge **La Scala, Milan Chorus and Orchestra / Gianandrea Gavazzeni**
EMI mono ② 567918-2 or Regis RRC2079 (131' · ADD · T/t). Recorded live 1957   Ⓜ/ⓈⒹⒹⒹ➤

This set comes from live performances at La Scala in the mid-1950s when the diva was at the height of her powers. Callas gives here an even more vital performance than on her studio recorded set. It was Callas's particular genius to find exactly the appropriate mode of expression for every role she tackled. Here we have Callas the tormented, guilty wife. But she also gives us a hundred different individual inflections to reflect the emotion of the moment: indeed, as John Steane points out in one of his illuminating notes, it's often a small aside that reveals as much about the character she's portraying as a big set-piece.

The context of an evening in the theatre makes this a more arresting, vivid interpretation on all sides than its studio counterpart of a year earlier, with Gianandrea Gavazzeni galvanising his fine cast to great things. As John Ardoin put it in his study of Callas's recordings: 'The La Scala performance is sung with more vivid colours, with accents more etched and a general intensification of Verdi's drama.' Here the sound picture is appreciably superior to that on earlier live sets which capture Callas in other roles at La Scala. The irresistible di Stefano is the soul of vital declamation as Riccardo. Ettore Bastianini's forthright Renato, the only role he sang in London and one of his best in an all too short career, and Giulietta Simionato's classic Ulrica are also huge assets. Other roles are filled with house singers of the day. An unbeatable set.

Un ballo in maschera
Plácido Domingo *ten* Riccardo **Piero Cappuccilli** *bar* Renato **Martina Arroyo** *sop* Amelia **Fiorenza Cossotto** *mez* Ulrica **Reri Grist** *sop* Oscar **Giorgio Giorgetti** *bass* Silvano **Gwynne Howell** *bass* Samuel **Richard Van Allan** *bass* Tom **Kenneth Collins** *ten* Judge **David Barrett** *bar* Servant

Haberdashers' Aske's School Girls' Choir; New Philharmonia Orchestra; Chorus of the Royal Opera House, Covent Garden / Riccardo Muti
EMI 566510-2 (127' · ADD · T/t). Recorded 1975 ⓂⒹ➤

This is the *Ballo* which, above all else, glories in Muti as an exuberant man of the theatre. The impetus with which he whips up the constituent parts of an ensemble into the vortex, and the juxtaposition of blasting *tutti* with slim, sweetly phrased woodwind detail, so typical of this opera, hits the ear more thrillingly than ever. So does the equally characteristic tugging undercurrent of the *ballo* against the intrigue of the *maschera*, activated by Muti with such acute perception and élan.

He provides pliant, springing support for all his singers too: Domingo, a warm, generous Riccardo, is every bit as happy with Muti as with Abbado. The same can't be said of Martina Arroyo, the weak link on this recording. Dramatically forceful but curiously cool and detached from the expressive nuancing of her part, she has little of the vulnerability of a Ricciarelli (Abbado), or the individuality of a Price (Solti). But, although this mid-price recording may not offer the most consistently luxurious vocal banquet, none the less, with Cossotto's stentorian Ulrica and Cappuccilli's staunch, resilient Renato, its strong sense of theatrical presence and its dramatic integrity will make it the chosen version for many new collectors.

Un ballo in maschera
Josephine Barstow *sop* Amelia **Plácido Domingo** *ten* Gustav **Leo Nucci** *bar* Renato **Sumi Jo** *sop* Oscar **Florence Quivar** *contr* Ulrica **Jean-Luc Chaignaud** *bass* Christiano **Kurt Rydl** *bass* Horn **Goran Simic** *bar* Ribbing **Wolfgang Witte** *ten* Judge **Adolf Tomaschek** *ten* Servant **Vienna Philharmonic Orchestra / Sir Georg Solti**
Stage director **John Schlesinger**
Video director **Brian Large**
TDK 📀 DV-CLOPUBIM. (145' · 4:3 · PCM stereo · 0) Recorded live at the Grosses Festspielhaus, Salzburg, on July 28, 1990   Ⓕ

The year 1990 was the last of the *ancien régime* at the Salzburg Festival before the revolution brought about by Gérard Mortier. In many ways it represented the *ne plus ultra* of the Karajan-influenced era; indeed, this production, first seen in 1989, should have been conducted by the old maestro had he not died some months before it was due to be staged – not, however, before he had had time to record it for DG.

John Schlesinger's bold, sumptuous production in William Dudley's evocative Swedish settings underline the mood of each scene. Gustav's study is a true trompe-l'oeil, with a model theatre (the monarch's pet project) in the foreground. Ulrica's cave, surrounded by rotten-looking tenements and the eerie gallows for the start of Act 2, is nicely counterpointed by a realistic Swedish house for the home of Renato – though we could have done without the slightly embarrassing presence of his little boy.

The finale is admittedly well over the top but succeeds in creating the fever pitch of the masked ball. Within this breathtaking scenery, Schlesinger occasionally over-eggs the pudding with too many extras and intrusive dancers, yet he cleverly maintains the principals in the foreground so that they are never overawed by the magnificence of the decor.

Solti, not always one's favoured conductor where Verdi is concerned, gives a carefully crafted and surely paced account of this inspired score, and he is eminently supportive of his distinguished cast. Domingo, in peak form, gives a commanding portrayal of the doomed monarch, by turns lightly insouciant in the early scenes, suitably impassioned with Amelia, tragic as the ruler dies; everything is executed with technical assurance and fine control of dynamics. On this night, after a squally scene in the soothsayer's den, Barstow finds her best Verdian form, pouring her heart and soul into Amelia's predicament in tone and phrasing always apt to the character's circumstance. The Act 3 prayer, 'Morrò, ma prima in grazia', is particularly fine. Her interpretation is a worthy souvenir of her under-recorded art. Nucci is also at his best. He delivers his whole role in exemplary voice, firm, steady in tone to support his supple phrasing: 'Eri tu' is the heart-rending experience it should be.

Florence Quivar also surpasses herself with her sturdy, steady Ulrica and, as the icing on the cake, Sumi Jo is a buoyant, charming, bright-voiced Oscar. With excellent conspirators, the cast is very near ideal.

It is a pity the picture isn't widescreen and that the sound recording is not always ideally balanced, but these minor drawbacks cannot prevent a strong recommendation.

Additional recommendation

Un ballo in maschera
Ricciarelli Amelia **Domingo** Riccardo **Bruson** Renato
Chorus and Orchestra of La Scala, Milan / Abbado
DG ② 453 148-2GTA2 (127' · ADD)   Ⓜ️🅱️➔

A satisfying and unified performance, largely because Abbado and his La Scala forces give us the sense of a real theatrical experience. Ricciarelli and Domingo give involved and expressive performances.

Un ballo in maschera
Shuard Amelia **Vickers** Gustavo III **Bastianini** bar
Renato **Royal Opera House Chor & Orch / Downes**
Royal Opera House mono ② ROHS009 (122' · ADD).
Recorded live   Ⓜ️🅾️

House-habitués know this as the Bastianini *Ballo*. It marked the baritone's debut at the Royal Opera House, to which he never returned. But the great performance is Vickers's. He was then in best vocal form, and already his intensity in such music by far exceeded that of any other tenor of our time. Amy Shuard also emerges well: a little rigid and severe in expression at first, but steadily gaining in freedom and humanity. Sir Edward Downes's firm but sensitive conducting is also very fine.

Don Carlo / Don Carlos

Don Carlo
Plácido Domingo ten Don Carlo **Montserrat Caballé** sop Elisabetta di Valois **Shirley Verrett** mez Eboli **Sherrill Milnes** bar Rodrigo **Ruggero Raimondi** bass Filippo II **Giovanni Foiani** bass Grand Inquisitor **Simon Estes** bass-bar Monk **Delia Wallis** mez Tebaldo **Ryland Davies** ten Conte di Lerma **John Noble** bar Herald **Maria-Rosa del Campo** sop Voice from Heaven **Ambrosian Opera Chorus; Royal Opera House Orchestra, Covent Garden / Carlo Maria Giulini**
EMI Great Recordings of the Century ③ 567401-2 (3h 29' · ADD · T/t). Recorded 1970   Ⓜ️🅾️🅾️🅾️🅱️➔

From the day that Giulini conducted the now legendary production of *Don Carlo* at Covent Garden in 1958, a recording of the opera by him looked a must. In fact, it was to be 12 years before EMI took the plunge, but the set was worth waiting for: it's the five-act version in Italian, without the cuts made at the Royal Opera, and well recorded and handsomely cast. Giulini himself had slowed down since the live performances, but the blend of majesty and lyric beauty that he brings to the opera is hard to resist. The music glows warmly in his hands, as befits one of Verdi's most human dramas.

His cast gathers together five of the leading singers of the 1970s. In particular, the trio of Caballé, Domingo and Milnes seemed to be rather predictably the names on almost every Italian opera recording at the time, but how glad we would be to have young singers like them today. Caballé, though occasionally sounding blowsy, is exquisite whenever quiet singing is called for, and Domingo is at his golden best throughout. Their murmured farewells at the monastery of San Giusto in Act 5 have never been surpassed. Verrett is a fiery Eboli (although it's a shame Giulini did not give her more pace in 'O don fatale'), and Milnes provides generous-hearted singing as Rodrigo. It's good to have an Italian bass as Philip II, but Raimondi lacks the black tone and fearsome presence of his notable predecessor in the role, Boris Christoff. Lovers of the opera will want to investigate the four-act version under Santini and also the five-act version in French under Pappano, both on EMI (which has more or less cornered the market for this opera). Otherwise, 30 years on, Giulini's splendid performance is as satisfying as any, probably still the number one recommendation.

Don Carlos (French version)
André Turp ten Don Carlos **Edith Tremblay** sop Elisabeth de Valois **Robert Savoie** bar Rodrigue **Joseph Rouleau** bass Philippe II **Richard Van Allan** bass Grand Inquisitor **Robert Lloyd** bass Monk **Michèle Vilma** mez Eboli **BBC Singers and Concert Orchestra / John Matheson**
Opera Rara ④ ORCV305 (3h 51' · ADD · S/T/t/N)
Recorded live 1972   Ⓕ

This is part of Opera Rara's invaluable issues of first versions of Verdi's operas, broadcast on BBC Radio 3 in the 1970s. It is given by a cast of largely Francophone singers, who make it sound – at last – like the truly French work it is.

We have the complete Fontainebleau scene, a short solo for Posa at the beginning of scene 2, a longer version of the Posa-Philippe scene in Act 2, the costume-changing of Elisabeth and Eboli, their duet before 'O don fatal' in Act 3, the whole of the ballet, the full Insurrection scene, and the longest version of the finale. That adds up to almost four hours. No wonder Verdi either made or sanctioned cuts. However, this enthralling set makes out the best case for this fullest of all versions, its considerable length quite forgotten on account of John Matheson's thoughtful, vital direction, every detail of the vast canvas given its due and played (and sung) finely by the assembled BBC musicians.

The Carlos, André Turp, often at Covent Garden, did nothing better than this portrayal of the sorely tested and unhappy Infante. His voice, full of emotional plangency, his well crafted phrasing and the sheer passion of his delivery make him ideal. As the tormented, dictatorial Philippe, Joseph Rouleau also surpasses himself vocally and dramatically, so we are at once angered by his tyrannical ways and saddened by his inner misery. Robert Savoie, the Rodrigue/Posa, does not have quite the vocal resources of his confrères, but he gives an honest, deeply felt account of a taxing part.

Edith Tremblay is a gloriously committed Elisabeth. She does not give a traditionally 'star' performance but one that is ideally aligned with the character. Her singing, especially of her big Act 5 solo, is full of natural, true feeling. The Eboli of Michèle Vilma is also a reading to treasure, replete with all the equivocal feelings of that erring character and sung with gratifying confidence. Richard Van Allan, the sole 'foreigner' in a main part, commands the French language and, with Rouleau as antagonist, makes the scene of the Grand Inquisitor and King, the clash of Church and State, the riveting confrontation it should be.

The recording is well balanced and has plenty of presence but careless digitalisation can lend a rather hard quality to some of the voices, although that is easily forgotten in the dedication of a unique occasion.

Don Carlo   **H**
Jon Vickers ten Don Carlo **Gré Brouwenstijn** sop
Elisabetta di Valois **Fedora Barbieri** mez Eboli **Tito Gobbi** bar Rodrigo **Boris Christoff** bass Filippo II
Michael Langdon bass Grand Inquisitor **Joseph Rouleau** bass Monk **Jeannette Sinclair** sop Tebaldo
Edgar Evans ten Conte di Lerma **Robert Allman** ten
Herald **Ava June** sop Voice from Heaven
Royal Opera House Chorus, Covent Garden /
Carlo Maria Giulini
Royal Opera House Heritage Series mono ③
ROHS003 (3h 22' · ADD · T/t/N)
Recorded live at the Royal Opera House, Covent Garden, London, on May 12, 1958

Includes Lord Harewood in conversation with
Roger Beardsley   Ⓜ ⊙⊙

The prestige of conductor Giulini and producer Visconti was of a special type: they were the aristocrats of their kind. And the cast, particularly with Gobbi and Christoff in their already famous roles, was as distinguished as any presented by Covent Garden since the war. This recording brings it back vividly and is so clear and faithful that it recreates in large measure all that was heard in these great performances. Chorus and orchestra must take a generous share of the praise. The recording also compels some adjustment of the remembered credits.

Barbieri's Eboli seemed at that period not quite to rank with the other principals. This was partly because it lay high for her voice and, though she comes through 'O don fatale' to win some of the evening's most enthusiastic applause, it was done only by omitting some top notes, and the recording suggests (as was probably not evident in the theatre) that at the end she had come very near to the limit of her resources. But, as we can hear now, it really was a magnificent performance of the part as a whole, and in dramatic commitment the intensity of the others is fully matched by her own.

Gobbi, so thoroughly identified with the role of Posa, is neither the most elegant of Verdi baritones nor the most lustrous in his production of the high notes, but his tones are so personal, the expression so warm in humanity, that he remains the great Rodrigo of memory. And Christoff is greatness itself. He too is utterly irreplaceable, so individual is the timbre and so authoritative the utterance. He sets a daunting standard for his fellow basses in the cast, but Langdon (Inquisitor) and Rouleau (Monk or Charles V) prove worthy colleagues.

But the opera, after all, is called Don Carlo, and Jon Vickers is its hero. Nothing about this recording is more moving than to hear this extraordinary singer as he was at that time. Nothing, that is, unless to find Gré Brouwenstijn so wonderfully brought back to life. She too was an aristocrat among the artists of her time. The duets of Elisabetta and Carlo are of the opera's essence, almost unbearable in their poignancy.

The omission of the Insurrection scene following Posa's death is regrettable: Lord Harewood explains in an illuminating interview with Roger Beardsley the thinking behind it, and in those days very few in the audience would have missed it, because they didn't know it existed! But this is not an occasion for regrets. Andrew Porter sums it up in his introductory essay: 'It does much to recapture the excitement of being there in 1958 and of demonstrating in a realisation at once scrupulous and impassioned a great opera that had been for too long undervalued.'

Don Carlos (sung in English)
Alastair Miles bass Philip II, King of Spain **Julian Gavin** ten Don Carlos **William Dazeley** bar Rodrigo, Marquis of Posa **John Tomlinson** bass The Grand

Inquisitor **Janice Watson** sop Elisabeth de Valois
Jane Dutton mez Princess of Eboli **Julia Sporsén**
sop Thibault **Clive Bayley** bass An Old Monk **Chorus
and Orchestra of Opera North / Richard Farnes**
Chandos ③ CHAN 3162 (167' · DDD)   Ⓕ◗

This is a four-act *Don Carlos* in English: no Fontainebleau therefore and, on records and on its
own terms, no competition. The absence of the
five-act opera's first scene involves loss, but
structurally there is a satisfaction in the balance
of first and last scenes both taking place at the
Monastery introduced by the solemnity of brass.
As for Andrew Porter's fine translation, in two
scenes it has special value for English-speakers,
both dialogues that need to be closely followed:
the King, first with Posa in Act 1, then with the
Inquisitor in Act 3.

Opera North have much of which they can be
justly proud. Under Richard Farnes, the orchestral playing will stand comparison with the
acknowledged best. The style impresses as bearing the imprint of a genuine Verdi conductor,
with playing where, at times, one feels as though
the instruments are contributing their own apt
dialogue to the drama.

Of the soloists we have to remember how
much is asked of them; and, indeed, much is
given. As so often happens, it is the baritone
whose singing falls most gratefully on the ear.
William Dazeley's voice is not remarkable for
either power or Italianate richness, but it is an
uncommonly pleasing one nevertheless and
thoroughly well produced. Julian Gavin's tenor
rings out powerfully in the upper register but
rather loses colour elsewhere: he sings the role,
however, with feeling and is able to communicate the sense of pain. With Alastair Miles we
have an artist whose years of good service have
begun to take their toll in a loosening of the
vibrations, yet his performance leaves a deep
impression and some of the phrases in his great
solo are beautifully taken. In the scene with the
Inquisitor, he and John Tomlinson have the
right kind of voice-relationship, but with Tomlinson the ageing is more troublesome, too
many of his notes lacking focus and control.

Neither of the principal women is well cast.
Jane Dutton as the Princess of Eboli has the
power and the range but her tone is uneven and
unsympathetic in character. Janice Watson is
sympathetic and within the natural scope of her
voice she sings her aria in the last act extremely
well, but the part calls for a different kind of
voice, one with a greater breadth of tone or a
warmer quality in moments of emotional
release.

Don Carlos (French version)
Roberto Alagna ten Don Carlos **Karita Mattila** sop
Elisabeth de Valois **Waltraud Meier** mez Eboli
Thomas Hampson bar Rodrigue **José van Dam**
bass-bar Philippe II **Eric Halfvarson** bass-bar Grand
Inquisitor **Csaba Airizer** bass Monk **Anat Efraty** sop
Thibault **Scot Weir** ten Comte de Lerme, Herald
Donna Brown sop Voice from Heaven

**Chorus of the Théâtre du Châtelet, Paris;
Orchestre de Paris / Antonio Pappano**
Stage director **Luc Bondy**
Video director **Yves André Hubert**
NVC Arts 📀 0630 16318-2 (3h 31' · 2-6)   Ⓕ○○

This performance appeared on VHS back in
March 1997. On widescreen television it
makes a far more arresting effect. The action
seems to be happening in the room with you.
That's due not only to the format but also to
director Luc Bondy's wish to portray the personal relationships, the characters' trials and
tribulations in the most intimate manner. In
contrast to most stagings of Verdi's epic, this
one turns all but the outdoor scenes, mainly
the Inquisition, into almost a domestic
drama.

For better or worse, the principals seem
very modern. José van Dam, a magnificent
and moving Philippe II, does sometimes remind
one of an out-of-sorts bank manager rather
than a ruler of an empire, with his troubled
wife, in the attractive person and voice of Mattila, as a workaday Queen. Charisma is excluded
by this interpretation. The relationship of
Carlos and Rodrigue, obviously a very close
one, is a touchy-feely affair, one that Alagna,
in a sincere, beautifully sung assumption, and
a palpitating Thomas Hampson, execute with
flair.

As ever, Meier isn't content with conventional
acting: her Eboli is a scheming and seductive
presence, consoling us with the intensity of her
singing with a voice a shade light for her part.
Indeed, on reappraising the musical side of the
performance, which was recorded live at the
Châtelet in Paris, it strikes you that all the voices
are a degree lighter than we're used to in the
piece, but that suits the French text, giving an
ease and fluidity to the vocal line that is, in truth,
its own justification.

Even more impressive on rehearing is Pappano's conducting, alive to every nuance of the
long work yet aware of its overall structure. In
the new medium the clarity and immediacy of
the picture is arresting. The sound, though a
shade soft in focus, is a great improvement on its
'ordinary' video counterpart. Listeners and
viewers who want to add this unforgettable work
to their collection need not hesitate.

Don Carlo
Luciano Pavarotti ten Don Carlo **Daniella Dessì** sop
Elisabetta di Valois **Luciana d'Intino** mez Eboli **Paolo
Coni** bar Rodrigo **Samuel Ramey** bass Filippo II
Alexander Anisimov bass Grand Inquisitor **Andrea
Silverstrelli** bass Monk **Marilena Laurenza** sop
Tebaldo **Orfeo Zanetti** ten Conte di Lerma **Mario
Bolognesi** ten Herald **Nuccia Focile** sop Voice from
Heaven **Chorus and Orchestra of La Scala, Milan /
Riccardo Muti**
Stage and video director **Franco Zeffirelli**
EMI 📀 599442-9 (3h 2' · NTSC · 4:3 · PCM stereo
5.1 & DTS 5.1 · 0). Recorded live at Teatro alla Scala,
Milan, December 1992   Ⓕ

If you want the edition of the work revised in Italian by Verdi, first performed in 1884, this is your only choice to date on DVD – and it proves a satisfying experience. The work in this form is tauter and more direct than the five-act French original caught on the DVD of the Châtelet production conducted by Pappano. Those who know Zeffirelli's style won't be surprised by the conventionally lavish production, but it effectively evokes the atmosphere of religious oppression and personal antagonisms Verdi so unerringly depicts.

The dark-hued, threatening setting fits Muti's energetic, rhythmically vital conception. He quickens the emotions in a peculiarly Italianate way, and throughout evinces a feeling for the colouring of the score. His reading is in turn a good background for some thoughtful and idiomatic singing.

Pavarotti delivers Carlo's music in a typically fervent manner, words ideally placed on the voice and his tone consistently firm and pliable. His girth makes him unconvincing as the small, lean, nervous Carlo of history, but his simple, sincere acting is its own advocate. Daniella Dessì looks the very image of the wronged, sympathetic Elisabetta and sings with feeling and good phrasing. Paolo Coni offers a concerned, upright Rodrigo, sung in warm tones though he sometimes loses focus under pressure.

Zeffirelli's video direction is well fashioned and the sound picture catches the aural ambience of La Scala. As a whole, this is a vivid experience.

Ernani

Ernani
Plácido Domingo ten Ernani **Mirella Freni** sop Elvira
Renato Bruson bar Don Carlo **Nicolai Ghiaurov** bass
De Silva **Jolanda Michieli** sop Giovanna **Gianfranco
Manganotti** ten Don Riccardo **Alfredo Giacomotti**
bass Iago **Chorus and Orchestra of La Scala, Milan /
Riccardo Muti**
EMI ② 381884-2 (128' · DDD · T/t)
Recorded live 1982   Ⓜ⤷

Renato Bruson's Don Carlo is an assumption that's as gripping dramatically as it is vocally. In his portrayal more than anywhere, the musical tension of *Ernani* becomes manifest, and everywhere Bruson offers superb Verdi singing. Domingo's Ernani is hardly less impressive and he benefits from being caught live on stage. His opening aria and cabaletta are full of delicate touches and obedience to the dynamic marks. In the last act, his recitative 'Tutto ora tace d'intorno' has great pathos, and his contributions to the final trio an overwhelming eloquence. Here, too, Freni achieves most, the etching-in of 'Il riso del tuo volto fa ch' io veda' a brief utterance of happiness, most affecting, and her desperate appeals to Silva for mercy sung with brio.

In her opening aria and cabaletta, the famous 'Ernani, Ernani', too much is asked of a voice not really meant by nature for this kind of heavy

duty, but none can quite match the sorrow and heartbreak of Elvira's predicament that Freni manages in the theatre. Ghiaurov, rusty as his voice had become, creates a great impression of dignity and implacable strength, and many of those qualities are carried over into his singing. 'Infelice' is delivered with mature nobility, 'Ah, io l'amo' is intensely moving. Ghiaurov is denied Silva's probably spurious cabaletta. Otherwise the work is given complete.

Muti conducts the score in exemplary manner. He has learnt when to allow his singers licence to phrase with meaning and when to press on. The La Scala chorus gives us the genuine sound of Italian voices in full flight, sounding much more inside their various assumptions than their rivals. The audience is occasionally in evidence, as are the on-stage effects, but the atmosphere of being in an opera house and taking part, as it were, in a real occasion has all the advantages over the aseptic feeling of a studio.

Additional recommendation

Ernani   Ⓗ
Del Monaco Ernani **Cerquetti** Elvira **Bastianini** Don
Carlo **Christoff** De Silva **Boni** Giovanna **Cesarini** Don
Riccardo **Neagu** Iago **Maggio Musicale Fiorentino
Chorus and Orch / Mitropoulos**
Bel Canto mono ② BCS5011 (118' · ADD · N)
Recorded live 1957   Ⓜ⭕

This is a performance to delight Verdians, Florence seriously challenging its La Scala rival on EMI. All four principals not only have voices of essential power but also have Verdian style as part of their interpretative make-up. Furthermore they're led by the legendary Mitropoulos. Mitropoulos sanctions a few regrettable cuts not tolerated by Muti. In other respects there's little to choose between these two live performances. For its age the sound is remarkably good and well worth investigating at mid-price.

Falstaff

Falstaff   Ⓗ
Tito Gobbi bar Falstaff **Rolando Panerai** bar Ford
Elisabeth Schwarzkopf sop Alice Ford **Anna Moffo**
sop Nannetta **Luigi Alva** ten Fenton **Fedora Barbieri**
mez Mistress Quickly **Nan Merriman** mez Meg Page
Tomaso Spataro ten Dr Caius **Renato Ercolani** ten
Bardolph **Nicola Zaccaria** bass Pistol **Philharmonia
Chorus and Orchestra / Herbert von Karajan**
EMI ② 377349-2 (120' · ADD · N/S)
Recorded 1956   Ⓑ⭕⭕⭕⤷

 This *Falstaff* still stands (with Toscanini) peerless in the catalogue. At its centre stands Tito Gobbi, and his is a presence large enough to encompass both the lord and the jester, the sensuous and the sensual, and the deep seriousness as well as the deep absurdity of his vision. Few Falstaffs have such a measure of the simplicity of his first monosyllables in the bustle around him; few find the poise as well as the confusion within his music. Karajan's recording is incomparable in its quartet of merry wives.

Schwarzkopf's Alice radiates both the 'gioia nell'aria' and the 'gioia nel' cor' of Verdi's writing, Fedora Barbieri's redoubtable Mistress Quickly, with her stentorian cries of 'Povera donna!', puts other readings in the shade; Anna Moffo's Nannetta, perfectly matched in timbre and agility with Luigi Alva's Fenton, is a constant delight. Above all, it's their corporate presence that works at such a distinctively higher level. Rolando Panerai is a magnificent Ford; his 'E sogno? o realtà?' is a high point of the performance.

This 1956 recording has been discreetly and skilfully doctored, but a little background hiss does remain. But one doesn't actually end up hearing it. This great recording is a-flutter with pungent solo detail, realising, with Nannetta, that the world is 'tutto deliro, sospiro e riso'. The episodes of the opera, its exits and entrances, its subjects and counter-subjects, pass with the unique sensibility of Verdi's final great exuberant fugue of life.

Falstaff   **H**

Giuseppe Valdengo *bar* Falstaff **Frank Guarrera** *bar* Ford **Herva Nelli** *sop* Alice Ford **Teresa Stich-Randall** *sop* Nannetta **Antonio Madasi** *ten* Fenton **Cloe Elmo** *contr* Mistress Quickly **Nan Merriman** *mez* Meg Page **Gabor Carelli** *ten* Dr Caius **John Carmen Rossi** *ten* Bardolph **Norman Scott** *bass* Pistol **Robert Shaw Chorale; NBC Symphony Orchestra / Arturo Toscanini**

RCA Gold Seal mono ② 74321 72372-2 (117' · ADD · T/t). Recorded 1950   Ⓜ❶❷❸❹→

 This *Falstaff* remains, as it always has been, one of the half a dozen greatest opera sets ever recorded. It's a miracle in every respect. How Toscanini loved Verdi and how he strained every sinew to fulfil this amazing score's variety in line, feeling and colour. Whether it's the clarity and discipline of the ensembles, the extraordinary care taken over orchestral detail or the alert control of dynamics, Toscanini is supreme, yet nothing is done for effect's sake; everything seems natural, inevitable, unforced, as though the score was being created anew before us with chamber-music finesse – and the atmosphere of a live performance adds to the feeling of immediacy. Nobody dares, or seems to want, to interrupt the magic being laid before him. Toscanini in his old age is matching the subtlety and vitality of the composer's own Indian summer – or one might be tempted to say spring, so delicate and effervescent does the scoring sound.

If, vocally, the main glory is the wonderful sense of ensemble gained through hours of hard rehearsals, individual contributions are almost all rewarding. Indeed, Valdengo's Falstaff, under Toscanini's tutelage, has not been surpassed on disc even by Gobbi. Flexibility, charm, exactness, refinement inform his beautifully and wisely sung portrayal. He's no less pointed and subtle in his encounter with Frank Guarrera's

imposing Ford. Another great joy of the set is the women's ensemble, their contribution the very epitome of smiling chatter. The Alice, Meg and Nannetta (Stich-Randall – none better), all sound, as they were, fresh and youthful. Herva Nelli is a lively and delightful Alice and Cloe Elmo's Quickly is as rich and ripe of voice and diction as any on disc, though a trifle coarse at times. The Fenton is sweet and Italianate in tone, but not as stylish as others. The smaller roles are all very much part of the team.

This set should certainly be a source of delightful revelation to a new generation of collectors who may have a wrong-headed view of what Toscanini was about. The remastering gives it clearer, more immediate sound than ever heard before from the originals.

Falstaff

Michele Pertusi *bar* Falstaff **Carlos Álvarez** *bar* Ford **Ana Ibarra** *sop* Alice Ford **Maria José Moreno** *sop* Nannetta **Bülent Bezdüz** *ten* Fenton **Jane Henschel** *contr* Mistress Quickly **Marina Domashenko** *mez* Meg Page **Alasdair Elliott** *ten* Dr Caius **Peter Hoare** *ten* Bardolph **Darren Jeffrey** *bass* Pistol **London Symphony Chorus and Orchestra / Sir Colin Davis**

LSO Live ② LSO0055 Ⓢ; ⚛ ② LSO0528 (119' · DSD/DDD · T/S/t/N). Recorded live   Ⓜ❶❷❸→

By all accounts the performances at the Barbican in London were among the most enjoyable of their kind in London for a long time, and certainly the enjoyment comes across on disc. The 'how' of it isn't so easily defined. It isn't the applause and occasional chuckles, though they help (comedy abhors a vacuum). It isn't even that, despite this being a concert rather than a staged event, the cast are performing entirely in character, and that they're doing so with zest and humorous intelligence. Rather it's as though a spirit of fun is in the air, breathed in by everyone, including the orchestra, who see the score's jokes and respond to its wit with the speed of light. Much of this must emanate from the maestro, who has every right to take pride in a brilliant achievement.

Michele Pertusi as Falstaff may lack Tito Gobbi's expressive resources, but he nevertheless has plenty of variety to offer. The grotesque acolytes and preposterous doctor play up well, and the lovers, Nannetta and Fenton, are a charming couple, convincingly young in voice and lyrical in style. Jane Henschel is a strong Mistress Quickly, better integrated into the ensemble than the riper plum-pudding dames who get the big laughs.

Falstaff has been well served on records ever since Toscanini set the standard high in 1950, but in few versions can the orchestra have played with more evident appreciation of the comedy on stage – it's almost as though the members of the LSO know the libretto by heart. This bids to become a firm favourite.

Falstaff

Christopher Purves *bar* Falstaff **Peter Hall** *ten*

Dr Caius **Alasdair Elliott** ten Bardolph **Paolo
Battaglia** bass Pistol **Jennifer Holloway** mez
Meg Page **Dina Kuznetsova** sop Alice Ford
Marie-Nicole Lemieux contr Mistress Quickly
Adriana Kucerova sop Nannetta **Bülent Bezdüz** ten
Fenton **Tassis Christoyannis** bar Ford
**Glyndebourne Chorus; London Philharmonic
Orchestra / Vladimir Jurowski**
Stage director **Richard Jones**
Opus Arte 🆅 OA1021D; 🆅 OABD7053D (136' ·
NTSC · 16:9 · 1080i · PCM stereo, 2.0 and DTS 5.1 · 0)
Recorded live in June 2009   Ⓕ🅞

A huge triumph for Glyndebourne, this, so deft
is the stagecraft, so happily assured the musical
touch. And the DVD carries the conviction of
doing full justice to all. If there is one scene in
which the Glyndebourne audience seems to
have an advantage over the armchair viewer, it is
the last. Midnight in Windsor Park always poses
problems and there are occasions where the
audience 'sees' the joke rather ahead. But Nannetta and the fairies are enchantingly moonlit
and the 'pizzica' sequence is resourcefully choreographed. And indeed all aspects of staging
(including Richard Jones's not always so welcome producing hand) work to happy effect.
The updating (to, at a guess, late wartime) is
unexpectedly refreshing and the characters
adapt naturally to their new conditions – Falstaff
as a kind of Evelyn Waugh figure crossed with
Fred Emney, and Mistress Quickly as a ripe
Arthur Marshall act. The settings – prize let-
tuces in Ford's garden, Sanderson chintzes in
the drawing room – raise a laugh and no objections. The cast is uniformly excellent, with
Christopher Purves's Falstaff much funnier than
most while being ever mindful of the opera
singer's first duty, which is to sing. Vladimir
Jurowski conducts so as to bring out all the
score's energy and wit without forcing the pace
or underlining the jokes. Possibly it is an excess
of producer's licence to offer him a pint in the
pause which follows 'Tutti gabbati', but he
drinks it down manfully and conducts the last
bars with relish.

Falstaff
Ambrogio Maestri bass-bar Falstaff **Roberto
Frontali** bar Ford **Barbara Frittoli** sop Alice Ford
Inva Mula sop Nannetta **Juan Diego Flórez** ten
Fenton **Bernadette Manca di Nissa** contr Mistress
Quickly **Anna Caterina Antonacci** mez Meg Page
Ernesto Gavazzi ten Dr Caius **Paolo Barbacini** ten
Bardolph **Luigi Roni** bass Pistol **Chorus and
Orchestra of La Scala, Milan / Riccardo Muti**
Stage director **Ruggero Cappuccio**
Video director **Pierre Cavasillas**
TDK Mediactive 🆅 DV-OPFAL (118' · 16:9 · 2.0 &
5.1 · 0)   Ⓕ🅞🅞

This performance derives from a special production of *Falstaff* at Verdi's birthplace to mark
the centenary of his death. It's a replica of staging given in the same theatre, the Teatro Verdi,
under Toscanini, in 1913, using facsimiles of the

original sets. Some may find the small stage and
traditional sets simply old-fashioned, but given a
superb cast perceptively directed by Ruggero
Cappuccio, what we see and hear is Verdi's
masterpiece presented in the most natural,
unforced way, with everyone on stage enjoying
themselves. The result is a warm-hearted,
unforced reading that makes the rival Graham
Vick production at Covent Garden look, by its
side, forced and contrived, not to mention the
inadequacies of the anti-Verdian Aix production
also on DVD. Muti's masterly traversal of the
score – at once prompt yet relaxed – adds to the
pleasure.

The cast is headed by Ambrogio Maestri, 31 at
the time, who in vocal and physical size is Italy's
answer to Bryn Terfel, Haitink's Falstaff, and as
with Terfel is a youngish man playing the ageing
Knight; but Maestri is very much a member of
an ensemble, not a star giving his interpretation.
He portrays the Fat Knight as still youthful in
his outlook and quite nimble afoot. He performs
it entirely without Terfel's (or Vick's) attempts
at vulgar exaggeration: everything emerges from
the text and music, and the singing itself is finely
modulated and easy on the ear.

He's surrounded by a group of Merry Wives as
ebullient and resourceful as any on audio or video
versions. Barbara Frittoli's scheming Alice is
nicely set of against Anna Caterina Antonacci's
witty Meg, while Bernadette Manca di Nissa
sings and acts Quickly truly, without the traditional guying of the part. Roberto Frontali's Ford
is much more in character than on the rival version and he parleys perfectly with Maestri's Falstaff. Juan Diego Flórez and Inva Mula as sweet-
voiced and handsome-looking lovers and excellent
comprimarios are all part of this highly recommendable DVD. Video direction and sound picture are exemplary. Don't miss its many delights.

Additional recommendations

Falstaff
Trimarchi Falstaff **Servile** Ford **Faulkner** Alice Ford
Dilbèr Nannetta **Comencini** Fenton **Chorus and
Orchestra of Hungarian State Opera / Humburg**
Naxos ② 8 660050/1 (120' · DDD · T/N)   Ⓢ🅓➤
Naxos's set does a good job at challenging the best
in the field. Humburg strikes just the right balance
between the high spirits and the delicacy in Verdi's
score. Trimarchi as Falstaff gives a reading full of
ripe understanding; his voice lies, as the role
requires, ideally poised between baritone and bass.
A very lovable portrait. This is a *Falstaff* to savour
and one that will bear repetition.

Falstaff
van Dam Falstaff **Stone** Ford **Madra** Alice Ford
Szmytka Nannetta **Dale** Fenton **La Monnaie Chorus
and Orch / Cambreling** Stage director **Pasqual**
Video director **Flédérick**
Warner Music Vision 🆅 5050467 4469-2-2
(130' · NTSC · 4:3 · 2.0 · 2-6)   Ⓕ🅞🅞
There can seldom have been so wholly satisfactory a
traversal of Verdi's closing masterpiece, on both dra-

matic and musical grounds, as this 1987 staging at Aix. Director Lluis Pasqual directs his principals with an eye for natural yet cleverly pointed movement. He's lucky to have José van Dam, at the height of his powers in 1987. This Falstaff is wholly believable as a mature lover and true knight, one who never plays the fool. He's surrounded by a cast on a similarly high level, headed by Barbara Madra's lively, quick-witted, beautifully sung Alice. Cambreling conducts a scrupulously prepared account of the score.

Falstaff

Bruson Falstaff **Nucci** Ford **Ricciarelli** Alice Ford **Hendricks** Nannetta **Gonzales** Fenton **Royal Opera House Chor & Orch / Giulini**
Stage director **Eyre** Video director **Large**
Warner Music Vision 50 51442 0494-2-8
(137' · NTSC · 4:3 · PCM stereo · 0).   Ⓕ

This *Falstaff* (it's a pleasure to report) is a delight from start to finish. Bruson is a magnificent Falstaff, whether from the twinkle in his eye or the radiant rotundity of his voice. He has a worthy Bardolph and Pistol too, both with an infallible feel for comedy. The wives are merry as it were from inner delight rather than as a dutiful part of an evening's work. Barbara Hendricks (a few low notes apart) makes an enchanting Nannetta, and Dalmacio Gonzales is a honey-toned Fenton. All do well, and although there's now a whole gallery of *Falstaffs* on film (some of them admirable), this will do very well.

Falstaff   Ⓗ

Taddei Falstaff **Colombo** Ford **Carteri** Alice Ford **Moffo** Nannetta **Alva** Fenton **RAI Chor & Orch Milan / Serafin** Video director **Graf**
Video Artists International 📀 VAIDVD4333
(118' · 4:3 black and white · PCM mono · 0)   Ⓕ

Vintage 1956 Italian television, black and white, with an occasional vertical line down the middle, and on the generally vivid soundtrack an occasional 'wow' – but all of this is nothing to the 'wow' of a performance. Splendidly cast, with not a weak link, conducted with benevolent mastery and produced so as to give the composer what he wanted. Taddei's smile is at the centre of everything, teeth white as his wig, more emblematic of the man even than his big belly. The Ford is also a fine singer, Scipione Colombo, courtly and vulpine in appearance, convincing in his wounded monologue. The merry wives take their centre not so much from the Alice Ford as from the Mistress Quickly and the ripe chest notes of Fedora Barbieri.

La forza del destino

La forza del destino   Ⓗ

Maria Caniglia sop Leonora **Galliano Masini** ten Don Alvaro **Carlo Tagliabue** bar Don Carlo **Tancredi Pasero** bass Padre Guardiano **Ebe Stignani** mez Preziosilla **Saturno Meletti** bar Melitone **Ernesto Dominici** bass Marquis of Calatrava **Giuseppe Nessi** ten Trabuco **Liana Avogadro** mez Curra **Italian Broadcasting Authority Chorus and Orchestra / Gino Marinuzzi**
Naxos Historical mono ③ 8 110206/7 (154' · ADD · N)
Recorded 1941   Ⓢ🅑➔

This is a fascinating, unmissable set in both historic and musical terms. Marinuzzi, a Toscanini coeval at La Scala, was chosen as conductor, and it's his only complete recording of an opera. The recording took place in May 1941 and was issued on 78rpm discs by Cetra. After the war Parlophone, which was then in charge of Cetra recordings in Britain, issued – in desultory fashion – a few separate discs. Sadly the whole version has never had the currency its great merits deserve, not at least as the first complete set (bar one traditionally cut scene) of the work and one with an entirely Italian cast. Now we have it to enjoy at super-budget price and in admirable transfers from original Cetra pressings by Ward Marston.

For the recording Marinuzzi had assembled a vintage cast of Italian singers of the day. Caniglia herself rightly considered her Leonora here as one of her finest recordings: one can hear why in her committed, vibrant and often very sensitive singing: she even attempts some of the refined *pianissimos* that graced the reading of this role by her near-contemporary, Zinka Milanov. It's a performance imbued with spiritual yearning – exactly what's wanted. By her side Masini's Alvaro is obviously a man of action with his blade-like, *spinto* tenor and sense of desperation at Alvaro's plight. If he's occasionally too lachrymose that's only a sign of his empathy with his role. As Alvaro's implacable antagonist, Don Carlo, Tagliabue provides dependable tone and an authentically styled interpretation of a kind seldom heard today. The pair's final and fatal encounter is one of the score's and the set's highlights.

Stignani, in her absolute prime, is a formidable Preziosilla, full in tone and clear in her passagework, exemplary in every way. Marston has made the recording as amenable as is possible. In any case it would be worth suffering much worse sound than this for such a satisfying traversal on all sides of this inspired score.

La forza del destino   Ⓗ

Stella Roman sop Leonora **Frederick Jagel** ten Don Alvaro **Lawrence Tibbett** bar Don Carlo **Ezio Pinza** bass Padre Guardiano **Irra Petina** mez Preziosilla **Salvatore Baccaloni** bass Melitone **Louis d'Angelo** bass Marquese **Thelma Votipka** mez Curra **Alessio de Paolis** ten Trabuco **Lorenzo Alvary** bass Mayor **John Gurney** bass Surgeon **Metropolitan Opera Chorus and Orchestra, New York / Bruno Walter**
Naxos Historical mono ③ 8 110038/40 (168' · AAD)
Recorded live 1943   Ⓢ

There has never been quite so electrifying a *Forza* as Walter's vital, brilliantly executed reading, which encapsulates the essence of the forthcoming drama. It confirms what few may know today, that Walter was a superb interpreter of Verdi. Yet this was the first time he had conducted *Forza*, so his lithe, finely honed reading is all the more remarkable. The other revelation is the Leonora of Stella Roman, a greatly underrated soprano brought to the Met in 1941, who yields few points to such notable interpreters of the part as Ponselle, Milanov and Tebaldi. They apart, you would go far to hear a Leonora so well equipped for the role, and so committed to it, one who uses her warm, generous voice to unerring effect in projecting the woman's dire predicament.

Padre Guardiano appears in the guise of Pinza, none better, and sounding, one uncertain high E apart, secure, concerned and authoritative. Jagel as Don Alvaro passes easily the test of the taxing aria of sad recollection at the start of Act 3. Tibbett as Don Carlo compels attention at every entry with his distinctive timbre and faultless style, but truth to tell the glorious tone had dulled since his great days in the 1930s and at times he sounds stretched by the part. Both his arias suffer cuts. Carlo's second (of three) duets with Alvaro is also excised as was then the custom, and *strettas* throughout are foreshortened. Baccaloni enjoys himself hugely as Melitone and obviously relishes his encounters with his superior, the Padre Guardiano, the two Italians revelling in the text. Petina is a lively but lightweight Preziosilla.

The sound is a bit crackly and restricted but good enough to enjoy an absorbing account of the score. This vivid version has much to commend it at the price.

La forza del destino (original St Petersburg version, 1862)
Martina Arroyo sop Leonora **Kenneth Collins** ten Don Alvaro **Peter Glossop** bar Don Carlo **Don Garrard** bass Padre Guardiano **Janet Coster** mez Preziosilla **Derek Hammond-Stroud** bar Melitone **Roderick Kennedy** bass Marquis **Kenneth Bowen** ten Trabuco **BBC Singers and Concert Orchestra / John Matheson**
Opera Rara ② ORCV304 (137' · DDD · T/t)　Ⓜ❶

This marks the final offering from Opera Rara's laudable restoration of BBC broadcasts from the 1970s and '80s of Verdi's first thoughts on specific operas, and it is quite up to the standard of the series. It differs only in being given without an audience, and was broadcast two years after the recording.

On disc we know the 1862 original *Forza* from Gergiev's Philips set recorded, appropriately enough, in St Petersburg. That version is by and large finely cast with Russian singers and excitingly conducted, but this one, featuring British artists and one North American, need hardly fear the comparison. John Matheson may be a slightly more measured interpreter than Gergiev but he is perhaps even more adept at disclosing the many subtleties in shaping the slightly sprawling score as a unified whole. His orchestra provides fine playing – special praise for the first clarinet before Alvaro's Act 3 solo – and the BBC Singers nicely characterise their roles.

Alvaro, an even more taxing role than in the better-known revised version for Milan, is superbly sung by Kenneth Collins: Bergonzi and Domingo apart, no other tenor in the late 20th century was as ideal for the part. Collins, a true *spinto*, makes light of the demands, and sings with unstinting strength and an innate

sense of Verdian style, a suitable souvenir of a singer so little represented on disc.

Martina Arroyo, also on Gardelli's EMI recording of 12 years earlier, is a profoundly sympathetic, even-voiced Leonora: she really sings her heart out. As the implacable Don Carlo, Peter Glossop remains an appreciable Verdian. His tone had loosened a little by 1981 but he splendidly conveys the avenging brother's wrath, particularly in his fiery encounter with Alvaro in Act 4.

Like Collins, Don Garrard and Derek Hammond-Stroud were then singing the revised version at the Coliseum. The much-admired Canadian bass sings with depth and authority as Padre Guardiano, and Hammond-Stroud in one of his favourite roles makes Melitone more than a mere *buffo* but rather a hot-headed, obtuse friar, as he should be. Janet Coster fills most of the considerable demands of Preziosilla's role and it is good to be reminded of the stalwart tenor Kenneth Bowen and of Roderick Kennedy's sturdy bass. All sing with exemplary Italian.

The recording has breadth and presence. The booklet is lavish though the skimpy note seriously underestimates the differences between this and the more famous revision, and it is a pity there are no biographies: the singers are hardly well known to most younger Verdi enthusiasts. But these complaints are of little consequence when the performance is so inspiriting and dedicated on all sides.

La forza del destino　　　　　　　　　　　Ⓗ
Antonietta Stella sop Leonora **Giuseppe di Stefano** ten Don Alvaro **Ettore Bastianini** bar Don Carlo **Walter Kreppel** bass Padre Guardiano **Giulietta Simionato** mez Preziosilla **Karl Dönch** bar Melitone **Ludwig Welter** bass Marquis **Hugo Meyer-Welfing** ten Trabuco **Harald Pröglhöf** bass Mayor **Franz Bierbach** bass Surgeon **Vienna State Opera Chorus and Orchestra / Dimitri Mitropoulos**
Orfeo d'Or mono Ⓜ ② C681 062I (151' · ADD · S/N)
Recorded live 1960　　　　　　　　　　　Ⓜ❶

Mitropoulos, who had only weeks to live, directs the work with that combination of sensitivity and drive that marked all his performances. With the Vienna State Opera Orchestra in glowing form, the results are very special. One quirk: rather than playing the Overture at the beginning, Mitropoulos places it after the first scene, a plan Verdi had but eventually abandoned. It works quite well, at least when played with the élan evident here.

Bastianini presents Don Carlo in all his menacing, vengeful fury with that dark-hued, immensely powerful baritone of his. As his antagonist he has di Stefano as Alvaro in his most eloquent, incisive and appealing form, relishing every word and note. If it's possible, the Leonora and Preziosilla are even better. Stella had a brief period when she was fully the equal of Tebaldi and here she is in the middle of it, singing the role as well as, if not better than any soprano on disc. Tebaldi-like in her full, Italianate tone, Caniglia-like in her identification with Leonora's plight, from start to finish she is magnificent, and she crowns her portrayal with a finely nuanced and felt 'Pace, pace' in the final act. Simionato was always one of the few mezzos who had the range and brio to fulfil the demands of Preziosilla's part, and she too is here at her appreciable best.

The rest of the cast is drawn from resident singers at the Staatsoper. Kreppel is a sound, full-bottomed bass who sings a sympathetic Padre Guardiano, especially fine in the long Act 2 duet with Leonora. But the rest are not half as idiomatic as their Italian counterparts in Florence, with Dönch comic as Melitone but in rather a Viennese way. Another drawback is the traditional cuts then imposed on the score; particularly heinous is the excising of Alvaro/Carlo duet in Act 3.

In this the performance's first official appearance, the sound is by and large excellent. Although there is no libretto, there are interesting notes in the booklet by Gottfried Kraus and Michael Gielen (on Mitropoulos).

La forza del destino Ⓗ
Renata Tebaldi sop Leonora **Franco Corelli** ten Don Alvaro **Ettore Bastianini** bar Don Carlo **Boris Christoff** bass Padre Guardiano **Oralia Dominguez** mez Preziosilla **Renato Capecchi** bar Melitone **Jorge Algorta** bass Marquis **Mariano Caruso** ten Trabuco **Anna di Stasio** mez Curra **Giuseppe Forgione** bass Mayor **Gianni Bardi** bass Surgeon
**Naples San Carlo Opera Chorus and Orchestra /
Francesco Molinari-Pradelli**
Hardy Classic Video 📀 HCD4002 (160' · NTSC · 4:3 · 1.0 · 0). Recorded live at the San Carlo Theatre, Naples, 1958. Includes interview with Tebaldi Ⓕ

Why is it that this performance in lo-fi and indifferent black-and-white picture, and in a distinctly old-fashioned staging, has become a legend among collectors of opera on video to the extent of becoming a VHS best-seller? The answer lies in the quality of execution of a once-in-a-lifetime cast, supported by idiomatic conducting and playing at the San Carlo in Naples back in 1958.

Tebaldi had already proved at the Maggio Musicale at Florence in 1953 under Mitropoulos that Leonora was to be among her most successful roles, and here she confirms the fact in spades with her lustrous, effortlessly shaped and eloquent traversal of the role.

By her side she has the incomparable Corelli, singing his first Don Alvaro, and revealing that his brilliant, exciting yet plangent tone is precisely the right instrument to project Alvaro's loves and sorrows. At this stage of his career his thrilling upper register and incisive delivery of the text were at their most potent, as he makes abundantly clear in aria and duet. As his antagonist, Bastianini sings with the kind of Verdian élan seemingly now extinct among his breed. He may not be the most subtle of Verdian baritones, but here his macho approach ideally suits Don Carlo's vengeful imprecations.

If that weren't enough vocal splendour for

one occasion, there's Christoff – yet another member of the cast at the peak of his career – intoning Padre Guardiano's dignified utterances in that unique if not always entirely Italianate manner of his. Renato Capecchi for long made the part of Melitone his own: one can see and hear why here in his amusing yet never overstated sense of the role's comic possibilities. The voices are caught with very little distortion in goodish sound. The original film has suffered some deterioration over the years, but its recent restoration yields far better results than was once the case on dim VHS copies: this DVD derives from RAI's original master copy. Pleasure is completed by the bonus of an interview with Tebaldi.

Additional recommendations

La forza del destino
Price Leonora **Domingo** Don Alvaro **Milnes** Don Carlo **John Alldis Choir; London Symphony Orchestra / Levine**
RCA ③ 74321 39502-2 (171' · DDD · T/t) Ⓜ
  A well-cast set and a strong recommendation. Leontyne Price followers will be tempted no doubt, but note she's past her prime here. The recording is uncut.

La forza del destino
Callas Leonora **Tucker** Don Alvaro **Tagliabue** Ⓗ
Don Carlo **Chorus and Orchestra of La Scala, Milan / Serafin**
EMI ③ 556323-2 (164' · ADD · T/t) Ⓕ🅓➤
  Callas is superb as Leonora and, Tagliabue aside, the rest of the cast turn in fine performances. Serafin does, however, make some cuts.

I Lombardi alla prima crociata

I Lombardi
June Anderson sop Giselda **Luciano Pavarotti** ten Oronte **Samuel Ramey** bass Pagano **Richard Leech** ten Arvino **Ildebrando d'Arcangelo** bass Pirro **Yanni Yannissis** bass Acciano **Jane Shaulis** mez Sofia **Anthony Dean Griffey** ten Prior **Patricia Racette** mez Viclinda **Chorus and Orchestra of the Metropolitan Opera, New York /James Levine**
Decca ② 455 287-2DHO2 (129' · DDD · T/t) Ⓕ🅓➤

Pavarotti appeared at the Met production of *I Lombardi* in 1993: this recording is the delayed result. He's in good voice and sings Oronte's aria with fine *legato*, binding the decorative turns of the cabaletta beautifully into the vocal line and throwing in a respectable top C to show us he still can. *I Lombardi* is a viscerally exciting opera. The first complete recording, conducted by Lamberto Gardelli (Philips), set a good benchmark in 1972, but that need not deter us from welcoming this lively newcomer. The Met Opera Orchestra plays with splendid precision and, as Turks and Crusaders, women of the harem and virgins, the Met Chorus has a high old time on both sides of *I Lombardi*'s war-zone. Levine himself has improved beyond recognition as a Verdian; this studio recording is well paced and has a good sense of theatre. Everything is swift and crisp.

The best role goes to the soprano Giselda, specially tailored for the delicate skills of Erminia Frezzolini. Among the current crop of Verdi sopranos, June Anderson is probably as plausible a modern Frezzolini as any. There's some lovely, pure-toned singing in her big scene at the end of Act 2 and her coloratura is shining bright, both in this cabaletta and later in 'In fondo all' alma'. Samuel Ramey makes a relatively lightweight Pagano, who alone decorates his second verses. In the second tenor role Richard Leech holds his own, although his voice doesn't take well to the microphone. Ildebrando d'Arcangelo proudly represents the younger generation of Italian singers in the small role of Pirro, and Patricia Racette sings brightly as Viclinda.

Gardelli's crusading first recording has a rough Italianate vigour that lovers of early Verdi will enjoy, but Levine and his forces more than hold their ground with pace and brilliance, and a bright, modern recording with on balance a better cast and the voices well forward.

Luisa Miller

Luisa Miller
Katia Ricciarelli sop Luisa **Plácido Domingo** ten Rodolfo **Renato Bruson** bar Miller **Gwynne Howell** bass Walter **Elena Obraztsova** cont Federica **Wladimiro Ganzarolli** bass Wurm **Audrey Michael** mez Laura **Luigi de Corato** ten Peasant **Chorus and Orchestra of the Royal Opera House, Covent Garden / Lorin Maazel**
DG 459 481-2GTA2 (133' · ADD). Recorded 1980 Ⓜ☐→

The strength of this DG reissue is the singing of the three principals. The production of *Luisa Miller* at the Royal Opera House, Covent Garden, on which the set was based, probably marked the high-point of Katia Ricciarelli's career. Maybe the recording caught her just a year too late, when some harsh sounds had started to intrude in her singing at *forte* above the stave, but the soft singing remains beautiful and the character is immensely touching. Domingo sings Rodolfo with a voice of metal as firm and glowing as bronze, even if he does not have the poetry of Bergonzi or the flair of Pavarotti. Bruson is heard in one of the best roles in his repertoire: the sympathetic music of the Miller calls for exactly the long, lyrical lines at which he excels, often spanning two phrases in a single breath where the average Verdi baritone would be left gasping. Howell makes a stately, but not very incisive Walter. Neither Ganzarolli nor Obraztsova had been in the Royal Opera stage production, and the decision to bring them into the cast solely for the recording was not justified by the results. Obraztsova's thick-voiced Federica is a liability, but the real stumbling-block is Maazel's insensitive conducting. Nevertheless, as a totality, this set remains the equal of any before us at the moment.

Macbeth

Macbeth
Piero Cappuccilli bar Macbeth **Shirley Verrett** mez Lady Macbeth **Nicolai Ghiaurov** bass Banquo **Plácido Domingo** ten Macduff **Antonio Savastano** ten Malcolm **Carlo Zardo** bass Doctor **Giovanni Foiani** bass Servant **Sergio Fontana** bass Herald **Alfredo Mariotti** bass Assassin **Stefania Malagú** mez Lady-in-waiting **Chorus and Orchestra of La Scala, Milan / Claudio Abbado**
DG ② 449 732-2 (154' · ADD · T/t). Recorded 1976 Ⓜ◯☐→

Verdi's lifelong admiration for Shakespeare resulted in only three operas based on his plays. *Macbeth*, the first, originally written in 1847, was extensively revised in 1865. Without losing the direct force of the original, Verdi added greater depth to is first ideas. Once derided as being un-Shakespearean, it's now recognised as a masterpiece for its psychological penetration as much as for its subtle melodic inspiration.

Abbado captures perfectly the atmosphere of dark deeds and personal ambition leading to tragedy projected by Verdi, and his reading holds the opera's disparate elements in the score under firm control, catching its interior tensions. He's well supported by his Scala forces. Shirley Verrett may not be ideally incisive or Italianate in accent as Lady Macbeth, but she peers into the character's soul most convincingly. As ever, truly inspired by Abbado, Cappuccilli is a suitably daunted and introverted Macbeth who sings a secure and unwavering *legato*. Domingo's upright Macduff and Ghiaurov's doom-laden Banquo are both admirable in their respective roles.

Macbeth
Peter Glossop bar Macbeth **Rita Hunter** sop Lady Macbeth **John Tomlinson** bass Banquo **Kenneth Collins** ten Macduff **Richard Greager** ten Malcolm **Christian du Plessis** bass Doctor **Michael George** bass Servant **Roger Heath** bass Assassin **Ludmilla Andrew** mez Lady-in-Waiting **BBC Singers; BBC Concert Orchestra / John Matheson**
Opera Rara ② ORCV301 (132' · DDD) Recorded 1979 Ⓕ◯◯

This recording started as a project engendered by the Verdi specialist Julian Budden to perform a number of Verdi operas in their original versions. Although Verdi's revisions of his first Shakespearean opera are mostly improvements, several aspects of the original score are worth reviving. Inevitably it's a more consistent whole, since the later amendments are in a changed and improved style. Lady Macbeth's second aria, 'Trionfai', is more basic and showy than its subtle successor, 'La luce langue'. The cabaletta to Macbeth's Act 3 aria is rousing and unusual, and was dropped in favour of another duet for Macbeth and his Lady. The chorus at the start of Act 4, replaced by a more distinctive piece, is in its own right a fine example of Risorgimento ardour, and the final scene, besides having Macbeth's effective aria as he lies mortally wounded, is tauter, if more blatant, than its successor.

What makes this issue most worthwhile, however, is the superb performance. John Matheson directs a vital, finely timed and well-integrated account of the score that catches all its astonishing originality. Rita Hunter is as accomplished and appropriate a Lady Macbeth as any on disc, bar the unique Callas for de Sabata. Peter Glossop's Verdian style is faultless, and his understanding of the part complete. Kenneth Collins delivers 'Ah, la paterno mano' in exemplary voice and style. John Tomlinson, then in pristine voice, is an imposing Banquo. Chorus and orchestra are hard to fault. The recording, slightly bass-heavy, has been transferred at rather a low level, but its balance is as good as you'd expect, given its origins. This is definitely an experience convinced Verdians should not miss.

Macbeth

Thomas Hampson *bar* Macbeth **Paoletta Marrocu** *sop* Lady Macbeth **Roberto Scandiuzzi** *bass* Banquo **Luis Lima** *ten* Macduff **Miroslav Christoff** *ten* Malcolm **Mihály Kálmándi** *bass* Doctor **Liuba Chuchrova** *mez* Lady-in-Waiting **Zürich Opera House Chorus and Orchestra / Franz Welser-Möst** *Stage director* **David Pountney** *Video director* **Thomas Grimm** TDK Mediactive ② DV-OPMAC (3h 6' · 16:9 · 2.0, 5.1 & DTS 5.1 · 2). Recorded live at the Opera House, Zürich, in 2001. Includes special feature, 'Macbeth – an Introduction'. Ⓕ**OO**

Here's yet another challenging and well-executed staging from the Zürich Opera, this one dating from 2001. David Pountney, in at least his third attempt at the work, presents the Shakespearean drama in predictably unorthodox manner, irritating in its overuse of distracting symbols, extras and props, but revelatory in its pointed treatment of the principal pair of characters. The production is at its most bizarre in the Witches' scenes, where a pack of maddened women disport themselves in an orgy of man-hating, but even when the effects are at their most outrageous a sense of a guiding hand is there to lend some sort of dramatic cohesion to the whole.

Pountney bases his concept on the erotic relationship, vividly delineated, between Macbeth and his spouse; their sex-dominated marriage is obviously the spur to their overweening ambition, with she – as ever – leading the way. Paoletta Marrocu, a Sardinian soprano with a growing reputation, throws caution to the winds in her energetic, purposeful, fierce attack on Lady Macbeth. From first to last it's a truly stunning performance both histrionically and vocally. Few sopranos, Callas undoubtedly is one, have sung the part so confidently and incisively in a powerful, lean yet strong voice unflinchingly projected. By her side Hampson's haunted Macbeth is a striking portrait of a man pushed to the limits in the cause of getting to the top. His voice may not

be truly Italianate in timbre, but he uses it here with such intelligence and force that one can overlook the want of a certain bite in his tone.

Welser-Möst presides over everything with an acute ear for the work's *tinta* and judges his speeds to a nicety, with admirable support from his own house's chorus and orchestra.

Additional recommendation

Macbeth Ⓗ
Mascherini Macbeth **Callas** Lady Macbeth **Tajo** Banquo **Chorus and Orchestra of La Scala, Milan / de Sabata**
EMI mono ② 566447-2 (139' · ADD · T/t) Recorded live Ⓜ **D**

Callas's portrayal of Lady Macbeth is definitive and Victor de Sabata's conducting electrifying. However, the rest of the cast aren't up to much, and the recorded sound is poor. A set for Callas fans only.

Nabucco

Nabucco

Tito Gobbi *bar* Nabucco **Bruno Prevedi** *ten* Ismaele **Carlo Cava** *bass* Zaccaria **Elena Suliotis** *sop* Abigaille **Dora Carral** *sop* Fenena **Anna d'Auria** *sop* Anna **Giovanni Foiani** *bass* High Priest of Baal **Walter Krautler** *ten* Abdallo **Vienna Opera Orchestra; Vienna State Opera Chorus / Lamberto Gardelli** Decca ② 417 407-2DH2 (121' · ADD · T/t) Recorded 1965 Ⓕ **OD**

The years have hardly lessened the excitement of listening to this vigorous, closely knit performance. One realises why we were all amazed by Suliotis's account of the role of Abigaille. Her singing seizes you by the throat through its raw depiction of malice and through its youthful, uninhibited power. With the benefit of hindsight one can hear how a voice treated so carelessly and unstintingly could not last long, and so it was to be; but we should be glad for the brightness of the meteor while it flashed all too briefly through the operatic firmament. As an interpretation, her Abigaille seems a little coarse set beside the refinements shown by Scotto for Muti on EMI. However, Suliotis can manage by nature what Scotto has to conjure up by art, and she's certainly a subtler artist than Dimitrova on the wayward Sinopoli/DG version.

Gobbi, nearing the end of his illustrious career in 1965, remains the most convincing interpreter on record of the crazed king. The voice may have become a shade hard and uningratiating, but his use of Italian and his colouring of his tone, finally his pathos, are certainly not rivalled by Cappuccilli (Sinopoli). Carlo Cava exudes implacable fury as old Zaccaria, but he's inclined to go through his tone at *forte*. Prevedi is more than adequate as Ismaele, Carral less than adequate as Fenena (here DG score with Valentini Terrani).

One of the main assets of the Decca remains Gardelli's prompt, unfussy, and yet thrillingly delivered interpretation, clearly conveyed to his excellent Viennese forces. It's much more steadily and convincingly paced than Sinopoli's reading. The recording is forward and has plenty of presence, but it now sounds a little boxy beside the greater spaciousness of the DG. But the panache of the Decca enterprise silences criticism (except when the minute cuts in Nabucco's part are conceived). It's a pleasure to hear the bold inspiration of Verdi's first triumph conveyed with such conviction.

Listen to the Act 1 finale and you're sure to be won over to the set as an entity.

Nabucco (sung in English)
Alan Opie bar Nabucco **Leonardo Capalbo** ten Ismael **Alastair Miles** bass Zachariah **Susan Patterson** sop Abigail **Jane Irwin** mez Fenena **Dean Robinson** bass High Priest **Paul Wade** ten Abdullah **Camilla Roberts** sop Anna
Opera North Chorus and Orchestra / David Parry
Chandos Opera in English ② CHAN3136
(126' · DDD · S/T/N)　　　　Ⓜ️ⓄⓄ➤

Opera in English is here fully justified by virtue of an excellent cast all-round who let us hear every word of the old, trusted translation by Norman Tucker and Tom Hammond, pioneers of giving works in the vernacular. But perhaps the most convincing reason for acquiring this set is the superb singing of the Opera North Chorus, who are in a sense this work's heroes. From start to finish they sing wholeheartedly and make the most of the text.

Heading the cast is Alan Opie, perhaps giving his best performance to date on disc. He reveals every facet of the troubled king's character. His early wilfulness, followed by madness and then his conversion to Jehovah, are all depicted with an unerring feeling for every word of the text. Of course the core of the opera comes in the great Act 3 duet with Abigail, then the noble solo 'Lord God of Judah', which Opie sings with proper sorrow and contrition.

In the duet he is partnered by Susan Patterson. She conveys every bit of the anti-heroine's scheming and unforgiving character, sings pretty much all of her taxing part with firm, full tone, then at the close shows suitable remorse in the Act 3 finale. As the one truly upright character, Zachariah, Alastair Miles proves his pre-eminence among British basses today in Verdi: every note of his two solos is sung with strength and a feeling for line, and he is as happy on high as below. Fenena is well served by Jane Irwin's lovely mezzo, shining forth in her Act 3 solo ending with a glorious high A. The one disappointment is the rather feeble Ismael, but he doesn't play a very big part in proceedings.

David Parry makes the most of Verdi's early, rudimentary style, conducting the piece for all its worth, supported finely by the Opera North Orchestra. We have the customary slightly over-reverberant Chandos sound, which at times favours the chorus and band at the expense of the soloists, but that is a minor blemish on a truly exemplary performance.

Nabucco
Leo Nucci bar Nabucco **Fabio Sartori** ten Ismaele **Carlo Colombara** bass Zaccaria **Maria Guleghina** sop Abigaille **Nino Surguladze** sop Fenena **Carlo Striuli** bass High Priest **Carlo Bosi** ten Abdallo **Patrizia Cigna** sop Anna
Verona Arena Chorus and Orchestra / Daniel Oren
Stage director **Denis Krief**
Video director **Tiziano Mancini**
Decca 📀 074 3245DH (141' · NTSC · 16:9 · HD · PCM stereo and DTS 5.1 stereo · 0)
Recorded live 2007　　　　　　　　　　　　Ⓕ

There is a good sense here of the fitness of things, and of their grandeur too. As the camera roves and observes the great arena before the show begins, one becomes probably more aware of its size than if one were there in person with the milling crowds trying to find a seat. For a roof there is the spacious firmament on high, and onstage a structure that might have been designed to fill the Tate Modern. Then, as the opera unfolds, Verdi's music fills the auditorium and merely human voices rise to their almost superhuman task.

Vocally, and perhaps dramatically, the opera is dominated by Abigaille, an outsize soprano whose music makes harder demands upon voice and technique than almost any comparable role in opera. Guleghina is the Abigaille of our time: powerful, intense, wide of range, agile in passagework, and when need arises capable of softness. If she were completely steady and if her timbre had an Italianate vibrancy and variety of coloration she would be ideal. As Nabucco, the veteran Nucci comes through with impressive authority and stamina, the middle of his voice still rich and ample. The High Priest, Zaccaria, the third major character, has one of the great bass roles in the Verdi repertoire: finely sung here by Carlo Colombara, firm, sonorous and noble in bearing.

Of the others, Fabio Sartori deserves mention, physically somewhat cumbersome, vocally full-bodied and incisive. Chorus and orchestra do the arena and its 2007 season credit, and the conductor, Daniel Oren, is well in control of his far-flung forces. The production team also wins its way through to grateful acknowledgment, despite the initial ill-will created by the blocks of scaffolding which suggest nothing more biblical than the local Ikea store in its early stages of construction. It has its uses, which include doing duty for the banks of the Euphrates, from which the Israelites sing (most beautifully) their immortal 'Va, pensiero'.

Otello

Otello
Plácido Domingo ten Otello **Cheryl Studer** sop Desdemona **Sergei Leiferkus** bar Iago **Ramón Vargas** ten Cassio **Michael Schade** ten Roderigo **Denyce Graves** mez Emilia **Ildebrando d'Arcangelo** bass Lodovico **Giacomo Prestia** bass Montano

Philippe Duminy *bass* Herald **Hauts-de-Seine Maîtrise; Chorus and Orchestra of the Opéra-Bastille, Paris / Myung-Whun Chung**
DG ② 439 805-2GH2 (132' · DDD · T/t)   Ⓕ**OOᗺ**

Just as *Othello* is a difficult play to bring off in the theatre, so *Otello* is a difficult opera to bring off out of it. For some years now, Domingo has been, on stage, the greatest Otello of our age. On record, though, he has had less success. Leiferkus and Domingo have worked closely together in the theatre; and it shows in scene after scene – nowhere more so than in the crucial sequence in Act 2 where Otello so rapidly ingests Iago's lethal poison. By bringing into the recording studio the feel and experience of a stage performance – meticulous study subtly modified by the improvised charge of the moment – both singers help defy the jinx that so often afflicts *Otello* on record. The skill of Leiferkus's performance is rooted in voice and technique: clear diction, a very disciplined rhythmic sense and a mastery of all ornament down to the most mordant of mordents. Above all, he's always there (usually stage right in this recording), steely-voiced, rabbiting on obsessively. We even hear his crucial interventions in the great Act 3 *concertato*.

Domingo is in superb voice; the sound seems golden as never before. Yet at the same time, it's a voice that's being more astutely deployed. To take that cruellest of all challenges to a studio-bound Otello, the great Act 3 soliloquy 'Dio! mi potevi', Domingo's performance is now simpler, more inward, more intense. It helps that his voice has darkened, winning back some of its russet baritonal colourings.

Chung's conducting is almost disarmingly vital. Verdi's scoring is more Gallic than Germanic. The score sounds very brilliant in the hands of the excellent Opéra-Bastille orchestra, and, in Act 4, very beautiful. Maybe Chung is wary of the emotional depths and, occasionally, the rhythmic infrastructure is muddled and unclear. And yet, the freshness is all gain. He's already a master of the big ensemble and the line of an act. Tension rarely slackens. On the rare occasions when it does, the mixing and matching of takes is probably to blame.

Studer's is a carefully drawn portrait of a chaste and sober-suited lady. Perhaps Verdi had a sweeter-voiced singer in mind for this paragon of 'goodness, resignation, and self-sacrifice' (Verdi's words, not Shakespeare's). Studer's oboe tones keep us at a certain distance, yet you'll look in vain for a better Desdemona. What's more, Studer is a singer who can single-mindedly focus the drama afresh, as she does more than once in Act 3. DG's recording is clear and unfussy and satisfyingly varied; Studer, in particular, is much helped by the beautifully open acoustic the engineers provide for the closing act. This is undoubtedly the best *Otello* on record since the early 1960s. It also happens to be the first time on disc that a great Otello at the height of his powers has been successfully caught in the context of a recording that can itself be generally considered worthy of the event, musically and technically.

VERDI OTELLO – IN BRIEF

Plácido Domingo *Otello* **Cheryl Studer** *Desdemona* **Sergei Leiferkus** *Iago* **Bastille Opera Chorus and Orchestra / Myung-Whun Chung**
DG ② 439 805-2GH2 (132' · DDD)   Ⓕ**OOᗺ**
Chung's high-octane conducting sets the standard for a marvellous set, with Domingo at his peak of vocal power and expression and Sergei Leiferkus a smooth-voiced, subtle Iago.

Jon Vickers *Otello* **Leonie Rysanek** *Desdemona* **Tito Gobbi** *Iago* **Rome Opera Chorus and Orchestra / Tullio Serafin**
RCA ② 09026 63180-2 (144' · ADD)   Ⓜ**O**
Jon Vickers is a heroically anguished Moor in his first recording, with Gobbi a marvellously rich and malevolent Iago, and Rysanek a large-voiced but vulnerable Desdemona. Serafin's conducting is splendidly powerful.

Jon Vickers *Otello* **Mirella Freni** *Desdemona* **Peter Glossop** *Iago* **Berlin Deutsche Oper Chorus; Berlin PO / Herbert von Karajan**
EMI ② 769308-2 (140' · ADD)   Ⓜ**ᗺ**
Karajan's recording comes up better on his spectacular film version, but since this isn't presently available the CD is still recommendable at mid-price, with Freni's deeply touching Desdemona and Peter Glossop's characterfully nasty Iago.

Otello   Ⓗ
Giovanni Martinelli *Otello* **Elisabeth Rethberg** *Desdemona* **Lawrence Tibbett** *Iago* **Metropolitan Opera Orchestra and Chorus, New York / Ettore Panizza**
Naxos Historical mono ② 8 111018/9 (150' · ADD)   Ⓢ**ᗺ**
Recorded live in 1938, this tremendous performance enshrines the magnificent Otello of Giovanni Martinelli: a towering characterisation that demands to be heard. Tibbett's Iago is comparably superb; only Rethberg is slightly under par.

Plácido Domingo *Otello* **Barbara Frittoli** *Desdemona* **Leo Nucci** *Iago* **Chorus and Orchestra of La Scala, Milan / Riccardo Muti**
TDK ᴅⱽᴰ DV-OPOTEL (140')   Ⓕ**O**
In this well-staged 2001 recording Domingo is in drier voice than in his younger selves, but still overwhelming. Barbara Frittoli is a deeply felt Desdemona. Muti conducts with spirit.

Plácido Domingo *Otello* **Renée Fleming** *Desdemona* **James Morris** *Iago* **Metropolitan Opera Chorus and Orchestra / James Levine**
DG ᴅⱽᴰ 073 092-9GH (142')   Ⓕ
A fine 1995 stage version from the Met, with Domingo a commanding Moor, Renée Fleming a beautiful Desdemona and James Morris, though not the most menacing Iago, credible and richly sung. Levine's conducting, while not as lively as Muti's, is still enjoyable.

Otello H

Giovanni Martinelli *ten* Otello **Elisabeth Rethberg** *sop* Desdemona **Lawrence Tibbett** *bar* Iago **Nicholas Massue** *ten* Cassio **Giovanni Paltrinieri** *ten* Roderigo **Thelma Votipka** *mez* Emilia **Nicola Moscona** *bass* Lodovico **George Cehanovsky** *bass* Montano **Metropolitan Opera Orchestra and Chorus, New York / Ettore Panizza**
Naxos Historical mono ② 8 111018/9 (150′ · ADD).
Recorded live 1938 ⓢ●●⭢

Not tall or ideally loud enough, his voice past its prime when (at over 50) he took the role into his repertoire, Giovanni Martinelli's Otello was a somewhat handicapped creation. He nevertheless wrung the heart, as Olin Downes (*New York Times*) put it, by conviction, subtlety and pathos: 'Mr Martinelli was Otello, in facial play and tragic bearing, the suggestion of great uncontrollable force and agony – a figure which never failed to evoke admiration and pity.'

On records he does more: almost every phrase comes to take the impress of his voice and style. The taut concentration of tone matches the emotional intensity; at every point a close and receptive study of the score has yielded its reward. Certainly there are things his voice would not do, but it was still an impressive instrument. At its best, as in the monologue, Martinelli's Otello remains finest of all.

The recording was pirated from radio and its transfer now is a triumph of Ward Marston's skill and hard work. He explains in a producer's note that the originals were not available for him to work on, but he has cleaned and restored so that the performance emerges more vividly than ever before. And what a performance!

The conductor Panizza was Toscanini's deputy in earlier years, and something of the master's energy is felt, in company with more flexibility and willingness to accommodate his singers. In Act 1 especially he makes frightening demands upon orchestra and chorus who, it must be said, meet them dauntlessly.

The recording, which places everything in such a bright light, is less than kind to Elisabeth Rethberg. Until recently hers had been a voice of special and most beautiful quality; but too many Aidas seem to have left their mark and the close recording catches an untoward hardness, though there is no mistaking the stylishness and a high degree of surviving mastery.

Tibbett's Iago is superbly caught, the best account of the role on records, not forgetting Gobbi. It is a mercurial portrayal, now genial, now ironic or insinuative, nakedly malignant. Like Martinelli, his response to every phrase is specific and vivid; and his voice resonates richly. It was for him the recording was made. Anyway, he deserves our gratitude twice over – for his own magnificent performance and for this inestimable gift to posterity.

Otello H

Ramón Vinay *ten* Otello **Gré Brouwenstijn** *sop* Desdemona **Otakar Kraus** *bar* Iago **John Lanigan**
ten Cassio **Raymond Nilsson** *ten* Roderigo **Noreen Berry** *mez* Emilia **Marian Nowakowski** *bass* Lodovico **Michael Langdon** *bass* Montano **Forbes Robinson** *bass* Herald **Royal Opera House Chorus and Orchestra, Covent Garden / Rafael Kubelík**
Royal Opera House Heritage Series mono ②
ROHS001 (140′ · ADD · T/t). Recorded live 1955 Ⓜ

This *Otello* of 1955, issued at long, long last, marked Rafael Kubelík's accession as music director and the first staging by the company of Verdi's tragedy. Excitement and expectation were high, and the performance was electrifying – after more than 50 years does it still sound as impressive?

Indeed it does, thanks not least to Kubelík's superb conducting. Even today he remains underrated as an opera conductor. Here he combines the dramatic drive of Toscanini with the more yielding approach of Serafin. While never losing an overview of the score, he brings out the myriad detail with an unerring ear for what matters: the two big ensembles are nicely contrasted with the plangent intricacies of Desdemona's Willow Song and 'Ave Maria'.

Vinay's Moor is an overwhelming interpretation – a terrifying portrayal of love, jealousy and anguish, sung in that peculiarly pained tone of his; Vinay's timbre tears at the heart so that one shares in his pain of the soul. Brouwenstijn is a most womanly and vulnerable Desdemona. In the love duet she is not quite at her best but in the devastating Act 3 duet she sings with tremenedous passion, and her Act 4 scena is notable for sweet tone, musical accuracy and, in the 'Ave Maria', a lovely *cantabile* and an exquisitely poised high A flat at its end.

At the time there was disappointment that the announced Iago, Tito Gobbi, was sacked by Kubelík because of his failure to turn up for rehearsals. He was replaced by the estimable house baritone of the day, Otakar Kraus, who brings an insinuating tone and plausible manner based on obedience to the text. From his singing alone one can almost visualise the bright-eyed, scheming villain. John Lanigan, the company's young lyric tenor of the day, provides a debonair Cassio. The rest are more than adequate.

The mono sound is dim at times and one would like a broader perspective, but one soon forgets these limitations in the immediacy of the performance. As well as any of its successors, it fulfils the exigent demands Verdi places on his cast and Vinay here surpasses even his own high standards.

Otello

Plácido Domingo *ten* Otello **Barbara Frittoli** *sop* Desdemona **Leo Nucci** *bar* Iago **Cesare Catani** *ten* Cassio **Antonello Ceron** *ten* Roderigo **Rossana Rinaldi** *mez* Emilia **Giovanni Battista Parodi** *bass* Lodovico **Cesare Lana** *bass* Montano **Ernesto Panariello** *bass* Herald **Giuseppe Verdi Conservatory Children's Choir, Milan; La Scala Children's Choir, Chorus and Orchestra, Milan / Riccardo Muti**
Stage director **Graham Vick**

Video director **Carlo Battistoni**
TDK Mediactive 📀 DV-OPOTEI (140' · 16:9 · PCM
Stereo, 5.1 & DTS 5.1· 0)　　　　　　Ⓕ**OO**

This is one of Graham Vick's most intelligent, detailed and involving productions housed in Ezio Frigero's superbly crafted and atmospheric set and clothed by Franca Squarciapino's traditional, beautifully wrought costumes. Here's proof, if proof were needed, that setting an opera in its period still works best provided you have such sensitive hands in control.

The thoughtful, often revelatory, handling of the principals often lends a new dimension to the work, especially with such eloquent singing actors as Plácido Domingo and Barbara Frittoli; remarkable is the strength of passion engendered by the fated lovers – blissful in Act 1, desperately tormented in Act 3.

At this late stage in his career Domingo was able to compensate for a voice that doesn't always obey his exemplary instincts with a moving portrayal of the Moor. His projection of his own near-disbelief in his agony and jealousy in Act 3, and again before the murder, is deeply affecting. So are Frittoli's facial expressions and body language, yielding and erotic in Act 1, making her Act 3 and final disillusion that much more terrifying to behold. Vocally Domingo sings with even more variety of dynamic and timbre than before. His pent-up fury in the big ensemble is truly frightening. Frittoli sings with many shades of tone and exquisite phrasing throughout, not least in her Act 4 solos, which she enacts with searing emotion. Leo Nucci's penny-plain, dully sung Iago isn't in the same league, and the young tenor taking Cassio lacks the requisite sweetness in the voice. The Emilia is admirable, as are the two basses. Muti leads the drama to its dreadful conclusion with his customary brio and care for incidentals. The video direction and the sound picture leave nothing to be desired.

Additional recommendations

Otello
Domingo Otello **Scotto** Desdemona **Milnes** Iago
National Philharmonic Orchestra; Ambrosian Opera Chorus / Levine
RCA ② 88697 44820-2 (134' · ADD)　　Ⓜ**O**

For some this is the finest of Domingo's several recorded Otellos. Also, Scotto's Desdemona is one of the most moving on disc. At mid-price this set is a real winner.

Otello
Vickers Otello **Rysanek** Desdemona **Gobbi** Iago
Rome Opera Chorus and Orchestra / Serafin
RCA ② 09026 63180-2 (144' · ADD)　　　Ⓜ

Tito Gobbi's Iago remains irreplaceable (except possibly for Giuseppe Valdengo's for Toscanini), and Jon Vickers is a superb Otello, more metallic and heroic than Domingo though not necessarily more sensitive.

Otello
Domingo Otello **Te Kanawa** Desdemona **Leiferkus** Iago **Chor & Orch of the Royal Opera / Solti**
Stage director **Moshinsky** *Video director* **Large**
Opus Arte 📀 OAR3102D (145' · NTSC · 4:3 · PCM stereo and 2.0 · 0)　　　　　Ⓜ**OO**

At Covent Garden, Elijah Moshinsky's production insists heavily on its religious agenda: Christ crucified looms at the back, dominant as in the east window of a cathedral. In the film version (because the camera roams) it is more a suggestive presence, less a directional imposition. It is moving to see how completely Domingo lives his role. Te Kanawa too shows herself alive to every suggestion of her music and words. Leiferkus is a powerful embodiment of malign will. Much could be written about Domingo's singing, and Te Kanawa's, and about Solti's conducting, but a video demands attention to the visual. Suffice to say that you can have the highest expectation and not be disappointed.

Otello　　　　　　　　　　　　　　　　Ⓗ
Del Monaco Otello **Carteri** Desdemona **Capecchi** Iago **Chor & Orch of RAI, Milan / Serafin**
Film director **Enriquez**
Hardy Classic Video 📀 HCD4004 (136' · NTSC · 4:3 Black & White · 1.0 · 0 · N). Recorded 1958　　Ⓕ

This film of *Otello* isn't to be overlooked, in spite of its age. Franco Enriquez was employed to achieve as much as was possible in terms of dramatic fluidity within the technical restrictions then applicable in the studio. Mario Del Monaco was then at the height of his powers, the reigning Otello of the time, and one of the role's most powerful exponents ever. By his side, Renato Capecchi sings a strongly voiced, highly articulate, intelligently shaped and believable Iago. But perhaps the most compelling performance of all is Rosanna Carteri's Desdemona. Love, fidelity and sincerity are conveyed in her eyes, indeed her whole being, and in her faultless vocal traversal of the role. Over all presides Serafin, conducting an unobtrusively correct and vital performance of a score he knew so well.

Rigoletto

Rigoletto　　　　　　　　　　　　　　Ⓗ
Leonard Warren *bar* Rigoletto **Bidú Sayão** *sop* Gilda **Jussi Björling** *ten* Duke **Norman Cordon** *bass* Sparafucile **Martha Lipton** *contr* Maddalena **William Hargrave** *bass* Monterone **Thelma Altman** *sop* Giovanna **Richard Manning** *ten* Borsa **George Cehanovsky** *bar* Marullo **Maxine Stellman** *mez* Countess Ceprano **John Baker** *bass* Count Ceprano **Metropolitan Opera Chorus and Orchestra, New York / Cesare Sodero**
Naxos Historical ② 8 110051/2 (116' · ADD)
Recorded live 1945　　　　　　　　　　Ⓢ**OO**

This performance marked the return of Björling to the Met after a wartime break of four years spent mostly in his native Sweden. And what a return it was: at 34 he was at the absolute peak of his powers and sings a Duke of Mantua imbued with supreme confidence and tremendous brio – just try the start of the Quartet. He and the

VERDI RIGOLETTO – IN BRIEF

Leonard Warren *Rigoletto* **Bidù Sayão** *Gilda* **H**
Jussi Björling *Duke* **Metropolitan Opera Chorus
and Orchestra / Cesare Sodero**
Naxos mono ② 8 110051/2 (116' · AAD) ⑤◐◑▷
A superb performance live from the New
York Met in this bargain-price 1945 set,
although the sound wouldn't make it every-
one's first choice.

Tito Gobbi *Rigoletto* **Maria Callas** *Gilda* **H**
Giuseppe di Stefano *Duke* **Chorus and
Orchestra of La Scala, Milan / Tullio Serafin**
EMI mono ② 556327-2 or Regis RRC2076
(118' · AAD) ⑤◐◑▷
Equally historic but in much finer sound,
though still mono, this 1955 version has the
great trio of principals with Serafin's dynamic
conducting; Regis adds a pair of bonus arias.

Renato Bruson *Rigoletto* **Edita Gruberová** *Gilda*
Neil Shicoff *Duke* **Santa Cecilia Academy
Chorus and Orchestra / Giuseppe Sinopoli**
Philips ② 462 158-2PM2 (128' · DDD) ⓂD▷
Renato Bruson and Edita Gruberová head a
good cast in a fine modern version, though
Neil Shicoff's Duke is sometimes rather
forced. Sinopoli's exciting reading is less
eccentric in its tempi than usual.

Piero Cappuccilli *Rigoletto* **Ileana Cotrubas**
Gilda **Plácido Domingo** *Duke* **Vienna State
Opera Chorus; Vienna PO / Carlo Maria Giulini**
DG ② 457 753-2GOR2 (128' · DDD) Ⓜ◐▷
Giulini's graceful, detailed conducting has
plenty of drama, still more so a strong cast
headed by Plácido Domingo, Piero Cappuccilli's restrained jester and Ileana Cotrubas's
meltingly vulnerable Gilda.

Robert Merrill *Rigoletto* **Anna Moffo** *Gilda*
Alfredo Kraus *Duke* **RCA Italiana Opera Chorus
and Orchestra / Sir Georg Solti**
RCA ② 82876 70785-2 (113' · ADD) Ⓜ
The 1960s Solti at high voltage may not suit
everyone, but this is an exciting and splendidly
cast set – Alfredo Kraus in his elegant prime,
Anna Moffo a beautifully girlish Gilda, Robert
Merrill's rich-voiced jester, uncharacteristically expressive, and for once, among the
supporting cast, the commanding Monterone
that Verdi required.

Paolo Gavanelli *Rigoletto* **Christine Schäfer** *Gilda*
Marcelo Álvarez *Duke* **Chorus and Orchestra of
the Royal Opera House / Edward Downes**
Opus Arte 🎞 OA0829D (169') Ⓕ
This highly modern but recognisable Covent
Garden staging, splendidly conducted by
Sir Edward Downes, stands out among
DVDs. Paolo Gavanelli is a magnificent
jester, Marcelo Álvarez a swaggering Duke
and Christine Schäfer's clear-voiced Gilda
detailed and moving.

house clearly revel in his display of tenor
strength, yet that power is always tempered by
innate artistry. If not a subtle interpreter, he's
always a thoughtful one, and never indulges
himself or his audience.

Similarly, Warren was, at the time, at the zenith
of his career. Vocally he's in total command of
the role and the house. His reading, although slightly
extroverted in some areas, evinces a firm tone, a
secure line and many shades of colour. He's at
his very best in his two duets with Gilda (sadly
and heinously cut about) and no wonder, given
the beautiful, plangent singing of Sayão, whose
'Caro nome' is so delicately phrased, touching
and keenly articulated. 'Tutte le feste' is still better, prompting Paul Jackson (who in general is
unjustifiably hard on the performance in *Saturday Afternoons at the old Met*, Duckworth: 1992)
to comment that Sayão's 'lovely, pliant, fully
rounded tones are immediately affecting'.
Indeed, in spite of the merits of the two male
principals, it's her truly memorable interpretation that makes this set essential listening.

All round, there are few recordings that match
this one for vocal distinction – perhaps only the
Serafin-Callas-Gobbi on EMI and the Giulini-
Cotrubas-Cappuccilli on DG. They are much
more expensive but boast superior sound. Björling and Warren both made later studio sets,
but neither matches his live contribution here,
off the stage.

The final virtue of this absorbing experience
is the conducting of the little-known Sodero.
His moderate – but never sluggish – tempi
allow for almost ideal articulation on all sides,
and his insistence on letting us hear the score so
clearly makes one regret even more all those
excisions then common in the opera house and
the studios.

Rigoletto **H**
Tito Gobbi *bar* Rigoletto **Maria Callas** *sop* Gilda
Giuseppe di Stefano *ten* Duke **Nicola Zaccaria** *bass*
Sparafucile **Adriana Lazzarini** *mez* Maddalena **Plinio
Clabassi** *bass* Monterone **Giuse Gerbino** *mez*
Giovanna **Renato Ercolani** *ten* Borsa **William Dickie**
bar Marullo **Elvira Galassi** *sop* Countess Ceprano
Carlo Forti *bass* Count Ceprano **Chorus and
Orchestra of La Scala, Milan / Tullio Serafin**
EMI mono ② 556327-2 or Regis RRC2076
(118' · ADD · N/T/t). Recorded 1955 Ⓜ/⑤◐◑

That one recording should continue to hold
sway over many other attractive comers after 55
years is simply a tribute to Callas, Gobbi, Serafin
and Walter Legge. Whatever the merits of its
successors, and they are many, no Rigoletto has
surpassed Gobbi in tonal variety, line, projection of character and understanding of what
Rigoletto is about; no Gilda has come anywhere
near Callas in meaningful phrasing – listen to
'Caro nome' or 'Tutte le feste' on any other set
if you're disbelieving – nor achieved such a careful differentiation of timbre before and after
her seduction; no conductor matches Serafin
in judging tempo and instrumental detail on a

nicety; nor benefited from a chorus and orchestra bred in the tradition of La Scala; no producer has equalled Legge in recording voices rather than the space round them. And di Stefano? Well, he may not be so stylish a Duke as some others, but the 'face' he gives his singing, and the sheer physical presence he conveys, not to mention his forward diction, are also unique in this opera. Nothing in this world is perfect, and so there are some small drawbacks here. Serafin sadly makes small cuts in the first Gilda-Rigoletto duet and omits entirely the Duke's cabaletta as used to be the practice in the theatre. Gobbi could be said not to have quite the weight of voice ideally called for by a Verdi baritone role. Finally, the recording, although immeasurably improved from previous issues of the set, still has one or two places of distortion obviously present on the original tape. In every other way, this remains the classic performance on record.

Rigoletto
Paolo Gavanelli bar Rigoletto **Christine Schäfer** sop Gilda **Marcelo Álvarez** ten Duke **Eric Halfvarson** bass Sparafucile **Graciela Araya** contr Maddalena **Giovanni Battista Parodi** bass Monterone **Elizabeth Sikora** sop Giovanna **Peter Auty** ten Borsa **Quentin Hayes** bar Marullo **Dervla Ramsay** mez Countess Ceprano **Graeme Broadbent** bass Count Ceprano **Andrea Hazell** mez Page **Nigel Cliffe** bass Usher **Royal Opera House Orchestra and Chorus, Covent Garden / Edward Downes**
Stage director **David McVicar**
Film director **Sue Judd**
Opus Arte Media 📀 OA0829D (169' · 16:9 · 5.1 · 0)
Ⓕ🔵

David McVicar's engrossing 2001 production of *Rigoletto* at Covent Garden caused something of a stir because of the frank licentiousness of the opening scene, including sex of all varieties. It's a bold and sensational beginning to the staging, depicting the Duke of Mantua as a libidinous and strident ruler of his ill-disciplined domain. Given that picture of the court, the contrast of Rigoletto's almost obsessive love for his daughter is all the more poignant.

That's the background to a performance of thrilling commitment on all sides, at whose centre is the arresting portrayal of Rigoletto from Paolo Gavanelli, probably the best acted and most sensitively sung, in terms of variety and colouring of tone, since Tito Gobbi essayed the role in the same house 35 years ago (even if he has an occasional tendency to lose pitch).

By comparison, Christine Schäfer's Gilda is a trifle cool at the start, but once ravished she comes to emotional life and is particularly moving in the final act. Her singing, though not Italianate in colour, is musically shaped and technically flawless. Marcelo Álvarez is the epitome of a selfish, macho ruler, and Eric Halfvarson a suitably sinister Sparafucile. Downes conducts a well-nigh faultless account. The only reservation concerns the sound. Too frequently the voices are too backwardly placed in relation

to the orchestra, but that shouldn't deter you from being part of a very special occasion.

Simon Boccanegra

Simon Boccanegra
Piero Cappuccilli bar Simon Boccanegra **Mirella Freni** sop Amelia **José Carreras** ten Gabriele **Nicolai Ghiaurov** bass Fiesco **José van Dam** bass-bar Paolo **Giovanni Foiani** bass Pietro **Antonio Savastano** ten Captain **Maria Fausta Gallamini** sop Maid **Chorus and Orchestra of La Scala, Milan / Claudio Abbado**
DG The Originals ② 449 752-2GOR2 (136' · ADD · T/t)
Recorded 1977
Ⓜ🔵🔵▶

This famous recording has become a classic, a studio performance following a series of performances at La Scala in the Strehler staging. The close, slightly claustrophobic recording exactly mirrors the mood of nefarious activities and intrigues following Boccanegra's rise to be Doge of Genoa, he and his lovely daughter victims of the dark deeds round them. In his plebeian being, clement exercise of authority and warm, fatherly love, Simon Boccanegra is made for Cappuccilli, who, under Abbado's tutelage, sings it not only *con amore* but with exemplary, delicately tinted tone and unbelievably long-breathed phrasing. As his daughter Amelia, Freni was just entering her quasi-*spinto* phase and expands her lyric voice easily into the greater demands of this more dramatic role. Similarly heavier duties hadn't yet tarnished the youthful ardour and sap in the tone of the 30-year-old Carreras. As the implacable Fiesco, Ghiaurov exudes vengeful command, and van Dam evil machinations as the villain Paolo. Over all presides Abbado in what remains one of his greatest recordings, alert to every facet of the wondrous score, timing every scene, in an opera tricky to pace, to near-perfection, and bringing theatrical drama into the home. This set should be essential to any reputable collection of Verdi.

Stiffelio

Stiffelio
José Carreras ten Stiffelio **Catherine Malfitano** sop Lina **Gwynne Howell** bass Jorg **Gregory Yurisich** bar Stankar **Adele Paxton** sop Dorotea **Robin Leggate** ten Raffaele di Leuthold **Lynton Atkinson** ten Federico di Frengel **Chorus and Orchestra of the Royal Opera House, Covent Garden / Edward Downes**
Stage director **Elijah Moshinsky**
Video director **Brian Large**
Opus Arte 📀 OAR3103D (122' · NTSC · 4:3 · 2.0 · 0)
Recorded live at the Royal Opera House, Covent Garden, London, on February 2 and 6, 1993   Ⓕ🔵🔵

In 2007 *Stiffelio* was reported sinking under the weight of a lavish production at the Metropolitan. At Covent Garden, the production team, led by Elijah Moshinsky, had much more the right idea and, in one decision of casting, the visual element is transformed. The opera has

VERDI LA TRAVIATA – IN BRIEF

Maria Callas Violetta **Alfredo Kraus** Alfredo Ⓗ
Mario Sereni Germont **San Carlos Theatre**
Lisbon Chorus and Orchestra / Franco Ghione
EMI ② 556330-2 (124' · ADD)   Ⓜ**OO**▷
Callas incarnates the doomed Violetta unlike
any rival, with Alfredo Kraus a poised,
plangent Alfredo, even if Ghione is not quite
their equal. The traditional cuts are made and
the live recording is not brilliant.

Ileana Cotrubas Violetta **Plácido Domingo**
Alfredo **Sherrill Milnes** Germont **Bavarian State**
Opera Chorus and Orchestra / Carlos Kleiber
DG ② 477 7115GOR2 (106' · ADD)   Ⓕ**O**▷
Cotrubas makes a more touching heroine than
Callas, vocally glorious and ardently sup-
ported by Domingo's Alfredo and Kleiber's
tautly dramatic conducting. Despite tradi-
tional cuts, a deeply moving performance.

Angela Gheorghiu Violetta **Frank Lopardo**
Alfredo **Leo Nucci** Germont **Chorus and**
Orchestra of the Royal Opera House /
Sir Georg Solti
Decca ② 448 119-2DHO2 (127' · DDD)   Ⓕ**O**▷
Decca **DVD** 071 431-9DH (135')   Ⓕ**O**
The famous performance that marked Gheor-
ghiu's debut appearance and one of Solti's
last. Splendidly recorded and alive – but do
consider the DVD. The production is lively
but unexceptional, with a decent supporting
cast, but it's still immensely involving.

Renata Scotto Violetta **Alfredo Kraus** Alfredo
Renato Bruson Germont **Philharmonia**
Orchestra / Riccardo Muti
EMI ② 509694-2 (114' · ADD)   Ⓕ**O**▷
Scotto gives a wonderfully characterised cen-
tral performance. Kraus again oozes style as
Alfredo and Bruson is perfect as his father.
Muti presides over everything with sensitiv-
ity to the work's dramatic ebb and flow.

Norah Amsellem Violetta **José Brós** Alfredo
Renato Bruson Germont **Chorus and Orchestra**
of the Teatro Real, Madrid / Jesús López Cobos
Opus Arte ② **DVD** OA0934D   Ⓕ**O**
A wonderfully sensitive updating of La traviata to wartime France. A fine cast acts and
sings magnificently.

Stefania Bonfadelli Violetta **Scott Piper** Alfredo
Renato Bruson Germont **Arturo Toscanini**
Foundation Chorus and Orchestra /
Plácido Domingo
TDK Mediactive **DVD** DV-OPLTR (205')   Ⓕ
Franco Zeffirelli brings his long expereince
of this opera to a largely young cast – Stefania
Bonfadelli is a lovely actress as well as a vocal
imaginative Violetta. Scott Piper imbues
Alfredo with considerable ardour. The vet-
eran Renato Bruson is a typically implacable
Germont. Domingo conducts efficiently.

only one female among the principals, and,
rather as in *Otello*, the action turns on her largely
passive character. She is Lina, wife of the minister of a Protestant community where the way of
life is simple and biblical law is strictly upheld.
At the Met she is played by Sharon Sweet whose
ample form and golden curls suggest (however
unjustly) an ungodly allowance of worldly pleasure. In her husband's absence she has 'fallen',
and Catherine Malfitano (the Lina at Covent
Garden) is attractive enough to make that seem
plausible while remaining in figure and demeanour one of the devout, and a 'pure' woman at
heart.

The other major difference in production is
one of scale. At the Metropolitan everything has
gone up in the world. The minister's house is
palatial, the modest gathering to celebrate his
return a full-scale ambassador's dinner party.
Lina's father is decked out in full military grandeur, while at Covent Garden he is clad in simple civilian dignity. Covent Garden's graveyard
is a matter of plain stones and crosses; the Met's
sports elaborate and (surely) abhorred images.
In every respect the London production is better, with unostentatious care taken over furnishings and each member of the chorus provided
with an identity.

The Stiffelio is Carreras in what was probably
the finest achievement among roles following
his serious illness. Gregory Yurisich sings magnificently as the father. Gwynne Howell is a
pillar of sonorous authority, and Robin Leggate,
having played Cassio so often, fits in perfectly as
his guilty counterpart. Edward Downes conducts with a sure and thoughtful touch.

La traviata

La traviata   Ⓗ
Maria Callas sop Violetta Valéry **Alfredo Kraus**
ten Alfredo Germont **Mario Sereni** bar Giorgio
Germont **Laura Zanini** mez Flora Bervoix **Piero De**
Palma ten Gastone **Alvaro Malta** bar Baron Douphol
Maria Cristina de Castro sop Annina **Alessandro**
Maddalena bass Doctor Grenvil **Vito Susca** bass
Marquis D'Obigny **Manuel Leitao** ten Messenger
Chorus and Orchestra of the Teatro Nacional de
San Carlos, Lisbon / Franco Ghione
EMI mono ② 556330-2 (124' · ADD · T/t) Recorded
live 1958   Ⓜ**OO**▷

Callas caught live is preferable to Callas
recorded in the studio, and Violetta was perhaps
her supreme role. The former Covent Garden
producer Ande Anderson pointedly commented
that, whereas other sopranos made you cry in
the final act of *Traviata*, Callas also made you
cry in the second, and one hears here what he
meant, as Callas's Violetta comes to the stark
realisation that she's going to have to give up her
one and only true beloved seemingly for ever.
The desperation that enters her voice at 'Non
sapete' is surpassed only by the sorrow and emptiness in the lead-in to 'Dite alla giovine', then
the fatalism of 'morro! la mia memoria', which

John Steane in his note that accompanies this essential CD reissue describes as being sung with such 'fullness of heart and voice'.

The final act is almost unbearable in its poignancy of expression: the reading of the letter so natural in its feeling of emptiness, the realisation that the doctor is lying so truthful, the sense of hollowness at what's possibly the opera's most moving moment, 'Ma se tornando …': 'If in returning you haven't saved my life, then nothing can save it'. All this and so much else suggests that Callas understood better than anyone else what this role is truly about.

But there's more to it even than that. Alfredo Kraus's Alfredo as heard here is as appealing as any on record. His Schipa-like tone at that stage in his career, his refinement of phrasing, especially in the duets with Callas, and his elegant yet ardent manner are exactly what the role requires. Mario Sereni may not quite be in the class of his colleagues but his Germont *père* is securely, sincerely and often perceptively sung and more acutely characterised than in his account of the part with de los Angeles. Almost as important, contrary to what you may read in some earlier reviews, Franco Ghione is an expert, knowledgeable conductor of this score, yielding to his singers yet prompt and dramatic when need be, and able to draw singing string tone from his excellent orchestra in the two preludes. So are there any drawbacks? Yes indeed; the prompter is all too audible, the audience coughs intrusively, particularly during the recitative at the start of Act 3, and the score is extensively cut in the manner traditional to pre-authentic days. Nevertheless, if it's to be but one *Traviata* in your collection, it must be this one.

La traviata
Angela Gheorghiu *sop* Violetta **Frank Lopardo** *ten* Alfredo **Leo Nucci** *bar* Germont **Leah-Marian Jones** *mez* Flora **Gillian Knight** *mez* Annina **Robin Leggate** *ten* Gaston **Richard Van Allan** *bass* Baron **Roderick Earle** *bass* Marquis **Mark Beesley** *bass* Doctor **Neil Griffiths** *ten* Giuseppe **Bryan Secombe** *bass* Messenger **Rodney Gibson** *ten* Servant **Chorus and Orchestra of the Royal Opera House, Covent Garden / Sir Georg Solti**
Decca ② 448 119-2DHO2 (127' · DDD · T/t)
Recorded live 1994   Ⓕ**O**▶

For Angela Gheorghiu, Violetta was the right role at the right time. The whole drama is there in her voice, every expression in the eyes and beat of the heart reflected in the way she shapes and colours Verdi's vocal lines. Her quiet singing is particularly lovely, affording subtle variations of tenderness and inner anxiety. When she does choose to make a point with force, as in her sudden warmth of feeling towards Giorgio Germont at 'Qual figlia m'abbracciate' or her chilling cry of 'Morro!', accompanied by a loud thump on the table, her ideas always hit home. A few moments of vocal weakness are accentuated by the microphone, mainly a tendency to go sharp and some hardness at the top of the voice that

was not troublesome in the theatre. Otherwise she's the most complete and moving Violetta we have had since her compatriot, Ileana Cotrubas.

These live performances were the first time that Sir Georg Solti, at the age of 82, had conducted a staged *La traviata* and he wanted two young singers who were also coming fresh to the opera. What was so spellbinding in the theatre was the touching intimacy they brought to their scenes together. Instead of the duets for Violetta and Alfredo turning into standard Italian operatic bawling, they became lovers' whispers. The effect comes across here in the cadenzas, where Gheorghiu and Frank Lopardo really seem to be listening to each other. Elsewhere, one is more aware than in the theatre that Lopardo's light tenor is far from being an idiomatic Italian voice. His idiosyncratic tone quality and un-Italian vowels can be problematical, as is some ungainly lifting up into notes. Leo Nucci, Decca's resident Verdi baritone at the time, makes a standard Giorgio Germont, not more, and apart from Leah-Marian Jones's energetic Flora, the smaller roles don't say a great deal for the Royal Opera's depth of casting.

Solti insisted that the opera be performed complete. But there's nothing studied about his conducting: the performance is fresh and alive from the first note to the last, the result of a lifetime's experience of how to pace a drama in the opera house. With the increasing number of live opera sets, a recommendation for *La traviata* is likely to be based on whether one is prepared to accept noises-off or not. Decca's recording is well balanced and vivid, dancing feet and banging doors included. Among the live sets, Giulini and Callas at La Scala in 1955 must be *hors concours*, but in rather awful sound. Muti's more recent La Scala set, in which he has to wrestle with Tiziana Fabbricini's wayward talents as Violetta, is the nearest comparison.

La traviata
Norah Amsellem *sop* Violetta **José Bros** *ten* Alfredo **Renato Bruson** *bar* Germont **Itxaro Mentxaka** *mez* Flora **Maria Espada** *sop* Annina **Emilio Sánchez** *ten* Gastone **David Rubiera** *bar* Baron **Marco Moncloa** *bar* Marquis **Chorus and Orchestra of the Teatro Real, Madrid / Jesús López Cobos**
Stage Director **Pier Luigi Pizzi**
Opus Arte ② **DVD** OA0934D (175' · NTSC · 16:9 · PCM stereo and DTS 5.1 · 0)
Recorded live at the Teatro Real, Madrid, in 2005   Ⓕ

Pier Luigi Pizzi's updating of *Traviata* to occupied Paris, first seen in 2003 in Madrid, might seem gratuitous, but because of his skill as designer and his experience directing singers, the new milieu hardly ever interferes, after the opening scene, with the central tragedy of Violetta's plight. That owes much to the freshness and immediacy of the portrayal by Norah Amsellem. From Violetta's first fevered entry to her agonising death she is totally absorbed in the role, acting and singing with the most eloquent feeling.

In the first scene we see her entering her soirée from her bedroom, the stage split in two – a slightly questionable idea – and she becomes infatuated with Alfredo in their Act 1 duet while on her lavish bed. It sounds gimmicky but as played by Amsellem and the sympathetic and stylishly sung Alfredo of José Bros it is totally convincing. The act ends with an all-consuming account of 'Ah! fors'è lui', both verses, shaped in long lines and phrased with unerring conviction so that one forgives harshness when she presses on her higher notes.

Act 2 scene 1 is set in the drawing-room of a 1930s-style country villa. Here the central encounter of Violetta and Germont *père* is the emotional centre of the work, as it should be, with Amsellem and Renato Bruson acting and reacting to each other with rewarding rapport. Bruson, at 69, sings with all the experience of his years and few signs of wear, and follows it with a masterly account of 'Di provenza'. In the second scene the whole company excels itself and the heroine is infinitely touching in 'Alfredo, Alfredo'.

In a stark, simple set for Act 3, this Violetta conveys her sorrow and terrified thoughts with inward passion. 'Addio del passato', again two verses, is notable for the length of line and exquisite phrasing Amsellem provides. She and Bros sing a near-ideal 'Parigi, o cara' before Violetta dies, a desperately tragic figure. Amsellem's slim figure and expressive face are notable assets in achieving her intelligent reading.

López-Cobos conducts an interpretation notable for yielding support of his singers combined with dramatic dash, and the Madrid orchestra play as though their lives depended on the results. No wonder this staging has received so much praise in Spain. Its preservation on DVD is welcome.

La traviata
Angela Gheorghiu *sop* Violetta **Natascha Petrinsky** *mez* Flora **Ramón Vargas** *ten* Alfredo Germont **Roberto Frontali** *bar* Giorgio Germont **Tiziana Tramonti** *sop* Annina **Enrico Cossutta** *ten* Gastone **Alessandro Paliaga** *bar* Barone Douphol **Piero Terranova** *bass* Marchese d'Obigny **Luigi Roni** *bass* Doctor Grenvil **Chorus and Orchestra of La Scala, Milan / Lorin Maazel**
Stage director **Liliana Cavani**
Video director **Paolo Longobardo**
ArtHaus Musik 📀 101 343 (134' · NTSC · 16:9 · PCM stereo, 5.1 and DTS 5.1 · 0)
Recorded live in 2007   Ⓕ❍

Nothing is perfect, always some stammer in the divine speech: we know that. But such blemishes as occur in the Scala production are incidental to its general excellence and to the greatness of Angela Gheorghiu's Violetta. She is a strangely variable quantity in the musical life of our time but here she is once again a true artist, the voice lovely as ever throughout most of its range, the expressive art in both singing and acting matured so that this portrayal is intensely mov-

ing and memorable. Here is a Violetta who rises to the great moments but whose every phrase and movement is intelligently guided and deeply felt. The internal argument in the solo of Act 1, for instance, develops with a marvellously subtle conflict of impulses, and though 'pleasure' wins at the end of it there has been just the right degree of forced gaiety to make it no surprise to find in Act 2 that love has prevailed after all.

The Germonts, son and father, are maddeningly stupid characters but decent, honest singers, the one (Ramón Vargas) not imaginative but capable of delicacy, the other (Roberto Frontali) clean-cut in his tone and modestly affecting in his aria. Maazel's conducting is a model of controlled flexibility, and the orchestra respond to him with unfailing precision. Visually, the production is a treat, the chorus handled unfussily as a collection of individuals, with the principal characters and their relationships given thoughtful and sensitive preparation.

To be ranked with the Los Angeles production with Fleming and Villazón (see above): we should count ourselves a favoured generation to have both or the choice of either.

La traviata
Renée Fleming *sop* Violetta **Rolando Villazón** *ten* Alfredo Germont **Renato Bruson** *bar* Giorgio Germont **Daniel Montenegro** *ten* Gastone **Philip Kraus** *bar* Baron **Lee Poulis** *bass* Marquis **James Creswell** *bass* Doctor **Suzanna Guzmán** *mez* Flora **Anna Alkhimova** *sop* Annina **Sal Malaki** *ten* Giuseppe
Los Angeles Opera Chorus and Orchestra / James Conlon
Stage director **Marta Domingo**
Video director **Brian Large**
DG 📀 074 3215DH (141' · NTSC · 16:9 · PCM stereo and DTS 5.1 · 0)   Ⓕ

La traviata
Teresa Stratas *sop* Violetta **Plácido Domingo** *ten* Alfredo Germont **Cornell MacNeil** *bar* Giorgio Germont **Maurizio Barbacini** *ten* Gastone **Allan Monk** *bar* Baron **Richard Oneto** *bass* Marquis **Robert Sommer** *bass* Doctor **Axelle Gall** *mez* Flora **Pina Cei** *sop* Annina **Luciano Brizi** *ten* Giuseppe
Metropolitan Opera Chorus and Orchestra / James Levine
Film director **Franco Zeffirelli**
DG 📀 073 4364GH (105' · NTSC · 4:3 · PCM stereo and DTS 5.1 · 0)   Ⓕ

'What about all this luxury?' Father Germont wants to know as he looks around him on arrival in Act 2. It's a fair question, and not only concerning the rural love-nest. If 'sumptuous' is (as we are assured) the word for the stage production at Los Angeles, a word has yet to be coined that will do justice to Zeffirelli's film version.

In their different ways both of these are unmissables. The Los Angeles performance is very moving; and the 1982 film has to be seen to be believed – which of course (again) is an equivocal form of recommendation. Each is committed to its medium, and perhaps some will find that a disqualification. In Los Angeles the audience makes its presence felt with generous and frequent applause, including (in two instances) at the rise of curtain. The film makes it clear from the start that every advantage is to be taken of freedom to roam: 'Look here upon this picture,' it seems to say, 'and on this…and this…and this.'

Both Violettas are distinguished and memorable, Fleming with one of the most lovely voices to be heard in the part, Stratas as one of the best actresses among singers. Fleming's warm, vibrant quality makes its mark from her very first phrase, and again from the start Stratas's face reflects all the shades by which hope and fear, the public image and the inner self may be expressed. Both meet the notoriously disparate vocal demands of the role, though Stratas's voice sounds worn on the high notes. In the last act Stratas's relative slightness of vocal and physical build works to her advantage. Both are fine in the developing emotions of the great duet with Germont *père*.

For all that Domingo and Villazón may seem to represent a kind of vocal continuum, their identities here are quite distinct, with Villazón the lighter, more volatile Alfredo, and, also, in musical detail sometimes the more refined. The fathers MacNeil and Bruson are quite unlike, MacNeil relatively coarse in character and singing, Bruson well past his prime as a singer but patrician in manner and still refulgent in the centre of his voice. At Los Angeles Conlon conducts level-headedly: Levine's flair is most evident in vigorous rhythmic passages such as the dances and the card game. In both videos the orchestra is less to the fore than it would be in a sound recording, and in the film is sometimes almost relegated to the status of background music. The film also makes cuts to the score, while the stage performance is complete with cabalettas for father and son and a second verse of 'Addio del passato' for Violetta.

Additional recommendations

La traviata
Bonfadelli Violetta **Piper** Alfredo **Bruson** Germont
Arturo Toscanini Foundation Chorus and Orchestra / Domingo Stage director **Zeffirelli**
TDK Mediactive 📀 DV-OPLTR (3h 25' · 16:9 · 2.0, 5.1 & DTS 5.1 · 0). Includes documentary, 'Making of La traviata', and Interviews   Ⓕ

    Lovingly directed and designed by the then 78-year-old Zeffirelli. Bonfadelli makes a very fine Violetta – it's a reading that demands to be seen and heard. Sound quality is beyond reproach, and though it may not surpass the López-Cobos DVD (reviewed above) it deserves a recommendation.

La traviata
Callas Violetta **di Stefano** Alfredo **Bastianini**   Ⓗ
Germont **Chorus and Orchestra of La Scala, Milan / Giulini**
EMI mono ② 566450-2 (124' · ADD) Recorded 1955 Ⓜ

    Surely the most famous recording of *Traviata*, with Callas an incomparable Violetta. The big let down, though, is Bastianini's Germont and the poor recorded sound.

Il trovatore

Il trovatore   Ⓗ
Maria Callas sop Leonora **Giuseppe di Stefano** ten Manrico **Rolando Panerai** bar Count di Luna **Fedora Barbieri** mez Azucena **Nicola Zaccaria** bass Ferrando **Luisa Villa** mez Ines **Renato Ercolani** ten Ruiz, Messenger **Giulio Mauri** bass Old Gypsy **Chorus and Orchestra of La Scala, Milan / Herbert von Karajan**
EMI ② 377365-2 (129' · ADD · N/S)
Recorded 1956.   ⒷⓄⓄⒹ▸

Callas and Karajan took the world by the ears in the 1950s with this *Il trovatore*. Leonora was one of Callas's finest stage roles, and this recording is wonderfully intense, with a dark concentrated loveliness of sound in the principal arias that puts one in mind of Muzio or Ponselle at their best. Walter Legge always managed to team Callas with the right conductor for the work in question. Often it was Serafin, but Karajan in *Il trovatore* is utterly compelling. This opera, like Beethoven's Seventh Symphony and Stravinsky's *The Rite of Spring*, is one of music's great essays in sustained rhythmic intensity; dramatically it deals powerfully in human archetypes. All this is realised by the young Karajan with that almost insolent mastery of score and orchestra which made him such a phenomenon at this period of is career. There are some cuts, but, equally, some welcome inclusions (such as the second verse of 'Di quella pira', sung by di Stefano with his own unique kind of *slancio*).

Although the EMI sound is very good, one or two climaxes suggest that in the heat of the moment, the engineer, Robert Beckett, let the needle run into the red and you might care to play the set in mono to restore that peculiar clarity and homogeneity of sound which are the mark of Legge's finest productions of the mono era. But whatever you do don't miss this set.

Il trovatore
Plácido Domingo ten Manrico **Leontyne Price** sop Leonora **Sherrill Milnes** bar Count di Luna **Fiorenza Cossotto** mez Azucena **Bonaldo Giaiotti** bass Ferrando **Elizabeth Bainbridge** mez Ines **Ryland Davies** ten Ruiz **Stanley Riley** bass Old Gypsy **Neilson Taylor** bar Messenger **Ambrosian Opera Chorus; New Philharmonia Orchestra / Zubin Mehta**
RCA Red Seal ② 74321 39504-2 (137' · ADD · T/t)
Recorded 1969   ⓂⓄ

The Leonora of Leontyne Price is the high-point of the Mehta recording: her velvety, sensuous articulation of what's certainly an 'immenso, eterno amor' is entirely distinctive

---

Giuseppe di Stefano *Manrico* **Maria Callas** Ⓗ
Leonora **Fedora Barbieri** *Azucena* **Chorus and Orchestra of La Scala, Milan / Herbert von Karajan**
EMI mono ② 556333-2 (129' · AAD) ⒻⓄⓄⒹ

A 1957 mono recording shouldn't put you off this, with its thrilling combination of Maria Callas and Giuseppe di Stefano in top form. Karajan is at his most dramatic, with the rest of the cast, notably Fedora Barbieri's Azucena, to match.

Plácido Domingo *Manrico* **Leontyne Price**
Leonora **Fiorenza Cossotto** *Azucena* **Ambrosian Opera Chorus, New Philharmonia Orchestra / Zubin Mehta**
RCA ② 74321 39504-2 (136' · AAD) ⓂⓄ

This is probably the best among several excellent modern recordings, with no weak links in its stellar cast. Mehta is more galvanic than usual. A rich, vivid recording.

Franco Corelli *Manrico* **Gabriella Tucci** *Leonora*
Giulietta Simionato *Azucena* **Rome Opera Chorus and Orchestra / Thomas Schippers**
HMV ② HMVD573413-2 (123' · ADD) Ⓢ

Vivid, fast-moving conducting and a less conventional cast – apart from its stars – give this a real sense of drama.

Jussi Björling *Manrico* **Zinka Milanov** *Leonora* Ⓗ
Fedora Barbieri *Azucena* **Robert Shaw Chorale, RCA Victor Orchestra / Renato Cellini**
RCA ② GD86643 (107' · AAD) Ⓜ

A 1952 mono recording that still carries plenty of excitement, with two quite extraordinary voices in Jussi Björling and the Met's great Verdi baritone Leonard Warren. Zinka Milanov is slightly less compelling, but Barbieri is a fine Azucena, and Cellini is more vital than many better-known interpreters.

Plácido Domingo *Manrico* **Rosalind Plowright**
Leonora **Brigitte Fassbaender** *Azucena* **Santa Cecilia Academy Chorus and Orchestra / Carlo Maria Giulini**
DG ② 477 5915GOR2 (140' · DDD) ⓂⒹ

'The thinking man's *Trovatore*', beautifully judged and detailed in both conducting and singing – yet intensely Italianate, with a cast conceding nothing to other versions.

Plácido Domingo *Manrico* **Raina Kabaivanska**
Leonora **Fiorenza Cossotto** *mez Azucena* **Vienna State Opera Chorus and Orchestra / Herbert von Karajan** *Stage director* **Herbert von Karajan** *Video director* **Günther Schneider-Siemssen**
TDK ② 🄳🅅🄳 DV-CLOPIT (151' · 4:3 · PCM stereo, 5.1 & DTS 5.1 · 0) ⒻⓄⓄ

Magnificently cast, superbly sung and sensitively directed, this 1978 Vienna production reveals why this was one of Karajan's favourite Verdi operas.

---

and dramatically astute. The New Philharmonia is a no less ardent exponent. Mehta's pacing may be uneven, his accompanying breathless, but he draws robust playing in bold primary colours to which the recording gives vivid presence.

The acoustic serves Manrico less well: he seems to be singing in the bath when we first overhear him. This, though, is a younger, simpler Domingo than the one we encounter elsewhere, and there are passages of wonderfully sustained intensity. Cossotto's Azucena is disappointing. All the vocal tricks and techniques are there, but it's very much a concert performance, and we're never entirely engaged.

Il trovatore Ⓗ
Peter Glossop *bar* Count di Luna **Gwyneth Jones**
sop Leonora **Giulietta Simionato** *mez* Azucena
Bruno Prevedi *ten* Manrico **Joseph Rouleau** *bass*
Ferrando **Elizabeth Bainbridge** *mez* Ines **John Dobson** *ten* Ruiz **William Clothier** *bar* Old Gypsy
Handel Owen *ten* Messenger
Chorus and Orchestra of the Royal Opera House, Covent Garden / Carlo Maria Giulini
Royal Opera House Heritage Series mono ②
ROHS011 (127' · ADD)
Recorded live at the Royal Opera House, Covent Garden, on November 26, 1964 Ⓜ

Leontyne Price being expected, prices were raised. When Price did not come and Gwyneth Jones was substituted the cast began to assume a more homely complexion than seemed right for a gala occasion, and absentees from the gallery began to feel complacent. As a result, many never heard Bruno Prevedi's Manrico. His 'Di quella pira' is not one for the book of legends, but the 'Ah si, ben mio' that precedes it deserved its applause, and the final scene is sung as by one inspired.

Gwyneth Jones is in best voice, before the loosening process had made itself evident and when her ample soprano was in its fullest bloom. She is technically in firm control and includes the Act 4 cabaletta, sung with assurance and scrupulous precision. Peter Glossop's performance is particularly moving. If lacking the brazen edge to battle it out with the brass in 'Per me ora fatale', he had all the warmth and generosity of tone to make a human being and not a paste-board villain of di Luna, and he sings his aria with the ease, range, power and beauty of the true Verdi baritone.

By 1964 Simionato's voice was too fragmented to capture with pleasure, but she still gives a performance on the grand lines. Otherwise the vocal heroes are the male chorus. For Giulini, his personal touch is felt more distinctively in the studio recording of 1983, but this performance is truer to the distinctive tensions and excitement of the opera itself.

Il trovatore
Plácido Domingo *ten* Manrico **Raina Kabaivanska**
sop Leonora **Piero Cappuccilli** *bar* Count di Luna

Fiorenza Cossotto *mez* Azucena **José van Dam** *bass*
Ferrando **Vienna State Opera Chorus and
Orchestra / Herbert von Karajan**
Stage director **Herbert von Karajan**
Video director **Günther Schneider-Siemssen**
TDK ② 📀 DV-CLOPIT (151' · 4:3 · PCM stereo, 5.1
& DTS 5.1 · 0) Recorded live at the Staatsoper,
Vienna, on May 1, 1978   Ⓕ**OO**

Never available before, this marvellous performance marked Karajan's long-awaited return to
the Vienna State Opera in 1978. It was also the
notorious occasion when Franco Bonisolli threw
a tantrum and walked out of the dress rehearsal.
He was replaced at the eleventh hour by
Domingo, who thereby completed a cast that
has hardly been bettered. Inspired no doubt by
the reception he receives on first entering the
pit, Karajan is at his most proactive, and the
singers react with real conviction to complement their exemplary singing.

The staging, Karajan's own, and the sets are
pretty conventional, but who cares when the score
is projected with such confidence and the voices
are of such rare quality? The youngish Domingo
is the feisty troubadour of the title to the life, and
he sings Manrico's taxing music as if that were the
easiest thing in the world. As his adversary, Count
di Luna, Piero Cappuccilli is in firm, supple voice,
giving a faultless account of 'Il balen' and fiercly
dramatic in the ensembles. Fiorenza Cossotto
offers her appreciable all to Azucena, a role she
made very much her own and one in which she's
yet to be surpassed. As Ferrando, José van Dam
launches the opera with tremendous authority.
Raina Kabaivanska, the Leonora, may not have
had a typically Verdian voice, but what she does
with her resources is remarkable, combining a
classic style – some beautifully etched phrasing –
with a poise as a vocal and dramatic actress that's
second to none, except perhaps Callas.

So it's one vocal treat after another, culminating in a superlative Act 4. Sound, picture and
direction are exemplary. This absorbing issue is
highly recommended to all admirers of Verdi
and great singing.

I Vespri siciliani

I Vespri siciliani   Ⓗ
Maria Callas *sop* Elena **Giorgio Kokolios-Bardi** *ten*
Arrigo **Enzo Mascherini** *bar* Montforte **Boris
Christoff** *bass* Procida **Bruno Carmassi** *bass*
Bethune **Mario Frosini** *bass* Vaudemont **Mafalda
Masini** *contr* Ninetta **Chorus and Orchestra of the
Maggio Musicale, Florence / Erich Kleiber**
Testament mono ② SBT2 1416 (159' · ADD)
Recorded live at the Teatro Comunale, Florence, on
May 26, 1951   Ⓕ

This recording, like Verdi's opera, has attracted
mixed reviews over the years. Composed for
Paris in 1855, *Les Vêpres siciliennes* has never
enjoyed the affection of critics or public in the
way the other 'mid-period' operas (*Boccanegra*,
Ballo and *Forza*) have.

This revival was one of the productions that
helped to spread Maria Callas's fame. At the
time, Lord Harewood wrote memorably in
Opera magazine about the tremendous force she
puts into the recitative in Act 1, in which the
Duchess Elena encourages the Sicilian popula-
tion to rebellion with the words 'Il vostro fato e
in vostra man' ('Your fate is in your own
hands').

Callas is terrific in the Act 1 aria and
cabaletta, as well as in the long duet with
Arrigo in Act 4, sung by Greek tenor Giorgio
Kokolios-Bardi. He had been one of Callas's
leading men at the National Opera in Athens,
and she particularly requested him for this
part. He's no Di Stefano but he gives a good
performance, especially of the aria in the
fourth act, 'Giorno di pianto'. In some ways
this opera is dominated by the two low male
voices – Boris Christoff is magnificent as the
gloomy, unforgiving Procida, while Enzo
Mascherini is in his element as the anguished
Guido di Montforte, who finds out too late
that his opponent is his own son.

Erich Kleiber is not usually associated with
the 19th-century Italian repertory but he
leads a vigorous performance, although there
are quite a few cuts. This tape (made for Walter Legge) does not include the Overture, so
the opera fits on two CDs. For Callas and
Christoff admirers, of course, this is an essential document. Although the sound quality is
variable, it is clearer than previous issues. The
Testament booklet is excellent, the libretto
available to download from the company's
website.

Tomás Luis de Victoria
Spanish 1548-1611

*Victoria sang as a choirboy at Ávila Cathedral.
When his voice broke he was sent to Rome where he
may have studied under Palestrina. He remained in
Italy until the 1580s during which time he served as
singer and organist at various churches and colleges.
He was also ordained as a priest while in Italy. He
returned to Spain as chaplain to Philip II's sister, the
Dowager Empress Maria, at the Descalzas Reales
convent, Madrid, from 1587 until her death in
1603; he remained there as organist until his
death, apart from a visit to Rome in 1594, when he
attended Palestrina's funeral.*

*The greatest composer of Renaissance Spain, his
reputation extended throughout Europe in his day.
Much of music – all written to sacred Latin texts –
was published, and the bulk of his output was Mass
and motet settings.*

Officium defunctorum

Officium defunctorum
Gabrieli Consort / Paul McCreesh
Archiv 447 095-2AH (60' · DDD · T/t)   Ⓕ**OO**▸

This is a remarkable recording. In some ways it's like a rediscovery, for here's an approach not too far from Pro Cantione Antiqua at its best and yet that group never recorded the work. The Gabrieli Consort adds chant to the Requiem Mass itself, thus creating more of a context for Victoria's magisterial work.

We have therefore the Epistle and preceding prayer, the Tract, Sequence, Gospel, Preface, Lord's Prayer and Postcommunion in addition to the polyphony; this also means, for example, that the *Kyrie* is sung nine-fold with alternating chant instead of simply three-fold only in polyphony. We can presume that the chant was taken from a suitable Spanish source by Luis Lozano Virumbrales, who's an expert in this field and the author of the insert-notes together with Paul McCreesh.

The performance itself is stately and imposing, with a tremendous homogeneity of sound: the use of an all-male choir, together with the added chant, lends it a tangibly monastic feel, though it would have been a fortunate monastery indeed that had falsettists of this quality. About the performance of the chant there are two points of interest: first, that it's doubled, like the polyphony, by a shawm, common Spanish practice at this period, and second, that McCreesh isn't afraid to have the falsettists singing the chant too.

The pace of the polyphony often seems unhurried, but never feels slow, and Westminster Cathedral Choir is faced with the hugely reverberant acoustics of its home building. From the beginning the singing is involving and incarnate, but the real magic comes nearer the end: from the *Agnus Dei* onwards one feels that the Gabrieli Consort have really got the measure of the music and is allowing it to speak through them. The final great responsory, the 'Libera me', is performed with heart-stopping power and conviction. McCreesh's approach shows how the Mass would have fitted into and complemented the liturgical framework without ever losing its own internal power and drama. A revelatory disc.

Masses

Missa O quam gloriosum. Missa Ave maris stella.
Motet – O quam gloriosum
Westminster Cathedral Choir / David Hill
Hyperion CDA66114 (57' · DDD)　　Ⓕ❍❍❍B⇢

This is likely to become one of your most cherished discs. It's notable for its spacious depth of sound, volatile unpredictability of interpretation, and above all the soaring *sostenuto* of the boy trebles, with their forward and slightly nasal tone quality. With their magnificently controlled *legato* lines, the Westminster boys treat Victoria's music as though it were some vast plainchant, with a passion that excites and uplifts. The choir is recorded in the exceptionally resonant Westminster Cathedral, at a distance and with great atmosphere.

Ave maris stella isn't one of Victoria's familiar Masses, quite simply because no music publisher

has made it available to choirs in a good, cheap edition. To have it rescued from obscurity is laudable in itself, but to have it sung with such poise and sensitivity is an unexpected double treat. Unlike *O quam gloriosum*, this is a work that thrills with echoes of Victoria's Spanish upbringing, of Morales and his predecessors, even of Josquin Desprez, whose own *Ave maris stella* Mass was brought to the cathedrals of the Iberian peninsula earlier in the century. The plainchant melody, familiar through Monteverdi's setting in the 1610 *Vespers*, completely dominates Victoria's music, for it's placed most often in huge treble lines that wheel high above the general texture. Magnificent as the early parts of the work are, nothing quite matches the final five-part *Agnus Dei*, sung here with admirable support and exquisitely shaped by David Hill. Recommended without reservation.

Missa Gaudeamus. Missa pro Victoria (both ed Dixon). Motets – Cum beatus Ignatius; Descendit angelus Domini; Doctor bonus amicus Dei Andreas; Ecce sacerdos magnus; Estote fortes in bello; Hic vir despiciens mundum; O decus apostolicum; Tu es Petrus; Veni, sponsa Christi (all ed Skinner)
The Cardinall's Musick / Andrew Carwood
ASV Gaudeamus CDGAU198 (78' · DDD · T/t)　　Ⓕ❍❍B⇢

There have been some fine recordings of Victoria's music in recent years, but none finer than this one at its best. The Cardinall's Musick has become known for its CDs of English Renaissance polyphony, but its approach, which joint directors Andrew Carwood and David Skinner describe as 'open and soloistic', works extremely well here, too. The two contrasted Mass settings are given the same highly expressive treatment as the motets, which, sung one to a part, have a madrigalian quality bringing out beautifully the natural, unforced rhetoric of Victoria's idiom.

The *Missa Gaudeamus*, based on a Morales motet, is scored for six voices. Performed with only two singers on each part, it sounds as rich and dark as the strongest chocolate; the overall blend is superb, clear and strikingly well balanced. With only two female voices on the upper part, the polyphonic texture isn't, as is so often the case, top-heavy; each strand carries equal weight, just as the densely contrapuntal writing demands. The final canonic *Agnus Dei* is sublime, and throughout – even in the longer movements – Carwood's sure-footed pacing allows the polyphony to ebb and flow like the swell of the sea.

The *Missa pro Victoria*, based on Janequin's chanson, *La guerre*, could hardly be more different in its forward-looking polychoral idiom. Here the writing is more condensed, more economical, but nevertheless highly dramatic. The ending of the *Gloria* is breathtaking, as is the magical opening of the Sanctus and the final 'dona nobis pacems' of the *Agnus Dei*. The clarion calls of the second *Kyrie* are equally striking. There are so many high spots on this disc that it's simply impossible to mention them all, and this is perhaps still more to the group's credit given that, as explained in the notes, a bout of flu among the singers can't have made for the easiest of recording sessions.

Victoria Missa Gaudeamus. Vidi speciosam
Frescobaldi Toccata per organo. Canzon dopo l'Epistola. Recercar dopo il Credo. Recercar: Sancta Maria Traditional Lectio libri Sapientiae **Anonymous** Assumpta est Maria in caelum. Gaudeamus omnes in Domino. Pater noster. Optimam partem elgit. Famulorum tuorum, quaesumus Domine. Mensae caelestis participes effecti. Propter veritatem. In illo tempore: intravit Jesus in quoddam castellum. Assumpta est Maria. Vere dignum et iustum est
**Lay Clerks of Westminster Cathedral /
Matthew Martin** with **Thomas Wilson** org
Hyperion CDA67748 (73' · DDD)   Ⓕ**ⓄⓄⓄ**Ⓓ▸

Westminster Cathedral's 19 Lay Clerks give a beautifully paced rendition of Victoria's rarely performed (and even less often recorded) *Missa Gaudeamus*. As was the case in The Cardinall's Musick's 1999 recording under Andrew Carwood (see above), the editions used are those prepared by Jon Dixon. He has also edited Victoria's sublime six-part motet *Vidi speciosam* which is used (in addition to the traditional plainsong chants) to augment the Ordinary movements of the Mass. Matthew Martin's tempi are consistently slower than Carwood's, though there is no sense of the music dragging. Rather, the singers are given the space to linger luxuriantly over their phrases.

Victoria's Mass setting for the Feast of the Assumption is based on a motet, *Iubilate Deo omnis terra*, composed in 1538 by Cristobal de Morales. On this recording it is presented in the context of a full choral and instrumental festal liturgical sequence, incorporating four organ pieces by Frescobaldi taken from his *Fiori musicale*, published in Venice in 1635. They are played by Thomas Wilson, the Cathedral's assistant organist, on a one-manual Goetze and Gwynn organ tuned to a meantone temperament. Organ and choir come together in the final Recercar: *Sancta Maria* by Frescobaldi.

The choral blend is – as might be expected – superb and exquisitely balanced. The countertenors soar to amazing heights without the slightest hint of strain. Background noises are kept to a minimum, apart from a faint electrical whirring in the right-hand channel during the chanted sections. This benchmark recording is another superb addition to both Hyperion's and Westminster Cathedral's illustrious Victoria discography.

Missa Dum complerentur. Dum complerentur. Veni Sancte Spiritus. Popule meus. Vexilla Regis. Veni Creator Spiritus. Pange lingua gloriosi. Lauda Sion
Westminster Cathedral Choir / James O'Donnell with **Joseph Cullen** org
Hyperion CDA66886 (70' · DDD· T/t)   Ⓕ**ⓄⓄ**▸

Westminster Cathedral Choir here makes a special contribution to the music of Tomás Luis de Victoria. The *Missa Dum complerentur*, for Pentecost, is based on Victoria's own motet; he adds an extra voice in the parody Mass setting and draws much on the opening material of the motet as well as its distinctive 'Alleluia' sections which ring out like a peal of bells – especially in this excellent performance. Indeed, the motet is finely conceived, with Victoria characteristically responding to the imagery of the text with changes of texture and pacing within the essentially contrapuntal idiom: a true master.

The choir, with its full-bodied sound and well-sustained vocal lines, has, over long years of tradition in singing this particular part of the repertory, achieved an almost intuitive feel for the flow of the music, which is perhaps as near as we'll ever get today to the authentic situation of professional church singers in Rome or the Spanish cathedrals in the 16th century. What we'll never know is whether the sonority – in particular the timbre of the boys' voices – resembles anything Victoria might have heard, that distinctive focus and intensity of tone well illustrated by the two Holy Week settings on the disc: the homophonic *Popule meus* and the hymn *Vexilla Regis*. This, and the two Pentecost hymns, are performed in *alternatim* with alternate verses in plainchant and polyphony. This is a superb and compelling disc that adds to our knowledge and appreciation of Victoria's art.

Officium Hebdomadae Sanctae

Officium Hebdomadae Sanctae – Dominica in ramis Palmarum; Feria sexta; Sabbato Sancto; Feria quinta. In Coena Domini. In Passione Domini
**La Colombina Ensemble; Schola Antiqua /
Juan Carlo Asensio**
Glossa ③ GCD922002/3 (3h 17' · DDD)   Ⓕ

Victoria's massive publication of 1585, the *Officium Hebdomadae Sanctae*, was never intended as a self-contained 'work': alongside the famous Tenebrae settings, it includes Lamentations for the three holy days, the Improperia ('Reproaches'), and music for Palm Sunday and for the St John and St Matthew Passions. Given the scale of these liturgies, a full CD re-creation is a practical impossibility.

Josep Cabré, director of La Colombina, therefore steers a pragmatic course, presenting enough of the surrounding plainchant to give a sense of its scale in relation to the polyphony. This sensible strategy works well, reconciling the complete presentation of the publication's contents with a more contextually sensitive approach. To the extent that both aims are fulfilled, this recording takes its place as one of the most significant contributions to Victoria's already impressive discography.

It's worth mentioning Victoria's use of a handful of simple recurring motifs (usually associated with specific words or phrases) that he would no doubt have expected his listeners to recognise. A recording such as this is probably the only way to experience the cumulative effect of such a strategy, now that actual liturgical performances within Holy Week are a thing of the past.

As to the performances, the polyphony is polished and involving in equal measure, although the emotional intensity associated with Victoria seems inversely proportional to the number of singers used. (They respond particularly well to the pieces scored for high voices, surely some of the most memorable music here.) While the inclusion of plainchant is both logical and effective, the manner in which it is sung is nearer to Solesmes than to the metrical approach that has sometimes been urged (and put into practice) for this period. The recording achieves a good presence, however, and enhances the performance's ambient qualities.

Louis Vierne   French 1870-1937

Born nearly blind, Vierne showed extraordinary musical promise. He joined César Franck's organ class at the Conservatoire in Paris and later became Widor's assistant at St Sulpice. In 1900 he was given post of organist at Notre Dame. Among his compositions are six organ symphonies as well as numerous songs and a large quantity of chamber music.

Organ Works

Symphonies Nos 1-6
Jeremy Filsell org
Signum Classics ③ SIGCD063 (3h 24' · DDD)
Played on the Cavaillé-Coll organ of St Ouen de
Rouen, France   Ⓕ

Vierne's six organ symphonies have very uneven representation in the catalogues. Most popular by far is the Third; and for 10 years the only widely available box-set was Ben van Oosten's (Dabringhaus und Grimm). In many ways this set was pretty well ideal, the only drawback being his lack of flair in the big toccata-like movements (such as the finale of No 1). Now Jeremy Filsell has brought just that kind of flair and panache to this set, recorded, interestingly, on the same instrument as Oosten's set.

It sounds quite different, though. The sound engineers have produced an altogether warmer and more all-embracing sound, giving the quieter movements (such as the enchanting Menuet of the Fourth Symphony) plenty of space to reveal their charms, while handling the monumental *pleno* in such a way that it still sends shivers down the spine without ever becoming overwhelming. The music, too, may be the same but Filsell seems to have a better sense of the musical architecture, especially in the later and more remote symphonies. As a result he convinces that the relative neglect, especially of the Fourth Symphony, is unwarranted; it may not be easy to communicate this music but it can be

done and Filsell does it wonderfully. The booklet-notes are exceptionally pretentious but all in all, Filsell has done both Vierne and discerning organ-lovers a great service.

Henri Vieuxtemps   Belgian 1820-1881

Vieuxtemps studied initially with his father, an amateur violinist, and he was soon giving concerts in Brussels and Liège. He travelled to Paris where he came into contact with Maria Malibran and her sister Pauline Viardot. He toured in 1833 and struck up friendships with Spohr and Schumann. During the following decade he travelled extensively and gained a great following, not only from his audiences but also from such eminent composers as Berlioz and Paganini.

His compositional ambitions were aided by study with Simon Sechter and Anton Reicha, and he wrote the first of his seven violin concertos shortly after. Extensive tours followed (taking in Russia – where he establshed a violin school at the St Petersburg Conservatory – and the US) and on returning to Brussels he accepted the post of professor at the Conservatory there. His most celebrated pupil was Eugène Ysaÿe. A stroke ended his performing career but he composed prolifically, mainly for string instruments.

Violin Concertos

Violin Concertos – No 4, Op 31; No 5, 'Grétry',
Op 37. Fantasia appassionata, Op 35
Viviane Hagner vn **Royal Flemish Philharmonic
Orchestra / Martyn Brabbins**
Hyperion CDA67798 (67' · DDD)   Ⓕ Ⓓ▸

Vieuxtemps's two best-known violin concertos have never been entirely neglected but there was a time when they were viewed as having little merit other than to demonstrate a violinist's prowess. Even the wonderful Heifetz recordings (Naxos) appeared with the opening *tuttis* drastically cut. Here, however, the watchwords are care and respect; the orchestra is beautifully balanced and recorded, Martyn Brabbins's direction is alert to Vieuxtemps's delicate Romanticism as well as his grand theatrical gestures, and Viviane Hagner, without quite matching Heifetz's freedom and eloquence, is a most resourceful and spirited advocate. She introduces subtle variety and takes us deep into the music. Her account is technically impressive, for instance in the hair-raising, slithering diminished-seventh chords in No 4's finale. Her performance of No 4 is, indeed, especially fine; the *Adagio religioso* creates a compelling emotional aura and the *Scherzo* is notable for precision and rhythmic élan.

The *Fantasia appassionata*, more lightweight than the concertos, still has some typically imaginative touches – the stark two-part texture at the start, the sophisticated orchestration of the concluding *Tarantella* – and reaches a high-point at the dreamlike *Adagio*, where the violin duets rapturously with horn and clarinet. As violin music it's both challenging and grateful, and Hagner makes the most of it.

Heitor Villa-Lobos   Brazilian 1887-1959

Villa-Lobos, having been taught to play the cello by his father, performed with popular musicians before travelling extensively. He went to Paris for most of the 1920s where his music, fusing a Western language with the luxuriousness of native Brazilian music, made a strong impression. On his return to Brazil, Villa-Lobos became a major mover in musical education, founding the Brazilian Academy of Music in Rio de Janeiro in 1945. It was at this time that he wrote his cycle of nine Bachianas Brasileiras for diverse combinations, marrying the spirit of Brazilian folk music with that of Bach. The Aria (Cantilena) from Bachianas Brasileira No 5 – a serene, ethereal melody sung to a wordless vocalise by a soprano floated over the accompaniment of eight plucked cellos – and The Little Train of the Caipira – a clever and colourful sound picture of a busy little train chugging through the Brazilian countryside – from No 2, are the most popular movements. His vast output includes operas, 12 symphonies, 17 string quartets, numerous songs and much piano music.

Chôros

Chôros – No 1[a]; No 4 [b]; No 6[d]; No 8[cd]; No 9[d]
[a]**Fabio Zanon** *gtr* [b]**Dante Yenque**,
[b]**Ozeas Arantes**, [b]**Samuel Hamzem** *hn*
[b]**Darren Coleman Milling** *bass tbn*
[c]**Linda Bustani**, [d]**Ilan Rechtman** *pfs*
[d]**São Paulo Symphony Orchestra / John Neschling**
BIS BIS-CD1450 (81' · DDD)   Ⓕ**O**➔

How many *Chôros* are there? Fourteen numbered examples (with two claimed as "lost"), two *Chôros bis*, a Wind Quintet *en forme de Chôros* and a concluding (!) choral-and-orchestral "Introduction to the *Chôros*", all more or less from the 1920s. No 6 (1926), which opens this second volume of BIS's survey, and No 9 (1929) may not have been written down until 1942 in time for their Rio premieres. Villa-Lobos was unreliable about many details of his work and these would not be unique in his output in being created only when performances finally materialised.

Whenever it was set down, the Sixth is a hugely engaging, if sprawling, orchestral fantasia and, like the Eighth (written and premiered between 1925 and 1927) and Ninth, was scored for large orchestra using exotic local percussion instruments. The Eighth is far more barbaric in character, tailored for the fad for primitivism then fashionable in Paris (where it was written), with parts for two pianos. Yet this is no concerto in disguise; although the first is a melodic soloist, the second is deployed as a percussive instrument and both orchestrally. BIS provides a clear balance.

Neschling and the São Paulo SO have the edge in the Ninth, which lies expressively between Nos 6 and 8. Separating these difficult orchestral works come the First for guitar (1920-21) and Fourth for brass (1926). There have been crisper performances of the latter, but Fabio Zanon's of the well known First is really rather good, languid and wistful, the tempi vibrantly elastic. This fine disc augurs well for what will presumably be the final instalment.

Bachianas Brasileiras

Bachianas Brasileiras Nos 2, 4 & 8
**Cincinnati Symphony Orchestra /
Jesús López-Cobos**
Telarc CD80393 (70' · DDD)   Ⓕ**O**

If any parallels existed between Bach and Brazilian idioms, they were largely in Villa-Lobos's mind – even the Fugue in No 8 of these *Bachianas Brasileiras* is totally un-Bach-like; so anyone coming fresh to these exotically coloured, rather sprawling works should not be misled by false expectations. But they're fascinating, indeed haunting, in a highly individual way. In view of the composer's sublime indifference to instrumental practicalities (as, for instance, the feasible length of a trombone *glissando*), his carelessness over detail in his scores, his Micawber-like trust that problems of balance he had created would be sorted out in performance, the chaotic state of the printed scores and orchestral parts of his music (littered as they are with wrong notes), and numerous misreadings in past performances, the only half-way reliable yardstick for conductors or critics is the composer's own recordings, made in the 1950s.

Compared to them, the present issue shows a number of differences. Chief of these is the warmer, more generalised sound, with less emphasis on clarity of detail. This works reasonably well in the Preludio of No 8, where concentration on the melodic line and the adoption of a slower tempo aid the movement's lyricism (likewise the more sentimental approach to the Aria of No 2). The Aria of No 8 is unquestionably more poetic and the Dansa of No 4 lighter; but in the most famous movement, the hilarious and ingenious 'Little Train of the Caipira' of No 2, the rasps near the start and the clatter of wheels on the track (evoked by the fiendishly difficult piano part) are far too subdued in favour of the 'big tune'.

López-Cobos deals persuasively with knotty questions of balance, such as in the middle section of No 3's Toccata, and brings to the fore the bell-like araponga bird's cry in No 4's Coral, but makes less of that movement's jungle screeches. He makes clear the thematic link between the sections of No 4's Aria, and seeks to overcome the repetitive pattern of its Preludio by taking a faster speed rather than by the wealth of tonal nuance the composer himself introduced. Perhaps such detailed comparisons are superfluous: enjoy, enjoy!

Bachianas Brasileiras – Nos 4, 5, 7 & 9.
Chôros No 10, 'Rasga o coração'
Renée Fleming sop **BBC Singers; New World
Symphony / Michael Tilson Thomas**
RCA Red Seal 09026 68538-2 (78' · DDD) ⓕⓞⒹ

In his booklet-note, the commentator here calls
Chôros No 10 the masterpiece of that quintessentially Brazilian series. It's certainly the most
ambitious, with very large orchestral and choral
forces in a complex mélange of urban street song
(a popular *schottisch* by Medeiros), chattering
native Indian chants and birdsong twitterings, of
mysterious jungle atmosphere, compulsive ostinato rhythms and virtuoso orchestral effects. The
present performance is excellent. The couplings
here are illuminating, consisting as they do of
more Villa-Lobos – four of his highly individual
tributes to Bach's influence. By far the best
known of the *Bachianas Brasileiras* is No 5, whose
Aria demonstrates the composer's ability to spin a
haunting long-flowing melody. Renée Fleming is
the sweet-toned soloist with the cello section of
this accomplished orchestra of young graduates
from American conservatoires: warmly lyrical as
she is, however, and brilliantly exact in the dart-
ings of the Dansa, her words aren't very distinct
even in the slow-moving Aria.

By his deeply expressive shaping of No 4's
Preludio Tilson Thomas avoids any satiety with
its extreme monothematicism, and in the second
movement secures coherent continuity despite
the (rather loud) insistent interventions of the
araponga bird's repeated note. He produces a
beautifully poetic tranquillity in the brief Prelude
of No 9 and complete lucidity and rhythmic
buoyancy in its Fugue. If that's the most Bachian
of the series, the much more substantial No 7 also
has its moments of homage: its first movement
has a fine breadth, and its finale is an impressive
and serious-minded large-scale fugue that begins
quietly and culminates in a grandiose blaze of
sound; but the busy Toccata is characteristically
and challengingly Brazilian, and the first part of
its Giga (before it goes all Hollywood) is delightfully fresh in this invigorating performance.

Solo Piano Works

Prole do bebê No 1. Cirandas. Hommage à Chopin
Sonia Rubinsky pf
Naxos 8 554489 (65' · DDD) ⓢⓞⒹ

Villa-Lobos's claim that his music was 'the fruit
of an immense, ardent and generous land' at
once disarms familiar criticism of extravagance
and formlessness. To regard such largesse
through the blinkered eyes of someone exclusively nurtured on a more restrained and economical diet is unacceptable. There may be tares
among the wheat but such strictures hardly apply
to the music in this Vol 1 which commences with
the enchanting *Prole do bebê*, Book 1 (the Second
Book is a tougher, altogether more astringent
and percussive experience, while a Third Book is
sadly lost). Intimately associated with Arthur

Rubinstein (who rearranged Villa-Lobos's miniatures, omitting some and ending 'O Polichinelo'
with an unmarked rip-roaring *glissando*), *Prole do
bebê* is here played complete. Sonia Rubinsky
makes light of a teasing rhythmic mix in 'Moren-
hina' (No 2) and in 'Caboclinha' (No 3) she relishes Villa-Lobos's audacity; his way of making
his seductive melody and rhythm surface through
a peal of church bells. Again, despite strong competition from Alma Petchersky on ASV in the no
less delightful *Cirandas*, Rubinsky scores an unequivocal success, ideally attuned to the central
and beguiling melody of 'Terezinha de Jesus'
(No 1) with its *forte e canto* instruction, and allowing the fight between the carnation and the rose
(No 4) to melt into a delicious love duet. Much
celebrated in her native Brazil and also in America, Sonia Rubinsky is excellently recorded.

Additional recommendation

Guia prático – Vol 1 (excs); Album 10; Album 11.
Ibericarabe. Suite infantil – No 1; No 2. Marqueza de
Santos – Gavota-Chôro; Valsinha-Brasileira
Rubinsky pf
Naxos 8 570504 (79' · DDD) ⓢⓞⓞⒹ
> Completists will obviously want the entire series,
> but with Volume 8 of the piano music of Villa-
> Lobos, Sonia Rubinsky reaches a triumphant end
> to a long, complex and luxuriant journey. And to an
> even greater extent than in the earlier issues she
> relishes every twist and turn of Brazil's ever-varied
> genius, playing with an enviable virtuosity, warmth
> and affection.

Choral Works

Missa São Sebastião. Bendita sabedoria. Praesepe[a].
Cor dulce, cor amabile. Panis angelicus. Sub tuum
praesidium. Ave Maria a 5. Ave Maria a 6. Pater
noster. Magnificat-alleluia[b]
[a]**Ansy Boothroyd**, [b]**Elizabeth McCormack** mez
Corydon Singers and Orchestra / Matthew Best
Hyperion CDA66638 (77' · DDD · T/t) ⓕⒹ

Asked to identify the composer of all these religious works except the Mass one would be most
unlikely to think of Villa-Lobos. That larger-
than-life exotic, that extravagantly experimental
and boisterous figure, the composer of such
chastely restrained music, the sweetly gentle *Cor
dulce*, the controlled fervour of the *Pater
noster*? Even the impressive and grandiose
Magnificat-alleluia gives no hint of its country of
origin. The one clue here might be that, of the
two *Ave Marias*, the (earlier) five-part setting is in
Portuguese. It's only the Mass that reveals all.
Amid its austere style and purely diatonic, contrapuntal idiom the *Sanctus* suddenly seems to come
from a different background: then one remembers that Sebastian is the patron saint of Rio de
Janeiro; and looking into the score one finds that
the liturgical heading of each movement is followed by a local one, the final *Agnus Dei* bearing
the subtitle 'Sebastian, protector of Brazil'.

This programme, all of unaccompanied music except for the *Magnificat-alleluia*, should not be listened to as a continuity if some feeling of sameness is to be avoided: the Corydon Singers are most efficient in all they do, but the outstanding performance is of the Mass.

Antonio Vivaldi
Italian 1678-1741

Even in the mid-20th century, Vivaldi's reputation as a composer was so small that not even the exact date of his birth or the place and date of his death had been established; his music was very rarely played in the 19th century. Now he's considered to be one of the most important figures of the Baroque era. He's certainly the most popular.

He was born in Venice when the city, though long past the height of its mercantile power, was the musical capital of Europe. His father was a violinist at San Marco and his son inherited his gift for the instrument, as well as his red hair (hence his nickname 'the Red Priest'). When he was 15 he began training for the priesthood but no sooner had he been ordained in 1703 than he was given a dispensation from saying Mass. Vivaldi was a lifelong asthmatic and complained of chest pains during services. The Church remained a useful backcloth for the remainder of his life but it seems that his priestly duties were never taken terribly seriously.

What he took only slightly more seriously was his position as maestro di violino (and later superintendent) of the Conservatorio dell'Ospedale della Pietà, one of the most famous musical centres in Venice, founded for the care and education of orphan girls. The standard of music-making was so high that many leading figures would perform in concert with the foundlings.

Vivaldi took up the post the year after becoming a priest and the year after that saw the publication of his first music. The next two decades of the century were incredibly productive: he established himself as one of the foremost violinists and composers in Europe, writing operas (at least one a year between 1713 and 1738, sometimes three or four) and instrumental works, including his two most famous sets of concertos (L'estro armonico, Op 3, and his Op 8 containing The Four Seasons). Between 1718 and 1721, Vivaldi left Venice to work in the service of Prince Philip of Hesse-Darmstadt, governor of Mantua, and here he met Anna Giraud (La Girò, she was called). She took the leading soprano role in many of Vivaldi's operas and, with her sister Paolina, became Vivaldi's travelling companion; both were rumoured to be his mistresses (strongly denied by Vivaldi).

During 1728 he had several audiences with the music-loving Emperor Charles VI. It was said that the Emperor spoke more with Vivaldi during the two weeks of their meetings than he had with ministers during the previous two years. Vivaldi dedicated his 12 concertos, La cetra, Op 9, to the Emperor.

The 1730s saw his powers wane. Philip of Hesse-Darmstadt died, the Church authorities took action against Vivaldi because of his lapsed priesthood and association with La Girò, and after that his contract with La Pietà was not renewed. His music began to fall out of favour and he left for Vienna in 1740, possibly with the intention of seeking a post with the Imperial Court of Vienna. It was not to be. Charles VI died in October 1740 and the once-wealthy Vivaldi, now ill and poverty-stricken, died some months later ignominiously. He was buried in a pauper's grave near St Stephen's – like another great composer of half a century later, Mozart.

Twenty-five years after Vivaldi's death, a certain Count Giacomo Durazzo acquired Vivaldi's scores from La Pietà. His heirs kept them secret, even stipulating that none of the works in their possession should be published or performed. It was not until the late 1920s, when the terms of the will were overthrown, that the treasures came to light.

Cello Concertos

Cello Concertos – in C minor, RV401; in B flat, RV423. Violin Concerto in F minor, 'Winter', RV297. Double Concerto in G minor, RV531[g]. Double Concerto, RV540[a]. Gloria, RV589 – Laudamus te[ag]. Juditha triumphans, RV645[a] – Noli ò cara, te adorantis[b]; Quanto magis generosa[f]. La fida ninfa, RV714[a] – Così sugl'occhi miei[bde]; Dite oihime[gh]. Il Giustino, RV717 – La gloria del mio sangue[abc] ([a]arr Koopman)
Yo-Yo Ma vc with [b]**Alfredo Bernardini**, [c]**Michel Henry** obs [d]**Wouter Verschuren** bn [e]**Margaret Faultless** vn [f]**Katherine McGillivray** va d'amore [g]**Jonathan Manson** vc [h]**Mike Fentross** lte **Amsterdam Baroque Orchestra / Ton Koopman** hpd/org
Sony Classical SK90916 (68' · DDD) ⒻⒹ→

It was only a matter of time before Yo-Yo Ma turned to Vivaldi, the first of the great composers to take the cello seriously as a soloist. Strange to relate, however, in this cheery get-together with Ton Koopman and the Amsterdam Baroque Orchestra, only three of its 11 pieces – the Double Concerto RV531 and the two solo concertos RV401 and 423 – were written for the cello. The others are all arrangements, from the appropriation of the slow movement of 'Winter' to the recasting of vocal numbers for colourful combinations of winds and strings, to the transformation of the beautiful Concerto for viola d'amore and lute, RV540, into a slightly less magical concerto for cello and organ.

Koopman, whose arrangements these are, claims that no one in Vivaldi's day would have thought twice about such things. Maybe he's right. RV540 apart, they're perfectly convincing, and you'd have to be a sour old grouch to object to them for long when they are played as expertly, as joyously and as lovingly as they are here. And, superb though Ma is on his 'baroqued' 1712 Stradivarius, each of the musicians, with special mentions going to Katherine McGillivray's exquisite viola d'amore and Jonathan Manson's cello, matching Ma all the way in RV531 and 'Laudamus te'.

An uncomplicated joy all round then, for its music, its performances and its recording, too, save only for the sometimes maddening prominence of the keyboard continuo.

Flute Concertos

Flute Concertos, Op 10.
Flute Concerto in C minor, RV441
Nicolaus Esterházy Sinfonia / Béla Drahos fl
Naxos 8 553101 (59' · DDD) ⓈO🅑➔

Vivaldi's flute concertos have certainly not been neglected on disc, and there's a wide choice of 'authentic' and middle-of-the-road versions played on both tranverse flute and recorder; this present selection is in the MOR vein and faces numerous competitors. In the flute concertos Béla Drahos is a superb soloist, as smooth as silk and agile as a kitten, and whose flights of fanciful embellishment might have won Vivaldi's approval. The Esterházy Sinfonia sounds a little beefy at times in its opening statements, but in the presence of the soloist its touch is appropriately light, and the third *Largo* ('Il sonno'), of Op 10 No 2, *La notte*, is impressively hushed. The outer movements of the bonus concerto, R441, dance on the lightest of feet; the work was originally written for the recorder, but on whichever instrument it's played, you wonder why it has no other currently listed recording. This present one would carry a warm recommendation even if it were not at bargain price.

Six Flute Concertos, Op 10.
Flute Concertos – RV429; RV440
Emmanuel Pahud fl
Australian Chamber Orchestra / Richard Tognetti
EMI 347212-2 (66' · DDD) 🅕🅑➔

Among the first flute concertos ever written, Vivaldi's Op 10 are also among the most imaginative. With vivid descriptive writing and everywhere unmistakably Vivaldian vitality and sparkle, they are surely a must for all flautists, Baroque and modern. Taking time off from the Berlin Philharmonic, 'modern' Emmanuel Pahud establishes a mastery of them that blasts out of the water any concerns about what kind of instrument he is using. His tone is light and liquid, his technical command complete and, more importantly, he is utterly at one with the music's character. Where some 'modern' players who dip into Baroque music work too hard, overburdening the music with stiff interpretative detail and resolutely showing off the embellishments they have learnt, Pahud's performances are natural and convincing, yet at the same time subtly stylish in matters of ornamentation, articulation and rhythm; the lilting first and second movements of No 5 are superbly poetic matchings of Baroque sensibility and technical control.

Not that he neglects the pictorial; he adds joyous extra bird-trills to *Il gardellino*, and enters deep into the spectral world of *La notte*, emerging from the impressionistic 'sleep' movement

into a finale in which we can almost feel the last phantoms of the night flying past our heads. In this he is keenly partnered by his excellent accompanists, and indeed the taut but far from unyielding contribution of the Australian Chamber Orchestra is of the highest order throughout. A disc to give nothing but pleasure.

Recorder Concertos

Recorder Concertos[d] – in C minor, RV441[b];
in F, RV442[a]; in C, RV443[b]; in C, RV444[b]; in A minor, RV445[b]. Chamber Concerto in D, 'La pastorella', RV95[bc]
[a]**László Czidra**,[b]**László Kecskeméti** recs [c]**Béla Horváth** ob [d]**István Hartenstein** bn [c]**Tamás Zalay** vn [c]**György Eder** vc [c]**Borbála Dobozy** hpd [d]**Nicolaus Esterházy Sinfonia**
Naxos 8 553829 (64' · DDD) Ⓢ🅑➔

This is claimed to be the first recording of the 'complete' recorder concertos of Vivaldi (RV441-45). Such archival primacy would be of little significance if the performances were substandard – but here they're high quality on all counts.

Kecskeméti bears the bulk of the soloist's burden, while Czidra appears only in RV442 (for treble recorder). Kecskeméti acquits himself on the same instrument with no less distinction in RV441 and, with no reflection on Czidra's manifest abilities, he could surely have made a clean sweep. Kecskeméti has the greatest 'showcase' opportunities, and he makes the most of them. His speed and clarity of articulation (as clean as a whistle, as it were) in the flanking movements are breathtaking and in some scale passages his sure-tongued choice of separate articulation gives life and variety – listen to the *Allegro molto* of RV443 and marvel! He adds embellishment where appropriate and in good taste. The basic five concertos alone would leave a disc somewhat under-filled and the choice of RV95, in which the recorder is featured, as a filler is a happy one. The Nicolaus Esterházy Sinfonia's contributions are happily light-footed. Excellent recording quality and bargain price are just extra reasons why this disc is a must-buy.

Vivaldi Recorder Concertos – in C minor, RV441; in G, RV443; in C, RV444 **Sammartini** Recorder Concerto in F **Telemann** Suite in A minor, TWV55:a2 🅟
Pamela Thorby recs
Sonnerie (Monica Huggett, Emilia Benjamin vns Katherine McGillivray va Alison McGillivray vc Sarah Groser violone Mathew Halls hpd/org)
Linn CKD217 (69' · DDD) 🅕O🅑➔

Pamela Thorby's work with the Palladian Ensemble has alone been sufficient to establish her as a world class performer, and the reputation of Sonnerie has long been sky-high. Their coming together offers a delightful prospect and though, as any sports-person knows, teams assembled from star players don't always work happily, this one lives up to its promise. Their material has a familiar look but their delivery of it is of rare quality and fully justifies this journey along oft-trodden paths.

The music trips off Thorby's tongue with the utmost fluency, cleanly articulated, and without any trace of the distressing sagging or wavering of pitch on long notes that haunts too many otherwise laudable performances by some others. No less notable is her enhancing embellishment, particularly though not exclusively in the slow movements. Sonnerie provide the perfect substrate for Thorby's excursions: stylish, precise and ideally balanced in the Linn recording.

Throughout, one has the impression of a single mind in control of two 'hands', soloist and *ripieno*. This recording is sheer pleasure and comes highly recommended.

Concertos, Op 3 – L'estro armonico

L'estro armonico   P
Europa Galante / Fabio Biondi vn
Virgin Classics Veritas ② 545315-2 (100' · DDD)
    Ⓕ**OO**Ⓑ→

No other set of Vivaldi's concertos contains the sheer variety on display in *L'estro armonico*. The catalogue has seldom been without a decent recording of these ceaselessly fascinating works, though none begins to approach this version in respect of fantasy and exuberance. Fabio Biondi and his Italian ensemble, Europa Galante, bring something entirely fresh and vital to oft-performed repertoire, illuminating well-trodden paths with affective articulation and eloquently voiced inflexions. Not all of their extravagant, Mediterranean gestures, perhaps, will find favour with listeners; indeed, some of Biondi's own embellishments can be a little inapposite. Tempi are well chosen, by and large, and ensemble is clear-textured and evenly balanced. The continuo group, which includes harpsichord, organ, archlute and Baroque guitar, makes an important contribution to the overall success.

This music is wonderful stuff, rejuvenating and immensely satisfying.

Violin Concertos, Op 4 – La stravaganza

Violin Concertos 'La stravaganza', Op 4 – No 1 in B flat, RV383a; No 2 in E minor, RV279; No 3 in G, RV301; No 4 in A minor, RV357; No 5 in A, RV347; No 6 in G minor, RV316a
Andrew Watkinson vn **City of London Sinfonia / Nicholas Kraemer**
Naxos 8 553323 (52' · DDD)   Ⓢ→

Violin Concertos, 'La stravaganza', Op 4 – No 7 in C, RV185; No 8 in D minor, RV249; No 9 in F, RV284; No 10 in C minor, RV196; No 11 in D minor, RV204; No 12 in G, RV298
Andrew Watkinson vn **City of London Sinfonia /**

Nicholas Kraemer
Naxos 8 553324 (46' · DDD)   Ⓢ→

La stravaganza is the second of the sets of concertos published during Vivaldi's lifetime. It was issued in about 1714 as the composer's Op 4 and, as with the greater number of his printed collections, contains 12 works. They are essentially violin concertos, although, to a much lesser extent than *L'estro armonico*, Vivaldi also provides on occasion solo parts for an additional violin or cello. These concertos have long been favourites, above all, perhaps, for the profusion of lyrically affecting slow movements, of which those belonging to Concertos Nos 1, 4, 5 and 12 are notably fine examples: in this music there's delicate nuance, poetic fantasy and sheer originality lying beneath the immediately recognisable hallmarks of the composer's outward style. Nicholas Kraemer is no stranger to this repertory having already recorded two of Vivaldi's other printed sets, Opp 8 and 9. Those, however, were with his period-instrument Raglan Baroque Players, whereas *La stravaganza* is played on instruments tuned to today's standard pitch. This, paradoxically, may be closer to the pitch which Vivaldi himself used rather than the lower Baroque pitch.

Listening to this music, so full of vitality, invention and expressive tenderness, leaves one feeling exhilarated. Andrew Watkinson plays with virtuoso flair, but senses the highly developed fantasy present in every one of the concertos. His embellishments are tasteful and restrained and his melodic line always clearly articulated. Tempi, for the most part, are effectively judged, though the almost unbearably beautiful *Largo* of the First Concerto, with its emotionally highly charged modulation towards the close, is perhaps a shade too slow.

The strings of the City of London Sinfonia sound tonally bright and unfailingly alert. Only in the *Adagio* of No 8 does the balance of the recording falter; the harpsichord's arpeggios (notably in the *Adagio molto* of 'Autumn') might have been allowed a little more prominence.

Violin Concertos 'La stravaganza', Op 4   P
Arte dei Suonatori / Rachel Podger vn
Channel Classics ② CCS19598 (103' · DDD);
② 🎧 CCSSA19503   Ⓕ**OOO**Ⓑ→

By the standards of the average Vivaldi violin concerto, the *La stravaganza* set is quite extravagant stuff, full of fantasy and experiment – novel sounds, ingenious textures, exploratory melodic lines, original types of figuration, unorthodox forms. It's heady music, and listening to its 12 concertos at a sitting isn't a mode of listening one would recommend.

Still less so in performances as high in voltage as the present ones. There's a current trend in Baroque performance to get away from the coolness and objectivity which for a long time were supposed (on the whole, mistakenly) to be a part of performing practice of the time, but possibly the pendulum has swung a little wildly the other way. Perhaps here it's intended to reflect Vivaldi's own notorious freedom of performance. But anyone who's admired earlier recordings with period instruments may find these a little extravagant and hard-hitting. And they aren't helped by the resonant acoustic of the church in Poland used for the recording, which produces a full and bright sound but a boomy bass and less clear a texture than might be ideal.

That said, however, these performances by Rachel Podger are crackling with vitality and executed with consistent brilliance as well as a kind of relish in virtuosity that catches the showy spirit, the self-conscious extravagance, of this particular set of works. There are plenty of movements here where her sheer digital dexterity is astonishing – for instance, the finale of No 6, with its scurrying figures, the second movement of No 7 or the finale of No 2 with its repetitive figures and leaping arpeggios. But perhaps even more enjoyable is the exquisitely fine detail of some of the slow movements. No 8 in D minor is perhapsthe wildest concerto of the lot, with its extraordinary lines in the first movement, the passionate, mysterious outer sections in the second and the powerful and original figuration inthe finale: that one has a performance to leave you breathless.

Another thing Podger is specially good at is the shaping of those numerous passages of Vivaldian sequences, which can be drearily predictable, but aren't so here because she knows just how to control the rhythmic tension and time the climax and resolution with logic and force. This set is certainly recommended as a fine example of a modern view of Baroque performance – and it sounds even better on SACD.

Violin Concertos, Op 8 (incl Four Seasons)

Violin Concertos, Op 8 – Nos 1-4, 'The Four Seasons': No 1 in E, 'Spring', RV269; No 2 in G minor, 'Summer', RV315; No 3 in F, 'Autumn', RV293; No 4 in F minor, 'Winter', RV297; **No 5** in E flat, RV253, **'La tempesta di mare'; No 6** in C, RV180, **'Il piacere'; No 7** in D minor, RV242; **No 8** in G minor, RV332; **No 9** in D minor, RV236; **No 10** in B flat, RV362, **'La caccia'; No 11** in D, RV210; **No 12** in C (two versions, RV178 & RV449)

The Four Seasons.   **P**
Violin Concertos in E flat, RV257; in B flat, RV376; in D, RV211
Giuliano Carmignola vn
Venice Baroque Orchestra / Andrea Marcon
Sony Classical 82796 90391-2 (72' · DDD)   Ⓕ**ⓄⓄ**Ⓓ→

Vivaldi's *Four Seasons*, like nature's, come and go in their various moods and meteorological vicissitudes. We've had ochre sunsets from Louis Kaufmann, Harnoncourt's Breughel-style rusticity and the provocative Nigel Kennedy, to mention but a scant few. Giuliano Carmignola's primary claim on our attentions (this is his second

shot at the piece) is, aside from a delightfully woody-sounding Baroque instrument, a keen narrative flair. He knows the musical period, understands principles of embellishment and doesn't hesitate to enrich his performances with added colour and with rhythmic thrust. 'Spring' arrives in rude high spirits, toying with birdsong (slowly at first then speeding up) and with thunder thrashing between violin desks. The violas' 'barking dog' is worryingly prominent (if you don't like dogs) and the finale contrasts a swelling *legato* against sparkly solo passagework. The 'impetuous weather of summer' has power enough to keep the National Grid up and running, and the diverse winds of the multifaceted opening *Allegro* of 'Autumn' and the way the harpsichord holds its own in the second and third movements are wonderful. The cruel weathers of 'Winter' inspire the expected bursts of virtuosity while the *Largo*'s raindrops unexpectedly seep through to the busy bass-line (most versions don't allow for the leak). Varieties of plucked continuo help fill out textures and Carmignola himself plays with immense brilliance. The three additional violin concertos are all said to be first recordings and reveal a rather different aspect of Vivaldi's style. Generally speaking, they sound more formal than the *Four Seasons*, almost pre-classical in RV257's opening *Andante molto e quasi allegro* and with sideways glances at Rameau in the opening of RV211 (which also includes a brief first-movement cadenza). Dance rhythms again predominate.

Great sound, full and forward and with every instrumental strand given its proper due. Thinking in terms only of the *Four Seasons*, good rivals are so plentiful that comparative discussion becomes less a question of 'who gets it right' than how you like your birds and storms. There are countless period-instrument options and almost as many that use modern instruments, but take heed of period performing practice. Up to now, the period favourites have been Il Giardino Armonico and Harnoncourt's Concentus Musicus Wien, and there's no reason why this new version shouldn't join their hallowed ranks.

The Four Seasons
Janine Jansen vn with **Henk Rubingh, Candida Thompson** vns **Julian Rachlin** va **Maarten Jansen** vc **Stacey Watton** db **Elizabeth Kenny** theorbo **Jan Jansen** org/hpd
Decca Ⓢ 475 6188DSA (39' · DDD)   Ⓕ**Ⓑ**→

There's so much to be said against it on extramusical grounds. The cynicism of the presentation, for a start: the booklet includes seven photographs of the beautiful Miss Jansen in four dresses, one of them a diaphanous décolleté number embroidered with butterflies. Then, opposite a black-and-white version of the latter in soft focus, there's a note by the violinist of numbing and ungrammatical banality. And Decca is charging full price for 39 minutes of music.

So to approach the music in a jaundiced frame of mind is understandable, and first impressions are not good: lush, squeeze-box phrasing in the opening *tutti* of 'Spring' and a distant harpsichord continuo put me in mind of old recordings by I Musici. Equally unstylish are the gratuitous *pizzicati* in the last movement of 'Autumn', where the frightened game is trying to escape horse and hound.

But the playing grows on you. Oddly enough, the absence of a *ripieno* string group doesn't make the performance small-scale. Janine Jansen and her colleagues play with splendid vigour in the outer movements, and Jansen herself weaves a line of great beauty in the *Largos* and the *Adagio*. There's a fair amount of *rubato*, especially in the first movement of 'Autumn', which certainly holds the attention. The dialogue between violin and organ continuo in the 'cuckoo' section of 'Summer' is a delight.

Vivaldi The Four Seasons'
Tartini Violin Sonata, 'Devil's Trill'
Academy of St Martin in the Fields / Joshua Bell vn
Sony Classical 88697 11013-2 (54' · DDD)   Ⓕ🅿️ⓄⒺ➡

A big-name violinist, the Academy of St Martin in the Fields, John Constable tinkling away on a ten-ton Goble – this *Seasons* is a bit like returning to old times. Any Vivaldi lover will have these iconic concertos in their collection already, probably several times over, but the merest glance at the packaging of this one will tell you that it is not aimed at them anyway. So what will the 'I want a *Four Seasons* but by somebody I've heard of' clientele get for their money? Well, mighty fine playing for certain: Bell has the lightness and quickness of Mercury in passagework, and a smooth and sweet lyricism no less divine in the slower sections. Not a single ugly noise emanates from his instrument, and he is well matched by the ASMF, their sound ample and softly comfortable yet clean and clear. It is doubtful if you will ever hear a more purely beautifully rapt ensemble rendition of the slow movement from *Spring*, for instance.

What is missing amid all this high-class musicianship is the inventive spark of excitement these pieces can provoke in so many players, especially through its descriptive elements. All right, not everyone has to give themselves over entirely to being dying stags, drunken peasants or barking dogs, but these performances would surely benefit from the greater rhythmic and dynamic flexibility a bit more pictorial imagining could bring. The fill-up is a thoughtful choice, however; Tartini's *Devil's Trill* Sonata, adroitly played with extra-romantic, stratospheric cadenza, as if to Bell the Devil were ne'er a foe.

Violin Concertos – Miscellaneous

Dresden Concertos – D, RV213; D, RV219; D, RV224; D minor, RV240; E flat, RV260; A, RV344; B minor, RV388
Cristiano Rossi vn
Accademia I Filarmonici / Alberto Martini
Naxos 8 554310 (67' · DDD)   Ⓢ➡

VIVALDI FOUR SEASONS – IN BRIEF

Concerto Italiano / Rinaldo Alessandrini   🅿️
Opus 111 ② OP30363 (103' · DDD)   ⒻⓄⓄ
A stunning new version of the *Four Seasons*, each season granted its own soloist. Theatricality and discipline are ideally combined in this unforgettable performance.

Enrico Onofri; Il Giardino Armonico   🅿️
Teldec 4509 96158-2 (61' · DDD)   ⒻⓄⓄ
Though a relatively small group, Il Giardino Armonico give as much vigour and sonority as you might wish, while allowing telling contributions from their continuo section.

Giuliano Carmignola; Venice Baroque Orchestra / Andrea Marcon   🅿️
Sony Classical 82796 90391-2 (72' · DDD)   ⒻⓄⓄ
A violinist of extraordinary technique and attractive tone and a truly imaginative interpretation. He's aided by the equally inventive playing of the orchestra, and the result is one of the most highly charged performances.

Gottfried von der Goltz; Freiburg Baroque Orchestra, Harp Consort   🅿️
Deutsche Harmonia Mundi 05472 77384-2 (66' · DDD)   Ⓕ
An imaginative performance which draws from a rich palette of continuo instruments – lirone, Baroque lute, cittern, archlute, guitar, theorbo, arch-cittern, harp and psaltery, together with harpsichord, organ and regal!

Andrew Manze; Amsterdam Baroque Orchestra / Ton Koopman   🅿️
Elatus 0927 46726-2 (57' · DDD)   Ⓕ
An 'authentic' performance for those who don't want their performance too spiced up. A straightforward account with subtle but telling individual touches by Manze.

ASMF / Joshua Bell
Sony Classical 88697 11013-2 (54' · DDD)   Ⓕ🅿️ⓄⒺ➡
Joshua Bell's performance exploys modern instruments, but the very stylish ones of the Academy of St Martin in the Fields at that. He plays with an appealing lightness of touch and draws ensemble playing of terrific elegance from his colleagues.

Anne-Sophie Mutter; Trondheim Soloists
DG 463 259-2GH (63' · DDD)   ⒻⓄⒺ➡
A nice halfway house between period manners and a more traditional interpretation. Quicksilver fiddling and a orchestra in total sympathy with their starry soloist make this a delight.

Janine Jansen *et al*
Decca Ⓐ 475 6188DSA (39' · DDD)   ⒻⒺ➡
A tremendous, small-scale interpretation from the young Janine Jansen and friends. A big hit on iTunes!

The Dresden link was forged by Vivaldi's friend and one-time pupil Johann Georg Pisendel. Pisendel visited Venice in 1716 when he appears to have struck up a warm friendship with Vivaldi, who dedicated several sonatas and concertos to him. The seven violin concertos on this disc have survived in manuscripts preserved in the Dresden Sächsische Landesbibliothek. Much of this music will be entirely new to most collectors. By and large these are pieces which do not wear their hearts on their sleeves. There are few extravagant flourishes and perhaps less than we might expect in the way of extrovert gesture. But there's no lack of brilliance in the solo violin writing – Pisendel's reputation as a virtuoso was hardly less than Vivaldi's – and, as ever, the music contains a profusion of effective rhythmic ideas. The solo violin parts are entrusted to Cristiano Rossi, who often, though not always, discovers the fantasy in Vivaldi's solo writing. The bowing is graceful and relaxed even if intonation is occasionally awry. The A major Concerto, RV344 affords a good instance of soloist and orchestra at their most persuasive. But the lyrically expressive violin melody against a dotted rhythm continuo of the *Largo* of RV224 is unquestionably the most alluring.

The more you hear this music, the more you're likely to be captivated by it. The recorded sound seems a little boxy and confined, but textures come through clearly all the same.

Concertos for Strings – RV111a; RV114; RV119;
RV121; RV127; RV146; RV152; RV156; RV157; 'Conca',
RV163; RV167; RV168
Venice Baroque Orchestra /
Andrea Marcon *hpd/org*
Archiv 474 5092AH (68' · DDD)   Ⓕ❶▷

This collection draws from Vivaldi's *Concerti per archi*, concertos for strings and continuo without the flamboyant writing for solo instruments found in the majority of the Red Priest's orchestral works. Across 68 minutes Vivaldi seems to have a seemingly inexhaustible arsenal of tricks, but it's never merely superficial. All the music on offer here is unmistakably Vivaldian: although there is common ground in many of these *concerti per archi*, they contain a dazzling kaleidoscope of moods and textures.

Andrea Marcon directs vivid, strongly etched performances that often reach fiery intensity. Things get off to a sizzling start with the precocious beginning of RV111a, and the opening *Allegro* of RV157 is a perfect illustration of Marcon's fondness for wonderfully incisive yet flowing continuo. But there are also notable moments of exquisite beauty, such as a gorgeously played *Largo* from RV127. The *Adagio* in RV121 is an evocative hushed moment graced with lovely theorbo playing. It is easy to notice the athleticism of the Venice Baroque Orchestra's vigorous playing of fast movements, yet it is equally significant that the group perform Vivaldi's slower music with tenderness.

Violin Concertos – 'Grosso Mogul', RV208;
'L'inquietudine', RV234; RV277; RV187.
Concerto grosso, RV580 Op 3 No 10.
Viktoria Mullova *vn* **Il Giardino Armonico /**
Giovanni Antonini
Onyx Classics ONYX4001 (54' · DDD)   Ⓕ▷

Viktoria Mullova isn't quite a Baroque violinist – her Strad is fitted with gut strings, she's using a Baroque bow and she plays very stylishly, but there's something about her sound that betrays the modern virtuoso. Her vibrato is modest but it's used in a way that harks back to her conventional Russian training. Much more important than rating her on a scale of authenticity, however, is to note that it's top-class violin playing: the rhythms are lively and poised, all the passagework is beautifully clear and exact.

The programme is excellent, too, in the way it shows the wide range of Vivaldi's imagination. The rarely encountered RV187 is a lovely piece, full of delightful original touches, in contrast to the better known *Grosso Mogul* which, despite its brilliance and its satisfying formal design, is oppressively short of significant ideas.

Il Giardino Armonico provide an immensely spirited accompaniment, four members taking the extra solo roles in Op 3 No 10 with great style. Vivaldi's music needs strong contrasts in performance; it should create a sense of amazement, which these accounts supply in a striking and convincing way. The prevalence of ferocious accents, ultra-short off-the-string bowing, and exaggerated dynamic shading is a little troubling: the strongest, swiftest bow stroke should retain the character of a gesture, rather than a hammer blow. But whether or not you agree, you're likely to enjoy the vigour, colourful variety and sheer expertise of these performances.

Violin Concertos – RV190; RV217; RV303; RV331;
RV325
Giuliano Carmignola *vn*
Venice Baroque Orchestra / Andrea Marcon
Archiv 477 6005AH (58' · DDD)   Ⓕ▷

Giuliano Carmignola and the Venice Baroque Orchestra here return to the all-Vivaldi format which has so far served them well. Given that the concertos on this release are advertised as world premiere recordings, that seems sensible enough. The mushrooming of the Vivaldi catalogue means that the excitement of hearing 'new' works can be as immediate as if he were still working among us today; and where we used to know but a handful of (mostly early) concertos, we are now becoming more aware of different stylistic periods, as well as the cross-fertilisation with other areas of his output.

Three of the works here show affinities with vocal works from the 1720s, when the brusque energy of the *L'estro armonico* concertos had been left behind in favour of something more dance-like; the other two are in the expansive, laid-back style of the 1730s. It is a little voyage of discovery, then, with the scenery including much harmonic resource and violinistic devilry. There are no surprises in the performances though: they are as purringly beautiful as ever from these artists. Carmignola dashes around Vivaldi's scampering passagework and giant leaps with an easy control and consistency of good tone, and the Venice Baroque Orchestra are worthy partners – their surging rivers of sound in the finale of RV325 give a real thrill. Indeed, while one can imagine violinists of the Manze or Biondi kind finding more drama or humour in this music, it is otherwise hard to find anything to fault in these Rolls-Royce performances.

Double Concertos – RV509; RV511; RV514; RV516; RV523; RV524
Giuliano Carmignola, Viktoria Mullova vns
Venice Baroque Orchestra / Andrea Marcon
Archiv 477 7466AH (59' · DDD)   ⒻⓄ▶

The Venice Baroque Orchestra have a frill-less way of going about their Vivaldi programming: no mixed running orders, no imaginative fillers, no clever links between different items, just single-minded concentration on one genre. This time the subject is double violin concertos, six of them and nothing else. Surprisingly, this is largely unexplored territory, not least as our performers have eschewed the four published examples of the Op 3 set in favour of works from the 24 surviving in Vivaldi's manuscripts. None is new to the catalogue, but none is exactly well known, and all the more welcome are they for that.

Vivaldi's approach to double-concerto writing was mostly to provide equal music for both soloists, who either play in euphonious parallel or alternate melody and accompaniment in short snatches. For this reason it is not only impossible to separate or differentiate the playing of Viktoria Mullova and Giuliano Carmignola here, but undesirable too. In this music they are as they should be: one living organism, both playing their Baroque violins with gorgeously burnished tone and an agile virtuosity which, freed from the macho pyrotechnics of the solo concertos, gains a relaxed and tender quality that reveals the poet in Vivaldi. And in those rare moments when there really is a difference, when one violin cuts loose with a glorious, yearning stretch of melody while the other accompanies with arpeggios or some such (as occurs in the finales of RV524 and 516), it warms like a sudden surge of blood through the veins.

Andrea Marcon and the VBO play their accompanimental role with their usual expert light touch, and the recording is spacious, clear and neatly balanced. A perfect Vivaldi treat.

'Concertos for the Emperor'
Violin Concertos – in C, RV189; in C minor, RV202; in F, 'Concerto per la solennità di San Lorenzo', RV286; in C, RV183; in E, 'L'amoroso', RV271; in E minor, 'Il favorito', RV277
The English Concert / Andrew Manze vn
Harmonia Mundi HMU90 7332 (79' · DDD)   Ⓕ

Vivaldi published his Op 9 concertos, *La cetra* ('The Lyre'), in 1727. Soon after, he presented Charles VI, the Habsburg emperor, with a manuscript set of concertos, also called *La cetra*. It was long supposed that these were the same concertos until someone looked at them more carefully, and noticed that 11 of the 12 were entirely different works. Vivaldi had simply used the same name again for a set of pieces he thought particularly well suited to the needs of the Viennese court. No one seems to have gathered them together for performance as a group until now. The six presented here show Vivaldi in his grandest and most magnificent vein, and exceptionally varied in mood.

The first item (No 2 of the set) is a dashing C major piece, with vigorous scales to catch the attention, then more contemplative minor-key music with much brilliant high writing for the soloist; there's a quietly eloquent slow movement, again with violin reaching its upper reaches; and in the finale, a lively, playful piece, the cadenza is positively stratospheric.

The second concerto (No 10) is entirely different, soft-toned, with a lovely E major glow, and a tenderness to the musical ideas untypical of Vivaldi. Then comes a big C minor work (No 7) with large gestures in its outer movements; in the finale there's a huge *crescendo* that makes the later Mannheim ones sound tame by comparison, with some elaborate violin coloratura.

The final concerto, in F major (No 4), is a big, ceremonial, stately piece, originally composed 'per la solennità di San Lorenzo', but it serves Charles VI pretty well, too, with a virtuoso finale to round it off. Perhaps the most powerful of the concertos, however, is No 11, full of nervous energy in its first movement, with an improvisatory violin line in its second above soft chords, and a strong reminiscence of the *Four Seasons* (not the only one here) in the finale.

This is an immensely enjoyable disc: the music very characteristic, but much freer of cliché than Vivaldi sometimes is. The violin-playing from Andrew Manze is of an extremely high order: rhythms beautifully springy, articulation clear and precise, intonation perfect, great refinement in the shaping of phrases, and a real command of the logic of the music. The orchestral support is strong and energetic, and the recorded quality first-rate. An outstanding CD in every way.

Concertos – 'L'inquietudine', RV234; 'La tempesta di mare', RV253; RV273; RV565. Sonata, 'La folia', RV63. Andromeda liberata – Sovvente il sole[a]
Chamber Orchestra of Europe / Daniel Hope vn
with [a]**Anne Sofie von Otter** mez
DG 477 7463GH (58' · DDD)   ⒻⓄ▶

Three cheers for Daniel Hope for making a high-profile Vivaldi release without recourse to *The Four Seasons*. Not that there is anything wrong with those marvellous pieces of course but the disc he has produced is surely a deeper way of signalling his love and understanding of the Red Priest. Vivaldi lovers will be familiar with some of the works here, but RV234 is not so well known, while real rarities are RV273, a delicious and long-limbed late work, and a spaciously atmospheric aria with obbligato violin from the opera *Andromeda liberata*.

Hope and the COE play them with the clarity and ensemble precision of a top-class Baroque orchestra, and with their sprightly bowing and general avoidance of vibrato, perhaps only the occasional sweetening of tone in Hope's top register really gives away that modern instruments are at work. There seems little doubt as to the kind of performances Hope has been influenced by, and the 'Baroque' feel is enhanced by a generous and active continuo section which even runs to a harp and a lirone. What results is Vivaldi that is enjoyable and without quirks, and perhaps all one would wish for is that final ounce of drive and energy the less reined-in playing of a Baroque orchestra can bring to faster movements. On the other hand, Hope's obvious relish for Vivaldi's stiller moments brings memorable results in the rich poetry of RV273 (real summer-night warmth here) and the captivatingly wistful 'Sovvento il sole', in which, though vocally less smooth-running than she has been in the past, guest soloist Anne Sofie von Otter catches the mood superbly. This is a disc made with love and intelligence – a powerful combination.

'The Rise of the North Italian Violin Concerto: 1690-1740'
'Vol 2 – Antonio Vivaldi: Virtuoso Impresario'
Vivaldi Violin Concertos – 'senza cantin', RV243; RV254; RV370. Concerto for Two Cellos and Strings, RV561. Concerto for Strings, RV134. La costanza trionfante degl'amori e de gl'odii, RV706[a] – Sento il cor brillarmi in petto; Hai sete di sangue; Amoroso caro sposo. La fida ninfa, RV714[a] – Dolce fiamma; Alma oppressa
[a]**Mhairi Lawson** sop
La Serenissima / Adrian Chandler vn
Avie AV2128 (77' · DDD · T/t)   Ⓕ

'Antonio Vivaldi: Virtuoso Impresario' examines links between Vivaldi's concertos and operas. Thus, the Concerto RV370 has origins partly in the opera *Ottone in villa*, RV134 was probably once the sinfonia to an oratorio, and RV254 shows signs of having started out life as an entr'acte. It should be said that the links are sometimes tenuous, but who could complain when the snippets of minutely detailed information which Adrian Chandler clearly commands encourage mixed programming so refreshingly different from the Vivaldian norm? It may not always bring us the Red Priest at his most inspired but it certainly shows a few sides to him that we do not always see – enough to confound daft comments about his lack of variety. For this is music brimming with ideas, from the unusual accompanimental texture of the slow movement of RV561, to the E-string-less experiment of RV243 (and the strange, off-beam harmonies of its slow movement), to RV134's excellent fugue. All are played with La Serenissima's customary bright energy and enthusiasm, to which qualities

are here added considerable subtlety of detail: listen to the way Chandler picks his way intelligently through the changing textural landscape of the first movement of RV243. Indeed, his playing throughout shows a smooth but vital tone, a fundamental likeability of sound and manner which is matched by soprano Mhairi Lawson in her five contrasted arias, all relative rarities dispatched with no-nonsense skill and aplomb. Here is further proof from this young British group that the Italian orchestras need not think to have Vivaldi to themselves just yet.

Double and Triple Concertos

Concertos – for Two Cellos in G minor, RV531; Ⓟ
for Two Violins, Two and Cellos in D, RV564; for Recorder – A minor, RV108; G, RV436. Trio Sonatas – D minor, 'La follia', RV63; C minor, RV83
Musica Alta Ripa
Dabringhaus und Grimm MDG309 0927-2 (56' · DDD)
                                                        ⒻⓄ

None of the pieces is new to the catalogue, but the playing is of a calibre that might entice readers to consider these alternative versions. The two largest works are the Concerto for two cellos and strings in G minor, and another, in D major, for two violins, two cellos and strings. Both fare well in the hands of sensitive performers such as these, and especially enjoyable is the beautifully inflected playing of the two solo cellists in the G minor work.

Albert Brüggen is an excellent cellist, and here (alongside partner Juris Teichmanis) he fulfils expectation raised by previous discs. Vivaldi wrote two concertos for pairs of solo violins and cellos; the other is RV575 – and both are satisfying pieces with beguiling slow movements. Melodically, this one gives pride of place to a solo violin in its centrally placed *Largo*, but one should nevertheless be allowed to hear more of the solo cello than is granted by this performance. The rhythmic élan of the finale is quite exhilarating. The two remaining concertos feature a recorder. One, RV436, is scored for transverse flute with strings, though a descant recorder has been substituted here. The other, RV108, is a chamber concerto for treble recorder, two violins and continuo. The soloist in each is Danya Segal, who brings the music to life with fluency and unpretentious eloquence. An attractive menu is completed by two strongly contrasting sonatas which, in their quite different ways, demonstrate Vivaldi's craftsmanship and invention in the medium.

This disc makes rewarding listening. The pieces have been chosen with real discernment and are played with virtuosity and an effective understanding of style.

Concerto for Multiple Instruments in C, RV557 Ⓟ
Double Concertos – Two Oboes in D minor, RV535; Oboe and Bassoon in G, RV545; Two Trumpets in C, RV537; Two Horns in F, RV538. Oboe Concerto in A minor, RV461. Bassoon Concerto in E minor, RV484

Ensemble Zefiro / Alfredo Bernardini
Astrée Naïve E8679 (64' · DDD)   Ⓕ Ⓞ Ⓞ 🅑➔

Ensemble Zefiro is one of the most remarkable
Baroque bands to emerge during the last decade or so, though we hear of it less often than it
deserves. Its specialised front line is its battery
of exceptionally gifted wind players, but the
support troops of strings and continuo are no
less worthy of commendation. In all technical
and musical respects they think, breathe and
act as one. Their dynamic range (from *sotto voce*
whisper to as many *f*s as you regard as adding
up to 'issimo') is put to vivid and impressive
use, whether terraced in *crescendos* or *diminuendos*, or in the finely judged squeezing of notes.
The *Allegros* are crisp, animated, joyously propulsive and full of Italian sunshine, and the
eloquent music-making of the oboe and bassoon soloists effortlessly conceals Vivaldi's
severe technical demands. It's perhaps the slow
movements that make the deepest impression:
how many times have we heard the same harmonic progressions but marvelled at Vivaldi's
ability to invest them with constantly new
charm and depth? There are appealing conversations in those of RV545 (oboe and bassoon),
RV535 (two oboes), RV557 (two recorders,
whose players aren't among the declared personnel in the booklet!) and RV538 (two cellos).
They are all marked by stylish embellishment,
and the last was an irresistible reminder of the
benchmark recording of the two-cello Concerto RV531 by Pleeth and Bylsma with the
AAM (L'Oiseau Lyre). Nicholas Anderson has
rightly described Alberto Grazzi as 'the poet of
the bassoon'; in this recording we have a veritable eisteddfod. This is a faultless and marvellous recording.

Concertos – for Viola d'amore and Lute in D minor, Ⓟ
RV540; for Cello in G, RV413; for Flute in G minor, 'La
notte', RV439; for Oboe in D minor, RV454; for Two
Horns in F, RV539; for Multiple Instruments – in D
minor, RV566; in F, 'Il Proteo ò sia il mondo rovescio',
RV572. Chamber Concerto in G minor, RV107.
Orchestra of the Age of Enlightenment
Linn CKD151 (74' · DDD)   Ⓕ Ⓞ 🅑➔

It's a nice idea for the Orchestra of the Age of
Enlightenment to record a disc of such varied
Vivaldian fare. The young women of the orchestra which Vivaldi directed at the Ospedale
della Pietà in Venice were as renowned for the
range of instruments they could wield as for
their virtuosity; so it seems neatly apposite that
the OAE, so full of capable soloists itself,
should use this music to celebrate its members'
own star qualities. And the mixture is a wide
one: three solo concertos; a rare Concerto for
two horns; the deservedly popular Concerto
for lute and viola d'amore, two concertos for
typically extravagant Vivaldian multiple line-
ups; and one of those chamber concertos in
which all the players are soloists. The OAE
play with great expertise and good taste

throughout. Judging by the list in the booklet,
they use a relatively large body of strings, but,
although this is noticeable, there's no feeling of
heaviness, and indeed the use of two double
basses gives the sound a substantial foundation
which is at the same time deliciously light on its
feet. There's a total of 16 soloists listed: among
the highlights are David Watkin's habitually
assured and intensely musical playing of the
Cello Concerto; Lisa Beznosiuk, sensitive as
ever in *La notte* (though struggling a bit against
the string sound); Andrew Clark and Roger
Montgomery, treading securely and confidently through the Concerto for two horns;
Anthony Robson, a little under the note sometimes but showing good breath control and
phrasing in the Oboe Concerto; and a fairy-
light performance of the Concerto for lute and
viola d'amore from Elizabeth Kenny and Catherine Mackintosh. The performances are all
directorless, and there was the odd place where
a guiding hand might have pepped things up
(or stopped the theorbo from twiddling so
much in the slow movement of the Cello Concerto), but in general this is a relaxed and convivial Vivaldi programme that one can simply
sit back and enjoy.

String Concertos

String Concertos – in C, RV110; in C, RV115;
in C minor, RV118; in D minor, 'Madrigalesco', RV129;
in E minor, RV134; in F, RV142; in G, RV145; in G,
'Alla rustica', RV151; in G minor, RV156; in A, RV158;
in A minor, RV161; in B flat, RV166; in B flat, RV167
Collegium Musicum 90 / Simon Standage vn
Chandos Chaconne CHAN0687 (62' · DDD)   Ⓕ Ⓞ 🅑➔

This third volume of Collegium Musicum 90's
survey of Vivaldi's string concertos offers a varied selection of works which bears testament to
their composer's untiring imagination. Vivaldi
composed more than 40 of these sparky little
miniatures, united by an (almost) uniform adoption of a three-movement format and by the lack
anywhere of any kind of soloist; for this reason
they're also sometimes known either as 'concertos for orchestra' or 'ripieno concertos'. None
lasts longer than eight minutes, and most come
in under five.

CM90 perform with accomplished ease,
attempting nothing outrageous but maintaining a
relaxed bonhomie and clear-cut eloquence entirely
suited to the music's modest aspirations. Theirs
isn't the taut Vivaldi sound we have become used
to hearing from other ensembles, but they have no
difficulty serving up lyrical sweetness or joyous
energy as required. Realistically and lucidly
recorded, the disc leaves little to be desired.

'The French Connection'
Concertos for Strings – RV114; RV119; RV157. Flute
Concertos[a] – RV432; RV438a. Bassoon Concertos[b] –
RV468 (fragment); RV488. Violin Concerto, RV211[c].
Chamber Concerto, RV100

[a]**Katy Bircher** *fl* [b]**Peter Whelen** *bn*
La Serenissima / Adrian Chandler [c]*vn*
Avie AV2178 (77' · DDD)   Ⓕ**OO**☐➤

Intriguing title? Well some, at least, of Vivaldi's own French connections are known: the French ambassador to Venice was among his patrons, and he supplied 12 concertos without soloist to an unknown Parisian collector. Adrian Chandler has taken three of these last as a starting-point for a full disc of flute, bassoon and violin concertos in which, he reckons, references to the French style are apparent. But is a dotted rhythm here, a chaconne there and a sprinkling of Rameau-ish moments enough to make Vivaldi sound French? Wisely, Chandler does not claim so, though his concession that 'Vivaldi's style is rarely unrecognisable' puts it mildly; Vivaldi seldom sounds like anyone else, even in the grand overture-like first movement of the Violin Concerto RV211, by some margin the most French-drenched piece on this disc. The chaconnes and melodic frou-frous found elsewhere may suggest Frenchness to one as sensitive to the composer's style as Chandler, but to the average listener they will surely sound like Vivaldi from head to toe.

But if this disc works hard to justify its title, what care we when the results make such enjoyable listening? The three solo instruments come and go in various combinations, always pleasing us and never outstaying their welcome. They are played with skill and taste, lapsing only when the bassoon overpowers the flute in the slow movement of RV438. The orchestral sound, as always with La Serenissima, achieves bright attractiveness and vivacity without feeling the need to pursue the taut energy of some other groups. And that's just fine.

Cello Sonatas

Cello Sonatas – E flat, RV39; E minor, RV40;   Ⓟ
G minor, RV42; A minor, RV44; B flat, RV45;
B flat, RV46
Pieter Wispelwey *vc* **Florilegium Ensemble**
(Elizabeth Kenny, William Carter *ltes/theorbos/gtrs*
Daniel Yeadon *vc* Neal Peres da Costa *hpd/org*)
Channel Classics CCS6294 (66' · DDD)   Ⓕ**O**

Vivaldi wrote with great imagination for the cello, and the sonatas, like the concertos, are plentifully endowed with affecting melodies – the third movement of the E minor Sonata is a superb example – and virtuoso gestures. It would seem, on the strength of these pieces, that Vivaldi possessed a rare sensibility to the expressive *cantabile* possibilities in writing for the cello. Certainly, few Baroque composers other than Bach and perhaps Geminiani realised the instrument's solo potential better than he. Wispelwey is a sensitive player who draws a warm if at times under-assertive sound from his instrument. Fast movements are clearly articulated, slow ones lyrically played with some feeling for the poetry of the music. The performances are thoughtful

and enlightened, with a continuo group that includes organ, harpsichord, cello, archlutes, theorbos and guitars in a variety of combinations. The quality of the recorded sound is fine.

Additional recommendation

Cello Sonatas – RV40; RV43; RV44; RV46; RV47
Dieltiens *vc* **Ensemble Explorations**
Et'cetera KTC4035 (77' · DDD)   Ⓕ
    If you've tended to consider Vivaldi's cello sonatas less interesting than most of his music, then these performances may persuade you to think again. The creative approach extends to every aspect of interpretation, continually throwing new light on the music. By refusing to accept routine attitudes to articulation and ornamentation, Dieltiens compels us to listen anew to typical Baroque turns of phrase and appreciate their rhetorical, expressive quality. Everywhere, the level of artistry is extremely high.

Violin Sonatas

12 Violin Sonatas, Op 2 – No 1 in G minor, RV27;
No 2 in A, RV31; No 3 in D minor, RV14; No 4 in F,
RV20; No 5 in B minor, RV36; No 6 in C, RV1
Elizabeth Wallfisch *vn* **Richard Tunnicliffe** *vc*
Malcolm Proud *hpd*
Hyperion CDA67467 (59' · DDD)   Ⓕ☐➤

Vivaldi's 12 violin sonatas, Op 2, were originally released in an edition by the Venetian music publisher Antonio Bortoli in 1709. They were highly regarded enough for Estienne Roger to publish his own edition in Amsterdam three years later, quickly followed by a pirated edition by John Walsh in London. Listening to this impressive new recording it's easy to understand why they were so appealing. Each of the six included here is packed with musical treasure. Elizabeth Wallfisch's delivery of the fast movements is dazzling, and her animated and witty playing in the Giga towards the end of the second sonata is stunning. More memorable still is her clean and lyrical expression in the simpler melodic movements. The slower *Andantes* that introduce each sonata are sensuously played, and suggest Vivaldi could articulate emotional depth beyond his Corellian model.

Richard Tunnicliffe and Malcolm Proud form an ideally sympathetic continuo section. In Bortoli's 1709 printed edition these sonatas were described as for violin and cello, without mention of a keyboard instrument. Following this clue, the third sonata is performed as a fabulous sinewy duet.

Gloria in excelsis Deo, RV588

Gloria – RV588; RV589. Introduzione al Gloria, 'Ostro
picta, armata spina', RV642
Monica Piccinini *sop* **Sara Mingardo** *contr*
Concerto Italiano / Rinaldo Alessandrini
Naïve OP30485 (67' · DDD)   Ⓕ**OO**☐➤

A dozen years after his celebrated recording of Vivaldi's *Gloria*, RV589, Alessandrini's re-recording of it as part of Naïve's Vivaldi Edition bears the traces of the realisation that anarchic speed is not, after all, the best way. This new performance, coupled with the other of Vivaldi's extant settings, still sets off at a brisker pace than most but it is no longer wilfully madcap: the articulate playing of Concerto Italiano permits enough room for the details to emerge, and Alessandrini nowadays seems to have enough confidence in his musicians (and in Vivaldi) to let the muscular expression of rhythms function without impatient snapping at the musical fabric. Another notable improvement from 1997 is his plangent choir. 'Et in terra' is perhaps a bit short on mystery and atmosphere but it ebbs and flows in an appealing way, and the fugal 'Propter magnam gloriam' is sung with plenty of muscle. 'Laudamus te' crackles with energy, and Anna Simboli's graceful 'Domine Deus Rex coelestis' features an elegant violin solo by Nicholas Robinson. Sara Mingardo treats 'Domine Deus Agnus Dei' like an operatic lament and her copious vibrato feels over-exaggerated (although Francesco Moi's organ realisation is spot on).

Concerto Italiano also delivers a zesty performance of Vivaldi's less famous *Gloria* setting (RV588). The choir's tuning and intonation can be a little frayed at the edges but the counterpoint in 'Qui tollis' is meticulously balanced, Mingardo is at her best in the heartfelt 'Qui sedes', and Alessandrini's spirited direction is irresistible. Both *Gloria* settings are preceded by short solo 'introduzioni'; *Ostro picta, armata spina* (RV642) is played with a charismatic spring in its step and the high florid soprano part is expertly dispatched by Monica Piccinini; it is peculiar that Naïve does not credit her on the cover but prominently names Mingardo, who provides only a little more than the equivalent service for the introduzione to RV588.

Gloria, RV588. Dixit Dominus, RV595.
Jubilate o amoeni chori. Nulla in mundo pax
Jane Archibald, Michele de Boer sops **Anita Krause** mez **Peter Mahon** counterten **Nils Brown** ten **Giles Tomkins** bass-bar **Aradia Ensemble / Kevin Mallon**
Naxos 8 557445; Ⓢ 🄜 6 110064 (69' · DDD · T/t)
Ⓢ🄳➤

In 1713 Vivaldi, teacher of the violin at the school of the Ospedale della Pietà in Venice, found himself taking on the responsibility for composing music for the Pietà's all-female choir. Here, in the first of a new series of recordings of all his sacred music on Naxos, are three works from around 1715: none is well known, but all are extremely attractive.

Dixit Dominus only came to light in the 1960s. Visitors came from all over Europe to hear the girls' singing and playing, and in 'Tecum principium', for two sopranos and two cellos, we can imagine their delight. The puzzle is how the 'male' parts were sung. Was the bass-line taken at pitch by deep-voiced women, or transposed upwards? The Aradia Chorus goes for the conventional lay-out, with a mixed alto line, and sings with admirable clarity and vigour.

Jane Archibald, who copes fearlessly with the coloratura of 'Dominus a dextris tuis', does equally well in the 'Alleluia' of *Nulla in mundo*, and tastefully decorates the reprise of the *da capo* siciliana with which the motet begins.

The oddity here is Vivaldi's integration of the alto motet, *Jubilate, o amoeni chori*, with a setting of the *Gloria*, RV588. Anita Krause is splendid, especially in the lilting 'Qui sedes'. Kevin Mallon is rather dogged in the Gloria's 'Et in terra pax', but elsewhere he conducts with a sure sense of style.

Gloria in D, RV589

Vivaldi Gloria[b]. Ostro picta, RV642[c]. Nisi Dominus, RV803[d] **Ruggieri** Gloria, RV ANH 23[a]
[ab]**Joanne Lunn, Carolyn Sampson** sops
[ab]**Joyce DiDonato** contr [ad]**Tuva Semmingsen** mezs
[abd]**Hilary Summers** contr [a]**Robin Blaze** counterten
The King's Consort Choir; The King's Consort / Robert King
Hyperion CDA66849 (77' · DDD · T/t) Ⓕ🄳➤

Robert King had the good fortune that a lost Vivaldi *Nisi Dominus* turned up just as his project to record the composer's complete sacred music reached its 10th and final volume. This is its premiere recording. As the work's authenticator, Michael Talbot, has pointed out, only Vivaldi would have dared to include solos for chalumeau, violin 'in tromba marina', viola d'amore, organ and cello in a single multi-sectional work. If, as it seems, this is one of the great colouristic experimenter's last sacred compositions, he certainly goes out with a bang. An atmospheric and loving performance gives a perfect start to its new life.

The other major work for this final volume is the famous *Gloria*, a fitting crown to the series. So much is good in it – boldness, brightness, expressive depth, melodic beauty – and it all comes through in this carefully judged interpretation. Carolyn Sampson is excellent in the short solo motet *Ostro picta*, a final reminder that high-quality solo singing has been one of the principal pleasures of this series. But King gives the final word to the members of his choir, who ably sing the stand-out solos in the intriguing *Gloria* by Giovanni Maria Ruggieri from which Vivaldi pinched his own concluding 'Cum Sancto Spiritu' fugue. With its bold strokes of originality and colour, it's easy to see how it could have impressed Vivaldi.

Psalms

Dixit Dominus in D, RV595[ab]. Domine ad adiuvandum me, RV593[a]. Credidi propter quod, RV605. Beatus vir in B flat, RV598[ab]. Beatus vir in C, RV597[abc] 🅿

^a**Susan Gritton,** ^b**Catrin Wyn-Davies** *sops* ^b**Catherine Denley** *mez* ^c**Charles Daniels** *ten* ^c**Neal Davies** *bass* ^c**Michael George** *bass* **Choir of The King's Consort; The King's Consort / Robert King**
Hyperion CDA66789 (70' · DDD · T/t)   (F)

Here are two of Vivaldi's most extended and impressive psalm settings. These are the single-choir *Dixit Dominus*, RV595 (Psalm 110), and double-choir *Beatus vir*, RV597 (Psalm 112). Vivaldi set both psalms more than once, and King's programme also includes the single-movement *Beatus vir*, RV598, as well as the response, *Domine ad adiuvandum me*, RV593, and the conservatively styled Vesper psalm, *Credidi propter quod*, RV605. The King's Consort Choir make a lively and warm-textured contribution; the solo line-up is also strong; with Susan Gritton and Catrin Wyn-Davies providing an evenly matched, lightly articulated partnership in their two duets. Neal Davies and Michael George are splendidly robust in their vigorous 'Potens in terra' duet from *Beatus vir* (RV597). Catherine Denley gives an appropriately strongly inflected account of 'Judicabit in nationibus' but is intimate and tender in her beautiful 'De torrente in via bibet' (from *Dixit*). The remaining soloist, Charles Daniels, delivers the virtuoso 'Peccator videbit' (*Beatus vir*, RV597) with lightness and comfortable agility. Although consisting of only three movements, the G major *Domine ad adiuvandum me* is easily on a level with the larger-scale pieces, its expressive warmth irresistible. This is a rewarding issue, spaciously recorded.

Dixit Dominus in D, RV594

Dixit Dominus in D, RV594^e. Lauda Jerusalem in   (P)
E minor, RV609^b. Magnificat in G minor, RV610^a.
Kyrie in G minor, RV587^c. Credo in E minor, RV591^d
^{abe}**Susan Gritton,** ^{abe}**Lisa Milne** *sops* ^{ae}**Catherine Denley** *mez* ^{ae}**Lynton Atkinson** *ten* ^e**David Wilson-Johnson** *bar* **The King's Consort Choristers and Choir; The King's Consort / Robert King**
Hyperion CDA66769 (63' · DDD · T/t)   (F)⊕+

King's 'super-group' featuring choristers drawn from seven English cathedral and collegiate choirs sounds better than ever – technically reliable, with a good, full sound – and are a credit to King's vision in bringing them together. This volume has five typically uplifting works, three of which – *Lauda Jerusalem*, *Dixit Dominus* and the G minor *Kyrie* – offer the opulent sound of double choir and orchestra. *Dixit Dominus* is the most substantial, a colourful 23-minute sequence of varied solos and choruses, with trumpets, oboes and two organs all chipping in, most notably in an awe-inspiring depiction of the Day of Judgement. The other two are perhaps less striking, though *Lauda Jerusalem* is certainly charming in its two-soprano interchanges. Highlights of the single-chorus works include another exquisite soprano duet and a fiery 'Fecit potentiam' in the *Magnificat*, and an extraordi-

nary 'Crucifixus' in the *Credo* which departs from the pain-wracked norm by seemingly depicting with lugubrious slow tread Christ's walk to Calvary. King manages very well in capturing the essence of Vivaldi's bold, sometimes disarmingly straightforward style. These tidy performances are driven with just the right amount of springy energy – neither too much nor too little – and are well recorded in the warm resonance of St Jude's Church, Hampstead in London.

Motets

Laudate pueri Dominum, RV600^a.   (P)
Salve regina, RV616^c. Sanctorum meritis, RV620^a. Sum in medio tempestatum, R632^b. Cur sagittas, cur tela, RV637^c
^a**Susan Gritton** *sop* ^b**Tuva Semmingsen** *mez*
^c**Nathalie Stutzmann** *contr* **The King's Consort / Robert King**
Hyperion CDA66829 (68' · DDD · T/t)   (F)⊕+

The best-known item here is the *Salve regina*, a piece which has been recorded on several occasions before, usually by countertenors. Vivaldi intended it for a woman, however, and here Nathalie Stutzmann is given the chance to show off the depth and dark nobility of her contralto voice. She strikes a suitably reverential tone, one which King's orchestral accompaniment matches perfectly – the opening ritornellos of the first and last sections are both exquisitely done.

The psalm *Laudate pueri* presents 23 minutes of attractive music without really doing much to set the pulse racing. More interesting are *Cur sagittas, cur tela* – which shows the soul maintaining stoical faith in the face of attack by 'the soldiers of hell' (with violins exuberantly chucking the arrows of the title), before enjoying the protected world of the believer – and the disc's star find, *Sum in medio tempestatum*. This is a bright, unashamedly operatic number, opening with a classic simile aria comparing the troubled soul to a storm-tossed ship, and going on to depict the safe haven that hoves into view when one has turned to Jesus. The virtuoso vocal writing is negotiated with stunning agility and lightness by mezzo Tuva Semmingsen.

Another well-executed Vivaldi disc, then, from King. The recorded sound is also just right.

In furore iustissimae irae, RV626^a. Laudate pueri (P)
Dominum, RV601^{ab}. Violin Concerto, 'per la Solennità di San Lorenzo', RV286^c. Double Concerto for Violin, Organ and Strings, RV541^{cd}. Sinfonia for Strings, 'Sinfonia al Santo Sepolcro', RV169
^a**Sandrine Piau** *sop* ^b**Marcello Gatti** *fl*
^c**Stefano Montanari** *vn* **Accademia Bizantina / Ottavio Dantone** ^d*org*
Naïve OP30416 (62' · DDD · T/t)   (F)

'*In furore* is the ideal score for any soprano who's spoiling for a fight – with herself!' So says Sandrine Piau in the booklet, and she could have added that it also makes a superb opener for any disc. The motet could have been made for a singer of Piau's avian lightness and agility, and sure enough she throws herself into it, bringing to it her usual precision and, with a technique that enables plenty of dazzling extra ornaments, winning personality.

With her energy and imagination, Piau manages to find contrast in the work, not just between its fearful opening movement and more penitential second, but on a local scale as well. In the *Laudate pueri*, an altogether more urbane offering, she sings with poise, expressive sophistication and tonal power. Piau's quickness of mind is matched by the orchestral playing of Accademia Bizantina, whose sound, typically for an Italian group, is deliciously grainy, allowing for an alert and intense approach to interpretative detail. Thus they never fail to enhance the mood of a particular number, a skill which they also put to good use in the disc's three orchestral works.

'Amor sacro'
In furore iustissimae irae, RV626. In turbato mare, RV627. Nulla in mundo pax, RV630. Sum in medio tempestatum, R632
Simone Kermes *sop*
Venice Baroque Orchestra / Andrea Marcon
Archiv 477 5980AH (67' · DDD · T/t) Ⓕ🅑➔

Opening with one of the composer's most thrillingly virtuoso motets, *In furore iustissimae irae*, the Venice Baroque Orchestra go on to one of his most beautiful, *Nulla in mundo pax*. And if the other two are less individually striking, they are nevertheless well worth hearing; *In turbato mare* opens with a stomach-churning depiction of those raging seas that are always tossing the soul so, and later conjures dread at mention of the 'horrors of death', while *Sum in medio tempestatum* treats a similar subject with a touch more mid-century leisure and politeness.

The disc is, of course, a vehicle for Simone Kermes, whose bright vocal talents have so far impressed in a number of Baroque operas but here make their solo recording debut. She proves more than a match for Vivaldi's typically athletic vocal demands – indeed adds to them in a number of tessitura-extending cadenzas – and makes much of the music's bold contrasts. Some may look for more innocence in the gentler music, where her mini-vibrato can sound rather knowing, but in general Kermes's performances give nothing but pleasure. The orchestra is forthright and exciting, with a satisfyingly full, organ-enriched sound, marred only by some of the cheesy lute embellishments. A straightforward Vivaldi disc, but one full of the strength of expertise.

Stabat mater in F minor, RV621

Vivaldi Stabat mater. Concerto, RV130, 'Sonata 🅟
al Santo Sepolcro', RV130 **Bach** Tilge, Höchster, meine
Sünden (Psalm 51), BWV1083[a] **Pergolesi** Salve regina

[a]**Emma Kirkby** *sop*
Theatre of Early Music / Daniel Taylor *counterten*
BIS 🔊 BIS-SACD1546 (75' · DDD · T/t) Ⓕ🅞🅞🅑➔

There are at least half a dozen recordings of Vivaldi's *Stabat mater* that one wouldn't want to be without but this profoundly beautiful version leaps straight into their ranks. The Theatre of Early Music band is small (just single strings and simple continuo) but its playing never feels underweight, and rhetorical qualities in the music are clear yet unforced. The opening *ritornello* is immaculately played, with an ideal atmosphere of hushed melancholy; the affinity between the instrumentalists and Taylor's gentle and deeply poetic singing is breathtaking. While some listeners may prefer gutsier or more 'operatic' voices, or more obviously dramatic styles of lamentation, Taylor's intelligent and stylish singing belongs in a select class alongside a few of the finest and sweetest voices of its type. There is plenty of understated dramatic weight in his interpretation of 'O quam tristis', and he tastefully moves through the few passages of more extended melismatic writing. 'Eja mater' is often a stumbling block, but here the sparsely accompanied texture is enchanting. It's beguilingly performed, and the Theatre of Early Music's dignified and flawless accompaniments play an equal part in the perfectly judged interpretation.

Pergolesi's *Salve regina* is also given an affecting rendition: the string playing has the perfect juxtaposition of piety and sensuality, and Taylor's soft singing is admirably communicative of the words. Violinist Adrian Butterfield leads an exquisite performance of the solemn Sonata 'al Santo Sepolcro', and the well chosen programme is rounded off by *Tilge, Höchster, meine Sünden* (Bach's creative yet respectful adaptation of Pergolesi's *Stabat mater*, using the text of Psalm 51), in which Emma Kirkby's delicate singing elegantly blends with Taylor's.

Stabat mater. Cessate, omai cessate, 🅟
RV684. Filiae mestae Jerusalem, RV638. String
Concertos – C, RV114; E flat, RV130, 'Sonata al Santo
Sepolcro'
Andreas Scholl *counterten*
Ensemble 415 / Chiara Banchini *vn*
Harmonia Mundi HMC90 1571 (52' · DDD · T/t)
Ⓕ🅞🅞🅞🅑➔

 Here's a very attractively prepared menu whose main course is the *Stabat mater* for countertenor and strings. Hors d'oeuvres and side-dishes consist of a *ripieno* concerto (RV114), a chamber cantata for countertenor and strings (RV684), a string sonata in E flat (RV130) and an introductory motet to a lost *Miserere* (RV638). Taken together, the pieces demonstrate something of Vivaldi's diverse style as a composer.

The chamber cantata, if closely related to the two sacred vocal items on the disc in respect of tonal colour, differs from them in character.

Conforming with the standard Italian cantata pattern at the time of two pairs of alternating recitative and *da capo* aria Vivaldi enlivens his pastoral idyll with two particularly affecting arias, the first with a palpitating *pizzicato* violin, the second a virtuoso vocal *tour de force* illustrating the plight of the forsaken lover. Andreas Scholl brings the whole thing off superbly with only a moment's faulty intonation at the close of the first aria. Unlike settings of the *Stabat mater* by Pergolesi and others, Vivaldi used only the first 10 of the 20 stanzas of the poem. His deeply expressive setting of the poem will be familiar to many readers, but few will have heard such an affecting performance as Scholl achieves here. The lyrical prayer of human yearning for faith contained in the 'Fac ut ardeat' movement is tenderly sung and here, as throughout the programme, sympathetically supported by Ensemble 415 under Chiara Banchini's experienced direction.

Vespers

Vespri Solenni per la Festa dell'Assunzione di Maria Vergine (ed Alessandrini/Delaméa) – Violin Concerto in C, RV581[9]; Concerto for Two Violins and Two Organs in F, RV584[h]; Domine ad adiuvandum me festina in G, RV593[b]; Introduzione al Dixit, RV635[b]; Dixit Dominus in D, RV594[abdef]; Laudate pueri in C minor, RV600[a]; Laetatus sum, RV607; Nisi Dominus in G minor, RV608[d]; Lauda Jerusalem in E minor, RV609[ab]; Magnificat in G minor, RV610a[abdef]; Salve regina in C minor, RV616[d]; Antiphons[c]
[a]**Gemma Bertagnolli,** [b]**Roberta Invernizzi,** [c]**Anna Simboli** sops [d]**Sara Mingardo** contr [e]**Gianluca Ferrarini** ten [f]**Matteo Bellotto** bar [g]**Antonio De Secondi,** [h]**Mauro Lopes Ferreira,** [h]**Francesca Vicari** vns [h]**Francesco Moi,** [h]**Ignazio Schifani** orgs
Concerto Italiano / Rinaldo Alessandrini
Opus 111 ③ OP30383 (153' · DDD · T/t)　Ⓕ❍❍❍

This isn't the 'Vivaldi Vespers', or even a reconstruction of a specific event, but a kind of 'sacred concert' in Vespers form, of the sort that Venetian churches in Vivaldi's time would mount in the name of worship. Whether he ever supplied all the music for any such occasion isn't clear, but he certainly set plenty of Vespers texts, enough at any rate for Rinaldo Alessandrini and scholar Frédéric Delaméa to put together this rich programme.

So this is music for a Vespers for the Feast of the Assumption as it might have been heard in one of Venice's more important churches, made up of Vivaldi's settings of the five Vespers psalms, a *Magnificat*, a *Salve regina*, a solo motet (*Ascende in laeta*) and a couple of orchestral concertos. Unmistakably Vivaldian in almost every bar, these pieces nevertheless show considerable variety; the psalms range from the opulence of *Dixit Dominus* for five soloists, two choirs and two choirs, to the expressive solo settings of *Laudate pueri* and *Nisi Dominus*, to the breezily functional choral treatments of *Laetatus sum* and *Lauda Jerusa-*

lem; *Ascende in laeta* is a virtuoso showpiece for soprano, and the *Salve regina* a sombre vehicle for contralto. The liturgical thread is supplied by plainchant antiphons, prettily rendered in a fascinating conjectural imitation of the 18th century's 'corrupt' manner, which is to say, with organ accompaniment and unabashed ornamentation.

Alessandrini's reading has an energy which is both forthright and controlled. His solo singers are of high quality; Roberta Invernizzi and Sara Mingardo are from the front rank of Italian Baroque singers, capable of expressive lyricism and thrilling virtuosity, but Gemma Bertagnolli is no less effective. The orchestra plays with inspiriting precision and life, but the choir could be improved on, and is poorly favoured in the recorded balance. Indeed, the recorded sound as a whole is a bit noisy, in places suffering a distant mechanical whir. Still, the overall effect is what counts most in a recording like this: the music has a vital sense of direction, resulting in two and a half hours of invigorating listening.

Chamber Cantatas

Cantatas – Alla caccia, alla caccia, RV670; Care selve amici prati, RV671; Elvira, anima mia, RV654. Chamber Concertos – in F, RV97; in G minor, 'La notte', RV104; in G minor, RV105.
Laura Polverelli mez **L'Astrée Ensemble**
Opus 111 OP30358 (55' · DDD · T/t)　Ⓕ❍

Whether Vivaldi wrote these cantatas for an exceptionally talented singer or just decided to give others a mischievously hard time isn't known; the fact remains that they're tough assignments. If Polverelli finds them so, she gives no sign of it. She's a mezzo with a cloudless upper register and a full-throated lower one, a wide and subtly nuanced range of volume, supple and pitch-perfect. These three chamber cantatas deal with various unhappy aspects of love, and she projects them without resorting to 'grand-operatic' excess. These are performances to treasure.

The chamber concertos show Vivaldi at his most happily inventive. All those on this disc have alternative versions, and if RV97 and 105 lack something of the verve of those by Giardino Armonico they're no less infectious.

The recording is clear and very well balanced, and the vocal texts are given in three languages, including English. A thoroughly enjoyable disc.

Alla caccia dell'alme, RV670. Care selve, RV671. Perfidissimo cor, RV674. Pianti, sospiri, RV676. Qual per ignoto, RV677. Orlando furioso, RV728 – Piangerò sinché l'onda. Tito Manlio, RV778 – Di verde ulivo. Cello Sonata, RV47
Philippe Jaroussky counterten
Ensemble Artaserse (Jérémie Papasergio bn Emilia Gliozzi vc Claire Antonini theo Yoko Nakamura hpd)
Virgin Classics 545721-2 (68' · DDD · T/t)　Ⓕ🄳➔

The countertenor Philippe Jaroussky soars as effortlessly as a bird, with no sense of strain: perhaps – for we can never know for certain – this is how the great castrati of the 18th century sounded. He was certainly convincing in the soprano role of Nero in the EuroArts DVD of Handel's *Agrippina*.

Little is known about the background to these cantatas. Each is in the familiar form of two *da capo* arias, separated and sometimes preceded by a recitative. The themes are equally familiar, generally concerned with the inconstancy or inaccessibility of the beloved, with reference to the storms, bright dawns and shipwrecks of *opera seria*. *Alla caccia dell'alme* describes 'barbarous Cloris' hunting souls and hearts, with predictable consequences for the victim. And there is a delightful surprise: no horn depicting the chase, of course: instead, here and elsewhere, we have the jolly bassoon of Jérémie Papasergio on the bass-line.

In fact the composition of the continuo group varies within each cantata and even during a movement: the 'A' section of the first aria in *Pianti, sospiri e dimandar mercede* features bassoon and lute, the 'B' section cello and harpsichord. This is justified by the quality of the playing but to switch from harpsichord to organ in the same piece seems to me fussy.

Philippe Jaroussky is sweet-toned and, as well as singing the divisions with wonderful control, he shows care for the meaning of the words. The aria from *Tito Manlio*, which really was written for contralto, finds him duetting with the cello obbligato of Emilia Gliozzi – superb!

Opera arias

'Amor profano'
L'olimpiade – Siam navi all'onde algenti. La fede tradita e vendicata – Sin nel placido soggiorno. Orlando furioso – Ah, fuggi rapido. Tito Manlio – Non m'affligge il tormento di morte; Dopo sì rei disastri; Combatta un gentil cor. Semiramide – Quegl'occhi luminosi. Il Tigrane – Squarciami pure il seno. Catone in Utica – Se in campo armato. Bajazet – Sinfonia. Griselda – Agitata da due venti. La verità in cimento – Amato ben, tu sei la mia speranza. Giustino – La farfalletta audace s'invola; Or che cinto ho il crin d'alloro
Simone Kermes sop
Venice Baroque Orchestra / Andrea Marcon
Archiv 477 6618AH (71' · DDD)   Ⓕ**Ⓞ➔**

Simone Kermes has once again teamed up with Andrea Marcon and his Venice Baroque Orchestra for a superbly balanced exploration of opera arias. The level of effort and intelligence in choosing the right repertoire is clearly manifest in this varied and stimulating anthology. There is a tangible variety of dramatic sentiments and instrumental colours: the introduction of solo cello, recorders, trumpets, solo trumpet and horns in occasional arias is perfectly timed to avoid too much textural monotony, and they make the experience livelier and entertaining. Each aria seems to have been meticulously placed in a sequence that pulls the listener through the contrasts in Vivaldi's operatic writing, which also means that the disc tells a story about the repertoire as well as giving Kermes and the Venetian players plenty of opportunities to show how well they can perform it.

Some of Kermes's dizzying cadenzas are perhaps excessive, but such extravagances are never dull. Her delivery of tempestuous coloratura arias is often exhilarating (the opening aria 'Siam navi all'onde algenti'). The Venice Baroque Orchestra's playing is also dazzling, sensitive and lyrical.

Five of the arias here are first recordings, including a robust heroic aria from *Orlando Furioso* – not Vivaldi's famous opera of that title but an earlier setting of the story that also featured music by Ristori – in which Kermes's rapid repeated notes are astonishing. The finest of the rare items is 'Quegl'occhi luminosi' (from *Semiramide*), which reminds us that, notwithstanding the flashy fast stuff, both singer and composer are often at their dramatic finest in ravishing slow music. 'Se in campo armato' (*Catone in Utica*) is tastefully played, with its vivacious trumpet-laden accompaniment excellently juxtaposed with a tender B section (although Kermes perhaps over-eggs the ornaments in the *da capo* repeat). The concluding aria 'Or che cinto ho il crin d'alloro' (*Giustino*) shows the musicians' infectious joy in the music, with an extrovert vocal line, exuberant horns, and snappy strings and continuo.

'Amor profano' is a role model of how a Baroque opera arias recital disc should be put together – with proper research, affection for the composer, and top-notch artistry.

Juditha triumphans – Armatae face. Farnace – Gelido in ogni vena; Forse, o caro, in questi accenti. Griselda – Ho il cor già lacero. L'incoronazione di Dario – Non mi lusinga vana speranza. L'Olimpiade – Mentre dormi, Amor fomenti. Orlando furioso – Nel profondo cieco mondo; Sol da te, mio dolce amore. Ottone in Villa – Misero spirto mio. Tito Manlio – Sonno, se pur sei sonno. La verita' in cimento – Solo quella guancia bella; Cara sorte di chi nata. Orlando finto pazzo – Lo stridor, l'orror d'Averno; Anderò, volerò, griderò. Arsilda, regina di Ponto – Tornar voglio al primo ardore
Magdalena Kožená mez
Venice Baroque Orchestra / Andrea Marcon
Archiv 477 8096AH (77' · DDD · T/t)   Ⓕ**ⓄⓄⓄ➔**

A third of the arias here have not been included in Naïve's Vivaldi Edition so far, which suggests that Kožená (presumably advised by Vivaldi scholar Frédéric Delaméa) has devoted some effort to exploring less familiar scores. In the booklet, Kožená remarks that Andrea Marcon and his Venetian accomplices 'have this music in their blood', and how entering the studio without having performed the pieces forced their music-making to be 'freshly baked'.

The decision to pack the programme with slower and subtler arias pays dividends: 'Sonno, se pur sei sonno' (*Tito Manlio*) is a quietly ravishing opener, 'Sol da te' (*Orlando furioso*) features beguiling flute-playing by Michele Favaro, and the disc concludes with an exquisite interpretation of 'Mentre dormi' (*L'Olimpiade*). Kožená's singing is often at its best; only her forced upward appoggiatura at the end of 'Non mi lusinga' is unconvincing. There is plenty of dramatic bite on offer even in slow music, especially in the compellingly taut 'Gelido in ogni vena' (based on the opening of 'Winter' from the *Four Seasons*), as Kožená eloquently conveys Farnace's icy shock that he has unwittingly condemned his son to death.

There haven't been many captivating Vivaldi opera aria anthologies, but this is definitely among the most intriguing, theatrically varied and convincing.

'Pyrotechnics'

Catone in Utica – Come in vano il mare irato; Chi può nelle sventure...Nella foresta. Semiramide – E prigioniero e re. La fida ninfa – Alma oppressa; Destin nemico...Destin avaro. Griselda – Agitata da due venti. Ipermestra – Vibro il ferro. Farnace – No, ch'amar non è fallo in cor guerriero...Quell'usignolo. Tito Manlio – Splender fra 'l cieco orror. Rosmira fedele – Vorrei dirti il mio dolore. Il labbro ti lusinga. Ricordati che sei. Sin nel placido soggiorno
Vivica Genaux *mez* **Europa Galante / Fabio Biondi**
Virgin Classics 694573-0 (75' · DDD)   Ⓕ➌➤

Pyrotechnics is what we are promised and that is exactly what we get for the majority of the disc's ample 75 minutes – more than enough to satisfy the most relentless pyromaniac. This enables Biondi and Genaux to devote their animated talents to conveying Vivaldi's art at its punchiest and snappiest.

Genaux's choice of repertoire, as is almost requisite with Vivaldi vocal projects, is guided by scholar Frédéric Delaméa, who provides an excellent essay. The inclusion of three genuine obscurities that cannot be confidently ascribed to any particular opera might appeal to avid collectors. Genaux's sure-footed rapid passagework is dazzling and her energised coloratura is happily wed to Europa Galante's zesty playing. Biondi's band is delicately poised on a knife-edge between eloquence and storminess in Griselda's 'Agitata da due venti'. By a few arias into the recital one begins to suspect that Vivaldi often says much the same thing in most of these selected scenes but it seems churlish to complain when he says it with such brio. However, it turns out that 'Pyrotechnics' covers a pleasing variety of styles: a few gentler arias are performed with graceful sensitivity – notably 'Quell'usignolo' from the 1738 revival of Farnace – and the hunting horns in 'Nella foresta' arrive just in the nick of time to prevent instrumental monotony. 'Sin nel placido soggiorno',

the loveliest of the three rarities, features charismatic recorders and forms a surprisingly understated and charming conclusion to proceedings. With Biondi ensuring that the music-making always feels fresh and Genaux on her most pleasing form, this is one of the better Vivaldi aria anthologies to have flared up in recent years.

'Arie ritrovate'

Arias from Orlando Furioso, Tito Manlio, La verità in cimento, Teuzzone and Scanderbeg
Sonia Prina *contr* **Stefano Montanari** *vn*
Accademia Bizantina / Ottavio Dantone
Naïve OP30443 (71' · DDD)   Ⓕ

Some of these arias are individual pieces in anthologies made by Vivaldi, or long-forgotten alternative opera arias that will not be recorded in the context of their parent work in Naïve's series.

'Con palme ed allori' is one of the few traces to have survived from *Scanderbeg*, an opera written to celebrate the reopening of the Teatro alla Pergola in Florence in June 1718. A martial aria with two trumpets, two oboes and strings, its spectacular boldness arrives just in time to inject some flamboyant theatricality after some less-than-striking alternative arias from *La verità in cimento*. However, all of the music is expertly crafted, and some of it is extraordinary, such as the beautiful 'Tu dormi in tante pene' from *Tito Manlio*. Sonia Prina has a firm grasp on melodic lines and a supple timbre. She reaffirms her status as an outstanding Baroque opera singer, and Ottavio Dantone lends excellent support from Accademia Bizantina.

Juditha triumphans, RV644

Juditha triumphans   ℗
Magdalena Kožená *mez* **Anke Herrmann** *sop*
Maria José Trullu, Marina Comparato, Tiziana Carraro *mezs* **Coro di Camera Accademia Nazionale di Santa Cecilia; Academia Montis Regalis / Alessandro de Marchi**
Opus 111 ② OP30314 (105' · DDD · T/t)   Ⓕ○○

Vivaldi's only surviving oratorio, *Juditha triumphans* (1716), with its strongly characterised roles and luxuriant orchestration, is a true Baroque masterpiece. Alessandro de Marchi has departed from other recent interpreters by daring to transpose the tenor and bass choral parts up an octave, as is widely believed was done by Vivaldi himself to accommodate the choir of the Ospedale della Pietà. The effect is breathtaking: the compressed, female choral textures positively gleam. From his superb cast of female soloists, de Marchi coaxes remarkable and dramatically convincing male vocal timbres. Maria José Trullu projects the various sides of Holofernes, who's depicted not merely as a monster but as capable of dignity and charm, even if ultimately incautious; she infuses her tone with a warmth and richness that countertenors might envy.

Magdalena Koená, the Bethulian widow Judith, casts a spell on those who only hear her: as well as Holofernes. She sings with poise almost throughout, as she enters the enemy camp, meets and seduces Holofernes, reflects on the transitoriness of life and prays for peace and strength before murdering the sleeping Holofernes. Only then, as she carries out her heroic – if horrific – mission does she fully convey her emotion.

The instrumentation offers a treasure trove of unusual and evocative instruments, even for the time: a pair of clarinets to characterise the dissolute Assyrian soldiers, recorders for 'nocturnal breezes' and a quartet of theorbos to depict the preparation of the feast. These and the more common obbligato and continuo instruments of the day are affectingly played by the musicians of the Academia Montis Regalis. At every turn there's ample evidence of the care de Marchi has lavished on this performance, and Robert King's by comparison seems less full-blooded and relatively static. Congratulations all round for an outstanding recording.

Bajazet

Bajazet   Ⓟ
Ildebrando D'Arcangelo bass-bar Bajazet **Patrizia Ciofi** sop Idaspe **David Daniels** counterten Tamerlano **Elīna Garanča** mez Andronico **Vivica Genaux** mez Irene **Marijana Mijanovic** mez Asteria
Europa Galante / Fabio Biondi vn
Virgin Classics ② 545676-2 (147' · DDD · T/t)
                Ⓟ**ⓄⓄⓄ**▷

 Vivaldi's *Bajazet*, based on the same libretto as Handel's *Tamerlano*, tells the story of the Tartar emperor Tamerlano and the Ottoman sultan Bajazet whom he's defeated. Vivaldi responds with sound dramatic sense. His recitatives especially show a conversational realism that allows them to be more than just a functional advancement of the plot; indeed, Bajazet's biggest moment is a powerful accompanied recitative.

Vivaldi works hard at characterisation, if by unusual means: *Bajazet* is partly a *pasticcio*, which is to say that it borrows and adapts arias from other operas written in the fashionable and suave Neapolitan style by composers such as Hasse and Giacomelli, who by the 1730s were beginning to dominate the operatic world. Vivaldi chose well. He'd have appreciated the crowd-pleasing virtuosity of an aria such as 'Qual guerriero in campo armato', originally written for Farinelli by his brother Riccardo Broschi; here it aptly expresses Irene's near-deranged indignation at being dumped by Tamerlano. Clever choices such as this make *Bajazet* a real opera, not just a hotch-potch.

The same can be said for the performers here. The cast has hardly a weak link: David

Daniels is in typically beautiful voice as Tamerlano, yet at the same time manages enough hardness to suggest the spiteful anger of the man; Elīna Garanča conveys a suitable measure of weakness as the indecisive Andronico; and Marijana Mijanovic's moving and dignified Asteria never looks like losing her moral high ground. Vivica Genaux gives a show-stopping display as Irene, and Patrizia Ciofi proves no less equal to the tough technical challenges set by the role of Andronico's friend Idaspe. Only Ildebrando D'Arcangelo as Bajazet disappoints slightly, failing to reach to the Sultan's defiant heart.

The orchestra's contribution, on the other hand, is a major bonus. Fabio Biondi has never been one to miss details, and he and his players bring out countless nuances in the score with their usual array of interpretative devices ranging from gentle cello chords in recitative to sparky off-beat accents and *pizzicatos*, and even some acid *sul ponticello*. There could hardly be a better way to bring this opera to life.

La fida ninfa

La fida ninfa
Sandrine Piau sop Licori **Veronica Cangemi** sop Morasto **Marie-Nicole Lemieux** sop Elpina **Lorenzo Regazzo** bass Oralto **Philippe Jaroussky** counterten Osmino **Topi Lehtipuu** ten Narete **Sara Mingardo** mez Giunone **Christian Senn** bass-bar Eolo
Ensemble Matheus / Jean-Christophe Spinosi
Naïve ③ OP30410 (3h 9' · DDD)   Ⓜ**ⓄⓄ**▷

La fida ninfa inaugurated Verona's new Teatro Filarmonico in 1732. Vivaldi scholar Frédéric Delaméa calls the opera a 'pastoral miniature', and notes that the quality of the Veronese orchestra and a cast of renowned singers stimulated 'the composer to take special care over the elaboration of his score'. There are lots of outstanding virtuoso arias and ensembles, but, more importantly, much of Vivaldi's music adroitly portrays the moods and situations of the characters in a typically tangled web of lovers' intrigues and mistaken identities.

Those familiar with Ensemble Matheus will expect the immediate plunge into fizzing energy, eccentric thwacking bowing from the string-players and over-exaggerated dynamic contrasts within the first few moments of the opening Sinfonia. In some obvious respects it is an exciting sound, although Jean-Christophe Spinosi's musical mannerisms are occasionally excessive and rob faster music of the affectionate warmth and sonorous depth that it could convey.

Much of the singing is marvellous. In 'Chi dal cielo' Lorenzo Regazzo sings with gusto and is boldly accompanied by a trumpet, strings and timpani. The principal male role Morasto is sung passionately by Veronica Cangemi. Sandrine Piau's limpid *messa di voce* and breathtaking technique in 'Selve annose', and her delivery of fiendish coloratura in 'Alma oppressa da sorte crudele', are astonishing even for her. Marie-

Nicole Lemieux and Philippe Jaroussky combine to charming effect in the lively duet 'Dimmi pastore'; Jaroussky's singing in the slow aria 'Ah, che non posso' is beautiful, and the two recorders in Lemieux's merry Arcadian aria 'Cento donzelle' play delightfully. 'Deh, ti piega', one of Vivaldi's finest arias for the tenor voice, is sung tenderly by Topi Lehtipuu.

This is probably Spinosi's most consistent opera recording yet and indicates that *La fida ninfa* is one of Vivaldi's best stage works.

Griselda

Griselda
Marie-Nicole Lemieux *contr* Griselda **Veronica Cangemi** *sop* Costanza **Simone Kermes** *sop* Ottone **Philippe Jaroussky** *counterten* Roberto Stefano Ferrari *ten* Gualtiero **Iestyn Davies** *counterten* Corrado
Ensemble Matheus / Jean-Christophe Spinosi
Naïve ③ OP30419 (155' · DDD · S/T/t/N)   Ⓕ**O**

Griselda was first performed at Venice's Teatro di San Samuele during spring 1735. Apostolo Zeno's libretto, based on a tale from Boccaccio's *Decameron*, was adapted for Vivaldi by Carlo Goldoni: Gualtiero is forced by political unrest and public criticism of his common-born wife Griselda to prove her noble worth by subjecting her to a torrent of cruel tests.

Marie-Nicole Lemieux's passionate performance of the title-role has vivid handling of text and emotive singing. Stefano Ferrari gets around Gualtiero's fiendish coloratura competently, and 'Tu vorresti col tuo pianto' is a rarity among Vivaldi's operas: a bona fide first-class tenor aria of real distinction, beauty and dramatic subtlety. Simone Kermes navigates Ottone's wide leaps in the slow aria 'Vede orgogliosa' with immaculate poise and tenderness, and in 'Dopo un'orrida' gleefully represents Ottone's premature exultation with some outstanding pyrotechnics. Veronica Cangemi provides some relaxed, attractive coloratura. Philippe Jaroussky's arias are consistently gorgeous but he is also surprisingly strong at the tempestuous 'Che legge tiranna'. Iestyn Davies is impressive in the colourful hunting aria 'Alle minaccie'.

Spinosi's pacing of the arias suggests sensible interpretation of Vivaldi's instructions. In extrovert arias one occasionally hears some contrived clattering bows from the strings but there is a substantial problem throughout the performance caused by underwhelming, pale playing from the lower strings. Three cellists and two basses play quietly most of the time, making the hushed *basso continuo* far too thin and rarely giving enough depth and texture to the dynamic width of Vivaldi's harmonic writing. One imagines the stronger musical sense that Alessandrini, Dantone or Sardelli might have brought to Griselda. Despite reservations about the top-heavy instrumental textures, this finely sung recording unveils another inventive opera.

L'Olimpiade

L'Olimpiade, RV725 (ed Alessandrini)   Ⓟ
Sara Mingardo *contr* Licida **Roberta Invernizzi** *sop* Megacle **Sonia Prina** *mez* Aristea **Marianna Kulikova** *mez* Argene **Laura Giordano** *sop* Aminta **Riccardo Novaro** *bar* Clistene **Sergio Foresti** *bass* Alcandro
Concerto Italiano / Rinaldo Alessandrini
Opus 111 ③ OP30316 (175' · DDD · T/t)   Ⓕ**OO**

More than 50 composers set Pietro Metastasio's libretto *L'Olimpiade* between 1733 and 1815, starting with Caldara and including along the way such names as Pergolesi, Galuppi, Cimarosa, Cherubini and Paisiello. The booklet-note for this new recording suggests that Vivaldi was trying to take on the newly fashionable Neapolitan composers at their own game, not only by setting a poem by their favourite librettist, but also by adopting some of their musical mannerisms. Maybe so, but there can be few composers with a more deeply ingrained personal style than our friend the Red Priest, and it's an unmistakably Vivaldian flavour which is the strongest in this thoroughly agreeable work.

Despite the public context – the story is played out against the backdrop of the Olympic Games – this is a drama which focuses on the personal predicaments of the principal characters, each of whom faces an interesting conflict between head and heart somewhere along the line. This is more apparent from Metastasio's words than from Vivaldi's music, to be honest, but that isn't to say that the composer has been unresponsive. The most effective and intimate moments occur in the recitatives, which are fluidly conversational and full of realistic interruptions, questions and exclamations, all of which Vivaldi handles with considerable dramatic skill.

Rinaldo Alessandrini's direction is typically unfussy and to the point, ever alert to the music's dramatic intent but without imposing himself on it unduly. The finest vocal performances come from Sara Mingardo, Roberta Invernizzi and Sonia Prina, but in truth no one is a weak link. The recitatives are effectively done, the arias thrown off with dash and aplomb, and everyone sounds as if they believe in the work.

Orlando finto pazzo

Orlando finto pazzo   Ⓟ
Antonio Abete *bass* Orlando **Gemma Bertagnolli** *sop* Ersilla **Marina Comparato** *mez* Tigrinda **Sonia Prina** *contr* Origille **Manuela Custer** *mez* Argillano **Martín Oro** *counterten* Grifone **Marianna Pizzolato** *mez* Brandimarte **Teatro Regio Chorus, Turin; Academia Montis Regalis / Alessandro de Marchi**
Opus 111 ③ OP30392 (207' · DDD · T/t)   Ⓕ**O**

Orlando finto pazzo ('Orlando feigns madness') was the second of Vivaldi's numerous operas, and his first for the Venetian stage. The story of Orlando's madness is taken not from the usual source, Ariosto's poem *Orlando furioso*, but Boiardo's earlier *Orlando innamorato*, a similarly tragicomic mix of love, intrigue and magic. In Ariosto's poem Orlando's madness is real, but here he pretends it for no obvious reason; in fact it's no more than a couple of episodes in a convoluted and unengaging plot built around a love-pentangle (no less), and further complicated by various disguises and rampant dissembling.

As it happens, Vivaldi doesn't on this evidence appear to have been a natural musical dramatist. Yet what makes this music worth hearing is his evident desire to make an operatic splash at his first major attempt: there's music of irrepressible zest and personality; this early attempt deploys all the fiery and ebullient energy of his concertos and allies it to vocal music of neck-tingling excitement. Like Haydn, Vivaldi may not have been a great opera composer, but he did write operas full of great music.

Alessandro de Marchi's joyous recording brings together a typical Italian Baroque cast for a performance and recording of skill and enthusiasm.

Orlando furioso

Orlando furioso   Ⓟ
Marie-Nicole Lemieux *contr* Orlando **Jennifer Larmore** *mez* Alcina **Veronica Cangemi** *sop* Angelica **Philippe Jaroussky** *counterten* Ruggiero **Lorenzo Regazzo** *bass-bar* Astolfo **Ann Hallenberg** *mez* Bradamante **Blandine Staskiewicz** *mez* Medoro **Les Eléments; Ensemble Matheus / Jean-Christophe Spinosi**
Opus 111 ③ OP30393 (183' · DDD · T/t)   ⒻＯＯ

Vivaldi's opera combines magic, heroism and comedy to tell of a seductive sorceress, a noble knight driven insane by love, a feisty fiancée who disguises herself as a man to rescue her bewitched lover, and a magic ring that helps ensure everything ends happily ever after. This recording bears the fruit of Vivaldi scholar Frédéric Delaméa's painstaking reconstruction of the original 1727 version. Marie-Nicole Lemieux's delivery of Orlando's anguished and often unhinged recitative is astonishingly good, full of conviction, passionate, and vocally brilliant. When his sanity is restored, she achieves a tangible lucidity that makes the drama wholly satisfying. Jennifer Larmore's sorceress Alcina is devious, vivacious, and venomous. Philippe Jaroussky's Ruggerio is adept at both delicacy and heroism and Ann Hallenberg is excellent as his fiancée Bradamante.

Ensemble Matheus provide bright ritornellos and intelligent accompaniments. The playing is often abrasive and intentionally percussive in fast music, but the performers also excel at the softer moments. Spinosi's direction is vividly theatrical, and recitatives are declaimed with aplomb, although sometimes it sounds as if characters cannot wait to interrupt with their next line.

Vivaldi's score has a dramatic stature greater than most of his other operas. He rarely devoted much attention to accompanied recitatives, but

here he composed several that are unusually extensive and adventurous. This is a magnificent achievement: if Vivaldi needed a champion to establish his credentials as an opera composer, then this recording is it.

Ottone in Villa

Ottone in Villa   Ⓟ
Monica Groop *mez* Ottone **Nancy Argenta** *sop* Caio Silio **Susan Gritton** *sop* Cleonilla **Sophie Daneman** *sop* Tullia **Mark Padmore** *ten* Decio **Collegium Musicum 90 / Richard Hickox**
Chandos Chaconne ② CHAN0614 (145' · DDD · T/t)   Ⓕ☞

This, Vivaldi's very first opera, was premiered in Vicenza in 1713 and was an instant hit. The story is a relatively uncomplicated one by the standards of Baroque opera, of amatory pretences and misunderstandings: it has been admirably summarised by Eric Cross (who has edited the work) as a 'light-weight, amoral entertainment in which the flirtatious Cleonilla consistently has the upper hand, and gullible Emperor Ottone (a far from heroic figure) never discovers the truth about the way he has been deceived'. The score proceeds in a succession of *secco* recitatives (with just a very occasional *accompagnato*) and *da capo* arias – which the present cast ornament very stylishly. There are no duets or ensembles except for a perfunctory final chorus in which the characters merely sing in unison; but there's an abundance of tuneful arias, and when Vivaldi can be bothered to write proper accompaniments to them – he often merely has violins doubling the voice, plus a bass-line – he can provide interesting imitative counterpoint. Several arias employ only the upper strings without cello and bass except in ritornellos. The small Vicenza theatre couldn't afford star singers, so only limited opportunities were provided for vocal virtuosity; but the present cast makes the most of its opportunities, both in display and in meditative mood. It isn't always easy to tell the three sopranos apart, but Susan Gritton well suggests the scheming minx Cleonilla; Nancy Argenta with her bright voice has the castrato role that includes several fine arias, and displays a *messa di voce* in an echo aria; and Sophie Daneman, in a breeches role, produces a wide range of colour. Monica Groop slightly under-characterises Ottone except when roused to dismiss Rome's anxiety at his dalliance. It's quite a relief to ear one male voice, and Mark Padmore is excellent. Richard Hickox keeps a firm rhythmic hand on everything and delivers quite the best and neatest Vivaldi operatic recording yet.

Richard Wagner   German 1813-1883

Wagner's mother, Johanna, was the daughter of a baker in Weissenfels (though some papers show that she may have been the illegitimate daughter of

Prince Friedrich Ferdinand Constantin of Weimar). At the time of Wagner's birth, she was married to a police registrar named Karl Friedrich Wagner who died when Richard was only six months old. Johanna had already been having an affair with Ludwig Geyer and had a daughter, Cäcilie, six months after they were married in 1814. Geyer proved to be a profound influence on the young Wagner and surrounded him with books and paintings and, of course, introduced him to the theatre and music. Geyer died when Wagner was only eight but the seeds had been sown. It was literature that was the initial attraction, though, not music. Wagner was only 11 when he wrote a drama, drawn from Shakespeare and the Greeks, in which 42 characters died in the first four acts, and some of whom reappeared as ghosts in the fifth act. His latent passion for music was aroused by a performance of Weber's Der Freischütz; when he heard Beethoven's Fidelio for the first time at the Gewandhaus, Leipzig, music became an obsession. He made arrangements of Beethoven's symphonies, began to absorb scores and produced his first compositions: two orchestral overtures. These were premiered in Leipzig in 1829, the first works of Wagner to be performed. And all this before he had had any formal training.

His future characters traits were beginning to emerge – a rebel, who was expelled from the Thomasschule in Leipzig and more concerned with duelling, drinking, gambling and women than his law studies at the University of Leipzig. During his brief sojourn there (he never took his degree) he became well known as a compulsive talker and for his dogmatic views. In 1831 he left to undertake six fruitful months of studying counterpoint with the cantor of the Thomasschule. His teacher, Theodor Weinlig, admitted that after that period there was nothing more he could teach him. As far as we know, this was the only professional instruction he ever received. He did not have any further music lessons. Then Wagner struck out on his own, writing a symphony and three operas – Die Hochzeit and Die Feen to his own bloodcurdling librettos and Das Liebesverbot based on Shakespeare's Measure for Measure.

At 22, Wagner was the conductor of a small opera house in Magdeburg. One reason for taking the job – the theatre was on the verge of bankruptcy – was his pursuit of a pretty young actress named Minna Planer. He was pursued by creditors claiming their gambling debts but in March 1836 the opera house produced Das Liebesverbot. It was such a fiasco that the theatre was empty at the second performance. It bankrupted the opera house. Wagner, overwhelmed with financial demands, left with Minna for a similar conducting post in Königsberg. They married in November 1836. The two of them then went on to Riga in Russian Poland to another opera post where they stayed unhappily for two years. Eventually, Wagner was dismissed, hounded by creditors, his passport confiscated and he was forced to flee Russia via a smugglers' route. At length, the couple arrived in Paris. From 1839 to 1842, he and Minna lived in abject poverty (on two occasions he was imprisoned for debt).

But then came his first taste of success. His opera Rienzi, which he had begun in 1837, was accepted for production at the Dresden Opera. The opera,

written in the approved Meyerbeer style, was a complete triumph and made Wagner's name known throughout Germany. Dresden next offered a production of Der fliegende Holländer, Wagner's first tentative steps towards a new style of opera. It resulted in complete failure but in February 1843 Wagner was made director of the Dresden Opera. In the following six years he raised the standard of performance there to unprecedented heights in a series of painstakingly produced performances, including, in October 1845, the premiere of his own Tannhäuser. By 1848 he had almost completed a third operatic masterpiece, Lohengrin.

That year was the year of revolution in Europe and its spirit had spread to Saxony by 1849. Wagner sided with the revolutionaries, producing radical pamphlets, making political speeches and sympathising with the rioters. When the revolution came to nothing he was forced to flee Germany and for the next 13 years lived in exile in Zürich. Here, he formulated his revolutionary ideas about opera and the 'music of the future': the concept of 'music drama' involving a synthesis of all the arts. The plan that began to occupy his mind was a giant project of four dramas in which all his theories would be realised, an opera cycle called Der Ring des Nibelungen. It took him a quarter of century to complete it.

Meanwhile, Franz Liszt had mounted the world premiere of Lohengrin (Weimar, 1850). Its fabulous success made Wagner the most famous living composer of German opera, though he was unable to attend any performances of his work there. At one time he lamented that he was just about the only German who had never seen a performance of Lohengrin. While working on The Ring, Wagner interrupted his labours with two other music dramas, Tristan und Isolde (1859) and Die Meistersinger von Nürnberg (1867). The friendship and generosity of a wealthy silk merchant, Otto Wesendonck, allowed him to live in a luxurious villa in Zürich while he was working on The Ring and Tristan. The friendship and generosity were repaid by Wagner having a passionate affair with Otto's wife, Mathilde. Much of Tristan was written under her influence; she may even have been the inspiration for the work, though it's just as likely that Wagner fell in love her because he was working on Tristan. Whatever, Tristan und Isolde is one of the most important works of the 19th century and its harmonic innovations exercised an enormous influence on the future of music, paving the way for Mahler and Schoenberg.

At length, the domestic situation in Zürich became impossible. Otto and Mathilde were fully aware of the situation and eventually Otto provided funds for Wagner and Minna to travel to Paris in 1859. Wagner's marriage had broken down irretrievably and soon a third married woman had entered his life. In 1862 Wagner fell in love with Cosima, the daughter of Franz Liszt and the wife of his friend and champion, the pianist and conductor Hans von Bülow. The mesmeric power Wagner exercised over his admirers is no better illustrated than by Bülow. First, Wagner and Cosima had an illegitimate daughter named Isolde; they then had a second illegitimate daughter, Eva. Only then, and after Minna had conveniently died in 1866, did Cosima desert her husband and set up house with Wagner. Throughout, Bülow remained devoted to Wagner and wrote to Cosima, 'You have preferred to devote your life and the treasures of your mind to one who is my superior. Far from blaming you I approve your action from every point of view and admit you are perfectly right'. Cosima was the woman for whom Wagner had been searching all his life, someone of great intelligence and independence of mind who would provide stability, adulation and understanding whenever it was needed. He remained with her for the rest of his life – well, nearly. After Wagner's death, the imperious Cosima, born in 1837, became the guardian of the Wagner shrine and survived until as late as 1930.

In the meantime, a political amnesty allowed Wagner to return to Germany in 1860. Four years later, his fortunes changed dramatically when the young King Ludwig II of Bavaria ascended the throne. He invited to Wagner to Munich and promised him unlimited support for all his projects. It's very likely he was in love with Wagner but, at any rate, a mutual admiration society flourished on a grand scale and, between 1865 and 1870, Munich was host to the world premieres of Tristan und Isolde, Die Meistersinger, Das Rheingold and Die Walküre (the last two being the first completed sections of The Ring). Ludwig's lavish support of Wagner soon brought him into conflict with the Bavarian Cabinet who advised that the whole economy would collapse if the King continued his patronage on such a reckless scale. They were also frightened by Wagner's political dabbling and his hold over the King, scandalised by his morals (everyone knew about his relationship with Cosima) and observed this arrogant musician with more than a little concern. Wagner retreated to a palatial estate on Lake Lucerne (paid for by Ludwig) where he was joined by Cosima. Here Eva was born (1867), and their first son Siegfried (1869). They eventually married in August 1870.

In 1871 Wagner announced plans for another Gargantuan scheme. Not a music-drama but a building, a special festival theatre where his works could be mounted under ideal conditions, produced to Wagner's own specifications. The council of the little Bavarian town of Bayreuth offered him a site and in May 1872 the cornerstone was laid. It was a huge undertaking and Wagner characteristically took to realising his dream with extraordinary vigour and determination. No setback troubled him – he persuaded wealthy patrons to provide part of the subsidy, he conducted concerts to help raise money, King Ludwig coughed up 100,000 talers and, eventually, the Bayreuth Festival Theatre was unveiled on August 13, 1876. The opening performance was the first complete presentation of the Ring cycle, Siegfried and Götterdämmerung (The Twilight of the Gods) receiving their world premieres. The event attracted world attention. Four thousand visitors were crammed into Bayreuth including the Emperor and Empress of Germany, the Emperor and Empress of Brazil, Grand Duke Vladimir of Russia along with other crowned heads and many of the greatest composers, including Tchaikovsky, Gounod, Saint-Saëns, Grieg and Liszt. Such novelties as gas lighting linked to electric projectors and a magic lantern

illuminating the Ride of the Valkyries matched the startling originality of the operas themselves. The festival made a huge deficit but at the closing party Wagner had the good grace to pay tribute to Liszt. He owed him, he said, everything. Today, the Bayreuth theatre remains a living shrine to Wagner's music and his vision.

Basking in his fame, relative wealth and security (though money worries continued to nag), living in the comfort of the Villa Wahnfried a few miles from the festival theatre in Bayreuth, Wagner settled down to other things. He had a final fling with a married woman. This time it was the beautiful daughter of the poet Théophile Gautier, Judith, wife of the poet Catulle Mendès. Judith Mendès, who was 40 years younger than Wagner, actually moved into the Villa Wahnfried (Cosima turned a blind eye) before returning to her husband in 1878. Wagner finished his last opera or 'consecrational play' Parsifal while producing a series of pamphlets and publications. In his all-embracing wisdom, he promulgated his lofty views on any number of topics. He believed the world could be save if everyone ate vegetables instead of meat; he ranted on about racial purity – the Jews were former cannibals, Christ was not a Jew but an Aryan, the Aryans had sprung from the gods, and so forth – all the things which led Hitler to say 'Whoever wants to understand National Socialist Germany must know Wagner.'

In August 1882 Wagner conducted a performance of Parsifal. It was his last public appearance as a conductor. He was exhausted and began to have premonitions of death. Later in the year he, Cosima and their children travelled to Venice for a lengthy holiday. As a birthday gift to his wife, Wagner conducted a private performance of his youthful symphony in December 1882. It was his last musical act. Six weeks later he died of a massive heart attack. His body was brought back to Bayreuth where it was buried in a vault in the garden of his villa to the strains of the funeral march from Götterdämmerung.

Incidentally, King Ludwig was faithful to the end to his 'divine friend', the man to whom he wrote, 'I can only adore you…an earthly being cannot requite a divine spirit'. His mental state deteriorated and he was committed to an asylum. On June 13, 1883, three months to the day after Wagner's death, Ludwig overpowered a psychiatrist who was escorting him on a walk and dragged him to the bottom of the Starnberg Lake, drowning himself in the process.

Orchestral Excerpts from Operas

Lohengrin – Prelude. Tannhäuser – Overture.　　**H**
Siegfried Idyll. Götterdämmerung – Siegfried's Rhine Journey; Siegfried's Funeral March
Lucerne Festival Orchestra; Vienna Philharmonic Orchestra / Wilhelm Furtwängler
Testament mono SBT1141 (61' · ADD)
Recorded late 1940s　　Ⓕ●

This is, as they say, something else. The *Lohengrin* Act 1 Prelude opens the disc of studio recordings, the only item of five with the Lucerne Festival Orchestra. The way the Swiss brass *crescendos* on the up-beat to the climactic delivery of the hymn must rate among the most elating of all Furtwängler moments. Why this and the *Tannhäuser* Overture have never been issued before remains a mystery, as probably do all the reasons why, in the latter piece, the Vienna Philharmonic sounds on fire for Furtwängler and on duty for, say, Knappertsbusch in 1953 (once available on a Decca LP). Siegfried's Rhine Journey evolves in one seamless sweep, barring the split-second but disconcerting rhythmic hiatus at the moment of take-off (4'51"). And mercifully, Furtwängler doesn't tag on the trite concert ending (as did Reiner and Toscanini), giving a chance to wonder at the uniquely resonant low brass sounds of the VPO. Then on to the Funeral March, every dark sound fully charting the depths, every phrase carrying special import, and, as in the *Siegfried Idyll*, the occasional passage reminding us of standards of tuning of the day. The latter account, Furtwängler's only recording of the piece, engages rather than diverts and charms, with Vienna string playing typically sweet and rapturous, and 'Siegfried, Hope of the World' tensely built to an almost delirious climax. Depth, presence and a naturally achieved clarity characterise all these recordings, and 78 sources only occasionally make their presence felt.

Der fliegende Holländer – Overture. Die Meistersinger von Nürnberg – Prelude, Act 1; Prelude, Act 3. Parsifal – Prelude; Good Friday Music. Tristan und Isolde – Prelude; Liebestod[a]
[a]Anja Kampe *sop* **Hallé Orchestra / Mark Elder**
Hallé CDHLL7517 (73' · DDD)　　　　Ⓜ**O▶**

Conductor, orchestra and recording team have gone to subtle lengths (including the use of two recording venues) to make a Wagner 'bleeding chunks' concert really work on disc. Like Rattle at the Royal Opera House before him, Elder has (re)calculated the crucial silences and the balancing of the brass and wind choirs in the *Parsifal* items to give them lift and presence outside the acoustic halo of the Bayreuth pit for which they were intended. The *Meistersinger* Act 3 Prelude makes use of 'period' string *portamentos* (the score's influence on Elgar's Second Symphony becoming even more apparent), while the same opera's Act 1 Prelude and the *Tristan* excerpts show clear touches of Elder's work with original instrument bands, eschewing Karajanesque symphonic gloss (and its 'big' 1970s sound) for the sake of increased mobility and presence of important inner part writing.

Anja Kampe is a clear, word-conscious, passionate Isolde, closely in tune with the 'house style' of these interpretations, while the final pages of this Liebestod (after the voice finishes) are attended to with a Boulez-like detail and fascination. Only the *Dutchman* Overture falls somewhat in between two stools – not quite the development of *Der Freischütz* that you might have expected after Elder's cunning reading of that score for ENO, nor the all-out nautical thriller provided in very different ways by Klemperer or Solti.

This is not a disc which blows you away at first hearing but one that repays careful and repeated listening. The recordings are in every way the handmaid of the performances.

'Wagner/Stokowski Symphonic Syntheses'
Parsifal – Symphonic Synthesis of Act 3.
Das Rheingold – Entrance of the Gods into Valhalla.
Die Walküre – Magic Fire Music; Ride of the Valkyries.
Tristan und Isolde – Symphonic Synthesis
Bournemouth Symphony Orchestra / José Serebrier
Naxos 8 570293 (74' · DDD)　　　　Ⓢ▶

It would be hard to imagine a more sumptuous disc. Stokowski, in these 'symphonic syntheses', enhances Wagner's already opulent orchestration with shrewdly added instrumental lines and with the vocal parts usually given to the strings. Then at times he thins the orchestration down for more transparent textures. José Serebrier conducts the Bournemouth SO in thrilling performances, passionate in a genuinely Stokowskian manner and treated to orchestral sound of demonstration quality.

Stokowski's aim was to provide more satisfying orchestral items in concerts than the popular 'bleeding chunks'. So in the most ambitious item, on *Tristan*, we have between the Prelude and Liebestod a rich orchestral version of the Love Duet. Where the end of the duet builds up to that chilling interruption from King Marke, Stokowski has it lead seamlessly into the equivalent passage in the Liebestod. It works superbly.

The selection starts excitingly with the Entry of the Gods into Valhalla and it is good to find Serebrier splendidly adding an anvil when Donner brings his hammer down. The *Parsifal* synthesis is limited to music from Act 3, thus ignoring the Good Friday Music. From *Die Walküre* comes the Magic Fire Music and, most excitingly, the Ride of the Valkyries. This is the finest of Naxos's Stokowski discs to date.

Additional recommendation

Der Ring des Nibelungen – orchestral highlights.
Coupled with Siegfried Idyll
Staatskapelle Dresden / Donald Runnicles
Warner Apex 2564 68043-4 (74 DDD)　　　Ⓑ**O**
　Recorded live, this is a splendid collection of orchestral highlights from *The Ring* (Ride of the Valkyries, Forest Murmurs, Siegfried's Rhine Journey and Funeral March among other things), with a suave reading of the *Siegfried Idyll* as coupling. Terrific sound too.

Wesendonck Lieder

Wesendonck Lieder. Tristan und Isolde – Prelude, Act 1; Mild und leise. Götterdämmerung – Dawn and Siegfried's Rhine Journey; Starke Scheite
Julia Varady *sop* **Deutsches Symphony Orchestra, Berlin / Dietrich Fischer-Dieskau**

Orfeo C467 981A (71' · DDD · T/t)   Ⓕ**OO**

This is a truly riveting recital of Wagner from Varady (magnificent singing) and Fischer-Dieskau. Varady's reading of the *Wesendonck Lieder* is remarkable, enthralling. There's nothing here of the slow, wallowing approach often favoured today. The feeling of the words is one of very present emotions. Try the final section of 'Stehe still!' starting 'Die Lippe verstummt' or the emphasis on the single word 'Smaragd' in 'Im Treibhaus' or the whole of a most beautifully etched 'Träume'. She's helped here by Fischer-Dieskau's refusal to indulge the music.

There have been few such warmly and intelligently sung versions of the Immolation. Maybe on stage Brünnhilde might have been beyond Varady; here there's not a sign of strain as she rides the orchestra, sympathetically supported by her husband. But what makes it stand out from performances by possibly better-endowed sopranos is her deep understanding of the text: again and again, nowhere more so than at 'Ruhe, ruhe, du Gott', where Varady's vibrating lower register is so effective, you feel the tingle factor coming to the fore. In the more heroic final sections, this Brünnhilde is like a woman transfigured. And transfiguration is a feature of Varady's concentrated, urgent Liebestod, her complete absorption with the text as much as with the music an object-lesson in great Wagner singing. The players of Fischer-Dieskau's Berlin orchestra cover themselves in glory. The recording is exemplary.

Der fliegende Holländer

Der fliegende Holländer
Theo Adam *bass-bar* Holländer **Anja Silja** *sop* Senta
Martti Talvela *bass* Daland **Ernst Kozub** *ten* Erik
Annelies Burmeister *mez* Mary **Gerhard Unger** *ten* Steuermann **BBC Chorus; New Philharmonia Orchestra / Otto Klemperer**
EMI Great Recordings of the Century ③ 567408-2
(152' · ADD · T/t). Recorded 1968   Ⓜ**O**➡

Klemperer's magisterial interpretation of this work was unavailable in any form for far too long so that its reissue was most welcome. As ever, Klemperer by and large justifies some moderate tempi by the way in which he sustains line and emphasises detail. Only once or twice – in the Spinning and Sailors' choruses – do you sense a lack of propulsion. Otherwise throughout there's a blazing intensity to the reading that brooks no denial. The storm and sea music in the Overture and thereafter is given stunning power, and the Dutchman's torture and passion is evoked in the orchestra. Indeed, the playing of the New Philharmonia is a bonus throughout. Klemperer catches as convincingly as anyone the elemental feeling of the work – the sense of the sea, basic passions and the interplay of character unerringly adumbrated.

There have been few baritones before or since Theo Adam who have sustained the line of the Dutchman so well and so intelligently

reached the heart of the matter where the text is concerned. Silja's bright, sometimes piercing timbre isn't to everyone's taste, but hers is a most moving portrayal of trust and loyalty and love unto death, the interpretation of an outstanding singing-actress. Martti Talvela, singing magnificently and suggesting a formidable presence, is a bluff, burly Daland. Ernst Kozub's Erik has its clumsy moments, but one admires the shining tone. Gerhard Unger offers an ardent, cleanly articulated Sailor. Annelies Burmeister is a ripe Mary. The overall sound is a shade on the dry side but doesn't detract from the enjoyment.

Der fliegende Holländer
Theo Adam *bass-bar* Holländer **Anja Silja** *sop* Senta
Martti Talvela *bass* Daland **James King** *ten* Erik
Kenneth Macdonald *ten* Steuermann **Annelies Burmeister** *mez* Mary **BBC Chorus; New Philharmonia Orchestra / Otto Klemperer**
Testament ② SBT2 1423 (151' · ADD)
Recorded live at the Royal Festival Hall, London, on March 19, 1968   Ⓕ**O**

Thanks to Testament, we now have the Royal Festival Hall performance, as broadcast by the BBC, to put alongside the Abbey Road recording (above – made by EMI at the same period) which might be justifiably deemed one of two or three great readings of the score on CD.

The two main characters are taken by the same singers, Theo Adam and Anja Silja. Martti Talvela and Annelies Burmeister can also be heard on both sets. The main difference is in the tenor department. James King, rather than Ernst Kozub, would probably have sung Erik in the studio if Decca had been willing to release him, and although this is a notoriously unrewarding part – especially when it has to be acted as well as sung – King's distinctive tonal combination of purity and weight was certainly a bonus in the Festival Hall, just as Kenneth Macdonald makes a fine Steersman. The most remarkable aspect of the performance nevertheless remains the empathy between Klemperer, Silja and Adam. Adam's Act 1 monologue seizes the dramatic high ground, but Silja raises the stakes still further with an electrifying account of Senta's Ballad, and the long duet which ends Act 2 has rarely been as intense and eloquent as it is here.

Live performance always brings risks: there is a split brass note early in Act 1, and Talvela loses his way briefly a little later on. But Klemperer's love of the music's raw edges and robust rhythms is evident throughout. Even at the stately tempo he adopts the Act 3 sailor's dance is so strongly projected that the tension never sags for a moment, and Klemperer's eccentric devotion to the three-act version of the score is far less damaging than it would be in a performance of lower voltage.

The recorded sound also comes up pretty well in this remastering. This extraordinarily 'live' reading of Wagner's windswept score now has the edge, even over the admirable studio alternative.

Additional recommendations

Hotter Holländer **Varnay** Senta **Glaz** Mary   **H**
Haysward Steuerman **Svanholm** Erik **Nilsson** Daland
**Metropolitan Opera Chorus and Orchestra, New
York / Reiner**
Naxos Historical mono ② 8 110189/90 (128' · ADD)
Recorded live 1950   **⑤●**

This performance marked the Met house debut
of Hans Hotter, and what a debut! Varnay and
Hotter seem to inspire each other to astonishing
feats of musical and dramatic truth. Among historic
recordings, this deserves a place up there with the
Clemens Krauss.

Der fliegende Holländer   **H**
Uhde Holländer *sop* **Lustig** Erik **Traxel**
Steuerman **Weber** Daland
Bayreuth Festival Chor & Orch / Keilberth
Testament ② SBT2 1384 (141' · ADD · S/T/t/N)
Recorded live 1955   **Ⓕ**

Keilberth achieves great unanimity of approach
from his players and absolutely superb singing
from the chorus (trained by the remarkable Wilhelm Pitz). The orchestra, perhaps because they
knew they were being recorded, play their hearts
out to create a fusion of notes and rhythm that is
really thrilling from start to finish. The singers are
no less inspired. Varnay, who was also Brünnhilde in
1955, brings to Senta a tireless dedication and vision
to match Uhde's hero. Ludwig Weber's earthy,
experienced Daland is another rewarding interpretation. All seem under the spell of the work
and the conductor in a reading that now has the
stereo sound it so richly deserves.

Lohengrin

Lohengrin
Jess Thomas *ten* Lohengrin **Elisabeth Grümmer** *sop*
Elsa **Christa Ludwig** *mez* Ortrud **Dietrich Fischer-
Dieskau** *bar* Telramund **Gottlob Frick** *bass* King
Henry **Otto Wiener** *bass* Herald **Vienna State
Opera Chorus; Vienna Philharmonic Orchestra /
Rudolf Kempe**
EMI Great Recordings of the Century ③ 567415-2
(3h 37' · ADD · T/t). Recorded 1963-64   **Ⓜ●●➒➔**

EMI's sound may have less presence and a narrower perspective than other versions, but neither the 'studio' ambience – the recording was
made in the Theater an der Wien – nor the
occasionally excessive prominence of the voices
prevents Kempe's reading from projecting a
strongly theatrical quality. However, it's the all-
round excellence of the cast, plus the bonus of an
uncut Act 3, which makes this the leading mid-
price recommendation.

Jess Thomas combines ardour and anguish as
well as any, and with Fischer-Dieskau a formidable (but never over-emphatic) antagonist, and
Gottlob Frick a majestic King Henry, the drama
of the opera's central conflict remains supremely
immediate and powerful. As Elsa and Ortrud,
Elisabeth Grümmer and Christa Ludwig are
ideal opposites, the former radiant yet quite

without the simpering overtones that afflict
some Elsas, the latter as potent in seductive
insinuation as in demonic ferocity. Not even
Ludwig can surpass the visceral intensity of
Astrid Varnay in the 1953 Bayreuth set under
Keilberth, and Keilberth's Telramund and Elsa
(Hermann Uhde and Eleanor Steber) are also
outstanding: yet Wolfgang Windgassen's
Lohengrin isn't as distinguished, nor as distinctive, as Jess Thomas's here. Even more importantly, Keilberth's reading lacks the visionary
quality that Kempe finds in the score. Ultimately, it's the power of that vision which raises
this performance above its rivals.

Lohengrin
Johan Botha *ten* Lohengrin **Adrianne Pieczonka**
sop Elsa **Kwangchul Youn** *bass* King Henry **Falk
Struckmann** *bar* Telramund **Petra Lang** *mez* Ortrud
Eike Wilm Schulte *bar* King's Herald
**North German Radio Chorus; Prague Chamber
Choir; West German Radio Chorus and Symphony
Orchestra, Cologne / Semyon Bychkov**
Profil ③ PH09004 (3h 34' · DDD · T/t)   **Ⓕ**

As a studio recording, this new Profil release can
claim a degree of rarity value. Also rare is its
inclusion of a segment of Lohengrin's 'In fernem Land' monologue which Wagner cut at the
time of the premiere, though this has previously
appeared in two of the best earlier recordings
(from Leinsdorf and Barenboim – see below).

The studio atmosphere means that there are
no obvious theatrical effects: no thumps and
bumps during fights, for example. But Semyon
Bychkov's impassioned conducting ensures that
there's no serious loss of theatricality; and even
in ordinary stereo the big ensembles sound
immensely imposing (the end of Act 2 overwhelming), which compensates to a degree for a
wide dynamic range that makes it difficult to set
a single suitable volume level throughout.

It can be argued that Wagner never settled on
a definitive version of Act 3. He was surely right
to cut the anticlimactic episode after Lohengrin
reveals his and his father's names, but despite its
inclusion here, Profil has failed to include the
text in a libretto whose usefulness is already
compromised by not having German, French
and English in parallel, as well as by a fusty English translation.

Fortunately, there are many positive factors
too. Bychkov's reading is admirable, with only
occasional exaggerations (including slowing up
towards the end of the Act 1 Prayer). Although
none of the cast surpasses the work's best exponents elsewhere, all are well worth hearing.
Johan Botha is ardent and mellifluous, lacking
only that finely spun, silvery thread of tone that
distinguished Jess Thomas in the role; nor does
Petra Lang – for all her sensitivity to the text –
quite set the stage ablaze as Astrid Varnay did.
Adrianne Pieczonka is occasionally shrill in
more strenuous passages, but there's an attractive tonal brightness that brings extra weight to
her Elsa. Underpinning it all are the excellent

Cologne forces, with Bychkov in the Act 1 Prelude conveying the 'awesome sweetness' that has to be brought to life if the drama is to work its magic. Not the best *Lohengrin* ever then, but it's good to have such a well characterised and sumptuously recorded new version.

Lohengrin
Klaus Florian Vogt ten Lohengrin **Solveig Kringelborn** sop Elsa **Waltraud Meier** mez Ortrud **Tom Fox** bar Telramund **Hans-Peter König** bass King Henry **Roman Trekel** bar Herald **Lyon National Opera Chorus; Mainz EuropaChor Akademie; Deutsches Symphonie-Orchester Berlin / Kent Nagano**
Stage director **Nikolaus Lehnhoff**
Video director **Thomas Grimm**
Opus Arte ③ 📀 OA0964D (4h 39' · NTSC · 16:9 · PCM stereo and DTS 5.1 · 0)
Recorded live 2006. Extra features include 'Never Shall Thou Ask of Me' – a documentary film by Reiner E Moritz, Illustrated Synopsis and Cast Gallery   Ⓕ

Nikolaus Lehnhoff's new *Lohengrin* is a calculated distillation of both the work's dramatic contents and its production history. The hand of his old master Wieland Wagner lies beneficially over the outer acts' terraced ranks of Brabantine courtiers and Saxon soldiers, as it does on the chessboard movements of the principals around a central disc. (The sets here are by the noted German architect Stephan Braunfels, whose recreation of a giant Svoboda staircase for the Act 2 processions is memorable.) The (swanless) appearance and departure of Lohengrin into a thin, central beam of light recall the imagery of Bayreuth's recent Keith Warner/Stefanos Lazaridis staging, while the promotion of Elsa to a constantly onstage narrator/dreamer continues an idea of Götz Friedrich's in an earlier Bayreuth production.

Yet, although Bettina Walter's costumes are modern-ish – somewhere between Juan Carlos's ceremonial Spain and a Hollywood *Prisoner of Zenda* – Lehnhoff's direction, as always, remains narrative-based and essentially traditional. Only once, in the bridal chamber scene of Act 3, does this director allow himself a conceit, showing Lohengrin, Wagner-like, at a reversed keyboard piano, composing and playing the wedding march. It's a strange and acute image, revealing at a stroke the hero's narcissistic and chauvinistic self-absorption.

Lehnhoff's accumulation of images is trenchantly delivered onstage by his two leading ladies, both wide-ranging, attention-holding actresses: Kringelborn in her vocal prime, strong, pure, never forcing; Meier in her vocal Indian summer, strong, impure, sometimes forcing, but always wholly in the service of this sexy, brainy Ortrud. Vogt, in his silver-blue zoot suit, is a charismatic enigma (hence ideal for this role), an apparently super-light voice but one with both stamina and sustaining power. The lower male voices also make their mark: Fox creates sympathy for this Macbeth without a brain;

Trekel's Herald has power and attitude; König is a subtly eponymous, weak liberal Henry. The chorus(es) sound undernourished, acting better than they keep together (in the tricky vocal helter-skelter of Lohengrin's arrival) with the pit. It sounds like early days for Kent Nagano at maintaining pace and flow through the weighty four-in-a-bar recitative-like passages.

Thomas Grimm gets his cameras in close, leaving the singers to track reactions to solo utterances but missing some crucial interplay. Within a natural sound spectrum, some tweaking has been done to pull out solo lines in ensemble, but the emotions of Lehnhoff's vision ring true and will give pleasure.

Additional recommendation

Lohengrin
Seiffert Lohengrin **Magee** Elsa **Polaski** Ortrud **Struckmann** Telramund **Pape** King Henry **Trekel** Herald **Staatskapelle Berlin / Barenboim**
Teldec ③ 3984 21484-2 (3h 31' · DDD · T/t)   Ⓕ
Barenboim manages to give an overriding unity to a work that can, in lesser hands, sprawl. As Lohengrin Seiffert's phrasing and sheer lyrical ardour make him a near-ideal white knight. His Elsa is Emily Magee, her tone full and refulgent, her interpretation deeply felt. Polaski makes a splendidly forceful and articulate Ortrud, only very occasionally sounding taxed by heavier passages. Pape is a model King Henry, pouring out his concerns in golden tone. Trekel is a strong Herald. The set is enhanced by a perfectly balanced and warm recording.

Die Meistersinger von Nürnberg

Die Meistersinger von Nürnberg
Thomas Stewart bar Hans Sachs **Sándor Kónya** ten Walther **Gundula Janowitz** sop Eva **Franz Crass** bass Pogner **Thomas Hemsley** bar Beckmesser **Gerhard Unger** ten David **Brigitte Fassbaender** mez Magdalene **Kieth Engen** bass Kothner **Horst Wilhelm** ten Vogelgesang **Richard Kogel** bass Nachtigall **Manfred Schmidt** ten Zorn **Friedrich Lenz** ten Eisslinger **Peter Baillie** ten Moser **Anton Diakov** bass Ortel **Karl Christian Kohn** bass Schwartz **Dieter Slembeck** bass Foltz **Raimund Grumbach** bass Nightwatchman **Bavarian Radio Chorus and Symphony Orchestra / Rafael Kubelík**
Calig ④ CAL50971/4 (4h 32' · ADD). Recorded 1967   Ⓕ ❌❌

There could be no more fitting memorial to Kubelík than the appearance of this, probably the most all-round satisfying *Meistersinger* in the era of stereo. It was recorded in 1967 by Bavarian Radio to mark the work's centenary the following year. Kubelík conducts an unforced, loving interpretation, showing a gratifying grasp of overall structure. As a whole the reading has an unobtrusive cohesion achieved within flexible tempi and dynamics. Everything proceeds at an even, well-judged pace with just the right surge of emotion at the climaxes. All this is conveyed unerringly to his own Bavarian Radio Symphony forces.

Stewart's Sachs is certainly his most successful performance on disc. He offers a finely moulded, deeply considered reading that relies on firm, evenly produced, mostly warm tone to create a darkish, philosophical poet-cobbler. Kónya is simply the most winning Walther on any set, superseding Sawallisch's excellent Heppner by virtue of a greater ardour in his delivery. Kónya pours out consistently warm, clear tone, his tenor hovering ideally between the lyric and the heroic. Nor are there many better Evas than the young Janowitz, certainly none with a lovelier voice. Franz Crass, a less pompous Pogner than some, sings his part effortlessly, with noble feeling. Hemsley, though singing his first Beckmesser, evinces a close affinity with the Town Clerk's mean-mindedness, and his German is faultless. Unger is a paragon among Davids, so eager in his responses and finding just the right timbre for the role. His Magdalene, again perfect casting, is the young Fassbaender. With a characterful Kothner in Engen, the requirements for a near-ideal *Meistersinger* ensemble are in place. As the recording doesn't betray its age this would undoubtedly be the first choice among stereo versions.

Die Meistersinger von Nürnberg
John Tomlinson bass Hans Sachs **Thomas Allen** bar Beckmesser **Gösta Winbergh** ten Walther **Nancy Gustafson** sop Eva **Catherine Wyn-Rogers** mez Magdalene **Herbert Lippert** ten David **Gwynne Howell** bass Pogner
Chorus and Orchestra of the Royal Opera House, Covent Garden / Bernard Haitink
Royal Opera House Heritage Series ④ ROHS008
(4h 25' · DDD). Recorded live on July 7, 1997   Ⓜ

The Mastersingers of Nuremberg
Norman Bailey bass-bar Hans Sachs **Derek Hammond-Stroud** bar Beckmesser **Alberto Remedios** ten Walther **Margaret Curphey** sop Eva **Ann Robson** mez Magdalene **Gregory Dempsey** ten David **Noel Mangin** bass Pogner
Chorus and Orchestra of Sadler's Wells Opera / Reginald Goodall
Chandos ④ CHAN3148 (293' · ADD)
Recorded live on February 10, 1968   ⓂOOOO▷

Both these new/old performances, stemming from live broadcasts at key moments in the two major London opera companies' histories, reflect the sense of community ensemble and Shakespearean mix of sacred and profane comedy which has become our particular national gift to Wagner's comedy.

The more recent performance is something of a coronation for Bernard Haitink's embattled but admired music directorship of the old Covent Garden. The performance, his happiest Wagner outing to date on disc, shows him to be a listening accompanist and precise balancer of orchestral textures. The discs too provide a souvenir of a memorable British double-act: John Tomlinson's Sachs (fully engaged as philosophical poet or virile, passionate shoemaker) and Thomas Allen's carefully drawn assumption of Beckmesser – pomposity and pathos founded on a vocal delivery which satisfies both demands for comedy and the stature appropriate to a senior member of the Mastersingers' Guild.

They are ably supported. Gösta Winbergh is a thinking man's knight who, like his bright and beautiful Evchen, Nancy Gustafson, is a great user of text as well as tone. Lippert is a fluent David, Gwynne Howell and Catherine Wyn-Rogers field a Pogner and Magdalene of uncommonly rich shadings – while the Masters' list is a veritable who's who of subtle, musical character actors. The recording has come up with a good sense of theatrical ping – apart from an oddly forward balance for the would-be eloping lovers in their Act 2 asides.

How happy one would be with this set in a competition-less world but other recorded maestros delve more profoundly into the text and theatricality of this score than Haitink chooses to do. One such is Reginald Goodall, whose 1968 Sadler's Wells performance(s) – legendary at least in British memory – has finally reached an official release on Chandos in Sir Peter Moores's Opera in English series. Here is one legend which hits the light of day as brightly as it shone 40 years ago. Goodall's understanding of what every beat of this score means, and his successful communication of that to his personally trained cast, is a thing of wonder. Climaxes (end of Act 1, the riot, the quintet etc) are immense; timers may tell us it's slow, but the pulse never flags.

Goodall's Walther, Alberto Remedios, once said that when he played Caruso's records at home he forgot to go out. The same compliment might be paid to this singer when he starts 'Am stillen Herd', or tells Sachs his morning dream in three parts, or delivers the prize song with a dream mixture of Italianate tone and line and German lyrical weight. OK, it's in English, and a rather quaint English – but it has to be heard. So does Norman Bailey's Sachs. He is a noble humanist, free (even in the gulling of Beckmesser) of petty concerns and stirred as opposed merely to being moody in yielding Evchen to Walther. His seamless delivery of the 'Flieder' monologue, natural authority in the 'Ein Kind war geboren' sequence and striking of the right blend of admonishment and advice in 'Verachtet mir die Meister nicht' all represent work on a Friedrich Schorr/Hans Hotter level. And, together with Goodall, Margaret Curphey makes Eva's predicaments and love always real rather than simply coy.

The plentiful laughter that can be heard is due to both the sharp theatrical pointing of Goodall's conducting and to the Eric Morecambe-like ability of Derek Hammond-Stroud's Beckmesser to be genuinely funny just by appearing. Hammond-Stroud's is a masterly comic performance at the other end of the pole to Allen's – but equally valid.

One can understand non-Anglophone readers smiling whimsically but this Chandos release genuinely becomes one of the miracles of the current Wagner discography.

Die Meistersinger von Nürnberg
Wolfgang Brendel bass-bar Hans Sachs **Gösta Winbergh** ten Walther **Eva Johansson** sop Eva
Victor von Halem bass Pogner **Elke Wilm Schulte** bar Beckmesser **Uwe Peper** ten David **Ute Walther** mez Magdalene **Lenus Carlson** bass Kothner **David Griffith** ten Vogelgesang **Barry McDaniel** bar Nachtigall **Volker Horn** ten Zorn **Peter Maus** ten Eisslinger **Otto Heuer** ten Moser **Ivan Sardi** bass Schwarz **Friedrich Molsberger** bass Foltz **Peter Edelmann** bass Nightwatchman **Berlin Opera Orchestra and Chorus / Rafael Frühbeck de Burgos**
Stage director **Götz Friedrich**
Video director **Brian Large**
Arthaus Musik **DVD** 100 152 (4h 26' · Region 0) Ⓕ**OO**

This has to be one of the most engrossing and satisfactory performances of *Die Meistersinger* in memory. Pleasure derives as much as anything from the sense of a complete integration of music and action in a staging that has been scrupulously rehearsed on all sides. This is a 1995 revival with the same cast as the 1993 original, and it's clear how keen the response of the singers to each other is.

The credit for one's profound enjoyment undoubtably goes to Götz Friedrich. Renowned for his handling of characters and their interaction on stage, his skills in that sphere have seldom if ever been more fruitfully displayed. The action and reaction of the masters in their Act 1 disputations, the subtle relationship between Sachs and Eva, the ebb and flow of the arguments between Sachs and Beckmesser, and the friendly interplay between Walther and Sachs, the disciple eagerly learning from the teacher in Act 1 scene 3, are all revelatory. In these and other scenes, more of the characters' humanity is expressed than has ever been shown before. This is operatic acting on the highest level of achievement.

Frühbeck de Burgos enhances the director's approach with his chamber-like treatment of the orchestra, allowing the singers' clear enunciation to be heard at all times. He's also to be commended for the discerning ebb and flow of his reading as a whole, which is at once lively and unforced. Wolfgang Brendel presents an affectionate, sympathetic, somewhat laid-back, ruminative Sachs, his voice lacking in warmth only at the bottom of his register, the sound more baritone than bass-orientated. As we know from Covent Garden, Winbergh is a well-nigh ideal Walther, singing his role with unwonted ease and lyrical breadth, responsive always to the text's meaning.

Johansson is a knowing, flirtatious Eva, forthcoming in voice and mien; her earthbound start of the Quintet comes as a disappointment after her gloriously outgoing 'O Sachs, mein Freund'. Schulte sings and acts Beckmesser to perfection, never resorting to caricature in

depicting the self-important, didactic town clerk and giving the role a wealth of nuance, always keeping to the notes. Peper is a well-routined, likeable David, von Halem an imposing, properly fatherly Pogner.

As a whole, this is a performance to treasure. It has admirably balanced sound and perceptive video direction by the ultra-experienced Brian Large. Recommended, though it probably bows to the Levine set (below).

Die Meistersinger von Nürnberg
James Morris bass Hans Sachs **Ben Heppner** ten Walther **Karita Mattila** sop Eva **René Pape** bass Pogner **Sir Thomas Allen** bass Beckmesser **Matthew Polenzani** ten David **Jill Grove** mez Magdalene **John Del Carlo** bass Kothner
Metropolitan Opera Chorus and Orchestra, New York / James Levine
Stage director **Otto Schenk**
Video director **Brian Large**
DG ② **DVD** 073 0949-2GH2 (4h 52' · NTSC · 16:9 · PCM stereo, 5.1 & DTS 5.1 · 0)
Recorded live at the Metropolitan Opera, New York, December 2001. Extras include picture gallery   Ⓕ**OO**

This most humane and intimate of all Wagner's operas is a natural for DVD, but we haven't yet had a wholly satisfactory version. However, this Met version, superbly recorded in widescreen, boasting a mouthwatering cast, largely fulfils the considerable expectations it raises.

Conducting and staging are solidly uncontroversial. Levine's rich, weighty Wagner style seems to suit *Meistersinger* better than *The Ring*. There are still some unexpected gear changes, but better integrated into a fluent, warm reading. Otto Schenk's production is almost aggressively traditional – lively enough, but one longs for some subtler spark of originality or insight, in the sets especially. A properly bustling Act 3 'Festweise' is welcome, instead of dull grandstands, but the Act 2 brawl is sadly shirked.

The singers are the best on DVD. With his clear, unbaritonal lyric Heldentenor, Ben Heppner is a convincingly poetic Walther; but the bulky face and frame lose credibility in Brian Large's vivid camera direction. Even the beautiful Karita Mattila's girlish antics look less appropriate, but she remains a stunning Eva, dramatic in power but with reserves of crystalline lyricism.

René Pape's Pogner looks no older than his 'daughter', a minor blemish on a finely resonant performance, but a blow to dramatic involvement. Sir Thomas Allen's minutely characterised, acidulous Beckmesser is properly malevolent yet unexpectedly mellifluous, hilarious without vocal distortions.

James Morris's Sachs is warm-hearted, quintessentially American and none the worse for that. His voice is more sinewy now and less steady, losing some of its rich tone and silken *legato*, but gaining in character. He's still not ideally expressive, though, making less of the cobbler-poet's visionary and temperamental side, and more telling as Eva and Walther's genial mentor than in the monologues. His fellow Mastersingers are well portrayed, though John Del Carlo could make more of Kothner, but the chorus and apprentices can't quite match Bayreuth's.

This amiable, large-scale performance is highly recommendable.

Additional recommendation

Die Meistersinger von Nürnberg   🅗
Schöffler Hans Sachs **Beirer** Walther **Seefried** Eva **Frick** mez Kundry **Pogner** Kunz Beckmesser **Dickie** David **Vienna State Opera Chorus and Orchestra / Fritz Reiner**
Orfeo d'Or mono ④ C667 054L (4h 18' · ADD)
Recorded live 1955   🅕

Paul Schöffler is the undoubted true hero of the evening, surely here giving the performance of a lifetime. This is a recording one would want to have for that alone, though indeed there are other as yet unmentioned attractions such as Murray Dickie's lively, clean-cut David and the sonorous Watchman of Frederick Guthrie. And the flexibility and warmth of Reiner's conducting does have an appeal of its own. Above all, the recording renews joyful contact with this adorable opera.

Parsifal

Parsifal   🅗
Jess Thomas ten Parsifal **George London** bass-bar Amfortas **Hans Hotter** bass-bar Gurnemanz **Irene Dalis** mez Kundry **Gustav Neidlinger** bass-bar Klingsor **Martti Talvela** bass Titurel **Niels Møller** ten First Knight **Gerd Nienstedt** bass Second Knight **Sona Cervená** mez First Squire, Sixth Flower Maiden **Ursula Boese** mez Second Squire **Gerhard Stolze** ten Third Squire **Georg Paskuda** ten Fourth Squire **Rita Bartos, Gundula Janowitz, Anja Silja, Elsa-Margrete Gardelli, Dorothea Siebert** sops Flower Maidens **Bayreuth Festival Chorus and Orchestra / Hans Knappertsbusch**
Philips ④ 475 7785POR4 (4h 10' · ADD · T/t)
Recorded live 1962   Ⓜ🅞🅞🅞↦

This is one of the greatest sets of all time. Every time one returns to it, its inspiration and distinction seem to have been enhanced. There have been many fine recordings of this great Eastertide opera, but none has so magnificently managed to capture the power, the spiritual grandeur, the human frailty and the almost unbearable beauty of the work as Hans Knappertsbusch. This live recording has a cast that has few equals. Hotter is superb, fleshing out Gurnemanz with a depth of insight that has never been surpassed. London's Amfortas captures the frightening sense of impotence and anguish with painful directness, while Thomas's Parsifal grows as the performance progresses and is no mean achievement. Dalis may lack that final degree of

sensuousness but she provides a fine interpretation nevertheless. Throughout the work, Knappertsbusch exercises a quite unequalled control over the proceedings; it's a fine testament to a great conductor. The Bayreuth acoustic is well reproduced, and this record is a profound and moving experience.

Parsifal
Norman Bailey bar Amfortas **Michael Langdon** bass Titurel **Louis Hendrikx** bass Gurnemanz **Jon Vickers** ten Parsifal **Donald McIntyre** bass Klingsor **Amy Shuard** sop Kundry **Edgar Evans** ten First Grail Knight **Dennis Wicks** bass Second Grail Knight **Nan Christie** sop **Delia Wallis** mez **David Lennox, John Dobson** tens Four Esquires **Kiri Te Kanawa, Maureen Keetch, Alison Hargan, Anne Pashley** sops **Anne Howells, Marjorie Biggar** mezs Flower Maidens
Chorus and Orchestra of the Royal Opera House, Covent Garden / Reginald Goodall
Royal Opera House Heritage Series ④ ROHS012
(4h 44' · ADD). Recorded live 1971   Ⓜ🅞🅞

Although Reginald Goodall was thoroughly familiar with Wagner's last opera from sitting in the pit for Hans Knappertsbusch's 1950s Bayreuth performances and from his own coaching work at Covent Garden, he actually made his debut conducting the work with the 1971 run from which this release derives. The planned cast was strong but illness led to four Gurnemanzes and two Klingsors being called upon to keep the curtain up.

By many accounts the opening night (with Gottlob Frick coming out of retirement as Gurnemanz) was a great evening – is there not some test recording of that around? The present performance, with the Belgian Louis Hendrikx returning as a careful, direct Gurnemanz, has passionate, well defined interpretations from Jon Vickers in the title-role, Donald MacIntyre as a rapaciously evil Klingsor (with superb German), Norman Bailey's sorrowful Amfortas and soaring contributions from solo flowers Kiri Te Kanawa and Anne Howells. Amy Shuard also makes her mark in a role especially suited to her dramatic, hard-edged soprano. Goodall's guidance of the music is replete with beautiful aperçus of balance and rhythm, not to mention much fine wind-playing. But, on this particular evening, the reading too often hangs fire. As interesting reviews of other Goodall performances have pointed out, the conductor's habits of following (rather than leading) singers he especially trusts, and his taking over of a German, especially Knappertsbusch-like, tradition of marking the end of paragraphs with lengthy, unwritten *Luftpausen* – in a score that already calls for many significant pauses – often elongate his reading to a point where Act 1, in the iconoclastic words of note-writer John Deathridge, 'verges on incoherence'.

In addition, Goodall's textures and instrumental colours here continually stress the work's pain and sadness. But it's not the whole story –

there's exciting psychological drama in this score too, of a *Tristan*-like heat and intensity.

Medici and ROH Heritage Series have done fine work in remastering these BBC tapes for release. Admirers of the conductor and collectors of the art of Jon Vickers will find a great deal of consummate music-making and singing here – but, without sounding mealy-mouthed, the story of Sir Reginald Goodall's *Parsifal* should not yet be over.

Parsifal
Peter Hofmann *ten* Parsifal **José van Dam** *bass-bar* Amfortas **Kurt Moll** *bass* Gurnemanz **Dunja Vejzovic** *mez* Kundry **Siegmund Nimsgern** *bass* Klingsor **Victor von Halem** *bass* Titurel **Claes Hakon Ahnsjö** *ten* First Knight **Kurt Rydl** *bass* Second Knight **Marjon Lambriks, Anne Gjevang** *mezs* **Heiner Hopfner** *ten* **Georg Tichy** *bass* Squires **Barbara Hendricks, Janet Perry, Inga Nielsen** *sops* **Audrey Michael** *mez* **Doris Soffel, Rohângiz Yachmi Caucig** *contrs* Flower Maidens **Hanna Schwarz** *mez* Voice from Above **Berlin Deutsche Opera Chorus; Berlin Philharmonic Orchestra / Herbert von Karajan**
DG ④ 413 347-2GH4 (256' · ADD · T/t)
Recorded 1979-80 ⓕ❍❍❍❽

Karajan's *Parsifal* seems to grow in stature as an interpretation on each rehearing; on its CD transfer it appears to have acquired a new depth, in terms of sound, because of the greater range of the recording and the greater presence of both singers and orchestra. As in practically all cases, CD offers a more immediate experience. Karajan's reading, a trifle stodgy in Act 1, grows in intensity and feeling with the work itself, reaching an almost terrifying force in the Prelude to Act 3 which is sustained to the end of the opera. Moll's Gurnemanz is a deeply expressive, softly moulded performance of notable beauty. Vejzovic, carefully nurtured by Karajan, gives the performance of her life as Kundry. Hofmann's tone isn't at all times as steady as a Parsifal's should be, but he depicts the character's anguish and eventual serenity in his sincere, inward interpretation. Van Dam is a trifle too placid as Amfortas, but his singing exhibits admirable power and fine steadiness. Nimsgern is the epitome of malice as Klingsor. The choral singing doesn't have quite the confidence of the superb orchestral playing, which has both qualities of Keats's imagining of beauty and truth in abundance.

Additional recommendations

Parsifal
Stewart Amfortas **Hagenau** Titurel **Hotter** Gurnemanz **Vickers** Parsifal **Neidlinger** Klingsor **Ericson** Kundry **Bayreuth Festival Chorus and Orchestra / Knappertsbusch**
Orfeo d'Or mono ④ C690 074L (4h 10' · ADD · S/N)
Recorded live 1964 ⓜ❍❍❍
The (to date) 11 released recordings of Hans Knappertsbusch's *Parsifal* performances at Bay-

reuth between 1951 and 1964 constitute a unique record of one conductor's work on a favoured score in a single theatre. This was not only Kna's last ever *Parsifal*, it was to be his last ever public performance. The performance is also vital for its preservation of Jon Vickers's Parsifal. In his second appearance on the Green Hill the Canadian tenor mixes great strength and great beauty of voice to an almost platonic ideal in the tricky Act 2 dialogue with Kundry.

Parsifal Ⓗ
Waechter Amfortas **Robinson** Titurel **Frick** Gurnemanz **Karl Liebl** *ten* Parsifal **Otakar Kraus** *bass* Klingsor **Gerda Lammers** *sop* Kundry **Covent Garden Opera Chorus and Orchestra / Rudolf Kempe**
Testament mono ④ SBT4 1455 (4h 4' · ADD)
Recorded live 1959 ⓕ
Rudolf Kempe's feeling for the long line never settles into mere rigidity and is matched by the outstanding blend of sensitivity and strength in the singing of Gottlob Frick. It is good to have such an impressive cast. Eberhard Wächter hits his most compelling form here. Karl Leibl lacks the youthful edge that Parsifal needs, but he avoids the stodginess and blandness that often afflict singers in the part. Gerda Lammers is an admirably un-gutteral Kundry, and to have Covent Garden stalwarts Otakar Kraus and Forbes Robinson in the cast reinforces the special qualities of this performance. If you can discount the sonic deficiencies and are prepared to allow a little time for the Kempe touch to make its very particular effect, you will be richly rewarded.

Rienzi

Rienzi
René Kollo *ten* Cola Rienzi **Siv Wennberg** *sop* Irene **Janis Martin** *sop* Adriano **Theo Adam** *bass* Paolo Orsini **Nikolaus Hillebrand** *bass* Steffano Colonna **Siegfried Vogel** *bass* Raimondo **Peter Schreier** *ten* Baroncelli **Günther Leib** *bass* Cecco del Vecchio **Ingeborg Springer** *sop* Messenger of Peace **Leipzig Radio Chorus; Dresden State Opera Chorus; Staatskapelle Dresden / Heinrich Hollreiser**
EMI ③ 567131-2 (3h 45' · ADD· T/t)
Recorded 1974-76 ⓜ❽

Rienzi is grand opera with a vengeance. Political imperatives count for more than mere human feelings, and politics means ceremony as well as warfare: marches, ballet music and extended choruses are much in evidence in this work, while even the solo arias often have the rhetorical punch of political harangues. It could all be an enormous bore. Yet the young Wagner, basing his work on Bulwer Lytton's story of the tragic Roman tribune, did manage to move beyond mere tub-thumping into a degree of intensity that – for those with ears to hear – prefigures the mature genius to come. In the end, Rienzi himself is more than just a political animal, and the existential anguish of Tannhäuser, Tristan and even Amfortas can be found glimmering in the distance. This performance isn't ideal in every respect, either musically, or as a recording. But its virtues outweigh its weaknesses by a considerable margin. Siv Wennberg was not in best voice at the time, but the other principals, notably René Kollo and Janis Martin, bring commendable stamina and conviction to their demanding roles. Above all Heinrich Hollreiser prevents the more routine material from sounding merely mechanical, and ensures that *Rienzi* has a truly Wagnerian sweep and fervour.

The Ring – Das Rheingold / Die Walküre

Das Rheingold
John Tomlinson bass Wotan **Linda Finnie** mez Fricka
Graham Clark ten Loge **Helmut Pampuch** ten Mime
Günter von Kannen bar Alberich **Eva Johansson**
sop Freia **Kurt Schreibmayer** ten Froh **Bodo**
Brinkmann bar Donner **Birgitta Svendén** mez Erda
Matthias Hölle bass Fasolt **Philip Kang** bass Fafner
Hilde Leidland sop Woglinde **Annette Küttenbaum**
mez Wellgunde **Jane Turner** mez Flosshilde
Bayreuth Festival Orchestra / Daniel Barenboim
Teldec ③ 4509 91185-2 (149' · DDD · T/t)
Recorded live 1991   Ⓕ**OO**

Die Walküre
Poul Elming ten Siegmund **Nadine Secunde** sop
Sieglinde **Anne Evans** sop Brünnhilde **John**
Tomlinson bass Wotan **Linda Finnie** mez Fricka,
Siegrune **Matthias Hölle** bass Hunding **Eva**
Johansson sop Gerhilde **Eva-Maria Bundschuh** sop
Helmwige **Ruth Floeren** sop Ortlinde **Shirley Close**
mez Waltraute **Hebe Dijkstra** mez Rossweisse
Birgitta Svendén mez Grimgerde **Hitomi Katagiri**
mez Schwertleite **Bayreuth Festival Orchestra /**
Daniel Barenboim
Teldec ④ 4509 91186-2 (3h 53' · DDD)
Recorded live 1992   Ⓕ**OO**

These are enthralling performances. Tomlinson's volatile Wotan is the most potent reading here. He manages to sing every word with insistent meaning and forceful declamation while maintaining a firm *legato*. His German is so idiomatic that he might have been speaking the language his whole life and he brings breadth and distinction of phrase to his solos at the close of both operas. Anne Evans has a single, important advantage over other recent Brünnhildes in that her voice is wholly free from wobble and she never makes an ugly sound. Hers is a light, girlish, honest portrayal, sung with unfailing musicality if not with the ultimate insights. Linda Finnie is an articulate, sharp-edged Fricka, and Graham Clark a sparky, incisive Loge. Nadine Secunde's impassioned Sieglinde is matched by the vital, exciting Siegmund of Poul Elming, and Matthias Hölle as both Hunding and Fasolt is another of those black basses of which Germany seems to have an inexhaustible supply. The whole is magnificently conducted by Barenboim, a more expansive Wagnerian than Böhm. By 1991 he had the full measure of its many facets, bringing immense authority and power to building its huge climaxes, yet finding all the

lightness of touch for the mercurial and/or diaphanous aspects of the score. He has the inestimable advantage of a Bayreuth orchestra at the peak of its form, surpassing – and this says much – even the Metropolitan orchestra for Levine. Similar qualities inform his interpretation of *Die Walküre*. Barenboim has now learnt how to match the epic stature of Wagner's mature works, how to pace them with an overview of the whole, and there's an incandescent, metaphysical feeling of a Furtwänglerian kind in is treatment of such passages as Wotan's anger and the Valkyrie ride. The orchestra is superb. It's backed by a recording of startling presence and depth, amply capturing the Bayreuth acoustic.

Das Rheingold   Ⓗ
Hans Hotter bass-bar Wotan **Georgine von**
Milinkovič mez Fricka **Rudolf Lustig** ten Loge **Paul**
Kuen ten Mime **Gustav Neidlinger** bass-bar Alberich
Hertha Wilfert sop Freia **Josef Traxel** ten Froh **Toni**
Blankenheim bar Donner **Maria von Ilosvay** mez Erda
Ludwig Weber bass Fasolt **Josef Greindl** bass Fafner
Jutta Vulpius sop Woglinde **Elisabeth Schärtel** mez
Wellgunde **Maria Graf** mez Flosshilde **Bayreuth**
Festival Orchestra / Joseph Keilberth
Testament ② SBT2 1390 (142' · ADD)
Recorded live 1955   Ⓕ

Here we are at the start of the revelatory Bayreuth *Ring* of 1955, and from the very first primordial sounds Joseph Keilberth establishes that this is to be a very special cycle. The opening scene is dominated by Gustav Neidlinger's nonpareil of an Alberich, who in the third scene becomes a frightening incarnation of malevolent power. But the Rhinemaidens aren't as steady as one might wish.

Scene 2 brings a kaleidoscope of authoritative interpretations, headed by Hans Hotter's commanding Wotan, a thoughtful portrait of an overweening, troubled figure sung with a Lieder-like attention to verbal detail. Georgine von Milinkovič is a suitably imposing Fricka and a convincing nag. Ludwig Weber's expressive, articulate Fasolt is partnered by Josef Greindl's louring Fafner. Rudolf Lustig's strongly sung Loge – no *comprimario* tenor he – is not the most fluent piece of singing, but he gives the text real meaning. Among the minor gods Josef Traxel stands out for his beautifully lyric Froh, luxury casting from one of the leading tenors then active in Germany. Maria von Ilosvay as Erda and Paul Kuen as Mime are just as characterful as in in *Siegfried*. Over all you have once again a sense of a truly experienced ensemble, each member of which plays to the other.

Once again, one is astounded by the ideal capturing of the Bayreuth acoustics and by the superlative playing of the orchestra, stimulated by Keilberth's astutely dramatic conducting.

Die Walküre
Poul Elming ten Siegmund **Nadine Secunde** sop
Sieglinde **Anne Evans** sop Brünnhilde **John**

Tomlinson *bass* Wotan **Linda Finnie** *mez* Fricka
Matthias Hölle *bass* Hunding **Eva Johansson** *sop*
Gerhilde **Eva-Maria Bundschuh** *sop* Helmwige **Ruth**
Floeren *sop* Ortlinde **Shirley Close** *mez* Waltraute
Hebe Dijkstra *mez* Rossweisse **Linda Finnie** *mez*
Siegrune **Birgitta Svendén** *mez* Grimgerde **Hitomi**
Katagiri *contr* Schwertleite **Bayreuth Festival**
Orchestra / Daniel Barenboim
Stage director **Harry Kupfer**
Video director **Horant H Hohlfeld**
Warner Classics ② 🅓🅥🅓 2564 62319-2
(3h 57' · NTSC · 16:9 · PCM stereo, 5.1 and
DTS 5.1 · 2/3/4/5)   Ⓕ

Wagner's most violent and personally anguished
drama plays here on designer Hans Schaver-
noch's 'road of history' – a stage so bare that it
makes Wieland Wagner's abstractions of the
1950s look scenically crowded. From his singing
actors director Harry Kupfer has secured performances of unremitting physical and emotional energy. Like Wagner's beloved philosopher Feuerbach, he believes that the gods were
created by humans in their own image. So in this
part of the tetralogy which is, surely, Wagner's
King Lear, John Tomlinson runs, dives, falls
and embraces, living out every part of the tragedy of his Walsung family (all of them red-
haired). It's an extraordinary *tour de force*, thrillingly sung off the text and the action.

This godfather's big dialogues with his wife
(Linda Finnie is his fur-collared, leather-great-
coated double, but all in black) and Erda-
daughter (Anne Evans, costumed likewise but
without fur) are not presented at all as the usual
stand-and-deliver displays of implacable will.
Fricka struggles to psych herself up to be
tough, clutching her still-loved husband in
stress at the sacrifice she is requiring. And in
Act 3, once Brünnhilde explains to her father
that it was the power of Siegmund's love for his
sister/bride that made her disobey his battle
orders, the two plot her punishment with
warm, almost incestuous smiles of complicity.
(Don't be alarmed; it's all in Wagner's text and
music.) Kupfer also has a strong line on Wagner's tricky-to-stage Act 1, showing the instant
attraction between Elming's freedom-fighter
Siegmund and Secunde's subtle psychological
portrait of Sieglinde, and emphatically marking the coming of spring by the disappearance
of the whole of Hunding's house bar the tree
with the sword.

This *Walküre* has made a belated bow on DVD
but its transfer is a visual and sonic success.
Video director Hohlfeld has mixed close-up and
distance well; only the Act 2 fight is confusing at
first view. There are no extras, only a moderately interesting interview with the director as
intellectual matter in the booklet and some
sloppy proofing of the German text in the subtitles.

Die Walküre   Ⓗ
Astrid Varnay *sop* Brünnhilde **Gré Brouwenstijn** *sop*
Sieglinde **Hans Hotter** *bass-bar* Wotan **Ramón**

Vinay *ten* Siegmund **Josef Greindl** *bass* Hunding
Georgine von Milinkovič *mez* Fricka, Grimgerde
Hertha Wilfert *sop* Gerhilde **Hilde Scheppan** *sop*
Helmwige **Elisabeth Schärtel** *mez* Waltraute **Maria**
von Ilosvay *mez* Schwertleite **Gerda Lammers** *sop*
Ortlinde **Jean Watson** *contr* Siegrune **Maria Graf**
mez Rossweisse **Bayreuth Festival Orchestra /**
Joseph Keilberth
Testament ④ SBT4 1391 (3h 38' · ADD · T/t)
Recorded live 1955   Ⓕ

Very properly, Hans Hotter, as Wotan, dominates this utterly absorbing and exciting account
of *Walküre*, the second instalment of the rediscovered Keilberth *Ring* at Bayreuth in 1955.
There exist several other incarnations of his
dominant reading but perhaps only that in the
Krauss cycle of 1953 reveals him in such superb
form. Whether arguing the moral toss with von
Milinkovič's harrying Fricka, sunk in deep desolation after his capitulation to his spouse (Wotan's
long narration so full of insights, not for a
moment dull), his fury at Brünnhilde's disobedi-
ence and his final relenting in an unforgettable
account of the Farewell, Hotter commands every
aspect of the role. His sonorous, wide-ranging
voice is matched by his verbal acuity, text and
tone in ideal accord. This, much more than his
portrayal in the Solti cycle, when his voice often
struggles with the part, is the performance to
judge him by.

As ever, his longstanding stage partnership with
the Brünnhilde of Astrid Varnay pays many dividends. She, too, is in prime form; she, too, melds
words and voice into a well-nigh perfect unity.
Not even a god could fail to response positively to
her appeals to be forgiven, and that follows a
warmly sung and deeply considered account of
the the Todesverkündigung in Act 2. That wonderfully moving scene also finds Ramón Vinay's
Siegmund in most eloquent form. As throughout
the first two acts, his singing benefits from his
attractively plangent tone and, in Act 1, his tale of
his sad plight. That, of course, turns to ecstasy in
the glorious love music that ends Act 1, where
Gré Brouwenstijn's womanly, vibrant Sieglinde is
a fit match. She is properly distraught and guilt-
ridden in Act 2 but – as so many lyrical sopranos
have found – the taxing passages in Act 3 prove a
shade beyond her.

In Act 1, Keilberth's direction takes a while
to catch fire. From the exciting start of Act 2
he is in his most persuasive form, he and his
fine orchestra projecting the manifold events
and changes of mood with a persuasively dramatic drive. The Ride of the Valkyries whizzes
along, Wotan's fury is frightening, the Magic
Fire music elating. Once more, he proves that
this was the year his *Ring* came into its own.

The recording is again amazingly lifelike,
catching the excitement of a notable occasion
on the Green Hill. The stage noises are
hardly ever distracting, nor should one be too
bothered by two or three moments when a
singer forgets his or her words. Altogether we
are here in the highest realm of Wagnerian
interpretation.

The Ring – Siegfried / Götterdämmerung

Siegfried
Heinz Kruse ten Siegfried **John Bröcheler** bass-bar
Wanderer **Jeannine Altmeyer** sop Brünnhilde
Graham Clark ten Mime **Henk Smit** bar Alberich
Anne Gjevang contr Erda **Carsten Stabell** bass
Fafner **Stefan Pangratz** treb Woodbird **Rotterdam
Philharmonic Orchestra / Hartmut Haenchen**
Stage director **Pierre Audi**
Video director **Misjel Vermeiren**
Opus Arte Ⓕ ③ 📀 OA0948D (4h 33' ·
NTSC · 16:9 · PCM stereo and DTS 5.1 · 0)
Recorded live at Het Muziektheater, Amsterdam, in
1999. Extra features include Illustrated Synopsis,
Cast Gallery and Introduction to Siegfried presented
by Michaël Zeeman

Götterdämmerung
Jeannine Altmeyer sop Brünnhilde **Heinz Kruse** ten
Siegfried **Kurt Rydl** bass Hagen **Wolfgang Schöne**
bass-bar Gunther **Eva-Maria Bundschuh** sop
Gutrune **Henk Smit** bass Alberich **Anne Gjevang**
mez Waltraute **Netherlands Philharmonic Orchestra
/ Hartmut Haenchen**
Stage director **Pierre Audi**
Video director **Hans Hulscher**
Opus Arte ③ 📀 OA0949D (4h 29' · NTSC · 16:9 ·
PCM stereo and DTS 5.1 · 0)
Recorded live at Het Muziektheater, Amsterdam,
in 1999. Extra features include Illustrated Synopsis,
Cast Gallery and Introduction to Götterdämmerung
presented by Michaël Zeeman   Ⓕ

The Pierre Audi Amsterdam *Ring* wholly justifies
Opus Arte's decision to follow up so soon its
uneven Harry Kupfer/Barcelona cycle. Audi and
designer George Tsypin work with a varying
series of thrillingly lit (Wolfgang Goebbel) acting
areas, Hartmut Haenchen's orchestra(s) constantly visible in a manner reminiscent of Baroque
theatre. There may be reservations about
Haenchen's straight, low-profile interpretation
of the music (given in the new critical edition,
here featuring colourful percussion and sound
effects, and some new brass pitches at the opening
of Act 3 of *Götterdämmerung*), or the harshness of
Eiko Ishioka's far from conventionally beautiful
Japanese theatrical costumes. But there can surely
be few about the freshness of Audi's theatrical
thinking, and his reinvention of 'deconstructionist' effects – Fafner as his own mouth; a fierily lit
and smoked platform to walk into; or the Wanderer's spear presented for Siegfried to break as a
huge, ceiling-high, world ash tree-like totem.
The visible Woodbird (at last, as Wagner wished,
taken by a boy) with his white, waif-like cockade
of hair is also a moving presence, especially at the
violent death of Mime.

Audi has cast and used his singing actors well.
Altmeyer goes from strength to strength, proving how right she was that Brünnhilde was her
role. Clark delivers another variation on his
widely travelled Mime, now older, more worried, perhaps more frightening. Gjevang, a
matchless Erda, then unveils a Waltraute that

for textual understanding, projection and sheer
intensity you'd have to have on a desert island.
Her Act 1 colleagues in *Götterdämmerung* –
Rydl's neurotic, exhibitionist Hagen and the
identical-looking Sebastian/Viola incestuous
Gibichungs of Bundschuh and Schöne – provide
compulsive acting too. And when Siegfried
comes to the rock with the tarnhelm? You'll
have to see (and hear!) for yourself.

A black mark, though, to Opus Arte for
forgetting (totally) the chorus in *Götterdämmerung* – viewers intrigued by their Cuprinol-
advertisement wooden-puppet look may want to
know who they are. The Netherlands Philharmonic lack, in the final pages of *Götterdämmerung*, the necessary lustrous string tone; in
Siegfried, their Rotterdam colleagues are idiomatically magnificent. If you're buying individually, the Audi *Götterdämmerung* is mandatory.

Götterdämmerung
Katarina Dalayman sop Brünnhilde **Lars Cleveman**
ten Siegfried **Attila Jun** bass Hagen **Andrew Shore**
bar Alberich **Peter Coleman-Wright** bass-bar
Gunther **Nancy Gustafson** sop Gutrune **Susan
Bickley** mez Waltraute **Miranda Keys** sop Yvonne
Howard mez **Ceri Williams** contr Norns **Katherine
Broderick** sop **Madeleine Shaw, Leah-Marian Jones**
mezs Rhinemaidens **Hallé Choir; BBC Symphony
Chorus; London Symphony Chorus; Royal Opera
Chorus and Extra Chorus; Hallé Orchestra /
Sir Mark Elder**
Hallé ⑤ CDHLD7525; MP3 disc CDHLM7530
(4h 44' · DDD). Recorded live 2009 Ⓢ/ⒻⓄⓄⒼ➔

Ⓖ Recorded live, this performance serves
as both culmination of, and progress
report on, Sir Mark Elder's first decade
with the Hallé. It gives the players, *in extenso*, the
chance to display their current skills and to show
how the Hallé has come to reacquire, under
Elder, its verve in Romantic 19th- and early-
20th-century scores.

Although Elder was an early student of both
Georg Solti and Edward Downes, relatively
quick Wagnerians, his own Wagner has more
parallels in texturing and overall *Klang* to the
1970s ENO *Ring* performances under Reginald
Goodall. There is evidence of how Elder has
absorbed Goodall-like detail and patience and
passed it on to his players: the wind playing
throughout, the needlepoint-accurate placing
and enunciation of the timpani part, or the
tricky string *concertato* under Gutrune's final,
vain attempt to denounce Brünnhilde in Act 3.

But Elder uses time to put distinct space or
style into a particular scene more than to make
grand, weighty effects. His Act 1 Gibich court,
characterfully inhabited by experienced vocal
actors Peter Coleman-Wright and Nancy Gustafson, is rather French in its instrumental
cadenzas and trills – a reference Wagner surely
intended. And much of Act 3's longer-than-
usual playing time is used, in the hunters' feast
scene that precedes Siegfried's murder, for careful observation of Wagner's pauses and tempo

changes to achieve a tension not normally attained until the Funeral March proper.

The situation of a concert performance – including here the splitting of the opera over two nights – allows for greater freshness of voice and accuracy in passages like Siegfried's exit aria in Act 2 ('Munter, ihr Mannen!') or the intervals Brünnhilde has to negotiate in her Act 2 accusations. Attila Jun not only sounds like one of the blackest Hagens since the Greindl/Frick heyday but can place his bleating sheep imitations and other cadential moments spot on the note. Rhinemaidens and Norns are rich individually and together. Susan Bickley makes Waltraute's tale a tragedy of loss more than a disguised plea for the ring, and Andrew Shore returns his Alberich from Bayreuth with interest.

The whole is topped by a serious and quite dark pair from Sweden. Lars Cleveman is a thinking, tragic Siegfried, well matching his conductor's conception of the work. His Brünnhilde, Katarina Dalayman, brings a good mixture of soprano and mezzo colours to the role, by turns steely and strong, or touchingly vulnerable. Her Immolation is unusually visionary and clear-sighted.

The recording quality plays to, or has used, the hall and the performance well, accommodating the large full chorus. There is a goodly space around the orchestra, the singers and important solos never sounding artificially engineered. Off- or near-stage perspectives are convincingly realised. This release on the Hallé's own label intriguingly offers the opera on either a single MP3 disc or a five-CD set, making the new performance competitive and immediately tempting as a second-option choice. In any event it's the most compelling and best-cast *Götterdämmerung* on disc since Barenboim's from Bayreuth.

Götterdämmerung   ⊞

Astrid Varnay *sop* Brünnhilde **Bernd Aldenhoff** *ten* Siegfried **Ludwig Weber** *bass* Hagen **Heinrich Pflanzl** *bass* Alberich **Hermann Uhde** *bar* Gunther **Martha Mödl** *sop* Gutrune, Third Norn **Elisabeth Höngen** *mez* Waltraute **Elisabeth Schwarzkopf** *sop* Woglinde **Hanna Ludwig** *sop* Wellgunde **Hertha Töpper** *mez* Flosshilde **Ruth Siewert** *mez* First Norn **Ira Malaniuk** *mez* Second Norn **Chorus and Orchestra of the Bayreuth Festival / Hans Knappertsbusch**

Testament mono ④ SBT4175 (4h 41' · ADD · T/t)
Recorded live 1951   Ⓕ**OOO**

Ⓖ   Testament awakened this sleeping Brünnhilde after half a century in Decca's vaults, held there because of an age-old dispute over rights between that company and EMI. This is a fitting memorial, alongside the exactly contemporaneous *Parsifal* (Teldec), to the phoenix-like reincarnation of Bayreuth post-war and to Wieland Wagner's genius as a producer and gatherer of all the talents to the Green Hill. The other hero of the occasion, as with *Parsifal*, is Knappertsbusch.

From the first bars of the Prologue he takes us right into the work, as concerned as three notable Norns (Mödl the most arresting of the three when prophesying the conflagration to come) with the inevitability of the tragic events portrayed within. He then takes us from Stygian gloom to mountain-top ecstasy with a masterly touch few equal. There we meet Varnay's youthful, vibrant, womanly heroine. Beside her is Aldenhoff's not-so-lovely Siegfried, yet once you become accustomed to his aggrandising, extrovert moments you hear a Heldentenor in the old mould, alive to every word and communicating with his audience. Later, arriving at Gibichung Hall, you meet the most forthright, articulate Gunther in Uhde. His greeting to Siegfried, 'Begrüsse froh, O Held', makes one realise why Uhde is pre-eminent in this role. Beside him is Weber's louring, gloating, ambitious Hagen. What intelligence there is in every bar he sings (try 'Ein Weib weiss ich' or the whole of the Watch). As Gutrune, Mödl isn't your usual sweet-toned milksop but a women not afraid to show her deep emotions. The great mezzo Höngen as Waltraute conveys with amazing immediacy Wotan's despair, and, with a shudder in her tone at 'Da brach sich sein Blick', the tenderness of his thoughts on his beloved Brünnhilde, making one feel it to be the most moving moment in the whole *Ring* and consoling us for occasionally grainy tone.

Throughout Act 2, Knappertsbusch is trenchant in characterising the tremendous conflicts depicted therein. Weber rouses the vassals with vigorous enthusiasm. Varnay is tremendous in her denunciations of Siegfried, Aldenhoff as vivid in his replies. Such immediacy can only be found in the opera house – damn the momentary lapses in ensemble, the few distractions when scenery is being moved or the audience coughs. In Act 3 the Rhinemaidens, led by Schwarzkopf, are too backwardly placed, the sole blot on the sound picture. In Siegfried's Narration, Aldenhoff captures the vitality of his earlier exploits, supported by gloriously rippling strings, and sings a fulsome death-song. Knappertsbusch, eagerly supported by Bayreuth's hand-picked orchestra (all individually named in the accompanying booklet), unleashes all the tremendous import of the Funeral March. Finally Varnay carries all before her, in better voice than later at Bayreuth, in a visionary account of the Immolation that rightly crowns a noble interpretation of her role and the whole work. The recording is superior even to that of the 1951 *Parsifal*, with only a few passages of uncertain balance to fault it, supporting an experience nobody ought to miss.

The Ring – complete

Das Rheingold   ⊞

George London *bass-bar* Wotan **Kirsten Flagstad** *sop* Fricka **Set Svanholm** *ten* Loge **Paul Kuen** *ten* Mime **Gustav Neidlinger** *bass-bar* Alberich **Claire Watson** *sop* Freia **Waldemar Kmentt** *ten* Froh

WAGNER'S RiNG CYCLE – IN BRIEF

Vienna PO / Sir Georg Solti H
Decca ⑭ 455 555-2DMO14 (14h 36' · ADD)
Ⓜ️OO

The first complete cycle is still the most clearly recommendable. Even if Solti's blazingly dynamic conducting isn't everyone's ideal, he unites the most consistently superb casting with John Culshaw's still magnificent recording. A classic of the recording era.

Staatskapelle Dresden / Marek Janowski
RCA ⑨ 82876 55709-2 (13h 59' · DDD) ⒷOO
Janowski makes this first digital version fresh, fast and straightforward, with several fine voices such as Jessye Norman and Peter Schreier, but also, unfortunately, Adam's now desiccated Wotan, and a rather studio-bound recording.

ENO / Sir Reginald Goodall
Chandos ⑭ CHAN3038/45/54/60 (16h 31' · DDD)
ⒷOO

Goodall's famously massive reading may shock some with its slowness, but it's beautifully detailed, with the immediacy of English, and offers some truly world-class performances. Recorded live, mostly in winter, hence some obtrusive coughing.

Berlin PO / Herbert von Karajan
DG ⑭ 457 780-2GOR14 (14h 58' · ADD) ⒷO
An underrated version, largely because Karajan's emphasis on orchestral and vocal beauty sometimes sounds mannered, and encompasses inconsistent and occasionally inadequate casting – particularly *Siegfried*. Nevertheless this is a well recorded and often magical set.

Bayreuth Festival Orch / Joseph Keilberth H
Testament SBT2 1390, SBT4 1391, SBT4 1392,
SBT4 1392 ⒻOOO
An astounding cycle, recorded in stereo live at Bayreuth in 1955, this has leapt to the top of the pile of historic *Ring*s. Keilberth shows what a superb Wagnerian he was and his cast is faultless.

Bayreuth Festival Orch / Christian Thielemann
Opus Arte ⑭ OACD9000BD (14h 57' · DDD)
ⒻO➔

Difficult to assess – and certainly outsung by many of the classic sets – this is a superb tribute to Thielemann's stewardship of the Wagner tradition at Bayreuth – this, from 2008.

Bayreuth Festival Orch / Daniel Barenboim
Warner Classics 2564 62091-2 ⒷOO
Vocally probaby the finest of modern *Ring* casts (with Tomlinson, Evans and Jerusalem on top form), Barenboim shows his long experience in every bar and draws some truly glorious playing from his fine orchestra.

Eberhard Waechter *bar* Donner **Jean Madeira** *contr*
Erda **Walter Kreppel** *bass* Fasolt **Kurt Böhme** *bass*
Fafner **Oda Balsborg** *sop* Woglinde **Hetty**
Plümacher *mez* Wellgunde **Ira Malaniuk** *mez*
Flosshilde

Die Walküre H
James King *ten* Siegmund **Régine Crespin** *sop*
Sieglinde **Birgit Nilsson** *sop* Brünnhilde **Hans Hotter**
bass-bar Wotan **Christa Ludwig** *mez* Fricka **Gottlob**
Frick *bass* Hunding **Vera Schlosser** *sop* Gerhilde
Berit Lindholm *sop* Helmwige **Helga Dernesch** *sop*
Ortlinde **Brigitte Fassbaender** *mez* Waltraute
Claudia Hellmann *sop* Rossweisse **Vera Little** *contr*
Siegrune **Marilyn Tyler** *sop* Grimgerde **Helen Watts**
contr Schwertleite

Siegfried H
Wolfgang Windgassen *ten* Siegfried **Hans Hotter**
bass-bar Wanderer **Birgit Nilsson** *sop* Brünnhilde
Gerhard Stolze *ten* Mime **Gustav Neidlinger** *bass-bar* Alberich **Marga Höffgen** *contr* Erda **Kurt Böhme**
bass Fafner **Joan Sutherland** *sop* Woodbird

Götterdämmerung H
Birgit Nilsson *sop* Brünnhilde **Wolfgang**
Windgassen *ten* Siegfried **Gottlob Frick** *bass* Hagen
Gustav Neidlinger *bass-bar* Alberich **Dietrich**
Fischer-Dieskau *bar* Gunther **Claire Watson** *sop*
Gutrune **Christa Ludwig** *mez* Waltraute **Gwyneth**
Jones *sop* Wellgunde **Lucia Popp** *sop* Woglinde
Maureen Guy *mez* Flosshilde **Helen Watts** *contr*
First Norn **Grace Hoffman** *mez* Second Norn **Anita**
Välkki *sop* Third Norn
Vienna State Opera Chorus; Vienna Philharmonic
Orchestra / Georg Solti
Decca ⑭ 455 555-2DMO14 (14h 36' · ADD · T/t)
Recorded 1958-65. Also available separately
Ⓜ️OO➔

As perspectives on the Solti/Culshaw enterprise lengthen, and critical reactions are kept alert by the regular appearance of new, or newly issued, and very different recordings, it may seem increasingly ironic that of all conductors the ultra-theatrical Solti should have been denied a live performance. There are indeed episodes in this recording that convey more of the mechanics of the studio than of the electricity of the opera house – the opening of *Die Walküre*, Act 2, and the closing scenes of *Siegfried* and *Götterdämmerung*, for example. Yet, in general, dramatic impetus and atmosphere are strongly established and well sustained, sometimes more powerfully than is usually managed in the theatre. As just one example one would instance the superb control with which the intensity of Donner's summoning up of the thunder in *Das Rheingold* is maintained across Froh's greeting to the rainbow bridge into Wotan's own great salutation. At the majestic climax of this scene the power of feeling conveyed by George London's fine performance counts for more than any 'artificiality' in the way the voice is balanced against the orchestra.

Equally memorable in a totally different context is Solti's management of the long transition in *Götterdämmerung* between Hagen's Watch and the appearance of Waltraute. Nothing could be less mannered or unnatural than Solti's grasp of perspective and feeling for the life of each phrase in this music. On CD the clarity of instrumental detail is consistently remarkable, and while not all the singers sound as if they're constantly in danger of being overwhelmed there are some vital episodes, especially those involving Windgassen and Nilsson. Awareness of what these artists achieved in other recordings strengthens the suspicion that they may have been giving more than we actually get here. Windgassen isn't allowed to dominate the sound picture in the way his part demands, and Nilsson can seem all-too relaxed within the comforting cocoon of the orchestral texture.

Factors like these, coupled with those distinctive Soltian confrontations between the hard-driven and the hammily protracted, have prevented the cycle from decisively seeing off its rivals over the years. It's questionable nevertheless whether any studio recording of *The Ring* could reasonably be expected to be more atmospheric, exciting or better performed than this one. The VPO isn't merely prominent, but excellent, and such interpretations as Svanholm's Loge, Neidlinger's Alberich and Frick's Hagen remain very impressive.

Above all, there's Hotter, whose incomparably authoritative, unfailingly alert and responsive Wotan stands up well when compared to his earlier Bayreuth accounts. Nowhere is he more commanding than in *Siegfried*, Act 1, where one even welcomes Stolze's mannerisms as Mime for the sparks they strike off the great bass-baritone. Earlier in this act the interplay of equally balanced instruments and voices in relatively intimate conversational phrases displays the Culshaw concept at its most convincing. He would have been astonished to hear what his successors have achieved in renewing his production through digital remastering. One now realises how much of the original sound was lost on the old pressings. In comparison with the 1980 Janowski/RCA version, the approaches are so different they almost seem like different experiences. Culshaw was intent on creating a theatre on record with all the well-known stage effects; the rival version eschews all such manifestations. In general, Janowski presents a much more intimate view of the work than Solti's.

However many other *Ring*s you may have, though, you'll need this one.

Der Ring des Nibelungen
Das Rheingold
Albert Dohmen *bass-bar* Wotan **Ralf Lukas** *bar* Donner **Clemens Bieber** *ten* Froh **Arnold Bezuyen** *ten* Loge **Kwangchul Youn** *bass* Fasolt **Hans-Peter König** *bar* Fafner **Andrew Shore** *bar* Alberich **Gerhard Siegel** *ten* Mime **Michelle Breedt** *mez* Fricka **Edith Haller** *sop* Freia **Christa Mayer** *contr* Erda **Fionnuala McCarthy** *sop* Woglinde **Ulrike Helzel** *sop* Wellgunde **Simone Schröder** *contr* Flosshilde

Die Walküre
Endrik Wottrich *ten* Siegmund **Kwangchul Youn** *bass* Hunding **Albert Dohmen** *bass-bar* Wotan **Eva-Maria Westbroek** *sop* Sieglinde **Linda Watson** *sop* Brünnhilde **Martina Dike** *mez* Fricka **Sonja Mühleck** *sop* Gerhilde **Anna Gabler** *sop* Ortlinde **Martina Dike** *mez* Waltraute **Simone Schröder** *contr* Schwertleite **Edith Haller** *sop* Helmwige **Wilke te Brummelstroete** *mez* Siegrune **Annette Küttenbaum** *mez* Grimgerde **Manuela Bress** *mez* Rossweisse

Siegfried
Stephen Gould *ten* Siegfried **Gerhard Siegel** *ten* Mime **Albert Dohmen** *bass-bar* Wanderer **Andrew Shore** *bar* Alberich **Hans-Peter König** *bar* Fafner **Christa Mayer** *contr* Erda **Linda Watson** *sop* Brünnhilde **Robin Johannsen** *sop* Woodbird

Götterdämmerung
Stephen Gould *ten* Siegfried **Ralf Lukas** *bar* Gunther **Hans-Peter König** *bass* Hagen **Andrew Shore** *bar* Alberich **Linda Watson** *sop* Brünnhilde **Edith Haller** *sop* Gutrune **Christa Mayer** *mez* Waltraute **Simone Schröder** *contr* First Norn **Martina Dike** *mez* Second Norn **Edith Haller** *sop* Third Norn **Fionnuala McCarthy** *sop* Woglinde **Ulrike Helzel** *sop* Wellgunde **Simone Schröder** *contr* Flosshilde
Chorus and Orchestra of the Bayreuth Festival / Christian Thielemann
Opus Arte Ⓕ ⑭ OACD9000BD (14h 57' · DDD)
Recorded live during the Bayreuth Festival in July and August, 2008

Ⓜ Ⓞ ➻

This new cycle, Opus Arte's first CD release, was assembled from performances of the latest Bayreuth stage production and becomes the fifth complete *Ring* commercially recorded live from Wagner's own theatre. This history has certainly impacted on the released audio result in which the casting, at least as heard here, is not always a match for Christian Thielemann's sovereign musical direction and preparation. The German word 'musizieren' – with its implications of both 'music-making' and 'working live' – might be a good verb for this conductor's work in finding and realising such a kaleidoscope of colours in *Rheingold*, or for his Karajan-like ability to bend and shape large structures, or for the style of his accompanying – try the Dawn duet in *Götterdämmerung* – which has a Lieder-pianist's response to his singers' texts and line. Thielemann also evidently knows how to make Bayreuth's eccentric pit work for him, and shows – as does the recording – a fine ear for balancing this score as played with the instruments of today. The small print, so to speak, of Wagner's scoring under the Rhinemaidens' climactic cries of 'Heia, Heia, Hahei' just before the gold is revealed, or the Nibelungs' carting gold around, is never lost to our ears through a wall of modern brass and percussion.

Over the years Thielemann's *Ring*, like all his Wagner, has been a continuous work in progress. He now revels in the lightness and impressionism of, say, Karajan or even Clemens

Krauss, mixed with a rather infectious sense of humour that, as in the score, is present even in the supposed heroics of the Valkyries' gathering or the forging of Nothung. This is a 'fast' *Ring*, but Thielemann's through-line for each scene convinces irrespective of the stopwatch.

The casting is uneven. It obviously represents an attempt to look for something new and fresh. The results seem hampered by some undercasting, a slightly eccentric selection in terms of blending with other voices and the inevitable fact that not all voices reproduce well. Albert Dohmen's Wotan is noble and intelligent but, even with this sensitive accompaniment, acoustic and recording, just one scale too small. The perimeters of the role's (essentially higher bass) tessitura do not lie well for him. Stephen Gould achieves an honest, sincerely sung, never belted Siegfried that is stretched by the big moments and rarely finds the juice or the ability to spin a line to thrill or to enchant us. Linda Watson, a committed, gamey stage performer, brings all the advantages of a former mezzo to the lower-lying or more meaty passages of *Walküre* and *Götterdämmerung* but is challenged by her higher-ranging *Siegfried* incarnation. Hans-Peter König's Hagen has a bluff, unmelodramatic straightforwardness but he rarely sounds frightening. Endrik Wottrich's Siegmund brings some credible dark colouring but the microphones are not kind to his rather nasal tone.

Of the other main players Eva-Maria Westbroek's detailed, tortured Sieglinde is a delight, as are Michelle Breedt's showy Fricka and Christa Mayer's young Erda (which comes off well in the *Siegfried* duet) and Waltraute. Gerhard Siegel's now much-travelled Mime is predictably efficient and accurate while Arnold Bezuyen's Loge sounds dry of tone but brings immense detail in dynamic and meaning. Andrew Shore's Alberich is a taste worth acquiring – about 100 per cent different in his kooky innocence, goblin- and working man-ness to the black, sleek, villainous Alberichs of yore.

It's hard to place this *Ring* – at present full-price – in a market made even more competitive today by the number of 'online' cycles to which keen Wagnerians will certainly have access. For Thielemann's work alone, the set is essential. The recordists have done their jobs well. As a vocal experience however, despite good Rhine-girls and Norns to add to the strengths above, this is no *bel canto* feast and is outsung by each of the classic Bayreuth sets.

Der Ring des Nibelungen
Casts include **Gré Brouwenstijn, Ilse Hollweg, Gerda Lammers, Paula Lenchner, Astrid Varnay, Lore Wissmann** sops **Maria von Ilosvay, Luisecharlotte Kamps, Jean Madeira, Georgine von Milinkovič, Elisabeth Schärtel** mezs **Paul Kuen, Ludwig Suthaus, Josef Traxel, Wolfgang Windgassen** tens **Alfons Herwig, Hermann Uhde** bars **Hans Hotter, Gustav Neidlinger** bass-bars **Josef Greindl, Arnold Van**

Mill basses **Bayreuth Festival Chorus and Orchestra / Hans Knappertsbusch**
Orfeo d'Or mono ⑬ C660 513Y (15h 13' · ADD · N). Recorded live in 1956   Ⓕ

During the pioneering post-war era at Bayreuth the conducting of the *Ring* was shared among the Ks – Karajan, Krauss, Knappertsbusch, Keilberth and Kempe. These conductors collectively had a knowledge and experience of the cycle not equalled before or since, with the sole exception of their contemporary Furtwängler, who returned after the war only to conduct Beethoven's Ninth.

Although they were brought up in the same, exemplary tradition, the Ks had very different ways of treating the *Ring*, as you can now discover given the availability of so many cycles on CD. Krauss in his superb 1953 cycle went for a lean, dramatic, often electrifying and elating approach. He shared the cycles with Keilberth in 1953 after Karajan refused to return to Bayreuth, and was scheduled to return in 1954. His sudden death left Keilberth solely in charge in 1954 and '55. We now have the elusive Keilberth cycle of 1955 from Testament, a version recorded by Decca but never issued. This now becomes the first stereo recording.

In 1956 Knappertsbusch, who had shared the 1951 cycles with Karajan returned to give what is generally agreed to be his most successful reading, taken as a whole. Unlike Krauss, Karajan and to a lesser extent Keilberth, the older conductor took a more measured view of the scores overall, one based on his preference for the long paragraph, well defined, almost pawky rhythms, and prominent ritardandi at points not always indicated in the score. At moments he seems to lose focus and let things run their own way where ensemble is concerned but, as a whole, especially in *Rheingold* and *Götterdämmerung*, his epic view of the score is almost unsurpassed. Even in the two middle operas there are moments of alternating quiet reflection and earthy energy that are very special.

He has at his command an ensemble of dedicated singers who had built their characterisations to a peak of achievement by 1956. Practically all are German-speaking and all have the art of acting with their voices in an immediate and communicative way, not to forget that they each had voices of a Wagnerian power too seldom found today.

Throughout *Rheingold* astonishment and delight are responses once more to the frightening power and presence of Gustav Neidlinger's trenchantly sung Alberich and by the detail, feeling and vocal authority of Hans Hotter's unsurpassed Wotan. Beside them an erstwhile Siegfried, Ludwig Suthaus, offers a Loge who gives every word, even syllable a distinctive colour and meaning, while Jean Madeira's Erda emits other-worldly authority. And any *Rheingold* that boasts Josef Traxel, then a leading lyric tenor in Germany, as Froh has a bonus.

Four singers heard in later operas are introduced here. Paul Kuen, another familiar figure, is Mime and provides character without exaggeration. Georgine von Milinkovič introduces us to an imperiously nagging Fricka and comes into her own in the next work. Josef Greindl is a formidable if unsubtle Fasolt, later a granite Hunding and a fearsome Hagen: no wonder, given so much work to do, he sometimes tires a little. Gré Brouwenstijn, a properly worried Freia, then gives us a Sieglinde who develops, in glorious tones, from an introvert to an extrovert when love strikes her. Beside her is Wolfgang Windgassen, standing in at the last moment for an ailing Vinay, and singing a Siegmund who is at once *bel canto* in line yet intensely eloquent. Incredibly, the next evening he is a tirelessly effective Siegfried.

Hotter is magnificent in Wotan's Act 2 monologue, here made to seem at the very heart of the whole cycle, and as ever deeply moving in his Act 3 Farewell, forgiving signs of vocal weariness at the start of the act. By then we have met and admired Astrid Varnay's very womanly yet heroic Brünnhilde. She occasionally overdoes the histrionics but by and large she has the character in her voice and bones in a way few other dramatic sopranos have managed.

In Siegfried Hotter manages ideally the humour of his Act 1 colloquy with Mime, his face-off with Neidlinger's Alberich in Act 2, and his desperation when meeting Madeira's implacable Erda at the start of Act 3. The awakening of Brünnhilde is not one of the conductor's best moments but the lovers give their all in the closing duet.

All the momentous climaxes of the cycle's finale find Kna at his most potent and involved, just as in 1951, and Varnay seconds him with her projection of all Brünnhilde's joy and sorrow. She also – incredibly – took on the Third Norn, at very short notice, Mödl having been taken suddenly ill. Madeira is heard again to advantage as both First Norn and Waltraute – would any singer do both today? Act 2 is simply tremendous. In this work Brouwenstijn returns as a vocally comely Gutrune, and Hermann Uhde, as in all the 1950s cycles, is an unsurpassed Gunther. With the Immolation one rightly feels that the earth has moved and that one has been through a life-enhancing experience, which is as it should be.

Music & Arts issued this cycle in 1998 but this is the first issue with the Bayreuth imprimatur, though the sound quality is only marginally superior here. Orchestral textures are sometimes muted but that has much to do with the opera house's layout. No texts or translations but a good booklet, which quotes one contemporary critic as saying this was undoubtedly the Festival's greatest moment to date. Allegiance to the 1953 Krauss set is not altered but there is much here that remains unsurpassed.

Der Ring des Nibelungen
Chorus and Orchestra of the Metropolitan Opera, New York / James Levine
Stage director **Otto Schenk**
Video director **Brian Large**

DG ⑦ 🔲 073 043-9GH7 (941' · 4:3 · 2.0 & 5.1* · 0)
*Dolby digital & DTS. Recorded live at the
Metropolitan Opera House 1989-90.   Ⓕ
Also available separately as below

Das Rheingold
James Morris *bass* Wotan **Christa Ludwig** *mez* Fricka **Siegfried Jerusalem** *ten* Loge **Heinz Zednik** *ten* Mime **Ekkehard Wlaschiha** *bass* Alberich **Mari Anne Häggander** *sop* Freia **Mark Baker** *ten* Froh **Alan Held** *bar* Donner **Birgitta Svendén** *mez* Erda **Jan-Hendrik Rootering** *bass* Fasolt **Matti Salminen** *bass* Fafner **Kaaren Erickson** *sop* Woglinde **Diane Kesling** *mez* Wellgunde **Meredith Parsons** *contr* Flosshilde
DG 🔲 073 036-9GH (163')   Ⓕ

Die Walküre
Gary Lakes *ten* Siegmund **Jessye Norman** *sop* Sieglinde **Hildegard Behrens** *sop* Brünnhilde **James Morris** *bass* Wotan **Christa Ludwig** *mez* Fricka **Kurt Moll** *bass* Hunding **Pyramid Sellers** *sop* Gerhilde **Katarina Ikonomu** *sop* Helmwige **Martha Thigpen** *sop* Ortlinde **Joyce Castle** *mez* Waltraute **Jacalyn Bower** *mez* Rossweise **Diane Kesling** *mez* Siegrune **Wendy Hillhouse** *mez* Grimgerde **Sondra Kelly** *contr* Schwertleite
DG ② 🔲 073 049-9GH2 (241')   Ⓕ

Siegfried
Siegfried Jerusalem *ten* Siegfried **James Morris** *bass* Wanderer **Hildegard Behrens** *sop* Brünnhilde **Heinz Zednik** *ten* Mime **Ekkehard Wlaschiha** *bass* Alberich **Birgitta Svendén** *mez* Erda **Fritz Hübner** *bass* Fafner **Dawn Upshaw** *sop* Woodbird
DG ②🔲 073 037-9GH2 (253')   Ⓕ

Götterdämmerung
Hildegard Behrens *sop* Brünnhilde **Siegfried Jerusalem** *ten* Siegfried **Matti Salminen** *bass* Hagen **Ekkehard Wlaschiha** *bass* Alberich **Anthony Raffell** *bass* Gunther **Hanna Lisowska** *sop* Gutrune **Christa Ludwig** *mez* Waltraute **Kaaren Erickson** *sop* Woglinde **Diane Kesling** *mez* Wellgunde **Meredith Parsons** *contr* Flosshilde **Gweneth Bean** *contr* First Norn **Joyce Castle** *mez* Second Norn **Andrea Gruber** *sop* Third Norn
DG ② 🔲 073 040-9GH2 (281')   Ⓕ🔵🔵

This Met cycle has plenty of strong points. It's the only one filmed version Wagner would have recognised – no small consideration. It's frequently assumed these days that he chose myth primarily to convey political allegory, but this is misleading. Myth inspired Wagner as directly as it did, say, Sibelius; and producers who ignore or mock this, like Patrice Chéreau on Pierre Boulez's rival set, miss a vital dimension. Here, Otto Schenk and designer Gunther Schneider-Siemssen preserve the Romantic imagery, often beautifully, as Brian Large's cameras reveal; but also unimaginatively, with too many tired compromises. Some, such as the Rhinemaidens' non-swimming contortions and the feeble dragon, are embarrassing, and the costumes often look poor on screen. Individual performances, too, sometimes don't fit into a satisfactory ensemble.

This set can also claim musical superiority; but again, not conclusively. Boulez mistakes speed for energy, drying out the richness of the score; Levine, with the magnificent Met orchestra, tends to wallow in it, especially in a disappointing *Rheingold*. Matters improve from *Walküre* onward, but he's prone to sudden wheelspinning accelerations, sometimes wrongfooting his singers. Boulez remains invisible at Bayreuth; Levine is too much with us, to the detriment of atmosphere. Nevertheless, his monumental approach does bring out *The Ring*'s sheer beauty and grandeur, where Boulez simply seems glib.

Levine's cast is superior, too, although the pivotal roles are the closest. Both Brünnhildes are splendid, spirited and deeply moving, but Boulez's Gwyneth Jones has the fuller voice; Hildegard Behrens, lithe and nervy, must force an essentially lyric instrument – quite successfully, but the effort shows. James Morris, aspiring to be a *bel canto* Wotan, has a richer voice than Boulez's Donald MacIntyre, but his diction and his acting are less incisive – partly the producer's fault in *Rheingold*; he improves thereafter. Siegfried Jerusalem, though, eclipses Boulez's inadequate Manfred Jung. More lyrical and vocally more heroic, he's a finer musician, less liable to strain and distort the line, and an impressive stage figure.

Jerusalem's surprisingly characterful Loge, despite his galia melon headgear, is probably the best thing in *Rheingold*. It's rewarding to hear the Narration in this kind of voice. Otherwise this is lacklustre. A superb Rhinemaiden trio is left earthbound, writhing unconvincingly round Ekkehard Wlaschiha's buffoonish Alberich, short on menace until the final curse. Christa Ludwig's once definitive Fricka looks and sounds tired. Levine's tempi in *Rheingold* rival those of Reginald Goodall, but without his structure and pacing; the Giants' entrance is marked *molto pesante*, not funereal. They, the Rhinemaidens and the lesser gods – especially Birgitta Svendén's keen-voiced Erda – outclass their betters.

Levine handles *Walküre* more successfully. Act 1, though, isn't a success. Gary Lakes's massive but rather lean-toned Siegmund is ill-matched with Jessye Norman, whose vocally searing Sieglinde is subverted by her *grande dame* manner, robbing the love scenes of any real involvement. Behrens, however, injects Act 2 with life, and though Ludwig's Fricka still sounds tired, Morris begins to make an impact, singing rather than declaiming the Narration. With a ringingly athletic Valkyrie band, Levine rushes the Ride, but brings the act to a moving Farewell.

Siegfried is visually and musically the best, with Levine at his liveliest, and a Romantic forest out of Altdorfer or von Schwind. Jerusalem's ardent hero may lack Heldentenor heft and suffer some constraint at the top but he carries off the forging and lyrical scenes with credit. The Wanderer often suits basses' range and personae, and Morris's commanding, world-weary god dominates Zednik's veteran Mime (mercifully not Chéreau's cute victim), Wlaschiha's now mordant Alberich

and Svendén's eerie Erda. Levine's protracted 'Awakening' stretches Behrens, but she and Jerusalem infuse the love duet with appealing life.

Levine's expansiveness suits *Götterdämmerung*, which opens with a powerful trio of Norns and a radiant Dawn duet. Chez Gibichung, though, the temperature drops, with Anthony Raffell (a fine Wotan) a miscast, bumbling Gunther, and Gutrune sadly unseductive. Matti Salminen's brutish Hagen, though richly sung, lacks the essential supernatural undertones. Ludwig is much better as Waltraute, but Jerusalem and especially Behrens carry the performance with involving intensity. The Immolation strains her voice, but remains satisfyingly cathartic, aided by appropriate stage spectacle, though Valhalla's downfall is disappointing.

All told, while this set may be less stimulating than the Boulez, it's also less distracting – without, as an eminent colleague once remarked, someone forever shouting in your ear. As well as the original digital stereo, remixed surround-sound tracks convincingly evoke extra ambience and detail. The image also remasters well, although you may want to turn up the colour.

Der Ring des Nibelungen
Chorus and Orchestra of the Royal Danish Opera / Michael Schønwandt
Stage director **Kasper Bech Holten**
Video director **Uffe Borgwardt**

Das Rheingold
Johan Reuter *bass-bar* Wotan **Hans Lewaetz** *bar* Donner **Johnny van Hal** *ten* Froh **Michael Kristensen** *ten* Loge **Stephen Milling** *bass* Fasolt **Christian Christiansen** *bar* Fafner **Sten Byriel** *bar* Alberich **Bengt-Ola Morgny** *ten* Mime **Randi Stene** *mez* Fricka **Anne Margrethe Dahl** *sop* Freia **Susanne Resmark** *contr* Erda **Dijna Mai-Mai** *sop* Woglinde **Ylva Kihlberg** *sop* Wellgunde **Hanna Fischer** *mez* Flosshilde

Die Walküre
Stig Andersen *ten* Siegmund **Gitta-Maria Sjöberg** *sop* Sieglinde **James Johnson** *bass-bar* Wotan **Iréne Theorin** *sop* Brünnhilde **Stephen Milling** *bass* Hunding **Randi Stene** *mez* Fricka **Emma Vetter** *sop* Helmwige **Carolina Sandgren** *sop* Ortlinde **Ylva Kihlberg** *sop* Gerhilde **Hanna Fischer** *mez* Waltraute **Anna Rydberg** *mez* Siegrune **Elisabeth Jansson** *mez* Rossweise **Elisabeth Halling** *mez* Grimgerde **Ulla Kudsk Jensen** *contr* Schwertleite

Siegfried
Stig Andersen *ten* Siegfried **Bengt-Ola Morgny** *ten* Mime **James Johnson** *bass-bar* Wotan **Sten Byriel** *bar* Alberich **Christian Christiansen** *bar* Fafner **Susanne Resmark** *contr* Erda **Iréne Theorin** *sop* Brünnhilde **Giselle Stille** *sop* Woodbird

Götterdämmerung
Stig Andersen *ten* Siegfried **Guido Paevatalu** *bar* Gunther **Peter Klaveness** *bass* Hagen **Sten Byriel** *bar* Alberich **Iréne Theorin** *sop* Brünnhilde **Ylva Kihlberg** *sop* Gutrune **Anna Bod** *mez* Waltraute

Susanne Resmark *contr* First Norn **Hanna Fischer** *mez* Second Norn **Anne Margrethe Dahl** *sop* Third Norn **Djina Mai-Mai** *sop* Woglinde **Elisabeth Meyer-Topsoe** *sop* Wellgunde **Ulla Kudsk Jensen** *contr* Flosshilde

Decca ⑦ **DVD** 074 3264DH7 (15h 20′ · NTSC · 16:9 · PCM stereo and DTS 5.1 · 0) Ⓟ**OOO**

The first of several wonders in this new set, collated from three cycles in the early summer of 2006, is the intuitive performing skill of a genuine house ensemble. Even the 'borrowed' Swedish and Norwegian artists, including the Brünnhilde and Hagen, are regulars in a company which inevitably casts the most demanding repertoire from its own – Copenhagen has achieved a class *Ring* with just one guest, James Johnson's *Walküre/Siegfried* Wotans. Moreover, if Stockholm is the Venice of the north, the Royal Danish Orchestra must be the Vienna Philharmonic of the north with its forward, rich woodwind timbres (a Nielsen sound, wholly suitable for Nibelung music) and cool-sweet string tone, the whole integrated, balanced and paced with a Kempe-like swiftness and attention to rhythmic detail by their chief Michael Schønwandt.

The assembled cut from the filming of the live performances (Uffe Borgwardt is the credited director of photography) is quite radical for a record of live opera. Like the curious spectator, these cameras want to look up the Rhinemaidens' flapper skirts, focus on props or the after-effects of violent action, or wonder how a scene looks from behind, from the wings, or even from beneath stage level in the orchestra pit. So the visual editing is busy, justifying allusions to the hand-held operation rediscovered by Danish art cinema directors. It gives the films a breathless close-up quality, the absolute inverse of the accustomed best-seat-in-the-stalls approach.

Kasper Bech Holten's production doesn't intentionally disturb realism and story-telling. There is a frame story – Brünnhilde is seen researching, in some giant sidestage Valhalla library store, the events of the past from the moment she betrayed Siegfried. But, in principle, this Copenhagen *Ring* follows a linear narrative. It's costumed and situated between (approximately) 1920 and the 1990s, and – through ever-ingenious lateral thinking – finds latter-day equivalents for Wagner's geography, properties and dramatic violence. Thus the Rhinegold itself is a beautiful, golden, naked swimming boy, whose heart is bloodily torn out by a serially drinking, lecherous Alberich when he is rejected by *les girls*. Once captured in Nibelheim, Alberich is chained up in a scary white-tiled torture room, surrendering the ring only when Wotan literally hacks off his entire lower arm. Loge, knowing too much at the end of *Rheingold*, is murdered by Wotan; Erda's life-support is turned off, sorrowfully, by Wotan in *Siegfried*; Alberich, having worn out Hagen, is dispatched at the end of their colloquy in *Götterdämmerung*; and, later in that same act, hos-

tages are executed by Hagen in 'celebration' of Gunther's wedding.

But don't get squeamish at the horror, or sniff at Quentin Tarantino-influenced trendiness. See instead how this director finds more heart-breaking emotion in Wagner's drama than almost any since Patrice Chéreau. In the last scene of *Walküre* Johnson's Wotan – a characterisation admirably unafraid of appearing less than godlike – searches the whole scene for a way out for Theorin's emotionally mobile Brünnhilde but has to end up (at that huge climax between the 'verses' of the Farewell) by tearing off her Valkyrie's black wings. Stig Andersen's Siegfried, sung with lyrical beauty, is seen desperately alone in the 'forest', stroking the bodies of Mime and Fafner whom he has killed and thus left himself stranded. Kasper Bech Holten is astute too at those potentially awkward moments of embarrassment and waiting and watching – watch the superb detail in the playing of his ensemble stars like Andersen (as both the Walsungs), Theorin, Byriel's unclichéd Alberich, Peter Klaveness's terrifying SS officer of a Hagen (although the voice cannot always equal his dramatic presence), Randı Stene's Fricka (Hillary Clinton with humour) or Guido Paevatalu's multifacetedly lazy, brutal coward of a Gunther.

In addition to the sheer zip of performance and filming, the sound picture is warm, resonant and true, the English subtitles give an unusually revealing and detailed insight into Wagner's text, and, winningly, the 'extra' item consists of a discussion between the stage director and his country's opera-loving head of state. But finally, can these performers, only some of them known on main stages outside Scandinavia, cut the mustard alongside the more international competition on six rival DVD productions? They most certainly can.

The Ring – complete in English

The Rhinegold (sung in English)
Norman Bailey *bar* Wotan **Katherine Pring** *mez* Fricka **Emile Belcourt** *ten* Loge **Gregory Dempsey** *ten* Mime **Derek Hammond-Stroud** *bar* Alberich **Lois McDonall** *sop* Freia **Robert Ferguson** *ten* Froh **Norman Welsby** *bar* Donner **Anne Collins** *contr* Erda **Robert Lloyd** *bass* Fasolt **Clifford Grant** *bass* Fafner **Valerie Masterson** *sop* Woglinde **Shelagh Squires** *mez* Wellgunde **Helen Attfield** *sop* Flosshilde **English National Opera Orchestra / Reginald Goodall**
Chandos Opera in English Series ③ CHAN3054 (174′ · ADD · N/t). Recorded live 1975 Ⓟ**O➔**

The Valkyrie (sung in English)
Alberto Remedios *ten* Siegmund **Margaret Curphey** *sop* Sieglinde **Rita Hunter** *sop* Brünnhilde **Norman Bailey** *bar* Wotan **Ann Howard** *contr* Fricka **Clifford Grant** *bass* Hunding **Katie Clarke** *sop* Gerhilde **Anne Evans** *sop* Helmwige **Ann Conoley** *sop* Ortlinde **Elizabeth Connell** *sop* Waltraute **Anne Collins** *contr* Rossweisse **Sarah Walker** *mez* Siegrune

Shelagh Squires *mez* Grimgerde **Helen Attfield** *sop*
Schwertleite **English National Opera Orchestra /
Reginald Goodall**
Chandos Opera in English Series ④ CHAN3038
(4h 9' · ADD · N/t). Recorded live 1976   ⑤O⭘➤

Siegfried (sung in English)
Alberto Remedios *ten* Siegfried **Norman Bailey**
bass-bar Wanderer **Rita Hunter** *sop* Brünnhilde
Gregory Dempsey *ten* Mime **Derek Hammond-
Stroud** *bar* Alberich **Anne Collins** *contr* Erda **Clifford
Grant** *bass* Fafner **Maurine London** *sop* Woodbird
Sadler's Wells Opera Orchestra / Reginald Goodall
Chandos ④ CHAN3045 (4h 39' · ADD · N/t)
Recorded live 1973   ⑤O⭘O➤

Twilight of the Gods (sung in English)
Alberto Remedios *ten* Siegfried **Norman Welsby**
bar Gunther **Aage Haugland** *bass* Hagen **Derek
Hammond-Stroud** *bar* Alberich **Rita Hunter** *sop*
Brünnhilde **Margaret Curphey** *sop* Gutrune
Katherine Pring *mez* Waltraute **Anne Collins** *contr*
First Norn **Gillian Knight** *mez* Second Norn **Anne
Evans** *sop* Third Norn **Valerie Masterson** *sop*
Woglinde **Shelagh Squires** *mez* Wellgunde **Helen
Attfield** *contr* Flosshilde **English National Opera
Orchestra and Chorus / Reginald Goodall**
Chandos Opera in English CHAN3060
(5h 12' · ADD · N/t). Recorded live 1977   ⑤O➤

Valkyrie: There's something inevitable, even
eternal about Goodall's long-breathed, full-
toned, often ideally articulated reading. The
ENO management's faith in him was handsomely repaid in his ability to convey his lifetime vision to is regular cast and eventually to
his audiences. On paper, tempi may look unacceptably slow; in practice there are very few
places – perhaps Siegmund's Spring song and
Sieglinde's reply – where they seem too tardy.
That's largely due to his ability to find the
Hauptstimme for every paragraph of the music,
indeed for a whole act and, perhaps even more,
to his ability to persuade players and singers
alike to sustain a long line. Listeners familiar
only with the Solti cycle will hardly recognise
this as the same work.

By 1976 all his singers were entirely inside
their respective roles and so able to project a
feeling of familiarity with their music that's evident in every bar. Like all the most satisfying
sets of the *Ring*, it benefits enormously from
being heard live in a theatre acoustic, and here
no compromises have to be made, so superb are
producer John Mordler's and his team's skills.
You seem to be seated in centre stalls imbibing
the performance. Rita Hunter bestrides the role
of Brünnhilde in a confident manner achieved in
relatively modern times only by Birgit Nilsson,
whose bright tone and effortless top Hunter's so
much resembles. She's also a thoughtful, very
human interpreter of the role, keen with her
words and investing them with the right import.
By her side Bailey confirms that he's as excellent
a Wotan as any since Hans Hotter. His reading
of the taxing part is virtually tireless and his
interpretation combines authority with fatherly

concern. Remedios's Siegmund remains one of
the most sweetly sung and appealing on disc. If
Curphey isn't quite in his class vocally, she offers
a deeply felt and sympathetic Sieglinde. Ann
Howard is, rightly, a termagant of a Fricka, with
a touch of asperity in her tone. Clifford Grant is
a sonorous, towering Hunding. The Valkyries,
comprising many of the most promising female
singers of the day (among them Elizabeth Connell and Anne Evans), acquit themselves very
well. All the cast benefit from Andrew Porter's
carefully wrought, very singable translation.
Overall, a hearty welcome back to a great
recording.

Siegfried: That Reginald Goodall idolised
Klemperer and Knappertsbusch is evident in
every aspect of this weighty, consistently
thought-through interpretation; indeed it consoles us for the cycle Klemperer never recorded.
The performance is also a reminder of what
those then in charge of the ENO – Stephen
Arlen, Lord Harewood and Edmund Tracey –
had the sense to realise: that here was a unique
opportunity to let a seasoned Wagnerian have
his head in terms of the time and trouble to
prepare a cycle in his own long time-scale. The
results are there for all to hear in the total
involvement of every member of the orchestra,
the lyrical lines of the singers, the superb
enunciation of the faultless translation.

Remedios's fresh, lyrical singing is a joy from
start to finish; nobody since has equalled him as
Siegfried. Dempsey's Mime is at once subtle,
funny yet menacing. Those who so praise Tomlinson as Wotan/Wanderer can't have heard
Bailey's better sung, articulate and eloquent
assumption, another reading not since surpassed.
To crown the performance we have Rita Hunter's glorious Brünnhilde, so luminously and
keenly sung, just about on a par with Nilsson in
the role. They are all wonderfully supported by
Goodall and his players. Only in some of Siegfried's Act 1 forging and his struggle with Fafner
might one ask for a shade more physical energy,
but that's a small price to pay for such understanding of Wagnerian structure.

Rhinegold and *Twilight of the Gods*: After more
than 25 years, these recordings remain gripping
for reasons similar to those applying to the other
sections of the English *Ring* reissued by Chandos. In spite of speeds that in other hands would
seem often unreasonably slow, or to an extent
because of them, Goodall's interpretation has an
unerring sense of lyrical and dramatic concentration, every paragraph, phrase and bar carefully considered and executed with loving care
by singers and players alike, all so closely
coached by their veteran conductor. Above all
there's the refined *legato* observed by all the
singers. And the sense of real-life occasion, the
theatre's acoustic clearly felt throughout.
Andrew Porter's wonderfully lucid translation is
given its full due by all the soloists, who once
more sound an utterly convincing team. In
Rhinegold the main honours are carried off by
Emile Belcourt's plausible, witty and articulate
Loge, Hammond-Stroud's imposing, strongly

sung Alberich, Robert Lloyd's sympathetic Fasolt and Bailey's ever-authoritative Wotan. With a pleasing trio of Rhinemaidens headed by Masterson's gleaming Woglinde, Clifford Grant's gloomy, louring Fafner and Anne Collins's deep-throated Erda, the strength of the ENO roster at the time is there for all to hear. In *Twilight*, Hunter and Remedios excel themselves as a more heroic than tragic pair, their singing steady, keen with words and very much in character following so many performances, by 1977, of the complete cycle. Aage Haugland offers a welcome souvenir of his career as a louring Hagen. Welsby uncovers the right touches of weak will for Gunther while Curphey is suitably alluring as sister Gutrune. Pring offers an appropriately urgent and strongly sung Waltraute. The Norns could hardly be more strongly cast.

By and large, the playing of the ENO Orchestra is of an equally consistent nature, responding to Goodall's long-breathed conducting with playing of beauty and strength adding up to a formidable traversal of the score. The recording, masterminded by John Mordler, need not fear comparison with anything more recent. Indeed the absence of unwanted reverberation and excessive sound effects is most welcome. What we get is the music unvarnished and truthful, for which many thanks again to the foresight of the ENO directors of the day and to Peter Moores for providing the wherewithal to execute it. Anyone wanting the work in the vernacular, who hasn't already acquired it in its previous incarnations, need not hesitate.

Tannhäuser

Tannhäuser
Peter Seiffert *ten* Tannhäuser **Jane Eaglen** *sop*
Elisabeth **Thomas Hampson** *bar* Wolfram **Waltraud Meier** *mez* Venus **René Pape** *bass* Hermann **Gunnar Gudbjörnsson** *ten* Walther **Hanno Müller-Brachmann** *bass-bar* Biterolf **Stephan Rügamer** *ten* Heinrich **Alfred Reiter** *bass* Reinmar **Dorothea Röschmann** *sop* Shepherd **Berlin State Opera Chorus; Berlin Staatskapelle / Daniel Barenboim**
Teldec ④ 8573 88064-2 (3h 15' · DDD · T/t)   Ⓕ**O**➜

This must be one of the most opulent recordings made of any opera. The truly remarkable range, perspective and balance of the sound is most appropriate for a work conceived on the grandest scale, yet it retains its focus in the more intimate scenes. The achievement of Barenboim's Berlin chorus, so important in this opera, and orchestra could hardly be bettered. The results are, if nothing else, an audio treat, surpassing the DG version's rather hit-and-miss engineering and the now slightly dated feel of the Decca. Indeed it's Konwitschny's 40-year-old set (EMI) that comes closest to the Teldec in terms of sonic breadth.

Domingo recorded Tannhäuser for DG (see below) but shied away from it on stage. The title-role, as many tenors admit, is a real killer. Seiffert is probably its most telling exponent: his performance that combines vocal assurance and

emotional involvement to create a vivid portrait of the hero torn between sacred and profane love. The objects of Tannhäuser's attention are impressively portrayed by Waltraud Meier and Jane Eaglen. Meier makes the most of the bigger opportunities and brings her customary tense expression to bear on Venus's utterance, while not quite effacing Christa Ludwig's voluptuous reading for Solti. Eaglen launches herself into the Hall of Song with a rather squally 'Dich teure Halle'; thereafter she sings with much of the inner feeling and prayerful dignity predicated by Wagner for his Elisabeth.

Hermann is a gift of a role for most German basses and René Pape takes his chances with his accustomed feeling for notes and text. Thomas Hampson delivers Wolfram's solos with the expected blend of mellifluous tone and verbal acuity, but his manner is a touch set apart and self-conscious, as if he has had to record these at separate sessions. One reservation about this Teldec set: Barenboim's penchant in meditative passages for very slow speeds. But he paces the Prelude, the huge ensemble at the end of Act 2 and all the Pilgrim's music with unerring skill.

It's unlikely that we shall ever hear a totally convincing account of what was, after all, Wagner's problem child among his mature works, but this new one has about as much going for it as any in recent times. If you want the Dresden version unaltered by later revisions, and there's something to be said for that choice, the Konwitschny has much to offer in terms of its conductor, sound and much of the solo work.

Tannhäuser (Paris version)
Plácido Domingo *ten* Tannhäuser **Cheryl Studer** *sop*
Elisabeth **Andreas Schmidt** *bar* Wolfram **Agnes Baltsa** *mez* Venus **Matti Salminen** *bass* Hermann **William Pell** *ten* Walther **Kurt Rydl** *bass* Biterolf **Clemens Biber** *ten* Heinrich **Oskar Hillebrandt** *bass* Reinmar **Barbara Bonney** *sop* Shepherd Boy **Chorus of the Royal Opera House, Covent Garden; Philharmonia Orchestra / Giuseppe Sinopoli**
DG ③ 427 625-2GH3 (176' · DDD · T/t)   Ⓕ**O**➜

Domingo's Tannhäuser is a success in almost every respect. He evokes the erotic passion of the Venusberg scene and brings to it just the right touch of nervous energy. This is boldly contrasted with the desperation and bitterness of the Rome Narration after the hero's fruitless visit to the Pope seeking forgiveness: Domingo's description of how Tannhäuser avoided every earthly delight on his pilgrimage is delivered with total conviction. In between he berates the slightly prissy attitude of his fellow knights on the Wartburg with the dangerous conceit of someone who knows a secret delight that they will never enjoy in their measured complacency. His tenor must be the steadiest and most resplendent ever to have tackled the part, although his German is far from idiomatic. Baltsa also has problems with her German, but she has the range and attack for an awkwardly lying part. It's obviously Sinopoli's concern throughout to bring out every last ounce of the drama in the piece, both in terms of orchestral detail and in his awareness in this opera of the longer line, often sustained by the upper strings. The Philharmonia's violins respond with their most eloquent playing. The kind of frisson Sinopoli offers is evident in the anticipatory excitement at the start of Act 2 and the iron control he maintains in the big ensemble later in the same act. Cheryl Studer's secure, beautiful voice has no difficulty coping with Sinopoli's deliberate tempi. She takes her part with total conviction, both vocal and interpretative, phrasing with constant intelligence. Andreas Schmidt is a mellifluous, concerned Wolfram, Salminen a rugged, characterful Landgrave and Barbara Bonney an ideally fresh Shepherd Boy.

The Covent Garden Chorus sings with consistent beauty of sound, and has been sensibly balanced with the orchestra. Domingo and Studer make this version a winner.

Additional recommendation

Tannhäuser   🄷
Windgassen Tannhäuser
Brouwenstijn Elisabeth **Fischer-Dieskau** Wolfram
Wilfert Venus **Greindl** Hermann **Traxel** Walther
Bayreuth Festival Chor & Orch / Cluytens
Orfeo d'Or mono ③ C643 043D (198' · ADD)
Recorded live 1955   Ⓜ

This is a revelatory interpretation of a work which isn't easy to bring off. André Cluytens had taken over at short notice, and he seems energised by the challenge. Contemporary reviews spoke of the bright, shining strings and the luminous texture of the orchestra, and of the 'intoxicating magic' of the whole concept. Director and conductor seem to have persuaded a fine cast to give of their very best. Wolfgang Windgassen is here in fresh voice. His true love, Elisabeth, is sung with total commitment and vibrant, outgoing voice by Gré Brouwenstijn. The mono sound is so good that you soon forget any limitations. This set enters the pantheon of great Bayreuth performances on disc.

Tannhäuser
Spas Wenkoff ten Tannhäuser **Gwyneth Jones** sop
Elizabeth, Venus **Bernd Weikl** bar Wolfram **Hans Sotin** bass Hermann **Franz Mazura** bar Biterolf
Robert Schunk ten Walther **Heinz Feldhoff** bass
Reinmar **John Pickering** ten Heinrich
**Chorus and Orchestra of the Bayreuth Festival /
Sir Colin Davis**
Stage director **Götz Friedrich**
Video director **Thomas Oloffson**
DG ② DVD 073 4446GH2 (3h 8' · NTSC · 4:3 · PCM
stereo and DTS 5.1 · 0)   Ⓕ🔘🔘

Tannhäuser (Paris version)
Robert Gambill ten Tannhäuser **Camilla Nylund** sop
Elisabeth **Waltraud Meier** sop Venus **Roman Trekel**
bar Wolfram **Stephen Milling** bass Hermann **Tom Fox** bar Biterolf **Marcel Reijans** ten Walther **Andreas**

Hörl bass Reinmar **Florian Hoffmann** ten Heinrich
**Deutsches Symphony Orchestra, Berlin /
Philippe Jordan**
Stage director **Nikolaus Lehnhoff**
Video director **Patrick Buttmann**
ArtHaus Musik ② DVD 101 351 (4h 23' · NTSC · 16:9 ·
PCM stereo, 5.1 and DTS 5.1 · 0)   Ⓕ

Thirty years separate these performances of *Tannhäuser*. The original video of the 1978 revival of Götz Friedrich's 1972 production was, we're told, 'the first complete film from Bayreuth', and this is its first DVD release. You're soon aware that it has not had the benefit of the latest technology: the lighting is not always well suited to the action and shifts between relatively close and relatively distant shots can appear awkward and arbitrary. The sound, too, is basic in its fixed focus, giving the voices too much prominence. All of this hardly matters, however, since the performance is electrifying, managing the difficult feat of doing justice to Wagner's inspiration without seeking to gainsay its gloriously hybrid nature.

Jürgen Rose's setting is austere, and one of the work's greatest moments, the astonishingly abrupt transition in Act 1 from the Venusberg to the idyllic countryside near the Wartburg, goes visually for too little. But the combination of Friedrich's tightly focused production and Sir Colin Davis's supremely flexible and energised conducting more than compensates. Davis is particularly in his element in the early stages of Act 2, to which he brings a Berliozian buoyancy, and what can sometimes seem almost comically tedious repetitions in the long processional chorus are anything but.

Adding to the lustre is the central trio of star performances. In 1978 Dame Gwyneth Jones was at her peak, taking time out from her definitive Bayreuth Brünnhilde to show how the roles of Venus and Elisabeth can be equally affecting, given maximum vocal and dramatic conviction. She weeps real tears in the mime that accompanies the Prelude to Act 3, as well she might, realising perhaps that she would never be better than this. Less sympathetically filmed, Spas Wenkoff still scores with the dogged power of his singing and acting, never out of character, never off the note, while Bernd Weikl is caught at his ardent, mellifluous best. With a fine supporting cast and the Bayreuth chorus and orchestra on top form, even those who resist the stylised eroticism of John Neumeier's choreography for the Bacchanale should find this set a memorable and moving experience.

The 2008 Baden-Baden version on ArtHaus Musik is, of course, technically superior as the film of a stage performance. It is not strictly comparable with the DG release anyway, since it offers the full post-*Tristan* Paris version, with the extended Venusberg music, while Bayreuth uses its own favoured hybrid – the Paris Bacchanale, before the singing starts, then the original Dresden version. Performances of the full Paris version are more likely to use different sopranos for the roles of Venus and Elisabeth, and it is one of the strengths of Baden-Baden 2008 to have two such different but excellent singers in these roles. Finnish soprano Camilla Nylund is new to me, and (like the Danish bass-baritone Stephen Milling, who comes close to upstaging most of his male colleagues as the Landgraf) is clearly a singer-actor of huge potential in this repertoire.

The solo singing is the outstanding feature of this new recording. Robert Gambill might have more of the 'mad axeman' about him than Bayreuth's Spas Wenkoff, but he has immense stamina and the presence to command the stage, especially during the big ensembles. Roman Trekel is a less spontaneous Wolfram than Weikl, his voice recorded with a degree of edginess that reduces its actual lyrical beauty. As with the remastered DG, the ArtHaus sound balance favours the voices at the expense of salient orchestral detail, but this drawback is much less bothersome than certain details of the production. In a setting even more austere than Bayreuth in 1978, Nikolaus Lehnhoff seems determined to drain the work of its Christian iconography and to nudge the audience with such deliberately incongruous props as a (non-functioning) microphone for the contestants in the Hall of Song. The production gets off to a bad start with a robotic, anti-erotic Bacchanale, and it is here that conductor Philippe Jordan's unsteady tempi, replete with pseudo-expressive over-emphases, first become apparent. Though it recurs, this problem is less pervasive than it might be, and Jordan is an alert supporter of his singers. But it is Colin Davis who has the fuller measure of this extraordinary score.

Tristan und Isolde

Tristan und Isolde
Plácido Domingo ten Tristan **Nina Stemme** sop Isolde **Mihoko Fujimura** sop Brangäne **René Pape** bass König Marke **Olaf Bär** bar Kurwenal **Jared Holt** ten Melot **Ian Bostridge** ten Shepherd **Matthew Rose** bar Helmsman **Rolando Villazón** ten Young Sailor **Royal Opera House Chorus and Orchestra, Covent Garden / Antonio Pappano**
EMI ③ 558006-5 (3h 46' · DDD · T/t)　Ⓕ❶❶🅱➔

Any major new recording of *Tristan und Isolde* is a big event, and this is bigger than most. As possibly the last studio recording on such a scale, it carries a weight of expectation, something doubled by an assumption which many never believed they'd hear: Plácido Domingo's Tristan. Of course, the 60-something tenor could never tackle this role on stage now, but it is not often one hears quite such a fantasy interpretation being realised on disc; even after Domingo's previous EMI releases of Wagnerian scenes, the idea of his recording this masterpiece in full seemed a little far-fetched. The advantage of the recording studio is that his Tristan never seems to tire and he gives an ardent account, characterised by the almost baritonal warmth of his voice. He may swallow the odd word but this is a committed and communicative performance, and he rises to the heights of Act 3.

Even so, it is the conducting of Antonio Pappano and the Isolde of Nina Stemme that truly put this in the highest league. Right from the start of the Prelude, which sounds languid without being really slow, Pappano draws a performance of glowing warmth. He moulds each detail but is never indulgent, with the result that the long spans all fall naturally into place. There is no need to over-stress Pappano's Italianate credentials, especially not when he conducts such an idiomatic Wagnerian performance, but they show themselves in the way he brings a *bel canto* quality to this music. This is a work that may have pushed the boundaries of tonality but it also reaches back to the world in which the composer served his operatic apprenticeship. Pappano's experience of *Tristan* in Brussels helps to make this sound like a 'lived-in' performance, and it must be hoped he will conduct it at Covent Garden.

Stemme is everything an Isolde needs to be: singing with radiant grandeur, she is rare in being able to sound sensuous even on the high notes. From her exciting first entry, she captures Isolde's temperament, and her Liebestod is notable for its beauty; her partnership with Domingo makes for a thrilling love duet. It is not often that a Brangäne sounds almost as glamorous, but Mihoko Fujimura sings with a warmly focused and even tone. René Pape is a noble and sonorous Marke, but Olaf Bär is less distinctive and occasionally woolly. As for the cameos, Rolando Villazón's Sailor is much less impressive than Ian Bostridge's ethereal and alert Shepherd. Even if this is not a recording to knock its legendary predecessors off their pedestals, it is an important addition to the discography and a stunning *Tristan* on today's terms. More than that: we'd think ourselves in operatic heaven if a live *Tristan* came close to this today.

Tristan und Isolde   **H**
Lauritz Melchior ten Tristan **Kirsten Flagstad** sop
Isolde **Sabine Kalter** contr Brangäne **Emanuel List**
bass King Marke **Herbert Janssen** bar Kurwenal **Frank
Sale** ten Melot **Octave Dua** ten Shepherd **Leslie
Horsman** bar Helmsman **Roy Devereux** ten Young
Sailor **Royal Opera House Chorus, Covent Garden;
London Philharmonic Orchestra / Fritz Reiner**
Naxos Historical mono ③ 8 110068/70 (3h 29' · ADD)
Recorded live 1936   ⑤**O**➔

This is an improved remastering by Ward Marston of a VAI set which received a warm welcome for preserving the rewarding partnership of Flagstad and Melchior, some would say unsurpassed in their respective roles and here on great form. The soprano, though at the start of her career in the part, is already a fully formed Isolde, and one marvels at Melchior, confirming his stature as the greatest Wagner tenor of all time. The rest of the cast are nothing special. Reiner, after a slow start, provides the right breadth and vitality to the work even when the

playing leaves a little to be desired. The then customary cuts are made in Acts 2 and 3. At super-bargain price (the VAI was at full price) this is an essential purchase for Wagnerians.

Tristan und Isolde
Wolfgang Windgassen ten Tristan **Birgit Nilsson**
sop Isolde **Christa Ludwig** mez Brangäne **Martti
Talvela** bass King Marke **Eberhard Waechter** bar
Kurwenal **Claude Heater** ten Melot **Erwin Wohlfahrt**
ten Shepherd **Gerd Nienstedt** bass Helmsman **Peter
Schreier** ten Sailor **Bayreuth Festival Chorus and
Orchestra / Karl Böhm**
DG The Originals ③ 449 772-2GOR3
(3h 39' · ADD · T/t). Recorded live 1966   Ⓜ**OOO**➔

Siegfried Jerusalem ten Tristan **Waltraud Meier**
mez Isolde **Marjana Lipovšek** mez Brangäne **Matti
Salminen** bass King Marke **Falk Struckmann** bar
Kurwenal **Johan Botha** ten Melot **Peter Maus** ten
Shepherd **Roman Trekel** bar Helmsman **Uwe
Heilmann** ten Sailor **Berlin State Opera Chorus;
Berlin Philharmonic Orchestra / Daniel Barenboim**
Teldec ③ 4509-94568-2 (3h 55' · DDD · T/t)
Recorded 1994   Ⓕ**O**

Böhm's recording is a live Bayreuth performance of distinction, for on stage are the most admired Tristan and Isolde of their time, and in the pit the 72-year-old conductor directs a performance which is unflagging in its passion and energy. He has a striking way in the Prelude and Liebestod of making the swell of passion seem like the movement of a great sea, sometimes with gentle motion, sometimes with the breaking of the mightiest of waves. Nilsson characterises strongly, and her voice with its cleaving-power can also soften beautifully. Windgassen's heroic performance in Act 3 is in some ways the crown of his achievements on record, even though the voice has dried and aged a little. Christa Ludwig is the ideal Brangäne, Waechter a suitably forthright Kurwenal and Talvela an expressive, noble-voiced Marke. Orchestra and chorus are at their finest.

Over several seasons of conducting the work at Bayreuth, Barenboim has thoroughly mastered the pacing and shaping of the score as a unified entity. Even more important, he has peered into the depths of both its construction and meaning, emerging with answers that satisfy on almost all counts, most tellingly so in the melancholic adumbration of Isolde's thoughts during her narration, in the sadly eloquent counterpoint of bass clarinet, lower strings and cor anglais underpinning King Marke's lament, and in the searingly tense support to Tristan's second hallucination. These are but the most salient moments in a reading that thoughtfully and unerringly reveals the inner parts of this astounding score. The obverse of this caring manner is a certain want of spontaneity, and a tendency to become a shade self-regarding. You occasionally miss the overwhelming force of Furtwängler's metaphysical account or the immediacy and excitement of Böhm's famous live Bayreuth reading. But the very mention of those conductors suggests that Barenboim can live in their world and survive the comparisons with his own perfectly valid interpretation. Besides, he has the most gloriously spacious yet well-focused recording so far of this opera, and an orchestra not only familiar with his ways but ready to execute them in a disciplined and sensitive manner. The recording also takes account of spatial questions, in particular the placing of the horns offstage at the start of Act 2.

Salminen delivers a classic account of Marke's anguished reproaches to Tristan, his singing at once sonorous, dignified and reaching to the heart, a reading on a par with that of his fellow countryman Talvela for Böhm. Meier's Isolde is a vitally wrought, verbally alert reading, which catches much of the venom of Act 1, the visceral excitement of Act 2, the lambent utterance of the Liebestod. Nothing she does is unmusical; everything is keenly intelligent, yet possibly her tone is too narrow for the role. Lipovšek's Brangäne tends to slide and swim in an ungainly fashion, sounding at times definitely overparted. Listening to Ludwig (Böhm) only serves to emphasise Lipovšek's deficiencies. Then it's often hard on the newer set to tell Isolde and Brangäne apart, so alike can be their timbre. As with his partner, Jerusalem sings his role with immaculate musicality; indeed, he may be the most accurate Tristan on disc where note values are concerned, one also consistently attentive to dynamics and long-breathed phrasing. On the other hand, although he puts a deal of feeling into his interpretation, he hasn't quite the intensity of utterance of either Windgassen (Böhm) or, even more, Suthaus (Furtwängler). His timbre is dry and occasionally rasping: in vocal terms alone Suthaus is in a class of his own. Yet, even with reservations about the Isolde and Tristan, this is a version that will undoubtedly hold a high place in any survey of this work, for which one performance can never hope to tell the whole story.

Tristan und Isolde
Robert Dean Smith ten Tristan **Iréne Theorin** sop Isolde **Robert Holl** bass King Marke **Jukka Rasilainen** bar Kurwenal **Ralf Lukas** ten Melot **Michelle Breedt** mez Brangäne **Clemens Bieber** ten A Young Sailor **Arnold Bezuyen** ten A Shepherd **Martin Snell** bar Helmsman **Bayreuth Festival Chorus and Orchestra / Peter Schneider**
Stage director **Christoph Marthaler**
Video director **Michael Beyer**
Opus Arte ③ 🟥 OA1033D; ② 🔷 OABD7067D (4h 49' · 16:9 · 1080i · PCM stereo DTS 5.0 · 0)
Recorded live 2009 ⒻⓄⓄⓄ

It's clear from about a minute after the curtain first parts on this Bayreuth Festival production that we are in very assured hands indeed onstage. Over a long period of work at Zürich's Schauspielhaus, Christoph Marthaler and his designer Anna Viebrock have invented a new aesthetic of 'modern dress' representations (often, as here,

1950s) of the great dramas from Aeschylus to Brecht, inevitably set in painstakingly detailed, often shabby, interior mid-European courtyards. Onto this design Marthaler grafts an intricate ground production that can be both as 'naturalistic' as conventional Chekhov (as here in the Brangäne/Isolde and Tristan/Isolde dialogues of Act 1) or as abstract and unrealistic as the hand-jive dances invented for ensemble work by Peter Sellars (seen here in Kurwenal's 'fight' with Melot in Act 3 and subsequent death).

The employment of the Marthaler/Viebrock aesthetic for Wagner's *Tristan* works in a manner that reinvents the wheels of both grand opera and 19th-century stage conventions about sex. For example, there are distinct 'stand and deliver' moments – after the potion has taken effect on the lovers in Act 1, in the Act 2 duet, and in Tristan's death-bed agonies. And growing sexual desire is expressed, 1950s movie-style (think Audrey Hepburn), by the loosening of a tie or a suit jacket, or the seductive removal of a glove, finger by finger. Brilliant, because these 'stagey' moments have been bought by Marthaler's attention to psychological detail.

As in all great stagings – and this surely is one – a list of unforgettable links between text, music and action soon accumulates. Two such are the shy little grin Isolde gives Tristan when they both realise in Act 1 that they're still alive and so in love, and the manner in which Marke questions Melot's boasting account of having delivered apparently concrete evidence of Tristan's infidelity ('Tatest du's? Wirklich?').

It's hard to know where to point the awards finger first in such a complete ensemble performance (and the revival director Anna-Sophia Mahler deserves credit too). But Iréne Theorin's multifaceted Isolde, Jukka Rasilainen's bullishly not-the-sharpest-tool-in-the-box Kurwenal and Robert Holl's insanely (or Schopenhauer-ily?) calm Marke have to be mentioned in dispatches. Musically everything is fine under the super-experienced Peter Schneider. The Blu-ray version catches perfectly the sometimes lurid colours and texture of Viebrock's work on both clothes and setting. Despite the ferocious competition, absolutely unmissable.

Tristan und Isolde
Robert Gambill ten Tristan **Nina Stemme** sop Isolde **Bo Skovhus** bar Kurwenal **René Pape** bass King Marke **Katarina Karnéus** mez Brangäne **Glyndebourne Chorus; London Philharmonic Orchestra / Jiří Bělohlávek**
Stage director **Nikolaus Lehnhoff**
Video director **Thomas Grimm**
Opus Arte ③ 🟥 OA0988D (5h 58' · NTSC · 16:9 · LPCM stereo and DTS 5.1 · 0)
Recorded live at Glyndebourne in 2007 ⒻⓄⓄ

The filming of each act begins annoyingly with a *Star Wars* storyline pan-in on the words 'Tristan und Isolde', 'Act 2' etc, using up the preludes. After that, however, comes a performance realised to Glyndebourne's highest standards – the chorus and stage brass are Bayreuth-level, the casting immaculate (they can all really sing these parts), and Bělohlávek's conducting balanced with a Goodall-like attention to the filigree detail of Wagner's new-wave scoring.

Old-style analyses of the music used to talk about the 'glance' motif. Lehnhoff's staging deploys a series of heartbreaking glances: Stemme's Isolde when Karnéus's Brangäne tells her she's taken the love draught, Stemme again when Tristan arrives in Act 2, Pape's Marke as he sees the lovers together and, at *Brokeback Mountain*-level, Skovhus's Kurwenal as he cradles Gambill's Tristan then breaks away, half in fear of his lord's death, half in fear of his feelings for him. In fact, has a Tristan ever been so deeply loved by his lady and squire as here, or felt so wretched at betraying his king? And is Skovhus actually the greatest Kurwenal yet recorded?

Roland Aeschlimann provides a geometrically attractive whorl of a standing set, concentric wooden circles telescoping towards a constantly varied horizon: a ship, a spaceship, everywhere, nowhere – perfect. The lighting (Robin Carter and Aeschlimann) has a genuine physical presence and seems to reinvent the colour blue. At the point of Isolde's almost belated arrival in Act 3, a surreal, Ingmar Bergman-like atmosphere permeates events: she arrives from behind on high as a figure of death and wraps him in a black cloak, while Skovhus's poignant Kurwenal gets a non-realistic, Brechtian centre-stage for his fights and death.

Additional recommendation

Tristan und Isolde
Jerusalem Tristan **Meier** Isolde **Hölle** King Marke **Struckmann** Kurwenal **Elming** Melot, A Young Sailor **Priew** Brangäne **Chor & Orch of the Bayreuth Festival / Barenboim** *Stage director* **Müller** *Video director* **Hohlfeld**
DG ② 📀 073 4439GH2 (3h 55' · NTSC · 16:9 · PCM stereo and DTS 5.1 · 0) 🄵 **OO**

This is a fine and intensely moving account of a supreme masterpiece of musical theatre. It is not perfect, but it is serious in its dramatic, theatrical intent. Müller's conception of the work is austere, not expecting setting or acting to get in the way of things which are best left to the music. Nowhere is this clearer than at the end, where Waltraud Meier sings the Liebestod from the front of the stage, with no semaphoring gestures and only facial expression and beautifully graded vocal projection to convey the essence of the drama. Her Tristan, Siegfried Jerusalem, is no less impressive. Add a marvellously sonorous Marke in Matthias Hölle, no weaknesses in the other roles, and the virtues stack up to something special.

Documentary

'Katharina Wagner's Baptism of Fire'
The road to her debut as director in Bayreuth

A film by **Dagmar Krauss**
ArtHaus Musik 📀 101 478 (82' · NTSC · 16:9 · 5.1 · 0) 🄵

Katharina, Wagner's great-granddaughter, is now, with her half-sister Eva, co-chief of the Bayreuth Festival. This documentary was made in 2007 about rehearsals for her festival production of *Die Meistersinger* – which was, effectively, an audition for that directorship, as well as being the first time since 1953 that a new member of the Wagner family had staged a Bayreuth show.

Katharina was deemed to have passed this test – with controversial colours. Her first two acts presented a wacky but relatively straightforward 'modern' view of the work. The arts in general, especially painting – as opposed to just music – were the subject of debate. Like a young Jackson Pollock, her Walther von Stolzing, a performance artist, attacked the serried ranks of the Masters' meeting tables and yellow Reclam pocket reference books, graffiti-ing away with a long-handled brush. Beckmesser was duly offended; a chain-smoking, informally dressed Sachs intrigued. But in the third act the director reversed the opera's traditional polarities. Beckmesser became the hero – a radical, obscene performance artist. Stolzing and Sachs (and Eva) sold out into a cosy, bourgeois world of Saturday night TV costumes and winner's cheques with uncomfortably national socialist overtones. Or that's how it was in 2007 – marked changes in this act have followed.

Dagmar Krauss's film, fluently shot and edited, shows the rehearsal process from director's introductory talk to the cast to first-night reception. Of course it has an 'official' Bayreuth imprimatur and is sympathetic, although not obsequious, to its young star (company tensions and one resignation are kept in). However, the decision to focus, in some detail, on the solving of production issues and problems – rather than the usual happy-clappy feigned bonhomie of rehearsal footage – makes the DVD valuable. It doesn't matter whether you think Katharina's concept is genius or rubbish, or even care much for Richard Wagner's music. This is an informative, pacy introduction to production work in progress.

A few comments about the presentation. The film runs 82 minutes but there are no chapter divisions. Credits on both booklet and DVD spine are minimalist: the cast are barely mentioned. The English language voice-over by the experienced Donald Arthur is a delight in its delivery and tone.

Sir William Walton   British 1902-1983

Both of Walton's parents were singers (his father was an organist, choirmaster and singing teacher) and at the age of 10 he won a place as a chorister at Christ Church, Oxford. He was encouraged in his youthful attempts at composition: when Sir Hubert Parry was shown some of his work he said, 'There's a lot in this chap, you must keep your eye on him'. Hugh Allen, the organist of New College, sponsored his admission to Christ College, enabling Walton to matriculate at the amazingly early age of 16.

While at Oxford he met the Sitwell family – Edith, Osbert and Sacheverell – who took him under their wing. For the next decade and more, Walton lived with them in their houses in Chelsea and Italy as a sort of adopted brother. He was only 19 when he composed the work that was to bring his name to public attention, Façade. The combination of Walton's witty, exuberant music and Edith Sitwell's nonsense verses were a cause célèbre after their first outing (the poetess 'declaiming' her own words through a megaphone and hidden behind a curtain).

Such hedonistic high spirits were not enough on which to build a serious career, though, and Walton soon proved that he was capable of great things with his Viola Concerto, the concert overture Portsmouth Point and, above all, the magnificent dramatic cantata Belshazzar's Feast and his fizzing Symphony No 1. He composed his first film score in 1934 (Escape Me Never) and discovered a medium to which his lyrico-dramatic gifts were ideally suited. It was during his work on the film of Shakespeare's As You Like It (1936) that he first met Laurence Olivier and the three Shakespeare films in which he collaborated with the great actor (Henry V, Hamlet and Richard III) put him in a class of his own as a film composer.

As early as 1939 Walton, 'the white hope of British music', pronounced prophetically, 'today's white hope is tomorrow's black sheep...I've just gone through the first halcyon periods and am just about ripe for my critical damnation'. Indeed, Walton wrote little during the decade after the Second World War. He had married the Argentinian Susana Gil in 1948 in Buenos Aires and shortly afterwards settled on the island of Ischia off the coast of Naples. His opera Troilus and Cressida (1954), the Cello Concerto (1956) and the Second Symphony (1960) were all coolly received by the critics, a reaction to his unfashionable late-Romanticism. By the time he died his music was once again coming back into fashion.

Cello Concerto

Cello Concerto[a] Violin Concerto[b]
[a]**Tim Hugh** vc [b]**Dong-Suk Kang** vn
English Northern Philharmonia / Paul Daniel
Naxos 8 554325 (60' · DDD)   Ⓢ Ⓞ ➤

Tim Hugh, outstanding in every way, gives a reading of the Concerto that's the most searching yet. More than direct rivals he finds a thoughtfulness, a sense of mystery, of inner meditation in Walton's great lyrical ideas – notably the main themes of the outer movements and the yearning melody of the central section of the second-movement *Scherzo*. Most strikingly, his *pianissimos* are more extreme. The openings of both the outer movements are more hushed than ever heard before on disc, with Hugh in inner intensity opting for broader speeds than usual. Not that he dawdles, as the overall timings of each movement make plain, and the bravura writing finds him equally con-

centrated, always sounding strong and spontaneous in the face of any technical challenges.

In the Violin Concerto Dong-Suk Kang plays immaculately with fresh, clean-cut tone, pure and true above the stave. Many will also applaud the way that Kang opts for speeds rather faster and more flowing than have latterly been favoured. That follows the example of Heifetz as the original interpreter, and Kang similarly relishes the bravura writing, not least in diamond-sharp articulation in the *Scherzo*.

Paul Daniel and the English Northern Philharmonia play with equal flair and sympathy. But though the recorded textures are commendably clear, the strings are too distantly balanced, lacking weight, so that moments where the violins are required to surge up warmly sound thin – hardly the fault of the players. An excellent coupling, though, with the Cello Concerto offering new depths of insight.

Additional recommendation

Walton Cello Concerto
Coupled with **Walton** Passacaglia **Bloch** Solo Cello Suite No 1 **Britten** Solo Cello Suite No 2, Op 80 – Ciaconna **Ligeti** Cello Sonata
Wispelwey vc **Sydney SO / Tate**
Onyx ONYX4042 (66' · DDD)   Ⓕ ➤

Peter Wispelwey here couples the Walton Concerto with a sequence of works for unaccompanied cello. As one would expect, his playing is flawless, though in the Walton, fast passages such as the central *Scherzo* are more successful in their brilliance than the slow, ruminative ones

---

Viola Concerto

Viola Concerto. Symphony No 2.
Johannesburg Festival Overture
Lars Anders Tomter va **English Northern Philharmonia / Paul Daniel**
Naxos 8 553402 (61' · DDD)   Ⓢ ➤

This disc opens with one of the wittiest, most exuberant performances of the *Johannesburg Festival Overture*: Daniel encourages the orchestra's virtuoso wind and brass soloists to point the jazz rhythms idiomatically, making the music sparkle. The Viola Concerto is just as delectably pointed, the whole performance magnetic. Tomter's tone, with its rapid-flicker vibrato, lacks the warmth of Kennedy's (reviewed below), but the vibrato is only obtrusive in that upper-middle register and his intonation is immaculate, his attack consistently clean, to match the crisp ensemble of the orchestra. Although he adopts relatively measured speeds both for the *Scherzo* and the jaunty opening theme of the finale, the rhythmic lift brings out the *scherzando* jollity of the latter all the more.

Daniel's keen observance of dynamic markings is again brought out in the stuttering fanfare theme of the *Scherzo*, with muted trumpets and trombones for once played *pianissimo* as marked.

The close of the slow epilogue has never been recorded with such a profound hush as here, subsiding in darkness, and the recording team is to be complimented on getting such beautiful sound, clean with plenty of bloom. Paul Daniel adopts a relatively broad tempo in the Symphony's first movement, and the flowing tempo for the central slow movement makes for a lighter, less passionate result too. The finale, with its brassy first statement of the Passacaglia theme, brings fine dynamic contrasts, but again Litton and others produce a fatter, weightier sound, which on balance is preferable. Yet Daniel's view is a very valid one, to round off most convincingly an invaluable addition to the Walton discography.

Walton Viola Concerto (original version)[a] **Rubbra**
Meditations on a Byzantine Hymn. Viola Concerto[a]
Lawrence Power va
[a]**BBC Scottish Symphony Orchestra / Ilan Volkov**
Hyperion CDA67587 (61' · DDD)   Ⓕ Ⓓ➔

It is good to welcome a modern recording of Walton's Viola Concerto in its original orchestration. When in 1938 Frederick Riddle, principal viola of the LSO, first recorded this seminal work, Walton had yet to slim down the orchestration to make the concerto more accessible. But even dedicated Waltonians may not notice much difference, particularly when in this fine recording the balance marginally favours the solo instrument. Yet as Leo Black suggests in his booklet-notes, the result 'perhaps conveys to a greater extent the freshness and grittiness of Walton's original conception'.

This was in many ways the breakthrough work in Walton's early career; it brought together in full maturity his distinctive mixture of yearning lyricism and jazzily syncopated writing. Lawrence Power serves the work superbly. Riddle's is arguably still the finest version (Dutton), with speeds marginally faster than modern versions, something not much approved by Walton. Yet Power is not much slower than Riddle in the *Andante comodo* first movement. In the finale differences in timing between Riddle and modern versions is greater, largely because of the expansive epilogue, which clearly echoes the accompanied cadenzas of Elgar's Violin Concerto.

The two Rubbra items here are welcome. His orchestration in the Concerto is never as clear as Walton's but it suits his musical idiom with its reliance on perfect fourths and other open intervals, as well as plainsong. The *Meditations on a Byzantine Theme*, the first recording in the version for unaccompanied viola, makes an apt extra. All told, a superb disc, much to be welcomed.

Violin Concerto

Violin Concerto. Viola Concerto
Nigel Kennedy vn/va
Royal Philharmonic Orchestra / André Previn
EMI Great Artists of the Century 562813-2 (72' · DDD)
                    Ⓕ Ⓞ Ⓞ ➔

Even next to the finest individual recordings of the two works, differently coupled, Kennedy provides formidable competition. Warmly expressive as Kennedy's mentor Menuhin was in both works, spaciously romantic and characteristically individual in every phrase, he was not a natural Waltonian, even with the composer to guide him. The comparison with Kennedy is fascinating. Not surprisingly, Kennedy's jazz sympathies give his playing a natural bite in the sharply syncopated passages so typical of Walton, matching Previn's similarly jazz-founded understanding.

The most controversial point of both interpretations of the Viola Concerto comes in the speed of the *Andante comodo* first movement. Kennedy is almost as slow as Menuhin and far slower than usual – but his pulse is steadier. The aching melancholy of that lovely opening, the dreamy quality of the second subject (*sognando* the marking) are caught more hauntingly. In the finale Kennedy's natural contrasting of the romantic and the *scherzando* sides of Walton are again most convincing, and the epilogue brings the most magic moment, when the *pianissimo* return of the first movement main theme is so hushed you hear it as though from the distance.

The marking *sognando* also comes at the opening of the Violin Concerto, and again Kennedy captures it beautifully. Kennedy's is a gloriously rich and red-blooded reading of the whole work, bringing ripe playing in the big romantic melodies balanced with formidable bravura in the contrasting passages written with Heifetz in mind.

For a coupling of two of the most beautiful string concertos written in the 20th century, this Kennedy record will set standards for many years to come. The recording is full and rounded, well-balanced with the soloist's wide dynamic range fully conveyed.

Symphonies

Symphony No 1 in B flat minor[a].
Violin Concerto[b]. Viola Concerto[c].
Cello Concerto[d]. Sinfonia concertante[e]
[b]**Jascha Heifetz** vn [c]**Yuri Bashmet** va [d]**Gregor Piatigorsky** vc [e]**Kathryn Stott** pf [ac]**London Symphony Orchestra / **[a]**André Previn, **[c]**Neeme Järvi; **[b]**Philharmonia Orchestra / William Walton; **[d]**Boston Symphony Orchestra / Charles Munch; **[e]**Royal Philharmonic Orchestra / Vernon Handley**
RCA Red Seal [b]mono ② 74321 92575-2 (145' · ADD/
[ce]DDD). Recorded [d]1959, [a]1966, [b]1950, [e]1989, [c]1998
                    Ⓜ Ⓞ Ⓞ

RCA's two-disc collection includes the premiere recording of the Cello Concerto with Piatigorsky – who commissioned the work – and the Boston Symphony under Charles Munch. Here is a high-powered reading, given an upfront recording, commendably full and open for 1959. Similarly Heifetz, who commissioned the Violin Concerto, remains supreme as an interpreter of that work, urgent beyond any rival as well as passionate. Here he plays with the composer conducting the Philharmonia. The 1950 mono recording has been nicely opened up, putting more air around the sound, making the absence of stereo a minimal drawback. The other two *concertante* works come in digital versions: Kathryn Stott adventurously going back to the original more elaborate version of the *Sinfonia concertante*, and Yuri Bashmet bringing his yearningly Slavonic temperament and masterly virtuosity to the Viola Concerto.

Bashmet's partners are the ideal combination of Previn and the LSO, and it's Previn's vintage version of the First Symphony with the LSO of an earlier generation that sets the seal on the whole package. Previn has never been matched, let alone surpassed. Also remarkable is the clarity, definition and sense of presence of the 1966 recording, with the stereo spectrum more sharply focused than in the digital recordings.

Symphony No 1. Partita
English Northern Philharmonia / Paul Daniel
Naxos 8 553180 (64' · DDD)　　　　⑤**OO**➔

Daniel demonstrates clearly here his natural affinity with Walton's music. In the sustained paragraphs of the First Symphony he knows unerringly how to build up tension to breaking point, before resolving it, and then building again – a quality vital above all in the first and third movements. He's freer than many in his use of *rubato* too, again often a question of building and resolving tension, as well as in the degree of elbow-room he allows for jazzy syncopations, always idiomatic. This symphony, with its heavy orchestration, would certainly have benefited from rather drier sound, but well-judged microphone balance allows ample detail through. Only occasionally do you feel a slight lack of body in high violin tone, a tiny reservation. Daniel's reading of the *Partita* brings out above all the work's joyfulness. It may not be quite as crisp in its ensemble as that of the dedicatees (Szell and the Cleveland Orchestra), but the degree of wildness, with dissonances underlined, proves a positive advantage in conveying enjoyment. In the slow movement Daniel at a relatively slow speed is markedly more expressive than those brilliant models, again a point which makes the performance more endearing.

Irrespective of price, this is a version of the much-recorded symphony that competes with the finest ever, and outshines most.

Additional recommendations

Symphony No 1
LSO / C Davis
LSO Live LSO0076; 💿 LSO0576 (46' · DDD)
Recorded live 2005　　　　⑤➔
When Sir Colin Davis conducted Walton's First Symphony at the Barbican it was greeted by ecstatic reviews – and rightly so. It was as though critics had suddenly rediscovered this iconic work. This new recording, the first version on SACD at a low price, finds a welcome place.

Symphony No 1[a]
Coupled with Belshazzar's Feast[b]
[b]**Noble** bar [b]**LPO Choir; Philharmonic Prom Orch / Boult**
Somm Céleste Series [a]mono SOMMCD094 (78' · ADD)
Recorded 1950s
Boult's interpretation of the Symphony impresses by dint of its thrusting energy, logic and cumulative grip. At the same time, it must be conceded that the orchestral playing falls some way short in terms of finesse. Nor is the early stereo Walthamstow Town Hall sound anything to write home about. Still, there's no missing the infectious commitment either here or in *Belshazzar's Feast*.

Symphony No 2[c]. Variations on a Theme by Hindemith[d]. Partita[c]. Violin Concerto[b]. Johannesburg Festival Overture[e]. Capriccio burlesco[e]. Belshazzar's Feast[a]
[a]**Walter Cassel** bar [b]**Zino Francescatti** vn [a]**Rutgers University Choir;** [cd]**Cleveland Orchestra / George Szell;** [ab]**Philadelphia Orchestra / Eugene Ormandy;** [e]**New York Philharmonic Orchestra / André Kostelanetz**
Sony Classical ② SB2K 89934 (143' · ADD)
Recorded 1959-73　　　　Ⓑ

Outstanding are the vintage Szell performances with the Cleveland Orchestra, in sheer brilliance never likely to be outshone. The composer himself was bowled over by Szell's 1961 Second Symphony, a work till then rather discounted, which drew an interpretation not just brilliant but passionate. In Szell's high-powered reading the *Hindemith* Variations, too, hang together superbly, and the *Partita*, a Cleveland commission, is scintillating from first to last.

André Kostelanetz turns the *Capriccio burlesco* into a sparkling comedy overture, a work he was the first to conduct, and the *Johannesburg Festival Overture* is made to sparkle too, arguably the finest of the Walton overtures. Both the Violin Concerto and *Belshazzar's Feast* are given expressive performances by Ormandy conducting the Philadelphia Orchestra. In the Concerto Zino Francescatti is powerful and passionate with his rapid, slightly nervy vibrato, while in *Belshazzar* choir and soloist are as committed as any British performers, even if their pronunciation of 'Isaiah' is pure American, the second syllable rhyming with 'day'. The sound is typically upfront and not as warm as it might be, though with plenty of atmosphere. Buy it for Szell's Second – an account Walton described as 'fantastic and stupendous'.

Spitfire Prelude and Fugue

Spitfire Prelude and Fugue. Sinfonia concertante[a]. Variations on a Theme by Hindemith. March – The History of the English Speaking Peoples
[a]**Peter Donohoe** pf
English Northern Philharmonia / Paul Daniel
Naxos 8 553869 (53' · DDD)　　　　⑤**OO**➔

Naxos opts for the original version of the *Sinfonia concertante* rather than Walton's revision, with piano writing and orchestration slimmed down. Walton himself, before he died, suggested such a return. As soloist Peter Donohoe plays with power and flamboyance, brought home the more when the piano is very forwardly balanced, too much so for a work which doesn't aim to be a full concerto, leaving the orchestra a little pale behind. Even so, hopefully this account, broad in the first movement, flowing in the central *Andante*, will persuade others to take it up, young man's music built on striking, colourful ideas, used with crisp concision.

Paul Daniel is splendid at interpreting the jazzy syncopations with the right degree of freedom, and in the *Spitfire Prelude and Fugue* he adds to the impact by taking the big march tune faster than many, similarly demonstrating that *The History of the English Speaking Peoples March*, buried for rather too long, is a match for Walton's other ceremonial marches. Best of all is the performance of the *Hindemith Variations*, given here with winning panache. The strings of the English Northern Philharmonia may not be as weighty as in some rival versions, but the articulation is brilliant, and the complex textures are all the more transparent. The fire and energy of the performance have never been surpassed on disc.

Façade

Walton Façade – An Entertainment[a]
Lambert Salome – Suite
[a]**Eleanor Bron,** [a]**Richard Stilgoe** spkrs
Nash Ensemble (Paul Watkins vc Philippa Davies fl
Richard Hosford cl John Wallace tpt Martin
Robertson [a]sax Simon Lembrick perc) /
David Lloyd-Jones
Hyperion CDA67239 (72' · DDD · T)   ⓕ❶➔

The *Façade* entertainment – poems by Edith Sitwell to music by the then-unknown William Walton – was an amorphous creation, a collection of settings built up over the years between 1922 and 1928. David Lloyd-Jones has devised an order for the 34 items (including the opening fanfare) which is arguably the best yet, avoiding the anticlimactic effect of *Façade 2* being separated. Eleanor Bron and Richard Stilgoe make an excellent pair of reciters, and the recording in a natural acoustic balances them well – not too close. They inflect the words more than Edith Sitwell and early interpreters did, but still keep a stylised manner, meticulously obeying the rhythms specified in the score. Not everyone will like the way Stilgoe adopts accents – Mummerset for 'Mariner Man' and 'Country Dance', Scots for 'Scotch Rhapsody', and something like southern-state American for the jazz rhythms of 'Old Sir Faulk' – but he's the most fluent *Façade* reciter on disc so far, with phenomenally clear articulation. Eleanor Bron is also meticulous over rhythm, in slower poems adopting a trance-like manner, which is effective and in style.

Under David Lloyd-Jones the brilliant sextet of players from the Nash Ensemble couldn't be more idiomatic.

Piano Quartet

Piano Quartet[a]. Violin Sonata[b]. Anon in Love[c].
Passacaglia[d]. Façade – Valse[e]
[c]**John Mark Ainsley** ten [c]**Craig Ogden** gtr
[a]**Nash Ensemble** ([b]Marianne Thorsen vn Lawrence
Power va [d]Paul Watkins vc [be]Ian Brown pf)
Hyperion CDA67340 (76' · DDD · T)   ⓕ❶➔

This excellent Hyperion issue brings together a wide-ranging group of Walton's chamber works, from his earliest major work, the Piano Quartet, originally written when he was 16, to his last instrumental piece, the *Passacaglia*, which he composed for Rostropovich when he was nearly 80. As a substantial bonus there's the little song-cycle for tenor and guitar, *Anon in Love*, as well as the two shorter pieces.

Helped by a spacious recording, the extra lightness and clarity brings an element of fantasy into such a movement as the *Scherzo* of the Piano Quartet and an extra tenderness into the lovely slow movement. Nowhere else does Walton so enthusiastically use modal thematic material, starting with the mysterious opening theme, which the Nash players take very reflectively at a speed much slower than the movement's main tempo, *Allegramente*. It's an astonishingly confident work for so young a composer, with adventurous writing for the strings that belies the fact that Walton was no string player.

The Violin Sonata, a more elusive work, long underestimated, is given an equally persuasive performance, with Marianne Thorsen, accompanied by Ian Brown, freely expressive. John Mark Ainsley is totally undaunted by the taxing vocal writing of *Anon in Love*, originally designed for Peter Pears. And Craig Ogden is an ideal accompanist, totally idiomatic, adding sparkle to the vigorous songs in this offbeat collection. Though Ian Brown gives a slightly sluggish account of *Façade*'s 'Valse' – in the awkward piano transcription ascribed to Walton himself – cellist Paul Watkins crowns the disc with a fine reading of the solo *Passacaglia*.

String Quartets

Piano Quartet in D minor[a]. String Quartet in A minor
[a]**Peter Donohoe** pf **Maggini Quartet** (Laurence
Jackson, David Angel vns Martin Outram va Michal
Kaznowski vc)
Naxos 8 554646 (58' · DDD)   ⓢ❶➔

The Maggini Quartet give refined and powerful performances in this Naxos release. The opening of the 1947 String Quartet is presented in hushed intimacy, making the contrast all the greater when Walton's richly lyrical writing emerges in full power. There's a tender, wistful quality here, which culminates in a rapt, intense account of the slow movement, where the world of late Beethoven comes much closer than most interpreters have appreciated. The poignancy of those two longer movements is then set against the clean bite of the second-movement *Scherzo* and the brief hectic finale, with their clear and transparent textures. With Peter Donohoe a powerful and incisive presence, and the Maggini Quartet again playing most persuasively, the early Piano Quartet is also given a performance of high contrasts, enhanced by a refined recording which conveys genuine *pianissimos* that are free from highlighting. If, in the first three movements, the pentatonic writing gives little idea of the mature Walton to come, some characteristic rhythmic and other devices are already apparent. It's in the finale that one gets the strongest Waltonian flavour in vigorously purposeful argument, though there the echoes are different, and Stravinsky's *Petrushka* is an obvious influence. The only reservation is that the piano is rather too forwardly balanced.

Belshazzar's Feast

Belshazzar's Feast[a]. Coronation Te Deum. Gloria[b]
[b]**Ameral Gunson** *contr* [b]**Neil Mackie** *ten* [a]**Gwynne Howell**, [b]**Stephen Roberts** *bars* **Bach Choir; Philharmonia Orchestra / Sir David Willcocks**
Chandos CHAN8760 (62' · DDD · T)   Ⓕ Ⓞ ☈

With Sir David Willcocks in charge of the choir which he directed since for nearly 40 years, one needn't fear that the composer's many near-impossible demands of the chorus in all three of these masterpieces won't be met with elegance and poise. In *Belshazzar* there's also a predictably fine balance of the forces to ensure that as much detail as possible is heard from both chorus and orchestra, even when Walton is bombarding us from all corners of the universe with extra brass bands and all manner of clamorous percussion in praise of pagan gods. Such supremely musical concerns bring their own rewards in a work that can often seem vulgar. The revelation here is the sustained degree of dramatic thrust, exhilaration and what Herbert Howells called 'animal joy' in the proceedings. How marvellous, too, to hear the work paced and scaled to avoid the impression of reduced voltage after the big moments. Gwynne Howell is the magnificently steady, firm and dark toned baritone. The *Gloria* and *Coronation Te Deum* are informed with the same concerns: accuracy and professional polish are rarely allowed to hinder these vital contributions to the British choral tradition. The recording's cathedral-like acoustic is as ideal for the *Te Deum*'s ethereal antiphonal effects, as it is for *Belshazzar*'s glorious spectacle; and Chandos matches Willcocks's care for balance, bar by bar.

Additional recommendation

Belshazzar's Feast
Coupled with Job

Terfel *bass-bar;* **BBC Singers; BBC SO / A Davis**
Warner Apex 0927 44394-2 (78' · DDD)   Ⓑ
Bryn Terfel makes an electrifying soloist in Davis's recommendable version of *Belshazzar*, and brings the important solo utterances vividly before us. Walton's rarely performed ballet is equally fine.

Belshazzar's Feast[b]   Ⓗ
Coupled with Viola Concerto[a]. Façade – Suite No 1[c]; Suite No 2[d]
[b]**Noble**, [a]**Riddle**; [b]**Huddersfield Choral Soc;** [a]**LSO;** [b]**Liverpool PO;** [cd]**LPO / Walton**
Pearl mono GEM0171 (76' · ADD)
Recorded [c]1936, [d]1938, [b]1943   Ⓜ Ⓞ Ⓞ
A fine CD transfer of Walton's own premiere recording of *Belshazzar's Feast* is coupled here with two other important first recordings of his. In some ways these have never been surpassed musically. That applies especially to the *Belshazzar* performance, made with lavish resources at the height of the war and with Dennis Noble unsurpassed as the baritone soloist.

Coronation Te Deum

Coronation Te Deum. A Litany: Drop, drop slow tears. Magnificat and Nunc dimittis. Where does the uttered music go?. Jubilate Deo. Henry V – Touch her soft lips and part; Passacaglia. Cantico del sole. The Twelve. Set me as a seal upon thine heart. Antiphon. Missa brevis
Christopher Whitton *org* **St John's College Choir, Cambridge / Christopher Robinson**
Naxos 8 555793 (66' · DDD)   Ⓢ Ⓞ Ⓞ ☈

This latest addition to Naxos's English Church Music series isn't just a first-rate bargain but provides a distinctive alternative to the Finzi Singers in the Chandos Walton Edition, in its use of boy trebles. The presence of boys' voices consistently brings extra freshness to the St John's Choir's performances, giving them the sort of bite one can imagine the composer having in mind, with Waltonian syncopations wonderfully idiomatic in their crisp articulation. Smaller in scale, with the organ set behind the choir, these more intimate readings also convey more clearly the impression of church performances, a clear advantage in the liturgical items above all, not just the delightful *Missa brevis*, but the *Jubilate*, and the *Magnificat* and *Nunc dimittis*. You might argue that this collegiate choir is on the small side for the big ceremonial *Te Deum* written for the Queen's Coronation in 1953, but there, more than ever, the freshness and bite make for extra clarity hard to achieve with bigger forces. With Robinson and the St John's Choir the words aren't just sharply defined but are given life, with subtle *rubato* and fine shading of dynamic.

Coronation Te Deum[ab]. A Queen's Fanfare[b]. A Litany (three versions). The Twelve[a]. Set me as a seal upon thine heart. Magnificat and Nunc dimittis[a]. Where does the uttered music go?. Jubilate Deo[a]. Missa

Brevis[a]. Cantico del sole. Make we joy now in this fest. King Herod and the Cock. All this time. What cheer?. Antiphon[ab]
[a]**James Vivian** org **Polyphony;**
[b]**The Wallace Collection / Stephen Layton**
Hyperion CDA67330 (77' · DDD · T/N) Ⓕ**O**➟

This disc has important bonuses that all Walton devotees will value. The inclusion of the Wallace Collection brings an immediate advantage in the first choral item, the *Coronation Te Deum*, when the extra bite of brass adds greatly to the impact of a piece originally designed for very large forces in Westminster Abbey. Brass also adds to the impact of the final item, *Antiphon*, one of Walton's very last works, setting George Herbert's hymn *Let all the world in every corner sing*. The new disc also includes Walton's four carols, which makes this as comprehensive a collection of Walton's shorter choral pieces as could be imagined. As for the performances and recording, the professional group, Polyphony, with sopranos very boyish, have many of the advantages that the St John's Choir offer on Naxos in bright choral sound set in an ecclesiastical atmosphere. The acoustic of Hereford Cathedral is a little washy in places, and the balance of some of the solo voices is odd at times, yet the merits of these performances far outweigh any slight reservations, with the professional singers a degree more warmly expressive than the all-male St John's Choir.

Troilus and Cressida

Troilus and Cressida
Judith Howarth sop Cressida **Arthur Davies** ten
Troilus **Clive Bayley** bass Calkas **Nigel Robson** ten
Pandarus **Alan Opie** bar Diomede **James Thornton**
bar Antenor **David Owen-Lewis** bass Horaste
Yvonne Howard mez Evadne **Peter Bodenham** ten
Priest **Keith Mills** ten Soldier **Bruce Budd** bass First
Watchman **Stephen Dowson** bass Second
Watchman **Brian Cookson** ten Third Watchman
**Chorus of Opera North; English Northern
Philharmonia / Richard Hickox**
Chandos ② CHAN9370/1 (133' · DDD · N/T)
Ⓕ**OOO**➟

Ⓖ   *Troilus and Cressida* is here powerfully presented as an opera for the central repertory, traditional in its red-blooded treatment of a big classical subject. Few operas since Puccini's have such a rich store of instantly memorable tunes as this. Walton wrote the piece in the wake of the first great operatic success of his rival, Benjamin Britten. What more natural than for Walton, by this time no longer an *enfant terrible* of British music but an Establishment figure, to turn his back on operas devoted like Britten's to offbeat subjects and to go back to an older tradition using a classical love story, based on Chaucer (not Shakespeare). As Richard Hickox suggests, fashion after 40 years matters little, and the success of the Opera North production in January 1995 indicated that at last the

time had come for a big, warmly Romantic, sharply dramatic work to be appreciated on its own terms.

This recording was made under studio conditions during the run of the opera in Leeds. The discs confirm what the live performances suggested, that Walton's tautening of the score, coupled with a restoration of the original soprano register for Cressida, proved entirely successful.

Hickox conducts a performance that's magnetic from beginning to end. The scene is atmospherically set in Act 1 by the chorus, initially off-stage, but then with the incisive Opera North chorus snapping out thrilling cries of 'We are accurs'd!'. The first soloist one hears is the High Priest, Calkas, Cressida's father, about to defect to the Greeks, and the role is superbly taken by the firm, dark-toned Clive Bayley. Troilus's entry and his declaration of love for Cressida bring Waltonian sensuousness and the first statements of the soaring Cressida theme. Arthur Davies isn't afraid of using his head voice for *pianissimos*, so contrasting the more dramatically with the big outbursts and his ringing top notes. This is a young-sounding hero, Italianate of tone. Similarly, Judith Howarth's Cressida is quite girlish, and she brings out the vulnerability of the character along with sweetness and warmth. After Calkas has defected to the Greeks, her cry of 'He has deserted us and Troy!' conveys genuine fear, with her will undermined.

All told, although some fine music has been cut, the tautened version is far more effective both musically and dramatically, with no longueurs. The role of Diomede, Cressida's Greek suitor, can seem one-dimensional, but Alan Opie in one of his finest performances on record sharpens the focus, making him a genuine threat, with the element of nobility fully allowed. As Antenor, James Thornton sings strongly but is less steady than the others, while Yvonne Howard is superb in the mezzo role of Evadne, Cressida's treacherous servant and confidante. Not just the chorus but the orchestra of Opera North respond with fervour.

Naturally and idiomatically they observe the Waltonian *rubato* and the lifting of jazzily syncopated rhythms which Hickox as a dedicated Waltonian instils, echoing the composer's own example. As for the recorded sound, the bloom of the acoustic enhances the score, helped by the wide dynamic range.

Peter Warlock   British 1894-1930

Peter Warlock (the nom de plume of Philip Heseltine) did not receive any official music education though he was soon mixing with composers such as Delius, Van Dieren, Moeran and Lambert. He edited English works of the Elizabethan era and wrote a large output of songs (including The Curlew for tenor and sextet). His output also includes choral music and a few instrumental pieces (the best-known – and his most performed work – is the Capriol Suite for strings, 1926, based on 16th-century dances).

Choral Works

Warlock A Cornish Carol. I saw a fair maiden.
Benedicamus Domino. The Full Heart. The Rich
Cavalcade. Corpus Christi. All the flowers of the
spring. As Dewe in Aprylle. Bethlehem Down.
Cornish Christmas Carol **Moeran** Songs of
Springtime. Phyllida and Corydon
Finzi Singers / Paul Spicer
Chandos CHAN9182 (76' · DDD · T)   ⒻⓄ▶

The Peter Warlock of the evergreen *Capriol
Suite* and the boisterous songs seems a world
away from the introverted and intense artist of
these unaccompanied choral carols. Perhaps
Warlock's real genius was an ability to create
profound expression in short musical structures,
but even the more outgoing pieces – the joyful
Benedicamus Domino and the *Cornish Christmas
Carol*, with its gentle hint at 'The First Nowell'
– have an artistic integrity which raises them
high above the level of the syrup of modern-day
carol settings. Given performances as openly
sincere and sensitive as these, few could be
unmoved. In the two Moeran madrigal suites
there's an indefinable Englishness – the result of
a deep awareness of tradition and love of the
countryside. The Finzi Singers' warm-toned,
richly expressive voices capture the very essence
of this uniquely lovely music.

Songs

The Wind from the West. To the Memory of a
F Great Singer. Take, O take those lips away. As ever I
saw. The bayley berith the bell away. There is a lady.
Lullaby. Sweet content. Late summer. The Singer.
Rest sweet nymphs. Sleep. A Sad Song. In an arbour
green. Autumn Twilight. I held love's head. Thou
gav'st me leave to kiss. Yarmouth Fair. Pretty Ring
Time. A Prayer to St Anthony. The Sick Heart. Robin
Goodfellow. Jillian of Berry. Fair and True. Ha'nacker
Mill. The Night. My Own Country. The First Mercy.
The Lover's Maze. Cradle Song. Sigh no more, ladies.
Passing by. The Contented Lover. The Fox
John Mark Ainsley ten **Roger Vignoles** pf
Hyperion CDA66736 (69' · DDD · T)   ⒻⓄ▶

Philip Heseltine, so strangely renamed, didn't
facilitate either the singing or the playing of his
songs. For the voice they have a way of passing
awkwardly between registers, and, though the
high notes aren't very high, they tend to be
uncomfortably placed. The pianist, caught for
long in a pool of chromatics, suddenly finds his
hands flying in both directions. Yet, for the
singer with the control of breath and command
of voice that John Mark Ainsley so splendidly
employs, and for a pianist with Roger Vignoles's
sureness of touch and insight, they must be wonderfully satisfying, for there's such a love of song
implicit in them and they speak with such a personal voice. The programme here is arranged
chronologically, 1911-30. Favourite sources are
early and Elizabethan poems, and the verse of

contemporaries such as Belloc, Symons and
Bruce Blunt. Even the earliest setting, 'The
Wind from the West', has the characteristic
touch of a lyrical impulse, directly responsive to
words, and a fastidious avoidance of strophic or
harmonic banality. Often a private unease works
within the chromaticism, as in the 'Cradle
Song', yet nothing could be more wholehearted
in gaiety when he's in the mood ('In an arbour
green', 'Robin Goodfellow', 'Jillian of Berry').
Ainsley sings with fine reserves of power as well
as softness; he phrases beautifully, and all the
nuance that's so essential for these songs (in
'Sleep', say) is most sensitively judged. Vignoles
is entirely at one with singer and composer.

Carl Maria von Weber
German 1786-1826

*Weber's father was a keen amateur violinist and
dreamt of his children becoming great musicians. His
niece Constanze was married to Mozart (making
Weber Mozart's first cousin by marriage). His son
did not, on the face of it, seem cut out for music – he
was born with a diseased hip and walked with a limp
all his life – but he was to become a precociously talented musician. Carl Maria's first teacher was his
stepbrother, a pupil of Haydn; his next was Haydn's
composer brother Michael.*

*By 14 Weber had composed his first opera (Das
Waldmädchen). By 1811 he had had a further three
produced. At the same time he had established himself
as a piano virtuoso and, two years later, was made
conductor of the German Opera in Prague. The King
of Saxony invited him to take charge of the German
Opera Theatre in Dresden and Weber opened his
first season there in 1817. Here he befriended a lawyer and writer called Friedrich Kind and suggested to
him the idea for what was to become his masterpiece,
Der Freischütz. Its composition occupied him for
three years. Spontini was the ruling master of opera
in Germany, dictating the Italian-French musical
tradition from the Berlin Opera against a rising
German nationalism. When Der Freischütz received
its triumphant premiere in 1821 the curtain had
been finally raised on the new Romantic movement.*

*After the moderate success of his next venture,
Euryanthe, Weber was obliged to go to Marienbad
for a cure for his tuberculosis, returning to begin
writing Oberon, commissioned by London's Covent
Garden. He was well enough in April 1826 to travel
to England for the premiere, which met with huge
success. Weber knew he was a doomed man and a few
months later he died. He was buried in London, his
remains later transferred to Dresden in 1844.*

Clarinet Concertos

Clarinet Concertos – No 1; No 2. Clarinet Concertino.
Clarinet Quintet (arr Kantorow)
Martin Fröst cl
Tapiola Sinfonietta / Jean-Jacques Kantorow
BIS ⊚ BIS-SACD1523 (74' · DDD/DSD)   ⒻⒹ▶

Martin Fröst's style of playing is well suited to Weber: he has a clear, fresh tone and fingers undefeated by even the most sensational of the applause music that ends some of these works. He is not afraid of considerable tempo variations within a movement, as Weber is on record as having wanted.

This all contributes to a charming, eloquent performance of the *Concertino*. However, the F minor Concerto (No 1) does not need its opening *Allegro* to be taken quite so fast for it to make its points, and the finale, here sounding like a brisk *allegro* verging on *presto*, is actually marked *Allegretto*, which gives the music more space and freedom. The slow movements of both concertos are played simply, without affectation, and Fröst remembers that the *alla polacca* of the finale of No 2 is a dance. He takes a bright lead in the Quintet; it is played here as a concerto with full strings, which is a pity but, given the *quatuor concertant* nature of the work, not as disastrous as it would be with Mozart. This is a fresh, amiable performance that responds to the music's varied nature.

Fröst also plays some cadenzas of his own, rejecting those which were later added by Carl Baermann, son of the much-admired dedicatee of the works, Heinrich Baermann. He further adds a few flourishes: unnecessarily, but there is no need to be too purist here. These are attractive, exhilarating performances, clearly recorded so as to do justice to the orchestral effects which were always part of Weber's exuberant invention.

Clarinet Concertos Nos 1 & 2.
Clarinet Quintet (orch version)
Fabio di Càsola cl **Russian Chamber Philharmonic, St Petersburg / Juri Gilbo**
Sony Classical 🎧 88697 37632-2 (67' · DDD) Ⓕ**O**▶

Such enticing works, admirable showpieces too, have received many recordings, but Fabio di Càsola's performances are dazzling and Juri Gilbo's persuasive partnership in slow movements is Romantic in the best Weberian operatic style. The twirly-whirly *Menuetto capriccio* of the arranged Quintet is deliciously done, and the closing *gioioso* is wonderfully infectious. The performances are capped by the bravura scales in the final jaunty *Allegro polacca* of Concerto No 2. The SACD sound is splendidly atmospheric, so this can be strongly recommended.

Additional recommendation

Clarinet Concertos Nos 1 & 2. Clarinet Concertino.
Clarinet Quintet
Kriikku cl **New Helsinki Qt; Finnish RSO / Oramo**
Ondine ODE895-2 (76' · DDD) Ⓕ**O**▶
  The formidable difficulties hold no terrors for Kriikku. He plays the First Concerto as a slightly tense, witty work, giving the *Adagio* a long-breathed lyricism and the finale humour as well as wit. The Second Concerto is treated as a more lyri-

cal and dramatic work, with an elegant *polacca* finale, and there's a beautiful length of phrasing in the *Andante*, as there is in the 'Fantasia' movement of the Quintet.

Overtures

Overtures – Euryanthe, J291; Peter Schmoll und seine Nachbarn, J8; Oberon, J306; Der Beherrscher der Geister, J122; Preciosa, J279; Silvana, J87; Abu Hassan, J106; Der Freischütz, J277. Turandot – Overture and Act 2 March, J75. Jubel-Ouvertüre, J245
New Zealand Symphony Orchestra / Antoni Wit
Naxos 8 570296 (76' · DDD) Ⓢ**OO**▶

Here are all six opera overtures, plus those for the incidental music to *Preciosa* and *Turandot*. *The Ruler of the Spirits* and *Jubel* are independent pieces, the latter celebratory and ending with a terrific orchestration of the tune we know as 'God Save the Queen', the former one of Weber's most brilliant pieces, one that really ought to feature more as a concert-opener. Antoni Wit goes at it with a will, and nimbly catches the good humour of the *Abu Hassan* overture, not least thanks to a lively oboe here and in *Peter Schmoll*. The orchestra also boasts a good horn section, very much called for in both *Oberon* and *Der Freischütz*. *Peter Schmoll* and *Silvana* are attractive examples of how early Weber began finding his voice as an orchestrator, in the case of *Schmoll* when still in his teens.

If only the sound were better, this would be an easy record to recommend. But as well as writing beautifully for wind, Weber makes demands on the richness and depth of the full orchestra and, especially in *Euryanthe* and *Oberon*, on the hurtling virtuosity of the strings. A crowded acoustic does not help clarity here, or in the busy figuration at the climax of *Jubel*. The seldom-played *Turandot*, with its quirky little oriental tune that caught Hindemith's ear for his *Weber Metamorphosis*, fares rather better.

Clarinet Quintet

Clarinet Quintet. Trio for Flute, Cello and Piano.
Piano Quartet.
Gaudier Ensemble (Richard Hosford cl Jaime Martin fl Marieke Blankestijn, Lesley Hatfield vns Iris Juda va Christoph Marks vc Susan Tomes pf)
Hyperion CDA67464 (73' · DDD) Ⓕ**B**▶

Weber's three pieces of chamber music make an attractive record, and the performances here are responsive to the works' particular problems. With the early Piano Quartet, the young virtuoso set himself some tricky tests, especially in the matter of balance. In the complicated middle section of the *Adagio*, for instance, there are leaping violin phrases, *forte*, against soft *piano* chords with a viola murmuring away to itself *pianissimo* in the middle. It works well here. In Susan Tomes's hands, the

Trio of the Minuet has a nice waltzing lilt and the finale blazes with energy. The players are willing to take liberties: though there is no warrant for the long *accelerando* in the finale of the Piano Trio, it is not the kind of thing Weber would have objected to, and both the pensive opening and the brooding melancholy of the 'Shepherd's Lament' are very much in the right spirit.

Richard Hosford is excellent in the Clarinet Quintet and is given a nice, clean acoustic for all the brilliant effects. There is, however, an oddity in the *Adagio* with the pairs of chromatic scales: the first, 'as loud as possible', is fine, but the second, *pianissimo*, is so quiet as to be barely audible, sounding as if it is drawn right away from the microphone. Hosford rounds it all off sensationally in the dazzling final pages. The only regret is that the players use the version, or something near it, prepared by the son of Weber's first performer, Heinrich Baermann. Carl Baermann claimed that this was the performing tradition but the evidence is insecure, and there is a good modern edition that comes closer to what must have been Weber's intentions. All the same, a very enjoyable disc.

Piano Sonatas

Piano Sonatas – No 1 in C, J138; No 2 in A flat, J199.
Rondo brillante in E flat, J252, 'La gaîté'. Invitation to the Dance, J260
Hamish Milne pf
CRD CRD3485 (76' · DDD)　　　　Ⓜ Ⓞ

Weber's piano music, once played by most pianists, has since suffered neglect and even the famous *Invitation to the Dance* is now more often heard in its orchestral form. Since he was a renowned pianist as well as a major composer, the neglect seems odd, particularly when other pianist composers such as Chopin and Liszt are at the centre of the concert repertory; but part of the trouble may lie in the difficulty of the music, reflecting his own huge hands and his tendency to write what the booklet-essay calls 'chords unplayable by others'. Hamish Milne makes out a real case for this music, and his playing of the two sonatas is idiomatic and resourceful, even if one can't banish the feeling that Weber all too readily used the melodic and harmonic formulae of 18th-century galanterie and simply dressed them up in 19th-century salon virtuosity. From this point of view, a comparison with Chopin's mature sonatas or Liszt's magnificent single essay in the form reveals Weber as a lightweight. A hearing of the first movement in the First Sonata will quickly tell you if this is how you may react, while in its *Presto* finale you may praise a Mendelssohnian lightness but also note a pomposity foreign to that composer. Leaving aside the musical quality of these sonatas, this is stylish playing which should win them friends. The *Rondo brillante* and *Invitation to the Dance* make no claim to be other than scintillating salon music, and are captivating in Milne's shapely and skilful performances. The recording is truthful and satisfying.

Der Freischütz

Der Freischütz
Peter Schreier ten Max (Hans Jörn Weber) **Gundula Janowitz** sop Agathe (Regina Jeske) **Edith Mathis** sop Aennchen (Ingrid Hille) **Theo Adam** bass Caspar (Gerhard Paul) **Bernd Weikl** bar Ottokar (Otto Mellies) **Siegfried Vogel** bass Cuno (Gerd Biewer) **Franz Crass** bass Hermit **Gerhard Paul** spkr Samiel **Günther Leib** bar Kilian (Peter Hölzel)
Leipzig Radio Chorus; Staatskapelle Dresden / Carlos Kleiber
DG The Originals ② 457 736-2GOR2 (130' · ADD · T/t)
Recorded 1973　　　　　Ⓕ Ⓞ Ⓞ Ⓓ

Carlos Kleiber's fine set of *Der Freischütz* earns reissue on CD for a number of reasons. One is the excellence of the actual recorded sound with a score that profits greatly from such attention. Weber's famous attention to details of orchestration is lovingly explored by a conductor who has taken the trouble to go back to the score in manuscript and observe the differences between that and most of the published versions. So not only do we hear the eerie sound of low flute thirds and the subtle contrast of unmuted viola with four-part muted violins in Agathe's 'Leise, leise', among much else, with a new freshness and point, but all the diabolical effects in the Wolf's Glen come up with a greater sense of depth, down to the grisliest detail. The beginning of the Overture, and the opening of the Wolf's Glen scene, steal upon us out of a primeval silence, as they should. All this would be of little point were the performance itself not of such interest. There's a good deal to argue about but this is because the performance is so interesting. Even if some of Kleiber's tempi are possibly unwise, they spring from a careful, thoughtful and musical mind.

The singing cast is excellent, with Gundula Janowitz an outstanding Agathe to a somewhat reflective Max from Peter Schreier, at his best when the hero is brought low by the devilish machinations; Edith Mathis is a pretty Aennchen, Theo Adam a fine, murky Caspar. The dialogue, spoken by actors, is slightly abbreviated and occasionally amended. Kleiber's reading produces much new insight to a magical old score.

Der Freischütz
Eberhard Waechter bar Ottokar **Gundula Janowitz** sop Agathe **Renate Holm** sop Aennchen **Manfred Jungwirth** bass Cuno **Karl Ridderbusch** bass Caspar **James King** ten Max
Vienna State Opera Chorus and Orchestra / Karl Böhm
Orfeo d'Or ② C732 072I (129' · ADD · S/N)
Recorded live 1972　　　　　　　　Ⓕ

Karl Böhm's *Freischütz* (1972) that has the natural ease of born kinship. His playing of the Overture sets the tone with sounds that breathe the sunlit forests; the Wolf's Glen scene tilts these into the lurking horror that is the dark side of the opera's coin.

The cast also inhabit their parts as if born into them. Gundula Janowitz floats her tone with ravishing effect in Agathe's 'Leise, leise' and in the later prayer, 'Und ob die Wolke'. Renate Holm sparkles alongside her, deliciously sending up the song about the 'ghostly' dog. Karl Ridderbusch is the blackest of Caspars, sinister yet not without a hint of pathos in this self-destroying soul. By the same token James King, much of whose career lay in German-speaking lands, has the heroic ring for Max but also the anxiety that has weakened his character. He earns the sonorous forgiveness of Franz Crass's Hermit. The smaller parts fit no less easily into this village community, Manfred Jungwirth making more than usual of Cuno.

There is a merry set of Bridesmaids, and Huntsmen who rejoice infectiously in the chase, though the Act 3 prelude anticipating their chorus is cut (so, reasonably, is a good deal of the dialogue). In the Wolf's Glen itself, there is too much in the way of shrieking winds and clattering hooves, when the music really does it all; but then this was a stage performance, and the scene meets with somewhat stunned applause. It never fails as a spine-chiller. Böhm handles everything beautifully, and unobtrusively, as if the work can be left to speak for itself, which of course is the art of real experience in the opera house. It is a most attractive performance. (The booklet excludes a text and translation.)

Anton Webern
Austrian 1883-1945

The son of an aristocratic mining engineer (Webern dropped the nobiliary 'von' when Austria became a republic after the First World War), it was while he was a student at the University of Vienna that he was introduced to Arnold Schoenberg. The relationship between the two was more disciple and friend than master and pupil and, having produced his official Op 1 (Passacaglia for Orchestra written in the conventional German idiom), he turned to atonalism. His Six Orchestral Pieces, Op 6 (1909, premiered 1913) created a scandal when they were first heard in Vienna. Concision and logic are emphasised – his Five Pieces for Orchestra (1913, first performed in 1969) takes only 10 minutes to perform while the fourth movement lasts a mere 19 seconds.

Accepting that he was never going to make a living as a popular composer, Webern's life, apart from a year in the army, was spent in conducting, private teaching and lecturing. His wife Wilhelmine, a cousin whom he married in 1911, bore him three daughters and a son, not helping his precarious financial situation. Whatever you think of his music, few composers have shown such fortitude and resoluteness in living with their artistic ideals and having abuse thrown at them, whatever they produced. When Schoenberg formalised his theories and gave 12-tone music a structure, Webern began writing longer works framed in strict classical forms; but the Anschluss of 1938 made his position difficult. He was denounced by the Nazis as a 'cul-

tural Bolshevik' and his music was banned in Austria and Germany.

Aged nearly 60, Webern was called up during the Second World War as an air-raid warden. In the spring of 1945 he learnt that his only son had been killed on the Yugoslav front. At Easter, he left his apartment in Mödling (Vienna) to travel to Mittersill near Salzburg where he had heard his son-in-law was involved in the black market. American soldiers had come to arrest him and when Webern stepped outside to smoke a cigar given to him by his son-in-law an American soldier bumped into him in the dark. Webern was ordered to stop, misunderstood the order, approached the soldier and was shot dead.

More than Berg and Schoenberg, Webern's music has exercised a tremendous influence on contemporary composers, especially Boulez and Stockhausen.

Complete Works, Opp 1-31

Passacaglia, Op 1 (**London Symphony Orchestra / Pierre Boulez**). Entflieht auf leichten Kähnen, Op 2 (**John Alldis Choir / Boulez**). Five Songs from 'Der siebente Ring', Op 3. Five Songs, Op 4 (**Heather Harper** sop **Charles Rosen** pf). Five Movements, Op 5 (**Juilliard Quartet**). Six Pieces, Op 6 (**LSO / Boulez**). Four Pieces, Op 7 (**Isaac Stern** vn **Rosen** pf). Two Songs, Op 8 (**Harper** sop **chamber ensemble / Boulez**). Six Bagatelles, Op 9 (**Juilliard Qt**). Five Pieces, Op 10 (**LSO / Boulez**). Three Little Pieces, Op 11 (**Gregor Piatigorsky** vc **Rosen** pf). Four Songs, Op 12 (**Harper** sop **Rosen** pf). Four Songs, Op 13. Six Songs, Op 14 (**Harper** sop **chamber ens / Boulez**). Five Sacred Songs, Op 15. Five Canons on Latin Texts, Op 16 (**Halina Lukomska** sop **chamber ens / Boulez**). Three Songs, Op 18 (**Lukomska** sop **John Williams** gtr **Colin Bradbury** cl **/ Boulez**). Two Songs, Op 19 (**John Alldis Ch, members LSO / Boulez**). String Trio, Op 20 (**members Juilliard Qt**). Symphony, Op 21 (**LSO / Boulez**). Quartet, Op 22 (**Robert Marcellus** cl **Abraham Weinstein** sax **Daniel Majeske** vn **Rosen** pf **/ Boulez**). Three Songs from 'Viae inviae', Op 23 (**Lukomska** sop **Rosen** pf). Concerto, Op 24 (**members LSO / Boulez**). Three Songs, Op 25 (**Lukomska** sop **Rosen** pf). Das Augenlicht, Op 26 (**John Alldis Ch, LSO / Boulez**). Piano Variations, Op 27 (**Rosen** pf). String Quartet, Op 28 (**Juilliard Qt**). Cantata No 1, Op 29 (**Lukomska** sop **John Alldis Ch; LSO / Boulez**). Variations, Op 30 (**LSO / Boulez**). Cantata No 2, Op 31 (**Lukomska** sop **Barry McDaniel** bar **John Alldis Ch; LSO / Boulez**). Five Movements, Op 5 – orchestral version (**LSO / Boulez**) Bach (orch Webern) Musikalischen Opfer, BWV1079 – Fuga (Ricercata) No 2 (**LSO / Boulez**) Schubert (orch Webern) Deutsche Tänze, D820 (**Frankfurt Radio Orchestra / Anton Webern**) (recorded live 1932) **Various artists**
Sony Classical ③ SM3K45845 (3h 43' · ADD · T/t).
Recorded 1967-72 Ⓜ●●●

Ⓖ Webern is as 'classic' to Boulez as Mozart or Brahms are to most other conductors, and when he's able to persuade performers to share his view the results can be remarkable – lucid in texture, responsive in expression. There are many sides to Webern, despite his well-nigh exclusive concern with miniature forms, and although this set isn't equally successful in realising them all, it leaves you in no doubt about the music's variety and emotional power, whether the piece is an ingenious canon-by-inversion or a simple, folk-like Lied. From a long list of performers one could single out Heather Harper and the Juilliard Quartet for special commendation; and the smooth confidence of the John Alldis Choir is also notable. The recordings were made over a five-year period, and have the typical CBS dryness of that time. Even so, in the finest performances which Boulez himself directs, that remarkable radiance of spirit so special to Webern is vividly conveyed. It's a fascinating bonus to hear Webern himself conducting his Schubert arrangements – music from another world, yet with an economy and emotional poise that Webern in his own way sought to emulate.

Miscellaneous works

Bach/Webern Musikalisches Opfer, BWV1079 – Ricercata a 6[e] **Webern** Zwei Lieder, Op 19[cd]. Five Movements, Op 5[d]. Zwei Lieder, Op 8[ae]. Five Pieces, Op 10[d]. Vier Lieder, Op 13[ae]. Sechs Lieder, Op 14[ae]. Fünf Geistliche Lieder, Op 15[ae]. Das Augenlicht, Op 26[cd]. Variations, Op 30[e]. Cantata No 2, Op 31[bcd]
[a]**Tony Arnold,** [b]**Claire Booth** sops
[b]**David Wilson-Johnson** bass [c]**Simon Joly Chorale;**
[d]**Philharmonia Orchestra;** [e]**Twentieth Century Classics Ensemble / Robert Craft**
Naxos 8 557531 (80' · DDD) ⑤Ⓓ➛

Now in his eighties, Robert Craft is re-recording Webern more than half a century after his pioneering CBS album. This instalment mixes early, middle and late compositions in an order that makes an effective programme when heard straight through. Both British and American artists are involved, and recordings were made in London and New York during 2007 and 2008.

Craft has not lost his edge: his admirably extensive booklet-notes detail the failings of Webern performance materials (a new, complete and definitive edition is at last being planned), and the inadequacies of other conductors (Boulez is shamed but not named). Whether or not adhering precisely to the published metronome markings is invariably a good thing, Craft's performances are certainly characterful and precise. It could be the recording process that has flattened out some of the dynamic shadings that he would surely have insisted on in actual performance; and other features of the sound – like an exceptionally prominent alto saxophone in the rarefied cantata *Das Augenlicht* – might have been an intentional interpretative nuance, jarring though it is.

The need for contrapuntal clarity could also explain the rather unatmospheric acoustic, more helpful to singers than instrumentalists. Soprano Tony Arnold is admirably mellifluous in the song sets, the wide-spanning lines given their full lyrical weight. Claire Booth and David Wilson-Johnson are no less impressive in Webern's last completed work, the Op 31 Cantata.

This disc also includes Webern's most strongly contrasted orchestral scores, the fugitive Op 10 Pieces and the craggy Variations, Op 30. Their effect in these sharply delineated performances – a quality no less apparent in the ultra-eccentric arrangement of Bach's *Ricercar* – may be more austere than affectionate, but the fierce originality and integrity of Webern's vision of musical perfection is never in doubt.

Passacaglia, Op 1

Webern Passacaglia. Five Pieces, Op 5. Six Pieces, Op 6. Im Sommerwind **Bach** (orch Webern) Musikalisches Opfer, BWV1079 – Ricercar a 6 **Schubert** (orch Webern) Deutsche Tänze, D820
Berlin Philharmonic Orchestra / Pierre Boulez
DG 447 099-2GH (67' · DDD) ⒻⓄ➛

With the exception of the Bach and Schubert arrangements, this is all relatively early, pre-serial Webern, yet Boulez devotes as much care and as much affection to the D minor *Passacaglia* and to the undeniably immature but irresistibly luscious *Im Sommerwind* as to the far more characteristic Op 5 and Op 6 pieces. Boulez doesn't imply that the mature Webern is present here in embryo; but he does perhaps make us ask how much of that later music is, like this, inspired by nature.

To be reminded of Brahms by the *Passacaglia* is no less appropriate. This is a Janus of a piece, looking back not only to Brahms's Fourth Symphony but beyond, and at the same time moving onwards from the delicate chamber passages in *Im Sommerwind* towards the 'orchestral chamber music' of Op 5 and Op 6. Boulez looks both ways too, with rich orchestral amplitude and expressive phrasing (very broad *rubato*) but he also notices Webern's already marked liking for transparent textures, quiet subtleties of string colour and the sound of the muted trumpet. And yes: heard in this context the shorter pieces are a logical progression. They are intensely expressive, with a wide range of emotion often within a few bars; no wonder Boulez prefers the earlier, richer scoring of Op 6. He obviously loves their Mahler-derived dissolution of the boundary between orchestral and chamber music, and encourages the orchestra to play with great tonal beauty. Those qualities recur in the Bach and Schubert arrangements. The recordings are warm and clean.

Five Pieces, Op 5

Webern String Quartet (arr Poppen). Five Pieces, Op 5. **Bach** Musical Offering, BWV1079 – Ricercar a 6 (orch Webern). Cantata No 4, Christ lag in Todesbanden, BWV4[a]
[a]**Hilliard Ensemble; Munich Chamber Orchestra / Christoph Poppen**
ECM New Series 461 912-2 (69' · DDD) ⒻⓄⓄⓄ➛

Ⓖ Symmetry, the cyclic evolution of a musical germ and the idea of birth in the midst of death: all are fundamental to this disc. Webern's motivically determined orchestration of the Ricercar from Bach's late *The Musical Offering*, where single lines change colour by the bar, opens and closes the programme. Christoph Poppen's orchestration of Webern's 1905 String Quartet soars and surges with an ardour that befits this early but significant masterpiece. Like Webern in Bach, Poppen knows how and where to taper his forces, while his players respond with obvious dedication. Bach's Cantata *Christ lag in Todesbanden* grows, as Herbert Glossner reminds us, from a 'primordial cell' of a single semitone motif. Eight stanzas each end with a 'Halleluja', as unalike in shade and meaning as the strands of Webern's 'Ricercar', so magnificent is the young Bach's handling of the texts. Poppen performs choral Bach with single voices; he also encourages a string playing style that largely dispenses with vibrato, so that when you cross from Webern's Quartet to Bach's BWV4 you could as well be switching to a period performance. The Hilliards sing beautifully, both solo and in ensemble, and the balance between voices and instruments is impeccable.

Some might balk at the sudden eruption of Webern's violent 'Heftig bewegt' on the heels of Bach's closing 'Halleluja', but the musical sense of having five 'symmetrical' Movements for String Quartet fall within the greater symmetry of the programme as a whole overrides any initial discomfort. Again, Poppen's finely tooled reading focuses in precise detail the mood and texture of each miniature so that the eventual return of Bach-Webern is indeed like a profound thought revisited by a changed mind.

Thomas Weelkes   English 1575?-1623

He was one of the most gifted of the madrigalists, and a major composer of English church music. As a vocal composer Weelkes's main deficiencies were a lack of response to the sound of words themselves, and uneven melodic invention. As a madrigalist he could not match Wilbye's ability for making his individual lines grow around the verbal phrase, and he lacked that composer's sensitive ear for the textural variety which may enhance the poetic shadings of the text; nor did he share Gibbons's mastery of vocal declamation. Weelkes's great strength lay in the vivid inventiveness of his very calculated musical imagery, and the commanding brilliance of a fully developed contrapuntal technique whose roots are more English than Italian.

O Jonathan. Rejoice in the Lord. All people, clap your hands. Te Deum & Jubilate (Eighth Service). O how amiable are thy dwellings. Christ Rising Again. When David Heard. Laboravi in gemitu meo. Magnificat & Nunc dimittis (Third Service). O vos omnes. Lord, to Thee I make my

moan. Give ear, O Lord. Hosanna to the Son of David
Tewkesbury Abbey Schola Cantorum /
Benjamin Nicholas
Delphian DCD34070 (60' · DDD)   Ⓕ

There remains an intensity of passionate utterance in the most striking of Weelkes's works, balanced by a sober moderation in much else. He himself, as we learn from contemporary accounts, was not characterised by either moderation or sobriety, at least in his latter years, coming to his choir 'from the Taverne or Ale house' cursing and swearing 'most dreadfully'. You would never guess as much from the decorous verse anthems and evening canticles, but the intensity of the lament *O Jonathan*, which opens the present recital, might suggest a less bridled temperament, as might the concentrated fervour of *Hosanna to the Son of David*, which closes it.

Under Benjamin Nicholas, director of Tewkesbury Abbey's Schola Cantorum, the choir has developed a strong style, remarkable for its sense of personal (or corporate) commitment as for the sonority of its tone and the assurance of its delivery. The trebles splendidly vindicate the tradition that places them at the heart of English cathedral music. The men's voices are also powerful and resonant and the total effect is rich and forthright. If anything, the 'standard' level of volume is set too high – it is not until the sixth item, *O how amiable are thy dwellings*, that we find reassurance that the choir can sing quietly. Fine solo work and neat organ playing are further assets, as is the introductory note by Dr Peter James.

Kurt Weill   German/American 1900-1950

Having composed a number of modishly modern orchestral works and got nowhere, Weill hit his stride as soon as he began writing for the theatre. In the Berlin of the 1920s he also found an appreciative audience for his short, sharp satirical operas. After Der Protagonist (1925) and Royal Palace (1926) he teamed up with the left-wing writer Bertolt Brecht. Their first success was the 'songspiel' Mahagonny (1927), subsequently remodelled as a three-act opera (Rise and Fall of the City of Mahagonny, 1929). But it was Brecht's adaptation of John Gay's The Beggar's Opera of 1728 that gave Weill by far his biggest – and most lasting – success. Under the title Die Dreigroschenoper it was produced all over Europe, receiving more than 4000 performances in about 120 German theatres after its premiere in 1928. With the stage peopled by pimps, prostitutes and low-life, Weill's haunting, rasping score and the venomous punch of the libretto, The Threepenny Opera retains its vivid association with the decadent years of the Weimar Republic.

Weill was the leading spokesman for the aesthetic vogue of Zeitkunst (music for the people), determined that his art should reflect contemporary life, that it should be accessible and that his theatre work should be unhampered by the restrictions of an opera house. His two-act opera *Der Jasager* ('The Yes-man'), written for schools to perform, has some claim to creating the educational genre of opera later taken up by Carl Orff and Benjamin Britten. But whatever his long-term aims, the Jewish-born Weill and his actress wife Lotte Lenya were forced to flee Nazi Germany in 1933. After a final collaboration with Brecht in Paris (*The Seven Deadly Sins*, 1933), Weill left for America and thereafter made his career on Broadway with a string of musicals and attempts at 'American opera', none of which have lasted the course. One of the first, however, *Knickerbocker Holiday* (1936), written with Maxwell Anderson, contains the unforgettable 'September Song' ('Oh it's a long, long time / From May to September…') which, as sang by Walter Huston, became almost as popular as 'Mack the Knife' from *The Threepenny Opera*.

Symphonies

Symphonies No 1 & 2. Lady in the Dark – Symphonic Nocturne (arr K Russell Bennett)
Bournemouth Symphony Orchestra / Marin Alsop
Naxos 8 557481 (74' · DDD)   ⑤🅑➔

Weill's Symphony No 2 is one of his most important works but it is not music calculated to cheer one up. Commissioned by the Princesse de Polignac in 1933, Weill completed it during the months immediately following his flight from Germany, after the Nazi seizure of power. Coming just after *Der Silbersee* and *Die sieben Todsünden*, it has a number of thematic similarities to those works but also seems to hint at some of Weill's later music, composed in America. A deeply pessimistic piece in its first two movements, it nevertheless ends on a questioning note that may express hope, or at least the energy to continue. The Bournemouth Symphony Orchestra under Marin Alsop give a satisfying performance.

Alsop achieves quite a triumph with the very early single-movement First Symphony, a student work never performed in the composer's lifetime: it's rarely played as confidently as here. The suite from *Lady In the Dark* is just a curiosity; without Ira Gershwin's lyrics the tunes don't sound particularly enticing. At least, though, it lightens the mood after some pretty relentless gloom. Excellent clear sound, at Naxos's price an easy recommendation.

Aufsteig und Fall der Stadt Mahagonny

Aufstieg und Fall der Stadt Mahagonny
Dame Gwyneth Jones *sop* Leokadja Begbick **Roy Cornelius Smith** *ten* Fatty **Wilbur Pauley** *bass* Trinity Moses **Catherine Malfitano** *sop* Jenny Smith **Jerry Hadley** *ten* Jimmy Mahoney **Udo Holdorf** *ten* Jake Schmidt **Dale Duesing** *bar* Pennybank Bill **Harry Peeters** *bass* Alaska Wolf Joe **Toby Spence** *ten* Tobby Higgins **Vienna State Opera Chorus; Vienna**

Radio Symphony Orchestra /
Dennis Russell Davies
Stage director **Peter Zadek**
Video director **Brian Large**
ArtHaus Musik 📀 100 092 (160' · 16:9 · 2.0 · 2, 5)   Ⓕ

Peter Zadek's production of Weill and Brecht's largest-scale opera was much criticised in 1998. It's possible to see in this DVD version that the Salzburg stage is really too big for the work, and that there's rather a lot of unnecessary action, much coming and going, walking about, and movement of furniture. However, Brian Large's filmed production makes such good use of close-ups that much of this is bypassed.

What makes this unmissable is Jerry Hadley's performance as Jim. From every point of view, dramatic, vocal and emotional, he encompasses the part so completely that you're totally gripped. The tension in his pose, his burning eyes, the physical daring of the interpretation command attention at every turn. At the end of Act 2, when Jenny sings 'Denn wie man sich bettet', Catherine Malfitano declaims the first verse as she's carried on Hadley's shoulders. Although the camera and the microphone are both harsh where Malfitano is concerned, she too gives such an involved and committed reading of the part that one has to forgive everything.

At no moment in her career would Gwyneth Jones's voice have been suitable for the role of the Widow Begbick, but she too is fascinating to watch, under-playing most of the time, so that when the trial scene arrives, the extra cruel edge she gives to gesture and song tells all the more. The other tremendous performance comes from Wilbur Pauley as a totally repellent Trinity Moses – his pose, Christ-like, after he's killed Joe in the boxing scene is horrific.

Dennis Russell Davies conducts a searing account of the score from the pit. The balance between voices and orchestra is sometimes very echoey, but this is inevitable on a stage as cavernous as Salzburg's.

Die Dreigroschenoper (The Threepenny Opera)

Die Dreigroschenoper
René Kollo Macheath **Ute Lemper** Polly Peachum **Milva** Jenny Smith **Mario Adorf** Peachum **Helga Dernesch** Frau Peachum **Wolfgang Reichmann** Brown **Susanne Tramper** Lucy Brown **Rolf Boysen** Street Singer **Berlin RIAS Chamber Choir and Sinfonietta / John Mauceri**
Decca 430 075-2DH (74' · DDD)   Ⓕ🅞➔

John Mauceri's presence makes itself felt immediately in the clarity of instrumental detail and the bounciness of the dance rhythms. Ute Lemper, too, is soon well in evidence in a splendidly shaped 'Barbara-Song'. There is also a superbly rounded Mrs Peachum in Helga Dernesch, whose 'Ballad of Sexual Dependency' is a *tour de force*. It is followed by an absolutely irresistible 'Zuhäter Ballade', in which the innocently spun out melody serves to accompany some wickedly expressive handling of the text by René Kollo as Macheath, and by the husky Milva (another impressive singing actress) as the whore Jenny. Kollo is no less impressive in his handling of Macheath's Epitaph, again tellingly accompanied by Mauceri. He has gone back to Weill's original manuscript material, has reconsidered tempi, and has ensured, for instance, that Macheath's music is properly sung by an operatic tenor.

Ultimately the old CBS recording retains a special magic of its own that makes it foolish to pretend to its devotees that this new recording should replace it – though it is currently out of the catalogue. On the other hand, there can scarcely be any doubt that it is to this new version that the uncommitted should be directed. The clearer Decca digital sound is obviously superior and the singing too is undeniably of a higher standard.

Die sieben Todsünden
(The Seven Deadly Sins)

Die sieben Todsünden[a]. Berlin im Licht[b]. La complainte de la Seine[b]. Es regnet[b]. Nannas Lied, 'Meine Herren, mit siebzehn Jahren'[b]. Youkali[b]. Wie lange noch?[b]
Brigitte Fassbaender mez [a]**Hans Sojer**, [a]**Karl-Heinz Brandt** tens [a]**Hidenori Komatsu** bar [a]**Ivan Urbas** bass [a]**North German Radio Philharmonic Orchestra, Hanover / Cord Garben** [b]pf
Harmonia Mundi HMA195 1420 (55' · DDD)   Ⓢ

Kurt Weill composed 'La complainte de la Seine' in 1934, while he was living in France. It was first sung and recorded by Lys Gauty. In the introduction to the first verse, Weill weaves in a quote from the marching theme at the end of *Die sieben Todsünden*. The two are neatly linked here, as Brigitte Fassbaender sings the chanson directly after the *ballet-chanté*. Of all the opera singers who have recorded *The Seven Deadly Sins*, Fassbaender has always been a favourite. She sings it in the original, higher key, and although some of the tempi chosen by Cord Garben seem a little slow, Fassbaender's luscious mezzo invests the work with a superb sense of world-weariness. All the other songs come from the cache of unpublished work that we first got to know in 1982 through Teresa Stratas's 'The Unknown Kurt Weill' (Nonesuch). Stratas gives the songs more urgency; Fassbaender seems relaxed by comparison, which is not to say that she doesn't extract every last ounce of irony from the lyrics, including one unique contribution from Jean Cocteau ('Es regnet'). The original issue had full texts and translations; here there are merely synopses. Nevertheless, at its modest price, this is highly recommended.

Street Scene

Street Scene
Ashley Putnam sop Anna Maurrant **Marc Embree**

bar Frank Maurrant **Teri Hansen** sop Rose Maurrant **Kip Wilborn** ten Sam Kaplan **Claudia Ashley** sop Nursemaid 1 **Muriel Costa-Greenspon** mez Nursemaid 2 **Yvette Bonner** sop Jennie Hildebrand **David Rae Smith** ten Abraham Kaplan **Janice Felty** mez Emma Jones **Heidi Eisenberg** mez Olga Olsen **Anthony Mee** ten Lippo Fiorentino **Ludwigshafen Theatre Chorus; Rhineland Palatinate State Philharmonic Orchestra / James Holmes**
Stage director **Francesca Zambello**
Film director **José Montes-Baquer**
ArtHaus Musik 📀 100 098 (143' · 16:9 · 2.0 · 2 & 5)
Recorded 1994   Ⓕ

Street Scene was the most ambitious product of Weill's American years. It's a kind of *Porgy and Bess* transferred to the slum tenements of New York during the Depression, mixing genuine operatic writing with unashamedly popular numbers. It's essentially a team opera, with many roles, portraying the ups and downs of urban life, including childbirth and death.

Ashley Putnam is visually too young for the role of Anna, perhaps, but vocally outstanding in her solo numbers. Teri Hansen initially sounds a shade constricted as her daughter Rose, but she's tender enough in her duet with Kip Wilborn as her lover Sam. Marc Embree is suitably menacing as husband Frank, Janice Felty a strong Emma, and Anthony Mee a delightful roly-poly Neapolitan. An undoubted star of the production is designer Adrienne Lobel, against whose magnificently solid and realistic set the action unfolds. Another is James Holmes, who brings out the score's darker, dramatic moments as much as its unashamed romanticism and jazz-inflected numbers.

This production reveals what a wonderful work it is – convincing both for its extended operatic writing and its marvellous tunes.

Mieczysław Weinberg
Polish/Russian 1919-1996

Also known by his Jewish name Moisei Samuilovich Vainberg, he studied at the Warsaw Conservatoire, and after moving to the USSR continued his studies at the conservatoire in Minsk. He wrote a lot of music, including 22 symphonies, 17 string quartets and seven operas.

Concertos

Clarinet Concerto, Op 104[a]. Fantasia, Op 52[b].
Flute Concertos[c] – No 1, Op 75; No 2, Op 148
[c]**Anders Jonhäll** fl [a]**Urban Claesson** cl
[b]**Claes Gunnarsson** vc
Gothenburg Symphony Orchestra / Thord Svedlund
Chandos 🔊 CHSA5064 (79' · DDD)   Ⓕ⬤↦

Appreciation of the Polish-born Mieczysław Weinberg has increased markedly over recent years. This collection of four concertos covers a fair proportion of the composer's maturity. The Cello Fantasia (1953) is a deftly through-composed design recalling the Myaskovsky Concerto in a melodic directness that yet conceals considerable expressive depths. The flute concertos are both lighter in content though not necessarily in manner: No 1 (1961) places its ruminative passacaglia between movements whose effervescence is often tempered by the ambivalent strains of klezmer, while No 2 (1987) places a brooding *Largo* between an *Allegro* that elides, Nielsen-like, between its frequently conflicting ideas and a finale whose valedictory allusions to the music of others are fitting in the context of one of Weinberg's last works.

Yet it is the Clarinet Concerto (1970) that is the real discovery here. On a substantial scale, it allows the soloist subtle dominance against a string orchestra that, in the first movement, evinces a sparseness often redolent of (though not indebted to) late Shostakovich and which, in the *Andante*, blends austerity with poetry to touching effect – before a finale whose dancing gait prevails in the face of more disruptive elements. The soloists are finely attuned to their respective concertos, and Thord Svedlund secures an incisive response from his Gothenburg forces. Excellent sound and a welcome addition to the Weinberg discography.

Judith Weir   British b1954

Weir studied composition with John Tavener and Robin Holloway before teaching for six years at the University of Glasgow and the RSAMD. From 1995 to 1998 she was the CBSO's Composer in Association; and from 1995 to 2000 she was artistic director of the Spitalfields Festival in London. Often drawing on sources from medieval history, as well as the traditional stories and music of her native Scotland, she is best known for her operas and theatre works, although she has also achieved considerable international renown for her extensive catalogue of orchestral and chamber works. Weir is now at work on a new opera which will receive its first performances at the Bregenz Festival, Austria, in 2011.

Operas

Blond Eckbert
Nicholas Folwell bar Blond Eckbert **Nerys Jones**
sop Bird **Anne-Marie Owens** mez Berthe
Christopher Ventris ten Walther, Hugh, Old Woman
**English National Opera Chorus and Orchestra /
Sian Edwards**
NMC Ancora NMCD106 (65' · DDD · S/T)   Ⓕ

Ludwig Tieck's novella *Der Blonde Eckbert* (1796) is a dark tale of incest and despair made even darker by the ironic framework of a bird's song extolling the peaceful solitude that can be found in nature. Judith Weir, writing her own libretto, has

seized on this essential contrast. While her bird sings eloquently, joyfully, her human characters articulate their growing awareness of the horrors that surround them in lines that are questing, often aggressive, though never shorn of the kind of lyricism that best represents vulnerability.

Unfolding over just 65 minutes to an ending suffused with a spirit of tragic radiance, the opera is a gripping, harrowing experience, and admiration of ENO for commissioning it is tempered only by regret at their failure to revive on a regular basis a work of such intense theatricality and musical approachability.

This recording (originally issued by Collins Classics) is not of one of the Coliseum performances but was made for a TV film shown on Channel 4. The balance strongly favours the voices and although most of the pungent, imaginative orchestral details still come across – with the use of brass and woodwind especially telling – the sound highlights a certain lack of nuance in Nicholas Folwell's account of the principal role and conveys little sense of stage movement or action. Nevertheless, Folwell and the rest of the small cast are persuasive, and the music is so immediate in its evocation of pastoral enchantment and menace that any studio-bound quality is far less of a hindrance than would often be the case.

The Consolations of Scholarship[a]. King Harald's Saga[b]. Piano Concerto[c]. Musicians Wrestle Everywhere[d]
[a]Janice Felty mez **[b]Judith Kellock** sop **[c]Xak Bjerken** pf **Ensemble X / [bcd]Mark Davis Scatterday, [a]Steven Stucky**
Albany TROY803 (65' · DDD · S/N)   Ⓕ

A 'grand opera in three acts' for a single unaccompanied soprano, lasting less than 15 minutes? You expect *King Harald's Saga* to be a joke, and there are indeed moments where the music seems to be echoing celebrated operatic extravagances, like Baba the Turk's cadenzas in Stravinsky's *The Rake's Progress*. But one of Judith Weir's great strengths is that she can combine irony with genuine depth of feeling, and in this early (1979) demonstration of benign iconoclasm she sets out a distinctive and appealing perspective on those alternatives to grand opera which music theatre has been exploring for most of the past century. Judith Kellock gives a finely judged performance.

Written six years later, *The Consolations of Scholarship* turns from Icelandic sagas to 14th-century Chinese plays. Here the singer is supported by a nine-strong instrumental ensemble which relishes the kind of bold, pungent textures that Weir would soon develop in her first 'proper' stage work, *A Night at the Chinese Opera* (1987). Indeed, so powerful is the instrumental writing that the voice's contribution – alternating between speech and song – sometimes has to struggle to cut through. A more forward balance for the otherwise excellent Janice Felty might have helped.

This admirable disc is completed by a pair of instrumental works from the mid-1990s. Appropriately, in view of its title, taken from American poet Emily Dickinson, *Musicians Wrestle Everywhere* reveals Weir at her most streetwise, the shapely modal lines and sharply delineated rhythms, as well as the wind-dominated scoring, suggesting a host of allusions ranging from Copland to John Adams and Louis Andriessen. The Piano Concerto is another exercise in puncturing pretension, making strong points about how both lyrical and brittle textures can interact with folk-like idioms in ways where nothing seems diluted or bland. Exemplary performances given resonant recordings, and strongly recommended.

Egon Wellesz   Austrian 1885-1974

Like his close friend Webern, Wellesz was a pupil of Schoenberg and Adler. Unlike Webern, though, he continued to pursue both creative and scholarly activities, before and after his move to England in 1938. He lectured at Oxford from 1943 and undertook research on Venetian opera, Viennese Baroque music and Byzantine chant, especially notation and hymnography. His compositions cover many genres and extend from a Schoenbergian style towards Bruckner (especially in the nine symphonies), Bartók (in his chamber music which includes nine string quartets) or Strauss (in the operas).

Symphonies

Symphonies – No 4, 'Sinfonia Austriaca', Op 70; No 6, Op 95; No 7, 'Contra torrentem', Op 102
Vienna Radio Symphony Orchestra /
Gottfried Rabl
CPO CPO999 808-2 (71' · DDD)   Ⓕ

Like his near-contemporaries Ernst Toch and Havergal Brian, Wellesz came late to the symphony, composing his first (1945), inspired by memories of Austria, at the age of 60. No 4 (1951-53) had similar inspiration and bears the sobriquet *Sinfonia Austriaca*. Although Wellesz used atonality or serialism throughout his life, he also used tonality if he felt it appropriate, mixing the disciplines as his expressive purposes demanded. No 4 is a case in point, essentially a pastoral (albeit vigorously so) tonal symphony employing varying degrees of 'free tonality' throughout, especially in the intense *Adagio*.

Wellesz's later symphonies employ a slow-fast-slow design, the slow outer spans tending to be varied in pulse, encasing vigorous central *scherzos*. No 6 (1965) is perhaps his best known, having been broadcast a few times over the years. A riveting work, it's one of his finest utterances, showcasing his mastery of symphonic cogency, formal construction and orchestration. As in the late symphonies of Vaughan Williams, Wellesz was constantly refining and exploring his sound world: if the harmonic language of the

Fourth is the most accessible to general listeners, the orchestration of the terser Seventh (1967) makes the earlier work seem pallid by comparison. Very strongly recommended.

String Quartets

String Quartets – No 3; No 4; No 6
Artis Quartet (Peter Schuhmayer, Johannes Meissl *vns* Herbert Kefer *va* Othmar Müller *vc*)
Nimbus NI5821 (63' · DDD)   Ⓕ

Viennese composer Egon Wellesz was very much a product of his times. Mahler's conducting was an early influence, while Schoenberg and von Hofmannsthal were influential associates. Once Hitler's hordes had conquered Europe he landed in Oxford where he became a Reader in Byzantine music. For a while the trauma of exile blocked Wellesz's creative impulse but he recovered well, and by the time of his death in 1972 had clocked up an impressively varied output. The quartets cover the length and breadth of Wellesz's career, the earliest here, the Third (1918), reflecting key Romantic and 'Impressionist' influences, the turbulent second movement starting out in the manner of Chausson, the rest more indebted perhaps to Debussy and early Schoenberg. There's also, in the fugal passages of the finale, a hint of Max Reger's playful counterpoint.

The curve of Wellesz's development reflects a trend similar to many of his contemporaries: early romanticism gives way, in the 1920s and beyond, to confrontational modernism eventually leading to a cooler, post-classical style. The Fourth Quartet (1922) is terse, aphoristic and tautly argued, each of its five movements shorter in length than you might expect, its style intense and inscrutable. Calum MacDonald's invaluable note suggests an audible prophecy of Berg's *Lyric Suite* and there some telling similarities to Bartók too.

The Sixth Quartet (1947) opens like a homage to Beethoven's *Coriolan* Overture and the classical axis remains in place more or less throughout, especially in the middle movements. Performance-wise one could hardly ask for more in the way of dedication or perception.

Samuel Sebastian Wesley
British 1810-1876

A grandson of Charles Wesley, the founder of Methodism, SS Wesley is one of the most significant composers of hymns. Between 1832 and his death he was organist at four different cathedrals.

Hymns

Ascribe unto the Lord. Blessed be the God and Father. Cast me not away from Thy presence. Let us lift up our heart. O give thanks unto the Lord. Thou

wilt keep him in perfect peace. Wash me throughly from my wickedness. The Wilderness and the solitary place. O God, whose nature and property
Choir of Clare College, Cambridge / Christopher Robinson with **James McVinnie** org
Naxos 8 570318 (75' · DDD)   ⑤🅾🅾▶

There are few lovelier anthems than Wesley's *Thou wilt keep him in perfect peace*; *Cast me not away* is worthy to stand with Purcell's *Hear my prayer*; and among his larger choral compositions *The Wilderness* retains an enviable place in the service-lists. For those who know *Ascribe unto the Lord* there will be many more for whom its final chorus, 'The Lord hath been mindful of us', is a firm favourite, satisfying in structure, vigorous in counterpoint, and sporting as its main themes two of the best melodies in the chorister's repertoire.

The Choir of Clare College, which many will remember for their fresh and accomplished singing under John Rutter, is here directed by Christopher Robinson, than whom none better. The Robinson touch is manifest in the marvellous phrase 'that the bones which thou hast broken may rejoice' (*Cast me not away*). Poor old Wesley had injured his in a fishing accident: he writes feelingly and the choir are with him. The 'ransomed of the Lord' passage in *The Wilderness* has terrific energy. And the soprano soloist in 'And sorrow and sighing' sings like an angel.

Charles-Marie Widor   French 1844-1937

'Widor's Toccata', a thrilling showpiece for organ, is the fifth and final movement of his Organ Symphony No 5 in F minor, Op 42 No 1, a relentless whirlwind of semiquavers with the pedals booming out the magisterial theme. It first appeared in 1878, quite eclipsing everything else Widor wrote, even though its musical content is really quite slight.

Widor, the doyen of French organists after the death of César Franck, recorded the Toccata himself at the age of 87 on the organ of Saint-Sulpice in Paris where he had been organist for an incredible 60 years. He wrote 10 other organ symphonies.

Organ Symphonies

Symphonies – No 9, 'Gothic'[a]; No 10, 'Roman'[b]
Jeremy Filsell org
ASV CDDCA1172 (63' · DDD)
Played on the organs of [a]St George's Chapel, Windsor, and [b]Liverpool Metropolitan Cathedral   Ⓕ

Jeremy Filsell here offers the two final and, some would say, most austere symphonies, and the disc is most welcome. Less welcome is the choice of St George's Chapel, Windsor, for No 9. It's a lovely organ and makes a huge noise, and the recording does it full justice. But it is so manifestly not French that it's hard to understand why it's been used. Of course great music transcends the

limitations of national characteristics but Widor's symphonies are so perfectly tailored to the unique sounds of a Cavaillé-Coll that to chose an instrument which is the very antithesis seems perverse. With the first movement we have the impression of a genial and portly uncle trying, without much success, to sound both stern and angry, while with the charming second movement, the warm, glutinous wash of sound is (like the booklet-notes) so self-indulgent that it clouds the musical message. Against this the Liverpool Metropolitan organ (for the Tenth Symphony) comes like a breath of fresh air, and while much of the detail is lost in the swimming-bath-like acoustic, with Filsell's wonderfully focused playing we do have a conclusion to this series which is both musically convincing and a pleasure to listen to.

Symphonies Nos 1-4, Op 13
Joris Verdin org
Ricercar ② RIC286 (90' · DDD). Played on the Cavaillé-Coll organ of Royaumont Abbey, France   Ⓑ

The misty acoustic, the puffy action noise and the heavy preponderance of eight- and 16-foot stops exude a suitably 19th-century atmosphere; and unreserved congratulations go to the engineers who have given us such an evocative sound-portrait of this fine Cavaillé-Coll (originally designed for a private house in 1864 and now moved to Royaumont Abbey). It has some truly lovely sounds – not least the delectable combination Joris Verdin conjures up for the 'Pastorale' of the Second Symphony.

Joris Verdin is faithful to the original edition of these four symphonies, first published as a group in 1872, and those familiar with the later performing versions of these works will immediately notice the differences; here the First Symphony has only five movements, the well known 'Marche ponitificale' as well as a 'Méditation' added later, while the Second possesses a gloriously nautical 'Scherzo' which was (sadly) later replaced by a 'Salve regina'. Recording these original versions is, however, not merely something of historic interest, it is an extremely worthwhile musical venture, and while students of Widor will find much to argue over, anyone with an ear for finely crafted music played with great panache and affection on a fine organ will not be disappointed here.

Henryk Wieniawski   Polish 1835-1880

After study at the Paris Conservatoire Wieniawski embarked on the career of a travelling virtuoso, giving concerts throughout Europe and in Russia. At the invitation of Anton Rubinstein he settled in St Petersburg (1860-72) where he laid the foundations for the Russian violin school. As a composer he wrote extensively for his own instrument, including two violin concertos. His last official position was as violin professor at the Brussels Conservatory (1875-77).

Violin Concerto No 1

Wieniawski Violin Concerto No 1 in F sharp minor, Op 14[b] **Beach** Romance, Op 23[a] **Debussy** Préludes – La fille aux cheveux de lin (arr A Hartmann)[a] **Elgar** Chanson de nuit, Op 15 No 1[a] **Kreisler** La Gitana[a] **Poldini** Marionnettes – Poupée valsante (arr Kreisler)[a] **Prokofiev** Tales of an Old Grandmother, Op 31 (arr Milstein)[a] – Andantino; Andante assai
Midori vn [a]**Robert McDonald** pf
[b]**St Louis Symphony Orchestra / Leonard Slatkin**
Sony Classical SK89700 (52' · DDD) (F)O☞

Wieniawski's First Violin Concerto has never matched No 2 in popularity, but Midori's involving performance makes one wonder why. Put it alongside Perlman's EMI version with the LPO under Ozawa, and – perhaps not surprisingly – her live account sounds more volatile and more freely expressive, with even the conventional passagework given an extra sparkle. She also chooses a more flowing *Larghetto* for the central 'Preghiera' (Prayer) slow movement, which brings out the songful lyricism more persuasively, with her first entry magically hushed, full of natural gravity. The dotted rhythms of the Rondo finale are then even more playful. The radio recording is full and forwardly balanced, but the range of dynamic and expression in Midori's playing is never compromised.

In the encore pieces, the range of dynamic is again remarkable. She plays the opening item, Hartmann's arrangement of Debussy's 'La fille aux cheveux de lin', with such delicacy she seems simply to be musing to herself, and her simple gravity in Elgar's *Chanson de nuit*, the last item, taken steadily, turns it into a sort of prayer. Such an approach could easily have lapsed into sentimentality, but emphatically not so here. A thoroughly enjoyable disc.

Hugo Wolf   Austrian 1860-1903

The fourth son of a leather merchant, an amateur musician who discouraged a musical career, Wolf was expelled from three different schools and was eventually thrown out of the Vienna Conservatory, which he'd entered in 1875, not because of his argumentative nature, his sullen disposition or the neglect of his studies – though all of these were true. He was the innocent victim of a malicious hoax: someone had sent a threatening letter to the director and signed it from Hugo Wolf.

All his life he lived in abject poverty. Unable to live at home, he had to depend on friends for lodgings and funds. He read music constantly and Wagner was his God – he met the great man once, aged 15, and showed him a song he had written. Wagner brushed the young hopeful aside telling him it was far too early for anyone to make judgements on whether one had talent or not.

When at last Wolf landed a job as assistant conductor to Karl Muck in Salzburg, he arrived with a bundle of clothes under one arm and a bust of Wagner under the other. Inevitably, the job lasted only a few months – he quarrelled with everyone – and he found himself once more back in Vienna. In 1884 he became the music critic of the Salonblatt and held on to this post for three years. His passionately held views made him many friends for he was devastatingly honest in his criticism and praise. He also made many powerful enemies.

But in 1888 Wolf had some encouragement. Some of his songs were issued by a small publishing house. This prompted an amazing outburst of creative energy and in one year he wrote 53 songs; a few months later he set 50 of Goethe's poems to music within the space of three and a half months. He himself could not believe what was happening – it was as if someone else was composing. He tackled German poems, Italian poems translated into German and Spanish poems translated into German. He had an innate ability to capture the spirit and character of each poem, combining Schumann's genius for striking exactly the right balance between vocal line and accompaniment with Schubert's grander rhetorical style. Wolf's gloomy life and intense personality are reflected in his music, certainly, but these elements by no means dominate. There is more passion, humour and sunshine than morbidity and Austrian weltschmerz.

In 1891 inspiration suddenly dried up like a stream in a drought. He was beside himself until he was able to write again at the end of the year. Again, for two years (1892-94) nothing came; then there was another burst in 1895. By then, there were some signs of recognition and even the formerly hostile dean of critics, Eduard Hanslick, had some kind things to say. Two Hugo Wolf Societies were formed in Berlin and Vienna. But this success was checked by the failure of Wolf's opera Der Corregidor at its premiere in Mannheim in 1896. When the Vienna Opera turned it down after initially agreeing to do it, something snapped and the syphilis he had contracted as a 17-year-old began to take hold. He was put in a sanatorium for a rest cure but on returning to Vienna from Italy he tried to commit suicide in the Traunsee. From 1898 for the remainder of his life he was confined in the Lower Austrian Mental Hospital. His body became more paralysed, his mind more confused.

Goethe Lieder

Goethe Lieder – Harfenspieler: I, Wer sich der   **H**
Einsamkeit ergibt; II, An die Türen; III, Wer nie sein Brot; Coptisches Lied I & II; Anakreons Grab; Ob der Koran von Ewigkeit sei?; So lang man nüchtern ist; Prometheus; Grenzen der Menschheit. Italienisches Liederbuch – Ein Ständchen Euch zu bringen; Schon streckt' ich aus; Geselle, woll'n wir uns in Kutten hüllen. Drei Gedichte von Michelangelo. Eichendorff Lieder – Der Musikant. Mörike Lieder – Der Tambour; Nimmersatte Liebe; Fussreise; Verborgenheit
Hans Hotter bass-bar **Gerald Moore** pf
Testament mono SBT1197 (70' · ADD · T/t)
Recorded 1951, 1953 & 1957 (F)OO

At last: a reissue of Hotter's 1953 Hugo Wolf recital, which forms the centrepiece of this release, and it's in far better, more immediate sound than on the original LP. Hotter's interpretations of 'Prometheus', 'Grenzen der Menschheit', the gloomy *Harfenspieler* Lieder and resigned Michelangelo settings – Wolf at his greatest – remain virtually unsurpassed. They were surely written with a bass-baritone of Hotter's calibre in mind and, quite apart from his vocal prowess, his verbal insights are once again remarkable, while the account of the naughty monks' exploits from the *Italian Songbook* remind us of Hotter the humorist. The earlier and later items that complete the CD disclose similar gifts, notably the delightful 'Der Tambour' – and 'Anakreons Grab', which, both in 1951 and 1957, matches the *Innigkeit* of Goethe's poem and Wolf's setting. Moore is a masterly partner in music that severely taxes the pianist. This disc is a must for Wolf enthusiasts.

Goethe Lieder – Mignon – I, Heiss mich nicht reden; II, Nur wer die Sehnsucht kennt; III, So lasst mich scheinen. Philine. Mignon, 'Kennst du das Land?'. Gutmann und Gutweib. Epiphanias. St Nepomuks Vorabend. Der Schäfer. Blumengruss. Gleich und Gleich. Die Spröde. Die Bekehrte. Frühling übers Jahr. Anakreons Grab. Dank des Paria. Phänomen. So lang man nüchtern ist. Hoch beglückt in deiner Liebe. Als ich auf dem Euphrat schiffte. Nimmer will ich dich verlieren!. Ganymed. Gretchen vor dem Andachtsbild der Mater Dolorosa. Wanderers Nachtlied
Geraldine McGreevy sop **Graham Johnson** pf
Hyperion CDA67130 (76' · DDD · T/t)　　　　Ⓕ𝔹➔

The first and abiding impression made by this recital is of air and grace. Graham Johnson's piano-playing is delightfully free yet exact. McGreevy's voice has a warmth in its still youthful glow; she also has the art of making it smile. In the first two Mignon songs she intensifies tone and emotion quite movingly; in 'Kennst du das Land?' she may be not quite *seeing* the mountain and caves of the third verse or feeling the awesome power of the 'Flut', and in 'Philine' she lacks the naughty zest for it. Yet always there are lovely things – as when she catches the expression of the statues as they put to Mignon their piteous question. She's also good (as are they both) at the boisterous 'Gutmann und Gutweib': a rarity that's lucky to find in Johnson so persuasive an advocate.

Italienisches Liederbuch

Italienisches Liederbuch
Christiane Oelze sop **Hans Peter Blochwitz** ten
Rudolf Jansen pf
Berlin Classics 0017482BC (78' · DDD · T)　　　Ⓕⓞ

These three excellent artists sensibly understate rather than overstate the songs' emotional content and where – about midway through the collection – the feelings become more immediate, the performers come forth with just the

right amount of added intensity. Christiane Oelze's fine-grained soprano, spirited readings and incisive diction fulfil just about every side of the songs assigned to her – from mocking, jealousy and anger to true love – and she wholly avoids the archness that afflicts some interpreters. Hans Peter Blochwitz, always a discerning Lieder singer, may have lost a little of his sweet tenor's bloom but compensates with a true understanding of the lyrical impulse that suffuses those wonderful love songs given to the male interpreter, especially the three successive, outright masterpieces beginning with 'Sterb' ich, so hüllt in Blumen'.

Rudolf Jansen deserves a notice to himself for his unravelling of all the intricacies of the often independent piano parts and for his outright mastery in giving the keyboard its due without ever stealing the thunder of the singers; his instrument is ideally balanced with the voices in a truthful recording. These songs are so remarkable that there will never be one definitive way of singing them. On another disc featuring a tenor, Schreier is a fuller-voiced, more 'interventionist' interpreter than Blochwitz: that pays huge dividends in some songs, less in others. In the end, the choice depends on a preference for one singer over another: Oelze and Blochwitz are probably favourite.

Mörike Lieder

Mörike Lieder – Der Genesene an die Hoffnung; Ein Stündlein wohl vor Tag; Der Tambour; Nimmersatte Liebe; Fussreise; Verborgenheit; Im Frühling; Auf einer Wanderung; Der Gärtner; In der Frühe; Gebet; Neue Liebe; Wo find' ich Trost?; Frage und Antwort; Lebe wohl; Heimweh; Denk' es, o Seele!; Der Jäger; Storchenbotschaft; Bei einer Trauung; Selbstgeständis; Abschied
Peter Schreier ten **Karl Engel** pf
Orfeo C142 981A (60' · DDD · T/t)　　　　Ⓕⓞ

Peter Schreier's ever-supple tenor, honed by keen-eyed intelligence and a verbal palate sharp enough to taste and try every last word, makes him a Wolf interpreter of the highest order. In this meticulously shaped programme of 22 of Wolf's eager settings of Mörike, one wonder appears after another. Schreier and his ever-sentient pianist, Karl Engel, move from a gentle awakening of love, which grows in intensity towards the innermost core of songs of doubt and fear, and on through a gallery of wonderfully dry, wry tableaux to the final farewell and the kicking of the critic downstairs. The first song here, 'Im Frühling', epitomises the equilibrium, security and entirety of performances which have grown from long-pondered consideration. The long, drowsy vowels and Schreier's sensitivity to the high-register placing of crucial words of longing all fuse into the slow-walking movement of cloud, wing, river, breeze, as language becomes expanded and enriched by tone. Schreier's remarkable steadiness of line in 'Verborgenheit' reveals the song's secrets only reluctantly: the fierce intensity of sudden illumination is all the more searing. Grotesquerie and poignancy coexist in 'Bei einer Trauung', and we feel every catch of the voice as Schreier turns weird and whimsical tale-teller in Storchenbotschaft.

Mörike Lieder – Der Genesene an die Hoffnung; Er ist's; Begegnung; Fussreise; Verborgenheit; Im Frühling; Auf einer Wanderung; Um Mitternacht; Auf ein altes Bild; In der Frühe; Wo find' ich Trost?; An die Geliebte; Peregrina I; Peregrina II; Lebe wohl; Heimweh; Denk' es, o Seele!; Der Feuerreiter; Die Geister am Mummelsee; Storchenbotschaft; Auftrag; Abschied
Roman Trekel bar **Oliver Pohl** pf
Oehms Classics OC305 (68' · DDD · T)   Ⓕ

There can be no better advocate of Hugo Wolf than Roman Trekel, now at the peak of his career as a Lieder interpreter, who presents this deeply satisfying recital of the best of the *Mörike Lieder*. These inspired songs need, above all, the kind of intense expression and intimate, detailed treatment that Trekel brings them. Performed as convincingly as they are here, they offer a particular frisson of individual accent that no other composer in the genre, whatever their other merits, quite equals: words and music seem as though they were written at one and the same time

Trekel achieves an ideal fusion of tonal security, sense of line and word-painting. In a comparatively long and complex Lied such as 'Im Frühling', he and the admirable Oliver Pohl traverse all the points of the expressive compass, and all the nuances of dynamics that belong to them. In that surpassingly sincere and beautiful love-song 'An die Geliebte' they build to the climax from 'Von Tiefe dann zu Tiefen' with a confidence that bespeaks long familiarity with the piece. Even better is the heartache they bring to 'Peregrina II' and 'Lebe wohl', where Wolf seems to enter into all the poet's suffering at the hands of a beloved. They also find the inner spirituality of the religion-inspired settings, such as 'Auf ein altes Bild' and 'Denk' es o Seele', the latter so compelling for saying so much in such a short time. In a quite different vein, they rise marvellously to the frenzied melodrama of 'Der Feuerreiter', always a challenge to singer and pianist and one that's surely met here.

A truthful recording adds to the disc's merits. Not so the notes, which omit any exposition of the songs and also English translations. Even so, this is a recital that ought to convert even Wolf heretics to the cause.

Mörike Lieder – Jägerlied; Der Tambour; Er ist's; Begegnung; Nimmersatte Liebe; Fussreise; Im Frühling; Auf einer Wanderung; Elfenlied; Der Gärtner; Um Mitternacht; Auf eine Christblume II; In der Frühe; Schlafendes Jesuskind; Gebet; An den Schlaf; An die Geliebte; Peregrina I; Peregrina II; Frage und Antwort; Lebe wohl; Denk' es, o Seele!; Lied eines Verliebten; Der Feuerreiter; Zur Warnung;

Bei einer Trauung
Wolfgang Holzmair bar **Imogen Cooper** pf
Wigmore Hall Live WHLIVE0029 (73' · DDD · T/t)
Recorded live in February 2008   Ⓜ

It was the subtle, impassioned, often humorous verses of the Swabian pastor-poet Eduard Mörike that, early in 1888, released Wolf from one of his recurrent creative impasses. The upshot was a richly varied anthology of 53 songs written in a characteristic frenzy of euphoria. At the Wigmore Hall in 2008 Wolfgang Holzmair and Imogen Cooper – always a rewarding Lieder partnership – performed 26 of them, plus an encore, 'Selbstgeständis', the ironic confession of a spoilt only child. With the exception of the sin-drenched religious songs ('Seufzer', 'Wo find' ich Trost?'), their programme encompassed virtually every aspect of the Mörike Songbook, from delicate character sketches and pantheistic nature lyrics to the demonic glitter of 'Der Feuerreiter' and the drolly acerbic song about a poet's hangover, 'Zur Warnung'.

These days Holzmair's light, tenorish – and distinctively Viennese – baritone can become tight under pressure, as at the central climax of an otherwise blithe, open-hearted 'Fussreise'. Occasionally his characteristic plangent vibrato can loosen into a quaver. But in close Wolfian collusion, he and Cooper are attentive alike to musical and poetic detail and the songs' larger shape. The enchanting 'Auf einer Wanderung' (where Cooper, typically, is minutely sensitive to Wolf's kaleidoscopic key shifts) has an ideal smiling eagerness, culminating in a rapt invocation to the Muses. Holzmair is graceful and ardent in another favourite, 'Der Gärtner', given a captivating lilt by Cooper, and both impassioned and truly *innig*, as Wolf asks, in 'Lebe wohl'.

On occasion Holzmair can resort to a semi-*Sprechgesang* where others preserve line and singing tone. Yet more often pleasure is virtually unalloyed. The recording sets the piano slightly further back than you may find ideal in Wolf, though the ear quickly adjusts. Presentation, as usual in this series, is first-rate, with texts and excellent translations by Richard Stokes, who also writes illuminatingly on the creative relationship between Mörike and Wolf.

Lieder

Eichendorff Lieder – Der Musikant; Verschwiegene Liebe; Das Ständchen; Nachtzauber; Seemanns Abschied. Goethe Lieder – Gutmann und Gutweib; Ganymed. Mörike Lieder – Der Genesene an die Hoffnung; Der Knabe und das Immlein; Begegnung; Nimmersatte Liebe; Verborgenheit; Im Frühling; Auf einer Wanderung; Um Mitternacht; Auf ein altes Bild; Gebet; An den Schlaf; An die Geliebte; Peregrina I; Peregrina II; Der Jäger; Lied eines Verliebten; Abschied
Ian Bostridge ten **Antonio Pappano** pf
EMI 342256-2 (72' · DDD · T/t) Ⓕ

Recordings of Wolf songs are rare today, ones sung by tenors even rarer, yet here comes one to delight the ear. Ian Bostridge's choice of songs is typically fastidious, his interpretation of them full of the intelligence, understanding and musicality we expect from him.

With Antonio Pappano in wonderfully supportive, positive form, they rise to inspired heights in the central group of Mörike settings – 'Im Frühling', 'Auf ein altes Bild', 'Gebet', 'An den Schlaf' and 'An die Geliebte'. In these contrasting songs of religious insight and deep love, Bostridge performs with a kind of inward concentration and then elatory spirit, coupled with his rapt palpitating tone, that precisely matches with Wolf's masterpieces. He is perhaps even better in the Goethe setting 'Ganymed', which can seldom if ever have received such a rapturous performance, and brings the recital to a satisfying close.

Against these wonders must be set songs where his syllabic emphasis and tendency to *Sprechgesang* lead to performances that sound mincing: 'Begegnung', 'Nimmersatte Liebe' (grossly overdone) and, earlier among the Eichendorff songs, 'Nachtzauber'. Here the wish to extract something from every word robs the songs of their natural flow, though among the Eichendorff settings, the over-familiar 'Verschwiegene Liebe' receives an unfettered and restorative reading.

Bostridge, with Pappano an always inventive partner, makes you hear the songs – like it or not – anew. One may not always capitulate to the results, but Wolf is a composer who, above all, benefits from two artists willing to live dangerously. They are helped by John Fraser's well balanced and full-bodied recording.

Oswald von Wolkenstein
German c1376-1445

Von Wolkenstein was a poet, composer and diplomat. As the repesentative of Sigismund, King of the Holy Roman Empire and of Hungary, he travelled through much of Europe. He is one of the most important composers of the early German Renaissance, and his melodies are of high quality. There are three main topics of his work: travel, God and sex.

Songs

'Songs of Myself'
Anonymous Parlamento. Mi, mi, sol, fa. Mit ganzem willen wünsch ich dir **Laufenberg** Bist grüsst maget reine **Wolkenstein** Es fügt sich. Herz, müt, leib, sel. Fröhlich zärtlich. Di molen van pariis[a]. Grasselik lif. Durch Barbarei, Arabia. Ach, senliches leiden. Des himels trone. Nu rue mit sorgen. Kom, liebster man. Jeloymors[b]. Der mai mit lieber zal. Vierhundert jar. Der oben swebt. Wes mich mein bühl
Andreas Scholl *counterten/bar* [a]**Pierre Des Molins**, [b]**Gilles Binchois** *tens* **Shield of Harmony** (Kathleen Dineen *sop/hp* Marc Lewon *citt/lte/viel/nyck* Margit Übellacker *dulce melos*) / **Crawford Young** *lte/citt*

Harmonia Mundi HMC90 2051 (81' · DDD · T/t)
Ⓕ OOOⒹ

This is a winner; and it will add enormously to Andreas Scholl's already enormous reputation. In the music of Oswald von Wolkenstein he has tackled one of the seriously difficult repertories of the Middle Ages, a couple of hundred years earlier than anything he has previously recorded. To do so he has assembled an excellent ensemble, with people who have specialised in this material for many years, and additionally enlisted the guidance of his former teacher, Richard Levitt, one of whose most enduring achievements is itself a record of music by Oswald.

Nobody is entirely clear how much Oswald was a composer – a suspiciously large portion of his known music is demonstrably borrowed from others – but he certainly ranks as one of the great linguistic innovators in German poetry and Scholl projects those texts magnificently, drawing on an inexhaustible range of colours and moods. His instrumental ensemble is based around plucked sounds, with an occasional use of vielle; and they are deployed with imagination as well as with a restraint that reflects the very latest position of musicological research on this music. Where the surviving music is monophonic, the newly devised accompaniments are eloquent as well as tactful; where there is written polyphony the scoring is impeccable. The result is an absolute ear-opener.

It is perhaps important also to salute the presence of Irish soprano Kathleen Dineen, who has hitherto had a fairly low profile in the CD catalogue but here sings two magnificent unaccompanied duets with Scholl as well as an unaccompanied solo song. This is a highly impressive, top-league debut.

Iannis Xenakis   Greek/French 1922-2001

Xenakis was a French composer of Greek parentage and Romanian birth. He was educated on Spetsai and at the Athens Polytechnic, where he studied engineering. In 1947 he arrived in Paris, where he became a member of Le Corbusier's architectural team, producing his first musical work, Metastasis, only in his early thirties. It was based on the design for the surfaces of the Philips pavilion to be built for the Brussels Exposition of 1958. It was a highly influential work but subsequently he explored mathematical and computer-based methods for composition. He also experimented with electronics in his later works.

Chamber Works

Atrées[a]. Morsima-Amorsima[b]. Nomos alpha[c]. Herma[d]. ST/4[e]. Polla ta dhina[f]. ST/10-1080262[g]. Akrata[h]. Achorripsis[i]
[b]**Jean-Claude Bernède** *vn* [b]**Paul Boufil**, [c]**Pierre Penassou** *vcs* [b]**Jacques Cazauran** *db*

1319

bdGeorges Pludermacher *pf* eQuatuor Bernède;
fMaîtrise de Notre Dame de Paris; afghiInstrumental
Ensemble of Contemporary Music, Paris /
abfghiKonstantin Simonovich
EMI ② 687674-2 (109' · ADD)   ⓈⓄ☞

These 40-year-old recordings still pack a considerable acoustic punch. Remastered to keep the original colours sharp without adding anachronistic atmosphere, they provide powerful testimony of the commitment of pioneering performers to difficult but memorable new music.

Apart from the brief and uncharacteristically scrappy *Achorripsis* (1957), all the works included were written between 1962 and 1966, when Xenakis was showing how then-new computer technology could set up a music whose rawness seemed like a calculatedly earthy slap in the face to Boulezian refinement. With many of the original artists involved in these recordings, high degrees of competence are evident, and nowhere more so than in the potent ritual of *Polla ta dhina*: a children's choir sing a Greek text (on one note, but with varied rhythms) while an instrumental ensemble weaves a dense, disruptive web around this stable centre. Sadly, the text as such – from Sophocles' *Antigone* – is not provided.

The redoubtable Konstantin Simonovich directs this, along with various purely instrumental scores, including the spectacularly polychromatic *ST/10*. The ensemble pieces *Atrées* and *Akrata* are no less spectacular in their contrasting ways. Then, in two of Xenakis's most demanding solo works, pianist Georges Pludermacher does battle with the untameable turbulence of *Herma* while Pierre Penassou tackles the longest and most enthralling item of all. *Nomos alpha* takes the cello apart and reassembles it in a structure that balances the varied recurrences of strongly contrasted materials to absorbing effect over an 18-minute span. The sound may have dated but the music radiates the timeless force of true modernity.

Knephas

A Colone. Nuits. Serment. Knephas. Medea
**New London Chamber Choir; Critical Band /
James Wood**
Hyperion CDA66980 (58' · DDD · T/t)   Ⓕ ⓄⓄⓄ☞

This enterprising release is a great success, showing just how varied – and unintimidating – Xenakis's music can be. The performances are nothing short of phenomenal in their technical assurance and emotional power, and the recording is also something special, giving the singers just the right degree of space and resonance to project the often complex textures with all the necessary precision. The earliest works offer different angles on the composer's ultra-expressionist idiom, with *Nuits* (1967) adopting a very direct way of representing its anguished lament for the martyrs of Greece's struggle for freedom after 1945. *Medea* (also 1967) uses much more text, and its chant-like style has affinities with

Stravinsky's *Les noces*, but the overall effect is much harsher, with abrasive yet imaginative instrumental writing. *A Colone* (1977) also has Stravinskian affinities, and the text (Sophocles's description of the delights of Colonus) prompts music which is uninhibitedly exuberant. This warmer, more celebratory side of Xenakis is carried over into *Serment* (1980), a short setting of a text derived from the Hippocratic Oath and not, one suspects, an entirely serious effort, though there's nothing trivial about it either. Finally, the superb *Knephas* ('Darkness') of 1990 begins in an appropriately unsparing manner, but ends with a hymnic apotheosis which recalls Messiaen in its harmonic character and warmth of atmosphere. Here is one of the 20th century's most important musical voices, and this recording does it full justice.

Eugene Ysaÿe   Belgian 1858-1931

One of the great violinists, Ysaÿe studied under Wieniawski in Brussels and Vieuxtemps in Paris. As professor at the Brussels Conservatory (1887-99) he initiated the Concerts Ysaÿe, appearing as violinist and conductor in contemporary French and Belgian music, meanwhile becoming renowned throughout Europe and in the USA (he was conductor of the Cincinnati SO from 1918 to 1922). As a composer he left a number of virtuoso works for violin, including six solo sonatas, his Op 27.

Violin Sonatas, Op 27

Solo Violin Sonatas
Thomas Zehetmair *vn*
ECM New Series 472 687-2 (66' · DDD)   Ⓕ ⓄⓄ☞

By tailoring his solo sonatas to fit the styles of six very different violinists Eugène Ysaÿe may have been acting as the ultimate critic, describing his subjects with musical illustrations rather than mere words. For example, there are the winking appoggiaturas in the finale of No 4, dedicated to Kreisler, which Thomas Zehetmair throws off with a mere flick of the wrist, or the rich chord structures of No 1, whose dedicatee, Joseph Szigeti, was a great Bach player. Bach is a particularly strong presence there, the key (G minor) and language so reminiscent of his first solo sonata. Again, the Jacques Thibaud piece, No 2 in A minor, has obsessive repetitions of the Prelude from Bach's E major Partita, played initially by Zehetmair with the lightest touch, though later repetitions gain in intensity. The sinister melding of Bach with the 'Dies irae' chant has to be one of the canniest masterstrokes of the period. There are stylistic parallels between No 2 and No 4, just as there were similarities between the players themselves.

The spicy Sixth Sonata recalls the Spanish fiddler Manuel Quiroga and takes on Latin influences, initially suggesting Ravel's *Tzigane* (composed at around the same time, though the similarity is probably coincidental) before shifting, a little later, to *habanera* mode.

As the ultimate thinking virtuoso, Zehetmair is an ideal interpreter of these pieces, delving between the notes, coaxing a wealth of colour, inflection and dynamic shading from each score, always with acute imagination. He is both explorer and demonstrator, his modes of attack as varied as his tone colouring. This is the best possible showcase for some marvellous if still undervalued music.

Riccardo Zandonai   Italian 1883-1944

Zandonai studied at the conservatory in Pesaro where one of his teachers was Mascagni (in 1935 Zandonai would become director of the conservatory). In 1902 he set a Pascoli poem, 'Il sogno di Rosetta', to some acclaim. In 1908, in Milan, he was heard by Arrigo Boito at a soirée, and Boito introduced him to Giulio Ricordi, one of Italy's foremost music publishers. Of his 13 operas, Francesca da Rimini is his best known work. Zandonai was the composer Puccini selected to complete Turandot but for whatever reason, the assignment went to Alfano.

Francesca da Rimini

Francesca da Rimini
Fabio Armiliato *ten* Paolo 'il Bello' **Daniela Dessì**
sop Francesca **Alberto Mastromarino** *bar* Giovanni
'lo Sciancato' **Giacinta Nicotra** *sop* Samaritana
Giuseppe Altomare *bar* Ostasio **Rosella Bevacqua**
sop Garsenda **Sabrina Modena** *mez* Adonella
Francesca Rinaldi *mez* Altichiara **Roberta Canzian**
sop Bianciofore **Angela Masi** *contr* La Schiava
Smaragdi **Ludovít Ludha** *ten* Malatestino
Dall'Occhio **Francesco Zingariello** *ten* Ser Toldo
Berardengo **Domenico Colaianni** *bass* Il Giullare
Alessandro Pucci *ten* Il Balestriere **Michelangelo
Brecciaroli** *bar* Un Prigioniero
**Vincenzo Bellini Lyric Chorus, Marchigiana;
Marchigiana Philharmonic Orchestra /
Maurizio Barbacini**
Stage director **Massimo Gasparon**
Video director **Michelangelo Rossi**
ArtHaus Musik 📀 101 363 (137' · NTSC · 4:3 · PCM
stereo, 5.1 and DTS 5.1 · 0)
Recorded live 2004   Ⓕ🔘🔘

This is just the sort of work for which a DVD issue is invaluable. One could travel the world and never find oneself in a city where the opera company was putting on Zandonai's most famous work. Premiered in 1914, it has had distinguished stagings (including one at the New York Met in 1984 with Scotto and Domingo, which is also on DVD from DG), but few and far between.

The tragic story of Francesca, married off against her will to the brutal Giovanni 'lo Sciancato' but all the time in love with his younger brother Paolo 'il Bello', is based on D'Annunzio's play, itself taken from an episode in Dante's *Inferno*. The title-role is a great challenge for the soprano: she is on stage for most of the evening. Daniela Dessì, understandably, begins slightly cautiously, but she rises splendidly to the great love duet at the end of Act 3, when the lovers read the story of Lancelot and Guinevere, and find their own passion cannot be denied.

Act 4 has a scene in which Francesca is taunted by the third brother, the scathing Malatestino, who is having a prisoner tortured offstage (shades of Act 2 of *Tosca*). He eventually exits and returns with the unfortunate victim's head, wrapped in a cloth. Ludovít Ludha is excellent in this part, as is Fabio Armiliato as Paolo. Alberto Mastromarino as Giovanni gets to hold the stage at the end: having murdered the lovers, he breaks his sword in half.

Massimo Gasparon's production is satisfyingly old-fashioned, his costumes evoking 14th-century Italy – heaven knows how many metres of brocade and silk were used. The big scene in Act 2, in which a battle is raging around the castle and Francesca refuses to hide but watches from a tower, is a bit difficult to show on the small screen, but the 'silent' duet at the end of Act 1, when Francesca sees Paolo for the first time and gives him a rose, is finely achieved. Zandonai's orchestral effects are fascinating, and Maurizio Barbacini and the Marchigiana orchestra make the most of them. Coming almost at the end of the age of *verismo*, *Francesca da Rimini* seems like a summing-up of all the influences that had weighed on Italian opera, and were ultimately to destroy it. It is a fascinating work – all the more enjoyable then to encounter it on DVD.

Jan Dismas Zelenka
Bohemian 1679-1745

A fine double-bass player who played in the royal orchestra at Dresden, Zelenka studied with Fux in Vienna and Lotti in Venice. From 1719 he remained in Dresden. Having gradually taken over the duties of the ailing Kapellmeister, Heinichen, he was made only church music composer (1735); Hasse was the new Kapellmeister. He composed mainly sacred works, among them three oratorios and 12 Masses.

Trio Sonatas

Trio Sonatas – No 2 in G minor, No 5 in F;   🅟
No 6 in C minor
Ensemble Zefiro (Paolo Grazzi, Alfredo Bernardini)
obs Alberto Grazzi *bn* Roberto Sensi *db* Rolf
Lislevand *theorbo* Rinaldo Alessandrini *hpd/org*)
Astrée Naïve E8511 (52' · DDD)   Ⓕ🔘

For sheer élan and spirit the Baroque instrumental players on this disc take some beating. Zelenka's six sonatas for two oboes, bassoon and continuo are among the most rewarding and at times most difficult pieces of Baroque chamber music in the oboe repertory. Indeed, pieces demanding such virtuosity from these instruments were probably without precedent at the time (1715). The writing is often such as to make us wonder if they were destined for friends or for enemies of the composer. Here, then, we're treated to some splendidly invigorating playing of music which offers a great deal beyond face value. The sounds of the solo instruments themselves, together with an effective continuo group of double bass, harpsichord/organ and theorbo are admirably captured in the recording.

The Lamentations of Jeremiah

The Lamentations of Jeremiah   Ⓟ
Michael Chance *counterten* **John Mark Ainsley**
ten **Michael George** *bass* **Chandos Baroque Players**
Hyperion Helios CDH55106 (73' · DDD · T/t)   Ⓑ

Between the incomparable settings by Thomas Tallis and the extremely austere one by Stravinsky (which he called *Threni*), the *Lamentations of Jeremiah* have attracted surprisingly few composers. Perhaps the predominantly sombre tone, without even the dramatic opportunities presented by the *Dies irae* in a *Requiem*, is off-putting. Be that as it may, Zelenka showed remarkable resourcefulness in his 1722 setting for the electoral chapel at Dresden, where he was Kapellmeister. His musical language is in many ways similar to that of JS Bach but there are also daring turns of phrase which are entirely personal. The six *Lamentations* feature each singer twice; this performance is intimate, slightly spacious in tempo and with a resonant acoustic.

Alexander Zemlinsky
Austrian 1871-1942

Zemlinsky studied at the Vienna Conservatory. In 1895 he became a close friend of Schoenberg's and received patronage from Mahler, who presented his opera Es war einmal at the Hofoper in 1900. His orchestral fantasy Die Seejungfrau dates from these years. By this time he was working as a theatre conductor in Vienna his later appointments were at the German theatre in Prague (1911-27) and the Kroll Opera in Berlin (1927-31). In 1933 he fled to Vienna, and then in 1938 to the USA. His output includes a number of operas, orchestral and chamber works.

Eine lyrische Symphonie, Op 18

Eine lyrische Symphonie
Christine Schäfer *sop* **Matthias Goerne** *bar*
Orchestre de Paris / Christoph Eschenbach
Capriccio 71 081 (52' · DDD/DSD · T/t)   Ⓕ

There have been several memorable recordings of Zemlinsky's masterpiece and this one, the first for many years, can be placed in their company. Christoph Eschenbach and his soloists clearly agree that the *Lyric Symphony* is not simply an orchestral song-cycle but a symphonic music-drama: the resulting performance has all the vividness and immediacy of a live event yet – equally importantly – excessive histrionics are avoided. This is music that needs no nudging or special pleading to exercise its power and poignancy.

Matthias Goerne has the combination of vocal heft and lyric mellifluousness necessary to sustain the demanding lines of the work's four odd-numbered episodes. Perhaps the third section, with its particularly sumptuous orchestral backcloth, could have taken a degree or two more of sheer vocal refinement, but overall Goerne does full justice to the heart-rending finale.

Christine Schäfer is especially convincing in the dramatic final stages of the second movement, and also in the Expressionistic sixth. Ideally, the fourth movement's gentle lover's plea might be even more rapt, more other-worldly than it is here. But this reading fits well with the interpretation as a whole. The voices are forwardly placed without loss of orchestral detail, and only in the brief, turbulent fifth movement might one feel that the instrumental sound needs more edge. Even so, the orchestral playing throughout is superb.

Additional recommendation

Eine florentinische Tragödie[a]. Eine lyrische Symphonie, Op 18[b]. Symphonische Gesänge[c]
Three Psalms
Vermillion *mez* **Kruse** *ten* **Dohmen** *bar* **Marc** *sop*
Hagegård *bar* **White** *bass* **Royal Concertgebouw Orchestra / Chailly**
Double Decca ② 473 734-2DF2 (156' · DDD)   ⓂⓄ⇨

A Florentine Tragedy is a disturbing, shocking piece, but to make its fullest impact it also needs to sound ravishingly beautiful. Zemlinsky's sumptuous scoring often demands an orchestra of the Royal Concertgebouw's stature, and in this reading it sounds quite magnificent. The recording leaves nothing to be desired: the colours are rich and clean. (Not currently listed on CD, but downloadable.)

CONDUCTORS

Sir John Barbirolli

Haydn Symphony No 83 in G minor, 'La poule'
Lehár Gold und Silber, Op 79 **J Strauss II**
Die Fledermaus – Overture. Kaiser-Walzer, Op 437.
Perpetuum mobile, Op 257. Tritsch-Tratsch-Polka,
Op 214 **R Strauss** Der Rosenkavalier Suite
Hallé Orchestra / Sir John Barbirolli
BBC Legends BBCL4038-2 (76' · ADD)
Recorded live 1969 Ⓜ ⓞⓞ

Among all the treasures rediscovered in the
BBC archives, this disc of a Barbirolli Prom
Concert of 1969 is among the most enticing. He
opens with one of his favourite Haydn symphonies, and only Beecham can match his delightful
characterisation of *The Hen* which Haydn makes
sure we hear several times in the course of a most
appealing first movement. As shaped by JB the
Andante combines an Elysian simplicity with
classical beauty of line, and the Minuet and
finale similarly match grace with exuberance.
There's surely no finer performance on disc.

Then comes the Johann Strauss section, with
Sir John himself vocalising in the Overture's
glorious waltz theme. But the highlight is a
richly contoured, magical account of the
Emperor Waltz, with all the mellow nobility of
line one associates with Bruno Walter, plus an
added touch of Barbirolli's Italianate sunshine.
The reprise is so lovely it would melt the hardest
heart. Then follows a fun performance of the
Tritsch-Tratsch-Polka, with outrageous agogic
tempo distortions and sudden pauses which
bring a couple of great bursts of laughter from
the Promenaders. But the best is yet to come.

With the *Rosenkavalier* suite the Hallé strings
and horns surpass themselves. The suite may be
no more than a comparatively inept pot-pourri,
but Sir John invests each section of the score with
such loving detail that you can only regret that he
never recorded the whole opera. The Prelude,
with its sexy, whooping horns, and a great passionate *tenuto* on the key moment of the lovers'
passionate embrace (behind the curtain), then
leads on to a wonderful feeling of tenderness as
their ardour gently subsides. Later the Presentation of the Rose scene, with exquisite oboe playing, is meltingly beautiful. After the great surge of
the Viennese waltz sequence, the closing section
and the sensuous duet that sees Octavian and
Sophie departing together is wonderfully affectionate, rudely interrupted by the explosive coda.

The encore is Lehár's *Gold and Silver*. Sir John
encourages his Promenaders to hum along gently so as not to overwhelm its famous lyrical
melody; he even manages to entice them into a
pianississimo when it's reprised. Prommers in the
late 1960s were just as appreciative but more
self-disciplined than they are today, and there's
no hint of vulgarity and much warmth in their
response. Sir John cuts the coda to make time

for his own witty little speech in appreciation of
their contribution, continuing with a warmly
expressed wish to return with his orchestra; this
alone is worth the price of an unforgettable disc,
recorded with great warmth and atmosphere.

Sir Thomas Beecham

The Beecham Collection – Delius Ⓗ
An Arabesk[dfh]. A Mass of Life – Part 2 No 3: Prelude[h].
Songs of Sunset – Parts 1-7[bdfh]; Part 8[cegi]. I-Brasil[ah]. Le
ciel est pardessus le toit[ei]. Cradle Song[ei]. Irmelin
Rose[ei]. Klein Venevil[eh]. The Nightingale[ei]. Twilight
Fancies[ei]. The Violet[eh]. The Violet[ei]. Wither[eh]
[a]**Dora Labbette** sop [b]**Olga Haley,** [c]**Nancy Evans**
mezzos [d]**Roy Henderson,** [e]**Redvers Llewellyn** bars
[f]**London Select Choir;** [g]**BBC Chorus;** [h]**London
Philharmonic Orchestra;** [i]**Royal Philharmonic
Orchestra / Sir Thomas Beecham** [i]pf
Somm Recordings mono SOMM-BEECHAM8
(74' · ADD). Recorded 1929-46 Ⓜ ⓞ

The Beecham Collection – Handel Ⓗ
Piano Concerto in A (arr Beecham)[a]. The Gods Go
a'Begging[b] – Introduction; Minuet; Hornpipe;
Musette; Tambourine; Gavotte; Sarabande; Fugato.
The Gods Go a'Begging[c] – Introduction; Larghetto;
Gavotte; Allegro; Ensemble; Bourrée The Origin of
Design[d]
[a]**Lady Betty Humby Beecham** pf [abd]**London
Philharmonic Orchestra;** [c]**Royal Philharmonic
Orchestra / Sir Thomas Beecham**
Somm Recordings mono SOMM-BEECHAM7
(75' · ADD). Recorded 1932-49 ⓞ

Thanks to Shirley, Lady Beecham, we have here
a splendid range of recordings from Sir Thomas's personal archive, most never issued
before. The great treasure is the live recording
of Delius's orchestral song-cycle to words by
Ernest Dowson, *Songs of Sunset*. The performance has been described as 'achingly beautiful',
and that's no exaggeration. Recorded at the
Leeds Festival in 1934, it presents a strikingly
different view of the work from that of other
interpreters on disc. Beecham conveys a virile
thrust and energy in the writing, partly opting
for faster speeds. Thanks to his magnetism,
arguments have a tautness that can otherwise
seem to ramble. Both in this, with its seven
linked sections, and in the single span of *An
Arabesk*, a setting of Jens Peter Jacobsen in
Philip Heseltine's translation, the line of the
argument is clarified. Roy Henderson is the
clean-cut, sensitive baritone soloist in both,
sounding very English, with Olga Haley a fresh,
bright mezzo soloist in the *Songs of Sunset*. What
prevented this inspired reading of the *Songs of
Sunset* from being issued before is that the test
pressing of the final climactic section is missing.
To complete the work, that final ensemble for
soloists and chorus together is taken from the
studio recording Beecham made for HMV in
1946, but which he rejected. With Nancy Evans
and Redvers Llewellyn as soloists, it makes an
excellent conclusion, with the chorus more

clearly focused than its predeccessor in 1934. What matters is that the choral sound in both has ample weight. There's some noise at the ends of 78 sides, but the full-bodied nature of the transfer makes that flaw easy to ignore.

Dora Labbette is the enchanting soprano soloist in all the separate songs, bright and silvery, attacking even the most exposed high notes with astonishing purity and precision, producing magical *pianissimos*. Four of the 10 come in the beautiful orchestral versions, with the rest accompanied at the piano by Beecham himself. He may not have been the most accomplished pianist, but his natural magnetism still shines out, not least in the striking early song, longer than the rest, *Twilight Fancies*.

The disc of his arrangements of Handel is just as distinctive, always elegant and warmly expressive. He defies latter-day taste if anything even more radically than Stokowski in his arrangements of Bach, yet is similarly winning. The 10 movements from the ballet *The Origin of Design* come from the very first recording sessions of Beecham's newly founded London Philharmonic in December 1932. The following month he re-recorded three of the movements, but this far bigger selection of movements was never issued – brilliantly performed, with the players on their toes, not least the soloist Leon Goossens. Sadly the 78 side containing the 'Serenade' is so damaged that the opening of the movement is omitted.

Seven of the movements from the later ballet *The Gods Go a'Begging*, made between 1933 and 1938, did get published, but all the rest, including the six movements from the same ballet recorded with the RPO in 1949, have never appeared in any format.

The oddity is the four-movement Piano Concerto that Beecham cobbled together from various Handel movements for his wife, the pianist Betty Humby. The result makes a curious confection, starting with a nine-minute 'Chaconne' in which grandly spacious sections punctuate energetic chaconne variations. The result is energetic, sounding less like Handel than 20th-century pastiche, with keyboard figuration and pianistic tricks unashamedly reflecting the Romantic concerto tradition. As in the Delius disc, transfers bring satisfyingly full-bodied sound, if with obvious limitations. What's clear throughout is the Beecham magic – wonderful control of phrasing and rhythm in performances that are light of touch and full of fun.

George Benjamin

'Horizon 2 – A Tribute to Olivier Messiaen'
Dalbavie La source d'un regard[a]
Dukas/G van Keulen La plainte, au loin, du faune[a]
Messiaen Chronochromie[a]. Les offrandes oubliées[a]
Zuidam Adam-Interludes[b]
Royal Concertgebouw Orchestra /
[a]**George Benjamin,** [b]**Ingo Metzmacher**
RCO Live ⎈ RCO09003 (73' · DDD/DSD)
Recorded live 2007 and 2008   ⒻⓄ

This second instalment in RCO Live's contemporary series is a contextualising tribute to Messiaen who featured strongly in the Royal Concertgebouw's 2007-08 season. At its heart, red in beak and claw, sits *Chronochromie* whose hard-edged block-built formalism still strikes fear in the uncommitted. Not so composer/conductor George Benjamin who knows this music as well as anyone and is an ardent exponent. The cacophonous 'Epôde' piles up 18 independent string lines to evoke Messiaen's most unexpected dawn chorus. Geert van Keulen's effective transcription of a Dukas piano piece written in memory of Debussy, and Messiaen's own early *Les offrandes oubliées*, put this implacable masterpiece in perspective.

Reminding us that Messiaen's own later work represents a retreat from modernist paradigms, the novelties are readily digestible too. Something of the master's synaesthetic perception of sound as colour is suggested by *La source d'un regard*, one of the compositions in which Marc-André Dalbavie drags elements of the 'spectral' movement of the French avant-garde in the direction of mainstream concert life. Less soporific than Saariaho, his luminous and tactile surfaces may or may not conceal a lack of substance but have the wow factor in spades.

Dubious about Messiaen's programmatic superstructures yet entranced by his music's ability to conjure ecstatic mysticism 'without New Age woolliness', Robert Zuidam (*b*1964) pays tribute with three eclectic, neo-tonal interludes culled from his subsequently completed opera, *Adam in Ballingschap*. A Dutch former Henze protégé and sometime musical prankster, Zuidam is probably best known to UK audiences for his (over-?) extended *McGonagall-Lieder*, giving new life to that famously talentless Scots versifier. The *Adam-Interludes* suggest that he will go deeper. The first piece is a disrupted processional. The second, borrowed from an ecstatic duet between Adam and Eve and yet more bejewelled, is actually permitted to climax. A *moto perpetuo*, bracing as well as shimmery, traditional but for its perversely anti-climactic final shrug, completes the triptych which Ingo Metzmacher directs with his customary skill.

Karl Böhm

'Karl Böhm in Rehearsal and Performance 3'
Schubert Symphony No 9, 'Great', D944
Vienna Symphony Orchestra / Karl Böhm
Video director **Henri Colpi**
Medici Arts 📀 207 2198
(120' · NTSC · 4:3 · PCM stereo · 0)   Ⓕ

Henri Colpi (1921-2006) directed *Une aussi longue absence* and was the film editor for *Last Year at Marienbad*, both from 1961. Five years later, Unitel chose wisely when looking for someone to shoot a Schubert symphony. It's hard to imagine Karl Böhm taking to *Nouvelle Vaguerie*, or to Karajan's favourite Clouzot, but Colpi does exactly what Clouzot and Karajan agree is the point of a music film (as reported in Richard Osborne's biography): to place 'the spectator in a privileged position whilst you tell him your story' (Clouzot) and to give him 'an added sense of the greatness of the music we are playing' (Karajan).

So, unlike many rehearsal films, the conductor and his men appear at ease while they are observed. Much of what Böhm does is simply to urge them to take greater care of the marks on the page: to distinguish between the controversial varieties of Schubert's accents, the *fortepiano*, *sforzando* and hairpin marks which are legion in the symphony. So often he wants the accents to do no more than prick the surface of the *piano* cloth.

The old battles are fought. 'You prodded me, but I don't want to get faster. Louder but not faster.' The balancing of winds with strings is not achieved without remark, but somehow effortless – a word to the oboe here, to the clarinet there, never to the strings – perhaps because of the reverberant but unspecified TV studio. Their parts are marked with 'his' interpretation and sometimes imperfectly so. He shouts to the trombones they've doubled in the *Scherzo*. They say they haven't. He says, well, it's too loud anyway, and why did you put your mouth to the trombone, from a sense of solidarity?

This is all routine work in the lab, and to some it will be chopped liver. It's not 'the making of an interpretation' – nor could it be – but the rehearsal reveals some hows, and a few whys, to the performance that follows: vibrant, unfussy, lacking the richness and refinement of Böhm's DG recording in Berlin but gaining some careless Viennese rapture in the process.

Gustavo Dudamel

'Fiesta'
Bernstein West Side Story – Mambo **Carreño**
Margariteña **E Castellanos** Santa Cruz de Pacairigua
Estévez Mediodía en el Llano **Ginastera** Estancia,
Op 8a – The Land Workers; Wheat Dance; The Peons
of the Hacienda; Malambo **Márquez** Danzón No 2
Revueltas Sensemayá **A Romero** Suite for Strings
No 1 – Fuga con Pajarillo
Simón Bolívar Youth Orchestra of Venezuela /
Gustavo Dudamel
DG 477 7457GH (76' · DDD)
Recorded live 2008   Ⓕ ❶❶❶❶▶

If curiosity overcomes you and you jump to the encore, the 'Mambo' section from Bernstein's *West Side Story*, you won't belive your ears! The Simón Bolívar Youth Orchestra's percussion section strike up the band with the swing, push and individuality of a dozen great jazz drummers and the brass section riff like they're plugged into the Venezuelan national grid.

These young musicians haven't needed to find a Latin American feel by learning notation. It already flows through their DNA and takes them beyond the notes, direct into the marrow of the music itself. And even when a piece is amiable rather than spectacular – Even-

cio Castellanos's *Santa Cruz de Pacairigua* being a case in point – their rhythmic nous and heightened melodic expressivity override the longueurs.

Content-wise the most robust pieces are Revueltas's *Sensemayá* and the dances from Ginastera's ballet *Estancia*. Revueltas's work already enjoys a cult status that Dudamel's understanding of its bold orchestral colourings and ritualistic power can only enhance. The Ginastera climaxes with the asymmetrical rhythmic trapdoors of 'Malambo', brass and percussion again to the fore, although the delicate oom-pahs and opulent string swells of the 'Wheat Dance' offer a rare moment of tranquillity. The warm horn and subtone string introduction to Antonio Estévez's *Mediodía en el Llano* also shows they can 'do' delicate, but inevitably it's the infectious hardcore Latin spirit that, once sampled, stays embedded in your imagination.

'El Sistema: Music to Change Life'
A film by Paul Smaczny and Maria Stodtmeier
Simón Bolívar Youth Orchestra of Venezuela /
Gustavo Dudamel
Medici Arts 🄳🅅🄳 205 6958 (109' · NTSC · 16:9 · PCM
stereo, 5.1 and DTS 5.1 · 0)   Ⓟ ❶❶❶

This inspiring film takes us behind the scenes of the worldwide phenomenon of the Simón Bolívar Youth Orchestra of Venezuela as it portrays the extraordinary story of El Sistema and how it operates from day to day from one of its many nuclei in one of the poorest parts of Caracas. Gustavo Dudamel and his dynamic orchestra are the outward manifestation of these music centres which were started back in 1975. Their founding father is José Antonio Abreu, composer, conductor and politician, who cuts an almost mystical figure in this stunningly photographed film. Working every hour that God has given, Abreu and his co-founder Frank de Polo and their dedicated and gifted staff have been teaching and performing music using traditional principles with the underprivileged and the handicapped. When one of his team queries such long hours, he replies, 'there'll be enough time in eternity'. They're supported by selfless parents and the other stars of this film, the children with their twinkling eyes and raven black hair. Their enthusiasm is infectious and poignant. Early on in the film we learn of the stark reality of their background: the gang culture, drug dealers and tatty environment.

No wonder they regard rehearsals as a haven from the violence of the street and the cramped conditions of home. Individual children are highlighted: a young boy blows the opening trumpet call of Mahler's Third without a blemish, a girl conducts Tchaikovsky with evident musical flair. Other scenes highlight Steffen Herrmann's finely tuned editing, camerawork and the beautifully chosen music for the soundtrack.

Riccardo Muti

'Europa Konzert 2009'
Martucci La canzone dei ricordi **Schubert** Symphony
No 9 in C major, 'Great', D944 **Verdi** La forza del
destino – Overture
Violeta Urmana sop
Berlin Philharmonic Orchestra / Riccardo Muti
Medici Arts 📀 205 7728 (90' · NTSC · 16:9 · 5.1 · 0)
Ⓕ ●

This concert comes from the San Carlo opera
house, Naples: Muti was born in Naples, and
Giuseppe Martucci, born in nearby Capua in
1856, died in Naples in 1909. Martucci was that
rare bird, a 19th-century Italian composer who
eschewed the composition of opera. But he certainly knew his Wagner: indeed, he conducted
the Italian premiere of *Tristan und Isolde* at Bologna in 1888. *La canzone dei ricordi* – 'The song of
memories' – was composed for voice and piano
around 1887 and orchestrated some 11 years
later. A seven-movement setting of a poem by
Rocco Emanuele Pagliara, it has its moments of
Tristan-esque yearning. The music is attractive,
without being terribly gripping. It's beautifully
constructed, the short last movement consisting
of fragments of the text recalled from the beginning. Equally fine is the orchestration: richly
scored strings for the first movement, grateful
solos for the oboe and cor anglais later on. Violeta Urmana sings passionately about love and
loss; in the royal box, President Berlusconi looks
impassive.

The concert begins with a stirring account of
the Overture to *La forza del destino*. The performance of Schubert's Ninth Symphony is as
smooth and well upholstered as a ride in a Rolls-
Royce. If the journey is comfortable, there are
still plenty of features to admire in the driving.
The symphony begins in stately fashion, the
inner parts in the violas and cellos lovingly
brought out. When, in the *Allegro*, Muti stops
conducting, the players continue with impressive precision. But, just before the end, the
woodwind statement of the theme from the
introduction is hard to hear: Schubert's fault,
but Muti's responsibility. (The exposition
repeats in the outer movements are not made;
neither are the second repeats in the *Scherzo* and
Trio.) Muti is at his most sensitive in the latter's
heart-stopping modulation into B flat. With
unobtrusive camerawork, this is a solid achievement.

Sir Simon Rattle

Beethoven Symphony No 7, Op 92 **Bruch** Violin
Concerto No 1, Op 26ᵃ **Stravinsky** Symphony in
Three Movements
ᵃVadim Repin vn
Berlin Philharmonic Orchestra / Sir Simon Rattle
Medici Arts 📀 205 6978 (92' · NTSC · 16:9 PCM
stereo, 5.1 and DTS 5.1 · 0)
Recorded live 2008 Ⓕ

The durability of recent BPO 'Europa' concerts
(played annually on May 1) has been compromised by dodgy acoustics – a Lisbon cathedral,
an Istanbul mosque, an Athenian amphitheatre.
The Great Hall of the Moscow Conservatoire,
on the other hand, seems to gather up the spectrum of this orchestra's sound and project it
through a lens of saturated intensity. The result
is not yet a caricature of its own assumed identity
but so highly coloured as to repel prolonged
exposure.

Rattle's interpretation of the Beethoven Seventh and the Stravinsky are recognisable from
recent EMI recordings but here more muscular
in assertion, more heavily set and even truculent
in outer movements. The piano in the *Symphony
in Three Movements* takes the part of a sardonic
commentator, sometimes an aggressor, and the
dominance of the tonic in the Beethoven has
seldom been subjected to such relentless threat.
Yet devotees to the wit of his earlier recording
with the CBSO may like to note the new balletic
delicacy of Rattle's approach to the slow movement of the Stravinsky, perhaps inspired by his
recent experiences of conducting *The Nutcracker*.

The sense of occasion is attested to by improvisatory touches to the Beethoven, including
some unusual woodwind nuances in the slow
introduction, the absence of an exposition
repeat and a surprising dash to the finish. The
concerto is too tender a flower to survive such a
parade of May Day firepower: Vadim Repin
struggles to impart the requisite intimacy but
Rattle and the orchestra struggle not to overpower him, and the contest is an unequal one.
The climax of the slow movement is all too readily reminiscent of the heights of the *Alpine Symphony* for which Strauss stole so grandiloquently
from Bruch. The Europa Concert is the Berlin
Philharmonic's show, and they let you know it.

Gennadi Rozhdestvensky

'Notes interdites'
Two Films by Bruno Monsaingeon – The Red Baton:
Scenes of Musical Life in Stalinist Russia. Gennadi
Rozhdestvensky: Conductor or Conjuror?
Schnittke Dead Souls
Prokofiev Zdravitsa
Victoria Postnikova pf **Russia State Symphonic
Capella and Orchestra / Gennadi Rozhdestvensky**
Medici Arts 📀 307 3498 (155' · NTSC · 4:3 · 2.1 · 0)
Ⓕ

Don't be deceived by the packaging or the DVD
menu. Here, directed by Bruno Monsaingeon,
are two 55-minute documentaries and two complete performances. In *The Red Baton* he has
assembled Soviet archive footage and interviews
with surviving players to remind us of the reali-
ties of music-making in an era so remote as to be
incomprehensible even to today's Russians. For
once there is no theory being proved or dis-
proved. Against a background of ceaseless
bureaucratic interference, graduating at times to

naked terror, paradoxically there developed a musical culture among the richest and most intense of the 20th century. That great survivor (and dissembler) Tikhon Khrennikov makes a cameo appearance but the bulk of recent testimony comes from Rudolf Barshai, who emigrated in the 1970s, and Gennadi Rozhdestvensky, who stayed to champion an inner world of music in which everyone could feel free.

The second film shows Rozhdestvensky in action at various stages of his career, accompanying the big beasts of Soviet music, defending himself against the familiar charge of underrehearsal and passing on his accumulated experience to a variety of orchestras and student practitioners. It says something that the love theme of Tchaikovsky's *Romeo and Juliet* still reduces him to tears. The complete performances, oddly billed as bonus tracks, are equally fascinating, not least the rarely heard Prokofiev cantata *Zdravitsa*, an ode to Stalin too explicit to find favour today. Taped in an empty hall, the sopranos sing a little flat. The melodic content is, more embarrassingly, top-notch.

The live rendition of the Schnittke, a film score souped up by Rozhdestvensky into a piece of performance art for himself, his orchestra and his wife, is surely the best record we have of a persona consciously designed to ensnare audiences and encourage musicians. The redoubtable Victoria Postnikova shines in a frantic parody of the octave cadenza from Tchaikovsky's First Piano Concerto.

Contemplating the events of 1948 can evoke tears, laughter too at the absurdity of it all. Whether or not Rozhdestvensky's ironic detachment helped him survive, it has made him one of the last great individualistic maestros of our age. His baton is still long, its movements unpredictable when not discarded altogether. And, unlike Stalin, he does not use a podium. Strongly recommended.

Leopold Stokowski

Bach/Stokowski Passacaglia and Fugue, BWV582[a]
Beethoven Symphony No 7, Op 92[b] **Ben-Haim** From Israel[c] **Gluck/Stokowski** Armide – Sicilienne[d]
Mendelssohn A Midsummer Night's Dream – Scherzo[e]
[e]**All-American Youth Orchestra;** [a]**International Festival Youth Orchestra;** [d]**Leopold Stokowski Symphony Orchestra;** [bc]**Symphony of the Air / Leopold Stokowski**
Cala CACD0551 (77' · ADD)   (F)

For most of the last century the need for an organisation to promote Leopold Stokowski would have seemed laughable, when the man himself was apparently doing a more than decent job. Thirty-five CDs later, this final release sponsored by the Leopold Stokowski Society is perhaps inevitably something of a ragbag of disparate character and quality, but also a rattle-bag of good yarns about the recording industry. EMI sat on the Beethoven (made in

1958) and Ben-Haim (1959) for years after acquiring them from United Artists. They are stereo in the way Fellini's *Giulietta degli Spiriti* is colour, manufactured from the audio equivalent of bri-nylon. This spangly quality brings to life the songs and dances *From Israel* without quite enticing me to hear beyond their local idiom. It also lends an authentically Stokowskian glow and throb to the strings in the slow movement of the Seventh Symphony, which is better played and balanced but lacks the vital fire of his performances with the Philadelphia and BBC Symphony orchestras (in 1927 and 1963).

Competition is stiffer still in his most imposing Bach arrangement, and one can think of at least three recordings that bring greater precision and attack to their rhetorical sweep. But again, thanks to the booklet data and essay, we can imagine Stoki with his multinational charges in a St Moritz ballroom, high summer of '69, and take our pleasure there. The AAYO again belie their weight of numbers in the *Midsummer Night's Dream Scherzo*, which is not stereo but binaural (simultaneously recorded on two mono decks) and brings a welcome, dry panache to Mendelssohn's wind writing. The solemn Gluck arrangement derives from the once-famed 1957 Capitol LP 'Music for Strings'. Its belated debut on CD makes a poignant envoi to an organisation that, once upon a time, could hardly have been credited.

INSTRUMENTALISTS

Piotr Anderszewski   *piano*

'Unquiet Traveller'
A film by Bruno Monsaingeon
Piotr Anderszewski *pf* with **Dorota Anderszewska** *vn* **Deutsche Kammerphilharmonie, Bremen;**
Philharmonia Orchestra / Gustavo Dudamel
Medici Arts ◾ 307 7938 (83' · NTSC · 16:9 · 2.0 · 0)
                                                 (P)○○○

This is a dazzling portrait of a pianist rapidly acquiring cult status. For many he is the most original and charismatic pianist of his generation, and like all true artists his life is a confusion of paradoxes. For Anderszewski, talking about music is a betrayal. Yet how he talks! Told he is an uncompromising pianist, he lives in fear of compromise, dreading concerto performances where responsibility is divided. Solo recitals are no less of a nightmare, a cruel form of exposure, recordings even more so as you strive for perfection, for an ever-elusive ideal. Of Hungarian-Polish birth, his nature veers from elation to depression, joy but also fear of the exigencies of a concert pianist's career. He speaks movingly of his greatest loves, of Bach, Beethoven, Chopin, Szymanowski and, most of all, Mozart. Hearing Mozart's Requiem at the Church of the Holy Cross in his beloved Warsaw was his first great inspiration and a reminder that Warsaw was raped and murdered first by the Nazis and then by the Russians. He stares masochistically at a photo album of old Warsaw, a rich and cosmopolitan city now standardised with the Chopin Airport as an example of unspeakable vulgarity. This leads to a stream-of-consciousness response to Chopin and of how his ultra-Polish soul comes clothed in a perfectly tailored suit. For him much of the Barcarolle is sufficiently rapturous to evoke a drunken gondolier, while the Third Ballade makes you think of young girls in white waking the streets of Paris. The C sharp minor Waltz, on the other hand, is 'noble'.

All this and so much more is filmed on a train as Anderszewski journeys from city to city, a born nomad now safely in the hands of his train-driver. There are superb examples of Bach (a razor-sharp Gigue from the First Partita), Mozart, Beethoven (the recording sessions for the First Concerto), Chopin, Schumann and Szymanowski, all played and described with a breathless and romantic wish to communicate at a bewildering number of different levels.

'Piotr Anderszewski at Carnegie Hall'
Bach Partita No 2, BWV826 **Bartók** Hungarian Folksongs from the Csík District, Sz35a **Beethoven** Piano Sonata No 31, Op 110 **Janáček** In the Mists **Schumann** Faschingsschwank aus Wien, Op 26
Piotr Anderszewski pf
Virgin Classics ② 267291-2 (85' · DDD)
Recorded live at the Stern Auditorium, Carnegie Hall, New York, on December 3, 2008   ℗Ⓞ➔

Some recital, this. Piotr Anderszewski establishes a commanding tone for the opening section of the Second Partita's Ouverture, hopping elegantly through the little march that leads on to a fast, immaculately voiced fugue. He uses the Courante's ornaments to 'lift' the melody line, and the play between a seamless *legato* and a gentle *staccato* accompaniment in the following Sarabande works wonderfully well. The Rondeau is again trippingly elegant, the closing Capriccio assertive in a way that balances it with the opening fugue.

Faschingsschwank aus Wien launches with a flourish: Anderszewski fractionally delays the opening's second chord in authentic Viennese style, while the *Scherzo* is full of telling though effective emphases, mostly along the lines of 'question and answer'. And yet in the ravishing Intermezzo he seems too aware of the notes (so many to negotiate). The finale works best, a fantastical sojourn dazzlingly negotiated.

Janáček's *In the Mists* is a given a peach of a performance, a sense of improvisation sitting securely at its heart. Each movement tells its own very personal story, or seems to, the third alternating idyll with searing drama. Anderszewski's mastery of simultaneously varied dynamics comes into play here but in Beethoven's Op 110 he can be just a little over-emphatic on detail – in particular the accompaniment that

underpins the first movement's principal theme. Throughout the recital the understandably enthusiastic Carnegie Hall audience is rather too keen to bound in at the end of each piece, a mild distraction on a recording that you hope to play again and again. This is an exceptional recital, and as ever the Carnegie Hall acoustic allows for a luminous piano tone.

Leif Ove Andsnes   *piano*

'Horizons'
Albéniz Tango, Op 165 No 2 **Antheil** Toccata No 2 **Bach/Busoni** Ten Chorale Preludes – Ich ruf zu dir, Herr **Chopin** Impromptu No 1, Op 29 **Debussy** Suite bergamasque – Clair de lune **Grieg** Humouresqe, Op 6 No 3. Folksong, Op 73 No 4 **Halvorsen/Andsnes** Chant de Veslemöy **Ibert** Dix Histoires – Le petite âne blanc **Chopin/Liszt** Meine Freuden, S480 No 5 **Liszt** Liebestraum No 3, S541. Valse impromptu, S213 **Mendelssohn** Song Without Words, Op 67 No 2 **Mompou** Cançións i danses I. Paisajes – El lago **C Scott** Lotusland, Op 47 No 1 **Scriabin** Impromptu No 1, Op 14 **Shostakovich** The Golden Age – Polka **Sibelius** Etude, Op 76 No 2 **Smetana** Am Seegestade (Concert Study), B119. **R Strauss/Gieseking** Ständchen, Op 17 No 2 **Trénet/'Mr Nobody'** Coin de rue
Leif Ove Andsnes pf
EMI 341682-2 (68' · DDD)   Ⓜ Ⓞ Ⓞ ➔

Andsnes here reveals a hitherto hidden side to his art – the salon charmer. Some of the pieces are favourites from his childhood, though it is not every nine-year-old who has tackled Sibelius's uncharacteristically jolly 'Staccato' Etude or mastered Chopin's First Impromptu with such fluency and grace. Appealing, too, is the drama and sweep he brings to Liszt's *Liebestraum* No 3 (though it will not suit everyone's taste) and his avoidance of cliché, while the Norwegian's own transcription of Halvorsen's *Chant de Veslemöy* (originally for violin), Ibert's *Le petit âne blanc* and Debussy's *Clair de lune* are played with a beguiling innocence, ravishing tonal finesse and – most important – palpable affection.

Bravura highlights include Gieseking's effulgent transcription of Richard Strauss's *Ständchen* and Smetana's *Am Seegestade* ('By the sea'), reminiscent of Raff's *La fileuse* and a rare example of a concert étude that opens in one key (B major) and closes a tone lower! Enterprisingly, Andsnes has tracked down a score of Charles Trénet's song *Coin de rue* transcribed by the coyly named 'Mr Nobody' whom I have no qualms about outing as none other than Alexis Weissenberg.

The whole recital is superbly recorded. As Andsnes himself says, 'It's great to see people walk away from a concert with a smile on their face'. This disc has the same effect.

Martha Argerich   *piano*

Debut Recital
Brahms Two Rhapsodies, Op 79 **Chopin** Scherzo

No 3 in C sharp minor, Op 39. Barcarolle in F sharp,
Op 60 **Liszt** Hungarian Rhapsody No 6 in D flat.
Piano Sonata in B minor, S178 **Prokofiev** Toccata in
D minor, Op 11 **Ravel** Jeux d'eau
Martha Argerich pf
DG The Originals 447 430-2GOR (71' · ADD)
Recorded 1960-71   Ⓜ🔴🔴🔴▷

Here, on this richly filled CD, is a
positive cornucopia of musical genius. Martha Argerich's 1961 disc
remains among the most spectacular of all
recorded debuts, an impression reinforced by
an outsize addition and encore: her 1972 Liszt
Sonata. True, there are occasional reminders
of her pianism at its most fraught and capricious (Chopin's *Barcarolle*) as well as tiny scat-
terings of inaccuracies, yet her playing always
blazes with a unique incandescence and character.

The Brahms *Rhapsodies* are as glowingly
interior as they're fleet. No more mercurial
Chopin *Scherzo* exists on record and if its savagery becomes flighty and skittish (with the
chorale's decorations sounding like manic bursts
of laughter), Argerich's fine-toned fluency will
make other, lesser pianists weep with envy.
Ravel's *Jeux d'eau* is gloriously indolent and
scintillating and the Prokofiev *Toccata* is spun off
in a manner that understandably provoked
Horowitz's awe and enthusiasm. Liszt's Sixth
Hungarian Rhapsody is a marvel of wit and daring
and the B minor Sonata is among the most dazzling ever perpetuated on disc. The recordings
have worn remarkably well and the transfers
have been expertly done.

'Live from the Lugano Festival 2008'
Arensky Piano Quintet, Op 51ª **Dvořák** Slavonic
Dancesᵇ – Op 46 Nos 1 & 7; Op 72 Nos 2 & 4
Janáček Concertinoᶜ **Mozart** Andante and Variations,
K501ᵈ **Piazzolla** Tre Tanghi (trans E Hubert)ᵉ. Las
cuatro estaciones (arr Bragato)ᶠ **Pletnev** Fantasia
elveticaᵍ **Rachmaninov** Suite No 1, Op 5ʰ **Ravel**
Introduction and Allegroⁱ **Saint-Saëns** Scherzo,
Op 87ʲ **Schumann** Violin Sonata No 2, Op 121ᵏ
Shostakovich Piano Trio No 1, Op 8ˡ
ᶜ**Corrado Giuffredi** cl ᶜ**Vincent Godel** bn ᶜ**Zora**
Slokar hn ᵏ**Renaud Capuçon**, ᵃᶜ**Lucia Hall**, ᶜ'ⁱ**Alissa**
Margulis, ᵃ**Dora Schwarzberg** vns ᵃᶜ**Nora Romanoff-**
Schwarzberg va ᶠ**Alexandre Debrus**, ᵃ**Mark**
Drobinsky, ˡ**Mischa Maisky** vcs ᶜᵈᵉᵍʰᵏ**Martha**
Argerich, ᶠ**Alexander Gurning**, ᵉ**Eduardo Hubert**,
ᵈ**Stephen Kovacevich**, ᵇ**Karin Lechner**, ᵇˡ**Lily Maisky**,
ᵍ**Alexander Mogilevsky**, ʲ**Akane Sakai**, ⁱ**Alessandro**
Stella, ⁱ**Giorgia Tomassi**, ᵃʰʲ**Lilya Zilberstein** pfs
ᵍ**Orchestra della Svizzera Italiana / Mikhail Pletnev**
EMI ③ 267051-2 (3h 40' · DDD)   Ⓢ🔴▷

'The Berlin Recital'
Bartók Violin Sonata No 1, Sz75. Solo Violin Sonata,
Sz117 **Kreisler** Liebesleid. Schön Rosmarin
Schumann Kinderszenen, Op 15. Violin Sonata No 2,
Op 121
Gidon Kremer vn **Martha Argerich** pf
EMI ② 693399-2 (117' · DDD)   Ⓕ🔴🔴▷

Anyone seeking evidence of how keenly Martha
Argerich can adjust her personality to suit the
interpretative preferences of her colleagues
need only compare these two versions of
Schumann's Second Violin Sonata from Lugano
in 2008 and Berlin in 2006. Argerich in Lugano
collaborates with Renaud Capuçon, darting
about the score as if treading hot coals, nimble,
at times breathless, and consistently appreciative
of Capuçon's malleable phrasing and warmly
brushed tone. The rapport with a more grainy,
acerbic-sounding Gidon Kremer (Berlin) is as
great but quite different in musical effect, even
though the two sets of movement timings match
(within seconds) and in both cases Argerich is
recognisably herself. But the contrasts in
approach are telling and at times fairly subtle.
For example, near the start of the Sonata's slow
movement, when the violinist switches from *pizzicato* to *arco* – in Gidon Kremer's case a transformation from genial troubadour to ghostly
apparition – Argerich anticipates the change by
stealthily, almost hesitantly, slowing the tempo.
This is Schumann at his most unhinged. While
the Capuçon/Argerich partnership goes for
colour and volatility, Kremer and Argerich (who
recorded the work some years ago for DG),
although equally exciting, are more darkly insistent, more appreciative perhaps of the music's
troubled soul. Rarely on disc have so many
superficial similarities gone hand in hand with as
many profound dissimilarities.

Both performances are riveting, and the two
very different acoustics (Lugano is far airier)
might have something to do with why Argerich
projects so differently in each case. Still, when
deciding which version to go for, potential purchasers are likely to view the two programming
contexts as crucial. The Lugano set, the latest in
series devoted to live recordings from the Festival, is full of memorable treats. It closes with a
kaleidoscopic half-hour *Fantasia elvetica* by
Mikhail Pletnev who also conducts the Svizzera
Italiana Orchestra, his two piano soloists for the
occasion Argerich and Alexander Mogilevsky.
Although stylistically eclectic (Respighi, Sibelius, Saint-Saëns, Poulenc and Shchedrin all
came to mind) the Fantasia is delightful: frothy,
listener-friendly and packed full of cheeky tunes.
Ravel's two-piano transcription of his *Introduction and Allegro* (Giorgia Tomassi, Alessandro
Stella) trades a delicate dreamscape for billowing virtuosity: the effect is rather like the piano
version of 'Une barque sur l'océan'. There are
piano duets or two-piano works by Mozart
(*Andante and Variations*, K501), Saint-Saëns (a
rather equivocal-sounding *Scherzo*, Op 87),
Rachmaninov (Suite No 1 with Argerich and
Lilya Zilberstein) and dances by Piazzolla and
Dvořák. We're also given Piazzolla's *Four Seasons* arranged for piano trio. Argerich leads a
tangy, rhythmically supple account of Janáček's
madcap Concertino, Lily and Mischa Maisky
join violinist Alissa Margulis for Shostakovich's
12-minute First Piano Trio and Zilberstein is
the pianist in Arensky's richly romantic Piano
Quintet in D. A sense of joy reigns throughout:

this music-making could happily serve as a corrective whenever some half-hearted studio-bound session dampens your spirits.

The Berlin concert with Argerich and Kremer is equally gripping but quite different. Argerich goes solo for a typically quixotic account of Schumann's *Kinderszenen*, each cameo following swiftly on the heels of the last, the style alert, playful, keenly attentive to inner voices and in the last two pieces appropriately poised. But for me the performances that make this Berlin concert absolutely indispensable are the two Bartók sonatas. The First Sonata's agitated badinage reaches fever pitch in the finale where Kremer swings in on a *glissando* and the two go hell for leather as one racy folk-style motif follows another. The Sonata's close is an absolute riot, so much so that the first encore, Kreisler's *Liebesleid*, limps in like an innocent bystander mistakenly targeted in a fight. True, *Schön Rosmarin* picks up the spirit but even Kreisler's charm cannot quite erase the recent memory of Bartók's unrelenting onslaught.

The first CD concludes with one of the finest ever recorded performances of Bartók's Solo Sonata, Kremer calling on his full repertoire of violinistic devices which include, in addition to the many called for in the score, a mastery of tonal colouring and a rhythmic grip that at times seem to transcend the limitations of the instrument. Kremer doesn't so much play as speak to you through the music and while his tone hasn't the alluring sweetness of, say, a (young) Menuhin, the sheer electricity of his interpretation more than compensates. Not once does the tension even begin to ease. What an artist!

'Evening Talks'
Martha Argerich pf
Medici Arts 📀 307 3428   Ⓕ

Pin down Martha Argerich's genius and she walks away with the pin. Most magisterially gifted of all pianists, her quixotic personality flashes in and out of the Medici Arts film 'Evening Talks', at once confiding and capricious as she reflects on the nature of her fraught and zigzag career. Camera-shy ('I'm not an exhibitionist like those people on Big Brother; they actually enjoy being filmed!'), she admits that if (heaven forbid) she was 'a Martha Argerich fan, she would love to see this movie'. Above all there is a sense of healing or recovery, a coming-to-terms with her gifts. For years, she confesses, her face clouding with memories, she felt like someone hurled into a swimming pool, unable to swim and with an increasing sense that her instinctive ability was not counterbalanced by reason or understanding. Catapulted into stardom, she travelled incessantly, met few people of her own age and became confused and depressed. And after reading a sizeable amount of Gide and Dostoevsky (both obsessed with the idea of the outlaw) she decided to 'transgress', to tell her agent that she had injured her hand before cutting her finger to avoid further public appearances.

Happily such harrowing talk is balanced by a growing sense of realism and confidence as depression shades into whimsy and, finally, stability. She confesses to a heavy debt to Friedrich Gulda, with whom she studied and who she idealised ('I never knew anyone so gifted or extraordinary'). From him she learnt about humour in early Beethoven while confessing that the trills in the central outburst of the slow movement of the Fourth Concerto unnerved her ('I could never play that piece'). Under his stern but often playful guidance she achieved a lighter view of life ('In Argentina we only did "feelings" and *bel canto*'). Gradually forgetting a time when she thought that one wrong note spelt the end of her career, she relished a jazz critic's comment – 'your Bach swings' – and Erroll Garner's response when he was told his jazz was influenced by Debussy ('Who was that dude?'). She accidentally learnt Prokofiev's Third Concerto while asleep, absorbing a neighbour's performance complete with inaccuracies. Today she rejoices in her appearances with a multitude of exceptionally talented musicians, cherishing their artistry and friendship. Her repertoire may have shrunk but this enables her to recreate endlessly her favoured works, to take risks and live dangerously. For her nothing is set in stone and the Schumann Piano Concerto, for example, is 'forever warm and still to be enjoyed'. A portrait of this elusive artist at all stages of her career, 'Evening Talks' comes triumphantly close to revealing the very essence of Martha Argerich.

Martha Argeich & Nelson Freire   *pianos*

Brahms Variations on a Theme by Joseph Haydn, Op 56b **Rachmaninov** Symphonic Dances, Op 45b **Ravel** La valse **Schubert** Grand Rondeau, D951
Martha Argerich, Nelson Freire pfs
DG 477 8570GH (72' · DDD)
Recorded live 2009   Ⓕ🔴🔴🔴▷

With musical elder-statesmanship comes the opportunity to revisit past repertoire and make new, potentially definitive records of one's interpretations. Martha Argerich, with her longtime friend and duet-partner Nelson Freire, does just that, offering a disc of her two-piano party pieces. Comparisons with previous recordings, though, are somewhat otiose as these are, like all of Argerich's music-making, performances in and of themselves, alive in the moment of creation. She delights nowadays in surrounding herself with like-minded chamber collaborators, challenging them (and herself) to ever greater feats of technique and expression.

How many times have we heard two-piano performances of the Brahms *St Antoni* Variations that open with the players out of sync, making it sound like a child's piano lesson? Argerich and Freire naturally, effortlessly put such solecisms to flight. After this chaste, almost didactic opening, the ensuing variations surge, muse, scamper; in the *Poco presto* variations we appreciate why Schoenberg admired Brahms so deeply; the pregnancy of the coda builds inexorably to its triumphant catharsis.

Rachmaninov's own virtuoso transcription of his *Symphonic Dances* (in which the players swap roles, so Freire takes the top line) demonstrates that two pianos can be (almost) as versatile as a romantic-size orchestra: of course, the full palette of woodwind colours is not available even to the 176-key two-Steinway behemoth; but Freire and Argerich tint and shade the music with the skill of a master orchestrator. The *Symphonic Dances*' ghostly waltz finds its image amplified and refracted in Ravel's nightmare scenario (Argerich on top once more), a thunderous climax to proceedings, echoed in the (hitherto preternaturally quiet) audience's explosive applause.

Providing repose among these three concert pieces is Schubert's very late (June 1828) *Grand Rondeau* in A major, for which the two players nuzzle up on one piano. Once again, in music that can sound dry and four-square in the wrong hands, Freire (*primo*) and Argerich show that theirs are indubitably the right hands, giving this characteristically modest but expansive piece expressive shape and structure.

This is a souvenir of what must have been a special evening at the Grosses Festspielhaus; but it's also so much more than that. To hear two musicians of this stature at the height of their recreative powers is never less than thrilling and thought-provoking.

Vladimir Ashkenazy *piano*

'Vladimir Ashkenazy: Master Musician'
Film director **Christopher Nupen**
Vladimir Ashkenazy pf/cond
Allegro Films **DVD** A09CND
(160' · NTSC · 4:3 · 2.0 · 0)   Ⓕ

Each of the four sections of this DVD is prefaced by one of the director's idiosyncratic chats to us viewers explaining the background to what we are about to see. Though these introductions are nothing if not self-regarding, Nupen has, to be fair, every right to be pleased with his achievements. He is a director in whose cultured and reassuring company musicians feel secure and relaxed.

The results are films of depth and real insight – and already of some historical importance. For instance, in the first one on the present volume, *The Vital Juices Are Russian*, we meet the young Ashkenazy in 1968 in the throes of moving his wife and small children from London to Iceland while fulfilling a hectic schedule of concerts – as a pianist, of course. The conducting phase of his career is celebrated in the brief second section, a nine-minute montage of four orchestral movements taken from various other Nupen/Ashkenazy films.

More substantial is the previously unpublished film of Ashkenazy's lengthy, thought-provoking introduction to Rachmaninov's *Corelli* Varia-

tions, followed by a live performance of the work in Lugano. The DVD ends with the customary Allegro Films makeweight compilation of 33 short extracts from its catalogue.

Alessio Bax *piano*

'Bach Transcribed'
Bach/Alessio Bax Keyboard Concerto No 5, BWV1056 – Largo **Bach/Busoni** Chaconne **Bach/Godowsky** Violin Sonata No 1. Cello Suite No 3 – Bourrée **Bach/Kempff** 'Zion hört die Wächter singen' from BWV140 **Bach/E Petri** Sheep May Safely Graze **Bach/Saint-Saëns** Violin Partita No 1 – Gavotte **Bach/Siloti** Air on the G String. Violin Sonata No 2 – Andante. Flute Sonata – Siciliano
Alessio Bax pf
Signum Classics SIGCD156 (60' · DDD)   ⒻⓄⓄ➼

In the realm of Romantic Bach transcriptions, Alessio Bax's stylistic perception and palette of tone-colours have considerably deepened in recent years, together with a level of technical control that gives new meaning to the word 'awesome'. *Legato* lines are full-bodied at all dynamic levels, while thick chords and rapid passagework betray not one speck of struggle. Furthermore, Bax retains tonal beauty and definition even in the loudest and most sonorous passages, achieved without the least banging.

Here, Godowsky's outrageously upholstered treatment of Bach's G minor Solo Violin Sonata receives its most effortless and imaginatively nuanced reading on disc. Bax's mesmerising melody/accompaniment distinction in Egon Petri's *Sheep May Safely Graze* makes Petri's venerable recording sound comparatively dry and matter-of-fact. Bax's sustaining power and subtle pedalling prevent his broad tempi for the Siloti *Air on the G String* and the Bach/Busoni Chaconne from dragging, although his gentle, rounded performance of Kempff's *Zion hört die Wächter singen* doesn't change my preference for Busoni's plainer transcription. Bax's own treatment of the F minor Keyboard Concerto's sublime slow movement captures this pianist at his lyrical apex. He replicates the *pizzicato* accompaniment to such tasteful and eloquent effect that you don't miss the string section. Signum's roomy, lifelike sound perfectly complements Bax's extraordinary pianism. A disc no 'hyphenated Bach' fan should miss.

Dennis Brain *horn*

Beethoven Quintet for Piano and Wind in E flat, Ⓗ
Op 16[a] **Brahms** Trio for Horn, Violin and Piano in E flat, Op 40[b] **Dukas** Villanelle[c] **Marais** Le Basque[d] (arr hn & pf) **Mozart** Quintet for Horn and Strings in E flat, K407/K386[e]
Dennis Brain hn [b]**Max Salpeter** vn [cd]**Wilfrid Parry**, [b]**Cyril Preedy** pfs [a]**Dennis Brain Wind Ensemble**; [e]**English String Quartet**
BBC Legends BBCL4048-2 (72' · ADD)
Recorded 1957   ⓂⓄⓄ

This is a marvellous record that does the fullest justice to the art of Dennis Brain, whom Boyd Neel called 'the finest Mozart player of his generation on any instrument'. This 1957 recording of the Mozart Horn Quintet surely bears that out. Brain has warm support from the English String Quartet, particularly in the lovely slow movement, but here his playing consistently dominates the ensemble lyrically, while the closing *Rondo* is sheer joy. So is Marais's delectable *Le Basque*. James Galway has subsequently made this piece his own on record, but Brain uses it as a witty encore, without showing off. Needless to say, the performance of the Brahms Horn Trio is very fine indeed. The infinitely sad, withdrawn atmosphere of the slow movement created by Brain's gentle soliloquy is unforgettable; and the infectious hunting-horn whooping of the finale carries all before it. The recording is distanced in a resonant acoustic and isn't ideally clear, but one soon forgets this.

The Dukas *Villanelle* is an arch-Romantic piece which all horn players feature for the want of something better, and Brain's ardour all but convinces us that it's fine music. But the highlight of the programme is the Beethoven piano and wind quintet, in which Brain shows himself the perfect chamber music partner. Without wishing to dominate, he can't help making his mark at every entry. And his colleagues join him to make a superb team. The recording is astonishingly real. The blending is so perfect, and Parry's pianism isn't only the bedrock of the performance – the playing itself is very beautiful indeed. In short, this is the performance against which all others must now be judged.

Julian Bream   *guitar, lute*

'Julian Bream plays Dowland and Bach'
Julian Bream *lte/gtr* with **The Golden Age Singers /
Margaret Field-Hyde**
DG mono ② 477 7550GOM2 (141' · ADD)   Ⓜ

When, in 1950, a teenage Julian Bream happened upon Peter Warlock's piano arrangements of some of John Dowland's lute pieces, it was love at first sight. For almost the next 30 years, Bream would devote himself to both the lute and the guitar before relinquishing the former in favour of the latter (although he was to return to the lute many years later).

This wonderful two-CD set takes in three LPs originally released by Westminster during the mid-1950s. As Tully Potter mentions in the booklet-notes, the solo Dowland and Bach LPs are especially significant for having been the first, for a plucked-string instrument, to be entirely devoted to a single composer. Also included is a selection of Dowland's ayres for lute and four voices, in which Bream is joined by the Golden Age Singers.

Ideas about what constitutes an authentic approach to early music fluctuate over time, but Art never goes out of fashion. Yes, Bream uses a wholly guitaristic technique on the lute (including the use of nails – but then Baroque lutenists like Piccinini also used them); yes, his phrasing and sense of timbre bear Segovia's influence to an uncommon degree. But Bream's genius transcends all. Whether it's in the astonishing intensity of Dowland's *Melancholy Galliard* and *Forlorn Hope Fancy* or in the finely proportioned sense of pace and drama in Bach's Chaconne, the impression is ultimately of a meeting of equals.

Alfred Brendel   *piano*

Haydn Piano Sonata in E flat, HobXVI/49
Mozart Piano Sonata No 14 in C minor, K457
Schubert Impromptu in G flat, D899 No 3
Alfred Brendel *pf*
Opus Arte 📀 OA0811D (155' · 16:9 ·
2.0 · 0) Includes documentary 'Man and Mask',
conversations with Sir Simon Rattle and poetry
readings   Ⓕ⒪

The main element in this double-disc tribute is the 70-minute portrait, 'Man and Mask', directed for television by Mark Kidel. This takes the great pianist to many of the haunts of his early life, as well as showing him relaxing at home in Hampstead. His first recital came in Graz in 1948, and received glowing notices, when he concentrated on works with fugues, including the Brahms *Handel* Variations and a sonata of his own which boasted a double-fugue at the end.

In Vienna he recalls making his first recording for Vox, a coupling of Balakirev's *Islamey*, Mussorgsky's *Pictures at an Exhibition* and Stravinsky's *Petrushka* suite. Later, on the day after his debut at Queen Elizabeth Hall, he had offers of recording contracts from three major companies. All this is amplified by clips from archive performances and a separate half-hour conversation with Sir Simon Rattle in rehearsal for Beethoven's Piano Concertos Nos 2 and 4, offering fascinating revelations from both pianist and conductor.

On the second disc comes a recital recorded at The Maltings, Snape, crowning this revealing issue with masterly performances of three of Brendel's favourite works.

'The Farewell Concerts'
Bach/Busoni Chorale Prelude, 'Nun komm' der
Heiden Heiland', BWV659 **Beethoven** Bagatelle,
Op 33 No 4. Piano Sonata No 13, Op 27 No 1
Haydn Variations in F minor, HobXVII/6
Mozart Piano Concerto No 9, K271. Piano Sonata
No 9, K533/494 **Schubert** Piano Sonata No 21, D960.
Impromptu, D899 No 3
Alfred Brendel *pf* **Vienna Philharmonic Orchestra /
Sir Charles Mackerras**
Decca ② 478 2116DH2 (141' · DDD) Ⓕ

There is much to glory in here. Brendel's Schubert, for instance. The final sonata was a moving choice in itself and the performance is all that you would expect: there's no grandstanding, no inordinately extreme tempi (à la late Richter) but throughout there's the sense that Brendel understands every aspect of Schubert's late masterpiece, has pondered it deeply, but the result is anything but ponderous. It starts so naturally it's as if you walked in on his performance, mid-stream, so to speak. The weighting of individual chords, the underlying pulse, the tempo – all grow from a decades-long familiarity. In the *Andante sostenuto* – and in the slow sections of the Beethoven sonata too – Brendel spins the musical line quite beautifully. It's a reminder that, for all his reputation as a cerebral musician, he's by no means a cool player. Beauty per se may not be his ultimate aim, but listening to the Schubert G flat major Impromptu, and the way he picks the melody out of the air, it's impossible to remain unmoved.

It's fitting that these discs should also include a Mozart concerto. Here we have his first great concerto, K271, with Brendel joined by his more recent Mozartian partner, Sir Charles Mackerras. It's a musical marriage made in heaven, especially when you add the VPO to the mix. Every phrase has such detail, such intricate colouring, yet, again, it's detailing that comes of long exposure to a work, built up over the years like a patina, rather than something superficially applied on a single level. The performance is unhurried but not in any way sluggish, and the slow movement is utterly glorious. You can hear faint vocalisations from Brendel, here and elsewhere, but they don't intrude unduly.

There is so much to admire throughout these two discs: his Mozart sonata is another treasure, and his soulful yet grand Bach/Busoni Chorale Prelude reminds us of repertoire from much earlier in his career, but perhaps the highlight is the Haydn – a composer absolutely made for Brendel's gifts (or should it be the other way round?). Rather than a sonata, we have here the F minor Variations, an apt example not only of Haydn's innovative formal genius but also a reminder that he, too, could write melodies to melt the heart. There is greatness to be found in every bar of these two discs, and that goes not only for the music but the musician too.

Renaud & Gautier Capuçon   *violin & cello*

'Inventions'
Bach/Neumann 20 Duos – selection **Bartók** Seven Hungarian Folkdances (arr Kraeute)[a] **Beffa** Masques I (Modéré). Masques II (Rythmiquement souple) **Eisler** Duo, Op 7 **Klein** Duo **Kreisler** Marche miniature viennoise **Martinů** Duo No 2, H371
Renaud Capuçon *vn* **Gautier Capuçon** *vc*
[a]**Aude Capuçon** *pf*
Virgin Classics 332626-2 (73' · DDD)   Ⓕ🅑➔

If you're put off by the idea of a whole CD of just violin and cello (Aude Capuçon only joins brothers Renaud and Gautier for the final three minutes), think again! There's an impressive

range both in the music, with its central-European theme, and the performances. The Bach transcriptions are splendidly spirited and stylish; one minor fault – difficult to avoid when playing Bach with a modern bow – is a tendency to exaggerate dynamic inflexions and the difference between long and short notes. The Bartók arrangements are wonderfully colourful and evocative; with such short pieces it's crucial to establish the character straight away, and the Capuçons do this every time.

The items by Karol Beffa were written expressly for the brothers. Each starts in meditative mood, with unclouded tonality, developing more complicated formulations as it proceeds, and each makes masterly use of the instruments' sonorities. The Martinů, dating from the year before his death in 1959, sounds remarkably full. The first movement is particularly attractive – if you imagine a mixture of Stravinsky and Dvořák, you'd be close. The Eisler, by contrast, is an early work, full of expressionistic outbursts, realised here with extreme vividness. The unfinished Duo by Gideon Klein (a young Holocaust victim) is rather more sober, intensely chromatic but not especially dissonant, and with powerfully concentrated melancholy expression.

All this music has a strong sense of time and place. Fritz Kreisler nostalgically evokes the Vienna of Johann Strauss, and here again the Capuçons get right into the idiom.

Shura Cherkassky   *piano*

Mendelssohn Andante and Rondo capriccioso, Op 14 **Schubert** Piano Sonata No 20, D959 **Schumann** Carnaval, Op 9 **Schumann/Tausig** Der Kontrabandiste, Op 74 No 10 **Tchaikovsky/ Rachmaninov** Cradle Songs, Op 16 No 1
Shura Cherkassky *pf*
BBC Legends BBCL4254-2 (77' · ADD)   Ⓕ
Recorded live at the Queen Elizabeth Hall, London, on November 1, 1970

'The Complete HMV Stereo Recordings'
Bach/Busoni Chaconne, BWV1004 **Beethoven** Bagatelle, Op 119 No 1 **Chasins** Three Chinese Pieces **Chopin** Mazurka No 7, Op 7 No 3. Waltz No 1, Op 18. Nocturne No 8, Op 27 No 2. Ballades – No 2, Op 38; No 3, Op 47 (two recordings) **Gershwin** Three Preludes (two recordings) **Liszt** Hungarian Rhapsody, S244 No 13. Valse de l'opéra Faust (Gounod), S407 **Litolff** Concerto symphonique No 4, Op 102 – Scherzo[a] **Lyadov** A Musical Snuffbox, Op 32 **Poulenc** Trois pièces – Toccata **Rachmaninov** Preludes, Op 23 – No 2; No 5 **Saint-Saëns/Godowsky** Le carnival des animaux – Le cygne **Schubert** Impromptu, D899 No 4
Shura Cherkassky *pf*
[a]**BBC Symphony Orchestra / Sir Malcolm Sargent**
First Hand Records Remasters ② FHR04 (119' · AAD)   Ⓑ
Recorded 1956/58

The live Queen Elizabeth Hall recital opens with quintessential Cherkassky. A more perfect rendition of Mendelssohn's *Andante and Rondo capric-*

cioso you are unlikely ever to hear, deftly executed with a bewitching feather-light delicacy. That said, Cherkassky in heavyweight German repertoire was always less clear cut. Here he plays Schubert's late A major Sonata, a work he visited infrequently. While it is the melody rather than the drama that attracts him, it is difficult not to fall under the beguiling spell of what you are hearing. *Carnaval*, too, for all its idiosyncratic moments, offers a masterclass in colouring and touch – who else can produce such a ravishing *pianissimo* or make an apparent *crescendo* and *decrescendo* on a single note? The Rachmaninov transcription (Cherkassky at his most melancholy) is new to the pianist's official discography.

First Hand's classily presented two-disc set of the complete HMV stereo recordings made in 1956 and 1958 is a treasure chest of Cherkassky rarities. Of the 20 works here, all released for the first time in stereo, 12 have never previously appeared on CD, among them the five Chopin titles and the Bach-Busoni Chaconne. While he was generally at his best in front of an audience, these studio recordings have the same vitality and spontaneity as his live performances. The Litolff *Scherzo* is a delicious musical soufflé while the *Hungarian Rhapsody* No 13 and the *Faust* Waltz (especially the stunning coda) are examples of pure pianistic *joie de vivre*. But above all – and this applies to both discs – are the sheer beauty of sound, individuality of conception and musical imagination that Cherkassky brings to whatever takes his fancy. Required listening for all students of the piano.

Stephen Cleobury   *organ*

'The Grand Organ of King's College, Cambridge'
Bach O Mensch, bewein' dein' Sünde gross, BWV622. Prelude and Fugue, BWV532 **Elgar** Chanson de matin, Op 15 No 2 **Gigout** Six Pièces – Grand choeur dialogué **Handel** Solomon, HWV67 – Arrival of the Queen of Sheba (arr Stainton de B Taylor) **Howells** Six Pieces – Master Tallis's Testament **Mendelssohn** Organ Sonata No 3, Op 65 **Reger** Seven Pieces, Op 145 – Weihnachten **Thalben-Ball** Elegy **Walton** Crown Imperial (arr Brewer) **S Wesley** 12 Short Pieces with a Voluntary added – Gavotte; Air
Stephen Cleobury org
Priory ② (**DVD** + CD) PRDVD3
(72' · 16:9 · PCM stereo and 5.1 · 0)   Ⓕ

King's College's director of music, Stephen Cleobury, guides us through the 79 stops of this much-enlarged, rebuilt and oft-heard instrument. It is good to be reminded of its capabilities as a solo instrument and not just as an accompanimental accessory to the College Choir. This film (made in May and June 2008) predates the most recent restoration work to the organ (in early 2009).

The filming and sound recording are up to Priory's excellent standards. Richard Knight's camerawork captures all the action, despite the cramped console environment, with plenty of

interesting shots of the pedalboard. Interior views of the Chapel are well-lit, varied and appropriate to the accompanying soundtrack. During Elgar's *Chanson de matin* and Thalben-Ball's *Elegy* the camera travels further afield across The Backs to Grantchester and the American Cemetery at Madingley.

Cleobury's playing is measured, smooth and beautifully synchronised with that tricky and cavernous acoustic. Nothing is overblown: flamboyance is eschewed. Instead, we can simply revel in the plummy weightiness of Reger, the beautiful lightness of the Queen of Sheba's semiquavers and the rolling timelessness of Master Tallis. Murrill's arrangement of Walton's *Crown Imperial* makes a fulsome finale with the tuba stop making its solitary appearance in the recital. The bonus features are also splendid. Particularly enjoyable is Cleobury's explanation of his approach to registration in each piece.

Imogen Cooper   *piano*

Beethoven Piano Sonata No 28, Op 101
Debussy 24 Préludes – Les terrasses des audiences
Mozart Piano Sonata No 8, K310 **Ravel** Miroirs
Imogen Cooper pf
Wigmore Hall Live WHLIVE0018 (78' · DDD)
Recorded live in 2007   Ⓕ

Throughout her live programme Imogen Cooper's poise and overall artistry make a refreshing change from a more overt, less subtle virtuosity. She captures all of Beethoven's speculative beauty at the start of his Op 101 Sonata, and if others are more fiercely energised in the second movement march, with its prophecy of Schumann's obsessive dotted rhythms, few are more stylish and refined. Again, if her view of Mozart's A minor Sonata could be thought sometimes self-consciously beautiful or manicured, there is no denying her calibre, never more so than in her urgent propulsion of the wind-swept finale.

Cooper studied with Kathleen Long in London and Jacques Février in Paris, which gives her Ravel a special distinction. Less animated or razor-sharp than others in 'Alborada del gracioso', she never forces the issue, and there is never a hint of the literalism that is the bane of many French pianists. 'Noctuelles', 'Oiseaux tristes' and 'La vallée des cloches' come beguilingly alive when played with such freedom and fantasy, yet always within a scrupulously true and accurate framework.

For her encore Cooper gives us Debussy's 'Les terraces des audiences', reminding you in every elusive phrase that subtlety and finesse are at the very heart of great French piano writing. The BBC's soft-grained sound is ideally attuned to this never less than beautiful recital.

Alfred Cortot   *piano*

'Encores'   Ⓗ
Albéniz Sous la palmera, Op 232 No 3

Brahms Wiegenlied, Op 49 No 4 **Chopin** Ballade No 1, Op 23. Berceuse, Op 57. Etude, 'Harp Study', Op 25 No 1. Impromptu No 2, Op 36. Waltz No 7, Op 64 No 2 **Handel** Keyboard Suite, Set 1 – No 5, HWV430 **Liszt** 19 Hungarian Rhapsodies, S244 – No 2; No 11. Paraphrase (on Verdi's Rigoletto), S434 **Schubert** Litanei auf das Fest Allerseelen, D343 **Weber** Aufforderung zum Tanze, J260 Op 65
Alfred Cortot pf
Naxos Historical mono 8 111261 (79' · ADD)
Recorded 1925-26   Ⓢ

Here, in recordings dating from 1925-26, is the very essence of Cortot, superbly remastered by Mark Obert-Thorn. A voice from another age, Cortot was addicted to his incomparable recreative art. Every bar and phrase of these performances induces a frenzy or delirium in the listener, setting the mind and senses reeling. Cortot may have 'discovered the opium in Chopin' (Daniel Barenboim) but he also discovered the opium in virtually everything else. His arrangement and playing of Schubert's *Litany* has all the poetic freedom and sumptuous tonal allure of the greatest singers and always you are made aware of his alternating simplicity, richness and intricacy of expression. Hear the cascades close to the end of Chopin's Second Impromptu and you may well agree that you have rarely heard such feline ease and facility. The mechanics (forced out of focus in the heat of the moment) could be erratic but the technique was scintillating in a way known to very few pianists. Cortot's Liszt Rhapsodies, decked out with an array of sly nudges and winks, are as flamboyant as any on record, and time and again you are made aware of his own dictum on music: 'my secret is, I can't have enough of it'. Above all, he reminds you of Liszt's celebrated description of a virtuoso as 'one called upon to make emotion weep, and sing, and sigh. To conjure scent and blossom, and breathe the breath of life'. A wild but enthralling fragment from Chopin's First Ballade is included (a complete version comes later) and there are two versions of both Liszt's 11th Hungarian Rhapsody and Weber's *Invitation to the Dance*.

Jacqueline du Pré   *cello*

Jacqueline du Pré: Les introuvables
Bach Cello Suites – No 1 in G, BWV1007; No 2 in D minor, BWV1008 (rec live 1962) **Beethoven** 12 Variations on Handel's 'See the conqu'ring hero comes', Wo045[i]. Seven Variations in E flat on Mozart's 'Bei Männern, welche Liebe fühlen', Wo046[i]. 12 Variations in F on 'Ein Mädchen oder Weibchen', Op 66[i] (rec live 1970). Cello Sonatas[c] – No 3 in A, Op 69; No 5 in D, Op 105 No 2 **Bruch** Kol Nidrei, Op 47[a] **Chopin** Cello Sonata, Op 65[i] **Delius** Cello Concerto[e] **Dvořák** Cello Concerto in B minor, B191[g]. Silent Woods, B182[g] **Elgar** Cello Concerto in E minor, Op 85[d] **Fauré** Elégie, Op 24[e] **Franck** Violin Sonata in A[i] (arr vc/pf) **Handel** Oboe Concerto in G minor, HWV287[b] (arr vc/pf Slatter: rec live 1961) **Haydn** Cello Concertos – No 1 in C[h]; No 2 in D[d] **Monn** (arr

Schoenberg) Cello Concerto in G minor[d] **Saint-Saëns** Cello Concerto No 1 in A minor, Op 33[f] **Schumann** Cello Concerto in A minor, Op 129[f]
Jacqueline du Pré vc [a]**Gerald Moore**, [b]**Ernest Lush**, [c]**Stephen Kovacevich** pfs [d]**London Symphony Orchestra / Sir John Barbirolli**; [e]**Royal Philharmonic Orchestra / Sir Malcolm Sargent**; [f]**New Philharmonia Orchestra**, [g]**Chicago Symphony Orchestra**, [h]**English Chamber Orchestra / Daniel Barenboim** pf
EMI ⑥ 568132-2 (357' · ADD)   ⒷOO

As the title suggests, this fine six-disc retrospective of Jacqueline du Pré's recording career – a mere 10 years long – was masterminded by French EMI. The wonder was that right from the start Jacqueline du Pré was mature in her artistry, and it's good that from the period even before the first official EMI sessions the collection includes three BBC recordings: Bach's Cello Suites Nos 1 and 2 and a Handel sonata arranged from the Oboe Concerto in G minor. Those early BBC recordings are inevitably flawed, but the sheer scale of the artistry is never in doubt. Of the handful of items recorded by EMI in July 1962 with Gerald Moore accompanying, only Bruch's *Kol Nidrei* is included.

The Delius was du Pré's first concerto recording, and she wasn't nearly as much at ease as she came to be later. The CD transfers don't minimise any of the flaws in the original recordings, notably the disappointing sound given to her Chicago recording of the Dvořák Concerto. Not only does the orchestra sound coarse and thin with a lot of background hiss, the cello is balanced far too close. Even so, the wide dynamic range of du Pré's playing is clearly represented, down to a whispered *pianissimo*. It was right to include it and also the cello sonata recordings of Chopin and Franck, the last she ever made, in December 1971. The tone may not have been quite so even, but the fire and warmth are undiminished.

All the concerto recordings are welcome, with the tear-laden quality in the slow movement of the Schumann matching that in the Elgar. It's good that her supreme Beethoven sonata recordings with Stephen Bishop (later Kovacevich) are included, both sparkling and darkly intense. From the Beethoven series recorded at the 1970 Edinburgh Festival by the BBC only the three sets of variations are included. A must for anyone who was ever magnetised by du Pré's playing.

James Ehnes   *violin*

Barber Violin Concerto, Op 14 **Korngold** Violin Concerto in D, Op 35 **Walton** Violin Concerto
James Ehnes vn **Vancouver Symphony Orchestra / Bramwell Tovey**
Onyx Classics ONYX4016 (79' · DDD)   Ⓕ

It's an inspired coupling, as well as a generous one, to have these three high-Romantic concertos together. James Ehnes gives superb performances, bringing out their full emotional thrust without vulgarity or exaggeration. His playing has always been impressive on disc, but here he excels himself in expressive range as well as tonal beauty, with expressive *rubato* perfectly controlled.

The concertos date from the late 1930s and '40s, and though at the time their Romanticism might have seemed outdated, the strength and memorability of the musical ideas in each amply justifies the composers' stance. In the Barber, Ehnes more than usually brings out the contrast between the first movement – improbably marked *Allegro* when the impression is of a slowish piece – and the *Andante* slow movement, strengthening the work's impact. The Korngold, drawing its striking main themes from some of the composer's film scores, is just as richly lyrical, prompting from Ehnes some ecstatic playing of the many stratospheric melodies above the stave, using a wide dynamic range with wonderfully delicate half-tones.

The Walton is just as memorable, for unlike most latter-day interpreters Ehnes has taken note of the example of the work's commissioner and dedicatee, Jascha Heifetz. Where the work is generally spread to well over half an hour, Ehnes takes exactly 30 minutes and the result is all the stronger. This is one of Walton's most richly inspired works, and Ehnes brings that out strongly, helped by the powerful playing of the Vancouver orchestra under Bramwell Tovey. Textures are not always as transparent as they might be but the power of the orchestral playing in all three works adds greatly to the impact of the performances. An outstanding disc in every way.

Rudolf Firkušný   *piano*

Chopin Mazurka, Op 63 No 3 **Martinů** Fantaisie et Toccata **Mussorgsky** Pictures at an Exhibition **Schubert** Three Pieces, D946 **Smetana** Furiant. Concert étude
Rudolf Firkušný *pf*
BBC Legends BBCL 4238-2 (76' · ADD)
Recorded live at the Queen Elizabeth Hall, London, on February 21, 1980   Ⓕ

Those inclined to think of Rudolf Firkušný as a stylish but understated pianist are in for a surprise. True, in Schubert's D946 pieces he remains a master of understatement. Playing with a patrician ease and grace, he none the less finds all of the Second Impromptu's central agitation, and if the quietly pulsing centre at the heart of No 3 sounds oddly diffident, he ends this whimsical caprice in dazzling style. In the Mussorgsky *Pictures* you sit back and listen to the highest musical quality caught, as it were, on the wing, but it is Firkušný's unleashing of power in the final pages of 'The Great Gate of Kiev' that hints at the sort of reserves he had up his sleeve when in his most outgoing mood.

For his Czech items (always at the heart of a Firkušný recital) he throws off Martinů's *Fantaisie and Toccata* with a special authenticity and aplomb, though even here he hardly prepares

you for his Smetana encores. Smetana's piano music bristles with every virtuoso challenge, and the sheer excitement of Firkušný's storm though the C major *Concert Study* (taken at a gloriously indiscreet, hair-raising speed) has the audience cheering him to the rafters. Chopin's Op 63 No 3 Mazurka is spun off with the most gentle lift to its phrases, another reminder of a pianist garlanded with honours, particularly in his homeland and in his adopted America. Firkušný was the sort of musician other musicians flocked to hear and since he made relatively few commerical recordings, this thrilling disc, finely mastered, is doubly welcome.

Leon Fleisher   *piano*

'Two Hands'
Bach Jesu, Joy of Man's desiring (arr Hess). Sheep may safely graze (arr E Petri) **Chopin** Mazurka No 32. Nocturne No 8, Op 27 No 2 **Debussy** Suite bergamasque – Clair de lune **D Scarlatti** Keyboard Sonata in E, Kk380 **Schubert** Piano Sonata No 21
Leon Fleisher *pf*
Vanguard Classics ATMCD1551 (74' · DDD) ⒫ⒹⒹ

This verges on the unbelievable. Leon Fleisher, now 75, who for more than 35 years couldn't use his right hand because of dystonia (a neurological disease 'characterised by involuntary muscle contractions which force certain parts of the body into abnormal, sometimes painful movements or positions'), recovers fully after treatment with botulinum toxin (more familiarly known as Botox). And he plays as if he'd never been incapacitated. Dexterity and dynamics are effortlessly controlled. Tone is evenly spread; bass-lines aren't weak, chords are cleanly articulated and inner voices have their place. Best of all, technique is coupled to an imaginative intellect that portrays the language of each composer in deep terms.

Schubert's sonata is very personal, running a gamut of feelings from resignation to gaiety but Fleisher (who repeats the first-movement exposition) also finds an undercurrent of toughness which he allows to burst forth in the finale. Yet there's a place for ease, for moments of stillness in the transcriptions of Bach; and it''s gratifying to hear Chopin hauntingly dark and shorn of glitter. Perhaps some glitter would have enlivened Scarlatti's sonata but Fleisher finds a contemplative side to the music that is often overlooked.

Good sound, though the piano is close and recorded level is higher in the Schubert. There are also breathing noises.

Emil Gilels   *piano*

Debussy Suite bergamasque – Clair de lune.   Ⓗ
Nocturnes – Fêtes (arr Borwick) **Godowsky** Renaissance, Book 2 – Gigue in E major, after Loeillet **Mendelssohn** Scherzo, Op 16 No 2. Songs Without Words, Book 3, Op 3 – No 18, 'Duetto', Op 38 No 6 **Mozart** Piano Sonata No 14, K457 **Rameau** Keyboard

Suite in E minor – Le rappel des oiseaux; La
villageoise **Ravel** Le tombeau de Couperin – Prélude;
Forlane; Toccata **Schumann** Toccata, Op 7.
Fantasiestücke, Op 12 – No 7, Traumes Wirren.
Spanisches Liederspiel, Op 74 – No 10, Der
Kontrabandiste (arr Tausig) **Smetana** Czech Dances –
No 2, Polka in A minor; No 3, Polka in F major
Emil Gilels pf
Naxos Historical mono 8 111350 (74' · ADD)
Recorded 1935-51   Ⓢ❍❍

Here, in performance after performance, is the
sort of playing that made Rubinstein, on hearing
the teenage Gilels in Russia, exclaim, 'if that boy
ever comes to America I might as well pack my
bags and retire'. Even in dated sound an 'elemental virtuoso gift' and a 'sonority rich in
noble metal' are omnipresent. And whether you
hear Gilels in his exquisite Rameau, the thunderous brilliance of his Godowsky or in the way
his decorations in Smetana's A minor Polka
shimmer like the beating of a hummingbird's
wings, you will hear a nonpareil pianism. True,
in years to come Gilels would find greater depth
than his enviably spruce and immaculately
turned Mozart conveys, but even here the playing is of an aristocratic distinction and finesse.

All in all these performances are a reminder of
this grandest of musical titans. Ward Marston's
transfers come up excellently and special thanks
go to Judith Rayner for the loan of discs from
her priceless collection.

Beethoven Piano Sonata No 27, Op 90 **Debussy**
Images – Reflets dans l'eau. Pour le piano **Prokofiev**
Piano Sonata No 3, Op 28ᵃ. Visions fugitives, Op 22ᵃ
– No 1, Largamente; No 3, Allegretto; No 5, Molto
giocoso; No 10, Ridiculosamente; No 11, Con
vivacita; No 17, Poetico **D Scarlatti** Keyboard
Sonatas – Kk27; Kk32; Kk125; Kk141; Kk466; Kk518;
Kk533 **Scriabin** Piano Sonata No 4, Op 30ᵃ
Emil Gilels pf
BBC Legends ᵃmono BBCL4261-2 (80' · ADD)
Recorded live ᵃ1957 & 1984   Ⓕ❍

Beethoven Piano Sonata No 21, 'Waldstein', Op 53.
12 Variations on a Russian Dance from Wranitzky's
'Das Waldmädchen', WoO71. 32 Variations on an
Original Theme, WoO80 **Weber** Piano Sonata No 2,
J199 Op 39
Emil Gilels pf
BBC Legends mono BBCL4260-2 (76' · ADD)
Recorded live 1968   Ⓕ❍❍

Here on two CDs is Emil Gilels, one of the
greatest pianists of the 20th century, in all his
imperious and aristocratic glory. The essential
qualities were a tone which his mentor Heinrich
Neuhaus considered be 'rich in noble metal,
20 carat gold, that we find in the voices of the
great singers', and of a warmth and humanity
that could reduce his outsize audiences to tears.
And so it is here in recitals all recorded in London.

Seven Scarlatti sonatas show him in an inimitable if unfashionable mood, slow and romanti-

cally free in the repeated notes of the D minor
Sonata, Kk141. His Debussy (including a first
commercial release of *Pour le piano*), once again,
sings and expands in a style far remote from a
more classic French performing tradition, and
his Beethoven, while not to everyone's taste, is
mesmeric in its imperturbable mastery. The
Waldstein Sonata in particular is more a calm
flow of events rather than a river in full spate,
though the *prestissimo* coda is a glorious virtuoso
dash to the finishing line. Both sets of variations
are given with a peerless pianistic grace and
mastery, and the virtuosity and charm of his
Weber A flat Sonata release all of its courtly
elegance. All of this is familiar Gilels repertoire;
yet hearing it again, live, and in such excellent
transfers is a reminder of a pianist as lovable as
he was formidable.

Augustin Hadelich   *violin*

'Flying Solo'
Bartók Solo Violin Sonata, Sz117 **Paganini** Çaprices
– No 4; No 9; No 21 **Ysaÿe** Solo Violin Sonatas,
Op 27 – No 3, 'Ballade'; No 5 **BA Zimmermann**
Violin Sonata
Augustin Hadelich vn
Avie AV2180 (64' · DDD)   Ⓕ❍❍➔

Augustin Hadelich (born 1984) here tackles a
programme of technically challenging works,
one, moreover, where each composer presents
different difficulties. He meets and surmounts
all obstacles, yet it's not technical wizardry that
most impresses but his musicianship. He makes
the musical sense of each piece crystal clear, and
his playing has an inner life; each phrase, each
note, is felt as it's played. The Bartók third
movement, 'Melodia', has constant expressive
variation of tone colour and emphasis, and the
sonata's Hungarian character comes out particularly strongly, due to Hadelich's idiomatic
rhythmic sense.

In the Fourth Paganini Caprice, Hadelich is
unusually successful in integrating the sustained
music with the intervening brilliant passages,
and the Ninth Caprice is delightfully buoyant –
it's good to hear this piece as Paganini wrote it,
without the traditional added harmonics near
the end. Of the Ysaÿe sonatas, No 3 is given an
appropriate sweeping narrative character, while
in No 5 Hadelich maintains a beautiful tranquillity for the initial portrayal of dawn and, in the
following 'Danse rustique' catches exactly the
poised rhythmic quality the composer asks for.
The Zimmermann makes a spectacular conclusion to the recital; Hadelich has clearly grasped
the full import of its intense, climactic final toccata.

Marc-André Hamelin   *piano*

'The Composer-Pianists'
Alkan Esquisses, Op 63 – No 46, Le premier billet-
doux; No 47, Scherzetto **Bach/Feinberg** Kommst du

nun, Jesu, vom Himmel herunter BWV650 **Busoni** Fantasia after J. S. Bach **Feinberg** Berceuse, Op 19a **Godowsky** Toccata in G flat, Op 13 **Hamelin** Etudes – No 9, 'd'après Rossini'; No 10, 'd'après Chopin'; No 12 (Prelude and Fugue) **Haydn/Alkan** Symphony No 94 in G, 'Surprise' – Andante **Medtner** Improvisation in B flat minor, Op 31 No 1 **Rachmaninov** Moment musical in E flat minor, Op 16 No 2. Etude-tableau in E flat, Op 33 No 4 **Scriabin** Poème tragique in B flat, Op 34. Deux Poèmes, Op 71 **Sorabji** Pastiche on Hindu Song from Rimsky-Korsakov's 'Sadko'
Marc-André Hamelin pf
Hyperion CDA67050 (68' · DDD)   ⓕ🅾🅾↦

Here is a cunning and potent mix of every conceivable form of pianistic and musical intricacy (it excludes the merely decorative, salon or ephemeral). Everything is of the most absorbing interest; everything is impeccably performed. Hamelin's richly inclusive programme ranges from Godowsky's Toccata, music of the most wicked, labyrinthine complexity, to three of his own projected cycle of 12 Etudes, among them a ferociously witty and demanding Prelude and Fugue and a reworking of Chopin's Op 10 No 5, full of black thoughts as well as black notes. Then there's Alkan's sinister absorption of the *Andante* from Haydn's *Surprise* Symphony (loyal to Haydn, Alkan's teasing perversity also makes such music peculiarly his own); a *Berceuse* by Samuel Feinberg that prompts Francis Pott, in his brilliantly illuminating notes, to question what sort of child would be lulled by such strangeness; some superb Medtner and Scriabin and a cloudy, profoundly expressive *Fantasia after JS Bach* by Busoni. Clearly among the most remarkable pianists of our time, Hamelin makes light of every technical and musical difficulty, easing his way through Godowsky's intricacy with yards to spare, registering every sly modulation of Alkan's 'Le premier billet-doux' and generating a white-hot intensity in Rachmaninov's admirably revised version of his Second *Moment musical*. Here, Hamelin's maintenance of a 'line' set within a hectically whirling complexity is something to marvel at. Taut, sinewy and impassioned, this performance is a worthy successor to Rachmaninov's own legendary disc. Every phrase and note is coolly appraised within its overall context and the results are audacious and immaculate as required. Hyperion's sound is superb.

'In a State of Jazz'
Antheil Jazz Sonata **Gulda** Prelude and Fugue. Play Piano Play – Exercise No 1; Exercise No 4; Exercise No 5 **Kapustin** Piano Sonata No 2 **Weissenberg** Six Arrangements of songs sung by Charles Trenet. Sonate en état de jazz
Marc-André Hamelin pf
Hyperion CDA67656 (69' · DDD)   ⓕ🅾

'In a State of Jazz' presents a form of fusion music where the influence of jazz is grafted onto

classical forms. So although Gulda, Kapustin and Weissenberg whirl us into heady jazz idioms, their work is notated rather than improvised. As Marc-André Hamelin tells us in the opening sentence of his brilliant accompanying essay, 'there is no jazz on this recording'.

Again, all three composers, temporarily stifled by classical norms and mores, sought a liberation that would send them soaring into what would once be considered alien territory. Weissenberg, for example, claims his *Sonata in a State of Jazz* is fuelled by 'intoxication, contamination and madness' while 'written in a state of indisputable sobriety'. Gulda, too, loved to escape from the confines of Carnegie Hall to the Birdland club in New York, jamming away into the small hours and claiming that he had left the past to join the vibrant living present and future. All this and much more makes for music that is arguably more brittle and sophisticated than uplifting, but it is played with such astounding agility and aplomb that you end up mesmerised by virtually every bar. Indeed, it is no exaggeration to say that no other pianist could approach Hamelin in such music. Notes pour and cascade like diamonds from his fingers and he has an inborn flair for the music's wild, free-wheeling melodies and rhythms, for its glittering whimsy and caprice.

Doubting Thomases should try the first movement of Kapustin's Second Sonata for crazed virtuoso exuberance and Trenet's 'Coin de rue' (cunningly arranged by Weissenberg) for teasing nostalgia. Superbly presented and recorded, this is a special addition to Hamelin's towering and unique discography.

Jascha Heifetz   *violin*

'Heifetz the Supreme'   Ⓗ
Bach Violin Partita No 2 in D minor, BWV1004 – Chaconne **Brahms** Violin Concerto in D, Op 77[a] **Bruch** Scottish Fantasy, Op 46[b] **Gershwin** (arr Heifetz) Three Preludes[c] **Glazunov** Violin Concerto in A minor, Op 82[d] **Sibelius** Violin Concerto in D minor, Op 47[e] **Tchaikovsky** Violin Concerto in D, Op 35[f]
Jascha Heifetz vn [c]**Brooks Smith** pf [aef]**Chicago Symphony Orchestra** / [af]**Fritz Reiner**; [b]**New Symphony Orchestra** / [b]**Sir Malcolm Sargent**; [d]**RCA Victor Symphony Orchestra** / [de]**Walter Hendl**
RCA Red Seal ③ 74321 63470-2 (154' · ADD) Recorded 1955-65   Ⓜ

For once a record company's hype is totally justified. Heifetz was and is supreme. He plays the Bach 'Chaconne', with an extraordinary range of dynamic and feeling, and a total grip on the structure. The subtlety of his bowing is a thing to marvel at. This is a superb anthology, excellently accompanied. How persuasively Reiner shapes the opening of the Brahms, and Sargent the *Scottish Fantasy*; how tenderly Heifetz plays the 'Canzonetta' of the Tchaikovsky, and then astonishes us with his quicksilver brilliance in the finale. Heifetz's first entry in the Sibelius is quite Elysian, and his tone in the slow movement sends shivers down the spine. He discovered all the Romantic charm in the Glazunov concerto, and virtually made it his own. And how good that the selection ends with Gershwin, sparklingly syncopated and bluesy by turns: nothing else here better shows the flexibility of the Heifetz bow arm, even if the microphones are too close.

Daniel Hope
violin

'Air – A Baroque Journey'
Anonymous Greensleeves to a Ground (arr Fourés) **Bach** Orchestral Suite No 3, BWV1068 – Air **Falconieri** Ciaccona. La suave melodia. Passacalle a 3 **Geminiani** Concerto grosso No 5 **Handel** Sarabanda, HWV437 (arr Fourés). **Leclair** Tambourin **B Marini** Per ogni sorte d'stromento, Op 22 – Passacalio a 3 & a 4 **D Ortiz** Ricercata segunda **Matteis** Diverse bizzarrie sopra la Vecchia sarabanda o pur Ciaccona. Ayrs for the Violin, Book 4 – Suite in F: Ground after the Scotch Humour **Pachelbel** Canon and Gigue **Telemann** Violin Concerto in A minor **Valente** Gagliarda napolitana (arr Fourés) **Westhoff** Sonate a Violino Solo – Sonata No 2: Imitazione del liuto; Sonata No 3: Imitazione delle campane. Sonata, 'La guerra' – La guerra cosi nominata di sua maestà **Daniel Hope, Lorenza Borrani, Lucy Gould** vns **Stewart Eaton** va **Jonathan Cohen, William Conway** vcs **Enno Senft** db **Kristian Bezuidenhout** hpd/org **Stefan Maass, Stephan Rath** lte/gtr/theo **Hans-Kristian Kjos Sørensen** perc
DG 477 8094GH (64' · DDD)   Ⓟ**ⓄⓄ**➡

To judge from his impeccably stylish performances, Daniel Hope has the music-making of period colleagues ringing in his ears; but although there's more than a touch of the Hespèrions, for instance, about his bubbling, percussion-enhanced accounts of Falconieri and Ortiz, it would be wrong to suggest that he's 'playing at Baroque' rather than creating something that's individual and true to himself.

For a start, his choice of music is clearly the product of much consideration, for alongside favourites such as the Pachelbel Canon and Bach's 'Air on a G String' (exquisitely performed with a one-to-a-part ensemble drawn from members of the COE), Hope homes in on single, characterful movements from relatively obscure larger works, including sonatas by the dazzling German Johann Paul von Westhoff, whom even period players have tended to neglect.

The concertos by Telemann and Geminiani are thoughtfully chosen, and there is also a handful of specially made arrangements. So what impression will be gained by new listeners following Hope and his excellent collaborators in this repertoire? He himself says he wants to emphasise the modern-ness of the music, and the exotic attraction some of these wandering composer-violinists must have had in person. In this he succeeds entirely, for this is an exciting disc with a heady, pied-piper power over the listener that comes from realising that the bright sense of discovery once felt by these composers

is being experienced just as much by their modern-day interpreters.

Vladimir Horowitz
piano

Original Jacket Collection
Vladimir Horowitz pf with various artists
Sony Classical (70 CDs) 88697 57500-2 (ADD/DDD)
Ⓢ**ⓄⓄⓄ**

For countless people, Horowitz has always been a pianistic god – a fallible deity, to be sure, but a paragon in terms of tonal colouring, technical brilliance, musical imagination and the ability to astonish and move audiences in equal measure. For younger readers it is difficult to explain just how celebrated Horowitz was. He died in 1989 but for many pianists his playing of certain composers and works remains the model to aspire to. He is still a palpable influence. 'Horowitzian' is a well-worn adjective in these pages.

The Original Jacket Collection is a joint venture between Sony and RCA. The 70 CDs contain most of Horowitz's American recordings issued on the RCA, Columbia, CBS and Sony labels between 1928 and 1989 (so no HMV or DG). Each disc is a facsimile of the original LP packaging including sleeve-notes (in microscopic typeface) but not the essays that came with LP box sets. An initial reaction is of open-jawed amazement – all these old friends from one's teenage years and beyond in miniaturised form. It is a beautifully produced and stunningly designed set of recordings. On closer inspection, however, all is not quite what it seems – and there are aspects of the project that could have been done better.

Space precludes an appraisal of the performances on all 70 discs. These have, in any case, been well covered in *Gramophone* over the years (a visit to **www.gramophone.net** is suggested). Horowitz collectors will have most of these recordings, with their more than 440 separate titles, but not the two complete recitals given on March 5, 1951, and November 12, 1967. These are previously unreleased (except for two short works from each concert) and include a Prokofiev Sonata No 7 and Chopin's Polonaise in C sharp minor, Op 26 No 1. The 1976 'Concert of the Century' celebrating the 85th anniversary of Carnegie Hall with Bernstein, Rostropovich, Fischer-Dieskau *et al* is here, as well as 'The Young Horowitz' LP back in the catalogue with the earliest American recordings and Kabalevsky's Sonata No 3. Omitted are the recently published recordings of Schumann's *Fantaisie* (1946), Balakirev's *Islamey* and Liszt's *St Francis Walking on the Water* (both revised by Horowitz and new to his discography), and other still-unreleased performances such as the Kreisler-Rachmaninov *Liebesleid*.

Inevitably, there is much duplication of repertoire, reflecting Horowitz's own musical preference over the years – two Mussorgsky *Pictures*, the two Tchaikovsky Firsts with Toscanini, two

Rach Threes (the glorious 1951 version with Reiner and the unfortunate 1978 travesty with Ormandy), four *Kinderszenens* and, an extreme example, Debussy's *Serenade for the Doll*, which appears six times. The historic 1965 'Carnegie Hall Return Concert' appears on CDs 42a/b and 57a/b, one version edited for clinkers, the other not. Buyers should be aware that these are not 70 CDs with 70- or even 60-plus minutes of music, inevitable if the producers were to preserve the integrity of the original LP format. Six discs have less than 30 minutes of music on them, 60 of them less than 50 minutes. The transfers appear to be the same as those previously released on CD.

The presentation is a disappointment. It is impossible to work out the criterion for how the collection has been ordered – and the classy-looking (CD size) 200-page hardback booklet doesn't help: 145 pages are taken up with track listings (left hand page) and, quite redundantly, each album cover in black-and-white (right hand page). These are followed by a brisk and sometimes contentious canter through Horowitz's recorded legacy written by reissue producer Jon M Samuels. There is no chronological list of recordings, nor any means of looking up a composer or piece of music to see which work Horowitz recorded when. An appendix with appropriate CD numbers would have been a simple and beneficial addition. Recording details for CD 2 are missing and a number of typos could have been eliminated with closer proof-reading.

At Carnegie Hall – The Private Collection [H]
Balakirev/Horowitz Islamey **Chopin** Barcarolle, Op 60 **Liszt/Horowitz** St François de Paule marchant sur les flots, S175 No 2 **Schumann** Fantasy, Op 17
Vladimir Horowitz pf
RCA Red Seal mono 88697 54812-2
(50' · ADD) (F)

At Carnegie Hall – The Private Collection [H]
Liszt Piano Sonata, S178
Mussorgsky/Horowitz Pictures at an Exhibition
Vladimir Horowitz pf
RCA Red Seal mono 88697 53885-2
(56' · ADD) (F)O

At Carnegie Hall – The Private Collection [H]
Beethoven Piano Sonatas – No 14, 'Moonlight', Op 27 No 2; No 21, 'Waldstein', Op 53
Haydn Piano Sonata No 62, HobXVI/52
Vladimir Horowitz pf
RCA Red Seal mono 88697 60474-2
(50' · ADD) (F)OO
All recorded live at Carnegie Hall, New York, 1945-50

Between 1945 and 1950 Vladimir Horowitz engaged the Carnegie Hall Recording Corporation to record all his solo recitals given in Carnegie Hall. Some selections from these recitals were released a number of years ago. The present discs are all of previously unpublished performances. A number (*Islamey*, for example)

have been floating around on the internet for a while. Contractual problems prevented their official release. Their appearance is a marvellous present not only to Horowitz fans but to pianophiles in general.

Be that as it may, these discs do not always show Horowitz in the best light. The prospect of hearing how the greatest pianistic mechanism of the day dispatches *Islamey*, one of the piano's ultimate digital challenges, fades from amazement to disappointment. After adhering faithfully to the text for two-thirds of the piece – breathtaking speed and clarity, unparalleled machine-gun octaves and a bewitching handling of the second (D major) theme – Horowitz goes his own way, rewriting the final pages to end with a run of his trademark interlocking double octaves. This is not quite as vulgar as his treatment of Liszt's *St Francis*, not so much walking *sur les flots* as riding on a turbocharged jet-ski and endangering marine life. Admire the technical accomplishment if you will but musically it is jejune and vacuous (and, again, rewritten). Both titles are new to Horowitz's discography. The Barcarolle is an acquired taste: it's fussy, unfocused and overwrought. The best of the disc is the Schumann in which Horowitz's narrative gifts and unique sound are heard at their best, even through some noisy surfaces. There is a cut of some 12 bars in the March. The later performance from the historic Carnegie Hall recital is less accurate but speaks more directly.

There are further cuts in Mussorgsky's *Pictures* and the Liszt Sonata. The former, from March 1949, is in Horowitz's two 'amplifications' familiar from his 1947 studio and 1951 live recordings and which, following Ravel, omit the 'Promenade' before 'Limoges'. Here he is on top form showing off a wealth of imaginative detail, acutely characterising each section and using the full sonority of the instrument. It's closer in conception to the 1947 account, but the more elaborate 1951 version, in a dead acoustic, while still impressive, seems more contained and less spontaneous. The Sonata, too, is glorious, halfway between his great first recording of the work in 1932 and the tortuous, grandiloquent affair from 1976. The microphone placement is noticeably different, however, as if from the back of the hall. Distance does not add enchantment to the sound and there is an unwarranted cut of 24 bars in the first 'movement'. Whether this was a bad decision by Horowitz or a lack of lacquer is not revealed by either producer Jon M Samuels or the fulsome notes by David Dubal.

The third disc contains the most consistently exalted music-making, though its repertoire is duplicated elsewhere in the Horowitz discography and, in truth, there is little to choose between earlier or later recordings of the three works. Haydn's late E flat Sonata was a novelty when Horowitz first recorded it in 1932. Sixteen years later it had clearly lost none of its appeal, sparingly pedalled, almost no repeats and with the pianist revelling in Haydn's joyous playfulness. The *Waldstein* gives the lie to those who feel Horowitz was not in tune with Beethoven, a powerful and stunningly articulated reading (listen to the left hand in the last movement – to say nothing of the handling of the infamous octave passage towards the end). After metronomic first and second movements of the *Moonlight* (but with what ravishing colours and tone, despite the swishy surface), the old master gives us a *Presto agitato* finale to remember. For my money, this 1947 live recording makes it preferable to the studio recordings of 1946, 1956 and 1972. Horowitz was often captured at his most inimitable and spontaneous in front of an audience which, for all their idiosyncrasies, is what makes the release of all three discs so valuable.

Stephen Hough   *piano*

'Stephen Hough's New Piano Album'
Chaminade Autrefois, Op 87 No 4. Pierrette, Op 41 **Godowsky** Triakontameron – Alt Wien **Hough** Etude de Concert. Musical Jewellery Box **Kálmán** Was weiss ein nie geküsster Rosenmund (arr Hough) **Liszt** Soirée de Vienne in A minor, S427 No 6 **Moszkowski** Etincelles, Op 36 No 6 **Pabst** Paraphrase on 'Sleeping Beauty' (arr Hough) **Paderewski** Mélodie in G flat, Op 16 No 2 **Rachmaninov** Humoresque in G, Op 10 No 5. Mélodie in E, Op 3 No 3 (1940 vers) **Rodgers** Carousel – The Carousel Waltz. The King and I – Hello, Young Lovers (all arr Hough) **Schubert** Moment musical in F minor, D780 No 3. Die schöne Müllerin, D795 – No 8, Morgengruss (all arr Godowsky) **Tchaikovsky** Dumka, Op 59. Humoresque in E minor, Op 10 No 2. Swan Lake, Op 20 – Pas de quatre (arr Wild) **Traditional** The Londonderry Air (arr Hough)
Stephen Hough *pf*
Hyperion CDA67043 (78' · DDD)   Ⓕ Ⓑ→

Stephen Hough fashions a viable programme culled from a bottomless piano bench of transcriptions, encores and other sundry ear-ticklers. Indeed, Hough proves that one can make a well-balanced meal using only desserts. Modern pianists, to be sure, are more calorie-conscious than their forebears, and Hough is no exception. It's not his way to emphasise inner voices or linger over juicy modulatory patterns, à la Hofmann, Moiseiwitsch, Horowitz, Cortot or Cherkassky. If Hough prefers to bind Godowsky's garish counterpoints with skimmed milk rather than double cream, he's cheeky (and smart!) enough to insert his own *ossias* into Moskowski's *Etincelles*, or to retool the Tchaikovsky/Pabst *Sleeping Beauty* Paraphrase to more brilliant pianistic effect. As in his previous 'Piano Albums', Hough serves up his own Rodgers & Hammerstein transcriptions. If the decorative note-spinning in 'Hello, Young Lovers' distracts from rather than enhances the eloquent original, the pianist's giddy romp through 'The Carousel Waltz' is a *tour de force* that brilliantly recaptures both the tender and tough-minded qualities inherent in the musical's book. Hough's own *Etude de Concert* gets plenty of finger-twisting mileage out of a rather unmemorable

theme, harmonised, however, with clever Gershwinisms. The unadorned Rachmaninov and Tchaikovsky selections are played with heartfelt simplicity and a lean yet singing sonority.

'Stephen Hough in Recital'
Beethoven Piano Sonata No 32, Op 111 **Chabrier** Feuillet d'album Leaf **Chopin** Waltzes – No 2, Op 34 No 1; No 7, Op 64 No 2 **Debussy** La plus que lente **Liszt** Mephisto Waltz No 1, 'Der Tanz in der Dorfschenke', S514. 4 Valse oubliées, S215 No 1 **Mendelssohn** Variations sérieuses, Op 54 **Saint-Saëns** Valse nonchalante, Op 110 **Traditional** Waltzing Matilda **Weber** Aufforderung zum Tanze, J260 Op 65
Stephen Hough *pf*
Hyperion CDA67686 (79' · DDD)   Ⓕ Ⓞ Ⓑ→

The menu for this sumptuous banquet, with its tasty hors d'oeuvre, substantial classic dish as the main course followed by a variety of unexpected and nourishing desserts, is perfectly balanced – enough to fill you without being bloated, and nothing that is hard to chew or liable to give you indigestion. But it is the different wines accompanying each course that make this meal special, that is to say the discriminating *premier cru* tone, touch (what magically hushed *pianissimos*) and masterly pedalling to which the diners are treated, each element adjusted to each composer yet all unmistakably Stephen Hough – vintage Hough at that, for here is a pianist at the height of his powers.

This is the sort of programme and style of playing redolent of the so-called Golden Áge of Rachmaninov, Hofmann, Godowsky, Cortot *et al* but which, in this earnest urtext era, is encountered all too infrequently. The Mendelssohn (with some seriously brisk tempi – try Variations 8 and 9) and a taut, crisply articulated account of Beethoven's Op 111 explore two aspects of variation form.

The 'second half' is devoted to waltz time, beginning with Weber's pioneering *Invitation* (1819), the earliest work in this recital. For some unaccountable reason it is rarely heard in its original form these days. Hough is at his finest – exuberant, seductive and scintillating by turns with the repeats (all are given) subtly varied second time round. After two delectably suave Chopin waltzes, Hough offers three contrasted Gallic takes on 3/4 time, imbuing each with the kind of affection and charm for which Cherkassky was famous. After this he cleverly takes us gently by the ear via Liszt's nostalgic *Valse oubliée* No 1 to the pianistic diablerie of his *Mephisto Waltz* No 1. Rounding off this masterclass is Hough's own witty transformation of *Waltzing Matilda* from its normal duple time to triple time. A great piano recording.

William Kapell   *piano*

'Kapell Rediscovered – The Australian Broadcasts'
Bach Suite, BWV818 **Chopin** Barcarolle, Op 60. Nocturne, Op 55 No 2. Scherzo No 1, Op 20

Debussy Suite Bergamasque **Mozart** Piano
Sonata No 16, K570 **Mussorgsky** Pictures at an
Exhibition **Prokofiev** Piano Sonata No 7, Op 83
Rachmaninov Piano Concerto No 3ᵃ **Traditional** God
Save the Queen
William Kapell pf
ᵃ**Victorian Symphony Orchestra /**
Sir Bernard Heinze
RCA Red Seal mono ② 82876 68560-2
(151' · ADD). Radio broadcasts live from Town Hall,
Melbourne, in July and October 1953　　　　Ⓜ

William Kapell was killed in a plane crash just
south of San Francisco in October 1953 – the
flight that was taking him home a week after he
had completed a triumphant three-month tour
of Australia. He was 31 years old. Several items
from this final trip have surfaced over the years
(the Rachmaninov, Mussorgsky and Chopin's
Second Sonata), but other rumoured recordings
never materialised – until 2003, when the titles
issued here were identified in a huge collection
of acetate discs recorded off-air by an Australian
music lover.

The surfaces are noisy, sometimes heavily
swishy and the sound is often horribly distorted
despite the best efforts of producer Jon M Samuels. His apologia notes that, because they did
not make it on to the acetates, a passage in the
final movement of the Rachmaninov had to be
patched (from a 1948 performance), and that the
first movement of the Bach Suite and final pages
of the Mussorgsky are taken from other sources.
You will not need to be told where these 'edits'
occur.

So, is it all worth persevering with? Oh yes.
This is the playing of a sublimely gifted artist.

Wilhelm Kempff　　　　　　　　　*piano*

Bach Chromatic Fantasia and Fugue in D minor,
BWV903 **Beethoven** Piano Sonata No 22 in F, Op 54
Schubert Piano Sonata No 12 in F minor, D625. Drei
Klavierstücke, D946. Impromptus, D899 – No 3 in G
flat; No 4 in A flat
Wilhelm Kempff pf
BBC Legends BBCL4045-2 (77' · ADD)
Recorded live 1969　　　　　　　　　Ⓜ❶❷❸

Ⓖ　Kempff's art was at its apogee at the
time of his 70th birthday in the autumn
of 1965; rigour and fantasy held in perfect poise. Bryce Morrison, who has provided
the notes for this BBC Legends release, and who
was present at this concert – and indeed many
other legendary recitals – recalls: 'If I were to
single out one musical experience that transcended all others, it would have to be Wilhelm
Kempff's 1969 Queen Elizabeth Hall recital. At
his greatest, as he undoubtedly was on this occasion, Kempff's playing seemed bathed in a
numinous light or halo of sound, his choice of
music by Bach, Beethoven, and Schubert seemingly improvised on the spot.'

Alfred Brendel has said of Kempff, 'he was an
Aeolian harp, ever ready to respond to whatever

interesting wind blew his way'. It's a remark that
applies especially well to Kempff's Schubert. He
has said that in his early years Schubert's music
was a book with seven seals. He played Schubert
Lieder, but it was not until much later, after the
First World War, that he entered the private
world of the piano sonatas. For him, Schubert's
'heavenly length' was never lengthy if seen in
proportion to the larger experience. 'If length
becomes evident as longueur,' Kempff has written, 'the fault lies with the interpreter (I speak
from my own experience…).'

Not here. The reading is wonderfully taut yet
touched with a rare ease of utterance. The enigmatic end is perfectly judged (and well 'heard' by
an audience whose applause merely stutters into
life). After the 'disconsolate lyricism' (BM's
phrase) of the sonata, the *Drei Klavierstücke* offer
more or less unalloyed pleasure, Kempff wing-
ing the music into life. The playing has charm,
dash and magic. He once said of Schubert's
piano music: 'It ought not to be subjected to the
glaring lights of the concert halls, as it's the confession of an extremely vulnerable spirit. Schubert reveals his innermost secrets to us *piano-
pianissimo*.' We hear this wonderfully well in
Kempff's playing of the first of his two encores,
the Impromptu in G flat, where his fabled *cantabile* comes even more mesmerisingly into its
own. An Aeolian harp indeed!

At the start of the recital, Kempff provides a
shrewdly voiced and somewhat Mendelssohnian
account of Bach's *Chromatic Fantasia and Fugue*.
It's a performance to free the fingers and light
the way ahead, the great work assuming the role
of warm-up man with as good a grace as can be
expected.

Arturo Benedetti Michelangeli　　　　*piano*

'The Early Recordings, Vol 1 – 1939-48'　　Ⓗ
Albéniz Malagueña, Op 71 No 8 **Bach** Italian
Concerto, BWV971 **Bach/Busoni** Chaconne **Brahms**
Variations on a Theme by Paganini, Op 35 **Galuppi**
Presto in B flat **Granados** Andaluza, Op 37 No 5
Marescotti Fantasque **Mompou** Canción y danza
No 1 **D Scarlatti** Keyboard Sonatas – Kk9; Kk11;
Kk27; Kk96 **Tomeoni** Allegro in G
Arturo Benedetti Michelangeli pf
Naxos Historical mono 8 111351 (80' · ADD)　　Ⓢ▷

Michelangeli ranks among the grandest of all
musical autocrats. And when his transcendent
mastery is complemented by warmth, wit and
charm, such additions are beyond price. Early in
his career he possessed a Romantic as well as magisterial charisma, and listening to his performance
of Bach's *Italian Concerto* with its wealth of colour,
nuance and resilience is to be reminded that a
human heart beat beneath that legendary froideur.
What sparkle, too, in Tomeoni's G major Allegro
and how he plays the arch-seducer to the manner
born in Albéniz's *Malagueña*. Granados's *Andaluza*
is heavily but irresistibly personalised, all fun and
fancy-free; hardly for lovers of a more 'correct'
Spanish style, while Marescotti's *Fantasque* is spun

off with a virtuosity as life-enhancing as it is thrilling. Michelangeli's reordering of the Brahms *Paganini* Variations is odd, but his performance remains of classic status. So, too, does his way with the Bach/Busoni Chaconne with his rapid tempi and lean, not-an-ounce-of-fat way with Busoni's *maestoso* instruction. This is an issue that all lovers of great artistry will pounce on, particularly when so enticingly offered at Naxos price.

'The Early Recordings, Vol 2 – 1939-51'   🄷
Beethoven Piano Sonata No 3, Op 2 No 3 **Chopin**
Scherzo No 2, Op 31. Berceuse, Op 57. Mazurkas –
No 25, Op 33 No 4; No 47, Op 68 No 2. Waltz No 9,
Op 69 No 1 **Mozart** Piano Concerto No 15, K450ᵃ
Arturo Benedetti Michelangeli pf
ᵃ**Pomeriggi Musicali Symphony Orchestra, Milan /
Ettore Gracis**
Naxos mono 8 112052 (74' · DDD) Ⓢ🄾🄾➍

This volume once more shows Michelangeli, among the greatest of all pianists, as an introvert who frequently masked his complex inner life with a curt military precision. Yet if he can bark orders he can also seduce you with sudden shafts of sunlight and affection. The second subject of Chopin's B flat minor Scherzo is as beguiling and heart-easing as you could wish and if the central section openly flouts Chopin's wish for continuity, becoming in effect a slow movement, it is made hypnotically personal and intense. Elsewhere, Michelangeli's explosive but flawlessly controlled force and energy are frightening in their perfection and one doubts whether a more masterly Second Scherzo exists on record. The Berceuse is a marvel of 'silvery fire', the recognisable de-synchronisation of the hands somehow made part and parcel of a unique personality. The B minor Mazurka, for long the pianist's favourite encore, and the Op 69 A flat Waltz, too, are marked with an indelible character as well as flashes of perversity light years away from, say, Rubinstein's patrician elegance.

Michelangeli's agility in the last two movements of Beethoven's Sonata No 3 has to be heard to be believed, though here and in one of Mozart's most delectable concertos you will need to look elsewhere for warmth and affection. The Mozart in particular can be chilly and unyielding, dressed, as it were, in stiff brocade. Transfer engineer Ward Marston has a hard time making the Milan orchestra sound acceptable but overall does his usual sterling service. An invaluable issue.

Lydia Mordkovitch   *violin*

Kabalevsky Improvisation, Op 21ᵇ **Khandoshkin**
Violin Sonataᵇ **Prokofiev** Five Pieces from
'Cinderella'ʳᵇ **Stravinsky** Russian Danceᵃ.
Russian Songᵃ **Volkonsky** Viola Sonata, Op 8ᵇ
Lydia Mordkovitch vn/va
ᵃ**John Milford,** ᵇ**Nicholas Walker** pfs
Chandos CHAN10526 (76' · DDD) Ⓕ🄳➍

Here is a fascinating programme of out-of-the-way Russian repertoire. Kabalevsky's *Improvisation*, like so much of his work, is a cocktail of Russian ingredients well adapted to the needs of aspiring Soviet fiddlers, and historically interesting as an example of a member of the apparat offering a model example of Socialist Realist instrumental music.

On a more ambitious scale, Andrey Volkonsky's Viola Sonata (1955-56) shows a young, independent-minded composer in the Thaw years, synthesising a style from the harsher pages of Bartók, Prokofiev and Shostakovich, and damn the consequences. Here recorded for the first time, the Sonata was composed for Rudolf Barshai and was performed several times by him with the composer. The Prokofievian toccata third movement comes off particularly well, but the slow finale – blankly desolate in a way prophetic of Shostakovich's Viola Sonata – presents an obstacle to its potential breakthrough into the modern repertoire.

Khandoshkin's solo violin music is a remarkably early example of Russian music with high-art aspirations, while its limitations compared to the likes of Bach and Biber weigh against its future outside the world of recordings. CD incarnations have come and gone over the years, and for those interested in the period, this one is therefore worth snapping up.

The transcriptions from Prokofiev's *Cinderella* and Stravinsky's *Petrushka* make an attractive conclusion to the disc, recorded with exemplary clarity. Not so exemplary is Lydia Mordkovitch's intonation, which is under strain throughout the programme, notably in the frequent passages of double-stopping. Yet she is a passionate advocate for everything she plays, her accompanists are excellent, and no collector of Russian/Soviet music would want to miss the chance to encounter Volkonsky's Viola Sonata, or to thank her and Chandos for the opportunity.

David Oistrakh   *violin*

Franck Violin Sonata **Ravel** Tzigane   🄷
Schumann (arr Kreisler) Fantasie, Op 131
Szymanowski Three Myths, Op 30
David Oistrakh vn **Vladimir Yampolsky** pf
Testament mono SBT1442 (70' · ADD) Ⓕ🄾🄾🄾

Here we have a fabulous unpublished programme that not only offers us new David Oistrakh repertoire but, in the case of the works we do already have from him, delivers performances that are sufficiently distinctive to warrant the duplication.

Take César Franck's Sonata, where Oistrakh's vibrato is more expressively intense than it often is on disc and where Vladimir Yampolsky transcends his familiar 'accompanist' role to assert an individual musical personality with playing that in its freedom and grandeur at times reminded me of Cortot, no less. Ravel's *Tzigane* is another winner – witty, spontaneous, incisive in its attack and, near the end, dangerously fast.

Other available Oistrakh *Tziganes* also deliver, musically speaking, but none sounds quite so thrillingly off the cuff.

And then there are the newcomers to Oistrakh's discography, all of them fine works. The Szymanowski *Myths* 'Narcissus' and 'Dryads and Pan' extend the experience we already have of Oistrakh in the opening 'Fountain of Arethusa' with seductive tone production, filigree passagework and a sense of play that perfectly matches Szymanowski's fantastical imagination. The late and rather discursive Schumann Fantasy in C, presented here with Fritz Kreisler's rich piano reduction, is a true *tour de force*, bittersweet one moment, boldly virtuoso the next and graced by a uniquely rounded musical sensibility that left the world the day David Oistrakh died.

Happily we still have the records, with this 1958 Bucharest recital being one of the finest of all. The sound is fairly good, the balance variable but never skewed. Utterly unmissable.

Nobuyuki Tsujii   *piano*

Beethoven Piano Sonata No 29, 'Hammerklavier', Op 106 **Chopin** Etudes, Op 10 Nos 1-6 **Liszt** La campanella, S140 No 3 **Musto** Improvisation / Fugue **Nobuyuki Tsujii** pf
Harmonia Mundi HMU90 7505 (69' · DDD)   ⓕⓞⓞ

This CD is of live performances from the preliminary and semi-final rounds of the Thirteenth Van Cliburn International Piano Competition. It is difficult not to be impressed by Nobuyuki Tsujii's technical accomplishment. His well drilled fingers make light work of the first six studies of Chopin's Op 10. The *Hammerklavier*, too, holds no terrors for him – resolutely brisk tempi, by and large exemplary textual clarity and a sound grasp of structure. The emotional depth of the work is beyond him at present. In the mesmerising section that prefaces the fugue, for example, all we get are the notes and dynamics, illustrative of a general lack of musical imagination throughout. Liszt's digitally demanding *La campanella* is tossed off with great brio and machine-gun repeated notes, while John Musto's piece, one of four new American works from which competitors could choose, is dispatched with marvellous fluency and not a little impish delight. Though it should have no bearing on the matter, the fact that Nobuyuki Tsujii has been blind from birth adds an extra dimension to his achievement.

Maurizio Pollini   *piano*

Boulez Piano Sonata No 2 **Prokofiev** Piano Sonata No 7 in B flat, Op 83 **Stravinsky** Three Movements from Petrushka **Webern** Piano Variations, Op 27 **Maurizio Pollini** pf
DG The Originals 447 431-2GOR (68' · ADD)
Recorded 1971-76   Ⓜⓞⓞⓞ▸

 Perfection needs to be pursued so that you can forget about it. Pollini's *Petrushka* movements are almost inhumanly accurate and fast; but what comes across is an exhilarating sense of abandon, plus an extraordinary cumulative excitement. The Prokofiev Seventh Sonata remains a benchmark recording not only for the athleticism of its outer movements but for the epic remorselessness of the central *Andante*. The Webern Variations are a magical fusion of intellectual passion and poetry, and the Boulez Sonata vividly reminds us why the European avant-garde was such a powerful force in the 1950s. These recordings are a monument to what it's possible for two hands to achieve on one musical instrument. The 'original-image bit-processing' has given a bit more brilliance and presence, as claimed, and another gain is the retention of atmosphere between movements.

Jonathan Plowright   *piano*

'Hommage à Chopin'
Balakirev Impromptu on the Themes of Two Preludes by Chopin **Bendel** Hommage à Chopin, Op 111 No 1 **L Berkeley** Three Mazurkas, Op 32 No 1 **Busoni** Variations on a Prelude of Chopin **B Godard** Hommage à Chopin, Op 66 No 2 **Godowsky** Walzermasken No 7, 'Profil (Chopin)' **Grieg** Studie, 'Hommage à Chopin', Op 73 No 5 **Honegger** Souvenir de Chopin **Leschetizky** Hommage à Chopin, Op 46 No 9 **Mompou** Variations sur un thème de Chopin **Nápravník** Notturno, 'La réminiscence de Chopin', Op 48 No 1 **Tchaikovsky** Un poco di Chopin, Op 72 No 15 **Villa-Lobos** Hommage à Chopin
Jonathan Plowright pf
Hyperion CDA67803 (80' · DDD)   ⓕⓞⓞ▸

Chopin's contemporaries were wary of paying him tribute, fearing his waspish tongue and sensing their inadequacy before such unnerving genius. Liszt in particular only offered his own adulation safely after Chopin's early death. Fortunately, later generations have been less cautious and here on this magnificent and richly enterprising disc you can hear Chopin's idiom refracted, as it were, through the prism of several richly diverse personalities. Balakirev audaciously links two contrasted Preludes, making the winsome B major (No 11) and storming E flat minor (No 14) somehow coalesce. Bendel turns for inspiration to the 'embalmed darkness' of the Nocturnes, and Grieg, while never less than true to his Nordic roots, captures his Polish master's Slavic tension and unease. Honegger and Chopin may seem an unlikely conjunction yet it is made with a special empathy and restraint, while Lennox Berkeley turns more to Szymanowski's Mazurkas than to Chopin's.

The most substantial offerings are from Mompou whose extended Variations reflect much of an inimitable magic later memorably verbalised by Wilfrid Mellers in his book *La jardin retrouvé*, while the sobriety of Chopin's C minor Prelude lends itself ideally to elaboration through Busoni's austere genius.

All of these multifaceted offerings (jewels as well as gemstones) show Jonathan Plowright as beguiling in intimacy as he is magisterial in virtuosity. Such quality will leave lesser pianists bemused, and Plowright has been immaculately recorded.

Ian Quinn *organ*

'Tender is the North'
Gade Three Tone Pieces, Op 22 **Másson** Larghetto
Nystedt Variations on 'Med Jesus vil eg fara', Op 4
Olsson Organ Sonata, Op 38 **Palmgren** Two Preludes
Sibelius Two Pieces, Op 111
Ian Quinn *org*
Chandos CHAN10581 (71' · DDD). Played on the
organ of Coventry Cathedral Ⓕ Ⓞ ➤

This must be one of the finest recordings of Coventry Cathedral's glorious Harrison and Harrison organ since Graham Barber's pioneering account of the Whitlock Sonata for Vista in 1979. By a happy coincidence Ian Quinn opens with Sibelius's monumental Two Pieces which were given their UK premiere by Whitlock in 1934. The *Intrada* of 1925 is a magnificent piece, as is the *Surusoitto* written in 1931 for the funeral of Sibelius's friend, the artist Akseli Gallen-Kallela.

Gade's *Three Tone Pieces* date from 1851. Mendelssohn springs to mind, especially in the charming central *Allegretto*. Equally endearing are Palmgren's exquisite pair of Preludes of 1908. Their very brevity makes one yearn for more organ music from his pen, but that's all there is!

Knut Nystedt's Variations were composed 70 years ago and are here receiving their long overdue premiere recording. Built on the Dupré tradition, the Norwegian folk-tune theme is treated with increasing levels of tonal sophistication and harmonic adventure. This impressive recital sheds new light on the treasures of Scandinavia. Quinn's playing is never less than enthralling and the organ – with Chandos's perfectly balanced engineering – has never sounded finer.

Michael Rabin *violin*

Bruch Violin Concerto No 1, Op 26[a] **Kroll** Banjo and
Fiddle[b] **Saint-Saëns** Havanaise, Op 83[c] **Sarasate**
Carmen Fantasy, Op 25[b]. Danzas españolas –
Malagueña, Op 21 No 1; Habanera, Op 21 No 2;
Zapateado, Op 23 No 2 **Tchaikovsky** Souvenir d'un
lieu cher, Op 42 – No 1 Méditation[b] **Wieniawski**
Caprice, Op 18 No 4 (arr Kreisler)[b]
Michael Rabin vn [b]**Lothar Broddack** pf [ac]**RIAS**
Symphony Orchestra, Berlin / Thomas Schippers
Audite AUDITE95 607 (70' · ADD)
Recorded [c]1962, [ab]1969 Ⓕ

Michael Rabin's was a talent that even among a plethora of great violinists was something rather

special, and we're lucky to have so many fine records that recall it, whether studio or live. Rabin died in 1972; he was 35 and victim of a neurological condition that necessitated debilitating medication. Rumours of psychological problems and drug mismanagement were rife, and yet in spite of these and other problems Rabin managed an impressive comeback, as this svelte but musically responsive account of Bruch's First Concerto amply proves. The line is mostly seamless, the tone warm and seductive, the bowing impeccably drawn. Thomas Schippers conducts a thoughtful if occasionally overweight accompaniment, somewhat muddily recorded although the violin sound is excellent. (The slow movement is occasionally troubled by an unobtrusive knocking.)

The shorter works include a brilliant account of Sarasate's *Carmen Fantasy* and a tenderly phrased Tchaikovsky *Méditation*. Also highly cherishable is the cheeky close to Kroll's *Banjo and Fiddle*. The other items relate the same happy impression, a technical wizard and an artist in total command of his instrument, someone who would surely have developed an extra musical dimension had he been granted another 30 or so years to do so. Sadly he wasn't but this well mastered programme of radio broadcasts is a valuable addition to Rabin's precious legacy.

Sergey Rachmaninov *piano*

Chopin Ballade No 3, Op 47. Nocturne No 2, Ⓗ
Op 9 No 2. Waltzes – No 7, Op 64 No 2; No 8, Op 64
No 3; No 14, Op *posth*. Piano Sonata No 2, Op 35
Liszt Polish Songs, S480 – No 1, Maiden's Wish (after
Chopin); No 6, 'Die Heimkehr' (after Chopin)
Schumann Carnaval, Op 9. Der Kontrabandiste,
Op 74 No 10
Sergey Rachmaninov pf
Naxos Historical mono 8 112020 (69' · ADD)
From RCA Victor originals, recorded 1925-42
Ⓢ Ⓞ Ⓞ Ⓞ ➤

Here is a reminder and a remembrance of a matchless idiosyncrasy and mastery, particularly when discs dating from 1925-42 are so superbly remastered by Ward Marston. Try this great pianist in Chopin's E flat Nocturne, Op 9 No 2, played in the style of the greatest Russian singers, with a melting *cantabile* and with a freedom and *rubato* that can make even the ever-elfin Cherkassky sound sober by comparison. The Op 64 Waltz in A flat dances with a gossamer lightness while the Third Ballade seems improvised on the spot. Today, Rachmaninov's operatic treatment of the Funeral March from the Second Sonata and his 'winds whistling over graveyards' alternative to Chopin's prescribed *sotto voce* in the finale may seem over-free, aberrations to be frowned on in our more puritan times. Yet even here you are conscious of a fierce musical integrity, one that scorns mere cleverness or difference for its own sake. The *Scherzo* from the same sonata has all of Rachmaninov's astonishing propulsion and pungent rhythmic drive; and in the final pages of Schumann's *Carnaval* the dancers are whirled into near oblivion. Rachmaninov could be gruff, tender, mordant (he includes 'Sphinxes', written in order to be ignored), dazzling, confiding and so much more. This is a superb first volume in what promises to be an invaluable series.

Sviatoslav Richter   *piano*

'The Russian Piano Tradition: The Neuhaus School'
Schubert Piano Sonatas – No 16, D845; No 17, D850.
Impromptu, D899 No 2
Sviatoslav Richter pf
APR mono APR5669 (78' · ADD)   Ⓕ

'Early Recordings, Vol 1 – 1948-1956'
Chopin Etude, Op 25 No 5 **Schubert** Impromptus –
D899 No 2; D935 No 2. Moment musical, D780 No 1
Schumann Fantasiestücke, Op 12 – No 1, Des
Abends; No 2, Aufschwung; No 3, Warum?; No 5, In
der Nacht; No 8, Ende von Lied. Humoreske, Op 20
Sviatoslav Richter pf
Naxos Historical mono 8 111352 (66' · ADD)   Ⓢ

Sviatoslav Richter's Schubert has always provoked controversy and APR's reissue of recordings dating from 1956-57 is a savage reminder of a pianist of uncompromising vision. Rhythms are held in a vice-like grip and there can rarely have been a more radical shift of simple-minded notions of Viennese charm and gentility. Certainly there is little sweetness from Richter, though his remorseless tread is unforgettably countered in the Trio of the A minor Sonata's *Scherzo* which is played with such poise and lucidity that it soars to ultimate heights of poetry. A suitably icy wind blows across the finale (a not-so-distant relation of the finale of Mozart's sonata in the same key) and even in the exultant, less despairing pages of the D major Sonata Richter's adamantine strength and rhythm are paramount. You may miss Kempff's beguiling lilt in the sing-a-song-of-sixpence finale or Gilels's emotionalism in the *con moto* but you can never be less than awed by such consummate if chilling mastery.

Naxos's issue of recordings dating from 1948-56 includes more austere Schubert (though the A flat Impromptu, D935, is an exception). But when you turn to Richter's Schumann you enter another world. Here this great pianist reminds you that Schumann has always been central to the repertoires of the finest Russian pianists. Rarely in its entire history can the *Humoreske* have been given with such energy and refinement, such poetry and fantasy. Try the *Einfach und zart* and the following Intermezzo with its joyous carillon of bells, or the final pages where Richter truly recalls 'magic casements, opening on the foam / Of perilous seas, in faery lands forlorn'. Five movements from the Op 12 *Fantasiestücke* complete the picture, and so too does Chopin's E minor Etude with Richter's slowly spiralling and assuaging view of the heavenly middle section.

Arthur Rubinstein   *piano*

Beethoven Piano Concerto No 4, Op 58[a]
Chopin Etude, Op 10 No 5[b]. Scherzo No 2, Op 31[c]
Saint-Saëns Piano Concerto No 2, Op 22[d]
Villa-Lobos Prole do bebê, Book 1[b] – Moreninha;
Pobrezinha; Polichinelle
Arthur Rubinstein pf [d]**BBC Symphony Orchestra /
Rudolf Schwarz;** [a]**London Philharmonic Orchestra /
Antal Dorati**
BBC Legends [abd]mono BBCL4216-2 (77' · ADD)
Recorded live in [d]1957, [b]1958, [a]1967, [c]1968   Ⓕ

One could hardly call this a disc of novel Rubinstein repertoire. All the works are familiar from his studio recordings and had been under his fingers for many years. Yet there is no better way of hearing this great artist than in front of an audience. All except the Villa-Lobos items and Chopin Etude come from performances in the Royal Festival Hall. We can overlook the less than glamorous sound and forgive the odd clinker here and there (what Rubinstein appearance would be complete without them?), for here is a pianist at the height of his considerable powers.

This performance of Beethoven's Fourth is imbued with a lifetime's experience. The Saint-Saëns, a work Rubinstein had played to the composer nearly 60 years earlier, could hardly be bettered (his second and preferred studio recording with Alfred Wallenstein was made just two months later). As a friend of Villa-Lobos we have authoritative versions of pieces he first recorded in 1931. The E minor Etude, too, was a special favourite, while the Scherzo, interrupted by applause from those who did not know the piece, is all patrician elegance.

Altogether marvellous – except for the printing of Jeremy Siepmann's thoughtful notes where the typesetter, who enjoys using the smallest possible font, is clearly a stranger to the convention of leaving a space after full stops. Why does this label insist on such unnecessary and irritating practices?

'The Legendary Moscow Recital'
Chopin Barcarolle, Op 60. Etudes – Op 10 No 4;
'Black Keys', Op 10 No 5; 'Harp Study', Op 25 No 1;
Op 25 No 5. Impromptu No 3, Op 51. Nocturne
No 8, Op 27 No 2. Piano Sonata No 2, Op 35.
Polonaises – No 5, Op 44; No 6, 'Heroic', Op 53
Debussy 24 Préludes – Ondine **Schumann** Des
Abends, Op 12 No 1 **Villa-Lobos** Prole do bebê,
Book 1 – Polichinelle
Arthur Rubinstein pf
Medici Arts 🅥 307 8548 (97' · NTSC · 4:3 · PCM
mono · 0). Recorded live at the Great Hall of the
Moscow Conservatory on October 1, 1964   Ⓕ

Considering his celebrity, longevity and huge studio recording legacy, there is very little film of Rubinstein in concert. Indeed, this is the only full solo recital one can recall and as such is immensely valuable, not least because the printed programme is devoted entirely to the composer with whom he was most closely associated and because, fine as are most of his studio recordings, Rubinstein played with a greater freedom and daring when in front of an audience.

The film of the occasion, preserved in the vaults of the Russian State television archives for nearly 50 years, provides a vivid reminder of this great artist's idiosyncrasies – the dignified, immobile posture, the expressionless face and the little tug at his lapels before the start of each item.

The playing, of course, is heart-warming, the kind that can absorb the odd fluff, though the memory lapse in the *Scherzo* of the Sonata is disconcerting (he has to make an unwritten repeat before ad libbing his way into the Trio). Everything seems so inevitable and right, whether in the caressing phrases of the Barcarolle or the bravura of the A flat Polonaise, the inevitable trademark conclusion to any Rubinstein recital. Aficionados will relish his only known performance of the *Aeolian Harp* Study, Op 25 No 1. (The bonuses are two short – 1'45" – silent films of excerpts from two Etudes shot in slow motion in Canada in 1928.)

Jordi Savall   *viol*

'The Celtic Viol'
Includes traditional Irish and Scottish pieces, selections from from Ryan's Mammoth Collection, William Marshall's 1822 Collection, Captain Simon Fraser's 1816 Collection, H Playford's Dancing Master 1696 and works by Gow, Laybourn Macpherson and O'Carolan
Jordi Savall *viol* **Andrew Lawrence-King** *hp*
Alia Vox ⦿ AVSA9865 (76' · DDD/DSD)   Ⓕ●◗

After a career spanning four decades, Jordi Savall still thirsts after new repertoire from the past and deeper musical insights. A breadth of musicianship and keen sense of humanity have enabled him to become a master of both courtly and common performing practices. This recording demonstrates how fine the line between them can sometimes be.

Elizabethan and Jacobean viol players improvised divisions on ground basses and it is our good fortune that examples and descriptions were written down (though there is still more we would wish to know). Much of the most popular instrumental music of that day – folk airs, dances, laments – was solely passed down from player to player, at least until some of the tunes found their way into printed collections.

Playing on five- and six-string treble viols and a five-string treble fiddle, Savall draws inspiration from the effects harvested from live and recorded performances. As always, his own playing is ravishingly beautiful and deeply poetic. He is joined on some tracks by Andrew Lawrence-King who delicately improvises counterpoint and accompaniments over drones on an Irish harp and psalterium. The repeated sections of the dances (reels) demand variation; elsewhere the music is strophic, even rhetorical, the changing implications of the 'story' giving rise to dif-

ferent ornamentation. There is also remarkable virtuoso display, especially in the quicker pieces, as one would expect.

For Savall, this recording is intended as 'a fervent tribute to the art of transmission', but therein lies the rub. This music stems from a living tradition, which has changed with the times, gathering fresh inspiration and wider influences. Savall brings to it a highly informed historical perspective but to some ears he may have blurred the distinctions, gentrifying a folk tradition. A thought-provoking recording.

Grigory Sokolov   *piano*

'Récital aux Champs-Elysées – Live in Paris'
A film by Bruno Monsaingeon
Bach/Siloti Prelude No 10, BWV855*a* **Beethoven** Piano Sonatas – No 9, Op 14 No 1; No 10, Op 14 No 2; No 15, 'Pastoral', Op 28 **Chopin** Mazurkas – No 3, Op 6 No 3; No 4, Op 6 No 4 **Couperin** Livres de clavecin, Book 3: 18th Ordre – Le tic-toc-choc, ou Les maillotins; Soeur Monique **Prokofiev** Piano Sonata No 7, Op 83 **Vardapet** Six Dances
Grigory Sokolov *pf*
Medici Arts 307 3888
(123' · NTSC · 16:9 · PCM stereo · 0)
Recorded live 2002   Ⓕ●●●

Some connoisseurs rate Grigory Sokolov (*b*1950) as the greatest living pianist. Most people have never heard (of) him and would find it hard to express an opinion one way or the other: he refuses to make studio recordings, and though all his recitals are taped, he's given his permission for only a handful to be released. His posthumous reputation will be enormous. Basically, you can only hear Sokolov by going to his concerts – or by buying this DVD, a rare relaxation of his stringent, not to say parsimonious, performance aesthetic. Like Richter, Sokolov prefers to play in near darkness, and for long sections of this recital the screen is largely black. The presence of an audience seems to be a necessary evil, if his cursory acknowledgement of those present at the Théâtre des Champs-Elysées on November 4, 2002, is anything to go by. Given all this, you may justifiably ask, 'Is there anything to watch, or shall I just close my eyes and listen?' In fact, Sokolov, a bulky, impassive figure, is fascinating to watch, playing as he does with dangerously high hand movements and expressive gestures.

As for the music-making, one simply bows in the presence of a master. Three Beethoven sonatas are played in an uninterrupted sequence with such beauty of tone, sculptured phrasing and cohesive narrative that criticism is silenced. After the interval comes *Six Dances* by the Armenian composer born Soghomon Soghomonyan (1869-1935; in 1893 he was renamed Komitas Vardapet after becoming a monk). Sparsely scored, bleak and pessimistic, you may find that they outstay their novelty value by some distance. Not so Prokofiev's Seventh Sonata, a coruscating, vehement reading that will make the hairs on the back of your neck stand on end.

Unmissable for all pianophiles. The encores are two delicious Chopin Mazurkas, Couperin's *Le tic-toc-choc* (rivetingly filmed in a single close-up frame) and Bach's Prelude in B minor arranged by Siloti. The DVD bears repeated viewing. One hopes that Sokolov will deign to let a wider audience hear more of him in the future.

Thomas Trotter   *organ*

'Sounds of St Giles'
Anonymous Four Renaissance Pieces **Bach** Trio Sonata No 1, BWV525 **Handel** Organ Concerto, HWV305a **F Holloway** Organ Symphony No 2, Op 47 – Scherzo **Litaize** Prélude et Danse fuguée **Rogg** Partita on the chorale 'Nun freut euch' **Stanley** Voluntary, Op 5 No 5 (Trumpet Voluntary) **Vaughan Williams** Three Preludes on Welsh Hymn-Tunes
Thomas Trotter org
Regent REGCD302 (67' · DDD)
Played on the Mander organ of St Giles Cripplegate, London   Ⓕ

The new Mander East organ has a mere 15 stops – not that you would know it from the extraordinary range of colours that Trotter conjures up. His own arrangement of Handel's Organ Concerto No 16 (itself an arrangement by Handel of his *Concerto a due cori* No 3) gets things off to a festive start. Four Renaissance pieces include the other-worldly *Sur 'La, Mi, Re'* with its three-note bass ostinato (A-E-D), echoed a fifth higher in the tenor with the right hand over the top playing a free melodic line. The dialogue for trumpet and flute in the Stanley Voluntary is set in high relief before the beautifully voiced trialogue of Bach's E flat Trio. The Baroque world is cleverly linked to the 20th century with Lionel Rogg's no less intricate (and intimate) variations on the chorale *Nun freut euch*, ending with a blazing Toccata.

After Vaughan Williams's three mellifluous (and very English) *Preludes on Welsh Hymn-Tunes* comes the delightful feather-light *Scherzo* from the Second Organ Symphony (1912) by the forgotten Frederick Holloway before the *pièce de résistance*, Gaston Litaize's *Prélude et Danse fuguée* (1964), a dazzling riot of cross-rhythms that test co-ordination to the limits. As much as an expression of what is achievable on a small organ, this disc underlines what a supreme stylist Trotter is. Superbly recorded.

Arcadi Volodos   *piano*

'Volodos in Vienna'
Bach Concerto, BWV596 – Sicilienne **Liszt** Années de pèlerinage, année 2: Italie, S161 – Après une lecture du Dante (Fantasia quasi sonata) **Ravel** Valses nobles et sentimentales **Schumann** Waldszenen, Op 82 **Scriabin** Danse languide, Op 51 No 4. Feuillet d'album, Op 45 No 1. Guirlandes, Op 73 No 1. Piano Sonata No 7, 'White Mass', Op 64. Preludes – Op 11 No 16; Op 37 No 1 **Tchaikovsky/Volodos** Children's Songs, Op 54 – No 10, Lullaby in a Storm

Arcadi Volodos pf
Sony Classical ② 88697 56887-2 (84' · DDD)
Recorded live 2009   Ⓜ ○○○⊕

 Arcadi Volodos has surely produced nothing finer on disc than this live recital, captured in Vienna in 2009. When Sony first signed Volodos they must have thought they were getting another great virtuoso-in-the-making. People were quick to point out the parallels with Horowitz in the astonishing feats on Volodos's first disc more than a decade ago, and who could forget his cheeky take on Mozart's 'Rondo alla turca'? It's striking that Sony has hung on to him despite his reluctance to play the fame game.

But with this latest release we're once again reminded that Volodos is a one-off. He has Sokolov's genius for making even the unpianistic pianistic, yet without his occasional eccentricities. He has the steel, combined with the velvety sound, and the sense of a companionable relationship with his instrument of Gilels. Yet there's fire aplenty too – witness his *Dante Sonata*, complete with the odd Volodosian touch (you'll recall from earlier discs that he likes to make pieces his own). No one quite achieves the incandescence of Ogdon in this work, but the sense that technically Volodos is in complete command, and that the piano is not in pain – even at the most extreme moments – is extraordinarily compelling. And through all the handfuls of notes he never loses sight of the work's form, the imperious left-hand theme that sweeps through the chorale-like texture done with complete assurance.

You couldn't be in Vienna without presenting a waltz or two, and here we get Ravel's skewed take on it. Volodos is less perfumed than some but there's a wonderful warmth to his sound as well as a sensitivity to the pieces' inner workings that delights. He attains the balance between lyricism and a pungent neo-classicism every bit as effectively as Casadesus in his classic reading. Right from the start, this is an uncompromisingly programmed recital, Volodos plunging his audience into the strange hinterland of Scriabin. Whether in the insistent lopsided gait of the *Danse languide* or the deep-toned Prelude No 16 from Op 11, he is spellbinding. And in the Seventh Sonata Volodos is wonderfully incense-laden and edgy.

Waldszenen is perhaps the finest jewel here, with Volodos bringing his story-telling genius to every piece. Its outwardly unassuming nature is deceptive, as the many great pianists who've been drawn to it have shown. But Volodos is absolutely up there with the best of them, Richter and Pires included.

The encores are supreme, from Volodos's Bach/Vivaldi *Sicilienne*, which is informed by a restrained beauty worthy of Gilels, a Tchaikovsky song rendered glorious even without voice yet its piano roulades never taking the limelight, and, finally, a telling return to Scriabin. The engineers have done wonders, in spite of the live conditions. Can there be a disc of finer piano playing this year?

Yuja Wang

Chopin Piano Sonata No 2, Op 35 **Ligeti** Etudes,
Book 1 – Fanfares; Book 2 – Der Zauberlehrling
Liszt Piano Sonata, S178 **Scriabin** Piano Sonata No 2,
'Sonata-fantasy', Op 19
Yuja Wang *pf*
DG 477 8140GH (73' · DDD)　　　Ⓢ❍❍❍❍▸

Make no mistake, 22-year-old Yuja Wang is a
wondrously gifted pianist whose debut album of
sonatas by Chopin, Liszt and Scriabin, with the
stimulating addition of two Ligeti Etudes, suggests a combination of blazing technique and a
rare instinct for poetry. Curtis-trained under
Gary Graffman, Wang tells us in an accompanying DVD of her special love for music of drama
and turbulence and how ever since first hearing
Pollini's recording of the Chopin Etudes she
dreamt of recording for DG.

In Scriabin's Second Sonata she is beautifully
sensitive to the moods, whether tranquil and
starlit or tempestuous, reflecting the composer's love of the Baltic Sea. She is fiery but never
reckless in Chopin's Second Sonata, off like the
proverbial greyhound at the first *doppio movimento*, and offers a dramatic bass emphasis at
the climax of the heaven-storming development. Her finale is truly *sotto voce* yet with the
widest variety of touch and expression, and for
the most part her playing, while sharply individual, is free from all distorting idiosyncrasy
or mannerism.

You wont hear anything on the scale of Richter
or Gilels in the Liszt Sonata but on the other
hand Wang is young, wonderfully talented and
trained, superbly recorded and, if this disc is
anything to go by, with the world at her feet. As
a crowning touch her Ligeti Etudes are both
musically and dazzlingly incisive. In the words
of the publicist, 'a star is born'.

'Transformation'

Brahms Variations on a Theme by Paganini, Op 35
Ravel La valse **D Scarlatti** Keyboard Sonatas – K380;
K466 **Stravinsky** Three Movements from Petrushka
Yuja Wang *pf*
DG 477 8795 (66' · DDD)　　　Ⓕ❍❍▸

Time was when many celebrated pianists
quailed before certain works. Not so today's
generation; and as on her previous DG album
(above – which understandably helped her to
win the *Gramophone* Young Artist of the Year
Award in 2009) Yuja Wang makes light of even
the fiercest complexity. In Stravinsky's *Petrushka*
her youthful verve and jagged accentuation
colour every bar of the 'Danse russe', and how
she relishes the puppets' quizzical mood-swings
from gaiety to desperation in 'Chez Pétrouchka'!
Here and most of all in 'La semaine grasse' she
has a dazzling way of lightening even the heaviest textures so that her entire performance
gleams with an astonishing brilliance and verve.
This is even truer of her Brahms *Paganini* Varia-

tions, making the reordering of both books a
marginal rather than serious consideration. Try
Variation 11 from Book 2 or the Variation coda
(No 14) to Book 1 and then hear her in Var 12
from Book 2 and you will find her as musically
beguiling as she is breathtakingly fleet. In Ravel's *La valse* her dynamics range from the merest
whisper to an elemental uproar (try the final
cataclysmic pages) and as if this was not enough
she gives us an oasis of calm in two Scarlatti
sonatas. For her, the second (K466 in F minor/
C major) is like 'air after rain' and it would be
hard to imagine playing of a more delicate emotional fervour. This entire recital leaves you in
no doubt that at 23 Yuja Wang is already among
the most brilliantly gifted of today's pianists.

ENSEMBLES

Alamire

'Henry's Music'

Anonymous King's Pavan. England be Glad.
Madame d'amours. Hec est preclarum **Benedictus
de Opitiis** Sub tuum presidium **Fayrfax** Lauda vivi
alpha et oo **Henry VIII** Consorts – VIII; XII; XIII. O My
Heart. Tandernaken. Helas madame. Though some
saith. Adieu madame. En vray amoure Jacotin Beati
omnes **Sampson** Salve radix. Psallite felices. Quam
pulcra est **Taverner** O Christe Jesu, pastor bone
Verdelot Nil majus superi vident
Andrew Lawrence King *hp*
Alamire; Quintessential / David Skinner
Obsidian CD705 (76' · DDD)　　　　　Ⓕ

This disc consists of pieces composed in
Henry VIII's honour by both English and continental composers, and a generous selection of
consort pieces and songs by the monarch himself. With the exception of the much-recorded
Tandernaken and the pleasant *Adieu madame*,
there's little to be said for Henry's slight, short-
winded compositions, which overuse a few stock
phrases. One does wonder how he got through
the two Masses he's reported to have written.

The occasional pieces written for him are a
mixed bag: Taverner's *O Christe Jesu*, albeit
originally in honour of Cardinal Wolsey, is the
best of them, followed by *Psallite felice* by Sampson (whose canonic curiosity *Salve radix* is also
worth hearing).

At nearly 17 minutes, *Lauda vivi alpha et oo*
dwarfs the rest, but it's a rather sprawling affair,
not Fayrfax's best. The choral contributions,
aided by a lucid acoustic, are secure and solid,
particularly the Sampson and Taverner pieces,
with the solo numbers slightly less convincing.
It might also be noted that *Lauda vivi* sounds
surprisingly restrained.

But the inclusion of Andrew Lawrence-King's
harp is a deft bit of programming, and the young

wind quintet Quintessential are similarly entertaining. Altogether it's a pleasing panorama of the optimistic, extrovert mood of the English court and its young ruler, before it all changed...

Brabant Ensemble

'Music from the Chirk Castle Part-Books'
Byrd O God give ear and do apply
Caustun Yield unto God the mighty Lord
Deane O Lord, Thou has dealt graciously.
The grace of our Lord Jesus Christ
Hooper Behold it is Christ **Mundy** Te Deum,
'for trebles'. Benedictus, 'for trebles' **R Parsons**
Deliver me from mine enemies. 'I am the resurrection
and the life saith the Lord', from the Burial Service
W Parsons The Litany, 'for trebles', 'O God the
Father of Heav'n' **Sheppard** Submit yourselves
one to another. O God be merciful unto us, and
bless us **Tallis** Christ rising again. With all our hearts.
Not every one that saith unto me **Tye** Blessed are all
they that fear the Lord
Brabant Ensemble / Stephen Rice
Hyperion CDA67695 (71' · DDD · T/t)　　Ⓕ**O**🅑➔

Here, the Brabant Ensemble turn their attention to English repertory of the same period: the Chirk Castle part-books' chequered history began in Wales, where they were copied for the choral establishment of a rich merchant turned landed gentry. One of the part-books was lost fairly early on, and has been reconstructed. It's been worth the effort, for although much of their repertory is known from other sources, a few significant pieces, here recorded for the first time, are not. These include two works by William Mundy, an English *Te Deum* and a *Benedictus*. Both are described as being 'for trebles' in the source; both are conceived on a large scale, and are undoubtedly significant additions to the repertoire. On that count alone this recording is self-recommending. An even greater name among the new additions is that of Tallis: his *Not every one that saith unto me* is brief indeed, but then how often is the discovery of an unfinished sketch by Mozart or Bach hailed as a 'significant find'?

A new departure it may be but the Brabant Ensemble is not on unfamiliar ground, for this is the repertory on which its singers cut their teeth. The predominant sonority is familiarly clear, transparent and assured, though in the lower range the voices are not quite so well defined as at the top. This soft centre is perhaps attributable to the sound recording, which is rather recessed and slightly unfocused. But for the sake of the new pieces alone, lovers of this repertory will welcome this enthusiastically.

Cambridge Singers

'The Sacred Flame'
Anerio Christus factus est **Bach** O Jesu Christ meins
Lebens Licht **Buxtehude** Magnificat **Gabrieli** Jubilate

Deo **Gesualdo** O vos omnes **Hassler** Dixit Maria
John IV of Portugal Crux fidelis **Josquin Desprez**
Ave Maria **Lassus** Ave verum corpus. Timor et tremor
Monteverdi Beatus vir. Cantate Domino. Christe
adoramus te **Palestrina** Exsultate Deo. Sicut cervus
Schütz Psalm 100. Selig sind die Toten **Sweelinck**
Laudate Dominum **Victoria** O vos omnes. Jesu dulcis
memoria
Cambridge Singers; La Nuova Musica /
John Rutter
Collegium COLCD134 (78' · DDD · T/t)　　Ⓕ**OO**🅑➔

This anthology spans the entire 16th and 17th centuries, employing singers and instrumentalists as required. Given its breadth of coverage it manages not to sound sprawling, and there are no weak links as regards either performance or programming. The decision to include *concertato* items (Monteverdi, Buxtehude and Bach) lends the project more variety than an entirely *a cappella* recital would have afforded. Many of the pieces one would expect to find are there indeed, and it's no disrespect to the Cambridge Singers to say that the performances are, again, much as one would expect: they don't disappoint, and in a few of the slightly less familiar pieces they surprise (as with the two short motets by Monteverdi, *Cantate Domino* and *Christe adoramus te*, or the almost bustling *Dixit Maria ad angeli* of Hassler). The instrumentalists from La Nuova Musica are sensible and sensitive accompanists, their light ornamentation in the Baroque pieces proving more than just a nod to the conventions of performance practice.

Clare College, Cambridge

'Illumina'
Anonymous Lumen ad revelationem **Byrd** O lux,
beata Trinitas **Grechaninov** The seven Days of the
Passion, Op 58 – O gladsome light **Harris** Bring us,
O Lord God **Hildegard of Bingen** O choruscans
stellarum **Holst** Nunc dimittis, H127 **Josquin**
Desprez Nunc dimittis **Ligeti** Lux aeterna **Palestrina**
Christe, qui lux es et dies. Lucis Creator optime
Rachmaninov Vespers, Op 37 – Nunc dimittis
Rautavaara Vigilia – Evening Hymn **Rutter** Hymn to
the Creator of Light **Tallis** O nata lux de lumine. Te
lucis ante terminum **Tchaikovsky** Vesper Service,
Op 52 – Hail, gladdening Light **Whyte** Christe, qui
lux es et dies **Wood** Hail, gladdening light
Clare College Choir, Cambridge / Timothy Brown
Collegium COLCD125 (76' · DDD · T/t)　　Ⓕ**O**🅑➔

Retrospectively the disc's final item, Ligeti's *Lux aeterna*, dominates the recital. Not only does it make an indelible impression, but it also casts its light over the entire programme and style of singing. To a listener who has not heard it before (a slightly smaller category than might be thought, as the piece was used in the film *2001: A Space Odyssey*) it may even come as the light on the road to Damascus, a blinding revelation of unknown choral sonorities. An extraordinary sound world is opening up, with long, finely ruled streams of light, a spectrum of colours wide as the distance from heaven to earth, and all mingling eventually within the cavern of a great bell. The challenge to singers (even when assisted by the reverberance of Ely Cathedral's Lady Chapel) is formidable indeed, and these young voices (with lungs and ears involved also) do marvellously well. And so they do throughout. The quality of choral tone here is remarkable: no thready sopranos, none of those bone-dry basses, but a sound that, though strictly disciplined in the matter of vibrato, is still fresh and natural. They achieve wonders of *crescendo*, as in William Harris's *Bring us, O Lord God*, and their opening chords (in Tallis's *O nata lux* for instance) are as if cut by the sharpest slicer ever made. Even so, this smooth, flawless beauty of sound is, in some contexts, like the modern beauty of the face of a heroine in some televised piece of period drama. Josquin Desprez's *Nunc dimittis* is an example: the singing is extremely beautiful, but conceptually (and not just in the women's voices) seems anachronistic. It's as though they have worked on their programme with the precept 'All choral music aspires to the condition of Ligeti'. A wondrous record, all the same.

The Clerks

'Don't Talk – Just Listen!'
C Fox A Spousal Verse. 20 Ways to Improve Your Life. Three Contrafacta **G Jackson** The Armed Man. Te Deum **Pitts** Thou wast present as on this day
Saxton Five Motets
The Clerks / Edward Wickham
Signum Classics SIGCD174 (61' · DDD)   Ⓕ

This group of contemporary vocal works was specially commissioned by The Clerks over the last 10 years and written to suit their forces, ranges and timbres.

Perhaps most substantial are the nine-part Five Motets by Robert Saxton, a polyphonically interesting and varied reflection on the central theme of an 'outward journey' and sense of 'return' symbolised by spiritual fulfilment. This cycle makes for rewarding repeated listening, not least for its detailed organisation (an insight of which is helpfully provided by the composer in the booklet-notes) and the rich, variegated texture of the vocal writing. Pitts's evocative Josquin-inspired *Thou wast present*, an intricate piece, is notable for the way in which a major triad stands at the centre of the structure and emerges luminously at the end. A mixture of archaic methods informs Jackson's *The Armed Man*, characterised not only by its use of the eponymous old French song but also through studied techniques of *cantus firmus*, hocketing and bi-textuality. Yet perhaps most memorable is the composer's use of Robert Palmer's First World War poem as a romantic foil (especially the compelling lyrical centre). The more opulent *Te Deum*, by contrast, reveals Jackson's more typical imaginative exploitation of luxuriant, multi-voiced sonorities.

Of the three works by Christopher Fox, which include the amusing cycle of aphorisms *20 Ways*

to Improve Your Life and the inventive *Three Contrafacta*, the most attractive is the shifting kaleidoscopic textures of the serene pastoral *A Spousal Verse*, a truly haunting miniature.

Hespèrion XXI

'The Forgotten Kingdom' –
Music from the Albigensian Crusade
Montserrat Figueras sop **Pascal Bertin** counterten
Lluis Vilamajó ten **Marc Mauillon** bar **Furio Zanasi**
bass **Andrew Lawrence-King** hp **La Capella Reial**
de Catalunya; Hespèrion XXI / Jordi Savall
Alia Vox ③ 🎵 AVSA9873 (3h 50' · DDD/DSD)   Ⓕ

Jordi Savall's latest 'Livre-CD' establishes a new gold standard for early music. Ostensibly intended as a 'small but intense tribute to the awakening of this the historical memory of Occitania', home of the Troubadours and a focus of resistance to the Church of Rome, it shows what international collaboration with fellow musicians and scholars – and EC funding – can achieve.

This epic project – nearly four hours of music and readings in Latin and Occitan (the Langue d'Oc), chronicling five centuries (c950-1463) – shines fresh light on the Cathars (dissidents calling themselves 'good Christian men and women'), who were hunted down and burnt at the stake – through the words and music of eye-witnesses. Their strophic sirventès, chansons and laments still touch us with their expressive power, authority and poignancy, especially when set alongside contemporary Roman texts. This is the fifth Livre-CD Savall has produced with Alia Vox: a substantial, beautifully illustrated book with 10 engaging essays and a detailed chronology as well as the song texts and readings – and three CDs.

For more than a decade, Savall and his Hespèrion colleagues have explored the related early music of oppressed people in a succession of recordings, amassing a wealth of knowledge and experience. For this project, Savall augmented his band with specialists on medieval Eastern European and Middle Eastern instruments – flutes, fiddles, lutes and zithers – to evoke a sense of a rich medieval soundscape. Their import can't be over-estimated: working with monophonic, often strophic music, they have created polyphony with drones, by doubling the vocal line, imitating and improvising on it, then providing introductions and ritornellos. They have taken pre-existing tunes and created instrumental fanfares, battle calls and laments, employing muffled drums to signal executions and bells to evoke the powerful presence of the Church. Savall takes ownership of the more elaborate versions of the Joan of Arc songs and the sombre final 'Homage to the "Good Men"' in which his own playing is sublime. Montserrat Figueras and the other vocal soloists and readers deliver superbly vivid performances. Altogether an impressive and deeply fascinating achievement.

King's Singers

'Sacred Bridges'
Anonymous Psalm 113, 'Laudate pueri Dominum'
Rossi Hebreo The Songs of Solomon – Psalm 118;
Psalm 124; Psalm 128 **Sweelinck** Pseaumes des
David, Premier livre – Ne vueilles pas, Ô Sire;
Pourquoy font bruit et s'assemblent les gens?;
Troisième livre – Mon Dieu, j'ay toy esperance **Ufkî**ᵃ,
Goudimel Psalm 5. Psalm 9 **Ufkî**ᵃ Psalm 2. Psalm 6
King's Singers; ᵃSarband
Signum Classics SIGCD065 (72' · DDD · T/t) ⒻⒹⒹⒹ→

Lately, TV arts/documentary schedules have
teemed with films on Islam, mostly over-simplify-
ing history to the point of distortion and suggesting a centuries-old conspiracy to deny the contribution Muslim civilisation made to European
culture. Viewers with an interest in early music
(and contemporary music, for that matter) may
have raised an eyebrow: if Islamic influence has
been concealed, it's been hidden in plain sight.

Especially in the context of fears of growing
Islamophobia after 9/11 and 7/7, any campaign
to foster understanding is commendable. This
CD reminds us of the common roots of Judaism,
Christianity and Islam, the importance of the
Psalms to each religion, and the connections
between the music of each. The programme
includes Rossi Hebreo's attempts to reconcile
Catholic liturgy with the Jewish tradition (from
which it ultimately sprang) and works by Ufkî, a
Polish Calvinist captive and convert to Islam
who recast melodies from the Genevan (Hugue-
not) Psalter in Turkish modes.

Sarband has collaborated with Concerto Köln
in intriguing explorations of the interaction
between European classical and Turkish music,
while the King's Singers have tackled an eclectic
repertoire ranging from Gesualdo to The Beatles,
so it's hardly surprising that the groups work well
together, meshing Reformation counterpoint
with 17th-century Ottoman music, comparing
and contrasting the incorporeal sounds of one
and the lithe rhythms of the other. They share the
pieces by Ufkî, Sarband performs an improvisation inspired by Psalm 2, and the King's Singers
take the rest of the tracks. Altogether a fascinating, attractive, beautifully performed album.

Kronos

'Black Angels'
Crumb Black Angels **Tallis** (arr Kronos Qt) Spem in
alium **Marta** Doom. A sigh **Ives** (arr Kronos Qt/Geist)
They are there! **Shostakovich** String Quartet No 8 in
C minor, Op 110
Kronos Quartet (David Harrington, John Sherba vns
Hank Dutt va Joan Jeanrenaud vc)
Nonesuch 7559 79242-2 (62' · DDD) ⒻⒹⒹⒹ→

This is very much the sort of imaginative programming we've come to expect from this talented young American quartet. With an overall
theme of war and persecution the disc opens
with George Crumb's *Black Angels*, for electric
string quartet. This work was inspired by the
Vietnam War and bears two inscriptions to that
effect – *in tempore belli* (in time of war) and 'Finished on Friday the 13th of March, 1970', and
it's described by Crumb as 'a kind of parable on
our troubled contemporary world'. The work is
divided into three sections which represent the
three stages of the voyage of the soul – fall from
grace, spiritual annihilation and redemption.

As with most of his works he calls on his instrumentalists to perform on a variety of instruments other than their own – here that ranges
from gongs, maracas and crystal glasses to vocal
sounds such as whistling, chanting and whispering. *Doom. A sigh* is the young Hungarian composer István Marta's disturbing portrait of a
Romanian village as they desperately fight to
retain their sense of identity in the face of dictatorship and persecution.

Marta's atmospheric blend of electronic
sound, string quartet and recorded folksongs
leaves one with a powerful and moving impression. At first sight Tallis's *Spem in alium* may
seem oddly out of place considering the overall
theme of this disc, but as the insert-notes point
out the text was probably taken from the story of
Judith, in which King Nebuchadnezzar's general Holofernes besieged the Jewish fortress of
Bethulia. Kronos's own arrangement of this
40–part motet (involving some multi-tracking)
certainly makes a fascinating alternative to the
original.

A particularly fine account of Shostakovich's
Eighth String Quartet (dedicated to the victims
of fascism and war) brings this thought-
provoking and imaginative recital to a close.
Performances throughout are outstanding, and
the recording first-class.

The Sixteen

'Renaissance: Music of Inner Peace'
Allegri Miserere mei **Anonymous** Veni creator
spiritus. Ubi caritas. Te lucis ante terminum. In
paradisum **Barber** Agnus Dei **Blow** Salvator mundi
Bruckner Locus iste **Byrd** Ave verum corpus.
Gradualia, Vol 1/i: Feast of All Saints – Offertory:
Iustorum animae. Mass for four voices – Agnus Dei
F Guerrero Ave Virgo sanctissima. Duo Seraphim
G Gabrieli Exultet jam angelica turba **Gibbons**
Hosanna to the Son of David **Górecki** Totus tuus
Josquin Ave Maria **Lassus** Ave regina coelorum.
Timor et tremor **Lotti** Crucifixus a 8 **Melgás** Salve
Regina **Monteverdi** Christe, adoramus te **Mouton**
Nesciens mater virgo virum **Palestrina** Missa Papae
Marcelli – Kyrie. Sicut cervus desiderat **Parsons** Ave
Maria **Poulenc** Salve regina **Purcell** Beati omnes qui
timent Dominum. Hear my prayer, O Lord **Sheppard**
Libera nos, salva nos I **Tallis** If ye love me. O nata lux
de lumine. Salvator mundi Domine. Adesto nunc
proprius **Tavener** The Lamb **Tomkins** When David
heard **Victoria** Salve regina **Weelkes** Hosanna to the
Son of David
The Sixteen / Harry Christophers
UCJ ② 986 6727 (150' · DDD) ⓂⒹⒹⒹ→

This splendid two-disc set features works from The Sixteen's repertory. Over a quarter of a century, under the direction of Harry Christophers, the group has never done anything that wasn't totally compelling in its musicianship and technical assurance.

Even the most casual collector is likely to have at least some of these pieces on disc already, but you'd have to look very hard to find performances to match any here. For example, they give us an electrifying account of Guerrero's *Duo seraphim*, while that great English Tudor classic, Weelkes's *Hosanna to the Son of David*, can rarely have been recorded with such fiery zeal. That mainstay of any half-decent church choir's repertoire, *Locus iste*, comes across here as freshly and as intensely moving as it must have sounded in 1869 when Bruckner wrote it. As for modern repertory, the subtlety brought to pieces by Górecki and Tavener elevates these already established choral classics.

For some this pair of discs will serve as conclusive proof that The Sixteen is the finest small choral group in existence. For others this matchless music-making will provide a source of endless satisfaction and enrichment.

Stile Antico

'Song of Songs'
Anonymous Nigra sum. Tota pulcra es amica mea. Dum esset rex – antiphon. Laeva ejus – antiphon. Speciosa facta es. Iam hiems transiit **Ceballos** Hortus conclusus **Clemens Non Papa** Ego flos campi **Gombert** Quam pulchra es **F Guerrero** Surge propera. Trahe me post te. Ego flos campi **Lassus** Veni dilecte mi **Lhéritier** Nigra sum **Palestrina** Motets, Book 4, 'Canticum canticorum' – Osculetur me; Nigra sum **Victoria** Vidi speciosam. Vadam, et circuibo civitatem. Secunda pars moteti **Vivanco** Veni dilecte mi
Stile Antico
Harmonia Mundi HMU80 7489 (78' · DDD)   Ⓕ Ⓞ ⊖➤

One expectation that such an album may raise in its listeners is an answer to the question of what common and special inspiration might composers have taken from contemplating this most erotic of Biblical texts. The symptoms of their reactions might be sensuous melismas, perhaps, and anguished suspensions, surging bass-lines and… let us draw a veil there. Such devices and stratagems are in abundance, whether chastely deployed in turn by Clemens and Palestrina or flaunted all at once in the selections of Guerrero and Gombert, though no more so than they would be on a programme of Marian or Lenten devotions; and these are just the opening four tracks.

That unfair calculation ignores the plainchant antiphons between each pair of motets. These interspersions work well – as they must in a genuinely liturgical context, as here, thanks to the quiet good taste and stylistically homogeneous approach of Stile Antico, with an especially winsome unanimity to the female-only *Tota pulchra es*.

Indeed, these are just the sort of performances one would hope to hear in church, which was

(one feels) the practical and creative laboratory for what is recorded: full but not strained singing, allowing an advantageous acoustic and the number (12) and freshness of voices to take care of blend and balance, with plenty left in reserve for the longer spans of the two magnificent Victoria anthems, *Vadam et circuibo* and *Vidi speciosam*.

Westminster Cathedral Choir

'From the Vaults of Westminster Cathedral'
Anonymous Rorate coeli. Ecce adventit dominator Dominus. Mass IX – Sanctus and Benedictus. Mass X – Kyrie; Gloria; Sanctus & Benedictus; Agnus Dei. Psalm 2. Dominus Dixit. Vidimus stellam. Marche des Rois mages **Bevan** Magnificat **Byrd** Lady Masses in Advent – Introit: Rorate coeli; Gradual: Tollite portas; Offertory: Ave Maria; Communion: Ecce Virgo concipiet **Lassus** Omnes de Saba **G Malcolm** Missa ad praesepe – Kyrie; Gloria; Agnus Dei **M Martin** Adam lay ybounden **Monteverdi** Messa a 4 – Gloria; Sanctus & Benedictus; Agnus Dei **Victoria** Descendit angelus Domini **C Wood** Nunc dimittis
Westminster Cathedral Choir / Martin Baker org with **Matthew Martin** org
Hyperion CDA67707 (78' · DDD · T/t) Ⓕ

The front cover gives little hint of what the disc might contain since the title simply states 'A Procession of Chant and Polyphony'. As it turns out, the programme processes from Advent through Christmas to Epiphany and the Presentation, each season featuring a setting of the Mass, interspersed with a thoroughly mixed collection of motets, carols and the evening canticles.

The earlier polyphonic works are splendidly sung. It was, after all, Westminster Cathedral's first director of music, Richard Runciman Terry, who almost single-handedly led the revival of Renaissance polyphony in London while also encouraging young, contemporary composers such as Howells, who produced his *Mass in the Dorian Mode* in 1912. The Monteverdi *Messa a 4* is especially virile and mellifluous.

It was a pleasant surprise to hear (for the first time) the *Missa ad praesepe* (Mass at the Crib) composed by one of Terry's successors, George Malcolm, in 1959. Its *Gloria* is especially lovely and memorable. Maurice Bevan's *Magnificat* is something of a throwback, stylistically, and pales somewhat when juxtaposed against Charles Wood's beautifully wrought *Nunc dimittis*.

Throughout, the choral singing under Martin Baker's direction glows resplendently, while still retaining its celebrated 'continental' edge. Another tremendous plus is the exhilarating, splashy, dynamic and fiery improvisations dished up by Matthew Martin on the Grand Organ. Who could fail to be moved by the image of lolloping camels in his cinematic concluding *Marche des Rois mages*?

The recording is up to Hyperion's exemplary high standards. What other treasures will the Westminster Vaults give up?

SINGERS

Victoria de los Angeles   *soprano*

Berlioz Les nuits d'été, Op 7[a] – Villanelle;
Le spectre de la rose; L'île inconnue **Brahms** Meine
Liebe ist grün, Op 63 No 5. Nachtigall, Op 97 No 1
Delibes Bonjour, Suzon! **Halffter** Dos Canciones
Handel Judas Maccabaeus, HWV63 – So shall the lute
and harp awake **Nin** Cantos populares españolas –
Montañesa; Paño murciano **Obradors** Chiquitita la
novia **Ravel** Vocalise en forme de habanera
A Scarlatti Le Violette **Schubert** Mein!, D795 No 11
Schumann Widmung, Op 25 No 1 **Stravinsky**
Pastorale **Valverde** Clavelitos **Vives** Canciones
epigramáticas – La presumida; El ritrato de Isabela
Victoria de los Angeles *sop* **Gerald Moore** *pf*
[a]**BBC Symphony Orchestra / Rudolf Schwarz**
BBC Legends mono BBCL4101–2 (62' · ADD)
Recorded live 1957   Ⓕ**OO**

When Victoria de los Angeles appeared at the
Edinburgh Festival in 1957, she was in her
prime, the voice as supple and sensitive as it was
beautiful. Everything she tackled seemed to be
touched by the magic of her attractive presence
and glorious singing.

Good as her account of Schumann's 'Widmung'
may be, it's when she gets to Brahms, perhaps her
favourite composer in this genre, that she's wholly
at home, the wistful sense of pain in 'Nachtigall'
caught to perfection. In the wordless pieces by
Stravinsky and Ravel she floats that warm yet
ethereal tone of hers with consummate ease, and
the long-breathed phrasing and excellent French
in Duparc's *mélodie* are enhanced by this artist's
innate skill in word-painting. For all that, audiences were always impatient for her to get to the
Spanish part of her programme, for in this field
she was unsurpassed as a singer and interpreter.
Many of these songs were also recorded by her in
the studio, but the live occasion gives these performances an extra frisson. The encores are even
better. An account of 'Clavelitos' is a superior
reading even to those famous ones available elsewhere. That's complemented by a delightfully
insouciant account of the Delibes song that she
didn't attempt on any other recorded occasion.

Gerald Moore, as was his wont, manages to
change idioms with his familiar virtuosity. As a
whole, this is an invaluable addition to the singer's extensive discography.

Dame Janet Baker   *mezzo-soprano*

'Scottish and English Folksongs'
Arne The Tempest – Where the bee sucks[a]
Beethoven Scottish Songs, Op 108[b] – No 5, The
sweetest lad was Jamie; No 7, Bonnie laddie,
highland laddie; No 20, Faithfu' Johnnie; WoO156[b] –
Cease your funning; Polly Stewart **Boyce** Tell me
lovely shepherd[c] **Campion** Third Booke of Ayres[d] – If
thou long'st so much to learne; Never love unlesse

you can; Oft have I sigh'd for him that heares me not.
Fourth Booke of Ayres[d] – Faine would I wed a faire
young man **Dowland** The First Book of Songs or
Ayres – Come againe[d] **Haydn** Scottish Folksong
Arrangements[e] – I'm o'er young to marry yet; John
Anderson; O can ye sew cushions; Sleepy Bodie; Up
in the morning early; The White Cockade; The brisk
young lad; O bonny lass; Duncan Gray; My boy
Tammy; Shepherds, I have lost my love; Green grow
the rashes; Love will find out the way; The birks of
Abergeldie; My ain kind dearie; Cumbernauld House;
Jamie come try me; The Flower of Edinburgh **Monro**
My lovely Celia[c] **Purcell** Lord, what is man?, Z192[c].
Sleep, Adam, sleep and take thy rest, Z195[c]
Dame Janet Baker *mez* [a]**Douglas Whittaker** *fl*
[be]**Yehudi Menuhin** *vn* [b]**Ross Pople** *vc* [ac]**Ambrose**
Gauntlett *vada* [d]**Robert Spencer** *lte* **George**
Malcolm [b]*hpd/*[a]*pf* [ac]**Martin Isepp** *hpd*
Testament SBT1241 (70' · ADD · T/t) Recorded 1967,
Ⓕ**OOO**

 'A Pageant of English Song' was Baker's first solo LP for EMI. Side 1, in
which she's accompanied by Martin
Isepp and Robert Spencer, is reissued on this
CD. Side 2, with Gerald Moore at the piano, can
be heard on a double CD on EMI.

Dame Janet was at the beginning of the high
summer of her career when this was recorded in
1967. Every recital, concert appearance or
opera role was an event. In the first song, Dowland's 'Come againe', each word is given the
perfect weight, with beautiful touches on the
repeated 'I sit, I sigh, I weep, I faint, I die'. The
jolly 'Never love unlesse you can', the melancholy 'Oft have I sigh'd' and the coquettish
'Faine would I wed' each has its own 'face',
Baker finding just the right expression in her
voice. The Scottish songs arranged by Haydn,
recorded eight years later, seem rather slight in
comparison. Nineteen of these arrangements
one after another seem rather too much of a
good thing.

The five Beethoven Scottish arrangements are
the best part of the 1975 session. 'Fathfu' Johnnie'
is a setting to place beside any great song of the
same period. The recording seems to favour
the instrumentalists somewhat, whereas in the
1967 selections, Baker's voice is always fresh and
forward.

Cecilia Bartoli   *mezzo-soprano*

'Sacrificium'
Araia Berenice – Cadrò, ma qual si mira **Caldara**
Sedecia – Profezie, di me diceste. La morte d'Abel
figura di quella dal nostro Redentore – Quel buon
pastor son io **Graun** Demofoonte – Misero
pargoletto. Adriano in Siria – Deh, tu bel Dio 'amor...
Ov'e il mio bene? **Leo** Zenobia in Palmira – Qual
farfalla **Porpora** Siface – Come nave in mezzo
all'onde; Usignolo sventurato. Germanico in
Germania – Parto, ma qual si mira. Semiramide
riconosciuta – In braccio a mille furie. Adelaide –
Nobil onda **Vinci** Farnace – Chi temea Giove
regnante

Bonus CD: Three Legendary Castrato Arias:
Broschi Artaserse – Son qual nave **Giacomelli**
Merope – Sposa, non mi conosci **Handel** Serse –
Ombra mai fu

Cecilia Bartoli *mez* **Il Giardino Armonico /
Giovanni Antonini**
Decca ② 478 1521DH (91' · DDD · N/T/t) Ⓜ**OO**➔

Those who remembered hearing the last castrato, Moreschi, sing at the Vatican in the
1900s, said that his discs really gave no idea of
the 'other-worldly' quality his voice
evoked, surrounded by the echo in the Sistine
Chapel. The thought sprung immediately to
mind, listening to the second track on this
new CD from Cecilia Bartoli and Il
Giardino Armonico, dedicated to the art of
the castrati. This is an aria from Caldara's
oratorio *Sedacia*, 'Profezie, di me diceste', in
which the holy man anticipates death and
everlasting peace.

Here Bartoli seems to capture some of the
mystery which shall ever remain where the
great castrato singers are concerned. Composed for Farinelli, as was Caldara's *La morte
d'Abel*, an aria from which concludes the recital,
it makes one ask what can be deduced from a
modern interpretation of what Farinelli's
admirers called 'a marvel…so perfect, so powerful, so sonorous'. Whatever the castrati may
or may not have sounded like, it is fairly certain
that their voices did not resemble that of a
modern mezzo-soprano. Bartoli's voice, even
when descending into the contralto register,
sounds essentially feminine. Her virtuoso skills
are given full rein in the display arias here,
especially those by Porpora such as the one that
opens the recital, 'Come nave in mezzo
all'onde' from *Siface*, and one by Leonardo
Vinci in which the orchestra is augmented by
thunderclaps, as the singer describes Jove's
anger.

It is more in the reflective, slow arias that Bartoli shows a greater sympathy with the sensual
mannerisms of the age. Farinelli's singing
enchanted the King of Spain every evening for
nearly 10 years. If he had sung the exquisite
string- and harp-accompanied 'Qual farfalla
innamorata' from Leonardo Leo's *Zenobia in
Palmira* with Bartoli's languid tone, it is easy to
understand how the melancholy ruler might
have been soothed.

Eleven of the arias here are claimed as world
premiere recordings, and there is a bonus CD
with some more familiar works, including
Handel's 'Ombra mai fu', composed for the
castrato Caffarelli. Giovanni Antonini and his
band provide the always effective accompaniments. There is such a huge quantity of music
from the 18th-century operatic repertory still
awaiting rediscovery that it is to the credit of all
involved in this project that it opens a window
on a too little-known world of performance.
The accompanying booklet has a 'Castrato
Compendium' in three languages, and some
startling illustrations.

Measha Brueggergosman *soprano*

'Surprise'
Bolcom 12 Cabaret Songs[b]: Vol 1 – Song of Black
Max (as told by the de Kooning boys); Amor;
Toothbrush Time; Surprise!; The Actor; George;
Vol 2 – The Total Stranger in the Garden
Satie La diva de l'empire[a]. L'omnibus automobile[a].
Tendrementa. Je te veux (arr Bolcom)[b]. Trois
Mélodies – Daphénéo (arr Caby)[b] **Schoenberg**
Cabaret Songs[b] – Galathea; Gigerlette; Der
genügsame Liebhaber; Einfältiges Lied; Mahnung;
Jedem das Seine; Seit ich so viele Weiber sah (all arr
Davin); Der Nachtwandler (arr Schoenberg)
Measha Brueggergosman *sop* [a]**William Bolcom** *pf*
[b]**BBC Symphony Orchestra / David Robertson**
DG 477 6589GH (60' · DDD) Ⓕ➔

William Bolcom's *Cabaret Songs* (there are 28 of
them in all) were composed for his wife Joan
Morris, who recorded them with the composer
at the piano in the 1970s. For Measha Brueg-
gosman's first solo recording, Bolcom has
orchestrated seven of them into a nifty little
song-cycle. The mood is generally slightly sinister, from the opening 'Surprise!' ('When she
tried to drink iodine from a paper cup'), through
a worrying tale of crime and punishment,
'Amor!', to the best-known of the songs, the
Weill-style 'Black Max'. This bears the subtitle
'As told by the de Kooning boys', and all the
verses by Bolcom's longtime lyricist and librett-
tist Arnold Weinstein have overtones of surreal-
ism and world-weary irony, suitable for one who
lived out his days in that seediest of grand hotels,
the Chelsea.

It's a brave man who sets out to orchestrate
Schoenberg, and Patrick Davin's reworkings of
the *Brettl-Lieder* inevitably have a softening
effect (just one, 'Der Nachtwandler', has
Schoenberg's own orchestration). Brueggergosman deals with them in a straightforward way,
without trying to overload them with charm or
significance.

The voice is a full soprano, well focused, with a
'snarling' edge used to great effect in the Bolcom songs. In the Schoenberg she employs a
more obviously operatic style, with a gentle
vibrato. The BBC Symphony Orchestra under
David Robertson play with considerable spirit,
above all in Bolcom's really gorgeous orchestration of Satie's 'Je te veux'. This and the other
chansons composed for Paulette Darty ('Ten-
drement' and 'La diva de l'empire') go well, but
'L'omnibus automobile' is taken too fast, so that
much of the crazy humour of Vincent Hyspa's
poem is lost. No matter, there is an enormous
amount to enjoy here from a hugely talented
singer.

'Night and Dreams'
Brahms Fünf Lieder, Op 106 – No 1, Ständchen
Debussy Beau soir **Duparc** Chanson triste. Phidylé
Falla Siete Canciones populares españolas – No 5,
Nana **Fauré** Three Songs, Op 23 – No 2, Notre

amour. Two Songs, Op 46 – No 2, Clair de lune **Hahn**
Chansons grises – No 5, L'heure exquise **Chausson**
Poème de l'amour et de la mer, Op 19 – Le temps
des lilas **Hime** Anoiteceu **Liszt** Oh! quand je dors,
S282 **Montsalvatge** Canciones negras – No 4,
Canción de cuna para dormir a un negrito **Mozart**
Abendempfindung an Laura, K523 **Poulenc**
Métamorphoses – No 2, C'est ainsi que tu es
Schubert Nachtstück, D672. An den Mond, D193
R Strauss Acht Lieder aus Letzte Blätter, Op 10 –
No 3, Die Nacht. Fünf Lieder, Op 41 – No 1,
Wiegenlied. Sechs Lieder, Op 17 – No 2, Ständchen
Warlock Sleep **Wolf** Spanisches Liederbuch – No 12,
In dem Schatten meiner Locken
Measha Brueggergosman sop **Justus Zeyen** pf
DG 477 8101GH (65' · DDD)   Ⓕ❍❍➔

In a programme that moves, as in dreams, from
land to land without seeming to notice, this
delicately attuned soprano and her ever-wakeful
pianist drift wherever Morpheus calls most
beguilingly. The lullabies, serenades, evocations
of moonlight and invocations to sleep are
sweetly voiced and extended to include the tender observation of a lover's repose or (in Fauré's
'Notre amour') the lively appreciation of love
itself. The 'exquisite hour' is not so drowsy as to
become merely soporific, and the expressive
range is perhaps surprisingly wide.

To all of these conditions the performers are
responsive and it is only at the very end that the
listener has any occasion to return betimes to
this critical earth. It may at some point have
occurred to us that in this multilingual tour of
dreamland not much English appears to be spoken and at the last moment, as if in awareness of
the fact, and as a kind of encore, Peter Warlock's
'Sleep' is tagged on. And then, strangely, these
sure-footed travellers quite lose their way. Like
nervous wayfarers by night, they move forward
in little jerks, sometimes too quickly but neither
in time with the poet's yearning heart or in tune
with the composer's plaintive progressions.

Otherwise all is well. There are many individual songs over which it would be pleasant to
linger but if it's to be just one, then let it be the
previously unknown Francis Hime (born 1939)
and his 'Anoiteceu'.

Maria Callas   *soprano*

Bellini Norma – Casta diva **Bizet** Carmen –   Ⓗ
L'amour est un oiseau rebelle; Près des remparts de
Séville; Les tringles des sistres **Catalani** La Wally –
Ebben?...Ne andrò lontana **Donizetti** Lucia di
Lammermoor – Spargi d'amaro pianto **Giordano**
Andrea Chénier – La mamma morta **Gluck** Orphée et
Eurydice – J'ai perdu mon Eurydice **Puccini** Gianni
Schicchi – O mio babbino caro. La bohème – Sì, mi
chiamano Mimì; Donde lieta uscì. Madama Butterfly
– Un bel dì vedremo. Tosca – Vissi d'arte **Rossini** Il
barbiere di Siviglia – Una voce poco fa **Saint-Saëns**
Samson et Dalila – Mon coeur s'ouvre à ta voix **Verdi**
La traviata – Ah, fors'è lui; Addio del passato
Maria Callas sop with **various artists**
EMI 557050-2 (74' · ADD · T/t)   Ⓕ❍❍➔

This single-disc collection comes with the subtitle 'Callas sings film', as half the items have been
chosen to link with film soundtracks. It may be
interesting to learn that 'Vissi d'arte' was used in
a film called *Copycat* or that the Habanera from
Carmen now has three film credits to its name, but
that's unlikely to sway the confirmed opera lover.
The more important factors will be the generous
length of the CD at 74 minutes and its full-price
tag, which is optimistic for what's in effect a sampler designed to encourage purchasers to investigate Callas's recordings further.

There's nothing cut-price about the performances. The 17 tracks on this disc are taken from
recordings that made operatic history in the
second half of the 20th century. It's particularly
heartening to find items from the 1954 Puccini
recital disc that Callas made with Serafin, where
the singing is perfectly schooled in every detail.
The two extracts from the live performance of
La traviata in Lisbon are welcome for showing
that Callas was as impressive live as on disc,
though it's a shame that 'Ah, fors'è lui' is shorn
of both its recitative and cabaletta.

Enrico Caruso   *tenor*

'Complete Recordings, Vol 5 – 1908-1910'   Ⓗ
Franchetti Germania – Studenti udite; Non, non
chiuder gli occhi vaghi **Geehl** For you alone **Gounod**
Faust – O merveille!ᵃ; Seigneur Dieu, que vois-je!ᵇ;
Eh! quoi! toujours seule?ᵇ; Il se fait tard!ᶜ; O nuit
d'amourᶜ; Mon coeur est pénétré d'épouvante!ᶜ;
Attends! Voici la rueᶜ; Que voulez-vous, messieurs?ᵈ;
Alerte! alerte!ᵉ **Leoncavallo** Pagliacci – No,
Pagliaccio non son **Mascagni** Cavalleria rusticanaᵍ –
O Lola ch'ai di latti fior di spino **Ponchielli** La
Gioconda – Cielo e mar! **Puccini** Madama Butterfly –
Amore o grillo; Non ve l'avevo detto?ᶠ **Tosti** Addio
Verdi Il trovatore – Mal reggendoʰ; Se m'ami ancorʰ.
Aida – Già i sacerdotiʰ; Misero appien mi festiʰ
ᵇᶜᵉ**Geraldine Farrar** sop ᵇ**Gabrielle Gilibert** mez
ʰ**Louise Homer** contr **Enrico Caruso** ten ᵈᶠ**Antonio
Scotti** bar ᵃᵇᵈᵉ**Marcel Journet** bass ᵍ**Francis Lapitino**
hp **Victor Orchestra**
Naxos Historical 8 110720 (79' · AAD)
Recorded 1910   Ⓢ

'Caruso in Opera, Vol 2'   Ⓗ
Arias from L'Africaine, Andrea Chénier, La bohème
(Leoncavallo and Puccini), Carmen, Cavalleria
rusticana, Don Pasquale, Eugene Onegin, La favorita,
Les Huguenots, Macbeth, Martha, Nero, La reine de
Saba, Rigoletto, Tosca & Il trovatore
Enrico Caruso ten with **various artists**
Nimbus Prima Voce mono NI7866 (79' · ADD)
Recorded 1905-20   Ⓢ

The 1906 recording of 'M'apparì' from *Martha*
comes first, and it introduces an aspect of Caruso's singing that rarely finds a place in the critical
commentaries: his subtlety. Partly, it's rhythmic.
The move-on and pull-back seems such an
instinctive process that we hardly notice it
(though no doubt a modern conductor would –
and check it immediately). It makes all the differ-

ence to the emotional life of the piece, the feeling of involvement and spontaneous development. Then there's the phrasing, marvellously achieved at the melody's reprise. The play of louder and softer tones, too, has every delicacy of fine graduation; and just as masterly is the more technical covering and (rare) opening of notes at the *passaggio*. An edition of the score which brought out all these features of Caruso's singing would be a densely annotated document. It would, even so, be a simplification, for accompanying all this is the dramatic and musical feeling, which defies analysis – and, of course, the voice.

That voice! You may feel you know all these records and hardly need to play them, yet there's scarcely an occasion when the beauty of it doesn't thrill with a sensation both old and new (the first 'Ah!' is one of recognition, the second of fresh wonder). So it is with the items here: excepting the *Eugene Onegin* aria, which remains external, and the late *L'Africaine* recording, with its saddening evidence of deterioration. The transfers are excellent.

Plácido Domingo — tenor

'Pasión Española'
Alonso Suspiros de España **Anta** La Cruz de Mayo **Lacosta** Porque te quiero. Cariño verdá **López–Quiroga y Miquel** ¡Ay, Maricruz!. Me embrujaste. Te lo juro yoª. ¡No me quieras tanto!. Ojos verdesª **Morales** Falsa monedaª. La bien pagá. El día que nací yo **Morales/Bosch** Antonio Vargas Heredia **Plácido Domingo** ten ª**José María Gallardo del Rey** gtr **Madrid Communidad Orchestra / Miguel Roa** DG 477 6590GH (54' · DDD) Ⓕ**O**➔

In this selection of coplas and pasodobles, the majority composed in the 1930s and '40s, Domingo uses his voice in a mostly baritonal range. These are the songs, as he writes in the notes, that he heard as a child in Spain, even before his family moved to Mexico: 'Since then I have had them in my mind's ear.'

The mood is for the most part highly emotional, drawing on a sort of fatalistic romanticism. Two of the most famous songs, composed by Juan Mostazo Morales to words by Perelló, 'Falsa moneda' and 'La bien pagá', were associated with Conchita Piquer, Imperio Argentina and Juan Valderrama, popular idols of the era, performing both before and after the Spanish Civil War. In these, and in more upbeat songs such as '¡Ay, Maricruz!' by Manuel López-Quiroga y Miquel, Domingo brings a fervent commitment to the story-telling. Each song is what he calls a 'mini-opera'.

Although originally they would have been accompanied by solo piano or guitar duettists, once the coplas transferred to the big screen – the huge repertory of popular Spanish musical films remains completely unknown in other centres – the sort of large-scale orchestration heard here became the norm. The Madrid orchestra under Miguel Roa provide elegant and idiomatic accompaniment.

Bernarda Fink — mezzo-soprano

'Il pianto de Maria'
Conti Il martiro di San Lorenzo – 'Sento già mancar la vita' **Ferrandini** Il pianto di Maria **Marini** Passacaglia a 4 **Monteverdi** Pianto della Madonna **Pisendel** Sonata **Vivaldi** Concerto for Strings, 'Madrigalesco', RV129. Sinfonia for Strings, 'Sinfonia al Santo Sepolcro', RV169. Sonata, 'Al Santo Sepolcro', RV130 **Bernarda Fink** mez **Il Giardino Armonico / Giovanni Antonini** L'Oiseau-Lyre 478 1466DH (61' · DDD · T/t) Ⓕ**O**➔

Most of the pieces in this excellent programme are connected with the events of Holy Week. The best-known is actually a rarity: Monteverdi's *Pianto della Madonna*, published in the *Selva morale e spirituale* of 1641, is a contrafactum – an adaptation to sacred words – of the *Lament from Arianna*, composed in 1608. It works well, and Bernarda Fink sings it with an affecting mixture of restraint and passion.

The Monteverdi is in Latin, whereas Giovanni Battista Ferrandini's *Il pianto di Maria*, at 25 minutes the longest piece on the disc, is in Italian. It's listed in the catalogue of Handel's works (HWV234) but many scholars have had their doubts on grounds of style. Laid out as a cantata, it consists of recitatives and *da capo* arias; but three recitatives move from *secco* to *accompagnato*, with vivid depictions of Christ's torture and of the earthquakes following his death. The first aria, string suspensions leading to the voice entering with slow, sustained notes, is meltingly beautiful.

Ferrandini was employed at the court in Munich; Francesco Bartolomeo Conti, the composer of the third vocal piece here, worked for the Habsburgs in Vienna. In the aria 'Sento già mancar la vita' St Lawrence, stretched out on the gridiron, calmly welcomes his death. Bernarda Fink is accompanied by the veiled tones of Giovanni Antonini's chalumeau, the effect curiously similar to the hushed appearance of Andromache and her son in Berlioz's *Les Troyens*.

With the Vivaldi Sonata and Sinfonia we are back in Holy Week. The instrumental pieces are done well, and this well planned disc is very desirable.

Gerald Finley — baritone

'Great Operatic Arias'
Adams Doctor Atomic – Batter My Heart **Bizet** Carmenª – You're most kind, and in return I toast you; Toreador, be ready! **Donizetti** Linda of Chamounix – In this valley we shared our childhood[b] **Mozart** Don Giovanni[c] – Come on, we're wasting time; There will my arms enfold you **Puccini** Tosca – Three agents, quick as you can now[d] **Rodgers** South Pacific – Some enchanted evening **Tchaikovsky** Iolanta – My only beloved Mathilde I claim **Turnage** The Silver Tassie – Oh bring to me a pint of wine **Verdi** Otello – Take it: take the path to your ruin; Yes,

I believed in God who has created me
Wagner Tannhäuser – Turning our gaze upon
this proud assembly; With dark foreboding
twilight casts her shadow; Look down, oh gentle
evening star. The Mastersingers of Nuremberg –
Do not disdain our Masters thus[e]
Weber Euryanthe – What refuge here?
Gerald Finley bar with [a]**Emma Brain-Gabbott**, [c]**Lucy
Crowe**, [a]**Kathryn Jenkin** sops [b]**Anne Marie Gibbons**,
[a]**Deborah Miles-Johnson** mezs
[d]**Matthew Long** ten [c]**Gareth Hancock** hpd
[ade]**Geoffrey Mitchell Choir; London Philharmonic
Orchestra / Edward Gardner**
Chandos Opera in English CHAN3167 (69' · DDD)
Ⓜ︎ⓄⓄ➍➤

All essentials for a recital are present here: the
featured artist in good voice, imagination capable of bringing 13 different characters to life
unseen (sometimes, as in the case of Tchaikovsky's Duke Robert, in barely three minutes),
apt recording decisions and on-the-pace accompaniment (delivered by ENO music chief
Edward Gardner, this time with the LPO, a
frequent Chandos project partner).

Both Gerald Finley and Gardner are natural
time-travellers in lyric theatre, be it in the
imaginative choice of Antonio's 'Ambo nati in
questa valle' from *Linda di Chamounix* or in
Richard Rodgers's 'Some enchanted evening'.
The latter is set here as a kind of encore and
nestles well musically next to Puccini's treatment of Scarpia's wholly different kind of love.
Its performance epitomises this programme:
unafraid to be romantic where necessary, but
with a just blend of control and detail to make
one hearing not enough.

The range of music covered gives the Canadian baritone the chance to give quite a calling-
card of his stage work. There is much imaginative detail in Iago's Credo, Lysiart, the
Donizetti, and the deceptively tricky *Tosca* Act 1
finale pitched at a convincingly monumental
tempo. Only in Hans Sachs's final address does
an uncompelling English translation and a slender choral sound limit the impact of Finley's
work.

Finally, as John Steane's informative and witty
note reminds us, there are two of what used to be
called 'creator records'. In the emotional John
Donne-based reverie from John Adams's *Doctor
Atomic* (where Finley was the first J Robert
Oppenheimer) the singer is superb and the glittering orchestration well caught by orchestra
and engineers. Then by way of complete contrast, there's Mark Anthony Turnage's *The Silver Tassie*, Finley in his bitter-sweet role of
Harry Heegan.

Ives Memories **Mussorgsky** Songs and Dances of
Death **Rautavaara** Three Sonnets – Shall I compare
thee? **Rorem** War Scenes **Tchaikovsky** Six Songs,
Op 25 – No 2, As o'er the burning ashes. Six Songs,
Op 38 – No 1, Don Juan's Serenade; No 2, It was in
the early spring; No 3, At the ball. Seven Songs,
Op 47 – No 6, Does the day reign?. Twelve Songs,

Op 60 – No 3, If only you knew; No 12, The mild stars
shone for us **W Charles** The Green-Eyed Dragon
Gerald Finley bass-bar **Julius Drake** pf
Wigmore Hall Live WHLIVE0025 (71' · DDD)
Recorded live 2007 Ⓜ︎Ⓓ➤

Aided by scrupulous support from Julius Drake,
Gerald Finley lavishes wonderfully rounded
treatment upon the sequence of seven Tchaikovsky songs that open proceedings. Be it in the
ardent swagger of 'Don Juan's Serenade', wistful
glow of 'At the ball' or meltingly lovely 'The
mild stars shone for us', Finley is not found
wanting. Not only do his top notes ring out with
thrilling projection (yet without a hint of hardness), he exhibits a grace, sensitivity and intelligence that ensure that the music never topples
into rampant self-pity.

There's a comparable authority and integrity
about these artists' interpretation of Mussorgsky's *Songs and Dances of Death*. Finley is in complete command of his very considerable resources,
distilling every ounce of pathos from the mother's
desperate pleadings in the opening 'Lullaby' and
conveying in full the grim implacability of 'The
Field-Marshal'. Ned Rorem's similarly declamatory *War Scenes* is also performed with total
understanding, while the last of the three encores,
Wolseley Charles's wickedly amusing 'The
Green-Eyed Dragon' (written in 1926 for Stanley
Holloway), predictably brings the house down. A
genuine treat, this, and not to be missed.

Renée Fleming   soprano

'Verismo'
Catalani La Wally – Ne mai dunque avrò pace?…
Ohime! **Cilea** Gloria – O mia cuna **Giordano** Fedora
– Tutto tramonta[a]. Siberia – Nel suo amore.
Leoncavallo La bohème[b] – Musette svaria sulla
bocca viva; Mimì Pinson la biondinetta. Zazà –
Angioletto il tuo nome?[c] **Mascagni** Iris – Un dì (ero
piccina). Lodoletta – Ah il suo nome…Flammen
perdonami **Puccini** Suor Angelica – Senza mamma.
La bohème – Sì, mi chiamano Mimì; Addio…Donde
lieta. Manon Lescaut – Sola perduta abbandonata.
Turandot – Tu che di gel cinta[d]. La rondine[e] – Ore
dolci e divine; Bevo al tuo fresco sorriso Zandonai
Conchita – Ier della fabbrica
Renée Fleming sop
with [be]**Saito Kaoru**, [ac]**Emma Latis**, [de]**Barbara
Vignudelli** sops [b]**Annalisa Dessi**, [e]**Lucia Mencaroni**
mezs [be]**Paolo Cauteruccio**, [ad]**Arturo Chacón-Cruz**,
[e]**Jonas Kaufmann** tens [b]**Gilles Armani**, [b]**Carlos
Gomez** bars [bd]**Marco Calabrese** bass **Giuseppe
Verdi Symphony Chorus and Orchestra, Milan /
Marco Armiliato**
Decca 478 1533DH (72' · DDD) Ⓟ︎ⓄⓄ➤

Renée Fleming, or her advisers, have chosen
well. They seek out pieces from the lyric repertoire and avoid the more violent emotions. Not
that Fleming's voice lacks the warmth and
darker tones that often carry a deeper human
appeal (the chest tones come movingly into play
as Mimì, with noble control of her feelings,

makes her simple arrangements in the Farewell). And there are times – Manon Lescaut's cries of protest at death's imminence – when the Italian tradition does expect a more forcefully vibrant tone and a more painfully raw show of emotion. But the feeling throughout is generous and true. Characterisation (as with the childlike heroines of Mascagni) infuses the voice without being applied like make-up. And the inclusion of some unexpected charmers – the solos from Leoncavallo's *Bohème* have the lilt of good operetta – is most welcome.

Care has been taken to supply other solo voices when these are part of the score, and indeed, in the final number we have the luxury 'extra' of Jonas Kaufmann's rich tenor to lead the bewitching ensemble from *La rondine*: the balance of the parts is not ideal but the piece remains irresistible, and it's good, after all the sighs and tears, to come out rejoicing.

Juan Diego Flórez   *tenor*

'Bel canto Spectacular'
Bellini I Puritani – Fini! Me lassa!...Vieni, fra queste braccia[b] **Donizetti** Don Pasquale – Povero Ernesto! L'elisir d'amore – Venti scudi[e]; Una furtiva lagrima. La Favorite – La maîtresse du roi?...Ange si pur. La fille du régiment – Ah! mes amis (Miei buoni amiche)[f]. Linda di Chamounix – Linda! Linda![a]; Da quel dì che t'incontra. Lucrezia Borgia – Partir degg'io... Io vuol Lucrezia; T'amo qual dama un angelo **Rossini** Otello – Ah vieni, nel tuo sangue vendicherò le offese[d]. Il viaggio a Reims – Di che son reo?[c]; D'alma celeste, oh Dio
Juan Diego Flórez *ten* with [a]Patricia Ciofi, [b]Anna Netrebko *sops* [c]Daniela Barcellona *mez* [d]Plácido Domingo *ten* [e]Mariusz Kwiecien, [f]Fernando Piqueras *bars* Cor de la Generalitat Valenciana; Orquesta de la Comunitat Valenciana / Daniel Oren
Decca 478 0315DH (77' · DDD)   (F)(P)➔
Also available as a special limited edition with DVD 478 0314

The opening track here is presumably Juan Diego Flórez's final word on the show-stopping aria from *La fille du régiment*. Having recorded it three times in French, he now offers it in Italian, although it hardly matters what language is being sung when it gets to the famous sequence of top Cs. It has become for him what 'Nessun dorma' was for Pavarotti – the aria every audience expects.

The rest of this attractive canter through the *bel canto* repertory finds our hero in robust form. This is very much a case of 'Flórez and friends'. Anna Netrebko contributes a touching Elvira to the great last-act duet from *I Puritani*, a very full version that culminates in those stratospheric phrases taking the tenor up to the high D. This is surely a role Flórez was born to sing. One could say the same about Carlo in *Linda di Chamounix*. Is there any more catchy Donizetti tune than the duet, 'Da quel dì che t'incontra'? Flórez and Patricia Ciofi are not undermined by

comparison with Sutherland and Pavarotti and the lovely solo from the same opera suits Flórez perfectly.

The two extracts from *L'elisir d'amore* are both winning, with Mariusz Kwiecien as an exceptionally vivid Belcore. Flórez has recorded 'Una furtiva lagrima' before – here he offers some new, attractive variations in the second verse. Rodrigo in Rossini's *Otello* was his first big success at Covent Garden, and a bonus track has him fighting it out with Plácido Domingo as the Moor. Somewhat more attractive is the long duet with Daniella Barcellona from *Il viaggio a Reims*. Flórez brings the CD to a rousing close with the extra aria from *Lucrezia Borgia* that Donizetti composed for Nicolai Ivanoff.

One gets the feeling this disc proved to be not only challenging but fun to record.

Elīna Garanča   *mezzo-soprano*

'Bel canto'
Bellini Adelson e Salvini – Dopo l'oscuro nembo. I Capuleti e i Montecchi[a] – Lieto del dolce incarco; La tremenda ultrice spada **Donizetti** L'assedio di Calais[b] – Al mio core oggetti amati; Io l'udio chiamarmi a nome; La speme un dolce palpito. Dom Sébastien – Sol adoré. Lucrezia Borgia – Il segreto per esser felici (Brindisi). Maria Stuarda[b] – Si, vuol di Francia il Rege (Elisabetta); Ah! quando all'ara scorgemi; In tal giorno di contento; Ah! dal ciel discenda un raggio. Roberto Devereux – All'afflitto è dolce il pianto **Rossini** Maometto Secondo – In questi estremi istanti. Tancredi – Oh patria!; Di tanti palpiti
Elīna Garanča *mez* with [b]Ekaterina Siurina *sop* [ab]Matthew Polenzani, [c]Adrian Sâmpetrean *tens* [ac]Ildebrando d'Arcangelo *bar* Teatro Comunale Philharmonic Orchestra, Bologna / Roberto Abbado
DG 477 7460GH (65' · DDD)   (F)(O)➔

Garanča begins with the best-known item, the Brindisi from the last act of *Lucrezia Borgia*, and if her voice is a little soft-grained for the reckless Maffio Orsini, she sings the song well. Strangely she sounds more masculine as Donizetti's Queen Elizabeth I in the entrance aria from *Maria Stuarda*. The gentle songs from *Adelson e Salvini* and *Dom Sébastien* make a nice contrast with the fireworks of 'Di tanti palpiti' from *Tancredi*.

Garanča is joined by Ekaterina Siurina in the spectacular duet from *L'assedio di Calais* – it's worth hearing the disc just for this – and they are aided here by Matthew Polenzani as well as in the trio from *Maometto Secondo*. Roberto Abbado and the Bologna orchestra provide the always sympathetic accompaniment (several of the items are performed 'from the original manuscript'). What of that long *bel canto* line? It is never allowed to overwhelm the dramatic situation of each scene but Garanča seems to find no difficulty in any of this music.

Véronique Gens
soprano

'Tragédiennes 2 – From Rameau to Berlioz'
Arriaga Herminie – Mais sur cette arène guerrière…
Il n'est plus…Dieux cruels **Berlioz** Les Troyens – Les
Grecs ont disparu…Malheureux Roi **Cherubini**
Médée – Ah! Nos peines seront communes **Gluck**
Alceste – Grands dieux soutenez mon courage…Ah!
Divinités implacables. Orphée et Eurydice – Air de
Furies; Ballet des ombres heureuses **Grétry**
Andromaque – C'est le seul espoir qui me reste…Si
fidèle au noeud qui l'engage **Piccini** Didon – Non, ce
n'est plus pour moi **Rameau** Les Paladins – Menuets I
& II; Entrée très gaye de Troubadours; Triste séjour;
Sarabande **Sacchini** Oedipe à Colone – Dieux, ce
n'est pas pour moi que ma voix vous implore.
Dardanus – Il me fuit…Rien ne peut émouvoir; Cesse
cruel amour de régner sur mon âme. Renaud – Hélas
vous le dirais-je… Ah! Que dis-tu
Véronique Gens sop
Les Talens Lyriques / Christophe Rousset Ⓕ❶❶Ⓓ→
Virgin Classics 216574-2 (67' · DDD · T/t) Ⓕ❶❶Ⓓ→

A very warm welcome this second 'Tragédiennes' volume from Véronique Gens and Christophe Rousset. The music chosen ranges from
the familiar to the extremely recherché. When
was the last time anyone had an opportunity to
see an opera by Sacchini or Piccini? Three of
Sacchini's *tragédies lyriques* are represented: *Renaud* (1783), *Dardanus* (1784) and *Oedipe à Colone*
(1786). The short scene for Antigone from
Oedipe is particularly impressive, the mood
changing from prayer to a passionate declaration
of intent as she vows to aid Oedipus in his sorrow.

Piccini's Dido seems to be just as tragic a figure
as those of Purcell or Berlioz, and Grétry's
Andromaque fumes against injustice with all the
passion that one would expect. The band plays
ballet music from Gluck's *Orphée* and Rameau's
Les Paladins, the latter providing a bridge into
the later works. One would not immediately
have thought of Gens as an ideal interpreter of
Néris, Medea's confidante in Cherubini's opera,
but she sings the aria, with its lovely oboe obbligato, with quiet dignity. The rarest item of all is
Herminie, a *scène lyrique* by Basque composer
Juan Crisóstomo de Arriaga, who was struck
down at the age of only 20, becoming known as
the Spanish Mozart. This second 'Tragédiennes'
volume is easily equal to the first and that must
be praise enough.

Susan Graham
mezzo-soprano

'Un frisson français'
Bachelet Chère nuit **Bizet** Chanson d'avril
Canteloube Chants d'Auvergne – Brezairola **Caplet**
Le corbeau et la renard **Chabrier** Les cigales
Chausson Les papillons, Op 2 No 3 **Debussy** Fêtes
galantes, Set 2 – Colloque sentimental **Duparc** Au
pays où se fait la guerre **Fauré** Vocalise-étude
Franck Nocturne **Gounod** Au rossignol **Hahn** A
Chloris **Honegger** Trois chansons de la petite sirène,

H63 **Lalo** Gitarre, Op 17 No 1 **Messiaen** Trois
Mélodies – La fiancée perdue **Paladilhe** Psyché
Poulenc La dame de Monte-Carlo **Ravel** Histoires
naturelles – Le paon **M Rosenthal** Chansons de
monsieur Bleu – La souris d'Angleterre **Roussel**
Réponse d'une épouse sage, Op 35 No 2 **Saint-
Saëns** Danse macabre **Satie** Trois Mélodies – Le
chapelier
Susan Graham mez **Malcolm Martineau** pf
Onyx ONYX4030 (78' · DDD) Ⓕ Ⓓ→

With Susan Graham in radiant form and Malcolm Martineau not just an accompanist but an
active partner in the project, 'Un frisson français' offers a unique survey of French *mélodie*
from the mid-19th century to the mid-20th:
22 songs…one per composer.

Martineau describes the plan as a 'tasting
menu', starting with Gounod, to whom he
ascribes the launching of the genre of French
mélodie. Even Ravel said that Gounod was 'the
true founder of the *mélodie* in France' and his
song 'Au rossignol' ('To the Nightingale') is
included in the first of five sections – 'founding
fathers', including Bizet, Franck, Lalo and
Saint-Saëns. It is fascinating to hear the original
version with piano of 'Danse macabre', Graham
marvellously biting.

Martineau describes the sequence as 'loosely
chronological', and one beauty of the scheme is
that rare and forgotten composers are included,
such as Paladilhe and Bachelet who are represented in late-Romantic *mélodies* with night and
nature dominating themes. The third group –
including Ravel and Debussy – takes us into the
20th century. Especially fascinating is André
Caplet's setting of 'Le corbeau et le renard'
('The Crow and the Fox') with elaborate piano
accompaniment.

Only rare songs are chosen for each composer
and perhaps Martineau chose some of them for
the colourful accompaniments, as in Chausson's
fluttering accompaniment for his picture of the
butterfly in 'Le papillon'. The fourth section has
childhood as a common theme and the climactic
section has only one song, much the longest,
Poulenc's 'La dame de Monte-Carlo', to words
by Jean Cocteau. It is like an encapsulated version of the operatic monodrama *La voix humaine*
with the singer on the verge of a breakdown.

A rich collection in excellent sound: no one is
likely to be disappointed.

Philippe Jaroussky
countertenor

'Opium'
Caplet Viens, une flûte invisible soupire^c **Chausson**
Le colibri, Op 2 No 7. Le temps de lilas. Les
papillons, Op 2 No 3. Les heures, Op 27 No 1.
Chaminade Sombrero. Mignonne **Debussy** Romance
No 2 **D'Indy** Lied maritime, Op 43 **Dukas** Sonnet
Dupont Les donneurs de sérénade **Fauré** Nell,
Op 18 No 1. Automne, Op 18 No 3 **Franck** Nocturne
Hahn A Chloris. Fêtes galantes (Mandoline).
12 Rondels – No 8, Quand je fus pris au pavillon.
Offrande. Chansons grises – No 5, L'heure exquise

Lekeu Trois Poèmes – No 1, Une tombe **Massenet**
Elégie[b]. Nuit d'Espagne **Saint-Saëns** Tournoiement,
'Songe d'opium', Op 26. Violons dans le soir[a]
Philippe Jaroussky counterten
Jérôme Ducros pf with [a]**Renaud Capuçon** vn
[b]**Gautier Capuçon** vc [c]**Emmanuel Pahud** fl
Virgin Classics 216621-2 (66' · DDD)   (F)●☺+

This is beautiful but it takes a bit of getting used
to. Philippe Jaroussky's countertenor (he has
often been called a male soprano), so well suited
to Vivaldi and Monteverdi, at first seems quite
wrong in the repertory of belle époque *mélodies*.
The song that gives the disc its title, *Tournoiement*, 'Songe d'Opium' by Saint-Saëns, with its
madly whirling accompaniment – splendidly
played by Jérôme Ducros – benefits from the
other-worldy sounds Jaroussky can produce.

Some of the better-known songs, for instance
Chausson's 'Le temps des lilas' and Hahn's
'Offrande' are so familiar as performed by rich-
voiced female singers that hearing just the initial
phrases one might suppose that the disc were
being played at an exaggeratedly high pitch.
However, there is no denying the accomplishment of Jaroussky's vocalism, although the basic
tone lacks warmth and variation at several key
moments. The selection is certainly adventurous,
including rarities such as Dukas's 'Sonnet',
d'Indy's 'Lied maritime', and two songs by composers who may be unfamiliar to many listeners:
'Sur une tombe', words and music by Guillaume
Lekeu (1870-94), the first of his *Trois Poèmes* of
1892, is a little elegy that begins gently but rises to
quite a passionate climax, while Gabriel Dupont's
'Les donneurs de sérénades' is yet another setting
of Verlaine's 'Mandoline' – Jaroussky gives a
wonderfully flirtatious performance. The songs
that require extra instruments are well served by
the trio of guest players, with Gautier Capuçon
especially eloquent in Massenet's 'Elégie'.

Jonas Kaufmann   *tenor*

Beethoven Fidelio – Gott! welch Dunkel hier!
Mozart Die Zauberflöte – Dies Bildnis ist bezaubernd
schön; Die Weisheitslehre dieser Knaben...Wie stark
ist nicht dein Zauberton[b] **Schubert** Fierrabras – Was
quälst du mich, O Missgeschick!...In tiefbewegter
Brust. Alfonso and Estrella – Schon, wenn es beginnt
zu tagen **Wagner** Lohengrin – In fernem Land[c]; Mein
lieber Schwan! Die Walküre – Winterstürme wichen
dem Wonnemond. Parsifal – Amfortas!...Die
Wunde![a]; Nur eine Waffe taugt
Jonas Kaufmann ten with [a]**Margarete Joswig** mez
[b]**Michael Volle** bass-bar [c]**Valdis Jansons** bass **Teatro
Regio Choir, Parma; Mahler Chamber Orchestra /
Claudio Abbado**
Decca 478 1463DH (69' · DDD)   (F)●●●●+

It should no longer come as a surprise, but however many times one has heard and admired
Jonas Kaufmann, the size of his voice can seem
astonishing whenever one returns to listen
again. Though he opens his new disc quietly, in
the rapt voice required for 'In fernem Land', his

tenor is immediately very striking for its body
and well supported control. Lohengrin – *bel
canto* Wagner, as it were – is the most recent role
Kaufmann has taken on in the theatre, and his
sense of story-telling here shows how he already
inhabits the part.

Indeed, the weight of his voice is reminiscent
more of a young Jon Vickers than Kaufmann's
acknowledged idol, Fritz Wunderlich. In his
'Bildnis' aria, the first of two from *Die Zauberflöte*
featured here, there is less of that Wunderlich-
like sweetness of tone by which most Taminos
are measured, and it's possible that Kaufmann
will be outgrowing this role soon.

Celebrated for his versatility, the German
tenor has been successful in key roles of the
French and Italian repertory, but here he shows
a special affinity for works in his native tongue.
The German Romantic theme is set already on
the CD cover, where he is portrayed as Caspar
David Friedrich's Wanderer. And that quintessential German Romantic work, *Fidelio*, is the
centrepiece of this disc: it receives a powerful
performance from both tenor (his opening
'Gott' is heart-piercing) and conductor.

Abbado has long been a champion of
Schubert's operas, and his accompaniments with
the Mahler Chamber Orchestra here are especially rewarding – not least in the wind-writing
in *Alfonso und Estrella*. Kaufmann has also sung
the title-role in *Fierrabras* widely, and it suits
both the tenor's power and his strong sense of
musical line.

Kaufmann ends where he began, with Wagner. Parsifal (Lohengrin's father) was his first
Wagner role, and Siegmund is just looming into
view. But his beautiful phrasing and controlled
singing in the 'Winterstürme' shows why he has
become the most sought-after tenor of his generation, and is a highlight of this exciting new
release.

Simon Keenlyside   *baritone*

Fauré Aubade, Op 6 No 1. En sourdine, Op 58 No 2.
Green, Op 58 No 3. Notre amour, Op 23 No 2. Fleur
jetée, Op 39 No 2. Spleen, Op 51 No 3. Madrigal,
Op 35. Le papillon et la fleur, Op 1 No 1 **Poulenc**
Banalités – No 2, Hôtel **Ravel** Histoires naturelles
Schubert An Silvia, D891. Einsiedelei, D337.
Verklärung, D59. Die Sterne D939. Himmelsfunken,
D651. Ständchen, D889 **Wolf** Mörike Lieder – Der
Knabe und das Immelein; Auf eine Christblume II; An
die Geliebte; Lied vom Winde; Lied eines Verliebten;
Gesang Weylas
Simon Keenlyside bar **Malcolm Martineau** pf
Wigmore Hall Live WHLIVE0031 (74' · DDD)
Recorded live 2008   (M)●+

There is not much suggestion of curiosity in
Simon Keenlyside's enquiries about the much-
commended Sylvia, and if he has any personal
feelings about the lady he conceals them behind
a somewhat severe exterior. That is the first
song of his opening Schubert group, and his last,
the famous 'Ständchen', rather similarly dis-

courages any sense of involvement. On the other hand, he sings both songs in such a way as to make it clear, if we did not know it already, that here is a singer with an unusually fine voice and full mastery of its usage: and for that is due more thanks than we (critics at any rate) usually show. In between these have come other songs, most memorably the sublime 'Himmelsfunken', that have more successfully engaged the imagination. Still, there has not as yet been much in the way of communication.

One sometimes wonders what difference it would make were the order of performance to be reversed. By the end of the recital we are on quite intimate terms, but they have been attained gradually, stage by stage. Hugo Wolf is at his most welcoming in 'Der Knabe und das Immelein' and Keenlyside is at his most responsive in 'An die Geliebte'. Then, after the interval, all is French. Fauré's 'Aubade' brings charm to the programme. 'En sourdine' matches tone to the half-closed eye, and the sleepy mood is sustained in 'Green'. Keenlyside is at his best in 'Notre amour' – and very French. In Ravel's *Histoires naturelles*, the words clear and well pointed, we listen intently as to a master story-teller.

In all this he has more than the support of the pianist, Malcolm Martineau: he has a collaborator in whom the life of texts as well as the music is experienced and communicated unfailingly. And often both artists perform uncannily as one. Incidentally, there are discrepancies, of order and content, between the programme here and as printed.

Magadalena Kožená
mezzo-soprano

'Songs My Mother Taught Me'
Dvořák Gypsy Melodies, Op 55[b]. Evening Songs, Op 3[b]. Moravian Duets, Op 32[ab] **Eben** Lute Songs[c] **Janáček** Moravian Folk Poetry[b]. Silesian Songs[b] **Martinů** Songs on Two Pages[b] **Novák** Fairytale of the Heart, Op 8[b] **Rösler** An die Entfernte[b] **Schulhoff** Folksongs and Dances from Těšín[b] **Traditional** If I were a strawberry plant[b]
Magdalena Kožená *mez* [a]Dorothea Röschmann *sop* [b]Malcolm Martineau *pf* [c]Michael Freimuth *gtr*
DG 477 6665GH (70' · DDD)   Ⓕ**ⓄⓄ**➔

Magdalena Kožená's heartwarming new album takes its title from one of the best-loved of all Czech songs, the centrepiece of Dvořák's *Gypsy Melodies*. Her smoothly phrased performance captures the nostalgia of this music, with which she is very much at home.

Singing in a language she really did learn from her mother, Kožená sounds at her most relaxed; there is no hint of the strain she has shown in some recent operatic work. She also suggests a fierce connection with these songs, abandoning herself into music that showcases well her glinting top and dusky lower notes. This is rich repertory, and Dvořák is not the earliest composer represented here. That honour goes to Jan Josef Rösler (1771-1813), with a Goethe setting (in

German). The programme stretches all the way to the lyrical Lute Songs of Petr Eben, who died in 2007.

Along the way we encounter the sophisticated music of Ervín Schulhoff and a lovely set by Vítězslav Novák. The mezzo opens with an unaccompanied folksong, and elsewhere benefits from the sympathetic partnership of Malcolm Martineau. But her programme is essentially framed with songs (and a couple of duets with Dorothea Röschmann) by Janáček, aptly since Kožená grew up in Brno. Miniatures by Martinů speak directly, as so often with this delightful composer.

Anna Netrebko
soprano

'Souvenirs'
Arditi Il bacio **Dvořák** Songs My Mother Taught Me, B104 No 4 **G Charpentier** Louise – Depuis le jour **Giménez** La Tempranica – La tarántula é un bich mú malo **Grieg** Peer Gynt, Op 23 – Solveig's Song **Guastavino** La rosa y el sauce **Hahn** L'Enamourée **Heuberger** Der Opernball – Im Chambre separée[c] **Kálmán** Die Csárdásfürstin – Heia, heia, in den Bergen ist mein Heimatland **Lehár** Giuditta – Meine Lippen, sie küssen **Lloyd Webber** Requiem – Pie Jesu[a] **Messager** Fortunio – Lorsque je n'étais qu'une enfant **Offenbach** Les contes d'Hoffmann – Belle nuit, ô nuit d'amour (Barcarolle)[b] **R Strauss** Cäcilie, Op 27 No 2. Wiegenlied, Op 41 No 1 **Rimsky-Korsakov** Not the wind, blowing from the heights, Op 43 No 2. Enslaved by the rose, the nightingale, Op 2 No 2 **Traditional** Schlof sche, mein Vögele
Anna Netrebko *sop* with [a]Andrew Swait *treb* [b]Elīna Garanča *mez* [c]Piotr Beczała *ten* Prague Philharmonic Choir; Prague Philharmonia / Emmanuel Villaume
DG 477 7639GH (62' · DDD)   Ⓕ**Ⓞ**➔

Something for everybody here. Netrebko is nothing if not adventurous in her choice of 'lollipops', and sings in nine languages. Inevitably the Russian items come off best: the lovely little Rimsky-Korsakov song about the wind whispering love into the poet's soul, and then the 'Oriental romance' of the rose and the nightingale. Both of these have been discreetly orchestrated for this disc by Andreas Tarkmann. The Yiddish lullaby 'Schlof sche, mein vögele' is done with great tenderness, as is the 'Pie Jesu' from Andrew Lloyd Webber's Requiem. This is one of three duets, Netrebko joined here by the boy soprano Andrew Swait. For the Barcarolle from *Les contes d'Hoffmann* she has Elīna Garanča on hand as Niklausse; they make a convincing pair of Venetian serenaders. Even better is 'Im Chambre separée' from Heuberger's *Der Opernball*, heard for once in its authentic form as a duet, taken slowly but done with great style, Piotr Beczała contributing a nice turn as the youthful Henri, eager to learn about the *demi-monde*.

Of the other operetta items Netrebko's raunchy 'Zapateado' from Giménez's *La Tempranica* is preferable to the rather effortful 'Heia, in den Bergen' from Kálmán's *Die Csárdásfürstin*. Two

French opera arias make a neat contrast: 'Depuis le jour' from *Louise*, very dreamy, the words well defined, and with a beautifully executed leap up to the exultant 'Je suis heureuse!' Then there is the little song from Messager's *Fortunio*, a moment of quietness sandwiched between Solveig's Song and 'Songs My Mother Taught Me' – this done in Czech, to the apparent delight of the Prague Philharmonie, conducted throughout with gentlemanly care by Emmanuel Villaume. Although the fireworks of Arditi's 'Il bacio' bring the disc to an exuberant finish, the introspective songs fare best.

Patricia Petibon
soprano

'Rosso – Italian Baroque Arias'

Handel Alcina – Tornami a vagheggiar; Ah! mio cor, schernito sei!. Rinaldo – Lascia ch'io pianga. Ariodante – Volate, amori; Neghittosi, or voi che fate?. Giulio Cesare – Piangerò la sorte mia **B Marcello** Arianna – Come mai puoi vedermi piangere? **Porpora** Lucio Papirio – Morte amara **Sartorio** Giulio Cesare in Egitto – Quando voglio. L'Orfeo – Orfeo, tu dormi **A Scarlatti** La Griselda – Se il mio dolor t'offende. Il Sedecia, re di Gerusalemme – Caldo sangue **Stradella** San Giovanni Battista – Queste lagrime e sospiri **Vivaldi** L'Olimpiade – Siam navi all'onde algenti
Patricia Petibon sop
Venice Baroque Orchestra / Andrea Marcon
DG 477 8763GH (75' · DDD) Ⓟ**ⓄⓄ**▸

This enterprisingly planned recital confirms Patricia Petibon as a singing actress with few peers in Baroque opera. Her nimble, flutey soprano has now acquired warmer, more sensuous tints; and she brings a memorable and distinct vocal personality to each of these assorted heroes, heroines, victims and villains *in extremis*. In an infectiously jaunty aria from Antonio Sartorio's *Giulio Cesare* she is the immortal seductress Cleopatra to the life, cajoling and insinuating to the accompaniment of castanets and thrumming Baroque guitar. She exudes a dangerous wheedling sweetness as Salome in a beautiful, suspension-laden aria from Stradella's lubricious oratorio *San Giovanni Battista*, and, at the other end of the spectrum, poignantly embodies the mingled sorrow and thirst for vengeance of the dying Ishmael (originally a castrato role) in Scarlatti's *Il Sedecia, re di Gerusalemme*.

Some may feel that in her quest for maximum drama Petibon occasionally resorts to effects more appropriate to Strauss's Elektra or Berg's Lulu than to these 18th-century creations. Take her bouts of deranged near-*Sprechgesang* in an aria from Scarlatti's *Griselda*, and her despairing sighing and slithering in the closing stages of Alcina's great lament, 'Ah! mio cor'. Yet for all the contentious style it is hard to resist the mesmeric intensity of Petibon's singing here.

Elsewhere the French soprano gives a dazzling account of coloratura showpiece 'Tornami a vagheggiar', enhancing Morgana's dizzy exuberance with stratospheric flights in the *da capo*.

Another virtuoso *tour de force* is Dalinda's 'Neghittosi, or voi che fate?' from *Ariodante*, where, egged on by hyperactively slashing archlutes, she hurls venom at the evil Polinesso, in the process unfurling some formidable chest tones. Typical, too, is the way Petibon makes Almirena's sarabande lament 'Lascia ch'io pianga' an emotional journey, with a surge of protest in the middle section and a new numbed, blanched tone in the *da capo*. Once or twice conductor Andrea Marcon favours over-fussy dynamic effects but for the most part his expert period band matches Petibon all the way in acuity and dramatic flair.

Irmgard Seefried
soprano

Brahms Die Trauernde, Op 7 No 5. Immer leiser wird mein Schlummer, Op 105 No 2. Nachtigall, Op 97 No 1. Wiegenlied, Op 49 No 4 **Cornelius** Brautlieder **Kienzl** Maria auf dem Berge, Op 55 No 3. Mai, Op 73 No 5 **Marx** Marienlied. Erinnerung. Lied eines Mädchens. Zigeuner. Sankta Maria **Mozart** Sehnsucht nach dem Frühlinqe, K596 **Schubert** Die Forelle, D550 **R Strauss** Morgen!, Op 27 No 4. Die Nacht, Op 10 No 3. Meinem Kinde, Op 37 No 3. Du meines Herzens Krönelein, Op 21 No 2. Ruhe, meine Seele!, Op 27 No 1. Allerseelen, Op 10 No 8. Schlagende Herzen, Op 29 No 2 **Wolf** Das verlassene Mägdlein. Der Gärtner. Im Frühling
Irmgard Seefried *sop* with Leopold Ludwig, **Ⓗ** Erik Werba, Viktor Graef *pfs*
Orfeo d'Or mono C598 091B (67' · ADD)
Recorded 1943-52 Ⓕ

A lovely collection: if you had to choose a single disc to represent Seefried in song you could not do better than this. The various groups of Lieder were taken from five occasions in Vienna and are said to be previously unpublished. The first, from 1943, the year of her debut at the State Opera, is the earliest; and the last, from 1952, has her, still young and fresh in tone, clearly an artist fully developed and in her prime.

Seefried had one of the strongest, most vivid personalities among singers. On stage as on the concert platform she was so much alive, her face expressive as her voice, it was as though she wore her own spotlight. Even now, in the course of this recital, sudden flashes rekindle the memory (the majestic phrases at the climax of 'Ruhe, meine Seele', for instance, brought her very close); yet the appeal of these performances does not depend on memory. The combination of freshness and warmth is one special quality; the close-knit, even texture of the voice another. The lesser-known songs are particularly attractive, with the five by Josef Marx infectious in their gaiety, boldness and warmth. Her style is very clean: she is sparing (but then very effective) in her use of *portamento*. But her personal warmth permeates the voice, and in these recordings one feels it as when she herself was part of our regular musical life half a century ago.

Dame Joan Sutherland *soprano*

'The Art of the Prima Donna' ⊞
Opera Arias from Artaxerxes, Die Entführung aus
dem Serail, Faust, Hamlet, Les Huguenots, Lakmé,
Norma[a], Otello, I Puritani, Rigoletto[a], Roméo et
Juliette, Samson, Semiramide[a], La Sonnambula
& La traviata
Dame Joan Sutherland *sop* [a]**Chorus and Orchestra
of the Royal Opera House, Covent Garden /
Francesco Molinari-Pradelli**
Decca Legends ② 467 115-2DL2 (109' · ADD · T/t)
Recorded 1960
Ⓜ❍❍❍Ⓓ→

'The Art of the Prima Donna', hardly
out of the catalogue since 1960, is now
remastered for Classic Sound. There
can't be many admirers who haven't already got
this, so for newcomers to Sutherland on disc one
can only say – listen and wonder. Her voice,
even throughout its range right up to the high E,
always keeping its natural quality, is heard at its
early fullness. Perhaps the best tracks of all are
'The soldier tir'd' from *Artaxerxes* and 'Let the
bright seraphim' from *Samson*, but every track is
beautiful. 'Casta diva' – her earliest attempt at it
– is her most limpid recording of this prayer,
'Bel raggio' from *Semiramide* has sparkling decorations, quite different from the ones she sang
on the complete recording six years later, and
the whole thing ends with the Jewel Song from
Faust. It was a big voice and sounded at its best in
larger theatres. It's difficult to imagine anyone,
coming to it for the first time, being disappointed.

Bryn Terfel *baritone*

'Bad Boys'
Beethoven Fidelio – Ha! Welch ein Augenblick!
Boito Mefistofele – Sono lo spirito che nega
Donizetti L'elisir d'amore – Udite, udite, o rustici
Gershwin Porgy and Bess – It ain't necessarily so
Gounod Faust – Le veau d'or est toujours debout!
Mozart Don Giovanni – Don Giovanni, a cenar teco
m'invitasti **Ponchielli** La Gioconda – O monumento!
Puccini Tosca – Tre sbirri, una carrozza[b] **Rossini** Il
barbiere di Siviglia – La calunnia è un venticello
Schönberg Les Misérables – There out in the
darkness **Sondheim** Sweeney Todd – Epiphany[a]
Sullivan Ruddigore – When the night wind howls
Verdi Otello – Vanne...Credo in un Dio crudel
Weber Der Freischütz – Schweig, schweig, damit
dich neimand warnt! **Weill** Der Dreigroschenoper –
Die Moritat von Mackie Messer
Bryn Terfel *bass-bar* with [a]**Anne Sofie von Otter**
mez [b]**Balcarras Craford** *bar* **Swedish Radio Choir;
Swedish Radio Symphony Orchestra / Paul Daniel**
DG 477 8091GH (58' · DDD)
Ⓕ❍❍❍Ⓓ→

The baddies always are more fun; in opera and
musical theatre they are that much larger than
life, too. Small wonder they prove (on the whole)
such a perfect fit for the world's most famous
bass-baritone. So enter Satan himself – aka Boito's Mefistofele – to call the tune and literally
whistle his contempt at all things good in nature.
Boito's showstopper has Bryn Terfel plumbing
the very depths of his bass extension and almost,
but not quite, slipping from song into growl.

It's a great start to his devilishly clever selection of 'Bad Boys' and – by way of delicious
contrast – it's followed by one whose purveyance
of evil takes an altogether more devious path.
Terfel's Chief of Police Scarpia – now well practised and celebrated – is the smoothest of opera-
tors using his oleaginous *legato* to lustful ends.
Paul Daniel (a perceptive collaborator) and the
Swedish RSO and Chorus back up his odious
insinuations with a resounding *Te Deum*.
Vocally, orchestrally and as a piece of engineering, it sounds mighty fine. Terfel, of course,
brings the smell of the theatre into everything
he does. Consider the deceptively subtle difference between Iago's 'Credo' and Barnaba's
more 'in your face' derision in his blacker-than-
black aria 'O monumento!' from *La Gioconda*.

Not everything is quite on the money. Gershwin's Sportin' Life really needs a reedier tenorial
sneer to the voice in 'It ain't necessarily so'.
Donizetti's roguish quack Dr Dulcamara too
needs a lighter touch.

Brecht's words for 'The Ballad of Mack the
Knife' casually slip off Terfel's cords like the
threats of a slickly attired bouncer and, speaking
of the threat of cold steel, Sweeney Todd's
'Epiphany' (with a flash of Anne Sofie von Otter's
cockney Mrs Lovett – not 'arf bad) is scary to
behold, though Terfel could surely have departed
from the written line where he hurls the promise
of vengeance at prospective customers.

The climax of the disc is the demise of Don
Giovanni with Terfel offering an unholy trinity
of all three characters.

Rolando Villazón *tenor*

'Cielo e mar'
Boito Mefistofele – Dai campi, dai prati; Giunto sul
passo estremo **Cilea** Adriana Lecouvreur – La
dolcissima effigie sorridente; L'anima ho stanca
Donizetti Poliuto – Veleno è l'aura ch'io respiro!;
Sfolgorò divino raggioa **Gomes** Fosca – Intenditi
con Dio!; Ah! Se tu sei fra gli angeli **Mercadante**
Il giuramento – La dea di tutti i cor!; Compita è omai;
Fu celeste quel contento **Pietri** Maristella – Io
conosco un giardino **Ponchielli** Il figliuol prodigo –
Il padre!... Il padre mio!; Tenda natal. La Gioconda –
Cielo e mar! **Verdi** Luisa Millera – Oh! fede negar
potessi; Quando le sere al placido; L'ara o l'avello
apprestami. Simon Boccanegra – O inferno! Amelia
qui!; Sento avvampar nell'anima
Rolando Villazón *ten* with [a]**Gianluca Alfano** *bar*
**Giuseppe Verdi Symphony Chorus and Orchestra,
Milan / Daniele Callegari**
DG 477 7224GH (57' · DDD)
Ⓕ❍Ⓓ→

This is a well chosen selection of tenor arias with a
few comparative rarities to offset the more obvious favourites. In its way it is a mini-history of a
century of Italian opera, from Donizetti's *Poliuto*

(1838) to Pietri's *Maristella* (1934). The Donizetti is the longest item and well though Villazón copes with this, it's hard to imagine him in this part, beloved of *tenore di forza* of the past including Tamagno and Corelli. In fact he has not sung any of these roles on stage yet; in a note he explains that the repertory here is something 'with more spontaneity…without the burden of history'.

Be that as it may, the parts for which he would seem to be destined are Gabriele Adorno in *Simon Boccanegra*, Rodolfo in *Luisa Miller* and Viscardo in *Il giuramento*. Mercadante's opera is based on the same Victor Hugo play as Ponchielli's *La Gioconda*, so it is a good idea to contrast these two very different interpretations of the same character.

The little romanza from Pietri's opera is the only piece by him that we ever get to hear. It was a favourite with Gigli, and several other tenors have recorded it. The aria from Brazilian composer Carlos Gomes's 1873 opera *Fosca* is a high-voltage outpouring of emotion, as is the aria for Azael in Ponchielli's *Il figliuol prodigo*.

Villazón sings them all with admirable intensity, his diction is excellent, and he can float a *pianissimo* when necessary, as in the opening 'Cielo e mar' from *La Gioconda* that gives the disc its title. Recording quality is first-rate, and the accompaniment is always sympathetic.

Various singers

'The NMC Songbook'
Includes songs by J Anderson, Bainbridge, Baker, G Barry, Basford, Bauld, Bawden, D Bedford, L Bedford, M Berkeley, Bingham, Birtwistle, Blake, Bryars, Burrell, Butler, G Carpenter, Cashian, Casken, Causton, J Cole, Cresswell, Crosse, Cutler, PM Davies, T Davies, C Dench, Dennehy, Dillon, Duddell, B Elias, Finnissy, Foskett, Fox, Fujikura, Gilbert, Goehr, Grange, Grant, Grime, Hall, B Harrison, S Harrison, J Harvey, M Hayes, Holloway, Holt, Horne, Howard, Hunt, Keeley, Kindsdottir, Leach, Lefanu, J Lloyd, MacMillan, MacRae, Marsh, PN Martin, C Matthews, D Matthews, Mayo, McCabe, Meredith, Molitor, Montague, Moore, Morley/C Matthews, Musgrave, Northcott, O'Regan, R Panufnik, Payne, Phibbs, J Philips, Poole, Powell, Powers, JD Roberts, Roxburgh, Rushton, Sackman, Sawer, Saxton, J Simpson, Skempton, Stoneham, Swayne, Turnage, Wallen, Watkins, Weir, J White, Wiegold, R Williams, H Wood and Woolrich
Artists include **Andrew Swait, Sam Harris** *trebs* **Elizabeth Atherton, Claire Booth, Ailish Tynan** *sops* **Susan Bickley, Loré Lixenberg, Jean Rigby** *mezs* **James Bowman, Michael Chance, Andrew Watts** *countertens* **Benjamin Hulett, Andrew Kennedy, Daniel Norman** *tens* **Omar Ebrahim, Richard Jackson, Stephan Loges, George Mosley, David Stout, Roderick Williams** *bars* **Gerald Barry, Errollyn Wallen** *vocs* **Andrew Ball, Iain Burnside, Michael Finnissy, Andrew Plant, Jonathan Powell, Huw Watkins, Andrew West** *pfs* **Jane Chapman** *hpd* **Lucy Wakeford** *hp* **Owen Gunnell** *perc* **Antonis Hatzinikolaou** *gtr*

NMC ④ NMCD150 (5h' · DDD · T)   Ⓕ ●●●●▷

 NMC's 20th anniversary celebrations may or may not 'kick-start a new interest in the genre' (Bayan Northcott) but the initiative gives us a useful snapshot of British Music now, even if certain tendencies are better represented than others.

There are full texts and the imaginative design concept reflects the disparity of the idiomatic options available. Whether tonal, atonal or pseudo-tonal, some of these are found as if by chance and loosely worn, others carefully nurtured and obsessively worked. Britten remains in some ways the key figure in that his example persuades many contributors to stick with conventionally accompanied solo voice(s). That said, his intuitive response to a text is less easily imitated than the externals of his style. Martin Butler's Blake setting upholds the tradition in its best and purest form. Other examples might lead you to conclude that dislocated consonance, high voicing and a certain infuriating feyness constitute the defining features of British song.

There's room for the provocateurs as well. Luke Stoneham gets away with an electronic soundscape while Gerald Barry turns in a gleefully graceless recitation of Oscar Wilde. Jonathan Cole has Roderick Williams perform a sequence of phonemes while guesting on balloon.

Is a song a song at all if its text is merely a jumping-off point, a colour without a context? Morgan Hayes's Dickensian passages, ideally chosen for such a project, are quickly sidelined amid dizzying virtuosity. Chris Dench is still sufficiently hard-core to represent what was once a New Complexity. Few others appear capable of writing fast music even in short bursts, hence perhaps Colin Matthews's decision to break up the sequence with instrumental interludes. In the tradition of Stanford's pseudonymous Karel Drofnatzki he may also be behind the modest haiku setting with its allusions to NMC marketing strategy. Call me old-fashioned but my own favourite items are those in which both the original text and the passion of a composer's response are intelligible in the finished product. In Hugh Wood's George Herbert setting, careful workmanship does not preclude a Tippettian sense of exaltation. There's a similar sense of engagement in Simon Holt's unaccompanied declamation (evoking a real-life incident in rural India) and Brian Elias's more subdued John Clare solo. The way in which the items are juxtaposed can be crucial too; the cooler limpidity of Howard Skempton and Gavin Bryars is doubly welcome in context.

The performers range from good to excellent. The recordings were almost all made in Hall One, Kings Place, an acclaimed venue where instrumental voices are unfailingly well projected. Human ones, less comfortable with its zingy resonance, can become a little hectoring.

But then only a critic or a fool would listen to the entire collection at a sitting. Much better to study at leisure what should prove to be an important cultural document.

THE INDEXES

INDEX OF COUPLINGS

H

T

INDEX TO ARTISTS

C

H

M

U

V

W